MERGENT'S SELECT COMMON STOCKS

2001

Edition

Published by:

MERGENT'S SELECT COMMON STOCKS

Table of Contents

INTRODUCTION

Welcome to ***Mergent's*** *Select Common Stocks*, our new annual guide to 1,000 New York Stock Exchange companies. Easy to use and eminently portable, this guide provides you with a wealth of information for casual browsing or instant research on companies in the news.

Here you'll find detailed profiles of 1,000 companies listed on the NYSE, the world's largest equities market with $12.37 trillion in market capitalization at 12/31/00. Here are the blue chips, the proven performers, the engines that drive the world's mightiest economy. These are the large-cap powerhouses, from **Exxon Mobil Corp.** to **Wal-Mart Stores, Inc.**, from **Citigroup Inc.** to **Sears, Roebuck & Co.**, from **Merck & Co., Inc.** to **Hewlett-Packard Co.**, from **Target Corp.** to **Generals Electric**, **Motors**, **Dynamics**, and **Mills.**

Nearly three-quarters of the companies profiled had revenues in excess of $1.00 billion in 2000. The top 50 in terms of revenue generated more than $3.00 trillion in sales in 2000, led by Exxon Mobil, riding the crest of rising energy prices and reflecting Exxon's acquisition of Mobil Corp. on 11/30/99. The 50 companies with the greatest assets held more than a total of $10.00 trillion in assets at the close of their most recent fiscal years. These are the companies for all seasons, the portfolio staples, the denizens of the Dow, the sultans of the S&P 500, the rockets of the Russell 1000.

Today's hot industries are well-represented. More than 50 oil and oil service companies are featured, as well as 27 natural gas companies. Eighteen drug companies and more than 30 healthcare and medical equipment providers are included. We have introduced a new category, Electricity Generation (Wholesale), to highlight a group of fast-growing energy providers, including **Calpine Corp.**, **Mirant Corp.**, and **NRG Energy Inc.** Providing ample evidence that technological innovation is not limited to tiny over-the-counter start-ups are more than 40 computer and computer software and services companies, as well as over 30 manufacturers of electronic components. In presenting a broad sweep of the economic landscape, we feature companies from some 100 industries, from **AAR Corporation** (aircraft engines) to **Zenith National Insurance Corp.** (property/casualty insurance).

According to the New York Stock Exchange, non-U.S. issuers are growing in importance on the NYSE. As of January 2001, there were 434 non-U.S. companies trading there, three times the number of just five years ago. Therefore, we have included some representative non-U.S. companies in this book, including **Sony Corp.** and **Honda Motor Co., Ltd.**, (Japan), **BP Amoco p.l.c.** (U.K.), **NorTel Networks Corp.** (Canada), **Norsk Hydro ASA** (Norway) and **Benetton Group S.P.A.**(Italy).

For each company profiled, you will find seven years of financial statistics and 15 years of stock performance data (when available). But, of course, by nature investors are future-oriented. Accordingly, each company's profile contains a Prospects section, in which our independent analysts note recent events and trends that could affect future earnings. As we proceed through another volatile year in the stock markets and the economy, it helps to have the facts.

Suzanne Wittebort
Assistant Vice President & Editor
Mergent, Inc.
Charlotte, NC
June, 2001

Top 50 Companies by Revenues

Rank	Company	2000 Revenue ($Mil.)
1.	Exxon Mobil Corp.	232,748.0
2.	Wal-Mart Stores, Inc.	193,295.0
3.	General Motors Corp.	184,632.0
4.	Ford Motor Co.	170,064.0
5.	BP Amoco p.l.c.	148,062.0
6.	General Electric Co.	129,853.0
7.	Citigroup Inc.	111,826.0
8.	Enron Corp.	100,789.0
9.	Intl. Business Machines	88,396.0
10.	Philip Morris Cos.	80,356.0
11.	AT&T Corp.	65,981.0
12.	Sony Corp.	64,860.6
13.	Verizon Communications	64,707.0
14.	Morgan (J.P.) Chase & Co.	60,065.0
15.	Honda Motor Co., Ltd.	59,158.7
16.	Bank of America Corp.	57,772.0
17.	SBC Communications	51,476.0
18.	Chevron Corp.	51,379.0
19.	Boeing Company (The)	51,321.0
20.	Texaco Inc.	50,100.0
21.	Duke Energy Corp.	49,318.0
22.	Kroger Company (The)	49,000.0
23.	Hewlett-Packard Co.	48,782.0
24.	Home Depot (The), Inc.	45,738.0
25.	Morgan Stanley Dean Witter	45,413.0
26.	Unilever, N.V.	45,297.4
27.	Merrill Lynch & Co., Inc.	44,872.0
28.	Fannie Mae	44,088.0
29.	American Intl. Group	42,440.0
30.	Compaq Computer Corp.	42,383.0
31.	Sears, Roebuck & Co.	40,937.0
32.	Merck & Co., Inc.	40,363.2
33.	Procter & Gamble Co.	39,951.0
34.	Conoco Inc.	39,287.0
35.	Motorola, Inc.	37,580.0
36.	Kmart Corp.	37,028.0
37.	Target Corp.	36,903.0
38.	Albertson's, Inc.	36,762.0
39.	McKesson HBOC, Inc.	36,734.0
40.	Berkshire Hathaway Inc.	33,976.0
41.	USX-Marathon Group	33,859.0
42.	Lucent Technologies Inc.	33,813.0
43.	Goldman Sachs Group	33,000.0
44.	Safeway Inc.	31,976.9
45.	MetLife, Inc.	31,947.0
46.	Penney (J.C.) Co., Inc.	31,846.0
47.	Ingram Micro Inc.	30,715.1
48.	Nortel Networks Corp.	30,293.0
49.	Cardinal Health, Inc.	29,870.6
50.	United Parcel Service, Inc.	29,771.0

Figures are for the most recent fiscal year for which data were available, up to and including fiscal years ending 1/31/01.

Top 50 Companies by Assets

Rank	Company	2000 Assets ($Mil.)	Rank	Company	2000 Assets ($Mil.)
1.	Citigroup Inc.	902,210.0	26.	BP Amoco p.l.c.	143,938.0
2.	Morgan (J.P.) Chase & Co.	715,348.0	27.	Berkshire Hathaway Inc.	135,792.0
3.	Fannie Mae	675,072.0	28.	American General Corp.	120,094.0
4.	Bank of America Corp.	642,191.0	29.	Allstate Corp. (The)	104,808.0
5.	Freddie Mac	459,297.0	30.	SunTrust Banks, Inc.	103,496.4
6.	General Electric Co.	437,006.0	31.	Lincoln National Corp.	99,844.1
7.	Morgan Stanley Dean Witter	426,794.0	32.	SBC Communications, Inc.	98,651.0
8.	Merrill Lynch & Co., Inc.	407,200.0	33.	CIGNA Corporation	95,088.0
9.	American Intl. Group	306,577.0	34.	Nationwide Finl. Services	93,178.6
10.	General Motors Corp.	303,100.0	35.	National City Corporation	88,534.6
11.	Goldman Sachs Group	289,760.0	36.	Intl. Business Machines	88,349.0
12.	Ford Motor Co.	284,421.0	37.	John Hancock Finl. Serv.	87,353.3
13.	Wells Fargo & Co.	272,426.0	38.	U.S. Bancorp	87,336.0
14.	Bank One Corp.	269,300.0	39.	Keycorp	87,270.0
15.	MetLife, Inc.	255,018.0	40.	Viacom Inc.	82,646.1
16.	First Union Corp.	254,170.0	41.	Philip Morris Cos.	79,067.0
17.	AT&T Corp.	242,223.0	42.	Wal-Mart Stores, Inc.	78,130.0
18.	Lehman Brothers Hldgs.	224,720.0	43.	Bank of New York Co.	77,114.0
19.	Washington Mutual, Inc.	194,716.0	44.	Household International	76,706.3
20.	FleetBoston Finl. Corp.	179,519.0	45.	Wachovia Corp.	74,031.7
21.	Hartford Finl. Services	171,532.0	46.	Qwest Communications Intl.	73,501.0
22.	Bear Stearns Cos., Inc.	171,166.5	47.	Loews Corporation	70,877.1
23.	Verizon Communications	164,735.0	48.	PNC Financial Serv. Group	69,844.0
24.	American Express Co.	154,423.0	49.	State Street Corp.	69,298.0
25.	Exxon Mobil Corp.	149,000.0	50.	Sony Corp.	66,029.8

Figures are for the most recent fiscal year for which data were available, up to and including fiscal years ending 1/31/01.

Top 50 Companies by Net Income

Rank	Company	2000 Net Income ($Mil.)	Rank	Company	2000 Net Income ($Mil.)
1.	Exxon Mobil Corp.	15,990.0	**26.**	Hewlett-Packard Co.	3,561.0
2.	Citigroup Inc.	13,519.0	**27.**	Procter & Gamble Co.	3,542.0
3.	General Electric Co.	12,735.0	**28.**	FleetBoston Finl. Corp.	3,420.0
4.	BP Amoco p.l.c.	11,870.0	**29.**	Berkshire Hathaway Inc.	3,328.0
5.	Verizon Communications	10,810.0	**30.**	Texas Instruments Inc.	3,087.0
6.	Philip Morris Cos.	8,510.0	**31.**	Goldman Sachs Group, Inc.	3,067.0
7.	Intl. Business Machines	8,093.0	**32.**	Lilly (Eli) & Co.	3,057.8
8.	SBC Communications	7,967.0	**33.**	United Parcel Service, Inc.	2,934.0
9.	Bank of America Corp.	7,517.0	**34.**	American Express Co.	2,810.0
10.	Merck & Co., Inc.	6,821.7	**35.**	Abbott Laboratories	2,786.0
11.	Wal-Mart Stores, Inc.	6,295.0	**36.**	Home Depot (The), Inc.	2,581.0
12.	Morgan (J.P.) Chase & Co.	5,727.0	**37.**	Honda Motor Co., Ltd.	2,545.4
13.	American Intl. Group	5,636.0	**38.**	Texaco Inc.	2,542.0
14.	Morgan Stanley Dean Witter	5,456.0	**39.**	Freddie Mac	2,539.0
15.	Ford Motor Co.	5,410.0	**40.**	Schering-Plough Corp.	2,423.0
16.	Chevron Corp.	5,185.0	**41.**	E.I. du Pont de Nemours	2,314.0
17.	Johnson & Johnson	4,800.0	**42.**	Allstate Corp. (The)	2,211.0
18.	AT&T Corp.	4,669.0	**43.**	PepsiCo Inc.	2,183.0
19.	General Motors Corp.	4,452.0	**44.**	Coca-Cola Co. (The)	2,177.0
20.	Fannie Mae	4,416.0	**45.**	Boeing Company (The)	2,128.0
21.	BellSouth Corp.	4,220.0	**46.**	McDonald's Corp.	1,977.3
22.	Bristol-Myers Squibb Co.	4,096.0	**47.**	ALLTEL Corp.	1,965.4
23.	Wells Fargo & Co.	4,026.0	**48.**	Cox Communications, Inc.	1,925.3
24.	Merrill Lynch & Co.	3,784.0	**49.**	Conoco, Inc.	1,902.0
25.	Pfizer Inc.	3,726.0	**50.**	Washington Mutual, Inc.	1,899.0

Figures are for the most recent fiscal year for which data were available, up to and including fiscal years ending 1/31/01.

Top 50 Companies by Net Profit Margin

Rank	Company	2000 Net Profit Margin %
1.	Cox Radio, Inc.	82.8
2.	Ambac Financial Group, Inc.	58.9
3.	Cox Communications, Inc.	54.9
4.	Spieker Properties, Inc.	44.2
5.	Cabletron Systems, Inc.	31.8
6.	Apache Corporation	31.6
7.	Chris-Craft Industries, Inc.	29.9
8.	Stilwell Financial, Inc.	29.5
9.	National Semiconductor	29.3
10.	UST, Inc.	28.6
11.	Lilly (Eli) & Co.	28.2
12.	Alliant Energy Corp.	27.9
13.	ALLTEL Corp.	27.8
14.	Eaton Vance Corp.	27.0
15.	Waddell & Reed Financial	26.7
16.	EOG Resources, Inc.	26.6
	Rouse Company (The)	26.6
18.	Moody's Corp.	26.3
19.	Texas Instruments Inc.	26.0
20.	Newfield Exploration Co.	25.6
21.	Carnival Corp.	25.3
22.	Schering-Plough Corp.	24.7
23.	Franklin Resources, Inc.	24.0
24.	Analog Devices, Inc.	23.6
25.	ALZA Corp.	23.3
26.	Overseas Shipholding Group	23.1
27.	Federated Investor Inc.	22.8
28.	Bristol-Myers Squibb Co.	22.5
29.	Medtronic, Inc.	21.9
30.	Advanced Micro Devices, Inc.	21.7
31.	Cypress Semiconductor Corp.	21.5
32.	Burlington Resources Inc.	21.4
	IDT Corp.	21.4
34.	Newhall Land & Farming Co.	21.3
35.	Vishay Intertechnology, Inc.	21.0
	Watson Pharmaceuticals, Inc.	21.0
37.	Micron Technology Inc.	20.5
38.	Kerr-McGee Corp.	20.4
39.	Abbott Laboratories	20.3
	CountryWide Credit Industries	20.3
41.	EMC Corp.	20.1
42.	Ocean Energy, Inc.	19.9
43.	DPL Inc.	19.8
44.	Waters Corp.	19.6
45.	Mylan Laboratories, Inc.	19.5
46.	ResMed Inc.	19.2
47.	Neuberger Berman Inc.	18.8
	Noble Drilling Corp.	18.8
49.	Marine Drilling Cos., Inc.	18.3
50.	Pioneer Natural Resources	18.0

Figures are for the most recent fiscal year for which data were available, up to and including fiscal years ending 1/31/01.

Top 50 Companies by Return on Assets

Rank	Company	2000 Return on Assets %	Rank	Company	2000 Return on Assets %
1.	Stilwell Financial, Inc.	42.0	26.	Abbott Laboratories	18.2
2.	Moody's Corp.	39.8	27.	Advanced Micro Devices	17.4
3.	Valassis	38.6		Texas Instruments Inc.	17.4
4.	Waddell & Reed Financial	32.9	29.	Avon Products, Inc.	17.2
5.	Intimate Brands, Inc.	29.7	30.	Merck & Co., Inc.	17.1
6.	Graco Inc.	29.5	31.	Catalina Marketing Corp.	16.9
7.	Eaton Vance Corp.	26.8		Mitchell Energy & Development	16.9
	UST, Inc.	26.8		Polaris Industries Inc.	16.9
9.	National Semiconductor	26.3	34.	EMC Corp.	16.8
10.	Deluxe Corp.	26.1	35.	Superior Industries Intl.	16.3
11.	Newhall Land & Farming Co.	24.3	36.	ALLTEL Corp.	16.1
12.	Bristol-Myers Squibb Co.	23.3	37.	Winnebago Industries, Inc.	15.7
13.	Waters Corp.	22.5	38.	Micron Technology Inc.	15.6
14.	Schering-Plough Corp.	22.4	39.	Johnson & Johnson	15.3
15.	Federated Investors Inc.	22.0	40.	Fairchild Semiconductor Intl.	14.9
	Teradyne, Inc.	22.0		Quaker Oats Co. (The)	14.9
17.	Wrigley (William) Jr. Co.	20.9	42.	Guidant Corp.	14.8
18.	Lilly (Eli) & Co.	20.8		Ralston Purina Co.	14.8
19.	Oxford Health Plans, Inc.	19.8	44.	Briggs & Stratton Corp.	14.7
20.	Medtronic, Inc.	19.4		Cabletron Systems, Inc.	14.7
21.	IDT Corp.	19.2		Colgate-Palmolive Co.	14.7
	ResMed Inc.	19.2	47.	DeVry Inc.	14.6
	Robert Half International	19.2	48.	Harley-Davidson, Inc.	14.3
24.	Vishay Intertechnology	18.6		RadioShack Corp.	14.3
25.	TJX Companies, Inc. (The)	18.3	50.	Total Systems Services, Inc.	14.2

Figures are for the most recent fiscal year for which data were available, up to and including fiscal years ending 1/31/01.

Top 50 Companies by Return on Equity

Rank	Company	2000 Return on Equity %	Rank	Company	2000 Return on Equity%
1.	Maytag Corp.	927.1	26.	Heinz (H.J.) Co.	55.8
2.	Campbell Soup Co.	521.2	27.	Georgia Gulf Corp.	54.1
3.	Amphenol Corp.	369.1	28.	Lilly (Eli) & Co.	50.6
4.	SunSource Inc.	216.5	29.	IDT Corp.	49.9
5.	Freeport-McMoRan Copper	203.0	30.	UniSource Energy Corp.	47.2
6.	UST, Inc.	163.3	31.	Merck & Co., Inc.	46.0
7.	International Game Technology	162.3	32.	Frontier Oil Corp.	45.7
8.	7-Eleven, Inc.	129.7	33.	Eaton Vance Corp.	45.5
9.	IMS Health, Inc.	112.2	34.	NL Industries, Inc.	45.1
10.	Federated Investors Inc.	105.1	35.	Bristol-Myers Squibb Co.	44.6
11.	Quaker Oats Co. (The)	101.7	36.	TJX Companies, Inc. (The)	44.2
12.	Ralston Purina Co.	99.5	37.	Pitney Bowes Inc.	43.8
13.	Waddell & Reed Finl., Inc.	98.2	38.	Plains All American Pipeline, L.P.	43.3
14.	Sara Lee Corp.	93.8	39.	Neuberger Berman Inc.	42.9
15.	Colgate-Palmolive Co.	72.5	40.	Gillette Company (The)	42.7
16.	Newhall Land & Farming Co.	71.6	41.	Radioshack Corp.	41.8
17.	Kellogg Co.	65.5	42.	Mitchell Energy & Development	41.5
18.	Intimate Brands, Inc.	65.0	43.	Eastman Kodak Co.	41.0
19.	Deluxe Corp.	64.5		Lyondell Chemical Co.	41.0
20.	Graco Inc.	63.2	45.	Black & Decker Corp.	40.7
21.	Stilwell Financial, Inc.	62.7	46.	Polaris Industries Inc.	40.4
22.	Oxford Health Plans, Inc.	62.2	47.	Schering-Plough Corp.	39.6
23.	Tupperware Corp.	60.5	48.	Intl. Business Machines	39.2
24.	Equifax Inc.	59.4	49.	Millipore Corp.	39.0
25.	Philip Morris Cos.	56.7	50.	ALLTEL Corp.	38.6

Figures are for the most recent fiscal year for which data were available, up to and including fiscal years ending 1/31/01.

Top 50 Companies by Recent Yield

Rank	Company	Yield %
1.	EOTT Energy Partners, L.P.	11.3
2.	iStar Financial Inc.	9.8
3.	Crescent Real Estate Equities Co.	9.2
4.	Mack-Cali Realty Corp.	9.1
	Plum Creek Timber Co.	9.1
6.	Post Properties, Inc.	8.5
	Thornburg Mortgage, Inc.	8.5
8.	Host Marriott Corp.	8.1
9.	Liberty Property Trust	7.9
	Simon Property Group, Inc.	7.9
11.	Puget Energy, Inc.	7.7
12.	Plains All American Pipeline, L.P.	7.6
13.	Duke-Weeks Realty Corp.	7.5
14.	Hunt Corp.	7.4
15.	National Presto Industries	7.3
16.	Ennis Business Forms, Inc.	7.1
17.	DQE, Inc.	7.0
18.	Apartment Invest. & Mgmt. Co.	6.8
	Cedar Fair, L.P.	6.8
20.	Hawaiian Electric Industries, Inc.	6.7
	ProLogis Trust	6.7
22.	Kansas City Power & Light	6.6
23.	Alliant Energy Corp.	6.5
	Archstone Communities Trust	6.5
	GPU, Inc.	6.5
	International Aluminum Corp.	6.5
	Kimco Realty Corp.	6.5
28.	Amcast Industrial Corp.	6.4
	CarrAmerica Realty Corp.	6.4
30.	AMB Property Corp.	6.3
	Dana Corp.	6.3
	Equity Office Properties	6.3
	Polymer Group, Inc.	6.3
34.	Equity Residential Prop. Trust	6.2
	WPS Resources Corp.	6.2
36.	RPM, Inc.	6.1
	UST, Inc.	6.1
38.	OGE Energy Corp.	6.0
	UGI Corp.	6.0
40.	Consolidated Edison, Inc.	5.9
	General Growth Properties	5.9
42.	Boston Properties, Inc.	5.8
	Vornado Realty Trust	5.8
44.	Ameren Corp.	5.7
	ArvinMeritor, Inc.	5.7
	Deluxe Corp.	5.7
	Lyondell Chemical Co.	5.7
	Oneok Inc.	5.7
	Southern Company (The)	5.7
50.	AvalonBay Communities, Inc.	5.6

Top 50 by 12-Month Price Score

Rank	Company	Price Score	Rank	Company	Price Score
1.	Standard Commercial Corp.	191.9	26.	Bergen Brunswig Corp.	146.4
2.	Oregon Steel Mills, Inc.	190.2	27.	Reynolds (R.J.) Tobacco Hldgs.	145.4
3.	DiMon Inc.	185.4	28.	Green Mountain Power Corp.	145.0
4.	EDO Corp.	182.7	29.	Webb (Del) Corp.	144.0
5.	Foster Wheeler Corp.	181.4	30.	USA Education, Inc.	143.9
6.	Fleming Companies, Inc.	172.7	31.	Total System Services, Inc.	143.8
	Service Corporation Intl.	172.7	32.	Block (H.R.), Inc.	143.1
8.	Group 1 Automotive, Inc.	169.0		Sodexho Marriott Services	143.1
9.	Hancock Fabrics, Inc.	168.6		Thornburg Mortgage, Inc.	143.1
10.	Blockbuster Inc.	165.5	35.	Jacobs Engineering Group	142.7
11.	Lab. Corp. of America Hldgs.	163.7	36.	Albany International Corp.	142.5
12.	Champion Enterprises, Inc.	163.4		International Game Technology	142.5
13.	Conseco, Inc.	160.4	38.	Dime Bancorp, Inc.	142.4
14.	Rite Aid Corp.	156.9	39.	Kmart Corp.	142.3
15.	Winn-Dixie Stores, Inc.	156.1	40.	Ryland Group, Inc. (The)	142.2
16.	CIT Group, Inc.	154.9	41.	Diagnostic Products Corp.	141.9
17.	Health Net, Inc.	153.0	42.	EMCOR Group, Inc.	141.4
18.	United Auto Group, Inc.	152.9	43.	Brown Shoe Company, Inc.	140.9
19.	Ameron International Corp.	150.8	44.	Genesco Inc.	140.6
20.	Frontier Oil Corp.	149.7	45.	Penney (J.C.) Company, Inc.	140.5
21.	AutoNation, Inc.	149.5	46.	Moore Corporation Ltd.	140.4
22.	NACCO Industries Inc.	148.8	47.	Ultramar Diamond Shamrock	140.3
23.	Loews Corp.	148.3	48.	Cendant Corp.	139.7
24.	Western Gas Resources, Inc.	148.2	49.	Philip Morris Cos.	139.5
25.	Manor Care, Inc.	146.7	50.	Freeport-McMoRan Copper	139.2

***Mergent's** 12-Month Price Scores are measures of company stock price performance for the previous 12 months relative to the New York Stock Exchange Composite Index. A score of 100 indicates that the stock exactly mirrored the price performance of the NYSE Composite Index for the period. A score of more than 100 means that the stock outperformed the index, while a score of less than 100 indicates that the stock did not do as well as the index. The higher the price score, the better the relative performance.*

*A more detailed definition of **Mergent's** Price Scores can be found on page 28a.*

Top 50 by Seven-Year Price Score

Rank	Company	Price Score	Rank	Company	Price Score
1.	EMC Corp.	249.4	**26.**	Tiffany & Co.	160.6
2.	Scientific-Atlanta Inc.	214.2	**27.**	Amphenol Corp.	159.3
3.	Jabil Circuit, Inc.	200.8	**28.**	Micron Technology Inc.	159.0
4.	Analog Devices, Inc.	199.6	**29.**	Texas Instruments Inc.	158.7
5.	AOL Time Warner Inc.	198.0	**30.**	Stryker Corp.	156.9
6.	Corning Inc.	192.6	**31.**	Titan Corp. (The)	156.0
7.	Forest Laboratories, Inc.	191.8	**32.**	Gallagher (Arthur J.) & Co.	155.8
8.	Price Communications Corp.	187.2	**33.**	SPX Corp.	154.2
9.	AES Corp.	182.7	**34.**	Walgreen Co.	152.8
10.	Kohl's Corp.	181.9	**35.**	Talbots (The), Inc.	152.3
11.	PerkinElmer, Inc.	178.1	**36.**	Best Buy Co., Inc.	151.7
12.	Allergen, Inc.	177.4	**37.**	Brown & Brown, Inc.	150.3
13.	Nortel Networks Corp.	176.9	**38.**	Genesco Inc.	149.6
14.	Eaton Vance Corp.	176.0	**39.**	Universal Health Services	149.5
15.	Dycom Industries, Inc.	174.1	**40.**	Cablevision Systems Corp.	149.3
16.	Dynegy Inc.	172.3		Citigroup Inc.	149.3
17.	Lehman Brothers Hldgs.	172.0	**42.**	CTS Corp.	148.6
18.	Enron Corp.	167.0	**43.**	Noble Drilling Corp.	147.9
19.	International Rectifier Corp.	166.9	**44.**	DeVry Inc.	147.0
20.	Harley-Davidson, Inc.	164.3	**45.**	Teradyne, Inc.	146.9
21.	Symbol Technologies, Inc.	164.0	**46.**	Legg Mason, Inc.	146.6
22.	BJ Services Co.	163.9		Mitchell Energy & Development	146.6
23.	Schwab (Charles) Corp.	163.4	**48.**	State Street Corp.	146.5
24.	Solectron Corp.	163.2	**49.**	Southwest Airlines Co.	146.2
25.	Morgan Stanley Dean Witter	160.9	**50.**	Merrill Lynch & Co., Inc.	146.1

***Mergent's** Seven-Year Price Scores are measures of company stock price performance for the previous seven years relative to the New York Stock Exchange Index Composite. A score of 100 indicates that the stock exactly mirrored the price performance of the NYSE Composite Index for the period. A score of more than 100 means that the stock outperformed the index, while a score of less than 100 indicates that the stock did not do as well as the index. The higher the price score, the better the relative performance.*

*A more detailed definition of **Mergent's** Price Scores can be found on page 28a.*

ADVERTISING
Catalina Marketing Corp.
* Interpublic Group of Companies, Inc.
Omnicom Group, Inc.
* True North Communications, Inc.
Valassis Communications, Inc.

AGRICULTURAL EQUIPMENT
* Deere & Company

AIRCRAFT & AEROSPACE
* AAR Corporation
Boeing Company
* GenCorp Inc.
United Technologies Corporation

AIRLINES
Alaska Air Group
AMR Corporation
Continental Airlines, Inc.
* Delta Air Lines, Incorporated
Southwest Airlines Co.
UAL Corp.
US Airways Group, Inc.

AMUSEMENTS
* Enesco Group Inc.
Hasbro, Inc.
* Mattel, Inc.
Russ Berrie and Company, Inc.

APPAREL
Angelica Corp.
Benetton Group S.P.A.
Burlington Coat Factory Warehouse Corp.
Intimate Brands, Inc.
Jones Apparel Group, Inc.
Kellwood Company
* Liz Claiborne, Inc.
Oxford Industries, Inc.
Phillips-Van Heusen Corporation
Polo Ralph Lauren
* Russell Corp.
* VF Corporation
Warnaco Group Inc.

AUTOMOBILE PARTS
American Axle & Manufacturing Holdings
Applied Industrial Technologies, Inc.
ArvinMeritor, Inc.
Autoliv, Inc.
* Barnes Group, Inc.
BorgWarner Inc.
* Cummins Engine Company, Inc.
* Dana Corporation
Delphi Automotive Systems Corp.
* Eaton Corporation
* Federal-Mogul Corporation
* Genuine Parts Company
Hayes Lemmerz International Inc.
ITT Industries, Inc.
* Johnson Controls, Inc.
Lear Corp.
* Smith (A.O.) Corporation
* SPX Corporation
Standard Motor Products, Inc.
Superior Industries International, Inc.
* The Timken Company
Tower Automotive Corp.
Wabtec Corp.

AUTOMOBILES & TRUCKS
* Ford Motor Company
* General Motors Corporation
* Harley-Davidson, Inc.
Honda Motor Co., Ltd.
Navistar International Corp.

BANKS–MAJOR
Bank of America Corporation
* Bank of New York Company Inc.
* Bank One Corporation
Capital One Financial Corp.
* First Union Corp.
MBNA Corp.
* Morgan (J.P.) Chase & Company, Inc.
* Wells Fargo & Company

BANKS–MID/ATLANTIC
* First Virginia Banks, Inc.
* M & T Bank Corporation
* Mellon Financial Corporation
* PNC Bank Corp.
* Valley National Bancorp
* Wilmington Trust Corp.

BANKS–MIDWEST
* Comerica, Inc.
Golden State Bancorp, Inc.
* KeyCorp.
* Marshall & Illsley Corporation
* National City Corporation
* North Fork Bancorp Inc.
* Pacific Century Financial
* TCF Financial Corporation
* U.S. Bancorp

BANKS–NORTHEAST
Charter One Financial, Inc.
* FleetBoston Financial Corp.
State Street Corp.

BANKS–SOUTH
* AmSouth Bancorporation
* BB&T Corporation
* First Tennessee National Corp.
* Hibernia Corp.
* SunTrust Banks, Inc.
Synovus Financial Corp.
Union Planters Corp.
* Wachovia Corporation

BANKS–WEST
* BancWest Corporation
City National Corporation
* UnionBanCal Corp.

BREWING
* Anheuser-Busch Companies, Inc.
Coors (Adolph) Co.

BUILDING MATERIALS & EQUIPMENT
* Ameron Inc.
International Aluminum Corp.
Martin Marietta Materials, Inc.

Masco Corporation
USG Corporation

CANDY & GUM

* Hershey Foods Corporation
Tootsie Roll Industries, Inc.
* Wrigley (Wm.) Jr. Company

CATALOG MERCHANDISING

Lands' End, Inc.

CEMENT & GYPSUM

* Lafarge Corporation
Texas Industries, Inc.

CHEMICALS

* Air Products & Chemicals, Inc.
* Avery Dennison Corporation
* Cabot Corporation
* Chemed Corporation
* Crompton Corporation
Cytec Industries
* The Dow Chemical Company
* Du Pont (E.I.) de Nemours & Co.
Eastman Chemical Co.
* Engelhard Corporation
* Ethyl Corporation
* Ferro Corporation
FMC Corporation
Georgia Gulf Corporation
* Goodrich (B.F.) Co.
* Grace (W.R.) & Company
Great Lakes Chemical Corp.
* Hercules, Incorporated
Imperial Chemical Industries PLC
* The Lubrizol Corporation
Lyondell Chemical Company
Millennium Chemicals Inc.
NCH Corporation
NL Industries, Inc.
* Olin Corporation
* PPG Industries, Inc.
Praxair, Inc.
Rohm & Haas Company
Solutia Inc.

COMPUTERS–COMPONENTS & PERIPHERAL EQUIPMENT

Agere Systems Inc.
Agilent Technologies, Inc.
Cabletron Systems, Inc.
Cypress Semiconductor Corp.
EMC Corp.
Fairchild Semiconductor International
Ingram Micro Inc.
International Rectifier Corp.
KEMET Corporation
LSI Logic Corp.
NCR Corporation
Quantum Corp.
SCI Systems, Inc.
Silicon Graphics, Inc.
Storage Technology Corp.
Symbol Technologies, Inc.
Systemax, Inc.
Western Digital Corp.

COMPUTERS–MAJOR

Compaq Computer Corp.
Gateway Inc.
* International Business Machines Corporation

COMPUTERS–SERVICES & SOFTWARE

Affiliated Computer Services, Inc.
AOL Time Warner, Inc.
Automatic Data Processing, Inc.
Avaya Inc.
Cadence Design Systems, Inc.
Ceridian Corporation
Computer Associates International, Inc.
Computer Sciences Corporation
Computer Task Group, Inc.
Convergys Corporation
Electronic Data Systems Corporation
First Data Corp.
Galileo International, Inc.
Gartner Group
Gerber Scientific Inc.
NOVA Corporation
Sungard Data Systems Inc.
Sybase, Inc.
Titan Corporation (The)
Total Systems Services Inc.
Unisys Corp.

CONGLOMERATES

* Alco Standard Corporation
Berkshire Hathaway Inc.
Loews Corporation
* Minnesota Mining and Manufacturing Company
Sequa Corporation
* Standex International Corp.
* Tenneco Automotive, Inc.
* Textron, Inc.
* TRW Inc.
Valhi, Inc.
Viad Corp.
* Vulcan Materials Company

CONTAINERS

* Ball Corporation
Crown Cork & Seal Company, Inc.
Owens-Illinois, Inc.

COPPER

* Phelps Dodge Corporation

COSMETICS, TOILETRIES & FRAGRANCES

Alberto-Culver Company
* Avon Products, Incorporated
* The Dial Corporation
The Estee Lauder Cos., Inc.
* Gillette Company
International Flavors & Fragrances, Inc.

DEFENSE SYSTEMS & EQUIPMENT

Curtiss-Wright Corp.
* EDO Corp.
General Dynamics Corporation
* Harris Corporation
Lockheed Martin Corporation
L-3 Communications Holdings, Inc.
Newport News Shipbuilding Inc.
Northrop Grumman Corp.
* Raytheon Company

TransTechnology Corporation
United Industrial Corp.

DISTILLING
* Brown-Forman Corp.
Constellation Brands, Inc.
* Fortune Brands, Inc.

DRUGS
* Abbott Laboratories
* Allergan, Inc.
Alpharma Inc.
Alza Corporation
* American Home Products Corp.
* Bristol-Myers Squibb Company
Carter-Wallace, Inc.
Forest Laboratories, Inc.
Genentech, Inc.
ICN Pharmaceuticals, Inc.
King Pharmaceuticals, Inc.
* Lilly (Eli) & Company
* Merck & Co., Inc.
Mylan Laboratories, Inc.
* Pfizer Incorporated
* Pharmacia Corporation
* Schering-Plough Corporation
Watson Pharmaceuticals, Inc.

ELECTRIC POWER - CENTRAL & SOUTHEASTERN
* Alliant Energy
* Ameren Corp.
* American Electric Power Co., Inc.
* CINergy Corp.
* CLECO Corp.
* CMS Energy Corporation
* DPL Inc.
* DQE, Inc.
* Duke Energy Corp.
* Entergy Corporation
* FPL Group, Inc.
* NiSource, Inc.
* Progressive Energy, Inc.
* SCANA Corporation
* The Southern Company
* TECO Energy Inc.
* Wisconsin Energy Corporation
* WPS Resources Corp.

ELECTRIC POWER - NORTHEASTERN
AES Corp.
* Allegheny Energy
Bangor Hydro-Electric Company
* CH Energy Group, Inc.
* Conectiv
* Consolidated Edison Co. of N.Y.
* Constellation Energy Group, Inc.
* Dominion Resources Inc.
DTE Energy Co.
* Energy East Corp.
Exelon Corporation
FirstEnergy Corp.
* GPU, Inc.
* Green Mountain Power Corp.
Niagara Mohawk Power Corporation
* Northeast Utilities
NSTAR
* Potomac Electric Power Company
* PPL Corporation
* Public Service Enterprise Group Inc.
* Rochester Gas & Electric Corporation

ELECTRIC POWER - WESTERN
* ALLETE Company
* Edison International
* Hawaiian Electric Industries, Inc.
* Idacorp, Inc.
* Kansas City Power & Light Company
* Montana Power Company
* Nevada Power Co.
* Northwestern Corp.
* Oklahoma Gas & Electric Company
* PG&E Corp.
* Pinnacle West Capital Corporation
* Puget Sound Power & Light Company
* Reliant Energy, Inc.
* Sierra Pacific Resources
* Texas Utilities Company
UniSource Energy
* UtiliCorp United Inc.
* The Washington Water Power Company
Western Resources, Inc.
Xcel Energy Inc.

ELECTRICAL EQUIPMENT
AMETEK, Inc.
Anixter Corp.
Baldor Electric Company
* Emerson Company
* General Electric Company
Harman International Industires, Inc.
Hewlett Packard Company
Hubbell Inc.
Lennox International Inc.
MagneTek, Inc.
Sony Corporation
* Thomas & Betts Corporation

ELECTRICITY GENERATION (WHOLESALE)
Calpine Corp.
Covanta Energy Corp.
Mirant Corp.
NRG Industries

ELECTRONIC COMPONENTS
Advanced Micro Devices, Inc.
Agere Systems Inc.
* Allen Telecom Inc.
Amphenol Corporation
Analog Devices Inc.
Arrow Electronics, Inc.
* Avnet, Incorporated
AVX Corporation
Cable Design Technologies Corp.
CommScope, Inc.
* CTS Corporation
Energizer Holdings Inc.
Esco Technologies, Inc.
Exide Corp.
Federal Signal Corp.
General Semiconductor, Inc.
Jabil Circuit, Inc.
MasTec, Inc.
MEMC Electronic Materials Inc.
Micron Technology Inc.
* Motorola, Inc.

National Semiconductor Corporation
Oak Industries Inc.
* Rockwell International Corporation
Safeguard Scientifics, Inc.
Scientific-Atlanta, Inc.
Solectron Corp.
Texas Instruments, Inc.
* Varian Medical Systems, Inc.
Vishay Intertechnology Inc.

ENGINEERING & CONSTRUCTION
Dravo Corp.
Dycom Industries Inc.
Fluor Corp.
* Foster Wheeler Corp.
Jacobs Engineering Group Inc.
Kaydon Corp.
URS Corp.

ENTERTAINMENT
Cablevision Systems Corp.
Fox Entertainment Group, Inc.
Metro Goldwin Mayer
Westwood One Inc.

EQUIPMENT & VEHICLE LEASING
Budget Group, Inc.
* Ryder Systems, Inc.
XTRA Corporation

FERTILIZER
IMC Global, Inc.
Norsk Hydro A.S.
Scotts Company

FINANCE
Alleghany Corp.
AMBAC Financial Group, Inc.
* American Express Co.
CIT Group, Inc.
* Citigroup Inc.
Countrywide Credit Industries, Inc.
Eaton Vance Corp.
* Fannie Mae
Federated Investors Inc.
* Freddie Mac
Heller Financial, Inc.
* Household International Inc.
iStar Financial Inc.
Metris Companies, Inc.
Morgan Stanley, Dean Witter & Co.
Providian Financial Corp.
Stewart Information Services
USA Education, Inc.

FLOOR COVERINGS
* Armstrong Holdings, Inc.
Mohawk Industries, Inc.

FOOD–GRAIN & AGRICULTURE
Archer Daniels Midland Company
* ConAgra Foods, Inc.
* International Multifoods Corp.
Pioneer Hi-Bred International, Inc.

FOOD PROCESSING
* Campbell Soup Company
* Chiquita Brands Int'l., Inc.
* Dean Foods Company
Dole Food Company Inc.
Earthgrains Company
Flowers Foods, Incorporated
* General Mills, Inc.
* Heinz (H.J.) Company
Hormel Foods Corporation
IBP, Inc.
Interstate Bakeries Corp.
* Kellogg Company
Krispy Kreme Doughnuts, Inc.
McCormick & Company, Inc.
* Quaker Oats Company
* Ralston Purina Group
* Sara Lee Corporation
Sensient Technologies Corp.
* The Smucker (J.M.) Co.
Tyson Foods, Inc.

FOOD SERVICES
Sodexho Marriott Services, Inc.

FOOD WHOLESALERS
* Fleming Companies, Inc.
* SUPERVALU
* Sysco Corp.
Suiza Foods Corp.

FOREST PRODUCTS
* Georgia-Pacific Group
* Louisiana-Pacific Corporation
* Mead Corporation
Plum Creek Timber Company
Pope & Talbot, Inc.
* Potlatch Corporation
* Weyerhaeuser Company
Willamette Industries, Inc.

FREIGHT TRANSPORTATION
Airborne Freight Corp.
* CNF Inc.
FedEx Corporation
Overseas Shipholding Group, Inc.
Pittston Company (The)
United Parcel Service, Inc.

FURNITURE & FIXTURES
Furniture Brands International
HON Industries Inc.
La-Z-Boy Chair Co.
Leggett & Platt, Inc.
Simpson Manufacturing
Thomas Industries, Inc.

GAMING
Aztar Corporation
Harrah's Entertainment, Inc.
International Game Technology
Mandalay Resorts Group
MGM Grand, Inc.
Park Place Entertainment Corporation
Pinnacle Entertainment, Inc.

GROCERY CHAINS
* Albertson's, Inc.
Great Atlantic & Pacific Tea Company, Inc.
* The Kroger Company
Ruddick Corp.
Safeway Inc.
* Weis Markets, Inc.
* Winn-Dixie Stores, Inc.

HARDWARE & TOOLS
* Black & Decker Corporation
MSC Industrial Direct Co., Inc.
* Newell Rubbermaid Inc.
Snap-on Inc.
* The Stanley Works

HEALTHCARE MANAGEMENT & SERVICES
Caremark RX, Inc.
Health Net, Inc.
* Humana Inc.
Laboratory Corp. of America Holdings
Mid Atlantic Medical Services
* Omnicare, Inc.
Trigon Healthcare, Inc.
UnitedHealth Group, Inc.
VISX, Inc.
WellPoint Health Networks, Inc.

HOMEBUILDING
Centex Corporation
Clayton Homes, Inc.
Horton (D.R.), Inc.
KB Home, Inc.
Lennar Corporation
Pulte Corporation
The Ryland Group, Inc.
Toll Brothers, Inc.

HOSPITALS & NURSING HOMES
Beverly Enterprises, Inc.
HCA The Healthcare Company
HCR Manor Care, Inc.
Health Management Associates, Inc.
HealthSouth Corporation
* Tenet Healthcare Corp.
Universal Health Services, Inc.

HOUSEHOLD APPLIANCES & UTENSILS
Applica Inc.
* Fedders Corp.
* Maytag Corporation
National Presto Industries, Inc.
* Oneida Ltd.
* Whirlpool Corporation
York International Corporation

INSURANCE–BROKERAGE
Brown & Brown, Inc.
* Marsh & McLennan Cos. Inc.
MBIA, Inc.

INSURANCE–COMBINED
* Aetna Inc.
Allmerica Financial Corporation
* American General Corp.
American International Group, Inc.
* Aon Corporation
Berkley (W.R.) Corp.
* CIGNA Corp.
Crawford & Co.
Gallagher (Arthur J.) & Co.
The Hartford Financial Services Group
* Jefferson-Pilot Corp.
Liberty Financial Cos., Inc.
* Lincoln National Corporation
* Old Republic International Corp.
St. Paul Companies, Inc.
21st Century Insurance Group
Unitrin, Inc.
Zenith National Insurance Corp.

INSURANCE–LIFE
* AFLAC Inc.
Conseco, Inc.
John Hancock Financial Services, Inc.
Liberty Corporation
MetLife Inc.
MONY Group, Inc. (The)
Nationwide Financial Services, Inc.
Protective Life Corp.
Torchmark Corp.
* UNUM Corporation

INSURANCE–MORTGAGE
PMI Group Inc.
Radian Group Inc.

INSURANCE–PROPERTY & CASUALTY
* Allstate Corp.
American Financial Group, Inc.
* The Chubb Corporation
CNA Financial Corp.
* Fidelity National Financial, Inc.
First American Corporation
Fremont General Corp.
MGIC Investment Corp.
The Progressive Corporation
Reinsurance Group of America, Inc.
Transatlantic Holdings, Inc.

INSURANCE–TITLE
LandAmerica Financial Group Inc.

JEWELRY
Movado Group, Inc.

MACHINERY & EQUIPMENT
Actuant Corporation
American Standard Companies, Inc.
Bairnco Corp.
* Briggs & Stratton Corporation
* Caterpillar Inc.
* Cooper Industries, Inc.
Crane Co.
Dover Corp.
Graco Inc.
IDEX Corporation
* Ingersoll-Rand Company
The Manitowoc Company
Mestek Inc.
NACCO Industries Inc.
Parker-Hannifin Corp.
* Pentair, Inc.
Thermo Electron Corp.
* The Toro Co.
Unova, Inc.

MAINTENANCE & SECURITY SERVICES
ABM Industries Inc.
Pittston Brinks Group
Wackenhut Corporation

MEASURING & CONTROL INSTRUMENTS
Applied Biosystems Group
Esterline Technologies Corporation
Fisher Scientific International, Inc.
* Millipore Corporation
PerkinElmer, Inc.
Starrett (L.S.) Company (The)
Steris Corp.

Tektronix, Inc.
* Teleflex Inc.
Teradyne, Inc.
Waters Corp.
Watts Industries, Inc.

MEDICAL & DENTAL EQUIPMENT & SUPPLIES

Acuson Corporation
AmeriSource Health Corp.
Apogent Technologies, Inc.
* Bard (C.R.), Inc.
* Baxter International Inc.
Beckman Coulter
* Becton, Dickinson & Company
Boston Scientific Corp.
Cooper Companies, Inc.
Diagnostic Products Corp.
Guidant Corporation
* Johnson & Johnson
Medtronic, Incorporated
Resmed Inc.
St. Jude Medical, Inc.
Stryker Corp.

METAL PRODUCTS

Amcast Industrial Corporation
Ampco-Pittsburgh Corporation
Commercial Metals Co.
* Harsco Corporation
Illinois Tool & Works, Inc.
* Kennametal, Inc.
Metals USA, Inc.
Precision Castparts Corp.
* SPS Technologies Inc.
Trinity Industries, Inc.

MINING & PROCESSING

* Alcan Aluminium Ltd.
* Aluminum Co. of America
AMCOL International
* Barrick Gold Corp.
* Brush Engineered Materials, Inc.
* Cleveland-Cliffs Inc.
Freeport-McMoRan Copper & Gold Inc.
* Homestake Mining Co.
IMCO Recycling Inc.
Inco Limited
Kaiser Aluminum Corp.
Minerals Technologies, Inc.
* Newmont Mining Corp.
Placer Dome Inc.

MOBILE HOMES

Champion Enterprises, Inc.
Coachman Industries, Inc.
Fleetwood Enterprises, Inc.
Monaco Coach Corp.
Skyline Corporation
Thor Industries, Inc.
Winnebago Industries, Inc.

MOTEL & HOTELS

Hilton Hotels Corporation
Host Marriott Corporation
Marriott International, Inc.
Starwood Hotels & Resorts
Wyndham International, Inc.

NATURAL GAS

Burlington Resources Inc.
Cabot Oil & Gas Corporation
Dynegy Inc.
El Paso Corp.
* Enron Corp.
EOTT Energy Partners, L.P.
KeySpan Corp.
Kinder Morgan, Inc.
* National Fuel Gas Company
* ONEOK Inc.
* Peoples Energy Corporation
Plains All American Pipeline, L.P.
Questar Corp.
* Southwestern Energy Company
* UGI Corp.
Valero Energy Corporation
* Westcoast Energy Inc.
Western Gas Resources, Inc.
The Williams Companies, Inc.

NATURAL GAS-DISTRIBUTORS

AGL Resources
ENERGEN Corp.
* Equitable Resources, Inc.
* Laclede Gas Company
* NICOR, Inc.
* Piedmont Natural Gas Company
* South Jersey Industries, Inc.
* WGL Holdings, Inc.

NEWSPAPERS

* Dow Jones & Company, Inc.
* Gannett Company, Inc.
Knight-Ridder Inc.
Lee Enterprises, Inc.
McClatchy Company
Scripps (E.W.) Company (The)
* Tribune Company
The Washington Post Company

OFFICE EQUIPMENT & SUPPLIES

Boise Cascade Office Products Corp.
Brady Corporation
* Diebold, Inc.
Ennis Business Forms, Inc.
Hunt Corporation
Lexmark International Group, Inc.
* Moore Corporation Ltd.
* Nashua Corporation
Office Depot, Inc.
OfficeMax, Inc.
* Pitney Bowes, Inc.
The Reynolds and Reynolds Company
Steelcase Inc.
Wallace Computer Services, Inc.
* Xerox Corporation

OIL

* Amerada Hess Corp.
Anadarko Petroleum Corp.
* Apache Corp.
* Ashland, Inc.
BP Amoco, P.L.C.
* Chevron Corporation
Conoco Inc.
EOG Resources, Inc.
* Exxon Mobil Corp.
Frontier Oil Corporation
* Kerr-McGee Corporation
Mitchell Energy & Development Corp.

Murphy Oil Corporation
Newfield Exploration Co.
Noble Affiliates Inc.
* Occidental Petroleum Corp.
Ocean Energy Inc.
* Pennzoil-Quaker State Co.
* Phillips Petroleum Co.
Pioneer Natural Resources Company
Royal Dutch Petroleum Company
* Sunoco, Inc.
Tesoro Petroleum Corp.
* Texaco, Inc.
Tosco Corp.
Ultramar Diamond Shamrock Corporation
* Unocal Corp.
* USX-Marathon Group

OIL SERVICES & EQUIPMENT
Atwood Oceanics, Inc.
Baker Hughes Inc.
BJ Services Co.
Cooper Cameron Corp.
Diamond Offshore Drilling, Inc.
Ensco International Inc.
Global Marine Inc.
Halliburton Company
Hanover Compressor Co.
Helmerich & Payne, Inc.
Marine Drilling Cos. Inc.
Maverick Tube Corp.
* McDermott International, Inc.
National-Oilwell Inc.
Noble Drilling Corporation
Pride International Inc.
Rowan Cos. Inc.
Schlumberger, Ltd.
Smith International, Inc.
Tidewater Inc.
Transocean Sedco Forex
Varco International Inc.
Weatherford International, Inc.

PAINTS & RELATED PRODUCTS
RPM Inc.
* Sherwin-Williams Company
The Valspar Corporation

PAPER
* Albany International Corp.
* Bemis Company Inc.
* Bowater, Inc.
* Chesapeake Corporation
Glatfelter (P.H.) Co.
* International Paper Co.
* Kimberly-Clark Corp.
Longview Fibre Company
Pactiv Corporation
Sonoco Products Company
* Temple-Inland Inc.
* Westvaco Corp.

PHOTO & OPTICAL
* Bausch & Lomb, Incorporated
CPI Corp.
* Eastman Kodak Company
* Polaroid Corporation

PLASTICS & PLASTIC PRODUCTS
Lamson & Sessions Co.
* Myers Industries Inc.
Sealed Air Corp.
PolyOne Corporation
Tupperware Corp.
West Co., Inc. (The)

POLLUTION CONTROL
* Donaldson Company, Inc.
Osmonics Incorporated
* Pall Corporation
Republic Services, Inc.
Waste Management, Inc.
Wellman, Inc.

PRINTING & ENGRAVING
* Banta Corporation
Consolidated Graphics, Inc.
Deluxe Corp.
* Donnelley (R.R.) & Sons Co., Inc.
The Harland (John H.) Co.

PUBLISHING
American Greetings Corp.
* Harcourt General, Inc.
Harte-Hanks, Inc.
* Houghton Mifflin Company
* McGraw-Hill Companies, Inc.
Meredith Corporation
Playboy Enterprises, Inc.
Primedia Inc.
Pulitzer Publishing Co.
The Reader's Digest Association, Inc.
Wiley (John) & Sons, Inc.

RAILROAD EQUIPMENT
* GATX Corp.

RAILROADS
Burlington Northern Santa Fe Corp.
* Canadian Pacific Ltd.
* CSX Corporation
Florida East Coast Industries, Inc.
Kansas City Southern Industries, Inc.
* Norfolk Southern Corporation
* Union Pacific Corp.

REAL ESTATE
AMB Property Corp.
Newhall Land and Farming Co.
* The Rouse Company
St. Joe Company
Webb (Del) Corporation

REAL ESTATE INVESTMENT TRUSTS
Apartment Investment and Management Co.
* Archstone Communities Trust
AvalonBay Communities Inc.
* Boston Properties Inc.
CarrAmerica Realty Corp.
Crescent Real Estate Equity Co.
* Duke-Weeks Realty Corp.
Dynex Capital, Inc.
* Equity Office Properties Trust
* Equity Residential Properties Trust
General Growth Properties, Inc.
* IndyMac Mortgage Holdings
* Liberty Property Trust
* Mack-Cali Realty Corp.
Post Properties Inc.
* Prologis Trust
Public Storage Inc.
Simon Property Group, Inc.
* Spieker Properties Inc.

* Thornburg Mortgage, Inc.
Vornado Realty Trust

RECREATION
* Brunswick Corporation
Callaway Golf Company
Carnival Corporation
* Cedar Fair, L.P.
Disney (Walt) Company
* Huffy Corp.
K2 Inc.
Six Flags Inc.

RESTAURANTS
Brinker International, Inc.
CKE Restaurants, Inc.
Darden Restaurants, Inc.
IHOP Corp.
Luby's Inc.
* McDonald's Corporation
Outback Steakhouse, Inc.
Ruby Tuesday, Inc.
TRICON Global Restaurants, Inc.
* Wendy's International, Inc.

RETAIL–DEPARTMENT STORES
* Dillard's, Inc.
Federated Department Stores, Inc.
Kohl's Corp.
May Department Stores Co.
* Penney (J.C.) Co., Inc.
Saks Incorporated
* Sears, Roebuck and Co.

RETAIL–DISCOUNT & VARIETY STORES
Big Lots Inc.
Dollar General Corp.
Family Dollar Stores, Inc.
K Mart Corp.
Payless ShoeSource Inc.
Shopko Stores, Inc.
* Target Corporation
* Venator Group, Inc.
Wal-Mart Stores, Inc.

RETAIL–DRUG STORES
Longs Drug Stores Corp.
* Rite Aid Corporation
* Walgreen Co.
CVS Corp.

RETAIL–SPECIALTY STORES
AnnTaylor Stores Corp.
Autonation, Inc.
Autozone, Inc.
Barnes & Noble, Inc.
Best Buy Co., Inc.
BJ's Wholesale Club, Inc.
Blockbuster, Inc.
Borders Group, Inc.
Circuit City Stores, Inc.
Claire's Stores, Inc.
The Gap, Inc.
Hancock Fabrics, Inc.
The Home Depot, Inc.
Jo-Ann Stores, Inc.
The Limited Inc.
* Lowe's Companies, Inc.
Neiman-Marcus Group, Inc.
Nordstrom, Inc.
* The Pep Boys–Manny, Moe & Jack
Pier 1 Imports, Inc.
* RadioShack Corporation
Sonic Automotive, Inc.
Talbots (The), Inc.
Tiffany & Co.
The TJX Companies, Inc.
Toys "R" Us
United Auto Group Inc.
Williams-Sonoma Inc.

SAVINGS & LOAN
Dime Bancorp
Golden West Financial Corp.
GreenPoint Financial Corp.
Washington Mutual, Inc.

SECURITIES BROKERAGE
The Bear Stearns Companies Inc.
E*TRADE Group, Inc.
Edwards (A.G.), Inc.
Franklin Resources, Inc.
Goldman Sachs Group, Inc. (The)
Legg Mason, Inc.
Lehman Brothers Holdings Inc.
* Merrill Lynch & Co., Inc.
Neuberger Berman Inc.
Raymond James Financial, Inc.
* Schwab (Charles) Corp. (The)
Stilwell Financial, Inc.
TD Waterhouse Group, Inc.
Waddell & Reed Financial, Inc.

SERVICES
Administaff, Inc.
Block (H&R), Inc.
Catalina Marketing Corp.
CDI Corp.
Cendant Corp.
ChoicePoint Inc.
Comdisco Inc.
DeVry, Inc.
DST Systems Inc.
The Dun & Bradstreet Corporation
* Equifax, Inc.
Hillenbrand Industries, Inc.
IMS Health, Inc.
Iron Mountain Inc.
Jenny Craig, Inc.
Labor Ready, Inc.
Manpower Inc.
Modis Professional Services, Inc.
Moody's Corporation
* National Service Industries, Inc.
Quanta Services, Inc.
Quest Diagnostics Inc.
Robert Half International Inc.
* Rollins, Inc.
Sabre Holding Corporation
Service Corp. International
* ServiceMaster Limited Partnership
Spherion Corporation

SHOE MANUFACTURING

* Brown Group, Inc.
Genesco, Inc.
Nike, Inc.
Reebok International Ltd.
* Stride Rite Corporation
Wolverine World Wide Corporation

SOAPS & CLEANERS

Church & Dwight Co., Inc.
* Clorox Co.
* Colgate-Palmolive Co.
* Ecolab, Inc.
* Procter & Gamble Co.
Unilever N.V.

SOFT DRINKS

* The Coca-Cola Company
Coca-Cola Enterprises, Inc.
Pepsi Bottling Group, Inc.
PepsiAmericas Inc.
* PepsiCo Inc.

STEEL

AK Steel Holding Corporation
Allegheny Technologies Inc.
* Bethlehem Steel Corp.
Birmingham Steel Corporation
* Carpenter Technology Corp.
* Nucor Corporation
Oregon Steel Mills, Inc.
* Quanex Corporation
Reliance Steel & Aluminum Co.
* Ryerson Tull, Inc.
USX U.S. Steel Group
Worthington Industries, Inc.

TELECOMMUNICATIONS

* ALLTEL Corp.
* AT&T Corporation
* BellSouth Corp.
BroadWing, Inc.
CenturyTel, Inc.
* Citizens Communications Company
Qwest Communications International, Inc.
* SBC Communications
* Sprint Corporation FON Group
* Verizon Communications

TELECOMMUNICATIONS-EQUIPMENT

American Tower Corporation
* Corning Inc.
General Cable Corp.
Lucent Technologies
* NorTel Networks Corp.
Superior Telecom, Inc.
Williams Communications Group

TELEVISION & RADIO BROADCASTING

Belo (A.H.) Corporation
Chris-Craft Industries, Inc.
Clear Channel Communications, Inc.
Cox Communications, Inc.
Cox Radio Inc.
Entercom Communications Corp.
Hearst-Argyle Television, Inc.
Hispanic Broadcasting Corp.
Univision Communications, Inc.
Viacom Inc.

TEXTILES

Cone Mills Corporation
Guilford Mills, Inc.
Polymer Group, Inc.
Springs Industries, Inc.
Unifi, Inc.
Westpoint Stevens, Inc.

TIRES & RUBBER GOODS

* Bandag Incorporated
* Carlisle Companies Incorporated
Cooper Tire & Rubber Co.
Danaher Corporation
* Goodyear Tire & Rubber Co.

TOBACCO

Dimon Incorporated
* Philip Morris Companies
R.J. Reynolds Tobacco Holdings, Inc.
* Standard Commercial Corp.
* Universal Corporation
* UST Inc.

WATER

* American Water Works Company
California Water Service Co.

WHOLESALERS–DISTRIBUTORS–JOBBERS

Bergen Brunswig Corp.
Grainger (W.W.), Inc.
* Handleman Company
Hughes Supply, Inc.
* McKesson HBOC, Inc.
Owens & Minor, Inc.
SunSource Inc.
Wesco International, Inc.

* Designates companies offering dividend reinvestment plans.

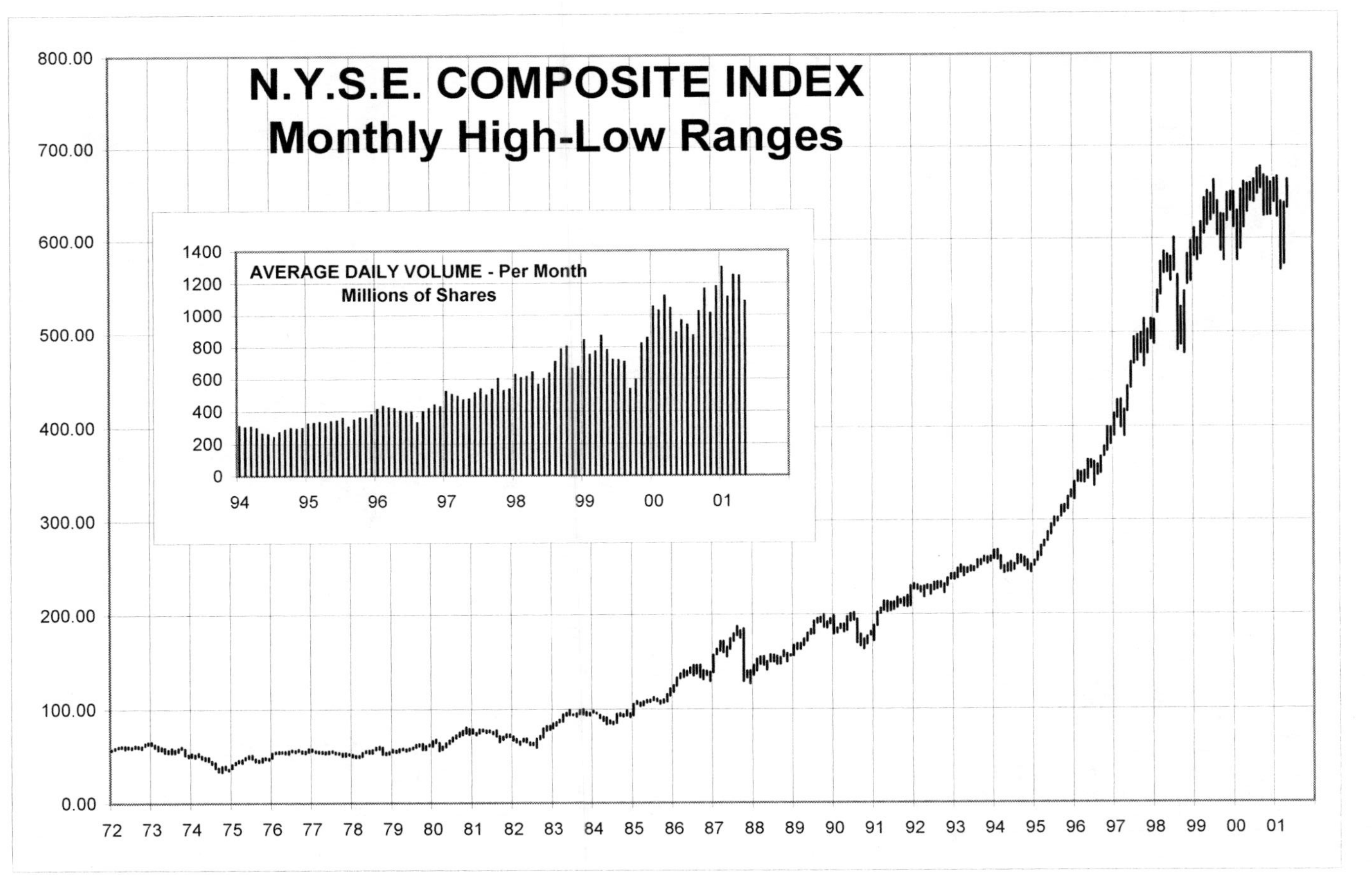
N.Y.S.E. COMPOSITE INDEX
Monthly High-Low Ranges
800.00
700.00
600.00
500.00
400.00
300.00
200.00
100.00
0.00
72 73 74 75 76 77 78 79 80 81 82 83 84 85 86 87 88 89 90 91 92 93 94 95 96 97 98 99 00 01
AVERAGE DAILY VOLUME - Per Month
Millions of Shares
1400
1200
1000
800
600
400
200
0
94 95 96 97 98 99 00 01

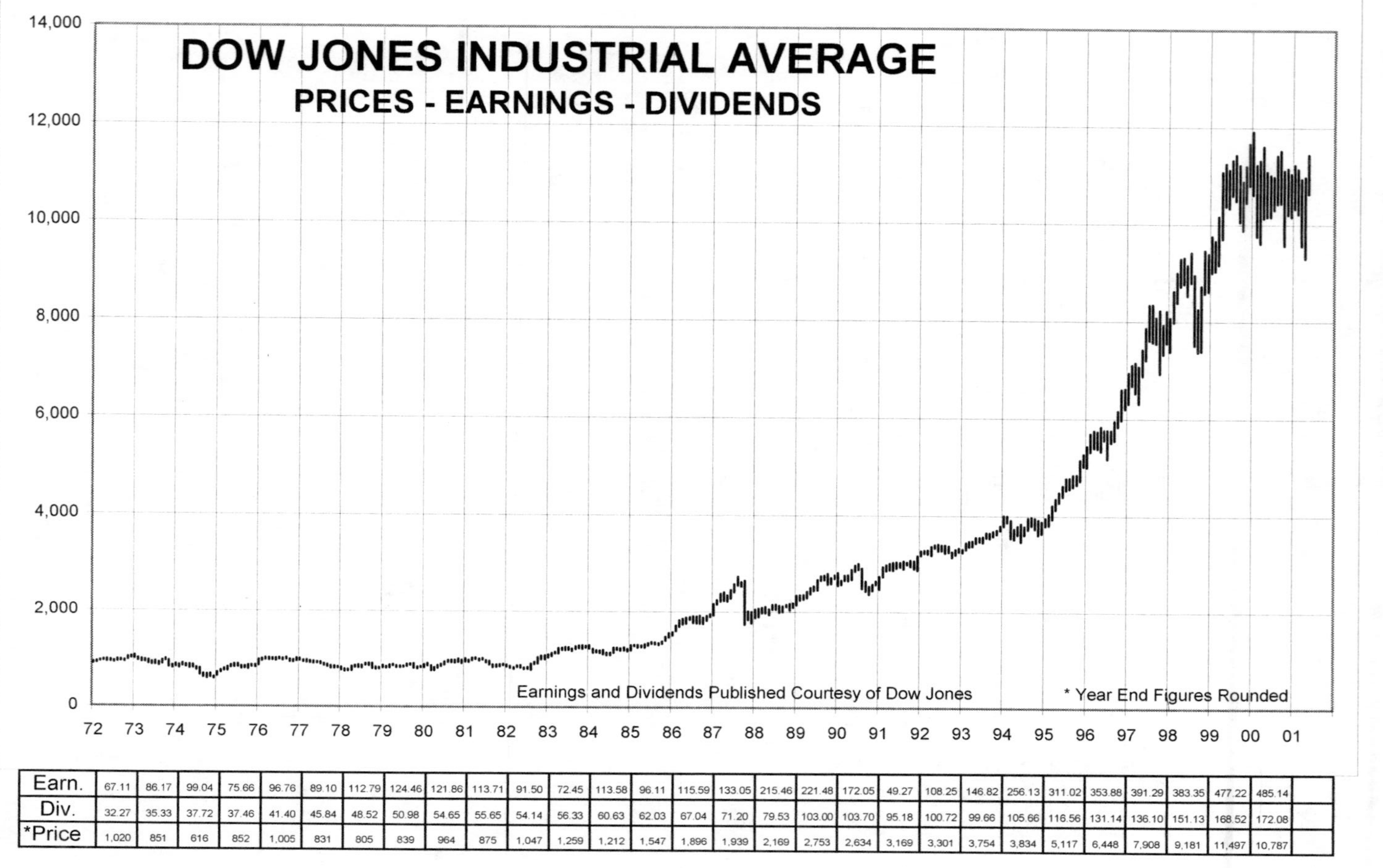

Earn.	67.11	86.17	99.04	75.66	96.76	89.10	112.79	124.46	121.86	113.71	91.50	72.45	113.58	96.11	115.59	133.05	215.46	221.48	172.05	49.27	108.25	146.82	256.13	311.02	353.88	391.29	383.35	477.22	485.14	
Div.	32.27	35.33	37.72	37.46	41.40	45.84	48.52	50.98	54.65	55.65	54.14	56.33	60.63	62.03	67.04	71.20	79.53	103.00	103.70	95.18	100.72	99.66	105.66	116.56	131.14	136.10	151.13	168.52	172.08	
*Price	1,020	851	616	852	1,005	831	805	839	964	875	1,047	1,259	1,212	1,547	1,896	1,939	2,169	2,753	2,634	3,169	3,301	3,754	3,834	5,117	6,448	7,908	9,181	11,497	10,787	

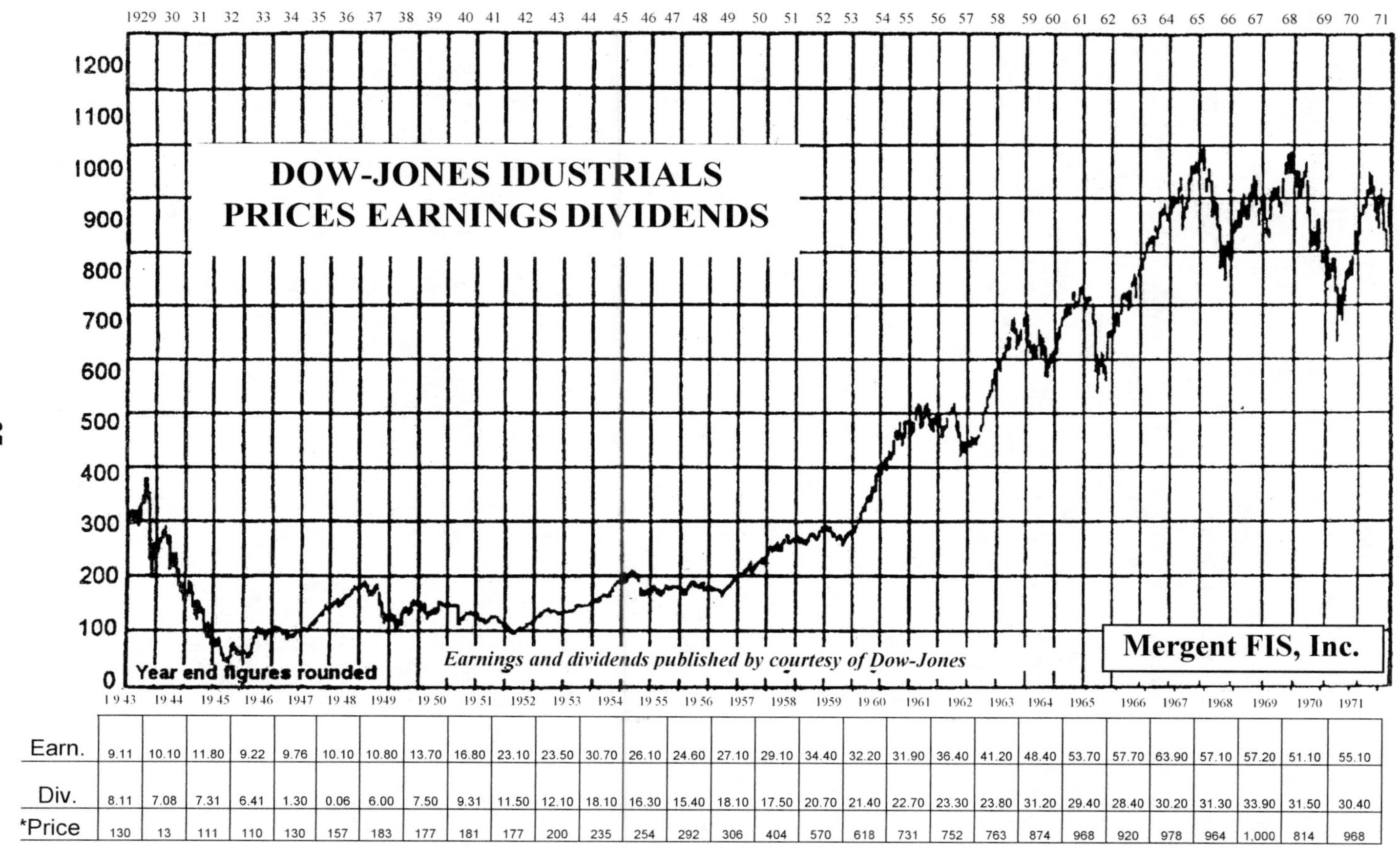

	1943	1944	1945	1946	1947	1948	1949	1950	1951	1952	1953	1954	1955	1956	1957	1958	1959	1960	1961	1962	1963	1964	1965	1966	1967	1968	1969	1970	1971
Earn.	9.11	10.10	11.80	9.22	9.76	10.10	10.80	13.70	16.80	23.10	23.50	30.70	26.10	24.60	27.10	29.10	34.40	32.20	31.90	36.40	41.20	48.40	53.70	57.70	63.90	57.10	57.20	51.10	55.10
Div.	8.11	7.08	7.31	6.41	1.30	0.06	6.00	7.50	9.31	11.50	12.10	18.10	16.30	15.40	18.10	17.50	20.70	21.40	22.70	23.30	23.80	31.20	29.40	28.40	30.20	31.30	33.90	31.50	30.40
*Price	130	13	111	110	130	157	183	177	181	177	200	235	254	292	306	404	570	618	731	752	763	874	968	920	978	964	1,000	814	968

HOW TO USE THIS BOOK

The presentation of background information plus current and historical data provides the answers to three basic questions for each company:

1. What does the company do?
   (See G.)
2. How has it done in the past?
   (See B, D, E, I, J.)
3. How is it doing now?
   (See D, E, F, H.)

The following information is highlighted:

A. CAPSULE STOCK INFORMATION – This section shows the stock symbol, plus the approximate yield afforded by the indicated dividend, based on a recent price, and the price earnings ratio calculated on earnings from the most recent four quarters.

B. LONG-TERM PRICE CHART – This chart illustrates the pattern of monthly stock price movements, fully adjusted for stock dividends and splits. The chart points out the degree of volatility in the price movement of the company's stock and reveals its long-term trend. It indicates areas of price support and resistance, plus other technical points to be considered by the investor. The bars at the base of the long-term price chart indicate the monthly trading volume.

C. PRICE SCORES – Below each company's price/volume chart are its ***Mergent's Price Scores***. These are basic measures of the stock's performance. Each stock is measured against the New York Stock Exchange Composite Index.

A score of 100 indicates that the stock did as well as the New York Stock Exchange Composite Index during the time period. A score of less than 100 means that the stock did not do as well; a score of more than 100 means that the stock outperformed the NYSE Composite Index. All stock prices are adjusted for splits and stock dividends. The time periods measured for each company conclude with the date of the recent price shown in the top-left corner of each company's profile.

The ***7 YEAR PRICE SCORE*** mirrors the common stock's price growth over the previous seven years. The higher the price score, the better the relative performance. It is based on the ratio of the latest 12-month average price to the current seven year average. This ratio is then indexed against the same ratio for the market as a whole (the New York Stock Exchange Composite Index), which is taken as 100.

The ***12 MONTH PRICE SCORE*** is a similar measurement but for a shorter period of time. It is based on the ratio of the latest two-month average price to the current 12-month average. As was done for the Long-Term Price Score, this ratio is also indexed to the same ratio for the market as a whole.

D. INTERIM EARNINGS (Per Share) – Figures are reported before effect of extraordinary items, discontinued operations and cumulative effects of accounting changes (unless otherwise noted). Each figure is for the quarterly period indicated, unless otherwise noted. These figures are essentially as reported by the company, although all figures are adjusted for all stock dividends and splits. See 'Earnings Per Share' below.

E. INTERIM DIVIDENDS (Per Share) – The cash dividends are the actual dollar amounts declared by the company. No adjustments have been made for stock dividends and splits. **Ex-Dividend Date**: a stockholder must purchase the stock prior to this date in order to be entitled to the dividend. The **Record Date** indicates the date on which the shareholder had to have been a holder of record in order to have qualified for the dividend. The **Payable Date** indicates the date the company paid or intends to pay the dividend. The cash amount shown in the first column is followed by a letter (example "Q" for quarterly) to indicate the frequency of the dividend.

Indicated Dividend – This is the annualized amount (fully adjusted for splits) of the latest regular cash dividend.

NYSE SYMBOL ILU
Rec. Pr. 46.50 (4/30/01) **A**

ILLUSTRATIVE INC.

YIELD	0.5%
P/E RATIO	29.4

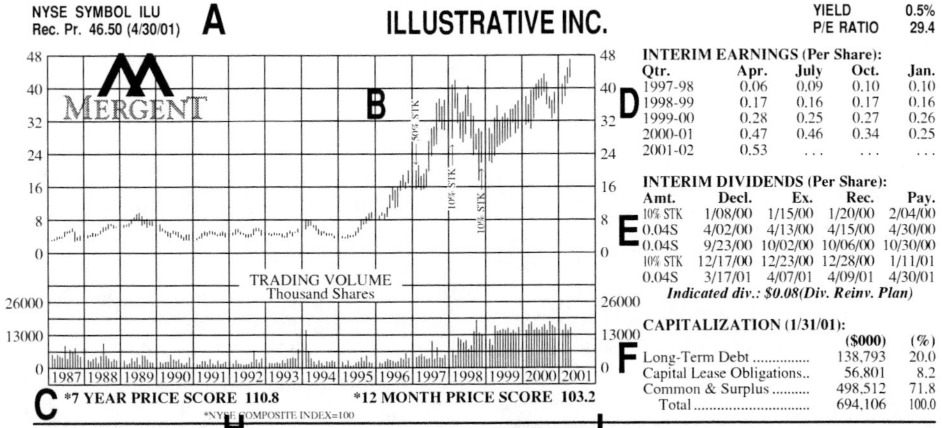

C *7 YEAR PRICE SCORE 110.8 *12 MONTH PRICE SCORE 103.2

*NYSE COMPOSITE INDEX=100

D **INTERIM EARNINGS (Per Share):**

Qtr.	Apr.	July	Oct.	Jan.
1997-98	0.06	0.09	0.10	0.10
1998-99	0.17	0.16	0.17	0.16
1999-00	0.28	0.25	0.27	0.26
2000-01	0.47	0.46	0.34	0.25
2001-02	0.53	...	...	...

E **INTERIM DIVIDENDS (Per Share):**

Amt.	Decl.	Ex.	Rec.	Pay.
10% STK	1/08/00	1/15/00	1/20/00	2/04/00
0.04S	4/02/00	4/13/00	4/15/00	4/30/00
0.04S	9/23/00	10/02/00	10/06/00	10/30/00
10% STK	12/17/00	12/23/00	12/28/00	1/11/01
0.04S	3/17/01	4/07/01	4/09/01	4/30/01

Indicated div.: $0.08(Div. Reinv. Plan)

F **CAPITALIZATION (1/31/01):**

	($000)	(%)
Long-Term Debt	138,793	20.0
Capital Lease Obligations..	56,801	8.2
Common & Surplus	498,512	71.8
Total	694,106	100.0

RECENT DEVELOPMENTS: H For the year ended 1/31/01, net income before an extraordinary gain improved to $46.8 million compared with net income of $22.3 million the year before. Total revenues increased to $1.15 billion from $614.1 million the year before. Increased revenues are contributing to improving margins at Bill's Burgers, Salads a Go Go, and Pizza Galore chains. Revenues from Company-owned restaurants climbed to $867.0 million from $712.8 billion.

PROSPECTS: I Growing revenues per restaurant across all the Company's chains bode well for future results. The Company is planning to open an additional 60 Bill's Burgers restaurants in 2001, and another 90 in 2002. Meanwhile, 80 Pizza Galore and 40 Salad a Go Go restaurants are planned to open in the Midwest in the second half of 2001. The Company is predicting earnings per share of $1.10 to $1.20 for the current fiscal year.

G BUSINESS

ILLUSTRATIVE INC., through its subsidiaries and franchisees, owns and/or operates 1,576 Bill's Burgers restaurants, featuring the Company's patented vegetarian Bill Burgers. The restaurants are located in all 50 states. In addition, the Company owns 582 Salad a Go Go restaurants and take-out facilities in 14 eastern and south-eastern states. The Company also owns and operates 312 Pizza Galore restaurants and 12 Seafood Symphony restaurants in North and South Carolina.

REVENUES

(01/31/01)	($000)	(%)
Co.-operated restaurants.............	1,022,453	88.9
Franchised & licensed.................	127,206	11.1
Total	1,149,659	100.0

J ANNUAL FINANCIAL DATA

	1/31/01	1/31/00	1/31/99	1/31/98	1/31/97	1/25/96	1/27/95
Earnings Per Share	**0.88**	**0.60**	**0.32**	**0.04**	**0.13**	**d0.09**	**0.40**
Cash Flow Per Share	**1.76**	**1.34**	**0.95**	**0.71**	**0.81**	**0.68**	**1.20**
Tang. Book Val. Per Share	**8.86**	**5.34**	**3.01**	**2.67**	**2.72**	**2.58**	**2.76**
Dividends Per Share	**0.07**	**0.06**	**0.05**	**0.04**	**0.03**	**0.02**	**0.01**
Dividend Payout %	**7.5**	**7.3**	**13.6**	**56.2**	**23.1**	**N.M.**	**2.5**
INCOME STATEMENT (IN MILLIONS):							
Total Revenues	1,149.7	614.1	465.4	443.7	460.4	502.6	533.6
Costs & Expenses	1,017.1	545.0	418.3	412.4	427.0	484.7	487.0
Depreciation & Amort.	46.4	27.1	21.4	22.8	22.8	25.2	26.6
Operating Income	86.2	42.0	25.7	8.6	10.5	d7.3	20.0
Net Interest Inc./(Exp.)	d16.9	d9.9	d10.0	d9.2	d10.4	d13.6	d16.7
Income Before Income Taxes	76.6	36.7	18.0	2.4	6.3	d7.3	18.9
Income Taxes	29.9	14.4	7.0	1.1	1.8	cr4.2	5.8
Net Income	46.8	22.3	11.0	1.3	4.4	d3.1	13.0
Cash Flow	93.2	49.4	32.3	24.0	27.3	22.1	39.6
Average Shs. Outstg. (000)	52,934	36,801	33,902	33,971	33,699	32,732	33,018
BALANCE SHEET (IN MILLIONS):							
Cash & Cash Equivalents	30.4	39.8	25.9	18.2	26.1	44.4	36.7
Total Current Assets	92.2	72.9	56.8	56.8	69.4	90.6	83.8
Net Property	674.6	242.9	155.7	163.8	146.8	150.6	175.0
Total Assets	957.4	401.2	246.8	244.3	242.1	268.9	292.6
Total Current Liabilities	176.5	83.9	61.3	71.6	66.6	91.4	92.3
Long-Term Obligations	195.6	81.9	70.6	69.9	63.3	80.3	102.1
Net Stockholders' Equity	498.5	214.8	101.2	88.5	92.1	84.7	89.7
Net Working Capital	d84.3	d11.0	d4.5	d14.7	2.9	d0.9	d8.5
Year-end Shs. Outstg. (000)	56,293	40,195	33,632	33,133	33,899	32,835	32,521
STATISTICAL RECORD: K							
Operating Profit Margin %	7.5	6.8	5.5	1.9	2.3	...	3.8
Net Profit Margin %	4.1	3.6	2.4	0.3	1.0	...	2.4
Return on Equity %	9.4	10.4	10.8	1.4	4.8	...	14.5
Return on Assets %	4.9	5.6	4.4	0.5	1.8	...	4.5
Debt/Total Assets %	20.4	20.4	28.6	28.6	26.1	29.8	34.9
Price Range	37 1/2-15 3/16	19-7	9 15/16-3 1/2	7 15/16-3 9/16	5 7/8-3 3/4	6 1/8-3 3/4	5 7/16-3 1/8
P/E Ratio	42.4-17.2	33.1-13.2	30.5-10.8	202.1-91.4	44.4-28.2	...	13.7-7.8
Average Yield %	0.3	0.3	0.7	0.4	...	...	...

Statistics are as originally reported. Adj. for stk. splits: 10% div., 1/99, 2/98; 3-for-2, 1/97

OFFICERS:
C. B. Dickens II, Chmn., C.E.O.
D. D. Alexander, President, C.O.O.
P. Patrick, Treas. & C.F.O.
B. I. Gussbus, Secretary
PRINCIPAL OFFICE: 800 N. Primrose Lane, Charlotte, NC 28200

TELEPHONE NUMBER: (704) 555-5796
FAX: (704) 555-3630
NO. OF EMPLOYEES: 46,500 (approx.)
SHAREHOLDERS: **L** 3,800 (approx.)
ANNUAL MEETING: In Jun.
INCORPORATED: NC, Dec., 1951

INSTITUTIONAL HOLDINGS:
No. of Institutions: 133
Shares Held: 44,571,077 (Adj.)
% Held: 78.2
INDUSTRY: Eating places (SIC: 5812)
TRANSFER AGENT(S): Wachovia Bank of N.C., Winston-Salem, NC

I

F. CAPITALIZATION – These are certain items in the company's capital account. Both the dollar amounts and their respective percentages are given.

Long-term Debt is the total amount of debt owed by the company which is due beyond one year.

Capital Lease Obligations is shown as a separate caption when indicated on the balance sheet as such.

Deferred Income Taxes represents the company's tax liability arising from accelerated depreciation and investment tax credit.

Preferred Stock is the sum of equity issues, exclusive of common stock, the holders of which have a prior claim, ahead of the common shareholders, to the income of the company while it continues to operate and to the assets in the event of dissolution.

Minority Interest in this instance is a capital item which reflects the share of ownership by an outside party in a consolidated subsidiary of the company.

Common and Surplus is the sum of the stated or par value of the common stock, plus additional paid-in capital and retained earnings less the dollar amount of treasury shares.

G. COMPANY BUSINESS – This section explains what the company does: the products or services it sells, its markets and production facilities.

H. RECENT DEVELOPMENTS – This section keeps you up to date on what has happened in the most recent quarter or fiscal year for which results are available. It provides analysis of recently released sales and earnings figures, including special charges and credits, and may also include results by sector, expense trends and ratios, and other current information.

I. PROSPECTS – This section looks forward and provides information that could significantly affect future earnings, including recent acquisitions, new product introductions, divestitures, expansions into new markets, demand trends, backlog levels, and each Company's own earnings estimate for the current year, when available.

J. ANNUAL FINANCIAL DATA – These figures are fully adjusted for all stock dividends and stock splits.

Earnings Per Share are as reported by the company except for adjustment for certain items as footnoted. Earnings per share reported after 12/15/97 are presented on a diluted basis, as described by Financial Accounting Standards Board Statement 128. Earnings per share reported prior to that date are shown on a primary basis.

Cash Flow Per Share is computed by dividing the total of net income and non-cash depreciation and amortization charges, less preferred dividends, by average shares outstanding.

Tangible Book Value Per Share is calculated by dividing stockholders equity minus intangibles by shares outstanding at fiscal year end. It demonstrates the underlying value of each common share if the company were to be liquidated as of that date.

Dividends Per Share represent the sum of all cash payments on a calendar year basis. Any fiscal year ending prior to June 30, for example, is shown with dividends for the prior calendar year.

Dividend Payout % is the percentage of cash paid out of **Earnings Per Share**.

K. INCOME STATEMENT, BALANCE SHEET AND STATISTICAL RECORD – Here is pertinent earnings and balance sheet information essential to analyzing a corporation's performance. The comparisons, each year shown as originally reported, provide the necessary historical perspective to intelligently review the various operating and financial trends. Generic definitions follow.

INCOME STATEMENT:

Total Revenues is the total income from operations including non-operating revenues.

Costs and Expenses is the total of all costs related to the operation of the business – including cost of sales, selling, and general and administrative expenses. Excluded items are depreciation, interest and non-operating expenses.

Depreciation and Amortization includes all non-cash charges such as depletion and amortization as well as depreciation.

Operating Income is the profit remaining after deducting depreciation as well as all operating costs and expenses from the company's net sales and revenues. This figure is *before* interest expenses, extraordinary gains and charges, and income and expense items of a non-operating nature.

Net Interest Income/(Expense) is the net amount of interest paid and received by a company during the fiscal year.

Income Before Income Taxes is the remaining income *after* deducting all costs, expenses, property charges, interest, etc. but *before* deducting income taxes.

Equity Earnings/Minority Interest is the net amount of profits allocated to minority owners or affiliates.

Income Taxes are shown as reported by the company and include both the amount of current taxes actually paid out and the amount deferred to future years.

Net Income is as reported by the corporation, before extraordinary gains and losses, discontinued operations and accounting changes, which are appropriately footnoted.

Cash Flow is the sum of net income and non-cash depreciation and amortization charges, less preferred dividends.

Average Shares Outstanding is the weighted average number of shares including common equivalent shares outstanding during the year, as reported by the corporation and fully adjusted for all stock dividends and splits. The use of *average shares* minimizes the distortion in *earnings per share* which could result from issuance of a large amount of stock or the company's purchase of a large amount of its own stock during the year.

BALANCE SHEET:

All balance sheet items are shown as reported by the corporation in its annual report. Because of the limited amount of space available and in an effort to simplify and standardize accounts, some items have been combined.

Cash & Cash Equivalents comprise unrestricted cash and temporary investments in marketable securities, such as U.S. Government securities, certificates of deposit and short-term investments.

Total Current Assets are all of the company's short-term assets, including cash, marketable securities, inventories, certain receivables, etc., as reported.

Net Property is total fixed assets, including all property, land, plants, buildings, equipment, fixtures, etc., less accumulated depreciation.

Total Assets represent the sum of all tangible and intangible assets as reported by the company.

Total Current Liabilities are all of the obligations of the company due within one year, as reported.

Long-term Obligations are total long-term debts (due beyond one year) reported by the company, including bonds, capital lease obligations, notes, mortgages, debentures, etc.

Net Stockholders' Equity is the sum of all capital stock accounts – stated values of preferred and common stock, paid-in capital, earned surplus (retained earnings), etc., net of all treasury stock.

Net Working Capital is derived by subtracting Current Liabilities from Current Assets.

Year-end Shares Outstanding are the number of shares outstanding as of the date of the company's annual report, exclusive of treasury stock and adjusted for subsequent stock dividends and splits.

STATISTICAL RECORD:

Operating Profit Margin indicates operating profit as a percentage of net sales or revenues.

Net Profit Margin is the percentage of total revenues remaining after the deduction of all non-extraordinary costs, including interest and taxes.

Return on Equity is one of several measures of profitability. It is the ratio of net income to net stockholders' equity, expressed as a percentage. This ratio illustrates how effectively the investment of the stockholders is being utilized to earn a profit.

Return on Assets is another means of measuring profitability. It is the ratio of net income to total assets, expressed as a percentage. This indicates how effectively the corporate assets are being used to generate profits.

Debt/Total Assets represents the ratio of long-term obligations to total assets as a percentage.

Price/Earnings Ratio is shown as a range. The figures are calculated by dividing the stock's highest price for the year and its lowest price by the year's earnings per share. Prices are for calendar years. Earnings used in the calculation for a particular calendar year are for the fiscal year in which the majority of the company's business took place. As a rule, for companies whose fiscal years end before June 30, the ratio is calculated by using the price range of the prior calendar year. For those with fiscal years ending on June 30 or later, the current year's price range is used.

Average Yield is the ratio (expressed as a percentage) of the annual dividend to the mean price of the common stock (average of the high and low for the year). Both prices and dividends are for calendar years.

EDITOR'S NOTE: In order to preserve the historical relationships between prices, earnings and dividends, figures are not restated to reflect subsequent events.

L. ADDITIONAL INFORMATION – For each stock, listings are provided for the company's officers, date of incorporation, its address, telephone number, fax number and website (when available), annual meeting date, the number of employees, the number of stockholders, institutional holdings, and transfer agent.

Institutional Holdings indicates the number of investment companies, insurance companies, bank trust and college endowment funds holding the stock and the total number of shares held as last reported. Coverage includes investment companies, mutual funds, insurance companies, and banks reporting under rule 13(F) to the Securities & Exchange Commission.

ABBREVIATIONS AND SYMBOLS

d .... Deficit
E .... Extra
M .... Monthly
N.M. .... Not Meaningful
p .... Preliminary
P.F. .... Pro Forma
Q .... Quarterly
r .... Revised
S .... Semi-annual
Sp .... Special Dividend
Y .... Year-end Dividend

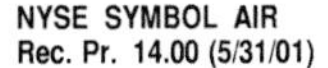

NYSE SYMBOL AIR
Rec. Pr. 14.00 (5/31/01)

AAR CORPORATION

YIELD 2.4%
P/E RATIO 24.6

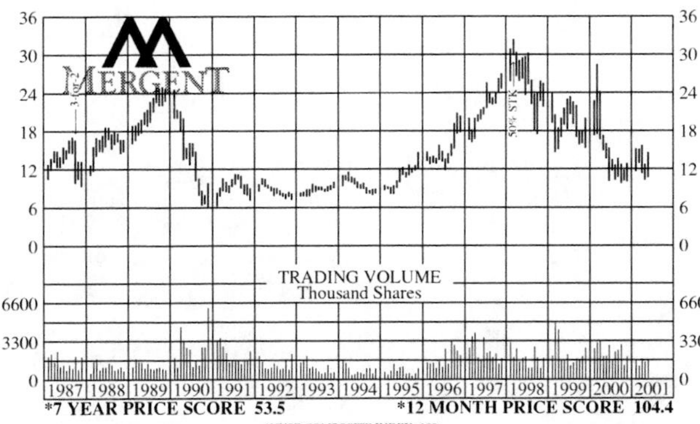

*7 YEAR PRICE SCORE 53.5 *12 MONTH PRICE SCORE 104.4

*NYSE COMPOSITE INDEX=100

INTERIM EARNINGS (Per Share):

Qtr.	Aug.	Nov.	Feb.	May
1996-97	0.20	0.21	0.24	0.26
1997-98	0.27	0.31	0.33	0.37
1998-99	0.34	0.36	0.37	0.42
1999-00	0.39	0.40	0.40	0.09
2000-01	0.12	0.16	0.20	...

INTERIM DIVIDENDS (Per Share):

Amt.	Decl.	Ex.	Rec.	Pay.
0.085Q	4/11/00	4/26/00	5/02/00	6/05/00
0.085Q	7/11/00	7/28/00	8/01/00	9/05/00
0.085Q	10/11/00	10/30/00	11/01/00	12/05/00
0.085Q	1/08/01	1/25/01	1/29/01	3/03/01
0.085Q	4/10/01	4/27/01	5/01/01	6/05/01

Indicated div.: $0.34 (Div. Reinv. Plan)

CAPITALIZATION (5/31/00):

	($000)	(%)
Long-Term Debt	180,447	31.3
Deferred Income Tax	56,020	9.7
Common & Surplus	339,515	58.9
Total	575,982	100.0

RECENT DEVELOPMENTS: For the quarter ended 2/28/01, net income totaled $5.4 million compared with $11.0 million in the prior year. Total sales slid 26.5% to $200.1 million from $272.3 million the year before. Gross profit was $35.7 million, or 17.9% of sales, versus $45.1 million, or 16.6% of sales, the year before. Operating income fell 39.7% to $12.5 million from $20.7 million the previous year.

PROSPECTS: Results are being negatively affected by difficult industry conditions including higher fuel prices, higher interest rates, and bankruptcies at certain airlines. These factors are being partially offset by continued strength in AIR's component repair and overhaul businesses. Going forward, the Company plans to increase its investment in assets supporting new generation aircraft including engines, auxiliary power units, avionics and landing gear.

BUSINESS

AAR CORPORATION provides aviation support to the worldwide aerospace/aviation industry and the United States and other governments. The Company is primarily involved in trading, manufacturing and overhaul within the aviation services business. The Aircraft and Engines Group purchases, sells and leases aircraft, engines and parts, and supplies aviation hardware. The Airframe and Accessories Group includes the maintenance of airframe and engine components, as well as certain types of aircraft overhaul and modification. The Manufacturing Group manufactures specialized aviation and industrial products with an emphasis on air cargo transport systems.

ANNUAL FINANCIAL DATA

	5/31/00	5/31/99	5/31/98	5/31/97	5/31/96	5/31/95	5/31/94
Earnings Per Share	**2 1.28**	**1.49**	**1.27**	**0.92**	**0.67**	**0.44**	**1 0.40**
Cash Flow Per Share	**1.98**	**2.10**	**1.77**	**1.41**	**1.09**	**0.87**	**0.81**
Tang. Book Val. Per Share	**11.19**	**10.44**	**9.90**	**9.65**	**8.28**	**7.85**	**7.68**
Dividends Per Share	**0.34**	**0.34**	**0.32**	**0.32**	**0.32**	**0.32**	**0.32**
Dividend Payout %	**26.6**	**22.8**	**25.2**	**34.8**	**48.0**	**72.7**	**80.0**
INCOME STATEMENT (IN MILLIONS):							
Total Revenues	3 1,024.3	918.0	782.1	589.3	505.0	451.4	407.8
Costs & Expenses	935.3	823.6	703.1	534.2	462.4	416.6	376.0
Depreciation & Amort.	18.4	17.1	14.3	12.3	10.1	10.3	9.9
Operating Income	70.7	77.4	64.7	42.9	32.4	24.4	21.8
Net Interest Inc./(Exp.)	d21.1	d17.6	d13.6	d9.9	d9.7	d9.7	d8.1
Income Before Income Taxes	49.5	59.8	51.2	33.0	22.8	14.7	13.7
Income Taxes	14.4	18.1	15.5	10.0	6.8	4.3	4.2
Net Income	2 35.2	41.7	35.7	23.0	16.0	10.5	1 9.5
Cash Flow	53.5	58.7	49.9	35.3	26.1	20.8	19.4
Average Shs. Outstg. (000)	27,103	28,006	28,174	25,026	23,967	23,898	23,856
BALANCE SHEET (IN MILLIONS):							
Cash & Cash Equivalents	1.2	8.3	17.2	51.7	33.6	22.5	18.1
Total Current Assets	511.3	508.2	468.4	414.1	338.0	321.6	307.7
Net Property	110.0	104.0	82.9	71.1	54.8	56.6	54.8
Total Assets	741.0	726.6	670.6	529.6	437.8	425.8	411.0
Total Current Liabilities	163.8	173.6	149.1	100.0	79.4	73.1	67.7
Long-Term Obligations	180.4	180.9	177.5	116.8	118.3	119.8	115.7
Net Stockholders' Equity	339.5	326.0	300.9	269.3	204.6	194.1	189.5
Net Working Capital	347.5	334.6	319.3	314.1	258.6	248.5	240.0
Year-end Shs. Outstg. (000)	26,865	27,381	27,704	27,306	23,997	23,942	23,859
STATISTICAL RECORD:							
Operating Profit Margin %	6.9	8.4	8.3	7.3	6.4	5.4	5.4
Net Profit Margin %	3.4	4.5	4.6	3.9	3.2	2.3	2.3
Return on Equity %	10.4	12.8	11.9	8.6	7.8	5.4	5.0
Return on Assets %	4.7	5.7	5.3	4.3	3.7	2.5	2.3
Debt/Total Assets %	24.4	24.9	26.5	22.1	27.0	28.1	28.2
Price Range	24.00-14.63	32.42-17.44	27.00-16.17	20.83-11.83	14.67-8.08	11.58-7.92	10.00-7.67
P/E Ratio	18.7-11.4	21.8-11.7	21.3-12.7	22.6-12.9	22.0-12.1	26.3-18.0	25.0-19.2
Average Yield %	1.8	1.4	1.5	2.0	2.8	3.3	3.6

Statistics are as originally reported. Adj. for 3-for-2 stk. split, 2/98. 1 Bef. $10,000 acctg. cr. 2 Incl. $4.0 mil ($0.11/sh) chg. to incr. bad debt reserves. 3 Incl. pass through sales of $66.8 mil.

OFFICERS:
I. A. Eichner, Chmn.
D. P. Storch, Pres., C.E.O.
T. J. Romenesko, V.P., C.F.O.
H. A. Pulsifer, V.P., Gen. Counsel, Sec.

INVESTOR CONTACT: Ann T. Baldwin, V.P.-Corp. Comm., (630) 227-2082

PRINCIPAL OFFICE: One AAR Place, 1100 North Wood Dale Road, Wood Dale, IL 60191

TELEPHONE NUMBER: (630) 227-2000
FAX: (630) 227-2019
WEB: www.aarcorp.com

NO. OF EMPLOYEES: 2,900 (avg.)

SHAREHOLDERS: 11,000 (approx.)

ANNUAL MEETING: In Oct.

INCORPORATED: DE, 1966

INSTITUTIONAL HOLDINGS:
No. of Institutions: 106
Shares Held: 20,722,067
% Held: 76.9

INDUSTRY: Aircraft engines and engine parts (SIC: 3724)

TRANSFER AGENT(S): First Chicago Trust Company of New York, Jersey City, NJ

NYSE SYMBOL ABT
Rec. Pr. 51.98 (5/31/01)

ABBOTT LABORATORIES

YIELD	1.6%
P/E RATIO	29.2

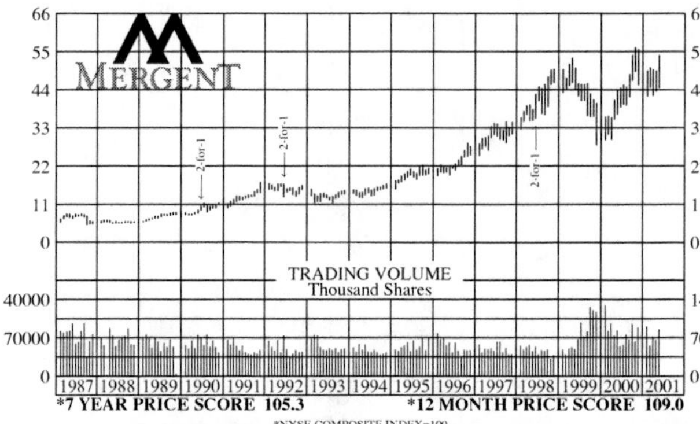

*7 YEAR PRICE SCORE 105.3 *12 MONTH PRICE SCORE 109.0

*NYSE COMPOSITE INDEX=100

INTERIM EARNINGS (Per Share):

Qtr.	Mar.	June	Sept.	Dec.
1997	0.35	0.34	0.31	0.37
1998	0.38	0.38	0.34	0.41
1999	0.43	0.42	0.38	0.43
2000	0.44	0.44	0.42	0.48

INTERIM DIVIDENDS (Per Share):

Amt.	Decl.	Ex.	Rec.	Pay.
0.19Q	6/09/00	7/12/00	7/14/00	8/15/00
0.19Q	9/07/00	10/11/00	10/13/00	11/15/00
0.19Q	12/08/00	1/10/01	1/15/01	2/15/01
0.21Q	2/09/01	4/10/01	4/12/01	5/15/01
0.21Q	6/08/01	7/11/01	7/13/01	8/15/01

Indicated div.: $0.84 (Div. Reinv. Plan)

CAPITALIZATION (12/31/00):

	($000)	(%)
Long-Term Debt	1,076,368	11.2
Common & Surplus	8,570,906	88.8
Total	9,647,274	100.0

RECENT DEVELOPMENTS: For the year ended 12/31/00, net earnings rose 13.9% to $2.79 billion compared with $2.45 billion in 1999. The 2000 results included a pre-tax gain of $138.5 million on the sale of business. Net sales grew 4.3% to $13.75 billion versus $13.18 billion the year before. Total sales in U.S. market increased 6.1% to $8.59 billion, while total international sales, including direct exports from the U.S. inched up 1.5% to $5.16 billion. Operating earnings improved 8.0% to $3.40 billion.

PROSPECTS: On 3/2/01, the Company announced that it has completed the acquisition of the pharmaceutical business of BASF for approximately $6.90 billion. The acquisition includes the global operations of Knoll. The addition should enable ABT to increase its pharmaceutical research and development spending and access monoclonal antibody technologies, broaden its global infrastructure and acquire late-stage and marketed products.

BUSINESS

ABBOTT LABORATORIES' principal business is the discovery, development, manufacture, and sale of human health care products and services. Pharmaceutical products include adult and pediatric pharmaceuticals and vitamins. This segment also includes consumer products, agricultural and chemical products, and bulk pharmaceuticals. Products in the hospital and laboratory segment include diagnostic systems, intravenous and irrigating fluids and related administration equipment, anesthetics, critical care equipment, and other specialty products. Products in the Ross segment include nutritional products such as SIMILAC and ENSURE.

BUSINESS LINE ANALYSIS

(12/31/2000)	REV (%)	INC (%)
Pharmaceutical	19.3	28.9
Diagnostics	21.9	9.5
Hospital	18.8	18.8
Ross	15.2	20.5
International	24.8	22.3
Total	100.0	100.0

ANNUAL FINANCIAL DATA

	12/31/00	12/31/99	12/31/98	12/31/97	12/31/96	12/31/95	12/31/94
Earnings Per Share	**2 1.78**	**1 1.57**	**1.51**	**1.34**	**1.21**	**1.06**	**0.94**
Cash Flow Per Share	**2.31**	**2.10**	**2.02**	**1.81**	**1.64**	**1.42**	**1.25**
Tang. Book Val. Per Share	**4.54**	**3.78**	**2.88**	**2.54**	**2.48**	**2.69**	**2.52**
Dividends Per Share	**0.74**	**0.66**	**0.59**	**0.53**	**0.47**	**0.41**	**0.37**
Dividend Payout %	**41.6**	**42.0**	**38.7**	**39.2**	**38.6**	**38.7**	**39.6**
INCOME STATEMENT (IN MILLIONS):							
Total Revenues	13,745.9	13,177.6	12,477.8	11,883.5	11,013.5	10,012.2	9,156.0
Costs & Expenses	9,517.9	9,200.2	8,575.7	8,305.3	7,710.3	7,062.9	6,501.3
Depreciation & Amort.	827.4	828.0	784.2	727.8	686.1	566.4	510.5
Operating Income	3,400.6	3,149.4	3,117.9	2,850.4	2,617.1	2,382.9	2,144.2
Net Interest Inc./(Exp.)	d23.2	d81.8	d104.1	d86.8	d50.9	d17.7	d12.8
Income Before Income Taxes	3,816.4	3,396.9	3,240.6	2,949.9	2,669.6	2,395.3	2,166.7
Income Taxes	1,030.4	951.1	907.4	855.5	787.5	706.6	650.0
Net Income	2 2,786.0	1 2,445.8	2,333.2	2,094.5	1,882.0	1,688.7	1,516.7
Cash Flow	3,613.4	3,273.8	3,117.5	2,822.2	2,568.1	2,255.1	2,027.2
Average Shs. Outstg. (000)	1,565,579	1,557,655	1,545,658	1,561,462	1,562,494	1,590,724	1,624,472
BALANCE SHEET (IN MILLIONS):							
Cash & Cash Equivalents	1,156.7	723.3	383.3	259.0	123.1	315.7	315.3
Total Current Assets	7,376.2	6,419.8	5,553.1	5,038.2	4,480.9	4,226.7	3,876.3
Net Property	4,816.9	4,770.1	4,738.8	4,569.7	4,461.5	4,249.5	3,920.9
Total Assets	15,283.3	14,471.0	13,216.2	12,061.1	11,125.6	9,412.6	8,523.7
Total Current Liabilities	4,297.5	4,516.7	4,962.1	5,034.5	4,343.7	3,790.3	3,475.9
Long-Term Obligations	1,076.4	1,336.8	1,339.7	938.0	932.9	435.2	287.1
Net Stockholders' Equity	8,570.9	7,427.6	5,713.7	4,998.7	4,820.2	4,396.8	4,049.4
Net Working Capital	3,078.7	1,903.0	591.0	3.7	137.2	436.4	400.5
Year-end Shs. Outstg. (000)	1,545,934	1,547,020	1,516,063	1,528,188	1,548,898	1,574,614	1,606,560
STATISTICAL RECORD:							
Operating Profit Margin %	24.7	23.9	25.0	24.0	23.8	23.8	23.4
Net Profit Margin %	20.3	18.6	18.7	17.6	17.1	16.9	16.6
Return on Equity %	32.5	32.9	40.8	41.9	39.0	38.4	37.5
Return on Assets %	18.2	16.9	17.7	17.4	16.9	17.9	17.8
Debt/Total Assets %	7.0	9.2	10.1	7.8	8.4	4.6	3.4
Price Range	56.25-29.38	53.31-27.94	50.06-32.53	34.88-24.88	28.69-19.06	22.38-15.31	17.00-12.69
P/E Ratio	31.6-16.5	34.0-17.8	33.2-21.5	26.0-18.6	23.8-15.8	21.1-14.4	18.2-13.6
Average Yield %	1.7	1.6	1.4	1.8	1.9	2.2	2.5

Statistics are as originally reported. Adjusted for 2-for-1 stock split, 5/98. 1 Incl. a nonrecurring pre-tax charge of $168.0 million relating to an FDA consent decree. 2 Incl. pre-tax gain of $138.5 mill. on sale of bus.

OFFICERS:
M. D. White, Chmn., C.E.O.
T. C. Freyman, Sr. V.P., Fin., C.F.O.
G. W. Linder, V.P., Treas.
J. M. De Lasa, Sr. V.P., Sec., Gen. Couns.

INVESTOR CONTACT: Catherine V. Babington, V.P., (847) 938-5633

PRINCIPAL OFFICE: 100 Abbott Park Road, Abbott Park, IL 60064-6400

TELEPHONE NUMBER: (847) 937-6100
FAX: (847) 937-1511
WEB: www.abbott.com

NO. OF EMPLOYEES: 60,571 (avg.)

SHAREHOLDERS: 101,272

ANNUAL MEETING: In Apr.

INCORPORATED: IL, Mar., 1900

INSTITUTIONAL HOLDINGS:
No. of Institutions: 991
Shares Held: 837,074,795
% Held: 54.0

INDUSTRY: Pharmaceutical preparations (SIC: 2834)

TRANSFER AGENT(S): EquiServe, Providence, RI

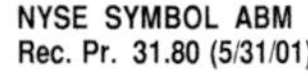

NYSE SYMBOL ABM
Rec. Pr. 31.80 (5/31/01)

ABM INDUSTRIES INCORPORATED

YIELD 2.1%
P/E RATIO 17.0

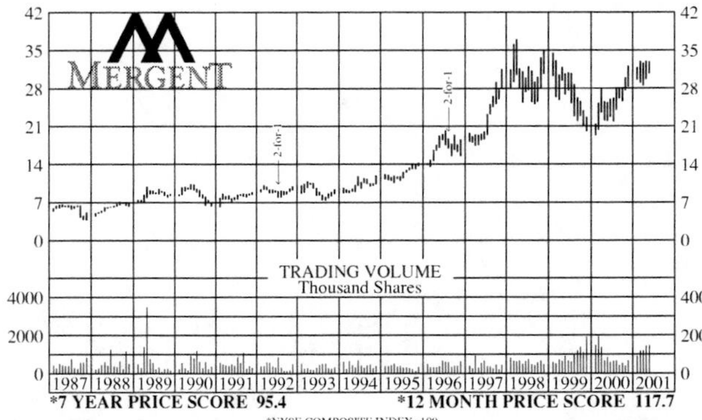

INTERIM EARNINGS (Per Share):

Qtr.	Jan.	April	July	Oct.
1996-97	0.20	0.26	0.34	0.40
1997-98	0.25	0.30	0.40	0.49
1998-99	0.29	0.35	0.46	0.55
1999-00	0.32	0.41	0.52	0.60
2000-01	0.34	...	...	...

INTERIM DIVIDENDS (Per Share):

Amt.	Decl.	Ex.	Rec.	Pay.
0.155Q	3/21/00	4/12/00	4/14/00	5/03/00
0.155Q	6/20/00	7/12/00	7/14/00	8/03/00
0.155Q	9/19/00	10/11/00	10/13/00	11/03/00
0.165Q	12/19/00	1/10/01	1/15/01	2/05/01
0.165Q	3/20/01	4/10/01	4/13/01	5/03/01

Indicated div.: $0.66

CAPITALIZATION (10/31/00):

	($000)	(%)
Long-Term Debt	36,811	10.2
Redeemable Pfd. Stock	6,400	1.8
Common & Surplus	316,309	88.0
Total	359,520	100.0

RECENT DEVELOPMENTS: For the quarter ended 1/31/01, net income increased 11.7% to $8.4 million compared with $7.5 million in 2000. Revenues were $470.4 million, up 9.8% from $428.6 million a year earlier. The improvement in results was primarily attributed to significant growth in the Company's multi-service and national account sales. In addition, outsourcing from the private sector, privatization by governmental agencies and ABM's active acquisition program contributed to strong overall growth.

PROSPECTS: On 4/5/01, the Company's subsidiary, American Building Maintenance, acquired all operations of CarpetMaster Cleaning, a regional provider of janitorial and related services in Albany and the surrounding Capital District of New York. On 3/26/01, American Sanitary Incorporated, a privately-owned distributor of building maintenance supplies and equipment, signed a letter of intent to acquire ABM's subsidiary, Easterday Janitorial Supply Company.

BUSINESS

ABM INDUSTRIES INCORPORATED is engaged in the business of providing commercial, industrial and institutional janitorial, window cleaning, engineering and building maintenance services. The Company is also engaged in the business of air conditioning, heating equipment, elevator and escalator installation, repair and servicing; lighting and outdoor signage installation and maintenance; parking facility operations; building security services; and janitorial supplies and equipment sales. Amtech group offers a wide range of mechanical, electrical and elevator services to retail and commercial businesses. Contributions to sales for fiscal 2000 were as follows: ABM Janitorial, 66.2%; Ampco System Parking, 10.4%; ABM Engineering, 9.4%; Amtech Lighting, 7.1%; and Amtech Elevator, 6.9%.

ANNUAL FINANCIAL DATA

	10/31/00	10/31/99	10/31/98	10/31/97	10/31/96	10/31/95	10/31/94
Earnings Per Share	**1.85**	**1.65**	**1.44**	**1.33**	**1.11**	**0.93**	**0.83**
Cash Flow Per Share	**2.86**	**2.54**	**2.31**	**2.15**	**1.85**	**1.55**	**1.37**
Tang. Book Val. Per Share	**8.97**	**7.65**	**6.24**	**4.76**	**4.51**	**3.87**	**3.48**
Dividends Per Share	**0.62**	**0.56**	**0.48**	**0.40**	**0.35**	**0.30**	**0.26**
Dividend Payout %	**33.5**	**33.9**	**33.3**	**30.1**	**31.5**	**32.4**	**31.2**
INCOME STATEMENT (IN MILLIONS):							
Total Revenues	1,807.6	1,629.7	1,501.8	1,252.5	1,086.9	965.4	884.6
Costs & Expenses	1,708.0	1,539.8	1,421.3	1,186.7	1,032.6	919.7	846.8
Depreciation & Amort.	23.5	20.7	19.6	16.1	13.7	11.5	9.3
Operating Income	76.0	69.2	61.0	49.6	40.7	34.2	28.5
Net Interest Inc./(Exp.)	d3.3	d2.0	d3.5	d2.7	d2.6	d2.7	d3.5
Income Before Income Taxes	72.7	67.2	57.5	47.0	38.1	31.4	25.1
Income Taxes	28.4	27.6	23.6	19.7	16.4	13.2	9.9
Net Income	44.3	39.7	33.9	27.2	21.7	18.2	15.2
Cash Flow	67.4	59.9	53.0	42.8	34.9	29.2	24.0
Average Shs. Outstg. (000)	23,709	23,748	23,161	20,143	19,123	19,180	17,816
BALANCE SHEET (IN MILLIONS):							
Cash & Cash Equivalents	2.0	2.1	1.8	1.8	1.6	1.8	7.4
Total Current Assets	436.8	367.6	324.3	291.5	233.8	209.9	189.4
Net Property	40.7	35.2	27.3	26.6	22.6	22.6	19.8
Total Assets	642.0	563.4	501.4	464.3	379.8	335.0	299.5
Total Current Liabilities	212.6	183.3	157.8	153.8	113.8	114.2	99.3
Long-Term Obligations	36.8	28.9	33.7	38.4	33.7	22.6	25.3
Net Stockholders' Equity	316.3	277.0	237.5	197.8	164.3	141.8	124.3
Net Working Capital	224.2	184.3	166.5	137.8	120.0	95.6	90.2
Year-end Shs. Outstg. (000)	22,999	22,407	21,601	20,464	19,489	18,732	18,098
STATISTICAL RECORD:							
Operating Profit Margin %	4.2	4.2	4.1	4.0	3.7	3.5	3.2
Net Profit Margin %	2.5	2.4	2.3	2.2	2.0	1.9	1.7
Return on Equity %	14.0	14.3	14.3	13.8	13.2	12.8	12.2
Return on Assets %	6.9	7.0	6.8	5.9	5.7	5.4	5.1
Debt/Total Assets %	5.7	5.1	6.7	8.3	8.9	6.7	8.4
Price Range	32.13-19.25	34.50-20.00	37.00-25.00	31.50-17.38	20.19-13.50	14.25-10.50	11.94-8.63
P/E Ratio	17.4-10.4	20.9-12.1	25.7-17.4	23.7-13.1	18.2-12.2	15.4-11.4	14.5-10.5
Average Yield %	2.4	2.1	1.5	1.6	2.1	2.4	2.5

Statistics are as originally reported. Adj. for stk. split: 2-for-1, 7/92 & 8/96.

OFFICERS:
M. H. Mandles, Chmn.
H. Slipsager, Pres., C.E.O.
J. E. Benton, C.O.O.
D. H. Hebble, Sr. V.P., C.F.O.

INVESTOR CONTACT: Henrik C. Slipslager, Investor Relations, (415) 733-4000

PRINCIPAL OFFICE: 160 Pacific Avenue, Suite 222, San Francisco, CA 94111

TELEPHONE NUMBER: (415) 733-4000
FAX: (415) 733-7333
WEB: www.abm.com

NO. OF EMPLOYEES: 60,000 (approx.)

SHAREHOLDERS: 5,490 (approx.)

ANNUAL MEETING: In Mar.

INCORPORATED: CA, Apr., 1955; reincorp., DE, May, 1985

INSTITUTIONAL HOLDINGS:
No. of Institutions: 102
Shares Held: 14,980,577
% Held: 63.1

INDUSTRY: Building maintenance services, nec (SIC: 7349)

TRANSFER AGENT(S): Mellon Investor Services LLC, San Francisco, CA

NYSE SYMBOL ATU
Rec. Pr. 14.70 (5/31/01)

ACTUANT CORPORATION

YIELD ...
P/E RATIO 9.7

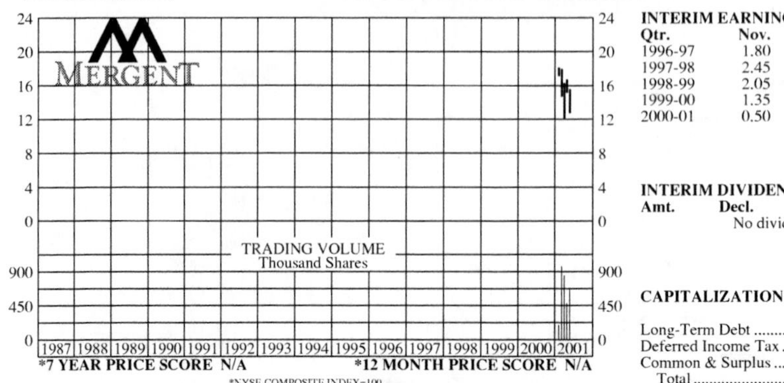

INTERIM EARNINGS (Per Share):

Qtr.	Nov.	Feb.	May	Aug.
1996-97	1.80	1.75	2.00	2.10
1997-98	2.45	2.05	2.75	d3.90
1998-99	2.05	2.40	2.55	2.90
1999-00	1.35	1.45	1.50	d0.85
2000-01	0.50	0.37	...	...

INTERIM DIVIDENDS (Per Share):

Amt.	Decl.	Ex.	Rec.	Pay.

No dividends paid.

CAPITALIZATION (8/31/00):

	($000)	(%)
Long-Term Debt	431,215	158.1
Deferred Income Tax	4,486	1.6
Common & Surplus	d162,955	-59.7
Total	272,746	100.0

RECENT DEVELOPMENTS: For the second quarter ended 2/28/01, net earnings were $3.1 million versus income from continuing operations of $11.9 million a year earlier. Results for 2000 included a corporate reorganization expense of $3.5 million. Net sales fell 38.4% to $113.3 million from $184.1 million in 1999. Excluding non-continuing businesses, sales in the tools & supplies segment declined 9.3% to $68.9 million and engineered solutions segment sales fell 22.4% to $44.4 million.

PROSPECTS: In an effort to reduce leverage, lower net financing costs, and create balance sheet flexibility, the Company has placed debt reduction as its top priority. During the recent quarter, ATU reduced its long-term debt by $10.1 million to $421.1 million and expects that its goal of $35.0 million in debt reduction for fiscal 2001 will be met and exceeded. For fiscal 2001, ATU expects sales in the range of $475.0 million to $485.0 million and diluted earnings per share in the range of $1.19 to $2.05.

BUSINESS

ACTUANT CORPORATION (formerly Applied Power Inc.) is a global manufacturer and marketer of a range of industrial products and systems, organized into two business segments: Tools & Supplies and Engineered Solutions. Tools & Supplies (45% of fiscal 2000 revenues) sells branded, specialized electrical and industrial tools to hydraulic and electrical wholesale distributors, to catalog houses and through various retail distribution channels. Engineered Solutions (55%) designs, manufacturers and markets customized motion control systems primarily for original equipment manufacturers in diversified niche markets. On 7/31/00, the Company completed the spin-off of its electronics business.

ANNUAL FINANCIAL DATA

	[7] 8/31/00	8/31/99	[1] 8/31/98	8/31/97	8/31/96	8/31/95	8/31/94
Earnings Per Share	[6] **3.50**	**9.90**	[2] **3.30**	**7.30**	**6.03**	[3] **4.55**	[4] **3.18**
Cash Flow Per Share	**6.28**	**19.41**	**9.24**	**11.42**	**9.80**	**7.90**	**6.83**
Tang. Book Val. Per Share	...	...	...	**11.64**	**14.05**	**11.92**	**7.39**
INCOME STATEMENT (IN THOUSANDS):							
Total Revenues	671,642	1,751,042	1,230,689	672,316	571,215	527,058	433,644
Costs & Expenses	564,826	1,484,649	1,107,300	575,770	488,690	456,375	372,029
Depreciation & Amort.	22,550	76,690	47,570	23,663	21,078	18,456	19,406
Operating Income	84,266	189,703	75,819	72,883	61,447	52,227	42,209
Net Interest Inc./(Exp.)	d37,670	d63,888	d28,531	d12,003	d12,510	d13,660	d16,454
Income Before Income Taxes	47,533	126,751	57,385	62,743	49,167	36,873	25,298
Income Taxes	19,488	47,354	30,698	20,705	15,438	11,868	8,402
Net Income	[6] 28,045	79,397	[2] 26,687	42,038	33,729	[3] 25,005	[4] 16,896
Cash Flow	50,595	156,087	74,257	65,701	54,807	43,461	36,302
Average Shs. Outstg.	8,062	8,040	8,035	5,751	5,593	5,498	5,316
BALANCE SHEET (IN THOUSANDS):							
Cash & Cash Equivalents	9,896	22,258	6,349	5,846	1,001	911	1,907
Total Current Assets	203,714	409,036	364,564	225,906	206,905	190,464	174,809
Net Property	49,168	273,902	225,170	90,580	76,236	68,435	67,745
Total Assets	416,981	1,624,846	1,174,722	463,592	381,241	332,946	317,402
Total Current Liabilities	126,243	323,665	260,708	128,274	107,729	97,447	101,965
Long-Term Obligations	431,215	808,438	512,557	101,663	76,548	74,156	77,956
Net Stockholders' Equity	d162,955	417,829	341,882	204,109	168,455	131,686	107,311
Net Working Capital	77,471	85,371	103,856	97,632	99,176	93,017	72,844
Year-end Shs. Outstg.	7,923	7,796	7,725	5,527	5,461	5,363	5,261
STATISTICAL RECORD:							
Operating Profit Margin %	12.5	10.8	6.2	10.8	10.8	9.9	9.7
Net Profit Margin %	4.2	4.5	2.2	6.3	5.9	4.7	3.9
Return on Equity %	...	19.0	7.8	20.6	20.0	19.0	15.7
Return on Assets %	6.7	4.9	2.3	9.1	8.8	7.5	5.3
Debt/Total Assets %	103.4	49.8	43.6	21.9	20.1	22.3	24.6

Statistics are as originally reported. Adj. for 1-for-5 split, 1/01; 100% stk. div., 2/98. [1] Refls. the 7/98 acq. of ZERO Corporation. [2] Incl. non-recurr. chrg. of $29.6 mill. [3] Bef. extraord. chrg. of $4.9 mill. [4] Bef. disc. oper. loss of $348,000, 8/31/94; $34.0 mill., 8/31/92. [5] Incl. non-recurr. chrg. $6.7 mill.; bef. disc. oper. loss $5.4 mill. & acctg. change chrg. of $4.4 mill. [6] Incl. contract termin. recov. of $1.4 mill., corp. reorg. exps. of $12.4 mill. & loss on disp. of prod. lines of $5.4 mill.; bef. extraord. gain of $38.5 mill. & disc. oper. income of $585,000. [7] Refls. 7/00 spin-off of electronics business.

OFFICERS:
R. G. Sim, Chmn.
R. C. Arzbaecher, Pres., C.E.O.
A. G. Lampereor, V.P., C.F.O.

INVESTOR CONTACT: A. E. Ertl, Inv. Rel., (414) 352-4160

PRINCIPAL OFFICE: 6100 North Baker Road, Milwaukee, WI 53209

TELEPHONE NUMBER: (414) 352-4160
FAX: (414) 247-5550
WEB: www.actuant.com

NO. OF EMPLOYEES: 2,135 (approx.)

SHAREHOLDERS: 5,248 (approx.)

ANNUAL MEETING: In Jan.

INCORPORATED: WI, 1910

INSTITUTIONAL HOLDINGS:
No. of Institutions: 76
Shares Held: 4,294,965
% Held: 54.1

INDUSTRY: Fluid power cylinders & actuators (SIC: 3593)

TRANSFER AGENT(S): Firstar Trust Company, Milwaukee, WI

NYSE SYMBOL ASF
Rec. Pr. 18.15 (3/31/01)

ADMINISTAFF, INC.

YIELD ...
P/E RATIO 31.8

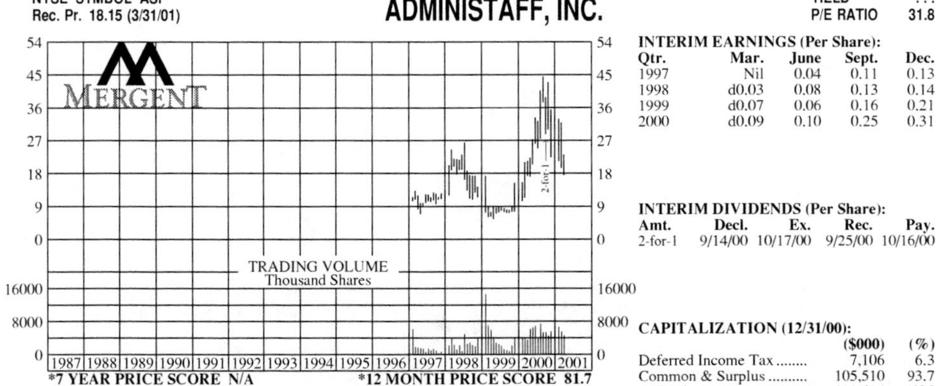

*7 YEAR PRICE SCORE N/A　　*12 MONTH PRICE SCORE 81.7

*NYSE COMPOSITE INDEX=100

INTERIM EARNINGS (Per Share):

Qtr.	Mar.	June	Sept.	Dec.
1997	Nil	0.04	0.11	0.13
1998	d0.03	0.08	0.13	0.14
1999	d0.07	0.06	0.16	0.21
2000	d0.09	0.10	0.25	0.31

INTERIM DIVIDENDS (Per Share):

Amt.	Decl.	Ex.	Rec.	Pay.
2-for-1	9/14/00	10/17/00	9/25/00	10/16/00

CAPITALIZATION (12/31/00):

	($000)	(%)
Deferred Income Tax........	7,106	6.3
Common & Surplus..........	105,510	93.7
Total..............................	112,616	100.0

RECENT DEVELOPMENTS: For the year ended 12/31/00, net income jumped 80.6% to $16.9 million compared with $9.4 million in the previous year. Results for 1999 included an after-tax nonrecurring charge of $920,000. Revenues increased 64.0% to $3.71 billion due to a 46.3% increase in the number of worksite employees paid by the customer per month and a 14.0% increase in fee payroll cost per worksite employee per month. Operating income more than doubled to $22.2 million.

PROSPECTS: As part of the Company's expansion strategy, ASF recently opened its third sales office in Chicago, Illinois, its fourth sales office in San Francisco, California, its fourth sales office in Houston, Texas and its first office in Boston, Massachusetts. The Company's long-term initiative is to open a total of 90 sales offices in 40 selected markets nationwide. Going forward, the Company expects results in 2001 to improve due to a decline in employment-related taxes.

BUSINESS

ADMINISTAFF, INC. serves as an off-site, full-service human resources department for small and medium-sized businesses throughout the United States. The Company's Personnel Management System includes employment administration, benefits and payroll administration, government compliance, recruiting and selection, employer liability management, owner support, employee recruiting and selection, performance management and training development services. The Company also offers Administaff Assistant®, an on-line resource for clients and worksite employees associated with ASF's services. Bizzport[sm], the Company's Internet portal, offers incentives to clients and employees through a chain of preferred providers. As of 4/11/01, ASF operates 34 sales offices in 18 major metropolitan markets.

QUARTERLY DATA

(12/31/00)($000)	Rev	Inc
1st Quarter.................	755,545	(2,471)
2nd Quarter................	864,450	2,800
3rd Quarter................	962,039	7,415
4th Quarter.................	1,126,497	9,156

ANNUAL FINANCIAL DATA

	12/31/00	12/31/99	12/31/98	12/31/97	12/31/96	12/31/95	12/31/94
Earnings Per Share	**0.58**	**1 0.34**	**0.31**	**0.27**	**0.12**	**0.05**	**0.19**
Cash Flow Per Share	**1.00**	**0.61**	**0.46**	**0.36**	**0.19**	**0.10**	**0.21**
Tang. Book Val. Per Share	**3.85**	**2.99**	**2.89**	**2.21**	**0.58**	**0.47**	**0.39**
INCOME STATEMENT (IN MILLIONS):							
Total Revenues	3,708.5	2,260.7	1,683.1	1,213.6	899.6	716.2	564.5
Costs & Expenses	3,674.3	2,242.6	1,667.6	1,201.6	891.4	712.9	558.0
Depreciation & Amort.	12.0	7.6	4.2	2.7	1.7	1.1	0.6
Operating Income	22.2	10.6	11.2	9.3	6.5	2.2	5.9
Net Interest Inc./(Exp.)	4.4	2.6	3.3	2.6	d0.3	...	...
Income Before Income Taxes	26.6	14.2	14.6	11.9	4.8	2.2	5.9
Income Taxes	9.7	4.9	5.5	4.5	2.2	1.1	2.2
Net Income	16.9	1 9.4	9.1	7.4	2.6	1.1	3.8
Cash Flow	28.9	17.0	13.4	10.1	4.3	2.2	4.3
Average Shs. Outstg. (000)	28,935	27,590	29,366	27,844	22,210	21,730	20,790
BALANCE SHEET (IN MILLIONS):							
Cash & Cash Equivalents	108.7	56.2	73.2	66.6	13.4	7.2	17.0
Total Current Assets	181.4	98.7	103.1	89.4	33.0	28.2	33.7
Net Property	52.4	44.4	31.0	16.7	11.6	9.1	5.4
Total Assets	242.8	147.7	142.8	109.5	48.4	39.5	41.1
Total Current Liabilities	130.2	62.9	50.7	42.8	28.4	23.5	24.9
Long-Term Obligations	...	...	...	...	4.1	4.6	4.7
Net Stockholders' Equity	105.5	80.5	86.9	63.8	13.3	10.7	8.1
Net Working Capital	51.2	35.8	52.5	46.6	4.6	4.7	8.8
Year-end Shs. Outstg. (000)	27,420	26,916	29,034	28,442	21,452	21,452	20,476
STATISTICAL RECORD:							
Operating Profit Margin %	0.6	0.5	0.7	0.8	0.7	0.3	1.0
Net Profit Margin %	0.5	0.4	0.5	0.6	0.3	0.2	0.7
Return on Equity %	16.0	11.6	10.5	11.7	19.6	10.4	46.7
Return on Assets %	7.0	6.3	6.4	6.8	5.4	2.8	9.2
Debt/Total Assets %	...	...	...	...	8.5	11.7	11.4
Price Range	44.56-10.38	17.25-5.56	26.47-10.81	13.25-6.88	...	...	...
P/E Ratio	76.8-17.9	50.7-16.4	85.4-34.9	50.0-25.9	...	...	...

Statistics are as originally reported. Adj. for 2-for-1 stk. split., 10/00. 1 Incl. after-tax nonrecurr. chrg. of $920,000.

OFFICERS:
P. J. Sarvadi, Pres., C.E.O.
R. G. Rawson, Exec. V.P., C.F.O., Treas.
J. H. Spurgin II, V.P., Gen. Couns., Sec.

INVESTOR CONTACT: Investor Relations Administator, (281) 348-3987

PRINCIPAL OFFICE: 19001 Crescent Springs Drive, Kingwood, TX 77339-3802

TELEPHONE NUMBER: (281) 358-8986
FAX: (281) 358-3354
WEB: www.administaff.com

NO. OF EMPLOYEES: 1,100 (approx.)

SHAREHOLDERS: 114

ANNUAL MEETING: In May

INCORPORATED: TX, 1986; reincorp., DE, 1996

INSTITUTIONAL HOLDINGS:
No. of Institutions: 118
Shares Held: 17,606,836
% Held: 64.2

INDUSTRY: Help supply services (SIC: 7363)

TRANSFER AGENT(S): Computershare Investor Services LLC, Chicago, IL

NYSE SYMBOL AMD
Rec. Pr. 28.25 (5/31/01)

ADVANCED MICRO DEVICES, INC.

YIELD ...
P/E RATIO 9.5

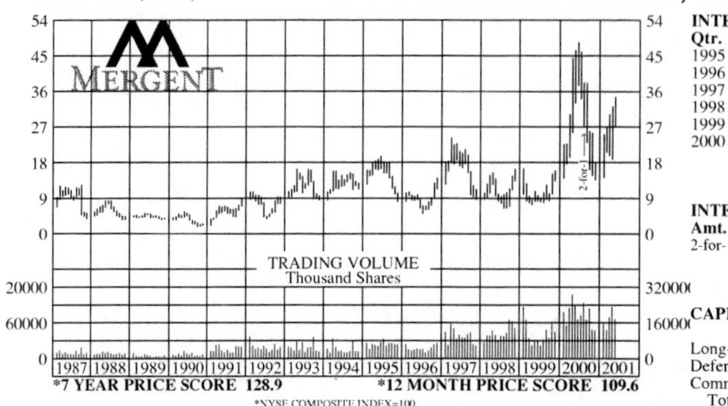

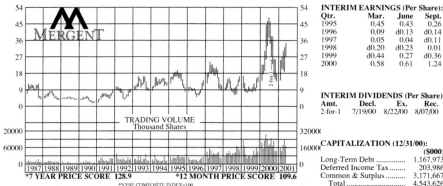

*7 YEAR PRICE SCORE 128.9 *12 MONTH PRICE SCORE 109.6
*NYSE COMPOSITE INDEX=100

INTERIM EARNINGS (Per Share):

Qtr.	Mar.	June	Sept.	Dec.
1995	0.45	0.43	0.26	0.26
1996	0.09	d0.13	d0.14	d0.08
1997	0.05	0.04	d0.11	d0.05
1998	d0.20	d0.23	0.01	0.08
1999	d0.44	0.27	d0.36	0.22
2000	0.58	0.61	1.24	0.53

INTERIM DIVIDENDS (Per Share):

Amt.	Decl.	Ex.	Rec.	Pay.
2-for-1	7/19/00	8/22/00	8/07/00	8/21/00

CAPITALIZATION (12/31/00):

	($000)	(%)
Long-Term Debt	1,167,973	25.7
Deferred Income Tax	203,986	4.5
Common & Surplus	3,171,667	69.8
Total	4,543,626	100.0

RECENT DEVELOPMENTS: For the year ended 12/31/00, income was $1.01 billion, before an extraordinary after-tax loss of $23.0 million, compared with a net loss of $88.9 million in 1999. Results for 2000 included pre-tax restructuring and other special charges of $38.2 million and a gain of $336.9 million on the sale the Legerity business. The 1999 results included a pre-tax gain of $432.1 million on the sale of the Vantis business. Net sales soared 62.5% to $4.64 billion from $2.88 billion in the prior year.

PROSPECTS: The Company benefited from increased demand for memory devices due to expanded unit sales of PCs in the business and consumer market as well as higher usage and functionality of cellular phones. Separately, AMD announced a three-year strategic agreement to supply Lucent Technologies with a significant portion of Lucent's flash memory device requirements. The flash memory will be used in Lucent's wireless, optical, and data networking products, systems and services.

BUSINESS

ADVANCED MICRO DEVICES designs, manufactures and markets complex integrated circuits. The Company's products include a wide variety of industry-standard integrated circuits, which are used in many diverse product applications such as telecommunications equipment, data and network communications equipment, consumer electronics, personal computers and workstations. In addition, the Company is involved in the production of non-volatile memory circuits or flash memory products, programmable logic devices and circuits for telecommunications, office automation and networking applications. Manufacturing facilities are located in the U.S., Bangkok, Japan, Thailand, Malaysia, England and Singapore.

BUSINESS LINE ANALYSIS

(12/31/2000)	REV (%)	INC (%)
Core Products	93.9	93.6
Voice Communications	3.0	3.9
Foundry Services	3.1	2.5
Total	100.0	100.0

ANNUAL FINANCIAL DATA

	12/31/00	12/26/99	12/27/98	12/28/97	12/29/96	12/31/95	12/25/94
Earnings Per Share	3 **2.95**	2 **d0.30**	1 **d0.36**	**d0.07**	**d0.25**	**1.43**	1 **1.51**
Cash Flow Per Share	**4.53**	**1.45**	**1.27**	**1.33**	**0.97**	**2.67**	**2.62**
Tang. Book Val. Per Share	**10.10**	**6.66**	**6.89**	**7.14**	**7.35**	**10.05**	**9.09**
Dividends Per Share	...	...	...	...	...	**0.01**	...
Dividend Payout %	...	...	...	...	...	**0.4**	...
INCOME STATEMENT (IN MILLIONS):							
Total Revenues	4,644.2	2,857.6	2,542.1	2,356.4	1,953.0	2,429.7	2,134.7
Costs & Expenses	3,176.4	2,663.0	2,238.3	2,052.6	1,873.7	1,818.9	1,405.5
Depreciation & Amort.	579.1	515.5	467.5	394.5	332.6	262.5	216.0
Operating Income	888.7	d320.9	d163.6	d90.7	d253.3	348.3	513.1
Net Interest Inc./(Exp.)	d60.0	d69.3	d66.5	d45.3	d14.8	d0.7	d1.8
Income Before Income Taxes	1,251.9	73.6	d207.4	d100.8	d208.8	378.3	469.6
Income Taxes	256.9	167.4	cr91.9	cr55.2	cr85.0	112.7	153.7
Equity Earnings/Minority Int.	11.0	4.8	11.6	24.6	54.8	34.9	d10.6
Net Income	3 1,006.1	2 d88.9	1 d104.0	d21.1	d68.9	300.5	1 305.3
Cash Flow	1,585.1	426.6	363.6	373.4	263.7	563.0	510.9
Average Shs. Outstg. (000)	350,000	294,136	287,336	280,906	271,374	211,150	195,020
BALANCE SHEET (IN MILLIONS):							
Cash & Cash Equivalents	1,293.2	596.5	697.0	467.0	386.2	490.6	377.9
Total Current Assets	2,657.7	1,409.9	1,562.0	1,175.3	1,029.1	1,096.8	986.6
Net Property	2,636.5	2,523.2	2,268.5	1,990.7	1,787.4	1,636.1	1,264.2
Total Assets	5,767.7	4,377.7	4,253.0	3,515.3	3,145.3	3,031.3	2,445.7
Total Current Liabilities	1,224.1	910.7	840.7	726.8	583.5	621.7	592.2
Long-Term Obligations	1,168.0	1,427.3	1,372.4	662.7	444.8	215.0	75.8
Net Stockholders' Equity	3,171.7	1,979.3	2,005.0	2,029.5	2,021.9	2,100.1	1,735.3
Net Working Capital	1,433.6	499.2	721.3	448.5	445.6	475.0	394.5
Year-end Shs. Outstg. (000)	314,137	297,313	290,954	284,246	275,160	209,038	190,834
STATISTICAL RECORD:							
Operating Profit Margin %	19.1	...	...	...	...	14.3	24.0
Net Profit Margin %	21.7	...	...	...	...	12.4	14.3
Return on Equity %	31.7	...	...	...	...	14.3	17.6
Return on Assets %	17.4	...	...	...	...	9.9	12.5
Debt/Total Assets %	20.3	32.6	32.3	18.9	14.1	7.1	3.1
Price Range	48.50-13.56	16.50-7.28	16.38-6.38	24.25-8.56	14.19-5.13	19.63-8.06	15.88-8.38
P/E Ratio	16.4-4.6	...	...	...	...	13.8-5.7	10.5-5.5

Statistics are as originally reported. Adj. for 2-for-1 stk. split, 8/21/00. 1 Incl. non-recurr. chrg. $11.3 mill., 12/98; $58.0 mill. & 12/94 2 Incl. non-recurr. chrg. $38.2 mill. and gain on sale of Vantis of $432.1 mill. 3 Incl. a pre-tax gain on sale of Legerity of $336.9 mill., pre-tax restruct. & other spec. chrg. of $38.2 mill. & excl. an after-tax extraord. loss of $23.0 mill.

OFFICERS:
W. J. Sanders III, Chmn., C.E.O.
H. d. Ruiz, Pres., C.O.O.
R. J. Rivet, Sr. V.P., C.F.O.

INVESTOR CONTACT: Toni Beckham, (408) 749-3127

PRINCIPAL OFFICE: One AMD Place, P.O. Box 3453, Sunnyvale, CA 94088-3453

TELEPHONE NUMBER: (408) 732-2400
FAX: (408) 982-6161
WEB: www.amd.com

NO. OF EMPLOYEES: 14,696 (approx.)

SHAREHOLDERS: 7,754

ANNUAL MEETING: In Apr.

INCORPORATED: DE, May, 1969

INSTITUTIONAL HOLDINGS:
No. of Institutions: 275
Shares Held: 142,554,613
% Held: 45.3

INDUSTRY: Semiconductors and related devices (SIC: 3674)

TRANSFER AGENT(S): First National Bank of Boston, Boston, MA

NYSE SYMBOL AES
Rec. Pr. 47.67 (4/30/01)

AES CORPORATION

YIELD ...
P/E RATIO 33.6

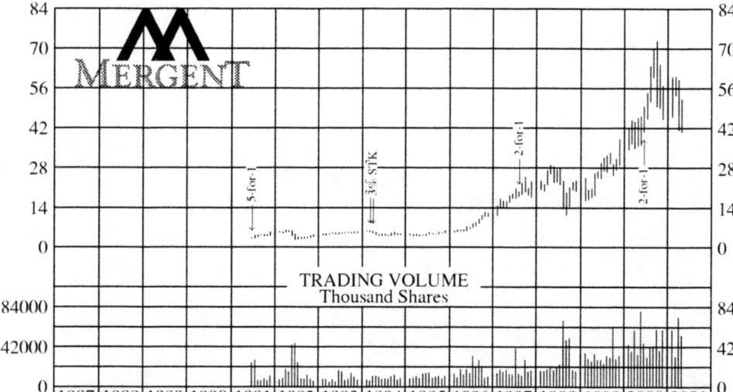

*7 YEAR PRICE SCORE 182.7 *12 MONTH PRICE SCORE 97.3

*NYSE COMPOSITE INDEX=100

INTERIM EARNINGS (Per Share):

Qtr.	Mar.	June	Sept.	Dec.
1996	0.10	0.10	0.11	0.11
1997	0.13	0.13	0.14	0.16
1998	0.19	0.20	0.22	0.25
1999	d0.04	0.18	0.15	0.30
2000	0.42	0.25	0.29	0.46

INTERIM DIVIDENDS (Per Share):

Amt.	Decl.	Ex.	Rec.	Pay.
2-for-1	4/18/00	6/02/00	5/01/00	6/01/00

CAPITALIZATION (12/31/00):

	($000)	(%)
Long-Term Debt	15,699,000	63.4
Deferred Income Tax	1,632,000	6.6
Minority Interest	1,382,000	5.6
Redeemable Pfd. Stock	1,228,000	5.0
Common & Surplus	4,811,000	19.4
Total	24,752,001	100.0

RECENT DEVELOPMENTS: For the year ended 12/31/00, the Company reported income of $648.0 million, before a net extraordinary loss of $7.0 million, versus income of $245.0 million, before a net extraordinary loss of $17.0 million, in the prior year. Sales and services revenues more than doubled to $6.69 billion compared with $3.25 billion in 1999. Operating income amounted to $1.62 billion, an increase of 74.6% versus $925.0 million a year earlier.

PROSPECTS: AES will acquire a 75.0% controlling interest in Kievoblenergo, an electric distribution company in the Ukraine, for about $45.9 million. On 3/27/01, AES completed its acquisition of IPALCO Enterprises, Inc., an Indianapolis based utility with 3,000 megawatts of generation and 433,000 customers. For 2001, AES expects earnings to be $1.75 to $1.90 per share, as well as grow at an average compounded annual growth rate of 25.0% to 30.0% over the next five years.

BUSINESS

AES CORPORATION is a public utility engaged in generating electricity by providing services to customers (generally electric utilities or regional electric companies) on a wholesale basis for further resale to end users. Sales by these generating companies are usually made under long-term contracts from power plants owned by AES subsidiaries and affiliates. As of 4/17/01, AES owns or has an interest in 160 power facilities, totaling over 58 gigawatts, in the United States, Argentina, Australia, Bangladesh, Brazil, Canada, Chile, China, Colombia, Dominican Republic, El Salvador, Georgia, Hungary, India, Italy, Kazakhstan, the Netherlands, Nigeria, Mexico, Oman, Pakistan, Panama, Sri Lanka, the United Kingdom and Venezuela. AES also distributes electricity in six countries through 14 distribution businesses.

REVENUES

(12/31/00)	Rev %	Inc %
Generation	53.0	79.4
Distribution	47.0	20.6
Total	100.0	100.0

ANNUAL FINANCIAL DATA

	12/31/00	12/31/99	12/31/98	12/31/97	12/31/96	12/31/95	12/31/94
Earnings Per Share	**1 0.71**	**1 0.31**	**1 0.42**	**1 0.28**	**0.20**	**0.18**	**0.16**
Cash Flow Per Share	**1.30**	**0.67**	**0.67**	**0.42**	**0.31**	**0.27**	**0.23**
Tang. Book Val. Per Share	**4.88**	**3.12**	**0.42**	**0.27**	**1.00**	**0.78**	**0.60**
INCOME STATEMENT (IN MILLIONS):							
Total Revenues	6,691.0	3,253.0	2,398.0	1,411.0	835.0	685.0	533.0
Costs & Expenses	4,494.0	2,050.0	1,469.0	929.0	492.0	382.0	258.0
Depreciation & Amort.	582.0	278.0	196.0	114.0	65.0	55.0	43.0
Operating Income	1,615.0	925.0	733.0	368.0	278.0	248.0	232.0
Net Interest Inc./(Exp.)	d1,054.0	d555.0	d418.0	d203.0	d120.0	d95.0	d99.0
Income Taxes	252.0	111.0	145.0	77.0	60.0	57.0	44.0
Equity Earnings/Minority Int.	356.0	d43.0	138.0	107.0	27.0	11.0	9.0
Net Income	1 648.0	1 245.0	1 307.0	1 188.0	125.0	107.0	98.0
Cash Flow	1,230.0	523.0	503.0	302.0	190.0	162.0	141.0
Average Shs. Outstg. (000)	946,200	785,000	756,000	711,200	606,400	608,000	616,000
BALANCE SHEET (IN MILLIONS):							
Gross Property	19,150.0	14,210.0	6,029.0	4,522.0	2,502.0	1,772.0	1,346.0
Accumulated Depreciation	1,304.0	763.0	525.0	373.0	282.0	222.0	162.0
Net Property	17,846.0	13,447.0	5,504.0	4,149.0	2,220.0	1,550.0	1,184.0
Total Assets	31,033.0	20,880.0	10,781.0	8,909.0	3,622.0	2,320.0	1,915.0
Long-Term Obligations	15,699.0	10,818.0	5,241.0	4,585.0	2,008.0	1,223.0	1,144.0
Net Stockholders' Equity	4,811.0	2,637.0	1,794.0	1,481.0	721.0	549.0	401.0
Year-end Shs. Outstg. (000)	962,000	828,000	722,268	699,200	618,400	600,000	600,000
STATISTICAL RECORD:							
Operating Profit Margin %	24.1	28.4	30.6	26.1	33.3	36.2	43.5
Net Profit Margin %	9.7	7.5	12.8	13.3	15.0	15.6	18.4
Net Inc./Net Property %	3.6	1.8	5.6	4.5	5.6	6.9	8.3
Net Inc./Tot. Capital %	2.6	1.4	3.6	2.5	3.9	5.1	5.4
Return on Equity %	13.5	9.3	17.1	12.7	17.3	19.5	24.4
Accum. Depr./Gross Prop. %	6.8	5.4	8.7	8.2	11.3	12.5	12.0
Price Range	72.81-34.25	38.19-16.41	29.00-11.50	24.81-11.19	12.53-5.25	6.00-4.00	5.95-3.94
P/E Ratio	102.5-48.2	123.2-52.9	69.5-27.5	89.4-40.3	61.9-25.9	34.1-22.7	36.6-24.2

Statistics are as originally reported. Adj. for stk. splits: 2-for-1, 6/00; 8/97; 3% div., 3/94; 3-for-2, 1/94. 1 Bef. extraordinary loss of $7.0 mill., 2000; $17.0 mill., 1999; gain of $4.0 mill., 1998; loss of $3.0 mill., 1997.

OFFICERS:
R. W. Sant, Chmn.
D. W. Bakke, Pres., C.E.O.
B. J. Sharp, Sr. V.P., C.F.O.
W. R. Luraschi, V.P., Gen. Couns., Sec.

INVESTOR CONTACT: Ken Woodcock, Sr. V.P., (703) 522-1315

PRINCIPAL OFFICE: 1001 North 19th Street, Arlington, VA 22209

TELEPHONE NUMBER: (703) 522-1315
FAX: (703) 528-4510
WEB: www.aesc.com

NO. OF EMPLOYEES: 14,500 (approx.)

SHAREHOLDERS: 1,092

ANNUAL MEETING: In Apr.

INCORPORATED: DE, Jan., 1981

INSTITUTIONAL HOLDINGS:
No. of Institutions: 460
Shares Held: 315,012,688
% Held: 63.1

INDUSTRY: Electric services (SIC: 4911)

TRANSFER AGENT(S): First Chicago Trust Company of New York, Jersey City, NJ

NYSE SYMBOL AET
Rec. Pr. 23.35 (5/31/01)

AETNA, INC.

YIELD	...
P/E RATIO	21.2

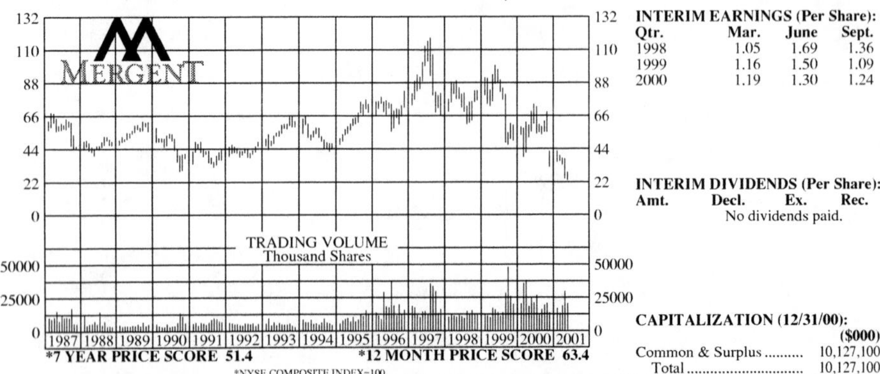

*7 YEAR PRICE SCORE 51.4 *12 MONTH PRICE SCORE 63.4

*NYSE COMPOSITE INDEX=100

INTERIM EARNINGS (Per Share):

Qtr.	Mar.	June	Sept.	Dec.
1998	1.05	1.69	1.36	1.31
1999	1.16	1.50	1.09	0.92
2000	1.19	1.30	1.24	d2.63

INTERIM DIVIDENDS (Per Share):

Amt.	Decl.	Ex.	Rec.	Pay.

No dividends paid.

CAPITALIZATION (12/31/00):

	($000)	(%)
Common & Surplus	10,127,100	100.0
Total	10,127,100	100.0

RECENT DEVELOPMENTS: For the year ended 12/31/00, the Company reported a loss from continuing operations of $127.4 million compared with net ncome of $399.4 million in the prior year. Results for 2000 included goodwill write-off of $310.2 million, severance and facilities charge of $142.5 million and net realized capital losses of $40.1 million. Results for 1999 included net realized capital gains of $62.5 million. Total revenues were $26.82 billion, up 21.3% versus $22.11 billion the year before.

PROSPECTS: Higher-than-expected costs resulting from increased patient use of outpatient, pharmacy and other services are continuing to plague the Company. As a result, AET expects a decline of up to 10.0% in its overall health-care membership this year due to Medicare market exits, commercial HMO product withdrawals in selected markets and membership attrition. Going forward, the Company's restructuring efforts and other changes are expected to help improve its financial performance by the end of 2003.

BUSINESS

AETNA, INC., is a health care benefits company with 19.3 million health members, 14.3 million dental members and 11.7 million group insurance members. The Company provides a full spectrum of health and dental products (ranging from managed care to indemnity products), group insurance products (including life, disability and long-term care insurance products) and certain specialty health products. The Company focuses on commercial customers, ranging from small employer groups to large, multi-site national accounts. The Company also has a large case pensions business that manages a variety of retirement products for qualified defined benefit and defined contribution plans of large customers. On 12/13/00, the Company was spun off from the "old" Aetna, with the simultaneous sale of the financial services and international businesses to ING Groep N.V. for $7.70 billion.

ANNUAL FINANCIAL DATA

	12/31/00	12/31/99	12/31/98
Earnings Per Share	**[1] d0.90**	...	...
Cash Flow Per Share	**3.26**	**6.11**	...
Tang. Book Val. Per Share	**16.99**	**14.48**	...
INCOME STATEMENT (IN MILLIONS):			
Total Revenues	26,818.9	22,109.7	16,589.0
Costs & Expenses	26,167.8	20,721.0	15,141.9
Depreciation & Amort.	587.9	488.4	466.9
Operating Income	63.2	900.3	980.2
Net Interest Inc./(Exp.)	d248.2	d232.7	d206.2
Income Before Income Taxes	d39.0	744.8	842.0
Income Taxes	88.4	345.4	391.6
Net Income	[1] d127.4	399.4	450.4
Cash Flow	460.5	887.8	917.3
Average Shs. Outstg. (000)	141,300	145,328	...
BALANCE SHEET (IN MILLIONS):			
Cash & Cash Equivalents	16,335.9	17,687.3	18,832.6
Total Current Assets	19,767.5	21,326.9	21,267.9
Net Property	390.0	473.0	413.1
Total Assets	47,445.7	52,421.9	53,355.2
Total Current Liabilities	10,003.4	10,821.9	8,946.6
Long-Term Obligations	...	2,093.9	1,593.3
Net Stockholders' Equity	10,127.1	10,703.2	11,429.5
Net Working Capital	9,764.1	10,505.0	12,321.3
Year-end Shs. Outstg. (000)	142,619	141,484	...
STATISTICAL RECORD:			
Operating Profit Margin %	0.2	4.1	5.9
Net Profit Margin %	...	1.8	2.7
Return on Equity %	...	3.7	3.9
Return on Assets %	...	0.8	0.8
Debt/Total Assets %	...	4.0	3.0
Price Range	73.69-31.88	99.88-46.50	89.38-60.19

Statistics are as originally reported. [1] Bef. inc. from disc. opers. of $254.5 mill., incl. one-time chrgs. of $452.7 mill. & net realized cap. loss of $40.1 mill.

OFFICERS:
W. H. Donaldson, Chmn.
J. W. Rowe, Pres., C.E.O.
L. E. Shaw Jr., Exec. V.P., Gen. Counsel

INVESTOR CONTACT: Investor Relations, (860) 273-0123

PRINCIPAL OFFICE: 151 Farmington Avenue, Hartford, CT 06156

TELEPHONE NUMBER: (860) 273-0123
FAX: (860) 240-6668
WEB: www.aetna.com

NO. OF EMPLOYEES: 41,000

SHAREHOLDERS: 15,845

ANNUAL MEETING: In April

INCORPORATED: PA, Dec., 1982

INSTITUTIONAL HOLDINGS:
No. of Institutions: 264
Shares Held: 111,578,313
% Held: 78.3

INDUSTRY: Insurance agents, brokers, & service (SIC: 6411)

TRANSFER AGENT(S): First Chicago Trust Company of New York, Jersey City, NJ

NYSE SYMBOL ACS
Rec. Pr. 72.00 (4/30/01)

AFFILIATED COMPUTER SERVICES, INC.

YIELD ...
P/E RATIO 31.9

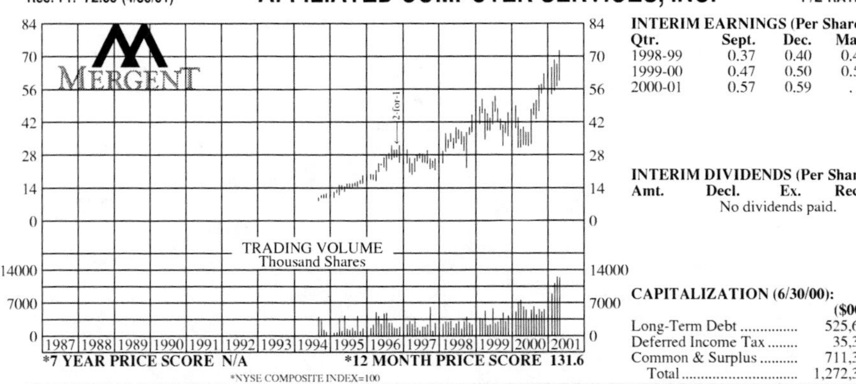

INTERIM EARNINGS (Per Share):

Qtr.	Sept.	Dec.	Mar.	June
1998-99	0.37	0.40	0.43	0.46
1999-00	0.47	0.50	0.53	0.57
2000-01	0.57	0.59	...	...

INTERIM DIVIDENDS (Per Share):

Amt.	Decl.	Ex.	Rec.	Pay.

No dividends paid.

CAPITALIZATION (6/30/00):

	($000)	(%)
Long-Term Debt	525,619	41.3
Deferred Income Tax	35,316	2.8
Common & Surplus	711,377	55.9
Total	1,272,312	100.0

RECENT DEVELOPMENTS: For the quarter ended 12/31/00, net income jumped 21.0% to $32.0 million versus $26.4 million in the corresponding quarter of 1999. Revenues were $500.9 million, up 5.2% from $476.0 million in the prior-year period. Operating income increased 24.9% to $56.7 million compared with $45.4 million the year before. Operating margins improved to 11.3% from 10.2% in the previous year.

PROSPECTS: The Company expects total revenues for fiscal 2001 to be about $2.10 billion, which excludes revenues of divested operations in the previous year. Additionally, the Company expects total revenue will reflect internal growth of about 14.0% to 15.0%. Operating margins and pre-tax margins are anticipated to be about 10.8% and 10.4%, respectively.

BUSINESS

AFFILIATED COMPUTER SERVICES, INC. provides a full range of information technology services to the commercial sector and federal government including business process outsourcing, technology outsourcing and systems integration services primarily in North America, as well as Central America, South America, Europe, Africa and the Middle East. The Company also provides services in loan and mortgage processing, claims processing, accounts payable processing, data capture, storage and retrieval services and trade marketing. Revenues for 2000 were derived: business process outsourcing, 48.3%; systems integration services, 30.8%; and technology outsourcing, 20.9%.

ANNUAL FINANCIAL DATA

	6/30/00	6/30/99	6/30/98	6/30/97	6/30/96	6/30/95	6/30/94
Earnings Per Share	**[1] 2.07**	**1.66**	**1.11**	**1.05**	**0.82**	**0.69**	**0.53**
Cash Flow Per Share	**3.48**	**2.75**	**2.02**	**1.91**	**1.34**	**1.15**	**0.90**
Tang. Book Val. Per Share	**0.88**	**...**	**1.71**	**1.50**	**1.72**	**1.05**	**...**
INCOME STATEMENT (IN MILLIONS):							
Total Revenues	1,962.5	1,642.2	1,189.1	624.5	396.5	313.2	271.1
Costs & Expenses	1,754.4	1,416.9	1,043.3	521.9	340.7	269.8	226.6
Depreciation & Amort.	84.8	66.7	47.5	31.3	15.0	11.8	8.5
Operating Income	123.4	158.6	98.3	71.4	40.8	31.5	24.8
Net Interest Inc./(Exp.)	d24.0	d17.6	d12.1	...	...	...	...
Income Before Income Taxes	195.3	145.5	94.1	65.0	39.9	29.8	20.2
Income Taxes	86.0	59.3	39.7	26.5	16.2	12.2	8.3
Net Income	[1] 109.3	86.2	54.4	38.5	23.8	17.6	11.9
Cash Flow	194.1	153.0	101.9	69.8	38.8	29.5	20.4
Average Shs. Outstg. (000)	55,806	55,668	50,487	36,567	28,880	25,616	22,826
BALANCE SHEET (IN MILLIONS):							
Cash & Cash Equivalents	44.5	32.8	84.0	21.3	34.7	49.7	49.4
Total Current Assets	771.9	415.9	365.1	168.2	168.8	114.4	99.2
Net Property	176.5	163.2	142.7	103.0	84.9	23.5	15.5
Total Assets	1,656.4	1,223.6	949.8	577.4	533.6	225.7	190.1
Total Current Liabilities	358.2	221.7	167.0	102.4	118.9	62.8	48.5
Long-Term Obligations	525.6	349.1	234.8	89.5	57.2	37.9	80.0
Net Stockholders' Equity	711.4	607.4	503.7	348.5	303.0	106.6	48.2
Net Working Capital	413.6	194.2	198.1	65.8	50.0	51.6	50.7
Year-end Shs. Outstg. (000)	49,581	49,245	48,238	35,902	23,380	26,584	20,798
STATISTICAL RECORD:							
Operating Profit Margin %	6.3	9.7	8.3	11.4	10.3	10.1	9.2
Net Profit Margin %	5.6	5.3	4.6	6.2	6.0	5.6	4.4
Return on Equity %	15.4	14.2	10.8	11.0	7.8	16.5	24.8
Return on Assets %	6.6	7.0	5.7	6.7	4.5	7.8	6.3
Debt/Total Assets %	31.7	28.5	24.7	15.5	10.7	16.8	42.1
Price Range	62.63-31.00	53.00-31.75	45.00-22.38	30.25-19.50	32.00-16.88	19.25-9.88	11.75-8.50
P/E Ratio	30.3-15.0	31.9-19.1	40.5-20.2	28.8-18.6	39.0-20.6	28.1-14.4	22.4-16.2

Statistics are as originally reported. [1] Incl. $72.0 mill. pre-tax non-recur. chgs. & $85.8 mill. pre-tax gain fr. divestitures.

OFFICERS:
D. Deason, Chmn.
J. A. Rich, Pres., C.E.O.
W. Edwards, C.F.O.

INVESTOR CONTACT: Investor Relations, (214) 841-8011

PRINCIPAL OFFICE: 2828 North Haskell, Dallas, TX 75204

TELEPHONE NUMBER: (214) 841-6111
FAX: (214) 841-8315
WEB: www.acs-inc.com

NO. OF EMPLOYEES: 18,500

SHAREHOLDERS: N/A

ANNUAL MEETING: In Oct.

INCORPORATED: DE, June, 1988

INSTITUTIONAL HOLDINGS:
No. of Institutions: 196
Shares Held: 43,686,512
% Held: 87.4

INDUSTRY: Data processing and preparation (SIC: 7374)

TRANSFER AGENT(S): FirstCity Transfer Co., Edison, NJ

NYSE SYMBOL AFL
Rec. Pr. 32.43 (5/31/01)

AFLAC INCORPORATED

YIELD 0.6%
P/E RATIO 25.5

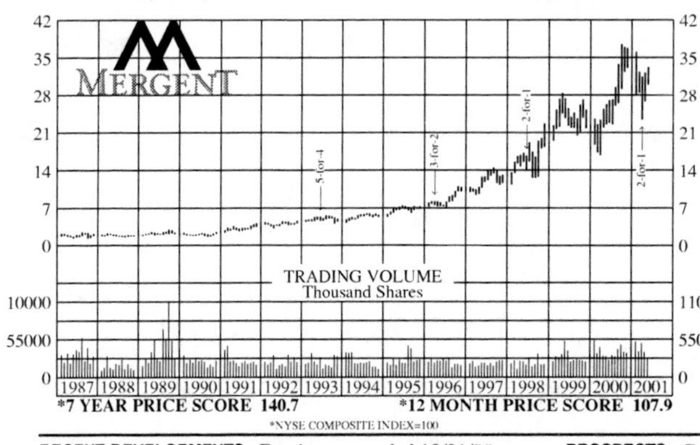

INTERIM EARNINGS (Per Share):

Qtr.	Mar.	June	Sept.	Dec.
1996	0.15	0.15	0.16	0.24
1997	0.16	0.54	0.17	0.18
1998	0.29	0.19	0.20	0.21
1999	0.36	0.24	0.26	0.19
2000	0.29	0.37	0.30	0.31

INTERIM DIVIDENDS (Per Share):

Amt.	Decl.	Ex.	Rec.	Pay.
0.085Q	7/25/00	8/15/00	8/17/00	9/01/00
0.085Q	10/24/00	11/14/00	11/16/00	12/01/00
0.085Q	1/29/01	2/13/01	2/15/01	3/01/01
2-for-1	2/13/01	3/19/01	2/27/01	3/16/01
0.05Q	2/13/01	5/15/01	5/17/01	6/01/01

Indicated div.: $0.20 (Div. Reinv. Plan)

CAPITALIZATION (12/31/00):

	($000)	(%)
Long-Term Debt	1,079,000	14.1
Deferred Income Tax	1,894,000	24.7
Common & Surplus	4,694,000	61.2
Total	7,667,000	100.0

RECENT DEVELOPMENTS: For the year ended 12/31/00, net earnings increased 20.3% to $687.0 million versus $571.0 million in 1999. Earnings for 2000 included a one-time benefitof $99.0 million and realized investment losses of $69.0 million. Earnings for 1999 included a benefit of $67.0 million and a non-recurring charge of $41.0 million. Total revenues improved 12.5% to $9.72 billion versus $8.64 billion a year earlier.

PROSPECTS: Going forward, the Company should be well positioned for continued strong business growth, led by a growing distribution system, increased brand awareness and high-quality insurance products. Moreover, AFL's solid presence in Japan, coupled with its extensive preparation for deregulation, should better position the Company for a more competitive market for supplement insurance products in Japan.

BUSINESS

AFLAC INC. is an international insurance organization whose principal subsidiary is American Family Life Assurance Company of Columbus. In addition to life, and health & accident insurance, AFL has pioneered cancer-expense and intensive-care insurance coverage. AFLAC's subsidiary Communicorp specializes in printing, advertising, audio-visuals, sales incentives, business meetings and mailings. As of 12/31/00, AFL insured more than 40.0 million people worldwide, and offers policies through more than 170,000 payroll accounts.

ANNUAL FINANCIAL DATA

	12/31/00	12/31/99	12/31/98	12/31/97	12/31/96	12/31/95	12/31/94
Earnings Per Share	**[2] 1.26**	**1.04**	**0.88**	**[1] 1.04**	**[1] 0.69**	**0.58**	**0.47**
Tang. Book Val. Per Share	**8.87**	**7.28**	**7.09**	**6.44**	**3.57**	**3.39**	**2.75**
Dividends Per Share	**0.17**	**0.14**	**0.13**	**0.11**	**0.10**	**0.08**	**0.07**
Dividend Payout %	**13.1**	**14.0**	**14.3**	**10.7**	**14.1**	**14.4**	**15.7**
INCOME STATEMENT (IN MILLIONS):							
Total Premium Income	8,239.0	7,264.0	5,943.0	5,873.7	5,910.0	6,070.8	5,180.7
Net Investment Income	1,550.0	1,369.0	1,138.0	1,077.7	1,022.0	1,025.0	838.8
Other Income	d69.0	7.0	23.0	299.3	168.2	94.8	91.2
Total Revenues	9,720.0	8,640.0	7,104.0	7,250.7	7,100.2	7,190.6	6,110.8
Policyholder Benefits	6,618.0	5,885.0	4,877.0	4,833.1	4,895.5	5,034.3	4,256.5
Income Before Income Taxes	1,012.0	778.0	551.0	864.8	650.0	601.0	504.3
Income Taxes	325.0	207.0	64.0	279.8	255.6	251.9	211.5
Net Income	[2] 687.0	571.0	487.0	[1] 585.0	[1] 394.4	349.1	292.8
Average Shs. Outstg. (000)	544,906	550,846	551,744	563,192	578,048	598,160	618,608
BALANCE SHEET (IN MILLIONS):							
Cash & Cash Equivalents	609.0	616.0	374.0	279.0	261.7	236.3	348.6
Premiums Due	301.0	270.0	272.0	215.7	227.0	321.1	303.7
Invst. Assets: Fixed-term	25,817.0	25,248.0	21,564.0	22,437.8	20,327.7	19,675.0	15,530.7
Invst. Assets: Equities	236.0	215.0	177.0	146.3	136.3	108.1	84.4
Invst. Assets: Loans	...	...	...	16.7	17.8	22.2	25.1
Invst. Assets: Total	31,558.0	31,408.0	26,620.0	22,644.2	20,746.5	20,040.8	15,976.1
Total Assets	37,232.0	37,041.0	31,222.0	29,454.0	25,022.8	25,338.0	20,287.1
Long-Term Obligations	1,079.0	1,111.0	596.0	523.2	353.5	327.3	184.9
Net Stockholders' Equity	4,694.0	3,868.0	3,770.0	3,430.5	2,125.6	2,134.1	1,751.8
Year-end Shs. Outstg. (000)	529,210	531,482	531,368	532,872	578,048	598,160	597,816
STATISTICAL RECORD:							
Return on Revenues %	7.1	6.6	6.9	8.1	5.6	4.9	4.8
Return on Equity %	14.6	14.8	12.9	17.1	18.6	16.4	16.7
Return on Assets %	1.8	1.5	1.6	2.0	1.6	1.4	1.4
Price Range	37.47-16.78	28.38-19.50	22.66-11.34	14.47-9.38	11.00-7.06	7.46-5.31	6.02-4.21
P/E Ratio	29.7-13.3	27.4-18.8	25.7-12.9	13.9-9.0	16.1-10.3	12.8-9.1	12.7-8.9
Average Yield %	0.6	0.6	0.7	0.9	1.1	1.3	1.5

Statistics are as originally reported. Adj. for stk. splits: 2-for-1, 3/01 & 6/98; 3-for-2, 3/96 [1] Incl. non-recurr. credit $267.2 mill., 12/97; $60.3 mill., 12/96 [2] Incl. one-time benefit of $99.0 mill. & realized invest. loss of $69.0 mill.

OFFICERS:
P. S. Amos, Chmn.
D. P. Amos, Vice-Chmn., Pres., C.E.O.
K. Cloninger III, Exec. V.P., C.F.O., Treas.

INVESTOR CONTACT: Kenneth S. Janke, Jr., Sr. V.P., Inv. Rel., (800) 235-2667

PRINCIPAL OFFICE: 1932 Wynnton Road, Columbus, GA 31999

TELEPHONE NUMBER: (706) 323-3431
FAX: (706) 596-3488
WEB: www.aflac.com

NO. OF EMPLOYEES: 5,278

SHAREHOLDERS: 67,995 (registered); 143,400 (common approx.)

ANNUAL MEETING: In May

INCORPORATED: GA, 1973

INSTITUTIONAL HOLDINGS:
No. of Institutions: 435
Shares Held: 278,449,547
% Held: 53.0

INDUSTRY: Accident and health insurance (SIC: 6321)

TRANSFER AGENT(S): AFLAC Incorporated

NYSE SYMBOL AGRA
Rec. Pr. 7.00 (5/31/01)

AGERE SYSTEMS INC

YIELD ...
P/E RATIO ...

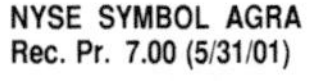

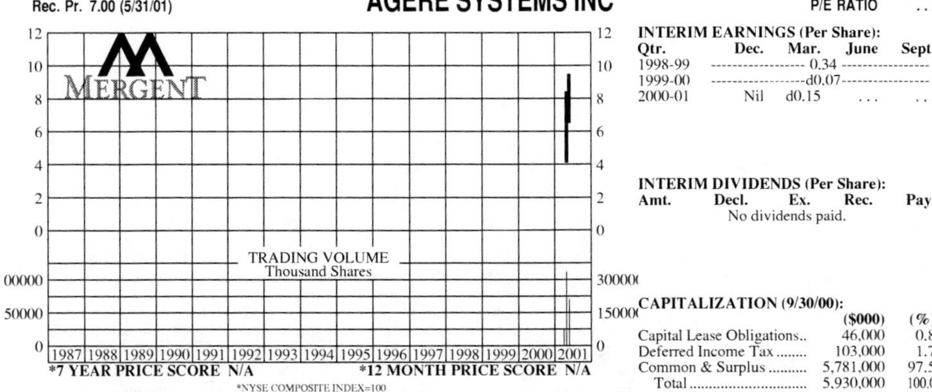

*7 YEAR PRICE SCORE N/A *12 MONTH PRICE SCORE N/A

*NYSE COMPOSITE INDEX=100

INTERIM EARNINGS (Per Share):

Qtr.	Dec.	Mar.	June	Sept.
1998-99		0.34		
1999-00		d0.07		
2000-01	Nil	d0.15	...	...

INTERIM DIVIDENDS (Per Share):

Amt.	Decl.	Ex.	Rec.	Pay.

No dividends paid.

CAPITALIZATION (9/30/00):

	($000)	(%)
Capital Lease Obligations..	46,000	0.8
Deferred Income Tax	103,000	1.7
Common & Surplus	5,781,000	97.5
Total	5,930,000	100.0

RECENT DEVELOPMENTS: For the quarter ended 3/31/01, the Company reported a net loss of $148.0 million compared with net income of $65.0 million in the year-earlier quarter. Results for the current quarter included a $112.0 million amortization of goodwill charge and a $36.0 million restructuring and separation charge. Results for 2000 included charges totaling $16.0 million. Total revenue rose 11.6% to $1.19 billion from $1.07 billion in the prior-year period.

PROSPECTS: AGRA anticipates revenues for the third quarter of fiscal 2001 to be between $950.0 million and $1.03 billion, which is 14.0% to 20.0% lower than in the second quarter. These estimates represent lower spending by telecommunications carriers and decreased demand from customers. Meanwhile, as part of an ongoing effort to align manufacturing capacity with customer demand and cut costs and expenses, AGRA will reduce its workforce by approximately 2,000 employees.

BUSINESS

AGERE SYSTEMS INC. designs, develops and manufactures optoelectronic components for communications networks, and integrated circuits for use in a broad range of communications and computer equipment. The Company operates in two segments: optoelectronic and integrated circuits. AGRA's optoelectronic components transmit, process, change, amplify and receive light that carries data and voice information over optical networks. AGRA provides optoelectronic components for use in both submarine and terrestrial networks, including high-speed transport networks, metropolitan networks, cable television networks and data communications networks. AGRA's integrated circuits are designed to perform a range of functions, including processing electronic signals, controlling electronic system functions and processing and storing data. AGRA also offers wireless local area networking products, which facilitate the transmission of data and voice signals within a localized area without cable or wires. The Company was spun off from Lucent Technologies Inc. in March 2001.

ANNUAL FINANCIAL DATA

	9/30/00	9/30/99	9/30/98
Earnings Per Share	**1 d0.07**	**1 2 0.34**	**1 0.29**
Cash Flow Per Share	**0.57**	**0.69**	**0.60**
Tang. Book Val. Per Share	**1.40**	...	...
INCOME STATEMENT (IN MILLIONS):			
Total Revenues	4,708.0	3,714.0	3,101.0
Costs & Expenses	3,886.0	2,837.0	2,314.0
Depreciation & Amort.	666.0	398.0	320.0
Operating Income	156.0	479.0	467.0
Net Interest Inc./(Exp.)	d58.0	d38.0	d21.0
Income Before Income Taxes	131.0	477.0	513.0
Income Taxes	207.0	158.0	210.0
Net Income	1 d76.0	1 2 319.0	1 303.0
Cash Flow	590.0	717.0	623.0
Average Shs. Outstg. (000)	1,035,000	1,035,000	1,035,000
BALANCE SHEET (IN MILLIONS):			
Total Current Assets	1,404.0	1,039.0	...
Net Property	1,883.0	1,716.0	...
Total Assets	7,067.0	3,020.0	...
Total Current Liabilities	976.0	820.0	...
Long-Term Obligations	46.0	64.0	...
Net Stockholders' Equity	5,781.0	1,962.0	...
Net Working Capital	428.0	219.0	...
Year-end Shs. Outstg. (000)	1,635,000	...	...
STATISTICAL RECORD:			
Operating Profit Margin %	3.3	12.9	15.1
Net Profit Margin %	...	8.6	9.8
Return on Equity %	...	16.3	...
Return on Assets %	...	10.6	...
Debt/Total Assets %	0.7	2.1	...

Statistics are as originally reported. 1 Incl. purchase in-process R&D chgs. $446.0 mill., 9/00; $17,000, 9/99; $48.0 mill., 9/98. 2 Bef. acctg. change credit of $32.0 mill.

OFFICERS:
J. A. Young, Chmn.
J. T. Dickson, Pres., C.E.O.
M. T. Greenquist, Exec. V.P., C.F.O.
J. F. Rankin, Sr. V.P., Gen. Couns., Sec.

INVESTOR CONTACT: Investor Relations, (610) 712-4323

PRINCIPAL OFFICE: 555 Union Boulevard, Allentown, PA 18109

TELEPHONE NUMBER: (610) 712-4323
WEB: www.agere.com

NO. OF EMPLOYEES: 17,400

SHAREHOLDERS: N/A

ANNUAL MEETING: N/A

INCORPORATED: DE, Aug., 2000

INSTITUTIONAL HOLDINGS:
No. of Institutions: 78
Shares Held: 174,165,700
% Held: 0.0

INDUSTRY: Semiconductors and related devices (SIC: 3674)

TRANSFER AGENT(S): The Bank of New York, New York, NY

NYSE SYMBOL A
Rec. Pr. 39.01 (4/30/01)

AGILENT TECHNOLOGIES, INC.

YIELD ...
P/E RATIO 22.4

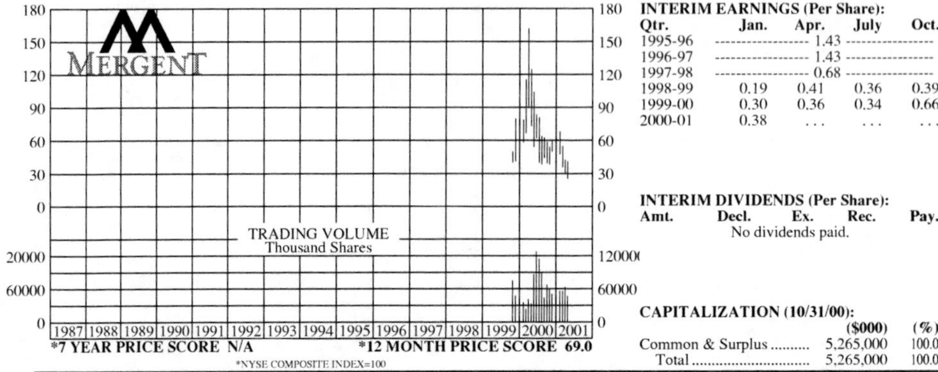

INTERIM EARNINGS (Per Share):

Qtr.	Jan.	Apr.	July	Oct.
1995-96		1.43		
1996-97		1.43		
1997-98		0.68		
1998-99	0.19	0.41	0.36	0.39
1999-00	0.30	0.36	0.34	0.66
2000-01	0.38	...	...	...

INTERIM DIVIDENDS (Per Share):

Amt.	Decl.	Ex.	Rec.	Pay.

No dividends paid.

CAPITALIZATION (10/31/00):

	($000)	(%)
Common & Surplus	5,265,000	100.0
Total	5,265,000	100.0

RECENT DEVELOPMENTS: For the quarter ended 1/31/01, net earnings jumped 36.6% to $179.0 million compared with net income of $131.0 million in 2000. Results for the first quarter of 2001 excluded a net charge of $16.0 million from a cumulative effect of an accounting change. Net revenue amounted to $2.84 billion, up 26.5% from $2.25 billion in the prior-year period. Operating earnings soared 63.2% to $279.0 million compared with $171.0 million the year before.

PROSPECTS: Results for the second quarter of 2001 may be hampered by the current economic slowdown, overcapacity and inventory adjustments made in many of the Company's key markets. As a result, the Company expects revenue growth to be between 10.0% and 15.0% for the full year. Separately, the Company sold a 40-acre parcel of surplus land in San Jose, CA. The sale resulted in a pre-tax gain of about $270.0 million. The Company plans to hold the remaining 30 acres of land for possible expansion.

BUSINESS

AGILENT TECHNOLOGIES, INC. is a global diversified technology company that provides applications to high-growth markets within the communications, electronics, healthcare and life sciences industries in 120 countries. A was incorporated in May 1999 as a wholly-owned subsidiary of Hewlett-Packard Company and was spun off in November 1999 as a separate entity. A operates in four business segments: test and measurement; semiconductor products; healthcare applications; and chemical analysis. The test and measurement unit (56.7% of 2000 revenues) provides test instruments and monitoring systems for electronic and communication devices. Semiconductor products (20.5%) consist of fiber optic communications devices. Healthcare applications (13.1%) provide patient monitoring, ultrasound imaging and cardiology products. The chemical analysis (9.7%) provides analytical instruments.

ANNUAL FINANCIAL DATA

	10/31/00	10/31/99	10/31/98	10/31/97	10/31/96
Earnings Per Share	**1.66**	**1.35**	**[1] 0.68**	**1.43**	**1.43**
Cash Flow Per Share	**2.75**	**2.60**	**1.93**	**2.51**	**2.48**
Tang. Book Val. Per Share	**10.37**	**8.90**	**7.95**	**8.18**	**...**
INCOME STATEMENT (IN MILLIONS):					
Total Revenues	10,773.0	8,331.0	7,952.0	7,785.0	7,379.0
Costs & Expenses	9,225.0	7,115.0	7,033.0	6,506.0	6,103.0
Depreciation & Amort.	495.0	475.0	477.0	409.0	401.0
Operating Income	1,053.0	741.0	442.0	870.0	875.0
Income Before Income Taxes	1,164.0	787.0	396.0	823.0	854.0
Income Taxes	407.0	275.0	139.0	280.0	312.0
Net Income	757.0	512.0	[1] 257.0	543.0	542.0
Cash Flow	1,252.0	987.0	734.0	952.0	943.0
Average Shs. Outstg. (000)	455,000	380,000	380,000	380,000	380,000
BALANCE SHEET (IN MILLIONS):					
Cash & Cash Equivalents	996.0	...	...	...	...
Total Current Assets	5,655.0	3,538.0	3,075.0	2,931.0	...
Net Property	1,741.0	1,387.0	1,481.0	1,623.0	...
Total Assets	8,425.0	5,444.0	4,987.0	5,006.0	...
Total Current Liabilities	2,758.0	1,681.0	1,599.0	1,523.0	...
Net Stockholders' Equity	5,265.0	3,382.0	3,022.0	3,110.0	...
Net Working Capital	2,897.0	1,857.0	1,476.0	1,408.0	...
Year-end Shs. Outstg. (000)	453,976	380,000	380,000	380,000	380,000
STATISTICAL RECORD:					
Operating Profit Margin %	9.8	8.9	5.6	11.2	11.9
Net Profit Margin %	7.0	6.1	3.2	7.0	7.3
Return on Equity %	14.4	15.1	8.5	17.5	...
Return on Assets %	9.0	9.4	5.2	10.8	...
Price Range	162.00-38.06	80.00-39.81	...	...	...
P/E Ratio	97.6-22.9	59.3-29.5	...	...	...

Statistics are as originally reported. [1] Incl. $163.0 mill. restr. chg.

OFFICERS:
G. Grinstein, Chmn.
E. W. Barnholt, Pres., C.E.O.
R. R. Walker, Exec. V.P., C.F.O.

INVESTOR CONTACT: Investor Relations, (650) 752-5000

PRINCIPAL OFFICE: 395 Page Mill Road, Palo Alto, CA 94304

TELEPHONE NUMBER: (650) 752-5000
FAX: (650) 752-5633
WEB: www.agilent.com

NO. OF EMPLOYEES: 47,000 (approx.)

SHAREHOLDERS: 85,921

ANNUAL MEETING: In Feb.

INCORPORATED: DE, May, 1999

INSTITUTIONAL HOLDINGS:
No. of Institutions: 739
Shares Held: 215,032,027
% Held: 47.1

INDUSTRY: Instruments to measure electricity (SIC: 3825)

TRANSFER AGENT(S): Computershare Investor Services, Chicago, IL

NYSE SYMBOL ATG
Rec. Pr. 23.50 (5/31/01)

AGL RESOURCES INC.

YIELD 4.6%
P/E RATIO 16.8

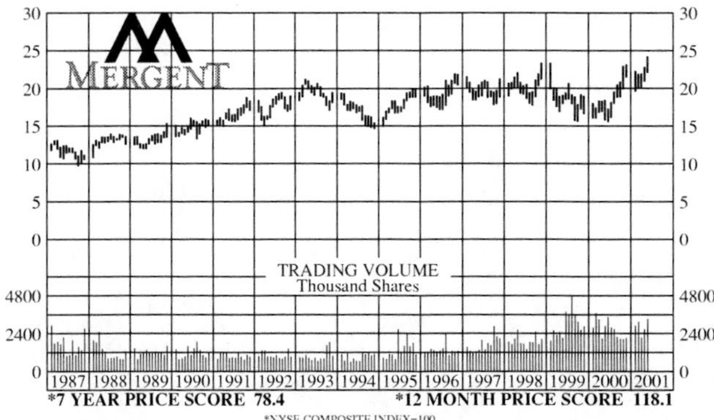

INTERIM EARNINGS (Per Share):

Qtr.	Dec.	Mar.	June	Sept.
1997-98	0.45	0.79	d0.02	0.19
1998-99	0.28	0.42	0.12	0.48
1999-00	0.30	0.41	0.26	0.32
2000-01	0.41	...	...	...

INTERIM DIVIDENDS (Per Share):

Amt.	Decl.	Ex.	Rec.	Pay.
0.27Q	5/09/00	5/17/00	5/19/00	6/01/00
0.27Q	8/08/00	8/16/00	8/18/00	9/01/00
0.27Q	10/31/00	11/15/00	11/17/00	12/01/00
0.27Q	1/26/01	2/14/01	2/16/01	3/01/01
0.27Q	4/26/01	5/16/01	5/18/01	6/01/01

Indicated div.: $1.08 (Div. Reinv. Plan)

CAPITALIZATION (9/30/00):

	($000)	(%)
Long-Term Debt	590,000	40.4
Capital Lease Obligations	1,000	0.1
Deferred Income Tax	249,600	17.1
Common & Surplus	620,900	42.5
Total	1,461,500	100.0

RECENT DEVELOPMENTS: For the first quarter ended 12/31/00, net income jumped 31.6% to $22.5 million compared with $17.1 million in the corresponding quarter of the previous year. Earnings growth was attributed to cost management initiatives, growth in ATG's customer base, colder weather, and the accelerated integration of the Virginia Natural Gas Inc. acquisition. Operating revenues soared 61.7% to $294.8 million from $182.3 million in the prior-year period.

PROSPECTS: On 2/13/01, the Company entered into an agreement with Alliance Data Systems to sell Utilipro, Inc., an integrated customer care and billing services provider for energy marketers in the U.S. Separately, the Virginia State Corporation Commission approved a filing made by Virginia Natural Gas Company and AGL Energy Services (AGLES) for AGLES to provide energy services to VNG for its approximately 230,000 customers in Virginia.

BUSINESS

AGL RESOURCES INC. (formerly Atlanta Gas Light Company) was formed 3/6/96 through a corporate restructuring for the primary purpose of becoming the parent holding company of Atlanta Gas Light Company (AGLC) and its subsidiaries. ATG's principal business is the distribution of natural gas through AGLC and its wholly-owned subsidiary, Chattanooga Gas Company, and in unregulated business activities through AGL Energy Services, Inc., AGL Investments, Inc. and their subsidiaries. ATG provides natural gas distribution services to 1.8 million customers in Georgia, Chattanooga, Tennessee, and southeastern Virginia. Revenues for 2000 were derived: 94.2% utility and 5.8% non-utility.

QUARTERLY DATA

(09/30/00)($000)	Rev	Inc
1st Quarter	182,300	33.5
2nd Quarter	160,100	37.5
3rd Quarter	131,800	38.4
4Th Quarter	133,200	28.4

ANNUAL FINANCIAL DATA

	9/30/00	9/30/99	9/30/98	9/30/97	9/30/96	9/30/95
Earnings Per Share	**1.29**	**1.29**	**1.41**	**1.37**	**1.37**	**[1] 0.50**
Cash Flow Per Share	**2.82**	**2.72**	**2.74**	**2.62**	**2.59**	**2.69**
Tang. Book Val. Per Share	**11.50**	**11.44**	**11.42**	**10.99**	**10.56**	...
Dividends Per Share	**1.08**	**1.08**	**1.08**	**1.08**	**1.07**	...
Dividend Payout %	**83.7**	**83.7**	**76.6**	**78.8**	**77.7**	...
INCOME STATEMENT (IN THOUSANDS):						
Total Revenues	607,400	1,068,600	1,338,600	1,287,600	1,228,600	1,068,500
Costs & Expenses	385,200	832,200	1,095,300	1,045,800	997,600	912,500
Depreciation & Amort.	84,400	81,800	75,700	70,300	67,500	62,500
Operating Income	137,800	154,600	167,600	171,500	163,500	93,500
Net Interest Inc./(Exp.)	d36,500	d70,600	d41,500	d41,900	d36,000	1,500
Income Taxes	37,200	39,100	38,800	46,800	47,500	16,700
Net Income	71,100	74,400	80,600	76,600	75,600	[1] 78,300
Cash Flow	155,500	156,200	156,300	146,900	143,100	140,800
Average Shs. Outstg.	55,200	57,400	57,100	56,100	55,300	52,400
BALANCE SHEET (IN THOUSANDS):						
Gross Property	2,459,700	2,391,000	2,239,500	2,174,900	1,441,600	...
Accumulated Depreciation	822,200	792,100	705,500	678,300	26,300	...
Net Property	1,637,500	1,598,900	1,534,000	1,496,600	1,415,300	...
Total Assets	2,019,900	1,969,300	1,981,800	1,936,600	1,823,100	1,674,600
Long-Term Obligations	591,000	610,000	660,000	660,000	554,500	554,500
Net Stockholders' Equity	620,900	661,500	654,100	622,100	588,300	557,300
Year-end Shs. Outstg.	54,000	57,800	57,300	56,600	55,700	...
STATISTICAL RECORD:						
Operating Profit Margin %	22.7	14.5	12.5	13.3	13.3	8.8
Net Profit Margin %	11.7	7.0	6.0	5.9	6.2	7.3
Net Inc./Net Property %	4.3	4.7	5.3	5.1	5.3	...
Net Inc./Tot. Capital %	4.9	5.0	5.3	5.2	5.5	6.7
Return on Equity %	11.5	11.2	12.3	12.3	12.9	14.0
Accum. Depr./Gross Prop. %	33.4	33.1	31.5	31.2	1.8	...
Price Range	23.19-15.50	23.38-15.56	23.38-17.69	21.63-17.75	22.00-17.13	20.00-14.88
P/E Ratio	18.0-12.0	18.1-12.1	16.6-12.5	15.8-13.0	16.1-12.5	40.0-29.7
Average Yield %	5.6	5.5	5.3	5.5	5.4	...

Statistics are as originally reported. Adjusted for 2-for-1 stock split, 12/95. [1] Before $2.9 mill. ($0.08 a sh.) gain from accounting adjustment, but incl. pre-tax restruct. charge of $70.3 mill.

OFFICERS:
D. R. Riddle, Chmn.
P. G. Rosput, Pres., C.E.O.
D. P. Weinstein, Sr. V.P., C.F.O.
P. R. Shlanta, Sr. V.P., Gen. Couns.

INVESTOR CONTACT: Melanie M. Pratt, (404) 584-3420

PRINCIPAL OFFICE: 817 West Peachtree Street, NW, Suite 1000, Atlanta, GA 30308

TELEPHONE NUMBER: (404) 584-9470
FAX: (404) 584-3945
WEB: www.aglresources.com

NO. OF EMPLOYEES: 1,938

SHAREHOLDERS: 621

ANNUAL MEETING: In Jan.

INCORPORATED: GA, Nov., 1995

INSTITUTIONAL HOLDINGS:
No. of Institutions: 153
Shares Held: 22,443,691
% Held: 41.4

INDUSTRY: Natural gas distribution (SIC: 4924)

TRANSFER AGENT(S): EquiServe Trust Company, N.A., Canton, MA

NYSE SYMBOL APD
Rec. Pr. 42.99 (4/30/01)

AIR PRODUCTS & CHEMICALS, INC.

YIELD 1.8%
P/E RATIO 44.8

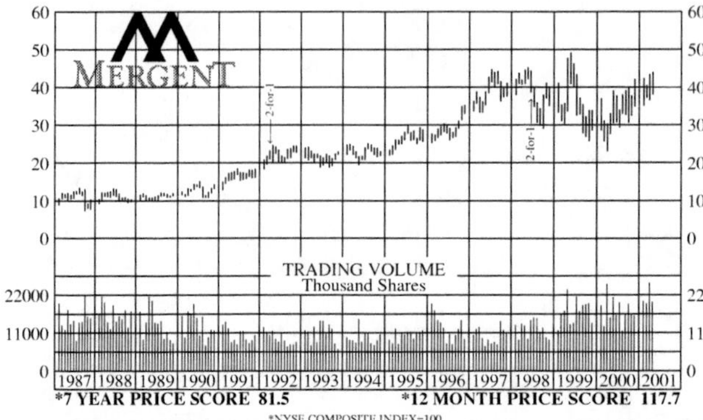

*7 YEAR PRICE SCORE 81.5 *12 MONTH PRICE SCORE 117.7

*NYSE COMPOSITE INDEX=100

INTERIM EARNINGS (Per Share):

Qtr.	Dec.	Mar.	June	Sept.
1997-98	0.72	0.55	0.63	0.59
1998-99	0.59	0.50	0.44	0.57
1999-00	0.23	0.22	d0.89	1.01
2000-01	0.62	...	...	...

INTERIM DIVIDENDS (Per Share):

Amt.	Decl.	Ex.	Rec.	Pay.
0.19Q	9/21/00	9/28/00	10/02/00	11/13/00
0.19Q	11/16/00	12/28/00	1/02/01	2/12/01
0.19Q	4/02/01	3/29/01	4/02/01	5/14/01

Indicated div.: $0.76 (Div. Reinv. Plan)

CAPITALIZATION (9/30/00):

	($000)	(%)
Long-Term Debt	2,615,800	41.3
Deferred Income Tax	781,800	12.3
Minority Interest	115,500	1.8
Common & Surplus	2,821,300	44.5
Total	6,334,400	100.0

RECENT DEVELOPMENTS: For the quarter ended 12/31/00, net income soared to $135.6 million compared with $50.6 million in the equivalent quarter of 1999. Results for 1999 included an after-tax charge of $70.6 million for currency hedges from the BOC Group transaction. Sales and other income totaled $1.45 billion, up 14.4% from $1.27 billion in the prior-year period. Industrial gas sales increased 27.0%, while gases operating income rose 25.0%.

PROSPECTS: The Company is cautious about estimates for fiscal 2001 due to the ongoing rise of natural gas prices and a slower global economy. Going into the third quarter, the Company expects prices for natural gas and other raw materials to stabilize, which should result in stronger third and fourth quarter results. As a result, the Company expects to report earnings growth of about 6.0% to 8.0% for fiscal 2001.

BUSINESS

AIR PRODUCTS & CHEMICALS, INC. is an international supplier of industrial and specialty gas products. Principal products of the industrial gases segment are oxygen, nitrogen, argon, hydrogen, carbon monoxide, carbon dioxide, synthesis gas, and helium. The chemical business consists of polymer chemicals, performance chemicals, and chemical intermediates. The equipment and services segment designs and manufactures cryogenic and gas processing equipment for air separation, gas processing, natural gas liquefaction, hydrogen purification, and nitrogen rejection. This segment also includes the continuing businesses from the environmental/energy segment (power generation and Pure Air).

BUSINESS LINE ANALYSIS

(09/30/2000)	Rev(%)	Inc(%)
Gases	63.4	77.8
Chemicals	32.4	21.1
Equipment	4.2	1.1
Total	100.0	100.0

ANNUAL FINANCIAL DATA

	9/30/00	9/30/99	9/30/98	9/30/97	9/30/96	9/30/95	9/30/94
Earnings Per Share	**[5] 0.57**	**[4] 2.09**	**[3] 2.48**	**1.95**	**[1] 1.86**	**[1] 1.65**	**[2] 1.03**
Cash Flow Per Share	**3.24**	**4.53**	**4.71**	**4.04**	**3.71**	**3.35**	**2.58**
Tang. Book Val. Per Share	**9.07**	**11.39**	**11.08**	**20.08**	**11.22**	**10.34**	**9.43**
Dividends Per Share	**0.74**	**0.70**	**0.64**	**0.57**	**0.54**	**0.51**	**0.47**
Dividend Payout %	**129.8**	**33.5**	**25.8**	**29.5**	**28.8**	**30.7**	**46.1**
INCOME STATEMENT (IN MILLIONS):							
Total Revenues	5,495.5	5,039.8	4,933.8	4,662.0	4,033.0	3,891.0	3,483.8
Costs & Expenses	4,089.0	3,787.9	3,599.4	3,477.5	3,030.0	2,907.0	2,644.9
Depreciation & Amort.	575.7	527.2	489.4	459.1	412.0	382.0	352.8
Operating Income	830.8	724.7	845.0	725.4	591.0	602.0	486.1
Net Interest Inc./(Exp.)	d196.7	d159.1	d162.8	d161.3	d129.0	d100.0	d81.6
Income Before Income Taxes	118.1	669.0	823.7	630.4	610.0	553.0	325.3
Income Taxes	cr13.7	203.4	276.9	201.1	193.0	185.0	91.8
Equity Earnings/Minority Int.	d7.6	d15.1	...	...	...	...	...
Net Income	[5] 124.2	[4] 450.5	[3] 546.8	429.3	[1] 417.0	[1] 368.0	[2] 233.5
Cash Flow	699.9	977.7	1,036.2	888.4	829.0	750.0	586.3
Average Shs. Outstg. (000)	216,200	216,000	220,100	220,100	223,400	224,000	227,200
BALANCE SHEET (IN MILLIONS):							
Cash & Cash Equivalents	94.1	132.0	61.5	52.5	79.0	87.0	99.9
Total Current Assets	1,805.0	1,782.4	1,641.7	1,624.3	1,375.0	1,332.0	1,177.7
Net Property	5,256.7	5,192.9	4,786.1	4,441.2	3,959.0	3,502.0	2,992.6
Total Assets	8,270.5	8,235.5	7,489.6	7,244.1	6,522.0	5,816.0	5,036.2
Total Current Liabilities	1,374.8	1,857.8	1,265.6	1,124.6	1,263.0	1,311.0	1,076.4
Long-Term Obligations	2,615.8	1,961.6	2,274.3	2,291.7	1,739.0	1,194.0	922.5
Net Stockholders' Equity	2,821.3	2,961.6	2,667.3	2,648.1	2,574.0	2,398.0	2,206.4
Net Working Capital	430.2	d75.4	376.1	499.7	112.0	21.0	101.3
Year-end Shs. Outstg. (000)	229,305	229,305	211,500	119,500	222,000	224,000	226,816
STATISTICAL RECORD:							
Operating Profit Margin %	15.1	14.4	17.1	15.6	14.7	15.5	14.0
Net Profit Margin %	2.3	8.9	11.1	9.2	10.3	9.5	6.7
Return on Equity %	4.4	15.2	20.5	16.2	16.2	15.3	10.6
Return on Assets %	1.5	5.5	7.3	5.9	6.4	6.3	4.6
Debt/Total Assets %	31.6	23.8	30.4	31.6	26.7	20.5	18.3
Price Range	42.25-23.00	49.25-25.69	45.34-29.00	44.81-33.19	35.31-25.19	29.81-21.94	25.19-19.38
P/E Ratio	74.1-40.3	23.6-12.3	18.3-11.7	23.0-17.0	19.0-13.5	18.1-13.3	24.5-18.8
Average Yield %	2.3	1.9	1.7	1.5	1.8	2.0	2.1

Statistics are as originally reported. Adj. for 2-for-1 split, 6/98. [1] Incl. $35.0 mil aft-tx gn, 1998; aft-tx gn $41.0 mil, 1996; $6.6 mil gn gas plt. sale, 1995. [2] Bef. $14.3 mil. acct. cr. & $74.5 mil. aft-tx chg for spl items. [3] Incl. $58.1 mil. after-tax gain fr. American Ref-Fuel Co. sale & contract settlements. [4] Incl. $28.3 mil. net chgs. & $23.6 mil. net gain. [5] Incl. $456.5 mil. aft-tx loss fr. currency hedges & $126.8 mil. gn fr. sale of bus.

OFFICERS:
J. P. Jones III, Chmn., Pres., C.E.O.
L. J. Daley, V.P., Fin., C.F.O., Contr.
W. D. Brown, V.P., Gen. Couns., Sec.

INVESTOR CONTACT: Alexander W. Masetti, Dir., Investor Relations, (610) 481-5775

PRINCIPAL OFFICE: 7201 Hamilton Boulevard, Allentown, PA 18195-1501

TELEPHONE NUMBER: (610) 481-4911
FAX: (610) 481-5900
WEB: www.airproducts.com
NO. OF EMPLOYEES: 17,500 (approx.)
SHAREHOLDERS: 11,639
ANNUAL MEETING: In Jan.
INCORPORATED: MI, Oct., 1940; reincorp., DE, June, 1940

INSTITUTIONAL HOLDINGS:
No. of Institutions: 409
Shares Held: 186,755,398
% Held: 87.0

INDUSTRY: Industrial gases (SIC: 2813)

TRANSFER AGENT(S): First Chicago Trust Company of New York, Jersey City, NJ

NYSE SYMBOL ABF
Rec. Pr. 9.16 (4/30/01)

AIRBORNE, INC.

YIELD 1.7%
P/E RATIO 32.7

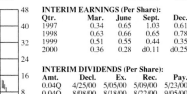

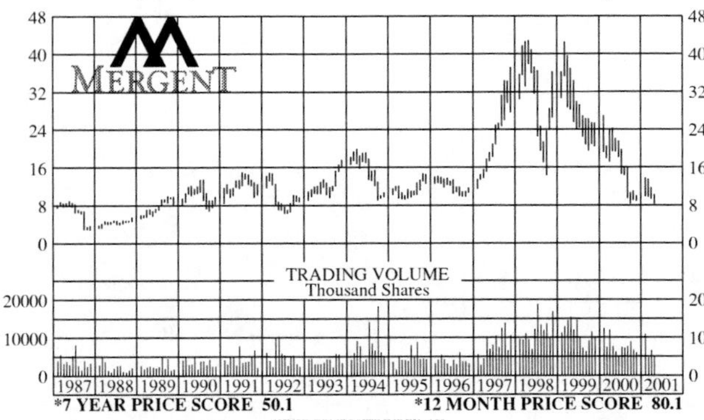

INTERIM EARNINGS (Per Share):

Qtr.	Mar.	June	Sept.	Dec.
1997	0.34	0.65	1.03	0.61
1998	0.63	0.66	0.65	0.78
1999	0.51	0.55	0.44	0.35
2000	0.36	0.28	d0.11	d0.25

INTERIM DIVIDENDS (Per Share):

Amt.	Decl.	Ex.	Rec.	Pay.
0.04Q	4/25/00	5/05/00	5/09/00	5/23/00
0.04Q	8/08/00	8/18/00	8/22/00	9/05/00
0.04Q	11/07/00	11/17/00	11/21/00	12/05/00
0.04Q	2/06/01	2/15/01	2/20/01	3/06/01
0.04Q	4/24/01	5/04/01	5/08/01	5/22/01

Indicated div.: $0.16

CAPITALIZATION (12/31/00):

	($000)	(%)
Long-Term Debt	322,230	24.6
Deferred Income Tax	125,444	9.6
Common & Surplus	862,855	65.8
Total	1,310,529	100.0

RECENT DEVELOPMENTS: For the year ended 12/31/00, the Company reported income of $14.3 million, before an accounting credit of $14.2 million, compared with net income of $91.2 million in the previous year. The decline in earnings primarily reflected the rising costs of jet fuel and the slow growth in ABF's core domestic shipments. Total revenues grew 4.4% to $3.28 billion from $3.14 billion in the prior year.

PROSPECTS: The Company anticipates continued slow shipment volume growth as a result of the weakened economy. However, shipment volume growth is expected to improve somewhat during the second half of 2001. Moreover, the Company will implement rate increases on its domestic business throughout 2001. The Company's objective is to increase revenues and return to operating profitability.

BUSINESS

AIRBORNE, INC. is the holding company for Airborne Express (formerly Airborne Freight Corporation), Sky Courier (formerly Airborne Forwarding Corp.), and ABX Air, Inc. Airborne Express serves the shipping needs of business customers worldwide. Airborne offers customers time-sensitive delivery of documents, letters, small packages, and freight throughout the U.S. and to more than 200 countries. On 12/21/00, ABF adopted a holding company structure.

REVENUES

(12/31/00)	($000)	(%)
Domestic	2,895,818	88.4
International	380,132	11.6
Total	3,275,950	100.0

ANNUAL FINANCIAL DATA

	12/31/00	12/31/99	12/31/98	12/31/97	12/31/96	12/31/95	12/31/94
Earnings Per Share	**[3] 0.30**	**[2] 1.85**	**2.72**	**2.44**	**[1] 1.28**	**1.11**	**1.81**
Cash Flow Per Share	**0.29**	**1.85**	**2.72**	**2.39**	**1.28**	**1.11**	**1.81**
Tang. Book Val. Per Share	**17.96**	**17.63**	**15.92**	**13.30**	**20.27**	**19.27**	**18.47**
INCOME STATEMENT (IN MILLIONS):							
Total Revenues	3,276.0	3,140.2	3,074.5	2,912.4	2,484.3	2,239.4	1,970.8
Costs & Expenses	3,233.3	2,980.2	2,840.1	2,687.2	2,401.4	2,170.4	1,881.8
Operating Income	42.6	160.0	234.5	225.3	79.2	69.0	88.9
Net Interest Inc./(Exp.)	d19.4	d17.3	d12.9	d27.8	d33.2	d29.3	d24.7
Income Before Income Taxes	23.2	147.4	221.6	197.5	45.9	39.6	64.3
Income Taxes	8.9	56.2	84.3	77.4	18.5	15.8	25.4
Net Income	[3] 14.3	[2] 91.2	137.3	120.1	[1] 27.4	23.8	38.8
Cash Flow	14.3	91.2	137.3	120.1	27.2	23.5	37.9
Average Shs. Outstg. (000)	48,647	49,269	50,561	50,339	21,282	21,204	21,001
BALANCE SHEET (IN MILLIONS):							
Cash & Cash Equivalents	40.4	28.7	18.7	25.5	35.8	17.9	10.3
Total Current Assets	373.5	470.1	435.8	426.6	415.2	352.1	293.3
Net Property	1,314.8	1,127.0	1,021.9	916.3	866.6	842.7	766.3
Total Assets	1,745.9	1,643.3	1,501.6	1,366.0	1,307.4	1,217.4	1,078.5
Total Current Liabilities	335.8	289.8	333.3	330.1	273.8	260.5	226.5
Long-Term Obligations	322.2	314.7	249.1	250.6	524.4	479.6	398.0
Net Stockholders' Equity	862.9	858.2	769.2	670.9	431.8	406.3	387.4
Net Working Capital	37.8	180.2	102.5	96.5	141.5	91.6	66.9
Year-end Shs. Outstg. (000)	48,035	48,685	48,321	50,429	21,306	21,083	20,971
STATISTICAL RECORD:							
Operating Profit Margin %	1.3	5.1	7.6	7.7	3.2	3.1	4.5
Net Profit Margin %	0.4	2.9	4.5	4.1	1.1	1.1	2.0
Return on Equity %	1.7	10.6	17.8	17.9	6.4	5.9	10.0
Return on Assets %	0.8	5.6	9.1	8.8	2.1	2.0	3.6
Debt/Total Assets %	18.5	19.2	16.6	18.3	40.1	39.4	36.9
Price Range	26.88-8.25	42.56-19.50	42.88-14.25	37.22-11.38	14.19-9.75	14.75-9.19	19.94-9.00
P/E Ratio	89.6-27.5	23.0-10.5	15.8-5.2	15.3-4.7	11.1-7.6	13.3-8.3	11.0-5.0

Statistics are as originally reported. Adj. for 2-for-1 stk. split, 2/98. [1] Incl. $3.7 mill. chrg. related to an airplane accident. [2] Incl. a gain of $4.6 mill. fr. the sale of securities. [3] Bef. acctg. chrg. of $14.2 mill.

OFFICERS:
R. S. Cline, Chmn., C.E.O.
C. D. Donaway, Pres., C.O.O.
L. H. Michael, Sr. V.P., C.F.O.

INVESTOR CONTACT: Lanny H. Michael, Sr. V.P., C.F.O., (206) 285-4600

PRINCIPAL OFFICE: 3101 Western Ave., Seattle, WA 98111-0662

TELEPHONE NUMBER: (206) 285-4600
FAX: (206) 281-7615
WEB: www.airborne.com

NO. OF EMPLOYEES: 16,000 full-time; 8,100 part-time

SHAREHOLDERS: 1,212

ANNUAL MEETING: In April

INCORPORATED: DE, May, 1968

INSTITUTIONAL HOLDINGS:
No. of Institutions: 79
Shares Held: 28,273,304
% Held: 58.8

INDUSTRY: Air courier services (SIC: 4513)

TRANSFER AGENT(S): The Bank of New York, New York, NY

NYSE SYMBOL AKS
Rec. Pr. 13.39 (5/31/01)

AK STEEL HOLDING CORPORATION

YIELD 1.9%
P/E RATIO 11.2

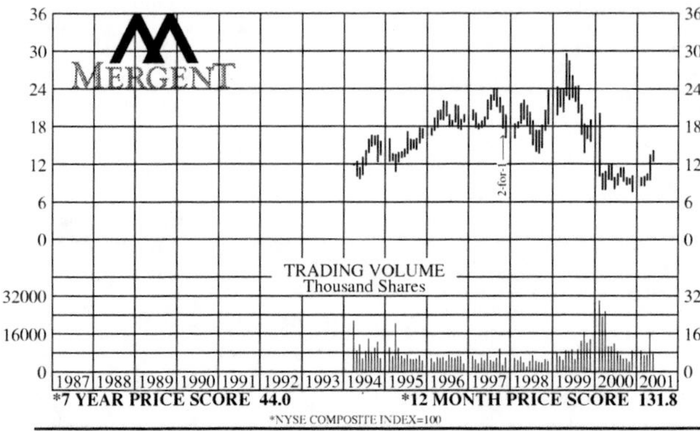

INTERIM EARNINGS (Per Share):

Qtr.	Mar.	June	Sept.	Dec.
1997	0.55	0.63	0.60	0.65
1998	0.47	0.56	0.16	0.73
1999	0.46	0.13	d0.04	d0.06
2000	0.24	0.44	0.38	0.14

INTERIM DIVIDENDS (Per Share):

Amt.	Decl.	Ex.	Rec.	Pay.
0.125Q	4/26/00	4/28/00	4/26/00	5/24/00
0.125Q	7/20/00	7/24/00	7/26/00	8/23/00
0.125Q	10/19/00	10/23/00	10/25/00	11/22/00
0.063Q	1/19/01	1/30/01	2/01/01	2/28/01
0.063Q	4/20/01	4/27/01	5/01/01	5/30/01

Indicated div.: $0.25 (Div. Reinv. Plan)

CAPITALIZATION (12/31/00):

	($000)	(%)
Long-Term Debt	1,387,600	51.3
Preferred Stock	12,500	0.5
Common & Surplus	1,306,800	48.3
Total	2,706,900	100.0

RECENT DEVELOPMENTS: For the year ended 12/31/00, net income was $132.4 million compared with income from continuing operations of $71.3 million in 1999. Results for 1999 included special charges and unusual losses of $99.7 million. Net sales were $4.52 billion, up 5.4% from $4.28 billion a year earlier. Steel shipments were essentially unchanged at 6.5 million tons compared with the prior year.

PROSPECTS: The Company is experiencing soaring energy costs, while spot market selling prices are plummeting. However, AKS is experiencing high productivity at every carbon and specialty plant. The Company's Mansfield Works established new annual production records in melting, casting and hot rolling. AKS' electrical steel tonnage shipping level is up significantly at its Zanesville and Butler Works locations.

BUSINESS

AK STEEL HOLDING CORPORATION operates through its wholly-owned subsidiary, AK Steel Corporation. AKS is a fully-integrated producer of flat-rolled carbon, stainless and electrical steels. In addition to its flat-rolled steel manufacturing and finishing operations, the Company owns and operates Sawhill Tubular, a manufacturer of a wide range of steel pipe and tubing products; Douglas Dynamics, L.L.C., the largest North American manufacturer of snowplows and ice control products for four-wheel drive light trucks; and the Greens Port Industrial Park on the Houston, Texas ship channel. On 9/30/99, the Company acquired Armco Inc.

REVENUES

(12/31/2000)	($000)	(%)
AK Holding	2448.3	58.7
Armco	1723.1	41.3
Total	4171.4	100.0

ANNUAL FINANCIAL DATA

	12/31/00	② 12/31/99	12/31/98	12/31/97	12/31/96	12/31/95	12/31/94
Earnings Per Share	**1.20**	**① 0.62**	**1.92**	**2.43**	**2.57**	**4.82**	**5.10**
Cash Flow Per Share	...	**2.90**	**3.56**	**3.60**	**3.97**	**6.18**	**6.44**
Tang. Book Val. Per Share	**0.01**	**10.32**	**15.75**	**14.46**	**14.59**	**13.04**	**8.61**
Dividends Per Share	**0.50**	**0.50**	**0.50**	**0.42**	**0.33**	**0.07**	...
Dividend Payout %	**41.7**	**80.6**	**26.0**	**17.5**	**12.6**	**1.6**	...
INCOME STATEMENT (IN MILLIONS):							
Total Revenues	4,517.2	4,284.8	2,393.6	2,440.5	2,301.8	2,257.3	2,016.6
Costs & Expenses	3,947.0	3,812.9	2,082.2	2,079.3	1,961.2	1,884.6	1,753.0
Depreciation & Amort.	232.0	227.1	97.8	79.8	76.1	74.6	70.7
Operating Income	338.2	244.8	213.6	281.4	264.5	298.1	192.9
Net Interest Inc./(Exp.)	d136.1	d123.7	d56.0	d76.3	d39.8	d35.6	d48.2
Income Before Income Taxes	210.1	141.9	176.2	241.5	237.0	281.5	152.0
Income Taxes	77.7	63.9	61.7	90.6	91.1	12.9	cr120.5
Equity Earnings/Minority Int.	...	d6.7	...	...	...	...	...
Net Income	132.4	① 71.3	114.5	150.9	145.9	268.6	272.5
Cash Flow	379.4	290.8	212.3	223.0	210.9	327.9	339.2
Average Shs. Outstg. (000)	...	102,900	59,600	62,000	53,186	53,030	52,684
BALANCE SHEET (IN MILLIONS):							
Cash & Cash Equivalents	86.8	54.4	83.0	606.1	739.3	312.8	261.8
Total Current Assets	1,521.8	1,432.5	807.5	1,221.6	1,365.7	887.2	884.5
Net Property	2,885.7	2,987.8	2,250.9	1,592.7	1,038.6	973.6	881.1
Total Assets	5,239.8	5,201.5	3,306.3	3,084.3	2,650.8	2,115.5	1,933.2
Total Current Liabilities	890.3	868.0	531.4	563.4	360.6	397.4	441.0
Long-Term Obligations	1,387.6	1,451.0	1,145.0	997.5	875.0	325.0	330.0
Net Stockholders' Equity	1,319.3	1,277.8	929.5	879.6	777.0	674.2	449.0
Net Working Capital	631.5	564.5	276.1	658.2	1,005.1	489.8	443.5
Year-end Shs. Outstg. (000)	107,650	110,640	59,023	60,809	53,240	51,678	52,122
STATISTICAL RECORD:							
Operating Profit Margin %	7.3	5.7	8.9	11.5	11.5	13.2	9.6
Net Profit Margin %	2.9	1.7	4.8	6.2	6.3	11.9	13.5
Return on Equity %	10.0	5.6	12.3	17.2	18.8	39.8	60.7
Return on Assets %	2.5	1.4	3.5	4.9	5.5	12.7	14.1
Debt/Total Assets %	26.5	27.9	34.6	32.3	33.0	15.4	17.1
Price Range	20.13-7.50	29.63-13.75	23.75-13.63	24.03-16.13	22.06-16.50	17.81-10.75	16.63-9.63
P/E Ratio	16.8-6.2	47.8-22.2	12.4-7.1	9.9-6.6	8.6-6.4	3.7-2.2	3.3-1.9
Average Yield %	3.6	2.3	2.7	2.1	1.7	0.5	...

Statistics are as originally reported. Adj. for 2-for-1 stock split, 11/17/97. ① Incl. an after-tax chrg. of $87.3 mill. for spec. chrgs. & other merger-related costs and excl. a gain of $7.5 mil. fr. discont. oper. and an extraord. loss of $13.4 mill. ② Reflects acquisition of Armco Inc.

OFFICERS:
R. M. Wardrop, Jr, Chmn., C.E.O.
J. L. Wareham, Pres.
J. L. Wainscott, Sr. V.P., C.F.O., Treas.
B. S. Harmon, V.P., Human Res., Sec.

INVESTOR CONTACT: James I. Wainscott, Sr. V.P., C.F.O., Treas., (513) 425-5392

PRINCIPAL OFFICE: 703 Curtis Street, Middletown, OH 45043

TELEPHONE NUMBER: (513) 425-5000
FAX: (513) 425-5220
WEB: www.aksteel.com

NO. OF EMPLOYEES: 11,500 (approx.)

SHAREHOLDERS: 17,545

ANNUAL MEETING: In May

INCORPORATED: DE, Dec., 1993

INSTITUTIONAL HOLDINGS:
No. of Institutions: 177
Shares Held: 76,414,929
% Held: 70.8

INDUSTRY: Blast furnaces and steel mills (SIC: 3312)

TRANSFER AGENT(S): The Fifth Third Bank, Cincinnati, OH

NYSE SYMBOL ALK
Rec. Pr. 28.73 (5/31/01)

ALASKA AIR GROUP, INC.

YIELD ...
P/E RATIO ...

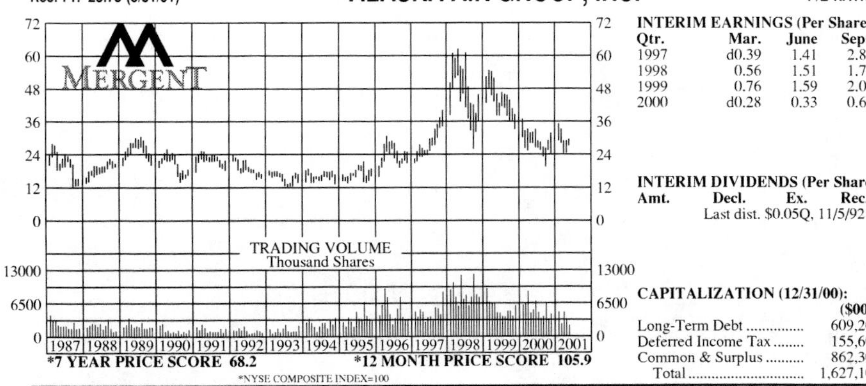

INTERIM EARNINGS (Per Share):

Qtr.	Mar.	June	Sept.	Dec.
1997	d0.39	1.41	2.85	0.73
1998	0.56	1.51	1.72	1.02
1999	0.76	1.59	2.07	0.64
2000	d0.28	0.33	0.60	d1.09

INTERIM DIVIDENDS (Per Share):

Amt.	Decl.	Ex.	Rec.	Pay.

Last dist. $0.05Q, 11/5/92

CAPITALIZATION (12/31/00):

	($000)	(%)
Long-Term Debt	609,200	37.4
Deferred Income Tax	155,600	9.6
Common & Surplus	862,300	53.0
Total	1,627,100	100.0

RECENT DEVELOPMENTS: For the year ended 12/31/00, loss totaled $13.4 million, before an accounting charge, versus net income of $134.2 million a year earlier. Results for 2000 included an after-tax special charge of $14.8 million related to ALK's frequent-flyer program. Total operating revenues grew 4.6% to $2.18 billion from $2.08 billion in 1999. Alaska Airlines' total operating revenues were up 4.1% to $1.75 billion, while Horizon Air's revenues rose 6.6% to $443.5 million.

PROSPECTS: Operating performance is continuing to be negatively affected by sharply higher fuel prices and increased labor and maintenance expenses. Meanwhile, Horizon Air is in the process of upgrading its fleet with new Dash 8-400 turboprop and CRJ700 Region Jet aircraft. Costs stemming from this transition are expected to constrain results during the current year. However, these new modern aircraft are expected to significantly increase efficiencies over the long term.

BUSINESS

ALASKA AIR GROUP, INC. is the holding company for Alaska Airlines, Inc. and Horizon Air Industries, Inc. Alaska Airlines (80% of 2000 revenues), operates a fleet of 95 aircraft and provides scheduled air transportation to 45 cities in Alaska, Washington, Oregon, California, Arizona, Nevada, Mexico and Russia. The carrier also serves 60 small communities in Alaska through subcontract agreements with local carriers. ALK acquired Jet America in 1986 and merged it with Alaska Airlines in October 1987. Horizon Air (20%), also acquired in 1986, provides air service to 40 destinations in Washington, Oregon, California, Idaho, Utah, Montana and Canada through its fleet of 62 aircraft.

REVENUES

(12/31/2000)	($000)	(%)
Passenger	2,032,300	93.4
Freight & Mail	87,600	4.0
Other Revenues	57,300	2.6
Total	2,177,200	100.0

ANNUAL FINANCIAL DATA

	12/31/00	12/31/99	12/31/98	12/31/97	12/31/96	12/31/95	12/31/94
Earnings Per Share	**[2] d0.51**	**[1] 5.06**	**[3] 4.81**	**3.53**	**[1] 2.65**	**1.28**	**1.68**
Cash Flow Per Share	**5.95**	**10.15**	**9.13**	**7.75**	**9.84**	**8.17**	**7.47**
Tang. Book Val. Per Share	**30.57**	**33.14**	**27.91**	**22.74**	**14.57**	**10.98**	**9.37**
INCOME STATEMENT (IN MILLIONS):							
Total Revenues	2,177.2	2,082.0	1,897.7	1,739.4	1,592.2	1,417.5	1,315.6
Costs & Expenses	2,027.0	1,747.2	1,570.5	1,497.0	1,401.1	1,248.8	1,163.0
Depreciation & Amort.	170.8	134.9	116.2	103.4	102.1	92.6	77.6
Operating Income	d20.6	199.9	211.0	139.0	89.0	75.7	75.0
Net Interest Inc./(Exp.)	3.8	14.1	7.6	d17.7	d26.3	d40.9	d38.8
Income Before Income Taxes	d15.7	220.7	204.4	123.6	64.3	34.0	41.0
Income Taxes	cr2.3	86.5	80.0	51.2	26.3	16.7	18.5
Net Income	[2] d13.4	[1] 134.2	[3] 124.4	72.4	[1] 38.0	17.7	22.5
Cash Flow	157.4	269.1	240.6	175.8	140.1	110.3	100.1
Average Shs. Outstg. (000)	26,440	26,507	26,367	22,689	14,241	13,500	13,400
BALANCE SHEET (IN MILLIONS):							
Cash & Cash Equivalents	461.7	329.0	306.6	212.7	101.8	135.1	104.9
Total Current Assets	805.7	581.9	528.8	424.6	300.2	338.4	272.6
Net Property	1,730.2	1,467.4	1,061.3	960.6	863.4	814.0	859.3
Total Assets	2,630.0	2,180.1	1,731.8	1,533.1	1,311.4	1,313.4	1,315.8
Total Current Liabilities	710.8	618.7	525.9	473.3	485.8	444.8	419.7
Long-Term Obligations	609.2	337.0	171.5	401.4	404.1	522.4	589.9
Net Stockholders' Equity	862.3	930.7	789.5	475.3	272.5	212.5	191.3
Net Working Capital	94.9	d36.8	2.9	d48.7	d185.6	d106.4	d147.1
Year-end Shs. Outstg. (000)	26,457	24,411	26,224	18,283	14,475	13,565	13,400
STATISTICAL RECORD:							
Operating Profit Margin %	...	9.6	11.1	8.0	5.6	5.3	5.7
Net Profit Margin %	...	6.4	6.6	4.2	2.4	1.2	1.7
Return on Equity %	...	14.4	15.8	15.2	13.9	8.3	11.8
Return on Assets %	...	6.2	7.2	4.7	2.9	1.3	1.7
Debt/Total Assets %	23.2	15.5	9.9	26.2	30.8	39.8	44.8
Price Range	36.88-19.50	54.69-33.19	62.56-26.00	40.13-20.75	30.75-15.88	21.38-13.50	18.88-13.13
P/E Ratio	...	10.8-6.6	13.0-5.4	11.4-5.9	11.6-6.0	16.7-10.5	11.2-7.8

Statistics are as originally reported. [1] Incl. $2.2 mil ($0.08/sh) after-tax gain from sale of Equant N.V., 1999; $3.6 mil gain from sale of assets, 1996. [2] Bef. $56.9 mil ($2.15/sh) acctg. change chg. and incl. $14.8 mil after-tax chg. related to the Company's frequent-flyer program. [3] Incl. $10.1 mil ($0.38/sh) after-tax chg. from legal settlement.

OFFICERS:
J. F. Kelly, Chmn., Pres., C.E.O.
H. G. Lehr, Sr. V.P.
K. Loveless, V.P., Gen. Couns., Sec.
B. D. Tilden, V.P., C.F.O.

INVESTOR CONTACT: Lou Cancelmi, (206) 433-3170

PRINCIPAL OFFICE: 19300 Pacific Highway South, Seattle, WA 98188

TELEPHONE NUMBER: (206) 431-7040
FAX: (206) 433-3379
WEB: www.alaskaair.com

NO. OF EMPLOYEES: 10,738 (avg.)

SHAREHOLDERS: 4,276

ANNUAL MEETING: In May

INCORPORATED: DE, May, 1985

INSTITUTIONAL HOLDINGS:
No. of Institutions: 121
Shares Held: 19,947,437
% Held: 75.4

INDUSTRY: Air transportation, scheduled (SIC: 4512)

TRANSFER AGENT(S): BankBoston, N.A., Boston, MA

NYSE SYMBOL AIN
Rec. Pr. 22.12 (5/31/01)

ALBANY INTERNATIONAL CORP.

YIELD ...
P/E RATIO 17.8

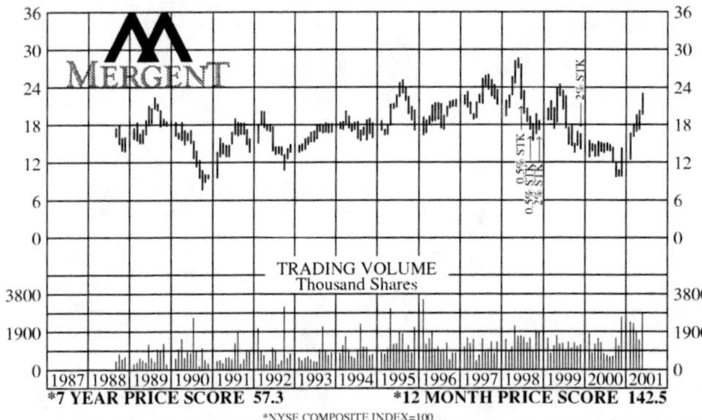

INTERIM EARNINGS (Per Share):

Qtr.	Mar.	June	Sept.	Dec.
1997	0.34	0.42	0.35	0.41
1998	0.34	0.33	0.35	d0.03
1999	0.37	0.30	0.35	d0.03
2000	0.33	0.31	0.30	0.30

INTERIM DIVIDENDS (Per Share):

Amt.	Decl.	Ex.	Rec.	Pay.
2% STK	11/05/98	12/02/98	12/04/98	1/06/99
2% STK	11/10/99	12/08/99	12/10/99	1/12/00

Dividend payment suspended.

CAPITALIZATION (12/31/00):

	($000)	(%)
Long-Term Debt	398,087	55.1
Common & Surplus	324,917	44.9
Total	723,004	100.0

RECENT DEVELOPMENTS: For the year ended 12/31/00, net income increased 26.0% to $38.1 million compared with $30.2 million in 1999. Results for 2000 included a $4.2 million charge related to relocating equipment in connection with the integration of Geschmay into the Company. Results for 1999 included non-recurring charges totaling $16.9 million. Net sales were $852.9 million, up 9.6% from $778.4 million a year earlier.

PROSPECTS: The Company continues to implement process improvements for its customers and suppliers. These improvements are geared to enhance customer service and production efficiencies while reducing inventories. These programs are expected to reduce inventory and accounts receivable $30.0 million by year-end 2001. Separately, pricing remains a challenge for AIN in its primary markets as paper industry consolidation continues.

BUSINESS

ALBANY INTERNATIONAL CORP. designs, manufactures and markets paper machine clothing for each section of the paper machine. AIN is the world's largest maker of paper machine clothing, the fabric upon which wood pulp is formed, pressed and dried in the production of paper and paperboard. These custom-designed engineered fabrics are essential to the papermaking process and are manufactured from monofilament and synthetic fiber material. AIN's principal manufacturing facilities are wholly-owned and located in the U.S., Canada, Brazil, Mexico, Australia, Finland, France, Germany, Great Britain, Sweden, Netherlands, China, Korea, South Africa and Italy.

BUSINESS LINE ANALYSIS

(12/31/2000)	Rev(%)	Inc(%)
Engineered Fabrics	82.9	92.9
High Performance Doors	12.2	5.0
All Other	4.9	2.1
Total	100.0	100.0

ANNUAL FINANCIAL DATA

	12/31/00	12/31/99	12/31/98	12/31/97	12/31/96	12/31/95	12/31/94
Earnings Per Share	**4 1.24**	**0.99**	**2 1.01**	**1.50**	**3 1.52**	**1.36**	**0.76**
Cash Flow Per Share	**3.27**	**28.36**	**2.57**	**2.87**	...	**3.35**	**2.53**
Tang. Book Val. Per Share	**5.30**	**4.18**	**8.46**	**9.51**	**8.87**	**8.50**	**7.92**
Dividends Per Share	...	...	**0.20**	**0.39**	**0.38**	**0.36**	**0.33**
Dividend Payout %	...	...	**19.8**	**26.3**	**25.0**	**26.2**	**43.8**
INCOME STATEMENT (IN MILLIONS):							
Total Revenues	852.9	778.4	722.7	710.1	692.8	652.6	567.6
Costs & Expenses	687.1	645.5	603.2	565.5	552.3	520.7	466.0
Depreciation & Amort.	62.2	55.9	48.8	45.0	45.2	43.1	38.6
Operating Income	103.6	77.0	70.6	99.6	95.3	88.9	62.9
Net Interest Inc./(Exp.)	d41.8	d25.6	d19.3	d15.5	1.5	0.6	d0.5
Income Before Income Taxes	62.6	51.9	51.7	79.6	79.4	69.9	41.8
Income Taxes	25.0	22.3	20.2	31.1	31.0	27.2	18.0
Equity Earnings/Minority Int.	0.5	0.6	0.2	0.5	0.2	0.4	0.1
Net Income	4 38.1	30.2	2 31.8	49.1	3 48.7	43.1	24.0
Cash Flow	100.3	864.5	80.6	94.1	110.9	106.3	79.7
Average Shs. Outstg. (000)	30,636	30,483	31,407	32,738	...	31,737	31,476
BALANCE SHEET (IN MILLIONS):							
Cash & Cash Equivalents	5.4	7.0	5.9	2.5	8.0	7.6	0.2
Total Current Assets	494.3	508.1	409.7	373.3	377.4	358.5	314.2
Net Property	387.7	435.2	325.1	321.6	339.5	342.2	320.7
Total Assets	1,112.3	1,206.8	866.4	796.9	824.7	796.5	721.4
Total Current Liabilities	222.0	177.0	220.0	170.4	173.1	123.9	112.8
Long-Term Obligations	398.1	521.3	181.1	173.7	187.1	245.3	232.8
Net Stockholders' Equity	324.9	325.4	314.9	343.1	328.8	302.3	271.9
Net Working Capital	272.3	331.1	189.7	202.9	204.3	234.6	201.4
Year-end Shs. Outstg. (000)	30,807	30,467	30,047	32,271	32,012	31,854	31,732
STATISTICAL RECORD:							
Operating Profit Margin %	12.2	9.9	9.8	14.0	13.8	13.6	11.1
Net Profit Margin %	4.5	3.9	4.4	6.9	7.0	6.6	4.2
Return on Equity %	11.7	9.3	10.1	14.3	14.8	14.2	8.8
Return on Assets %	3.4	2.5	3.7	6.2	5.9	5.4	3.3
Debt/Total Assets %	35.8	43.2	20.9	21.8	22.7	30.8	32.3
Price Range	15.50-9.63	24.51-13.48	28.73-15.44	26.11-18.79	22.01-16.30	25.22-16.30	20.22-15.35
P/E Ratio	12.5-7.8	24.8-13.6	28.4-15.3	17.4-12.5	14.5-10.7	18.5-12.0	26.6-20.2
Average Yield %	...	...	0.9	1.8	2.0	1.7	1.9

Statistics are as originally reported. Class A & B common shares. Adj. for stk. split: 0.5%, 7/98 and 10/98; 2.0%, 1/99 and 1/00. 1 Bef. extraord. credit of $1.0 mill. ($0.04 a sh.) and acctg. chg. of $7.3 mill. ($0.29 a sh.). 2 Incl. a net restruct. chrg. of $419,000, 1993, $20.2 million,1998. 3 Bef. extraord. loss of $1.3 mill. ($0.04 a sh.). 4 Incl. chrg. of $4.2 mill. for equip. relocation.

OFFICERS:
F. L. McKone, Chmn., C.E.O.
F. R. Schmeler, Pres., C.O.O.
M. C. Nahl, Sr. V.P., C.F.O.

INVESTOR CONTACT: Charles B. Buchanan, V.P. & Sec., (518) 445-2284

PRINCIPAL OFFICE: 1373 Broadway, P.O. Box 1907, Albany, NY 12204

TELEPHONE NUMBER: (518) 445-2200
FAX: (518) 445-2265
WEB: www.albint.com
NO. OF EMPLOYEES: 7,164
SHAREHOLDERS: 6,500 (approx.)
ANNUAL MEETING: In May
INCORPORATED: NY, 1895; reincorp., DE, Aug., 1983

INSTITUTIONAL HOLDINGS:
No. of Institutions: 101
Shares Held: 20,889,104
% Held: 67.8

INDUSTRY: Broadwoven fabric mills, manmade (SIC: 2221)

TRANSFER AGENT(S): Computershare Investor Services, Chicago, IL

NYSE SYMBOL ACV
Rec. Pr. 40.74 (4/30/01)

ALBERTO-CULVER COMPANY

YIELD 0.8%
P/E RATIO 23.1

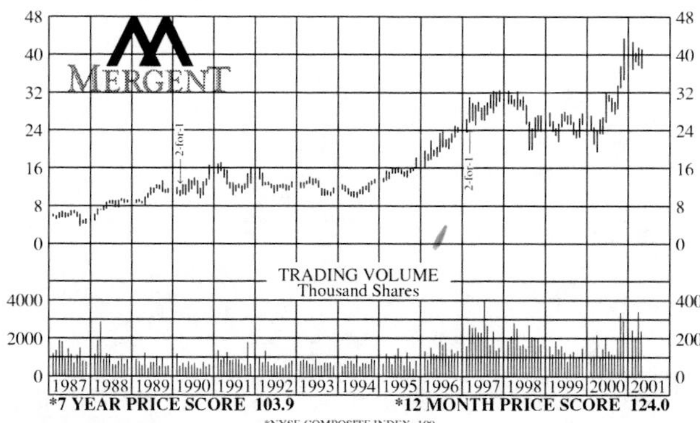

INTERIM EARNINGS (Per Share):

Qtr.	Dec.	Mar.	June	Sept.
1996-97	0.47	0.31	0.33	0.38
1997-98	0.32	0.32	0.35	0.38
1998-99	0.32	0.35	0.40	0.44
1999-00	0.37	0.40	0.45	0.50
2000-01	0.41	...	...	...

INTERIM DIVIDENDS (Per Share):

Amt.	Decl.	Ex.	Rec.	Pay.
0.075Q	4/27/00	5/04/00	5/08/00	5/20/00
0.075Q	7/27/00	8/03/00	8/07/00	8/20/00
0.075Q	10/26/00	11/02/00	11/06/00	11/20/00
0.083Q	1/25/01	2/01/01	2/05/01	2/20/01
0.083Q	4/26/01	5/03/01	5/07/01	5/21/01

Indicated div.: $0.33

CAPITALIZATION (9/30/00):

	($000)	(%)
Long-Term Debt	340,948	33.6
Deferred Income Tax	38,349	3.8
Common & Surplus	636,481	62.7
Total	1,015,778	100.0

RECENT DEVELOPMENTS: For the quarter ended 12/31/00, net earnings declined 12.0% to $23.6 million compared with $26.8 million in the prior-year quarter. Earnings for 1999 included a non-recurring gain of $6.0 million. Net sales totaled $593.6 million, an increase of 12.9% versus $525.8 million a year earlier. Gross profit fell to 50.8% of net sales compared with 51.1% of net sales in the 1999 quarter.

PROSPECTS: Going forward, Alberto-Culver North America should continue to benefit from improved execution, sharper focus on the Company's core brands, innovative marketing and stronger relationships with ACV's trading partners. In addition, the Company will continue implementing programs globally to position ACV's Alberto-Culver International business for continued sales growth and improved profit margins in the future.

BUSINESS

ALBERTO-CULVER COMPANY and its consolidated subsidiaries operate three principal business segments. The Company's consumer products business includes two segments, Alberto-Culver North America and Alberto-Culver International, which are engaged in developing, manufacturing, distributing and marketing branded consumer products worldwide. Alberto-Culver North America includes ACV's consumer products in the U.S. and Canada, while Alberto-Culver International sells consumer products in more than 120 other countries. ACV's third segment, Specialty Distribution - Sally, consists of Sally Beauty Company, a specialty distributor of professional beauty supplies with 2,063 stores as of 12/31/00 in the United States, Germany, the United Kingdom, Canada and Japan. Name brands sold by the Company include ALBERTO VO5 hair care products and ST. IVES SWISS FORMULA hair and skin products.

ANNUAL FINANCIAL DATA

	9/30/00	9/30/99	9/30/98	9/30/97	9/30/96	9/30/95	9/30/94
Earnings Per Share	**[1] 1.83**	**1.51**	**1.37**	**[1] 1.49**	**[1] 1.11**	**0.95**	**0.79**
Cash Flow Per Share	**2.71**	**2.25**	**1.94**	**2.17**	**1.70**	**1.39**	**1.16**
Tang. Book Val. Per Share	**5.16**	**5.81**	**5.75**	**5.57**	**4.33**	**5.08**	**4.93**
Dividends Per Share	**0.30**	**0.26**	**0.24**	**0.20**	**0.18**	**0.16**	**0.14**
Dividend Payout %	**16.4**	**17.2**	**17.5**	**13.4**	**16.2**	**16.9**	**17.8**
INCOME STATEMENT (IN MILLIONS):							
Total Revenues	2,247.2	1,975.9	1,834.7	1,775.3	1,590.4	1,358.2	1,216.1
Costs & Expenses	2,024.0	1,787.3	1,655.6	1,592.0	1,445.4	1,242.8	1,118.3
Depreciation & Amort.	49.6	42.2	38.1	38.9	32.9	24.7	20.9
Operating Income	173.5	146.5	141.0	144.4	112.1	90.8	76.9
Net Interest Inc./(Exp.)	d19.2	d12.7	d8.6	d8.2	d12.1	d6.5	d5.9
Income Before Income Taxes	154.3	133.8	132.4	136.1	100.0	84.2	71.1
Income Taxes	51.1	47.5	49.3	50.7	37.3	31.6	27.0
Net Income	[1] 103.2	86.3	83.1	[1] 85.4	[1] 62.7	52.7	44.1
Cash Flow	152.8	128.5	121.2	124.4	95.7	77.3	65.0
Average Shs. Outstg. (000)	56,410	57,162	62,420	57,202	56,426	55,698	56,084
BALANCE SHEET (IN MILLIONS):							
Cash & Cash Equivalents	115.0	57.8	73.3	87.6	71.6	147.0	50.4
Total Current Assets	740.5	645.6	591.6	580.3	512.7	536.5	401.8
Net Property	240.1	238.8	223.5	191.0	175.9	157.8	132.9
Total Assets	1,389.8	1,184.5	1,068.2	1,000.1	909.3	815.1	610.2
Total Current Liabilities	340.8	336.4	313.6	311.3	286.6	234.8	216.0
Long-Term Obligations	340.9	225.2	171.8	149.4	161.5	183.1	43.0
Net Stockholders' Equity	636.5	568.8	534.0	497.0	425.1	370.9	327.0
Net Working Capital	399.7	309.2	277.9	269.0	226.1	301.7	185.7
Year-end Shs. Outstg. (000)	55,939	55,726	57,210	56,142	55,630	55,458	55,360
STATISTICAL RECORD:							
Operating Profit Margin %	7.7	7.4	7.7	8.1	7.0	6.7	6.3
Net Profit Margin %	4.6	4.4	4.5	4.8	3.9	3.9	3.6
Return on Equity %	16.2	15.2	15.6	17.2	14.8	14.2	13.5
Return on Assets %	7.4	7.3	7.8	8.5	6.9	6.5	7.2
Debt/Total Assets %	24.5	19.0	16.1	14.9	17.8	22.5	7.0
Price Range	43.50-19.38	27.88-21.56	32.44-19.75	32.56-23.56	25.00-16.25	18.25-12.94	13.69-9.69
P/E Ratio	23.8-10.6	18.5-14.3	23.7-14.4	21.9-15.8	22.5-14.6	19.3-13.7	17.4-12.3
Average Yield %	1.0	1.1	0.9	0.7	0.9	1.0	1.2

Statistics are as originally reported. Adj. for stk. split: 2-for-1, 2/97 [1] Incl. non-recurr. gain $6.0 mill., 9/00; credit, $15.6 mill., 9/97, $9.8 mill., 9/96

OFFICERS:
L. H. Lavin, Chmn.
B. E. Lavin, Vice-Chmn., Treas., Sec.
C. L. Bernick, Vice-Chmn., Asst. Sec.
H. B. Bernick, Pres., C.E.O.

INVESTOR CONTACT: Bernice E. Lavin, Sec. & Treas., (708) 450-3000

PRINCIPAL OFFICE: 2525 Armitage Avenue, Melrose Park, IL 60160

TELEPHONE NUMBER: (708) 450-3000
FAX: (708) 450-3419
WEB: www.alberto.com

NO. OF EMPLOYEES: 15,300 (approx.)

SHAREHOLDERS: 923 (class A com.); 944 (class B com.).

ANNUAL MEETING: In Jan.

INCORPORATED: DE, Jan., 1961

INSTITUTIONAL HOLDINGS:
No. of Institutions: 157
Shares Held: 14,556,633
% Held: 25.8

INDUSTRY: Toilet preparations (SIC: 2844)

TRANSFER AGENT(S): EquiServe L.P., Providence, RI

NYSE SYMBOL ABS
Rec. Pr. 28.70 (5/31/01)

ALBERTSON'S, INC.

YIELD 2.6%
P/E RATIO 15.7

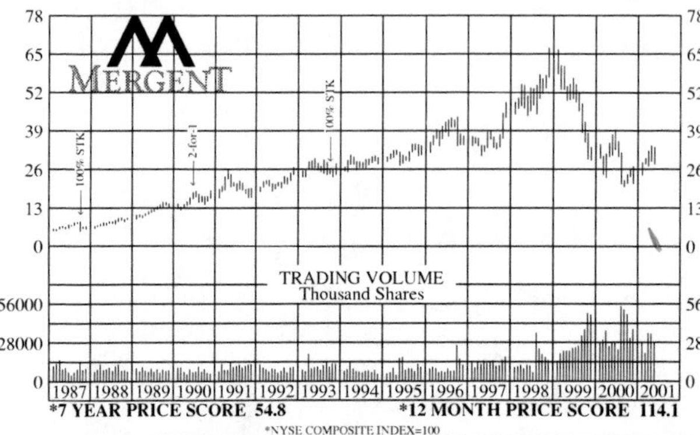

INTERIM EARNINGS (Per Share):

Qtr.	Apr.	July	Oct.	Jan.
1997-98	0.44	0.44	0.50	0.71
1998-99	0.45	0.52	0.56	0.77
1999-00	0.56	d0.49	0.31	0.62
2000-01	0.42	0.46	0.41	0.54

INTERIM DIVIDENDS (Per Share):

Amt.	Decl.	Ex.	Rec.	Pay.
0.19Q	6/14/00	7/12/00	7/14/00	8/10/00
0.19Q	9/08/00	10/12/00	10/16/00	11/10/00
0.19Q	12/06/00	1/10/01	1/15/01	2/10/01
0.19Q	3/15/01	4/11/01	4/16/01	5/10/01
0.19Q	6/13/01	7/12/01	7/16/01	8/10/01

Indicated div.: $0.76 (Div. Reinv. Plan)

CAPITALIZATION (2/1/01):

	($000)	(%)
Long-Term Debt	5,715,000	48.6
Capital Lease Obligations	227,000	1.9
Deferred Income Tax	116,000	1.0
Common & Surplus	5,694,000	48.5
Total	11,752,000	100.0

RECENT DEVELOPMENTS: For the 52 weeks ended 2/1/01, net earnings was $765.0 million, up 79.2% versus income of $427.0 million, before an extraordinary after-tax charge of $23.0 million, in the corresponding 53-week period the year before. Results in the recent period included after-tax merger-related and one-time charges of $105.0 million. Sales slid 1.9% to $36.76 billion from $37.48 billion a year earlier.

PROSPECTS: The Company is continuing to develop and implement expense reduction programs designed to lower store-level labor, supplies and office costs. ABS anticipates reducing distribution and selling, general and administrative expenses by $250.0 million in 2001. Meanwhile, the Company is hoping to increase its market share in existing markets through focused marketing and merchandising programs, aggressive remodels and new store openings.

BUSINESS

ALBERTSON'S, INC. is one of the largest retail food-drug chains in the United States. As of 4/24/01, ABS operated 2,536 stores in 36 states under three different formats: combination food-drug, conventional, and warehouse. Combination food-drug units, ranging between 35,000 sq. ft. and 82,000 sq. ft., consist of grocery, general merchandise, and meat and produce departments, along with pharmacy, lobby/video, floral, and bakery service departments. The Company's stores are operated under the Albertson's, Jewel Osco, Acme Markets, Sav-on and Osco Drug banners, while warehouse stores are operated primarily under the "Max Food and Drug" banner. Retail operations are supported by 12 Company-owned distribution centers. On 6/23/99, the Company acquired American Stores Company.

ANNUAL FINANCIAL DATA

	2/1/01	[4] 2/3/00	1/28/99	1/29/98	1/30/97	2/1/96	2/2/95
Earnings Per Share	**[5] 1.83**	**[3] 1.00**	**[2] 2.30**	**2.08**	**1.96**	**1.84**	**[1] 1.65**
Cash Flow Per Share	**4.22**	**3.17**	**3.82**	**3.40**	**3.13**	**2.83**	**2.54**
Tang. Book Val. Per Share	**9.85**	**9.72**	**10.84**	**9.85**	**8.96**	**7.75**	**6.65**
Dividends Per Share	**0.75**	**0.71**	**0.67**	**0.63**	**0.58**	**0.50**	**0.42**
Dividend Payout %	**41.0**	**71.0**	**29.1**	**30.3**	**29.6**	**27.2**	**25.5**
INCOME STATEMENT (IN MILLIONS):							
Total Revenues	36,762.0	37,478.0	16,005.1	14,689.5	13,776.7	12,585.0	11,894.6
Costs & Expenses	34,099.0	35,326.0	14,656.6	13,469.1	12,632.8	11,526.4	10,925.0
Depreciation & Amort.	1,001.0	912.0	375.4	328.8	294.3	251.5	226.5
Operating Income	1,662.0	1,240.0	973.2	891.7	849.6	807.2	743.1
Net Interest Inc./(Exp.)	d385.0	d353.0	d107.1	d82.6	d64.6	d55.6	d62.1
Income Before Income Taxes	1,274.0	899.0	894.8	826.9	794.8	758.5	678.7
Income Taxes	509.0	472.0	327.7	310.1	301.1	293.5	261.3
Net Income	[5] 765.0	[3] 427.0	[2] 567.2	516.8	493.8	465.0	[1] 417.4
Cash Flow	1,766.0	1,339.0	942.5	845.6	788.1	716.4	643.8
Average Shs. Outstg. (000)	418,000	423,000	246,808	248,497	251,710	253,080	253,633
BALANCE SHEET (IN MILLIONS):							
Cash & Cash Equivalents	57.0	231.0	80.6	108.1	90.9	69.1	50.2
Total Current Assets	4,300.0	4,582.0	1,833.9	1,627.9	1,475.9	1,283.0	1,189.6
Net Property	9,622.0	8,913.0	3,974.0	3,383.4	3,054.6	2,697.5	2,309.4
Total Assets	16,078.0	15,701.0	6,234.0	5,218.6	4,714.6	4,135.9	3,621.7
Total Current Liabilities	3,395.0	4,055.0	1,378.8	1,275.5	1,055.1	1,088.5	1,095.4
Long-Term Obligations	5,942.0	4,992.0	1,684.5	1,130.6	1,051.8	732.3	512.3
Net Stockholders' Equity	5,694.0	5,702.0	2,810.5	2,419.5	2,247.0	1,952.5	1,687.9
Net Working Capital	905.0	527.0	455.1	352.3	420.8	194.5	94.2
Year-end Shs. Outstg. (000)	405,000	424,000	245,697	245,736	250,690	251,919	253,984
STATISTICAL RECORD:							
Operating Profit Margin %	4.5	3.3	6.1	6.1	6.2	6.4	6.2
Net Profit Margin %	2.1	1.1	3.5	3.5	3.6	3.7	3.5
Return on Equity %	13.4	7.5	20.2	21.4	22.0	23.8	24.7
Return on Assets %	4.8	2.7	9.1	9.9	10.5	11.2	11.5
Debt/Total Assets %	37.0	31.8	27.0	21.7	22.3	17.7	14.1
Price Range	39.25-20.06	66.63-29.00	67.13-44.00	48.63-30.50	43.75-31.50	34.63-27.25	30.88-25.13
P/E Ratio	21.4-11.0	66.6-29.0	29.2-19.1	23.4-14.7	22.3-16.1	18.8-14.8	18.7-15.2
Average Yield %	2.5	1.5	1.2	1.6	1.5	1.6	1.5

Statistics are as originally reported. [1] Bef. $17 mil ($0.07/sh) chg. for acctg. adj. [2] Incl. $24.4 mil pre-tax impairment chg. for store closures. [3] Bef. $23.3 mil ($0.05/sh) extraord. chg. & incl. one-time pre-tax chgs. totaling $689.0 mil related to the acq. of American Stores Company and a litigation settlement. [4] Refl. acquis. of American Stores Co. in 6/99. [5] Incl. $105.0 mil ($0.25/sh) one-time after-tax chg.

OFFICERS:
L. R. Johnston, Chmn., C.E.O.
P. Lynch, Pres., C.O.O.
T. R. Saldin, Exec. V.P., Gen. Couns.

PRINCIPAL OFFICE: 250 Parkcenter Blvd., P.O. Box 20, Boise, ID 83726

TELEPHONE NUMBER: (208) 395-6200
FAX: (208) 395-6777
WEB: www.albertsons.com

NO. OF EMPLOYEES: 235,000 (approx.)

SHAREHOLDERS: 32,000 (approx.)

ANNUAL MEETING: In June

INCORPORATED: DE, Apr., 1969

INSTITUTIONAL HOLDINGS:
No. of Institutions: 401
Shares Held: 272,479,270
% Held: 67.3

INDUSTRY: Grocery stores (SIC: 5411)

TRANSFER AGENT(S): Mellon Investor Services, Ridgefield Park, NJ

NYSE SYMBOL AL
Rec. Pr. 44.80 (5/31/01)

ALCAN INC.

YIELD 1.3%
P/E RATIO 16.8

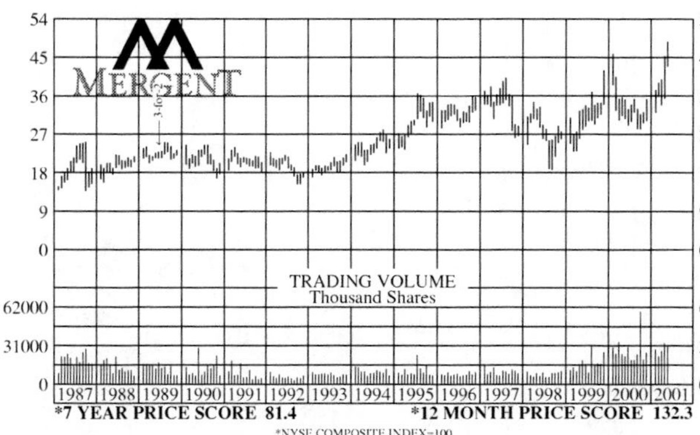

*7 YEAR PRICE SCORE 81.4 *12 MONTH PRICE SCORE 132.3

*NYSE COMPOSITE INDEX=100

INTERIM EARNINGS (Per Share):

Qtr.	Mar.	June	Sept.	Dec.
1997	0.62	0.50	0.34	0.56
1998	0.50	0.37	0.46	0.38
1999	0.16	0.32	0.71	0.87
2000	0.78	0.70	0.85	0.34

INTERIM DIVIDENDS (Per Share):

Amt.	Decl.	Ex.	Rec.	Pay.
0.15Q	2/10/00	2/22/00	2/24/00	3/20/00
0.15Q	4/27/00	5/18/00	5/22/00	6/20/00
0.15Q	7/27/00	8/17/00	8/21/00	9/20/00
0.15Q	10/26/00	11/16/00	11/20/00	12/18/00
0.15Q	2/15/01	2/21/01	2/23/01	3/20/01

Indicated div.: $0.60

CAPITALIZATION (12/31/00):

	($000)	(%)
Long-Term Debt	3,195,000	23.3
Deferred Income Tax	1,227,000	9.0
Minority Interest	244,000	1.8
Preferred Stock	160,000	1.2
Common & Surplus	8,867,000	64.8
Total	13,693,000	100.0

RECENT DEVELOPMENTS: For the year ended 12/31/00, net income amounted to $602.0 million versus $460.0 million in the corresponding period of the prior year. Results for 2000 included pre-tax non-cash merger-related charges of $60.0 million and a pre-tax net non-operating gain of $31.0 million. The 1999 results included pre-tax net operating gains of $37.0 million. Total revenues increased 23.2% to $9.24 billion from $7.50 billion the year before.

PROSPECTS: On 1/31/01, AL completed the acquisition of the Gove alumina refinery and related bauxite mine in Australia. AL now owns 100.0% of the Gove assets, which have a total annual capacity of 1.8 million tonnes of low-cost aluminum. Separately, AL's post-merger integration of Alusuisse Group Ltd. is progressing very well, as indicated with the recently announced 33.0% jump in expected synergies to $200.0 million.

BUSINESS

ALCAN INC. (formerly Alcan Aluminum Limited), a Canadian corporation, is the parent company of a multinational industrial group engaged in all aspects of the aluminum packaging industries. Through subsidiaries, joint ventures and related companies on six contents, Alcan's activities include bauxite mining, alumina refining, power generation, aluminum smelting, manufacturing, recycling and packaging, as well as research and development. Alcan is composed of four business groups, which include Primary Metal, Aluminum Fabrication, Americas and Asia, Europe and Global Packaging.

ANNUAL FINANCIAL DATA

	12/31/00	12/31/99	12/31/98	12/31/97	12/31/96	12/31/95	12/31/94
Earnings Per Share	**[6] 2.50**	**2.06**	**[5] 1.71**	**[4] 2.02**	**[3] 1.74**	**[2] 2.30**	**[1] 0.34**
Cash Flow Per Share	**6.99**	**6.25**	**5.41**	**5.99**	**5.32**	**5.24**	**2.50**
Tang. Book Val. Per Share	**18.46**	**24.65**	**23.71**	**21.43**	**20.57**	**19.84**	**19.17**
Dividends Per Share	**0.60**	**0.60**	**0.60**	**0.60**	**0.60**	**0.45**	**0.30**
Dividend Payout %	**24.0**	**29.1**	**35.1**	**29.7**	**34.5**	**19.6**	**88.2**
INCOME STATEMENT (IN MILLIONS):							
Total Revenues	9,244.0	7,503.0	8,020.0	7,865.0	7,689.0	9,387.0	8,325.0
Costs & Expenses	7,816.0	6,340.0	6,905.0	6,676.0	6,625.0	8,058.0	7,654.0
Depreciation & Amort.	545.0	477.0	462.0	436.0	431.0	447.0	431.0
Operating Income	883.0	686.0	653.0	753.0	633.0	882.0	240.0
Income Before Income Taxes	883.0	686.0	653.0	753.0	633.0	882.0	240.0
Income Taxes	254.0	211.0	210.0	248.0	212.0	340.0	112.0
Equity Earnings/Minority Int.	5.0	d15.0	d44.0	d37.0	d11.0	1.0	d32.0
Net Income	[6] 602.0	460.0	[5] 399.0	[4] 468.0	[3] 410.0	[2] 543.0	[1] 96.0
Cash Flow	1,137.0	928.0	851.0	894.0	825.0	966.0	506.0
Average Shs. Outstg. (000)	248,200	219,100	227,400	227,000	226,200	225,300	224,300
BALANCE SHEET (IN MILLIONS):							
Cash & Cash Equivalents	261.0	315.0	615.0	608.0	546.0	66.0	27.0
Total Current Assets	4,656.0	2,890.0	3,429.0	3,241.0	3,113.0	3,005.0	2,821.0
Net Property	10,033.0	6,434.0	5,897.0	5,458.0	5,470.0	5,672.0	5,534.0
Total Assets	18,407.0	9,849.0	9,901.0	9,466.0	9,228.0	9,702.0	9,989.0
Total Current Liabilities	3,840.0	1,746.0	1,384.0	1,424.0	1,303.0	1,448.0	1,384.0
Long-Term Obligations	3,195.0	1,011.0	1,537.0	1,241.0	1,319.0	1,711.0	2,206.0
Net Stockholders' Equity	9,027.0	5,541.0	5,519.0	5,074.0	4,864.0	4,835.0	4,661.0
Net Working Capital	816.0	1,144.0	2,045.0	1,817.0	1,810.0	1,557.0	1,437.0
Year-end Shs. Outstg. (000)	317,921	218,315	226,000	227,300	226,600	225,913	224,685
STATISTICAL RECORD:							
Operating Profit Margin %	9.6	9.1	8.1	9.6	8.2	9.4	2.9
Net Profit Margin %	6.5	6.1	5.0	6.0	5.3	5.8	1.2
Return on Equity %	6.7	8.3	7.2	9.2	8.4	11.2	2.1
Return on Assets %	3.3	4.7	4.0	4.9	4.4	5.6	1.0
Debt/Total Assets %	17.4	10.3	15.5	13.1	14.3	17.6	22.1
Price Range	45.94-28.19	42.00-22.94	34.50-18.69	40.31-26.06	36.13-28.38	36.63-23.38	28.13-19.75
P/E Ratio	18.4-11.3	20.4-11.1	20.2-10.9	20.0-12.9	20.8-16.3	15.9-10.2	82.7-58.1
Average Yield %	1.6	1.8	2.3	1.8	1.9	1.5	1.3

Statistics are as originally reported. All figures are in U.S. dollars unless otherwise noted. [1] Incl. one-time net gain of $2.0 mill. [2] Bef. extra. loss of $280.0 mill. [3] Incl. net gain. of $8.0 mill. fr. sale of bus. [4] Incl. net gains of $36.0 mill., pre-tax spec. chg. of $30.0 mill. & excl. net extra. chg. of $17.0 mill. [5] Incl. spec. net gains of $148.0 mill., a net chg. of $120.0 mill. & a chrg. of $9.0 mill. [6] Incl. pre-tax non-cash merger rel. chrgs. of $60.0 mill. & net non-oper. gain of $31.0 mill.

OFFICERS:
J. R. Evans, Chmn.
T. Engen, C.E.O
S. Thadhani, Exec. V.P., C.F.O.

INVESTOR CONTACT: Michael Hanley, (514) 848-8368

PRINCIPAL OFFICE: 1188 Sherbrooke Street West, Montreal, Quebec, Canada

TELEPHONE NUMBER: (514) 848-8000
FAX: (514) 848-8115
WEB: www.alcan.com
NO. OF EMPLOYEES: 53,000 (approx.)
SHAREHOLDERS: 19,640 (com); 780 (preference)
ANNUAL MEETING: In Apr.
INCORPORATED: CAN, June, 1902

INSTITUTIONAL HOLDINGS:
No. of Institutions: 227
Shares Held: 130,212,924
% Held: 40.9

INDUSTRY: Secondary nonferrous metals (SIC: 3341)

TRANSFER AGENT(S): CIBC Mellon Trust Company, Montreal, Quebec, Canada

NYSE SYMBOL AA
Rec. Pr. 43.15 (5/31/01)

ALCOA, INC.

YIELD 1.4%
P/E RATIO 23.7

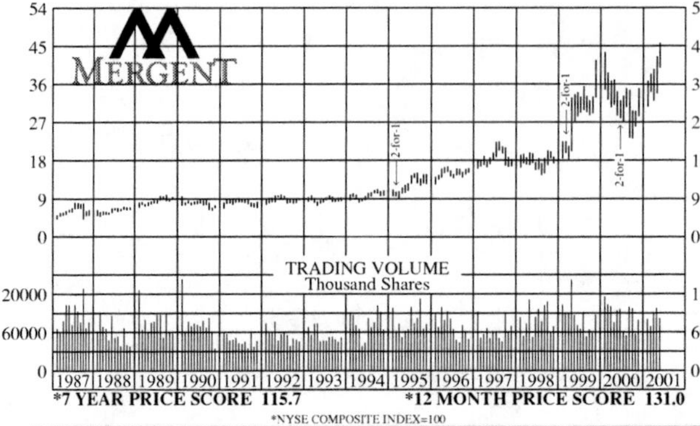

*7 YEAR PRICE SCORE 115.7 *12 MONTH PRICE SCORE 131.0

*NYSE COMPOSITE INDEX=100

INTERIM EARNINGS (Per Share):

Qtr.	Mar.	June	Sept.	Dec.
1997	0.23	0.30	0.33	0.31
1998	0.31	0.31	0.31	0.30
1999	0.30	0.33	0.35	0.45
2000	0.48	0.47	0.42	0.45

INTERIM DIVIDENDS (Per Share):

Amt.	Decl.	Ex.	Rec.	Pay.
2-for-1	1/10/00	6/12/00	5/26/00	6/09/00
0.125Q	7/14/00	8/02/00	8/04/00	8/25/00
0.125Q	9/14/00	11/01/00	11/03/00	11/25/00
0.15Q	1/12/01	1/31/01	2/02/01	2/25/01
0.15Q	3/09/01	5/02/01	5/04/01	5/25/01

Indicated div.: $0.60 (Div. Reinv. Plan)

CAPITALIZATION (12/31/00):

	($000)	(%)
Long-Term Debt [1]	4,987,000	26.4
Deferred Income Tax	969,000	5.1
Minority Interest	1,514,000	8.0
Preferred Stock	56,000	0.3
Common & Surplus	11,366,000	60.2
Total	18,892,000	100.0

RECENT DEVELOPMENTS: For the year ended 12/31/00, net income soared 41.3% to $1.49 billion versus $1.05 billion in the previous year. Total sales jumped 40.4% to $23.09 billion from $16.45 billion a year earlier. Income from operations climbed 44.3% to $1.87 billion from $1.30 billion in 1999. Shipments of aluminum products increased 20.5% to 5.4 million from 4.5 million the prior year.

PROSPECTS: On 1/25/01, the Company completed the sale of Reynolds Australia Alumina, Ltd. LLC, which holds a 56.0% interest in the Worsley alumina refinery located in Western Australia for approximately $1.49 billion. Separately, the Company and ATK have reached a definitive agreement under which AA will sell its Thiokol Propulsion business for approximately $685.0 million.

BUSINESS

ALCOA, INC. (formerly Aluminum Co. of America) is a major integrated producer of aluminum products. Principal operations include the mining and processing of bauxite, the refining of alumina from bauxite, the smelting of aluminum from alumina, the processing of aluminum and aluminum alloys into mill products and finished products, and the recycling of used aluminum products. Alcoa has operations around the world including Latin America, and the Far East. In 2000, revenues were derived as follows: alumina and chemicals, 9.2%; primary metals, 16.4%; flat-rolled products, 23.7%; engineered products, 23.9%; packaging and consumer, 9.1% and other, 17.7%. In 2000, AA shipped 5,398,000 metric tons of aluminum.

ANNUAL FINANCIAL DATA

	12/31/00	12/31/99	12/31/98	12/31/97	12/31/96	12/31/95	12/31/94
Earnings Per Share	**[5] 1.81**	**1.41**	**[4] 1.21**	**[3] 1.16**	**[2] 0.74**	**1.11**	**[1] 0.62**
Cash Flow Per Share	**3.29**	**2.62**	**2.43**	**2.24**	**1.83**	**2.14**	**1.59**
Tang. Book Val. Per Share	**6.20**	**6.71**	**6.25**	**5.76**	**6.39**	**5.37**	**4.96**
Dividends Per Share	**0.50**	**0.40**	**0.34**	**0.24**	**0.33**	**0.23**	**0.20**
Dividend Payout %	**27.6**	**28.5**	**28.4**	**21.1**	**45.2**	**20.3**	**32.3**
INCOME STATEMENT (IN MILLIONS):							
Total Revenues	23,090.0	16,447.0	15,489.4	13,481.7	13,128.4	12,654.9	10,391.5
Costs & Expenses	18,632.0	13,502.0	12,830.5	11,081.0	10,949.9	10,318.4	8,693.8
Depreciation & Amort.	1,219.0	901.0	856.2	753.6	764.2	730.3	688.8
Operating Income	3,239.0	2,044.0	1,802.7	1,647.1	1,414.3	1,606.2	1,008.9
Net Interest Inc./(Exp.)	d427.0	d195.0	d197.9	d140.9	d133.7	d119.8	d106.7
Income Before Income Taxes	2,812.0	1,849.0	1,604.8	1,601.7	1,081.7	1,470.2	822.5
Income Taxes	942.0	553.0	513.5	528.7	360.7	445.9	219.2
Equity Earnings/Minority Int.	d381.0	d242.0	d238.3	d267.9	d206.1	d233.8	d160.2
Net Income	[5] 1,489.0	1,054.0	[4] 853.0	[3] 805.1	[2] 514.9	790.5	[1] 443.1
Cash Flow	2,706.0	1,953.0	1,707.1	1,556.6	1,277.0	1,518.7	1,129.8
Average Shs. Outstg. (000)	823,200	747,200	703,234	695,440	697,336	712,072	711,524
BALANCE SHEET (IN MILLIONS):							
Cash & Cash Equivalents	371.0	314.0	381.6	906.4	616.6	1,062.4	624.7
Total Current Assets	7,578.0	4,800.0	5,025.1	4,416.9	4,281.2	4,741.7	4,153.2
Net Property	12,850.0	9,133.0	9,133.5	6,666.5	7,077.5	6,929.7	6,689.4
Total Assets	31,691.0	17,066.0	17,462.5	13,070.6	13,449.9	15,615.4	13,863.8
Total Current Liabilities	7,954.0	3,003.0	3,268.3	2,452.5	2,373.4	2,652.2	2,553.5
Long-Term Obligations	4,987.0	2,657.0	2,877.0	1,457.2	1,689.8	1,215.5	1,029.8
Net Stockholders' Equity	11,422.0	6,318.0	6,055.9	4,419.4	4,462.4	4,444.7	3,999.2
Net Working Capital	d376.0	1,797.0	1,756.8	1,964.4	1,907.8	2,089.5	1,599.7
Year-end Shs. Outstg. (000)	865,517	735,498	733,618	673,104	690,040	705,256	714,848
STATISTICAL RECORD:							
Operating Profit Margin %	14.0	12.4	11.6	12.2	10.8	12.7	9.7
Net Profit Margin %	6.4	6.4	5.5	6.0	3.9	6.2	4.3
Return on Equity %	13.0	16.7	14.1	18.2	11.5	17.8	11.1
Return on Assets %	4.7	6.2	4.9	6.2	3.8	5.1	3.2
Debt/Total Assets %	15.7	15.6	16.5	11.1	12.6	7.8	7.4
Price Range	43.63-23.13	41.69-17.97	20.31-14.50	22.41-16.06	16.56-12.28	15.06-9.22	11.28-8.03
P/E Ratio	24.1-12.8	29.6-12.7	16.8-12.0	19.4-13.9	22.5-16.7	13.6-8.3	18.2-13.0
Average Yield %	1.5	1.3	2.0	1.3	2.3	1.9	2.1

Statistics are as originally reported. Adjusted for 2-for-1 stock split, 6/00, 2/99 & 2/95. [1] Incl. non-recurr. net gains of $300.2 mill. & non-recurr. net chgs. of $117.9 mill. & bef. $67.9 mill. chg. for early retire. of debr. [2] Incl. spec. net chgs. of $123.3 mill. & nonrecurr. losses of $47.1 mill. [3] Incl. net loss of $12.7 mill. for marking to market certain alum. commodity contracts & a net gain of $43.9 mill. for the sale of assets. [4] Incl. a net loss of $2.7 mill. as a result of marking to market certain alum. commodity contracts. [5] Bef. acctg. chrg. of $5.0 mill.

OFFICERS:
A. J. Belda, Chmn., C.E.O.
R. B. Kelson, Exec. V.P., C.F.O.
L. R. Purtell, Exec. V.P., Gen. Couns.

INVESTOR CONTACT: Charles D. McLane, Inv. Rel., (412) 553-2231

PRINCIPAL OFFICE: 201 Isabella Street, Pittsburgh, PA 15212-5858

TELEPHONE NUMBER: (412) 553-4545
FAX: (412) 553-4498
WEB: www.alcoa.com
NO. OF EMPLOYEES: 142,000
SHAREHOLDERS: 265,300 (approx. of record)
ANNUAL MEETING: In Apr.
INCORPORATED: PA, 1888

INSTITUTIONAL HOLDINGS:
No. of Institutions: 590
Shares Held: 657,649,614
% Held: 75.9

INDUSTRY: Primary aluminum (SIC: 3334)

TRANSFER AGENT(S): First Chicago Trust Company of New York, Jersey City, NJ

NYSE SYMBOL Y
Rec. Pr. 208.80 (5/31/01)

ALLEGHANY CORPORATION

YIELD ...
P/E RATIO 47.2

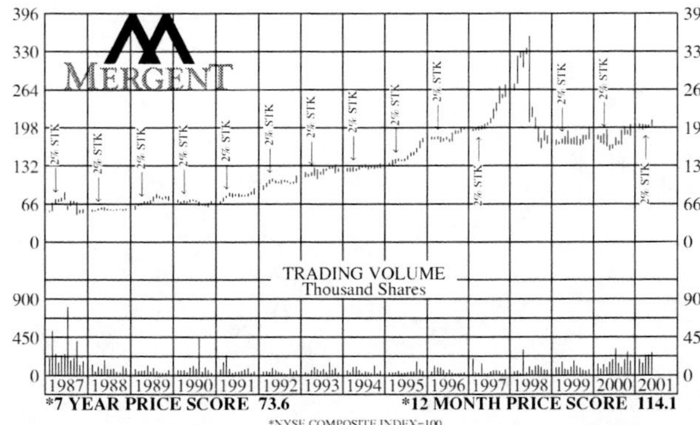

*7 YEAR PRICE SCORE 73.6 *12 MONTH PRICE SCORE 114.1

*NYSE COMPOSITE INDEX=100

INTERIM EARNINGS (Per Share):

Qtr.	Mar.	June	Sept.	Dec.
1996	2.20	2.99	2.61	3.59
1997	0.92	2.26	2.11	2.03
1998	1.68	2.25	2.61	1.75
1999	2.05	2.75	7.47	0.87
2000	d4.48	14.61	1.18	d6.87

INTERIM DIVIDENDS (Per Share):

Amt.	Decl.	Ex.	Rec.	Pay.
2% STK	3/22/00	3/30/00	4/03/00	4/28/00
2% STK	3/21/01	3/29/01	4/02/01	4/27/01

CAPITALIZATION (12/31/00):

	($000)	(%)
Long-Term Debt	228,343	16.4
Common & Surplus	1,165,074	83.6
Total	1,393,417	100.0

RECENT DEVELOPMENTS: For the year ended 12/31/00, earnings from continuing operations fell 50.0% to $34.0 million from $67.9 million a year earlier. Results excluded income from discontinued operations of $34.9 million and $32.2 million for 2000 and 1999, respectively. Earnings for 2000 included a gain of $136.7 million on the sale of a subsidiary. Total revenues decreased 21.7% to $945.2 million, from $1.21 billion in 1999. Comparisons were made with restated prior-year figures.

PROSPECTS: On 2/1/01, the Company announced the completion of the acquisition of its financial services operating unit Alleghany Asset Management, Inc. by a subsidiary of ABN AMRO North America Holding Company. Under the terms of the transaction, Alleghany received $825.0 million in cash. The Company expects to report an after-tax gain on the sale in excess of $65.00 per share of the Company's common stock.

BUSINESS

ALLEGHANY CORPORATION is engaged, through its subsidiary Alleghany Underwriting Holdings Ltd., in the property and casualty insurance and reinsurance businesses. The Company is also engaged, through its subsidiaries World Minerals Inc., Celite Corporation and Harborlite Corporation, in the industrial minerals business. The Company conducts a steel fastener importing and distribution business through its subsidiary Heads & Threads International LLC. Through its subsidiary Alleghany Properties, Inc., The Company owns and manages properties in California. On 2/1/01, the Company sold Alleghany Asset Management, Inc., its financial services business. On 5/10/00, the Company sold its Underwriters Re Group, Inc. property and casualty reinsurance and insurance business. As of 3/31/01, the Company owned 4.6% of Burlington Northern Santa Fe Corp.

BUSINESS LINE ANALYSIS

(12/31/00)	Rev (%)	Inc (%)
Property & Casualty Insurance	43.8	(484.0)
Mining & Filtration	21.8	21.5
Industrial Fasteners	14.3	26.1
Corporate Activities	20.1	536.4
Total	100.0	100.0

ANNUAL FINANCIAL DATA

	12/31/00	12/31/99	12/31/98	[2] 12/31/97	12/31/96	12/31/95	12/31/94
Earnings Per Share	[1][3] 4.51	12.94	8.26	[1] 6.71	11.36	11.15	[1] 9.06
Cash Flow Per Share	7.03	17.17	10.65	9.87	18.10	16.92	14.99
Tang. Book Val. Per Share	161.55	145.62	165.81	204.93	185.19	175.38	136.61
INCOME STATEMENT (IN MILLIONS):							
Total Revenues	945.2	1,376.2	919.0	796.7	2,062.2	1,784.8	1,827.1
Costs & Expenses	914.4	1,149.1	777.3	675.1	1,851.4	1,590.6	1,660.0
Depreciation & Amort.	19.0	32.8	18.4	24.2	51.6	44.1	44.8
Operating Income	11.8	194.2	123.3	97.3	159.2	150.1	122.3
Net Interest Inc./(Exp.)	d24.0	d32.3	d32.3	d32.1	d32.1	d29.0	d29.3
Income Before Income Taxes	d12.1	161.9	91.0	65.2	127.1	121.1	93.0
Income Taxes	cr46.1	61.8	27.6	13.8	40.0	35.8	24.6
Net Income	[1][3] 34.0	100.1	63.4	[1] 51.4	87.0	85.3	[1] 68.4
Cash Flow	53.0	132.9	81.8	75.6	138.6	129.4	113.2
Average Shs. Outstg. (000)	7,535	7,740	7,679	7,657	7,658	7,652	7,546
BALANCE SHEET (IN MILLIONS):							
Cash & Cash Equivalents	19.1	1,220.9	1,384.1	1,324.7	2,177.3	1,877.9	1,686.5
Total Current Assets	1,076.5	2,857.4	2,550.0	2,059.6	2,946.9	2,670.5	2,412.1
Net Property	165.8	207.6	208.7	193.3	287.2	272.3	202.9
Total Assets	2,707.6	4,485.0	4,282.4	3,700.4	4,500.6	4,122.5	3,587.9
Long-Term Obligations	228.3	408.0	439.8	389.6	447.5	331.7	335.1
Net Stockholders' Equity	1,165.1	1,107.9	1,247.4	1,570.9	1,423.3	1,320.6	1,021.2
Net Working Capital	1,076.5	2,857.4	2,550.0	2,059.6	2,946.9	2,670.5	2,412.1
Year-end Shs. Outstg. (000)	7,212	7,608	7,523	7,666	7,685	7,530	7,475
STATISTICAL RECORD:							
Operating Profit Margin %	1.3	14.1	13.4	12.2	7.7	8.4	6.7
Net Profit Margin %	3.6	7.3	6.9	6.5	4.2	4.8	3.7
Return on Equity %	2.9	9.0	5.1	3.3	6.1	6.5	6.7
Return on Assets %	1.3	2.2	1.5	1.4	1.9	2.1	1.9
Debt/Total Assets %	8.4	9.1	10.3	10.5	9.9	8.0	9.3
Price Range	203.07-157.84	198.60-166.77	356.68-162.08	273.28-192.16	196.78-172.76	180.70-132.31	135.75-121.45
P/E Ratio	45.0-35.0	15.4-12.9	43.2-19.6	40.7-28.6	17.3-15.2	16.2-11.9	15.0-13.4

Statistics are as originally reported. Adj. for all 2% stk. divs. through 4/27/01 [1] Bef. disc. oper. gain $34.9 mill.,12/00; $32.7 mill., 12/98; $54.3 mill., 12/97; $69.1 mill., 12/94 [2] Reflects the spin-off of Chicago Title and Trust Co. [3] Incl. non-recurr. gain $136.7 mill.

OFFICERS:
F. Kirby, Chmn.
J. J. Burns Jr., Pres., C.E.O., C.O.O.
D. B. Cuming, Sr. V.P., C.F.O.

INVESTOR CONTACT: R.M. Hart, Inv. Rel., (212) 752-1356

PRINCIPAL OFFICE: 375 Park Avenue, New York, NY 10152

TELEPHONE NUMBER: (212) 752-1356
FAX: (212) 759-8149
WEB: www.alleghanyfunds.com

NO. OF EMPLOYEES: 2,083 (avg.)

SHAREHOLDERS: 1,625 (approx. common)

ANNUAL MEETING: In April

INCORPORATED: DE, 1984

INSTITUTIONAL HOLDINGS:
No. of Institutions: 113
Shares Held: 4,182,158
% Held: 57.6

INDUSTRY: Title insurance (SIC: 6361)

TRANSFER AGENT(S): Computershare Investor Services, Chicago, IL

NYSE SYMBOL AYE
Rec. Pr. 51.16 (4/30/01)

ALLEGHENY ENERGY, INC.

YIELD 3.2%
P/E RATIO 18.0

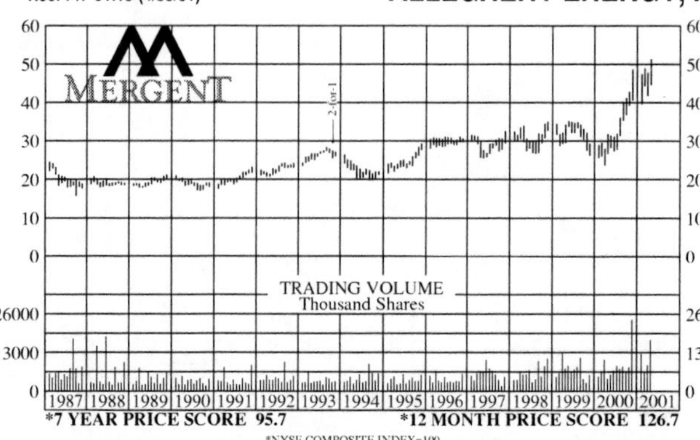

*7 YEAR PRICE SCORE 95.7 *12 MONTH PRICE SCORE 126.7

*NYSE COMPOSITE INDEX=100

INTERIM EARNINGS (Per Share):

Qtr.	Mar.	June	Sept.	Dec.
1997	0.64	0.42	0.61	0.63
1998	0.64	0.44	0.68	0.39
1999	0.80	0.55	0.63	0.66
2000	0.78	0.65	0.69	0.72

INTERIM DIVIDENDS (Per Share):

Amt.	Decl.	Ex.	Rec.	Pay.
0.43Q	6/01/00	6/08/00	6/12/00	6/30/00
0.43Q	9/07/00	9/14/00	9/18/00	9/29/00
0.43Q	12/07/00	12/14/00	12/18/00	12/29/00
0.43Q	3/01/01	3/08/01	3/12/01	3/30/01
0.43Q	6/07/01	6/14/01	6/18/01	6/29/01

Indicated div.: $1.72 (Div. Reinv. Plan)

CAPITALIZATION (12/31/00):

	($000)	(%)
Long-Term Debt	2,559,510	48.6
Deferred Income Tax	888,303	16.9
Preferred Stock	74,000	1.4
Common & Surplus	1,740,681	33.1
Total	5,262,494	100.0

RECENT DEVELOPMENTS: For the year ended 12/31/00, income before an extraordinary charge climbed 2.1% to $313.7 million compared with $307.2 million in 1999. Results for 2000 excluded an extraordinary charge of $77.0 million. Results for 1999 excluded an extraordinary charge of $17.0 million, a reacquired debt extraordinary charge of $10.0 million, a merger-related charge of $11.8 million, and generation project costs of $10.0 million. Total revenues jumped 42.8% to $4.01 billion from $2.81 billion.

PROSPECTS: The Company is targeting earnings per share growth in excess of 10.0% per year through 2004. In addition, the Company expects its power plants will produce at 72.0% capacity in 2001, which is up over 70.0% from 1999. Earnings per share for full-year 2001 are expected to range between $3.10 to $3.30, and if the acquisition of 1,710 megawatts of generating assets in the Midwest is completed, earnings may range between $3.50 and $3.70 per share.

BUSINESS

ALLEGHENY ENERGY, INC. (formerly Allegheny Power System, Inc.) is an electric utility holding company that derives substantially all of its income from the electric utility operations of its regulated subsidiaries, Allegheny Power, Monongahela Power Co., Allegheny Energy Supply Company, LLC, The Potomac Edison Co., and West Penn Power Co. The principal markets for AYE's electric sales are in the states of PA, WVA, MD, VA, and OH. AYE also has a wholly-owned non-utility subsidiary, Allegheny Ventures, which is involved primarily in energy-related businesses. As of 12/31/00, AYE provided electric service to 3.0 million customers in an area of 29,000 square miles with a population of about three million.

ANNUAL FINANCIAL DATA

	12/31/00	12/31/99	12/31/98	12/31/97	12/31/96	12/31/95	12/31/94
Earnings Per Share	[5] **2.84**	[4] **2.45**	[3] **2.15**	**2.30**	[2] **1.73**	[2] **2.00**	[1] **1.86**
Cash Flow Per Share	**4.97**	**4.57**	**4.36**	**4.48**	**3.91**	**4.14**	**3.75**
Tang. Book Val. Per Share	**13.80**	**14.97**	**16.49**	**16.92**	**16.28**	**16.11**	**14.62**
Dividends Per Share	**1.72**	**1.72**	**1.72**	**1.72**	**1.69**	**1.65**	**1.64**
Dividend Payout %	**60.6**	**70.2**	**80.0**	**74.8**	**97.7**	**82.5**	**88.2**
INCOME STATEMENT (IN MILLIONS):							
Total Revenues	4,011.9	2,808.4	2,576.4	2,369.5	2,327.6	2,647.8	2,451.7
Costs & Expenses	3,010.2	1,863.9	1,649.0	1,420.9	1,430.2	1,712.8	1,597.7
Depreciation & Amort.	235.2	246.3	270.4	265.8	263.2	256.3	223.9
Maintenance Exp.	230.3	223.5	217.6	230.6	243.3	256.6	241.9
Operating Income	536.2	474.6	439.5	452.2	390.9	422.1	388.1
Net Interest Inc./(Exp.)	d222.9	d181.7	d177.0	d184.1	d179.1	d177.9	d156.4
Net Income	[5] 313.7	[4] 285.4	[3] 263.0	281.3	[2] 210.0	[2] 239.7	[1] 219.8
Cash Flow	548.8	531.7	533.4	547.0	473.3	496.0	443.6
Average Shs. Outstg. (000)	110,436	116,237	122,436	122,208	121,141	119,864	118,272
BALANCE SHEET (IN MILLIONS):							
Gross Property	9,507.0	8,839.7	8,629.7	8,451.4	8,206.2	7,812.7	7,586.8
Accumulated Depreciation	3,967.6	3,632.6	3,395.6	3,155.2	2,910.0	2,700.1	2,529.4
Net Property	5,539.3	5,207.2	5,234.1	5,296.2	5,296.2	5,112.6	5,057.4
Total Assets	7,697.0	6,852.4	6,747.8	6,654.1	6,618.5	6,447.3	6,362.2
Long-Term Obligations	2,559.5	2,254.5	2,179.3	2,193.2	2,397.1	2,273.2	2,178.5
Net Stockholders' Equity	1,814.7	1,769.3	2,204.0	2,427.0	2,339.2	2,300.0	2,359.4
Year-end Shs. Outstg. (000)	110,436	110,436	122,436	122,436	121,840	120,701	119,293
STATISTICAL RECORD:							
Operating Profit Margin %	13.4	16.9	17.1	19.1	16.8	15.9	15.8
Net Profit Margin %	7.8	10.2	10.2	11.9	9.0	9.1	9.0
Net Inc./Net Property %	5.7	5.5	5.0	5.3	4.0	4.7	4.3
Net Inc./Tot. Capital %	6.0	5.8	5.0	5.1	3.8	4.4	4.2
Return on Equity %	17.3	16.1	11.9	12.5	9.7	11.3	10.7
Accum. Depr./Gross Prop. %	41.7	41.1	39.3	37.3	35.5	34.6	33.3
Price Range	48.75-23.63	35.19-26.19	34.94-26.63	32.59-25.50	31.13-28.00	29.25-21.50	26.50-19.75
P/E Ratio	171.6-83.2	14.4-10.7	16.2-12.4	14.2-11.1	18.0-16.2	14.6-10.7	14.2-10.6
Average Yield %	4.8	5.6	5.6	5.9	5.7	6.5	7.1

Statistics are as originally reported. [1] Incl. net chg. of $5.3 mill. & bef. cumulative effect of acctg. chg. [2] Incl. after-tax chgs. from restr. activity of $62.6 mill., 1996; $14.1 mill., 1995. [3] Excl. $275.4 mill. after-tax extraord. chg. rel. to write-off by West Penn Power for deregul. in PA. [4] Excl. $27.0 mill. extra chgs., $11.8 mill. merger-related chgs. & $10.0 mill. chg. [5] Excl. $77.0 mill. extraord. chg.

OFFICERS:
A. J. Noia, Chmn., Pres., C.E.O.
M. P. Morrell, Sr. V.P., C.F.O.
R. F. Binder, V.P., Treas.

INVESTOR CONTACT: Cynthia A. Shoop, Inv. Rel., (301) 665-2718

PRINCIPAL OFFICE: 10435 Downsville Pike, Hagerstown, MD 21740-1766

TELEPHONE NUMBER: (301) 790-3400
FAX: (301) 665-2746
WEB: www.alleghenyenergy.com

NO. OF EMPLOYEES: 4,817

SHAREHOLDERS: 40,589

ANNUAL MEETING: In May

INCORPORATED: MD, Dec., 1925

INSTITUTIONAL HOLDINGS:
No. of Institutions: 319
Shares Held: 52,662,359
% Held: 47.7

INDUSTRY: Electric services (SIC: 4911)

TRANSFER AGENT(S): Mellon Investor Services, Ridgefield Park, NJ

NYSE SYMBOL ATI
Rec. Pr. 18.24 (4/30/01)

ALLEGHENY TECHNOLOGIES INCORPORATED

YIELD 4.4%
P/E RATIO 11.5

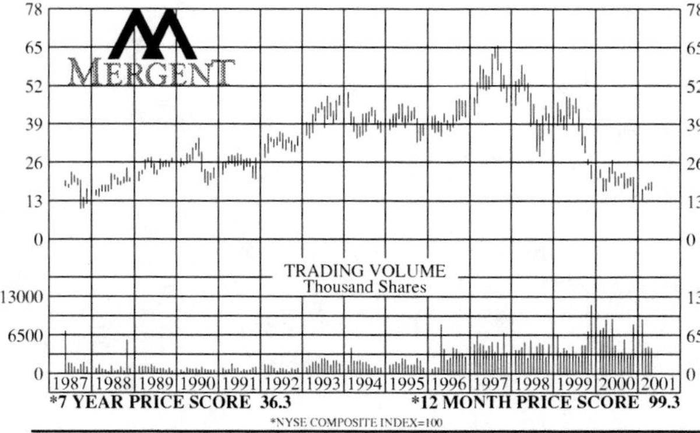

INTERIM EARNINGS (Per Share):

Qtr.	Mar.	June	Sept.	Dec.
1997	0.72	1.00	0.74	0.94
1998	0.28	0.76	0.66	0.74
1999	0.62	0.60	0.40	0.14
2000	0.47	0.53	0.52	0.07

INTERIM DIVIDENDS (Per Share):

Amt.	Decl.	Ex.	Rec.	Pay.
0.20Q	5/11/00	5/25/00	5/30/00	6/13/00
0.20Q	8/10/00	8/24/00	8/28/00	9/12/00
0.20Q	11/09/00	11/22/00	11/27/00	12/12/00
0.20Q	2/08/01	2/22/01	2/26/01	3/13/01
0.20Q	5/03/01	5/24/01	5/29/01	6/12/01

Indicated div.: $0.80 (Div. Reinv. Plan)

CAPITALIZATION (12/31/00):

	($000)	(%)
Long-Term Debt	490,600	29.1
Deferred Income Tax	158,700	9.4
Common & Surplus	1,039,200	61.5
Total	1,688,500	100.0

RECENT DEVELOPMENTS: For the year ended 12/31/00, net income increased 19.4% to $132.5 million compared with income from continuing operations of $111.0 million in 1999. Earnings included non-recurring items that resulted in net special charges of $15.0 million and $7.9 million in 2000 and 1999, respectively. Sales were $2.46 billion, up 7.2% from $2.30 billion a year earlier.

PROSPECTS: In an attempt to improve performance, ATI initiated a company-wide cost-reduction program of $110.0 million. As part of the program, ATI estimates annual cost savings of $7.0 million beginning in the second quarter of 2001 via idling a high-cost titanium sponge production facility at the Oremet plant in Oregon.

BUSINESS

ALLEGHENY TECHNOLOGIES INCORPORATED (formerly Allegheny Teledyne Inc.) is a diversified producer of specialty materials including stainless steel, nickel-based and cobalt-based alloys and superalloys, titanium and titanium alloys, specialty steel alloys, zirconium and related alloys, and tungsten-based specialty materials. The Company consists of the following operating units: Allegheny Ludlum; Allvac; Oremet-Wah Chang; Allegheny Rodney Strip Division; Titanium Industries; Rome Metals; Metalworking Products; Casting Service and Portland Forge. On 11/30/99, the Company completed the spin-offs of Teledyne Technologies Incorporated and Water Pik Technologies, Inc.

ANNUAL FINANCIAL DATA

	12/31/00	12/31/99	[4] 12/31/98	12/31/97	12/31/96	12/31/95	12/31/94
Earnings Per Share	[5] 1.60	[5] 1.16	[3] 2.44	[2] 3.34	[1] 2.56	[1] 3.12	0.12
Cash Flow Per Share	2.89	2.15	3.53	4.44	3.79	4.38	1.33
Tang. Book Val. Per Share	10.51	11.02	11.12	9.52	7.96	7.16	...
Dividends Per Share	0.80	1.28	1.28	1.28	0.32	...	...
Dividend Payout %	50.0	110.3	52.4	38.3	12.5	...	...
INCOME STATEMENT (IN MILLIONS):							
Total Revenues	2,460.4	2,296.1	3,923.4	3,745.1	3,815.6	4,048.1	3,457.3
Costs & Expenses	2,132.0	2,017.3	3,412.6	3,225.6	3,369.4	3,533.4	3,280.5
Depreciation & Amort.	99.7	95.3	109.0	98.5	105.3	110.9	108.4
Operating Income	228.7	183.5	401.8	421.0	340.9	403.8	68.4
Net Interest Inc./(Exp.)	d34.4	d25.9	d19.3	d19.6	d34.7	d37.6	d44.0
Income Before Income Taxes	208.8	174.2	391.2	475.2	384.7	440.9	29.2
Income Taxes	76.3	63.2	150.0	177.6	158.2	164.1	19.4
Net Income	[5] 132.5	[5] 111.0	[3] 241.2	[2] 297.6	[1] 226.5	[1] 276.8	9.8
Cash Flow	232.2	206.3	350.2	396.1	329.8	386.1	118.2
Average Shs. Outstg. (000)	80,300	95,900	99,100	89,200	87,041	88,193	88,781
BALANCE SHEET (IN MILLIONS):							
Cash & Cash Equivalents	26.2	50.7	74.8	50.3	62.5	112.6	...
Total Current Assets	1,022.8	1,033.5	1,364.5	1,228.7	1,199.8	1,235.9	...
Net Property	872.0	912.4	1,003.6	687.7	731.4	755.9	...
Total Assets	2,776.2	2,750.6	3,175.5	2,604.5	2,606.4	2,628.9	...
Total Current Liabilities	413.5	540.0	622.3	561.5	585.8	556.1	...
Long-Term Obligations	490.6	200.3	446.8	326.1	443.4	561.1	...
Net Stockholders' Equity	1,039.2	1,200.2	1,339.9	999.7	871.5	785.8	...
Net Working Capital	609.3	493.5	742.2	667.2	614.0	679.8	...
Year-end Shs. Outstg. (000)	80,340	90,368	97,437	87,165	87,195	87,243	...
STATISTICAL RECORD:							
Operating Profit Margin %	9.3	8.0	10.2	11.2	8.9	10.0	2.0
Net Profit Margin %	5.4	4.8	6.1	7.9	5.9	6.8	0.3
Return on Equity %	12.8	9.2	18.0	29.8	26.0	35.2	...
Return on Assets %	4.8	4.0	7.6	11.4	8.7	10.5	...
Debt/Total Assets %	17.7	7.3	14.1	12.5	17.0	21.3	...
Price Range	26.81-12.50	48.38-20.25	59.13-28.00	65.75-42.00	47.50-34.75	46.00-32.75	49.75-34.00
P/E Ratio	16.8-7.8	41.7-17.5	24.2-11.5	19.7-12.6	18.6-13.6	14.7-10.5	414.2-283.1
Average Yield %	4.1	3.7	2.9	2.4	0.8	...	...

Statistics are as originally reported. Adj. for stk. split: 1-for-2, 11/99. [1] Excl. extraord. chrg. of an undisclosed amount, 1995; $13.5 mill. ($0.08/sh.), 1996. [2] Incl. merger and restr. costs of $10.4 mill. [3] Incl. merger and restr. costs of $67.8 mill. [4] Results for 1998 and earlier are for Allegheny Teledyne Inc. prior to the spin-off of Teledyne Technologies Inc. and Water Pik Technologies, Inc. [5] Bef. extraord. gain $129.6 mill. and disc. oper. inc. of $59.6 mill., 1999; incl. non-recurring chrg. of $15.0 mill., 2000; $7.9 mill., 1999.

OFFICERS:
R. P. Bozzone, Chmn., Pres., C.E.O.
J. D. Walton, Sr. V.P., Gen. Couns., Sec.
R. J. Harshman, V.P., Fin., C.F.O.

INVESTOR CONTACT: R. J. Harshman, (412) 394-2861

PRINCIPAL OFFICE: 1000 Six PPG Place, Pittsburgh, PA 15222-5479

TELEPHONE NUMBER: (412) 394-2800
FAX: (412) 394-2805
WEB: www.alleghenytechnologies.com

NO. OF EMPLOYEES: 11,400 (approx.)

SHAREHOLDERS: 7,990 (approx.)

ANNUAL MEETING: In May

INCORPORATED: DE, 1996

INSTITUTIONAL HOLDINGS:
No. of Institutions: 183
Shares Held: 38,842,545
% Held: 48.5

INDUSTRY: Semiconductors and related devices (SIC: 3674)

TRANSFER AGENT(S): Mellon Investor Services, Ridgefield Park, NJ

NYSE SYMBOL ALN
Rec. Pr. 12.00 (5/31/01)

ALLEN TELECOM INC.

YIELD	...
P/E RATIO	31.6

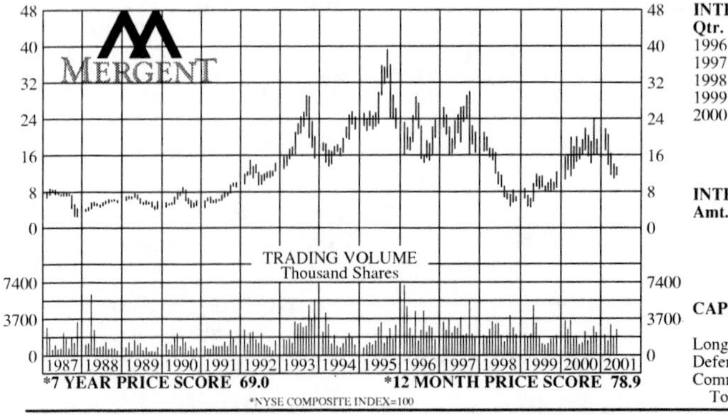

*7 YEAR PRICE SCORE 69.0 *12 MONTH PRICE SCORE 78.9

*NYSE COMPOSITE INDEX=100

INTERIM EARNINGS (Per Share):

Qtr.	Mar.	June	Sept.	Dec.
1996	0.16	0.19	0.13	0.25
1997	0.26	0.25	0.29	0.08
1998	0.23	d0.41	0.10	d0.12
1999	d0.05	Nil	0.10	d0.23
2000	0.02	0.08	0.15	0.13

INTERIM DIVIDENDS (Per Share):

Amt.	Decl.	Ex.	Rec.	Pay.

No dividends paid.

CAPITALIZATION (12/31/00):

	($000)	(%)
Long-Term Debt	134,639	35.5
Deferred Income Tax	9,168	2.4
Common & Surplus	234,981	62.0
Total	378,788	100.0

RECENT DEVELOPMENTS: For the year ended 12/31/00, income from continuing operations was $10.8 million versus a loss from continuing operations of $5.2 million in 1999. Results for 2000 and 1999 excluded net gains of $1.3 million and $2.4 million, respectively, from discontinued operations. Also, the 1999 results included a pre-tax non-recurring charge of $12.3 million. Sales advanced 16.8% to $392.6 million. Wireless equipment segment sales rose 17.2% to $367.5 million, while wireless engineering services segment sales grew 11.3% to $25.1 million.

PROSPECTS: On 2/5/01, ALN announced that its MIKOM division received an $8.8 million order from Orange UK for GSM1800 EDGE compatible radio frequency boosters that balance and enhance the uplink and downlink connections in a mobile phone network. The order should be fullfilled during the first three quarters of 2001. On 1/23/01, ALN announced its intent to acquire Smith-Woolley Telecoms. The acquisition should enhance ALN's service offerings with the addition of cell site development in the U.K. and Europe.

BUSINESS

ALLEN TELECOM INC. is a supplier of wireless equipment to the global telecommunications infrastructure market. The FOREM division supplies sophisticated filters, duplexers, combiners, amplifiers and microwave radios to an array of OEM customers. The MIKOM division provides repeaters and other products that enhance both the coverage and the capacity of a wireless system. Tekmar Sistemi specializes in multi-band, multi-technology fiber optic in-building coverage systems. Telia manufacturers a complete range of advanced power amplifiers. Decibel Products and Antenna Specialists manufacture land-based and mobile antennas in frequency bands that cover all of the traditional wireless networks. Grayson Wireless supplies measurement and signal processing systems for testing the overall performance of a wireless network and provides geolocation services. Comsearch offers engineering and consulting services for wireless operators.

BUSINESS LINE ANALYSIS

(12/31/2000)	REV (%)	INC (%)
Communications Equipment	93.6	89.6
Engineering & Consulting	6.4	10.4
Total	100.0	100.0

ANNUAL FINANCIAL DATA

	12/31/00	12/31/99	12/31/98	12/31/97	12/31/96	12/31/95	12/31/94
Earnings Per Share	**[5] 0.38**	**[4] d0.19**	**[1] d0.21**	**[3] 0.88**	**[2] 0.76**	**[1] 0.95**	**0.74**
Cash Flow Per Share	**1.23**	**0.71**	**0.70**	**1.60**	**1.44**	**1.51**	**1.15**
Tang. Book Val. Per Share	**3.78**	**3.81**	**3.97**	**4.91**	**5.08**	**4.87**	**6.01**
INCOME STATEMENT (IN THOUSANDS):							
Total Revenues	392,608	333,697	388,004	432,508	369,498	315,377	216,313
Costs & Expenses	341,181	309,403	371,185	363,011	301,700	250,621	173,519
Depreciation & Amort.	24,020	24,930	24,633	19,733	18,487	15,118	10,793
Operating Income	27,407	d636	d7,814	49,764	49,311	49,638	32,001
Net Interest Inc./(Exp.)	d9,033	d8,146	d6,805	d3,051	d6,558	d1,821	d1,294
Income Before Income Taxes	18,374	d5,412	d8,554	46,713	46,526	47,817	30,707
Income Taxes	7,530	cr1,844	cr5,310	17,723	19,665	19,270	10,973
Equity Earnings/Minority Int.	d91	d1,650	d2,268	d5,009	d6,305	d3,027	d523
Net Income	[5] 10,753	[4] d5,218	[1] d5,512	[3] 23,981	[2] 20,556	[1] 25,520	19,211
Cash Flow	34,773	19,712	19,121	43,714	39,043	40,638	30,004
Average Shs. Outstg.	28,270	27,660	27,370	27,340	27,060	26,900	26,100
BALANCE SHEET (IN THOUSANDS):							
Cash & Cash Equivalents	10,539	22,085	19,900	30,775	23,879	15,706	55,240
Total Current Assets	217,125	204,150	202,963	242,036	199,180	177,814	178,191
Net Property	41,279	49,253	61,582	60,543	51,942	77,124	56,860
Total Assets	473,022	451,430	465,585	514,433	410,512	363,565	357,716
Total Current Liabilities	84,494	76,088	69,498	131,021	104,802	84,443	70,251
Long-Term Obligations	134,639	120,905	128,677	97,915	49,957	47,058	44,910
Net Stockholders' Equity	234,981	240,912	250,081	260,822	225,951	210,377	224,181
Net Working Capital	132,631	128,062	133,465	111,015	94,378	93,371	107,940
Year-end Shs. Outstg.	28,022	27,882	29,759	27,292	26,763	26,560	26,107
STATISTICAL RECORD:							
Operating Profit Margin %	7.0	...	...	11.5	13.3	15.7	14.8
Net Profit Margin %	2.7	...	...	5.5	5.6	8.1	8.9
Return on Equity %	4.6	...	...	9.2	9.1	12.1	8.6
Return on Assets %	2.3	...	...	4.7	5.0	7.0	5.4
Debt/Total Assets %	28.5	26.8	27.6	19.0	12.2	12.9	12.6
Price Range	24.00-10.56	12.38-4.50	21.13-4.69	30.00-16.00	28.88-14.25	39.38-21.25	25.63-13.50
P/E Ratio	63.1-27.8	...	...	34.1-18.2	38.0-18.7	41.4-22.4	34.6-18.2

Statistics are as originally reported. [1] Bef. disc. oper gain: 1998, $7.1 mill.; 1995, $7.1 mill. ($0.27/sh) [2] Bef. disc. opers. loss $7.5 mill.; Incl. non-recurr. chrg. $2.7 mill. for write-off of R&D. [3] Bef. extraord. chrg. $632,000; Incl. special tax chrg. $6.0 mill. [4] Bef. disc. opers. gain of $2.4 mill.; Incl. net restruct chrg. of $19.4 mill. [5] Incl. net pre-tax chrgs. of $500,000 & bef. gain fr. disc. opers. of $1.3 mill.

OFFICERS:
P. W. Colburn, Chmn.
R. G. Paul, Pres., C.E.O.
R. A. Youdelman, Exec. V.P., C.F.O.
INVESTOR CONTACT: Dianne McCormick, Dir., Investor Relations, (216) 765-5855
PRINCIPAL OFFICE: 25101 Chagrin Blvd., Beachwood, OH 44122

TELEPHONE NUMBER: (216) 765-5855
FAX: (216) 765-0410
WEB: www.allentele.com
NO. OF EMPLOYEES: 2,500 (avg.)
SHAREHOLDERS: 1,698
ANNUAL MEETING: In Apr.
INCORPORATED: DE, Feb., 1969

INSTITUTIONAL HOLDINGS:
No. of Institutions: 97
Shares Held: 23,487,999
% Held: 83.6
INDUSTRY: Radio & TV communications equipment (SIC: 3663)
TRANSFER AGENT(S): Fifth Third Bank, Cincinnati, OH

NYSE SYMBOL AGN
Rec. Pr. 89.70 (5/31/01)

ALLERGAN, INC.

YIELD 0.4%
P/E RATIO 55.7

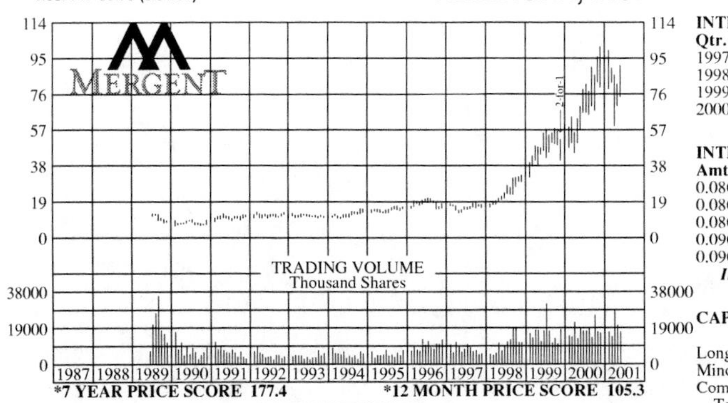

***7 YEAR PRICE SCORE 177.4** ***12 MONTH PRICE SCORE 105.3**

*NYSE COMPOSITE INDEX=100

INTERIM EARNINGS (Per Share):

Qtr.	Mar.	June	Sept.	Dec.
1997	0.14	0.17	0.33	0.35
1998	d0.94	0.26	d0.24	0.22
1999	0.26	0.35	0.35	0.44
2000	0.33	0.39	0.41	0.48

INTERIM DIVIDENDS (Per Share):

Amt.	Decl.	Ex.	Rec.	Pay.
0.08Q	4/27/00	5/24/00	5/26/00	6/16/00
0.08Q	7/26/00	8/23/00	8/25/00	9/15/00
0.08Q	10/20/00	11/15/00	11/17/00	12/08/00
0.09Q	1/31/01	2/14/01	2/16/01	3/16/01
0.09Q	4/25/01	5/16/01	5/18/01	6/15/01

Indicated div.: $0.36 (Div. Reinv. Plan)

CAPITALIZATION (12/31/00):

	($000)	(%)
Long-Term Debt	584,700	40.1
Minority Interest	600	0.0
Common & Surplus	873,800	59.9
Total	1,459,100	100.0

RECENT DEVELOPMENTS: For the year ended 12/31/00, net income advanced 14.3% to $215.1 million versus $188.2 million the year before. Net sales climbed 15.6% to $1.63 billion from $1.41 billion in 1999. Net sales of specialty pharmaceuticals rose 19.4% to $983.5 million from $823.6 million, while net sales of medical devices and over-the-counter product lines slipped 0.6% to $579.1 million.

PROSPECTS: The Company has signed an agreement with Photochemical Co., Ltd. for the right to develop and commercialize ATX-S10, a light-activated modified porphyrin compound used for photodynamic therapy of age-related macular degeneration. Going forward, the Company anticipates 2001 sales in the range of $1.7 million to $1.8 million.

BUSINESS

ALLERGAN, INC. is an international provider of specialty therapeutic products principally in the areas of eye and skin care. The specialty pharmaceutical division's eye-care segment develops, manufactures and markets a broad range of prescription ophthalmic products designed to treat diseases and disorders of the eye, including glaucoma, inflammation, infection, allergy and ophthalmic muscle disorders. The skin-care segment markets a line of skin-care products primarily to dermatologists in the United States. The surgical division markets intraocular lenses, surgically related pharmaceuticals, and other ophthalmic surgical products. The optical division markets a broad range of products worldwide for use with all types of contact lenses, including cleaners and disinfecting solutions.

REVENUES

(12/31/2000)	($000)	(%)
Specialty Pharmaceuticals	983,500	63.0
Opthalmic Surgical	250,400	16.0
Contact Lens Care	328,700	21.0
Total	1,562,600	100.0

ANNUAL FINANCIAL DATA

	12/31/00	12/31/99	12/31/98	12/31/97	12/31/96	12/31/95	12/31/94
Earnings Per Share	**1.61**	**[5] 1.39**	**[4] d0.69**	**[3] 0.98**	**[2] 0.59**	**[1] 0.56**	**0.87**
Cash Flow Per Share	**2.26**	**2.00**	**d0.03**	**1.58**	**1.21**	**1.09**	**1.32**
Tang. Book Val. Per Share	**5.62**	**3.73**	**3.98**	**4.81**	**3.90**	**3.05**	**3.98**
Dividends Per Share	**0.32**	**0.28**	**0.26**	**0.26**	**0.25**	**0.24**	**0.21**
Dividend Payout %	**19.9**	**20.1**	**...**	**26.7**	**41.5**	**42.0**	**24.3**
INCOME STATEMENT (IN MILLIONS):							
Total Revenues	1,625.5	1,452.4	1,296.1	1,149.0	1,156.9	1,067.2	947.2
Costs & Expenses	1,242.3	1,106.5	1,296.4	920.2	966.0	877.2	732.8
Depreciation & Amort.	86.8	82.4	86.8	79.8	80.3	68.7	57.8
Operating Income	296.4	263.5	d87.1	149.0	110.6	121.3	156.6
Net Interest Inc./(Exp.)	4.1	d0.8	d4.7	...	0.6	d3.9	d2.8
Income Before Income Taxes	303.8	269.0	d57.7	157.1	108.0	125.2	158.9
Income Taxes	88.1	80.7	32.8	29.0	31.3	51.7	46.2
Equity Earnings/Minority Int.	d0.6	d0.1	0.3	0.2	0.4	d1.0	d2.0
Net Income	215.1	[5] 188.2	[4] d90.2	[3] 128.3	[2] 77.1	[1] 72.5	110.7
Cash Flow	301.9	270.6	d3.4	208.1	157.4	141.2	168.5
Average Shs. Outstg. (000)	133,800	135,200	131,200	131,600	130,200	129,600	127,800
BALANCE SHEET (IN MILLIONS):							
Cash & Cash Equivalents	773.9	162.9	181.6	180.9	112.0	102.3	130.7
Total Current Assets	1,326.3	697.5	661.2	636.4	599.7	522.3	485.5
Net Property	351.6	330.3	324.9	357.8	348.5	357.5	314.8
Total Assets	1,971.0	1,339.1	1,334.4	1,398.9	1,349.8	1,316.3	1,059.8
Total Current Liabilities	432.5	419.9	368.5	363.3	375.3	331.6	323.7
Long-Term Obligations	584.7	208.8	201.1	142.5	170.0	266.7	83.7
Net Stockholders' Equity	873.8	634.5	696.0	841.4	749.8	668.9	603.3
Net Working Capital	893.8	277.6	292.7	273.1	224.4	190.7	161.8
Year-end Shs. Outstg. (000)	131,681	129,819	132,234	130,586	131,026	129,066	119,878
STATISTICAL RECORD:							
Operating Profit Margin %	18.2	18.1	...	13.0	9.6	11.4	16.5
Net Profit Margin %	13.2	13.0	...	11.2	6.7	6.8	11.7
Return on Equity %	24.6	29.7	...	15.2	10.3	10.8	18.3
Return on Assets %	10.9	14.1	...	9.2	5.7	5.5	10.4
Debt/Total Assets %	29.7	15.6	15.1	10.2	12.6	20.3	7.9
Price Range	101.13-44.50	57.81-31.69	33.25-15.88	18.59-12.94	21.00-15.00	16.88-12.88	15.44-10.00
P/E Ratio	62.8-27.6	41.6-22.8	...	19.1-13.3	35.6-25.4	30.1-23.0	17.8-11.6
Average Yield %	0.4	0.6	1.1	1.6	1.4	1.6	1.7

Statistics are as originally reported. Adjusted for a 2-for-1 stock split 12/99. [1] Incl. an unusual exp. of $50.0 mill. [2] Incl. a restruct. chrg. $70.1 mill. & asset write-offs $7.4 mill. [3] Incl. an inven. adj. chg. $14.0 mill. & a one-time gain $9.5 mill. [4] Incl. a pre-tax restruct. chg. $74.8 mill. & total pre-tax chrgs. $240.9 mill. [5] Incl. a pre-tax restr. gain $9.6 mill., a pre-tax asset write-off gain $1.4 mill., a net gain on invests. $14.0 mill., & a pre-tax chg. $6.9 mill.

OFFICERS:
H. W. Boyer Ph.D., Chmn.
D. E. Pyott, Pres., C.E.O.
E. K. Brandt, Corp. V.P., C.F.O.

INVESTOR CONTACT: Jeffrey L. Edwards, Sr. V.P., Treas./Tax/Inv. Rel., (714) 246-4636

PRINCIPAL OFFICE: 2525 Dupont Drive, Irvine, CA 92612

TELEPHONE NUMBER: (714) 246-4500
FAX: (714) 246-6987
WEB: www.allergan.com

NO. OF EMPLOYEES: 6,181

SHAREHOLDERS: 11,000 (approx.)

ANNUAL MEETING: In Apr.

INCORPORATED: CA, 1948; reincorp., DE, 1977

INSTITUTIONAL HOLDINGS:
No. of Institutions: 322
Shares Held: 116,389,701
% Held: 88.3

INDUSTRY: Pharmaceutical preparations (SIC: 2834)

TRANSFER AGENT(S): First Chicago Trust Company of New York, Jersey City, NJ

NYSE SYMBOL ALE
Rec. Pr. 24.37 (4/30/01)

ALLETE

YIELD 4.4%
P/E RATIO 11.5

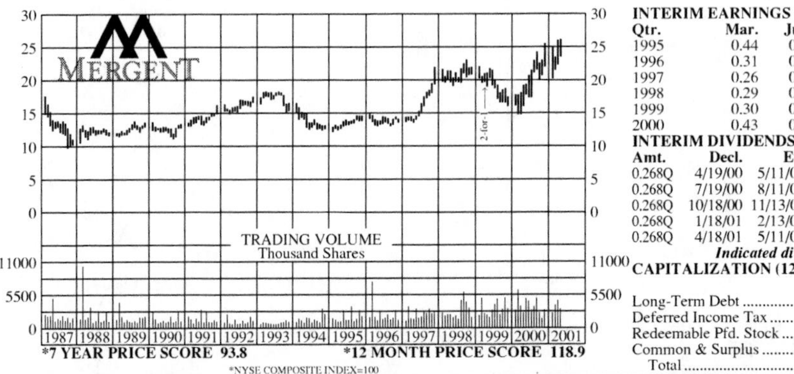

INTERIM EARNINGS (Per Share):

Qtr.	Mar.	June	Sept.	Dec.
1995	0.44	0.18	0.26	0.16
1996	0.31	0.25	0.29	0.30
1997	0.26	0.30	0.37	0.31
1998	0.29	0.36	0.40	0.31
1999	0.30	0.02	0.50	0.15
2000	0.43	0.92	0.50	0.27

INTERIM DIVIDENDS (Per Share):

Amt.	Decl.	Ex.	Rec.	Pay.
0.268Q	4/19/00	5/11/00	5/15/00	6/01/00
0.268Q	7/19/00	8/11/00	8/15/00	9/01/00
0.268Q	10/18/00	11/13/00	11/15/00	12/01/00
0.268Q	1/18/01	2/13/01	2/15/01	3/01/01
0.268Q	4/18/01	5/11/01	5/15/01	6/01/01

Indicated div.: $1.07

CAPITALIZATION (12/31/00):

	($000)	(%)
Long-Term Debt	952,300	46.4
Deferred Income Tax	125,100	6.1
Redeemable Pfd. Stock	75,000	3.7
Common & Surplus	900,800	43.9
Total	2,053,200	100.0

RECENT DEVELOPMENTS: For the year ended 12/31/00, net income more than doubled to $148.6 million versus $68.0 million in the prior year. Earnings for 2000 included income from investment in Capital Re and related disposition of ACE Limited of $48.0 million, while earnings for 1999 included loss form investment in Capital Re and related disposition of ACE Limited of $34.5 million. Total operating revenue improved 17.7% to $1.33 billion from $1.13 billion the year before.

PROSPECTS: On 4/11/01, the Company's subsidiary, ALLETE Properties, announced that it had a firm contract to sell the Tarpon Point Marina and the surrounding 150 acres of development property in Cape Coral, Florida to the Grosse Point Development Company for $29.0 million. The final closing is scheduled for June 2001. This transaction is expected to be a significant contributor to earnings in the second quarter of 2001.

BUSINESS

ALLETE (formerly Minnesota Power, Inc.) operates in four business segments: Electric Services, which include electric and gas services, coal mining and telecommunications; Automotive Services, which include a network of vehicle auctions, a finance company, an auto transport company, a vehicle remarketing company, a company that provides field information services and a company that provides Internet-based parts location and insurance adjustment audit services; Water Services, which include water and wastewater services; and Investments, which includes real estate operations, investments in emerging technologies related to the electric utility industry and a securities portfolio. Revenues in 2000 were derived: 44.3% electric operations; 8.9% water services; 41.0% automotive services; and 5.8% investments.

REVENUES

(12/31/2000)	($000)	(%)
Energy Services	586,080	45.7
Automotive Services	546,120	42.6
Water Services	119,880	9.4
Investments	29,290	2.3
Total	1,281,370	100.0

ANNUAL FINANCIAL DATA

	12/31/00	12/31/99	12/31/98	12/31/97	12/31/96	12/31/95	12/31/94
Earnings Per Share	**3 2.11**	**2 0.97**	**1.35**	**1.24**	**1.14**	**1 1.03**	**1.03**
Cash Flow Per Share	**3.36**	**2.09**	**2.52**	**2.39**	**2.25**	**2.08**	**1.80**
Tang. Book Val. Per Share	**5.73**	**8.50**	**8.51**	**7.31**	**6.58**	**7.16**	**8.99**
Dividends Per Share	**1.07**	**1.07**	**1.02**	**1.02**	**1.02**	**1.02**	**1.01**
Dividend Payout %	**50.7**	**110.3**	**75.8**	**82.6**	**89.5**	**99.0**	**98.0**
INCOME STATEMENT (IN MILLIONS):							
Total Revenues	1,331.9	1,131.8	1,039.7	953.6	846.9	672.9	637.8
Costs & Expenses	1,006.1	923.2	816.2	752.6	688.2	550.4	511.4
Depreciation & Amort.	86.7	76.9	75.0	70.8	65.1	59.6	54.2
Operating Income	239.1	131.7	148.5	130.2	93.6	63.0	82.8
Income Before Income Taxes	233.1	125.7	142.5	124.2	88.9	63.0	72.2
Income Taxes	84.5	57.7	54.0	46.6	19.6	1.2	21.5
Net Income	3 148.6	2 68.0	88.5	77.6	69.2	1 61.9	61.3
Cash Flow	235.3	142.9	161.5	146.4	131.9	118.2	101.7
Average Shs. Outstg. (000)	70,100	68,400	64,200	61,200	58,618	56,966	56,478
BALANCE SHEET (IN MILLIONS):							
Cash & Cash Equivalents	310.1	281.1	259.3	181.4	126.9	71.6	101.0
Total Current Assets	731.0	564.5	487.5	385.3	332.1	252.0	266.1
Net Property	1,479.7	1,258.8	1,550.6	1,525.7	1,523.7	1,448.7	1,080.4
Total Assets	2,914.0	2,312.6	2,317.1	2,188.9	2,146.0	1,947.6	1,807.8
Total Current Liabilities	707.0	398.3	346.0	342.6	337.0	256.8	182.8
Long-Term Obligations	952.3	712.8	747.2	760.4	694.4	639.5	601.3
Net Stockholders' Equity	900.8	817.3	1,564.3	1,441.9	1,411.8	1,272.2	1,211.6
Net Working Capital	24.0	166.2	141.5	42.7	d4.9	d4.8	83.3
Year-end Shs. Outstg. (000)	74,700	73,500	72,400	67,200	65,516	62,936	62,494
STATISTICAL RECORD:							
Operating Profit Margin %	18.0	11.6	14.3	13.7	11.1	9.4	13.0
Net Profit Margin %	11.2	6.0	8.5	8.1	8.2	9.2	9.6
Return on Equity %	16.5	8.3	10.8	11.4	11.1	10.1	10.4
Return on Assets %	5.1	2.9	3.8	3.5	3.2	3.2	2.8
Debt/Total Assets %	32.7	30.8	32.2	34.7	32.4	32.8	33.3
Price Range	25.50-14.75	22.09-16.00	23.13-19.03	22.00-13.50	14.88-13.00	14.63-12.13	16.50-12.38
P/E Ratio	12.1-7.0	22.8-16.5	17.2-14.1	17.8-10.9	13.0-11.4	14.2-11.8	16.0-12.0
Average Yield %	5.3	5.6	4.8	5.7	7.3	7.6	7.0

Statistics are as originally reported. Adj. for stk. splits: 2-for-1, 3/99 1 Bef. disc. opers. gain $2.8 mill. 2 Incl. $24.1 mill. non-cash chrg. associated with the final valuation of the acquisition of Capital Re by Ace Limited, which was completed 12/30/99. 3 Incl. income from investment and related disposition of $49.0 mill.

OFFICERS:
E. L. Russell, Chmn., Pres., C.E.O.
D. G. Gartzke, Sr. V.P., C.F.O.
J. K. Vizanko, Treas.
P. R. Halverson, V.P., Sec., Gen. Couns.

INVESTOR CONTACT: Timothy J. Thorp, Dir., Inv. Rel., (218) 723-3953

PRINCIPAL OFFICE: 30 West Superior Street, Duluth, MN 55802-2093

TELEPHONE NUMBER: (218) 279-5000
FAX: (218) 720-2502
WEB: www.mnpower.com

NO. OF EMPLOYEES: 9,000 full-time (approx.); 4,000 part-time (approx.)

SHAREHOLDERS: 38,000 (common)

ANNUAL MEETING: In May

INCORPORATED: MN, 1906

INSTITUTIONAL HOLDINGS:
No. of Institutions: 175
Shares Held: 19,939,486
% Held: 26.5

INDUSTRY: Electric and other services combined (SIC: 4931)

TRANSFER AGENT(S): Company and Wells Fargo Bank, Duluth, MN

NYSE SYMBOL LNT
Rec. Pr. 30.75 (5/31/01)

ALLIANT ENERGY CORPORATION

YIELD 6.5%
P/E RATIO 6.4

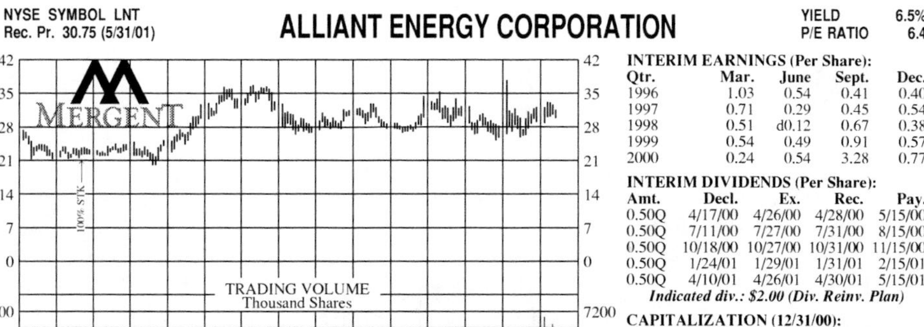

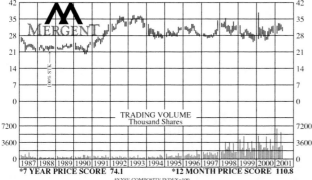

*7 YEAR PRICE SCORE 74.1 *12 MONTH PRICE SCORE 110.8
*NYSE COMPOSITE INDEX=100

INTERIM EARNINGS (Per Share):

Qtr.	Mar.	June	Sept.	Dec.
1996	1.03	0.54	0.41	0.40
1997	0.71	0.29	0.45	0.54
1998	0.51	d0.12	0.67	0.38
1999	0.54	0.49	0.91	0.57
2000	0.24	0.54	3.28	0.77

INTERIM DIVIDENDS (Per Share):

Amt.	Decl.	Ex.	Rec.	Pay.
0.50Q	4/17/00	4/26/00	4/28/00	5/15/00
0.50Q	7/11/00	7/27/00	7/31/00	8/15/00
0.50Q	10/18/00	10/27/00	10/31/00	11/15/00
0.50Q	1/24/01	1/29/01	1/31/01	2/15/01
0.50Q	4/10/01	4/26/01	4/30/01	5/15/01

Indicated div.: $2.00 (Div. Reinv. Plan)

CAPITALIZATION (12/31/00):

	($000)	(%)
Long-Term Debt	1,910,116	38.3
Deferred Income Tax	931,675	18.7
Preferred Stock	113,790	2.3
Common & Surplus	2,037,472	40.8
Total	4,993,053	100.0

RECENT DEVELOPMENTS: For the year ended 12/31/00, LNT reported income of $382.0 million, before an after-tax accounting credit of $16.7 million, versus net income of $196.6 million a year earlier. Results for 2000 included a non-cash net gain of $204.0 million. Operating revenues rose 13.0% to $2.40 billion. Electric utility operating revenue climbed 6.4% to $1.65 billion, while gas utility operating revenue grew 32.0% to $414.9 million. Non-regulated and other operating revenues rose 29.4% to $342.0 million.

PROSPECTS: LNT plans to combine the newly-acquired companies of EUA Cogenex and Energy Assets to form Cogenex, a new subsidiary providing on-site energy services, central plan construction and operations, demand-side management programs, performance contracting and peaking generation to the eastern and mid-western sections of the U.S. Separately, LNT expects earnings will grow 7.0% to 10.0% annually. Going forward, LNT expects its diversified business to generate 25.0% of its total earnings.

BUSINESS

ALLIANT ENERGY CORPORATION was formed as the result of a three-way merger involving IES Industries Inc., Interstate Power Company and WPL Holdings, Inc. in April 1998. The Company is a diversified holding company for Wisconsin Power and Light (WP&L), IES Utilities Inc. (IES), Interstate Power Company (IPC) and Alliant Energy Resources. Through its public utilities of WP&L, IES, IPC, the Company provides electric, natural gas, water, and steam energy to more than two million customers in Iowa, Illinois, Minnesota, and Wisconsin. Alliant Energy Resources is a non-utility business dealing with telecommunications and real estate development.

REVENUES

(12/31/00)	($000)	(%)
Electric Utility	1,648,036	68.5
Gas Utility	414,948	17.3
Non-regulated & other	342,000	14.2
Total	2,404,984	100.0

ANNUAL FINANCIAL DATA

	12/31/00	12/31/99	[4] 12/31/98	12/31/97	12/31/96	12/31/95	12/31/94
Earnings Per Share	[6] 4.82	[5] 2.51	[3] 1.26	1.99	[2][3] 2.38	[1] 2.33	2.13
Cash Flow Per Share	8.89	6.08	4.89	5.25	5.52	5.38	5.00
Tang. Book Val. Per Share	25.79	27.29	20.69	19.73	19.74	19.41	19.43
Dividends Per Share	2.00	2.00	2.00	2.00	1.97	1.94	1.92
Dividend Payout %	41.5	79.7	158.7	100.5	82.8	83.3	90.1
INCOME STATEMENT (IN MILLIONS):							
Total Revenues	2,405.0	2,198.0	2,130.9	919.3	932.8	807.3	816.2
Costs & Expenses	1,368.4	1,121.7	1,102.7	510.0	533.6	408.6	433.3
Depreciation & Amort.	322.3	279.1	279.5	115.7	96.7	94.1	88.2
Maintenance Exp.	...	115.4	122.7	48.1	46.5	42.0	41.2
Operating Income	381.1	376.5	283.3	128.6	141.5	146.0	130.0
Net Interest Inc./(Exp.)	d173.6	d136.2	d129.4	d42.5	d42.0	d43.6	d36.7
Income Taxes	238.8	120.5	58.1	28.7	41.8	36.1	35.4
Net Income	[6] 382.0	[5] 196.6	[3] 96.7	61.3	[2][3] 73.2	[1] 71.6	65.3
Cash Flow	704.3	475.7	376.2	177.0	169.9	165.7	153.5
Average Shs. Outstg. (000)	79,193	78,395	76,912	30,782	30,790	30,774	30,671
BALANCE SHEET (IN MILLIONS):							
Gross Property	6,382.4	6,151.4	5,910.0	2,291.5	2,188.6	2,079.7	2,055.7
Accumulated Depreciation	3,296.5	3,077.5	2,852.6	1,065.7	967.4	887.6	808.9
Net Property	3,719.3	3,486.0	3,456.8	1,356.1	1,369.8	1,355.8	1,389.5
Total Assets	6,733.8	6,075.7	4,959.3	1,861.8	1,900.5	1,872.4	1,805.9
Long-Term Obligations	1,910.1	1,512.8	1,556.9	457.5	362.6	430.4	448.1
Net Stockholders' Equity	2,151.3	2,269.2	1,719.8	667.5	667.3	657.4	657.8
Year-end Shs. Outstg. (000)	79,010	78,984	77,630	30,789	30,774	30,774	30,774
STATISTICAL RECORD:							
Operating Profit Margin %	15.8	17.1	13.3	14.0	15.2	18.1	15.9
Net Profit Margin %	27.9	20.9	18.5	6.7	7.8	8.9	8.0
Net Inc./Net Property %	18.0	13.2	11.4	4.5	5.3	5.2	4.7
Net Inc./Tot. Capital %	13.4	9.6	9.9	6.4	5.6	5.2	4.8
Return on Equity %	17.8	8.7	5.6	9.2	11.0	10.9	9.9
Accum. Depr./Gross Prop. %	51.7	50.0	48.3	46.5	44.2	42.7	39.3
Price Range	37.75-25.75	32.38-25.19	35.38-28.00	34.44-26.75	32.88-27.50	31.75-27.25	32.88-26.38
P/E Ratio	7.8-5.3	12.9-10.0	28.1-22.2	17.3-13.4	13.8-11.6	13.6-11.7	15.4-12.4
Average Yield %	6.3	6.9	6.3	6.5	6.5	6.6	6.5

Statistics are as originally reported. Financial data reflects WPL Holdings, Inc. prior to the 1998 merger. [1] Bef. disc oper. loss $13.2 mill. ($0.43) [2] Incl. non-recurr. credit $0.11/sh. [3] Incl. non-recurr. charge of $54.0 mill. [4] Reflects the consumation of the merger on 4/21/98 [5] Incl. gains totaling $50.3 mill. [6] Bef. net acctg. credit of $16.7 mill. & Incl. non-cash gain of $204.0 mill.

OFFICERS:
E. B. Davis Jr., Chmn., Pres., C.E.O.
T. M. Walker, Exec. V.P., C.F.O.
E. M. Gleason, V.P., Treas., Corp. Sec.

INVESTOR CONTACT: Joni Aeschbach, Mgr., Shareowners Svs, (608) 252-3321

PRINCIPAL OFFICE: 222 West Washington Avenue, Madison, WI 53703

TELEPHONE NUMBER: (608) 252-3311
FAX: (608) 252-3397
WEB: www.alliant-energy.com

NO. OF EMPLOYEES: 7,882

SHAREHOLDERS: 60,883 (approx.)

ANNUAL MEETING: In May

INCORPORATED: WI, Apr., 1981

INSTITUTIONAL HOLDINGS:
No. of Institutions: 195
Shares Held: 20,007,823
% Held: 25.3

INDUSTRY: Electric and other services combined (SIC: 4931)

TRANSFER AGENT(S): The Company

NYSE SYMBOL AW
Rec. Pr. 16.88 (5/31/01)

ALLIED WASTE INDUSTRIES, INC.

YIELD ...
P/E RATIO 52.7

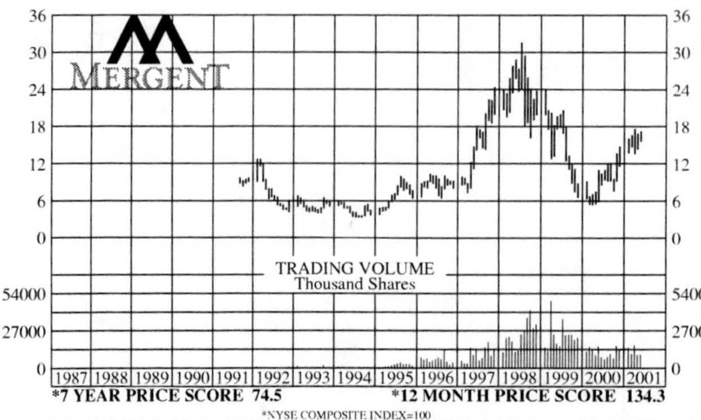

*7 YEAR PRICE SCORE 74.5 *12 MONTH PRICE SCORE 134.3

*NYSE COMPOSITE INDEX=100

INTERIM EARNINGS (Per Share):

Qtr.	Mar.	June	Sept.	Dec.
1997	0.08	0.15	0.17	0.18
1998	0.20	d0.05	0.08	d1.50
1999	0.21	0.29	d1.84	0.08
2000	0.04	0.16	0.02	0.10

INTERIM DIVIDENDS (Per Share):

Amt.	Decl.	Ex.	Rec.	Pay.

No dividends paid.

CAPITALIZATION (12/31/00):

	($000)	(%)
Long-Term Debt	9,907,006	84.9
Preferred Stock	1,069,827	9.2
Common & Surplus	697,832	6.0
Total	11,674,665	100.0

RECENT DEVELOPMENTS: For the year ended 12/31/00, the Company reported income of $137.7 million, before an after-tax extraordinary loss of $13.3 million, compared with a loss of $221.2 million, before an extraordinary loss, in 1999. Results included acquisition related and unusual costs of $127.3 million and $588.9 million in 2000 and 1999, respectively. Revenues were $5.71 billion, up 7.1% from $3.34 billion a year earlier.

PROSPECTS: Looking ahead, the Company expects revenues for 2001 to range from $5.85 billion to $5.95 billion. Earnings before interest, taxes, depreciation and amortization (EBITDA) is expected to range between $2.08 billion and $2.15 billion. The expected increase in both revenues and EBITDA from 2000 levels should reflect the effect of, among other things, the rollover of net divestitures completed in 2000 and lower commodity prices.

BUSINESS

ALLIED WASTE INDUSTRIES, INC. is a non-hazardous solid waste management company that operates as a vertically integrated company that provides collection, transfer, disposal and recycling services for residential, commercial and industrial customers. As of 12/31/00, the Company operated 338 collection companies, 151 transfer stations, 164 active landfills, and 75 recycling facilities within 40 states. On 12/30/96, AW acquired substantially all of the non-hazardous solid waste management business conducted by Laidlaw Inc. On 8/2/99, the Company acquired Browning-Ferris Industries, Inc.

REVENUES

(12/31/2000)	($000)	(%)
Collection	4,227,680	61.7
Disposal	1,993,276	29.1
Recycling	384,027	5.6
Other	242,196	3.6
Total	6,847,179	100.0

ANNUAL FINANCIAL DATA

	12/31/00	[4] 12/31/99	12/31/98	12/31/97	12/31/96	12/31/95	12/31/94
Earnings Per Share	**[1][5] 0.29**	**[3] d1.69**	**[1][2] d0.54**	**[1] 0.57**	**[1] d1.15**	**0.17**	**[1] d0.66**
Cash Flow Per Share	**3.89**	**0.72**	**0.45**	**1.78**	**d0.61**	**0.89**	**0.23**
Tang. Book Val. Per Share	**...**	**...**	**5.04**	**...**	**...**	**1.19**	**0.62**
INCOME STATEMENT (IN MILLIONS):							
Total Revenues	5,707.5	3,341.1	1,575.6	875.0	246.7	169.9	97.4
Costs & Expenses	3,824.9	2,769.2	1,296.0	579.9	268.7	116.2	80.9
Depreciation & Amort.	674.0	384.1	180.0	113.5	31.5	23.4	12.0
Operating Income	1,208.5	187.8	29.9	181.6	d59.3	30.3	4.5
Net Interest Inc./(Exp.)	d878.2	d435.8	d84.4	d92.0	d7.1	d9.0	d10.5
Income Before Income Taxes	381.2	d227.3	d54.5	90.7	d66.4	21.3	d5.9
Income Taxes	237.5	cr8.8	43.8	37.1	cr0.4	9.6	cr0.8
Equity Earnings/Minority Int.	d6.0	d2.8	...	...	...	...	...
Net Income	[1][5] 137.7	[3] d221.2	[1][2] d98.3	[1] 53.6	[1] d66.0	11.6	[1] d5.1
Cash Flow	743.2	135.1	81.7	166.7	d35.6	28.7	3.1
Average Shs. Outstg. (000)	191,122	187,801	182,796	93,444	58,423	32,108	13,313
BALANCE SHEET (IN MILLIONS):							
Cash & Cash Equivalents	122.1	121.4	39.7	11.9	50.1	4.0	4.2
Total Current Assets	1,271.7	2,248.4	499.9	187.5	709.8	53.3	34.3
Net Property	3,860.5	3,738.4	1,776.0	1,287.2	706.8	302.4	193.6
Total Assets	14,513.6	14,963.1	3,752.6	2,448.7	2,317.5	458.7	315.0
Total Current Liabilities	1,599.8	2,629.5	454.9	232.5	682.7	90.6	43.6
Long-Term Obligations	9,907.0	9,628.7	2,161.7	1,401.9	1,148.5	186.4	153.6
Net Stockholders' Equity	1,767.7	1,639.6	930.1	596.2	275.6	136.3	84.8
Net Working Capital	d328.0	d381.1	45.0	d45.1	27.1	d37.3	d9.3
Year-end Shs. Outstg. (000)	196,109	184,495	184,495	103,564	75,479	40,093	14,090
STATISTICAL RECORD:							
Operating Profit Margin %	21.2	5.6	1.9	20.8	...	17.9	4.6
Net Profit Margin %	2.4	...	...	6.1	...	6.8	...
Return on Equity %	7.8	...	...	9.0	...	8.5	...
Return on Assets %	0.9	...	...	2.2	...	2.5	...
Debt/Total Assets %	68.3	64.3	57.6	57.3	49.6	40.6	48.8
Price Range	14.75-5.31	24.06-6.50	31.63-16.13	24.38-7.25	10.38-6.44	10.00-3.75	6.00-3.25
P/E Ratio	41.0-14.8	...	...	42.8-12.7	...	58.8-22.0	...

Statistics are as originally reported. [1] Bef. extraord. chrg. 12/31/00: $13.3 mill.; 12/31/98: $124.8 mill.; 12/31/97: $53.2 mill.; 12/31/96: $13.4 mill.; 12/31/94: $3.1 mill. [2] Incl. acq.-rel. and unusual chgs. of $247.9 million and asset impairment chg. of $69.7 million. [3] Excl. extraord. loss of $3.2 mill. and acctg. charge of $64.3 mill.; incl. acq. related costs and unusual costs of $588.9 mill. [4] Incl. the Browning-Ferris Industries, Inc. acquisition. [5] Incl. acq.-rel. and unusual chgs. of $127.3 mill. & excl. extraord. loss of $13.3 mill.

OFFICERS:
T. H. Van Weelden, Chmn., C.E.O.
L. Henk, Pres., C.O.O.
T. W. Ryan, Exec. V.P., C.F.O.

INVESTOR CONTACT: Investor Relations, (480) 627-2700

PRINCIPAL OFFICE: 15880 North Greenway-Hayden Loop, Suite 100, Scottsdale, AZ 85260

TELEPHONE NUMBER: (480) 627-2700
FAX: (480) 423-9424
WEB: www.awin.com

NO. OF EMPLOYEES: 28,000 (approx.)

SHAREHOLDERS: 772 (approx. record)

ANNUAL MEETING: In May

INCORPORATED: TX, June, 1987; reincorp., DE, July, 1989

INSTITUTIONAL HOLDINGS:
No. of Institutions: 193
Shares Held: 117,286,094
% Held: 59.5

INDUSTRY: Refuse systems (SIC: 4953)

TRANSFER AGENT(S): American Stock Transfer & Trust, New York, NY

NYSE SYMBOL AFC
Rec. Pr. 50.50 (4/30/01)

ALLMERICA FINANCIAL CORP.

YIELD 0.5%
P/E RATIO ...

*7 YEAR PRICE SCORE N/A *12 MONTH PRICE SCORE 91.4

*NYSE COMPOSITE INDEX=100

INTERIM EARNINGS (Per Share):

Qtr.	Mar.	June	Sept.	Dec.
1996	0.94	0.85	0.93	0.91
1997	0.32	0.75	1.04	1.58
1998	1.11	1.00	0.13	1.10
1999	2.67	1.21	1.08	1.25
2000	0.56	0.88	1.16	1.11

INTERIM DIVIDENDS (Per Share):

Amt.	Decl.	Ex.	Rec.	Pay.
0.25A	7/27/99	10/28/99	11/01/99	11/15/99
0.25A	7/25/00	10/30/00	11/01/00	11/15/00

Indicated div.: $0.25

CAPITALIZATION (12/31/00):

	($000)	(%)
Long-Term Debt	199,500	6.9
Redeemable Pfd. Stock	300,000	10.3
Common & Surplus	2,409,100	82.8
Total	2,908,600	100.0

RECENT DEVELOPMENTS: For the year ended 12/31/00, net income was $199.9 million versus income from continued operations of $345.1 million in 1999. Earnings for 1999 excluded losses totaling $49.3 million related to discontinued operations and the disposal of the Company's group life and health insurance business. Results for 2000 included net realized investment losses of $87.8 million and restructuring costs of $13.5 million. Results for 1999 included net realized investment gains of $63.0 million. Total revenues declined 1.8% to $3.09 billion.

PROSPECTS: During the year, the Company's Asset Accumulation business produced higher profits, achieved increased variable annuity sales over the prior year and introduced several new products. These new products should create growth opportunities for the Company in the future. In the Risk Management business, the Company should continue to benefit from solid premium growth, and is making significant progress toward a more competitive expense structure.

BUSINESS

ALLMERICA FINANCIAL CORP., is a non-insurance holding company for a diversified group of insurance and financial services companies including First Allmerica Financial Life Insurance Company, Allmerica Financial Life Insurance and Annuity Company, Allmerica Asset Management, Inc., Allmerica Property & Casualty Companies, Inc., The Hanover Insurance Company, Citizens Insurance Corporation and Citizens Company of America. The Company offers financial products and services in the areas of risk management and asset accumulation through three operating segments; Risk Management, Allmerica Financial Services and Allmerica Asset Management. The Company's Risk Management segment consists primarily of its property and casualty operations. The Company's Allmerica Financial Services segment provides investment-oriented life insurance and annuities to upper income individuals and small businesses. The Allmerica Asset Management segment offers stable value products such as guaranteed investment contracts to ERISA-qualified retirement plans as well as other non-ERISA institutional buyers.

ANNUAL FINANCIAL DATA

	12/31/00	12/31/99	12/31/98	12/31/97	12/31/96	12/31/95	12/31/94
Earnings Per Share	**[7] 3.70**	**[6] 6.21**	**[5] 3.33**	**[4] 3.52**	**[3] 3.63**	**[2] 2.61**	...
Cash Flow Per Share	**4.12**	**6.83**	**3.70**	**4.09**	**4.52**	**4.12**	...
Tang. Book Val. Per Share	**45.71**	**41.33**	**41.96**	**39.69**	**34.43**	**31.42**	...
Dividends Per Share	**0.25**	**0.25**	**0.20**	**0.20**	**0.20**	...	...
Dividend Payout %	**6.8**	**4.0**	**6.0**	**5.7**	**5.5**	...	...
INCOME STATEMENT (IN MILLIONS):							
Total Revenues	3,087.9	3,145.2	3,432.5	3,006.4	3,274.7	3,218.2	2,788.5
Costs & Expenses	2,846.5	2,643.0	3,131.0	2,634.8	2,898.3	2,879.4	2,779.0
Depreciation & Amort.	22.8	34.2	21.9	31.6	44.7	57.7	...
Operating Income	218.6	468.0	279.6	340.0	331.7	281.1	9.5
Income Before Income Taxes	218.6	468.0	279.6	340.0	331.7	301.8	9.5
Income Taxes	2.7	106.9	49.1	84.7	75.2	82.7	...
Equity Earnings/Minority Int.	d16.0	d16.0	d29.3	d62.7	d74.6	d73.1	31.1
Net Income	[7] 199.9	[6] 345.1	[5] 201.2	[4] 192.6	[3] 181.9	[2] 146.0	[1] 40.6
Cash Flow	222.7	379.3	223.1	224.2	226.6	203.7	40.6
Average Shs. Outstg. (000)	54,000	55,500	60,300	54,800	50,100	49,400	...
BALANCE SHEET (IN MILLIONS):							
Cash & Cash Equivalents	279.2	442.2	550.3	215.1	178.5	289.5	146.6
Total Current Assets	2,422.0	2,447.3	2,216.6	1,809.8	1,680.3	1,896.8	371.4
Total Assets	31,588.0	30,769.6	27,607.9	22,549.0	18,997.7	17,757.7	10,502.8
Total Current Liabilities	1,568.2	964.1	987.6	754.3	726.8	724.0	179.1
Long-Term Obligations	199.5	199.5	199.5	202.1	202.2	202.3	...
Net Stockholders' Equity	2,409.1	2,240.2	2,458.6	2,381.3	1,724.7	1,574.2	610.4
Net Working Capital	853.8	1,483.2	1,229.0	1,055.5	953.5	1,172.8	192.3
Year-end Shs. Outstg. (000)	52,700	54,200	58,600	60,000	50,100	50,100	...
STATISTICAL RECORD:							
Operating Profit Margin %	7.1	14.9	8.1	11.3	10.1	8.7	0.3
Net Profit Margin %	6.5	11.0	5.9	6.4	5.6	4.5	1.5
Return on Equity %	8.3	15.4	8.2	8.1	10.5	9.3	6.7
Return on Assets %	0.6	1.1	0.7	0.9	1.0	0.8	0.4
Debt/Total Assets %	0.6	0.6	0.7	0.9	1.1	1.1	...
Price Range	74.25-35.06	64.81-46.06	75.25-38.38	50.50-32.63	34.38-24.75	28.63-23.88	...
P/E Ratio	20.1-9.5	10.4-7.4	22.6-11.5	14.3-9.3	9.5-6.8	11.0-9.1	...
Average Yield %	0.5	0.5	0.4	0.5	0.7	...	...

Statistics are as originally reported. [1] Incl. equity in net inc. of unconsol. affil. of $38.0 mill. [2] Incl. equity in net inc. of unconsol. affil. of $93.2 mill. [3] Incl. net realized invest. loss $900,000. [4] Incl. net realized invest. loss $200,000. [5] Incl. net realized invest. gain $1.7 mill. [6] Incl. net realized invest. loss $400,000. [7] Incl. net realized invest. losses of $87.8 mill. & restruct. costs of $13.5 mill.

OFFICERS:
J. F. O'Brien, Chmn., Pres., C.E.O.
E. J. Parry III, V.P., C.F.O., Treas.
J. K. Huber, V.P., Gen. Couns.

INVESTOR CONTACT: Henry P. St. Cyr, V.P., Inv. Rel., (508) 855-2959

PRINCIPAL OFFICE: 440 Lincoln Street, Worcester, MA 01653

TELEPHONE NUMBER: (508) 855-1000
FAX: (508) 853-6332
WEB: www.allmerica.com

NO. OF EMPLOYEES: 5,700 (approx.)

SHAREHOLDERS: 42,167

ANNUAL MEETING: In May

INCORPORATED: DE, 1995

INSTITUTIONAL HOLDINGS:
No. of Institutions: 230
Shares Held: 32,582,284
% Held: 61.3

INDUSTRY: Fire, marine, and casualty insurance (SIC: 6331)

TRANSFER AGENT(S): First Chicago Trust Company of New York, Jersey City, NJ

NYSE SYMBOL ALL
Rec. Pr. 45.02 (5/31/01)

ALLSTATE CORPORATION (THE)

YIELD 1.7%
P/E RATIO 15.3

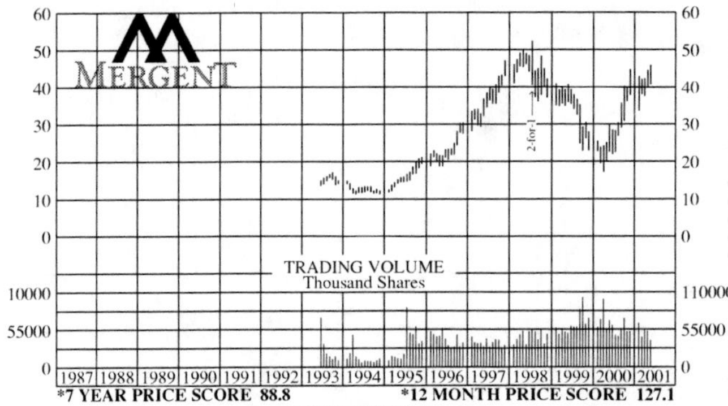

TRADING VOLUME
Thousand Shares

*7 YEAR PRICE SCORE 88.8 *12 MONTH PRICE SCORE 127.1
*NYSE COMPOSITE INDEX=100

INTERIM EARNINGS (Per Share):

Qtr.	Mar.	June	Sept	Dec.
1996	0.47	0.86	0.33	0.67
1997	0.87	0.74	0.95	1.01
1998	1.10	1.05	0.86	0.93
1999	1.27	0.95	0.62	0.54
2000	0.73	0.61	0.87	0.74

INTERIM DIVIDENDS (Per Share):

Amt.	Decl.	Ex.	Rec.	Pay.
0.17Q	5/18/00	5/26/00	5/31/00	7/03/00
0.17Q	7/13/00	8/29/00	8/31/00	10/02/00
0.17Q	11/09/00	11/28/00	11/30/00	1/02/01
0.19Q	2/15/01	2/26/01	2/28/01	4/02/01
0.19Q	5/15/01	5/29/01	5/31/01	7/02/01

Indicated div.: $0.76 (Div. Reinv. Plan)

CAPITALIZATION (12/31/00):

	($000)	(%)
Long-Term Debt	3,112,000	14.4
Deferred Income Tax	348,000	1.6
Redeemable Pfd. Stock	750,000	3.5
Common & Surplus	17,451,000	80.6
Total	21,661,000	100.0

RECENT DEVELOPMENTS: For the year ended 12/31/00, net income decreased 18.7% to $2.21 billion compared with $2.72 billion in 1999. Results included after-tax net realized capital gains of $248.0 million and $691.0 million in 2000 and 1999, respectively. Also, results for 2000 included restructuring charges of $38.0 million, while the prior year included restructuring charges of $53.0 million and acquisition charges of $63.0 million. Total revenues climbed 8.1% to $29.13 billion versus $26.96 billion in the previous year.

PROSPECTS: During the year, the Company continued to see positive results from its strategic initiatives to improve the profitability of its Property-Liability business. Going forward, ALL will continue to launch its multi-access strategy, which allows customers to reach the Company how, when and where they want to be served. On 5/8/01, ALL acquired Sterling Collision Centers Inc., which operates a network of 39 collision repair stores in seven states, for an undisclosed amount.

BUSINESS

THE ALLSTATE CORPORATION is a holding company for Allstate Insurance Company. Its business is conducted principally through Allstate Insurance Company, Allstate Life Insurance Company and their subsidiaries. The Company is engaged, principally in the United States and Canada, in the personal property and casualty insurance business and the life insurance and savings business. ALL operates in four business segments: personal property and casualty, life and savings, discontinued lines and coverages, and corporate and other business. On 6/30/95, Sears, Roebuck and Company distributed its 80.3% ownership in ALL's common stock to Sears shareholders. In 1999, the Company acquired American Heritage Life Investment Corp. and the personal lines business of CNA Financial Corp.

ANNUAL FINANCIAL DATA

	12/31/00	12/31/99	12/31/98	12/31/97	12/31/96	12/31/95	12/31/94
Earnings Per Share	**3 2.95**	**2 3.38**	**3.94**	**3.56**	**2.32**	**2.12**	**0.54**
Tang. Book Val. Per Share	**22.26**	**19.51**	**21.08**	**18.36**	**15.22**	**14.15**	**9.38**
Dividends Per Share	**0.66**	**0.58**	**0.53**	**0.36**	**0.42**	**0.39**	**0.36**
Dividend Payout %	**22.4**	**17.3**	**13.3**	**10.1**	**18.4**	**18.4**	**66.7**
INCOME STATEMENT (IN MILLIONS):							
Total Premium Income	24,076.0	21,735.0	20,826.0	20,106.0	19,702.0	18,908.0	17,861.0
Net Investment Income	4,633.0	4,112.0	3,890.0	3,861.0	3,813.0	3,627.0	3,401.0
Other Income	425.0	1,112.0	1,163.0	982.0	784.0	258.0	202.0
Total Revenues	29,134.0	26,959.0	25,879.0	24,949.0	24,299.0	22,793.0	21,464.0
Income Before Income Taxes	3,047.0	3,907.0	4,745.0	4,434.0	2,669.0	2,421.0	227.0
Income Taxes	795.0	1,148.0	1,422.0	1,324.0	619.0	573.0	cr256.0
Equity Earnings/Minority Int.	d41.0	d39.0	d29.0	d5.0	25.0	56.0	...
Net Income	3 2,211.0	2 2,720.0	3,294.0	3,105.0	2,075.0	1,904.0	483.0
Average Shs. Outstg. (000)	748,700	803,800	836,600	874,000	896,400	898,000	900,000
BALANCE SHEET (IN MILLIONS):							
Cash & Cash Equivalents	60,980.0	55,540.0	53,818.0	51,080.0	47,211.0	45,362.0	30,101.0
Premiums Due	6,154.0	6,347.0	5,014.0	5,007.0	5,070.0	4,993.0	5,912.0
Invst. Assets: Fixed-term	...	...	...	...	...	...	8,008.0
Invst. Assets: Equities	6,086.0	6,738.0	6,421.0	6,765.0	5,561.0	6,150.0	4,852.0
Invst. Assets: Loans	4,599.0	4,068.0	3,458.0	3,002.0	3,146.0	3,280.0	3,234.0
Invst. Assets: Total	74,483.0	69,645.0	66,525.0	62,548.0	58,329.0	56,505.0	48,179.0
Total Assets	104,808.0	98,119.0	87,691.0	80,918.0	74,508.0	70,029.0	61,371.0
Long-Term Obligations	3,112.0	2,186.0	1,353.0	1,497.0	1,386.0	1,228.0	869.0
Net Stockholders' Equity	17,451.0	16,601.0	17,240.0	15,610.0	13,452.0	12,680.0	8,427.0
Year-end Shs. Outstg. (000)	728,000	787,000	818,000	850,000	884,000	896,000	898,000
STATISTICAL RECORD:							
Return on Revenues %	7.6	10.1	12.7	12.4	8.5	8.4	2.3
Return on Equity %	12.7	16.4	19.1	19.9	15.4	15.0	5.7
Return on Assets %	2.1	2.8	3.8	3.8	2.8	2.7	0.8
Price Range	44.75-17.19	41.00-22.88	52.38-36.06	47.19-28.13	30.44-18.69	21.19-11.75	14.94-11.31
P/E Ratio	15.2-5.8	12.1-6.8	13.3-9.2	13.3-7.9	13.1-8.1	10.0-5.5	27.7-20.9
Average Yield %	2.1	1.8	1.2	1.0	1.7	2.4	2.7

Statistics are as originally reported. Adj. for stk. split: 2-for-1, 7/98 1 Bef. acctg. change chrg. $326.0 mill. 2 Incl. non-recurr. chrg. $116.0 mill. 3 Incl. restruc. chrg. $38.0 mill.

OFFICERS:
E. M. Liddy, Chmn., Pres., C.E.O.
J. L. Carl, V.P., C.F.O.
R. W. Pike, V.P., Sec.

INVESTOR CONTACT: Investor Relations, (800) 416-8803

PRINCIPAL OFFICE: 2775 Sanders Road, Northbrook, IL 60062

TELEPHONE NUMBER: (847) 402-5000
FAX: (847) 402-0169
WEB: www.allstate.com

NO. OF EMPLOYEES: 52,000 (approx.)

SHAREHOLDERS: 172,064

ANNUAL MEETING: In May

INCORPORATED: DE, Nov., 1992

INSTITUTIONAL HOLDINGS:
No. of Institutions: 586
Shares Held: 444,403,486
% Held: 61.3

INDUSTRY: Fire, marine, and casualty insurance (SIC: 6331)

TRANSFER AGENT(S): First Chicago Trust Company of New York, Jersey City, NJ

NYSE SYMBOL AT
Rec. Pr. 54.61 (4/30/01)

ALLTEL CORPORATION

YIELD 2.4%
P/E RATIO 8.8

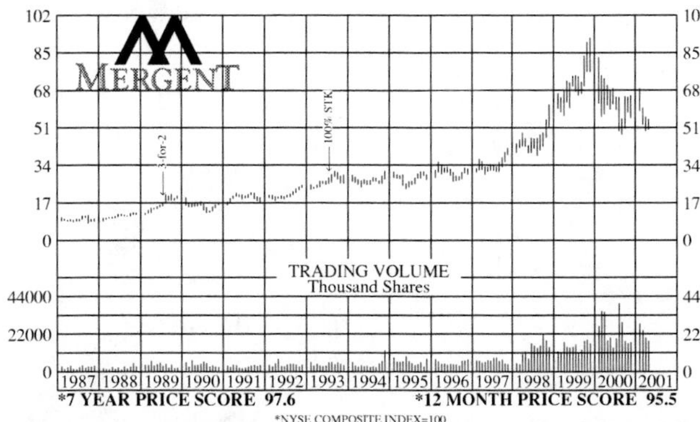

*7 YEAR PRICE SCORE 97.6 *12 MONTH PRICE SCORE 95.5

*NYSE COMPOSITE INDEX=100

INTERIM EARNINGS (Per Share):

Qtr.	Mar.	June	Sept.	Dec.
1997	0.54	0.92	0.65	0.59
1998	0.66	1.06	0.57	0.55
1999	0.59	0.67	0.47	0.73
2000	0.68	3.15	1.53	0.83

INTERIM DIVIDENDS (Per Share):

Amt.	Decl.	Ex.	Rec.	Pay.
0.32Q	4/20/00	6/07/00	6/09/00	7/03/00
0.32Q	7/20/00	9/07/00	9/11/00	10/03/00
0.33Q	10/26/00	12/06/00	12/08/00	1/03/01
0.33Q	1/25/01	2/22/01	2/26/01	4/03/01
0.33Q	4/26/01	6/06/01	6/08/01	7/03/01

Indicated div.: $1.32 (Div. Reinv. Plan)

CAPITALIZATION (12/31/00):

	($000)	(%)
Long-Term Debt	4,611,700	46.5
Deferred Income Tax	217,000	2.2
Preferred Stock	500	0.0
Common & Surplus	5,094,900	51.3
Total	9,924,100	100.0

RECENT DEVELOPMENTS: For the year ended 12/31/00, net income was $1.97 billion, before an accounting charge of $36.6 million, versus net income of $783.6 million in 1999. Results for 2000 and 1999 included gains from disposal of assets and other non-recurring items totaling $1.93 billion and $43.1 million. Also, results for 2000 and 1999 included non-recurring charges of $25.4 million and $90.5 million, respectively. Revenues rose 9.4% to $7.07 billion.

PROSPECTS: Prospects are mixed. AT should benefit from its October 2000 purchase of wireless properties in South Louisiana, including New Orleans and Baton Rouge. However, net wireless customer additions generated internally, or excluding customers that were acquired, fell 11.4% to 142,475 for the quarter ended 12/31/00 versus 160,767 net customer additions a year earlier. Also, the average revenue per customer per month slipped 4.4% to $47.55.

BUSINESS

ALLTEL CORPORATION, with more than 10.0 million communication customers in 24 states, as of 12/31/00, provides information services to telecommunications, financial and mortgage clients in 55 countries and territories. AT owns subsidiaries that provide wireless and wireline local, long-distance, network access and Internet services, wide-area paging service and information processing management services and advanced application software. ALLTEL Communications Products, Inc. operates nine warehouses and 23 counter-sales showrooms across the U.S. and is a major distributor of telecommunications equipment and materials. ALLTEL Communications Products supplies equipment to affiliated and non-affiliated communications companies, business systems suppliers, railroads, governments, and retail and industrial companies. On 7/2/99, the Company acquired Aliant Communications Inc. for $1.80 billion.

BUSINESS LINE ANALYSIS

(12/31/2000)	REV (%)	INC (%)
Wireless	45.1	43.3
Wireline	23.6	45.7
Emerging business	5.4	(4.0)
Information services	17.3	13.6
Other operations	8.6	1.4
Total	100.0	100.0

ANNUAL FINANCIAL DATA

	12/31/00	12/31/99	12/31/98	12/31/97	12/31/96	12/31/95	12/31/94
Earnings Per Share	**[5] 6.20**	**[4] 2.47**	**[1] 1.89**	**[2] 2.70**	**[2] 1.53**	**1.86**	**[3] 1.43**
Cash Flow Per Share	**9.31**	**5.19**	**4.44**	**5.10**	**3.75**	**4.02**	**3.34**
Tang. Book Val. Per Share	**5.92**	**7.03**	**5.82**	**8.67**	**8.88**	**7.64**	**5.96**
Dividends Per Share	**1.28**	**1.22**	**1.16**	**1.10**	**1.04**	**0.96**	**0.88**
Dividend Payout %	**20.6**	**49.4**	**61.4**	**40.7**	**68.0**	**51.6**	**61.5**
INCOME STATEMENT (IN MILLIONS):							
Total Revenues	7,067.0	6,302.3	5,194.0	3,263.6	3,192.4	3,109.7	2,961.7
Costs & Expenses	4,411.1	3,915.0	3,597.9	2,065.8	2,176.7	2,015.9	1,965.9
Depreciation & Amort.	988.4	862.2	707.1	450.8	424.1	409.8	362.0
Operating Income	1,667.5	1,525.1	889.0	[2] 747.0	[2] 591.6	684.0	633.9
Net Interest Inc./(Exp.)	d310.8	d280.2	d263.7	d130.2	d130.8	d138.2	d137.1
Income Before Income Taxes	3,350.7	1,330.9	972.3	828.7	461.4	571.8	436.5
Income Taxes	1,385.3	547.2	446.9	320.8	169.7	217.2	164.8
Equity Earnings/Minority Int.	23.3	d11.6	12.7	...	...	d8.7	...
Net Income	[5] 1,965.4	[4] 783.6	[1] 525.5	[2] 507.9	[2] 291.7	354.6	[3] 271.8
Cash Flow	2,953.7	1,644.9	1,231.7	957.6	714.8	763.3	632.5
Average Shs. Outstg. (000)	317,200	316,814	277,276	187,689	190,370	190,072	189,454
BALANCE SHEET (IN MILLIONS):							
Cash & Cash Equivalents	67.2	17.6	55.5	16.2	13.9	21.4	26.1
Total Current Assets	1,780.7	1,167.2	980.8	665.8	709.5	731.2	692.7
Net Property	6,549.0	5,734.5	4,828.1	3,190.5	3,041.5	2,972.8	2,963.2
Total Assets	12,182.0	10,774.2	9,374.2	5,633.4	5,359.2	5,073.1	4,713.9
Total Current Liabilities	1,515.9	1,194.0	1,206.5	637.3	590.7	569.3	605.6
Long-Term Obligations	4,611.7	3,750.4	3,491.8	1,874.2	1,756.1	1,761.6	1,846.2
Net Stockholders' Equity	5,095.4	4,205.7	3,270.9	2,208.5	2,097.1	1,935.6	1,625.4
Net Working Capital	264.8	d26.8	d225.7	28.6	118.8	162.0	87.1
Year-end Shs. Outstg. (000)	312,984	314,258	281,198	183,673	187,200	189,268	187,981
STATISTICAL RECORD:							
Operating Profit Margin %	23.6	24.2	17.1	22.9	18.5	22.0	21.4
Net Profit Margin %	27.8	12.4	10.1	15.6	9.1	11.4	9.2
Return on Equity %	38.6	18.6	16.1	23.0	13.9	18.3	16.7
Return on Assets %	16.1	7.3	5.6	9.0	5.4	7.0	5.8
Debt/Total Assets %	37.9	34.8	37.2	33.3	32.8	34.7	39.2
Price Range	82.94-47.75	91.81-56.31	61.38-38.25	41.63-29.75	35.63-26.63	31.13-23.25	31.38-24.00
P/E Ratio	13.4-7.7	37.2-22.8	32.5-20.2	15.4-11.0	23.3-17.4	16.7-12.5	21.9-16.8
Average Yield %	2.0	1.6	2.3	3.1	3.3	3.5	3.2

Statistics are as originally reported. [1] Incl. one-time pre-tax net chrg. of $10.8 mill. [2] Incl. non-recurr. credit 12/31/97: $189.7 mill.; chrg. 12/31/96: $74.2 mill. [3] Bef. write-dwn. of $32.0 mill on assets. [4] Incl. one-time chrgs. of $90.5 mill. [5] Incl. one-time chrgs. of $25.4 mill. & pre-tax gain of $1.93 bill. on disposal of assets and oth. non-recurr. items; bef. acctg. chge. chrg. of $36.6 mill. ($0.12/sh.)

OFFICERS:
J. T. Ford, Chmn., C.E.O.
D. E. Foster, Vice-Chmn.
S. T. Ford, Pres., C.O.O.

INVESTOR CONTACT: Kerry Brooks, V.P., Inv. Rel., (501) 905-8991

PRINCIPAL OFFICE: One Allied Drive, Little Rock, AR 72202

TELEPHONE NUMBER: (501) 905-8000
FAX: (501) 905-0962
WEB: www.alltel.com

NO. OF EMPLOYEES: 27,257 (avg.)

SHAREHOLDERS: 255,000 (approx.)

ANNUAL MEETING: In April

INCORPORATED: OH, June, 1960; reincorp., DE, 1990

INSTITUTIONAL HOLDINGS:
No. of Institutions: 527
Shares Held: 165,795,878
% Held: 53.0

INDUSTRY: Telephone communications, exc. radio (SIC: 4813)

TRANSFER AGENT(S): First Union National Bank of North Carolina, Charlotte, NC

NYSE SYMBOL ALO
Rec. Pr. 25.65 (5/31/01)

ALPHARMA INC.

YIELD 0.7%
P/E RATIO 16.5

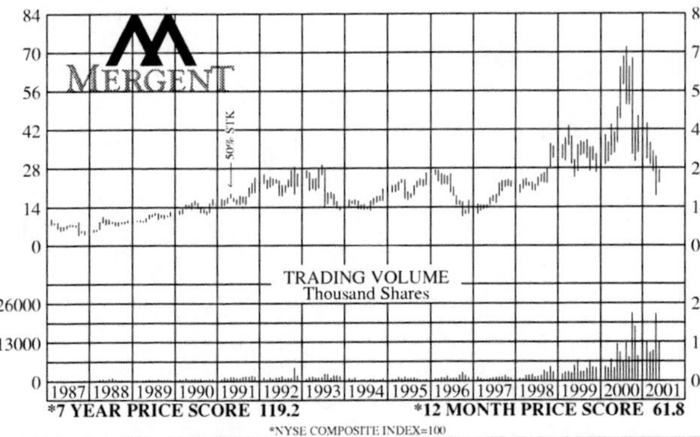

*7 YEAR PRICE SCORE 119.2 *12 MONTH PRICE SCORE 61.8

*NYSE COMPOSITE INDEX=100

INTERIM EARNINGS (Per Share):

Qtr.	Mar.	June	Sept.	Dec.
1997	0.10	0.16	0.22	0.26
1998	0.21	0.09	0.28	0.32
1999	0.27	0.28	0.38	0.41
2000	0.35	0.24	0.48	0.48

INTERIM DIVIDENDS (Per Share):

Amt.	Decl.	Ex.	Rec.	Pay.
0.045Q	5/26/00	7/12/00	7/14/00	7/28/00
0.045Q	10/02/00	10/11/00	10/13/00	10/27/00
0.045Q	12/14/00	1/10/01	1/12/01	1/26/01
0.045Q	3/29/01	4/10/01	4/12/01	4/27/01
0.045Q	5/30/01	7/11/01	7/13/01	7/27/01

Indicated div.: $0.18

CAPITALIZATION (12/31/00):

	($000)	(%)
Long-Term Debt	504,445	36.1
Deferred Income Tax	29,404	2.1
Common & Surplus	861,932	61.8
Total	1,395,781	100.0

RECENT DEVELOPMENTS: For the twelve months ended 12/31/00, net income soared 65.4% to $61.1 million compared with $37.0 million in the previous year. Results for 2000 included after-tax one-time charges of $4.0 million related to the acquisition and interim financing of Roche MFA business. Total revenues increased 25.5% to $919.5 million from $732.4 million in the prior year.

PROSPECTS: Looking ahead, the Company expects both of its business segments to contribute to its growth in 2001. ALO confirmed it goal of earnings per share growth for 2001 to be about 25.0%. Separately, ALO's focus is still to expand into U.S. solid dose capabilities and to increase critical mass in some areas of its international pharmaceutical business.

BUSINESS

ALPHARMA INC. (formerly A. L. Pharma Inc.) is a multinational pharmaceutical company that develops, manufactures and markets specialty generic and proprietary human pharmaceuticals and animal health products. The Human Pharmaceuticals segment is comprised of the U.S. Pharmaceuticals, International Pharmaceuticals, and Fine Chemicals Divisions. The Animal Health segment is comprised of the Animal Health and Aquatic Animal Health Divisions. The Human Pharmaceuticals segment accounted for 65.4% of 2000 revenues and the Animal Health segment, 34.6%. The Company conducts business worldwide and has a significant presence in North America, Europe and the Far East. The U.S. generated 43.0% of 2000 Pharmaceutical revenues and international markets accounted for 57.0%.

BUSINESS LINE ANALYSIS

(12/31/2000)	REV (%)	INC (%)
IPD	33.4	27.4
USPD	25.2	17.4
FCD	6.8	16.8
AHD	33.1	40.5
AAHD	1.5	(2.1)
Total	100.0	100.0

ANNUAL FINANCIAL DATA

	12/31/00	12/31/99	12/31/98	12/31/97	12/31/96	12/31/95	12/31/94
Earnings Per Share	**[5] 1.60**	**1.34**	**[4] 0.92**	**0.76**	**[3] d0.53**	**[2] 0.86**	**[1] d0.08**
Cash Flow Per Share	**2.65**	**2.58**	**2.37**	**2.12**	**0.92**	**2.29**	**1.16**
Tang. Book Val. Per Share	**6.15**	...	...	**3.50**	**3.04**	**3.55**	**2.43**
Dividends Per Share	**0.18**	**0.18**	**0.18**	**0.18**	**0.18**	**0.18**	**0.18**
Dividend Payout %	**11.2**	**13.4**	**19.6**	**23.7**	...	**20.9**	...
INCOME STATEMENT (IN THOUSANDS):							
Total Revenues	919,523	742,176	604,584	500,288	486,184	520,882	469,263
Costs & Expenses	721,153	592,247	501,468	422,482	450,761	437,379	426,512
Depreciation & Amort.	64,836	50,418	38,120	30,908	31,503	31,022	26,773
Operating Income	133,534	99,511	64,996	46,898	3,920	52,481	15,978
Net Interest Inc./(Exp.)	d45,183	d39,174	d25,613	d18,581	d19,976	d21,282	d13,923
Income Before Income Taxes	84,921	61,787	38,983	27,750	d16,226	30,228	1,736
Income Taxes	23,778	22,236	14,772	10,342	cr4,765	11,411	3,439
Net Income	[5] 61,143	39,551	[4] 24,211	17,408	[3] d11,461	[2] 18,817	[1] d1,703
Cash Flow	125,979	89,969	62,331	48,316	20,042	49,839	25,070
Average Shs. Outstg.	47,479	34,848	26,279	22,780	21,715	21,754	21,666
BALANCE SHEET (IN THOUSANDS):							
Cash & Cash Equivalents	72,931	17,655	14,414	10,997	15,944	18,351	15,512
Total Current Assets	614,463	386,123	335,484	273,677	274,859	282,886	250,499
Net Property	345,042	244,413	244,132	199,560	209,803	212,176	202,903
Total Assets	1,624,480	1,164,517	908,936	631,866	613,407	634,853	592,318
Total Current Liabilities	206,438	165,856	170,437	133,926	155,651	169,284	154,650
Long-Term Obligations	504,445	591,784	429,034	223,975	233,781	219,451	220,036
Net Stockholders' Equity	861,932	354,604	267,279	238,473	186,042	205,190	181,288
Net Working Capital	408,025	220,267	165,047	139,751	119,208	113,602	95,849
Year-end Shs. Outstg.	40,214	29,613	27,255	25,343	21,765	21,663	21,596
STATISTICAL RECORD:							
Operating Profit Margin %	14.5	13.4	10.8	9.4	0.8	10.1	3.4
Net Profit Margin %	6.6	5.3	4.0	3.5	...	3.6	...
Return on Equity %	7.1	11.2	9.1	7.3	...	9.2	...
Return on Assets %	3.8	3.4	2.7	2.8	...	3.0	...
Debt/Total Assets %	31.1	50.8	47.2	35.4	38.1	34.6	37.1
Price Range	71.94-29.19	43.38-24.56	36.94-18.94	23.88-11.38	27.38-10.63	26.38-16.50	20.63-12.63
P/E Ratio	45.0-18.2	32.4-18.3	40.1-20.6	31.4-15.0	...	30.7-19.2	...
Average Yield %	0.4	0.5	0.6	1.0	0.9	0.8	1.1

Statistics are as originally reported. [1] Bef. extraord. chrg. $683,000 ($0.03 a sh.) & incl. chrgs. $17.0 mill. ($0.79 a sh.). [2] Incl. a pre-tax gain of $2.8 mill. [3] Incl. after-tax chrgs. $7.5 mill. rel. to the prod. of rationalization plans. [4] Incl. an after-tax chg. $3.1 mill. rel. to the acq. of Cox Pharmaceuticals. [5] Incl. an after-tax chg. $4.0 mill. rel. to the acq. of Roche MFA bus.

OFFICERS:
E. W. Sissener, Chmn.
I. Wilk, Pres., C.E.O.
J. Smith, V.P., C.F.O.

INVESTOR CONTACT: David R Jackson, Inv. Rel., (201) 947-7774

PRINCIPAL OFFICE: One Executive Drive, P.O. Box 1399, Ft. Lee, NJ 07024

TELEPHONE NUMBER: (201) 947-7774
FAX: (201) 947-4879
WEB: www.alpharma.com

NO. OF EMPLOYEES: 3,500 (approx.)

SHAREHOLDERS: 2,142 (class A); 1 (class B)

ANNUAL MEETING: In May

INCORPORATED: DE, Sept., 1983

INSTITUTIONAL HOLDINGS:
No. of Institutions: 184
Shares Held: 33,727,447
% Held: 83.9

INDUSTRY: Pharmaceutical preparations (SIC: 2834)

TRANSFER AGENT(S): BankBoston, N.A. c/o EquiServe Limited Partnership, Boston, MA

NYSE SYMBOL AZA
Rec. Pr. 47.15 (5/31/01)

ALZA CORPORATION

YIELD . . .
P/E RATIO 47.6

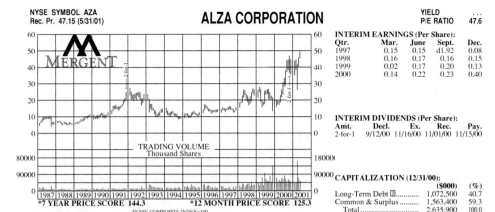

MERGENT

TRADING VOLUME
Thousand Shares

1987 1988 1989 1990 1991 1992 1993 1994 1995 1996 1997 1998 1999 2000 2001

*7 YEAR PRICE SCORE 144.3 *12 MONTH PRICE SCORE 125.3

*NYSE COMPOSITE INDEX=100

INTERIM EARNINGS (Per Share):

Qtr.	Mar.	June	Sept.	Dec.
1997	0.15	0.15	d1.92	0.08
1998	0.16	0.17	0.16	0.15
1999	0.02	0.17	0.20	0.13
2000	0.14	0.22	0.23	0.40

INTERIM DIVIDENDS (Per Share):

Amt.	Decl.	Ex.	Rec.	Pay.
2-for-1	9/12/00	11/16/00	11/01/00	11/15/00

CAPITALIZATION (12/31/00):

	($000)	(%)
Long-Term Debt [2]	1,072,500	40.7
Common & Surplus	1,563,400	59.3
Total	2,635,900	100.0

RECENT DEVELOPMENTS: For the year ended 12/31/00, AZA reported income of $230.7 million, before an accounting charge of $7.4 million, compared with net income of $91.0 million in the previous year. Earnings for 2000 included a pre-tax charge of $12.4 million for acquisitions of in-process research and development. Total revenues increased 25.5% to $988.5 million from $795.9 million the year before.

PROSPECTS: On 2/5/01, the Company acquired certain marketing rights to the Flexeril® product and trademark from Merck and Co., Inc. Separately, AZA has received approval in Canada to market CAELYX® for the treatment of advanced ovarian cancer. Going forward, AZA will concentrate on new product approvals, product development partnerships, and the expansion of its commercial pharmaceutical organization.

BUSINESS

ALZA CORPORATION is a research-based pharmaceutical company specializing in drug delivery technologies. The Company applies its delivery technologies to develop pharmaceutical products with enhanced therapeutic value for its own portfolio and for many of the world's leading pharmaceutical companies. The Company's sales and marketing efforts are currently focused in urology, oncology and central nervous system products. The Company's two primary drug delivery systems are transdermal (through the skin) and oral. Transdermal products include NICODERM, a smoking cessation product, and TESTODERM, a treatment for testosterone-deficient men. Oral products include PROCARDIA XL, a treatment for angina and hypertension, and GLUCOTROL XL, a product for Type II diabetes.

REVENUES

(12/31/2000)	($000)	(%)
Net Sales	607,200	61.4
Royalties, Fees & Other	281,200	28.5
Research & Development	100,100	10.1
Total	988,500	100.0

ANNUAL FINANCIAL DATA

	12/31/00	12/31/99	12/31/98	12/31/97	12/31/96	12/31/95	12/31/94
Earnings Per Share	**[5] 0.97**	**[4] 0.44**	**0.63**	**[3] d1.53**	**[2] 0.54**	**[1] 0.44**	**0.36**
Cash Flow Per Share	**1.14**	**0.76**	**0.80**	**d1.34**	**0.61**	**0.53**	**0.44**
Tang. Book Val. Per Share	**6.58**	**3.38**	**2.61**	**1.76**	**3.53**	**2.75**	**2.22**
INCOME STATEMENT (IN MILLIONS):							
Total Revenues	988.5	795.9	584.5	464.4	466.0	350.6	278.8
Costs & Expenses	656.3	581.0	332.3	635.1	251.9	194.6	152.4
Depreciation & Amort.	76.5	65.7	47.9	33.3	22.0	15.3	13.7
Operating Income	255.7	149.2	204.3	d204.0	192.1	140.7	112.7
Net Interest Inc./(Exp.)	d58.0	d58.1	d56.3	d55.0	d43.0	d23.9	d19.4
Income Before Income Taxes	256.7	132.7	172.8	d211.4	149.1	116.8	93.3
Income Taxes	26.0	41.7	60.5	49.7	56.7	44.4	35.2
Net Income	[5] 230.7	[4] 91.0	112.3	[3] d261.1	[2] 92.4	[1] 72.4	58.1
Cash Flow	307.2	156.7	160.2	d227.8	114.4	87.7	71.8
Average Shs. Outstg. (000)	269,900	207,000	201,000	170,200	188,400	165,218	164,572
BALANCE SHEET (IN MILLIONS):							
Cash & Cash Equivalents	1,013.4	217.4	170.7	174.2	999.8	419.0	344.9
Total Current Assets	1,275.1	432.7	389.0	358.0	1,174.8	578.1	492.4
Net Property	421.4	417.8	361.0	310.4	307.8	277.0	245.5
Total Assets	2,921.6	1,852.5	1,576.3	1,369.2	1,613.7	937.2	806.3
Total Current Liabilities	150.6	134.9	118.1	104.6	67.2	67.9	56.0
Long-Term Obligations	1,072.5	939.2	922.6	902.6	882.3	363.0	345.5
Net Stockholders' Equity	1,563.4	691.8	455.2	301.2	596.7	454.6	364.5
Net Working Capital	1,124.5	297.8	270.9	253.4	1,107.6	510.1	436.4
Year-end Shs. Outstg. (000)	237,500	204,400	174,600	171,000	169,200	165,012	164,086
STATISTICAL RECORD:							
Operating Profit Margin %	25.9	18.7	35.0	. . .	41.2	40.1	40.4
Net Profit Margin %	23.3	11.4	19.2	. . .	19.8	20.7	20.8
Return on Equity %	14.8	13.2	24.7	. . .	15.5	15.9	15.9
Return on Assets %	7.9	4.9	7.1	. . .	5.7	7.7	7.2
Debt/Total Assets %	36.7	50.7	58.5	65.9	54.7	38.7	42.9
Price Range	47.00-15.94	27.88-13.25	27.00-15.44	16.25-12.38	17.44-12.00	13.50-9.06	15.38-8.50
P/E Ratio	48.4-16.4	63.3-30.1	42.9-24.5	. . .	32.3-22.2	30.7-20.6	43.3-23.9

Statistics are as originally reported. Adj. for 2-for-1 stk split, 11/00 [1] Incl. gain from reversal of reserve $7.0 mill. & a chrg $7.0 mill. for pymt. to U.S. Bioscience. [2] Incl. after-tax non-recurr. gain $9.0 mill. [3] Incl. non-recurr. pre-tax chrgs totaling $368.7 mill. [4] Incl. total pre-tax chrgs. $61.0 mill. [5] Bef. acctg. chg. $7.4 mill., incl. in-process res. & dev. chrg. $12.4.

OFFICERS:
E. Mario, Chmn., C.E.O.
M. K. Fust, Sr. V.P., C.F.O.
B. C. Cozadd, Exec. V.P., C.O.O.

INVESTOR CONTACT: Patty Eisenhaur, (650) 233-5222

PRINCIPAL OFFICE: 1900 Charleston Road, P.O. Box 7210, Mountain View, CA 94039-7210

TELEPHONE NUMBER: (650) 564-2000
FAX: (650) 564-5121
WEB: www.alza.com

NO. OF EMPLOYEES: 2,442 (avg.)

SHAREHOLDERS: 7,062 (approx.)

ANNUAL MEETING: In June

INCORPORATED: CA, Jun., 1968; reincorp., DE, May, 1968

INSTITUTIONAL HOLDINGS:
No. of Institutions: 450
Shares Held: 192,694,911
% Held: 80.6

INDUSTRY: Pharmaceutical preparations (SIC: 2834)

TRANSFER AGENT(S): EquiServe, L.P., Canton, MA

NYSE SYMBOL AMB
Rec. Pr. 24.90 (4/30/01)

AMB PROPERTY CORP.

YIELD 6.3%
P/E RATIO 18.6

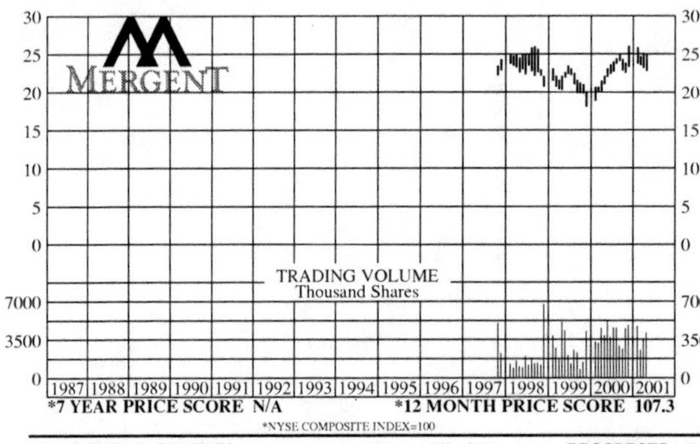

*7 YEAR PRICE SCORE N/A   *12 MONTH PRICE SCORE 107.3

*NYSE COMPOSITE INDEX=100

INTERIM EARNINGS (Per Share):

Qtr.	Mar.	June	Sept.	Dec.
1998	0.32	0.32	0.32	0.30
1999	0.30	0.50	0.60	0.58
2000	0.34	0.33	0.39	0.28

INTERIM DIVIDENDS (Per Share):

Amt.	Decl.	Ex.	Rec.	Pay.
0.37Q	5/24/00	6/30/00	7/05/00	7/17/00
0.37Q	9/11/00	10/02/00	10/04/00	10/16/00
0.37Q	12/01/00	12/08/00	12/12/00	12/22/00
0.395Q	2/27/01	4/02/01	4/04/01	4/16/01
0.395Q	5/22/01	7/02/01	7/05/01	7/16/01

Indicated div.: $1.58

CAPITALIZATION (12/31/00):

	($000)	(%)
Long-Term Debt	1,836,276	42.9
Minority Interest	674,378	15.8
Preferred Stock	96,100	2.2
Common & Surplus	1,671,830	39.1
Total	4,278,584	100.0

RECENT DEVELOPMENTS: For the year ended 12/31/00, net income totaled $121.8 million compared with income of $180.3 million, before an extraordinary charge of $4.2 million, in the previous year. Results included a gain from the disposition of real estate of $7.0 million and $53.8 million in 2000 and 1999, respectively. Total revenue improved 6.6% to $477.7 million versus $448.2 million in 1999. Rental revenue increased 5.6% to $464.2 million, while investment management and other income more than doubled to $8.3 million.

PROSPECTS: Going forward, the Company will continue to focus on its strategy of disposing of nearly $1.00 billion in retail assets, while placing emphasis on industrial real estate located in supply-constrained markets nationwide. Accordingly, the Company disposed of $176.0 million in non-core assets and exited three non-core markets during 2000. Also, the Company acquired $730.0 million in industrial properties and completed $144.0 million in renovation and development projects.

BUSINESS

AMB PROPERTY CORP. is an owner and operator of industrial real estate properties. The Company, through its 93.6%-owned subsidiary, AMB Property, L.P., is engaged in the acquisition, ownership, operation, management, renovation, expansion and development of primarily industrial properties in target markets nationwide. These properties are mainly located in major distribution areas near airports, seaports and freeway systems. As of 12/31/00, AMB owned managed and had renovation and development projects totaling 1,005 buildings and 91.6 million square feet in 27 metropolitan markets. Approximately 57.0% of AMB's industrial properties are located in the six largest distribution/hub markets in the U.S., including the San Francisco Bay Area, Southern California, Dallas/Fort Worth, Chicago and the Northern New Jersey/New York area.

QUARTERLY DATA

(12/31/00)($000)	REV	INC
1st Quarter	110,323	31,045
2nd Quarter	113,479	30,007
3rd Quarter	121,371	34,846
4th Quarter	132,534	25,884

ANNUAL FINANCIAL DATA

	12/31/00	12/31/99	12/31/98	12/31/97	12/31/96	12/31/95	12/31/94
Earnings Per Share	[3] **1.35**	[2] **1.97**	**1.27**	**1.38**	...	...	...
Tang. Book Val. Per Share	**19.87**	**20.36**	**19.43**	**19.42**	...	...	...
Dividends Per Share	**1.48**	**1.74**	**1.03**	**0.13**	...	...	...
Dividend Payout %	**109.6**	**88.4**	**80.9**	**9.7**	...	...	...
INCOME STATEMENT (IN THOUSANDS):							
Rental Income	464,164	439,658	354,658	26,465	166,415	106,180	50,893
Total Income	477,707	448,183	358,887	56,062	167,953	108,249	51,682
Costs & Expenses	131,480	133,146	108,003	29,454	56,159	37,673	17,094
Depreciation	96,258	67,505	57,464	4,195	28,591	17,524	8,812
Interest Expense	90,270	88,681	69,670	3,528	26,867	20,533	12,023
Income Before Income Taxes	161,531	212,604	123,750	18,885	54,865	32,519	13,753
Equity Earnings/Minority Int.	d39,749	d34,011	d11,157	d657	d465	12	d559
Net Income	[3] 121,782	[2] 178,593	112,593	18,228	[1] 54,400	32,531	13,194
Average Shs. Outstg.	84,155	86,347	86,235	13,168	...	...	...
BALANCE SHEET (IN THOUSANDS):							
Cash & Cash Equivalents	42,722	137,019	25,137	39,968	33,120	110,474	...
Total Real Estate Investments	4,126,708	3,393,452	3,483,361	2,438,846	1,554,387	984,955	...
Total Assets	4,425,626	3,621,550	3,562,885	2,506,255	1,622,559	1,117,181	...
Long-Term Obligations	1,836,276	1,270,037	1,368,196	685,652	548,134	254,067	...
Total Liabilities	2,657,696	1,792,291	1,797,525	838,225	594,958	279,982	...
Net Stockholders' Equity	1,767,930	1,829,259	1,765,360	1,668,030	1,027,601	837,199	...
Year-end Shs. Outstg.	84,139	85,133	85,918	85,875	...	...	...
STATISTICAL RECORD:							
Net Inc.+Depr./Assets %	4.9	6.8	4.8	0.9	5.1	4.5	...
Return on Equity %	6.9	9.8	6.4	1.1	5.3	3.9	...
Return on Assets %	2.8	4.9	3.2	0.7	3.4	2.9	...
Price Range	26.06-18.81	23.50-18.00	26.00-20.75	24.31-22.25	...	...	...
P/E Ratio	19.3-13.9	11.9-9.1	20.5-16.3	17.6-16.1	...	...	...
Average Yield %	6.6	8.4	4.4	0.6	...	...	...

Statistics are as originally reported. [1] Bef. loss of $1.5 mill. from disc. ops. [2] Bef. extraord. chrg. of $2.5 mill.; incls. gain of $53.6 mill. from divest. of real estate. [3] Incls. gain of $7.0 mill. from dispos. of real estate.

OFFICERS:
H. R. Moghadam, Chmn., C.E.O.
W. B. Baird, Pres.
M. A. Coke, Exec. V.P., C.F.O.

INVESTOR CONTACT: Victoria A. Robinson, Dir. Inv. Relations (877) 285-3111

PRINCIPAL OFFICE: Pier 1, Bay 1, San Francisco, CA 94111

TELEPHONE NUMBER: (415) 394-9000
FAX: (415) 394-9001
WEB: www.amb.com

NO. OF EMPLOYEES: 145

SHAREHOLDERS: 235 (approx.)

ANNUAL MEETING: In May

INCORPORATED: MD, 1983

INSTITUTIONAL HOLDINGS:
No. of Institutions: 138
Shares Held: 65,927,450
% Held: 77.6

INDUSTRY: Real estate investment trusts (SIC: 6798)

TRANSFER AGENT(S): Boston EquiServe, Boston, MA

NYSE SYMBOL ABK
Rec. Pr. 56.05 (5/31/01)

AMBAC FINANCIAL GROUP, INC.

YIELD 0.6%
P/E RATIO 16.4

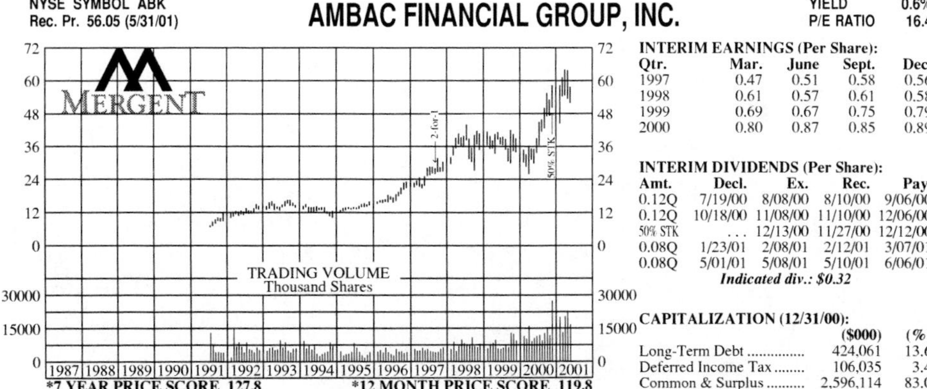

***7 YEAR PRICE SCORE 127.8** ***12 MONTH PRICE SCORE 119.8**

*NYSE COMPOSITE INDEX=100

INTERIM EARNINGS (Per Share):

Qtr.	Mar.	June	Sept.	Dec.
1997	0.47	0.51	0.58	0.56
1998	0.61	0.57	0.61	0.58
1999	0.69	0.67	0.75	0.79
2000	0.80	0.87	0.85	0.89

INTERIM DIVIDENDS (Per Share):

Amt.	Decl.	Ex.	Rec.	Pay.
0.12Q	7/19/00	8/08/00	8/10/00	9/06/00
0.12Q	10/18/00	11/08/00	11/10/00	12/06/00
50% STK	...	12/13/00	11/27/00	12/12/00
0.08Q	1/23/01	2/08/01	2/12/01	3/07/01
0.08Q	5/01/01	5/08/01	5/10/01	6/06/01

Indicated div.: $0.32

CAPITALIZATION (12/31/00):

	($000)	(%)
Long-Term Debt	424,061	13.6
Deferred Income Tax	106,035	3.4
Common & Surplus	2,596,114	83.0
Total	3,126,210	100.0

RECENT DEVELOPMENTS: For the year ended 12/31/00, the Company reported net income of $366.2 million compared with $307.9 million in the prior year. Total revenues were $621.3 million versus $533.3 million the year before. Net premiums written climbed 4.9% to $492.3 million from $383.4 million in 1999. Net premiums earned grew 17.7% to $311.3 million from $264.4 million a year earlier. As of 9/30/00, total assets amounted to $11.35 billion.

PROSPECTS: Results benefited from brisk business activity in the final quarter of the year, particularly in the municipal market where the Company concluded several transactions. With regard to the California utility crisis, ABK currently has just under $150.0 million in combined net par insured exposure, approximately divided evenly between Southern California Edison and Pacific Gas & Electric. Going forward, the Company believes that the likelihood of any material permanent loss to ABK is very low.

BUSINESS

AMBAC FINANCIAL GROUP, Inc. is a holding company whose subsidiaries provide financial guarantee products and other financial services to clients in both the public and private sectors worldwide. The Company provides financial guarantees for municipal and structured finance obligations through its principal operating subsidiary, Ambac Assurance Corporation. Through its financial services subsidiaries, the Company provides investment agreements, interest rate swaps, investment advisory and cash management services, primarily to states, municipalities and their authorities.

REVENUES

(12/31/00)	($000)	(%)
Financial Guarantee Insurance	565,421	91.0
Financial Services	53,565	8.6
Other	2,324	0.4
Total	621,310	100.0

ANNUAL FINANCIAL DATA

	12/31/00	12/31/99	12/31/98	12/31/97	12/31/96	12/31/95	12/31/94
Earnings Per Share	**3.41**	**2.87**	**2.37**	**2.09**	**2.63**	**1.59**	**1.34**
Cash Flow Per Share	**3.32**	**2.86**	**1.43**	**1.14**	**1.74**	**1.04**	**0.52**
Tang. Book Val. Per Share	**24.60**	**19.23**	**19.98**	**17.85**	**15.34**	**13.35**	**9.83**
Dividends Per Share	**0.31**	**0.28**	**0.25**	**0.23**	**0.20**	**0.18**	**0.17**
Dividend Payout %	**9.0**	**9.7**	**10.7**	**11.0**	**7.8**	**11.6**	**12.3**
INCOME STATEMENT (IN MILLIONS):							
Total Revenues	621.3	533.3	358.3	282.1	193.5	195.7	149.8
Costs & Expenses	79.6	61.3	55.2	44.9	40.6	32.7	26.0
Depreciation & Amort.	d9.4	d1.5	d2.5	d1.3	0.4	5.1	9.5
Operating Income	551.1	473.5	305.6	238.5	152.6	157.9	114.3
Net Interest Inc./(Exp.)	d37.5	d62.3	d68.3	d49.3	d31.9	d26.1	d29.4
Income Before Income Taxes	482.1	404.7	328.9	286.0	375.5	214.2	179.9
Income Taxes	116.0	96.7	74.9	63.0	99.2	46.6	38.8
Equity Earnings/Minority Int.	...	...	...	...	0.6	d0.2	1.5
Net Income	366.2	307.9	155.2	123.3	181.6	104.3	45.3
Cash Flow	356.8	306.4	152.7	122.0	182.0	109.4	54.8
Average Shs. Outstg. (000)	107,415	107,049	106,995	106,841	104,895	105,303	105,621
BALANCE SHEET (IN MILLIONS):							
Cash & Cash Equivalents	554.7	337.5	380.1	231.0	321.4	429.1	230.4
Total Current Assets	848.5	1,462.9	1,548.9	786.7	607.9	858.2	452.3
Total Assets	10,120.3	11,345.1	11,212.3	8,249.7	5,876.0	5,309.3	4,293.3
Total Current Liabilities	5,024.0	7,081.4	6,874.1	4,660.6	2,847.9	2,564.3	2,076.8
Long-Term Obligations	424.1	424.0	423.9	223.9	223.8	223.7	223.7
Net Stockholders' Equity	2,596.1	2,018.5	2,096.1	1,872.5	1,615.0	1,404.0	1,033.5
Net Working Capital	d4,175.4	d5,618.5	d5,325.2	d3,874.0	d2,240.0	d1,706.1	d1,624.5
Year-end Shs. Outstg. (000)	105,551	104,937	104,913	104,921	105,270	105,192	105,093
STATISTICAL RECORD:							
Operating Profit Margin %	88.7	88.8	85.3	84.6	78.8	80.7	76.3
Net Profit Margin %	58.9	57.7	43.3	43.7	93.9	53.3	30.3
Return on Equity %	14.1	15.3	7.4	6.6	11.2	7.4	4.4
Return on Assets %	3.6	2.7	1.4	1.5	3.1	2.0	1.1
Debt/Total Assets %	4.2	3.7	3.8	2.7	3.8	4.2	5.2
Price Range	58.31-25.92	42.00-29.79	43.96-27.25	31.71-20.67	23.17-15.17	15.96-12.17	15.00-10.08
P/E Ratio	17.1-7.6	14.6-10.4	18.5-11.5	15.2-9.9	8.8-5.8	10.0-7.6	11.2-7.5
Average Yield %	0.7	0.8	0.7	0.9	1.1	1.3	1.3

Statistics are as originally reported. Adj. for stk. splits: 50% div., 12/00; 2-for-1, 9/97

OFFICERS:
P. B. Lassiter, Chmn., Pres., C.E.O.
F. J. Bivona, Exec. V.P., C.F.O.

INVESTOR CONTACT: Brian S. Moore, Managing Dir., External Relations, (800) 221-1854

PRINCIPAL OFFICE: One State Street Plaza, New York, NY 10004

TELEPHONE NUMBER: (212) 668-0340
FAX: (212) 509-9190
WEB: www.ambac.com

NO. OF EMPLOYEES: 364 (avg.)

SHAREHOLDERS: 75

ANNUAL MEETING: In May

INCORPORATED: DE, April, 1991

INSTITUTIONAL HOLDINGS:
No. of Institutions: 298
Shares Held: 101,077,267
% Held: 95.7

INDUSTRY: Surety insurance (SIC: 6351)

TRANSFER AGENT(S): Citibank, N.A., New York, NY

NYSE SYMBOL AIZ
Rec. Pr. 8.80 (5/31/01)

AMCAST INDUSTRIAL CORPORATION

YIELD 6.4%
P/E RATIO 25.9

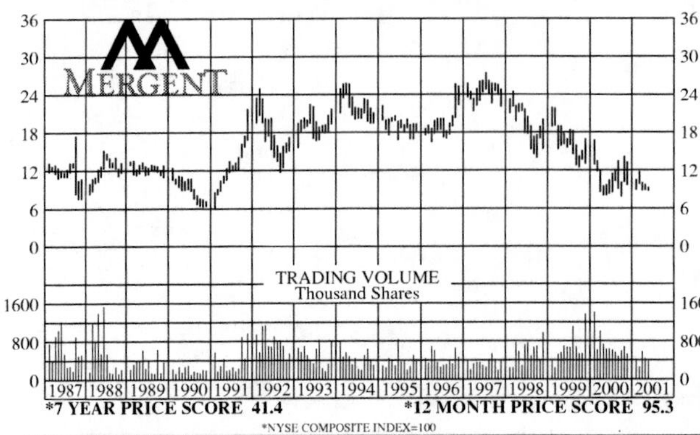

INTERIM EARNINGS (Per Share):

Qtr.	Nov.	Feb.	May	Aug.
1997	0.48	0.24	0.50	0.28
1998	0.44	0.57	0.58	0.10
1999	1.09	0.49	0.41	0.12
2000	0.17	0.08	0.21	0.04
2001	0.01	...	...	...

INTERIM DIVIDENDS (Per Share):

Amt.	Decl.	Ex.	Rec.	Pay.
0.14Q	2/25/00	3/08/00	3/10/00	3/27/00
0.14Q	5/30/00	6/07/00	6/09/00	6/26/00
0.14Q	8/31/00	9/07/00	9/11/00	9/29/00
0.14Q	10/25/00	12/05/00	12/07/00	12/22/00
0.14Q	2/15/01	3/06/01	3/08/01	3/26/01

Indicated div.: $0.56 (Div. Reinv. Plan)

CAPITALIZATION (8/31/00):

	($000)	(%)
Long-Term Debt	147,273	44.0
Deferred Income Tax	31,275	9.3
Common & Surplus	155,954	46.6
Total	334,502	100.0

RECENT DEVELOPMENTS: For the quarter ended 12/3/00, net income decreased 93.7% to $82,000 compared with income of $1.3 million, before an accounting credit of $983,000, in the equivalent 1999 quarter. The decline in earnings reflected a softening in the economy and cautiousness on the part of some customers regarding inventory levels. Net sales were $137.9 million, down 5.6% from $146.1 million a year earlier.

PROSPECTS: Current weak market demand is depressing sales for AIZ's Engineered Components segment. AIZ's Flow Control Products segment is being adversely affected by slowness in construction markets and increased price competition. Thus, AIZ has trimmed its automotive work force 25.0% to synchronize sales volume and manpower levels. Moreover, inventories will be aggressively reduced to bring them into line over the next few months.

BUSINESS

AMCAST INDUSTRIAL CORPORATION is a manufacturer of technology-intensive metal products in the U.S. The Company's two primary businesses are Engineered Components for original equipment manufacturers and brand name Flow Control Products marketed through national distribution channels. The Engineered Components group primarily serves automotive and aerospace manufacturers. Flow Control Products include specialty fittings, valves, filters and equipment for plumbing, air conditioning and refrigeration systems. Amcast serves three major sectors of the economy: automotive, construction, and industrial. Engineered Components contributed 75.8% to fiscal 2000 revenues, while Flow Control Products contributed 24.2%.

REVENUES

(08/31/2000)	($000)	(%)
Flow Control Products	147,697	24.2
Engineered Components	462,958	75.8
Total	610,655	100.0

ANNUAL FINANCIAL DATA

	8/31/00	8/31/99	8/31/98	8/31/97	8/31/96	8/31/95	8/31/94
Earnings Per Share	**4 0.38**	**3 2.11**	**2 1.81**	**1 1.50**	**1.85**	**2.02**	**1.72**
Cash Flow Per Share	**4.14**	**3.56**	**2.68**	**3.86**	**3.88**	**3.71**	**3.24**
Tang. Book Val. Per Share	**12.64**	**12.23**	**10.67**	**13.23**	**15.50**	**14.52**	**13.03**
Dividends Per Share	**0.56**	**0.56**	**0.56**	**0.56**	**0.56**	**0.54**	**0.50**
Dividend Payout %	**147.3**	**26.5**	**30.9**	**37.3**	**30.3**	**26.7**	**29.1**
INCOME STATEMENT (IN THOUSANDS):							
Total Revenues	610,655	588,933	574,414	387,051	343,934	328,231	271,856
Costs & Expenses	556,099	520,500	516,391	339,346	299,178	286,867	235,824
Depreciation & Amort.	32,999	31,346	32,113	20,463	17,428	14,392	12,812
Operating Income	21,557	46,110	37,958	27,242	27,328	26,972	23,220
Net Interest Inc./(Exp.)	d12,929	d13,182	d15,045	d5,135	d2,348	d1,387	d1,594
Income Before Income Taxes	5,422	31,538	22,975	20,005	24,731	26,098	22,067
Income Taxes	2,058	12,221	6,210	7,022	8,805	8,927	7,613
Equity Earnings/Minority Int.	d3,206	d1,390	62	d2,102	d249	513	441
Net Income	4 3,364	3 1,271	2 d7,331	1 12,983	15,926	17,171	14,454
Cash Flow	36,363	32,617	24,782	33,446	33,354	31,563	27,266
Average Shs. Outstg.	8,792	9,162	9,250	8,674	8,606	8,509	8,425
BALANCE SHEET (IN THOUSANDS):							
Cash & Cash Equivalents	3,062	6,928	7,022	9,608	5,413	1,286	15,414
Total Current Assets	181,919	203,057	222,651	203,225	109,221	102,861	97,426
Net Property	226,857	256,758	260,117	235,244	138,606	105,623	73,654
Total Assets	480,386	533,486	563,450	508,918	269,217	229,367	194,161
Total Current Liabilities	126,926	134,102	135,722	176,965	51,447	55,016	48,836
Long-Term Obligations	147,273	174,061	217,199	145,304	58,783	29,687	13,910
Net Stockholders' Equity	155,954	170,766	160,814	158,226	136,164	124,205	110,163
Net Working Capital	54,993	68,955	86,929	26,260	57,774	47,845	48,590
Year-end Shs. Outstg.	8,406	8,955	9,207	9,177	8,618	8,556	8,454
STATISTICAL RECORD:							
Operating Profit Margin %	3.5	7.8	6.6	7.0	7.9	8.2	8.5
Net Profit Margin %	0.6	0.2	...	3.4	4.6	5.2	5.3
Return on Equity %	2.2	0.7	...	8.2	11.7	13.8	13.1
Return on Assets %	0.7	0.2	...	2.6	5.9	7.5	7.4
Debt/Total Assets %	30.7	32.6	38.5	28.6	21.8	12.9	7.2
Price Range	16.81-7.81	22.00-12.38	24.50-13.88	27.50-21.25	25.75-16.38	22.25-16.75	25.88-19.38
P/E Ratio	44.2-20.6	10.4-5.9	13.5-7.7	18.3-14.2	13.9-8.9	11.0-8.3	15.0-11.3
Average Yield %	4.5	3.3	2.9	2.3	2.7	2.8	2.2

Statistics are as originally reported. 1 Incl. pre-tax chrg. of $3.5 mill. for overstated inventory values at the Amcast Precision unit. 2 Bef. a chrg. of $8.6 million for the cum. effect of an acctg. change. 3 Incl. gain of $9.0 mill. 4 Incl. restruct. chrg. of $721,000. Bef. acctg. chrg. of $983,000.

OFFICERS:
L. W. Ladehoff, Chmn.
B. O. Pond, Jr., Pres., C.E.O.
M. R. Higgins, Treas.
D. G. Daly, V.P., Gen. Couns., Sec.

INVESTOR CONTACT: Michael R. Higgins, Investor Relations, (937) 291-7015

PRINCIPAL OFFICE: 7887 Washington Village Drive, Dayton, OH 45459

TELEPHONE NUMBER: (937) 291-7000
FAX: (937) 291-7005
WEB: www.amcast.com

NO. OF EMPLOYEES: 4,530 (approx.)

SHAREHOLDERS: 6,483 (approx.)

ANNUAL MEETING: In Dec.

INCORPORATED: OH, 1869

INSTITUTIONAL HOLDINGS:
No. of Institutions: 45
Shares Held: 2,837,077
% Held: 33.8

INDUSTRY: Valves and pipe fittings, nec (SIC: 3494)

TRANSFER AGENT(S): First Chicago Trust Company of New York, Jersey City, NJ

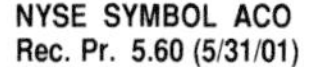

NYSE SYMBOL ACO
Rec. Pr. 5.60 (5/31/01)

AMCOL INTERNATIONAL CORPORATION

YIELD 1.1%
P/E RATIO . . .

INTERIM EARNINGS (Per Share):

Qtr.	Mar.	June	Sept.	Dec.
1997	0.11	0.15	0.24	0.23
1998	0.12	0.20	0.24	0.23
1999	0.21	0.29	0.34	d0.02
2000	0.21	0.15	0.10	d0.19

INTERIM DIVIDENDS (Per Share):

Amt.	Decl.	Ex.	Rec.	Pay.
14.00Q	6/06/00	7/03/00	6/16/00	6/30/00
0.01Q	8/02/00	8/17/00	8/21/00	9/06/00
0.01Q	11/13/00	11/30/00	12/04/00	1/03/01
0.01Q	2/06/01	2/14/01	2/19/01	3/02/01
0.015Q	5/17/01	5/23/01	5/28/01	6/08/01

Indicated div.: $0.06

CAPITALIZATION (12/31/00):

	($000)	(%)
Long-Term Debt	51,334	27.6
Minority Interest	4	0.0
Common & Surplus	134,907	72.4
Total	186,245	100.0

RECENT DEVELOPMENTS: For the year ended 12/31/00, ACO reported income from continuing operations of $3.3 million versus loss from continuing operations of $8.3 million in 1999. Results for 2000 and 1999 included after-tax nonrecurring charges of $13.0 million and $10.0 million, respectively. Results excluded after-tax gains of $323.4 million in 2000 and $30.5 million in 1999 from discontinued operations. Net sales dropped 4.1% to $304.1 million.

PROSPECTS: The Company announced that its board of directors has completed its review of strategic alternatives to enhance shareholder value. Based on the results of the review, it has been determined that the most appropriate strategy is for AMCOL to remain independent and to focus on operating strategies for its remaining businesses. ACO continues to evaluate the spin-off of its Nanocor subsidiary, various alternatives for funding Nanocar's operations.

BUSINESS

AMCOL INTERNATIONAL CORPORATION'S (formerly American Colloid Co.) business may be generally divided into two principal categories: minerals and environmental. ACO produces sodium and calcium bentonite clays used for a variety of industrial and consumer applications, including cat litter. Environmental products and technologies service the wastewater treatment, groundwater monitoring/drilling, soil sealing/landfill lining and commercial construction markets. The Company also operates a long-haul trucking business, primarily concentrated in the Great Plains and Midwestern U.S. On 6/1/00, ACO sold its absorbent polymer segment to BASF AG for $656.5 million.

ANNUAL FINANCIAL DATA

	12/31/00	12/31/99	12/31/98	12/31/97	12/31/96	12/31/95	12/31/94
Earnings Per Share	**2 0.11**	**1 0.82**	**0.78**	**0.72**	**0.52**	**0.60**	**0.52**
Cash Flow Per Share	**0.74**	**2.19**	**1.94**	**1.82**	**1.47**	**1.32**	**1.02**
Tang. Book Val. Per Share	**4.67**	**6.93**	**5.77**	**5.39**	**5.12**	**4.69**	**4.47**
Dividends Per Share	**0.30**	**0.26**	**0.23**	**0.20**	**0.19**	**0.17**	**0.15**
Dividend Payout %	**272.7**	**31.7**	**28.8**	**27.8**	**35.9**	**27.8**	**29.5**
INCOME STATEMENT (IN THOUSANDS):							
Total Revenues	304,065	552,052	521,530	477,060	405,347	347,688	265,443
Costs & Expenses	281,589	471,411	446,188	403,679	345,103	294,002	227,010
Depreciation & Amort.	18,996	37,208	33,122	31,912	27,907	21,289	14,442
Operating Income	3,480	43,433	42,220	41,469	32,337	32,397	23,991
Net Interest Inc./(Exp.)	d3,241	d6,396	d7,933	d8,628	d8,450	d6,727	d2,332
Income Before Income Taxes	10,365	35,699	34,427	32,443	23,217	26,887	22,203
Income Taxes	7,532	13,913	12,350	11,399	7,979	9,082	6,828
Equity Earnings/Minority Int.	470	448	8	. . .	d13	d34	d92
Net Income	2 3,303	1 22,234	22,085	21,044	15,225	17,771	15,283
Cash Flow	22,299	59,442	55,207	52,956	43,132	39,060	29,725
Average Shs. Outstg.	29,957	27,199	28,386	29,125	29,295	29,519	29,231
BALANCE SHEET (IN THOUSANDS):							
Cash & Cash Equivalents	178,606	3,815	2,758	3,077	3,054	1,888	10,389
Total Current Assets	269,787	164,770	164,076	150,270	148,475	126,337	105,839
Net Property	80,152	172,408	171,478	175,324	180,876	175,211	141,420
Total Assets	374,128	349,007	357,864	351,009	350,708	322,366	261,047
Total Current Liabilities	177,939	59,715	74,083	67,241	51,870	35,882	36,617
Long-Term Obligations	51,334	93,914	96,268	94,425	118,855	117,016	71,458
Net Stockholders' Equity	134,907	186,440	172,914	175,943	167,404	155,494	141,319
Net Working Capital	91,848	105,055	89,993	83,029	96,605	90,455	69,222
Year-end Shs. Outstg.	28,781	26,852	26,869	28,474	28,497	28,701	28,521
STATISTICAL RECORD:							
Operating Profit Margin %	1.1	7.9	8.1	8.7	8.0	9.3	9.0
Net Profit Margin %	1.1	4.0	4.2	4.4	3.8	5.1	5.8
Return on Equity %	2.4	11.9	12.8	12.0	9.1	11.4	10.8
Return on Assets %	0.9	6.4	6.2	6.0	4.3	5.5	5.9
Debt/Total Assets %	13.7	26.9	26.9	26.9	33.9	36.3	27.4
Price Range	17.69-2.88	17.88-8.25	16.38-8.00	17.25-10.17	11.33-7.17	12.17-7.92	16.83-7.00
P/E Ratio	160.7-26.1	21.8-10.1	21.0-10.3	24.0-14.1	21.8-13.8	20.3-13.2	32.4-13.5
Average Yield %	2.9	2.0	1.8	1.5	2.0	1.7	1.3

Statistics are as originally reported. Adj. for stk. splits: 3-for-2, 12/1/97. 1 Incl. a net charge of $8.8 mill. rel. to intangible assets assoc. with ACO's environmental and U.K. cat litter operations & a net chrg. of $1.3 mill. for the write-down of assets assoc. with ACO's wastewater cleaning and testing business. 2 Excl. net gain of $316.3 mill. on disp. on absorbent polymers segment & incl. an after-tax chrg. for asset impair. and bus. realignment of $13.0 mill.

OFFICERS:
J. Hughes, Chmn.
L. E. Washow, Pres., C.E.O., C.O.O.

INVESTOR CONTACT: Jennifer B. Melsheimer, (847) 394-8730

PRINCIPAL OFFICE: One North Arlington, 1500 West Shure Drive, Suite 500, Arlington Heights, IL 60004-7803

TELEPHONE NUMBER: (847) 394-8730
FAX: (847) 506-6199
WEB: www.amcol.com
NO. OF EMPLOYEES: 1,064 (avg.)
SHAREHOLDERS: 3,284
ANNUAL MEETING: In May
INCORPORATED: SD, 1924; reincorp., DE, 1959

INSTITUTIONAL HOLDINGS:
No. of Institutions: 49
Shares Held: 8,320,184
% Held: 29.8

INDUSTRY: Clay and related minerals, nec (SIC: 1459)

TRANSFER AGENT(S): Computershare Investor Services, Chicago, IL

NYSE SYMBOL AHC
Rec. Pr. 85.64 (5/31/01)

AMERADA HESS CORPORATION

YIELD 1.4%
P/E RATIO 7.5

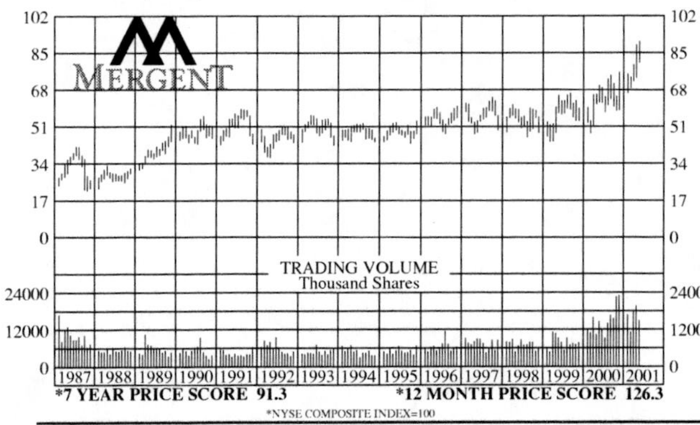

*7 YEAR PRICE SCORE 91.3 *12 MONTH PRICE SCORE 126.3
*NYSE COMPOSITE INDEX=100

INTERIM EARNINGS (Per Share):

Qtr.	Mar.	June	Sept.	Dec.
1997	0.05	0.45	0.25	d0.67
1998	d0.14	d0.24	d0.70	d4.70
1999	0.79	0.86	1.75	1.45
2000	2.47	2.24	2.86	3.83

INTERIM DIVIDENDS (Per Share):

Amt.	Decl.	Ex.	Rec.	Pay.
0.15Q	6/07/00	6/15/00	6/19/00	6/30/00
0.15Q	9/06/00	9/14/00	9/18/00	9/29/00
0.15Q	12/18/00	12/14/00	12/18/00	1/03/01
0.30Q	3/07/01	3/15/01	3/19/01	3/30/01
0.30Q	6/06/01	6/14/01	6/18/01	6/29/01

Indicated div.: $1.20 (Div. Reinv. Plan)

CAPITALIZATION (12/31/00):

	($000)	(%)
Long-Term Debt	1,985,000	31.1
Deferred Income Tax	510,000	8.0
Common & Surplus	3,883,000	60.9
Total	6,378,000	100.0

RECENT DEVELOPMENTS: For the year ended 12/31/00, net income soared to $1.02 billion versus $438.0 million a year earlier. Results for 2000 included a net gain of $60.0 million on the termination of AHC's proposed acquisition of LASMO plc, partially offset by a non-recurring charge of $24.0 million. Results for 1999 included special charges of $131.0 million. Total revenues surged 64.5% to $12.28 billion from $7.46 billion in 1999, reflecting sharply higher crude oil, natural gas and refined product selling prices.

PROSPECTS: Prospects are positive, reflecting rising production and strong crude oil and natural gas prices. Separately, on 1/29/01, AHC announced that it has an agreement to buy 53 company-operated retail outlets, located primarily in the Boston metropolitan area and southern New Hampshire, from Gibbs Oil Company Limited Partnership. Also, on 2/20/01, AHC announced it had reached an agreement to purchase the exploration and production assets of LLOG Exploration Company for $750.0 million.

BUSINESS

AMERADA HESS CORPORATION and its subsidiaries explore for, produce, purchase, transport and sell crude oil and natural gas. These exploration and production activities take place in the U.S., United Kingdom, Norway, Denmark, Gabon, Algeria, Azerbaijan, Indonesia, Thailand, Malaysia, Brazil and other countries. AHC also manufactures, purchases, transports, trades and markets refined petroleum and other energy products. AHC owns 50.0% of a refinery joint venture in the U.S. Virgin Islands, and another facility, terminals and retail outlets located on the East Coast of the U.S. As of 12/31/00, retail sales were performed through 929 HESS gas stations, of which approximately 540 had HESS-MART convenience stores. Total proved reserves in 2000 were 755.0 million barrels of crude oil and 1,807.0 million cubic feet of natural gas. In 2000, revenues were derived as follows: crude oil, 18.2%; natural gas, 28.9%; petroleum products, 45.0% and other 7.9%.

ANNUAL FINANCIAL DATA

	12/31/00	12/31/99	12/31/98	12/31/97	12/31/96	12/31/95	12/31/94
Earnings Per Share	**[4] 11.38**	**[3] 4.85**	**[2] d5.12**	**[1] 0.08**	**[1] 7.09**	**[1] d4.24**	**0.79**
Cash Flow Per Share	**19.33**	**12.03**	**2.26**	**7.38**	**15.50**	**5.36**	**10.81**
Tang. Book Val. Per Share	**43.76**	**33.51**	**29.26**	**35.16**	**36.35**	**28.60**	**33.33**
Dividends Per Share	**0.60**	**0.60**	**0.60**	**0.60**	**0.60**	**0.60**	**0.45**
Dividend Payout %	**5.3**	**12.4**	**...**	**749.1**	**8.5**	**...**	**57.0**
INCOME STATEMENT (IN MILLIONS):							
Total Revenues	12,277.0	7,461.4	6,621.1	8,340.0	8,929.7	7,524.8	6,698.8
Costs & Expenses	9,729.0	5,824.7	6,114.0	7,324.0	6,967.1	6,152.7	5,289.9
Depreciation & Amort.	714.0	648.7	661.8	672.7	783.2	893.1	927.9
Operating Income	1,834.0	988.0	d154.7	343.3	1,179.4	479.0	481.0
Net Interest Inc./(Exp.)	d162.0	d158.2	d152.9	d136.1	d165.5	d247.5	d245.1
Income Before Income Taxes	1,672.0	701.8	d514.1	126.6	1,013.9	d352.6	235.8
Income Taxes	649.0	264.2	cr55.2	119.1	353.8	41.8	162.1
Net Income	[4] 1,023.0	[3] 437.6	[2] d458.9	[1] 7.5	[1] 660.1	[1] d394.4	73.7
Cash Flow	1,737.0	1,086.3	202.9	680.2	1,443.3	498.7	1,001.6
Average Shs. Outstg. (000)	89,878	90,280	89,585	92,163	93,111	93,002	92,689
BALANCE SHEET (IN MILLIONS):							
Cash & Cash Equivalents	312.0	40.9	73.8	91.2	112.5	56.1	53.1
Total Current Assets	4,115.0	1,827.6	1,886.7	2,203.6	2,426.8	1,962.5	1,721.7
Net Property	4,323.0	4,051.7	4,191.9	5,190.8	4,907.3	5,369.7	6,366.0
Total Assets	10,274.0	7,727.7	7,883.0	7,934.6	7,784.5	7,756.4	8,337.9
Total Current Liabilities	3,538.0	1,578.9	1,796.8	1,739.9	1,737.0	1,604.6	1,201.4
Long-Term Obligations	1,985.0	2,286.7	2,476.1	2,003.0	1,711.8	2,587.4	3,235.2
Net Stockholders' Equity	3,883.0	3,038.2	2,643.4	3,215.7	3,383.6	2,660.4	3,099.6
Net Working Capital	577.0	248.7	89.9	463.8	689.9	358.0	520.2
Year-end Shs. Outstg. (000)	88,744	90,676	90,357	91,451	93,073	93,011	92,996
STATISTICAL RECORD:							
Operating Profit Margin %	14.9	13.2	...	4.1	13.2	6.4	7.2
Net Profit Margin %	8.3	5.9	...	0.1	7.4	...	1.1
Return on Equity %	26.3	14.4	...	0.2	19.5	...	2.4
Return on Assets %	10.0	5.7	...	0.1	8.5	...	0.9
Debt/Total Assets %	19.3	29.6	31.4	25.2	22.0	33.4	38.8
Price Range	76.25-47.81	66.31-43.75	61.06-46.00	64.50-47.38	60.50-47.50	53.63-43.25	52.63-43.75
P/E Ratio	6.7-4.2	13.7-9.0	...	805.2-591.4	8.5-6.7	...	66.6-55.4
Average Yield %	1.0	1.1	1.1	1.1	1.1	1.2	0.9

Statistics are as originally reported. [1] Incls. non-recurr. net chrg. 12/31/97: $16.8 mill.; net credit 12/31/96: $424.4 mill.; net chrg. 12/31/95: $381.1 mill. [2] Incls. loss of $25.7 mill. fr. sale of assets & asset impair. chrg. of $206.5 mill. [3] Incls. one-time cr. of $176.0 mill. fr. asset sales; inc. tax benefit of $54.6 mill. & asset impair. chrg. of $99.5 mill. [4] Incls. net gain of $60.0 mill. on acq. termin. & non-recurr. chrg. of $24.0 mill.

OFFICERS:
J. B. Hess, Chmn., C.E.O.
W. S. Laidlaw, Pres., C.O.O.
J. Y. Schreyer, Exec. V.P., C.F.O.

INVESTOR CONTACT: C.T. Tursi, Inv. Rel., (212) 536-8593

PRINCIPAL OFFICE: 1185 Avenue of the Americas, New York, NY 10036

TELEPHONE NUMBER: (212) 997-8500
FAX: (212) 536-8390
WEB: www.hess.com

NO. OF EMPLOYEES: 9,891 (avg.)

SHAREHOLDERS: 7,709

ANNUAL MEETING: In May

INCORPORATED: DE, Feb., 1920

INSTITUTIONAL HOLDINGS:
No. of Institutions: 298
Shares Held: 66,526,280
% Held: 74.9

INDUSTRY: Petroleum refining (SIC: 2911)

TRANSFER AGENT(S): The Bank of New York, New York, NY

NYSE SYMBOL AEE
Rec. Pr. 44.60 (5/31/01)

AMEREN CORPORATION

YIELD 5.7%
P/E RATIO 13.4

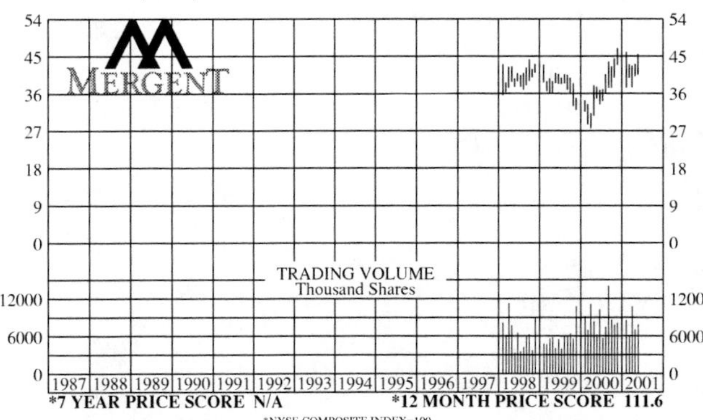

*7 YEAR PRICE SCORE N/A *12 MONTH PRICE SCORE 111.6

*NYSE COMPOSITE INDEX=100

INTERIM EARNINGS (Per Share):

Qtr.	Mar.	June	Sept.	Dec.
1996	0.42	0.53	1.58	0.18
1997	0.33	0.58	1.57	0.34
1998	0.29	0.61	1.73	0.19
1999	0.40	0.63	1.82	d0.04
2000	0.45	0.83	1.87	0.19

INTERIM DIVIDENDS (Per Share):

Amt.	Decl.	Ex.	Rec.	Pay.
0.635Q	4/25/00	6/06/00	6/08/00	6/30/00
0.635Q	8/25/00	9/07/00	9/11/00	9/29/00
0.635Q	10/13/00	12/07/00	12/11/00	12/29/00
0.635Q	2/09/01	3/06/01	3/08/01	3/30/01
0.635Q	4/24/01	6/06/01	6/08/01	6/29/01

Indicated div.: $2.54 (Div. Reinv. Plan)

CAPITALIZATION (12/31/00):

	($000)	(%)
Long-Term Debt	2,745,068	35.6
Deferred Income Tax	1,540,536	20.0
Minority Interest	3,940	0.1
Preferred Stock	235,197	3.0
Common & Surplus	3,196,671	41.4
Total	7,721,412	100.0

RECENT DEVELOPMENTS: For the year ended 12/31/00, net income advanced 18.7% to $457.1 million compared with $385.1 million in the previous year. Results for 2000 included an after-tax nonrecurring charge of $15.0 million, while 1999 results included an after-tax nonrecurring charge of $31.0 million. Also, results for 2000 and 1999 included credits of $65.0 million ad $33.0 million associated with the alternative rate regulation plan. Operating revenues rose 9.4% to $3.86 billion.

PROSPECTS: AEE, the Missouri Public Service Commission staff, and other parties, submitted filings to the Missouri Public Service Commission requesting an extension of the experimental alternative regulation plan, which expired on 6/30/01. AEE's filing included requests to extend the current plan with modifications, such as retail electric rate reductions and additional customer credits. Separately, AEE anticipates earnings for 2001 to range between $3.30 and $3.45 per share

BUSINESS

AMEREN CORPORATION was formed on 12/31/97 upon the merger of Union Electric Company, now known as AmerenUE, and Central Illinois Public Service Company (CIPSCO, Inc.), now known as AmerenCIPS. AEE companies provide energy services to 1.5 million electric and 300,000 natural gas customers throughout its 44,500 square mile territory in Missouri and Illinois. AEE also operates AmerenEnergy, Inc., an energy marketing and trading affiliate; CIPSCO Investment Co., which manages nonutility investments; and Ameren Services, which provides support services to the corporation and its subsidiaries.

QUARTERLY DATA

(12/31/00) ($000)	Rev	Inc
1st Quarter	825,376	108,578
2nd Quarter	940,304	159,206
3rd Quarter	1,195,411	305,685
4th Quarter	894,758	66,841

ANNUAL FINANCIAL DATA

	12/31/00	12/31/99	12/31/98	12/31/97	12/31/96	12/31/95
Earnings Per Share	**[3] 3.33**	**2.81**	**[2] 2.82**	**[1] 2.82**	**2.71**	**2.72**
Cash Flow Per Share	**6.30**	**5.55**	**5.55**	**5.57**	**5.42**	**5.33**
Tang. Book Val. Per Share	**23.30**	**22.52**	**22.27**	**22.00**	**21.98**	...
Dividends Per Share	**2.54**	**2.54**	**2.54**	...	...	...
Dividend Payout %	**76.3**	**90.4**	**90.1**	...	...	...
INCOME STATEMENT (IN MILLIONS):						
Total Revenues	3,855.8	3,523.6	3,318.2	3,326.5	3,328.4	3,235.9
Costs & Expenses	2,440.7	2,213.8	2,059.6	2,057.0	2,078.9	1,992.5
Depreciation & Amort.	406.9	376.4	375.3	377.2	371.4	358.0
Maintenance Exp.	367.9	370.9	312.0	310.2	302.2	307.5
Operating Income	640.3	562.5	571.2	582.1	575.9	577.9
Net Interest Inc./(Exp.)	d171.4	d161.2	d174.6	d177.9	d172.9	d172.6
Net Income	[3] 457.1	385.1	[2] 386.5	[1] 386.5	371.7	372.9
Cash Flow	864.0	761.5	761.8	763.7	743.0	730.8
Average Shs. Outstg. (000)	137,215	137,215	137,215	137,215	137,215	137,215
BALANCE SHEET (IN MILLIONS):						
Gross Property	13,910.0	13,056.5	12,530.9	12,272.5	11,975.2	...
Accumulated Depreciation	6,204.4	5,891.3	5,602.8	5,285.4	5,024.0	...
Net Property	7,705.7	7,165.2	6,928.0	6,987.1	6,951.1	...
Total Assets	9,714.4	9,177.6	8,847.4	8,827.5	8,932.6	...
Long-Term Obligations	2,745.1	2,448.4	2,289.4	2,506.1	2,335.5	...
Net Stockholders' Equity	3,431.9	3,324.9	3,291.3	3,254.2	3,314.9	...
Year-end Shs. Outstg. (000)	137,215	137,215	137,215	137,215	137,215	137,215
STATISTICAL RECORD:						
Operating Profit Margin %	16.6	16.0	17.2	17.5	17.3	17.9
Net Profit Margin %	11.9	10.9	11.6	11.6	11.2	11.5
Net Inc./Net Property %	5.9	5.4	5.6	5.5	5.3	...
Net Inc./Tot. Capital %	5.9	5.3	5.4	5.3	5.1	...
Return on Equity %	13.3	11.6	11.7	11.9	11.2	...
Accum. Depr./Gross Prop. %	44.6	45.1	44.7	43.1	42.0	...
Price Range	46.94-27.56	42.94-32.00	44.31-35.56	...	...	...
P/E Ratio	14.1-8.3	15.3-11.4	15.7-12.6	...	...	...
Average Yield %	6.8	6.8	6.4	...	...	...

Statistics are as originally reported. Results prior to 1997 are reported on a pro forma basis [1] Bef. extraord. chrg. $51.8 mil. ($0.38/sh.); incl. nonrecurr. chrg. of $25.0 mill. [2] Incl. after-tax nonrecurr. chrg. of $31.0 mill. [3] Incl. after-tax nonrecurr. chrg. $15.0 mill. & credit of $65.0 mill. assoc. with the alternative rate regulation plan.

OFFICERS:
C. W. Mueller, Chmn., Pres., C.E.O.
J. E. Birdsong, Treas.
S. R. Sullivan, V.P., Gen. Couns., Sec.

INVESTOR CONTACT: Ameren Services Company, Investor Services Department, (800) 255-2237

PRINCIPAL OFFICE: 1901 Chouteau Avenue, P.O. Box 66149, St. Louis, MO 63166-6149

TELEPHONE NUMBER: (314) 621-3222
FAX: (314) 554-2888
WEB: www.ameren.com

NO. OF EMPLOYEES: 7,342

SHAREHOLDERS: 107,587

ANNUAL MEETING: In Apr.

INCORPORATED: MO, Aug., 1995

INSTITUTIONAL HOLDINGS:
No. of Institutions: 272
Shares Held: 58,140,584
% Held: 42.4

INDUSTRY: Electric services (SIC: 4911)

TRANSFER AGENT(S): Ameren Services Company, St. Louis, MO

NYSE SYMBOL AWA
Rec. Pr. 10.21 (4/30/01)

AMERICA WEST HOLDING CORPORATION

YIELD ...
P/E RATIO 85.1

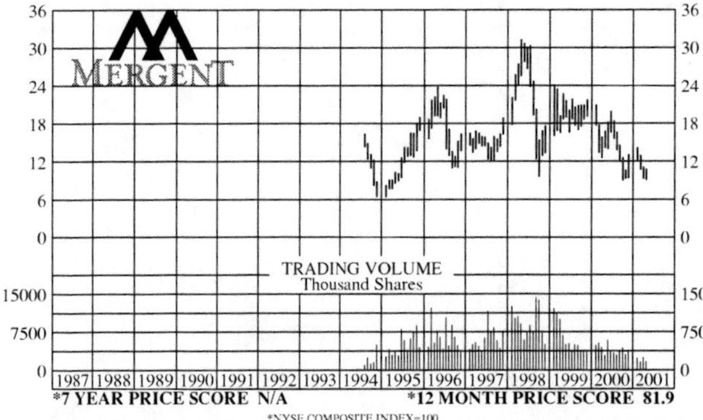

*7 YEAR PRICE SCORE N/A *12 MONTH PRICE SCORE 81.9

*NYSE COMPOSITE INDEX=100

INTERIM EARNINGS (Per Share):

Qtr.	Mar.	June	Sept.	Dec.
1998	0.53	0.86	0.49	0.52
1999	0.63	1.06	0.57	0.77
2000	0.40	0.91	0.04	d1.23

INTERIM DIVIDENDS (Per Share):

Amt.	Decl.	Ex.	Rec.	Pay.

No dividends paid.

CAPITALIZATION (12/31/00):

	($000)	(%)
Long-Term Debt	145,578	17.1
Deferred Income Tax	40,545	4.8
Common & Surplus	667,073	78.2
Total	853,196	100.0

RECENT DEVELOPMENTS: For the year ended 12/31/00, net income declined to $7.7 million compared with $119.4 million in the previous year. Results were dampened by higher operating expenses which rose 17.5% to $2.36 billion versus $2.01 billion in the preceding year. Total operating revenues increased 6.0% to $2.34 billion from $2.21 billion in the prior year. Passenger revenues rose 7.5% to $2.18 billion, while cargo revenues dropped 10.9% to $37.4 million. Other revenues fell 9.6% to $127.2 million.

PROSPECTS: On 4/18/01, the Company's subsidiary, America West Airlines announced a cost reduction plan which includes the reduction of overhead and a slowing of the airline's growth through the return of five older, leased aircraft. As a result, the annualized expense budget will be reduced by approximately $75.0 million. The capital reductions will be realized in 2001, while approximately $25.0 million of the $75.0 million of cost reduction will occur in 2001.

BUSINESS

AMERICA WEST HOLDINGS CORPORATION is an aviation and travel company that operates through two wholly-owned subsidiaries, America West Airlines and The Leisure Company. America West Airlines is the nation's ninth largest commercial air carrier, serving 92 destinations with more than 900 daily departures in the U.S., Canada and Mexico. Along with its codeshare partners, America West Airlines serves more than 180 destinations worldwide. The Leisure Company offers tour packages, as its principal business is inclusive vacation packaging and charter air transportation service.

REVENUES

(12/31/2000)	($000)	(%)
Passenger	2,179,811	93.0
Cargo	37,377	1.6
Other	127,166	5.4
Total	2,344,354	100.0

ANNUAL FINANCIAL DATA

	12/31/00	12/31/99	12/31/98	12/31/97	12/31/96	12/31/95	12/31/94
Earnings Per Share	**0.22**	[1] **3.03**	[1] **2.40**	**1.63**	[2][3] **0.21**	[2][3] **1.18**	**0.17**
Cash Flow Per Share	**5.54**	**7.57**	**5.80**	**4.41**	**2.43**	**2.87**	**0.69**
Tang. Book Val. Per Share	**20.43**	**14.38**	**14.43**	**14.87**	**13.59**	**14.36**	**13.55**
INCOME STATEMENT (IN MILLIONS):							
Total Revenues	2,344.4	2,210.9	2,023.3	1,875.0	1,739.5	1,550.6	469.8
Costs & Expenses	2,166.9	1,827.3	1,660.6	1,585.0	1,499.4	1,303.4	407.8
Depreciation & Amort.	190.1	179.0	153.6	128.1	106.3	82.0	23.1
Operating Income	d12.6	204.6	209.1	161.8	68.7	154.7	38.9
Net Interest Inc./(Exp.)	0.5	d9.8	d12.9	d21.6	d34.0	d43.6	d18.8
Income Before Income Taxes	24.7	206.2	194.3	140.0	34.5	108.4	19.7
Income Taxes	17.1	86.8	85.8	65.0	24.9	53.6	11.9
Net Income	7.7	[1] 119.4	[1] 108.6	75.0	[2][3] 9.6	[2][3] 54.8	7.8
Cash Flow	197.8	298.4	262.2	203.1	115.9	136.8	30.9
Average Shs. Outstg. (000)	35,688	39,432	45,208	46,071	47,635	47,666	45,127
BALANCE SHEET (IN MILLIONS):							
Cash & Cash Equivalents	194.8	127.8	135.8	172.3	176.6	224.4	182.6
Total Current Assets	431.1	338.0	302.1	323.9	351.8	365.4	293.5
Net Property	754.3	707.7	762.0	695.4	670.6	602.1	554.5
Total Assets	1,568.5	1,507.2	1,525.0	1,546.8	1,597.7	1,588.7	1,545.1
Total Current Liabilities	614.2	498.8	535.3	485.9	522.7	435.8	341.4
Long-Term Obligations	145.6	155.2	207.9	272.8	330.1	374.0	465.6
Net Stockholders' Equity	667.1	714.2	669.5	683.6	622.8	649.5	595.4
Net Working Capital	d183.1	d160.8	d233.2	d162.0	d170.9	d70.4	d47.9
Year-end Shs. Outstg. (000)	32,657	49,662	46,380	45,982	45,826	45,229	43,936
STATISTICAL RECORD:							
Operating Profit Margin %	...	9.3	10.3	8.6	3.9	10.0	8.3
Net Profit Margin %	0.3	5.4	5.4	4.0	0.6	3.5	1.7
Return on Equity %	1.2	16.7	16.2	11.0	1.5	8.4	1.3
Return on Assets %	0.5	7.9	7.1	4.8	0.6	3.4	0.5
Debt/Total Assets %	9.3	10.3	13.6	17.6	20.7	23.5	30.1
Price Range	20.94-8.94	24.13-16.00	31.31-9.56	18.88-12.00	23.75-10.88	19.00-6.38	16.38-6.38
P/E Ratio	95.1-40.6	8.0-5.3	13.0-4.0	11.6-7.4	113.0-51.8	16.1-5.4	96.3-37.5

Statistics are as originally reported. [1] Incl. Leisure Company expense, 1999, $52.9 mill.; 1998, $39.5 mill. [2] Incl. nonrecurr. special chrg., 1996, $65.1 mill.; 1995, $10.5 mill. [3] Bef. extraord. chrg., 1996, $1.1 mill.; 1995, $984,000

OFFICERS:
W. A. Franke, Chmn., Pres., C.E.O.
T. K. MacGillivray, Sr. V.P., C.F.O.

PRINCIPAL OFFICE: 111 West Rio Salado Parkway, Tempe, AZ 85281

TELEPHONE NUMBER: (480) 693-0800
FAX: (602) 997-9875
WEB: www.americawest.com
NO. OF EMPLOYEES: 11,337 full-time; 2,809 part-time
SHAREHOLDERS: 3 (class A); 7,844 (approx. class B)
ANNUAL MEETING: In May
INCORPORATED: DE, Sept., 1981

INSTITUTIONAL HOLDINGS:
No. of Institutions: 91
Shares Held: 24,544,195
% Held: 73.0

INDUSTRY: Air transportation, scheduled (SIC: 4512)

TRANSFER AGENT(S): Computershare Investor Services, Los Angeles, CA

NYSE SYMBOL AXL
Rec. Pr. 9.25 (3/31/01)

AMERICAN AXLE & MANUFACTURING HOLDINGS, INC.

YIELD ...
P/E RATIO 3.6

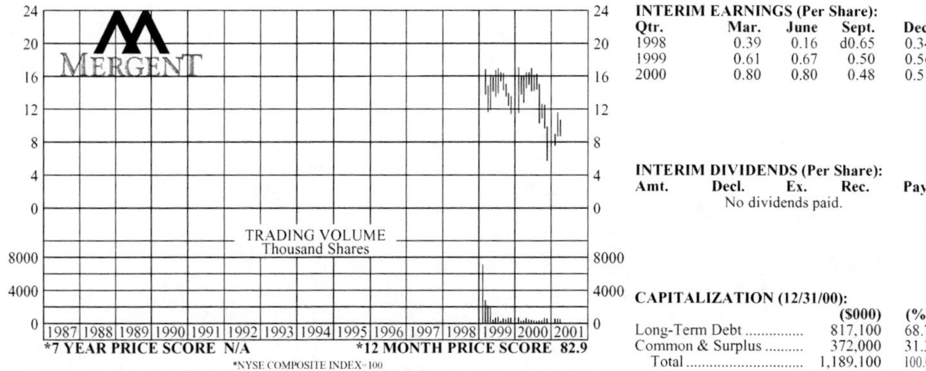

*7 YEAR PRICE SCORE N/A *12 MONTH PRICE SCORE 82.9

*NYSE COMPOSITE INDEX=100

INTERIM EARNINGS (Per Share):

Qtr.	Mar.	June	Sept.	Dec.
1998	0.39	0.16	d0.65	0.34
1999	0.61	0.67	0.50	0.56
2000	0.80	0.80	0.48	0.51

INTERIM DIVIDENDS (Per Share):

Amt.	Decl.	Ex.	Rec.	Pay.

No dividends paid.

CAPITALIZATION (12/31/00):

	($000)	(%)
Long-Term Debt	817,100	68.7
Common & Surplus	372,000	31.3
Total	1,189,100	100.0

RECENT DEVELOPMENTS: For the year ended 12/31/00, the Company reported net income of $129.2 million, an increase of 11.8% versus $115.6 million in the previous year. Net sales rose 3.9% to $3.07 billion compared with $2.95 billion a year earlier. Operating income grew 9.1% to $259.4 million due to strong demand for value-added technology products, operating efficiencies, and successful production start-ups at manufacturing facilities located in Guanajuato, Mexico and Cheektowaga, New York.

PROSPECTS: On 1/11/01, AXL was awarded a new forging contract with Stanadyne Automotive. Beginning in 2001, MSP Industries Corporation, an AXL subsidiary, will manufacture forgings for a new Stanadyne diesel engine fuel pump shaft. During 2000, AXL was awarded contracts with 10 customers to forge and machine more than 30 components. These new contracts should generate revenues of more than $60.0 million on an annual basis. In 2001, AXL expects earnings to reach $2.02 per share.

BUSINESS

AMERICAN AXLE & MANUFACTURING HOLDINGS, INC., formerly the final drive and forge business unit of General Motors, is the parent company of Colfor Manufacturing, Inc., MSP Industries Corporation and Albion Automotive Holdings Limited. The Company, through its subsidiaries, is a Tier 1 supplier of driveline systems, chassis systems and forged products for trucks, buses, passenger cars and sport utility vehicles. The Company's driveline products include axles, propeller shafts, chassis components, forged products and other products for rear-wheel drive passenger cars. Albion Automotive (Holdings) Limited supplies front steerable and rear axles, driving heads, crankshafts, chassis components and transmission parts used in medium-duty trucks and buses for customers located in the United Kingdom and Europe. AXL operates 17 manufacturing facilities located in the U.S., Brazil, Mexico and the United Kingdom.

QUARTERLY DATA

(12/31/00)($000)	Rev	Inc
1st Quarter	835,900	40,100
2nd Quarter	819,700	40,000
3rd Quarter	675,500	24,200
4th Quarter	738,400	24,900

ANNUAL FINANCIAL DATA

	12/31/00	12/31/99	12/31/98	[2] 12/31/97	[2] 12/31/96	[2] 12/31/95
Earnings Per Share	**2.60**	**2.34**	**0.08**	**[1] 0.43**	**0.58**	**0.85**
Cash Flow Per Share	**4.77**	**4.14**	**1.67**	**0.83**	**1.01**	**1.15**
Tang. Book Val. Per Share	**8.51**	**5.69**	**1.24**	**4.54**	**11.88**	**...**
INCOME STATEMENT (IN MILLIONS):						
Total Revenues	3,069.5	2,953.1	2,040.6	2,147.5	2,022.3	1,968.1
Costs & Expenses	2,702.2	2,621.5	1,921.6	1,981.1	1,892.7	1,833.9
Depreciation & Amort.	107.9	89.5	68.8	50.2	36.1	25.2
Operating Income	259.4	242.1	50.2	116.1	93.5	108.9
Net Interest Inc./(Exp.)	d58.8	d54.6	d44.3	d1.8	9.4	9.1
Income Before Income Taxes	203.4	183.4	5.6	94.2	98.3	118.0
Income Taxes	74.2	67.8	2.1	38.9	36.6	47.4
Net Income	129.2	115.6	3.5	[1] 55.3	61.7	70.6
Cash Flow	237.1	205.1	72.3	105.3	84.2	95.8
Average Shs. Outstg. (000)	49,700	49,500	43,200	126,508	83,054	83,054
BALANCE SHEET (IN MILLIONS):						
Cash & Cash Equivalents	35.2	140.2	4.5	17.3	126.0	...
Total Current Assets	500.6	509.5	294.0	289.2	340.7	...
Net Property	1,200.1	929.0	829.3	649.8	419.4	...
Total Assets	1,902.5	1,677.1	1,226.2	1,017.7	771.2	...
Total Current Liabilities	510.3	446.7	362.9	386.0	237.5	...
Long-Term Obligations	817.1	774.9	693.4	507.0	2.4	...
Net Stockholders' Equity	372.0	263.7	40.4	37.2	450.2	...
Net Working Capital	d9.7	62.8	d68.9	d96.8	103.3	...
Year-end Shs. Outstg. (000)	43,700	46,357	32,456	8,209	21,053	...
STATISTICAL RECORD:						
Operating Profit Margin %	8.5	8.2	2.5	5.4	4.6	5.5
Net Profit Margin %	4.2	3.9	0.2	2.6	3.1	3.6
Return on Equity %	34.7	43.8	8.7	148.4	13.7	...
Return on Assets %	6.8	6.9	0.3	5.4	8.0	...
Debt/Total Assets %	42.9	46.2	56.5	49.8	0.3	...
Price Range	17.13-5.75	17.38-11.38	...	...	...	...
P/E Ratio	6.6-2.2	7.4-4.9	...	...	...	...

Statistics are as originally reported. [1] Incl. pre-tax nonrecurr. chrg. $15.9 mill. [2] Financials for American Axle & Manufacturing of Michigan, Inc.

OFFICERS:
R. E. Dauch, Chmn., C.E.O.
J. D. Robinson, Pres., C.O.O.
R. J. Adams, Exec. V.P., C.F.O.

INVESTOR CONTACT: Robert A. Krause, Investor Relations, (313) 974-3074

PRINCIPAL OFFICE: 1840 Holbrook Avenue, Detroit, MI 48212-3488

TELEPHONE NUMBER: (313) 974-2000
FAX: (313) 974-3090
WEB: www.aam.com

NO. OF EMPLOYEES: 11,654 (approx.)

SHAREHOLDERS: 350 (approx.)

ANNUAL MEETING: In May

INCORPORATED: DE, 1998

INSTITUTIONAL HOLDINGS:
No. of Institutions: 43
Shares Held: 5,796,321
% Held: 13.2

INDUSTRY: Motor vehicle parts and accessories (SIC: 3714)

TRANSFER AGENT(S): First Chicago Trust Company, a Division of EquiServe, Jersey City, NJ

NYSE SYMBOL AEP
Rec. Pr. 50.20 (5/31/01)

AMERICAN ELECTRIC POWER COMPANY, INC.

YIELD 4.8%
P/E RATIO 24.5

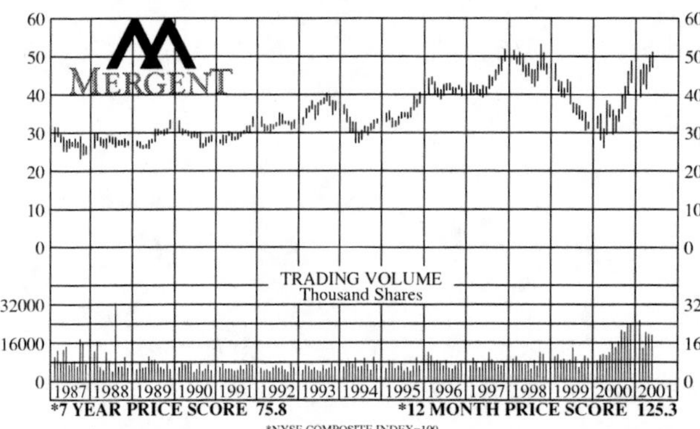

*7 YEAR PRICE SCORE 75.8 *12 MONTH PRICE SCORE 125.3

*NYSE COMPOSITE INDEX=100

INTERIM EARNINGS (Per Share):

Qtr.	Mar.	June	Sept.	Dec.
1996	0.96	0.60	0.87	0.71
1997	0.92	0.64	1.07	0.66
1998	0.79	0.62	1.02	0.38
1999	0.79	0.46	0.90	0.55
2000	0.53	d0.06	1.25	0.33

INTERIM DIVIDENDS (Per Share):

Amt.	Decl.	Ex.	Rec.	Pay.
0.60Q	4/26/00	5/08/00	5/10/00	6/09/00
0.60Q	7/26/00	8/08/00	8/10/00	9/08/00
0.60Q	10/25/00	11/08/00	11/10/00	12/08/00
0.60Q	1/24/01	2/07/01	2/09/01	3/09/01
0.60Q	4/25/01	5/08/01	5/10/01	6/08/01

Indicated div.: $2.40 (Div. Reinv. Plan)

CAPITALIZATION (12/31/00):

	($000)	(%)
Long-Term Debt	9,602,000	41.7
Deferred Income Tax	4,875,000	21.2
Redeemable Pfd. Stock	334,000	1.5
Preferred Stock	161,000	0.7
Common & Surplus	8,054,000	35.0
Total	23,026,000	100.0

RECENT DEVELOPMENTS: For the year ended 12/31/00, the Company reported income from continuing operations of $302.0 million versus income from continuing operations of $986.0 million in 1999. Results for 2000 and 1999 excluded after-tax extraordinary losses of $35.0 million and $14.0 million, respectively. Total revenues advanced 10.4% to $13.69 billion. Revenues from domestic electric utility operations grew 10.1% to $10.83 billion, while worldwide electric and gas operations increased 11.6% to $2.87 billion.

PROSPECTS: On 1/11/01, AEP announced that it has executed a definitive agreement to acquire Houston Pipe Line Company. Recently, AEP agreed to sell its Frontera plant to TECO Power Services for about $265.0 million in cash. The sale was required by the Federal Energy Regulatory Commission to address market power issues related to AEP's acquisition of Central and South West Corp. Going forward, AEP plans to separate its regulated and nonregulated businesses by the beginning of 2002.

BUSINESS

AMERICAN ELECTRIC POWER COMPANY, INC. is a holding company that controls one of the largest electric systems in the country, providing energy to 4.8 million customers in parts of Arkansas, Indiana, Kentucky, Louisiana, Michigan, Ohio, Oklahoma, Tennessee, Texas, Virginia and West Virginia. AEP's electric utility subsidiaries own or lease generating stations with total generating capacity of more than 38,000 megawatts. The Company serves more than 4.0 million customers outside the U.S. through holdings in Australia, Brazil, China, Mexico and the U.K. The Company has expanded its business to non-regulated energy activities through several subsidiaries including AEP Energy Services, Inc., AEP Resources, Inc., AEP Resources Service Company, and AEP Communications. On 6/15/00, AEP acquired Central and South West Corporation.

BUSINESS LINE ANALYSIS

(12/31/00)	Rev	Rev
Domestic regulated electric	10,827	79.1
Worldwide electric & gas	2,867	20.9
Total	13,694	100.0

ANNUAL FINANCIAL DATA

	12/31/00	12/31/99	12/31/98	12/31/97	12/31/96	12/31/95	12/31/94
Earnings Per Share	**3 0.94**	**2 2.69**	**2.81**	**1 3.28**	**3.14**	**2.85**	**2.71**
Cash Flow Per Share	**5.12**	**5.61**	**6.14**	**6.56**	**6.59**	**6.25**	**5.75**
Tang. Book Val. Per Share	**20.72**	**25.79**	**25.24**	**24.62**	**24.15**	**23.25**	**22.83**
Dividends Per Share	**2.40**	**2.40**	**2.40**	**2.40**	**2.40**	**2.40**	**2.40**
Dividend Payout %	**255.3**	**89.2**	**85.4**	**73.2**	**76.4**	**84.2**	**88.6**
INCOME STATEMENT (IN MILLIONS):							
Total Revenues	13,694.0	6,916.0	6,345.9	5,879.8	5,849.2	5,670.3	5,504.7
Costs & Expenses	10,321.0	5,048.0	3,895.7	3,450.6	3,350.1	3,260.4	3,249.7
Depreciation & Amort.	1,347.0	563.0	634.3	620.2	646.1	631.5	561.2
Maintenance Exp.	...	...	542.9	483.3	502.8	541.8	544.3
Operating Income	2,026.0	1,305.0	956.7	984.5	1,008.0	964.5	932.2
Net Interest Inc./(Exp.)	...	...	d419.1	d405.8	d381.3	d400.1	d389.0
Income Taxes	597.0	260.0	316.2	341.3	342.2	272.0	217.2
Net Income	3 302.0	2 520.0	536.2	1 620.4	587.4	529.9	500.0
Cash Flow	1,649.0	1,083.0	1,170.5	1,240.6	1,233.5	1,161.4	1,061.2
Average Shs. Outstg. (000)	322,000	193,000	190,774	189,039	187,321	185,847	184,666
BALANCE SHEET (IN MILLIONS):							
Gross Property	38,088.0	22,205.0	20,146.3	19,596.5	18,970.2	18,496.0	18,174.6
Accumulated Depreciation	15,695.0	9,150.0	8,416.4	7,963.6	7,549.8	7,111.1	6,826.5
Net Property	22,393.0	13,055.0	12,571.3	11,695.1	11,420.4	11,384.8	11,348.1
Total Assets	54,548.0	21,488.0	19,483.2	16,615.3	15,885.5	15,902.3	15,712.7
Long-Term Obligations	9,602.0	6,336.0	6,799.6	5,129.5	4,796.8	4,920.3	4,686.6
Net Stockholders' Equity	8,215.0	5,170.0	4,887.8	4,724.0	4,635.7	4,488.0	4,462.9
Year-end Shs. Outstg. (000)	322,019	194,103	191,816	189,989	188,235	186,635	185,235
STATISTICAL RECORD:							
Operating Profit Margin %	14.8	18.9	15.1	16.7	17.2	17.0	16.9
Net Profit Margin %	2.2	7.5	8.4	10.6	10.0	9.3	9.1
Net Inc./Net Property %	1.3	4.0	4.3	5.3	5.1	4.7	4.4
Net Inc./Tot. Capital %	1.3	3.6	3.7	4.9	4.7	4.2	4.1
Return on Equity %	3.7	10.1	11.0	13.1	12.7	11.8	11.2
Accum. Depr./Gross Prop. %	41.2	41.2	41.8	40.6	39.8	38.4	37.6
Price Range	48.94-25.94	48.19-30.56	53.31-42.06	52.00-39.13	44.75-38.63	40.63-31.25	37.38-27.25
P/E Ratio	52.1-27.6	17.9-11.4	19.0-15.0	15.9-11.9	14.3-12.3	14.3-11.0	13.8-10.1
Average Yield %	6.4	6.1	5.0	5.3	5.8	6.7	7.4

Statistics are as originally reported. 1 Bef. extraord. chrg. of $109.4 mill. ($0.58/sh) 2 Incl. a chrg of $0.43 per share from restart efforts net of deferrals under Indiana and Michigan settle. agree. 3 Bef. net after-tax extraord. loss of $35.0 mill. & incl. spec. chrgs. of $264.0 mill.

OFFICERS:
E. L. Draper Jr., Chmn., Pres., C.E.O.
T. V. Shockely III, Vice-Chmn.
H. W. Fayne, Exec. V.P., C.F.O.

INVESTOR CONTACT: Bette Jo Rozsa, (614) 223-2840

PRINCIPAL OFFICE: 1 Riverside Plaza, Columbus, OH 43215-2373

TELEPHONE NUMBER: (614) 223-1000
FAX: (614) 223-1823
WEB: www.aep.com
NO. OF EMPLOYEES: 26,376 (avg.)
SHAREHOLDERS: 160,000 (approx.)
ANNUAL MEETING: In Apr.
INCORPORATED: NY, Dec., 1906; reincorp., NY, Feb., 1925

INSTITUTIONAL HOLDINGS:
No. of Institutions: 409
Shares Held: 198,246,047
% Held: 61.6

INDUSTRY: Electric services (SIC: 4911)

TRANSFER AGENT(S): EquiServe, First Chicago Division, Jersey City, NJ

NYSE SYMBOL AXP
Rec. Pr. 42.44 (4/30/01)

AMERICAN EXPRESS COMPANY

YIELD 0.8%
P/E RATIO 20.6

*7 YEAR PRICE SCORE 131.0 *12 MONTH PRICE SCORE 82.4

*NYSE COMPOSITE INDEX=100

INTERIM EARNINGS (Per Share):

Qtr.	Mar.	June	Sept.	Dec.
1996	0.27	0.31	0.32	0.41
1997	0.31	0.36	0.37	0.35
1998	0.33	0.41	0.42	0.39
1999	0.42	0.47	0.47	0.44
2000	0.48	0.54	0.54	0.50

INTERIM DIVIDENDS (Per Share):

Amt.	Decl.	Ex.	Rec.	Pay.
0.08Q	5/22/00	7/05/00	7/07/00	8/10/00
0.08Q	9/25/00	10/04/00	10/06/00	11/10/00
0.08Q	11/27/00	1/03/01	1/05/01	2/09/01
0.08Q	3/26/01	4/04/01	4/06/01	5/10/01
0.08Q	5/23/01	7/03/01	7/06/01	8/10/01

Indicated div.: $0.32 (Div. Reinv. Plan)

CAPITALIZATION (12/31/00):

	($000)	(%)
Long-Term Debt	4,711,000	28.7
Common & Surplus	11,684,000	71.3
Total	16,395,000	100.0

RECENT DEVELOPMENTS: For the year ended 12/31/00, net income totaled $2.81 billion, up 13.5% versus $2.48 billion in the prior year. Consolidated revenues increased 22.8% to $23.68 billion from $19.28 billion the year before. Travel Related Services net revenues grew 14.5% to $17.44 billion, while net income improved 14.0% to $1.93 billion. American Express Financial Advisors' net revenues rose 12.9% to $4.22 billion and net income climbed 10.4% to $1.03 billion.

PROSPECTS: On 3/30/01, the Company announced that it has completed its acquisition of SierraCities.com Inc., an equipment finance company, for approximately $107.5 million. This acquisition should significantly expand AXP's existing equipment financing business and enhance its ability to provide products and services to small companies. Going forward, earnings for 2001 are expected to be hampered by the continued decline in the equity markets.

BUSINESS

AMERICAN EXPRESS COMPANY operates in three primary divisions and is a leader in charge cards, travelers checks, travel products and services, financial planning and international banking. The Travel Related Services division (78% of 2000 revenues) provides, among other things, global network services, the American Express® Card and other consumer and corporate lending products, and corporate and consumer travel products and services. The Financial Advisors division (19%) provides financial planning and advice, a variety of investment products, personal insurance, and retail brokerage services. The American Express Bank (3%) provides financial services for corporations, financial institutions and retail customers, including American Express Travelers Cheques.

ANNUAL FINANCIAL DATA

	12/31/00	12/31/99	12/31/98	12/31/97	12/31/96	12/31/95	12/31/94
Earnings Per Share	**2.07**	**1.81**	**1.54**	**1.38**	**2 1.30**	**1.04**	**1 0.89**
Cash Flow Per Share	**2.07**	**1.81**	**1.54**	**1.39**	**1.30**	**1.05**	**0.90**
Tang. Book Val. Per Share	**8.81**	**7.53**	**7.18**	**6.84**	**6.01**	**5.53**	**4.19**
Dividends Per Share	**0.32**	**0.30**	**0.30**	**0.30**	**0.30**	**0.30**	**0.32**
Dividend Payout %	**15.2**	**16.6**	**19.4**	**21.7**	**23.1**	**28.9**	**35.5**
INCOME STATEMENT (IN MILLIONS):							
Total Revenues	23,675.0	21,278.0	19,132.0	17,760.0	16,237.0	15,841.0	14,282.0
Costs & Expenses	18,413.0	16,789.0	15,208.0	14,086.0	12,457.0	12,416.0	11,380.0
Operating Income	5,262.0	4,489.0	3,924.0	3,674.0	3,780.0	3,425.0	2,902.0
Net Interest Inc./(Exp.)	d1,354.0	d1,051.0	d999.0	d924.0	d1,116.0	d1,242.0	d1,011.0
Income Before Income Taxes	3,908.0	3,438.0	2,925.0	2,750.0	2,664.0	2,183.0	1,891.0
Income Taxes	1,098.0	963.0	784.0	759.0	763.0	619.0	511.0
Net Income	2,810.0	2,475.0	2,141.0	1,991.0	2 1,901.0	1,564.0	1 1,380.0
Cash Flow	2,810.0	2,475.0	2,141.0	1,991.0	1,895.0	1,549.0	1,348.0
Average Shs. Outstg. (000)	1,360,000	1,368,000	1,389,000	1,437,000	1,456,800	1,494,000	1,526,445
BALANCE SHEET (IN MILLIONS):							
Cash & Cash Equivalents	8,487.0	7,471.0	4,092.0	4,179.0	2,677.0	3,200.0	3,433.0
Total Current Assets	39,030.0	33,938.0	26,316.0	25,953.0	23,168.0	23,114.0	20,580.0
Net Property	2,506.0	1,996.0	1,637.0	1,533.0	1,675.0	1,783.0	1,840.0
Total Assets	154,423.0	148,517.0	126,933.0	120,003.0	108,512.0	107,405.0	97,006.0
Total Current Liabilities	63,522.0	56,346.0	44,199.0	40,524.0	38,396.0	37,926.0	34,322.0
Long-Term Obligations	4,711.0	5,995.0	7,019.0	7,873.0	6,552.0	7,570.0	7,162.0
Net Stockholders' Equity	11,684.0	10,095.0	9,698.0	9,574.0	8,528.0	8,220.0	6,433.0
Net Working Capital	d24,492.0	d22,408.0	d17,883.0	d14,571.0	d15,228.0	d14,812.0	d13,742.0
Year-end Shs. Outstg. (000)	1,326,000	1,340,700	1,351,500	1,399,200	1,418,700	1,449,324	1,487,598
STATISTICAL RECORD:							
Operating Profit Margin %	22.2	21.1	20.5	20.7	23.3	21.6	20.3
Net Profit Margin %	11.9	11.6	11.2	11.2	11.7	9.9	9.7
Return on Equity %	24.0	24.5	22.1	20.8	22.3	19.0	21.5
Return on Assets %	1.8	1.7	1.7	1.7	1.8	1.5	1.4
Debt/Total Assets %	3.1	4.0	5.5	6.6	6.0	7.0	7.4
Price Range	63.00-39.83	56.29-31.62	39.54-22.33	30.50-17.87	20.12-12.87	15.04-9.67	11.04-8.42
P/E Ratio	30.4-19.2	31.1-17.5	25.6-14.5	22.0-12.9	15.5-9.9	14.5-9.3	12.4-9.4
Average Yield %	0.6	0.7	1.0	1.2	1.8	2.4	3.3

Statistics are as originally reported. Adj. for stk. split: 3-for-1, 5/00 1 Bef. disc. oper gain $33.0 mill. 2 Incl. non-recurr. credit $162.0 mill.

OFFICERS:
H. Golub, Chmn.
K. I. Chenault, Pres., C.E.O.
G. L. Crittenden, Exec. V.P., C.F.O.

INVESTOR CONTACT: Investor Relations, (212) 640-2000

PRINCIPAL OFFICE: World Financial Center, 200 Vesey Street, New York, NY 10285

TELEPHONE NUMBER: (212) 640-2000
FAX: (212) 619-9230
WEB: www.americanexpress.com

NO. OF EMPLOYEES: 89,000 (approx.)

SHAREHOLDERS: 53,884

ANNUAL MEETING: In April

INCORPORATED: NY, June, 1965

INSTITUTIONAL HOLDINGS:
No. of Institutions: 916
Shares Held: 871,150,658
% Held: 65.3

INDUSTRY: Misc. business credit institutions (SIC: 6159)

TRANSFER AGENT(S): Mellon Investor Services, Ridgefield Park, NJ

NYSE SYMBOL AFG
Rec. Pr. 26.59 (4/30/01)

AMERICAN FINANCIAL GROUP, INC.

YIELD 3.8%
P/E RATIO . . .

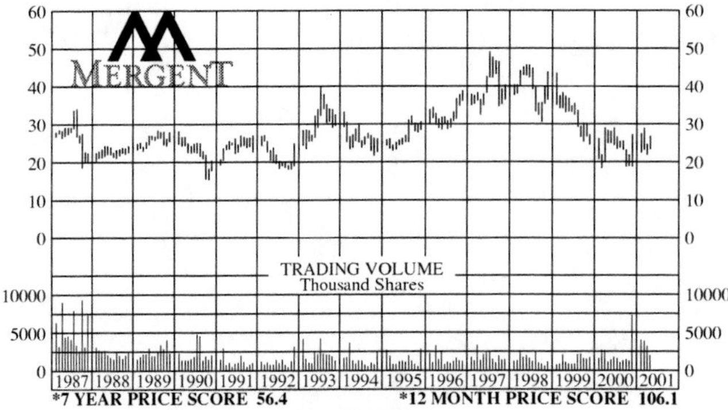

MERGENT

TRADING VOLUME
Thousand Shares

1987 1988 1989 1990 1991 1992 1993 1994 1995 1996 1997 1998 1999 2000 2001

*7 YEAR PRICE SCORE 56.4 *12 MONTH PRICE SCORE 106.1

*NYSE COMPOSITE INDEX=100

INTERIM EARNINGS (Per Share):

Qtr.	Mar.	June	Sept.	Dec.
1996	1.35	0.96	2.00	0.02
1997	1.03	1.03	0.57	0.68
1998	1.08	0.65	0.91	d0.63
1999	0.96	0.74	0.48	0.24
2000	0.76	0.28	d0.38	d1.43

INTERIM DIVIDENDS (Per Share):

Amt.	Decl.	Ex.	Rec.	Pay.
0.25Q	4/05/00	4/12/00	4/15/00	4/25/00
0.25Q	7/05/00	7/12/00	7/15/00	7/25/00
0.25Q	10/02/00	10/11/00	10/15/00	10/25/00
0.25Q	1/02/01	1/10/01	1/15/01	1/25/01
0.25Q	4/02/01	4/10/01	4/15/01	4/25/01

Indicated div.: $1.00 (Div. Reinv. Plan)

CAPITALIZATION (12/31/00):

	($000)	(%)
Long-Term Debt	779,956	27.5
Minority Interest	508,033	17.9
Common & Surplus	1,548,530	54.6
Total	2,836,519	100.0

RECENT DEVELOPMENTS: For the year ended 12/31/00, the Company reported a loss of $47.0 million, before an accounting charge of $9.1 million, versus income of $146.9 million, before an extraordinary loss of $1.7 million and an accounting charge of $3.8 million, in 1999. Operating revenues amounted to $3.82 billion, up 13.6% versus $3.31 billion a year earlier. Property and casualty net premiums-written jumped 16.6% to $2.64 billion. The combined ratio was 108.0% versus 102.0% in the prior year.

PROSPECTS: On 4/2/01, AFG's insurance subsidiary, Great American Insurance Company, announced the completion of the sale of its Japanese Division to Mitsui Marine and Fire Insurance Company of America, for $22.0 million. This transaction should enable Great American to redirect statutory capital and surplus to other strategically targeted areas. AFG expects to record a net after-tax loss of $6.0 million from this sale.

BUSINESS

AMERICAN FINANCIAL GROUP, INC. (formerly American Premier Group, Inc.) is a holding company for American Premier Underwriters, Inc., which acquired American Financial Corporation on 4/3/95. American Premier Underwriters, Inc. is a specialty property and casualty insurance company. Principal operations are conducted by a group of non-standard private passenger automobile insurance companies and by Republic Indemnity Company of America, a California workers' compensation insurance company. American Financial Corporation is engaged primarily in multi-line property and casualty insurance businesses and in the sale of tax-deferred annuities.

ANNUAL FINANCIAL DATA

	12/31/00	12/31/99	12/31/98	12/31/97	12/31/96	[3] 12/31/95	12/31/94
Earnings Per Share	[5] d0.80	[4] 2.44	[2] 2.01	[2] 3.28	[2] 4.31	[2] 3.87	[1] 0.02
Tang. Book Val. Per Share	6.92	5.94	15.93	13.78	13.49	11.74	22.95
Dividends Per Share	1.00	1.00	1.00	. . .	. . .	. . .	. . .
Dividend Payout %	. . .	41.0	49.7	. . .	. . .	. . .	. . .
INCOME STATEMENT (IN MILLIONS):							
Total Premium Income	2,725.3	2,334.7	2,869.1	2,945.9	2,948.1	2,648.7	1,557.9
Other Income	1,092.0	999.7	1,180.9	1,074.8	1,167.3	980.9	209.5
Total Revenues	3,817.3	3,334.5	4,050.0	4,020.7	4,115.4	3,629.6	1,767.4
Income Before Income Taxes	109.9	302.1	204.8	319.6	353.2	246.9	41.2
Income Taxes	29.0	98.2	79.6	120.1	91.3	56.5	40.4
Equity Earnings/Minority Int.	d127.8	d56.9	. . .	. . .	. . .	. . .	. . .
Net Income	[5] d47.0	[4] 147.0	[2] 125.2	[2] 199.5	[2] 262.0	[2] 190.4	[1] 0.8
Average Shs. Outstg. (000)	59,074	60,210	62,185	60,748	60,801	47,620	48,000
BALANCE SHEET (IN MILLIONS):							
Cash & Cash Equivalents	11,012.7	10,822.5	11,243.5	11,557.0	10,961.3	10,641.4	287.5
Premiums Due	213.5	217.2	220.5	513.7	568.8	631.4	438.7
Invst. Assets: Fixed-term	. . .	. . .	. . .	. . .	. . .	. . .	2,421.6
Invst. Assets: Equities	. . .	. . .	. . .	. . .	. . .	. . .	11.7
Invst. Assets: Total	10,574.0	10,431.9	10,946.8	11,299.9	10,513.0	10,097.0	2,684.1
Total Assets	16,415.5	16,054.1	15,845.2	15,755.3	15,051.1	14,953.9	4,194.0
Long-Term Obligations	780.0	732.7	592.4	580.7	517.9	882.1	507.3
Net Stockholders' Equity	1,548.5	1,340.0	1,716.2	1,662.7	1,554.4	1,440.1	1,548.7
Year-end Shs. Outstg. (000)	67,410	58,420	60,928	61,049	61,072	60,139	46,282
STATISTICAL RECORD:							
Return on Revenues %	. . .	4.4	3.1	5.0	6.4	5.2	. . .
Return on Equity %	. . .	11.0	7.3	12.0	16.9	13.2	0.1
Return on Assets %	. . .	0.9	0.8	1.3	1.7	1.3	. . .
Price Range	29.00-18.38	43.63-24.50	45.75-30.50	49.25-32.38	38.88-28.50	32.13-22.88	33.25-21.63
P/E Ratio	. . .	17.9-10.0	22.8-15.2	15.0-9.9	9.0-6.6	8.3-5.9	1,654.2-1,075.9
Average Yield %	4.2	2.9	2.6	. . .	. . .	. . .	. . .

Statistics are as originally reported. [1] Bef. disc. oper. loss $0.5 mill. [2] Bef. extraord. chrg. 1998, $0.7 mill.; 1997, $7.2 mill.; 1996, $28.7 mill.; credit 1995, $0.8 mill. [3] Refl. the merger of American Financial Corp. and American Premier Underwriters, Inc. [4] Incl. a net gain $14.0 mill. & excl. a loss $3.8 mill. for an acctg. change & an extraord. loss $1.7 mill. [5] Excl. loss of $9.1 mill. for acctg. chrg.

OFFICERS:
C. H. Lindner, Chmn., C.E.O.
K. E. Lindner, Co-Pres.
S. C. Lindner, Co-Pres.
C. H. Lindner III, Co-Pres.

INVESTOR CONTACT: Investor Relations, (513) 579-6739

PRINCIPAL OFFICE: One East Fourth Street, Suite 919, Cincinnati, OH 45202

TELEPHONE NUMBER: (513) 579-2121
FAX: (513) 579-0108
WEB: www.amfnl.com

NO. OF EMPLOYEES: 10,600 (approx.)

SHAREHOLDERS: 14,200 (approx.)

ANNUAL MEETING: In May

INCORPORATED: OH, 1994

INSTITUTIONAL HOLDINGS:
No. of Institutions: 134
Shares Held: 31,750,103
% Held: 47.1

INDUSTRY: Fire, marine, and casualty insurance (SIC: 6331)

TRANSFER AGENT(S): Securities Transfer Company, Cincinnati, OH

NYSE SYMBOL AGC
Rec. Pr. 45.23 (5/31/01)

AMERICAN GENERAL CORPORATION

YIELD 2.1%
P/E RATIO 22.8

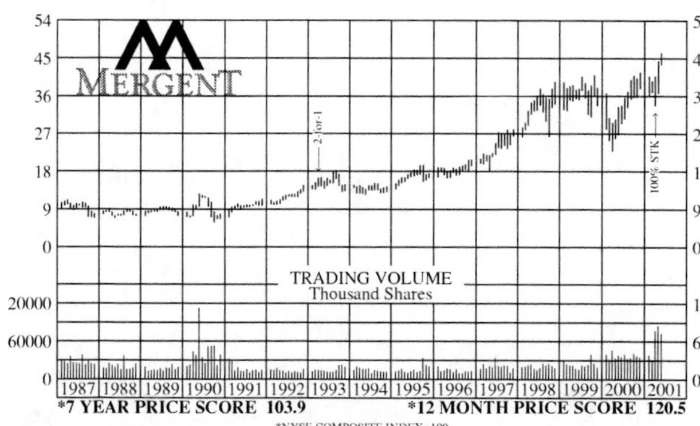

INTERIM EARNINGS (Per Share):

Qtr.	Mar.	June	Sept.	Dec.
1996	0.41	0.40	0.41	0.17
1997	0.44	d0.25	0.46	0.46
1998	0.48	0.51	0.49	Nil
1999	0.56	0.57	0.58	0.51
2000	0.56	0.19	0.63	0.60

INTERIM DIVIDENDS (Per Share):

Amt.	Decl.	Ex.	Rec.	Pay.
0.44Q	7/27/00	8/08/00	8/10/00	9/01/00
0.44Q	11/02/00	11/14/00	11/16/00	12/01/00
0.48Q	1/23/01	2/06/01	2/08/01	3/01/01
100% STK	1/23/01	3/02/01	2/08/01	3/01/01
0.24Q	4/26/01	5/08/01	5/10/01	6/01/01

Indicated div.: $0.96 (Div. Reinv. Plan)

CAPITALIZATION (12/31/00):

	($000)	(%)
Long-Term Debt	14,092,000	64.3
Common & Surplus	7,820,000	35.7
Total	21,912,000	100.0

RECENT DEVELOPMENTS: For the year ended 12/31/00, net income fell 11.3% to $1.00 billion compared with $1.13 billion in 1999. Results included realized investment losses of $114.0 million and $12.0 million in 2000 and 1999, respectively. Results for 2000 and 1999 also included non-recurring items of $193.0 million and $36.0 million, respectively. Total revenues amounted to $11.06 billion compared with $10.68 billion a year earlier. Operating earnings jumped 11.1% to $1.31 billion from $1.18 billion.

PROSPECTS: On 5/11/01, the Company announced that it has entered into a definitive agreement to be acquired by American International Group, Inc. Under the terms of the transaction, the Company's shareholders will receive $46.00 per AGC share held in AIG common stock, subject to a collar mechanism. Simultaneously, the Company terminated its previous merger agreement with Prudential plc, and paid Prudential the $600.0 million termination fee specified in that agreement. The transaction is expected to be completed by the end of the year.

BUSINESS

AMERICAN GENERAL CORPORATION, with assets of $120.09 billion at 12/31/00, is one of the nation's largest consumer financial service organizations. It is a provider of retirement annuities, consumer loans, and life insurance. Variable Annuity Life Insurance Co., AGC's retirement annuity company, which contributed 39% of 2000 division earnings, is a provider of retirement plans for teachers and other employees of not-for-profit organizations. The consumer finance companies, 15%, offer a wide range of credit-related products and services. The life insurance segment, 46%, emphasizes the sale and service of both traditional and interest-sensitive life insurance and annuities. On June 30, 1997, AGC acquired USLIFE Corp. During 1998, AGC acquired Western National Corp.

ANNUAL FINANCIAL DATA

	12/31/00	12/31/99	[2] 12/31/98	12/31/97	12/31/96	12/31/95	12/31/94
Earnings Per Share	[1] 1.98	[1] 2.20	[1] 1.48	[1] 1.10	1.38	1.32	1.23
Tang. Book Val. Per Share	12.73	9.74	14.29	14.03	12.26	12.80	7.04
Dividends Per Share	0.88	0.80	0.75	0.70	0.65	0.62	0.58
Dividend Payout %	44.4	36.4	50.7	63.9	47.3	47.0	47.3
INCOME STATEMENT (IN MILLIONS):							
Total Premium Income	3,839.0	3,772.0	3,605.0	3,362.0	1,968.0	1,753.0	1,210.0
Net Investment Income	5,453.0	5,232.0	5,095.0	4,020.0	3,271.0	3,095.0	2,493.0
Other Income	1,771.0	1,675.0	1,551.0	1,545.0	1,608.0	1,604.0	1,138.0
Total Revenues	11,063.0	10,679.0	10,251.0	8,927.0	6,847.0	6,452.0	4,841.0
Policyholder Benefits	5,500.0	5,313.0	5,159.0	4,332.0	3,156.0	3,047.0	2,224.0
Income Before Income Taxes	1,674.0	1,887.0	1,323.0	1,073.0	964.0	850.0	802.0
Income Taxes	568.0	664.0	459.0	447.0	347.0	286.0	289.0
Equity Earnings/Minority Int.	...	...	d11.0	...	40.0	43.0	...
Net Income	[1] 1,003.0	[1] 1,131.0	[1] 764.0	[1] 542.0	577.0	545.0	513.0
Average Shs. Outstg. (000)	508,800	518,400	523,000	498,400	402,000	410,000	418,000
BALANCE SHEET (IN MILLIONS):							
Cash & Cash Equivalents	671.0	970.0	995.0	569.0	309.0	264.0	254.0
Invst. Assets: Fixed-term	64,132.0	60,625.0	62,731.0	47,747.0	38,490.0	37,213.0	25,700.0
Invst. Assets: Loans	18,114.0	17,091.0	15,354.0	13,440.0	4,698.0	4,646.0	3,848.0
Invst. Assets: Total	84,054.0	79,365.0	79,520.0	62,018.0	44,805.0	43,311.0	30,971.0
Total Assets	120,094.0	115,447.0	105,107.0	80,620.0	59,024.0	53,235.0	38,601.0
Long-Term Obligations	14,092.0	13,326.0	11,606.0	9,182.0	9,163.0	9,193.0	8,926.0
Net Stockholders' Equity	7,820.0	6,420.0	8,871.0	7,583.0	5,621.0	5,801.0	3,457.0
Year-end Shs. Outstg. (000)	500,700	496,200	503,600	486,000	406,000	408,000	406,000
STATISTICAL RECORD:							
Return on Revenues %	9.1	10.6	7.5	6.1	8.4	8.4	10.6
Return on Equity %	12.8	17.6	8.6	7.1	10.3	9.4	14.8
Return on Assets %	0.8	1.0	0.7	0.7	1.0	1.0	1.3
Price Range	41.72-22.81	41.09-30.94	39.50-26.16	28.13-18.25	20.88-16.44	19.56-13.75	15.25-12.44
P/E Ratio	21.1-11.5	18.7-14.1	26.7-17.7	25.7-16.7	15.2-12.0	14.8-10.4	12.4-10.2
Average Yield %	2.7	2.2	2.3	3.0	3.5	3.7	4.2

Statistics are as originally reported. Adj. for stk. split: 2-for-1, 3/01 [1] Incl. non-recurr. chrg. $193.0 mill., 12/00; $36.0 mill., 12/99; $56.0 mill., 12/98; $435.0 mill., 12/97 [2] Includes results of Western National Corporation, acquired on 2/25/98.

OFFICERS:
R. M. Devlin, Chmn., Pres., C.E.O.
J. A. Graf, Sr. Vice-Chmn.

INVESTOR CONTACT: Investor Relations, (800) 242-1111

PRINCIPAL OFFICE: 2929 Allen Parkway, Houston, TX 77019-2155

TELEPHONE NUMBER: (713) 522-1111
FAX: (713) 523-8531
WEB: www.americangeneral.com

NO. OF EMPLOYEES: 15,900 (approx.)

SHAREHOLDERS: 35,181

ANNUAL MEETING: In April
INCORPORATED: TX, Feb., 1980

INSTITUTIONAL HOLDINGS:
No. of Institutions: 507
Shares Held: 337,882,627
% Held: 67.7

INDUSTRY: Life insurance (SIC: 6311)

TRANSFER AGENT(S): First Chicago Trust Company of New York, Jersey City, NJ

NYSE SYMBOL AM
Rec. Pr. 11.51 (4/30/01)

AMERICAN GREETINGS CORPORATION

YIELD 3.5%
P/E RATIO . . .

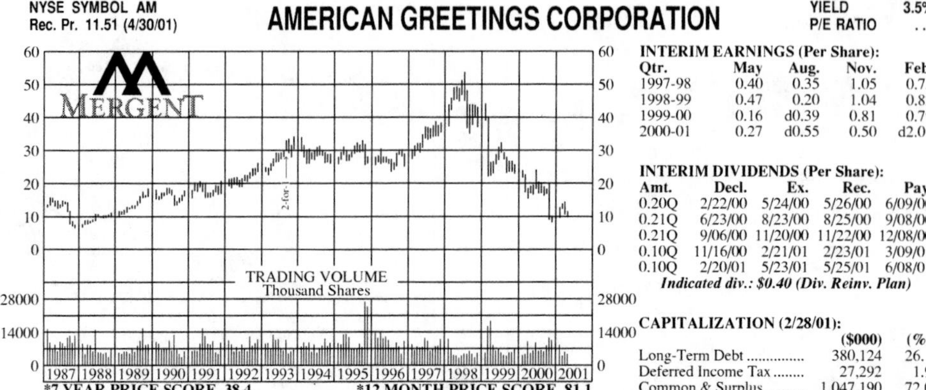

INTERIM EARNINGS (Per Share):

Qtr.	May	Aug.	Nov.	Feb.
1997-98	0.40	0.35	1.05	0.75
1998-99	0.47	0.20	1.04	0.82
1999-00	0.16	d0.39	0.81	0.79
2000-01	0.27	d0.55	0.50	d2.01

INTERIM DIVIDENDS (Per Share):

Amt.	Decl.	Ex.	Rec.	Pay.
0.20Q	2/22/00	5/24/00	5/26/00	6/09/00
0.21Q	6/23/00	8/23/00	8/25/00	9/08/00
0.21Q	9/06/00	11/20/00	11/22/00	12/08/00
0.10Q	11/16/00	2/21/01	2/23/01	3/09/01
0.10Q	2/20/01	5/23/01	5/25/01	6/08/01

Indicated div.: $0.40 (Div. Reinv. Plan)

CAPITALIZATION (2/28/01):

	($000)	(%)
Long-Term Debt	380,124	26.1
Deferred Income Tax	27,292	1.9
Common & Surplus	1,047,190	72.0
Total	1,454,606	100.0

RECENT DEVELOPMENTS: For the year ended 2/28/01, AM reported a loss of $92.7 million, before an after-tax accounting charge of $21.1 million, versus net income of $90.0 million in the previous year. Earnings for 2000 and 1999 included one-time, after-tax charges of $176.0 million and $4.8 million, respectively. Results for 2000 were adversely affected by consumer price resistance and continued retail inventory pressure. Net sales increased 15.8% to $2.52 billion from $2.18 billion a year earlier.

PROSPECTS: The Company announced plans to reduce its workforce by 13.0%, or 1,500, to lower costs and meet demand for cheaper cards. Moreover, AM intends to decrease product lines and consolidate six facilities. The restructuring, which is expected to be completed by the end of fiscal 2002, will result in a pre-tax charge of $200.0 million to $220.0 million. Beginning in fiscal 2003, the new structure should result in ongoing pre-tax savings of approximately $90.0 million.

BUSINESS

AMERICAN GREETINGS CORPORATION designs, manufactures and sells everyday and seasonal greeting cards and other social expression products. Greeting cards, gift wrap, paper party goods, candles, balloons, stationery and giftware are manufactured and sold in the U.S. by the Company, Plus Mark, Inc., Carlton Cards Retail, Inc. and Quality Greeting Card Distributing Company. AM also manufactures and sells its products in Canada, the United Kingdom, France, Mexico, Australia, New Zealand, and in South Africa. In March 1998, AM acquired U.K.-based Camden Graphics Corp. In May 1998, the Company acquired U.K.-based Hanson White Ltd. On 3/2/00, AM acquired Gibson Greetings, Inc.

ANNUAL FINANCIAL DATA

	2/28/01	2/29/00	2/28/99	2/28/98	2/28/97	2/29/96	2/28/95
Earnings Per Share	**2 d1.46**	**4 1.37**	**4 2.53**	**3 2.55**	**2.23**	**1 1.54**	**2.00**
Cash Flow Per Share	**0.08**	**2.35**	**3.48**	**3.43**	**3.10**	**2.56**	**2.92**
Tang. Book Val. Per Share	**12.87**	**14.18**	**15.57**	**18.90**	**18.16**	**16.53**	**15.61**
Dividends Per Share	**0.82**	**0.78**	**0.74**	**0.70**	**0.66**	**0.60**	**0.53**
Dividend Payout %	**. . .**	**56.9**	**29.2**	**27.4**	**29.6**	**39.0**	**26.5**
INCOME STATEMENT (IN MILLIONS):							
Total Revenues	2,518.8	2,175.2	2,205.7	2,212.1	2,172.3	2,012.0	1,878.4
Costs & Expenses	2,250.0	1,932.3	1,826.5	1,830.8	1,822.7	1,737.3	1,566.0
Depreciation & Amort.	98.1	64.3	67.0	65.9	64.6	75.3	68.4
Operating Income	170.8	178.5	312.2	315.4	285.1	199.3	244.0
Net Interest Inc./(Exp.)	d55.4	d34.3	d29.3	d23.0	d30.7	d24.3	d16.9
Income Before Income Taxes	98.6	140.6	281.6	292.4	254.3	175.0	227.2
Income Taxes	191.3	50.6	101.4	102.4	87.2	59.9	78.4
Net Income	2 d92.7	4 90.0	4 180.2	3 190.1	167.1	1 115.1	148.8
Cash Flow	5.4	154.3	247.3	256.0	231.7	190.5	217.2
Average Shs. Outstg. (000)	63,646	65,592	71,104	74,546	74,819	74,529	74,305
BALANCE SHEET (IN MILLIONS):							
Cash & Cash Equivalents	51.7	61.0	144.6	47.6	35.1	30.1	87.2
Total Current Assets	1,205.7	1,100.7	1,145.8	1,023.2	1,004.9	970.2	893.4
Net Property	477.2	447.4	434.8	447.6	462.8	440.3	448.8
Total Assets	2,712.1	2,518.0	2,419.3	2,145.9	2,135.1	2,005.8	1,761.8
Total Current Liabilities	1,111.3	582.5	417.7	517.2	442.7	453.8	362.3
Long-Term Obligations	380.1	442.1	463.2	148.8	219.6	231.1	74.5
Net Stockholders' Equity	1,047.2	1,252.4	1,346.6	1,345.2	1,361.7	1,235.0	1,159.5
Net Working Capital	94.5	518.2	728.1	506.0	562.1	516.3	531.2
Year-end Shs. Outstg. (000)	63,489	77,803	77,783	71,182	74,982	74,708	74,302
STATISTICAL RECORD:							
Operating Profit Margin %	6.8	8.2	14.2	14.3	13.1	9.9	13.0
Net Profit Margin %	. . .	4.1	8.2	8.6	7.7	5.7	7.9
Return on Equity %	. . .	7.2	13.4	14.1	12.3	9.3	12.8
Return on Assets %	. . .	3.6	7.4	8.9	7.8	5.7	8.4
Debt/Total Assets %	14.0	17.6	19.1	6.9	10.3	11.5	4.2
Price Range	24.06-8.19	44.31-22.00	53.75-35.00	38.75-27.38	30.50-23.50	33.00-25.50	34.00-25.88
P/E Ratio	. . .	32.3-16.1	21.2-13.8	15.2-10.7	13.7-10.5	21.4-16.6	17.0-12.9
Average Yield %	5.1	2.4	1.7	2.1	2.4	2.1	1.8

Statistics are as originally reported. Adj. for 2-for-1 stock split, 6/93. 1 Incl. $52.1 mill. asset impairment loss. 2 Excl. acct. chrgs. of $21.1 mill., 2/01; $17.2 mill., 2/94. 3 Incl. pre-tax gain of $22.1 mill. resulting from the divestiture of Acme Frame Products and Wilhold, Inc. 4 Incl. pre-tax restructuring chrg. of $38.9 mill., 2/00; $13.9 mill., 2/99.

OFFICERS:
M. Weiss, Chmn., C.E.O.
J. C. Spira, Pres., C.O.O.
W. S. Meyer, Sr. V.P., C.F.O.
D. A. Cable, V.P., Treas.

INVESTOR CONTACT: Dale A. Cable, V.P. & Treas., (216) 252-7300

PRINCIPAL OFFICE: One American Road, Cleveland, OH 44144

TELEPHONE NUMBER: (216) 252-7300
FAX: (216) 252-6778
WEB: www.americangreetings.com
NO. OF EMPLOYEES: 11,700 full-time (approx.); 27,000 part-time (approx.)
SHAREHOLDERS: 28,800 (approx. record class A); 202 (approx. record class B)
ANNUAL MEETING: In June
INCORPORATED: OH, Jan., 1944

INSTITUTIONAL HOLDINGS:
No. of Institutions: 176
Shares Held: 50,308,895
% Held: 79.2

INDUSTRY: Greeting cards (SIC: 2771)

TRANSFER AGENT(S): National City Bank, Cleveland, OH

NYSE SYMBOL AHP
Rec. Pr. 63.30 (5/31/01)

AMERICAN HOME PRODUCTS CORPORATION

YIELD 1.5%
P/E RATIO . . .

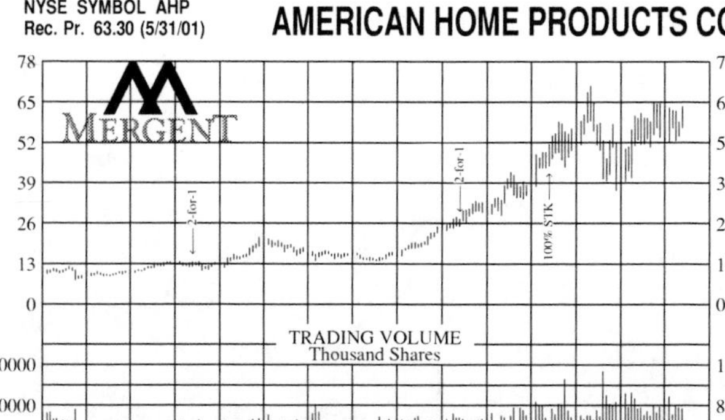

*7 YEAR PRICE SCORE 108.0 *12 MONTH PRICE SCORE 107.3

*NYSE COMPOSITE INDEX=100

INTERIM EARNINGS (Per Share):

Qtr.	Mar.	June	Sept.	Dec.
1997	0.45	0.36	0.34	0.44
1998	0.74	0.39	0.46	0.26
1999	0.49	0.30	d2.20	0.45
2000	1.32	0.31	0.58	d2.91

INTERIM DIVIDENDS (Per Share):

Amt.	Decl.	Ex.	Rec.	Pay.
0.23Q	4/27/00	5/10/00	5/12/00	6/01/00
0.23Q	7/20/00	8/09/00	8/11/00	9/01/00
0.23Q	9/21/00	11/09/00	11/13/00	12/01/00
0.23Q	1/23/01	2/09/01	2/13/01	3/01/01
0.23Q	4/26/01	5/09/01	5/11/01	6/01/01

Indicated div.: $0.92 (Div. Reinv. Plan)

CAPITALIZATION (12/31/00):

	($000)	(%)
Long-Term Debt	2,394,790	45.9
Preferred Stock	55	0.0
Common & Surplus	2,818,038	54.1
Total	5,212,883	100.0

RECENT DEVELOPMENTS: For the year ended 12/31/00, AHP reported a loss from continuing operations of $901.0 million versus a loss from continuing operations of $1.21 billion in 1999. Results for 2000 included a pre-tax non-recurring charge of $8.25 billion. Results also reflect a pre-tax gain of $2.06 billion, a credit of $1.71 billion and excluded a loss on disposal of $1.57 billion. Net revenue rose 11.6% to $13.26 billion.

PROSPECTS: The Company anticipates taking no further charges related to the litigation over the diet drugs REDUX and PONDIMIN. AHP is seeking market approval for Alesse® to treat moderate acne vulgaris in women of reproductive age with no known contraindications to oral contraceptive therapy. AHP believes it will be able to achieve earnings in the range of $2.15 to $2.20 per share.

BUSINESS

AMERICAN HOME PRODUCTS CORPORATION is engaged in the discovery, development, manufacture, distribution and sale of products in two segments: Pharmaceuticals and Consumer Health Care. Pharmaceuticals include branded and generic human ethical pharmaceuticals, biologicals, nutritionals, and animal biologicals and pharmaceuticals. Consumer Health Care products include analgesics, cough/cold/allergy remedies, vitamin, mineral and nutritional supplements, herbal products, and hemorrhoidal, antacid and asthma relief items sold over-the-counter. Pharmaceuticals accounted for 81.4% of 2000 sales and Consumer Health Care, 18.6%.

ANNUAL FINANCIAL DATA

	12/31/00	12/31/99	12/31/98	12/31/97	12/31/96	12/31/95	12/31/94
Earnings Per Share	**7 d0.69**	**6 d0.94**	**5 1.85**	**4 1.56**	**3 1.48**	**1 2 1.36**	**1 1.24**
Cash Flow Per Share	**d0.28**	**d0.42**	**2.35**	**2.09**	**2.00**	**1.90**	**1.49**
Tang. Book Val. Per Share	. . .	. . .	**1.23**	**0.31**	. . .	. . .	. . .
Dividends Per Share	**0.92**	**0.91**	**0.87**	**0.83**	**0.78**	**0.76**	**0.73**
Dividend Payout %	. . .	. . .	**47.0**	**53.2**	**52.9**	**55.7**	**59.2**
INCOME STATEMENT (IN MILLIONS):							
Total Revenues	13,262.8	13,550.2	13,462.7	14,196.0	14,088.3	13,376.1	8,966.2
Costs & Expenses	16,954.8	14,817.0	9,875.4	10,249.9	10,453.6	10,364.6	6,655.9
Depreciation & Amort.	535.0	682.3	664.7	702.0	658.1	679.2	306.2
Operating Income	d4,227.1	d1,949.2	2,922.6	3,244.1	2,976.7	2,332.3	2,004.2
Net Interest Inc./(Exp.)	d57.6	d213.9	d207.2	d370.7	d433.0	d514.9	d8.8
Income Before Income Taxes	d1,101.0	d1,925.6	3,585.5	2,814.7	2,755.5	2,438.7	2,029.8
Income Taxes	cr200.0	cr698.5	1,111.1	771.6	872.1	758.3	501.5
Net Income	7 d901.0	6 d1,227.1	5 2,474.3	4 2,043.1	3 1,883.4	1 2 1,680.4	1 1,528.3
Cash Flow	d366.0	d544.8	3,138.9	2,745.1	2,541.4	2,359.6	1,834.3
Average Shs. Outstg. (000)	1,306,474	1,308,876	1,336,641	1,312,975	1,270,852	1,239,340	1,229,652
BALANCE SHEET (IN MILLIONS):							
Cash & Cash Equivalents	2,985.3	2,413.3	1,301.5	1,099.7	1,544.1	2,020.1	1,944.2
Total Current Assets	10,180.8	9,738.1	7,955.6	7,361.3	7,470.4	7,986.1	7,821.2
Net Property	5,034.8	4,565.0	4,289.7	4,296.9	4,036.7	3,960.3	3,811.9
Total Assets	21,092.5	23,906.3	21,079.1	20,825.1	20,785.3	21,362.9	21,674.8
Total Current Liabilities	9,742.1	7,110.2	4,210.7	4,327.0	4,337.6	4,556.2	4,618.1
Long-Term Obligations	2,394.8	3,668.6	3,859.2	5,031.9	6,020.6	7,808.8	9,973.2
Net Stockholders' Equity	2,818.1	6,214.7	9,614.8	8,741.7	7,045.9	5,657.9	4,443.6
Net Working Capital	438.8	2,627.9	3,744.9	3,034.3	3,132.8	3,429.9	3,203.2
Year-end Shs. Outstg. (000)	1,311,774	1,303,916	1,312,399	1,300,754	1,279,966	1,254,800	1,223,924
STATISTICAL RECORD:							
Operating Profit Margin %	. . .	. . .	21.7	22.9	21.1	17.4	22.4
Net Profit Margin %	. . .	. . .	18.4	14.4	13.4	12.6	17.0
Return on Equity %	. . .	. . .	25.7	23.4	26.7	29.7	34.4
Return on Assets %	. . .	. . .	11.7	9.8	9.1	7.9	7.1
Debt/Total Assets %	11.4	15.3	18.3	24.2	29.0	36.6	46.0
Price Range	65.25-39.38	70.25-36.50	58.75-37.75	42.44-28.50	33.25-23.53	24.97-15.44	16.81-13.84
P/E Ratio	. . .	. . .	31.8-20.4	27.2-18.3	22.5-15.9	18.4-11.4	13.5-11.1
Average Yield %	1.8	1.7	1.8	2.3	2.8	3.7	4.8

Statistics are as originally reported. Adj. for 2-for-1 stock split, 5/98 & 5/96. 1 Incl. one-time chg. of $308.3 mil., 1995; & $97.0 mil., 1994. 2 Incl. Amer. Cyanamid Co., a non-recurr. gain of $623.9 mil. & a spl. restr. chg. of $117.2 mil. 3 Incl. net gain on sale of bus. of $706.3 mil. & spl. chgs. of $697.9 mil. 4 Incl. a spec. net chg. of $180.0 mill. 5 Incl. a net gain of $330.8 mill. & a net restr. chg. of $343.6 mill. 6 Incl. a net spec. chg. of $53.0 mill. & a net chg. of $3.29 bill. 7 Incl. net pre-tax nonrecurr. chrg. of $8.25 bill.

OFFICERS:
J. R. Stafford, Chmn., C.E.O.
R. Essner, Pres., C.O.O.
K. J. Martin, Sr. V.P., C.F.O.

INVESTOR CONTACT: Thomas G. Cavanagh, V.P., Inv. Rel., (973) 660-5706

PRINCIPAL OFFICE: Five Giralda Farms, Madison, NJ 07940-0874

TELEPHONE NUMBER: (973) 660-5000
FAX: (973) 660-5012
WEB: www.ahp.com

NO. OF EMPLOYEES: 48,036 (avg.)

SHAREHOLDERS: 57,885 (record)

ANNUAL MEETING: In Apr.

INCORPORATED: DE, Feb., 1926

INSTITUTIONAL HOLDINGS:
No. of Institutions: 991
Shares Held: 871,397,432
% Held: 66.3

INDUSTRY: Pharmaceutical preparations (SIC: 2834)

TRANSFER AGENT(S): Mellon Investor Services, Ridgefield Park, NJ

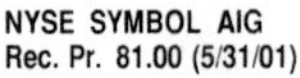

NYSE SYMBOL AIG
Rec. Pr. 81.00 (5/31/01)

AMERICAN INTERNATIONAL GROUP, INC.

YIELD 0.2%
P/E RATIO 29.9

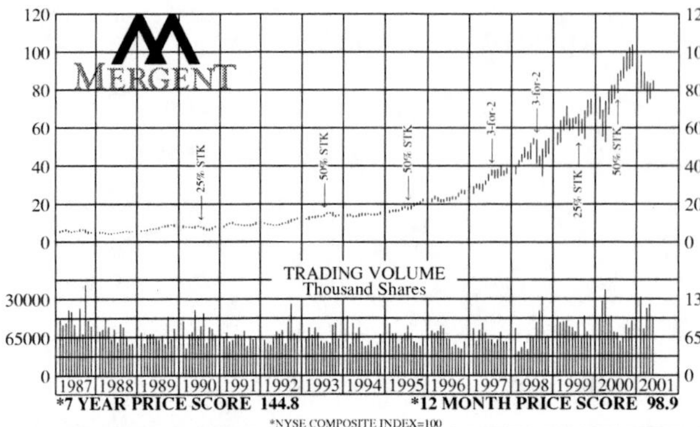

*7 YEAR PRICE SCORE 144.8 *12 MONTH PRICE SCORE 98.9

*NYSE COMPOSITE INDEX=100

INTERIM EARNINGS (Per Share):

Qtr.	Mar.	June	Sept.	Dec.
1996	0.27	0.29	0.29	0.31
1997	0.31	0.33	0.33	0.36
1998	0.36	0.38	0.38	0.41
1999	0.41	0.67	0.54	0.56
2000	0.57	0.90	0.60	0.64

INTERIM DIVIDENDS (Per Share):

Amt.	Decl.	Ex.	Rec.	Pay.
0.037Q	5/17/00	8/30/00	9/01/00	9/15/00
0.037Q	9/14/00	11/29/00	12/01/00	12/15/00
0.037Q	11/15/00	2/28/01	3/02/01	3/16/01
0.037Q	3/13/01	5/30/01	6/01/01	6/15/01
0.042Q	5/16/01	8/07/01	8/09/01	9/14/01

Indicated div.: $0.17

CAPITALIZATION (12/31/00):

	($000)	(%)
Long-Term Debt	20,672,000	32.8
Minority Interest	1,465,000	2.3
Redeemable Pfd. Stock	1,347,000	2.1
Common & Surplus	39,619,000	62.8
Total	63,103,000	100.0

RECENT DEVELOPMENTS: For the year ended 12/31/00, net income increased 11.5% to $5.64 billion versus $5.06 billion in 1999. Total revenues increased 12.4% to $42.44 billion from $37.75 billion in the previous year. Total premium income improved 12.8% to $31.02 billion versus $27.49 billion a year earlier. General Insurance net premiums written improved 8.0% to $17.53 billion and operating income grew 1.3% to $3.52 billion. Premium income and other considerations from the life insurance segment increased 20.2% to $29.60 billion.

PROSPECTS: On 5/11/01, the Company announced that it has entered into a definitive agreement to acquire American General Corporation in a transaction valued at approximately $23.00 billion. The acquisition, which strengthens AIG's U.S. life insurance and annuities businesses, is expected to add approximately 8.0% to 10.0% to AIG's earnings and yield about $400.0 million in pre-tax savings in the first year following completion of the deal. The acquisition is expected to be completed by year end.

BUSINESS

AMERICAN INTERNATIONAL GROUP, INC. is a U.S.-based international insurance and financial services organization and an underwriter of commercial and industrial insurance in the United States. AIG's global businesses also include financial services and asset management, including aircraft leasing, financial products, trading and market making, consumer finance, institutional, retail and direct investment fund asset management, real estate investment management, and retirement savings products. Approximately 50% of AIG's revenues during 2000 were derived from its foreign operations. Major insurance subsidiaries are: American Home Assurance Co., National Union Fire Insurance Co. of Pittsburgh, PA., and New Hampshire Insurance Co. On 1/1/99, AIG acquired SunAmerica Inc. for $18.00 billion.

ANNUAL FINANCIAL DATA

	12/31/00	12/31/99	12/31/98	12/31/97	12/31/96	12/31/95	12/31/94
Earnings Per Share	**2.41**	**2.15**	**1.90**	**1.68**	**1.46**	**1.26**	**1.09**
Tang. Book Val. Per Share	**16.98**	**14.33**	**13.78**	**12.20**	**11.13**	**9.91**	**8.22**
Dividends Per Share	**0.14**	**0.13**	**0.11**	**0.10**	**0.09**	**0.08**	**0.07**
Dividend Payout %	**5.8**	**5.9**	**5.9**	**6.0**	**6.0**	**6.1**	**6.3**
INCOME STATEMENT (IN MILLIONS):							
Total Premium Income	31,017.0	27,486.0	24,345.0	22,346.7	20,833.1	19,443.9	17,011.2
Other Income	11,423.0	10,265.0	6,507.0	5,600.7	5,041.2	4,386.1	3,781.7
Total Revenues	42,440.0	37,751.0	30,852.0	27,947.4	25,874.3	23,829.9	20,792.8
Policyholder Benefits	7,186.0	6,919.0	6,036.0	5,607.0	5,451.1	4,936.7	4,076.5
Income Before Income Taxes	8,349.0	7,512.0	5,529.0	4,698.9	4,013.2	3,465.9	2,952.0
Income Taxes	2,458.0	2,219.0	1,594.0	1,366.6	1,116.0	955.5	776.5
Equity Earnings/Minority Int.	d255.0	d238.0	d112.0	81.7	56.1	45.4	26.3
Net Income	5,636.0	5,055.0	3,766.0	3,332.3	2,897.3	2,510.4	2,175.5
Average Shs. Outstg. (000)	2,343,000	2,350,500	1,978,125	1,982,768	1,987,221	1,999,780	2,003,396
BALANCE SHEET (IN MILLIONS):							
Cash & Cash Equivalents	53,692.0	43,995.0	36,784.0	28,972.3	22,963.9	19,285.6	15,601.1
Premiums Due	42,012.0	37,898.0	35,652.0	33,109.0	29,937.1	29,610.3	27,721.5
Invst. Assets: Fixed-term	102,010.0	90,142.0	61,906.0	51,326.7	48,148.0	42,441.1	35,018.4
Invst. Assets: Equities	6,125.0	6,002.0	5,565.0	5,209.3	5,989.6	5,294.9	5,002.7
Invst. Assets: Loans	12,243.0	12,134.0	8,247.0	7,919.8	7,876.8	7,860.5	5,353.1
Invst. Assets: Total	173,524.0	152,204.0	114,526.0	94,970.6	87,696.9	76,934.5	62,796.8
Total Assets	306,577.0	268,238.0	194,398.0	163,970.7	148,431.0	134,136.4	114,346.1
Long-Term Obligations	20,672.0	2,344.0	1,620.0	13,885.4	13,299.3	9,915.3	8,194.6
Net Stockholders' Equity	39,619.0	33,306.0	27,131.0	24,001.1	22,044.2	19,827.1	16,421.7
Year-end Shs. Outstg. (000)	2,332,713	2,323,692	1,968,750	1,967,394	1,980,454	2,000,464	1,998,683
STATISTICAL RECORD:							
Return on Revenues %	13.3	13.4	12.2	11.9	11.2	10.5	10.5
Return on Equity %	14.2	15.2	13.9	13.9	13.1	12.7	13.2
Return on Assets %	1.8	1.9	1.9	2.0	2.0	1.9	1.9
Price Range	103.75-52.38	75.25-51.00	54.74-34.60	40.02-25.25	27.59-20.89	22.64-15.19	15.92-12.92
P/E Ratio	43.0-21.7	35.0-23.7	28.7-18.2	23.8-15.0	18.9-14.3	18.0-12.1	14.7-11.9
Average Yield %	0.2	0.2	0.3	0.3	0.4	0.4	0.5

Statistics are as originally reported. Adj. for stk. splits: 25% div., 7/30/99; 3-for-2, 7/98, 7/97, 7/95

OFFICERS:
M. R. Greenberg, Chmn., C.E.O.
T. R. Tizzio, Sr. Vice-Chmn.
E. E. Matthews, Vice-Chmn.
INVESTOR CONTACT: Investor Relations, (212) 770-7000
PRINCIPAL OFFICE: 70 Pine Street, New York, NY 10270

TELEPHONE NUMBER: (212) 770-7000
FAX: (212) 344-6828
WEB: www.aig.com
NO. OF EMPLOYEES: 61,000 (approx.)
SHAREHOLDERS: 32,000 (approx.)
ANNUAL MEETING: In May
INCORPORATED: DE, June, 1967

INSTITUTIONAL HOLDINGS:
No. of Institutions: 1,099
Shares Held: 1,332,064,371
% Held: 57.1
INDUSTRY: Fire, marine, and casualty insurance (SIC: 6331)
TRANSFER AGENT(S): First Chicago Trust Company of New York, Jersey City, NJ

NYSE SYMBOL ASD
Rec. Pr. 60.25 (4/30/01)

AMERICAN STANDARD COMPANIES, INC.

YIELD ...
P/E RATIO 13.9

TRADING VOLUME Thousand Shares

*7 YEAR PRICE SCORE N/A *12 MONTH PRICE SCORE 128.8

*NYSE COMPOSITE INDEX=100

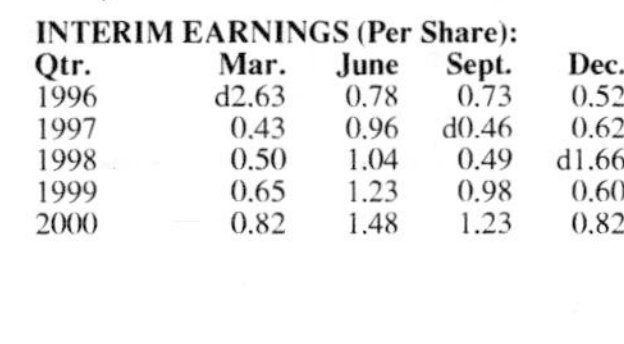

INTERIM EARNINGS (Per Share):

Qtr.	Mar.	June	Sept.	Dec.
1996	d2.63	0.78	0.73	0.52
1997	0.43	0.96	d0.46	0.62
1998	0.50	1.04	0.49	d1.66
1999	0.65	1.23	0.98	0.60
2000	0.82	1.48	1.23	0.82

INTERIM DIVIDENDS (Per Share):

Amt.	Decl.	Ex.	Rec.	Pay.
	No dividends paid.			

CAPITALIZATION (12/31/00):

	($000)	(%)
Long-Term Debt	2,375,566	117.1
Deferred Income Tax	45,215	2.2
Common & Surplus	d392,903	-19.4
Total	2,027,878	100.0

RECENT DEVELOPMENTS: For the year ended 12/31/00, net income increased 19.3% to $315.0 million compared with $264.0 million a year earlier. Results for 2000 included a restructuring and asset impairment charge of $70.0 million, partially offset by a gain of $57.0 million on the 12/18/00 sale of the Company's Calorex water heater business to Grupo Industrial Saltillo (GISSA). GISSA will sell water heaters in the U.S. and Canada under the AMERICAN STANDARD brand name. Total sales advanced 5.7% to $7.60 billion from $7.19 billion in 1999.

PROSPECTS: Results going forward should be supported by new applications to existing customers, acceleration of sales in new product lines, geographic expansion and ASD's recently announced operational restructuring plan. The restructuring plan, implemented to eliminate redundant work, enhance productivity and improve profitability, is expected to generate about $50.0 million in annualized cost savings, with initial benefits starting in late 2001. For full-year 2001, ASD is targeting 5.0% to 6.0% sales growth and an increase of 13.0% to 17.0% in earnings per share.

BUSINESS

AMERICAN STANDARD COMPANIES, INC. is a global manufacturer of air conditioning systems and services for commercial, institutional and residential buildings; plumbing fixtures and fittings for bathrooms and kitchens; and vehicle control systems for medium-sized and heavy trucks, buses trailers and utility vehicles. The Company's brand names include TRANE and AMERICAN STANDARD for air conditioning systems, AMERICAN STANDARD, IDEAL STANDARD, STANDARD, PORCHER, JADO, ARMITAGE SHANKS and DOLOMITE for plumbing products, and WABCO for vehicle control systems. On 2/2/99, the Company acquired Armitage/Dolomite for approximately $427.0 million.

BUSINESS LINE ANALYSIS

(12/31/2000)	Rev(%)	Inc(%)
Air Conditioning Products	62.2	63.2
Plumbing Products	23.7	19.3
Vehicle Control Products	14.1	17.5
Total	100.0	100.0

ANNUAL FINANCIAL DATA

	12/31/00	12/31/99	12/31/98	12/31/97	12/31/96	12/31/95	12/31/94
Earnings Per Share	[6] **4.36**	[5] **3.63**	[1] **0.46**	[2] **1.57**	[3] **d0.60**	[4] **1.90**	[4] **d1.29**
Cash Flow Per Share	**7.32**	**6.42**	**3.04**	**3.73**	**1.27**	**3.82**	**1.28**
INCOME STATEMENT (IN MILLIONS):							
Total Revenues	7,598.4	7,189.5	6,653.9	6,007.5	5,804.6	5,221.5	4,457.5
Costs & Expenses	6,734.1	6,348.1	6,110.0	5,414.5	5,403.2	4,637.9	4,058.8
Depreciation & Amort.	213.4	202.1	190.0	164.0	145.5	143.4	154.4
Operating Income	650.9	639.4	353.8	429.0	255.8	440.2	244.3
Net Interest Inc./(Exp.)	d198.7	d187.8	d188.4	d192.2	d198.2	d213.3	d259.4
Income Before Income Taxes	509.4	451.5	165.4	236.8	57.6	226.9	d15.2
Income Taxes	194.2	187.4	131.8	116.9	104.3	85.1	62.5
Net Income	[6] 315.2	[5] 264.1	[1] 33.6	[2] 119.9	[3] d46.7	[4] 141.8	[4] d77.7
Cash Flow	528.6	466.2	223.6	283.8	98.8	285.2	76.7
Average Shs. Outstg. (000)	72,198	72,666	73,672	76,167	77,987	74,672	59,933
BALANCE SHEET (IN MILLIONS):							
Cash & Cash Equivalents	85.4	61.2	64.8	28.8	59.7	...	92.7
Total Current Assets	1,878.5	1,725.6	1,591.3	1,393.3	1,386.4	1,206.2	1,064.5
Net Property	1,382.7	1,414.2	1,241.0	1,139.2	1,006.0	924.5	812.7
Total Assets	4,744.7	4,686.0	4,156.2	3,764.1	3,519.7	3,430.9	3,156.1
Total Current Liabilities	1,806.6	2,286.6	2,350.6	1,841.2	1,236.9	1,306.6	1,078.7
Long-Term Obligations	2,375.6	1,886.7	1,527.5	1,550.8	1,741.8	1,770.1	2,152.3
Net Stockholders' Equity	d392.9	d496.5	d701.0	d609.8	d380.4	d390.1	d797.6
Net Working Capital	72.0	d561.1	d759.3	d447.9	149.5	d100.4	d14.2
Year-end Shs. Outstg. (000)	69,533	70,743	69,925	71,963	78,573	76,733	60,932
STATISTICAL RECORD:							
Operating Profit Margin %	8.6	8.9	5.3	7.1	4.4	8.4	5.5
Net Profit Margin %	4.1	3.7	0.5	2.0	...	2.7	...
Return on Assets %	6.6	5.6	0.8	3.2	...	4.1	...
Debt/Total Assets %	50.1	40.3	36.8	41.2	49.5	51.6	68.2
Price Range	49.75-34.31	49.44-31.13	49.25-21.63	51.63-34.63	39.75-25.50	32.00-19.63	...
P/E Ratio	11.4-7.9	13.6-8.6	107.0-47.0	32.9-22.1	...	16.8-10.3	...

Statistics are as originally reported. [1] Incls. one-time restr. chrg. of $197.0 mill. [2] Incls. non-recurr. pre-tax chrg. of $90.0 mill.; bef. extraord. chrg. of $24.0 mill. [3] Incls. non-recurr. chrg. $235.2 mill. [4] Bef. extraord. chrg. 12/31/95: $30.0 mill. ($0.40/sh.); chrg. 12/31/94: $8.7 mill. ($0.15/sh.) [5] Incls. restruct. chrgs. of $15.0 mill. [6] Incls. restruct. & asset impair. chrg. of $70.0 mill. and $57.0 mill. gain on sale of business.

OFFICERS:
F. Poses, Chmn., C.E.O.
G. P. D'Aloia, Sr. V.P., C.F.O.
J. P. McGrath, Sr. V.P., Sec., Gen. Counsel,

PRINCIPAL OFFICE: One Centennial Avenue, P.O. Box 6820, Piscataway, NJ 08855

TELEPHONE NUMBER: (732) 980-6000
FAX: (732) 980-6300
WEB: www.americanstandard.com
NO. OF EMPLOYEES: 61,000 (approx.)
SHAREHOLDERS: 36,000 (approx.)
ANNUAL MEETING: In May
INCORPORATED: DE, 1988

INSTITUTIONAL HOLDINGS:
No. of Institutions: 192
Shares Held: 52,878,138
% Held: 76.3

INDUSTRY: Refrigeration and heating equipment (SIC: 3585)

TRANSFER AGENT(S): Citibank, NA, New York, NY

NYSE SYMBOL AMT
Rec. Pr. 24.74 (5/31/01)

AMERICAN TOWER CORPORATION

YIELD ...
P/E RATIO ...

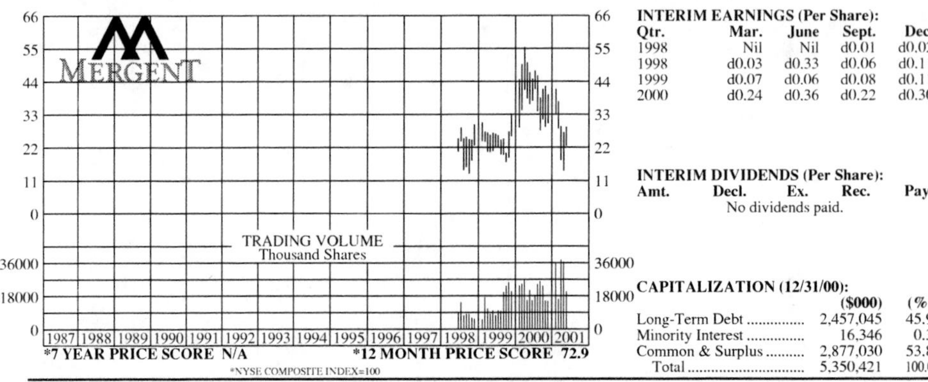

INTERIM EARNINGS (Per Share):

Qtr.	Mar.	June	Sept.	Dec.
1998	Nil	Nil	d0.01	d0.02
1998	d0.03	d0.33	d0.06	d0.11
1999	d0.07	d0.06	d0.08	d0.11
2000	d0.24	d0.36	d0.22	d0.30

INTERIM DIVIDENDS (Per Share):

Amt.	Decl.	Ex.	Rec.	Pay.

No dividends paid.

CAPITALIZATION (12/31/00):

	($000)	(%)
Long-Term Debt	2,457,045	45.9
Minority Interest	16,346	0.3
Common & Surplus	2,877,030	53.8
Total	5,350,421	100.0

RECENT DEVELOPMENTS: For the year ended 12/31/00, AMT posted a loss of $190.3 million, before extraordinary losses on extinguishment of debt of $4.3 million, compared with a loss of $49.4 million, before extraordinary losses of $1.4 million, in the prior year. Results for 2000 included note conversion charges of $17.0 million. Total operating revenues increased to $735.3 million from $258.1 million in 1999.

PROSPECTS: In December 2000, AMT signed a definitive agreement with ALLTEL Corporation to acquire the rights to 2,193 communications towers through a 15-year agreement to sublease for consideration of up to $658.0 million. Under the terms of the sublease agreement, AMT will have the option to purchase the towers at the end of the 15-year term. AMT will also have the option to acquire the rights to about 200 additional towers, for cash consideration of up to $300,000 per tower.

BUSINESS

AMERICAN TOWER CORPORATION is an independent owner, operator and developer of broadcast and wireless communications sites in North America and Mexico. As of 12/31/00, AMT operated a network of approximately 13,600 multi-user sites in the U.S., Mexico and Canada, including approximately 300 broadcast tower sites. Of these sites, approximately 12,600 are owned or leased sites and approximately 1,000 are managed or lease-sublease sites. The Company's network encompasses 48 states and the District of Columbia. Operating segments include rental and management (37.8% of 2000 revenues), network development services (42.4%), and satellite and fiber network access services (19.8%). AMT was spun off from American Radio Systems Corporation on 6/4/98.

ANNUAL FINANCIAL DATA

	12/31/00	12/31/99	12/31/98	12/31/97	12/31/96	12/31/95
Earnings Per Share	**2 d1.13**	**1 d0.33**	**1 d0.48**	**1 d0.03**	...	...
Cash Flow Per Share	**0.64**	**0.58**	**0.20**	**0.10**	...	...
Tang. Book Val. Per Share	**2.06**	**4.76**	**3.45**	**4.06**	...	...
INCOME STATEMENT (IN MILLIONS):						
Total Revenues	735.3	258.1	103.5	17.5	2.9	0.2
Costs & Expenses	537.9	162.5	77.7	10.1	2.2	0.3
Depreciation & Amort.	299.0	136.6	54.0	6.5	1.0	0.1
Operating Income	d101.6	d41.1	d28.1	0.9	d0.3	d0.2
Net Interest Inc./(Exp.)	d144.2	d27.5	d23.2	d3.0	...	...
Income Before Income Taxes	d249.9	d49.1	d42.4	d2.0	d0.4	d0.2
Income Taxes	cr59.7	0.2	cr4.5	cr0.5	...	cr0.1
Net Income	2 d190.3	1 d49.4	1 d37.9	1 d1.6	d0.5	d0.1
Cash Flow	108.7	87.3	16.0	4.9	0.5	d0.1
Average Shs. Outstg. (000)	168,715	149,749	79,786	48,692	...	...
BALANCE SHEET (IN MILLIONS):						
Cash & Cash Equivalents	128.1	25.2	186.2	4.6	2.4	...
Total Current Assets	471.2	139.4	207.6	8.7	2.7	...
Net Property	2,296.7	1,092.3	449.5	117.6	19.7	...
Total Assets	5,660.7	3,018.9	1,502.3	255.4	37.1	...
Total Current Liabilities	297.8	125.0	115.6	11.0	2.1	...
Long-Term Obligations	2,457.0	736.1	279.5	90.1	4.4	...
Net Stockholders' Equity	2,877.0	2,145.1	1,091.7	153.2	29.7	...
Net Working Capital	173.4	14.4	92.0	d2.3	0.5	...
Year-end Shs. Outstg. (000)	180,399	155,670	108,294	35,634	...	...
STATISTICAL RECORD:						
Operating Profit Margin %	...	...	...	5.3	...	...
Debt/Total Assets %	43.4	24.4	18.6	35.3	11.9	...
Price Range	55.50-27.63	33.25-17.13	29.63-13.25	...	...	...

Statistics are as originally reported. 1 Bef. extraord. loss of $1.4 mill. ($0.01/sh.), 1999; $8.9 mill. ($0.11/sh.), 1998; $694,000 ($0.01/sh.), 1997. 2 Bef. extraord. loss of $4.3 mill. ($0.02/sh.); incls. non-recurr. chrg. of $17.0 mill.

OFFICERS:
S. B. Dodge, Chmn., Pres., C.E.O.
J. L. Winn, C.F.O., Treas.
D. C. Wiest, C.O.O.

INVESTOR CONTACT: Anne Alter, Director of Investor Relations, (617) 375-7500

PRINCIPAL OFFICE: 116 Huntington Avenue, Boston, MA 02116

TELEPHONE NUMBER: (617) 375-7500
FAX: (617) 375-7575
WEB: www.americantower.com

NO. OF EMPLOYEES: 3,300 (approx.)

SHAREHOLDERS: 662 (class A)

ANNUAL MEETING: In May

INCORPORATED: DE, July, 1995

INSTITUTIONAL HOLDINGS:
No. of Institutions: 194
Shares Held: 147,769,600
% Held: 77.5

INDUSTRY: Communication services, nec (SIC: 4899)

TRANSFER AGENT(S): Computershare Investor Services, Chicago, IL

NYSE SYMBOL AWK
Rec. Pr. 32.25 (3/31/01)

AMERICAN WATER WORKS COMPANY, INC.

YIELD 2.9%
P/E RATIO 20.0

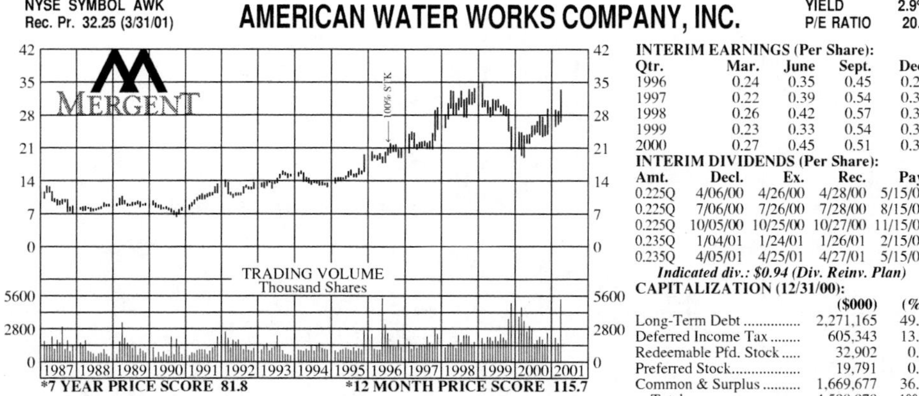

INTERIM EARNINGS (Per Share):

Qtr.	Mar.	June	Sept.	Dec.
1996	0.24	0.35	0.45	0.27
1997	0.22	0.39	0.54	0.31
1998	0.26	0.42	0.57	0.33
1999	0.23	0.33	0.54	0.33
2000	0.27	0.45	0.51	0.38

INTERIM DIVIDENDS (Per Share):

Amt.	Decl.	Ex.	Rec.	Pay.
0.225Q	4/06/00	4/26/00	4/28/00	5/15/00
0.225Q	7/06/00	7/26/00	7/28/00	8/15/00
0.225Q	10/05/00	10/25/00	10/27/00	11/15/00
0.235Q	1/04/01	1/24/01	1/26/01	2/15/01
0.235Q	4/05/01	4/25/01	4/27/01	5/15/01

Indicated div.: $0.94 (Div. Reinv. Plan)

CAPITALIZATION (12/31/00):

	($000)	(%)
Long-Term Debt	2,271,165	49.4
Deferred Income Tax	605,343	13.2
Redeemable Pfd. Stock	32,902	0.7
Preferred Stock	19,791	0.4
Common & Surplus	1,669,677	36.3
Total	4,598,878	100.0

RECENT DEVELOPMENTS: For the year ended 12/31/00, net income advanced 19.3% to $161.1 million compared with $135.0 million a year earlier. Results for 1999 included a net nonrecurring charge of $12.9 million. Operating revenues grew 7.1% to $1.35 billion. Revenues benefited from customer growth, rate increases and cost-savings initiatives, partially offset by the adverse affect of cooler-than-normal temperatures and frequent participation.

PROSPECTS: AWK is awaiting regulatory approval for 15 acquisitions, which should add about 100,000 people to AWK's service area. The Company is also awaiting regulatory approval for the pending acquisitions of SJW Corp. and the water and wastewater assets of Citizens Communication Company. Going forward, revenues should benefit from rate increases. Also, AWK anticipates additional revenues of $32.0 million during 2001 from six pending rate cases.

BUSINESS

AMERICAN WATER WORKS COMPANY, INC. is engaged in the ownership of companies providing water supply service. The Company and its subsidiaries constitute the American Water System, which has been functioning for 48 years. The American Water Works Service Company, a subsidiary, provides professional and staff services to affiliated companies. AWK established American Commonwealth Management Services Company to provide management services to water and sewer systems. The American Water Capital Corporation is the primary funding vehicle for the Company and its subsidiaries. As of 5/4/01, AWK's subsidiary operating companies provide water service to 10.0 million people in more than 1,300 communities in 23 states.

QUARTERLY DATA

(12/31/00)	Rev($000)	Inc($000)
1st Quarter	307,759	90,448
2nd Quarter	346,409	120,011
3rd Quarter	364,125	136,135
4th Quarter	332,297	109,584

ANNUAL FINANCIAL DATA

	12/31/00	12/31/99	12/31/98	12/31/97	12/31/96	12/31/95	12/31/94
Earnings Per Share	**1.61**	**2 1.40**	**1.58**	**1.45**	**1.31**	**1 1.32**	**1.17**
Cash Flow Per Share	**3.41**	**3.11**	**3.20**	**2.88**	**2.68**	**2.62**	**2.43**
Tang. Book Val. Per Share	**16.92**	**15.85**	**15.32**	**14.28**	**13.49**	**12.07**	**11.23**
Dividends Per Share	**0.90**	**0.86**	**0.82**	**0.76**	**0.70**	**0.64**	**0.54**
Dividend Payout %	**55.9**	**61.4**	**51.9**	**52.4**	**53.4**	**48.5**	**46.1**
INCOME STATEMENT (IN MILLIONS):							
Total Revenues	1,350.6	1,260.9	1,017.8	954.2	894.6	802.8	770.2
Costs & Expenses	717.9	675.6	528.1	507.8	498.7	471.6	456.9
Depreciation & Amort.	176.6	165.6	129.8	112.5	101.9	87.0	80.6
Operating Income	456.2	419.6	359.9	333.9	294.0	244.3	182.8
Net Interest Inc./(Exp.)	d188.7	d170.4	d150.5	d142.7	d133.1	d108.7	d106.7
Income Taxes	105.3	91.4	83.3	74.7	63.8	57.6	49.9
Net Income	161.1	2 138.9	131.0	119.1	101.7	1 92.1	78.7
Cash Flow	333.9	300.6	256.8	227.7	199.6	175.0	155.3
Average Shs. Outstg. (000)	97,988	96,544	80,298	79,144	74,609	66,764	63,836
BALANCE SHEET (IN MILLIONS):							
Gross Property	6,554.5	6,143.7	4,945.0	4,527.7	4,188.9	3,510.6	3,219.6
Accumulated Depreciation	1,276.4	1,152.6	848.5	755.4	682.8	590.8	535.1
Net Property	5,371.5	5,084.5	4,153.2	3,828.1	3,560.1	2,962.6	2,726.1
Total Assets	6,134.8	5,952.2	4,708.3	4,314.3	4,032.2	3,403.1	3,206.7
Long-Term Obligations	2,271.2	2,393.1	2,106.0	1,870.8	1,716.4	1,384.6	1,308.0
Net Stockholders' Equity	1,689.5	1,562.1	1,257.1	1,160.3	1,075.8	836.9	751.4
Year-end Shs. Outstg. (000)	98,691	97,304	80,895	79,993	78,421	67,826	65,318
STATISTICAL RECORD:							
Operating Profit Margin %	33.8	33.3	35.4	35.0	32.9	30.4	23.7
Net Profit Margin %	11.9	11.0	12.9	12.5	11.4	11.5	10.2
Net Inc./Net Property %	3.0	2.7	3.2	3.1	2.9	3.1	2.9
Net Inc./Tot. Capital %	3.5	3.0	3.4	3.4	3.1	3.5	3.2
Return on Equity %	9.5	8.9	10.4	10.3	9.5	11.0	10.5
Accum. Depr./Gross Prop. %	19.5	18.8	17.2	16.7	16.3	16.8	16.6
Price Range	29.38-18.94	34.75-20.50	33.75-25.25	29.69-19.88	22.00-17.75	19.63-13.38	16.13-12.63
P/E Ratio	18.2-11.8	24.8-14.6	21.4-16.0	20.5-13.7	16.8-13.5	14.9-10.1	13.8-10.8
Average Yield %	3.7	3.1	2.8	3.1	3.5	3.9	3.8

Statistics are as originally reported. Adj. for stk. splits: 2-for-1, 8/96 1 Incl. non-recurr. cr. of $3.9 mill. ($0.06/sh.) 2 Incl. after-tax nonrecurr. chrg. of $20.5 mill.

OFFICERS:
M. Ware, Chmn.
A. P. Terracciano, Vice-Chmn.
J. J. Barr, Pres., C.E.O.
E. C. Wolf, V.P., C.F.O.

INVESTOR CONTACT: James E. Harrison, VP, Investor Relations, (856) 346-8200

PRINCIPAL OFFICE: 1025 Laurel Oak Rd., P.O. Box 1770, Voorhees, NJ 08043

TELEPHONE NUMBER: (856) 346-8200
FAX: (856) 346-8300
WEB: www.amwater.com

NO. OF EMPLOYEES: 5,050

SHAREHOLDERS: 41,391

ANNUAL MEETING: In May

INCORPORATED: DE, Aug., 1936

INSTITUTIONAL HOLDINGS:
No. of Institutions: 187
Shares Held: 32,168,795
% Held: 32.5

INDUSTRY: Water supply (SIC: 4941)

TRANSFER AGENT(S): BankBoston N.A., Boston, MA

NYSE SYMBOL AAS
Rec. Pr. 57.71 (5/31/01)

AMERISOURCE HEALTH CORPORATION

YIELD ...
P/E RATIO 29.3

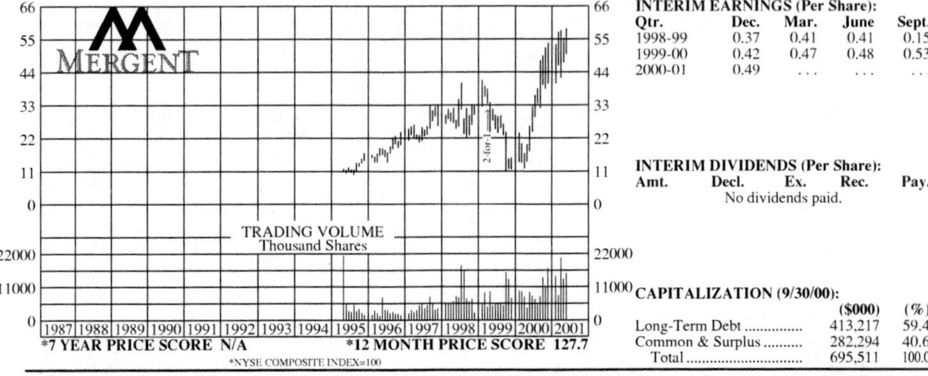

*7 YEAR PRICE SCORE N/A *12 MONTH PRICE SCORE 127.7
*NYSE COMPOSITE INDEX=100

INTERIM EARNINGS (Per Share):

Qtr.	Dec.	Mar.	June	Sept.
1998-99	0.37	0.41	0.41	0.15
1999-00	0.42	0.47	0.48	0.53
2000-01	0.49	...	...	...

INTERIM DIVIDENDS (Per Share):

Amt.	Decl.	Ex.	Rec.	Pay.

No dividends paid.

CAPITALIZATION (9/30/00):

	($000)	(%)
Long-Term Debt	413,217	59.4
Common & Surplus	282,294	40.6
Total	695,511	100.0

RECENT DEVELOPMENTS: For the first quarter ended 12/31/00, net income increased 21.3% to $26.2 million versus $21.6 million in the corresponding period of the previous year. Total revenues jumped 16.5% to $3.31 billion from $2.84 billion in the prior-year period. Operating revenue advanced 16.9% to $3.31 billion from $2.83 billion. Revenue from bulk deliveries to customer warehouses plummeted 95.8% to $444,000 from $10.6 million in 1999.

PROSPECTS: On 1/31/01, the Company announced that it has recently signed new customer agreements totaling more than $450.0 million in annualized revenue. The new revenue is divided about equally between the Company's institutional business, made up of the Health Systems and Alternate Site customer groups, and its retail business, which includes Chain Drugstores and Independent Community Pharmacies.

BUSINESS

AMERISOURCE HEALTH CORPORATION, through its subsidiary AmeriSource Corporation, is a full-service wholesale distributor of pharmaceutical products and related healthcare services. The Company serves its customers nationwide through 21 drug distribution facilities and three specialty products distribution facilities. The Company is the primary source of supply for its customers, and offers a broad range of services designed to enhance the operating efficiencies and competitive positions of its customers and its suppliers. AAS' 15,000 customers include hospitals and managed care facilities (accounting for 48% of operating revenue in fiscal 2000), independent community pharmacies (39%) and chain drug stores, including pharmacy departments of supermarkets and mass merchandisers (13%).

QUARTERLY DATA

(09/30/2000)($000)	Rev	Inc
1st Quarter	2,839,382	21,599
2nd Quarter	2,842,203	24,299
3rd Quarter	2,931,706	25,120
4th Quarter	3,031,730	27,996

ANNUAL FINANCIAL DATA

	9/30/00	9/30/99	9/30/98	9/30/97	9/30/96	9/30/95	9/30/94
Earnings Per Share	**(5) 1.90**	**(4) 1.38**	**(3) 1.04**	**(2) 0.98**	**(2) 0.93**	**(2) 0.77**	**(1) d5.84**
Cash Flow Per Share	**2.24**	**1.76**	**1.38**	**1.27**	**1.18**	**1.05**	**d5.34**
Tang. Book Val. Per Share	**4.81**	**2.88**	**1.55**	**0.26**	...	...	...
INCOME STATEMENT (IN MILLIONS):							
Total Revenues	11,645.0	9,807.4	8,668.8	7,815.9	5,551.7	4,668.9	4,301.8
Costs & Expenses	11,426.0	9,628.2	8,527.3	7,682.0	5,442.2	4,561.0	4,385.0
Depreciation & Amort.	17.4	20.2	16.5	14.3	11.6	10.1	14.8
Operating Income	201.6	159.0	124.9	119.6	97.9	97.8	d97.9
Net Interest Inc./(Exp.)	d41.9	d39.7	d42.1	d41.6	d36.0	d52.3	d62.6
Income Before Income Taxes	159.7	119.3	82.8	78.0	61.9	45.5	d164.6
Income Taxes	60.7	48.4	32.3	30.6	19.3	17.3	7.8
Net Income	(5) 99.0	(4) 70.9	(3) 50.5	(2) 47.4	(2) 42.7	(2) 28.2	(1) d172.4
Cash Flow	116.4	91.1	67.1	61.8	54.2	38.3	d157.7
Average Shs. Outstg. (000)	52,020	51,683	48,550	48,542	46,062	36,666	29,500
BALANCE SHEET (IN MILLIONS):							
Cash & Cash Equivalents	120.8	59.5	85.5	68.9	71.2	46.8	25.3
Total Current Assets	2,320.6	1,920.0	1,418.3	1,624.7	1,115.1	773.2	651.7
Net Property	65.0	64.4	60.8	67.5	51.7	45.2	41.2
Total Assets	2,458.6	2,060.6	1,552.3	1,745.0	1,188.0	838.7	711.6
Total Current Liabilities	1,751.5	1,327.3	1,015.2	1,130.1	785.8	530.0	518.4
Long-Term Obligations	413.2	558.7	453.8	589.8	433.7	435.8	487.6
Net Stockholders' Equity	282.3	166.3	75.3	14.3	d36.8	d135.7	d300.7
Net Working Capital	569.1	592.7	403.1	494.6	329.3	243.2	133.4
Year-end Shs. Outstg. (000)	58,731	57,812	48,458	54,296	53,948	50,968	26,728
STATISTICAL RECORD:							
Operating Profit Margin %	1.7	1.6	1.4	1.5	1.8	2.1	...
Net Profit Margin %	0.9	0.7	0.6	0.6	0.8	0.6	...
Return on Equity %	35.1	42.6	67.1	331.6	...	...	...
Return on Assets %	4.0	3.4	3.3	2.7	3.6	3.4	...
Debt/Total Assets %	16.8	27.1	29.2	33.8	36.5	52.0	68.5
Price Range	53.69-12.00	41.38-11.00	40.38-22.23	33.16-20.63	24.13-13.94	17.13-9.88	...
P/E Ratio	28.3-6.3	30.0-8.0	38.8-21.4	34.0-21.2	26.1-15.1	22.2-12.8	...

Statistics are as originally reported. Adj. for 2-for-1 split 3/99 (1) Bef. extraord. loss $656,000 and acctg. chrg. $34.6 mill., but incl. non-recurr chrg. $179.8 mill. (2) Bef. extraord. loss $2.0 mill., 1997; $7.2 mill., 1996; $18.0 mill., 1995 (3) Incl. non-recurr. chrg. $26.7 mill. (4) Bef. extraord. loss $3.4 mill., but incl. non-recurr chrg. $14.9 mill. (5) Incl. one-time credit of $1.1 mill.

OFFICERS:
R. D. Yost, Chmn., C.E.O.
K. J. Hilzinger, Pres., C.O.O.
G. L. James III, V.P., C.F.O.

INVESTOR CONTACT: Michael N. Kilpatriac, V.P. Inv. Rel., (610) 727-7118

PRINCIPAL OFFICE: 1300 Morris Drive, Suite 100, Chesterbrook, PA 19087-5594

TELEPHONE NUMBER: (610) 727-7000
FAX: (610) 647-0141
WEB: www.amerisource.com

NO. OF EMPLOYEES: 3,550 full-time (approx.); 150 part-time (approx.)

SHAREHOLDERS: 278 (class A); 2 (class B); 3 (class C)

ANNUAL MEETING: In Mar.

INCORPORATED: DE, 1988

INSTITUTIONAL HOLDINGS:
No. of Institutions: 209
Shares Held: 53,060,315
% Held: 100.9

INDUSTRY: Drugs, proprietaries, and sundries (SIC: 5122)

TRANSFER AGENT(S): Mellon Investor Services, Pittsburgh, PA

NYSE SYMBOL AMN
Rec. Pr. 70.25 (5/31/01)

AMERON INTERNATIONAL CORPORATION

YIELD 1.8%
P/E RATIO 11.0

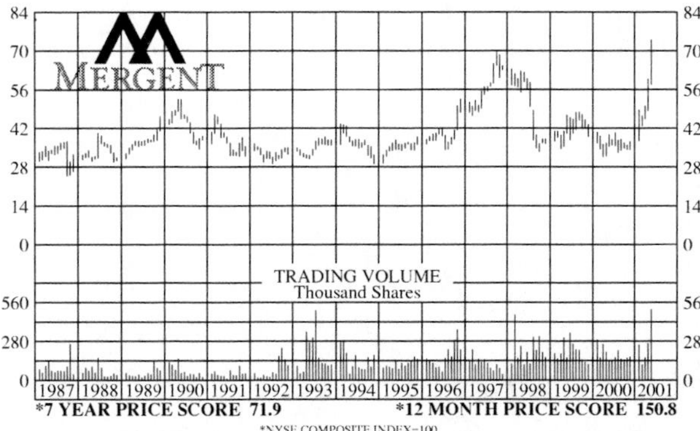

*7 YEAR PRICE SCORE 71.9 *12 MONTH PRICE SCORE 150.8

*NYSE COMPOSITE INDEX=100

INTERIM EARNINGS (Per Share):

Qtr.	Feb.	May	Aug.	Nov.
1996-97	0.23	1.30	1.72	1.48
1997-98	d0.23	1.09	1.51	2.71
1998-99	0.25	1.50	1.98	1.62
1999-00	0.24	1.55	2.02	2.60

INTERIM DIVIDENDS (Per Share):

Amt.	Decl.	Ex.	Rec.	Pay.
0.32Q	3/24/00	4/25/00	4/27/00	5/16/00
0.32Q	6/21/00	7/25/00	7/27/00	8/15/00
0.32Q	9/22/00	10/24/00	10/26/00	11/21/00
0.32Q	1/11/01	1/23/01	1/25/01	2/20/01
0.32Q	3/23/01	4/24/01	4/26/01	5/15/01

Indicated div.: $1.28 (Div. Reinv. Plan)

CAPITALIZATION (11/30/00):

	($000)	(%)
Long-Term Debt	140,718	43.5
Common & Surplus	182,430	56.5
Total	323,148	100.0

RECENT DEVELOPMENTS: For the year ended 11/30/00, net income advanced 13.8% to $25.3 million compared with $22.3 million in 1999. Sales rose 1.0% to $550.7 million, led by higher sales from AMN's Fiberglass-Composite Pipe group, which benefited from higher demand for oil field piping worldwide and continued strong performance from its operations in Asia. Results for the Infrastructure Products group were also improved.

PROSPECTS: Demand for oil field piping remains robust, which should result in continued growth for the Fiberglass-Composite Pipe group. Also, the Water Transmission group is expected to continue to perform at a consistently high level in 2001. Meanwhile, AMN expects sales and market conditions for the Performance Coatings & Finishes group to rebound to more favorable levels in 2001.

BUSINESS

AMERON INTERNATIONAL CORPORATION (formerly Ameron, Inc.) consists of four business segments. The Water Transmission group includes concrete cylinder pipe, prestressed concrete cylinder pipe, steel pipe and reinforced concrete pipe. The Performance Coatings & Finishes group develops, manufactures and markets high-performance coatings and surfacer systems on a world-wide basis. Fiberglass-Composite Pipe group develops, manufactures and markets filament-wound and molded fiberglass pipe and fittings. The Infrastructure Products group, which is comprised of the Ameron Hawaii & Poles Products division, includes ready-mix concrete, crushed and sized basaltic aggregates, dune sand, concrete pipe and box culverts, primarily to the construction industry in Hawaii. The Company operates businesses in North America, South America, Europe, Australasia and Asia. It also participates in several joint venture companies in the U.S., Saudia Arabia, Kuwait, Egypt and Mexico.

ANNUAL FINANCIAL DATA

	11/30/00	11/30/99	11/30/98	11/30/97	11/30/96	11/30/95	11/30/94
Earnings Per Share	**6.41**	**5.54**	**2 5.08**	**4.73**	**3.87**	**3.15**	**1 2.75**
Cash Flow Per Share	**10.97**	**10.26**	**3.81**	**8.80**	**8.00**	**7.25**	**6.79**
Tang. Book Val. Per Share	**42.20**	**41.96**	**37.02**	**35.38**	**44.47**	**33.86**	**31.71**
Dividends Per Share	**1.28**	**1.28**	**1.28**	**1.28**	**1.28**	**1.28**	**1.28**
Dividend Payout %	**20.0**	**23.1**	**25.2**	**27.1**	**33.1**	**40.6**	**46.5**
INCOME STATEMENT (IN THOUSANDS):							
Total Revenues	550,661	545,081	552,146	533,506	496,940	481,405	417,682
Costs & Expenses	506,691	496,278	503,580	484,222	454,552	444,234	384,619
Depreciation & Amort.	18,022	18,986	18,699	16,676	16,445	16,226	15,855
Operating Income	25,948	29,817	41,810	32,608	25,943	20,945	27,593
Net Interest Inc./(Exp.)	d12,244	d12,938	d15,077	d11,855	d10,752	d11,371	d11,191
Income Before Income Taxes	33,793	32,755	31,917	31,246	23,707	17,642	16,402
Income Taxes	8,448	10,482	11,171	11,874	8,297	5,190	6,971
Equity Earnings/Minority Int.	12,664	...	...	...	...	...	1,359
Net Income	25,345	22,273	2 d3,140	19,372	15,410	12,452	1 10,790
Cash Flow	43,367	41,259	15,559	36,048	31,855	28,678	26,645
Average Shs. Outstg.	3,953	4,023	4,084	4,095	3,982	3,955	3,924
BALANCE SHEET (IN THOUSANDS):							
Cash & Cash Equivalents	11,514	10,521	16,376	9,848	18,381	12,923	9,030
Total Current Assets	263,970	242,654	273,690	241,292	223,623	206,838	188,091
Net Property	145,196	149,597	157,918	127,678	125,687	114,116	112,953
Total Assets	478,449	458,967	499,689	433,225	411,666	371,381	350,856
Total Current Liabilities	128,344	115,141	126,830	87,265	101,765	92,380	87,086
Long-Term Obligations	140,718	135,237	165,308	140,917	112,598	91,565	92,847
Net Stockholders' Equity	182,430	178,120	167,168	152,982	144,798	134,572	124,807
Net Working Capital	135,626	127,513	146,860	154,027	121,858	114,458	101,005
Year-end Shs. Outstg.	3,992	3,869	4,030	4,005	2,985	3,956	3,936
STATISTICAL RECORD:							
Operating Profit Margin %	4.7	5.5	7.6	6.1	5.2	4.4	6.6
Net Profit Margin %	4.6	4.1	...	3.6	3.1	2.6	2.6
Return on Equity %	13.9	12.5	...	12.7	10.6	9.3	8.6
Return on Assets %	5.3	4.9	...	4.5	3.7	3.4	3.1
Debt/Total Assets %	29.4	29.5	33.1	32.5	27.4	24.7	26.5
Price Range	40.50-31.63	47.94-34.50	63.50-33.38	70.00-46.38	52.50-34.13	39.00-29.13	43.50-29.00
P/E Ratio	6.3-4.9	8.7-6.2	12.5-6.6	14.8-9.8	13.6-8.8	12.4-9.2	15.8-10.5
Average Yield %	3.5	3.1	2.6	2.2	3.0	3.8	3.5

Statistics are as originally reported. 1 Incl. an after-tax gain from the sale of a subsidiary of $1.8 mill. ($0.46/sh.) 2 Incl. non-recur. gain of $26.9 mill. & asset write-downs and other chrgs. of $21.7 mill.

OFFICERS:
J. S. Marlen, Chmn., Pres., C.E.O.
G. Wagner, Sr. V.P., C.F.O.
J. Solis, Sr. V.P., Gen. Couns., Sec.

INVESTOR CONTACT: Gary Wagner, (626) 683-4000

PRINCIPAL OFFICE: 245 South Los Robles Ave., Pasadena, CA 91101

TELEPHONE NUMBER: (626) 683-4000
FAX: (626) 683-4000
WEB: www.ameron.com

NO. OF EMPLOYEES: 3,100 (approx.)

SHAREHOLDERS: 1,326 (record)

ANNUAL MEETING: In Mar.

INCORPORATED: DE, Apr., 1929; reincorp., DE, Mar., 1986

INSTITUTIONAL HOLDINGS:
No. of Institutions: 41
Shares Held: 1,892,451
% Held: 48.9

INDUSTRY: Concrete block and brick (SIC: 3271)

TRANSFER AGENT(S): First Chicago Trust Company of New York, Jersey City, NJ

NYSE SYMBOL AME
Rec. Pr. 27.61 (4/30/01)

AMETEK, INC.

YIELD 0.9%
P/E RATIO 13.1

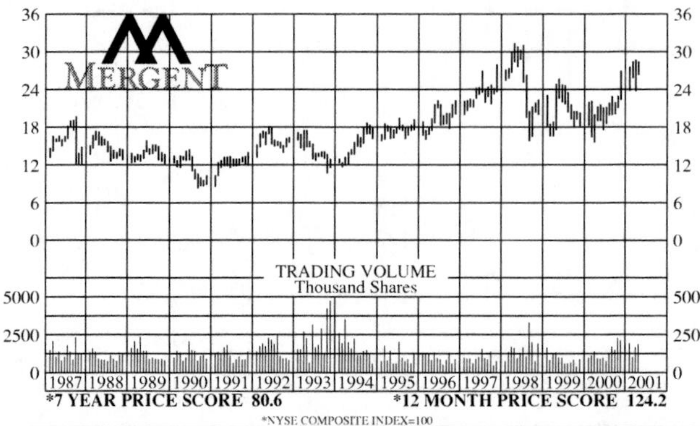

*7 YEAR PRICE SCORE 80.6 *12 MONTH PRICE SCORE 124.2

*NYSE COMPOSITE INDEX=100

INTERIM EARNINGS (Per Share):

Qtr.	Mar.	June	Sept.	Dec.
1996	0.86	1.02	0.94	1.04
1997	0.97	0.97	1.12	0.40
1998	0.44	0.45	0.42	0.19
1999	0.45	0.47	0.47	0.46
2000	0.52	0.53	0.53	0.53

INTERIM DIVIDENDS (Per Share):

Amt.	Decl.	Ex.	Rec.	Pay.
0.06Q	5/10/00	6/14/00	6/16/00	6/30/00
0.06Q	8/23/00	9/13/00	9/15/00	9/29/00
0.06Q	11/15/00	12/06/00	12/08/00	12/22/00
0.06Q	2/21/01	3/14/01	3/16/01	3/30/01
0.06Q	5/23/01	6/13/01	6/15/01	6/29/01

Indicated div.: $0.24

CAPITALIZATION (12/31/00):

	($000)	(%)
Long-Term Debt	233,616	45.4
Common & Surplus	280,838	54.6
Total	514,454	100.0

RECENT DEVELOPMENTS: For the year ended 12/31/00, net income increased 12.8% to $68.5 million versus $60.8 million a year earlier. Net sales rose 10.8% to $1.02 billion. Sales from AME's Electronic Instruments segment rose 13.0% to $509.5 million and operating income increased 12.6% to $78.8 million, led by recent acquisitions and strength in several core markets, including the aerospace, power and process businesses. Sales from the Electromechanical segment gained 8.7% to $515.2 million, while operating income jumped 14.8% to $77.6 million.

PROSPECTS: The Company's near-term prospects are clouded by the slowing U.S. economy. Consequently, AME has accelerated cost-reduction efforts across the Company, including a more aggressive movement of production to low-cost locales, the resizing of several businesses, and general expense reductions company-wide. Accordingly, the Company is projecting revenue growth for full-year 2001 to be in the mid to high single-digit percentage level. AME also foresees positive earnings per share growth, driven by strength in the second half of 2001.

BUSINESS

AMETEK, INC. manufactures electric motors and electronic instruments through its operations in North America, South America, Europe and Asia. AME's products are produced and sold worldwide through its Electronic Instruments group and the Electromechanical group. The Electronic Instruments group builds technologically advanced monitoring, sensing, calibration, and display devices for the aerospace, heavy vehicle and process industries. The Electromechanical group is the world's largest producer of air-moving electric motors for vacuum cleaners and other floorcare products. This group also produces brushless air-moving motors for aerospace, mass-transit, medical and computer markets and specialty metals for electronics, telecommunications, consumer, automotive and other markets.

BUSINESS LINE ANALYSIS

(12/31/2000)	REV (%)	INC (%)
Electromechanical	50.3	49.6
Electronic Instruments	49.7	50.4
Total	100.0	100.0

ANNUAL FINANCIAL DATA

	12/31/00	12/31/99	12/31/98	12/31/97	12/31/96	12/31/95	12/31/94
Earnings Per Share	**2.11**	**1.85**	**1 1.50**	**2 1.49**	**1.57**	**3 1.31**	**4 1.05**
Cash Flow Per Share	**3.44**	**3.05**	**2.63**	**2.45**	**2.64**	**2.34**	**2.05**
Tang. Book Val. Per Share	...	...	**0.77**	**3.25**	**3.96**	**2.65**	**2.11**
Dividends Per Share	**0.24**	**0.24**	**0.24**	**0.12**	...	...	...
Dividend Payout %	**11.4**	**13.0**	**16.0**	**8.1**	...	...	...
INCOME STATEMENT (IN MILLIONS):							
Total Revenues	1,024.7	924.8	927.5	847.8	868.7	837.5	808.0
Costs & Expenses	845.5	766.4	792.7	722.9	738.7	713.7	691.3
Depreciation & Amort.	43.3	39.6	38.4	32.9	34.9	34.5	37.3
Operating Income	135.9	118.8	96.4	92.0	95.1	89.3	79.3
Net Interest Inc./(Exp.)	d29.2	d24.8	d23.7	d18.2	d19.1	d20.2	d21.6
Income Before Income Taxes	106.1	94.5	77.4	78.2	78.7	69.3	61.8
Income Taxes	37.6	33.7	26.9	27.9	27.5	25.5	22.8
Net Income	68.5	60.8	1 50.4	2 50.3	51.2	3 43.8	4 39.0
Cash Flow	111.8	100.4	88.8	83.1	86.1	78.2	76.3
Average Shs. Outstg. (000)	32,534	32,925	33,741	33,879	32,671	33,426	37,126
BALANCE SHEET (IN MILLIONS):							
Cash & Cash Equivalents	15.3	15.4	16.9	10.0	9.5	12.7	17.7
Total Current Assets	303.1	256.1	267.8	248.5	247.0	249.3	254.0
Net Property	214.0	219.6	214.4	186.4	192.4	176.8	175.1
Total Assets	859.0	768.2	699.8	555.2	537.9	526.7	502.0
Total Current Liabilities	297.7	262.7	233.9	178.7	186.0	210.7	183.2
Long-Term Obligations	233.6	231.8	227.0	152.3	150.3	150.4	190.3
Net Stockholders' Equity	280.8	216.2	174.0	159.0	129.5	87.1	73.2
Net Working Capital	5.4	d6.6	33.9	69.7	61.0	38.7	70.7
Year-end Shs. Outstg. (000)	32,445	31,963	32,091	33,000	32,706	32,858	34,707
STATISTICAL RECORD:							
Operating Profit Margin %	13.3	12.8	10.4	10.8	10.9	10.7	9.8
Net Profit Margin %	6.7	6.6	5.4	5.9	5.9	5.2	4.8
Return on Equity %	24.4	28.1	29.0	31.6	39.5	50.3	53.3
Return on Assets %	8.0	7.9	7.2	9.1	9.5	8.3	7.8
Debt/Total Assets %	27.2	30.2	32.4	27.4	27.9	28.6	37.9
Price Range	26.94-15.50	25.75-16.50	31.38-15.75	28.00-19.88	22.25-16.00	19.50-15.75	18.75-11.63
P/E Ratio	12.8-7.3	13.9-8.9	20.9-10.5	18.8-13.3	14.2-10.2	14.9-12.0	17.9-11.1
Average Yield %	1.1	1.1	1.0	0.5	...	...	...

Statistics are as originally reported. 1 Bef. extraord. chrg. of $8.7 mill.; incls. one-time chrg. of $8.0 mill. 2 Bef. inc. of $149,000 from disc. ops. 3 Bef. inc. from disc. ops. of $11.2 mill. ($0.33/sh.), extraord. chrg. $2.7 mill. & non-recurr. credit of $10.4 mill. 4 Bef. extraor. chrg. of $11.8 mill. and acctg. adj. credit of $3.8 mill.

OFFICERS:
F. S. Hermance, Chmn., C.E.O.
J. J. Molinelli, Exec. V.P., C.F.O.
D. D. Saunders, V.P., Treas.

INVESTOR CONTACT: W. J. Burke, (610) 889-5249

PRINCIPAL OFFICE: 37 North Valley Road, Paoli, PA 19301-0801

TELEPHONE NUMBER: (610) 647-2121
FAX: (610) 647-0211
WEB: www.ametek.com

NO. OF EMPLOYEES: 8,100 (approx.)

SHAREHOLDERS: 2,800 (approx.)

ANNUAL MEETING: In May

INCORPORATED: DE, Mar., 1930

INSTITUTIONAL HOLDINGS:
No. of Institutions: 146
Shares Held: 22,149,629
% Held: 67.6

INDUSTRY: Motors and generators (SIC: 3621)

TRANSFER AGENT(S): American Stock Transfer & Trust Company, New York, NY

NYSE SYMBOL AP
Rec. Pr. 10.50 (5/31/01)

AMPCO-PITTSBURGH CORPORATION

YIELD 3.8%
P/E RATIO 6.3

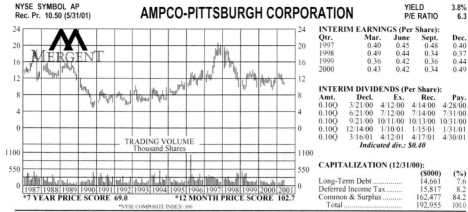

MERGENT

TRADING VOLUME
Thousand Shares

1987 1988 1989 1990 1991 1992 1993 1994 1995 1996 1997 1998 1999 2000 2001

*7 YEAR PRICE SCORE 69.0 *12 MONTH PRICE SCORE 102.7

*NYSE COMPOSITE INDEX=100

INTERIM EARNINGS (Per Share):

Qtr.	Mar.	June	Sept.	Dec.
1997	0.40	0.45	0.48	0.40
1998	0.49	0.44	0.34	0.37
1999	0.36	0.42	0.36	0.44
2000	0.43	0.42	0.34	0.49

INTERIM DIVIDENDS (Per Share):

Amt.	Decl.	Ex.	Rec.	Pay.
0.10Q	3/21/00	4/12/00	4/14/00	4/28/00
0.10Q	6/21/00	7/12/00	7/14/00	7/31/00
0.10Q	9/21/00	10/11/00	10/13/00	10/31/00
0.10Q	12/14/00	1/10/01	1/15/01	1/31/01
0.10Q	3/16/01	4/12/01	4/17/01	4/30/01

Indicated div.: $0.40

CAPITALIZATION (12/31/00):

	($000)	(%)
Long-Term Debt	14,661	7.6
Deferred Income Tax	15,817	8.2
Common & Surplus	162,477	84.2
Total	192,955	100.0

RECENT DEVELOPMENTS: For the year ended 12/31/00, net income increased 6.9% to $16.2 million from $15.1 million in 1999. Net sales were $228.0 million, up 6.5% from $214.2 million the year before, primarily due to a full year of sales from the Davy Roll Company Limited. Sales for the Forged and Cast Rolls segment rose 8.1% to $113.1 million. The Air and liquid Processing segment reported a 9.0% increase in sales to $80.3 million. Plastics Processing Machinery sales declined 3.5% to $34.6 million.

PROSPECTS: In the near-term, AP expects further deterioration in the profits of its Forged and Cast Rolls group. AP has modified production schedules to reduce labor and energy expense and is working with suppliers to lower procurement costs. In addition, on 3/6/01, AP announced that the operations of its forged hardened steel roll finishing plant in Belgium will be phased out and then permanently closed. Meanwhile, AP should continue to benefit from the strong performanc of its Air and Liquid Processing group.

BUSINESS

AMPCO-PITTSBURGH CORPORATION is a producer of finned tube heat exchange coils, air handling systems, pumps for construction, power generation, refrigeration, and chemical processing. AP also produces feed screws, barrels, heat transfer and chill rolls & forged hardened steel and cast rolls. The Company conducts business through three segments: Forged and Cast Rolls, Air and Liquid Processing, and Plastics Processing Machinery. Business in the Forged and Cast Rolls segment is conducted through Union Electric Steel Corporation, The Davy Roll Company Limited, Formet Limited and Turner Chilled Rolls Limited. The Air and Liquid Processing segment is comprised of Aerofin Corporation, Buffalo Air Handling Company, and Buffalo Pumps, Inc. The Plastics Processing Machinery segment is comprised of New Castle Industries, Inc. and its subsidiaries, and F. R. Gross Company.

BUSINESS LINE ANALYSIS

(12/31/2000)	Rev (%)	Inc (%)
Forged & Cast Rolls	49.6	49.6
Air and Liquid Processing	35.2	40.7
Plastics Processing Machinery	15.2	9.7
Total	100.0	100.0

ANNUAL FINANCIAL DATA

	12/31/00	12/31/99	12/31/98	12/31/97	12/31/96	12/31/95	12/31/94
Earnings Per Share	**1.68**	**1.58**	**1.64**	**[1] 1.73**	**[1] 1.29**	**0.94**	**[2] 0.66**
Cash Flow Per Share	**2.46**	**2.38**	**2.42**	**2.42**	**1.94**	**1.54**	**1.21**
Tang. Book Val. Per Share	**16.92**	**15.91**	**14.86**	**13.51**	**12.49**	**11.71**	**10.75**
Dividends Per Share	**0.40**	**0.40**	**0.36**	**0.34**	**0.15**	**0.10**	**0.10**
Dividend Payout %	**23.8**	**25.3**	**21.9**	**19.7**	**11.6**	**10.6**	**15.1**
INCOME STATEMENT (IN THOUSANDS):							
Total Revenues	228,028	211,827	187,853	173,906	162,403	143,785	113,836
Costs & Expenses	198,518	181,382	157,128	145,273	138,182	123,926	100,225
Depreciation & Amort.	7,425	7,631	7,523	6,672	6,152	5,683	5,251
Operating Income	22,085	22,814	23,202	21,961	18,068	14,176	8,360
Net Interest Inc./(Exp.)	d922	...	...	...	...	...	...
Income Before Income Taxes	21,942	22,690	23,622	25,905	18,770	13,975	10,192
Income Taxes	5,750	7,546	7,955	9,365	6,380	4,925	3,870
Net Income	16,192	15,144	15,667	[1] 16,540	[1] 12,390	9,050	[2] 6,322
Cash Flow	23,617	22,776	23,189	23,212	18,543	14,733	11,574
Average Shs. Outstg.	9,601	9,586	9,578	9,578	9,578	9,578	9,578
BALANCE SHEET (IN THOUSANDS):							
Cash & Cash Equivalents	17,861	16,323	33,108	21,696	29,920	22,523	24,722
Total Current Assets	120,755	118,583	107,694	96,703	99,243	91,962	79,751
Net Property	93,439	88,721	76,776	72,535	57,328	55,152	49,744
Total Assets	244,464	235,808	211,811	196,845	188,170	171,424	151,912
Total Current Liabilities	34,620	40,292	26,423	23,759	26,169	25,019	20,258
Long-Term Obligations	14,661	14,661	12,586	12,586	12,586	1,350	...
Net Stockholders' Equity	162,477	152,620	142,299	129,416	119,667	112,135	102,971
Net Working Capital	86,135	78,291	81,271	72,944	73,074	66,943	59,493
Year-end Shs. Outstg.	9,603	9,590	9,578	9,578	9,578	9,578	9,578
STATISTICAL RECORD:							
Operating Profit Margin %	9.7	10.8	12.4	12.6	11.1	9.9	7.3
Net Profit Margin %	7.1	7.1	8.3	9.5	7.6	6.3	5.6
Return on Equity %	10.0	9.9	11.0	12.8	10.4	8.1	6.1
Return on Assets %	6.6	6.4	7.4	8.4	6.6	5.3	4.2
Debt/Total Assets %	6.0	6.2	5.9	6.4	6.7	0.8	...
Price Range	12.94-9.19	14.13-9.19	19.63-9.88	20.63-11.13	14.00-10.00	11.38-7.75	9.88-6.13
P/E Ratio	7.7-5.5	8.9-5.8	12.0-6.0	11.9-6.4	10.9-7.8	12.1-8.2	15.0-9.3
Average Yield %	3.6	3.4	2.4	2.1	1.3	1.0	1.3

Statistics are as originally reported. [1] Incl. gain on sale of invstmnts. of $519,000, 1996; and $2.3 mill., 1997. [2] Incl. pre-tax gains of $2.6 mill. on sale of Amersham shas. and net gain of $1.0 mill. fr. sale of int. in U.S. Biochem. Corp.

OFFICERS:
L. Berkman, Chmn.
R. A. Paul, Pres., C.E.O.
R. J. Siddons, Exec. V.P., C.O.O.
D. Johnson, V.P., Contr., Treas.

INVESTOR CONTACT: Rose Goover, V.P., Sec., (412) 456-4418

PRINCIPAL OFFICE: 600 Grant Street, Suite 4600, Pittsburgh, PA 15219

TELEPHONE NUMBER: (412) 456-4400
FAX: (412) 456-4404
WEB: www.ampcopgh.com

NO. OF EMPLOYEES: 1,817

SHAREHOLDERS: 1,027

ANNUAL MEETING: In Apr.

INCORPORATED: PA, Mar., 1929

INSTITUTIONAL HOLDINGS:
No. of Institutions: 25
Shares Held: 4,964,055
% Held: 51.7

INDUSTRY: Pumps and pumping equipment (SIC: 3561)

TRANSFER AGENT(S): Mellon Investor Services, Pittsburgh, PA

NYSE SYMBOL APH
Rec. Pr. 50.63 (5/31/01)

AMPHENOL CORPORATION

YIELD ...
P/E RATIO 20.1

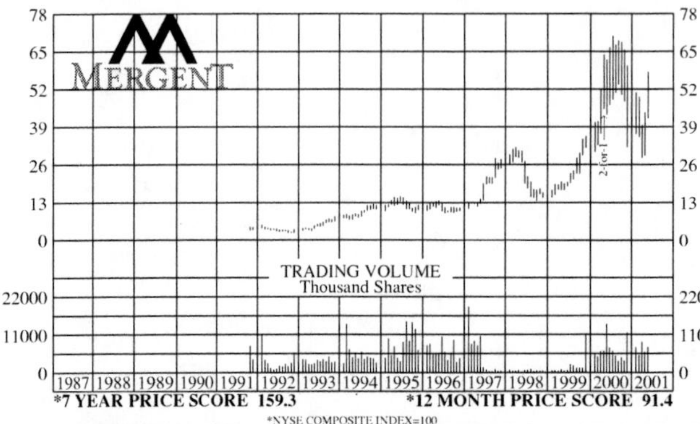

*7 YEAR PRICE SCORE 159.3 *12 MONTH PRICE SCORE 91.4

*NYSE COMPOSITE INDEX=100

INTERIM EARNINGS (Per Share):

Qtr.	Mar.	June	Sept.	Dec.
1996	0.18	0.19	0.18	0.19
1997	0.20	0.25	0.24	0.27
1998	0.27	0.29	0.23	0.23
1999	0.23	0.29	0.32	0.37
2000	0.48	0.61	0.67	0.76

INTERIM DIVIDENDS (Per Share):

Amt.	Decl.	Ex.	Rec.	Pay.
2-for-1	3/15/00	4/26/00	3/23/00	4/25/00

CAPITALIZATION (12/31/00):

	($000)	(%)
Long-Term Debt	700,216	96.0
Common & Surplus	29,234	4.0
Total	729,450	100.0

RECENT DEVELOPMENTS: For the year ended 12/31/00, net income amounted to $107.9 million compared with income of $44.3 million, before a net extraordinary charge of $8.7 million, in the previous year. Earnings were driven by strong top-line growth in the Company's major market sectors as well as its geographic regions. Net sales increased 34.5% to $1.36 billion versus $1.01 billion in the prior year. Sales growth was led by strong demand for interconnect products and coaxial cable.

PROSPECTS: Revenues continue to be driven by strong demand in the communications markets for coaxial cable and interconnect products, products used in handsets and wireless network infrastructure, internet equipment and upgrades, and expansion of HFC broadband communications networks. Separately, APH continues to focus on expanding its product lines in high-growth markets such as communications and voice, video and data communications technologies.

BUSINESS

AMPHENOL CORPORATION designs, maunfactures and markets electrical, electronic and fiber optic connectors, interconnect systems, coaxial and flat-ribbon cable. The primary end markets for the Company's products are communications systems for the converging technologies of voice, video and data communications, commercial and military aerospace electronics applications; and automotive and mass transportation applications and industrial factory automation equipment. The Company manufactures and assembles its products at facilities located in North America, South America, Europe, Asia and Australia.

QUARTERLY DATA

(12/31/00)($000)	Rev	Inc
1st Quarter	300,049	20,264
2nd Quarter	335,510	26,210
3rd Quarter	354,694	28,834
4th Quarter	369,449	32,596

ANNUAL FINANCIAL DATA

	12/31/00	12/31/99	12/31/98	12/31/97	12/31/96	12/31/95	12/31/94
Earnings Per Share	2.52	[1] 1.21	1.02	[2] 0.92	0.73	0.67	[1] 0.46
Cash Flow Per Share	3.57	2.37	2.08	1.53	1.04	0.97	0.76
Tang. Book Val. Per Share	...	...	...	...	0.16	0.02	...
INCOME STATEMENT (IN MILLIONS):							
Total Revenues	1,359.7	1,010.6	918.9	884.3	776.2	783.2	692.7
Costs & Expenses	1,070.2	807.1	731.1	694.5	608.7	620.1	559.8
Depreciation & Amort.	45.1	42.8	38.0	34.4	29.5	28.4	28.8
Operating Income	244.4	160.7	149.7	155.4	138.0	134.7	104.1
Net Interest Inc./(Exp.)	d61.7	d79.3	d81.2	d64.7	d24.6	d25.5	d30.4
Income Before Income Taxes	173.2	76.2	64.0	87.2	109.7	104.6	69.5
Income Taxes	65.3	31.9	27.5	35.9	42.1	41.8	27.1
Net Income	107.9	[1] 44.3	36.5	[2] 51.3	67.6	62.9	[1] 42.4
Cash Flow	153.0	87.1	74.5	85.6	97.1	91.3	71.2
Average Shs. Outstg. (000)	42,879	36,664	35,885	56,006	93,300	94,608	93,224
BALANCE SHEET (IN MILLIONS):							
Cash & Cash Equivalents	24.6	12.9	3.1	4.7	4.0	12.0	...
Total Current Assets	412.7	335.2	287.7	254.8	233.8	225.7	...
Net Property	161.0	120.0	126.8	111.6	102.1	94.7	...
Total Assets	1,004.3	836.4	807.4	737.2	710.7	689.9	...
Total Current Liabilities	242.5	145.9	124.2	117.3	96.9	104.4	...
Long-Term Obligations	700.2	745.7	952.5	937.3	219.5	195.2	...
Net Stockholders' Equity	29.2	d81.2	d292.3	d343.1	360.5	344.1	...
Net Working Capital	170.1	189.3	163.5	137.5	136.9	121.3	...
Year-end Shs. Outstg. (000)	41,687	41,232	35,725	35,066	89,440	94,640	...
STATISTICAL RECORD:							
Operating Profit Margin %	18.0	15.9	16.3	17.6	17.8	17.2	15.0
Net Profit Margin %	7.9	4.4	4.0	5.8	8.7	8.0	6.1
Return on Equity %	369.1	...	...	...	18.7	18.3	...
Return on Assets %	10.7	5.3	4.5	7.0	9.5	9.1	...
Debt/Total Assets %	69.7	89.2	118.0	127.1	30.9	28.3	...
Price Range	70.38-30.31	35.75-14.72	32.00-13.50	28.25-10.75	13.81-9.38	15.19-9.38	12.56-7.06
P/E Ratio	27.9-12.0	29.5-12.2	31.4-13.2	30.9-11.7	19.0-12.9	22.8-14.1	27.6-15.5

Statistics are as originally reported. Adj. for 2-for-1 stk. split, 4/00. [1] Bef. extraord. chrg. of $8.7 mill., 1999; $4.1 mill., 1994. [2] Bef. extraord. chrg. of $24.5 mill. & incl. nonrecurr. chrg. of $2.5 mill.

OFFICERS:
M. H. Loeffler, Chmn., Pres., C.E.O.
E. G. Jepsen, Exec. V.P., C.F.O.
D. G. Reardon, Treas., Contr.
E. C. Wetmore, Sec., Gen. Couns.

INVESTOR CONTACT: Edward G. Jepsen, Exec. V.P., C.F.O., (203) 265-8650

PRINCIPAL OFFICE: 358 Hall Avenue, Wallingford, CT 06492

TELEPHONE NUMBER: (203) 265-8900
FAX: (203) 265-8746
WEB: www.amphenol.com

NO. OF EMPLOYEES: 8,000 (approx.)

SHAREHOLDERS: 95

ANNUAL MEETING: In May

INCORPORATED: DE, Nov., 1991

INSTITUTIONAL HOLDINGS:
No. of Institutions: 147
Shares Held: 20,994,712
% Held: 50.4

INDUSTRY: Electronic connectors (SIC: 3678)

TRANSFER AGENT(S): Boston EquiServe L.P., Canton, MA

NYSE SYMBOL AMR
Rec. Pr. 38.99 (5/31/01)

AMR CORPORATION

YIELD ...
P/E RATIO 8.2

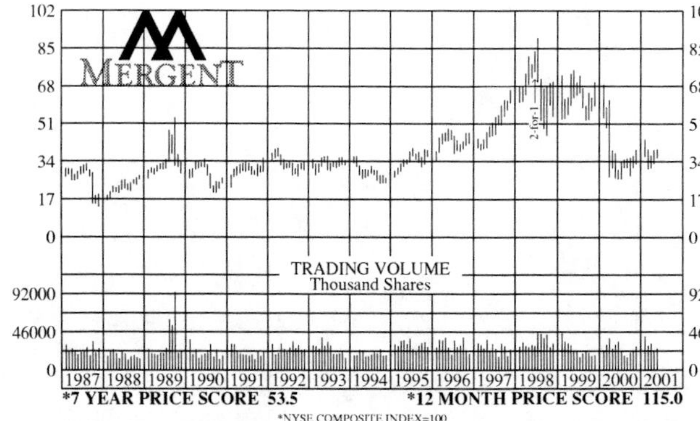

*7 YEAR PRICE SCORE 53.5 *12 MONTH PRICE SCORE 115.0

*NYSE COMPOSITE INDEX=100

INTERIM EARNINGS (Per Share):

Qtr.	Mar.	June	Sept.	Dec.
1997	0.83	1.63	1.78	1.17
1998	1.62	2.30	2.48	1.09
1999	0.57	1.70	1.76	1.37
2000	0.57	1.96	1.96	0.29

INTERIM DIVIDENDS (Per Share):

Amt.	Decl.	Ex.	Rec.	Pay.

No dividends paid.

CAPITALIZATION (12/31/00):

	($000)	(%)
Long-Term Debt	4,151,000	27.6
Capital Lease Obligations	1,323,000	8.8
Deferred Income Tax	2,385,000	15.9
Common & Surplus	7,176,000	47.7
Total	15,035,000	100.0

RECENT DEVELOPMENTS: For the year ended 12/31/00, earnings from continuing operations totaled $779.0 million, up 18.8% versus income from continuing operations of $656.0 million the year before. Results in 2000 included a $36.0 million after-tax gain from the sale of priceline.com warrants. Total operating revenues climbed 11.1% to $19.70 billion from $17.73 billion a year earlier. Operating income advanced 19.5% to $1.38 billion.

PROSPECTS: On 4/9/01, American Airlines, Inc. announced that it has completed its acquisition of substantially all the assets of Trans World Airlines, Inc. for approximately $742.0 million in cash and the assumption of about $3.50 billion of aircraft operating leases. The acquisition is expected to significantly improve American's east/west operations by providing an important new hub in St. Louis, Missouri.

BUSINESS

AMR CORPORATION, the parent company of American Airlines, Inc., operates in three major lines of business. The Air Transportation Group consists of American's Passenger and Cargo divisions and AMR Eagle, Inc., a regional airline operator. The Company provides scheduled jet service to more than 240 destinations in 49 countries. AMR Management Services Group provides airline and airport ground services, management consulting and training, and investment service activities. At 12/31/00, AMR operated a fleet of 978 jet aircraft. On 3/15/00, the Company spun off Sabre, Inc. to AMR shareholders. On 4/9/01, AMR acquired Trans World Airlines, Inc.

REVENUES

(12/31/00)	($000)	(%)
Passenger-Amer. Airlines	16,377,000	83.1
Passenger-AMR Eagle	1,452,000	7.4
Cargo	721,000	3.6
Other revenues	1,153,000	5.9
Total revenues	19,703,000	100.0

ANNUAL FINANCIAL DATA

	12/31/00	12/31/99	12/31/98	12/31/97	12/31/96	12/31/95	12/31/94
Earnings Per Share	**[5] 4.81**	**[4] 4.17**	**[4] 7.48**	**[3] 5.39**	**[2] 6.32**	**1.24**	**[1] 1.13**
Cash Flow Per Share	**12.23**	**11.13**	**14.82**	**12.25**	**13.42**	**9.44**	**10.48**
Tang. Book Val. Per Share	**47.19**	**44.21**	**39.58**	**34.01**	**29.25**	**21.45**	**19.24**
INCOME STATEMENT (IN MILLIONS):							
Total Revenues	19,703.0	17,730.0	19,205.0	18,570.0	17,753.0	16,910.0	16,137.0
Costs & Expenses	17,120.0	15,482.0	15,580.0	15,400.0	14,710.0	14,636.0	13,881.0
Depreciation & Amort.	1,202.0	1,092.0	1,287.0	1,244.0	1,204.0	1,259.0	1,250.0
Operating Income	1,381.0	1,156.0	2,338.0	1,926.0	1,839.0	1,015.0	1,006.0
Net Interest Inc./(Exp.)	d162.0	d186.0	d128.0	d261.0	d419.0	d607.0	d569.0
Income Before Income Taxes	1,287.0	1,006.0	2,164.0	1,646.0	1,633.0	353.0	370.0
Income Taxes	508.0	350.0	858.0	661.0	528.0	162.0	142.0
Net Income	[5] 779.0	[4] 656.0	[4] 1,306.0	[3] 985.0	[2] 1,105.0	191.0	[1] 228.0
Cash Flow	1,981.0	1,748.0	2,593.0	2,229.0	2,309.0	1,450.0	1,593.0
Average Shs. Outstg. (000)	162,000	157,000	175,000	182,000	172,000	153,600	152,000
BALANCE SHEET (IN MILLIONS):							
Cash & Cash Equivalents	2,233.0	1,791.0	2,073.0	2,434.0	1,811.0	901.0	777.0
Total Current Assets	5,179.0	4,424.0	4,875.0	5,071.0	4,470.0	3,137.0	3,118.0
Net Property	18,636.0	16,287.0	14,386.0	13,257.0	13,305.0	13,565.0	13,898.0
Total Assets	26,213.0	24,374.0	22,303.0	20,915.0	20,497.0	19,556.0	19,486.0
Total Current Liabilities	6,990.0	5,864.0	5,639.0	5,617.0	5,566.0	4,632.0	4,914.0
Long-Term Obligations	5,474.0	5,689.0	4,200.0	3,889.0	4,542.0	7,052.0	7,878.0
Net Stockholders' Equity	7,176.0	6,858.0	6,698.0	6,216.0	5,668.0	3,720.0	3,380.0
Net Working Capital	d1,811.0	d1,440.0	d764.0	d546.0	d1,096.0	d1,495.0	d1,796.0
Year-end Shs. Outstg. (000)	152,063	148,245	161,351	173,198	182,000	152,800	151,800
STATISTICAL RECORD:							
Operating Profit Margin %	7.0	6.5	12.2	10.4	10.4	6.0	6.2
Net Profit Margin %	4.0	3.7	6.8	5.3	6.2	1.1	1.4
Return on Equity %	10.9	9.6	19.5	15.8	19.5	5.1	6.7
Return on Assets %	3.0	2.7	5.9	4.7	5.4	1.0	1.2
Debt/Total Assets %	20.9	23.3	18.8	18.6	22.2	36.1	40.4
Price Range	68.75-26.00	75.44-52.56	89.94-45.63	66.28-39.13	48.75-34.00	40.13-26.69	36.38-24.06
P/E Ratio	14.3-5.4	18.1-12.6	12.0-6.1	12.3-7.3	7.7-5.4	32.4-21.5	32.2-21.3

Statistics are as originally reported. Adj. for 2-for-1 stk. split, 6/98. [1] Bef. $29 mil loss from early retirmnt. of debt & incl. $334 mil in restr. chgs. [2] Bef. $89 mil extraord. chg. & incl. $251 mil non-recur. net gain. [3] Incl. $20 mil pre-tax chg. & special items after-tax cr. of $13 mil. [4] Bef. $329 mil ($2.09/sh) gain fr. disc. ops., 1999; $8 mil ($0.04/sh) income fr. disc. ops., 1998. [5] Bef. $43 mil ($0.27/sh) income fr. disc. ops. and $9 mil ($0.05/sh) extraord. chg. & incl. $36 mil ($0.21/sh) after-tax gain fr. sale of priceline.com warrants.

OFFICERS:
D. J. Carty, Chmn., Pres., C.E.O.
R. W. Baker, Vice-Chmn.
T. W. Horton, Sr. V.P., C.F.O.

INVESTOR CONTACT: Linda Dill, Dir., Inv. Rel., (817) 967-2970

PRINCIPAL OFFICE: 4333 Amon Carter Blvd., Ft. Worth, TX 76155

TELEPHONE NUMBER: (817) 963-1234
FAX: (817) 967-9641
WEB: www.amrcorp.com

NO. OF EMPLOYEES: 103,000 (approx.)

SHAREHOLDERS: 13,250 (approx.)

ANNUAL MEETING: In May

INCORPORATED: DE, Oct., 1982

INSTITUTIONAL HOLDINGS:
No. of Institutions: 312
Shares Held: 132,500,644
% Held: 86.3

INDUSTRY: Air transportation, scheduled (SIC: 4512)

TRANSFER AGENT(S): First Chicago Trust Company of New York, Jersey City, NJ

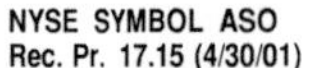

NYSE SYMBOL ASO
Rec. Pr. 17.15 (4/30/01)

AMSOUTH BANCORPORATION

YIELD 4.9%
P/E RATIO 20.2

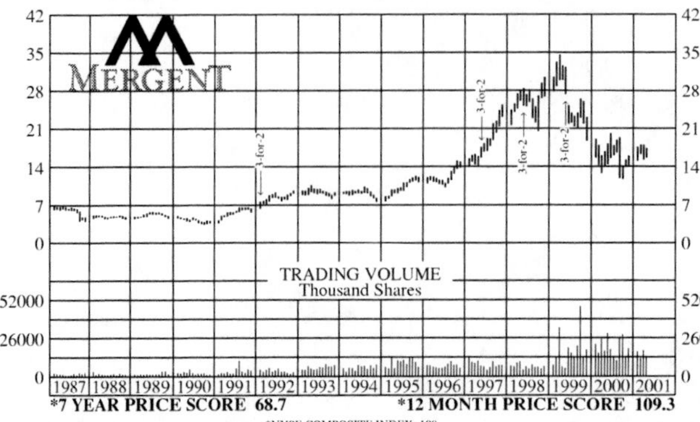

*7 YEAR PRICE SCORE 68.7 *12 MONTH PRICE SCORE 109.3

*NYSE COMPOSITE INDEX=100

INTERIM EARNINGS (Per Share):

Qtr.	Mar.	June	Sept.	Dec.
1997	0.29	0.30	0.31	0.32
1998	0.34	0.36	0.37	0.38
1999	0.39	0.42	0.44	d0.16
2000	0.35	0.26	d0.10	0.34

INTERIM DIVIDENDS (Per Share):

Amt.	Decl.	Ex.	Rec.	Pay.
0.20Q	4/20/00	6/12/00	6/14/00	7/01/00
0.20Q	7/20/00	9/11/00	9/13/00	10/02/00
0.21Q	10/18/00	12/11/00	12/13/00	1/02/01
0.21Q	1/22/01	3/15/01	3/19/01	4/02/01
0.21Q	4/19/01	6/14/01	6/18/01	7/02/01

Indicated div.: $0.84 (Div. Reinv. Plan)

CAPITALIZATION (12/31/00):

	($000)	(%)
Total Deposits	26,623,304	75.4
Long-Term Debt	5,883,405	16.7
Common & Surplus	2,813,407	8.0
Total	35,320,116	100.0

RECENT DEVELOPMENTS: For the year ended 12/31/00, net income declined 3.3% to $329.1 million from $340.5 million in the prior year. Earnings for 2000 and 1999 included pre-tax merger-related costs of $110.2 million and $301.4 million, respectively. Net interest income fell 8.5% to $1.38 billion. Provision for loan losses increased 37.4% to $227.6 million. Non-interest income dropped 21.0% to $669.5 million. Non-interest expense, excluding merger-related costs, declined 6.7% to $1.26 billion.

PROSPECTS: ASO announced that it is expanding its Internet banking through the creation of an e-Commerce group. This will allow the Company to expand and improve its on-line offerings across all of ASO's lines of business. The new e-Commerce group will also be responsible for the development of e-products and Internet alliance partner selection and management. The revision of the Company's Web site includes a complete suite of Internet banking services.

BUSINESS

AMSOUTH BANCORPORATION is headquartered in Birmingham, Alabama. As of 12/31/00, ASO had assets of $38.94 billion and operated 600 branch banking offices and 1,250 ATMs in the following southeastern states: Alabama, Florida, Tennessee, Mississippi, Georgia, and Louisiana. ASO's affiliates, AmSouth N.A., AmSouth Bank of Florida, AmSouth Bank of Tennessee, AmSouth Bank of Georgia and AmSouth Bank of Alabama, AmSouth Investment Services and AmSouth Leasing Corp., provide a full line of traditional and nontraditional financial services including consumer and commercial banking, mortgage lending, trust services and investment management. On 10/1/99, ASO acquired First American Corp.

LOAN DISTRIBUTION

(12/31/2000)	($000)	(%)
Commercial	9,077,937	36.9
Commercial Real Estate	4,840,124	19.7
Consumer	10,698,374	43.4
Total	24,616,435	100.0

ANNUAL FINANCIAL DATA

	12/31/00	[5] 12/31/99	12/31/98	12/31/97	12/31/96	12/31/95	12/31/94
Earnings Per Share	[6] 0.86	[4] 0.86	[3] 1.45	1.21	[2] 0.96	[1] 0.89	0.67
Tang. Book Val. Per Share	7.53	7.56	8.05	7.64	7.38	7.16	6.69
Dividends Per Share	0.80	0.67	0.53	0.50	0.47	0.45	0.41
Dividend Payout %	93.0	78.3	36.9	41.0	49.5	50.7	62.2
INCOME STATEMENT (IN MILLIONS):							
Total Interest Income	3,070.4	2,932.8	1,462.5	1,377.8	1,353.8	1,275.1	1,047.7
Total Interest Expense	1,691.3	1,424.8	763.6	701.5	701.4	679.4	480.4
Net Interest Income	1,379.1	1,507.9	699.0	676.3	652.4	595.7	567.3
Provision for Loan Losses	227.6	165.6	58.1	67.4	65.2	40.1	30.1
Non-Interest Income	669.5	847.6	346.6	266.0	235.3	231.8	179.0
Non-Interest Expense	1,366.4	1,648.5	582.1	526.2	534.2	512.1	522.9
Income Before Taxes	454.6	541.4	405.3	348.7	288.3	275.2	193.3
Net Income	[6] 329.1	[4] 340.5	[3] 262.7	226.2	[2] 182.7	[1] 175.0	127.3
Average Shs. Outstg. (000)	384,677	396,515	181,922	186,179	191,042	196,634	190,779
BALANCE SHEET (IN MILLIONS):							
Cash & Due from Banks	1,278.7	1,563.3	619.6	658.5	648.5	651.6	616.6
Securities Avail. for Sale	1,920.9	6,016.7	3,033.5	2,509.1	2,294.4	2,482.8	389.4
Total Loans & Leases	25,088.2	26,436.4	12,869.9	12,342.8	12,168.6	11,819.8	11,496.1
Allowance for Credit Losses	852.2	533.1	283.7	284.4	267.4	255.0	237.4
Net Loans & Leases	24,236.0	25,903.3	12,586.2	12,058.5	11,901.2	11,564.8	11,258.7
Total Assets	38,936.0	43,406.6	19,794.1	18,622.3	18,407.3	17,738.8	16,778.0
Total Deposits	26,623.3	27,912.4	13,283.8	12,945.2	12,467.6	13,408.8	13,067.1
Long-Term Obligations	5,883.4	5,603.5	3,239.8	1,633.2	1,435.7	447.8	386.1
Total Liabilities	36,122.6	40,447.3	18,474.1	17,237.0	17,011.4	16,355.3	15,467.5
Net Stockholders' Equity	2,813.4	2,959.2	1,427.6	1,385.2	1,395.8	1,383.5	1,310.5
Year-end Shs. Outstg. (000)	373,807	391,374	177,377	181,208	189,081	193,269	195,939
STATISTICAL RECORD:							
Return on Equity %	11.7	11.5	18.4	16.3	13.1	12.6	9.7
Return on Assets %	0.8	0.8	1.3	1.2	1.0	1.0	0.8
Equity/Assets %	7.0	6.8	7.2	7.4	7.6	7.8	7.8
Non-Int. Exp./Tot. Inc. %	66.7	70.0	55.7	55.8	60.2	61.9	70.1
Price Range	20.06-11.69	34.59-18.75	30.42-20.46	25.36-14.00	15.07-10.19	12.26-7.63	10.33-7.52
P/E Ratio	23.3-13.6	40.2-21.8	21.0-14.1	20.9-11.5	15.8-10.6	13.8-8.6	15.5-11.3
Average Yield %	5.0	2.5	2.1	2.5	3.8	4.5	4.6

Statistics are as originally reported. Adj. for 3-for-2 splits 5/99, 4/98, 4/97. [1] Incl. pre-tax gain on the sale of 3rd party mtg. servicing portfolio to G.E. Capital Services, Inc. & $22.0 mill. in add'l. exps. rel. to the consol. & workforce reduction. [2] Incl. SAIF pre-tax chrg. of $24.2 mill. [3] Incl. $28.0 mill. gain fr. sale of assets. [4] Incl. net gain fr. sale of businesses of $8.6 mill. & merger-rel. chrgs. of $301.4 mill. [5] Refl. acquis. of First American Corp. in 10/99. [6] Incl. pre-tax merger-rel. costs of $110.2 mill. & a gain of $538,000 on the sale of businesses.

OFFICERS:
C. D. Ritter, Chmn., Pres., C.E.O.
S. D. Gibson, Vice-Chmn., C.F.O.
S. A. Yoder, Exec. V.P., Gen. Couns., Sec.

INVESTOR CONTACT: M. List Underwood, Jr., Exec. V.P.-Corp. Fin., (205) 801-0265

PRINCIPAL OFFICE: 1900 Fifth Avenue North, Birmingham, AL 35203

TELEPHONE NUMBER: (205) 320-7151
FAX: (205) 326-4072
WEB: www.amsouth.com

NO. OF EMPLOYEES: 12,296

SHAREHOLDERS: 32,338 (approx.)

ANNUAL MEETING: In April

INCORPORATED: DE, Nov., 1970

INSTITUTIONAL HOLDINGS:
No. of Institutions: 269
Shares Held: 122,945,278
% Held: 32.8

INDUSTRY: State commercial banks (SIC: 6022)

TRANSFER AGENT(S): The Bank of New York, New York, NY

NYSE SYMBOL APC
Rec. Pr. 62.61 (5/31/01)

ANADARKO PETROLEUM CORPORATION

YIELD 0.3%
P/E RATIO 17.2

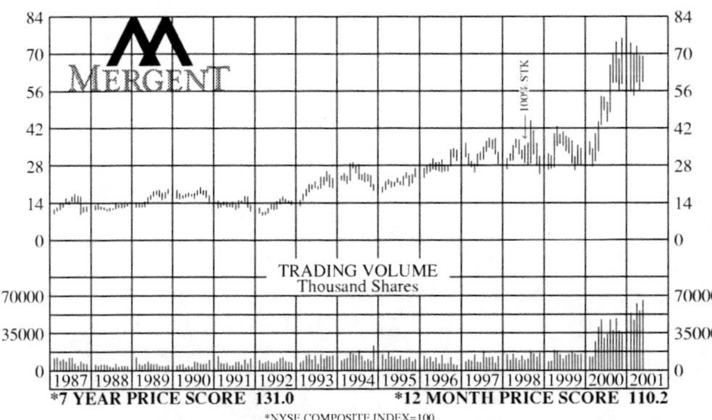

INTERIM EARNINGS (Per Share):

Qtr.	Mar.	June	Sept.	Dec.
1996	0.18	0.15	0.21	0.32
1997	0.29	0.12	0.15	0.35
1998	0.06	0.02	d0.02	d0.47
1999	d0.19	0.06	0.15	0.22
2000	0.37	0.48	1.03	1.75

INTERIM DIVIDENDS (Per Share):

Amt.	Decl.	Ex.	Rec.	Pay.
0.05Q	4/27/00	6/12/00	6/14/00	6/28/00
0.05Q	7/31/00	9/11/00	9/13/00	9/27/00
0.05Q	10/30/00	12/11/00	12/13/00	12/27/00
0.05Q	2/01/01	3/12/01	3/14/01	3/28/01
0.05Q	4/26/01	6/11/01	6/13/01	6/27/01

Indicated div.: $0.20

CAPITALIZATION (12/31/00):

	($000)	(%)
Long-Term Debt	3,984,000	27.7
Deferred Income Tax	3,633,000	25.2
Preferred Stock	200,000	1.4
Common & Surplus	6,586,000	45.7
Total	14,403,000	100.0

RECENT DEVELOPMENTS: For the year ended 12/31/00, income soared to $824.0 million, before an accounting charge of $17.0 million, versus $43.0 million a year earlier. Results for 2000 and 1999 included impairment charges related to international properties of $50.0 million and $24.0 million, respectively. Results for 2000 also included after-tax merger expenses of $43.0 million. Total revenues surged to $5.69 billion from $1.77 billion in 1999.

PROSPECTS: On 2/1/01, APC approved a capital-spending program totaling $2.83 billion for 2001, representing a 63.8% increase over capital outlays in 2000. Given the expected strong future demand for natural gas in North America, APC's primary focus for the 2001 budget will be to find new natural gas reserves and increase gas production in the Lower 48, the Gulf of Mexico and in Canada.

BUSINESS

ANADARKO PETROLEUM CORPORATION ranks among the nation's largest independent oil and gas exploration and production companies with 2.06 billion energy equivalent barrels of proved energy reserves. APC's major areas of operations are located in the U.S., primarily in Texas, Louisiana, the mid-continent and Rocky Mountain regions, Alaska and in the shallow and deep waters of the Gulf of Mexico, as well as in Canada, Algeria, Guatemala, Venezuela and other international areas. Exploration activity is underway in Tunisia, West Africa, the former Soviet Republic of Georgia, Australia and the North Atlantic Margin. APC also owns and operates gas gathering systems in its core producing areas. In addition, the Company engages in the minerals business through non-operated joint venture and royalty arrangements in several coal, industrial minerals and trona (natural soda ash) mines located on lands within and adjacent to its Land Grant holdings in Wyoming. At 12/31/00, proved reserves amounted to: natural gas, 6.09 trillion cubic feet; crude oil, condensate and natural gas liquids, 1.05 billion barrels. On 7/14/00, APC acquired Union Pacific Resources Group Inc.

ANNUAL FINANCIAL DATA

	5 12/31/00	12/31/99	12/31/98	12/31/97	12/31/96	12/31/95	12/31/94
Earnings Per Share	**4 4.25**	**3 0.25**	**d0.41**	**0.89**	**1 0.85**	**0.18**	**1 0.35**
Cash Flow Per Share	**7.45**	**2.01**	**1.30**	**2.56**	**2.28**	**1.59**	**1.83**
Tang. Book Val. Per Share	**20.80**	**10.30**	**8.65**	**9.17**	**8.52**	**7.58**	**7.64**
Dividends Per Share	**0.20**	**0.20**	**0.19**	**0.15**	**0.15**	**0.15**	**0.15**
Dividend Payout %	**4.7**	**80.0**	**. . .**	**16.9**	**17.6**	**83.3**	**42.8**
INCOME STATEMENT (IN MILLIONS):							
Total Revenues	5,686.0	701.1	560.3	673.2	569.0	434.0	482.5
Costs & Expenses	3,642.0	302.4	362.0	268.7	204.4	203.1	219.7
Depreciation & Amort.	625.0	219.8	205.6	201.1	169.0	166.5	174.1
Operating Income	1,419.0	178.9	d7.4	203.4	195.6	64.5	88.7
Net Interest Inc./(Exp.)	d93.0	d74.1	d57.7	d41.0	d39.0	d36.4	d26.1
Income Before Income Taxes	1,426.0	104.8	d65.1	164.4	157.8	29.3	64.7
Income Taxes	602.0	62.2	cr22.9	57.0	57.1	8.2	23.6
Net Income	4 824.0	3 42.6	d42.2	107.3	1 100.7	21.0	1 41.1
Cash Flow	1,438.0	251.4	156.4	308.4	269.7	187.5	215.2
Average Shs. Outstg. (000)	193,000	125,187	120,103	120,254	118,494	117,870	117,552
BALANCE SHEET (IN MILLIONS):							
Cash & Cash Equivalents	199.0	44.8	17.0	8.9	14.6	17.1	6.5
Total Current Assets	1,973.0	355.9	229.9	219.0	269.8	163.2	138.6
Net Property	13,011.0	3,681.2	3,381.5	2,754.8	2,297.5	2,088.8	1,986.1
Total Assets	16,669.0	4,098.4	3,633.0	2,992.5	2,584.0	2,267.0	2,142.1
Total Current Liabilities	1,676.0	387.2	288.7	252.3	285.3	190.5	128.2
Long-Term Obligations	3,984.0	1,443.3	1,425.4	955.7	731.0	674.0	629.3
Net Stockholders' Equity	6,786.0	1,534.6	1,259.5	1,116.8	1,014.1	909.7	899.6
Net Working Capital	297.0	d31.2	d58.8	d33.3	d15.4	d27.3	10.5
Year-end Shs. Outstg. (000)	253,303	129,620	122,436	121,772	119,052	120,032	117,714
STATISTICAL RECORD:							
Operating Profit Margin %	25.0	25.5	. . .	30.2	34.4	14.9	18.4
Net Profit Margin %	14.5	6.1	. . .	15.9	17.7	4.8	8.5
Return on Equity %	12.1	2.8	. . .	9.6	9.9	2.3	4.6
Return on Assets %	4.9	1.0	. . .	3.6	3.9	0.9	1.9
Debt/Total Assets %	23.9	35.2	39.2	31.9	28.3	29.7	29.4
Price Range	75.95-27.56	42.75-26.25	44.88-24.75	38.38-25.38	34.44-23.38	27.06-17.81	29.25-18.50
P/E Ratio	17.9-6.5	170.9-105.0	. . .	43.1-28.5	40.5-27.5	150.3-98.9	83.5-52.8
Average Yield %	0.4	0.6	0.5	0.5	0.5	0.7	0.6

Statistics are as originally reported. Adj. for 2-for-1 stk. split, 7/98. 1 Incls. non-recurr. credit 12/31/96: $12.3 mill.; chrg. 12/31/94: $6.6 mill.; pre-tax chrg. 12/31/92: $21.0 mill. 2 Bef. acctg. change credit of $77.4 mill. 3 Incls. non-cash pre-tax chrg. of $24.0 mill. 4 Incls. aft.-tax merger-rel. chrges. of $43.0 mill. (0.22/sh.) & an impair. chrg. of $50.0 mill. rel. to int'l. prop.; bef. acctg. chge. chrg. of $17.0 mill. ($0.09/sh.) 5 Incls. results for Union Pacific Resources Group Inc.

OFFICERS:
R. J. Allison Jr., Chmn., C.E.O.
J. N. Seitz, Pres., C.O.O.
M. E. Rose, Exec. V.P., C.F.O.

INVESTOR CONTACT: Paul Taylor, V.P., Investor Relations, (281) 873-3855

PRINCIPAL OFFICE: 17001 Northchase Drive, Houston, TX 77060-2141

TELEPHONE NUMBER: (281) 875-1101
FAX: (281) 874-3385
WEB: www.anadarko.com

NO. OF EMPLOYEES: 3,500 (approx.)

SHAREHOLDERS: 22,000

ANNUAL MEETING: In April

INCORPORATED: DE, 1985

INSTITUTIONAL HOLDINGS:
No. of Institutions: 561
Shares Held: 199,530,650
% Held: 79.6

INDUSTRY: Crude petroleum and natural gas (SIC: 1311)

TRANSFER AGENT(S): Mellon Investor Services, Ridgefield Park, NJ

NYSE SYMBOL ADI
Rec. Pr. 44.55 (5/31/01)

ANALOG DEVICES, INC.

YIELD ...
P/E RATIO 24.2

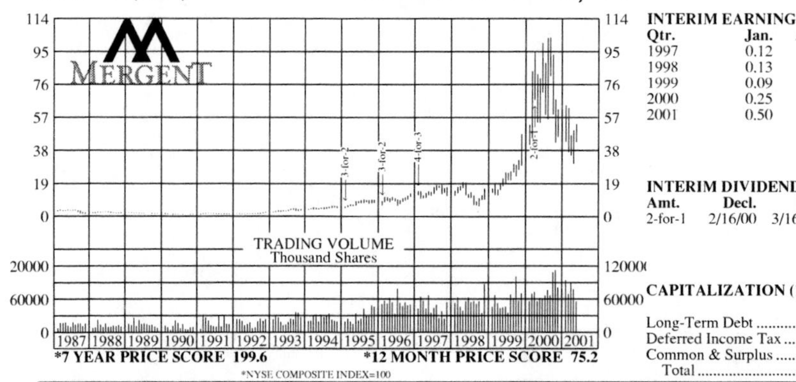

*7 YEAR PRICE SCORE 199.6 *12 MONTH PRICE SCORE 75.2

*NYSE COMPOSITE INDEX=100

INTERIM EARNINGS (Per Share):

Qtr.	Jan.	April	July	Oct.
1997	0.12	0.13	0.14	0.15
1998	0.13	0.14	0.03	0.08
1999	0.09	0.11	0.15	0.20
2000	0.25	0.32	0.50	0.52
2001	0.50	...	...	...

INTERIM DIVIDENDS (Per Share):

Amt.	Decl.	Ex.	Rec.	Pay.
2-for-1	2/16/00	3/16/00	2/28/00	3/15/00

CAPITALIZATION (10/28/00):

	($000)	(%)
Long-Term Debt	1,212,960	34.0
Deferred Income Tax	51,205	1.4
Common & Surplus	2,303,650	64.6
Total	3,567,815	100.0

RECENT DEVELOPMENTS: For the quarter ended 2/3/01, net income more than doubled to $190.4 million versus $93.0 million in the corresponding period of the prior year. Results for 2000 included a pre-tax charge of $9.5 million for write-off of in-process research and development. Net sales surged 57.5% to $772.3 million, mainly due to a 61.0% improvement in analog products revenue and a 48.0% increase in DSP products revenue.

PROSPECTS: Going forward, the Company believes gross margins as a percentage of sales will remain strong, based on a more favorable product mix. Meanwhile, the Company anticipates fiscal 2001 revenues could grow approximately 20.0% to 25.0%, assuming inventories come into balance and production builds in some key high-volume communication programs.

BUSINESS

ANALOG DEVICES, INC. is a semiconductor company that manufactures precision high-performance linear and mixed signal integrated circuits. These devices are used to condition, amplify and otherwise process analog signals from sensors that measure real-world phenomena such as temperature, pressure and velocity and convert those signals into digital form that microprocessors and computers can read. ADI also manufactures a family of integrated circuits used for digital signal processing applications (DSP). Additional products include board-level subsystems and signal processing components. Most of the Company's products are sold to OEMs that incorporate them into equipment, instruments and systems used by end-users.

REVENUES

10/28/2000($000)	($000)	(%)
North America	1,722,056	66.8
Europe	504,669	19.6
Asia	350,822	13.6
Total	2,577,547	100.0

ANNUAL FINANCIAL DATA

	10/28/00	10/30/99	10/31/98	11/1/97	11/2/96	10/28/95	10/29/94
Earnings Per Share	**1 1.59**	**0.55**	**0.36**	**0.52**	**0.52**	**0.38**	**0.24**
Cash Flow Per Share	**2.00**	**0.94**	**0.69**	**0.79**	**0.75**	**0.58**	**0.44**
Tang. Book Val. Per Share	**5.90**	**4.53**	**3.47**	**3.31**	**2.66**	**2.09**	**2.50**
INCOME STATEMENT (IN MILLIONS):							
Total Revenues	2,577.5	1,450.4	1,230.6	1,243.5	1,193.8	941.5	773.5
Costs & Expenses	1,653.8	1,064.9	945.3	906.5	882.8	719.7	610.4
Depreciation & Amort.	156.7	142.6	127.6	103.6	83.8	64.1	61.3
Operating Income	767.1	242.9	157.7	233.4	227.1	157.8	101.8
Net Interest Inc./(Exp.)	57.6	18.7	5.6	3.7	5.2	3.9	d2.0
Income Before Income Taxes	865.7	257.5	150.5	235.9	230.7	159.4	96.9
Income Taxes	258.6	60.7	31.0	57.7	58.8	40.2	22.4
Equity Earnings/Minority Int.	...	d1.1	d9.8	...	...	...	...
Net Income	1 607.1	196.8	119.5	178.2	171.9	119.3	74.5
Cash Flow	763.8	339.4	247.0	281.8	255.7	183.4	135.8
Average Shs. Outstg. (000)	381,157	362,904	355,750	354,926	342,578	317,437	309,085
BALANCE SHEET (IN MILLIONS):							
Cash & Cash Equivalents	2,235.3	762.4	304.9	340.6	299.9	151.1	181.8
Total Current Assets	3,168.0	1,379.1	903.5	895.4	820.3	526.0	505.5
Net Property	779.2	642.8	703.4	661.6	583.3	432.0	281.8
Total Assets	4,411.3	2,218.4	1,861.7	1,763.9	1,515.7	1,001.6	815.9
Total Current Liabilities	649.9	479.3	320.9	274.4	270.2	254.4	206.2
Long-Term Obligations	1,213.0	16.2	340.8	348.9	353.7	80.0	80.1
Net Stockholders' Equity	2,303.7	1,616.0	1,128.4	1,088.1	862.8	656.0	521.9
Net Working Capital	2,518.1	899.8	582.7	621.0	550.0	271.6	299.3
Year-end Shs. Outstg. (000)	357,924	349,775	320,620	323,812	317,490	305,419	200,672
STATISTICAL RECORD:							
Operating Profit Margin %	29.8	16.7	12.8	18.8	19.0	16.8	13.2
Net Profit Margin %	23.6	13.6	9.7	14.3	14.4	12.7	9.6
Return on Equity %	26.4	12.2	10.6	16.4	19.9	18.2	14.3
Return on Assets %	13.8	8.9	6.4	10.1	11.3	11.9	9.1
Debt/Total Assets %	27.5	0.7	18.3	19.8	23.3	8.0	9.8
Price Range	103.00-41.31	47.25-12.19	19.81-6.00	18.34-10.31	13.32-6.38	9.88-5.00	6.13-3.90
P/E Ratio	64.8-26.0	85.9-22.2	55.8-16.9	35.3-19.8	25.9-12.4	26.3-13.3	25.5-16.2

Statistics are as originally reported. Adj. for stk. splits: 100% div., 3/00; 50% div., 1/95; 3-for-2, 11/95 1 Incl. pre-tax chrg. of $9.5 mill. for in-process R&D write-off.

OFFICERS:
R. Stata, Chmn.
J. G. Fishman, Pres., C.E.O.
J. E. McDonough, V.P., C.F.O.

INVESTOR CONTACT: James O. Fishbeck, Dir. Corp. Comm., (800) 262-5643

PRINCIPAL OFFICE: One Technology Way, P.O. Box 9106, Norwood, MA 02062-9106

TELEPHONE NUMBER: (781) 329-4700
FAX: (781) 326-8703
WEB: www.analog.com

NO. OF EMPLOYEES: 9,100 (approx.)

SHAREHOLDERS: 4,600 (approx.)

ANNUAL MEETING: In Mar.

INCORPORATED: MA, Jan., 1965

INSTITUTIONAL HOLDINGS:
No. of Institutions: 475
Shares Held: 276,978,151
% Held: 77.0

INDUSTRY: Semiconductors and related devices (SIC: 3674)

TRANSFER AGENT(S): BankBoston, NA, Boston, MA

NYSE SYMBOL AGL
Rec. Pr. 13.26 (4/30/01)

ANGELICA CORPORATION

YIELD 2.4%
P/E RATIO 17.4

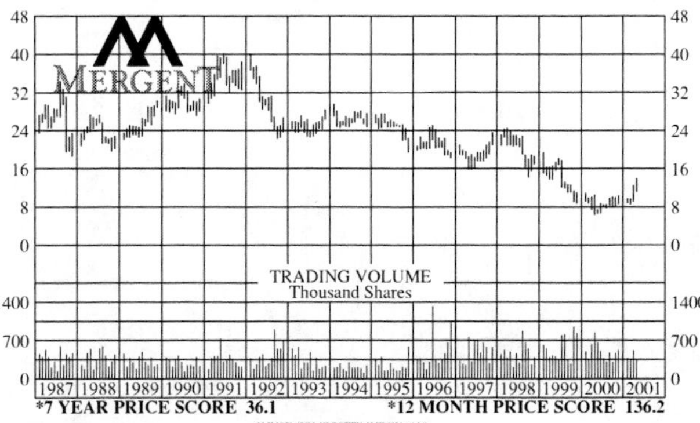

INTERIM EARNINGS (Per Share):

Qtr.	Apr.	July	Oct.	Jan.
1996-97	0.33	0.30	0.20	0.05
1997-98	0.22	0.14	d1.29	0.18
1998-99	0.26	0.20	0.31	0.22
1999-00	0.29	0.15	0.07	0.10
2000-01	0.18	0.21	0.23	0.14

INTERIM DIVIDENDS (Per Share):

Amt.	Decl.	Ex.	Rec.	Pay.
0.08Q	5/24/00	6/13/00	6/15/00	7/01/00
0.08Q	8/30/00	9/13/00	9/15/00	10/01/00
0.08Q	11/29/00	12/13/00	12/15/00	1/01/01
0.08Q	2/28/01	3/13/01	3/15/01	4/01/01
0.08Q	5/30/01	6/13/01	6/15/01	7/01/01

Indicated div.: $0.32 (Div. Reinv. Plan)

CAPITALIZATION (1/27/01):

	($000)	(%)
Long-Term Debt	60,963	26.4
Deferred Income Tax	5,897	2.6
Common & Surplus	164,319	71.1
Total	231,179	100.0

RECENT DEVELOPMENTS: For the year ended 1/27/01, net income climbed 24.9% to $6.6 million from $5.3 million in the previous year. Total revenues declined 2.1% to $458.6 million from $468.4 million in 1999. Revenue from textile services slipped slightly to $243.3 million, while the segment's operating earnings improved 7.7% to $14.5 million. Manufacturing and marketing revenues decreased 4.5% to $148.8 million, while operating earnings grew 14.4% to $6.1 million. Retail sales rose 2.3% to $92.7 million, while retail operating earnings fell 24.7% to $2.5 million.

PROSPECTS: Earnings from the Company's textile services segment were fueled by better management of linen costs and improved plant productivity, despite substantial increases in energy costs in both the third and fourth quarters. These energy costs are expected to negatively affect the AGL's performance throughout the remainder of this year. Meanwhile, earnings in the manufacturing and marketing segment grew over the prior year as efforts to lower costs through increased non-domestic contract sourcing continued to be successful.

BUSINESS

ANGELICA CORPORATION provides rental and laundry services of textiles and garments primarily to health care institutions; manufactures and markets uniforms for institutions and businesses; and operates a national chain of nearly 300 retail uniform and shoe stores. Principal markets are: health services, including hospitals, nurses and other health care professionals; hospitality, including hotels and restaurants; commerce, including retailers and transportation companies; industry, including manufacturers, food processors and high technology companies. AGL operates directly in Canada and the U.K. through Angelica International, Ltd.

ANNUAL FINANCIAL DATA

	1/27/01	1/29/00	1/30/99	1/31/98	1/25/97	1/27/96	1/28/95
Earnings Per Share	**0.76**	**0.61**	**0.99**	**1 d0.75**	**0.88**	**1 0.13**	**1.44**
Cash Flow Per Share	**2.56**	**2.52**	**2.91**	**1.14**	**2.72**	**2.07**	**3.29**
Tang. Book Val. Per Share	**18.61**	**18.17**	**18.30**	**17.59**	**19.85**	**19.81**	**20.77**
Dividends Per Share	**0.64**	**0.96**	**0.96**	**0.96**	**0.96**	**0.94**	**0.94**
Dividend Payout %	**84.2**	**157.4**	**97.0**	**...**	**109.1**	**726.4**	**65.3**
INCOME STATEMENT (IN THOUSANDS):							
Total Revenues	458,646	462,941	491,645	526,524	489,219	487,014	472,832
Costs & Expenses	424,656	428,910	447,709	506,868	447,277	455,372	423,711
Depreciation & Amort.	15,635	16,643	17,316	17,322	16,875	17,794	16,883
Operating Income	18,355	17,388	26,620	2,334	25,067	13,848	32,238
Net Interest Inc./(Exp.)	d8,097	d8,635	d9,726	d10,702	d9,588	d9,104	d7,906
Income Before Income Taxes	10,454	8,372	14,342	d11,126	12,938	1,855	21,254
Income Taxes	3,868	3,098	5,450	cr4,228	4,916	714	8,183
Net Income	6,586	5,274	8,892	1 d6,898	8,022	1 1,141	13,071
Cash Flow	22,221	21,917	26,208	10,424	24,897	18,935	29,954
Average Shs. Outstg.	8,681	8,686	9,014	9,153	9,157	9,140	9,107
BALANCE SHEET (IN THOUSANDS):							
Cash & Cash Equivalents	20,311	15,651	6,876	2,833	2,122	11,029	2,211
Total Current Assets	205,717	189,312	197,389	229,411	232,412	226,581	219,917
Net Property	85,120	92,187	101,631	108,193	102,830	90,794	97,650
Total Assets	326,284	319,595	339,090	378,709	374,104	353,227	353,548
Total Current Liabilities	81,268	48,190	61,318	87,412	69,397	45,538	69,183
Long-Term Obligations	60,963	87,916	90,910	96,742	97,417	100,103	69,683
Net Stockholders' Equity	164,319	163,412	165,803	174,108	189,241	189,530	196,660
Net Working Capital	124,449	141,122	136,071	141,999	163,015	181,043	150,734
Year-end Shs. Outstg.	8,542	8,676	8,671	9,472	9,131	9,142	9,119
STATISTICAL RECORD:							
Operating Profit Margin %	4.0	3.8	5.4	0.4	5.1	2.8	6.8
Net Profit Margin %	1.4	1.1	1.8	...	1.6	0.2	2.8
Return on Equity %	4.0	3.2	5.4	...	4.2	0.6	6.6
Return on Assets %	2.0	1.7	2.6	...	2.1	0.3	3.7
Debt/Total Assets %	18.7	27.5	26.8	25.5	26.0	28.3	19.7
Price Range	10.94-6.31	19.38-8.69	24.50-14.13	23.63-15.75	25.13-18.13	27.50-19.38	29.50-24.50
P/E Ratio	14.4-8.3	31.8-14.2	24.7-14.3	...	28.5-20.6	211.4-148.9	20.5-17.0
Average Yield %	7.4	6.8	5.0	4.9	4.4	4.0	3.5

Statistics are as originally reported. 1 Incl. non-recurr chrg. 1997, $14.7 mill.; 1995, $14.1 mill.

OFFICERS:
D. W. Hubble, Chmn., Pres., C.E.O.
T. M. Armstrong, Sr. V.P., C.F.O.
J. W. Shaffer, V.P., Treas.

INVESTOR CONTACT: Investor Relations, (314) 854-3800

PRINCIPAL OFFICE: 424 South Woods Mill Road, Chesterfield, MO 63017-3406

TELEPHONE NUMBER: (314) 854-3800
FAX: (314) 854-3870
WEB: www.angelica-corp.com
NO. OF EMPLOYEES: 6,760 full-time (approx.); 840 part-time (approx.)
SHAREHOLDERS: 1,273 (of record)
ANNUAL MEETING: In May
INCORPORATED: MO, March, 1968

INSTITUTIONAL HOLDINGS:
No. of Institutions: 44
Shares Held: 5,339,585
% Held: 62.2

INDUSTRY: Miscellaneous personal services, nec (SIC: 7299)

TRANSFER AGENT(S): UMB Bank, Kansas City, MO

NYSE SYMBOL BUD
Rec. Pr. 39.99 (4/30/01)

ANHEUSER-BUSCH COMPANIES, INC.

YIELD 1.7%
P/E RATIO 23.7

MERGENT

TRADING VOLUME
Thousand Shares

1987 1988 1989 1990 1991 1992 1993 1994 1995 1996 1997 1998 1999 2000 2001

*7 YEAR PRICE SCORE 120.5 *12 MONTH PRICE SCORE 109.6

*NYSE COMPOSITE INDEX=100

INTERIM EARNINGS (Per Share):

Qtr.	Mar.	June	Sept.	Dec.
1997	0.26	0.38	0.40	0.15
1998	0.27	0.40	0.42	0.18
1999	0.33	0.45	0.49	0.21
2000	0.38	0.52	0.56	0.23

INTERIM DIVIDENDS (Per Share):

Amt.	Decl.	Ex.	Rec.	Pay.
0.33Q	7/26/00	8/07/00	8/09/00	9/11/00
2-for-1	7/26/00	9/19/00	8/17/00	9/18/00
0.165Q	10/25/00	11/07/00	11/09/00	12/11/00
0.165Q	1/16/01	2/07/01	2/09/01	3/09/01
0.165Q	4/25/01	5/07/01	5/09/01	6/11/01

Indicated div.: $0.66 (Div. Reinv. Plan)

CAPITALIZATION (12/31/00):

	($000)	(%)
Long-Term Debt	5,374,500	49.4
Deferred Income Tax	1,372,900	12.6
Common & Surplus	4,128,900	38.0
Total	10,876,300	100.0

RECENT DEVELOPMENTS: For the year ended 12/31/00, net income increased 10.7% to $1.55 billion compared with $1.40 billion in the previous year. Net sales rose 4.8% to $12.26 billion from $11.70 billion the year before. Results for 2000 reflected solid volume increases in domestic beer operations and strong revenue per barrel growth. The improvement in earnings also resulted from the strong performance of BUD's subsidiary, Grupo Modelo.

PROSPECTS: The Company is implementing the second stage of its revenue enhancement strategy for 2001. Selected price increases and discount reductions have been put into effect in markets representing 35.0% of BUD's domestic volume. This is in addition to the 40.0% covered in the first stage of the initiative. Meanwhile, BUD has an earnings per share growth goal of 12.0% for 2001.

BUSINESS

ANHEUSER-BUSCH COMPANIES, INC. is a diversified corporation whose chief subsidiary is Anheuser-Busch, Inc., the world's largest brewer. Beer is sold under brand names including BUDWEISER MICHELOB BUSCH and NATURAL LIGHT. BUD is also the country's second largest theme park operator. Theme park operations are conducted through BUD's subsidiary, Busch Entertainment Corporation, which currently owns nine theme parks. BUD also engages in packaging, malt and rice production, international beer and non-beer beverages. BUD owns approximately 50.0% of Grupo Modelo, S.A. de C.V., a Mexican brewer.

REVENUES

(12/31/2000)	($000)	(%)
Domestic Beer	11,490.5	76.0
Int'l Beer	647.8	4.2
Package	2,012.2	13.3
Entertainment	837.9	5.5
Other	122.8	1.0
Total	15,111.2	100.0

ANNUAL FINANCIAL DATA

	12/31/00	12/31/99	12/31/98	12/31/97	12/31/96	12/31/95	12/31/94
Earnings Per Share	**1.69**	**1.47**	**1.27**	**[3] 1.18**	**[2] 1.14**	**[1] 0.86**	**0.98**
Cash Flow Per Share	**2.56**	**2.29**	**2.02**	**1.86**	**1.73**	**1.41**	**1.57**
Tang. Book Val. Per Share	**4.11**	**4.25**	**4.42**	**4.15**	**4.05**	**4.36**	**3.82**
Dividends Per Share	**0.63**	**0.58**	**0.54**	**0.50**	**0.46**	**0.42**	**0.38**
Dividend Payout %	**37.3**	**39.5**	**42.7**	**42.4**	**40.3**	**48.8**	**38.9**
INCOME STATEMENT (IN MILLIONS):							
Total Revenues	12,261.8	11,703.7	11,245.8	11,066.2	10,883.7	10,340.5	12,053.8
Costs & Expenses	8,963.6	8,624.4	8,382.1	8,329.5	8,260.7	7,982.0	9,527.2
Depreciation & Amort.	803.5	777.0	738.4	683.7	593.9	565.6	627.5
Operating Income	2,494.7	2,302.3	2,125.3	2,053.0	2,029.1	1,792.9	1,899.1
Net Interest Inc./(Exp.)	d313.8	d285.3	d259.7	d211.2	d187.9	d191.7	d196.0
Income Before Income Taxes	2,179.9	2,007.6	1,852.6	1,832.5	1,892.9	1,461.7	1,707.1
Income Taxes	828.3	762.9	704.3	703.6	736.8	575.1	675.0
Equity Earnings/Minority Int.	200.0	157.5	85.0	50.3	...	...	...
Net Income	1,551.6	1,402.2	1,233.3	[3] 1,179.2	[2] 1,156.1	[1] 886.6	1,032.1
Cash Flow	2,355.1	2,179.2	1,971.7	1,862.9	1,750.0	1,452.2	1,659.6
Average Shs. Outstg. (000)	919,700	953,600	975,000	999,400	1,011,600	1,031,600	1,056,400
BALANCE SHEET (IN MILLIONS):							
Cash & Cash Equivalents	159.9	152.1	224.8	147.3	93.6	93.6	156.4
Total Current Assets	1,547.9	1,600.6	1,640.4	1,583.9	1,465.8	1,510.6	1,861.6
Net Property	8,243.8	7,964.6	7,849.0	7,750.6	7,208.2	6,763.0	7,547.7
Total Assets	13,084.5	12,640.4	12,484.3	11,727.1	10,463.6	10,590.9	11,045.4
Total Current Liabilities	1,675.7	1,987.2	1,730.3	1,500.7	1,430.9	1,242.0	1,669.0
Long-Term Obligations	5,374.5	4,880.6	4,718.6	4,365.6	3,270.9	3,270.1	3,078.4
Net Stockholders' Equity	4,128.9	3,921.5	4,216.0	4,041.8	4,029.1	4,433.9	4,415.5
Net Working Capital	d127.8	d386.6	d89.9	83.2	34.9	268.6	192.6
Year-end Shs. Outstg. (000)	903,600	922,200	953,200	974,040	994,714	1,015,904	1,029,160
STATISTICAL RECORD:							
Operating Profit Margin %	20.3	19.7	18.9	18.6	18.6	17.3	15.8
Net Profit Margin %	12.7	12.0	11.0	10.7	10.6	8.6	8.6
Return on Equity %	37.6	35.8	29.3	29.2	28.7	20.0	23.4
Return on Assets %	11.9	11.1	9.9	10.1	11.0	8.4	9.3
Debt/Total Assets %	41.1	38.6	37.8	37.2	31.3	30.9	27.9
Price Range	49.88-27.31	42.00-32.22	34.13-21.47	24.13-19.25	22.50-16.19	17.00-12.69	13.84-11.78
P/E Ratio	29.5-16.2	28.6-21.9	27.0-17.0	20.4-16.3	19.7-14.2	19.8-14.8	14.2-12.0
Average Yield %	1.6	1.6	1.9	2.3	2.4	2.8	3.0

Statistics are as originally reported. Adj. for 2-for-1 stk. split, 9/00 & 9/96. [1] Incl. $160.0 mill. pre-tax write off & excl. disc. oper. loss of $244.3 mill. [2] Incl. $54.7 mill. gain fr. the sale of the St. Louis Cardinals & bef. disc. oper. gain of $33.8 mill. [3] Bef. acctg. change chrge. of $10.0 mill., 1997.

OFFICERS:
A. A. Busch III, Chmn., Pres.
W. R. Baker, V.P., C.F.O.
J. Jacob, Exec. V.P., C.O.O.

INVESTOR CONTACT: C. Ramirez, Investor Relations, (314) 577-9629

PRINCIPAL OFFICE: One Busch Place, St. Louis, MO 63118

TELEPHONE NUMBER: (314) 577-2000
FAX: (314) 577-2900
WEB: www.anheuser-busch.com

NO. OF EMPLOYEES: 23,725

SHAREHOLDERS: 58,614

ANNUAL MEETING: In April

INCORPORATED: DE, April, 1979

INSTITUTIONAL HOLDINGS:
No. of Institutions: 695
Shares Held: 554,193,213
% Held: 61.8

INDUSTRY: Malt beverages (SIC: 2082)

TRANSFER AGENT(S): Mellon Investor Services, Ridgefield Park, NJ

NYSE SYMBOL AXE
Rec. Pr. 29.90 (5/31/01)

ANIXTER INTERNATIONAL INC.

YIELD	...
P/E RATIO	14.5

***7 YEAR PRICE SCORE 100.4** ***12 MONTH PRICE SCORE 108.9**

*NYSE COMPOSITE INDEX=100

INTERIM EARNINGS (Per Share):

Qtr.	Mar.	June	Sept.	Dec.
1997	0.23	0.22	0.24	0.26
1998	0.35	0.44	0.24	0.07
1999	0.19	0.33	1.06	0.31
2000	0.44	0.62	0.59	0.41

INTERIM DIVIDENDS (Per Share):

Amt.	Decl.	Ex.	Rec.	Pay.
		No dividends paid.		

CAPITALIZATION (12/29/00):

	($000)	(%)
Long-Term Debt	451,900	44.9
Common & Surplus	554,900	55.1
Total	1,006,800	100.0

RECENT DEVELOPMENTS: For the year ended 12/29/00, net income jumped 12.9% to $78.7 million versus income from continuing operations of $69.7 million in the previous year. Net sales increased 29.6% to $3.51 billion from $2.71 billion in the prior year. The increase in sales and earnings was attributed to improved performance from AXE's international businesses. Gross profit advanced 22.8% to $821.9 million from $669.3 million in 1999.

PROSPECTS: In the enterprise network market, AXE will continue to caplitalized on the trends that are driving the need for increased bandwidth and network reliability. In the service provider market, AXE will work with product manufacturers to positionthe distribution channel as the most cost-effective way to get product to certain customers. In the specialty wire and cable market, AXE will stay aggresively focused on original equipment manufacturers.

BUSINESS

ANIXTER INTERNATIONAL INC. (formerly Itel Corp.) distributes networking and cable products for network infrastructure requirements through Anixter Inc., a supplier of wiring systems, networking and Internet products for voice, data and video networks and electrical power applications in North America, Europe, Asia and Latin America. Anixter stocks and/or sells a full line of these products from a network of 94 locations in the U.S., 18 in Canada, 14 in the U.K., 27 in Continental Europe, 16 in Latin America, 4 in Australia, and 14 in Asia as of 3/29/01. Anixter sells about 87,000 products to 85,000 active customers and works with over 1,600 active suppliers.

GEOGRAPHIC DATA

(12/31/2000)	REV(%)	INC(%)
United States	69.8	76.2
Europe	16.7	13.0
Canada.......................	8.1	10.3
Asia Pacific & Latin America	5.4	0.5
Total	100.0	100.0

ANNUAL FINANCIAL DATA

	12/29/00	12/31/99	1/1/99	1/2/98	1/3/97	12/31/95	12/31/94
Earnings Per Share	**2.03**	**[4] 1.83**	**[3] 0.99**	**[2] 0.95**	**0.73**	**0.71**	**[1] 1.44**
Cash Flow Per Share	**2.59**	**2.51**	**1.58**	**1.62**	**1.27**	**1.10**	**0.97**
Tang. Book Val. Per Share	**8.38**	**6.33**	**4.24**	**5.79**	**5.26**	**5.07**	**12.10**
INCOME STATEMENT (IN MILLIONS):							
Total Revenues	3,514.4	2,670.0	2,348.5	2,805.2	2,475.3	2,194.8	1,732.6
Costs & Expenses	3,297.2	2,531.2	2,234.7	2,662.2	2,360.0	2,073.5	1,646.8
Depreciation & Amort.	27.4	26.0	26.8	31.9	26.9	21.7	16.0
Operating Income	189.8	112.8	87.0	111.1	88.4	99.6	69.8
Net Interest Inc./(Exp.)	d43.3	d34.9	d31.7	d33.5	d29.9	d24.8	d33.0
Income Before Income Taxes	134.6	78.2	76.5	79.6	64.8	74.4	70.0
Income Taxes	55.9	8.5	31.8	34.3	28.7	35.3	23.8
Net Income	78.7	[4] 69.7	[3] 44.7	[2] 45.3	36.1	39.1	[1] 46.2
Cash Flow	106.1	95.7	71.5	77.2	63.0	60.8	62.2
Average Shs. Outstg. (000)	40,889	38,078	45,263	47,775	49,717	55,410	64,090
BALANCE SHEET (IN MILLIONS):							
Cash & Cash Equivalents	20.8	17.5	20.5	10.6	18.2	10.5	14.2
Total Current Assets	1,334.4	1,121.1	920.4	1,014.0	868.5	781.0	620.8
Net Property	56.5	53.1	57.6	64.3	61.6	49.2	33.4
Total Assets	1,686.0	1,434.7	1,335.1	1,440.7	1,261.0	1,184.7	1,110.9
Total Current Liabilities	646.8	495.5	341.0	448.1	313.5	331.9	266.5
Long-Term Obligations	451.9	468.0	543.6	468.8	468.4	333.7	280.5
Net Stockholders' Equity	554.9	456.4	411.5	477.0	435.5	449.0	543.9
Net Working Capital	687.6	625.6	579.4	565.9	555.0	449.1	354.3
Year-end Shs. Outstg. (000)	37,655	35,924	41,878	47,297	48,007	52,488	29,426
STATISTICAL RECORD:							
Operating Profit Margin %	5.4	4.2	3.7	4.0	3.6	4.5	4.0
Net Profit Margin %	2.2	2.6	1.9	1.6	1.5	1.8	2.7
Return on Equity %	14.2	15.3	10.9	9.5	8.3	8.7	8.5
Return on Assets %	4.7	4.9	3.3	3.1	2.9	3.3	4.2
Debt/Total Assets %	26.8	32.6	40.7	32.5	37.1	28.2	25.2
Price Range	37.38-17.56	23.75-10.63	22.75-11.88	19.69-12.00	20.00-12.63	22.06-16.63	18.13-11.38
P/E Ratio	18.4-8.7	13.0-5.8	23.0-12.0	20.7-12.6	27.4-17.3	31.1-23.4	12.6-7.9

Statistics are as originally reported. Adjusted for 2-for-1 stock split, 10/95. [1] Bef. inc. fr. dis. opers. of $200.7 mill. [2] Incl. nonrecurr. gain of $1.2 mill. in conj. with the merger of AXE's ANTEC affiliate with TSX Corp. [3] Incl. an after-tax gain of $24.3 million assoc./w. the sale of 2.2 million shares of ANTEC common stock & excl. a gain of $20.9 million from disc. opers. [4] Incl. a net restr. chg. of $1.8 mill. for staff reduct. & facil. consol. in Latin America, a gain of $24.3 mill. from the rev. of certain tax liabil. assoc./w completing IRS audits for a number of open years, & excl. a net gain of $54.5 mill. for. disc.

OFFICERS:
S. Zell, Chmn.
R. W. Grubbs, Pres., C.E.O.
D. J. Letham, Sr. V.P., C.F.O.

INVESTOR CONTACT: Dennis Letham, Sr. V.P., C.F.O., (847) 677-2600

PRINCIPAL OFFICE: 4711 Golf Road, Skokie, IL 60076

TELEPHONE NUMBER: (847) 677-2600
FAX: (847) 677-8557
WEB: www.anixter.com

NO. OF EMPLOYEES: 5,900 (approx.)

SHAREHOLDERS: 4,081 (record)

ANNUAL MEETING: In May

INCORPORATED: DE, Dec., 1967

INSTITUTIONAL HOLDINGS:
No. of Institutions: 158
Shares Held: 23,293,831
% Held: 62.6

INDUSTRY: Communications equipment, nec (SIC: 3669)

TRANSFER AGENT(S): Mellon Investor Services, Ridgefield Park, NJ.

NYSE SYMBOL ANN
Rec. Pr. 34.12 (5/31/01)

ANNTAYLOR STORES CORPORATION

YIELD ...
P/E RATIO 19.6

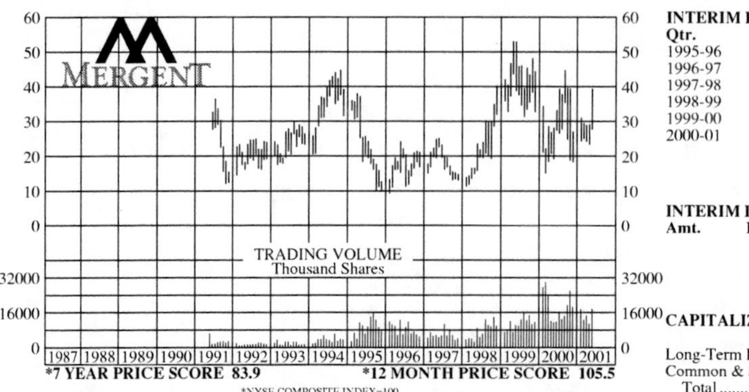

*7 YEAR PRICE SCORE 83.9 *12 MONTH PRICE SCORE 105.5

*NYSE COMPOSITE INDEX=100

INTERIM EARNINGS (Per Share):

Qtr.	Apr.	July	Oct.	Jan.
1995-96	0.15	d0.16	0.03	d0.05
1996-97	0.08	0.03	0.13	0.12
1997-98	0.25	0.04	0.08	0.09
1998-99	0.25	0.27	0.50	0.42
1999-00	0.51	0.39	0.65	0.50
2000-01	0.38	0.45	0.78	0.13

INTERIM DIVIDENDS (Per Share):

Amt.	Decl.	Ex.	Rec.	Pay.

No dividends paid.

CAPITALIZATION (2/3/01):

	($000)	(%)
Long-Term Debt	116,210	16.8
Common & Surplus	574,029	83.2
Total	690,239	100.0

RECENT DEVELOPMENTS: For the 53 weeks ended 2/3/01, net income was $52.4 million, down 20.0% versus income of $65.5 million, before an extraordinary charge, in the corresponding 52-week period the year before. Results in the recent year included one-time pre-tax charges of $10.7 million. Net sales totaled $1.23 billion, up 13.7% compared with $1.08 billion a year earlier. Comparable-store sales, on a 52-week basis, slipped 0.5% year-over-year. As a percentage of net sales, gross profit was 49.5% versus 50.6% in the prior year.

PROSPECTS: The Company plans to increase its selection of more classic-styled merchandise during the fall and holiday 2001 seasons after seeing sales growth decline in late 2000 and early 2001 as ANN shifted to more contemporary fashions. In fiscal 2001, the Company anticipates opening approximately 20 new Ann Taylor stores and about 70 new Ann Taylor Loft stores. Capital expenditures related to this store expansion program are expected to total approximately $67.4 million, including store refurbishing and refixturing costs.

BUSINESS

ANNTAYLOR STORES CORPORATION is a specialty retailer of women's apparel, shoes and accessories sold primarily under the Ann Taylor brand name. Its product line includes career and casual separates, weekend wear, dresses, tops accessories, and shoes. The Company's Ann Taylor stores, which sell better-quality women's fashions, are primarily located in malls and upscale specialty retail centers. ANN also operates Ann Taylor Loft stores, which sell moderately-priced merchandise under the Ann Taylor Loft label. In addition, the Company operates Ann Taylor Factory stores in factory outlet centers. These stores serve primarily as a clearance vehicle for merchandise from Ann Taylor stores. As of 5/5/01, ANN operated 488 stores in 42 states, the District of Columbia and Puerto Rico and an online store.

QUARTERLY DATA

(2/3/01)($000)	Rev	Inc
1st Quarter	277,068	11,282
2nd Quarter	306,252	13,426
3rd Quarter	305,876	23,877
4th Quarter	343,580	3,778

ANNUAL FINANCIAL DATA

	2/3/01	1/29/00	1/30/99	1/31/98	2/1/97	2/3/96	1/28/95
Earnings Per Share	**[2] 1.76**	**[1] 2.08**	**1.44**	**[1] 0.47**	**[2] 0.36**	**d0.04**	**[1] 1.40**
Cash Flow Per Share	**3.19**	**3.41**	**2.57**	**2.02**	**1.87**	**1.18**	**2.33**
Tang. Book Val. Per Share	**9.59**	**7.24**	**4.34**	**2.08**	**1.13**	**0.53**	**0.13**
INCOME STATEMENT (IN MILLIONS):							
Total Revenues	1,232.8	1,084.5	911.9	781.0	798.1	731.1	658.8
Costs & Expenses	1,087.3	916.8	780.1	691.1	715.2	677.5	559.9
Depreciation & Amort.	47.2	43.3	40.3	39.9	36.5	28.4	21.6
Operating Income	98.2	124.4	91.6	50.0	46.5	25.3	77.3
Net Interest Inc./(Exp.)	d4.8	d7.4	d18.1	d20.0	d24.4	d21.0	d14.2
Income Before Income Taxes	93.4	115.7	72.9	29.5	21.6	4.3	62.9
Income Taxes	41.0	50.2	33.6	17.5	13.0	5.2	30.3
Net Income	[2] 52.4	[1] 65.5	39.3	[1] 12.0	[2] 8.7	d0.9	[1] 32.6
Cash Flow	99.6	108.8	79.6	51.9	45.2	27.5	54.2
Average Shs. Outstg. (000)	31,221	31,849	31,006	25,693	24,104	23,209	23,286
BALANCE SHEET (IN MILLIONS):							
Cash & Cash Equivalents	32.0	35.1	67.0	31.4	7.0	1.3	1.6
Total Current Assets	313.8	271.6	298.5	210.1	196.5	198.7	168.1
Net Property	220.0	173.6	151.8	139.6	143.4	153.9	96.3
Total Assets	848.1	765.1	775.4	683.7	688.1	678.7	598.3
Total Current Liabilities	141.0	120.2	129.8	87.9	77.7	112.2	65.9
Long-Term Obligations	116.2	114.5	104.0	105.2	130.9	232.2	200.0
Net Stockholders' Equity	574.0	515.6	432.7	384.1	370.6	325.7	326.1
Net Working Capital	172.8	151.4	168.7	122.2	118.8	86.5	102.2
Year-end Shs. Outstg. (000)	28,823	28,570	26,018	25,645	25,587	23,083	23,107
STATISTICAL RECORD:							
Operating Profit Margin %	8.0	11.5	10.0	6.4	5.8	3.5	11.7
Net Profit Margin %	4.2	6.0	4.3	1.5	1.1	...	5.0
Return on Equity %	9.1	12.7	9.1	3.1	2.3	...	10.0
Return on Assets %	6.2	8.6	5.1	1.8	1.3	...	5.5
Debt/Total Assets %	13.7	15.0	13.4	15.4	19.0	34.2	33.4
Price Range	44.88-15.00	53.06-31.19	40.25-11.25	25.25-13.00	24.25-9.25	38.00-9.88	44.88-20.50
P/E Ratio	25.5-8.5	25.5-15.0	27.9-7.8	53.7-27.7	67.3-25.7	...	32.1-14.6

Statistics are as originally reported. [1] Bef. $962,000 ($0.03/sh) extraord. loss, 1/00; $173,000 ($0.01/sh), 1/98; $868,000 ($0.04/sh), 1/95. [2] Incl. $10.7 mil one-time pre-tax chgs., 2/01; & $4.0 mil ($0.16/sh) after-tax chg. for store closings & employee contract obligs., 2/97.

OFFICERS:
J. P. Spainhour, Chmn., C.E.O.
B. Erdos, Sr. Exec. V.P., C.O.O.
J. M. Smith, Sr. V.P., C.F.O., Treas.

INVESTOR CONTACT: Doreen Dempsey, Dir., Inv. Rel., (212) 541-3484

PRINCIPAL OFFICE: 142 West 57th Street, New York, NY 10019

TELEPHONE NUMBER: (212) 541-3300
FAX: (212) 541-3379
WEB: www.anntaylor.com
NO. OF EMPLOYEES: 4,400 full-time (approx.); 4,600 part-time (approx.)
SHAREHOLDERS: 562
ANNUAL MEETING: In May
INCORPORATED: DE, 1988

INSTITUTIONAL HOLDINGS:
No. of Institutions: 149
Shares Held: 31,491,808
% Held: 108.7

INDUSTRY: Women's clothing stores (SIC: 5621)

TRANSFER AGENT(S): Continental Stock Transfer & Trust Company, New York, NY

NYSE SYMBOL AOL
Rec. Pr. 50.5 (4/30/01)

AOL TIME WARNER INC.

YIELD ...
P/E RATIO 114.8

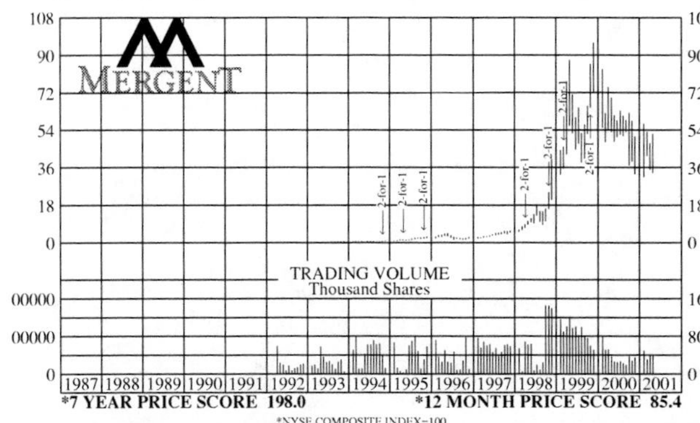

INTERIM EARNINGS (Per Share):

Qtr.	Sept.	Dec.	Mar.	June
1997-98	0.01	0.02	0.01	0.02
1998-99	0.05	0.06	0.17	0.07
1999-00	0.07	0.10	0.17	0.13
2000-01	0.13	0.01	...	...

INTERIM DIVIDENDS (Per Share):

Amt.	Decl.	Ex.	Rec.	Pay.
2-for-1	10/28/99	11/23/99	11/08/99	11/22/99

CAPITALIZATION (6/30/00):

	($000)	(%)
Long-Term Debt	1,630,000	20.9
Common & Surplus	6,161,000	79.1
Total	7,791,000	100.0

RECENT DEVELOPMENTS: For the quarter ended 12/31/00, net income fell 86.8% to $37.0 million compared with $280.0 million in the equivalent quarter of 1999. Results for 1999 included merger and restructuring charges of $5.0 million. Total revenues jumped 27.3% to $2.06 billion from $1.62 billion in the prior-year period. Advertising, commerce and other revenues increased 65.0% to $741.0 million, while subscription services revenues rose 15.6% to $1.23 billion.

PROSPECTS: On 1/11/01, the Company announced that it has completed its merger with Time Warner Inc. creating a major Internet-powered media and communications company. The new company, AOL Time Warner Inc., will increase the development of interactive media and attempt to capitalize on opportunities in digital music, interactive television and broadband Internet services. Going forward, the Company expects to meet its goal of more than $40.00 billion in revenues for fiscal 2001.

BUSINESS

AOL TIME WARNER INC. (formerly America Online, Inc.) was formed from the merger between America Online, Inc. and Time Warner, Inc. in January 2001. AOL classifies its business interests into the following categories: interactive services, which consists of the development and operation of branded interactive services such as AOL, CompuServe and Netscape; cable systems, which includes interests in cable television systems including Time Warner Cable; publishing, including interests in magazines, including TIME, FORTUNE and SPORTS ILLUSTRATED; books, and direct marketing; music, including Warner Music Group and its labels Atlantic, Elektra, London-Sire, Rhino, Warner Bros. Records and Warner Music International; television networks, including WTBS Superstation, TNT, Cartoon Networks, CNN News Group, Home Box Office and the WB Television Network; and filmed entertainment, including Warner Bros. and New Line Cinema.

ANNUAL FINANCIAL DATA

	6/30/00	6/30/99	6/30/98	6/30/97	6/30/96	6/30/95	6/30/94
Earnings Per Share	**[4] 0.48**	**[3] 0.30**	**[2] 0.04**	**[1] d0.33**	**0.02**	**d0.06**	**0.04**
Cash Flow Per Share	**0.58**	**0.39**	**0.09**	**d0.25**	**0.11**	**0.04**	**0.03**
Tang. Book Val. Per Share	**2.44**	**1.17**	**0.12**	**0.04**	**0.31**	**0.13**	**0.11**
Dividend Payout %	...	...	**0.2**	...	...	...	...
INCOME STATEMENT (IN MILLIONS):							
Total Revenues	6,886.0	4,777.0	2,600.0	1,685.2	1,093.9	394.3	115.7
Costs & Expenses	5,201.0	4,097.0	2,422.0	2,067.1	869.2	341.5	76.0
Depreciation & Amort.	287.0	222.0	100.0	123.8	159.4	72.1	20.4
Operating Income	1,398.0	458.0	78.0	d505.6	65.2	d19.3	4.2
Net Interest Inc./(Exp.)	...	...	...	...	...	2.9	...
Income Before Income Taxes	2,014.0	1,096.0	92.0	d499.3	62.3	d18.5	10.0
Income Taxes	782.0	334.0	...	...	32.5	15.2	3.8
Net Income	[4] 1,232.0	[3] 762.0	[2] 92.0	[1] d499.3	29.8	d33.6	6.2
Cash Flow	1,519.0	984.0	192.0	d375.6	189.3	38.4	38.0
Average Shs. Outstg. (000)	2,603,000	2,554,000	2,072,000	1,529,712	1,729,552	1,087,552	1,104,560
BALANCE SHEET (IN MILLIONS):							
Cash & Cash Equivalents	3,415.0	1,424.0	631.0	124.6	129.1	64.1	67.7
Total Current Assets	4,428.0	1,979.0	930.0	323.5	270.6	132.9	105.3
Net Property	991.0	657.0	363.0	233.1	101.3	70.5	18.4
Total Assets	10,673.0	5,348.0	2,214.0	846.7	958.8	406.5	155.2
Total Current Liabilities	2,395.0	1,725.0	894.0	554.5	289.9	133.3	40.4
Long-Term Obligations	1,630.0	348.0	372.0	50.0	19.3	19.5	5.8
Net Stockholders' Equity	6,161.0	3,033.0	598.0	128.0	512.5	217.9	98.9
Net Working Capital	2,033.0	254.0	36.0	d231.0	d19.3	d0.5	65.0
Year-end Shs. Outstg. (000)	2,316,495	2,201,788	1,757,128	1,603,024	1,482,016	1,201,760	927,360
STATISTICAL RECORD:							
Operating Profit Margin %	20.3	9.6	3.0	...	6.0	...	3.6
Net Profit Margin %	17.9	16.0	3.5	...	2.7	...	5.3
Return on Equity %	20.0	25.1	15.4	...	5.8	...	17.7
Return on Assets %	11.5	14.2	4.2	...	3.1	...	11.3
Debt/Total Assets %	15.3	6.5	16.8	5.9	2.0	4.8	3.9
Price Range	83.38-32.75	95.81-32.50	40.00-5.16	5.71-1.98	4.44-1.40	2.89-0.77	0.91-0.37
P/E Ratio	173.7-68.2	319.3-108.3	907.0-116.9	...	245.2-77.3	...	435.3-177.7

Statistics are as originally reported. Adj. for 2-for-1 split, 11/94, 4/95, 11/95, 3/98, 11/98, 2/99 & 11/99. [1] Incl. $1.0 mill. non-recur. chg., 1998; $482.6 mill., 1997. [2] Incl. $132.0 mill. restr., acq. R&D, & settlement chgs. [3] Incl. $567.0 mill. net gain & $120.0 mill. net chgs. [4] Incl. $15.0 mill. merger & restr. chgs.

OFFICERS:
S. M. Case, Chmn.
G. Levin, C.E.O.
R. W. Pittman, Pres., Co-C.O.O.

INVESTOR CONTACT: Richard E. Hanlon, VP -Investor Relations, (703) 448-8700

PRINCIPAL OFFICE: 22000 AOL Way, Dulles, VA 20166-9323

TELEPHONE NUMBER: (703) 265-1000
FAX: (703) 265-1101
WEB: www.aol.com

NO. OF EMPLOYEES: 15,000 (avg.)

SHAREHOLDERS: 42,800 (approx. record); 3,000,000 (approx. beneficial)

ANNUAL MEETING: In Oct.

INCORPORATED: DE, May, 1985

INSTITUTIONAL HOLDINGS:
No. of Institutions: 701
Shares Held: 1,046,181,719
% Held: 0.0

INDUSTRY: Information retrieval services (SIC: 7375)

TRANSFER AGENT(S): EquiServe Trust Company, N.A., Boston, MA

NYSE SYMBOL AOC
Rec. Pr. 33.24 (4/30/01)

AON CORPORATION

YIELD 2.7%
P/E RATIO 18.3

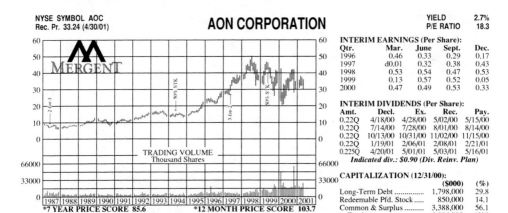

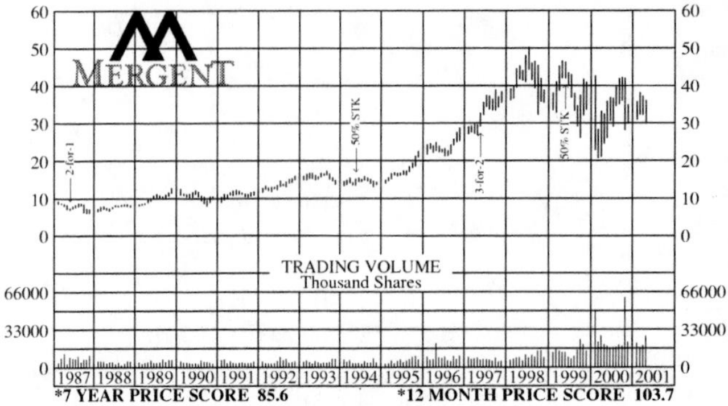

TRADING VOLUME
Thousand Shares

*7 YEAR PRICE SCORE 85.6 *12 MONTH PRICE SCORE 103.7

*NYSE COMPOSITE INDEX=100

INTERIM EARNINGS (Per Share):

Qtr.	Mar.	June	Sept.	Dec.
1996	0.46	0.33	0.29	0.17
1997	d0.01	0.32	0.38	0.43
1998	0.53	0.54	0.47	0.53
1999	0.13	0.57	0.52	0.05
2000	0.47	0.49	0.53	0.33

INTERIM DIVIDENDS (Per Share):

Amt.	Decl.	Ex.	Rec.	Pay.
0.22Q	4/18/00	4/28/00	5/02/00	5/15/00
0.22Q	7/14/00	7/28/00	8/01/00	8/14/00
0.22Q	10/13/00	10/31/00	11/02/00	11/15/00
0.22Q	1/19/01	2/06/01	2/08/01	2/21/01
0.225Q	4/20/01	5/01/01	5/03/01	5/16/01

Indicated div.: $0.90 (Div. Reinv. Plan)

CAPITALIZATION (12/31/00):

	($000)	(%)
Long-Term Debt	1,798,000	29.8
Redeemable Pfd. Stock	850,000	14.1
Common & Surplus	3,388,000	56.1
Total	6,036,000	100.0

RECENT DEVELOPMENTS: For the year ended 12/31/00, AOC reported income of $481.0 million, before a $7.0 million accounting charge, versus net income of $352.0 million in 1999. Earnings included special charges of $82.0 million in 2000 and $313.0 million in 1999. Total revenues climbed 4.3% to $7.38 billion. Revenues from brokerage commissions and fees grew 6.6% to $4.95 billion. Premiums and other revenue rose 3.6% to $1.92 billion, while investment income fell 12.0% to $508.0 million.

PROSPECTS: On 12/8/00, AGC agreed to purchase the global captive management and risk finance consulting operations of International Risk Management Group Ltd. Separately, AOC's subsidiary, Cambridge Integrated Services Group, Inc., completed a definitive agreement with Reliance Insurance Company to provide claims management services for the majority of Reliance's outstanding insurance policies.

BUSINESS

AON CORPORATION is a holding company whose subsidiaries operate in three distinct segments: Insurance Brokerage and Other Services, Consulting, and Insurance Underwriting. The Insurance Brokerage and Other Services segment consists principally of Aon's retail, reinsurance, specialty and wholesale brokerage operations. The Consulting segment provides a full range of employee benefits, human resources, compensation, and change management services. The Insurance Underwriting segment is comprised of direct sales life and accident and health, warranty, specialty and other insurance products.

ANNUAL FINANCIAL DATA

	12/31/00	12/31/99	12/31/98	12/31/97	12/31/96	12/31/95	12/31/94
Earnings Per Share	**[3] 1.82**	**[2] 1.33**	**2.07**	**1.12**	**[1] 1.10**	**[1] 1.14**	**1.40**
Tang. Book Val. Per Share	...	...	...	...	**4.93**	**4.38**	**2.88**
Dividends Per Share	**0.87**	**0.81**	**0.73**	**0.68**	**0.63**	**0.60**	**0.56**
Dividend Payout %	**47.8**	**61.1**	**35.4**	**60.7**	**57.3**	**52.1**	**40.1**
INCOME STATEMENT (IN MILLIONS):							
Total Premium Income	1,921.0	1,854.0	1,706.0	1,608.9	1,526.7	1,426.5	1,933.7
Other Income	5,454.0	5,216.0	4,787.0	4,141.7	2,361.5	2,039.2	2,223.2
Total Revenues	7,375.0	7,070.0	6,493.0	5,750.6	3,888.2	3,465.7	4,156.9
Policyholder Benefits	1,037.0	973.0	896.0	842.3	789.5	698.5	1,304.9
Income Before Income Taxes	854.0	635.0	931.0	541.6	445.6	458.0	537.6
Income Taxes	333.0	243.0	349.0	203.1	153.8	154.0	177.6
Equity Earnings/Minority Int.	d40.0	d40.0	d41.0	d39.7	...	...	...
Net Income	[3] 481.0	[2] 352.0	541.0	298.8	[1] 291.8	[1] 303.7	360.0
Average Shs. Outstg. (000)	263,000	262,700	259,350	255,750	247,950	244,575	238,898
BALANCE SHEET (IN MILLIONS):							
Cash & Cash Equivalents	3,443.0	3,199.0	2,944.0	2,782.4	1,676.4	1,053.6	1,292.0
Premiums Due	8,230.0	7,346.0	6,543.0	6,183.1	4,555.2	2,844.3	2,519.7
Invst. Assets: Fixed-term	2,337.0	2,497.0	3,103.0	3,143.6	2,826.1	7,687.1	7,144.1
Invst. Assets: Loans	...	...	...	...	87.2	858.3	782.4
Invst. Assets: Total	6,019.0	6,184.0	6,452.0	5,922.1	5,212.8	10,639.1	9,782.5
Total Assets	22,251.0	21,132.0	19,688.0	18,691.2	13,722.7	19,735.8	17,921.9
Long-Term Obligations	1,798.0	1,011.0	580.0	637.1	521.2	554.3	561.0
Net Stockholders' Equity	3,388.0	3,051.0	3,017.0	2,822.1	2,832.9	2,673.7	2,257.4
Year-end Shs. Outstg. (000)	261,339	253,753	256,191	251,957	249,525	243,675	242,316
STATISTICAL RECORD:							
Return on Revenues %	6.5	5.0	8.3	5.2	7.5	8.8	8.7
Return on Equity %	14.2	11.5	17.9	10.6	10.3	11.4	15.9
Return on Assets %	2.2	1.7	2.7	1.6	2.1	1.5	2.0
Price Range	42.75-20.69	46.67-26.06	50.38-32.17	38.96-26.78	28.78-21.11	22.61-13.95	15.89-13.00
P/E Ratio	23.5-11.4	35.1-19.6	24.3-15.5	34.8-23.9	26.1-19.2	19.8-12.2	11.4-9.3
Average Yield %	2.7	2.2	1.8	2.1	2.5	3.3	3.9

Statistics are as originally reported. Adj. for stk. splits: 3-for-2, 5/99; 5/97; 5/94 [1] Bef. disc. oper. gain 1996, $43.4 mill.; 1995, $99.1 mill. [2] Incl. non-recurr. chrg. $313.0 mill. [3] Bef. acctg. change chrg. of $7.0 mill., but incl. special chrgs. of $82.0 mill.

OFFICERS:
P. G. Ryan, Chmn., C.E.O.
M. D. O'Halleran, Pres., C.O.O.
H. N. Medvin, Exec. V.P., C.F.O.
D. M. Aigotti, Treas.

INVESTOR CONTACT: Sean P. O'Neill, V.P., Financial Relations, (312) 701-3983

PRINCIPAL OFFICE: 123 North Wacker Drive, Chicago, IL 60606

TELEPHONE NUMBER: (312) 701-3000
FAX: (312) 701-3080
WEB: www.aon.com

NO. OF EMPLOYEES: 51,000 (approx.)

SHAREHOLDERS: 13,650 (approx.)

ANNUAL MEETING: In April

INCORPORATED: IL, Oct., 1949; reincorp., DE, 1979

INSTITUTIONAL HOLDINGS:
No. of Institutions: 334
Shares Held: 153,061,815
% Held: 58.6

INDUSTRY: Accident and health insurance (SIC: 6321)

TRANSFER AGENT(S): First Chicago Trust Company of New York, Jersey City, NJ

NYSE SYMBOL APA
Rec. Pr. 63.96 (4/30/01)

APACHE CORPORATION

YIELD 0.4%
P/E RATIO 11.2

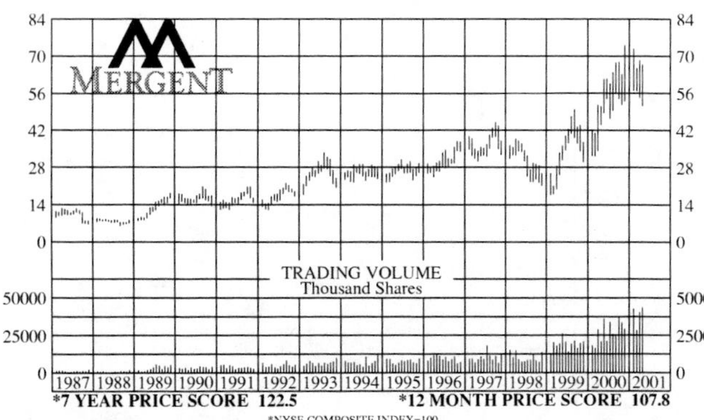

*7 YEAR PRICE SCORE 122.5 *12 MONTH PRICE SCORE 107.8

*NYSE COMPOSITE INDEX=100

INTERIM EARNINGS (Per Share):

Qtr.	Mar.	June	Sept.	Dec.
1997	0.59	0.29	0.34	0.50
1998	0.18	0.09	0.03	d1.64
1999	d0.04	0.28	0.59	0.80
2000	0.96	1.18	1.58	1.96

INTERIM DIVIDENDS (Per Share):

Amt.	Decl.	Ex.	Rec.	Pay.
0.07Q	5/06/99	6/28/99	6/30/99	7/30/99
0.07Q	8/11/99	9/28/99	9/30/99	10/29/99
0.07Q	9/29/99	12/29/99	12/31/99	1/31/00
0.07Q	2/22/00	3/29/00	3/31/00	4/28/00
0.14Q	9/22/00	11/13/00	11/15/00	12/15/00

2 *Indicated div.: $0.28 (Div. Reinv. Plan)*

CAPITALIZATION (12/31/00):

	($000)	(%)
Long-Term Debt	2,193,258	33.0
Deferred Income Tax	699,833	10.5
Preferred Stock	306,594	4.6
Common & Surplus	3,448,046	51.9
Total	6,647,731	100.0

RECENT DEVELOPMENTS: For the year ended 12/31/00, net income soared to $720.6 million, before an after-tax accounting charge of $7.5 million, versus $200.9 million the prior year. Total revenues surged 99.2% to $2.28 billion as higher prices and increased oil and natural gas production contributed to APA's enhanced results. Separately, APA expects to spend about $1.00 billion, excluding acquisitions, on exploration and development for 2001, about 30.0% higher than the previous year.

PROSPECTS: On 3/23/01, the Company announced that it has completed the acquisition of Repsol YPF assets in Egypt's Western Desert and, with partner Shell Overseas Holdings, the acquisition of Fletcher Challenge Energy, for a combined cost to APA of approximately $1.00 billion. On 12/29/00, the Company announced that it has acquired Canadian properties from Canadian affiliates of Phillips Petroleum Company for approximately $490.0 million.

BUSINESS

APACHE CORPORATION is an independent energy company that explores for, develops and produces natural gas, crude oil and natural gas liquids. In North America, APA's exploration and production interests are focused on the Gulf of Mexico, the Anadarko Basin, the Permian Basin, the Gulf Coast and the Western Sedimentary Basin of Canada. Outside of North America, Apache has exploration and production interests offshore Western Australia and in Egypt, and exploration interests in Poland and offshore The People's Republic of China. As of 12/31/00, total proved reserves were: oil, natural gas liquids and condensate 522.5 million barrels; and natural gas 3.38 trillion cubic feet.

BUSINESS LINE ANALYSIS

(12/31/2000)	Rev(%)	Inc(%)
United States	60.0	57.6
Canada	14.5	15.2
Egypt	15.7	17.8
Australia	9.8	9.4
Total	100.0	100.0

ANNUAL FINANCIAL DATA

	12/31/00	12/31/99	12/31/98	12/31/97	12/31/96	12/31/95	12/31/94
Earnings Per Share	**3 5.73**	**1.72**	**d1.34**	**1.65**	**1.42**	**1 0.28**	**0.70**
Cash Flow Per Share	**10.32**	**5.85**	**5.09**	**5.47**	**5.15**	**4.49**	**4.56**
Tang. Book Val. Per Share	**27.89**	**20.71**	**17.42**	**18.53**	**16.86**	**14.11**	**13.28**
Dividends Per Share	**0.28**	**0.28**	**0.28**	**0.28**	**0.28**	**0.28**	**0.28**
Dividend Payout %	**4.9**	**16.3**	**...**	**17.0**	**19.7**	**100.0**	**40.0**
INCOME STATEMENT (IN MILLIONS):							
Total Revenues	2,283.0	1,300.4	877.3	1,178.0	977.4	750.7	545.2
Costs & Expenses	387.3	559.0	362.3	457.5	395.1	344.8	213.9
Depreciation & Amort.	586.3	447.7	630.5	387.9	320.3	302.2	236.5
Operating Income	1,309.5	293.7	d115.5	332.6	262.1	103.7	94.7
Net Interest Inc./(Exp.)	d106.6	50.7	d70.5	d72.3	d61.6	d70.6	d30.7
Income Before Income Taxes	1,203.7	344.6	d187.6	258.6	200.2	33.1	64.5
Income Taxes	483.1	143.7	cr58.2	103.7	78.8	12.9	21.6
Equity Earnings/Minority Int.	0.9	0.2	d1.6	d1.7	d0.3	...	0.5
Net Income	3 720.6	200.9	d129.4	154.9	121.4	1 20.2	42.8
Cash Flow	1,286.9	634.1	499.1	542.8	441.7	322.4	279.4
Average Shs. Outstg. (000)	124,716	108,354	98,066	99,254	85,777	71,792	61,317
BALANCE SHEET (IN MILLIONS):							
Cash & Cash Equivalents	37.2	13.2	14.5	9.7	13.2	13.6	15.1
Total Current Assets	630.0	343.1	227.0	348.3	268.2	208.3	134.9
Net Property	6,812.5	5,115.9	3,727.5	3,733.2	3,100.1	2,401.6	1,685.4
Total Assets	7,482.0	5,502.5	3,996.1	4,138.6	3,432.4	2,681.5	1,879.0
Total Current Liabilities	553.3	336.8	305.8	343.8	309.7	230.3	147.8
Long-Term Obligations	2,193.3	1,879.7	1,343.3	1,501.4	1,235.7	1,072.1	657.5
Net Stockholders' Equity	3,754.6	2,669.4	1,801.8	1,729.2	1,518.5	1,091.8	816.2
Net Working Capital	76.7	6.3	d78.8	4.5	d41.5	d22.0	d12.9
Year-end Shs. Outstg. (000)	123,635	113,996	97,769	93,305	90,059	77,379	61,440
STATISTICAL RECORD:							
Operating Profit Margin %	57.4	22.6	...	28.2	26.8	13.8	17.4
Net Profit Margin %	31.6	15.4	...	13.1	12.4	2.7	7.9
Return on Equity %	19.2	7.5	...	9.0	8.0	1.9	5.2
Return on Assets %	9.6	3.7	...	3.7	3.5	0.8	2.3
Debt/Total Assets %	29.3	34.2	33.6	36.3	36.0	40.0	35.0
Price Range	74.19-32.13	49.81-17.63	38.75-21.06	45.06-30.13	37.88-24.38	31.00-22.25	29.25-22.25
P/E Ratio	12.9-5.6	29.0-10.2	...	27.3-18.3	26.7-17.2	110.7-79.4	41.8-31.8
Average Yield %	0.5	0.8	0.9	0.7	0.9	1.1	1.1

Statistics are as originally reported. 1 Incls. non-recurr. pre-tax chrg. 12/31/95: $10.0 mill. 2 Dividend payment schedule changed from quarterly basis to an annual basis. 3 Bef. an after-tax acctg. chge. chrg. of $7.5 mill. ($0.07/sh.)

OFFICERS:
R. Plank, Chmn., C.E.O.
G. S. Farris, Pres., C.O.O.
R. B. Plank, Exec. V.P., C.F.O.

INVESTOR CONTACT: Robert J. Dye, V.P., Investor Relations, (713) 296-6662

PRINCIPAL OFFICE: One Post Oak Central, 2000 Post Oak Blvd., Suite 100, Houston, TX 77056-4400

TELEPHONE NUMBER: (713) 296-6000
FAX: (713) 296-6490
WEB: www.apachecorp.com

NO. OF EMPLOYEES: 1,546 (avg.)

SHAREHOLDERS: 10,000 (approx. common); 62,000 (approx. beneficial)

ANNUAL MEETING: In May

INCORPORATED: DE, Dec., 1954

INSTITUTIONAL HOLDINGS:
No. of Institutions: 410
Shares Held: 100,765,871
% Held: 81.4

INDUSTRY: Crude petroleum and natural gas (SIC: 1311)

TRANSFER AGENT(S): Wells Fargo Bank Minnesota, N.A., South St. Paul, MN

NYSE SYMBOL AIV
Rec. Pr. 45.87 (5/31/01)

APARTMENT INVESTMENT & MANAGEMENT CO.

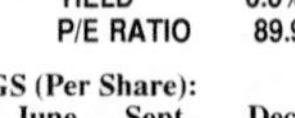
YIELD 6.8%
P/E RATIO 89.9

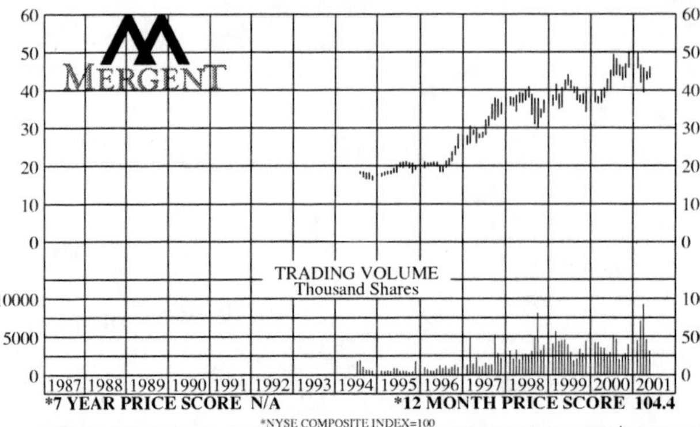

INTERIM EARNINGS (Per Share):

Qtr.	Mar.	June	Sept.	Dec.
1997	0.28	0.26	0.25	0.29
1998	0.43	0.19	0.19	0.05
1999	0.01	0.14	0.07	0.15
2000	0.17	d0.04	0.20	0.18

INTERIM DIVIDENDS (Per Share):

Amt.	Decl.	Ex.	Rec.	Pay.
0.70Q	4/20/00	5/03/00	5/05/00	5/12/00
0.70Q	7/20/00	8/02/00	8/04/00	8/11/00
0.70Q	10/18/00	11/01/00	11/03/00	11/10/00
0.78Q	1/24/01	1/31/01	2/02/01	2/09/01
0.78Q	4/19/01	5/02/01	5/04/01	5/11/01

Indicated div.: $3.12

CAPITALIZATION (12/31/00):

	($000)	(%)
Long-Term Debt	4,031,375	57.3
Minority Interest	471,687	6.7
Redeemable Pfd. Stock	32,330	0.5
Preferred Stock	837,717	11.9
Common & Surplus	1,663,940	23.6
Total	7,037,049	100.0

RECENT DEVELOPMENTS: For the year ended 12/31/00, net income jumped 28.0% to $99.2 million compared with $77.5 million in the previous year. Results included a gain on the disposition of properties of $26.3 million versus a loss of $1.8 million in the prior year. Total income surged 90.6% to $1.10 billion versus $577.4 million in 1999. Rental and other property revenues nearly doubled to $1.06 billion from $533.9 million in the preceding year. Management fees and other income increased 26.5% to $49.7 million.

PROSPECTS: During the fourth quarter, the Company completed $897.0 million in acquisitions, depositions, and mortgage-financing transactions. AIV acquired eight properties for $99.0 million and purchased $77.0 million of limited partnership interests. Also, AIV sold 28 apartment communities and one commercial property for a total of $233.0 million. Separately, the Company completed the acquisition of Oxford Tax-Exempt Fund II Limited Partnership, which holds tax-exempt bonds and taxable securities that are secured primarily by mortgaged on 17 properties.

BUSINESS

APARTMENT INVESTMENT & MANAGEMENT COMPANY is a self-administered and self-managed real estate investment trust engaged in the ownership, acquisition, development, expansion and management of multi-family apartment properties. The Company has 25 regional operating centers, which hold a geographically diversified portfolio of apartment communities. The Company, through its subsidiaries, operates 1,720 properties, including approximately 326,000 apartment units, and serves approximately one million residents. The Company's properties are located in 47 states, the District of Columbia and Puerto Rico.

ANNUAL FINANCIAL DATA

	12/31/00	12/31/99	12/31/98	12/31/97	12/31/96	12/31/95	12/31/94
Earnings Per Share	[1] **0.52**	[1] **0.38**	[1] **0.80**	[1] [2] **1.08**	[1] **1.04**	**0.86**	**0.42**
Tang. Book Val. Per Share	**23.32**	**24.27**	**20.26**	**19.34**	**14.10**	**13.59**	**14.63**
Dividends Per Share	**2.80**	**2.50**	**2.25**	**1.85**	**1.70**	**1.66**	**0.29**
Dividend Payout %	**538.4**	**657.7**	**281.2**	**171.3**	**163.4**	**193.0**	**69.0**
INCOME STATEMENT (IN MILLIONS):							
Rental Income	1,051.0	533.9	377.1	193.0	100.5	74.9	24.9
Total Income	1,100.7	577.4	401.2	206.9	108.9	83.1	28.1
Costs & Expenses	485.2	268.7	190.2	98.7	48.6	39.8	14.1
Depreciation	330.0	137.6	93.4	39.1	20.3	15.6	4.9
Interest Expense	269.8	140.1	89.4	51.4	24.8	13.3	1.6
Income Before Income Taxes	108.3	91.9	63.4	29.1	15.8	15.0	7.7
Equity Earnings/Minority Int.	d9.1	d10.9	1.1	d0.2	d2.8	d1.6	d0.6
Net Income	[1] 99.2	[1] 81.0	[1] 64.5	[1] [2] 28.9	[1] 13.0	13.4	7.1
Average Shs. Outstg. (000)	69,063	63,446	47,624	24,436	12,427	9,579	...
BALANCE SHEET (IN MILLIONS):							
Cash & Cash Equivalents	284.0	186.2	127.1	61.3	29.0	19.4	19.4
Total Real Estate Investments	6,099.2	4,096.2	2,601.0	1,510.2	751.9	448.4	390.6
Total Assets	7,699.9	5,685.0	4,268.3	2,100.5	827.7	478.7	416.7
Long-Term Obligations	4,031.4	2,375.1	1,242.4	755.4	317.6	239.7	119.7
Total Liabilities	5,198.2	3,422.1	2,365.7	1,055.2	611.9	309.7	276.4
Net Stockholders' Equity	2,501.7	2,262.8	1,902.6	1,045.3	215.7	169.0	140.3
Year-end Shs. Outstg. (000)	71,337	66,803	48,451	40,602	15,305	12,433	9,589
STATISTICAL RECORD:							
Net Inc.+Depr./Assets %	5.6	3.8	3.7	3.2	4.0	6.1	2.9
Return on Equity %	4.0	3.6	3.4	2.8	6.0	7.9	5.1
Return on Assets %	1.3	1.4	1.5	1.4	1.6	2.8	1.7
Price Range	50.06-36.31	44.13-34.06	41.00-30.00	38.00-25.50	28.38-18.38	21.25-17.13	18.63-16.25
P/E Ratio	96.3-69.8	116.1-89.6	51.2-37.5	35.2-23.6	27.3-17.7	24.7-19.9	44.3-38.7
Average Yield %	6.5	6.4	6.3	5.8	7.3	8.7	1.7

Statistics are as originally reported. [1] Incl. diposition of property gain, $26.3 mill., 12/00; loss, $1.8 mill., 12/99; gain, $4.7 mill., 12/98; $2.7 mill., 12/97; $44,000, 12/96 [2] Bef. extraord. chrg. $269,000.

OFFICERS:
T. Considine, Chmn., C.E.O.
P. K. Kompaniez, Vice-Chmn., Pres.
P. J. McAuliffe, Exec. V.P., C.F.O.

INVESTOR CONTACT: Katie Murphee, V.P. Inv. Rel., (303) 691-4440

PRINCIPAL OFFICE: 2000 S. Colorado Blvd., Tower Two, Denver, CO 80222

TELEPHONE NUMBER: (303) 757-8101
FAX: (303) 757-8735
WEB: www.aimco.com

NO. OF EMPLOYEES: 9,500 (approx.)

SHAREHOLDERS: 2,776 (class A common)

ANNUAL MEETING: In June

INCORPORATED: MD, Jan., 1994

INSTITUTIONAL HOLDINGS:
No. of Institutions: 152
Shares Held: 47,967,999
% Held: 65.4

INDUSTRY: Real estate investment trusts (SIC: 6798)

TRANSFER AGENT(S): BankBoston, Boston, MA

NYSE SYMBOL AOT
Rec. Pr. 24.34 (5/31/01)

APOGENT TECHNOLOGIES, INC.

YIELD . . .
P/E RATIO 29.3

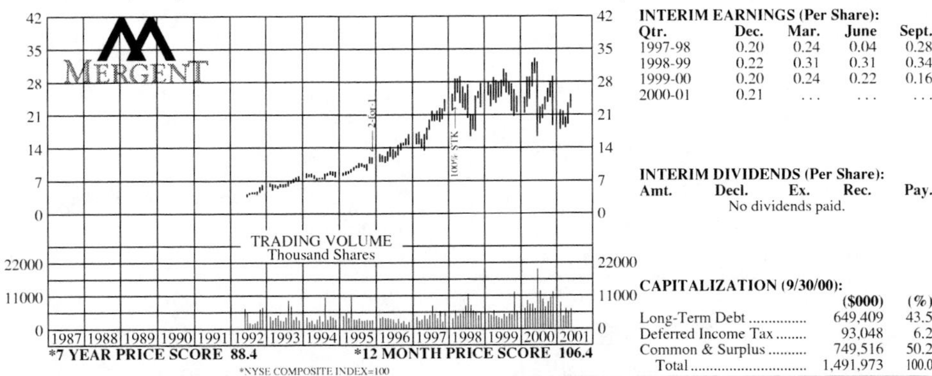

INTERIM EARNINGS (Per Share):

Qtr.	Dec.	Mar.	June	Sept.
1997-98	0.20	0.24	0.04	0.28
1998-99	0.22	0.31	0.31	0.34
1999-00	0.20	0.24	0.22	0.16
2000-01	0.21	. . .	. . .	. . .

INTERIM DIVIDENDS (Per Share):

Amt.	Decl.	Ex.	Rec.	Pay.

No dividends paid.

CAPITALIZATION (9/30/00):

	($000)	(%)
Long-Term Debt	649,409	43.5
Deferred Income Tax	93,048	6.2
Common & Surplus	749,516	50.2
Total	1,491,973	100.0

RECENT DEVELOPMENTS: For the three months ended 12/31/00, income from continuing operations advanced 8.3% to $22.2 million compared with net income of $20.5 million in the corresponding quarter of 1999. The 2000 results excluded a net loss from discontinued operations of $11.0 million and an extraordinary loss of $700,000. Net sales climbed 7.8% to $220.8 million from $204.9 million in the year-earlier period.

PROSPECTS: Looking ahead, the Company continues to expect more favorable internal growth rates during fiscal 2001 of approximately 4.0%, 11.0%, and 9.0% in the next three quarters consistent with its objective of 7.0% overall internal growth for the year. In addition, the Company expects diluted earnings per share for fiscal year 2001 to be $1.00.

BUSINESS

APOGENT TECHNOLOGIES, INC. (formerly Sybron International Corp.) manufactures value-added products for the labware and life sciences, clinical and industrial, diagnostics and microbiology, and laboratory equipment industries. AOT's products include: reusuable and disposable plastic products; products for critical packaging applications; microscope slides, cover glass, glass tubes and vials; stains and reagents; diagnostic test kits, cultural media, diagnostic reagents, and other products used in detecting causes of various infections or diseases; heating, stirring and temperature control apparatus; systems for producing ultra pure water; constant temperature equipment; and furnaces, fluorometers, spectrophotometers and strip chart recorders. On 12/11/00, the Company spun off its dental business.

BUSINESS LINE ANALYSIS

(9/30/2000)	Rev(%)	Inc(%)
Laboratory & Life Science	40.0	39.0
Clinical & Industrial..	24.7	25.9
Diagnostics & Microbiolog	24.1	25.1
Laboratoy Equipment	11.2	10.0
Total	100.0	100.0

ANNUAL FINANCIAL DATA

	9/30/00	9/30/99	9/30/98	9/30/97	9/30/96	9/30/95	9/30/94
Earnings Per Share	**[4][5] 0.81**	**[3] 1.18**	**[2] 0.75**	**0.83**	**[1] 0.60**	**0.55**	**0.46**
Cash Flow Per Share	**1.44**	**1.80**	**1.30**	**1.32**	**1.06**	**0.91**	**0.79**
INCOME STATEMENT (IN MILLIONS):							
Total Revenues	863.6	1,103.2	960.7	795.1	674.5	519.2	439.7
Costs & Expenses	604.0	772.4	712.6	566.3	493.6	376.3	317.3
Depreciation & Amort.	66.6	66.5	57.1	48.9	44.1	33.7	30.4
Operating Income	193.0	264.3	191.0	180.0	136.7	109.1	92.0
Net Interest Inc./(Exp.)	d49.4	d57.1	d56.9	d43.2	d35.2	d23.0	d19.7
Income Before Income Taxes	144.3	206.5	134.1	135.9	100.9	84.9	70.9
Income Taxes	57.6	81.2	56.0	54.0	43.3	33.1	27.9
Equity Earnings/Minority Int.	. . .	. . .	. . .	. . .	. . .	d0.3	d0.3
Net Income	[4][5] 86.7	[3] 125.3	[2] 78.0	81.9	[1] 57.6	51.8	43.0
Cash Flow	153.3	191.7	135.1	130.7	101.7	85.5	73.4
Average Shs. Outstg. (000)	106,803	106,570	103,964	98,956	95,834	93,956	92,676
BALANCE SHEET (IN MILLIONS):							
Cash & Cash Equivalents	12.4	18.5	22.5	17.2	10.9	9.2	11.2
Total Current Assets	510.5	492.0	445.8	359.8	282.6	248.4	185.9
Net Property	208.1	245.2	224.5	190.3	170.2	148.1	100.0
Total Assets	1,792.4	1,842.9	1,545.1	1,182.7	938.6	782.6	564.2
Total Current Liabilities	241.1	191.9	220.3	144.3	138.8	138.2	95.6
Long-Term Obligations	649.4	875.3	790.1	645.7	481.0	406.5	223.6
Net Stockholders' Equity	749.5	625.3	470.0	367.0	283.1	227.3	176.8
Net Working Capital	269.4	300.0	225.4	215.5	143.9	110.3	90.2
Year-end Shs. Outstg. (000)	105,192	104,024	101,005	96,344	93,850	93,056	92,784
STATISTICAL RECORD:							
Operating Profit Margin %	22.3	24.0	19.9	22.6	20.3	21.0	20.9
Net Profit Margin %	10.0	11.4	8.1	10.3	8.5	10.0	9.8
Return on Equity %	11.6	20.0	16.6	22.3	20.3	22.8	24.3
Return on Assets %	4.8	6.8	5.1	6.9	6.1	6.6	7.6
Debt/Total Assets %	36.2	47.5	51.1	54.6	51.3	51.9	39.6
Price Range	33.06-16.38	30.81-20.69	29.13-16.38	24.25-13.38	16.88-10.81	12.06-8.06	9.06-6.88
P/E Ratio	40.8-20.2	26.1-17.5	38.8-21.8	29.4-16.2	28.1-18.0	21.9-14.7	19.6-14.8

Statistics are as originally reported. Adj. for stk. split: 2-for-1, 12/95; 100%, 2/98. [1] Incl. pre-tax restruct. chrg. of $7.5 mill. [2] Incl. pre-tax mgr., trans. & integrat. exp. of $10.5 mill. & restruct, chrg. of $23.3 mill. [3] Incls. restr. chrg. of $932,000 & mgr., trans. & integrat. chrg. of $2.6 mill.; excl. after-tax gain of $17.3 mill. [4] Excl. income of $41.6 mill. from disc. opers. [5] Excl. net loss of $11.0 mill. from disc. oper., extraord. loss of $700,000 & restruct. chrg. of $10.3 mill.

OFFICERS:
K. F. Yontz, Chmn.
F. H. Jellinek Jr., Pres., C.E.O.

INVESTOR CONTACT: Tricia Mintzlaff, Inv. Rel., (603) 433-6131

PRINCIPAL OFFICE: 48 Congress Street, Portsmouth, NH 03801

TELEPHONE NUMBER: (603) 433-6131
FAX: (603) 274-6561
WEB: www.sybron.com

NO. OF EMPLOYEES: 6,000 (approx.)

SHAREHOLDERS: 413

ANNUAL MEETING: In Jan.

INCORPORATED: NY, 1965; reincorp., WI, 1987

INSTITUTIONAL HOLDINGS:
No. of Institutions: 200
Shares Held: 89,105,228
% Held: 84.6

INDUSTRY: Dental equipment and supplies (SIC: 3843)

TRANSFER AGENT(S): Fleet National Bank c/o EquiServe, Providence, RI

NYSE SYMBOL APN
Rec. Pr. 8.49 (5/31/01)

APPLICA INC.

YIELD ...
P/E RATIO ...

TRADING VOLUME
Thousand Shares

*7 YEAR PRICE SCORE 42.8 *12 MONTH PRICE SCORE 102.9

*NYSE COMPOSITE INDEX=100

INTERIM EARNINGS (Per Share):

Qtr.	Mar.	June	Sept.	Dec.
1995	0.02	0.05	0.05	d0.23
1996	0.02	d0.03	0.10	0.12
1997	0.02	0.10	0.43	0.45
1998	0.06	d0.38	1.58	0.02
1999	d0.30	d0.47	0.59	0.84
2000	d0.13	d0.01	0.35	d1.14

INTERIM DIVIDENDS (Per Share):

Amt.	Decl.	Ex.	Rec.	Pay.

No dividends paid.

CAPITALIZATION (12/31/00):

	($000)	(%)
Long-Term Debt	260,147	44.5
Common & Surplus	324,474	55.5
Total	584,621	100.0

RECENT DEVELOPMENTS: For the year ended 12/31/00, the Company reported a net loss of $21.2 million versus net income of $16.8 million in 1999. Results for 2000 included a repositioning charge of $34.1 million, while results for 1999 included a repositioning credit of $1.5 million. Sales and other revenues grew 4.2% to $748.8 million from $718.3 million in the prior year. Gross profit as a percentage of revenues totaled 27.4% compared with 32.6% the year before. Operating profit fell 82.4% to $10.3 million from $58.8 million a year earlier.

PROSPECTS: The Company is being negatively affected by the slow down in the U.S. economy and a reduction in inventories by many of its key customers, as well as rising material and energy costs. Going forward, the Company will continue to take steps to more effectively manage its assets, while looking to take advantage of future growth opportunities. Meanwhile, APN remains optimistic that it will benefit from the growth of its Black and Decker branded products, as well as cost synergy and manufacturing efficiency programs put into place.

BUSINESS

APPLICA INC. (formerly Windmere-Durable Holdings, Inc.) is engaged in three business units: consumer products North America, consumer products international and manufacturing. The consumer products North America and International segments distribute kitchen electric, personal care and home environment products under licensed brand names such as Black & Decker (which was acquired in June 1998), as well as the Windmere and private label brand names. The consumer products international segment products are marketed throughout all countries in Latin America except for Brazil. The manufacturing segment includes APN's operations located in Bao An County, Guangdong Province of the Peoples' Republic of China and in Queretaro, Mexico. The majority of the Company's products are manufactured in these two facilities. As of 12/31/00, APN owned a 50.0% equity interest in Newtech Electronics Industries, Inc., which designs and markets consumer electronics.

ANNUAL FINANCIAL DATA

	12/31/00	12/31/99	12/31/98	12/31/97	12/31/96	12/31/95	12/31/94
Earnings Per Share	[4] **d0.92**	[3] **0.72**	[1] **1.33**	**1.00**	[2] **0.22**	[1] **d0.11**	[1] **1.17**
Cash Flow Per Share	**0.73**	**2.12**	**2.26**	**1.38**	**0.59**	**0.25**	**1.46**
Tang. Book Val. Per Share	**4.34**	**15.17**	**14.67**	**10.53**	**9.61**	**9.87**	**10.20**
Dividends Per Share	...	...	...	**0.10**	**0.20**	**0.20**	**0.15**
Dividend Payout %	...	...	...	**10.0**	**90.9**	...	**12.8**
INCOME STATEMENT (IN THOUSANDS):							
Total Revenues	748,751	718,309	474,356	261,885	197,004	187,777	181,112
Costs & Expenses	700,464	627,056	444,529	240,494	190,310	186,351	154,677
Depreciation & Amort.	37,945	32,494	20,117	7,363	6,393	6,181	5,230
Operating Income	10,342	58,759	9,710	14,029	300	d4,755	21,205
Net Interest Inc./(Exp.)	d30,301	d27,109	d16,632	d3,351	d1,346	d578	d552
Income Before Income Taxes	d22,758	21,020	40,368	20,758	3,672	d3,165	23,131
Income Taxes	cr1,542	4,177	11,616	923	cr280	cr1,281	2,595
Equity Earnings/Minority Int.	...	...	...	...	...	...	1
Net Income	[4] d21,216	[3] 16,843	[1] 28,752	19,835	[2] 3,951	[1] d1,884	[1] 20,537
Cash Flow	16,729	49,337	48,868	27,198	10,345	4,298	25,767
Average Shs. Outstg.	22,947	23,325	21,612	19,776	17,620	17,227	17,589
BALANCE SHEET (IN THOUSANDS):							
Cash & Cash Equivalents	16,857	13,768	20,415	8,224	8,780	17,768	15,488
Total Current Assets	400,295	388,784	398,847	179,960	155,016	147,188	150,848
Net Property	78,200	75,983	76,077	37,199	32,760	30,485	28,449
Total Assets	707,935	712,673	742,737	281,847	237,279	188,012	197,124
Total Current Liabilities	123,314	125,469	131,413	73,882	49,452	19,563	21,567
Long-Term Obligations	260,147	243,571	272,370	16,070	19,885	2,852	3,667
Net Stockholders' Equity	324,474	343,397	324,018	190,821	167,695	164,931	170,625
Net Working Capital	276,981	263,315	267,434	106,078	105,565	127,626	129,281
Year-end Shs. Outstg.	23,080	22,641	22,091	18,119	17,445	16,713	16,734
STATISTICAL RECORD:							
Operating Profit Margin %	1.4	8.2	2.0	5.4	0.2	...	11.7
Net Profit Margin %	...	2.3	6.1	7.6	2.0	...	11.3
Return on Equity %	...	4.9	8.9	10.4	2.4	...	12.0
Return on Assets %	...	2.4	3.9	7.0	1.7	...	10.4
Debt/Total Assets %	36.7	34.2	36.7	5.7	8.4	1.5	1.9
Price Range	19.44-3.00	17.25-4.69	37.38-4.06	26.69-12.00	16.75-6.88	10.13-5.75	12.00-6.75
P/E Ratio	...	24.0-6.5	28.1-3.1	26.7-12.0	76.1-31.2	...	10.3-5.8
Average Yield %	...	...	...	0.5	1.7	2.5	1.6

Statistics are as originally reported. [1] Incl. non-recur. chrg. 1998, $9.9 mill.; 1995, $8.0 mill.; credit 1994, $21.2 mill. [2] Bef. extraord. credit $3.5 mill. [3] Incl. gain $994,000 and after-tax chrg. $8.3 mill. [4] Incl. repositioning chrg. of $34.1 mill.

OFFICERS:
D. M. Friedson, Chmn., C.E.O.
H. D. Schulman, Pres.

INVESTOR CONTACT: Investor Relations, (305) 362-2611

PRINCIPAL OFFICE: 5980 Miami Lakes Dr., Miami Lakes, FL 33014

TELEPHONE NUMBER: (305) 362-2611
FAX: (305) 364-0502
WEB: www.windmere.com

NO. OF EMPLOYEES: 17,000 (approx.)

SHAREHOLDERS: 1,000 (approx.)

ANNUAL MEETING: In May

INCORPORATED: FL, Oct., 1963

INSTITUTIONAL HOLDINGS:
No. of Institutions: 66
Shares Held: 12,576,664
% Held: 54.4

INDUSTRY: Electric housewares and fans (SIC: 3634)

TRANSFER AGENT(S): American Stock Transfer & Trust Company, New York, NY

NYSE SYMBOL ABI
Rec. Pr. 32.06 (4/30/01)

APPLIED BIOSYSTEMS GROUP - APPLERA CORP.

YIELD 0.5%
P/E RATIO 32.1

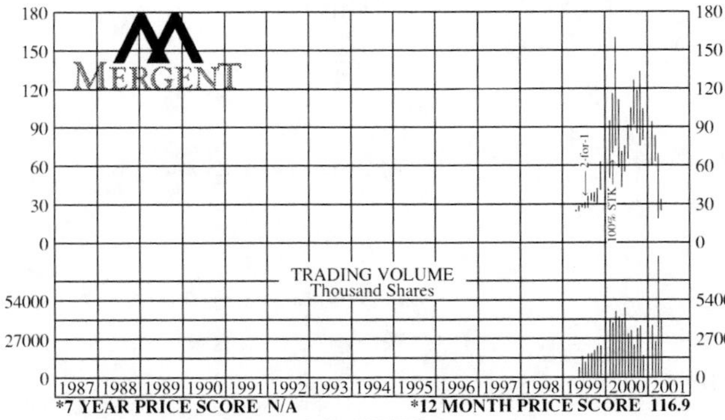

*7 YEAR PRICE SCORE N/A *12 MONTH PRICE SCORE 116.9

*NYSE COMPOSITE INDEX=100

INTERIM EARNINGS (Per Share):

Qtr.	Sept.	Dec.	Mar.	June
1998-99		0.72		
1999-00	0.14	0.21	0.26	0.26
2000-01	0.22	0.26	...	...

INTERIM DIVIDENDS (Per Share):

Amt.	Decl.	Ex.	Rec.	Pay.
0.043Q	3/17/00	5/30/00	6/01/00	7/03/00
0.043Q	8/17/00	8/30/00	9/01/00	10/02/00
0.043Q	11/16/00	11/29/00	12/01/00	1/02/01
0.043Q	1/18/01	2/27/01	3/01/01	4/02/01
0.043Q	3/23/01	5/30/01	6/01/01	7/02/01

Indicated div.: $0.17

CAPITALIZATION (6/30/00):

	($000)	(%)
Long-Term Debt	36,115	3.7
Common & Surplus	934,364	96.3
Total	970,479	100.0

RECENT DEVELOPMENTS: For the quarter ended 12/31/00, net income jumped 32.4% to $58.0 million versus $43.8 million in the equivalent quarter of 1999. Results for 2000 and 1999 included pre-tax gains from the sale of investments of $3.0 million and $25.8 million, respectively. Net revenues were $411.0 million, up 22.4% from $335.9 million in the prior-year period. Gross margin rose 17.9% to $213.1 million.

PROSPECTS: In fiscal 2001, the Company expects revenues and earnings to grow 20.0% year over year, including foreign currency translations. Operating margins are expected to fluctuate by quarter depending on currency, seasonal and other factors including product mix. Overall, the Company expects fiscal 2001 margins will be similar to the margins in fiscal 2000. Separately, the Company signed a technology access agreement with Agilent Technologies.

BUSINESS

APPLIED BIOSYSTEMS GROUP (formerly PE Biosystems Group), a subsidiary of Applera Corporation, develops and markets instrument-based systems, reagents, software, and contract services to the life science industry and research community. Customers use these tools to analyze nucleic acids (DNA and RNA), small molecules, and proteins to make scientific discoveries leading to the development of new pharmaceuticals, and to conduct standardized testing. On 5/5/99, The Perkin-Elmer Corporation changed its name to PE Corporation and created two new classes of common stock, PE Biosystems Group and Celera Genomics Group. On 11/30/00, the name of PE Corporation was changed to Applera Corporation and the name of PE Biosystems Group was changed to the Applied Biosystems Group.

ANNUAL FINANCIAL DATA

	6/30/00	6/30/99	6/30/98	6/30/97
Earnings Per Share	**4 0.86**	**3 1.44**	...	...
Cash Flow Per Share	**1.11**	**1.87**	...	...
Tang. Book Val. Per Share	**4.46**	**5.20**	...	...
Dividends Per Share	**0.17**	**0.17**	**0.17**	**0.17**
Dividend Payout %	**19.8**	**11.8**	...	...
INCOME STATEMENT (IN MILLIONS):				
Total Revenues	1,388.1	1,221.7	940.1	767.5
Costs & Expenses	1,120.4	989.5	851.4	641.7
Depreciation & Amort.	54.5	44.3	35.3	25.4
Operating Income	213.2	187.9	53.4	100.3
Net Interest Inc./(Exp.)	10.5	d2.2	1.0	3.0
Income Before Income Taxes	275.7	192.4	59.2	170.0
Income Taxes	89.5	30.7	29.5	37.3
Equity Earnings/Minority Int.	...	d13.4	d5.6	...
Net Income	4 186.2	3 148.4	2 24.0	1 132.7
Cash Flow	240.8	192.7	59.3	158.1
Average Shs. Outstg. (000)	217,016	103,104	...	...
BALANCE SHEET (IN MILLIONS):				
Cash & Cash Equivalents	394.6	236.5	84.1	...
Total Current Assets	997.8	918.3	651.1	...
Net Property	230.9	182.2	159.1	...
Total Assets	1,698.1	1,347.6	1,128.9	...
Total Current Liabilities	602.7	643.6	362.0	...
Long-Term Obligations	36.1	31.5	33.7	...
Net Stockholders' Equity	934.4	534.3	565.5	...
Net Working Capital	395.2	274.7	289.1	...
Year-end Shs. Outstg. (000)	209,420	102,707	...	...
STATISTICAL RECORD:				
Operating Profit Margin %	15.4	15.4	5.7	13.1
Net Profit Margin %	13.4	12.1	2.6	17.3
Return on Equity %	19.9	27.8	4.2	...
Return on Assets %	11.0	11.0	2.1	...
Debt/Total Assets %	2.1	2.3	3.0	...
Price Range	160.00-42.81	62.94-23.81	...	...
P/E Ratio	186.0-49.8	43.7-16.5	...	...
Average Yield %	0.2	0.4	...	...

Statistics are as originally reported. Adj. for 2-for-1 split, 7/99. Adj. for 100% stk. div., 2/00. 1 Excls. income from disc. ops. of $27.9 mill. 2 Incl. $28.9 mill. pre-tax acquired research and develop. chg. & $44.0 mill. net restr. chg., bef. income of $40.7 mill. from disc. ops. 3 Incl. $1.5 mill. chg. for merger costs, $6.1 mill. gain, excl. $79.1 mill. gain on disp. of disc. ops. 4 Incl. $2.1 mill. spl. chg. fr. merger costs & $48.6 mill. gain fr. sale of investments.

OFFICERS:
T. L. White, Chmn.
M. W. Hunkapiller, Pres.
D. L. Winger, Sr. V.P., C.F.O.

INVESTOR CONTACT: Peter Dworkin, V.P., Investor Relations, (203) 544-2479

PRINCIPAL OFFICE: 761 Main Avenue, Norwalk, CT 06859-0001

TELEPHONE NUMBER: (203) 762-1000
FAX: (203) 762-6000
WEB: www.appliedbiosystems.com
NO. OF EMPLOYEES: 4,036 (approx.)
SHAREHOLDERS: 6,534 (approx.)
ANNUAL MEETING: In Oct.
INCORPORATED: NY, Dec., 1939; reincorp., DE, 1998

INSTITUTIONAL HOLDINGS:
No. of Institutions: 445
Shares Held: 169,102,819
% Held: 80.8

INDUSTRY: Measuring & controlling devices, nec (SIC: 3829)

TRANSFER AGENT(S): BankBoston, N.A., c/o Boston EquiServe, Boston, MA

NYSE SYMBOL AIT
Rec. Pr. 18.91 (4/30/01)

APPLIED INDUSTRIAL TECHNOLOGIES, INC.

YIELD 2.5%
P/E RATIO 11.4

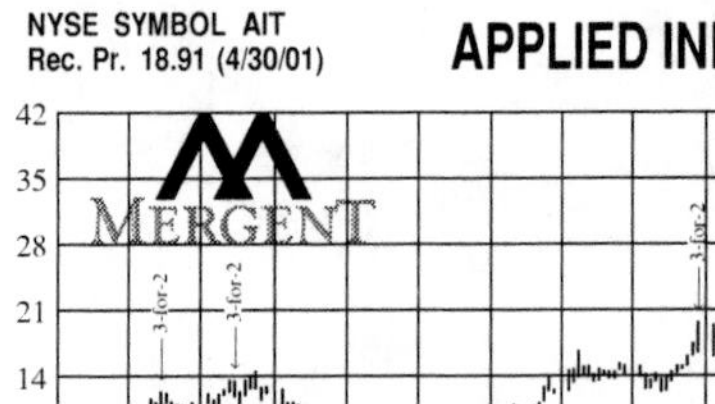

*7 YEAR PRICE SCORE 70.6 *12 MONTH PRICE SCORE 106.6

*NYSE COMPOSITE INDEX=100

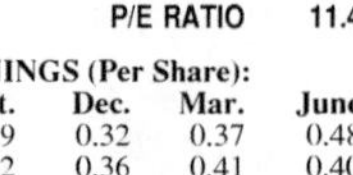

INTERIM EARNINGS (Per Share):

Qtr.	Sept.	Dec.	Mar.	June
1996-97	0.29	0.32	0.37	0.48
1997-98	0.22	0.36	0.41	0.40
1998-99	0.06	0.20	0.30	0.37
1999-00	0.28	0.30	0.40	0.53
2000-01	0.36	0.37	...	...

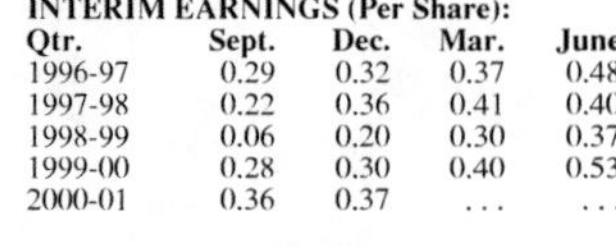

INTERIM DIVIDENDS (Per Share):

Amt.	Decl.	Ex.	Rec.	Pay.
0.12Q	4/20/00	5/11/00	5/15/00	5/31/00
0.12Q	7/20/00	8/11/00	8/15/00	8/31/00
0.12Q	10/17/00	11/13/00	11/15/00	11/30/00
0.12Q	1/12/01	2/12/01	2/14/01	2/28/01
0.12Q	4/19/01	5/11/01	5/15/01	5/31/01

Indicated div.: $0.48 (Div. Reinv. Plan)

CAPITALIZATION (6/30/00):

	($000)	(%)
Long-Term Debt	112,168	27.3
Common & Surplus	299,331	72.7
Total	411,499	100.0

RECENT DEVELOPMENTS: For the second quarter ended 12/31/00, net income amounted to $7.4 million, up 18.1% versus $6.2 million in the comparable prior-year period. Earnings benefited from a favorable business mix and the Company's continued focus on asset management. Net sales advanced 6.8% to $405.4 million compared with $379.7 million in the second quarter of 1999. Operating income rose 21.9% to $14.7 million versus $12.0 million a year earlier.

PROSPECTS: In 2001, sales should benefit from the acquisition of Dynavest Corporation, which is expected to contribute revenues of $72.0 million on an annual basis. However, sales may be hindered by a decline in manufacturing activity in various industries served by the Company. Separately, AIT and Hall Holdings, Inc. formed iSource Performance Materials to distribute APL's regulated performance materials and chemicals that require special handling and shipping.

BUSINESS

APPLIED INDUSTRIAL TECHNOLOGIES, INC. distributes industrial, fluid power, fabricated rubber products and engineered systems. In addition, the Company offers rubber and fluid power shop services as well as engineering, design and fabrication services related to electrical, gearing and material handling systems. The Company offers technical application support for its products and provides applications to help customers minimize downtime and reduce procurement and maintenance costs. The Company operates over 470 Service Centers, eight distribution centers and over 30 mechanical, fluid power and industrial rubber service shops in 47 states, Canada and Puerto Rico. AIT operates under the names of Air and Hydraulics Engineering, Dees Fluid Power, Dynavest, Engineered Sales, Elect-Air Tool Company, Fornaciari Company, HyPower, Rafael Benitez Carrillo and Power Hydraulic

ANNUAL FINANCIAL DATA

	6/30/00	6/30/99	6/30/98	6/30/97	6/30/96	6/30/95	6/30/94
Earnings Per Share	**1.50**	**[2] 0.93**	**1.38**	**[1] 1.47**	**1.27**	**0.98**	**0.75**
Cash Flow Per Share	**2.61**	**1.98**	**2.34**	**2.25**	**2.10**	...	...
Tang. Book Val. Per Share	**11.57**	**10.96**	**10.92**	**10.88**	**9.91**	**9.17**	**8.86**
Dividends Per Share	**0.48**	**0.48**	**0.48**	**0.44**	**0.39**	**0.33**	**0.29**
Dividend Payout %	**32.0**	**51.6**	**34.8**	**29.9**	**30.5**	**34.1**	**39.3**
INCOME STATEMENT (IN MILLIONS):							
Total Revenues	1,571.7	1,527.9	1,491.4	1,160.3	1,143.7	1,054.8	936.3
Costs & Expenses	1,491.0	1,462.8	1,411.9	1,095.2	1,079.0	1,003.9	892.1
Depreciation & Amort.	23.0	22.7	21.0	14.4	15.4	14.0	16.4
Operating Income	57.7	42.5	58.5	50.6	49.3	36.9	27.8
Net Interest Inc./(Exp.)	d7.2	d9.9	d8.7	d5.5	d8.4	d7.3	d6.2
Income Before Income Taxes	50.5	32.6	49.8	45.1	40.8	29.7	21.7
Income Taxes	19.5	12.7	19.7	18.0	17.5	12.8	9.0
Net Income	31.0	[2] 19.9	30.1	[1] 27.1	23.3	16.9	12.7
Cash Flow	54.0	42.6	51.1	41.5	38.8	30.9	29.1
Average Shs. Outstg. (000)	20,687	21,546	21,827	18,465	18,455	...	...
BALANCE SHEET (IN MILLIONS):							
Cash & Cash Equivalents	12.3	19.2	9.3	22.4	9.2	4.8	10.9
Total Current Assets	415.0	389.2	414.9	285.5	295.1	265.4	249.2
Net Property	97.2	107.2	113.1	90.8	86.3	79.3	80.1
Total Assets	594.7	574.3	606.1	394.1	404.1	359.2	343.5
Total Current Liabilities	159.9	132.1	193.1	120.7	143.2	111.8	104.6
Long-Term Obligations	112.2	126.0	90.0	51.4	62.9	74.3	80.0
Net Stockholders' Equity	299.3	293.6	294.5	207.6	189.3	165.4	150.5
Net Working Capital	255.1	257.1	221.8	164.7	152.0	153.6	144.6
Year-end Shs. Outstg. (000)	20,078	21,101	22,102	18,620	18,566	17,532	16,979
STATISTICAL RECORD:							
Operating Profit Margin %	3.7	2.8	3.9	4.4	4.3	3.5	3.0
Net Profit Margin %	2.0	1.3	2.0	2.3	2.0	1.6	1.4
Return on Equity %	10.4	6.8	10.2	13.1	12.3	10.2	8.4
Return on Assets %	5.2	3.5	5.0	6.9	5.8	4.7	3.7
Debt/Total Assets %	18.9	21.9	14.8	13.0	15.6	20.7	23.3
Price Range	21.00-14.31	19.06-11.13	29.31-12.00	34.81-18.25	22.50-16.00	19.75-12.22	16.67-12.33
P/E Ratio	14.0-9.5	20.5-12.0	21.2-8.7	23.7-12.4	17.8-12.6	20.2-12.5	22.3-16.5
Average Yield %	2.7	3.2	2.3	1.7	2.0	2.1	2.0

Statistics are as originally reported. Adj. for stk. splits: 3-for-2, 12/95, 9/97. [1] Incl. non-recurr. chg. $4.0 mill [2] Incl. pretax restruct. & other spec. chrgs. totaling $5.4 mill.

OFFICERS:
D. L. Pugh, Chmn., C.E.O.
G. Rein, Pres., C.O.O.
R. C. Stinson, V.P., Gen. Couns., Sec.

INVESTOR CONTACT: John R. Whitten, V.P., C.F.O. & Treas., (216) 426-4000

PRINCIPAL OFFICE: One Applied Plaza, Cleveland, OH 44115

TELEPHONE NUMBER: (216) 426-4000
FAX: (216) 426-4884
WEB: www.appliedindustrial.com

NO. OF EMPLOYEES: 4,847 (avg.)

SHAREHOLDERS: 6,467

ANNUAL MEETING: In Oct.

INCORPORATED: DE, Nov., 1928; reincorp., OH, Oct., 1988

INSTITUTIONAL HOLDINGS:
No. of Institutions: 91
Shares Held: 13,544,760
% Held: 68.4

INDUSTRY: Industrial supplies (SIC: 5085)

TRANSFER AGENT(S): Computershare Investor Services, Chicago, IL

NYSE SYMBOL ADM
Rec. Pr. 13.50 (5/31/01)

ARCHER DANIELS MIDLAND COMPANY

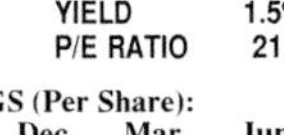

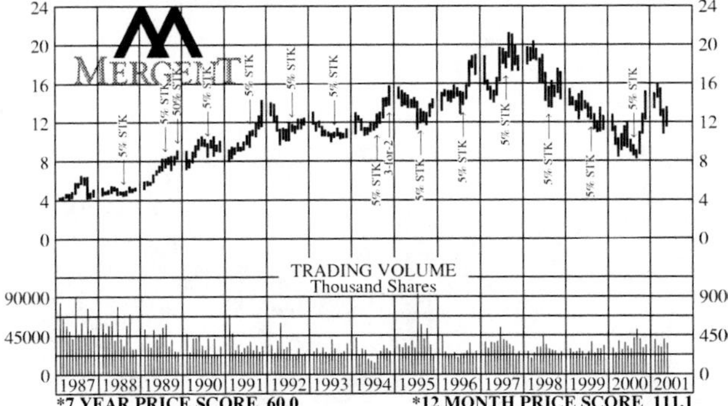

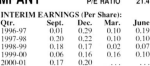

INTERIM EARNINGS (Per Share):

Qtr.	Sept.	Dec.	Mar.	June
1996-97	0.01	0.29	0.10	0.19
1997-98	0.20	0.22	0.10	0.10
1998-99	0.18	0.17	0.02	0.07
1999-00	0.06	0.16	0.16	0.10
2000-01	0.17	0.20	...	...

INTERIM DIVIDENDS (Per Share):

Amt.	Decl.	Ex.	Rec.	Pay.
0.05Q	7/27/00	8/09/00	8/11/00	9/04/00
5% STK	7/27/00	8/24/00	8/28/00	9/25/00
0.05Q	10/26/00	11/08/00	11/10/00	12/04/00
0.05Q	1/23/01	1/31/01	2/02/01	3/05/01
0.05Q	5/03/01	5/09/01	5/11/01	6/04/01

Indicated div.: $0.20

CAPITALIZATION (6/30/00):

	($000)	(%)
Long-Term Debt	3,277,218	32.9
Deferred Income Tax	560,772	5.6
Common & Surplus	6,110,243	61.4
Total	9,948,233	100.0

RECENT DEVELOPMENTS: For the quarter ended 12/31/00, net earnings advanced 22.3% to $124.6 million from $101.9 million a year earlier. Net sales and other operating income totaled $4.94 billion, up 7.1% compared with $4.62 billion the year before. Gross profit climbed 2.5% to $416.3 million, or 8.4% of net sales, from $406.3 million, or 8.8% of net sales, in the prior year. Earnings from operations increased 10.7% to $228.9 million from $206.8 million the previous year.

PROSPECTS: Results are benefiting from strong demand for ethanol, coupled with ADM's restructuring efforts in 2000, which helped reduce costs and improve manufacturing efficiencies. The Company plans to expand its ethanol production capacity in 2001 to 930.0 million gallons from 875.0 million gallons the year before. Also, ADM may begin to use corn oil as fuel for its grain-drying facilities to reduce energy costs and help offset an oversupply of vegetable oil in the marketplace.

BUSINESS

ARCHER DANIELS MIDLAND COMPANY is engaged in the business of processing and merchandising agricultural commodities. ADM is one of the largest domestic processors of oil seeds and vegetable oil, and one of the largest flour millers and corn refiners in the U.S. ADM's corn wet milling operations produce corn syrups, high fructose syrups, glucose, corn starches and ethyl alcohol (ethanol). Other operations include storage of grain, shelling of peanuts, production of consumer food products and formula feeds, production of malt products and refining of sugar. ADM Investor Services provides the Company and other commercial firms with commodity hedging services and is a futures commission merchant.

ANNUAL FINANCIAL DATA

	6/30/00	6/30/99	6/30/98	6/30/97	6/30/96	6/30/95	6/30/94
Earnings Per Share	**[4] 0.47**	**[3] 0.43**	**[2] 0.62**	**[2] 0.57**	**[1] 1.04**	**1.15**	**0.69**
Cash Flow Per Share	**1.49**	**1.38**	**1.47**	**1.30**	**1.67**	**1.74**	**1.23**
Tang. Book Val. Per Share	**9.86**	**9.59**	**9.95**	**9.37**	**9.26**	**8.75**	**7.29**
Dividends Per Share	**0.193**	**0.184**	**0.175**	**0.167**	**0.159**	**0.10**	**0.054**
Dividend Payout %	**41.1**	**42.8**	**28.2**	**29.3**	**15.3**	**8.7**	**7.8**
INCOME STATEMENT (IN MILLIONS):							
Total Revenues	12,876.8	14,283.3	16,108.6	13,853.3	13,314.0	12,671.9	11,374.4
Costs & Expenses	11,739.0	13,130.2	14,828.3	12,752.3	11,980.4	11,052.0	10,233.9
Depreciation & Amort.	647.6	622.2	560.1	475.5	419.2	406.8	374.1
Operating Income	490.2	531.0	720.3	625.4	914.4	1,213.1	766.4
Income Before Income Taxes	353.2	419.8	610.0	644.4	1,054.4	1,181.5	738.3
Income Taxes	52.3	138.5	206.4	267.1	358.5	385.6	254.2
Net Income	[4] 300.9	[3] 281.3	[2] 403.6	[2] 377.3	[1] 695.9	795.9	484.1
Cash Flow	948.5	903.5	963.7	852.8	1,115.1	1,202.7	858.1
Average Shs. Outstg. (000)	637,409	652,694	653,378	657,478	668,583	690,805	697,245
BALANCE SHEET (IN MILLIONS):							
Cash & Cash Equivalents	931.4	903.6	725.5	728.0	1,354.8	1,119.3	1,335.5
Total Current Assets	6,162.4	5,789.6	5,451.7	4,284.3	4,384.7	3,712.6	3,910.8
Net Property	5,277.1	5,567.2	5,322.7	4,708.6	4,114.3	3,762.3	3,538.6
Total Assets	14,423.1	14,029.9	13,833.5	11,354.4	10,449.9	9,756.9	8,746.9
Total Current Liabilities	4,332.9	3,840.3	3,717.3	2,248.8	1,633.6	1,172.4	1,127.0
Long-Term Obligations	3,277.2	3,191.9	2,847.1	2,344.9	2,003.0	2,070.1	2,021.4
Net Stockholders' Equity	6,110.2	6,240.6	6,504.9	6,050.1	6,144.8	5,854.2	5,045.4
Net Working Capital	1,829.4	1,949.3	1,734.4	2,035.6	2,751.1	2,540.3	2,783.8
Year-end Shs. Outstg. (000)	619,698	650,801	653,916	645,671	663,449	668,740	692,376
STATISTICAL RECORD:							
Operating Profit Margin %	3.8	3.7	4.5	4.5	6.9	9.6	6.7
Net Profit Margin %	2.3	2.0	2.5	2.7	5.2	6.3	4.3
Return on Equity %	4.9	4.5	6.2	6.2	11.3	13.6	9.6
Return on Assets %	2.1	2.0	2.9	3.3	6.7	8.2	5.5
Debt/Total Assets %	22.7	22.8	20.6	20.7	19.2	21.2	23.1
Price Range	15.19-8.19	15.48-10.89	20.41-13.44	21.27-13.99	19.03-12.83	15.67-11.19	15.76-10.60
P/E Ratio	32.3-17.4	36.1-25.4	33.0-21.7	37.3-24.5	18.3-12.4	13.6-9.7	22.8-15.3
Average Yield %	1.7	1.4	1.0	0.9	1.0	0.7	0.4

Statistics are as originally reported. Adj. for all stk. divs. & splits through 9/00. [1] Incl. $0.04/sh net chg. [2] Incl. $48 mil ($0.07/sh) chg. for fines & litig. costs & $0.04/sh gain fr secs. transactions, 1998; & $0.18/sh net chg., 1997. [3] Excl. $15.3 mil ($0.02/sh) extraord. chg. & incl. $63.0 mil ($0.10/sh) gain fr. secs. transactions. [4] Incl. $72.0 mil ($0.11/sh) chg. for plant closings, $60.0 mil ($0.10/sh) tax credit & $6.0 mil ($0.01/sh) after-tax gain fr. secs. transactions.

OFFICERS:
G. A. Andreas, Chmn., C.E.O.
J. D. McNamara, Pres.
D. J. Schmalz, V.P., C.F.O.

PRINCIPAL OFFICE: 4666 Faries Parkway, Box 1470, Decatur, IL 62525

TELEPHONE NUMBER: (217) 424-5200
FAX: (217) 424-5381
WEB: www.admworld.com

NO. OF EMPLOYEES: 22,753 (avg.)

SHAREHOLDERS: 29,911

ANNUAL MEETING: In Oct.

INCORPORATED: DE, May, 1923

INSTITUTIONAL HOLDINGS:
No. of Institutions: 339
Shares Held: 371,283,258
% Held: 58.7

INDUSTRY: Soybean oil mills (SIC: 2075)

TRANSFER AGENT(S): Hickory Point Bank & Trust, Decatur, IL

NYSE SYMBOL ASN
Rec. Pr. 25.78 (4/30/01)

ARCHSTONE COMMUNITIES TRUST

YIELD 6.5%
P/E RATIO 14.6

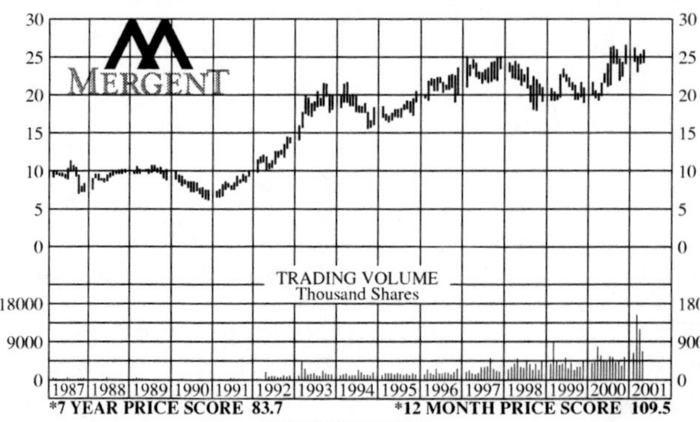

*7 YEAR PRICE SCORE 83.7 *12 MONTH PRICE SCORE 109.5

*NYSE COMPOSITE INDEX=100

INTERIM EARNINGS (Per Share):

Qtr.	Mar.	June	Sept.	Dec.
1997	0.51	0.38	d0.50	0.26
1998	0.42	0.25	0.36	0.43
1999	0.27	0.36	0.46	0.37
2000	0.28	0.57	0.61	0.31

INTERIM DIVIDENDS (Per Share):

Amt.	Decl.	Ex.	Rec.	Pay.
0.385Q	4/25/00	5/10/00	5/12/00	5/26/00
0.385Q	8/08/00	8/14/00	8/16/00	8/30/00
0.385Q	...	11/10/00	11/14/00	11/29/00
0.41Q	12/07/00	2/12/01	2/14/01	2/28/01
0.41Q	12/07/00	5/15/01	5/17/01	5/31/01

Indicated div.: $1.64 (Div. Reinv. Plan)

CAPITALIZATION (12/31/00):

	($000)	(%)
Long-Term Debt	2,470,785	51.3
Minority Interest	93,337	1.9
Preferred Stock	286,856	6.0
Common & Surplus	1,964,750	40.8
Total	4,815,728	100.0

RECENT DEVELOPMENTS: For the year ended 12/31/00, earnings were $262.3 million, before an extraordinary charge of $911,000, compared with earnings of $229.4 million, before an extraordinary charge of $1.1 million, in 1999. Results for 2000 and 1999 included gains of $93.1 million and $62.1 million, respectively, from the disposition of investments. Total revenues increased 8.4% to $723.2 million versus $667.0 million in the previous year.

PROSPECTS: The Company is benefiting from stronger growth in same-store revenues, particularly in California and the greater Washington D.C. metropolitan area, where approximately 38.4% of its capital is invested. ASN also continues to perform well in the Atlanta market. Separately, the Company recently expanded its testing of Lease Rent Optimizer (LRO), a revenue management software program, to six communities in Denver, Atlanta and Austin, Texas.

BUSINESS

ARCHSTONE COMMUNITIES TRUST is a major real estate investment trust company focused on the operation, development, acquisition, redevelopment and long-term ownership of apartment communities in markets and sub-markets with high barriers to entry throughout the United States. The Company's apartment communities are located in markets that include 31 of the nation's 50 largest metropolitan markets. As of 12/31/00, the Company's portfolio consisted of 229 communities, representing 70,685 units, including 8,176 units in its development pipeline.

QUARTERLY DATA

(12/31/2000)	Rev ($000)	Inc ($000)
1st Quarter	177,016	43,197
2nd Quarter	184,813	46,882
3rd Quarter	187,889	49,971
4th Quarter	173,516	36,416

ANNUAL FINANCIAL DATA

	12/31/00	12/31/99	12/31/98	12/31/97	12/31/96	12/31/95	12/31/94
Earnings Per Share	**1.78**	[1][2] **1.47**	[1][3] **1.49**	[1][4] **0.65**	[1][2] **1.47**	[1] **0.93**	**0.66**
Tang. Book Val. Per Share	**15.99**	**16.33**	**16.44**	**14.04**	**13.27**	**13.03**	**12.10**
Dividends Per Share	**1.54**	**1.48**	**1.39**	**1.63**	**1.24**	**1.15**	**1.00**
Dividend Payout %	**86.5**	**100.7**	**93.3**	**250.0**	**84.3**	**123.6**	**151.5**
INCOME STATEMENT (IN MILLIONS):							
Rental Income	688.5	637.8	484.5	335.1	322.0	262.5	183.5
Interest Income	...	...	...	16.7	2.0	2.4	2.6
Total Income	723.2	666.9	513.6	355.7	326.2	264.9	186.1
Costs & Expenses	403.1	367.2	283.4	278.1	187.3	146.5	114.8
Depreciation	143.7	132.4	96.3	52.9	44.9	36.7	24.6
Income Before Income Taxes	269.5	229.4	199.5	72.9	131.6	84.3	46.7
Equity Earnings/Minority Int.	d7.2	...	...	...	...	...	...
Net Income	262.3	[1][2] 229.4	[1][3] 199.5	[1][4] 72.9	[1][2] 131.6	[1] 84.3	46.7
Average Shs. Outstg. (000)	137,730	139,829	125,825	90,230	73,057	67,052	46,734
BALANCE SHEET (IN MILLIONS):							
Cash & Cash Equivalents	12.4	78.8	101.0	4.9	5.6	26.9	8.1
Total Real Estate Investments	4,912.3	4,916.7	4,664.0	2,475.2	2,055.8	1,773.9	1,250.1
Total Assets	5,019.7	5,302.4	5,059.9	2,805.7	2,282.4	1,841.0	1,295.8
Long-Term Obligations	2,470.8	2,465.1	2,172.4	1,127.2	907.4	487.1	395.6
Total Liabilities	2,768.1	2,734.9	2,431.6	1,265.3	1,014.9	565.3	455.1
Net Stockholders' Equity	2,251.6	2,567.5	2,628.3	1,540.4	1,267.5	1,275.7	840.6
Year-end Shs. Outstg. (000)	122,838	139,008	143,313	92,634	75,346	72,211	50,456
STATISTICAL RECORD:							
Net Inc.+Depr./Assets %	8.1	6.8	5.8	4.5	7.7	6.6	5.5
Return on Equity %	11.6	8.9	7.6	4.7	10.4	6.6	5.6
Return on Assets %	5.2	4.3	3.9	2.6	5.8	4.6	3.6
Price Range	26.56-19.25	23.50-18.94	24.50-17.88	25.13-21.00	23.63-19.00	20.50-16.38	21.75-15.50
P/E Ratio	14.9-10.8	16.0-12.9	16.4-12.0	38.6-32.3	16.1-12.9	22.0-17.6	32.9-23.5
Average Yield %	6.7	7.0	6.6	7.0	5.8	6.2	5.4

Statistics are as originally reported. [1] Incl. from the disposition of investments: gain, 2000, $93.1 mill.; 1999, $62.1 mill.; 1998, $65.5 mill.; 1997, $48.2 mill.; 1996, $37.5 mill.; 1995, $2.6 mill. [2] Bef. extraord. chrg. 2000, $911,000; 1999, $1.1 mill.; 1996, $870,000. [3] Bef. extraord. chrg. of $1.5 mill.; Incls. one-time chrg. of $2.2 mill. [4] Incls. one-time chrg. of $71.7 mill.

OFFICERS:
R. S. Sellers, Chmn., C.E.O.
C. E. Mueller Jr., Sr. V.P., C.F.O.
C. Brower, Sr. V.P., Gen. Coun., Sec.

INVESTOR CONTACT: Investor Relations, (800) 982-9293

PRINCIPAL OFFICE: 7670 South Chester St., Suite 100, Englewood, CO 80112

TELEPHONE NUMBER: (303) 708-5959
FAX: (303) 708-5999
WEB: www.archstonecommunities.com

NO. OF EMPLOYEES: 2,000 (approx.)

SHAREHOLDERS: 3,200 (approx.) (approx. 18,900 beneficial holders common)

ANNUAL MEETING: In May

INCORPORATED: MD, 1982

INSTITUTIONAL HOLDINGS:
No. of Institutions: 177
Shares Held: 73,504,410
% Held: 60.9

INDUSTRY: Real estate investment trusts (SIC: 6798)

TRANSFER AGENT(S): Mellon Investor Services, Ridgefield Park, NJ.

NYSE SYMBOL ARW
Rec. Pr. 25.18 (5/31/01)

ARROW ELECTRONICS, INC.

YIELD ...
P/E RATIO 7.0

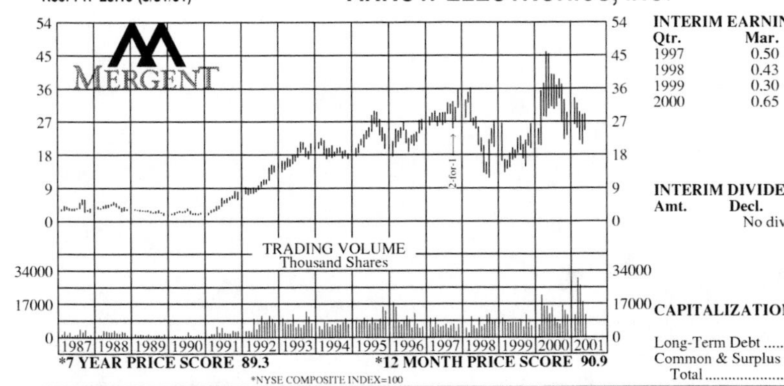

*7 YEAR PRICE SCORE 89.3 *12 MONTH PRICE SCORE 90.9

*NYSE COMPOSITE INDEX=100

INTERIM EARNINGS (Per Share):

Qtr.	Mar.	June	Sept.	Dec.
1997	0.50	0.52	0.09	0.53
1998	0.43	0.37	0.37	0.34
1999	0.30	0.16	0.38	0.46
2000	0.65	0.84	1.02	1.09

INTERIM DIVIDENDS (Per Share):

Amt.	Decl.	Ex.	Rec.	Pay.

No dividends paid.

CAPITALIZATION (12/31/00):

	($000)	(%)
Long-Term Debt	3,027,671	61.3
Common & Surplus	1,913,748	38.7
Total	4,941,419	100.0

RECENT DEVELOPMENTS: For the twelve months ended 12/31/00, net income more than doubled to $357.3 million compared with $124.2 million in the previous year. Results for 1999 included a pre-tax charge of $24.6 million associated with the acquisition and integration of the electronics distribution group of Bell Industries and Richey Electronics. Sales improved 39.2% to $12.96 billion from $9.31 billion in the prior year.

PROSPECTS: The Company signed a franchise agreement with Broadcom Corporation which covers distribution of Broadcom's silicon products in North and South America. Going forward, the Company should continue to benefit from the strength of its components businesses, despite the impact of cancellations and rescheduled orders among a small slice of its customer base.

BUSINESS

ARROW ELECTRONICS, INC. distributes electronic components and computer products. ARW serves more than 200,000 original equipment manufacturers, contract manufacturers and commercial customers in 39 countries. ARW's electronics distribution network encompasses over 225 selling locations supported by 23 primary distribution centers as of 12/31/00. Through its subsidiaries, ARW is the largest electronics distributor in Europe and Asia/Pacific. Through its network, Arrow offers a wide range of value-added services designed to help its customers reduce time to market, lower total cost of ownership, and enhance overall competitiveness.

REVENUES

(12/31/2000)	($000)	(%)
Electronic Components	9,851,041	76.0
Computer Products	3,108,209	24.0
Total	12,959,250	100.00

ANNUAL FINANCIAL DATA

	12/31/00	12/31/99	12/31/98	12/31/97	12/31/96	12/31/95	12/31/94
Earnings Per Share	**3.62**	**3 1.29**	**1.50**	**2 1.64**	**1.98**	**2.11**	**1 1.20**
Cash Flow Per Share	**4.63**	**2.11**	**2.07**	**2.11**	**2.36**	**2.47**	**1.52**
Tang. Book Val. Per Share	**6.88**	**6.15**	**8.01**	**7.38**	**12.08**	**8.06**	**5.45**
INCOME STATEMENT (IN MILLIONS):							
Total Revenues	12,959.3	9,312.6	8,344.7	7,763.9	6,534.6	5,919.4	4,649.2
Costs & Expenses	12,075.7	8,895.3	7,937.1	7,342.2	6,094.5	5,461.0	4,363.4
Depreciation & Amort.	99.5	78.6	55.1	47.1	39.5	35.2	29.8
Operating Income	784.1	338.7	352.5	374.7	400.6	423.2	256.0
Net Interest Inc./(Exp.)	d171.3	d106.3	d81.1	d67.1	d38.0	d46.4	d36.2
Income Before Income Taxes	610.1	231.2	272.3	308.4	362.6	379.3	219.8
Income Taxes	248.2	101.8	115.0	131.6	144.7	153.1	91.2
Equity Earnings/Minority Int.	d6.6	d6.4	d10.5	d12.3	d15.3	d21.2	d16.7
Net Income	357.9	3 124.2	145.8	2 163.7	202.7	202.5	1 111.9
Cash Flow	457.4	202.8	200.9	210.7	242.2	237.7	141.7
Average Shs. Outstg. (000)	98,833	96,045	97,113	99,769	102,760	96,162	93,268
BALANCE SHEET (IN MILLIONS):							
Cash & Cash Equivalents	55.5	44.9	158.9	112.7	136.4	93.9	105.6
Total Current Assets	5,764.2	3,157.9	2,860.8	2,630.3	2,120.1	2,104.7	1,558.2
Net Property	316.5	223.7	154.8	114.2	115.2	117.3	89.8
Total Assets	7,604.5	4,483.3	3,839.9	3,537.9	2,710.4	2,701.0	2,038.8
Total Current Liabilities	2,570.9	1,324.7	1,165.1	1,196.5	846.1	886.7	689.5
Long-Term Obligations	3,027.7	1,533.4	1,040.2	823.1	344.6	451.7	349.4
Net Stockholders' Equity	1,913.7	1,550.5	1,487.3	1,360.8	1,358.5	1,195.9	837.9
Net Working Capital	3,193.3	1,833.3	1,695.7	1,433.9	1,274.0	1,218.1	868.8
Year-end Shs. Outstg. (000)	98,411	95,945	95,628	96,938	80,254	101,296	92,334
STATISTICAL RECORD:							
Operating Profit Margin %	6.1	3.6	4.2	4.8	6.1	7.1	5.5
Net Profit Margin %	2.8	1.3	1.7	2.1	3.1	3.4	2.4
Return on Equity %	18.7	8.0	9.8	12.0	14.9	16.9	13.4
Return on Assets %	4.7	2.8	3.8	4.6	7.5	7.5	5.5
Debt/Total Assets %	39.8	34.2	27.1	23.3	12.7	16.7	17.1
Price Range	46.00-20.50	26.56-13.19	36.25-11.75	36.00-25.13	27.69-17.63	29.88-17.56	22.56-16.81
P/E Ratio	12.7-5.7	20.6-10.2	24.2-7.8	21.9-15.3	14.0-8.9	14.2-8.3	18.8-14.0

Statistics are as originally reported. Adj. for stk. splits: 2-for-1, 10/97 1 Incl. non-recurr. chrg. $45.4 mill. fr. integration of Gasts/FA Distributing Inc. 2 Incl. realignment chrgs. of $59.6 mill. 3 Incl. one-time chrg. of $24.6 mill. for the acq. and integration of the electronics distrib. group of Bell industries and Richey Electronics.

OFFICERS:
S. P. Kaufman, Chmn.
F. M. Scricco, Pres., C.E.O., C.O.O.
S. R. Leno, Sr. V.P., C.F.O.

INVESTOR CONTACT: Robert E. Klatell, Sr. V.P., C.F.O., (516) 391-1830

PRINCIPAL OFFICE: 25 Hub Drive, Melville, NY 11747

TELEPHONE NUMBER: (516) 391-1300
FAX: (516) 391-1640
WEB: www.arrow.com

NO. OF EMPLOYEES: 12,200 (avg.)

SHAREHOLDERS: 3,200 (approx.)

ANNUAL MEETING: In May

INCORPORATED: NY, Nov., 1946

INSTITUTIONAL HOLDINGS:
No. of Institutions: 250
Shares Held: 98,622,512
% Held: 100.4

INDUSTRY: Electronic parts and equipment (SIC: 5065)

TRANSFER AGENT(S): Mellon Investor Services, Ridgefield Park, NJ

NYSE SYMBOL ARM
Rec. Pr. 15.50 (5/31/01)

ARVINMERITOR, INC.

YIELD 5.7%
P/E RATIO 6.8

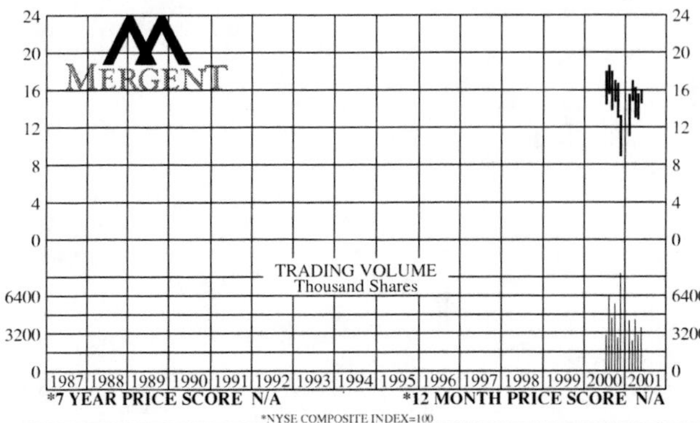

INTERIM EARNINGS (Per Share):

Qtr.	Dec.	Mar.	June	Sept.
1997-98	0.47	0.64	0.68	0.34
1998-99	0.58	0.72	0.56	0.95
1999-00	1.94	1.22	0.86	0.35
2000-01	d0.15	...	...	...

INTERIM DIVIDENDS (Per Share):

Amt.	Decl.	Ex.	Rec.	Pay.
0.22Q	7/19/00	8/10/00	8/14/00	9/05/00
0.22Q	11/08/00	11/16/00	11/20/00	12/11/00
0.22Q	2/14/01	2/22/01	2/26/01	3/19/01
0.22Q	4/11/01	5/17/01	5/21/01	6/11/01

Indicated div.: $0.88 (Div. Reinv. Plan)

CAPITALIZATION (9/30/00):

	($000)	(%)
Long-Term Debt	1,537,000	61.5
Minority Interest	96,000	3.8
Redeemable Pfd. Stock	74,000	3.0
Common & Surplus	793,000	31.7
Total	2,500,000	100.0

RECENT DEVELOPMENTS: For the first quarter ended 12/31/00, the Company reported a net loss of $10.0 million versus income of $97.0 million in the comparable prior-year period. Results for fiscal 2001 included pre-tax nonrecurring charges of $46.0 million related to the Company's restructuring initiatives. The fiscal 2000 results included nonrecurring items that resulted in a net pre-tax gain of $109.0 million. Sales rose 46.0% to $1.66 billion, while operating income fell 89.4% to $18.0 million.

PROSPECTS: ARM announced the termination of Arvin-Kayaba LLC, its North American joint venture with Kayaba Industry Co. Ltd. Separately, ARM will report pre-tax restructuring charges of $90.0 million in fiscal 2001. Revenues are expected to decline about 10.0% in fiscal 2001 due to curtailments in vehicle production by major automobile manufacturers. In addition, ARM has lowered its fiscal 2001 earnings estimates to be in the range of $2.00 to $2.30 per share.

BUSINESS

ARVINMERITOR, INC. was formed through the acquisition of Arvin Industries, Inc. by Meritor Automotive, Inc. on 7/7/00. The Company is a global provider of integrated automotive systems, modules and components to light vehicle, commercial truck, trailer and specialty original manufacturers and related aftermarket customers. ARM also offers coil coating services for the transportation, appliance, construction and furniture industries. The Light Vehicle Systems segment includes exhaust systems, aperture systems and undercarriage systems. The Commercial Vehicle segment consists of drivetrain systems and components, including axles, brakes, and drivelines. The Light Vehicle Aftermarket segment includes exhaust, ride control, filter products and accessories. The Other segment encompases the business units that are not focused on automotive products.

BUSINESS LINE ANALYSIS

(09/30/2000)	REV (%)	INC (%)
Light Vehicle Systems	39.4	39.6
Commercial Vehicle System	55.7	58.8
Light Vehicle Aftermarket	4.1	1.6
Other	0.8	0.0
Total	100.0	100.0

ANNUAL FINANCIAL DATA

	9/30/00	[2] 9/30/99	9/30/98
Earnings Per Share	[3] **4.12**	[1] **3.75**	**2.84**
Cash Flow Per Share	**7.18**	**6.27**	**4.81**
Tang. Book Val. Per Share	**0.54**	...	...
Dividends Per Share	**0.44**	...	...
Dividend Payout %	**10.7**	...	...
INCOME STATEMENT (IN MILLIONS):			
Total Revenues	5,153.0	4,450.0	3,836.0
Costs & Expenses	4,562.0	3,962.0	3,436.0
Depreciation & Amort.	162.0	131.0	102.0
Operating Income	429.0	357.0	298.0
Net Interest Inc./(Exp.)	d89.0	d61.0	d39.0
Income Before Income Taxes	369.0	333.0	256.0
Income Taxes	141.0	129.0	102.0
Equity Earnings/Minority Int.	d10.0	d10.0	d7.0
Net Income	[3] 218.0	[1] 194.0	147.0
Cash Flow	380.0	325.0	249.0
Average Shs. Outstg. (000)	52,900	51,800	51,800
BALANCE SHEET (IN MILLIONS):			
Cash & Cash Equivalents	116.0	68.0	...
Total Current Assets	2,189.0	1,332.0	...
Net Property	1,348.0	766.0	...
Total Assets	4,720.0	2,796.0	...
Total Current Liabilities	1,725.0	1,124.0	...
Long-Term Obligations	1,537.0	802.0	...
Net Stockholders' Equity	793.0	348.0	...
Net Working Capital	464.0	208.0	...
Year-end Shs. Outstg. (000)	67,900	68,800	...
STATISTICAL RECORD:			
Operating Profit Margin %	8.3	8.0	7.8
Net Profit Margin %	4.2	4.4	3.8
Return on Equity %	27.5	55.7	...
Return on Assets %	4.6	6.9	...
Debt/Total Assets %	32.6	28.7	...
Price Range	18.63-8.88	...	...
P/E Ratio	4.5-2.2	...	...
Average Yield %	3.2	...	...

Statistics are as originally reported. [1] Incl. one-time chrg. 1999, $4.0 mill.; 1997, $29.0 mill.; 1996 $36.0 mill. [2] Financials for 1999 and prior are for Meritor Automotive, Inc. [3] Incl. pre-tax restr. chrg. of $26.0 mill., merger exp. of $10.0 mill. and $89.0 mill. gain on the sale of assets.

OFFICERS:
L. D. Yost, Chmn., C.E.O.
V. W. Hunt, Vice Chmn., Pres
V. G. Baker II, Gen Couns., Sec.

INVESTOR CONTACT: Paul R. Ryder, V.P., Investor Relations, (248) 435-4702

PRINCIPAL OFFICE: 2135 West Maple Road, Troy, MI 48084-7186

TELEPHONE NUMBER: (248) 435-1000
FAX: (248) 435-1393
WEB: www.arvinmeritor.com

NO. OF EMPLOYEES: 36,000

SHAREHOLDERS: 44,793

ANNUAL MEETING: In Feb.

INCORPORATED: IN, July, 2000

INSTITUTIONAL HOLDINGS:
No. of Institutions: 172
Shares Held: 29,893,727
% Held: 45.6

INDUSTRY: Motor vehicle parts and accessories (SIC: 3714)

TRANSFER AGENT(S): EquiServe First Chicago Trust Company Division, Jersey City, NJ

NYSE SYMBOL ASH
Rec. Pr. 43.06 (4/30/01)

ASHLAND, INC.

YIELD 2.6%
P/E RATIO 9.8

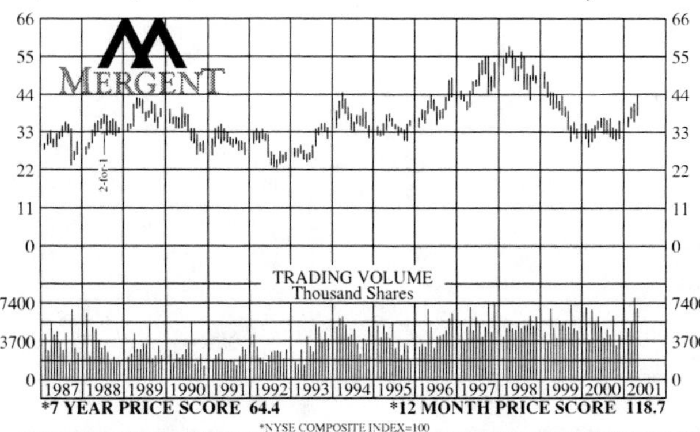

INTERIM EARNINGS (Per Share):

Qtr.	Dec.	Mar.	June	Sept.
1996-97	0.47	0.03	1.57	0.62
1997-98	0.68	0.37	1.59	Nil
1998-99	d0.14	1.16	1.35	1.57
1999-00	0.55	0.35	1.83	1.38
2000-01	0.84	...	...	...

INTERIM DIVIDENDS (Per Share):

Amt.	Decl.	Ex.	Rec.	Pay.
0.275Q	5/18/00	5/25/00	5/30/00	6/15/00
0.275Q	7/19/00	8/22/00	8/24/00	9/15/00
0.275Q	11/02/00	11/16/00	11/20/00	12/15/00
0.275Q	1/24/01	2/21/01	2/23/01	3/15/01
0.275Q	5/17/01	5/24/01	5/29/01	6/15/01

Indicated div.: $1.10 (Div. Reinv. Plan)

CAPITALIZATION (9/30/00):

	($000)	(%)
Long-Term Debt	1,899,000	45.7
Deferred Income Tax	288,000	6.9
Common & Surplus	1,965,000	47.3
Total	4,152,000	100.0

RECENT DEVELOPMENTS: For the quarter ended 12/31/00, net income was $59.0 million versus income from continuing operations of $40.0 million a year earlier. Total revenues rose 3.3% to $2.01 billion. Refining and marketing operating income surged to $109.0 million from $33.0 million. However, APAC segment operating income fell 65.8% to $13.0 million and Ashland Distribution operating income declined 23.1% to $10.0 million. Ashland Specialty Chemical operating income fell 37.9% to $18.0 million.

PROSPECTS: Prospects are mixed. The slowing U.S. economy, particularly in the automotive and construction markets, could pressure certain parts of Ashland Specialty Chemical and Ashland Distribution. However, continued strong supply and demand fundamentals for Midwest petroleum markets should lead to solid results from ASH's refining and marketing unit. Results for APAC should also improve, provided normal spring and summer weather patterns prevail.

BUSINESS

ASHLAND, INC. is a diversified energy company with operations in five industry segments. APAC performs contract construction work, bridge construction, and produces asphaltic and ready-mix concrete, and other aggregate. Ashland Distribution distributes chemicals, plastics and fiber reinforcements. Ashland Specialty Chemical manufactures and sells a variety of specialty chemicals. Valvoline is a marketer of motor oil, automotive chemicals, automotive appearance products, antifreeze, filters, rust preventives, and coolants. Services include 630 Valvoline Instant Oil Change centers in 34 states. Refining and marketing operations are conducted through 38%-owned Marathon Ashland Petroleum LLC, a joint venture formed on 1/1/98 with Marathon Oil Company. On 3/27/00, ASH distributed 17.4 million shares of its Arch Coal Inc. common stock to ASH shareholders in the form of a taxable dividend. ASH sold its remaining 4.8 million shares on 2/2/2001.

ANNUAL FINANCIAL DATA

	9/30/00	9/30/99	9/30/98	9/30/97	9/30/96	9/30/95	9/30/94
Earnings Per Share	**3 4.10**	**3.89**	**2.63**	**1 3.80**	**2.97**	**0.08**	**2.94**
Cash Flow Per Share	**7.45**	**6.91**	**4.99**	**10.63**	**7.51**	**7.94**	**7.97**
Tang. Book Val. Per Share	**20.40**	**27.50**	**25.39**	**25.39**	**21.89**	**19.61**	**20.03**
Dividends Per Share	**1.10**	**1.10**	**1.10**	**1.10**	**1.10**	**1.10**	**1.02**
Dividend Payout %	**26.8**	**28.3**	**41.8**	**28.9**	**37.0**	**1,373.3**	**34.9**
INCOME STATEMENT (IN MILLIONS):							
Total Revenues	8,436.0	7,251.0	2 6,933.0	14,319.0	12,968.0	12,239.0	10,382.0
Costs & Expenses	7,528.0	6,401.0	6,305.0	13,257.0	12,235.0	11,554.0	9,707.0
Depreciation & Amort.	237.0	228.0	181.0	572.0	371.0	487.0	308.0
Operating Income	671.0	622.0	447.0	490.0	362.0	198.0	367.0
Net Interest Inc./(Exp.)	d188.0	d140.0	d130.0	d170.0	d169.0	d171.0	d117.0
Income Before Income Taxes	483.0	482.0	317.0	335.0	217.0	34.0	272.0
Income Taxes	191.0	192.0	114.0	119.0	73.0	cr13.0	75.0
Equity Earnings/Minority Int.	...	...	...	d9.0	16.0	d16.0	22.0
Net Income	3 292.0	290.0	203.0	1 192.0	136.0	24.0	197.0
Cash Flow	529.0	518.0	384.0	755.0	488.0	492.0	486.0
Average Shs. Outstg. (000)	71,000	75,000	77,000	71,000	65,000	62,000	61,000
BALANCE SHEET (IN MILLIONS):							
Cash & Cash Equivalents	67.0	110.0	34.0	268.0	77.0	52.0	40.0
Total Current Assets	2,131.0	2,059.0	1,828.0	2,995.0	2,665.0	2,575.0	2,171.0
Net Property	1,422.0	1,292.0	1,161.0	3,891.0	3,285.0	3,570.0	2,816.0
Total Assets	6,771.0	6,424.0	6,082.0	7,777.0	7,089.0	6,992.0	5,815.0
Total Current Liabilities	1,699.0	1,396.0	1,361.0	2,261.0	2,198.0	2,094.0	1,688.0
Long-Term Obligations	1,899.0	1,627.0	1,507.0	1,639.0	1,784.0	1,828.0	1,391.0
Net Stockholders' Equity	1,965.0	2,200.0	2,137.0	2,024.0	1,521.0	1,362.0	1,302.0
Net Working Capital	432.0	663.0	467.0	734.0	467.0	481.0	483.0
Year-end Shs. Outstg. (000)	70,000	72,000	76,000	75,000	64,000	64,000	61,000
STATISTICAL RECORD:							
Operating Profit Margin %	8.0	8.6	6.4	3.4	2.8	1.6	3.5
Net Profit Margin %	3.5	4.0	2.9	1.3	1.0	0.2	1.9
Return on Equity %	14.9	13.2	9.5	9.5	8.9	1.8	15.1
Return on Assets %	4.3	4.5	3.3	2.5	1.9	0.3	3.4
Debt/Total Assets %	28.0	25.3	24.8	21.1	25.2	26.1	23.9
Price Range	37.19-28.63	50.63-30.31	57.94-42.25	55.00-39.25	48.88-34.25	38.38-30.38	44.50-31.25
P/E Ratio	9.1-7.0	13.0-7.8	22.0-16.1	14.5-10.3	16.5-11.5	479.1-379.2	15.1-10.6
Average Yield %	3.3	2.7	2.2	2.3	2.6	3.2	2.7

Statistics are as originally reported. 1 Bef. cr. of $96.0 mill. fr. disc. ops. & extraord. chrg. of $9.0 mill. 2 Refl. formation of Marathon Ashland Petroleum LLC (MAP). ASH accounts for its invest. in MAP using the equity method of acctg. 3 Bef. disc. oper. loss of $218.0 mill. (3.07/sh.) & an extraord. loss of $4.0 mill. ($0.05/sh.)

OFFICERS:
P. W. Chellgren, Chmn., C.E.O.
J. M. Quin, Sr. V.P., C.F.O.
D. L. Hausrath, V.P., Gen. Couns.

INVESTOR CONTACT: R. C. Hughes, Dir., Inv. Rel., (859) 815-4095

PRINCIPAL OFFICE: 50 E. RiverCenter Blvd., Covington, KY 41012-0391

TELEPHONE NUMBER: (859) 815-3333
FAX: (859) 329-5188
WEB: www.ashland.com

NO. OF EMPLOYEES: 25,800 (approx.)

SHAREHOLDERS: 19,600 (approx.)

ANNUAL MEETING: In Jan.

INCORPORATED: KY, Oct., 1936

INSTITUTIONAL HOLDINGS:
No. of Institutions: 213
Shares Held: 48,994,868
% Held: 70.4

INDUSTRY: Petroleum refining (SIC: 2911)

TRANSFER AGENT(S): National City Bank, Cleveland, OH

NYSE SYMBOL T
Rec. Pr. 22.28 (4/30/01)

AT&T CORP.

YIELD 0.7%
P/E RATIO 23.0

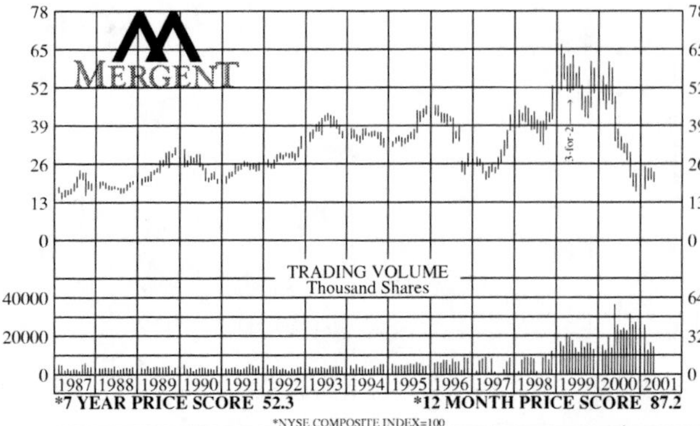

*7 YEAR PRICE SCORE 52.3 *12 MONTH PRICE SCORE 87.2

*NYSE COMPOSITE INDEX=100

INTERIM EARNINGS (Per Share):

Qtr.	Mar.	June	Sept.	Dec.
1996	0.60	0.63	0.56	0.51
1997	0.46	0.39	0.47	0.54
1998	0.53	d0.06	0.77	0.75
1999	0.38	0.49	0.50	0.36
2000	0.54	0.53	0.35	d0.45

INTERIM DIVIDENDS (Per Share):

Amt.	Decl.	Ex.	Rec.	Pay.
0.22Q	3/14/00	3/29/00	3/31/00	5/01/00
0.22Q	6/21/00	6/28/00	6/30/00	8/01/00
0.22Q	9/25/00	9/27/00	9/29/00	11/01/00
0.037Q	12/20/00	12/27/00	12/29/00	2/01/01
0.037Q	3/21/01	3/28/01	3/30/01	5/01/01

Indicated div.: $0.15 (Div. Reinv. Plan)

CAPITALIZATION (12/31/00):

	($000)	(%)
Long-Term Debt	33,092,000	18.1
Deferred Income Tax	36,713,000	20.1
Minority Interest	4,883,000	2.7
Redeemable Pfd. Stock	4,710,000	2.6
Common & Surplus	103,198,000	56.5
Total	182,596,001	100.0

RECENT DEVELOPMENTS: For the year ended 12/31/00, net income for AT&T Common Stock Group, which excludes the results from the Company's equity interest in Liberty Media Group, totaled $3.18 billion versus $5.45 billion a year earlier. Results for 2000 and 1999 included restructuring and other charges of $7.03 billion and $1.51 billion, respectively. Revenues advanced 5.4% to $65.98 billion from $62.60 billion in 1999.

PROSPECTS: Near-term prospects are mixed. AT&T Wireless and, to a lesser degree AT&T Broadband, should continue to post healthy revenue growth. However, AT&T Consumer revenues will likely decline, and flat revenues are expected at AT&T Business. Meanwhile, the AT&T Broadband initial public offering is scheduled for fall of 2001, followed by the distribution of the AT&T Consumer tracking stock to T shareholders later in 2001.

BUSINESS

AT&T CORP. is a global company that provides voice, data and video communications services and products, serving more than 80.0 million customers including consumers, large and small businesses, and government entities. The Company and its subsidiaries furnish domestic long distance, international long distance, regional, local and wireless telecommunications services and cable television, and provide billing, directory and calling card services to support its communications operations. Also, AT&T is a supplier of data and Internet services for businesses and is the largest direct Internet service provider to consumers in the U.S. On 3/9/99, the Company acquired Tele-Communications, Inc., a provider of domestic cable and telecommunications services, and its interests in At Home Corp. On 6/15/00, the Company acquired MediaOne Group in a transaction valued at approximately $44.00 billion.

REVENUES

(12/31/2000)	($000)	(%)
Business services	28,488,000	43.1
Consumer services	18,976,000	28.7
Wireless services	10,448,000	15.8
Broadband	8,217,000	12.4
Total	66,129,000	100.0

ANNUAL FINANCIAL DATA

	12/31/00	12/31/99	12/31/98	12/31/97	12/31/96	12/31/95	12/31/94
Earnings Per Share	[5][6] **0.88**	[4][5] **1.74**	[1] **1.94**	[2] **1.83**	[2] **2.31**	[3] **0.06**	[3] **2.01**
Cash Flow Per Share	**4.21**	**3.45**	**3.65**	**3.39**	**3.44**	**2.09**	**3.73**
Tang. Book Val. Per Share	**15.45**	**19.69**	**6.68**	**5.88**	**5.02**	**3.85**	**5.81**
Dividends Per Share	**0.88**	**0.88**	**0.88**	**0.88**	**0.88**	**0.88**	**0.88**
Dividend Payout %	**100.0**	**50.6**	**45.4**	**48.2**	**38.0**	**1,464.2**	**43.8**
INCOME STATEMENT (IN MILLIONS):							
Total Revenues	65,981.0	62,391.0	53,223.0	51,319.0	52,184.0	79,609.0	75,094.0
Costs & Expenses	51,437.0	44,093.0	41,107.0	40,524.0	40,634.0	73,549.0	63,025.0
Depreciation & Amort.	10,267.0	7,439.0	4,629.0	3,827.0	2,740.0	4,845.0	4,039.0
Operating Income	4,277.0	10,859.0	7,487.0	6,968.0	8,810.0	1,215.0	8,030.0
Net Interest Inc./(Exp.)	d3,183.0	d1,651.0	d427.0	d191.0	d334.0	d738.0	d748.0
Income Before Income Taxes	2,608.0	6,685.0	8,307.0	7,193.0	8,866.0	935.0	7,518.0
Income Taxes	3,342.0	3,257.0	3,072.0	2,721.0	3,258.0	796.0	2,808.0
Equity Earnings/Minority Int.	5,403.0	d2,022.0	...	...	...	...	...
Net Income	[6] 4,669.0	[4] 3,428.0	[1] 5,235.0	[2] 4,472.0	[2] 5,608.0	[3] 139.0	[3] 4,710.0
Cash Flow	14,642.0	10,867.0	9,864.0	8,299.0	8,348.0	4,984.0	8,749.0
Average Shs. Outstg. (000)	3,545,000	3,152,000	2,700,000	2,445,000	2,424,000	2,388,000	2,346,000
BALANCE SHEET (IN MILLIONS):							
Cash & Cash Equivalents	2,228.0	1,024.0	3,160.0	145.0	134.0	908.0	1,208.0
Total Current Assets	17,087.0	13,884.0	14,118.0	16,179.0	18,310.0	39,509.0	37,611.0
Net Property	51,161.0	39,618.0	26,903.0	22,710.0	19,794.0	22,264.0	22,035.0
Total Assets	242,223.0	169,406.0	59,550.0	58,635.0	55,552.0	88,884.0	79,262.0
Total Current Liabilities	50,867.0	28,207.0	15,442.0	16,942.0	16,318.0	39,372.0	30,930.0
Long-Term Obligations	33,092.0	21,591.0	5,556.0	6,826.0	7,883.0	11,635.0	11,358.0
Net Stockholders' Equity	103,198.0	78,927.0	25,522.0	22,647.0	20,295.0	17,274.0	17,921.0
Net Working Capital	d33,780.0	d14,323.0	d1,324.0	d763.0	1,992.0	137.0	6,681.0
Year-end Shs. Outstg. (000)	3,760,151	3,196,000	2,631,000	2,436,000	2,434,500	2,394,008	2,353,509
STATISTICAL RECORD:							
Operating Profit Margin %	6.5	17.4	14.1	13.6	16.9	1.5	10.7
Net Profit Margin %	7.1	5.5	9.8	8.7	10.7	0.2	6.3
Return on Equity %	4.5	4.3	20.5	19.7	27.6	0.8	26.3
Return on Assets %	1.9	2.0	8.8	7.6	10.1	0.2	5.9
Debt/Total Assets %	13.7	12.7	9.3	11.6	14.2	13.1	14.3
Price Range	60.81-16.50	66.67-41.50	52.67-32.25	42.67-20.50	45.92-22.17	45.67-31.75	38.09-31.50
P/E Ratio	69.1-18.7	38.3-23.8	27.1-16.6	23.4-11.2	19.9-9.6	759.9-528.3	19.0-15.7
Average Yield %	2.3	1.6	2.1	2.8	2.6	2.3	2.5

Statistics are as originally reported. Adj. for 3-for-2, stk. split, 4/15/99 [1] Incl. non-recurr. pre-tax chrg. of $2.51 bill.; bef. gain of $1.29 bill. fr. disc. ops. & extraord. chrg. of $137.0 mill. [2] Bef. disc. ops. credit 12/31/97: $166.0 mill.; credit 12/31/96: $300.0 mill. [3] Incl. non-recurr. chrg. 12/31/95: $7.85 bill.; 12/31/94: $169.0 mill. [4] Incl. non-recurr. chrg. of $1.51 bill. [5] Refl. AT&T Common Stock Group [6] Incl. restr. & other chgs. of $7.03 bill.

OFFICERS:
C. M. Armstrong, Chmn., C.E.O.
D. W. Dorman, Pres.
C. H. Noski, C.F.O.

INVESTOR CONTACT: Investor Relations, (908) 221-3655

PRINCIPAL OFFICE: 32 Avenue Of The Americas, New York, NY 10013-2412

TELEPHONE NUMBER: (212) 387-5400
FAX: (908) 221-2528
WEB: www.att.com

NO. OF EMPLOYEES: 166,000 (approx.)

SHAREHOLDERS: 4,800,000 (approx.)

ANNUAL MEETING: In May

INCORPORATED: NY, Mar., 1885

INSTITUTIONAL HOLDINGS:
No. of Institutions: 927
Shares Held: 1,605,015,522
% Held: 42.8

INDUSTRY: Telephone communications, exc. radio (SIC: 4813)

TRANSFER AGENT(S): BankBoston, NA, Boston, MA

NYSE SYMBOL ATW
Rec. Pr. 42.88 (5/31/01)

ATWOOD OCEANICS, INC.

YIELD ...
P/E RATIO 22.9

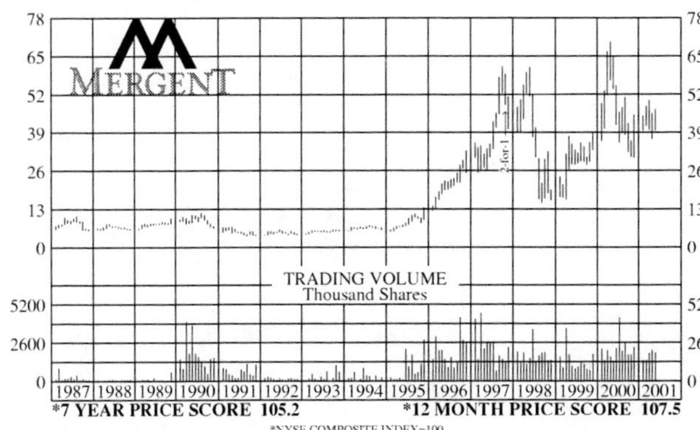

*7 YEAR PRICE SCORE 105.2 *12 MONTH PRICE SCORE 107.5
*NYSE COMPOSITE INDEX=100

INTERIM EARNINGS (Per Share):

Qtr.	Dec.	Mar.	June	Sept.
1994-95	0.13	0.10	0.24	0.07
1995-96	0.05	0.10	0.18	0.53
1996-97	0.29	0.23	0.27	0.37
1997-98	0.63	0.84	0.72	0.65
1998-99	0.49	0.64	0.53	0.35
1999-00	0.36	0.43	0.37	0.49
2000-01	0.58	...	...	...

INTERIM DIVIDENDS (Per Share):

Amt.	Decl.	Ex.	Rec.	Pay.

No dividends paid.

CAPITALIZATION (9/30/00):

	($000)	(%)
Long-Term Debt	46,000	16.8
Deferred Income Tax	10,390	3.8
Common & Surplus	218,205	79.5
Total	274,595	100.0

RECENT DEVELOPMENTS: For the three months ended 12/31/00, net income increased 59.1% to $8.0 million compared with $5.1 million in the corresponding year-earlier period. Results benefited from changes in the Company's depreciation policy related to certain rigs. The changes, which went into effect on 10/1/00, reduced depreciation expenses by approximately $1.7 million. Total contract revenues increased 26.5% to $39.4 million from $31.2 million a year earlier.

PROSPECTS: ATW's prospects are positive, reflecting increasing international exploration and development spending by companies seeking to capitalize on the historically high prices of crude oil and natural gas. During fiscal year 2001, ATW is planning additional upgrades of the ATWOOD HUNTER estimated to cost between $40.0 million and $50.0 million and the ATWOOD EAGLE estimated to cost $80.0 million. Separately, on 12/5/00, ATW purchased the semisubmersible unit SEASCOUT for $4.5 million.

BUSINESS

ATWOOD OCEANICS, INC., together with its wholly-owned subsidiaries, is engaged in contract drilling of exploratory and developmental oil and natural gas wells in offshore areas and related support, management and consulting services. Most of the Company's contract drilling operations are conducted outside the U.S. as the Company is actively involved in operations in the territorial waters of Australia, Israel, Malaysia, India, Egypt, and the Phillipines. Presently, the Company owns three third-generation semisubmersibles, one second-generation semisubmersible, one jack-up, one second-generation semisubmersible tender assist rig, one submersible and one modular, self-contained platform rig, and a 50.0% interest in a new generation platform rig. ATW also provides supervisory, labor and consulting services to two operator owned platform rigs in Australia.

REVENUES

(09/30/00)	($000)	(%)
Contract drilling	131,387	97.7
Contract management	3,127	2.3
Total	134,514	100.0

ANNUAL FINANCIAL DATA

	9/30/00	9/30/99	9/30/98	9/30/97	9/30/96	9/30/95	9/30/94
Earnings Per Share	**1.66**	**2.01**	**2.84**	**1.16**	**0.86**	**0.54**	**0.47**
Cash Flow Per Share	**3.82**	**3.78**	**4.13**	**1.94**	**1.63**	**1.41**	**1.55**
Tang. Book Val. Per Share	**15.79**	**14.06**	**12.02**	**9.06**	**7.89**	**7.16**	**6.53**
INCOME STATEMENT (IN THOUSANDS):							
Total Revenues	134,514	150,009	151,809	89,082	79,455	72,231	68,794
Costs & Expenses	67,296	77,308	72,189	54,351	56,049	54,882	48,121
Depreciation & Amort.	30,027	24,470	18,023	10,518	10,346	11,563	14,149
Operating Income	37,191	48,231	61,597	24,213	13,060	5,786	6,524
Net Interest Inc./(Exp.)	d3,907	d4,172	d3,599	d1,212	d2,522	d132	d2,892
Income Before Income Taxes	35,898	46,507	60,319	25,378	15,843	8,932	6,935
Income Taxes	12,750	18,787	20,955	9,759	4,475	1,872	726
Equity Earnings/Minority Int.	...	...	...	...	...	908	3,303
Net Income	23,148	27,720	39,364	15,619	11,368	7,060	6,209
Cash Flow	53,175	52,190	57,387	26,137	21,714	18,623	20,358
Average Shs. Outstg.	13,916	13,791	13,884	13,474	13,328	13,182	13,164
BALANCE SHEET (IN THOUSANDS):							
Cash & Cash Equivalents	19,740	20,105	11,621	19,264	17,565	11,984	16,119
Total Current Assets	64,917	50,532	51,587	47,051	44,170	34,266	38,472
Net Property	224,107	218,914	205,632	143,923	91,124	91,427	82,845
Total Assets	313,251	293,604	281,737	215,330	159,309	152,853	153,460
Total Current Liabilities	17,484	19,013	26,723	19,502	18,019	20,505	13,301
Long-Term Obligations	46,000	54,000	72,000	58,750	26,540	35,569	50,294
Net Stockholders' Equity	218,205	192,229	163,766	122,689	105,554	94,892	85,959
Net Working Capital	47,433	31,519	24,864	27,549	26,151	13,761	25,171
Year-end Shs. Outstg.	13,823	13,675	13,625	13,546	13,382	13,258	13,164
STATISTICAL RECORD:							
Operating Profit Margin %	27.6	32.2	40.6	27.2	16.4	8.0	9.5
Net Profit Margin %	17.2	18.5	25.9	17.5	14.3	9.8	9.0
Return on Equity %	10.6	14.4	24.0	12.7	10.8	7.4	7.2
Return on Assets %	7.4	9.4	14.0	7.3	7.1	4.6	4.0
Debt/Total Assets %	14.7	18.4	25.6	27.3	16.7	23.3	32.8
Price Range	69.88-30.20	38.81-16.13	61.38-15.06	61.63-25.38	32.75-12.25	13.50-5.19	7.44-5.50
P/E Ratio	42.1-18.2	19.3-8.0	21.6-5.3	53.1-21.9	38.3-14.3	25.0-9.6	15.8-11.7

Statistics are as originally reported. Adj. for 2-for-1 stk. split, 11/97.

OFFICERS:
J. R. Irwin, Pres., C.E.O.
J. M. Holland, Sr. V.P., Sec.

INVESTOR CONTACT: James M. Holland, Sr. Vice Pres. & Sec., (281) 749-7804

PRINCIPAL OFFICE: 15835 Park Ten Place Dr., Houston, TX 77218

TELEPHONE NUMBER: (281) 492-2929
FAX: (281) 492-0345
WEB: www.atwd.com

NO. OF EMPLOYEES: 850 (approx.)

SHAREHOLDERS: 750 (approx.)

ANNUAL MEETING: In Feb.

INCORPORATED: TX, Oct., 1968

INSTITUTIONAL HOLDINGS:
No. of Institutions: 101
Shares Held: 10,212,291
% Held: 73.8

INDUSTRY: Drilling oil and gas wells (SIC: 1381)

TRANSFER AGENT(S): Continental Stock Transfer & Trust Company, New York, NY

NYSE SYMBOL ALV
Rec. Pr. 18.65 (5/31/01)

AUTOLIV, INC.

YIELD 2.4%
P/E RATIO 11.2

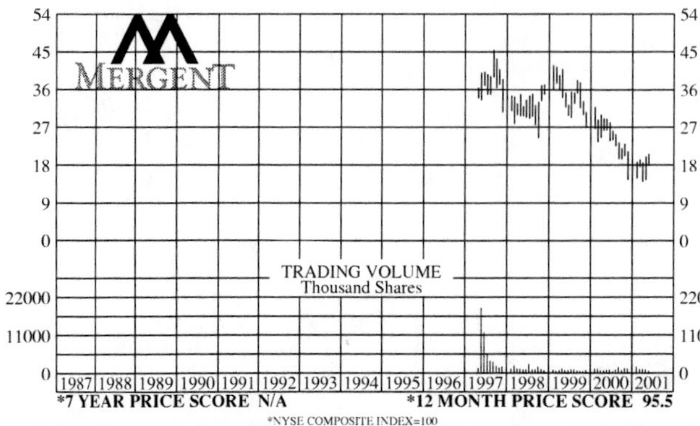

INTERIM EARNINGS (Per Share):

Qtr.	Mar.	June	Sept.	Dec.
1997	0.52	d7.97	0.34	0.45
1998	0.41	0.50	0.37	0.56
1999	0.43	0.50	0.42	0.60
2000	0.54	0.54	0.39	0.20

INTERIM DIVIDENDS (Per Share):

Amt.	Decl.	Ex.	Rec.	Pay.
0.11Q	5/04/00	8/08/00	8/10/00	9/07/00
0.11Q	8/11/00	11/07/00	11/09/00	12/07/00
0.11Q	12/07/00	1/30/01	2/01/01	3/01/01
0.11Q	2/16/01	5/08/01	5/10/01	6/07/01
0.11Q	4/25/01	8/07/01	8/09/01	9/06/01

Indicated div.: $0.44

CAPITALIZATION (12/31/00):

	($000)	(%)
Long-Term Debt	737,400	27.6
Minority Interest	22,000	0.8
Common & Surplus	1,910,100	71.6
Total	2,669,500	100.0

RECENT DEVELOPMENTS: For the year ended 12/31/00, net income fell 15.6% to $168.7 million compared with $199.9 million in the previous year. The decrease in earnings was primarily attributed to weaker demand, resulting from cutbacks in North American vehicle production by major automobile makers. Total net sales rose 8.0% to $4.12 billion. Sales of airbag products increased 8.1% to $2.93 billion, while sales of seat belt products grew 7.7% to $1.18 billion. Operating income declined 7.9% to $339.5 million.

PROSPECTS: The Company began the implementation of a comprehensive action program to reduce costs, eliminate unutilized capacity and improve cash flow. In addition, the Company will consolidate operations in the U.S. and Europe by phasing out, down-sizing and closing certain plants. On 12/29/00, ALV completed the sale of the aerospace unit of OEA Merger Corporation, an ALV subsidiary, to BFGoodrich Company.

BUSINESS

AUTOLIV, INC. is a major supplier to major automobile manufacturers worldwide of occupant protection systems with a broad range of product offerings through its two principal operating subsidiaries. Autoliv AB, Inc. is Swedish-based company that develops and manufactures seat belt pretensioners, frontal airbags, side-impact airbags, steering wheels and seat sub-systems. Autoliv ASP, Inc. develops and manufactures seat belts, steering wheels, airbag modules, inflators and cushions. ALV operates 80 production facilities in 30 countries.

QUARTERLY DATA

(12/31/00) ($000)	REV	INC
1st Quarter	1,084,000	55,200
2nd Quarter	1,074,200	55,100
3rd Quarter	954,800	38,900
4th Quarter	1,003,100	19,500

ANNUAL FINANCIAL DATA

	12/31/00	12/31/99	12/31/98	12/31/97
Earnings Per Share	**1.67**	**1.95**	**1.84**	**[1] d6.70**
Cash Flow Per Share	**4.34**	**4.43**	**4.07**	**d4.82**
Tang. Book Val. Per Share	**1.75**	**3.28**	**1.92**	**0.09**
Dividends Per Share	**0.44**	**0.44**	**0.44**	**0.22**
Dividend Payout %	**26.3**	**22.6**	**23.9**	...
INCOME STATEMENT (IN MILLIONS):				
Total Revenues	4,116.1	3,812.2	3,488.7	2,739.6
Costs & Expenses	3,507.5	3,190.2	2,906.6	3,030.0
Depreciation & Amort.	269.1	253.4	228.0	162.6
Operating Income	339.5	368.6	354.1	d453.0
Net Interest Inc./(Exp.)	d53.2	d43.5	d48.0	d33.8
Income Before Income Taxes	290.6	329.7	312.5	d477.3
Income Taxes	117.2	132.0	123.9	99.1
Equity Earnings/Minority Int.	d0.4	6.8	6.1	6.3
Net Income	168.7	199.9	188.3	[1] d579.6
Cash Flow	437.8	453.3	416.3	d417.0
Average Shs. Outstg. (000)	100,900	102,400	102,300	86,500
BALANCE SHEET (IN MILLIONS):				
Cash & Cash Equivalents	82.2	119.2	118.5	152.0
Total Current Assets	1,349.0	1,181.5	1,131.8	974.2
Net Property	867.2	834.6	868.6	727.2
Total Assets	4,067.8	3,646.5	3,668.1	3,430.5
Total Current Liabilities	1,255.9	1,104.6	1,062.7	999.5
Long-Term Obligations	737.4	470.4	628.6	611.8
Net Stockholders' Equity	1,910.1	1,931.0	1,846.0	1,704.0
Net Working Capital	93.1	76.9	69.1	d25.3
Year-end Shs. Outstg. (000)	97,800	102,300	102,300	102,200
STATISTICAL RECORD:				
Operating Profit Margin %	8.2	9.7	10.1	...
Net Profit Margin %	4.1	5.2	5.4	...
Return on Equity %	8.8	10.4	10.2	...
Return on Assets %	4.1	5.5	5.1	...
Debt/Total Assets %	18.1	12.9	17.1	17.8
Price Range	31.81-14.50	41.88-27.25	37.25-24.44	45.50-30.50
P/E Ratio	19.0-8.7	21.5-14.0	20.2-13.3	...
Average Yield %	1.9	1.3	1.4	0.6

Statistics are as originally reported. [1] Incl. gain of $732.3 mill. fr. write-off of acqd. R&D.

OFFICERS:
S. J. Steward, Chmn.
L. Westerberg, Pres., C.E.O.
M. Lindquist, V.P., C.F.O.

INVESTOR CONTACT: Patrick Jarobe, Dir., Inv. Rel., (248) 475-0407

PRINCIPAL OFFICE: 3350 Airport Road, Ogden, UT 84405

TELEPHONE NUMBER: (801) 625-9200
FAX: (801) 625-4911
WEB: www.autoliv.com

NO. OF EMPLOYEES: 22,580

SHAREHOLDERS: 60,000 (approx.)

ANNUAL MEETING: In Apr.

INCORPORATED: DE, 1996

INSTITUTIONAL HOLDINGS:
No. of Institutions: 88
Shares Held: 11,790,823
% Held: 12.1

INDUSTRY: Motor vehicle parts and accessories (SIC: 3714)

TRANSFER AGENT(S): First Chicago Trust Company EquiServe, Inc., Jersey City, NJ

NYSE SYMBOL ADP
Rec. Pr. 54.25 (4/30/01)

AUTOMATIC DATA PROCESSING, INC.

YIELD 0.8%
P/E RATIO 39.9

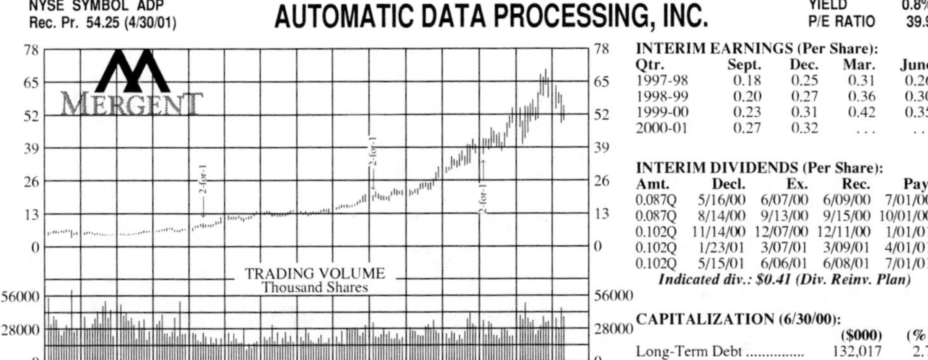

*7 YEAR PRICE SCORE 134.0 *12 MONTH PRICE SCORE 98.1
*NYSE COMPOSITE INDEX=100

INTERIM EARNINGS (Per Share):

Qtr.	Sept.	Dec.	Mar.	June
1997-98	0.18	0.25	0.31	0.26
1998-99	0.20	0.27	0.36	0.30
1999-00	0.23	0.31	0.42	0.35
2000-01	0.27	0.32	...	...

INTERIM DIVIDENDS (Per Share):

Amt.	Decl.	Ex.	Rec.	Pay.
0.087Q	5/16/00	6/07/00	6/09/00	7/01/00
0.087Q	8/14/00	9/13/00	9/15/00	10/01/00
0.102Q	11/14/00	12/07/00	12/11/00	1/01/01
0.102Q	1/23/01	3/07/01	3/09/01	4/01/01
0.102Q	5/15/01	6/06/01	6/08/01	7/01/01

Indicated div.: $0.41 (Div. Reinv. Plan)

CAPITALIZATION (6/30/00):

	($000)	(%)
Long-Term Debt	132,017	2.7
Deferred Income Tax	151,337	3.1
Common & Surplus	4,582,818	94.2
Total	4,866,172	100.0

RECENT DEVELOPMENTS: For the quarter ended 12/31/00, net earnings climbed 4.0% to $207.4 million versus $199.5 million in the corresponding quarter of 1999. Results for 2000 included a $27.0 million after-tax write-down of the Company's investment in Bridge Information Systems, Inc. Total revenues were $1.68 billion, up 12.8% from $1.49 billion in the prior-year period. Revenues in the Brokerage segment increased 17.8% to $370.0 million due to the recent acquisition of Cunningham Graphics.

PROSPECTS: ADP® Dealer Services Group announced the acquisition of Traver Technologies, Ltd., a provider of front-end training and consulting packages to about 300 dealerships in North America. The acquisition strengthens the Company existing dealer consulting businesses of Performance Inc., Mike Nicholes, Inc. and ASC. Separately, the Company is forecasting revenue growth of 13.0% to 15.0% and earnings per share growth of 16.0% to 18.0% for fiscal year 2001.

BUSINESS

AUTOMATIC DATA PROCESSING, INC. is an independent computer services firm with over 500,000 clients. AUD's Employer Services group (57.6% of 2000 revenues) serves employers with payroll, human resources, tax deposit and reporting services. Brokerage Services (23.5% of revenues) provides high quality, high speed securities transaction processing, investor support tools, market data services, and investor communications related services to the financial community worldwide. ADP Dealer Services (11.7% of revenues) is the world's largest provider of computing, data and professional services to auto and truck dealers in the U.S., Canada, Europe, Asia and Latin America. Other Service groups (7.2% of revenues) include claims services and ADP international.

ANNUAL FINANCIAL DATA

	6/30/00	6/30/99	6/30/98	6/30/97	6/30/96	6/30/95	6/30/94
Earnings Per Share	**1.31**	[3] **1.10**	**0.99**	[2] **0.88**	**0.79**	**0.69**	[1] **0.59**
Cash Flow Per Share	**1.74**	**1.52**	**1.37**	**1.27**	**1.14**	**0.99**	**0.86**
Tang. Book Val. Per Share	**4.71**	**3.97**	**2.90**	**2.30**	**1.86**	**2.41**	**1.92**
Dividends Per Share	**0.35**	**0.30**	**0.27**	**0.23**	**0.20**	**0.16**	**0.14**
Dividend Payout %	**26.7**	**27.7**	**26.8**	**26.1**	**25.5**	**23.4**	**23.6**
INCOME STATEMENT (IN MILLIONS):							
Total Revenues	6,287.5	5,540.1	4,798.1	4,112.2	3,566.6	2,893.7	2,469.0
Costs & Expenses	4,668.1	4,163.7	3,645.2	3,136.9	2,699.8	2,162.6	1,853.5
Depreciation & Amort.	284.3	272.8	244.6	223.4	201.6	172.5	148.3
Operating Income	1,335.1	1,103.6	908.2	751.8	665.1	558.6	467.2
Net Interest Inc./(Exp.)	d13.1	d19.1	d24.0	d27.8	d29.7	d24.3	d20.8
Income Before Income Taxes	1,289.6	1,084.5	884.2	724.0	635.4	534.3	446.3
Income Taxes	448.8	387.7	278.9	210.5	180.7	139.5	112.2
Net Income	840.8	[3] 696.8	605.3	[2] 513.5	454.7	394.8	[1] 334.1
Cash Flow	1,125.1	969.6	849.9	736.9	656.3	567.4	482.4
Average Shs. Outstg. (000)	646,098	636,892	620,822	581,980	577,934	570,224	563,560
BALANCE SHEET (IN MILLIONS):							
Cash & Cash Equivalents	1,824.4	1,092.5	897.2	1,024.9	636.2	697.6	590.6
Total Current Assets	3,064.5	2,194.3	1,829.3	1,805.3	1,454.3	1,211.1	985.4
Net Property	597.3	579.3	583.7	519.3	468.3	416.0	395.8
Total Assets	16,850.8	5,824.8	5,175.4	4,382.8	3,839.9	3,201.1	2,705.6
Total Current Liabilities	1,296.7	1,286.4	1,221.0	1,019.9	835.6	543.2	478.2
Long-Term Obligations	132.0	145.8	192.1	401.2	403.7	390.2	373.0
Net Stockholders' Equity	4,582.8	4,007.9	3,406.5	2,660.6	2,315.3	2,096.6	1,691.3
Net Working Capital	1,767.8	907.9	608.3	785.5	618.7	667.9	507.2
Year-end Shs. Outstg. (000)	628,746	623,627	604,212	585,698	575,242	576,336	562,796
STATISTICAL RECORD:							
Operating Profit Margin %	21.2	19.9	18.9	18.3	18.6	19.3	18.9
Net Profit Margin %	13.4	12.6	12.6	12.5	12.7	13.6	13.5
Return on Equity %	18.3	17.4	17.8	19.3	19.6	18.8	19.8
Return on Assets %	5.0	12.0	11.7	11.7	11.8	12.3	12.3
Debt/Total Assets %	0.8	2.5	3.7	9.2	10.5	12.2	13.8
Price Range	69.94-40.00	54.81-36.25	42.16-28.78	31.34-19.75	22.88-17.81	20.59-14.38	14.94-11.91
P/E Ratio	53.4-30.5	49.8-33.0	42.6-29.1	35.6-22.4	29.1-22.7	29.7-20.7	25.2-20.1
Average Yield %	0.6	0.7	0.7	0.9	1.0	0.9	1.0

Statistics are as originally reported. Adj. for 2-for-1 stk. split, 1/99 & 1/96. [1] Excl. acctg. chg. of $4.8 mill. [2] Incl. non-recur. chg. of $11.7 mill. [3] Incl. about $37.0 pre-tax gain, $40.0 mill. provision for taxes, & $14.0 mill. net non-recur. adjustment.

OFFICERS:
A. F. Weinbach, Chmn., C.E.O.
G. C. Butler, Pres., C.O.O.
R. J. Haviland, V.P., C.F.O.

INVESTOR CONTACT: Investor Relations, (973) 994-5000

PRINCIPAL OFFICE: One ADP Blvd., Roseland, NJ 07068-1728

TELEPHONE NUMBER: (973) 994-5000
FAX: (973) 994-5390
WEB: www.adp.com

NO. OF EMPLOYEES: 40,000 (approx.)

SHAREHOLDERS: 33,985

ANNUAL MEETING: In Nov.

INCORPORATED: DE, June, 1961

INSTITUTIONAL HOLDINGS:
No. of Institutions: 777
Shares Held: 450,206,375
% Held: 70.9

INDUSTRY: Data processing and preparation (SIC: 7374)

TRANSFER AGENT(S): Mellon Investor Services, Ridgefield Park, NJ

NYSE SYMBOL AN
Rec. Pr. 11.65 (5/31/01)

AUTONATION, INC.

YIELD ...
P/E RATIO 12.7

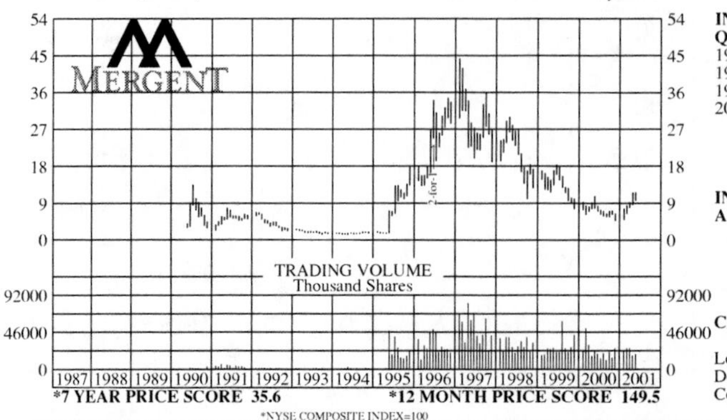

INTERIM EARNINGS (Per Share):

Qtr.	Mar.	June	Sept.	Dec.
1997	0.08	0.17	0.28	d0.07
1998	0.17	0.27	0.38	0.22
1999	0.11	0.21	0.22	d0.71
2000	0.18	0.27	0.26	0.21

INTERIM DIVIDENDS (Per Share):

Amt.	Decl.	Ex.	Rec.	Pay.

No dividends paid.

CAPITALIZATION (12/31/00):

	($000)	(%)
Long-Term Debt	850,400	15.3
Deferred Income Tax	877,200	15.7
Common & Surplus	3,842,500	69.0
Total	5,570,100	100.0

RECENT DEVELOPMENTS: For the year ended 12/31/00, income from continuing operations was $328.1 million versus a loss from continuing operations of $31.5 million the prior year. Results for 2000 included a $3.8 million pre-tax asset impairment gain, while the 1999 results included a $416.4 million pre-tax restructuring and asset impairment charge. Total revenues grew 2.5% to $20.61 billion from $20.11 billion the year before. New vehicle sales climbed 8.8% to $12.49 billion, while used car sales slid 12.9% to $3.86 billion.

PROSPECTS: The Company is focusing on boosting sales of used cars, along with growing its parts and service and finance and insurance businesses, to help offset anticipated weaker demand for new vehicles, due to slowing economic conditions in the U.S. Meanwhile, results are benefiting from improved operating efficiencies and reductions in corporate overhead. The Company is targeting full-year 2001 earnings from continuing operations of between $0.85 and $0.90 per share.

BUSINESS

AUTONATION, INC. (formerly Republic Industries, Inc.) operates over 400 automotive retail franchises in 17 states, which sell new and used vehicles under a wide range of regional brand names. AN also operates more than 350 Web sites that offer a large selection of new and used vehicles for sale. The Company provides financing, secondary customer referral programs, vehicle protection and maintenance programs and insurance through AutoNation Financial Services. On 4/28/99, the Company completed the sale of Republic Services, Inc., a provider of non-hazardous solid waste collection and disposal services in the U.S. In December, 1999, AN closed its chain of used-car megastore outlets. On 6/30/00, AN spun off ANC Rental Corporation, comprised of the Alamo Rent-A-Car, National Car Rental and CarTemps USA vehicle rental companies.

ANNUAL FINANCIAL DATA

	12/31/00	12/31/99	12/31/98	[5] 12/31/97	[4] 12/31/96	12/31/95	12/31/94
Earnings Per Share	[1][2] 0.91	[1][2] d0.07	[2] 0.71	[1][2] 0.46	[1][3] d0.12	[2] 0.19	[2] 0.16
Cash Flow Per Share	1.28	0.21	2.94	2.79	2.15	0.31	0.24
Tang. Book Val. Per Share	2.65	4.72	6.44	4.34	4.05	2.21	1.41
INCOME STATEMENT (IN MILLIONS):							
Total Revenues	20,609.6	20,111.8	16,118.2	10,305.6	2,365.5	260.3	48.8
Costs & Expenses	19,751.0	20,004.2	14,531.4	9,102.4	1,827.5	202.7	34.5
Depreciation & Amort.	133.8	123.0	1,051.6	1,003.6	540.5	21.0	4.7
Operating Income	724.8	d15.4	535.2	199.6	d2.4	36.6	9.5
Net Interest Inc./(Exp.)	d233.2	d14.3	d11.8	1.4	d12.9	0.1	d1.0
Income Before Income Taxes	525.0	d27.5	522.7	315.4	d10.2	36.7	8.5
Income Taxes	196.9	4.0	188.1	115.2	17.7	13.5	...
Net Income	[1][2] 328.1	[1][2] d31.5	[2] 334.6	[1][2] 200.2	[1][3] d27.9	[2] 23.2	[2] 8.5
Cash Flow	461.9	91.5	1,386.2	1,203.8	512.6	44.2	13.3
Average Shs. Outstg. (000)	361,400	429,800	470,900	430,900	238,866	140,950	54,834
BALANCE SHEET (IN MILLIONS):							
Cash & Cash Equivalents	82.2	369.3	217.3	148.0	63.6	159.8	2.7
Total Current Assets	4,176.2	4,300.9	8,406.3	6,825.8	2,584.8	206.8	14.2
Net Property	1,538.1	1,360.4	2,043.6	2,096.9	846.4	187.5	85.5
Total Assets	8,830.0	9,613.4	13,925.8	10,527.3	3,776.1	542.1	132.4
Total Current Liabilities	3,141.3	3,164.5	5,540.4	4,262.6	2,228.1	63.9	10.1
Long-Term Obligations	850.4	836.1	2,315.6	2,333.6	170.6	...	14.9
Net Stockholders' Equity	3,842.5	4,601.2	5,424.2	3,484.3	1,276.2	436.4	88.0
Net Working Capital	1,034.9	1,136.4	2,865.9	2,563.2	356.8	142.9	4.1
Year-end Shs. Outstg. (000)	348,085	375,363	458,130	432,706	258,866	152,112	54,372
STATISTICAL RECORD:							
Operating Profit Margin %	3.5	...	3.3	1.9	...	14.1	19.5
Net Profit Margin %	1.6	...	2.1	1.9	...	8.9	17.4
Return on Equity %	8.5	...	6.2	5.7	...	5.3	9.7
Return on Assets %	3.7	...	2.4	1.9	...	4.3	6.4
Debt/Total Assets %	9.6	8.7	16.6	22.2	4.5	...	11.3
Price Range	10.75-4.63	18.38-7.50	30.00-10.00	44.38-19.00	34.63-13.19	18.06-1.50	2.06-1.25
P/E Ratio	11.8-5.1	...	42.2-14.1	96.4-41.3	...	97.6-8.1	13.3-8.1

Statistics are as originally reported. Adj. for 2-for-1 stk. split, 6/96. [1] Incl. $3.8 mil pre-tax asset impairment gain, 2000; $390.2 mil one-time pre-tax chg., 1999; $179.1 mil chg., 1997; $38.3 mil chg., 1996. [2] Bef. $1.8 mil disc. ops. gain, 2000; $314.4 mil ($0.73/sh) gain, 1999; $164.9 mil ($0.35/sh) gain, 1998; $239.5 mil ($0.56/sh) gain, 1997; $293,000 loss, 1995; $2.7 mil ($0.05/sh) gain, 1994. [3] Bef. $31.6 mil ($0.13/sh) extraord. chg. [4] Incl. results of Alamo Rent-A-Car, Inc., acq. on 11/25/96. [5] Incl. results of National Car Rental System, Inc., acq. on 2/25/97.

OFFICERS:
H. W. Huizenga, Chmn.
M. J. Jackson, C.E.O.
M. E. Maroone, Pres., C.O.O.
C. T. Monaghan, C.F.O.

PRINCIPAL OFFICE: 110 S.E. 6th Street, Ft. Lauderdale, FL 33301

TELEPHONE NUMBER: (954) 769-6000
FAX: (954) 779-3884
WEB: www.autonation.com
NO. OF EMPLOYEES: 31,000 (approx.)
SHAREHOLDERS: 3,700 (approx.)
ANNUAL MEETING: In May
INCORPORATED: OK, Nov., 1980; reincorp., DE, May, 1991

INSTITUTIONAL HOLDINGS:
No. of Institutions: 111
Shares Held: 100,925,113
% Held: 29.9

INDUSTRY: Automotive dealers, nec (SIC: 5599)

TRANSFER AGENT(S): EquiServe, Jersey City, NJ

NYSE SYMBOL AZO
Rec. Pr. 33.07 (5/31/01)

AUTOZONE, INC.

YIELD	. . .
P/E RATIO	15.9

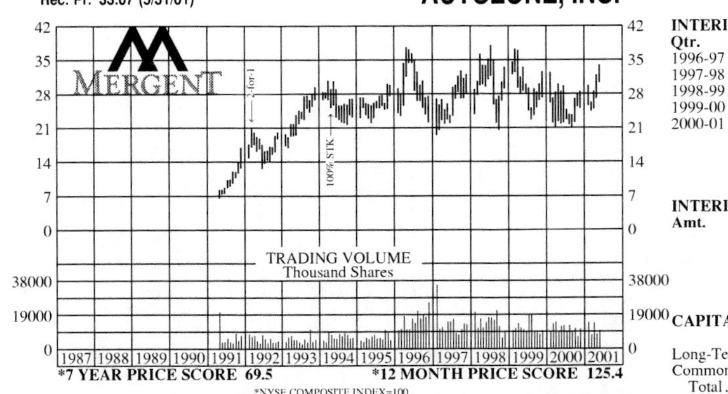

INTERIM EARNINGS (Per Share):

Qtr.	Nov.	Feb.	May	Aug.
1996-97	0.25	0.19	0.30	0.53
1997-98	0.31	0.22	0.35	0.60
1998-99	0.34	0.24	0.39	0.67
1999-00	0.40	0.28	0.50	0.84
2000-01	0.46	0.28	. . .	. . .

INTERIM DIVIDENDS (Per Share):

Amt.	Decl.	Ex.	Rec.	Pay.

No dividends paid.

CAPITALIZATION (8/26/00):

	($000)	(%)
Long-Term Debt	1,249,937	55.7
Common & Surplus	992,179	44.3
Total	2,242,116	100.0

RECENT DEVELOPMENTS: For the twelve weeks ended 2/10/01, net income slid 18.8% to $31.7 million from $39.1 million the year before. Net sales rose 5.4% to $974.0 million from $924.2 million the previous year. Comparable-store sales increased 2.0%. Gross profit was $397.3 million, or 40.8% of net sales, versus $388.4 million, or 42.0% of net sales, in the prior year. Operating profit slipped 3.4% to $77.3 million from $80.0 million the previous year.

PROSPECTS: Results are being negatively affected by weakening economic conditions and higher energy and gas prices. During the current year, the Company is targeting earnings per share in the range of $2.25 to $2.30 and anticipates earnings per share will grow by 15.0% in fiscal 2002. These expectations are based on same-store sales growth of between 2.0% and 4.0% during the second half of fiscal 2001 and for fiscal 2002.

BUSINESS

AUTOZONE, INC. operates a chain of retail stores that offer a wide assortment of new and remanufactured automotive replacement parts for domestic and foreign cars, vans and light trucks, as well as spark plugs, chemicals, motor oil, maintenance items and various other automotive accessories. AZO sells its products primarily to the do-it-yourself market through its chain of 2,972 AutoZone stores in 42 states and 13 AutoZone stores in Mexico. AZO also sells heavy-duty truck parts through 49 TruckPro stores in 15 states and automotive diagnostic and repair software through ALLDATA. AZO acquired TruckPro in May 1998 and Chief Auto Parts in June 1998.

ANNUAL FINANCIAL DATA

	8/26/00	8/28/99	8/29/98	8/30/97	8/31/96	8/26/95	8/27/94
Earnings Per Share	**2.00**	**1.63**	**1.48**	**1.29**	**1.13**	**0.93**	**0.78**
Cash Flow Per Share	**2.95**	**2.48**	**2.11**	**1.81**	**1.55**	**1.25**	**1.00**
Tang. Book Val. Per Share	**5.49**	**6.83**	**7.37**	**7.00**	**5.65**	**4.54**	**3.51**
INCOME STATEMENT (IN MILLIONS):							
Total Revenues	4,482.7	4,116.4	3,242.9	2,691.4	2,242.6	1,808.1	1,508.0
Costs & Expenses	3,843.9	3,554.8	2,764.0	2,292.3	1,910.2	1,532.1	1,284.2
Depreciation & Amort.	126.8	128.5	96.6	77.8	63.5	48.3	33.1
Operating Income	512.0	433.1	382.3	321.4	268.9	227.7	190.7
Net Interest Inc./(Exp.)	d76.8	d45.3	d18.2	d8.8	d2.0	0.6	2.2
Income Before Income Taxes	435.2	387.8	364.1	312.5	267.0	228.3	193.0
Income Taxes	167.6	143.0	136.2	117.5	99.8	89.5	76.6
Net Income	267.6	244.8	227.9	195.0	167.2	138.8	116.4
Cash Flow	394.4	373.3	324.5	272.8	230.7	187.1	149.5
Average Shs. Outstg. (000)	133,869	150,257	154,070	150,726	148,476	149,302	148,726
BALANCE SHEET (IN MILLIONS):							
Cash & Cash Equivalents	7.0	5.9	6.6	4.7	3.9	6.4	56.2
Total Current Assets	1,186.8	1,225.1	1,117.1	778.8	613.1	447.8	424.4
Net Property	1,758.4	1,638.5	1,427.5	1,081.1	862.9	644.2	436.1
Total Assets	3,333.2	3,284.8	2,748.1	1,884.0	1,498.4	1,111.8	882.1
Total Current Liabilities	1,034.5	1,000.6	859.8	592.5	612.9	417.5	339.0
Long-Term Obligations	1,249.9	888.3	545.1	198.4	. . .	. . .	4.0
Net Stockholders' Equity	992.2	1,323.8	1,302.1	1,075.2	865.6	684.7	528.4
Net Working Capital	152.2	224.5	257.3	186.3	0.2	30.3	85.4
Year-end Shs. Outstg. (000)	121,510	144,353	152,086	151,313	150,137	147,052	145,417
STATISTICAL RECORD:							
Operating Profit Margin %	11.4	10.5	11.8	11.9	12.0	12.6	12.6
Net Profit Margin %	6.0	5.9	7.0	7.2	7.5	7.7	7.7
Return on Equity %	27.0	18.5	17.5	18.1	19.3	20.3	22.0
Return on Assets %	8.0	7.5	8.3	10.4	11.2	12.5	13.2
Debt/Total Assets %	37.5	27.0	19.8	10.5	. . .	. . .	0.5
Price Range	32.50-21.00	37.31-22.56	38.00-20.50	32.81-19.50	37.63-22.13	30.13-22.00	30.75-21.63
P/E Ratio	16.2-10.5	22.9-13.8	25.7-13.9	25.4-15.1	33.3-19.6	32.4-23.7	39.4-27.7

Statistics are as originally reported.

OFFICERS:
S. Odland, Chmn., C.E.O.
T. D. Vargo, Pres., C.O.O.
R. J. Hunt, Exec. V.P., C.F.O.
H. L. Goldsmith, Sr. V.P., Sec., Gen. Couns.

INVESTOR CONTACT: Sheila Stuewe, Asst. treas., (901) 325-4458

PRINCIPAL OFFICE: 123 South Front Street, Memphis, TN 38103-3607

TELEPHONE NUMBER: (901) 495-6500
FAX: (901) 495-8300
WEB: www.autozone.com

NO. OF EMPLOYEES: 29,000 full-time (approx.); 14,000 part-time (approx.)

SHAREHOLDERS: 3,561 (approx. record)

ANNUAL MEETING: In Dec.

INCORPORATED: DE, May, 1986; reincorp., NV, Dec., 1991

INSTITUTIONAL HOLDINGS:
No. of Institutions: 220
Shares Held: 67,929,801
% Held: 60.8

INDUSTRY: Auto and home supply stores (SIC: 5531)

TRANSFER AGENT(S): EquiServe, Jersey City, NJ

NYSE SYMBOL AVB
Rec. Pr. 45.40 (4/30/01)

AVALONBAY COMMUNITIES, INC.

YIELD 5.6%
P/E RATIO 18.1

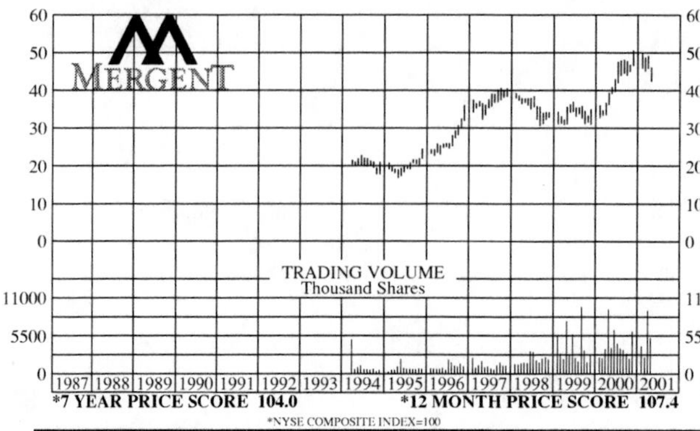

*7 YEAR PRICE SCORE 104.0 *12 MONTH PRICE SCORE 107.4
*NYSE COMPOSITE INDEX=100

INTERIM EARNINGS (Per Share):

Qtr.	Mar.	June	Sept.	Dec.
1996	0.19	0.20	0.28	0.31
1997	0.33	0.33	0.36	0.37
1998	0.34	0.34	0.37	0.34
1999	0.10	0.80	0.37	0.78
2000	0.55	0.60	0.71	0.99

INTERIM DIVIDENDS (Per Share):

Amt.	Decl.	Ex.	Rec.	Pay.
0.56Q	3/10/00	3/30/00	4/03/00	4/17/00
0.56Q	6/20/00	6/28/00	6/30/00	7/17/00
0.56Q	9/22/00	9/27/00	9/29/00	10/16/00
0.56Q	12/11/00	12/27/00	12/29/00	1/16/01
0.64Q	2/21/01	3/27/01	3/30/01	4/16/01

Indicated div.: $2.56

CAPITALIZATION (12/31/00):

	($000)	(%)
Long-Term Debt	1,335,000	34.9
Minority Interest	49,501	1.3
Preferred Stock	183	0.0
Common & Surplus	2,442,310	63.8
Total	3,826,994	100.0

RECENT DEVELOPMENTS: For the year ended 12/31/00, net income improved 22.2% to $210.6 million compared with $172.3 million in the previous year. Results for 1999 included non-recurring charges of $16.8 million. Total revenues jumped 13.3% to $573.4 million from $506.0 million in the prior year. Rental income totaled $571.9 million, an increase of 13.4% from $504.6 million the year before. Management fees declined 10.6% to $1.1 million, while other income jumped 69.9% to $401,000.

PROSPECTS: For 2001, the Company plans to invest approximately $460.0 million in the development and redevelopment of communities. Also, the Company expects to generate gross proceeds from the sale of communities in the range of $225.0 million to $275.0 million. Moreover, the Company anticipates estimated same-store community revenue growth to range from 7.0% to 8.0%, while operating expenses and capitalized overhead are expected to increase approximately 15.0% for 2001.

BUSINESS

AVALONBAY COMMUNITIES, INC. is a real estate investment trust company focused on developing, redeveloping, acquiring and managing luxury apartment communities in high barrier-to-entry markets of the United States. These markets include Northern California, Southern California and the Northeast, Mid-Atlantic, Midwest and Northwest regions of the country. As of December 31, 2000, the Company owned or held interest in 138 apartment communities containing 40,631 apartment homes in twelve states and the District of Columbia, of which ten communities are under construction and four are under reconstruction. In addition, the Company holds future development rights for 34 communities.

BUSINESS LINE ANALYSIS

(12/31/00)	REV (%)	INC (%)
Stable Communities	55.1	55.6
Developed Communities	17.6	18.6
Redeveloped Communities	6.3	5.7
Other Communities	21.0	20.1
Total	100.0	100.0

ANNUAL FINANCIAL DATA

	12/31/00	12/31/99	12/31/98	12/31/97	12/31/96	12/31/95	12/31/94
Earnings Per Share	**2.53**	**[2] 2.00**	**1.37**	**[2] 1.40**	**[1] 1.05**	**0.91**	**0.65**
Tang. Book Val. Per Share	**36.35**	**36.04**	**36.62**	**30.39**	**21.69**	**20.58**	**17.04**
Dividends Per Share	**2.20**	**2.05**	**1.02**	...	...	...	...
Dividend Payout %	**87.0**	**102.5**	**74.4**	...	...	...	...
INCOME STATEMENT (IN MILLIONS):							
Rental Income	571.9	503.1	352.0	121.9	80.4	52.1	31.1
Total Income	573.4	504.5	352.9	126.0	82.6	53.5	32.0
Costs & Expenses	286.2	277.9	187.4	59.6	43.4	30.7	16.2
Depreciation	122.6	109.8	78.4	27.0	18.7	13.7	8.4
Income Before Income Taxes	210.1	171.4	94.3	39.4	20.5	11.5	7.5
Equity Earnings/Minority Int.	0.5	0.9	0.2	d0.5	d0.3	...	...
Net Income	210.6	[2] 172.3	94.4	[2] 38.9	[1] 20.1	11.5	7.5
Average Shs. Outstg. (000)	68,141	66,111	50,147	22,472	14,985	11,554	11,544
BALANCE SHEET (IN MILLIONS):							
Cash & Cash Equivalents	92.2	30.5	26.8	4.8	1.9	1.7	5.7
Total Real Estate Investments	4,200.0	4,041.3	3,890.9	1,294.5	697.8	463.7	375.8
Total Assets	4,397.2	4,154.7	4,030.2	1,317.7	711.9	477.2	390.0
Long-Term Obligations	1,335.0	1,163.6	1,039.0	...	...	...	...
Total Liabilities	1,954.7	1,784.4	1,690.8	525.0	299.6	239.6	193.3
Net Stockholders' Equity	2,442.5	2,370.3	2,339.5	792.7	412.3	237.6	196.7
Year-end Shs. Outstg. (000)	67,192	65,758	63,887	26,078	19,008	11,544	11,544
STATISTICAL RECORD:							
Net Inc.+Depr./Assets %	7.6	6.8	4.3	5.0	5.5	5.3	4.1
Return on Equity %	8.6	7.3	4.0	4.9	4.9	4.8	3.8
Return on Assets %	4.8	4.1	2.3	3.0	2.8	2.4	1.9
Price Range	50.63-32.63	37.00-30.81	39.25-30.50	40.63-32.13	36.00-22.63	24.50-16.75	22.75-17.75
P/E Ratio	20.0-12.9	18.5-15.4	28.6-22.3	29.0-22.9	34.3-21.5	26.9-18.4	35.0-27.3
Average Yield %	5.3	6.0	2.9	...	...	...	...

Statistics are as originally reported. [1] Bef. extraord. chrg. $511,000 [2] Incl. non-recurr. chrg. $16.8 mill., 12/99; $710,000, 12/97

OFFICERS:
R. L. Michaux, Chmn., C.E.O.
B. Blair, Pres., C.O.O.
T. J. Sargeant, Exec. V.P., C.F.O.

INVESTOR CONTACT: Thomas J. Sargeant, Exec. V.P., C.F.O., (703) 317-4635.

PRINCIPAL OFFICE: 2900 Eisenhower Avenue, Suite 300, Alexandria, VA 22314

TELEPHONE NUMBER: (703) 329-6300
FAX: (703) 329-1459
WEB: www.avalonbay.com

NO. OF EMPLOYEES: 500 (approx.)

SHAREHOLDERS: 928

ANNUAL MEETING: In May

INCORPORATED: CA, 1978; reincorp., MD, July, 1995

INSTITUTIONAL HOLDINGS:
No. of Institutions: 196
Shares Held: 67,914,455
% Held: 101.3

INDUSTRY: Real estate investment trusts (SIC: 6798)

TRANSFER AGENT(S): First Union National Bank, Charlotte, NC

NYSE SYMBOL AV
Rec. Pr. 13.00 (3/31/01)

AVAYA INC.

YIELD ...
P/E RATIO ...

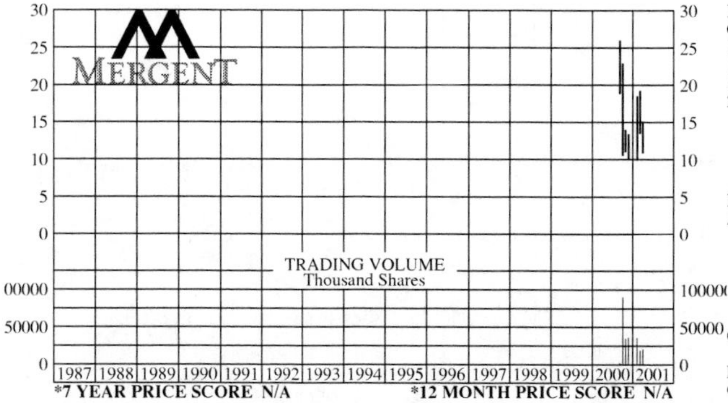

*7 YEAR PRICE SCORE N/A *12 MONTH PRICE SCORE N/A
*NYSE COMPOSITE INDEX=100

INTERIM EARNINGS (Per Share):

Qtr.	Dec.	Mar.	June	Sept.
1997-98		0.17		
1998-99		1.03		
1999-00		d1.39		
2000-01	0.03	...	...	...

INTERIM DIVIDENDS (Per Share):

Amt.	Decl.	Ex.	Rec.	Pay.

No dividends paid.

CAPITALIZATION (9/30/00):

	($000)	(%)
Long-Term Debt	713,000	48.3
Common & Surplus	764,000	51.7
Total	1,477,000	100.0

RECENT DEVELOPMENTS: For the three months ended 12/31/00, net income totaled $16.0 million compared with $69.0 million a year earlier. Results for 2000 included pre-tax business restructuring-related charges of $23.0 million and after-tax one-time and start-up expenses of $35.0 million associated with the Company's spin-off from Lucent Technologies. The Company expects to incur additional one-time and start-up expenses throughout fiscal 2001. Revenues declined 3.5% to $1.79 billion from $1.85 billion in 1999.

PROSPECTS: AV continues to progress with the restructuring of its business, eliminating or consolidating 131 locations worldwide or 500,000 square feet of space, as part of its goal to reduce real estate holdings by 30.0% in 2001. In addition, AV has consolidated data centers and servers and is eliminating and replacing legacy applications. Strong growth from the Company's data networking and connectivity solutions businesses, coupled with the benefits from ongoing restructuring initiatives, enhance AV's future prospects.

BUSINESS

AVAYA INC. is a provider of communications systems and software. Operations are divided into three segments: communications solutions, services and connectivity solutions. The communications segment is comprised of voice communications systems and software for businesses, services for customer and business relationships management, networking products and product installation services. The services segment offers maintenance and other services. The connectivity solutions segment produces structured cabling systems and electronic cabinets. AV was spun off from Lucent Technologies Inc. on 9/30/00.

REVENUES

(9/30/2000)	($000)	(%)
Communications Solutions	4,323,000	56.3
Services	1,958,000	25.4
Connectivity Solutions	1,397,000	18.2
Corporate & Other	2,000	0.1
Total	7,680,000	100.0

ANNUAL FINANCIAL DATA

	9/30/00	9/30/99	9/30/98
Earnings Per Share	**[1] d1.39**	**1.03**	**0.17**
Cash Flow Per Share	**d0.58**	**1.46**	**0.91**
Tang. Book Val. Per Share	**1.99**	**5.47**	...
INCOME STATEMENT (IN MILLIONS):			
Total Revenues	7,680.0	8,268.0	7,754.0
Costs & Expenses	7,903.0	7,687.0	7,252.0
Depreciation & Amort.	220.0	212.0	193.0
Operating Income	d443.0	369.0	309.0
Net Interest Inc./(Exp.)	d76.0	d90.0	d94.0
Income Before Income Taxes	d448.0	307.0	240.0
Income Taxes	cr73.0	121.0	197.0
Net Income	[1] d375.0	186.0	43.0
Cash Flow	d155.0	398.0	236.0
Average Shs. Outstg. (000)	269,000	273,000	260,000
BALANCE SHEET (IN MILLIONS):			
Cash & Cash Equivalents	271.0	194.0	107.0
Total Current Assets	3,362.0	3,043.0	3,065.0
Net Property	966.0	676.0	613.0
Total Assets	5,037.0	4,239.0	4,177.0
Total Current Liabilities	2,589.0	1,597.0	1,540.0
Long-Term Obligations	713.0	...	...
Net Stockholders' Equity	764.0	1,817.0	1,795.0
Net Working Capital	773.0	1,446.0	1,525.0
Year-end Shs. Outstg. (000)	282,028	278,293	...
STATISTICAL RECORD:			
Operating Profit Margin %	...	4.5	4.0
Net Profit Margin %	...	2.2	0.6
Return on Equity %	...	10.2	2.4
Return on Assets %	...	4.4	1.0
Debt/Total Assets %	14.2	...	...
Price Range	26.00-10.00	...	...

Statistics are as originally reported. [1] Incls. nonrecurr. chrgs. of $757.0 mill. for restruct. & separation fr. Lucent Technologies Inc.

OFFICERS:
P. F. Russo, Chmn.
D. K. Peterson, Vice-Chmn., Pres., C.E.O.
G. K. McGuire Sr., C.F.O.
P. F. Craven, V.P., General Counsel, Sec.

PRINCIPAL OFFICE: 211 Mount Airy Road, Basking Ridge, NJ 07920

TELEPHONE NUMBER: (908) 953-6000
WEB: www.avaya.com

NO. OF EMPLOYEES: 31,000 (approx.)

SHAREHOLDERS: 1,406,847 (approx.)

ANNUAL MEETING: N/A

INCORPORATED: DE, Feb., 2000

INSTITUTIONAL HOLDINGS:
No. of Institutions: 370
Shares Held: 100,353,436
% Held: 35.5

INDUSTRY: Communication services, nec (SIC: 4899)

TRANSFER AGENT(S): Bank of New York, New York, NY

NYSE SYMBOL AVY
Rec. Pr. 56.07 (4/30/01)

AVERY DENNISON CORPORATION

YIELD 2.1%
P/E RATIO 19.7

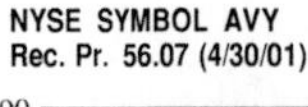

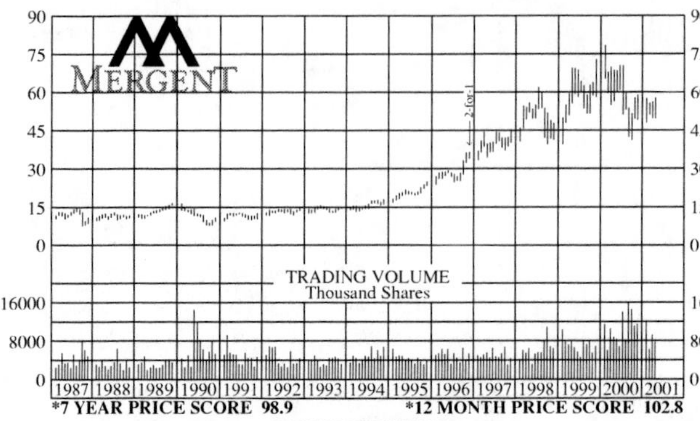

***7 YEAR PRICE SCORE 98.9** ***12 MONTH PRICE SCORE 102.8**

*NYSE COMPOSITE INDEX=100

INTERIM EARNINGS (Per Share):

Qtr.	Mar.	June	Sept.	Dec.
1997	0.47	0.48	0.51	0.52
1998	0.52	0.55	0.54	0.54
1999	0.18	0.63	0.65	0.67
2000	0.70	0.73	0.73	0.69

INTERIM DIVIDENDS (Per Share):

Amt.	Decl.	Ex.	Rec.	Pay.
0.27Q	4/27/00	6/05/00	6/07/00	6/21/00
0.27Q	7/27/00	9/01/00	9/06/00	9/20/00
0.30Q	10/26/00	12/04/00	12/06/00	12/20/00
0.30Q	1/25/01	3/05/01	3/07/01	3/21/01
0.30Q	4/26/01	6/04/01	6/06/01	6/20/01

Indicated div.: $1.20 (Div. Reinv. Plan)

CAPITALIZATION (12/30/00):

	($000)	(%)
Long-Term Debt	772,900	44.8
Deferred Income Tax	94,000	5.4
Common & Surplus	858,700	49.8
Total	1,725,600	100.0

RECENT DEVELOPMENTS: For the year ended 12/30/00, net income jumped 31.6% to $283.5 million compared with $215.4 million in 1999. Results for 1999 included a restructuring charge of $65.0 million. Net sales were $3.89 billion, up 3.3% from $3.77 million in the prior-year. Operating income increased 29.0% to $426.3 million compared with $330.4 million in the previous year. Unit volume increased 8.6% over the prior year. Results benefited from the Company's extensive restructuring program.

PROSPECTS: The Company anticipates volume growth to be soft through the first half of 2001 due to a slowing North American economy. However, AVY expects economic conditions to improve during the second half of 2001 and report full-year revenue growth of 4.0% to 6.0% and earnings per share growth in the range of $2.90 to $3.05. Separately, the Company acquired Dunsirn Industries Inc., a provider of non-pressure-sensitive materials to the narrow Web printing industry and customized slitting and distribution services.

BUSINESS

AVERY DENNISON CORPORATION is a worldwide manufacturer of pressure-sensitive adhesives and materials, office products and converted products. A portion of self-adhesive material is converted into labels and other products through embossing, printing, stamping and die-cutting, and some are sold in unconverted form as base materials, tapes and reflective sheeting. AVY also manufactures and sells a variety of office products and other items not involving pressure-sensitive components, such as notebooks, three-ring binders, organization systems, felt-tip markers, glues, fasteners, business forms, tickets, tags, and imprinting equipment. Sales for 2000 were derived: pressure-sensitive adhesives and materials, 53.0%; and consumer and converted products, 47.0%.

ANNUAL FINANCIAL DATA

	12/30/00	1/1/00	1/2/99	12/27/97	12/28/96	12/30/95	12/31/94
Earnings Per Share	**2.84**	**[2] 2.13**	**2.15**	**1.93**	**[1] 1.68**	**[1] 1.35**	**0.98**
Cash Flow Per Share	**4.41**	**3.61**	**3.37**	**3.03**	**2.76**	**2.36**	**1.91**
Tang. Book Val. Per Share	**4.21**	**4.18**	**6.88**	**6.87**	**6.72**	**8.91**	**6.84**
Dividends Per Share	**1.11**	**0.99**	**0.87**	**0.72**	**0.62**	**0.56**	**0.49**
Dividend Payout %	**39.1**	**46.5**	**40.5**	**37.3**	**36.9**	**41.1**	**50.5**
INCOME STATEMENT (IN MILLIONS):							
Total Revenues	3,893.5	3,768.2	3,459.9	3,345.7	3,222.5	3,113.9	2,856.7
Costs & Expenses	3,255.7	3,244.0	2,961.4	2,886.0	2,801.1	2,737.0	2,538.3
Depreciation & Amort.	156.9	150.4	127.2	116.8	113.4	107.9	102.5
Operating Income	480.9	373.8	371.3	342.9	308.0	269.0	215.9
Net Interest Inc./(Exp.)	d54.6	d43.4	d34.6	d31.7	d37.4	d44.3	d43.0
Income Before Income Taxes	426.3	330.4	336.7	311.2	270.6	224.7	172.9
Income Taxes	142.8	115.0	113.4	106.4	94.7	81.0	63.5
Net Income	283.5	[2] 215.4	223.3	205.3	[1] 175.9	[1] 143.7	109.4
Cash Flow	440.4	365.8	350.5	321.6	289.3	251.6	211.9
Average Shs. Outstg. (000)	99,800	101,300	104,100	106,100	105,000	106,500	111,100
BALANCE SHEET (IN MILLIONS):							
Cash & Cash Equivalents	11.4	6.9	18.5	3.3	3.8	27.0	3.1
Total Current Assets	982.4	956.0	802.0	793.5	804.5	800.1	676.9
Net Property	1,079.0	1,043.5	1,035.6	985.3	962.7	907.4	831.6
Total Assets	2,699.1	2,592.5	2,142.6	2,046.5	2,036.7	1,963.6	1,763.1
Total Current Liabilities	800.7	850.4	664.3	629.9	693.9	672.5	554.1
Long-Term Obligations	772.9	617.5	465.9	404.1	370.7	334.0	347.3
Net Stockholders' Equity	858.7	843.5	869.9	884.0	890.8	1,123.4	935.1
Net Working Capital	181.7	105.6	137.7	163.6	110.6	127.6	122.8
Year-end Shs. Outstg. (000)	110,245	98,800	100,000	102,400	103,600	106,100	107,100
STATISTICAL RECORD:							
Operating Profit Margin %	12.4	9.9	10.7	10.2	9.6	8.6	7.6
Net Profit Margin %	7.3	5.7	6.5	6.1	5.5	4.6	3.8
Return on Equity %	33.0	26.6	26.8	24.5	21.1	17.6	15.0
Return on Assets %	10.5	8.3	10.4	10.0	8.6	7.3	6.2
Debt/Total Assets %	28.6	23.8	21.7	19.7	18.2	17.0	19.7
Price Range	78.50-41.13	73.00-39.38	62.06-39.44	45.31-33.38	36.50-23.75	25.06-16.56	18.00-13.19
P/E Ratio	27.6-14.5	34.3-18.5	28.9-18.3	23.5-17.3	21.7-14.1	18.6-12.3	18.4-13.5
Average Yield %	1.9	1.8	1.7	1.8	2.1	2.7	3.2

Statistics are as originally reported. Adj. for 2-for-1 split, 12/96. [1] Incl. non-recur. chgs. of $2.1 mill., 1996; $1.5 mill., 1995. [2] Incl. $65.0 mill. one-time restr. chg.

OFFICERS:
P. M. Neal, Chmn., C.E.O.
D. A. Scarborough, Pres., C.O.O.
D. R. O'Bryant, Sr. V.P., Fin. and C.F.O.

INVESTOR CONTACT: Cynthia S. Guenther, Inv. Rel., (626) 304-2204

PRINCIPAL OFFICE: 150 North Orange Grove Boulevard, Pasadena, CA 91103

TELEPHONE NUMBER: (626) 304-2000
FAX: (626) 792-7312
WEB: www.averydennison.com

NO. OF EMPLOYEES: 17,900 (avg.)

SHAREHOLDERS: 12,987

ANNUAL MEETING: In Apr.

INCORPORATED: DE, Sept., 1946

INSTITUTIONAL HOLDINGS:
No. of Institutions: 369
Shares Held: 78,554,478
% Held: 71.3

INDUSTRY: Paper coated and laminated, nec (SIC: 2672)

TRANSFER AGENT(S): First Chicago Trust Company of New York, Jersey City, NJ

NYSE SYMBOL AVA
Rec. Pr. 19.90 (4/30/01)

AVISTA CORPORATION

YIELD 2.4%
P/E RATIO 14.3

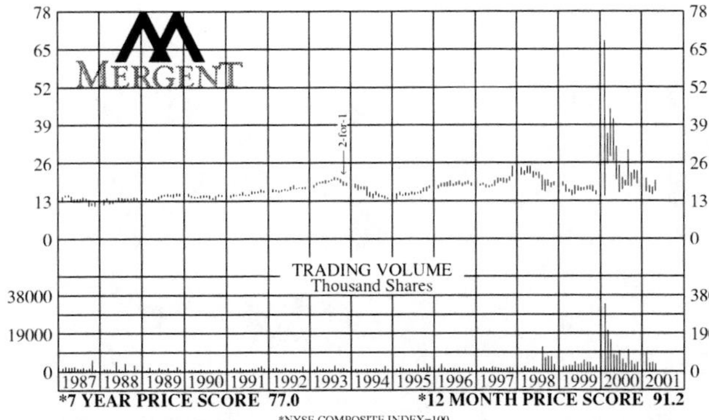

INTERIM EARNINGS (Per Share):

Qtr.	Mar.	June	Sept.	Dec.
1996	0.42	0.54	0.22	0.17
1997	0.29	0.28	0.31	0.40
1998	0.57	0.27	0.14	0.30
1999	0.34	0.08	0.52	d0.98
2000	d0.28	d0.47	0.72	1.42

INTERIM DIVIDENDS (Per Share):

Amt.	Decl.	Ex.	Rec.	Pay.
0.12Q	5/12/00	5/19/00	5/23/00	6/15/00
0.12Q	8/11/00	8/18/00	8/22/00	9/15/00
0.12Q	11/10/00	11/17/00	11/21/00	12/15/00
0.12Q	2/08/01	2/21/01	2/23/01	3/15/01
0.12Q	5/11/01	5/18/01	5/22/01	6/15/01

Indicated div.: $0.48 (Div. Reinv. Plan)

CAPITALIZATION (12/31/00):

	($000)	(%)
Long-Term Debt	679,806	34.2
Deferred Income Tax	446,310	22.5
Redeemable Pfd. Stock	135,000	6.8
Common & Surplus	724,224	36.5
Total	1,985,340	100.0

RECENT DEVELOPMENTS: For the year ended 12/31/00, net income more than tripled to $91.7 million, compared with $26.0 million in the prior year. Earnings included asset impairment and restructuring charges of $9.8 million and $42.9 million in 2000 and 1999, respectively. Revenues rose nearly 1.0% to $7.91 billion. The Energy Trading and Marketing division fueled earnings growth with $161.8 million in net income.

PROSPECTS: Going forward, earnings for the Company's electric and gas utility business for the full year 2001 are estimated to be in a range of $0.90 to $1.00 per share. The Company's consolidated earnings for the full year 2001 will likely reflect the negative impact of efforts to support its technology businesses, and expectations for a reduced contribution from Avista Energy as AVA continues to minimize the risk profile for this business.

BUSINESS

AVISTA CORPORATION (formerly The Washington Water Power Company), is an energy, information and technology company with utility and subsidiary operations located throughout North America. The Company's operations are organized into four lines of business: Avista Utilities, Energy Trading and Marketing, Information and Technology, and Pentzer and Other. Avista Utilities represents the regulated utility operations that are responsible for retail electric and natural gas distribution, electric transmission services, electric generation and production, electric wholesale marketing and electric commodity trading. Avista Capital owns all of the Company's non-regulated energy and non-energy businesses. The Energy Trading and Marketing line of business includes Avista Energy, Inc., Avista Power, LLC and Avista-STEAG, LLC. The Information and Technology line of business includes Avista Advantage, Avista Labs and Avista Communications. The Pentzer and Other line of business includes Pentzer Corporation, Avista Development, Inc. and Avista Services, Inc.

ANNUAL FINANCIAL DATA

	12/31/00	12/31/99	12/31/98	12/31/97	12/31/96	12/31/95	12/31/94
Earnings Per Share	**[5] 1.47**	**[4] 0.12**	**1.28**	**[2] 1.96**	**[1] 1.35**	**1.41**	**1.28**
Cash Flow Per Share	**3.12**	**2.12**	**2.57**	**3.20**	**2.64**	**2.64**	**2.39**
Tang. Book Val. Per Share	**15.34**	**11.04**	**12.06**	**13.38**	**12.70**	**12.82**	**12.45**
Dividends Per Share	**0.48**	**0.48**	**1.05**	**1.24**	**1.24**	**1.24**	**1.24**
Dividend Payout %	**32.7**	**399.7**	**82.0**	**63.3**	**91.8**	**87.9**	**96.9**
INCOME STATEMENT (IN MILLIONS):							
Total Revenues	7,911.5	7,905.0	[3] 3,684.0	1,302.2	945.0	755.0	670.8
Costs & Expenses	7,632.1	7,797.2	3,440.6	1,042.8	685.9	497.6	455.8
Depreciation & Amort.	75.9	76.5	70.5	69.9	72.1	67.6	59.5
Operating Income	203.4	31.4	172.8	189.5	186.9	189.8	155.5
Net Interest Inc./(Exp.)	d68.7	d65.1	d69.1	d18.9	d63.3	d58.0	d49.4
Income Taxes	73.5	16.7	43.3	61.1	49.5	52.4	44.7
Net Income	[5] 91.7	[4] 26.0	78.1	[2] 114.8	[1] 83.5	87.1	77.2
Cash Flow	143.9	81.1	140.3	179.3	147.6	145.6	128.0
Average Shs. Outstg. (000)	46,103	38,213	54,604	55,960	55,960	55,173	53,538
BALANCE SHEET (IN MILLIONS):							
Gross Property	2,238.8	2,215.6	2,140.7	2,068.5	1,990.3	1,903.7	1,829.6
Accumulated Depreciation	720.5	714.8	669.8	635.3	592.4	546.2	500.6
Net Property	1,518.3	1,500.8	1,470.9	1,433.1	1,397.9	1,357.4	1,329.0
Total Assets	12,563.9	3,713.5	3,253.6	2,411.8	2,177.3	2,098.9	1,994.3
Long-Term Obligations	679.8	718.2	730.0	762.2	764.5	738.3	721.1
Net Stockholders' Equity	724.2	656.8	757.3	748.8	760.7	767.1	727.5
Year-end Shs. Outstg. (000)	47,209	35,648	40,454	55,960	55,960	55,948	54,421
STATISTICAL RECORD:							
Operating Profit Margin %	2.6	0.4	4.7	14.5	19.8	25.1	23.2
Net Profit Margin %	1.2	0.3	2.1	8.8	8.8	11.5	11.5
Net Inc./Net Property %	6.0	1.7	5.3	8.0	6.0	6.4	5.8
Net Inc./Tot. Capital %	4.6	1.4	3.9	5.7	4.4	4.6	4.2
Return on Equity %	12.7	4.0	10.3	15.3	11.0	11.4	10.6
Accum. Depr./Gross Prop. %	32.2	32.3	31.3	30.7	29.8	28.7	27.4
Price Range	68.00-14.63	19.56-14.63	24.88-16.13	24.81-17.38	19.88-17.13	18.13-13.50	18.88-13.63
P/E Ratio	46.3-9.9	162.9-121.8	19.4-12.6	12.7-8.9	14.7-12.7	12.9-9.6	14.7-10.6
Average Yield %	1.2	2.8	5.1	5.9	6.7	7.8	7.6

Statistics are as originally reported. [1] Incl. non-recurr. chrg. $21.4 mill. [2] Incl. non-recurr. after-tax gain $41.0 mill. [3] Reflects the start-up of National Energy Trading and Marketing operations. [4] Incl. one-time chrg. of $42.9 mill. & a net gain of $57.5 mill. [5] Incl. restruct. chrg. $9.8 mill.

OFFICERS:
G. G. Ely, Pres., C.E.O.
J. E. Eliassen, Sr. V.P., C.F.O.
R. R. Peterson, V.P., Treas.
T. L. Syms, V.P., Corp. Sec.

INVESTOR CONTACT: Investor Relations, (509) 495.8725

PRINCIPAL OFFICE: 1411 East Mission Ave., Spokane, WA 99202-2600

TELEPHONE NUMBER: (509) 489-0500
FAX: (509) 482-4361
WEB: www.avistacorp.com

NO. OF EMPLOYEES: 2,260 (avg.)

SHAREHOLDERS: 19,066 (approx.)

ANNUAL MEETING: In May

INCORPORATED: WA, March, 1989

INSTITUTIONAL HOLDINGS:
No. of Institutions: 124
Shares Held: 21,394,596
% Held: 45.3

INDUSTRY: Electric and other services combined (SIC: 4931)

TRANSFER AGENT(S): The Bank of New York, New York, NY

NYSE SYMBOL AVT
Rec. Pr. 24.64 (5/31/01)

AVNET, INC.

YIELD 1.2%
P/E RATIO 8.8

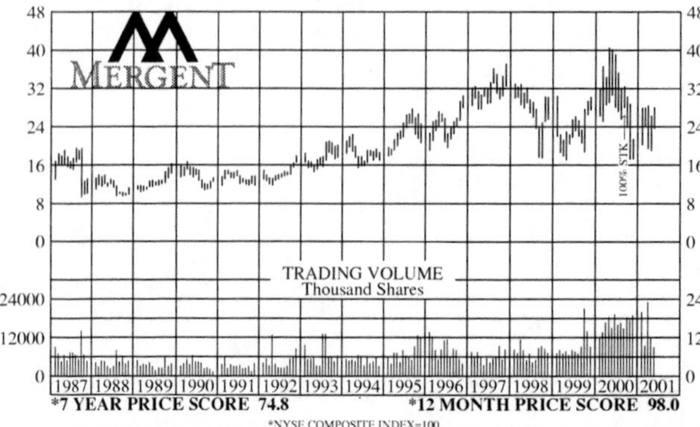

*7 YEAR PRICE SCORE 74.8 *12 MONTH PRICE SCORE 98.0

*NYSE COMPOSITE INDEX=100

INTERIM EARNINGS (Per Share):

Qtr.	Sept.	Dec.	Mar.	June
1995-96	0.51	0.54	0.56	0.55
1996-97	0.49	0.53	0.55	0.57
1997-98	0.51	0.64	0.52	0.22
1998-99	0.21	0.37	0.37	1.51
1999-00	0.32	0.19	0.47	0.74
2000-01	0.81	0.78	...	...

INTERIM DIVIDENDS (Per Share):

Amt.	Decl.	Ex.	Rec.	Pay.
0.15Q	7/28/00	9/13/00	9/15/00	10/02/00
100% STK	9/05/00	9/29/00	9/18/00	9/28/00
0.075Q	11/20/00	12/13/00	12/15/00	1/02/01
0.075Q	1/30/01	3/14/01	3/16/01	4/02/01
0.075Q	5/25/01	6/13/01	6/15/01	7/02/01

Indicated div.: $0.30 (Div. Reinv. Plan)

CAPITALIZATION (6/30/00):

	($000)	(%)
Long-Term Debt	1,438,610	43.1
Common & Surplus	1,901,971	56.9
Total	3,340,581	100.0

RECENT DEVELOPMENTS: For the quarter ended 12/29/00, net income was $72.2 million versus $15.1 million the year before, partially due to the acquisition of EBV Group and RKE Systems. Results for fiscal 2000 included after-tax special charges totaling $17.6 million. Sales jumped 61.3% to $3.39 billion. Electronics Marketing segment sales grew 44.9% to $2.18 billion, while Computer Marketing segment sales rose 56.7% to $720.2 million. Revenues for the Avnet Applied Computing segment more than tripled to $487.7 million.

PROSPECTS: Recently, AVT acquired two companies, EBV Group and RKE Systems, from German-based E.ON AG for approximately $740.0 million. Going forward, results should continue to be positively affected by the transaction. Separately, the EM group opened a 35,000 square foot logistics and material management and warehouse facility located in Guadalajara, Mexico. On 3/22/01, AVT agreed to acquire Kent Electronics Corporation in a stock-for-stock merger transaction valued at approximately $550.0 million.

BUSINESS

AVNET, INC. is an industrial distributor of electronic components and computer products. The Electronics Marketing (EM) group engages in global marketing, assembly and processing of electronic and electromechanical components and certain computer products. In addition, the EM group offers value-added services such as inventory replacement systems, kitting, connector and cable assembly and semiconductor programming. The Computer Marketing (CM) group distributes computer products to value-added resellers and end users internationally. The Applied Computing (AC) group markets original equipment manufacturer system- and sub-system level components. The Corporate services group performs non-sales and marketing back-office functions. AVT serves customers in 63 countries.

REVENUES

(06/30/00)	($000)	(%)
Electronics Marketing	6,638,200	72.4
Computer Marketing	1,863,500	20.3
Avner Applied Computing	670,500	7.3
Total	9,172,200	100.0

ANNUAL FINANCIAL DATA

	6/30/00	7/2/99	6/26/98	6/27/97	6/28/96	6/30/95	7/1/94
Earnings Per Share	**3 1.75**	**2.43**	**2 1.90**	**2.13**	**2.16**	**1.66**	**1 1.08**
Cash Flow Per Share	**2.66**	**3.16**	**2.54**	**2.70**	**...**	**2.04**	**1.47**
Tang. Book Val. Per Share	**11.83**	**14.38**	**11.72**	**12.47**	**11.64**	**10.05**	**13.63**
Dividends Per Share	**0.30**	**0.30**	**0.30**	**0.30**	**0.30**	**0.30**	**0.30**
Dividend Payout %	**17.1**	**12.3**	**15.8**	**14.1**	**13.9**	**18.1**	**27.8**
INCOME STATEMENT (IN MILLIONS):							
Total Revenues	9,172.2	6,350.0	5,916.3	5,390.6	5,207.8	4,300.0	3,552.5
Costs & Expenses	8,762.7	6,124.5	5,594.5	5,013.5	4,815.3	4,001.7	3,351.1
Depreciation & Amort.	75.6	52.3	50.5	49.4	43.5	36.9	31.8
Operating Income	334.0	173.2	271.2	327.7	349.0	261.5	169.6
Net Interest Inc./(Exp.)	d84.3	d52.1	d40.0	d26.1	d25.9	d23.2	d14.7
Income Before Income Taxes	254.5	375.3	267.3	313.4	325.0	243.4	154.8
Income Taxes	109.4	200.8	115.9	130.7	136.8	103.1	66.7
Net Income	3 145.1	174.5	2 151.4	182.8	188.3	140.3	1 88.1
Cash Flow	220.7	226.7	202.0	232.2	231.8	177.1	119.9
Average Shs. Outstg. (000)	83,124	71,834	79,646	86,098	...	86,842	81,694
BALANCE SHEET (IN MILLIONS):							
Cash & Cash Equivalents	167.2	312.0	82.6	59.3	47.8	49.3	53.9
Total Current Assets	3,873.3	2,313.3	2,068.4	1,896.4	1,813.1	1,524.3	1,264.1
Net Property	289.9	194.0	155.5	181.5	176.9	145.6	115.1
Total Assets	5,244.4	2,984.7	2,733.7	2,594.1	2,521.7	2,125.6	1,787.7
Total Current Liabilities	1,903.8	795.9	607.1	577.5	519.2	467.2	376.1
Long-Term Obligations	1,438.6	791.2	810.7	514.4	497.2	419.0	303.1
Net Stockholders' Equity	1,902.0	1,397.6	1,315.9	1,502.2	1,505.2	1,239.4	1,108.5
Net Working Capital	1,969.5	1,517.5	1,461.3	1,319.0	1,293.9	1,057.1	888.0
Year-end Shs. Outstg. (000)	88,361	70,382	72,926	82,210	86,842	81,584	81,318
STATISTICAL RECORD:							
Operating Profit Margin %	3.6	2.7	4.6	6.1	6.7	6.1	4.8
Net Profit Margin %	1.6	2.7	2.6	3.4	3.6	3.3	2.5
Return on Equity %	7.6	12.5	11.5	12.2	12.5	11.3	7.9
Return on Assets %	2.8	5.8	5.5	7.0	7.5	6.6	4.9
Debt/Total Assets %	27.4	26.5	29.7	19.8	19.7	19.7	17.0
Price Range	40.56-17.19	30.47-17.00	33.13-17.47	37.25-27.56	30.56-19.00	27.81-17.88	22.50-15.38
P/E Ratio	23.2-9.8	12.5-7.0	17.4-9.2	17.5-13.0	14.2-8.8	16.8-10.8	20.8-14.2
Average Yield %	1.0	1.3	1.2	0.9	1.2	1.3	1.6

Statistics are as originally reported. Adj. for 2-for-1 stk. split, 9/00. 1 Incl. non-recurr. chrg. $22.7 mill. fr restruc. 2 Incl. non-recurr. gain $33.8 mill. 3 Incl. after-tax spec. chrgs. of $30.4 mill., 6/00; $21.6 mill., 12/00.

OFFICERS:
R. Vallee, Chmn., C.E.O.
R. Sadowski, Sr. V.P., C.F.O.
D. R. Birk, Sr. V.P., Sec., Gen. Couns.

INVESTOR CONTACT: John J. Hovis, Sr V.P., Investor Relations, (480) 643-7291

PRINCIPAL OFFICE: 2211 South 47th Street, Phoenix, AZ 85034

TELEPHONE NUMBER: (480) 643-2000
FAX: (480) 643-7370
WEB: www.avnet.com

NO. OF EMPLOYEES: 11,500 (avg.)

SHAREHOLDERS: 5,500 (approx. record)

ANNUAL MEETING: In Nov.

INCORPORATED: NY, July, 1955

INSTITUTIONAL HOLDINGS:
No. of Institutions: 235
Shares Held: 84,218,504
% Held: 91.2

INDUSTRY: Electronic parts and equipment (SIC: 5065)

TRANSFER AGENT(S): The Bank of New York, New York, NY

NYSE SYMBOL AVP
Rec. Pr. 42.32 (4/30/01)

AVON PRODUCTS, INC.

YIELD 1.8%
P/E RATIO 20.8

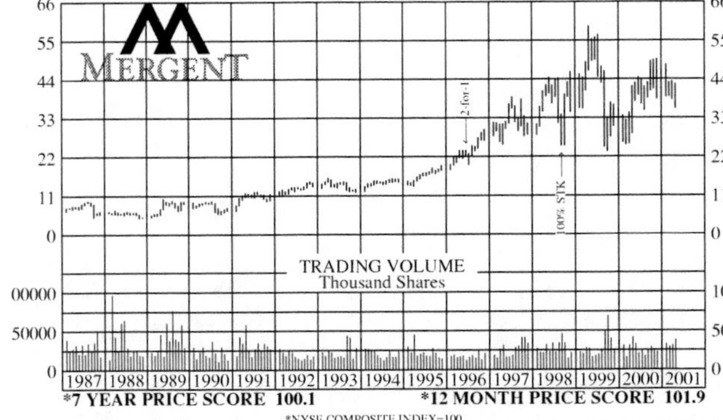

*7 YEAR PRICE SCORE 100.1 *12 MONTH PRICE SCORE 101.9

*NYSE COMPOSITE INDEX=100

INTERIM EARNINGS (Per Share):

Qtr.	Mar.	June	Sept.	Dec.
1996	0.14	0.32	0.24	0.50
1997	0.16	0.36	0.26	0.51
1998	d0.12	0.42	0.16	0.56
1999	d0.19	0.46	0.34	0.58
2000	0.31	0.52	0.39	0.81

INTERIM DIVIDENDS (Per Share):

Amt.	Decl.	Ex.	Rec.	Pay.
0.185Q	5/04/00	5/15/00	5/17/00	6/01/00
0.185Q	8/02/00	8/14/00	8/16/00	9/01/00
0.185Q	11/02/00	11/14/00	11/16/00	12/01/00
0.19Q	2/01/01	2/13/01	2/15/01	3/01/01
0.19Q	5/03/01	5/14/01	5/16/01	6/01/01

Indicated div.: $0.76 (Div. Reinv. Plan)

CAPITALIZATION (12/31/00):

	($000)	(%)
Long-Term Debt	1,108,200	120.0
Deferred Income Tax	31,300	3.4
Common & Surplus	d215,800	-23.4
Total	923,700	100.0

RECENT DEVELOPMENTS: For the year ended 12/31/00, the Company reported income of $485.1 million, before an accounting change charge of $6.7 million, compared with net income of $302.4 million in the prior year. Earnings for 1999 included a special charge of $105.2 million. Total revenues totaled $5.71 billion, an increase of 8.0% versus $5.29 billion the year before. Operating profit climbed 43.6% to $788.7 million from $549.4 million in the previous year.

PROSPECTS: Going foward, AVP is targeting mid-single digit sales growth, after an estimated negative foreign currency impact of 6.0%. In local currency terms, AVP is targeting double-digit sales growth for 2001. In addition, the Company also expects double-digit earnings growth to result in earnings per share of $2.10 to $2.12 per share. Separately, AVP plans to continue to increase strategic spending in 2001 for a total of $40.0 million to $50.0 million.

BUSINESS

AVON PRODUCTS, INC. is a diversified company that concentrates on the direct selling of beauty products through Avon U.S. and Avon International. In the direct selling beauty business, sales are currently made directly to consumers principally through Avon representatives in 139 countries. Products sold include cosmetics, fragrances, toiletries, fashion jewelry and accessories, gift and decorative products, home entertainment, and health and nutrition products. Avon product lines include such recognizable brands as ANEW, SKIN-SO-SOFT, AVON COLOR, FAR AWAY, RARE GOLD, PERCEIVE AND AVON SKIN CARE. The products are sold by a worldwide total of approximately 3.4 million representatives, over 452,000 of whom are in the United States. In 2000, contributions to net sales by geographic area consisted of: North America, 37.9%; Latin America, 32.4%; Europe, 15.6% and Pacific, 14.1%.

ANNUAL FINANCIAL DATA

	12/31/00	12/31/99	12/31/98	12/31/97	12/31/96	12/31/95	12/31/94
Earnings Per Share	**[3] 2.02**	**[4] 1.17**	**[2] 1.02**	**1.27**	**1.19**	**[1] 1.05**	**[1][3] 0.94**
Cash Flow Per Share	**2.40**	**1.49**	**1.29**	**1.54**	**1.43**	**1.26**	**1.14**
Tang. Book Val. Per Share	...	...	**1.09**	**1.08**	**0.91**	**0.71**	**0.67**
Dividends Per Share	**0.74**	**0.72**	**0.68**	**0.63**	**0.58**	**0.53**	**0.47**
Dividend Payout %	**36.6**	**61.5**	**66.7**	**49.6**	**48.7**	**50.0**	**50.6**
INCOME STATEMENT (IN MILLIONS):							
Total Revenues	5,714.6	5,289.1	5,212.7	5,079.4	4,814.2	4,492.1	4,266.5
Costs & Expenses	4,828.8	4,656.7	4,667.5	4,469.5	4,204.9	3,926.3	3,715.2
Depreciation & Amort.	97.1	83.0	72.0	72.1	64.5	58.3	55.7
Operating Income	788.7	549.4	473.2	537.8	544.8	507.5	495.6
Net Interest Inc./(Exp.)	d76.2	d32.1	d18.8	d18.8	d25.5	d21.9	d28.7
Income Before Income Taxes	691.0	506.6	455.9	534.9	510.4	465.0	433.8
Income Taxes	201.7	204.2	190.8	197.9	191.4	176.4	163.5
Equity Earnings/Minority Int.	d4.2	...	4.9	1.8	d1.1	d2.5	d5.5
Net Income	[3] 485.1	[4] 302.4	[2] 270.0	338.8	317.9	[1] 286.1	[1][3] 264.8
Cash Flow	582.2	385.4	342.0	410.9	382.4	344.4	320.5
Average Shs. Outstg. (000)	242,950	259,370	265,950	267,000	267,400	272,960	282,360
BALANCE SHEET (IN MILLIONS):							
Cash & Cash Equivalents	122.7	117.4	105.6	141.9	184.5	151.4	214.8
Total Current Assets	1,545.7	1,337.8	1,341.4	1,344.0	1,349.6	1,215.0	1,150.3
Net Property	768.4	734.8	669.9	611.0	566.6	537.8	528.4
Total Assets	2,826.4	2,528.6	2,433.5	2,272.9	2,222.4	2,052.8	1,978.3
Total Current Liabilities	1,359.3	1,712.8	1,329.5	1,355.9	1,391.3	1,245.3	1,141.0
Long-Term Obligations	1,108.2	701.4	201.0	102.2	104.5	114.2	116.5
Net Stockholders' Equity	d215.8	d406.1	285.1	285.0	241.7	192.7	185.6
Net Working Capital	186.4	d375.0	11.9	d11.9	d41.7	d30.3	9.3
Year-end Shs. Outstg. (000)	354,536	237,895	262,520	263,628	265,640	270,468	276,296
STATISTICAL RECORD:							
Operating Profit Margin %	13.8	10.4	9.1	10.6	11.3	11.3	11.6
Net Profit Margin %	8.5	5.7	5.2	6.7	6.6	6.4	6.2
Return on Equity %	...	...	94.7	118.9	131.5	148.5	142.7
Return on Assets %	17.2	12.0	11.1	14.9	14.3	13.9	13.4
Debt/Total Assets %	39.2	27.7	8.3	4.5	4.7	5.6	5.9
Price Range	49.75-25.25	59.13-23.31	46.25-25.00	39.00-25.31	29.75-18.16	19.59-13.50	15.91-12.09
P/E Ratio	24.6-12.5	50.5-19.9	45.3-24.5	30.7-19.9	25.0-15.3	18.7-12.9	17.0-12.9
Average Yield %	2.0	1.7	1.9	2.0	2.4	3.2	3.4

Statistics are as originally reported. Adj. for stk. splits: 2-for-1, 9/98; 6/96 [1] Bef. disc. oper. loss 1995, $29.6 mill.; 1994, $25.0 mill. [2] Incl. non-recurr. chrg. 1998, $70.5 mill. [3] Bef. acctg. change chrg. 2000, $6.7 mill.; 1994, $45.2 mill. [4] Incl. pre-tax special chrg. of $105.2 mill.

OFFICERS:
S. C. Gault, Chmn.
S. J. Kropf, Pres., C.O.O.
R. J. Corti, Exec. V.P., C.F.O.

INVESTOR CONTACT: Carol Murray-Negron, V.P., Inv. Rel., (212) 282-5320

PRINCIPAL OFFICE: 1345 Avenue of the Americas, New York, NY 10105-0196

TELEPHONE NUMBER: (212) 282-5000
FAX: (212) 282-6035
WEB: www.avon.com

NO. OF EMPLOYEES: 43,000 (avg.)

SHAREHOLDERS: 22,964

ANNUAL MEETING: In May

INCORPORATED: NY, Jan., 1916

INSTITUTIONAL HOLDINGS:
No. of Institutions: 382
Shares Held: 198,646,957
% Held: 83.5

INDUSTRY: Toilet preparations (SIC: 2844)

TRANSFER AGENT(S): First Chicago Trust Company of New York, Jersey City, NJ

NYSE SYMBOL AVX
Rec. Pr. 18.70 (5/31/01)

AVX CORPORATION

YIELD 0.8%
P/E RATIO 8.0

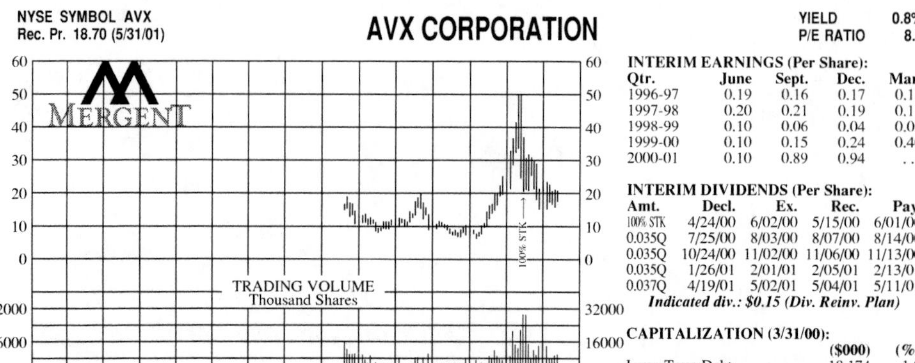

INTERIM EARNINGS (Per Share):

Qtr.	June	Sept.	Dec.	Mar.
1996-97	0.19	0.16	0.17	0.18
1997-98	0.20	0.21	0.19	0.17
1998-99	0.10	0.06	0.04	0.05
1999-00	0.10	0.15	0.24	0.40
2000-01	0.10	0.89	0.94	...

INTERIM DIVIDENDS (Per Share):

Amt.	Decl.	Ex.	Rec.	Pay.
100% STK	4/24/00	6/02/00	5/15/00	6/01/00
0.035Q	7/25/00	8/03/00	8/07/00	8/14/00
0.035Q	10/24/00	11/02/00	11/06/00	11/13/00
0.035Q	1/26/01	2/01/01	2/05/01	2/13/01
0.037Q	4/19/01	5/02/01	5/04/01	5/11/01

Indicated div.: $0.15 (Div. Reinv. Plan)

CAPITALIZATION (3/31/00):

	($000)	(%)
Long-Term Debt	18,174	1.8
Deferred Income Tax	4,894	0.5
Common & Surplus	982,021	97.7
Total	1,005,089	100.0

RECENT DEVELOPMENTS: For the quarter ended 12/31/00, net income amounted to $166.1 million versus $42.5 million in the comparable quarter of fiscal 2000. Results for fiscal 2000 included income of $3.0 million related to a settlement for defective materials from a supplier. Earnings benefited from higher average selling prices driven by strong demand of passive electronic components, particularly in the telecommunications and information technology markets. Net sales jumped 70.4% to $709.5 million.

PROSPECTS: Sales growth continues to be driven by strong demand for passive components and a favorable pricing environment. Over the next year, earnings should benefit from strong worldwide demand for electronic components, cost-saving initiatives, and the conversion to base metals from palladium metals in the production of certain mutli-layer ceramic capacitors. Going forward, the Company plans to significantly offset increasing material costs by reducing its reliance on palladium metals.

BUSINESS

AVX CORPORATION is a manufacturer and supplier of a broad line of passive electronic components and related products. A substantial portion of AVX's electronic component sales are of ceramic and tantalum capacitors, both in leaded and surface-mount versions. Capacitors are used in virtually all electronic products and applications to store, filter and regulate electrical energy. The Company also manufactures and sells electronic connectors and distributes and sells certain passive components and connectors. In fiscal 2000, sales were derived as follows: U.S., 40.5%; Europe, 26.5%; Asia, 31.8%; and other, 1.2%. AVX is 70.0% owned by Kyocera.

ANNUAL FINANCIAL DATA

	3/31/00	3/31/99	3/31/98	3/31/97	3/31/96	3/31/95	3/31/94
Earnings Per Share	**0.90**	**0.24**	**0.76**	**0.69**	**0.79**	**0.44**	**[1] 0.21**
Cash Flow Per Share	**1.46**	**0.78**	**1.26**	**1.16**	**1.19**	**0.79**	**0.53**
Tang. Book Val. Per Share	**5.21**	**4.36**	**4.63**	**3.96**	**3.34**	**2.43**	**2.10**
Dividends Per Share	**0.13**	**0.13**	**0.12**	**0.11**	**0.03**	...	...
Dividend Payout %	**14.4**	**53.1**	**15.5**	**15.6**	**3.2**	...	...
INCOME STATEMENT (IN MILLIONS):							
Total Revenues	1,630.3	1,245.5	1,267.7	1,126.2	1,207.8	988.9	795.5
Costs & Expenses	1,309.8	1,097.4	993.3	872.0	933.2	818.1	684.7
Depreciation & Amort.	99.3	94.7	87.7	82.2	69.9	60.6	55.2
Operating Income	221.2	53.3	186.7	171.9	204.7	110.2	55.6
Net Interest Inc./(Exp.)	6.8	5.7	9.3	5.5	2.7	d0.2	d2.0
Income Before Income Taxes	232.1	60.7	197.4	178.4	209.1	111.2	55.0
Income Taxes	75.2	19.2	62.8	57.1	71.3	36.3	19.8
Net Income	156.9	41.5	134.7	121.3	137.7	74.9	[1] 35.2
Cash Flow	256.2	136.2	222.3	203.6	207.6	135.5	90.4
Average Shs. Outstg. (000)	174,977	174,168	176,560	176,000	174,350	171,600	171,600
BALANCE SHEET (IN MILLIONS):							
Cash & Cash Equivalents	175.7	173.1	201.9	188.6	131.6	43.8	26.9
Total Current Assets	846.8	663.5	722.2	638.5	561.1	397.0	321.2
Net Property	372.8	304.2	282.3	271.6	266.5	232.0	209.2
Total Assets	1,308.3	1,058.0	1,048.7	949.3	867.5	670.7	574.0
Total Current Liabilities	282.7	192.3	169.4	181.8	203.2	172.0	131.7
Long-Term Obligations	18.2	12.7	8.4	12.2	8.5	9.5	10.4
Net Stockholders' Equity	982.0	830.6	850.9	732.0	624.0	456.3	400.8
Net Working Capital	564.1	471.3	552.8	456.7	357.9	225.0	189.5
Year-end Shs. Outstg. (000)	174,493	172,510	176,367	176,000	176,000	171,600	171,600
STATISTICAL RECORD:							
Operating Profit Margin %	13.6	4.3	14.7	15.3	16.9	11.1	7.0
Net Profit Margin %	9.6	3.3	10.6	10.8	11.4	7.6	4.4
Return on Equity %	16.0	5.0	15.8	16.6	22.1	16.4	8.8
Return on Assets %	12.0	3.9	12.8	12.8	15.9	11.2	6.1
Debt/Total Assets %	1.4	1.2	0.8	1.3	1.0	1.4	1.8
Price Range	25.22-6.28	11.69-6.75	19.81-8.84	13.75-8.00	19.00-10.56	...	...
P/E Ratio	28.0-7.0	48.7-28.1	26.1-11.6	19.9-11.6	24.0-13.4	...	...
Average Yield %	0.8	1.4	0.8	1.0	0.2	...	...

Statistics are as originally reported. Adj. for stk. split., 2-for-1, 6/00. [1] Bef. acctg. change chrg. $5.0 mill.

OFFICERS:
B. P. Rosen, Chmn., C.E.O.
J. S. Gilbertson, Pres., C.O.O.
K. P. Cummings, C.F.O., V.P., Treas., Sec.

INVESTOR CONTACT: Investor Relations, (843) 946-0466

PRINCIPAL OFFICE: P.O. Box 867, Myrtle Beach, SC 29578

TELEPHONE NUMBER: (843) 946-0466
FAX: (843) 448-6091
WEB: www.avxcorp.com

NO. OF EMPLOYEES: 18,000 (approx.)

SHAREHOLDERS: 372 (approx.)

ANNUAL MEETING: In July

INCORPORATED: DE, 1972

INSTITUTIONAL HOLDINGS:
No. of Institutions: 146
Shares Held: 39,231,718
% Held: 22.5

INDUSTRY: Electronic connectors (SIC: 3678)

TRANSFER AGENT(S): The American Stock Transfer and Trust Company, New York, NY

NYSE SYMBOL AZR
Rec. Pr. 12.97 (4/30/01)

AZTAR CORPORATION

YIELD ...
P/E RATIO 10.6

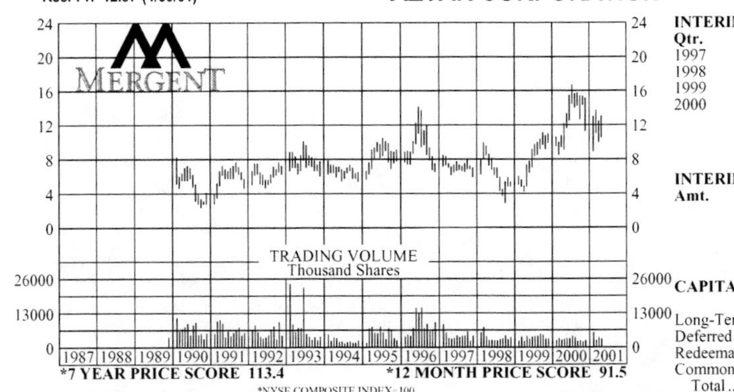

INTERIM EARNINGS (Per Share):

Qtr.	Mar.	June	Sept.	Dec.
1997	0.05	0.07	0.07	d0.11
1998	0.01	0.08	0.12	0.03
1999	0.06	0.13	0.18	0.10
2000	0.25	0.51	0.34	0.12

INTERIM DIVIDENDS (Per Share):

Amt.	Decl.	Ex.	Rec.	Pay.

No dividends paid.

CAPITALIZATION (12/28/00):

	($000)	(%)
Long-Term Debt	463,011	51.6
Deferred Income Tax	5,153	0.6
Redeemable Pfd. Stock	6,400	0.7
Common & Surplus	422,706	47.1
Total	897,270	100.0

RECENT DEVELOPMENTS: For the year ended 12/28/00, AZR reported net income of $53.1 million versus income of $22.1 million, before an after-tax extraordinary loss of $15.7 million, in the prior year. Total revenues increased 6.0% to $848.1 million from $800.3 million the year before. Casino revenues grew 4.7% to $677.1 million. Rooms revenues advanced 11.6% to $72.8 million, while food and beverage revenues rose 7.0% to $57.0 million.

PROSPECTS: The Company announced that it will spend $225.0 million on a major addition to its Tropicana resort in Atlantic City, adding 500 rooms and as many as 50 shops, clubs and restaurants. The expanded facilities will be in a new tower with 200,000 square feet of entertainment space and 20,000 square feet of convention space. AZR expects construction on the tower to begin by the end of 2001 and to be completed in the second half of 2003.

BUSINESS

AZTAR CORPORATION operates in the major domestic gaming markets with casino/hotel facilities in Atlantic City, New Jersey, and in Las Vegas and Laughlin, Nevada. In addition, AZR operates riverboat casinos in Caruthersville, Missouri and Evansville, Indiana. The Tropicana Casino and Resort (formerly TropWorld) encompasses 12 acres and has 220 yards of ocean beach frontage along the Boardwalk in Atlantic City. The Tropicana Resort and Casino is located on a 34-acre site on the southeast corner of the Strip and Tropicana Avenue in Las Vegas. The Ramada Express Hotel and Casino is located on 28 acres in Laughlin, Nevada.

REVENUES

(12/28/00)	($000)	(%)
Casino	677,121	79.8
Rooms	72,829	8.6
Food & Beverage	57,033	6.7
Other	41,105	4.9
Total	848,088	100.0

ANNUAL FINANCIAL DATA

	12/28/00	12/31/99	12/31/98	1/1/98	1/2/97	12/28/95	12/29/94
Earnings Per Share	**5 1.23**	**1 0.46**	**1 0.23**	**4 0.08**	**3 4 0.47**	**3 d0.14**	**1 0.42**
Cash Flow Per Share	**2.54**	**1.69**	**1.44**	**1.26**	**1.73**	**0.97**	**1.47**
Tang. Book Val. Per Share	**10.92**	**9.96**	**10.02**	**9.82**	**9.76**	**9.40**	**9.65**
INCOME STATEMENT (IN MILLIONS):							
Total Revenues	848.1	800.3	806.1	782.4	777.5	572.9	541.4
Costs & Expenses	677.5	655.0	668.8	660.7	666.1	487.4	432.5
Depreciation & Amort.	55.1	55.7	55.7	54.2	52.5	42.8	39.5
Operating Income	115.5	89.6	81.6	67.4	58.9	42.7	69.4
Net Interest Inc./(Exp.)	d40.6	d51.3	d57.4	d60.5	d56.2	d47.8	d46.6
Income Before Income Taxes	70.7	34.4	19.9	2.3	d2.1	d10.2	18.7
Income Taxes	17.6	12.2	8.4	cr2.2	cr22.7	cr5.2	1.9
Equity Earnings/Minority Int.	d4.2	d4.0	d4.3	d4.6	d4.8	d5.1	d4.2
Net Income	5 53.1	1 22.1	1 11.5	4 4.4	3 4 20.6	3 d5.0	1 16.8
Cash Flow	107.7	77.3	66.6	58.0	72.4	37.1	55.6
Average Shs. Outstg. (000)	42,577	46,197	46,614	46,687	42,172	39,026	38,196
BALANCE SHEET (IN MILLIONS):							
Cash & Cash Equivalents	48.1	54.2	58.6	46.1	44.1	26.5	52.1
Total Current Assets	107.2	117.6	121.8	118.8	113.3	73.1	93.8
Net Property	839.6	866.2	887.4	902.9	927.1	853.7	756.3
Total Assets	1,011.7	1,049.0	1,077.7	1,091.5	1,119.6	1,013.2	915.4
Total Current Liabilities	94.1	89.3	100.4	124.7	120.2	102.1	72.7
Long-Term Obligations	463.0	497.6	487.5	491.9	527.0	496.4	430.2
Net Stockholders' Equity	422.7	427.9	454.1	444.0	439.3	359.7	361.4
Net Working Capital	13.1	28.3	21.4	d5.9	d6.9	d28.9	21.1
Year-end Shs. Outstg. (000)	38,697	42,945	45,338	45,199	45,000	38,266	37,459
STATISTICAL RECORD:							
Operating Profit Margin %	13.6	11.2	10.1	8.6	7.6	7.5	12.8
Net Profit Margin %	6.3	2.8	1.4	0.6	2.7	...	3.1
Return on Equity %	12.6	5.2	2.5	1.0	4.7	...	4.7
Return on Assets %	5.3	2.1	1.1	0.4	1.8	...	1.8
Debt/Total Assets %	45.8	47.4	45.2	45.1	47.1	49.0	47.0
Price Range	16.69-8.50	11.13-4.19	9.94-2.88	8.50-5.88	14.13-6.50	10.50-5.63	7.88-5.38
P/E Ratio	13.6-6.9	24.2-9.1	43.2-12.5	106.1-73.3	30.0-13.8	...	18.7-12.8

Statistics are as originally reported. 1 Bef. extra. chrg. $15.7 mill., 1999; $1.3 mill., 1998; chrg. $2.7 mill., 1994. 2 Bef. disc. ops. credit of $1.3 mill., acct. chng. credit of $7.5 mill. & extra. loss of $5.3 mill. 3 Incl. pre-opening expen. of $2.9 mill., 1996; & $7.7 mill., 1995. 4 Incl. tax benefits of $2.2 mill., 1997 & $22.6 mill., 1996. 5 Incl. a non-recurr. tax benef. of $7.5 mill.

OFFICERS:
P. E. Rubeli, Chmn., Pres., C.E.O.
R. M. Haddock, Exec. V.P., C.F.O.
N. W. Armstrong Jr., V.P., Admin., Sec.
N. A. Ciarfalia, Treas.

INVESTOR CONTACT: Joe Cole, Vice-Pres., Corp. Commun., (602) 381-4111

PRINCIPAL OFFICE: 2390 East Camelback Road, Suite 400, Phoenix, AZ 85016-3452

TELEPHONE NUMBER: (602) 381-4100
FAX: (602) 381-4107
WEB: www.aztar.com

NO. OF EMPLOYEES: 10,400 (approx.)

SHAREHOLDERS: 7,656

ANNUAL MEETING: In May

INCORPORATED: DE, June, 1989

INSTITUTIONAL HOLDINGS:
No. of Institutions: 123
Shares Held: 28,907,473
% Held: 76.0

INDUSTRY: Amusement and recreation, nec (SIC: 7999)

TRANSFER AGENT(S): Mellon Investor Services, Los Angeles, CA

NYSE SYMBOL BZ
Rec. Pr. 6.50 (5/31/01)

BAIRNCO CORP.

YIELD 3.1%
P/E RATIO 6.1

*7 YEAR PRICE SCORE 79.1 *12 MONTH PRICE SCORE 100.9

*NYSE COMPOSITE INDEX=100

INTERIM EARNINGS (Per Share):

Qtr.	Mar.	June	Sept.	Dec.
1995	0.18	0.20	0.18	0.19
1996	0.21	0.22	0.20	0.22
1997	0.23	0.25	0.23	0.23
1998	0.24	0.18	0.14	d0.40
1999	0.28	0.29	0.25	0.26
2000	0.32	0.33	0.26	0.16

INTERIM DIVIDENDS (Per Share):

Amt.	Decl.	Ex.	Rec.	Pay.
0.05Q	5/19/00	6/01/00	6/05/00	6/29/00
0.05Q	8/18/00	8/31/00	9/05/00	9/28/00
0.05Q	11/17/00	12/01/00	12/05/00	1/02/01
0.05Q	2/16/01	3/01/01	3/05/01	3/30/01
0.05Q	5/18/01	5/31/01	6/04/01	6/29/01

Indicated div.: $0.20

CAPITALIZATION (12/31/00):

	($000)	(%)
Long-Term Debt	37,456	38.6
Deferred Income Tax	6,967	7.2
Common & Surplus	52,709	54.3
Total	97,132	100.0

RECENT DEVELOPMENTS: For the year ended 12/31/00, net income totaled $8.2 million versus $8.6 million a year earlier. Results for 2000 included a provision for litigation of $1.0 million. Earnings were negatively affected by BZ's Kasco segment. Kasco's U.S. operations experienced significant competitive pressures, while its European operations posted lower operating results due to the negative currency translation effect of the strong U.S. dollar and reduced meat consumption. Revenues rose 11.0% to $187.5 million.

PROSPECTS: Near-term prospects are likely to be pressured by lower results being experienced at the Company's Kasco business unit. Kasco continued to make changes to its structure during the fourth quarter of 2000 in an effort to reduce costs and return the business to profitability during 2001. Separately, on 1/10/01, BZ announced that it has purchased selected net assets of Viscor, Inc., whose engineered-coated products include transfer adhesives, single and double-coated foam and film tapes, and other custom coated products.

BUSINESS

BAIRNCO CORP. is a diversified multinational company that operates two businesses segments. Engineered materials and components are designed, manufactured and sold under the Arlon brand identity to electronic, industrial and commercial markets. These products are based on common technologies in coating, laminating, polymers and dispersion chemistry. Replacement products and services are manufactured and distributed under the Kasco brand identity, principally to supermarkets, meat and deli operations, and meat, poultry and fish processing plants throughout the U.S., Canada and Europe. Kasco also manufactures small band saw blades for cutting metal and wood, and large band saw blades for use at lumber mills. In Canada and France, in addition to providing its replacement products, Kasco also distributes equipment to the supermarket and food processing industries.

BUSINESS LINE ANALYSIS

(12/31/2000)	Rev(%)	Inc(%)
Arlon	77.5	99.5
Kasco	22.5	0.5
Total	100.0	100.0

ANNUAL FINANCIAL DATA

	12/31/00	12/31/99	12/31/98	12/31/97	12/31/96	12/31/95	12/31/94
Earnings Per Share	**2 1.07**	**1.08**	**1 0.18**	**0.94**	**0.85**	**0.75**	**0.69**
Cash Flow Per Share	**2.26**	**1.99**	**0.94**	**1.63**	**1.49**	**1.35**	**1.31**
Tang. Book Val. Per Share	**5.46**	**4.92**	**4.18**	**4.99**	**4.41**	**3.94**	**3.41**
Dividends Per Share	**0.20**	**0.20**	**0.20**	**0.20**	**0.20**	**0.20**	**0.20**
Dividend Payout %	**18.7**	**18.5**	**111.0**	**21.3**	**23.5**	**26.7**	**29.0**
INCOME STATEMENT (IN THOUSANDS):							
Total Revenues	187,513	168,881	156,456	158,708	150,234	150,507	145,522
Costs & Expenses	162,872	146,514	145,239	136,600	128,973	129,560	125,366
Depreciation & Amort.	9,097	7,365	6,688	6,516	6,305	6,314	6,502
Operating Income	15,544	15,002	4,529	15,592	14,956	14,633	13,654
Net Interest Inc./(Exp.)	d3,481	d2,104	d1,998	d1,834	d1,725	d2,026	d2,144
Income Before Income Taxes	12,063	12,898	2,531	13,758	13,231	12,607	11,510
Income Taxes	3,830	4,257	937	4,987	4,896	4,826	4,255
Net Income	2 8,233	8,641	1 1,594	8,771	8,335	7,781	7,255
Cash Flow	17,330	16,006	8,282	15,287	14,640	14,095	13,757
Average Shs. Outstg.	7,678	8,038	8,818	9,350	9,851	10,436	10,500
BALANCE SHEET (IN THOUSANDS):							
Cash & Cash Equivalents	945	660	822	1,217	855	608	1,478
Total Current Assets	70,303	63,209	60,846	57,943	52,500	51,342	52,131
Net Property	47,341	39,682	41,402	39,913	38,276	34,449	36,289
Total Assets	135,769	119,145	118,555	109,286	102,600	98,196	102,772
Total Current Liabilities	35,377	29,953	27,587	22,231	22,159	22,992	25,854
Long-Term Obligations	37,456	26,591	33,471	27,291	24,717	21,236	26,864
Net Stockholders' Equity	52,709	50,167	46,438	52,469	49,464	48,024	43,997
Net Working Capital	34,926	33,256	33,259	35,712	30,341	28,350	26,277
Year-end Shs. Outstg.	7,308	7,797	8,283	8,994	9,414	10,124	10,500
STATISTICAL RECORD:							
Operating Profit Margin %	8.3	8.9	2.9	9.8	10.0	9.7	9.4
Net Profit Margin %	4.4	5.1	1.0	5.5	5.5	5.2	5.0
Return on Equity %	15.6	17.2	3.4	16.7	16.9	16.2	16.5
Return on Assets %	6.1	7.3	1.3	8.0	8.1	7.9	7.1
Debt/Total Assets %	27.6	22.3	28.2	25.0	24.1	21.6	26.1
Price Range	8.00-6.00	8.00-4.63	11.50-5.50	11.38-6.38	8.50-5.50	6.13-3.88	5.50-3.00
P/E Ratio	7.5-5.6	7.4-4.3	63.9-30.5	12.1-6.8	10.0-6.5	8.2-5.2	8.0-4.3
Average Yield %	2.9	3.2	2.4	2.3	2.9	4.0	4.7

Statistics are as originally reported. 1 Incl. one-time pre-tax chrg. of $7.5 mill. 2 Incl. litigation prov. of $1.0 mill.

OFFICERS:
L. E. Fichthorn III, Chmn., C.E.O.
J. W. Lambert, V.P., Treas.
L. D. Smith, V.P., Sec.

INVESTOR CONTACT: James W. Lambert, V.P., Treas., (407) 875-2222

PRINCIPAL OFFICE: 300 Primera Blvd., Suite 432, Lake Mary, FL 32746

TELEPHONE NUMBER: (407) 875-2222
FAX: (407) 875-3398
WEB: www.bairnco.com
NO. OF EMPLOYEES: 926
SHAREHOLDERS: 1,246 (approx. record)
ANNUAL MEETING: In April
INCORPORATED: NY, April, 1981; reincorp., DE, Sept., 1991

INSTITUTIONAL HOLDINGS:
No. of Institutions: 14
Shares Held: 2,600,645
% Held: 35.6

INDUSTRY: Plastics materials and resins (SIC: 2821)

TRANSFER AGENT(S): Trust Company Bank, Atlanta, GA.

NYSE SYMBOL BHI
Rec. Pr. 39.29 (4/30/01)

BAKER HUGHES INC.

YIELD 1.2%
P/E RATIO 126.7

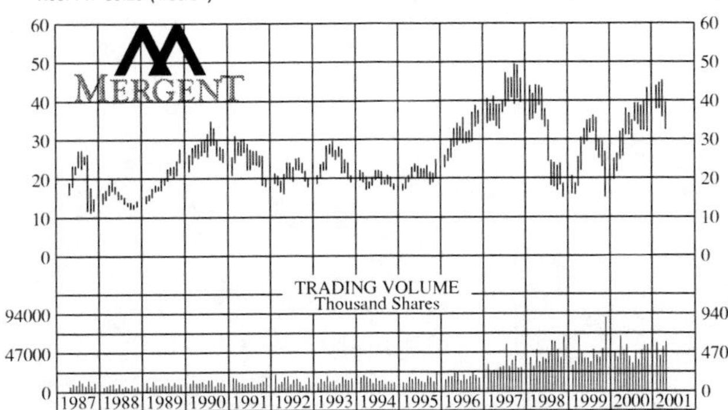

***7 YEAR PRICE SCORE 90.9** ***12 MONTH PRICE SCORE 110.4**

*NYSE COMPOSITE INDEX=100

INTERIM EARNINGS (Per Share):

Qtr.	Dec.	Mar.	June	Sept.
1996-97	0.35	0.39	0.56	d0.49
Qtr.	**Mar.**	**June**	**Sept.**	**Dec.**
1997	...	...	...	0.34
1998	0.35	0.36	d1.65	0.02
1999	0.14	0.22	0.05	d0.25
2000	0.04	0.19	0.20	d0.12

INTERIM DIVIDENDS (Per Share):

Amt.	Decl.	Ex.	Rec.	Pay.
0.115Q	4/26/00	5/04/00	5/08/00	5/26/00
0.115Q	7/26/00	8/03/00	8/07/00	8/25/00
0.115Q	10/25/00	11/02/00	11/06/00	11/24/00
0.115Q	1/24/01	2/01/01	2/05/01	2/23/01
0.115Q	4/25/01	5/03/01	5/07/01	5/25/01

Indicated div.: $0.46

CAPITALIZATION (12/31/00):

	($000)	(%)
Long-Term Debt	2,049,600	39.0
Deferred Income Tax	158,600	3.0
Common & Surplus	3,046,700	58.0
Total	5,254,900	100.0

RECENT DEVELOPMENTS: For the year ended 12/31/00, net income totaled $102.3 million versus $33.3 million a year earlier. Results for 2000 included net unusual charges of $69.6 million and a gain of $14.1 million on trading securities. Results for 1999 included a merger-related credit of $1.6 million, net unusual charges of $4.8 million, and a gain of $31.5 million on trading securities. Revenues rose 5.9% to $5.23 billion. Prior year amounts have been reclassified to reinstate Baker Process as a continuing operation.

PROSPECTS: Although the outlook for North American gas-directed exploration and production spending remains strong, capacity constraints of service companies and the availability of rigs and crews could moderate future activity growth. BHI noted that the spending increases for 2001 that its customers have announced have been about 15.0% to 20.0%, with the majority of the gains likely to be directed outside of North America. As a result, BHI is projecting full-year earnings per share to be between $1.10 and $1.20.

BUSINESS

BAKER HUGHES INC. is engaged in oilfield and process industries. BHI also manufactures and sells other products and provides services to industries that are not related to the oilfield or continuous process industries. The oilfield services segment supplies wellbore related products, services and systems to the worldwide oil and gas industry. Through its six oilfield service operations, Baker Atlas, Baker Hughes INTEQ, Baker Oil Tools, Baker Petrolite, Centrilift and Hughes Christensen, BHI provides equipment, products and services for drilling, formation evaluation, completion and production of oil and gas wells. The Baker Process division provides a broad range of separation equipment and systems to concentrate product or separate and remove waste material in the mineral, industrial, pulp and paper and municipal industries. BHI also owns 30.0% of the Western GECO seismic venture, which was formed in November 2000 with Schlumberger Limited. On 8/10/98, the Company acquired Western Atlas, Inc.

REVENUES

(12/31/00)	($000)	(%)
Oilfield	4,910,800	93.8
Process	323,000	6.2
Total	5,233,800	100.0

ANNUAL FINANCIAL DATA

	12/31/00	12/31/99	[1] 12/31/98	[6] 12/31/97	9/30/97	9/30/96	9/30/95
Earnings Per Share	[5] 0.31	[4] 0.16	[2] d0.92	0.34	[3] 0.71	1.23	[3] 0.67
Cash Flow Per Share	2.14	2.52	1.43	...	1.93	2.30	1.94
Tang. Book Val. Per Share	4.64	4.17	3.98	6.26	9.16	6.45	5.21
Dividends Per Share	0.46	0.46	0.46	0.46	0.46	0.46	0.46
Dividend Payout %	148.3	287.3	...	135.3	64.8	37.4	68.6
INCOME STATEMENT (IN MILLIONS):							
Total Revenues	5,233.8	4,546.7	6,311.9	1,572.9	3,685.4	3,027.7	2,637.5
Costs & Expenses	4,227.3	3,561.5	5,689.3	1,228.6	3,239.5	2,565.2	2,227.0
Depreciation & Amort.	611.5	778.4	758.3	141.7	186.0	155.8	154.5
Operating Income	395.0	206.8	d135.7	202.6	259.9	306.7	255.9
Net Interest Inc./(Exp.)	d168.5	d154.0	d145.4	d23.4	d46.8	d52.1	d50.8
Income Before Income Taxes	236.0	84.3	d281.1	179.2	213.1	298.9	205.1
Income Taxes	133.7	32.0	16.3	68.0	104.0	122.5	85.1
Equity Earnings/Minority Int.	d4.6	...	...	...	...	...	...
Net Income	[5] 102.3	[4] 52.3	[2] d297.4	111.2	[3] 109.1	176.4	[3] 120.0
Cash Flow	713.8	830.7	364.6	252.9	295.1	332.2	266.5
Average Shs. Outstg. (000)	332,900	329,900	321,700	...	153,100	144,406	141,326
BALANCE SHEET (IN MILLIONS):							
Cash & Cash Equivalents	34.6	16.9	16.6	41.9	8.6	7.7	6.8
Total Current Assets	2,486.6	2,329.8	2,724.5	2,919.8	2,220.5	1,716.4	1,564.8
Net Property	1,378.7	2,010.2	2,292.3	1,979.0	982.9	599.0	575.1
Total Assets	6,452.7	7,039.8	7,810.8	7,230.6	4,756.3	3,297.4	3,166.6
Total Current Liabilities	987.8	1,000.2	1,309.9	1,417.1	936.3	635.3	580.1
Long-Term Obligations	2,049.6	2,706.0	2,726.3	1,605.3	771.8	673.6	798.4
Net Stockholders' Equity	3,046.7	3,071.1	3,199.4	3,519.0	2,604.6	1,689.2	1,513.6
Net Working Capital	1,498.8	1,329.6	1,414.6	1,502.7	1,284.2	1,081.1	984.7
Year-end Shs. Outstg. (000)	333,700	329,800	327,100	316,800	169,100	144,553	142,237
STATISTICAL RECORD:							
Operating Profit Margin %	7.5	4.5	...	12.9	7.1	10.1	9.7
Net Profit Margin %	2.0	1.2	...	7.1	3.0	5.8	4.5
Return on Equity %	3.4	1.7	...	3.2	4.2	10.4	7.9
Return on Assets %	1.6	0.7	...	1.5	2.3	5.3	3.8
Debt/Total Assets %	31.8	38.4	34.9	22.2	16.2	20.4	25.2
Price Range	43.38-19.63	36.25-15.00	44.13-15.00	49.63-32.63	49.63-32.63	38.88-22.75	24.88-16.75
P/E Ratio	139.9-63.3	226.4-93.7	...	145.9-95.9	69.9-45.9	31.6-18.5	37.1-25.0
Average Yield %	1.5	1.8	1.6	1.1	1.1	1.5	2.2

Statistics are as originally reported. [1] Refl. acq. of Western Atlas, Inc. [2] Incl. chrgs. totaling $414.1 mill. [3] Bef. acctg. chrg. 9/30/97, $12.1 mill.; chrg. 9/30/95, $14.6 mill. [4] Incl. credit of $7.2 mill.; bef. loss of $19.0 mill. fr. disc. ops. [5] Incl. net unusual chrg. of $69.6 mill. & $14.1 mill. gain on trading securities. [6] 3 mos. only due to fiscal yr.-end chge.

OFFICERS:
M. E. Wiley, Chmn., Pres., C.E.O.
G. S. Finley, Sr. V.P., C.F.O.
A. J. Szescila, Sr. V.P., C.O.O.

INVESTOR CONTACT: Gary R. Flaharty, Dir., Investor Relations, (713) 439-8039

PRINCIPAL OFFICE: 3900 Essex Lane, Houston, TX 77027-5177

TELEPHONE NUMBER: (713) 439-8600
FAX: (713) 739-8699
WEB: www.bakerhughes.com

NO. OF EMPLOYEES: 24,500 (avg.)

SHAREHOLDERS: 30,700 (approx. record)

ANNUAL MEETING: In Apr.

INCORPORATED: DE, Apr., 1987

INSTITUTIONAL HOLDINGS:
No. of Institutions: 399
Shares Held: 284,351,743
% Held: 84.9

INDUSTRY: Oil and gas field machinery (SIC: 3533)

TRANSFER AGENT(S): Mellon Investor Services, Ridgefield Park, NJ

NYSE SYMBOL BEZ
Rec. Pr. 21.00 (5/31/01)

BALDOR ELECTRIC COMPANY

YIELD 2.5%
P/E RATIO 15.8

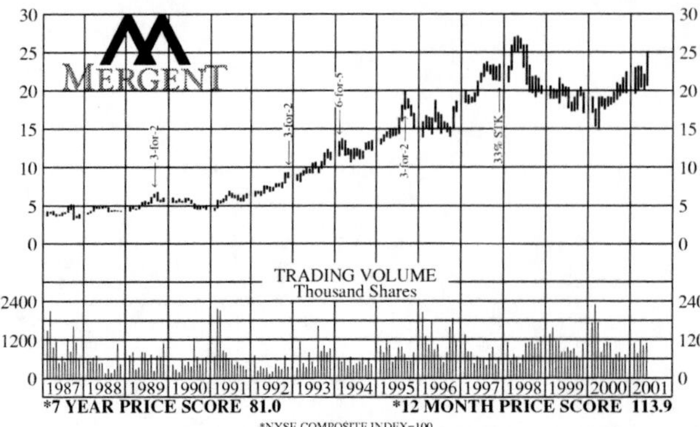

***7 YEAR PRICE SCORE 81.0** ***12 MONTH PRICE SCORE 113.9**

*NYSE COMPOSITE INDEX=100

INTERIM EARNINGS (Per Share):

Qtr.	Mar.	June	Sept.	Dec.
1997	0.26	0.28	0.28	0.28
1998	0.31	0.30	0.29	0.27
1999	0.29	0.30	0.30	0.30
2000	0.35	0.36	0.33	0.29

INTERIM DIVIDENDS (Per Share):

Amt.	Decl.	Ex.	Rec.	Pay.
0.12Q	5/01/00	6/07/00	6/09/00	6/30/00
0.13Q	8/15/00	9/13/00	9/15/00	9/29/00
0.13Q	11/16/00	12/08/00	12/12/00	1/02/01
0.13Q	2/05/01	3/07/01	3/09/01	3/30/01
0.13Q	4/28/01	6/06/01	6/08/01	6/29/01

Indicated div.: $0.52 (Div. Reinv. Plan)

CAPITALIZATION (12/30/00):

	($000)	(%)
Long-Term Debt	99,832	26.5
Deferred Income Tax	16,683	4.4
Common & Surplus	260,845	69.1
Total	377,360	100.0

RECENT DEVELOPMENTS: For the twelve months ended 12/30/00, net income improved 5.8% to $46.3 million from $43.7 million in 1999. Net sales jumped 6.1% to $623.1 million from $585.6 million in the previous year. Gross profit climbed 6.3% to $197.4 million from $185.7 million the year before. Operating profit advanced 6.1% to $85.8 million versus $80.8 million in the prior year. Earnings before income taxes increased 5.0% to $74.0 million.

PROSPECTS: The Company announced it has received Food and Drug Administration approval to market the Bard Stinger Ablation Catheter for the treatment of cardiac arrhythmias. Separately, the Company announced that it will not exercise its option to acquire the capital stock of Endologix, Inc. Going forward, BEZ is moving aggressively to introduce additional new products, expand their sales force, and add customers in new markets.

BUSINESS

BALDOR ELECTRIC COMPANY designs, manufactures and markets a line of electric motors, adjustable speed drives and soft starters that are used with electric motors. The electric motors BEZ makes range from 1/50 HP through 700 HP D.C. and ½ HP through 800 HP A.C. The Company sells industrial control products, which include servo products, DC controls, and inverter and vector drives. BEZ's motors and drives are designed, manufactured and marketed for general purposes and individual customer requirements and specifications.

QUARTERLY DATA

(12/30/2000)($000)	REV	INC
1st Quarter	158,019	12,220
2nd Quarter	163,190	12,535
3rd Quarter	155,376	11,485
4th Quarter	144,657	10,023

ANNUAL FINANCIAL DATA

	12/30/00	1/1/00	1/2/99	1/3/98	12/28/96	12/30/95	12/31/94
Earnings Per Share	**1.34**	**1.19**	**1.17**	**1.09**	**0.97**	**0.84**	**0.70**
Cash Flow Per Share	**1.91**	**1.79**	**1.71**	**1.61**	**1.45**	**1.24**	**1.04**
Tang. Book Val. Per Share	**7.72**	**7.48**	**7.21**	**6.76**	**5.73**	**5.69**	**5.03**
Dividends Per Share	**0.49**	**0.43**	**0.40**	**0.35**	**0.29**	**0.25**	**0.20**
Dividend Payout %	**36.6**	**36.1**	**34.2**	**31.7**	**29.5**	**29.5**	**28.8**
INCOME STATEMENT (IN THOUSANDS):							
Total Revenues	623,080	579,262	591,425	559,783	505,372	475,699	419,820
Costs & Expenses	515,634	475,737	487,802	463,829	420,590	398,742	356,420
Depreciation & Amort.	19,838	20,767	20,511	19,337	17,277	15,583	13,121
Operating Income	87,608	82,758	83,112	76,617	67,505	61,374	50,279
Net Interest Inc./(Exp.)	d3,840	d2,790	d1,721	d2,124	d2,668	d1,260	d1,279
Income Before Income Taxes	74,021	70,523	71,952	65,635	57,192	52,946	43,212
Income Taxes	27,758	26,800	27,342	25,270	22,019	20,641	16,853
Net Income	46,263	43,723	44,610	40,365	35,173	32,305	26,359
Cash Flow	66,101	64,490	65,121	59,702	52,450	47,888	39,480
Average Shs. Outstg.	34,570	36,077	38,067	37,063	36,291	38,521	38,004
BALANCE SHEET (IN THOUSANDS):							
Cash & Cash Equivalents	15,005	42,908	38,789	21,475	25,842	34,809	34,844
Total Current Assets	262,421	272,330	256,488	219,440	218,157	212,095	181,172
Net Property	138,820	124,802	123,137	104,097	95,364	89,071	81,502
Total Assets	464,978	423,941	411,926	355,889	325,486	313,462	283,155
Total Current Liabilities	87,618	88,374	80,362	78,172	71,182	67,026	62,622
Long-Term Obligations	99,832	56,305	57,015	27,929	45,027	25,255	26,303
Net Stockholders' Equity	260,845	266,109	264,292	243,434	200,325	211,377	184,262
Net Working Capital	174,803	183,956	176,126	141,268	146,975	145,069	118,550
Year-end Shs. Outstg.	33,769	35,592	36,677	36,029	34,935	37,160	36,620
STATISTICAL RECORD:							
Operating Profit Margin %	14.1	14.3	14.1	13.7	13.4	12.9	12.0
Net Profit Margin %	7.4	7.5	7.5	7.2	7.0	6.8	6.3
Return on Equity %	17.7	16.4	16.9	16.6	17.6	15.3	14.3
Return on Assets %	9.9	10.3	10.8	11.3	10.8	10.3	9.3
Debt/Total Assets %	21.5	13.3	13.8	7.8	13.8	8.1	9.3
Price Range	22.50-14.88	21.69-17.00	27.19-19.06	23.82-18.19	18.76-13.88	19.88-12.94	13.75-10.63
P/E Ratio	16.8-11.1	18.2-14.3	23.2-16.3	21.8-16.7	19.4-14.3	23.7-15.4	19.8-15.3
Average Yield %	2.6	2.2	1.7	1.6	1.8	1.5	1.6

Statistics are as originally reported. Adj. for a 3-for-2 stock split 12/92 & 9/95; 6-for-5, 1/94; 4-for-3, 12/97.

OFFICERS:
R. S. Boreham Jr., Chmn.
R. L. Qualls, Vice-Chmn.
J. A. McFarland, Pres., C.E.O.
R. E. Tucker, C.F.O., Treas.

INVESTOR CONTACT: Lloyd G. Davis, V.P., C.F.O., Sec. & Treas., (501) 646-4711

PRINCIPAL OFFICE: 5711 R. S. Boreham, Jr. Street, P.O. Box 2400, Ft. Smith, AR 72908-2400

TELEPHONE NUMBER: (501) 646-4711
FAX: (501) 648-5752
WEB: www.baldor.com

NO. OF EMPLOYEES: 4,066

SHAREHOLDERS: 5,715

ANNUAL MEETING: In Apr.

INCORPORATED: MO, Mar., 1920

INSTITUTIONAL HOLDINGS:
No. of Institutions: 108
Shares Held: 10,282,530
% Held: 30.3

INDUSTRY: Motors and generators (SIC: 3621)

TRANSFER AGENT(S): Continental Stock Transfer & Trust Company, New York, NY

NYSE SYMBOL BLL
Rec. Pr. 46.00 (4/30/01)

BALL CORPORATION

YIELD 1.3%
P/E RATIO 21.7

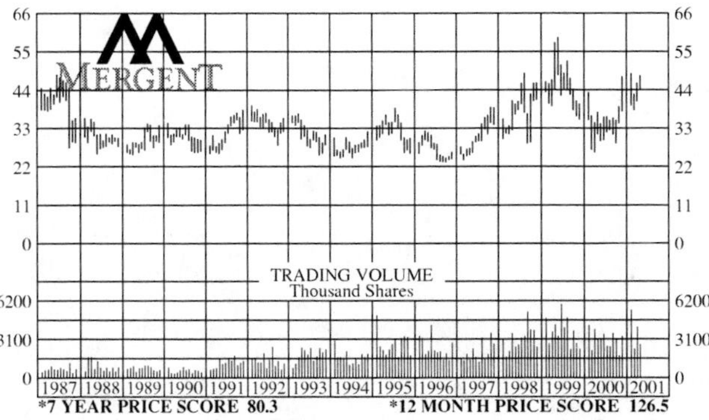

INTERIM EARNINGS (Per Share):

Qtr.	Mar.	June	Sept.	Dec.
1997	0.21	0.67	0.73	0.23
1998	0.14	0.57	0.75	d0.61
1999	0.47	0.96	1.13	0.59
2000	0.62	d0.55	1.43	0.62

INTERIM DIVIDENDS (Per Share):

Amt.	Decl.	Ex.	Rec.	Pay.
0.15Q	7/26/00	8/30/00	9/01/00	9/15/00
0.15Q	10/25/00	11/29/00	12/01/00	12/15/00
0.15Q	1/24/01	2/27/01	3/01/01	3/15/01
0.15Q	4/25/01	5/30/01	6/01/01	6/15/01

Indicated div.: $0.60 (Div. Reinv. Plan)

CAPITALIZATION (12/31/00):

	($000)	(%)
Long-Term Debt	1,293,400	65.0
Minority Interest	14,900	0.7
Preferred Stock	53,400	2.7
Common & Surplus	629,000	31.6
Total	1,990,700	100.0

RECENT DEVELOPMENTS: For the twelve months ended 12/31/00, net earnings fell 34.5% to $68.2 million compared with $104.2 million in 1999. Results for 2000 included a charge of $76.4 million for business consolidation costs and other charges. Total net sales slipped 1.1% to $3.66 billion from $3.71 billion in the prior year. Sales for the packaging segment slipped to $3.30 billion.

PROSPECTS: During 2000, BLL confronted challenging industry environments in both the packaging and aerospace segments. These challenges were met through improved management of the Company's businesses, which included aggressive cost reductions. The actions taken in 2000 and previous years should better position the Company in the competitive markets it serves.

BUSINESS

BALL CORPORATION is a manufacturer of metal and plastic packaging, primarily for beverages and foods, and a supplier of aerospace and other technologies and services to commercial and governmental customers. The packaging segment (90.1% of 2000 sales) includes metal packaging, comprised primarily of two-piece beverage containers and two and three-piece food containers; and PET (polyethylene terephthalate) plastic beverage and food containers. The aerospace and technologies segment (9.9% of 2000 sales) consists of two divisions: the aerospace systems division and the telecommunication products division.

ANNUAL FINANCIAL DATA

	12/31/00	12/31/99	12/31/98	12/31/97	12/31/96	12/31/95	12/31/94
Earnings Per Share	**[5] 2.14**	**3.15**	**[4] 0.91**	**[3] 1.74**	**[2] 0.34**	**[1] d0.72**	**[1] 2.35**
Cash Flow Per Share	**7.24**	**8.15**	**5.64**	**5.35**	**3.42**	**3.06**	**6.63**
Tang. Book Val. Per Share	**...**	**...**	**...**	**20.43**	**19.00**	**17.78**	**14.98**
Dividends Per Share	**0.60**	**0.60**	**0.60**	**0.60**	**0.60**	**0.60**	**0.60**
Dividend Payout %	**28.0**	**19.0**	**65.9**	**34.5**	**176.4**	**...**	**25.5**
INCOME STATEMENT (IN MILLIONS):							
Total Revenues	3,664.7	3,584.2	2,896.4	2,388.5	2,184.4	2,591.7	2,593.4
Costs & Expenses	3,296.5	3,142.5	2,635.9	2,131.6	2,028.0	2,456.1	2,305.6
Depreciation & Amort.	159.1	162.9	154.6	117.5	93.5	113.6	127.0
Operating Income	209.1	278.8	105.9	139.4	62.9	22.0	160.8
Net Interest Inc./(Exp.)	d95.2	d107.6	d78.6	d53.5	d33.3	d37.8	d41.0
Income Before Income Taxes	113.9	171.2	27.3	85.9	29.6	d15.8	119.8
Income Taxes	42.8	64.9	8.8	32.0	7.2	cr0.1	44.7
Equity Earnings/Minority Int.	d2.9	d2.1	13.5	4.4	d9.3	d2.9	d2.1
Net Income	[5] 68.2	104.2	[4] 32.0	[3] 58.3	[2] 13.1	[1] d18.6	[1] 73.0
Cash Flow	224.7	264.4	183.8	173.0	103.7	91.9	196.8
Average Shs. Outstg. (000)	31,017	32,450	32,592	32,311	30,314	30,024	29,662
BALANCE SHEET (IN MILLIONS):							
Cash & Cash Equivalents	25.6	35.8	34.0	25.5	169.2	5.1	10.4
Total Current Assets	969.3	895.8	885.6	798.1	766.6	592.7	698.1
Net Property	1,003.7	1,121.2	1,174.4	919.5	699.0	628.6	779.9
Total Assets	2,649.8	2,732.1	2,854.8	2,090.1	1,700.8	1,612.5	1,759.8
Total Current Liabilities	659.1	670.1	687.6	837.8	511.0	497.5	499.7
Long-Term Obligations	1,293.4	1,351.4	1,520.5	566.4	407.7	320.4	377.0
Net Stockholders' Equity	682.4	690.9	622.3	634.2	604.4	582.7	616.7
Net Working Capital	310.2	225.7	198.0	d39.7	255.6	95.2	198.4
Year-end Shs. Outstg. (000)	28,049	29,817	30,455	30,220	30,519	30,115	29,867
STATISTICAL RECORD:							
Operating Profit Margin %	5.7	7.8	6.2	5.8	2.9	0.8	6.2
Net Profit Margin %	1.9	2.9	1.1	2.4	0.6	...	2.8
Return on Equity %	10.0	15.1	5.1	9.2	4.1	...	12.1
Return on Assets %	2.6	3.8	1.1	2.8	0.8	...	4.1
Debt/Total Assets %	48.8	49.5	53.3	27.1	24.0	19.9	21.4
Price Range	47.94-26.00	59.13-35.38	48.94-28.63	39.00-23.75	32.25-23.13	38.75-25.75	32.13-24.38
P/E Ratio	22.4-12.1	18.8-11.2	53.8-31.5	22.4-13.6	94.8-68.0	...	13.7-10.4
Average Yield %	1.6	1.3	1.5	1.9	2.2	1.9	2.1

Statistics are as originally reported. [1] Incl. $1.4 mill. non-recur. net chg., 1994; Incl. net loss on disp. of bus. & $118.2 mill. oth., 1995. [2] Bef. $11.1 mill. income fr. disc. ops. & incl. $21.0 mill. loss on disp. of bus. [3] Incl. $9.0 mill. gain. [4] Incl. $73.9 mill. chg. for relocation & $600,000 loss fr. deprec. of Thai currency and excl. $12.1 mill. chg. for debt refinan. & $3.3 mill. for acct. costs. [5] Incl. $76.4 mill. chg. fr. bus. consolidation costs & other chgs.

OFFICERS:
G. A. Sissel, Chmn.
R. D. Hoover, Pres., C.E.O.
R. J. Seabrook, Sr. V.P., C.F.O.

INVESTOR CONTACT: Ann T. Scott, Mgr., Inv. Rel., (303) 469-3131

PRINCIPAL OFFICE: 10 Longs Peak Drive, Broomfield, CO 80021-2510

TELEPHONE NUMBER: (303) 469-3131
FAX: (303) 460-2127
WEB: www.ball.com

NO. OF EMPLOYEES: 11,200 (approx.)

SHAREHOLDERS: 6,178 (record)

ANNUAL MEETING: In Apr.

INCORPORATED: IN, 1922

INSTITUTIONAL HOLDINGS:
No. of Institutions: 173
Shares Held: 20,982,784
% Held: 76.4

INDUSTRY: Metal cans (SIC: 3411)

TRANSFER AGENT(S): First Chicago Trust Company of New York, Jersey City, NJ

NYSE SYMBOL BWE
Rec. Pr. 24.95 (4/30/01)

BANCWEST CORPORATION

YIELD 2.2%
P/E RATIO 14.4

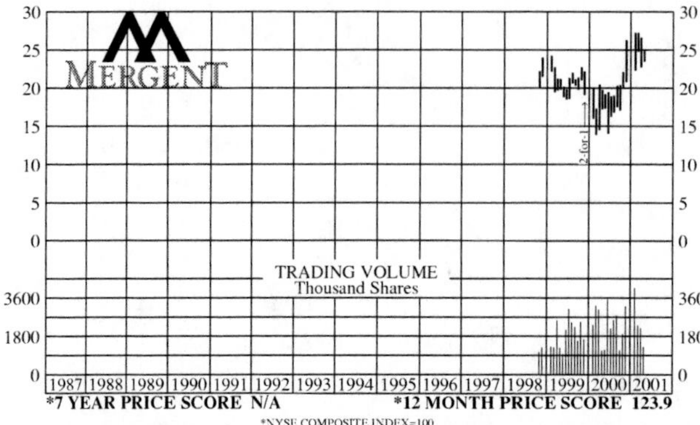

*7 YEAR PRICE SCORE N/A *12 MONTH PRICE SCORE 123.9

*NYSE COMPOSITE INDEX=100

INTERIM EARNINGS (Per Share):

Qtr.	Mar.	June	Sept.	Dec.
1998	0.34	0.35	0.36	0.37
1999	0.35	0.37	0.30	0.32
2000	0.40	0.43	0.45	0.45

INTERIM DIVIDENDS (Per Share):

Amt.	Decl.	Ex.	Rec.	Pay.
0.17Q	5/18/00	5/30/00	6/01/00	6/15/00
0.17Q	8/17/00	8/30/00	9/01/00	9/15/00
0.17Q	11/16/00	11/29/00	12/01/00	12/15/00
0.19Q	2/15/01	2/27/01	3/01/01	3/15/01
0.19Q	5/17/01	5/30/01	6/01/01	6/15/01

Indicated div.: $0.76 (Div. Reinv. Plan)

CAPITALIZATION (12/31/00):

	($000)	(%)
Total Deposits	14,128,139	82.7
Long-Term Debt	967,423	5.7
Common & Surplus	1,989,493	11.6
Total	17,085,055	100.0

RECENT DEVELOPMENTS: For the year ended 12/31/00, net income increased 25.5% to $216.4 million from $172.4 million in 1999. Earnings for 2000 and 1999 included pre-tax nonrecurring costs of $1.3 million and $17.5 million, respectively. Net interest income grew 8.4% to $746.9 million. Total non-interest income grew 9.3% to $216.1 million. Total non-interest expense, including the above costs, declined slightly to $534.0 million from $535.1 million in the previous year.

PROSPECTS: On 2/19/01, the Company announced that its subsidiary, Bank of the West, completed its acquisition of 23 locations in metropolitan Albuquerque and Las Cruces, New Mexico from First Security Corporation. As a result of the transaction, which represents the Company's market entry into New Mexico, Bank of the West will rank third in deposit share among commercial banks in the state. On 1/12/01, Bank of the West acquired seven former Las Vegas branches of First Security Bank.

BUSINESS

BANCWEST CORPORATION (formerly First Hawaiian, Inc.), with assets of $18.46 billion as of 12/31/00, is a bank holding company that operates a general commercial banking business and other businesses related to banking. Through its principal subsidiaries, Bank of the West and First Hawaiian Bank, the Company provides commercial and consumer banking services, engages in commercial and equipment and vehicle leasing and offers trust and insurance products. BancWest Corporation's subsidiaries operate 229 offices in the states of California, Hawaii, Oregon, Washington, Idaho and Nevada, and in Guam and Saipan.

LOAN DISTRIBUTION

(12/31/2000)	($000)	(%)
Comm, Fin & Agric	2,604,590	18.6
Commercial Real Estate	2,618,312	18.7
Real Estate Construction	405,542	2.9
Residential Real Estate	2,360,167	16.9
Consumer	3,599,954	25.8
Lease Financing	2,038,516	14.6
Foreign	344,750	2.5
Total	13,971,831	100.0

ANNUAL FINANCIAL DATA

	12/31/00	12/31/99	12/31/98	12/31/97	12/31/96	12/31/95	12/31/94
Earnings Per Share	**[1] 1.73**	**[1] 1.38**	**[1] 1.08**	**1.32**	**1.28**	**1.22**	**1.13**
Tang. Book Val. Per Share	**10.71**	**9.34**	**15.20**	**9.74**	**9.06**	**8.95**	**8.36**
Dividends Per Share	**0.68**	**0.64**	**0.62**	**0.62**	**0.60**	**0.59**	**0.59**
Dividend Payout %	**39.3**	**46.0**	**57.4**	**47.0**	**46.9**	**48.4**	**52.2**
INCOME STATEMENT (IN MILLIONS):							
Total Interest Income	1,309.9	1,135.7	684.4	592.5	574.1	560.0	475.8
Total Interest Expense	562.9	446.9	290.2	258.0	252.8	265.3	179.7
Net Interest Income	746.9	688.8	394.2	334.5	321.3	294.7	296.1
Provision for Loan Losses	60.4	55.3	28.6	17.2	23.6	38.1	22.9
Non-Interest Income	216.1	197.6	119.6	98.5	87.5	94.9	86.7
Non-Interest Expense	534.0	535.1	353.8	292.2	269.3	229.3	248.3
Income Before Taxes	368.6	296.1	131.5	123.6	115.8	122.1	111.5
Net Income	[1] 216.4	[1] 172.4	[1] 76.6	84.3	80.3	77.0	72.5
Average Shs. Outstg. (000)	125,050	124,699	142,784	127,500	125,596	126,940	129,036
BALANCE SHEET (IN MILLIONS):							
Cash & Due from Banks	873.6	810.0	615.2	282.9	333.5	304.1	262.9
Securities Avail. for Sale	1,960.8	1,868.0	1,347.0	778.1	1,140.7	1,175.3	152.0
Total Loans & Leases	13,971.8	12,524.0	11,340.0	6,238.7	5,806.7	5,259.5	5,533.6
Allowance for Credit Losses	172.4	161.4	149.6	82.6	85.2	78.7	61.3
Net Loans & Leases	13,799.4	12,362.6	d149.6	6,156.1	5,721.5	5,180.8	5,472.3
Total Assets	18,457.1	16,681.0	15,050.0	8,093.1	8,002.2	7,564.5	7,535.1
Total Deposits	14,128.1	12,878.0	11,260.3	6,089.2	5,936.7	5,358.3	5,152.2
Long-Term Obligations	967.4	801.8	730.0	318.7	205.7	238.8	219.3
Total Liabilities	16,467.6	14,838.3	13,382.0	7,361.4	7,296.3	6,915.0	6,907.2
Net Stockholders' Equity	1,989.5	1,842.7	1,667.9	731.7	705.9	649.5	627.9
Year-end Shs. Outstg. (000)	124,551	124,611	126,220	125,380	127,096	124,580	128,104
STATISTICAL RECORD:							
Return on Equity %	10.9	9.4	4.6	11.5	11.4	11.9	11.5
Return on Assets %	1.2	1.0	1.0	1.0	1.0	1.0	1.0
Equity/Assets %	10.8	11.0	11.1	9.0	8.8	8.6	8.3
Non-Int. Exp./Tot. Inc. %	55.5	60.4	68.9	67.5	65.9	58.9	64.9
Price Range	26.31-13.88	24.25-18.50	24.00-20.00	...	...	...	...
P/E Ratio	15.2-8.0	17.6-13.4	...	...	...	...	...
Average Yield %	3.4	3.0	2.8	...	...	...	...

Statistics are as originally reported. Adj. for 2-for-1 stk. split, 12/99. [1] Incl. restruct., merger-related & other non-recurr. costs of $1.3 mill., 2000; $17.5 mill., 1999; $25.5 mill., 1998.

OFFICERS:
W. A. Dods Jr., Chmn., C.E.O.
D. J. McGrath, Pres., C.O.O.
H. H. Karr, Exec. V.P., C.F.O.

INVESTOR CONTACT: Howard H. Karr, Exec. V.P. & C.F.O., (808) 525-8800

PRINCIPAL OFFICE: 999 Bishop Street, Honolulu, HI 96813

TELEPHONE NUMBER: (808) 525-7000
FAX: (808) 525-5733
WEB: www.bancwestcorp.com

NO. OF EMPLOYEES: 5,009

SHAREHOLDERS: 4,679 One holder of class A common stock.

ANNUAL MEETING: In April

INCORPORATED: DE, July, 1974

INSTITUTIONAL HOLDINGS:
No. of Institutions: 133
Shares Held: 26,491,233
% Held: 21.3

INDUSTRY: State commercial banks (SIC: 6022)

TRANSFER AGENT(S): American Stock Transfer & Trust Company, New York, NY

NYSE SYMBOL BDG
Rec. Pr. 26.30 (5/31/01)

BANDAG, INC.

YIELD 4.6%
P/E RATIO 9.1

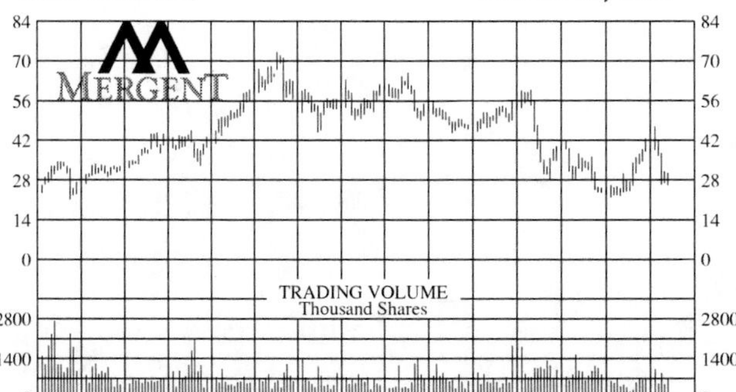

*7 YEAR PRICE SCORE 54.9 *12 MONTH PRICE SCORE 91.7

*NYSE COMPOSITE INDEX=100

INTERIM EARNINGS (Per Share):

Qtr.	Mar.	June	Sept.	Dec.
1996	0.65	0.83	1.02	0.94
1997	0.60	0.76	1.04	2.92
1998	0.40	0.62	0.77	0.84
1999	0.46	0.73	0.82	0.38
2000	0.48	0.85	0.86	0.71

INTERIM DIVIDENDS (Per Share):

Amt.	Decl.	Ex.	Rec.	Pay.
0.295Q	5/02/00	6/15/00	6/19/00	7/21/00
0.295Q	8/29/00	9/18/00	9/20/00	10/20/00
0.305Q	11/14/00	12/18/00	12/20/00	1/19/01
0.305Q	3/13/01	3/15/01	3/19/01	4/20/01
0.305Q	5/15/01	6/15/01	6/19/01	7/20/01

Indicated div.: $1.22 (Div. Reinv. Plan)

CAPITALIZATION (12/31/00):

	($000)	(%)
Long-Term Debt	105,163	18.1
Deferred Income Tax	2,494	0.4
Common & Surplus	474,157	81.5
Total	581,814	100.0

RECENT DEVELOPMENTS: For the year ended 12/31/00, net earnings advanced 15.3% to $60.3 million versus $52.3 million a year earlier. Results for 1999 included an after-tax nonrecurring charge of $7.7 million primarily due to restructuring of BDG's North American retread business. Total revenues slipped 1.3% to $1.01 billion from $1.03 billion in 1999. Net sales slipped 1.6% to $996.1 million. Revenues reflected softening of the North American retread market due to an over-abundant supply of new truck tires.

PROSPECTS: Going forward, sales volumes may continue to be hampered by softening of the North American retread market due to sluggish new truck demand. The lack of demand continues to increase competitive pressures. The Company may find it difficult to recover rising costs of energy and raw materials and achieve results comparable to 2000 due to increased competition. Meanwhile, BDG should continue to benefit from market acceptance of new products.

BUSINESS

BANDAG, INC. is engaged in the manufacture of precured tread rubber, equipment, and supplies for the retreading of truck and bus tires by a patented cold-bonding reaction. The Company also does some custom processing of rubber compounds. Revenues are generated by nearly 1,300 franchised dealers in the U.S. and abroad who are licensed to produce and market cold process retreads utilizing the Bandag process. BDG's wholly-owned subsidiary, Tire Management Solutions, Inc. (TMS), provides tire management systems outsourcing for commercial truck fleets. Tire Distribution Systems, Inc. (TDS), also a wholly-owned subsidiary, sells and services new and retread tires.

QUARTERLY DATA

(12/31/00)($000)	Rev	Inc
1st Quarter	224,289	10,013
2nd Quarter	249,116	17,6142
3rd Quarter	269,905	17,914
4th Quarter	252,749	14,764

ANNUAL FINANCIAL DATA

	12/31/00	12/31/99	12/31/98	12/31/97	12/31/96	12/31/95	12/31/94
Earnings Per Share	**2.90**	**2 2.40**	**2 2.63**	**1 5.33**	**3.44**	**3.82**	**3.51**
Cash Flow Per Share	**5.33**	**4.87**	**4.91**	**6.93**	**4.89**	**5.18**	**4.83**
Tang. Book Val. Per Share	**20.03**	**18.62**	**19.14**	**17.00**	**17.85**	**16.60**	**16.95**
Dividends Per Share	**1.18**	**1.14**	**1.10**	**1.00**	**0.90**	**0.80**	**0.70**
Dividend Payout %	**40.7**	**47.5**	**41.8**	**18.8**	**26.2**	**20.9**	**19.9**
INCOME STATEMENT (IN MILLIONS):							
Total Revenues	1,013.4	1,027.9	1,079.5	931.7	769.0	755.3	665.7
Costs & Expenses	854.9	872.3	917.8	688.6	602.4	563.6	478.4
Depreciation & Amort.	50.5	53.8	51.4	36.9	34.6	34.6	35.3
Operating Income	108.1	101.8	110.3	206.3	132.0	157.1	152.0
Net Interest Inc./(Exp.)	d8.7	d9.7	d10.8	d3.3	d1.2	d2.0	d2.1
Income Before Income Taxes	99.4	92.1	99.5	202.9	130.8	155.1	149.8
Income Taxes	39.0	39.8	40.2	80.9	49.2	58.1	55.8
Net Income	60.3	2 52.3	2 59.3	1 122.0	81.6	97.0	94.0
Cash Flow	110.8	106.1	110.7	158.9	116.2	131.6	129.3
Average Shs. Outstg. (000)	20,778	21,764	22,559	22,908	23,746	25,420	26,801
BALANCE SHEET (IN MILLIONS):							
Cash & Cash Equivalents	93.4	60.1	47.6	198.0	33.5	40.8	83.4
Total Current Assets	427.2	428.1	439.1	599.0	341.7	328.5	344.9
Net Property	177.2	198.0	213.0	197.6	145.1	144.9	151.8
Total Assets	714.5	722.4	755.7	899.9	588.3	554.2	582.1
Total Current Liabilities	132.7	154.1	174.9	306.5	139.2	122.0	113.3
Long-Term Obligations	105.2	111.2	109.8	123.2	10.1	11.9	12.3
Net Stockholders' Equity	474.2	454.1	495.7	463.4	410.9	404.1	442.8
Net Working Capital	294.4	274.1	264.2	292.5	202.5	206.4	231.6
Year-end Shs. Outstg. (000)	20,562	20,771	21,955	22,813	22,923	24,178	26,123
STATISTICAL RECORD:							
Operating Profit Margin %	10.7	9.9	10.2	22.1	17.2	20.8	22.8
Net Profit Margin %	6.0	5.1	5.5	13.1	10.6	12.8	14.1
Return on Equity %	12.7	11.5	12.0	26.3	19.9	24.0	21.2
Return on Assets %	8.4	7.2	7.8	13.6	13.9	17.5	16.1
Debt/Total Assets %	14.7	15.4	14.5	13.7	1.7	2.1	2.1
Price Range	42.63-21.88	41.63-23.50	59.75-28.31	55.75-45.00	55.88-44.50	65.88-49.00	63.50-49.13
P/E Ratio	14.7-7.5	17.3-9.8	22.7-10.8	10.5-8.4	16.2-12.9	17.2-12.8	18.1-14.0
Average Yield %	3.7	3.5	2.5	2.0	1.8	1.4	1.2

Statistics are as originally reported. 1 Incl. nonrecurr. gain of $78.6 mill. on sale of secur. 2 Incl. nonrecurr. chrg. of $13.5 mill., 1999; $4.2 mill., 1998.

OFFICERS:
M. G. Carver, Chmn., Pres., C.E.O.
W. W. Heidbreder, V.P., C.F.O., Sec.
L. A. Carver, Treas.

INVESTOR CONTACT: Warren W. Heidbreder, V.P., C.F.O., Sec., (319) 262-1260

PRINCIPAL OFFICE: 2905 North Highway 61, Muscatine, IA 52761-5886

TELEPHONE NUMBER: (563) 262-1400
FAX: (563) 262-1284
WEB: www.bandag.com

NO. OF EMPLOYEES: 4,330 (approx.)

SHAREHOLDERS: 1,966 (common); 1,100 (class A); 291 (Class B)

ANNUAL MEETING: In May

INCORPORATED: IA, Dec., 1957

INSTITUTIONAL HOLDINGS:
No. of Institutions: 95
Shares Held: 5,252,738
% Held: 25.4

INDUSTRY: Tires and inner tubes (SIC: 3011)

TRANSFER AGENT(S): BankBoston, NA, Boston, MA

NYSE SYMBOL BGR
Rec. Pr. 26.45 (5/31/01)

BANGOR HYDRO-ELECTRIC COMPANY

YIELD 3.0%
P/E RATIO 17.9

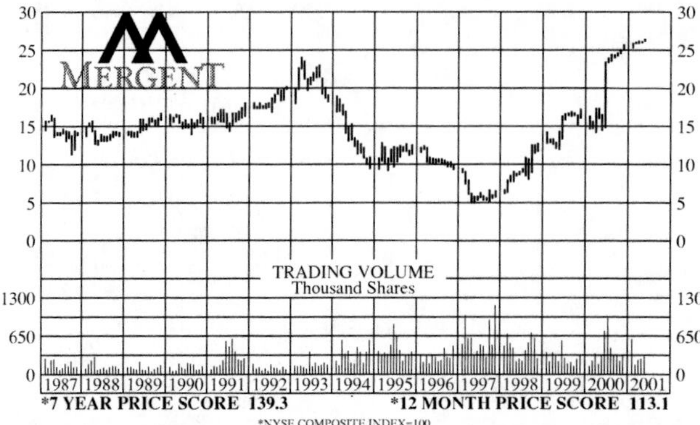

INTERIM EARNINGS (Per Share):

Qtr.	Mar.	June	Sept.	Dec.
1997	0.05	d0.19	d0.07	d0.03
1998	0.28	0.27	0.36	0.48
1999	0.53	0.43	0.65	0.74
2000	0.53	0.17	0.53	0.25

INTERIM DIVIDENDS (Per Share):

Amt.	Decl.	Ex.	Rec.	Pay.
0.20Q	3/15/00	3/29/00	3/31/00	4/20/00
0.20Q	6/21/00	6/29/00	7/03/00	7/20/00
0.20Q	9/20/00	9/28/00	10/02/00	10/20/00
0.20Q	12/20/00	12/28/00	1/02/01	1/20/01
0.20Q	3/21/01	3/28/01	3/30/01	4/20/01

Indicated div.: $0.80

CAPITALIZATION (12/31/00):

	($000)	(%)
Long-Term Debt	161,960	43.1
Deferred Income Tax	71,423	19.0
Preferred Stock	4,734	1.3
Common & Surplus	137,420	36.6
Total	375,537	100.0

RECENT DEVELOPMENTS: For the year ended 12/31/00, net income fell 39.3% to $11.1 million compared with $18.3 million in 1999. Results for 2000 included non-recurring charges totaling $4.1 million and a gain of $736,342 related to the sale of Penobscot Natural Gas. Total revenues were $212.3 million, up 7.2% from $198.0 million in the prior year.

PROSPECTS: On 1/24/01, the Federal Energy Regulatory Commission approved the proposed acquisition of the Company by Emera Inc. Under the agreement, Emera will acquire all of the outstanding common stock shares of BGR for $205.0 million. The merger is still pending approval from the U.S. Securities and Exchange Commission and is expected to be completed during the first half of 2001.

BUSINESS

BANGOR HYDRO-ELECTRIC COMPANY is a public utility engaged in the purchase, transmission, distribution and sale of electric energy and other energy-related services. The Company has a service area of 5,275 square miles with a population of about 192,000 people and owns about 580 miles of transmission lines and about 4,500 miles of distribution lines. BGR serves about 107,000 customers in portions of the Maine counties of Penobscot, Hancock, Washington, Waldo, Piscataquis, and Aroostook. The Company also purchases energy at wholesale and sells energy to retail customers and other utilities for resale. Electric revenues for 2000 were derived: residential, 45.2%; commercial, 34.7%; industrial, 18.6%; lighting, 1.4%; and wholesale, 0.1%. In July 1999, the Company sold Penobscot Hydro Company, a wholly-owned subsidiary, to PP&L Global.

ANNUAL FINANCIAL DATA

	12/31/00	12/31/99	12/31/98	12/31/97	12/31/96	12/31/95	12/31/94
Earnings Per Share	**[2] 1.30**	**[1] 2.08**	**1.33**	**d0.24**	**1.33**	**0.36**	**0.84**
Cash Flow Per Share	**4.73**	**6.05**	**5.74**	**4.75**	**5.69**	**3.39**	**28.32**
Tang. Book Val. Per Share	**18.66**	**18.02**	**16.14**	**14.47**	**14.71**	**14.13**	**14.71**
Dividends Per Share	**0.75**	**0.30**	...	**0.18**	**0.72**	**1.02**	**1.32**
Dividend Payout %	**57.7**	**14.4**	...	...	**54.1**	**283.3**	**157.1**
INCOME STATEMENT (IN THOUSANDS):							
Total Revenues	212,338	197,995	195,144	187,324	187,374	184,914	264,411
Costs & Expenses	157,241	128,682	126,082	126,765	119,167	139,261	56,094
Depreciation & Amort.	28,673	33,156	33,926	36,770	31,965	21,984	10,333
Operating Income	26,424	36,158	35,136	23,789	36,241	23,669	17,332
Net Interest Inc./(Exp.)	d15,935	d20,683	d24,963	d25,467	d26,425	d20,092	d11,183
Net Income	[2] 11,102	[1] 18,281	11,465	d387	11,283	4,336	188,109
Cash Flow	39,509	50,491	44,147	35,008	41,711	24,619	196,789
Average Shs. Outstg.	8,354	8,348	7,693	7,363	7,336	7,264	6,948
BALANCE SHEET (IN THOUSANDS):							
Gross Property	321,625	312,639	366,905	353,020	336,387	318,525	298,758
Accumulated Depreciation	86,684	84,825	101,633	96,595	87,736	81,934	75,667
Net Property	234,941	227,814	265,272	256,426	248,651	236,592	223,091
Total Assets	532,220	543,950	605,688	600,583	556,629	566,076	381,250
Long-Term Obligations	161,960	183,300	263,028	221,643	274,221	288,075	116,367
Net Stockholders' Equity	142,154	137,456	123,598	111,292	113,055	107,926	110,392
Year-end Shs. Outstg.	7,363	7,363	7,363	7,363	7,363	7,302	7,185
STATISTICAL RECORD:							
Operating Profit Margin %	12.4	18.3	18.0	12.7	19.3	12.8	6.6
Net Profit Margin %	5.2	9.2	5.9	...	6.0	2.3	71.1
Net Inc./Net Property %	4.7	8.0	4.3	...	4.5	1.8	84.3
Net Inc./Tot. Capital %	3.0	4.7	2.4	...	2.4	0.9	60.9
Return on Equity %	7.8	13.3	9.3	...	10.0	4.0	170.4
Accum. Depr./Gross Prop. %	27.0	27.1	27.7	27.4	26.1	25.7	25.3
Price Range	25.75-14.13	17.31-11.88	12.81-6.13	9.50-4.88	12.50-9.25	12.88-9.13	19.00-9.38
P/E Ratio	19.8-10.9	8.3-5.7	9.6-4.6	...	9.4-7.0	35.8-25.3	22.6-11.2
Average Yield %	3.8	2.1	...	2.5	6.6	9.3	9.3

Statistics are as originally reported. [1] Incl. $3.5 mill. net gains. [2] Incl. chgs. totaling $4.1 mill. & a gain of $736,342 fr. sale of bus.

OFFICERS:
R. S. Briggs, Chmn., Pres., C.E.O.
F. S. Samp, V.P., Fin. & Law, C.F.O.
C. R. Lee, Sr. V.P., C.O.O.

INVESTOR CONTACT: Shareholder Services Dept., (207) 990-6936

PRINCIPAL OFFICE: 33 State Street, Bangor, ME 04401

TELEPHONE NUMBER: (207) 945-5621
FAX: (207) 990-6993
WEB: www.bhe.com

NO. OF EMPLOYEES: 427

SHAREHOLDERS: 6,222

ANNUAL MEETING: In May

INCORPORATED: ME, Aug., 1924

INSTITUTIONAL HOLDINGS:
No. of Institutions: 52
Shares Held: 3,150,188
% Held: 42.8

INDUSTRY: Electric services (SIC: 4911)

TRANSFER AGENT(S): BankBoston, N.A., c/o EquiServe, Boston, MA

NYSE SYMBOL BAC
Rec. Pr. 56.00 (4/30/01)

BANK OF AMERICA CORPORATION

YIELD 4.0%
P/E RATIO 12.4

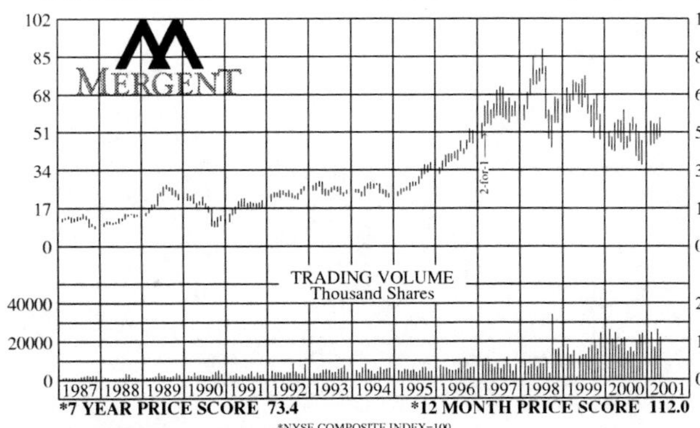

INTERIM EARNINGS (Per Share):

Qtr.	Mar.	June	Sept.	Dec.
1997	0.97	1.05	1.11	1.12
1998	0.51	1.43	0.21	0.66
1999	1.08	1.07	1.23	1.10
2000	1.33	1.23	1.10	0.85

INTERIM DIVIDENDS (Per Share):

Amt.	Decl.	Ex.	Rec.	Pay.
0.50Q	4/25/00	5/31/00	6/02/00	6/23/00
0.50Q	7/26/00	8/30/00	9/01/00	9/22/00
0.56Q	10/25/00	11/29/00	12/01/00	12/20/00
0.56Q	1/24/01	2/28/01	3/02/01	3/23/01
0.56Q	4/25/01	5/30/01	6/01/01	6/22/01

Indicated div.: $2.24 (Div. Reinv. Plan)

CAPITALIZATION (12/31/00):

	($000)	(%)
Total Deposits	364,244,000	76.0
Long-Term Debt	67,547,000	14.1
Preferred Stock	72,000	0.0
Common & Surplus	47,556,000	9.9
Total	479,419,000	100.0

RECENT DEVELOPMENTS: For the year ended 12/31/00, net income declined 4.6% to $7.52 billion. Earnings for 2000 and 1999 included after-tax charges of $346.0 million and $358.0 million, respectively, related to growth initiatives and mergers. Net interest income grew 1.1% to $18.44 billion. Provision for credit losses rose 39.3% to $2.54 billion. Total non-interest income rose 1.4% to $14.51 billion. Other non-interest expense grew 5.4% to $18.08 billion.

PROSPECTS: The Company continues to successfully implement its customer-focused strategy to expand relationships and increase revenues. As a result, BAC expects earnings per share in 2001 to range from $5.10 to $5.20 compared with earnings per share of $4.52 in 2000. Return on equity is expected to range from 16.5% to 18.0%. BAC will continue to invest in such areas as e-commerce, payments and asset management.

BUSINESS

BANK OF AMERICA CORPORATION (formerly NationsBank Corporation), is a bank holding company with $642.19 billion in total assets as of 12/31/00. The Company was formed on 9/30/98 as a result of BankAmerica merging into NationsBank. The Company adopted its present name on 4/29/99. BAC provides financial products and services to more than 30 million households and two million businesses, as well as providing international corporate financial services for business transactions in 190 countries. The Company maintains full-service operations in 21 states and the District of Columbia.

LOAN DISTRIBUTION

(12/31/2000)	($000)	(%)
Commercial	203,542,000	51.9
Residential Mortgage	84,394,000	21.5
Home Equity Lines	21,598,000	5.5
Direct/Indirect Consumer	40,457,000	10.3
Consumer Finance	25,800,000	6.6
Bankcard	14,094,000	3.6
Foreign Consumer	2,308,000	0.6
Total	392,193,000	100.0

ANNUAL FINANCIAL DATA

	12/31/00	12/31/99	[3] 12/31/98	12/31/97	12/31/96	12/31/95	12/31/94
Earnings Per Share	[2] 4.52	[2] 4.48	[2] 2.90	4.17	[1] 4.00	3.56	3.06
Tang. Book Val. Per Share	19.00	15.66	16.68	14.86	18.43	19.08	16.64
Dividends Per Share	2.06	1.85	1.59	1.37	1.20	1.04	0.94
Dividend Payout %	45.6	41.3	54.8	32.9	30.0	29.2	30.7
INCOME STATEMENT (IN MILLIONS):							
Total Interest Income	43,258.0	37,323.0	38,588.0	16,579.0	13,796.0	13,220.0	10,529.0
Total Interest Expense	24,816.0	19,086.0	20,290.0	8,681.0	7,467.0	7,773.0	5,318.0
Net Interest Income	18,442.0	18,237.0	18,298.0	7,898.0	6,329.0	5,447.0	5,211.0
Provision for Loan Losses	2,535.0	1,820.0	2,920.0	800.0	605.0	382.0	310.0
Non-Interest Income	14,514.0	14,309.0	13,206.0	5,155.0	3,713.0	3,107.0	2,584.0
Non-Interest Expense	18,083.0	18,511.0	20,536.0	7,457.0	5,803.0	5,136.0	cr12.0
Income Before Taxes	11,788.0	12,215.0	8,048.0	4,796.0	3,634.0	2,991.0	2,555.0
Net Income	[2] 7,517.0	[2] 7,882.0	[2] 5,165.0	3,077.0	[1] 2,375.0	1,995.0	1,690.0
Average Shs. Outstg. (000)	1,664,929	1,760,058	1,775,760	737,791	590,216	544,959	550,000
BALANCE SHEET (IN MILLIONS):							
Securities Avail. for Sale	113,140.0	124,945.0	124,942.0	72,120.0	32,809.0	39,578.0	20,125.0
Total Loans & Leases	392,193.0	370,662.0	357,328.0	146,417.0	125,031.0	119,020.0	105,033.0
Allowance for Credit Losses	6,838.0	6,828.0	7,122.0	5,407.0	4,716.0	4,150.0	3,848.0
Net Loans & Leases	385,355.0	363,834.0	350,206.0	141,010.0	120,315.0	114,870.0	101,185.0
Total Assets	642,191.0	632,574.0	617,679.0	264,562.0	185,794.0	187,298.0	169,604.0
Total Deposits	364,244.0	347,273.0	357,260.0	138,194.0	106,498.0	100,691.0	100,470.0
Long-Term Obligations	67,547.0	55,486.0	45,888.0	27,204.0	22,985.0	17,775.0	8,488.0
Total Liabilities	594,563.0	588,142.0	571,741.0	243,225.0	172,085.0	174,497.0	158,593.0
Net Stockholders' Equity	47,628.0	44,432.0	45,938.0	21,337.0	13,709.0	12,801.0	11,011.0
Year-end Shs. Outstg. (000)	1,613,632	1,677,273	1,724,484	712,188	573,000	549,000	552,000
STATISTICAL RECORD:							
Return on Equity %	15.8	17.7	11.2	14.4	17.3	15.6	15.3
Return on Assets %	1.2	1.2	0.8	1.2	1.3	1.1	1.0
Equity/Assets %	7.4	7.0	7.4	8.1	7.4	6.8	6.5
Non-Int. Exp./Tot. Inc. %	56.5	56.9	65.2	57.1	57.8	60.0	d0.2
Price Range	61.00-36.31	76.38-47.63	88.44-44.00	71.69-48.00	52.63-32.19	37.38-22.31	28.69-21.69
P/E Ratio	13.5-8.0	17.0-10.6	30.5-15.2	17.2-11.5	13.2-8.0	10.5-6.3	9.4-7.1
Average Yield %	4.2	3.0	2.4	2.3	2.8	3.5	3.7

Statistics are as originally reported. Adj. for 2-for-1 stk. split, 2/97. [1] Incl. aft.-tax merger-rel. chgs. of $77.0 mill. [2] Incl. merg.-rel. & restr. chgs. of $346.0 mill., 2000; $358.0 mill., 1999; $1.80 bill., 1998. [3] Refl. merger of NationsBank Corp. & BankAmerica Corp. on 9/30/98.

OFFICERS:
K. D. Lewis, Chmn., Pres., C.E.O.
J. H. Hance Jr., Vice-Chmn., C.F.O.

INVESTOR CONTACT: Jane Smith, Manager, Shareholder Relations, (704) 386-5681

PRINCIPAL OFFICE: Bank of America Corporate Center, Charlotte, NC 28255

TELEPHONE NUMBER: (888) 279-3457
FAX: (704) 388-9278
WEB: www.bankofamerica.com

NO. OF EMPLOYEES: 142,724

SHAREHOLDERS: 256,883

ANNUAL MEETING: In April

INCORPORATED: NC, July, 1968; reincorp., DE, Sept., 1998

INSTITUTIONAL HOLDINGS:
No. of Institutions: 838
Shares Held: 891,834,572
% Held: 55.5

INDUSTRY: National commercial banks (SIC: 6021)

TRANSFER AGENT(S): Mellon Investor Services, Ridgefield Park, NJ

NYSE SYMBOL BK
Rec. Pr. 50.20 (4/30/01)

BANK OF NEW YORK COMPANY, INC. (THE)

YIELD 1.4%
P/E RATIO 26.0

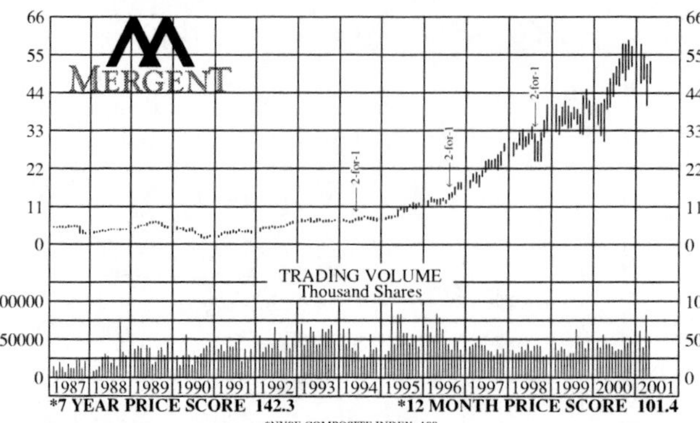

INTERIM EARNINGS (Per Share):

Qtr.	Mar.	June	Sept.	Dec.
1997	0.33	0.34	0.35	0.38
1998	0.37	0.38	0.39	0.40
1999	0.41	0.42	1.02	0.44
2000	0.46	0.48	0.49	0.50

INTERIM DIVIDENDS (Per Share):

Amt.	Decl.	Ex.	Rec.	Pay.
0.16Q	4/11/00	4/18/00	4/21/00	5/04/00
0.16Q	7/11/00	7/19/00	7/21/00	8/03/00
0.18Q	10/10/00	10/18/00	10/20/00	11/02/00
0.18Q	1/09/01	1/17/01	1/19/01	2/01/01
0.18Q	4/10/01	4/18/01	4/20/01	5/03/01

Indicated div.: $0.72 (Div. Reinv. Plan)

CAPITALIZATION (12/31/00):

	($000)	(%)
Total Deposits	56,376,000	84.1
Long-Term Debt	3,036,000	4.5
Redeemable Pfd. Stock	1,500,000	2.2
Preferred Stock	1,000	0.0
Common & Surplus	6,151,000	9.2
Total	67,064,000	100.0

RECENT DEVELOPMENTS: For the year ended 12/31/00, net income dropped 17.8% to $1.43 billion from $1.74 billion in the prior year. Results for 1999 included a $1.02 billion gain on the sale of BNY Financial Corp. Net interest income grew 9.9% to $1.87 billion from $1.70 billion the year before. Total non-interest income, including the BNYFC gain, decreased 11.0% to $3.11 billion. Total non-interest expense grew 19.1% to $2.51 billion.

PROSPECTS: The Company should continue to perform well as BK continues to focus on high-growth, fee-based businesses. Fee revenue should continue to be strong across all product lines, particularly in global custody, depositary receipts, unit investment trust, and mutual funds. Separately, BK entered into an alliance with Agricultural Bank of China. BK will provide consultancy services as it prepares to launch open-end mutual funds in China.

BUSINESS

THE BANK OF NEW YORK COMPANY, INC. is a bank holding company with assets, as of 12/31/00, of $77.11 billion. BK provides a broad range of banking and other financial services to corporations and individuals worldwide through six basic businesses: securities servicing and cash processing; trust, investment management and private banking; corporate banking; asset-based lending; retail banking and financial market services. BK's primary subsidiaries are the Bank of New York, BNY Holdings (Delaware) Corporation, and The Bank of New York (Delaware). BK has operating centers in London, Brussels, Dublin, Singapore and Luxembourg and 29 non-U.S. branch and representative offices in 26 countries and provides securities servicing in 99 markets.

LOAN DISTRIBUTION

(12/31/2000)	($000)	(%)
Commercial & Industrial	13,785,000	38.7
Real Estate	6,070,000	17.0
Banks & Oth Finl Institut	2,014,000	5.7
Purch or Carrying Securs	2,697,000	7.6
Asset Based Lease	2,212,000	6.2
Consumer & Oth Loans	2,222,000	6.2
Foreign Loans	6,645,000	18.6
Total	35,645,000	100.0

ANNUAL FINANCIAL DATA

	12/31/00	12/31/99	12/31/98	12/31/97	12/31/96	12/31/95	12/31/94
Earnings Per Share	**1.92**	[4] **2.27**	**1.53**	[3] **1.36**	**1.24**	[1] [2] **1.14**	[1] **0.98**
Tang. Book Val. Per Share	**8.30**	**6.95**	**7.05**	**6.67**	**6.50**	**6.46**	**5.58**
Dividends Per Share	**0.66**	**0.58**	**0.54**	**0.49**	**0.42**	**0.34**	**0.27**
Dividend Payout %	**34.4**	**25.5**	**35.3**	**36.2**	**34.0**	**29.7**	**27.9**
INCOME STATEMENT (IN MILLIONS):							
Total Interest Income	4,377.0	3,473.0	3,510.0	3,560.0	3,583.0	3,831.0	2,962.0
Total Interest Expense	2,507.0	1,772.0	1,859.0	1,705.0	1,622.0	1,802.0	1,245.0
Net Interest Income	1,870.0	1,701.0	1,651.0	1,855.0	1,961.0	2,029.0	1,717.0
Provision for Loan Losses	105.0	135.0	20.0	280.0	600.0	330.0	162.0
Non-Interest Income	3,109.0	3,493.0	2,283.0	2,137.0	2,130.0	1,491.0	1,289.0
Non-Interest Expense	2,510.0	2,107.0	1,928.0	1,874.0	1,835.0	1,708.0	1,646.0
Income Before Taxes	2,364.0	2,952.0	1,986.0	1,838.0	1,656.0	1,482.0	1,198.0
Equity Earnings/Minority Int.	d113.0	d112.0	d95.0	d65.0	d2.0	...	...
Net Income	1,429.0	[4] 1,739.0	1,192.0	[3] 1,104.0	1,020.0	[1] [2] 914.0	[1] 749.0
Average Shs. Outstg. (000)	745,000	765,000	781,000	808,000	840,000	848,000	808,000
BALANCE SHEET (IN MILLIONS):							
Cash & Due from Banks	3,125.0	3,276.0	3,999.0	5,769.0	6,032.0	4,711.0	2,903.0
Securities Avail. for Sale	18,700.0	14,743.0	7,088.0	8,117.0	5,430.0	4,434.0	2,661.0
Total Loans & Leases	39,699.0	40,014.0	40,756.0	37,042.0	38,484.0	38,661.0	33,953.0
Allowance for Credit Losses	4,054.0	3,062.0	3,006.0	2,556.0	2,379.0	1,730.0	1,662.0
Net Loans & Leases	35,645.0	36,952.0	37,750.0	34,486.0	36,105.0	36,931.0	32,291.0
Total Assets	77,114.0	74,756.0	63,503.0	59,961.0	55,765.0	53,720.0	48,879.0
Total Deposits	56,376.0	55,751.0	44,632.0	41,357.0	39,343.0	35,918.0	34,091.0
Long-Term Obligations	3,036.0	2,811.0	2,086.0	1,809.0	1,816.0	1,848.0	1,774.0
Total Liabilities	70,962.0	69,613.0	58,055.0	54,959.0	50,638.0	48,488.0	44,583.0
Net Stockholders' Equity	6,152.0	5,143.0	5,448.0	5,002.0	5,127.0	5,232.0	4,296.0
Year-end Shs. Outstg. (000)	741,068	740,214	773,119	750,000	772,000	792,000	748,000
STATISTICAL RECORD:							
Return on Equity %	23.2	33.8	21.9	22.1	19.9	17.5	17.4
Return on Assets %	1.9	2.3	1.9	1.8	1.8	1.7	1.5
Equity/Assets %	8.0	6.9	8.6	8.3	9.2	9.7	8.8
Non-Int. Exp./Tot. Inc. %	52.0	42.2	51.3	48.6	45.9	50.2	55.0
Price Range	59.38-29.75	45.19-31.81	40.56-24.00	29.28-16.38	18.06-10.88	12.25-7.13	8.31-6.24
P/E Ratio	30.9-15.5	19.9-14.0	26.5-15.7	21.6-12.1	14.6-8.8	10.7-6.2	8.5-6.4
Average Yield %	1.5	1.5	1.7	2.1	2.9	3.5	3.8

Statistics are as originally reported. Adj. for 2-for-1 split, 8/98, 8/96 & 5/94. [1] Incl. $58.0 mill. aft.-tax gain on sale ARCS Inc. mtg. svcs. ptf., 1995; $22.0 mill. pre-tax gain on sale of interest in Wing Hang Bank, 1994. [2] Incl. $13.0 mill. chg. from settlement of litigation. [3] Incl. a pre-tax gain of $177.0 million from the sale of BK's credit card operations & a $100.0 million provision for credit losses. [4] Incl. a pre-tax gain of $1.02 bill. on the sale of BNY Financial Corp.

OFFICERS:
T. A. Renyi, Chmn., C.E.O.
A. R. Griffith, Vice-Chmn.
G. L. Hassell, Pres.
B. W. Van Saun, Sr. Exec. V.P., C.F.O.

INVESTOR CONTACT: Shareholder Relations, (800) 432-0140

PRINCIPAL OFFICE: One Wall Street, New York, NY 10286

TELEPHONE NUMBER: (212) 495-1784
FAX: (212) 495-2546
WEB: www.bankofny.com

NO. OF EMPLOYEES: 18,861 (avg.)

SHAREHOLDERS: 28,719

ANNUAL MEETING: In May

INCORPORATED: NY, July, 1968

INSTITUTIONAL HOLDINGS:
No. of Institutions: 656
Shares Held: 452,347,244
% Held: 61.4

INDUSTRY: State commercial banks (SIC: 6022)

TRANSFER AGENT(S): The Bank of New York, New York, NY

NYSE SYMBOL ONE
Rec. Pr. 37.77 (4/30/01)

BANK ONE CORPORATION

YIELD 2.2%
P/E RATIO . . .

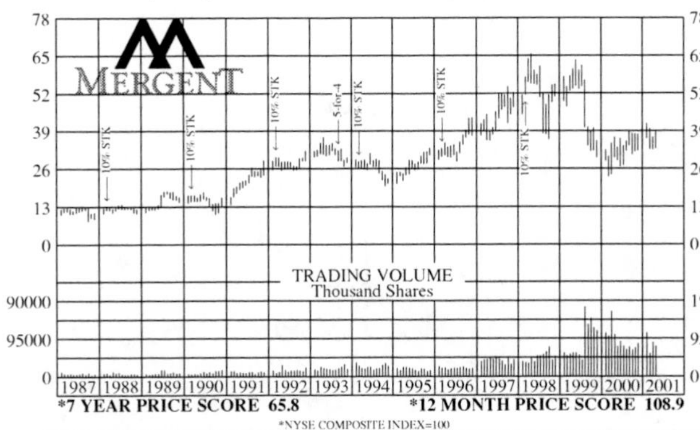

INTERIM EARNINGS (Per Share):

Qtr.	Mar.	June	Sept.	Dec.
1997	0.78	0.02	0.66	0.79
1998	0.79	0.68	0.89	0.19
1999	0.96	0.83	0.79	0.36
2000	0.60	d1.11	0.50	d0.44

INTERIM DIVIDENDS (Per Share):

Amt.	Decl.	Ex.	Rec.	Pay.
0.42Q	4/18/00	6/13/00	6/15/00	7/01/00
0.21Q	7/19/00	9/13/00	9/15/00	10/01/00
0.21Q	10/17/00	12/13/00	12/15/00	1/01/01
0.21Q	1/16/01	3/13/01	3/15/01	4/01/01
0.21Q	4/16/01	6/13/01	6/15/01	7/01/01

Indicated div.: $0.84 (Div. Reinv. Plan)

CAPITALIZATION (12/31/00):

	($000)	(%)
Total Deposits	167,077,000	73.7
Long-Term Debt	40,911,000	18.1
Preferred Stock	190,000	0.1
Common & Surplus	18,445,000	8.1
Total	226,623,000	100.0

RECENT DEVELOPMENTS: For the year ended 12/31/00, ONE reported a net loss of $511.0 million compared with net income of $3.48 billion the year before, reflecting the weakened economy and credit quality. Earnings for 2000 and 1999 included pre-tax merger-related and restructuring charges of $161.0 million and $554.0 million, respectively. Net interest income fell 2.1% to $8.84 billion. Total non-interest income declined 41.4% to $5.09 billion.

PROSPECTS: ONE is implementing a waste-reduction program that will lower the expense base by an annualized $500.0 million, while providing for investments in technology and customer service. ONE continues to progress on its Texas/Louisiana system conversion project. ONE also continues to improve its commercial customer profitability system. Results should benefit from the increased number of Internet-enabled banking platform PCs to 14,500.

BUSINESS

BANK ONE CORPORATION (formerly Banc One Corporation)with assets of more than $269.30 billion as of 12/31/00, is a bank holding company. The Company, formed on 10/1/98, is a result of the acquisition of First Chicago NBD Corporation by Banc One Corporation, and is the nation's fourth-largest bank holding company, the largest VISA credit card issuer, and the third-largest bank lender to small businesses. ONE offers a variety of financial services to corporate, retail and trust customers. The Company operates more than 1,800 banking centers and a nationwide network of ATMs. ONE also operates affiliates that engage in data processing, venture capital, merchant banking, trust, investment management, brokerage, equipment leasing, consumer finance and insurance.

LOAN DISTRIBUTION

(12/31/2000)	($000)	(%)
Commercial loans	100,460,000	57.7
Consumer loans	69,047,000	39.6
Credit card loans	4,744,000	2.7
Total	174,251,000	100.0

ANNUAL FINANCIAL DATA

	12/31/00	12/31/99	12/31/98	12/31/97	12/31/96	12/31/95	12/31/94
Earnings Per Share	**[3] d0.45**	**[3] 2.95**	**[3] 2.61**	**[3] 1.99**	**[2] 2.94**	**2.65**	**[1] 2.00**
Tang. Book Val. Per Share	**15.56**	**17.03**	**17.02**	**14.74**	**16.95**	**16.38**	**14.68**
Dividends Per Share	**1.47**	**1.64**	**1.49**	**1.35**	**1.21**	**1.10**	**1.00**
Dividend Payout %	**. . .**	**55.6**	**56.9**	**67.6**	**41.2**	**41.5**	**50.1**
INCOME STATEMENT (IN MILLIONS):							
Total Interest Income	20,078.0	17,294.0	17,524.0	9,383.2	8,044.9	7,100.9	6,437.5
Total Interest Expense	11,242.0	8,273.0	8,177.0	3,990.9	3,189.4	2,971.5	2,248.8
Net Interest Income	8,836.0	9,021.0	9,347.0	5,392.3	4,855.5	4,129.4	4,188.6
Provision for Loan Losses	3,398.0	1,249.0	1,408.0	1,211.1	788.1	457.5	242.3
Non-Interest Income	5,090.0	8,692.0	8,071.0	3,835.9	2,227.5	1,870.0	1,419.6
Non-Interest Expense	11,447.0	11,490.0	11,545.0	6,048.8	4,184.2	3,631.6	3,847.1
Income Before Taxes	d1,080.0	4,974.0	4,465.0	1,968.3	2,110.7	1,910.3	1,518.9
Net Income	[3] d511.0	[3] 3,479.0	[3] 3,108.0	[3] 1,305.7	[2] 1,426.5	1,277.9	[1] 1,005.1
Average Shs. Outstg. (000)	1,154,000	1,178,000	1,189,000	655,700	480,620	476,655	492,930
BALANCE SHEET (IN MILLIONS):							
Cash & Due from Banks	17,291.0	16,076.0	19,878.0	7,727.4	6,350.8	5,501.3	5,073.4
Securities Avail. for Sale	5,110.0	11,324.0	12,299.0	15,306.2	14,983.9	15,075.1	13,857.6
Total Loans & Leases	174,251.0	163,877.0	155,398.0	82,052.8	74,193.9	65,328.7	61,992.9
Allowance for Credit Losses	4,110.0	2,285.0	2,271.0	1,325.9	1,075.1	938.0	897.2
Net Loans & Leases	170,141.0	161,592.0	153,127.0	80,726.9	73,118.8	64,390.7	61,095.7
Total Assets	269,300.0	269,425.0	261,496.0	115,901.3	101,848.1	90,454.0	88,922.6
Total Deposits	167,077.0	162,278.0	161,542.0	77,414.3	72,373.1	67,320.2	68,090.1
Long-Term Obligations	40,911.0	35,435.0	22,298.0	11,066.4	4,189.5	2,720.4	1,866.4
Total Liabilities	250,665.0	249,335.0	240,936.0	105,525.3	93,201.1	82,256.5	81,357.7
Net Stockholders' Equity	18,635.0	20,090.0	20,560.0	10,376.0	8,647.0	8,197.5	7,564.9
Year-end Shs. Outstg. (000)	1,159,829	1,147,343	1,177,310	644,500	469,989	470,416	480,353
STATISTICAL RECORD:							
Return on Equity %	. . .	17.3	15.1	12.6	16.5	15.6	13.3
Return on Assets %	. . .	1.3	1.2	1.1	1.4	1.4	1.1
Equity/Assets %	6.9	7.5	7.9	9.0	8.5	9.1	8.5
Non-Int. Exp./Tot. Inc. %	82.2	64.9	66.3	65.5	59.1	60.5	68.6
Price Range	39.00-23.19	63.56-29.75	65.63-36.06	54.43-35.68	43.52-28.41	33.16-20.77	31.41-19.94
P/E Ratio	. . .	21.5-10.1	25.1-13.8	27.4-17.9	14.8-9.7	12.5-7.8	15.7-10.0
Average Yield %	4.7	3.5	2.9	3.0	3.4	4.1	3.9

Statistics are as originally reported. Adj. for 10% stk. div. 2/98, 3/96, 3/94. [1] Incl. $40.0 mill. chrg. for acq. of Liberty Bancorp, mtg. loan ctr. consol. & liti. costs. [2] Incl. one-time SAIF chrg. of $34.3 mill. [3] Incl. pre-tax merger-rel. & restr. chrgs.: $161.0 mill., 2000; $554.0 mill., 1999; $1.06 bill., 1998; $337.3 mill., 1997.

OFFICERS:
J. Dimon, Chmn., C.E.O.
C. W. Scharf, Exec. V.P., C.F.O.

INVESTOR CONTACT: Jay S. Gould, Director - Investor Relations, (312) 732-4812

PRINCIPAL OFFICE: 1 Bank One Plaza, Chicago, IL 60670

TELEPHONE NUMBER: (312) 732-4000
FAX: (312) 732-1704
WEB: www.bankone.com

NO. OF EMPLOYEES: 80,778 (avg.)

SHAREHOLDERS: 119,152

ANNUAL MEETING: In May

INCORPORATED: DE, April, 1998

INSTITUTIONAL HOLDINGS:
No. of Institutions: 646
Shares Held: 689,213,973
% Held: 59.4

INDUSTRY: National commercial banks (SIC: 6021)

TRANSFER AGENT(S): First Chicago Trust Company of New York, Jersey City, NJ

NYSE SYMBOL BN
Rec. Pr. 26.10 (4/30/01)

BANTA CORPORATION

YIELD 2.3%
P/E RATIO 11.1

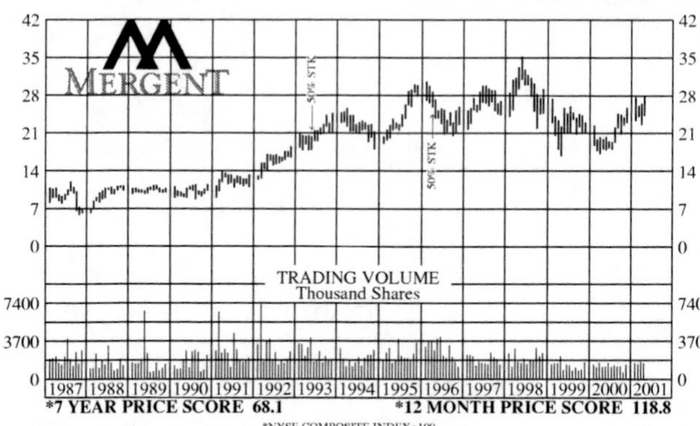

INTERIM EARNINGS (Per Share):

Qtr.	Mar.	June	Sept.	Dec.
1997	0.33	0.42	0.19	0.50
1998	0.37	0.45	0.55	0.43
1999	0.35	d0.97	0.65	0.59
2000	0.39	0.50	0.78	0.69

INTERIM DIVIDENDS (Per Share):

Amt.	Decl.	Ex.	Rec.	Pay.
0.15Q	4/26/00	7/12/00	7/14/00	8/01/00
0.15Q	7/25/00	10/18/00	10/20/00	11/01/00
0.15Q	12/05/00	1/17/01	1/19/01	2/01/01
0.15Q	1/30/01	4/10/01	4/13/01	5/01/01
0.15Q	4/24/01	7/11/01	7/13/01	8/01/01

Indicated div.: $0.60 (Div. Reinv. Plan)

CAPITALIZATION (12/30/00):

	($000)	(%)
Long-Term Debt	179,202	31.2
Deferred Income Tax	24,106	4.2
Common & Surplus	370,912	64.6
Total	574,220	100.0

RECENT DEVELOPMENTS: For the year ended 12/31/00, net income climbed 7.8% to $58.7 million versus $54.5 million in 1999. Net sales were $1.54 billion, up 20.3% from $1.28 billion in the prior year. Gross profit rose 16.6% to $310.5 million from $266.4 million the year before. Operating earnings increased 11.1% to $114.8 million versus $103.4 million in the previous year. Results benefited from healthy print markets and BN's strong supply-chain management business.

PROSPECTS: For the year 2001, the Company expects to increase total revenue 8.0% to 10.0% and earnings per share to range between $2.53 to $2.58. Production at many of the Company's print facilities has been hampered by a soft economy. The educational market is expected to remain strong in 2001 and contribute to higher earnings. Meanwhile, the publication segment should benefit from ongoing gains in market share.

BUSINESS

BANTA CORPORATION is a North American provider of a broad range of printing and digital imaging services. BN operates in three business segments: print, turnkey services, and healthcare. The print segment provides products and services to publishers of educational and general books and special interest magazines. The print segment also supplies direct marketing materials and consumer and business catalogs. The turnkey services segment provides supply-chain management, product assembly, fulfillment and product localization services to technology companies. The healthcare products is primarily engaged in the production of disposable products used in outpatient clinics, dental offices and hospitals. Sales (and operating income) for 2000 were derived: printing and digital imaging, 70.9% (79.2%); supply-chain management, 22.6% (15.4%); and healthcare, 6.5% (5.4%).

ANNUAL FINANCIAL DATA

	12/30/00	1/1/00	1/2/99	1/3/98	12/28/96	12/31/95	12/31/94
Earnings Per Share	**2.35**	**[1] 0.59**	**1.80**	**[1] 1.44**	**1.63**	**1.75**	**1.56**
Cash Flow Per Share	**5.38**	**3.10**	**4.06**	**3.50**	**3.49**	**3.42**	**2.92**
Tang. Book Val. Per Share	**12.41**	**12.31**	**11.83**	**11.80**	**12.29**	**16.83**	**15.29**
Dividends Per Share	**0.60**	**0.56**	**0.51**	**0.47**	**0.44**	**0.37**	**0.35**
Dividend Payout %	**25.5**	**94.9**	**28.3**	**32.6**	**26.8**	**21.3**	**22.2**
INCOME STATEMENT (IN MILLIONS):							
Total Revenues	1,537.7	1,278.3	1,335.8	1,202.5	1,083.8	1,022.7	811.3
Costs & Expenses	1,347.2	1,161.7	1,171.4	1,060.8	933.3	873.7	686.5
Depreciation & Amort.	75.7	68.2	66.9	62.1	58.3	51.1	41.5
Operating Income	114.8	48.4	97.5	79.5	92.2	97.9	83.4
Net Interest Inc./(Exp.)	d16.8	d12.4	d10.8	d11.1	d10.2	d9.9	d5.9
Income Before Income Taxes	96.6	34.6	86.1	70.8	84.2	89.1	78.7
Income Taxes	37.9	18.6	33.2	27.5	33.3	35.5	31.5
Net Income	58.7	[1] 16.0	52.9	[1] 43.3	50.9	53.6	47.2
Cash Flow	134.5	84.2	119.8	105.4	109.2	104.6	88.7
Average Shs. Outstg. (000)	24,980	27,177	29,475	30,113	31,249	30,624	30,366
BALANCE SHEET (IN MILLIONS):							
Cash & Cash Equivalents	27.7	27.7	26.6	16.4	57.4	27.1	0.4
Total Current Assets	406.7	355.9	354.6	365.7	347.5	310.8	248.4
Net Property	344.3	327.4	318.6	338.4	319.9	313.7	293.7
Total Assets	854.5	773.3	770.0	781.2	719.2	678.8	577.8
Total Current Liabilities	240.3	245.4	196.5	200.4	127.8	122.9	147.0
Long-Term Obligations	179.2	113.5	120.6	130.1	133.7	135.0	67.8
Net Stockholders' Equity	370.9	353.8	409.9	414.1	420.6	387.1	331.6
Net Working Capital	166.4	110.5	158.1	165.3	219.6	188.0	101.4
Year-end Shs. Outstg. (000)	24,567	23,943	28,261	29,793	30,969	20,560	20,126
STATISTICAL RECORD:							
Operating Profit Margin %	7.5	3.8	7.3	6.6	8.5	9.6	10.3
Net Profit Margin %	3.8	1.3	4.0	3.6	4.7	5.2	5.8
Return on Equity %	15.8	4.5	12.9	10.5	12.1	13.8	14.2
Return on Assets %	6.9	2.1	6.9	5.5	7.1	7.9	8.2
Debt/Total Assets %	21.0	14.7	15.7	16.6	18.6	19.9	11.7
Price Range	25.70-17.19	27.38-16.75	35.25-21.81	29.88-21.63	30.67-20.50	30.08-19.00	25.67-18.00
P/E Ratio	10.9-7.3	46.4-28.4	19.6-12.1	20.7-15.0	18.8-12.6	17.2-10.9	16.5-11.5
Average Yield %	2.8	2.5	1.8	1.8	1.7	1.5	1.6

Statistics are as originally reported. Adj. for 50% stk. div., 3/1/96. [1] Incl. restr. charges of $55.0 mill., 1/00; $13.5 mill., 1/98.

OFFICERS:
D. D. Belcher, Chmn., C.E.O.
S. A. Streeter, Pres., C.O.O.
G. A. Henseler, Exec. V.P., C.F.O.

INVESTOR CONTACT: Gerald A. Henseler, Exec. V.P., (920) 751-7777

PRINCIPAL OFFICE: 225 Main Street, Box 8003, Menasha, WI 54952-8003

TELEPHONE NUMBER: (920) 751-7777
FAX: (920) 751-7790
WEB: www.banta.com

NO. OF EMPLOYEES: 8,000 (approx.)

SHAREHOLDERS: 1,987 (record)

ANNUAL MEETING: In Apr.

INCORPORATED: WI, 1901

INSTITUTIONAL HOLDINGS:
No. of Institutions: 140
Shares Held: 20,277,381
% Held: 82.5

INDUSTRY: Commercial printing, nec (SIC: 2759)

TRANSFER AGENT(S): Firstar Bank, N.A., Milwaukee, WI.

NYSE SYMBOL BCR
Rec. Pr. 56.45 (5/31/01)

BARD (C.R.), INC.

YIELD 1.5%
P/E RATIO 27.0

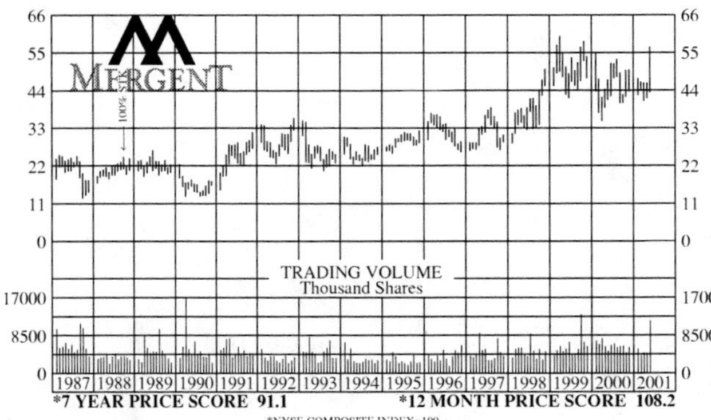

INTERIM EARNINGS (Per Share):

Qtr.	Mar.	June	Sept.	Dec.
1997	0.46	0.46	d0.07	0.42
1998	0.44	0.71	0.42	3.03
1999	0.51	0.55	0.58	0.64
2000	0.62	0.65	0.66	0.16

INTERIM DIVIDENDS (Per Share):

Amt.	Decl.	Ex.	Rec.	Pay.
0.20Q	4/19/00	4/27/00	5/01/00	5/12/00
0.21Q	7/12/00	7/20/00	7/24/00	8/04/00
0.21Q	10/11/00	10/19/00	10/23/00	11/03/00
0.21Q	12/13/00	1/18/01	1/22/01	2/02/01
0.21Q	4/18/01	4/26/01	4/30/01	5/11/01

Indicated div.: $0.84 (Div. Reinv. Plan)

CAPITALIZATION (12/31/00):

	($000)	(%)
Long-Term Debt	204,300	25.0
Common & Surplus	613,900	75.0
Total	818,200	100.0

RECENT DEVELOPMENTS: For the year ended 12/31/00, net income climbed 9.5% to $106.9 million from $118.1 million in 1999. Results for 2000 and 1999 included gains from dispositions of cardiology businesses of $15.4 million and $9.2 million, respectively. Net sales rose 6.0% to $1.10 billion. Vascular net sales grew 6.6% to $241.2 million, while urology net sales grew 2.1% to $361.2 million. Oncology net sales jumped 6.3% to $253.0 million.

PROSPECTS: On 5/30/00, the Company and Tyco International entered into a definitive agreement, pursuant to which a subsidiary of Tyco will acquire BCR for approximately $3.20 billion, including the assumption of debt. Under the terms of the agreement, shareholders of BCR will receive Tyco stock equivalent to $60.00 per BCR share. The deal is expected to close near the end of 2001.

BUSINESS

BARD (C.R.), INC. is a multinational developer, manufacturer and marketer of health care products. The Company engages in the design, manufacture, packaging, distribution and sale of medical, surgical, diagnostic and patient-care devices. Bard holds strong positions in cardiovascular, urological, surgical and general health care products. BCR products are marketed worldwide to hospitals, individual health care professionals, extended care facilities, alternate site facilities and the home, employing a combination of direct delivery and medical specialty distributors. Hospitals, physicians and nursing homes purchase approximately 90.0% of the Company's products as of 12/31/00. The Vascular Group accounted for 22.0% of 2000 sales; Urology, 32.9%; Oncology, 23.0%; Surgery, 16.6%; and other, 5.5%.

ANNUAL FINANCIAL DATA

	12/31/00	12/31/99	12/31/98	12/31/97	12/31/96	12/31/95	12/31/94
Earnings Per Share	**[5] 2.09**	**[5] 2.28**	**[4] 4.51**	**[3] 1.26**	**[2] 1.62**	**[1] 1.53**	**[1] 1.44**
Cash Flow Per Share	**3.06**	**3.22**	**5.56**	**2.26**	**2.63**	**2.42**	**2.20**
Tang. Book Val. Per Share	**5.06**	**4.67**	**4.05**	**2.62**	**2.71**	**4.36**	**3.35**
Dividends Per Share	**0.82**	**0.78**	**0.74**	**0.70**	**0.66**	**0.62**	**0.58**
Dividend Payout %	**39.2**	**34.2**	**16.4**	**55.6**	**40.7**	**40.5**	**40.3**
INCOME STATEMENT (IN MILLIONS):							
Total Revenues	1,098.8	1,036.5	1,164.7	1,213.5	1,194.4	1,137.8	1,018.2
Costs & Expenses	854.9	797.5	947.3	991.8	976.0	947.3	827.9
Depreciation & Amort.	49.6	49.1	58.7	57.3	57.4	50.6	39.6
Operating Income	194.3	189.9	158.7	164.4	161.0	139.9	150.7
Net Interest Inc./(Exp.)	d19.3	d19.3	d26.4	d32.9	d26.4	d24.2	d15.1
Income Before Income Taxes	154.0	173.3	464.4	104.9	102.7	123.5	103.0
Income Taxes	47.1	55.2	212.1	32.6	10.2	36.7	28.1
Net Income	[5] 106.9	[5] 118.1	[4] 252.3	[3] 72.3	[2] 92.5	[1] 86.8	[1] 74.9
Cash Flow	156.5	167.2	311.0	129.6	149.9	137.4	114.5
Average Shs. Outstg. (000)	51,222	51,882	55,970	57,273	57,090	56,731	52,005
BALANCE SHEET (IN MILLIONS):							
Cash & Cash Equivalents	119.7	95.9	42.4	60.7	78.0	51.3	34.2
Total Current Assets	526.6	529.1	488.5	563.5	576.9	503.9	428.0
Net Property	155.5	169.7	172.7	206.4	226.1	214.2	199.9
Total Assets	1,089.2	1,126.4	1,079.8	1,279.3	1,332.5	1,091.0	958.4
Total Current Liabilities	224.5	352.5	302.8	310.6	336.2	273.3	364.6
Long-Term Obligations	204.3	158.4	160.0	340.7	342.8	198.4	78.3
Net Stockholders' Equity	613.9	574.3	567.6	573.1	601.5	564.6	439.8
Net Working Capital	302.1	176.6	185.7	252.9	240.7	230.6	63.4
Year-end Shs. Outstg. (000)	50,909	50,782	51,498	56,785	56,986	57,101	52,048
STATISTICAL RECORD:							
Operating Profit Margin %	17.7	18.3	13.6	13.5	13.5	12.3	14.8
Net Profit Margin %	9.7	11.4	21.7	6.0	7.7	7.6	7.4
Return on Equity %	17.4	20.6	44.5	12.6	15.4	15.4	17.0
Return on Assets %	9.8	10.5	23.4	5.7	6.9	8.0	7.8
Debt/Total Assets %	18.8	14.1	14.8	26.6	25.7	18.2	8.2
Price Range	54.94-35.00	59.88-41.69	50.25-28.50	39.00-26.38	37.38-25.88	32.25-25.50	30.50-22.25
P/E Ratio	26.3-16.7	26.3-18.3	11.1-6.3	30.9-20.9	23.1-16.0	21.1-16.7	21.2-15.5
Average Yield %	1.8	1.5	1.9	2.1	2.1	2.1	2.2

Statistics are as originally reported. [1] Incl. one-time chg. of $17.7 mill., 1995; ch$16.9 mill., 1994. [2] Incl. net nonrecurr. chgs. of $12.9 mill. [3] Incl. pre-tax restruct chg. of $44.1 mill. & a nonrecurr. net gain of $3.9 mill. [4] Incl. net gain of $163.8 mill. fr. the sale of cardiology bus. & several nonrecur. chgs. total. $25.9 mill. [5] Incl. gain fr. the sale cardiology bus. of $9.2 mill., 1999; $15.4 mill., 2000

OFFICERS:
W. H. Longfield, Chmn., C.E.O.
C. Slacik, Sr. V.P., C.F.O.

INVESTOR CONTACT: Earle L. Parker, V.P. & Chief Inv. Rel. Off., (908) 277-8059

PRINCIPAL OFFICE: 730 Central Ave, Murray Hill, NJ 07974

TELEPHONE NUMBER: (908) 277-8000
FAX: (908) 277-8278
WEB: www.crbard.com

NO. OF EMPLOYEES: 8,100 (approx.)

SHAREHOLDERS: 6,701

ANNUAL MEETING: In Apr.

INCORPORATED: NJ, Feb., 1972

INSTITUTIONAL HOLDINGS:
No. of Institutions: 245
Shares Held: 39,603,087
% Held: 78.0

INDUSTRY: Surgical and medical instruments (SIC: 3841)

TRANSFER AGENT(S): First Chicago Trust Company of New York, Jersey City, NJ

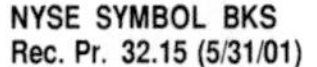

NYSE SYMBOL BKS
Rec. Pr. 32.15 (5/31/01)

BARNES & NOBLE, INC.

YIELD ...
P/E RATIO ...

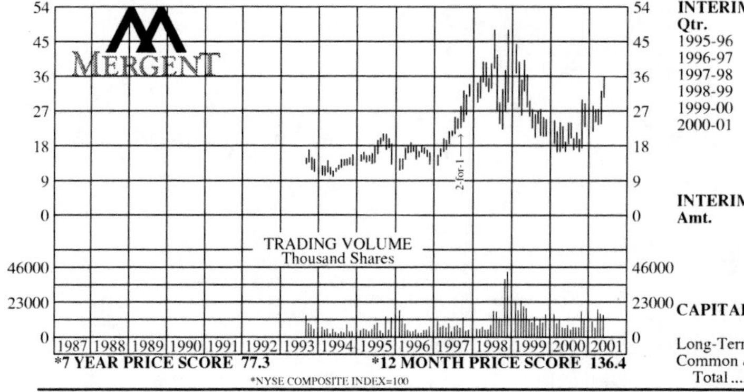

*7 YEAR PRICE SCORE 77.3 *12 MONTH PRICE SCORE 136.4

*NYSE COMPOSITE INDEX=100

INTERIM EARNINGS (Per Share):

Qtr.	Apr.	July	Oct.	Jan.
1995-96	d0.09	d0.04	d0.06	d0.63
1996-97	d0.08	d0.04	d0.04	0.90
1997-98	d0.06	d0.02	Nil	0.98
1998-99	d0.05	d0.08	d0.07	1.47
1999-00	d0.02	0.33	0.05	1.48
2000-01	d0.06	d0.13	d0.08	d0.52

INTERIM DIVIDENDS (Per Share):

Amt.	Decl.	Ex.	Rec.	Pay.

No dividends paid.

CAPITALIZATION (2/3/01):

	($000)	(%)
Long-Term Debt	666,900	46.2
Common & Surplus	777,677	53.8
Total	1,444,577	100.0

RECENT DEVELOPMENTS: For the 53 weeks ended 2/3/01, the Company reported a net loss of $52.0 million versus earnings of $129.0 million, before a $4.5 million accounting charge, in the comparable 52-week period the year before. Results in the recent period included a $106.8 million pre-tax impairment charge, while prior-year results included a $25.0 million pre-tax gain from the formation of Barnes & Noble.com. Sales climbed 25.5% to $4.38 billion from $3.49 billion a year earlier. Gross profit was $1.21 billion, up 20.3% versus $1.00 billion the previous year.

PROSPECTS: The Company expects sales at Babbage's will accelerate during the second half of 2001 due to the launch of major new video game platforms by Nintendo and Microsoft, along with increased availability of PlayStation 2. The rapidly growing video game market is expected to fuel significant increases in operating profitability by the fourth quarter of 2001 and into the following year. Meanwhile, BKS is targeting consolidated earnings of $1.61 per share for fiscal 2001 and a comparable-store sales increase of 4.0% to 5.0% at its core Barnes & Noble superstores.

BUSINESS

BARNES & NOBLE, INC. is a retailer of trade books, mass market paperbacks, children's books, off-price bargain books and magazines. As of 5/24/01, the Company operated 568 Barnes & Noble and 335 B. Dalton bookstores. BKS also publishes books under its own imprint for exclusive sale through its retail stores, mail-order catalogs, and Web site. On 10/28/99, BKS acquired Babbage's Etc., a computer software retailer that operates 966 stores under the Babbage's, Software Etc., GameStop and Funco names. BKS owns approximately 40.0% of Barnes & Noble.com. On 6/19/00, BKS acquired Funco, Inc., a video game retailer that operates 407 stores.

BUSINESS LINE ANALYSIS

(2/3/2001)	REV (%)	INC (%)
Bookstores	82.7	95.5
Video Games & Software	17.3	4.5
Total	100.0	100.0

ANNUAL FINANCIAL DATA

	2/3/01	1/29/00	1/30/99	1/31/98	2/1/97	1/27/96	1/28/95
Earnings Per Share	**4 d0.81**	**3 1.81**	**2 1.29**	**1 0.93**	**0.74**	**d0.85**	**0.41**
Cash Flow Per Share	**1.47**	**3.39**	**2.53**	**2.05**	**1.63**	**d0.04**	**1.03**
Tang. Book Val. Per Share	**6.43**	**8.37**	**8.61**	**6.50**	**5.46**	**4.60**	**3.72**
INCOME STATEMENT (IN MILLIONS):							
Total Revenues	4,375.8	3,486.0	3,005.6	2,796.9	2,448.1	1,976.9	1,622.7
Costs & Expenses	4,095.7	3,141.2	2,728.3	2,571.0	2,266.8	1,961.9	1,515.3
Depreciation & Amort.	146.3	112.7	88.7	78.6	61.7	50.2	38.9
Operating Income	133.8	232.1	188.6	147.3	119.7	d35.2	68.5
Net Interest Inc./(Exp.)	d53.5	d23.8	d24.4	d37.7	d38.3	d28.1	d23.0
Income Before Income Taxes	d33.0	218.6	156.6	109.6	81.4	d63.3	45.6
Income Taxes	19.0	89.6	64.2	44.9	30.2	cr10.3	20.1
Net Income	4 d52.0	3 129.0	2 92.4	1 64.7	51.2	d53.0	25.5
Cash Flow	94.4	241.7	181.1	143.3	112.9	d2.8	64.4
Average Shs. Outstg. (000)	64,341	71,354	71,677	69,836	69,152	62,434	62,688
BALANCE SHEET (IN MILLIONS):							
Cash & Cash Equivalents	26.0	24.2	31.1	12.7	12.4	9.3	55.4
Total Current Assets	1,455.3	1,241.5	1,088.3	977.6	867.0	848.2	613.9
Net Property	566.2	568.0	510.3	482.1	434.8	319.9	243.6
Total Assets	2,557.5	2,413.8	1,807.6	1,591.2	1,446.6	1,315.3	1,026.4
Total Current Liabilities	935.1	922.9	772.3	712.8	654.3	621.7	457.9
Long-Term Obligations	666.9	431.6	249.1	284.8	290.0	262.4	190.0
Net Stockholders' Equity	777.7	846.4	678.8	531.8	456.0	400.2	358.2
Net Working Capital	520.2	318.7	316.0	264.7	212.7	226.5	156.0
Year-end Shs. Outstg. (000)	65,044	65,528	68,759	67,922	66,376	65,918	60,166
STATISTICAL RECORD:							
Operating Profit Margin %	3.1	6.7	6.3	5.3	4.9	...	4.2
Net Profit Margin %	...	3.7	3.1	2.3	2.1	...	1.6
Return on Equity %	...	15.2	13.6	12.2	11.2	...	7.1
Return on Assets %	...	5.3	5.1	4.1	3.5	...	2.5
Debt/Total Assets %	26.1	17.9	13.8	17.9	20.0	19.9	18.5
Price Range	29.94-16.31	44.38-20.06	48.00-22.19	33.94-12.88	18.88-11.63	21.13-13.06	15.69-10.00
P/E Ratio	...	24.5-11.1	37.2-17.2	36.5-13.8	25.5-15.7	...	38.7-24.7

Statistics are as originally reported. Adj. for 2-for-1 stk. split, 9/97. 1 Bef. $11.5 mil ($0.17/sh) extraord. chg. 2 Incl. $4.5 mil ($0.06/sh) net loss from the Company's equity interest in barnesandnoble.com. 3 Bef. $4.5 mil ($0.07/sh) acctg. chrg. & incl. $25.0 mil non-recur. pre-tax gain from formation of barnesandnoble.com. 4 Incl. $92.4 mil ($1.44/sh) impairment chg.

OFFICERS:
L. Riggio, Chmn., C.E.O.
S. Riggio, Vice-Chmn.
M. O'Connell, C.F.O.

INVESTOR CONTACT: Maria Florez, Dir., Inv. Rel., (212) 633-4009

PRINCIPAL OFFICE: 122 Fifth Avenue, New York, NY 10011

TELEPHONE NUMBER: (212) 633-3300
FAX: (212) 366-5186
WEB: www.barnesandnoble.com
NO. OF EMPLOYEES: 48,000 (avg.)
SHAREHOLDERS: 2,032 (approx.)
ANNUAL MEETING: In June
INCORPORATED: DE, Nov., 1986

INSTITUTIONAL HOLDINGS:
No. of Institutions: 175
Shares Held: 41,179,641
% Held: 63.2

INDUSTRY: Book stores (SIC: 5942)

TRANSFER AGENT(S): The Bank of New York, New York, NY

NYSE SYMBOL B
Rec. Pr. 21.25 (5/31/01)

BARNES GROUP INC.

YIELD 3.8%
P/E RATIO 11.2

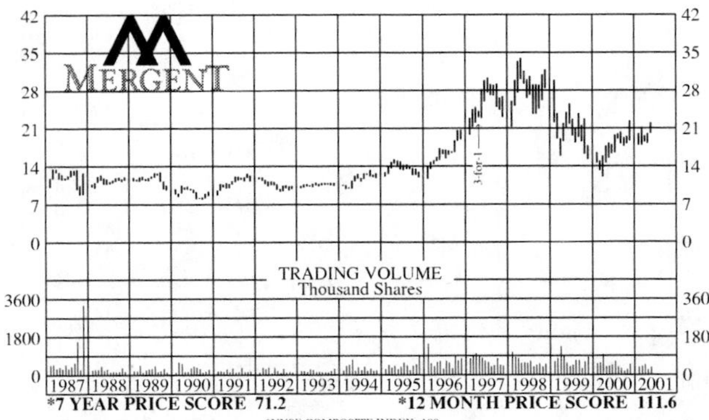

INTERIM EARNINGS (Per Share):

Qtr.	Mar.	June	Sept.	Dec.
1996	0.34	0.43	0.44	0.43
1997	0.49	0.53	0.50	0.47
1998	0.58	0.23	0.52	0.36
1999	0.50	0.41	0.45	0.08
2000	0.50	0.49	0.49	0.41

INTERIM DIVIDENDS (Per Share):

Amt.	Decl.	Ex.	Rec.	Pay.
0.20Q	4/12/00	5/26/00	5/31/00	6/09/00
0.20Q	7/13/00	8/28/00	8/30/00	9/08/00
0.20Q	10/12/00	11/27/00	11/29/00	12/08/00
0.20Q	2/07/01	2/27/01	3/01/01	3/12/01
0.20Q	4/12/01	5/30/01	6/01/01	6/11/01

Indicated div.: $0.80 (Div. Reinv. Plan)

CAPITALIZATION (12/31/00):

	($000)	(%)
Long-Term Debt	230,000	53.3
Common & Surplus	201,333	46.7
Total	431,333	100.0

RECENT DEVELOPMENTS: For the year ended 12/31/00, net income amounted to $35.7 million, up 24.7% compared with $28.6 million in the previous year. Net sales advanced 18.9% to $740.0 million versus $622.4 million the year before. Sales at Associated Spring increased 15.8% to $327.3 million, reflecting strong sales volumes of mechanical springs and nitrogen gas springs. Barnes Aerospace sales climbed 11.0% to $135.1 million, while Barnes Distribution sales grew 26.3% to $291.1 million.

PROSPECTS: Going forward, revenues should benefit from recent acquisitions and product expansion into international markets. The recent acquisitions of Kratz-Wilde Machine Company, Apex Manufacturing Inc., Allegheny-Teledyne and Curtis Industries, Inc. are starting to contribute to earnings at Barnes Distribution and Barnes Aerospace. As a result, these businesses are expected to report higher earnings in 2001. On 1/11/01, the Company announced that it acquired Euro Stock Springs & Components Limited.

BUSINESS

BARNES GROUP INC. is a diversified company that manufactures and provides products and services to industrial markets. Barnes Distribution (38.7% of 2000 revenues; 19.9% of operating profits) distributes high-strength fasteners, automotive replacement parts, spray chemicals, adhesives, sealants and welding supplies for maintenance and repair to the industrial aftermarket. Barnes Distribution services customers under the brand names of Bowman Distribution, Curtis Industries, Mechanics Choice, Raymond, Motalink and Autoliaison. Associated Spring (43.4%; 67.8%) is the largest manufacturer of precision springs and customer made metal parts for the automotive, home appliance, farm machinery, heavy construction and electronics industries. The Barnes Aerospace group (17.9%; 12.3%) produces machine components for the primary engine manufacturers serving the commercial aircraft and defense industries.

QUARTERLY DATA

(12/31/2000)	Rev	Inc
1st Quarter	173,000	9,400
2nd Quarter	188,500	9,100
3rd Quarter	190,600	9,300
4th Quarter	187,900	7,900

ANNUAL FINANCIAL DATA

	12/31/00	12/31/99	12/31/98	12/31/97	12/31/96	12/31/95	12/31/94
Earnings Per Share	**1.90**	**1.46**	**1.69**	**1.96**	**[1] 1.63**	**1.40**	**1.07**
Cash Flow Per Share	**3.85**	**3.01**	**3.08**	**3.32**	**2.97**	**2.76**	**2.31**
Tang. Book Val. Per Share	**2.45**	**4.88**	**8.59**	**8.04**	**6.89**	**5.53**	**4.49**
Dividends Per Share	**0.79**	**0.75**	**0.69**	**0.65**	**0.60**	**0.53**	**0.48**
Dividend Payout %	**41.6**	**51.4**	**41.1**	**33.2**	**36.7**	**38.1**	**45.3**
INCOME STATEMENT (IN THOUSANDS):							
Total Revenues	740,032	622,356	651,183	642,660	594,989	592,509	569,197
Costs & Expenses	641,212	546,504	567,531	548,771	513,047	516,955	508,815
Depreciation & Amort.	35,871	30,602	28,431	28,123	26,626	26,750	23,733
Operating Income	62,949	45,250	55,221	65,766	55,316	48,804	36,649
Net Interest Inc./(Exp.)	d15,140	d6,093	d4,106	d4,864	d4,981	d5,274	d5,133
Income Before Income Taxes	48,590	42,698	54,663	64,502	52,310	45,450	33,922
Income Taxes	12,925	14,086	20,169	24,079	19,742	17,966	13,606
Net Income	35,665	28,612	34,494	40,423	[1] 32,568	27,484	20,316
Cash Flow	71,536	59,214	62,925	68,546	59,194	54,234	44,049
Average Shs. Outstg.	18,568	19,643	20,426	20,656	19,923	19,641	19,062
BALANCE SHEET (IN THOUSANDS):							
Cash & Cash Equivalents	23,303	43,632	42,772	32,530	23,986	17,868	22,023
Total Current Assets	241,348	219,185	207,228	203,017	190,298	172,816	175,537
Net Property	163,766	145,105	139,247	133,830	131,071	122,870	112,569
Total Assets	636,941	516,282	418,904	407,978	389,956	361,549	351,956
Total Current Liabilities	126,846	116,020	100,344	89,925	80,822	77,536	87,212
Long-Term Obligations	230,000	140,000	51,000	62,205	74,951	77,491	79,839
Net Stockholders' Equity	201,333	180,614	188,674	180,859	157,164	128,841	107,139
Net Working Capital	114,502	103,165	106,884	113,092	109,476	95,280	88,325
Year-end Shs. Outstg.	18,607	18,851	19,835	20,154	19,992	19,665	19,287
STATISTICAL RECORD:							
Operating Profit Margin %	8.5	7.3	8.5	10.2	9.3	8.2	6.4
Net Profit Margin %	4.8	4.6	5.3	6.3	5.5	4.6	3.6
Return on Equity %	17.7	15.8	18.3	22.4	20.7	21.3	19.0
Return on Assets %	5.6	5.5	8.2	9.9	8.4	7.6	5.8
Debt/Total Assets %	36.1	27.1	12.2	15.2	19.2	21.4	22.7
Price Range	22.38-12.00	30.00-15.25	34.00-21.25	30.38-19.79	20.67-11.67	15.25-11.96	13.29-9.83
P/E Ratio	11.8-6.3	20.5-10.4	20.1-12.6	15.5-10.1	12.7-7.1	10.9-8.5	12.5-9.2
Average Yield %	4.6	3.3	2.5	2.6	3.7	3.9	4.2

Statistics are as originally reported. Adj. for stk splits: 3-for-1, 4/97 [1] Incl. non-recurr. chrg. $1.3 mill.

OFFICERS:
Thomas Barnes, Chmn.
E. M. Carpenter, Pres. & C.E.O.
W. C. Denninger, Sr. V.P., C.F.O.

INVESTOR CONTACT: Phillip J. Penn, Investor Relations, (860) 583-7070

PRINCIPAL OFFICE: 123 Main Street, Bristol, CT 06011-0489

TELEPHONE NUMBER: (860) 583-7070
FAX: (860) 589-3507
WEB: www.barnesgroupinc.com

NO. OF EMPLOYEES: 5,600 (approx.)

SHAREHOLDERS: 3,931

ANNUAL MEETING: In Apr.

INCORPORATED: DE, Jan., 1925

INSTITUTIONAL HOLDINGS:
No. of Institutions: 75
Shares Held: 8,250,213
% Held: 44.3

INDUSTRY: Fabricated metal products, nec (SIC: 3499)

TRANSFER AGENT(S): Mellon Investor Services, L.L.C., Ridgefield Park, NJ

NYSE SYMBOL ABX
Rec. Pr. 16.50 (5/31/01)

BARRICK GOLD CORP.

YIELD 1.3%
P/E RATIO . . .

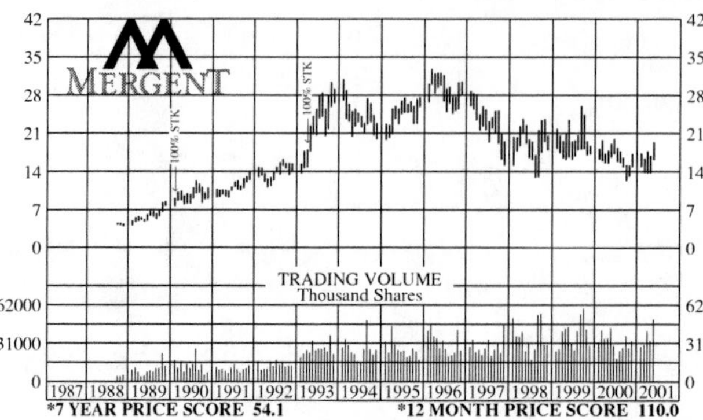

*7 YEAR PRICE SCORE 54.1 *12 MONTH PRICE SCORE 110.0
*NYSE COMPOSITE INDEX=100

INTERIM EARNINGS (Per Share):

Qtr.	Mar.	June	Sept.	Dec.
1997	0.15	0.31	0.50	0.20
1998	0.20	0.38	0.58	0.79
1999	0.23	0.43	0.63	0.83
2000	0.18	0.18	0.22	d2.51

INTERIM DIVIDENDS (Per Share):

Amt.	Decl.	Ex.	Rec.	Pay.
0.10S	5/04/99	5/26/99	5/31/99	6/15/99
0.10S	11/17/99	11/26/99	11/30/99	12/15/99
0.11S	5/16/00	5/26/00	5/31/00	6/15/00
0.11S	11/16/00	11/28/00	11/30/00	12/15/00
0.11S	5/08/01	5/29/01	5/31/01	6/15/01

Indicated div.: $0.22 (Div. Reinv. Plan)

CAPITALIZATION (12/31/00):

	($000)	(%)
Long-Term Debt	676,000	16.8
Deferred Income Tax	335,000	8.3
Common & Surplus	3,023,000	74.9
Total	4,034,000	100.0

RECENT DEVELOPMENTS: For the year ended 12/31/00, the Company reported a net loss of $766.0 million compared with net income of $331.0 million in the prior year. The decline in earnings was attributed to higher costs and expenses and a provision for mining assets, despite a mark-to-market gain on ABX's Premium Gold Sales program. Total revenues dropped 5.2% to $1.36 billion from $1.43 billion in the previous year.

PROSPECTS: In 2001, ABX expects total production to rise to 3.8 million ounces at a total cash cost of $156.00 per ounce. Separately, the Bulyanhulu Mine in Tanzania is on schedule for start up in early April and is expected to produce 400,000 ounces annually at costs of $130.00 per ounce. Futhermore, production plans are currently being reviewed to potentially increase the annual rate to 500,000 ounces.

BUSINESS

BARRICK GOLD CORP. is an international gold producer with five mines in the United States, Canada, Chile, and Peru, and three other mines under development. The Company engages in gold mining and other related activities including exploration, development, mining and processing. As of 12/31/00, proven and probable reserves were $58.5 million ounces of gold. As of 12/31/00, the Company had gold production of 3.7 million ounces and gold sold of 3.7 million ounces. In the fourth quarter of 1999, ABX ceased operations at its Bullfrog Mine.

REVENUES

(12/31/2000)	($000)	(%)
Gold Sales	1,330,000	98.0
Interest & Other Income	27000	2.0
Total	1,357000	100.0

ANNUAL FINANCIAL DATA

	12/31/00	12/31/99	12/31/98	12/31/97	12/31/96	12/31/95	12/31/94
Earnings Per Share	**d1.93**	**0.83**	**0.79**	**d0.33**	**0.60**	**0.83**	**0.81**
Cash Flow Per Share	**d1.08**	**1.75**	**1.33**	**0.17**	**1.10**	**1.34**	**1.16**
Tang. Book Val. Per Share	**7.63**	**10.49**	**9.53**	**8.91**	**9.39**	**8.26**	**7.41**
Dividends Per Share	**0.22**	**0.20**	**0.18**	**0.16**	**0.14**	**0.12**	**0.10**
Dividend Payout %	**. . .**	**24.1**	**22.8**	**. . .**	**23.3**	**14.5**	**12.3**
INCOME STATEMENT (IN MILLIONS):							
Total Revenues	1,357.0	1,432.0	1,298.0	1,294.0	1,318.0	1,308.0	954.0
Costs & Expenses	626.0	595.0	681.0	755.0	790.0	715.0	501.0
Depreciation & Amort.	339.0	385.0	216.0	188.0	183.0	181.0	106.0
Operating Income	392.0	452.0	401.0	351.0	345.0	412.0	347.0
Net Interest Inc./(Exp.)	d6.0	d11.0	. . .	. . .	d10.0	d21.0	d11.0
Income Before Income Taxes	d944.0	441.0	443.0	d80.0	290.0	391.0	336.0
Income Taxes	cr178.0	110.0	142.0	43.0	72.0	98.0	85.0
Net Income	d766.0	331.0	301.0	d123.0	218.0	293.0	251.0
Cash Flow	d427.0	716.0	517.0	65.0	401.0	474.0	357.0
Average Shs. Outstg. (000)	396,000	410,000	390,000	373,000	363,000	354,000	309,000
BALANCE SHEET (IN MILLIONS):							
Cash & Cash Equivalents	623.0	500.0	416.0	292.0	245.0	285.0	458.0
Total Current Assets	865.0	744.0	611.0	446.0	483.0	509.0	657.0
Net Property	3,565.0	4,488.0	3,991.0	3,824.0	3,991.0	3,004.0	2,769.0
Total Assets	4,535.0	5,353.0	4,655.0	4,306.0	4,515.0	3,557.0	3,474.0
Total Current Liabilities	354.0	304.0	233.0	193.0	192.0	223.0	289.0
Long-Term Obligations	676.0	525.0	500.0	500.0	500.0	100.0	283.0
Net Stockholders' Equity	3,023.0	4,154.0	3,592.0	3,324.0	3,501.0	2,949.0	2,617.0
Net Working Capital	511.0	440.0	378.0	253.0	291.0	286.0	368.0
Year-end Shs. Outstg. (000)	396,000	396,000	377,000	373,000	373,000	357,000	353,000
STATISTICAL RECORD:							
Operating Profit Margin %	28.9	31.6	30.9	27.1	26.2	31.5	36.4
Net Profit Margin %	. . .	23.1	23.2	. . .	16.5	22.4	26.3
Return on Equity %	. . .	8.0	8.4	. . .	6.2	9.9	9.6
Return on Assets %	. . .	6.2	6.5	. . .	4.8	8.2	7.2
Debt/Total Assets %	14.9	9.8	10.7	11.6	11.1	2.8	8.1
Price Range	20.00-12.31	26.00-16.13	23.69-12.88	28.75-15.13	32.88-24.63	27.63-19.75	31.00-19.88
P/E Ratio	. . .	31.3-19.4	30.0-16.3	. . .	54.8-41.0	33.3-23.8	38.3-24.5
Average Yield %	1.4	0.9	1.0	0.7	0.5	0.5	0.4

Statistics are as originally reported.

OFFICERS:
P. Munk, Chmn.
A. A. MacNaughton, Vice-Chmn.
J. K. Carrington, Vice-Chmn., C.O.O.
R. Oliphant, Pres., C.E.O.

INVESTOR CONTACT: Richard Young, V.P. Inv. Rel., (416) 307-7431

PRINCIPAL OFFICE: Royal Bank Plaza, South Tower, 200 Bay Street, Suite 2700, Toronto, Ontario, Canada

TELEPHONE NUMBER: (416) 861-9911
FAX: (416) 861-2492
WEB: www.barrick.com

NO. OF EMPLOYEES: N/A

SHAREHOLDERS: 13,615

ANNUAL MEETING: In May

INCORPORATED: CAN, 1983

INSTITUTIONAL HOLDINGS:
No. of Institutions: 244
Shares Held: 182,495,048
% Held: 46.1

INDUSTRY: Gold ores (SIC: 1041)

TRANSFER AGENT(S): CIBC Mellon Trust Company, Toronto, Canada; Mellon Investor Services, Ridgefield Park, New Jersey

NYSE SYMBOL BOL
Rec. Pr. 47.30 (5/31/01)

BAUSCH & LOMB, INC.

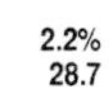

YIELD 2.2%
P/E RATIO 28.7

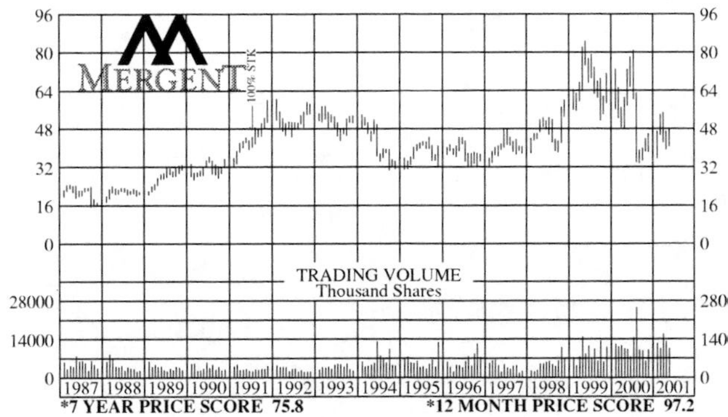

INTERIM EARNINGS (Per Share):

Qtr	Mar.	June	Sept.	Dec.
1997	0.39	0.54	0.25	0.29
1998	d0.89	0.98	0.65	d0.77
1999	0.39	0.49	0.71	0.29
2000	0.68	0.64	0.27	0.06

INTERIM DIVIDENDS (Per Share):

Amt.	Decl.	Ex.	Rec.	Pay.
0.26Q	5/02/00	5/30/00	6/01/00	7/03/00
0.26Q	7/25/00	8/30/00	9/01/00	10/02/00
0.26Q	10/30/00	11/29/00	12/01/00	1/02/01
0.26Q	2/27/01	3/07/01	3/09/01	4/02/01
0.26Q	5/01/01	5/30/01	6/01/01	7/02/01

Indicated div.: $1.04 (Div. Reinv. Plan)

CAPITALIZATION (12/30/00):

	($000)	(%)
Long-Term Debt [1]	763,100	35.0
Deferred Income Tax	159,600	7.3
Minority Interest	217,000	10.0
Common & Surplus [2]	1,039,400	47.7
Total	2,179,100	100.0

RECENT DEVELOPMENTS: For the year ended 12/30/00, income from continuing operations declined 20.2% to $82.0 million versus income of $102.7 million in 1999. The 2000 results included pre-tax charges of $57.5 million and excluded an after-tax gain of $1.4 million from early extinguishment of debt. Total net sales inched up 0.9% to $1.77 billion.

PROSPECTS: Going forward, BOL should continue to benefit from restructuring actions that are expected to generate savings of approximately $20.0 million in 2001 and $40.0 million annually thereafter. Separately, BOL and VISX entered into a settlement and license agreement underwhich VISX has licensed its patents relating to refracturing excimer lasers to the Company.

BUSINESS

BAUSCH & LOMB, INC. is a global eye-care company. The Company operates three product lines: Vision Care, Surgical, and Pharmaceuticals. The Vision Care business includes contact lenses and lens care products. The Surgical business offers a line of products for ophthalmic surgery. The Pharmaceuticals business develops and markets prescription and over-the-counter drugs used to treat a wide range of eye conditions, including glaucoma, eye allergies, conjunctivitis, and dry eye. Bausch & Lomb products are available in more than 100 countries around the world. Revenues for 2000 were derived: Vision Care, 57.7%; Pharmaceuticals, 15.5%; and Surgical, 26.8%.

ANNUAL FINANCIAL DATA

	12/30/00	12/25/99	12/26/98	12/27/97	12/28/96	12/30/95	12/31/94
Earnings Per Share	**[5] 1.49**	**[8] 1.79**	**[7] 0.45**	**[6] 0.89**	**[4] [5] 1.47**	**[3] 1.94**	**0.23**
Cash Flow Per Share	**4.20**	**4.42**	**3.35**	**2.90**	**3.47**	**3.76**	**1.89**
Tang. Book Val. Per Share	**4.18**	**11.05**	**1.52**	**7.45**	**8.86**	**9.62**	**8.79**
Dividends Per Share	**1.04**	**1.04**	**1.04**	**1.04**	**1.04**	**1.00**	**0.93**
Dividend Payout %	**69.8**	**58.1**	**231.1**	**116.8**	**70.7**	**51.3**	**404.2**
INCOME STATEMENT (IN MILLIONS):							
Total Revenues	1,772.4	1,756.1	2,362.8	1,915.7	1,926.8	1,932.9	1,850.6
Costs & Expenses	1,482.8	1,385.7	2,075.3	1,655.7	1,622.7	1,617.0	1,657.5
Depreciation & Amort.	147.7	156.2	163.8	112.0	113.3	105.3	99.3
Operating Income	141.9	214.2	123.7	148.0	190.8	210.6	93.8
Net Interest Inc./(Exp.)	d68.5	d88.4	d100.8	d56.0	d51.7	d45.8	d41.4
Income Before Income Taxes	160.7	185.0	130.4	118.0	168.9	211.8	90.3
Income Taxes	65.5	66.6	79.4	45.6	63.7	78.1	52.8
Equity Earnings/Minority Int.	d13.2	d15.7	d25.8	d23.0	d22.1	d21.7	d24.1
Net Income	[5] 82.0	[8] 102.7	[7] 25.2	[6] 49.4	[4] [5] 83.1	[3] 112.0	13.5
Cash Flow	229.7	258.9	189.0	161.4	196.4	217.3	112.7
Average Shs. Outstg. (000)	54,724	58,639	56,367	55,654	56,552	57,852	59,739
BALANCE SHEET (IN MILLIONS):							
Cash & Cash Equivalents	827.7	952.1	429.2	183.7	167.8	194.6	232.5
Total Current Assets	1,645.7	1,810.3	1,586.8	1,090.2	947.6	930.4	954.0
Net Property	494.8	524.8	725.0	580.2	566.7	550.4	542.8
Total Assets	3,085.9	3,273.5	3,491.7	2,772.9	2,603.4	2,550.1	2,457.7
Total Current Liabilities	808.7	619.6	812.4	887.3	929.1	859.5	676.5
Long-Term Obligations	763.1	977.0	1,281.3	510.8	236.3	191.0	289.5
Net Stockholders' Equity	1,039.4	1,234.0	845.0	818.4	881.9	929.3	914.4
Net Working Capital	837.0	1,190.7	774.4	202.9	18.5	70.9	277.4
Year-end Shs. Outstg. (000)	53,473	56,763	56,827	55,209	55,403	56,941	58,992
STATISTICAL RECORD:							
Operating Profit Margin %	8.0	12.2	5.2	7.7	9.9	10.9	5.1
Net Profit Margin %	4.6	5.8	1.1	2.6	4.3	5.8	0.7
Return on Equity %	7.9	8.3	3.0	6.0	9.4	12.1	1.5
Return on Assets %	2.7	3.1	0.7	1.8	3.2	4.4	0.5
Debt/Total Assets %	24.7	29.8	36.7	18.4	9.1	7.5	11.8
Price Range	80.88-33.56	84.75-51.38	60.00-37.75	47.88-32.50	44.50-32.50	44.50-30.88	53.88-30.63
P/E Ratio	54.3-22.5	47.3-28.7	133.3-83.9	53.8-36.5	30.3-22.1	22.9-15.9	234.1-133.1
Average Yield %	1.8	1.5	2.1	2.6	2.7	2.6	2.2

Statistics are as originally reported. Adjusted for 2-for-1 stock split, 6/91. [1] Incl. cap. lse. obligs. [2] Incl. Cl. B. common. [3] Incl. net nonrecurr. chgs. of $10.8 mill. [4] Incl. restruct. chg. of $15.1 mill., 1996; $33.7 mill, 2000. [5] Incl. a net nonrecurr. gain of $1.5 mill., an after-tax chg. of $16.1 mill. [6] Incl. net nonrecurr. chgs. of $76.2 mill. [7] Incl. a net non recurr. chgs. of $84.2 mill. [8] Incl. a pre-tax gain of $6.7 mill. fr., an after-tax restr. chg. of $34.2 mill., excl. a net gain of $342.1 mill.

OFFICERS:
W. M. Carpenter, Chmn., C.E.O.
S. C. McCluski, Sr. V.P., C.F.O.

INVESTOR CONTACT: Angela J. Panzarella, V.P., Inv. Rel., (716) 338-6025

PRINCIPAL OFFICE: One Bausch & Lomb Place, Rochester, NY 14604-2701

TELEPHONE NUMBER: (716) 338-6000
FAX: (716) 338-6007
WEB: www.bausch.com

NO. OF EMPLOYEES: 12,400 (approx.)

SHAREHOLDERS: 6,700 (approx.)

ANNUAL MEETING: In May

INCORPORATED: NY, Mar., 1908

INSTITUTIONAL HOLDINGS:
No. of Institutions: 223
Shares Held: 46,284,557
% Held: 86.4

INDUSTRY: Ophthalmic goods (SIC: 3851)

TRANSFER AGENT(S): Mellon Investor Services, South Hackensack, NJ

NYSE SYMBOL BAX
Rec. Pr. 49.38 (5/31/01)

BAXTER INTERNATIONAL INC.

YIELD 1.2%
P/E RATIO 20.0

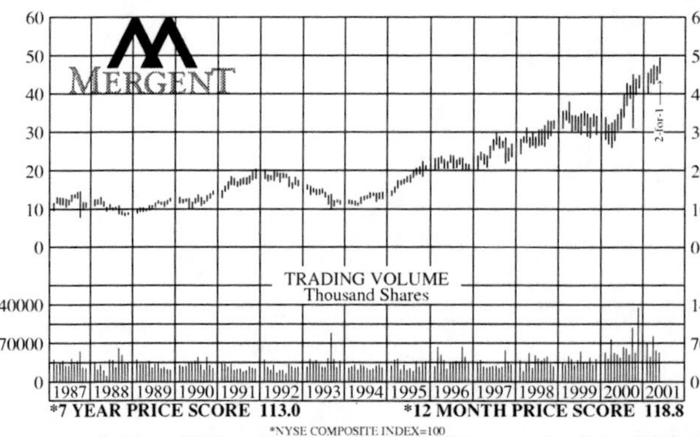

INTERIM EARNINGS (Per Share):

Qtr.	Mar.	June	Sept.	Dec.
1997	d0.37	0.29	0.29	0.32
1998	0.29	0.31	d0.22	0.37
1999	0.31	0.35	0.34	0.39
2000	0.33	0.08	0.39	0.45

INTERIM DIVIDENDS (Per Share):

Amt.	Decl.	Ex.	Rec.	Pay.
0.291Q	5/04/99	6/09/99	6/11/99	7/01/99
0.291Q	9/20/99	9/22/99	9/24/99	10/01/99
0.291Q	11/16/99	12/08/99	12/10/99	1/03/00
1.164A	11/14/00	12/13/00	12/15/00	1/08/01
2-for-1	2/28/01	5/31/01	5/09/01	5/30/01

Indicated div.: $0.58 (Adj.; Div. Reinv. Plan)

CAPITALIZATION (12/31/00):

	($000)	(%)
Long-Term Debt [4]	1,726,000	38.0
Deferred Income Tax	160,000	3.5
Common & Surplus	2,659,000	58.5
Total	4,545,000	100.0

RECENT DEVELOPMENTS: For the year ended 12/31/00, net income declined 5.3% to $738.0 million versus $779.0 million in 1999. Results for 2000 included pre-tax nonrecurring charges totaling $286.0 million and net special charges of $13.0 million. The 1999 results excluded a net accounting charge of $27.0 million. Net sales rose 8.1% to $6.90 billion from $6.38 billion a year earlier. Operating income fell 12.1% to $1.01 billion.

PROSPECTS: In 2001, BAX should benefit from a strong product pipeline and the acquisitions of Althin Medical A.B. and North American Vaccine, Inc. BAX continues to make significant progress in the development of products through collaborations with Cerus Corporation, Arriva Pharmaceuticals, Pharming Group and XOMA Ltd. For 2001, BAX anticipates sales and earnings growth to reach the low double digits.

BUSINESS

BAXTER INTERNATIONAL INC. develops, distributes, and manufactures products and technologies related to the blood and circulatory system. Operations are divided into three business segments. The I.V. Systems/Medical Products segment develops technologies and systems to improve intravenous medication delivery and distributes medical products. The BioScience segment develops biopharmaceutical and blood collection and separation products and technologies. The Renal segment develops products and provides services for the treatment of end-stage kidney disease. BAX manufactures products in 29 countries and sells them in over 100 countries. BAX's products are used by hospitals, clinical and medical research laboratories, blood and dialysis centers, rehabilitation centers, nursing homes, doctors' offices and by patients, at home, under physician supervision.

QUARTERLY DATA

(12/31/2000) (000)	Rev	Inc
1st Quarter	1,583,000	191,000
2nd Quarter	1,694,000	48,000
3rd Quarter	1,687,000	231,000
4th Quarter	1,932,000	270,000

ANNUAL FINANCIAL DATA

	12/31/00	12/31/99	12/31/98	12/31/97	12/31/96	12/31/95	12/31/94
Earnings Per Share	[8] **1.24**	[7] **1.35**	[6] **0.55**	[5] **0.53**	[4] **1.06**	[3] **0.67**	**1.07**
Cash Flow Per Share	**1.91**	**1.99**	**1.28**	**1.25**	**1.70**	**1.30**	**2.00**
Tang. Book Val. Per Share	**2.42**	**4.18**	**1.79**	**1.78**	**2.06**	**4.79**	**2.54**
Dividends Per Share	**0.15**	**0.58**	**0.58**	**0.56**	[2] **0.58**	**0.55**	**0.51**
Dividend Payout %	**11.8**	**43.1**	**105.4**	**105.7**	**54.7**	**82.0**	**47.7**
INCOME STATEMENT (IN MILLIONS):							
Total Revenues	6,896.0	6,380.0	6,599.0	6,138.0	5,438.0	5,048.0	9,324.0
Costs & Expenses	5,538.0	4,858.0	5,479.0	5,615.0	4,179.0	4,001.0	7,777.0
Depreciation & Amort.	405.0	372.0	426.0	398.0	348.0	336.0	524.0
Operating Income	1,011.0	1,150.0	694.0	686.0	911.0	711.0	1,023.0
Net Interest Inc./(Exp.)	d85.0	d87.0	d161.0	d163.0	d103.0	d96.0	d193.0
Income Before Income Taxes	946.0	1,052.0	549.0	523.0	793.0	524.0	801.0
Income Taxes	208.0	273.0	234.0	223.0	218.0	153.0	205.0
Net Income	[8] 738.0	[7] 779.0	[6] 315.0	[5] 300.0	[4] 575.0	[3] 371.0	596.0
Cash Flow	1,143.0	1,173.0	741.0	698.0	923.0	707.0	1,120.0
Average Shs. Outstg. (000)	598,000	590,000	578,000	556,000	544,000	544,000	560,000
BALANCE SHEET (IN MILLIONS):							
Cash & Cash Equivalents	579.0	606.0	709.0	465.0	761.0	476.0	471.0
Total Current Assets	3,651.0	3,819.0	4,651.0	3,870.0	3,480.0	2,911.0	4,340.0
Net Property	2,807.0	2,650.0	2,673.0	2,360.0	1,843.0	1,749.0	2,562.0
Total Assets	8,733.0	9,644.0	10,085.0	8,707.0	7,596.0	9,437.0	10,002.0
Total Current Liabilities	3,372.0	2,700.0	2,988.0	2,557.0	2,445.0	2,154.0	2,766.0
Long-Term Obligations	1,726.0	2,601.0	3,096.0	2,635.0	1,695.0	2,372.0	2,341.0
Net Stockholders' Equity	2,659.0	3,348.0	2,839.0	2,619.0	2,504.0	3,704.0	3,720.0
Net Working Capital	279.0	1,119.0	1,663.0	1,313.0	1,035.0	757.0	1,574.0
Year-end Shs. Outstg. (000)	586,000	580,000	572,000	561,000	544,000	544,000	564,000
STATISTICAL RECORD:							
Operating Profit Margin %	14.7	18.0	10.5	11.2	16.8	14.1	11.0
Net Profit Margin %	10.7	12.2	4.8	4.9	10.6	7.3	6.4
Return on Equity %	27.8	23.3	11.1	11.5	23.0	10.0	16.0
Return on Assets %	8.5	8.1	3.1	3.4	7.6	3.9	6.0
Debt/Total Assets %	19.8	27.0	30.7	30.3	22.3	25.1	23.4
Price Range	45.13-25.88	38.00-28.41	33.00-24.25	30.13-19.94	24.06-19.88	22.38-13.38	14.44-10.81
P/E Ratio	36.5-20.9	28.1-21.0	60.5-44.5	56.8-37.6	22.8-18.8	33.4-20.0	13.6-10.2
Average Yield %	0.4	1.8	2.0	1.1	2.7	3.0	4.0

Statistics are as originally reported. Adj. for 2-for-1 stk. split, 5/01. [1] 1 sh. of Allegiance Corp. for each sh. held. effective 10/1/96. [2] Incl. lease obligs. [3] Excl. inc. fr. disc. opers. of $278.0 mill. & pre-tax nonrecurr. chgs. of $133.0 mill. [4] Excl. inc. fr. disc. opers. of $94.0 mill. [5] Excl. disc. opers. of Allegiance Corp. [6] Incl. pre-tax nonrecurr. chrgs. of $425.0 mill. [7] Excl. net nonrecurr. net gain of $18.0 mill. [8] Incl. a pre-tax nonrecurr. net chrgs. $299.0 mill.

OFFICERS:
H. M. Jansen Kraemer Jr., Chmn.,C.E.O.
B. P. Anderson, Sr. V.P., C.F.O.
S. J. Meyer, Treas.

INVESTOR CONTACT: Neville J. Jehareijah, V.P., Financial Relations, (847) 948-4550

PRINCIPAL OFFICE: One Baxter Parkway, Deerfield, IL 60015-4633

TELEPHONE NUMBER: (847) 948-2000
FAX: (847) 948-2964
WEB: www.baxter.com

NO. OF EMPLOYEES: 43,000 (approx.)

SHAREHOLDERS: 58,800 (approx.)

ANNUAL MEETING: In May

INCORPORATED: DE, Oct., 1931

INSTITUTIONAL HOLDINGS:
No. of Institutions: 611
Shares Held: 432,318,756 (Adj.)
% Held: 73.0

INDUSTRY: Surgical and medical instruments (SIC: 3841)

TRANSFER AGENT(S): First Chicago Trust Company of New York, Jersey City, NJ

NYSE SYMBOL BBT
Rec. Pr. 35.42 (4/30/01)

BB&T CORPORATION

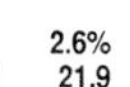

YIELD 2.6%
P/E RATIO 21.9

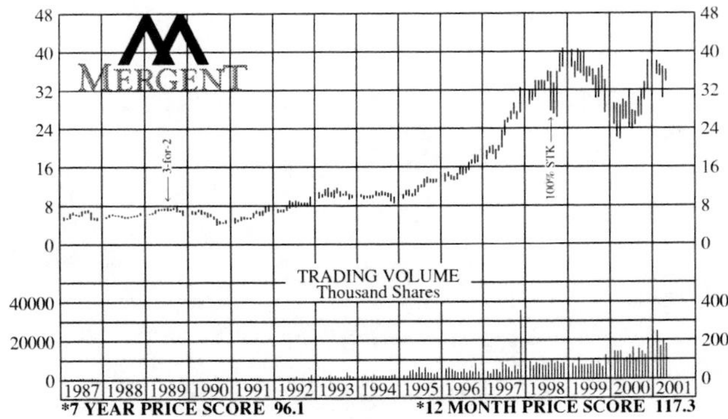

***7 YEAR PRICE SCORE 96.1** ***12 MONTH PRICE SCORE 117.3**
*NYSE COMPOSITE INDEX=100

INTERIM EARNINGS (Per Share):

Qtr.	Mar.	June	Sept.	Dec.
1997	0.75	0.45	0.71	0.69
1998	0.39	0.42	0.44	0.46
1999	0.44	0.49	0.44	0.47
2000	0.46	0.48	0.12	0.56

INTERIM DIVIDENDS (Per Share):

Amt.	Decl.	Ex.	Rec.	Pay.
0.20Q	2/22/00	4/12/00	4/14/00	5/01/00
0.23Q	6/27/00	7/12/00	7/14/00	8/01/00
0.23Q	8/22/00	10/11/00	10/13/00	11/01/00
0.23Q	12/19/00	1/10/01	1/12/01	2/01/01
0.23Q	2/27/01	4/10/01	4/13/01	5/01/01

Indicated div.: $0.92 (Div. Reinv. Plan)

CAPITALIZATION (12/31/00):

	($000)	(%)
Total Deposits	38,014,501	74.3
Long-Term Debt	8,354,672	16.3
Common & Surplus	4,785,925	9.4
Total	51,155,098	100.0

RECENT DEVELOPMENTS: For the year ended 12/31/00, net income dropped 11.2% to $626.4 million from $705.6 million in the prior year. Results for 2000 and 1999 included after-tax non-recurring charges of $248.6 million and $61.7 million, respectively. Net interest income increased 4.3% to $2.02 billion from $1.93 billion the year before. Non-interest income declined 11.2% to $777.0 million. Non-interest expense increased 6.9% to $1.76 billion. Comparisons were made with restated 1999 figures.

PROSPECTS: On 1/24/01, BBT agreed to acquire F&M National Corp. of Winchester, Virginia in a transaction valued at $1.17 billion. F&M has $4.00 billion in assets and operates 185 offices throughout Virginia, West Virginia and Maryland. The acquisition is expected to close in the third quarter of 2001. BBT also agreed to acquire Virginia Capital Bancshares, Inc. As a result of both acquisitions, BBT's assets will increase to more than $11.00 billion and BBT will rank fourth in market share in Virginia.

BUSINESS

BB&T CORPORATION, a multi-bank holding company with assets of $59.34 billion as of 12/31/00, owns 854 banking offices in the Carolinas, Virginia, West Virginia, Tennessee, Kentucky, Georgia, Maryland and Washington, D.C. BBT's largest subsidiary is Branch Banking and Trust Company (BB&T-NC). BB&T-NC's subsidiaries include BB&T Leasing Corp., BB&T Investment Services, BB&T Insurance Services and W.E. Stanley, Inc. BBT's other subsidiaries include Prime Rate Premium Finance Corp., Inc., Laureate Capital Corp., Branch Banking and Trust Co. of South Carolina and Branch Banking and Trust Co. of Virginia. On 1/13/00, BBT acquired Premier Bancshares, Inc. On 7/7/00, BBT acquired One Valley Bancorp Inc.

LOAN DISTRIBUTION

(12/31/00)	($000)	(%)
Comm, Financial & Agricultural	5,894	14.0
Real Estate-Construction	3,789	9.0
Real Estate-Mortgage	22,428	53.6
Consumer	5,368	12.8
Leases	4,454	10.6
Total	41,934	100.0

ANNUAL FINANCIAL DATA

	12/31/00	12/31/99	12/31/98	12/31/97	12/31/96	12/31/95	12/31/94
Earnings Per Share	**[6] 1.55**	**[5] 1.83**	**[4] 1.71**	**[3] 1.30**	**[2] 1.28**	**[1] 0.83**	**1.19**
Tang. Book Val. Per Share	**11.92**	**9.66**	**9.51**	**8.22**	**7.91**	**8.08**	**7.12**
Dividends Per Share	**0.86**	**0.75**	**0.66**	**0.58**	**0.50**	**0.43**	**0.37**
Dividend Payout %	**55.5**	**41.0**	**38.6**	**44.6**	**39.1**	**51.8**	**31.1**
INCOME STATEMENT (IN MILLIONS):							
Total Interest Income	4,339.7	3,115.8	2,481.2	2,122.9	1,606.6	1,548.2	578.4
Total Interest Expense	2,322.0	1,534.1	1,233.8	1,023.4	778.1	806.6	255.7
Net Interest Income	2,017.6	1,581.7	1,247.4	1,099.5	828.5	741.5	322.7
Provision for Loan Losses	127.4	92.1	80.3	89.9	53.7	31.4	7.2
Non-Interest Income	777.0	761.4	528.0	474.9	297.4	226.4	83.0
Non-Interest Expense	1,761.5	1,346.9	961.4	937.1	654.1	672.3	231.2
Income Before Taxes	905.7	904.1	733.7	547.4	418.2	264.2	167.3
Net Income	[6] 626.4	[5] 612.8	[4] 501.8	[3] 359.9	[2] 283.7	[1] 178.1	109.6
Average Shs. Outstg. (000)	398,916	335,298	293,571	276,440	220,972	207,964	87,658
BALANCE SHEET (IN MILLIONS):							
Cash & Due from Banks	1,471.0	1,138.8	938.8	839.6	638.7	582.6	264.7
Securities Avail. for Sale	13,878.6	10,575.3	8,031.8	6,549.4	5,136.8	5,201.3	992.0
Total Loans & Leases	41,933.8	30,152.2	23,375.2	20,012.0	14,524.6	13,636.2	5,434.9
Allowance for Credit Losses	3,001.5	1,627.8	1,024.6	495.2	344.0	241.1	70.6
Net Loans & Leases	38,932.4	28,524.5	22,350.7	19,516.9	14,180.7	13,395.0	5,364.3
Total Assets	59,340.2	43,481.0	34,427.2	29,177.6	21,246.6	20,492.9	8,756.1
Total Deposits	38,014.5	27,251.1	23,046.9	20,210.1	14,953.9	14,684.1	6,165.1
Long-Term Obligations	8,354.7	5,491.7	4,736.9	3,283.0	2,051.8	1,383.9	197.5
Total Liabilities	54,554.3	40,281.8	31,668.7	26,940.0	19,517.4	18,818.9	8,123.8
Net Stockholders' Equity	4,785.9	3,199.2	2,758.5	2,237.6	1,729.2	1,674.1	632.3
Year-end Shs. Outstg. (000)	401,649	331,170	290,211	272,104	218,594	206,714	88,318
STATISTICAL RECORD:							
Return on Equity %	13.1	19.2	18.2	16.1	16.4	10.6	17.3
Return on Assets %	1.1	1.4	1.5	1.2	1.3	0.9	1.3
Equity/Assets %	8.1	7.4	8.0	7.7	8.1	8.2	7.2
Non-Int. Exp./Tot. Inc. %	58.5	57.4	54.4	59.6	58.3	68.2	57.1
Price Range	38.25-21.69	40.63-27.19	40.75-26.25	32.50-17.50	18.50-12.88	14.00-9.38	11.00-8.44
P/E Ratio	24.7-14.0	22.2-14.9	23.8-15.3	25.0-13.5	14.5-10.1	16.9-11.3	9.2-7.1
Average Yield %	2.9	2.2	2.0	2.3	3.2	3.7	3.8

Statistics are as originally reported. Adj. for 100% stock div., 8/98. [1] Incl. $108.0 pre-tax merger-rel. chgs., $19.8 mill. in sec. losses, & $12.3 mill. gain on the sale of divest. deposits. [2] Incl. one-time after-tax SAIF chg. of $21.3 mill. [3] Incl. $42.7 mill. in after-tax UCB merger-rel. chgs. [4] Incl. after-tax merger costs of $10.9 mill. [5] Incl. non-recurr. chrg. of $46.2 mill. [6] Incl. aft.-tax nonrecurr. chrgs. of $248.6 mill.

OFFICERS:
J. A. Allison IV, Chmn., C.E.O.
K. S. King, Pres.
S. E. Reed, Sr. Exec. V.P., C.F.O.
H. G. Williamson, C.O.O.

INVESTOR CONTACT: Thomas A. Nicholson Jr., Senior Vice Pres, (336) 733-3058

PRINCIPAL OFFICE: 200 West Second Street, Winston-Salem, NC 27101

TELEPHONE NUMBER: (336) 733-2000
FAX: (336) 671-2399
WEB: www.bbandt.com

NO. OF EMPLOYEES: 17,500 (approx.)

SHAREHOLDERS: 68,703

ANNUAL MEETING: In April

INCORPORATED: NC, 1897; reincorp., NC, 1968

INSTITUTIONAL HOLDINGS:
No. of Institutions: 308
Shares Held: 98,812,421
% Held: 24.2

INDUSTRY: National commercial banks (SIC: 6021)

TRANSFER AGENT(S): Branch Banking & Trust Company, Wilson, NC

NYSE SYMBOL BSC
Rec. Pr. 50.30 (4/30/01)

BEAR STEARNS COMPANIES, INC. (THE)

YIELD 1.1%
P/E RATIO 11.1

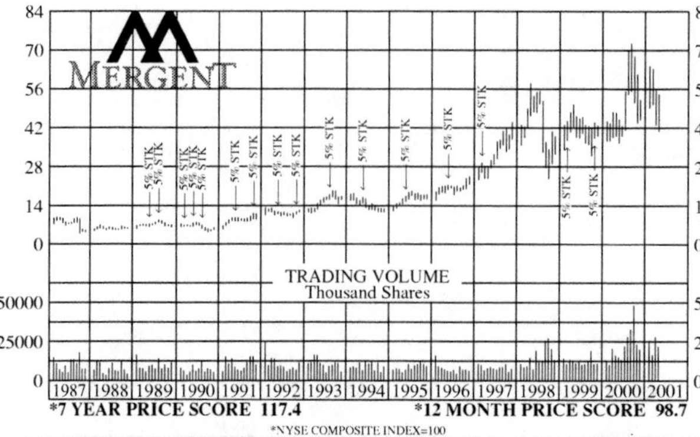

*7 YEAR PRICE SCORE 117.4 *12 MONTH PRICE SCORE 98.7

*NYSE COMPOSITE INDEX=100

INTERIM EARNINGS (Per Share):

Qtr.	Sept.	Dec.	Mar.	June
1997-98	1.01	1.01	1.05	1.11
1998-99	0.36	0.80	1.35	1.76
1999-00	0.95	1.64	...	...
Qtr.	**Feb.**	**May**	**Aug.**	**Nov.**
2000	1.89	0.77	1.32	1.36
2001	1.10	...	...	...

INTERIM DIVIDENDS (Per Share):

Amt.	Decl.	Ex.	Rec.	Pay.
0.10E	3/15/00	4/12/00	4/14/00	4/28/00
0.15Q	6/14/00	7/13/00	7/17/00	7/31/00
0.15Q	9/14/00	10/13/00	10/17/00	10/31/00
0.15Q	1/04/01	1/12/01	1/17/01	1/31/01
0.15Q	3/30/01	4/11/01	4/16/01	4/30/01

Indicated div.: $0.60

CAPITALIZATION (11/30/00):

	($000)	(%)
Long-Term Debt	20,095,888	78.0
Preferred Stock	800,000	3.1
Common & Surplus	4,854,288	18.9
Total	25,750,176	100.0

RECENT DEVELOPMENTS: For the quarter ended 2/23/01, BSC reported income of $166.0 million, before an accounting charge of $6.3 million, versus net income of $278.2 million in the prior-year period. Total revenues fell 20.2% to $2.15 billion. Revenues, net of interest expense, decreased 19.4% to $1.21 billion. Interest and dividends revenues slipped 20.7% to $1.09 billion. Principal transactions revenues fell 7.4% to $599.5 million.

PROSPECTS: Going forward, BSC's global clearing business should continue to grow and provide a solid base for recurring earnings. Increases in mergers and acquisitions should continue to offset the impact of a challenging market environment, while the Company's institutional equities and fixed income businesses should continue to perform well. Separately, BSC acquired a 49.8% interest in Wagner Stott Mercator, LLC, a specialist firm on the NYSE.

BUSINESS

THE BEAR STEARNS COMPANIES, INC. is the parent company of Bear, Stearns and Company Inc., a worldwide investment banking, securities trading and brokerage firm. The firm's business includes corporate finance and mergers and acquisitions, public finance, institutional equities and fixed income sales and trading, private client services and asset management. Through its wholly-owned subsidiary, Bear Stearns Securities Corp., it provides professional and correspondent clearing services. The revenue breakdown for the fiscal year ended 11/26/00 was commissions, 11.7%; principal transactions, 21.9%; investment banking, 9.9%; interest & dividends, 54.9%; and other, 1.6%.

BUSINESS LINE ANALYSIS

(11/30/2000)	REV (%)	INC (%)
Capital Markets	66.6	60.2
Global Clearing Services	20.4	31.2
Wealth Management	13.0	8.6
Total	100.0	100.0

ANNUAL FINANCIAL DATA

	11/30/00	[2] 11/26/99	6/30/99	6/30/98	6/30/97	6/30/96	6/30/95
Earnings Per Share	**[3] 5.35**	**1.78**	**4.27**	**[1] 4.17**	**3.81**	**2.97**	**1.40**
Cash Flow Per Share	**5.84**	**2.01**	**4.63**	**4.47**	**4.17**	**3.27**	**1.69**
Tang. Book Val. Per Share	**44.54**	**34.97**	**33.07**	**28.39**	**21.90**	**17.72**	**13.43**
Dividends Per Share	**0.55**	**0.56**	**0.56**	**0.54**	**0.54**	**0.51**	**0.48**
Dividend Payout %	**10.3**	**31.7**	**13.2**	**13.0**	**14.1**	**17.3**	**34.5**
INCOME STATEMENT (IN MILLIONS):							
Total Revenues	10,276.6	3,470.3	7,882.0	7,979.9	6,077.3	4,963.9	3,753.6
Costs & Expenses	8,951.4	2,954.0	6,684.8	6,801.3	4,973.9	4,059.1	3,306.2
Depreciation & Amort.	153.6	62.7	133.1	115.1	89.7	69.9	59.3
Operating Income	1,171.5	453.6	1,064.1	1,063.5	1,013.7	834.9	388.1
Income Before Income Taxes	1,171.5	453.6	1,064.1	1,063.5	1,013.7	834.9	388.1
Income Taxes	398.3	167.8	391.1	403.1	400.4	344.3	147.5
Net Income	[3] 773.2	285.8	673.0	[1] 660.4	613.3	490.6	240.6
Cash Flow	887.7	332.2	766.7	744.6	679.2	536.0	274.7
Average Shs. Outstg. (000)	152,034	165,584	165,483	166,456	163,002	164,113	162,901
BALANCE SHEET (IN MILLIONS):							
Cash & Cash Equivalents	103,939.8	101,760.0	93,925.7	92,088.8	71,749.8	55,958.5	45,582.9
Total Current Assets	122,657.2	119,563.5	110,255.1	108,122.1	81,956.2	65,051.9	52,382.4
Net Property	542.6	504.0	486.7	448.0	379.5	331.9	312.9
Total Assets	171,166.5	162,038.0	153,894.3	154,495.9	121,433.5	92,085.2	74,597.2
Total Current Liabilities	144,134.7	140,157.1	133,137.2	135,316.3	108,722.4	82,051.8	67,580.8
Long-Term Obligations	20,095.9	15,911.4	14,647.1	13,296.0	8,120.3	6,043.6	4,059.9
Net Stockholders' Equity	5,654.3	4,941.9	4,955.5	4,291.5	3,246.4	2,745.4	2,352.5
Net Working Capital	d21,477.5	d20,593.6	d22,882.1	d27,194.2	d26,766.2	d16,999.9	d15,198.4
Year-end Shs. Outstg. (000)	108,982	118,439	125,662	123,003	129,646	130,248	142,623
STATISTICAL RECORD:							
Operating Profit Margin %	11.4	13.1	13.5	13.3	16.7	16.8	10.3
Net Profit Margin %	7.5	8.2	8.5	8.3	10.1	9.9	6.4
Return on Equity %	13.7	5.8	13.6	15.4	18.9	17.9	10.2
Return on Assets %	0.5	0.2	0.4	0.4	0.5	0.5	0.3
Debt/Total Assets %	11.7	9.8	9.5	8.6	6.7	6.6	5.4
Price Range	72.50-36.50	50.48-31.91	50.48-31.91	58.05-23.58	44.05-23.22	24.51-15.73	19.23-11.95
P/E Ratio	13.6-6.8	28.4-17.9	11.8-7.5	13.9-5.7	11.6-6.1	8.3-5.3	13.8-8.6
Average Yield %	1.0	1.4	1.4	1.3	1.6	2.5	3.1

Statistics are as originally reported. Adj. for all stk. dividends thru 11/99. [1] Includes special charges of $108.0 million related to an increase in litigation reserves. [2] For five months due to change in fiscal year-end. [3] Incl. an after-tax charge of $96.0 mill. related to increased legal reserves following a jury verdict.

OFFICERS:
A. C. Greenberg, Chmn.
J. E. Cayne, Pres., C.E.O.
S. L. Molinaro Jr., Sr. V.P., Fin., C.F.O.

INVESTOR CONTACT: Elizabeth Ventura, Investor Relations, (212) 272-9251

PRINCIPAL OFFICE: 245 Park Avenue, New York, NY 10167

TELEPHONE NUMBER: (212) 272-2000
FAX: (212) 272-4785
WEB: www.bearstearns.com

NO. OF EMPLOYEES: 11,201 (avg.)

SHAREHOLDERS: 2,462

ANNUAL MEETING: In Mar.

INCORPORATED: DE, Aug., 1985

INSTITUTIONAL HOLDINGS:
No. of Institutions: 314
Shares Held: 64,574,597
% Held: 60.4

INDUSTRY: Security brokers and dealers (SIC: 6211)

TRANSFER AGENT(S): Mellon Investor Services, New York, NY

NYSE SYMBOL BEC
Rec. Pr. 37.75 (5/31/01)

BECKMAN COULTER, INC.

YIELD 0.9%
P/E RATIO 18.5

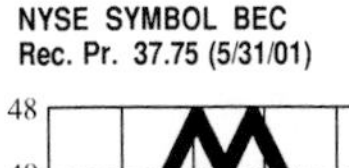

*7 YEAR PRICE SCORE 116.3 *12 MONTH PRICE SCORE 103.6

*NYSE COMPOSITE INDEX=100

INTERIM EARNINGS (Per Share):

Qtr.	Mar.	June	Sept.	Dec.
1997	0.27	0.36	0.34	d5.82
1998	d0.15	0.16	0.24	0.32
1999	0.29	0.44	0.41	0.65
2000	0.35	0.53	0.47	0.69

INTERIM DIVIDENDS (Per Share):

Amt.	Decl.	Ex.	Rec.	Pay.
0.16Q	8/04/00	8/16/00	8/18/00	9/07/00
0.17Q	10/05/00	10/18/00	10/20/00	11/10/00
100% STK	10/05/00	12/08/00	11/15/00	12/07/00
0.085Q	2/01/01	2/14/01	2/16/01	3/07/01
0.085Q	4/05/01	5/09/01	5/11/01	5/31/01

Indicated div.: $0.34

CAPITALIZATION (12/31/00):

	($000)	(%)
Long-Term Debt	862,800	69.8
Deferred Income Tax	28,800	2.3
Common & Surplus	343,900	27.8
Total	1,235,500	100.0

RECENT DEVELOPMENTS: For the year ended 12/31/00, net income advanced 18.4% to $125.5 million compared with $106.0 million in 1999. Results included pre-tax restructuring gains of $2.4 million in 2000 and $200,000 in 1999, respectively. Earnings were boosted by strong demand for genome research testing. Sales amounted to $1.89 billion, an increase of 4.3% versus $1.81 billion a year earlier. Operating income grew 7.4% to $232.6 million.

PROSPECTS: Earnings growth should continue to be fueled by new products, including the Biomeck® FX laboratory automation workstation, the CEQ™ 2000XL DNA analysis system and automated and free prostate specific antigen testing for the Access® System. For 2001, the Company anticipates sales growth to be in the range of 5.0% to 7.0% and earnings growth to be in the range of 13.0% to 15.0%.

BUSINESS

BECKMAN COULTIER, INC. (formerly Beckman Instruments Inc.) designs, manufactures, sells, and services laboratory systems for biological analysis and investigation into life processes. The Company targets two markets: the life sciences laboratory market and the hospital and clinical diagnostic laboratory market. Customers such as universities, research institutions, pharmaceutical companies, hospitals and clinical laboratories use Beckman products across the entire spectrum of biologically-based endeavors, from basic scientific research to daily analysis of blood samples. Beckman markets its products in approximately 130 countries. BEC's products are used in all phases of the battle against disease to improve methodologies for biological discovery and diagnosis of disease.

BUSINESS LINE ANALYSIS

(12/31/2000)	Rev (%)	Inc (%)
Clinical Diagnostics	78.0	77.1
Life Science Research	22.0	22.9
Total	100.0	100.0

ANNUAL FINANCIAL DATA

	12/31/00	12/31/99	12/31/98	12/31/97	12/31/96	12/31/95	12/31/94
Earnings Per Share	**2.03**	**5 1.79**	**4 0.57**	**3 d4.79**	**1.29**	**2 0.85**	**1 0.84**
Cash Flow Per Share	**4.23**	**4.20**	**3.17**	**d2.81**	**2.81**	**2.22**	**2.09**
Tang. Book Val. Per Share	...	...	...	...	**7.13**	**5.97**	**5.66**
Dividends Per Share	**0.33**	**0.32**	**0.31**	**0.30**	**0.26**	**0.22**	**0.20**
Dividend Payout %	**16.0**	**17.9**	**53.5**	...	**20.2**	**25.9**	**23.8**
INCOME STATEMENT (IN MILLIONS):							
Total Revenues	1,886.9	1,808.7	1,718.2	1,198.0	1,028.0	930.1	888.6
Costs & Expenses	1,518.2	1,448.5	1,451.0	1,325.9	817.7	767.9	730.9
Depreciation & Amort.	136.1	143.7	152.4	109.1	87.8	79.1	70.1
Operating Income	232.6	216.5	114.8	d237.0	122.5	83.1	87.6
Net Interest Inc./(Exp.)	d65.6	d66.0	d74.4	d23.3	d12.3	d8.1	d8.1
Income Before Income Taxes	181.9	154.7	46.6	d251.9	111.5	72.4	74.9
Income Taxes	56.4	48.7	13.1	12.5	36.8	23.5	27.6
Net Income	125.5	5 106.0	4 33.5	3 d264.4	74.7	2 48.9	1 47.3
Cash Flow	261.6	249.7	185.9	d155.3	162.5	128.0	117.4
Average Shs. Outstg. (000)	61,800	59,400	58,600	55,200	57,800	57,614	56,158
BALANCE SHEET (IN MILLIONS):							
Cash & Cash Equivalents	29.6	34.4	24.7	33.5	42.7	34.4	44.9
Total Current Assets	927.8	966.4	956.6	976.7	579.4	533.3	512.0
Net Property	298.2	305.9	309.4	410.9	263.5	252.1	232.6
Total Assets	2,018.2	2,110.8	2,133.3	2,331.0	960.1	907.8	829.1
Total Current Liabilities	501.1	575.9	719.3	894.9	279.3	251.2	268.8
Long-Term Obligations	862.8	980.7	982.2	1,181.3	176.6	162.7	117.3
Net Stockholders' Equity	343.9	227.9	126.9	81.8	398.9	347.9	317.0
Net Working Capital	426.7	390.5	237.3	81.8	300.1	282.1	243.2
Year-end Shs. Outstg. (000)	59,700	58,000	56,800	55,200	55,952	58,248	56,010
STATISTICAL RECORD:							
Operating Profit Margin %	12.3	12.0	6.7	...	11.9	8.9	9.9
Net Profit Margin %	6.7	5.9	1.9	...	7.3	5.3	5.3
Return on Equity %	36.5	46.5	26.4	...	18.7	14.1	14.9
Return on Assets %	6.2	5.0	1.6	...	7.8	5.4	5.7
Debt/Total Assets %	42.8	46.5	46.0	50.7	18.4	17.9	14.1
Price Range	42.44-22.78	27.88-19.75	32.47-20.03	26.16-18.69	20.56-16.00	17.94-13.00	16.25-11.50
P/E Ratio	20.9-11.2	15.6-11.1	57.0-35.1	...	15.9-12.4	21.1-15.3	19.3-13.7
Average Yield %	1.0	1.3	1.2	1.3	1.4	1.4	1.4

Statistics are as originally reported. Adj. for 2-for-1 stk. split., 12/00. 1 Bef. acctg. chrg. of $5.1 mill. & nonrecurr. chrgs. of $11.3 mill. 2 Incl. nonrecurr. chrgs. of $30.8 mill. 3 Incl. a $0.05 per share dilution for exps. & incl. after-tax chgs. total. $318.4 mill. 4 Incl. after-tax chrgs. total. $110.9 mill. 5 Incl. a pre-tax restruct. gain of $2.4 mill., 2000; $200,000, 1999.

OFFICERS:
J. P. Wareham, Chmn., Pres., C.E.O.
A. I. Khalifa, V.P., C.F.O.
J. T. Glover, V.P., Treas.

INVESTOR CONTACT: Jeanie Herbert, Mgr. Inv. Rel., (714) 773-7620

PRINCIPAL OFFICE: 4300 N. Harbor Blvd., Fullerton, CA 92835

TELEPHONE NUMBER: (714) 871-4848
FAX: (714) 773-8283
WEB: www.beckmancoulter.com

NO. OF EMPLOYEES: 9,520 (approx.)

SHAREHOLDERS: 6,551 (approx.)

ANNUAL MEETING: In Apr.

INCORPORATED: DE, July, 1988

INSTITUTIONAL HOLDINGS:
No. of Institutions: 205
Shares Held: 49,219,079
% Held: 82.3

INDUSTRY: Analytical instruments (SIC: 3826)

TRANSFER AGENT(S): First Chicago Trust Company of New York, Jersey City, NJ

NYSE SYMBOL BDX
Rec. Pr. 34.33 (5/31/01)

BECTON, DICKINSON AND COMPANY

YIELD 1.1%
P/E RATIO 24.0

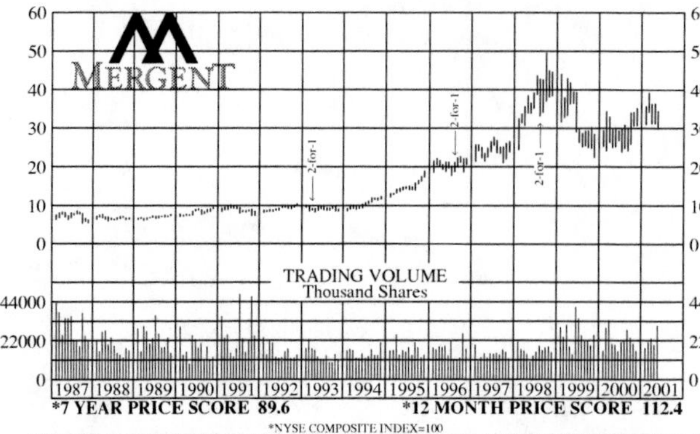

INTERIM EARNINGS (Per Share):

Qtr.	Dec.	Mar.	June	Sept.
1997-98	0.25	d0.05	0.36	0.34
1998-99	0.29	0.34	0.12	0.29
1999-00	0.29	0.45	0.43	0.32
2000-01	0.23	...	...	...

INTERIM DIVIDENDS (Per Share):

Amt.	Decl.	Ex.	Rec.	Pay.
0.093Q	5/23/00	6/07/00	6/09/00	6/30/00
0.093Q	7/25/00	9/06/00	9/08/00	9/29/00
0.095Q	11/28/00	12/08/00	12/12/00	1/02/01
0.095Q	1/23/01	3/07/01	3/09/01	3/30/01
0.095Q	5/22/01	6/06/01	6/08/01	6/29/01

Indicated div.: $0.38 (Div. Reinv. Plan)

CAPITALIZATION (9/30/00):

	($000)	(%)
Long-Term Debt	779,569	27.6
Deferred Income Tax	86,494	3.1
Preferred Stock	43,570	1.5
Common & Surplus	1,912,428	67.8
Total	2,822,061	100.0

RECENT DEVELOPMENTS: For the quarter ended 12/31/00, net income decreased 19.5% to $60.6 million compared with $75.3 million in the corresponding quarter of the previous year. Revenues slipped 1.9% to $843.3 million. Revenues were negatively affected by foreign exchange translation and the impact of remaining inventory reductions at the trade level following the discontinuation of certain distributor incentive programs.

PROSPECTS: On 12/20/00, BDX announced a definitive agreement to acquire Gentest Corporation, a privately-held company serving the life sciences market in the areas of drug metabolism and toxicology testing of pharmaceutical candidates. The acquisition should expand BDX's presence in the areas of reagents and systems for pharmaceutical drug discovery research. Meanwhile, BDX will look to invest in promising product initiatives to drive revenue growth.

BUSINESS

BECTON, DICKINSON AND COMPANY is principally engaged in the manufacture and sale of a broad line of medical supplies and devices and diagnostic systems used by health care professionals, medical research institutions and the general public. The Company's operations consist of two worldwide business segments: medical supplies and devices, and diagnostic systems. Major products in the medical supplies segment are hypodermic products, specially designed devices for diabetes care, prefillable drug delivery systems, infusion therapy products, elastic support products and thermometers. Major products in the diagnostic systems segment are clinical and industrial microbiology products, sample collection products, flow cytometry systems, tissue culture labware and hematology instruments.

BUSINESS LINE ANALYSIS

(9/30/2000)	Rev (%)	Inc (%)
Medical Systems	54.3	59.6
Biosciences	30.9	20.6
Preanalytical Solutions	14.8	19.8
Total	100.0	100.0

ANNUAL FINANCIAL DATA

	9/30/00	9/30/99	9/30/98	9/30/97	9/30/96	9/30/95	9/30/94
Earnings Per Share	**4 1.49**	**1.04**	**2 3 0.90**	**1.21**	**1.10**	**0.90**	**0.76**
Cash Flow Per Share	**2.59**	**2.02**	**1.78**	**2.08**	**1.91**	**1.66**	**1.47**
Tang. Book Val. Per Share	**3.80**	**2.74**	**3.30**	**4.11**	**4.43**	**3.19**	**2.98**
Dividends Per Share	**0.37**	**0.34**	**0.29**	**0.26**	**0.23**	**0.21**	**0.19**
Dividend Payout %	**24.8**	**32.7**	**32.2**	**21.5**	**20.9**	**22.9**	**24.3**
INCOME STATEMENT (IN MILLIONS):							
Total Revenues	3,618.3	3,418.4	3,116.9	2,810.5	2,769.8	2,712.5	2,559.5
Costs & Expenses	2,815.3	2,714.3	2,482.7	2,150.2	2,138.0	2,108.1	2,030.7
Depreciation & Amort.	288.3	258.9	228.7	209.8	200.5	207.8	203.7
Operating Income	514.8	445.2	405.4	450.5	431.2	396.7	325.0
Net Interest Inc./(Exp.)	d74.2	d72.1	d56.3	d39.4	d37.4	d42.8	d47.6
Income Before Income Taxes	519.9	372.7	340.9	422.6	393.7	349.6	296.2
Income Taxes	127.0	96.9	104.3	122.6	110.2	97.9	69.0
Net Income	4 392.9	275.7	2 3 236.6	300.1	283.4	251.7	227.2
Cash Flow	678.7	532.0	462.7	507.2	481.3	456.8	428.2
Average Shs. Outstg. (000)	263,239	264,580	262,128	245,230	253,418	276,804	293,332
BALANCE SHEET (IN MILLIONS):							
Cash & Cash Equivalents	54.8	64.6	90.6	141.0	165.1	240.0	178.8
Total Current Assets	1,660.7	1,683.7	1,542.8	1,312.6	1,276.8	1,327.5	1,326.6
Net Property	1,576.1	1,431.1	1,302.7	1,250.7	1,244.1	1,281.0	1,376.3
Total Assets	4,505.1	4,437.0	3,846.0	3,080.3	2,889.8	3,332.0	3,528.1
Total Current Liabilities	1,353.5	1,329.3	1,091.9	678.2	766.1	720.0	678.3
Long-Term Obligations	779.6	954.2	765.2	665.4	468.2	557.6	669.2
Net Stockholders' Equity	1,956.0	1,768.7	1,613.8	1,385.4	1,325.2	1,398.4	1,481.7
Net Working Capital	307.1	354.4	450.8	634.4	510.7	607.5	648.2
Year-end Shs. Outstg. (000)	253,496	250,798	247,843	244,168	247,220	260,300	281,112
STATISTICAL RECORD:							
Operating Profit Margin %	14.2	13.0	13.0	16.0	15.6	14.6	12.7
Net Profit Margin %	10.9	8.1	7.6	10.7	10.2	9.3	8.9
Return on Equity %	20.1	15.6	14.7	21.7	21.4	18.0	15.3
Return on Assets %	8.7	6.2	6.2	9.7	9.8	7.6	6.4
Debt/Total Assets %	17.3	21.5	19.9	21.6	16.2	16.7	19.0
Price Range	35.31-23.75	44.19-22.38	49.63-24.38	27.81-20.94	22.75-17.69	19.00-12.00	12.47-8.50
P/E Ratio	23.7-15.9	42.5-21.5	55.1-27.1	23.0-17.3	20.7-16.1	21.2-13.4	16.4-11.2
Average Yield %	1.3	1.0	0.8	1.1	1.1	1.3	1.8

Statistics are as originally reported. Adj. for 2-for-1 stock split, 2/93 & 8/96. 1 Bef. acctg. adj. charge of $141.1 mill. 2 Incl. nonrecurr. chrgs. of $97.9 mill. 3 Incl. nonrecurr. chrgs. of $110.0 mill. 4 Incl. a one-time pre-tax spec. chrg. of $57.5 mill. & net gains on invest. of $76.2 mill.

OFFICERS:
E. J. Ludwig, Pres. C.E.O.
J. R. Considine, Exec. V.P., C.F.O.
B. M. Healy, V.P., Gen. Couns., Corp. Sec.

INVESTOR CONTACT: Dean Paranicas, Inv. Rel., (201) 847-7102

PRINCIPAL OFFICE: 1 Becton Drive, Franklin Lakes, NJ 07417-1880

TELEPHONE NUMBER: (201) 847-6800
FAX: (201) 847-6475
WEB: www.bd.com

NO. OF EMPLOYEES: 25,000 (approx.)

SHAREHOLDERS: 10,690 (approx.)

ANNUAL MEETING: In Feb.

INCORPORATED: NJ, Nov., 1906

INSTITUTIONAL HOLDINGS:
No. of Institutions: 394
Shares Held: 206,089,194
% Held: 80.3

INDUSTRY: Surgical and medical instruments (SIC: 3841)

TRANSFER AGENT(S): First Chicago Trust Company of New York, Jersey City, NJ

NYSE SYMBOL BLS
Rec. Pr. 40.92 (3/31/01)

BELLSOUTH CORPORATION

YIELD 1.9%
P/E RATIO 18.3

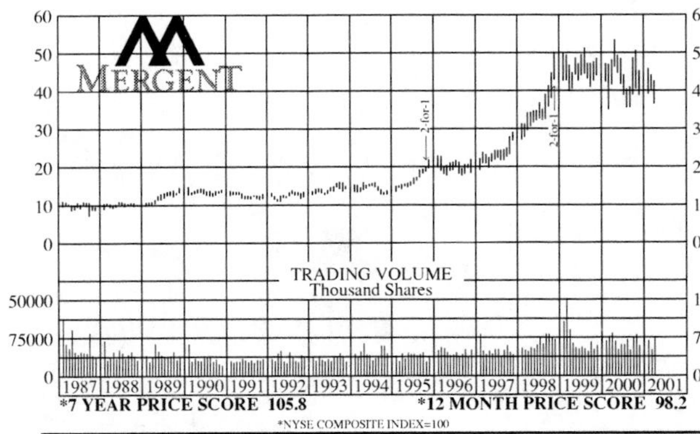

INTERIM EARNINGS (Per Share):

Qtr	Mar.	June.	Sept.	Dec.
1996	0.49	0.32	0.32	0.32
1997	0.35	0.33	0.60	0.37
1998	0.45	0.41	0.41	0.51
1999	0.32	0.51	0.53	0.55
2000	0.53	0.56	0.55	0.59

INTERIM DIVIDENDS (Per Share):

Amt.	Decl.	Ex.	Rec.	Pay.
0.19Q	6/27/00	7/11/00	7/13/00	8/01/00
0.19Q	9/25/00	10/10/00	10/12/00	11/01/00
0.19Q	11/27/00	1/09/01	1/11/01	2/01/01
0.19Q	2/26/01	4/10/01	4/12/01	5/01/01

Indicated div.: $0.76 (Div. Reinv. Plan)

CAPITALIZATION (12/31/00):

	($000)	(%)
Long-Term Debt	12,463,000	37.8
Deferred Income Tax	3,580,000	10.9
Common & Surplus	16,912,000	51.3
Total	32,955,000	100.0

RECENT DEVELOPMENTS: For the year ended 12/31/00, net income increased 22.4% to $4.22 billion versus $3.45 billion in the prior-year period. Results for 2000 included a net non-recurring credit of $65.0 million, while results for 1999 included a net non-recurring charge of $377.0 million. Total operating revenues rose 3.7% to $26.15 billion from $25.22 billion in the corresponding period a year earlier. Results were driven by strength in BLS's data, wireless and international operations.

PROSPECTS: BLS continues to accelerate its broadband deployment and is now targeting a total of 600,000 Digital Subscriber Line high-speed Internet access customers by 12/31/01 versus 215,000 in 2000. Separately, on 12/5/00, BLS shareholders approved a plan for the creation of the BellSouth Latin America Group tracking stock, which is intended to reflect the separate performance of BLS' operations in Latin America. Issuance is dependent on market conditions and other factors.

BUSINESS

BELLSOUTH CORPORATION is one of seven regional holding companies divested by AT&T on 1/1/84. Through its BellSouth Telecommunications Inc. subsidiary, BLS provides wireline communications services, including local exchange, network access and intraLATA long distance services throughout its nine-state territory in Alabama, Florida, Georgia, Kentucky, Louisiana, Mississippi, North Carolina, South Carolina and Tennessee. The Company's international operations consist primarily of wireless service providers operating in 15 countries in Latin America, Asia and Europe. BLS also owns a group a companies that publish, print, sell advertising in and perform related services concerning alphabetical and classified telephone directories in both paper and electronic formats. As of 12/31/00, BLS owned more than 54.2 million access lines. In April 2000, BLS contributed its wireless operations to a joint venture with SBC Communications and formed Cingular Wireless, a provider of wireless voice and data communications services in the U.S. BLS owns about 40% of Cingular, which has over 19.0 million U.S. wireless subscribers.

ANNUAL FINANCIAL DATA

	12/31/00	12/31/99	12/31/98	12/31/97	12/31/96	12/31/95	12/31/94
Earnings Per Share	**5 2.23**	**4 1.80**	**1 1.78**	**2 1.65**	**2 1.44**	**3 0.79**	**1.09**
Cash Flow Per Share	**4.84**	**4.24**	**3.97**	**3.64**	**3.31**	**2.53**	**2.73**
Tang. Book Val. Per Share	**6.81**	**5.86**	**6.79**	**6.66**	**5.98**	**5.18**	**6.52**
Dividends Per Share	**0.76**	**0.76**	**0.72**	**0.72**	**0.72**	**0.70**	**0.69**
Dividend Payout %	**34.1**	**42.2**	**40.4**	**43.8**	**50.0**	**88.8**	**63.5**
INCOME STATEMENT (IN MILLIONS):							
Total Revenues	26,151.0	25,224.0	23,123.0	20,561.0	19,040.0	17,886.0	16,844.0
Costs & Expenses	14,332.0	14,116.0	12,862.0	11,221.0	10,542.0	11,139.0	9,528.0
Depreciation & Amort.	4,935.0	4,671.0	4,357.0	3,964.0	3,719.0	3,455.0	3,259.0
Operating Income	6,884.0	6,437.0	5,904.0	5,376.0	4,779.0	3,292.0	4,057.0
Net Interest Inc./(Exp.)	d1,328.0	d1,030.0	d837.0	d761.0	d721.0	d724.0	d601.0
Income Before Income Taxes	5,908.0	5,657.0	5,751.0	5,421.0	4,608.0	2,588.0	3,593.0
Income Taxes	2,378.0	2,040.0	2,224.0	2,151.0	1,745.0	1,024.0	1,243.0
Equity Earnings/Minority Int.	690.0	d169.0	...	...	...	...	d190.0
Net Income	5 4,220.0	4 3,448.0	1 3,527.0	2 3,270.0	2 2,863.0	3 1,564.0	2,160.0
Cash Flow	9,155.0	8,119.0	7,884.0	7,234.0	6,582.0	5,019.0	5,419.0
Average Shs. Outstg. (000)	1,891,000	1,916,000	1,984,000	1,990,000	1,988,000	1,986,000	1,988,000
BALANCE SHEET (IN MILLIONS):							
Cash & Cash Equivalents	1,098.0	1,392.0	3,187.0	2,587.0	1,229.0	1,782.0	658.0
Total Current Assets	7,406.0	7,387.0	8,706.0	8,117.0	6,298.0	6,505.0	4,729.0
Net Property	24,157.0	24,631.0	23,940.0	22,861.0	21,825.0	21,092.0	25,164.0
Total Assets	50,925.0	43,453.0	39,410.0	36,301.0	32,568.0	31,880.0	34,400.0
Total Current Liabilities	13,270.0	13,395.0	9,150.0	8,783.0	6,441.0	7,390.0	6,498.0
Long-Term Obligations	12,463.0	9,113.0	8,715.0	7,348.0	8,116.0	7,924.0	7,435.0
Net Stockholders' Equity	16,912.0	14,815.0	16,110.0	15,165.0	13,249.0	11,825.0	14,368.0
Net Working Capital	d5,864.0	d6,008.0	d444.0	d666.0	d143.0	d885.0	d1,769.0
Year-end Shs. Outstg. (000)	1,872,000	1,883,000	1,950,000	1,984,000	1,982,000	1,988,000	1,984,000
STATISTICAL RECORD:							
Operating Profit Margin %	26.3	25.5	25.5	26.1	25.1	18.4	24.1
Net Profit Margin %	16.1	13.7	15.3	15.9	15.0	8.7	12.8
Return on Equity %	25.0	23.3	21.9	21.6	21.6	13.2	15.0
Return on Assets %	8.3	7.9	8.9	9.0	8.8	4.9	6.3
Debt/Total Assets %	24.5	21.0	22.1	20.2	24.9	24.9	21.6
Price Range	53.50-34.94	51.31-39.75	50.00-27.06	29.06-19.06	22.94-17.63	21.94-13.41	15.88-12.63
P/E Ratio	24.0-15.7	28.5-22.1	28.1-15.2	17.7-11.6	15.9-12.2	27.9-17.1	14.6-11.6
Average Yield %	1.7	1.7	1.9	3.0	3.6	3.9	4.8

Statistics are as originally reported. Adj. for 2-for-1 stk. splits, 12/98 & 11/95. 1 Incls. gain of $335.0 mill. fr. sale of assets. 2 Incls. non-recurr. pre-tax credit 12/31/97: $787.0 mill.; after-tax credit 12/31/96: $344.0 mill. 3 Bef. extraord. chrgs. of $2.72 bill. ($2.75/sh.) 4 Incls. non-recurr. chrg. $320.0 mill. 5 Incls. non-recurr. credit of $65.0 mill.

OFFICERS:
F. D. Ackerman, Chmn., Pres., C.E.O.
J. A. Drummond, Vice-Chmn.
R. M. Dykes, Exec. V.P., C.F.O.

INVESTOR CONTACT: P. Kushner, Investor Relations, (404) 249-2365

PRINCIPAL OFFICE: 1155 Peachtree Street N.E., Atlanta, GA 30309-3610

TELEPHONE NUMBER: (404) 249-2000
FAX: (404) 249-2071
WEB: www.bellsouth.com

NO. OF EMPLOYEES: 103,900 (approx.)

SHAREHOLDERS: 891,893

ANNUAL MEETING: In Apr.

INCORPORATED: GA, Dec., 1983

INSTITUTIONAL HOLDINGS:
No. of Institutions: 876
Shares Held: 872,911,578
% Held: 46.6

INDUSTRY: Telephone communications, exc. radio (SIC: 4813)

TRANSFER AGENT(S): Mellon Investor Services, LLC, Ridgefield Park, NJ

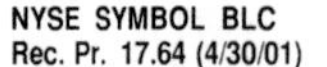

NYSE SYMBOL BLC
Rec. Pr. 17.64 (4/30/01)

BELO CORPORATION

YIELD 1.5%
P/E RATIO 13.5

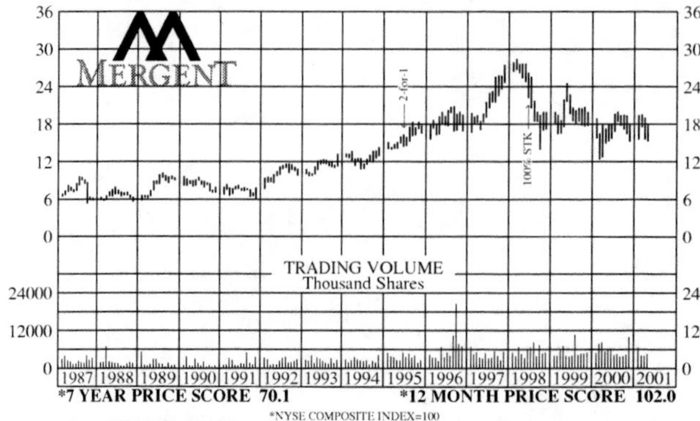

INTERIM EARNINGS (Per Share):

Qtr.	Mar.	June	Sept.	Dec.
1996	0.17	0.30	0.21	0.39
1997	0.19	0.21	0.12	0.19
1998	0.11	0.24	0.08	0.10
1999	0.11	0.67	0.14	0.58
2000	0.13	0.27	0.15	0.76

INTERIM DIVIDENDS (Per Share):

Amt.	Decl.	Ex.	Rec.	Pay.
0.07Q	2/11/00	5/10/00	5/12/00	6/02/00
0.07Q	7/28/00	8/09/00	8/11/00	9/01/00
0.07Q	9/29/00	11/08/00	11/10/00	12/01/00
0.075Q	12/01/00	2/07/01	2/09/01	3/02/01
0.075Q	2/09/01	5/09/01	5/11/01	6/01/01

Indicated div.: $0.30

CAPITALIZATION (12/31/00):

	($000)	(%)
Long-Term Debt	1,789,600	50.5
Deferred Income Tax	404,221	11.4
Common & Surplus	1,349,408	38.1
Total	3,543,229	100.0

RECENT DEVELOPMENTS: For the year ended 12/31/00, net income fell 15.4% to $150.8 million versus $178.3 million in 1999. Earnings for 2000 and 1999 included gains on the sale of subsidiaries of $104.6 million and $117.8 million, respectively. Total net operating revenues amounted to $1.59 billion, up 10.8% from $1.43 billion the year before. Broadcasting revenues rose 16.8% to $699.5 million, while newspaper publishing revenues jumped 6.8% to $872.7 million. Interactive media revenues climbed 59.5% to $10.4 million.

PROSPECTS: On 1/25/01, BLC agreed to purchase KTTU-TV, the UPN affiliate in the Tucson, Arizona television market, for $18.0 million. In December, the Company announced that it will create a southwest operating cluster consisting of BLC's television stations, newspapers and cable news operations in Arizona and California. Going forward, BLC will be challenged by a soft advertising environment, higher newsprint costs, and continued investment in Belo Interactive.

BUSINESS

BELO (A.H.) CORPORATION is a media company, with a diversified group of television broadcasting, newspaper publishing, interactive media and cable news operations in several markets and regions, including Texas, the Pacific Northwest, the Southwest, Rhode Island, and the mid-Atlantic region. The Company owns and operates 17 network-affiliated television stations; five daily newspapers, including The Dallas Morning News, The Providence Journal and The Press-Enterprise in Riverside, California; six local or regional cable news channels; and Belo Productions, Inc. The Company also manages three television stations through local marketing agreements. Six of the Company's stations are in the top 17 U.S. television markets. The Company's television group reaches 13.7% of all U.S. television households. In 2000, newspaper publishing accounted for 54.7% of revenues, broadcasting 43.8%, interactive media, 0.6% and other, 0.9%.

ANNUAL FINANCIAL DATA

	12/31/00	12/31/99	12/31/98	12/31/97	12/31/96	12/31/95	12/31/94
Earnings Per Share	**1 1.29**	**1 1.50**	**0.52**	**0.71**	**1.06**	**0.84**	**0.85**
Cash Flow Per Share	**2.87**	**2.91**	**1.80**	**1.86**	**1.84**	**1.59**	**1.43**
Dividends Per Share	**0.28**	**0.26**	**0.24**	**0.22**	**0.20**	**0.16**	**0.15**
Dividend Payout %	**21.7**	**17.3**	**46.1**	**31.0**	**19.4**	**18.7**	**17.6**
INCOME STATEMENT (IN MILLIONS):							
Total Revenues	1,588.8	1,434.0	1,407.3	1,248.4	824.3	735.3	628.1
Costs & Expenses	1,101.1	1,000.5	1,014.8	872.6	593.5	539.3	450.7
Depreciation & Amort.	185.0	169.0	159.4	135.0	65.2	59.4	46.4
Operating Income	302.7	264.5	233.1	240.8	165.6	136.6	131.0
Net Interest Inc./(Exp.)	d132.8	d110.6	d107.6	d90.8	d27.6	d30.0	d16.1
Income Before Income Taxes	266.8	276.5	130.5	154.1	144.0	111.0	107.9
Income Taxes	116.0	98.1	65.6	71.2	56.5	44.4	39.0
Net Income	1 150.8	1 178.3	64.9	83.0	87.5	66.6	68.9
Cash Flow	335.8	347.3	224.3	218.0	152.7	126.0	115.3
Average Shs. Outstg. (000)	117,198	119,177	124,836	117,122	83,020	79,292	80,892
BALANCE SHEET (IN MILLIONS):							
Cash & Cash Equivalents	87.7	45.6	19.5	11.9	13.8	12.8	9.3
Total Current Assets	421.0	352.0	275.8	277.0	171.9	165.3	130.3
Net Property	637.6	655.0	626.8	608.3	370.8	361.8	312.2
Total Assets	3,893.3	3,976.3	3,539.1	3,623.0	1,224.1	1,154.0	913.8
Total Current Liabilities	302.7	259.8	180.7	214.5	89.3	81.7	83.7
Long-Term Obligations	1,789.6	1,849.5	1,634.0	1,614.0	631.9	557.4	330.4
Net Stockholders' Equity	1,349.4	1,389.8	1,248.1	1,326.0	370.5	388.5	382.5
Net Working Capital	118.3	92.1	95.0	62.5	82.6	83.6	46.6
Year-end Shs. Outstg. (000)	109,854	118,656	118,925	124,694	72,520	76,484	79,444
STATISTICAL RECORD:							
Operating Profit Margin %	19.1	18.4	16.6	19.3	20.1	18.6	20.9
Net Profit Margin %	9.5	12.4	4.6	6.6	10.6	9.1	11.0
Return on Equity %	11.2	12.8	5.2	6.3	23.6	17.1	18.0
Return on Assets %	3.9	4.5	1.8	2.3	7.1	5.8	7.5
Debt/Total Assets %	46.0	46.5	46.2	44.6	51.6	48.3	36.2
Price Range	20.00-12.31	24.50-16.38	28.47-13.94	27.56-16.63	20.88-15.50	18.38-13.91	14.31-10.78
P/E Ratio	15.5-9.5	16.3-10.9	54.7-26.8	38.8-23.4	19.8-14.7	21.9-16.6	16.8-12.7
Average Yield %	1.7	1.3	1.1	1.0	1.1	1.0	1.2

Statistics are as originally reported. Adj. for stk. splits: 2-for-1, 6/98 and 5/95 1 Incl. gains on sale of subsidiaries & invest. $104.6 mill., 12/00; $117.8 mill., 12/99

OFFICERS:
R. W. Decherd, Chmn., Pres., C.E.O.
D. A. Shive, Exec. V.P., C.F.O.

INVESTOR CONTACT: Carey P. Hendrickson, V.P., Investor Relations, (214) 977-6626

PRINCIPAL OFFICE: 400 South Record Street, Dallas, TX 75265-5237

TELEPHONE NUMBER: (214) 977-6606
FAX: (214) 977-6603
WEB: www.belo.com
NO. OF EMPLOYEES: 7,245 (approx.)
SHAREHOLDERS: 8,721 (approx. series A); 603 (approx. series B)
ANNUAL MEETING: In May
INCORPORATED: DE, May, 1987

INSTITUTIONAL HOLDINGS:
No. of Institutions: 189
Shares Held: 55,908,481
% Held: 51.1

INDUSTRY: Newspapers (SIC: 2711)

TRANSFER AGENT(S): BankBoston, N.A., Boston, MA

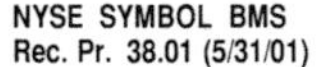

NYSE SYMBOL BMS
Rec. Pr. 38.01 (5/31/01)

BEMIS COMPANY, INC.

YIELD 2.6%
P/E RATIO 15.6

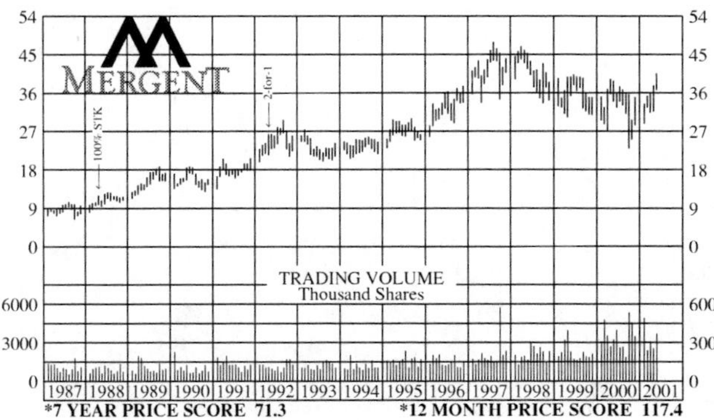

*7 YEAR PRICE SCORE 71.3 *12 MONTH PRICE SCORE 117.4

*NYSE COMPOSITE INDEX=100

INTERIM EARNINGS (Per Share):

Qtr.	Mar.	June	Sept.	Dec.
1997	0.37	0.52	0.47	0.64
1998	0.41	0.56	0.52	0.60
1999	0.35	0.60	0.59	0.63
2000	0.55	0.66	0.60	0.63

INTERIM DIVIDENDS (Per Share):

Amt.	Decl.	Ex.	Rec.	Pay.
0.24Q	5/04/00	5/17/00	5/19/00	6/01/00
0.24Q	8/03/00	8/14/00	8/16/00	9/01/00
0.24Q	10/26/00	11/13/00	11/15/00	12/01/00
0.25Q	2/01/01	2/14/01	2/16/01	3/01/01
0.25Q	5/03/01	5/16/01	5/18/01	6/01/01

Indicated div.: $1.00 (Div. Reinv. Plan)

CAPITALIZATION (12/31/00):

	($000)	(%)
Long-Term Debt 1	437,952	32.6
Deferred Income Tax	103,621	7.7
Minority Interest	1,570	0.1
Common & Surplus	798,757	59.5
Total	1,341,900	100.0

RECENT DEVELOPMENTS: For the year ended 12/31/00, net income increased 13.8% to $130.6 million. Net sales advanced 10.3% to $2.16 billion. Flexible Packaging segment operating profit advanced 18.0%, while operating profit for the Pressure Sensitive Materials group fell 9.0%. For the quarter ended 12/31/00, net income increased slightly to $33.4 million from $33.3 million in the equivalent 1999 quarter.

PROSPECTS: BMS' flexible packaging business should continue to benefit from its multi-layered coextruded structures and polyethylene product lines as its customers attempt to gain market share with new packaging initiatives. Within the pressure-sensitive materials business, results are being hampered by soft demand and increasing raw material costs. As a result, BMS has initiated programs to improve the pricing of its products and reduce overhead.

BUSINESS

BEMIS COMPANY, INC. is a manufacturer of flexible packaging products and pressure-sensitive materials, selling to customers throughout the United States, Canada, and Europe, with a growing presence in Asia Pacific, South America, and Mexico. Flexible packaging products include a broad range of consumer and industrial packaging consisting of high-barrier products that include advanced multi-layer coextruded, coated and laminated film structures; polyethylene products; and paper products. Pressure-Sensitive Materials include roll label products, graphics and distribution products, and technical and industrial products. In 2000, sales were as follows: flexible packaging, 77%, and pressure-sensitive materials, 23%.

ANNUAL FINANCIAL DATA

	12/31/00	12/31/99	12/31/98	12/31/97	12/31/96	12/31/95	12/31/94
Earnings Per Share	**2.44**	**2.18**	**2.09**	**2.00**	**1.90**	**1.63**	**1.40**
Cash Flow Per Share	**4.46**	**4.04**	**3.76**	**3.46**	**3.14**	**2.74**	**2.40**
Tang. Book Val. Per Share	**9.52**	**13.91**	**12.83**	**12.08**	**10.83**	**9.76**	**8.16**
Dividends Per Share	**0.96**	**0.92**	**0.88**	**0.80**	**0.72**	**0.64**	**0.54**
Dividend Payout %	**39.3**	**42.2**	**42.1**	**40.0**	**37.9**	**39.3**	**38.6**
INCOME STATEMENT (IN MILLIONS):							
Total Revenues	2,164.6	1,918.0	1,848.0	1,877.2	1,655.4	1,523.4	1,390.5
Costs & Expenses	1,811.5	1,602.1	1,550.5	1,603.1	1,413.9	1,317.1	1,209.6
Depreciation & Amort.	108.1	97.7	88.9	78.9	66.2	58.0	51.8
Operating Income	245.0	218.2	208.5	195.3	175.4	148.3	129.1
Net Interest Inc./(Exp.)	d31.6	d21.2	d21.9	d18.9	d13.4	d11.5	d8.4
Income Before Income Taxes	211.5	185.9	181.9	175.0	162.8	136.1	118.1
Income Taxes	80.9	71.1	70.5	67.4	61.7	50.9	45.3
Equity Earnings/Minority Int.	d0.5	d4.2	d4.4	d5.4	d4.7	d3.8	d3.4
Net Income	130.6	114.8	111.4	107.6	101.1	85.2	72.8
Cash Flow	238.7	212.5	200.3	186.4	167.3	143.2	124.6
Average Shs. Outstg. (000)	53,553	52,657	53,324	53,880	53,252	52,311	51,953
BALANCE SHEET (IN MILLIONS):							
Cash & Cash Equivalents	28.9	18.2	23.7	13.8	10.2	22.0	12.7
Total Current Assets	640.0	583.6	517.9	516.4	466.9	442.3	418.9
Net Property	825.8	776.2	740.1	685.2	583.5	534.6	461.3
Total Assets	1,888.6	1,532.1	1,453.1	1,362.6	1,168.8	1,030.6	923.3
Total Current Liabilities	495.1	253.3	242.8	251.2	214.4	219.2	210.8
Long-Term Obligations	438.0	372.3	371.4	316.8	241.1	166.4	171.7
Net Stockholders' Equity	798.8	725.9	670.8	639.9	567.1	512.8	418.0
Net Working Capital	144.9	330.3	275.2	265.2	252.5	223.1	208.1
Year-end Shs. Outstg. (000)	52,602	52,189	52,269	52,968	52,361	52,567	51,211
STATISTICAL RECORD:							
Operating Profit Margin %	11.3	11.4	11.3	10.4	10.6	9.7	9.3
Net Profit Margin %	6.0	6.0	6.0	5.7	6.1	5.6	5.2
Return on Equity %	16.4	15.8	16.6	16.8	17.8	16.6	17.4
Return on Assets %	6.9	7.5	7.7	7.9	8.6	8.3	7.9
Debt/Total Assets %	23.2	24.3	25.6	23.2	20.6	16.1	18.6
Price Range	39.31-22.94	40.38-30.19	46.94-33.50	47.94-33.63	37.63-25.63	30.00-23.00	25.75-20.50
P/E Ratio	16.1-9.4	18.5-13.8	22.5-16.0	24.0-16.8	19.8-13.5	18.4-14.1	18.4-14.6
Average Yield %	3.1	2.6	2.2	2.0	2.3	2.4	2.3

Statistics are as originally reported. Adj. for stk. splits: 2-for-1, 3/92. 1 Incl. capital lease obligations.

OFFICERS:
J. H. Roe, Chmn.
R. F. Mlnarik, Vice-Chmn.
J. H. Curler, Pres., C.E.O.
B. R. Field, III, Sr. V.P., C.F.O., Treas.

INVESTOR CONTACT: Robert F. Kleiber, Dir.-Investor Relations, (612) 376-3030

PRINCIPAL OFFICE: 222 South 9th Street, Suite 2300, Minneapolis, MN 55402-4099

TELEPHONE NUMBER: (612) 376-3000
FAX: (612) 340-6174
WEB: www.bemis.com

NO. OF EMPLOYEES: 10,969 (avg.)

SHAREHOLDERS: 5,005

ANNUAL MEETING: In May

INCORPORATED: MO, May, 1885

INSTITUTIONAL HOLDINGS:
No. of Institutions: 203
Shares Held: 31,254,229
% Held: 59.2

INDUSTRY: Paper coated & laminated, packaging (SIC: 2671)

TRANSFER AGENT(S): Wells Fargo Investor Services, South St. Paul, MN

NYSE SYMBOL BNG
Rec. Pr. 30.35 (5/31/01)

BENETTON GROUP S.P.A.

YIELD ...
P/E RATIO N.A.

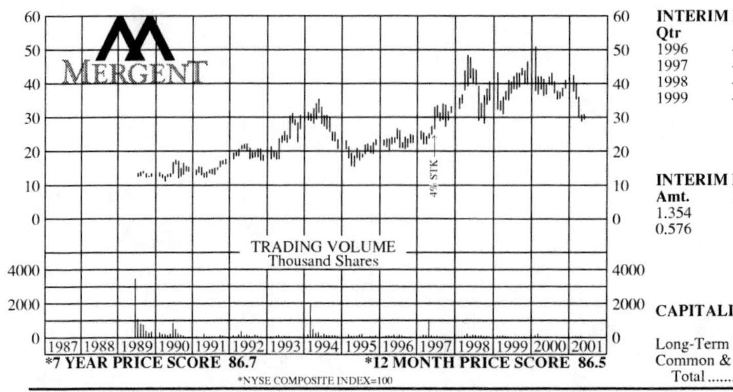

*7 YEAR PRICE SCORE 86.7 *12 MONTH PRICE SCORE 86.5

*NYSE COMPOSITE INDEX=100

INTERIM EARNINGS (Per Share):

Qtr	Mar.	June	Sept.	Dec.
1996		1.97		
1997		1.96		
1998		1.94		
1999		1.78		

INTERIM DIVIDENDS (Per Share):

Amt.	Decl.	Ex.	Rec.	Pay.
1.354	...	5/17/00	5/19/00	6/05/00
0.576	...	5/21/01	5/23/01	6/05/01

CAPITALIZATION (12/31/99):

	($000)	(%)
Long-Term Debt	457,301	29.5
Common & Surplus	1,090,625	70.5
Total	1,547,926	100.0

RECENT DEVELOPMENTS: For the year ended 12/31/00, net income amounted to $235.5 million (471.00 billion lire) versus $161.1 million (322.20 billion lire) in the previous year. Earnings for 2000 included a gain of $73.0 million (145.90 billion lire) from the sale of the Formula One team, while earnings for 1999 included a loss of $11.2 million (22.40 billion lire). Revenues rose to $1.95 billion (3.91 trillion lire) versus $1.92 billion (3.84 trillion lire) in 1999. Income from operations was $299.2 million (598.40 billion lire) versus $305.6 million (611.20 billion lire) a year ago.

PROSPECTS: On 6/4/01, BNG announced plans to increase the number of its "Mega Store" outlets in Japan from the current four to ten by 2002. The six new outlets will be located in Sapporo, Sendai, Nagoya, Fukuoka, Tokyo and Osaka. The Company runs a total of 230 outlets across Japan and intends to expand the scale of each shop and upgrade them as well. Separately, BNG announced that it has no intention of selling its Sports division despite having received offers.

BUSINESS

BENETTON GROUP S.P.A. manufactures and markets fashion apparel in wool, cotton and woven fabrics in addition to sports equipment, sportswear and casual wear for men, women and children. The Company offers casual wear mainly under UNITED COLORS OF BENETTON, SISLEY, and UNDERCOLORS. BNG also sells sportswear and equipment, including shoes and accessories, under the brands PLAYLIFE, NORDICA, PRINCE, ROLLERBLADE and KIL-LERLOOP. BNG's products are sold through a network of about 6,000 stores which are nearly all independently owned and are located in approximately 120 countries. BNG licenses its trademarks for products, such as watches, sunglasses and other fashion accessories, manufactured and sold by other companies. As of 1/3/01, the Benetton family, through Edizione Holding S.p.A., owned approximately 69.4% of the Company's shares.

ANNUAL FINANCIAL DATA

	12/31/99	12/31/98	12/31/97	12/31/96	12/31/95	12/31/94	12/31/93
Earnings Per Share	**1.78**	**1.94**	**1.96**	**1.97**	**1.51**	**1.45**	**1.53**
Cash Flow Per Share	**2.74**	**3.10**	**2.89**	**2.73**	**2.21**	**2.11**	**2.19**
Tang. Book Val. Per Share	**8.63**	**10.70**	**11.04**	**14.16**	**11.14**	**10.21**	**7.89**
Dividends Per Share	**1.67**	**0.40**	**0.38**	**0.35**	**0.32**	**0.33**	**0.31**
Dividend Payout %	**94.0**	**20.5**	**19.3**	**17.6**	**20.9**	**22.6**	**20.3**
INCOME STATEMENT (IN MILLIONS):							
Total Revenues	1,943.2	2,260.6	2,181.2	1,968.5	1,774.2	1,705.8	1,669.2
Costs & Expenses	1,550.2	1,886.2	1,803.9	1,626.3	1,449.5	1,417.5	1,372.3
Depreciation & Amort.	87.7	105.4	83.3	66.4	60.6	57.4	54.5
Operating Income	305.3	269.0	294.0	275.8	264.1	231.0	242.4
Net Interest Inc./(Exp.)	d137.9	d210.3	d212.3	d313.5	d355.4	d327.3	d359.7
Income Before Income Taxes	256.4	253.7	322.1	320.0	246.7	214.6	209.9
Income Taxes	92.2	78.6	141.8	144.6	113.2	90.3	82.9
Equity Earnings/Minority Int.	d3.1	0.9	d6.1	d3.4	d1.3	1.8	d2.2
Net Income	161.1	175.9	174.1	171.9	132.2	126.1	124.8
Cash Flow	248.9	281.3	257.4	238.4	192.7	183.5	179.4
BALANCE SHEET (IN MILLIONS):							
Cash & Cash Equivalents	405.0	799.7	840.9	866.8	574.1	416.5	510.6
Total Current Assets	1,580.4	2,202.1	2,416.1	2,139.9	1,752.6	1,586.2	1,576.2
Net Property	482.4	462.8	420.3	414.6	370.8	356.2	354.3
Total Assets	2,553.3	3,098.4	3,279.5	2,705.0	2,302.2	2,122.3	2,036.4
Total Current Liabilities	907.1	1,070.8	1,092.9	1,066.4	893.0	728.6	885.2
Long-Term Obligations	457.3	565.1	726.9	257.3	301.3	388.7	398.4
Net Stockholders' Equity	1,090.6	1,349.9	1,339.6	1,291.8	1,017.5	928.8	676.4
Net Working Capital	673.3	1,131.3	1,323.2	1,073.5	859.6	857.6	691.0
Year-end Shs. Outstg. (000)	90,779	90,750	89,100	87,250	87,300	86,800	82,000
STATISTICAL RECORD:							
Operating Profit Margin %	15.7	11.9	13.5	14.0	14.9	13.5	14.5
Net Profit Margin %	8.3	7.8	8.0	8.7	7.4	7.4	7.5
Return on Equity %	14.8	13.0	13.0	13.3	13.0	13.6	18.5
Return on Assets %	6.3	5.7	5.3	6.4	5.7	5.9	6.1
Debt/Total Assets %	17.9	18.2	22.2	9.5	13.1	18.3	19.6
Price Range	46.56-30.88	48.44-28.25	34.00-22.00	26.68-19.95	23.44-15.39	35.46-20.67	31.25-17.55
P/E Ratio	26.2-17.3	24.9-14.5	17.4-11.2	13.5-10.1	15.5-10.2	24.4-14.2	20.5-11.5
Average Yield %	4.3	1.0	1.3	1.5	1.6	1.2	1.3

Statistics are as originally reported. All figures are in U.S. dollars unless otherwise noted. Exchange rates: $1=L2,000.00, 12/31/00; $1=L2,000.00, 12/99; $1=L1,666.67, 12/98; $1=L1,666.67, 12/97; $1=L1,428.6, 12/96; $1=L1,666.67, 12/95; $1=L1,666.67, 12/94. All per share figures, prices & ratios calculated using ADRs. One ADR=20 ordinary shrs.

OFFICERS:
L. Benetton, Chmn.
G. Benetton, Dep. Chmn.
L. de Puppi, Man. Dir.

INVESTOR CONTACT: Investor Relations, (212) 483-4491 (U.S.)

PRINCIPAL OFFICE: Villa Minelli, Ponzano Veneto, TV, Italy

TELEPHONE NUMBER: (212) 483-4491 (NY)
WEB: www.benetton.it

NO. OF EMPLOYEES: 6,585

SHAREHOLDERS: 9,640

ANNUAL MEETING: In April

INCORPORATED: ITA, 1965

INSTITUTIONAL HOLDINGS:
No. of Institutions: 9
Shares Held: 470,788
% Held: 0.5

INDUSTRY: Women's and misses' outerwear, nec (SIC: 2339)

DEPOSITARY BANKS(S): Morgan Guaranty Trust Co., New York, NY

NYSE SYMBOL BBC
Rec. Pr. 20.60 (5/31/01)

BERGEN BRUNSWIG CORPORATION

YIELD 0.2%
P/E RATIO ...

*7 YEAR PRICE SCORE 69.8 *12 MONTH PRICE SCORE 146.4

*NYSE COMPOSITE INDEX=100

INTERIM EARNINGS (Per Share):

Qtr.	Dec.	Mar.	June	Sept.
1996-97	0.18	0.20	0.22	0.20
1997-98	0.21	0.18	0.26	d0.63
1998-99	0.27	0.35	0.26	d0.21
1999-00	0.16	0.18	0.15	d4.05
2000-01	0.16	...	...	...

INTERIM DIVIDENDS (Per Share):

Amt.	Decl.	Ex.	Rec.	Pay.
0.01Q	5/09/00	5/11/00	5/15/00	6/05/00
0.01Q	8/11/00	8/17/00	8/21/00	9/05/00
0.01Q	11/17/00	11/24/00	11/28/00	12/06/00
0.01Q	2/15/01	2/21/01	2/23/01	3/01/01
0.01Q	5/10/01	5/16/01	5/18/01	6/01/01

Indicated div.: $0.04

CAPITALIZATION (9/30/00):

	($000)	(%)
Long-Term Debt	1,067,282	51.1
Redeemable Pfd. Stock	300,000	14.4
Common & Surplus	723,249	34.6
Total	2,090,531	100.0

RECENT DEVELOPMENTS: For the quarter ended 12/31/00, net earnings totaled $21.4 million, up 2.3% versus earnings from continuing operations of $20.9 million a year earlier. Total net sales and other revenues rose 4.0% to $5.85 billion from $5.63 billion the year before. Prior-year results benefited from unusually strong drug sales stemming from concerns about Y2K-related distribution problems. Operating earnings grew 11.1% to $74.3 million from $66.9 million in the prior year.

PROSPECTS: On 3/19/01, the Company and AmeriSource Health Corporation announced they have entered into an agreement to merge and form a new company, called AmeriSource-Bergen Corporation, which will have annual revenues of about $35.00 billion. Under the terms of the agreement, each share of BBC common stock will be converted into 0.37 shares of AmeriSource-Bergen common stock. The deal is expected to be completed during the summer of 2001.

BUSINESS

BERGEN BRUNSWIG CORPORATION is a major supplier of pharmaceuticals and specialty healthcare products, as well as information management systems and consulting services. The Company provides its products and services to hospitals, nursing homes, physicians, drug stores, manufacturers and patients. Through its subsidiaries, the Company provides product distribution, logistics, pharmacy management programs, and Internet fulfillment services designed to help reduce costs and improve patient outcomes throughout the healthcare industry.

ANNUAL FINANCIAL DATA

	9/30/00	9/30/99	9/30/98	9/30/97	9/30/96	9/30/95	9/30/94
Earnings Per Share	**[2] d3.58**	**0.59**	**[1] 0.03**	**[1] 0.81**	**0.73**	**0.64**	**0.58**
Cash Flow Per Share	**d2.87**	**1.19**	**0.40**	**1.21**	**1.12**	**0.99**	**0.90**
Tang. Book Val. Per Share	**0.48**	**...**	**3.65**	**3.13**	**2.40**	**1.79**	**1.43**
Dividends Per Share	**0.10**	**0.30**	**0.26**	**0.23**	**0.19**	**0.19**	**0.18**
Dividend Payout %	**...**	**50.8**	**847.2**	**28.3**	**26.2**	**29.8**	**31.5**
INCOME STATEMENT (IN MILLIONS):							
Total Revenues	22,942.9	21,245.5	17,121.7	11,660.5	9,942.7	8,447.6	7,483.8
Costs & Expenses	23,157.6	20,971.5	16,978.3	11,450.5	9,748.9	8,273.4	7,336.4
Depreciation & Amort.	94.9	66.0	37.5	40.8	38.4	34.2	31.3
Operating Income	d309.6	208.1	105.9	169.2	155.4	140.0	116.0
Net Interest Inc./(Exp.)	d112.0	d74.1	d40.0	d30.8	d30.2	d30.5	d17.9
Income Before Income Taxes	d426.6	133.9	65.9	138.4	125.3	109.5	98.1
Income Taxes	40.3	58.5	62.8	56.8	51.7	45.5	42.0
Equity Earnings/Minority Int.	d14.1	d4.9	...	...	...	...	...
Net Income	[2] d481.0	75.4	[1] 3.1	[1] 81.7	73.5	63.9	56.1
Cash Flow	d386.1	141.5	40.6	122.4	111.9	98.1	87.5
Average Shs. Outstg. (000)	134,504	119,095	102,620	101,428	99,948	99,503	96,710
BALANCE SHEET (IN MILLIONS):							
Cash & Cash Equivalents	94.0	116.4	79.0	57.3	21.4	64.4	5.3
Total Current Assets	3,517.5	3,467.9	2,500.8	2,155.5	1,932.2	1,843.9	1,445.4
Net Property	208.5	240.4	144.8	138.4	142.7	153.1	136.3
Total Assets	4,571.4	5,535.4	3,003.2	2,707.1	2,489.8	2,405.5	1,995.1
Total Current Liabilities	2,452.0	2,697.9	1,909.4	1,624.3	1,491.6	1,328.4	1,191.1
Long-Term Obligations	1,067.3	993.3	448.3	418.2	398.0	539.3	320.5
Net Stockholders' Equity	723.2	1,495.5	629.1	644.9	579.0	519.3	461.9
Net Working Capital	1,065.5	770.0	591.4	531.2	440.6	515.5	254.3
Year-end Shs. Outstg. (000)	134,789	134,206	102,882	100,830	100,155	99,573	97,690
STATISTICAL RECORD:							
Operating Profit Margin %	...	1.0	0.6	1.5	1.6	1.7	1.6
Net Profit Margin %	...	0.4	...	0.7	0.7	0.8	0.7
Return on Equity %	...	5.0	0.5	12.7	12.7	12.3	12.2
Return on Assets %	...	1.4	0.1	3.0	3.0	2.7	2.8
Debt/Total Assets %	23.3	17.9	14.9	15.4	16.0	22.4	16.1
Price Range	17.70-4.50	37.75-6.44	35.00-16.81	23.03-11.05	13.20-9.65	11.65-7.70	7.95-5.24
P/E Ratio	...	64.0-10.9	N.M.	28.6-13.7	18.0-13.2	18.1-12.0	13.7-9.0
Average Yield %	0.9	1.4	1.0	1.3	1.7	2.0	2.8

Statistics are as originally reported. Adj. for stk. split, 2-for-1, 12/98; 5-for-4, 6/97; & 5% div., 1/95. [1] Incl. $110.2 mil pre-tax non-recur. chg., 1998; & $5.8 mil chg., 1997. [2] Bef. $271.8 mil ($2.02/sh) loss fr. disc. opers. & incl. $526.3 mil pre-tax non-recur. chg.

OFFICERS:
R. E. Martini, Chmn., C.E.O.
N. F. Dimick, Exec. V.P., C.F.O.
M. A. Montevideo, Treas.
M. A. Sawdei, Exec. V.P., Sec.

INVESTOR CONTACT: Donna Dolan, V.P.-Corp. Fin., (714) 385-4226

PRINCIPAL OFFICE: 4000 Metropolitan Drive, Orange, CA 92868-3510

TELEPHONE NUMBER: (714) 385-4000
FAX: (714) 385-1442
WEB: www.bergenbrunswig.com

NO. OF EMPLOYEES: 10,300 (approx.)

SHAREHOLDERS: N/A

ANNUAL MEETING: In Feb.

INCORPORATED: NJ, Feb., 1956

INSTITUTIONAL HOLDINGS:
No. of Institutions: 194
Shares Held: 96,351,443
% Held: 71.3

INDUSTRY: Drugs, proprietaries, and sundries (SIC: 5122)

TRANSFER AGENT(S): Mellon Investor Services, Ridgefield Park, NJ

NYSE SYMBOL BER
Rec. Pr. 43.50 (5/31/01)

BERKLEY (W. R.) CORPORATION

YIELD 1.2%
P/E RATIO 31.5

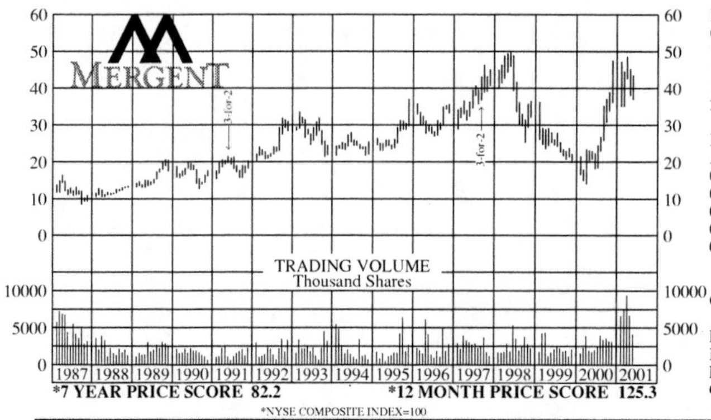

*7 YEAR PRICE SCORE 82.2 *12 MONTH PRICE SCORE 125.3
*NYSE COMPOSITE INDEX=100

INTERIM EARNINGS (Per Share):

Qtr.	Mar.	June	Sept.	Dec.
1997	0.90	0.63	0.80	0.74
1998	0.78	0.70	0.36	d0.14
1999	0.07	0.22	d0.02	d1.59
2000	0.17	0.26	0.27	0.68

INTERIM DIVIDENDS (Per Share):

Amt.	Decl.	Ex.	Rec.	Pay.
0.13Q	5/09/00	6/14/00	6/16/00	7/03/00
0.13Q	8/08/00	9/14/00	9/18/00	10/02/00
0.13Q	11/07/00	12/13/00	12/15/00	1/02/01
0.13Q	3/13/01	3/19/01	3/21/01	4/02/01
0.13Q	5/15/01	6/13/01	6/15/01	7/02/01

Indicated div.: $0.52

CAPITALIZATION (12/31/00):

	($000)	(%)
Long-Term Debt	370,158	28.9
Minority Interest	31,877	2.5
Redeemable Pfd. Stock	198,169	15.5
Common & Surplus	680,896	53.1
Total	1,281,100	100.0

RECENT DEVELOPMENTS: For the year ended 12/31/00, net income totaled $36.2 million compared with a loss of $34.0 million, before an extraordinary gain and accounting charge, in the prior year. Results for 2000 and 1999 included a restructuring charge of $1.9 million and $11.5 million, respectively. Total revenues advanced 6.4% to $1.78 billion from $1.67 billion the year before. Premiums earned improved 5.4% to $1.49 billion, while net investment income climbed 10.6% to $210.4 million.

PROSPECTS: The improved results in 2000 reflect the impact of more favorable market conditions, including higher prices, higher investment income and improved operating efficiencies. Separately, BER began redirecting its reinsurance business away from the property sub-segments, which expose the Company to weather-related and other natural catastrophes, and decided to withdraw altogether from the Latin American and Caribbean market.

BUSINESS

W.R. BERKLEY CORPORATION is an insurance holding company that, through its subsidiaries, operates in all segments of the property casualty insurance business. The Company's operating units are grouped in five segments according to market served: Regional Property Casualty Insurance, Reinsurance, Specialty Insurance, Alternative Markets and International. The Company's regional insurance operations are conducted primarily in the New England, Mid-Atlantic, Midwest and Southern sections of the United States. The reinsurance, specialty insurance, and alternative insurance operations are conducted on a nationwide basis. Presently, international operations are conducted primarily in Argentina and the Philippines.

ANNUAL FINANCIAL DATA

	12/31/00	12/31/99	12/31/98	12/31/97	12/31/96	12/31/95	12/31/94
Earnings Per Share	**3 1.39**	**2 d1.34**	**1 1.76**	**3.02**	**2.56**	**1.91**	**0.96**
Tang. Book Val. Per Share	**23.75**	**20.11**	**29.60**	**29.56**	**27.37**	**28.43**	**21.54**
Dividends Per Share	**0.52**	**0.51**	**0.47**	**0.40**	**0.34**	**0.31**	**0.29**
Dividend Payout %	**37.4**	**...**	**26.7**	**13.1**	**13.3**	**16.4**	**29.9**
INCOME STATEMENT (IN MILLIONS):							
Total Premium Income	1,491.0	1,414.4	1,278.4	1,111.7	981.2	803.3	655.0
Other Income	290.3	259.3	304.1	288.6	243.9	218.6	175.8
Total Revenues	1,781.3	1,673.7	1,582.5	1,400.3	1,225.2	1,021.9	830.8
Policyholder Benefits	1,094.4	1,085.8	914.8	734.4	669.2	571.0	486.1
Income Before Income Taxes	40.9	d79.2	62.8	129.2	115.0	82.7	30.8
Income Taxes	2.5	cr45.8	5.5	30.7	25.1	17.6	cr1.6
Equity Earnings/Minority Int.	d2.2	d0.6	1.4	0.5	0.3	d4.3	2.8
Net Income	3 36.2	2 d34.5	1 51.2	91.2	76.4	49.8	24.7
Average Shs. Outstg. (000)	25,991	25,927	29,115	30,185	29,792	26,121	25,773
BALANCE SHEET (IN MILLIONS):							
Cash & Cash Equivalents	0.9	20.1	16.1	21.7	19.3	10.2	5.5
Premiums Due	1,399.1	1,259.8	1,120.3	764.3	683.9	654.7	1,318.8
Invst. Assets: Fixed-term	2,619.2	2,516.5	2,866.1	2,817.1	2,517.1	2,290.1	1,618.3
Invst. Assets: Equities	83.8	61.4	65.9	86.2	93.9	101.6	69.3
Invst. Assets: Total	2,703.0	2,577.9	2,931.9	2,903.4	2,611.0	2,391.6	1,687.6
Total Assets	5,022.1	4,784.8	4,983.4	4,599.3	4,073.3	3,618.7	3,582.3
Long-Term Obligations	370.2	394.8	394.4	390.4	390.1	319.3	331.0
Net Stockholders' Equity	680.9	591.8	861.2	947.2	879.6	929.7	597.5
Year-end Shs. Outstg. (000)	25,656	25,617	26,504	29,568	29,454	30,252	25,167
STATISTICAL RECORD:							
Return on Revenues %	2.0	...	3.2	6.5	6.2	4.9	3.0
Return on Equity %	5.3	...	5.9	9.6	8.7	5.4	4.1
Return on Assets %	0.7	...	1.0	2.0	1.9	1.4	0.7
Price Range	47.63-14.00	36.25-19.81	49.88-25.25	46.38-28.79	35.83-26.83	37.00-23.00	28.00-21.67
P/E Ratio	34.3-10.1	...	28.3-14.3	15.4-9.5	14.0-10.5	19.4-12.1	29.2-22.6
Average Yield %	1.7	1.8	1.3	1.1	1.1	1.0	1.2

Statistics are as originally reported. Adj. for stk. split: 3-for-2, 9/18/97 1 Incl. non-recurr. chrg. $11.5 mill. 2 Bef. acctg. change chrg. $3.3 mill. and extraord. gain $735,000 3 Incl. a restructuring charge of $1.9 mill.

OFFICERS:
W. R. Berkley, Chmn., Pres., C.E.O.
E. G. Ballard, Sr. V.P., C.F.O., Treas.
C. T. Finnegan III, Sr. V.P., Gen. Couns. Insur., Sec.

INVESTOR CONTACT: Eugene G. Ballard, Sr. V.P., C.F.O., (203) 629-3000

PRINCIPAL OFFICE: 165 Mason Street, P.O. Box 2518, Greenwich, CT 06836-2518

TELEPHONE NUMBER: (203) 629-3000
FAX: (203) 629-3492
WEB: www.wrberkley.com

NO. OF EMPLOYEES: 4,426

SHAREHOLDERS: 671 (approx.)

ANNUAL MEETING: In May

INCORPORATED: DE, Jan., 1970

INSTITUTIONAL HOLDINGS:
No. of Institutions: 123
Shares Held: 23,157,132
% Held: 79.9

INDUSTRY: Fire, marine, and casualty insurance (SIC: 6331)

TRANSFER AGENT(S): Mellon Investor Services, New York, NY

NYSE SYMBOL BRKB
Rec. Pr. 2275.00 (4/30/01)

BERKSHIRE HATHAWAY INC.

YIELD ...
P/E RATIO 31.2

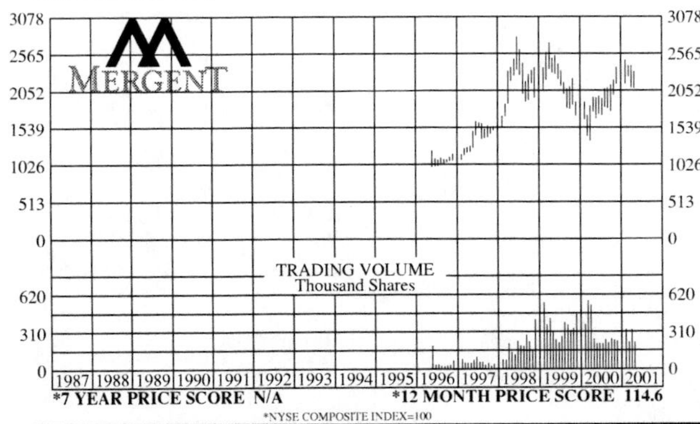

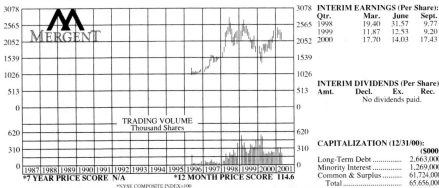

***7 YEAR PRICE SCORE N/A** ***12 MONTH PRICE SCORE 114.6**

*NYSE COMPOSITE INDEX=100

INTERIM EARNINGS (Per Share):

Qtr.	Mar.	June	Sept.	Dec.
1998	19.40	31.57	9.77	14.80
1999	11.87	12.53	9.20	0.57
2000	17.70	14.03	17.43	23.67

INTERIM DIVIDENDS (Per Share):

Amt.	Decl.	Ex.	Rec.	Pay.

No dividends paid.

CAPITALIZATION (12/31/00):

	($000)	(%)
Long-Term Debt	2,663,000	4.1
Minority Interest	1,269,000	1.9
Common & Surplus	61,724,000	94.0
Total	65,656,000	100.0

RECENT DEVELOPMENTS: For the year ended 12/31/00, net income more than doubled to $3.33 billion compared with $1.56 billion in the previous year. Results included realized investment gains of $3.96 billion and $1.37 billion in 2000 and 1999, respectively. Total revenues jumped 41.4% to $33.98 billion versus $24.03 billion in the comparable period a year earlier. Insurance premiums earned increased 35.2% to $19.34 billion, while sales and services revenues improved 12.4% to $7.33 billion. Interest, dividend and other investment income rose 16.1% to $2.69 billion.

PROSPECTS: On 2/27/01, the Company completed the acquisition of Johns Manville Corporation, a manufacturer and marketer of building products, for approximately $1.80 billion. As a result of the acquisition, Johns Manville will become a subsidiary of the Company. Separately on 1/2/01, the Company acquired Benjamin Moore & Co., a manufacturer and retailer of premium paints, stains, and industrial coatings. Going forward, the Company will continue to focus on its aggressive acquisition program.

BUSINESS

BERKSHIRE HATHAWAY INC. is engaged in diverse business activities including the property and casualty insurance business. The Company's insurance and reinsurance business activities are conducted through 36 domestic and 16 foreign-based insurance companies including GEICO and General RE. BRK's non-insurance subsidiaries operate in a wide range of industries. FlightSafety International provides training of aircraft and ship operators. Executive Jet provides fractional ownership programs for general aviation aircraft. Nebraska Furniture Mart, R.C. Willey Home Furnishings, Star Furniture, and Jordans Furniture are retailers of home furnishings. Borsheims, Helzberg Diamond Shops and Ben Bridge Jeweler are retailers of fine jewelry. Scott Fetzer is a diversified manufacturer and distributor of commercial and industrial products. On 1/2/01, the Company acquired Johns Manville Corp. and Benjamin Moore & Co. In 2000, BRK acquired CORT Business Services, MidAmerican Energy Holdings (76.0% owned) and Shaw Industries (87.3% owned). Also, BRK has substantial equity stakes in The Coca-Cola Co., American Express Co., The Gillette Co., Wells Fargo & Co., WESCO, and The Washington Post Co.

ANNUAL FINANCIAL DATA

	12/31/00	12/31/99	12/31/98	12/31/97	12/31/96	12/31/95	12/31/94
[1] Earnings Per Share	**72.83**	**34.17**	**75.40**	**51.40**	**68.83**	**20.37**	**14.00**
Tang. Book Val. Per Share	**935.84**	**865.47**	**202.27**	**789.89**	**561.53**	**480.66**	**336.02**
INCOME STATEMENT (IN MILLIONS):							
Total Premium Income	19,343.0	14,306.0	5,481.0	4,761.0	4,118.0	957.5	923.2
Net Investment Income	2,686.0	2,314.0	1,049.0	916.0	778.0	474.8	426.1
Other Income	11,947.0	7,408.0	7,302.0	4,753.0	5,604.0	3,055.4	2,498.2
Total Revenues	33,976.0	24,028.0	13,832.0	10,430.0	10,500.0	4,487.7	3,847.5
Policyholder Benefits	17,332.0	12,518.0	4,040.0	3,420.0	3,089.0	612.0	565.3
Income Before Income Taxes	5,587.0	2,450.0	4,314.0	2,827.0	3,706.0	1,008.8	662.2
Income Taxes	2,018.0	852.0	1,457.0	898.0	1,197.0	270.3	158.7
Equity Earnings/Minority Int.	d241.0	d41.0	d27.0	d28.0	d20.0	d13.3	d8.7
Net Income	3,328.0	1,557.0	2,830.0	1,901.0	2,489.0	725.2	494.8
Average Shs. Outstg. (000)	45,690	45,600	37,530	36,990	36,150	35,610	35,340
BALANCE SHEET (IN MILLIONS):							
Cash & Cash Equivalents	5,263.0	3,835.0	13,582.0	1,002.4	1,339.8	2,703.8	273.9
Premiums Due	11,764.0	8,558.0	7,224.0	1,711.5	1,523.2	718.9	580.6
Invst. Assets: Fixed-term	32,567.0	30,222.0	21,246.0	10,297.8	6,446.9	835.2	1,820.7
Invst. Assets: Equities	37,619.0	39,508.0	39,761.0	36,247.7	27,750.6	22,000.3	15,236.5
Invst. Assets: Total	73,542.0	69,730.0	61,007.0	46,545.5	34,197.5	23,658.2	18,080.6
Total Assets	135,792.0	131,416.0	122,237.0	56,110.9	43,409.5	29,928.8	21,338.2
Long-Term Obligations	2,663.0	2,465.0	2,385.0	2,266.7	1,944.4	1,061.7	810.7
Net Stockholders' Equity	61,724.0	57,761.0	57,403.0	31,455.2	23,426.3	17,217.1	11,874.9
Year-end Shs. Outstg. (000)	1,526	1,521	6,420	1,198	1,206	1,194	1,178
STATISTICAL RECORD:							
Return on Revenues %	9.8	6.5	20.5	18.2	23.7	16.2	12.9
Return on Equity %	5.4	2.7	4.9	6.0	10.6	4.2	4.2
Return on Assets %	2.5	1.2	2.3	3.4	5.7	2.4	2.3
P/E Ratio	1.1-0.6	2.6-1.7	1.2-0.7	1.1-0.7	0.6-0.5	...	...

Statistics are as originally reported. [1] Earnings per share data represents B share.

OFFICERS:
W. E. Buffett, Chmn., C.E.O.
C. T. Munger, Vice-Chmn.
M. D. Hamburg, V.P., C.F.O.

PRINCIPAL OFFICE: 1440 Kiewit Plaza, Omaha, NE 68131

TELEPHONE NUMBER: (402) 346-1400
WEB: www.berkshirehathaway.com

NO. OF EMPLOYEES: 112,000 (approx.)

SHAREHOLDERS: 8,800 (approx. class A); 14,000 (approx. class B)

ANNUAL MEETING: In Apr.

INCORPORATED: DE, Aug., 1973

INSTITUTIONAL HOLDINGS:
No. of Institutions: 455
Shares Held: 2,373,850 (B shares only)
% Held: N/A

INDUSTRY: Fire, marine, and casualty insurance (SIC: 6331)

TRANSFER AGENT(S): Fleet National Bank, N.A. c/o EquiServe, Providence, RI

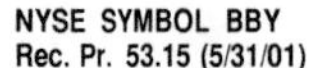

NYSE SYMBOL BBY
Rec. Pr. 53.15 (5/31/01)

BEST BUY CO., INC.

YIELD ...
P/E RATIO 28.6

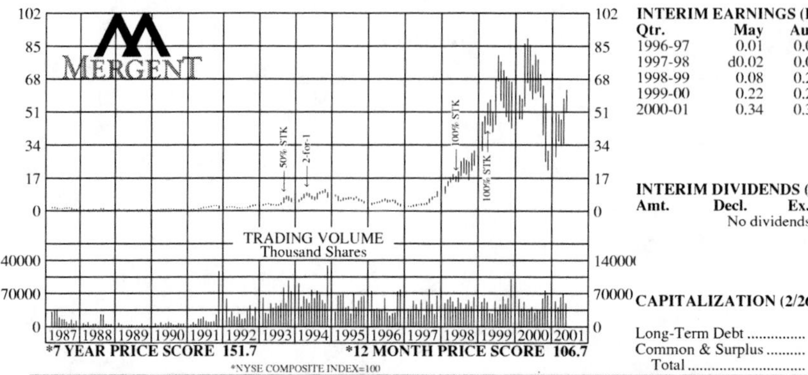

*7 YEAR PRICE SCORE 151.7 *12 MONTH PRICE SCORE 106.7

*NYSE COMPOSITE INDEX=100

INTERIM EARNINGS (Per Share):

Qtr.	May	Aug.	Nov.	Feb.
1996-97	0.01	0.03	d0.07	0.05
1997-98	d0.02	0.04	0.15	0.33
1998-99	0.08	0.21	0.26	0.52
1999-00	0.22	0.28	0.37	0.78
2000-01	0.34	0.36	0.27	0.89

INTERIM DIVIDENDS (Per Share):

Amt.	Decl.	Ex.	Rec.	Pay.
No dividends paid.				

CAPITALIZATION (2/26/00):

	($000)	(%)
Long-Term Debt	14,860	1.3
Common & Surplus	1,095,985	98.7
Total	1,110,845	100.0

RECENT DEVELOPMENTS: For the fiscal year ended 3/3/01, net earnings rose 14.1% to $395.8 million from $347.1 million the year before. Earnings were hurt by a slowdown in consumer spending and increased promotional activity. Revenues advanced 22.7% to $15.33 billion from $12.49 billion a year earlier. Comparable-store sales rose 4.9% year-over-year. Gross profit totaled $3.06 billion, or 20.0% of revenues, versus $2.39 billion, or 19.2% of revenues, the previous year. Operating income climbed 12.1% to $604.3 million from $539.3 million in the prior year.

PROSPECTS: The Company's efforts to expand its market share are expected to fuel earnings growth going forward. During fiscal 2002, BBY plans to open approximately 60 stores, including about 20 of its smaller market stores. In addition, the Company plans to remodel or relocate approximately seven stores during the year. Comparable-store sales are expected to increase modestly in fiscal 2002, while gross profit margins are anticipated to benefit from continued expansion of the digital product cycle and a more profitable product assortment.

BUSINESS

BEST BUY CO., INC. is one of the nation's largest consumer-electronics and major-appliance specialty retailers. The Company sells nationally-recognized, name-brand consumer electronics, personal computers and home-office products, major appliances, entertainment software and photographic equipment through more than 400 Best Buy stores in 41 states, primarily in the central United States. In addition, the Company operates approximately 1,300 music and video retail stores through its Musicland Stores Corporation subsidiary under the names Sam Goody, Suncoast, On Cue, and Media Play.

ANNUAL FINANCIAL DATA

	2/26/00	2/27/99	2/28/98	3/1/97	3/2/96	2/25/95	2/26/94
Earnings Per Share	**1.63**	**1.07**	**0.52**	**[2] 0.01**	**0.28**	**0.33**	**[1] 0.25**
Cash Flow Per Share	**2.15**	**1.44**	**0.83**	**0.39**	**0.59**	**0.55**	**0.39**
Tang. Book Val. Per Share	**5.47**	**5.23**	**3.12**	**2.53**	**2.52**	**2.23**	**1.87**
INCOME STATEMENT (IN MILLIONS):							
Total Revenues	12,494.0	10,077.9	8,358.2	7,770.7	7,217.4	5,079.6	3,006.5
Costs & Expenses	11,845.2	9,635.0	8,099.8	7,650.6	7,040.0	4,919.1	2,906.9
Depreciation & Amort.	109.5	78.4	71.6	66.8	54.9	38.6	22.4
Operating Income	539.3	364.5	186.9	53.2	122.6	121.9	77.2
Net Interest Inc./(Exp.)	23.3	0.4	d33.0	d50.3	d43.6	d27.9	d8.8
Income Before Income Taxes	562.6	364.9	153.9	2.9	79.0	94.1	68.4
Income Taxes	215.5	140.5	59.4	1.1	31.0	36.4	26.7
Net Income	347.1	224.4	94.5	[2] 1.7	48.0	57.7	[1] 41.7
Cash Flow	456.6	302.8	166.0	68.6	102.9	96.2	64.1
Average Shs. Outstg. (000)	212,580	210,006	200,252	174,328	174,560	173,884	165,344
BALANCE SHEET (IN MILLIONS):							
Cash & Cash Equivalents	750.7	785.8	520.1	89.8	86.4	144.7	59.9
Total Current Assets	2,238.5	2,063.1	1,710.3	1,385.0	1,560.5	1,240.7	764.6
Net Property	698.1	423.6	332.9	331.6	311.0	237.5	172.7
Total Assets	2,995.3	2,512.5	2,056.3	1,734.3	1,890.8	1,507.1	952.5
Total Current Liabilities	1,785.0	1,386.9	1,033.7	817.6	973.7	631.6	402.0
Long-Term Obligations	14.9	30.5	210.4	216.6	206.3	227.2	210.8
Net Stockholders' Equity	1,096.0	1,064.1	557.7	438.3	431.6	376.1	311.4
Net Working Capital	453.4	676.2	676.6	567.5	586.8	609.0	362.6
Year-end Shs. Outstg. (000)	200,379	203,621	178,504	173,148	171,368	168,864	166,968
STATISTICAL RECORD:							
Operating Profit Margin %	4.3	3.6	2.2	0.7	1.7	2.4	2.6
Net Profit Margin %	2.8	2.2	1.1	...	0.7	1.1	1.4
Return on Equity %	31.7	21.1	16.9	0.4	11.1	15.3	13.4
Return on Assets %	11.6	8.9	4.6	0.1	2.5	3.8	4.4
Debt/Total Assets %	0.5	1.2	10.2	12.5	10.9	15.1	22.1
Price Range	80.50-30.88	31.13-9.00	10.25-1.97	6.56-2.44	8.41-4.00	11.31-4.75	7.86-2.70
P/E Ratio	49.4-18.9	29.1-8.4	19.7-3.8	649.8-241.3	30.6-14.5	34.0-14.3	31.1-10.7

Statistics are as originally reported. Adj. for 2-for-1 stk. split, 3/99, 5/98, & 4/94. [1] Bef. $425,000 ($0.01/sh) acctg. chg. [2] Incl. $25 mil pre-tax chg. for write-down of inventory.

OFFICERS:
R. M. Schulze, Chmn., C.E.O.
B. H. Anderson, Vice-Chmn., Pres., C.O.O.
A. U. Lenzmeier, Exec. V.P., C.F.O.

INVESTOR CONTACT: Susan Hoff, Sr. V.P.-Corp. & Pub. Aff., (952) 947-2443

PRINCIPAL OFFICE: 7075 Flying Cloud Dr., Eden Prairie, MN 55344

TELEPHONE NUMBER: (952) 947-2000
FAX: (952) 947-2422
WEB: www.bestbuy.com
NO. OF EMPLOYEES: 55,000 (approx.)
SHAREHOLDERS: 1,940
ANNUAL MEETING: In June
INCORPORATED: MI, 1966; reincorp., MN, 1966

INSTITUTIONAL HOLDINGS:
No. of Institutions: 294
Shares Held: 120,849,960
% Held: 58.2

INDUSTRY: Radio, TV, & electronic stores (SIC: 5731)

TRANSFER AGENT(S): First Chicago Trust Company of New York, Jersey City, NJ

NYSE SYMBOL BS
Rec. Pr. 2.76 (5/31/01)

BETHLEHEM STEEL CORPORATION

YIELD . . .
P/E RATIO . . .

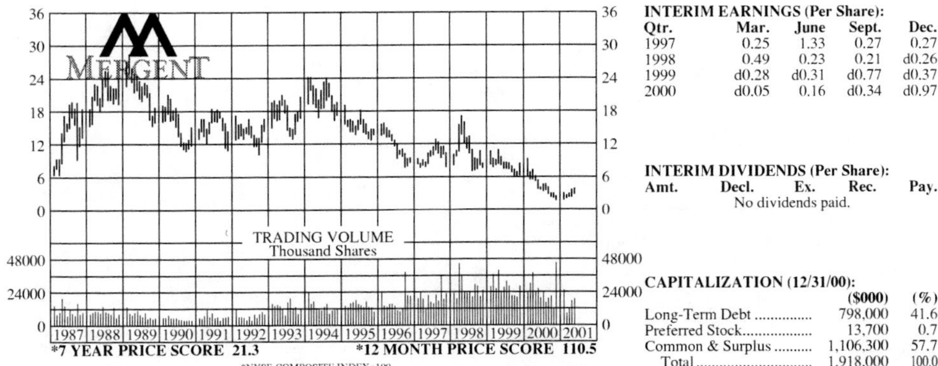

*7 YEAR PRICE SCORE 21.3 *12 MONTH PRICE SCORE 110.5

*NYSE COMPOSITE INDEX=100

INTERIM EARNINGS (Per Share):

Qtr.	Mar.	June	Sept.	Dec.
1997	0.25	1.33	0.27	0.27
1998	0.49	0.23	0.21	d0.26
1999	d0.28	d0.31	d0.77	d0.37
2000	d0.05	0.16	d0.34	d0.97

INTERIM DIVIDENDS (Per Share):

Amt.	Decl.	Ex.	Rec.	Pay.

No dividends paid.

CAPITALIZATION (12/31/00):

	($000)	(%)
Long-Term Debt	798,000	41.6
Preferred Stock	13,700	0.7
Common & Surplus	1,106,300	57.7
Total	1,918,000	100.0

RECENT DEVELOPMENTS: For the year ended 12/31/00, BS incurred a net loss of $118.4 million compared with a loss of $183.2 million in 1999. Earnings for 2000 included non-recurring items that resulted in a net after-tax gain of $17.0 million. Results were adversely affected by competitive market conditions caused by high levels of steel imports, high customer inventories and the slowing economy. Net sales advanced 2.6% to $4.20 billion compared $4.09 billion in 1999.

PROSPECTS: The Company continues to believe that the U.S. will have moderate growth and low inflation this year. BS continues to be concerned about the high levels of steel imports which entered the Company's markets in 2000 in quantities second only to the record levels experienced in 1998. BS believes that imports in 2001 will be somewhat lower than 2000 levels given the recent favorable trade case rulings involving hot-rolled sheet products and the extremely low current market prices for steel.

BUSINESS

BETHLEHEM STEEL CORPORATION is an integrated steel producer engaged primarily in the manufacture and sale of a wide variety of steel mill products. These products include hot-rolled, cold-rolled and coated sheets, tin mill products, carbon and alloy plates, rail, specialty blooms, carbon and alloy bars and large-diameter pipe. The Company's principal steel operations include the Burns Harbor Division, the Sparrows Point Division and the Pennsylvania Steel Technologies Division. During 2000, the Company's former Bethlehem Lukens Plate Division was consolidated into the Sparrows Point and Burns Harbor Divisions. Bethlehem also has iron ore operations, railroad and trucking operations and lake shipping operations. During 1997, the Company sold its steel-related operations.

QUARTERLY DATA

(12/31/00)($000s)	REV	INC
1st Quarter	1,161,700	3,100
2nd Quarter	1,116,400	31,600
3rd Quarter	1,013,600	(34,800)
4th Quarter	904,900	(118,200)

ANNUAL FINANCIAL DATA

	12/31/00	12/31/99	12/31/98	12/31/97	12/31/96	12/31/95	12/31/94
Earnings Per Share	**1 d1.21**	**d1.72**	**1 0.64**	**1 2.03**	**1 d3.15**	**1.24**	**0.35**
Cash Flow Per Share	**0.77**	**0.25**	**2.65**	**3.70**	**d0.74**	**3.80**	**2.81**
Tang. Book Val. Per Share	**5.99**	**7.02**	**8.62**	**10.63**	**7.08**	**6.87**	**6.51**
INCOME STATEMENT (IN MILLIONS):							
Total Revenues	4,196.6	3,914.8	4,477.8	4,631.2	4,679.0	4,867.5	4,819.4
Costs & Expenses	4,010.9	3,835.9	4,041.8	4,026.2	4,738.7	4,314.6	4,424.7
Depreciation & Amort.	260.3	257.5	246.5	231.0	268.7	284.0	261.1
Operating Income	d74.6	d178.6	189.5	374.0	d328.4	268.9	133.6
Net Interest Inc./(Exp.)	d68.8	d43.6	d45.4	d38.3	d47.4	d52.3	d39.1
Income Before Income Taxes	d143.4	d222.2	144.1	335.7	d375.8	216.6	94.5
Income Taxes	cr25.0	cr39.0	24.0	55.0	cr67.0	37.0	14.0
Net Income	1 d118.4	d183.2	1 120.1	1 280.7	1 d308.8	179.6	80.5
Cash Flow	101.2	33.1	324.9	470.1	d82.0	421.2	298.5
Average Shs. Outstg. (000)	131,747	130,199	122,585	127,039	111,286	110,708	106,053
BALANCE SHEET (IN MILLIONS):							
Cash & Cash Equivalents	109.7	99.4	137.8	252.4	136.6	180.0	159.5
Total Current Assets	1,146.4	1,209.4	1,494.8	1,464.0	1,488.4	1,525.8	1,569.1
Net Property	2,870.5	2,899.7	2,655.7	2,357.7	2,419.8	2,714.2	2,759.3
Total Assets	5,467.0	5,536.2	5,621.5	4,802.6	5,109.9	5,700.3	5,782.4
Total Current Liabilities	927.2	1,033.4	985.2	910.8	957.4	1,049.6	1,011.2
Long-Term Obligations	798.0	754.1	627.7	451.6	497.4	546.8	668.4
Net Stockholders' Equity	1,120.0	1,277.1	1,489.5	1,215.0	966.0	1,238.3	1,155.8
Net Working Capital	219.2	176.0	509.6	553.2	531.0	476.2	557.9
Year-end Shs. Outstg. (000)	129,773	131,470	130,196	112,991	111,833	110,707	109,886
STATISTICAL RECORD:							
Operating Profit Margin %	. . .	. . .	4.2	8.1	. . .	5.5	2.8
Net Profit Margin %	. . .	. . .	2.7	6.1	. . .	3.7	1.7
Return on Equity %	. . .	. . .	8.1	23.1	. . .	14.5	7.0
Return on Assets %	. . .	. . .	2.1	5.8	. . .	3.2	1.4
Debt/Total Assets %	14.6	13.6	11.2	9.4	9.7	9.6	11.6
Price Range	9.31-1.63	10.94-5.88	17.13-7.00	12.88-7.63	15.88-7.63	19.13-12.63	24.25-16.25
P/E Ratio	. . .	. . .	26.8-10.9	6.3-3.8	. . .	15.4-10.2	69.3-46.4

Statistics are as originally reported. 1 Incl. pre-tax non-recurr. gain, 2000, $20.9 mill.; gain, 1998, $35.0 mill.; loss, 1997, $135.0 mill.; gain, 1996, $465.0 mill.

OFFICERS:
D. R. Dunham, Chmn., Pres., C.E.O.
G. L. Millenbruch, Vice Chmn., C.F.O.
W. H. Graham, V.P., Gen. Couns., Sec.

INVESTOR CONTACT: Investor Relations, (610) 694-2424

PRINCIPAL OFFICE: 1170 Eighth Avenue, Bethlehem, PA 18016-7699

TELEPHONE NUMBER: (610) 694-2424
FAX: (610) 694-1509
WEB: www.bethsteel.com

NO. OF EMPLOYEES: 14,700 (avg.)

SHAREHOLDERS: 31,350

ANNUAL MEETING: In Apr.

INCORPORATED: DE, July, 1919

INSTITUTIONAL HOLDINGS:
No. of Institutions: 101
Shares Held: 51,091,611
% Held: 39.4

INDUSTRY: Blast furnaces and steel mills (SIC: 3312)

TRANSFER AGENT(S): First Chicago Trust Company of New York, Jersey City, NJ

NYSE SYMBOL BEV
Rec. Pr. 9.00 (5/31/01)

BEVERLY ENTERPRISES, INC.

YIELD . . .
P/E RATIO . . .

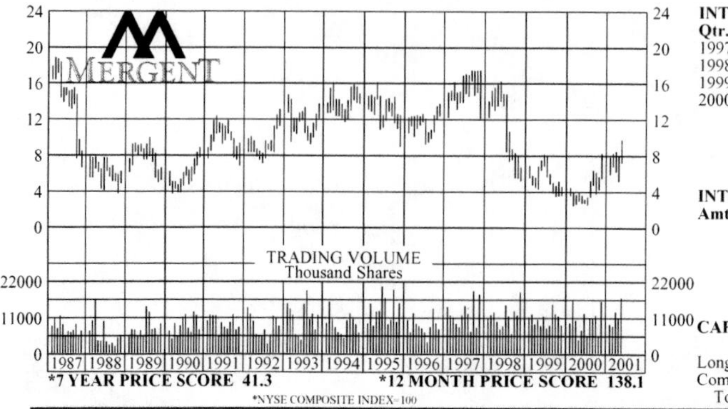

INTERIM EARNINGS (Per Share):

Qtr.	Mar.	June	Sept.	Dec.
1997	0.19	0.21	0.26	d0.07
1998	0.17	0.20	0.21	d0.90
1999	0.06	d1.13	0.08	d0.32
2000	0.06	0.08	d0.22	d0.45

INTERIM DIVIDENDS (Per Share):

Amt.	Decl.	Ex.	Rec.	Pay.

No dividends paid.

CAPITALIZATION (12/31/00):

	($000)	(%)
Long-Term Debt [1]	564,247	49.1
Common & Surplus	583,993	50.9
Total	1,148,240	100.0

RECENT DEVELOPMENTS: For the year ended 12/31/00, the Company reported a net loss of $54.5 million compared with a net loss $134.6 million in the previous year. Results for 2000 and 1999 included a pre-tax charge for asset impairments, workforce reductions and other unusual items of $90.2 million and $28.4 million, respectively. Total revenues rose 3.5% to $2.64 billion from $2.55 billion the year before. BEV reported operating income of $3.3 million in 2000 versus an operating loss of $141.1 million in 1999.

PROSPECTS: The Company expects to increase its 2001 revenues by approximately $30.0 million as a result of the passage of the latest Medicare provider relief package. However, this increase is expected to be more than offset by significant increases in several major expense categories. The Company plans to focus on cost control and operating effectiveness in an effort to increase operating earnings by at least 10.0% in 2001.

BUSINESS

BEVERLY ENTERPRISES, INC. is a long-term health care company operating nursing facilities, subacute units, institutional pharmacies, retirement living centers, and home health centers. The Company also provides ancillary services, which include occupational, physical, speech, respiratory and IV therapy, as well as sales of pharmaceutical products. The patient population is made up of Medicaid, Medicare and other patients. Changes in the patient mix can significantly affect earnings. BEV also operates retirement living projects and villas, which are affiliated with nearby nursing facilities operated by the Company, as well as durable medical equipment outlets and pharmacies.

QUARTERLY DATA

(12/31/2000) ($000)	Rev	Inc
1st Quarter	646,927	6,621
2nd Quarter	655,888	8,522
3rd Quarter	665,889	(22,471)
4th Quarter	659,556	(46,814)

ANNUAL FINANCIAL DATA

	12/31/00	12/31/99	12/31/98	12/31/97	12/31/96	12/31/95	12/31/94
Earnings Per Share	**[5] d0.53**	**[5] d1.31**	**[5] d0.24**	**[4] 0.57**	**[2] 0.50**	**[3] d0.16**	**[2] 0.79**
Cash Flow Per Share	**0.47**	**d0.32**	**0.69**	**1.63**	**1.61**	**1.01**	**1.86**
Tang. Book Val. Per Share	**3.66**	**4.01**	**5.46**	**7.21**	**5.10**	**4.27**	**4.76**
INCOME STATEMENT (IN MILLIONS):							
Total Revenues	2,628.3	2,551.0	2,822.9	3,230.3	3,281.0	3,242.8	2,983.8
Costs & Expenses	2,522.4	2,590.1	2,711.8	2,928.9	2,955.7	3,056.7	2,711.3
Depreciation & Amort.	102.6	102.1	96.1	110.2	108.7	108.0	93.0
Operating Income	3.3	d141.1	15.1	191.2	216.6	78.1	179.6
Net Interest Inc./(Exp.)	d80.0	d72.6	d65.9	d82.7	d91.1	d84.2	d64.8
Income Before Income Taxes	d76.8	d213.7	d50.9	108.5	125.5	d6.2	114.8
Income Taxes	cr22.3	cr79.1	cr25.9	49.9	73.5	2.0	37.9
Net Income	[5] d54.5	[5] d134.6	[5] d24.9	[4] 58.6	[2] 52.0	[3] d8.1	[2] 76.9
Cash Flow	48.1	d32.6	71.1	168.8	160.0	93.0	161.6
Average Shs. Outstg. (000)	102,452	102,491	103,762	103,422	99,646	92,233	87,087
BALANCE SHEET (IN MILLIONS):							
Cash & Cash Equivalents	25.9	24.7	17.3	105.2	69.8	56.3	68.0
Total Current Assets	443.4	493.8	696.0	626.3	697.2	716.6	652.3
Net Property	1,063.2	1,110.1	1,120.3	1,158.3	1,248.8	1,190.0	1,200.6
Total Assets	1,876.0	1,982.9	2,160.5	2,073.5	2,525.1	2,506.5	2,322.6
Total Current Liabilities	532.7	388.1	357.2	344.0	379.0	473.5	409.6
Long-Term Obligations	564.2	746.2	878.3	686.9	1,106.3	988.9	918.0
Net Stockholders' Equity	584.0	641.1	776.2	862.5	861.1	820.3	827.2
Net Working Capital	d89.3	105.7	338.8	282.3	318.2	243.0	242.7
Year-end Shs. Outstg. (000)	103,757	102,496	102,388	105,890	99,009	98,646	85,649
STATISTICAL RECORD:							
Operating Profit Margin %	0.1	. . .	0.5	5.9	6.6	2.4	6.0
Net Profit Margin %	. . .	. . .	. . .	1.8	1.6	. . .	2.6
Return on Equity %	. . .	. . .	. . .	6.8	6.0	. . .	9.3
Return on Assets %	. . .	. . .	. . .	2.8	2.1	. . .	3.3
Debt/Total Assets %	30.1	37.6	40.7	33.1	43.8	39.5	39.5
Price Range	8.25-2.50	8.19-3.50	16.25-5.25	17.50-12.13	13.75-9.25	16.13-9.00	16.13-11.75
P/E Ratio	. . .	. . .	. . .	30.7-21.3	27.5-18.5	. . .	20.4-14.9

Statistics are as originally reported. [1] Incl. debs. conv. into com. [2] Bef. an extraord. chg. of $1.7 mill., 1996; $2.4 mill., 1994. [3] Incl. pre-tax chg. of $68.1 mill. for acctg. changes, 1995. [4] Incl. pre-tax trans. costs of $40.0 mill. [5] Incl. pre-tax non-recurr. chrgs. of $181.7 mill., 1998; $243.2 mill., 1999; $90.2 mill., 2000.

OFFICERS:
D. R. Banks, Chmn., C.E.O.
W. R. Floyd, Pres. C.E.O.
S. A. Tabakin, Exec. V.P., C.F.O.

INVESTOR CONTACT: Jim Griffith, Inv. Rel., (501) 452-6712

PRINCIPAL OFFICE: One Thousand Beverly Way, Fort Smith, AR 72919

TELEPHONE NUMBER: (501) 201-2000
FAX: (501) 452-5131
WEB: www.beverlynet.com

NO. OF EMPLOYEES: 64,000 (approx.)

SHAREHOLDERS: 5,249

ANNUAL MEETING: In May

INCORPORATED: DE, Feb., 1987

INSTITUTIONAL HOLDINGS:
No. of Institutions: 127
Shares Held: 81,972,061
% Held: 79.1

INDUSTRY: Skilled nursing care facilities (SIC: 8051)

TRANSFER AGENT(S): The Bank of New York, New York, NY

NYSE SYMBOL BLI
Rec. Pr. 12.98 (5/31/01)

BIG LOTS, INC.

YIELD	...
P/E RATIO	20.6

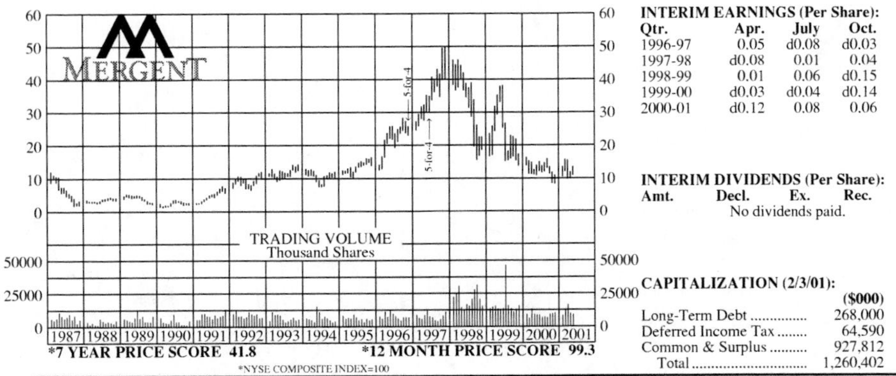

INTERIM EARNINGS (Per Share):

Qtr.	Apr.	July	Oct.	Jan.
1996-97	0.05	d0.08	d0.03	1.26
1997-98	d0.08	0.01	0.04	0.60
1998-99	0.01	0.06	d0.15	1.06
1999-00	d0.03	d0.04	d0.14	1.06
2000-01	d0.12	0.08	0.06	0.61

INTERIM DIVIDENDS (Per Share):

Amt.	Decl.	Ex.	Rec.	Pay.
No dividends paid.				

CAPITALIZATION (2/3/01):

	($000)	(%)
Long-Term Debt	268,000	21.3
Deferred Income Tax	64,590	5.1
Common & Surplus	927,812	73.6
Total	1,260,402	100.0

RECENT DEVELOPMENTS: For the 53 weeks ended 2/3/01, income from continuing operations was $98.3 million versus income from continuing operations of $92.7 million in the corresponding 52-week period the year before. Total sales grew 11.7% to $3.28 billion from $2.93 billion a year earlier. Comparable-store sales from continuing operations, including all stores open two years at the beginning of the fiscal year, grew 3.7% year over year. Operating profit rose 9.3% to $185.5 million. Comparisons were made with restated prior-year results.

PROSPECTS: On 5/16/01, the Company changed its corporate name to Big Lots, Inc. BLI plans to change its store names nationally to Big Lots by the end of 2002. Separately, BLI completed the sale of its K*B Toys division to an affiliate of Bain Capital, Inc. for approximately $305.0 million. The sale of this division should help BLI sharpen its focus on growing its core close-out business and is expected to provide greater predictability and consistency to earnings through the elimination of the seasonal toy operations.

BUSINESS

BIG LOTS, INC. (formerly Consolidated Stores Corporation) is a retailer of close-out merchandise. As of 5/30/01, the Company operated 1,306 stores under the names Big Lots, Big Lots Furniture, Odd Lots, Pic 'N' Save, and Mac Frugal's Bargains*Close-outs. The Company's stores offer substantial savings on a wide variety of name-brand consumer products, including food items, health and beauty aids, electronics, housewares, tools, paint, lawn and garden, hardware, sporting goods, toys and softlines. On 1/16/98, BLI acquired Mac Frugal's Bargains*Close-outs, Inc. On 12/7/00, BLI completed the sale of its K*B Toy division.

QUARTERLY DATA

(2/3/2001) ($000)	REV	INC
1st Quarter	723,139	(13,177)
2nd Quarter	708,518	(62,679)
3rd Quarter	733,495	(400,018)
4th Quarter	1,111,936	95,222

ANNUAL FINANCIAL DATA

	2/3/01	1/29/00	1/30/99	1/31/98	2/1/97	2/3/96	1/28/95
Earnings Per Share	**4 0.87**	**0.85**	**3 0.97**	**2 0.77**	**1 1.35**	**0.85**	**0.74**
Cash Flow Per Share	**1.43**	**1.74**	**1.71**	**1.47**	**1.92**	**1.24**	**1.09**
Tang. Book Val. Per Share	**8.28**	**11.71**	**10.79**	**9.60**	**8.15**	**5.22**	**4.30**
INCOME STATEMENT (IN MILLIONS):							
Total Revenues	3,277.1	4,700.2	4,193.7	4,055.3	2,647.5	1,512.3	1,278.6
Costs & Expenses	3,029.3	4,429.3	3,906.0	3,743.3	2,402.6	1,370.3	1,153.4
Depreciation & Amort.	62.3	100.5	84.0	79.2	48.4	30.0	26.5
Operating Income	185.5	170.4	203.7	232.9	196.5	112.0	98.7
Net Interest Inc./(Exp.)	d22.9	d25.3	d24.3	d25.7	d16.8	d8.0	d7.2
Income Before Income Taxes	162.5	145.1	179.4	162.2	179.9	102.3	92.0
Income Taxes	64.2	57.3	69.9	76.3	66.5	37.9	36.8
Equity Earnings/Minority Int.	...	8.3	...	...	...	...	...
Net Income	4 98.3	96.1	3 109.4	2 85.9	1 113.3	64.4	55.2
Cash Flow	160.6	196.6	193.4	165.1	161.7	94.4	81.7
Average Shs. Outstg. (000)	112,414	112,952	112,800	112,063	84,041	76,411	75,120
BALANCE SHEET (IN MILLIONS):							
Cash & Cash Equivalents	30.7	96.3	75.9	41.7	30.0	13.0	40.4
Total Current Assets	1,100.6	1,419.7	1,335.2	1,107.5	926.5	452.0	381.3
Net Property	481.9	730.0	683.4	613.5	380.1	177.3	161.5
Total Assets	1,585.4	2,186.8	2,042.5	1,746.4	1,330.5	639.8	551.6
Total Current Liabilities	325.0	710.8	459.9	525.3	457.2	198.2	170.7
Long-Term Obligations	268.0	60.5	295.6	115.3	151.3	25.0	40.0
Net Stockholders' Equity	927.8	1,300.1	1,181.9	1,034.5	682.1	389.6	315.2
Net Working Capital	775.6	708.9	875.2	582.2	469.3	253.9	210.6
Year-end Shs. Outstg. (000)	112,079	111,000	109,524	107,796	83,698	74,650	73,228
STATISTICAL RECORD:							
Operating Profit Margin %	5.7	3.6	4.9	5.7	7.4	7.4	7.7
Net Profit Margin %	3.0	2.0	2.6	2.1	4.3	4.3	4.3
Return on Equity %	10.6	7.4	9.3	8.3	16.6	16.5	17.5
Return on Assets %	6.2	4.4	5.4	4.9	8.5	10.1	10.0
Debt/Total Assets %	16.9	2.8	14.5	6.6	11.4	3.9	7.3
Price Range	16.38-8.25	38.13-13.69	46.13-15.50	50.00-24.50	28.32-12.40	16.40-10.08	12.96-7.36
P/E Ratio	18.8-9.5	44.8-16.1	47.5-16.0	64.9-31.8	20.9-9.2	19.4-11.9	17.6-10.0

Statistics are as originally reported. Adj. for 5-for-4 stk. split, 6/97 & 12/96. 1 Bef. $1.9 mil ($0.03/sh) extraord. chg.; $8.6 mil ($0.10/sh) loss fr. discont. opers.; & $18.9 mil ($0.22/sh) loss fr. disp. of opers. 2 Incl. pre-tax merger-related chg. of $45.0 mil 3 Bef. $12.6 mil ($0.11/sh) acctg. chg. 4 Bef. $479.0 mil ($4.26/sh) loss fr. discont. opers.

OFFICERS:
M. J. Potter, Chmn., Pres., C.E.O.
A. J. Bell, Vice-Chmn., C.A.O., acting C.F.O.
J. A. McGrady, V.P., Treas.

PRINCIPAL OFFICE: 300 Phillipi Road, P.O. Box 28512, Columbus, OH 43228-0512

TELEPHONE NUMBER: (614) 278-6800
FAX: (614) 278-6666
WEB: www.biglots.com
NO. OF EMPLOYEES: 16,162 full-time; 29,514 part-time
SHAREHOLDERS: 1,652
ANNUAL MEETING: In May
INCORPORATED: DE, 1983

INSTITUTIONAL HOLDINGS:
No. of Institutions: 185
Shares Held: 106,896,164
% Held: 94.4

INDUSTRY: Department stores (SIC: 5311)

TRANSFER AGENT(S): National City Bank, Cleveland, OH

NYSE SYMBOL BIR
Rec. Pr. 1.05 (4/30/01)

BIRMINGHAM STEEL CORPORATION

YIELD ...
P/E RATIO ...

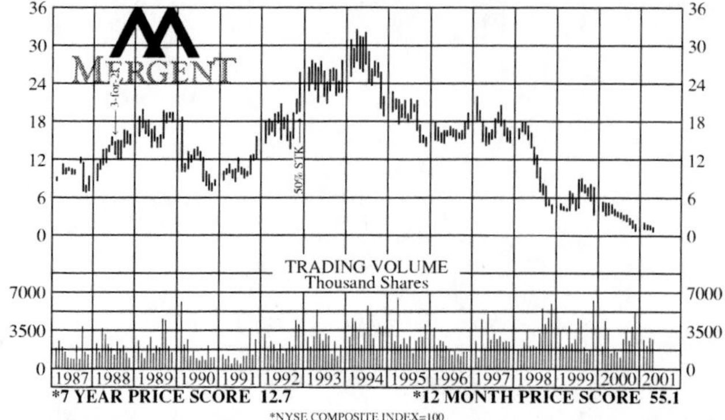

*7 YEAR PRICE SCORE 12.7 *12 MONTH PRICE SCORE 55.1
*NYSE COMPOSITE INDEX=100

INTERIM EARNINGS (Per Share):

Qtr.	Sept.	Dec.	Mar.	June
1997-98	0.24	0.09	d0.14	d0.14
1998-99	0.03	d0.17	d0.53	d0.78
1999-00	0.19	d5.74	d0.85	d0.47
2000-01	d0.49	d0.56	...	...

INTERIM DIVIDENDS (Per Share):

Amt.	Decl.	Ex.	Rec.	Pay.
0.025Q	4/20/99	4/28/99	4/30/99	5/10/99
0.025Q	7/20/99	7/28/99	7/30/99	8/09/99
0.025Q	10/20/99	10/27/99	10/29/99	11/09/99

Dividend payment suspended.

CAPITALIZATION (6/30/00):

	($000)	(%)
Long-Term Debt [1]	594,090	76.0
Common & Surplus	188,015	24.0
Total	782,105	100.0

RECENT DEVELOPMENTS: For the quarter ended 12/31/00, BIR incurred a loss from continuing operations of $17.3 million versus a loss from continuing operations of $41.7 million in 1999. Results included a nonrecurring gain of $46,000 and a nonrecurring charge of $28.5 million in the current and prior-year period. Net sales were $148.6 million, down 12.4% from $169.6 million a year earlier.

PROSPECTS: On 4/24/01, the Company announced that unless one of the two parties actively negotiating to buy American Steel & Wire, its Cleveland, Ohio plant, completes a purchase within the next 60 days, operations at the facility will be permanently suspended. The shutdown of the plant would generate annualized cash savings of $20.0 million.

BUSINESS

BIRMINGHAM STEEL CORPORATION operates non-union mini-mills located across the U.S. that produce primarily steel reinforcing bar and merchant products on a low-cost basis. The Company also specializes in manufacturing high-quality steel rod and wire from semi-finished billets at its American Steel and Wire subsidiary. BIR's carbon steel rebar products are sold primarily to independent fabricators for use in the construction industry. The Company's merchant products, which include rounds, flats, squares, strip, angles and channel, are sold to fabricators, steel service centers and original equipment manufacturers for use in general industrial applications. BIR divested its mine roof support business in 1995.

REVENUES

(06/30/2000)	($000)	(%)
Rebar/Merchant	719,286	77.1
SBQ	213,260	22.9
Total	932,546	100.0

ANNUAL FINANCIAL DATA

	6/30/00	6/30/99	6/30/98	6/30/97	6/30/96	6/30/95	[2] 6/30/94
Earnings Per Share	**[8] d7.51**	**[7] 0.11**	**[6] 0.05**	**0.50**	**[5] d0.08**	**[4] 1.74**	**[3] 0.86**
Cash Flow Per Share	**d5.58**	**1.48**	**2.02**	**2.07**	**1.14**	**2.84**	**1.99**
Tang. Book Val. Per Share	**6.07**	**7.77**	**15.57**	**15.89**	**15.67**	**16.13**	**14.94**
Dividends Per Share	...	**0.10**	**0.33**	**0.40**	**0.40**	**0.40**	**0.40**
Dividend Payout %	...	**90.8**	**648.7**	**80.0**	...	**23.0**	**46.5**
INCOME STATEMENT (IN MILLIONS):							
Total Revenues	932.5	709.9	1,136.0	978.9	832.5	885.6	702.9
Costs & Expenses	1,089.1	618.2	1,043.3	894.2	792.1	768.0	633.0
Depreciation & Amort.	58.2	40.2	58.2	45.8	34.7	32.3	27.7
Operating Income	d214.7	51.5	34.5	38.9	5.7	85.2	42.2
Net Interest Inc./(Exp.)	d51.7	d24.2	d29.0	d20.2	d12.0	d8.9	d11.1
Income Before Income Taxes	d267.3	18.1	2.8	24.7	d2.4	85.8	35.8
Income Taxes	cr41.0	14.8	1.2	10.3	cr0.2	35.1	14.6
Equity Earnings/Minority Int.	8.0	5.5	1.6	2.3	...	...	...
Net Income	[8] d226.3	[7] 3.3	[6] 1.6	14.4	[5] d2.2	[4] 50.6	[3] 21.2
Cash Flow	d168.2	43.5	59.8	60.3	32.5	83.0	48.9
Average Shs. Outstg. (000)	30,118	29,481	29,674	29,091	28,566	29,162	24,595
BALANCE SHEET (IN MILLIONS):							
Cash & Cash Equivalents	0.9	0.9	0.9	1.0	6.7	4.3	28.9
Total Current Assets	278.4	270.9	394.0	366.9	328.0	303.0	275.8
Net Property	638.3	439.6	757.5	761.6	544.0	411.7	374.9
Total Assets	959.9	877.5	1,244.8	1,211.0	928.0	756.8	689.9
Total Current Liabilities	135.7	160.5	156.3	138.0	116.4	96.1	62.7
Long-Term Obligations	594.1	469.1	558.8	526.1	307.5	142.5	142.5
Net Stockholders' Equity	188.0	230.7	460.6	471.5	448.2	459.7	439.0
Net Working Capital	142.7	110.4	237.7	228.9	211.6	206.9	213.1
Year-end Shs. Outstg. (000)	30,977	29,686	29,589	29,680	28,609	28,496	29,389
STATISTICAL RECORD:							
Operating Profit Margin %	...	7.3	3.0	4.0	0.7	9.6	6.0
Net Profit Margin %	...	0.5	0.1	1.5	...	5.7	3.0
Return on Equity %	...	1.4	0.4	3.1	...	11.0	4.8
Return on Assets %	...	0.4	0.1	1.2	...	6.7	3.1
Debt/Total Assets %	61.9	53.5	44.9	43.4	33.1	18.8	20.7
Price Range	5.44-0.75	9.06-3.25	18.00-3.50	22.00-14.13	19.38-14.50	22.75-14.00	32.63-18.75
P/E Ratio	...	82.3-29.5	359.3-69.9	44.0-28.2	...	13.1-8.0	37.9-21.8
Average Yield %	...	1.6	3.0	2.2	2.4	2.2	1.6

Statistics are as originally reported. [1] Incl. capital lease oblig. [2] Incl. results of American Steel & Wire, acq. in Nov. 1993. [3] Bef. an acctg. chrg. of $380,000. [4] Incl. pre-tax non-recurr. chrgs. of $28.0 mill. [5] Incl. pre-oper. start-up & unus. exp. of $15.2 mill. [6] Incl. a nonrecurr. pretax chrg. of $14.5 mill. Incl. pre-tax gains of $6.3 mill. [7] Incl. pre-oper. start-up exp. of $10.9 mill. & nonrecurr. pre-tax gains of $5.1 mill. [8] Excl. disc. oper. gain $173.2 mill. and an extraord. loss of $1.7 mill., but incl. a non-recurr. loss $210.5 mill.

OFFICERS:
J. D. Correnti, Chmn., C.E.O.
J. A. Todd, Jr., Vice-Chmn., C.A.O.
J. D. Garrett, V.P., C.F.O.

INVESTOR CONTACT: J. Daniel Garrett, V.P., C.F.O., (205) 970-1213

PRINCIPAL OFFICE: 1000 Urban Center Parkway, Suite 300, Birmingham, AL 35242

TELEPHONE NUMBER: (205) 970-1200
FAX: (205) 970-1352
WEB: www.birminghamsteel.com

NO. OF EMPLOYEES: 2,126 (avg.)

SHAREHOLDERS: 1,470

ANNUAL MEETING: In Oct.

INCORPORATED: DE, 1983

INSTITUTIONAL HOLDINGS:
No. of Institutions: 28
Shares Held: 9,959,086
% Held: 32.0

INDUSTRY: Blast furnaces and steel mills (SIC: 3312)

TRANSFER AGENT(S): First Union National Bank, Charlotte, NC

NYSE SYMBOL BJS
Rec. Pr. 37.50 (5/31/01)

BJ SERVICES COMPANY

YIELD ...
P/E RATIO 38.7

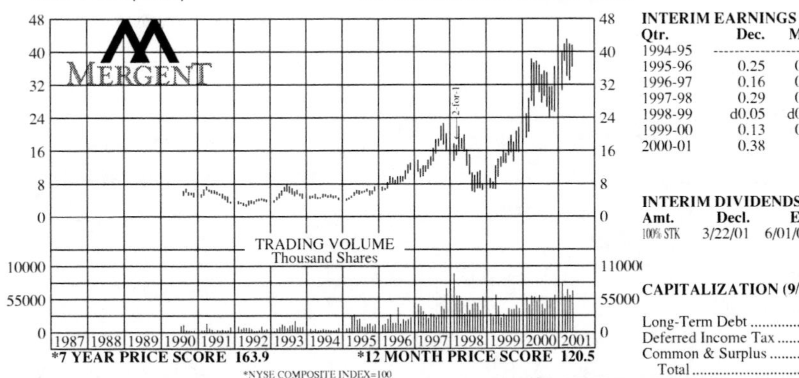

*7 YEAR PRICE SCORE 163.9 *12 MONTH PRICE SCORE 120.5
*NYSE COMPOSITE INDEX=100

INTERIM EARNINGS (Per Share):

Qtr.	Dec.	Mar.	June	Sept.
1994-95		0.12		
1995-96	0.25	0.25	0.34	0.47
1996-97	0.16	0.08	0.16	0.23
1997-98	0.29	0.24	0.22	0.01
1998-99	d0.05	d0.08	d0.12	0.03
1999-00	0.13	0.18	0.16	0.25
2000-01	0.38	...	...	...

INTERIM DIVIDENDS (Per Share):

Amt.	Decl.	Ex.	Rec.	Pay.
100% STK	3/22/01	6/01/01	5/17/01	5/31/01

CAPITALIZATION (9/30/00):

	($000)	(%)
Long-Term Debt	141,981	10.8
Deferred Income Tax	7,966	0.6
Common & Surplus	1,169,771	88.6
Total	1,319,718	100.0

RECENT DEVELOPMENTS: For the three months ended 12/31/00, net income soared to $63.5 million compared with $20.5 million in the prior period due to improvements in U.S. drilling activity and pricing, and stronger-than-expected international revenues. Revenues jumped 38.0% to $489.7 million from $354.8 million a year earlier. Operating income margins improved to 20.6% from 10.6% the year before reflecting improved U.S. pricing, better equipment utilization, and labor and equipment efficiencies.

PROSPECTS: Results in the current environment of higher natural gas and crude oil prices are being driven by strong demand for the Company's value-added technologies that result in increased production. BJS noted that the stronger activity levels have also allowed the Company to capture most of its September 2000 price increase. As a result of the positive outlook, BJS has raised its full-year fiscal 2001 projections to a split adjusted $1.55 per share versus its previous estimate of $1.25 per share.

BUSINESS

BJ SERVICES COMPANY is a provider of pressure pumping and other oilfield services for the worldwide petroleum industry. Pressure pumping services consist of cementing and stimulation services used in the completion of new oil and natural gas wells and in remedial work of existing wells, both onshore and offshore. Other oilfield services include product and equipment sales for pressure pumping services, tubular services provided to the oil and gas exploration and production industry, commissioning and inspection services provided to refineries, pipelines and offshore platforms and specialty chemical services. Effective 6/28/99, BJS acquired Fracmaster Ltd. for total consideration of $78.4 million.

BUSINESS LINE ANALYSIS

(09/30/2000)($000)	Rev (%)	Inc (%)
U.S./Mexico Pressure Pump	47.8	62.1
Int'l Pressure Pumping	40.5	30.0
Other Oilfield Services	11.7	7.9
Total	100.0	100.0

ANNUAL FINANCIAL DATA

	9/30/00	9/30/99	9/30/98	9/30/97	9/30/96	9/30/95	9/30/94
Earnings Per Share	**0.70**	**1 d0.21**	**0.72**	**0.66**	**0.32**	**0.12**	**0.17**
Cash Flow Per Share	**1.30**	**0.50**	**1.29**	**1.20**	**0.85**	**0.61**	**0.58**
Tang. Book Val. Per Share	**4.20**	**2.72**	**2.82**	**2.90**	**1.80**	**2.45**	**2.69**
INCOME STATEMENT (IN MILLIONS):							
Total Revenues	1,555.4	1,131.3	1,527.5	1,466.6	965.3	633.7	434.5
Costs & Expenses	1,258.1	1,006.6	1,211.6	1,193.8	816.9	554.1	390.5
Depreciation & Amort.	102.0	99.8	91.5	90.4	66.1	42.1	25.3
Operating Income	195.2	14.8	197.8	182.4	74.9	20.3	18.7
Net Interest Inc./(Exp.)	d18.4	d30.8	d24.9	d29.8	d25.6	d14.3	d6.7
Income Before Income Taxes	175.3	d44.9	172.1	154.4	52.6	8.8	12.8
Income Taxes	57.3	cr15.2	54.7	46.5	12.1	cr1.1	2.0
Net Income	118.0	1 d29.7	117.4	107.9	40.5	9.9	10.8
Cash Flow	220.0	70.1	208.9	198.3	106.5	52.0	36.1
Average Shs. Outstg. (000)	168,700	141,578	162,526	164,992	125,524	85,504	62,660
BALANCE SHEET (IN MILLIONS):							
Cash & Cash Equivalents	6.5	3.9	1.6	3.9	2.9	1.8	3.2
Total Current Assets	506.4	439.0	451.8	474.7	418.1	256.9	158.4
Net Property	585.4	659.7	602.0	540.4	558.2	416.8	198.8
Total Assets	1,785.2	1,824.8	1,743.7	1,726.8	1,709.2	989.7	410.1
Total Current Liabilities	337.1	445.1	513.1	385.3	292.0	204.3	121.1
Long-Term Obligations	142.0	422.8	241.9	298.6	523.0	259.6	74.7
Net Stockholders' Equity	1,169.8	877.1	900.1	960.2	841.7	466.8	189.9
Net Working Capital	169.3	d6.2	d61.3	89.4	126.1	52.7	37.3
Year-end Shs. Outstg. (000)	165,296	142,356	140,868	154,124	152,356	111,808	62,684
STATISTICAL RECORD:							
Operating Profit Margin %	12.6	1.3	12.9	12.4	7.8	3.2	4.3
Net Profit Margin %	7.6	...	7.7	7.4	4.2	1.6	2.5
Return on Equity %	10.1	...	13.0	11.2	4.8	2.1	5.7
Return on Assets %	6.6	...	6.7	6.2	2.4	1.0	2.6
Debt/Total Assets %	8.0	23.2	13.9	17.3	30.6	26.2	18.2
Price Range	38.38-19.06	21.72-6.72	21.91-5.94	22.69-9.56	13.13-6.28	7.38-3.88	5.63-4.06
P/E Ratio	54.8-27.2	...	30.4-8.2	34.6-14.6	41.7-19.9	64.1-33.7	33.1-23.9

Statistics are as originally reported. Adj. for stk. splits, 3-for-1, 2/98; 2-for-1, 5/01 1 Incl. nonrecurr. pre-tax chrgs. of $39.7 mill.

OFFICERS:
J. W. Stewart, Chmn., Pres., C.E.O.
M. McShane, Sr. V.P., C.F.O.
M. D. Fitzgerald, V.P., Contr., C.A.O.

INVESTOR CONTACT: Robert C. Coons, Corp. Comm. Mgr., (713) 462-4239

PRINCIPAL OFFICE: 5500 N.W. Central Drive, Houston, TX 77210-4442

TELEPHONE NUMBER: (713) 462-4239
FAX: (713) 895-5603
WEB: www.bjservices.com

NO. OF EMPLOYEES: 9,265 (avg.)

SHAREHOLDERS: 2,028 (approx.)

ANNUAL MEETING: In Jan.

INCORPORATED: DE, 1990

INSTITUTIONAL HOLDINGS:
No. of Institutions: 282
Shares Held: 161,758,888 (Adj.)
% Held: 98.5

INDUSTRY: Oil and gas field services, nec (SIC: 1389)

TRANSFER AGENT(S): The Bank of New York, New York, NY

NYSE SYMBOL BJ
Rec. Pr. 48.75 (5/31/01)

BJ'S WHOLESALE CLUB, INC.

YIELD ...
P/E RATIO 27.5

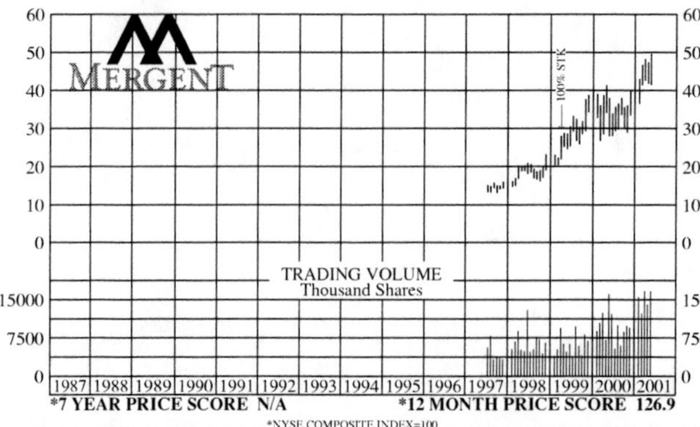

INTERIM EARNINGS (Per Share):

Qtr.	Apr.	July	Oct.	Jan.
1997-98		0.91		
1998-99	0.14	0.24	0.19	0.50
1999-00	0.19	0.34	0.31	0.63
2000-01	0.24	0.42	0.37	0.74

INTERIM DIVIDENDS (Per Share):

Amt.	Decl.	Ex.	Rec.	Pay.

No dividends paid.

CAPITALIZATION (2/3/01):

	($000)	(%)
Capital Lease Obligations..	1,828	0.3
Deferred Income Tax	7,895	1.2
Common & Surplus	664,915	98.6
Total	674,638	100.0

RECENT DEVELOPMENTS: For the 53 weeks ended 2/3/01, net income climbed 18.3% to $131.5 million from $111.1 million in the corresponding 52-week period the year before. Total revenues advanced 17.3% to $4.93 billion from $4.21 billion the previous year. Comparable-club sales were up 5.1% year-over-year. Operating income was $207.9 million, up 17.1% compared with $177.5 million a year earlier. During 2000, the Company opened eleven new clubs and fifteen new gas stations.

PROSPECTS: The Company is continuing to expand its base of clubs in both existing and new markets. During 2001, BJ plans to open fourteen new warehouse clubs, including two relocations of existing units. The Company is focusing on new market development in the Southeast and plans to open between seven and nine new clubs in the Carolinas and Florida in 2001. BJ anticipates building a new distribution facility in the Southeast to help support expansion and future growth in the region.

BUSINESS

BJ'S WHOLESALE CLUB, INC. sells brand name food and general merchandise at discounted prices through warehouse clubs in the eastern United States. As of 4/6/01, BJ operated 118 clubs and two distribution centers in 15 states. In addition, the Company has gas stations in operation at 34 of its clubs. BJ sells food items such as frozen foods, fresh meat, dairy products, dry grocery items, fresh produce and flowers, canned goods, and household paper products and cleaning supplies. General merchandise includes office supplies and equipment, consumer electronics, small appliances, auto accessories, tires, jewelry, housewares, health and beauty aids, computer software, books, greeting cards, apparel, tools, toys, and seasonal items. The customers at the Company's warehouse clubs are generally limited to members who pay an annual fee of $40.

QUARTERLY DATA

(2/3/2001)($000)	REV	INC
1st Quarter	1,021,073	18,094
2nd Quarter	1,177,253	31,220
3rd Quarter	1,151,506	27,391
4th Quarter	1,478,441	54,796

ANNUAL FINANCIAL DATA

	2/3/01	1/29/00	1/30/99	1/31/98	1/25/97	1/27/96	1/28/95
Earnings Per Share	**1.77**	**1.47**	**1 1.07**	**0.91**	...	...	...
Cash Flow Per Share	**2.51**	**2.09**	**1.61**	**1.40**	...	...	...
Tang. Book Val. Per Share	**9.18**	**7.85**	**6.57**	**5.95**	**4.21**	**3.39**	...
INCOME STATEMENT (IN MILLIONS):							
Total Revenues	4,932.1	4,206.2	3,552.2	3,226.5	2,922.8	2,529.6	2,293.1
Costs & Expenses	4,669.3	3,982.2	3,377.5	3,068.4	2,784.5	2,419.8	2,206.8
Depreciation & Amort.	55.0	46.5	40.9	37.4	33.8	27.2	21.8
Operating Income	207.9	177.5	133.8	120.6	104.6	82.7	64.5
Net Interest Inc./(Exp.)	6.0	3.8	1.0	d8.7	d16.8	d14.8	d13.7
Income Before Income Taxes	213.8	181.3	134.8	111.9	87.7	67.9	50.8
Income Taxes	82.3	70.2	53.0	43.6	34.1	26.4	19.9
Net Income	131.5	111.1	1 81.8	68.3	53.6	41.6	30.9
Cash Flow	186.4	157.6	122.6	105.7	87.4	68.7	52.7
Average Shs. Outstg. (000)	74,381	75,391	76,096	75,488	...	...	...
BALANCE SHEET (IN MILLIONS):							
Cash & Cash Equivalents	120.4	60.4	12.3	12.7	...	...	...
Total Current Assets	694.6	580.7	456.6	404.2	341.9	317.5	...
Net Property	525.0	481.3	440.1	396.5	385.2	350.8	...
Total Assets	1,233.7	1,073.4	907.6	811.6	737.2	676.7	...
Total Current Liabilities	514.6	447.2	347.6	279.2	278.9	240.3	...
Long-Term Obligations	1.8	2.1	32.2	44.9	150.7	184.5	...
Net Stockholders' Equity	664.9	577.4	485.0	446.3	275.6	222.0	...
Net Working Capital	179.9	133.5	109.0	125.0	62.9	77.2	...
Year-end Shs. Outstg. (000)	72,463	73,543	73,805	75,008	65,482	65,482	...
STATISTICAL RECORD:							
Operating Profit Margin %	4.2	4.2	3.8	3.7	3.6	3.3	2.8
Net Profit Margin %	2.7	2.6	2.3	2.1	1.8	1.6	1.3
Return on Equity %	19.8	19.2	16.9	15.3	19.5	18.7	...
Return on Assets %	10.7	10.4	9.0	8.4	7.3	6.1	...
Debt/Total Assets %	0.1	0.2	3.6	5.5	20.4	27.3	...
Price Range	41.38-26.75	38.75-20.25	23.16-14.63	16.00-13.00	...	...	...
P/E Ratio	23.4-15.1	26.4-13.8	21.6-13.7	17.7-14.4	...	...	...

Statistics are as originally reported. Adj. for 2-for-1 stk. split, 3/99. 1 Bef. $19.3 mil ($0.25/sh) acctg. chg., 1/99.

OFFICERS:
H. J. Zarkin, Chmn.
J. J. Nugent, Pres., C.E.O.
F. D. Forward, Exec. V.P., C.F.O.
S. M. Gallivan, V.P., Gen. Couns., Sec.

INVESTOR CONTACT: Eileen H. Kirrane, Asst. V.P., Inv. Rel., (508) 651-6650

PRINCIPAL OFFICE: One Mercer Road, Natick, MA 01760

TELEPHONE NUMBER: (508) 651-7400
FAX: (508) 651-6114
WEB: www.bjs.com

NO. OF EMPLOYEES: 14,700 (approx.)

SHAREHOLDERS: 2,300 (approx.)

ANNUAL MEETING: In May

INCORPORATED: DE, Nov., 1996

INSTITUTIONAL HOLDINGS:
No. of Institutions: 264
Shares Held: 65,793,087
% Held: 90.4

INDUSTRY: Variety stores (SIC: 5331)

TRANSFER AGENT(S): The First Chicago Trust Company of New York, Jersey City, NJ

NYSE SYMBOL BDK
Rec. Pr. 39.65 (5/31/01)

BLACK & DECKER CORPORATION

YIELD 1.2%
P/E RATIO 11.9

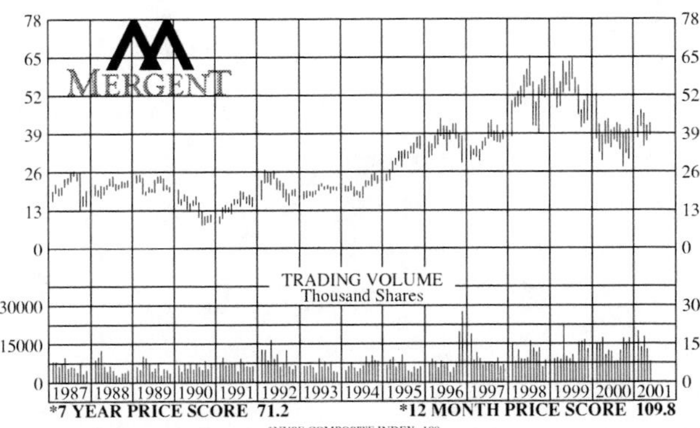

*7 YEAR PRICE SCORE 71.2 *12 MONTH PRICE SCORE 109.8

*NYSE COMPOSITE INDEX=100

INTERIM EARNINGS (Per Share):

Qtr.	Mar.	June	Sept.	Dec.
1997	0.27	0.47	0.60	1.00
1998	d10.21	0.61	0.72	1.03
1999	0.44	0.80	0.85	1.31
2000	0.69	0.97	1.03	0.64

INTERIM DIVIDENDS (Per Share):

Amt.	Decl.	Ex.	Rec.	Pay.
0.12Q	4/25/00	6/14/00	6/16/00	6/30/00
0.12Q	7/24/00	9/13/00	9/15/00	9/29/00
0.12Q	10/19/00	12/13/00	12/15/00	12/29/00
0.12Q	2/08/01	3/14/01	3/16/01	3/30/01
0.12Q	4/25/01	6/13/01	6/15/01	6/29/01

Indicated div.: $0.48 (Div. Reinv. Plan)

CAPITALIZATION (12/31/00):

	($000)	(%)
Long-Term Debt	798,500	46.6
Deferred Income Tax	221,000	12.9
Common & Surplus	692,400	40.4
Total	1,711,900	100.0

RECENT DEVELOPMENTS: For the year ended 12/31/00, net income declined 6.1% to $282.0 million versus $300.3 million in 1999. Earnings were adversely affected by the slowdown in the U.S. economy and inventory reductions of key retailers. Sales were $4.56 billion, up slightly from $4.52 billion in 1999. Results for 2000 included restructuring costs of $39.1 million and a gain on sale of business of $20.1 million.

PROSPECTS: BDK is taking immediate action to more closely align its business structure to the weaker economic environment. BDK will attempt to reduce costs and invest in new products both internally and through strategic acquisitions. BDK initiated a strategic repositioning plan on 1/26/98 to intensify focus on core operations and improve operating performance. The restructuring is expected to generate approximately $20.0 million in savings in 2002.

BUSINESS

BLACK & DECKER CORPORATION is a global marketer and manufacturer of products used in and around the home and for commercial applications. The Power Tools and Accessories (PT&A) segment manufactures and sells consumer and professional power tools and accessories, electric cleaning and lighting products, and electric lawn and garden tools and offers product service. During 1998, the Company divested its household products businesses; however, it retained the cleaning and lighting products businesses. Consequently, the PT&A segment also sells the retained household products business, as well as sells plumbing products to customers outside the U.S. and Canada. The Hardware and Home Improvement segment manufactures and sells security hardware and manufactures plumbing products as well as sells plumbing products to customers in the U.S. and Canada. The Fastening and Assembly Systems segment manufactures and sells fastening and assembly systems.

ANNUAL FINANCIAL DATA

	12/31/00	12/31/99	12/31/98	12/31/97	12/31/96	[1] 12/31/95	12/31/94
Earnings Per Share	[6] 3.34	[5] 3.40	[4] d8.22	2.35	[3] 1.64	[2] 2.33	1.37
Cash Flow Per Share	5.28	5.21	d4.04	4.57	4.09	4.81	3.91
Tang. Book Val. Per Share	...	0.66	...	...	...	...	...
Dividends Per Share	0.48	0.48	0.48	0.48	0.48	0.40	0.40
Dividend Payout %	14.4	14.1	...	20.4	29.3	17.2	29.2
INCOME STATEMENT (IN MILLIONS):							
Total Revenues	4,560.8	4,520.5	4,559.9	4,940.5	4,914.4	4,766.1	5,248.3
Costs & Expenses	3,914.2	3,824.2	4,985.4	4,237.0	4,342.9	4,133.3	4,641.0
Depreciation & Amort.	163.4	160.0	155.2	214.2	214.6	206.7	213.6
Operating Income	503.3	536.3	d466.2	489.3	356.9	426.1	393.7
Net Interest Inc./(Exp.)	d104.2	d95.8	114.4	d124.6	d135.4	d184.4	d188.1
Income Before Income Taxes	404.6	441.3	d588.3	349.5	202.7	225.5	190.1
Income Taxes	122.6	141.0	166.5	122.3	43.5	9.0	62.7
Net Income	[6] 282.0	[5] 300.3	[4] d754.8	227.2	[3] 159.2	[2] 216.5	127.4
Cash Flow	445.4	460.3	d370.8	441.4	364.7	411.6	329.4
Average Shs. Outstg. (000)	84,400	88,400	91,800	96,500	91,300	87,900	84,300
BALANCE SHEET (IN MILLIONS):							
Cash & Cash Equivalents	135.0	147.3	87.9	246.8	141.8	131.6	65.9
Total Current Assets	1,962.0	1,911.4	1,751.8	2,078.8	1,804.2	2,106.6	1,833.2
Net Property	748.1	739.6	727.6	915.1	905.8	866.8	858.1
Total Assets	4,089.7	4,012.7	3,852.5	5,360.7	5,153.5	5,545.3	5,433.7
Total Current Liabilities	1,632.3	1,572.7	1,374.7	1,372.6	1,506.6	1,786.9	1,879.8
Long-Term Obligations	798.5	847.1	1,148.9	1,623.7	1,415.8	1,704.5	1,723.2
Net Stockholders' Equity	692.4	801.1	574.0	1,791.4	1,632.4	1,423.2	1,169.4
Net Working Capital	329.7	338.7	377.1	706.2	297.6	319.7	d46.6
Year-end Shs. Outstg. (000)	80,343	87,190	87,498	94,843	94,249	86,448	84,689
STATISTICAL RECORD:							
Operating Profit Margin %	11.0	11.9	...	9.9	7.3	8.9	7.5
Net Profit Margin %	6.2	6.6	...	4.6	3.2	4.5	2.4
Return on Equity %	40.7	37.5	...	12.7	9.8	15.2	10.9
Return on Assets %	6.9	7.5	...	4.2	3.1	3.9	2.3
Debt/Total Assets %	19.5	21.1	29.8	30.3	27.5	30.7	31.7
Price Range	52.38-27.56	64.63-41.00	65.50-37.94	43.44-29.63	44.25-29.00	38.13-22.88	25.75-17.00
P/E Ratio	15.7-8.3	19.0-12.1	...	18.5-12.6	27.0-17.7	16.4-9.8	18.8-12.4
Average Yield %	1.2	0.9	0.9	1.3	1.3	1.3	1.9

Statistics are as originally reported. [1] Reflects sale of PRC Inc. [2] Bef. extraord. chrg. of $30.9 mill. and inc. fr. disc. opers. of $38.4 mill. [3] Excl. inc. fr. discont. oper. of $70.4 mill.; incl. non-recurr. chrg. $91.3 mill. [4] Incl. gain of $114.5 million before tax; a write-off chrg. of $900.0 mill. for goodwill; and restruct. chrg. of $164.7 mill. [5] Incl. nonrecurr. after-tax gain of $13.1 million from the sale of a business. [6] Incl. restruct. and exit costs of $39.1 mill. and a gain on the sale of a business of $20.1 mill.

OFFICERS:
N. D. Archibald, Chmn., Pres., C.E.O.
M. D. Mangan, Sr. V.P., C.F.O.
M. M. Rothleitner, V.P., Treas.

INVESTOR CONTACT: V. P. Shelley, Mgr.-Investor Relations, (410) 716-3979

PRINCIPAL OFFICE: 701 East Joppa Rd., Towson, MD 21286

TELEPHONE NUMBER: (410) 716-3900
FAX: (410) 716-2610
WEB: www.bdk.com

NO. OF EMPLOYEES: 23,600 (approx.)

SHAREHOLDERS: 16,646

ANNUAL MEETING: In Apr.

INCORPORATED: MD, Sept., 1910

INSTITUTIONAL HOLDINGS:
No. of Institutions: 286
Shares Held: 70,669,811
% Held: 87.5

INDUSTRY: Power-driven handtools (SIC: 3546)

TRANSFER AGENT(S): EquiServe, Jersey City, NJ

NYSE SYMBOL HRB
Rec. Pr. 59.64 (5/31/01)

BLOCK (H & R), INC.

YIELD 2.0%
P/E RATIO 24.6

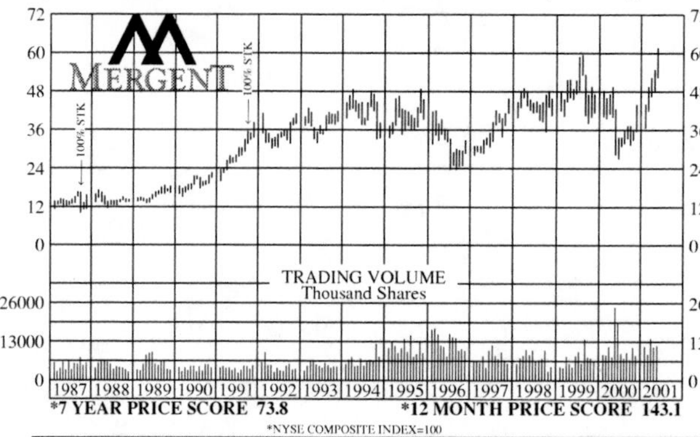

*7 YEAR PRICE SCORE 73.8 *12 MONTH PRICE SCORE 143.1

*NYSE COMPOSITE INDEX=100

INTERIM EARNINGS (Per Share):

Qtr.	July	Oct.	Jan.	Apr.
1996-97	d0.50	d0.71	d0.24	1.90
1997-98	d0.37	d0.29	d0.17	2.37
1998-99	d0.26	d0.31	d0.03	3.03
1999-00	d0.38	d0.46	d0.07	3.45
2000-01	d0.55	d0.54	0.06	...

INTERIM DIVIDENDS (Per Share):

Amt.	Decl.	Ex.	Rec.	Pay.
0.275Q	5/31/00	6/08/00	6/12/00	7/03/00
0.30Q	6/29/00	9/07/00	9/11/00	10/02/00
0.30Q	11/28/00	12/08/00	12/12/00	1/02/01
0.30Q	2/27/01	3/08/01	3/12/01	4/02/01
0.30Q	5/23/01	6/07/01	6/11/01	7/02/01

Indicated div.: $1.20

CAPITALIZATION (4/30/00):

	($000)	(%)
Long-Term Debt	872,396	41.7
Common & Surplus	1,218,589	58.3
Total	2,090,985	100.0

RECENT DEVELOPMENTS: For the quarter ended 1/31/01, net income was $5.6 million compared with a net loss of $7.1 million in the comparable prior-year period. Earnings benefited from disciplined expense control, strong performance from HRB's mortgage and e-commerce businesses and the early start of the tax filing season. Revenues advanced 29.0% to $661.4 million. Revenues benefited from double-digit growth in each of the Company's domestic lines of business, led by a 37.6% increase in HRB's U.S. tax operations.

PROSPECTS: HRB expects to achieve annual revenue growth of 10.0% to 15.0%. On 2/26/01, HRB announced that it has entered into an agreement with Yahoo! Inc., a global Internet communications, commerce and media company. Under the terms of the agreement, HRB will supply tax content and services on the Yahoo! Tax Center, a portal for tax information and filing on the Internet. Over the next five years, the number of people preparing and filing returns via the Internet are expected to double to 40.0 million.

BUSINESS

H&R BLOCK, INC. is a diversified company offering tax preparation, mortgage services and financial products and services. As of 5/30/01, H&R Block Tax Services Inc. offers tax return preparation and electronic filing services for 19.2 million customers through more than 10,000 offices primarily in the U.S., Canada, Australia and the United Kingdom. H&R Block Financial Advisors provide consumers with financial planning and investment products. Option One Mortgage Corporation and H&R Block Mortgage Corporation offer a range of home mortgage products. Through RSM McGladrey Inc. and HRB Business Services Inc., the Company offers accounting, tax and consulting services. Block Financial Corporation offers consumer financial products and services, including online tax preparation over the Internet. On 12/1/99, HRB acquired Olde Financial Corp. and Financial Marketing Services Inc.

REVENUES

(04/30/00)	($000)	(%)
Service revenues	1,924,911	78.5
Product sales	271,896	11.1
Royalties	137,162	5.6
Other Revenue	117,974	4.8
Total	2,451,943	100.0

ANNUAL FINANCIAL DATA

	4/30/00	4/30/99	4/30/98	4/30/97	4/30/96	4/30/95	4/30/94
Earnings Per Share	**2.55**	**[2] 2.36**	**[1] 1.62**	**0.45**	**[1] 1.18**	**1.01**	**[1] 1.54**
Cash Flow Per Share	**4.03**	**3.10**	**2.14**	**3.17**	**1.49**	**1.65**	**2.07**
Tang. Book Val. Per Share	**1.13**	**6.02**	**9.66**	**8.83**	**9.64**	**5.80**	**5.97**
Dividends Per Share	**1.02**	**0.85**	**0.80**	**1.28**	**1.26**	**1.15**	**1.03**
Dividend Payout %	**40.2**	**36.0**	**49.4**	**284.4**	**106.6**	**114.1**	**66.9**
INCOME STATEMENT (IN MILLIONS):							
Total Revenues	2,451.9	1,644.7	1,306.8	1,929.7	894.4	1,360.3	1,238.7
Costs & Expenses	1,901.1	1,215.0	995.0	1,624.2	664.5	1,072.6	898.4
Depreciation & Amort.	147.2	74.6	55.8	287.6	32.5	67.7	57.1
Operating Income	403.6	355.1	256.0	17.8	197.5	220.0	283.2
Income Before Income Taxes	412.3	383.5	280.9	38.6	197.5	220.0	283.2
Income Taxes	160.4	145.7	106.7	14.6	72.4	112.7	119.2
Equity Earnings/Minority Int.	...	...	...	23.8	...	...	...
Net Income	251.9	[2] 237.8	[1] 174.2	47.8	[1] 125.1	107.3	[1] 164.0
Cash Flow	399.1	312.4	229.9	335.4	157.6	174.9	221.1
Average Shs. Outstg. (000)	98,929	100,821	107,573	105,840	106,059	105,871	106,769
BALANCE SHEET (IN MILLIONS):							
Cash & Cash Equivalents	442.3	250.1	1,247.0	680.2	418.6	353.5	514.4
Total Current Assets	3,863.5	1,087.4	2,143.3	1,270.0	1,262.9	635.5	699.8
Net Property	260.7	114.2	77.3	420.3	51.5	227.4	165.2
Total Assets	5,699.4	1,910.2	2,904.1	1,906.3	1,417.6	1,078.0	1,074.7
Total Current Liabilities	3,520.4	553.8	1,276.9	713.1	339.7	358.7	336.2
Long-Term Obligations	872.4	249.7	249.7	...	...	...	...
Net Stockholders' Equity	1,218.6	1,062.0	1,341.6	999.1	1,039.6	685.9	707.9
Net Working Capital	343.1	533.6	866.4	556.9	923.2	276.8	363.6
Year-end Shs. Outstg. (000)	108,973	108,973	108,973	104,078	103,418	104,683	107,149
STATISTICAL RECORD:							
Operating Profit Margin %	16.5	21.6	19.6	0.9	22.1	16.2	22.9
Net Profit Margin %	10.3	14.5	13.3	2.5	14.0	7.9	13.2
Return on Equity %	20.7	22.4	13.0	4.8	12.0	15.6	23.2
Return on Assets %	4.4	12.4	6.0	2.5	8.8	9.9	15.3
Debt/Total Assets %	15.3	13.1	8.6	...	...	...	...
Price Range	59.50-38.00	49.06-35.31	45.75-28.00	42.13-23.63	48.88-33.38	48.75-33.00	42.75-31.88
P/E Ratio	23.3-14.9	20.8-15.0	28.2-17.3	93.6-52.5	41.4-28.3	48.3-32.7	27.8-20.7
Average Yield %	2.1	2.0	2.2	3.9	3.1	2.8	2.8

Statistics are as originally reported. [1] Bef. disc. oper. gain 1998, $218.0 mill.; 1996, $52.1 mill.; 1994, $36.5 mill. [2] Bef. disc. oper. loss $22.4 mill.

OFFICERS:
H. W. Bloch, Chmn.
M. A. Ernst, Pres., C.O.O.
F. J. Cotroneo, Sr. V.P., C.F.O.

INVESTOR CONTACT: Mark Barnett, Dir., Inv. Rel., (816) 701-4443

PRINCIPAL OFFICE: 4400 Main Street, Kansas City, MO 64111

TELEPHONE NUMBER: (816) 753-6900
FAX: (816) 932-8390
WEB: www.hrblock.com

NO. OF EMPLOYEES: 10,000 (approx.)

SHAREHOLDERS: 33,305

ANNUAL MEETING: In Sept.

INCORPORATED: MO, 1955

INSTITUTIONAL HOLDINGS:
No. of Institutions: 310
Shares Held: 73,549,995
% Held: 80.5

INDUSTRY: Tax return preparation services (SIC: 7291)

TRANSFER AGENT(S): Mellon Investor Services, Ridgefield Park, NJ

NYSE SYMBOL BBI
Rec. Pr. 21.51 (5/31/01)

BLOCKBUSTER INC.

YIELD 0.4%
P/E RATIO . . .

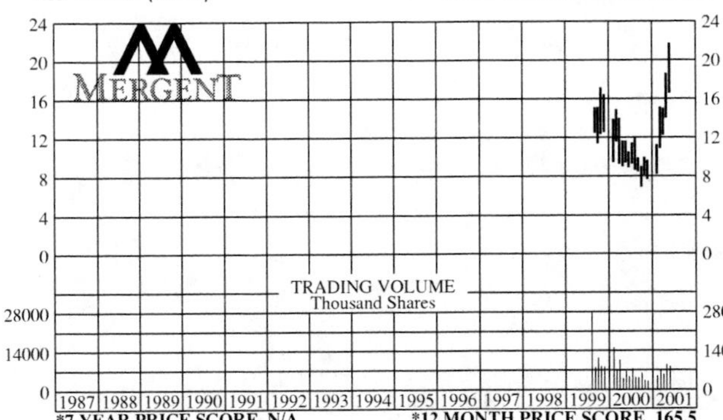

*7 YEAR PRICE SCORE N/A *12 MONTH PRICE SCORE 165.5

*NYSE COMPOSITE INDEX=100

INTERIM EARNINGS (Per Share):

Qtr.	Mar.	June	Sept.	Dec.
1998	0.11	d2.21	d0.15	d0.09
1999	d0.02	d0.28	d0.12	d0.04
2000	d0.02	d0.16	d0.11	d0.14

INTERIM DIVIDENDS (Per Share):

Amt.	Decl.	Ex.	Rec.	Pay.
0.02Q	5/23/00	6/01/00	6/05/00	6/19/00
0.02Q	7/26/00	8/24/00	8/28/00	9/18/00
0.02Q	9/27/00	11/09/00	11/13/00	12/04/00
0.02Q	1/30/01	2/14/01	2/19/01	3/12/01
0.02Q	5/22/01	5/31/01	6/04/01	6/18/01

Indicated div.: $0.08

CAPITALIZATION (12/31/00):

	($000)	(%)
Long-Term Debt	1,039,000	14.1
Capital Lease Obligations	97,500	1.3
Deferred Income Tax	207,200	2.8
Common & Surplus	6,008,400	81.7
Total	7,352,100	100.0

RECENT DEVELOPMENTS: For the year ended 12/31/00, net loss totaled $75.9 million compared with a net loss of $69.2 million a year earlier. Total revenues climbed 11.1% to $4.96 billion from $4.46 billion the year before. Rental revenues grew 10.7% to $4.16 billion, while merchandise sales advanced 14.6% to $704.8 million. Worldwide same-store revenues were up 5.6% year over year. Gross profit was $2.92 billion, or 59.0% of total revenues, versus $2.70 billion, or 60.5% of total revenues, the previous year. Operating income slid 37.8% to $75.7 million.

PROSPECTS: During 2001, BBI anticipates opening between 200 and 250 new company-operated stores, primarily in the U.S., significantly fewer than the 524 net store additions in 2000 due to a slower rate of competitor store growth. Capital expenditures in 2001 are expected to be about $150.0 million to $175.0 million, a decline of nearly 30.0% from 2000, reflecting the reduction in the number of new stores. Meanwhile, revenues should benefit from the Company's focus on expanding the selection of DVDs in its stores.

BUSINESS

BLOCKBUSTER INC. is a major renter of home videocassettes, DVDs and video games throughout the Americas, Europe, Asia and Australia. As of 3/31/01, BBI operated 4,295 company-operated stores in the United States; 1,988 company-operated international stores; and 1,440 franchised and/or joint venture stores. The Company's stores offer a wide selection of pre-recorded videos and DVDs for rent or purchase, along with video games for use with Sony PlayStation, Nintendo and other video game platforms. The Company also rents video game consoles, as well as VHS and DVD players, in most of its domestic company-operated stores, and sells other complementary products. As of 2/28/01, Viacom International Inc. owned 82.3% of BBI's Class A common stock and all of its Class B common stock.

REVENUES

(12/13/00)	($000)	(%)
Rental Revenues	4,161,700	83.9
Merchandise Sales	704,800	14.2
Other Revenues	93,600	1.9
Total	4,960,100	100.0

ANNUAL FINANCIAL DATA

	12/31/00	12/31/99	12/31/98	12/31/97	12/31/96
Earnings Per Share	**d0.43**	**d0.44**	**d2.34**	**d2.21**	**[1] 0.54**
Cash Flow Per Share	**6.39**	**6.39**	**8.21**	**6.28**	**7.13**
Tang. Book Val. Per Share	**1.14**	**0.85**	. . .	**9.90**	. . .
Dividends Per Share	**0.08**	**0.02**	. . .	. . .	. . .
INCOME STATEMENT (IN MILLIONS):					
Total Revenues	4,960.1	4,463.5	3,893.4	3,313.6	2,942.1
Costs & Expenses	3,689.7	3,274.4	2,733.8	2,305.8	1,725.6
Depreciation & Amort.	1,194.7	1,067.4	1,518.8	1,222.4	948.9
Operating Income	75.7	121.7	d359.2	d214.6	267.6
Net Interest Inc./(Exp.)	d109.2	d116.1	d23.7	d27.1	d18.4
Income Before Income Taxes	d31.8	5.4	d394.7	d269.3	249.2
Income Taxes	45.4	71.8	cr59.4	30.0	167.4
Equity Earnings/Minority Int.	1.3	d2.8	d1.3	d18.9	d4.0
Net Income	d75.9	d69.2	d336.6	d318.2	[1] 77.8
Cash Flow	1,118.8	998.2	1,182.2	904.2	1,026.7
Average Shs. Outstg. (000)	175,000	156,100	144,000	144,000	144,000
BALANCE SHEET (IN MILLIONS):					
Cash & Cash Equivalents	194.2	119.6	99.0	129.6	. . .
Total Current Assets	799.5	712.6	631.7	627.9	. . .
Net Property	1,079.4	1,148.3	995.3	1,085.2	. . .
Total Assets	8,548.9	8,540.8	8,274.8	8,731.0	. . .
Total Current Liabilities	1,123.2	1,131.4	846.2	713.1	. . .
Long-Term Obligations	1,136.5	1,138.4	1,715.2	331.3	. . .
Net Stockholders' Equity	6,008.4	6,125.0	5,637.9	7,617.6	. . .
Net Working Capital	d323.7	d418.8	d214.5	d85.2	. . .
Year-end Shs. Outstg. (000)	175,000	175,000	144,000	144,000	144,000
STATISTICAL RECORD:					
Operating Profit Margin %	1.5	2.7	. . .	. . .	9.1
Net Profit Margin %	. . .	. . .	. . .	. . .	2.6
Debt/Total Assets %	13.3	13.3	20.7	3.8	. . .
Price Range	14.88-6.88	17.13-11.38	. . .	. . .	. . .
Average Yield %	0.7	0.1	. . .	. . .	. . .

Statistics are as originally reported. [1] Incl. $50.2 mil restr. chg.

OFFICERS:
J. F. Antioco, Chmn., Pres., C.E.O.
L. J. Zine, Exec. V.P., C.F.O.
E. Stead, Exec. V.P., Gen. Couns., Sec.

INVESTOR CONTACT: Mary Bell, V.P., Inv. Rel., (214) 854-3863

PRINCIPAL OFFICE: 1201 Elm Street, Dallas, TX 75270

TELEPHONE NUMBER: (214) 854-3000
FAX: (214) 854-4848
WEB: www.blockbuster.com

NO. OF EMPLOYEES: 95,800 (approx.)

SHAREHOLDERS: 273 (cl. A); 1 (cl. B)

ANNUAL MEETING: In May

INCORPORATED: DE, Oct., 1989

INSTITUTIONAL HOLDINGS:
No. of Institutions: 87
Shares Held: 28,309,539
% Held: 16.2

INDUSTRY: Video tape rental (SIC: 7841)

TRANSFER AGENT(S): First Chicago Trust Company of New York, Jersey City, NJ

NYSE SYMBOL BMC
Rec. Pr. 24.19 (4/30/01)

BMC SOFTWARE, INC.

YIELD	...
P/E RATIO	51.5

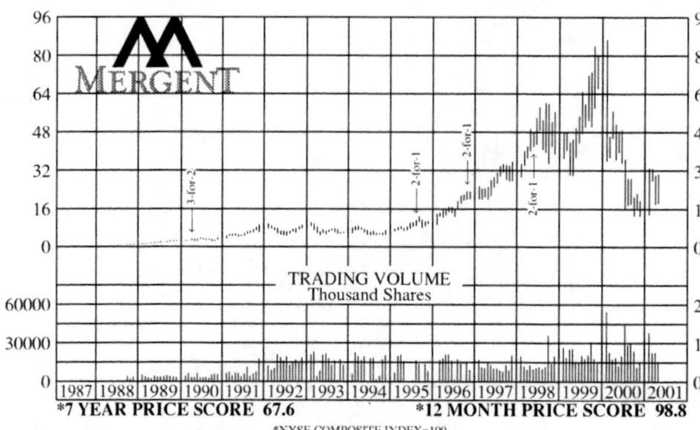

INTERIM EARNINGS (Per Share):

Qtr.	June	Sept.	Dec.	Mar.
1996-97	0.13	0.17	0.23	0.25
1997-98	d0.05	0.21	0.30	0.31
1998-99	0.26	0.33	0.44	0.40
1999-00	0.07	0.23	0.27	0.39
2000-01	0.04	d0.05	0.09	...

INTERIM DIVIDENDS (Per Share):

Amt.	Decl.	Ex.	Rec.	Pay.

No dividends paid.

CAPITALIZATION (3/31/00):

	($000)	(%)
Common & Surplus	1,780,900	100.0
Total	1,780,900	100.0

RECENT DEVELOPMENTS: For the third quarter ended 12/31/00, net income plunged 68.4% to $21.9 million compared with net income of $69.2 million in the corresponding 1999 quarter. Earnings for 2000 included $2.4 million in merger related and compensation charges. Results for 1999 included a $16.6 million settlement charge. Total revenues declined 9.6% to $385.5 million from $426.4 million in the prior-year quarter. License revenues dropped 20.6% to $228.9 million.

PROSPECTS: On 2/28/01, EMC acquired Perform, SA, a French Web-based network optimization software developer. BMC will offer two products from the Perform acquisition. Pricing for PATROL Dashboard will start at $10,000, while pricing for PATROL Visualis™ will begin at approximately $40,000. As a result of the acquisition, BMC is adding a PATROL Network Management Line of Business to its extended line of PATROL products.

BUSINESS

BMC SOFTWARE, INC. is a worldwide developer and vendor of more than 100 software solutions for automating application and data management across host-based and open systems environments. The Company's products are primarily designed to facilitate database and network management, maintenance and recovery and to increase the speed and efficiency of data-communications. The Company has more than 10,000 customers and 821,000 software licenses worldwide. In March 1999, BMCS acquired Boole & Babbage Inc. In April 1999, the Company acquired New Dimensions Software, Ltd.

ANNUAL FINANCIAL DATA

	3/31/00	3/31/99	3/31/98	3/31/97	3/31/96	3/31/95	3/31/94
Earnings Per Share	**[1] 0.96**	**[2] 1.46**	**[1] 0.77**	**0.77**	**0.51**	**0.38**	**[1] 0.27**
Cash Flow Per Share	**1.89**	**1.77**	**1.03**	**0.92**	**0.57**	**0.47**	**0.34**
Tang. Book Val. Per Share	**5.14**	**5.27**	**3.41**	**2.57**	**1.72**	**1.47**	**1.19**
INCOME STATEMENT (IN MILLIONS):							
Total Revenues	1,719.2	1,303.9	730.6	563.2	428.9	345.0	288.5
Costs & Expenses	1,213.1	811.8	446.4	313.7	266.9	217.6	194.2
Depreciation & Amort.	235.6	76.8	58.0	32.5	14.4	18.8	14.4
Operating Income	270.5	415.2	226.2	217.0	147.6	108.6	79.9
Net Interest Inc./(Exp.)	40.9	62.7	30.4	20.1	15.4	11.7	10.7
Income Before Income Taxes	311.4	477.9	256.6	237.1	163.0	120.3	90.6
Income Taxes	68.9	113.7	90.7	73.2	57.5	42.8	34.1
Net Income	[1] 242.5	[2] 364.2	[1] 165.9	163.9	105.6	77.5	[1] 56.5
Cash Flow	478.1	441.0	223.9	196.4	120.0	96.3	70.9
Average Shs. Outstg. (000)	253,000	248,647	216,590	214,310	209,144	203,904	209,216
BALANCE SHEET (IN MILLIONS):							
Cash & Cash Equivalents	255.2	454.2	128.3	139.0	130.2	93.8	80.3
Total Current Assets	896.2	873.4	373.9	248.4	228.0	182.9	160.7
Net Property	337.5	244.4	163.0	116.3	107.9	101.3	93.2
Total Assets	2,962.1	2,282.7	1,248.5	844.2	608.2	502.6	417.5
Total Current Liabilities	883.9	650.9	335.5	204.7	184.2	147.7	127.1
Net Stockholders' Equity	1,780.9	1,345.8	767.3	554.0	388.0	313.1	259.8
Net Working Capital	12.3	222.6	38.3	43.7	43.8	35.2	33.6
Year-end Shs. Outstg. (000)	244,600	234,573	206,328	200,326	210,080	202,000	205,952
STATISTICAL RECORD:							
Operating Profit Margin %	15.7	31.8	31.0	38.5	34.4	31.5	27.7
Net Profit Margin %	14.1	27.9	22.7	29.1	24.6	22.5	19.6
Return on Equity %	13.6	27.1	21.6	29.6	27.2	24.8	21.7
Return on Assets %	8.2	16.0	13.3	19.4	17.4	15.4	13.5
Price Range	84.06-30.00	60.25-29.25	35.63-19.81	23.38-9.31	12.88-6.75	8.88-5.03	10.52-4.84
P/E Ratio	87.6-31.2	41.3-20.0	46.3-25.7	30.6-12.2	25.5-13.4	23.3-13.2	38.9-17.9

Statistics are as originally reported. Adj. for stk. splits: 2-for-1, 5/15/98; 2-for-1, 11/18/96; 2-for-1, 8/14/95. [1] Incl. non-recurr. chrg., $150.3 mill., 3/00; $7.3 mill., 3/98; $32.0 mill., 3/94. [2] Bef. acctg. change chrg. of $1.5 mill., but incl. non-recurr. chrg. $38.3 mill.

OFFICERS:
M. P. Watson Jr., Chmn., Pres., C.E.O.
W. M. Austin, Sr. V.P., C.F.O.

INVESTOR CONTACT: John W. Cox, Director of Investor Relations, (800) 841-2031

PRINCIPAL OFFICE: 2101 CityWest Boulevard, Houston, TX 77042-2827

TELEPHONE NUMBER: (713) 918-8800
FAX: (713) 918-8000
WEB: www.bmc.com

NO. OF EMPLOYEES: 6,677

SHAREHOLDERS: 1,723

ANNUAL MEETING: In Aug.

INCORPORATED: TX, 1980; reincorp., DE, July, 1988

INSTITUTIONAL HOLDINGS:
No. of Institutions: 301
Shares Held: 161,291,763
% Held: 66.2

INDUSTRY: Prepackaged software (SIC: 7372)

TRANSFER AGENT(S): Fleet National Bank, Boston, MA

NYSE SYMBOL BA
Rec. Pr. 62.89 (5/31/01)

BOEING COMPANY (THE)

YIELD 1.1%
P/E RATIO 25.8

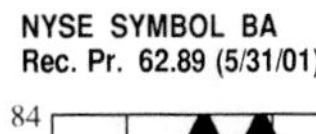

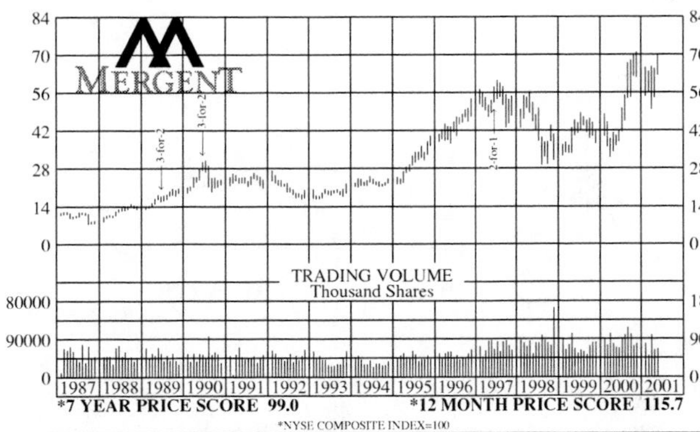

INTERIM EARNINGS (Per Share):

Qtr.	Mar.	June	Sept.	Dec.
1997	0.55	0.48	d0.72	d0.51
1998	0.05	0.26	0.36	0.48
1999	0.50	0.75	0.52	0.74
2000	0.48	0.71	0.70	0.55

INTERIM DIVIDENDS (Per Share):

Amt.	Decl.	Ex.	Rec.	Pay.
0.14Q	5/01/00	5/10/00	5/12/00	6/02/00
0.14Q	6/26/00	8/09/00	8/11/00	9/01/00
0.14Q	10/30/00	11/08/00	11/10/00	12/01/00
0.17Q	12/11/00	2/07/01	2/09/01	3/02/01
0.17Q	5/01/01	5/09/01	5/11/01	6/01/01

Indicated div.: $0.68 (Div. Reinv. Plan)

CAPITALIZATION (12/31/00):

	($000)	(%)
Long-Term Debt	7,567,000	40.7
Common & Surplus	11,020,000	59.3
Total	18,587,000	100.0

RECENT DEVELOPMENTS: For the year ended 12/31/00, net earnings slipped 7.8% to $2.13 billion from $2.31 billion the year before. Results in 2000 included pre-tax non-recurring charges of $616.0 million primarily related to in-process research and development and employee benefit expenses, along with costs related to a Delta III demonstration launch. The 1999 earnings included a pre-tax gain of $87.0 million. Sales and other operating revenues slid 11.5% to $51.32 billion, due primarily to lower sales in the Commercial Airplanes segment.

PROSPECTS: The Company is targeting annual revenues of $57.00 billion in 2001, rising to more than $62.00 billion in the following year. The Company is forecasting commercial aircraft deliveries in 2001 and 2002 of about 530 each year, up from 489 in 2000. Meanwhile, anticipated operating profit margin of 8.5% in 2001 is expected to improve to more than 9.0% in 2002. BA is considering several initiatives that will help lower costs, including the possible closure of its Renton, Washington-based facility that builds the Company's 737 and 757 jetliners.

BUSINESS

THE BOEING COMPANY is a major commercial aerospace and defense concern, operating in three main business segments. The Commercial Airplanes segment (60.6% of 2000 revenues) principally involves development, production and marketing of commercial aircraft and provides related support services mainly to commercial customers. Operations in the Military Aircraft and Missiles segment (23.7%) involve research, development, production and modification of military aircraft, including fighter, transport and attack aircraft, helicopters and missiles. The Space and Communications segment (15.7%) provides research, development, production, modification for space systems, missile defense systems, satellite launching vehicles, rocket engines, and information and battle management systems. On 8/1/97, the Company acquired McDonnell Douglas Corp. On 10/6/00, BA acquired the space and communications operations of Hughes Electronics Corporation.

ANNUAL FINANCIAL DATA

	12/31/00	12/31/99	12/31/98	12/31/97	12/31/96	12/31/95	12/31/94
Earnings Per Share	**[2] 2.44**	**[2] 2.49**	**[2] 1.15**	**[2] d0.18**	**[2] 1.60**	**[1] 0.58**	**1.26**
Cash Flow Per Share	**4.14**	**4.50**	**2.96**	**1.22**	**3.23**	**2.08**	**2.93**
Tang. Book Val. Per Share	**6.63**	**10.15**	**10.25**	**10.56**	**11.75**	**14.39**	**14.22**
Dividends Per Share	**0.56**	**0.56**	**0.56**	**0.56**	**0.55**	**0.50**	**0.50**
Dividend Payout %	**22.9**	**22.5**	**48.7**	**...**	**34.2**	**86.9**	**39.8**
INCOME STATEMENT (IN MILLIONS):							
Total Revenues	51,321.0	57,993.0	56,154.0	45,800.0	22,681.0	19,515.0	21,924.0
Costs & Expenses	46,848.0	53,182.0	52,898.0	44,697.0	20,336.0	17,580.0	19,631.0
Depreciation & Amort.	1,479.0	1,645.0	1,622.0	1,458.0	991.0	1,033.0	1,142.0
Operating Income	3,058.0	3,170.0	1,567.0	d355.0	1,354.0	302.0	1,151.0
Net Interest Inc./(Exp.)	d445.0	d431.0	d453.0	d513.0	d145.0	d151.0	d130.0
Income Before Income Taxes	2,999.0	3,324.0	1,397.0	d341.0	1,363.0	360.0	1,143.0
Income Taxes	871.0	1,015.0	277.0	cr163.0	268.0	cr33.0	287.0
Equity Earnings/Minority Int.	64.0	4.0	d67.0	...	...	...	...
Net Income	[2] 2,128.0	[2] 2,309.0	[2] 1,120.0	[2] d178.0	[2] 1,095.0	[1] 393.0	856.0
Cash Flow	3,607.0	3,954.0	2,742.0	1,280.0	2,086.0	1,426.0	1,998.0
Average Shs. Outstg. (000)	871,300	925,900	976,700	970,100	688,000	684,000	682,000
BALANCE SHEET (IN MILLIONS):							
Cash & Cash Equivalents	1,010.0	3,454.0	2,462.0	5,149.0	5,258.0	3,730.0	2,643.0
Total Current Assets	15,864.0	15,712.0	16,610.0	19,263.0	15,080.0	13,178.0	10,414.0
Net Property	8,814.0	8,245.0	8,589.0	8,391.0	6,813.0	6,456.0	6,802.0
Total Assets	42,028.0	36,147.0	37,024.0	38,024.0	27,254.0	22,098.0	22,578.0
Total Current Liabilities	18,289.0	13,656.0	13,774.0	14,152.0	8,642.0	7,415.0	6,827.0
Long-Term Obligations	7,567.0	5,980.0	6,103.0	6,123.0	3,980.0	2,344.0	2,603.0
Net Stockholders' Equity	11,020.0	11,462.0	12,316.0	12,953.0	10,941.0	9,898.0	9,700.0
Net Working Capital	d2,425.0	2,056.0	2,836.0	5,111.0	6,438.0	5,763.0	3,587.0
Year-end Shs. Outstg. (000)	875,485	909,513	976,000	1,000,000	720,000	688,000	682,000
STATISTICAL RECORD:							
Operating Profit Margin %	6.0	5.5	2.8	...	6.0	1.5	5.2
Net Profit Margin %	4.1	4.0	2.0	...	4.8	2.0	3.9
Return on Equity %	19.3	20.1	9.1	...	10.0	4.0	8.8
Return on Assets %	5.1	6.4	3.0	...	4.0	1.8	3.8
Debt/Total Assets %	18.0	16.5	16.5	16.1	14.6	10.6	11.5
Price Range	70.94-32.00	48.50-32.56	56.25-29.00	60.50-43.00	53.75-37.06	40.00-22.19	25.06-21.06
P/E Ratio	29.1-13.1	19.5-13.1	48.9-25.2	...	33.7-23.2	69.6-38.6	20.0-16.8
Average Yield %	1.1	1.4	1.3	1.1	1.2	1.6	2.2

Statistics are as originally reported. Adj. for 2-for-1 stk. split, 6/97. [1] Incl. $600 mil non-recur. pre-tax chg. for spcl. retirmnt. program. [2] Incl. $616 mil ($0.44/sh) pre-tax non-recur. chg., 2000; $87 mil pre-tax gain, 1999; $219 mil non-recur. chg., 1998; $1.90 bil net non-recur. chg., 1997; $6 mil gain, 1996.

OFFICERS:
P. M. Condit, Chmn., C.E.O.
H. C. Stonecipher, Pres., C.O.O.
M. M. Sears, Sr. V.P., C.F.O.
W. Skowronski, V.P.-Fin., Treas.

PRINCIPAL OFFICE: 7755 East Marginal Way South, Seattle, WA 98108

TELEPHONE NUMBER: (206) 655-2121
FAX: (206) 655-3987
WEB: www.boeing.com
NO. OF EMPLOYEES: 198,000 (approx.)
SHAREHOLDERS: 146,886
ANNUAL MEETING: In Apr.
INCORPORATED: DE, July, 1934

INSTITUTIONAL HOLDINGS:
No. of Institutions: 701
Shares Held: 503,162,163
% Held: 60.3

INDUSTRY: Aircraft (SIC: 3721)

TRANSFER AGENT(S): EquiServe, Providence, RI

NYSE SYMBOL BCC
Rec. Pr. 34.98 (4/30/01)

BOISE CASCADE CORPORATION

YIELD 1.7%
P/E RATIO 12.8

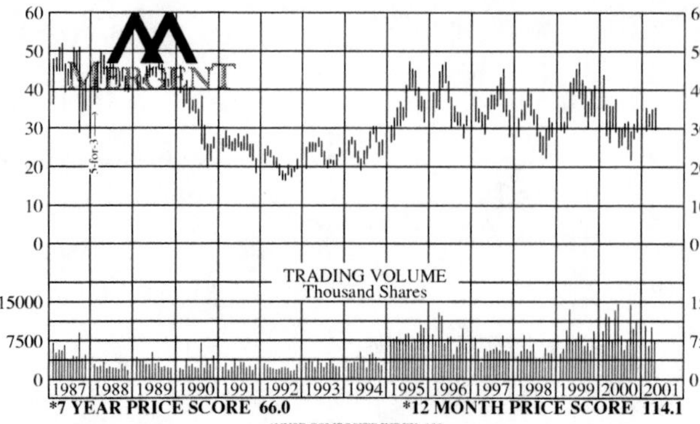

INTERIM EARNINGS (Per Share):

Qtr.	Mar.	June	Sept.	Dec.
1997	d0.51	d0.53	d0.23	0.02
1998	d0.18	d1.20	0.72	d0.25
1999	0.26	0.92	0.74	1.18
2000	0.60	0.46	1.33	0.34

INTERIM DIVIDENDS (Per Share):

Amt.	Decl.	Ex.	Rec.	Pay.
0.15Q	12/08/00	12/27/00	1/01/01	1/15/01
0.15Q	2/09/01	3/28/01	4/01/01	4/15/01
0.15Q	4/20/01	6/27/01	7/01/01	7/15/01

Indicated div.: $0.60 (Div. Reinv. Plan)

CAPITALIZATION (12/31/00):

	($000)	(%)
Long-Term Debt [1]	1,822,687	45.9
Deferred Income Tax	383,646	9.7
Minority Interest	9,469	0.2
Preferred Stock	210,961	5.3
Common & Surplus	1,546,011	38.9
Total	3,972,774	100.0

RECENT DEVELOPMENTS: For the year 12/31/00, net income declined 10.6% to $178.6 million compared with $199.8 million in the prior year. The decline in net income was primarily attributed to lower structural panel and lumber prices in BCC's building products segment and lower operating margins in its office products segment. Sales were $7.81 billion, up 9.2% from $7.15 billion a year earlier.

PROSPECTS: In the office products segment, BCC plans to grow sales from initiatives that will address new market segments, sell more products to existing customers, and increase geographic coverage. In the building products segment, BCC expects market conditions to remain flat. Within BCC's paper segment, results should improve; however, they may be tempered by higher energy costs.

BUSINESS

BOISE CASCADE CORPORATION is an integrated paper and forest products company with domestic and international operations. BCC manufactures and distributes paper, corrugated containers and wood products, distributes office products and building materials, and owns and manages timberlands to support those operations. BCC's segments consist of Paper & Paper Products, Building Products, and Office Products. BCC owns or controls 2.3 million acres of timberland in the Pacific Northwest, the upper Midwest, and the South. Other operations consist of information services, leasing, transportation and insurance. In 1996, BCC completed the sale of its coated publication paper business for about $639.0 million in cash. In 1995, BCC spun off Boise Cascade Office Products (BCOP). Effective 4/20/00, BCC purchased the minority public shares of BCOP for a total of $216.1 million, and BCOP became a wholly-owned subsidiary of BCC.

ANNUAL FINANCIAL DATA

	12/31/00	12/31/99	12/31/98	12/31/97	12/31/96	12/31/95	12/31/94
Earnings Per Share	**2.73**	**[5] 3.06**	**[4] d0.75**	**d1.19**	**d0.63**	**[3] 5.93**	**[2] d3.08**
Cash Flow Per Share	**7.76**	**7.96**	**4.30**	**3.90**	**4.81**	**10.50**	**6.16**
Tang. Book Val. Per Share	**19.93**	**15.77**	**12.17**	**13.01**	**31.35**	**32.65**	**15.74**
Dividends Per Share	**0.60**	**0.60**	**0.60**	**0.60**	**0.60**	**0.60**	**0.60**
Dividend Payout %	**22.0**	**19.6**	**...**	**...**	**...**	**10.1**	**...**
INCOME STATEMENT (IN MILLIONS):							
Total Revenues	7,806.7	6,952.7	6,162.1	5,493.1	5,108.2	5,074.2	4,140.4
Costs & Expenses	7,064.9	6,165.3	5,734.9	5,123.8	4,732.7	4,192.7	3,751.3
Depreciation & Amort.	297.7	289.0	282.7	256.6	258.3	272.9	254.3
Operating Income	444.0	498.4	136.9	102.4	152.1	655.6	91.7
Net Interest Inc./(Exp.)	d145.3	d142.4	d157.6	d131.3	d124.9	d132.2	d146.1
Income Before Income Taxes	298.3	355.9	d21.3	d28.9	31.3	589.4	d64.7
Income Taxes	116.3	142.4	cr2.7	cr9.3	12.0	231.3	cr2.1
Equity Earnings/Minority Int.	d3.4	d13.8	d9.8	d10.7	d10.3	d6.3	...
Net Income	178.6	[5] 199.8	[4] d28.4	d30.4	d20.0	[3] 385.0	[2] d65.3
Cash Flow	460.3	471.6	240.1	196.7	188.1	529.0	173.9
Average Shs. Outstg. (000)	61,413	61,419	60,907	60,621	48,277	55,028	38,110
BALANCE SHEET (IN MILLIONS):							
Cash & Cash Equivalents	62.8	66.9	74.4	63.6	260.9	51.5	29.5
Total Current Assets	1,577.3	1,531.1	1,368.4	1,353.7	1,355.4	1,313.2	918.3
Net Property	2,872.8	2,851.7	2,841.7	2,902.7	2,846.8	2,987.6	2,891.6
Total Assets	5,266.9	5,138.4	4,966.7	4,969.9	4,710.7	4,656.2	4,294.1
Total Current Liabilities	1,014.4	1,124.7	1,130.1	893.7	932.6	769.9	657.8
Long-Term Obligations	1,822.7	1,717.3	1,733.9	1,902.7	1,526.1	1,578.8	1,856.1
Net Stockholders' Equity	1,757.0	1,614.1	1,428.4	1,612.5	2,072.7	2,122.3	1,364.9
Net Working Capital	562.9	406.4	238.3	459.9	422.8	543.3	260.4
Year-end Shs. Outstg. (000)	57,337	57,158	56,338	61,909	48,476	47,760	38,284
STATISTICAL RECORD:							
Operating Profit Margin %	5.7	7.2	2.2	1.9	3.0	12.9	2.2
Net Profit Margin %	2.3	2.9	...	...	...	7.6	...
Return on Equity %	10.2	12.4	...	...	...	18.1	...
Return on Assets %	3.4	3.9	...	...	...	8.3	...
Debt/Total Assets %	34.6	33.4	34.9	38.3	32.4	33.9	43.2
Price Range	43.94-21.75	47.19-28.75	40.38-22.25	45.56-27.75	47.25-27.38	47.50-26.25	30.50-19.00
P/E Ratio	16.1-8.0	15.4-9.4	...	...	...	8.0-4.4	...
Average Yield %	1.8	1.6	1.9	1.6	1.6	1.6	2.4

Statistics are as originally reported. [1] Incl. cv. subord. debs. and guarantee of 8.5% ESOP debt. [2] Incl. chrg. of $27 mill. rel. to sale of secur. [3] Incl. gains of $66.2 mill. from the IPO of Boise Cascade Office Products Corp.; $183 mill. fr. the divestment of BCC's int. in Rainy River Forest Products. [4] Incl. pre-tax nonrecurr. chrg. of $92.3 mill., but bef. accts. gain of $8.6 mill. [5] Incl. nonrecurr. items that reulted in a net gain of a $51.5 mill.

OFFICERS:
G. J. Harad, Chmn., C.E.O.
T. Crumley, Sr. V.P., C.F.O.
I. Littman, V.P., Treas.
J. Holleran, V.P., Gen. Couns.

INVESTOR CONTACT: Investor Relations, (208) 384-6390

PRINCIPAL OFFICE: 1111 West Jefferson Street, P.O. Box 50, Boise, ID 83728-0001

TELEPHONE NUMBER: (208) 384-6161
FAX: (208) 384-7189
WEB: www.bc.com

NO. OF EMPLOYEES: 25,257 (avg.)

SHAREHOLDERS: 15,461 (approx.)

ANNUAL MEETING: In Apr.

INCORPORATED: DE, Apr., 1931

INSTITUTIONAL HOLDINGS:
No. of Institutions: 206
Shares Held: 51,214,008
% Held: 89.3

INDUSTRY: Paper mills (SIC: 2621)

TRANSFER AGENT(S): Wells Fargo Bank Minnesota, South St. Paul, MN

NYSE SYMBOL BGP
Rec. Pr. 18.27 (5/31/01)

BORDERS GROUP, INC.

YIELD ...
P/E RATIO 33.2

***7 YEAR PRICE SCORE N/A** ***12 MONTH PRICE SCORE 133.0**

*NYSE COMPOSITE INDEX=100

INTERIM EARNINGS (Per Share):

Qtr.	Apr.	July	Oct.	Jan.
1996-97	d0.05	d0.03	d0.04	0.82
1997-98	Nil	0.01	Nil	0.96
1998-99	0.05	0.03	d0.01	1.06
1999-00	d0.05	d0.03	d0.02	1.23
2000-01	d0.01	d0.02	d0.06	0.64

INTERIM DIVIDENDS (Per Share):

Amt.	Decl.	Ex.	Rec.	Pay.

No dividends paid.

CAPITALIZATION (1/28/01):

	($000)	(%)
Long-Term Debt	15,000	1.7
Common & Surplus	846,500	98.3
Total	861,500	100.0

RECENT DEVELOPMENTS: For the year ended 1/28/01, income from continuing operations totaled $73.8 million compared with income from continuing operations of $94.0 million a year earlier. Results in the recent period included a one-time pre-tax charge of $36.2 million related to asset impairments and other writedowns. Sales advanced 10.2% to $3.27 billion from $2.97 billion the year before. Comparable-store sales at Borders locations rose 2.3%, while comparable-store sales at Waldenbooks stores slipped 2.9%.

PROSPECTS: The Company is focusing on improving comparable-store sales and continuing with its store expansion program. In 2001, comparable-store sales at domestic Borders stores are expected to grow 3.0% to 4.0%, while comparable-store sales at Waldenbooks are expected to decline by 1.0% to 2.0%. During 2001, BGP anticipates opening between 25 and 30 new domestic Borders stores and five or six international locations. The Company is targeting earnings, excluding one-time charges, of $1.38 to $1.40 per share in 2001.

BUSINESS

BORDERS GROUP, INC. is the second largest operator of book and music superstores and the largest operator of mall-based bookstores, based on both sales and number of stores. As of 4/29/01, the Company operated 339 superstores under the Borders name in the U.S., as well as 15 stores located in the United Kingdom, Australia, New Zealand, Singapore, and Puerto Rico. The Company also operates 862 mall-based and other bookstores primarily under the Waldenbooks name, and 32 bookstores under the Books etc. name in the United Kingdom. BGP is also an on-line retailer of books, music and video through its Borders Online, Inc. subsidiary.

ANNUAL FINANCIAL DATA

	1/28/01	1/23/00	1/24/99	1/25/98	1/26/97	1/28/96	1/22/95
Earnings Per Share	**[2] 0.92**	**1.13**	**1.12**	**0.98**	**0.70**	**[1] d2.53**	**[1] 0.24**
Cash Flow Per Share	**2.11**	**2.18**	**1.92**	**1.64**	**1.22**	**d2.03**	**0.76**
Tang. Book Val. Per Share	**9.70**	**8.76**	**7.84**	**6.48**	**6.23**	**5.74**	**8.12**
INCOME STATEMENT (IN MILLIONS):							
Total Revenues	3,271.2	2,999.2	2,595.0	2,266.0	1,958.8	1,749.0	1,511.0
Costs & Expenses	3,040.8	2,748.3	2,361.0	2,073.2	1,812.8	1,907.4	1,421.6
Depreciation & Amort.	95.3	84.7	66.7	54.8	42.9	42.0	45.6
Operating Income	135.1	166.2	167.3	138.0	103.1	d200.4	43.8
Net Interest Inc./(Exp.)	d13.1	d17.9	d16.2	d7.2	d7.0	d4.6	d1.0
Income Before Income Taxes	122.0	148.3	151.1	130.8	96.1	d205.0	42.8
Income Taxes	48.2	58.0	59.0	50.6	38.2	6.1	21.9
Net Income	[2] 73.8	90.3	92.1	80.2	57.9	[1] d211.1	[1] 20.9
Cash Flow	169.1	175.0	158.8	135.0	100.8	d169.4	66.4
Average Shs. Outstg. (000)	80,288	80,218	82,503	82,241	82,554	83,358	87,260
BALANCE SHEET (IN MILLIONS):							
Cash & Cash Equivalents	59.1	41.6	42.8	65.1	42.6	36.5	237.0
Total Current Assets	1,335.1	1,198.2	1,133.3	1,018.4	846.4	740.2	816.2
Net Property	562.3	558.2	493.8	373.7	289.2	243.5	244.2
Total Assets	2,047.1	1,914.8	1,766.6	1,534.9	1,211.0	1,052.3	1,355.9
Total Current Liabilities	1,117.9	1,027.9	988.8	881.4	634.5	542.9	558.2
Long-Term Obligations	15.0	16.2	6.3	5.2	6.2	8.1	10.9
Net Stockholders' Equity	846.5	802.6	715.1	598.1	511.4	472.0	726.3
Net Working Capital	217.2	170.3	144.5	137.0	211.9	197.3	258.0
Year-end Shs. Outstg. (000)	77,688	77,688	77,695	75,396	75,858	75,318	57,520
STATISTICAL RECORD:							
Operating Profit Margin %	4.1	5.5	6.4	6.1	5.3	...	2.9
Net Profit Margin %	2.3	3.0	3.5	3.5	3.0	...	1.4
Return on Equity %	8.7	11.3	12.9	13.4	11.3	...	2.9
Return on Assets %	3.6	4.7	5.2	5.2	4.8	...	1.5
Debt/Total Assets %	0.7	0.8	0.4	0.3	0.5	0.8	0.8
Price Range	17.88-10.88	25.75-11.75	41.75-17.88	32.31-17.06	19.63-8.19	10.94-6.94	...
P/E Ratio	19.4-11.8	22.8-10.4	37.3-16.0	33.0-17.4	28.0-11.7	...	...

Statistics are as originally reported. Adj. for stk. split, 2-for-1, 3/97. [1] Incl. $63.1 mil pre-tax non-recur. chg., 1/96; $6.4 mil, 1/95. [2] Bef. $30.2 mil ($0.38/sh) loss fr discont. oper. & incl. $36.2 pre-tax chg. fr asset impairments and other writedowns.

OFFICERS:
R. F. DiRomualdo, Chmn.
G. P. Josefowicz, Pres., C.E.O.
E. Wilhelm, Sr. V.P.-Fin., C.F.O.

INVESTOR CONTACT: Sherry Pringle, (734) 477-1794

PRINCIPAL OFFICE: 100 Phoenix Drive, Ann Arbor, MI 48108

TELEPHONE NUMBER: (734) 477-1100
FAX: (734) 477-4538
WEB: www.borders.com
NO. OF EMPLOYEES: 17,000 full-time (approx.); 13,000 part-time (approx.)
SHAREHOLDERS: 4,163
ANNUAL MEETING: In May
INCORPORATED: DE, Aug., 1994

INSTITUTIONAL HOLDINGS:
No. of Institutions: 159
Shares Held: 64,049,023
% Held: 80.1

INDUSTRY: Book stores (SIC: 5942)

TRANSFER AGENT(S): First Chicago Trust Company of New York, Chicago, IL

NYSE SYMBOL BWA
Rec. Pr. 45.25 (5/31/01)

BORGWARNER INC.

YIELD ...
P/E RATIO 12.8

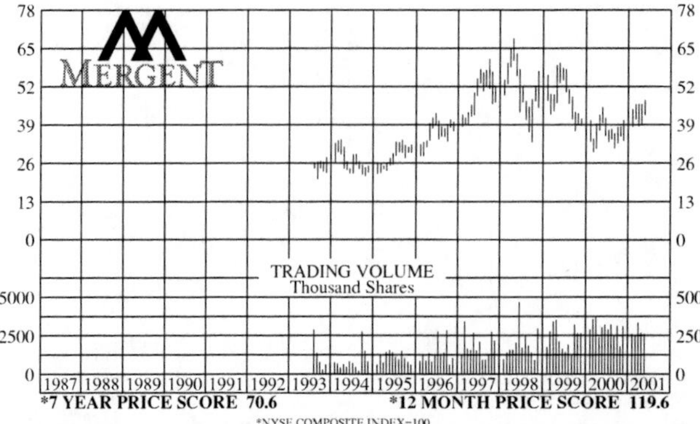

*7 YEAR PRICE SCORE 70.6 *12 MONTH PRICE SCORE 119.6

*NYSE COMPOSITE INDEX=100

INTERIM EARNINGS (Per Share):

Qtr.	Mar.	June	Sept.	Dec.
1996	0.52	0.93	0.80	d0.47
1997	1.05	1.25	0.91	1.14
1998	1.10	0.83	0.73	1.35
1999	1.32	1.35	1.02	1.36
2000	1.53	1.51	0.20	0.30

INTERIM DIVIDENDS (Per Share):

Amt.	Decl.	Ex.	Rec.	Pay.
0.15Q	7/23/99	7/29/99	8/02/99	8/16/99
0.15Q	10/20/99	10/28/99	11/01/99	11/15/99
0.15Q	1/21/00	1/28/00	2/01/00	2/15/00
0.15Q	4/10/00	4/27/00	5/01/00	5/15/00

CAPITALIZATION (12/31/00):

	($000)	(%)
Long-Term Debt	740,400	40.3
Minority Interest	10,300	0.6
Common & Surplus	1,087,100	59.2
Total	1,837,800	100.0

RECENT DEVELOPMENTS: For the year ended 12/31/00, net income was $94.0 million, down 28.9% versus $132.3 million in 1999. Results for 2000 included a pre-tax nonrecurring charge of $62.9 million related to the Company's restructuring initiatives. Earnings were adversely affected by the impact of a weak Euro on strong European sales and weaker automobile production during the second half of 2000. Net sales rose 7.6% to $2.65 billion from $2.46 billion a year earlier.

PROSPECTS: Production cuts by major North American automobile manufacturers are expected to continue to pressure earnings through the first half of 2001. The Company curtailed production and implemented temporary layoffs in its manufacturing facilities to bring costs in line with softening demand. These actions are expected to generate cost savings of $19.0 million in 2001. For the second half of 2001, the Company anticipates improved results as car and truck inventories are reduced.

BUSINESS

BORGWARNER INC. (formerly BorgWarner Automotive, Inc.) is a global supplier of highly engineered systems and components, primarily for automotive powertrain applications. These products are manufactured and sold worldwide, primarily to original equipment manufacturers of passenger cars, sport utility vehicles and light trucks, including Ford, DaimlerChrysler, General Motors, Toyota, Caterpillar, Navistar, PSA and VW Group. BWA operates 46 manufacturing facilities in 13 countries serving auto makers in North America, Europe, and Asia. BWA's operating segments include TorqTransfer Systems, Transmission Systems, Morse TEC, Cooling Systems and Air/Fluid Systems. BWA acquired Eaton Corp.'s Fluid Power division on 10/1/99.

BUSINESS LINE ANALYSIS

(12/31/00)	Rev (%)	Inc (%)
Air/Fluid Systems	16.7	12.8
Cooling Systems	11.0	11.5
Morse TEC	34.6	45.8
TorqTransfer Systems	20.6	13.4
Transmission Systems	17.1	16.5
Total	100.0	100.0

ANNUAL FINANCIAL DATA

	12/31/00	12/31/99	12/31/98	12/31/97	12/31/96	12/31/95	12/31/94
Earnings Per Share	**2 3.54**	**5.07**	**4.00**	**4.31**	**1 1.77**	**3.15**	**2.75**
Cash Flow Per Share	**9.04**	**9.81**	**7.87**	**7.95**	**5.37**	**6.44**	**5.76**
Tang. Book Val. Per Share	...	...	**9.27**	**6.29**	**3.10**	**12.45**	**10.24**
Dividends Per Share	**0.30**	**0.60**	**0.60**	**0.60**	**0.60**	**0.60**	**0.55**
Dividend Payout %	**8.5**	**11.8**	**15.0**	**13.9**	**33.9**	**19.0**	**20.0**
INCOME STATEMENT (IN MILLIONS):							
Total Revenues	2,645.9	2,458.6	1,836.8	1,767.0	1,540.1	1,329.1	1,223.4
Costs & Expenses	2,247.2	2,091.8	1,585.8	1,507.4	1,328.2	1,142.7	1,040.5
Depreciation & Amort.	145.5	123.4	91.6	87.1	84.8	77.6	70.5
Operating Income	253.2	243.4	159.4	172.5	127.1	108.8	112.4
Net Interest Inc./(Exp.)	d62.6	d49.2	d26.9	d24.6	d21.4	d14.2	d13.9
Income Before Income Taxes	148.8	207.0	140.7	157.9	54.7	111.2	107.7
Income Taxes	54.8	74.7	46.0	54.7	12.9	37.0	43.3
Equity Earnings/Minority Int.	21.1	12.8	8.2	10.0	10.5	16.6	9.2
Net Income	2 94.0	132.3	94.7	103.2	1 41.8	74.2	64.4
Cash Flow	239.5	255.7	186.3	190.3	126.6	151.8	134.9
Average Shs. Outstg. (000)	26,487	26,078	23,676	23,934	23,564	23,562	23,424
BALANCE SHEET (IN MILLIONS):							
Cash & Cash Equivalents	21.4	21.7	44.0	13.4	11.5	12.1	14.9
Total Current Assets	410.6	558.3	376.1	306.9	253.1	207.5	195.3
Net Property	807.2	796.0	634.5	611.7	534.2	523.0	462.3
Total Assets	2,765.9	2,970.7	1,846.1	1,736.3	1,623.6	1,335.2	1,240.3
Total Current Liabilities	529.9	659.8	454.1	395.2	337.9	252.5	247.8
Long-Term Obligations	740.4	846.3	248.5	270.4	279.3	103.1	86.8
Net Stockholders' Equity	1,087.1	1,057.5	777.3	693.7	628.8	600.0	534.9
Net Working Capital	d119.3	d101.5	d78.0	d88.3	d84.8	d45.0	d52.5
Year-end Shs. Outstg. (000)	26,225	26,724	23,387	23,543	23,586	23,055	21,705
STATISTICAL RECORD:							
Operating Profit Margin %	9.6	9.9	8.7	9.8	8.3	8.2	9.2
Net Profit Margin %	3.6	5.4	5.2	5.8	2.7	5.6	5.3
Return on Equity %	8.6	12.5	12.2	14.9	6.6	12.4	12.0
Return on Assets %	3.4	4.5	5.1	5.9	2.6	5.6	5.2
Debt/Total Assets %	26.8	28.5	13.5	15.6	17.2	7.7	7.0
Price Range	45.00-29.75	60.00-36.75	68.38-33.06	61.50-38.38	43.00-28.38	33.88-22.38	34.00-21.63
P/E Ratio	12.7-8.4	11.8-7.2	17.1-8.3	14.3-8.9	24.3-16.0	10.8-7.1	12.4-7.9
Average Yield %	0.8	1.2	1.2	1.2	1.7	2.1	2.0

Statistics are as originally reported. 1 Incl. non-recurr. chrg. $35.0 mill. for the sale of assets 2 Incl. pre-tax nonrecurr. chrg. of $62.9 mill.

OFFICERS:
J. F. Fiedler, Chmn., C.E.O.
G. E. Strickler, Exec. V.P., C.F.O.
J. L. Obermayer, V.P, Treas.
L. H. Horiszny, V.P., Sec., Gen. Couns.

INVESTOR CONTACT: Mary Brevard, Dir. Investor Relations, (312) 322-8683

PRINCIPAL OFFICE: 200 South Michigan Avenue, Chicago, IL 60604

TELEPHONE NUMBER: (312) 322-8500
FAX: (312) 322-8683
WEB: www.bwauto.com

NO. OF EMPLOYEES: 14,000 (approx.)

SHAREHOLDERS: 3,084 (approx. record)

ANNUAL MEETING: In Apr.

INCORPORATED: DE, 1987

INSTITUTIONAL HOLDINGS:
No. of Institutions: 171
Shares Held: 22,720,787
% Held: 86.4

INDUSTRY: Motor vehicle parts and accessories (SIC: 3714)

TRANSFER AGENT(S): Mellon Investor Services, New York, NY

NYSE SYMBOL BXP
Rec. Pr. 39.88 (5/31/01)

BOSTON PROPERTIES, INC.

YIELD 5.8%
P/E RATIO 20.0

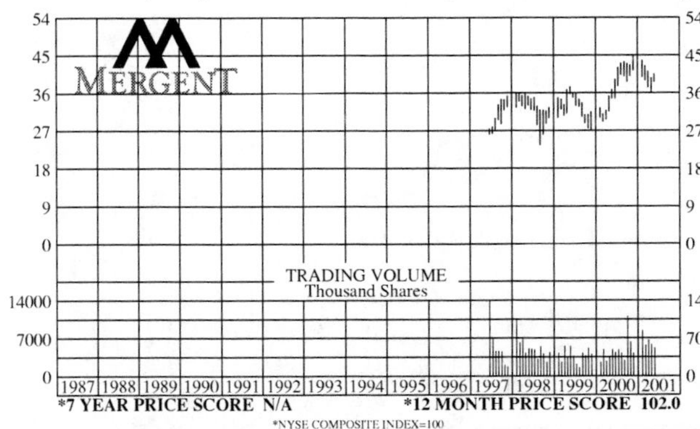

*7 YEAR PRICE SCORE N/A *12 MONTH PRICE SCORE 102.0

*NYSE COMPOSITE INDEX=100

INTERIM EARNINGS (Per Share):

Qtr.	Mar.	June	Sept.	Dec.
1998	0.36	0.48	0.40	0.37
1999	0.39	0.41	0.40	0.51
2000	0.45	0.50	0.52	0.52

INTERIM DIVIDENDS (Per Share):

Amt.	Decl.	Ex.	Rec.	Pay.
0.53Q	5/03/00	6/28/00	6/30/00	7/28/00
0.53Q	9/18/00	9/27/00	9/29/00	10/27/00
0.53Q	12/15/00	12/27/00	12/29/00	1/29/01
0.53Q	3/20/01	3/28/01	3/30/01	4/30/01
0.58Q	5/02/01	6/27/01	6/29/01	7/30/01

Indicated div.: $2.32

CAPITALIZATION (12/31/00):

	($000)	(%)
Long-Term Debt	3,414,891	56.5
Minority Interest	877,715	14.5
Redeemable Pfd. Stock	100,000	1.7
Common & Surplus	1,647,727	27.3
Total	6,040,333	100.0

RECENT DEVELOPMENTS: For the quarter ended 12/31/00, income before an extraordinary loss of $334,000 totaled $153.3 million versus net income of $119.8 million in 1999. Results included a net loss of $234,000 in 2000 and a gain of $6.5 million in 1999 on sales of real estate. Total revenue jumped 11.8% to $879.4 million versus $786.6 million a year earlier. Total rental revenue increased 12.2% to $858.9 million, while interest and other revenue jumped 33.2% to $8.6 million. Development and management services revenue fell 19.5% to $11.8 million.

PROSPECTS: On 4/25/01, BXP announced that it has completed its acquisition, through a joint venture with affiliates of Allied Partners, of the 59-story 1.6 million-square-foot Citigroup Center in New York City for approximately $755.0 million, including closing costs and mortgage-recording taxes. The Company will manage and lease the property, bringing to a total of 4.5 million square feet of office space that BXP owns and manages in Midtown Manhattan. Meanwhile, BXP is currently constructing two towers in Times Square that will total 2.3 million square feet.

BUSINESS

BOSTON PROPERTIES, INC. is a fully integrated, self-administered and self-managed real estate investment trust. The Company develops, redevelops, acquires, manages, operates and owns a diverse portfolio of office, industrial and hotel properties. The Company is one of the largest owners and developers of office properties in the United States, concentrated in four core markets: Boston, Washington DC, Midtown Manhattan and San Francisco. As of December 31, 2000, Boston Properties owned 144 properties totaling approximately 37.6 million square feet, including 15 properties currently under construction totaling 4.5 million square feet.

ANNUAL FINANCIAL DATA

	12/31/00	12/31/99	12/31/98	12/31/97	12/31/96	12/31/95
Earnings Per Share	**1 2 2.01**	**2 1.71**	**1 1.61**	**1 0.70**	...	...
Tang. Book Val. Per Share	**19.02**	**15.57**	**14.93**	**4.52**	...	...
Dividends Per Share	**1.96**	**1.73**	**1.64**	**0.44**	...	...
Dividend Payout %	**97.5**	**100.9**	**101.9**	**62.8**	...	...
INCOME STATEMENT (IN MILLIONS):						
Rental Income	715.4	646.9	419.8	126.4	169.4	155.6
Total Income	879.4	786.6	513.8	145.6	269.9	248.7
Costs & Expenses	300.4	278.7	173.0	46.8	115.7	109.8
Depreciation	133.2	120.1	75.4	21.7	36.2	33.8
Interest Expense	...	...	...	38.3	109.4	108.8
Income Before Income Taxes	230.3	189.3	140.6	38.9	8.7	d3.7
Equity Earnings/Minority Int.	d77.0	d69.5	d42.0	d11.4	d0.4	d0.3
Net Income	1 2 153.3	2 119.8	1 98.6	1 27.4	1 8.3	d4.0
Average Shs. Outstg. (000)	72,741	66,776	61,308	39,108	...	...
BALANCE SHEET (IN MILLIONS):						
Cash & Cash Equivalents	288.0	12.0	12.2	17.6	9.0	25.9
Total Assets	6,226.5	5,434.8	5,235.1	1,672.5	896.5	922.8
Long-Term Obligations	3,414.9	3,321.6	3,088.7	1,332.3	1,442.5	1,401.4
Total Liabilities	4,578.7	4,377.2	4,286.6	1,497.5	1,473.1	1,429.4
Net Stockholders' Equity	1,647.7	1,057.6	948.5	175.0	d576.6	d506.7
Year-end Shs. Outstg. (000)	86,630	67,910	63,528	38,694	...	...
STATISTICAL RECORD:						
Net Inc.+Depr./Assets %	4.6	4.4	3.3	2.9	5.0	...
Return on Equity %	9.3	11.3	10.4	15.7	...	...
Return on Assets %	2.5	2.2	1.9	1.6	0.9	...
Price Range	44.88-29.00	37.50-27.25	36.06-23.44	35.25-26.06	...	...
P/E Ratio	22.3-14.4	21.9-15.9	22.4-14.6	50.3-37.2	...	...
Average Yield %	5.3	5.3	5.5	1.4	...	...

Statistics are as originally reported. 1 Excl. an extraord. chrg., $5.5 mill., 2/98; gain, $7.9 mill., 12/97; chrg., $994,000, 12/96 2 Incl. gain on sale of real estate, $234,000, 12/00; $6.5 mill., 12/99

OFFICERS:
M. B. Zuckerman, Chmn.
E. H. Linde, Pres., C.E.O.
D. T. Linde, Sr. V.P., C.F.O.

INVESTOR CONTACT: Investor Relations, (617) 236-3300

PRINCIPAL OFFICE: 800 Boylston Street, Boston, MA 02199

TELEPHONE NUMBER: (617) 236-3300
FAX: (617) 536-3128
WEB: www.bostonproperties.com

NO. OF EMPLOYEES: 600 (avg.)

SHAREHOLDERS: 468 (approx.)

ANNUAL MEETING: In May

INCORPORATED: DE, March, 1997

INSTITUTIONAL HOLDINGS:
No. of Institutions: 197
Shares Held: 72,819,116
% Held: 80.8

INDUSTRY: Subdividers and developers, nec (SIC: 6552)

TRANSFER AGENT(S): EquiServe, Canton, MA

NYSE SYMBOL BSX
Rec. Pr. 17.32 (5/31/01)

BOSTON SCIENTIFIC CORPORATION

YIELD ...
P/E RATIO 18.8

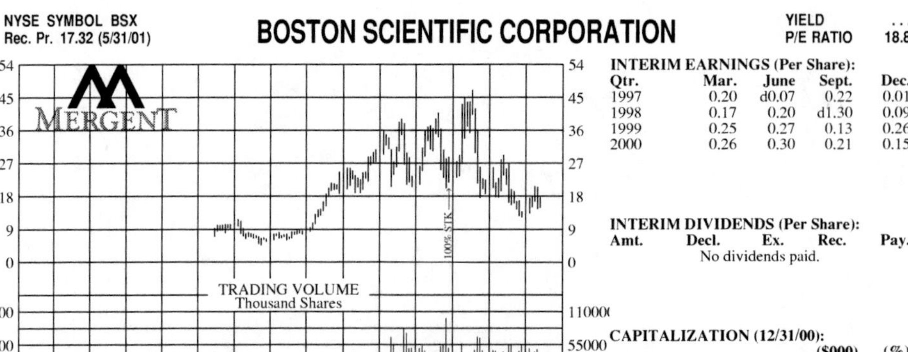

*7 YEAR PRICE SCORE 54.3 *12 MONTH PRICE SCORE 103.8
*NYSE COMPOSITE INDEX=100

INTERIM EARNINGS (Per Share):

Qtr.	Mar.	June	Sept.	Dec.
1997	0.20	d0.07	0.22	0.01
1998	0.17	0.20	d1.30	0.09
1999	0.25	0.27	0.13	0.26
2000	0.26	0.30	0.21	0.15

INTERIM DIVIDENDS (Per Share):

Amt.	Decl.	Ex.	Rec.	Pay.

No dividends paid.

CAPITALIZATION (12/31/00):

	($000)	(%)
Long-Term Debt	562,000	22.4
Capital Lease Obligations	12,000	0.5
Common & Surplus	1,935,000	77.1
Total	2,509,000	100.0

RECENT DEVELOPMENTS: For the twelve months ended 12/31/00, net income was $373.0 million compared with $371.0 million in the prior year. Results for 2000 included a pre-tax special charge of $58.0 million, while the 1999 results included a pre-tax special credit of $10.0 million. Net sales decreased 6.3% to $2.66 billion from $2.84 billion in the previous year. The decline in sales was attributed to issues related to its coronary stent and balloon pipeline.

PROSPECTS: BSX announced that it is launching its new Maverick® Balloon Dialation Catheter in the U.S. BSX believes the new catheter will set a new standard for balloon angioplasty. Separately, BSX received U.S. FDA approval to market the full product line of the NIROYAL™ Elite Monorail™ Coronary Stent System. Meanwhile, BSX signed a definitive agreement to acquire Interventional Technologies, Inc., a developer, manufacturer and marketer of minimally invasive devices for use for use in intervention cardiology, for about $345.0 million.

BUSINESS

BOSTON SCIENTIFIC CORPORATION is a developer, manufacturer and marketer of medical devices. The Company sells a broad range of products that are used by physicians to perform less invasive medical specialties, including cardiology, gastroenterology, pulmonary medicine, radiology, urology and vascular surgery. Less invasive procedures provide effective alternatives to traditional surgery by reducing procedural trauma, complexity, cost and recovery time. BSX's products are generally inserted into the human body through natural openings or small incisions in the skin and can be guided to most areas of the anatomy to diagnose and treat a wide range of medical problems.

QUARTERLY DATA

(12/31/2000) ($000)	REV	INC
1st Quarter	679,000	106,000
2nd Quarter	695,000	122,000
3rd Quarter	652,000	85,000
4th Quarter	638,000	60,000

ANNUAL FINANCIAL DATA

	12/31/00	12/31/99	12/31/98	12/31/97	12/31/96	12/31/95	12/31/94
Earnings Per Share	**7 0.91**	**6 0.92**	**5 d0.68**	**4 0.35**	**3 0.46**	**1 2 0.02**	**0.41**
Cash Flow Per Share	**1.36**	**1.33**	**d0.35**	**0.62**	**0.63**	**0.13**	**0.45**
Tang. Book Val. Per Share	**3.98**	**3.44**	**1.25**	**1.74**	**1.70**	**1.74**	**1.57**
INCOME STATEMENT (IN MILLIONS):							
Total Revenues	2,664.0	2,842.0	2,233.6	1,872.3	1,462.0	1,129.2	448.9
Costs & Expenses	1,903.0	1,975.0	2,312.4	1,516.6	1,091.1	1,014.8	309.8
Depreciation & Amort.	181.0	178.0	128.6	86.7	61.4	39.5	9.1
Operating Income	580.0	689.0	d207.4	269.0	309.5	74.9	130.0
Net Interest Inc./(Exp.)	d70.0	d118.0	d67.6	d14.3	d11.2	d9.6	d2.0
Income Before Income Taxes	527.0	562.0	d275.3	258.7	297.0	83.8	129.0
Income Taxes	154.0	191.0	cr10.9	98.3	129.9	77.4	49.2
Net Income	7 373.0	6 371.0	5 d264.4	4 160.4	3 167.1	1 2 6.4	79.7
Cash Flow	554.0	549.0	d135.8	247.1	228.5	46.0	88.8
Average Shs. Outstg. (000)	408,322	411,351	390,836	399,776	362,586	355,068	196,018
BALANCE SHEET (IN MILLIONS):							
Cash & Cash Equivalents	60.0	78.0	75.4	80.3	80.5	150.8	118.4
Total Current Assets	992.0	1,055.0	1,266.6	1,064.0	748.9	537.1	263.8
Net Property	567.0	604.0	679.9	499.0	347.2	253.8	113.2
Total Assets	3,427.0	3,572.0	3,892.7	1,967.8	1,512.1	1,075.3	431.8
Total Current Liabilities	819.0	1,055.0	1,619.7	808.0	463.8	270.5	73.7
Long-Term Obligations	574.0	678.0	1,363.8	46.3	...	13.2	8.9
Net Stockholders' Equity	1,935.0	1,724.0	821.1	986.2	916.3	752.5	340.0
Net Working Capital	173.0	...	d353.0	256.0	285.1	266.6	190.1
Year-end Shs. Outstg. (000)	399,848	409,049	394,186	387,622	356,916	353,308	194,160
STATISTICAL RECORD:							
Operating Profit Margin %	21.8	24.2	...	14.4	21.2	6.6	29.0
Net Profit Margin %	14.0	13.1	...	8.6	11.4	0.6	17.8
Return on Equity %	19.3	21.5	...	16.3	18.2	0.9	23.5
Return on Assets %	10.9	10.4	...	8.2	11.1	0.6	18.5
Debt/Total Assets %	16.7	19.0	35.0	2.4	...	1.2	2.1
Price Range	29.19-12.19	47.06-17.56	40.84-20.13	39.22-20.50	30.75-18.88	24.69-8.31	8.94-5.94
P/E Ratio	32.1-13.4	51.1-19.1	...	112.0-58.6	66.8-41.0	1,228.2-413.6	22.1-14.7

Statistics are as originally reported. Adj. for 2-for-1 stk. split 11/30/98. 1 Incl. after-tax and spec. chgs. of $195.3 mill. 2 Incl. acquired opers. of Meadox Medicals, Inc. Heart Technology, Inc., Scimed Life Systems, Inc., and Cardiovascular Imaging Systems, Inc.. 3 Incl. pre-tax nonrecurr. & spec. charges rel. to acqs. of $128.3 mill. 4 Incl. after-tax merger-rel. exps. of $192.0 mill. & excl. a net chg. of $21.1 mill. 5 Incl. spec. provs. $84.0 mill. & spec. credits of $20.0 mill. 6 Incl. a net credit of $10.0 mill. 7 Incl. a net chrg. of $58.0 mill.

OFFICERS:
P. M. Nicholas, Chmn.
J. R. Tobin, Pres., C.E.O.
L. C. Best, Sr. V.P., C.F.O.
INVESTOR CONTACT: Investor Relation, (508) 650-8555
PRINCIPAL OFFICE: One Boston Scientific Place, Natick, MA 01760-1537

TELEPHONE NUMBER: (508) 650-8000
FAX: (508) 647-2200
WEB: www.bsci.com
NO. OF EMPLOYEES: 13,720 (avg.)
SHAREHOLDERS: 10,082 (approx.)
ANNUAL MEETING: In May
INCORPORATED: DE, 1979

INSTITUTIONAL HOLDINGS:
No. of Institutions: 308
Shares Held: 185,885,557
% Held: 45.9
INDUSTRY: Surgical and medical instruments (SIC: 3841)
TRANSFER AGENT(S): EquiServe, L.P., Boston, MA

NYSE SYMBOL BOW
Rec. Pr. 48.50 (4/30/01)

BOWATER INC.

YIELD 1.6%
P/E RATIO 16.0

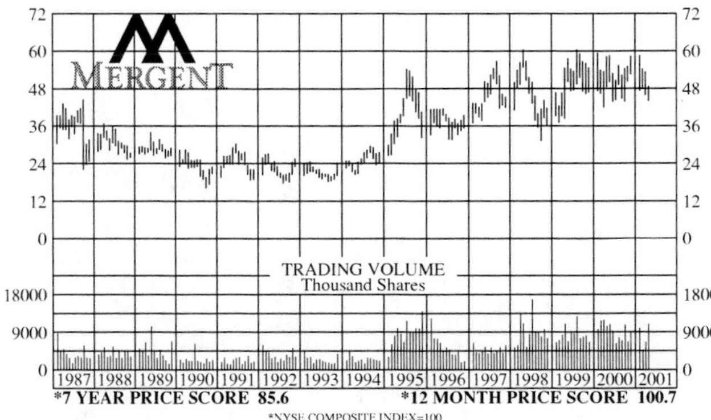

***7 YEAR PRICE SCORE 85.6** ***12 MONTH PRICE SCORE 100.7**

*NYSE COMPOSITE INDEX=100

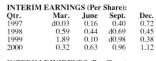

INTERIM EARNINGS (Per Share):

Qtr.	Mar.	June	Sept.	Dec.
1997	d0.03	0.16	0.40	0.72
1998	0.59	0.44	d0.69	0.45
1999	1.89	0.10	d0.98	0.38
2000	0.32	0.63	0.96	1.12

INTERIM DIVIDENDS (Per Share):

Amt.	Decl.	Ex.	Rec.	Pay.
0.20Q	5/10/00	6/08/00	6/12/00	7/03/00
0.20Q	7/26/00	9/07/00	9/11/00	10/02/00
0.20Q	11/08/00	12/07/00	12/11/00	1/02/01
0.20Q	1/31/01	3/08/01	3/12/01	4/02/01
0.20Q	5/09/01	6/07/01	6/11/01	7/02/01

Indicated div.: $0.80 (Div. Reinv. Plan)

CAPITALIZATION (12/31/00):

	($000)	(%)
Long-Term Debt	1,304,700	34.9
Deferred Income Tax	508,100	13.6
Minority Interest	123,600	3.3
Common & Surplus	1,797,100	48.1
Total	3,733,500	100.0

RECENT DEVELOPMENTS: For the year ended 12/31/00, net income increased 102.5% to $159.4 million compared with $78.7 million a year earlier. Net sales were $2.33 billion, up 9.3% from $2.13 billion a year earlier. Results for 1999 included an impairment of asset charge of $92.0 million. Results included a net gain on the sale of assets of $7.3 million in 2000 and $225.4 million in 1999.

PROSPECTS: On 1/8/01, the Company terminated negotiations with Sepoong Corporation and its major creditor, Chohung Bank, to acquire the Sepoong paper mill located in Kunsan, South Korea. BOW noted that there were unacceptable delays in satisfying certain conditions contemplated when the parties signed the previously announced preliminary letter of intent in September 2000.

BUSINESS

BOWATER INC. is a global producer of newsprint. In addition, the Company makes coated and uncoated groundwood papers, bleached kraft pulp and lumber products. BOW has nine pulp and paper mills in the United States, Canada and South Korea. The Company also owns and operates a coating operation and three sawmills that produce softwood dimension lumber. These operations are supported by 1.8 million acres of timberlands owned or leased in the United States and Canada and over 14.0 million acres of timber cutting rights in Canada. BOW completed the sale of its Great Northern Paper, Inc. subsidiary for $250.0 million in the third quarter of 1999. The Company is one of the world's largest consumers of recycled newspapers and magazines.

ANNUAL FINANCIAL DATA

	12/31/00	12/31/99	12/31/98	12/31/97	12/31/96	12/31/95	12/31/94
Earnings Per Share	**6 3.02**	**4 5 1.41**	**4 d0.44**	**1.25**	**3 4.71**	**2 5.60**	**1 d0.59**
Cash Flow Per Share	**62.45**	**52.14**	**52.55**	**5.48**	**8.96**	**10.16**	**4.47**
Tang. Book Val. Per Share	**18.50**	**14.80**	**15.98**	**27.89**	**27.93**	**23.91**	**17.43**
Dividends Per Share	**0.80**	**0.80**	**0.80**	**0.80**	**0.75**	**0.60**	**0.60**
Dividend Payout %	**26.5**	**56.7**	**...**	**64.0**	**15.9**	**10.7**	**...**
INCOME STATEMENT (IN MILLIONS):							
Total Revenues	2,333.7	2,134.7	1,995.0	1,484.5	1,718.3	2,001.1	1,359.0
Costs & Expenses	1,675.2	1,590.5	1,623.2	1,179.0	1,242.7	1,277.7	1,148.5
Depreciation & Amort.	295.2	300.2	229.6	169.8	174.4	174.2	168.4
Operating Income	363.3	244.0	142.2	135.7	301.2	549.3	42.1
Net Interest Inc./(Exp.)	d119.6	d119.0	d80.9	d45.9	d50.3	d71.6	d90.6
Income Before Income Taxes	239.4	155.8	16.8	89.5	353.2	464.6	d6.8
Income Taxes	70.3	71.5	27.1	33.1	124.4	183.1	cr4.8
Equity Earnings/Minority Int.	d9.5	d5.6	d8.2	d2.7	d24.7	d23.2	d2.8
Net Income	6 159.4	4 5 78.7	4 d18.5	53.7	3 204.1	2 258.2	1 d4.8
Cash Flow	3,297.1	2,867.6	2,501.5	220.9	365.8	414.5	146.7
Average Shs. Outstg. (000)	52,800	55,000	47,600	40,812	42,261	42,567	36,566
BALANCE SHEET (IN MILLIONS):							
Cash & Cash Equivalents	20.4	26.8	59.5	405.5	430.7	264.6	154.8
Total Current Assets	615.6	532.5	695.4	718.4	753.8	674.0	513.8
Net Property	2,981.1	2,581.3	2,885.2	1,554.5	1,636.7	1,711.0	1,785.0
Total Assets	5,004.1	4,552.2	5,091.4	2,745.8	2,865.5	2,908.2	2,851.4
Total Current Liabilities	951.4	397.8	772.5	194.7	253.9	285.3	210.6
Long-Term Obligations	1,304.7	1,454.6	1,534.6	757.1	759.0	816.5	1,116.9
Net Stockholders' Equity	1,797.1	1,770.8	1,777.0	1,154.2	1,171.1	1,095.4	887.4
Net Working Capital	d335.8	134.7	d77.1	523.7	499.9	388.7	303.2
Year-end Shs. Outstg. (000)	50,277	60,828	51,936	40,474	41,013	39,100	36,698
STATISTICAL RECORD:							
Operating Profit Margin %	15.6	11.4	7.1	9.1	17.5	27.4	3.1
Net Profit Margin %	6.8	3.7	...	3.6	11.9	12.9	...
Return on Equity %	8.8	4.4	...	4.7	17.4	23.6	...
Return on Assets %	3.2	1.7	...	2.0	7.1	8.9	...
Debt/Total Assets %	26.1	32.0	30.1	27.6	26.5	28.1	39.2
Price Range	59.56-21.75	60.56-36.94	60.50-31.19	57.00-36.88	41.63-31.50	54.38-26.38	29.63-20.38
P/E Ratio	19.7-13.9	42.9-26.2	...	45.6-29.5	8.8-6.7	9.7-4.7	...
Average Yield %	1.6	1.6	1.7	1.7	2.1	1.5	2.4

Statistics are as originally reported. 1 Incl. gains of $43.1 mill. fr. the sale of timberlands. 2 Incl. gains of $2.2 mill., chrgs. of $30 mill., restruct. chrgs. of $24 mill., bef. $7.1 mill. extraord. chrg. 3 Bef. an extraord. chrg. of $3.9 mill. ($0.09 a sh.); incl. pre-tax of $98.1 mill. 4 Incl. a chrg. of $120.0 mill. to reduce the book value of assets at the Millinocket, Maine paper mill, 1998; $92.0 mill., Great Northern Paper, Inc., 1999. 5 Incl. a pre-tax gain of $225.4 million. 6 Incl. nonrecurr. gain of $7.3 mill.

OFFICERS:
A. M. Nemirow, Chmn., Pres., C.E.O.
D. G. Maffucci, Sr. V.P., C.F.O.
A. Barash, Sr. V.P., Gen. Couns.

INVESTOR CONTACT: Donald J. D'Antuono, V.P. Corp. Development, (864) 282-9370

PRINCIPAL OFFICE: 55 East Camperdown Way, P. O. Box 1028, Greenville, SC 29602

TELEPHONE NUMBER: (864) 271-7733
FAX: (864) 282-9482
WEB: www.bowater.com

NO. OF EMPLOYEES: 6,400

SHAREHOLDERS: 4,284

ANNUAL MEETING: In May

INCORPORATED: DE, 1964

INSTITUTIONAL HOLDINGS:
No. of Institutions: 195
Shares Held: 46,889,070
% Held: 93.1

INDUSTRY: Paper mills (SIC: 2621)

TRANSFER AGENT(S): The Bank of New York, New York, NY

NYSE SYMBOL BP
Rec. Pr. 53.39 (5/31/01)

BP AMOCO P.L.C.

YIELD ...
P/E RATIO ...

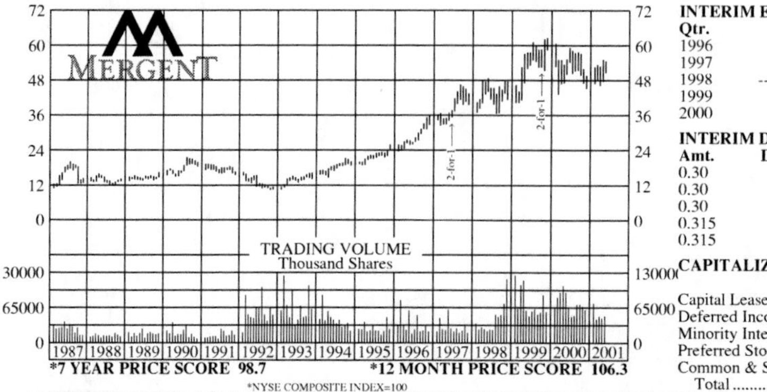

INTERIM EARNINGS (Per Share):

Qtr.	Mar.	June	Sept.	Dec.
1996	0.60	0.50	0.62	0.42
1997	0.52	0.64	0.59	0.51
1998	---------------- 1.02 ----------------			
1999	0.21	0.51	0.58	0.53
2000	0.95	0.83	0.92	0.63

INTERIM DIVIDENDS (Per Share):

Amt.	Decl.	Ex.	Rec.	Pay.
0.30	...	2/23/00	2/25/00	3/24/00
0.30	...	5/17/00	5/19/00	6/12/00
0.30	...	8/16/00	8/18/00	9/11/00
0.315	...	11/15/00	11/17/00	12/11/00
0.315	...	2/21/01	2/23/01	3/19/01

CAPITALIZATION (12/31/00):

	($000)	(%)
Capital Lease Obligations..	14,772,000	16.3
Deferred Income Tax	1,822,000	2.0
Minority Interest	585,000	0.6
Preferred Stock..................	21,000	0.0
Common & Surplus	73,395,000	81.0
Total	90,595,000	100.0

RECENT DEVELOPMENTS: For the twelve months ended 12/31/00, net income increased to $11.87 billion versus $5.01 billion a year earlier. Results for 2000 and 1999 included a profit of $220.0 million and a loss of $337.0 million, respectively, on the sale of fixed assets and businesses and termination of operations. Results for 1999 also included a restructuring charge of $1.94 billion. Revenues rose 77.2% to $148.06 billion from $83.57 billion in 1999.

PROSPECTS: On 6/3/01, BP announced the signing of an agreement for the Company to take a significant interest in a major Saudi Arabian gas development and hydrocarbons project. BP will share stakes with Shell, ExxonMobil and Phillips in the integrated Core Venture 1 project to find and develop gas reserves. Subject to negotiations, BP expects to invest up to $3.75 billion of the $15.00 billion cost of the project. ExxonMobil will lead the consortium.

BUSINESS

BP AMOCO, P.L.C. was formed through the 1/4/99 merger of British Petroleum Company, P.L.C. and U.S.-based Amoco Corp., creating one of the three largest energy companies in the world in terms of revenues, market value and oil and natural gas reserves. Principal operations include oil and natural gas exploration, development and production; oil supply, trading, refining and marketing; and chemicals manufacturing and marketing. Exploration and production activities are conducted in 25 countries; production operations in 21 countries. Operating assets include 24 wholly- or partly-owned refinery facilities and 29,000 service stations. The Company conducts its chemicals operations on 55 sites worldwide. On 4/18/00, BP completed its acquisition of Atlantic Richfield Company (ARCO).

ANNUAL FINANCIAL DATA

	[6] 12/31/00	12/31/99	12/31/98	[2] 12/31/97	12/31/96	12/31/95	12/31/94
Earnings Per Share	**[5] 3.27**	**[4] 1.55**	**[1] 1.03**	**[3] 2.20**	**[3] 2.34**	**[3] 0.95**	**1.37**
Tang. Book Val. Per Share	**2.54**	**2.05**	**4.00**	**3.78**	**3.55**	**3.04**	**2.89**
Dividends Per Share	**1.22**	**1.52**	**1.21**	**1.36**	**0.86**	**0.64**	**0.44**
Dividend Payout %	**37.3**	**98.1**	**117.5**	**61.8**	**36.8**	**67.4**	**32.1**
INCOME STATEMENT (IN MILLIONS):							
Total Revenues	148,062.0	83,566.0	68,304.0	72,960.6	75,796.7	56,072.6	51,826.5
Costs & Expenses	132,711.0	76,244.0	63,923.0	66,556.0	69,567.7	51,662.1	48,167.6
Operating Income	15,351.0	7,322.0	4,381.0	6,404.6	6,229.0	4,410.5	3,659.0
Net Interest Inc./(Exp.)	d1,770.0	d1,316.0	d1,053.0	d496.9	d696.4	d773.4	d848.2
Income Before Income Taxes	16,934.0	7,026.0	4,843.0	6,120.9	6,213.7	3,022.1	3,569.8
Income Taxes	4,972.0	1,880.0	1,520.0	1,960.8	1,875.8	1,287.4	1,083.0
Equity Earnings/Minority Int.	1,508.0	1,020.0	1,284.0	d13.4	d13.6	7.8	d18.8
Net Income	[5] 11,870.0	[4] 5,008.0	[1] 3,260.0	[3] 4,146.6	[3] 4,324.4	[3] 1,742.5	2,468.0
Average Shs. Outstg. (000)	21,783,000	19,497,000	9,596,000	5,702,000	5,613,000	5,538,000	5,474,000
BALANCE SHEET (IN MILLIONS):							
Cash & Cash Equivalents	1,831.0	1,551.0	875.0	278.7	259.3	613.4	294.2
Total Current Assets	40,119.0	23,477.0	17,226.0	16,274.3	18,219.3	15,130.9	13,923.8
Net Property	75,173.0	52,631.0	54,465.0	32,970.0	31,865.1	30,342.5	30,350.0
Total Assets	143,938.0	89,561.0	84,500.0	55,193.9	55,193.3	50,242.7	48,652.7
Total Current Liabilities	37,147.0	23,275.0	18,166.0	16,984.4	17,990.5	15,065.7	13,441.8
Long-Term Obligations	14,772.0	9,644.0	10,918.0	5,390.6	5,886.7	7,392.3	8,928.3
Net Stockholders' Equity	73,416.0	43,281.0	41,786.0	23,691.2	21,681.1	18,347.1	17,304.2
Net Working Capital	2,972.0	202.0	d940.0	d710.1	228.8	65.2	482.0
Year-end Shs. Outstg. (000)	22,258,746	19,484,024	9,683,000	5,763,000	5,650,000	5,575,000	5,575,000
STATISTICAL RECORD:							
Operating Profit Margin %	10.4	8.8	6.4	8.8	8.2	7.9	7.1
Net Profit Margin %	8.0	6.0	4.8	5.7	5.7	3.1	4.8
Return on Equity %	16.2	11.6	7.8	17.5	19.9	9.5	14.3
Return on Assets %	8.2	5.6	3.9	7.5	7.8	3.5	5.1
Debt/Total Assets %	10.3	10.8	12.9	9.8	10.7	14.7	18.4
Price Range	60.63-43.13	62.63-40.19	48.66-36.50	46.50-32.44	35.94-23.63	25.97-18.91	21.31-14.59
P/E Ratio	18.5-13.2	40.4-25.9	47.2-35.4	21.1-14.7	15.4-10.1	27.3-19.9	15.6-10.6
Average Yield %	2.3	3.0	2.8	3.5	2.9	2.8	2.4

Statistics are as originally reported. All figures are in U.S. dollars unless otherwise noted. All per sh. figs. & ratios are calculated using ADRs. One ADR=six ordinary shares. Exchange rates are as follows: $1US=£0.67, 12/31/00; £0.62, 12/31/99; £0.61, 12/31/98; £0.71, 12/31/97; £0.59, 12/31/96; £0.64, 12/31/95; £0.64, 12/31/94 [1] Incl. cr. of $623.0 mil [2] Prior results refl. ops. of British Petroleum only. [3] Incl. chrgs. 12/31/97, $57.0 mil; 12/31/96, $733.0 mil; 12/31/95, $1.41 bil [4] Incl. aft.-tax chrgs. of $2.05 bil [5] Incl. gain of $222.0 mil [6] Refl. acq. of Atlantic Richfield Company

OFFICERS:
P.D. Sutherland, Chmn.
J. Browne, Group Chief Exec.
J. G. S. Buchanan, C.F.O.

INVESTOR CONTACT: Investor Relations, (216) 584-4101 (U.S.)

PRINCIPAL OFFICE: Britannic House, 1 Finsbury Circus, London, United Kingdom

TELEPHONE NUMBER: (216) 584-4101 (U.S.)
WEB: www.bp.com

NO. OF EMPLOYEES: 98,000 (avg.)

SHAREHOLDERS: 365,905 (ordinary); 2051 (preference)

ANNUAL MEETING: In Apr.

INCORPORATED: U.K., 1909

INSTITUTIONAL HOLDINGS:
No. of Institutions: 833
Shares Held: 582,465,709
% Held: 15.5

INDUSTRY: Crude petroleum and natural gas (SIC: 1311)

DEPOSITARY BANKS(S): Morgan Guaranty Trust Company of New York, Boston, MA

NYSE SYMBOL BRC
Rec. Pr. 31.50 (5/31/01)

BRADY CORPORATION

YIELD 2.3%
P/E RATIO 16.2

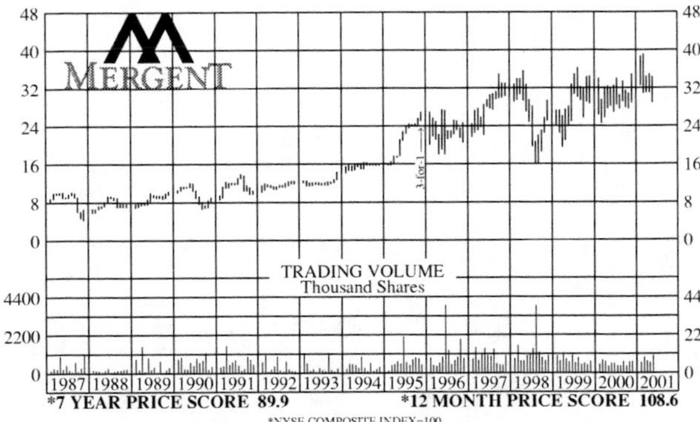

INTERIM EARNINGS (Per Share):

Qtr.	Oct.	Jan.	Apr.	July
1996-97	0.30	0.31	0.43	0.40
1997-98	0.37	0.31	0.44	0.11
1998-99	0.38	0.35	0.57	0.43
1999-00	0.54	0.43	0.51	0.57
2000-01	0.49	0.37	...	...

INTERIM DIVIDENDS (Per Share):

Amt.	Decl.	Ex.	Rec.	Pay.
0.17Q	5/16/00	7/06/00	7/10/00	7/31/00
0.18Q	9/12/00	10/05/00	10/10/00	10/31/00
0.18Q	11/15/00	1/09/01	1/11/01	1/31/01
0.18Q	2/20/01	4/06/01	4/10/01	4/30/01
0.18Q	5/15/01	7/09/01	7/11/01	7/31/01

Indicated div.: $0.72 (Div. Reinv. Plan)

CAPITALIZATION (7/31/00):

	($000)	(%)
Long-Term Debt	4,157	1.4
Preferred Stock	2,855	1.0
Common & Surplus	288,369	97.6
Total	295,381	100.0

RECENT DEVELOPMENTS: For the three months ended 1/31/01, net income totaled $8.6 million, down 12.3% compared with $9.8 million in the previous year. Net sales grew 3.4% to $133.7 million from $129.2 million a year earlier. U.S. sales increased 7.3%, while international sales slipped 0.9%, reflecting unfavorable foreign currency exchange rates. Operating income slid 8.6% to $14.1 million from $15.4 million the year before.

PROSPECTS: Earnings are being constrained by continued weakness in foreign currencies compared with the U.S. dollar, coupled with sluggish economic conditions, especially in the industrial segment of the U.S. Meanwhile, the Company is implementing several cost-control initiatives including freezing hiring, cutting overtime and reducing the use of contract workers, to help offset sluggish sales.

BUSINESS

BRADY CORPORATION (formerly W.H. Brady Co.) is an international manufacturer and marketer of identification and material solutions designed to help companies improve safety, security, productivity and performance. BRC's array of labels are used in applications ranging from marking wires and cables in facilities, electrical, telecommunication and transportation equipment to marking electronic components and printed circuit boards that require identification for purposes such as maintenance, work-in-process or asset tracking. Offerings ranging from signs, pipemakers, lockout/tagout devices, labels and tags to services including consulting, product installation and training enable companies to comply with safety and environmental regulations.

ANNUAL FINANCIAL DATA

	7/31/00	7/31/99	7/31/98	7/31/97	7/31/96	7/31/95	7/31/94
Earnings Per Share	**2.05**	**[1] 1.73**	**[1] 1.23**	**1.44**	**1.27**	**1.28**	**0.85**
Cash Flow Per Share	**2.84**	**2.41**	**1.83**	**1.05**	**0.88**	**1.71**	**1.29**
Tang. Book Val. Per Share	**8.95**	**8.87**	**7.87**	**7.64**	**6.96**	**7.69**	**6.54**
Dividends Per Share	**0.69**	**0.65**	**0.61**	**0.54**	**0.43**	**0.30**	**0.24**
Dividend Payout %	**33.7**	**37.6**	**49.6**	**37.5**	**33.9**	**23.5**	**27.8**
INCOME STATEMENT (IN THOUSANDS):							
Total Revenues	541,077	470,862	455,150	426,081	359,542	314,362	255,841
Costs & Expenses	453,953	391,941	395,932	361,562	307,775	264,618	216,931
Depreciation & Amort.	17,833	15,149	13,288	14,151	10,602	9,159	9,435
Operating Income	69,291	63,772	45,930	50,368	41,165	40,585	29,475
Net Interest Inc./(Exp.)	d578	d445	d403	d256	d302	d555	d410
Income Before Income Taxes	76,131	64,782	46,165	51,271	45,433	44,639	29,902
Income Taxes	28,930	25,198	18,129	19,564	17,406	16,728	11,362
Net Income	47,201	[1] 39,584	[1] 28,036	31,707	28,027	27,911	18,540
Cash Flow	64,775	54,474	41,065	45,599	38,370	36,811	27,716
Average Shs. Outstg.	22,933	22,683	22,602	43,816	43,694	21,681	21,678
BALANCE SHEET (IN THOUSANDS):							
Cash & Cash Equivalents	60,784	75,466	65,609	65,329	49,281	89,067	66,107
Total Current Assets	203,183	203,169	184,053	187,969	156,111	164,472	131,763
Net Property	80,660	66,984	67,165	62,442	65,649	58,573	64,343
Total Assets	398,134	351,120	311,824	291,662	261,835	230,005	202,509
Total Current Liabilities	87,099	73,285	58,667	57,245	46,423	34,534	31,740
Long-Term Obligations	4,157	1,402	3,716	3,890	1,809	1,903	1,855
Net Stockholders' Equity	291,224	260,564	233,373	206,547	189,263	170,823	145,129
Net Working Capital	116,084	129,884	125,386	130,724	109,688	129,938	100,023
Year-end Shs. Outstg.	20,962	20,835	22,496	21,941	21,863	21,831	21,738
STATISTICAL RECORD:							
Operating Profit Margin %	12.8	13.5	10.1	11.8	11.4	12.9	11.5
Net Profit Margin %	8.7	8.4	6.2	7.4	7.8	8.9	7.2
Return on Equity %	16.2	15.2	12.0	15.4	14.8	16.3	12.8
Return on Assets %	11.9	11.3	9.0	10.9	10.7	12.1	9.2
Debt/Total Assets %	1.0	0.4	1.2	1.3	0.7	0.8	0.9
Price Range	34.94-24.50	36.31-19.50	35.75-16.25	35.00-21.63	27.50-18.00	27.00-15.67	16.33-14.08
P/E Ratio	17.0-12.0	21.0-11.3	29.1-13.2	24.3-15.0	21.7-14.2	21.1-12.3	19.2-16.6
Average Yield %	2.3	2.3	2.3	1.9	1.9	1.4	1.6

Statistics are as originally reported. Adj. for stk. splits: 3-for-1, 12/95. [1] Incl. $611,000 non-recur. pre-tax gain, 1999; $5.4 mil chrg., 1998

OFFICERS:
K. M. Hudson, Pres., C.E.O.
F. M. Jaehnert, V.P., C.F.O.
T. E. Scherer, V.P., Contr., Asst. Sec.
P. J. Lettenberger, Sec.

INVESTOR CONTACT: Laurie Spiegelberg Bernardy, V.P., Corp. Comm., (414) 438-6880

PRINCIPAL OFFICE: 6555 West Good Hope Road, Milwaukee, WI 53223-0571

TELEPHONE NUMBER: (414) 358-6600
FAX: (414) 438-6910
WEB: www.bradycorp.com

NO. OF EMPLOYEES: 3,100 (approx.)

SHAREHOLDERS: 391 (class A); 2 (class B); 4,000 (beneficial)

ANNUAL MEETING: In Nov.

INCORPORATED: WI, 1939

INSTITUTIONAL HOLDINGS:
No. of Institutions: 99
Shares Held: 14,757,392
% Held: 64.6

INDUSTRY: Signs and advertising specialities (SIC: 3993)

TRANSFER AGENT(S): Firstar Bank, N.A., Milwaukee, WI

NYSE SYMBOL BGG
Rec. Pr. 40.50 (4/30/01)

BRIGGS & STRATTON CORPORATION

YIELD 3.1%
P/E RATIO 10.9

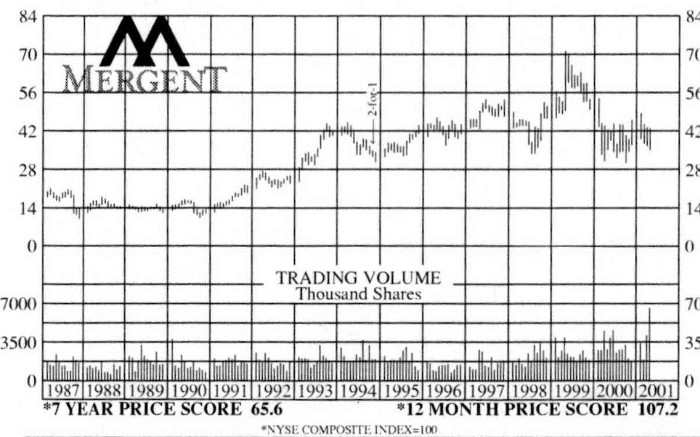

*7 YEAR PRICE SCORE 65.6 *12 MONTH PRICE SCORE 107.2

*NYSE COMPOSITE INDEX=100

INTERIM EARNINGS (Per Share):

Qtr.	Sept.	Dec.	Mar.	June
1995-96	d0.11	0.82	1.57	0.91
1996-97	d0.18	0.58	1.60	0.13
1997-98	d0.10	0.41	1.45	1.13
1998-99	0.19	1.05	1.79	1.51
1999-00	1.10	1.77	1.84	1.24
2000-01	d0.29	0.92	. . .	. . .

INTERIM DIVIDENDS (Per Share):

Amt.	Decl.	Ex.	Rec.	Pay.
0.30Q	4/19/00	5/30/00	6/01/00	6/30/00
0.31Q	8/02/00	8/22/00	8/24/00	10/02/00
0.31Q	10/16/00	11/29/00	12/01/00	1/02/01
0.31Q	1/17/01	2/27/01	3/01/01	4/02/01
0.31Q	4/18/01	5/30/01	6/01/01	6/29/01

Indicated div.: $1.24 (Div. Reinv. Plan)

CAPITALIZATION (7/2/00):

	($000)	(%)
Long-Term Debt	98,512	19.2
Deferred Income Tax	4,011	0.8
Common & Surplus	409,465	80.0
Total	511,988	100.0

RECENT DEVELOPMENTS: For the three months ended 12/31/00, net income declined 51.6% to $19.9 million compared with $41.1 million in the prior-year quarter. Net sales fell 12.9% to $367.8 million from $422.2 million in the corresponding year-earlier period. Results were negatively influenced by the effect of a strong dollar on exports to Europe, a shift in sales mix to smaller engines that contribute less gross profit dollars, lower production levels and greater interest expense.

PROSPECTS: Near-term results are likely to be pressured by continued weakness in the Euro compared with the prior year, higher interest expense and the projected lower utilization of production facilities resulting from the Company reducing its finished goods inventory. In addition, results in 2001 could be constrained by the negative effects of the slowing U.S. economy. Accordingly, the Company is now projecting earnings for fiscal 2001 to range between $70.0 and $75.0 million.

BUSINESS

BRIGGS & STRATTON CORPORATION is a producer of air cooled gasoline engines for outdoor power equipment. The Company designs, manufactures, markets and services these products for original equipment manufacturers (OEMs) worldwide. These engines are primarily aluminum alloy gasoline engines ranging from 3 through 25 horsepower. BGG's engines are used primarily by the lawn and garden equipment industry. The lawn and garden equipment applications include walk-behind lawn mowers, riding lawn mowers and garden tillers. Briggs & Stratton engines are marketed under various brand names including CLASSIC™, SPRINT™, QUATTRO™, QUANTUM®, INTEK™, IC®, INDUSTRIAL PLUS™ and VANGUARD™. On 2/27/95, the Company spun off its automotive lock business, Strattec Security Corporation. Dividends have been paid since 1929.

QUARTERLY DATA

(7/02/2000)($000)	Rev	Inc
First Quarter	298,933	25,703
Second Quarter	422,238	41,144
Third Quarter.............	468,678	42,056
Fourth Quarter...........	400,708	27,570

ANNUAL FINANCIAL DATA

	7/2/00	6/27/99	6/28/98	6/29/97	6/30/96	7/2/95	7/3/94
Earnings Per Share	**2 5.97**	**4.52**	**2.85**	**2.16**	**3.19**	**3.62**	**1 3.54**
Cash Flow Per Share	**8.22**	**6.64**	**4.78**	**3.68**	**4.68**	**5.16**	**5.03**
Tang. Book Val. Per Share	**18.51**	**15.45**	**12.87**	**13.40**	**17.17**	**15.19**	**13.96**
Dividends Per Share	**1.21**	**1.17**	**1.13**	**1.10**	**1.06**	**1.01**	**0.91**
Dividend Payout %	**20.3**	**25.9**	**39.6**	**50.9**	**33.2**	**27.9**	**25.7**
INCOME STATEMENT (IN MILLIONS):							
Total Revenues	1,590.6	1,501.7	1,327.6	1,316.4	1,287.0	1,339.7	1,285.5
Costs & Expenses	1,334.0	1,272.0	1,155.2	1,169.3	1,090.6	1,125.5	1,070.8
Depreciation & Amort.	51.4	49.6	47.7	43.4	43.0	44.4	43.0
Operating Income	205.2	180.1	124.7	103.7	153.4	169.8	171.7
Net Interest Inc./(Exp.)	d21.3	d17.0	d19.4	d9.9	d10.1	d8.6	d9.0
Income Before Income Taxes	216.6	169.8	113.1	99.3	149.1	170.4	169.7
Income Taxes	80.2	63.7	42.5	37.7	56.6	65.6	67.2
Net Income	2 136.5	106.1	70.6	61.6	92.4	104.8	1 102.5
Cash Flow	187.8	155.7	118.4	104.9	135.4	149.3	145.4
Average Shs. Outstg. (000)	22,842	23,459	24,775	28,551	28,927	28,927	28,927
BALANCE SHEET (IN MILLIONS):							
Cash & Cash Equivalents	17.0	60.8	84.5	112.9	150.6	170.6	221.1
Total Current Assets	472.0	459.1	382.0	418.4	452.7	453.3	482.8
Net Property	395.6	404.5	391.9	396.3	374.2	343.3	285.9
Total Assets	930.2	875.9	793.4	842.2	838.2	798.5	777.4
Total Current Liabilities	312.8	282.5	222.9	214.0	190.2	197.3	206.7
Long-Term Obligations	98.5	113.3	128.1	142.9	60.0	75.0	75.0
Net Stockholders' Equity	409.5	365.9	316.5	351.1	500.5	439.5	403.8
Net Working Capital	159.2	176.6	159.1	204.4	262.5	256.1	276.0
Year-end Shs. Outstg. (000)	21,746	23,200	23,824	25,414	28,927	28,927	28,927
STATISTICAL RECORD:							
Operating Profit Margin %	12.9	12.0	9.4	7.9	11.9	12.7	13.4
Net Profit Margin %	8.6	7.1	5.3	4.7	7.2	7.8	8.0
Return on Equity %	33.3	29.0	22.3	17.5	18.5	23.8	25.4
Return on Assets %	14.7	12.1	8.9	7.3	11.0	13.1	13.2
Debt/Total Assets %	10.6	12.9	16.1	17.0	7.2	9.4	9.6
Price Range	53.88-30.38	71.13-46.69	52.44-33.63	53.63-42.63	46.88-36.50	44.13-32.25	45.13-30.50
P/E Ratio	9.0-5.1	15.7-10.3	18.4-11.8	24.8-19.7	14.7-11.4	12.2-8.9	12.7-8.6
Average Yield %	2.9	2.0	2.6	2.3	2.5	2.6	2.4

Statistics are as originally reported. Adj. for 2-for-1 stk. split, 11/94. 1 Bef. acctg. chg. of $32.6 mill.; incls. non-recurr. credit of $2.8 mill. 2 Incl. non-recurr. gain $16.5 mill.

OFFICERS:
F. P. Stratton Jr., Chmn., C.E.O.
J. S. Shiely, Pres., C.O.O.
J. E. Brenn, Sr. V.P., C.F.O.
C. R. Twinem, Treas.

INVESTOR CONTACT: G. R. Thompson, V.P., Corp. Comm., (414) 259-5312

PRINCIPAL OFFICE: 12301 West Wirth Street, Wauwatosa, WI 53222

TELEPHONE NUMBER: (414) 259-5333
FAX: (414) 259-9594
WEB: www.briggsandstratton.com

NO. OF EMPLOYEES: 7,233 (avg.)

SHAREHOLDERS: 4,345

ANNUAL MEETING: In Oct.

INCORPORATED: WI, Oct., 1924; reincorp., WI, Oct., 1992

INSTITUTIONAL HOLDINGS:
No. of Institutions: 184
Shares Held: 17,421,829
% Held: 80.7

INDUSTRY: Internal combustion engines, nec (SIC: 3519)

TRANSFER AGENT(S): Firstar Trust Company, Milwaukee, WI

NYSE SYMBOL EAT
Rec. Pr. 24.55 (5/31/01)

BRINKER INTERNATIONAL, INC.

YIELD ...
P/E RATIO 20.3

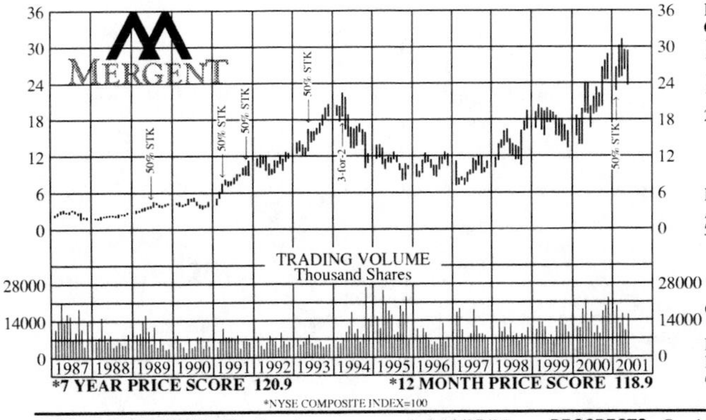

TRADING VOLUME
Thousand Shares

*7 YEAR PRICE SCORE 120.9 *12 MONTH PRICE SCORE 118.9
*NYSE COMPOSITE INDEX=100

INTERIM EARNINGS (Per Share):

Qtr.	Sept.	Dec.	Mar.	June
1996-97	0.14	0.10	0.12	0.19
1997-98	0.17	0.13	0.16	0.23
1998-99	0.21	0.17	0.21	0.27
1999-00	0.27	0.25	0.29	0.36
2000-01	0.35	0.21	...	...

INTERIM DIVIDENDS (Per Share):

Amt.	Decl.	Ex.	Rec.	Pay.
50% STK	12/08/00	1/17/01	1/03/01	1/16/01

CAPITALIZATION (6/28/00):

	($000)	(%)
Long-Term Debt	110,323	12.5
Deferred Income Tax	7,667	0.9
Common & Surplus	762,208	86.6
Total	880,198	100.0

RECENT DEVELOPMENTS: For the quarter ended 12/27/00, net income advanced 26.7% to $32.2 million compared with $25.4 million a year earlier. Revenues rose 12.0% to $583.3 million, due to higher comparable same-store sales for the Company's CHILI'S and MACARONI GRILL restaurants, which grew 6.0% and 3.4%, respectively. Meanwhile, comparable same-store sales for ON THE BORDER restaurants were down 4.6%. Operating income rose 20.6% to $52.5 million from $43.5 million in 1999.

PROSPECTS: On 11/20/00, the Company announced it has reached an agreement with NE Restaurant Company, Inc. to acquire 40 CHILI'S and seven ON THE BORDER restaurants from the franchise partner in a transaction valued at about $93.0 million. In addition, EAT will acquire four future CHILI'S restaurant sites currently under construction as well as development rights for both brands in Massachusetts, Connecticut, Vermont, New Hampshire, Rhode Island, Maine and areas of New York State.

BUSINESS

BRINKER INTERNATIONAL, INC. (formerly Chili's, Inc.) operates and develops full-service restaurants. As of 12/27/00, the Company owned, operated or franchised 1,109 restaurants under the names CHILI'S GRILL & BAR, ROMANO'S MACARONI GRILL, ON THE BORDER MEXICAN GRILL & CANTINA, COZYMEL'S COASTAL MEXICAN GRILL, MAGGIANO'S LITTLE ITALY, CORNER BAKERY CAFE, EATZI'S MARKET & BAKERY, WILDFIRE and BIG BOWL. CHILI'S operates full-service restaurants, featuring a casual atmosphere and limited menu of broadly appealing food items. ROMANO'S operates upscale and casual full-service Italian-theme restaurants. ON THE BORDER is a full-service, casual, Tex-Mex theme restaurant featuring Southwest specialties. COZYMEL'S restaurants are casual and upscale, authentic Mexican restaurants.

QUARTERLY DATA

(06/28/00)($000)	Rev	Inc
1st Quarter	511,033	27,106
2nd Quarter	520,900	25,422
3rd Quarter	551,191	28,602
4th Quarter	576,713	36,710

ANNUAL FINANCIAL DATA

	6/28/00	6/30/99	6/24/98	6/25/97	6/26/96	6/28/95	6/29/94
Earnings Per Share	**1.17**	**2 0.83**	**0.68**	**0.54**	**1 0.29**	**0.65**	**0.55**
Cash Flow Per Share	**2.08**	**1.64**	**1.54**	**1.24**	**0.85**	**1.18**	**1.01**
Tang. Book Val. Per Share	**6.99**	**5.94**	**5.23**	**4.55**	**4.62**	**4.53**	**3.84**
INCOME STATEMENT (IN MILLIONS):							
Total Revenues	2,159.8	1,870.6	1,574.4	1,335.3	1,163.0	1,042.2	878.5
Costs & Expenses	1,871.4	1,634.0	1,370.1	1,159.7	1,055.1	874.8	732.3
Depreciation & Amort.	92.8	82.4	86.4	78.8	64.6	58.6	51.5
Operating Income	195.7	154.2	117.9	96.9	43.3	108.9	94.6
Net Interest Inc./(Exp.)	d10.7	d9.2	d11.0	d9.5	d4.6	d0.6	d0.4
Income Before Income Taxes	181.5	130.5	105.5	91.0	52.1	111.4	95.4
Income Taxes	63.7	45.3	36.4	30.5	17.8	38.7	33.8
Net Income	117.8	2 85.2	69.1	60.5	1 34.4	72.7	61.6
Cash Flow	210.6	167.6	155.5	139.3	99.0	131.3	113.1
Average Shs. Outstg. (000)	101,115	102,185	101,175	112,200	116,853	111,425	111,858
BALANCE SHEET (IN MILLIONS):							
Cash & Cash Equivalents	12.3	12.6	31.2	47.7	27.1	38.8	3.6
Total Current Assets	103.6	103.2	105.5	112.4	88.4	94.0	47.2
Net Property	888.1	813.4	708.6	749.6	611.2	568.1	434.2
Total Assets	1,162.3	1,085.6	989.4	996.9	888.8	732.8	558.7
Total Current Liabilities	231.0	190.1	198.1	155.7	123.4	96.4	103.4
Long-Term Obligations	110.3	183.2	147.3	287.5	117.8	103.1	5.7
Net Stockholders' Equity	762.2	661.4	593.7	523.7	608.2	496.8	417.3
Net Working Capital	d127.4	d87.0	d92.6	d43.3	d35.0	d2.4	d56.2
Year-end Shs. Outstg. (000)	98,800	98,849	98,889	97,836	115,884	108,111	106,545
STATISTICAL RECORD:							
Operating Profit Margin %	9.1	8.2	7.5	7.3	3.7	10.4	10.8
Net Profit Margin %	5.5	4.6	4.4	4.5	3.0	7.0	7.0
Return on Equity %	15.5	12.9	11.6	11.6	5.7	14.6	14.8
Return on Assets %	10.1	7.9	7.0	6.1	3.9	9.9	11.0
Debt/Total Assets %	9.5	16.9	14.9	28.8	13.3	14.1	1.0
Price Range	28.88-13.83	20.42-13.25	19.50-10.00	11.92-7.08	12.67-8.50	13.92-7.92	22.45-10.00
P/E Ratio	24.7-11.9	24.5-15.9	28.7-14.7	22.1-13.1	43.2-29.0	21.3-12.1	40.6-18.1

Statistics are as originally reported. Adj. for stk. splits: 50.0%, 1/01; 3-for-2, 3/94 1 Incl. non-recurr. chrg. $50.0 mill. & credit $9.3 mill. 2 Bef. acctg. charge of $6.4 mill.

OFFICERS:
R. A. McDougall, Chmn., C.E.O.
D. H. Brooks, Pres., C.O.O.
C. Sonsteby, Exec. V.P., C.F.O.

INVESTOR CONTACT: Charles M. Stosteby, Sr. V.P., Inv. Rel., (972) 770-9406

PRINCIPAL OFFICE: 6820 LBJ Freeway, Dallas, TX 75240

TELEPHONE NUMBER: (972) 980-9917
FAX: (972) 770-9593
WEB: www.brinker.com

NO. OF EMPLOYEES: 68,000 (approx.)

SHAREHOLDERS: 1,254

ANNUAL MEETING: In Nov.

INCORPORATED: DE, Sept., 1983

INSTITUTIONAL HOLDINGS:
No. of Institutions: 235
Shares Held: 136,785,956 (Adj.)
% Held: 91.4

INDUSTRY: Eating places (SIC: 5812)

TRANSFER AGENT(S): Mellon Investor Services, LLC, Dallas, TX

NYSE SYMBOL BMY
Rec. Pr. 54.24 (5/31/01)

BRISTOL-MYERS SQUIBB COMPANY

YIELD 2.0%
P/E RATIO 26.5

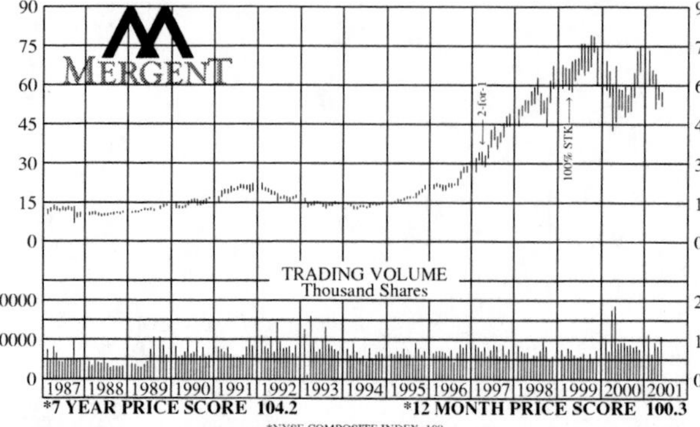

*7 YEAR PRICE SCORE 104.2 *12 MONTH PRICE SCORE 100.3

*NYSE COMPOSITE INDEX=100

INTERIM EARNINGS (Per Share):

Qtr.	Mar.	June	Sept.	Dec.
1997	0.41	0.37	0.43	0.39
1998	0.46	0.41	0.48	0.21
1999	0.53	0.47	0.54	0.52
2000	0.56	0.50	0.45	0.54

INTERIM DIVIDENDS (Per Share):

Amt.	Decl.	Ex.	Rec.	Pay.
0.245Q	6/06/00	7/05/00	7/07/00	8/01/00
0.245Q	9/12/00	10/04/00	10/06/00	11/01/00
0.275Q	12/05/00	1/03/01	1/05/01	2/01/01
0.275Q	3/06/01	4/04/01	4/06/01	5/01/01
0.275Q	6/05/01	7/03/01	7/06/01	8/01/01

Indicated div.: $1.10 (Div. Reinv. Plan)

CAPITALIZATION (12/31/00):

	($000)	(%)
Long-Term Debt	1,336,000	12.7
Common & Surplus	9,180,000	87.3
Total	10,516,000	100.0

RECENT DEVELOPMENTS: For the year ended 12/31/00, BMY posted income from continuing operations of $4.10 billion versus income from continuing operations of $3.79 billion in the previous year. Results for 2000 included a provision for restructuring of $386.0 million, a pre-tax gain of $160.0 million on the sale of businesses and excluded a gain of $375.0 million on discontinued operations. Net sales jumped 7.9% to $18.22 billion from $16.88 billion the year before.

PROSPECTS: On 2/22/01, the Company announced its intention to separate its orthopaedics subsidiary Zimmer, Inc. into an independent publicly traded entity, through a tax-free distribution to BMY shareholders. The Company expects to establish Zimmer as an independent publicly traded company by 9/30/01. Separately, on 2/6/01, the Company announced that it will conduct clinical studies to access the safety and efficacy of GLUCOVANCE® in children aged 10 and over with type 2 diabetes.

BUSINESS

BRISTOL-MYERS SQUIBB COMPANY, through its divisions and subsidiaries, is a major producer and distributor of medicines. Major products include PRAVACHOL (10.0% of 2000 sales), a cholesterol-lowering agent; GLUCOPHAGE (9.5%), an oral medication for treatment of non-insulin dependent (type 2) diabetes; and TAXOL (8.7%), an anticancer agent. As of 12/31/00, the Company had 54 product lines with more than $50.0 million in annual sales, including 31 with more than $100.0 million in annual sales. On 9/28/00, BMY announced the planned divestiture of its Clairol and Zimmer businesses in 2001.

ANNUAL FINANCIAL DATA

	12/31/00	12/31/99	12/31/98	12/31/97	12/31/96	12/31/95	12/31/94
Earnings Per Share	[4] **2.05**	**2.06**	[3] **1.55**	[2] **1.57**	**1.42**	[1] **0.90**	**0.91**
Cash Flow Per Share	**2.42**	**2.39**	**1.85**	**1.86**	**1.68**	**1.12**	**1.07**
Tang. Book Val. Per Share	**3.96**	**3.61**	**3.01**	**2.82**	**2.53**	**2.28**	**2.35**
Dividends Per Share	**0.98**	**0.86**	**0.78**	**0.76**	**0.75**	**0.74**	**0.73**
Dividend Payout %	**47.8**	**41.7**	**50.3**	**48.4**	**52.8**	**82.7**	**80.7**
INCOME STATEMENT (IN MILLIONS):							
Total Revenues	18,216.0	20,222.0	18,284.0	16,701.0	15,065.0	13,767.0	11,984.0
Costs & Expenses	11,992.0	13,691.0	12,337.0	11,897.0	10,593.0	10,014.0	8,435.0
Depreciation & Amort.	746.0	678.0	625.0	591.0	519.0	448.0	328.0
Operating Income	5,478.0	5,853.0	5,322.0	4,213.0	3,953.0	3,305.0	3,221.0
Net Interest Inc./(Exp.)	...	...	d67.0	d12.0	17.0	42.0	56.0
Income Before Income Taxes	5,478.0	5,767.0	4,268.0	4,482.0	4,013.0	2,402.0	2,555.0
Income Taxes	1,382.0	1,600.0	1,127.0	1,277.0	1,163.0	590.0	713.0
Net Income	[4] 4,096.0	4,167.0	[3] 3,141.0	[2] 3,205.0	2,850.0	[1] 1,812.0	1,842.0
Cash Flow	4,842.0	4,845.0	3,766.0	3,796.0	3,369.0	2,260.0	2,170.0
Average Shs. Outstg. (000)	1,997,000	2,027,000	2,031,000	2,042,000	2,008,000	2,024,000	2,036,000
BALANCE SHEET (IN MILLIONS):							
Cash & Cash Equivalents	3,385.0	2,957.0	2,529.0	1,794.0	2,185.0	2,178.0	2,423.0
Total Current Assets	9,824.0	9,267.0	8,782.0	7,736.0	7,528.0	7,018.0	6,710.0
Net Property	4,548.0	4,621.0	4,429.0	4,156.0	3,964.0	3,760.0	3,666.0
Total Assets	17,578.0	17,114.0	16,272.0	14,977.0	14,685.0	13,929.0	12,910.0
Total Current Liabilities	5,632.0	5,537.0	5,791.0	5,032.0	5,050.0	4,806.0	4,274.0
Long-Term Obligations	1,336.0	1,342.0	1,364.0	1,279.0	966.0	635.0	644.0
Net Stockholders' Equity	9,180.0	8,645.0	7,576.0	7,219.0	6,570.0	5,823.0	5,705.0
Net Working Capital	4,192.0	3,730.0	2,991.0	2,704.0	2,478.0	2,212.0	2,436.0
Year-end Shs. Outstg. (000)	1,953,535	1,980,806	1,988,000	1,986,000	2,002,000	2,020,000	2,028,000
STATISTICAL RECORD:							
Operating Profit Margin %	30.1	28.9	29.1	25.2	26.2	24.0	26.9
Net Profit Margin %	22.5	20.6	17.2	19.2	18.9	13.2	15.4
Return on Equity %	44.6	48.2	41.5	44.4	43.4	31.1	32.3
Return on Assets %	23.3	24.3	19.3	21.4	19.4	13.0	14.3
Debt/Total Assets %	7.6	7.8	8.4	8.5	6.6	4.6	5.0
Price Range	74.88-42.44	79.25-57.25	67.63-44.16	49.09-26.63	29.09-19.50	21.78-14.44	15.25-12.50
P/E Ratio	36.5-20.7	38.5-27.8	43.6-28.5	31.3-17.0	20.5-13.7	24.3-16.1	16.8-13.8
Average Yield %	1.7	1.3	1.4	2.0	3.1	4.1	5.3

Statistics are as originally reported. Adj. for 2-for-1 stk. split, 2/97 & 2/99. [1] Incl. spec. after-tax chg. of $590.0 mill. & $98.0 mill. prov. for litigation. [2] Incl. pre-tax prov. of $225.0 mill. for restr. & $225.0 mill. gain on sale of a bus. [3] Incl. spec. chg. of $800.0 mill., pre-tax prov. for restr. of $201.0 mill., & gain of $201.0 mill. [4] Bef. inc. fr. disc. ops. of $615.0 mill.; Incl. a pre-tax prov. of $508.0 mill. & gain of $160.0 mill.

OFFICERS:
C. A. Heimbold Jr., Chmn., C.E.O.
P. R. Dolan, Pres., C.E.O. -Designate

INVESTOR CONTACT: Investor Relations, (212) 546-4000

PRINCIPAL OFFICE: 345 Park Avenue, New York, NY 10154-0037

TELEPHONE NUMBER: (212) 546-4000
FAX: (212) 546-4020
WEB: www.bms.com

NO. OF EMPLOYEES: 44,000 (approx.)

SHAREHOLDERS: 114,096 (approx.)

ANNUAL MEETING: In May

INCORPORATED: DE, Aug., 1933

INSTITUTIONAL HOLDINGS:
No. of Institutions: 1,122
Shares Held: 1,195,408,838
% Held: 61.3

INDUSTRY: Pharmaceutical preparations (SIC: 2834)

TRANSFER AGENT(S): Mellon Investor Services, Ridgefield Park, NJ

NYSE SYMBOL BRW
Rec. Pr. 24.80 (4/30/01)

BROADWING, INC.

YIELD ...
P/E RATIO ...

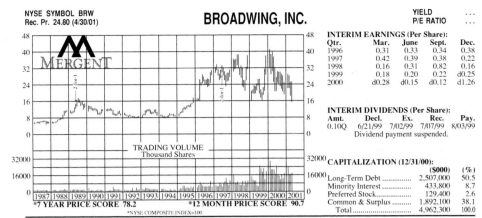

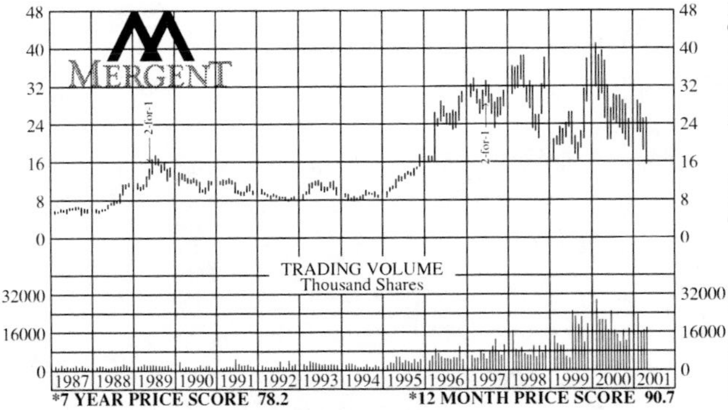

MERGENT

TRADING VOLUME
Thousand Shares

1987 1988 1989 1990 1991 1992 1993 1994 1995 1996 1997 1998 1999 2000 2001

*7 YEAR PRICE SCORE 78.2 *12 MONTH PRICE SCORE 90.7

*NYSE COMPOSITE INDEX=100

INTERIM EARNINGS (Per Share):

Qtr.	Mar.	June	Sept.	Dec.
1996	0.31	0.33	0.34	0.38
1997	0.42	0.39	0.38	0.22
1998	0.16	0.31	0.82	0.16
1999	0.18	0.20	0.22	d0.25
2000	d0.28	d0.15	d0.12	d1.26

INTERIM DIVIDENDS (Per Share):

Amt.	Decl.	Ex.	Rec.	Pay.
0.10Q	6/21/99	7/02/99	7/07/99	8/03/99

Dividend payment suspended.

CAPITALIZATION (12/31/00):

	($000)	(%)
Long-Term Debt	2,507,000	50.5
Minority Interest	433,800	8.7
Preferred Stock	129,400	2.6
Common & Surplus	1,892,100	38.1
Total	4,962,300	100.0

RECENT DEVELOPMENTS: For the year ended 12/31/00, BRW posted a loss from continuing operations of $376.5 million versus income from continuing operations of $34.6 million a year earlier. Results for 2000 included a restructuring credit of $800,000 and a net loss on investments of $356.3 million. Results for 1999 included a restructuring charge of $10.8 million. Revenues totaled $2.05 billion compared with $1.10 billion in 1999.

PROSPECTS: Results are being driven by growth from BRW's Broadband Services segment, which includes 11 fully operational Web-hosting centers offering an array of services from optical transport to Web hosting and managed services. Also, demand for asymmetrical digital subscriber line (ASDL) service remains positive. BRW's ASDL offerings include high-speed Internet access, pay-per-use movies, streaming media, and high-speed gaming.

BUSINESS

BROADWING, INC. (formerly Cincinnati Bell, Inc.) is a full service provider of wireline and wireless telecommunications services. The Broadband segment utilizes BRW's optical network consisting of more than 18,000 route miles to provide broadband transport, Internet services and switched long distance. The Broadband segment offers data collocation, information technology consulting, network construction and other services. The Local Communications segment provides local telephone service, network access, data transport, high-speed Internet access, switched long distance and other products and services. The Wireless segment is comprised of the operations of the Company's CBW subsidiary, an 80.1%-owned venture, as of 12/31/00, with AT&T PCS, Inc. The Other Communications segment combines the operations of BRW's Cincinnati Bell Any Distance, Cincinnati Bell Directory, ZoomTown.com and Cincinnati Bell Public Communications Inc. On 12/31/98, the Company spun off Convergys Corporation. On 11/9/99, Cincinnati Bell Inc. acquired IXC Communications, Inc. to form Broadwing, Inc.

ANNUAL FINANCIAL DATA

	12/31/00	12/31/99	12/31/98	12/31/97	12/31/96	12/31/95	12/31/94
Earnings Per Share	**[8] d1.82**	**[6] 0.24**	**[1] 0.59**	**[2] 1.41**	**[3] 1.35**	**[4] d0.19**	**[5] 0.58**
Cash Flow Per Share	**0.35**	**1.44**	**1.40**	**2.75**	**2.61**	**1.03**	**1.75**
Tang. Book Val. Per Share	**...**	**...**	**0.28**	**2.83**	**3.18**	**2.29**	**2.69**
Dividends Per Share	**...**	**0.30**	**0.40**	**0.40**	**0.40**	**0.40**	**0.40**
Dividend Payout %	**...**	**124.9**	**67.8**	**28.4**	**29.6**	**...**	**69.6**
INCOME STATEMENT (IN MILLIONS):							
Total Revenues	2,050.1	1,131.1	885.1	1,756.8	1,573.7	1,336.1	1,228.2
Costs & Expenses	1,551.3	806.3	595.1	1,244.3	1,124.1	956.0	903.0
Depreciation & Amort.	459.7	181.0	111.1	185.4	172.8	162.2	154.1
Operating Income	39.1	143.8	180.0	313.1	306.5	46.7	165.4
Net Interest Inc./(Exp.)	d163.6	d61.7	d24.2	d35.5	d33.9	d52.8	d49.5
Income Before Income Taxes	d542.1	71.3	126.1	296.9	284.7	d19.6	117.6
Income Taxes	cr165.6	33.3	44.3	103.3	99.7	5.7	42.1
Net Income	[8] d376.5	[6] 38.0	[1] 81.8	[2] 193.6	[3] 185.0	[4] d25.3	[5] 75.5
Cash Flow	75.1	216.9	192.9	379.0	357.8	136.9	229.6
Average Shs. Outstg. (000)	211,700	150,700	138,200	137,700	137,178	132,542	130,886
BALANCE SHEET (IN MILLIONS):							
Cash & Cash Equivalents	37.9	80.0	10.1	9.9	2.0	2.9	78.4
Total Current Assets	462.7	413.4	197.4	450.0	390.6	341.4	398.6
Net Property	2,966.2	2,500.9	698.2	703.2	985.8	993.9	1,036.2
Total Assets	6,477.6	[7] 6,508.6	1,041.0	1,498.7	1,670.9	1,591.7	1,723.4
Total Current Liabilities	727.3	568.1	405.3	534.9	512.3	453.3	383.3
Long-Term Obligations	2,507.0	2,136.0	366.8	269.2	279.5	386.8	528.3
Net Stockholders' Equity	2,021.5	2,361.4	142.1	579.7	634.4	478.1	552.4
Net Working Capital	d264.6	d154.7	d207.9	d84.9	d121.7	d111.9	15.3
Year-end Shs. Outstg. (000)	215,530	200,872	136,382	136,100	135,200	133,400	131,896
STATISTICAL RECORD:							
Operating Profit Margin %	1.9	12.7	20.3	17.8	19.5	3.5	13.5
Net Profit Margin %	...	3.4	9.2	11.0	11.8	...	6.1
Return on Equity %	...	1.6	57.6	33.4	29.2	...	13.7
Return on Assets %	...	0.6	7.9	12.9	11.1	...	4.4
Debt/Total Assets %	38.7	32.8	35.2	18.0	16.7	24.3	30.7
Price Range	41.06-19.06	37.88-16.06	38.63-20.88	33.75-23.06	30.81-15.88	17.63-8.44	10.06-7.69
P/E Ratio	...	157.7-66.9	65.5-35.4	23.9-16.4	22.8-11.8	...	17.5-13.4
Average Yield %	...	1.1	1.3	1.4	1.7	3.1	4.5

Statistics are as originally reported. Adj. for 2-for-1 stk. split, 5/97 [1] Bef. inc. fr. disc. ops. of $69.1 mil. & extraord. chrg. of $1.0 mil. [2] Incl. chrgs. of $9.7 mil.; bef. extraord. chrg. of $210.0 mil. [3] Incl. non-recur. cr. of $17.4 mil. [4] Incl. non-recur. chrg. of $84.1 mil.; bef. extraord. chrg. of $7.0 mil. [5] Bef. acctg. adj. chg. of $2.9 mil. [6] Bef. extraord. chrg. of $6.6 mil. [7] Refl. acq. of IXC Communications, Inc. [8] Incl. non-recur. cr. of $800,000, net loss on invest. of $356.3 mil.; bef. disc. ops. of $200,000 & oth. chrgs. of $800,000

OFFICERS:
J. D. Kiggen, Chmn.
R. G. Ellenberger, Pres., C.E.O.
K. W. Mooney, Exec. V.P., C.F.O.

INVESTOR CONTACT: M. W. Boher, Investor Relations, (513) 397-9904

PRINCIPAL OFFICE: 201 East Fourth Street, Cincinnati, OH 45202

TELEPHONE NUMBER: (513) 397-9900
FAX: (513) 397-1081
WEB: www.broadwing.com

NO. OF EMPLOYEES: 6,400 (approx.)

SHAREHOLDERS: 105,000 (approx.)

ANNUAL MEETING: In Mar.

INCORPORATED: OH, July, 1873

INSTITUTIONAL HOLDINGS:
No. of Institutions: 272
Shares Held: 117,491,974
% Held: 53.9

INDUSTRY: Telephone communications, exc. radio (SIC: 4813)

TRANSFER AGENT(S): Fifth Third Bank, Cincinnati, OH

NYSE SYMBOL BRO
Rec. Pr. 42.40 (4/30/01)

BROWN & BROWN, INC.

YIELD 0.7%
P/E RATIO 36.6

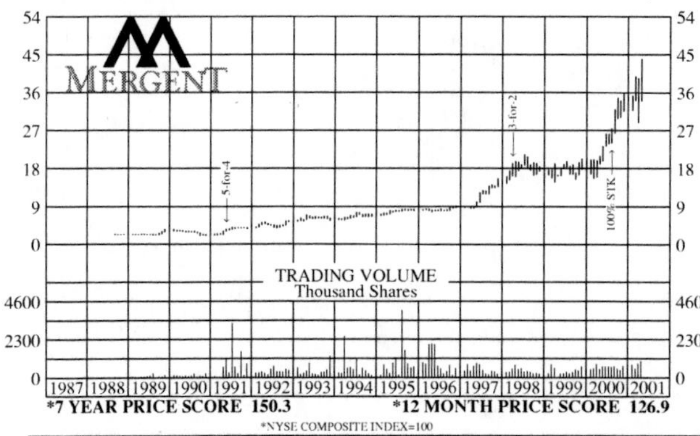

*7 YEAR PRICE SCORE 150.3 *12 MONTH PRICE SCORE 126.9
*NYSE COMPOSITE INDEX=100

INTERIM EARNINGS (Per Share):

Qtr	Mar.	June	Sept.	Dec.
1996	0.17	0.13	0.17	0.17
1997	0.20	0.16	0.20	0.20
1998	0.24	0.18	0.23	0.23
1999	0.27	0.21	0.26	0.26
2000	0.31	0.25	0.30	0.30

INTERIM DIVIDENDS (Per Share):

Amt.	Decl.	Ex.	Rec.	Pay.
0.13Q	7/26/00	8/07/00	8/09/00	8/23/00
100% STK	7/26/00	8/24/00	8/09/00	8/23/00
0.075Q	10/25/00	11/06/00	11/08/00	11/22/00
0.075Q	1/24/01	2/05/01	2/07/01	2/21/01
0.075Q	4/18/01	5/02/01	5/04/01	5/18/01

Indicated div.: $0.30

CAPITALIZATION (12/31/00):

	($000)	(%)
Long-Term Debt	2,736	2.2
Common & Surplus	121,911	97.8
Total	124,647	100.0

RECENT DEVELOPMENTS: For the year ended 12/31/00, net income increased 23.9% to $33.2 million versus $26.8 million in the prior year. Total revenues were $209.7 million, up 11.3% from $188.4 million a year earlier. Commissions and fees grew 11.5% to $204.9 million, while investment income jumped 38.4% to $3.9 million. However, other income fell 49.8% to $954,000 from $1.9 million in 1999.

PROSPECTS: On 2/15/01, BRO announced it has acquired Spencer & Associates, Inc., a commercial and personal lines insurance agency serving the Melbourne and Titusville, Florida area. On 4/9/01, the Company announced the acquisition of The Harris Agency, an independent insurance agency with clients in the Washington, D.C., metropolitan area.

BUSINESS

BROWN & BROWN, INC. (formerly Poe & Brown, Inc.) is a diversified insurance brokerage and agency that markets and sells primarily property and casualty insurance products and services to its clients. The Company's business is divided into four divisions: the Retail Division, which markets and sells a broad range of insurance products to commercial, professional and individual clients; the National Programs Division, which develops and administers property and casualty insurance and employee benefits coverage solutions for professional and commercial groups and trade associations nationwide; the Service Division, which provides insurance-related services such as third-party administration and consultation for workers' compensation and employee benefit self-insurance markets; and the Brokerage Division, which markets and sells excess and surplus commercial insurance primarily through non-affiliated independent agents and brokers. The Company conducts all of its operations in the United States.

REVENUES

(12/31/2000)	($000)	(%)
Retail	146,647	69.7
Programs	21,653	10.3
Service	18,825	9.0
Brokerage	23,170	11.0
Total	210,295	100.0

ANNUAL FINANCIAL DATA

	12/31/00	12/31/99	12/31/98	12/31/97	12/31/96	12/31/95	12/31/94
Earnings Per Share	**1.16**	**0.99**	**0.86**	**0.74**	**0.63**	**0.57**	**0.52**
Cash Flow Per Share	**1.62**	**1.42**	**1.21**	**1.05**	**0.92**	**0.82**	**0.77**
Tang. Book Val. Per Share	**0.70**	**0.41**	**0.18**	**1.05**	**0.66**	**0.68**	**0.45**
Dividends Per Share	**0.27**	**0.23**	**0.20**	**0.18**	**0.16**	**0.16**	**0.14**
Dividend Payout %	**23.3**	**23.2**	**23.8**	**23.9**	**25.8**	**28.2**	**26.9**
INCOME STATEMENT (IN THOUSANDS):							
Total Revenues	209,706	176,413	153,791	129,191	118,680	106,365	99,507
Costs & Expenses	141,982	119,712	106,365	83,525	78,448	71,537	67,343
Depreciation & Amort.	13,156	11,809	9,381	8,051	7,471	6,487	6,304
Operating Income	54,568	44,892	38,045	37,615	32,761	28,341	25,860
Net Interest Inc./(Exp.)	d590	d684	d560	d5,977	d5,715	d5,012	d5,508
Income Before Income Taxes	53,978	44,208	37,485	31,638	27,046	23,329	20,352
Income Taxes	20,792	17,036	14,432	12,251	10,548	8,530	7,067
Net Income	33,186	27,172	23,053	19,387	16,498	14,799	13,285
Cash Flow	46,342	38,981	32,434	27,438	23,969	21,286	19,589
Average Shs. Outstg.	28,663	27,472	26,862	26,175	26,049	26,097	25,572
BALANCE SHEET (IN THOUSANDS):							
Cash & Cash Equivalents	57,983	37,940	42,920	49,025	32,873	29,658	23,782
Total Current Assets	148,758	112,937	121,946	117,680	103,120	92,547	86,287
Net Property	14,210	14,337	13,698	11,863	12,085	10,412	8,286
Total Assets	276,719	235,163	230,513	194,129	179,743	151,121	139,335
Total Current Liabilities	144,476	119,514	118,866	102,798	97,394	81,843	78,318
Long-Term Obligations	2,736	3,909	17,207	4,093	5,300	7,023	7,430
Net Stockholders' Equity	121,911	103,026	84,208	77,142	67,286	54,412	44,044
Net Working Capital	4,282	d6,577	3,080	14,882	5,726	10,704	7,969
Year-end Shs. Outstg.	28,699	27,440	26,996	26,214	25,968	26,046	25,656
STATISTICAL RECORD:							
Operating Profit Margin %	26.0	25.4	24.7	29.1	27.6	26.6	26.0
Net Profit Margin %	15.8	15.4	15.0	15.0	13.9	13.9	13.4
Return on Equity %	27.2	26.4	27.4	25.1	24.5	27.2	30.2
Return on Assets %	12.0	11.6	10.0	10.0	9.2	9.8	9.5
Debt/Total Assets %	1.0	1.7	7.5	2.1	2.9	4.6	5.3
Price Range	35.88-15.63	20.31-14.66	21.25-14.40	15.67-8.50	9.17-7.58	8.42-6.75	7.58-5.67
P/E Ratio	30.9-13.5	20.5-14.8	24.7-16.7	21.2-11.5	14.5-12.0	14.8-11.9	14.6-10.9
Average Yield %	1.0	1.3	1.2	1.5	2.0	2.1	2.1

Statistics are as originally reported. Adj. for stk. splits: 2-for-1, 8/00; 3-for-2, 2/98;

OFFICERS:
J. H. Brown, Chmn., Pres., C.E.O.
C. T. Walker, V.P., C.F.O., Treas.
L. Gramming, V.P., Sec., Gen. Couns.

INVESTOR CONTACT: Cory T. Walker, V.P., C.F.O., (904) 239-7250

PRINCIPAL OFFICE: 220 South Ridgewood Ave., Daytona Beach, FL 32114

TELEPHONE NUMBER: (904) 252-9601
FAX: (904) 239-5729
WEB: www.brown-n-brown.com

NO. OF EMPLOYEES: 1,614

SHAREHOLDERS: 802 (record)

ANNUAL MEETING: In April

INCORPORATED: FL, 1959

INSTITUTIONAL HOLDINGS:
No. of Institutions: 79
Shares Held: 14,594,531
% Held: 49.1

INDUSTRY: Insurance agents, brokers, & service (SIC: 6411)

TRANSFER AGENT(S): First Union National Bank, Charlotte, NC

NYSE SYMBOL BWS
Rec. Pr. 19.95 (5/31/01)

BROWN SHOE COMPANY, INC.

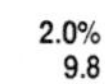

YIELD	2.0%
P/E RATIO	9.8

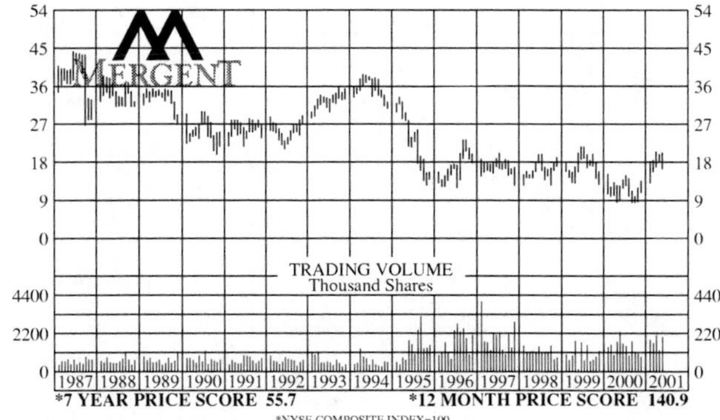

*7 YEAR PRICE SCORE 55.7 *12 MONTH PRICE SCORE 140.9

*NYSE COMPOSITE INDEX=100

INTERIM EARNINGS (Per Share):

Qtr.	Apr.	July	Oct.	Jan.
1996	0.03	0.31	0.73	0.08
1997	0.09	0.20	d0.75	d0.72
1998	0.22	0.24	0.72	0.14
1999	0.35	0.58	0.81	0.22
2000	0.36	0.51	0.88	0.29

INTERIM DIVIDENDS (Per Share):

Amt.	Decl.	Ex.	Rec.	Pay.
0.10Q	5/25/00	6/01/00	6/05/00	7/01/00
0.10Q	9/14/00	9/21/00	9/25/00	10/02/00
0.10Q	12/07/00	12/14/00	12/18/00	1/02/01
0.10Q	3/08/01	3/15/01	3/19/01	4/02/01
0.10Q	5/24/01	5/31/01	6/04/01	7/02/01

Indicated div.: $0.40

CAPITALIZATION (2/3/01):

	($000)	(%)
Long-Term Debt	152,037	35.4
Deferred Income Tax	7,678	1.8
Common & Surplus	269,972	62.8
Total	429,687	100.0

RECENT DEVELOPMENTS: For the year ended 2/3/01, net income grew 2.4% to $36.4 million compared with $35.5 million in 1999. Net sales totaled $1.68 billion, up 5.7% versus $1.59 billion the year before. Results reflected improved product offering at both retail and wholesale. At Famous Footwear, sales increased 11.4% to $1.03 billion, while Naturalizer retail sales rose 9.1% to $203.5 million. BWS' wholesale business reported a 4.9% decrease in sales to $447.6 million. Gross profit as a percentage of net sales improved to 40.5% versus 39.3% the year before.

PROSPECTS: On 5/21/01, BWS announced the launch of two footwear e-tailing sites: Shoes.com and FamousFootwear.com. Both sites will be managed by Shoes.com, Inc., a company jointly owned by Brown Shoe, The Walking Company and private investors. Going forward, the Famous Footwear brand will continue with its program of opening larger, more productive stores. The Company will continue to invest in a new image and marketing of its Naturalizer brand, and is targeting significant gains in market share over the next three years.

BUSINESS

BROWN SHOE COMPANY, INC. (formerly Brown Group, Inc.) is a $1.68 billion dollar footwear company with worldwide operations. The Company's retail footwear segment manufactures, supplies and sells women's and children's footwear and operates shoe stores and leased retail shoe departments in department stores. This segment includes the operations of Famous Footwear, which as of 12/31/00 had approximately 925 stores, and Naturalizer, which had 481 stores as of 12/31/00, in the U.S. & Canada. The Company's wholesale brands are sold in department stores, multi-line shoe stores and branded specialty stores through its Brown Branded, Brown Pagoda and Canada Wholesale divisions. These brands include: NATURALIZER, LIFESTRIDE, NIGHTLIFE, LS STUDIO, AIRSTEP, BUSTER BROWN, CONNIE, LARRY STUART and WILDCATS. The division also licenses brands including DR. SCHOLL'S BARBIE, DIGIMON, RUGRATS and SAMMY SOSA. Brown Pagoda Division of Brown Shoe, markets branded and private label footwear to an extensive network of both mass-merchandise, mid-tier and department stores throughout the U.S.

ANNUAL FINANCIAL DATA

	2/3/01	1/29/00	1/30/99	1/31/98	2/1/97	2/3/96	1/28/95
Earnings Per Share	**2.04**	**1.96**	**1.32**	**d1.19**	**1.15**	[1][2] **0.04**	[1] **1.91**
Cash Flow Per Share	**3.38**	**3.37**	**2.82**	**0.32**	**2.61**	**1.40**	**3.16**
Tang. Book Val. Per Share	**15.46**	**13.69**	**11.95**	**11.04**	**13.19**	**12.92**	**13.90**
Dividends Per Share	**0.40**	**0.40**	**0.40**	**1.00**	**1.00**	**1.45**	**1.60**
Dividend Payout %	**19.6**	**20.4**	**30.3**	**...**	**86.9**	**3,616.0**	**83.8**
INCOME STATEMENT (IN MILLIONS):							
Total Revenues	1,684.9	1,592.5	1,538.5	1,567.2	1,525.1	1,455.9	1,461.6
Costs & Expenses	1,589.6	1,500.1	1,450.1	1,521.4	1,454.0	1,419.2	1,376.1
Depreciation & Amort.	24.0	25.5	26.9	26.7	25.9	23.8	22.1
Operating Income	71.3	66.9	61.5	19.1	45.2	12.9	63.4
Net Interest Inc./(Exp.)	d18.8	d17.3	d19.4	d21.8	d18.1	d16.0	d14.3
Income Before Income Taxes	52.4	51.8	37.6	d2.2	27.2	d4.7	60.0
Income Taxes	16.0	16.3	13.9	18.7	6.9	cr5.4	26.4
Net Income	36.4	35.5	23.7	d20.9	20.3	[1][2] 0.7	[1] 33.6
Cash Flow	60.3	61.0	50.6	5.8	46.2	24.5	55.7
Average Shs. Outstg. (000)	17,846	18,125	17,943	17,841	17,699	17,483	17,639
BALANCE SHEET (IN MILLIONS):							
Cash & Cash Equivalents	50.5	34.2	45.5	50.1	38.7	35.1	18.9
Total Current Assets	562.7	487.8	497.4	538.5	564.8	505.3	479.0
Net Property	90.6	84.6	82.2	82.7	85.4	87.7	92.9
Total Assets	740.1	650.3	655.2	695.0	722.4	661.1	636.5
Total Current Liabilities	296.2	217.8	246.4	278.1	263.8	295.9	219.8
Long-Term Obligations	152.0	162.0	172.0	197.0	197.0	105.5	133.2
Net Stockholders' Equity	270.0	249.9	217.2	199.2	237.0	231.6	249.7
Net Working Capital	266.5	270.0	250.9	260.4	301.0	209.4	259.2
Year-end Shs. Outstg. (000)	17,461	18,263	18,168	18,049	17,970	17,931	17,970
STATISTICAL RECORD:							
Operating Profit Margin %	4.2	4.2	4.0	1.2	3.0	0.9	4.3
Net Profit Margin %	2.2	2.2	1.5	...	1.3	...	2.3
Return on Equity %	13.5	14.2	10.9	...	8.6	0.3	13.4
Return on Assets %	4.9	5.5	3.6	...	2.8	0.1	5.3
Debt/Total Assets %	20.5	24.9	26.3	28.3	27.3	16.0	20.9
Price Range	15.19-8.44	21.75-12.69	20.00-12.44	20.13-12.44	23.38-11.88	33.38-12.50	38.88-30.63
P/E Ratio	7.4-4.1	11.1-6.5	15.2-9.4	...	20.3-10.3	832.3-311.7	20.4-16.0
Average Yield %	3.4	2.3	2.5	6.1	5.7	6.3	4.6

Statistics are as originally reported. [1] Bef. disc. oper. gain 2/3/96, $2.6 mill.; 1/28/95, $5.8 mill. [2] Bef. non-recurr. chrg. $3.6 mill.

OFFICERS:
R. A. Fromm, Chmn., Pres., C.E.O.
A. M. Rosen, C.F.O., Treas.
R. D. Pickle, V.P., Gen. Couns., Sec.

INVESTOR CONTACT: Investor Relations, (314) 854-4000

PRINCIPAL OFFICE: 8300 Maryland Ave., St. Louis, MO 63105-3693

TELEPHONE NUMBER: (314) 854-4000
FAX: (314) 854-4274
WEB: www.brownshoe.com

NO. OF EMPLOYEES: 11,900 (approx.)

SHAREHOLDERS: 5,800 (approx.)

ANNUAL MEETING: In May

INCORPORATED: NY, Jan., 1913

INSTITUTIONAL HOLDINGS:
No. of Institutions: 98
Shares Held: 10,795,945
% Held: 61.8

INDUSTRY: Women's footwear, except athletic (SIC: 3144)

TRANSFER AGENT(S): First Chicago Trust Company of New York, Jersery City, NJ

NYSE SYMBOL BFB
Rec. Pr. 60.80 (4/30/01)

BROWN-FORMAN CORPORATION

YIELD 2.0%
P/E RATIO 18.1

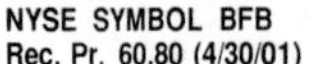

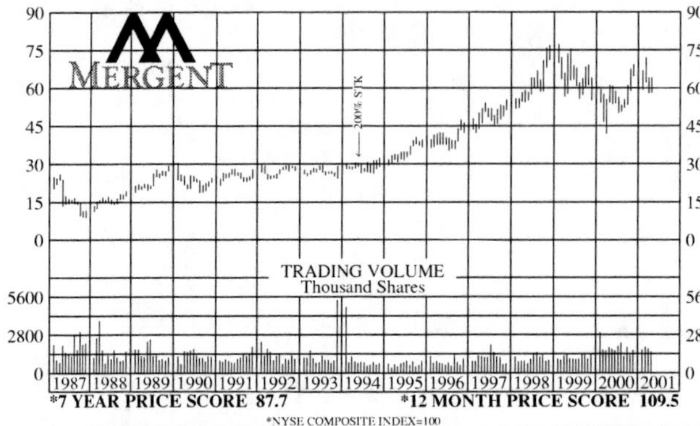

INTERIM EARNINGS (Per Share):

Qtr.	July	Oct.	Jan.	Apr.
1997-98	0.50	0.88	0.66	0.63
1998-99	0.54	0.97	0.72	0.70
1999-00	0.56	1.06	0.80	0.76
2000-01	0.62	1.17	0.80	...

INTERIM DIVIDENDS (Per Share):

Amt.	Decl.	Ex.	Rec.	Pay.
0.31Q	5/25/00	6/07/00	6/09/00	7/01/00
0.31Q	7/27/00	9/01/00	9/06/00	10/01/00
0.33Q	11/15/00	12/04/00	12/06/00	1/01/01
0.33Q	1/25/01	3/06/01	3/08/01	4/01/01
0.33Q	5/24/01	6/05/01	6/07/01	7/01/01

Indicated div.: $1.32 (Div. Reinv. Plan)

CAPITALIZATION (4/30/00):

	($000)	(%)
Long-Term Debt	41,000	3.5
Deferred Income Tax	95,000	8.0
Common & Surplus	1,048,000	88.5
Total	1,184,000	100.0

RECENT DEVELOPMENTS: For the quarter ended 1/31/01, net income increased 2.7% to $56.3 million from $54.8 million in the prior-year period. Net sales improved to $559.4 million from $557.3 million the year before. Sales from the wine and spirits segment rose to $394.0 million from $393.0 million a year earlier. Sales for the consumer durables segment grew to $165.4 million from $164.3 million in the previous year.

PROSPECTS: BFB anticipates moderate earnings growth for the remainder of fiscal 2001, resulting from a slowing U.S. economy, recent weak performance from HARTMANN LUGGAGE, and a continued movement toward lower beverage trade inventories. However, the Company's outlook for long-term growth remains positive, based upon favorable demographic trends and benefits from sustained brand investments.

BUSINESS

BROWN-FORMAN CORPORATION, with assets as of 1/31/01 of $1.86 billion, operates in two business segments: wines and spirits and consumer durables. The wines and spirits segment includes the production, importing and marketing of wines and distilled spirits under brand names of JACK DANIEL'S, SOUTHERN COMFORT, CANADIAN MIST, KORBEL CALIFORNIA CHAMPAGNES, and FETZER VINEYARDS CALIFORNIA WINES. The consumer durables segment includes tableware and flatware sold under the LENOX, GORHAM, DANSK, and KIRK STEFF brand names, as well as HARTMANN luggage. In fiscal 2000, sales (operating income) were as follows: 72.3% (87.3%), wine and spirits; and 27.7% (12.7%) consumer durables.

ANNUAL FINANCIAL DATA

	4/30/00	4/30/99	4/30/98	4/30/97	4/30/96	4/30/95	4/30/94
Earnings Per Share	**3.18**	**2.93**	**2.67**	**2.45**	**2.31**	**2.15**	**[1] 2.04**
Cash Flow Per Share	**4.08**	**3.74**	**3.42**	**3.17**	**2.99**	**2.78**	**2.63**
Tang. Book Val. Per Share	**11.36**	**9.53**	**8.04**	**6.73**	**5.26**	**3.94**	**2.50**
Dividends Per Share	**1.18**	**1.12**	**1.08**	**1.04**	**0.99**	**0.95**	**0.91**
Dividend Payout %	**37.1**	**38.2**	**40.4**	**42.4**	**42.9**	**44.0**	**44.4**
INCOME STATEMENT (IN MILLIONS):							
Total Revenues	2,134.0	2,030.0	1,924.0	1,841.0	1,807.0	1,679.6	1,628.5
Costs & Expenses	1,724.0	1,653.0	1,566.0	1,504.0	1,487.0	1,368.4	1,342.1
Depreciation & Amort.	62.0	55.0	51.0	50.0	46.0	43.5	46.0
Operating Income	348.0	322.0	307.0	287.0	274.0	267.8	240.4
Net Interest Inc./(Exp.)	d5.0	d4.0	d11.0	d14.0	d17.0	d20.7	d13.2
Income Before Income Taxes	343.0	318.0	296.0	273.0	257.0	247.1	257.2
Income Taxes	125.0	116.0	111.0	104.0	97.0	98.4	96.2
Net Income	218.0	202.0	185.0	169.0	160.0	148.6	[1] 161.1
Cash Flow	280.0	257.0	235.0	218.0	205.0	191.7	207.1
Average Shs. Outstg. (000)	68,600	68,700	69,000	69,014	68,996	68,996	78,657
BALANCE SHEET (IN MILLIONS):							
Cash & Cash Equivalents	180.0	171.0	78.0	58.0	54.0	62.5	30.5
Total Current Assets	1,020.0	999.0	869.0	802.0	768.0	697.9	649.9
Net Property	376.0	348.0	281.0	292.0	281.0	252.2	246.0
Total Assets	1,802.0	1,735.0	1,494.0	1,428.0	1,381.0	1,285.6	1,233.8
Total Current Liabilities	522.0	517.0	382.0	399.0	303.0	285.6	281.1
Long-Term Obligations	41.0	53.0	50.0	63.0	211.0	246.8	299.1
Net Stockholders' Equity	1,048.0	917.0	817.0	730.0	634.0	545.8	463.7
Net Working Capital	498.0	482.0	487.0	403.0	465.0	412.3	368.9
Year-end Shs. Outstg. (000)	68,512	68,506	68,996	68,996	68,996	68,996	70,174
STATISTICAL RECORD:							
Operating Profit Margin %	16.3	15.9	16.0	15.6	15.2	15.9	14.8
Net Profit Margin %	10.2	10.0	9.6	9.2	8.9	8.8	9.9
Return on Equity %	20.8	22.0	22.6	23.2	25.2	27.2	34.7
Return on Assets %	12.1	11.6	12.4	11.8	11.6	11.6	13.1
Debt/Total Assets %	2.3	3.1	3.3	4.4	15.3	19.2	24.2
Price Range	77.25-54.94	76.88-51.75	55.38-42.00	47.50-35.25	40.75-29.38	32.50-26.13	29.58-24.33
P/E Ratio	24.3-17.3	26.2-17.7	20.7-15.7	19.4-14.4	17.6-12.7	15.1-12.2	14.5-11.9
Average Yield %	1.8	1.7	2.2	2.5	2.8	3.2	3.4

Statistics are as originally reported. Adj. for 200% stk. div. 5/94. [1] Bef. acct. chge. of $32.5 mill. ($0.41 per sh.) & gain fr. sale of bus. of $30.1 mill. ($0.67 per sh.).

OFFICERS:
O. Brown II, Chmn., C.E.O.
W. M. Street, Vice-Chmn., Pres.
P. A. Wood, Exec. V.P., C.F.O.
M. Crutcher, Sr. V.P., Gen. Coun., Sec.

INVESTOR CONTACT: John Bridendall, Sr. V.P.-Corp. Dev., (502) 774-7290

PRINCIPAL OFFICE: 850 Dixie Highway, Louisville, KY 40210

TELEPHONE NUMBER: (502) 585-1100
FAX: (502) 774-7876
WEB: www.brown-forman.com

NO. OF EMPLOYEES: 6,000 full-time (approx.); 1,400 part-time (approx.)

SHAREHOLDERS: 3,728 (Class A common); 4,749 (Class B common)

ANNUAL MEETING: In July

INCORPORATED: KY, 1901; reincorp., DE, 1933

INSTITUTIONAL HOLDINGS:
No. of Institutions: 187
Shares Held: 28,144,431
% Held: 41.1

INDUSTRY: Wines, brandy, and brandy spirits (SIC: 2084)

TRANSFER AGENT(S): First Chicago Trust Company of New York, Jersey City, NJ

NYSE SYMBOL BC
Rec. Pr. 22.60 (5/31/01)

BRUNSWICK CORPORATION

YIELD 2.2%
P/E RATIO 9.7

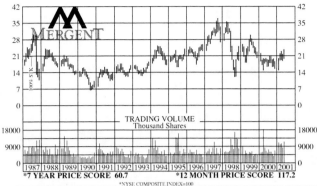

*7 YEAR PRICE SCORE 60.7 *12 MONTH PRICE SCORE 117.2
*NYSE COMPOSITE INDEX=100

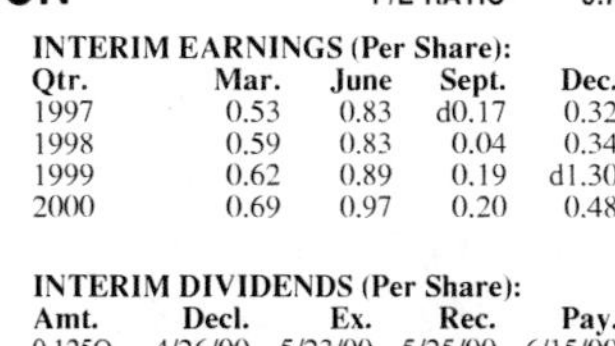

INTERIM EARNINGS (Per Share):

Qtr.	Mar.	June	Sept.	Dec.
1997	0.53	0.83	d0.17	0.32
1998	0.59	0.83	0.04	0.34
1999	0.62	0.89	0.19	d1.30
2000	0.69	0.97	0.20	0.48

INTERIM DIVIDENDS (Per Share):

Amt.	Decl.	Ex.	Rec.	Pay.
0.125Q	4/26/00	5/23/00	5/25/00	6/15/00
0.125Q	7/26/00	8/23/00	8/25/00	9/15/00
0.125Q	10/24/00	11/20/00	11/22/00	12/15/00
0.125Q	2/06/01	2/22/01	2/26/01	3/15/01
0.125Q	5/01/01	5/23/01	5/25/01	6/15/01

Indicated div.: $0.50 (Div. Reinv. Plan)

CAPITALIZATION (12/31/00):

	($000)	(%)
Long-Term Debt	601,800	31.9
Deferred Income Tax	215,400	11.4
Common & Surplus	1,067,100	56.6
Total	1,884,300	100.0

RECENT DEVELOPMENTS: For the year ended 12/31/00, income from continuing operations increased 41.3% to $202.2 million compared with income from continuing operations of $143.1 million in 1999. Earnings included non-recurring after-tax charges of $40.0 million and $71.4 million for 2000 and 1999, respectively. Net sales were $3.81 billion, up 7.6% from $3.54 billion a year earlier.

PROSPECTS: BC is forecasting a decline of about 7.0% in demand for domestic marine products at the retail level. Consequently, in January 2001, BC announced that it will close four boat manufacturing plants, which will reduce boat revenues by about 10.0%. The cessation of the four plants will cost BC between $5.0 million to $7.0 million. BC will then have 18 boat plants throughout the U.S. as well as interests internationally after the closings.

BUSINESS

BRUNSWICK CORPORATION is a global marketer and manufacturer of consumer brands including MERCURY and MARINER outboard engines; MERCURY MERCRUISER sterndrives and inboard engines; SEA RAY, BAYLINER and MAXUM pleasure boats; BAJA high-performance boats; BOSTON WHALER and TROPHY offshore fishing boats; PRINCECRAFT deck and pontoon boats; LIFE FITNESS, HAMMER STRENGTH and PARABODY fitness equipment; BRUNSWICK bowling centers, equipment and consumer products; and BRUNSWICK billiards tables.

BUSINESS LINE ANALYSIS

(12/31/2000)	REV(%)	INC(%)
Marine Engine	42.9	55.5
Boat	38.3	29.8
Recreation	18.8	14.7
Total	100.0	100.0

ANNUAL FINANCIAL DATA

	12/31/00	12/31/99	12/31/98	12/31/97	12/31/96	12/31/95	12/31/94
Earnings Per Share	[2][6] **2.28**	[5] **0.41**	[4] **1.80**	[3] **1.51**	**1.88**	[1][2] **1.39**	**1.35**
Cash Flow Per Share	**3.96**	**2.20**	**3.42**	**3.07**	**3.19**	**2.65**	**2.60**
Tang. Book Val. Per Share	**6.40**	**6.99**	**5.35**	**4.75**	**7.18**	**6.58**	**5.41**
Dividends Per Share	**0.50**	**0.50**	**0.50**	**0.50**	**0.50**	**0.50**	**0.44**
Dividend Payout %	**21.9**	**121.9**	**27.8**	**33.1**	**26.6**	**36.0**	**32.6**
INCOME STATEMENT (IN MILLIONS):							
Total Revenues	3,811.9	4,283.8	3,945.2	3,657.4	3,160.3	3,041.4	2,700.1
Costs & Expenses	3,266.0	4,006.9	3,445.3	3,229.7	2,725.8	2,701.3	2,370.3
Depreciation & Amort.	148.8	165.6	159.7	156.9	129.7	120.5	119.8
Operating Income	397.1	111.3	340.2	270.8	304.8	219.6	210.0
Net Interest Inc./(Exp.)	d67.6	d61.0	d62.7	d51.3	d33.4	d32.5	d28.5
Income Before Income Taxes	323.3	55.0	283.8	236.2	290.3	208.1	198.4
Income Taxes	121.1	17.1	105.2	85.0	104.5	73.9	69.4
Net Income	[2][6] 202.2	[5] 37.9	[4] 178.6	[3] 151.2	185.8	[1][2] 134.2	129.0
Cash Flow	351.0	203.5	338.3	308.1	315.5	254.7	248.8
Average Shs. Outstg. (000)	88,700	92,600	99,000	100,300	98,800	96,200	95,700
BALANCE SHEET (IN MILLIONS):							
Cash & Cash Equivalents	125.2	100.8	126.1	85.6	242.1	355.5	203.4
Total Current Assets	1,831.8	1,578.2	1,454.4	1,366.0	1,241.8	1,277.6	1,057.5
Net Property	803.2	881.8	845.1	783.0	685.4	598.9	565.4
Total Assets	3,396.5	3,354.8	3,351.5	3,241.4	2,802.4	2,360.5	2,122.3
Total Current Liabilities	1,247.9	1,088.4	1,036.4	948.2	831.1	680.4	621.3
Long-Term Obligations	601.8	622.5	635.4	645.5	455.4	312.8	318.8
Net Stockholders' Equity	1,067.1	1,300.2	1,311.3	1,315.0	1,197.7	1,043.1	910.7
Net Working Capital	583.9	489.8	418.0	417.8	410.7	597.2	436.2
Year-end Shs. Outstg. (000)	87,344	91,811	91,800	99,481	98,466	97,905	95,451
STATISTICAL RECORD:							
Operating Profit Margin %	10.4	2.6	8.6	7.4	9.6	7.2	7.8
Net Profit Margin %	5.3	0.9	4.5	4.1	5.9	4.4	4.8
Return on Equity %	18.9	2.9	13.6	11.5	15.5	12.9	14.2
Return on Assets %	6.0	1.1	5.3	4.7	6.6	5.7	6.1
Debt/Total Assets %	17.7	18.6	19.0	19.9	16.3	13.3	15.0
Price Range	22.13-14.75	30.00-18.06	35.69-12.00	37.00-23.13	25.88-17.25	24.00-16.25	25.38-17.00
P/E Ratio	9.7-6.5	73.2-44.0	19.8-6.7	24.5-15.3	13.8-9.2	17.3-11.7	18.8-12.6
Average Yield %	2.7	2.1	2.1	1.7	2.3	2.5	2.1

Statistics are as originally reported. [1] Incl. a nonrecur. chrg. of $24.4 mill. [2] Bef. discont. oper. loss of $7.0 mill., 1995; $298.0 mill., 2000. [3] Incl. strategic chrg. of $63.0 mill. & bef. acctg. adj. chrg. of $700,000. [4] Incl. strategic chrg. of $60.0 mill. Bef. after-tax gain of $7.7 mill. fr. discont. oper. [5] Incl. a litigation charge of $116.0 mill. and strategic chrg. of $151.0 mill. [6] Incl. nonrecurr. after-tax chrg. of $40.0 mill.

OFFICERS:
G. W. Buckley, Chmn., C.E.O.
V. J. Reich, Sr. V.P., C.F.O.
P. B. Hamilton, Exec. V.P.

INVESTOR CONTACT: Investor Relations, (847) 735-4294

PRINCIPAL OFFICE: One North Field Court, Lake Forest, IL 60045-4811

TELEPHONE NUMBER: (847) 735-4700
FAX: (847) 735-4765
WEB: www.brunswickcorp.com

NO. OF EMPLOYEES: 23,200 (approx.)

SHAREHOLDERS: 13,800 (approx.)

ANNUAL MEETING: In May

INCORPORATED: DE, Dec., 1907

INSTITUTIONAL HOLDINGS:
No. of Institutions: 228
Shares Held: 64,619,611
% Held: 73.8

INDUSTRY: Boat building and repairing (SIC: 3732)

TRANSFER AGENT(S): Brunswick Shareholder Services, Lake Forest, IL

NYSE SYMBOL BW
Rec. Pr. 20.00 (4/30/01)

BRUSH ENGINEERED MATERIALS INC.

YIELD 2.4
P/E RATIO 23.3

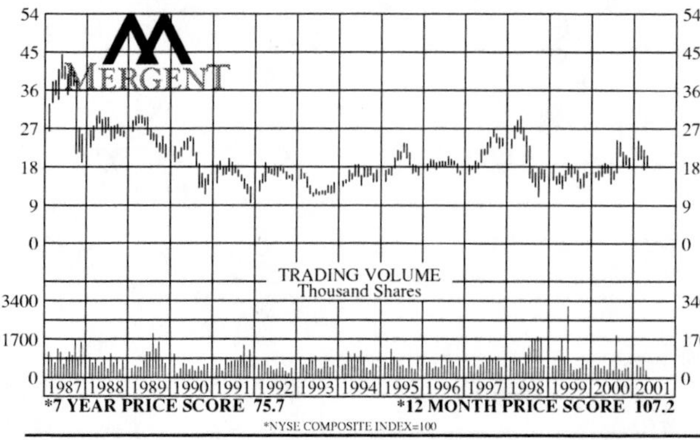

INTERIM EARNINGS (Per Share):

Qtr.	Mar.	June	Sept.	Dec.
1995	0.42	0.40	0.20	0.24
1996	0.32	0.51	0.28	0.41
1997	0.39	0.45	0.24	0.46
1998	0.37	d0.80	0.01	d0.02
1999	0.15	0.20	d0.03	0.08
2000	0.14	0.24	0.25	0.23

INTERIM DIVIDENDS (Per Share):

Amt.	Decl.	Ex.	Rec.	Pay.
0.12Q	5/04/99	6/16/99	6/18/99	7/05/99
0.12Q	9/16/99	9/23/99	9/27/99	10/04/99
0.12Q	12/07/99	12/16/99	12/20/99	1/04/00
0.12Q	3/07/00	3/22/00	3/24/00	4/07/00
0.12Q	5/01/01	6/20/01	6/22/01	7/06/01

Indicated div.: $0.48

CAPITALIZATION (12/31/00):

	($000)	(%)
Long-Term Debt	43,305	14.9
Deferred Income Tax	17,148	5.9
Common & Surplus	229,907	79.2
Total	290,360	100.0

RECENT DEVELOPMENTS: For the year ended 12/31/00, net income more than doubled to $14.2 million compared with $6.4 million a year earlier. Net sales advanced 23.7% to $563.7 million versus $455.7 million in 1999. Sales in the Metals Systems segment rose 23.5% to $378.2 million, while Microelectronic segment sales grew 27.4% to $179.1 million. Sales continue to be driven by strong demand in the telecommunications, computer, optical media and automotive electronics markets.

PROSPECTS: The Company announced that it has completed the second phase of its reorganization plan, which involved the formation of three new entities, Brush Resources Inc., Zentrix Technologies, Inc., and Brush Ceramic Products, Inc. Brush Resources, Inc. and Zentrix are wholly-owned subsidiaries of Brush Engineered Materials Inc. Separately, BW expects sales growth to be in the double digits in 2001.

BUSINESS

BRUSH ENGINEERED MATERIALS INC. (formerly Brush Wellman Inc.) is an international producer and supplier of high-performance engineered materials. The Company's Brush Wellman Inc. subsidiary, is the only fully-integrated producer of beryllium, beryllium-containing alloys and beryllia ceramic in the world, for use primarily in the defense and aerospace markets. In addition, the Company produces engineered material systems and precious metal and specialty alloy products for use in computers, telecommunications, automotive electronics, aerospace, undersea cables and other applications. The Company operates two primary business segments: the Metal Systems Group, which is comprised of Bush Wellman Inc. and Technical Materials, Inc. and the Microelectronics Group, which is comprised of Williams Advanced Materials Inc., Zentrix Technologies, Inc., and Brush Ceramic Products Inc., which are wholly-owned subsidiaries of the Company.

BUSINESS LINE ANALYSIS

(12/31/2000)	REV (%)	INC (%)
Metal Systems	67.9	76.2
Microelectronics	32.1	23.8
Total	100.0	100.0

ANNUAL FINANCIAL DATA

	12/31/00	12/31/99	12/31/98	12/31/97	12/31/96	12/31/95	12/31/94
Earnings Per Share	**0.86**	**0.40**	**[1] d0.44**	**1.56**	**1.52**	**1.26**	**[2] 1.14**
Cash Flow Per Share	**2.13**	**1.67**	**0.89**	**2.70**	**2.66**	**2.36**	**2.22**
Tang. Book Val. Per Share	**13.92**	**13.51**	**13.60**	**14.45**	**13.46**	**12.46**	**11.60**
Dividends Per Share	**0.24**	**0.48**	**0.48**	**0.45**	**0.41**	**0.34**	**0.23**
Dividend Payout %	**27.9**	**120.0**	**...**	**28.8**	**27.0**	**27.0**	**20.2**
INCOME STATEMENT (IN THOUSANDS):							
Total Revenues	563,690	455,707	409,892	433,801	376,279	369,618	345,878
Costs & Expenses	519,826	424,370	398,670	379,082	323,437	322,490	303,192
Depreciation & Amort.	20,878	20,779	21,535	18,695	18,537	18,042	17,588
Operating Income	22,986	10,558	d10,313	36,024	34,305	29,086	25,098
Net Interest Inc./(Exp.)	d4,652	d4,173	d1,249	d553	d1,128	d1,653	d2,071
Income Before Income Taxes	18,334	6,385	d11,562	35,471	33,177	27,433	23,027
Income Taxes	4,169	cr54	cr4,430	9,874	8,686	6,744	4,477
Net Income	14,165	6,439	[1] d7,132	25,597	24,491	20,689	[2] 18,550
Cash Flow	35,043	27,218	14,403	44,292	43,028	38,731	36,138
Average Shs. Outstg.	16,449	16,280	16,268	16,429	16,148	16,409	16,243
BALANCE SHEET (IN THOUSANDS):							
Cash & Cash Equivalents	4,314	99	1,938	7,170	31,749	29,553	20,441
Total Current Assets	250,079	224,255	194,524	178,911	197,233	191,747	181,217
Net Property	170,460	155,689	164,469	173,622	130,220	121,194	116,763
Total Assets	452,506	424,491	403,690	383,852	355,779	331,853	317,133
Total Current Liabilities	106,692	99,424	93,532	78,312	69,061	66,591	65,923
Long-Term Obligations	43,305	42,305	32,105	17,905	18,860	16,996	18,527
Net Stockholders' Equity	229,907	220,638	221,811	236,813	219,257	200,302	186,940
Net Working Capital	143,387	124,831	100,992	100,599	128,172	125,156	115,294
Year-end Shs. Outstg.	16,514	16,327	16,304	16,383	16,291	16,071	16,122
STATISTICAL RECORD:							
Operating Profit Margin %	4.1	2.3	...	8.3	9.1	7.9	7.3
Net Profit Margin %	2.5	1.4	...	5.9	6.5	5.6	5.4
Return on Equity %	6.2	2.9	...	10.8	11.2	10.3	9.9
Return on Assets %	3.1	1.5	...	6.7	6.9	6.2	5.8
Debt/Total Assets %	9.6	10.0	8.0	4.7	5.3	5.1	5.8
Price Range	24.31-14.00	19.06-12.88	30.00-10.94	26.81-16.13	20.50-16.13	23.63-14.50	18.63-13.38
P/E Ratio	28.3-16.3	47.6-32.2	...	17.2-10.3	13.5-10.6	18.7-11.5	16.3-11.7
Average Yield %	1.3	3.0	2.3	2.1	2.2	1.8	1.4

Statistics are as originally reported. [1] Incl. a nonrecurring pre-tax charge of $22.6 mill. [2] Incl. pre-tax charge of $2.0 mill. ($0.09 a sh.)

OFFICERS:
G. D. Harnett, Chmn., Pres., C.E.O.
J. D. Grampa, V.P., Fin., C.F.O.
J. J. Pallam, V.P., Gen. Couns.

INVESTOR CONTACT: Investor Relations, (216) 486-4200

PRINCIPAL OFFICE: 17876 St. Clair Avenue, Cleveland, OH 44110

TELEPHONE NUMBER: (216) 486-4200
FAX: (216) 383-4091
WEB: www.beminc.com

NO. OF EMPLOYEES: 2,500 (avg.)

SHAREHOLDERS: 2,064 (record)

ANNUAL MEETING: In May

INCORPORATED: OH, Jan., 1931

INSTITUTIONAL HOLDINGS:
No. of Institutions: 77
Shares Held: 11,379,149
% Held: 68.7

INDUSTRY: Primary nonferrous metals, nec (SIC: 3339)

TRANSFER AGENT(S): National City Bank, Cleveland, OH

NYSE SYMBOL BD
Rec. Pr. 2.75 (4/30/01)

BUDGET GROUP, INC.

YIELD ...
P/E RATIO ...

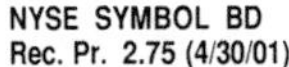

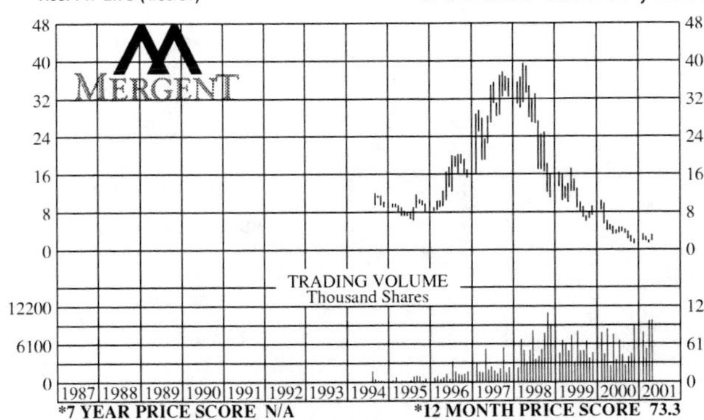

INTERIM EARNINGS (Per Share):

Qtr.	Mar.	June	Sept.	Dec.
1998	d0.12	0.16	1.38	d1.84
1999	d0.64	0.42	0.86	d2.05
2000	d0.80	0.27	0.30	d15.07

INTERIM DIVIDENDS (Per Share):

Amt.	Decl.	Ex.	Rec.	Pay.

No dividends paid.

CAPITALIZATION (12/31/00):

	($000)	(%)
Long-Term Debt	3,456,597	102.7
Common & Surplus	d90,395	-2.7
Total	3,366,202	100.0

RECENT DEVELOPMENTS: For the year ended 12/31/00, loss from continuing operations was $570.3 million compared with $49.9 million in 1999. Results for 2000 and 1999 excluding an estimated loss of $34.4 million and $14.3 million, respectively, from the disposal of business segments. Results for 1999 also excluded a loss of $327,000 from discontinued operations. Operating revenues climbed 3.7% to $2.44 billion from $2.35 billion in the prior year.

PROSPECTS: The Company expects pre-tax income for 2001 domestic car and truck rental operations to be about $5.0 million. This represents an improvement of about $65.0 million over 2000. The negative effect on earnings from the international division is expected to decrease throughout the year as BD completes its re-franchising plan. The full effect of the re-franchising strategy in Europe should result in improved earnings in 2002.

BUSINESS

BUDGET GROUP, INC. is engaged in the rental of cars, trucks, passenger vans and recreational vehicles through owned and franchised operations and the sale of new and used vehicles. The Company is the parent company for several brand-name rental businesses. The car rental division consists of Budget Rent a Car Corporation and Premier Car Rental LLC. The truck rental division consists of Budget Truck Rental and Ryder TRS Inc. The truck division also provides a range of other products and services, including renting automobile towing equipment and other moving accessories. BD provides a variety of liability-limiting products such as physical damage waivers, personal accident and cargo protection and supplemental liability protection.

ANNUAL FINANCIAL DATA

	12/31/00	12/31/99	12/31/98	12/31/97	12/31/96	12/31/95	12/31/94
Earnings Per Share	**3 d15.31**	**2 d1.37**	**1 d0.12**	**1.60**	**0.47**	**0.05**	**0.10**
Cash Flow Per Share	**4.09**	**15.85**	**17.19**	**12.88**	**7.40**	**4.85**	**2.30**
Tang. Book Val. Per Share	...	...	...	...	**2.10**	...	**1.91**
INCOME STATEMENT (IN MILLIONS):							
Total Revenues	2,436.4	2,349.5	2,616.2	1,303.8	357.4	149.7	38.6
Costs & Expenses	1,998.6	1,568.2	1,855.2	831.3	256.4	105.0	26.1
Depreciation & Amort.	722.6	627.4	554.7	301.1	65.7	30.6	8.2
Operating Income	d284.9	153.9	206.3	171.3	35.3	14.2	4.4
Net Interest Inc./(Exp.)	d263.0	d208.8	d190.2	d108.0	d26.2	d13.2	d3.8
Income Before Income Taxes	d547.8	d55.0	6.6	63.3	7.8	1.0	0.6
Income Taxes	3.7	cr23.8	0.3	26.4	3.3	0.7	0.3
Equity Earnings/Minority Int.	d18.7	d18.7	d10.0	...	...	...	...
Net Income	3 d570.3	2 d49.9	1 d3.6	36.9	4.5	0.3	0.4
Cash Flow	152.4	577.5	551.1	338.1	70.2	30.9	8.3
Average Shs. Outstg. (000)	37,255	36,430	32,067	26,245	9,488	6,369	3,704
BALANCE SHEET (IN MILLIONS):							
Cash & Cash Equivalents	74.8	58.0	557.7	439.7	116.8	68.1	33.6
Total Current Assets	411.0	474.2	1,063.9	803.8	195.9	118.9	39.1
Net Property	169.0	215.5	229.3	140.2	18.5	12.5	5.2
Total Assets	4,519.9	5,082.5	5,134.1	3,574.8	616.1	407.3	161.2
Total Current Liabilities	862.0	585.1	517.1	418.4	31.1	24.0	5.9
Long-Term Obligations	3,456.6	3,637.7	3,635.1	2,610.0	454.7	319.0	127.2
Net Stockholders' Equity	d90.4	567.5	650.6	438.0	92.0	39.6	26.9
Net Working Capital	d450.9	d110.9	546.8	385.4	164.8	94.9	33.2
Year-end Shs. Outstg. (000)	37,255	39,130	35,825	25,805	9,320	7,157	5,973
STATISTICAL RECORD:							
Operating Profit Margin %	...	6.5	7.9	13.1	9.9	9.5	11.4
Net Profit Margin %	...	...	...	2.8	1.3	0.2	1.0
Return on Equity %	...	...	...	8.4	4.9	0.9	1.4
Return on Assets %	...	...	...	1.0	0.7	0.1	0.2
Debt/Total Assets %	76.5	71.6	70.8	73.0	73.8	78.3	78.9
Price Range	10.44-1.19	17.25-6.00	39.50-11.00	37.75-16.00	20.25-8.25	11.75-6.19	12.00-9.00
P/E Ratio	...	...	...	23.6-10.0	43.1-17.5	234.5-123.5	119.9-89.9

Statistics are as originally reported. 1 Incl. $14.4 mill. restr. chg. and excl. $8.1 mill. fr. disc. ops. & $26.6 mill. net loss fr. extraordinary chg. 2 Incl. $105.4 mill. non-recur. chg. & excl. $14.7 mill. fr. disc. ops. 3 Excl. $34.4 mill. estimated loss fr. bus. segments.

OFFICERS:
S. Miller, Chmn., C.E.O.
J. D. Congdon, Vice-Chmn.
M. Sotir, Pres., C.O.O.
W. S. Johnson, Exec. V.P., C.F.O.

INVESTOR CONTACT: Sarah Lewensohn, (630) 955-7602

PRINCIPAL OFFICE: 125 Basin Street, Suite 210, Daytona Beach, FL 32114

TELEPHONE NUMBER: (904) 238-7035
FAX: (904) 238-7461
WEB: www.budget.com

NO. OF EMPLOYEES: 12,400 (approx.)

SHAREHOLDERS: 344 (Class A common); 3 (Class B common)

ANNUAL MEETING: In May

INCORPORATED: DE, Dec., 1992

INSTITUTIONAL HOLDINGS:
No. of Institutions: 36
Shares Held: 15,014,993
% Held: 40.3

INDUSTRY: Passenger car rental (SIC: 7514)

TRANSFER AGENT(S): Mellon Investor Services, Ridgefield Park, NJ

NYSE SYMBOL BCF
Rec. Pr. 19.56 (5/31/01)

BURLINGTON COAT FACTORY WAREHOUSE CORP.

YIELD 0.1%
P/E RATIO 11.2

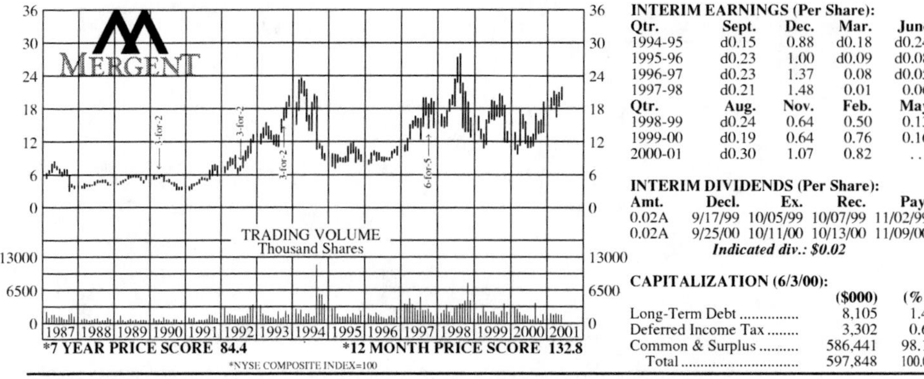

INTERIM EARNINGS (Per Share):

Qtr.	Sept.	Dec.	Mar.	June
1994-95	d0.15	0.88	d0.18	d0.24
1995-96	d0.23	1.00	d0.09	d0.08
1996-97	d0.23	1.37	0.08	d0.05
1997-98	d0.21	1.48	0.01	0.06
Qtr.	**Aug.**	**Nov.**	**Feb.**	**May**
1998-99	d0.24	0.64	0.50	0.13
1999-00	d0.19	0.64	0.76	0.16
2000-01	d0.30	1.07	0.82	...

INTERIM DIVIDENDS (Per Share):

Amt.	Decl.	Ex.	Rec.	Pay.
0.02A	9/17/99	10/05/99	10/07/99	11/02/99
0.02A	9/25/00	10/11/00	10/13/00	11/09/00

Indicated div.: $0.02

CAPITALIZATION (6/3/00):

	($000)	(%)
Long-Term Debt	8,105	1.4
Deferred Income Tax	3,302	0.6
Common & Surplus	586,441	98.1
Total	597,848	100.0

RECENT DEVELOPMENTS: For the three months ended 3/3/01, net income rose 3.9% to $36.1 million from $34.8 million in the previous year. Total revenues grew 5.3% to $732.3 million from $695.2 million a year earlier. The increase in revenues reflected a 5.2% improvement to $722.7 million in net sales, as well as a 13.5% increase to $9.6 million in other income. Comparable-store sales were up 3.4% from the prior-year quarter.

PROSPECTS: Results are benefiting from improvements in initial margins, along with a lower level of promotional activity. Going forward, sales may be positively affected by the launch of THE CHRISTOPHER LOWELL COLLECTION, a line of comforters, sheets, bathroom accessories, rugs, towels, shower curtains, window treatments, candles and other decorative items, as well as the CHRISTOPHER LOWELL DESIGNER PAINT COLLECTION.

BUSINESS

BURLINGTON COAT FACTORY WAREHOUSE CORP. operates 295 stores in 42 states as of 3/21/01, which sell off-price apparel for men, women and children. The Company operates stores under the names Burlington Coat Factory Warehouse, Cohoes Fashions, Decelle, Luxury Linens, Totally 4 Kids, Fit For Men, and Baby Depot. Cohoes Fashions offers merchandise in the middle to higher price range. Decelle offers merchandise in the moderate price range for the entire family. Luxury Linens is a specialty store for linens, bath shop items, gifts and accessories. Totally 4 Kids is a moderate to upscale concept store offering maternity wear, baby furniture, children's wear, children's books, toys, computer softwear for kids and educational tapes. Fit For Men specializes in special size menswear. Baby Depot specializes in infant and toddler apparel, furnishings and accessories.

ANNUAL FINANCIAL DATA

	6/3/00	5/29/99	① 5/30/98	6/28/97	6/29/96	7/1/95	7/2/94
Earnings Per Share	**1.37**	**1.02**	**1.34**	**1.18**	**0.59**	**0.31**	**0.93**
Cash Flow Per Share	**2.26**	**1.76**	**1.96**	**1.81**	**1.21**	**0.84**	**1.37**
Tang. Book Val. Per Share	**13.16**	**11.81**	**10.89**	**9.30**	**8.38**	**7.88**	**7.57**
Dividends Per Share	**0.02**	**0.02**	**0.02**	**0.02**	...	...	...
Dividend Payout %	**1.5**	**2.0**	**1.2**	**1.4**	...	...	...
INCOME STATEMENT (IN MILLIONS):							
Total Revenues	2,226.2	2,005.7	1,813.9	1,776.8	1,610.9	1,597.0	1,480.7
Costs & Expenses	2,079.7	1,888.7	1,671.7	1,641.9	1,520.2	1,532.2	1,376.9
Depreciation & Amort.	41.0	35.0	29.6	31.0	29.9	26.3	21.5
Operating Income	105.5	81.9	112.6	103.8	60.7	38.5	82.3
Net Interest Inc./(Exp.)	d5.4	d5.8	d6.8	d8.1	d11.7	d13.6	d9.9
Income Before Income Taxes	100.1	76.1	105.8	95.8	49.0	24.9	72.4
Income Taxes	37.7	28.4	42.1	39.2	20.0	10.1	27.0
Net Income	62.5	47.8	63.6	56.5	29.0	14.9	45.4
Cash Flow	103.5	82.8	93.3	87.6	58.9	41.2	66.9
Average Shs. Outstg. (000)	45,708	46,964	47,520	48,254	48,877	48,853	48,758
BALANCE SHEET (IN MILLIONS):							
Cash & Cash Equivalents	127.8	107.0	154.0	157.4	73.6	14.5	21.2
Total Current Assets	693.5	651.7	680.6	557.1	488.6	496.7	528.8
Net Property	318.3	252.2	222.8	209.9	206.6	224.5	184.6
Total Assets	1,046.0	941.6	909.8	775.1	704.7	735.3	725.4
Total Current Liabilities	433.1	318.9	312.1	237.4	200.5	251.3	250.2
Long-Term Obligations	8.1	53.0	60.9	62.3	74.9	83.3	91.4
Net Stockholders' Equity	586.4	548.2	516.1	460.2	413.7	385.0	369.9
Net Working Capital	260.4	332.8	368.5	319.7	288.1	245.5	278.6
Year-end Shs. Outstg. (000)	44,567	46,400	47,379	49,511	49,398	48,854	48,834
STATISTICAL RECORD:							
Operating Profit Margin %	4.7	4.1	6.2	5.8	3.8	2.4	5.6
Net Profit Margin %	2.8	2.4	3.5	3.2	1.8	0.9	3.1
Return on Equity %	10.7	8.7	12.3	12.3	7.0	3.9	12.3
Return on Assets %	6.0	5.1	7.0	7.3	4.1	2.0	6.3
Debt/Total Assets %	0.8	5.6	6.7	8.0	10.6	11.3	12.6
Price Range	20.75-10.75	28.06-12.75	20.00-10.21	20.00-10.21	11.15-7.81	11.98-7.08	23.65-8.54
P/E Ratio	15.1-7.8	27.5-12.5	14.9-7.6	17.0-8.7	18.8-13.2	38.9-23.0	25.3-9.2
Average Yield %	0.1	0.1	0.1	0.1	...	...	...

Statistics are as originally reported. Adj. for stk. splits: 6-for-5, 10/97. ① Results for 11 months only to reflect change in fiscal year to the Saturday nearest the last day in May. Fourth quarter results are for two months due to year-end change.

OFFICERS:
M. G. Milstein, Pres., C.E.O.
M. Mesa, Exec. V.P.
H. Milstein, Exec. V.P., Sec.

INVESTOR CONTACT: Bernard Bradsky, V.P. & Treas., (609) 387-7800

PRINCIPAL OFFICE: 1830 Route 130 North, Burlington, NJ 08016

TELEPHONE NUMBER: (609) 387-7800
FAX: (609) 387-7071
WEB: www.coat.com

NO. OF EMPLOYEES: 21,000 (approx.)

SHAREHOLDERS: 317 (record)

ANNUAL MEETING: In Oct.

INCORPORATED: DE, Apr., 1983

INSTITUTIONAL HOLDINGS:
No. of Institutions: 105
Shares Held: 14,712,381
% Held: 33.2

INDUSTRY: Family clothing stores (SIC: 5651)

TRANSFER AGENT(S): American Stock Transfer & Trust Company, New York, NY

NYSE SYMBOL BNI
Rec. Pr. 29.40 (4/30/01)

BURLINGTON NORTHERN SANTA FE CORPORATION

YIELD 1.6%
P/E RATIO 12.4

INTERIM EARNINGS (Per Share):

Qtr.	Mar.	June	Sept.	Dec.
1996	0.40	0.45	0.53	0.52
1997	0.32	0.50	0.60	0.46
1998	0.56	0.58	0.66	0.63
1999	0.50	0.50	0.75	0.69
2000	0.55	0.53	0.64	0.65

INTERIM DIVIDENDS (Per Share):

Amt.	Decl.	Ex.	Rec.	Pay.
0.12Q	7/20/00	9/07/00	9/11/00	10/02/00
0.12Q	9/21/00	12/08/00	12/12/00	1/02/01
0.01RR	12/11/00	3/08/01	3/12/01	4/02/01
0.12Q	1/18/01	3/08/01	3/12/01	4/02/01
0.12Q	4/19/01	6/07/01	6/11/01	7/02/01

Indicated div.: $0.48 (Div. Reinv. Plan)

CAPITALIZATION (12/31/00):

	($000)	(%)
Long-Term Debt	6,614,000	32.2
Deferred Income Tax	6,422,000	31.3
Common & Surplus	7,480,000	36.5
Total	20,516,000	100.0

RECENT DEVELOPMENTS: For the year ended 12/31/00, net income fell 13.8% to $980.0 million versus $1.14 billion a year earlier. Results for 2000 included a pre-tax merger charge of $20.0 million, while results for 1999 included a non-recurring gain of $50.0 million. Also, results for 2000 and 1999 included gains of $29.0 million and $26.0 million, respectively, from property dispositions. Total revenues rose to $9.21 billion from $9.19 billion in 1999 as intermodal, carload and automotive sectors gains were partially offset by lower coal and agricultural revenues.

PROSPECTS: Prospects are clouded by the slowing U.S. economy that could put additional pressure on freight revenues, which slipped 1.9% to $2.32 billion for the quarter ended 12/31/00. In particular, the automotive industry's outlook for 2001 has been reduced and the chemical industry has also shown signs of weakness, due in part to sharply higher commodity costs. Looking forward, BNI's continued focus on cost containment, coupled with expansion into new markets and services, should enable the Company to gain market share, enhancing its long-term outlook.

BUSINESS

BURLINGTON NORTHERN SANTA FE CORPORATION, created through the merger of Burlington Northern, Inc. and Santa Fe Pacific Corp. on September 22, 1995, owns one of the largest railroad networks in the United States, with more than 33,500 route miles stretching across 28 states and two Canadian provinces, as of 12/31/00, to provide single-line service to shippers. The Company's principal subsidiary, The Burlington Northern and Santa Fe Railway Company (BNSF), transports a wide range of products and commodities, including the transportation of containers and trailers or intermodal, coal and agricultural commodities. Other significant aspects of BNSF's business include the transportation of chemicals, forest products, consumer goods, metals, minerals, automobiles and automobile parts.

REVENUES

(12/31/2000)	($000)	(%)
Intermodal	2,654,000	28.8
Carload	2,577,000	28.0
Coal	2,131,000	23.1
Agricultural Commodities	1,257,000	13.7
Automotive	493,000	5.4
Other Revenues	93,000	1.0
Total	9,205,000	100.0

ANNUAL FINANCIAL DATA

	12/31/00	12/31/99	12/31/98	12/31/97	12/31/96	12/31/95	[3] 12/31/94
Earnings Per Share	[5] 2.36	2.44	2.43	[1] 1.88	1.90	[2] 0.55	[4] 1.49
Cash Flow Per Share	4.52	4.36	4.17	3.52	3.52	2.24	2.91
Tang. Book Val. Per Share	19.10	17.98	16.52	14.53	12.95	11.22	7.10
Dividends Per Share	0.48	0.48	0.42	0.40	0.40	0.40	0.40
Dividend Payout %	20.3	19.7	17.3	21.3	21.1	72.3	26.8
INCOME STATEMENT (IN MILLIONS):							
Total Revenues	9,205.0	9,100.0	8,941.0	8,413.0	8,187.0	6,183.0	4,995.0
Costs & Expenses	6,202.0	5,998.0	5,951.0	5,873.0	5,679.0	5,137.0	3,780.0
Depreciation & Amort.	895.0	897.0	832.0	773.0	760.0	520.0	362.0
Operating Income	2,108.0	2,205.0	2,158.0	1,767.0	1,748.0	526.0	853.0
Net Interest Inc./(Exp.)	d453.0	d387.0	d354.0	d344.0	d301.0	d220.0	d155.0
Income Before Income Taxes	1,585.0	1,819.0	1,849.0	1,404.0	1,440.0	334.0	695.0
Income Taxes	605.0	682.0	694.0	519.0	551.0	136.0	269.0
Net Income	[5] 980.0	1,137.0	1,155.0	[1] 885.0	889.0	[2] 198.0	[4] 426.0
Cash Flow	1,875.0	2,034.0	1,987.0	1,658.0	1,649.0	697.0	766.0
Average Shs. Outstg. (000)	415,200	466,800	476,200	471,000	468,000	320,190	270,561
BALANCE SHEET (IN MILLIONS):							
Cash & Cash Equivalents	11.0	22.0	25.0	31.0	47.0	50.0	27.0
Total Current Assets	976.0	1,066.0	1,206.0	1,234.0	1,331.0	1,264.0	1,012.0
Net Property	22,369.0	21,681.0	20,662.0	19,211.0	17,633.0	16,001.0	6,311.0
Total Assets	24,375.0	23,700.0	22,690.0	21,336.0	19,846.0	18,269.0	7,592.0
Total Current Liabilities	2,186.0	2,075.0	2,197.0	2,060.0	2,311.0	2,369.0	1,447.0
Long-Term Obligations	6,614.0	5,655.0	5,188.0	5,181.0	4,546.0	4,153.0	1,877.0
Net Stockholders' Equity	7,480.0	8,172.0	7,770.0	6,812.0	5,981.0	5,037.0	2,237.0
Net Working Capital	d1,210.0	d1,009.0	d991.0	d826.0	d980.0	d1,105.0	d435.0
Year-end Shs. Outstg. (000)	391,592	454,559	470,475	468,912	462,000	448,815	267,672
STATISTICAL RECORD:							
Operating Profit Margin %	22.9	24.2	24.1	21.0	21.4	8.5	17.1
Net Profit Margin %	10.6	12.5	12.9	10.5	10.9	3.2	8.5
Return on Equity %	13.1	13.9	14.9	13.0	14.9	3.9	19.0
Return on Assets %	4.0	4.8	5.1	4.1	4.5	1.1	5.6
Debt/Total Assets %	27.1	23.9	22.9	24.3	22.9	22.7	24.7
Price Range	29.56-19.06	37.94-22.88	35.71-26.88	33.65-23.42	30.04-24.50	28.25-15.17	22.21-15.50
P/E Ratio	12.5-8.1	15.5-9.4	14.7-11.1	17.9-12.5	15.8-12.9	51.1-27.4	14.9-10.4
Average Yield %	2.0	1.6	1.3	1.4	1.5	1.8	2.1

Statistics are as originally reported. Adj. for 3-for-1 stk. split, 9/98 [1] Incls. non-recurr. chrg. of $57.0 mill. [2] Bef. extrord. chrg. of $6.0 mill.; acctg. adj. chrg. of $100.0 mill.; incls. pre-tax chrg. of $735.0 mill. [3] Figures are for Burlington Northern Inc. [4] Bef. acctg. adj. chg. of $10.0 mill. [5] Incls. pre-tax merg.-rel. chrg. of $20.0 mill. & prop. disp. gain of $29.0 mill.

OFFICERS:
R. D. Krebs, Chmn.
M. K. Rose, Pres., C.E.O.
T. N. Hund, Exec. V.P., C.F.O., Treas.
INVESTOR CONTACT: Marsha K. Morgan, V.P., Corp. Sec., (817) 352-6452
PRINCIPAL OFFICE: 2650 Lou Menk Drive, Fort Worth, TX 76131-2830

TELEPHONE NUMBER: (817) 333-2000
FAX: (817) 333-2377
WEB: www.bnsf.com
NO. OF EMPLOYEES: 39,600 (approx.)
SHAREHOLDERS: 44,000 (approx.)
ANNUAL MEETING: In Apr.
INCORPORATED: DE, Dec., 1994

INSTITUTIONAL HOLDINGS:
No. of Institutions: 399
Shares Held: 315,724,877
% Held: 80.4
INDUSTRY: Railroads, line-haul operating (SIC: 4011)
TRANSFER AGENT(S): First Chicago Trust Company of New York, Jersey City, NJ

NYSE SYMBOL BR
Rec. Pr. 47.21 (4/30/01)

BURLINGTON RESOURCES INC.

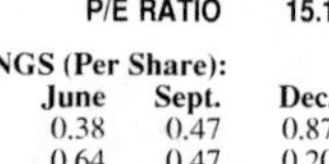
YIELD 1.2%
P/E RATIO 15.1

*7 YEAR PRICE SCORE 75.0 *12 MONTH PRICE SCORE 118.6

*NYSE COMPOSITE INDEX=100

INTERIM EARNINGS (Per Share):

Qtr.	Mar.	June	Sept.	Dec.
1996	0.30	0.38	0.47	0.87
1997	0.88	0.64	0.47	0.20
1998	0.27	0.13	0.08	Nil
1999	d0.05	0.08	0.23	d0.38
2000	0.35	0.43	0.93	1.41

INTERIM DIVIDENDS (Per Share):

Amt.	Decl.	Ex.	Rec.	Pay.
0.138Q	4/19/00	6/07/00	6/09/00	7/05/00
0.138Q	7/20/00	9/06/00	9/08/00	10/02/00
0.138Q	10/18/00	12/06/00	12/08/00	1/03/01
0.138Q	1/17/01	3/07/01	3/09/01	4/02/01
0.138Q	4/18/01	6/06/01	6/08/01	7/03/01

Indicated div.: $0.55

CAPITALIZATION (12/31/00):

	($000)	(%)
Long-Term Debt	2,301,000	36.4
Deferred Income Tax	266,000	4.2
Common & Surplus	3,750,000	59.4
Total	6,317,000	100.0

RECENT DEVELOPMENTS: For the year ended 12/31/00, net income increased to $675.0 million versus $1.0 million a year earlier. Results for 1999 included an after-tax charge of $140.0 million for impairment of oil and gas properties and an after-tax charge of $26.0 million for merger costs related to the acquisition of Poco Petroleums Ltd. Revenues advanced 36.1% to $3.15 billion from $2.31 billion in 1999. Separately, on 12/6/00, BR announced its 2001 capital budget of approximately $1.10 billion, excluding acquisitions, an increase about 10.0% versus 2000.

PROSPECTS: On 1/17/01, BR announced two separate transactions to acquire properties in the Western Canadian Sedimentary Basin. In the first transaction, which closed on 1/16/01 with an effective date of 8/1/00, BR acquired properties from Petrobank Energy for about $57.0 million. In the second transaction, BR will acquire assets, including producing and undeveloped acreage as well as compressor stations and gathering lines, from ATCO Viking-Kinsella for $328.0 million. This transaction, which is effective 12/31/00, is expected to close by mid 2001.

BUSINESS

BURLINGTON RESOURCES INC. is a holding engaged, through its principal subsidiaries, Burlington Resources Oil & Gas LP (formerly known as Burlington Resources Oil & Gas Company), The Louisiana Land and Exploration Company, and Burlington Resources Canada Energy Ltd. (formerly known as Poco Petroleums Ltd.), and their affiliated companies, in the exploration for and the development of and production and marketing of crude oil and natural gas. The Company has properties in the U.S., Canada, the United Kingdom, South America and China. At 12/31/00, total proved reserves were 8.24 trillion cubic feet of natural gas, and 347.4 millions of barrels of oil. On 11/18/99, the Company completed its acquisition of Poco Petroleums Ltd. in a transaction valued at about $2.50 billion. In October 1997, BR completed a merger with The Louisiana Land and Exploration Company valued at approximately $3.00 billion.

ANNUAL FINANCIAL DATA

	12/31/00	12/31/99	12/31/98	[1] 12/31/97	12/31/96	12/31/95	12/31/94
Earnings Per Share	3.12	[2] 0.01	0.48	[2] 1.79	2.02	[2] d2.20	[3] 1.20
Cash Flow Per Share	6.38	2.91	3.50	4.84	4.77	0.73	3.81
Tang. Book Val. Per Share	17.40	15.03	19.86	17.07	18.68	17.54	20.30
Dividends Per Share	0.55	0.55	0.55	0.55	0.55	0.55	0.55
Dividend Payout %	17.6	5,445.5	114.6	30.7	27.2	...	45.8
INCOME STATEMENT (IN MILLIONS):							
Total Revenues	3,147.0	2,065.0	1,637.0	2,000.0	1,293.0	872.5	1,054.8
Costs & Expenses	1,252.0	1,198.0	885.0	959.0	529.0	967.1	542.4
Depreciation & Amort.	704.0	631.0	534.0	538.0	346.0	372.6	337.4
Operating Income	1,191.0	236.0	218.0	503.0	418.0	d467.2	175.0
Net Interest Inc./(Exp.)	d197.0	d211.0	d148.0	d142.0	d113.0	d108.9	d90.3
Income Before Income Taxes	967.0	23.0	95.0	411.0	307.0	d576.7	90.3
Income Taxes	292.0	22.0	9.0	92.0	52.0	cr297.1	cr64.0
Net Income	675.0	[2] 1.0	86.0	[2] 319.0	255.0	[2] d279.6	[3] 154.2
Cash Flow	1,379.0	632.0	620.0	857.0	601.0	93.0	491.7
Average Shs. Outstg. (000)	216,000	217,000	177,000	177,000	126,000	127,000	129,000
BALANCE SHEET (IN MILLIONS):							
Cash & Cash Equivalents	132.0	89.0	...	235.0	68.0	20.5	19.9
Total Current Assets	1,011.0	667.0	456.0	678.0	442.0	265.0	266.1
Net Property	6,307.0	6,357.0	5,358.0	5,040.0	3,780.0	3,767.2	4,357.4
Total Assets	7,506.0	7,191.0	5,917.0	5,821.0	4,316.0	4,142.8	4,808.6
Total Current Liabilities	758.0	648.0	494.0	538.0	368.0	321.9	262.0
Long-Term Obligations	2,301.0	2,769.0	1,938.0	1,748.0	1,347.0	1,350.3	1,309.1
Net Stockholders' Equity	3,750.0	3,246.0	3,018.0	3,016.0	2,333.0	2,220.4	2,568.0
Net Working Capital	253.0	19.0	d38.0	140.0	74.0	d56.9	4.1
Year-end Shs. Outstg. (000)	215,569	215,970	151,955	176,709	124,919	126,574	126,509
STATISTICAL RECORD:							
Operating Profit Margin %	37.8	11.4	13.3	25.2	32.3	...	16.6
Net Profit Margin %	21.4	...	5.3	16.0	19.7	...	14.6
Return on Equity %	18.0	...	2.8	10.6	10.9	...	6.0
Return on Assets %	9.0	...	1.5	5.5	5.9	...	3.2
Debt/Total Assets %	30.7	38.5	32.8	30.0	31.2	32.6	27.2
Price Range	52.88-25.75	47.63-29.50	49.63-29.44	54.50-39.75	53.50-35.13	42.25-33.63	49.63-33.13
P/E Ratio	16.9-8.3	N.M.	103.4-61.3	30.4-22.2	26.5-17.4	...	41.4-27.6
Average Yield %	1.4	1.4	1.4	1.2	1.2	1.4	1.3

Statistics are as originally reported. [1] Refls. acq. of Louisiana Land & Exploration Co. [2] Incls. non-recurr. chrgs. 12/31/99: $262.0 mill.; 12/31/97: $40.0 mill.; chrg. 12/31/95: $304.0 mill. [3] Revs. in '94 incl. net amts. from sale of NGLs.

OFFICERS:
B. S. Shackouls, Chmn., Pres., C.E.O.
S. J. Shapiro, Sr. V.P., C.F.O.
D. D. Hawk, V.P., Treas.

INVESTOR CONTACT: J. Carrara, Inv. Rel., (713) 624-9548

PRINCIPAL OFFICE: 5051 Westheimer, Suite 1400, Houston, TX 77056

TELEPHONE NUMBER: (713) 624-9500
FAX: (713) 624-9645
WEB: www.br-inc.com

NO. OF EMPLOYEES: 1,783

SHAREHOLDERS: 17,856

ANNUAL MEETING: In Apr.

INCORPORATED: DE, 1988

INSTITUTIONAL HOLDINGS:
No. of Institutions: 457
Shares Held: 177,890,149
% Held: 82.4

INDUSTRY: Natural gas transmission (SIC: 4922)

TRANSFER AGENT(S): Fleet National Bank, Providence, RI

NYSE SYMBOL CDT
Rec. Pr. 14.20 (5/31/01)

CABLE DESIGN TECHNOLOGIES CORP.

YIELD ...
P/E RATIO 10.8

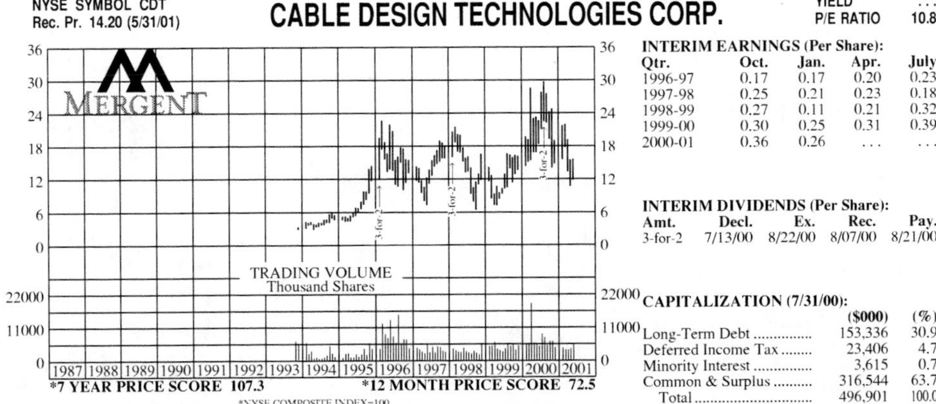

*7 YEAR PRICE SCORE 107.3 *12 MONTH PRICE SCORE 72.5

*NYSE COMPOSITE INDEX=100

INTERIM EARNINGS (Per Share):

Qtr.	Oct.	Jan.	Apr.	July
1996-97	0.17	0.17	0.20	0.23
1997-98	0.25	0.21	0.23	0.18
1998-99	0.27	0.11	0.21	0.32
1999-00	0.30	0.25	0.31	0.39
2000-01	0.36	0.26	...	...

INTERIM DIVIDENDS (Per Share):

Amt.	Decl.	Ex.	Rec.	Pay.
3-for-2	7/13/00	8/22/00	8/07/00	8/21/00

CAPITALIZATION (7/31/00):

	($000)	(%)
Long-Term Debt	153,336	30.9
Deferred Income Tax	23,406	4.7
Minority Interest	3,615	0.7
Common & Surplus	316,544	63.7
Total	496,901	100.0

RECENT DEVELOPMENTS: For the second quarter ended 1/31/01, net income was $11.5 million, up 10.6% from $10.4 million a year earlier. Net sales rose 13.7% to $202.6 million from $178.2 million in 1999. Network Communication segment sales grew 17.0% to $140.2 million, reflecting higher shipments of gigabit network, central office and fiber optic connectivity products. Specialty Electronic segment sales grew 7.8% to $62.4 million due to strong demand for automation and process control cable products.

PROSPECTS: The Company continues to ramp up the production capabilities of certain plants located in Canada, Germany, Mexico and the eastern U.S. to better meet the increasing demand for CDT's central office, metro loop, connectivity automation and process controls products. Going forward, the Company anticipates business growth to continue through the spring and summer months. However, this growth may be tempered by difficult economic conditions in the U.S.

BUSINESS

CABLE DESIGN TECHNOLOGIES CORP. is a manufacturer of technologically advanced electronic data transmission cables for network, communications, specialty electronics, and automation and process control applications, including complete voice and data wiring solutions, fiber optic connective products and other components required to build high performance telecommunications infrastructures. The Company's products are manufactured or distributed under the trade names Montrose/CDT, Phalo/CDT, West Penn/CDT, Mohawk/CDT, Manhattan/CDT, X-Mark/CDT, Dearborn/CDT, Thermax/CDT, Barcel/CDT, NORDX/CDT, NORCOM/CDT in Canada, NEK/CDT and Orebro/CDT in Sweden, Anglo American/CDT and Raydex/CDT in the U.K., Cekan/CDT in Denmark, and HEW-Kabel/CDT in Germany and ITC/CDT in Italy.

BUSINESS LINE ANALYSIS

(07/31/00)	Rev (%)	Inc (%)
Network Communication	68.3	60.3
Specialty Electronics	31.7	39.7
Total	100.0	100.0

ANNUAL FINANCIAL DATA

	7/31/00	7/31/99	7/31/98	7/31/97	7/31/96	7/31/95	7/31/94
Earnings Per Share	**4 1.25**	**3 0.91**	**2 0.86**	**0.87**	**1 0.38**	**0.38**	**1 0.29**
Cash Flow Per Share	**1.73**	**1.34**	**1.16**	**1.11**	**0.52**	**0.48**	**0.39**
Tang. Book Val. Per Share	**5.42**	**3.96**	**3.95**	**3.60**	**3.56**	**0.55**	**0.08**
INCOME STATEMENT (IN THOUSANDS):							
Total Revenues	797,824	683,999	651,668	516,996	357,352	188,941	145,389
Costs & Expenses	673,031	584,594	564,169	444,319	319,837	155,513	120,228
Depreciation & Amort.	21,449	18,830	14,045	10,075	5,988	3,815	3,360
Operating Income	103,344	80,575	73,454	62,602	31,527	29,613	21,801
Net Interest Inc./(Exp.)	d11,770	d13,346	d8,560	d5,338	d5,362	d5,111	d5,247
Income Before Income Taxes	90,211	66,364	65,816	57,322	25,894	24,507	16,896
Income Taxes	35,291	26,723	25,335	21,287	10,013	9,794	6,758
Net Income	4 54,920	3 39,641	2 40,481	36,035	1 15,881	14,713	1 10,138
Cash Flow	76,369	58,471	54,526	46,110	21,869	18,528	13,498
Average Shs. Outstg.	44,086	43,694	46,982	41,397	41,911	38,435	34,837
BALANCE SHEET (IN THOUSANDS):							
Cash & Cash Equivalents	16,454	11,424	11,143	9,017	16,097	2,210	2,242
Total Current Assets	326,160	305,985	276,545	247,545	208,456	72,371	60,617
Net Property	205,880	201,586	160,891	127,568	89,519	30,147	26,331
Total Assets	615,353	595,100	503,560	429,499	320,105	117,006	102,719
Total Current Liabilities	109,450	142,221	101,869	85,520	72,682	30,870	21,370
Long-Term Obligations	153,336	171,727	136,052	126,661	73,068	52,696	63,828
Net Stockholders' Equity	316,544	252,102	244,898	205,125	165,457	31,865	16,243
Net Working Capital	216,710	163,764	174,676	162,025	135,774	41,501	39,247
Year-end Shs. Outstg.	43,495	42,233	45,690	42,201	40,622	32,886	32,771
STATISTICAL RECORD:							
Operating Profit Margin %	13.0	11.8	11.3	12.1	8.8	15.7	15.0
Net Profit Margin %	6.9	5.8	6.2	7.0	4.4	7.8	7.0
Return on Equity %	17.3	15.7	16.5	17.6	9.6	46.2	62.4
Return on Assets %	8.9	6.7	8.0	8.4	5.0	12.6	9.9
Debt/Total Assets %	24.9	28.9	27.0	29.5	22.8	45.0	62.1
Price Range	29.75-14.00	16.63-7.25	21.50-6.42	19.00-7.28	22.67-10.00	14.45-4.30	5.85-2.89
P/E Ratio	23.8-11.2	18.3-8.0	25.0-7.5	21.8-8.3	60.0-26.4	37.8-11.2	20.2-10.0

Statistics are as originally reported. Adj. for 3-for-2 stk. splits, 8/00, 12/95 & 1/98. 1 Bef. extraord. charges of $596,000, 1996; $4.0 million, 1994. 2 Incl. non-recur. chrg. of $6.1 mill. 3 Incl. non-recur. chrg. of $4.9 mill. 4 Incl. non-recur. gain of $189,000.

OFFICERS:
B. C. Cressey, Chmn.
P. M. Olson, Pres., C.E.O.
K. O. Hale, V.P., C.F.O.
C. B. Fromm, V.P., General Couns., Sec.

INVESTOR CONTACT: Kenneth O. Hale, V.P., C.F.O., (412) 937-2300

PRINCIPAL OFFICE: Foster Plaza 7, 661 Andersen Drive, Pittsburgh, PA 15220

TELEPHONE NUMBER: (412) 937-2300
FAX: (412) 937-9690
WEB: www.cdtc.com

NO. OF EMPLOYEES: 3,900 (approx.)

SHAREHOLDERS: 180

ANNUAL MEETING: In Dec.

INCORPORATED: DE, May, 1988

INSTITUTIONAL HOLDINGS:
No. of Institutions: 155
Shares Held: 34,643,026
% Held: 79.1

INDUSTRY: Nonferrous wiredrawing & insulating (SIC: 3357)

TRANSFER AGENT(S): Fleet National Bank, Boston, MA

NYSE SYMBOL CS
Rec. Pr. 15.68 (4/30/01)

CABLETRON SYSTEMS, INC.

YIELD	...
P/E RATIO	12.7

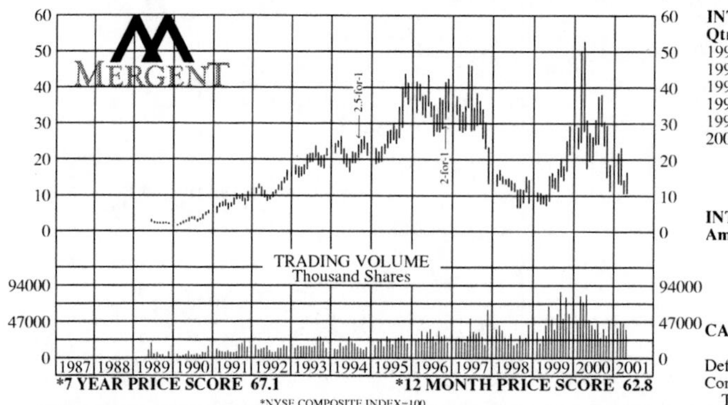

*7 YEAR PRICE SCORE 67.1 *12 MONTH PRICE SCORE 62.8
*NYSE COMPOSITE INDEX=100

INTERIM EARNINGS (Per Share):

Qtr.	May	Aug.	Nov.	Feb.
1995-96	0.34	0.37	0.39	0.05
1996-97	0.44	0.25	0.46	0.39
1997-98	0.38	0.37	0.13	d1.67
1998-99	d0.93	0.09	d0.50	d0.05
1999-00	d0.13	0.07	0.14	2.23
2000-01	d0.21	d0.60	d0.19	...

INTERIM DIVIDENDS (Per Share):

Amt.	Decl.	Ex.	Rec.	Pay.

No dividends paid.

CAPITALIZATION (2/29/00):

	($000)	(%)
Deferred Income Tax	459,863	17.6
Common & Surplus	2,147,439	82.4
Total	2,607,302	100.0

RECENT DEVELOPMENTS: For the three months ended 12/2/00, the Company reported a net loss of $32.4 million versus net income of $42.6 million in 1999. Results for 2000 included a stock-based compensation charge of $3.5 million. Net sales were $248.9 million, down 33.0% from $371.7 million in the prior-year period. CS' subsidiary, Enterasys Networks, reported a 19.6% improvement in revenues to $205.8 million reflecting key customer wins. Gross profit decreased 29.7% to $123.9 million.

PROSPECTS: On 1/31/01, the Company announced that it has completed the acquisition of Indus River Networks for about $170.0 million including the transfer of 4.1 million of CS' common and CS stock convertible into about 1.0% of Enterasys Network stock. Indus is a developer of managed remote networking applications that focus on scalability, security, dependability and policy management requirements of large corporations. Indus will be integrated with Enterasys Networks.

BUSINESS

CABLETRON SYSTEMS, INC. develops, manufactures, markets, installs and supports a wide range of standard-based Local Area Network (LAN) and Wide Area Network (WAN) connectivity hardware and software products. CS's approach to networking is based on a strategy known as Synthesis, a strategic framework that combines infrastructure products and technologies, automated management tools, and support services to allow users to smoothly migrate from traditional router-based internetworks to switch-based virtual enterprise internetworks. CS also produces and supports other networking products, such as adapter cards, other interconnection equipment, wiring cable, and file server products, and provides a wide range of networking services.

ANNUAL FINANCIAL DATA

	2/29/00	2/28/99	2/28/98	2/28/97	2/29/96	2/28/95	2/28/94
Earnings Per Share	**[5] 2.46**	**[4] d1.47**	**[3] d0.81**	**1.43**	**[2] 1.15**	**[1] 1.14**	**0.84**
Cash Flow Per Share	**3.12**	**d0.78**	**d0.39**	**1.75**	**1.37**	**1.32**	**0.96**
Tang. Book Val. Per Share	**10.99**	**5.17**	**6.02**	**6.92**	**5.38**	**4.11**	**2.96**
INCOME STATEMENT (IN MILLIONS):							
Total Revenues	1,459.6	1,411.3	1,377.3	1,406.6	1,069.7	810.7	598.1
Costs & Expenses	1,320.8	1,353.3	1,133.4	973.5	724.4	545.5	403.3
Depreciation & Amort.	123.5	114.7	65.3	49.7	32.1	26.8	17.3
Operating Income	d5.8	d291.6	d239.1	320.3	227.6	238.4	177.5
Net Interest Inc./(Exp.)	18.6	15.1	18.6	19.4	17.1	9.6	5.8
Income Before Income Taxes	759.0	d276.5	d220.5	339.7	224.6	248.0	183.3
Income Taxes	294.8	cr31.1	cr93.4	117.6	80.2	86.0	64.1
Net Income	[5] 464.3	[4] d245.4	[3] d127.1	222.1	[2] 164.4	[1] 162.0	119.2
Cash Flow	587.7	d130.7	d61.8	271.8	196.5	188.8	136.6
Average Shs. Outstg. (000)	188,618	167,432	157,686	155,207	143,678	142,988	142,036
BALANCE SHEET (IN MILLIONS):							
Cash & Cash Equivalents	573.0	273.4	324.1	380.2	253.5	244.6	163.7
Total Current Assets	1,007.4	840.4	1,034.2	890.6	624.3	471.1	326.5
Net Property	125.0	188.5	244.7	204.6	150.0	116.8	79.5
Total Assets	3,166.5	1,566.5	1,606.3	1,306.9	951.3	689.9	499.1
Total Current Liabilities	559.2	469.5	472.8	214.3	164.4	96.3	70.7
Net Stockholders' Equity	2,147.4	1,089.8	989.0	1,081.5	777.8	587.5	423.8
Net Working Capital	448.2	370.9	561.4	676.3	460.0	374.8	255.8
Year-end Shs. Outstg. (000)	183,585	172,184	158,267	156,305	144,468	142,938	142,760
STATISTICAL RECORD:							
Operating Profit Margin %	...	...	...	22.8	21.3	29.4	29.7
Net Profit Margin %	31.8	...	...	15.8	15.4	20.0	19.9
Return on Equity %	21.6	...	...	20.5	21.1	27.6	28.1
Return on Assets %	14.7	...	...	18.6	17.3	23.5	23.9
Price Range	29.31-7.19	17.13-6.63	46.50-13.25	43.56-26.50	43.88-18.69	26.50-16.52	23.80-14.90
P/E Ratio	11.9-2.9	...	...	30.5-18.5	38.1-16.2	23.3-14.6	28.3-17.7

Statistics are as originally reported. Adj. for 2.5-for-1 split, 9/94; 2-for-1 split, 11/96. [1] Incl. $52.3 mill. ($0.36/sh.) after-tax non-recur. purch. & rel. expenses. [2] Incl. $63.0 mill. pre-tax non-recur. chg. [3] Incl. $257.0 mill. after-tax realign. & one-time acq. chgs. [4] Incl. $213.8 mill. after-tax spl. chgs. for in-process R&D and $10.7 mill. after-tax chg. for equip. [5] Incl. a gain of $705.1 mill. fr. the sale of FlowPoint subsidairy and chgs. of $21.1 mill. for restr. & $41.3 mill. for amort. of intangs.

OFFICERS:
P. Patel, Chmn., Pres., C.E.O.
D. J. Kirkpatrick, Exec. V.P., C.F.O.
M. D. Myerow, Sec.

INVESTOR CONTACT: J. Kim, (603) 337-2247

PRINCIPAL OFFICE: 35 Industrial Way, Rochester, NH 03867

TELEPHONE NUMBER: (603) 332-9400
FAX: (603) 332-8007
WEB: www.cabletron.com

NO. OF EMPLOYEES: 4,456 (approx.)

SHAREHOLDERS: 2,821 (approx.)

ANNUAL MEETING: In July

INCORPORATED: DE, 1988

INSTITUTIONAL HOLDINGS:
No. of Institutions: 234
Shares Held: 124,909,490
% Held: 67.6

INDUSTRY: Computer peripheral equipment, nec (SIC: 3577)

TRANSFER AGENT(S): BankBoston, NA, c/o Boston EquiServe, Boston, MA

NYSE SYMBOL CVC
Rec. Pr. 68.75 (4/30/01)

CABLEVISION SYSTEMS CORPORATION

YIELD ...
P/E RATIO 52.9

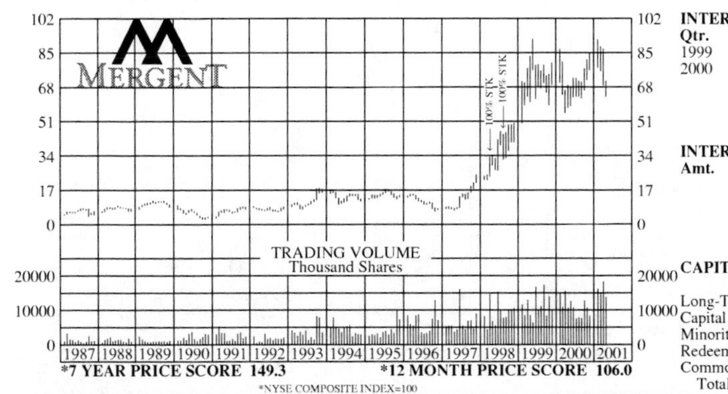

*7 YEAR PRICE SCORE 149.3 *12 MONTH PRICE SCORE 106.0

*NYSE COMPOSITE INDEX=100

INTERIM EARNINGS (Per Share):

Qtr.	Mar.	June	Sept.	Dec.
1999	d1.57	d1.10	d1.17	d1.28
2000	d0.67	d0.99	d0.23	3.19

INTERIM DIVIDENDS (Per Share):

Amt.	Decl.	Ex.	Rec.	Pay.

No dividends paid.

CAPITALIZATION (12/31/00):

	($000)	(%)
Long-Term Debt	3,741,856	108.2
Capital Lease Obligations	114,173	3.3
Minority Interest	587,985	17.0
Redeemable Pfd. Stock	1,544,294	44.7
Common & Surplus	d2,529,879	-73.2
Total	3,458,429	100.0

RECENT DEVELOPMENTS: For the year ended 12/31/00, net income jumped to $229.3 million compared with a net loss of $800.6 million in the previous year. Results for 2000 included a gain on sale of cable assets and programming interests of $1.21 billion. Total revenues increased 11.9% to $4.41 billion versus $3.94 billion in the prior year. Operating loss totaled $33.0 million, down from $174.1 million in the preceding year.

PROSPECTS: On 4/3/01, the Company and Metro Goldwyn-Mayer Inc. announced that MGM Networks has completed its acquisition of a 20.0% stake in four of Rainbow's national networks: AMC, Bravo, The Independent Film Channel and WE: Women's Entertainment, for approximately $825.0 million. Meanwhile, the Company will continue to focus on investing in its cable, commercial telephone and new media businesses in 2001.

BUSINESS

CABLEVISION SYSTEMS CORPORATON is one of the nation's major telecommunications and entertainment companies. The Company consists of the Cablevision NY Group (NYSE: CVC) and the Rainbow Media Group (NYSE: RMG). CVC is comprised of cable television operations serving approximately 3.0 million subscribers located in the New York metropolitan area, as well as Madison Square Garden, Radio City Entertainment, THE WIZ consumer electronics stores in 42 locations in the New York metropolitan area and Clearview Cinemas with 290 motion picture theatre screens in the New York metropolitan area. RMG includes five national networks, Rainbow's interest in the national Fox Sports Net, and five Fox Sports Net regional sports channels outside the New York market.

REVENUES

(12/31/2000)	($000)	(%)
Telecommunication Service	2,328,194	50.8
Rainbow Media	484,816	10.6
MSG	876,397	19.1
Retail Electronics	693,354	15.1
All Other	200,499	4.4
Total	4,583,260	100.0

ANNUAL FINANCIAL DATA

	12/31/00	12/31/99	12/31/98	12/31/97	12/31/96	12/31/95	12/31/94
Earnings Per Share	**1 1.29**	**d5.12**	**1 d3.16**	**1 d0.12**	**d4.63**	**1 d3.54**	**2 d3.43**
Cash Flow Per Share	**7.23**	**0.66**	**2.07**	**4.97**	**d0.59**	**0.02**	**d0.33**
INCOME STATEMENT (IN MILLIONS):							
Total Revenues	4,411.0	3,943.0	3,265.1	1,949.4	1,315.1	1,078.1	837.2
Costs & Expenses	3,415.5	3,213.9	2,533.8	1,360.7	839.6	659.2	484.1
Depreciation & Amort.	1,028.6	903.2	742.6	507.5	401.2	339.4	290.4
Operating Income	d33.0	d174.1	d11.3	81.2	74.4	79.4	62.7
Net Interest Inc./(Exp.)	d562.6	d465.7	d402.4	d363.2	d265.0	d311.9	d261.8
Income Before Income Taxes	410.6	d660.8	d286.5	224.5	d240.6	d215.8	d228.9
Equity Earnings/Minority Int.	d181.4	d139.8	d162.0	d87.9	d91.4	d101.7	d86.3
Net Income	1 229.3	d800.6	1 d448.5	1 136.7	d332.1	1 d317.5	2 d315.2
Cash Flow	1,257.8	102.6	294.1	495.4	d58.7	1.7	d31.2
Average Shs. Outstg. (000)	173,913	156,503	142,016	99,608	99,308	95,304	93,776
BALANCE SHEET (IN MILLIONS):							
Cash & Cash Equivalents	37.9	62.7	173.8	410.1	11.6	15.3	...
Total Current Assets	1,135.3	973.9	1,059.4	959.5	293.7	295.9	...
Net Property	3,285.7	2,752.5	2,506.8	1,831.2	1,391.0	1,026.4	...
Total Assets	8,273.3	7,130.3	7,061.1	5,625.1	3,034.7	2,502.3	...
Total Current Liabilities	4,814.9	4,360.1	4,068.0	3,594.3	2,226.5	1,517.7	...
Long-Term Obligations	3,856.0	3,840.2	3,306.1	2,453.7	1,664.5	2,164.6	...
Net Stockholders' Equity	d2,529.9	d3,067.1	d2,611.7	d2,378.8	d2,374.3	d1,891.7	...
Net Working Capital	d3,679.5	d3,386.2	d3,008.6	d2,634.7	d1,932.8	d1,221.8	...
Year-end Shs. Outstg. (000)	174,922	173,211	151,494	100,284	99,352	103,132	...
STATISTICAL RECORD:							
Operating Profit Margin %	...	...	...	4.2	5.7	7.4	7.5
Net Profit Margin %	5.2	...	...	7.0	...	...	...
Return on Assets %	2.8	...	...	2.4	...	...	...
Debt/Total Assets %	46.6	53.9	46.8	43.6	54.8	86.5	...
Price Range	86.88-55.00	91.88-49.88	50.25-21.78	24.56-6.78	15.09-6.25	17.44-12.19	16.97-9.75
P/E Ratio	67.3-42.6	...	...	...	...	...	...

Statistics are as originally reported. Adj. for 100% stk. div., 8/98 & 3/98. 1 Incl. gain on sales of programs int. & cable assets, 2000, $1.21 bill.; 1998, $170.9 mill.; 1997, $372.1 mill.; 1995, $36.0 mill. 2 Incl. restruct. expenses of $4.3 mill.

OFFICERS:
C. F. Dolan, Chmn.
R. S. Lemle, Vice-Chmn., Sec., Gen. Couns.
W. J. Bell, Vice-Chmn.
J. L. Dolan, Pres., C.E.O.

INVESTOR CONTACT: Investor Relations, (516) 803-2270

PRINCIPAL OFFICE: 1111 Stewart Avenue, Bethpage, NY 11714-3581

TELEPHONE NUMBER: (516) 803-2300
FAX: (516) 803-2273
WEB: www.cablevision.com

NO. OF EMPLOYEES: 14,578 full-time; 3,530 part-time

SHAREHOLDERS: 1,006 (record class A); 25 (record class B)

ANNUAL MEETING: In June

INCORPORATED: DE, Mar., 1998

INSTITUTIONAL HOLDINGS:
No. of Institutions: 213
Shares Held: 70,049,426
% Held: 40.0

INDUSTRY: Cable and other pay TV services (SIC: 4841)

TRANSFER AGENT(S): Mellon Investor Services, Ridgefield Park, NJ

NYSE SYMBOL CBT
Rec. Pr. 32.51 (4/30/01)

CABOT CORPORATION

YIELD 1.6%
P/E RATIO 19.2

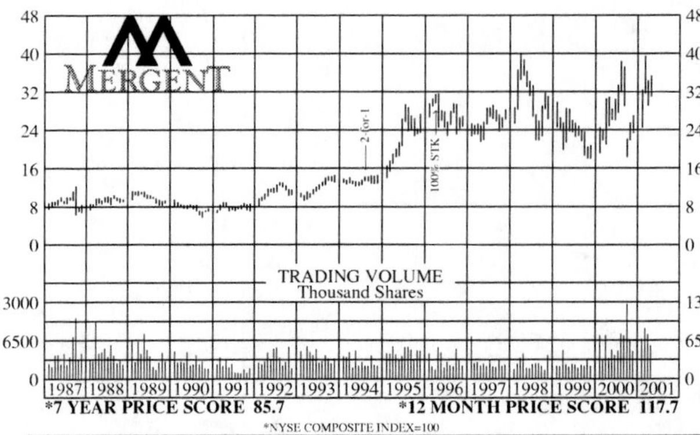

INTERIM EARNINGS (Per Share):

Qtr.	Dec.	Mar.	June	Sept.
1997-98	0.41	0.50	0.44	0.26
1998-99	0.43	0.45	0.30	0.13
1999-00	0.50	0.57	0.44	0.31
2000-01	0.37	...	...	...

INTERIM DIVIDENDS (Per Share):

Amt.	Decl.	Ex.	Rec.	Pay.
0.11Q	7/14/00	8/23/00	8/25/00	9/08/00
0.11Q	11/10/00	11/21/00	11/24/00	12/08/00
0.11Q	1/12/01	2/21/01	2/23/01	3/09/01
0.13Q	5/11/01	5/23/01	5/25/01	6/08/01

Indicated div.: $0.52 (Div. Reinv. Plan)

CAPITALIZATION (9/30/00):

	($000)	(%)
Long-Term Debt	329,000	22.0
Deferred Income Tax	90,000	6.0
Minority Interest	31,000	2.1
Preferred Stock	75,000	5.0
Common & Surplus	972,000	64.9
Total	1,497,000	100.0

RECENT DEVELOPMENTS: For the quarter ended 12/31/00, net income slipped 9.7% to $28.0 million versus income from continuing operations of $31.0 million in 1999. Results for 1999 excluded net income of $7.0 million from discontinued operations. Total revenues were $406.0 million, up 7.4% from $378.0 million in the prior-year period. Operating profit fell 33.9% to $39.0 million versus $59.0 million in the previous year.

PROSPECTS: The Company expects demand for its tantalum products will remain strong since the market for tantalum has become very tight. CBT expects its average selling price for tantalum products for fiscal 2001 to increase by 35.0% to 45.0% and increase again by 30.0% to 45.0% in fiscal 2002 due to several new long-term contracts with principal customers. The average total cost per unit of tantalum will increase by 35.0% to 45.0% in fiscal 2001.

BUSINESS

CABOT CORPORATION is a global company with businesses in chemicals, performance materials, specialty fluids, microelectronic materials, and liquefied natural gas. As of 12/31/00, CBT and its affiliates had 45 manufacturing facilities in 23 countries. The Company manufactures, markets and distributes fine powders through four specialty chemical businesses: carbon black; fumed silica; plastics; and inkjet colorants. In September 2000, CBT spun off Cabot Microelectronics Corporation. In July 2000, the Company sold Cabot Liquefied Natural Gas. As of 12/31/00, CBT owns an approximately 41.4% interest in Aearo Corporation (formerly Cabot Safety Holdings Corp.). Revenues for fiscal 2000 were derived: chemicals group, 85.3%; performance materials, 13.5%; and specialty fluids, 1.3%.

ANNUAL FINANCIAL DATA

	9/30/00	9/30/99	9/30/98	9/30/97	9/30/96	9/30/95	9/30/94
Earnings Per Share	**[4] 1.46**	**[3] 1.31**	**[2] 1.61**	**1.27**	**[1] 2.60**	**[1] 2.17**	**[1] 0.98**
Cash Flow Per Share	**3.21**	**3.00**	**3.13**	**2.82**	**3.93**	**3.39**	**2.12**
Tang. Book Val. Per Share	**14.05**	**9.10**	**9.01**	**8.83**	**8.76**	**7.97**	**3.08**
Dividends Per Share	**0.44**	**0.44**	**0.43**	**0.40**	**0.37**	**0.41**	**0.27**
Dividend Payout %	**30.1**	**33.6**	**26.7**	**31.5**	**14.2**	**18.9**	**27.5**
INCOME STATEMENT (IN MILLIONS):							
Total Revenues	1,523.0	1,699.0	1,652.8	1,636.7	1,865.2	1,840.9	1,686.6
Costs & Expenses	1,194.0	1,369.0	1,317.9	1,333.7	1,499.4	1,458.7	1,417.7
Depreciation & Amort.	129.0	125.0	115.4	109.9	97.0	94.2	87.4
Operating Income	200.0	205.0	219.5	193.1	268.7	288.0	181.5
Net Interest Inc./(Exp.)	d33.0	d46.0	d42.0	d43.2	d41.7	d35.6	d41.7
Income Before Income Taxes	157.0	136.0	168.0	117.0	279.8	256.0	118.3
Income Taxes	57.0	49.0	60.5	42.1	98.2	101.1	45.0
Equity Earnings/Minority Int.	8.0	10.0	14.1	17.8	12.4	17.0	5.3
Net Income	[4] 108.0	[3] 97.0	[2] 121.6	92.7	[1] 194.1	[1] 171.9	[1] 78.7
Cash Flow	234.0	219.0	233.8	199.4	287.8	262.6	162.5
Average Shs. Outstg. (000)	73,000	73,000	74,600	70,730	73,237	77,452	76,498
BALANCE SHEET (IN MILLIONS):							
Cash & Cash Equivalents	638.0	35.0	39.6	39.2	58.1	90.8	80.9
Total Current Assets	1,190.0	659.0	618.9	611.2	709.8	677.9	606.4
Net Property	806.0	1,024.0	978.0	922.3	903.0	706.5	694.5
Total Assets	2,134.0	1,842.0	1,805.2	1,823.6	1,857.6	1,654.3	1,616.8
Total Current Liabilities	494.0	450.0	536.3	541.4	527.7	402.4	475.1
Long-Term Obligations	329.0	419.0	316.3	285.5	321.5	306.4	307.8
Net Stockholders' Equity	1,047.0	706.0	705.5	727.8	744.9	685.0	562.5
Net Working Capital	696.0	209.0	82.6	69.8	182.1	275.5	131.3
Year-end Shs. Outstg. (000)	67,700	67,124	67,242	69,482	71,589	74,764	135,550
STATISTICAL RECORD:							
Operating Profit Margin %	13.1	12.1	13.3	11.8	14.4	15.6	10.8
Net Profit Margin %	7.1	5.7	7.4	5.7	10.4	9.3	4.7
Return on Equity %	10.3	13.7	17.2	12.7	26.1	25.1	14.0
Return on Assets %	5.1	5.3	6.7	5.1	10.4	10.4	4.9
Debt/Total Assets %	15.4	22.7	17.5	15.7	17.3	18.5	19.0
Price Range	38.44-18.19	29.81-17.94	39.94-21.75	29.25-21.50	31.63-22.75	29.38-14.00	14.63-12.19
P/E Ratio	26.3-12.5	22.8-13.7	24.8-13.5	23.0-16.9	12.2-8.7	13.5-6.5	14.9-12.4
Average Yield %	1.6	1.8	1.4	1.6	1.4	1.9	2.0

Statistics are as originally reported. Adj. for 2-for-1 split, 3/96 & 7/94. [1] Incl. $69.7 mill. ($0.55/sh.) net pre-tax gain, 1996; $32.6 mill., 1995; $6.2 mill., 1994. [2] Incl. $60.0 mill. asset impairment chg., $25.0 mill. pre-tax chg. & $90.3 mill. pre-tax gain. [3] Incl. $110.9 mill. pre-tax chgs. & $9.9 mill. pre-tax gain fr. sale of securities. [4] Incl. $10.0 mill. chg. fr. cost reduction efforts & excl. $36.0 mill. net inc. fr. disc. ops. & $309.0 mill. gain fr. sale of bus.

OFFICERS:
S. W. Bodman, Chmn.
K. F. Burnes, Pres., C.E.O.
R. L. Culver, Exec. V.P., C.F.O.

INVESTOR CONTACT: Eduardo E. Cordero, Investor Relations, (617) 342-6216

PRINCIPAL OFFICE: Two Seaport lane, Suite 1300, Boston, MA 02210

TELEPHONE NUMBER: (617) 345-0100
FAX: (617) 342-6103
WEB: www.cabot-corp.com

NO. OF EMPLOYEES: 4,500 (approx.)

SHAREHOLDERS: 1,700 (approx.)

ANNUAL MEETING: In Mar.

INCORPORATED: DE, 1960

INSTITUTIONAL HOLDINGS:
No. of Institutions: 186
Shares Held: 46,054,788
% Held: 69.4

INDUSTRY: Carbon black (SIC: 2895)

TRANSFER AGENT(S): Fleet National Bank, c/o EquiServe, Providence, RI

NYSE SYMBOL COG
Rec. Pr. 30.80 (5/31/01)

CABOT OIL & GAS CORPORATION

YIELD 0.5%
P/E RATIO 29.9

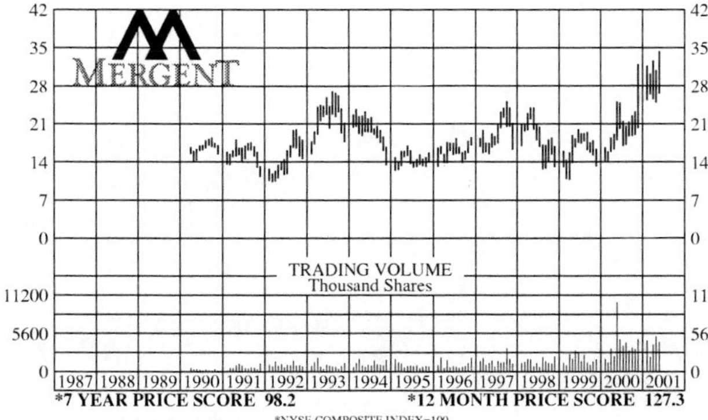

INTERIM EARNINGS (Per Share):

Qtr.	Mar.	June	Sept.	Dec.
1995	d0.36	d0.23	d3.22	d0.24
1996	0.23	0.04	0.13	0.27
1997	0.42	0.09	0.10	0.38
1998	0.12	0.09	d0.10	d0.03
1999	d0.13	Nil	0.15	0.19
2000	0.18	0.05	0.21	0.59

INTERIM DIVIDENDS (Per Share):

Amt.	Decl.	Ex.	Rec.	Pay.
0.04Q	5/09/00	5/17/00	5/19/00	5/26/00
0.04Q	7/31/00	8/09/00	8/11/00	8/25/00
0.04Q	10/27/00	11/08/00	11/10/00	11/24/00
0.04Q	1/30/01	2/07/01	2/09/01	2/23/01
0.04Q	5/04/01	5/16/01	5/18/01	5/25/01

Indicated div.: $0.16

CAPITALIZATION (12/31/00):

	($000)	(%)
Long-Term Debt	253,000	41.9
Deferred Income Tax	108,174	17.9
Common & Surplus	242,505	40.2
Total	603,679	100.0

RECENT DEVELOPMENTS: For the year ended 12/31/00, net income rose to $25.5 million versus $8.5 million a year earlier. Results for 2000 included bad debt expense of $2.1 million and a $39,000 loss on the sale of assets. Results for 1999 included a $4.0 million gain on the sale of assets. Net operating revenues advanced 25.4% to $368.7 million. Results were driven by significantly higher natural gas and crude oil prices. Realized natural gas prices surged 43.7% to $3.19 per thousand cubic feet (Mcf), while crude oil jumped 55.7% to $26.81 per barrel.

PROSPECTS: Strong natural gas prices and rising production levels brighten COG's near-term outlook. In an attempt to lock in the recent strength in natural gas prices, the Company has hedged about half of its gas production from February 2001 through October 2001 at a $5.50 per Mcf floor and a ceiling of $9.55 per Mcf. Separately, COG has set its capital budget for 2001 at $167.0 million, about 37.0% higher than the prior year. Of the total program, COG has earmarked $112.0 million for drilling, 42.0% for exploration wells and 58.0% for development wells.

BUSINESS

CABOT OIL & GAS CORPORATION is engaged in the exploration, development, acquisition and exploitation of oil and gas properties located in four areas of the United States including the onshore Texas and Louisiana Gulf Coast, The Rocky Mountains, Appalachia, and The Mid-Continent or Anadarko Basin. Cabot Oil & Gas was organized in 1989 as the successor to the oil and gas business of Cabot Corporation, founded in 1891. As of 12/31/00, COG's proved reserves totaled 1.02 trillion cubic feet equivalent, 94% of which was natural gas.

REVENUES

(12/31/2000)	($000)	(%)
Natural Gas		
Production	194,185	52.7
Brokered Natural Gas	141,085	38.3
Crude Oil &		
Condensate	25,544	6.9
Other	7,837	2.1
Total	368,651	100.0

ANNUAL FINANCIAL DATA

	12/31/00	12/31/99	12/31/98	12/31/97	12/31/96	12/31/95	12/31/94
Earnings Per Share	**1 1.06**	**0.21**	**0.08**	**0.97**	**0.67**	**d4.05**	**d0.25**
Cash Flow Per Share	**2.99**	**2.36**	**1.72**	**2.67**	**2.54**	**d1.97**	**2.07**
Tang. Book Val. Per Share	**8.31**	**7.52**	**7.31**	**7.46**	**7.03**	**6.48**	**10.67**
Dividends Per Share	**0.16**	**0.16**	**0.16**	**0.16**	**0.16**	**0.16**	**0.16**
Dividend Payout %	**15.1**	**76.2**	**199.8**	**16.5**	**23.9**	...	...
INCOME STATEMENT (IN THOUSANDS):							
Total Revenues	368,651	181,873	159,606	185,127	163,061	213,923	237,067
Costs & Expenses	250,354	92,968	91,490	80,738	73,270	282,861	171,093
Depreciation & Amort.	53,441	53,357	41,186	40,598	42,689	47,206	51,040
Operating Income	64,817	39,498	27,403	63,852	48,787	d116,758	15,013
Net Interest Inc./(Exp.)	d22,878	d25,818	d18,598	d17,961	d17,409	d24,885	d16,651
Income Before Income Taxes	41,939	13,680	8,805	45,891	31,378	d141,643	d1,638
Income Taxes	16,467	5,161	3,501	17,557	10,554	cr55,025	cr643
Net Income	1 25,472	8,519	5,304	28,334	20,824	d86,618	d995
Cash Flow	82,662	58,474	43,088	63,829	57,947	d44,965	45,596
Average Shs. Outstg.	27,665	24,726	25,106	23,922	22,807	22,775	22,018
BALANCE SHEET (IN THOUSANDS):							
Cash & Cash Equivalents	7,574	1,679	2,200	1,784	1,367	3,029	3,773
Total Current Assets	110,269	66,640	71,115	70,533	79,637	52,348	52,019
Net Property	623,174	590,301	629,908	469,399	480,511	474,371	634,934
Total Assets	735,634	659,480	704,160	541,805	561,341	528,155	688,352
Total Current Liabilities	118,108	89,938	99,034	85,872	72,617	60,881	53,740
Long-Term Obligations	253,000	277,000	327,000	183,000	248,000	249,000	268,363
Net Stockholders' Equity	242,505	186,496	182,668	184,062	160,704	147,856	243,082
Net Working Capital	d7,839	d23,298	d27,919	d15,339	7,020	d8,533	d1,721
Year-end Shs. Outstg.	29,192	24,771	24,960	24,667	22,847	22,783	22,757
STATISTICAL RECORD:							
Operating Profit Margin %	17.6	21.7	17.2	34.5	29.9	...	6.3
Net Profit Margin %	6.9	4.7	3.3	15.3	12.8	...	...
Return on Equity %	10.5	4.6	2.9	15.4	13.0	...	...
Return on Assets %	3.5	1.3	0.8	5.2	3.7	...	...
Debt/Total Assets %	34.4	42.0	46.4	33.8	44.2	47.1	39.0
Price Range	32.00-14.06	20.00-10.75	24.00-12.63	25.19-15.38	18.50-13.13	17.00-12.38	23.75-13.38
P/E Ratio	30.2-13.3	95.2-51.2	299.6-157.6	26.0-15.8	27.6-19.6	...	...
Average Yield %	0.7	1.0	0.9	0.8	1.0	1.1	0.9

Statistics are as originally reported. 1 Incls. bad debt exp. of $2.1 mill. & loss on sale of assets of $39,000.

OFFICERS:
R. R. Seegmiller, Chmn., Pres., C.E.O.
S. C. Schroeder, V.P., C.F.O.,Treas.
L. A. Machesney, V.P., Corp. Sec.

INVESTOR CONTACT: Scott C. Schroeder, V.P., C.F.O., Treas., (281) 589-4993

PRINCIPAL OFFICE: 1200 Enclave Parkway, Houston, TX 77077

TELEPHONE NUMBER: (281) 589-4600
FAX: (281) 589-4653
WEB: www.cabotog.com

NO. OF EMPLOYEES: 323 (avg.)

SHAREHOLDERS: 942

ANNUAL MEETING: In May

INCORPORATED: DE, Dec., 1989

INSTITUTIONAL HOLDINGS:
No. of Institutions: 140
Shares Held: 26,402,420
% Held: 89.7

INDUSTRY: Crude petroleum and natural gas (SIC: 1311)

TRANSFER AGENT(S): Bank Boston N.A., Boston, MA

NYSE SYMBOL CDN
Rec. Pr. 20.70 (4/30/01)

CADENCE DESIGN SYSTEMS, INC.

YIELD . . .
P/E RATIO 115.0

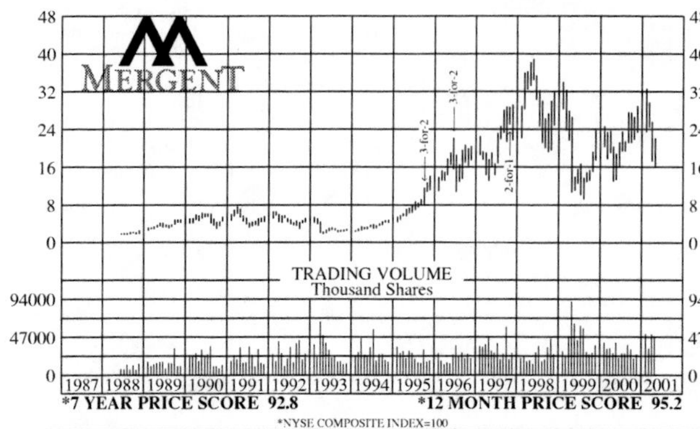

INTERIM EARNINGS (Per Share):

Qtr.	Mar.	June	Sept.	Dec.
1998	d0.01	0.23	d0.34	0.19
1999	0.20	d0.01	d0.17	d0.09
2000	d0.05	0.02	0.05	0.16

INTERIM DIVIDENDS (Per Share):

Amt.	Decl.	Ex.	Rec.	Pay.

No dividends paid.

CAPITALIZATION (12/30/00):

	($000)	(%)
Long-Term Debt	3,298	0.4
Minority Interest	11,612	1.3
Common & Surplus	909,465	98.4
Total	924,375	100.0

RECENT DEVELOPMENTS: For the year ended 12/30/00, net income amounted to $50.0 million compared with a net loss of $14.1 million in 1999. Results for 2000 and 1999 included unusual charges of $59.3 million and $6.8 million, respectively. Results for 1999 also included a charge of $11.4 million from the amortization of deferred stock. Total revenue was $1.28 billion, up 17.0% from $1.09 billion in the prior-year. Tality® Corporation, an operating unit of CDN, contributed $199.0 million to total revenues.

PROSPECTS: The Company anticipates total revenue growth for the full year to be about 18.0%, with product revenue increasing about 30.0%. Service revenue is expected to continue to be negatively affected by the economy. The operating margin for the year is anticipated to be in the range of 20.0%. Going forward, the Company will continue to invest in research and development and customer relations, while managing costs.

BUSINESS

CADENCE DESIGN SYSTEMS, INC. provides software and other technology and offers design and methodology services for the product development requirements of the world's electronics companies. The Company licenses its electronic design automation software technology and provides a range of professional services to companies ranging from consulting services to helping customers optimize their product development processes. CDN is a supplier of end-to-end products and services that are used by companies to design and develop complex chips and electronic systems including semiconductors, computer systems and peripherals, telecommunications and networking equipment, mobile and wireless devices, automotive electronics, and consumer products. Revenues for 2000 were derived: product, 49.0%; services, 26.3%; and maintenance, 24.7%.

ANNUAL FINANCIAL DATA

	12/30/00	1/1/00	1/2/99	1/3/98	12/28/96	12/31/95	12/31/94
Earnings Per Share	**[1] [3] 0.19**	**[1] d0.06**	**[1] 0.14**	**[1] [2] 0.77**	**[1] 0.16**	**0.52**	**[1] 0.19**
Cash Flow Per Share	**0.98**	**0.62**	**0.58**	**1.08**	**0.44**	**0.77**	**0.39**
Tang. Book Val. Per Share	**2.35**	**2.36**	**2.84**	**3.34**	**2.31**	**0.62**	**0.79**
INCOME STATEMENT (IN MILLIONS):							
Total Revenues	1,279.6	1,093.3	1,216.1	926.4	741.5	548.4	429.1
Costs & Expenses	1,009.3	942.2	1,008.5	637.2	598.5	384.5	340.8
Depreciation & Amort.	206.8	163.9	102.4	56.6	51.7	46.0	44.3
Operating Income	63.4	d12.7	105.2	232.5	91.3	117.9	44.0
Net Interest Inc./(Exp.)	. . .	. . .	. . .	. . .	2.4	2.6	. . .
Income Before Income Taxes	68.0	d11.4	112.7	258.8	90.5	135.1	48.9
Income Taxes	18.0	2.7	80.7	78.4	61.4	37.8	12.2
Net Income	[1] [3] 50.0	[1] d14.1	[1] 32.0	[1] [2] 180.4	[1] 29.0	97.3	[1] 36.6
Cash Flow	256.8	149.8	134.4	237.0	80.8	143.3	76.1
Average Shs. Outstg. (000)	262,696	242,037	233,647	219,552	183,180	185,896	197,610
BALANCE SHEET (IN MILLIONS):							
Cash & Cash Equivalents	137.0	118.8	209.8	304.2	285.5	96.6	96.9
Total Current Assets	556.8	479.9	579.7	609.1	491.1	206.9	191.9
Net Property	368.9	330.4	262.7	197.4	160.9	124.1	122.1
Total Assets	1,477.3	1,459.7	1,406.0	1,023.9	717.0	374.0	361.0
Total Current Liabilities	491.6	421.6	327.9	268.8	231.6	200.4	164.4
Long-Term Obligations	3.3	25.0	136.4	1.6	20.3	1.6	2.1
Net Stockholders' Equity	909.5	986.1	876.2	741.4	431.2	132.2	173.6
Net Working Capital	65.3	58.4	251.8	340.3	259.6	6.5	27.5
Year-end Shs. Outstg. (000)	243,662	243,328	204,291	214,405	173,222	157,128	170,584
STATISTICAL RECORD:							
Operating Profit Margin %	5.0	. . .	8.6	25.1	12.3	21.5	10.3
Net Profit Margin %	3.9	. . .	2.6	19.5	3.9	17.7	8.5
Return on Equity %	5.5	. . .	3.7	24.3	6.7	73.6	18.3
Return on Assets %	3.4	. . .	2.3	17.6	4.0	26.0	10.1
Debt/Total Assets %	0.2	1.7	9.7	0.2	2.8	0.4	0.6
Price Range	28.94-13.00	34.13-9.19	39.00-19.13	29.13-13.06	22.19-10.69	14.13-4.28	4.83-2.28
P/E Ratio	152.2-68.4	. . .	278.4-136.5	35.5-15.9	138.6-66.8	27.0-8.2	26.0-12.2

Statistics are as originally reported. [1] Incl. unusual chg. of $14.7 mill., 1994; $100.5 mill., 1996; $44.1 mill., 1997; $263.6 mill., 1998; $59.3 mill., 1999; and $6.8 mill., 2000. [2] Excl. $12.3 mill. chg. fr. cumul. effect of acctg. method. [3] Incl. $11.4 mill. amort. of deferred stock chg.

OFFICERS:
D. L. Lucas, Chmn.
H. R. Bingham, Pres, C.E.O.
W. Potter, Sr. V.P., C.F.O.

INVESTOR CONTACT: Investor Relations, (408) 236-5972

PRINCIPAL OFFICE: 2655 Seely Road, Building 5, San Jose, CA 95134

TELEPHONE NUMBER: (408) 943-1234
FAX: (408) 944-0747
WEB: www.cadence.com

NO. OF EMPLOYEES: 5,650 (approx.)

SHAREHOLDERS: 1,464 (Approx.); 42,007 (approx. beneficial owners)

ANNUAL MEETING: In May

INCORPORATED: DE, May, 1988

INSTITUTIONAL HOLDINGS:
No. of Institutions: 233
Shares Held: 202,483,134
% Held: 82.7

INDUSTRY: Prepackaged software (SIC: 7372)

TRANSFER AGENT(S): Mellon Investor Services, South Hackensack, NJ

NYSE SYMBOL CWT
Rec. Pr. 24.75 (5/31/01)

CALIFORNIA WATER SERVICE GROUP

YIELD 4.5%
P/E RATIO 19.0

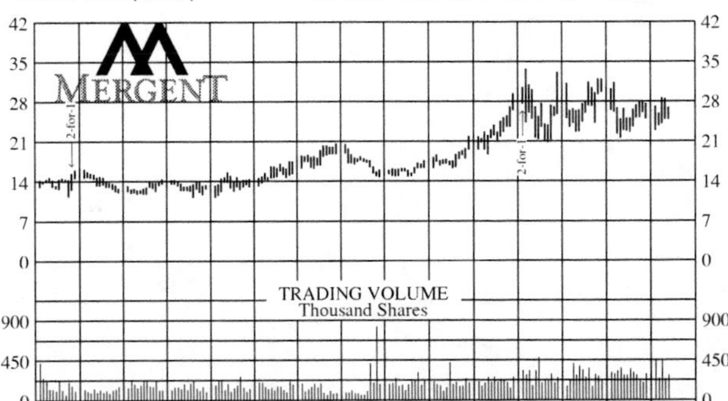

*7 YEAR PRICE SCORE 83.9   *12 MONTH PRICE SCORE 109.1

*NYSE COMPOSITE INDEX=100

INTERIM EARNINGS (Per Share):

Qtr.	Mar.	June	Sept.	Dec.
1996	0.09	0.46	0.69	0.27
1997	0.23	0.70	0.62	0.28
1998	0.12	0.28	0.72	0.33
1999	0.20	0.44	0.62	0.30
2000	0.09	0.38	0.60	0.23

INTERIM DIVIDENDS (Per Share):

Amt.	Decl.	Ex.	Rec.	Pay.
0.275Q	4/19/00	4/27/00	5/01/00	5/15/00
0.275Q	7/19/00	7/28/00	8/01/00	8/15/00
0.275Q	10/18/00	10/30/00	11/01/00	11/15/00
0.279Q	1/24/01	1/30/01	2/01/01	2/15/01
0.279Q	4/18/01	4/27/01	5/01/01	5/15/01

Indicated div.: $1.12 (Div. Reinv. Plan)

CAPITALIZATION (12/31/00):

	($000)	(%)
Long-Term Debt	187,098	45.1
Deferred Income Tax	25,620	6.2
Preferred Stock	3,475	0.8
Common & Surplus	198,834	47.9
Total	415,027	100.0

RECENT DEVELOPMENTS: For the year ended 12/31/00, net income amounted to $20.0 million, down 9.1% from $22.0 million in 1999. Earnings were adversely affected by higher production costs due to increased customer usage and rate increases implemented by wholesale suppliers in seven districts. Operating revenues rose 4.2% to $244.8 million compared with $234.9 million a year earlier. Net operating income inched up to $33.2 million versus $33.0 million the year before.

PROSPECTS: CWT has agreed to acquire the water and wastewater assets of Rio Grande Utility Corporation for $2.3 million plus the assumption of $3.1 million in debt. Separately, as part of a five-year meter reading agreement with Los Alamos County, New Mexico, CWT will read the county's 8,300 electric, 7,200 gas and 6,700 water meters each month for an annual fee of about $185,000. Meanwhile, CWT completed the acquistion of Buhl, EPTCO, Nish and Tulco Water Systems.

BUSINESS

CALIFORNIA WATER SERVICE GROUP is a public utility water company that, as of 3/27/01, owns and operates 21 water systems serving 80 communities in California, New Mexico and Washington. CWT is the parent company of California Water Service Co., New Mexico Water Service Co., CWS Utility Services and Washington Water Service Co. The sole business of the Company consists of the production, purchase, storage, purification, distribution and sale of water for domestic, industrial, public, and irrigation uses, and for fire protection. Annual water production totals nearly 105 billion gallons with 50% derived from purchased surface sources and 50% pumped from more than 500 Company-owned wells. In September 1999, Washington Water Service Co., was formed as a new subsidiary.

REVENUES

(12/31/00)	($000)	(%)
Residential	171,234	69.9
Business	44,211	18.1
Industrial	11,014	4.5
Public Authorities	11,609	4.7
Other	6,738	2.8
Total	244,806	100.0

ANNUAL FINANCIAL DATA

	12/31/00	12/31/99	12/31/98	12/31/97	12/31/96	12/31/95	12/31/94
Earnings Per Share	**1.31**	**1.53**	**1.45**	**1.83**	**1.51**	**1.17**	**1.22**
Cash Flow Per Share	**2.53**	**2.76**	**2.61**	**2.93**	**2.52**	**2.09**	**2.17**
Tang. Book Val. Per Share	**13.13**	**13.70**	**13.38**	**13.00**	**12.22**	**11.72**	**11.56**
Dividends Per Share	**1.10**	**1.08**	**1.07**	**1.05**	**1.04**	**1.02**	**0.99**
Dividend Payout %	**84.0**	**70.9**	**73.8**	**57.6**	**69.1**	**87.5**	**81.1**
INCOME STATEMENT (IN THOUSANDS):							
Total Revenues	244,806	206,440	186,273	195,324	182,764	165,086	157,271
Costs & Expenses	170,079	138,669	122,056	124,036	119,265	110,686	103,353
Depreciation & Amort.	18,368	15,802	14,563	13,670	12,665	11,436	10,958
Maintenance Exp.	11,592	9,183	9,030	9,319	8,317	7,722	7,855
Operating Income	33,196	30,610	30,074	34,349	30,367	25,392	25,505
Net Interest Inc./(Exp.)	d14,646	d13,201	d12,446	d11,902	d11,907	d11,462	d11,384
Income Taxes	11,571	12,176	10,550	13,950	12,150	9,850	9,600
Net Income	19,963	19,919	18,395	23,305	19,067	14,698	14,408
Cash Flow	38,179	35,568	32,805	36,822	31,579	25,981	25,213
Average Shs. Outstg.	15,173	12,936	12,619	12,619	12,580	12,506	11,676
BALANCE SHEET (IN THOUSANDS):							
Gross Property	851,281	737,352	680,690	647,648	618,432	584,392	559,180
Accumulated Depreciation	269,273	221,998	202,385	187,241	174,844	162,217	151,285
Net Property	582,008	515,354	478,305	460,407	443,588	422,175	407,895
Total Assets	666,605	587,618	548,499	531,297	512,390	484,883	464,228
Long-Term Obligations	187,098	156,572	136,345	139,205	142,153	145,540	128,944
Net Stockholders' Equity	202,309	180,657	172,279	167,540	157,701	150,424	147,922
Year-end Shs. Outstg.	15,146	12,936	12,619	12,619	12,620	12,538	12,494
STATISTICAL RECORD:							
Operating Profit Margin %	13.6	14.8	16.1	17.6	16.6	15.4	16.2
Net Profit Margin %	8.2	9.6	9.9	11.9	10.4	8.9	9.2
Net Inc./Net Property %	3.4	3.9	3.8	5.1	4.3	3.5	3.5
Net Inc./Tot. Capital %	4.8	5.6	5.5	7.0	5.9	4.7	5.0
Return on Equity %	9.9	11.0	10.7	13.9	12.1	9.8	9.7
Accum. Depr./Gross Prop. %	31.6	30.1	29.7	28.9	28.3	27.8	27.1
Price Range	31.38-21.50	32.00-22.56	33.75-20.75	29.38-18.63	21.88-16.25	17.63-14.81	20.50-14.69
P/E Ratio	23.9-16.4	20.9-14.7	23.3-14.3	16.1-10.2	14.5-10.8	15.1-12.7	16.8-12.0
Average Yield %	4.2	4.0	3.9	4.4	5.5	6.3	5.6

Statistics are as originally reported. Adj. for stk. split: 2-for-1, 1/98

OFFICERS:
R. W. Foy, Chmn.
P. C. Nelson, Pres., C.E.O.
G. F. Feeney, V.P., C.F.O., Treas.

INVESTOR CONTACT: Gerald F. Feeney, (408) 367-8216

PRINCIPAL OFFICE: 1720 North First Street, San Jose, CA 95112-4598

TELEPHONE NUMBER: (408) 367-8200
FAX: (408) 437-9185
WEB: www.calwater.com

NO. OF EMPLOYEES: 797 (avg.)

SHAREHOLDERS: 11,000 (approx.)

ANNUAL MEETING: In Apr.

INCORPORATED: CA, Dec., 1926

INSTITUTIONAL HOLDINGS:
No. of Institutions: 62
Shares Held: 2,320,611
% Held: 15.3

INDUSTRY: Water supply (SIC: 4941)

TRANSFER AGENT(S): BankBoston Corp., Boston, MA

NYSE SYMBOL ELY
Rec. Pr. 22.71 (5/31/01)

CALLAWAY GOLF COMPANY

YIELD ...
P/E RATIO 19.6

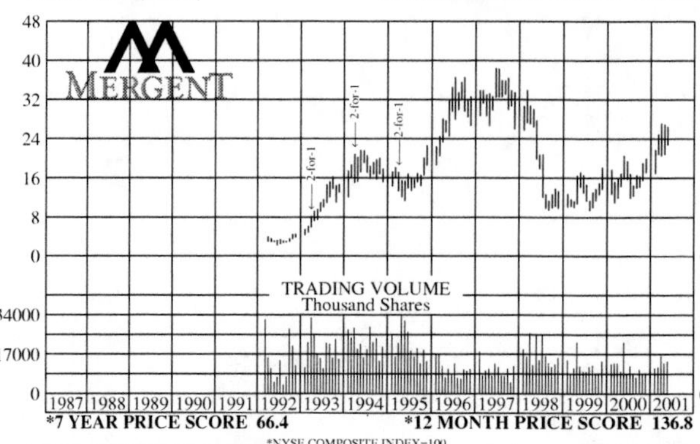

*7 YEAR PRICE SCORE 66.4 *12 MONTH PRICE SCORE 136.8

*NYSE COMPOSITE INDEX=100

INTERIM EARNINGS (Per Share):

Qtr.	Mar.	June	Sept.	Dec.
1997	0.34	0.66	0.52	0.34
1998	0.16	0.30	0.08	d0.93
1999	0.18	0.35	0.25	0.00
2000	0.22	0.62	0.28	0.04

INTERIM DIVIDENDS (Per Share):

Amt.	Decl.	Ex.	Rec.	Pay.
0.07Q	5/03/00	5/12/00	5/16/00	6/06/00
0.07Q	8/23/00	8/31/00	9/05/00	9/26/00
0.07Q	11/09/00	11/20/00	11/22/00	12/13/00
0.07Q	2/08/01	2/16/01	2/21/01	3/14/01
0.07Q	5/02/01	5/11/01	5/15/01	6/05/01

Indicated div.: $0.28(Div. Reinv. Plan)

CAPITALIZATION (12/31/00):

	($000)	(%)
Common & Surplus	511,744	100.0
Total	511,744	100.0

RECENT DEVELOPMENTS: For the year ended 12/31/00, net income advanced 50.1% to $83.0 million compared with $55.3 million in 1999. Results for 2000 included a one-time tax benefit of $0.05 per share associated with consolidation of the Company's club and ball operations. Results for 1999 included a restructuring gain of $5.9 million and nonrecurring costs of $5.7 million. Net sales were $840.4 million, up 16.9% from $719.0 million a year earlier.

PROSPECTS: Looking ahead, the Company expects revenues and gross margins for fiscal 2001 to be approximately $900.0 million and 50.0%, respectively. Pre-tax profit for the year should be approximately 19.0% of net revenues, while earnings per share should be in the range of $1.51 to $1.56. Meanwhile, ELY's efforts to expand profitability during fiscal 2001 will include focusing on the golf ball business, introducing new products and targeting products to average golfers.

BUSINESS

CALLAWAY GOLF COMPANY designs, manufactures, and markets innovative golf clubs. The Company's golf clubs are sold at premium prices to average and skilled golfers on the basis of performance, ease of use and appearance. Primary products currently include BIG BERTHA® Metal Woods and Irons, including BIG BERTHA ERC™ II FORGED TITANIUM DRIVERS, BIG BERTHA HAWK EYE® VFT™ TITANIUM DRIVERS, and FAIRWAY WOODS, BIG BERTHA STEELHEAD PLUS™ STAINLESS STEEL DRIVERS and FAIRWAY WOODS, HAWK EYE TUNGSTEN INJECTED™ TITANIUM IRONS, STEELHEAD™ X-14® and STEELHEAD X-14 PRO SERIES STAINLESS STEEL IRONS, and BOBBY JONES® and CARLSBAD SERIES™ PUTTERS. ELY also makes and sells ODYSSEY® PUTTERS, including WHITE HOT™, TRIHOT™, and DUAL FORCE® PUTTERS. Callaway Golf Ball Company, a wholly-owned subsidiary of ELY, makes and sells the Callaway Golf® Rule 35™ FIRMFEEL™ and SOFTFEEL golf ball.

ANNUAL FINANCIAL DATA

	12/31/00	12/31/99	12/31/98	12/31/97	12/31/96	12/31/95	12/31/94
Earnings Per Share	[4] **1.14**	[3] **0.78**	[2] **d0.38**	[1] **1.85**	**1.73**	**1.40**	**1.07**
Cash Flow Per Share	**1.71**	**1.35**	**0.13**	**2.12**	**1.91**	**1.55**	**1.15**
Tang. Book Val. Per Share	**5.38**	**4.98**	**4.33**	**4.97**	**4.97**	**3.17**	**2.74**
Dividends Per Share	**0.28**	**0.28**	**0.28**	**0.28**	**0.24**	**0.20**	**0.10**
Dividend Payout %	**24.1**	**35.9**	**...**	**15.1**	**13.9**	**14.3**	**9.4**
INCOME STATEMENT (IN THOUSANDS):							
Total Revenues	837,627	714,471	697,621	842,927	678,512	553,287	448,729
Costs & Expenses	675,323	594,685	701,875	614,330	475,993	388,125	316,015
Depreciation & Amort.	40,249	39,877	35,885	19,408	12,691	10,778	6,184
Operating Income	122,055	79,909	d40,139	209,189	189,828	154,384	126,530
Net Interest Inc./(Exp.)	7,267	5,588	1,240	4,576	5,767	4,017	2,536
Income Before Income Taxes	129,322	85,497	d38,899	213,765	195,595	158,401	129,405
Income Taxes	47,366	30,175	cr12,335	81,061	73,258	60,665	51,383
Net Income	[4] 81,956	[3] 55,322	[2] d26,564	[1] 132,704	122,337	97,736	78,022
Cash Flow	122,205	95,199	9,321	152,112	135,028	108,514	84,206
Average Shs. Outstg.	71,412	70,397	69,463	71,698	70,661	69,855	73,104
BALANCE SHEET (IN THOUSANDS):							
Cash & Cash Equivalents	102,596	112,602	45,618	26,204	108,457	59,157	54,356
Total Current Assets	342,469	310,472	323,606	281,786	311,513	209,705	187,390
Net Property	134,712	142,214	172,794	142,503	91,346	69,034	50,619
Total Assets	630,934	616,783	655,827	561,714	428,428	289,975	243,622
Total Current Liabilities	109,306	105,274	184,008	72,384	61,052	62,834	56,598
Net Stockholders' Equity	511,744	499,934	453,096	481,425	362,267	224,934	186,414
Net Working Capital	233,163	205,198	139,598	209,402	250,461	146,871	130,792
Year-end Shs. Outstg.	74,143	76,302	75,098	74,252	72,855	70,912	68,094
STATISTICAL RECORD:							
Operating Profit Margin %	14.6	11.2	...	24.8	28.0	27.9	28.2
Net Profit Margin %	9.8	7.7	...	15.7	18.0	17.7	17.4
Return on Equity %	16.0	11.1	...	27.6	33.8	43.5	41.9
Return on Assets %	13.0	9.0	...	23.6	28.6	33.7	32.0
Price Range	20.63-10.94	18.19-9.31	33.94-9.38	38.50-25.88	36.63-18.50	22.63-11.25	21.69-12.06
P/E Ratio	18.1-9.6	23.3-11.9	...	20.8-14.0	21.2-10.7	16.2-8.0	20.4-11.3
Average Yield %	...	1.0	1.3	0.9	0.9	1.2	0.6

Statistics are as originally reported. Adj. for stk. split: 2-for-1, 3/95, 3/94 & 3/93. [1] Incl. nonrecur. chrg. of $12 mill. for the settlement of litigaion between the Company & a former employee. [2] Incl. restruct. chrg. of $54.2 mill. and reserves for excess inventory chrg. of $30.0 mill. [3] Incl. restruct. chrg. of $5.9 mill. [4] Incl. one-time tax benefit of $0.05 per share assoc. with consol. of ELY'S club and ball operations.

OFFICERS:
E. Callaway, Chmn., Pres., C.E.O.
B. J. Holiday, Exec. V.P., C.F.O.
S. McCracken, Sr. Exec. V.P., Sec.

INVESTOR CONTACT: Krista Mallory, Dir., Investor Relations, (760) 931-1771

PRINCIPAL OFFICE: 2180 Rutherford Road, Carlsbad, CA 92008-8815

TELEPHONE NUMBER: (760) 931-1771
FAX: (760) 931-8013
WEB: www.callawaygolf.com

NO. OF EMPLOYEES: 2,600 (approx.)

SHAREHOLDERS: 9,000 (approx.)

ANNUAL MEETING: In May

INCORPORATED: CA, Sept., 1982; reincorp., DE, July, 1999

INSTITUTIONAL HOLDINGS:
No. of Institutions: 179
Shares Held: 44,937,107
% Held: 60.6

INDUSTRY: Sporting and athletic goods, nec (SIC: 3949)

TRANSFER AGENT(S): Mellon Investor Services, Ridgefield Park, NJ

NYSE SYMBOL CPN
Rec. Pr. 56.99 (4/30/01)

CALPINE CORPORATION

YIELD ...
P/E RATIO 51.8

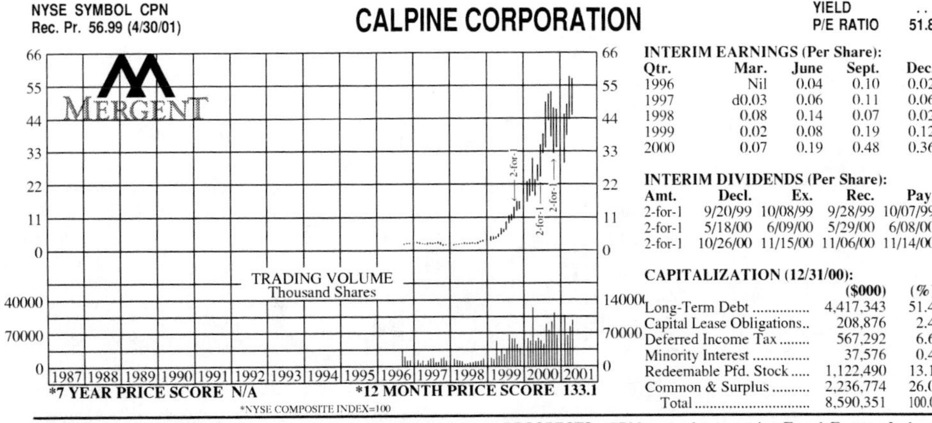

*7 YEAR PRICE SCORE N/A *12 MONTH PRICE SCORE 133.1

*NYSE COMPOSITE INDEX=100

INTERIM EARNINGS (Per Share):

Qtr.	Mar.	June	Sept.	Dec.
1996	Nil	0.04	0.10	0.02
1997	d0.03	0.06	0.11	0.06
1998	0.08	0.14	0.07	0.02
1999	0.02	0.08	0.19	0.12
2000	0.07	0.19	0.48	0.36

INTERIM DIVIDENDS (Per Share):

Amt.	Decl.	Ex.	Rec.	Pay.
2-for-1	9/20/99	10/08/99	9/28/99	10/07/99
2-for-1	5/18/00	6/09/00	5/29/00	6/08/00
2-for-1	10/26/00	11/15/00	11/06/00	11/14/00

CAPITALIZATION (12/31/00):

	($000)	(%)
Long-Term Debt	4,417,343	51.4
Capital Lease Obligations	208,876	2.4
Deferred Income Tax	567,292	6.6
Minority Interest	37,576	0.4
Redeemable Pfd. Stock	1,122,490	13.1
Common & Surplus	2,236,774	26.0
Total	8,590,351	100.0

RECENT DEVELOPMENTS: For the twelve months ended 12/31/00, income before an extraordinary charge soared to $324.7 million compared with $96.2 million in 1999. Results for 2000 and 1999 excluded a net extraordinary charge of $796,000 and $793,000, respectively. Total revenue more than tripled to $2.28 billion from $847.7 million in the prior year. Gross profit jumped to $724.1 million compared with $285.9 million in the previous year. Income from operations surged to $602.4 million.

PROSPECTS: CPN agreed to acquire Encal Energy Ltd., a natural gas and petroleum exploration and development company, through a stock-for-stock exchange valued at about $1.20 billion, including the assumption of debt. Upon completion of the acquisition, CPN will gain about 1.0 trillion cubic feet of natural gas reserves and access to firm gas transportation capacity from western Canada to California and the eastern U.S. The acquisition enhances CPN's natural gas-fired electric generating assets.

BUSINESS

CALPINE CORPORATION is an independent power company engaged in the development, acquisition, ownership and operation of power generation facilities, and the sale of electricity predominantly to utility or other third-party end users in the U.S. The Company is focused on clean, efficient combined-cycle, natural gas-fired generation and is a producer of renewable geothermal energy. As of 12/31/00, CPN owned interest in 44 power plants, which have an aggregate capacity of 4,273 megawatts. The Company also had 24 plants under construction totaling 13,400 megawatts and 24 plants in announced development totaling 14,200 megawatts. During 2000, the Company completed construction of five facilities totaling nearly 1,500 megawatts of power generation facilities in New England, Texas and the Midwest.

ANNUAL FINANCIAL DATA

	3 12/31/00	12/31/99	12/31/98	12/31/97	12/31/96	12/31/95	12/31/94
Earnings Per Share	2 1.11	2 0.43	2 0.27	0.21	0.16	0.07	1 0.07
Cash Flow Per Share	1.66	0.82	0.71	0.48	0.47	0.29	2.33
Tang. Book Val. Per Share	7.88	3.82	1.78	1.50	1.28	0.29	1.80
INCOME STATEMENT (IN MILLIONS):							
Total Revenues	2,282.8	847.7	555.9	276.3	214.6	132.1	94.8
Costs & Expenses	1,538.8	534.0	335.0	132.3	111.2	63.5	42.6
Depreciation & Amort.	141.6	87.2	74.3	46.8	36.6	25.9	20.3
Operating Income	602.4	226.5	146.7	97.2	66.8	42.7	31.8
Net Interest Inc./(Exp.)	d16.8	d67.1	d74.4	d47.2	d45.3	d32.2	d23.9
Income Taxes	219.0	62.0	27.1	18.5	9.1	5.0	3.9
Equity Earnings/Minority Int.	d2.7	...	...	...	...	...	...
Net Income	2 324.7	2 96.2	2 46.3	34.7	18.7	7.4	1 6.0
Cash Flow	466.3	183.5	120.6	81.5	55.3	33.3	26.4
Average Shs. Outstg. (000)	280,776	222,644	169,312	168,128	117,440	113,208	11,309
BALANCE SHEET (IN MILLIONS):							
Gross Property	7,787.5	3,093.5	1,298.3	868.1	750.7	508.3	369.5
Accumulated Depreciation	328.5	227.1	204.0	148.4	100.7	60.5	34.0
Net Property	7,459.1	2,866.4	1,094.3	719.7	650.1	447.8	335.5
Total Assets	9,737.3	3,991.6	1,728.9	1,381.0	1,030.2	554.5	421.4
Long-Term Obligations	4,626.2	2,006.2	1,065.9	742.9	563.6	321.8	307.1
Net Stockholders' Equity	2,236.8	964.6	287.0	240.0	203.1	25.2	18.6
Year-end Shs. Outstg. (000)	283,715	252,216	161,288	160,480	158,744	86,304	10,388
STATISTICAL RECORD:							
Operating Profit Margin %	26.4	26.7	26.4	35.2	31.1	32.3	33.5
Net Profit Margin %	14.2	11.4	8.3	12.6	8.7	5.6	6.4
Net Inc./Net Property %	4.4	3.4	4.2	4.8	2.9	1.6	1.8
Net Inc./Tot. Capital %	3.8	2.7	3.1	3.1	2.2	1.7	1.6
Return on Equity %	14.5	10.0	16.1	14.5	9.2	29.2	32.3
Accum. Depr./Gross Prop. %	4.2	7.3	15.7	17.1	13.4	11.9	9.2
Price Range	52.97-16.09	16.38-3.16	3.45-1.59	2.87-1.55	2.50-2.00	...	...
P/E Ratio	47.7-14.5	37.9-7.3	12.6-5.8	13.9-7.5	15.7-12.6	...	...

Statistics are as originally reported. Adj. for 5.194-for-1 split, 9/96. Adj. for 2-for-1 split, 10/99, 6/00 & 11/00. 1 Incl. $1.0 mill. provision for write-off of project costs. 2 Excl. net extraord. chgs. of $641,000, 1998; $793,000, 1999; $796,000, 2000. 3 Revs. refl. CPN's strategy to acq. & build low-cost power generation plants in key mkts. in the U.S.

OFFICERS:
P. Cartwright, Chmn., Pres., C.E.O.
A. Curtis, Exec. V.P., C.F.O.
D. Fishback, Sr. V.P., C.I.O.

INVESTOR CONTACT: Investor Relations, (408) 995-5115

PRINCIPAL OFFICE: 50 West San Fernando Street, San Jose, CA 95113

TELEPHONE NUMBER: (408) 995-5115
FAX: (408) 995-0505
WEB: www.calpine.com

NO. OF EMPLOYEES: 1,883

SHAREHOLDERS: 547

ANNUAL MEETING: In May

INCORPORATED: CA, June, 1984; reincorp., DE, Sept., 1996

INSTITUTIONAL HOLDINGS:
No. of Institutions: 440
Shares Held: 265,405,055
% Held: 88.0

INDUSTRY: Electric services (SIC: 4911)

TRANSFER AGENT(S): First Chicago Trust Company of New York, Jersey City, NJ

NYSE SYMBOL CPB
Rec. Pr. 29.54 (5/31/01)

CAMPBELL SOUP COMPANY

YIELD 3.0%
P/E RATIO 18.7

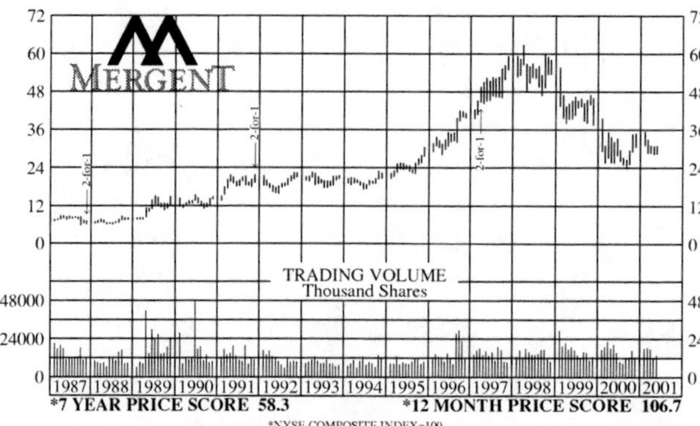

*7 YEAR PRICE SCORE 58.3 *12 MONTH PRICE SCORE 106.7

*NYSE COMPOSITE INDEX=100

INTERIM EARNINGS (Per Share):

Qtr.	Oct.	Jan.	Apr.	July
1996-97	0.18	0.59	0.34	0.42
1997-98	0.58	0.67	d0.08	0.40
1998-99	0.58	0.49	0.37	0.18
1999-00	0.54	0.65	0.32	0.14
2000-01	0.47	0.65	...	...

INTERIM DIVIDENDS (Per Share):

Amt.	Decl.	Ex.	Rec.	Pay.
0.225Q	3/22/00	4/05/00	4/07/00	5/01/00
0.225Q	6/22/00	7/05/00	7/07/00	7/31/00
0.225Q	9/28/00	10/04/00	10/06/00	10/31/00
0.225Q	11/16/00	1/03/01	1/05/01	1/31/01
0.225Q	3/22/01	4/04/01	4/06/01	4/30/01

Indicated div.: $0.90 (Div. Reinv. Plan)

CAPITALIZATION (7/30/00):

	($000)	(%)
Long-Term Debt	1,218,000	89.9
Common & Surplus	137,000	10.1
Total	1,355,000	100.0

RECENT DEVELOPMENTS: For the quarter ended 1/28/01, net earnings totaled $271.0 million, down 3.6% versus $281.0 million in the prior year. Net sales grew 2.1% to $1.96 billion from $1.92 billion the previous year. Sales of Soups and Sauces rose 1.8% to $1.39 billion from $1.36 billion the year before. Biscuits and Confectionery sales climbed 5.1% to $440.5 million from $419.1 million a year earlier. Away From Home sales were $146.2 million, up 2.2% versus $143.0 million the prior year. Operating earnings slipped 2.0% to $491.0 million.

PROSPECTS: On 1/29/01, CPB announced that it has agreed to purchase several soup and sauce businesses in Europe from Unilever for about $950.0 million. The acquisition of these businesses, which have combined annual sales of more than $400.0 million, is subject to European regulatory approval and other customary conditions. Meanwhile, the Company intends to increase marketing spending above planned spending levels in its core U.S. businesses in the second half of fiscal 2001, reflecting the success of these initiatives in the first half of the year.

BUSINESS

CAMPBELL SOUP COMPANY is a major manufacturer of prepared convenience foods. CPB is also involved in the fresh foods, refrigerated foods, candy and mail order businesses. Well-known brand names include CAMPBELL'S, SWANSON, PEPPERIDGE FARM, V-8, PACE, PREGO, and GODIVA chocolates. Products sold by CPB under these brand names include: canned foods such as ready-to-serve soups, juices, gravies, pasta, meat and vegetables; frozen foods such as dinners, breakfasts and entrees; other items including salsa, pickles and relishes, various condiments, chocolate, salads and confectionery items. For fiscal year 2000, sales were derived: Soup and Sauces, 68.0%; Biscuits and Confectionery, 23.1%; Away From Home (including the foodservice business), 8.4%; and Other, 0.5%.

ANNUAL FINANCIAL DATA

	7/30/00	8/1/99	8/2/98	8/3/97	7/28/96	7/30/95	7/31/94
Earnings Per Share	**1.65**	**2 1.63**	**3 1.50**	**2 1.51**	**1 1.61**	**1.40**	**1.26**
Cash Flow Per Share	**2.23**	**2.20**	**2.07**	**2.21**	**2.27**	**1.99**	**1.76**
Tang. Book Val. Per Share	...	...	...	...	**1.64**	**1.20**	**2.78**
Dividends Per Share	**0.90**	**0.90**	**0.84**	**0.77**	**0.69**	**0.62**	**0.56**
Dividend Payout %	**54.5**	**55.2**	**56.0**	**51.0**	**42.9**	**44.3**	**44.6**
INCOME STATEMENT (IN MILLIONS):							
Total Revenues	6,267.0	6,424.0	6,696.0	7,964.0	7,678.0	7,278.0	6,690.0
Costs & Expenses	4,751.0	4,899.0	5,187.0	6,370.0	6,035.0	5,837.0	5,408.0
Depreciation & Amort.	251.0	255.0	261.0	328.0	326.0	294.0	255.0
Operating Income	1,265.0	1,270.0	1,248.0	1,266.0	1,317.0	1,147.0	1,027.0
Net Interest Inc./(Exp.)	d188.0	d173.0	d175.0	d159.0	d120.0	d105.0	d64.0
Income Before Income Taxes	1,077.0	1,097.0	1,073.0	1,107.0	1,197.0	1,042.0	963.0
Income Taxes	363.0	373.0	384.0	394.0	395.0	344.0	333.0
Net Income	714.0	2 724.0	3 689.0	2 713.0	1 802.0	698.0	630.0
Cash Flow	965.0	979.0	950.0	1,041.0	1,128.0	992.0	885.0
Average Shs. Outstg. (000)	432,000	445,000	460,000	472,000	498,000	498,000	502,000
BALANCE SHEET (IN MILLIONS):							
Cash & Cash Equivalents	27.0	6.0	16.0	26.0	34.0	53.0	96.0
Total Current Assets	1,168.0	1,294.0	1,440.0	1,583.0	1,618.0	1,581.0	1,601.0
Net Property	1,644.0	1,726.0	1,723.0	2,560.0	2,681.0	2,584.0	2,401.0
Total Assets	5,196.0	5,522.0	5,633.0	6,459.0	6,632.0	6,315.0	4,992.0
Total Current Liabilities	3,032.0	3,146.0	2,803.0	2,981.0	2,229.0	2,164.0	1,665.0
Long-Term Obligations	1,218.0	1,330.0	1,169.0	1,153.0	744.0	857.0	560.0
Net Stockholders' Equity	137.0	235.0	874.0	1,520.0	2,618.0	2,312.0	1,961.0
Net Working Capital	d1,864.0	d1,852.0	d1,363.0	d1,398.0	d611.0	d583.0	d64.0
Year-end Shs. Outstg. (000)	439,000	429,000	448,000	458,000	494,000	498,000	496,638
STATISTICAL RECORD:							
Operating Profit Margin %	20.2	19.8	18.6	15.9	17.2	15.8	15.4
Net Profit Margin %	11.4	11.3	10.3	9.0	10.4	9.6	9.4
Return on Equity %	521.2	308.1	78.8	46.9	30.6	30.2	32.1
Return on Assets %	13.7	13.1	12.2	11.0	12.1	11.1	12.6
Debt/Total Assets %	23.4	24.1	20.8	17.9	11.2	13.6	11.2
Price Range	39.63-23.75	55.75-37.44	62.88-46.69	59.44-39.38	42.13-28.00	30.63-20.50	23.00-17.13
P/E Ratio	24.0-14.4	34.2-23.0	41.9-31.1	39.4-26.1	26.2-17.4	21.9-14.6	18.3-13.6
Average Yield %	2.8	1.9	1.5	1.6	2.0	2.4	2.8

Statistics are as originally reported. Adj. for 2-for-1 stk. split, 3/97. 1 Incl. $0.05/sh non-recur. gain, 1996. 2 Incl. $36.0 mil pre-tax restr. chg., 1999; & $160.1 mil ($0.34/sh) after-tax restr. chg., 1997. 3 Incl. $262 mil pre-tax restr. chg.; bef. $11 mil acctg. chg.; & bef. $54 mil loss from discont. opers.

OFFICERS:
P. E. Lippencott, Chmn.
D. R. Conant, Pres., C.E.O.
R. A. Schiffner, Sr. V.P., C.F.O.

INVESTOR CONTACT: Leonard F. Griehs, V.P., Investor Relations, (609) 342-6428

PRINCIPAL OFFICE: Campbell Place, Camden, NJ 08103-1799

TELEPHONE NUMBER: (609) 342-4800
FAX: (609) 342-3878
WEB: www.campbellsoup.com

NO. OF EMPLOYEES: 24,500 (avg.)

SHAREHOLDERS: 38,722

ANNUAL MEETING: In Nov.

INCORPORATED: NJ, Nov., 1922

INSTITUTIONAL HOLDINGS:
No. of Institutions: 311
Shares Held: 115,661,267
% Held: 28.3

INDUSTRY: Canned specialties (SIC: 2032)

TRANSFER AGENT(S): EquiServe, Jersey City, NJ

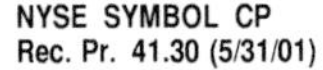

NYSE SYMBOL CP
Rec. Pr. 41.30 (5/31/01)

CANADIAN PACIFIC LTD.

YIELD . . .
P/E RATIO . . .

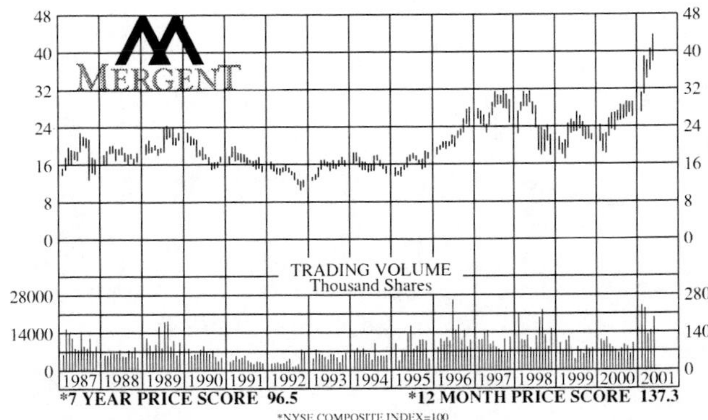

*7 YEAR PRICE SCORE 96.5 *12 MONTH PRICE SCORE 137.3
*NYSE COMPOSITE INDEX=100

INTERIM EARNINGS (Per Share[7]):

Qtr.	Mar.	June	Sept.	Dec.
1996	0.40	0.53	0.73	0.74
1997	0.52	0.70	0.68	0.81
1998	0.48	0.51	0.61	0.73
1999	0.35	d0.32	0.80	0.93
2000	0.93	1.19	1.48	1.92

INTERIM DIVIDENDS (Per Share):

Amt.	Decl.	Ex.	Rec.	Pay.
0.14Q	3/13/00	3/23/00	3/27/00	4/28/00
0.14Q	6/12/00	6/23/00	6/27/00	7/28/00
0.14Q	7/19/00	9/25/00	9/27/00	10/30/00
0.14Q	12/11/00	12/22/00	12/27/00	1/29/01
0.14Q	3/12/01	3/23/01	3/27/01	4/30/01

Indicated div.: $0.56

CAPITALIZATION (12/31/00):

	($000)	(%)
Long-Term Debt	2,689,884	22.7
Deferred Income Tax	2,283,559	19.2
Minority Interest	515,145	4.3
Preferred Stock	146,784	1.2
Common & Surplus	6,228,646	52.5
Total	11,864,017	100.0

RECENT DEVELOPMENTS: For the year ended 12/31/00, net income surged to C$1.77 billion ($1.18 billion) versus C$593.9 million ($411.2 million) in 1999. Results for 1999 included an after-tax non-recurring charge of C$302.0 million ($209.1 million). Revenues rose 41.7% to C$16.10 billion ($10.74 billion), driven by improved profitability across each of CP's business units.

PROSPECTS: On 2/13/01, CP announced its intention to divide the Company into five separate companies, all of which will be publicly traded. Under the proposed reorganization, CP intends to distribute its 86.0% investment in PanCanadian Petroleum and its 100.0% interest in each of Canadian Pacific Railway, CP Ships, and Fording to holders of the Company's common shares.

BUSINESS

CANADIAN PACIFIC LTD. is a diversified operating company active in transportation, energy and hotels. CP's group of companies includes: Canadian Pacific Railway, which provides rail and intermodal freight transportation services over a 14,000-mile rail network extending from Montreal to Vancouver and throughout the U.S. Midwest and Northeast; CP Ships, which provides international ocean and inland transportation for containerized cargo; PanCanadian Petroleum, which is active in the exploration, development, production and marketing of natural gas, crude oil and natural gas liquids; Fording, which is a producer of export coal; and Canadian Pacific Hotels & Resorts, Canada's largest hotel management company operating 71 properties with over 30,000 rooms in Canada, the United States, Mexico, Bermuda, and Barbados. In addition to hotel management, Canadian Pacific Hotels & Resorts holds real estate interests in 20 properties and a 34% investment interest in the Legacy Hotels Real Estate Investment Trust, which owns 19 hotels.

ANNUAL FINANCIAL DATA

	12/31/00	12/31/99	12/31/98	12/31/97	12/31/96	12/31/95	12/31/94
Earnings Per Share	**3.78**	[6] **1.30**	[5] **1.58**	[4] **1.91**	[3] **1.77**	[1][2] **d1.33**	[1] **0.92**
Cash Flow Per Share	**6.45**	**3.56**	**2.13**	**1.32**	**2.01**	**2.48**	**1.79**
Tang. Book Val. Per Share	**19.84**	**17.08**	**15.89**	**15.48**	**13.50**	**12.49**	**14.18**
Dividends Per Share	**0.56**	**0.56**	**0.52**	**0.48**	**0.48**	**0.32**	**0.32**
Dividend Payout %	**14.8**	**43.0**	**32.9**	**25.2**	**27.1**	**. . .**	**34.8**
INCOME STATEMENT (IN MILLIONS):							
Total Revenues	10,743.0	7,870.6	6,708.8	6,658.5	6,348.9	5,823.8	5,033.6
Costs & Expenses	7,742.8	6,258.7	5,039.6	4,758.2	4,641.1	5,507.6	3,665.5
Depreciation & Amort.	850.0	749.4	716.4	670.5	688.0	698.0	574.0
Operating Income	2,150.2	862.5	952.8	1,229.8	1,019.7	d381.8	794.1
Net Interest Inc./(Exp.)	d214.3	d190.1	d165.7	d135.7	d172.0	d262.6	d287.4
Income Before Income Taxes	1,853.7	640.8	736.4	1,077.1	828.0	d740.7	458.8
Income Taxes	543.5	168.7	193.6	388.0	209.4	cr289.1	129.0
Equity Earnings/Minority Int.	d101.3	d33.5	d13.2	d29.8	d8.8	d3.2	d18.3
Net Income	1,208.8	[6] 438.6	[5] 529.6	[4] 659.4	[3] 609.8	[1][2] d454.8	[1] 311.5
Cash Flow	2,050.6	1,180.7	716.4	455.2	691.7	846.7	605.2
Average Shs. Outstg. (000)	317,900	331,500	335,800	345,400	344,400	342,100	337,500
BALANCE SHEET (IN MILLIONS):							
Cash & Cash Equivalents	603.4	388.6	405.0	417.3	717.4	820.0	917.6
Total Current Assets	2,535.4	1,900.8	1,742.4	2,240.4	1,952.4	1,787.8	1,867.3
Net Property	11,854.9	10,902.2	9,986.1	8,914.2	8,094.7	8,896.2	9,038.3
Total Assets	16,123.4	14,068.2	12,999.5	12,071.7	11,124.3	11,754.2	12,056.8
Total Current Liabilities	3,354.9	2,505.2	2,692.6	2,194.7	2,249.3	2,071.8	1,541.0
Long-Term Obligations	2,689.9	2,417.0	2,180.8	1,870.8	1,941.1	3,235.1	3,384.6
Net Stockholders' Equity	6,375.4	5,725.3	5,285.9	5,274.9	4,682.4	4,285.0	4,857.9
Net Working Capital	d819.5	d604.4	d950.2	45.8	d296.9	d283.9	326.3
Year-end Shs. Outstg. (000)	314,000	326,300	332,700	340,700	346,900	342,300	341,800
STATISTICAL RECORD:							
Operating Profit Margin %	20.0	11.0	14.2	18.5	16.1	. . .	15.8
Net Profit Margin %	11.3	5.6	7.9	9.9	9.6	. . .	6.2
Return on Equity %	19.0	7.7	10.0	12.5	13.0	. . .	6.4
Return on Assets %	7.5	3.1	4.1	5.5	5.5	. . .	2.6
Debt/Total Assets %	16.7	17.2	16.8	15.5	17.4	27.5	28.1
Price Range	29.31-18.25	27.13-17.00	31.56-17.88	31.69-22.63	28.13-18.00	18.88-13.38	18.50-14.00
P/E Ratio	7.8-4.8	20.8-13.1	20.0-11.3	16.6-11.9	15.9-10.2	. . .	20.1-15.2
Average Yield %	2.4	2.5	2.1	1.8	2.1	2.0	2.0

Statistics are as originally reported. All figures are in U.S dollars unless noted. Exchange rates: US$1=C$1.50, 12/31/00, US$1=C$1.44, 12/31/99; C$1.51, 12/31/98; C$1.44, 12/31/97; C$1.37, 12/31/96; C$1.36, 12/31/95; C$1.40, 12/31/94. [1] Bef. disc. ops. loss 12/31/95, C$202.9 mil; loss 12/31/94, C$16.7 mil [2] Incl. chrg. of C$1.09 bil [3] Bef. loss fr. disc. ops. of C$5.0 mil; incls. cr. of C$92.9 mil [4] Bef. gain of C$309.1 mil fr. disc. ops.; incls. chrg. of C$51.0 mil [5] Incl. gain of C$20.0 mil [6] Incl. restr. chrg. of C$302.0 mil [7] In Canadian dollars

OFFICERS:
D. P. O'Brien, Chmn., Pres., C.E.O.
M. A. Grandin, Exec. V.P., C.F.O.
R. B. Hodgins, V.P., Treas.

INVESTOR CONTACT: S. M. McIntosh, V.P., Corp. Comm. & Inv. Rel., (403) 218-8055

PRINCIPAL OFFICE: 1800 Bankers Hall East, 855 2nd St. S.W., Calgary, Alberta, Canada

TELEPHONE NUMBER: (403) 218-8000
FAX: (403) 218-8005
WEB: www.cp.ca

NO. OF EMPLOYEES: 45,521 (avg.)

SHAREHOLDERS: 34,210

ANNUAL MEETING: In Apr.

INCORPORATED: Canada, Feb., 1881

INSTITUTIONAL HOLDINGS:
No. of Institutions: 203
Shares Held: 138,951,123
% Held: 44.0

INDUSTRY: Railroads, line-haul operating (SIC: 4011)

TRANSFER AGENT(S): Computershare Trust Company of Canada

NYSE SYMBOL COF
Rec. Pr. 65.11 (5/31/01)

CAPITAL ONE FINANCIAL CORP.

YIELD 0.2%
P/E RATIO 29.1

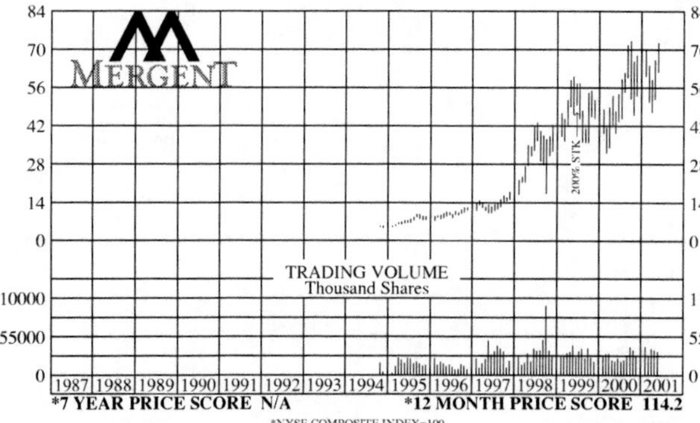

INTERIM EARNINGS (Per Share):

Qtr	Mar.	June	Sept.	Dec.
1996	0.19	0.19	0.19	0.20
1997	0.21	0.19	0.24	0.29
1998	0.32	0.32	0.33	0.35
1999	0.39	0.41	0.45	0.47
2000	0.51	0.54	0.58	0.61

INTERIM DIVIDENDS (Per Share):

Amt.	Decl.	Ex.	Rec.	Pay.
0.027Q	4/27/00	5/08/00	5/10/00	5/22/00
0.027Q	7/20/00	8/07/00	8/09/00	8/21/00
0.027Q	10/17/00	11/06/00	11/08/00	11/20/00
0.027Q	1/18/01	2/06/01	2/08/01	2/20/01
0.027Q	4/26/01	5/07/01	5/09/01	5/21/01

Indicated div.: $0.11 (Div. Reinv. Plan)

CAPITALIZATION (12/31/00):

	($000)	(%)
Total Deposits	8,379,025	58.2
Long-Term Debt	4,050,597	28.1
Common & Surplus	1,962,514	13.6
Total	14,392,136	100.0

RECENT DEVELOPMENTS: For the year ended 12/31/00, net income increased 29.3% to $469.6 million compared with $363.1 million in the prior year. Total interest income climbed 50.0% to $2.39 billion versus $1.59 billion a year earlier. Net interest income totaled $1.59 billion, up 50.9% from $1.05 billion in 1999. Provision for loan losses rose 87.5% to $718.2 million from $382.9 million the year before. Total non-interest income grew 27.9% to $3.03 billion from $2.37 billion in the previous year.

PROSPECTS: The Company is benefiting from loan growth in all segments, increased revenues and new customers added. For example, for the year ended 12/31/00, loan balance rose 45.9% to $29.50 billion versus the year before and new accounts increased 42.5% to 33.8 million compared with the prior year. Also, on-line account originations and on-line accounts serviced for fiscal 2000 surpassed COF's goal of one million originations and two million accounts serviced on-line.

BUSINESS

CAPITAL ONE FINANCIAL CORP. is a holding company whose subsidiaries provide a variety of financial products and services to consumers. The Company's subsidiary Capital One Bank offers credit card products. Capital One, F.S.B. provides certain consumer lending and deposit services. Capital One Services, Inc. provides various operating and administrative services. Prior to November 22, 1994, the Company operated as the credit card division of Signet Bank. The Company is among the largest providers of MasterCard and Visa credit cards in the world. Also, the Company provides financial service on the Internet, with on-line accounts, real-time account numbering and on-line retail deposits. The Company's subsidiaries collectively had 33.8 million accounts and $29.50 billion in managed loans as of 12/31/00.

ANNUAL FINANCIAL DATA

	12/31/00	12/31/99	12/31/98	12/31/97	12/31/96	12/31/95	12/31/94
Earnings Per Share	**2.24**	**1.72**	**1.32**	**0.93**	**0.77**	**0.63**	**0.48**
Tang. Book Val. Per Share	**9.94**	**7.69**	**6.45**	**4.55**	**3.72**	**3.02**	**2.39**
Dividends Per Share	**0.11**	**0.11**	**0.11**	**0.11**	**0.11**	**0.08**	**...**
Dividend Payout %	**4.8**	**6.2**	**8.1**	**11.4**	**13.9**	**12.6**	**...**
INCOME STATEMENT (IN MILLIONS):							
Total Interest Income	2,389.9	1,593.5	1,111.5	718.0	660.5	457.4	258.7
Total Interest Expense	801.0	540.9	424.3	334.8	295.0	249.4	93.7
Net Interest Income	1,588.9	1,052.6	687.3	383.1	365.5	208.0	165.0
Provision for Loan Losses	718.2	382.9	267.0	262.8	167.2	65.9	30.7
Non-Interest Income	3,034.4	2,372.4	1,488.3	1,069.1	763.4	553.0	396.9
Non-Interest Expense	3,147.7	2,465.0	1,464.6	884.0	713.2	497.4	384.3
Income Before Taxes	757.5	577.0	443.9	305.5	248.5	197.7	146.8
Net Income	469.6	363.1	275.2	189.4	155.3	126.5	95.3
Average Shs. Outstg. (000)	209,449	210,683	208,765	202,953	202,764	199,779	198,201
BALANCE SHEET (IN MILLIONS):							
Cash & Due from Banks	74.5	134.1	16.0	5.0	48.7	51.7	93.9
Securities Avail. for Sale	1,696.8	1,856.4	1,796.8	1,242.7	865.0	413.0	99.1
Total Loans & Leases	15,112.7	9,913.5	6,157.1	4,861.7	4,343.9	2,921.7	2,228.5
Allowance for Credit Losses	527.0	342.0	231.0	183.0	118.5	72.0	68.5
Net Loans & Leases	14,585.7	9,571.5	5,926.1	4,678.7	4,225.4	2,849.7	2,159.9
Total Assets	18,889.3	13,336.4	9,419.4	7,078.3	6,467.4	4,759.3	3,092.0
Total Deposits	8,379.0	3,783.8	2,000.0	1,313.7	943.0	696.0	452.2
Long-Term Obligations	4,050.6	4,180.5	3,739.4	3,632.8	3,994.2	2,491.9	22.0
Total Liabilities	16,926.8	11,820.8	8,149.0	6,185.0	5,727.1	4,160.1	2,617.4
Net Stockholders' Equity	1,962.5	1,515.6	1,270.4	893.3	740.4	599.2	474.6
Year-end Shs. Outstg. (000)	197,369	197,046	196,979	196,107	198,975	198,525	198,201
STATISTICAL RECORD:							
Return on Equity %	23.9	24.0	21.7	21.2	21.0	21.1	20.1
Return on Assets %	2.5	2.7	2.9	2.7	2.4	2.7	3.1
Equity/Assets %	10.4	11.4	13.5	12.6	11.4	12.6	15.3
Non-Int. Exp./Tot. Inc. %	68.1	72.0	67.3	60.9	63.2	65.4	68.4
Price Range	73.25-32.06	60.24-35.81	43.31-16.85	17.96-10.17	12.29-7.25	9.87-5.12	5.54-4.62
P/E Ratio	32.7-14.3	35.0-20.8	32.8-12.8	19.2-10.9	16.0-9.5	15.6-8.1	11.5-9.6
Average Yield %	0.2	0.2	0.4	0.8	1.1	1.1	...

Statistics are as originally reported. Adj. for stk. split: 3-for-1, 6/99

OFFICERS:
R. D. Fairbank, Chmn., C.E.O.
N. W. Morris, Pres., C.O.O.
J. G. Finneran Jr., Sr. V.P., Gen. Couns., Sec.

INVESTOR CONTACT: Paul Paquin, V.P., Inv. Rel., (703) 205-1039

PRINCIPAL OFFICE: 2980 Fairview Park Dr., Suite 1300, Falls Church, VA 22042-4525

TELEPHONE NUMBER: (703) 205-1000
FAX: (703) 205-1755
WEB: www.capitalone.com

NO. OF EMPLOYEES: 19,247

SHAREHOLDERS: 10,019

ANNUAL MEETING: In April

INCORPORATED: DE, July, 1994

INSTITUTIONAL HOLDINGS:
No. of Institutions: 391
Shares Held: 133,868,756
% Held: 64.6

INDUSTRY: Personal credit institutions (SIC: 6141)

TRANSFER AGENT(S): First Chicago Trust Company of New York, Jersey City, NJ

NYSE SYMBOL CAH
Rec. Pr. 71.99 (5/31/01)

CARDINAL HEALTH, INC.

YIELD 0.1%
P/E RATIO 39.8

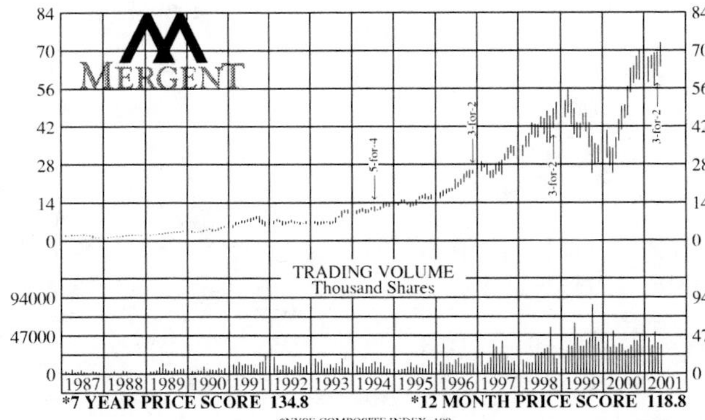

INTERIM EARNINGS (Per Share):

Qtr.	Sept.	Dec.	Mar.	June
1996-97	0.18	0.17	0.15	0.25
1997-98	0.22	0.27	0.22	0.26
1998-99	0.29	0.33	0.19	0.35
1999-00	0.29	0.41	0.45	0.46
2000-01	0.41	0.49	...	...

INTERIM DIVIDENDS (Per Share):

Amt.	Decl.	Ex.	Rec.	Pay.
0.03Q	8/09/00	9/27/00	10/01/00	10/15/00
0.03Q	11/01/00	12/27/00	1/01/01	1/15/01
0.03Q	2/14/01	3/28/01	4/01/01	4/15/01
3-for-2	2/27/01	4/23/01	3/04/01	4/20/01
0.025Q	5/09/01	6/27/01	7/01/01	7/15/01

Indicated div.: $0.10

CAPITALIZATION (6/30/00):

	($000)	(%)
Long-Term Debt	1,485,800	27.2
Common & Surplus	3,981,200	72.8
Total	5,467,000	100.0

RECENT DEVELOPMENTS: For the quarter ended 12/31/00, net earnings climbed 20.6% to $209.2 million from $173.5 million the year before. Results for the recent and prior-year periods included after-tax merger-related charges of $5.4 million and $3.4 million, respectively. Total revenue, including bulk deliveries to customer warehouses, advanced 30.3% to $9.64 billion from $7.40 billion the previous year. Gross margin totaled $809.0 million, or 8.4% of total revenue, versus $721.9 million, or 9.8% of total revenues, a year earlier.

PROSPECTS: On 2/14/00, CAH completed its acquisition of Bindley Western Industries, Inc., a wholesale distributor of pharmaceuticals with annual revenues of about $5.80 billion, for approximately $2.20 billion in stock. The acquisition will give the Company a substantial presence in the fast-growing area of nuclear medicine. Bindley Western operates 32 nuclear pharmacies that prepare unit-dose pharmaceuticals using radioactive materials. Synergies stemming from the acquisition are expected to exceed $100.0 million annually within three years.

BUSINESS

CARDINAL HEALTH, INC. (formerly Cardinal Distribution, Inc.) is a holding company whose subsidiaries offer a broad array of products and services for health-care providers and manufacturers. Services include pharmaceutical packing and distribution, drug delivery systems development, automated dispensing systems manufacturing, hospital pharmacy management, retail pharmacy franchising, and healthcare information systems development. On 8/7/98, the Company acquired R.P. Scherer, a manufacturer of drug delivery systems. On 2/3/99, CAH completed the acquisition of Allegiance Corporation, a distributor and manufacturer of medical and laboratory products.

ANNUAL FINANCIAL DATA

	6/30/00	6/30/99	6/30/98	6/30/97	6/30/96	6/30/95	[2] 6/30/94
Earnings Per Share	**[1] 1.59**	**[1] 1.09**	**[1] 0.99**	**[1] 0.74**	**[1] 0.51**	**0.60**	**[1] 0.25**
Cash Flow Per Share	**2.17**	**1.65**	**1.24**	**0.95**	**0.66**	**0.75**	**0.38**
Tang. Book Val. Per Share	**7.28**	**6.14**	**4.99**	**4.93**	**3.94**	**3.87**	**2.89**
Dividends Per Share	**0.07**	**0.07**	**0.05**	**0.04**	**0.04**	**0.04**	**0.03**
Dividend Payout %	**4.6**	**6.1**	**5.5**	**6.0**	**6.9**	**6.0**	**12.6**
INCOME STATEMENT (IN MILLIONS):							
Total Revenues	29,870.6	25,033.6	15,918.1	10,968.0	8,862.4	7,806.1	5,790.4
Costs & Expenses	28,429.7	23,923.1	15,437.8	10,582.4	8,615.2	7,621.2	5,687.5
Depreciation & Amort.	245.9	233.5	64.3	51.3	32.5	21.2	17.0
Operating Income	1,195.0	877.0	416.0	334.4	214.8	163.6	86.0
Net Interest Inc./(Exp.)	...	d99.4	d23.0	d28.0	d23.9	d19.3	d18.1
Income Before Income Taxes	1,077.8	759.2	402.5	312.3	202.1	146.5	70.8
Income Taxes	398.1	302.9	155.4	131.2	90.2	61.5	35.6
Net Income	[1] 679.7	[1] 456.3	[1] 247.1	[1] 181.1	[1] 111.9	85.0	[1] 35.1
Cash Flow	925.6	689.8	311.4	232.4	144.4	106.2	50.9
Average Shs. Outstg. (000)	426,600	418,500	250,756	245,516	218,258	142,341	132,948
BALANCE SHEET (IN MILLIONS):							
Cash & Cash Equivalents	504.6	165.2	305.0	243.1	342.1	63.2	54.9
Total Current Assets	6,870.6	5,146.6	3,228.7	2,503.7	2,239.8	1,674.7	1,287.1
Net Property	1,626.9	1,540.5	331.4	276.7	153.5	95.2	60.0
Total Assets	10,264.9	8,289.0	3,961.1	3,108.5	2,681.1	1,841.8	1,395.6
Total Current Liabilities	4,261.5	2,959.0	1,844.1	1,408.8	1,385.7	1,073.4	816.0
Long-Term Obligations	1,485.8	1,223.9	272.6	277.8	265.1	209.3	210.1
Net Stockholders' Equity	3,981.2	3,463.0	1,625.2	1,332.2	930.7	548.2	368.5
Net Working Capital	2,609.1	2,187.6	1,384.5	1,095.0	854.1	601.3	471.1
Year-end Shs. Outstg. (000)	414,750	410,850	300,580	245,412	212,645	141,564	127,690
STATISTICAL RECORD:							
Operating Profit Margin %	4.0	3.5	2.6	3.0	2.4	2.1	1.5
Net Profit Margin %	2.3	1.8	1.6	1.7	1.3	1.1	0.6
Return on Equity %	17.1	13.2	15.2	13.6	12.0	15.5	9.5
Return on Assets %	6.6	5.5	6.2	5.8	4.2	4.6	2.5
Debt/Total Assets %	14.5	14.8	6.9	8.9	9.9	11.4	15.1
Price Range	69.96-24.67	55.50-24.67	50.92-30.97	35.00-22.89	26.00-15.54	17.22-12.30	14.30-9.84
P/E Ratio	43.9-15.5	50.8-22.6	51.6-31.4	47.4-31.0	50.7-30.3	28.9-20.7	56.1-38.6
Average Yield %	0.2	0.2	0.1	0.2	0.2	0.2	0.3

Statistics are as originally reported. Adj. for 3-for-2 stk. split, 4/01, 10/98 & 12/96. [1] Incl. $49.8 mil ($0.12/sh) net merger costs, 6/00; $117.6 mil ($0.28/sh), 6/99; $41 mil, 6/98; $40.2 mil, 6/97; $47.8 mil, 6/96; & $28.2 mil, 6/94. [2] Changed fiscal year end to 6/30 from 3/31.

OFFICERS:
R. D. Walter, Chmn., C.E.O.
J. C. Kane, Vice-Chmn., Pres., C.O.O.
R. J. Miller, Exec. V.P., C.F.O.

INVESTOR CONTACT: Debra Dendahl Haley, Dir., Inv. Rel., (614) 757-7481

PRINCIPAL OFFICE: 7000 Cardinal Place, Dublin, OH 43017

TELEPHONE NUMBER: (614) 757-5000
FAX: (614) 717-6000
WEB: www.cardinal.com

NO. OF EMPLOYEES: 42,200 (approx.)

SHAREHOLDERS: 21,800 (approx.)

ANNUAL MEETING: In Nov.

INCORPORATED: OH, July, 1982

INSTITUTIONAL HOLDINGS:
No. of Institutions: 589
Shares Held: 337,570,640 (Adj.)
% Held: 76.2

INDUSTRY: Drugs, proprietaries, and sundries (SIC: 5122)

TRANSFER AGENT(S): EquiServe Trust Company, Jersey City, NJ

NYSE SYMBOL CMX
Rec. Pr. 16.28 (5/31/01)

CAREMARK RX, INC.

YIELD ...
P/E RATIO 37.9

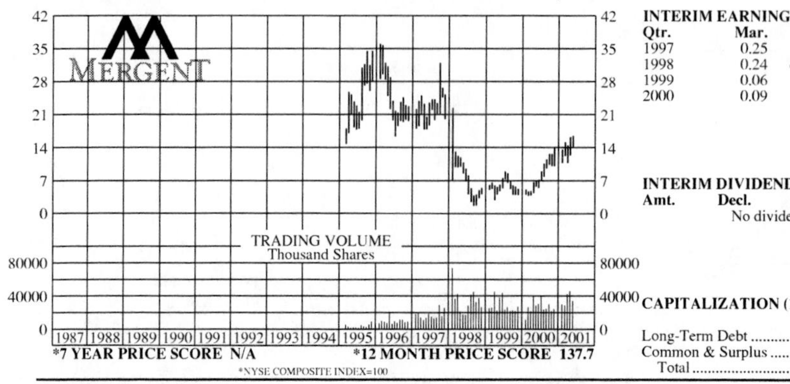

INTERIM EARNINGS (Per Share):

Qtr.	Mar.	June	Sept.	Dec.
1997	0.25	0.27	0.29	d4.23
1998	0.24	d0.12	0.04	0.06
1999	0.06	0.06	0.07	0.10
2000	0.09	0.09	0.11	0.14

INTERIM DIVIDENDS (Per Share):

Amt.	Decl.	Ex.	Rec.	Pay.

No dividends paid.

CAPITALIZATION (12/31/00):

	($000)	(%)
Long-Term Debt	733,347	...
Common & Surplus	d969,064	...
Total	d235,717	100.0

RECENT DEVELOPMENTS: For the year ended 12/31/00, income from continuing operations soared 63.6% to $91.4 million versus income from continuing operations of $55.9 million in 1999. Results for 2000 and 1999 excluded losses from discontinued operations of $268.0 million and $199.3 million, respectively. Net revenue jumped 33.9% to $4.43 billion from $3.31 billion a year earlier.

PROSPECTS: The Company and iScribe, Inc., a healthcare technology company that develops mobile, handheld, wireless technology services for physicians, will partner to introduce physicians and CMX's clients to iScribe's electronic prescribing technology. Meanwhile, the Company should continue to benefit from CMX's strong operating performance, led by its robust book of net new business for 2001.

BUSINESS

CAREMARK RX, INC. (formerly MedPartners, Inc.) is a major U.S. pharmaceutical services company that provides prescription benefit management (PBM), therapeutic pharmaceutical services (CT services), and associated disease management programs. MDM provides PBM services for clients throughout the U.S., including corporations, insurance companies, unions, government employee groups and managed care organizations. MDM's CT services are designed to meet the healthcare needs of individuals with certain chronic diseases or conditions. These services include the design, development and management of comprehensive programs comprising drug therapy, physician support and patient education. The Company acquired Caremark International Inc. on 9/5/96.

QUARTERLY DATA

(12/31/2000)($000)	Rev	Inc
1st Quarter	1,052,548	(181,215)
2nd Quarter	1,084,456	19,012
3rd Quarter	1,089,362	23,648
4th Quarter	1,203,778	(38,000)

ANNUAL FINANCIAL DATA

	12/31/00	12/31/99	12/31/98	12/31/97	[3] 12/31/96	12/31/95	12/31/94
Earnings Per Share	[7] 0.43	[6] 0.29	[5] 0.16	[4] d3.73	[1] d0.58	d0.30	d0.14
Cash Flow Per Share	0.55	0.40	0.29	d3.09	d0.05	0.24	d0.03
Tang. Book Val. Per Share	...	...	...	...	0.49	1.09	...
INCOME STATEMENT (IN MILLIONS):							
Total Revenues	4,430.1	3,307.8	2,634.0	6,331.2	4,813.5	725.7	75.2
Costs & Expenses	4,194.6	3,106.3	2,471.4	6,220.7	4,495.6	683.0	74.9
Depreciation & Amort.	25.4	22.1	24.7	120.4	81.9	17.5	1.2
Operating Income	210.2	179.4	137.9	d9.9	235.9	25.2	d1.0
Net Interest Inc./(Exp.)	d97.0	d115.3	d78.8	d55.7	d23.9	d6.0	d0.6
Income Before Income Taxes	113.2	64.1	49.6	d771.8	d95.1	d44.5	d1.6
Income Taxes	8.5	5.0	18.9	cr78.0	cr5.3	cr34.9	...
Net Income	[7] 91.4	[6] 55.9	[5] 30.8	[4] d693.7	[1] d89.8	d9.6	d1.6
Cash Flow	99.1	74.7	55.5	d573.3	d7.9	7.8	d0.4
Average Shs. Outstg. (000)	214,025	194,950	189,927	185,830	155,364	32,513	11,288
BALANCE SHEET (IN MILLIONS):							
Cash & Cash Equivalents	2.4	6.8	23.1	215.8	123.8	26.6	4.8
Total Current Assets	453.3	534.7	1,185.6	1,313.0	947.1	135.2	33.4
Net Property	110.3	108.2	115.8	530.0	505.1	105.5	13.9
Total Assets	685.5	770.8	1,862.1	2,890.5	2,266.0	355.0	56.3
Total Current Liabilities	635.2	563.4	1,100.5	1,237.3	776.8	115.8	16.7
Long-Term Obligations	733.3	1,230.0	1,735.1	1,470.6	715.7	131.2	21.4
Net Stockholders' Equity	d969.1	d1,281.5	d1,144.2	90.9	739.5	104.9	d1.9
Net Working Capital	d181.9	d28.8	85.1	75.7	170.3	19.3	16.7
Year-end Shs. Outstg. (000)	230,755	191,140	199,032	188,449	165,281	32,422	9,841
STATISTICAL RECORD:							
Operating Profit Margin %	4.7	5.4	5.2	...	4.9	3.5	...
Net Profit Margin %	2.1	1.7	1.2	...	...	...	...
Return on Assets %	13.3	7.3	1.7	...	...	...	...
Debt/Total Assets %	107.0	159.6	93.2	50.9	31.6	37.0	38.0
Price Range	13.94-3.75	9.00-2.88	22.38-1.63	32.00-17.88	36.00-16.38	34.50-14.75	...
P/E Ratio	32.4-8.7	31.0-9.9	139.8-10.1	...	...	...	...

Statistics are as originally reported. [1] Incl. pre-tax merger exps. of $308.7 mill. and excl. loss fr. disc. opers. of $68.7 mill. [3] Reflects the acq. of Caremark International, Inc. [4] Incl. a pre-tax merger exp. of $59.4 mill., a pre-tax chg. of $664.7 mill. for restruct. & impair. chgs., a net loss of $96.0 mill. fr. disc. opers. and a net chg. of $30.9 mill. for the cum. effect of a change in acctg. prin. [5] Incl. a pre-tax restruct. chrg. of $9.5 mill.; excl. a loss of $1.28 bill. fr. disc. oper. and a loss of $6.3 mill. fr. cum. eff. of chg. in account. prin. [6] Bef. loss from disc. oper. of $199.3 mill. [7] Bef. loss from disc. oper. of $268.0 mill.

OFFICERS:
E. M. Crawford, Chmn., C.E.O.
J. H. Dickerson Jr., Pres., C.O.O.
H. A. McLure, Exec. V.P., C.F.O.

INVESTOR CONTACT: Peter J. Clemens IV, Sr. V.P., (205) 733-8996

PRINCIPAL OFFICE: 3000 Galleria Tower, Suite 1000, Birmingham, AL 35244

TELEPHONE NUMBER: (205) 733-8996
FAX: (205) 733-9780
WEB: www.caremark.com

NO. OF EMPLOYEES: 3,474 (avg.)

SHAREHOLDERS: 20,700

ANNUAL MEETING: In May

INCORPORATED: DE, Jan., 1993

INSTITUTIONAL HOLDINGS:
No. of Institutions: 209
Shares Held: 202,587,656
% Held: 90.4

INDUSTRY: Health and allied services, nec (SIC: 8099)

TRANSFER AGENT(S): First Chicago Trust Company of New York, Jersey City, NJ

NYSE SYMBOL CSL
Rec. Pr. 32.62 (3/31/01)

CARLISLE COMPANIES INC.

YIELD 2.0%
P/E RATIO 10.4

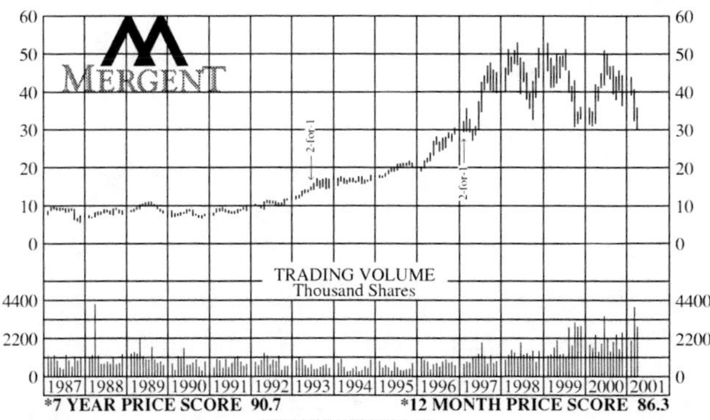

*7 YEAR PRICE SCORE 90.7 *12 MONTH PRICE SCORE 86.3

*NYSE COMPOSITE INDEX=100

INTERIM EARNINGS (Per Share):

Qtr.	Mar.	June	Sept.	Dec.
1996	0.35	0.53	0.50	0.42
1997	0.43	0.68	0.63	0.54
1998	0.62	0.80	0.73	0.62
1999	0.71	0.91	0.81	0.70
2000	0.83	1.04	0.92	0.35

INTERIM DIVIDENDS (Per Share):

Amt.	Decl.	Ex.	Rec.	Pay.
0.18Q	5/03/00	5/15/00	5/17/00	6/01/00
0.20Q	8/02/00	8/15/00	8/17/00	9/01/00
0.20Q	11/01/00	11/14/00	11/16/00	12/01/00
0.20Q	2/07/01	2/14/01	2/16/01	3/01/01
0.20Q	5/02/01	5/15/01	5/17/01	6/01/01

Indicated div.: $0.80 (Div. Reinv. Plan)

CAPITALIZATION (12/31/00):

	($000)	(%)
Long-Term Debt	281,864	34.0
Common & Surplus	547,879	66.0
Total	829,743	100.0

RECENT DEVELOPMENTS: For the year ended 12/31/00, net income amounted to $96.2 million compared with $95.8 million in the previous year. Results for 1999 included a pre-tax nonrecurring gain of $685,000. Net sales advanced 9.9% to $1.77 billion versus $1.61 billion a year earlier. Sales of Industrial Components advanced 21.6% to $641.7 million, while General Industry sales rose 15.5% to $420.0 million. Meanwhile, sales of Construction Materials climbed 0.4% to $407.0 million, while Automotive Comonents sales declined 3.8% to $302.4 million.

PROSPECTS: For the first half of 2001, earnings will continue to struggle with lower pricing and higher material costs as competitors attempt to retain sales volume in a declining market. In an attempt to increase profit margins, CSL announced the closure of two plants, six regional support offices and staff reductions. CSL's outlook is optimistic for the second half of 2001. Sales should benefit from a portfolio of new products, customers and markets from recent acquisitions of Bontech Engineering A/S in Denmark, Scheffers and Stork Friesland BV.

BUSINESS

CARLISLE COMPANIES INC. produces and sells a diverse line of products for industry, primarily of rubber, plastic and metal content. The Construction Materials segment manufactures membranes and accessories necessary for rubber and plastic roofing systems for non-residential flat roofs. The Industrial Components segment manufactures and distributes tire and wheel assemblies, heavy-duty friction and braking products and high-performance wire/cable and cable assemblies. The Automotive Components segment manufactures highly engineered plastic and rubber components for tier 1 suppliers and other manufacturers in the automotive industry. The General Industry consists of several businesses that produce specialty trailers, payload trailers and dump bodies, stainless steel in-plant processing equipment, food service products and cheesemaking systems. In January 1999, CSL divested its perishable cargo business.

ANNUAL FINANCIAL DATA

	12/31/00	12/31/99	12/31/98	12/31/97	12/31/96	12/31/95	12/31/94
Earnings Per Share	**3.14**	**[1] 3.13**	**2.77**	**2.28**	**1.80**	**1.41**	**1.15**
Cash Flow Per Share	**5.09**	**4.67**	**4.24**	**3.53**	**2.76**	**2.15**	**1.86**
Tang. Book Val. Per Share	**9.79**	**10.63**	**8.85**	**7.48**	**6.55**	**7.71**	**7.44**
Dividends Per Share	**0.76**	**0.68**	**0.60**	**0.53**	**0.47**	**0.42**	**0.38**
Dividend Payout %	**24.2**	**21.7**	**21.7**	**23.0**	**25.8**	**29.8**	**33.0**
INCOME STATEMENT (IN MILLIONS):							
Total Revenues	1,771.1	1,611.3	1,517.5	1,260.6	1,017.5	822.5	692.7
Costs & Expenses	1,536.1	1,396.0	1,320.7	1,094.4	890.6	723.2	609.3
Depreciation & Amort.	59.5	47.4	45.2	38.8	29.8	23.2	21.9
Operating Income	175.4	167.9	151.6	127.4	97.1	76.1	61.4
Net Interest Inc./(Exp.)	d28.0	d19.2	d22.7	d16.5	d9.1	d6.1	d4.6
Income Before Income Taxes	150.9	155.5	140.3	116.8	92.0	72.9	58.8
Income Taxes	54.7	59.7	55.4	46.1	36.4	28.8	23.2
Net Income	96.2	[1] 95.8	84.9	70.7	55.7	44.1	35.6
Cash Flow	155.7	143.2	130.1	109.4	85.4	67.3	57.5
Average Shs. Outstg. (000)	30,599	30,635	30,674	31,025	30,953	31,266	30,960
BALANCE SHEET (IN MILLIONS):							
Cash & Cash Equivalents	9.0	10.4	3.9	1.7	8.3	3.2	71.0
Total Current Assets	576.5	541.0	478.5	417.5	345.9	281.9	273.2
Net Property	402.6	349.5	354.8	294.2	264.2	193.1	158.2
Total Assets	1,305.7	1,080.7	1,022.9	861.2	742.5	542.4	485.3
Total Current Liabilities	399.9	240.4	255.3	226.1	170.6	128.2	108.6
Long-Term Obligations	281.9	281.7	273.5	209.6	315.5	72.7	69.1
Net Stockholders' Equity	547.9	478.1	406.9	348.8	307.5	273.3	247.9
Net Working Capital	176.5	300.7	223.2	191.4	175.3	153.7	164.7
Year-end Shs. Outstg. (000)	30,251	30,128	30,179	30,351	30,351	30,638	30,826
STATISTICAL RECORD:							
Operating Profit Margin %	9.9	10.4	10.0	10.1	9.5	9.3	8.9
Net Profit Margin %	5.4	5.9	5.6	5.6	5.5	5.4	5.1
Return on Equity %	17.6	20.0	20.9	20.3	18.1	16.1	14.4
Return on Assets %	7.4	8.9	8.3	8.2	7.5	8.1	7.3
Debt/Total Assets %	21.6	26.1	26.7	24.3	42.5	13.4	14.2
Price Range	51.00-30.94	52.94-30.63	53.06-32.56	47.75-27.00	30.50-19.00	21.81-17.25	18.06-15.13
P/E Ratio	16.2-9.9	16.9-9.8	19.2-11.8	20.9-11.8	16.9-10.6	15.5-12.2	15.7-13.2
Average Yield %	1.9	1.6	1.4	1.4	1.9	2.2	2.3

Statistics are as originally reported. Adj. for 2-for-1 split: 1/97. [1] Incl. non-recurr. gain of $685,000.

OFFICERS:
S. P. Munn, Chmn.
D. J. Hall, Vice-Chmn., C.O.O
R. D. McKinnish, Pres., C.E.O.

INVESTOR CONTACT: Investor Relations, (800) 897-9071

PRINCIPAL OFFICE: 250 South Clinton Street, Suite 201, Syracuse, NY 13202-1258

TELEPHONE NUMBER: (315) 474-2500
FAX: (315) 474-2008
WEB: www.carlisle.com
NO. OF EMPLOYEES: 11,710 (approx.)
SHAREHOLDERS: 2,396 (record)
ANNUAL MEETING: In Apr.
INCORPORATED: DE, Sept., 1917; reincorp., DE, May, 1986

INSTITUTIONAL HOLDINGS:
No. of Institutions: 162
Shares Held: 15,847,495
% Held: 52.4

INDUSTRY: Tires and inner tubes (SIC: 3011)

TRANSFER AGENT(S): Computershare Investor Service, Chicago, IL

NYSE SYMBOL CCL
Rec. Pr. 28.23 (5/31/01)

CARNIVAL CORPORATION

YIELD 1.5%
P/E RATIO 18.1

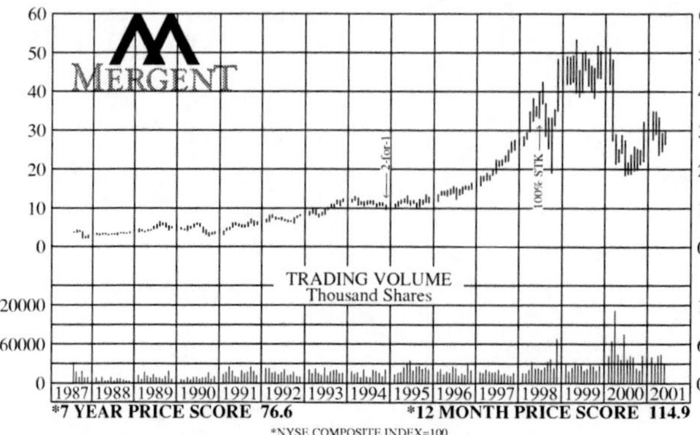

*7 YEAR PRICE SCORE 76.6 *12 MONTH PRICE SCORE 114.9

*NYSE COMPOSITE INDEX=100

INTERIM EARNINGS (Per Share):

Qtr.	Feb.	May	Aug.	Nov.
1996-97	0.15	0.22	0.50	0.26
1997-98	0.19	0.27	0.58	0.37
1998-99	0.26	0.33	0.67	0.40
1999-00	0.28	0.34	0.67	0.33
2000-01	0.22	...	...	...

INTERIM DIVIDENDS (Per Share):

Amt.	Decl.	Ex.	Rec.	Pay.
0.105Q	4/14/00	5/26/00	5/31/00	6/14/00
0.105Q	7/19/00	8/29/00	8/31/00	9/14/00
0.105Q	10/20/00	11/28/00	11/30/00	12/14/00
0.105Q	1/11/01	2/22/01	2/26/01	3/14/01
0.105Q	4/19/01	5/29/01	5/31/01	6/14/01

Indicated div.: $0.42 (Div. Reinv. Plan)

CAPITALIZATION (11/30/00):

	($000)	(%)
Long-Term Debt [1]	2,099,077	26.3
Common & Surplus	5,870,617	73.7
Total	7,969,694	100.0

RECENT DEVELOPMENTS: For the quarter ended 2/28/01, net income fell 25.4% to $128.0 million compared with $171.5 million in the equivalent 1999 quarter. The decline in earnings was primarily attributed to significantly higher net revenue yields during the 2000 quarter, which largely resulted from the unusually high-priced "Millennium sailings" over the New Year's period last year. Revenues were $1.01 billion, up 22.2% from $824.9 million a year earlier.

PROSPECTS: As part of CCL's ongoing efforts to increase its presence in the European market, the Company finalized contracts for the construction of two new 105,000-ton ships for its Costa Cruises brand and also transferred Carnival Cruise Lines' 1,022-passenger Tropicale to the Costa fleet. In addition, The Costa Tropicale is currently undergoing a major refit in Italy and is expected to begin operating seven-day Mediterranean cruises in June 2001.

BUSINESS

CARNIVAL CORPORATION (formerly Carnival Cruise Lines, Inc.) is a major multiple-night cruise company. The Company offers a broad range of major cruise brands serving the contemporary cruise market through Carnival Cruise Lines, the premium cruise market through Holland America Line and the luxury cruise market through Cunard Line, Seabourn Cruise Line and Windstar Cruises. CCL also owns in Costa Crociere S.p.A., an Italian cruise company, and Airtours plc, an integrated leisure travel group of companies, which also operates cruise ships. Costa and Airtours' Sun Cruises target the contemporary cruise market. In April 1995, the Company sold its 49% equity interest in Epirotiki Line, a Greek cruise operator, for $25.0 million.

ANNUAL FINANCIAL DATA

	11/30/00	11/30/99	11/30/98	11/30/97	11/30/96	11/30/95	11/30/94
Earnings Per Share	**[2] 1.60**	**1.66**	**1.40**	**1.20**	**0.98**	**0.80**	**0.68**
Cash Flow Per Share	**1.04**	**1.03**	**0.87**	**0.70**	**0.61**	**1.02**	**0.87**
Tang. Book Val. Per Share	**8.37**	**8.86**	**6.46**	**5.71**	**4.77**	**3.72**	**3.00**
Dividends Per Share	**0.42**	**0.38**	**0.32**	**0.24**	**0.19**	**0.16**	**0.14**
Dividend Payout %	**26.2**	**22.6**	**22.5**	**20.0**	**19.4**	**19.8**	**21.1**
INCOME STATEMENT (IN MILLIONS):							
Total Revenues	3,778.5	3,573.2	3,086.0	2,500.6	2,258.5	1,998.2	1,806.0
Costs & Expenses	2,507.8	2,309.9	1,988.8	1,619.2	1,516.1	1,379.7	1,251.7
Depreciation & Amort.	287.7	243.7	200.7	167.3	145.0	128.4	110.6
Operating Income	983.0	1,019.7	896.5	714.1	597.4	490.0	443.7
Net Interest Inc./(Exp.)	d24.9	d5.0	d47.5	d47.2	d45.5	d48.7	d42.7
Income Before Income Taxes	966.6	1,044.0	850.8	672.3	575.3	460.5	391.8
Income Taxes	1.1	2.8	3.8	6.2	9.0	9.4	10.1
Equity Earnings/Minority Int.	...	d14.0	d11.1	...	...	...	...
Net Income	[2] 965.5	1,027.2	835.9	666.1	566.3	451.1	381.8
Cash Flow	1,253.1	1,270.9	1,036.6	833.3	711.3	579.5	492.4
Average Shs. Outstg. (000)	1,201,577	1,228,484	1,193,485	1,190,624	1,170,448	568,440	565,488
BALANCE SHEET (IN MILLIONS):							
Cash & Cash Equivalents	189.3	544.6	143.2	149.7	124.1	103.8	124.2
Total Current Assets	549.5	791.6	370.3	336.0	290.9	256.4	240.4
Net Property	8,001.3	6,410.5	5,768.1	4,327.4	4,099.0	3,414.8	3,071.4
Total Assets	9,831.3	8,286.4	7,179.3	5,426.8	5,101.9	4,105.5	3,669.8
Total Current Liabilities	1,715.3	1,404.9	1,135.1	786.1	662.7	594.7	565.0
Long-Term Obligations	2,099.1	867.5	1,563.0	1,015.3	1,316.6	1,150.0	1,161.9
Net Stockholders' Equity	5,870.6	5,931.2	4,285.5	3,605.1	3,030.9	2,344.9	1,928.9
Net Working Capital	d1,165.8	d613.3	d764.8	d450.1	d371.8	d338.3	d324.5
Year-end Shs. Outstg. (000)	617,568	616,966	595,448	594,408	589,380	569,690	565,064
STATISTICAL RECORD:							
Operating Profit Margin %	25.8	28.5	29.1	28.6	26.5	24.5	24.6
Net Profit Margin %	25.3	28.7	27.1	26.6	25.1	22.6	21.1
Return on Equity %	16.4	17.3	19.5	18.5	18.7	19.2	19.8
Return on Assets %	9.8	12.4	11.6	12.3	11.1	11.0	10.4
Debt/Total Assets %	21.4	10.5	21.8	18.7	25.8	28.0	31.7
Price Range	51.25-18.31	53.50-38.13	48.50-19.00	27.63-15.69	16.56-11.63	13.56-10.00	13.06-9.56
P/E Ratio	32.0-11.4	32.2-23.0	34.6-13.6	23.0-13.1	16.9-11.9	17.1-12.6	19.3-14.2
Average Yield %	1.2	0.8	0.9	1.1	1.3	1.3	1.3

Statistics are as originally reported. All figures are in U.S. dollars unless otherwise noted. Adj. for stock splits; 2-for-1, 6/12/98 and 12/14/94. [1] Incl. zero coupon convert. deb. [2] Incl. nonrecurr. chrg. of $24.0 mill.

OFFICERS:
M. Arison, Chmn., C.E.O.
H. S. Frank, Vice-Chmn., C.O.O.
G. R. Cahill, Sr. V.P. Finance, C.F.O.
L. Zemnick, V.P., Treasurer

INVESTOR CONTACT: Investor Relations, (305) 599-2600

PRINCIPAL OFFICE: Carnival Place, 3655 N.W. 87th Avenue, Miami, FL 33178-2428

TELEPHONE NUMBER: (305) 599-2600
FAX: (305) 471-4700
WEB: www.carnivalcorp.com

NO. OF EMPLOYEES: 4,300 full-time; 2,100 part-time

SHAREHOLDERS: 4,763 (approx.)

ANNUAL MEETING: In Apr.

INCORPORATED: PAN, Nov., 1974

INSTITUTIONAL HOLDINGS:
No. of Institutions: 391
Shares Held: 239,328,194
% Held: 40.9

INDUSTRY: Water passenger transportation, nec (SIC: 4489)

TRANSFER AGENT(S): First Union National Bank, Charlotte, NC

NYSE SYMBOL CRS
Rec. Pr. 26.20 (4/30/01)

CARPENTER TECHNOLOGY CORPORATION

YIELD 5.0%
P/E RATIO 11.1

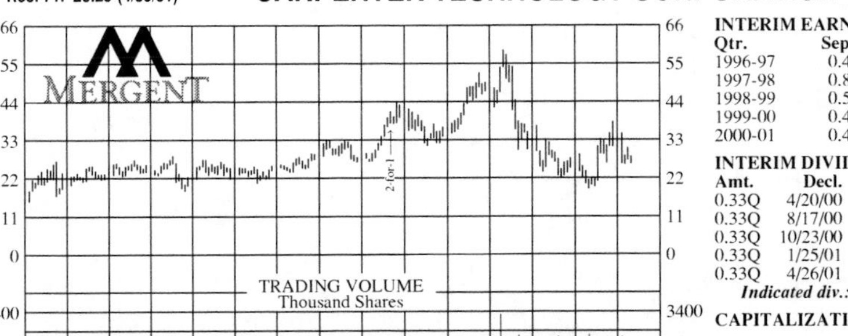

*7 YEAR PRICE SCORE 60.1 *12 MONTH PRICE SCORE 105.3

*NYSE COMPOSITE INDEX=100

INTERIM EARNINGS (Per Share):

Qtr.	Sept.	Dec.	Mar.	June
1996-97	0.46	0.79	0.86	1.14
1997-98	0.85	0.89	1.02	1.08
1998-99	0.51	0.53	0.04	0.50
1999-00	0.44	0.55	0.52	0.80
2000-01	0.48	0.57	...	...

INTERIM DIVIDENDS (Per Share):

Amt.	Decl.	Ex.	Rec.	Pay.
0.33Q	4/20/00	4/28/00	5/02/00	6/01/00
0.33Q	8/17/00	8/25/00	8/29/00	9/07/00
0.33Q	10/23/00	10/31/00	11/02/00	12/07/00
0.33Q	1/25/01	2/02/01	2/06/01	3/01/01
0.33Q	4/26/01	5/04/01	5/08/01	6/07/01

Indicated div.: $1.32 (Div. Reinv. Plan)

CAPITALIZATION (6/30/00):

	($000)	(%)
Long-Term Debt 1	352,300	30.3
Deferred Income Tax	158,000	13.6
Preferred Stock	26,000	2.2
Common & Surplus	627,600	53.9
Total	1,163,900	100.0

RECENT DEVELOPMENTS: For the quarter ended 12/31/00, net income rose 4.7% to $13.3 million compared with $12.7 million in the 1999 quarter. Earnings for 2000 included a non-operating charge of $0.06 per diluted share related to the decrease in the value of certain investments. Net sales were $288.7 million, up 13.7% from $254.0 million a year earlier. Results were positively affected by the stronger aerospace and power generation markets.

PROSPECTS: For the fiscal year ended 6/30/01, CRS anticipates diluted earnings per share to be in the range of $2.40 to $2.60. Separately, the Company's SAO unit is implementing an energy surcharge on all orders shipped after 1/31/01 in an effort to address the effect of the slowdown in the automobile industry, lower volumes and margins for certain stainless steel products, and increasing energy costs.

BUSINESS

CARPENTER TECHNOLOGY CORPORATION is an international manufacturer of high performance alloys, specialty metals, and advanced materials for use in the aerospace, automotive, electronic, medical and consumer products industries. The Company primarily processes basic raw materials such as chromium, nickel, titanium, iron scrap and other metal alloying elements through various melting, hot forming and cold working facilities to produce finished products in the form of billet, bar, rod, wire, narrow strip, special shapes and hollow forms in many sizes and finishes, and produces certain metal powders and fabricated metal products. In addition, ceramic and metal injection molded products are produced from various raw materials using molding, heating and other processes. The Company has more than 14,000 customers in the United States, Europe, Asia and Mexico.

REVENUES

(6/30/2000)	($000)	(%)
Specialty Metals	968,000	88.1
Engineered Products	130,800	11.9
Total	1,098,000	100.0

ANNUAL FINANCIAL DATA

	6/30/00	6/30/99	6/30/98	6/30/97	6/30/96	6/30/95	6/30/94
Earnings Per Share	**2.31**	**3 1.58**	**3.84**	**3.30**	**3.51**	**2.81**	**2 2.28**
Cash Flow Per Share	**5.53**	**4.45**	**6.55**	**5.70**	**5.72**	**4.90**	**4.17**
Tang. Book Val. Per Share	**20.73**	**19.47**	**20.26**	**16.24**	**15.75**	**13.47**	**12.99**
Dividends Per Share	**1.32**	**1.32**	**1.32**	**1.32**	**1.32**	**1.26**	**1.20**
Dividend Payout %	**57.1**	**83.5**	**34.4**	**40.0**	**37.6**	**44.8**	**52.6**
INCOME STATEMENT (IN MILLIONS):							
Total Revenues	1,095.8	1,036.7	1,176.7	939.0	865.3	757.5	628.8
Costs & Expenses	927.5	871.8	950.5	783.3	714.5	635.0	521.0
Depreciation & Amort.	68.3	65.7	58.2	41.0	35.2	32.5	29.0
Operating Income	100.0	99.2	168.0	114.8	115.6	90.1	78.8
Net Interest Inc./(Exp.)	d33.4	d29.3	d29.0	d19.9	d18.9	d14.5	d15.5
Income Before Income Taxes	79.9	55.8	136.9	97.9	95.2	74.6	62.7
Income Taxes	26.6	18.7	52.9	37.9	35.0	27.1	24.4
Equity Earnings/Minority Int.	...	...	...	d1.2	d7.0	d3.0	d0.9
Net Income	53.3	3 37.1	84.0	60.0	60.1	47.5	2 38.3
Cash Flow	119.8	101.3	140.6	99.4	93.8	78.4	65.7
Average Shs. Outstg. (000)	22,000	23,100	21,700	17,703	16,677	16,327	16,130
BALANCE SHEET (IN MILLIONS):							
Cash & Cash Equivalents	9.5	5.5	52.4	18.6	13.2	20.1	5.4
Total Current Assets	483.0	422.7	645.5	402.2	324.5	240.4	171.2
Net Property	789.9	750.4	644.1	513.6	419.5	403.6	391.8
Total Assets	1,745.9	1,607.8	1,698.9	1,223.0	912.0	831.8	729.9
Total Current Liabilities	394.4	294.5	349.1	258.0	172.0	134.2	98.5
Long-Term Obligations	352.3	355.0	370.7	244.7	188.0	194.8	83.9
Net Stockholders' Equity	653.6	632.5	659.5	449.3	309.1	263.9	239.1
Net Working Capital	88.6	128.2	296.4	144.2	152.5	106.3	72.7
Year-end Shs. Outstg. (000)	21,964	21,900	22,700	19,482	16,617	16,292	16,180
STATISTICAL RECORD:							
Operating Profit Margin %	9.1	9.6	14.3	12.2	13.4	11.9	12.5
Net Profit Margin %	4.9	3.6	7.1	6.4	7.0	6.3	6.1
Return on Equity %	8.2	5.9	12.7	13.4	19.5	18.0	16.0
Return on Assets %	3.1	2.3	4.9	4.9	6.6	5.7	5.2
Debt/Total Assets %	20.2	22.1	21.8	20.0	20.6	23.4	11.5
Price Range	38.25-18.75	37.13-22.19	58.94-30.00	52.44-34.75	42.00-31.25	44.00-26.63	33.19-26.56
P/E Ratio	16.6-8.1	23.5-14.0	15.3-7.8	15.9-10.5	12.0-8.9	15.7-9.5	14.6-11.6
Average Yield %	4.6	4.5	3.0	3.0	3.6	3.6	4.0

Statistics are as originally reported. Adj. for stk. split: 2-for-1, 9/95. 1 Incl. cap. lease oblig. 2 Bef. extraord. chrg. of $2.0 mill. ($0.12/sh.) 3 Incl. special chrgs. of $14.2 mill.

OFFICERS:
R. W. Cardy, Chmn., C.E.O.
D. M. Draeger, Pres., C.O.O.
T. E. Geremski, Sr. V.P., C.F.O.

INVESTOR CONTACT: Robert J. Dickson, Investor Relations, (610) 208-2165

PRINCIPAL OFFICE: 1047 N. Park Road, Wyomissing, PA 19610-1339

TELEPHONE NUMBER: (610) 208-2000
FAX: (610) 208-2361
WEB: www.cartech.com

NO. OF EMPLOYEES: 5,700 (approx.)

SHAREHOLDERS: 5,984

ANNUAL MEETING: In Oct.

INCORPORATED: DE, 1968

INSTITUTIONAL HOLDINGS:
No. of Institutions: 135
Shares Held: 12,391,086
% Held: 56.2

INDUSTRY: Blast furnaces and steel mills (SIC: 3312)

TRANSFER AGENT(S): First Chicago Trust Company of New York, Jersey City, NJ

NYSE SYMBOL CRE
Rec. Pr. 28.75 (4/30/01)

CARRAMERICA REALTY CORPORATION

YIELD 6.4%
P/E RATIO 17.4

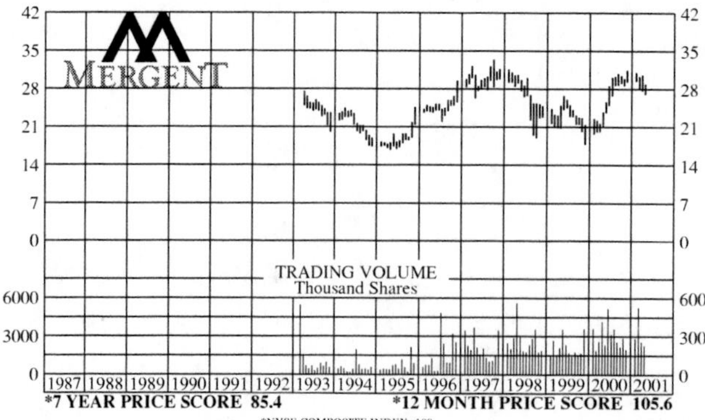

*7 YEAR PRICE SCORE 85.4 *12 MONTH PRICE SCORE 105.6

*NYSE COMPOSITE INDEX=100

INTERIM EARNINGS (Per Share):

Qtr.	Mar.	June	Sept.	Dec.
1998	0.59	0.30	0.37	0.09
1999	0.30	0.19	0.18	0.23
2000	0.36	0.31	0.60	0.25

INTERIM DIVIDENDS (Per Share):

Amt.	Decl.	Ex.	Rec.	Pay.
0.463Q	5/05/00	5/17/00	5/19/00	6/02/00
0.463Q	8/04/00	8/16/00	8/18/00	9/01/00
0.463Q	11/02/00	11/15/00	11/17/00	12/01/00
0.463Q	2/02/01	2/14/01	2/16/01	3/02/01
0.463Q	5/03/01	5/16/01	5/18/01	6/01/01

Indicated div.: $1.85

CAPITALIZATION (12/31/00):

	($000)	(%)
Long-Term Debt	1,211,158	41.1
Minority Interest	89,687	3.0
Preferred Stock	93	0.0
Common & Surplus	1,646,613	55.9
Total	2,947,551	100.0

RECENT DEVELOPMENTS: For the year ended 12/31/00, income from continuing operations totaled $147.2 million compared with $96.3 million in 1999. Results excluded income from discontinued operations of $32.3 million in 2000 versus a loss of $7.9 million in 1999. Results also excluded an extraordinary gain on the sale of assets and other provisions of $36.4 million and $54.8 million in 2000 and 1999. Total revenues increased 8.2% to $558.0 million.

PROSPECTS: The Company will continue to focus on its goal of achieving long-term sustainable per share cash flow growth by acquiring, developing, owning and operating office properties primarily in high-growth markets while maintaining and enhancing a national operating system that provides corporate users of office space with a mix of products and services.

BUSINESS

CARRAMERICA REALTY CORPORATION is a fully integrated, self-administered and self-managed publicly-traded real estate investment trust that focuses primarily on the acquisition, development, ownership and operation of office properties in growth markets across the United States. As of 12/31/00, the Company and its affiliates own, directly or through joint ventures, interests in a portfolio of 283 operating office properties and have 13 office buildings under development in eight key growth markets. The Company's markets include Atlanta, Austin, Chicago, Dallas, Denver, Los Angeles/Orange County, Phoenix, Portland, Salt Lake City, San Diego, San Francisco Bay Area, Seattle, and metropolitan Washington, D.C.

REVENUES

(12/31/2000)	($000)	(%)
Minimum base rent	448,068	80.3
Recoveries from tenants	64,344	11.5
Parking & other charges	19,447	3.5
Real estate service	26,172	4.7
Total	558,031	100.0

ANNUAL FINANCIAL DATA

	12/31/00	12/31/99	12/31/98	12/31/97	12/31/96	12/31/95	12/31/94
Earnings Per Share	**[5] 1.65**	**[1] 0.90**	**[3] 1.32**	**[2] 1.23**	**[2][4] 0.90**	**[4] 0.90**	**1.06**
Tang. Book Val. Per Share	**25.15**	**25.01**	**21.92**	**25.16**	**17.90**	**6.96**	**7.87**
Dividends Per Share	**1.85**	**1.85**	**1.85**	**1.75**	**1.75**	**1.76**	**1.74**
Dividend Payout %	**112.1**	**205.5**	**140.1**	**142.3**	**194.4**	**195.5**	**163.9**
INCOME STATEMENT (IN MILLIONS):							
Total Income	558.0	515.9	602.6	359.4	166.7	100.9	99.2
Costs & Expenses	314.5	295.2	382.5	203.9	101.1	66.1	68.3
Depreciation	128.5	119.7	111.0	77.0	38.3	18.5	14.4
Income Before Income Taxes	126.9	114.6	144.5	86.4	29.1	17.4	17.8
Income Taxes	...	0.8	1.9	...	...	...	...
Equity Earnings/Minority Int.	d8.6	d12.4	d10.8	d7.6	d4.2	d5.3	d5.7
Net Income	[5] 147.2	[1] 96.3	[3] 126.5	[2] 78.7	[2][4] 24.8	[4] 12.1	12.1
Average Shs. Outstg. (000)	67,649	67,982	68,778	59,597	32,000	13,338	15,879
BALANCE SHEET (IN MILLIONS):							
Cash & Cash Equivalents	64.2	64.4	85.1	41.9	35.9	11.5	20.4
Total Real Estate Investments	2,432.1	2,744.4	2,731.1	2,212.8	1,356.3	381.7	337.7
Total Assets	3,072.8	3,479.1	3,793.5	2,744.1	1,536.6	458.9	407.9
Long-Term Obligations	1,211.2	1,603.4	1,704.4	1,025.1	655.4	317.4	254.9
Total Liabilities	1,426.1	1,792.4	1,979.1	1,191.4	749.1	363.3	301.9
Net Stockholders' Equity	1,646.7	1,686.7	1,814.4	1,552.7	787.5	95.5	106.0
Year-end Shs. Outstg. (000)	65,018	66,826	71,760	59,994	43,789	13,409	13,248
STATISTICAL RECORD:							
Net Inc.+Depr./Assets %	9.0	6.2	6.3	5.7	4.1	6.7	6.5
Return on Equity %	8.9	5.7	7.0	5.1	3.1	12.6	11.4
Return on Assets %	4.8	2.8	3.3	2.9	1.6	2.6	3.0
Price Range	31.50-19.69	26.75-17.75	31.69-19.00	33.44-26.25	29.50-21.88	24.63-16.75	24.50-17.38
P/E Ratio	19.1-11.9	29.7-19.7	24.0-14.4	27.2-21.3	32.8-24.3	27.4-18.6	23.1-16.4
Average Yield %	7.2	8.3	7.3	5.9	6.8	8.5	8.3

Statistics are as originally reported. [1] Bef. loss from discont. oper. of $7.9 mill. and extraord. gain on sale of assets of $54.8 mill. incl. $4.5 mill. loss on treas. stock. [2] Bef. extraord. loss, 1997, $608,000; 1996, $484,000. [3] Incl. $13.7 mill. gain on treas. stock. [4] Incl. loss on write off of investments, 1996, $2.3 mill.; 1995, $1.9 mill. [5] Bef. inc. from disc. oper. of $32.3 mill. and extraord. gain on sale of assets of $36.4 mill.

OFFICERS:
T. A. Carr, Chmn., Pres., C.E.O.
R. F. Katchuk, C.F.O.
S. E. Riffee, Sr. V.P., Treas., Contr.
L. A. Madrid, Gen. Couns. & Corp. Sec.

INVESTOR CONTACT: Investor Relations, (202) 729-7500

PRINCIPAL OFFICE: 1850 K Street N.W., Washington, DC 20006

TELEPHONE NUMBER: (202) 729-7500
FAX: (202) 729-1080
WEB: www.carramerica.com

NO. OF EMPLOYEES: 800 (approx.)

SHAREHOLDERS: 419

ANNUAL MEETING: In May

INCORPORATED: MD, July, 1992

INSTITUTIONAL HOLDINGS:
No. of Institutions: 119
Shares Held: 30,434,371
% Held: 46.7

INDUSTRY: Real estate investment trusts (SIC: 6798)

TRANSFER AGENT(S): BankBoston NA, Boston, MA

NYSE SYMBOL CAR
Rec. Pr. 19.15 (5/31/01)

CARTER-WALLACE, INC.

YIELD 1.7%
P/E RATIO 18.1

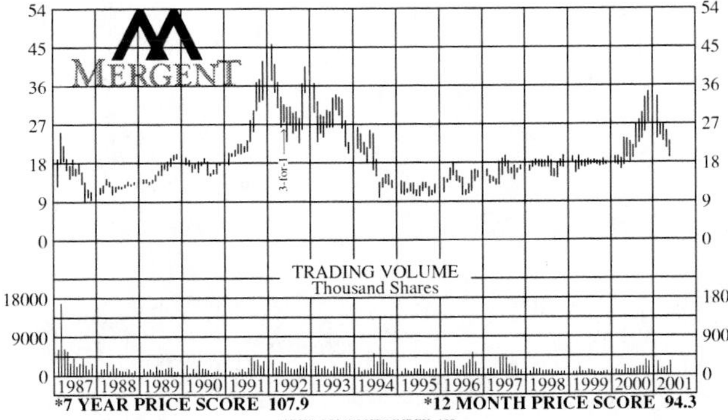

INTERIM EARNINGS (Per Share):

Qtr.	June	Sept.	Dec.	Mar.
1997-98	0.20	0.10	0.15	0.14
1998-99	0.01	0.13	0.17	0.11
1999-00	0.29	0.20	0.30	0.15
2000-01	0.48	0.17	0.26	...

INTERIM DIVIDENDS (Per Share):

Amt.	Decl.	Ex.	Rec.	Pay.
0.08Q	4/13/00	5/01/00	5/03/00	5/30/00
0.08Q	7/19/00	8/04/00	8/08/00	9/01/00
0.08Q	10/26/00	11/10/00	11/14/00	12/06/00
0.08Q	1/25/01	2/14/01	2/16/01	3/12/01
0.08Q	4/19/01	5/07/01	5/09/01	6/05/01

Indicated div.: $0.32

CAPITALIZATION (3/31/00):

	($000)	(%)
Long-Term Debt	59,541	13.2
Common & Surplus	391,038	86.8
Total	450,579	100.0

RECENT DEVELOPMENTS: For the quarter ended 12/31/00, net income decreased 10.2% to $12.5 million versus $14.0 million in the year-earlier quater. Results for 2000 included a $6.1 million pre-tax charge related to the acceleration of certain pension and other costs. Revenues rose 2.3% to $199.4 million from $194.9 million the year before. Net sales for the Domestic Consumer Products segment rose 5.3% to $71.9 million, while sales for the Domestic Health Care segment grew 4.6% to $70.0 million. Sales for the International segment fell 4.6% to $54.3 million.

PROSPECTS: Sales of pharmaceutical products in the Domestic Health Care segment continue to be affected by generic competition, while international sales are being affected by unfavorable foreign exchange rates, despite higher unit sales and selling price increases. However, domestic consumer and health care products sales should continue to grow modestly. Meanwhile, CAR will look to benefit from increased research and development spending in the Domestic Health Care segment.

BUSINESS

CARTER-WALLACE, INC. manufactures and markets consumer products such as personal care items, pet products and non-prescription drugs. Its professional products include ethical pharmaceuticals and diagnostics used in the determination of pregnancy, rheumatic fever, and mononucleosis. Well-known brands are ARRID anti-perspirant sprays, creams and roll-ons, PEARL DROPS tooth polish, NAIR depilatories, CARTERS PILLS laxative, and pet products such as LINATONE food supplements, THERALIN vitamin supplements, and VICTORY flea collars. The Company's TROJAN products have more than a 65% share of the condom market according to CAR. Domestic consumer products accounted for 40.6% of fiscal 2000 net sales, health care, 27.5%; and international, 31.7%.

ANNUAL FINANCIAL DATA

	3/31/00	3/31/99	3/31/98	3/31/97	3/31/96	3/31/95	3/31/94
Earnings Per Share	**0.94**	**0.62**	**0.59**	**0.58**	**0.16**	**2 d1.22**	**1 0.58**
Cash Flow Per Share	**1.64**	**1.22**	**1.13**	**1.08**	**0.70**	**d0.62**	**1.18**
Tang. Book Val. Per Share	**6.15**	**4.72**	**4.96**	**4.87**	**4.34**	**4.27**	**6.30**
Dividends Per Share	**0.24**	**0.20**	**0.16**	**0.16**	**0.16**	**0.33**	**0.33**
Dividend Payout %	**25.5**	**32.3**	**27.1**	**27.6**	**99.9**	**...**	**57.4**
INCOME STATEMENT (IN THOUSANDS):							
Total Revenues	760,644	684,672	668,925	656,181	667,477	669,978	670,263
Costs & Expenses	641,937	599,385	588,938	576,895	616,766	717,054	597,015
Depreciation & Amort.	30,675	26,749	24,736	23,337	24,920	27,842	27,442
Operating Income	88,032	58,538	55,251	55,949	25,791	d74,918	45,806
Net Interest Inc./(Exp.)	d4,614	d4,492	d4,308	d4,186	d3,889	d2,512	d1,976
Income Before Income Taxes	71,036	46,244	44,755	45,349	12,797	d87,030	37,382
Income Taxes	27,704	18,035	17,454	18,593	5,247	cr30,762	10,773
Net Income	43,332	28,209	27,301	26,756	7,550	2 d56,268	1 26,609
Cash Flow	74,007	54,958	52,037	50,093	32,470	d28,426	54,051
Average Shs. Outstg.	45,019	45,180	46,093	46,389	46,160	46,108	45,900
BALANCE SHEET (IN THOUSANDS):							
Cash & Cash Equivalents	103,788	81,252	77,487	53,791	71,219	58,286	56,194
Total Current Assets	374,018	329,590	319,938	301,156	336,773	303,317	315,426
Net Property	149,410	150,596	150,223	154,844	139,273	137,608	157,059
Total Assets	762,236	721,952	693,613	685,922	718,925	680,224	628,562
Total Current Liabilities	168,571	170,041	174,223	158,184	199,690	202,721	130,267
Long-Term Obligations	59,541	64,861	48,887	51,025	55,928	23,115	9,309
Net Stockholders' Equity	391,038	359,156	349,650	349,154	332,896	327,139	393,508
Net Working Capital	205,447	159,549	145,715	142,972	137,083	100,596	185,159
Year-end Shs. Outstg.	43,278	47,205	45,384	46,341	46,375	46,179	44,955
STATISTICAL RECORD:							
Operating Profit Margin %	11.6	8.5	8.3	8.5	3.9	...	6.8
Net Profit Margin %	5.7	4.1	4.1	4.1	1.1	...	4.0
Return on Equity %	11.1	7.9	7.8	7.7	2.3	...	6.8
Return on Assets %	5.7	3.9	3.9	3.9	1.1	...	4.2
Debt/Total Assets %	7.8	9.0	7.0	7.4	7.8	3.4	1.5
Price Range	19.63-15.50	19.69-14.38	19.75-12.75	18.00-10.38	13.88-10.13	26.38-9.88	36.63-20.13
P/E Ratio	20.9-16.5	31.7-23.2	33.5-21.6	31.0-17.9	86.7-63.2	...	63.1-34.7
Average Yield %	1.4	1.2	1.0	1.1	1.3	1.8	1.2

Statistics are as originally reported. 1 Incl. nonrecurr. chgs. of $129.3 mill. 2 Incl. nonrecurr. chgs. of $42.0 mill.

OFFICERS:
H. H. Hoyt Jr., Chmn., C.E.O.
R. Levine, Pres., C.O.O.
P. A. Veteri, Exec. V.P., C.F.O.

INVESTOR CONTACT: Ruder Finn, Inc., (800) 984-1777

PRINCIPAL OFFICE: 1345 Avenue of the Americas, New York, NY 10105

TELEPHONE NUMBER: (212) 339-5000
FAX: (212) 239-5100
WEB: www.pearldrops.com
NO. OF EMPLOYEES: 3,320 (approx.)
SHAREHOLDERS: 1,913 (common); 1,142 (class B common).
ANNUAL MEETING: In July
INCORPORATED: DE, Nov., 1968

INSTITUTIONAL HOLDINGS:
No. of Institutions: 110
Shares Held: 16,700,317
% Held: 36.9

INDUSTRY: Pharmaceutical preparations (SIC: 2834)

TRANSFER AGENT(S): The Bank of New York, New York, NY

NYSE SYMBOL POS
Rec. Pr. 33.40 (5/31/01)

CATALINA MARKETING CORPORATION

YIELD ...
P/E RATIO 33.4

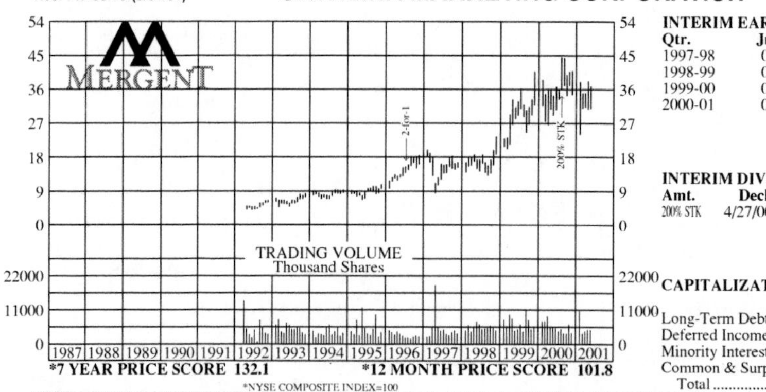

INTERIM EARNINGS (Per Share):

Qtr.	June	Sept.	Dec.	Mar.
1997-98	0.10	0.14	0.20	0.14
1998-99	0.12	0.11	0.21	0.22
1999-00	0.15	0.20	0.29	0.25
2000-01	0.20	0.26	0.29	0.25

INTERIM DIVIDENDS (Per Share):

Amt.	Decl.	Ex.	Rec.	Pay.
200% STK	4/27/00	8/18/00	7/26/00	8/17/00

CAPITALIZATION (3/31/00):

	($000)	(%)
Long-Term Debt	10,814	6.7
Deferred Income Tax	8,380	5.2
Minority Interest	1,228	0.8
Common & Surplus	141,045	87.4
Total	161,467	100.0

RECENT DEVELOPMENTS: For the year ended 3/31/01, net income advanced 13.2% to $58.1 million compared with $51.3 million in the previous year. Revenue increased 19.1% to $417.9 million from $350.9 million in the prior year. This increase reflected revenue growth of 28.0% in the Company's core domestic business compared with the year before. Income from operations improved 10.3% to $94.0 million.

PROSPECTS: In fiscal 2002, the Company anticipates its revenue and earnings growth will both range from 20.0% to 25.0%. On 4/10/01, the Company entered into an agreement under which Albertson's, Inc. will expand the Catalina Marketing Network® into all of its food divisions, expanding the network by more than 870 stores. This should enable POS to achieve its goal of 1,000 net installations for fiscal 2002.

BUSINESS

CATALINA MARKETING CORPORATION provides a wide range of strategic targeted marketing services for consumer goods companies, pharmaceutical manufacturers and their respective retailers. The targeted marketing services of the Company are provided by interrelated operating groups that strive to influence the purchasing behavior of consumers wherever and whenever they make purchasing decisions. Through the Company's operating groups, POS is able to reach consumers internationally and domestically in-store, using incentives, loyalty programs, sampling and advertising messages; and at-home, through direct mailings and on-line. The Company is composed of three business groups: Catalina Marketing Services Worldwide, Health Services Marketing and Emerging Businesses. The products and services offered by POS originate from the Catalina Marketing Network®, the Company's proprietary, electronic marketing system.

ANNUAL FINANCIAL DATA

	3/31/00	3/31/99	3/31/98	3/31/97	3/31/96	3/31/95	3/31/94
Earnings Per Share	**0.89**	**0.66**	**0.58**	**0.44**	**0.37**	**0.29**	**0.21**
Cash Flow Per Share	**1.49**	**1.14**	**1.00**	**0.74**	**0.61**	**0.54**	**0.40**
Tang. Book Val. Per Share	**1.29**	**1.55**	**1.29**	**1.33**	**1.22**	**0.94**	**0.76**
INCOME STATEMENT (IN THOUSANDS):							
Total Revenues	350,922	264,783	217,150	172,143	134,155	113,254	91,448
Costs & Expenses	230,476	169,468	140,324	110,536	84,886	69,863	61,335
Depreciation & Amort.	35,175	27,404	23,934	18,264	14,461	15,215	11,569
Operating Income	85,271	67,911	52,892	43,343	34,808	28,176	18,544
Income Before Income Taxes	84,676	65,577	51,929	44,567	36,217	27,929	19,216
Income Taxes	34,041	27,969	19,058	17,880	14,855	11,259	7,634
Equity Earnings/Minority Int.	713	...	...	554	666	559	1,088
Net Income	51,348	37,608	32,871	27,241	22,028	17,229	12,670
Cash Flow	86,523	65,012	56,805	45,505	36,489	32,444	24,239
Average Shs. Outstg.	57,957	57,027	57,078	61,473	59,766	60,384	61,164
BALANCE SHEET (IN THOUSANDS):							
Cash & Cash Equivalents	13,765	13,942	18,434	13,698	25,778	30,729	26,863
Total Current Assets	115,372	95,481	63,567	61,749	65,291	57,405	51,182
Net Property	115,000	87,686	70,513	69,578	46,253	37,440	32,944
Total Assets	303,752	221,047	157,066	154,696	114,187	96,556	85,476
Total Current Liabilities	142,285	90,335	61,521	53,466	40,461	39,925	40,194
Long-Term Obligations	10,814	4,083	430	869	...	...	...
Net Stockholders' Equity	141,045	120,933	90,042	96,938	71,222	55,494	44,858
Net Working Capital	d26,913	5,146	2,046	8,283	24,830	17,480	10,988
Year-end Shs. Outstg.	54,603	55,167	55,137	58,818	58,488	58,800	59,124
STATISTICAL RECORD:							
Operating Profit Margin %	24.3	25.6	24.4	25.2	25.9	24.9	20.3
Net Profit Margin %	14.6	14.2	15.1	15.8	16.4	15.2	13.9
Return on Equity %	36.4	31.1	36.5	28.1	30.9	31.0	28.2
Return on Assets %	16.9	17.0	20.9	17.6	19.3	17.8	14.8
Debt/Total Assets %	3.6	1.8	0.3	0.6	...	...	...
Price Range	40.83-20.19	23.50-13.12	20.00-8.37	18.50-9.73	10.81-6.67	9.37-6.87	8.37-4.75
P/E Ratio	46.0-22.8	35.6-19.9	34.7-14.5	41.7-22.0	29.4-18.1	32.9-24.1	40.4-22.9

Statistics are as originally reported. Adj. for stk. split: 200% stk. div., 8/00; 2-for-1, 6/96.

OFFICERS:
D. D. Granger, Chmn., Pres., C.E.O.
J. P. Port, C.F.O., Sr. V.P.
C. W. Wolf, Treas., V.P.

INVESTOR CONTACT: Investor Relations, (727) 579-5000

PRINCIPAL OFFICE: 11300 9th St. North, St. Petersburg, FL 33716

TELEPHONE NUMBER: (727) 579-5000
FAX: (727) 570-8507
WEB: www.catalinamktg.com

NO. OF EMPLOYEES: 1,430

SHAREHOLDERS: 604 (approx.)

ANNUAL MEETING: In July

INCORPORATED: CA, 1983; reincorp., DE, Mar., 1992

INSTITUTIONAL HOLDINGS:
No. of Institutions: 198
Shares Held: 47,809,231
% Held: 86.1

INDUSTRY: Advertising agencies (SIC: 7311)

TRANSFER AGENT(S): Mellon Investor Services, Los Angeles, CA

NYSE SYMBOL CAT
Rec. Pr. 50.20 (4/30/01)

CATERPILLAR INC.

YIELD 2.5%
P/E RATIO 16.7

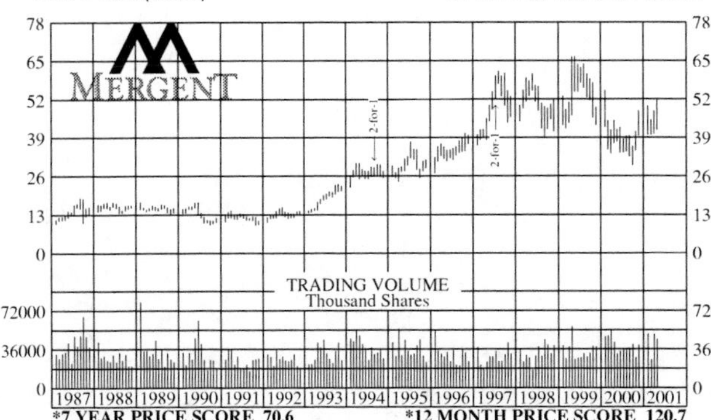

***7 YEAR PRICE SCORE 70.6** ***12 MONTH PRICE SCORE 120.7**

*NYSE COMPOSITE INDEX=100

INTERIM EARNINGS (Per Share):

Qtr.	Mar.	June	Sept.	Dec.
1996	0.77	0.97	0.81	1.00
1997	1.04	1.15	1.03	1.20
1998	1.15	1.20	0.92	0.83
1999	0.57	0.78	0.61	0.67
2000	0.73	0.90	0.62	0.76

INTERIM DIVIDENDS (Per Share):

Amt.	Decl.	Ex.	Rec.	Pay.
0.325Q	4/12/00	4/19/00	4/24/00	5/20/00
0.34Q	6/14/00	7/18/00	7/20/00	8/19/00
0.34Q	10/11/00	10/18/00	10/20/00	11/20/00
0.34Q	12/13/00	1/18/01	1/22/01	2/20/01
0.34Q	4/11/01	4/19/01	4/23/01	5/19/01

Indicated div.: $1.36 (Div. Reinv. Plan)

CAPITALIZATION (12/31/00):

	($000)	(%)
Long-Term Debt	11,334,000	66.9
Common & Surplus	5,600,000	33.1
Total	16,934,000	100.0

RECENT DEVELOPMENTS: For the year ended 12/31/00, net income increased 11.3% to $1.05 billion compared with $946.0 million a year earlier. CAT attributed the improvement primarily to higher physical volume, improved price realization (excluding currency), manufacturing efficiencies and a favorable income tax adjustment, partially offset by foreign exchange losses, resulting from the strong U.S. dollar. Total sales and revenues climbed 2.4% to $20.18 billion from $19.70 billion in 1999.

PROSPECTS: CAT expects 2001 earnings will decline approximately 5.0% to 10.0% from 2000 due to expected North American sales volume decreases and continuing global pricing pressures. In an effort to improve the Company's long-term cost structure, CAT will increase its strategic investments. Separately, on 1/11/01, CAT announced that it has purchased Pioneer Machinery, Inc., a supplier of forestry products equipment. CAT will also purchase an affiliated used equipment company, Ironmart, Inc., and finance company, Federal Financial Services, Inc.

BUSINESS

CATERPILLAR INC. operates in three principal lines of business. The machinery division designs, manufactures and markets construction, mining, agricultural and forestry machinery. Products include track and wheel tractors and loaders, pipelayers, backhoe loaders, mining shovels, log loaders, off-highway trucks, paving products, skid steer loaders, and related parts. The engines division designs, manufactures and markets engines for Caterpillar machinery; on-highway trucks and locomotives; marine, petroleum, construction, industrial, agricultural, and other applications; electric power generation systems; and related parts. Engines range from 5 to over 22,000 horsepower, and turbines range from 1,340 to 18,000 horsepower. The financial products division, provides financing to customers and dealers for the purchase and lease of Caterpillar and noncompetitive related equipment, as well as some financing for Caterpillar sales to dealers. The financial products division also provides various forms of insurance to customers and dealers.

ANNUAL FINANCIAL DATA

	12/31/00	12/31/99	12/31/98	12/31/97	12/31/96	12/31/95	12/31/94
Earnings Per Share	**3.02**	**2.63**	**4.11**	**4.37**	**3.54**	**2.86**	**2.35**
Cash Flow Per Share	**5.95**	**5.26**	**6.46**	**6.31**	**5.33**	**4.59**	**4.03**
Tang. Book Val. Per Share	**11.92**	**11.09**	**10.89**	**12.10**	**10.22**	**8.29**	**6.68**
Dividends Per Share	**1.33**	**1.25**	**1.10**	**0.90**	**0.75**	**0.60**	**0.23**
Dividend Payout %	**44.0**	**47.5**	**26.8**	**20.6**	**21.2**	**21.0**	**9.6**
INCOME STATEMENT (IN MILLIONS):							
Total Revenues	20,175.0	19,702.0	20,977.0	18,949.0	16,522.0	16,072.0	14,328.0
Costs & Expenses	16,728.0	16,703.0	17,370.0	15,420.0	13,539.0	13,416.0	12,001.0
Depreciation & Amort.	1,022.0	945.0	865.0	738.0	696.0	682.0	683.0
Operating Income	2,425.0	2,054.0	2,742.0	2,791.0	2,287.0	1,974.0	1,644.0
Net Interest Inc./(Exp.)	d980.0	d829.0	d753.0	d592.0	d510.0	d484.0	d410.0
Income Before Income Taxes	1,528.0	1,421.0	2,174.0	131.0	1,941.0	1,615.0	1,273.0
Income Taxes	447.0	455.0	665.0	796.0	613.0	501.0	354.0
Equity Earnings/Minority Int.	d28.0	d20.0	4.0	48.0	33.0	22.0	36.0
Net Income	1,053.0	946.0	1,513.0	1,665.0	1,361.0	1,136.0	955.0
Cash Flow	2,075.0	1,891.0	2,378.0	2,403.0	2,057.0	1,818.0	1,638.0
Average Shs. Outstg. (000)	348,898	359,367	368,130	381,000	386,000	396,000	406,000
BALANCE SHEET (IN MILLIONS):							
Cash & Cash Equivalents	334.0	548.0	360.0	292.0	487.0	638.0	419.0
Total Current Assets	12,521.0	11,734.0	11,459.0	9,814.0	8,783.0	7,647.0	7,409.0
Net Property	5,588.0	5,201.0	4,866.0	4,058.0	3,767.0	3,644.0	3,776.0
Total Assets	28,464.0	26,635.0	25,128.0	20,756.0	18,728.0	16,830.0	16,250.0
Total Current Liabilities	8,568.0	8,178.0	7,565.0	6,379.0	7,013.0	6,049.0	5,498.0
Long-Term Obligations	11,334.0	9,928.0	9,404.0	6,942.0	4,532.0	3,964.0	4,270.0
Net Stockholders' Equity	5,600.0	5,465.0	5,131.0	4,679.0	4,116.0	3,388.0	2,911.0
Net Working Capital	3,953.0	3,556.0	3,894.0	3,435.0	1,770.0	1,598.0	1,911.0
Year-end Shs. Outstg. (000)	343,397	353,748	357,198	368,000	380,000	388,000	400,000
STATISTICAL RECORD:							
Operating Profit Margin %	12.0	10.4	13.1	14.7	13.8	12.3	11.5
Net Profit Margin %	5.2	4.8	7.2	8.8	8.2	7.1	6.7
Return on Equity %	18.8	17.3	29.5	35.6	33.1	33.5	32.8
Return on Assets %	3.7	3.6	6.0	8.0	7.3	6.7	5.9
Debt/Total Assets %	39.8	37.3	37.4	33.4	24.2	23.6	26.3
Price Range	55.13-29.56	66.44-42.00	60.75-39.06	61.63-36.25	40.50-27.00	37.63-24.13	30.38-22.19
P/E Ratio	18.3-9.8	25.3-16.0	14.8-9.5	14.1-8.3	11.5-7.6	13.2-8.4	12.9-9.4
Average Yield %	3.1	2.3	2.2	1.8	2.2	1.9	0.9

Statistics are as originally reported. Adj. for 2-for-1 stk. split, 9/94 & 7/97.

OFFICERS:
G. Barton, Chmn., C.E.O.
R. R. Atterbury, III, V.P., Couns., Sec.
F. L. Pheeters, V.P., C.F.O.

INVESTOR CONTACT: J. Hawkinson, Corp. Public Affairs, (309) 675-4715

PRINCIPAL OFFICE: 100 N.E. Adams Street, Peoria, IL 61629

TELEPHONE NUMBER: (309) 675-1000
FAX: (309) 675-4332
WEB: www.CAT.com
NO. OF EMPLOYEES: 68,440
SHAREHOLDERS: 36,253 (record)
ANNUAL MEETING: In Apr.
INCORPORATED: CA, Apr., 1925; reincorp., DE, May, 1986

INSTITUTIONAL HOLDINGS:
No. of Institutions: 467
Shares Held: 219,741,414
% Held: 64.0

INDUSTRY: Construction machinery (SIC: 3531)

TRANSFER AGENT(S): First Chicago Trust Company of New York, Jersey City, NJ

NYSE SYMBOL CDI
Rec. Pr. 16.70 (5/31/01)

CDI CORP.

YIELD ...
P/E RATIO 9.7

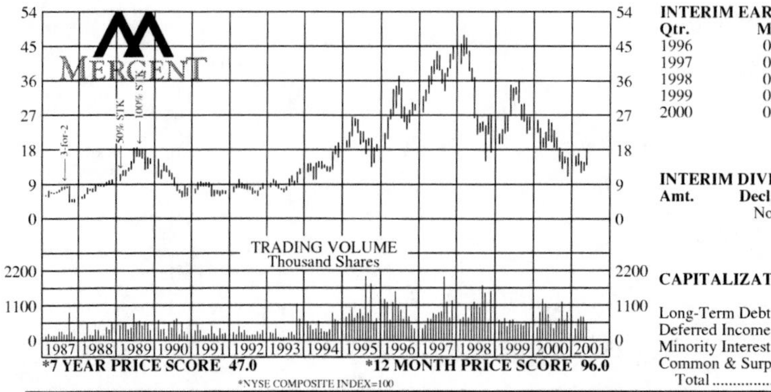

***7 YEAR PRICE SCORE 47.0** ***12 MONTH PRICE SCORE 96.0**

*NYSE COMPOSITE INDEX=100

INTERIM EARNINGS (Per Share):

Qtr.	Mar.	June	Sept.	Dec.
1996	0.44	0.53	0.65	0.52
1997	0.54	0.60	0.69	0.53
1998	0.54	0.47	0.63	0.62
1999	0.62	0.65	0.70	0.64
2000	0.62	0.67	0.59	d0.15

INTERIM DIVIDENDS (Per Share):

Amt.	Decl.	Ex.	Rec.	Pay.
		No dividends paid.		

CAPITALIZATION (12/31/00):

	($000)	(%)
Long-Term Debt	49,623	13.1
Deferred Income Tax	1,272	0.3
Minority Interest	3,144	0.8
Common & Surplus	325,795	85.8
Total	379,834	100.0

RECENT DEVELOPMENTS: For the year ended 12/31/00, net income amounted to $33.0 million versus income from continuing operations of $46.7 million a year earlier. The 2000 results included pre-tax nonrecurring charges totaling $11.7 million. Revenues rose 7.2% to $1.72 billion. Technical Services revenues grew 6.1% to $985.9 million. Information Technology revenues increased 7.3% to $355.7 million. Todays Staffing revenues climbed 4.8% to $238.9 million. Meanwhile, Management Recruiters' revenues jumped 20.7% to $136.8 million.

PROSPECTS: During 2001, the Company anticipates an increase in operating costs totaling $8.7 million associated with its information systems and health care benefits. The Company plans to reduce corporate spending in an attempt to offset these higher costs. Meanwhile, results should benefit from strong demand for higher-margin engineering services as well as a projected increase in new hires. For 2001, the Company expects earnings to be approximately $2.00 per share.

BUSINESS

CDI CORP. is a provider of personnel services in the United States and Canada. The Technical Services segment provides technical services and temporary engineering, technical and scientific personnel to a broad range of clients in the industry and to the U.S. Government. The Information Technology segment provides information technology services to commercial clients. Todays Staffing provides temporary clerical and marketing support personnel services to commercial clients. Management Recruiters includes contingency search and recruiting services for permanent employment of management, technical and sales personnel. CDI and its franchisees operate more than 1,400 offices in 28 countries.

REVENUES

(12/31/00)	($000)	(%)
Info Technology Services	355,693	20.7
Technical Services	985,891	57.3
Management Recruiters	136,752	8.0
Todays Staffing	238,908	14.0
Total	1,717,244	100.0

ANNUAL FINANCIAL DATA

	12/31/00	12/31/99	12/31/98	12/31/97	12/31/96	12/31/95	12/31/94
Earnings Per Share	**[2] 1.73**	**[1] 2.60**	**[1] 2.25**	**[1] 2.36**	**[1] 2.14**	**[1] 1.55**	**1.13**
Cash Flow Per Share	**2.97**	**3.56**	**2.98**	**2.96**	**2.70**	**2.17**	**1.85**
Tang. Book Val. Per Share	**12.35**	**10.72**	**10.10**	**10.02**	**8.14**	**7.33**	**5.93**
INCOME STATEMENT (IN MILLIONS):							
Total Revenues	1,717.2	1,601.9	1,540.5	1,496.8	1,374.9	1,270.5	1,097.6
Costs & Expenses	1,633.8	1,497.6	1,450.0	1,405.5	1,290.0	1,202.2	1,042.5
Depreciation & Amort.	23.7	18.3	14.5	12.1	11.2	12.4	14.2
Operating Income	59.8	86.0	76.1	79.1	73.7	55.8	40.9
Net Interest Inc./(Exp.)	d5.2	d2.1	d1.4	d2.3	d3.5	d4.5	d4.1
Income Before Income Taxes	54.6	83.9	74.7	76.8	70.2	51.4	36.8
Income Taxes	20.7	33.0	29.5	28.7	27.6	20.6	14.4
Equity Earnings/Minority Int.	d0.9	d1.2	d1.0	d1.2	d0.2	d0.1	...
Net Income	[2] 33.0	[1] 49.7	[1] 44.2	[1] 46.9	[1] 42.5	[1] 30.7	22.4
Cash Flow	56.7	68.0	58.7	59.1	53.6	43.1	36.5
Average Shs. Outstg. (000)	19,104	19,116	19,683	19,929	19,872	19,831	19,779
BALANCE SHEET (IN MILLIONS):							
Cash & Cash Equivalents	11.4	11.4	7.0	7.0	6.1	4.5	5.2
Total Current Assets	402.8	373.7	332.8	289.6	288.0	271.8	224.4
Net Property	66.1	53.3	39.5	26.4	25.5	30.5	43.1
Total Assets	572.0	531.7	435.8	348.8	340.2	312.2	297.7
Total Current Liabilities	179.1	155.0	145.6	121.3	106.9	110.1	96.2
Long-Term Obligations	49.6	65.7	35.1	...	48.9	67.9	58.8
Net Stockholders' Equity	325.8	293.8	241.1	215.8	176.9	145.4	138.9
Net Working Capital	223.7	218.7	187.2	168.3	181.1	161.7	128.2
Year-end Shs. Outstg. (000)	19,065	19,072	19,034	19,924	19,829	19,820	19,715
STATISTICAL RECORD:							
Operating Profit Margin %	3.5	5.4	4.9	5.3	5.4	4.4	3.7
Net Profit Margin %	1.9	3.1	2.9	3.1	3.1	2.4	2.0
Return on Equity %	10.1	16.9	18.3	21.7	24.0	21.1	16.1
Return on Assets %	5.8	9.3	10.2	13.5	12.5	9.8	7.5
Debt/Total Assets %	8.7	12.3	8.0	...	14.4	21.7	19.8
Price Range	25.88-11.00	36.00-19.50	47.94-15.00	45.19-27.75	37.25-18.00	26.63-13.50	19.88-10.25
P/E Ratio	15.0-6.4	13.8-7.5	21.3-6.7	19.1-11.8	17.4-8.4	17.2-8.7	17.6-9.1

Statistics are as originally reported. [1] Bef. disc. oper., inc. 1999, $2.8 mill.; 1998, $1.3 mill., loss 1997, $9.3 mill.; 1996, $11.1 mill.; 1995, $25.5 mill. [2] Incl. pre-tax nonrecurr. chrgs. of $11.7 mill.

OFFICERS:
W. R. Garrison, Chmn.
A. M. Levantin, Acting Pres. and C.E.O.
G. L. Cowan, Exec. V.P., C.F.O.

INVESTOR CONTACT: Investor Relations, (215) 569-2200

PRINCIPAL OFFICE: 1717 Arch Street, 35th Floor, Philadelphia, PA 19103-2768

TELEPHONE NUMBER: (215) 569-2200
FAX: (215) 569-1750
WEB: www.cdicorp.com

NO. OF EMPLOYEES: 32,360 (approx.)

SHAREHOLDERS: 517

ANNUAL MEETING: In May

INCORPORATED: PA, Sept., 1950

INSTITUTIONAL HOLDINGS:
No. of Institutions: 76
Shares Held: 6,470,521
% Held: 33.9

INDUSTRY: Help supply services (SIC: 7363)

TRANSFER AGENT(S): Mellon Investor Services, Ridgefield Park, NJ

NYSE SYMBOL FUN
Rec. Pr. 22.80 (5/31/01)

CEDAR FAIR, L.P.

YIELD 6.8%
P/E RATIO 15.1

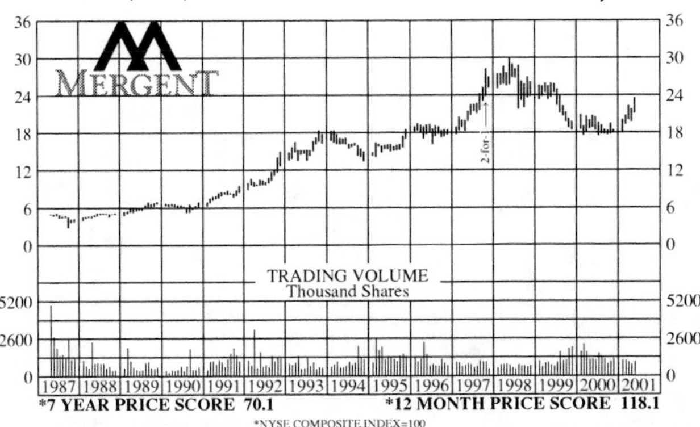

INTERIM EARNINGS (Per Share):

Qtr.	Mar.	June	Sept.	Dec.
1997	d0.37	0.31	1.81	d0.28
1998	d0.44	0.37	1.79	d0.14
1999	d0.41	0.37	1.83	d0.15
2000	d0.51	0.36	1.83	d0.17

INTERIM DIVIDENDS (Per Share):

Amt.	Decl.	Ex.	Rec.	Pay.
0.375Q	3/06/00	4/03/00	4/05/00	5/15/00
0.375Q	6/19/00	7/03/00	7/06/00	8/15/00
0.39Q	9/25/00	10/02/00	10/04/00	11/15/00
0.39Q	12/20/00	1/02/01	1/04/01	2/15/01
0.39Q	3/09/01	4/02/01	4/04/01	5/15/01

Indicated div.: $1.56 (Div. Reinv. Plan)

CAPITALIZATION (12/31/00):

	($000)	(%)
Long-Term Debt	300,000	47.6
Common & Surplus	330,589	52.4
Total	630,589	100.0

RECENT DEVELOPMENTS: For the year ended 12/31/00, net income declined 9.3% to $77.8 million from $85.8 million in the equivalent 1999 quarter. Results for 2000 included nonrecurring costs to terminate general partner fees of $7.8 million. Net revenues were $472.9 million, up 8.0% from $438.0 million a year earlier. Interest expense increased 38.9% to $21.4 million due to higher interest rates, as well as increased borrowings for several 1999 acquisitions.

PROSPECTS: Going forward, FUN is investing $38.0 million in capital improvements at its nine properties. The major projects include the construction of Talon, a suspended coaster, at Dorney Park; the addition of an upscale camping complex at Cedar Point; and the introduction of Camp Snoopy and the Peanuts characters at World of Fun. Separately, FUN expects net income to grow in the mid-single digit range in 2001.

BUSINESS

CEDAR FAIR, L.P. is a limited partnership managed by Cedar Fair Management Company. The partnership owns and operates five amusement parks: Cedar Point, located on Lake Erie in Sandusky, OH; Knott's Berry Farm, located in Buena Park, CA; Dorney Park & Wildwater Kingdom, located in South Whitehall Township, PA; Valleyfair, located in Shakopee, Minnesota; and Worlds of Fun and Oceans of Fun, located in Kansas City, Missouri. The partnership's water parks are located in Chula Visa, California and adjacent to Cedar Point, Knott's Berry Farm and Worlds of Fun. The parks are family-oriented, with recreational facilities for people of all ages, and provide environments with rides and entertainment. All principal rides and attractions are owned and operated by the Partnership. The Company has two hotels: Breakers Tower at Cedar Point and the Buena Park Hotel. FUN also operates Knott's Camp Snoopy at the Mall of America in Bloomington, Minnesota under a management contract.

ANNUAL FINANCIAL DATA

	12/31/00	12/31/99	12/31/98	12/31/97	12/31/96	12/31/95	12/31/94
Earnings Per Share	**1 1.50**	**1.63**	**1.58**	**1.47**	**1.59**	**1.45**	**1.40**
Cash Flow Per Share	**2.27**	**2.31**	**2.20**	**1.95**	**2.02**	**1.83**	**1.75**
Tang. Book Val. Per Share	**6.31**	**6.56**	**6.38**	**5.24**	**3.47**	**3.06**	**2.33**
Dividends Per Share	**1.50**	**1.39**	**1.28**	**1.26**	**1.18**	**1.13**	**1.03**
Dividend Payout %	**100.2**	**85.1**	**81.3**	**85.5**	**73.9**	**78.0**	**73.9**
INCOME STATEMENT (IN THOUSANDS):							
Total Revenues	472,920	438,001	419,500	264,137	250,523	218,197	198,358
Costs & Expenses	317,832	286,194	274,827	166,306	150,330	128,442	115,382
Depreciation & Amort.	39,572	35,082	32,065	21,528	19,072	16,742	14,960
Operating Income	115,516	116,755	112,608	76,303	81,121	73,013	68,016
Net Interest Inc./(Exp.)	d21,357	d15,371	d14,660	d7,845	d6,942	d6,877	d7,293
Income Before Income Taxes	94,159	101,384	97,948	68,458	74,179	66,136	62,825
Income Taxes	16,353	15,580	14,507	...	...	...	...
Net Income	1 77,806	85,804	83,441	68,458	74,179	66,136	62,825
Cash Flow	117,378	120,856	115,506	89,986	93,251	82,878	77,785
Average Shs. Outstg.	51,679	52,390	52,414	46,265	46,116	45,214	44,534
BALANCE SHEET (IN THOUSANDS):							
Cash & Cash Equivalents	2,392	638	1,137	2,520	1,279	111	350
Total Current Assets	25,378	24,184	20,967	21,954	11,730	9,805	8,198
Net Property	728,919	674,640	600,044	567,137	281,638	253,840	204,331
Total Assets	764,143	708,961	631,325	599,619	304,104	274,717	223,982
Total Current Liabilities	114,024	86,559	77,231	62,426	39,241	37,648	33,602
Long-Term Obligations	300,000	261,200	200,350	189,750	87,600	80,000	71,400
Net Stockholders' Equity	330,589	349,986	341,991	285,381	169,994	151,476	115,054
Net Working Capital	d88,646	d62,375	d56,264	d40,472	d27,511	d27,843	d25,404
Year-end Shs. Outstg.	50,813	51,798	51,980	52,403	45,920	45,920	44,480
STATISTICAL RECORD:							
Operating Profit Margin %	24.4	26.7	26.8	28.9	32.4	33.5	34.3
Net Profit Margin %	16.5	19.6	19.9	25.9	29.6	30.3	31.7
Return on Equity %	23.5	24.5	24.4	24.0	43.6	43.7	54.6
Return on Assets %	10.2	12.1	13.2	11.4	24.4	24.1	28.0
Debt/Total Assets %	39.3	36.8	31.7	31.6	28.8	29.1	31.9
Price Range	20.88-17.44	26.00-18.44	30.13-21.75	28.25-17.69	19.50-16.13	18.56-14.06	18.31-13.38
P/E Ratio	13.9-11.6	15.9-11.3	19.1-13.8	19.2-12.0	12.3-10.1	12.8-9.7	13.1-9.6
Average Yield %	7.8	6.2	5.0	5.5	6.6	6.9	6.5

Statistics are as originally reported. Adj. for stk. split: 2-for-1, 11/7/97. 1 Incl. nonrecurr. chrg. of $7.8 mill. to terminate general partner fees.

OFFICERS:
R. L. Kinzel, Pres., C.E.O.
B. A. Jackson, Corp. V.P., C.F.O.
T. W. Salamone, Treas.

INVESTOR CONTACT: Brian C. Witherow, Dir.-Investor Relations, (419) 627-2173

PRINCIPAL OFFICE: One Cedar Point Drive, Sandusky, OH 44870-5259

TELEPHONE NUMBER: (419) 626-0830
FAX: (419) 627-2234
WEB: www.cedarfair.com

NO. OF EMPLOYEES: 1,400 (approx.)

SHAREHOLDERS: 11,000 (approx.)

ANNUAL MEETING: N/A

INCORPORATED: MN, 1983; reincorp., DE, 1987

INSTITUTIONAL HOLDINGS:
No. of Institutions: 100
Shares Held: 10,036,919
% Held: 19.8

INDUSTRY: Amusement parks (SIC: 7996)

TRANSFER AGENT(S): American Stock Transfer & Trust Company, New York, NY

NYSE SYMBOL CD
Rec. Pr. 19.18 (5/31/01)

CENDANT CORPORATION

YIELD ...
P/E RATIO 23.1

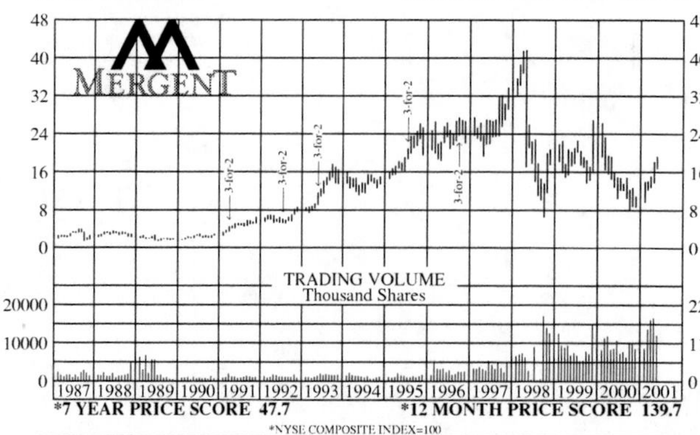

INTERIM EARNINGS (Per Share):

Qtr.	Mar.	June	Sept.	Dec.
1997	0.21	d0.02	0.31	d0.42
1998	0.21	0.18	0.13	d0.36
1999	0.22	1.08	0.27	d2.06
2000	0.17	0.24	0.25	0.17

INTERIM DIVIDENDS (Per Share):

Amt.	Decl.	Ex.	Rec.	Pay.

No dividends paid.

CAPITALIZATION (12/31/00):

	($000)	(%)
Long-Term Debt	3,988,000	42.9
Deferred Income Tax	476,000	5.1
Redeemable Pfd. Stock	2,058,000	22.1
Common & Surplus	2,774,000	29.8
Total	9,296,000	100.0

RECENT DEVELOPMENTS: For the year ended 12/31/00, income from continuing operations was $576.0 million versus a loss from continuing operations of $333.0 million in 1999. Results for 2000 and 1999 included net nonrecurring charges totaling $99.0 million and $1.98 billion, respectively. Also, results for 2000 excluded a net extraordinary loss of $2.0 million, a net accounting charge of $56.0 million and a net gain of $84.0 million from discontinued operations. Net revenues declined 13.1% to $3.93 billion.

PROSPECTS: On 3/1/01, the Company completed the acquisition of Avis Group Holdings, Inc., for about $937.0 million. Separately, CD acquired Fairfield Communities, Inc., for about $690.0 million in cash. Both acquisitions are expected to be immediately accretive to CD's earnings per share. In addition, CD expects to record a pre-tax gain in excess of $525.0 million from the sale of its Internet real estate portal, Move.com to Homestore.com, Inc. For 2001, CD expects earnings of $1.00 per share.

BUSINESS

CENDANT CORPORATION, which was formed in December 1997 through the merger of CUC International and HFS Incorporated, operates through four principal operating segments. The travel segment facilitates vacation timeshare exchanges and franchises hotel and car rental businesses. The real estate segment assists in employee relocation, provides home buyers with mortgages and franchises real estate brokerage businesses. The direct marketing segment provides an array of services through more than 20 membership clubs. The diversified services segment offers car park services, tax preparation services, consumer software in various multimedia forms, information technology services, credit information services and financial products. CD owns approximately 87.0% of Move.com, which provides on-line relocation, real estate, and home-related services.

REVENUES

(12/31/00)	($000)	(%)
Service Fees	3,783,000	96.3
Other revenues	147,000	3.7
Total	3,930,000	100.0

ANNUAL FINANCIAL DATA

	12/31/00	12/31/99	12/31/98	[1] 12/31/97	1/31/97	1/31/96	1/31/95
Earnings Per Share	[5] 0.78	[4] d0.30	[3] 0.18	[2] 0.06	0.41	0.37	0.30
Cash Flow Per Share	1.39	1.12	1.98	2.41	2.14	1.43	1.25
Tang. Book Val. Per Share	...	...	...	0.89	2.02	1.05	0.63
INCOME STATEMENT (IN MILLIONS):							
Total Revenues	3,930.0	5,402.0	5,283.8	5,314.7	2,347.7	1,415.0	1,044.7
Costs & Expenses	2,325.0	5,707.0	3,339.5	1,809.5	1,196.7	690.4	474.8
Depreciation & Amort.	483.0	1,069.0	1,582.6	1,996.3	704.3	453.9	378.8
Operating Income	1,122.0	d1,374.0	361.7	1,508.9	446.6	270.7	191.1
Net Interest Inc./(Exp.)	d145.0	d199.0	d113.9	d66.3	9.5	d0.9	0.1
Income Before Income Taxes	969.0	d574.0	315.0	294.7	276.2	266.3	190.5
Income Taxes	309.0	cr406.0	104.5	239.3	112.1	103.0	72.9
Equity Earnings/Minority Int.	d84.0	d61.0	d50.6	...	...	...	...
Net Income	[5] 576.0	[4] d229.0	[3] 159.9	[2] 55.4	164.1	172.1	118.2
Cash Flow	1,059.0	840.0	1,742.5	2,051.7	868.4	626.0	497.0
Average Shs. Outstg. (000)	762,000	751,000	880,400	851,700	405,073	438,075	397,913
BALANCE SHEET (IN MILLIONS):							
Cash & Cash Equivalents	967.0	1,164.0	1,008.7	149.5	622.3	270.0	180.6
Total Current Assets	2,384.0	4,592.0	4,546.9	2,575.3	1,430.1	767.7	503.9
Net Property	1,273.0	1,347.0	1,432.8	...	145.6	61.4	35.1
Total Assets	14,516.0	15,149.0	20,216.5	14,851.2	2,473.4	1,141.3	768.2
Total Current Liabilities	1,911.0	5,610.0	2,871.7	1,742.8	481.4	149.8	109.5
Long-Term Obligations	3,988.0	4,759.0	10,259.7	6,950.9	23.5	14.4	15.0
Net Stockholders' Equity	2,774.0	2,206.0	4,835.6	4,477.5	1,255.1	727.2	440.1
Net Working Capital	473.0	d1,018.0	1,675.2	832.5	948.7	617.9	394.4
Year-end Shs. Outstg. (000)	737,888	706,548	833,281	831,788	402,875	431,597	386,505
STATISTICAL RECORD:							
Operating Profit Margin %	28.5	...	6.8	28.4	19.0	19.1	18.3
Net Profit Margin %	14.7	...	3.0	1.0	7.0	12.2	11.3
Return on Equity %	20.8	...	3.3	1.2	13.1	23.7	26.9
Return on Assets %	4.0	...	0.8	0.4	6.6	15.1	15.4
Debt/Total Assets %	27.5	31.4	50.7	46.8	0.9	1.3	2.0
Price Range	26.31-8.13	26.94-13.63	41.69-6.50	33.81-19.25	27.42-18.33	26.17-14.50	15.95-11.11
P/E Ratio	33.7-10.4	...	231.5-36.1	562.6-320.3	67.7-45.3	70.1-38.9	53.9-37.5

Statistics are as originally reported. Adj. for stk. splits through 10/96 [1] Results refl. fiscal yr.-end change fr. merger of CUC Intl. & HFS Inc. Results prior to 12/31/97 were for CUC Intl. [2] Incl. non-recurr. chrg. $1.15 bill. [3] Bef. disc. oper. inc. of $379.7 mill., but incl. non-recurr. chrg. $838.3 mill. [4] Incl. one-time chrgs. totaling $3.03 bill. rel. to lit. settlement, term. acquis., and other unusual chrgs. & bef. gain of $174.1 mill. fr. sale of disc. ops. [5] Bef. after-tax acctg. chrg. of $56.0 mill., net gain of $84.0 mill. fr. disc. ops. & after-tax extraord. loss of $2.0 mill. & incl. net pre-tax nonrecurr. chrg. of $99.0 mill.

OFFICERS:
H. R. Silverman, Chmn., Pres., C.E.O.
J. E. Buckman, Vice-Chmn., Gen. Couns.

INVESTOR CONTACT: Samuel J. Levenson, Sr. V.P., Investor Relations, (212) 413-1834

PRINCIPAL OFFICE: 9 West 57th Street, New York, NY 10019

TELEPHONE NUMBER: (212) 413-1800
FAX: (212) 413-1924
WEB: www.cendant.com
NO. OF EMPLOYEES: 28,000 (approx.)
SHAREHOLDERS: 9,171 (approx.)
ANNUAL MEETING: In May
INCORPORATED: DE, 1973; reincorp., DE, 1974

INSTITUTIONAL HOLDINGS:
No. of Institutions: 432
Shares Held: 571,133,321
% Held: 67.0

INDUSTRY: Miscellaneous personal services, nec (SIC: 7299)

TRANSFER AGENT(S): Mellon Investor Service, South Hackensack, NJ

NYSE SYMBOL CTX
Rec. Pr. 43.15 (4/30/01)

CENTEX CORPORATION

YIELD 0.4%
P/E RATIO 10.6

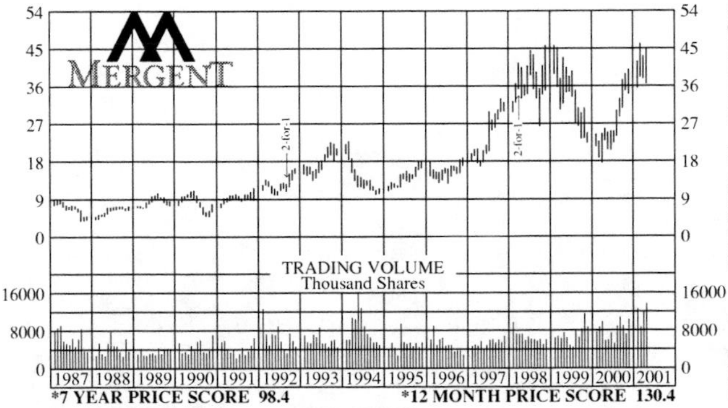

MERGENT

TRADING VOLUME
Thousand Shares

***7 YEAR PRICE SCORE 98.4** ***12 MONTH PRICE SCORE 130.4**

*NYSE COMPOSITE INDEX=100

INTERIM EARNINGS (Per Share):

Qtr.	June	Sept.	Dec.	Mar.
1996-97	0.38	0.48	0.47	0.49
1997-98	0.45	0.60	0.61	0.71
1998-99	0.78	0.91	0.96	1.10
1999-00	0.95	1.07	1.04	1.17
2000-01	0.81	0.98	1.12	...

INTERIM DIVIDENDS (Per Share):

Amt.	Decl.	Ex.	Rec.	Pay.
0.04Q	5/30/00	6/13/00	6/15/00	7/13/00
0.04Q	8/24/00	8/31/00	9/05/00	10/03/00
0.04Q	11/27/00	12/08/00	12/12/00	1/09/01
0.04Q	3/01/01	3/09/01	3/13/01	4/10/01
0.04Q	5/23/01	6/08/01	6/12/01	7/11/01

Indicated div.: $0.16

CAPITALIZATION (3/31/00):

	($000)	(%)
Long-Term Debt [1]	751,160	32.7
Minority Interest	129,352	5.6
Common & Surplus	1,419,349	61.7
Total	2,299,861	100.0

RECENT DEVELOPMENTS: For the quarter ended 12/31/00, net income advanced 8.4% to $68.5 million from $63.2 million in the equivalent 1999 quarter. Earnings benefited from an increase in Centex Homes' closings, which grew 18.9% to $4,893 units. Revenues rose 14.7% to $1.64 billion from $1.43 billion a year earlier. Total Home Building revenues increased 17.4% to $1.07 billion, while Financial Services revenues advanced 13.8% to $121.3 million.

PROSPECTS: During the fourth quarter of fiscal 2001, the Company acquired the home building businesses of The Selective Group, based in Farmington Hills, Michigan, and CityHomes, a builder of upscale urban townhomes in Dallas, TX. Separately, Centex HomeTeam Pest Control acquired four pest management companies, three in Florida and one in North Carolina.

BUSINESS

CENTEX CORPORATION has operations in home building, investment real estate, financial services, construction products and contracting and construction services. The Financial Services segment consists of CTX's mortgage banking operations. As of 4/25/01, CTX owned approximately 65.2% of publicly-held Centex Construction Products, Inc., which manufactures cement, concrete and aggregate, and gypsum wallboard. Centex Development Co., L.P. conducts CTX's real estate development activities. In 2001, sales (and operating income) were derived as follows: Home Building, which includes conventional and manufactured housing, 66.8% (66.6%); Investment Real Estate, 0.5% (8.5%); Financial Services, 6.9% (3.3%); Construction Products, 6.6% (16.6%); Contracting and Construction Services, 19.2% (5.0%).

ANNUAL FINANCIAL DATA

	3/31/00	3/31/99	3/31/98	3/31/97	3/31/96	3/31/95	3/31/94
Earnings Per Share	**4.22**	**3.75**	**2.36**	**1.81**	**0.92**	**1.52**	**[2] 1.30**
Cash Flow Per Share	**5.02**	**4.33**	**2.78**	**2.04**	**1.13**	**1.63**	**1.60**
Tang. Book Val. Per Share	**19.66**	**16.43**	**14.40**	**12.62**	**12.71**	**11.90**	**10.56**
Dividends Per Share	**0.16**	**0.15**	**0.11**	**0.10**	**0.10**	**0.10**	**0.10**
Dividend Payout %	**3.8**	**4.1**	**4.7**	**5.5**	**10.9**	**6.6**	**7.7**
INCOME STATEMENT (IN MILLIONS):							
Total Revenues	5,956.4	5,154.8	3,975.5	3,785.0	3,103.0	3,277.5	3,214.5
Costs & Expenses	5,425.8	4,691.8	3,674.7	3,576.0	3,028.3	3,201.2	3,059.8
Depreciation & Amort.	49.0	36.2	25.6	13.5	12.5	6.4	19.6
Operating Income	481.6	426.9	275.1	195.4	62.2	69.9	135.0
Income Before Income Taxes	416.9	373.3	231.6	16.7	87.8	145.8	135.0
Income Taxes	159.7	141.3	86.8	57.2	34.4	53.5	49.9
Equity Earnings/Minority Int.	d64.8	d53.6	d43.4	d31.7	25.6	16.6	...
Net Income	257.1	232.0	144.8	106.6	53.4	92.2	[2] 85.2
Cash Flow	306.1	268.1	170.4	120.1	65.9	98.7	104.8
Average Shs. Outstg. (000)	60,929	61,854	61,265	58,858	58,182	60,654	65,580
BALANCE SHEET (IN MILLIONS):							
Cash & Cash Equivalents	139.6	111.3	98.3	31.3	14.0	23.8	154.5
Total Current Assets	2,549.1	2,090.9	1,540.9	1,387.8	1,500.3	1,426.1	1,522.5
Net Property	360.6	313.7	296.0	293.1	37.1	41.3	188.9
Total Assets	4,038.7	4,334.7	3,416.2	2,678.8	2,337.0	2,049.7	2,580.4
Total Current Liabilities	1,688.0	2,645.3	1,952.0	1,365.2	1,276.5	1,132.2	1,613.6
Long-Term Obligations	751.2	284.3	237.7	236.8	321.0	222.5	222.8
Net Stockholders' Equity	1,419.3	1,197.6	991.2	835.8	722.8	668.2	668.7
Net Working Capital	861.1	d554.3	d411.1	22.6	223.8	293.8	d91.0
Year-end Shs. Outstg. (000)	59,388	59,388	59,532	58,032	56,850	56,142	63,328
STATISTICAL RECORD:							
Operating Profit Margin %	8.1	8.3	6.9	5.2	2.0	2.1	4.2
Net Profit Margin %	4.3	4.5	3.6	2.8	1.7	2.8	2.6
Return on Equity %	18.1	19.4	14.6	12.8	7.4	13.8	12.7
Return on Assets %	6.4	5.4	4.2	4.0	2.3	4.5	3.3
Debt/Total Assets %	18.6	6.6	7.0	8.8	13.7	10.9	8.6
Price Range	45.75-22.38	45.75-26.38	33.00-16.75	18.88-12.63	18.00-10.94	22.88-10.06	22.63-13.38
P/E Ratio	10.8-5.3	12.2-7.0	14.0-7.1	10.4-7.0	19.7-12.0	15.0-6.6	17.4-10.3
Average Yield %	0.5	0.4	0.4	0.6	0.7	0.6	0.6

Statistics are as originally reported. Adj. for stk. split: 2-for-1, 2/98. [1] Incl. subordinated debentures. [2] Incl. a net gain of $37.5 mill. on the sale of interest in Centex Construction Products, Inc.

OFFICERS:
L. E. Hirsh, Chmn., C.E.O.
D. W. Quinn, Vice-Chmn., C.F.O.
R. G. Smerge, Exec. V.P., Sec., Gen. Couns.

INVESTOR CONTACT: R. G. Smerge, (214) 981-5000

PRINCIPAL OFFICE: 2728 N. Harwood, Dallas, TX 75201-1516

TELEPHONE NUMBER: (214) 981-5000
FAX: (214) 981-6859
WEB: www.centex.com

NO. OF EMPLOYEES: 13,368

SHAREHOLDERS: 3,295 (approx.)

ANNUAL MEETING: In July

INCORPORATED: NV, Nov., 1968; reincorp., DE, 1953

INSTITUTIONAL HOLDINGS:
No. of Institutions: 245
Shares Held: 50,781,549
% Held: 85.6

INDUSTRY: Operative builders (SIC: 1531)

TRANSFER AGENT(S): Mellon Investor Services, Ridgefield Park, NJ

NYSE SYMBOL CTL
Rec. Pr. 27.18 (4/30/01)

CENTURYTEL, INC.

YIELD 0.7%
P/E RATIO 16.7

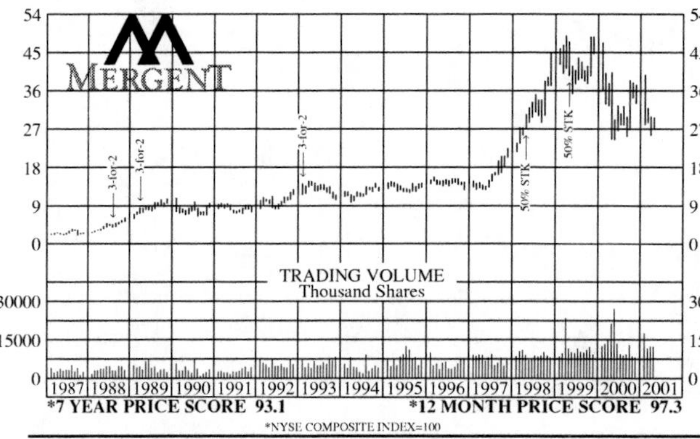

*7 YEAR PRICE SCORE 93.1 *12 MONTH PRICE SCORE 97.3

*NYSE COMPOSITE INDEX=100

INTERIM EARNINGS (Per Share):

Qtr.	Mar.	June	Sept.	Dec.
1997	0.25	0.61	0.30	0.73
1998	0.41	0.46	0.39	0.37
1999	0.43	0.38	0.46	0.43
2000	0.35	0.41	0.47	0.40

INTERIM DIVIDENDS (Per Share):

Amt.	Decl.	Ex.	Rec.	Pay.
0.048Q	5/23/00	5/31/00	6/02/00	6/16/00
0.048Q	8/22/00	8/30/00	9/01/00	9/15/00
0.048Q	11/16/00	11/29/00	12/01/00	12/15/00
0.05Q	2/28/01	3/08/01	3/12/01	3/23/01
0.05Q	5/22/01	5/30/01	6/01/01	6/15/01

Indicated div.: $0.20 (Div. Reinv. Plan)

CAPITALIZATION (12/31/00):

	($000)	(%)
Long-Term Debt	3,050,292	60.0
Preferred Stock	7,975	0.2
Common & Surplus	2,024,104	39.8
Total	5,082,371	100.0

RECENT DEVELOPMENTS: For the year ended 12/31/00, net income fell 3.5% to $231.5 million from $239.8 million a year earlier, primarily due to increased interest expense related to acquisition financing. Results for 2000 and 1999 included gains on sales of assets of $20.6 million and $62.8 million, respectively. Total revenues increased 10.1% to $1.85 billion from $1.68 billion in 1999. Telephone operations revenues rose 11.4% to $1.25 billion and wireless operation revenues advanced 5.0% to $443.6 million.

PROSPECTS: Prospects for 2001 are limited, despite growth initiatives that include increased availability of digital subscriber line service, continued integration of the Verizon access lines and the deployment of new services in a number of the newly acquired markets. Factors weighing on 2001 results consist of estimated Competitive Local Exchange Carrier startup losses of $15.0 million, additional interest expense due to the Verizon acquisitions, and lower than anticipated telephone revenues.

BUSINESS

CENTURYTEL, INC. (formerly Century Telephone Enterprises, Inc.) is a regional diversified telecommunications company that is primarily engaged in providing integrated communications services including local exchange, wireless, long distance, Internet access and security monitoring services. As of 12/31/00, Century's telephone subsidiaries provided service to over 1.8 million customers in 21 states. Century Cellunet, Inc. provides mobile communications services. Century Business Communications, Inc. offers mailing, direct marketing and creative services, database management, workflow analysis and systems consultation. Century Telecommunications, Inc. provides long-distance service and operator services on a regional basis. Interactive Communications, Inc. provides interactive information services. On 12/1/97, CTL acquired Pacific Telecom, Inc. for nearly $2.20 billion. On 7/31/00, CTL acquired certain assets from Verizon Communications for approximately $1.10 billion.

BUSINESS LINE ANALYSIS

(12/31/2000)	REV (%)	INC (%)
Telephone	67.9	71.6
Wireless	24.0	22.4
Other	8.1	6.0
Total	100.0	100.0

ANNUAL FINANCIAL DATA

	12/31/00	12/31/99	12/31/98	12/31/97	12/31/96	12/31/95	12/31/94
Earnings Per Share	**[3] 1.63**	**[3] 1.70**	**[1] 1.64**	**[2] 1.87**	**[2] 0.96**	**0.88**	**0.84**
Cash Flow Per Share	**4.37**	**4.16**	**3.98**	**3.02**	**1.94**	**1.75**	**1.63**
Tang. Book Val. Per Share	**...**	**1.39**	**...**	**...**	**3.61**	**2.95**	**1.71**
Dividends Per Share	**0.19**	**0.18**	**0.17**	**0.16**	**0.16**	**0.15**	**0.14**
Dividend Payout %	**11.7**	**10.6**	**10.6**	**8.8**	**16.7**	**16.8**	**17.0**
INCOME STATEMENT (IN MILLIONS):							
Total Revenues	1,845.9	1,676.7	1,577.1	901.5	749.7	644.8	540.2
Costs & Expenses	932.5	819.8	768.7	474.3	394.4	328.2	275.1
Depreciation & Amort.	388.1	348.8	328.6	159.5	132.0	113.8	95.7
Operating Income	525.4	508.1	479.8	267.8	223.3	202.9	169.4
Net Interest Inc./(Exp.)	d183.3	d150.6	d167.6	d56.5	d44.7	d43.6	d42.6
Income Before Income Taxes	386.2	429.3	387.5	408.3	203.6	183.1	161.5
Income Taxes	154.7	189.5	158.7	152.4	74.6	68.3	61.3
Equity Earnings/Minority Int.	16.8	d0.2	20.1	22.3	20.3	12.0	15.7
Net Income	[3] 231.5	[3] 239.8	[1] 228.8	[2] 256.0	[2] 129.1	114.8	100.2
Cash Flow	619.1	588.2	556.9	415.0	260.7	228.4	195.9
Average Shs. Outstg. (000)	141,864	141,432	140,105	137,412	134,829	130,806	120,150
BALANCE SHEET (IN MILLIONS):							
Cash & Cash Equivalents	19.0	56.6	5.7	26.0	8.4	8.5	7.2
Total Current Assets	376.5	286.1	226.2	283.5	109.2	95.3	81.2
Net Property	2,959.3	2,256.5	2,351.5	2,258.4	1,149.0	1,047.8	947.1
Total Assets	6,393.3	4,705.4	4,935.5	4,709.2	2,028.5	1,862.4	1,643.3
Total Current Liabilities	743.4	309.2	304.8	322.1	144.1	139.9	286.7
Long-Term Obligations	3,050.3	2,078.3	2,558.0	2,609.5	625.9	622.9	518.6
Net Stockholders' Equity	2,032.1	1,848.0	1,531.5	1,300.3	1,028.2	888.4	650.2
Net Working Capital	d366.9	d23.1	d78.6	d38.6	d34.9	d44.6	d205.4
Year-end Shs. Outstg. (000)	140,667	139,946	138,083	136,656	134,683	133,007	120,542
STATISTICAL RECORD:							
Operating Profit Margin %	28.5	30.3	30.4	29.7	29.8	31.5	31.4
Net Profit Margin %	12.5	14.3	14.5	28.4	17.2	17.8	18.6
Return on Equity %	11.4	13.0	14.9	19.7	12.6	12.9	15.4
Return on Assets %	3.6	5.1	4.6	5.4	6.4	6.2	6.1
Debt/Total Assets %	47.7	44.2	51.8	55.4	30.9	33.4	31.6
Price Range	47.31-24.44	49.00-35.19	45.17-21.56	22.42-12.67	15.78-12.67	14.72-12.00	14.33-9.72
P/E Ratio	29.0-15.0	28.8-20.7	27.5-13.1	12.0-6.8	16.5-13.2	16.8-13.7	17.1-11.6
Average Yield %	0.5	0.4	0.5	0.9	1.1	1.1	1.2

Statistics are as originally reported. Adj. for stk. splits: 50%, 3/99 & 3/98 [1] Incl. non-recurr. pre-tax credit of $49.9 mill. [2] Incl. pre-tax credit 12/31/97: $169.9 mill.; credit 12/31/96, $815,000. [3] Incl. pre-tax gain on sales of assets of $20.6 mill., 2000; $62.8 mill., 1999.

OFFICERS:
C. M. Williams, Chmn.
G. F. Post III, Vice-Chmn., Pres., C.E.O.
R. S. Ewing Jr., Exec. V.P., C.F.O.

INVESTOR CONTACT: Jeff Glover, V.P., Investor Relations, (800) 833-1188

PRINCIPAL OFFICE: 100 CenturyTel Dr., Monroe, LA 71203

TELEPHONE NUMBER: (318) 388-9000
FAX: (318) 789-8656
WEB: www.centurytel.com

NO. OF EMPLOYEES: 6,860 (approx.)

SHAREHOLDERS: 5,550 (approx.)

ANNUAL MEETING: In May

INCORPORATED: LA, Apr., 1968

INSTITUTIONAL HOLDINGS:
No. of Institutions: 311
Shares Held: 95,649,112
% Held: 67.8

INDUSTRY: Telephone communications, exc. radio (SIC: 4813)

TRANSFER AGENT(S): Computershare Investor Services, LLC, Chicago, IL

NYSE SYMBOL CEN
Rec. Pr. 18.50 (4/30/01)

CERIDIAN CORPORATION

YIELD ...
P/E RATIO 34.3

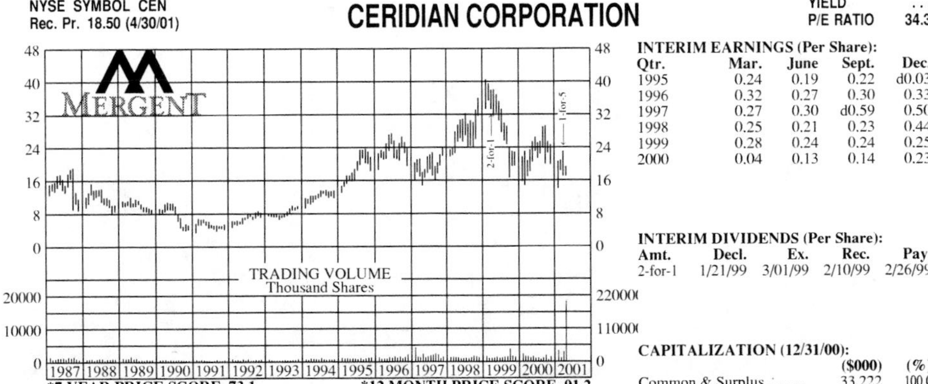

INTERIM EARNINGS (Per Share):

Qtr.	Mar.	June	Sept.	Dec.
1995	0.24	0.19	0.22	d0.03
1996	0.32	0.27	0.30	0.33
1997	0.27	0.30	d0.59	0.50
1998	0.25	0.21	0.23	0.44
1999	0.28	0.24	0.24	0.25
2000	0.04	0.13	0.14	0.23

INTERIM DIVIDENDS (Per Share):

Amt.	Decl.	Ex.	Rec.	Pay.
2-for-1	1/21/99	3/01/99	2/10/99	2/26/99

CAPITALIZATION (12/31/00):

	($000)	(%)
Common & Surplus	33,222	100.0
Total	33,222	100.0

RECENT DEVELOPMENTS: For the year ended 12/31/00, earnings from continuing operations fell 23.9% to $79.5 million versus $104.4 million in 1999. Results for 2000 and 1999 excluded discontinued operations of $20.7 million and $40.9 million, respectively. Revenues were $1.18 billion, up 4.3% from $1.13 billion in 1999. Revenues from Human Resource Services rose 4.7% to $866.9 million. Comparisons were made with restated prior-year figures.

PROSPECTS: On 3/30/01, Ceridian Corporation (old) completed the tax-free spin-off of its Arbitron business into a separate, publicly-traded company called Arbitron, Inc. As a result, shares of CEN and Arbitron began trading separately on 4/2/01. Going forward, the Company expects revenues from the transportation side of its business will not be as robust due to the increasing softness in the freight market. Nevertheless, CEN anticipates earnings per share for 2001 to be in the range of $0.65 and $0.70.

BUSINESS

CERIDIAN CORPORATION was formed as a result of the 3/30/01 spin-off of the human resources division, human resource services, and Comdata subsidiaries of Ceridian Corporation (old). The Company provides information services (IS) and consists of the Human Resources Group and Comdata Holdings Corp. CEN provides products and services to customers in the human resources, trucking, and electronic media markets. IS businesses collect, manage and analyze data and process transactions on behalf of customers, report information resulting from such activities to customers, and provide customers with related software applications and services. In 1998, CEN sold its Defense Electronics operations and acquired Tapscan. Revenues in 2000 were derived: human resource services, 73.7%; and Comdata, 26.3%.

ANNUAL FINANCIAL DATA

	12/31/00	12/31/99	12/31/98	12/31/97	12/31/96	[2] 12/31/95	12/31/94
Earnings Per Share	[5] 0.54	1.01	[4] 1.11	[3] 0.23	1.20	[1] 0.61	0.72
Cash Flow Per Share	1.14	1.53	1.46	0.60	1.81	1.16	1.07
Tang. Book Val. Per Share	...	...	1.72	2.26	...	...	0.59
INCOME STATEMENT (IN MILLIONS):							
Total Revenues	1,175.7	1,342.3	1,162.1	1,074.8	1,495.6	1,333.0	916.3
Costs & Expenses	925.2	1,007.1	894.1	834.3	1,220.0	1,101.3	810.4
Depreciation & Amort.	87.6	77.4	51.2	60.9	73.9	63.4	32.9
Operating Income	162.9	257.8	216.8	179.6	201.7	168.3	73.0
Net Interest Inc./(Exp.)	d35.1	d18.3	6.1	d8.9	d3.4	d18.5	9.0
Income Before Income Taxes	127.8	238.4	229.7	d138.6	196.2	116.2	85.2
Income Taxes	48.3	89.5	65.3	cr174.0	14.3	18.7	6.6
Equity Earnings/Minority Int.	...	...	...	...	d4.4	d4.1	0.3
Net Income	[5] 79.5	148.9	[4] 164.4	[3] 35.4	181.9	[1] 97.5	78.6
Cash Flow	167.1	226.3	215.6	96.3	242.8	147.9	98.5
Average Shs. Outstg. (000)	146,734	147,964	147,597	159,482	141,170	138,704	91,730
BALANCE SHEET (IN MILLIONS):							
Cash & Cash Equivalents	158.6	81.4	101.8	268.0	169.2	151.7	171.4
Total Current Assets	460.9	645.3	633.7	720.1	613.6	570.8	346.1
Net Property	160.4	192.8	91.3	79.6	129.0	120.9	97.8
Total Assets	2,088.0	2,059.9	1,289.7	1,243.3	1,251.1	1,126.1	690.3
Total Current Liabilities	473.9	451.7	436.7	478.8	624.8	605.6	306.8
Long-Term Obligations	500.3	611.1	54.2	0.8	142.1	205.3	17.5
Net Stockholders' Equity	936.2	842.7	650.6	588.3	346.3	150.0	186.5
Net Working Capital	241.5	193.6	197.0	241.3	d11.2	d34.8	39.3
Year-end Shs. Outstg. (000)	145,754	144,734	143,514	147,884	159,536	134,554	91,030
STATISTICAL RECORD:							
Operating Profit Margin %	13.9	19.2	18.7	16.7	13.5	12.6	8.0
Net Profit Margin %	6.8	11.1	14.1	3.3	12.2	7.3	8.6
Return on Equity %	8.5	17.7	25.3	6.0	52.5	65.0	42.1
Return on Assets %	3.8	7.2	12.7	2.8	14.5	8.7	11.4
Debt/Total Assets %	24.5	29.7	4.2	0.1	11.4	18.2	2.5
Price Range	29.19-14.75	40.50-16.63	36.00-21.75	23.88-14.75	27.44-18.50	23.75-13.06	13.75-9.25
P/E Ratio	54.1-27.3	40.1-16.5	32.4-19.6	106.1-65.5	23.0-15.5	38.9-21.4	19.2-12.9

Statistics are as originally reported. Adj. for 2-for-1 split, 2/99. Fins. for 12/99 & prior years refl. the ops. of Ceridian Corp. (old). [1] Excl. $38.9 mill. extraord. loss. [2] Incl. Comdata & Resumix results, acq. in 1995. [3] Incl. $189.7 mill. one-time chg. [4] Incl. $24.3 mill. gain fr. sale of bus. & land and excl. $25.4 mill. gain fr. disc. ops. [5] Excl. $20.7 mill. from disc. ops.

OFFICERS:
R. L. Turner, Chmn., Pres., C.E.O.
J. R. Eickloff, Exec. V.P., C.F.O.
G. M. Nelson, V.P., Gen. Couns., Sec.

INVESTOR CONTACT: Craig Manson, V.P. of Inv. Rel., (952) 853-6022

PRINCIPAL OFFICE: 3311 East Old Shakopee Rd., Minneapolis, MN 55425

TELEPHONE NUMBER: (952) 853-8100
FAX: (952) 853-3932
WEB: www.ceridian.com

NO. OF EMPLOYEES: 9,600

SHAREHOLDERS: 12,400

ANNUAL MEETING: In May

INCORPORATED: MN, July, 1957; reincorp., DE, 1968

INSTITUTIONAL HOLDINGS:
No. of Institutions: 220
Shares Held: 138,658,290
% Held: 95.2

INDUSTRY: Commercial nonphysical research (SIC: 8732)

TRANSFER AGENT(S): The Bank of New York, New York, NY

NYSE SYMBOL CHG
Rec. Pr. 43.50 (5/31/01)

CH ENERGY GROUP, INC.

YIELD 5.0%
P/E RATIO 14.1

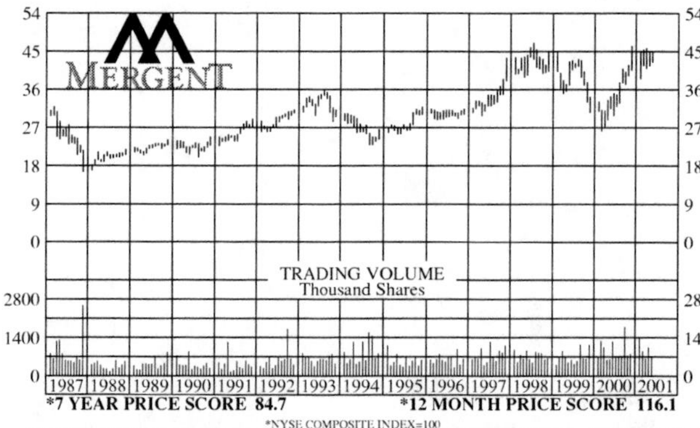

INTERIM EARNINGS (Per Share):

Qtr.	Mar.	June	Sept.	Dec.
1997	1.18	0.55	0.72	0.52
1998	1.06	0.54	0.77	0.52
1999	1.09	0.51	0.77	0.51
2000	1.07	0.47	0.87	0.68

INTERIM DIVIDENDS (Per Share):

Amt.	Decl.	Ex.	Rec.	Pay.
0.54Q	3/24/00	4/06/00	4/10/00	5/01/00
0.54Q	6/23/00	7/06/00	7/10/00	8/01/00
0.54Q	9/19/00	10/05/00	10/10/00	11/01/00
0.54Q	12/15/00	1/08/01	1/10/01	2/01/01
0.54Q	3/23/01	4/06/01	4/10/01	5/01/01

Indicated div.: $2.16 (Div. Reinv. Plan)

CAPITALIZATION (12/31/00):

	($000)	(%)
Long-Term Debt	320,369	30.5
Deferred Income Tax	194,828	18.5
Preferred Stock	56,030	5.3
Common & Surplus	480,742	45.7
Total	1,051,969	100.0

RECENT DEVELOPMENTS: For the year ended 12/31/00, net income rose 4.9% to $51.0 million compared with $48.6 million in 1999. Total operating revenues jumped 43.7% to $749.9 million from $567.1 million in the prior year. Electric operating revenues increased 24.3% to $531.8 million, while gas operating revenues improved 13.7% to $107.0 million. Energy sales benefited from the growing economy of the Mid-Hudson region in spite of cooler than normal summer weather in 2000.

PROSPECTS: CHG expects earnings per share for 2001 will be up 5.0% over 2000 to $3.25. Of this total, $2.30 is expected to come from Central Hudson Gas & Electric Corporation, $0.45 from Central Hudson Energy Services, Inc., and $0.50 from the investment income from proceeds received from the sale of the utility's fossil-fueled electric generating plants. Separately, CHG completed the sale of its interest in the Roseton and Danskammer electric generating plants in the Town of Newburgh, NY to Dynegy Inc.

BUSINESS

CH ENERGY GROUP, INC. (formerly Central Hudson Gas & Electric Corp.) became the holding company of Central Hudson Gas & Electric Corporation and Central Hudson Energy Services, Inc. on 12/15/99. CHG generates, purchases, and distributes electricity, and purchases and distributes gas to communities along the Hudson River. CHG serves a population of approximately 600,000 in a 2,600 square-mile area in the Mid-Hudson Valley region of New York State. Electric service is available throughout the territory, and natural gas is provided in the following cities: Poughkeepsie, Beacon, Newburgh, Kingston and the Village of Catskill. The Company's territory reflects a diversified economy, including manufacturing industries, research firms, farms, governmental agencies, public and private institutions, resorts, and wholesale and retail trade operations.

ANNUAL FINANCIAL DATA

	12/31/00	12/31/99	12/31/98	12/31/97	12/31/96	12/31/95	12/31/94
Earnings Per Share	**3.05**	**[1] 2.88**	**2.90**	**2.97**	**2.99**	**2.74**	**2.68**
Cash Flow Per Share	**6.36**	**5.92**	**5.77**	**5.75**	**5.61**	**5.35**	**5.29**
Tang. Book Val. Per Share	**25.20**	**28.29**	**28.00**	**27.60**	**26.87**	**25.96**	**25.34**
INCOME STATEMENT (IN MILLIONS):							
Total Revenues	749.9	521.9	503.5	520.3	514.0	512.2	515.7
Costs & Expenses	616.1	371.9	356.3	374.3	362.1	366.5	365.2
Depreciation & Amort.	55.3	51.2	49.0	48.3	47.1	45.4	44.6
Maintenance Exp.	...	28.2	26.9	27.6	28.9	29.4	32.7
Operating Income	78.5	70.6	71.3	70.1	75.8	70.9	73.1
Net Interest Inc./(Exp.)	d33.9	d29.6	d27.4	d26.4	d27.7	d28.4	d30.6
Income Taxes	1.0	1.2	cr1.1	cr3.0	cr1.6	cr0.4	cr1.2
Net Income	51.0	[1] 48.6	52.5	51.9	51.4	52.7	45.8
Cash Flow	106.3	99.8	98.3	100.2	98.5	93.0	85.3
Average Shs. Outstg. (000)	16,716	16,862	17,034	17,435	17,549	17,380	17,102
BALANCE SHEET (IN MILLIONS):							
Gross Property	1,639.8	1,598.7	1,561.0	1,526.2	1,490.4	1,454.1	1,416.8
Accumulated Depreciation	708.9	677.3	632.8	593.4	550.7	517.0	485.8
Net Property	930.9	921.4	928.2	932.8	939.6	937.1	931.1
Total Assets	1,531.0	1,335.9	1,316.0	1,252.1	1,249.1	1,250.1	1,309.4
Long-Term Obligations	320.4	335.5	356.9	361.8	362.0	389.2	389.4
Net Stockholders' Equity	536.8	540.4	528.2	533.1	527.7	510.3	517.8
Year-end Shs. Outstg. (000)	16,362	16,862	16,862	17,285	17,555	17,496	17,238
STATISTICAL RECORD:							
Operating Profit Margin %	10.5	13.5	14.2	13.5	14.8	13.8	14.2
Net Profit Margin %	6.8	9.3	10.4	10.0	10.0	10.3	8.9
Net Inc./Net Property %	5.5	5.3	5.7	5.6	5.5	5.6	4.9
Net Inc./Tot. Capital %	4.8	4.5	4.8	4.7	4.7	4.8	4.0
Return on Equity %	9.5	9.0	9.9	9.7	9.7	10.3	8.8
Accum. Depr./Gross Prop. %	43.2	42.4	40.5	38.9	37.0	35.6	34.3
Price Range	46.31-26.13	45.00-30.56	47.06-38.88	43.56-29.75	31.50-28.75	31.88-25.38	30.38-22.88
P/E Ratio	15.2-8.6	15.6-10.6	16.2-13.4	14.7-10.0	10.5-9.6	11.6-9.3	11.3-8.5
Average Yield %	6.0	...	...	...	...	...	...

Statistics are as originally reported. [1] Incl. $432,000 non-recur. chg. fr. favorable ins. settlement & $455,000 non-recur. chg.

OFFICERS:
P. J. Ganci, Chmn., Pres., C.E.O.
S. V. Lant, C.F.O., Treas.
C. E. Meyer, Exec. V.P.

INVESTOR CONTACT: Denise D. VanBuren, Inv. Rel., (914) 471-8323

PRINCIPAL OFFICE: 284 South Avenue, Poughkeepsie, NY 12601-4879

TELEPHONE NUMBER: (845) 452-2000
FAX: (845) 486-5782
WEB: www.centralhud.com

NO. OF EMPLOYEES: 1,075

SHAREHOLDERS: 19,419

ANNUAL MEETING: In Apr.

INCORPORATED: NY, Dec., 1926

INSTITUTIONAL HOLDINGS:
No. of Institutions: 125
Shares Held: 6,731,094
% Held: 41.1

INDUSTRY: Electric and other services combined (SIC: 4931)

TRANSFER AGENT(S): First Chicago Trust Company of New York, Jersey City, NJ

NYSE SYMBOL CHB
Rec. Pr. 10.62 (5/31/01)

CHAMPION ENTERPRISES, INC.

YIELD . . .
P/E RATIO . . .

*7 YEAR PRICE SCORE 27.6 *12 MONTH PRICE SCORE 163.4

*NYSE COMPOSITE INDEX=100

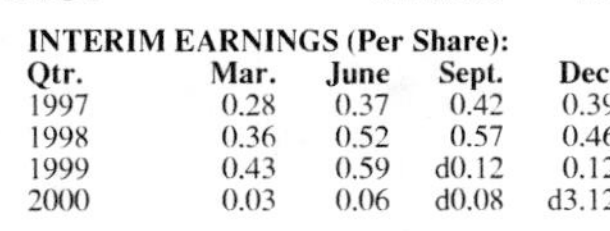

INTERIM EARNINGS (Per Share):

Qtr.	Mar.	June	Sept.	Dec.
1997	0.28	0.37	0.42	0.39
1998	0.36	0.52	0.57	0.46
1999	0.43	0.59	d0.12	0.12
2000	0.03	0.06	d0.08	d3.12

INTERIM DIVIDENDS (Per Share):

Amt.	Decl.	Ex.	Rec.	Pay.

No dividends paid.

CAPITALIZATION (12/30/00):

	($000)	(%)
Long-Term Debt	225,634	43.2
Common & Surplus	296,809	56.8
Total	522,443	100.0

RECENT DEVELOPMENTS: For the year ended 12/31/00, the Company reported a net loss of $147.3 million compared with net income of $50.0 million in the equivalent 1999 quarter. Results included pre-tax nonrecurring charges of $198.3 million for 2000 and $33.6 million for 1999. Total net sales declined 25.1% to $1.92 billion compared with $2.56 billion a year earlier.

PROSPECTS: Through its Genesis Homes initiative, CHB is creating innovative homes and marketing programs targeting local builders and developers. CHB's sales goal in 2001 for Genesis is 4,000 homes through 500 local builders. CHB is experiencing improved retail traffic as well as lower interest rates from the industry's consumer finance companies.

BUSINESS

CHAMPION ENTERPRISES, INC. operates primarily in the manufactured housing industry. Champion has 53 home-building facilities in the U.S. and western Canada. Company-operated retail housing centers total 260 locations. Champion homes are sold by 3,500 independent retail locations, including more than 1,000 Alliance of Champions locations. The Company produces a broad range of single and multi-section homes under various trade names and brand names in a variety of floor plans and price ranges. Homes manufactured by the Company usually include two to four bedrooms, a living room or family room, dining room, kitchen and two full bathrooms. The completed home contains carpeting, cabinets, appliances, wall and window coverings and electrical, heating and plumbing systems. The homes can also come equipped with optional features such as fireplaces and skylights.

ANNUAL FINANCIAL DATA

	12/30/00	1/1/00	1/2/99	1/3/98	12/28/96	12/30/95	12/31/94
Earnings Per Share	**2 d3.12**	**2 1.02**	**1.91**	**1 1.45**	**2 1.09**	**1.01**	**1 0.82**
Cash Flow Per Share	**d2.27**	**1.80**	**2.46**	**1.80**	**1.39**	**1.20**	**0.94**
Tang. Book Val. Per Share	**0.48**	. . .	. . .	**3.45**	**2.14**	**1.02**	**1.40**
INCOME STATEMENT (IN MILLIONS):							
Total Revenues	1,921.7	2,488.7	2,254.3	1,675.1	1,644.1	797.9	615.7
Costs & Expenses	2,074.6	2,343.2	2,135.8	1,541.5	1,513.4	736.7	575.1
Depreciation & Amort.	40.3	37.9	26.9	17.1	14.9	6.2	3.9
Operating Income	d193.2	107.6	170.3	116.4	115.8	55.0	36.7
Net Interest Inc./(Exp.)	d27.2	d25.5	d13.5	0.9	0.4	d1.5	0.2
Income Before Income Taxes	d220.3	82.0	156.8	117.4	94.2	53.5	34.1
Income Taxes	cr73.0	32.0	62.6	46.6	40.6	21.2	8.9
Net Income	2 d147.3	2 50.0	94.2	1 70.8	2 53.6	32.3	1 25.2
Cash Flow	d107.0	87.9	121.1	87.9	68.5	38.4	29.1
Average Shs. Outstg. (000)	47,252	48,889	49,284	48,875	49,363	31,926	30,932
BALANCE SHEET (IN MILLIONS):							
Cash & Cash Equivalents	50.1	12.8	23.8	60.3	19.4	15.0	23.0
Total Current Assets	376.5	453.7	385.6	229.5	216.7	108.5	97.8
Net Property	207.3	222.9	191.0	143.5	122.6	39.4	30.1
Total Assets	942.1	1,182.9	1,021.7	501.3	472.4	235.9	171.2
Total Current Liabilities	342.9	429.2	393.7	183.4	195.2	104.5	79.1
Long-Term Obligations	225.6	224.4	121.6	1.8	1.2	18.3	12.9
Net Stockholders' Equity	296.8	444.3	405.2	280.4	226.6	113.1	79.3
Net Working Capital	33.7	24.5	d8.1	46.1	21.5	4.0	18.8
Year-end Shs. Outstg. (000)	47,357	47,304	48,270	46,600	47,695	30,604	30,212
STATISTICAL RECORD:							
Operating Profit Margin %	. . .	4.3	7.6	7.0	7.0	6.9	6.0
Net Profit Margin %	. . .	2.0	4.2	4.2	3.3	4.0	4.1
Return on Equity %	. . .	11.3	23.2	25.2	23.6	28.5	31.8
Return on Assets %	. . .	4.2	9.2	14.1	11.3	13.7	14.7
Debt/Total Assets %	24.0	19.0	11.9	0.4	0.2	7.8	7.5
Price Range	8.56-2.31	27.38-7.88	30.00-17.50	21.25-13.75	26.13-11.88	15.50-6.81	10.19-4.38
P/E Ratio	. . .	26.8-7.7	15.7-9.2	14.7-9.5	24.0-10.9	15.3-6.7	12.5-5.4

Statistics are as originally reported. Adj. for stk. split: 2-for-1, 5/95 & 5/96. 1 Bef. discont. oper. gain $1.9 mill., 12/31/94; gain $4.5 mill., 1/3/98. 2 Incl. non-recurr. pretax chrg. $22.0 mill., 1996; $33.6 mill., 1999; $198.3 mill., 2000.

OFFICERS:
W. R. Young, Jr., Chmn., Pres., C.E.O.
J. J. Collins, Sr. V.P., Gen. Couns.
P. C. Surles, C.O.O.

INVESTOR CONTACT: Colleen T. Bauman, Asst. V.P., Investor Relations, Libby A. Argiri, Mgr., Investor Relations

PRINCIPAL OFFICE: 2701 Cambridge Court, Suite 300, Auburn Hills, MI 48326

TELEPHONE NUMBER: (248) 340-9090
FAX: (800) 758-5804
WEB: www.championhomes.com

NO. OF EMPLOYEES: 12,000 (approx.)

SHAREHOLDERS: 6,000 (approx.); 8,000 (beneficial)

ANNUAL MEETING: In May

INCORPORATED: MI, June, 1953

INSTITUTIONAL HOLDINGS:
No. of Institutions: 82
Shares Held: 38,075,067
% Held: 80.1

INDUSTRY: Mobile homes (SIC: 2451)

TRANSFER AGENT(S): American Stock Transfer & Trust Company, New York, NY

NYSE SYMBOL CF
Rec. Pr. 29.30 (4/30/01)

CHARTER ONE FINANCIAL, INC.

YIELD 2.7%
P/E RATIO 14.7

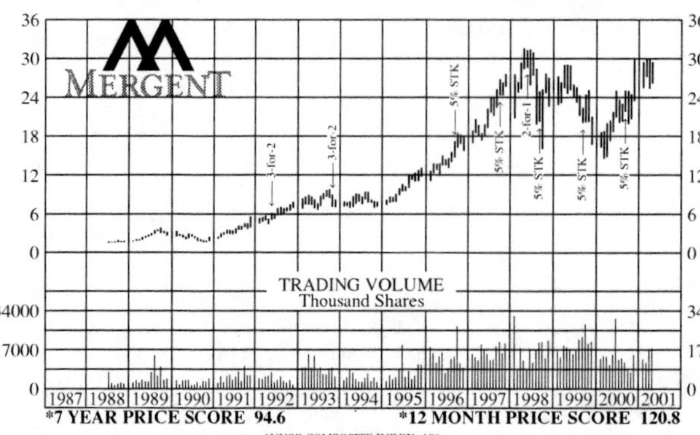

*7 YEAR PRICE SCORE 94.6 *12 MONTH PRICE SCORE 120.8

*NYSE COMPOSITE INDEX=100

INTERIM EARNINGS (Per Share):

Qtr.	Mar.	June	Sept.	Dec.
1997	0.34	0.37	0.36	d0.07
1998	0.39	0.42	0.43	0.24
1999	0.45	0.47	0.46	0.09
2000	0.50	0.47	0.51	0.52

INTERIM DIVIDENDS (Per Share):

Amt.	Decl.	Ex.	Rec.	Pay.
0.18Q	7/18/00	8/03/00	8/07/00	8/21/00
5% STK	7/18/00	9/12/00	9/14/00	9/30/00
0.18Q	10/19/00	11/01/00	11/03/00	11/20/00
0.18Q	1/23/01	2/02/01	2/06/01	2/20/01
0.20Q	4/18/01	5/03/01	5/07/01	5/21/01

Indicated div.: $0.80 (Div. Reinv. Plan)

CAPITALIZATION (12/31/00):

	($000)	(%)
Total Deposits	19,605,671	61.9
Long-Term Debt	9,636,277	30.4
Common & Surplus	2,456,204	7.7
Total	31,698,152	100.0

RECENT DEVELOPMENTS: For the year ended 12/31/00, CF reported net income of $434.0 million versus income of $335.5 million, before an extraordinary charge of $1.6 million, in 1999. Earnings for 2000 and 1999 included pre-tax merger expenses of $29.5 million and $63.5 million, respectively, as well as a non-recurring net gain of $9.3 million and a net loss of $57.0 million, respectively. Comparisons were made with restated 1999 results due to the acquisition of St. Paul Bancorp, Inc. in October 1999.

PROSPECTS: On 1/23/01, the Company entered into a definitive agreement to acquire Alliance Bancorp in a stock transaction valued at about $245.0 million. As a result of the acquisition, which should close in the third quarter of 2001, CF will have the sixth largest retail banking operation in the Chicago metropolitan region with about $5.00 billion in deposits. Separately, CF anticipates earnings per share of $2.30 and retail banking revenue of nearly $300.0 million for 2001.

BUSINESS

CHARTER ONE FINANCIAL, INC. is a bank holding company whose principal line of business is consumer banking, which includes retail banking, mortgage banking and other related financial services. As of 12/31/00, the Company had $32.97 billion in total assets. The Company has approximately 420 branch locations in Ohio, Michigan, Illinois, New York, Vermont and Massachusetts. Additionally, Charter One Mortgage Corp., the Company's mortgage banking subsidiary, operates 36 loan production offices across 13 states, and Charter One Auto Finance Corp., the Company's indirect auto finance subsidiary, generates loans in 10 states. On 10/1/99, CF acquired St. Paul Bancorp, Inc. On 11/5/99, CF acquired fourteen Vermont National Bank offices from Chittenden Corporation.

LOAN DISTRIBUTION

(12/31/2000)	($000)	(%)
Real-Estate-Mortgage	12,247,390	54.5
Automobile	3,046,038	13.6
Retail Consumer Loans	4,583,770	20.4
Leases	1,778,021	7.9
Corporate Banking	802,379	3.6
Total	22,457,598	100.0

ANNUAL FINANCIAL DATA

	12/31/00	12/31/99	12/31/98	12/31/97	12/31/96	12/31/95	12/31/94
Earnings Per Share	[3] **2.00**	[1] [2] **1.46**	[1] [2] **1.47**	[1] [2] **1.01**	**1.15**	[1] **0.31**	[2] **1.20**
Tang. Book Val. Per Share	**10.97**	**10.05**	**9.41**	**8.55**	**8.04**	**7.62**	**6.75**
Dividends Per Share	**0.68**	**0.57**	**0.48**	**0.41**	**0.35**	**0.29**	**0.23**
Dividend Payout %	**33.8**	**39.1**	**32.5**	**40.6**	**30.6**	**95.7**	**19.2**
INCOME STATEMENT (IN MILLIONS):							
Total Interest Income	2,247.1	2,128.5	1,760.4	1,377.7	1,004.5	1,087.4	395.6
Total Interest Expense	1,344.1	1,194.4	1,031.3	850.7	621.1	769.6	217.5
Net Interest Income	903.0	934.1	729.1	527.0	383.4	317.8	178.1
Provision for Loan Losses	54.2	35.2	29.5	40.9	4.0	1.0	2.8
Non-Interest Income	392.9	230.6	211.6	110.8	57.1	d47.8	28.1
Non-Interest Expense	604.0	633.3	492.5	373.9	244.0	215.7	102.1
Income Before Taxes	637.7	496.1	418.7	223.0	192.5	53.2	101.3
Net Income	[3] 434.0	[1] [2] 335.5	[1] [2] 277.0	[1] [2] 151.1	127.7	[1] 34.0	[2] 67.6
Average Shs. Outstg. (000)	217,592	228,738	188,239	149,924	110,938	111,484	56,387
BALANCE SHEET (IN MILLIONS):							
Cash & Due from Banks	530.8	689.1	334.1	214.7	152.3	163.1	126.8
Securities Avail. for Sale	4,087.2	4,193.1	2,299.2	1,070.2	265.4	1,843.0	99.4
Total Loans & Leases	24,297.4	22,545.8	17,688.0	12,360.1	8,295.0	6,842.9	3,635.6
Allowance for Credit Losses	347.3	623.2	185.3	. . .	194.6	168.6	93.1
Net Loans & Leases	23,950.2	21,922.6	17,502.7	12,360.1	8,100.3	6,674.3	3,542.5
Total Assets	32,971.4	31,464.8	24,467.3	19,760.3	13,904.6	13,578.9	5,756.7
Total Deposits	19,605.7	19,074.0	15,165.1	10,219.2	7,841.2	7,012.5	4,368.2
Long-Term Obligations	9,636.3	9,226.2	6,186.1	5,370.5	3,194.3	3,163.1	1,318.7
Total Liabilities	30,515.2	29,421.4	22,592.1	18,383.4	12,975.9	12,734.5	5,761.1
Net Stockholders' Equity	2,456.2	2,397.7	1,875.1	1,376.9	928.7	844.4	369.1
Year-end Shs. Outstg. (000)	208,228	219,721	182,352	150,394	107,527	109,439	54,635
STATISTICAL RECORD:							
Return on Equity %	17.7	14.0	14.8	11.0	13.8	4.0	18.3
Return on Assets %	1.3	1.1	1.1	0.8	0.9	0.3	1.1
Equity/Assets %	7.4	7.6	7.7	7.0	6.7	6.2	6.4
Non-Int. Exp./Tot. Inc. %	46.6	54.4	52.4	58.6	55.4	79.9	49.5
Price Range	30.00-14.52	29.14-16.67	31.64-15.99	27.64-16.92	18.41-11.07	13.08-7.39	9.40-6.95
P/E Ratio	15.0-7.3	20.0-11.4	21.5-10.9	27.5-16.8	16.0-9.6	42.6-24.1	7.8-5.8
Average Yield %	3.0	2.5	2.0	1.8	2.4	2.9	2.8

Statistics are as originally reported. Adj. for stk. splits: 5% stk. div., 9/00, 9/99; 9/98; 2-for-1, 5/98; 5% stk. div., 10/97; 5% stk. div., 9/96 [1] Incl. non-recurr. chrg. $37.5 mill., 1995; $60.6 mill., 1997; $55.7 mill., 1998; $63.5 mill., 1999. [2] Bef. extraord. credit $7.0 mill., 1994; chrg. $2.7 mill., 1997; chrg. $61.7 mill., 1998; chrg. $1.6 mill., 1999. [3] Incl. pre-tax merger expenses of $29.5 mill. & non-recurr. net gains of $9.3 mill.

OFFICERS:
C. J. Koch, Chmn., Pres., C.E.O.
H. G. Chorbajian, Vice-Chmn.
L. S. Simon, Vice-Chmn.

INVESTOR CONTACT: Ellen L. Batkie, Senior V.P., (800) 262-6301

PRINCIPAL OFFICE: 1215 Superior Avenue, Cleveland, OH 44114

TELEPHONE NUMBER: (216) 566-5300
FAX: (216) 566-1465
WEB: www.charterone.com

NO. OF EMPLOYEES: 7,000 (approx.)

SHAREHOLDERS: 20,100

ANNUAL MEETING: In Apr.

INCORPORATED: DE, 1987

INSTITUTIONAL HOLDINGS:
No. of Institutions: 268
Shares Held: 126,515,353
% Held: 60.8

INDUSTRY: Federal savings institutions (SIC: 6035)

TRANSFER AGENT(S): EquiServe, Providence, RI

NYSE SYMBOL CHE
Rec. Pr. 35.10 (5/31/01)

CHEMED CORPORATION

YIELD 1.3%
P/E RATIO 17.0

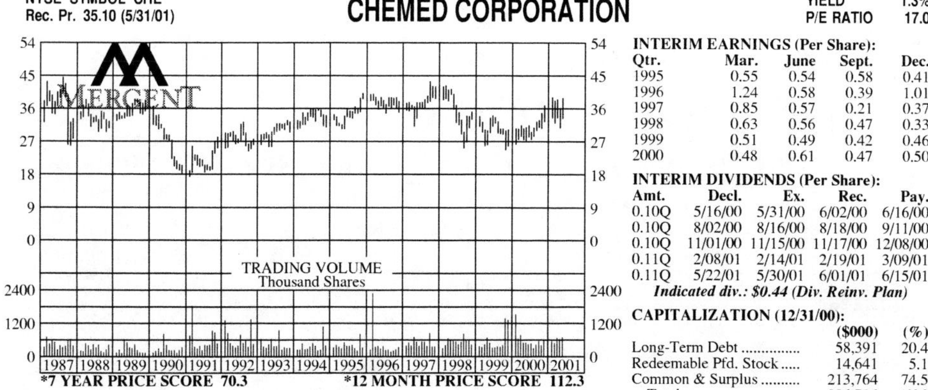

INTERIM EARNINGS (Per Share):

Qtr.	Mar.	June	Sept.	Dec.
1995	0.55	0.54	0.58	0.41
1996	1.24	0.58	0.39	1.01
1997	0.85	0.57	0.21	0.37
1998	0.63	0.56	0.47	0.33
1999	0.51	0.49	0.42	0.46
2000	0.48	0.61	0.47	0.50

INTERIM DIVIDENDS (Per Share):

Amt.	Decl.	Ex.	Rec.	Pay.
0.10Q	5/16/00	5/31/00	6/02/00	6/16/00
0.10Q	8/02/00	8/16/00	8/18/00	9/11/00
0.10Q	11/01/00	11/15/00	11/17/00	12/08/00
0.11Q	2/08/01	2/14/01	2/19/01	3/09/01
0.11Q	5/22/01	5/30/01	6/01/01	6/15/01

Indicated div.: $0.44 (Div. Reinv. Plan)

CAPITALIZATION (12/31/00):

	($000)	(%)
Long-Term Debt	58,391	20.4
Redeemable Pfd. Stock	14,641	5.1
Common & Surplus	213,764	74.5
Total	286,796	100.0

RECENT DEVELOPMENTS: For the year ended 12/31/00, net income climbed 4.5% to $20.6 million compared with $19.7 million in 1999. Results for 2000 and 1999 included after-tax gains of $2.3 million and $3.0 million, respectively, from the sales of investments. Service revenues and sales rose 10.4% to $500.7 million from $453.6 million in the prior year. Revenues for Roto-Rooter rose 15.8% to $281.1 million.

PROSPECTS: During 2000, Roto-Rooter completed three franchise acquisitions, which contributed $9.1 million to the year's revenues. Going forward, Roto-Rooter should benefit from its broadened sales of equipment and products to the plumbing and drain cleaning industry, as well as increased sales of drain care products. Meanwhile, Service America should benefit from the elimination of unprofitable contracts and investments in its infrastructure.

BUSINESS

CHEMED CORPORATION is a diversified corporation with strategic positions in plumbing and drain cleaning (Roto-Rooter Inc., 100% owned); residential appliance and AC services (Service America Systems, Inc.); home healthcare services (Patient Care Inc., 100% owned); and computer software and related services (Cadre Computer). In 2000, sales and service revenues from continuing operations were: Roto-Rooter, 56%; Patient Care, 27%; and Service America, 15%, and Cadre Computer, 2%. During 2000, Roto-Rooter completed three purchase business combinations. CHE sold National Sanitary Supply Co. and The Omnia Group in 1997. Also, the Company acquired Priority Care, Inc. in April 1997.

ANNUAL FINANCIAL DATA

	12/31/00	12/31/99	12/31/98	12/31/97	12/31/96	12/31/95	12/31/94
Earnings Per Share	**6 2.07**	**6 1.87**	**5 1.97**	**4 1.71**	**1 3.23**	**1 3 2.07**	**2 1.47**
Cash Flow Per Share	**4.27**	**3.79**	**3.68**	**3.22**	**5.14**	**3.92**	**3.08**
Tang. Book Val. Per Share	**3.36**	**3.48**	**5.23**	**7.09**	**1.37**	**7.21**	**13.04**
Dividends Per Share	**0.40**	**2.12**	**2.12**	**2.09**	**2.08**	**2.06**	**2.04**
Dividend Payout %	**19.3**	**113.4**	**107.6**	**122.2**	**64.4**	**99.5**	**138.8**
INCOME STATEMENT (IN THOUSANDS):							
Total Revenues	500,685	453,593	381,283	341,729	683,817	699,165	645,027
Costs & Expenses	443,772	406,679	344,659	307,084	633,588	648,536	601,814
Depreciation & Amort.	23,445	20,129	17,284	15,163	18,847	18,205	15,807
Operating Income	33,468	26,785	19,340	19,482	31,382	32,424	27,406
Net Interest Inc./(Exp.)	d6,736	d6,858	d6,793	d10,552	d8,950	d8,466	d8,807
Income Before Income Taxes	33,246	30,953	32,125	27,881	57,385	40,959	29,774
Income Taxes	12,662	11,257	12,216	10,804	21,866	15,614	10,954
Equity Earnings/Minority Int.	...	...	...	...	d3,791	d4,906	d4,288
Net Income	6 20,584	6 19,696	5 19,909	4 17,077	1 31,728	1 3 20,439	2 14,532
Cash Flow	44,029	39,825	37,193	32,240	50,575	38,644	30,339
Average Shs. Outstg.	10,305	10,514	10,100	10,014	9,836	9,861	9,856
BALANCE SHEET (IN THOUSANDS):							
Cash & Cash Equivalents	24,326	31,536	58,056	87,095	31,897	48,224	24,239
Total Current Assets	106,470	111,802	124,631	177,468	192,359	219,437	183,319
Net Property	75,177	71,728	61,721	53,089	83,259	77,131	77,116
Total Assets	421,375	421,303	429,704	448,838	559,350	531,868	505,483
Total Current Liabilities	106,942	98,428	91,098	94,365	124,548	145,004	142,666
Long-Term Obligations	58,391	78,580	80,407	83,720	158,168	85,368	92,133
Net Stockholders' Equity	213,764	212,044	223,356	228,120	217,891	208,657	263,292
Net Working Capital	d472	13,374	33,533	83,103	67,811	74,433	40,653
Year-end Shs. Outstg.	9,850	10,396	10,415	10,078	9,952	9,850	9,865
STATISTICAL RECORD:							
Operating Profit Margin %	6.7	5.9	5.1	5.7	4.6	4.6	4.2
Net Profit Margin %	4.1	4.3	5.2	5.0	4.6	2.9	2.3
Return on Equity %	9.6	9.3	8.9	7.5	14.6	9.8	5.5
Return on Assets %	4.9	4.7	4.6	3.8	5.7	3.8	2.9
Debt/Total Assets %	13.9	18.7	18.7	18.7	28.3	16.1	18.2
Price Range	36.88-26.13	34.06-24.63	42.38-25.13	43.50-31.00	40.13-34.63	40.25-30.38	36.13-30.25
P/E Ratio	17.8-12.6	18.2-13.2	21.5-12.8	25.4-18.1	12.4-10.7	19.4-14.7	24.6-20.6
Average Yield %	1.3	7.2	6.3	5.6	5.6	5.8	6.1

Statistics are as originally reported. 1 Bef disc. ops: cr$2.7 mil ($0.28/sh), 1995; cr$600,000 ($0.06/sh), 1996. 2 Excl. $29.3 mil sale of sec. disc. oper & oth chgs. 3 Incl. $1.5 mil non-recur pre-tax exp. 4 Incl. $7.7 mil aft-tx cap gains; bef $13.2 mil gain for disc. ops. 5 Incl. $7.7 mill. after-tax gains fr. sale of investments & after-tax costs with pooling of int. combo. 6 Incl. $2.3 mill. after-tax gains, 2000; $2.9 mill., 1999.

OFFICERS:
E. L. Hutton, Chmn., C.E.O.
K. J. McNamara, Pres.
T. S. O'Toole, Exec. V.P., Treas.

INVESTOR CONTACT: Timothy S. O'Toole, Exec. V.P. & Treas., (800) 224-3633

PRINCIPAL OFFICE: 2600 Chemed Ctr., 255 East Fifth St., Cincinnati, OH 45202-4726

TELEPHONE NUMBER: (513) 762-6900
FAX: (513) 762-6919
WEB: www.chemed.com

NO. OF EMPLOYEES: 7,591

SHAREHOLDERS: 3,783 (approx.)

ANNUAL MEETING: In May

INCORPORATED: DE, Apr., 1970

INSTITUTIONAL HOLDINGS:
No. of Institutions: 100
Shares Held: 6,285,259
% Held: 62.8

INDUSTRY: Chemicals & allied products, nec (SIC: 5169)

TRANSFER AGENT(S): Wells Fargo Shareowner Services, South St. Paul, MN

NYSE SYMBOL CSK
Rec. Pr. 22.30 (5/31/01)

CHESAPEAKE CORPORATION

YIELD 3.9%
P/E RATIO 76.9

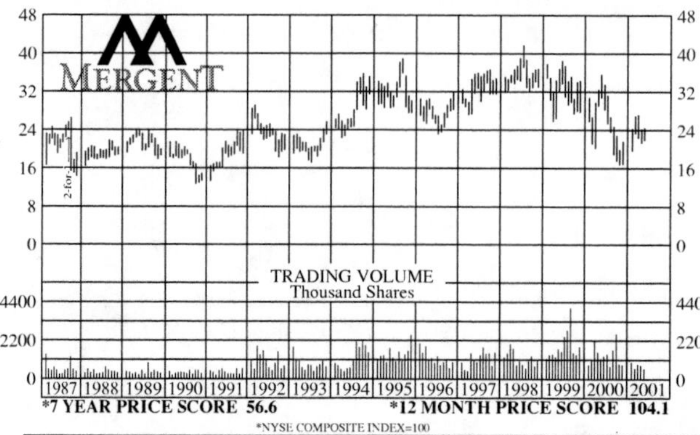

*7 YEAR PRICE SCORE 56.6 *12 MONTH PRICE SCORE 104.1

*NYSE COMPOSITE INDEX=100

INTERIM EARNINGS (Per Share):

Qtr.	Mar.	June	Sept.	Dec.
1997	d0.15	1.57	0.41	0.34
1998	0.37	0.49	0.60	0.10
1999	0.39	0.39	3.16	9.50
2000	0.14	0.11	d0.11	0.15

INTERIM DIVIDENDS (Per Share):

Amt.	Decl.	Ex.	Rec.	Pay.
0.22Q	3/10/00	4/12/00	4/14/00	5/15/00
0.22Q	6/13/00	7/12/00	7/14/00	8/15/00
0.22Q	8/07/00	10/11/00	10/13/00	11/15/00
0.22Q	12/12/00	1/10/01	1/12/01	2/15/01
0.22Q	2/21/01	4/10/01	4/12/01	5/15/01

Indicated div.: $0.88 (Div. Reinv. Plan)

CAPITALIZATION (12/31/00):

	($000)	(%)
Long-Term Debt	634,700	52.5
Deferred Income Tax	226,200	18.7
Common & Surplus	349,200	28.9
Total	1,210,100	100.0

RECENT DEVELOPMENTS: For the year ended 12/31/00, income from continuing operations declined 75.7% to $11.2 million. Results included after-tax restructuring and other losses of $4.7 million in 2000 and $20.1 million in 1999. Results for 1999 also included an after-tax gain of $48.0 million. Net sales from continuing operations were $654.7 million, up 65.0% from $396.7 million.

PROSPECTS: On 1/22/01, CSK announced that it has agreed to sell its interest in Georgia-Pacific Tissue, LLC to Georgia-Pacific Corporation. CSK will receive about $235.0 million for certain indemnifiable deferred tax liabilities for its 5.0% ownership interest and its agreement to terminate the joint venture.

BUSINESS

CHESAPEAKE CORPORATION is primarily focused on specialty packaging and merchandising services. CSK is the largest North American producer of temporary and permanent point-of-purchase displays. CSK also produces European folding carton, leaflet and label supplies, and, in specific U.S. markets, produces customized, corrugated packaging. CSK has over 75 manufacturing locations in North America, Europe, Africa and Asia. CSK operates in four business segments: European Specialty Packaging, Merchandising and Specialty Packaging, Plastic Packaging and Land Development. In 1999, CSK contributed substantially all the assets of its Wisconsin Tissue business to a joint venture with Georgia-Pacific. In 1999, CSK sold its tissue, building products, and timberlands businesses for $242.0 million.

ANNUAL FINANCIAL DATA

	12/31/00	12/31/99	12/31/98	12/31/97	12/31/96	12/31/95	12/31/94
Earnings Per Share	**[6] 0.70**	**[5] 12.29**	**[4] 1.57**	**[3] 2.18**	**1.27**	**[2] 3.88**	**[1] 1.58**
Cash Flow Per Share	**d10.82**	**16.27**	**4.46**	**5.42**	**5.09**	**7.04**	**4.66**
Tang. Book Val. Per Share	**...**	**14.59**	**18.27**	**19.81**	**20.05**	**19.68**	**16.53**
Dividends Per Share	**0.88**	**0.88**	**0.80**	**0.80**	**0.80**	**0.76**	**0.72**
Dividend Payout %	**125.7**	**7.2**	**51.0**	**36.7**	**63.0**	**19.6**	**45.6**
INCOME STATEMENT (IN MILLIONS):							
Total Revenues	654.7	1,162.0	950.4	1,021.0	1,158.6	1,233.7	990.5
Costs & Expenses	541.4	1,041.2	821.9	925.7	994.1	996.6	836.1
Depreciation & Amort.	73.6	81.2	62.3	75.8	90.2	75.8	73.3
Operating Income	39.7	39.6	66.2	19.5	74.3	161.3	81.1
Net Interest Inc./(Exp.)	d28.1	d30.4	d18.9	d22.0	d33.9	d30.8	d31.1
Income Before Income Taxes	17.6	433.2	55.8	85.2	47.1	141.6	58.2
Income Taxes	6.4	182.4	21.8	34.3	17.0	48.2	20.6
Net Income	[6] 11.2	[5] 250.8	[4] 34.0	[3] 50.9	30.1	[2] 93.4	[1] 37.6
Cash Flow	d173.2	332.0	96.3	126.7	120.3	169.2	110.9
Average Shs. Outstg. (000)	16,000	20,400	21,568	23,360	23,645	24,051	23,775
BALANCE SHEET (IN MILLIONS):							
Cash & Cash Equivalents	31.2	306.6	62.4	73.3	9.8	5.2	33.2
Total Current Assets	308.3	610.9	313.4	308.3	325.8	281.6	271.6
Net Property	372.2	355.7	543.2	508.3	863.5	780.9	646.4
Total Assets	1,540.9	1,373.2	979.4	913.0	1,290.2	1,146.3	1,013.1
Total Current Liabilities	271.8	319.9	157.6	133.4	166.8	139.3	127.3
Long-Term Obligations	634.7	224.4	270.4	264.3	499.4	393.6	364.0
Net Stockholders' Equity	349.2	551.7	441.3	422.0	469.1	468.3	393.3
Net Working Capital	36.5	291.0	155.8	174.9	159.0	142.3	144.3
Year-end Shs. Outstg. (000)	15,100	17,500	21,400	21,300	23,400	23,800	23,800
STATISTICAL RECORD:							
Operating Profit Margin %	10.0	3.4	7.0	1.9	6.4	13.1	8.2
Net Profit Margin %	...	21.6	3.6	5.0	2.6	7.6	3.8
Return on Equity %	...	45.5	7.7	12.1	6.4	19.9	9.6
Return on Assets %	...	18.3	3.5	5.6	2.3	8.1	3.7
Debt/Total Assets %	41.2	16.3	27.6	28.9	38.7	34.3	35.9
Price Range	35.75-16.75	38.63-25.75	41.75-31.75	36.75-27.13	31.75-23.13	39.00-27.50	35.88-22.25
P/E Ratio	51.1-23.9	3.1-2.1	26.6-20.2	16.9-12.4	25.0-18.2	10.1-7.1	22.7-14.1
Average Yield %	3.4	2.7	2.2	2.5	2.9	2.3	2.5

Statistics are as originally reported. [1] Incl. $700,000 chrg. of extended use of the LIFO invent. acctg. method. [2] Incl. chrg. of $8 mill. & gain of $1.8 mill. [3] Incl. $49.1 mill. gain & $10.8 mill. restruct. chrg.; excl. $2.3 mill. extraord. loss. [4] Bef. acctg. gain of $13.3 mill., but incl. non-recurr. chrgs. of $8.8 mill. [5] Incl. after-tax nonrecurr. gain of $242.0 mill. on sale of tissue, building products and timberlands bus. [6] Incl. after-tax nonrecurr. chrg. of $4.7 mill., but excl. an after-tax extraord. loss of $1.5 mill. and an after-tax loss of $33.8 million from disc. opers.

OFFICERS:
T. H. Johnson, Chmn., Pres., C.E.O.
W. T. Tolley, Sr. V.P., C.F.O.
J. P. Causey, Jr., Sr. V.P., Sec., Gen. Couns.

INVESTOR CONTACT: Joel Mostrom, Inv. Rel., (804) 697-1147

PRINCIPAL OFFICE: 1021 E. Cary Street, P.O. Box 2350, Richmond, VA 23218-2350

TELEPHONE NUMBER: (804) 697-1000
FAX: (804) 697-1199
WEB: www.cskcorp.com

NO. OF EMPLOYEES: 8,720

SHAREHOLDERS: 5,696

ANNUAL MEETING: In Apr.

INCORPORATED: VA, Oct., 1918

INSTITUTIONAL HOLDINGS:
No. of Institutions: 82
Shares Held: 6,812,949
% Held: 45.0

INDUSTRY: Paper mills (SIC: 2621)

TRANSFER AGENT(S): Computershare Investor Services, Chicago, IL

NYSE SYMBOL CHV
Rec. Pr. 96.56 (4/30/01)

CHEVRON CORPORATION

YIELD 2.7%
P/E RATIO 12.1

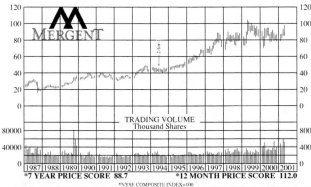

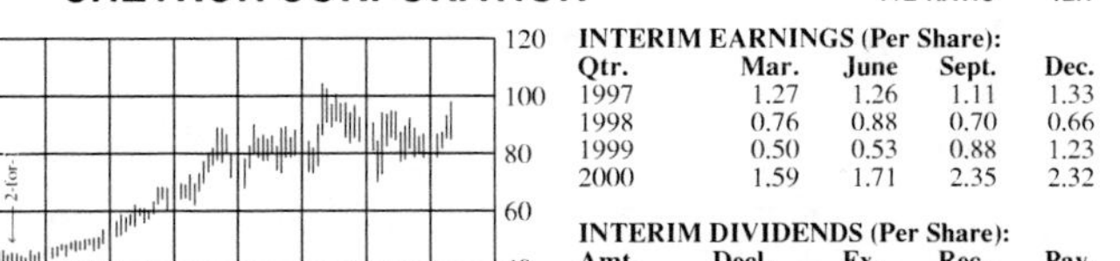

*7 YEAR PRICE SCORE 88.7 *12 MONTH PRICE SCORE 112.0
*NYSE COMPOSITE INDEX=100

INTERIM EARNINGS (Per Share):

Qtr.	Mar.	June	Sept.	Dec.
1997	1.27	1.26	1.11	1.33
1998	0.76	0.88	0.70	0.66
1999	0.50	0.53	0.88	1.23
2000	1.59	1.71	2.35	2.32

INTERIM DIVIDENDS (Per Share):

Amt.	Decl.	Ex.	Rec.	Pay.
0.65Q	4/26/00	5/17/00	5/19/00	6/12/00
0.65Q	7/26/00	8/16/00	8/18/00	9/11/00
0.65Q	10/25/00	11/15/00	11/17/00	12/11/00
0.65Q	1/31/01	2/14/01	2/16/01	3/12/01
0.65Q	4/25/01	5/16/01	5/18/01	6/11/01

Indicated div.: $2.60 (Div. Reinv. Plan)

CAPITALIZATION (12/31/00):

	($000)	(%)
Long-Term Debt	4,872,000	16.2
Capital Lease Obligations	281,000	0.9
Deferred Income Tax	4,908,000	16.4
Common & Surplus	19,925,000	66.4
Total	29,986,000	100.0

RECENT DEVELOPMENTS: For the year ended 12/31/00, net income soared to $5.19 billion versus $2.07 billion a year earlier. Results for 2000 and 1999 included net non-recurring special charges of $252.0 million and $216.0 million, respectively. Total revenues jumped 42.5% to $51.38 billion from $36.06 billion in 1999. Total exploration and production operating income surged to $4.49 billion from $1.58 billion in the prior year, due to higher prices for both crude oil and natural gas.

PROSPECTS: On 1/18/01, CHV announced a $6.00 billion capital and exploratory spending program for 2001, a 16.4% increase from the prior year. CHV's 2001 capital budget includes $3.70 billion for worldwide exploration and production, about $1.40 billion for worldwide refining, marketing and transportation, and about $650.0 million for investments in power and natural gas facilities and distribution, and in technology. Meanwhile, the Company continues to make progress with its proposed merger with Texaco Corporation.

BUSINESS

CHEVRON CORPORATION is engaged in fully integrated petroleum operations, chemical operations, coal mining and energy services. CHV operates in the U.S and approximately 100 other countries. Petroleum operations consist of exploring for, developing and producing of crude oil and natural gas; refining crude oil into finished petroleum products; marketing crude oil, natural gas and the many products derived from petroleum; and transporting crude oil, natural gas and petroleum products by pipelines, marine vessels, motor equipment and rail car. Chemical operations include the manufacture and marketing of commodity petrochemicals, plastics for industrial uses and fuel and lubricating oil additives. As of 12/31/00, net proved developed reserves were: crude oil, condensate and natural gas liquids, 5,001 million barrels; and natural gas, 9,552 billion cubic feet.

BUSINESS LINE ANALYSIS

(12/31/00)	Rev (%)	Inc (%)
Exploration & Production	28.1	86.6
Refining, Marketing, & Tr	66.2	12.6
Chemicals	4.9	0.8
Other	0.7	0
Total	100.0	100.0

ANNUAL FINANCIAL DATA

	12/31/00	12/31/99	12/31/98	12/31/97	12/31/96	12/31/95	12/31/94
Earnings Per Share	**[3] 7.97**	**[2] 3.14**	**2.04**	**4.95**	**[1] 3.99**	**[1] 1.43**	**2.60**
Cash Flow Per Share	**12.34**	**7.48**	**5.57**	**8.44**	**7.39**	**6.61**	**6.33**
Tang. Book Val. Per Share	**31.08**	**27.04**	**25.81**	**26.64**	**23.82**	**22.02**	**22.39**
Dividends Per Share	**2.60**	**2.48**	**2.44**	**2.28**	**2.08**	**1.93**	**1.85**
Dividend Payout %	**32.6**	**79.0**	**119.6**	**46.1**	**52.1**	**134.6**	**71.2**
INCOME STATEMENT (IN MILLIONS):							
Total Revenues	51,379.0	36,060.0	30,329.0	41,262.0	43,126.0	36,529.0	35,414.0
Costs & Expenses	39,551.0	29,600.0	25,998.0	33,836.0	36,573.0	31,511.0	30,274.0
Depreciation & Amort.	2,848.0	2,866.0	2,320.0	2,300.0	2,216.0	3,381.0	2,431.0
Operating Income	8,980.0	3,594.0	2,011.0	5,126.0	4,337.0	1,637.0	2,709.0
Net Interest Inc./(Exp.)	d460.0	d472.0	d405.0	d312.0	d364.0	d401.0	d346.0
Income Before Income Taxes	9,270.0	3,648.0	1,834.0	5,502.0	4,740.0	1,789.0	2,803.0
Income Taxes	4,085.0	1,578.0	495.0	2,246.0	2,133.0	859.0	1,110.0
Equity Earnings/Minority Int.	750.0	526.0	228.0	688.0	767.0	553.0	440.0
Net Income	[3] 5,185.0	[2] 2,070.0	1,339.0	3,256.0	[1] 2,607.0	[1] 930.0	1,693.0
Cash Flow	8,033.0	4,936.0	3,659.0	5,556.0	4,823.0	4,311.0	4,124.0
Average Shs. Outstg. (000)	651,100	659,500	657,100	658,400	653,000	652,000	652,000
BALANCE SHEET (IN MILLIONS):							
Cash & Cash Equivalents	2,630.0	2,032.0	1,413.0	1,670.0	1,637.0	1,394.0	1,306.0
Total Current Assets	8,213.0	8,297.0	6,297.0	7,006.0	7,942.0	7,867.0	7,591.0
Net Property	22,894.0	25,317.0	23,729.0	22,671.0	21,496.0	21,696.0	22,173.0
Total Assets	41,264.0	40,668.0	36,540.0	35,473.0	34,854.0	34,330.0	34,407.0
Total Current Liabilities	7,674.0	8,889.0	7,166.0	6,946.0	8,907.0	9,445.0	9,392.0
Long-Term Obligations	5,153.0	5,485.0	4,393.0	4,431.0	3,988.0	4,521.0	4,128.0
Net Stockholders' Equity	19,925.0	17,749.0	17,034.0	17,472.0	15,623.0	14,355.0	14,596.0
Net Working Capital	539.0	d592.0	d869.0	60.0	d965.0	d1,578.0	d1,801.0
Year-end Shs. Outstg. (000)	641,060	656,346	660,000	655,900	656,000	652,000	652,000
STATISTICAL RECORD:							
Operating Profit Margin %	17.5	10.0	6.6	12.4	10.1	4.5	7.6
Net Profit Margin %	10.1	5.7	4.4	7.9	6.0	2.5	4.8
Return on Equity %	26.0	11.7	7.9	18.6	16.7	6.5	11.6
Return on Assets %	12.6	5.1	3.7	9.2	7.5	2.7	4.9
Debt/Total Assets %	12.5	13.5	12.0	12.5	11.4	13.2	12.0
Price Range	94.88-69.94	104.44-73.13	90.19-67.75	89.19-61.75	68.38-51.00	53.63-43.38	47.31-39.88
P/E Ratio	11.9-8.8	33.3-23.3	44.2-33.2	18.0-12.5	17.1-12.8	37.5-30.3	18.2-15.3
Average Yield %	3.2	2.8	3.1	3.0	3.5	4.0	4.2

Statistics are as originally reported. Adj. for 2-for-1 stk. split, 5/94 [1] Incls. nonrecurr. chrg. 12/31/96: $44.0 mill.; chrgs. totaling 12/31/95: $1.03 bill. [2] Incls. special chrgs. of $216.0 mill. [3] Incls. spec. chrgs. of $252.0 mill.

OFFICERS:
D. J. O'Reilly, Chmn., C.E.O.
R. H. Matzke, Vice-Chmn.
J. S. Watson, V.P., C.F.O.

INVESTOR CONTACT: Peter Trueblood, Mgr., Inv. Rel., (415) 894-5690

PRINCIPAL OFFICE: 575 Market Street, San Francisco, CA 94105-2586

TELEPHONE NUMBER: (415) 894-7700
FAX: (415) 894-6017
WEB: www.chevron.com
NO. OF EMPLOYEES: 34,610
SHAREHOLDERS: 107,000 (approx.)
ANNUAL MEETING: In Apr.
INCORPORATED: DE, Jan., 1926

INSTITUTIONAL HOLDINGS:
No. of Institutions: 869
Shares Held: 351,540,485
% Held: 54.8

INDUSTRY: Petroleum refining (SIC: 2911)

TRANSFER AGENT(S): Mellon Investor Services, Ridgefield Park, NJ

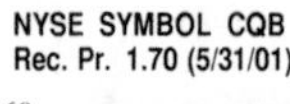

NYSE SYMBOL CQB
Rec. Pr. 1.70 (5/31/01)

CHIQUITA BRANDS INTERNATIONAL, INC.

YIELD ...
P/E RATIO ...

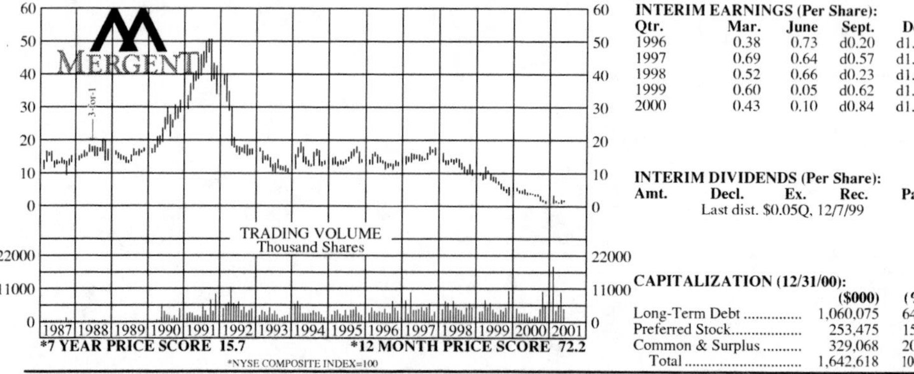

INTERIM EARNINGS (Per Share):

Qtr.	Mar.	June	Sept.	Dec.
1996	0.38	0.73	d0.20	d1.65
1997	0.69	0.64	d0.57	d1.01
1998	0.52	0.66	d0.23	d1.62
1999	0.60	0.05	d0.62	d1.25
2000	0.43	0.10	d0.84	d1.40

INTERIM DIVIDENDS (Per Share):

Amt.	Decl.	Ex.	Rec.	Pay.

Last dist. $0.05Q, 12/7/99

CAPITALIZATION (12/31/00):

	($000)	(%)
Long-Term Debt	1,060,075	64.5
Preferred Stock	253,475	15.4
Common & Surplus	329,068	20.0
Total	1,642,618	100.0

RECENT DEVELOPMENTS: For the year ended 12/31/00, net loss totaled $94.9 million versus a net loss of $58.4 million the year before. Results in 2000 included one-time pre-tax charges of $20.1 million from asset write-downs in the Fresh Produce segment. The 1999 results included a $9.0 million pre-tax workforce reduction charge. Net sales slid 11.8% to $2.25 billion from $2.56 billion a year earlier. Operating income, including the aforementioned charges, fell 35.0% to $27.3 million from $42.0 million in 1999.

PROSPECTS: The Company announced plans to restructure its outstanding debt to help resolve upcoming debt maturities and improve financial liquidity. The proposed restructuring initiatives, which are subject to bondholder approval, include the conversion of a significant portion of CQB's outstanding $862.0 million public debt into common equity. If bondholders support the initiatives, the Company will likely apply to restructure through the Chapter 11 bankruptcy process.

BUSINESS

CHIQUITA BRANDS INTERNATIONAL, INC. (formerly United Brands Co.) is a marketer, producer and distributor of fresh and prepared food products. The Fresh Produce segment includes the production, transportation, distribution and marketing of CHIQUITA bananas and a wide variety of other fresh fruits and vegetables. The Processed Foods segment consists of the production, distribution and marketing of the Company's private-label and branded canned vegetables, branded fruit and vegetable juices and beverages, processed bananas and edible oil based consumer products. American Financial Group, Inc. owns approximately 36% of the Company.

REVENUES

(12/31/2000)	($000)	(%)
Fresh Produce	1,787,334	79.3
Processed Food	466,436	20.7
Total	2,253,770	100.0

ANNUAL FINANCIAL DATA

	12/31/00	12/31/99	12/31/98	12/31/97	12/31/96	4 12/31/95	12/31/94
Earnings Per Share	6 d1.68	2 d1.15	d0.55	d0.29	5 d0.72	3 0.37	1 d1.07
Cash Flow Per Share	d0.22	0.33	0.98	1.31	1.03	2.32	1.27
Tang. Book Val. Per Share	2.47	4.09	5.36	5.91	5.57	6.68	5.86
Dividends Per Share	...	0.20	0.20	0.20	0.20	0.20	0.20
Dividend Payout %	...	...	...	...	...	54.0	...
INCOME STATEMENT (IN MILLIONS):							
Total Revenues	2,253.8	2,555.8	2,720.4	2,433.7	2,435.2	2,566.0	3,961.7
Costs & Expenses	2,128.9	2,416.5	2,542.6	2,242.0	2,254.5	2,285.6	3,729.8
Depreciation & Amort.	97.5	97.3	99.1	91.6	96.5	104.6	122.2
Operating Income	27.4	42.0	78.6	100.2	84.3	175.8	109.8
Net Interest Inc./(Exp.)	d115.5	d92.5	d95.9	d92.4	d102.0	d135.4	d146.6
Income Before Income Taxes	d87.9	d50.1	d9.9	8.5	d16.7	41.9	d35.2
Income Taxes	7.0	8.3	8.5	8.2	11.0	13.9	13.5
Net Income	6 d94.9	2 d58.4	d18.4	0.3	5 d27.7	3 28.0	1 d48.7
Cash Flow	d14.5	21.8	63.6	75.0	56.8	124.3	66.2
Average Shs. Outstg. (000)	66,498	65,768	64,663	57,025	55,167	53,670	52,033
BALANCE SHEET (IN MILLIONS):							
Cash & Cash Equivalents	96.9	97.9	88.9	125.7	285.6	271.4	178.9
Total Current Assets	846.5	902.9	840.2	783.5	844.3	876.8	918.2
Net Property	1,071.3	1,177.8	1,122.8	1,151.4	1,139.7	1,182.1	1,433.9
Total Assets	2,416.8	2,596.1	2,509.1	2,401.6	2,466.9	2,623.5	2,902.0
Total Current Liabilities	612.9	488.4	531.4	483.1	464.3	509.9	653.8
Long-Term Obligations	1,060.1	1,227.0	1,002.6	962.0	1,178.2	1,242.0	1,364.9
Net Stockholders' Equity	582.5	705.3	794.0	780.1	724.3	672.2	644.8
Net Working Capital	233.6	414.4	308.8	300.3	380.0	366.9	264.4
Year-end Shs. Outstg. (000)	66,706	65,922	65,448	61,168	55,841	54,769	49,301
STATISTICAL RECORD:							
Operating Profit Margin %	1.2	1.6	2.9	4.1	3.5	6.8	2.8
Net Profit Margin %	...	...	...	...	...	1.1	...
Return on Equity %	...	...	...	...	...	4.2	...
Return on Assets %	...	...	...	...	...	1.1	...
Debt/Total Assets %	43.9	47.3	40.0	40.1	47.8	47.3	47.0
Price Range	5.69-0.88	12.06-3.38	16.25-9.31	18.13-12.63	16.50-11.13	18.13-12.13	19.38-11.25
P/E Ratio	...	...	...	...	...	49.0-32.8	...
Average Yield %	...	2.6	1.6	1.3	1.4	1.3	1.3

Statistics are as originally reported. 1 Incl. $57.2 mil ($1.10/sh) non-recur. loss & bef. $22.8 mil ($0.44/sh) extraord. loss. 2 Incl. $9.0 mil ($0.14/sh) pre-tax chg. 3 Bef. $7.6 mil ($0.14/sh) extraord. loss, bef. $11.2 mil ($0.21/sh) loss fr disc. opers. & incl. $19.3 mil ($0.36/sh) gain fr asset sale. 4 Refl. disp. of meat div. 5 Incl. $70.3 ($1.27/sh) non-recur. loss & bef. $23 mil ($0.41/sh) extraord. loss. 6 Incl. $20.1 mil ($0.30/sh) non-recur. chg.

OFFICERS:
C. H. Lindner, Chmn., C.E.O.
S. G. Warshaw, Pres., C.O.O.
J. B. Riley, Sr. V.P., C.F.O.

INVESTOR CONTACT: Joseph W. Hagin, II, V.P., Corp. Affairs, (513) 784-6366

PRINCIPAL OFFICE: 250 East Fifth St., Cincinnati, OH 45202

TELEPHONE NUMBER: (513) 784-8000
FAX: (513) 784-8030
WEB: www.chiquita.com

NO. OF EMPLOYEES: 30,000 (approx.)

SHAREHOLDERS: 5,205

ANNUAL MEETING: In Sept.

INCORPORATED: NJ, Mar., 1899

INSTITUTIONAL HOLDINGS:
No. of Institutions: 43
Shares Held: 32,270,802
% Held: 48.4

INDUSTRY: Fruits and tree nuts, nec (SIC: 0179)

TRANSFER AGENT(S): Securities Transfer Company, Cincinnati, OH

NYSE SYMBOL CPS
Rec. Pr. 37.10 (4/30/01)

CHOICEPOINT, INC.

YIELD ...
P/E RATIO 51.5

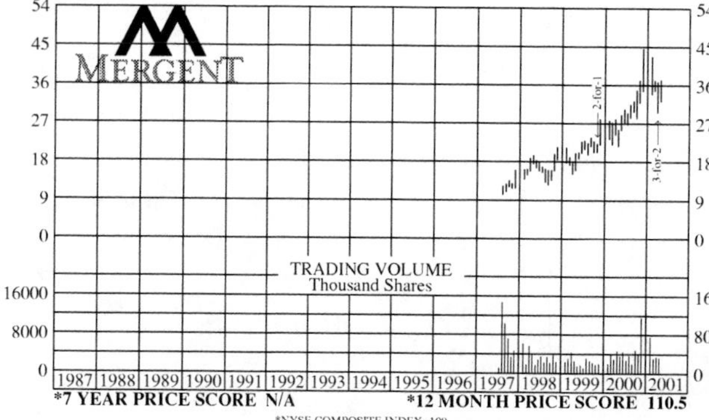

*7 YEAR PRICE SCORE N/A *12 MONTH PRICE SCORE 110.5
*NYSE COMPOSITE INDEX=100

INTERIM EARNINGS (Per Share):

Qtr.	Mar.	June	Sept.	Dec.
1998	0.17	0.19	0.18	0.25
1999	0.20	0.21	0.23	0.24
2000	0.24	d0.10	0.28	0.30

INTERIM DIVIDENDS (Per Share):

Amt.	Decl.	Ex.	Rec.	Pay.
2-for-1	10/20/99	11/26/99	11/10/99	11/24/99
3-for-2	1/31/01	3/08/01	2/16/01	3/07/01

CAPITALIZATION (12/31/00):

	($000)	(%)
Long-Term Debt	141,638	26.1
Common & Surplus	401,069	73.9
Total	542,707	100.0

RECENT DEVELOPMENTS: For the year ended 12/31/00, net income improved 3.9% to $43.8 million compared with $42.2 million in the previous year. Results for 2000 and 1999 included merger costs and unusual items of $28.9 million and $2.4 million, respectively. Results for 1999 also included a $2.5 million gain on the sale of a business. Total revenues jumped 16.9% to $593.5 million versus $507.9 million in the preceding year.

PROSPECTS: On February 1, 2001, the Company acquired BTi Employee Screening Services Inc., a pre-employment background screening organization serving a client base that includes Fortune 500 companies, institutions, and mid-sized and small businesses. Separately, on February 9, 2001, CPS signed an agreement to acquire ABI Consulting Inc., a third party administrator of workplace drug and alcohol testing programs.

BUSINESS

CHOICEPOINT, INC. is a provider of risk management and fraud prevention information and related technology to the insurance industry. The Company also offers risk management and fraud prevention services to organizations in other industries. The Company operates in two primary service groups: Insurance services and Business & Government services. Insurance services include automated direct marketing, underwriting and claims information, such as motor vehicle reports, the Company's Comprehensive Loss Underwriting Exchange database services, vehicle registration services, credit reports, modeling services, ChoicePointLink™, and driver's license information. Business & Government services include risk management and fraud prevention services and related technology solutions, shareholder locator services and database marketing services to Fortune 1000 corporations, asset-based lenders, legal and professional service providers, health care service providers and local, state and federal government agencies.

BUSINESS LINE ANALYSIS

(12/31/2000)	REV (%)	INC (%)
Insurance	50.2	52.0
Business & Government...........	49.8	48.0
Total	100.0	100.0

ANNUAL FINANCIAL DATA

	12/31/00	12/31/99	12/31/98	12/31/97	12/31/96	12/31/95	12/31/94
Earnings Per Share	[1] **0.69**	[1][2] **0.87**	[1][2] **0.79**	[1][2] **0.64**	...	...	...
Cash Flow Per Share	**1.54**	**1.71**	**1.48**	**1.27**	...	...	...
Tang. Book Val. Per Share	**0.50**	...	...	...	...	...	...
INCOME STATEMENT (IN THOUSANDS):							
Total Revenues	593,533	430,143	406,475	417,321	366,481	328,990	284,566
Costs & Expenses	449,861	314,142	314,035	343,606	300,216	283,741	257,956
Depreciation & Amort.	53,619	37,913	31,032	27,638	18,654	13,321	10,033
Operating Income	90,053	78,088	61,408	46,077	47,611	31,928	16,577
Net Interest Inc./(Exp.)	d11,743	d11,142	d7,748	d6,649	d6,597	d5,830	d2,638
Income Before Income Taxes	78,310	69,459	62,467	53,466	41,014	26,098	13,939
Income Taxes	34,488	30,070	27,048	24,522	17,734	11,233	7,327
Net Income	[1] 43,822	[1][2] 39,389	[1][2] 35,419	[1][2] 28,944	23,280	[1] 14,865	6,612
Cash Flow	97,441	77,302	66,451	56,582	41,934	28,186	16,645
Average Shs. Outstg.	63,104	45,287	45,018	44,673	...	...	...
BALANCE SHEET (IN THOUSANDS):							
Cash & Cash Equivalents	44,909	40,085	18,883	35,858	1,726	645	...
Total Current Assets	178,329	155,841	143,606	146,119	91,931	78,159	...
Net Property	68,792	52,559	55,279	42,985	35,407	19,796	...
Total Assets	704,439	532,872	534,199	359,971	301,824	200,779	...
Total Current Liabilities	106,339	88,362	124,960	77,238	44,965	40,420	...
Long-Term Obligations	141,638	187,195	191,697	95,457	1,051	...	...
Net Stockholders' Equity	401,069	202,911	159,572	127,745	196,327	104,641	...
Net Working Capital	71,990	67,479	18,646	68,881	46,966	37,739	...
Year-end Shs. Outstg.	61,566	43,607	43,980	43,923	...	...	...
STATISTICAL RECORD:							
Operating Profit Margin %	15.2	18.2	15.1	11.0	13.0	9.7	5.8
Net Profit Margin %	7.4	9.2	8.7	6.9	6.4	4.5	2.3
Return on Equity %	10.9	19.4	22.2	22.7	11.9	14.2	...
Return on Assets %	6.2	7.4	6.6	8.0	7.7	7.4	...
Debt/Total Assets %	20.1	35.1	35.9	26.5	0.3	...	...
Price Range	44.67-21.67	27.96-15.13	21.50-12.46	16.04-10.25	...	...	...
P/E Ratio	64.7-31.4	32.2-17.4	27.3-15.8	25.1-16.0	...	...	...

Statistics are as originally reported. Adj. for 2-for-1 stk. spl., 11/99 & 3-for-2 stk. spl., 3/01. [1] Incl. non-recurr. chrgs., $28.9 mill., 2000; $1.6 mill., 1999; $3.8 mill., 1998; $6.2 mill., 1997; $9.2 mill., 1995. [2] Incl. net gain on sale of businesses $2.5 mill., 1999; $8.8 mill., 1998; $14.0 mill., 1997

OFFICERS:
D. V. Smith, Chmn., Pres., C.E.O.
M. S. Wood, C.F.O.
D. E. Trine, Treas., Corp. Contr.
J. M. de Janes, Sec., Gen. Couns.

INVESTOR CONTACT: John Mongelli, Investor Relations, (770) 752-6171

PRINCIPAL OFFICE: 1000 Alderman Drive, Alpharetta, GA 30005

TELEPHONE NUMBER: (770) 752-6000
FAX: (770) 752-6250
WEB: www.choicepoint.net

NO. OF EMPLOYEES: 4,200 (approx.)

SHAREHOLDERS: 4,632 (approx. record)

ANNUAL MEETING: In May

INCORPORATED: GA, 1997

INSTITUTIONAL HOLDINGS:
No. of Institutions: 203
Shares Held: 43,613,285
% Held: 71.6

INDUSTRY: Credit reporting services (SIC: 7323)

TRANSFER AGENT(S): SunTrust Bank, Atlanta, GA

NYSE SYMBOL CCN
Rec. Pr. 69.49 (5/31/01)

CHRIS-CRAFT INDUSTRIES, INC.

YIELD ...
P/E RATIO 19.4

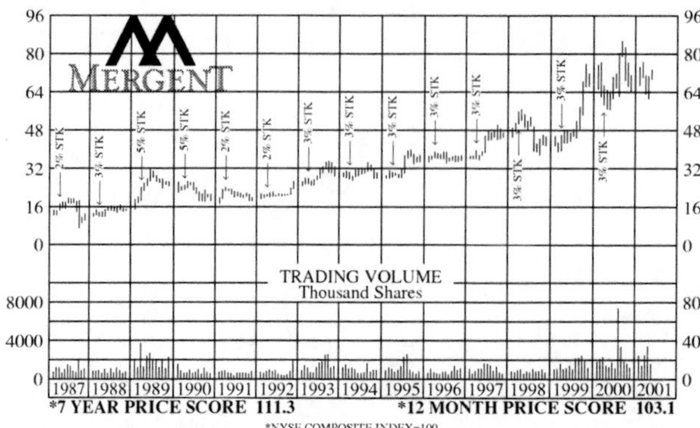

*7 YEAR PRICE SCORE 111.3 *12 MONTH PRICE SCORE 103.1

*NYSE COMPOSITE INDEX=100

INTERIM EARNINGS (Per Share):

Qtr.	Mar.	June	Sept.	Dec.
1996	0.01	0.08	d0.05	d0.03
1997	2.13	0.28	0.13	0.09
1998	0.04	0.27	0.33	0.02
1999	0.02	0.15	0.17	0.61
2000	0.07	0.46	0.43	2.62

INTERIM DIVIDENDS (Per Share):

Amt.	Decl.	Ex.	Rec.	Pay.
3% STK	3/16/00	3/29/00	3/31/00	4/14/00

CAPITALIZATION (12/31/00):

	($000)	(%)
Minority Interest	553,394	25.7
Preferred Stock	4,075	0.2
Common & Surplus	1,598,127	74.1
Total	2,155,596	100.0

RECENT DEVELOPMENTS: For the year ended 12/31/00, net income jumped to $158.0 million from $42.4 million in 1999. Earnings for 2000 included an impairment charge of $10.0 million. Earnings for 2000 and 1999 included an equity loss and other expenses related to United Paramount Network of $35.7 million and $97.3 million, respectively. Operating revenues increased 7.6% to $528.8 million. Operating revenues from television stations grew 7.7% to $528.8 million. Operating income amounted to $115.2 million, up 22.3% from $94.2 million the year before.

PROSPECTS: In August 2000, the Company, BHC Communications, Inc. and United Television, Inc. agreed to be acquired by News Corporation and Fox Television Stations for consideration comprising a cash payment of $2.13 billion and approximately 73.0 million American Depository Receipts representing 292.0 million News Corporation preferred shares. Recently, the deal was approved by CCN's shareholders. The merger remains subject to approval by the U.S. Federal Communications Commission

BUSINESS

CHRIS-CRAFT INDUSTRIES, INC. is engaged in television broadcasting. The Company's television broadcasting division is operated by 80%-owned broadcasting subsidiary, BHC Communications, Inc., which owns and operates ten television stations, three wholly-owned by BHC and seven owned by United Television, Inc. (UTV) (57.9% owned by BHC). BHC, along with the Paramount Television Group of Viacom, Inc. created the United Paramount Network, a fifth television network, which premiered in January 1995. Chris-Craft Industrial Products, Inc., the wholly-owned subsidiary of Chris-Craft that constitutes its industrial division, is primarily engaged in manufacturing plastic flexible films and distributing containment systems to the healthcare industry. In 1992, CCN acquired Pinelands, Inc., owner of WWOR, for $313.0 million.

QUARTERLY DATA

(12/31/2000)($000)	REV	INC
1st Quarter	127,834	2,935
2nd Quarter	138,040	20,389
3rd Quarter	124,668	19,266
4th Quarter	138,300	115,423

ANNUAL FINANCIAL DATA

	12/31/00	12/31/99	12/31/98	12/31/97	12/31/96	12/31/95	12/31/94
Earnings Per Share	**[1] 3.48**	**0.94**	**0.67**	**[1] 2.14**	**0.01**	**0.63**	**1.87**
Cash Flow Per Share	**6.42**	**3.72**	**4.05**	**6.05**	**3.36**	**3.85**	**5.45**
Tang. Book Val. Per Share	**31.55**	**27.63**	**28.95**	**41.35**	**28.96**	**31.12**	**29.32**
INCOME STATEMENT (IN MILLIONS):							
Total Revenues	528.8	491.5	467.1	464.6	465.7	472.1	481.4
Costs & Expenses	279.5	273.2	261.8	254.3	247.3	252.0	250.8
Depreciation & Amort.	134.1	124.1	110.6	114.8	115.1	109.4	122.8
Operating Income	115.2	94.2	94.7	95.5	103.3	110.6	107.8
Income Before Income Taxes	217.7	103.0	86.4	242.6	38.8	65.3	163.8
Income Taxes	cr1.1	32.3	32.5	99.6	19.5	17.6	57.3
Equity Earnings/Minority Int.	d96.5	d125.6	d113.0	d136.9	d164.8	d155.0	d45.7
Net Income	[1] 158.0	42.4	29.5	[1] 93.5	0.8	22.0	64.7
Cash Flow	291.7	166.1	139.7	207.9	115.4	130.9	187.0
Average Shs. Outstg. (000)	45,475	44,830	34,545	34,433	34,445	34,095	34,406
BALANCE SHEET (IN MILLIONS):							
Cash & Cash Equivalents	1,445.1	1,359.7	1,415.5	1,501.9	1,395.2	1,523.4	1,520.5
Total Current Assets	1,858.8	1,645.1	1,656.7	1,749.5	1,668.4	1,757.9	1,769.0
Net Property	67.2	65.0	51.6	47.4	49.9	49.9	51.6
Total Assets	2,552.2	2,346.0	2,245.4	2,226.4	2,137.3	2,203.9	2,232.2
Total Current Liabilities	278.4	291.2	268.8	263.0	250.3	226.5	243.6
Net Stockholders' Equity	1,602.2	1,441.8	1,408.5	1,383.2	1,288.9	1,319.0	1,306.2
Net Working Capital	1,580.4	1,353.9	1,388.0	1,486.6	1,418.1	1,531.4	1,525.4
Year-end Shs. Outstg. (000)	36,050	34,792	33,665	25,092	33,157	31,831	33,093
STATISTICAL RECORD:							
Operating Profit Margin %	21.8	19.2	20.3	20.6	22.2	23.4	22.4
Net Profit Margin %	29.9	8.6	6.3	20.1	0.2	4.7	13.4
Return on Equity %	9.9	2.9	2.1	6.8	0.1	1.7	5.0
Return on Assets %	6.2	1.8	1.3	4.2	...	1.0	2.9
Price Range	85.31-56.44	75.97-38.94	56.91-37.53	50.34-35.46	39.10-34.10	39.90-27.74	34.76-26.80
P/E Ratio	24.5-16.2	80.7-41.3	84.9-56.0	23.6-16.6	4,425.1-3,859.4	63.2-44.0	18.6-14.4

Statistics are as originally reported. Adj. for stk. splits: 3% div., 4/00; 4/99; 4/98; 4/97; 4/96; 4/95; 4/94 [1] Incl. non-recurr. chrg. $10.0 mill., 12/00; gain $153.9 mill., 12/97

OFFICERS:
H. J. Siegel, Chmn., Pres.
J. K. Merkel, Sr. V.P., Treas.
B. C. Kelly, Sr. V.P., Gen Couns., Sec.

INVESTOR CONTACT: Brian C. Kelly, Sec., (212) 421-0200

PRINCIPAL OFFICE: 767 Fifth Avenue, New York, NY 10153

TELEPHONE NUMBER: (212) 421-0200
FAX: (212) 935-8462
WEB: www.cclife.org
NO. OF EMPLOYEES: 1,412
SHAREHOLDERS: 2,328 (common); 1,468(class B)
ANNUAL MEETING: In May
INCORPORATED: DE, Jan., 1928

INSTITUTIONAL HOLDINGS:
No. of Institutions: 151
Shares Held: 18,712,871
% Held: 53.2

INDUSTRY: Television broadcasting stations (SIC: 4833)

TRANSFER AGENT(S): Mellon Investor Services, Ridgefield Park, NJ

NYSE SYMBOL CB
Rec. Pr. 75.35 (5/31/01)

CHUBB CORPORATION (THE)

YIELD 1.8%
P/E RATIO 18.8

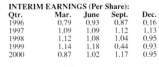

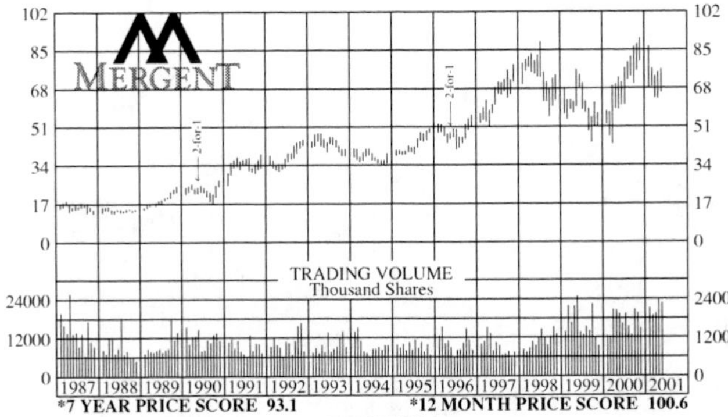

TRADING VOLUME
Thousand Shares

*7 YEAR PRICE SCORE 93.1 *12 MONTH PRICE SCORE 100.6

*NYSE COMPOSITE INDEX=100

INTERIM EARNINGS (Per Share):

Qtr.	Mar.	June	Sept.	Dec.
1996	0.79	0.93	0.87	0.16
1997	1.09	1.09	1.12	1.13
1998	1.12	1.08	1.04	0.95
1999	1.14	1.18	0.44	0.93
2000	0.87	1.02	1.17	0.95

INTERIM DIVIDENDS (Per Share):

Amt.	Decl.	Ex.	Rec.	Pay.
0.33Q	9/08/00	9/20/00	9/22/00	10/10/00
0.33Q	12/01/00	12/13/00	12/15/00	1/03/01
0.34Q	3/02/01	3/20/01	3/22/01	4/05/01
0.34Q	6/01/01	6/13/01	6/15/01	7/03/01

Indicated div.: $1.36 (Div. Reinv. Plan)

CAPITALIZATION (12/31/00):

	($000)	(%)
Long-Term Debt	753,800	9.7
Common & Surplus	6,981,700	90.3
Total	7,735,500	100.0

RECENT DEVELOPMENTS: For the year ended 12/31/00, net income was $714.6 million, up 15.1% from $621.1 million in 1999. Earnings included after-tax realized investment gains of $33.5 million and $55.8 million in 2000 and 1999, respectively. Net premiums written increased 11.1% to $6.33 billion versus $5.70 billion a year earlier. Personal insurance net premiums written jumped 13.0% to $1.72 billion, while total standard commercial insurance net premiums written declined 3.0% to $1.79 billion. Net specialty commercial premiums written grew 21.0% to $2.82 billion.

PROSPECTS: CB is benefiting from stronger premium growth in both its personal and specialty commercial product lines. Standard commercial premiums written were down 3.0% for the year as a result of declines in the multiple peril and casualty lines. However, progress is being made to accelerate rate increases and shed underperforming accounts. The combined loss and expense ratio for the standard commercial segment was 114.0% in 2000 compared with 123.6% in 1999.

BUSINESS

THE CHUBB CORPORATION offers commercial and personal property and casualty insurance. It also maintains operations in life and health insurance, and real estate development. The Company operates more than 120 offices throughout North America, Europe, South America and the Pacific Rim. For the year ended 12/31/00, property and casualty accounted for 97% of total revenues; real estate, 1%; and other, 2%. In 2000, the combined loss and expense ratio after policyholders' dividends was 100.4%.

ANNUAL FINANCIAL DATA

	12/31/00	12/31/99	12/31/98	12/31/97	12/31/96	12/31/95	12/31/94
Earnings Per Share	**4.01**	**3.66**	**4.19**	**4.39**	**[1] 2.75**	**3.93**	**2.98**
Tang. Book Val. Per Share	**37.13**	**32.85**	**34.78**	**32.11**	**31.24**	**30.14**	**24.46**
Dividends Per Share	**1.31**	**1.27**	**1.22**	**1.14**	**1.05**	**0.96**	**0.91**
Dividend Payout %	**32.7**	**34.8**	**29.1**	**26.0**	**38.4**	**24.6**	**30.4**
INCOME STATEMENT (IN MILLIONS):							
Total Premium Income	6,145.9	5,652.0	5,303.8	5,157.4	4,569.3	4,770.1	4,612.6
Other Income	1,105.6	1,077.6	1,046.0	1,506.6	1,111.3	1,319.1	1,097.0
Total Revenues	7,251.5	6,729.6	6,349.8	6,664.0	5,680.5	6,089.2	5,709.5
Policyholder Benefits	4,127.7	3,942.0	3,493.7	3,307.0	3,010.8	3,219.2	3,271.6
Income Before Income Taxes	851.0	710.1	849.7	974.1	546.9	900.1	639.4
Income Taxes	136.4	89.0	142.7	204.6	60.7	203.4	110.9
Net Income	714.6	621.1	707.0	769.5	[1] 486.2	696.6	528.5
Average Shs. Outstg. (000)	178,300	169,800	168,600	176,200	174,402	179,884	180,900
BALANCE SHEET (IN MILLIONS):							
Cash & Cash Equivalents	1,079.1	1,223.3	352.5	736.6	280.6	496.4	816.5
Premiums Due	1,409.8	1,234.7	1,199.3	1,144.4	984.9	872.9	787.2
Invst. Assets: Fixed-term	15,564.4	14,519.1	13,318.9	12,453.4	11,158.8	12,602.8	10,722.7
Invst. Assets: Equities	830.6	769.2	1,092.2	871.1	646.3	587.8	642.2
Invst. Assets: Loans	...	...	...	...	...	212.3	202.7
Invst. Assets: Total	18,128.8	17,188.3	15,501.3	14,839.6	13,685.0	15,630.0	14,118.7
Total Assets	25,026.7	23,537.0	20,746.0	19,615.6	19,938.9	22,996.5	20,723.1
Long-Term Obligations	753.8	759.2	607.5	398.6	1,070.5	1,156.0	1,285.6
Net Stockholders' Equity	6,981.7	6,271.8	5,644.1	5,657.1	5,462.9	5,262.7	4,247.0
Year-end Shs. Outstg. (000)	174,919	175,490	162,267	176,200	174,861	174,602	173,642
STATISTICAL RECORD:							
Return on Revenues %	9.9	9.2	11.1	11.5	8.6	11.4	9.3
Return on Equity %	10.2	9.9	12.5	13.6	8.9	13.2	12.4
Return on Assets %	2.9	2.6	3.4	3.9	2.4	3.0	2.6
Price Range	90.25-43.25	76.38-44.00	88.81-55.38	78.50-51.13	56.25-40.88	50.31-38.06	41.56-34.31
P/E Ratio	22.5-10.8	20.9-12.0	21.2-13.2	17.9-11.6	20.5-14.9	12.8-9.7	14.0-11.5
Average Yield %	2.0	2.1	1.7	1.8	2.2	2.2	2.4

Statistics are as originally reported. Adj. for stk. split: 2-for-1, 5/96 [1] Bef. disc. oper. gain $26.5 mill.

OFFICERS:
D. R. O'Hare, Chmn., C.E.O.
J. J. Degnan, Pres.
D. B. Kelso, Exec. V.P., C.F.O.

INVESTOR CONTACT: Mary Jane Murphy, Asst. Sec., (908) 903-3579

PRINCIPAL OFFICE: 15 Mountain View Rd., P.O. Box 1615, Warren, NJ 07061-1615

TELEPHONE NUMBER: (908) 903-2000
FAX: (908) 903-2003
WEB: www.chubb.com

NO. OF EMPLOYEES: 12,400 (approx.)

SHAREHOLDERS: 6,600 (approx.)

ANNUAL MEETING: In April

INCORPORATED: NJ, June, 1967

INSTITUTIONAL HOLDINGS:
No. of Institutions: 449
Shares Held: 129,238,956
% Held: 73.7

INDUSTRY: Fire, marine, and casualty insurance (SIC: 6331)

TRANSFER AGENT(S): First Chicago Trust Company of New York, Jersey City, NJ

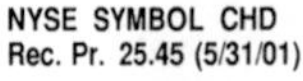

NYSE SYMBOL CHD
Rec. Pr. 25.45 (5/31/01)

CHURCH & DWIGHT COOMPANY, INC.

YIELD 1.1%
P/E RATIO 30.3

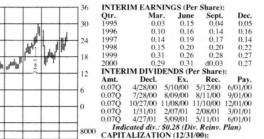

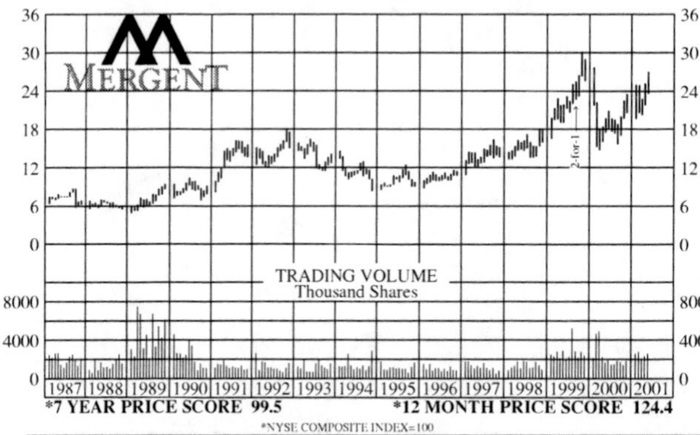

INTERIM EARNINGS (Per Share):

Qtr.	Mar.	June	Sept.	Dec.
1995	0.03	0.15	0.04	0.05
1996	0.10	0.16	0.14	0.16
1997	0.14	0.19	0.17	0.14
1998	0.15	0.20	0.20	0.22
1999	0.31	0.26	0.28	0.27
2000	0.29	0.31	d0.03	0.27

INTERIM DIVIDENDS (Per Share):

Amt.	Decl.	Ex.	Rec.	Pay.
0.07Q	4/28/00	5/10/00	5/12/00	6/01/00
0.07Q	7/28/00	8/09/00	8/11/00	9/01/00
0.07Q	10/27/00	11/08/00	11/10/00	12/01/00
0.07Q	1/31/01	2/07/01	2/08/01	3/01/01
0.07Q	4/27/01	5/09/01	5/11/01	6/01/01

Indicated div.: $0.28 (Div. Reinv. Plan)

CAPITALIZATION (12/31/00):

	($000)	(%)
Long-Term Debt	20,136	7.3
Deferred Income Tax	17,852	6.5
Minority Interest	3,455	1.3
Common & Surplus	234,650	85.0
Total	276,093	100.0

RECENT DEVELOPMENTS: For the year ended 12/31/00, net income decreased 26.0% to $33.6 million compared with $45.4 million in the prior year. Results for 1999 included a gain on the sale of mineral rights of $11.8 million. Net sales totaled $795.7 million, an increase of 7.5% versus $740.2 million a year earlier. Total consumer business sales climbed 8.0% to $634.1 million from $586.9 million in 1999. Total specialty products sales grew 3.8% to $186.6 million from $179.7 million the year before.

PROSPECTS: On 5/21/01, CHD acquired USA Detergents, its partner in the ARMUS LLC joint venture, in an all-cash transaction valued at $120.0 million, including the assumption of debt. CHD expects the acquisition to increase its laundry products sales to $400 million a year and contribute significantly to 2002 earnings. On 5/8/01, CHD signed a definitive agreement to acquire the consumer products business of Carter-Wallace, Inc. in a partnership with private equity group, Kelso & Company, for a total price of $739.0 million, including the assumption of debt.

BUSINESS

CHURCH & DWIGHT COMPANY, INC. is the world's leading producer of sodium bicarbonate, popularly known as baking soda. The Company sells its products, primarily under the ARM & HAMMER trademark, to consumers through supermarkets, drug stores and mass merchandisers and to industrial customers and distributors. CHD operates two business divisions. Consumer Products (77% of 2000 sales) produces ARM & HAMMER products such as baking soda, carpet and room deodorizers, dental care products and laundry products. Specialty Products (23%) produces sodium bicarbonate and related products for the food, pharmaceuticals, animal feed and industrial markets. On 12/2/99, CHD acquired CLEAN SHOWER® and SCRUB FREE®.

ANNUAL FINANCIAL DATA

	12/31/00	12/31/99	12/31/98	12/31/97	12/31/96	12/31/95	12/31/94
Earnings Per Share	**0.84**	**[2] 1.11**	**0.76**	**0.62**	**0.55**	**[1] 0.26**	**[1] 0.16**
Cash Flow Per Share	**1.43**	**1.57**	**1.17**	**0.97**	**0.89**	**0.60**	**0.45**
Tang. Book Val. Per Share	**3.93**	**3.59**	**4.39**	**4.61**	**4.25**	**3.84**	**3.94**
Dividends Per Share	**0.28**	**0.26**	**0.24**	**0.23**	**0.22**	**0.22**	**0.22**
Dividend Payout %	**33.3**	**23.4**	**31.8**	**37.4**	**40.4**	**84.6**	**141.8**
INCOME STATEMENT (IN THOUSANDS):							
Total Revenues	795,725	730,036	684,393	574,906	527,771	485,759	491,048
Costs & Expenses	720,110	643,100	625,397	530,192	486,884	464,252	477,831
Depreciation & Amort.	23,454	19,256	16,503	14,158	13,624	13,138	11,743
Operating Income	52,161	67,680	42,493	30,556	27,263	8,369	1,474
Net Interest Inc./(Exp.)	d2,824	d1,544	d1,305	754	1,192	d6	d235
Income Before Income Taxes	52,161	72,703	46,186	38,687	33,171	16,292	9,732
Income Taxes	18,315	26,821	15,897	14,181	11,943	6,140	3,615
Equity Earnings/Minority Int.	2,724	5,841	5,276	6,057	5,140	7,389	7,874
Net Income	33,559	[2] 45,357	30,289	24,506	21,228	[1] 10,152	[1] 6,117
Cash Flow	57,013	64,613	46,792	38,664	34,852	23,290	17,860
Average Shs. Outstg.	39,933	41,043	40,050	39,942	39,068	39,134	39,412
BALANCE SHEET (IN THOUSANDS):							
Cash & Cash Equivalents	24,563	23,765	18,231	18,942	27,913	16,382	7,635
Total Current Assets	162,527	175,783	166,808	149,443	135,519	119,175	124,312
Net Property	168,570	182,219	161,712	142,343	138,371	144,339	138,460
Total Assets	455,632	476,306	391,438	351,014	307,971	293,180	295,587
Total Current Liabilities	149,138	140,608	124,237	126,231	98,754	97,101	99,776
Long-Term Obligations	20,136	58,107	29,630	6,815	7,500	7,500	7,500
Net Stockholders' Equity	234,650	226,733	194,838	179,341	165,312	153,682	153,941
Net Working Capital	13,389	35,175	42,571	23,212	36,765	22,074	24,536
Year-end Shs. Outstg.	38,378	39,856	38,622	38,874	38,904	39,050	39,054
STATISTICAL RECORD:							
Operating Profit Margin %	6.6	9.3	6.2	5.3	5.2	1.7	0.3
Net Profit Margin %	4.2	6.2	4.4	4.3	4.0	2.1	1.2
Return on Equity %	14.3	20.0	15.5	13.7	12.8	6.6	4.0
Return on Assets %	7.4	9.5	7.7	7.0	6.9	3.5	2.1
Debt/Total Assets %	4.4	12.2	7.6	1.9	2.4	2.6	2.5
Price Range	27.75-14.69	30.19-16.50	18.00-13.28	16.38-10.81	11.63-8.75	12.44-8.50	14.63-8.31
P/E Ratio	33.0-17.5	27.2-14.9	23.8-17.6	26.6-17.6	21.3-16.1	47.8-32.7	94.3-53.6
Average Yield %	1.3	1.1	1.5	1.7	2.2	2.1	1.9

Statistics are as originally reported. Adj. for 2-for-1 split, 9/99 [1] Incl. non-recurr. chrg. 1995, $4.0 mill.; 1994, $6.5 mill. [2] Incl. pre-tax impairment chrg. of $6.2 mill.

OFFICERS:
D. C. Minton, Chmn.
R. A. Davies III, Pres., C.E.O.
Z. Eiref, V.P., C.F.O.
M. A. Bilawsky, V.P., Gen. Couns., Sec.

PRINCIPAL OFFICE: 469 N. Harrison Street, Princeton, NJ 08543-5297

TELEPHONE NUMBER: (609) 683-5900
FAX: (609) 497-7269
WEB: www.churchdwight.com

NO. OF EMPLOYEES: 1,439

SHAREHOLDERS: 10,000 (approx.)

ANNUAL MEETING: In May

INCORPORATED: DE, 1925

INSTITUTIONAL HOLDINGS:
No. of Institutions: 136
Shares Held: 21,591,558
% Held: 55.6

INDUSTRY: Alkalies and chlorine (SIC: 2812)

TRANSFER AGENT(S): Mellon Investor Services, Ridgefield Park, NJ

NYSE SYMBOL CI
Rec. Pr. 106.70 (4/30/01)

CIGNA CORPORATION

YIELD 1.2%
P/E RATIO 17.5

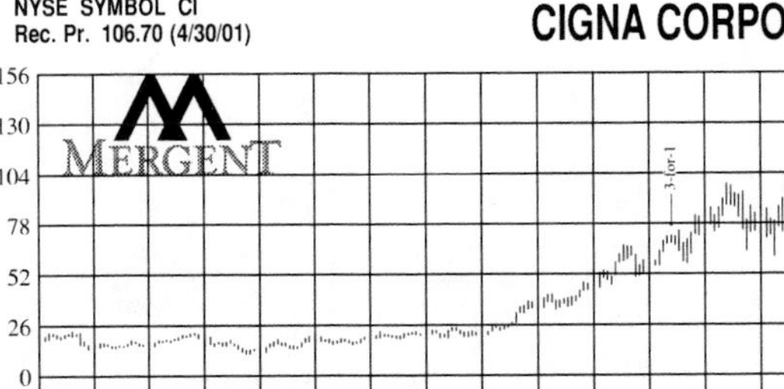

*7 YEAR PRICE SCORE 129.3 *12 MONTH PRICE SCORE 105.6
*NYSE COMPOSITE INDEX=100

INTERIM EARNINGS (Per Share):

Qtr.	Mar.	June	Sept.	Dec.
1996	1.03	1.00	1.23	1.36
1997	1.29	1.24	1.24	1.09
1998	2.27	1.42	1.19	1.14
1999	1.34	1.48	d0.68	1.63
2000	1.60	0.99	1.74	1.76

INTERIM DIVIDENDS (Per Share):

Amt.	Decl.	Ex.	Rec.	Pay.
0.31Q	4/26/00	6/08/00	6/12/00	7/10/00
0.31Q	7/26/00	9/08/00	9/12/00	10/10/00
0.31Q	12/11/00	12/20/00	12/22/00	1/10/01
0.32Q	2/28/01	3/09/01	3/13/01	4/10/01
0.32Q	4/25/01	6/08/01	6/12/01	7/10/01

Indicated div.: $1.28 (Div. Reinv. Plan)

CAPITALIZATION (12/31/00):

	($000)	(%)
Long-Term Debt	1,163,000	17.1
Common & Surplus	5,626,000	82.9
Total	6,789,000	100.0

RECENT DEVELOPMENTS: For the year ended 12/31/00, net income totaled $987.0 million compared with income from continuing operations of $699.0 million in 1999. Results for 1999 included a gain of $66.0 million related to the sale of a partial interest in CI's Japanese life insurance operation. Results also included realized investment gains of $7.0 million and $8.0 million in 2000 and 1999, respectively and net investment income of $2.94 billion and $2.96 billion in 2000 and 1999, respectively. Total revenues increased 6.8% to $20.00 billion.

PROSPECTS: Results should continue to benefit from rate increases and the 7.2% increase in covered lives to 14.3 million at 12/31/00, versus 13.4 million a year earlier. As of 1/1/01, CI substantially exited the Medicare business. Premiums and premium equivalents for 2000 included $905.0 million for Medicare operations. Meanwhile, the international segment is benefiting from solid growth in the life insurance and group benefits business in Japan and certain other Asian countries.

BUSINESS

CIGNA CORPORATION is a provider of health care products and services, group life, accident and disability insurance, retirement products and services and investment management. The Employee Health Care, Life and Disability Benefits segment offers a wide range of traditional indemnity products and services and is a provider of managed care and cost containment products and services to 14.3 million members as of 12/31/00. The Employee Retirement Benefits and Investment Services segment provides investment products and professional services, and had $55.20 billion in assets under management as of 12/31/00. CI's International Life, Health and Employee Benefits segment provides individual and group life, accident and health, health care and employee benefits outside the U.S. Other operations include reinsurance business. On 11/98, CI sold its individual life insurance and annuity business. On 7/2/99, CI sold its property and casualty businesses.

REVENUES

(12/31/2000)	($000)	(%)
Premiums & Fees	16,328,000	81.7
Net Investment Income	2,942,000	14.7
Other Revenues	717,000	3.6
Total	19,994,000	100.0

ANNUAL FINANCIAL DATA

	12/31/00	12/31/99	12/31/98	12/31/97	12/31/96	12/31/95	12/31/94
Earnings Per Share	**6.08**	1 2 **8.99**	**6.05**	**4.88**	**4.62**	**0.95**	**2.55**
Tang. Book Val. Per Share	**24.66**	**25.69**	**32.21**	**28.46**	**27.66**	**27.96**	**21.51**
Dividends Per Share	**1.23**	**1.19**	**1.14**	**1.10**	**1.05**	**1.01**	**1.01**
Dividend Payout %	**20.2**	**13.2**	**18.8**	**22.5**	**22.8**	**106.3**	**39.7**
INCOME STATEMENT (IN MILLIONS):							
Total Premium Income	16,328.0	15,079.0	16,413.0	14,935.0	13,916.0	13,914.0	13,912.0
Other Income	3,666.0	3,702.0	5,024.0	5,103.0	5,034.0	5,041.0	4,480.0
Total Revenues	19,994.0	18,781.0	21,437.0	20,038.0	18,950.0	18,955.0	18,392.0
Policyholder Benefits	13,487.0	12,522.0	13,861.0	13,029.0	12,473.0	13,855.0	12,926.0
Income Before Income Taxes	1,497.0	1,219.0	2,010.0	1,650.0	1,601.0	251.0	805.0
Income Taxes	510.0	520.0	718.0	564.0	545.0	40.0	251.0
Net Income	987.0	1 2 699.0	1,292.0	1,086.0	1,056.0	211.0	554.0
Average Shs. Outstg. (000)	159,810	197,248	213,447	223,000	222,000	222,000	216,000
BALANCE SHEET (IN MILLIONS):							
Cash & Cash Equivalents	2,372.0	3,182.0	3,336.0	2,837.0	2,607.0	2,672.0	2,546.0
Premiums Due	11,241.0	10,399.0	19,255.0	12,806.0	13,514.0	13,254.0	13,736.0
Invst. Assets: Fixed-term	24,776.0	22,944.0	32,634.0	36,358.0	34,933.0	36,241.0	30,817.0
Invst. Assets: Equities	569.0	585.0	1,043.0	854.0	701.0	661.0	1,806.0
Invst. Assets: Loans	12,755.0	12,816.0	15,784.0	18,112.0	18,223.0	18,117.0	15,325.0
Invst. Assets: Total	39,808.0	38,295.0	50,707.0	56,578.0	56,534.0	57,710.0	50,919.0
Total Assets	95,088.0	95,333.0	114,612.0	108,199.0	98,932.0	95,903.0	86,102.0
Long-Term Obligations	1,163.0	1,359.0	1,431.0	1,465.0	1,021.0	1,066.0	1,389.0
Net Stockholders' Equity	5,626.0	6,315.0	9,119.0	8,690.0	7,208.0	7,157.0	5,811.0
Year-end Shs. Outstg. (000)	152,005	169,697	205,650	216,000	222,000	216,000	216,000
STATISTICAL RECORD:							
Return on Revenues %	4.9	3.7	6.0	5.4	5.6	1.1	3.0
Return on Equity %	17.5	11.1	14.2	12.5	14.7	2.9	9.5
Return on Assets %	1.0	0.7	1.1	1.0	1.1	0.2	0.6
Price Range	136.75-60.75	98.63-63.44	82.38-56.00	66.92-44.71	47.79-33.58	38.33-20.75	24.67-19.00
P/E Ratio	22.5-10.0	11.0-7.1	13.6-9.3	13.7-9.2	10.4-7.3	40.2-21.8	9.7-7.4
Average Yield %	1.2	1.5	1.6	2.0	2.6	3.4	4.6

Statistics are as originally reported. Adj. for stk. split: 3-for-1, 5/98 1 Bef. acctg. change chrg. $91.0 mill. 2 Bef. disc. oper. gain $1.17 bill.

OFFICERS:
H. E. Hanway, Chmn., Pres., C.E.O.
J. G. Stewart, Exec. V.P., C.F.O.
T. J. Wagner, Exec. V.P., Gen. Couns.

INVESTOR CONTACT: Shareholder Services, (215) 761-3516

PRINCIPAL OFFICE: One Liberty Place, 1650 Market Street, Philadelphia, PA 19192-1550

TELEPHONE NUMBER: (215) 761-1000
FAX: (215) 761-5515
WEB: www.cigna.com

NO. OF EMPLOYEES: 43,200 (approx.)

SHAREHOLDERS: 10,947

ANNUAL MEETING: In April

INCORPORATED: DE, Nov., 1981

INSTITUTIONAL HOLDINGS:
No. of Institutions: 483
Shares Held: 129,311,041
% Held: 85.0

INDUSTRY: Fire, marine, and casualty insurance (SIC: 6331)

TRANSFER AGENT(S): First Chicago Trust Company of New York, Jersey City, NJ

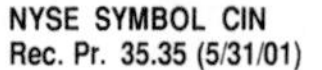

NYSE SYMBOL CIN
Rec. Pr. 35.35 (5/31/01)

CINERGY CORPORATION

YIELD 5.1%
P/E RATIO 14.1

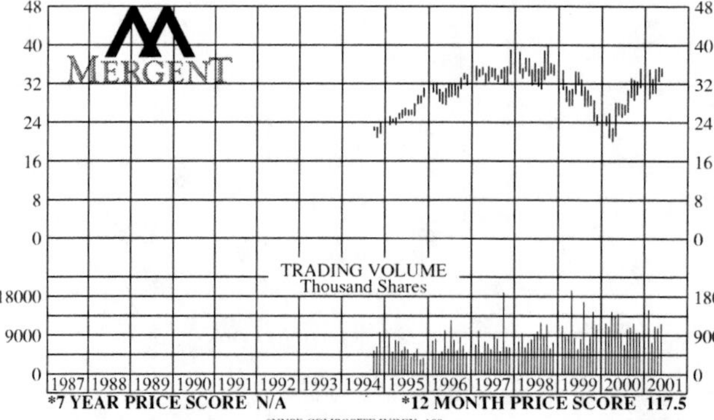

*7 YEAR PRICE SCORE N/A *12 MONTH PRICE SCORE 117.5
*NYSE COMPOSITE INDEX=100

INTERIM EARNINGS (Per Share):

Qtr.	Mar.	June	Sept.	Dec.
1996	0.70	0.35	0.63	0.44
1997	0.72	0.35	0.53	0.70
1998	0.67	d0.16	0.69	0.45
1999	0.80	0.37	0.76	0.60
2000	0.87	0.47	0.58	0.58

INTERIM DIVIDENDS (Per Share):

Amt.	Decl.	Ex.	Rec.	Pay.
0.45Q	4/27/00	5/02/00	5/04/00	5/15/00
0.45Q	7/19/00	7/27/00	7/31/00	8/15/00
0.45Q	10/12/00	10/19/00	10/23/00	11/15/00
0.45Q	1/17/01	1/25/01	1/29/01	2/15/01
0.45Q	5/01/01	5/04/01	5/08/01	5/15/01

Indicated div.: $1.80 (Div. Reinv. Plan)

CAPITALIZATION (12/31/00):

	($000)	(%)
Long-Term Debt	2,876,367	41.6
Deferred Income Tax	1,185,968	17.2
Redeemable Pfd. Stock	62,834	0.9
Common & Surplus	2,788,961	40.3
Total	6,914,130	100.0

RECENT DEVELOPMENTS: For the year ended 12/31/00, net income slipped 1.0% to $399.5 million compared with $403.6 million the year before. Results for 2000 included nonrecurring items that resulted in a one-time charge of $0.11 per share. The 1999 results included a pre-tax gain of $99.3 million. Operating revenues amounted to $8.42 billion, an increase of 41.8% versus $5.94 billion in the previous year. Electric operating revenues advanced 24.8% to $5.38 billion, while gas operating revenues jumped 84.3% to $2.94 billion.

PROSPECTS: On 2/5/01, CIN reorganized under a new corporate structure with three business units. The Energy Merchant unit includes power plant development, power production and CIN's combined heat and process steam operations. The regulated businesses unit operates gas and electric transmission and distribution services and is responsible for regulatory business planning. The Power Technology and Infrastructure Services unit manages a portfolio of strategic investments and the outsourcing of services to improve energy systems.

BUSINESS

CINERGY CORPORATION is the parent company of the Cincinnati Gas and Electric Company and PSI Energy, Inc. CIN provides electricity, natural gas, and other energy services through three business units: the Energy Merchant unit, the Regulated Business unit and the Power Technology and Infrastructure Services unit. The Company provides electric and gas service in Southwestern Ohio and adjacent areas in Kentucky and Indiana. CIN is one of the largest non-nuclear electric generating companies in the United States. As of 4/26/01, the Company had 16,500 megawatts of owned capacity and served approximately 1.5 million electric customers and 500,000 gas customers in Indiana, Ohio and Kentucky. Operating revenue breakdown in 2000 was: 63.9% electric, 34.9% gas and 1.1% other. In January 2000, Vestar was formed as a new subsidiary.

REVENUES

(12/31/00)	($000)	(%)
Electric	5,384	63.9
Gas	2,942	35.0
Other	96	1.1
Total	8,422	100.0

ANNUAL FINANCIAL DATA

	12/31/00	12/31/99	12/31/98	12/31/97	12/31/96	12/31/95	12/31/94
Earnings Per Share	**[4] 2.50**	**[3] 2.53**	**1.65**	**[2] 1.59**	**[1] 2.12**	**2.22**	**1.30**
Cash Flow Per Share	**4.83**	**4.77**	**3.69**	**4.51**	**4.00**	**4.14**	**3.43**
Tang. Book Val. Per Share	**17.54**	**16.70**	**16.02**	**16.10**	**16.39**	**16.17**	**15.56**
Dividends Per Share	**1.80**	**1.80**	**1.80**	**1.80**	**1.74**	**1.72**	**0.10**
Dividend Payout %	**72.0**	**71.1**	**109.1**	**113.2**	**82.1**	**77.5**	**7.9**
INCOME STATEMENT (IN MILLIONS):							
Total Revenues	8,422.0	5,937.9	5,876.3	4,352.8	3,242.7	3,023.4	2,924.2
Costs & Expenses	7,186.4	4,890.8	4,984.4	3,348.7	2,207.8	1,974.8	1,988.3
Depreciation & Amort.	374.0	353.8	325.5	289.1	282.8	279.8	294.4
Maintenance Exp.	...	...	...	176.5	193.9	182.2	201.0
Operating Income	861.6	693.2	566.4	538.6	558.3	586.7	440.5
Net Interest Inc./(Exp.)	d224.5	d234.8	d243.6	d176.4	d184.4	d205.8	d206.9
Income Taxes	251.6	208.7	117.2	cr35.9	cr19.5	cr7.4	cr10.6
Equity Earnings/Minority Int.	5.0	157.3	51.5	60.4	25.4	...	...
Net Income	[4] 399.5	[3] 403.6	261.0	[2] 422.6	[1] 366.0	368.0	211.5
Cash Flow	773.4	757.5	586.5	711.7	630.3	647.8	505.9
Average Shs. Outstg. (000)	160,000	158,863	159,000	157,685	157,678	156,620	147,426
BALANCE SHEET (IN MILLIONS):							
Gross Property	11,186.0	10,677.3	10,384.7	10,097.4	9,881.5	9,617.3	9,362.7
Accumulated Depreciation	4,555.6	4,259.9	4,040.2	3,800.3	3,591.9	3,367.4	3,163.8
Net Property	6,630.4	6,417.5	6,344.4	6,297.1	6,289.6	6,249.9	6,198.9
Total Assets	12,329.7	9,616.9	10,298.8	8,858.2	8,848.5	8,220.1	8,149.8
Long-Term Obligations	2,876.4	2,989.2	2,604.5	2,150.9	2,535.0	2,530.8	2,715.3
Net Stockholders' Equity	2,789.0	2,653.7	2,541.2	2,539.2	2,584.5	2,548.8	2,414.3
Year-end Shs. Outstg. (000)	158,968	158,923	158,664	157,745	157,679	157,670	155,198
STATISTICAL RECORD:							
Operating Profit Margin %	10.2	11.7	9.6	12.4	17.2	19.4	15.1
Net Profit Margin %	4.7	6.8	4.4	9.7	11.3	12.2	7.2
Net Inc./Net Property %	6.0	6.3	4.1	6.7	5.8	5.9	3.4
Net Inc./Tot. Capital %	5.8	5.8	4.1	6.9	5.7	5.6	3.2
Return on Equity %	14.3	15.2	10.3	16.6	14.2	14.4	8.8
Accum. Depr./Gross Prop. %	40.7	39.9	38.9	37.6	36.3	35.0	33.8
Price Range	35.25-20.00	34.88-23.44	39.88-30.81	39.13-32.00	34.25-27.50	31.13-23.38	24.00-20.75
P/E Ratio	14.1-8.0	13.8-9.3	24.2-18.7	24.6-20.1	16.2-13.0	14.0-10.5	18.5-16.0
Average Yield %	6.5	6.2	5.1	5.1	5.6	6.3	0.5

Statistics are as originally reported. [1] Incl. non-recurr. chrg. 1993, $233.0 mill.; 1996, $0.24/sh. [2] Bef. extraord. chrg. $109.4 mill. ($0.69/sh.) [3] Incl. pre-tax $99.3 gain on sale of assets. [4] Incl. one-time chrg. of $0.11 per share.

OFFICERS:
J. E. Rogers, Chmn., Pres., C.E.O.
R. F. Duncan, Exec. V.P., C.F.O.
L. Gamblin, V.P., Treas.
INVESTOR CONTACT: Steve Schrader, Investor Relations, (513) 287-1083
PRINCIPAL OFFICE: 139 E. Fourth St., Cincinnati, OH 45202

TELEPHONE NUMBER: (513) 287-1099
FAX: (513) 287-2875
WEB: www.cinergy.com
NO. OF EMPLOYEES: 8,362
SHAREHOLDERS: 61,049
ANNUAL MEETING: In May
INCORPORATED: DE, Oct., 1994

INSTITUTIONAL HOLDINGS:
No. of Institutions: 282
Shares Held: 115,360,723
% Held: 72.6

INDUSTRY: Electric and other services combined (SIC: 4931)

TRANSFER AGENT(S): The Company

NYSE SYMBOL CC
Rec. Pr. 15.01 (5/31/01)

CIRCUIT CITY GROUP

YIELD 0.5%
P/E RATIO 20.8

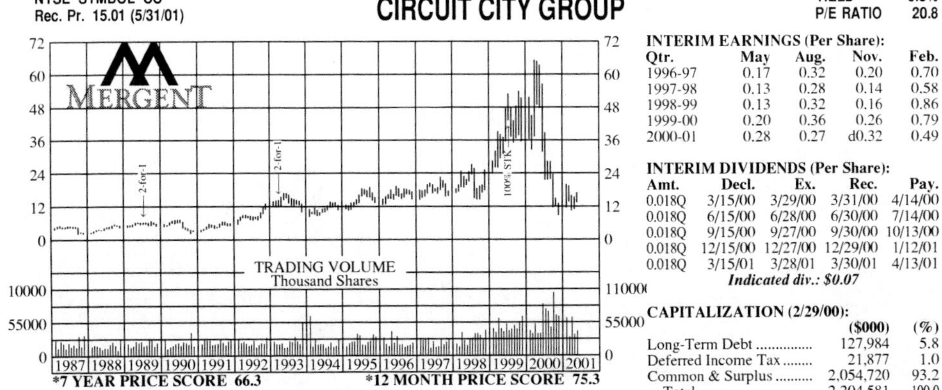

*7 YEAR PRICE SCORE 66.3 *12 MONTH PRICE SCORE 75.3

*NYSE COMPOSITE INDEX=100

INTERIM EARNINGS (Per Share):

Qtr.	May	Aug.	Nov.	Feb.
1996-97	0.17	0.32	0.20	0.70
1997-98	0.13	0.28	0.14	0.58
1998-99	0.13	0.32	0.16	0.86
1999-00	0.20	0.36	0.26	0.79
2000-01	0.28	0.27	d0.32	0.49

INTERIM DIVIDENDS (Per Share):

Amt.	Decl.	Ex.	Rec.	Pay.
0.018Q	3/15/00	3/29/00	3/31/00	4/14/00
0.018Q	6/15/00	6/28/00	6/30/00	7/14/00
0.018Q	9/15/00	9/27/00	9/30/00	10/13/00
0.018Q	12/15/00	12/27/00	12/29/00	1/12/01
0.018Q	3/15/01	3/28/01	3/30/01	4/13/01

Indicated div.: $0.07

CAPITALIZATION (2/29/00):

	($000)	(%)
Long-Term Debt	127,984	5.8
Deferred Income Tax	21,877	1.0
Common & Surplus	2,054,720	93.2
Total	2,204,581	100.0

RECENT DEVELOPMENTS: For the year ended 2/28/01, net earnings totaled $149.2 million compared with earnings from continuing operations of $327.6 million the year before. Results in the recent period included one-time pre-tax charges totaling $30.0 million related to CC's exit from the appliance business. Net sales and operating revenues slipped 1.3% to $10.46 billion from $10.60 billion a year earlier. Comparable-store sales were down 4.0%, due primarily to the Company's exit from the appliance business, which was completed during the third quarter.

PROSPECTS: The Company plans to implement a new store remodeling format that should help eliminate costly changes that have little impact on sales and can be completed within 60 days. CC expects to remodel 20 to 25 stores to reflect this new format, rather than the 140 initially anticipated, relocate 10 to 15 stores and open between 15 and 20 new stores in the fiscal year that began on 3/1/01. New and expanded merchandise selections should more than offset the sales lost by the Company's exit from the appliance business.

BUSINESS

CIRCUIT CITY GROUP was formed on 2/4/97 by the redesignation of Circuit City Stores, Inc. common stock and an initial public offering of CarMax Group (NYSE: KMX) common stock. CC is a specialty retailer of brand-name electronic equipment and consumer appliances including VCRs, cameras, stereo systems, compact disc players, and telephones. As of 4/2/01, CC operates 593 Circuit City Superstores and 34 mall-based Circuit City Express Stores throughout the U.S. The Company holds a 74.7% interest in CarMax Group, which operates 40 used car superstores and 21 new car franchises.

ANNUAL FINANCIAL DATA

	2/29/00	2/28/99	2/28/98	2/28/97	2/29/96
Earnings Per Share	**1 1.60**	**1.48**	**1.13**	**1.40**	**1.86**
Cash Flow Per Share	**2.25**	**2.78**	**2.26**	**2.40**	**2.68**
Tang. Book Val. Per Share	**10.08**	**18.05**	**16.60**	**15.55**	**...**
Dividends Per Share	**0.07**	**0.07**	**0.07**	**0.07**	**0.06**
Dividend Payout %	**4.4**	**4.7**	**6.2**	**4.6**	**3.0**
INCOME STATEMENT (IN MILLIONS):					
Total Revenues	10,599.4	9,338.1	7,996.6	7,153.6	6,753.3
Costs & Expenses	9,925.7	8,916.9	7,635.4	6,796.8	6,357.0
Depreciation & Amort.	132.9	130.3	111.7	97.3	79.0
Operating Income	540.8	291.0	249.4	259.5	317.3
Net Interest Inc./(Exp.)	d13.8	d21.9	d25.1	d23.5	d21.3
Income Before Income Taxes	527.0	269.1	224.3	236.0	295.9
Income Taxes	200.2	102.6	85.8	90.2	111.3
Equity Earnings/Minority Int.	0.9	d18.1	d26.5	d9.1	d5.2
Net Income	1 327.6	148.4	112.1	136.7	179.4
Cash Flow	460.5	278.7	223.8	234.0	258.4
Average Shs. Outstg. (000)	204,321	100,406	99,204	97,311	96,573
BALANCE SHEET (IN MILLIONS):					
Cash & Cash Equivalents	634.0	248.2	90.2	32.2	...
Total Current Assets	2,516.9	2,053.4	1,913.7	1,880.4	...
Net Property	753.3	801.8	834.3	793.9	...
Total Assets	3,537.4	3,134.8	3,061.6	3,008.3	...
Total Current Liabilities	1,210.0	881.9	850.3	854.4	...
Long-Term Obligations	128.0	286.9	396.9	430.3	...
Net Stockholders' Equity	2,054.7	1,825.5	1,648.3	1,526.7	...
Net Working Capital	1,306.9	1,171.5	1,063.5	1,026.0	...
Year-end Shs. Outstg. (000)	203,868	101,160	99,282	98,178	...
STATISTICAL RECORD:					
Operating Profit Margin %	5.1	3.1	3.1	3.6	4.7
Net Profit Margin %	3.1	1.6	1.4	1.9	2.7
Return on Equity %	15.9	8.1	6.8	9.0	...
Return on Assets %	9.3	4.7	3.7	4.5	...
Debt/Total Assets %	3.6	9.2	13.0	14.3	...
Price Range	53.88-23.69	27.25-14.41	22.75-14.31	19.38-12.50	19.00-10.50
P/E Ratio	33.7-14.8	18.4-9.7	20.1-12.7	13.8-8.9	10.2-5.6
Average Yield %	0.2	0.3	0.4	0.4	0.4

Statistics are as originally reported. Adj. for 2-for-1 stk. split, 7/99. 1 Bef. loss from disc. Digital Video Express ops. $130.2 mil ($0.64/sh).

OFFICERS:
R. L. Sharp, Chmn., C.E.O.
W. A. McCollough, Pres., C.O.O.
M. T. Chalifoux, Exec. V.P., C.F.O., Sec.

INVESTOR CONTACT: Ann M. Collier, V.P. Fin. & Pub. Rel., (804) 527-4058

PRINCIPAL OFFICE: 9950 Mayland Drive, Richmond, VA 23233

TELEPHONE NUMBER: (804) 527-4000
FAX: (804) 527-4164
WEB: www.circuitcity.com

NO. OF EMPLOYEES: 53,284 (avg.)

SHAREHOLDERS: 8,308

ANNUAL MEETING: In June

INCORPORATED: VA, Sept., 1949

INSTITUTIONAL HOLDINGS:
No. of Institutions: 269
Shares Held: 147,874,146
% Held: 71.9

INDUSTRY: Radio, TV, & electronic stores (SIC: 5731)

TRANSFER AGENT(S): Wells Fargo Shareowner Services, South St. Paul, MN

NYSE SYMBOL CIT
Rec. Pr. 36.70 (4/30/01)

CIT GROUP, INC.

YIELD 1.1%
P/E RATIO 15.7

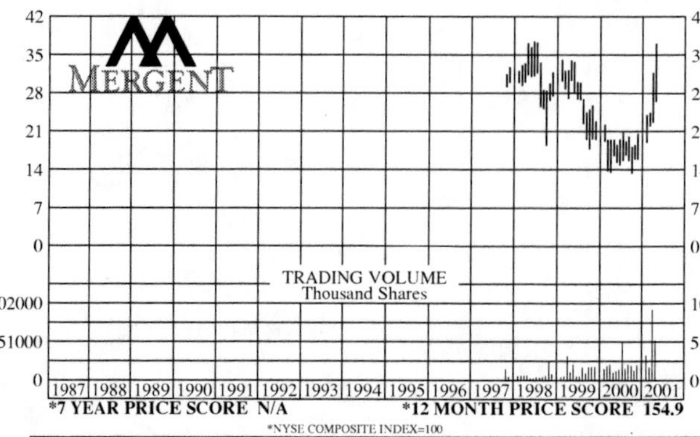

*7 YEAR PRICE SCORE N/A *12 MONTH PRICE SCORE 154.9

*NYSE COMPOSITE INDEX=100

INTERIM EARNINGS (Per Share):

Qtr.	Mar.	June	Sept.	Dec.
1997	0.44	0.59	0.48	0.44
1998	0.50	0.51	0.53	0.54
1999	0.57	0.59	0.60	0.49
2000	0.55	0.58	0.60	0.61

INTERIM DIVIDENDS (Per Share):

Amt.	Decl.	Ex.	Rec.	Pay.
0.10Q	4/27/00	5/08/00	5/10/00	5/31/00
0.10Q	7/27/00	8/08/00	8/10/00	8/31/00
0.10Q	10/26/00	11/08/00	11/10/00	11/30/00
0.10Q	1/25/01	2/05/01	2/07/01	2/28/01
0.10Q	4/26/01	5/07/01	5/09/01	5/31/01

Indicated div.: $0.40 (Div. Reinv. Plan)

CAPITALIZATION (12/31/00):

	($000)	(%)
Long-Term Debt	37,965,100	84.6
Deferred Income Tax	646,800	1.4
Redeemable Pfd. Stock	250,000	0.6
Common & Surplus	6,007,200	13.4
Total	44,869,100	100.0

RECENT DEVELOPMENTS: For the year ended 12/31/00, net income increased 57.1% to $611.6 million compared with $389.4 million in the previous year. Net finance income more than doubled to $2.75 billion from $1.27 billion the year before. Finance income soared to $5.25 billion from $2.57 billion in 1999. Interest expenses jumped 93.1% to $2.50 billion compared with $1.30 billion the year before. Operating revenue surged to $2.38 billion versus $1.27 billion a year earlier.

PROSPECTS: On 3/13/01, the Company and Tyco International Ltd. announced that they have entered into a definitive agreement under which Tyco will acquire CIT in a tax-free stock-for-stock exchange. Under the terms of the agreement, CIT shareholders will receive 0.6907 Tyco shares for each share of CIT. The transaction is valued at $35.02 per CIT share, for an aggregate value of approximately $9.20 billion. The transaction is expected to close on 6/1/01.

BUSINESS

CIT GROUP, INC. is a diversified finance organization with $54.90 billion in managed assets as of 12/31/00. CIT provides secured commercial and consumer financing primarily in the United States to smaller, middle-market and larger businesses and to individuals through a nationwide distribution network. CIT operates three segments: Equipment Financing and Leasing, Commercial Finance and Consumer. Each segment operates through strategic business units, which market products and services to satisfy the financing needs of specific customers, industries and markets. At 12/31/00, the Equipment Financing and Leasing segment represented 52.04% of total financing and leasing assets, Vendor Technology Finance 21.05%, Commercial Finance 19.93% and Structured Finance 6.98%. Dai-Ichi Kangyo Bank owns a 44% stake in CIT.

ANNUAL FINANCIAL DATA

	12/31/00	[2] 12/31/99	12/31/98	12/31/97	12/31/96	12/31/95	12/31/94
Earnings Per Share	**2.33**	**2.22**	**2.08**	**[1] 1.95**	...	...	...
Cash Flow Per Share	**7.69**	**4.52**	**3.28**	**3.01**	...	...	...
Tang. Book Val. Per Share	**16.15**	**15.46**	**16.66**	**14.91**	...	...	...
Dividends Per Share	**0.40**	**0.40**	**0.30**	...	...	...	...
Dividend Payout %	**17.2**	**18.0**	**14.4**	...	...	...	...
INCOME STATEMENT (IN MILLIONS):							
Total Revenues	6,160.4	2,916.7	2,270.5	2,130.5	1,890.3	1,713.9	1,438.2
Costs & Expenses	3,747.0	1,897.7	1,531.6	1,457.5	1,334.2	1,260.1	1,037.8
Depreciation & Amort.	1,408.7	402.8	195.9	168.6	140.3	88.7	75.4
Operating Income	1,004.7	616.2	543.0	504.4	415.8	365.1	325.1
Income Before Income Taxes	1,004.7	616.2	543.0	504.4	415.8	365.1	325.1
Income Taxes	373.9	207.6	185.0	178.0	155.7	139.8	123.9
Equity Earnings/Minority Int.	d19.2	d19.2	d19.2	d16.3	...	...	...
Net Income	611.6	389.4	338.8	[1] 310.1	260.1	225.3	201.1
Cash Flow	2,020.3	792.2	534.7	478.7	400.4	314.0	276.5
Average Shs. Outstg. (000)	262,697	175,161	163,189	159,154	...	...	...
BALANCE SHEET (IN MILLIONS):							
Cash & Cash Equivalents	812.1	1,073.4	73.6	140.4	103.1	161.5	6.6
Total Current Assets	812.1	1,073.4	73.6	140.4	103.1	161.5	6.6
Net Property	7,190.6	6,125.9	2,774.1	1,905.6	1,402.1	1,113.0	867.9
Total Assets	48,689.8	45,081.1	24,303.1	20,464.1	18,932.5	17,420.3	15,963.5
Total Current Liabilities	3,820.7	3,392.4	1,996.4	1,862.7	1,728.1	1,466.8	1,348.1
Long-Term Obligations	37,965.1	35,373.5	18,651.4	15,314.9	14,605.7	13,570.1	12,395.8
Net Stockholders' Equity	6,007.2	5,554.4	2,701.6	2,432.9	2,075.4	1,914.2	1,793.0
Net Working Capital	d3,008.6	d2,319.0	d1,922.8	d1,722.3	d1,625.0	d1,305.3	d1,341.5
Year-end Shs. Outstg. (000)	250,260	239,540	162,176	163,174	1	1	1
STATISTICAL RECORD:							
Operating Profit Margin %	16.3	21.1	23.9	23.7	22.0	21.3	22.6
Net Profit Margin %	9.9	13.4	14.9	14.6	13.8	13.1	14.0
Return on Equity %	10.2	7.0	12.5	12.7	12.5	11.8	11.2
Return on Assets %	1.3	0.9	1.4	1.5	1.4	1.3	1.3
Debt/Total Assets %	78.0	78.5	76.7	74.8	77.1	77.9	77.7
Price Range	22.25-13.31	34.19-17.69	37.50-18.38	32.81-29.13	...	...	...
P/E Ratio	9.5-5.7	15.4-8.0	18.0-8.8	16.8-14.9	...	...	...
Average Yield %	2.2	1.5	1.1	...	...	...	...

Statistics are as originally reported. [1] Incl. gain of $58.0 mill. from sale on eqty. int. acquired. [2] Incl. ops. of Newcourt Credit Group Inc.

OFFICERS:
A. R. Gamper Jr., Chmn., Pres., C.E.O.
J. M. Leone, Exec. V.P., C.F.O.

INVESTOR CONTACT: James J. Egan, Exec. V.P., Inv. Rel., (973) 535-5911

PRINCIPAL OFFICE: 1211 Avenue of the Americas, New York, NY 10036

TELEPHONE NUMBER: (212) 536-1390
WEB: www.citgroup.com

NO. OF EMPLOYEES: 7,355 (approx.)

SHAREHOLDERS: 19,984

ANNUAL MEETING: In May

INCORPORATED: DE, Aug., 1979

INSTITUTIONAL HOLDINGS:
No. of Institutions: 226
Shares Held: 148,346,861
% Held: 56.6

INDUSTRY: Short-term business credit (SIC: 6153)

TRANSFER AGENT(S): The Bank of New York , New York, NY

NYSE SYMBOL C
Rec. Pr. 51.25 (5/31/01)

CITIGROUP INC.

YIELD 1.1%
P/E RATIO 19.3

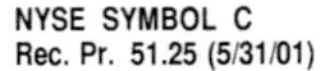

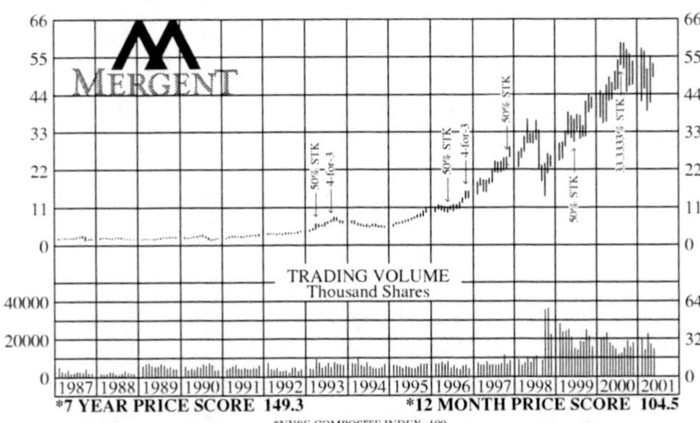

INTERIM EARNINGS (Per Share):

Qtr.	Mar.	June	Sept.	Dec.
1996	0.26	0.29	0.29	0.32
1997	0.34	0.37	0.43	0.15
1998	0.46	0.47	0.11	0.14
1999	0.52	0.53	0.53	0.56
2000	0.78	0.65	0.67	0.55

INTERIM DIVIDENDS (Per Share):

Amt.	Decl.	Ex.	Rec.	Pay.
33.333% STK	7/19/00	8/28/00	8/07/00	8/25/00
0.14Q	7/19/00	8/03/00	8/07/00	8/25/00
0.14Q	10/17/00	11/02/00	11/06/00	11/22/00
0.14Q	1/16/01	2/01/01	2/05/01	2/23/01
0.14Q	4/17/01	5/03/01	5/07/01	5/25/01

Indicated div.: $0.56 (Div. Reinv. Plan)

CAPITALIZATION (12/31/00):

	($000)	(%)
Long-Term Debt	111,778,000	61.1
Redeemable Pfd. Stock	4,920,000	2.7
Preferred Stock	1,745,000	1.0
Common & Surplus	64,461,000	35.2
Total	182,904,000	100.0

RECENT DEVELOPMENTS: For the year ended 12/31/00, net income advanced 18.9% to $13.52 billion from $11.37 billion in 1999. Results included after-tax non-recurring charges of $621.0 million in 2000. Global consumer segment earnings increased 21.8% to $5.29 billion, while global corporate and investment bank earnings rose 27.5% to $6.37 billion. Revenues grew 18.6% to $111.83 billion.

PROSPECTS: Going forward, the Company will focus on tailoring its investment, insurance and consumer finance products to the needs of the emerging middle class around the world. On 5/17/01, the Company agreed to acquire Grupo Financiero Banamex-Accival, Mexico's second-largest financial group, for approximately $12.50 billion. The acquisition is expected to close in the fourth quarter of 2001.

BUSINESS

CITIGROUP INC., (formerly Travelers Group Inc.) was formed on 10/8/98 by the merger of Travelers and Citicorp. The Company consists of businesses that produce a broad range of financial services -- asset management, banking and consumer finance, credit and charge cards, insurance, investments, investment banking and trading -- and use diverse channels to make them available to consumer and corporate customers around the world. Among its businesses are Citibank, Commercial Credit, Primerica Financial Services, Salomon Smith Barney, Salomon Smith Barney Asset Management, Travelers Life & Annuity, and Travelers Property Casualty. On 1/18/00, the Company acquired Shroders PLC. On 11/30/00, the Company acquired Associates First Capital Corporation.

ANNUAL FINANCIAL DATA

	12/31/00	12/31/99	5 12/31/98	4 12/31/97	12/31/96	12/31/95	3 12/31/94
Earnings Per Share	7 2.62	6 2.15	1 1.22	1 1.27	1 2 1.15	1 2 0.81	1 0.64
Tang. Book Val. Per Share	12.84	10.64	8.94	6.99	4.95	4.74	3.04
Dividends Per Share	0.52	0.41	0.28	0.20	0.15	0.13	0.10
Dividend Payout %	19.8	18.9	22.8	15.7	13.0	16.5	14.9
INCOME STATEMENT (IN MILLIONS):							
Total Premium Income	12,429.0	10,441.0	9,850.0	8,995.0	7,633.0	4,977.0	7,590.0
Net Investment Income	64,939.0	44,900.0	46,239.0	17,618.0	6,712.0	5,474.0	4,667.0
Other Income	34,458.0	26,664.0	20,342.0	10,996.0	7,000.0	6,132.0	6,208.0
Total Revenues	111,826.0	82,005.0	76,431.0	37,609.0	21,345.0	16,583.0	18,465.0
Policyholder Benefits	10,147.0	8,671.0	8,365.0	7,714.0	7,366.0	5,017.0	7,797.0
Income Before Income Taxes	21,143.0	15,948.0	9,269.0	5,012.0	3,398.0	2,521.0	2,149.0
Income Taxes	7,525.0	5,703.0	3,234.0	1,696.0	1,051.0	893.0	823.0
Equity Earnings/Minority Int.	d99.0	d251.0	d228.0	d212.0	d47.0	...	...
Net Income	7 13,519.0	1 6 9,994.0	1 5,807.0	1 3,104.0	1 2 2,300.0	1 2 1,628.0	1 1,326.0
Average Shs. Outstg. (000)	5,122,200	4,591,332	4,630,399	2,359,799	1,916,399	1,904,399	1,931,999
BALANCE SHEET (IN MILLIONS):							
Cash & Cash Equivalents	253,011.0	235,968.0	228,513.0	253,499.0	83,611.0	61,163.0	61,019.0
Premiums Due	36,237.0	32,677.0	30,905.0	30,939.0	22,408.0	16,584.0	17,282.0
Securities Avail. for Sale	132,513.0	109,155.0	119,845.0	139,732.0	56,463.0	39,696.0	34,137.0
Invst. Assets: Loans	367,022.0	244,206.0	221,958.0	10,816.0	8,071.0	7,238.0	6,885.0
Total Assets	902,210.0	716,937.0	668,641.0	386,555.0	151,067.0	114,475.0	115,297.0
Total Deposits	300,586.0	261,091.0	228,649.0	...	...	...	...
Long-Term Obligations	111,778.0	47,092.0	48,671.0	28,352.0	11,327.0	9,190.0	7,075.0
Net Stockholders' Equity	66,206.0	49,686.0	42,708.0	20,893.0	13,085.0	11,710.0	8,640.0
Year-end Shs. Outstg. (000)	5,022,222	4,490,032	4,515,999	2,289,999	1,912,800	1,895,999	1,904,000
STATISTICAL RECORD:							
Return on Revenues %	12.1	12.2	7.6	8.3	10.8	9.8	7.2
Return on Equity %	20.4	20.1	13.6	14.9	17.6	13.9	15.3
Return on Assets %	1.5	1.4	0.9	0.8	1.5	1.4	1.2
Price Range	59.13-35.34	43.69-24.50	36.75-14.25	28.69-14.58	15.83-9.42	10.65-5.40	7.19-5.06
P/E Ratio	22.6-13.5	20.4-11.4	30.2-11.7	22.6-11.5	13.8-8.2	13.1-6.7	11.2-7.9
Average Yield %	1.1	1.2	1.1	0.9	1.2	1.7	1.6

Statistics are as originally reported. Adj. for stk. splits: 33.3% stk. div., 8/25/00; 3-for-2, 5/99; 11/97 & 5/96; 4-for-3, 8/00 & 11/96. 1 Incl. non-recurr. credit 1999, $47.0 mill.; 1998, $795.0 mill.; chrg. 1997, $255.4 mill.; credit 1996, $397.0 mill.; 1995, $117.0 mill. 2 Bef. disc. ops. gain. 1996, $31.0 mill.; 1995, $206.0 mill. 3 Results reflect merger of Primerica & Old Travelers in 12/93. 4 Results reflect the acquisition of Salomon Inc. in 11/97 5 Results prior to fourth quarter of 1998 are for Travelers Group. 6 BEf, acctg. chrg. 1999, $127.0 mill. 7 Incl. restruct. & merger related items of $621.0 mill.

OFFICERS:
S. I. Weill, Chmn., C.E.O.
D. C. Maughan, Vice-Chmn.
W. R. Rhodes, Vice-Chmn.
P. J. Collins, Vice-Chmn.

INVESTOR CONTACT: Leah Johnson, Investor Relations (212) 559-1000

PRINCIPAL OFFICE: 399 Park Avenue, New York, NY 10043

TELEPHONE NUMBER: (212) 559-1000
FAX: (212) 816-8913
WEB: www.citigroup.com

NO. OF EMPLOYEES: 242,000 (approx.)

SHAREHOLDERS: 250,300 (approx.)

ANNUAL MEETING: In April

INCORPORATED: DE, Dec., 1993

INSTITUTIONAL HOLDINGS:
No. of Institutions: 1,231
Shares Held: 3,148,933,194
% Held: 62.7

INDUSTRY: Fire, marine, and casualty insurance (SIC: 6331)

TRANSFER AGENT(S): Citibank Shareholder Services, Jersey City, NJ

NYSE SYMBOL CZN
Rec. Pr. 11.50 (4/30/01)

CITIZENS COMMUNICATIONS CO.

YIELD . . .
P/E RATIO . . .

*7 YEAR PRICE SCORE 97.6 *12 MONTH PRICE SCORE 94.0

*NYSE COMPOSITE INDEX=100

INTERIM EARNINGS (Per Share):

Qtr.	Mar.	June	Sept.	Dec.
1996	0.16	0.18	0.19	0.20
1997	0.13	d0.50	0.09	0.32
1998	0.12	0.06	0.06	0.01
1999	0.21	0.03	0.05	0.26
2000	0.03	0.01	0.01	d0.15

INTERIM DIVIDENDS (Per Share):

Amt.	Decl.	Ex.	Rec.	Pay.
No dividends paid.				

CAPITALIZATION (12/31/00):

	($000)	(%)
Long-Term Debt	3,062,289	57.9
Deferred Income Tax	490,487	9.3
Redeemable Pfd. Stock	20,250	0.4
Common & Surplus	1,720,001	32.5
Total	5,293,027	100.0

RECENT DEVELOPMENTS: For the year ended 12/31/00, CZN posted a loss from continuing operations of $40.1 million versus income of $136.6 million a year earlier. Results for 2000 and 1999 included acquisition assimilation expenses of $39.9 million and $3.9 million, respectively. Revenues rose 12.8% to $1.80 billion. Effective 9/30/00, CZN reclassified its gas segment as an asset held for sale and is no longer including the segment in the results of discontinued operations.

PROSPECTS: Future results should benefit from CZN's sharpened business focus and the pending acquisition of approximately 1.7 million telephone access lines, which is expected to be completed in the second half of 2001. Separately, on 4/23/01, CZN and Atmos Energy Corporation received approval from the Louisiana Public Service Commission for CZN to transfer the assets of Louisiana Gas Service Company and LGS Natural Gas Company to Atmos for a purchase price of $365.0 million. The closing of the transaction is expected by mid 2001.

BUSINESS

CITIZENS COMMUNICATIONS CO. (formerly Citizens Utilities Co.) is a telecommunications company providing wireline communications services primarily to rural areas, small and medium sized cities and towns throughout the U.S. as an incumbent local exchange carrier. In addition, CZN provides competitive local exchange carrier services to business customers and to other communications carriers in the western U.S. through its 85%-owned subsidiary as of 12/31/00, Electric Lightwave Inc. The Company serves 1.4 million access lines 17 states as of 12/31/00. CZN also provides public services including natural gas transmission and distribution, electric transmission and distribution and water distribution and wastewater treatment services to primarily rural and suburban customers throughout the U.S.

REVENUES

(12/31/2000)	($000)	(%)
Local Exchange Carrier	963,743	53.4
Electric Lightwave Inc.	243,977	13.4
Gas	374,751	20.8
Electric	223,072	12.4
Total	1,805,543	100.0

ANNUAL FINANCIAL DATA

	12/31/00	12/31/99	12/31/98	12/31/97	12/31/96	12/31/95	12/31/94
Earnings Per Share	**4 d0.11**	**3 0.45**	**1 0.23**	**2 0.04**	**0.73**	**0.65**	**0.70**
Cash Flow Per Share	**1.15**	**1.89**	**1.22**	**0.94**	**1.60**	**1.34**	**1.26**
Tang. Book Val. Per Share	**4.09**	**7.30**	**6.90**	**6.58**	**6.64**	**6.42**	**5.43**
INCOME STATEMENT (IN MILLIONS):							
Total Revenues	1,802.4	1,087.4	1,542.4	1,393.6	1,306.5	1,069.0	916.0
Costs & Expenses	1,333.0	699.8	1,106.4	1,142.0	817.1	655.9	572.7
Depreciation & Amort.	347.5	379.6	257.8	235.8	193.7	158.9	115.2
Operating Income	121.8	8.1	178.2	15.8	295.7	254.2	228.1
Net Interest Inc./(Exp.)	d187.4	d87.0	d112.2	d109.3	d92.7	d87.8	d72.7
Income Before Income Taxes	d50.0	187.9	87.9	23.7	269.4	226.4	208.3
Income Taxes	cr16.1	64.6	22.3	7.4	84.9	66.8	64.3
Net Income	4 d40.1	117.1	1 3 59.4	2 10.1	184.5	159.5	144.0
Cash Flow	307.5	496.7	317.2	245.9	372.4	318.5	259.2
Average Shs. Outstg. (000)	266,931	262,392	259,621	260,824	233,364	237,095	206,016
BALANCE SHEET (IN MILLIONS):							
Cash & Cash Equivalents	70.1	37.1	31.9	35.2	24.2	17.9	123.0
Total Current Assets	2,262.7	308.6	414.0	377.3	369.8	252.7	314.1
Net Property	3,509.8	d1,569.9	4,048.6	3,667.8	3,138.1	2,908.0	2,569.7
Total Assets	6,955.0	5,771.7	5,292.9	4,872.9	4,523.1	3,918.2	3,576.6
Total Current Liabilities	992.5	467.0	507.7	417.9	409.5	503.7	879.2
Long-Term Obligations	3,062.3	2,107.5	1,900.2	1,706.5	1,509.7	1,187.0	994.2
Net Stockholders' Equity	1,720.0	1,919.9	1,792.8	1,679.2	1,678.2	1,559.9	1,156.9
Net Working Capital	1,270.2	d158.4	d93.7	d40.6	d39.7	d251.0	d565.1
Year-end Shs. Outstg. (000)	265,768	262,925	259,885	255,049	252,835	243,019	213,136
STATISTICAL RECORD:							
Operating Profit Margin %	6.8	0.7	11.6	1.1	22.6	23.8	24.9
Net Profit Margin %	. . .	10.8	3.9	0.7	14.1	14.9	15.7
Return on Equity %	. . .	6.1	3.3	0.6	11.0	10.2	12.4
Return on Assets %	. . .	8.9	1.1	0.2	4.1	4.1	4.0
Debt/Total Assets %	44.0	36.5	35.9	35.0	33.4	30.3	27.8
Price Range	19.00-12.50	14.31-7.25	11.20-6.89	11.72-7.62	11.24-9.46	11.99-9.13	14.43-10.44
P/E Ratio	. . .	31.8-16.1	48.7-29.9	292.3-190.1	7.7-6.5	9.3-7.1	10.3-7.5

Statistics are as originally reported. Adj. for all stk. splits & divs. thru 12/98 1 Bef. acctg. chg. chrg. of $2.3 mill. 2 Incl. non-recurr. pre-tax chrg. of $78.7 mill. 3 Bef. disc. oper. gain of $27.4 mill. 4 Incl. acq. & assimilation exp. of $39.9 mill.; bef. inc. fr. disc. ops. of $11.7 mill. ($0.04/sh.)

OFFICERS:
L. Tow, Chmn., C.E.O.
R. J. Graf, Vice-Chmn., Pres., C.O.O.
S. N. Schneider, Vice-Chmn., Exec. V.P.
INVESTOR CONTACT: Brigid M. Smith, Asst. V.P., Corp. Comm. (203) 614-5042
PRINCIPAL OFFICE: 3 High Ridge Park, Stamford, CT 06905

TELEPHONE NUMBER: (203) 614-5600
FAX: (203) 614-4602
WEB: www.czn.net
NO. OF EMPLOYEES: 7,191 (approx.)
SHAREHOLDERS: 37,753 (approx.)
ANNUAL MEETING: In May
INCORPORATED: DE, Nov., 1935

INSTITUTIONAL HOLDINGS:
No. of Institutions: 216
Shares Held: 134,427,815
% Held: 51.1
INDUSTRY: Telephone communications, exc. radio (SIC: 4813)
TRANSFER AGENT(S): Illinois Stock Transfer Company, Chicago, IL

NYSE SYMBOL CYN
Rec. Pr. 42.63 (5/31/01)

CITY NATIONAL CORPORATION

YIELD 1.7%
P/E RATIO 15.7

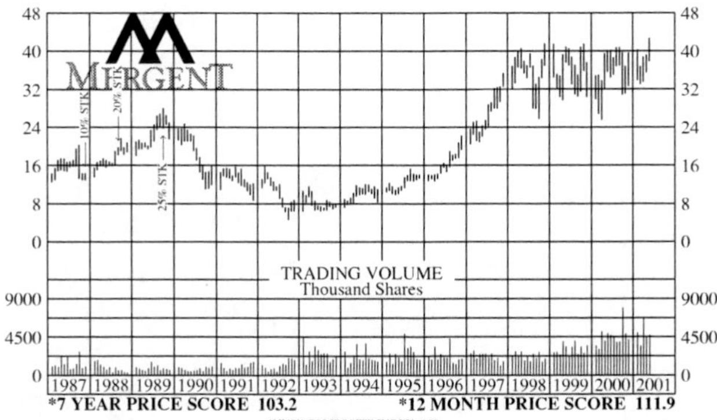

INTERIM EARNINGS (Per Share):

Qtr.	Mar.	June	Sept.	Dec.
1997	0.38	0.41	0.44	0.45
1998	0.46	0.49	0.53	0.52
1999	0.55	0.55	0.60	0.60
2000	0.66	0.68	0.70	0.68

INTERIM DIVIDENDS (Per Share):

Amt.	Decl.	Ex.	Rec.	Pay.
0.175Q	4/27/00	5/08/00	5/10/00	5/22/00
0.175Q	7/27/00	8/07/00	8/09/00	8/21/00
0.175Q	10/26/00	11/06/00	11/08/00	11/20/00
0.185Q	1/25/01	2/05/01	2/07/01	2/20/01
0.185Q	4/25/01	5/07/01	5/09/01	5/21/01

Indicated div.: $0.74

CAPITALIZATION (12/31/00):

	($000)	(%)
Total Deposits	7,408,670	87.3
Long-Term Debt	332,058	3.9
Common & Surplus	743,648	8.8
Total	8,484,376	100.0

RECENT DEVELOPMENTS: For the year ended 12/31/00, net income rose 21.8% to $131.7 million from $108.1 million in 1999. Net interest income grew 26.2% to $406.5 million from $322.0 million a year earlier. Provision for credit losses was $21.5 million compared with none the year before. Total non-interest income rose 25.5% to $109.5 million from $87.2 million in the prior year. Total non-interest expense increased 21.9% to $294.8 million.

PROSPECTS: In 2001, CYN estimates earnings per diluted share growth to be 8.0% to 11.0%, while growth in non-interest income will range from 15.0% to 20.0%. CYN expects non-interest expense to increase 5.0% to 8.0%. Also, CYN anticipates a provision for credit losses of approximately $30.0 million to $45.0 million may be required in 2001, based on CYN's assessment of the credit quality of the portfolio.

BUSINESS

CITY NATIONAL CORPORATION, with assets of $9.10 billion as of 12/31/00, conducts its business through City National Bank. The Bank operates more than 48 banking offices in Los Angeles, Orange, San Diego, Riverside, Ventura, San Bernardino, San Mateo and San Francisco counties, as well as a loan production office in Sacramento. CYN is engaged in one operating segment: providing private and business banking, including investment and trust services. The Bank offers a broad range of loans, deposit, cash management, international banking, and other products and services. The Bank also manages and offers mutual funds under the name of CNI Charter Funds. On 2/29/00, CYN acquired The Pacific Bank, N.A. On 1/4/01, CYN acquired Reed, Conner & Birdwell, an investment management firm.

LOAN DISTRIBUTION

(12/31/2000)	($000)	(%)
Commercial	3,248,253	49.8
Real Estate Mortgage	1,479,862	22.7
Residential First Mtge	1,273,711	19.5
Real Estate Construction	452,301	6.9
Installment	73,018	1.1
Total	6,527,145	100.0

ANNUAL FINANCIAL DATA

	12/31/00	12/31/99	12/31/98	12/31/97	12/31/96	12/31/95	12/31/94
Earnings Per Share	**2.72**	**[1] 2.30**	**[1] 2.00**	**[1] 1.68**	**[1] 1.52**	**[2] 1.08**	**[1] 0.81**
Tang. Book Val. Per Share	**11.50**	**9.78**	**10.61**	**9.83**	**8.90**	**8.12**	**7.32**
Dividends Per Share	**0.70**	**0.66**	**0.56**	**0.44**	**0.36**	**0.26**	**0.05**
Dividend Payout %	**25.7**	**28.7**	**28.0**	**26.2**	**23.7**	**24.1**	**6.2**
INCOME STATEMENT (IN MILLIONS):							
Total Interest Income	646.3	470.4	423.9	358.0	282.1	217.6	181.8
Total Interest Expense	239.8	148.4	130.3	104.3	82.4	55.3	38.4
Net Interest Income	406.5	322.0	293.7	253.7	199.7	162.3	143.4
Provision for Loan Losses	21.5	...	...	...	...	...	6.0
Non-Interest Income	109.5	87.2	67.7	53.4	44.0	34.6	32.8
Non-Interest Expense	294.8	241.8	211.3	181.8	144.6	118.1	117.5
Income Before Taxes	199.7	167.4	150.0	125.3	99.1	78.8	52.7
Net Income	131.7	[1] 108.1	[1] 96.2	[1] 80.1	[1] 66.6	[2] 48.8	[1] 37.2
Average Shs. Outstg. (000)	48,393	46,938	48,141	47,809	43,888	45,198	45,626
BALANCE SHEET (IN MILLIONS):							
Cash & Due from Banks	386.8	233.2	285.8	327.4	331.0	339.7	298.7
Securities Avail. for Sale	1,593.9	1,129.8	1,047.0	637.5	648.0	895.1	116.0
Total Loans & Leases	6,527.1	5,490.7	4,530.4	3,825.2	2,845.6	2,355.0	1,653.8
Allowance for Credit Losses	135.4	134.1	135.3	137.8	130.1	131.5	105.3
Net Loans & Leases	6,391.7	5,356.6	4,395.1	3,687.5	2,715.5	2,223.5	1,548.4
Total Assets	9,096.7	7,213.6	6,427.8	5,252.0	4,216.5	4,157.6	3,012.8
Total Deposits	7,408.7	5,669.4	4,887.4	4,228.3	3,386.5	3,248.0	2,417.8
Long-Term Obligations	332.1	303.5	323.3	50.0	34.8	25.0	...
Total Liabilities	8,353.0	6,642.0	5,866.0	4,743.4	3,815.7	3,790.6	2,682.1
Net Stockholders' Equity	743.6	571.6	561.8	508.7	400.7	367.0	330.7
Year-end Shs. Outstg. (000)	47,630	45,457	46,007	46,137	43,908	45,193	45,193
STATISTICAL RECORD:							
Return on Equity %	17.7	18.9	17.1	15.8	16.6	13.3	11.2
Return on Assets %	1.4	1.5	1.5	1.5	1.6	1.2	1.2
Equity/Assets %	8.2	7.9	8.7	9.7	9.5	8.8	11.0
Non-Int. Exp./Tot. Inc. %	57.1	59.1	58.5	59.2	59.3	60.0	66.7
Price Range	40.81-25.50	41.56-29.63	41.63-25.75	35.38-20.38	22.25-12.63	15.38-9.75	12.13-7.13
P/E Ratio	15.0-9.4	18.1-12.9	20.8-12.9	21.1-12.1	14.6-8.3	14.2-9.0	15.0-8.8
Average Yield %	2.1	1.9	1.7	1.6	2.1	2.1	0.5

Statistics are as originally reported. [1] Incl. a gain on the sale of assets of $2.1 mill., 1999; $1.8 mill., 1998; $1.6 mill., 1997; $1.1 mill., 1996; $1.5 mill., 1994.

OFFICERS:
B. Goldsmith, Chmn.
R. Goldsmith, Vice-Chmn., C.E.O.
G. H. Benter Jr., Pres.

INVESTOR CONTACT: Frank P. Pekny, Exec. V.P., C.F.O. & Treas.

PRINCIPAL OFFICE: 400 North Roxbury Drive, Beverly Hills, CA 90210

TELEPHONE NUMBER: (310) 888-6000
FAX: (310) 858-3334
WEB: www.cnb.com

NO. OF EMPLOYEES: 2,034

SHAREHOLDERS: 1,953 (approx.)

ANNUAL MEETING: In April

INCORPORATED: DE, Oct., 1968

INSTITUTIONAL HOLDINGS:
No. of Institutions: 188
Shares Held: 26,829,633
% Held: 56.2

INDUSTRY: National commercial banks (SIC: 6021)

TRANSFER AGENT(S): City National Bank, Beverly Hills, CA

NYSE SYMBOL CKR
Rec. Pr. 2.65 (5/31/01)

CKE RESTAURANTS, INC.

YIELD ...
P/E RATIO ...

INTERIM EARNINGS (Per Share):

Qtr.	May	Aug.	Nov.	Jan.
1996-97	0.15	0.15	0.15	0.15
1997-98	0.25	0.23	0.25	0.24
1998-99	0.43	0.42	0.31	0.23
1999-00	0.36	0.20	0.06	d1.22
2000-01	d0.05	d0.22	d0.58	d2.94

INTERIM DIVIDENDS (Per Share):

Amt.	Decl.	Ex.	Rec.	Pay.
0.04S	9/29/99	9/30/99	10/04/99	10/28/99
0.04S	4/07/00	4/17/00	4/19/00	5/04/00

No action taken on 11/4/00 dividend.

CAPITALIZATION (1/31/01):

	($000)	(%)
Long-Term Debt	465,985	52.0
Capital Lease Obligations	81,173	9.1
Common & Surplus	349,557	39.0
Total	896,715	100.0

RECENT DEVELOPMENTS: For the year ended 1/29/01, CKR reported a net loss of $194.1 million versus a loss of $29.4 million in the prior year. Results for 2001 included a loss on property sold or held for sale of $46.4 million, while 2000 results included a $15.2 million gain on property sold or held for sale. Results also included charges of $98.3 million and $42.0 million for store closure and asset impairment expenses in 2001 and 2000, respectively. Total revenues fell 10.3% to $1.78 billion.

PROSPECTS: The Company will continue to focus on reducing general and administrative expenses and streamlining corporate business processes to achieve additional savings. Accordingly, CKR has sold about 400 Hardee's and Carl's Jr. stores. On 3/14/01, the Company announced that it has signed a purchase agreement with an affiliate of Jacobson Partners, to purchase CKR's Taco Bueno subsidiary for $72.5 million. The transaction is expected to close in the second quarter of 2001.

BUSINESS

CKE RESTAURANTS, INC., through its subsidiaries, franchisees and licensees, operates 970 Carl's Jr. quick-service restaurants, including Carl's Jr./Green Burrito dual-brand locations, in 13 Western states and Mexico; 2,603 Hardee's quick-service restaurants in 32 states and 11 foreign countries; and 125 Taco Bueno quick-service restaurants in Texas and Oklahoma. As of 1/31/01, more than 90.0% of the restaurants are Company-operated. In September 1998, the Company sold its wholly-owned subsidiary, JB's Family Restaurants, Inc.

REVENUES

(01/31/01)	($000)	(%)
Co.-operated restaurants	1,569,504	87.9
Franchised & licensed	215,078	12.1
Total	1,784,582	100.0

ANNUAL FINANCIAL DATA

	1/31/01	1/31/00	1/31/99	1/31/98	1/31/97	1/31/96	1/31/95
Earnings Per Share	**[3] d3.84**	**[2] d0.57**	**[1] 1.39**	**0.97**	**0.66**	**0.36**	**0.04**
Cash Flow Per Share	**d1.73**	**1.45**	**2.67**	**1.94**	**1.48**	**1.05**	**0.78**
Tang. Book Val. Per Share	**6.71**	**10.48**	**11.32**	**9.74**	**5.88**	**3.31**	**2.94**
Dividends Per Share	**0.04**	**0.08**	**0.07**	**0.07**	**0.04**	**0.04**	**0.02**
Dividend Payout %	...	...	**5.2**	**6.8**	**6.6**	**12.3**	**51.1**
INCOME STATEMENT (IN MILLIONS):							
Total Revenues	1,784.6	1,990.1	1,892.0	1,149.7	614.1	465.4	443.7
Costs & Expenses	1,810.6	1,837.8	1,646.7	1,017.1	545.0	418.3	412.4
Depreciation & Amort.	107.0	104.5	77.1	46.4	27.1	21.4	22.8
Operating Income	d133.0	47.9	168.2	86.2	42.0	25.7	8.6
Net Interest Inc./(Exp.)	d69.8	d63.3	d43.5	d16.9	d9.9	d10.0	d9.2
Income Before Income Taxes	d205.3	d47.5	124.1	76.6	36.7	18.0	2.4
Income Taxes	cr11.1	cr18.1	49.6	29.9	14.4	7.0	1.1
Net Income	[3] d194.1	[2] d29.4	[1] 74.5	46.8	22.3	11.0	1.3
Cash Flow	d87.1	75.0	151.6	93.2	49.4	32.3	24.0
Average Shs. Outstg. (000)	50,501	51,668	56,714	48,122	33,455	30,820	30,883
BALANCE SHEET (IN MILLIONS):							
Cash & Cash Equivalents	16.9	36.5	46.3	30.4	39.8	25.9	18.2
Total Current Assets	190.7	128.1	134.3	92.2	72.9	56.8	56.8
Net Property	774.3	1,136.0	1,022.1	674.6	242.9	155.7	163.8
Total Assets	1,214.0	1,568.5	1,496.9	957.4	401.2	246.8	244.3
Total Current Liabilities	214.0	211.9	201.6	176.5	83.9	61.3	71.6
Long-Term Obligations	547.2	726.3	613.3	195.6	81.9	70.6	69.9
Net Stockholders' Equity	349.6	545.8	586.8	498.5	214.8	101.2	88.5
Net Working Capital	d23.3	d83.8	d67.4	d84.3	d11.0	d4.5	d14.7
Year-end Shs. Outstg. (000)	52,086	52,086	51,850	51,175	36,541	30,575	30,121
STATISTICAL RECORD:							
Operating Profit Margin %	...	2.4	8.9	7.5	6.8	5.5	1.9
Net Profit Margin %	...	...	3.9	4.1	3.6	2.4	0.3
Return on Equity %	...	...	12.7	9.4	10.4	10.8	1.4
Return on Assets %	...	...	5.0	4.9	5.6	4.4	0.5
Debt/Total Assets %	45.1	46.3	41.0	20.4	20.4	28.6	28.6
Price Range	8.25-1.94	30.31-5.69	42.05-15.00	37.50-15.19	19.97-7.99	9.92-3.51	7.92-3.58
P/E Ratio	...	...	30.2-10.8	38.5-15.6	30.1-12.0	27.8-9.8	183.8-83.1
Average Yield %	0.8	0.4	0.3	0.3	0.3	0.7	0.4

Statistics are as originally reported. Adj. for stk. splits: 10% div., 1/99, 2/98; 3-for-2, 1/97 [1] Bef. extraord. gain of $3.3 mill. [2] Incl. nonrecurr. chrg. of $42.0 mill.; bef. extraord. gain of $290,000. [3] Incl. $46.4 mill. loss fr. property sold or held for sale.

OFFICERS:
W. P. Foley II, Chmn.
D. D. Lane, Vice-Chmn.
A. F. Puzder, Pres., C.E.O.
D. J. Lacey, Exec. V.P., C.F.O.

INVESTOR CONTACT: Loren C. Pannier, Sr. V.P., Investor Relations, (714) 774-5796

PRINCIPAL OFFICE: 401 W. Carl Karcher Way, Anaheim, CA 92801

TELEPHONE NUMBER: (714) 774-5796
FAX: (714) 490-3630
WEB: www.ckr.com

NO. OF EMPLOYEES: 35,500 (approx.)

SHAREHOLDERS: 1,900 (approx.)

ANNUAL MEETING: In June

INCORPORATED: CA, Feb., 1966; reincorp., DE,

INSTITUTIONAL HOLDINGS:
No. of Institutions: 31
Shares Held: 20,862,944
% Held: 41.3

INDUSTRY: Eating places (SIC: 5812)

TRANSFER AGENT(S): Mellon Investor Services, Los Angeles, CA

NYSE SYMBOL CLE
Rec. Pr. 19.05 (4/30/01)

CLAIRE'S STORES, INC.

YIELD	0.9%
P/E RATIO	14.5

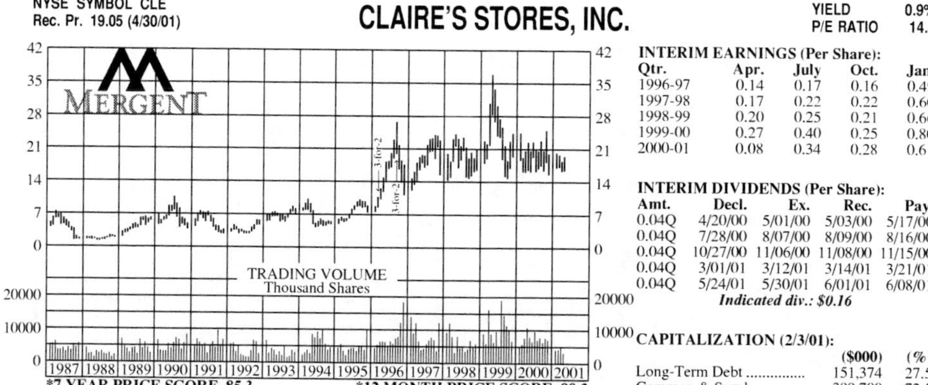

*7 YEAR PRICE SCORE 85.3 *12 MONTH PRICE SCORE 99.3

*NYSE COMPOSITE INDEX=100

INTERIM EARNINGS (Per Share):

Qtr.	Apr.	July	Oct.	Jan.
1996-97	0.14	0.17	0.16	0.49
1997-98	0.17	0.22	0.22	0.60
1998-99	0.20	0.25	0.21	0.66
1999-00	0.27	0.40	0.25	0.80
2000-01	0.08	0.34	0.28	0.61

INTERIM DIVIDENDS (Per Share):

Amt.	Decl.	Ex.	Rec.	Pay.
0.04Q	4/20/00	5/01/00	5/03/00	5/17/00
0.04Q	7/28/00	8/07/00	8/09/00	8/16/00
0.04Q	10/27/00	11/06/00	11/08/00	11/15/00
0.04Q	3/01/01	3/12/01	3/14/01	3/21/01
0.04Q	5/24/01	5/30/01	6/01/01	6/08/01

Indicated div.: $0.16

CAPITALIZATION (2/3/01):

	($000)	(%)
Long-Term Debt	151,374	27.5
Common & Surplus	399,700	72.5
Total	551,074	100.0

RECENT DEVELOPMENTS: For the 53 weeks ended 2/3/01, net income totaled $65.0 million, down 26.1% compared with $87.9 million in the coresponding 52-week period the year before. Results in the prior-year period included a one-time pre-tax charge of $8.7 million from asset impairment, partially offset by a one-time pre-tax $3.9 million gain on investments. Net sales climbed 25.2% to $1.06 billion from $846.9 million the previous year. Same-store sales, on a comparable 52-week basis, slipped 1.0% year-over-year.

PROSPECTS: Earnings are being negatively affected by higher-than-usual promotional activity, as the Company takes steps to clear out inventories to make room for new Spring merchandise. Meanwhile, CLE is in the process of implementing a new image and product selection at its Afterthoughts stores in an effort to differentiate these stores from the Company's Claire's Accessories locations. In fiscal 2001, CLE is targeting sales growth of about 4.0% and net earnings of approximately $83.0 million.

BUSINESS

CLAIRE'S STORES, INC. is a mall-based retailer of fashion accessories, including costume jewelry, hair ornaments and earrings, and apparel for pre-teens and teenagers. At 3/31/01, the Company operated 3,021 stores in North America, Japan, the United Kingdom, Ireland, Switzerland, Austria, France and Germany under the trade names CLAIRE'S ACCESSORIES, AFTERTHOUGHTS, THE ICING, MR. RAGS and VELVET PIXIES. The Company sold its graphic art products subsidiary, Decor, in March of 1992. On 12/1/99, CLE acquired 768 Afterthoughts stores. In January 1999, the Company discontinued Just Nikki, Inc.

REVENUES

(2/3/2001)	($000)	(%)
Jewelry	473,989	44.7
Accessories	475,203	44.8
Apparel	111,225	10.5
Total	1,060,417	100.0

ANNUAL FINANCIAL DATA

	2/3/01	1/29/00	1/30/99	1/31/98	2/1/97	2/3/96	1/28/95
Earnings Per Share	**1.30**	**[2] 1.71**	**[1] 1.40**	**1.19**	**0.95**	**0.66**	**0.51**
Cash Flow Per Share	**2.18**	**2.27**	**1.83**	**1.54**	**1.28**	**0.98**	**0.81**
Tang. Book Val. Per Share	**4.27**	**3.65**	**6.01**	**5.20**	**4.31**	**3.23**	**2.61**
Dividends Per Share	**0.16**	**0.16**	**0.15**	**0.12**	**0.09**	**0.05**	**0.05**
Dividend Payout %	**12.3**	**9.4**	**10.7**	**10.1**	**9.5**	**8.1**	**10.0**
INCOME STATEMENT (IN MILLIONS):							
Total Revenues	1,060.4	846.9	661.9	500.2	440.2	344.9	301.4
Costs & Expenses	906.1	678.0	527.7	396.9	355.1	282.3	250.0
Depreciation & Amort.	44.1	28.8	21.9	17.2	15.8	15.0	13.9
Operating Income	110.2	140.1	112.3	86.0	69.3	47.6	37.6
Net Interest Inc./(Exp.)	d9.9	3.5	6.3	7.1	3.0	2.0	0.9
Income Before Income Taxes	100.2	138.8	113.7	93.1	72.3	49.6	38.5
Income Taxes	35.3	50.9	42.1	34.9	27.2	18.7	14.6
Net Income	65.0	[2] 87.9	[1] 71.7	58.2	45.1	30.9	23.9
Cash Flow	109.1	116.8	93.5	75.4	60.9	45.9	37.7
Average Shs. Outstg. (000)	50,101	51,334	51,108	49,062	47,591	47,025	46,755
BALANCE SHEET (IN MILLIONS):							
Cash & Cash Equivalents	111.7	140.9	153.3	132.4	93.4	59.3	48.5
Total Current Assets	259.8	290.0	239.6	198.5	151.0	103.8	78.7
Net Property	171.1	166.8	115.5	87.5	72.7	69.3	70.3
Total Assets	668.5	702.1	394.3	306.3	242.9	187.8	158.6
Total Current Liabilities	100.1	96.9	69.1	46.5	42.9	30.5	30.0
Long-Term Obligations	151.4	192.0	...	...	...	...	3.0
Net Stockholders' Equity	399.7	398.8	314.2	251.6	194.5	152.9	122.2
Net Working Capital	159.7	193.2	170.5	152.0	108.1	73.2	48.7
Year-end Shs. Outstg. (000)	45,820	51,133	50,806	48,370	45,109	47,339	46,773
STATISTICAL RECORD:							
Operating Profit Margin %	10.4	16.5	17.0	17.2	15.7	13.8	12.5
Net Profit Margin %	6.1	10.4	10.8	11.6	10.3	9.0	7.9
Return on Equity %	16.3	22.1	22.8	23.1	23.2	20.2	19.5
Return on Assets %	9.7	12.5	18.2	19.0	18.6	16.5	15.0
Debt/Total Assets %	22.6	27.3	...	...	...	...	1.9
Price Range	24.94-15.63	36.88-14.75	24.13-14.31	24.00-12.13	26.63-7.56	10.22-5.00	10.28-4.22
P/E Ratio	19.2-12.0	21.6-8.6	17.2-10.2	20.2-10.2	28.0-8.0	15.5-7.6	20.1-8.3
Average Yield %	0.8	0.6	0.8	0.7	0.5	0.7	0.7

Statistics are as originally reported. Adj. for 3-for-2 stk. split, 9/96 & 2/96. [1] Bef. loss from disc. ops. $9.4 mill. ($0.18/sh). [2] Incl. $5.5 mil ($0.11/sh) non-recur. after-tax restr. chg.

OFFICERS:
R. Schaefer, Chmn., Pres., C.E.O.
M. Schaefer, Vice-Chmn.
E. B. Schaefer, Vice-Chmn.
I. D. Kaplan, Sr. V.P., C.F.O., Treas.

INVESTOR CONTACT: Sonia Rohan, Dir., Inv. Rel., (212) 594-3127

PRINCIPAL OFFICE: 3 S.W. 129th Avenue, Pembroke Pines, FL 33027

TELEPHONE NUMBER: (954) 433-3900
FAX: (954) 433-3999
WEB: www.clairestores.com
NO. OF EMPLOYEES: 20,500 (approx.)
SHAREHOLDERS: 1,707 (approx.)(com.); 604 (Cl. A com.)
ANNUAL MEETING: In June
INCORPORATED: DE, Oct., 1961; reincorp., FL, June, 2000

INSTITUTIONAL HOLDINGS:
No. of Institutions: 140
Shares Held: 32,579,895
% Held: 66.8

INDUSTRY: Women's accessory & specialty stores (SIC: 5632)

TRANSFER AGENT(S): First Union National Bank, Charlotte, NC

NYSE SYMBOL CMH
Rec. Pr. 13.92 (4/30/01)

CLAYTON HOMES, INC.

YIELD 0.5%
P/E RATIO 14.8

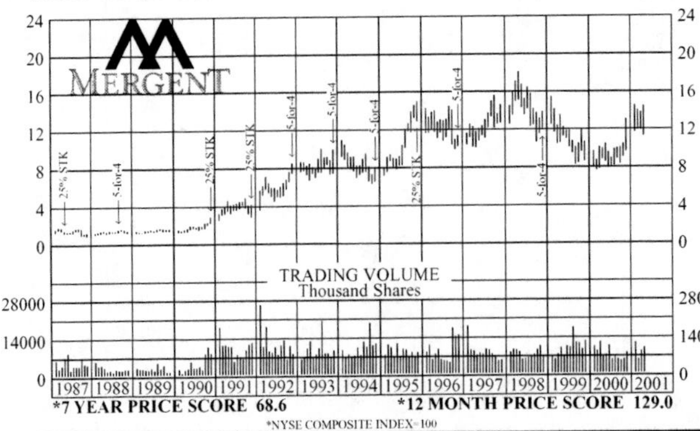

*7 YEAR PRICE SCORE 68.6 *12 MONTH PRICE SCORE 129.0

*NYSE COMPOSITE INDEX=100

INTERIM EARNINGS (Per Share):

Qtr.	Sept.	Dec.	Mar.	June
1996-97	0.18	0.18	0.18	0.27
1997-98	0.20	0.21	0.21	0.30
1998-99	0.22	0.24	0.24	0.36
1999-00	0.25	0.25	0.26	0.27
2000-01	0.21	0.20	...	...

INTERIM DIVIDENDS (Per Share):

Amt.	Decl.	Ex.	Rec.	Pay.
0.016Q	4/19/00	6/26/00	6/28/00	7/19/00
0.016Q	7/26/00	9/25/00	9/27/00	10/18/00
0.016Q	11/01/00	12/22/00	12/27/00	1/17/01
0.016Q	1/25/01	3/26/01	3/28/01	4/18/01
0.016Q	4/25/01	6/25/01	6/27/01	7/18/01

Indicated div.: $0.06 (Div. Reinv. Plan)

CAPITALIZATION (6/30/00):

	($000)	(%)
Long-Term Debt [1]	99,216	8.7
Common & Surplus	1,036,375	91.3
Total	1,135,591	100.0

RECENT DEVELOPMENTS: For the quarter ended 12/31/00, net income decreased 22.0% to $27.5 million compared with $35.2 million the year before. Revenue was $284.9 million, down 7.9% from $309.2 million a year earlier. Total homes sold decreased 16.5% to 6,128. As of 12/31/00, CMH's order backlog (consisting of Company-owned and independent retail orders) was $9.1 million versus $13.6 million a year earlier.

PROSPECTS: The Company continues to operate in an excess capacity industry environment where more than 80 plants have closed during the second quarter. More manufactured housing plants are expected to close in the coming months. Although the Company has no intentions of closing any of its facilities, it will be operating on reduced schedules in the near-term.

BUSINESS

CLAYTON HOMES, INC. builds, sells, finances and insures manufactured homes, and owns and operates residential manufactured housing communities in 33 states. The Manufacturing group is a producer of homes with 20 plants supplying 716 independent and Company-owned retail centers. The Retail group sells, installs and services factory built homes. As of 12/31/00, company-owned retail centers numbered 310 in 23 states. Financial Services provides financing and insurance for homebuyers of Company-owned and selected independent retail sales centers through Vanderbilt Mortgage and Finance, a wholly-owned subsidiary. The Communities group owns and operates 77 manufactured housing communities with 20,435 homesites in 12 states.

ANNUAL FINANCIAL DATA

	6/30/00	6/30/99	6/30/98	6/30/97	6/30/96	6/30/95	6/30/94
Earnings Per Share	**1.03**	**1.06**	**0.92**	**0.80**	**0.71**	**[3] 0.58**	**[2] 0.48**
Cash Flow Per Share	**1.20**	**1.18**	**1.02**	**0.89**	**0.79**	**0.64**	**0.53**
Tang. Book Val. Per Share	**7.54**	**6.66**	**5.93**	**5.09**	**4.38**	**3.69**	**3.93**
Dividends Per Share	**0.06**	**0.06**	**0.06**	**0.06**	**0.05**	**0.04**	**...**
Dividend Payout %	**6.2**	**6.0**	**7.0**	**8.0**	**7.2**	**7.0**	**...**
INCOME STATEMENT (IN MILLIONS):							
Total Revenues	1,293.3	1,344.3	1,127.8	1,021.7	928.7	758.1	628.2
Costs & Expenses	1,042.7	1,075.2	896.4	821.1	749.9	617.9	512.9
Depreciation & Amort.	23.7	17.8	14.7	13.1	11.2	8.3	6.7
Operating Income	227.0	251.3	216.6	187.5	167.7	131.9	108.6
Net Interest Inc./(Exp.)	1.6	d5.3	5.5	5.2	4.6	3.9	...
Income Before Income Taxes	228.6	246.0	222.1	192.7	172.3	135.8	108.3
Income Taxes	84.6	91.0	84.4	73.2	65.5	48.8	39.0
Net Income	144.0	155.0	137.7	119.5	106.8	[3] 87.0	[2] 69.6
Cash Flow	167.7	172.8	152.4	132.6	118.0	95.3	76.3
Average Shs. Outstg. (000)	139,815	145,931	149,504	149,346	149,183	148,286	143,845
BALANCE SHEET (IN MILLIONS):							
Cash & Cash Equivalents	43.9	2.7	1.7	89.7	47.4	49.4	38.9
Total Current Assets	939.4	895.0	1,006.0	687.8	573.7	481.3	470.4
Net Property	305.5	291.5	261.5	214.1	184.3	166.0	129.9
Total Assets	1,506.4	1,417.2	1,457.8	1,045.8	886.4	761.2	770.5
Total Current Liabilities	122.8	130.6	138.6	99.5	91.1	63.9	55.8
Long-Term Obligations	99.2	96.5	247.6	22.8	30.3	48.7	70.7
Net Stockholders' Equity	1,036.4	947.8	881.0	754.5	650.2	544.2	462.2
Net Working Capital	816.6	764.4	867.5	588.3	482.7	417.3	414.5
Year-end Shs. Outstg. (000)	137,499	142,373	148,520	148,121	148,580	147,598	117,656
STATISTICAL RECORD:							
Operating Profit Margin %	17.6	18.7	19.2	18.4	18.1	17.4	17.3
Net Profit Margin %	11.1	11.5	12.2	11.7	11.5	11.5	11.1
Return on Equity %	13.9	16.4	15.6	15.8	16.4	16.0	15.1
Return on Assets %	9.6	10.9	9.4	11.4	12.0	11.4	9.0
Debt/Total Assets %	6.6	6.8	17.0	2.2	3.4	6.4	9.2
Price Range	13.06-7.69	15.44-8.25	18.13-10.63	15.63-10.13	14.50-9.94	14.00-7.19	10.94-6.31
P/E Ratio	12.7-7.5	14.6-7.8	19.7-11.6	19.5-12.6	20.3-13.9	25.6-12.3	22.8-13.1
Average Yield %	0.6	0.5	0.4	0.5	0.4	0.4	...

Statistics are as originally reported. Adj. for stk. split: 25% stk. divs.,12/94, 12/95, 12/96 & 12/98. [1] Incl. debentures conv. into common stock. [2] Bef. an acctg. cr. of $3.0 mill. [3] Incl. a $4.8 mill. pretax gain from the sale of CMH's interest in two communities.

OFFICERS:
J. L. Clayton, Chmn.
K. T. Clayton, Pres., C.E.O.
A. W. Krupacs, V.P.
G. A. Hamilton, V.P., Controller

INVESTOR CONTACT: Investor Relations, (865) 380-3206

PRINCIPAL OFFICE: 5000 Clayton Road, Maryville, TN 37804

TELEPHONE NUMBER: (865) 380-3000
FAX: (865) 380-3750
WEB: www.clayton.net

NO. OF EMPLOYEES: 7,429 (avg.)

SHAREHOLDERS: 11,380 (of record)

ANNUAL MEETING: In Nov.

INCORPORATED: TN, May, 1968; reincorp., DE.

INSTITUTIONAL HOLDINGS:
No. of Institutions: 172
Shares Held: 66,190,791
% Held: 48.0

INDUSTRY: Mobile homes (SIC: 2451)

TRANSFER AGENT(S): American Stock Transfer & Trust Company, New York, NY

NYSE SYMBOL CCU
Rec. Pr. 55.80 (4/30/01)

CLEAR CHANNEL COMMUNICATIONS, INC.

YIELD ...
P/E RATIO 62.0

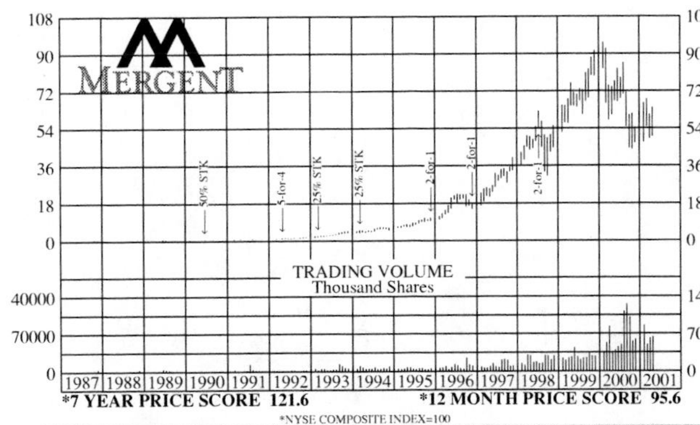

*7 YEAR PRICE SCORE 121.6 *12 MONTH PRICE SCORE 95.6

*NYSE COMPOSITE INDEX=100

INTERIM EARNINGS (Per Share):

Qtr.	Mar.	June	Sept.	Dec.
1996	0.04	0.09	0.02	0.10
1997	0.05	0.08	0.10	0.11
1998	0.02	0.11	0.05	0.04
1999	d0.05	0.35	Nil	d0.03
2000	d0.12	0.09	0.96	d0.33

INTERIM DIVIDENDS (Per Share):

Amt.	Decl.	Ex.	Rec.	Pay.

No dividends paid.

CAPITALIZATION (12/31/00):

	($000)	(%)
Long-Term Debt	10,100,028	21.4
Deferred Income Tax	6,771,198	14.3
Minority Interest	61,745	0.1
Common & Surplus	30,347,173	64.2
Total	47,280,144	100.0

RECENT DEVELOPMENTS: For the year ended 12/31/00, net income amounted to $248.8 million compared with income of $85.7 million, before an extraordinary loss, in 1999. Results for 2000 included non-cash compensation expense of $16.0 million and a gain on the sale of assets of $783.7 million. Results for 1999 included a gain on the sale of assets of $138.7 million. Net revenue jumped 99.6% to $5.35 billion versus $2.68 billion the year before.

PROSPECTS: On 1/31/00, CCU signed a definitive agreement to purchase Texas-based KJOL (AM) from Radio One, Inc. for approximately $16.0 million. On 2/16/01, Nassau Broadcasting Partners, L.P., completed the acquisition of Pennsylvania-based WODE (FM) and WEEX (AM) from CCU. CCU will also pay $12.0 million to Nassau and will acquire New Jersey-based WNNJ (AM), WNNJ (FM), WSUS (FM), and WHCY (FM).

BUSINESS

CLEAR CHANNEL COMMUNICATIONS, INC. is a diversified media company that owns or programs radio and television stations and is one of the largest domestic outdoor advertising companies. As of 3/31/01, CCU operated, or was affiliated with, more than 1,170 radio stations, 17 television stations and more than 700,000 outdoor advertising displays in 45 countries. Also, CCU has equity interests in over 240 radio stations internationally. CU owns a 50% equity interest in the Australian Radio Network Pty. Ltd., which operates radio stations in Australia; a one-third equity interest in the New Zealand Radio Network, which operates radio stations throughout New Zealand; a 32.3% non-voting equity interest in Heftel Broadcasting Corporation, a domestic Spanish-language radio broadcaster; and a 30% equity interest in American Tower Corporation, a domestic provider of wireless transmission sites. On 5/4/99, CCU acquired Jacor Communications, Inc. On 8/1/00, CCU acquired SFX Entertainment, Inc. On 9/30/00, CCU acquired AMFM Inc.

ANNUAL FINANCIAL DATA

	[3] 12/31/00	12/31/99	12/31/98	12/31/97	12/31/96	12/31/95	12/31/94
Earnings Per Share	[2] **0.57**	[1] **0.26**	**0.22**	**0.34**	**0.25**	**0.23**	**0.16**
Cash Flow Per Share	**3.83**	**2.54**	**1.51**	**1.06**	**0.66**	**0.55**	**0.41**
Tang. Book Val. Per Share	...	...	**0.35**	...	...	...	...
INCOME STATEMENT (IN MILLIONS):							
Total Revenues	5,345.3	2,678.2	1,350.9	697.1	351.7	243.8	173.1
Costs & Expenses	3,607.3	1,687.4	787.8	398.6	191.8	127.4	95.7
Depreciation & Amort.	1,433.1	737.1	322.2	130.9	60.8	45.0	34.5
Operating Income	304.9	253.7	240.9	167.6	99.1	71.4	42.9
Net Interest Inc./(Exp.)	d383.1	d192.3	d135.8	d75.1	d30.1	d20.8	d7.7
Income Before Income Taxes	713.5	220.2	117.9	104.1	71.2	52.7	36.4
Income Taxes	464.7	150.6	72.4	47.1	28.4	20.7	14.4
Equity Earnings/Minority Int.	25.2	16.1	8.5	6.6	d5.2	2.9	...
Net Income	[2] 248.8	[1] 85.7	54.0	63.6	37.7	32.0	22.0
Cash Flow	1,681.9	822.7	376.3	194.5	98.5	77.0	56.5
Average Shs. Outstg. (000)	438,711	324,408	249,123	183,030	149,298	140,402	138,652
BALANCE SHEET (IN MILLIONS):							
Cash & Cash Equivalents	505.5	76.7	36.5	24.7	16.7	5.4	6.8
Total Current Assets	2,343.2	925.1	410.0	198.6	113.2	70.5	53.9
Net Property	4,255.2	2,478.1	1,915.8	746.3	147.8	99.9	85.3
Total Assets	50,056.5	16,821.5	7,539.9	3,455.6	1,324.7	563.0	411.6
Total Current Liabilities	2,128.6	685.5	258.1	86.9	43.5	36.0	27.7
Long-Term Obligations	10,100.0	4,093.5	2,323.6	1,540.4	725.1	334.2	238.2
Net Stockholders' Equity	30,347.2	10,084.0	4,483.4	1,746.8	513.4	163.7	130.5
Net Working Capital	214.7	239.6	151.8	111.8	69.7	34.5	26.3
Year-end Shs. Outstg. (000)	585,651	338,610	263,698	196,389	153,930	138,371	137,843
STATISTICAL RECORD:							
Operating Profit Margin %	5.7	9.5	17.8	24.0	28.2	29.3	24.8
Net Profit Margin %	4.7	3.2	4.0	9.1	10.7	13.1	12.7
Return on Equity %	0.8	0.8	1.2	3.6	7.3	19.6	16.9
Return on Assets %	0.5	0.5	0.7	1.8	2.8	5.7	5.3
Debt/Total Assets %	20.2	24.3	30.8	44.6	54.7	59.4	57.9
Price Range	95.50-43.88	91.50-52.00	62.31-31.00	39.94-16.81	22.63-10.19	11.06-6.27	6.50-3.93
P/E Ratio	167.5-77.0	351.8-199.9	283.1-140.8	119.2-50.2	90.5-40.7	48.5-27.5	41.1-24.8

Statistics are as originally reported. Adj. for stk. splits: 2-for-1, 7/98, 12/96 & 12/95; 25% div., 2/94 [1] Incl. gain on sale of stations of $138.7 mill. & excl. extraord. loss of $13.2 mill. [2] Incl. non-cash compen. exp. of $16.0 mill. & gain on sale of assets of $783.4 mill. [3] Reflect the acqs. of SFX Entertainment, Inc. and AMFM Inc. on 8/1/00 and 9/30/00, respectively

OFFICERS:
L. L. Mays, Chmn., C.E.O.
M. P. Mays, Pres., C.O.O.
R. T. Mays, Exec. V.P., C.F.O.
W. A. Ripperton Riordan, Exec. V.P., C.O.O.

INVESTOR CONTACT: Terri A. Hunter, V.P., Inv. Rel., (210) 822-2828

PRINCIPAL OFFICE: 200 East Basse Road, San Antonio, TX 78209-8328

TELEPHONE NUMBER: (210) 822-2828
FAX: (210) 822-2299
WEB: www.clearchannel.com

NO. OF EMPLOYEES: 56,350 (approx.)

SHAREHOLDERS: 3,120 (approx. record)

ANNUAL MEETING: In April

INCORPORATED: TX, 1974

INSTITUTIONAL HOLDINGS:
No. of Institutions: 483
Shares Held: 406,319,452
% Held: 69.2

INDUSTRY: Radio broadcasting stations (SIC: 4832)

TRANSFER AGENT(S): Bank of New York, New York, NY

NYSE SYMBOL CNL
Rec. Pr. 23.25 (5/31/01)

CLECO CORPORATION

YIELD 3.7%
P/E RATIO 16.7

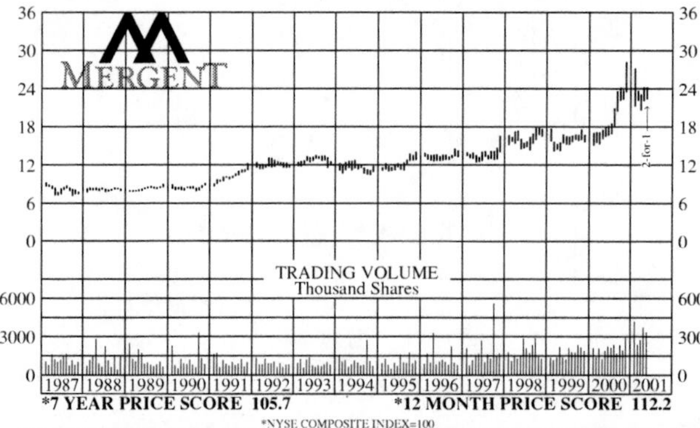

*7 YEAR PRICE SCORE 105.7 *12 MONTH PRICE SCORE 112.2

*NYSE COMPOSITE INDEX=100

INTERIM EARNINGS (Per Share):

Qtr.	Mar.	June	Sept.	Dec.
1997	0.16	0.24	0.48	0.23
1998	0.15	0.32	0.48	0.19
1999	0.18	0.30	0.54	0.18
2000	0.22	0.36	0.63	0.18

INTERIM DIVIDENDS (Per Share):

Amt.	Decl.	Ex.	Rec.	Pay.
0.425Q	7/28/00	8/02/00	8/04/00	8/15/00
0.425Q	10/27/00	11/01/00	11/03/00	11/15/00
0.425Q	1/26/01	2/01/01	2/05/01	2/15/01
0.435Q	4/27/01	5/03/01	5/07/01	5/15/01
2-for-1	2/26/01	5/22/01	5/07/01	5/21/01

Indicated div.: $0.87 (Adj.; Div. Reinv. Plan)

CAPITALIZATION (12/31/00):

	($000)	(%)
Long-Term Debt	659,135	45.5
Deferred Income Tax	308,958	21.3
Preferred Stock	15,096	1.0
Common & Surplus	464,919	32.1
Total	1,448,108	100.0

RECENT DEVELOPMENTS: For the year ended 12/31/00, the Company reported income from continuing operations of $69.3 million compared with income from continuing operations of $58.1 million in 1999. Results excluded after-tax losses of $6.9 million in 2000 and $1.3 million in 1999 from discontinued operations. The 2000 results also excluded an after-tax extraordinary gain of $2.5 million. Total operating revenues rose 7.3% to $820.0 million.

PROSPECTS: On 4/2/01, CNL has sold substantially all of the assets of Utility Construction & Technology Solutions LLC, its wholly-owned electric services subsidiary. The transaction should enable CNL to focus on its utility wire and wholesale energy operations. CNL expects to reach an agreement with a potential buyer in the near future. Separately, revenues should continue to benefit from the successful debut of CNL's Evangeline Power Station.

BUSINESS

CLECO CORPORATION, under an energy services holding structure, is the parent company of Cleco Power LLC and Cleco Midstream Resources LLC. Cleco Power LLC is a regulated electric utility company that, as of 5/29/01, provides electricity to approximately 250,000 customers in Lousiana. Cleco Midstream Resources LLC is a nonregulated regional energy services group that develops and operates electric power generation facilities; invests in and develops natural gas pipelines and other gas-related assets; and provides energy services to organizations that operate electric utility systems. The other segment consists of a shared services subsidiary, an investment subsidiary, a retail subsidiary, Utility Construction and Technology Solutions, LLC.

QUARTERLY DATA

(12/31/00)($000)	Rev	Inc
1st Quarter	119,166	25,917
2nd Quarter	146,793	32,837
3rd Quarter	205,728	38,680
4th Quarter	163,913	24,390

ANNUAL FINANCIAL DATA

	12/31/00	12/31/99	12/31/98	12/31/97	12/31/96	12/31/95	12/31/94
Earnings Per Share	**[1] 1.46**	**1.19**	**1.12**	**1.09**	**1.12**	**1.04**	**0.96**
Cash Flow Per Share	**2.57**	**2.19**	**2.11**	**2.02**	**2.07**	**1.94**	**1.81**
Tang. Book Val. Per Share	**10.33**	**9.77**	**9.45**	**9.10**	**8.76**	**8.41**	**7.61**
Dividends Per Share	**0.84**	**0.41**	**0.81**	**0.79**	**0.77**	**0.75**	**0.73**
Dividend Payout %	**58.1**	**35.0**	**72.3**	**72.5**	**68.8**	**72.1**	**76.0**
INCOME STATEMENT (IN MILLIONS):							
Total Revenues	820.0	768.2	515.2	456.2	435.4	394.4	379.6
Costs & Expenses	582.3	576.2	328.9	280.5	264.6	231.3	226.3
Depreciation & Amort.	55.2	49.5	49.1	45.9	42.7	40.6	38.3
Maintenance Exp.	35.3	29.9	30.3	23.3	23.5	22.6	24.7
Operating Income	147.2	112.5	80.3	78.8	78.4	74.7	70.4
Net Interest Inc./(Exp.)	d42.7	d27.9	d27.0	d28.2	d27.8	d28.0	d26.1
Income Taxes	35.0	27.2	26.7	27.7	26.2	25.2	19.9
Net Income	[1] 69.3	56.8	53.8	52.5	52.1	48.7	45.0
Cash Flow	122.7	104.3	100.7	96.3	92.8	87.2	81.3
Average Shs. Outstg. (000)	47,655	47,697	47,734	47,728	44,906	44,862	44,830
BALANCE SHEET (IN MILLIONS):							
Gross Property	1,836.9	1,767.3	1,641.5	1,544.2	1,428.1	1,371.2	1,322.6
Accumulated Depreciation	604.1	555.7	551.7	518.7	475.2	441.7	410.5
Net Property	1,232.8	1,211.6	1,089.8	1,025.6	952.9	929.5	912.1
Total Assets	1,845.7	1,704.7	1,429.0	1,361.0	1,321.8	1,266.0	1,178.2
Long-Term Obligations	659.1	579.6	343.0	365.9	340.9	360.8	336.6
Net Stockholders' Equity	480.0	452.5	437.5	420.1	402.9	385.1	369.4
Year-end Shs. Outstg. (000)	44,991	44,884	44,962	44,926	44,906	44,854	47,684
STATISTICAL RECORD:							
Operating Profit Margin %	18.0	14.6	15.6	17.3	18.0	18.9	18.6
Net Profit Margin %	8.5	7.4	10.4	11.5	12.0	12.3	11.9
Net Inc./Net Property %	5.6	4.7	4.9	5.1	5.5	5.2	4.9
Net Inc./Tot. Capital %	4.8	3.9	4.7	4.6	4.8	4.4	4.8
Return on Equity %	14.4	12.5	12.3	12.5	12.9	12.6	12.2
Accum. Depr./Gross Prop. %	32.9	31.4	33.6	33.6	33.3	32.2	31.0
Price Range	28.25-15.06	17.75-14.13	18.06-14.31	16.56-12.38	14.63-12.56	14.06-11.00	12.81-10.44
P/E Ratio	19.4-10.4	15.0-11.9	16.1-12.8	15.2-11.4	13.1-11.3	13.5-10.6	13.3-10.9
Average Yield %	3.9	2.6	2.5	2.7	2.8	3.0	3.1

Statistics are as originally reported. Adj. for 2-for-1 stock split 5/21/01. [1] Bef. extraord. gain of $2.5 mill. & disc. opers. loss $6.9 mill.

OFFICERS:
D. M. Eppler, Chmn., Pres., C.E.O.
T. J. Howlin, Sr. V.P., C.F.O.
K. F. Nolen, Treas., Sec.

INVESTOR CONTACT: Rodney J. Hamilton, Dir. Inv. Rel., (318) 484-7400

PRINCIPAL OFFICE: 2030 Donahue Ferry Rd., Pineville, LA 71360-5226

TELEPHONE NUMBER: (318) 484-7400
FAX: (318) 484-7465
WEB: www.cleco.com

NO. OF EMPLOYEES: 992

SHAREHOLDERS: 9,289

ANNUAL MEETING: In Apr.

INCORPORATED: LA, Dec., 1932

INSTITUTIONAL HOLDINGS:
No. of Institutions: 156
Shares Held: 24,012,992
% Held: 53.4

INDUSTRY: Electric services (SIC: 4911)

TRANSFER AGENT(S): First Chicago Trust Company of New York, Jersey City, NJ

NYSE SYMBOL CLF
Rec. Pr. 20.30 (5/31/01)

CLEVELAND-CLIFFS INC.

YIELD 2.0%
P/E RATIO 11.7

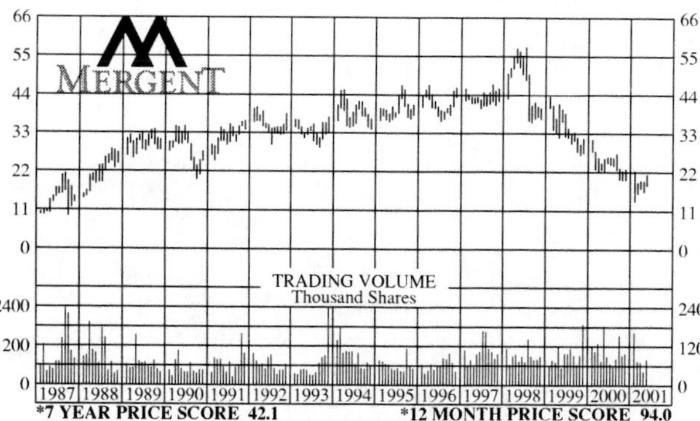

*7 YEAR PRICE SCORE 42.1 *12 MONTH PRICE SCORE 94.0
*NYSE COMPOSITE INDEX=100

INTERIM EARNINGS (Per Share):

Qtr.	Mar.	June	Sept.	Dec.
1997	0.26	1.14	1.86	1.56
1998	0.04	1.48	1.78	1.76
1999	0.24	0.70	d0.96	0.45
2000	d0.32	1.04	0.60	0.42

INTERIM DIVIDENDS (Per Share):

Amt.	Decl.	Ex.	Rec.	Pay.
0.375Q	5/09/00	5/17/00	5/19/00	6/01/00
0.375Q	7/12/00	8/10/00	8/14/00	9/01/00
0.375Q	11/14/00	11/21/00	11/24/00	12/01/00
0.10Q	1/09/01	2/09/01	2/13/01	3/01/01
0.10Q	5/08/01	5/16/01	5/18/01	6/01/01

Indicated div.: $0.40 (Div. Reinv. Plan)

CAPITALIZATION (12/31/00):

	($000)	(%)
Long-Term Debt	70,000	14.1
Minority Interest	23,900	4.8
Common & Surplus	402,000	81.1
Total	495,900	100.0

RECENT DEVELOPMENTS: For the year ended 12/31/00, net income more than tripled to $18.1 million versus $4.8 million in the previous year. Earnings included non-recurring items that resulted in after-tax special gains of $8.0 million and $4.4 million in 2000 and 1999, respectively. The increase in earnings reflected significant production curtailments in 1999 and elevated pellet sales volume. Total revenues rose 22.6% to $455.0 million versus $371.0 million in the previous year.

PROSPECTS: For 2001, the Company's outlook regarding pellet sales volume and production levels at managed mines is uncertain. The Company announced production curtailments at the Hibbing and Northshore mines to reduce its inventory levels. Earnings are expected to be adversely affected by idle expenses associated with lower operating levels at these mines. Meanwhile, CLF expects losses at Cliffs and Associates Limited for the first half of 2001 to be higher than 2000 due to modifications at the Trinidad plant.

BUSINESS

CLEVELAND-CLIFFS INC. produces and sells iron ore pellets; controls, develops, and leases reserves to mine owners; manages and owns interests in mines; sells iron ore; and owns interests in ancillary companies providing services to the mines. The Company's five iron ore mines produce multiple grades of pellets for partners and customers representing integrated steel products in the United States, Canada and Europe. The Company is developing a significant ferrous metallics business through Cliffs and Associates Limited, which consists of a facility located in Trinidad and Tobago, that produces and markets hot briquetted iron to the steel industry.

QUARTERLY DATA

(12/31/2000)($000)	REV	INC
1st Quarter	36,300	(3,500)
2nd Quarter	152,400	11,000
3rd Quarter	152,500	6,300
4th Quarter	113,800	4,300

ANNUAL FINANCIAL DATA

	12/31/00	12/31/99	12/31/98	12/31/97	12/31/96	12/31/95	12/31/94
Earnings Per Share	**(4) 1.73**	**0.43**	**5.06**	**(3) 4.80**	**(2) 5.26**	**(1) 5.10**	**3.54**
Cash Flow Per Share	**4.20**	**2.46**	**6.88**	**6.44**	**6.78**	**6.53**	**4.73**
Tang. Book Val. Per Share	**39.73**	**38.25**	**39.84**	**36.18**	**32.58**	**28.91**	**25.59**
Dividends Per Share	**1.50**	**1.50**	**1.45**	**1.30**	**1.30**	**1.30**	**1.23**
Dividend Payout %	**86.7**	**348.8**	**28.7**	**27.1**	**24.7**	**25.5**	**34.6**
INCOME STATEMENT (IN THOUSANDS):							
Total Revenues	455,000	361,400	503,900	455,700	518,100	473,100	388,900
Costs & Expenses	373,300	312,600	396,400	352,700	392,000	354,700	301,400
Depreciation & Amort.	25,600	22,500	20,300	18,900	17,600	16,800	14,400
Operating Income	56,100	26,300	87,200	84,100	108,500	101,600	73,100
Net Interest Inc./(Exp.)	d4,900	d3,700	d400	d2,600	d4,600	d6,500	d6,600
Income Before Income Taxes	16,600	4,700	71,800	72,600	95,500	71,600	57,500
Income Taxes	cr1,500	cr100	14,400	17,700	34,500	10,700	14,700
Net Income	(4) 18,100	4,800	57,400	(3) 54,900	(2) 61,000	(1) 60,900	42,800
Cash Flow	43,700	27,300	77,700	73,800	78,600	77,700	57,200
Average Shs. Outstg.	10,400	11,100	11,300	11,456	11,600	11,900	12,100
BALANCE SHEET (IN THOUSANDS):							
Cash & Cash Equivalents	29,900	67,600	130,300	115,900	169,400	148,800	141,400
Total Current Assets	248,000	217,100	259,900	265,800	300,800	292,700	269,100
Net Property	272,700	153,900	150,000	134,000	127,700	120,000	110,400
Total Assets	727,800	679,700	723,500	694,300	673,700	644,600	616,500
Total Current Liabilities	102,200	73,700	89,200	91,800	105,500	103,500	99,600
Long-Term Obligations	70,000	70,000	70,000	70,000	70,000	70,000	70,000
Net Stockholders' Equity	402,000	407,300	446,200	409,200	370,400	342,000	309,600
Net Working Capital	145,800	143,400	170,700	174,000	195,300	189,200	169,500
Year-end Shs. Outstg.	10,119	10,647	11,200	11,309	11,370	11,829	12,100
STATISTICAL RECORD:							
Operating Profit Margin %	12.3	7.3	17.3	18.5	20.9	21.5	18.8
Net Profit Margin %	4.0	1.3	11.4	12.0	11.8	12.9	11.0
Return on Equity %	4.5	1.2	12.9	13.4	16.5	17.8	13.8
Return on Assets %	2.5	0.7	7.9	7.9	9.1	9.4	6.9
Debt/Total Assets %	9.6	10.3	9.7	10.1	10.4	10.9	11.4
Price Range	31.38-19.69	43.56-26.81	57.69-36.06	47.13-40.00	46.88-36.25	46.75-36.13	45.50-34.00
P/E Ratio	18.1-11.4	101.3-62.3	11.4-7.1	9.8-8.3	8.9-6.9	9.2-7.1	12.9-9.6
Average Yield %	5.9	4.3	3.1	3.0	3.1	3.1	3.1

Statistics are as originally reported. (1) Bef. extraord. chg. of $3.1 mill. (2) Incl. a $1.3 mill. after-tax prop. insur. recov. assoc./w an ore train derailment. (3) Incl. an after-tax credit of $3.2 mill. assoc./w the rev. of an excess accrual for Savage River Mine closedown obligs. & a $5.6 mill. credit fr. the settle. of prior years' tax issues. (4) Incl. after-tax spec. gain of $8.0 mill.

OFFICERS:
J. S. Brinzo, Chmn., C.E.O.
T. J. O'Neil, Pres., C.O.O.

INVESTOR CONTACT: Fred Rice, Dir., Inv. Rel., (800) 214-0739

PRINCIPAL OFFICE: 1100 Superior Avenue, Cleveland, OH 44114-2589

TELEPHONE NUMBER: (216) 694-5700
FAX: (216) 694-4880
WEB: www.cleveland-cliffs.com

NO. OF EMPLOYEES: 5,645 (avg.)

SHAREHOLDERS: 2,579

ANNUAL MEETING: In May

INCORPORATED: OH, Feb., 1985

INSTITUTIONAL HOLDINGS:
No. of Institutions: 87
Shares Held: 8,135,586
% Held: 80.3

INDUSTRY: Iron ores (SIC: 1011)

TRANSFER AGENT(S): First Chicago Trust Company of New York, Jersey City, NJ

NYSE SYMBOL CLX
Rec. Pr. 34.64 (5/31/01)

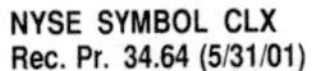

CLOROX COMPANY (THE)

YIELD 2.4%
P/E RATIO 20.5

TRADING VOLUME
Thousand Shares

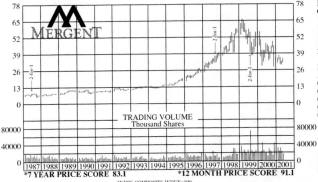

*7 YEAR PRICE SCORE 83.1 *12 MONTH PRICE SCORE 91.1

*NYSE COMPOSITE INDEX=100

INTERIM EARNINGS (Per Share):

Qtr.	Sept.	Dec.	Mar.	June
1996-97	0.32	0.22	0.32	0.36
1997-98	0.36	0.24	0.36	0.47
1998-99	0.41	0.28	0.09	0.21
1999-00	0.36	0.32	0.44	0.52
2000-01	0.42	0.31	...	...

INTERIM DIVIDENDS (Per Share):

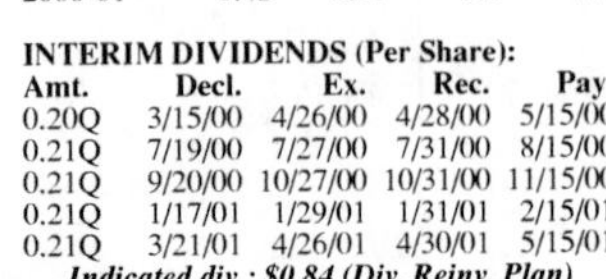

Amt.	Decl.	Ex.	Rec.	Pay.
0.20Q	3/15/00	4/26/00	4/28/00	5/15/00
0.21Q	7/19/00	7/27/00	7/31/00	8/15/00
0.21Q	9/20/00	10/27/00	10/31/00	11/15/00
0.21Q	1/17/01	1/29/01	1/31/01	2/15/01
0.21Q	3/21/01	4/26/01	4/30/01	5/15/01

Indicated div.: $0.84 (Div. Reinv. Plan)

CAPITALIZATION (6/30/00):

	($000)	(%)
Long-Term Debt	590,000	22.6
Deferred Income Tax	224,000	8.6
Common & Surplus	1,794,000	68.8
Total	2,608,000	100.0

RECENT DEVELOPMENTS: For the quarter ended 12/31/00, net earnings declined 15.8% to $64.0 million compared with $76.0 million in the prior-year quarter. Results for 2000 and 1999 included restructuring charges and asset impairment charges of $4.0 million and $6.0 million, respectively. Results for 2000 also included charges of $12.0 million related to inventory and related costs. Net sales fell 5.8% to $899.0 million versus $954.0 million a year earlier.

PROSPECTS: On 4/9/01, the Company announced it has terminated its agreement to form a joint venture with Bombril S.A., a Brazilian cleaning utensils and household cleaners business. The Company will continue searching for opportunities in Latin America, a key element of CLX's long-term growth strategy. Going forward, the Company expects volume and sales to grow in the low single-digit range, and earnings to be flat in fiscal 2001 versus the prior fiscal year.

BUSINESS

THE CLOROX COMPANY is a manufacturer and marketer of household products, both domestic and international, and products for institutional markets. CLX operates in four business segments: U.S. Home Care and Cleaning, U.S. Specialty Products, U.S. Food, Food Preparation and Storage, and International. The U.S. Home Care and Cleaning segment includes the Company's household cleaning bleach and other home care products as well as the Company's professional products business. These products include SOFT SCRUB, CLOROX, TUFFY, FORMULA 409, LIQUID PLUMR, PINE - SOL, TILEX, and SOS. The U.S. Specialty Products segment includes the Company's charcoal, automotive care, cat litter, insecticide and firelog categories. Brand names include ARMOR ALL, STP and KINGSFORD CHARCOAL. The U.S. Food, Food Preparation and Storage segment includes the Company's dressings, sauces, BRITA, GLAD, and GLADWARE businesses. These products include HIDDEN VALLEY dressings, SCOOP AWAY, JONNY CAT and FRESH STEP cat litters. The International segment, which includes the Company's overseas operations, exports and Puerto Rico, primarily focuses on the laundry, household cleaning and insecticide categories. On 1/29/99, the Company acquired First Brands Corp. for $2.00 billion.

ANNUAL FINANCIAL DATA

	6/30/00	[2] 6/30/99	6/30/98	6/30/97	6/30/96	6/30/95	6/30/94
Earnings Per Share	[3] **1.64**	[3] **1.03**	**1.41**	**1.21**	**1.07**	**0.95**	[1] **0.84**
Cash Flow Per Share	**2.48**	**1.87**	**2.06**	**1.82**	**1.63**	**1.43**	**1.27**
Tang. Book Val. Per Share	**1.10**	**0.31**	...	...	**1.11**	**1.68**	**1.82**
Dividends Per Share	**0.82**	**0.76**	**0.68**	**0.61**	**0.56**	**0.51**	**0.47**
Dividend Payout %	**50.0**	**73.8**	**48.2**	**50.6**	**51.9**	**53.4**	**55.5**
INCOME STATEMENT (IN MILLIONS):							
Total Revenues	4,083.0	4,003.0	2,741.3	2,532.7	2,217.8	1,984.2	1,836.9
Costs & Expenses	3,138.0	3,250.0	2,065.6	1,939.9	1,686.3	1,521.2	1,416.9
Depreciation & Amort.	201.0	202.0	137.6	126.4	116.5	103.9	94.1
Operating Income	744.0	551.0	538.1	466.4	415.0	359.1	325.9
Net Interest Inc./(Exp.)	d98.0	d97.0	d69.7	d55.6	d38.3	d25.1	d18.4
Income Before Income Taxes	622.0	430.0	471.9	416.0	370.4	337.9	306.6
Income Taxes	228.0	184.0	174.0	166.6	148.3	137.1	126.6
Net Income	[3] 394.0	[3] 246.0	298.0	249.4	222.1	200.8	[1] 180.0
Cash Flow	595.0	448.0	435.5	375.8	338.6	304.7	274.1
Average Shs. Outstg. (000)	239,614	240,002	211,270	206,584	207,740	212,588	215,200
BALANCE SHEET (IN MILLIONS):							
Cash & Cash Equivalents	245.0	132.0	89.7	101.0	90.8	137.3	115.9
Total Current Assets	1,454.0	1,116.0	798.7	673.5	573.8	600.3	504.3
Net Property	1,079.0	1,054.0	596.3	570.6	551.4	525.0	532.6
Total Assets	4,353.0	4,132.0	3,030.0	2,778.0	2,178.9	1,906.7	1,697.6
Total Current Liabilities	1,541.0	1,368.0	1,225.1	892.7	623.9	479.3	375.8
Long-Term Obligations	590.0	702.0	316.3	565.9	356.3	253.1	216.1
Net Stockholders' Equity	1,794.0	1,570.0	1,085.2	1,036.0	932.8	943.9	909.4
Net Working Capital	d87.0	d252.0	d426.4	d219.2	d50.0	121.0	128.4
Year-end Shs. Outstg. (000)	235,361	235,311	207,370	206,390	205,032	209,608	213,488
STATISTICAL RECORD:							
Operating Profit Margin %	18.2	13.8	19.6	18.4	18.7	18.1	17.7
Net Profit Margin %	9.6	6.1	10.9	9.8	10.0	10.1	9.8
Return on Equity %	22.0	15.7	27.5	24.1	23.8	21.3	19.8
Return on Assets %	9.1	6.0	9.8	9.0	10.2	10.5	10.6
Debt/Total Assets %	13.6	17.0	10.4	20.4	16.4	13.3	12.7
Price Range	56.38-28.38	66.47-37.50	58.75-37.19	40.19-24.31	27.56-17.50	19.81-13.81	14.88-11.75
P/E Ratio	34.4-17.3	64.5-36.4	41.7-26.4	33.3-20.2	25.8-16.4	21.0-14.6	17.7-14.0
Average Yield %	1.9	1.5	1.4	1.9	2.5	3.0	3.5

Statistics are as originally reported. Adj. for stk. splits: 2-for-1, 8/99 and 9/97. [1] Bef. disc. oper. gain $32.1 mill. [2] Incl. results of First Brands Corp. [3] Incl. one-time chrgs. $21.0 mill., 6/00; $180.0 mill., 6/99.

OFFICERS:
G. C. Sullivan, Chmn., C.E.O.
G. E. Johnston, Pres., C.O.O.
K. M. Rose, V.P., C.F.O.
P. D. Bewley, Sr. V.P., Gen., Couns., Sec.

INVESTOR CONTACT: Steve Silberblatt, Investor Relations, (510) 271-7291

PRINCIPAL OFFICE: 1221 Broadway, Oakland, CA 94612-1888

TELEPHONE NUMBER: (510) 271-7000
FAX: (510) 832-1463
WEB: www.clorox.com

NO. OF EMPLOYEES: 11,000 (approx.)

SHAREHOLDERS: 15,554 (approx.)

ANNUAL MEETING: In Nov.

INCORPORATED: DE, 1986

INSTITUTIONAL HOLDINGS:
No. of Institutions: 365
Shares Held: 121,358,332
% Held: 51.3

INDUSTRY: Polishes and sanitation goods (SIC: 2842)

TRANSFER AGENT(S): First Chicago Trust Company of New York, Jersey City, NJ

NYSE SYMBOL CMS
Rec. Pr. 30.52 (4/30/01)

CMS ENERGY CORPORATION

YIELD 4.8%
P/E RATIO 84.8

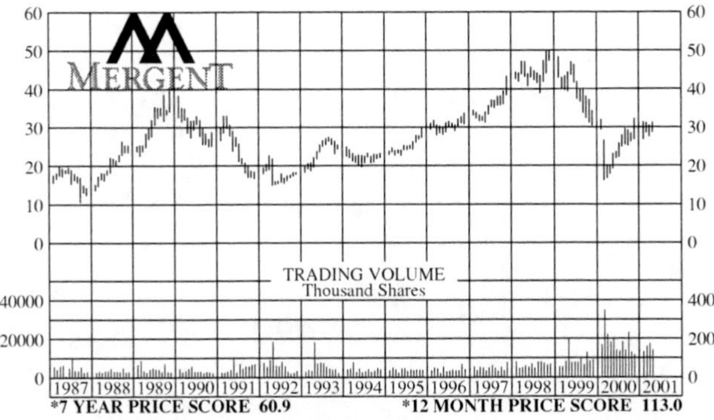

*7 YEAR PRICE SCORE 60.9 *12 MONTH PRICE SCORE 113.0
*NYSE COMPOSITE INDEX=100

INTERIM EARNINGS (Per Share):

Qtr.	Mar.	June	Sept.	Dec.
1997	0.79	0.55	0.70	0.59
1998	0.72	0.62	0.80	0.44
1999	0.80	0.67	0.78	d0.08
2000	---------------- 0.36 ----------------			

INTERIM DIVIDENDS (Per Share):

Amt.	Decl.	Ex.	Rec.	Pay.
0.365Q	7/28/00	8/08/00	8/10/00	8/22/00
0.365Q	10/23/00	10/31/00	11/02/00	11/22/00
0.365Q	1/29/01	2/05/01	2/07/01	2/22/01
0.365Q	4/27/01	5/03/01	5/07/01	5/22/01

Indicated div.: $1.46 (Div. Reinv. Plan)

CAPITALIZATION (12/31/00):

	($000)	(%)
Long-Term Debt	7,464,000	66.9
Capital Lease Obligations	54,000	0.5
Deferred Income Tax	749,000	6.7
Minority Interest	88,000	0.8
Redeemable Pfd. Stock	395,000	3.5
Preferred Stock	44,000	0.4
Common & Surplus	2,361,000	21.2
Total	11,155,000	100.0

RECENT DEVELOPMENTS: For the year ended 12/31/00, income from continuing operations was $41.0 million, before an accounting charge of $5.0 million, compared with $277.0 million in 1999. Results for 2000 included a net loss of $268.0 million from the write-down of the Company's investment in Loy Yang Power located in Australia. The 1999 results included a net investment loss of $49.0 million. Operating revenue jumped 47.4% to $9.00 billion.

PROSPECTS: On 2/9/01, CMS completed its Jorf Lasfar power plant, a coal-fueled facility, located in Morocco. The facility generates over half of Morocco's total electricity supply with its 1,356 megawatts of capacity. On 12/14/00, the Company announced the sale its 48.0% ownership interest in the Edeersa Electric Distribution utility to PSEG Global in a transaction valued at about $107.3 million. The sale is part of CMS's asset optimization program.

BUSINESS

CMS ENERGY CORPORATION is a holding company for Consumers Energy Company and CMS Enterprises Company. Consumers Energy Company provides natural gas and electricity to residents of the lower Michigan peninsula. Combined electric and gas operations serve two-thirds of Michigan's 9.5 million residents. CMS Enterprises Company offers several domestic and international energy businesses through its subsidiaries including: natural gas transmission, storage and processing; independent power production; oil and gas exploration and production; international energy distribution; and energy marketing, services and trading.

REVENUES

(12/31/00)	($000)	(%)
Electric utility	2,676,000	29.7
Gas utility	1,196,000	13.3
Natural gas, store & products	906,000	10.1
Independent power products	500,000	5.5
Oil & gas explore & products	131,000	1.5
Marketing, serv & trading	3,294,000	36.6
Other	295,000	3.3
Total	8,998,000	100.0

ANNUAL FINANCIAL DATA

	12/31/00	12/31/99	12/31/98	12/31/97	12/31/96	12/31/95	12/31/94
Earnings Per Share	**④ 0.32**	**③ 2.42**	**② 2.62**	**2.61**	**2.45**	**① 2.27**	**2.09**
Cash Flow Per Share	**6.30**	**7.91**	**7.25**	**7.99**	**7.22**	**7.02**	**7.34**
Tang. Book Val. Per Share	**12.13**	**13.49**	**17.79**	**19.59**	**16.52**	**14.84**	**12.72**
Dividends Per Share	**1.46**	**1.39**	**1.26**	**1.14**	**1.02**	**0.90**	**0.78**
Dividend Payout %	**456.1**	**57.4**	**48.1**	**43.7**	**41.6**	**39.6**	**37.3**
INCOME STATEMENT (IN MILLIONS):							
Total Revenues	8,998.0	6,103.0	5,141.0	4,787.0	4,333.0	3,890.0	3,619.0
Costs & Expenses	7,302.0	4,345.0	3,655.0	3,346.0	2,982.0	2,624.0	2,471.0
Depreciation & Amort.	671.0	630.0	535.0	521.0	482.0	477.0	452.0
Maintenance Exp.	298.0	216.0	176.0	174.0	178.0	186.0	192.0
Operating Income	727.0	912.0	775.0	746.0	691.0	603.0	504.0
Net Interest Inc./(Exp.)	d590.0	d519.0	d336.0	d306.0	d265.0	d243.0	d205.0
Income Taxes	60.0	64.0	100.0	117.0	139.0	118.0	104.0
Equity Earnings/Minority Int.	d3.0	...	...	...	...	...	...
Net Income	④ 41.0	③ 277.0	② 242.0	268.0	240.0	① 204.0	179.0
Cash Flow	712.0	907.0	777.0	789.0	722.0	681.0	631.0
Average Shs. Outstg. (000)	113,100	114,700	107,200	98,700	100,000	97,000	86,000
BALANCE SHEET (IN MILLIONS):							
Gross Property	14,087.0	14,278.0	11,253.0	10,705.0	10,147.0	9,701.0	9,125.0
Accumulated Depreciation	6,252.0	6,157.0	5,213.0	5,270.0	4,867.0	4,627.0	4,299.0
Net Property	7,835.0	8,121.0	6,040.0	5,435.0	5,280.0	5,074.0	4,826.0
Total Assets	15,851.0	15,462.0	11,310.0	9,793.0	8,616.0	8,143.0	7,384.0
Long-Term Obligations	7,518.0	7,799.0	5,004.0	3,520.0	2,945.0	3,012.0	2,817.0
Net Stockholders' Equity	2,405.0	2,500.0	2,312.0	2,215.0	2,058.0	1,825.0	1,463.0
Year-end Shs. Outstg. (000)	121,201	116,038	116,557	100,900	103,000	99,000	87,000
STATISTICAL RECORD:							
Operating Profit Margin %	8.1	14.9	15.1	15.6	15.9	15.5	13.9
Net Profit Margin %	0.5	4.5	4.7	5.6	5.5	5.2	4.9
Net Inc./Net Property %	0.5	3.4	4.0	4.9	4.5	4.0	3.7
Net Inc./Tot. Capital %	0.4	2.4	3.0	4.0	4.1	3.7	3.7
Return on Equity %	1.7	11.1	10.5	12.1	11.7	11.2	12.2
Accum. Depr./Gross Prop. %	44.4	43.1	46.3	49.2	48.0	47.7	47.1
Price Range	32.25-16.06	48.44-30.31	50.13-38.75	43.38-31.13	33.75-27.81	30.00-22.63	25.00-19.63
P/E Ratio	100.7-50.2	20.0-12.5	19.1-14.8	16.6-11.9	13.8-11.4	13.2-10.0	12.0-9.4
Average Yield %	6.0	3.5	2.8	3.1	3.3	3.4	3.5

Statistics are as originally reported. ① Incl. non-recurr. credit $15.0 mill. ② Bef. acctg. chrg. credit $43.0 mill. ③ Incl. special net chrg. of $49.0 mill. ($0.45/sh.) and a one-time chrg. of $84.0 mill. ($0.26/sh.) ④ Bef. acctg. chrg. $5.0 mill. & incl. net loss of $268.0 mill. fr. sale of an investment.

OFFICERS:
W. T. McCormick Jr., Chmn., C.E.O.
V. J. Fryling, Pres., C.O.O.
A. M. Wright, Exec. V.P., C.F.O.
R. A. Kershner, Sr. V.P., General Couns.

INVESTOR CONTACT: Investor Relations, (517) 788-2590

PRINCIPAL OFFICE: Fairlane Plaza South, Ste. 1100, 330 Town Center Drive, Dearborn, MI 48126

TELEPHONE NUMBER: (313) 436-9200
FAX: (313) 436-9225
WEB: www.cmsenergy.com

NO. OF EMPLOYEES: 11,599 full-time; 53 part-time

SHAREHOLDERS: 66,783

ANNUAL MEETING: In May

INCORPORATED: MI, 1987

INSTITUTIONAL HOLDINGS:
No. of Institutions: 239
Shares Held: 86,144,572
% Held: 65.5

INDUSTRY: Electric and other services combined (SIC: 4931)

TRANSFER AGENT(S): Investor Services Department, Jackson, MI

NYSE SYMBOL CNA
Rec. Pr. 35.31 (4/30/01)

CNA FINANCIAL CORPORATION

YIELD ...
P/E RATIO 5.3

INTERIM EARNINGS (Per Share):

Qtr.	Mar.	June	Sept.	Dec.
1996	1.77	1.08	1.28	1.04
1997	0.95	1.26	1.47	1.49
1998	1.25	1.12	d0.09	d0.80
1999	0.91	0.82	0.15	d1.68
2000	0.76	1.80	3.00	1.06

INTERIM DIVIDENDS (Per Share):

Amt.	Decl.	Ex.	Rec.	Pay.

No dividends paid.

CAPITALIZATION (12/31/00):

	($000)	(%)
Long-Term Debt	2,729,000	21.7
Minority Interest	217,000	1.7
Common & Surplus	9,647,000	76.6
Total	12,593,000	100.0

RECENT DEVELOPMENTS: For the year ended 12/31/00, the Company reported net income of $1.21 billion compared with income of $47.0 million, before an accounting change charge, in 1999. Results included realized investment gains of $860.0 million and $192.0 million in 2000 and 1999, respectively. Results for 1999 also included after-tax restructuring and other related charges of $54.0 million. Net premium earned declined 13.2% to $6.78 billion versus $7.81 billion in the prior year.

PROSPECTS: On 1/4/01, CNA, the insurance unit of the Company, announced the closing of the sale of its life reinsurance business to MARC, the U.S. life subsidiary of Munich Re. The transaction will help CNA to narrow its focus on its core business-to-business insurance services. The financial terms of the transaction were not disclosed. Going forward, the discipline of simplifying and sharpening CNA's business focus should drive strategies that are expected to benefit customers and shareholders.

BUSINESS

CNA FINANCIAL CORPORATION'S principal business is as a multiple-line insurer, underwriting property, casualty, life, accident and health coverages and pension products and annuities. Property and casualty insurance operations are conducted by Continental Casualty Co. and its affiliates, and life insurance operations are conducted primarily by Continental Assurance Co. The Company also provides services that include risk management, information services, health care management and claims administration. The Company acquired The Continental Corporation on 5/10/95. Loews Corporation owns 87% of CNA Financial Corp.'s outstanding common stock as of 12/31/00.

REVENUES

(12/31/2000)	($000)	(%)
Premiums	11,474,000	80.3
Net Investment Income	2,080,000	14.5
Other Revenues	739,000	5.2
Total	14,293,000	100.0

ANNUAL FINANCIAL DATA

	12/31/00	12/31/99	12/31/98	12/31/97	12/31/96	12/31/95	12/31/94
Earnings Per Share	**6.61**	**2 0.19**	**1 1.49**	**5.17**	**5.17**	**4.05**	**0.17**
Tang. Book Val. Per Share	**50.91**	**45.88**	**45.89**	**40.66**	**35.02**	**33.06**	**23.62**
INCOME STATEMENT (IN MILLIONS):							
Total Premium Income	11,474.0	13,282.0	13,375.0	13,362.0	13,479.0	11,735.1	9,474.4
Other Income	4,140.0	3,121.0	3,699.0	3,710.0	3,508.8	2,964.6	1,525.1
Total Revenues	15,614.0	16,403.0	17,074.0	17,072.0	16,987.8	14,699.7	10,999.5
Policyholder Benefits	9,831.0	11,900.0	11,717.0	11,268.0	11,370.6	9,951.7	8,450.3
Income Before Income Taxes	1,810.0	d11.0	349.0	1,358.0	1,345.0	1,042.4	d134.0
Income Taxes	568.0	cr88.0	47.0	392.0	380.2	285.4	cr170.5
Equity Earnings/Minority Int.	d28.0	d30.0	d20.0	...	...	...	...
Net Income	1,214.0	2 47.0	1 282.0	966.0	964.8	757.0	36.5
Average Shs. Outstg. (000)	183,600	184,200	184,900	185,400	185,400	185,394	185,394
BALANCE SHEET (IN MILLIONS):							
Cash & Cash Equivalents	7,298.0	7,118.0	6,224.0	6,081.0	6,969.9	4,863.8	5,938.5
Premiums Due	14,862.0	13,059.0	12,598.0	12,822.0	13,008.7	12,789.4	7,401.2
Invst. Assets: Fixed-term	26,652.0	27,248.0	30,073.0	29,548.0	27,720.6	30,444.7	20,827.7
Invst. Assets: Total	34,801.0	35,250.0	36,849.0	35,900.0	35,135.2	35,597.7	26,815.4
Total Assets	62,068.0	61,219.0	62,432.0	61,269.0	60,456.7	59,901.8	44,320.4
Long-Term Obligations	2,729.0	2,881.0	3,160.0	2,897.0	2,764.9	2,767.9	911.8
Net Stockholders' Equity	9,647.0	8,938.0	9,157.0	8,309.0	7,059.8	6,735.5	4,545.9
Year-end Shs. Outstg. (000)	183,264	184,407	183,890	185,394	185,394	185,394	185,394
STATISTICAL RECORD:							
Return on Revenues %	7.8	0.3	1.7	5.7	5.7	5.1	0.3
Return on Equity %	12.6	0.5	3.1	11.6	13.7	11.2	0.8
Return on Assets %	2.0	0.1	0.5	1.6	1.6	1.3	0.1
Price Range	41.94-24.56	45.31-33.00	53.31-34.50	44.08-32.13	39.17-31.92	41.08-21.58	27.42-20.00
P/E Ratio	6.3-3.7	238.3-173.7	35.8-23.2	8.5-6.2	7.6-6.2	10.2-5.3	161.2-117.6

Statistics are as originally reported. Adj. for stk. split: 3-for-1, 6/98 1 Incl. restruct. chrg. $246.0 mill. 2 Incl. restruct. chrg. $54.0 mill.; bef. acctg. change chrg. $177.0 mill.

OFFICERS:
E. J. Noha, Chmn.
L. A. Tisch, C.E.O.
R. V. Deutsch, Sr. V.P., C.F.O.
J. D. Kantor, Sr. V.P., Gen. Couns., Sec.

INVESTOR CONTACT: Donald P. Lofe, Jr., V.P., (312) 822-3993

PRINCIPAL OFFICE: CNA Plaza, Chicago, IL 60685

TELEPHONE NUMBER: (312) 822-5000
FAX: (312) 822-6419
WEB: www.cna.com

NO. OF EMPLOYEES: 19,100 (approx.)

SHAREHOLDERS: 2,540

ANNUAL MEETING: In May

INCORPORATED: DE, Sept., 1967

INSTITUTIONAL HOLDINGS:
No. of Institutions: 108
Shares Held: 177,304,539
% Held: 96.7

INDUSTRY: Fire, marine, and casualty insurance (SIC: 6331)

TRANSFER AGENT(S): First Chicago Trust Company of New York, Jersey City, NJ

NYSE SYMBOL CNF
Rec. Pr. 30.66 (4/30/01)

CNF INC.

YIELD 1.3%
P/E RATIO 11.5

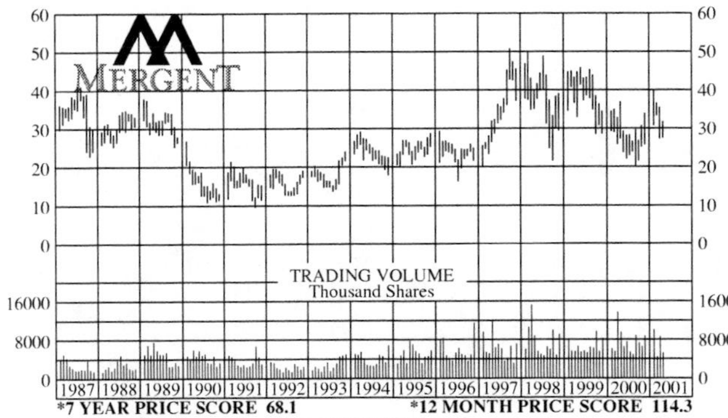

*7 YEAR PRICE SCORE 68.1 *12 MONTH PRICE SCORE 114.3

*NYSE COMPOSITE INDEX=100

INTERIM EARNINGS (Per Share):

Qtr.	Mar.	June	Sept.	Dec.
1997	0.43	0.59	0.75	0.51
1998	0.33	0.73	0.78	0.61
1999	0.74	0.86	0.77	0.97
2000	0.69	0.80	0.48	0.70

INTERIM DIVIDENDS (Per Share):

Amt.	Decl.	Ex.	Rec.	Pay.
0.10Q	5/01/00	5/11/00	5/15/00	6/15/00
0.10Q	6/26/00	8/11/00	8/15/00	9/15/00
0.10Q	10/02/00	11/13/00	11/15/00	12/15/00
0.10Q	1/29/01	2/13/01	2/15/01	3/15/01
0.10Q	4/30/01	5/11/01	5/15/01	6/15/01

Indicated div.: $0.40 (Div. Reinv. Plan)

CAPITALIZATION (12/31/00):

	($000)	(%)
Long-Term Debt	424,116	22.7
Capital Lease Obligations	110,533	5.9
Deferred Income Tax	144,463	7.7
Redeemable Pfd. Stock	125,000	6.7
Preferred Stock	8	0.0
Common & Surplus	1,061,914	56.9
Total	1,866,034	100.0

RECENT DEVELOPMENTS: For the year ended 12/31/00, CNF reported income of $151.3 million, before an accounting charge of $2.7 million, versus income of $187.5 million in 1999. Earnings for 2000 and 1999 excluded a loss of $13.5 million and a gain of $3.0 million, respectively, from discontinued operations. Earnings for 2000 included a net after-tax loss of $8.6 million. Earnings for 1999 included various after-tax gains of $20.4 million. Total revenues rose 10.6% to $5.57 billion from $5.04 billion in the prior year.

PROSPECTS: Going forward, the Company expects to be negatively affected by the slowing U.S. economy. However, the pricing environment at Con-Way and Emery Worldwide should remain firm. At Menlo Logistics, revenue and operating income are expected to continue to increase at approximately 20.0% annually. CNF anticipates start-up costs for Vector SCM, a joint venture with General Motors formed in December 2000, to be approximately $6.0 million.

BUSINESS

CNF INC. (formerly CNF Transportation, Inc.) is a provider of regional less-than-truckload trucking, heavy air freight, contract logistics, and trailer manufacturing. CNF's four principal subsidiaries include: Con-Way Transportation Services, which provides regional LTL trucking services in all 50 states; Emery Worldwide, which provides domestic and international air freight services, as well as nightly air transportation services to the U.S. Postal Service; Menlo Logistics, a contract logistics company; and Road Systems, Inc., which manufactures and rebuilds trailers. CNF also provides other transportation services, including truckload services, ocean forwarding and customs brokerage.

BUSINESS LINE ANALYSIS

(12/31/2000)($000)	REV (%)	INC (%)
Con-Way Transportation	36.7	78.4
Emery Worldwide	46.8	9.8
Menlo Logistics	16.0	11.5
Other Segments	0.5	0.3
Total	100.0	100.0

ANNUAL FINANCIAL DATA

	12/31/00	12/31/99	12/31/98	12/31/97	[2] 12/31/96	12/31/95	12/31/94
Earnings Per Share	[3][5] 2.65	[4] 3.35	2.45	2.19	[3] 1.59	1.10	[1] 1.11
Cash Flow Per Share	6.10	6.87	5.48	4.59	3.71	4.39	5.02
Tang. Book Val. Per Share	16.59	14.49	10.61	8.03	9.87	14.67	16.30
Dividends Per Share	0.40	0.40	0.40	0.40	0.40	0.41	...
Dividend Payout %	15.1	11.9	16.3	18.3	25.2	37.3	...
INCOME STATEMENT (IN MILLIONS):							
Total Revenues	5,572.4	5,592.8	4,941.5	4,266.8	3,662.2	5,281.1	4,680.5
Costs & Expenses	5,084.4	5,031.4	4,477.8	3,871.4	3,374.3	4,989.1	4,392.5
Depreciation & Amort.	198.0	202.3	173.1	130.5	95.7	148.1	145.8
Operating Income	290.0	359.1	290.5	264.9	192.1	143.9	142.2
Net Interest Inc./(Exp.)	d30.0	d26.0	d32.6	d39.6	d39.8	d34.3	d27.9
Income Before Income Taxes	261.2	337.1	250.4	221.8	147.1	110.9	111.9
Income Taxes	109.9	146.6	111.4	100.9	67.0	53.5	51.6
Net Income	[3][5] 151.3	[4] 190.5	139.0	120.9	[3] 80.2	57.4	[1] 60.3
Cash Flow	341.1	384.6	304.0	243.5	167.3	194.6	187.0
Average Shs. Outstg. (000)	55,901	56,019	55,514	53,077	45,063	44,362	37,216
BALANCE SHEET (IN MILLIONS):							
Cash & Cash Equivalents	104.5	146.3	73.9	97.6	82.1	86.3	95.7
Total Current Assets	1,240.3	1,200.2	1,100.4	1,009.4	815.9	1,151.6	1,031.5
Net Property	1,106.5	1,131.0	984.5	879.8	752.6	1,076.0	944.6
Total Assets	3,244.9	3,049.0	2,689.4	2,421.5	2,081.9	2,750.1	2,472.7
Total Current Liabilities	958.9	1,049.2	900.6	806.1	815.1	959.2	877.2
Long-Term Obligations	534.6	433.4	467.6	473.5	477.2	495.5	397.9
Net Stockholders' Equity	1,061.9	967.9	776.4	658.1	508.3	722.4	673.6
Net Working Capital	281.4	151.1	199.7	203.2	0.8	192.3	154.2
Year-end Shs. Outstg. (000)	48,656	48,450	47,875	47,392	44,566	43,902	36,354
STATISTICAL RECORD:							
Operating Profit Margin %	5.2	6.4	5.9	6.2	5.2	2.7	3.0
Net Profit Margin %	2.7	3.4	2.8	2.8	2.2	1.1	1.3
Return on Equity %	14.2	19.7	17.9	18.4	15.8	7.9	9.0
Return on Assets %	4.7	6.2	5.2	5.0	3.9	2.1	2.4
Debt/Total Assets %	16.5	14.2	17.4	19.6	22.9	18.0	16.1
Price Range	36.88-20.19	45.88-28.38	49.94-21.56	50.88-20.25	29.38-16.25	28.75-20.25	29.25-17.88
P/E Ratio	13.9-7.6	13.7-8.5	20.4-8.8	23.2-9.2	18.5-10.2	26.1-18.4	26.3-16.1
Average Yield %	1.4	1.1	1.1	1.1	1.8	1.7	...

Statistics are as originally reported. [1] Bef. extra. chg. of $5.5 mill. [2] Refl. spin-off of Consolidated Freightways Corp. [3] Bef. loss from disc. ops. of $13.5 mill., 2000; $52.6 mill., 1996. [4] Incl. various pre-tax net gains of $26.6 mill. [5] Incl. various after-tax losses of $10.1 mill.

OFFICERS:
D. E. Moffitt, Chmn.
G. L. Quesnel, Pres., C.E.O., Interim C.F.O.
E. G. Schmoller, Sr. V.P., Sec., Gen. Couns.

INVESTOR CONTACT: James R. Allen, Investor Relations, (650) 494-2900

PRINCIPAL OFFICE: 3240 Hillview Ave., Palo Alto, CA 94304

TELEPHONE NUMBER: (650) 494-2900
FAX: (650) 813-0160
WEB: www.cnf.com

NO. OF EMPLOYEES: 28,700 (approx.)

SHAREHOLDERS: 8,802

ANNUAL MEETING: In April

INCORPORATED: WA, Aug., 1929; reincorp., DE, 1958

INSTITUTIONAL HOLDINGS:
No. of Institutions: 187
Shares Held: 40,052,499
% Held: 82.2

INDUSTRY: Trucking, except local (SIC: 4213)

TRANSFER AGENT(S): First Chicago Trust Company of New York, Jersey City, NJ

NYSE SYMBOL COA
Rec. Pr. 9.98 (5/31/01)

COACHMEN INDUSTRIES, INC.

YIELD 2.0%
P/E RATIO 66.5

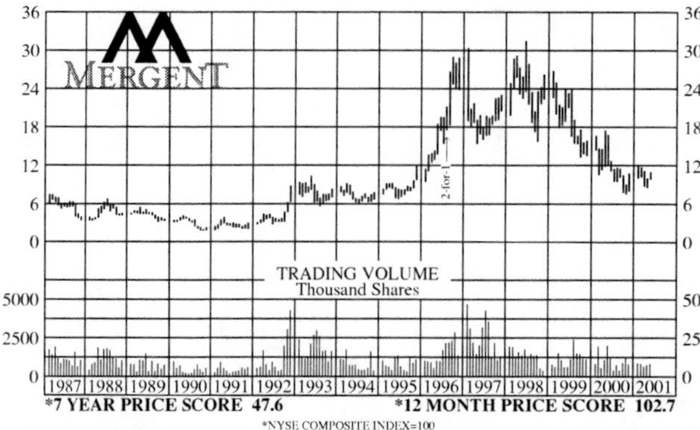

INTERIM EARNINGS (Per Share):

Qtr.	Mar.	June	Sept.	Dec.
1997	0.26	0.37	0.44	0.36
1998	0.36	0.53	0.59	0.43
1999	0.43	0.58	0.58	0.24
2000	0.26	0.24	0.15	d0.50

INTERIM DIVIDENDS (Per Share):

Amt.	Decl.	Ex.	Rec.	Pay.
0.05Q	5/05/00	5/23/00	5/25/00	6/15/00
0.05Q	7/27/00	8/15/00	8/17/00	9/07/00
0.05Q	10/20/00	11/08/00	11/10/00	12/01/00
0.05Q	2/01/01	2/20/01	2/22/01	3/15/01
0.05Q	5/03/01	5/22/01	5/24/01	6/14/01

Indicated div.: $0.20

CAPITALIZATION (12/31/00):

	($000)	(%)
Long-Term Debt	11,795	5.1
Deferred Income Tax	3,370	1.5
Common & Surplus	214,949	93.4
Total	230,114	100.0

RECENT DEVELOPMENTS: For the year ended 12/31/00, net income declined 92.7% to $2.2 million compared with $29.5 million in 1999. Earnings for 2000 included pre-tax gain of $891,000 from the sale of property. Net sales were $710.0 million, down 16.2% from $847.0 million a year earlier. Recreational vehicle segment sales declined 22.1% to $538.4 million, while sales in the modular housing and building segment rose 10.1% to $171.6 million.

PROSPECTS: COA's acquisition of KanBuild, Inc. should be completed during February 2001. KanBuild is a modular home producer with year 2000 revenues of $30.0 million and pretax earnings of $1.8 million. Separately, the Company has made significant progress on its strategic plans and has taken steps anticipating changing market conditions that should improve profitability.

BUSINESS

COACHMEN INDUSTRIES, INC. is a full-line manufacturer of recreational vehicles and modular homes. COA's recreational vehicles are marketed under various brand names, including COACHMEN, SHASTA, and VIKING, through approximately 1,300 independent dealers located in 49 states and internationally and through eight Company-owned dealerships. The recreational vehicle companies of COA include Coachmen Recreational Vehicle Co., Georgie Boy Manufacturing, Inc., Viking Recreational Vehicle Co., and Shasta Industries. The vehicle segment consists of the manufacture and distribution of Class A and Class C motorhomes, travel trailers, fifth wheel trailers, camping trailers, truck campers, and truck conversions and related parts and supplies. The housing segment consists of factory produced modular homes. The Company's modular homes are manufactured by COA's All American Homes operation, which sells homes through approximately 300 builders, by COA's Mod-U-Kraf Homes, Inc., and Miller Building Systems. The Company produces a variety of fiberglass and termoformed plastic products through PRODESIGN.

ANNUAL FINANCIAL DATA

	12/31/00	12/31/99	12/31/98	12/31/97	12/31/96	12/31/95	12/31/94
Earnings Per Share	**[4] 0.14**	**[3] 1.80**	**1.92**	**1.42**	**[2] 1.94**	**[1] 1.18**	**[1] 1.01**
Cash Flow Per Share	**0.86**	**2.36**	**2.38**	**1.82**	**2.16**	**1.46**	**1.21**
Tang. Book Val. Per Share	**12.67**	**13.47**	**12.11**	**10.70**	**7.92**	**5.75**	**5.03**
Dividends Per Share	**0.20**	**0.20**	**0.20**	**0.20**	**0.23**	**0.14**	**0.12**
Dividend Payout %	**142.8**	**11.1**	**10.4**	**14.1**	**12.1**	**11.9**	**11.9**
INCOME STATEMENT (IN THOUSANDS):							
Total Revenues	709,975	847,024	756,030	661,591	606,474	515,862	394,024
Costs & Expenses	696,245	797,108	702,153	619,498	561,179	485,073	368,424
Depreciation & Amort.	11,214	9,273	7,948	6,833	5,623	4,130	3,100
Operating Income	2,516	40,643	45,928	35,260	39,672	26,659	22,500
Net Interest Inc./(Exp.)	d751	918	3,092	2,431	43	d1,836	d814
Income Before Income Taxes	2,887	45,041	50,291	38,826	41,483	27,957	22,812
Income Taxes	723	15,539	17,228	14,063	14,146	10,408	8,028
Net Income	[4] 2,164	[3] 29,502	33,063	24,763	[2] 27,337	[1] 17,549	[1] 14,784
Cash Flow	13,378	38,775	41,011	31,595	32,960	21,679	17,885
Average Shs. Outstg.	15,639	16,421	17,261	17,401	15,281	14,882	14,744
BALANCE SHEET (IN THOUSANDS):							
Cash & Cash Equivalents	21,351	36,819	54,289	87,281	66,949	17,521	20,284
Total Current Assets	173,950	190,822	185,411	189,938	163,913	101,722	89,153
Net Property	84,163	74,678	63,072	46,602	39,857	31,747	19,211
Total Assets	296,446	285,766	268,476	259,062	227,448	150,249	125,021
Total Current Liabilities	57,713	55,719	45,718	49,676	38,522	41,135	37,819
Long-Term Obligations	11,795	8,346	10,191	12,591	14,841	12,118	7,023
Net Stockholders' Equity	214,949	213,646	205,458	190,136	167,656	91,037	74,756
Net Working Capital	116,237	135,103	139,693	140,262	125,391	60,588	51,334
Year-end Shs. Outstg.	15,703	15,528	16,585	17,302	20,528	14,938	14,798
STATISTICAL RECORD:							
Operating Profit Margin %	0.4	4.8	6.1	5.3	6.5	5.2	5.7
Net Profit Margin %	0.3	3.5	4.4	3.7	4.5	3.4	3.8
Return on Equity %	1.0	13.8	16.1	13.0	16.3	19.3	19.8
Return on Assets %	0.7	10.3	12.3	9.6	12.0	11.7	11.8
Debt/Total Assets %	4.0	2.9	3.8	4.9	6.5	8.1	5.6
Price Range	17.50-7.50	26.88-13.25	31.50-15.69	30.38-15.38	29.00-9.44	11.88-6.69	9.19-5.88
P/E Ratio	124.9-53.5	14.9-7.4	16.4-8.2	21.4-10.8	14.9-4.9	10.1-5.7	9.1-5.8
Average Yield %	1.6	1.0	0.8	0.9	1.2	1.5	1.6

Statistics are as originally reported. Adj. for 2-for-1 stock split, 8/28/96. [1] Incl. gains on the sale of property of $2.9 mill., 1995; & $88,902, 1994. [2] Bef. acctg. adj. of $2.3 mill. [3] Incl. a pre-tax charge of $709,000 for acctg. change. [4] Incls. gain of $891,000 from the sale of property.

OFFICERS:
C. C. Skinner, Chmn., C.E.O., Pres.
R. M. Lavers, Exec. V.P., Interim C.F.O.

INVESTOR CONTACT: Melanie A. DeMorrow, Asst. V.P., Shareholder Rel., (219) 262-0123

PRINCIPAL OFFICE: 2831 Dexter Drive, Elkhart, IN 46514

TELEPHONE NUMBER: (219) 262-0123
FAX: (219) 262-8823
WEB: wwww.coachmen.com

NO. OF EMPLOYEES: 4,149 (avg.)

SHAREHOLDERS: 2,011

ANNUAL MEETING: In May

INCORPORATED: IN, Dec., 1964

INSTITUTIONAL HOLDINGS:
No. of Institutions: 73
Shares Held: 11,156,071
% Held: 70.8

INDUSTRY: Motor homes (SIC: 3716)

TRANSFER AGENT(S): First Chicago Trust Company of New York, New York, NY

NYSE SYMBOL KO
Rec. Pr. 46.19 (4/30/01)

COCA-COLA COMPANY (THE)

YIELD	1.6%
P/E RATIO	52.5

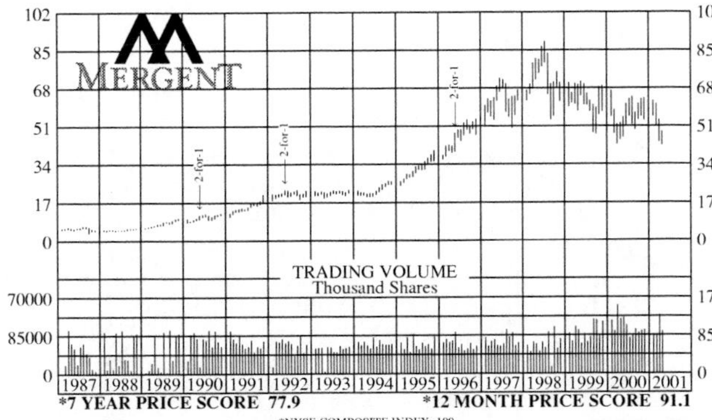

*7 YEAR PRICE SCORE 77.9 *12 MONTH PRICE SCORE 91.1

*NYSE COMPOSITE INDEX=100

INTERIM EARNINGS (Per Share):

Qtr.	Mar.	June	Sept.	Dec.
1997	0.40	0.53	0.41	0.33
1998	0.35	0.48	0.36	0.24
1999	0.30	0.38	0.32	d0.02
2000	d0.02	0.37	0.43	0.10

INTERIM DIVIDENDS (Per Share):

Amt.	Decl.	Ex.	Rec.	Pay.
0.17Q	4/19/00	6/13/00	6/15/00	7/01/00
0.17Q	7/20/00	9/13/00	9/15/00	10/01/00
0.17Q	10/18/00	11/29/00	12/01/00	12/15/00
0.18Q	2/15/01	3/13/01	3/15/01	4/01/01
0.18Q	4/17/01	6/13/01	6/15/01	7/01/01

Indicated div.: $0.72 (Div. Reinv. Plan)

CAPITALIZATION (12/31/00):

	($000)	(%)
Long-Term Debt	835,000	7.9
Deferred Income Tax	358,000	3.4
Common & Surplus	9,316,000	88.6
Total	10,509,000	100.0

RECENT DEVELOPMENTS: For the year ended 12/31/00, net income declined 10.4% to $2.18 billion versus $2.43 billion in 1999. Results for 2000 and 1999 included non-recurring charges of $1.44 billion and $813.0 million, respectively. Net operating revenues rose 3.3% to $20.46 billion. On 2/21/01, KO and The Procter & Gamble Company announced a stand-alone enterprise focused on marketing juices, juice-based beverages and snacks on a global basis. KO and P&G will each own 50.0% of the new company.

PROSPECTS: On 1/30/00, KO and Nestle S.A. announced the further development of their existing joint venture partnership, Coca-Cola and Nestle Refreshments, which will be renamed Beverage Partners Worldwide (BPW). In addition to its present coffee and tea-based product lines, BPW, which currently operates in 24 countries, will also participate in the fast growing herbal beverage sector, as well as market beverages with a healthful positioning.

BUSINESS

THE COCA-COLA COMPANY is engaged in the manufacturing, distributing and marketing of soft drink concentrates and syrups. Principal beverage products are: COCA-COLA, COCA-COLA CLASSIC, DIET COKE, CHERRY COKE, FANTA, SPRITE, MR. PIBB, MELLO YELLOW, BARQ'S ROOT BEER, POWERADE, FRUITOPIA, DASANI plus other assorted diet and caffeine-free versions. The Minute Maid Company produces, distributes and markets principally juice and juice-drink products. Popular brands include MINUTE MAID, FIVE ALIVE, BRIGHT & EARLY, BACARDI brand tropical fruit mixers and HI-C. Additionally, Coca-Cola Nestle Refreshments, KO's joint venture with Nestle S.A., markets ready-to-drink teas and coffees in certain countries. As of 12/31/00, KO held an approximate 40% interest in Coca-Cola Enterprises, Inc., a soft drink bottling concern.

GEOGRAPHIC DATA

(12/31/2000)	REV(%)	INC(%)
North America	38.8	29.5
Africa & Middle East	3.6	1.7
Europe & Eurasia	21.5	29.6
Latin America	10.7	19.2
Asia Pacific	25.4	20.0
Total	100.0	100.0

ANNUAL FINANCIAL DATA

	12/31/00	12/31/99	12/31/98	12/31/97	12/31/96	12/31/95	12/31/94
Earnings Per Share	3 **0.88**	2 **0.98**	**1.42**	1 **1.64**	**1.40**	**1.18**	**0.99**
Cash Flow Per Share	**1.19**	**1.30**	**1.67**	**1.89**	**1.59**	**1.36**	**1.15**
Tang. Book Val. Per Share	**2.98**	**3.06**	**3.19**	**2.66**	**2.18**	**1.78**	**1.79**
Dividends Per Share	**0.68**	**0.64**	**0.60**	**0.56**	**0.50**	**0.44**	**0.39**
Dividend Payout %	**77.3**	**65.3**	**42.3**	**34.1**	**35.7**	**37.3**	**39.4**
INCOME STATEMENT (IN MILLIONS):							
Total Revenues	20,458.0	19,805.0	18,813.0	18,868.0	18,546.0	18,018.0	16,172.0
Costs & Expenses	15,994.0	15,031.0	13,201.0	13,241.0	14,152.0	13,538.0	12,053.0
Depreciation & Amort.	773.0	792.0	645.0	626.0	479.0	454.0	411.0
Operating Income	3,691.0	3,982.0	4,967.0	1 5,001.0	3,915.0	4,026.0	3,708.0
Net Interest Inc./(Exp.)	d102.0	d77.0	d58.0	d47.0	d48.0	d27.0	d18.0
Income Before Income Taxes	3,399.0	3,819.0	5,198.0	6,055.0	4,596.0	4,328.0	3,728.0
Income Taxes	1,222.0	1,388.0	1,665.0	1,926.0	1,104.0	1,342.0	1,174.0
Equity Earnings/Minority Int.	d289.0	d184.0	32.0	155.0	211.0	169.0	134.0
Net Income	3 2,177.0	2 2,431.0	3,533.0	1 4,129.0	3,492.0	2,986.0	2,554.0
Cash Flow	2,950.0	3,223.0	4,178.0	4,755.0	3,971.0	3,440.0	2,965.0
Average Shs. Outstg. (000)	2,487,000	2,487,000	2,496,000	2,515,000	2,494,000	2,524,000	2,580,000
BALANCE SHEET (IN MILLIONS):							
Cash & Cash Equivalents	1,892.0	1,812.0	1,807.0	1,843.0	1,658.0	1,315.0	1,531.0
Total Current Assets	6,620.0	6,480.0	6,380.0	5,969.0	5,910.0	5,450.0	5,205.0
Net Property	4,168.0	4,267.0	3,669.0	3,743.0	3,550.0	4,336.0	4,080.0
Total Assets	20,834.0	21,623.0	19,145.0	16,940.0	16,161.0	15,041.0	13,873.0
Total Current Liabilities	9,321.0	9,856.0	8,640.0	7,379.0	7,406.0	7,348.0	6,177.0
Long-Term Obligations	835.0	854.0	687.0	801.0	1,116.0	1,141.0	1,426.0
Net Stockholders' Equity	9,316.0	9,513.0	8,403.0	7,311.0	6,156.0	5,392.0	5,235.0
Net Working Capital	d2,701.0	d3,376.0	d2,260.0	d1,410.0	d1,496.0	d1,898.0	d972.0
Year-end Shs. Outstg. (000)	2,484,761	2,471,575	2,466,000	2,471,000	2,481,000	2,504,598	2,551,866
STATISTICAL RECORD:							
Operating Profit Margin %	18.0	20.1	26.4	26.5	21.1	22.3	22.9
Net Profit Margin %	10.6	12.3	18.8	21.9	18.8	16.6	15.8
Return on Equity %	23.4	25.6	42.0	56.5	56.7	55.4	48.8
Return on Assets %	10.4	11.2	18.5	24.4	21.6	19.9	18.4
Debt/Total Assets %	4.0	3.9	3.6	4.7	6.9	7.6	10.3
Price Range	66.88-42.88	70.88-47.31	88.94-53.63	72.63-50.00	54.25-36.06	40.19-24.38	26.75-19.44
P/E Ratio	76.0-48.7	72.3-48.3	62.6-37.8	44.3-30.5	38.7-25.8	34.1-20.7	27.0-19.6
Average Yield %	1.2	1.1	0.8	0.9	1.1	1.4	1.7

Statistics are as originally reported. Adj. for 2-for-1 stk. split, 5/96 1 Incls. non-recurr. pre-tax net gain of $290.0 mill. 2 Incls. non-recurr. chrg. of $813.0 mill. 3 Incls. non-recurr. chrgs. of $1.04 bill. ($0.29/sh.) & asset writedown of $405.0 mill. ($0.16/sh.)

OFFICERS:
D. N. Daft, Chmn., C.E.O.
G. P. Fayard, Sr. V.P., C.F.O.
J. R. Gladden, Exec. V.P., Gen. Couns.

INVESTOR CONTACT: Institutional Investor Inquires, (404) 676-5766

PRINCIPAL OFFICE: One Coca-Cola Plaza, Atlanta, GA 30313

TELEPHONE NUMBER: (404) 676-2121
FAX: (404) 676-6792
WEB: www.coca-cola.com

NO. OF EMPLOYEES: 36,900 (approx.)

SHAREHOLDERS: 380,581 (record)

ANNUAL MEETING: In Apr.

INCORPORATED: DE, Sept., 1919

INSTITUTIONAL HOLDINGS:
No. of Institutions: 973
Shares Held: 1,315,661,827
% Held: 52.9

INDUSTRY: Bottled and canned soft drinks (SIC: 2086)

TRANSFER AGENT(S): First Chicago Trust Company of New York, Jersey City, NJ

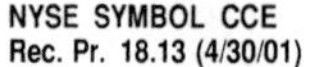

NYSE SYMBOL CCE
Rec. Pr. 18.13 (4/30/01)

COCA-COLA ENTERPRISES INC.

YIELD 0.9%
P/E RATIO 33.0

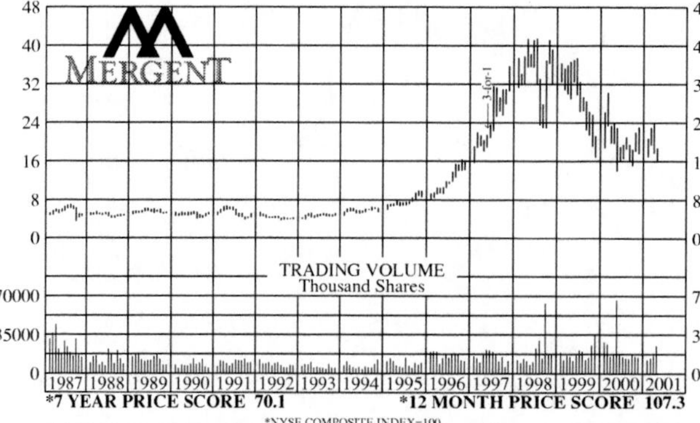

*7 YEAR PRICE SCORE 70.1 *12 MONTH PRICE SCORE 107.3

*NYSE COMPOSITE INDEX=100

INTERIM EARNINGS (Per Share):

Qtr.	Mar.	June	Sept.	Dec.
1996	0.01	0.15	0.10	0.02
1997	d0.09	0.29	0.29	d0.05
1998	d0.13	0.27	0.28	d0.09
1999	d0.15	0.08	0.24	d0.04
2000	d0.08	0.29	0.30	0.04

INTERIM DIVIDENDS (Per Share):

Amt.	Decl.	Ex.	Rec.	Pay.
0.04Q	4/14/00	6/16/00	6/20/00	7/03/00
0.04Q	7/18/00	9/15/00	9/19/00	10/02/00
0.04Q	10/17/00	11/29/00	12/01/00	12/15/00
0.04Q	2/20/01	3/16/01	3/20/01	4/02/01
0.04Q	4/20/01	6/15/01	6/19/01	7/02/01

Indicated div.: $0.16 (Div. Reinv. Plan)

CAPITALIZATION (12/31/00):

	($000)	(%)
Long-Term Debt	10,348,000	57.6
Deferred Income Tax	4,774,000	26.6
Preferred Stock	44,000	0.2
Common & Surplus	2,790,000	15.5
Total	17,956,000	100.0

RECENT DEVELOPMENTS: For the year ended 12/31/00, net income was $236.0 million versus $59.0 million in the prior year. Results for 2000 included a non-recurring charge of $12.0 million related to Great Britain, insurance proceeds of $20.0 million related to the 1999 product recall in Europe, and a $14.0 million non-recurring reduction in income tax expense. Results for 1999 included non-recurring production recall costs of $103.0 million. Net operating revenues rose 2.4% to $14.75 billion from $14.41 billion in 1999.

PROSPECTS: CCE's prospects remain clouded by weak case bottle and can volume growth, specifically in North America. On the positive side, North America and European case bottle and can volume in the recent quarter advanced 2.0% and 6.5%, respectively, compared with the year-ago period. Moreover, the Company expects these positive trends to accelerate in 2001 on the strength of enhanced national marketing programs from The Coca-Cola Company, CCE's local brand-building initiatives and more moderate, market-based price increases.

BUSINESS

COCA-COLA ENTERPRISES INC. markets, produces and distributes products of The Coca-Cola Company. CCE also distributes AW, CANADA DRY, DR PEPPER and several other beverage brands in North America, and APPLETISE, BUXTON, NESTEA and several other beverage brands in Europe. The Company, involved in the liquid nonalcoholic refreshment business, extends its product line beyond traditional carbonated soft drink categories to beverages such as still and sparkling waters, juices, isotonics, coffee-based drinks and teas. CCE's bottling territories in North America are located in 46 states of the U.S., the District of Columbia and all ten provinces of Canada. CCE also has bottling territories in Europe, including Great Britain, Belgium, Luxembourg, Monaco, the Netherlands and continental France. In 2000, CCE sold approximately 3.80 billion cases (24 eight-ounce servings or 192 ounces per case) of products in bottle, can and fountain containers. As of 2/21/01, The Coca-Cola Company owned approximately 40.0% of CCE's outstanding common shares.

ANNUAL FINANCIAL DATA

	12/31/00	12/31/99	12/31/98	[2] 12/31/97	12/31/96	12/31/95	12/31/94
Earnings Per Share	[5] 0.54	[4] 0.13	[1] 0.35	[1] 0.43	[3] 0.28	0.21	0.17
Cash Flow Per Share	3.48	3.22	3.03	2.67	1.97	1.58	1.35
Tang. Book Val. Per Share	6.67	6.83	5.95	4.69	3.65	3.45	3.28
Dividends Per Share	0.16	0.16	0.14	0.08	0.03	0.02	0.02
Dividend Payout %	29.6	123.0	41.4	19.4	11.9	7.9	9.6
INCOME STATEMENT (IN MILLIONS):							
Total Revenues	14,750.0	14,406.0	13,414.0	11,278.0	7,921.0	6,773.0	6,011.0
Costs & Expenses	12,363.0	12,219.0	11,425.0	9,612.0	6,749.0	5,776.0	5,110.0
Depreciation & Amort.	1,261.0	1,348.0	1,120.0	946.0	627.0	529.0	461.0
Operating Income	1,126.0	839.0	869.0	720.0	545.0	468.0	440.0
Net Interest Inc./(Exp.)	d791.0	d751.0	d701.0	d536.0	d351.0	d326.0	d310.0
Income Before Income Taxes	333.0	88.0	169.0	178.0	194.0	145.0	127.0
Income Taxes	97.0	29.0	56.0	65.0	80.0	63.0	58.0
Net Income	[5] 236.0	[4] 59.0	[1] 113.0	[1] 113.0	[3] 114.0	82.0	69.0
Cash Flow	1,494.0	1,404.0	1,232.0	1,057.0	733.0	609.0	528.0
Average Shs. Outstg. (000)	429,000	436,000	406,000	396,000	373,000	386,000	390,000
BALANCE SHEET (IN MILLIONS):							
Cash & Cash Equivalents	294.0	141.0	68.0	45.0	47.0	8.0	22.0
Total Current Assets	2,631.0	2,581.0	2,285.0	1,813.0	1,319.0	982.0	810.0
Net Property	5,783.0	5,594.0	4,891.0	3,862.0	2,812.0	2,158.0	1,963.0
Total Assets	22,162.0	22,730.0	21,132.0	17,487.0	11,234.0	9,064.0	8,738.0
Total Current Liabilities	3,094.0	3,614.0	3,397.0	3,032.0	1,690.0	859.0	1,089.0
Long-Term Obligations	10,348.0	10,153.0	9,605.0	7,760.0	4,814.0	4,138.0	3,896.0
Net Stockholders' Equity	2,834.0	2,924.0	2,438.0	1,814.0	1,508.0	1,359.0	1,297.0
Net Working Capital	d463.0	d1,033.0	d1,112.0	d1,219.0	d371.0	123.0	d279.0
Year-end Shs. Outstg. (000)	418,069	421,317	401,455	386,554	376,305	385,653	387,000
STATISTICAL RECORD:							
Operating Profit Margin %	7.6	5.8	6.5	6.4	6.9	6.9	7.3
Net Profit Margin %	1.6	0.4	0.8	1.0	1.4	1.2	1.1
Return on Equity %	8.3	2.0	4.6	6.2	7.6	6.0	5.3
Return on Assets %	1.1	0.3	0.5	0.6	1.0	0.9	0.8
Debt/Total Assets %	46.7	44.7	45.5	44.4	42.9	45.7	44.6
Price Range	30.25-14.00	37.50-16.81	41.56-22.88	35.81-15.71	16.38-8.00	9.96-5.92	6.50-4.67
P/E Ratio	56.0-25.9	288.2-129.2	118.7-65.3	83.3-36.5	58.5-28.6	47.4-28.2	37.6-27.0
Average Yield %	0.7	0.6	0.5	0.3	0.3	0.2	0.3

Statistics are as originally reported. Adj. for 3-for-1 stk. split, 5/97 [1] Bef. income tax rate chge. benefit 12/31/98: $29.0 mill.; benefit 12/31/97, $58.0 mill. [2] Incl. results fr. acqs. of Coke Canada & Coke New York [3] Incl. non-recur. cr. of $10.0 mill. [4] Incl. non-recur. chrg. of $103.0 mill. [5] Incl. non-recur. chrg. of $12.0. mill. & insur. proceeds of $20.0 mill.

OFFICERS:
S. K. Johnston Jr., Chmn., C.E.O.
J. R. Alm, Pres., C.O.O.
V. R. Palmer, Sr. V.P., Treas.

INVESTOR CONTACT: Helene Krupp, Investor Relations, (770) 989-3246

PRINCIPAL OFFICE: 2500 Windy Ridge Parkway, Atlanta, GA 30339

TELEPHONE NUMBER: (770) 989-3000
FAX: (770) 989-3788
WEB: www.cokecce.com

NO. OF EMPLOYEES: 67,000 (approx.)

SHAREHOLDERS: 16,144

ANNUAL MEETING: In Apr.

INCORPORATED: DE, 1944

INSTITUTIONAL HOLDINGS:
No. of Institutions: 199
Shares Held: 142,657,498
% Held: 33.9

INDUSTRY: Bottled and canned soft drinks (SIC: 2086)

TRANSFER AGENT(S): EquiServe, Jersey City, NJ

NYSE SYMBOL CL
Rec. Pr. 56.64 (5/31/01)

COLGATE-PALMOLIVE COMPANY

YIELD 1.1%
P/E RATIO 33.3

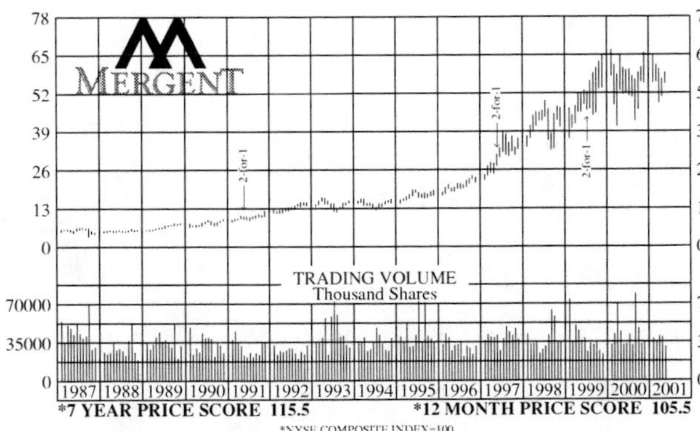

*7 YEAR PRICE SCORE 115.5 *12 MONTH PRICE SCORE 105.5
*NYSE COMPOSITE INDEX=100

INTERIM EARNINGS (Per Share):

Qtr.	Mar.	June	Sept.	Dec.
1996	0.24	0.25	0.27	0.30
1997	0.28	0.29	0.31	0.32
1998	0.30	0.31	0.33	0.37
1999	0.33	0.36	0.38	0.41
2000	0.38	0.42	0.44	0.46

INTERIM DIVIDENDS (Per Share):

Amt.	Decl.	Ex.	Rec.	Pay.
0.158Q	3/09/00	4/24/00	4/26/00	5/15/00
0.158Q	7/13/00	7/24/00	7/26/00	8/15/00
0.158Q	10/12/00	10/24/00	10/26/00	11/15/00
0.158Q	1/11/01	1/24/01	1/26/01	2/15/01
0.158Q	3/08/01	4/24/01	4/26/01	5/15/01

Indicated div.: $0.63 (Div. Reinv. Plan)

CAPITALIZATION (12/31/00):

	($000)	(%)
Long-Term Debt	2,536,900	57.0
Deferred Income Tax	447,300	10.0
Preferred Stock	354,100	8.0
Common & Surplus	1,114,000	25.0
Total	4,452,300	100.0

RECENT DEVELOPMENTS: For the year ended 12/31/00, net income increased 13.5% to $1.06 billion compared with $937.3 million in 1999. Net sales totaled $9.36 billion, up 2.6% versus $9.12 billion in the prior year. In North America, unit volume and sales grew 8.0%. Latin American unit volume and sales improved 6.0%. In Europe, unit volume climbed 4.0%, while sales fell 7.0% reflecting the weak Euro. In the Asia/Africa region, unit volume rose 7.0%, and sales advanced 2.0%.

PROSPECTS: On 12/29/00, the Company announced the sale of its Viva detergent business in Mexico to Henkel, the German consumer products and chemical company, effective January 2001. The sale of this non-core brand is consistent with the Company's strategy to de-emphasize detergents while investing in its high margin personal care and oral care businesses, which have been exhibiting healthy volume growth both in Mexico and around the world.

BUSINESS

COLGATE-PALMOLIVE COMPANY is a consumer products company that markets its products in over 200 countries. The Company operates five segments. Oral, Personal, Fabric and Household Surface Care accounted for 88.0% of 1999 revenues and consists of toothpastes, toothbrushes, soaps, shampoos, baby products, deodorants, detergents, cleaners, shave products and other similar items under brand names including COLGATE, PALMOLIVE, MENNEN, SOFT SOAP, IRISH SPRINGS, PROTEX, SORRISO, KOLYNOS, AJAX, AXION, SOUPLINE, SUAVITEL and FAB. Pet Nutrition, 12%, consists of pet food products manufactured and marketed by Hill's Pet Nutrition. Hill's markets pet foods primarily under SCIENCE DIET, which is sold by authorized pet supply retailers, breeders and veterinarians for every day nutritional needs, and PRESCRIPTION DIET for dogs and cats with disease conditions.

ANNUAL FINANCIAL DATA

	12/31/00	12/31/99	12/31/98	12/31/97	12/31/96	12/31/95	12/31/94
Earnings Per Share	**1.70**	**1.47**	**1.31**	**1.14**	**1.05**	**[1] 0.26**	**[1] 0.96**
Cash Flow Per Share	**2.23**	**2.00**	**1.82**	**1.63**	**1.62**	**0.81**	**1.39**
Dividends Per Share	**0.63**	**0.59**	**0.55**	**0.53**	**0.47**	**0.44**	**0.39**
Dividend Payout %	**37.1**	**40.1**	**42.1**	**46.7**	**44.8**	**169.2**	**40.3**
INCOME STATEMENT (IN MILLIONS):							
Total Revenues	9,357.9	9,118.2	8,971.6	9,056.7	8,749.0	8,358.2	7,587.9
Costs & Expenses	7,227.3	7,138.2	7,157.1	7,378.6	7,186.9	7,392.9	6,303.4
Depreciation & Amort.	337.8	340.2	330.3	319.9	316.3	300.3	235.1
Operating Income	1,792.8	1,639.8	1,484.2	1,358.2	1,245.8	665.0	1,049.4
Net Interest Inc./(Exp.)	d173.3	d171.6	d172.9	d183.5	d197.4	d205.4	d86.7
Income Before Income Taxes	1,567.2	1,394.6	1,250.1	1,102.3	954.6	363.5	879.9
Income Taxes	503.4	457.3	401.5	361.9	319.6	191.5	299.7
Net Income	1,063.8	937.3	848.6	740.4	635.0	[1] 172.0	[1] 580.2
Cash Flow	1,401.6	1,256.5	1,158.0	1,039.2	929.9	450.7	793.7
Average Shs. Outstg. (000)	627,300	638,800	648,400	650,200	586,400	580,800	584,800
BALANCE SHEET (IN MILLIONS):							
Cash & Cash Equivalents	212.5	235.2	194.5	205.3	307.8	256.6	217.5
Total Current Assets	2,347.2	2,354.8	2,244.9	2,196.5	2,372.3	2,360.2	2,177.7
Net Property	2,528.3	2,551.1	2,589.2	2,441.0	2,428.9	2,155.2	1,988.1
Total Assets	7,252.3	7,423.1	7,685.2	7,538.7	7,901.5	7,642.3	6,142.4
Total Current Liabilities	2,244.1	2,273.5	2,114.4	1,959.5	1,904.3	1,753.1	1,529.2
Long-Term Obligations	2,536.9	2,243.3	2,300.6	2,340.3	2,786.8	2,992.0	1,751.5
Net Stockholders' Equity	1,468.1	1,833.7	2,085.6	2,178.6	2,034.1	1,679.8	1,822.9
Net Working Capital	103.1	81.3	130.5	237.0	468.0	607.1	648.5
Year-end Shs. Outstg. (000)	732,853	578,863	585,420	591,280	588,536	583,200	577,616
STATISTICAL RECORD:							
Operating Profit Margin %	19.2	18.0	16.5	15.0	14.2	8.0	13.8
Net Profit Margin %	11.4	10.3	9.5	8.2	7.3	2.1	7.6
Return on Equity %	72.5	51.1	40.7	34.0	31.2	10.2	31.8
Return on Assets %	14.7	12.6	11.0	9.8	8.0	2.3	9.4
Debt/Total Assets %	35.0	30.2	29.9	31.0	35.3	39.2	28.5
Price Range	66.75-40.50	65.00-36.56	49.44-32.53	39.34-22.50	24.13-17.22	19.34-14.50	16.34-12.38
P/E Ratio	39.3-23.8	44.2-24.9	37.9-24.9	34.7-19.8	23.0-16.4	74.4-55.7	17.1-13.0
Average Yield %	1.2	1.2	1.3	1.7	2.3	2.6	2.7

Statistics are as originally reported. Adj. for stk. splits: 2-for-1, 6/99 & 5/97 [1] Incl. non-recurr. chrg. $369.2 mill., 12/95; $5.2 mill., 12/94

OFFICERS:
R. Mark, Chmn., C.E.O.
W. S. Shanahan, Pres., C.O.O.

INVESTOR CONTACT: Bina Thompson, Inv. Rel., (212) 310-3072

PRINCIPAL OFFICE: 300 Park Ave., New York, NY 10022-7499

TELEPHONE NUMBER: (212) 310-2000
FAX: (212) 310-3284
WEB: www.colgate.com

NO. OF EMPLOYEES: 38,300 (approx.)

SHAREHOLDERS: 42,300 (com.); 247 (pfd.)

ANNUAL MEETING: In May

INCORPORATED: DE, July, 1923

INSTITUTIONAL HOLDINGS:
No. of Institutions: 688
Shares Held: 372,242,381
% Held: 66.0

INDUSTRY: Toilet preparations (SIC: 2844)

TRANSFER AGENT(S): First Chicago Trust Company of New York, Jersey City, NJ

NYSE SYMBOL CDO
Rec. Pr. 2.16 (5/31/01)

COMDISCO, INC.

YIELD 4.6%
P/E RATIO 1.6

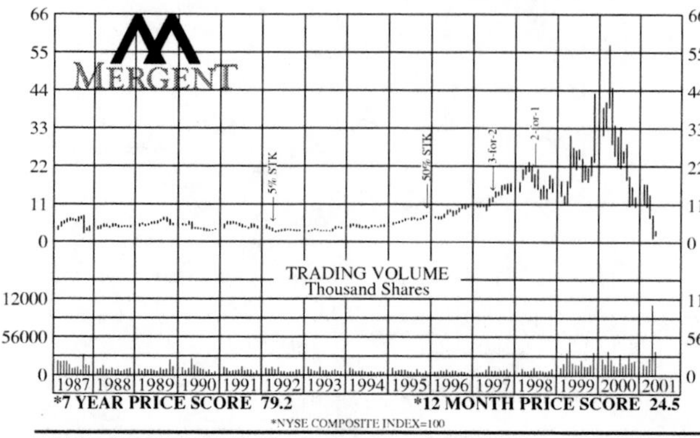

*7 YEAR PRICE SCORE 79.2 *12 MONTH PRICE SCORE 24.5

*NYSE COMPOSITE INDEX=100

INTERIM EARNINGS (Per Share):

Qtr.	Dec.	Mar.	June	Sept.
1997-98	0.22	0.23	0.24	0.25
1998-99	0.24	d0.37	0.22	0.19
1999-00	0.26	0.26	0.10	0.44
2000-01	0.55	...	...	...

INTERIM DIVIDENDS (Per Share):

Amt.	Decl.	Ex.	Rec.	Pay.
0.025Q	1/25/00	2/09/00	2/11/00	3/13/00
0.025Q	4/25/00	5/10/00	5/12/00	6/12/00
0.025Q	7/25/00	8/09/00	8/11/00	9/11/00
0.025Q	11/08/00	11/09/00	11/13/00	12/11/00
0.025Q	1/31/01	2/07/01	2/09/01	3/12/01

Indicated div.: $0.10

CAPITALIZATION (9/30/00):

	($000)	(%)
Long-Term Debt	4,147,000	71.9
Deferred Income Tax	404,000	7.0
Common & Surplus	1,214,000	21.1
Total	5,765,000	100.0

RECENT DEVELOPMENTS: For the quarter ended 12/31/00, CDO reported income from continuing operations of $86.0 million versus income from continuing operations of $59.0 million in the corresponding prior-year period. Fiscal 2001 results excluded a net accounting charge of $2.0 million, while results for fiscal 2000 excluded a net loss from discontinued operations of $17.0 million. Total revenue grew 3.8% to $909.0 million. Leasing revenue fell 16.5% to $491.0 million, while venture revenue jumped 81.6% to $256.0 million.

PROSPECTS: On 1/9/01, CDO announced plans to exit the managed network services business in order to focus on its high-growth lines of business, including continuity, Web hosting and data storage services. Separately, the Company expanded its portfolio of security management services to include services that enable healthcare organizations to meet compliances of the Health Insurance Portability and Accountability Act of 1996. Going forward, revenues should benefit from an alliance with Veriprise Wireless Corporation.

BUSINESS

COMDISCO, INC. is a provider of global technology services to help its customers maximize technology functionality, predictability and availability. The services include equipment leasing, continuity and desktop management applications. These services are designed to provide asset and technological planning as well as data and voice availability and recovery to users of high technology equipment. CDO operates in three principal operating segments: leasing, technology services and ventures. The ventures division represents the Company's retained interest in its venture financing business.

REVENUES

(9/30/00)	($000)	(%)
Leasing and Sales	2,699,000	69.8
Services	637,000	16.5
Other	531,000	13.7
Total	3,867,000	100.0

ANNUAL FINANCIAL DATA

	9/30/00	9/30/99	9/30/98	9/30/97	9/30/96	9/30/95	9/30/94
Earnings Per Share	**1.58**	**[1] 0.30**	**0.93**	**0.78**	**0.67**	**0.58**	**0.26**
Cash Flow Per Share	**1.58**	**0.30**	**0.93**	**0.78**	**0.67**	**0.58**	**0.25**
Tang. Book Val. Per Share	**7.96**	**6.94**	**6.44**	**5.24**	**4.73**	**4.39**	**3.88**
Dividends Per Share	**0.10**	**0.10**	**0.10**	**0.10**	**0.07**	**0.08**	**0.08**
Dividend Payout %	**6.3**	**33.3**	**10.8**	**12.6**	**10.5**	**14.4**	**31.1**
INCOME STATEMENT (IN MILLIONS):							
Total Revenues	3,867.0	4,159.0	3,243.0	2,819.0	2,431.0	2,240.0	2,098.0
Costs & Expenses	3,115.0	3,747.0	2,677.0	2,309.0	1,985.0	1,798.0	1,666.0
Operating Income	752.0	412.0	566.0	510.0	446.0	442.0	432.0
Net Interest Inc./(Exp.)	d354.0	d337.0	d326.0	d299.0	d262.0	d274.0	d263.0
Income Before Income Taxes	398.0	75.0	240.0	211.0	184.0	168.0	89.0
Income Taxes	143.0	27.0	87.0	80.0	70.0	64.0	36.0
Net Income	255.0	[1] 48.0	153.0	131.0	114.0	104.0	53.0
Cash Flow	255.0	48.0	151.0	123.0	106.0	96.0	44.0
Average Shs. Outstg. (000)	161,782	161,787	163,000	158,000	159,000	165,000	174,000
BALANCE SHEET (IN MILLIONS):							
Cash & Cash Equivalents	370.0	433.0	93.0	82.0	56.0	115.0	88.0
Total Current Assets	1,678.0	1,244.0	598.0	501.0	429.0	424.0	402.0
Net Property	3,448.0	3,745.0	4,258.0	3,711.0	2,991.0	2,270.0	1,864.0
Total Assets	8,754.0	7,807.0	7,063.0	6,350.0	5,591.0	5,039.0	4,807.0
Total Current Liabilities	1,507.0	1,098.0	1,443.0	1,194.0	1,267.0	772.0	677.0
Long-Term Obligations	4,147.0	4,236.0	3,318.0	2,918.0	2,145.0	1,796.0	1,364.0
Net Stockholders' Equity	1,214.0	1,060.0	979.0	865.0	799.0	776.0	741.0
Net Working Capital	171.0	146.0	d845.0	d693.0	d838.0	d348.0	d275.0
Year-end Shs. Outstg. (000)	152,569	152,792	152,000	148,000	150,000	156,000	165,000
STATISTICAL RECORD:							
Operating Profit Margin %	19.4	9.9	17.5	18.1	18.3	19.7	20.6
Net Profit Margin %	6.6	1.2	4.7	4.6	4.7	4.6	2.5
Return on Equity %	21.0	4.5	15.6	15.1	14.3	13.4	7.2
Return on Assets %	2.9	0.6	2.2	2.1	2.0	2.1	1.1
Debt/Total Assets %	47.4	54.3	47.0	46.0	38.4	35.6	28.4
Price Range	57.25-10.13	43.00-10.75	23.28-12.44	17.03-9.13	11.00-6.63	7.92-4.89	5.39-3.95
P/E Ratio	36.2-6.4	143.3-35.8	25.0-13.4	21.8-11.7	16.5-9.9	13.7-8.5	21.0-15.3
Average Yield %	0.3	0.4	0.6	0.8	0.8	1.3	1.7

Statistics are as originally reported. Adj. for stk. splits: 2-for-1, 6/98; 3-for-2, 6/97; 11/95.
[1] Incl. one-time chrg. of $485.0 mill. for sale of assets.

OFFICERS:
P. A. Hewes, Pres., C.E.O.
J. J. Vosicky, Exec. V.P., C.F.O.

INVESTOR CONTACT: James J. Hyland, V.P., Investor Rel., (847) 518-5779

PRINCIPAL OFFICE: 6111 North River Road, Rosemont, IL 60018

TELEPHONE NUMBER: (847) 698-3000
FAX: (847) 518-5854
WEB: www.comdisco.com

NO. OF EMPLOYEES: 3,500 (approx.)

SHAREHOLDERS: 1,900 (approx.)

ANNUAL MEETING: In Feb.

INCORPORATED: DE, June, 1971

INSTITUTIONAL HOLDINGS:
No. of Institutions: 199
Shares Held: 62,634,327
% Held: 41.4

INDUSTRY: Computer rental & leasing (SIC: 7377)

TRANSFER AGENT(S): Mellon Investor Services, New York, NY

NYSE SYMBOL CMA
Rec. Pr. 51.43 (4/30/01)

COMERICA, INC.

YIELD 3.1%
P/E RATIO 11.1

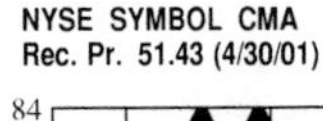

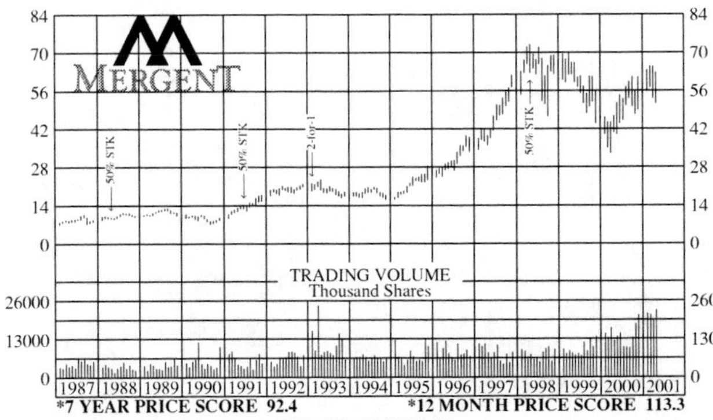

*7 YEAR PRICE SCORE 92.4 *12 MONTH PRICE SCORE 113.3

*NYSE COMPOSITE INDEX=100

INTERIM EARNINGS (Per Share):

Qtr.	Mar.	June	Sept.	Dec.
1997	0.73	0.77	0.82	0.85
1998	0.88	0.92	0.95	0.97
1999	0.98	1.03	1.05	1.08
2000	1.10	1.15	1.18	1.20

INTERIM DIVIDENDS (Per Share):

Amt.	Decl.	Ex.	Rec.	Pay.
0.40Q	5/19/00	6/13/00	6/15/00	7/01/00
0.40Q	7/25/00	9/13/00	9/15/00	10/01/00
0.40Q	11/28/00	12/13/00	12/15/00	1/01/01
0.44Q	1/23/01	3/13/01	3/15/01	4/01/01
0.44Q	5/22/01	6/13/01	6/15/01	7/01/01

Indicated div.: $1.76 (Div. Reinv. Plan)

CAPITALIZATION (12/31/00):

	($000)	(%)
Total Deposits	27,168,012	69.2
Long-Term Debt	8,088,661	20.6
Preferred Stock	250,000	0.6
Common & Surplus	3,757,266	9.6
Total	39,263,939	100.0

RECENT DEVELOPMENTS: For the year ended 12/31/00, net income rose 11.4% to $749.3 million from $672.6 million in the prior year. Earnings for 2000 and 1999 included pre-tax net gains of $47.6 million and $21.3 million, respectively, on the sales of businesses. Net interest income grew 7.2% to $1.66 billion. Total non-interest income, including the above net gains, advanced 15.2% to $825.9 million. Total non-interest expenses increased 6.4% to $1.19 billion.

PROSPECTS: On 1/23/01, the Company entered into a definitive agreement to acquire Alliance Bancorp in a stock transaction valued at about $245.0 million. As a result of the acquisition, which should close in the third quarter of 2001, CF will have the sixth largest retail banking operation in the Chicago metropolitan region with about $5.00 billion in deposits. Separately, CF anticipates earnings per share of $2.30 and retail banking revenue of nearly $300.0 million for 2001.

BUSINESS

COMERICA, INC. is a bank holding company headquartered in Detroit, Michigan. The Company, as of 12/31/00, had assets of $41.99 billion and total deposits of $27.17 billion. The Company operates banking subsidiaries in Michigan, Texas and California, banking operations in Florida, and businesses in several other states. CMA is a diversified financial services provider, offering a broad range of financial products and services for businesses and individuals. The Company also operates banking subsidiaries in Canada and Mexico.

LOAN DISTRIBUTION

(12/31/2000)	($000)	(%)
Commercial	22,729,464	63.1
International	2,571,156	7.1
Real Estate		
Construction	2,310,000	6.4
Commercial		
Mortgage	5,271,078	14.6
Residental Mortgage	806,561	2.2
Consumer	1,436,773	4.0
Lease financing	934,914	2.6
Total	36,060,345	100.0

ANNUAL FINANCIAL DATA

	12/31/00	12/31/99	12/31/98	12/31/97	12/31/96	12/31/95	12/31/94
Earnings Per Share	**[2] 4.63**	**4.14**	**[1] 3.72**	**3.19**	**[1] 2.37**	**2.36**	**2.19**
Tang. Book Val. Per Share	**23.94**	**20.60**	**17.94**	**16.02**	**14.77**	**15.17**	**13.64**
Dividends Per Share	**1.56**	**1.40**	**1.25**	**1.12**	**0.99**	**0.89**	**0.80**
Dividend Payout %	**33.7**	**33.8**	**33.5**	**35.1**	**41.7**	**37.9**	**36.6**
INCOME STATEMENT (IN MILLIONS):							
Total Interest Income	3,261.6	2,672.7	2,616.8	2,647.4	2,562.8	2,613.9	2,091.9
Total Interest Expense	1,602.8	1,125.6	1,155.5	1,204.6	1,150.5	1,314.0	861.8
Net Interest Income	1,658.9	1,547.1	1,461.3	1,442.8	1,412.3	1,299.9	1,230.1
Provision for Loan Losses	145.0	114.0	113.0	146.0	114.0	86.5	56.0
Non-Interest Income	825.9	716.9	603.1	528.0	507.0	498.7	450.2
Non-Interest Expense	1,188.4	1,117.0	1,020.0	1,008.0	1,159.0	1,086.4	1,042.2
Income Before Taxes	1,151.4	1,033.1	931.4	816.7	646.2	625.7	582.1
Net Income	[2] 749.3	672.6	[1] 607.1	530.5	[1] 417.2	413.4	387.2
Average Shs. Outstg. (000)	156,398	158,397	158,757	161,040	172,281	175,341	177,240
BALANCE SHEET (IN MILLIONS):							
Cash & Due from Banks	1,496.7	1,202.0	1,773.1	1,927.1	1,901.8	2,028.4	1,822.3
Securities Avail. for Sale	2,843.1	3,352.4	2,821.8	4,208.9	4,800.0	6,870.0	2,910.6
Total Loans & Leases	36,060.3	32,693.3	30,604.9	28,895.0	26,206.7	24,442.3	22,209.2
Allowance for Credit Losses	538.1	476.5	452.4	424.1	367.2	341.3	326.2
Net Loans & Leases	35,522.2	32,216.8	30,152.5	28,470.9	25,839.5	24,100.9	21,883.1
Total Assets	41,985.2	38,653.3	36,600.8	36,292.4	34,102.5	35,469.9	33,429.9
Total Deposits	27,168.0	23,291.4	24,313.1	22,586.3	22,367.2	23,167.2	22,432.3
Long-Term Obligations	8,088.7	8,579.9	5,282.3	7,286.4	4,241.8	4,644.4	4,097.9
Total Liabilities	37,977.9	35,178.7	33,554.2	33,530.6	31,590.5	32,862.1	31,038.1
Net Stockholders' Equity	4,007.3	3,474.6	3,046.6	2,761.8	2,615.6	2,607.7	2,391.8
Year-end Shs. Outstg. (000)	156,944	156,518	155,881	156,815	160,211	171,906	175,368
STATISTICAL RECORD:							
Return on Equity %	18.7	19.4	19.9	19.2	15.9	15.9	16.2
Return on Assets %	1.8	1.7	1.7	1.5	1.2	1.2	1.2
Equity/Assets %	9.5	9.0	8.3	7.6	7.7	7.4	7.2
Non-Int. Exp./Tot. Inc. %	47.8	49.3	49.4	51.1	60.4	60.4	62.0
Price Range	61.13-32.94	70.00-44.00	73.00-46.50	61.88-34.17	39.58-24.17	28.50-16.08	20.83-16.08
P/E Ratio	13.2-7.1	16.9-10.6	19.6-12.5	19.4-10.7	16.7-10.2	12.1-6.8	9.5-7.4
Average Yield %	3.3	2.5	2.1	2.3	3.1	4.0	4.3

Statistics are as originally reported. Adj. for 50% stk. div., 4/98. [1] Incl. merger-related or restructuring charges: $6.8 mill., 1998; $90.0 mill., 1996. [2] Incl. a pre-tax net gain of $47.6 million on the sales of businesses.

OFFICERS:
E. A. Miller, Chmn., Pres., C.E.O.
R. W. Babb Jr., Vice-Chmn., C.F.O.

INVESTOR CONTACT: Judith S. Love, Investor Relations, (313) 222-2840

PRINCIPAL OFFICE: 500 Woodward Ave., Detroit, MI 48226

TELEPHONE NUMBER: (313) 222-3300
FAX: (313) 222-6091
WEB: www.comerica.com

NO. OF EMPLOYEES: 8,911 full-time; 1,450 part-time

SHAREHOLDERS: 17,257 (approx.)

ANNUAL MEETING: In May

INCORPORATED: DE, 1973

INSTITUTIONAL HOLDINGS:
No. of Institutions: 379
Shares Held: 96,318,855
% Held: 54.3

INDUSTRY: National commercial banks (SIC: 6021)

TRANSFER AGENT(S): Wells Fargo Shareowner Services, South St. Paul, MN

NYSE SYMBOL CMC
Rec. Pr. 25.45 (5/31/01)

COMMERCIAL METALS COMPANY

YIELD 2.0%
P/E RATIO 14.0

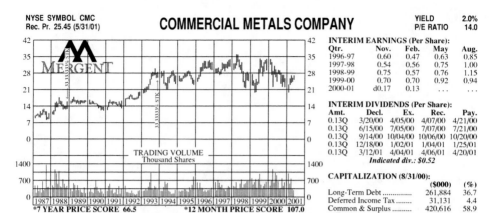

TRADING VOLUME
Thousand Shares

*7 YEAR PRICE SCORE 66.5 *12 MONTH PRICE SCORE 107.0

*NYSE COMPOSITE INDEX=100

INTERIM EARNINGS (Per Share):

Qtr.	Nov.	Feb.	May	Aug.
1996-97	0.60	0.47	0.63	0.85
1997-98	0.54	0.56	0.75	1.00
1998-99	0.75	0.57	0.76	1.15
1999-00	0.70	0.70	0.92	0.94
2000-01	d0.17	0.13	...	...

INTERIM DIVIDENDS (Per Share):

Amt.	Decl.	Ex.	Rec.	Pay.
0.13Q	3/20/00	4/05/00	4/07/00	4/21/00
0.13Q	6/15/00	7/05/00	7/07/00	7/21/00
0.13Q	9/14/00	10/04/00	10/06/00	10/20/00
0.13Q	12/18/00	1/02/01	1/04/01	1/25/01
0.13Q	3/12/01	4/04/01	4/06/01	4/20/01

Indicated div.: $0.52

CAPITALIZATION (8/31/00):

	($000)	(%)
Long-Term Debt	261,884	36.7
Deferred Income Tax	31,131	4.4
Common & Surplus	420,616	58.9
Total	713,631	100.0

RECENT DEVELOPMENTS: For the quarter ended 2/28/01, net income decreased 84.0% to $1.7 million compared with $10.4 million in 2000. Net sales were $578.3 million, down 9.3% from $637.6 million a year earlier. The decline in results was primarily attributed to lower selling prices across the board, coupled with inventories that were reduced out of necessity. Also, operating costs were elevated by sharply higher electricity and natural gas prices.

PROSPECTS: On 2/13/01, CMC acquired the operating assets and trade name of Allform Inc., a supplier of concrete-related forms and supplies including rental tilt-up accessories. Allform, headquartered in Tampa, Florida, services commerical, highway, industrial and residential contractors throughout Central Florida. Looking ahead, CMC expects 2001 second half results to improve over first half as its operating levels improve.

BUSINESS

COMMERCIAL METALS COMPANY'S businesses are organized into three segments and operates through a network of over 120 locations. The Manufacturing segment consists of the CMC Steel Group and the Howell Metal Company subsidiary, a manufacturer of copper tubing. The Recycling segment is engaged in processing secondary (scrap) metals for recycling into new metal products through 43 recycling plants and the Commercial Metals Railroad Salvage Company. The Marketing and Trading segment is involved in buying and selling primary and secondary metals and other commodities and products through a global network of trading offices.

ANNUAL FINANCIAL DATA

	8/31/00	8/31/99	8/31/98	8/31/97	8/31/96	8/31/95	8/31/94
Earnings Per Share	**[2] 3.25**	**[1] 3.22**	**2.82**	**2.53**	**3.01**	**[1] 2.52**	**1.75**
Cash Flow Per Share	**7.92**	**6.78**	**5.96**	**5.49**	**5.72**	**5.04**	**3.77**
Tang. Book Val. Per Share	**31.93**	**29.05**	**26.18**	**24.04**	**22.20**	**19.72**	**17.01**
Dividends Per Share	**0.52**	**0.52**	**0.52**	**0.52**	**0.49**	**0.48**	**0.48**
Dividend Payout %	**16.0**	**16.1**	**18.4**	**20.6**	**16.3**	**19.0**	**27.4**
INCOME STATEMENT (IN MILLIONS):							
Total Revenues	2,661.4	2,251.4	2,367.6	2,258.4	2,322.4	2,116.8	1,666.2
Costs & Expenses	2,476.2	2,088.8	2,214.5	2,124.6	2,178.1	1,994.1	1,578.0
Depreciation & Amort.	66.6	52.1	47.5	43.7	41.6	38.1	30.1
Operating Income	118.7	110.6	105.6	90.1	102.7	75.2	49.7
Net Interest Inc./(Exp.)	d27.3	d19.6	d18.1	d14.6	d15.8	d15.2	d9.3
Income Before Income Taxes	73.3	75.0	68.1	61.0	72.9	58.0	40.9
Income Taxes	27.0	27.9	25.4	22.4	26.9	19.8	14.7
Net Income	[2] 46.3	[1] 47.1	42.7	38.6	46.0	[1] 38.2	26.2
Cash Flow	112.8	99.2	90.2	82.3	87.6	67.0	47.9
Average Shs. Outstg. (000)	14,250	14,627	15,121	15,005	15,306	15,151	14,956
BALANCE SHEET (IN MILLIONS):							
Cash & Cash Equivalents	20.1	44.7	31.0	33.0	24.3	21.0	38.3
Total Current Assets	715.0	662.3	673.5	585.3	539.5	534.1	446.1
Net Property	407.5	402.3	318.5	247.3	222.7	209.7	156.8
Total Assets	1,172.9	1,079.0	1,002.6	839.1	766.8	748.1	604.9
Total Current Liabilities	439.2	371.7	426.1	278.1	264.1	268.4	271.0
Long-Term Obligations	261.9	265.6	173.8	185.2	146.5	158.0	72.1
Net Stockholders' Equity	420.6	418.5	381.4	354.9	335.1	303.2	242.8
Net Working Capital	275.8	290.7	247.4	307.1	275.4	265.7	175.1
Year-end Shs. Outstg. (000)	13,173	14,406	14,570	14,761	15,096	15,370	14,275
STATISTICAL RECORD:							
Operating Profit Margin %	4.5	4.9	4.5	4.0	4.4	4.0	3.5
Net Profit Margin %	1.7	2.1	1.8	1.7	2.0	1.8	1.6
Return on Equity %	11.0	11.3	11.2	10.9	13.7	9.5	7.3
Return on Assets %	3.9	4.4	4.3	4.6	6.0	5.1	4.3
Debt/Total Assets %	22.3	24.6	17.3	22.1	19.1	21.1	11.9
Price Range	33.94-22.00	34.19-19.69	36.00-21.56	33.88-27.13	33.50-24.38	29.00-23.00	29.13-21.00
P/E Ratio	10.4-6.8	10.6-6.1	12.8-7.6	13.4-10.7	11.1-8.1	11.5-9.1	16.6-12.0
Average Yield %	1.9	1.9	1.8	1.7	1.7	1.8	1.9

Statistics are as originally reported. [1] Incl. a litigation chrg. of $6.7 mill., 1995; $3.3 mill., 1999. [2] Incl. nonrecurr. chrg. of $1.2 mill.

OFFICERS:
S. A. Rabin, Chmn., Pres., C.E.O.
W. B. Larson, V.P., C.F.O.
D. M. Sudbury, V.P., Gen. Couns., Sec.

INVESTOR CONTACT: Debbie L. Okie, Dir., Public Relations, (214) 689-4354

PRINCIPAL OFFICE: 7800 Stemmons Freeway, Dallas, TX 75247

TELEPHONE NUMBER: (214) 689-4300
FAX: (214) 689-5886
WEB: www.commercialmetals.com

NO. OF EMPLOYEES: 8,378 (approx.)

SHAREHOLDERS: 2,646 (approx.)

ANNUAL MEETING: In Jan.

INCORPORATED: DE, 1946

INSTITUTIONAL HOLDINGS:
No. of Institutions: 88
Shares Held: 5,913,944
% Held: 45.6

INDUSTRY: Blast furnaces and steel mills (SIC: 3312)

TRANSFER AGENT(S): Mellon Investor Services, L.L.C., Ridgefield Park, NJ

NYSE SYMBOL CTV
Rec. Pr. 18.88 (4/30/01)

COMMSCOPE, INC.

YIELD ...
P/E RATIO 11.8

INTERIM EARNINGS (Per Share):

Qtr.	Mar.	June	Sept.	Dec.
1996	0.23	0.24	0.29	0.30
1997	0.26	0.24	0.14	Nil
1998	0.13	0.17	0.23	0.26
1999	0.21	0.33	0.38	0.39
2000	0.32	0.42	0.43	0.43

INTERIM DIVIDENDS (Per Share):

Amt.	Decl.	Ex.	Rec.	Pay.
		No dividends paid.		

CAPITALIZATION (12/31/00):

	($000)	(%)
Long-Term Debt	225,316	36.1
Deferred Income Tax	24,006	3.8
Common & Surplus	374,520	60.0
Total	623,842	100.0

RECENT DEVELOPMENTS: For the year ended 12/31/00, net income increased 24.7% to $84.9 million compared with $68.1 million in 1999. Net sales totaled $950.0 million, up 26.9% versus $748.9 million a year earlier. CATV/video sales improved 32.0% to $733.1 million, while wireless and other telecom sales advanced 26.0% to $131.6 million. Local area network sales declined slightly to $85.3 million.

PROSPECTS: On 4/2/01, the Company announced that it has eliminated approximately 500 permanent positions or about 13.0% of its workforce and cut temporary workers in response to the ongoing economic slowdown. Separately, CTV is uncertain about earnings for the remainder of 2001. The current slowdown in the economy continues to affect worldwide telecommunications capital spending for both wired and wireless communications networks.

BUSINESS

COMMSCOPE, INC., manufactures and sells cable for three broad product categories: cable television and other video applications, local area network applications, and wireless and other telecommunications applications. The Company is a worldwide designer, manufacturer and marketer of a broad line of coaxial cables and other high-performance electronic and fiber-optic cable products for cable television, telephony, Internet access and wireless communications. The Company is also a manufacturer of broadband cable for hybrid fiber coaxial applications. In addition, the Company is a supplier of coaxial, twisted pair and fiber-optic cables for premise wiring (local area networks). The Company's products are used in cable television networks, telephone central offices, satellite television systems and security surveillance. The Company has approximately 2,300 customers in more than 76 countries.

REVENUES

(12/31/2000)	($000)	(%)
CATV/Video Products.................	733,100	77.1
Wireless & Other Telecom.................	131,600	13.9
LAN Products...........	85,300	9.0
Total	950,000	100.0

ANNUAL FINANCIAL DATA

	12/31/00	12/31/99	12/31/98	12/31/97	12/31/96	12/31/95	12/31/94
Earnings Per Share	**1.60**	**1.31**	**0.79**	**0.70**	...	...	...
Cash Flow Per Share	**2.15**	**1.87**	**1.29**	**1.20**	...	...	...
Tang. Book Val. Per Share	**3.98**	**2.02**	**0.41**	...	...	...	...
INCOME STATEMENT (IN THOUSANDS):							
Total Revenues	950,026	748,914	571,733	599,216	572,212	485,160	445,328
Costs & Expenses	768,176	602,102	476,101	498,357	453,006	382,678	341,136
Depreciation & Amort.	35,799	29,295	24,662	21,677	18,952	17,219	16,422
Operating Income	146,051	117,517	70,970	79,182	100,254	85,263	87,770
Net Interest Inc./(Exp.)	d9,655	d9,626	d14,890	d13,485	d9,990	d8,665	d12,281
Income Before Income Taxes	136,880	108,627	60,214	61,514	92,103	76,713	75,485
Income Taxes	51,993	40,550	20,983	24,056	34,981	29,382	30,389
Net Income	84,887	68,077	39,231	37,458	57,122	47,331	45,096
Cash Flow	120,686	97,372	63,893	59,135	76,074	64,550	61,518
Average Shs. Outstg.	56,047	52,050	49,521	49,238	...	...	...
BALANCE SHEET (IN THOUSANDS):							
Cash & Cash Equivalents	7,704	30,223	4,129	3,330	...	...	...
Total Current Assets	289,663	215,179	144,412	155,835	157,982	115,532	...
Net Property	251,356	181,488	135,082	133,235	117,022	90,587	...
Total Assets	721,182	582,535	465,327	483,539	479,885	412,378	...
Total Current Liabilities	80,559	68,227	50,430	43,049	50,762	42,624	...
Long-Term Obligations	225,316	198,402	181,800	265,800	10,800	10,800	...
Net Stockholders' Equity	374,520	281,344	203,972	150,032	393,560	339,177	...
Net Working Capital	209,104	146,952	93,982	112,786	107,220	72,908	...
Year-end Shs. Outstg.	51,264	50,889	50,254	49,109	240	240	...
STATISTICAL RECORD:							
Operating Profit Margin %	15.4	15.7	12.4	13.2	17.5	17.6	19.7
Net Profit Margin %	8.9	9.1	6.9	6.3	10.0	9.8	10.1
Return on Equity %	22.7	24.2	19.2	25.0	14.5	14.0	...
Return on Assets %	11.8	11.7	8.4	7.7	11.9	11.5	...
Debt/Total Assets %	31.2	34.1	39.1	55.0	2.3	2.6	...
Price Range	50.13-15.25	46.38-15.88	20.75-8.75	19.00-10.38	...	...	...
P/E Ratio	31.3-9.5	35.4-12.1	26.3-11.1	27.1-14.8	...	...	...

Statistics are as originally reported.

OFFICERS:
F. M. Drendel, Chmn., C.E.O.
B. D. Garrett, Pres., C.O.O.
J. L. Leonhardt, Exec. V.P., C.F.O.
F. B. Wyatt II, V.P., Gen. Couns., Sec.

INVESTOR CONTACT: Philip M. Armstrong, Jr, Dir., Inv. Rel., (828) 323-4848

PRINCIPAL OFFICE: 1375 Lenoir-Rhyne Blvd., Hickory, NC 28602

TELEPHONE NUMBER: (828) 324-2200
FAX: (828) 328-3400
WEB: www.commscope.com

NO. OF EMPLOYEES: 4,000 (approx.)

SHAREHOLDERS: 706 (approx.)

ANNUAL MEETING: In May

INCORPORATED: DE, Jan., 1997

INSTITUTIONAL HOLDINGS:
No. of Institutions: 164
Shares Held: 40,197,896
% Held: 78.2

INDUSTRY: Radio & TV communications equipment (SIC: 3663)

TRANSFER AGENT(S): Mellon Investor Services, Ridgefield Park, NJ

NYSE SYMBOL CPQ
Rec. Pr. 15.99 (5/31/01)

COMPAQ COMPUTER CORPORATION

YIELD 0.6%
P/E RATIO 48.5

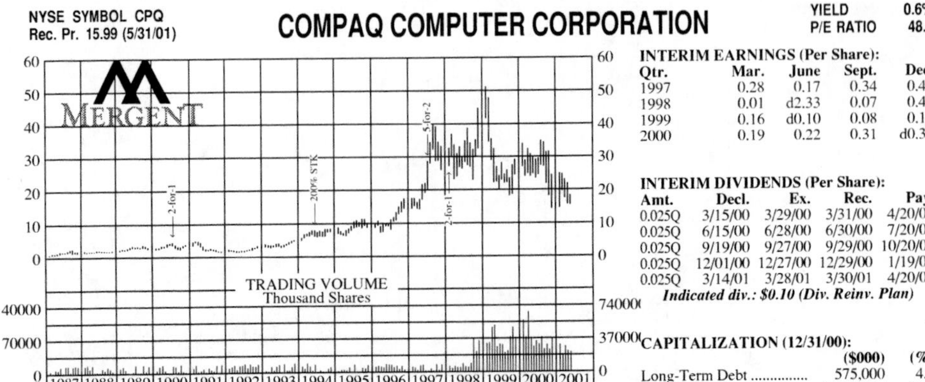

*7 YEAR PRICE SCORE 84.9 *12 MONTH PRICE SCORE 80.0

*NYSE COMPOSITE INDEX=100

INTERIM EARNINGS (Per Share):

Qtr.	Mar.	June	Sept.	Dec.
1997	0.28	0.17	0.34	0.43
1998	0.01	d2.33	0.07	0.43
1999	0.16	d0.10	0.08	0.19
2000	0.19	0.22	0.31	d0.39

INTERIM DIVIDENDS (Per Share):

Amt.	Decl.	Ex.	Rec.	Pay.
0.025Q	3/15/00	3/29/00	3/31/00	4/20/00
0.025Q	6/15/00	6/28/00	6/30/00	7/20/00
0.025Q	9/19/00	9/27/00	9/29/00	10/20/00
0.025Q	12/01/00	12/27/00	12/29/00	1/19/01
0.025Q	3/14/01	3/28/01	3/30/01	4/20/01

Indicated div.: $0.10 (Div. Reinv. Plan)

CAPITALIZATION (12/31/00):

	($000)	(%)
Long-Term Debt	575,000	4.5
Common & Surplus	12,080,000	95.5
Total	12,655,000	100.0

RECENT DEVELOPMENTS: For the year ended 12/31/00, income, before the cumulative effect of an accounting charge of $26.0 million, climbed 4.6% to $595.0 million versus net income of $569.0 million in 1999. Results for 2000 and 1999 included a gain of $86.0 million in 2000 and a charge of $868.0 million in 1999 for restructuring and other activities. Total revenues were $42.4 billion, up 10.0% from $38.53 billion in the prior year. Revenues from products grew 11.8% to $35.7 million.

PROSPECTS: CPQ expects market conditions to be challenging during the first half of 2001. As a result, CPQ will continue to develop new products and integrate them into applications. For the full year 2001, CPQ anticipates to achieve earnings per share growth in the range of 20.0% to 25.0%. Separately, CPQ will provide end-to-end business services to The Mead Corporation, a paper and forest products company. Under the agreement, CPQ will provide Mead with enterprise-wide industry-standard products.

BUSINESS

COMPAQ COMPUTER CORPORATION designs, develops, manufactures and markets a wide range of personal computing products, including desktop personal computers, portable computers, and tower PC servers and peripheral products that store and manage data in network environments. In addition to its core products, CPQ provides NT professional workstations, Internet products and services, mobile computing for home and schools, high-speed network connections, and computer equipment financing. Compaq products are sold in more than 200 countries. On 8/18/99, CMGI, Inc. became an indirectly-owned affiliate of the Company through a strategic partnership that allows both companies to pursue cooperative Internet-related business opportunities.

ANNUAL FINANCIAL DATA

	12/31/00	12/31/99	12/31/98	12/31/97	12/31/96	12/31/95	12/31/94
Earnings Per Share	**[5] 0.34**	**[4] 0.34**	**[3] d1.71**	**[2] 1.19**	**0.94**	**[1] 0.58**	**0.65**
Cash Flow Per Share	**1.15**	**1.14**	**d1.15**	**1.53**	**1.15**	**0.73**	**0.77**
Tang. Book Val. Per Share	**7.15**	**8.74**	**6.73**	**6.21**	**4.49**	**3.45**	**2.82**
Dividends Per Share	**0.10**	**0.08**	**0.06**	...	...	...	...
Dividend Payout %	**29.4**	**23.5**	...	...	...	...	...
INCOME STATEMENT (IN MILLIONS):							
Total Revenues	42,383.0	38,525.0	31,169.0	24,584.0	18,109.0	14,755.0	10,866.0
Costs & Expenses	38,437.0	36,083.0	33,007.0	21,304.0	15,947.0	13,258.0	9,431.0
Depreciation & Amort.	1,407.0	1,402.0	893.0	545.0	285.0	214.0	169.0
Operating Income	2,539.0	1,040.0	d2,731.0	2,735.0	1,877.0	1,283.0	1,266.0
Income Before Income Taxes	875.0	934.0	d2,662.0	2,758.0	1,876.0	1,188.0	1,172.0
Income Taxes	280.0	365.0	81.0	903.0	563.0	399.0	305.0
Net Income	[5] 595.0	[4] 569.0	[3] d2,743.0	[2] 1,855.0	1,313.0	[1] 789.0	867.0
Cash Flow	2,002.0	1,971.0	d1,850.0	2,400.0	1,598.0	1,003.0	1,036.0
Average Shs. Outstg. (000)	1,742,000	1,735,000	1,608,000	1,564,000	1,391,500	1,368,000	1,343,000
BALANCE SHEET (IN MILLIONS):							
Cash & Cash Equivalents	2,569.0	3,302.0	4,091.0	6,762.0	3,993.0	745.0	471.0
Total Current Assets	15,111.0	13,849.0	15,167.0	12,017.0	9,169.0	6,527.0	5,158.0
Net Property	3,431.0	3,249.0	2,902.0	1,985.0	1,172.0	1,110.0	944.0
Total Assets	24,856.0	27,277.0	23,051.0	14,631.0	10,760.0	8,040.0	6,350.0
Total Current Liabilities	11,549.0	11,838.0	10,733.0	5,202.0	3,852.0	2,680.0	2,013.0
Long-Term Obligations	575.0	...	...	...	300.0	300.0	300.0
Net Stockholders' Equity	12,080.0	14,834.0	11,351.0	9,429.0	6,144.0	4,614.0	3,674.0
Net Working Capital	3,562.0	2,011.0	4,434.0	6,815.0	5,317.0	3,847.0	3,145.0
Year-end Shs. Outstg. (000)	1,689,000	1,698,000	1,687,000	1,519,000	1,368,000	1,335,500	1,305,000
STATISTICAL RECORD:							
Operating Profit Margin %	6.0	2.7	...	11.1	10.4	8.7	11.7
Net Profit Margin %	1.4	1.5	...	7.5	7.3	5.3	8.0
Return on Equity %	4.9	3.8	...	19.7	21.4	17.1	23.6
Return on Assets %	2.4	2.1	...	12.7	12.5	10.1	14.1
Debt/Total Assets %	2.3	...	...	...	2.9	3.8	4.9
Price Range	34.88-14.30	51.25-18.25	44.75-22.94	39.78-14.20	17.43-7.18	11.35-6.23	8.43-4.83
P/E Ratio	102.5-42.0	150.7-53.7	...	33.4-11.9	18.5-7.6	19.7-10.8	13.0-7.5
Average Yield %	0.4	0.2	0.2	...	...	...	...

Statistics are as originally reported. Adj. for 2-for-1 split, 1/98; 3-for-1 split, 6/94; 5-for-2 split, 11/97. [1] Incl. $241.0 mill. ($0.44/sh.) non-tax deduct. chg. [2] Incl. $252.0 mill. non-recur. chg. [3] Incl. $3.20 bill. chg. for in-process tech. & $393.0 mill. restr. & asset impairment chgs. [4] Incl. $868.0 mill. restr. chg. & $1.18 bill. gain fr. sale of bus. [5] Incl. $86.0 mill. restr. chg. & excl. $26.0 mill. cumulative effect of an acctg. change.

OFFICERS:
M. D. Capellas, Chmn., Pres., C.E.O.
J. J. Greene Jr., Sr. V.P., C.F.O.
T. C. Siekman, Sr. V.P., Gen. Couns.

INVESTOR CONTACT: Investor Relations, (800) 433-2391

PRINCIPAL OFFICE: 20555 State Highway 249, Houston, TX 77070-2698

TELEPHONE NUMBER: (281) 370-0670
FAX: (281) 514-0570
WEB: www.compaq.com

NO. OF EMPLOYEES: 70,100 full-time (approx.); 24,500 part-time (approx.)

SHAREHOLDERS: 91,000 (approx. record)

ANNUAL MEETING: In Apr.

INCORPORATED: DE, Feb., 1982

INSTITUTIONAL HOLDINGS:
No. of Institutions: 654
Shares Held: 955,558,501
% Held: 56.6

INDUSTRY: Electronic computers (SIC: 3571)

TRANSFER AGENT(S): BankBoston, N.A., c/o EquiServe, Boston, MA

NYSE SYMBOL CA
Rec. Pr. 32.19 (4/30/01)

COMPUTER ASSOCIATES INTERNATIONAL, INC.

YIELD 0.3%
P/E RATIO 33.2

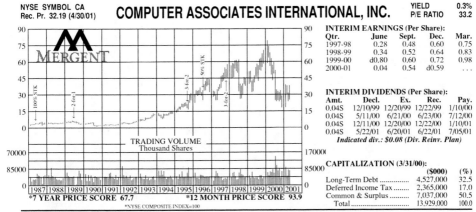

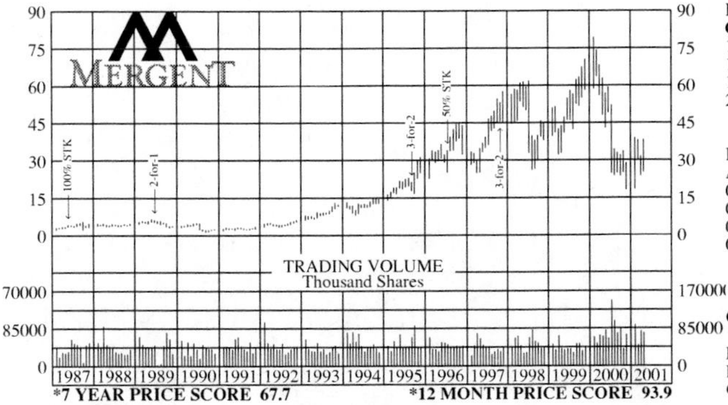

TRADING VOLUME
Thousand Shares

*7 YEAR PRICE SCORE 67.7 *12 MONTH PRICE SCORE 93.9

*NYSE COMPOSITE INDEX=100

INTERIM EARNINGS (Per Share):

Qtr.	June	Sept.	Dec.	Mar.
1997-98	0.28	0.48	0.60	0.75
1998-99	0.34	0.52	0.64	0.83
1999-00	d0.80	0.60	0.72	0.98
2000-01	0.04	0.54	d0.59	...

INTERIM DIVIDENDS (Per Share):

Amt.	Decl.	Ex.	Rec.	Pay.
0.04S	12/10/99	12/20/99	12/22/99	1/10/00
0.04S	5/11/00	6/21/00	6/23/00	7/12/00
0.04S	12/11/00	12/20/00	12/22/00	1/10/01
0.04S	5/22/01	6/20/01	6/22/01	7/05/01

Indicated div.: $0.08 (Div. Reinv. Plan)

CAPITALIZATION (3/31/00):

	($000)	(%)
Long-Term Debt	4,527,000	32.5
Deferred Income Tax	2,365,000	17.0
Common & Surplus	7,037,000	50.5
Total	13,929,000	100.0

RECENT DEVELOPMENTS: For the quarter ended 12/31/00, the Company reported a net loss of $342.0 million compared with net income of $401.0 million in the equivalent quarter of 1999. Results for 1999 included a special charge of $37.0 million from the write-down of an investment in CHS Electronics, Inc. Total revenue fell 53.2% to $783.0 million from $1.67 billion in the prior-year period. CA announced that $629.0 million of the total contract value concluded in the quarter was not recognized as revenue.

PROSPECTS: Future results should benefit from the Company's new business model, a progressive software portfolio and its reputation for innovative applications. In addition, the new business model should reflect higher revenue streams and visibility into the Company's operations. Meanwhile, the residual value earned in the third quarter of fiscal 2001 and each quarter thereafter should strengthen shareholder value through enhanced visibility and stability of future revenue streams.

BUSINESS

COMPUTER ASSOCIATES INTERNATIONAL, INC. is a business software company that delivers the end-to-end infrastructure to enable e-business through technology, education and services. CA provides software applications for all types of businesses throughout the world. The Company has a portfolio of more than 800 products, including enterprise management, database and application development, as well as products that provide the infrastructure for e-business and e-commerce over the Internet. Many of CA's products provide tools to measure and improve computer hardware and software performance and programmer productivity. In 1999, CA acquired Computer Management Sciences, Inc. and PLATINUM Technology International, Inc. In March 2000, CA acquired Sterling Software, Inc. for $3.30 billion.

ANNUAL FINANCIAL DATA

	3/31/00	3/31/99	3/31/98	3/31/97	3/31/96	3/31/95	3/31/94
Earnings Per Share	[4] 1.25	[3] 1.11	[2] 2.06	0.65	[1] d0.11	[1] 0.76	[1] 1.04
Cash Flow Per Share	2.32	1.69	2.68	1.39	0.64	1.22	1.58
Tang. Book Val. Per Share	...	1.65	2.00	...	0.32	1.65	2.03
Dividends Per Share	0.08	0.08	0.07	0.06	0.06	0.05	0.04
Dividend Payout %	6.4	7.2	3.2	9.6	...	6.6	3.4
INCOME STATEMENT (IN MILLIONS):							
Total Revenues	6,103.0	5,253.0	4,719.0	4,040.0	3,504.6	2,623.0	2,148.5
Costs & Expenses	3,580.0	2,724.0	2,353.0	2,582.0	3,130.1	1,660.6	1,313.4
Depreciation & Amort.	594.0	325.0	349.0	424.0	404.3	257.7	206.3
Operating Income	1,929.0	2,204.0	2,017.0	1,034.0	d29.8	704.7	628.8
Net Interest Inc./(Exp.)	d339.0	d123.0	d143.0	d102.0	d70.8	d8.1	d1.8
Income Before Income Taxes	1,590.0	1,010.0	1,874.0	932.0	d100.6	696.6	627.0
Income Taxes	894.0	384.0	705.0	566.0	cr44.3	264.7	225.7
Net Income	[4] 696.0	[3] 626.0	[2] 1,169.0	366.0	[1] d56.4	[1] 431.9	[1] 401.3
Cash Flow	1,290.0	951.0	1,518.0	790.0	348.0	689.6	607.6
Average Shs. Outstg. (000)	557,000	562,000	566,000	568,500	543,000	567,000	385,713
BALANCE SHEET (IN MILLIONS):							
Cash & Cash Equivalents	1,387.0	536.0	310.0	199.0	201.2	301.2	368.2
Total Current Assets	3,992.0	2,631.0	2,255.0	1,780.0	1,447.7	1,147.6	999.2
Net Property	829.0	598.0	459.0	438.0	420.3	344.0	304.6
Total Assets	17,493.0	8,070.0	6,706.0	6,084.0	5,016.0	3,269.4	2,491.6
Total Current Liabilities	3,004.0	1,863.0	1,876.0	1,727.0	1,501.5	847.9	548.6
Long-Term Obligations	4,527.0	2,032.0	1,027.0	1,663.0	944.5	50.5	71.4
Net Stockholders' Equity	7,037.0	2,729.0	2,481.0	1,503.0	1,481.7	1,578.1	1,243.1
Net Working Capital	988.0	768.0	379.0	53.0	d53.8	299.7	450.6
Year-end Shs. Outstg. (000)	589,392	535,703	546,052	542,955	360,309	567,000	385,713
STATISTICAL RECORD:							
Operating Profit Margin %	31.6	42.0	42.7	25.6	...	26.9	29.3
Net Profit Margin %	11.4	11.9	24.8	9.1	...	16.5	18.7
Return on Equity %	9.9	22.9	47.1	24.4	...	27.4	32.3
Return on Assets %	4.0	7.8	17.4	6.0	...	13.2	16.1
Debt/Total Assets %	25.9	25.2	15.3	27.3	18.8	1.5	2.9
Price Range	70.63-32.13	61.94-26.00	57.50-24.83	45.25-22.56	31.33-13.89	15.07-8.11	13.11-5.96
P/E Ratio	56.5-25.7	55.8-23.4	27.9-12.1	69.9-34.9	...	19.8-10.7	12.6-5.7
Average Yield %	0.2	0.2	0.2	0.2	0.3	0.4	0.4

Statistics are as originally reported. Adj. for 3-for-2 split, 8/95, 7/96 & 11/97. [1] Incl. after-tax write-off for purch. R&D of: $154.6 mill., 1994; $808.0 mill., 1995; $598.0 mill., 1996. [2] Excl. $33.8 mill. pre-tax chg. rel. to CSC tender offer. [3] Incl. $1.07 bill. chg. rel. to the vesting of stock ownership. [4] Incl. $796.0 mill. in-process R&D chg. & $50.0 mill. non-cash asset write-down chg.

OFFICERS:
C. B. Wang, Chmn.
S. Kumar, Pres., C.E.O., C.O.O.
I. Zar, Exec. V.P., C.F.O.

INVESTOR CONTACT: Investor Relations, (631) 342-5601

PRINCIPAL OFFICE: One Computer Associates Plaza, Islandia, NY 11749

TELEPHONE NUMBER: (631) 342-5224
FAX: (631) 342-5329
WEB: www.ca.com

NO. OF EMPLOYEES: 21,000 (approx.)

SHAREHOLDERS: 10,000 (approx.)

ANNUAL MEETING: In Aug.

INCORPORATED: DE, June, 1974

INSTITUTIONAL HOLDINGS:
No. of Institutions: 435
Shares Held: 300,390,024
% Held: 52.1

INDUSTRY: Prepackaged software (SIC: 7372)

TRANSFER AGENT(S): Mellon Investor Services, Ridgefield Park, NJ

NYSE SYMBOL CSC
Rec. Pr. 35.63 (4/30/01)

COMPUTER SCIENCES CORPORATION

YIELD ...
P/E RATIO 14.7

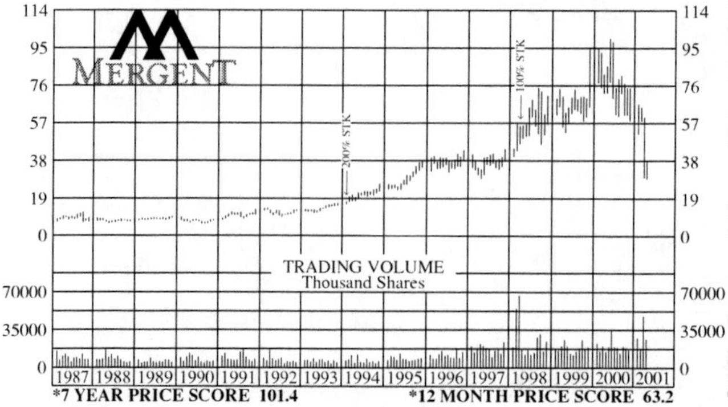

TRADING VOLUME
Thousand Shares

*7 YEAR PRICE SCORE 101.4 *12 MONTH PRICE SCORE 63.2

*NYSE COMPOSITE INDEX=100

INTERIM EARNINGS (Per Share):

Qtr.	June	Sept.	Dec.	Mar.
1995-96	0.25	0.27	0.32	0.42
1996-97	0.29	0.09	0.37	0.49
1997-98	0.34	0.37	0.44	0.50
1998-99	0.40	0.45	0.54	0.72
1999-00	0.48	0.55	0.48	0.84
2000-01	0.56	0.64	0.38	...

INTERIM DIVIDENDS (Per Share):

Amt.	Decl.	Ex.	Rec.	Pay.

No dividends paid.

CAPITALIZATION (3/31/00):

	($000)	(%)
Long-Term Debt	652,367	17.3
Deferred Income Tax	83,796	2.2
Common & Surplus	3,043,974	80.5
Total	3,780,137	100.0

RECENT DEVELOPMENTS: For the quarter ended 12/29/00, net income fell 20.3% to $65.6 million versus $82.3 million in the equivalent quarter of 1999. Results for 2000 and 1999 included after-tax special charges of $57.3 million and $29.8 million, respectively. Special charges for 2000 were related to the December 2000 acquisition of Mynd Corporation. Revenues increased 12.9% to $2.66 billion from $2.36 billion in the prior year.

PROSPECTS: The Company is focusing on a plethora of opportunities in the federal market, which over the next 26 months should amount to about $22.00 billion. These opportunities are expected to stem the federal government moving toward the private sector for commercial practices as it emphasizes its modernization efforts. Separately, CSC has been selected as one of more than 40 companies that will compete for a $19.50 billion contract.

BUSINESS

COMPUTER SCIENCES CORPORATION offers a broad array of professional services to industry and government and specializes in the application of advanced and complex information technology to achieve its customers' strategic objectives. CSC's services include: outsourcing, which includes operating all or a portion of a customer's technology infrastructure, including systems analysis, applications development, network operations and data center management; systems integration, which includes designing, developing, implementing and integrating complete information systems; and information technology and management consulting and other professional services. Revenues for the year ended 3/31/00 were derived as follows: U.S. Commercial, 38.9%; Europe, 27.0%; other international, 9.9%; Department of Defense, 15.7%; and civil agencies, 8.5%.

ANNUAL FINANCIAL DATA

	3/31/00	4/2/99	4/3/98	3/28/97	3/29/96	3/31/95	4/1/94
Earnings Per Share	[3] **2.37**	**2.11**	[2] **1.64**	[1] **1.23**	[1] **1.24**	**1.05**	**0.89**
Cash Flow Per Share	**5.59**	**4.85**	**4.08**	**6.72**	**6.88**	**5.35**	**4.31**
Tang. Book Val. Per Share	**11.18**	**9.92**	**8.52**	**12.73**	**14.08**	**11.70**	**8.22**
INCOME STATEMENT (IN MILLIONS):							
Total Revenues	9,370.7	7,660.0	6,600.8	5,616.0	4,242.4	3,372.5	2,582.7
Costs & Expenses	8,131.9	6,669.7	5,751.9	4,898.3	3,728.6	2,996.8	2,292.0
Depreciation & Amort.	545.7	445.0	386.9	333.2	252.1	172.6	130.7
Operating Income	693.1	545.3	462.1	384.5	261.8	203.1	159.9
Net Interest Inc./(Exp.)	d40.5	d33.9	d42.1	d32.3	d30.4	d25.6	d10.9
Income Before Income Taxes	611.5	511.4	190.9	303.3	231.4	173.7	149.1
Income Taxes	208.6	170.2	cr69.5	110.9	89.7	63.0	58.2
Net Income	[3] 402.9	341.2	[2] 260.4	[1] 192.4	[1] 141.7	110.7	90.9
Cash Flow	948.6	786.2	647.2	525.7	393.8	283.4	221.6
Average Shs. Outstg. (000)	169,749	161,949	158,526	156,394	114,428	105,950	102,770
BALANCE SHEET (IN MILLIONS):							
Cash & Cash Equivalents	260.4	602.6	274.7	110.7	104.9	155.3	126.8
Total Current Assets	2,766.3	2,669.0	1,982.6	1,612.4	1,144.3	1,081.5	857.1
Net Property	1,274.9	1,086.9	957.2	888.1	640.8	530.1	393.0
Total Assets	5,874.1	5,007.7	4,046.8	3,580.9	2,595.8	2,333.7	1,806.4
Total Current Liabilities	1,984.0	2,081.4	1,214.8	1,087.1	760.4	777.9	661.2
Long-Term Obligations	652.4	397.9	736.1	630.8	405.5	310.3	273.3
Net Stockholders' Equity	3,044.0	2,399.9	2,001.3	1,669.6	1,305.7	1,148.6	805.7
Net Working Capital	782.4	587.6	767.8	525.3	383.8	303.6	195.9
Year-end Shs. Outstg. (000)	167,508	159,140	156,978	153,186	112,060	110,342	101,212
STATISTICAL RECORD:							
Operating Profit Margin %	7.4	7.1	7.0	6.8	6.2	6.0	6.2
Net Profit Margin %	4.3	4.5	3.9	3.4	3.3	3.3	3.5
Return on Equity %	13.2	14.2	13.0	11.5	10.9	9.6	11.3
Return on Assets %	6.9	6.8	6.4	5.4	5.5	4.7	5.0
Debt/Total Assets %	11.1	7.9	18.2	17.6	15.6	13.3	15.1
Price Range	94.63-52.38	74.88-39.97	43.88-28.94	43.25-32.06	37.63-23.25	26.31-15.81	16.71-11.67
P/E Ratio	39.9-22.1	35.5-18.9	26.8-17.6	35.2-26.1	30.3-18.7	25.2-15.1	18.9-13.2

Statistics are as originally reported. Adj. for 3-for-1 split, 1/94; 100% stk. split, 3/98. Fiscal yr. ends 3/31 of the following yr. [1] Incl. $35.3 mill. ($0.23/sh.) non-recur. chg., 1996; cr$1.7 mill., 1997. [2] Incl. $13.9 mill. after-tax spl. chg. rel. to an unsolicited take-over attempt. [3] Incl. after-tax spl. chgs. of $29.8 mill., 1999; $57.3 mill., 2000.

OFFICERS:
V. B. Honeycutt, Chmn., Pres., C.E.O.
L. J. Level, V.P., C.F.O.
H. D. Fisk, V.P., Gen. Couns., & Sec.

INVESTOR CONTACT: Bill Lackey, Investor Relations, (310) 615-1700

PRINCIPAL OFFICE: 2100 East Grand Ave., El Segundo, CA 90245

TELEPHONE NUMBER: (310) 615-0311
FAX: (310) 640-2648
WEB: www.csc.com

NO. OF EMPLOYEES: 58,000 (approx.)

SHAREHOLDERS: 9,630

ANNUAL MEETING: In Aug.

INCORPORATED: NV, Apr., 1959

INSTITUTIONAL HOLDINGS:
No. of Institutions: 436
Shares Held: 122,683,822
% Held: 72.8

INDUSTRY: Computer integrated systems design (SIC: 7373)

TRANSFER AGENT(S): Mellon Investor Services, Ridgefield Park, NJ

NYSE SYMBOL CTG
Rec. Pr. 5.75 (5/31/01)

COMPUTER TASK GROUP, INC.

YIELD . . .
P/E RATIO . . .

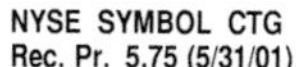

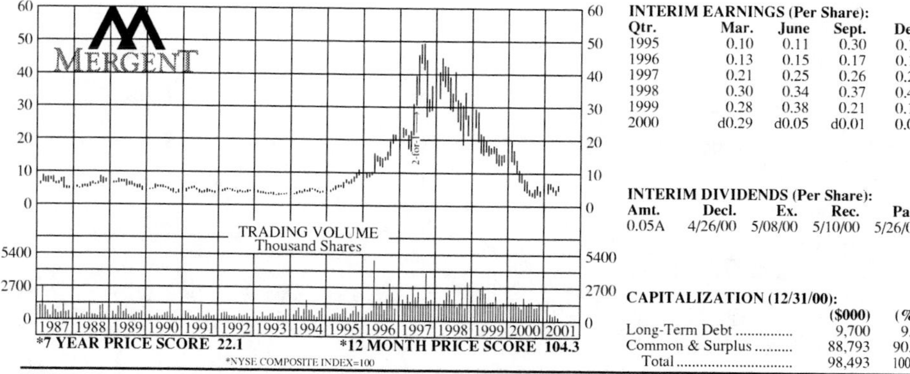

*7 YEAR PRICE SCORE 22.1 *12 MONTH PRICE SCORE 104.3

*NYSE COMPOSITE INDEX=100

INTERIM EARNINGS (Per Share):

Qtr.	Mar.	June	Sept.	Dec.
1995	0.10	0.11	0.30	0.12
1996	0.13	0.15	0.17	0.18
1997	0.21	0.25	0.26	0.29
1998	0.30	0.34	0.37	0.41
1999	0.28	0.38	0.21	0.13
2000	d0.29	d0.05	d0.01	0.01

INTERIM DIVIDENDS (Per Share):

Amt.	Decl.	Ex.	Rec.	Pay.
0.05A	4/26/00	5/08/00	5/10/00	5/26/00

CAPITALIZATION (12/31/00):

	($000)	(%)
Long-Term Debt	9,700	9.8
Common & Surplus	88,793	90.2
Total	98,493	100.0

RECENT DEVELOPMENTS: For the year ended 12/31/00, the Company reported a net loss of $5.7 million compared with net income of $16.7 million in 1999. Results for 2000 included a restructuring charge of $4.2 million. Total revenues were $345.7 million, down 26.8% from $472.0 million in the prior year. Operating loss was $5.6 million compared with operating income of $30.8 million the year before. A very challenging business environment hampered results for information technology service providers.

PROSPECTS: In an effort to better position the Company for renewed growth in revenues and earnings, CTG has restructured its sales and delivery organizations to help drive top line growth. The Company has removed three brands previously used in the North American market and is focusing on one team. In addition, the Company has introduced new global practices to leverage relationships with third-party partners. Separately CTG anticipates 2001 revenues to be between $380.0 million and $395.0 million.

BUSINESS

COMPUTER TASK GROUP, INC. is an information technology services company that provides IT services to Fortune 500 and other companies through strategic partnerships in each of the following areas: Business Consulting, Development & Integration, and Managed Support. CTG works with customers to develop effective business solutions through information systems and technology. CTG's professional staff may support a customer's software development team on a specific application or project or may manage the project entirely for the customer. CTG's range of services extends from flexible staffing provided on a per diem basis to managing multi-million dollar technology projects. Revenues (and operating income) for 2000 were derived: North America, 82.2% (77.1%) and Europe, 17.8% (22.9%).

ANNUAL FINANCIAL DATA

	12/31/00	12/31/99	12/31/98	12/31/97	12/31/96	12/31/95	12/31/94
Earnings Per Share	**5 d0.35**	**4 1.00**	**1.42**	**1.01**	**0.63**	**3 0.62**	**2 0.26**
Cash Flow Per Share	**0.25**	**1.51**	**1.72**	**1.32**	**1.05**	**0.97**	**0.58**
Tang. Book Val. Per Share	**0.48**	**0.52**	**3.89**	**2.51**	**3.24**	**2.72**	**2.22**
Dividends Per Share	**0.05**	**0.05**	**0.05**	**0.05**	**0.05**	**0.05**	**0.05**
Dividend Payout %	**. . .**	**5.0**	**3.5**	**5.0**	**8.0**	**8.1**	**19.2**
INCOME STATEMENT (IN THOUSANDS):							
Total Revenues	345,676	472,008	467,838	407,588	365,076	339,407	301,559
Costs & Expenses	341,625	432,695	422,985	373,204	338,907	320,511	297,891
Depreciation & Amort.	9,696	8,480	5,002	5,428	7,651	6,146	5,888
Operating Income	d5,645	30,833	39,851	28,956	18,518	12,750	d2,220
Income Before Income Taxes	d8,679	29,864	40,757	30,268	18,504	12,041	8,130
Income Taxes	cr3,018	13,163	16,712	12,406	7,424	1,265	3,333
Net Income	5 d5,661	4 16,701	24,045	17,862	11,080	3 10,776	2 4,797
Cash Flow	4,035	25,181	29,047	23,290	18,731	16,922	10,685
Average Shs. Outstg.	16,272	16,680	16,913	17,615	17,786	17,400	18,532
BALANCE SHEET (IN THOUSANDS):							
Cash & Cash Equivalents	2,562	10,684	57,748	25,033	41,516	16,545	5,112
Total Current Assets	66,065	97,319	137,334	88,873	101,182	78,769	68,193
Net Property	13,784	13,483	13,146	12,445	12,380	17,981	17,790
Total Assets	162,367	199,159	156,809	107,741	121,281	104,766	95,490
Total Current Liabilities	53,521	62,117	62,473	41,771	39,651	29,260	29,346
Long-Term Obligations	9,700	31,380	. . .	. . .	. . .	3,640	6,114
Net Stockholders' Equity	88,793	94,924	83,449	55,326	71,504	61,476	50,658
Net Working Capital	12,544	35,202	74,861	47,102	61,531	49,509	38,847
Year-end Shs. Outstg.	20,871	20,876	20,748	20,751	20,672	20,596	19,974
STATISTICAL RECORD:							
Operating Profit Margin %	. . .	6.5	8.5	7.1	5.1	3.8	. . .
Net Profit Margin %	. . .	3.5	5.1	4.4	3.0	3.2	1.6
Return on Equity %	. . .	17.6	28.8	32.3	15.5	17.5	9.5
Return on Assets %	. . .	8.4	15.3	16.6	9.1	10.3	5.0
Debt/Total Assets %	6.0	15.8	. . .	. . .	. . .	3.5	6.4
Price Range	20.00-2.69	29.50-12.31	45.00-18.50	49.38-16.56	21.75-8.38	11.00-4.06	5.19-3.31
P/E Ratio	. . .	29.5-12.3	31.7-13.0	48.9-16.4	34.8-13.4	17.9-6.6	19.9-12.7
Average Yield %	0.4	0.2	0.2	0.2	0.3	0.7	1.2

Statistics are as originally reported. Adj. for 2-for-1 split, 5/97. 1 Incl. $37.1 mill. ($1.31/sh.) net chg. for restr. & interest expense. 2 Incl. $11.3 mill. pre-tax gain fr. sale of assets & $7.7 mill. chg. for severance pkg. & exp. reduction. 3 Incl. $3.2 mill. ($0.18/sh.) non-recur. tax benefit. 4 Incl. $2.5 mill. non-recur. chg. for arbitration award. 5 Incl. $4.2 mill. restr. chg.

OFFICERS:
D. L. Jennings, Chmn., Pres., C.E.O.
J. R. Boldt, V.P., C.E.O., Treas.
P. P. Radetich, Sec., Gen. Couns.

INVESTOR CONTACT: James R. Boldt, (716) 887-7221

PRINCIPAL OFFICE: 800 Delaware Avenue, Buffalo, NY 14209

TELEPHONE NUMBER: (716) 882-8000
FAX: (716) 887-7456
WEB: www.ctg.com

NO. OF EMPLOYEES: 4,000 (approx.)

SHAREHOLDERS: 3,362

ANNUAL MEETING: In May

INCORPORATED: NY, Mar., 1966

INSTITUTIONAL HOLDINGS:
No. of Institutions: 58
Shares Held: 9,720,671
% Held: 46.6

INDUSTRY: Computer programming services (SIC: 7371)

TRANSFER AGENT(S): Bank Boston, c/o Boston EquiServe, Boston, MA

NYSE SYMBOL CAG
Rec. Pr. 20.85 (5/31/01)

CONAGRA FOODS, INC.

YIELD 4.3%
P/E RATIO 20.2

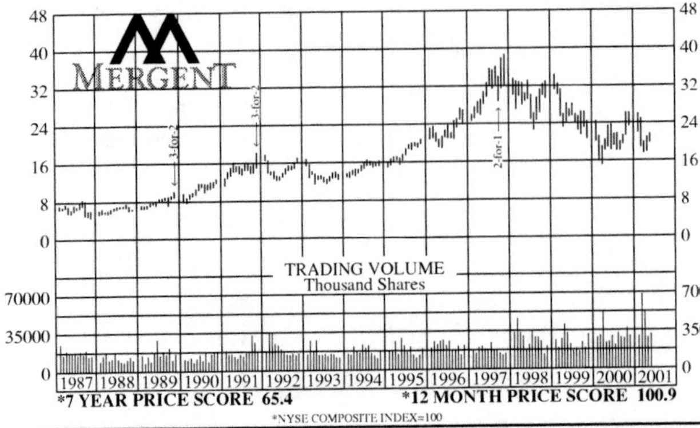

*7 YEAR PRICE SCORE 65.4   *12 MONTH PRICE SCORE 100.9

*NYSE COMPOSITE INDEX=100

INTERIM EARNINGS (Per Share):

Qtr.	Aug.	Nov.	Feb.	May
1996-97	0.21	0.41	0.32	0.41
1997-98	0.48	0.46	0.30	0.36
1998-99	0.23	0.46	0.36	d0.30
1999-00	0.21	0.39	0.30	d0.04
2000-01	0.30	0.58	0.19	...

INTERIM DIVIDENDS (Per Share):

Amt.	Decl.	Ex.	Rec.	Pay.
0.203Q	4/10/00	4/26/00	4/28/00	6/01/00
0.203Q	7/17/00	7/27/00	7/31/00	9/01/00
0.225Q	9/28/00	10/25/00	10/27/00	12/01/00
0.225Q	12/07/00	1/31/01	2/02/01	3/01/01
0.225Q	4/09/01	5/02/01	5/04/01	6/01/01

Indicated div.: $0.90 (Div. Reinv. Plan)

CAPITALIZATION (5/28/00):

	($000)	(%)
Long-Term Debt	2,566,800	46.4
Common & Surplus	2,964,100	53.6
Total	5,530,900	100.0

RECENT DEVELOPMENTS: For the 13 weeks ended 2/25/01, net income was $98.5 million, down 31.3% versus $143.4 million the year before. Results in the prior-year period included pre-tax restructuring charges totaling $84.6 million. Net sales rose 8.9% to $6.43 billion from $5.90 billion a year earlier, reflecting strong growth in the Packaged Foods segment. Operating profit slid 29.9% to $327.6 million from $467.6 million the previous year.

PROSPECTS: Results are benefiting from the acquisitions in 2000 of CHEF BOYARDEE, BUMBLE BEE, PAM, and GULDEN'S. CAG expects most of its current fiscal year earnings growth to occur during the fourth quarter, as CAG plans to support the roll-out of several new products during the third quarter with an aggressive marketing campaign. CAG is targeting double-digit annual earnings growth over the long term.

BUSINESS

CONAGRA FOODS, INC. (formerly ConAgra, Inc.) operates in three industry segments: Refrigerated Foods (49.3% of fiscal 2000 sales) produces and markets branded processed meats, beef and pork products, and chicken and turkey products. Packaged Foods (30.4%) includes shelf-stable and frozen foods, dairy products, and products for foodservice markets. Major brands include: HEALTHY CHOICE, BANQUET, CHEF BOYARDEE, WESSON, HUNT'S, ORVILLE REDENBACHER'S, SLIM JIM, PETER PAN, PARKAY, VAN CAMP'S, PAM, SWISS MISS, EGG BEATERS, REDDI-WIP, ACT II, FLEISCHMANN'S, BUMBLE BEE, BUTTERBALL, and ARMOUR. Agricultural Products (20.3%) provides crop protection chemicals, fertilizers and seeds, and processes, distributes and trades ingredients for food products and meat and poultry production.

ANNUAL FINANCIAL DATA

	5/28/00	5/30/99	5/31/98	5/25/97	5/26/96	5/28/95	5/29/94
Earnings Per Share	**[2] 0.86**	**[2] 0.75**	**[1] 1.36**	**1.34**	**[2] 0.40**	**1.03**	**0.91**
Cash Flow Per Share	**1.98**	**1.80**	**2.33**	**2.24**	**1.28**	**1.85**	**1.71**
Tang. Book Val. Per Share	**1.22**	**1.02**	**0.85**	**0.08**	**...**	**0.15**	**...**
Dividends Per Share	**0.74**	**0.65**	**0.56**	**0.49**	**0.43**	**0.37**	**0.32**
Dividend Payout %	**85.9**	**86.3**	**41.5**	**36.8**	**108.8**	**36.3**	**35.6**
INCOME STATEMENT (IN MILLIONS):							
Total Revenues	25,385.8	24,594.3	23,840.5	24,002.1	24,821.6	24,108.9	23,512.2
Costs & Expenses	23,557.6	22,654.8	22,073.8	22,293.4	23,192.4	22,632.5	22,174.8
Depreciation & Amort.	536.5	499.8	446.3	413.8	407.9	375.8	368.4
Operating Income	1,291.7	1,439.7	1,320.4	1,294.9	1,221.3	1,100.6	969.0
Net Interest Inc./(Exp.)	d303.4	d316.6	d299.3	d277.2	d304.9	d278.1	d254.2
Income Before Income Taxes	666.1	682.3	1,021.1	1,017.7	408.6	825.9	720.0
Income Taxes	253.1	323.9	393.1	402.7	219.7	330.3	282.9
Equity Earnings/Minority Int.	...	...	...	...	...	3.4	5.2
Net Income	[2] 413.0	[2] 358.4	[1] 628.0	615.0	[2] 188.9	495.6	437.1
Cash Flow	949.5	858.2	1,074.3	1,028.8	588.2	847.4	781.5
Average Shs. Outstg. (000)	478,600	476,700	461,300	459,000	459,000	458,000	457,000
BALANCE SHEET (IN MILLIONS):							
Cash & Cash Equivalents	157.6	62.8	95.2	105.8	113.7	60.0	452.4
Total Current Assets	5,966.5	5,656.1	5,487.4	5,205.0	5,566.9	5,140.2	5,143.3
Net Property	3,584.0	3,614.2	3,395.8	3,242.5	2,820.5	2,796.0	2,586.3
Total Assets	12,295.8	12,146.1	11,702.8	11,277.1	11,196.6	10,801.0	10,721.8
Total Current Liabilities	5,489.2	5,386.4	5,070.2	4,989.6	5,193.7	3,964.9	4,752.8
Long-Term Obligations	2,566.8	2,543.1	2,487.4	2,355.7	2,262.9	2,520.0	2,206.8
Net Stockholders' Equity	2,964.1	2,908.8	2,778.9	2,471.7	2,255.5	2,495.4	2,226.9
Net Working Capital	477.3	269.7	417.2	215.4	373.2	1,175.3	390.5
Year-end Shs. Outstg. (000)	492,212	488,173	459,076	476,126	486,312	491,394	496,390
STATISTICAL RECORD:							
Operating Profit Margin %	5.1	5.9	5.5	5.4	4.9	4.6	4.1
Net Profit Margin %	1.6	1.5	2.6	2.6	0.8	2.1	1.9
Return on Equity %	13.9	12.3	22.6	24.9	8.4	19.9	19.6
Return on Assets %	3.4	3.0	5.4	5.5	1.7	4.6	4.1
Debt/Total Assets %	20.9	20.9	21.3	20.9	20.2	23.3	20.6
Price Range	34.38-20.63	33.63-22.56	38.75-24.50	27.38-18.81	20.88-14.88	16.56-12.75	16.81-11.38
P/E Ratio	40.0-24.0	44.8-30.1	28.5-18.0	20.4-14.0	52.8-37.6	16.1-12.4	18.6-12.6
Average Yield %	2.7	2.3	1.8	2.1	2.4	2.6	2.3

Statistics are as originally reported. Adj. for 2-for-1 stk. split, 10/97. [1] Bef. $14.8 mil ($0.03/sh) chg. for acctg. change. [2] Incl. $621.4 mil pre-tax, non-recur. chg., 2000; $337.9 mil ($0.71/sh) after-tax, non-recur chg., 1999; & $356.3 mil ($0.78/sh) after-tax, non-recur. chg., 1996.

OFFICERS:
B. C. Rohde, Chmn., Pres., C.E.O.
J. P. O'Donnell, Exec. V.P., C.F.O., Sec.
K. W. Gerhardt, Sr. V.P., Chief Info. Off.

INVESTOR CONTACT: Shareholder Services, (800) 214-0349

PRINCIPAL OFFICE: One ConAgra Drive, Omaha, NE 68102-5001

TELEPHONE NUMBER: (402) 595-4000
FAX: (402) 978-4447
WEB: www.conagra.com
NO. OF EMPLOYEES: 85,000 (approx.)
SHAREHOLDERS: 34,000 (record); 160,000 (approx. beneficial)
ANNUAL MEETING: In Sept.
INCORPORATED: NE, Sept., 1919; reincorp., DE, Dec., 1975

INSTITUTIONAL HOLDINGS:
No. of Institutions: 402
Shares Held: 311,948,085
% Held: 58.1

INDUSTRY: Meat packing plants (SIC: 2011)

TRANSFER AGENT(S): Wells Fargo Shareowner Services, St. Paul, MN

NYSE SYMBOL COE
Rec. Pr. 1.39 (5/31/01)

CONE MILLS CORPORATION

YIELD . . .
P/E RATIO . . .

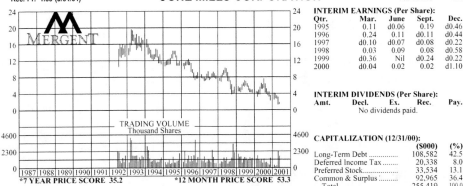

TRADING VOLUME
Thousand Shares

*7 YEAR PRICE SCORE 35.2 *12 MONTH PRICE SCORE 53.3

*NYSE COMPOSITE INDEX=100

INTERIM EARNINGS (Per Share):

Qtr.	Mar.	June	Sept.	Dec.
1995	0.11	d0.06	0.19	d0.46
1996	0.24	0.11	d0.11	d0.44
1997	d0.10	d0.07	d0.08	d0.22
1998	0.03	0.09	0.08	d0.58
1999	d0.36	Nil	d0.24	d0.22
2000	d0.04	0.02	0.02	d1.10

INTERIM DIVIDENDS (Per Share):

Amt.	Decl.	Ex.	Rec.	Pay.

No dividends paid.

CAPITALIZATION (12/31/00):

	($000)	(%)
Long-Term Debt	108,582	42.5
Deferred Income Tax	20,338	8.0
Preferred Stock	33,534	13.1
Common & Surplus	92,965	36.4
Total	255,419	100.0

RECENT DEVELOPMENTS: For the year ended 12/31/00, the Company reported a loss of $25.3 million, before an accounting change charge, compared with a loss of $18.0 million, before an accounting change charge, in 1999. Earnings for 2000 and 1999 included restructuring and impairment of assets charges of $38.5 million and $16.0 million, respectively. Earnings were negatively affected by the shutdown of the Company's Raytex wide-print plant. Net sales grew slightly to $617.7 million versus $616.3 million a year earlier.

PROSPECTS: Recently, COE announced two initiatives aimed at improving earnings in 2001. The initiatives are the expansion of the Parras Cone joint venture denim plant in Parras, Mexico, and the shutdown of COE's Raytex top-of-bed fabrics printing plant in Marion, South Carolina. The Parras Cone expansion should allow COE to keep up with the substantial growth in demand for sourcing of denim jeans for U.S. markets from Mexico. The closing of the Raytex plant will eliminate significant operating losses.

BUSINESS

CONE MILLS CORPORATION is the largest producer of denim fabrics in the world and is the largest printer of home furnishings fabrics in the U.S. The Company operates in three business segments: demin & khaki, commission finishing and decorative fabrics. All manufacturing is performed in the U.S. and at Parras Cone, a joint venture plant in Mexico. Sales and marketing activities are conducted through a worldwide distribution network. Products for the apparel market include denims and specialty sportswear fabrics. Some of Cone's major denim customers are Levi Strauss, Ralph Lauren (Polo), Guess, and The Gap. Products for home furnishings include commissioned finishing services and Cone Decorative Fabrics, a designer and distributor of printed and jacquard woven decorative fabrics.

ANNUAL FINANCIAL DATA

	12/31/00	1/2/00	1/3/99	12/28/97	12/29/96	12/31/95	1/1/95
Earnings Per Share	**[1][3] d1.14**	**[1][3] d0.83**	**[1] d0.37**	**[1] d0.47**	**[1] d0.19**	**d0.22**	**[2] 1.20**
Cash Flow Per Share	**d0.20**	**0.23**	**0.80**	**0.63**	**1.01**	**1.03**	**2.15**
Tang. Book Val. Per Share	**3.64**	**4.81**	**5.69**	**6.09**	**6.53**	**6.71**	**7.24**
INCOME STATEMENT (IN THOUSANDS):							
Total Revenues	617,721	616,321	728,626	716,853	745,939	910,217	806,167
Costs & Expenses	614,102	605,953	705,917	696,467	703,310	843,420	719,518
Depreciation & Amort.	24,001	26,912	30,364	28,715	29,806	31,373	24,046
Operating Income	d20,382	d16,544	d7,655	d8,329	12,823	35,424	62,603
Net Interest Inc./(Exp.)	d16,971	d12,921	d12,113	d11,674	d14,897	d14,518	d7,310
Income Before Income Taxes	d42,609	d30,458	d19,768	d20,003	d2,074	20,906	55,293
Income Taxes	cr14,624	cr10,740	cr7,907	cr8,001	cr2,311	7,306	19,764
Equity Earnings/Minority Int.	2,716	1,684	5,210	2,637	d2,458	d16,856	223
Net Income	[1][3] d25,269	[1][3] d18,034	[1] d6,651	[1] d9,365	[1] d2,221	d3,256	[2] 35,752
Cash Flow	d5,121	5,831	20,800	16,369	24,687	25,427	57,138
Average Shs. Outstg.	25,481	25,462	25,929	26,140	27,179	27,380	27,834
BALANCE SHEET (IN THOUSANDS):							
Cash & Cash Equivalents	2,876	1,267	639	856	1,018	336	1,158
Total Current Assets	155,545	165,560	167,746	179,547	204,418	233,892	213,239
Net Property	192,901	221,458	238,666	251,887	250,678	267,208	237,741
Total Assets	423,216	472,797	488,517	506,646	529,986	584,320	524,077
Total Current Liabilities	153,631	150,323	103,710	121,166	119,571	150,872	117,573
Long-Term Obligations	108,582	119,115	161,385	139,656	149,968	161,782	126,108
Net Stockholders' Equity	126,499	158,127	183,082	198,000	210,251	222,125	236,880
Net Working Capital	1,914	15,237	64,036	58,381	84,847	83,020	95,666
Year-end Shs. Outstg.	25,522	25,480	25,432	26,202	26,301	27,380	27,404
STATISTICAL RECORD:							
Operating Profit Margin %	...	...	...	...	1.7	3.9	7.8
Net Profit Margin %	...	...	...	...	...	...	4.4
Return on Equity %	...	...	...	...	...	...	15.1
Return on Assets %	...	...	...	...	...	...	6.8
Debt/Total Assets %	25.7	25.2	33.0	27.6	28.3	27.7	24.1
Price Range	7.63-2.25	7.19-4.13	10.25-3.81	9.38-7.00	12.38-7.25	14.38-10.63	17.25-11.13
P/E Ratio	...	...	...	...	...	...	14.4-9.3

Statistics are as originally reported. [1] Incl. non-recurr. chrg. 2000, $38.5 mill.; 1999, $16.0 mill.; 1998, $19.3 mill.; 1997, $5.2 mill.; 1996, $5.2 mill. [2] Bef. disc. oper. gain 1994, $0.4 mill. [3] Bef. acctg. change chrg. $825,000, 2000; $1.0 mill., 1999

OFFICERS:
D. L. Trogdon, Chmn.
J. L. Bakane, Pres., C.E.O.
G. L. Smith, Exec. V.P., C.F.O.

INVESTOR CONTACT: David E. Bray, Treasurer, (336) 379-6220

PRINCIPAL OFFICE: 3101 North Elm Street, Greensboro, NC 27408

TELEPHONE NUMBER: (336) 379-6220
FAX: (336) 379-6287
WEB: www.cone.com

NO. OF EMPLOYEES: 4,300 (approx.)

SHAREHOLDERS: 322 (approximately)

ANNUAL MEETING: In May

INCORPORATED: NC, 1891

INSTITUTIONAL HOLDINGS:
No. of Institutions: 46
Shares Held: 6,225,916
% Held: 24.4

INDUSTRY: Broadwoven fabric mills, cotton (SIC: 2211)

TRANSFER AGENT(S): First Union National Bank, Charlotte, NC

NYSE SYMBOL CIV
Rec. Pr. 22.50 (5/31/01)

CONECTIV

YIELD 3.9%
P/E RATIO 11.4

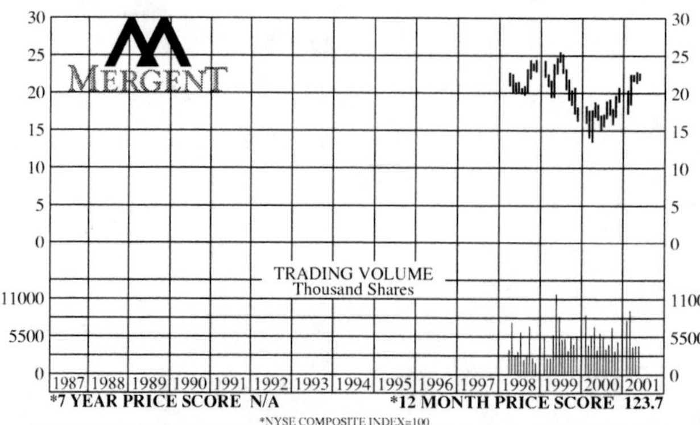

*7 YEAR PRICE SCORE N/A *12 MONTH PRICE SCORE 123.7

*NYSE COMPOSITE INDEX=100

INTERIM EARNINGS (Per Share):

Qtr.	Mar.	June	Sept.	Dec.
1998	d0.06	0.37	0.83	0.24
1999	0.47	0.31	d2.89	d0.15
2000	0.41	0.20	1.01	0.35

INTERIM DIVIDENDS (Per Share):

Amt.	Decl.	Ex.	Rec.	Pay.
0.22Q	6/27/00	7/10/00	7/12/00	7/31/00
0.22Q	9/26/00	10/11/00	10/13/00	10/31/00
0.22Q	12/05/00	1/09/01	1/11/01	1/31/01
0.22Q	3/26/01	4/10/01	4/12/01	4/30/01

Indicated div.: $0.88 (Div. Reinv. Plan)

CAPITALIZATION (12/31/00):

	($000)	(%)
Long-Term Debt	2,021,789	47.0
Capital Lease Obligations	13,744	0.3
Deferred Income Tax	823,094	19.1
Redeemable Pfd. Stock	188,950	4.4
Preferred Stock	95,933	2.2
Common & Surplus	1,160,269	27.0
Total	4,303,779	100.0

RECENT DEVELOPMENTS: For the year ended 12/31/00, net income soared to $170.8 million versus a net loss of $198.1 million in 1999. Results for 2000 included a net gain of $12.8 million from the sale of an interest in nuclear plants and an after-tax non-recurring charge of $23.4 million. Results for 1999 included an after-tax non-recurring charge of $383.3 million. Total operating revenues rose 34.3% to $5.03 billion from $3.74 billion in 1999. Results were somewhat offset by lower regulated revenues.

PROSPECTS: CIV and Potomac Electric Power Company announced a merger agreement in which Potomac will acquire CIV for a combination of cash and stock valued at $2.20 billion. The merger will create the largest electricity delivery company in the mid-Atlantic region. The merger is expected to be completed in early 2002. Separately, CIV expects to continue to grow its earnings as it develops additional new mid-merit plants to meet the growing demand for power.

BUSINESS

CONECTIV was formed through the merger of Delmarva Power & Light Company and Atlantic Energy, Inc. on 3/1/98. Conectiv is the newly-established parent company to Delmarva Power and Atlantic Energy, which will operate under their traditional names. CIV serves approximately one million utility customers in Delaware, Maryland, New Jersey and Virginia. CIV's non-utility businesses include Conectiv Resource Partners, Inc., which provides a variety of support services to Conectiv subsidiaries; Conectiv Communications, Inc., which provides local and long-distance telephone services; and Conectiv Services Inc., a provider of heating, ventilation, and air conditioning services.

ANNUAL FINANCIAL DATA

	12/31/00	12/31/99	12/31/98	12/31/97	12/31/96	12/31/95	12/31/94
Earnings Per Share	**3 1.97**	**2 1.14**	**1 1.50**	**1.69**	**1.77**	**1.79**	**1.67**
Cash Flow Per Share	**5.08**	**4.11**	**4.11**	**1.74**	**3.98**	**17.53**	**17.40**
Tang. Book Val. Per Share	**9.22**	**8.38**	**14.33**	...	...	...	...
Dividends Per Share	**0.88**	**1.21**	**1.16**	...	...	...	...
Dividend Payout %	**44.7**	**106.1**	**77.0**	...	...	...	...
INCOME STATEMENT (IN MILLIONS):							
Total Revenues	5,029.1	3,744.9	3,071.6	2,525.9	1,168.7	1,055.7	1,033.4
Costs & Expenses	3,630.6	2,469.4	1,890.8	1,554.7	506.3	...	...
Depreciation & Amort.	283.1	294.9	261.5	...	134.1	...	...
Maintenance Exp.	627.7	635.0	532.4	529.0	277.9	...	...
Operating Income	487.8	345.6	386.9	442.2	250.4	254.4	233.2
Net Interest Inc./(Exp.)	d212.6	d177.2	d149.4	d150.0	d70.3	...	...
Income Taxes	133.5	105.8	105.8	130.4	78.3	...	...
Net Income	3 170.8	2 113.6	1 153.2	185.9	107.3	107.5	98.9
Cash Flow	453.9	408.5	414.7	185.9	241.4	1,055.7	1,033.4
Average Shs. Outstg. (000)	89,428	99,430	100,899	107,063	60,698	60,217	59,377
BALANCE SHEET (IN MILLIONS):							
Gross Property	5,643.2	5,369.5	6,369.3	6,253.3	...	...	...
Accumulated Depreciation	2,180.0	2,097.5	2,499.9	2,305.0	...	...	...
Net Property	3,463.3	3,272.0	4,077.6	4,128.5	...	...	...
Total Assets	6,478.0	6,138.5	6,087.7	5,929.4	2,931.9	2,866.7	2,669.8
Long-Term Obligations	2,035.5	30.4	1,783.2	1,932.4	924.6	874.7	794.2
Net Stockholders' Equity	1,256.2	1,234.1	2,032.1	1,957.9	70.0	...	...
Year-end Shs. Outstg. (000)	88,471	91,748	100,517	...	...	...	...
STATISTICAL RECORD:							
Operating Profit Margin %	9.7	9.2	12.6	17.5	21.4	24.1	22.6
Net Profit Margin %	3.4	3.0	5.0	7.4	9.2	10.2	9.6
Net Inc./Net Property %	4.9	3.5	3.8	4.5	...	...	...
Net Inc./Tot. Capital %	4.0	5.2	3.2	3.8	9.9	...	...
Return on Equity %	13.6	9.2	7.5	9.5	153.2	...	...
Accum. Depr./Gross Prop. %	38.6	39.1	39.2	36.9	...	...	...
Price Range	20.75-13.44	25.50-16.25	24.50-19.69	...	...	...	...
P/E Ratio	10.5-6.8	22.4-14.3	16.3-13.1	...	...	...	...
Average Yield %	5.1	5.8	5.2	...	...	...	...

Statistics are as originally reported. 1 Incl. $8.6 mill. after-tax credit fr. gain on settlement. 2 Bef. extraord. loss $311.7 mill., but incl. $71.6 mill. non-recur. chgs. 3 Incl. $12.8 mill. net gain fr. sale of nuclear plants & $23.4 mill. net non-recur. chg.

OFFICERS:
H. E. Cosgrove, Chmn., C.E.O.
T. S. Shaw, Pres., C.O.O.
J. C. van Roden, Sr. V.P., C.F.O.

INVESTOR CONTACT: Robert K. Marshall, Investor Relations, (302) 429-3114

PRINCIPAL OFFICE: 800 King Street, P.O. Box 231, Wilmington, DE 19899

TELEPHONE NUMBER: (302) 429-3114
FAX: (302) 429-3328
WEB: www.conectiv.com

NO. OF EMPLOYEES: 3,573 (avg.)

SHAREHOLDERS: 62,318 (com.); 28,249 (class A com.)

ANNUAL MEETING: In Mar.

INCORPORATED: DE, 1998

INSTITUTIONAL HOLDINGS:
No. of Institutions: 170
Shares Held: 33,213,288
% Held: 37.5

INDUSTRY: Electric and other services combined (SIC: 4931)

TRANSFER AGENT(S): The Bank of New York, New York, NY

NYSE SYMBOL COCB
Rec. Pr. 30.42 (4/30/01)

CONOCO INC.

YIELD 2.5%
P/E RATIO 10.1

MERGENT

TRADING VOLUME
Thousand Shares

*7 YEAR PRICE SCORE N/A
*12 MONTH PRICE SCORE 114.1
*NYSE COMPOSITE INDEX=100

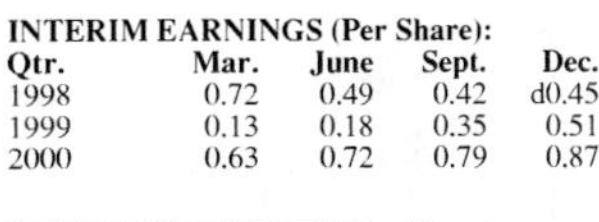

INTERIM EARNINGS (Per Share):

Qtr.	Mar.	June	Sept.	Dec.
1998	0.72	0.49	0.42	d0.45
1999	0.13	0.18	0.35	0.51
2000	0.63	0.72	0.79	0.87

INTERIM DIVIDENDS (Per Share):

Amt.	Decl.	Ex.	Rec.	Pay.
0.19Q	4/25/00	5/08/00	5/10/00	6/10/00
0.19Q	7/24/00	8/08/00	8/10/00	9/10/00
0.19Q	10/23/00	11/08/00	11/10/00	12/10/00
0.19Q	1/22/01	2/07/01	2/10/01	3/10/01
0.19Q	4/23/01	5/08/01	5/10/01	6/10/01

Indicated div.: $0.76

CAPITALIZATION (12/31/00):

	($000)	(%)
Long-Term Debt	4,138,000	34.4
Deferred Income Tax	1,911,000	15.9
Minority Interest	337,000	2.8
Common & Surplus	5,628,000	46.8
Total	12,014,000	100.0

RECENT DEVELOPMENTS: For the year ended 12/31/00, net income soared to $1.90 billion versus $744.0 million in 1999. Results included net non-recurring charges of $46.0 million and $38.0 million for 2000 and 1999, respectively. Total revenues surged 43.9% to $39.29 billion from $27.31 billion a year earlier. Upstream earnings jumped to $1.85 billion from $845.0 million in 1999, while downstream earnings rose 66.2% to $394.0 million from $237.0 million in 1999.

PROSPECTS: Prospects are enhanced by strong natural gas and crude oil prices, healthy refining and natural gas liquids margins, and higher production volumes. Overall, COC's total production for 2000 rose 2.8% to 654,000 barrels of oil equivalent per day, aided by various acquisitions, additional production from the Ursa field in the Gulf of Mexico and the Vampire field in the U.K. Accordingly, the Company now expects to exceed the high end of the range for reserve replacement in 2000, earlier estimated to be between 125% to 135% of oil and gas produced.

BUSINESS

CONOCO INC. is an integrated global energy company organized into three operating segments. Upstream activities include exploring for, developing, producing and selling of crude oil, natural gas and natural gas liquids. Downstream activities include refining crude oil and other feedstocks into petroleum products, buying and selling crude oil and refined products and transporting, distributing and marketing petroleum products. Emerging businesses activities include the development of new businesses beyond the Company's traditional operations. COC operates in over 40 countries. As of 12/31/00, COC owned or had equity interests in nine refineries worldwide, with a total crude distillation capacity of about 904,000 barrels per day. Additionally, the Company had a marketing network of approximately 8,100 outlets in the U.S., Europe and Asia Pacific. As of 12/31/00, COC had proved worldwide reserves of 2,647 million barrels-of-oil-equivalent, 38% of which were natural gas. The Company was acquired by DuPont in 1981, and spun off as an independent company by DuPont on 10/28/98.

ANNUAL FINANCIAL DATA

	12/31/00	12/31/99	12/31/98	12/31/97	12/31/96	12/31/95
Earnings Per Share	**1 3.00**	**1.17**	**0.95**	...	...	...
Cash Flow Per Share	**5.06**	**3.05**	**3.29**	...	...	...
Tang. Book Val. Per Share	**9.03**	**7.28**	**7.07**	...	...	...
Dividends Per Share	**0.76**	**0.71**	...	...	...	...
Dividend Payout %	**25.3**	**60.7**	...	...	...	...
INCOME STATEMENT (IN MILLIONS):						
Total Revenues	39,287.0	27,309.0	23,168.0	26,263.0	24,416.0	20,518.0
Costs & Expenses	34,190.0	24,588.0	21,162.0	22,941.0	21,356.0	18,028.0
Depreciation & Amort.	1,301.0	1,193.0	1,113.0	1,179.0	1,085.0	1,067.0
Operating Income	3,796.0	1,528.0	893.0	2,143.0	1,975.0	1,423.0
Net Interest Inc./(Exp.)	d338.0	d311.0	d199.0	d36.0	d74.0	d74.0
Income Before Income Taxes	3,458.0	1,217.0	694.0	2,107.0	1,901.0	1,349.0
Income Taxes	1,556.0	473.0	244.0	1,010.0	1,038.0	774.0
Net Income	1 1,902.0	744.0	450.0	1,097.0	863.0	575.0
Cash Flow	3,203.0	1,937.0	1,563.0	2,276.0	1,948.0	1,642.0
Average Shs. Outstg. (000)	633,000	636,000	475,000	...	...	...
BALANCE SHEET (IN MILLIONS):						
Cash & Cash Equivalents	342.0	317.0	394.0	1,154.0	853.0	...
Total Current Assets	3,411.0	3,068.0	2,770.0	4,207.0	3,658.0	...
Net Property	12,207.0	11,235.0	11,413.0	10,828.0	10,082.0	...
Total Assets	18,127.0	16,375.0	16,075.0	17,062.0	15,226.0	...
Total Current Liabilities	4,187.0	3,758.0	2,725.0	3,640.0	2,796.0	...
Long-Term Obligations	4,138.0	4,080.0	4,689.0	1,556.0	2,388.0	...
Net Stockholders' Equity	5,628.0	4,555.0	4,438.0	7,896.0	6,579.0	...
Net Working Capital	d776.0	d690.0	45.0	567.0	862.0	...
Year-end Shs. Outstg. (000)	623,433	625,583	628,000	...	...	...
STATISTICAL RECORD:						
Operating Profit Margin %	9.7	5.6	3.9	8.2	8.1	6.9
Net Profit Margin %	4.8	2.7	1.9	4.2	3.5	2.8
Return on Equity %	33.8	16.3	10.1	13.9	13.1	...
Return on Assets %	10.5	4.5	2.8	6.4	5.7	...
Debt/Total Assets %	22.8	24.9	29.2	9.1	15.7	...
Price Range	29.94-19.00	29.38-20.75	...	...	...	...
P/E Ratio	10.0-6.3	25.1-17.7	...	...	...	...
Average Yield %	3.1	2.8	...	...	...	...

Statistics are as originally reported. 1 Incls. net non-recurr. chrgs. of $46.0 mill.

OFFICERS:
A. W. Dunham, Chmn., Pres., C.E.O.
R. W. Goldman, Sr. V.P., C.F.O.
R. A. Harrington, Sr. V.P., Gen. Couns.

INVESTOR CONTACT: Sondra Fowler, Inv. Rel., (281) 293-4595

PRINCIPAL OFFICE: 600 North Dairy Ashford Rd., Houston, TX 77079

TELEPHONE NUMBER: (281) 293-1000
FAX: (281) 293-1440
WEB: www.conoco.com
NO. OF EMPLOYEES: 17,600 (avg.)
SHAREHOLDERS: 6,077 (Class B)
ANNUAL MEETING: In May
INCORPORATED: UT, 1875; reincorp., DE, Oct., 1998

INSTITUTIONAL HOLDINGS:
No. of Institutions: 429
Shares Held: 359,345,809
% Held: 57.6

INDUSTRY: Crude petroleum and natural gas (SIC: 1311)

TRANSFER AGENT(S): First Chicago Trust Company of New York, Jersey City, NJ

NYSE SYMBOL CNC
Rec. Pr. 19.03 (4/30/01)

CONSECO, INC.

YIELD 1.1%
P/E RATIO ...

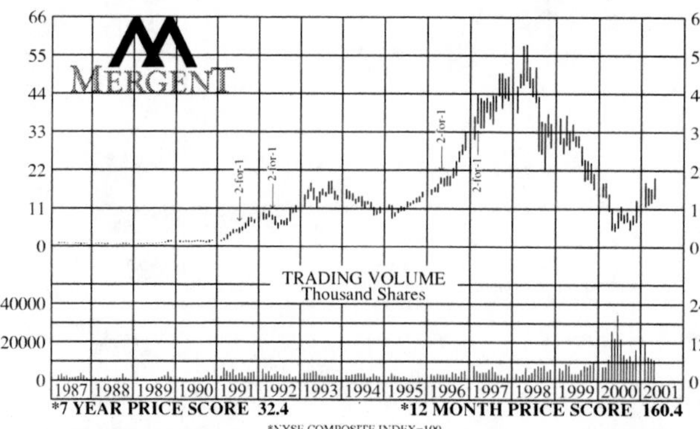

*7 YEAR PRICE SCORE 32.4 *12 MONTH PRICE SCORE 160.4
*NYSE COMPOSITE INDEX=100

INTERIM EARNINGS (Per Share):

Qtr.	Mar.	June	Sept.	Dec.
1996	0.60	0.44	0.55	0.54
1997	0.51	0.64	0.73	0.81
1998	0.81	d0.88	0.85	0.86
1999	0.92	0.90	0.58	0.52
2000	0.22	d1.25	d1.32	d1.16

INTERIM DIVIDENDS (Per Share):

Amt.	Decl.	Ex.	Rec.	Pay.
0.14Q	5/26/99	6/16/99	6/18/99	7/01/99
0.15Q	7/28/99	9/16/99	9/20/99	10/01/99
0.15Q	10/27/99	12/16/99	12/20/99	1/03/00
0.05Q	2/23/00	3/16/00	3/20/00	4/03/00
0.05Q	6/16/00	6/22/00	6/26/00	7/03/00

Indicated div.: $0.20

CAPITALIZATION (12/31/00):

	($000)	(%)
Long-Term Debt	7,865,900	64.3
Preferred Stock	486,800	4.0
Common & Surplus	3,887,600	31.8
Total	12,240,300	100.0

RECENT DEVELOPMENTS: For the year ended 12/31/00, loss before an extraordinary charge was $1.13 billion versus net income of $595.0 million in 1999. Results included impairment charges of $515.7 million and $554.3 million in 2000 and 1999, respectively. Results for 2000 included special charges of $699.3 million. Results for 2000 excluded an after-tax extraordinary charge of $5.0 million and an after-tax accounting change charge of $55.3 million. Total revenues fell to $8.30 billion from $8.34 billion in 1999.

PROSPECTS: On 4/23/01, the Company announced it would cut 2,000 jobs, or 14% of its overall work force, over the next 21 months as it farms out some call-center and back-office services to India. At the same time, CNC also announced it would buy the firm providing the services in India, exlService, for approximately $52.6 million in stock. The transaction is expected to save more than $30.0 million in annual costs, and should produce about $0.11 a share in pre-tax profits as early as next year.

BUSINESS

CONSECO, INC. is a specialized financial services holding company with subsidiaries operating throughout the United States. The Company's insurance subsidiaries develop, market and administer supplemental health insurance, annuity, individual life insurance and other insurance products. The Company's finance subsidiaries originate, securitize and service manufactured housing, home equity, retail credit and floorplan loans.

REVENUES

(12/31/2000)	($000)	(%)
Insurance & Fee-Based	5,103,400	61.3
Finance Segment	2,416,900	29.0
Corporate & Other	805,300	9.7
Total	8,325,600	100.0

ANNUAL FINANCIAL DATA

	12/31/00	12/31/99	12/31/98	12/31/97	12/31/96	12/31/95	12/31/94
Earnings Per Share	**3 4 d3.51**	**1.79**	**1.53**	**1 2 2.67**	**1 2 2.12**	**1 2.37**	**1 1.29**
Tang. Book Val. Per Share	**0.27**	**3.51**	**3.82**	**0.73**	**3.70**	**...**	**...**
Dividends Per Share	**0.25**	**0.57**	**0.52**	**0.22**	**0.06**	**0.07**	**0.13**
Dividend Payout %	**...**	**31.8**	**33.7**	**8.2**	**2.7**	**3.1**	**9.7**
INCOME STATEMENT (IN MILLIONS):							
Total Premium Income	4,220.3	4,040.5	3,948.8	3,410.8	1,654.2	1,465.0	1,285.6
Other Income	4,076.1	4,295.2	3,767.2	2,157.6	1,413.1	1,390.3	511.5
Total Revenues	8,296.4	8,335.7	7,716.0	5,568.4	3,067.3	2,855.3	1,797.1
Policyholder Benefits	4,071.0	3,815.9	3,580.5	2,185.7	1,173.3	1,075.5	915.4
Income Before Income Taxes	d1,361.8	1,150.9	1,045.7	1,003.1	493.6	418.5	324.4
Income Taxes	cr376.2	423.1	445.6	376.6	179.8	87.0	111.0
Equity Earnings/Minority Int.	d145.3	d132.8	d90.4	d52.3	d34.9	d109.0	5.9
Net Income	3 4 d1,130.9	595.0	509.7	1 2 574.2	1 2 278.9	1 222.5	1 154.4
Average Shs. Outstg. (000)	325,953	332,893	332,701	210,179	126,812	86,094	105,392
BALANCE SHEET (IN MILLIONS):							
Cash & Cash Equivalents	1,663.6	1,686.9	1,704.7	990.5	281.6	189.9	295.4
Premiums Due	17,804.4	10,773.0	4,034.3	934.7	513.0	84.8	240.7
Invst. Assets: Fixed-term	21,755.1	22,203.8	21,827.3	22,773.7	17,307.1	12,963.3	7,067.1
Invst. Assets: Equities	248.3	312.7	376.4	228.9	99.7	36.6	39.6
Invst. Assets: Loans	1,885.8	1,938.6	1,815.8	1,767.2	1,345.5	906.6	386.7
Invst. Assets: Total	25,017.6	26,431.6	28,289.4	26,278.4	19,293.5	14,187.6	8,074.5
Total Assets	58,589.2	52,185.9	43,599.9	35,914.8	25,612.7	17,297.5	10,811.9
Long-Term Obligations	7,865.9	7,164.3	5,321.5	2,354.9	1,094.9	1,456.1	802.9
Net Stockholders' Equity	4,374.4	5,556.2	5,273.6	3,890.1	3,086.0	1,111.7	747.0
Year-end Shs. Outstg. (000)	325,318	327,679	315,844	186,666	167,128	81,032	88,740
STATISTICAL RECORD:							
Return on Revenues %	...	7.1	6.6	10.3	9.1	7.8	8.6
Return on Equity %	...	10.7	9.7	14.8	9.0	20.0	20.7
Return on Assets %	...	1.1	1.2	1.6	1.1	1.3	1.4
Price Range	18.50-4.50	37.88-16.56	58.13-21.94	50.06-30.75	33.13-14.91	15.78-8.13	16.56-8.97
P/E Ratio	...	21.2-9.3	38.0-14.3	18.7-11.5	15.6-7.0	6.7-3.4	12.9-7.0
Average Yield %	2.2	2.1	1.3	0.5	0.2	0.6	1.0

Statistics are as originally reported. Adj. for stk. splits: 2-for-1, 2/97, 4/96 1 Bef. extraord. chrg. 1998, $30.3 mill.; 1997, $6.9 mill.; 1996, $26.5 mill.; 1995, $2.1 mill.; 1994, $4.0 mill. 2 Incl. non-recurr. chrg. 1998, $688.0 mill.; 1997, $71.7 mill.; 1996, $49.8 mill. 3 Incl. impairment chrg. of $515.7 mill. and special chrg. $699.3 mill. 4 Excl. extraord. chrg. $5.0 mill. & cum. effect on account. chng. $55.3 mill. & incl. spec. chrg. $699.3 mill.

OFFICERS:
G. C. Wendt, Chmn., C.E.O.
T. J. Kilian, Pres., C.O.O.
C. B. Chokel, C.F.O.
J. S. Adams, Sr. V.P., C.A.O., Treas.

INVESTOR CONTACT: Tommy Hill, Inv. Rel., (317) 817-2893

PRINCIPAL OFFICE: 11825 N. Pennsylvania St., Carmel, IN 46032

TELEPHONE NUMBER: (317) 817-6100
FAX: (800) 344-6452
WEB: www.conseco.com

NO. OF EMPLOYEES: 14,300 (approx.)

SHAREHOLDERS: 170,200 (approx.)

ANNUAL MEETING: In June

INCORPORATED: IN, Aug., 1979

INSTITUTIONAL HOLDINGS:
No. of Institutions: 293
Shares Held: 177,374,778
% Held: 52.5

INDUSTRY: Accident and health insurance (SIC: 6321)

TRANSFER AGENT(S): First Union National Bank, Charlotte, NC

NYSE SYMBOL ED
Rec. Pr. 37.41 (4/30/01)

CONSOLIDATED EDISON, INC.

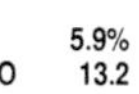

YIELD 5.9%
P/E RATIO 13.2

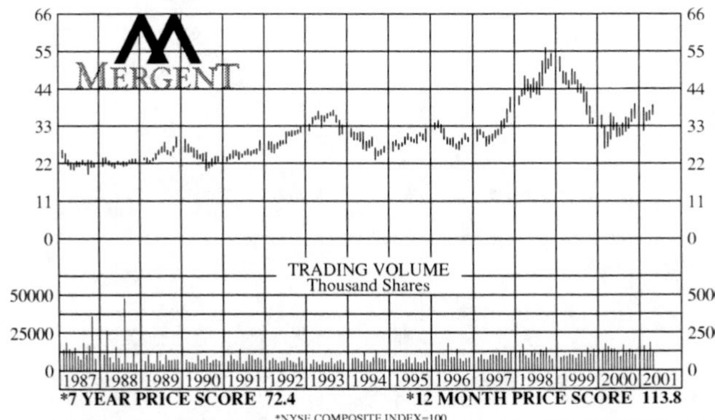

***7 YEAR PRICE SCORE 72.4** ***12 MONTH PRICE SCORE 113.8**

*NYSE COMPOSITE INDEX=100

INTERIM EARNINGS (Per Share):

Qtr.	Mar.	June	Sept.	Dec.
1997	0.69	0.18	1.49	0.59
1998	0.73	0.26	1.49	0.56
1999	0.76	0.30	1.50	0.57
2000	0.88	0.33	1.32	0.30

INTERIM DIVIDENDS (Per Share):

Amt.	Decl.	Ex.	Rec.	Pay.
0.545Q	4/20/00	5/15/00	5/17/00	6/15/00
0.545Q	7/20/00	8/14/00	8/16/00	9/15/00
0.545Q	10/19/00	11/13/00	11/15/00	12/15/00
0.55Q	1/18/01	2/12/01	2/14/01	3/15/01
0.55Q	4/19/01	5/14/01	5/16/01	6/15/01

Indicated div.: $2.20 (Div. Reinv. Plan)

CAPITALIZATION (12/31/00):

	($000)	(%)
Long-Term Debt	5,415,409	40.2
Capital Lease Obligations	31,504	0.2
Deferred Income Tax	2,302,764	17.1
Redeemable Pfd. Stock	37,050	0.3
Preferred Stock	212,563	1.6
Common & Surplus	5,472,389	40.6
Total	13,471,679	100.0

RECENT DEVELOPMENTS: For the year ended 12/31/00, net income fell 13.9% to $615.2 million compared with $714.2 million in 1999. Total operating revenues increased 25.9% to $9.43 billion from $7.49 billion in the prior year. Results for 2000 included a charge of about $84.9 million from replacement power costs related to the Indian Point 2 nuclear generating plant. Electric operating revenues grew 20.0% to $6.95 billion.

PROSPECTS: The Company anticipates earnings for 2001 to be in the range of $3.20 to $3.30 per share, excluding the effects of the proposed merger with Northeast Utilities. Future results should benefit from the sale of ED's nuclear plant and related assets for $602.0 million and 9.2 acres of property for an anticipated price of $576.0 million to $680.0 million.

BUSINESS

CONSOLIDATED EDISON, INC. (formerly Consolidated Edison Company of New York) provides a range of energy-related products and services through six subsidiaries. Consolidated Edison Company of New York is a regulated utility providing electric, gas and steam service to New York City and Westchester County, New York. Orange and Rockland Utilities, Inc. is a regulated utility serving customers in southeastern New York state and adjacent sections of New Jersey and northeastern Pennsylvania. Con Edison Solutions is a retail energy services company and Con Edison Energy is a wholesale energy supply company. Con Edison Development is an infrastructure development company and Con Edison Communications is a telecommunications infrastructure company.

ANNUAL FINANCIAL DATA

	12/31/00	12/31/99	12/31/98	12/31/97	12/31/96	12/31/95	12/31/94
Earnings Per Share	**[1] 2.83**	**3.13**	**3.04**	**2.95**	**2.93**	**2.93**	**2.98**
Cash Flow Per Share	**5.51**	**5.49**	**5.25**	**5.09**	**5.04**	**4.87**	**4.78**
Tang. Book Val. Per Share	**26.39**	**25.90**	**25.88**	**25.18**	**24.37**	**23.51**	**22.62**
Dividends Per Share	**2.18**	**2.14**	**2.12**	**2.10**	**2.08**	**2.04**	**2.00**
Dividend Payout %	**77.0**	**68.4**	**69.7**	**71.2**	**71.0**	**69.6**	**67.1**
INCOME STATEMENT (IN MILLIONS):							
Total Revenues	9,431.4	7,491.3	7,093.0	7,121.3	6,959.7	6,536.9	6,373.1
Costs & Expenses	7,370.8	5,507.4	5,043.8	5,098.3	4,991.1	4,527.6	4,408.4
Depreciation & Amort.	586.4	526.2	518.5	502.8	496.4	455.8	422.4
Maintenance Exp.	458.0	438.0	477.4	474.8	458.6	512.1	506.2
Operating Income	1,016.1	1,019.8	1,053.3	1,045.4	1,013.6	1,041.4	1,036.2
Net Interest Inc./(Exp.)	d407.4	d337.6	d325.8	d333.1	d323.5	d329.0	d305.2
Income Taxes	cr10.6	cr26.9	cr2.2	cr3.2	cr1.0	1.1	0.4
Net Income	[1] 615.2	714.2	729.7	712.8	694.1	723.9	734.3
Cash Flow	1,169.2	1,226.8	1,231.3	1,197.3	1,184.6	1,144.1	1,121.0
Average Shs. Outstg. (000)	212,186	223,442	234,308	235,082	234,977	234,930	234,754
BALANCE SHEET (IN MILLIONS):							
Gross Property	17,020.5	16,002.8	16,033.9	15,557.2	15,251.6	14,766.1	14,297.4
Accumulated Depreciation	5,234.7	4,733.6	4,726.2	4,392.4	4,285.7	4,037.0	3,828.6
Net Property	11,893.4	11,353.8	11,406.5	11,267.1	11,067.3	10,814.4	10,561.2
Total Assets	16,767.2	15,531.5	14,381.4	14,722.5	14,057.2	13,949.9	13,728.4
Long-Term Obligations	5,446.9	4,559.1	4,087.4	4,228.8	4,281.3	3,962.5	4,078.3
Net Stockholders' Equity	5,685.0	5,624.6	6,238.2	6,163.5	5,965.7	6,062.7	5,853.3
Year-end Shs. Outstg. (000)	188,816	192,452	232,833	235,490	234,994	234,956	234,905
STATISTICAL RECORD:							
Operating Profit Margin %	10.8	13.6	14.9	14.7	14.6	15.9	16.3
Net Profit Margin %	6.3	9.5	10.3	10.0	10.0	11.1	11.5
Net Inc./Net Property %	5.0	6.3	6.4	6.3	6.3	6.7	7.0
Net Inc./Tot. Capital %	4.4	5.7	5.7	5.6	5.5	5.8	6.0
Return on Equity %	10.5	12.7	11.7	11.6	11.6	11.9	12.5
Accum. Depr./Gross Prop. %	30.8	29.6	29.5	28.2	28.1	27.3	26.8
Price Range	39.50-26.19	53.44-33.56	56.13-39.06	41.50-27.00	34.75-25.88	32.25-25.50	32.38-23.00
P/E Ratio	14.4-9.6	17.1-10.7	18.5-12.8	14.1-9.2	11.9-8.8	11.0-8.7	10.9-7.7
Average Yield %	6.6	4.9	4.5	6.1	6.9	7.1	7.2

Statistics are as originally reported. [1] Incl. approx. $84.9 mill. chg. fr. replacement power costs.

OFFICERS:
E. R. McGrath, Chmn., C.E.O.
K. Burke, Pres., C.O.O.
J. S. Freilich, Exec. V.P., C.F.O.

INVESTOR CONTACT: Jan C. Childress, Dir. of Inv. Rel., (212) 460-6611

PRINCIPAL OFFICE: 4 Irving Place, New York, NY 10003

TELEPHONE NUMBER: (212) 460-4600
FAX: (212) 475-0734
WEB: www.conedison.com

NO. OF EMPLOYEES: 13,231 (avg.)

SHAREHOLDERS: 108,999

ANNUAL MEETING: In May

INCORPORATED: NY, Nov., 1884

INSTITUTIONAL HOLDINGS:
No. of Institutions: 303
Shares Held: 94,548,523
% Held: 44.6

INDUSTRY: Electric and other services combined (SIC: 4931)

TRANSFER AGENT(S): The Bank of New York, New York, NY

NYSE SYMBOL CGX
Rec. Pr. 16.33 (5/31/01)

CONSOLIDATED GRAPHICS, INC.

YIELD ...
P/E RATIO 7.4

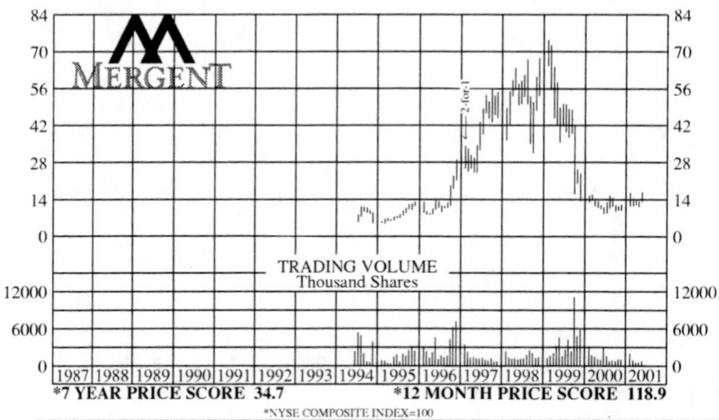

*7 YEAR PRICE SCORE 34.7 *12 MONTH PRICE SCORE 118.9

*NYSE COMPOSITE INDEX=100

INTERIM EARNINGS (Per Share):

Qtr.	June	Sept.	Dec.	Mar.
1998-99		2.28		
1999-00	0.70	0.68	0.56	0.58
2000-01	0.59	0.61	0.42	...

INTERIM DIVIDENDS (Per Share):

Amt.	Decl.	Ex.	Rec.	Pay.

No dividends paid.

CAPITALIZATION (3/31/00):

	($000)	(%)
Long-Term Debt	261,407	49.0
Common & Surplus	272,531	51.0
Total	533,938	100.0

RECENT DEVELOPMENTS: For the quarter ended 12/31/00, net income fell 37.9% to $5.5 million compared with $8.9 million in the equivalent quarter of 1999. Sales were $171.2 million, up 8.1% from $158.4 million in the prior-year period. The increase in sales was due to the incremental revenue contribution of three acquisitions during fiscal 2000, and internal growth generated by CGX's focused efforts to build market share, add to its national account base and pursue its electronic media initiatives.

PROSPECTS: Results may continue to be hampered by the general economic slowdown and soft commercial print demand. As a result, CGX has implemented several initiatives designed to reduce costs and strengthen operations. Meanwhile, CGX continues to focus on its e-commerce products and services marketed through CGXmedia, particularly the Custom Ordering Interactive Network and Online Private Asset Library products.

BUSINESS

CONSOLIDATED GRAPHICS, INC. is a provider of general commercial printing services with printing operations in 25 states as of 12/31/00. The majority of the Company's sales are derived from traditional printing services, including electronic prepress, printing, finishing, storage and delivery of high-quality, custom-designed products. These products include multicolor product and capability brochures, shareholder communications, catalogs, training manuals, point-of-purchase marketing materials, trading cards and direct mail pieces. The Company has a diverse customer base, including both national and local corporations, mutual fund companies, advertising agencies, graphic design firms, catalog retailers and direct mail distributors. The Company also offers an extensive and growing range of digital and Internet-based services marketed through CGXmedia.

ANNUAL FINANCIAL DATA

	3/31/00	3/31/99	3/31/98	3/31/97	3/31/96	3/31/95	3/31/94
Earnings Per Share	**2.51**	**2.28**	**1.40**	**0.83**	**[1] 0.36**	**0.46**	**0.53**
Cash Flow Per Share	**4.65**	**3.72**	**2.17**	**1.31**	**0.70**	**0.88**	...
Tang. Book Val. Per Share	**5.39**	**6.33**	**5.95**	**4.85**	**3.78**	**3.49**	**1.60**
INCOME STATEMENT (IN THOUSANDS):							
Total Revenues	624,895	435,961	231,282	144,082	85,133	57,166	48,643
Costs & Expenses	514,408	355,098	187,859	119,936	74,360	45,776	40,737
Depreciation & Amort.	32,881	20,209	10,040	5,814	3,782	4,089	1,571
Operating Income	77,606	60,654	33,383	18,332	6,991	7,301	6,335
Net Interest Inc./(Exp.)	d13,476	d7,745	d3,720	d2,305	d860	d427	d1,018
Income Before Income Taxes	64,130	52,909	29,663	16,027	6,131	6,874	5,317
Income Taxes	25,651	20,634	11,273	5,927	2,146	2,392	1,806
Net Income	38,479	32,275	18,390	10,100	[1] 3,985	4,482	3,511
Cash Flow	71,360	52,484	28,430	15,914	7,767	8,526	4,525
Average Shs. Outstg.	15,336	14,126	13,112	12,166	11,068	9,721	...
BALANCE SHEET (IN THOUSANDS):							
Cash & Cash Equivalents	8,197	6,538	5,268	3,636	3,086	1,707	2,102
Total Current Assets	161,460	130,519	71,479	43,096	31,503	24,260	16,593
Net Property	310,344	230,733	135,892	85,643	50,591	35,504	19,910
Total Assets	677,277	489,654	237,645	135,720	87,809	60,288	36,809
Total Current Liabilities	99,730	80,758	43,610	21,016	12,648	10,463	8,675
Long-Term Obligations	261,407	170,574	73,030	39,321	20,105	8,820	13,470
Net Stockholders' Equity	272,531	214,454	105,332	66,447	49,876	38,170	8,981
Net Working Capital	61,730	49,761	27,869	22,080	18,855	13,797	7,918
Year-end Shs. Outstg.	13,708	14,650	12,960	12,450	11,855	10,934	5,596
STATISTICAL RECORD:							
Operating Profit Margin %	12.4	13.9	14.4	12.7	8.2	12.8	13.0
Net Profit Margin %	6.2	7.4	8.0	7.0	4.7	7.8	7.2
Return on Equity %	14.1	15.0	17.5	15.2	8.0	11.7	39.1
Return on Assets %	5.7	6.6	7.7	7.4	4.5	7.4	9.5
Debt/Total Assets %	38.6	34.8	30.7	29.0	22.9	14.6	36.6
Price Range	74.50-13.31	67.63-31.50	56.19-23.88	29.00-8.13	13.06-4.75	11.25-4.88	...
P/E Ratio	29.7-5.3	29.7-13.8	40.1-17.1	34.9-9.8	36.3-13.2	24.5-10.6	...

Statistics are as originally reported. Adj. for 2-for-1 stock split, 1/10/97. [1] Incl. restr. chg. of $1.5 mill.

OFFICERS:
J. R. Davis, Chmn., C.E.O.
C. F. White, Pres., C.O.O.
W. M. Rose, Exec. V.P., C.F.O.

INVESTOR CONTACT: Wayne M. Rose, Exec. V.P., C.F.O., (713) 787-0977

PRINCIPAL OFFICE: 5858 Westheimer Road, Suite 200, Houston, TX 77057

TELEPHONE NUMBER: (713) 787-0977
FAX: (713) 787-5013
WEB: www.consolidatedgraphics.com

NO. OF EMPLOYEES: 5,000 (avg.)

SHAREHOLDERS: 193 (of record); 7,000 (approx., beneficial)

ANNUAL MEETING: In July

INCORPORATED: TX, 1985

INSTITUTIONAL HOLDINGS:
No. of Institutions: 59
Shares Held: 4,686,769
% Held: 36.0

INDUSTRY: Commercial printing, nec (SIC: 2759)

TRANSFER AGENT(S): American Stock Transfer & Trust Company, New York, NY

NYSE SYMBOL STZ
Rec. Pr. 38.65 (5/31/01)

CONSTELLATION BRANDS, INC.

YIELD ...
P/E RATIO 12.4

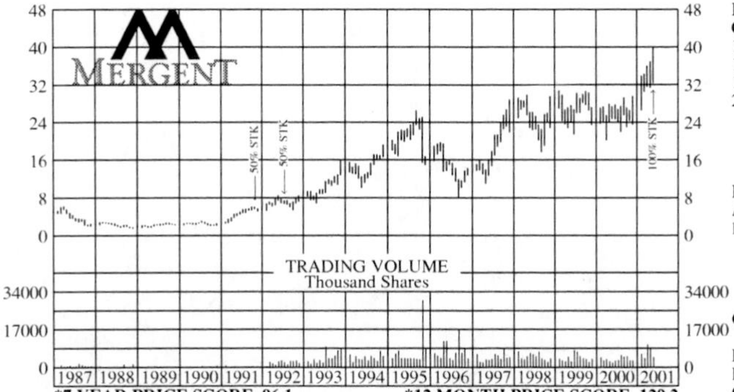

TRADING VOLUME
Thousand Shares

*7 YEAR PRICE SCORE 96.1 *12 MONTH PRICE SCORE 129.2

*NYSE COMPOSITE INDEX=100

INTERIM EARNINGS (Per Share):

Qtr.	May	Aug.	Nov.	Feb.
1997-98	0.26	0.32	0.45	0.33
1998-99	0.35	0.42	0.54	0.17
1999-00	0.30	0.57	0.80	0.42
2000-01	0.48	0.70	0.94	0.99

INTERIM DIVIDENDS (Per Share):

Amt.	Decl.	Ex.	Rec.	Pay.
100% STK	4/12/01	5/15/01	4/30/01	5/14/01

CAPITALIZATION (2/29/00):

	($000)	(%)
Long-Term Debt	1,237,135	66.0
Deferred Income Tax	116,447	6.2
Common & Surplus	520,840	27.8
Total	1,874,422	100.0

RECENT DEVELOPMENTS: For the year ended 2/28/01, net income rose 25.8% to $97.3 million from $77.4 million in the prior year. Net sales improved 2.4% to $2.40 billion from $2.34 billion a year earlier. Net sales for Barton increased 12.8% to $945.1 million, while net sales for Canandaigua Wine fell 3.3% to $688.4 million. Net sales from Matthew Clark decreased 5.3% to $691.1 million, and net sales for Franciscan advanced 49.9% to $93.1 million.

PROSPECTS: On 4/10/01, the Company entered into an agreement to acquire Sonoma, California-based Ravenswood Winery, a premium wine producer, for approximately $148.0 million. Going forward, the Company expects diluted earnings per share will range from $2.98 and $3.03 in fiscal 2001. This estimate includes the expected effect of the proposed acquisition of Ravenswood.

BUSINESS

CONSTELLATION BRANDS, INC. (formerly Canandaigua Brands, Inc.) is a producer, marketer and distributor of more than 180 premier branded beverage alcohol products in North America and the U.K. STZ's business is broken into four divisions: Barton Inc. (beer and distilled spirits), Canandaigua Wine Co. (wine and grape juice concentrate), Franciscan Estates (premium wines), and Matthew Clark plc (wine and cider in the U.K.). STZ's key products include: Beer: Corona, Modelo Especial, Pacifico, Negra Modelo, St. Pauli Girl, Tsingtao, Peroni, Double Diamond, Tetley's English Ale and Point in the U.S.; Wine: Almaden, Inglenook, Richards Wild Irish Rose, Arbor Mist, Paul Masson, Taylor, J. Roget, Marcus James, Estate Cellars, Dunnewood, Vina Santa Carolina and Mystic Cliffs in the U.S., and Stowells of Chelsea, QC, Stones and Concord in the U.K.; Distilled Spirits: Barton, Fleischmann's, Canadian LTD, Chi-Chi's and Inver House in the U.S.; Cider: Blackthorn, Olde English and Diamond White in the U.K.

ANNUAL FINANCIAL DATA

	2/29/00	2/28/99	2/28/98	2/28/97	1 2/29/96	8/31/95	8/31/94
Earnings Per Share	**4 2.09**	**3 1.65**	**1.31**	**0.71**	**2 0.09**	**2 1.07**	**2 0.37**
Cash Flow Per Share	**3.85**	**2.69**	**2.19**	**1.52**	**0.43**	**1.61**	**0.81**
Tang. Book Val. Per Share	**14.32**	**12.11**	**11.08**	**9.66**	**9.08**	**8.98**	**6.38**
INCOME STATEMENT (IN MILLIONS):							
Total Revenues	2,340.5	1,497.3	1,212.8	1,135.0	535.0	906.5	629.6
Costs & Expenses	2,040.3	1,312.5	1,062.2	1,021.2	497.1	794.5	578.8
Depreciation & Amort.	65.2	39.0	33.5	32.0	14.0	20.7	13.8
Operating Income	235.0	145.9	117.1	81.8	24.0	91.3	37.0
Net Interest Inc./(Exp.)	d106.1	d41.5	d32.2	d34.0	d17.3	d24.6	d18.1
Income Before Income Taxes	129.0	104.4	84.9	47.8	6.7	66.7	18.9
Income Taxes	51.6	42.5	34.8	20.1	3.4	25.7	7.2
Net Income	4 77.4	3 61.9	50.1	27.7	2 3.3	2 41.0	2 11.7
Cash Flow	142.5	100.9	83.6	59.6	17.3	61.7	25.5
Average Shs. Outstg. (000)	36,998	37,508	38,210	39,314	40,012	38,296	31,568
BALANCE SHEET (IN MILLIONS):							
Cash & Cash Equivalents	34.3	27.6	1.2	10.0	3.3	4.2	1.5
Total Current Assets	996.0	855.7	564.3	501.0	518.0	401.5	454.0
Net Property	543.0	428.8	244.0	249.6	250.6	217.5	194.3
Total Assets	2,348.8	1,793.8	1,073.2	1,020.9	1,054.6	785.9	826.6
Total Current Liabilities	438.2	415.3	283.3	246.6	300.0	174.8	238.2
Long-Term Obligations	1,237.1	831.7	309.2	338.9	327.6	198.9	289.1
Net Stockholders' Equity	520.8	435.3	415.2	364.7	356.5	351.9	204.2
Net Working Capital	557.8	440.5	281.0	254.4	218.1	226.8	215.8
Year-end Shs. Outstg. (000)	36,379	35,942	37,472	37,754	39,246	39,168	32,014
STATISTICAL RECORD:							
Operating Profit Margin %	10.0	9.7	9.7	7.2	4.5	10.1	5.9
Net Profit Margin %	3.3	4.1	4.1	2.4	0.6	4.5	1.9
Return on Equity %	14.9	14.2	12.1	7.6	0.9	11.7	5.7
Return on Assets %	3.3	3.5	4.7	2.7	0.3	5.2	1.4
Debt/Total Assets %	52.7	46.4	28.8	33.2	31.1	25.3	35.0
Price Range	30.75-21.44	29.88-17.63	28.81-10.94	19.75-7.88	26.50-14.88	26.50-14.88	19.25-10.13
P/E Ratio	14.7-10.3	18.1-10.7	22.0-8.3	28.0-11.2	311.4-174.8	24.8-13.9	52.0-27.4

Statistics are as originally reported. Adj. for stk. splits: 2-for-1, 5/01. 1 For 6 mos. ended 2/29/96 due to fiscal yr-end change. 2 Incl. non-recurr. chrg. of $2.4 mill., 2/96; $2.2 mill., 8/95; $24.0 mill., 8/94. 3 Bef. extraord. loss of $11.4 mill.; incl. nonrecurr. chrg. of $2.6 mill. 4 Incl. pre-tax nonrecurr. chrgs. of approx. $6.0 mill.

OFFICERS:
R. Sands, Chmn., Pres., C.E.O.
T. S. Summer, Exec. V.P., C.F.O.
T. J. Mullin, Exec. V.P., Gen. Couns.

INVESTOR CONTACT: Lynn Fetterman, Sr. V.P., (716) 394-7900

PRINCIPAL OFFICE: 300 Willowbrook Office Park, Fairport, NY 14450

TELEPHONE NUMBER: (716) 218-2169
FAX: (716) 394-4839
WEB: www.cbrands.com

NO. OF EMPLOYEES: 4,500 (approx.)

SHAREHOLDERS: 940 (Cl. A com.); 273 (Cl. B com.)

ANNUAL MEETING: In July

INCORPORATED: DE, 1972

INSTITUTIONAL HOLDINGS:
No. of Institutions: 184
Shares Held: 29,758,562
% Held: 72.2

INDUSTRY: Wines, brandy, and brandy spirits (SIC: 2084)

TRANSFER AGENT(S): Mellon Investor Services, Ridgefield Park, NJ

NYSE SYMBOL CEG
Rec. Pr. 47.74 (4/30/01)

CONSTELLATION ENERGY GROUP, INC.

YIELD 1.0%
P/E RATIO 20.8

*7 YEAR PRICE SCORE 99.4 *12 MONTH PRICE SCORE 116.8

*NYSE COMPOSITE INDEX=100

INTERIM EARNINGS (Per Share):

Qtr.	Mar.	June	Sept.	Dec.
1997	1.66	1.36	1.53	0.12
1998	0.50	0.39	1.08	0.09
1999	0.55	0.45	0.91	0.26
2000	0.48	0.26	0.98	0.57

INTERIM DIVIDENDS (Per Share):

Amt.	Decl.	Ex.	Rec.	Pay.
0.42Q	5/19/00	6/08/00	6/12/00	7/03/00
0.42Q	6/29/00	9/07/00	9/11/00	10/02/00
0.42Q	10/20/00	12/07/00	12/11/00	1/02/01
0.12Q	2/16/01	3/08/01	3/12/01	4/02/01
0.12Q	5/18/01	6/07/01	6/11/01	7/02/01

Indicated div.: $0.48 (Div. Reinv. Plan)

CAPITALIZATION (12/31/00):

	($000)	(%)
Long-Term Debt	3,159,300	40.3
Deferred Income Tax	1,339,500	17.1
Preferred Stock	190,000	2.4
Common & Surplus	3,153,000	40.2
Total	7,841,800	100.0

RECENT DEVELOPMENTS: For the year ended 12/31/00, net income rose 5.8% to $345.3 million compared with income of $326.4 million, before an extraordinary after-tax charge of $66.3 million, in 1999. Results for 2000 included a deregulation transition charge of $15.0 million, and an after-tax charge of $4.2 million for a targeted voluntary special early retirement program. Earnings for 1999 included net after-tax non-recurring items totaling $45.4 million. Total revenues climbed 2.4% to $3.88 billion.

PROSPECTS: Going forward, the Company expects to achieve stronger earnings as CEG continues to increase its electric generating assets. The Company expects to add 1,050 megawatts of gas-fired peaking capacity during the summer of 2001. On 12/12/00, CEG agreed to acquire 100.0% of Unit 1 and 82.0% of Unit 2 of the Nine Mile Point nuclear plants for $815.0 million. The acquisition is expected to be accretive to CEG's earnings.

BUSINESS

CONSTELLATION ENERGY GROUP, INC. (formerly Baltimore Gas & Electric Co.) is the holding company for Baltimore Gas and Electric Company (BGE) and Constellation Enterprises, Inc. As of 12/31/00, BGE provided service to more than 1.1 million electric customers and more than 590,000 natural gas customers in Central Maryland. Constellation Enterprises is a holding company for several diversified businesses engaged in energy services. Constellation Nuclear is a wholly-owned subsidiary of CEG. The energy services, which includes wholesale generation and power marketing and retail energy businesses are Constellation Power Source, Inc.; Constellation Power, Inc. and Constellation Energy Source, Inc. Revenues in 2000 were derived: electric, 55.0%; natural gas, 15.6%; and non-regulated businesses, 29.4%.

ANNUAL FINANCIAL DATA

	12/31/00	12/31/99	12/31/98	12/31/97	12/31/96	12/31/95	12/31/94
Earnings Per Share	**5 2.30**	**3 4 2.18**	**3 2.06**	**1 3 1.72**	**2 1.85**	**1 2.02**	**1 1.93**
Cash Flow Per Share	**5.80**	**5.56**	**4.95**	**4.41**	**4.44**	**4.58**	**4.32**
Tang. Book Val. Per Share	**20.95**	**20.05**	**19.98**	**19.40**	**19.35**	**19.07**	**18.42**
Dividends Per Share	**1.68**	**1.68**	**1.68**	**1.62**	**1.58**	**1.54**	**1.50**
Dividend Payout %	**73.0**	**77.1**	**81.5**	**70.9**	**85.4**	**76.2**	**77.7**
INCOME STATEMENT (IN MILLIONS):							
Total Revenues	3,878.5	3,786.2	3,358.1	3,307.6	3,153.2	2,934.8	2,783.0
Costs & Expenses	2,513.5	2,334.2	2,010.1	2,008.7	1,926.5	1,691.9	1,631.8
Depreciation & Amort.	524.8	505.9	429.4	396.8	383.2	379.0	351.1
Maintenance Exp.	...	186.2	177.5	178.5	174.1	168.3	164.9
Operating Income	840.2	759.9	741.1	723.6	669.5	695.7	635.3
Net Interest Inc./(Exp.)	d271.4	d255.0	d240.9	d230.0	d198.4	d197.0	d190.2
Income Taxes	230.1	186.4	178.2	158.0	166.3	169.5	153.9
Net Income	5 345.3	3 4 326.4	3 327.7	1 3 282.8	2 310.8	1 338.0	1 323.6
Cash Flow	870.1	832.3	735.3	650.9	655.4	676.4	634.8
Average Shs. Outstg. (000)	150,000	149,600	148,500	147,700	147,560	147,527	147,100
BALANCE SHEET (IN MILLIONS):							
Gross Property	10,442.1	8,989.2	8,744.2	8,494.9	8,195.7	7,979.4	7,722.2
Accumulated Depreciation	3,798.1	3,466.1	3,087.5	2,843.4	2,613.4	2,481.8	2,305.4
Net Property	6,644.0	5,523.1	5,656.7	5,651.5	5,582.4	5,497.6	5,416.8
Total Assets	12,384.6	9,683.8	9,195.0	8,773.4	8,551.0	8,316.7	8,143.5
Long-Term Obligations	3,159.3	2,575.4	3,128.1	2,988.9	2,758.8	2,598.3	2,584.9
Net Stockholders' Equity	3,343.0	3,183.0	3,171.5	3,075.5	3,067.1	3,081.9	2,927.1
Year-end Shs. Outstg. (000)	150,532	149,246	149,246	147,700	147,667	147,527	147,527
STATISTICAL RECORD:							
Operating Profit Margin %	21.7	20.1	22.1	21.9	21.2	23.7	22.8
Net Profit Margin %	8.9	8.6	9.8	8.6	9.9	11.5	11.6
Net Inc./Net Property %	5.2	5.9	5.8	5.0	5.6	6.1	6.0
Net Inc./Tot. Capital %	4.4	4.6	4.3	3.8	4.3	4.7	4.7
Return on Equity %	10.3	10.3	10.3	9.2	10.1	11.0	11.1
Accum. Depr./Gross Prop. %	36.4	38.6	35.3	33.5	31.9	31.1	29.9
Price Range	52.06-27.06	31.50-24.69	35.25-29.25	34.31-24.75	29.50-25.00	29.00-22.00	25.50-20.50
P/E Ratio	22.6-11.8	14.4-11.3	17.1-14.2	19.9-14.4	15.9-13.5	14.4-10.9	13.2-10.6
Average Yield %	4.2	6.0	5.2	5.5	5.8	6.0	6.5

Statistics are as originally reported. 1 Incl. $37.5 mill. net write-offs, 1997; $9.7 mill., 1995; $11.0 mill., 1994. 2 Incl. $62.0 mill. one-time disallow. for energy during nuclear outages in 1989-91. 3 Incl. $45.4 mill. in spl. chgs. & the write-down of invtmts., 1999; $23.7 mill., 1998; $46.0 mill., 1997. 4 Excl. $66.3 mill. extraord. chg. 5 Incl. after-tax chg. of $150.0 mill. for CEG's trans. to deregul. of electric bus. & a $4.2 mill. net chg. for voluntary early retirement program.

OFFICERS:
C. H. Poindexter, Chmn., C.E.O.
E. P. Grubman, Co.- Pres.
C. W. Shivery, Co. - Pres.

INVESTOR CONTACT: Investor Relations, (410) 234-5000

PRINCIPAL OFFICE: 250 W. Pratt Street, Baltimore, MD 21201

TELEPHONE NUMBER: (410) 234-5000
FAX: (410) 234-5367
WEB: www.constellationenergy.com

NO. OF EMPLOYEES: 7,000 (avg.)

SHAREHOLDERS: 58,650

ANNUAL MEETING: In Apr.

INCORPORATED: MD, June, 1906

INSTITUTIONAL HOLDINGS:
No. of Institutions: 327
Shares Held: 78,169,698
% Held: 51.7

INDUSTRY: Electric and other services combined (SIC: 4931)

TRANSFER AGENT(S): Computershare Investor Services, Chicago, IL

NYSE SYMBOL CAL
Rec. Pr. 49.17 (5/31/01)

CONTINENTAL AIRLINES, INC.

YIELD ...
P/E RATIO 8.8

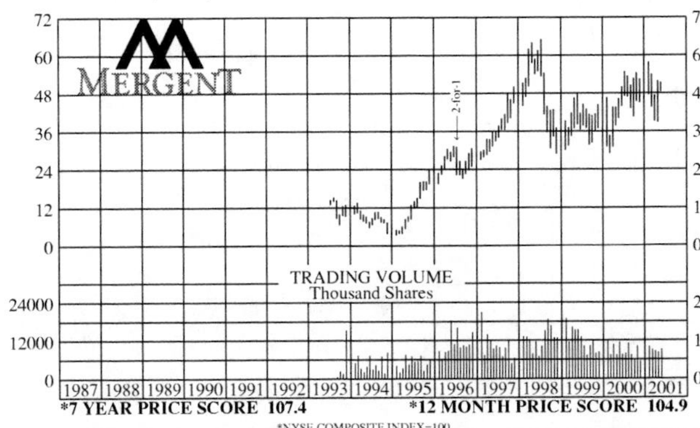

*7 YEAR PRICE SCORE 107.4 *12 MONTH PRICE SCORE 104.9

*NYSE COMPOSITE INDEX=100

INTERIM EARNINGS (Per Share):

Qtr.	Mar.	June	Sept.	Dec.
1996	1.60	3.05	0.42	0.82
1997	1.28	2.22	1.97	1.26
1998	1.06	2.11	0.97	0.91
1999	1.19	1.80	1.53	2.42
2000	0.21	2.46	2.24	0.70

INTERIM DIVIDENDS (Per Share):

Amt.	Decl.	Ex.	Rec.	Pay.

No dividends paid.

CAPITALIZATION (12/31/00):

	($000)	(%)
Long-Term Debt	3,374,000	56.1
Deferred Income Tax	787,000	13.1
Redeemable Pfd. Stock	692,000	11.5
Common & Surplus	1,160,000	19.3
Total	6,013,000	100.0

RECENT DEVELOPMENTS: For the year ended 12/31/00, income, before a net extraordinary charge of $6.0 million, totaled $348.0 million, down 28.7% compared with income of $488.0 million, before an accounting charge, the year before. Results included net one-time gains of $6.0 million and $117.0 million in 2000 and 1999, respectively. Total operating revenue climbed 14.6% to $9.90 billion from $8.64 billion a year earlier. Operating income rose 14.0% to $684.0 million. The passenger load factor, or percentage of seats filled, increased to 74.5% from 73.2% in 1999.

PROSPECTS: The Company is is adding 15 to 20 new gates at Bush Intercontinental Airport in Houston, Texas to help support CAL's growing international traffic. The new gates, which will accommodate both domestic and international flights, are expected to be phased in beginning as early as December 2002, with completion anticipated in mid-2003. Initially, the new gates will be used to grow the Company's domestic operations while the airport completes construction of a new Federal Inspection Service facility, scheduled to open in 2004.

BUSINESS

CONTINENTAL AIRLINES, INC. is a major U.S. air carrier engaged in the business of transporting passengers, cargo and mail. CAL, together with its wholly-owned subsidiaries Continental Express, Inc. and Continental Micronesia, Inc., flies to 136 domestic and 92 international destinations and offers additional connecting service through alliances with domestic and foreign carriers. CAL provides service to Europe, Mexico, Central America and South America, and through its Guam hub, provides service in the western Pacific, including Japan. Major hubs include Newark, Houston, Cleveland and Guam. Through its alliance with Northwest Airlines, Inc., CAL's domestic route system connects with Northwest's hubs in Minneapolis, Detroit and Memphis.

REVENUES

(12/31/2000)	($000)	(%)
Passenger	9,308,000	94.0
Cargo & Mail	360,000	3.7
Other	231,000	2.3
Total	9,899,000	100.0

ANNUAL FINANCIAL DATA

	12/31/00	12/31/99	12/31/98	12/31/97	12/31/96	12/31/95	12/31/94
Earnings Per Share	**[4] 5.54**	**[1][3] 6.64**	**[1][2] 5.06**	**[2] 5.03**	**[1][2] 4.97**	**[1] 3.60**	**d11.88**
Cash Flow Per Share	**11.94**	**11.47**	**8.48**	**7.91**	**8.83**	**7.31**	**d6.94**
Tang. Book Val. Per Share	**1.35**	**7.06**	**0.19**	...	...	...	...
INCOME STATEMENT (IN MILLIONS):							
Total Revenues	9,899.0	8,639.0	7,951.0	7,213.0	6,360.0	5,825.0	5,670.0
Costs & Expenses	8,813.0	7,679.0	6,956.0	6,243.0	5,581.0	5,187.0	5,423.0
Depreciation & Amort.	402.0	360.0	294.0	254.0	254.0	253.0	258.0
Operating Income	684.0	600.0	701.0	716.0	525.0	385.0	d11.0
Net Interest Inc./(Exp.)	d107.0	d107.0	d64.0	d75.0	d117.0	d176.0	d201.0
Income Before Income Taxes	571.0	798.0	648.0	640.0	428.0	310.0	d651.0
Income Taxes	222.0	310.0	248.0	237.0	86.0	78.0	cr42.0
Equity Earnings/Minority Int.	...	...	...	...	d3.0	d6.0	d4.0
Net Income	[4] 348.0	[1][3] 488.0	[1][2] 387.0	[2] 389.0	[1][2] 325.0	[1] 224.0	d613.0
Cash Flow	750.0	848.0	659.0	641.0	574.0	468.0	d361.0
Average Shs. Outstg. (000)	62,800	73,900	80,300	81,000	65,000	64,000	52,000
BALANCE SHEET (IN MILLIONS):							
Cash & Cash Equivalents	1,395.0	1,590.0	1,399.0	1,025.0	1,061.0	747.0	396.0
Total Current Assets	2,459.0	2,606.0	2,354.0	1,728.0	1,634.0	1,315.0	990.0
Net Property	5,163.0	4,173.0	3,065.0	2,225.0	1,596.0	1,461.0	1,593.0
Total Assets	9,201.0	8,223.0	7,086.0	5,830.0	5,206.0	4,821.0	4,601.0
Total Current Liabilities	2,980.0	2,775.0	2,442.0	2,285.0	2,104.0	1,984.0	2,408.0
Long-Term Obligations	3,374.0	3,055.0	2,480.0	1,568.0	2,992.0	3,010.0	2,240.0
Net Stockholders' Equity	1,160.0	1,593.0	1,193.0	916.0	581.0	305.0	103.0
Net Working Capital	d521.0	d169.0	d88.0	d557.0	d470.0	d669.0	d1,418.0
Year-end Shs. Outstg. (000)	58,450	65,481	64,800	59,000	57,000	54,000	54,000
STATISTICAL RECORD:							
Operating Profit Margin %	6.9	6.9	8.8	9.9	8.3	6.6	...
Net Profit Margin %	3.5	5.6	4.9	5.4	5.1	3.8	...
Return on Equity %	30.0	30.6	32.4	42.5	55.9	73.4	...
Return on Assets %	3.8	5.9	5.5	6.7	6.2	4.6	...
Debt/Total Assets %	36.7	37.2	35.0	26.9	57.5	62.4	48.7
Price Range	54.81-29.00	48.00-30.00	65.13-28.88	50.19-27.00	31.44-19.44	23.75-3.25	13.63-3.75
P/E Ratio	9.9-5.2	7.2-4.5	12.9-5.7	10.0-5.4	6.3-3.9	6.6-0.9	...

Statistics are as originally reported. Adj. for 2-for-1 stk. split, 7/96. [1] Incl. $132 mil after-tax gain, 1999; $77 mil after-tax fleet disposition chrg., 1998; $59.5 mil chrg., 1996; & $108 mil pre-tax gain, 1995. [2] Bef. $4 mil ($0.07/sh) after-tax extraord. chrg., 2000; $4 mil ($0.04/sh) after-tax extraord. chrg., 1998; $4 mil ($0.04/sh) after-tax extraord. loss, 1997; $6 mil ($0.12/sh) after-tax extraord. loss, 1996. [3] Bef. $33 mil ($0.44/sh) acctg. change chrg. [4] Bef. $6.0 mil ($0.09/sh) extraord. chg. & incl. $6 mil after-tax gain fr sale of invest. in America West.

OFFICERS:
G. Bethune, Chmn., C.E.O.
G. D. Brenneman, Pres., C.O.O.
L. W. Kellner, Exec. V.P., C.F.O.

INVESTOR CONTACT: Diane Schad, Staff V.P.-Fin., (713) 324-5242

PRINCIPAL OFFICE: 1600 Smith Street, Dept. HQSEO, Houston, TX 77002

TELEPHONE NUMBER: (713) 324-2950
FAX: (713) 520-6329
WEB: www.flycontinental.com
NO. OF EMPLOYEES: 54,300 (approx.)
SHAREHOLDERS: 509 (Cl. B)
ANNUAL MEETING: In May
INCORPORATED: DE, 1985

INSTITUTIONAL HOLDINGS:
No. of Institutions: 137
Shares Held: 54,587,971
% Held: 101.8

INDUSTRY: Air transportation, scheduled (SIC: 4512)

TRANSFER AGENT(S): Computershare Investor Services, Chicago, IL

NYSE SYMBOL CVG
Rec. Pr. 36.50 (4/30/01)

CONVERGYS CORPORATION

YIELD ...
P/E RATIO 29.7

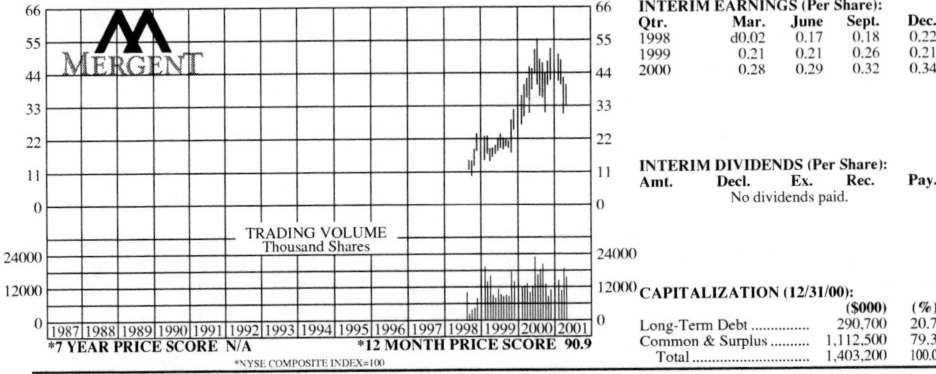

INTERIM EARNINGS (Per Share):

Qtr.	Mar.	June	Sept.	Dec.
1998	d0.02	0.17	0.18	0.22
1999	0.21	0.21	0.26	0.21
2000	0.28	0.29	0.32	0.34

INTERIM DIVIDENDS (Per Share):

Amt.	Decl.	Ex.	Rec.	Pay.

No dividends paid.

CAPITALIZATION (12/31/00):

	($000)	(%)
Long-Term Debt	290,700	20.7
Common & Surplus	1,112,500	79.3
Total	1,403,200	100.0

RECENT DEVELOPMENTS: For the year ended 12/31/00, net income soared 42.1% to $194.7 million versus $137.0 million in 1999. Results for 2000 and 1999 included charges of $300,000 and $13.9 million, respectively, from year 2000 programming. Also, results for 1999 included $2.0 million in purchased research and development charges and $6.9 million in special charges. Total revenues rose 22.7% to $2.16 billion from $1.76 billion in the prior year. Operating income jumped 39.4% to $327.9 million.

PROSPECTS: Going forward, the Company anticipates total revenue growth to be at or above 15.0%. Moreover, revenue growth for the Information Management Group is expected to range between 12.0% to 14.0%, while revenue growth in the Customer Management Group should range between 18.0% to 24.0%. Earnings per share for 2001 is expected to be about $1.52. Separately, CVG renewed its billing contract with Sprint Personal Communication Services, which serves approximately 10.0 million subscribers.

BUSINESS

CONVERGYS CORPORATION is a provider of outsourced information and customer management services. CVG develops long-term strategic relationships with clients in the telecommunications, cable, broadband, satellite broadcasting, Internet services, utilities, technology, financial services, consumer products, healthcare and pharmaceutical industries. CVG operates through two subsidiaries: the Information Management Group, which provides outsourced billing and information services; and the Customer Management Group, which provides outsourced marketing and customer support services. CVG was spun off from Cincinnati Bell Inc. (now Broadwing, Inc.) on 12/31/98. Revenues for 2000 were derived from the Information Management Group, 36%, and the Customer Management Group, 64%.

ANNUAL FINANCIAL DATA

	12/31/00	12/31/99	12/31/98	12/31/97	12/31/96	12/31/95
Earnings Per Share	**2 1.23**	**1 0.89**	**0.57**	**0.63**	**0.57**	**d0.03**
Cash Flow Per Share	**2.25**	**1.73**	**1.28**	**1.08**	**0.95**	**0.31**
Tang. Book Val. Per Share	**2.41**	**1.13**	**0.29**	**1.85**	**1.22**	...
INCOME STATEMENT (IN MILLIONS):						
Total Revenues	2,162.5	1,762.9	1,447.2	987.5	842.4	644.7
Costs & Expenses	1,673.8	1,397.4	1,206.0	812.4	671.4	567.6
Depreciation & Amort.	160.8	130.3	101.3	61.0	51.8	45.9
Operating Income	327.9	235.2	139.9	114.1	119.2	31.2
Net Interest Inc./(Exp.)	d32.9	d32.5	d33.9	d5.4	d6.0	d7.4
Income Before Income Taxes	317.0	222.5	130.6	130.6	124.8	19.4
Income Taxes	122.3	85.5	49.6	44.0	46.8	22.9
Net Income	2 194.7	1 137.0	81.0	86.6	78.0	d3.5
Cash Flow	355.5	267.3	182.3	147.6	129.8	42.4
Average Shs. Outstg. (000)	158,000	154,500	142,900	137,000	137,000	137,000
BALANCE SHEET (IN MILLIONS):						
Cash & Cash Equivalents	28.2	30.8	3.8	2.1	2.3	...
Total Current Assets	481.1	297.9	360.5	265.8	234.8	...
Net Property	392.6	335.6	249.8	130.0	123.0	...
Total Assets	1,779.5	1,579.5	1,450.9	654.4	619.2	...
Total Current Liabilities	359.0	387.4	697.9	216.6	232.4	...
Long-Term Obligations	290.7	250.3	...	1.2	8.3	...
Net Stockholders' Equity	1,112.5	927.2	731.5	430.8	364.2	...
Net Working Capital	122.1	d89.5	d337.4	49.2	2.4	...
Year-end Shs. Outstg. (000)	154,800	153,000	151,950	137,000	137,000	137,000
STATISTICAL RECORD:						
Operating Profit Margin %	15.2	13.3	9.7	11.6	14.2	4.8
Net Profit Margin %	9.0	7.8	5.6	8.8	9.3	...
Return on Equity %	17.5	14.8	11.1	20.1	21.4	...
Return on Assets %	10.9	8.7	5.6	13.2	12.6	...
Debt/Total Assets %	16.3	15.8	...	0.2	1.3	...
Price Range	55.44-26.63	31.75-14.50	23.75-9.63	...	...	...
P/E Ratio	45.1-21.6	35.7-16.3	41.7-16.9	...	...	...

Statistics are as originally reported. 1 Incl. $6.9 mill. special chgs. 2 Incl. $300,000 chg. fr. year 2000 programming.

OFFICERS:
J. F. Orr, Chmn., Pres., C.E.O.
S. G. Rolls, C.F.O.
W. D. Basket III, Gen. Couns., Sec.

INVESTOR CONTACT: Ron Harris, Director, Investor Relations, (888) 284-9900

PRINCIPAL OFFICE: 201 East Fourth Street, Cincinnati, OH 45202

TELEPHONE NUMBER: (513) 723-7000
FAX: (513) 421-8624
WEB: www.convergys.com

NO. OF EMPLOYEES: 41,000 (avg.)

SHAREHOLDERS: 18,849 (record)

ANNUAL MEETING: In Apr.

INCORPORATED: OH, May, 1998

INSTITUTIONAL HOLDINGS:
No. of Institutions: 339
Shares Held: 97,693,358
% Held: 62.9

INDUSTRY: Computer integrated systems design (SIC: 7373)

TRANSFER AGENT(S): The Fifth Third Bank, Corporate Trust Services, Cincinnati, OH

NYSE SYMBOL CAM
Rec. Pr. 63.06 (4/30/01)

COOPER CAMERON CORPORATION

YIELD ...
P/E RATIO 126.1

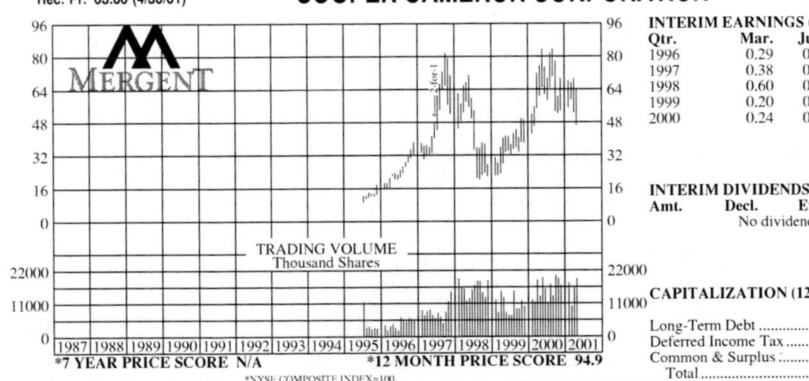

INTERIM EARNINGS (Per Share):

Qtr.	Mar.	June	Sept.	Dec.
1996	0.29	0.49	0.72	0.90
1997	0.38	0.66	0.76	0.89
1998	0.60	0.81	0.58	0.49
1999	0.20	0.17	0.29	0.13
2000	0.24	0.29	0.15	d0.18

INTERIM DIVIDENDS (Per Share):

Amt.	Decl.	Ex.	Rec.	Pay.
	No dividends paid.			

CAPITALIZATION (12/31/00):

	($000)	(%)
Long-Term Debt	188,060	17.6
Deferred Income Tax	38,453	3.6
Common & Surplus	842,279	78.8
Total	1,068,792	100.0

RECENT DEVELOPMENTS: For the year ended 12/31/00, net income declined to $27.7 million versus $43.0 million the previous year. Results for 2000 included net nonrecurring charges of $77.4 million, about $22.7 million of which reflected asset writedowns and accruable costs related primarily to Cooper Energy Services' decision to exit the Superior engine business. Results for 1999 included net nonrecurring charges of $10.6 million. Total revenues fell 6.0% to $1.39 billion. Results for 1999 included CAM's Rotating business, which was sold in September 1999.

PROSPECTS: Near-term prospects are positive, reflecting solid demand from CAM's Cameron segment due to higher worldwide exploration and production activity. For the quarter ended 12/31/00, CAM's total orders and backlogs rose 26.1% to $383.1 million, led by a 29.4% increase to $233.7 million at Cameron. Looking forward, awards for large-scale subsea projects could lead to significantly improved future results. CAM currently has more than $1.20 billion of project bids outstanding.

BUSINESS

COOPER CAMERON CORPORATION is an international manufacturer of oil and gas pressure control equipment with operations organized into four separate business segments. Cameron (60.5% of 2000 revenues) is an international manufacturer of oil and gas pressure control equipment, including wellheads, chokes, blowout preventers and assembled systems for oil and gas drilling, production and transmission used in onshore, offshore and subsea applications. Cooper Cameron Valves (15.9%) provides a full range of ball valves, gate valves, butterfly valves and accessories. Cooper Energy Services (16.2%) designs, manufacturers, markets and services compression and power equipment including engines, integral engine compressors, reciprocating compressors, turbochargers and ignition systems. Cooper Turbocompressor (7.4%) provides centrifugal air compressors and aftermarket productions to manufacturing companies and chemical process industries worldwide.

ANNUAL FINANCIAL DATA

	12/31/00	12/31/99	12/31/98	12/31/97	12/31/96	12/31/95	12/31/94
Earnings Per Share	**[1] 0.50**	**[1] 0.78**	**[1] 2.48**	**2.53**	**[1] 2.41**	**[1] d19.87**	...
Cash Flow Per Share	**1.87**	**2.31**	**3.80**	**3.71**	**2.50**	**d8.55**	**1.33**
Tang. Book Val. Per Share	**10.75**	**8.57**	**9.22**	**7.61**	**5.01**	**3.78**	...
INCOME STATEMENT (IN MILLIONS):							
Total Revenues	1,386.7	1,464.8	1,882.1	1,806.1	1,388.2	1,144.0	1,110.1
Costs & Expenses	1,172.2	1,271.7	1,559.2	1,512.3	1,205.5	1,062.9	1,016.5
Depreciation & Amort.	75.3	83.7	72.5	65.9	62.5	71.8	70.2
Operating Income	139.2	109.3	250.4	228.0	120.2	9.4	23.4
Net Interest Inc./(Exp.)	d18.0	d27.8	d32.7	d28.6	d20.9	d23.3	d20.0
Income Before Income Taxes	43.8	70.9	195.7	199.4	92.0	d496.4	3.3
Income Taxes	16.1	27.9	59.6	58.8	27.8	3.7	7.1
Net Income	[1] 27.7	[1] 43.0	[1] 136.2	140.6	[1] 64.2	[1] d500.1	d3.7
Cash Flow	103.0	126.7	208.6	206.4	126.7	d428.3	66.5
Average Shs. Outstg. (000)	55,013	54,848	54,902	55,606	50,690	50,092	50,000
BALANCE SHEET (IN MILLIONS):							
Cash & Cash Equivalents	16.6	8.2	21.3	11.6	9.1	12.1	...
Total Current Assets	688.0	704.6	966.3	960.8	810.0	528.8	628.4
Net Property	403.2	419.6	490.6	395.5	369.5	346.6	384.1
Total Assets	1,493.9	1,470.7	1,823.6	1,643.2	1,480.7	1,135.4	1,710.4
Total Current Liabilities	346.0	421.8	529.8	528.8	444.8	316.7	276.4
Long-Term Obligations	188.1	195.9	364.4	328.8	347.5	234.8	374.8
Net Stockholders' Equity	842.3	714.1	780.3	642.1	516.1	423.6	878.1
Net Working Capital	342.0	282.7	436.4	432.0	365.1	212.0	352.0
Year-end Shs. Outstg. (000)	54,012	50,568	52,782	52,758	51,212	50,292	...
STATISTICAL RECORD:							
Operating Profit Margin %	10.0	7.5	13.3	12.6	8.7	0.8	2.1
Net Profit Margin %	2.0	2.9	7.2	7.8	4.6	...	...
Return on Equity %	3.3	6.0	17.4	21.9	12.4	...	...
Return on Assets %	1.9	2.9	7.5	8.6	4.3	...	...
Debt/Total Assets %	12.6	13.3	20.0	20.0	23.5	20.7	21.9
Price Range	83.88-42.38	50.00-22.25	71.00-20.13	81.75-30.25	38.25-15.94	17.75-9.25	...
P/E Ratio	167.7-84.7	64.1-28.5	28.6-8.1	32.3-12.0	15.9-6.6	...	...

Statistics are as originally reported. Adj. for 2-for-1 stk. split, 6/97 [1] Incls. net nonrecurr. chrg. of $77.4 mill., 2000; $10.6 mill., 1999; $22.0 mill., 1998; $7.3 mill., 1996; $41.5 mill., 1995.

OFFICERS:
S. R. Erikson, Chmn., Pres., C.E.O.
T. R. Hix, Sr. V.P., C.F.O.
W. C. Lemmer, V.P., Sec., Gen. Couns.

INVESTOR CONTACT: R. S. Amann, (713) 513-3344

PRINCIPAL OFFICE: 515 Post Oak Boulevard, Suite 1200, Houston, TX 77027

TELEPHONE NUMBER: (713) 513-3300
FAX: (713) 513-3320
WEB: www.coopercameron.com

NO. OF EMPLOYEES: 7,300 (approx.)

SHAREHOLDERS: 1,801 (approx. of record)

ANNUAL MEETING: In May

INCORPORATED: DE, Nov., 1994

INSTITUTIONAL HOLDINGS:
No. of Institutions: 197
Shares Held: 48,115,866
% Held: 88.9

INDUSTRY: Oil and gas field machinery (SIC: 3533)

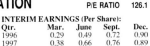

TRANSFER AGENT(S): First Chicago Trust Company of New York, Jersey City, NJ

NYSE SYMBOL COO
Rec. Pr. 45.70 (5/31/01)

COOPER COMPANIES, INC.

YIELD 0.4%
P/E RATIO 21.6

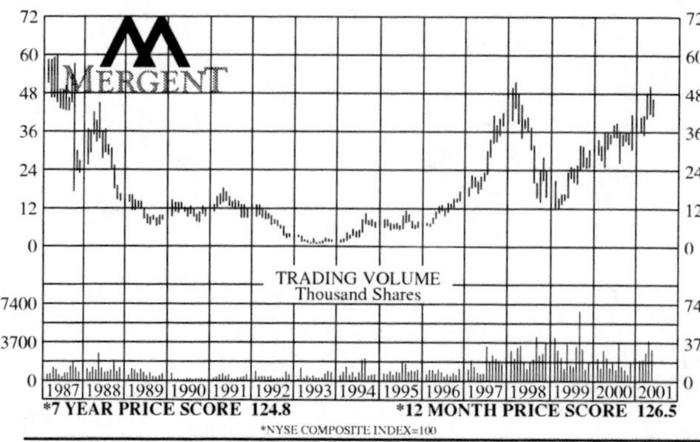

INTERIM EARNINGS (Per Share):

Qtr.	Jan.	Apr.	July	Oct.
1997-98	0.39	0.55	0.68	2.45
1998-99	0.18	0.38	0.46	0.53
1999-00	0.34	0.47	0.59	0.63
2000-01	0.43	...	...	...

INTERIM DIVIDENDS (Per Share):

Amt.	Decl.	Ex.	Rec.	Pay.
0.02Q	2/29/00	3/13/00	3/15/00	4/05/00
0.02Q	5/19/00	6/13/00	6/15/00	7/05/00
0.02Q	8/30/00	9/13/00	9/15/00	10/05/00
0.02Q	12/05/00	12/13/00	12/15/00	1/05/01
0.05Q	5/18/01	6/13/01	6/15/01	7/05/01

Indicated div.: $0.20

CAPITALIZATION (10/31/00):

	($000)	(%)
Long-Term Debt	40,257	16.9
Common & Surplus	198,438	83.1
Total	238,695	100.0

RECENT DEVELOPMENTS: For the first quarter ended 1/31/01, net income was $6.3 million versus income of $4.8 million, before an accounting charge of $432,000, a year earlier. Net sales advanced 21.0% to $48.9 million from $40.4 million the year before. CooperVision business unit revenues increased 11.3% to $35.6 million, reflecting a 26.0% increase in customer demand for disposable-planned replacement toric contact lenses.

PROSPECTS: The CooperVision (CVI) contact lens unit should benefit from the introduction of value-added aspheric and cosmetic contact lenses in all major European markets. In addition, Rohto Pharmaceuticals, Inc., which markets CVI's conventional spherical and toric lenses under the Rohto i Q trade name in Japan, plans to introduce a lens material designed for bi-weekly replacement during 2002.

BUSINESS

COOPER COMPANIES, INC. and its subsidiaries develop, manufacture and market specialty healthcare products. The Company operates in two businesses. CooperVision markets a broad range of contact lenses that correct visual defects, specializing in toric lenses that correct astigmatism. CooperVision markets its products primarily in North America and Europe. CooperSurgical markets diagnostic products, surgical instruments and accessories to the women's healthcare market, primarily in the United States. Revenues (and operating income) for 2000 were derived: CooperVision, 76.9% (88.2%) and CooperSurgical, 23.1% (11.8%).

ANNUAL FINANCIAL DATA

	10/31/00	10/31/99	10/31/98	10/31/97	10/31/96	10/31/95	10/31/94
Earnings Per Share	**[4] 2.03**	**[3] 1.54**	**[2] 3.79**	**3.70**	**1.41**	**[1] 0.01**	**d0.47**
Cash Flow Per Share	**2.63**	**1.99**	**4.34**	**4.03**	**1.70**	**0.29**	**d0.06**
Tang. Book Val. Per Share	**6.06**	**5.95**	**4.22**	**5.06**	...	...	...
Dividends Per Share	**0.08**	**0.04**	...	...	...	...	...
Dividend Payout %	**3.9**	**2.6**	...	...	...	...	...
INCOME STATEMENT (IN THOUSANDS):							
Total Revenues	197,317	165,328	147,192	141,473	109,131	97,090	95,645
Costs & Expenses	141,714	118,077	109,076	111,417	88,936	85,829	91,023
Depreciation & Amort.	8,734	8,440	8,416	4,267	3,352	3,253	4,199
Operating Income	46,869	38,811	29,700	25,789	16,843	8,008	423
Net Interest Inc./(Exp.)	d4,744	d6,330	d6,253	d4,214	d5,312	d4,741	d4,533
Income Before Income Taxes	42,127	32,712	23,087	21,784	12,115	230	d9,297
Income Taxes	12,727	10,711	cr34,723	cr26,606	cr4,488	115	cr4,600
Net Income	[4] 29,400	[3] 22,001	[2] 57,810	48,390	16,603	[1] 115	d4,697
Cash Flow	38,134	30,441	66,226	52,657	19,955	3,368	d587
Average Shs. Outstg.	14,510	15,286	15,269	13,071	11,761	11,576	10,193
BALANCE SHEET (IN THOUSANDS):							
Cash & Cash Equivalents	14,608	20,922	7,333	18,249	6,837	11,207	10,320
Total Current Assets	112,685	100,461	116,077	68,569	42,495	41,228	43,505
Net Property	47,933	40,319	34,234	39,523	34,674	34,062	34,787
Total Assets	322,565	285,873	296,041	175,298	102,909	91,992	95,058
Total Current Liabilities	65,275	41,896	46,701	33,617	33,308	39,613	42,256
Long-Term Obligations	40,257	57,067	78,677	9,125	47,920	43,490	46,184
Net Stockholders' Equity	198,438	164,143	145,253	111,533	15,330	d1,749	d3,654
Net Working Capital	47,410	58,565	69,376	34,952	9,187	1,615	1,249
Year-end Shs. Outstg.	14,460	14,058	14,426	14,798	11,671	11,576	11,282
STATISTICAL RECORD:							
Operating Profit Margin %	23.8	23.5	20.2	18.2	15.4	8.2	0.4
Net Profit Margin %	14.9	13.3	39.3	34.2	15.2	0.1	...
Return on Equity %	14.8	13.4	39.8	43.4	108.3	...	...
Return on Assets %	9.1	7.7	19.5	27.6	16.1	0.1	...
Debt/Total Assets %	12.5	20.0	26.6	5.2	46.6	47.3	48.6
Price Range	41.50-25.00	31.88-11.75	51.69-14.00	42.00-15.88	17.38-6.38	11.26-5.26	10.51-1.32
P/E Ratio	20.4-12.3	20.7-7.6	13.6-3.7	11.4-4.3	12.3-4.5	1,115.0-520.3	...
Average Yield %	0.2	0.2	...	...	...	...	...

Statistics are as originally reported. Adj. for 1-for-3 rev. split, 9/95. [1] Incl. $1.5 mill. for restruct & $3.4 mill. for settle. of dispute. [2] Excl. $22.3 mill. loss on sale of ops. & $18.0 mill. loss fr. disc. ops. [3] Excl. a gain of $3.1mill. from disc. ops. [4] Bef. after-tax acctg. chrg. of $432,000.

OFFICERS:
A. E. Rubenstein, Chmn.
A. T. Bender, Pres., C.E.O.
R. S. Weiss, Exec. V.P., C.F.O., Treas.

INVESTOR CONTACT: B. Norris Battin, Inv. Rel., (925) 460-3600

PRINCIPAL OFFICE: 6140 Stoneridge Mall Road, Ste. 590, Pleasanton, CA 94588

TELEPHONE NUMBER: (925) 460-3600
FAX: (925) 460-3620
WEB: www.coopercos.com

NO. OF EMPLOYEES: 2,100 (approx.)

SHAREHOLDERS: 1,719

ANNUAL MEETING: In Mar.

INCORPORATED: DE, Mar., 1980

INSTITUTIONAL HOLDINGS:
No. of Institutions: 135
Shares Held: 12,251,077
% Held: 84.1

INDUSTRY: Ophthalmic goods (SIC: 3851)

TRANSFER AGENT(S): American Stock Transfer & Trust Company, New York, NY

NYSE SYMBOL CBE
Rec. Pr. 37.37 (4/30/01)

COOPER INDUSTRIES, INC.

YIELD 3.7%
P/E RATIO 9.8

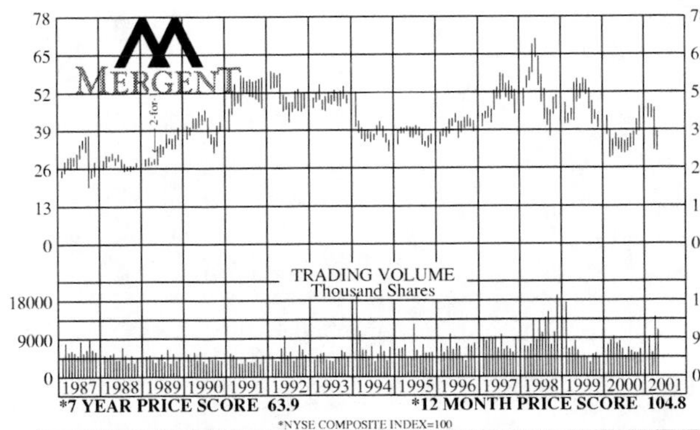

INTERIM EARNINGS (Per Share):

Qtr.	Mar.	June	Sept.	Dec.
1995	0.48	0.71	0.62	0.68
1996	0.58	0.82	0.72	0.81
1997	0.71	0.88	0.84	0.90
1998	0.76	0.88	0.59	1.27
1999	0.80	0.92	0.89	0.89
2000	0.89	0.99	0.97	0.95

INTERIM DIVIDENDS (Per Share):

Amt.	Decl.	Ex.	Rec.	Pay.
0.35Q	4/25/00	6/08/00	6/12/00	7/03/00
0.35Q	8/01/00	9/12/00	9/14/00	10/02/00
0.35Q	11/07/00	11/29/00	12/01/00	1/02/01
0.35Q	2/14/01	2/27/01	3/01/01	4/02/01
0.35Q	4/24/01	6/07/01	6/11/01	7/02/01

Indicated div.: $1.40 (Div. Reinv. Plan)

CAPITALIZATION (12/31/00):

	($000)	(%)
Long-Term Debt	1,300,800	40.6
Common & Surplus	1,904,200	59.4
Total	3,205,000	100.0

RECENT DEVELOPMENTS: For the year ended 12/31/00, net income increased 7.7% to $357.4 million versus $331.9 million a year earlier. Results for 1999 included non-recurring charges of $3.7 million. Revenues rose 15.3% to $4.46 billion from $3.87 billion in 1999. Electrical Products revenues jumped 19.5% to $3.66 billion, driven primarily by the continued expansion of electronics markets and recent acquisitions. Tools & Hardware revenues eased to $800.7 million from $808.0 million.

PROSPECTS: Near-term results could be limited by the slowing U.S. economy; however, CBE expects gradual improvement throughout 2001. Recent initiatives include reducing production costs through the relocation of Eagle Electric's manufacturing operations to Mexico, realignment of CBE's lighting fixture domestic manufacturing facilities and the completion of a new factory in Mexico to serve U.S. and Latin American markets, consolidation of CBE's U.S. tool manufacturing facilities and startup of a new plant in Mexico targeting markets in Latin and South America.

BUSINESS

COOPER INDUSTRIES, INC. operates in two business segments: Electrical Products and Tools & Hardware. The Electrical Products segment (82.0% of 2000 revenues) manufactures, markets and sells electrical and circuit protection products, including fittings, support systems, enclosures, wiring devices, plugs, receptacles, lighting fixtures, fuses, emergency lighting, fire detection systems and security products for use in residential, commercial and industrial construction, maintenance and repair applications. This segment also manufactures, markets and sells products for use by utilities and in industry for electrical power transmission and distribution. The Tools & Hardware segment (18.0%) manufactures, markets and sells hand tools for industrial, construction and consumer markets; automated assembly systems for industrial markets; and electric and pneumatic industrial power tools for general industry, primarily automotive and aerospace manufacturers. On 10/9/98, CBE completed the sale of its former Automotive Products division to Federal-Mogul Corporation for $1.90 billion.

ANNUAL FINANCIAL DATA

	12/31/00	12/31/99	4 12/31/98	12/31/97	12/31/96	12/31/95	12/31/94
Earnings Per Share	**3.80**	**3.50**	**1 2.93**	**2 3.26**	**2.93**	**3 2.52**	**3 2.10**
Cash Flow Per Share	**5.65**	**5.05**	**4.13**	**5.23**	**5.11**	**4.48**	**4.31**
Tang. Book Val. Per Share	...	**0.04**	**0.91**	**1.55**	...	...	**4.76**
Dividends Per Share	**1.38**	**1.32**	**1.32**	**1.32**	**1.32**	**1.32**	**1.32**
Dividend Payout %	**36.3**	**37.7**	**45.0**	**40.5**	**45.0**	**52.4**	**62.9**
INCOME STATEMENT (IN MILLIONS):							
Total Revenues	4,459.9	3,868.9	3,651.2	5,288.8	5,283.7	4,810.9	4,588.0
Costs & Expenses	3,635.3	3,143.8	2,969.8	4,359.1	4,500.4	3,980.6	3,811.0
Depreciation & Amort.	174.4	147.6	137.5	219.6	233.8	218.8	199.0
Operating Income	650.2	577.5	543.9	710.1	549.5	611.5	578.0
Net Interest Inc./(Exp.)	d100.3	d55.2	d101.9	d90.4	d142.1	d151.0	d73.3
Income Before Income Taxes	549.9	518.6	523.6	626.7	558.0	478.0	504.7
Income Taxes	192.5	186.7	187.7	232.1	242.6	197.4	211.9
Net Income	357.4	331.9	1 335.9	2 394.6	315.4	3 280.6	3 292.8
Cash Flow	531.8	479.5	473.4	614.2	549.2	499.4	438.5
Average Shs. Outstg. (000)	94,150	94,942	114,658	117,459	107,579	111,510	114,218
BALANCE SHEET (IN MILLIONS):							
Cash & Cash Equivalents	26.4	26.9	20.4	30.3	16.1	17.7	25.3
Total Current Assets	1,735.1	1,466.6	1,417.3	2,136.7	2,098.1	2,127.3	2,100.2
Net Property	870.4	768.0	710.5	1,198.8	1,241.3	1,232.1	1,187.5
Total Assets	4,789.3	4,143.4	3,779.1	6,052.5	5,950.4	6,063.9	6,400.7
Total Current Liabilities	1,173.6	1,085.8	970.7	1,385.1	1,381.3	1,382.4	1,333.1
Long-Term Obligations	1,300.8	894.5	774.5	1,272.2	1,737.7	1,865.3	1,361.9
Net Stockholders' Equity	1,904.2	1,743.1	1,563.6	2,576.6	1,890.2	1,716.4	2,741.1
Net Working Capital	561.5	380.8	446.6	751.6	716.8	744.9	767.1
Year-end Shs. Outstg. (000)	93,539	94,200	94,249	120,161	107,877	107,877	116,923
STATISTICAL RECORD:							
Operating Profit Margin %	14.6	14.9	14.9	13.4	10.4	12.7	12.6
Net Profit Margin %	8.0	8.6	9.2	7.5	6.0	5.8	6.4
Return on Equity %	18.8	19.0	21.5	15.3	16.7	16.3	10.7
Return on Assets %	7.5	8.0	8.9	6.5	5.3	4.6	4.6
Debt/Total Assets %	27.2	21.6	20.5	21.0	29.2	30.8	21.3
Price Range	47.00-29.38	56.75-39.63	70.38-36.88	58.63-40.00	44.63-34.13	40.50-32.88	52.25-31.63
P/E Ratio	12.4-7.7	16.2-11.3	24.0-12.6	18.0-12.3	15.2-11.6	16.1-13.0	24.9-15.1
Average Yield %	3.6	2.7	2.5	2.7	3.4	3.6	3.1

Statistics are as originally reported. 1 Incls. one-time pre-tax credit of $81.6 mill.; bef. income of $87.1 mill. from disc. ops. 2 Incls. non-recurr. pre-tax gain of $9.1 mill. 3 Bef. loss from disc. ops. 12/31/95: $186.6 mill. ($1.67/sh.); loss 12/31/94: $313.4 mill. ($2.75/sh.) 4 Refls. sale of Automotive division.

OFFICERS:
H. J. Riley Jr., Chmn., Pres., C.E.O.
D. B. McWilliams, Sr. V.P., C.F.O.
R. E. Jackson Jr., C.O.O.

INVESTOR CONTACT: Richard F. Bajenski, V.P., Inv. Rel., (713) 209-8610

PRINCIPAL OFFICE: 600 Travis, Suite 5800, Houston, TX 77002-1001

TELEPHONE NUMBER: (713) 209-8400
FAX: (713) 209-8996
WEB: www.cooperindustries.com

NO. OF EMPLOYEES: 34,250 (approx.)

SHAREHOLDERS: 27,945

ANNUAL MEETING: In Apr.

INCORPORATED: OH, Jan., 1919

INSTITUTIONAL HOLDINGS:
No. of Institutions: 257
Shares Held: 68,903,552
% Held: 73.7

INDUSTRY: Commercial lighting fixtures (SIC: 3646)

TRANSFER AGENT(S): First Chicago Trust Company of New York, Jersey City, NJ

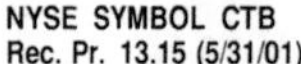

NYSE SYMBOL CTB
Rec. Pr. 13.15 (5/31/01)

COOPER TIRE & RUBBER COMPANY

YIELD 3.2%
P/E RATIO 10.1

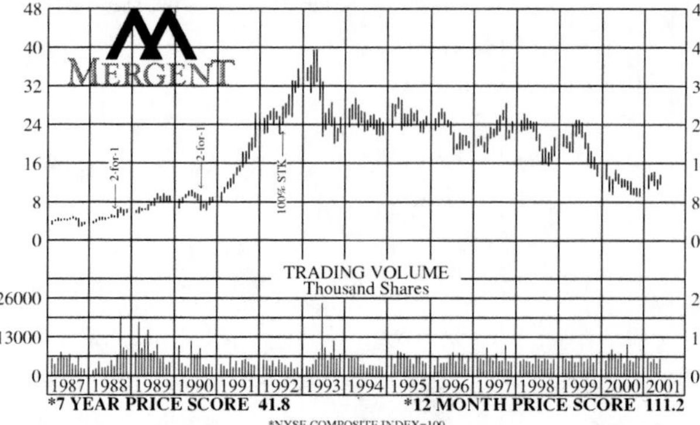

*7 YEAR PRICE SCORE 41.8 *12 MONTH PRICE SCORE 111.2

*NYSE COMPOSITE INDEX=100

INTERIM EARNINGS (Per Share):

Qtr.	Mar.	June	Sept.	Dec.
1996	0.28	0.30	0.32	0.40
1997	0.31	0.40	0.40	0.44
1998	0.34	0.41	0.39	0.50
1999	0.41	0.50	0.46	0.42
2000	0.41	0.48	0.32	0.09

INTERIM DIVIDENDS (Per Share):

Amt.	Decl.	Ex.	Rec.	Pay.
0.105Q	5/03/00	5/31/00	6/02/00	6/30/00
0.105Q	7/20/00	9/06/00	9/08/00	9/29/00
0.105Q	11/20/00	11/28/00	11/30/00	12/22/00
0.105Q	2/09/01	3/01/01	3/05/01	3/30/01
0.105Q	5/01/01	5/30/01	6/01/01	6/29/01

Indicated div.: $0.42 (Div. Reinv. Plan)

CAPITALIZATION (12/31/00):

	($000)	(%)
Long-Term Debt	1,036,960	50.5
Deferred Income Tax	62,447	3.0
Common & Surplus	952,556	46.4
Total	2,051,963	100.0

RECENT DEVELOPMENTS: For the year ended 12/31/00, net income fell 28.6% to $96.7 million compared with $135.5 million in the previous year. Results for 2000 included pre-tax restructuring and other nonrecurring charges totaling $38.7 million associated with the shutdown and consolidation of operations. Net sales jumped 58.1% to $3.47 billion versus $2.20 billion in 1999. Tire segment net sales grew 15.8% to $1.80 billion, primarily due to the acquisition of Oliver Rubber. Net sales in the Automotive segment more than doubled to $1.70 billion.

PROSPECTS: During 2001, CTB plans to complete the majority of its restructuring initiatives that are designed to improve efficiencies and reduce costs of its worldwide operations. As part of the restructuring plan, CTB reorganized its tire group into three new divisions, consisting of the North American Tire division, the International Tire division and the Commercial Products division. CTB plans to close or downsize 22 facilities by the end of 2001. Separately, revenues should benefit from more than $350.0 million in new business.

BUSINESS

COOPER TIRE & RUBBER COMPANY specializes in manufacturing and marketing rubber products for consumers and industrial users. Products for the tire group include automobile, motorcycle and truck tires, inner tubes, tread rubber and equipment. In the automotive group, the Company supplies original equipment of sealing, trim, vibration control products and fluid handling systems to the automotive industry in North America, Europe, Australia and South America. CTB markets its products nationally and internationally through well-established channels of distribution. Represented among its customers are automobile manufacturing companies, independent distributors and dealers, oil companies, large retail chains and industrial manufacturers. The Standard Products Company was acquired 10/27/99.

BUSINESS LINE ANALYSIS

(12/31/00)	Rev(%)	Inc(%)
Tire	51.5	72.8
Automotive	48.5	27.2
Total	100.0	100.0

ANNUAL FINANCIAL DATA

	12/31/00	12/31/99	12/31/98	12/31/97	12/31/96	12/31/95	12/31/94
Earnings Per Share	**1 1.31**	**1.79**	**1.64**	**1.55**	**1.30**	**1.35**	**1.54**
Cash Flow Per Share	**3.88**	**3.44**	**2.97**	**2.75**	**2.22**	**2.11**	**2.20**
Tang. Book Val. Per Share	**7.07**	**7.15**	**11.45**	**10.58**	**9.67**	**8.95**	**7.92**
Dividends Per Share	**0.42**	**0.42**	**0.39**	**0.35**	**0.31**	**0.27**	**0.23**
Dividend Payout %	**32.1**	**23.5**	**23.8**	**22.6**	**23.8**	**20.0**	**14.9**
INCOME STATEMENT (IN MILLIONS):							
Total Revenues	3,472.4	2,196.3	1,879.8	1,814.4	1,620.2	1,497.5	1,405.5
Costs & Expenses	3,031.1	1,831.7	1,563.1	1,508.5	1,369.6	1,253.4	1,139.1
Depreciation & Amort.	188.8	125.6	103.2	95.5	76.8	63.3	55.6
Operating Income	252.5	239.1	213.4	210.4	173.7	180.8	210.8
Net Interest Inc./(Exp.)	d97.5	d24.4	d15.2	d15.7	d1.7	d0.7	d2.7
Income Before Income Taxes	160.2	215.5	198.2	194.8	172.1	180.1	208.1
Income Taxes	63.4	80.0	71.3	72.4	64.2	67.3	79.6
Net Income	1 96.7	135.5	127.0	122.4	107.9	112.8	128.5
Cash Flow	285.5	261.1	230.2	217.9	184.7	176.1	184.1
Average Shs. Outstg. (000)	73,585	75,837	77,598	79,128	83,214	83,646	83,623
BALANCE SHEET (IN MILLIONS):							
Cash & Cash Equivalents	45.8	71.1	42.0	52.9	19.5	23.2	103.3
Total Current Assets	1,031.2	945.4	569.5	554.6	443.6	430.6	454.7
Net Property	1,285.4	1,227.1	885.3	860.4	792.4	678.9	549.6
Total Assets	2,922.0	2,757.6	1,541.3	1,496.0	1,273.0	1,143.7	1,039.7
Total Current Liabilities	606.5	395.9	193.0	200.3	187.5	158.4	151.6
Long-Term Obligations	1,037.0	1,046.5	205.3	205.5	69.5	28.6	33.6
Net Stockholders' Equity	952.6	975.6	867.9	833.6	786.6	748.8	662.1
Net Working Capital	424.7	549.6	376.5	354.3	256.1	272.2	303.1
Year-end Shs. Outstg. (000)	72,544	75,810	75,791	78,760	81,367	83,662	83,634
STATISTICAL RECORD:							
Operating Profit Margin %	7.3	10.9	11.4	11.6	10.7	12.1	15.0
Net Profit Margin %	2.8	6.2	6.8	6.7	6.7	7.5	9.1
Return on Equity %	10.2	13.9	14.6	14.7	13.7	15.1	19.4
Return on Assets %	3.3	4.9	8.2	8.2	8.5	9.9	12.4
Debt/Total Assets %	35.5	37.9	13.3	13.7	5.5	2.5	3.2
Price Range	16.00-9.19	25.00-13.25	26.25-15.44	28.44-18.00	27.38-17.88	29.63-22.25	29.50-21.63
P/E Ratio	12.2-7.0	14.0-7.4	16.0-9.4	18.3-11.6	21.1-13.7	21.9-16.5	19.2-14.0
Average Yield %	3.3	2.2	1.9	1.5	1.4	1.0	0.9

Statistics are as originally reported. 1 Incl. pre-tax nonrecurr. chrg. of $38.7 mill.

OFFICERS:
T. A. Dattilo, Chmn., Pres., C.E.O.
P. G. Weaver, V.P., C.F.O.
R. D. Teeple, V.P., Sec., Gen. Couns.

INVESTOR CONTACT: Roger S. Hendriksen, Dir. Investor Relations, (419) 424-4768

PRINCIPAL OFFICE: Lima and Western Avenues, Findlay, OH 45840

TELEPHONE NUMBER: (419) 423-1321
FAX: (419) 424-4305
WEB: www.coopertire.com

NO. OF EMPLOYEES: 21,185 (avg.)

SHAREHOLDERS: 4,704

ANNUAL MEETING: In May

INCORPORATED: DE, Mar., 1930

INSTITUTIONAL HOLDINGS:
No. of Institutions: 182
Shares Held: 44,764,059
% Held: 61.7

INDUSTRY: Tires and inner tubes (SIC: 3011)

TRANSFER AGENT(S): Fifth Third Bank, Cincinnati, OH

NYSE SYMBOL RKY
Rec. Pr. 52.00 (4/30/01)

COORS (ADOLPH) COMPANY

YIELD 1.6%
P/E RATIO 17.7

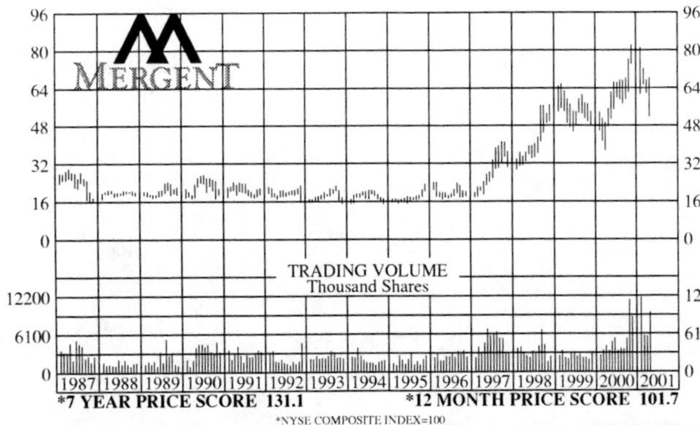

*7 YEAR PRICE SCORE 131.1 *12 MONTH PRICE SCORE 101.7
*NYSE COMPOSITE INDEX=100

INTERIM EARNINGS (Per Share):

Qtr.	Mar.	June	Sept.	Dec.
1997	0.21	1.36	0.47	0.15
1998	0.26	1.06	0.24	0.25
1999	0.32	1.23	0.58	0.33
2000	0.40	1.29	0.92	0.32

INTERIM DIVIDENDS (Per Share):

Amt.	Decl.	Ex.	Rec.	Pay.
0.185Q	5/11/00	5/26/00	5/31/00	6/15/00
0.185Q	8/17/00	8/29/00	8/31/00	9/15/00
0.185Q	11/16/00	11/28/00	11/30/00	12/15/00
0.185Q	2/16/01	2/26/01	2/28/01	3/15/01
0.205Q	5/17/01	5/29/01	5/31/01	6/15/01

Indicated div.: $0.82

CAPITALIZATION (12/31/00):

	($000)	(%)
Long-Term Debt	105,000	9.3
Deferred Income Tax	89,986	8.0
Common & Surplus	932,389	82.7
Total	1,127,375	100.0

RECENT DEVELOPMENTS: For the 53 weeks ended 12/31/00, net income advanced 18.8% to $109.6 million from $92.3 million in the prior year. Earnings for 2000 and 1999 included pre-tax special charges of $15.2 million and $5.7 million, respectively. Net sales grew 8.0% to $2.41 billion from $2.24 billion in the previous year. Sales volume totaled 23.0 million barrels, up 4.7% from the year before. Distributor sales to retail increased approximately 6.5% compared with the prior year.

PROSPECTS: On 1/2/01, RKY finalized a joint venture with Molson, Inc., a Canadian brewer, to import, market, sell and distribute Molson's brands of beer in the U.S. The joint venture has the exclusive rights to Molson brands currently sold in the U.S., including Molson Canadian, Molson Golden and Molson Ice, as well as future Molson brands that may be developed for export to the U.S. RKY paid Molson $65.0 million for a 49.9% interest in the venture.

BUSINESS

ADOLPH COORS COMPANY, through its principal operating subsidiary Coors Brewing Company (CBC), produces, markets and sells malt-based beverages. CBC currently has 13 brands in its portfolio, of which four are premium products that make up the Coors family of beers: COORS LIGHT®, ORIGINAL COORS®, COORS DRY® and COORS NON-ALCOHOLIC®. CBC produces and markets COORS EXTRA GOLD® and ZIMA®, a malt-based, above-premium beverage. CBC also offers specialty, above-premium beers, including WINTERFEST® and BLUEMOON™ ales. In addition, CBC sells licensed products, including GEORGE KILLIAN'S® products, and popular-priced products, including KEYSTONE® products. RKY also owns London-based Coors Brewing International, Ltd. and Coors Canada, Inc.

GEOGRAPHIC DATA

(12/31/2000)($000)	Rev	Inc
1st Quarter	505,429	14,819
2nd Quarter	669,813	48,344
3rd Quarter	657,076	34,492
4th Quarter	582,097	11,962

ANNUAL FINANCIAL DATA

	12/31/00	12/26/99	12/27/98	12/28/97	12/29/96	12/31/95	12/25/94
Earnings Per Share	**1 2.93**	**1 2.46**	**1 1.81**	**1 2.16**	**1.14**	**1.13**	**1.52**
Cash Flow Per Share	**6.38**	**5.77**	**4.89**	**5.24**	**4.33**	**4.35**	**4.67**
Tang. Book Val. Per Share	**24.32**	**22.06**	**20.51**	**19.36**	**18.30**	**17.59**	**13.77**
Dividends Per Share	**0.72**	**0.65**	**0.60**	**0.55**	**0.50**	**0.50**	**0.50**
Dividend Payout %	**24.6**	**26.2**	**33.1**	**25.5**	**43.9**	**44.2**	**32.9**
INCOME STATEMENT (IN MILLIONS):							
Total Revenues	2,414.4	2,056.6	1,899.5	1,822.2	1,732.2	1,675.4	1,662.7
Costs & Expenses	2,134.5	1,790.9	1,679.9	1,557.6	1,530.1	1,472.6	1,433.7
Depreciation & Amort.	129.3	123.8	115.8	117.2	121.1	122.8	120.8
Operating Income	150.6	142.0	103.8	147.4	81.0	79.9	108.2
Net Interest Inc./(Exp.)	14.9	6.9	2.3	d4.2	d11.1	d10.5	d9.9
Income Before Income Taxes	169.5	150.7	111.1	146.9	75.0	73.3	104.2
Income Taxes	59.9	58.4	43.3	64.6	31.6	30.1	46.1
Net Income	1 109.6	1 92.3	1 67.8	1 82.3	43.4	43.2	58.1
Cash Flow	238.9	230.5	183.6	199.4	164.5	166.0	178.9
Average Shs. Outstg. (000)	37,450	37,457	37,515	38,056	37,991	38,170	38,283
BALANCE SHEET (IN MILLIONS):							
Cash & Cash Equivalents	192.5	277.0	256.2	211.0	110.9	32.4	27.2
Total Current Assets	497.8	612.8	549.0	517.2	416.6	362.5	355.2
Net Property	735.8	714.0	714.4	733.1	814.1	887.4	922.2
Total Assets	1,629.3	1,546.4	1,460.6	1,412.1	1,362.5	1,386.9	1,371.6
Total Current Liabilities	379.3	392.7	383.9	359.1	292.4	323.7	380.2
Long-Term Obligations	105.0	105.0	105.0	145.0	176.0	195.0	131.0
Net Stockholders' Equity	932.4	841.5	774.8	736.6	715.5	695.0	674.2
Net Working Capital	118.4	220.1	165.1	158.0	124.2	38.9	d25.0
Year-end Shs. Outstg. (000)	37,131	36,722	36,655	36,859	37,922	37,997	47,460
STATISTICAL RECORD:							
Operating Profit Margin %	6.2	6.9	5.5	8.1	4.7	4.8	6.5
Net Profit Margin %	4.5	5.2	3.6	4.5	2.5	2.6	3.5
Return on Equity %	11.8	12.7	8.7	11.2	6.1	6.2	8.6
Return on Assets %	6.7	6.9	4.6	5.8	3.2	3.1	4.2
Debt/Total Assets %	6.4	6.8	7.2	10.3	12.9	14.1	9.6
Price Range	82.31-37.38	65.81-45.25	56.75-29.25	41.25-17.50	24.25-16.75	23.25-15.13	20.88-14.75
P/E Ratio	28.1-12.8	26.8-18.4	31.4-16.2	19.1-8.1	21.3-14.7	20.6-13.4	13.7-9.7
Average Yield %	1.2	1.2	1.4	1.9	2.4	2.6	2.8

Statistics are as originally reported. 1 Incl. non-recurr. chrg. $15.2 mill., 2000; $5.7 mill., 1999; chrge. $19.4 mill., 1998; credit $31.5 mill., 1997.

OFFICERS:
W. K. Coors, Chmn.
J. Coors, Vice-Chmn.
P. H. Coors, Pres., C.E.O.
T. V. Wolf, Sr. V.P., C.F.O.

INVESTOR CONTACT: Dave Dunnewald, Investor Relations, (303) 279-6565

PRINCIPAL OFFICE: 12th & Ford Streets, Golden, CO 80401

TELEPHONE NUMBER: (303) 279-6565
FAX: (303) 425-7967
WEB: www.coorsinvestor.com

NO. OF EMPLOYEES: 5,850 (approx.)

SHAREHOLDERS: 2,921 (approx. class B common)

ANNUAL MEETING: In May

INCORPORATED: CO, 1913

INSTITUTIONAL HOLDINGS:
No. of Institutions: 224
Shares Held: 19,302,426
% Held: 52.4

INDUSTRY: Malt beverages (SIC: 2082)

TRANSFER AGENT(S): BankBoston, N.A., Canton, MA

NYSE SYMBOL GLW
Rec. Pr. 18.92 (5/31/01)

CORNING INC.

YIELD 1.3%
P/E RATIO 41.1

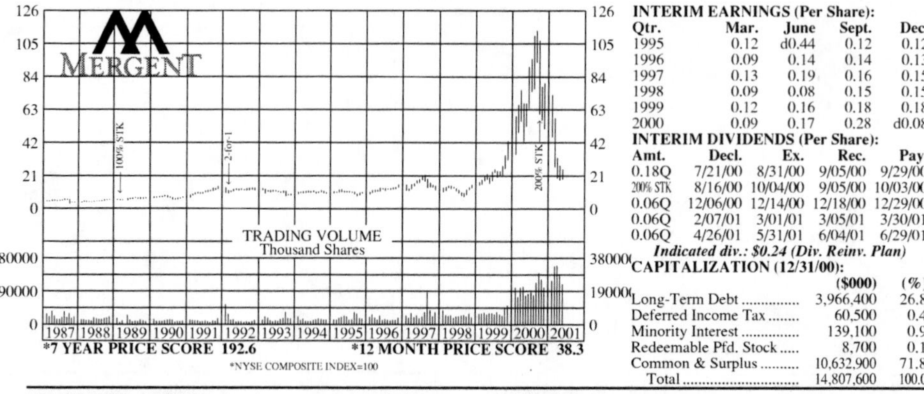

*7 YEAR PRICE SCORE 192.6 *12 MONTH PRICE SCORE 38.3
*NYSE COMPOSITE INDEX=100

INTERIM EARNINGS (Per Share):

Qtr.	Mar.	June	Sept.	Dec.
1995	0.12	d0.44	0.12	0.12
1996	0.09	0.14	0.14	0.13
1997	0.13	0.19	0.16	0.15
1998	0.09	0.08	0.15	0.15
1999	0.12	0.16	0.18	0.18
2000	0.09	0.17	0.28	d0.08

INTERIM DIVIDENDS (Per Share):

Amt.	Decl.	Ex.	Rec.	Pay.
0.18Q	7/21/00	8/31/00	9/05/00	9/29/00
200% STK	8/16/00	10/04/00	9/05/00	10/03/00
0.06Q	12/06/00	12/14/00	12/18/00	12/29/00
0.06Q	2/07/01	3/01/01	3/05/01	3/30/01
0.06Q	4/26/01	5/31/01	6/04/01	6/29/01

Indicated div.: $0.24 (Div. Reinv. Plan)

CAPITALIZATION (12/31/00):

	($000)	(%)
Long-Term Debt	3,966,400	26.8
Deferred Income Tax	60,500	0.4
Minority Interest	139,100	0.9
Redeemable Pfd. Stock	8,700	0.1
Common & Surplus	10,632,900	71.8
Total	14,807,600	100.0

RECENT DEVELOPMENTS: For the year ended 12/31/00, net income from continuing operations was $409.5 million versus $511.0 million in 1999. Results for 2000 and 1999 included non-recurring charges of $245.0 million and $27.8 million, respectively. Results for 2000 also included acquisition-related charges of $462.6 million, while results for 1999 included a nonrecurring charge of $1.4 million. Total revenues rose 51.1% to $7.27 billion.

PROSPECTS: Near-term results are expected to be pressured by the slowing telecommunications market. The Company noted that the capital spending outlook for network carriers continues to soften and is now affecting all of its telecommunications businesses, including optical fiber. In response, GLW is accelerating its efforts to reduce spending and initiate workforce reductions, which as of the first quarter of 2001 totaled about 4,300.

BUSINESS

CORNING INCORPORATED is a global, technology-based corporation operating in three business segments. The telecommunications segment (72.1% of 2000 revenues) produces optical fiber and cable, optical hardware and equipment, photonic modules and components and optical networking devices for the worldwide telecommunications industry. The advanced materials segment (15.3%) manufactures specialized products with unique properties for customer applications utilizing glass, glass ceramic and polymer technologies. Businesses within this segment include environmental products, life science products, semiconductor materials and optical and lighting products. The information display segment (12.6%) manufactures glass panels and funnels for televisions and CRTs, liquid crystal display glass for flat panel displays and projection video lens assemblies. On 12/31/96, Corning spun off its health care services segment. On 4/1/98, Corning sold its consumer housewares business to an affiliate of Borden, Inc.

REVENUES

(12/31/2000)	($000)	(%)
Telecommunications	5,120,700	72.1
Advanced Materials	1,086,000	15.3
Information Display	894,100	12.6
Total	7,100,800	100.0

ANNUAL FINANCIAL DATA

	12/31/00	12/31/99	12/31/98	12/31/97	12/31/96	12/31/95	1/1/95
Earnings Per Share	**⑤ 0.46**	**④ 0.64**	**③ 0.46**	**0.62**	**② 0.50**	**① d0.08**	**① 0.44**
Cash Flow Per Share	**1.34**	**1.15**	**0.85**	**1.03**	**0.93**	**0.48**	**0.98**
Tang. Book Val. Per Share	**3.29**	**2.59**	**1.72**	**1.27**	**0.92**	**1.00**	**1.25**
Dividends Per Share	**0.24**	**0.24**	**0.24**	**0.24**	**0.24**	**0.24**	**0.23**
Dividend Payout %	**52.2**	**37.3**	**51.8**	**38.9**	**48.0**	**...**	**52.3**
INCOME STATEMENT (IN MILLIONS):							
Total Revenues	7,273.1	4,368.1	3,572.1	4,129.1	3,684.5	5,346.1	4,799.2
Costs & Expenses	5,198.5	3,245.9	2,722.1	3,006.7	2,801.9	4,348.8	3,853.4
Depreciation & Amort.	764.9	380.7	298.0	321.6	288.1	377.4	338.4
Operating Income	1,309.7	741.5	552.0	800.8	594.5	619.9	607.4
Net Interest Inc./(Exp.)	d106.6	d79.9	d56.7	d85.0	d69.1	d117.8	d110.4
Income Before Income Taxes	691.4	620.8	439.6	678.2	487.3	465.9	459.5
Income Taxes	407.1	188.6	132.8	227.2	163.2	154.7	170.1
Equity Earnings/Minority Int.	125.2	47.0	34.4	2.5	32.5	d348.3	d2.0
Net Income	⑤ 409.5	④ 476.9	③ 327.5	439.8	② 342.9	① d50.8	① 281.3
Cash Flow	1,174.4	857.6	625.5	761.4	631.0	326.6	619.7
Average Shs. Outstg. (000)	879,300	743,100	731,700	736,200	681,300	679,800	635,400
BALANCE SHEET (IN MILLIONS):							
Cash & Cash Equivalents	1,793.8	253.4	45.4	101.3	223.2	214.9	161.3
Total Current Assets	4,634.4	1,782.5	1,310.3	1,424.2	1,418.7	1,834.3	1,726.3
Net Property	4,679.0	3,103.1	2,684.9	2,427.6	1,977.7	2,031.6	1,890.6
Total Assets	17,525.7	6,012.2	4,981.9	4,811.4	4,321.3	5,987.1	6,022.7
Total Current Liabilities	1,948.7	1,906.5	1,279.3	1,017.3	861.4	1,311.1	1,141.8
Long-Term Obligations	3,966.4	1,288.7	998.3	1,134.1	1,208.5	1,393.0	1,405.6
Net Stockholders' Equity	10,632.9	2,227.2	1,505.6	1,246.5	961.1	2,103.0	2,263.0
Net Working Capital	2,685.7	d124.0	31.0	406.9	557.3	523.2	584.5
Year-end Shs. Outstg. (000)	1,000,000	736,200	694,500	694,800	686,100	689,400	684,600
STATISTICAL RECORD:							
Operating Profit Margin %	18.0	17.0	15.5	19.4	16.1	11.6	12.7
Net Profit Margin %	5.6	10.9	9.2	10.7	9.3	...	5.9
Return on Equity %	3.9	21.4	21.8	35.3	35.7	...	12.4
Return on Assets %	2.3	7.9	6.6	9.1	7.9	...	4.7
Debt/Total Assets %	22.6	21.4	20.0	23.6	28.0	23.3	23.3
Price Range	113.28-34.33	43.02-14.92	15.23-7.62	21.71-11.25	15.42-9.29	12.46-8.04	11.69-9.21
P/E Ratio	246.2-74.6	66.9-23.2	32.9-16.5	35.2-18.2	30.8-18.6	...	26.6-20.9
Average Yield %	0.3	0.8	2.1	1.5	1.9	2.3	2.2

Statistics are as originally reported. Adj. for 3-for-1 stk. split, 10/00 ① Incl. $40.5 mil aft.-tax restr. chrg. & $365.5 mil equity loss for Dow Corning invt., 1995; & $82.3 mil spec. chrg., 1994 ② Bef. loss fr. disc. ops. of $167.3 mil ③ Bef. loss fr. disc. ops. of $66.5 mil; incl. aft.-tax chrg. of $26.3 mil ④ Bef. loss fr. disc. ops. of $4.8 mil; incl. aft.-tax gain of $8.1 mil ⑤ Bef. loss fr. disc. ops. of $12.5 mil; incl. non-recurr. chrgs. of $707.6 mil

OFFICERS:
R. G. Ackerman, Chmn.
N. E. Garrity, Vice-Chmn.
J. W. Loose, Pres., C.E.O.

INVESTOR CONTACT: K. M. Dietz, Dir., Inv. Rel., (607) 974-8217

PRINCIPAL OFFICE: One Riverfront Plaza, Corning, NY 14831

TELEPHONE NUMBER: (607) 974-9000
FAX: (607) 974-8688
WEB: www.corning.com

NO. OF EMPLOYEES: 40,300 (avg.)

SHAREHOLDERS: 20,200

ANNUAL MEETING: In June

INCORPORATED: NY, Dec., 1936

INSTITUTIONAL HOLDINGS:
No. of Institutions: 719
Shares Held: 610,449,053
% Held: 65.6

INDUSTRY: Communications equipment, nec (SIC: 3669)

TRANSFER AGENT(S): Computershare Investor Services, Chicago, IL

NYSE SYMBOL CCR
Rec. Pr. 38.73 (5/31/01)

COUNTRYWIDE CREDIT INDUSTRIES

YIELD 1.0%
P/E RATIO 12.3

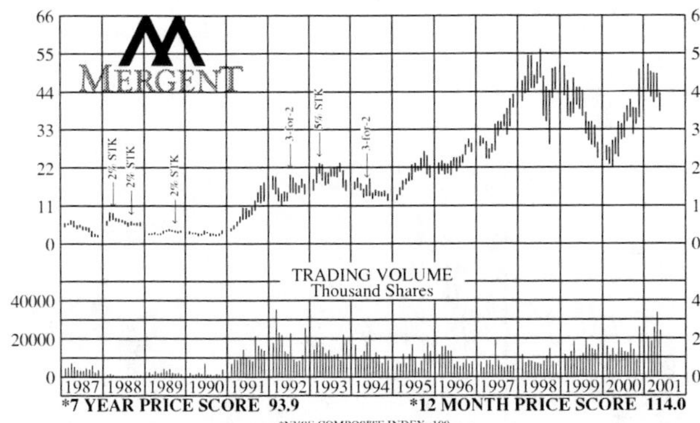

*7 YEAR PRICE SCORE 93.9 *12 MONTH PRICE SCORE 114.0

*NYSE COMPOSITE INDEX=100

INTERIM EARNINGS (Per Share):

Qtr.	May	Aug.	Nov.	Feb.
1996-97	0.58	0.60	0.62	0.63
1997-98	0.64	0.99	0.71	0.74
1998-99	0.78	0.81	0.84	0.86
1999-00	0.88	0.91	0.87	0.87
2000-01	0.72	0.77	0.80	...

INTERIM DIVIDENDS (Per Share):

Amt.	Decl.	Ex.	Rec.	Pay.
0.10Q	3/24/00	4/07/00	4/11/00	4/28/00
0.10Q	6/02/00	7/11/00	7/13/00	7/31/00
0.10Q	9/26/00	10/11/00	10/13/00	10/31/00
0.10Q	12/27/00	1/10/01	1/12/01	1/31/01
0.10Q	3/29/01	4/09/01	4/11/01	4/30/01

Indicated div.: $0.40

CAPITALIZATION (2/29/00):

	($000)	(%)
Long-Term Debt	9,782,625	70.2
Deferred Income Tax	1,272,311	9.1
Common & Surplus	2,887,879	20.7
Total	13,942,815	100.0

RECENT DEVELOPMENTS: For the quarter ended 11/30/00, net income declined 5.1% to $95.4 million versus $100.6 million in the prior-year quarter. Earnings for 1999 included a gain on the sale of a subsidiary of $4.4 million. Earnings were negatively affected by increased amortization and impairment. Total revenues amounted to $520.6 million, up 17.5% versus $443.1 million the year before. Loan production revenue grew 34.6% to $256.4 million. Net interest expense was $2.3 million in 2000 versus net interest income of $14.1 million a year earlier.

PROSPECTS: Going forward, the Company should benefit from the current market environment. Refinance activity has risen in recent months, creating growth in the Company's pipeline of loans-in-process. If refinance activity continues at these levels, the anticipated seasonal decline in purchase volume expected in the fourth fiscal quarter may be offset. The Company's consumer businesses, primarily driven by CCR's mortgage activities, should also remain strong due to escalating refinance mortgage activity.

BUSINESS

COUNTRYWIDE CREDIT INDUSTRIES, INC. is a holding company which, through its principal subsidiary, Countrywide Home Loans, Inc. (CHL) is engaged primarily in the mortgage banking business, and as such originates, purchases, sells and services mortgage loans. The Company's mortgage loans are principally prime credit quality first-lien mortgage loans secured by single-family residences. The Company also offers home equity loans both in conjunction with newly produced prime credit quality first mortgages and as a separate product. In addition, the Company offers sub-prime credit quality first-lien single-family mortgage loans. Also, the Company offers products and services complementary to its mortgage banking business.

ANNUAL FINANCIAL DATA

	2/29/00	2/28/99	2/28/98	2/28/97	2/29/96	2/28/95	2/28/94
Earnings Per Share	**2 3.52**	**3.29**	**1 3.09**	**2.44**	**1.95**	**0.96**	**1.97**
Cash Flow Per Share	**5.63**	**12.37**	**8.53**	**3.78**	**5.68**	**2.28**	**4.83**
Tang. Book Val. Per Share	...	...	...	...	...	...	**0.48**
Dividends Per Share	**0.38**	**0.32**	**0.32**	**0.32**	**0.32**	**0.31**	**0.27**
Dividend Payout %	**10.8**	**9.7**	**10.4**	**13.1**	**16.4**	**32.6**	**13.6**
INCOME STATEMENT (IN MILLIONS):							
Total Revenues	2,018.7	1,979.0	1,509.0	1,112.5	860.7	602.7	755.6
Costs & Expenses	1,140.4	284.4	336.7	548.8	161.2	333.5	198.6
Depreciation & Amort.	247.0	1,062.8	606.7	141.8	373.4	121.8	257.9
Operating Income	631.2	631.8	565.5	421.9	326.2	147.3	299.1
Income Before Income Taxes	631.2	631.8	565.5	421.9	326.2	147.3	299.1
Income Taxes	221.0	246.4	220.6	164.5	130.5	58.9	119.6
Net Income	2 410.2	385.4	1 345.0	257.4	195.7	88.4	179.5
Cash Flow	657.3	1,448.2	951.7	399.1	569.1	210.2	436.6
Average Shs. Outstg. (000)	116,688	117,045	111,526	105,677	100,270	92,087	90,501
BALANCE SHEET (IN MILLIONS):							
Cash & Cash Equivalents	2,043.9	58.7	10.7	18.3	16.4	17.6	4.0
Total Current Assets	2,043.9	58.7	10.7	1,470.2	929.1	958.6	643.3
Net Property	410.9	311.7	226.3	190.1	141.0	145.6	145.6
Total Assets	15,822.3	15,648.3	12,219.2	8,089.3	8,657.7	5,579.7	5,585.5
Total Current Liabilities	1,379.5	1,601.4	1,282.9	828.8	743.2	305.3	537.6
Long-Term Obligations	9,782.6	9,935.8	7,475.2	4,713.3	6,097.5	3,963.1	3,859.2
Net Stockholders' Equity	2,887.9	2,518.9	2,087.9	1,611.5	1,319.8	942.6	880.1
Net Working Capital	664.4	d1,542.7	d1,272.2	641.5	185.9	653.3	105.7
Year-end Shs. Outstg. (000)	113,463	112,619	109,206	106,096	102,242	91,370	91,064
STATISTICAL RECORD:							
Operating Profit Margin %	31.3	31.9	37.5	37.9	37.9	24.4	39.6
Net Profit Margin %	20.3	19.5	22.9	23.1	22.7	14.7	23.8
Return on Equity %	14.2	15.3	16.5	16.0	14.8	9.4	20.4
Return on Assets %	2.6	2.5	2.8	3.2	2.3	1.6	3.2
Debt/Total Assets %	61.8	63.5	61.2	58.3	70.4	71.0	69.1
Price Range	51.44-24.63	56.25-28.63	43.25-24.38	30.25-19.75	26.75-12.50	19.08-12.38	23.33-15.24
P/E Ratio	14.6-7.0	17.1-8.7	14.0-7.9	12.4-8.1	13.7-6.4	19.9-12.9	11.8-7.7
Average Yield %	1.0	0.8	0.9	1.3	1.6	2.0	1.4

Statistics are as originally reported. Adj. for stk. splits: 3-for-2, 5/94 1 Incl. non-recurr. credit $57.4 mill. 2 Incl. non-recurr. gain $25.0 mill.

OFFICERS:
A. R. Mozilo, Chmn., Pres., C.E.O.
C. M. Garcia, C.F.O., C.A.O.,
S. L. Kurland, C.O.O.

INVESTOR CONTACT: Nancy Parker, Corp. V.P.; Inv. Rel., (818) 225-3550

PRINCIPAL OFFICE: 4500 Park Granada, Calabasas, CA 91302

TELEPHONE NUMBER: (818) 225-3000
FAX: (818) 304-5979
WEB: www.countrywide.com
NO. OF EMPLOYEES: 10,572 (avg.)
SHAREHOLDERS: 2,174
ANNUAL MEETING: In July
INCORPORATED: NY, March, 1969; reincorp., DE.

INSTITUTIONAL HOLDINGS:
No. of Institutions: 291
Shares Held: 97,974,312
% Held: 83.2

INDUSTRY: Mortgage bankers and correspondents (SIC: 6162)

TRANSFER AGENT(S): Bank of New York, New York, NY

NYSE SYMBOL COV
Rec. Pr. 21.77 (5/31/01)

COVANTA ENERGY CORPORATION

YIELD ...
P/E RATIO ...

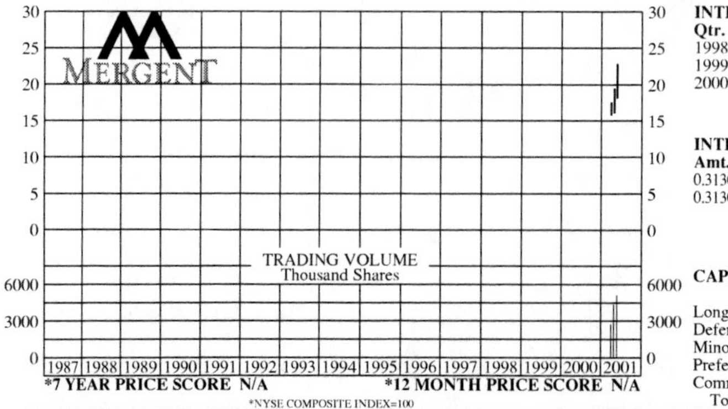

INTERIM EARNINGS (Per Share):

Qtr.	Mar.	June	Sept.	Dec.
1998	0.23	0.52	0.55	0.40
1999	0.21	0.49	0.17	d1.31
2000	d0.08	d0.21	0.05	d1.49

INTERIM DIVIDENDS (Per Share):

Amt.	Decl.	Ex.	Rec.	Pay.
0.313Q	1/21/99	3/11/99	3/15/99	4/05/99
0.313Q	5/20/99	6/10/99	6/14/99	7/06/99

Div. payments suspended.

CAPITALIZATION (12/31/00):

	($000)	(%)
Long-Term Debt	1,749,164	75.0
Deferred Income Tax	315,931	13.6
Minority Interest	34,290	1.5
Preferred Stock	36	0.0
Common & Surplus	231,520	9.9
Total	2,330,941	100.0

RECENT DEVELOPMENTS: For the year ended 12/31/00, COV reported a loss from continuing operations of $85.6 million versus a loss of $36.3 million, before an accounting charge of $3.8 million, in 1999. Earnings for 2000 and 1999 excluded losses of $143.7 million and $41.9 million, respectively, from discontinued operations, and included net nonrecurring charges of $120.7 million and $21.2 million, respectively. Revenues fell 0.7% to $1.02 billion.

PROSPECTS: In 2001, the Company expects its core energy business will generate earnings per share in the range of $1.18 to $1.22, and base earnings before interest and taxes in the range of $120.0 million to $123.0 million. COV should benefit from a full year's operations of the Quezon facility, and partial year operations of two new generating plants located in Asia, and one plant located in Europe.

BUSINESS

COVANTA ENERGY CORPORATION (formerly Ogden Corporation) is a global developer, owner and operator of independent power projects and related infrastructure. The Company's independent power business develops, structures, owns, operates and maintains projects that generate power for sale to utilities and industrial users worldwide. The Company's waste-to-energy facilities convert municipal solid waste into energy for numerous communities, predominantly in the U.S. The Company also offers single-source design/build/operate capabilities for water and wastewater treatment infrastructures. As of 3/8/01, OG has sold a large majority of its entertainment and aviation businesses, which are being accounted for as discontinued operations.

QUARTERLY DATA

(12/31/2000)($000)	Rev	Inc
1st Quarter	239,016	(29,484)
2nd Quarter	264,982	(76,903)
3rd Quarter	254,737	(34,371)
4th Quarter	261,267	(88,527)

ANNUAL FINANCIAL DATA

	12/31/00	12/31/99	12/31/98	12/31/97	12/31/96	12/31/95	12/31/94
Earnings Per Share	**[5] d1.73**	**[1][4] d0.74**	**[3] 1.70**	**[3] 1.49**	**[3] 1.30**	**[2] 0.15**	**[1] 1.55**
Cash Flow Per Share	**0.50**	**1.19**	**3.75**	**3.36**	**3.62**	**2.37**	**3.63**
Tang. Book Val. Per Share	**2.58**	**6.64**	**5.85**	**7.42**	**6.64**	**6.29**	**7.45**
Dividends Per Share	...	**0.94**	**1.25**	**1.25**	**1.25**	**1.25**	**1.25**
Dividend Payout %	...	...	**73.5**	**83.9**	**96.1**	**832.8**	**80.6**
INCOME STATEMENT (IN MILLIONS):							
Total Revenues	1,020.0	1,000.4	1,692.4	1,749.7	2,031.1	2,185.0	2,110.2
Costs & Expenses	989.3	928.1	1,428.8	1,507.6	1,797.6	2,026.0	1,870.2
Depreciation & Amort.	110.3	94.9	114.3	104.4	115.3	109.6	90.5
Operating Income	d79.6	d22.6	149.2	137.7	118.2	49.4	149.5
Net Interest Inc./(Exp.)	d35.3	d30.7	d15.9	d8.6	d13.4	d15.4	d10.9
Income Before Income Taxes	d115.0	d37.0	153.0	130.8	109.6	40.5	139.4
Income Taxes	cr34.1	cr6.9	61.8	53.1	46.2	34.2	61.9
Net Income	[5] d85.6	[1][4] d36.3	[3] 87.0	[3] 75.7	[3] 64.5	[2] 7.4	[1] 67.8
Cash Flow	24.6	58.5	201.2	179.9	179.6	116.9	158.2
Average Shs. Outstg. (000)	49,534	49,235	53,674	53,617	49,663	49,385	43,610
BALANCE SHEET (IN MILLIONS):							
Cash & Cash Equivalents	371.0	204.7	416.4	289.6	242.2	206.0	308.7
Total Current Assets	803.3	1,179.5	954.4	832.1	886.2	926.4	995.9
Net Property	1,789.4	1,841.8	1,987.6	1,947.5	1,851.3	1,879.2	1,884.8
Total Assets	3,295.5	3,727.1	3,922.8	3,639.3	3,597.5	3,652.7	3,644.9
Total Current Liabilities	633.5	675.3	624.8	525.9	541.5	510.5	512.9
Long-Term Obligations	1,749.2	1,884.4	1,907.5	1,927.3	1,958.7	2,044.2	2,047.0
Net Stockholders' Equity	231.6	443.1	549.1	566.1	550.9	547.0	596.8
Net Working Capital	169.9	504.2	329.7	306.1	344.6	415.8	483.0
Year-end Shs. Outstg. (000)	49,645	49,468	48,946	47,160	49,775	49,468	48,777
STATISTICAL RECORD:							
Operating Profit Margin %	...	...	8.8	7.9	5.8	2.3	7.1
Net Profit Margin %	...	...	5.1	4.3	3.2	0.3	3.2
Return on Equity %	...	...	15.8	13.4	11.7	1.4	11.4
Return on Assets %	...	...	2.2	2.1	1.8	0.2	1.9
Debt/Total Assets %	53.1	50.6	48.6	53.0	54.4	56.0	56.2
Price Range	17.50-7.25	28.00-8.44	32.50-23.00	28.31-18.38	23.88-17.63	24.13-18.38	24.38-17.75
P/E Ratio	...	...	19.1-13.5	19.0-12.3	18.4-13.6	160.7-122.4	15.7-11.5
Average Yield %	...	5.1	4.5	5.4	6.0	5.9	5.9

Statistics are as originally reported. [1] Bef. acct. chrg. of $3.8 mill., 1999; $1.5 mill., 1994; $5.3 mill., 1993; & $5.2 mill., 1992. [2] Incl. after-tax chrgs. of $48.9 mill. [3] Incl. pre-tax gain fr. the sale of businesses: $49.2 mill., 1998; $34.5 mill., 1997; $13.2 mill., 1996. [4] Bef. disc. opers. loss of $41.9 mill. & incl. a net chrg. of $3.4 mill. [5] Bef. disc. opers. loss of $128.9 mill.; incl. non-recurr. chrgs. of $34.3 mill.

OFFICERS:
S. G. Mackin, Pres., C.E.O.
E. W. Moneypenny, Exec. V.P., C.F.O.
L. M. Walters, V.P., Treas.
L. H. Coit, Sr. V.P., Gen. Couns.

INVESTOR CONTACT: Louise M. Walters, Investor Relations, (973) 882-7260

PRINCIPAL OFFICE: 40 Lane Road, Fairfield, NJ 07004

TELEPHONE NUMBER: (973) 882-9000
FAX: (973) 882-9121
WEB: www.covantaenergy.com

NO. OF EMPLOYEES: 4,700 (approx.)

SHAREHOLDERS: 5,123 (approx.); 699 (approx. pref.)

ANNUAL MEETING: In May

INCORPORATED: DE, Aug., 1939

INSTITUTIONAL HOLDINGS:
No. of Institutions: 139
Shares Held: 34,159,148
% Held: 68.7

INDUSTRY: Electric services (SIC: 4911)

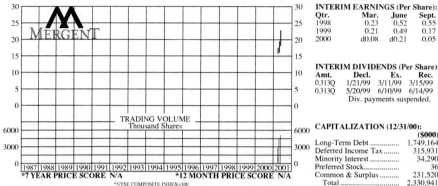

TRANSFER AGENT(S): Mellon Investor Services, Ridgefield Park, NJ

NYSE SYMBOL COX
Rec. Pr. 43.25 (5/31/01)

COX COMMUNICATIONS, INC.

YIELD	...
P/E RATIO	13.8

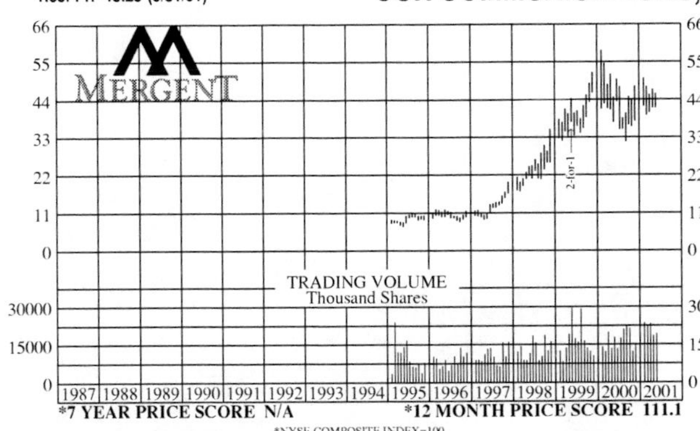

*7 YEAR PRICE SCORE N/A *12 MONTH PRICE SCORE 111.1

*NYSE COMPOSITE INDEX=100

INTERIM EARNINGS (Per Share):

Qtr.	Mar.	June	Sept.	Dec.
1996	0.02	0.05	d0.05	d0.11
1997	d0.07	0.12	d0.15	d0.15
1998	d0.19	d0.02	1.95	0.56
1999	0.45	0.90	0.02	0.18
2000	1.74	0.15	1.37	d0.12

INTERIM DIVIDENDS (Per Share):

Amt.	Decl.	Ex.	Rec.	Pay.
No dividends paid.				

CAPITALIZATION (12/31/00):

	($000)	(%)
Long-Term Debt	8,543,762	44.9
Minority Interest	126,447	0.7
Redeemable Pfd. Stock	1,155,411	6.1
Preferred Stock	4,836	0.0
Common & Surplus	9,211,437	48.4
Total	19,041,893	100.0

RECENT DEVELOPMENTS: For the year ended 12/31/00, net income more than doubled to $1.93 billion compared with $881.9 million in 1999. Results for 1999 included a gain on the sale and exchange of cable television systems of $77.4 million. Results for 2000 and 1999 included a net gain on investments of $3.28 billion and $1.57 billion, respectively. Total revenues were $3.51 billion, up 51.3% versus $2.32 billion a year earlier. Video revenues improved 44.7% to $2.77 billion.

PROSPECTS: Going forward, the Company will continue to focus on implementing its core business strategy, which has driven results and sustained growth in COX's advance telecommunications services. In addition, the Company will continue to expand its operations to meet market needs and rising consumer demand. The Company expects operating cash flow to improve by 12.0% to 13.0% in 2001 versus 2000, and total revenues to increase by 14.0% to 16.0% in 2001.

BUSINESS

COX COMMUNICATIONS, INC. serves approximately 6.2 million customers nationwide, making COX the nation's fifth largest cable television company. A full-service provider of telecommunications products, the Company offers a variety of services, including COX CABLE; local and long distance telephone services under the COX DIGITAL TELEPHONE brand; high-speed Internet access under the brands COX@HOME, ROAD RUNNER and COX EXPRESS; advanced digital video programming services under the COX DIGITAL CABLE brand; and commercial voice and data services via COX BUSINESS SERVICES. The Company is an investor in telecommunications companies including Sprint PCS and Excite@Home, as well as programming networks including Discovery Channel, The Learning Channel, Outdoor Life and Speedvision.

ANNUAL FINANCIAL DATA

	12/31/00	12/31/99	12/31/98	12/31/97	12/31/96	12/31/95	12/31/94
Earnings Per Share	**3.16**	**1.51**	**1 2.30**	**1 d0.25**	**1 d0.09**	...	...
Cash Flow Per Share	**5.20**	**2.74**	**3.13**	**0.50**	**0.52**	...	...
Tang. Book Val. Per Share	...	**2.25**	**2.55**	...	...	...	...
INCOME STATEMENT (IN MILLIONS):							
Total Revenues	3,506.9	2,318.1	1,716.8	1,610.4	1,460.3	1,286.2	736.3
Costs & Expenses	2,129.6	1,339.6	1,057.7	1,000.5	903.4	792.9	467.8
Depreciation & Amort.	1,236.5	715.7	457.7	404.5	335.2	267.3	128.8
Operating Income	140.8	262.9	201.4	205.3	221.7	226.0	139.8
Net Interest Inc./(Exp.)	d550.8	d305.7	d223.3	d202.1	d146.1	d132.3	d46.1
Income Before Income Taxes	2,872.1	1,480.5	2,093.5	d190.0	d28.5	203.7	52.3
Income Taxes	877.0	580.0	822.8	cr53.5	23.0	99.9	25.8
Equity Earnings/Minority Int.	d69.8	d18.6	...	...	...	...	...
Net Income	1,925.3	881.9	1 1,270.7	1 d136.5	1 d51.6	103.8	26.6
Cash Flow	3,161.7	1,597.6	1,728.3	268.0	283.6	371.1	155.3
Average Shs. Outstg. (000)	608,549	583,082	552,422	541,002	540,482	...	...
BALANCE SHEET (IN MILLIONS):							
Cash & Cash Equivalents	78.4	33.3	30.6	232.5	42.3	39.2	3.3
Total Current Assets	436.8	293.8	196.7	376.5	164.9	157.1	45.2
Net Property	5,916.4	4,038.2	2,652.2	1,979.1	1,531.8	1,213.9	664.3
Total Assets	24,720.8	26,614.5	12,878.1	6,556.6	5,784.6	5,555.3	1,874.7
Total Current Liabilities	5,306.8	7,147.7	3,183.6	939.6	515.3	490.2	185.9
Long-Term Obligations	8,543.8	6,375.8	3,920.2	3,148.8	2,823.9	2,392.7	750.0
Net Stockholders' Equity	9,216.3	11,535.6	5,376.6	2,357.3	2,261.3	2,332.0	834.8
Net Working Capital	d4,870.1	d6,853.8	d2,986.9	d563.0	d350.4	d333.2	d140.7
Year-end Shs. Outstg. (000)	599,825	603,767	554,710	542,150	540,526	540,328	200
STATISTICAL RECORD:							
Operating Profit Margin %	4.0	11.3	11.7	12.7	15.2	17.6	19.0
Net Profit Margin %	54.9	38.0	74.0	...	...	8.1	3.6
Return on Equity %	20.9	7.6	23.6	...	...	4.5	3.2
Return on Assets %	7.8	3.3	9.9	...	...	1.9	1.4
Debt/Total Assets %	34.6	24.0	30.4	48.0	48.8	43.1	40.0
Price Range	58.38-31.69	52.00-32.00	35.38-17.19	19.97-9.00	12.06-8.31	10.75-7.00	...
P/E Ratio	18.5-10.0	34.4-21.2	15.4-7.5	...	...	...	...

Statistics are as originally reported. Adj. for stk. split: 2-for-1, 12/99 1 Incl. gain on issuance of stk. by affiliated companies: 1998, $165.3 mill.; 1997, $90;8 mill., 1996, $50.1 mill.

OFFICERS:
J. C. Kennedy, Chmn.
J. O. Robbins, Pres., C.E.O.
J. W. Hayes, Exec. V.P., C.F.O.

INVESTOR CONTACT: Frank Loomans, Inv. Relations, (404) 843-5377

PRINCIPAL OFFICE: 1400 Lake Hearn Drive NE, Atlanta, GA 30319

TELEPHONE NUMBER: (404) 843-5000
FAX: (404) 843-5030
WEB: www.cox.com

NO. OF EMPLOYEES: 19,000 (approx.)

SHAREHOLDERS: 6,290 (class A common)

ANNUAL MEETING: In May

INCORPORATED: DE, May, 1994

INSTITUTIONAL HOLDINGS:
No. of Institutions: 298
Shares Held: 144,632,711
% Held: 24.1

INDUSTRY: Cable and other pay TV services (SIC: 4841)

TRANSFER AGENT(S): First Chicago Trust Company of New York, Jersey City, NJ

NYSE SYMBOL CXR
Rec. Pr. 25.80 (4/30/01)

COX RADIO, INC.

YIELD	...
P/E RATIO	7.9

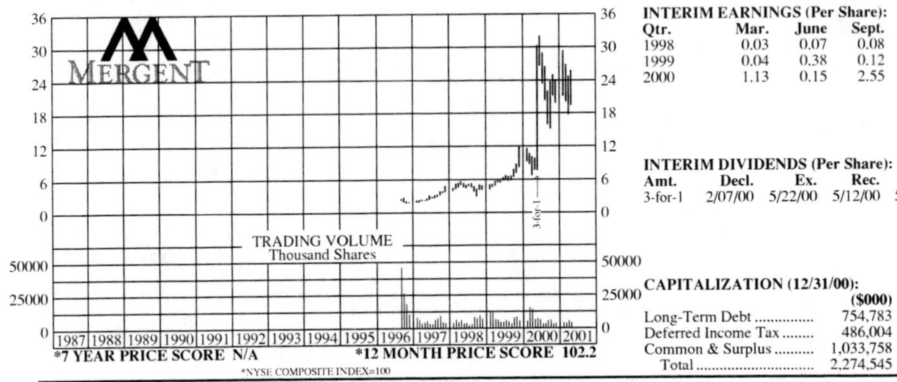

*7 YEAR PRICE SCORE N/A *12 MONTH PRICE SCORE 102.2

*NYSE COMPOSITE INDEX=100

INTERIM EARNINGS (Per Share):

Qtr.	Mar.	June	Sept.	Dec.
1998	0.03	0.07	0.08	0.08
1999	0.04	0.38	0.12	0.10
2000	1.13	0.15	2.55	0.05

INTERIM DIVIDENDS (Per Share):

Amt.	Decl.	Ex.	Rec.	Pay.
3-for-1	2/07/00	5/22/00	5/12/00	5/19/00

CAPITALIZATION (12/31/00):

	($000)	(%)
Long-Term Debt	754,783	33.2
Deferred Income Tax	486,004	21.4
Common & Surplus	1,033,758	45.4
Total	2,274,545	100.0

RECENT DEVELOPMENTS: For the year ended 12/31/00, net income skyrocketed to $305.9 million compared with $55.3 million in the corresponding year. Results for 2000 included an unusual after-tax gain of $244.6 million stemming from a transaction in which CXR exchanged two Los Angeles stations for 13 stations in Miami, Atlanta, Jacksonville and Stamford/Norwalk, Connecticut. Total revenues increased 22.9% to $369.4 million from $300.5 million in 1999.

PROSPECTS: As it integrates recent acquisitions, the Company expects net revenue growth in 2001 in the range of 10.0% and 12.0% over 2000. In addition, the Company anticipates cash flow per share growth of between 15.0% and 20.0% over 2000. Also, the Company expects accelerating net revenue and broadcast cash flow growth for the second half of 2001. In February 2001, the Company acquired WDYL-FM of Richmond, VA and WJMZ-FM and WPEK-FM of Greenville, SC.

BUSINESS

COX RADIO, INC. is the fourth-largest radio broadcasting company in the United States, based on net revenues. The Company, upon completion of all pending transactions, will own or operate, or provide sales and marketing services, for 83 stations (68 FM and 15 AM) clustered in 18 markets, including major markets such as Atlanta, Houston, Miami, Tampa, Orlando and San Antonio. The Company is an indirect majority-owned subsidiary of Cox Enterprises, Inc. Cox Enterprises indirectly owns approximately 63% of the Company's common stock and has approximately 94% of the voting power in the Company as of 12/31/00.

REVENUES

(12/31/2000)	($000)	(%)
Local	267,563	72.4
National	84,499	22.9
Other	17,342	4.7
Total	369,404	100.0

ANNUAL FINANCIAL DATA

	12/31/00	12/31/99	12/31/98	12/31/97	12/31/96	12/31/95	12/31/94
Earnings Per Share	**1 3.26**	**0.64**	**0.27**	**0.58**	**0.23**	**0.02**	...
Cash Flow Per Share	**3.71**	**0.97**	**0.54**	**0.79**	**0.35**	**0.19**	...
Tang. Book Val. Per Share	...	...	...	...	**1.15**	...	...
INCOME STATEMENT (IN MILLIONS):							
Total Revenues	369.4	300.5	261.2	199.6	132.9	123.6	111.5
Costs & Expenses	cr239.6	153.4	175.4	185.8	99.2	95.8	79.0
Depreciation & Amort.	43.0	29.1	23.4	17.5	8.1	7.2	7.0
Operating Income	566.0	117.9	62.4	45.5	27.6	20.5	25.6
Net Interest Inc./(Exp.)	d32.5	d22.8	...	...	...	...	...
Income Before Income Taxes	534.5	94.8	45.1	84.5	24.7	14.4	20.1
Income Taxes	228.5	39.6	22.0	34.8	9.8	6.2	8.9
Net Income	1 305.9	55.3	23.0	49.7	14.9	8.2	11.2
Cash Flow	348.9	84.4	46.4	d31.1	19.0	15.4	18.2
Average Shs. Outstg. (000)	93,936	86,637	86,556	85,482	65,286	81,570	...
BALANCE SHEET (IN MILLIONS):							
Cash & Cash Equivalents	7.0	14.7	6.5	6.2	10.6	1.7	1.9
Total Current Assets	107.2	93.9	68.1	60.7	43.7	35.6	33.5
Net Property	75.6	56.6	51.9	46.1	27.1	28.0	26.3
Total Assets	2,317.8	986.6	753.1	654.6	261.7	191.8	180.0
Total Current Liabilities	40.8	42.1	29.2	27.2	14.8	13.0	12.5
Long-Term Obligations	754.8	437.2	300.2	235.7	...	125.1	120.3
Net Stockholders' Equity	1,033.8	378.7	313.0	287.3	235.8	47.2	40.4
Net Working Capital	66.4	51.8	38.9	33.5	28.9	22.6	21.0
Year-end Shs. Outstg. (000)	99,427	86,628	85,650	85,227	84,945	1,800	1,800
STATISTICAL RECORD:							
Operating Profit Margin %	153.2	39.2	23.9	22.8	20.8	16.6	22.9
Net Profit Margin %	82.8	18.4	8.8	24.9	11.2	6.6	10.0
Return on Equity %	29.6	14.6	7.4	17.3	6.3	17.3	27.7
Return on Assets %	13.2	5.6	3.1	7.6	5.7	4.3	6.2
Debt/Total Assets %	32.6	44.3	39.9	36.0	...	65.2	66.8
Price Range	32.00-6.72	11.89-4.15	5.71-2.92	4.83-1.89	2.74-1.72	...	...
P/E Ratio	9.8-2.1	18.7-6.5	21.4-10.9	8.3-3.2	11.9-7.5	...	...

Statistics are as originally reported. Adj. for 3-for-1 stk. spl., 5/00 1 Incl. after-tax gain $244.6 mill.

OFFICERS:
D. E. Easterly, Chmn.
R. F. Neil, Pres., C.E.O.
N. Johnston, V.P., C.F.O.

INVESTOR CONTACT: Charles Odom, (404) 843-5000

PRINCIPAL OFFICE: 1400 Lake Hearn Drive, Atlanta, GA 30319

TELEPHONE NUMBER: (404) 843-5000
FAX: (404) 843-5890
WEB: www.coxradio.com

NO. OF EMPLOYEES: 1,616 full-time; 641 part-time

SHAREHOLDERS: 345 (1 class B)

ANNUAL MEETING: In May

INCORPORATED: DE, 1996

INSTITUTIONAL HOLDINGS:
No. of Institutions: 100
Shares Held: 35,007,300
% Held: 35.2

INDUSTRY: Radio broadcasting stations (SIC: 4832)

TRANSFER AGENT(S): First Chicago Trust Company of New York, Jersey City, NJ

NYSE SYMBOL CPY
Rec. Pr. 19.70 (5/31/01)

CPI CORP.

YIELD 2.8%
P/E RATIO 10.4

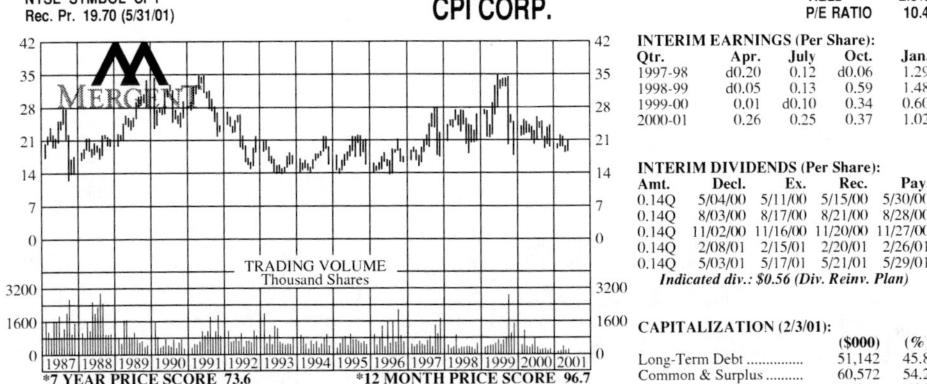

*7 YEAR PRICE SCORE 73.6 *12 MONTH PRICE SCORE 96.7
*NYSE COMPOSITE INDEX=100

INTERIM EARNINGS (Per Share):

Qtr.	Apr.	July	Oct.	Jan.
1997-98	d0.20	0.12	d0.06	1.29
1998-99	d0.05	0.13	0.59	1.48
1999-00	0.01	d0.10	0.34	0.60
2000-01	0.26	0.25	0.37	1.02

INTERIM DIVIDENDS (Per Share):

Amt.	Decl.	Ex.	Rec.	Pay.
0.14Q	5/04/00	5/11/00	5/15/00	5/30/00
0.14Q	8/03/00	8/17/00	8/21/00	8/28/00
0.14Q	11/02/00	11/16/00	11/20/00	11/27/00
0.14Q	2/08/01	2/15/01	2/20/01	2/26/01
0.14Q	5/03/01	5/17/01	5/21/01	5/29/01

Indicated div.: $0.56 (Div. Reinv. Plan)

CAPITALIZATION (2/3/01):

	($000)	(%)
Long-Term Debt	51,142	45.8
Common & Surplus	60,572	54.2
Total	111,714	100.0

RECENT DEVELOPMENTS: For the twelve months ended 2/3/01, the Company reported income from continuing operations of $15.1 million compared with income from continuing operations of $3.2 million in 1999. Results for 2000 and 1999 excluded net losses of $4.1 million and $6.4 million from discontinued operations, respectively. Total net sales inched up 0.4% to $320.4 million from $319.1 million the year before.

PROSPECTS: On 4/24/01, the Company entered into an agreement to sell its Wall Decor business, operating under the name "Prints Plus", to TRU Retail, Inc., a corporation formed by the management of Prints Plus, for approximately $4.0 million in cash and $12.0 million in 9.0% preferred stock of the new wall decor company. The parties expect to complete the transaction in the Summer of 2001. The Wall Decor segment has been treated as a discontinued operation since 1999.

BUSINESS

CPI CORP. develops and markets consumer services and related products through a network of small retail locations. Within the Portraits Studio segment, the Company operates 1,027 Sears Portrait Studios throughout the U.S., Canada and Puerto Rico as of 2/3/001. Sears Portrait Studios provide professional portraits of babies, children, adults and family groups. The Company also provides photo accessories, such as picture frames and photo albums, and services that include the Portrait PreviewSystem® and Smile Savers Plan®. In 2000, the Company formed a wholly-owned subsidiary, Centrics Technology, Inc., that is committed to the full-time development of business computer software for both the Portrait Studio segment and other third-party business, and is treating this business as a separate segment, the Technology Development Segment. Within the Technology Development segment, the Company markets an Internet-based mail-order photofinishing business under the name searsphoto.com and offers software programs primarily for retail service industry use, software consulting and custom software development under the name Centrics Technology, Inc.

ANNUAL FINANCIAL DATA

	2/3/01	2/5/00	2/6/99	2/7/98	2/1/97	2/3/96	2/4/95
Earnings Per Share	**[5] 1.87**	**[5] 0.32**	**[4] 2.15**	**[4] 1.07**	**[3] 1.06**	**[2][3] 1.26**	**[1] 1.05**
Cash Flow Per Share	**4.89**	**2.67**	**4.29**	**3.36**	**3.87**	**4.19**	**3.74**
Tang. Book Val. Per Share	**3.39**	**9.28**	**6.57**	**5.83**	**11.90**	**8.88**	**8.19**
Dividends Per Share	**0.56**	**0.56**	**0.56**	**0.56**	**0.56**	**0.56**	**0.56**
Dividend Payout %	**29.9**	**174.9**	**26.0**	**52.3**	**52.8**	**44.4**	**53.3**
INCOME STATEMENT (IN THOUSANDS):							
Total Revenues	320,380	319,135	389,510	366,701	467,034	526,651	533,155
Costs & Expenses	269,873	288,901	338,215	311,348	408,716	453,972	467,866
Depreciation & Amort.	24,382	23,499	21,935	27,155	37,946	41,007	37,896
Operating Income	26,125	6,735	29,360	28,198	20,372	31,672	27,393
Net Interest Inc./(Exp.)	d2,854	d1,693	d918	d2,001	d3,769	d4,597	d4,338
Income Before Income Taxes	23,176	4,918	33,759	20,897	22,799	27,638	23,528
Income Taxes	8,112	1,721	11,815	8,184	8,436	9,979	8,706
Net Income	[5] 15,064	[5] 3,197	[4] 21,944	[4] 12,713	[3] 14,363	[2][3] 17,659	[1] 14,822
Cash Flow	39,446	26,696	43,879	39,868	52,309	58,666	52,718
Average Shs. Outstg.	8,075	10,010	10,217	11,871	13,518	13,989	14,101
BALANCE SHEET (IN THOUSANDS):							
Cash & Cash Equivalents	38,820	49,546	76,000	15,292	21,923	8,331	14,350
Total Current Assets	70,402	81,464	113,671	94,405	63,685	72,825	81,982
Net Property	72,603	84,923	111,148	124,718	130,762	167,944	159,126
Total Assets	175,912	199,263	234,693	228,761	246,720	300,488	300,481
Total Current Liabilities	49,562	42,094	35,776	47,442	50,847	64,013	69,767
Long-Term Obligations	51,142	59,637	59,559	59,482	44,888	54,804	59,742
Net Stockholders' Equity	60,572	81,257	116,516	102,092	139,525	174,168	169,513
Net Working Capital	20,840	39,370	77,895	46,963	12,838	8,812	12,215
Year-end Shs. Outstg.	17,886	8,761	17,730	17,499	11,686	13,867	13,821
STATISTICAL RECORD:							
Operating Profit Margin %	8.2	2.1	7.5	7.7	4.4	6.0	5.1
Net Profit Margin %	4.7	1.0	5.6	3.5	3.1	3.4	2.8
Return on Equity %	24.9	3.9	18.8	12.5	10.3	10.1	8.7
Return on Assets %	8.6	1.6	9.4	5.6	5.8	5.9	4.9
Debt/Total Assets %	29.1	29.9	25.4	26.0	18.2	18.2	19.9
Price Range	25.94-19.13	34.88-17.69	27.44-18.13	28.00-15.44	21.25-13.63	22.13-13.75	21.88-14.00
P/E Ratio	13.9-10.2	109.0-55.3	12.8-8.4	26.2-14.4	20.0-12.9	17.6-10.9	20.8-13.3
Average Yield %	2.5	2.1	2.5	2.6	3.2	3.1	3.1

Statistics are as originally reported. [1] Excl. net loss of $3.3 mill. fr. disc. opers. [2] Incl. a gain of $6.2 mill. fr. the sale of its 51% interest in Fox Studio, Inc. [3] Incl. a loss of $485,000 on CPY's joint venture, 1996; $1.8 mill., 1997 & an after-tax chg. of $2.6 mill. rel to the sale of CPY's 49% int. in the Fox Studio, Inc. joint venture. [4] Incl. a pre-tax gains of $1.2 mill. in 1998, $5.0 mill. in 1999. [5] Bef. loss fr. disc. opers. of $4.1 mill., 2001; $6.4 mill., 2000.

OFFICERS:
J. D. Pierson, Chmn., C.E.O.
R. Isaak, Pres.
B. C. Arthur, Exec. V.P., Treas.
J. E. Nelson, Sec., Gen. Couns.

INVESTOR CONTACT: Investor Relations, (314) 231-1575

PRINCIPAL OFFICE: 1706 Washington Avenue, St. Louis, MO 63103-1790

TELEPHONE NUMBER: (314) 231-1575
FAX: (314) 231-8150
WEB: www.cpicorp.com

NO. OF EMPLOYEES: 2,700 full-time; 4,500 part-time

SHAREHOLDERS: 1,908 (approx.)

ANNUAL MEETING: In June

INCORPORATED: DE, Apr., 1982

INSTITUTIONAL HOLDINGS:
No. of Institutions: 60
Shares Held: 6,144,271
% Held: 79.9

INDUSTRY: Photographic studios, portrait (SIC: 7221)

TRANSFER AGENT(S): Computershare Investor Services, Chicago, IL

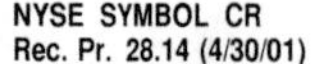
NYSE SYMBOL CR
Rec. Pr. 28.14 (4/30/01)

CRANE CO.

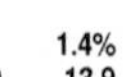
YIELD 1.4%
P/E RATIO 13.9

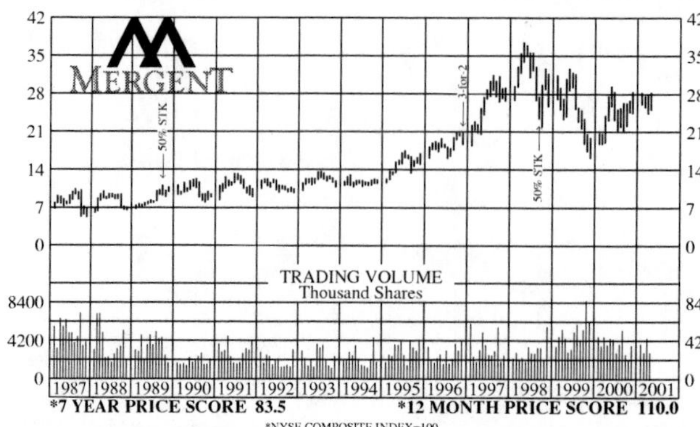

INTERIM EARNINGS (Per Share):

Qtr.	Mar.	June	Sept.	Dec.
1995	0.19	0.29	0.31	0.31
1996	0.27	0.32	0.39	0.36
1997	0.33	0.42	0.45	0.43
1998	0.43	0.53	0.53	0.51
1999	0.49	0.57	0.27	0.22
2000	0.45	0.78	0.35	0.44

INTERIM DIVIDENDS (Per Share):

Amt.	Decl.	Ex.	Rec.	Pay.
0.10Q	5/22/00	5/30/00	6/01/00	6/13/00
0.10Q	8/14/00	8/30/00	9/01/00	9/12/00
0.10Q	10/23/00	11/29/00	12/01/00	12/12/00
0.10Q	1/22/01	2/28/01	3/02/01	3/12/01
0.10Q	5/21/01	5/30/01	6/01/01	6/11/01

Indicated div.: $0.40 (Div. Reinv. Plan)

CAPITALIZATION (12/31/00):

	($000)	(%)
Long-Term Debt	213,790	25.2
Deferred Income Tax	28,386	3.3
Common & Surplus	606,763	71.5
Total	848,939	100.0

RECENT DEVELOPMENTS: For the twelve months ended 12/31/00, net income totaled $123.7 million versus income from continuing operations of $100.9 million in the previous year. Results for 2000 and 1999 included gains from the sale of investments of $28.9 million and $2.6 million, respectively. Total net sales declined 4.0% to $1.49 billion from $1.55 billion in the prior year. Order backlog at 12/31/00 rose 31.8% to $503.6 million, while orders advanced 7.8% to $1.60 billion.

PROSPECTS: CR remains positive on its full-year 2001 earnings outlook, with the Company projecting a 10.0% to 15.0% gain in operating results versus fiscal 2000, excluding gains from investments. However, near-term results will likely be pressured by the effects of the slowing U.S. economy. Separately, on 4/3/01, CR announced it had completed the acquisition of the Industrial Flow Group of Alfa Laval Holding AB for about $37.0 million. CR also announced the acquisition of the assets of the Valve Repair Division of Groth Corporation for about $3.4 million.

BUSINESS

CRANE CO. is a diversified manufacturer of engineered industrial products. The Company manufactures products serving truck/trailer and recreational vehicle, pharmaceutical, chemical processing, pulp and paper, ultra pure water and waste management industries, as well as aerospace, fluid handling, automated merchandising, and other industrial markets.

BUSINESS LINE ANALYSIS

(12/31/2000)	Rev (%)	Inc (%)
Engineered Materials.	22.9	25.5
Merchandising Systems	14.8	16.1
Aerospace	23.3	43.1
Fluid Handling	30.9	16.4
Controls	8.1	(1.1)
Total	100.0	100.0

ANNUAL FINANCIAL DATA

	12/31/00	12/31/99	12/31/98	12/31/97	12/31/96	12/31/95	12/31/94
Earnings Per Share	**3 2.03**	**2 1.50**	**2.00**	**1.63**	**1 1.34**	**1.11**	**0.83**
Cash Flow Per Share	**2.92**	**2.40**	**2.88**	**2.42**	**2.05**	**1.82**	**1.48**
Tang. Book Val. Per Share	**4.11**	**3.10**	**3.33**	**3.81**	**2.95**	**2.14**	**1.38**
Dividends Per Share	**0.40**	**0.40**	**0.37**	**0.33**	**0.33**	**0.33**	**0.33**
Dividend Payout %	**19.7**	**26.7**	**18.3**	**20.5**	**24.9**	**30.0**	**40.3**
INCOME STATEMENT (IN MILLIONS):							
Total Revenues	1,491.2	1,553.7	2,268.5	2,036.8	1,847.7	1,782.3	1,653.5
Costs & Expenses	1,251.9	1,322.8	1,968.1	1,784.8	1,632.2	1,590.6	1,498.9
Depreciation & Amort.	55.3	61.3	61.5	55.4	49.4	48.8	44.7
Operating Income	184.0	169.6	238.9	196.6	166.2	142.9	109.9
Net Interest Inc./(Exp.)	d20.7	d18.1	d25.0	d20.7	d20.9	d24.9	d20.6
Income Before Income Taxes	190.4	155.8	214.6	175.8	145.0	121.5	91.2
Income Taxes	66.6	54.9	76.2	63.1	52.9	45.1	35.3
Net Income	3 123.7	2 100.9	138.4	112.8	1 92.1	76.3	55.9
Cash Flow	179.0	162.2	199.9	168.2	141.5	125.1	100.6
Average Shs. Outstg. (000)	61,399	67,460	69,368	69,384	68,895	68,724	67,829
BALANCE SHEET (IN MILLIONS):							
Cash & Cash Equivalents	10.9	3.2	15.9	7.0	11.6	5.5	2.1
Total Current Assets	500.2	505.2	699.0	607.8	540.0	498.0	480.2
Net Property	246.1	256.6	307.6	273.8	258.3	243.9	263.0
Total Assets	1,143.9	1,175.4	1,454.7	1,185.9	1,088.9	998.4	1,008.0
Total Current Liabilities	232.0	233.5	351.2	295.8	253.9	241.3	244.3
Long-Term Obligations	213.8	286.8	359.1	260.7	267.8	281.1	331.3
Net Stockholders' Equity	606.8	568.1	643.2	532.5	462.7	374.7	328.0
Net Working Capital	268.2	271.6	347.8	311.9	286.2	256.8	235.9
Year-end Shs. Outstg. (000)	60,426	62,802	68,495	68,313	68,490	67,781	67,606
STATISTICAL RECORD:							
Operating Profit Margin %	12.3	10.9	10.5	9.7	9.0	8.0	6.6
Net Profit Margin %	8.3	6.5	6.1	5.5	5.0	4.3	3.4
Return on Equity %	20.4	17.8	21.5	21.2	19.9	20.4	17.1
Return on Assets %	10.8	8.6	9.5	9.5	8.5	7.6	5.5
Debt/Total Assets %	18.7	24.4	24.7	22.0	24.6	28.2	32.9
Price Range	29.50-18.63	32.75-16.06	37.58-21.75	31.50-18.33	21.00-16.00	17.56-11.50	13.11-10.72
P/E Ratio	14.5-9.2	21.8-10.7	18.8-10.9	19.4-11.3	15.7-11.9	15.8-10.4	15.9-13.0
Average Yield %	1.7	1.6	1.2	1.3	1.8	2.3	2.8

Statistics are as originally reported. Adj. for 50% stk. div., 9/98 1 Incls. non-recurr. chrg. 12/31/96: $2.3 mill. 2 Bef. inc. of $13.7 mill. from disc. ops. & incl. pre-tax spec. chgs. of $35.0 mill. 3 Incl. gain from the sale of investments of $28.9 mill. ($0.26/sh.)

OFFICERS:
R. S. Evans, Chmn.
E. C. Fast, Pres., C.E.O.
M. L. Raithel, V.P., C.F.O.

INVESTOR CONTACT: Shareholder Relations, (888) 272-6327

PRINCIPAL OFFICE: 100 First Stamford Place, Stamford, CT 06902

TELEPHONE NUMBER: (203) 363-7300
FAX: (203) 363-7295
WEB: www.craneco.com

NO. OF EMPLOYEES: 9,000 (approx.)

SHAREHOLDERS: 4,800 (approx.)

ANNUAL MEETING: In Apr.

INCORPORATED: DE, May, 1985

INSTITUTIONAL HOLDINGS:
No. of Institutions: 179
Shares Held: 31,039,671
% Held: 51.2

INDUSTRY: Fluid power valves & hose fittings (SIC: 3492)

TRANSFER AGENT(S): EquiServe/First Chicago Trust Division, Jersey City, NJ

NYSE SYMBOL CRDB
Rec. Pr. 10.50 (5/31/01)

CRAWFORD & COMPANY

YIELD 5.3%
P/E RATIO 16.7

*7 YEAR PRICE SCORE 65.1 *12 MONTH PRICE SCORE 109.2

*NYSE COMPOSITE INDEX=100

INTERIM EARNINGS (Per Share):

Qtr.	Mar.	June	Sept.	Dec.
1996	0.20	0.20	0.21	0.23
1997	0.12	0.27	0.29	0.25
1998	0.23	0.24	d0.04	0.12
1999	0.20	0.21	0.16	0.21
2000	0.21	0.22	0.20	d0.11

INTERIM DIVIDENDS (Per Share):

Amt.	Decl.	Ex.	Rec.	Pay.
0.138Q	4/26/00	5/03/00	5/05/00	5/19/00
0.138Q	7/26/00	8/04/00	8/08/00	8/18/00
0.138Q	10/25/00	11/01/00	11/03/00	11/17/00
0.14Q	1/30/01	2/08/01	2/12/01	2/27/01
0.14Q	4/24/01	5/02/01	5/04/01	4/18/01

Indicated div.: $0.56

CAPITALIZATION (12/31/00):

	($000)	(%)
Long-Term Debt	36,662	14.2
Deferred Income Tax	3,941	1.5
Common & Surplus	217,767	84.3
Total	258,370	100.0

RECENT DEVELOPMENTS: For the year ended 12/31/00, net income fell 35.4% to $25.3 million compared with $39.3 million in 1999. Earnings for 2000 and 1999 included nonrecurring charges of $16.7 million and $5.2 million, respectively. Revenues totaled $712.2 million, up 1.5% versus $701.9 million the year before. Domestic revenues climbed slightly to $519.2 million from $523.3 million, while revenues from international operations rose 8.1% to $193.0 million.

PROSPECTS: The Company is being negatively affected by the poor performance of the property and casualty insurance market over the past couple of years. Going forward, the Company will actively pursue outsourcing arrangements with companies, in an effort to produce sustainable growth in 2001. For instance, the Company's managed care revenues in this market continued to grow in the 2000 fourth quarter as a result of a strategic outsourcing arrangement with a large insurance company.

BUSINESS

CRAWFORD & COMPANY is a diversified services firm organized into three business units: Risk Management Services (RMS), Healthcare Management (HCM) and Claims Services. RMS primarily fulfills corporate market needs by providing risk management and claims adjusting services including risk management information systems and services through the subsidiary, Crawford Risk Sciences Group. HCM offers a full range of managed care services for both the corporate and insurance markets. Claims Service is responsible for handling claims support to the insurance industry through the complete investigation, evaluation, disposition and management of losses. The Company operates over 700 offices in 65 countries. In 1999, the Company acquired the Garden City Group, which manages class action litigation settlements

ANNUAL FINANCIAL DATA

	12/31/00	12/31/99	12/31/98	12/31/97	12/31/96	12/31/95	12/31/94
Earnings Per Share	**[1] 0.52**	**0.78**	**[1] 0.54**	**[1] 0.93**	**0.84**	**0.69**	**0.76**
Cash Flow Per Share	**0.93**	**1.11**	**0.83**	**1.23**	**1.15**	**1.01**	**1.04**
Tang. Book Val. Per Share	**2.79**	**3.35**	**3.46**	**3.30**	**3.38**	**3.19**	**3.07**
Dividends Per Share	**0.55**	**0.52**	**0.50**	**0.44**	**0.39**	**0.36**	**0.33**
Dividend Payout %	**105.7**	**66.7**	**92.6**	**47.3**	**46.0**	**52.2**	**43.9**
INCOME STATEMENT (IN THOUSANDS):							
Total Revenues	712,174	701,926	667,271	692,322	633,625	607,577	587,781
Costs & Expenses	646,399	621,154	609,790	604,715	545,939	530,332	504,818
Depreciation & Amort.	20,149	17,028	14,798	15,423	15,716	16,865	14,912
Operating Income	45,626	63,744	42,683	72,184	71,970	60,380	68,051
Net Interest Inc./(Exp.)	d4,476	...	...	...	...	...	...
Income Before Income Taxes	41,150	63,744	42,683	72,184	71,970	60,380	68,051
Income Taxes	15,802	24,480	16,395	27,697	29,160	24,360	27,450
Equity Earnings/Minority Int.	...	...	1,177	2,502	...	...	...
Net Income	[1] 25,348	39,264	[1] 27,465	[1] 46,989	42,810	36,020	40,601
Cash Flow	45,497	56,292	42,263	62,412	58,526	52,885	55,513
Average Shs. Outstg.	48,933	50,498	50,938	50,687	51,032	52,277	53,585
BALANCE SHEET (IN THOUSANDS):							
Cash & Cash Equivalents	22,136	17,716	8,423	55,380	55,485	46,398	57,734
Total Current Assets	263,725	267,836	251,146	278,814	246,896	234,380	243,639
Net Property	42,797	48,891	42,943	39,192	31,637	36,448	37,448
Total Assets	458,351	474,028	433,269	428,866	378,085	366,983	362,894
Total Current Liabilities	157,639	157,990	140,574	124,569	110,652	95,054	117,619
Long-Term Obligations	36,662	16,053	1,854	731	376	9,412	9,962
Net Stockholders' Equity	217,767	250,279	240,051	215,005	221,536	220,860	213,153
Net Working Capital	106,086	109,846	110,572	154,245	136,244	139,326	126,020
Year-end Shs. Outstg.	48,451	50,718	50,903	49,393	50,111	51,792	52,544
STATISTICAL RECORD:							
Operating Profit Margin %	6.4	9.1	6.4	10.4	11.4	9.9	11.6
Net Profit Margin %	3.6	5.6	4.1	6.8	6.8	5.9	6.9
Return on Equity %	11.6	15.7	11.4	21.9	19.3	16.3	19.0
Return on Assets %	5.5	8.3	6.3	11.0	11.3	9.8	11.2
Debt/Total Assets %	8.0	3.4	0.4	0.2	0.1	2.6	2.7
Price Range	14.13-11.00	16.38-10.13	20.63-12.00	22.88-13.88	16.00-9.75	11.83-9.67	11.33-9.58
P/E Ratio	27.2-21.1	21.0-13.0	38.2-22.2	24.6-14.9	19.0-11.6	17.1-14.0	14.9-12.6
Average Yield %	4.4	3.9	3.1	2.4	3.0	3.3	3.2

Statistics are as originally reported. Adj. for stk. split: 3-for-2, 3/97 [1] Incl. non-recurr. chrg. $16.7 mill., 12/00; $3.0 mill., 12/98; $13.0 mill., 12/97

OFFICERS:
A. L. Meyers Jr., Chmn., C.E.O.
G. L. Davis, Pres., C.O.O.
J. F. Giblin, C.F.O., Exec. V.P.
J. F. Osten, Exec. V.P., Gen. Couns.

INVESTOR CONTACT: Christy Taylor, Inv. Rel., (800) 241-2541

PRINCIPAL OFFICE: 5620 Glenridge Dr., N.E., Atlanta, GA 30342

TELEPHONE NUMBER: (404) 256-0830
FAX: (404) 847-4359
WEB: www.crawfordandcompany.com

NO. OF EMPLOYEES: 7,825

SHAREHOLDERS: 1,884 (approx. class A); 855 (approx. class B).

ANNUAL MEETING: In April

INCORPORATED: GA, May, 1943

INSTITUTIONAL HOLDINGS:
No. of Institutions: 40
Shares Held: 17,193,035
% Held: 35.5

INDUSTRY: Management consulting services (SIC: 8742)

TRANSFER AGENT(S): SunTrust Bank, Atlanta, GA

NYSE SYMBOL CEI
Rec. Pr. 23.79 (4/30/01)

CRESCENT REAL ESTATE EQUITIES COMPANY

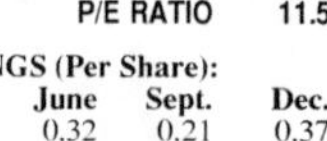

YIELD 9.2%
P/E RATIO 11.5

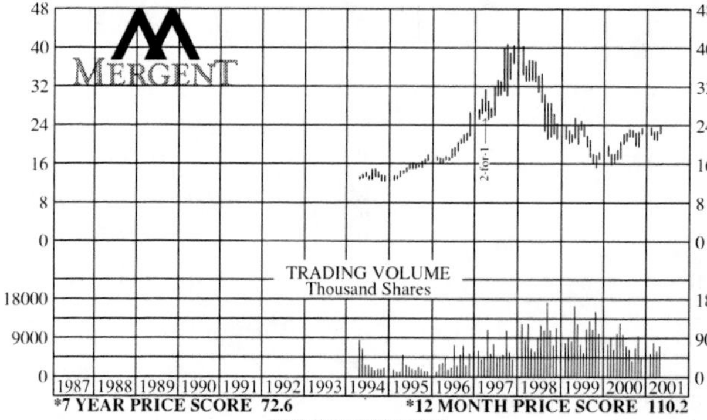

*7 YEAR PRICE SCORE 72.6 *12 MONTH PRICE SCORE 110.2
*NYSE COMPOSITE INDEX=100

INTERIM EARNINGS (Per Share):

Qtr.	Mar.	June	Sept.	Dec.
1998	0.33	0.32	0.21	0.37
1999	0.24	0.39	d0.88	0.19
2000	0.41	0.27	0.70	0.69

INTERIM DIVIDENDS (Per Share):

Amt.	Decl.	Ex.	Rec.	Pay.
0.55Q	4/10/00	4/26/00	4/28/00	5/15/00
0.55Q	7/14/00	7/27/00	7/31/00	8/15/00
0.55Q	10/13/00	10/27/00	10/31/00	11/15/00
0.55Q	1/15/01	1/29/01	1/31/01	2/15/01
0.55Q	4/13/01	4/26/01	4/30/01	5/15/01

Indicated div.: $2.20

CAPITALIZATION (12/31/00):

	($000)	(%)
Long-Term Debt	1,718,443	45.4
Minority Interest	337,505	8.9
Preferred Stock	200,000	5.3
Common & Surplus	1,531,327	40.4
Total	3,787,275	100.0

RECENT DEVELOPMENTS: For the year ended 12/31/00, income before an extraordinary loss of $3.9 million totaled $252.1 million versus net income of $11.0 million in the comparable period. Results for the current fiscal year included a net gain on property sales of $119.6 million. Results for 1999 included non-recurring charges totaling $193.8 million. Total revenues declined 3.7% to $718.4 million compared with $746.3 million in the previous year.

PROSPECTS: Going forward, CEI should continue to benefit from strong demand in its core office markets. Separately, CEI will continue to evaluate its four business-class hotels for disposition over the next couple of years. In addition, CEI should benefit from its ten-year joint-venture arrangement with Booth Creek Ski Holdings, Inc. Meanwhile, CEI continues to actively market its 21 remaining behavioral healthcare facilities.

BUSINESS

CRESCENT REAL ESTATE EQUITIES COMPANY operates as a real estate investment trust. CEI provides management, leasing and development services. The Company operates in five investment segments: Office, Resorts and Hotels, Residential Development, Temperature-controlled Logistics, and Behavioral Healthcare. The office segment consists of 78 office properties, with 28.7 million square feet of rentable space in major metropolitan markets across the Southwest. The resort and hotel segment is comprised of three luxury resorts and spas and two Canyon Ranch destination fitness resorts and spas. The residential development segment consists of five residential corporations that currently own 19 properties through joint venture or partnership agreements. The temperature-controlled logistics segment consists of 89 facilities in growth areas and major distribution cities across the country. The behavioral healthcare segment consists of 21 properties, all of which are up for sale. CEI's other investments include four full-service hotels.

ANNUAL FINANCIAL DATA

	12/31/00	12/31/99	12/31/98	12/31/97	12/31/96	12/31/95	3 12/31/94
Earnings Per Share	1 2 2.05	2 d0.06	1.21	1.20	1 0.72	0.66	1 2 0.28
Tang. Book Val. Per Share	12.57	15.28	17.84	18.62	11.97	12.67	7.33
Dividends Per Share	2.20	2.20	1.69	1.29	1.13	1.02	0.40
Dividend Payout %	107.3	...	139.7	107.9	156.9	156.5	141.0
INCOME STATEMENT (IN MILLIONS):							
Rental Income	693.5	720.8	671.7	430.4	202.0	123.5	49.1
Interest Income	24.9	25.5	26.7	17.0	6.9	6.5	1.3
Total Income	718.4	746.3	698.3	447.4	208.9	130.0	50.3
Costs & Expenses	283.5	467.3	277.7	171.7	78.5	49.8	20.8
Depreciation	133.3	141.9	124.6	77.9	43.3	30.6	15.2
Interest Expense	203.2	192.0	152.2	86.4	42.9	18.8	3.5
Income Before Income Taxes	303.1	13.3	183.2	135.0	48.0	36.4	11.6
Equity Earnings/Minority Int.	24.7	65.9	21.7	6.1	d5.7	d3.5	0.3
Net Income	1 2 252.1	2 11.0	165.6	117.3	1 38.4	27.4	1 2 12.6
Average Shs. Outstg. (000)	128,732	137,892	127,402	97,847	53,282	41,742	32,050
BALANCE SHEET (IN MILLIONS):							
Cash & Cash Equivalents	133.5	160.9	157.1	108.2	62.5	39.1	42.3
Total Assets	4,531.8	4,950.6	5,043.4	4,180.0	1,730.9	964.2	538.4
Long-Term Obligations	1,718.4	2,088.9	1,658.2	1,360.1	627.8	424.5	...
Total Liabilities	2,800.4	2,893.8	2,620.9	1,982.7	865.8	557.6	303.1
Net Stockholders' Equity	1,731.3	2,056.8	2,422.5	2,197.3	865.2	406.5	235.3
Year-end Shs. Outstg. (000)	121,819	121,537	124,555	117,978	72,292	32,094	32,094
STATISTICAL RECORD:							
Net Inc.+Depr./Assets %	8.5	3.1	5.8	4.7	4.7	6.0	5.0
Return on Equity %	14.6	0.5	6.8	5.3	4.4	6.7	5.4
Return on Assets %	5.6	0.2	3.3	2.8	2.2	2.8	2.3
Price Range	23.44-15.75	25.50-15.13	40.38-21.06	40.75-25.13	26.63-16.06	17.94-12.50	15.00-12.25
P/E Ratio	11.4-7.7	...	33.4-17.4	34.0-20.9	37.0-22.3	27.4-19.1	53.6-43.7
Average Yield %	11.2	10.8	5.5	3.9	5.3	6.7	2.9

Statistics are as originally reported. 1 Bef. extraord. charge, 2000, $3.9 mill.; 1996, $1.3 mill.; 1994, $949,000. 2 Incl. non-recurr. gain, 2000, $119.6 mill.; chrgs., 1999, $193.8 mill.; 1994, $1.9 mill. 3 For the period from 5/5/94

OFFICERS:
R. E. Rainwater, Chmn.
J. C. Goff, C.E.O.
J. R. Crenshaw, Sr. V.P., C.F.O.

INVESTOR CONTACT: Investor Relations, (817) 321-2100

PRINCIPAL OFFICE: 777 Main St., Suite 2100, Fort Worth, TX 76102-5325

TELEPHONE NUMBER: (817) 321-2100
FAX: (817) 321-2000
WEB: www.cei-crescent.com

NO. OF EMPLOYEES: 707

SHAREHOLDERS: 1,177 (approx.)

ANNUAL MEETING: In June

INCORPORATED: MD, Feb., 1994

INSTITUTIONAL HOLDINGS:
No. of Institutions: 152
Shares Held: 62,126,284
% Held: 57.9

INDUSTRY: Real estate investment trusts (SIC: 6798)

TRANSFER AGENT(S): Boston EquiServe, L.P., Boston, MA

NYSE SYMBOL CLJ
Rec. Pr. 26.01 (4/30/01)

CRESTLINE CAPITAL CORP.

YIELD	...
P/E RATIO	9.7

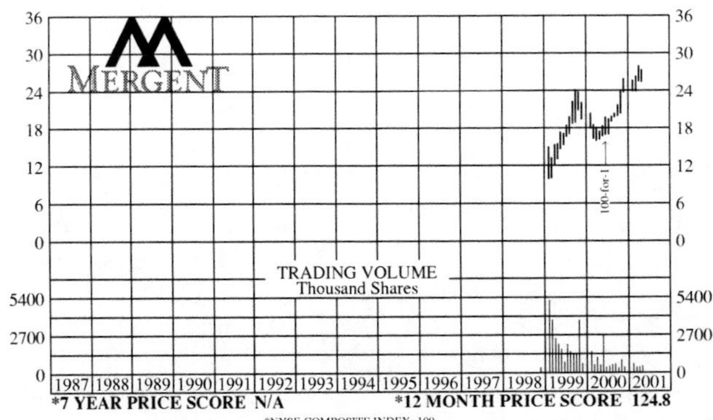

*7 YEAR PRICE SCORE N/A *12 MONTH PRICE SCORE 124.8
*NYSE COMPOSITE INDEX=100

INTERIM EARNINGS (Per Share):

Qtr.	Mar.	June	Sept.	Dec.
1999	0.35	0.53	0.51	0.53
2000	0.57	0.65	0.51	0.94

INTERIM DIVIDENDS (Per Share):

Amt.	Decl.	Ex.	Rec.	Pay.
1-for-100	...	6/23/00	...	...
100-for-1	...	6/23/00	...	...

CAPITALIZATION (12/29/00):

	($000)	(%)
Long-Term Debt	428,602	47.2
Deferred Income Tax	67,866	7.5
Common & Surplus	412,088	45.4
Total	908,556	100.0

RECENT DEVELOPMENTS: For the year ended 12/29/00, the Company reported income from continuing operations of $44.5 million, before a net extraordinary gain of $253,000, versus net income of $39.9 million in the prior year. Earnings reflected strong performances from the Company's hotel management and senior living businesses. Total revenues advanced 8.3% to $4.82 billion compared with $4.45 billion in the corresponding period of 1999.

PROSPECTS: On 1/11/01, CLJ announced that it has completed the sale of leases held by the Company on certain full-service hotels owned by Host Marriott in an all-cash transaction valued at approximately $201.0 million. The transaction will transfer ownership of lessee entities owned by CLJ to a subsidiary of Host Marriott. The proceeds will be used to continue implementation of CLJ's dual strategy of growing its hotel management business and repurchasing its stock.

BUSINESS

CRESTLINE CAPITAL CORP. is the parent company of Crestline Hotels & Resorts, Inc., which is engaged in the ownership, management and leasing of hotels and the ownership of senior living communities. The Company manages of 34 properties independently under the brand names of MARRIOTT, HYATT, HILTON, SHERATON, RENAISSANCE, CROWNE PLAZA, HILTON GARDEN INN, HOLIDAY INN, COURTYARD by MARRIOTT and RESIDENCE INN. In addition, the Company also leases 116 full-service hotels and subleases 71 limited service hotels from Host Marriott Corporation. The 31 senior living communities owned by the Company are managed by Marriott International under long-term agreements. CLJ owns 82.0% of a general partnership interest in an upscale extended-stay hotel portfolio, consisting of 10 Residence Inn hotels. On 12/29/98, CLJ was spun off from Host Marriott Corporation.

REVENUES

(12/31/2000)	($000)	(%)
Hotel Rooms	2,936,069	61.0
Hotel Food & Beverage	1,288,117	26.7
Other Hotel	326,128	6.8
Senior Living	261,886	5.4
Other revenues & Equity in affiliates	4,957	0.1
Total	4,817,157	100.0

ANNUAL FINANCIAL DATA

	12/29/00	12/31/99	1/1/99	1/2/98
Earnings Per Share	**[1] 2.67**	**1.91**	**0.27**	...
Cash Flow Per Share	**4.52**	**3.09**	**1.22**	...
Tang. Book Val. Per Share	**26.42**	**23.30**	**20.95**	...
INCOME STATEMENT (IN MILLIONS):				
Total Revenues	4,817.2	4,447.1	241.3	36.9
Costs & Expenses	4,663.1	4,311.8	183.5	10.3
Depreciation & Amort.	30.7	24.5	20.6	10.6
Operating Income	123.4	110.8	37.2	16.0
Net Interest Inc./(Exp.)	d30.4	d26.8	d20.8	d13.1
Income Before Income Taxes	76.1	67.6	10.0	0.6
Income Taxes	31.6	27.7	4.1	0.2
Net Income	[1] 44.5	39.9	5.9	0.4
Cash Flow	75.3	64.4	26.5	11.0
Average Shs. Outstg. (000)	16,665	20,840	21,656	...
BALANCE SHEET (IN MILLIONS):				
Cash & Cash Equivalents	35.5	36.8	66.8	28.3
Total Current Assets	35.5	36.8	66.8	28.3
Net Property	745.5	745.6	655.7	633.8
Total Assets	1,017.4	964.9	858.8	663.5
Total Current Liabilities	12.5	16.9	6.4	20.4
Long-Term Obligations	428.6	395.9	308.2	349.9
Net Stockholders' Equity	412.1	400.7	459.3	227.1
Net Working Capital	23.0	19.9	60.3	7.9
Year-end Shs. Outstg. (000)	15,600	17,200	21,926	...
STATISTICAL RECORD:				
Operating Profit Margin %	2.6	2.5	15.4	43.3
Net Profit Margin %	0.9	0.9	2.5	1.0
Return on Equity %	10.8	10.0	1.3	0.2
Return on Assets %	4.4	4.1	0.7	0.1
Debt/Total Assets %	42.1	41.0	35.9	52.7
Price Range	25.94-15.88	24.13-9.81	...	...
P/E Ratio	9.7-5.9	12.6-5.1	...	...

Statistics are as originally reported. Adj. for stk. splits, 1-for-100 & 100-for-1, 6/23/00.
[1] Bef. net extraord. gain of $253,000.

OFFICERS:
B. D. Wardinski, Chmn., Pres., C.E.O.
J. L. Francis, Exec. V.P., C.F.O.
L. K. Harvey, Sr. V.P., Treas., Contr.

INVESTOR CONTACT: Shareholder Relations, (800) 524-4458

PRINCIPAL OFFICE: 6600 Rockledge Drive, Bethesda, MD 20817

TELEPHONE NUMBER: (240) 694-2000
FAX: (240) 694-2099
WEB: www.crestlinecapital.com

NO. OF EMPLOYEES: 3,837

SHAREHOLDERS: 27,039 (approx.)

ANNUAL MEETING: In June

INCORPORATED: MD, Nov., 1998

INSTITUTIONAL HOLDINGS:
No. of Institutions: 62
Shares Held: 13,138,493
% Held: 85.4

INDUSTRY: Hotels and motels (SIC: 7011)

TRANSFER AGENT(S): Bank of New York, New York, NY

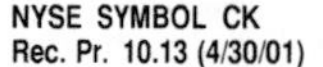

NYSE SYMBOL CK
Rec. Pr. 10.13 (4/30/01)

CROMPTON CORPORATION

YIELD 2.0%
P/E RATIO 13.0

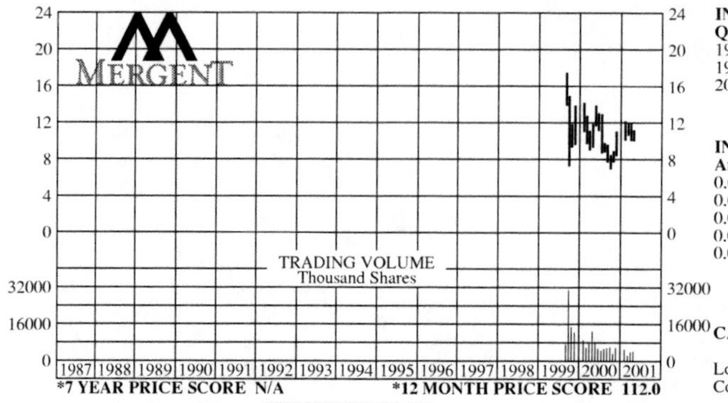

*7 YEAR PRICE SCORE N/A *12 MONTH PRICE SCORE 112.0

*NYSE COMPOSITE INDEX=100

INTERIM EARNINGS (Per Share):

Qtr.	Mar.	June	Sept.	Dec.
1998	0.42	0.52	0.40	1.11
1999	0.86	0.57	d2.21	d0.77
2000	0.26	0.36	0.19	d0.03

INTERIM DIVIDENDS (Per Share):

Amt.	Decl.	Ex.	Rec.	Pay.
0.05Q	4/25/00	5/03/00	5/05/00	5/26/00
0.05Q	7/25/00	8/02/00	8/04/00	8/25/00
0.05Q	10/31/00	11/08/00	11/10/00	11/24/00
0.05Q	1/30/01	2/07/01	2/09/01	2/23/01
0.05Q	4/24/01	5/02/01	5/04/01	5/25/01

Indicated div.: $0.20

CAPITALIZATION (12/31/00):

	($000)	(%)
Long-Term Debt	1,479,394	66.2
Common & Surplus	753,976	33.8
Total	2,233,370	100.0

RECENT DEVELOPMENTS: For the twelve months ended 12/31/00, net earnings were $89.3 million compared with a loss of $159.4 million, before an extraordinary charge, in 1999. Results for 2000 included a $15.0 million charge from facility shutdown costs. Results for 1999 included charges totaling $254.3 million. Net sales jumped 45.2% to $3.04 billion from $2.09 billion in the prior year.

PROSPECTS: The chemical industry continues to be hampered by the slowing U.S. economy, the high level of raw material and energy costs, and the strong U.S. dollar. These factors are expected to continue into 2001, but are anticipated to improve during the second half of the year. Meanwhile, the Company is continuing the divestiture process of the Refined Products and Industrial Specialties businesses.

BUSINESS

CROMPTON CORPORATION (formerly CK Witco Corporation) was formed on 9/1/99 through the merger of Crompton & Knowles Corporation and Witco Corporation. The Company is a worldwide producer and marketer of specialty chemicals and equipment. These products include polymers, polymer additives and polymer processing equipment, rubber chemicals, dyes, organosilicones, industrial specialties, petroleum and performance additives, refined products, and crop protection chemicals. The Company does business in more than 120 countries. Major subsidiaries include: Witco; Uniroyal Chemical; Davis-Standard Corporation; and Crompton & Knowles Colors Inc.

ANNUAL FINANCIAL DATA

	12/31/00	12/31/99	12/31/98	12/31/97	[1] 12/31/96
Earnings Per Share	**[6] 0.78**	**[5] d1.91**	**[4] 2.42**	**[3] 1.22**	**[2] d0.31**
Cash Flow Per Share	**2.36**	**d0.51**	**3.48**	**2.28**	**0.84**
Dividends Per Share	**0.20**	**0.05**	...	...	...
Dividend Payout %	**25.6**	...	...	...	...
INCOME STATEMENT (IN MILLIONS):					
Total Revenues	3,038.4	2,092.4	1,796.1	1,851.2	1,804.0
Costs & Expenses	2,599.5	1,984.9	1,497.3	1,547.0	1,617.8
Depreciation & Amort.	182.0	116.6	80.5	79.9	82.6
Operating Income	268.3	1.4	218.3	224.3	103.6
Net Interest Inc./(Exp.)	d120.5	d69.8	d78.5	d103.3	d114.2
Income Before Income Taxes	142.4	d116.4	298.7	148.7	d9.3
Income Taxes	53.1	42.9	115.5	56.7	12.7
Net Income	[6] 89.3	[5] d159.4	[4] 183.2	[3] 92.1	[2] d22.1
Cash Flow	271.3	d42.7	263.8	171.9	60.5
Average Shs. Outstg. (000)	115,165	83,507	75,700	75,358	...
BALANCE SHEET (IN MILLIONS):					
Cash & Cash Equivalents	20.8	10.5	12.1	10.6	...
Total Current Assets	1,076.9	1,119.8	597.8	715.0	...
Net Property	1,182.1	1,262.3	473.4	474.9	...
Total Assets	3,528.3	3,726.6	1,408.9	1,548.8	1,657.2
Total Current Liabilities	715.5	978.0	394.4	363.1	...
Long-Term Obligations	1,479.4	1,309.8	646.9	896.3	...
Net Stockholders' Equity	754.0	759.9	66.7	d20.1	...
Net Working Capital	361.4	141.8	203.4	352.0	...
Year-end Shs. Outstg. (000)	112,475	116,835	...	...	...
STATISTICAL RECORD:					
Operating Profit Margin %	8.8	0.1	12.2	12.1	5.7
Net Profit Margin %	2.9	...	10.2	5.0	...
Return on Equity %	11.8	...	274.7	...	...
Return on Assets %	2.5	...	13.0	5.9	...
Debt/Total Assets %	41.9	35.1	45.9	57.9	...
Price Range	14.19-6.94	17.50-7.25	...	...	...
P/E Ratio	18.2-8.9	...	...	...	...
Average Yield %	1.9	0.4	...	...	...

Statistics are as originally reported. Results for 1998 and earlier are for Crompton & Knowles Corp. [1] Incl. results of Uniroyal Chem. Corp., acq. in 8/96. [2] Excl. $441,000 extraord. chg. and incl. $85.0 merg. chgs. & $30.0 mill. spl. provision. [3] Excl. $5.2 mill. extraord. loss. [4] Excl. $21.5 mill. extraord. loss and incl. $5.0 mill. net chg. & $92.1 mill. net gain. [5] Bef. $15.7 mill. extraord. loss and incl. $26.8 mill. gain, $195.0 mill. acq. in-process R&D chg., $20.6 mill. merger chg., & $65.5 mill. loss. [6] Incl. $15.0 mill. chg.

OFFICERS:
V. A. Calarco, Chmn., Pres., C.E.O.
P. Barna, Sr. V.P., C.F.O.
J. R. Jespen, V.P., Treas.

INVESTOR CONTACT: William A. Kuser, Investor Relations, (203) 552-2000

PRINCIPAL OFFICE: One American Lane, Greenwich, CT 06831-2559

TELEPHONE NUMBER: (203) 552-2000
FAX: (203) 353-5424
WEB: www.cromptoncorp.com

NO. OF EMPLOYEES: 8,300 (approx.)

SHAREHOLDERS: 6,371

ANNUAL MEETING: In Apr.

INCORPORATED: DE, Sept., 1999

INSTITUTIONAL HOLDINGS:
No. of Institutions: 153
Shares Held: 83,824,648
% Held: 74.4

INDUSTRY: Industrial organic chemicals, nec (SIC: 2869)

TRANSFER AGENT(S): Mellon Investor Services, Ridgefield Park, NJ

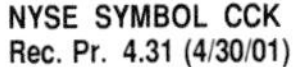

NYSE SYMBOL CCK
Rec. Pr. 4.31 (4/30/01)

CROWN CORK & SEAL CO., INC.

YIELD ...
P/E RATIO ...

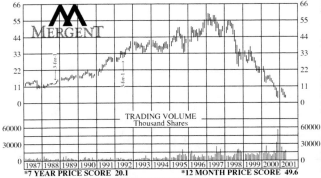

TRADING VOLUME
Thousand Shares

*7 YEAR PRICE SCORE 20.1 *12 MONTH PRICE SCORE 49.6

*NYSE COMPOSITE INDEX=100

INTERIM EARNINGS (Per Share):

Qtr.	Mar.	June	Sept.	Dec.
1997	0.26	0.98	0.62	0.31
1998	0.29	0.95	d0.20	d0.37
1999	0.21	0.77	0.91	d0.57
2000	0.17	d0.03	0.35	d1.89

INTERIM DIVIDENDS (Per Share):

Amt.	Decl.	Ex.	Rec.	Pay.
0.25Q	10/29/99	11/02/99	11/04/99	11/20/99
0.25Q	12/16/99	1/31/00	2/02/00	2/22/00
0.25Q	2/25/00	5/02/00	5/04/00	5/22/00
0.25Q	7/27/00	8/03/00	8/07/00	8/21/00
0.25Q	10/26/00	11/02/00	11/06/00	11/20/00

Dividend suspended.

CAPITALIZATION (12/31/00):

	($000)	(%)
Long-Term Debt	5,049,000	68.7
Minority Interest	195,000	2.7
Common & Surplus	2,109,000	28.7
Total	7,353,000	100.0

RECENT DEVELOPMENTS: For the year ended 12/31/00, CCK reported a net loss of $174.0 million compared with net income of $181.0 million in 1999. Results for 2000 and 1999 included a provision of $333.0 million and $156.0 million, respectively, for restructuring and other charges. Results for 2000 and 1999 also included a $1.0 million gain and a loss of $18.0 million, respectively, from the sale of assets. Net sales slipped 8.9% to $7.29 billion.

PROSPECTS: The Company announced the availability of the SuperEnd™ beverage can end, which utilizes less metal while improving the quality of the end through improved seams and increased strength. The Company recently completed the conversion of its end manufacturing line in Dayton, Ohio with a capacity of 1.80 billion SuperEnd™ units per year. CCK has sped up its implementation schedule in response to customer demand.

BUSINESS

CROWN CORK & SEAL CO. is a global manufacturer of packaging products for consumer goods. Products include metal cans and plastic containers for food, beverage, household, personal care and other products; packaging for health and beauty care applications; closures, pumps and dispensing systems; composite containers; and machinery for beverage filling, material handling and can making. CCK operates 223 plants located in 50 countries. Net sales (and operating income) in 2000 by division were: North America, 51.3% (43.0%); Europe, 44.4% (68.7%); Asia-Pacific, 4.3% (4.4%); and Other, 0% (d16.1%).

REVENUES

(12/31/2000)	($000)	(%)
Metal Beverage Cans & Ends	2,339	32.1
Metal Food Cans & Ends	2,135	29.3
Other Metal Packaning	1,243	17.1
Plastic Packaging	1,495	20.5
Other Products	77	1.0
Total	7,289	100.0

ANNUAL FINANCIAL DATA

	12/31/00	12/31/99	12/31/98	12/31/97	[1] 12/31/96	12/31/95	12/31/94
Earnings Per Share	[7] d1.40	[6] 1.36	[5] 0.71	[3][5] 2.15	[3][4] 2.16	[4] 0.83	[2] 1.47
Cash Flow Per Share	2.52	5.30	4.67	5.83	7.97	3.87	3.83
Tang. Book Val. Per Share	...	...	...	...	...	4.05	2.72
Dividends Per Share	1.00	1.00	1.00	1.00	1.00	...	...
Dividend Payout %	...	73.5	140.8	46.5	46.3	...	...
INCOME STATEMENT (IN MILLIONS):							
Total Revenues	7,289.0	7,732.0	8,300.0	8,494.6	8,331.9	5,053.8	4,452.2
Costs & Expenses	6,629.0	6,564.0	7,210.0	7,187.9	7,159.5	4,561.4	3,949.5
Depreciation & Amort.	495.0	522.0	533.0	540.0	495.9	256.3	218.3
Operating Income	165.0	646.0	557.0	766.7	676.5	236.1	284.4
Net Interest Inc./(Exp.)	d373.0	d342.0	d363.0	d339.9	d305.8	d136.1	d91.6
Income Before Income Taxes	d217.0	309.0	180.0	457.0	431.0	109.5	182.7
Income Taxes	cr58.0	105.0	74.0	147.7	134.4	24.9	55.6
Equity Earnings/Minority Int.	d15.0	d23.0	d1.0	d7.7	d12.6	d9.7	3.9
Net Income	[7] d174.0	[6] 181.0	[5] 105.0	[3][5] 301.6	[3][4] 309.2	[4] 94.3	[2] 123.2
Cash Flow	319.0	688.0	621.0	818.2	760.1	331.2	349.3
Average Shs. Outstg. (000)	126,800	129,800	132,900	140,300	103,500	90,650	89,087
BALANCE SHEET (IN MILLIONS):							
Cash & Cash Equivalents	382.0	267.0	284.0	205.6	160.4	68.1	43.5
Total Current Assets	2,913.0	2,841.0	3,168.0	3,147.2	3,291.9	1,708.9	1,605.6
Net Property	2,969.0	3,255.0	3,743.0	3,663.9	3,717.3	2,005.9	1,816.5
Total Assets	11,159.0	11,545.0	12,469.0	12,305.7	12,590.2	5,051.7	4,781.3
Total Current Liabilities	2,261.0	3,414.0	4,710.0	4,049.3	6,123.4	1,947.2	2,220.1
Long-Term Obligations	5,049.0	3,573.0	3,188.0	3,301.4	3,923.5	1,490.1	2,179.0
Net Stockholders' Equity	2,109.0	2,891.0	2,975.0	3,529.2	3,563.3	1,461.2	1,365.2
Net Working Capital	652.0	d573.0	d1,542.0	d902.1	d2,831.5	d238.3	d614.5
Year-end Shs. Outstg. (000)	125,622	121,081	122,337	128,399	128,411	90,233	89,360
STATISTICAL RECORD:							
Operating Profit Margin %	2.3	8.4	6.7	9.0	8.1	4.7	6.4
Net Profit Margin %	...	2.3	1.3	3.6	3.7	1.9	2.8
Return on Equity %	...	6.3	3.5	8.5	8.7	6.5	9.6
Return on Assets %	...	1.6	0.8	2.5	2.5	1.9	2.6
Debt/Total Assets %	45.2	30.9	25.6	26.8	31.2	29.5	45.6
Price Range	24.19-2.94	37.50-19.69	55.19-24.00	59.75-43.56	55.50-40.63	50.63-33.50	41.88-33.50
P/E Ratio	...	27.6-14.5	77.7-33.8	27.8-20.3	25.7-18.8	61.0-40.4	28.5-22.8
Average Yield %	7.4	3.5	2.5	1.9	2.1	...	...

Statistics are as originally reported. [1] Incl. ops. of CarnaudMetalbox. [2] Incl. Tri Valley Growers' can mfg. facilities results & $73.2 mill. after-tax restr. chg. [3] Incl. $6.1 mill. gain on sale of assets, 1997; $23.8 mill., 1996. [4] Incl. $303.7 mill. restr. chg., 1998; $39.8 mill., 1996; $67.0 mill., 1995. [5] Bef. $7.6 mill. acct. chg. [6] Incl. $17.4 mill. gain fr. sale of assets & $155.9 mill. restr. chgs. [7] Incl. $333.0 mill. net chg. fr. restr. and $1.0 mill. gain fr. sale of assets.

OFFICERS:
W. J. Avery, Chmn.
J. W. Conway, Pres., C.E.O., C.O.O.

INVESTOR CONTACT: Cecile Prevot, Corp. Comm., (215) 552-3770

PRINCIPAL OFFICE: One Crown Way, Philadelphia, PA 19154

TELEPHONE NUMBER: (215) 698-5100
FAX: (215) 676-7245
WEB: www.crowncork.com
NO. OF EMPLOYEES: 34,618 (avg.)
SHAREHOLDERS: 5,555
ANNUAL MEETING: In Apr.
INCORPORATED: NY, Dec., 1927; reincorp., PA, Aug., 1989

INSTITUTIONAL HOLDINGS:
No. of Institutions: 159
Shares Held: 88,026,630
% Held: 70.1

INDUSTRY: Metal cans (SIC: 3411)

TRANSFER AGENT(S): First Chicago Trust Company of New York, Jersey City, NJ

NYSE SYMBOL CSX
Rec. Pr. 35.07 (4/30/01)

CSX CORPORATION

YIELD 3.4%
P/E RATIO 39.4

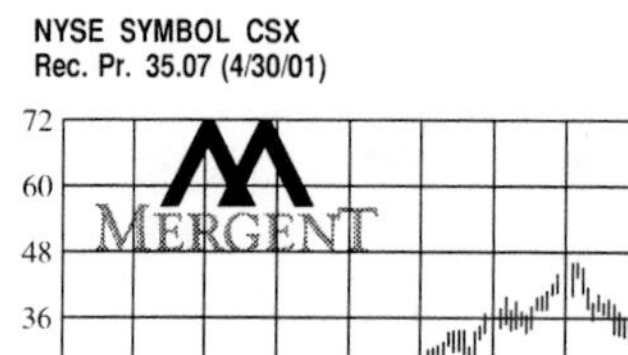

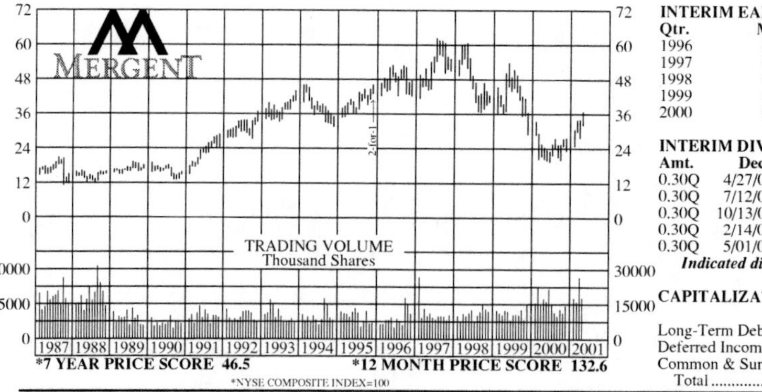

*7 YEAR PRICE SCORE 46.5 *12 MONTH PRICE SCORE 132.6

*NYSE COMPOSITE INDEX=100

INTERIM EARNINGS (Per Share):

Qtr.	Mar.	June	Sept.	Dec.
1996	0.69	1.11	1.04	1.17
1997	0.70	1.04	0.95	0.97
1998	0.41	0.68	0.88	0.51
1999	0.36	0.53	d0.54	d0.12
2000	0.12	0.23	0.28	0.26

INTERIM DIVIDENDS (Per Share):

Amt.	Decl.	Ex.	Rec.	Pay.
0.30Q	4/27/00	5/23/00	5/25/00	6/15/00
0.30Q	7/12/00	8/23/00	8/25/00	9/15/00
0.30Q	10/13/00	11/21/00	11/24/00	12/15/00
0.30Q	2/14/01	2/22/01	2/26/01	3/15/01
0.30Q	5/01/01	5/23/01	5/25/01	6/15/01

Indicated div.: $1.20 (Div. Reinv. Plan)

CAPITALIZATION (12/29/00):

	($000)	(%)
Long-Term Debt	5,810,000	38.2
Deferred Income Tax	3,384,000	22.2
Common & Surplus	6,017,000	39.6
Total	15,211,000	100.0

RECENT DEVELOPMENTS: For the year ended 12/31/00, earnings from continuing operations totaled $186.0 million versus income from continuing operations of $32.0 million last year. Results for 2000 and 1999 excluded net gains from discontinued operations of $379.0 million and $19.0 million, respectively. Results for 2000 also excluded an after-tax charge of $49.0 million from the cumulative effect of a change in accounting. Operating revenue totaled $8.19 billion versus $10.38 billion in 1999.

PROSPECTS: Higher fuel costs and the slowing U.S. economy could pressure results as key sectors, specifically automotive, chemical, paper and steel, experience weakness. However, cost reductions and pricing initiatives, coupled with improvement in railroad efficiency, brighten CSX's future prospects. On 2/1/01, CSX announced the formation of TRANSFLO℠ Corporation, a business unit that will provide rail-centric transloading, materials management and distribution services across North America.

BUSINESS

CSX CORPORATION is an international, multimodal transportation company with interests in rail freight, intermodal, container-shipping, and barging. The rail system, CSX Transportation Inc., operates over a 22,700 route-mile network in 23 states, the District of Columbia and two Canadian provinces. CSX Intermodal Inc. operates a network of dedicated intermodal facilities across North America. CSX Lines provides domestic ocean liner service and operates 16 U.S.-flagged vessels and 27,000 containers along six service routes. CSX World Terminals operates terminals in Hong Kong, China, Australia, Europe, Russia and the Dominican Republic. As of 12/31/00, CSX also owned a 34% equity investment in American Commercial Lines Inc. Non-transportation interests include CSX Real Property Inc. and one resort property. On 6/1/99, CSX took over the operation of the acquired Conrail, Inc. assets.

ANNUAL FINANCIAL DATA

	12/29/00	12/31/99	12/25/98	12/26/97	12/27/96	12/29/95	12/30/94
Earnings Per Share	**[3] 0.88**	**[2] 0.24**	**2.51**	**[1] 3.72**	**4.00**	**[1] 2.94**	**3.12**
Cash Flow Per Share	**3.72**	**3.16**	**5.45**	**6.74**	**6.89**	**5.80**	**5.88**
Tang. Book Val. Per Share	**28.28**	**26.35**	**27.08**	**26.41**	**23.02**	**20.20**	**17.85**
Dividends Per Share	**1.20**	**1.20**	**1.20**	**1.08**	**1.04**	**0.92**	**0.88**
Dividend Payout %	**136.3**	**499.8**	**47.8**	**29.0**	**26.0**	**31.3**	**28.2**
INCOME STATEMENT (IN MILLIONS):							
Total Revenues	8,191.0	10,811.0	9,898.0	10,621.0	10,536.0	10,504.0	9,608.0
Costs & Expenses	6,786.0	9,582.0	8,108.0	8,392.0	8,394.0	8,732.0	7,799.0
Depreciation & Amort.	600.0	621.0	630.0	646.0	620.0	600.0	577.0
Operating Income	805.0	608.0	1,160.0	1,583.0	1,522.0	1,172.0	1,232.0
Net Interest Inc./(Exp.)	d543.0	d521.0	d506.0	d451.0	d249.0	d270.0	d281.0
Income Before Income Taxes	277.0	139.0	773.0	1,183.0	1,316.0	974.0	1,006.0
Income Taxes	91.0	88.0	236.0	384.0	461.0	356.0	354.0
Net Income	[3] 186.0	[2] 51.0	537.0	[1] 799.0	855.0	[1] 618.0	652.0
Cash Flow	786.0	672.0	1,167.0	1,445.0	1,475.0	1,218.0	1,229.0
Average Shs. Outstg. (000)	211,314	212,696	214,196	214,445	214,000	210,000	209,000
BALANCE SHEET (IN MILLIONS):							
Cash & Cash Equivalents	684.0	974.0	533.0	690.0	682.0	660.0	535.0
Total Current Assets	2,046.0	2,563.0	1,984.0	2,175.0	2,072.0	1,935.0	1,665.0
Net Property	12,642.0	12,257.0	12,645.0	12,406.0	11,906.0	11,297.0	11,044.0
Total Assets	20,491.0	20,720.0	20,427.0	19,957.0	16,965.0	14,282.0	13,724.0
Total Current Liabilities	3,280.0	3,473.0	2,600.0	2,707.0	2,757.0	2,991.0	2,505.0
Long-Term Obligations	5,810.0	6,196.0	6,432.0	6,416.0	4,331.0	2,222.0	2,618.0
Net Stockholders' Equity	6,017.0	5,756.0	5,880.0	5,766.0	4,995.0	4,242.0	3,731.0
Net Working Capital	d1,234.0	d910.0	d616.0	d532.0	d685.0	d1,056.0	d840.0
Year-end Shs. Outstg. (000)	212,738	218,445	217,119	218,310	217,000	210,000	209,000
STATISTICAL RECORD:							
Operating Profit Margin %	9.8	5.6	11.7	14.9	14.4	11.2	12.8
Net Profit Margin %	2.3	0.5	5.4	7.5	8.1	5.9	6.8
Return on Equity %	3.1	0.9	9.1	13.9	17.1	14.6	17.5
Return on Assets %	0.9	0.2	2.6	4.0	5.0	4.3	4.8
Debt/Total Assets %	28.4	29.9	31.5	32.1	25.5	15.6	19.1
Price Range	33.44-19.50	53.94-28.81	60.75-36.50	62.44-41.25	53.13-42.13	46.13-34.69	46.19-31.56
P/E Ratio	38.0-22.2	224.6-120.0	24.2-14.5	16.8-11.1	13.3-10.5	15.7-11.8	14.8-10.1
Average Yield %	4.5	2.9	2.5	2.1	2.2	2.3	2.3

Statistics are as originally reported. Adj. for 2-for-1 stk. split, 12/95 [1] Incls. non-recurr. chrgs. 12/31/97: $97.0 mill.; net chrg. 12/31/95: $206.0 mill. [2] Incls. non-recurr. after-tax chrgs. of $34.0; non-recurr. after-tax gain of $17.0 mill.; non-recurr. chrg. of $271.0 mill.; Bef. acctg. change chrg. of $49.0 mill. [3] Bef. income fr. disc. opers. of $379.0 mill. ($1.79/sh.)

OFFICERS:
J. W. Snow, Chmn., Pres., C.E.O.
A. R. Carpenter, Vice-Chmn.
P. R. Goodwin, Vice-Chmn., Exec. V.P., C.F.O.

INVESTOR CONTACT: K. L. Kennedy, Admin.-Shareholder Serv., (804) 782-1465

PRINCIPAL OFFICE: 901 East Cary St., Richmond, VA 23219-4031

TELEPHONE NUMBER: (804) 782-1400
FAX: (804) 782-1409
WEB: www.csx.com

NO. OF EMPLOYEES: 45,355

SHAREHOLDERS: 49,083

ANNUAL MEETING: In May

INCORPORATED: VA, 1980

INSTITUTIONAL HOLDINGS:
No. of Institutions: 278
Shares Held: 165,498,360
% Held: 77.7

INDUSTRY: Railroads, line-haul operating (SIC: 4011)

TRANSFER AGENT(S): Computershare Investor Services, Chicago, IL

NYSE SYMBOL CTS
Rec. Pr. 24.00 (4/30/01)

CTS CORP.

YIELD	0.5%
P/E RATIO	8.2

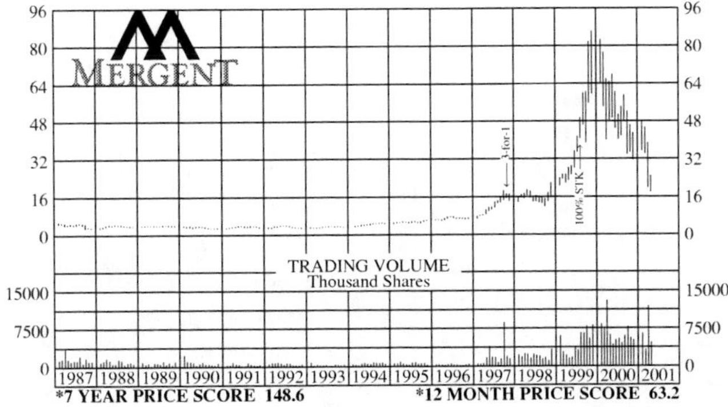

***7 YEAR PRICE SCORE 148.6** ***12 MONTH PRICE SCORE 63.2**

*NYSE COMPOSITE INDEX=100

INTERIM EARNINGS (Per Share):

Qtr.	Mar.	June	Sept.	Dec.
1997	0.22	0.27	0.24	d0.01
1998	0.28	0.33	0.29	0.35
1999	0.08	0.51	0.56	0.66
2000	0.68	0.71	0.76	0.79

INTERIM DIVIDENDS (Per Share):

Amt.	Decl.	Ex.	Rec.	Pay.
0.03Q	5/31/00	6/28/00	6/30/00	7/28/00
0.03Q	8/18/00	9/27/00	9/29/00	10/30/00
0.03Q	10/20/00	12/27/00	12/29/00	1/29/01
0.03Q	1/22/01	3/28/01	3/30/01	4/27/01
0.03Q	4/18/01	6/27/01	6/29/01	7/27/01

Indicated div.: $0.12 (Div. Reinv. Plan)

CAPITALIZATION (12/31/00):

	($000)	(%)
Long-Term Debt	178,000	38.8
Deferred Income Tax	34,612	7.5
Common & Surplus	246,357	53.7
Total	458,969	100.0

RECENT DEVELOPMENTS: For the twelve months ended 12/31/00, income from continuing operations soared 63.9% to $84.3 million compared with net earnings of $51.5 million in the previous year. The 1999 results included a pre-tax charge of $12.9 million for acquired in-process research and development. Net sales advanced 28.0% to $866.5 million. Electronic component sales climbed 5.8% to $536.7 million, while electronic assemblies sales rocketed 94.3% to $329.8 million. Operating earnings surged 55.4% to $128.6 million.

PROSPECTS: On 2/13/01, the Company announced that its CTS Automotive Products division has been awarded a new seat position sensor business by a seat component supplier for use in minivans. The contract represents both a new application and a new customer for CTS seat sensor products. Total sales from the contract are expected to exceed $9.0 million over the life of the program. Looking ahead, CTS expects the wireless handset and automotive markets will show significant growth in 2001.

BUSINESS

CTS CORP. designs, manufactures, assembles and sells a line of electronic components and electronic assemblies serving original equipment manufacturers. The electronic components segment consists principally of automotive sensors used in commercial or consumer vehicles and frequency control devices. The electronic assemblies segment consists principally of flex cable assemblies used in the disk drive market, hybrid microcircuits used in the healthcare market, cursor controls for computers and interconnect products, and connectors used in the telecommunications industry. On 2/26/99, CTS acquired Motorola's Component Products Division, which operates under the name RF Integrated Modules (formerly CTS Wireless Communications).

BUSINESS LINE ANALYSIS

(12/31/00)	Rev (%)	Inc (%)
Electronic Components	61.9	76.3
Electronic Assemblies	38.1	23.7
Total	100.0	100.0

ANNUAL FINANCIAL DATA

	12/31/00	12/31/99	12/31/98	12/31/97	12/31/96	12/31/95	12/31/94
Earnings Per Share	**4 2.94**	**3 1.80**	**2 1.17**	**1 0.72**	**0.67**	**0.55**	**0.45**
Cash Flow Per Share	**4.49**	**2.99**	**1.82**	**1.24**	**1.07**	**0.92**	**0.81**
Tang. Book Val. Per Share	**6.56**	**4.06**	**4.55**	**5.15**	**5.17**	**4.53**	**4.08**
Dividends Per Share	**0.12**	**0.12**	**0.12**	**0.12**	**0.11**	**0.10**	**0.07**
Dividend Payout %	**4.1**	**6.7**	**10.3**	**16.8**	**16.4**	**18.2**	**14.8**
INCOME STATEMENT (IN THOUSANDS):							
Total Revenues	866,523	677,076	370,441	415,151	321,297	300,157	268,707
Costs & Expenses	693,568	560,373	301,678	363,038	275,386	260,986	236,787
Depreciation & Amort.	44,325	33,907	19,155	16,965	12,491	11,683	11,236
Operating Income	128,630	82,796	49,608	35,148	33,420	27,488	20,684
Net Interest Inc./(Exp.)	d12,204	d9,079	d1,053	d486	432	d369	d57
Income Before Income Taxes	117,127	74,055	49,441	35,097	33,602	27,684	21,487
Income Taxes	32,796	22,587	15,368	12,284	12,432	10,520	7,520
Net Income	4 84,331	3 51,468	2 34,073	1 22,813	21,170	17,164	13,967
Cash Flow	128,656	85,375	53,228	39,778	33,661	28,847	25,203
Average Shs. Outstg.	28,675	28,589	29,228	31,952	31,350	31,302	31,020
BALANCE SHEET (IN THOUSANDS):							
Cash & Cash Equivalents	20,564	24,219	16,273	39,847	44,957	37,271	24,922
Total Current Assets	305,696	254,297	118,583	185,733	138,201	126,113	110,667
Net Property	224,861	139,692	67,186	76,027	56,103	50,696	50,777
Total Assets	672,929	522,652	293,189	329,581	249,372	227,127	206,826
Total Current Liabilities	202,891	154,461	82,377	92,352	51,391	50,962	44,792
Long-Term Obligations	178,000	162,000	42,000	63,474	11,220	13,714	15,595
Net Stockholders' Equity	246,357	164,764	123,839	147,496	166,232	146,253	131,855
Net Working Capital	102,805	99,836	36,206	93,381	86,810	75,151	65,875
Year-end Shs. Outstg.	27,781	27,462	27,242	28,626	31,350	31,302	31,074
STATISTICAL RECORD:							
Operating Profit Margin %	14.8	12.2	13.4	8.5	10.4	9.2	7.7
Net Profit Margin %	9.7	7.6	9.2	5.5	6.6	5.7	5.2
Return on Equity %	34.2	31.2	27.5	15.5	12.7	11.7	10.6
Return on Assets %	12.5	9.8	11.6	6.9	8.5	7.6	6.8
Debt/Total Assets %	26.5	31.0	14.3	19.3	4.5	6.0	7.5
Price Range	82.75-31.50	86.25-20.44	21.94-11.81	18.63-6.79	7.83-6.00	6.29-4.56	5.10-3.25
P/E Ratio	28.1-10.7	47.9-11.4	18.8-10.1	26.0-9.5	11.7-8.9	11.4-8.3	11.3-7.2
Average Yield %	0.2	0.2	0.7	0.9	1.6	1.8	1.6

Statistics are as originally reported. Adj. for 2-for-1 split, 8/99; 3-for-1 split, 11/97. 1 Incl. $10.5 mill. ($0.67/sh.) after-tax non-recur. chrg. 2 Bef. disc. oper. gain $3.4 mill. 3 Incl. $12.9 mill pre-tax non-recurr. chrg. 4 Bef. loss of $529,000 from disc. opers.

OFFICERS:
J. P. Walker, Chmn., C.E.O.
D. K. Schwanz, Pres., C.O.O.
G. T. Newhart, V.P., Interim C.F.O.

INVESTOR CONTACT: George T. Newhart, (219) 293-7511

PRINCIPAL OFFICE: 905 West Blvd. North, Elkhart, IN 46514

TELEPHONE NUMBER: (219) 293-7511
FAX: (219) 293-6146
WEB: www.ctscorp.com
NO. OF EMPLOYEES: 9,060
SHAREHOLDERS: 1,520 (approx.)
ANNUAL MEETING: In Apr.
INCORPORATED: IN, Feb., 1929

INSTITUTIONAL HOLDINGS:
No. of Institutions: 167
Shares Held: 18,035,230
% Held: 64.9

INDUSTRY: Electronic resistors (SIC: 3676)

TRANSFER AGENT(S): State Street Bank and Trust Company, Boston, MA

NYSE SYMBOL CUM
Rec. Pr. 41.40 (4/30/01)

CUMMINS INC.

YIELD 2.9%
P/E RATIO 197.1

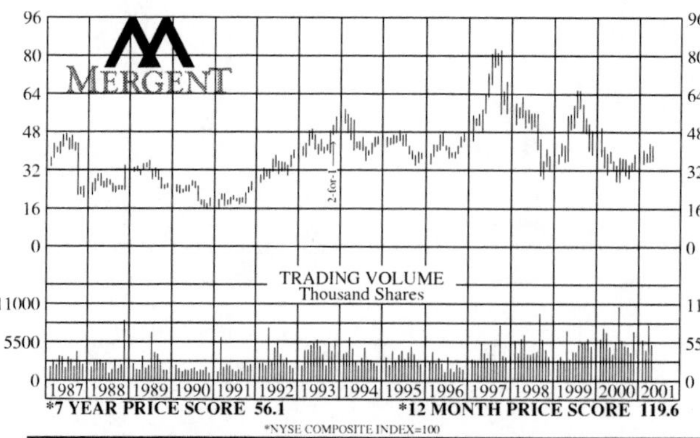

INTERIM EARNINGS (Per Share):

Qtr.	Mar.	June	Sept.	Dec.
1996	1.21	1.10	0.67	1.03
1997	1.06	1.39	1.40	1.66
1998	0.18	1.38	d2.86	0.75
1999	0.63	1.50	1.35	0.65
2000	1.09	1.62	0.66	d3.16

INTERIM DIVIDENDS (Per Share):

Amt.	Decl.	Ex.	Rec.	Pay.
0.30Q	4/04/00	5/30/00	6/01/00	6/15/00
0.30Q	7/11/00	8/30/00	9/01/00	9/15/00
0.30Q	10/10/00	11/29/00	12/01/00	12/15/00
0.30Q	2/13/01	2/27/01	3/01/01	3/15/01
0.30Q	4/03/01	5/30/01	6/01/01	6/15/01

Indicated div.: $1.20 (Div. Reinv. Plan)

CAPITALIZATION (12/31/00):

	($000)	(%)
Long-Term Debt	1,032,000	42.3
Minority Interest	72,000	3.0
Common & Surplus	1,336,000	54.8
Total	2,440,000	100.0

RECENT DEVELOPMENTS: For the twelve months ended 12/31/00, net earnings plunged 95.0% to $8.0 million compared with $160.0 million in the prior year. Results for 2000 and 1999 included pre-tax restructuring, asset impairment and other nonrecurring charges of $160.0 million and $60.0 million, respectively. Net sales fell to $6.60 billion from $6.64 billion in 1999. Engine revenues fell 4.1% to $4.05 billion. Power generation revenues rose 2.9% to $1.40 billion, while Filtration and Other sales climbed 8.9% to $1.15 billion.

PROSPECTS: CUM anticipates its Power Generation and Filtration and Other businesses will remain strong and profitable, despite challenges expected in the Engine business. The Company estimates earnings for 2001 to be approximately half the level reported for the year 2000. Separately, CUM has announced a number of longer-term restructuring activities throughout the Company. These actions, when fully implemented, should save the Company approximately $55.0 million per year.

BUSINESS

CUMMINS INC. (formerly Cummins Engine Company Inc.) is a worldwide designer and manufacturer of in-line and V-type engines and produces a broad range of engine-related components and power systems. The Company's principal market is the North American heavy-truck industry. Cummins operates in three business segments. The Engine Group (61.4% of 2000 sales) offers diesel engines for heavy-duty trucks, medium-duty trucks, and bus and light commercial vehicles. The Power Generation Group (21.1% of 2000 sales) offers diesel, natural gas, and gasoline-fueled power generation sets. The Filtration Group and Other segment (17.5% of 2000 sales) offers technical solutions including engine filters, hydraulic fluids and air.

REVENUES

(12/31/00)($000)	Rev	Inc
Engine	4,050,000	(107,000)
Power Generation	1,395,000	84,000
Filtration & Other	1,152,000	112,000
Total	6,597,000	89,000

ANNUAL FINANCIAL DATA

	12/31/00	12/31/99	12/31/98	12/31/97	12/31/96	12/31/95	12/31/94
Earnings Per Share	**[1] 0.20**	**[1] 4.13**	**[1] d0.55**	**5.48**	**4.01**	**[1] 5.52**	**6.11**
Cash Flow Per Share	**6.49**	**10.18**	**4.62**	**9.56**	**7.76**	**9.02**	**9.19**
Tang. Book Val. Per Share	**23.72**	**25.66**	**21.14**	**33.49**	**33.30**	**29.43**	**25.78**
Dividends Per Share	**1.20**	**1.13**	**1.10**	**1.07**	**1.00**	**1.00**	**0.63**
Dividend Payout %	**599.7**	**27.2**	**...**	**19.6**	**24.9**	**18.1**	**10.2**
INCOME STATEMENT (IN MILLIONS):							
Total Revenues	6,597.0	6,639.0	6,266.0	5,625.0	5,257.0	5,245.0	4,737.2
Costs & Expenses	6,278.0	6,074.0	5,893.0	5,191.0	4,900.0	4,904.0	4,302.0
Depreciation & Amort.	240.0	233.0	199.0	158.0	149.0	143.0	127.7
Operating Income	79.0	332.0	174.0	276.0	208.0	198.0	307.5
Net Interest Inc./(Exp.)	d86.0	d75.0	d71.0	d26.0	d18.0	d13.0	d17.5
Income Before Income Taxes	3.0	221.0	d6.0	286.0	214.0	177.0	293.5
Income Taxes	cr19.0	55.0	4.0	74.0	54.0	cr47.0	40.5
Equity Earnings/Minority Int.	d14.0	d6.0	d11.0	...	...	...	d0.1
Net Income	[1] 8.0	[1] 160.0	[1] d21.0	212.0	160.0	[1] 224.0	252.9
Cash Flow	248.0	393.0	178.0	370.0	309.0	367.0	380.6
Average Shs. Outstg. (000)	38,200	38,600	38,500	38,700	39,800	40,700	41,400
BALANCE SHEET (IN MILLIONS):							
Cash & Cash Equivalents	62.0	74.0	38.0	49.0	108.0	60.0	146.9
Total Current Assets	1,830.0	2,180.0	1,876.0	1,710.0	1,553.0	1,388.0	1,297.8
Net Property	1,598.0	1,630.0	1,671.0	1,532.0	1,286.0	1,148.0	1,089.9
Total Assets	4,500.0	4,697.0	4,542.0	3,765.0	3,369.0	3,056.0	2,706.3
Total Current Liabilities	1,223.0	1,314.0	1,071.0	1,055.0	1,021.0	1,053.0	840.0
Long-Term Obligations	1,032.0	1,092.0	1,137.0	522.0	283.0	117.0	154.9
Net Stockholders' Equity	1,336.0	1,429.0	1,272.0	1,422.0	1,312.0	1,183.0	1,072.6
Net Working Capital	607.0	866.0	805.0	655.0	532.0	335.0	457.8
Year-end Shs. Outstg. (000)	41,400	41,500	42,000	42,100	39,400	40,200	41,600
STATISTICAL RECORD:							
Operating Profit Margin %	1.2	5.0	2.8	4.9	4.0	3.8	6.5
Net Profit Margin %	0.1	2.4	...	3.8	3.0	4.3	5.3
Return on Equity %	0.6	11.2	...	14.9	12.2	18.9	23.6
Return on Assets %	0.2	3.4	...	5.6	4.7	7.3	9.3
Debt/Total Assets %	22.9	23.2	25.0	13.9	8.4	3.8	5.7
Price Range	50.00-27.06	65.69-34.56	62.75-28.31	83.00-44.25	47.75-34.50	48.63-34.00	57.63-35.88
P/E Ratio	249.9-135.2	15.9-8.4	...	15.1-8.1	11.9-8.6	8.8-6.2	9.4-5.9
Average Yield %	3.1	2.2	2.4	1.7	2.4	2.4	1.3

Statistics are as originally reported. [1] Incl. non-recurr. chrg. $77.0 mill., 1995; $161.0 mill., 1998 & $60.0 mill., 1999; $160.0 mill., 2000

OFFICERS:
T. M. Solso, Chmn., Pres., C.E.O.
T. Linebarger, V.P., C.F.O.

INVESTOR CONTACT: Dorothy Brown Smith, (812) 377-7719

PRINCIPAL OFFICE: 500 Jackson Street, Box 3005, Columbus, IN 47202-3005

TELEPHONE NUMBER: (812) 377-5000
FAX: (812) 377-4937
WEB: www.cummins.com

NO. OF EMPLOYEES: 28,000 (avg.)

SHAREHOLDERS: 4,800 (approx.)

ANNUAL MEETING: In Apr.

INCORPORATED: IN, Feb., 1919

INSTITUTIONAL HOLDINGS:
No. of Institutions: 199
Shares Held: 19,853,649
% Held: 48.0

INDUSTRY: Internal combustion engines, nec (SIC: 3519)

TRANSFER AGENT(S): First Chicago Trust Company of New York, Jersey City, NJ

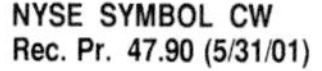

NYSE SYMBOL CW
Rec. Pr. 47.90 (5/31/01)

CURTISS-WRIGHT CORPORATION

YIELD 1.1%
P/E RATIO 11.9

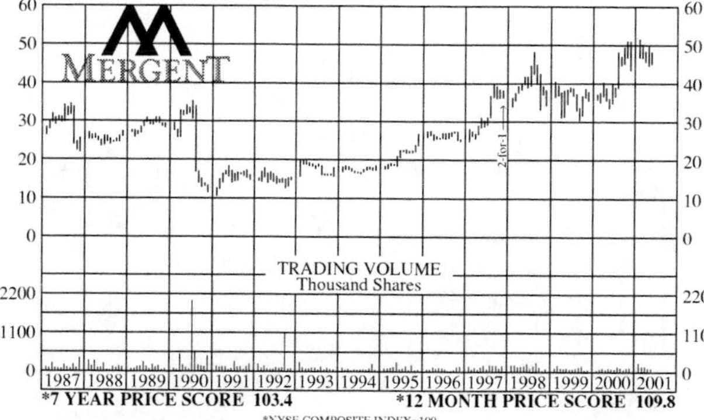

INTERIM EARNINGS (Per Share):

Qtr.	Mar.	June	Sept.	Dec.
1996	0.32	0.51	0.44	0.31
1997	0.49	0.69	0.79	0.77
1998	0.64	0.75	0.66	0.78
1999	0.78	0.79	1.38	0.87
2000	0.91	1.05	1.09	0.99

INTERIM DIVIDENDS (Per Share):

Amt.	Decl.	Ex.	Rec.	Pay.
0.13Q	4/11/00	7/12/00	7/14/00	7/28/00
0.13Q	9/18/00	10/12/00	10/16/00	10/30/00
0.13Q	11/20/00	11/29/00	12/01/00	12/15/00
0.13Q	2/02/01	4/10/01	4/12/01	4/26/01
0.13Q	4/24/01	7/11/01	7/13/01	7/27/01

Indicated div.: $0.52 (Div. Reinv. Plan)

CAPITALIZATION (12/31/00):

	($000)	(%)
Long-Term Debt	24,730	7.3
Deferred Income Tax	21,689	6.4
Common & Surplus	290,224	86.2
Total	336,643	100.0

RECENT DEVELOPMENTS: For the year ended 12/31/00, net income advanced 5.2% to $41.1 million from $39.0 million in the previous year. Earnings for 2000 and 1999 included nonrecurring items that resulted in net after-tax gains of $3.2 million and $5.0 million, respectively. Net sales grew 12.4% to $329.6 million from $293.3 million in the prior year. Operating income increased 2.0% to $52.2 million versus $51.2 million in 1999.

PROSPECTS: CW entered 2001 with a strengthened balance sheet due to significantly reduced inventory levels. Hence, CW is well-positioned to pursue strategic acquisitions and fund organic health programs. On 12/15/00, Metal Improvement Company, a subsidiary of the Company, acquired the commercial heat-treating business of Electric Furnace Co. in Salem, Ohio, which expands CW's network of heat-treating facilities in North America.

BUSINESS

CURTISS-WRIGHT CORPORATION designs, develops and manufactures flight control actuation systems and components for the aerospace industry and provides metal-treating services such as shot peening and heat treating. In addition, the Company designs, manufactures, refurbishes and tests highly engineered valves of various types and sizes. The Company reports its operations in three segments: Motion Control, Metal Treatment, and Flow Control. Operations are conducted through 37 metal treatment service facilities located in North America and Europe, and component overhaul facilities located in Florida, North Carolina, Denmark and Singapore.

BUSINESS LINE ANALYSIS

(12/31/2000)	Rev(%)	Inc(%)
Motion Control..........	38.4	31.3
Metal Treatment........	32.0	47.8
Flow Control	29.6	20.9
Total	100.0	100.0

ANNUAL FINANCIAL DATA

	12/31/00	12/31/99	12/31/98	12/31/97	12/31/96	12/31/95	12/31/94
Earnings Per Share	**[5] 4.03**	**[4] 3.82**	**[3] 2.82**	**[2] 2.71**	**1.59**	**1.80**	**[1] 1.93**
Cash Flow Per Share	**5.44**	**5.08**	**3.76**	**3.59**	**2.47**	**2.73**	**3.01**
Tang. Book Val. Per Share	**24.23**	**20.72**	**19.51**	**19.76**	**18.04**	**16.95**	**15.69**
Dividends Per Share	**0.52**	**0.52**	**0.52**	**0.51**	**0.50**	**0.50**	**0.50**
Dividend Payout %	**12.9**	**13.6**	**18.4**	**18.6**	**31.5**	**27.9**	**25.9**
INCOME STATEMENT (IN THOUSANDS):							
Total Revenues	329,575	293,263	249,413	219,395	170,536	167,551	166,189
Costs & Expenses	263,044	229,242	203,405	176,979	142,408	129,998	126,148
Depreciation & Amort.	14,346	12,864	9,661	9,097	8,946	9,512	10,883
Operating Income	52,185	51,157	36,347	33,319	19,182	28,041	29,158
Net Interest Inc./(Exp.)	d1,743	d1,289	d485	d387	d387	d549	d401
Income Before Income Taxes	65,971	63,309	47,580	41,899	24,129	27,492	28,757
Income Taxes	24,897	24,264	18,527	14,014	8,020	9,323	9,210
Net Income	[5] 41,074	[4] 39,045	[3] 29,053	[2] 27,885	16,109	18,169	[1] 19,547
Cash Flow	55,420	51,909	38,714	36,982	25,055	27,681	30,430
Average Shs. Outstg.	10,194	10,215	10,305	10,291	10,158	10,124	10,122
BALANCE SHEET (IN THOUSANDS):							
Cash & Cash Equivalents	71,458	35,107	72,253	68,755	61,991	78,763	76,445
Total Current Assets	202,072	180,370	198,573	171,380	157,833	153,625	144,343
Net Property	90,453	94,578	74,511	65,883	63,962	56,269	60,438
Total Assets	409,416	387,126	352,740	284,708	267,164	246,201	238,694
Total Current Liabilities	52,293	55,932	67,810	38,629	42,416	33,054	36,014
Long-Term Obligations	24,730	34,171	20,162	10,347	10,347	10,347	9,047
Net Stockholders' Equity	290,224	258,355	229,593	204,853	183,363	172,179	158,769
Net Working Capital	149,779	124,438	130,763	132,751	115,417	120,571	108,329
Year-end Shs. Outstg.	10,017	10,040	10,191	10,175	10,162	10,156	10,122
STATISTICAL RECORD:							
Operating Profit Margin %	15.8	17.4	14.6	15.2	11.2	16.7	17.5
Net Profit Margin %	12.5	13.3	11.6	12.7	9.4	10.8	11.8
Return on Equity %	14.2	15.1	12.7	13.6	8.8	10.6	12.3
Return on Assets %	10.0	10.1	8.2	9.8	6.0	7.4	8.2
Debt/Total Assets %	6.0	8.8	5.7	3.6	3.9	4.2	3.8
Price Range	51.13-33.44	40.63-30.38	48.38-33.06	39.88-24.75	27.63-24.81	26.88-17.56	18.63-16.31
P/E Ratio	12.7-8.3	10.6-8.0	17.2-11.7	14.7-9.1	17.4-15.7	15.0-9.8	9.6-8.5
Average Yield %	1.2	1.5	1.3	1.6	1.9	2.3	2.9

Statistics are as originally reported. Adj. for 2-for-1 stock split, 12/97. [1] Bef acct. chrg. of $244,000 [2] Incl. gain of $2.0 mill. fr. the sale of excess real estate. [3] Incl. aft.-tax chgs. of $1.3 mill. fr. consol. chgs. & insur. claim proceeds. [4] Incl. an after-tax gain of $7.4 mill. rel. to an insur. claim settlement & a chrg. of $2.3 mill. rel. to consol. of facilities. [5] Incl. net after-tax gains of $3.2 mill.

OFFICERS:
M. R. Benante, Chmn., C.E.O.
G. Nachman, Exec. V.P.
G. J. Benschip, Treas.

INVESTOR CONTACT: Gary Benschip, Treasurer, (201) 896-8520

PRINCIPAL OFFICE: 1200 Wall Street West, Lyndhurst, NJ 07071

TELEPHONE NUMBER: (201) 896-8400
FAX: (201) 438-5680
WEB: www.curtisswright.com

NO. OF EMPLOYEES: 2,286 (avg.)

SHAREHOLDERS: 3,564

ANNUAL MEETING: In May

INCORPORATED: DE, Aug., 1929

INSTITUTIONAL HOLDINGS:
No. of Institutions: 52
Shares Held: 8,244,469
% Held: 82.0

INDUSTRY: Metal heat treating (SIC: 3398)

TRANSFER AGENT(S): Mellon Investor Services LLC, South Hackensack, NJ

NYSE SYMBOL CVS
Rec. Pr. 54.90 (5/31/01)

CVS CORPORATION

YIELD 0.4%
P/E RATIO 30.0

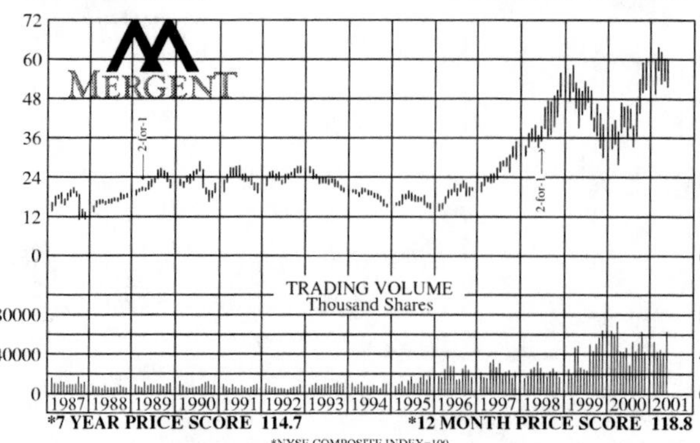

INTERIM EARNINGS (Per Share):

Qtr.	Mar.	June	Sept.	Dec.
1997	0.26	d0.69	0.21	0.31
1998	0.34	0.03	0.25	0.36
1999	0.40	0.40	0.30	0.46
2000	0.47	0.46	0.39	0.51

INTERIM DIVIDENDS (Per Share):

Amt.	Decl.	Ex.	Rec.	Pay.
0.058Q	4/19/00	4/20/00	4/25/00	5/04/00
0.058Q	7/12/00	7/20/00	7/24/00	8/04/00
0.058Q	9/13/00	10/19/00	10/23/00	11/03/00
0.058Q	1/10/01	1/19/01	1/23/01	2/05/01
0.058Q	3/07/01	4/20/01	4/24/01	5/04/01

Indicated div.: $0.23 (Div. Reinv. Plan)

CAPITALIZATION (12/30/00):

	($000)	(%)
Long-Term Debt	536,800	11.0
Deferred Income Tax	28,000	0.6
Preferred Stock	267,500	5.5
Common & Surplus	4,037,100	82.9
Total	4,869,400	100.0

RECENT DEVELOPMENTS: For the 52 weeks ended 12/30/00, net earnings climbed 17.5% to $746.0 million from $635.1 million in the corresponding 53-week period the year before. Results in the recent period included an $11.5 million after-tax non-recurring gain stemming from a litigation settlement. Net sales grew 11.0% to $20.09 billion from $18.10 billion a year earlier. Operating profit rose 16.5% to $1.32 billion from $1.14 billion in 1999.

PROSPECTS: Long-term revenue and earnings growth should be fueled by the Company's plans to expand into new, high-growth markets. On 2/6/01, the Company announced plans to enter two new U.S. drugstore markets, Phoenix, Arizona and Las Vegas, Nevada. The Company anticipates opening stores in Las Vegas by the end of 2001, while the first CVS stores in Phoenix are scheduled to open during the first half of 2002.

BUSINESS

CVS CORPORATION (formerly Melville Corporation) operates a chain of 4,124 drug stores in 31 states and the District of Columbia. CVS emerged as a stand-alone chain drug company following a restructuring program in which Melville Corporation divested its non-drug store operations and created two publicly-traded independent companies, CVS and Footstar, Inc. In addition to prescription drugs and services, CVS offers a broad selection of general merchandise, including over-the-counter drugs, greeting cards, film and photofinishing services, beauty and cosmetics, seasonal merchandise and convenience foods. In May 1997, CVS acquired Revco D.S., Inc. and in March 1998, CVS acquired Arbor Drugs Inc.

QUARTERLY DATA

(12/30/2000) ($000)	Rev	Inc
1st Quarter	4,739,500	191,300
2nd Quarter	4,942,800	186,500
3rd Quarter	4,916,400	158,700
4th Quarter	5,488,800	209,500

ANNUAL FINANCIAL DATA

	12/30/00	1/1/00	12/31/98	[4] 12/31/97	[6] 12/31/96	[7] 12/31/95	12/31/94
Earnings Per Share	[5] 1.83	1.55	[5] 0.98	[3] 0.07	[2] 1.06	[1] d3.01	1.38
Cash Flow Per Share	2.52	2.20	1.56	0.72	1.70	d1.84	2.44
Tang. Book Val. Per Share	8.20	6.88	5.40	3.96	3.87	4.84	7.54
Dividends Per Share	0.23	0.23	0.22	0.22	0.22	0.76	0.76
Dividend Payout %	12.6	14.8	22.9	313.8	20.8	...	55.3
INCOME STATEMENT (IN MILLIONS):							
Total Revenues	20,087.5	18,098.3	15,273.6	12,738.2	5,528.1	9,689.1	11,285.6
Costs & Expenses	18,468.2	16,684.9	14,251.7	12,312.2	5,094.8	10,203.5	10,468.6
Depreciation & Amort.	296.6	277.9	249.7	226.2	133.7	228.4	206.3
Operating Income	1,322.7	1,135.5	772.2	199.8	299.6	d742.8	610.7
Net Interest Inc./(Exp.)	d79.3	d59.1	d60.9	d44.8	d23.2	d55.0	d32.6
Income Before Income Taxes	1,243.4	1,076.4	711.3	155.0	403.4	d797.8	578.1
Income Taxes	497.4	441.3	314.9	117.7	163.8	cr182.1	218.7
Net Income	[5] 746.0	635.1	[5] 396.4	[3] 37.3	[2] 239.6	[1] d615.7	307.5
Cash Flow	1,028.0	898.3	632.5	249.8	358.8	d404.2	496.7
Average Shs. Outstg. (000)	408,000	408,900	405,200	346,000	211,400	210,400	210,962
BALANCE SHEET (IN MILLIONS):							
Cash & Cash Equivalents	337.3	230.0	180.8	168.5	603.3	304.6	117.0
Total Current Assets	4,936.6	4,608.0	4,349.2	3,685.0	1,972.7	2,559.9	2,650.5
Net Property	1,742.1	1,601.0	1,351.2	958.2	606.5	1,114.4	1,526.9
Total Assets	7,949.5	7,275.4	6,736.2	5,636.9	2,831.8	3,961.6	4,735.5
Total Current Liabilities	2,964.1	2,889.9	3,183.3	2,855.0	1,181.9	1,797.7	1,642.7
Long-Term Obligations	536.8	558.5	275.7	272.6	303.7	327.7	331.3
Net Stockholders' Equity	4,304.6	3,679.7	3,110.6	2,361.4	1,245.1	1,547.8	2,381.6
Net Working Capital	1,972.5	1,718.1	1,165.9	830.0	790.8	762.2	1,007.8
Year-end Shs. Outstg. (000)	392,322	391,996	390,211	344,800	213,200	210,212	211,284
STATISTICAL RECORD:							
Operating Profit Margin %	6.6	6.3	5.1	1.6	5.4	...	5.4
Net Profit Margin %	3.7	3.5	2.6	0.3	4.3	...	2.7
Return on Equity %	17.3	17.3	12.7	1.6	19.2	...	12.9
Return on Assets %	9.4	8.7	5.9	0.7	8.5	...	6.5
Debt/Total Assets %	6.8	7.7	4.1	4.8	10.7	8.3	7.0
Price Range	60.44-27.75	58.38-30.00	56.00-30.44	35.00-19.50	23.00-13.63	19.94-14.31	20.81-14.75
P/E Ratio	33.0-15.2	37.7-19.4	57.1-31.1	499.3-278.2	21.7-12.9	...	15.1-10.7
Average Yield %	0.5	0.5	0.5	0.8	1.2	4.4	4.3

Statistics are as originally reported. Adj. for 2-for-1 stk. split, 6/98. [1] Bef. $547,000 gain fr disc. ops. & $42 mil acctg. cr., incl. $799 mil restr. chg. [2] Bef. $164.2 mil ($0.78/sh) loss fr disc. ops., incl. $121.4 mil ($0.34/sh) gain fr sale of secs. & $148 mil ($0.70/sh) restr. chg. [3] Bef. $17.1 mil ($0.05/sh) extraord. chg. & $17.5 mil gain fr disc. ops., incl. $442.7 mil merger & restr. chg. [4] Refls incl. of Revco ops. [5] Incl. $11.5 mil ($0.03/sh) after-tax gain, 2000; $158.3 mil pre-tax chg., 1998. [6] Refls. sale of Kay-Bee Center, Inc. [7] Refls. sale of Marshalls.

OFFICERS:
T. M. Ryan, Chmn., Pres., C.E.O.
D. B. Rickard, Exec. V.P., C.F.O.

INVESTOR CONTACT: Nancy R. Cristal, V.P.-Inv. Rel., (800) 201-0938

PRINCIPAL OFFICE: One CVS Drive, Woonsocket, RI 02895

TELEPHONE NUMBER: (401) 765-1500
FAX: (401) 762-2137
WEB: www.cvs.com
NO. OF EMPLOYEES: 99,000 (approx.)
SHAREHOLDERS: 12,100 (approx.)
ANNUAL MEETING: In Apr.
INCORPORATED: NY, May, 1914; reincorp., DE, Nov., 1996

INSTITUTIONAL HOLDINGS:
No. of Institutions: 544
Shares Held: 335,531,798
% Held: 85.4

INDUSTRY: Drug stores and proprietary stores (SIC: 5912)

TRANSFER AGENT(S): The Bank of New York, New York, NY

NYSE SYMBOL CY
Rec. Pr. 21.15 (5/31/01)

CYPRESS SEMICONDUCTOR CORP.

YIELD ...
P/E RATIO 10.4

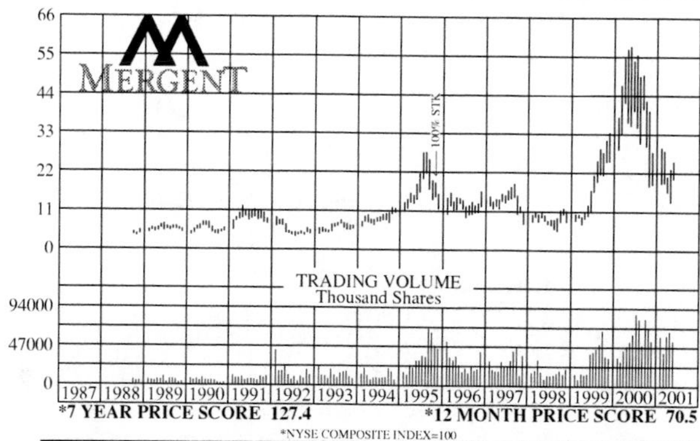

*7 YEAR PRICE SCORE 127.4 *12 MONTH PRICE SCORE 70.5

*NYSE COMPOSITE INDEX=100

INTERIM EARNINGS (Per Share):

Qtr.	Mar.	June	Sept.	Dec.
1997	0.06	0.07	0.08	Nil
1998	d1.03	d0.11	d0.01	d0.07
1999	0.09	0.08	0.23	0.39
2000	0.41	0.49	0.45	0.68

INTERIM DIVIDENDS (Per Share):

Amt.	Decl.	Ex.	Rec.	Pay.

No dividends paid.

CAPITALIZATION (12/31/00):

	($000)	(%)
Long-Term Debt	570,500	28.5
Deferred Income Tax	103,604	5.2
Common & Surplus	1,327,668	66.3
Total	2,001,772	100.0

RECENT DEVELOPMENTS: For the year ended 12/31/00, net income more than tripled to $277.3 million versus $88.1 million in 1999. Results for 2000 included acquisition-related costs of $56.2 million and a restructuring credit of $485,000. The 1999 results included a net nonrecurring charge of $34.1 million. Revenues jumped 72.8% to $1.29 billion versus $745.0 million in the previous year. Operating income amounted to $328.8 million versus $51.6 million in 1999.

PROSPECTS: On 3/1/01, CY completed its acquisition of International Microcircuits, Inc. (IMI), a supplier of timing technology integrated circuits, in an all-cash transaction valued at $125.0 million. The acquisition should enhance CY's product porfolio with complementary products, including programmable clocks, clock distribution products, electromagnetic interference suppression devices and application-specific products. The acquisition should be accretive to earnings beginning in 2002.

BUSINESS

CYPRESS SEMICONDUCTOR CORP. is a global supplier of high-performance digital and mixed-signal integrated circuits to a broad range of markets, including data communications, telecommunications, computation, consumer products and industrial control. CY structures its business into four business segments with two product lines. CY's business segments include: wide area networks (WAN), storage networks (SN), wireless terminals and wireless infrastructure. The Company's memory products line primarily consists of static random access memory products. The Company's portfolio of non-memory products consists of programmable logic products and programming software, programmable-skew clocking, data communications products, computer products, microcontrollers and non-volatile memory products.

REVENUES

(12/31/00)	($000)	(%)
Memory Products	638,111	49.6
Non-memory Products	649,676	50.4
Total	1,287,787	100.0

ANNUAL FINANCIAL DATA

	12/31/00	1/2/00	1/3/99	12/29/97	12/30/96	1/1/96	1/2/95
Earnings Per Share	**[1][3] 2.03**	**[1][3] 0.81**	**[2] d1.24**	**0.21**	**[1] 0.63**	**[2] 1.15**	**0.61**
Cash Flow Per Share	**2.97**	**1.79**	**d7.55**	**1.41**	**1.83**	**1.90**	**1.18**
Tang. Book Val. Per Share	**10.57**	**6.32**	**5.76**	**7.10**	**6.30**	**5.79**	**4.54**
INCOME STATEMENT (IN MILLIONS):							
Total Revenues	1,287.8	705.5	554.9	544.4	528.4	596.1	406.4
Costs & Expenses	808.2	544.2	1,245.4	410.7	346.4	369.5	281.9
Depreciation & Amort.	150.7	108.5	113.7	115.3	100.4	67.4	46.7
Operating Income	328.8	52.8	d127.3	18.3	81.6	159.2	77.8
Net Interest Inc./(Exp.)	d23.6	d9.6	d10.9	d7.2	d6.9	d6.2	d4.0
Income Before Income Taxes	370.2	95.9	d124.9	24.0	83.5	161.4	80.1
Income Taxes	92.9	4.8	cr14.0	5.6	30.5	58.9	29.6
Net Income	[1][3] 277.3	[1][3] 91.1	[2] d787.8	18.4	[1] 53.0	[2] 102.5	50.5
Cash Flow	428.0	199.5	d674.1	133.8	153.4	169.8	97.2
Average Shs. Outstg. (000)	144,228	111,735	89,338	94,648	83,661	89,347	82,313
BALANCE SHEET (IN MILLIONS):							
Cash & Cash Equivalents	884.6	270.6	152.2	201.6	93.8	161.6	193.3
Total Current Assets	1,282.8	537.4	283.7	398.1	281.4	351.6	317.1
Net Property	571.5	357.2	347.7	442.7	437.6	336.6	201.6
Total Assets	2,361.8	1,117.2	756.3	956.3	794.0	750.7	555.7
Total Current Liabilities	299.4	192.8	99.6	93.1	155.4	161.1	91.2
Long-Term Obligations	570.5	160.0	160.0	175.0	98.2	95.9	93.7
Net Stockholders' Equity	1,327.7	698.0	489.1	643.5	510.7	472.1	353.0
Net Working Capital	983.4	344.6	184.1	305.0	126.0	190.6	226.0
Year-end Shs. Outstg. (000)	125,659	110,516	84,859	90,684	81,098	81,501	77,821
STATISTICAL RECORD:							
Operating Profit Margin %	25.5	7.5	...	3.4	15.4	26.7	19.1
Net Profit Margin %	21.5	12.9	...	3.4	10.0	17.2	12.4
Return on Equity %	20.9	13.0	...	2.9	10.4	21.7	14.3
Return on Assets %	11.7	8.2	...	1.9	6.7	13.7	9.1
Debt/Total Assets %	24.2	14.3	21.2	18.3	12.4	12.8	16.9
Price Range	58.00-18.25	33.50-7.38	12.00-5.50	18.94-7.38	16.63-9.13	27.75-10.75	12.06-6.56
P/E Ratio	28.6-9.0	41.4-9.1	...	90.1-35.1	26.4-14.5	24.1-9.3	19.8-10.8

Statistics are as originally reported. Adj. for 2-for-1 stk. split. [1] Incl. special credit of $485,000, 2000; $3.8 mill., 1999; $7.0 mill., 1996. [2] Incl. restruct. & other nonrecurr. costs of $58.9 mill., 1998; $17.8 mill., 1995. [3] Incl. acq.-related nonrecurr. chrg. of $56.2 mill., 2000; $37.9 mill., 1999.

OFFICERS:
E. Benhamou, Chmn.
T. J. Rodgers, Pres., C.E.O.
E. Hernandez, Exec. V.P., C.F.O.

INVESTOR CONTACT: Investor Relations Dept., (408) 943-2911

PRINCIPAL OFFICE: 3901 North First Street, San Jose, CA 95134-1599

TELEPHONE NUMBER: (408) 943-2600
FAX: (408) 943-2741
WEB: www.cypress.com

NO. OF EMPLOYEES: 4,435

SHAREHOLDERS: 88,000 (approx.)

ANNUAL MEETING: In May

INCORPORATED: CA, Dec., 1982; reincorp., DE, Feb., 1987

INSTITUTIONAL HOLDINGS:
No. of Institutions: 253
Shares Held: 73,050,072
% Held: 57.5

INDUSTRY: Semiconductors and related devices (SIC: 3674)

TRANSFER AGENT(S): EquiServe, L.P., Canton, MA

NYSE SYMBOL CYT
Rec. Pr. 32.71 (4/30/01)

CYTEC INDUSTRIES, INC.

YIELD ...
P/E RATIO 7.9

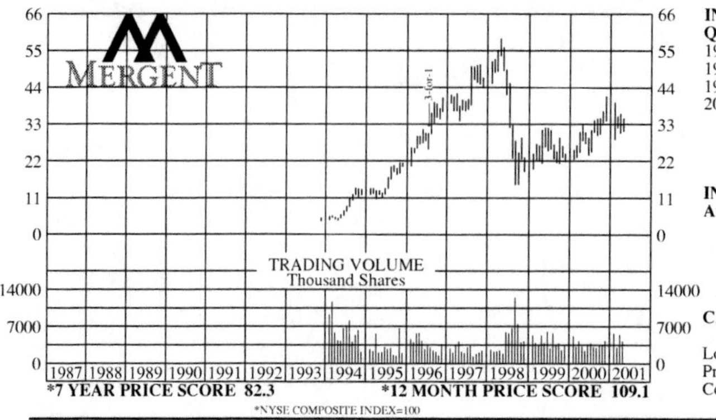

INTERIM EARNINGS (Per Share):

Qtr.	Mar.	June	Sept.	Dec.
1997	0.56	0.59	0.60	0.65
1998	0.66	0.73	0.59	0.71
1999	0.63	0.63	0.79	0.68
2000	0.74	0.95	0.65	1.82

INTERIM DIVIDENDS (Per Share):

Amt.	Decl.	Ex.	Rec.	Pay.
No dividends paid.				

CAPITALIZATION (12/31/00):

	($000)	(%)
Long-Term Debt	311,200	33.6
Preferred Stock	100	0.0
Common & Surplus	616,100	66.4
Total	927,400	100.0

RECENT DEVELOPMENTS: For the year ended 12/31/00, net earnings jumped 46.4% to $177.6 million versus $121.3 million in 1999. Results for 2000 included an after-tax gain of $8.7 million related to insurance settlements, an after-tax gain of $57.8 million from the sale of the Paper Chemical business, and an after-tax expense of $10.6 million for restructuring and other charges. Results for 1999 included a reduction of $8.0 million in income tax expense and a charge of $2.5 million. Net sales climbed 3.3% to $1.49 billion.

PROSPECTS: Near-term earnings may be hampered by increases in raw material prices and slowing in parts of the U.S. and Asian economies. The Company's Water and Industrial Process Chemicals division is well positioned to meet its 2001 growth goals due to ongoing opportunities to expand in CYT's global markets through technology, acquisitions and volume growth. However, slowing economic growth may reduce sales to the plastics, automotive and industrial coating markets.

BUSINESS

CYTEC INDUSTRIES, INC. develops manufactures and markets water and industrial process chemicals, specialty material, building block chemicals and performance products. The water and industrial process chemicals product category was responsible for 25.9% of 2000 revenues. The products include water treating, paper mining and phosphine chemicals. The specialty materials product category accounted for 26.4% of 2000 revenues. The products include aerospace adhesives and advanced composites; acrylic plastics and methyl methcrylate; refinery and styrene catalysts and other specialty materials. Building block chemicals (17.2% of revenues) include acrylonitrile, acrylamide, melamine methanol, and other building block chemicals. Performance products (30.5% of revenues) include specialty resins, polymer additives, surfactants, specialty monomers and urethane systems.

ANNUAL FINANCIAL DATA

	12/31/00	12/31/99	12/31/98	12/31/97	12/31/96	12/31/95	12/31/94
Earnings Per Share	4 **4.15**	3 **2.73**	2 **2.68**	1 **2.39**	**2.01**	**1.80**	**1.05**
Cash Flow Per Share	**6.41**	**4.86**	**4.56**	**4.05**	**3.79**	**6.54**	**3.60**
Tang. Book Val. Per Share	**5.77**	**2.66**	**1.88**	**2.03**	**6.53**	**6.49**	**1.64**
INCOME STATEMENT (IN MILLIONS):							
Total Revenues	1,492.5	1,412.5	1,444.5	1,290.6	1,259.6	1,260.1	1,101.3
Costs & Expenses	1,219.3	1,132.4	1,171.8	1,092.6	1,034.5	1,047.5	946.8
Depreciation & Amort.	96.6	95.1	87.2	78.8	89.0	89.9	86.0
Operating Income	176.6	185.0	185.5	119.2	136.1	122.7	68.5
Net Interest Inc./(Exp.)	d25.1	d26.9	d22.4	d5.7	d4.0	d1.0	d0.2
Income Before Income Taxes	271.1	173.0	197.9	149.7	142.1	132.1	80.6
Income Taxes	93.5	51.7	73.2	36.1	56.9	cr136.2	34.7
Equity Earnings/Minority Int.	15.0	5.6	20.3	12.3	14.9	13.9	10.1
Net Income	4 177.6	3 121.3	2 124.7	1 113.6	100.1	282.2	56.1
Cash Flow	274.2	216.4	211.9	192.4	189.1	166.2	127.4
Average Shs. Outstg. (000)	42,745	44,505	46,480	47,554	49,913	56,903	39,450
BALANCE SHEET (IN MILLIONS):							
Cash & Cash Equivalents	56.8	12.0	1.7	6.4	20.4	12.0	97.7
Total Current Assets	567.8	491.1	477.6	452.8	416.3	404.0	439.0
Net Property	616.2	655.7	667.5	629.7	582.2	605.7	586.7
Total Assets	1,719.4	1,759.9	1,730.6	1,614.1	1,261.1	1,293.8	1,199.4
Total Current Liabilities	358.9	366.1	394.4	375.0	312.8	317.7	320.1
Long-Term Obligations	311.2	422.5	419.5	324.0	89.0	66.0	...
Net Stockholders' Equity	616.2	505.8	431.0	387.4	314.4	342.9	83.3
Net Working Capital	208.9	125.0	83.2	77.8	103.5	86.3	118.9
Year-end Shs. Outstg. (000)	40,166	41,610	43,190	45,137	45,494	50,034	39,384
STATISTICAL RECORD:							
Operating Profit Margin %	11.8	13.1	12.8	9.2	10.8	9.7	6.2
Net Profit Margin %	11.9	8.6	8.6	8.8	7.9	22.4	5.1
Return on Equity %	28.8	24.0	28.9	29.3	31.8	82.3	67.3
Return on Assets %	10.3	6.9	7.2	7.0	7.9	21.8	4.7
Debt/Total Assets %	18.1	24.0	24.2	20.1	7.1	5.1	...
Price Range	41.31-22.38	31.94-19.50	58.56-14.88	50.94-33.88	40.88-20.38	21.42-10.58	13.96-4.21
P/E Ratio	10.0-5.4	11.7-7.1	21.9-5.6	21.3-14.2	20.3-10.1	11.9-5.9	13.3-4.0

Statistics are as originally reported. Adj. for 3-for-1 stk. split, 7/96. 1 Incl. $71.0 mill. pre-tax restr. chgs., $24.4 mill. gain for reversal of tax valu. allowance, & $13.6 mill. gain rel. to divest. of product line. 2 Incl. $2.8 mill. after-tax gain fr. sale of bus. 3 Incl. $8.0 mill. income exp., $2.5 mill. external chg. & $600,000 restr. chgs. 4 Incl. $8.7 mill. net gain fr. ins. settlement, $57.8 mill. net gain fr. sale of bus., and $10.6 mill. net expense for restr. chgs.

OFFICERS:
D. Lilley, Chmn., Pres., C.E.O.
J. P. Cronin, Exec. V.P., C.F.O.
E. F. Jackman, V.P., Gen. Couns., Sec.

INVESTOR CONTACT: David M. Drillock, Contr., (973) 357-3100

PRINCIPAL OFFICE: Five Garret Mountain Plaza, West Paterson, NJ 07424

TELEPHONE NUMBER: (973) 357-3100
FAX: (973) 357-3061
WEB: www.cytec.com

NO. OF EMPLOYEES: 4,800 (approx.)

SHAREHOLDERS: 14,500 (approx.)

ANNUAL MEETING: In May

INCORPORATED: DE, Dec., 1993

INSTITUTIONAL HOLDINGS:
No. of Institutions: 192
Shares Held: 30,168,734
% Held: 75.1

INDUSTRY: Chemical preparations, nec (SIC: 2899)

TRANSFER AGENT(S): Mellon Investor Services, Ridgefield Park, NJ

NYSE SYMBOL DCN
Rec. Pr. 19.63 (4/30/01)

DANA CORPORATION

YIELD 6.3%
P/E RATIO 9.3

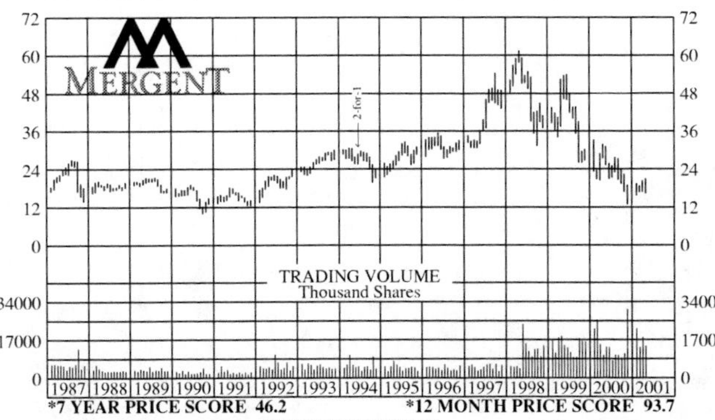

INTERIM EARNINGS (Per Share):

Qtr.	Mar.	June	Sept.	Dec.
1997	0.90	0.90	0.93	0.70
1998	0.89	1.08	0.59	0.81
1999	0.84	1.14	0.97	Nil
2000	1.54	0.95	0.19	d0.57

INTERIM DIVIDENDS (Per Share):

Amt.	Decl.	Ex.	Rec.	Pay.
0.31Q	7/17/00	8/30/00	9/01/00	9/15/00
0.31Q	10/16/00	11/29/00	12/01/00	12/15/00
0.31Q	2/12/01	2/27/01	3/01/01	3/15/01
0.31Q	4/17/01	5/30/01	6/01/01	6/15/01

Indicated div.: $1.24 (Div. Reinv. Plan)

CAPITALIZATION (12/31/00):

	($000)	(%)
Long-Term Debt	2,649,000	49.1
Minority Interest	121,000	2.2
Common & Surplus	2,628,000	48.7
Total	5,398,000	100.0

RECENT DEVELOPMENTS: For the twelve months ended 12/31/00, net income decreased 34.9% to $334.0 million compared with $513.0 million in the previous year. Results for 2000 and 1999 included restructuring and integration charges of $173.0 million and $181.0 million, respectively. Total revenues dropped 5.0% to $12.69 billion from $13.35 billion in 1999. Net sales fell 6.4% to $12.32 billion from $13.16 billion, while revenue from lease financing and other income shot up 92.8% to $374.0 million.

PROSPECTS: DCN eliminated 10,000 jobs to counter a slowdown in the auto industry. In addition, DCN reorganized its former Heavy Truck strategic business unit, renaming it the Commercial Vehicle Systems strategic business unit. The reorganization should expand capabilities, introduce more proprietary technology, and provide value-added products, systems, and services. Separately, DCN agreed to sell the assets of its Fluid Systems operation in Dallas, Texas to Standard Motor Products, Inc.

BUSINESS

DANA CORPORATION manufactures and markets vehicle components and provides services for original equipment markets, distribution markets and financial services. The Vehicular segment includes axles, frames, transmissions, universal joints, clutches and engine parts. The Industrial segment manufactures and markets various products, including products for off-highway motor vehicles. The Lease Financing segment consists of Dana Credit Corporation, which includes leasing companies and real estate development and management. Within these segments DCN operates seven components: Automotive Systems, Automotive Aftermarket, Commercial Vehicle, Off-Highway Systems, Engine Systems, Fluid Systems, and Leasing Services. DCN operates 300 major facilities in 35 countries.

QUARTERLY DATA

(12/31/00)($000)	REV	INC
1st Quarter	3,468,000	245,000
2nd Quarter	3,296,000	144,000
3rd Quarter	2,865,000	29,000
4th Quarter	2,688,000	(84,000)

ANNUAL FINANCIAL DATA

	12/31/00	12/31/99	12/31/98	12/31/97	12/31/96	12/31/95	12/31/94
Earnings Per Share	**1 2.18**	**1 3.08**	**1 3.20**	**1 1.94**	**3.01**	**2.84**	**2.31**
Cash Flow Per Share	**5.60**	**6.20**	**6.12**	**4.68**	**5.74**	**5.27**	**4.45**
Tang. Book Val. Per Share	**17.76**	**18.12**	**17.74**	**15.89**	**10.76**	**8.08**	**6.69**
Dividends Per Share	**1.24**	**1.24**	**1.14**	**1.04**	**0.98**	**0.90**	**0.83**
Dividend Payout %	**56.9**	**40.3**	**35.6**	**53.6**	**32.6**	**31.7**	**35.9**
INCOME STATEMENT (IN MILLIONS):							
Total Revenues	12,691.0	13,353.0	12,838.7	12,402.4	7,890.7	7,794.5	6,740.5
Costs & Expenses	11,381.0	11,818.0	11,201.6	11,096.5	6,961.6	6,889.1	6,024.9
Depreciation & Amort.	523.0	519.0	487.7	450.3	278.4	245.8	210.6
Operating Income	787.0	1,016.0	1,149.4	855.6	650.7	659.6	505.0
Net Interest Inc./(Exp.)	d323.0	d279.0	d279.6	d251.4	d159.0	d146.4	d113.4
Income Before Income Taxes	464.0	737.0	820.2	604.2	491.7	513.2	391.6
Income Taxes	171.0	251.0	315.6	293.8	166.3	181.2	157.4
Equity Earnings/Minority Int.	41.0	27.0	29.5	9.7	d19.4	d43.9	d6.0
Net Income	1 334.0	1 513.0	1 534.1	1 320.1	306.0	288.1	228.2
Cash Flow	857.0	1,032.0	1,021.8	770.4	584.4	533.9	438.8
Average Shs. Outstg. (000)	153,000	166,498	167,000	164,600	101,800	101,300	98,689
BALANCE SHEET (IN MILLIONS):							
Cash & Cash Equivalents	179.0	111.0	246.9	677.0	227.8	66.6	112.2
Total Current Assets	4,323.0	4,801.0	4,337.0	4,285.3	2,209.8	2,023.0	1,812.8
Net Property	3,509.0	3,450.0	3,303.8	2,776.7	1,824.8	1,649.5	1,347.2
Total Assets	11,236.0	11,123.0	10,137.5	9,511.1	6,775.4	6,279.4	5,725.5
Total Current Liabilities	4,331.0	3,888.0	3,986.6	3,794.0	1,837.1	1,964.4	1,722.4
Long-Term Obligations	2,649.0	2,732.0	1,717.9	1,789.8	1,697.7	1,315.1	1,186.5
Net Stockholders' Equity	2,628.0	2,957.0	2,939.2	2,602.4	1,428.7	1,164.6	939.8
Net Working Capital	d8.0	913.0	350.4	491.3	372.7	58.6	90.4
Year-end Shs. Outstg. (000)	148,000	163,151	165,700	163,800	103,000	101,500	98,800
STATISTICAL RECORD:							
Operating Profit Margin %	6.2	7.6	9.0	6.9	8.2	8.5	7.5
Net Profit Margin %	2.6	3.8	4.2	2.6	3.9	3.7	3.4
Return on Equity %	12.7	17.3	18.2	12.3	21.4	24.7	24.3
Return on Assets %	3.0	4.6	5.3	3.4	4.5	4.6	4.0
Debt/Total Assets %	23.6	24.6	16.9	18.8	25.1	20.9	20.7
Price Range	33.25-12.81	54.06-26.00	61.50-31.31	54.38-30.63	35.50-27.25	32.63-21.38	30.69-19.63
P/E Ratio	15.3-5.9	17.6-8.4	19.2-9.8	28.0-15.8	11.8-9.1	11.5-7.5	13.3-8.5
Average Yield %	5.4	3.1	2.5	2.4	3.1	3.3	3.3

Statistics are as originally reported. Adj. for stk. splits: 2-for-1, 6/15/94 1 Includes non-recurr. chrgs. $327.6 mill., 12/97; $167.3 mill., 12/98; $181.0 mill., 12/99; $173.0 mill., 12/00

OFFICERS:
J. M. Magliochetti, Chmn., Pres., C.E.O., C.O.O.
R. Richter, V.P., C.F.O.

INVESTOR CONTACT: Greg Smietanski, Dir.-Inv. Rel., (800) 537-8823

PRINCIPAL OFFICE: 4500 Dorr Street, Toledo, OH 43615

TELEPHONE NUMBER: (419) 535-4500
FAX: (419) 535-4643
WEB: www.dana.com

NO. OF EMPLOYEES: 79,300 (approx.)

SHAREHOLDERS: 35,620 (record)

ANNUAL MEETING: In Apr.

INCORPORATED: NJ, 1905; reincorp., VA, Oct., 1916

INSTITUTIONAL HOLDINGS:
No. of Institutions: 255
Shares Held: 120,056,297
% Held: 81.2

INDUSTRY: Motor vehicle parts and accessories (SIC: 3714)

TRANSFER AGENT(S): Mellon Investor Services, LLC, Ridgefield Park, NJ

NYSE SYMBOL DHR
Rec. Pr. 56.01 (4/30/01)

DANAHER CORPORATION

YIELD 0.1%
P/E RATIO 25.1

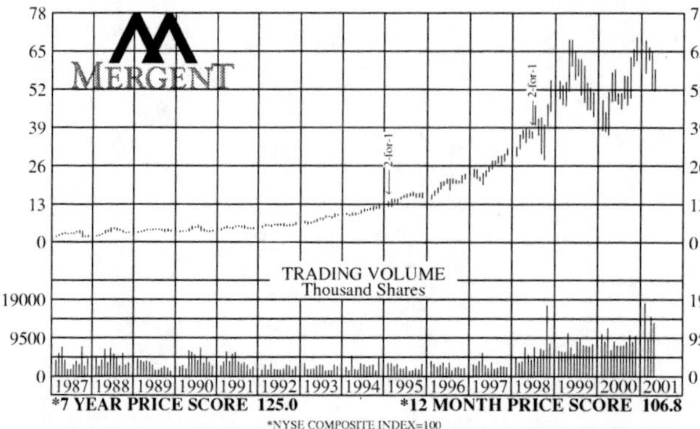

***7 YEAR PRICE SCORE 125.0** ***12 MONTH PRICE SCORE 106.8**

*NYSE COMPOSITE INDEX=100

INTERIM EARNINGS (Per Share):

Qtr.	Mar.	June	Sept.	Dec.
1996	0.23	0.27	0.28	0.29
1997	0.26	0.32	0.35	0.36
1998	0.32	0.38	0.20	0.42
1999	0.39	0.45	0.42	0.51
2000	0.49	0.56	0.58	0.60

INTERIM DIVIDENDS (Per Share):

Amt.	Decl.	Ex.	Rec.	Pay.
0.015Q	3/03/00	3/29/00	3/31/00	4/28/00
0.015Q	6/16/00	6/28/00	6/30/00	7/31/00
0.02Q	9/18/00	9/27/00	9/29/00	10/31/00
0.02Q	12/05/00	12/27/00	12/29/00	1/31/01
0.02Q	...	3/28/01	3/30/01	4/27/01

Indicated div.: $0.08

CAPITALIZATION (12/31/00):

	($000)	(%)
Long-Term Debt	713,557	26.9
Common & Surplus	1,942,333	73.1
Total	2,655,890	100.0

RECENT DEVELOPMENTS: For the year ended 12/31/00, net income increased 23.9% to $324.2 million compared with $261.6 million in the previous year. The 1999 results included a one-time pre-tax charge of $11.8 million associated with acquisition of Hach Company. Net sales advanced 18.2% to $3.78 billion from $3.20 billion in the prior year. Process/Environment Control segment sales were strong, allowing the Company to realize 6.0% core volume growth. Operating profit jumped 20.6% to $552.1 million.

PROSPECTS: On 1/2/01, the Company completed the previously announced acquisition of United Power Corporation. The acquisition of United Power should allow DHR to offer the customer a broader selection power quality products, particularly for the rapidly expanding data center market. Separately, the Company purchased the Zellweger Analytics water analysis business from Zellweger Luwa, AG for about $40.0 million. DHR expects the effect of the acquisition to be neutral to 2001 earnings.

BUSINESS

DANAHER CORPORATION is a manufacturer of industrial and consumer products, with emphasis on proprietary technology, and operates through two business segments. The process/environmental controls segment produces and sells compact, professional electronic test tools, underground storage tank leak detection systems and motion, position, speed, temperature, level and position instruments and sensing devices, power switches and controls, liquid flow, and quality measuring devices. The tools and components segment produces and distributes general purpose mechanics' hand tools and automotive specialty tools. Other products include tool boxes and storage devices, diesel engine retarders, and wheel service equipment.

BUSINESS LINE ANALYSIS

(12/31/00)	REV (%)	INC (%)
Process/Environmental	64.6	66.9
Tools & Components	35.4	33.1
Total	100.0	100.0

ANNUAL FINANCIAL DATA

	12/31/00	12/31/99	12/31/98	12/31/97	12/31/96	12/31/95	12/31/94
Earnings Per Share	**2.23**	**[3] 1.79**	**1.32**	**[2] 1.29**	**[1] 1.07**	**[1] 0.89**	**0.70**
Cash Flow Per Share	**3.26**	**2.66**	**2.10**	**1.92**	**1.64**	**1.37**	**1.08**
Tang. Book Val. Per Share	**0.55**	**3.40**	**0.50**	**0.60**	**0.06**	**...**	**0.31**
Dividends Per Share	**0.07**	**0.06**	**0.05**	**0.05**	**0.04**	**0.04**	**0.03**
Dividend Payout %	**2.9**	**3.4**	**4.0**	**3.9**	**4.0**	**4.5**	**4.3**
INCOME STATEMENT (IN MILLIONS):							
Total Revenues	3,777.8	3,197.2	2,910.0	2,051.0	1,811.9	1,486.8	1,288.7
Costs & Expenses	3,075.9	2,612.8	2,434.5	1,708.0	1,517.1	1,248.0	1,098.3
Depreciation & Amort.	149.7	126.4	108.7	76.1	68.6	58.5	44.6
Operating Income	552.1	458.0	366.8	266.9	226.1	180.3	145.8
Net Interest Inc./(Exp.)	d29.2	d16.7	d24.9	d13.1	d16.4	d7.2	d9.3
Income Before Income Taxes	522.9	429.6	301.1	253.8	209.8	173.1	136.5
Income Taxes	198.7	167.9	118.2	99.0	81.8	67.3	54.9
Net Income	324.2	[3] 261.6	182.9	[2] 154.8	[1] 128.0	[1] 105.8	81.7
Cash Flow	473.9	388.0	291.6	230.9	196.6	164.3	126.2
Average Shs. Outstg. (000)	145,499	146,089	138,885	120,512	119,910	119,726	116,654
BALANCE SHEET (IN MILLIONS):							
Cash & Cash Equivalents	176.9	260.3	41.9	33.3	26.4	7.9	2.0
Total Current Assets	1,474.3	1,202.1	886.9	618.3	546.7	466.5	388.7
Net Property	575.5	500.2	471.0	335.2	319.6	291.9	273.1
Total Assets	4,031.7	3,047.1	2,738.7	1,879.7	1,765.1	1,486.0	1,134.9
Total Current Liabilities	1,018.5	708.8	688.7	524.2	474.6	404.1	396.2
Long-Term Obligations	713.6	341.0	412.9	162.7	219.6	268.6	116.5
Net Stockholders' Equity	1,942.3	1,777.0	1,351.8	916.9	800.3	586.3	476.1
Net Working Capital	455.8	493.3	198.2	94.1	72.2	62.3	d7.5
Year-end Shs. Outstg. (000)	142,013	142,440	135,107	105,440	117,778	117,006	106,784
STATISTICAL RECORD:							
Operating Profit Margin %	14.6	14.3	12.6	13.0	12.5	12.1	11.3
Net Profit Margin %	8.6	8.2	6.3	7.5	7.1	7.1	6.3
Return on Equity %	16.7	14.7	13.5	16.9	16.0	18.0	17.1
Return on Assets %	8.0	8.6	6.7	8.2	7.2	7.1	7.2
Debt/Total Assets %	17.7	11.2	15.1	8.7	12.4	18.1	10.3
Price Range	69.81-36.44	69.00-42.75	55.25-28.00	32.00-19.50	23.31-14.63	17.19-12.13	13.28-9.00
P/E Ratio	31.3-16.3	38.5-23.9	41.9-21.2	24.9-15.2	21.9-13.7	19.4-13.7	19.0-12.9
Average Yield %	0.1	0.1	0.1	0.2	0.2	0.3	0.3

Statistics are as originally reported. Adj. for stk. splits: 2-for-1; 1/95, 5/98 [1] Bef disc. opers. gain $2.6 mill., 1995 & $79.8 mill, 1996 [2] Incl. non-recurr. credit $6.0 mill. from sale of investment. [3] Incls. one-time after-tax chrg. of $11.8 mill. for acqs.

OFFICERS:
S. M. Rales, Chmn.
H. L. Culp Jr., Pres., C.E.O.
P. W. Allender, Exec. V.P., C.F.O., Sec.

INVESTOR CONTACT: Patrick W. Allender, Exec. V.P., C.F.O., Sec., (202) 828-0850

PRINCIPAL OFFICE: 1250 24th St N.W., Suite 800, Washington, DC 20037

TELEPHONE NUMBER: (202) 828-0850
FAX: (202) 828-0860
WEB: www.danaher.com

NO. OF EMPLOYEES: 24,000 (avg.)

SHAREHOLDERS: 3,200 (approx.)

ANNUAL MEETING: In May

INCORPORATED: DE, 1987

INSTITUTIONAL HOLDINGS:
No. of Institutions: 304
Shares Held: 75,631,103
% Held: 53.1

INDUSTRY: Hardware, nec (SIC: 3429)

TRANSFER AGENT(S): SunTrust Bank, Atlanta, GA

NYSE SYMBOL DRI
Rec. Pr. 27.90 (5/31/01)

DARDEN RESTAURANTS, INC.

YIELD 0.3%
P/E RATIO 17.9

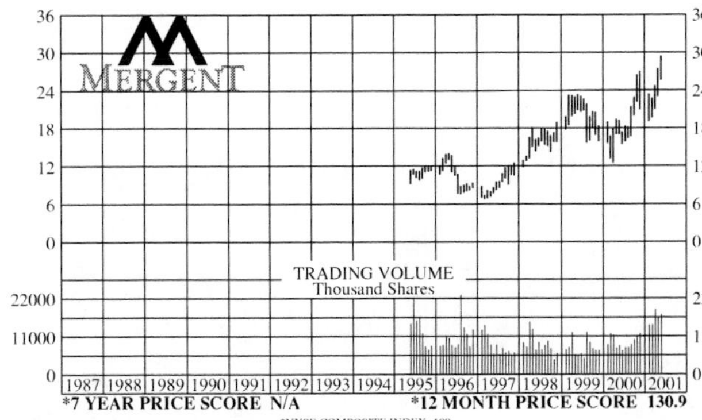

*7 YEAR PRICE SCORE N/A   *12 MONTH PRICE SCORE 130.9

*NYSE COMPOSITE INDEX=100

INTERIM EARNINGS (Per Share):

Qtr.	Aug.	Nov.	Feb.	May
1996-97	0.13	d0.07	0.10	d0.75
1997-98	0.16	0.05	0.20	0.28
1998-99	0.24	0.11	0.27	0.37
1999-00	0.35	0.18	0.36	0.46
2000-01	0.46	0.24	0.40	...

INTERIM DIVIDENDS (Per Share):

Amt.	Decl.	Ex.	Rec.	Pay.
0.04S	9/23/99	10/06/99	10/11/99	11/01/99
0.04S	3/30/00	4/06/00	4/10/00	5/01/00
0.04S	9/20/00	10/05/00	10/10/00	11/01/00
0.04S	3/21/01	4/06/01	4/10/01	5/01/01

Indicated div.: $0.08 (Div. Reinv. Plan)

CAPITALIZATION (5/28/00):

	($000)	(%)
Long-Term Debt	304,073	22.6
Deferred Income Tax	79,102	5.9
Common & Surplus	960,470	71.5
Total	1,343,645	100.0

RECENT DEVELOPMENTS: For the thirteen weeks ended 2/25/01, net earnings advanced 5.6% to $49.5 million versus $46.9 million in prior-year quarter. Net sales jumped 7.8% to $988.6 million from $917.5 million in the previous year. Red Lobster sales rose 6.2% to $539.8 million, while same-restaurant sales climbed 5.5%. Olive Garden sales grew 6.8% to $422.6 million, while same-restaurant sales rose 5.6%.

PROSPECTS: During the twelve months ended 2/25/01, DRI opened four Red Lobster, five Olive Garden, nine Bahama Breeze and four Smokey Bones BBQ Sports Bar restaurants, bringing DRI's total number up to 1,148. Going forward, the Company expects to open three additional Bahama Breeze restaurants and four new Smokey Bones BBQ Sports Bars in fiscal 2001. Results look promising for The Olive Garden and Red Lobster due menu mix and pricing.

BUSINESS

DARDEN RESTAURANTS, INC. and its subsidiaries, as of 2/25/01, operated a total of 1,148 restaurant locations in 49 states, including 655 Red Lobster locations, 469 The Olive Garden locations, 19 Bahama Breeze locations and five Smokey Bones BBQ restaurants. In addition, the Company operates 37 restaurants in Canada, including 32 Red Lobster unites and five The Olive Garden units. All of the restaurants in North America are Company-operated. Red Lobster is a full-service, seafood-specialty restaurant offering a menu featuring fresh fish, shrimp, crab, lobster, scallops, and other seafood in a casual atmosphere. The Olive Garden is a full-service Italian restaurant featuring recipes from both northern and southern Italy. Bahama Breeze has a Caribbean theme. Smokey Bones, a BBQ and sportsbar prototype restaurant, is DRI's latest test concept.

ANNUAL FINANCIAL DATA

	5/28/00	5/30/99	5/31/98	5/25/97	5/26/96	5/28/95	5/29/94
Earnings Per Share	**[3] 1.34**	**[3] 0.99**	**0.67**	**[1] d0.59**	**[1] 0.47**	**[1] 0.33**	**[2] 0.77**
Cash Flow Per Share	**2.37**	**1.91**	**1.54**	**0.32**	**1.33**	**1.19**	**1.56**
Tang. Book Val. Per Share	**7.86**	**7.30**	**7.23**	**7.40**	**7.75**	**7.42**	...
Dividends Per Share	**0.08**	**0.08**	**0.08**	**0.08**	**0.04**	...	...
Dividend Payout %	**6.0**	**8.1**	**11.9**	...	**8.5**	...	...
INCOME STATEMENT (IN MILLIONS):							
Total Revenues	3,701.3	3,458.1	3,287.0	3,171.8	3,191.8	3,163.3	2,963.0
Costs & Expenses	3,268.6	3,092.5	2,982.3	3,163.3	2,920.1	2,940.8	2,626.2
Depreciation & Amort.	136.4	130.2	131.0	140.7	136.5	135.5	124.7
Operating Income	296.3	235.4	173.8	d132.2	135.1	87.0	212.1
Net Interest Inc./(Exp.)	d22.4	d19.5	d20.1	d22.3	d21.4	d21.9	d18.4
Income Before Income Taxes	273.9	215.9	153.7	d154.5	113.7	65.1	193.7
Income Taxes	97.2	75.3	52.0	cr63.5	39.4	12.7	70.6
Net Income	[3] 176.7	[3] 140.5	101.7	[1] d91.0	[1] 74.4	[1] 52.4	[2] 123.1
Cash Flow	313.1	270.7	232.7	49.7	210.9	187.9	247.8
Average Shs. Outstg. (000)	131,900	141,400	151,400	155,600	158,700	158,000	159,100
BALANCE SHEET (IN MILLIONS):							
Cash & Cash Equivalents	26.1	41.0	33.5	25.5	30.3	20.1	17.7
Total Current Assets	290.5	327.7	397.5	337.4	288.0	307.6	249.7
Net Property	1,578.5	1,473.5	1,490.3	1,533.3	1,702.9	1,738.0	1,564.2
Total Assets	1,971.4	1,905.7	1,984.7	1,963.7	2,088.5	2,113.4	1,859.1
Total Current Liabilities	606.9	534.2	558.7	480.6	445.3	517.2	347.3
Long-Term Obligations	304.1	314.1	310.6	313.2	301.2	303.8	3.9
Net Stockholders' Equity	960.5	964.0	1,019.8	1,081.2	1,222.6	1,174.0	1,427.9
Net Working Capital	d316.4	d206.5	d161.1	d143.2	d157.3	d209.6	d97.6
Year-end Shs. Outstg. (000)	122,192	132,120	141,146	146,042	157,711	158,178	...
STATISTICAL RECORD:							
Operating Profit Margin %	8.0	6.8	5.3	...	4.2	2.8	7.2
Net Profit Margin %	4.8	4.1	3.1	...	2.3	1.7	4.2
Return on Equity %	18.4	14.6	10.0	...	6.1	4.5	8.6
Return on Assets %	9.0	7.4	5.1	...	3.6	2.5	6.6
Debt/Total Assets %	15.4	16.5	15.6	15.9	14.4	14.4	0.2
Price Range	23.38-15.63	18.94-11.75	12.50-6.75	14.00-7.50	12.13-9.13	...	...
P/E Ratio	17.4-11.7	19.1-11.9	18.7-10.1	...	25.8-19.4	...	...
Average Yield %	0.4	0.5	0.8	0.7	0.4	...	...

Statistics are as originally reported. [1] Incl. non-recurr. chrg. 5/25/97, $229.9 mill.; 5/26/96, $75.0 mill.; 5/28/95, $99.3 mill. [2] Bef. acctg. change credit $3.7 mill. [3] Incls. restr. chrg. of $8.5 mill., 5/30/99; $8.5 mill., 5/28/00.

OFFICERS:
J. R. Lee, Chmn., C.E.O.
B. Sweatt III, Pres., Exec. V.P.
C. Otis Jr., Sr. V.P., C.F.O.

INVESTOR CONTACT: Investor Relations, (800) 832-7336

PRINCIPAL OFFICE: 5900 Lake Ellenor Drive, Orlando, FL 32809

TELEPHONE NUMBER: (407) 245-4000
FAX: (407) 850-5296
WEB: www.darden.com

NO. OF EMPLOYEES: 122,300 (avg.)

SHAREHOLDERS: 31,896 (record)

ANNUAL MEETING: In Sept.

INCORPORATED: FL, Mar., 1995

INSTITUTIONAL HOLDINGS:
No. of Institutions: 274
Shares Held: 85,360,240
% Held: 72.3

INDUSTRY: Eating places (SIC: 5812)

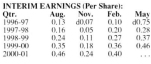

TRANSFER AGENT(S): First Union National Bank, Charlotte, NC

NYSE SYMBOL DF
Rec. Pr. 40.20 (5/31/01)

DEAN FOODS COMPANY

YIELD 2.2%
P/E RATIO 15.5

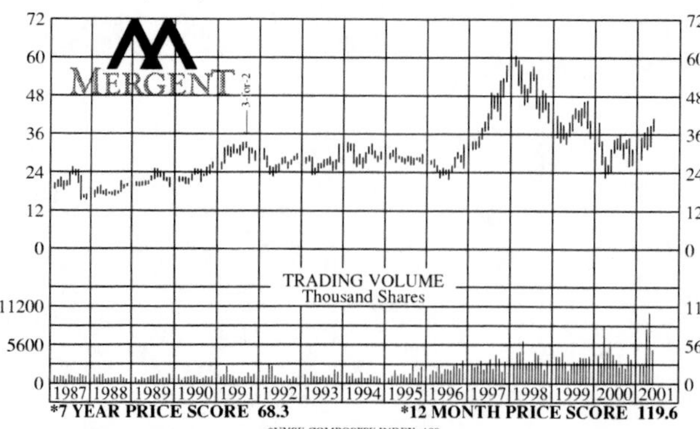

INTERIM EARNINGS (Per Share):

Qtr.	Aug.	Nov.	Feb.	May
1996-97	0.45	0.47	0.51	0.73
1997-98	0.53	0.66	0.60	0.81
1998-99	0.56	0.58	0.08	0.52
1999-00	0.70	0.68	0.67	0.72
2000-01	0.74	0.66	0.47	...

INTERIM DIVIDENDS (Per Share):

Amt.	Decl.	Ex.	Rec.	Pay.
0.225Q	7/28/00	8/23/00	8/25/00	9/15/00
0.225Q	9/26/00	11/21/00	11/24/00	12/15/00
0.225Q	1/26/01	2/21/01	2/23/01	3/15/01
0.225Q	3/23/01	5/23/01	5/25/01	6/15/01

Indicated div.: $0.90 (Div. Reinv. Plan)

CAPITALIZATION (5/28/00):

	($000)	(%)
Long-Term Debt	758,725	50.1
Deferred Income Tax	99,410	6.6
Common & Surplus	657,685	43.4
Total	1,515,820	100.0

RECENT DEVELOPMENTS: For the quarter ended 2/25/01, net income totaled $16.7 million, down 33.7% versus $25.2 million the year before. Net sales climbed 11.9% to $1.09 billion from $976.8 million a year earlier. Sales from the Dairy segment rose 9.0% to $806.6 million from $739.7 million in the prior year. Specialty Foods segment sales grew 11.4% to $185.4 million, while National Refrigerated Products segment sales advanced 43.3% to $101.3 million. Operating earnings slipped 15.8% to $45.9 million.

PROSPECTS: On 4/5/01, the Company announced that it has signed an agreement to be acquired by Suiza Foods Corporation in a transaction valued at $2.50 billion, including the assumption of $1.00 billion of debt. Under the terms of the deal, DF shareholders will receive consideration consisting of $21.00 per share in cash and 0.429 shares of Suiza common stock. The transaction, which is expected to be completed in the third quarter of calendar 2001, is subject to shareholder and regulatory approvals.

BUSINESS

DEAN FOODS COMPANY is a food processor and distributor engaged primarily in three business segments, Dairy Products, Specialty Food Products and National Refrigerated Products. The Dairy Products segment includes fluid milk and cultured products and ice cream and frozen desserts. The Specialty Food Products segment includes non-dairy creamers, aseptic products, pickles, relishes and specialty sauces. The National Refrigerated Products segment includes extended shelf-life products such as whipping creams and coffee creamers as well as DEAN'S dips, MARIE'S salad dressings, and LAND O' LAKES fresh dairy products. In the fiscal year ended 5/28/00, sales were derived: Dairy, 75.5%; Specialty Foods, 17.5%; and National Refrigerated Products, 7.0%.

ANNUAL FINANCIAL DATA

	5/28/00	5/30/99	5/31/98	5/25/97	5/26/96	5/28/95	5/29/94
Earnings Per Share	**4 2.77**	**3 1.74**	**2.13**	**2.16**	**1 d1.24**	**2.01**	**2 1.78**
Cash Flow Per Share	**5.58**	**3.91**	**3.58**	**4.00**	**0.68**	**3.76**	**3.34**
Tang. Book Val. Per Share	**2.65**	**4.20**	**7.12**	**11.36**	**10.26**	**12.14**	**10.79**
Dividends Per Share	**0.86**	**0.82**	**0.78**	**0.74**	**0.70**	**0.66**	**0.62**
Dividend Payout %	**31.0**	**47.1**	**36.6**	**34.3**	**...**	**32.8**	**34.8**
INCOME STATEMENT (IN MILLIONS):							
Total Revenues	4,065.6	3,755.1	2,735.8	3,018.4	2,814.3	2,630.2	2,431.2
Costs & Expenses	3,735.5	3,513.9	2,512.9	2,774.2	2,629.7	2,403.1	2,236.3
Depreciation & Amort.	107.6	87.9	60.4	74.1	77.0	70.0	61.9
Operating Income	222.6	153.3	162.5	170.1	d42.4	157.1	133.1
Net Interest Inc./(Exp.)	d49.3	d38.0	d18.8	d24.4	d27.0	d20.7	d14.7
Income Before Income Taxes	173.3	115.3	143.7	145.7	d69.4	136.4	118.3
Income Taxes	67.2	45.0	55.8	59.0	cr19.7	56.3	47.6
Net Income	4 106.1	3 70.3	88.0	86.7	1 d49.7	80.1	2 70.8
Cash Flow	213.7	158.3	148.4	160.8	27.4	150.1	132.6
Average Shs. Outstg. (000)	38,311	40,482	41,395	40,188	40,122	39,890	39,737
BALANCE SHEET (IN MILLIONS):							
Cash & Cash Equivalents	26.6	16.0	11.9	4.4	10.4	4.8	11.0
Total Current Assets	600.4	582.1	420.2	562.1	584.4	518.9	460.2
Net Property	815.3	764.9	551.1	527.2	525.7	570.1	543.2
Total Assets	2,003.5	1,911.9	1,607.2	1,217.4	1,222.2	1,202.4	1,109.2
Total Current Liabilities	449.1	439.5	352.9	354.1	398.5	303.9	367.3
Long-Term Obligations	758.7	631.3	558.2	211.9	221.7	224.7	136.2
Net Stockholders' Equity	657.7	716.4	619.3	567.7	507.7	584.5	524.8
Net Working Capital	151.3	142.7	67.3	208.0	185.9	215.0	92.9
Year-end Shs. Outstg. (000)	35,485	39,276	39,970	40,283	40,133	40,078	39,789
STATISTICAL RECORD:							
Operating Profit Margin %	5.5	4.1	5.9	5.6	...	6.0	5.5
Net Profit Margin %	2.6	1.9	3.2	2.9	...	3.0	2.9
Return on Equity %	16.1	9.8	14.2	15.3	...	13.7	13.5
Return on Assets %	5.3	3.7	5.5	7.1	...	6.7	6.4
Debt/Total Assets %	37.9	33.0	34.7	17.4	18.1	18.7	12.3
Price Range	46.56-32.94	60.69-39.50	57.75-31.00	32.75-21.75	31.75-26.25	33.50-25.25	32.88-23.13
P/E Ratio	16.8-11.9	34.9-22.7	27.1-14.6	15.2-10.1	...	16.7-12.6	18.5-13.0
Average Yield %	2.2	1.6	1.8	2.7	2.4	2.2	2.2

Statistics are as originally reported. 1 Incl. non-recur. chg. $97.7 mil. 2 Bef. $1.2 mil chg. for acctg. adj. 3 Bef. $80.9 mil ($2.03/sh) gain from discont. opers. & incl. $11.0 mil ($0.27/sh) net one-time plant closure costs. 4 Incl. $3.8 mil ($0.10/sh) net one-time plant closure costs.

OFFICERS:
H. M. Dean, Chmn., C.E.O.
B. A. Klein, V.P.-Fin., C.F.O.

INVESTOR CONTACT: LuAnn Lilja, Dir., Corporate Communications, (847) 233-5459

PRINCIPAL OFFICE: 3600 North River Road, Franklin Park, IL 60131

TELEPHONE NUMBER: (847) 678-1680
FAX: (847) 233-5501
WEB: www.deanfoods.com
NO. OF EMPLOYEES: 13,000 full-time (approx.); 300 part-time (approx.)
SHAREHOLDERS: 8,272 (approx.)
ANNUAL MEETING: In Sept.
INCORPORATED: IL, June, 1925; reincorp., DE, May, 1968

INSTITUTIONAL HOLDINGS:
No. of Institutions: 169
Shares Held: 15,350,000
% Held: 43.1

INDUSTRY: Fluid milk (SIC: 2026)

TRANSFER AGENT(S): Mellon Investor Services, Chicago, IL

NYSE SYMBOL DE
Rec. Pr. 37.36 (5/31/01)

DEERE & COMPANY

YIELD 2.4%
P/E RATIO 17.5

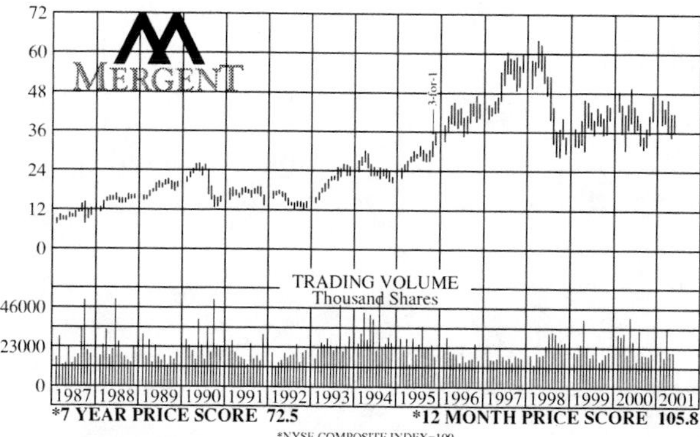

*7 YEAR PRICE SCORE 72.5 *12 MONTH PRICE SCORE 105.8
*NYSE COMPOSITE INDEX=100

INTERIM EARNINGS (Per Share):

Qtr.	Jan.	Apr.	July	Oct.
1996-97	0.69	1.25	1.00	0.84
1997-98	0.81	1.45	1.19	0.71
1998-99	0.21	0.65	0.29	d0.13
1999-00	0.16	0.87	0.72	0.30
2000-01	0.24	...	...	...

INTERIM DIVIDENDS (Per Share):

Amt.	Decl.	Ex.	Rec.	Pay.
0.22Q	5/31/00	6/28/00	6/30/00	8/01/00
0.22Q	8/30/00	9/27/00	9/30/00	11/01/00
0.22Q	12/06/00	12/27/00	12/31/00	2/01/01
0.22Q	2/28/01	3/28/01	3/31/01	5/01/01
0.22Q	5/30/01	6/27/01	6/30/01	8/01/01

Indicated div.: $0.88 (Div. Reinv. Plan)

CAPITALIZATION (10/31/00):

	($000)	(%)
Long-Term Debt	4,764,300	52.1
Deferred Income Tax	74,600	0.8
Common & Surplus	4,301,900	47.1
Total	9,140,800	100.0

RECENT DEVELOPMENTS: For the quarter ended 1/31/01, net income surged 47.4% to $56.0 million from $38.0 million the year before. Total net sales and revenues rose 14.6% to $2.68 billion from $2.34 billion a year earlier. Net sales of agricultural equipment climbed 18.6% to $1.23 billion, while net sales of construction equipment jumped 32.5% to $448.0 million. Net sales of commercial and consumer equipment slipped 13.0% to $429.0 million. Credit revenues increased 21.9% to $367.0 million.

PROSPECTS: In 2001, the Company anticipates worldwide sales will increase 9.0% compared with 2000, including an expected 10.0% increase in sales during the second quarter. Results are expected to be driven by the introduction of new products and services, coupled with the Company's initiatives focused on improving profitability. During the first quarter of 2001, DE acquired McGinnis Farms, Inc., which should help expand DE's operations into the fast-growing commercial landscape and irrigation industries.

BUSINESS

DEERE & COMPANY manufactures and distributes agricultural equipment, lawn and grounds care products, and industrial equipment for construction, forestry, and public works. The Company also provides credit and health care products. The farm equipment segment produces a full range of equipment including: tractors; tillage, soil preparation, planting and harvesting machinery; and crop-handling equipment. The industrial equipment segment produces crawler dozers and loaders; four-wheel-drive loaders; elevating scrapers; motor graders; excavators; log skidders; and tree harvesting equipment. The lawn and garden operation manufactures and distributes mowers, golf course equipment and other outdoor power products.

BUSINESS LINE ANALYSIS

(10/31/2000)	Rev (%)	Inc (%)
Agricultural Equipment	45.4	41.4
Comml & Consumer Equipment	22.7	16.5
Construction Equipment	16.8	19.8
Credit Revenues	10.1	26.3
Other Revenues	5.0	(4.0)
Total	100.0	100.0

ANNUAL FINANCIAL DATA

	10/31/00	10/31/99	10/31/98	10/31/97	10/31/96	10/31/95	10/31/94
Earnings Per Share	**2.06**	**1.02**	**4.16**	**3.78**	**3.14**	**2.71**	**2.34**
Cash Flow Per Share	**4.80**	**3.21**	**5.86**	**5.23**	**4.33**	**3.80**	**3.32**
Tang. Book Val. Per Share	**15.56**	**16.25**	**16.63**	**15.94**	**12.72**	**10.61**	**8.80**
Dividends Per Share	**0.88**	**0.88**	**0.88**	**0.80**	**0.80**	**0.75**	**0.68**
Dividend Payout %	**42.7**	**86.3**	**21.2**	**21.2**	**25.5**	**27.7**	**29.2**
INCOME STATEMENT (IN MILLIONS):							
Total Revenues	13,136.8	11,750.9	13,821.5	12,791.4	11,229.4	10,290.5	9,029.8
Costs & Expenses	11,034.9	10,315.9	11,324.1	10,496.5	9,229.2	8,522.3	7,549.2
Depreciation & Amort.	647.9	513.3	418.0	365.6	311.4	283.1	256.7
Operating Income	1,454.0	921.7	2,079.4	1,929.3	1,688.8	1,485.1	1,223.9
Net Interest Inc./(Exp.)	d676.5	d556.6	d519.4	d422.2	d402.2	d392.4	d303.0
Income Before Income Taxes	777.5	365.1	1,560.0	1,507.1	1,286.6	1,092.7	920.9
Income Taxes	293.8	134.7	553.9	550.9	479.8	397.8	332.2
Equity Earnings/Minority Int.	1.8	8.8	15.3	3.9	10.5	11.2	14.9
Net Income	485.5	239.2	1,021.4	960.1	817.3	706.1	603.6
Cash Flow	1,133.4	752.5	1,439.4	1,325.7	1,128.7	989.2	860.3
Average Shs. Outstg. (000)	236,000	234,400	245,700	253,700	260,547	260,494	259,263
BALANCE SHEET (IN MILLIONS):							
Cash & Cash Equivalents	419.1	611.0	1,177.0	1,149.6	1,160.9	1,193.4	1,371.7
Total Current Assets	15,997.6	13,857.5	14,638.1	13,163.0	12,047.3	11,272.8	10,168.9
Net Property	1,912.0	1,782.0	1,700.0	1,524.0	1,352.0	1,336.0	1,314.0
Total Assets	20,469.1	17,577.6	18,001.5	16,320.0	14,653.1	13,848.0	12,781.1
Total Current Liabilities	8,825.1	7,081.3	8,351.3	6,780.5	5,980.3	5,773.1	5,036.8
Long-Term Obligations	4,764.3	3,806.2	2,791.7	2,622.8	2,425.4	2,175.8	2,053.9
Net Stockholders' Equity	4,301.9	4,094.3	4,079.8	4,147.2	3,557.2	3,085.4	2,557.9
Net Working Capital	7,172.5	6,776.2	6,286.8	6,382.5	6,067.0	5,499.7	5,132.1
Year-end Shs. Outstg. (000)	234,556	233,805	232,310	250,293	257,266	261,975	258,438
STATISTICAL RECORD:							
Operating Profit Margin %	11.1	7.8	15.0	15.1	15.0	14.4	13.6
Net Profit Margin %	3.7	2.0	7.4	7.5	7.3	6.9	6.7
Return on Equity %	11.3	5.8	25.0	23.2	23.0	22.9	23.6
Return on Assets %	2.4	1.4	5.7	5.9	5.6	5.1	4.7
Debt/Total Assets %	23.3	21.7	15.5	16.1	16.6	15.7	16.1
Price Range	49.63-30.31	45.94-30.19	64.13-28.38	60.50-39.88	47.13-33.00	36.00-21.67	30.29-20.42
P/E Ratio	24.1-14.7	45.0-29.6	15.4-6.8	16.0-10.5	15.0-10.5	13.3-8.0	13.0-8.7
Average Yield %	2.2	2.3	1.9	1.6	2.0	2.6	2.7

Statistics are as originally reported. Adj. for 3-for-1 stk. split, 11/95.

OFFICERS:
R. W. Lane, Chmn., Pres., C.E.O.
N. J. Jones, Sr. V.P., C.F.O.
F. S. Cottrell, Sr. V.P., Gen. Couns., Sec.

INVESTOR CONTACT: Marie Ziegler, Director, Investor Relations, (309) 765-4491

PRINCIPAL OFFICE: One John Deere Place, Moline, IL 61265

TELEPHONE NUMBER: (309) 765-8000
FAX: (309) 765-9929
WEB: www.deere.com

NO. OF EMPLOYEES: 43,700 (approx.)

SHAREHOLDERS: 33,241

ANNUAL MEETING: In Feb.

INCORPORATED: DE, Apr., 1958

INSTITUTIONAL HOLDINGS:
No. of Institutions: 386
Shares Held: 183,170,223
% Held: 78.0

INDUSTRY: Farm machinery and equipment (SIC: 3523)

TRANSFER AGENT(S): The Bank of New York, New York, NY

NYSE SYMBOL DPH
Rec. Pr. 14.90 (4/30/01)

DELPHI AUTOMOTIVE SYSTEMS CORPORATION

YIELD 1.9%
P/E RATIO 7.9

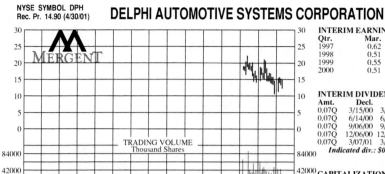

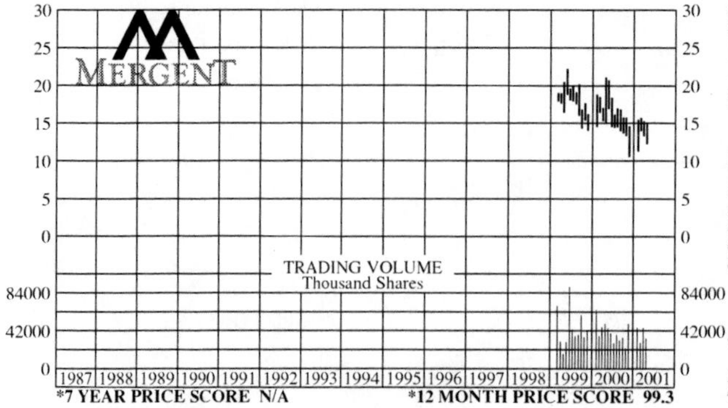

TRADING VOLUME
Thousand Shares

*7 YEAR PRICE SCORE N/A　　*12 MONTH PRICE SCORE 99.3

*NYSE COMPOSITE INDEX=100

INTERIM EARNINGS (Per Share):

Qtr.	Mar.	June	Sept.	Dec.
1997	0.62	0.80	0.16	d1.12
1998	0.51	0.18	d0.38	0.19
1999	0.55	0.70	0.24	0.48
2000	0.51	0.75	0.26	0.36

INTERIM DIVIDENDS (Per Share):

Amt.	Decl.	Ex.	Rec.	Pay.
0.07Q	3/15/00	3/22/00	3/24/00	4/24/00
0.07Q	6/14/00	6/22/00	6/26/00	7/25/00
0.07Q	9/06/00	9/14/00	9/18/00	10/16/00
0.07Q	12/06/00	12/14/00	12/18/00	1/18/01
0.07Q	3/07/01	3/15/01	3/19/01	4/16/01

Indicated div.: $0.28 (Div. Reinv. Plan)

CAPITALIZATION (12/31/00):

	($000)	(%)
Long-Term Debt	1,623,000	30.1
Common & Surplus	3,766,000	69.9
Total	5,389,000	100.0

RECENT DEVELOPMENTS: For the year ended 12/31/00, net income amounted to $1.06 billion compared with $1.08 billion in the previous year. Results for 2000 included an after-tax, one-time, non-cash charge of $32.0 million from acquisistion-related in-process research and development. Total net sales slipped to $29.14 billion from $29.19 billion the year before. General Motors sales fell 7.3% to $20.67 billion, while sales to other customers jumped 23.0% to $8.47 million. Operating income rose 3.7% to $1.74 billion.

PROSPECTS: DPH announced its intentions to sell, close or consolidate nine plants, downsize the workforce at more than 40 other facilities plus exit selected products. The restructuring plan will reduce worldwide employment by about 11,500 positions. The plan includes exiting about $900.0 million of DHP's businesses previously announced to be under portfolio review. Separately, DPH completed the purchase of the Vehicle Switch/Electronics Division of Eaton Corp. for $300.0 million.

BUSINESS

DELPHI AUTOMOTIVE SYSTEMS CORPORATION is a supplier of components, integrated systems and modules to the automotive industry. The Company provides its products directly to automotive manufacturers and to the worldwide aftermarket for replacement parts, and to other industrial customers. The Company operates its business along three major product sectors: Electronics and Mobile Communication; Safety, Thermal and Electrical Architecture; and Dynamics and Propulsion. As of 12/31/00, DPH operated 53 customer centers and sales offices and 31 technical centers, 190 wholly-owned manufacturing centers and 44 joint-ventures. On 2/10/99, General Motors spun off a portion of DPH. GM retained ownership of 82.3% of DPH's common stock.

REVENUES

(12/31/00)	($000)	(%)
General Motors & affiliates	20,665,000	70.9
Other customers	8,474,000	29.1
Total	29,139,000	100.0

ANNUAL FINANCIAL DATA

	12/31/00	12/31/99	12/31/98	12/31/97	12/31/96	12/31/95	12/31/94
Earnings Per Share	**[1] 1.88**	**1.95**	**d0.20**	**0.46**	**1.83**	**2.81**	**2.10**
Cash Flow Per Share	**3.55**	**3.50**	**2.17**	**4.70**	**3.65**	**4.47**	...
Tang. Book Val. Per Share	**6.73**	**5.69**	**0.02**	...	**1.98**	...	...
Dividends Per Share	**0.28**	**0.14**	...	...	...	...	...
Dividend Payout %	**14.9**	**7.2**	...	...	...	...	...
INCOME STATEMENT (IN MILLIONS):							
Total Revenues	29,139.0	29,192.0	28,479.0	31,447.0	31,032.0	31,661.0	31,044.0
Costs & Expenses	26,510.0	26,654.0	27,598.0	29,125.0	28,916.0	28,750.0	28,960.0
Depreciation & Amort.	936.0	856.0	1,102.0	1,970.0	843.0	773.0	...
Operating Income	1,693.0	1,682.0	d221.0	352.0	1,273.0	2,138.0	2,084.0
Net Interest Inc./(Exp.)	d183.0	d132.0	d277.0	d287.0	d276.0	d293.0	d310.0
Income Before Income Taxes	1,667.0	1,721.0	d266.0	259.0	1,112.0	1,946.0	1,877.0
Income Taxes	605.0	638.0	cr173.0	44.0	259.0	639.0	644.0
Net Income	[1] 1,062.0	1,083.0	d93.0	215.0	853.0	1,307.0	1,233.0
Cash Flow	1,998.0	1,939.0	1,009.0	2,185.0	1,696.0	2,080.0	1,233.0
Average Shs. Outstg. (000)	563,568	554,633	465,000	465,000	465,000	465,000	...
BALANCE SHEET (IN MILLIONS):							
Cash & Cash Equivalents	760.0	1,556.0	1,000.0	1,000.0	1,000.0	...	...
Total Current Assets	8,603.0	9,811.0	6,405.0	6,378.0	6,204.0	...	...
Net Property	5,718.0	5,106.0	4,965.0	4,600.0	5,241.0	...	...
Total Assets	18,521.0	18,350.0	15,506.0	15,026.0	15,390.0	...	14,494.0
Total Current Liabilities	6,243.0	6,737.0	4,061.0	4,066.0	3,755.0	...	...
Long-Term Obligations	1,623.0	1,640.0	3,137.0	3,341.0	3,352.0	...	...
Net Stockholders' Equity	3,766.0	3,200.0	9.0	d413.0	922.0	...	120.0
Net Working Capital	2,360.0	3,074.0	2,344.0	2,312.0	2,449.0	...	...
Year-end Shs. Outstg. (000)	559,800	562,000	565,000	465,000	465,000	465,000	...
STATISTICAL RECORD:							
Operating Profit Margin %	5.8	5.8	...	1.1	4.1	6.8	6.7
Net Profit Margin %	3.6	3.7	...	0.7	2.7	4.1	4.0
Return on Equity %	28.2	33.8	...	...	92.5	...	1,027.5
Return on Assets %	5.7	5.9	...	1.4	5.5	...	8.5
Debt/Total Assets %	8.8	8.9	20.2	22.2	21.8	...	...
Price Range	21.13-10.50	22.25-14.00	...	...	...	...	...
P/E Ratio	11.2-5.6	11.4-7.2	...	...	...	...	...
Average Yield %	1.8	0.8	...	...	...	...	...

Statistics are as originally reported. [1] Incl. non-recurr. after-tax chrg. $32.0 mill.

OFFICERS:
J. T. Battenberg III, Chmn., Pres., C.E.O.
A. S. Dawes, Exec. V.P., C.F.O.
J. G. Blahnik, V.P., Treas.

INVESTOR CONTACT: Investor Relations, (248) 813-2000

PRINCIPAL OFFICE: 5725 Delphi Drive, Troy, MI 48098-2815

TELEPHONE NUMBER: (248) 813-2000
FAX: (248) 813-2670
WEB: www.delphiauto.com

NO. OF EMPLOYEES: 38,000 full-time (approx.); 173,000 part-time (approx.)

SHAREHOLDERS: 417,341 (record)

ANNUAL MEETING: In May

INCORPORATED: DE, 1998

INSTITUTIONAL HOLDINGS:
No. of Institutions: 382
Shares Held: 370,892,873
% Held: 66.3

INDUSTRY: Motor vehicle parts and accessories (SIC: 3714)

TRANSFER AGENT(S): The Bank of New York, New York, NY

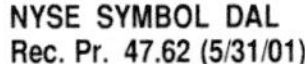

NYSE SYMBOL DAL
Rec. Pr. 47.62 (5/31/01)

DELTA AIR LINES, INC.

YIELD 0.2%
P/E RATIO 6.7

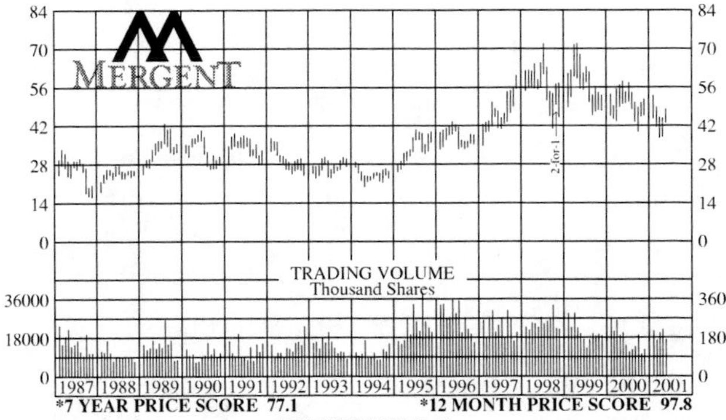

*7 YEAR PRICE SCORE 77.1 *12 MONTH PRICE SCORE 97.8
*NYSE COMPOSITE INDEX=100

INTERIM EARNINGS (Per Share):

Qtr.	Sept.	Dec.	Mar.	June
1997-98	1.67	1.20	1.23	2.26
1998-99	2.08	1.29	1.42	2.40
1999-00	2.38	2.50	1.67	3.51
Qtr.	**Mar.**	**June**	**Sept.**	**Dec.**
2000	...	...	1.77	0.12

INTERIM DIVIDENDS (Per Share):

Amt.	Decl.	Ex.	Rec.	Pay.
0.025Q	7/27/00	8/07/00	8/09/00	9/01/00
0.025Q	10/25/00	11/06/00	11/08/00	12/01/00
0.025Q	1/25/01	2/05/01	2/07/01	3/01/01
0.025Q	4/26/01	5/07/01	5/09/01	6/01/01

Indicated div.: $0.10 (Div. Reinv. Plan)

CAPITALIZATION (12/31/00):

	($000)	(%)
Long-Term Debt	5,797,000	45.7
Capital Lease Obligations	99,000	0.8
Deferred Income Tax	1,220,000	9.6
Preferred Stock	460,000	3.6
Common & Surplus	5,117,000	40.3
Total	12,693,000	100.0

RECENT DEVELOPMENTS: For the year ended 12/31/00, earnings, before an accounting charge of $100.0 million, totaled $928.0 million, versus earnings of $1.26 billion, before an accounting charge of $54.0 million, the year before. Results in 2000 and 1999 included pre-tax charges of $108.0 million and $469.0 million, respectively. These charges were offset by one-time pre-tax gains of $301.0 million and $927.0 million in 2000 and 1999, respectively. Total operating revenues increased 12.5% to $16.74 billion.

PROSPECTS: On 4/22/01, the Company announced that it had reached a tentative contract agreement with its pilots, averting a possible strike. The agreement, if ratified by the pilots' union, will expire on 5/1/05 and ends labor talks that began in September 1999. Meanwhile, the Company is scaling back its previously planned capacity expansion in 2001 to between 2.0% and 2.5% from 3.5% to 4.0% in an effort to cut costs. In April 2001, DAL began daily service to Buenos Aires, Argentina from Atlanta.

BUSINESS

DELTA AIR LINES, INC. is a major air carrier providing scheduled passenger and cargo service through a network of routes throughout the U.S. and abroad. Delta, Delta Express, Delta Shuttle, the Delta Connection carriers and Delta's Worldwide Partners operate 5,183 flights each day to 354 cities in 65 countries. As of 12/31/00, the Company owned or leased 605 aircraft. On 5/11/99, the Company acquired ASA Holdings, Inc., the parent of Atlantic Southeast Airlines. DAL acquired various assets of Pan Am Corp. in 1991.

ANNUAL FINANCIAL DATA

	[6] 12/31/00	6/30/00	6/30/99	6/30/98	6/30/97	6/30/96	6/30/95
Earnings Per Share	[5] 7.05	[4] 9.90	7.20	6.34	[3] 5.65	[1] 0.71	[2] 2.04
Cash Flow Per Share	16.05	18.15	13.47	11.77	10.39	6.79	7.55
Tang. Book Val. Per Share	23.30	19.04	23.64	18.94	15.55	13.19	9.91
Dividends Per Share	0.10	0.10	0.10	0.10	0.10	0.10	0.10
Dividend Payout %	1.4	1.0	1.4	1.6	1.8	14.1	4.9
INCOME STATEMENT (IN MILLIONS):							
Total Revenues	16,741.0	15,888.0	14,711.0	14,138.0	13,590.0	12,455.0	12,194.0
Costs & Expenses	13,917.0	13,454.0	11,880.0	11,584.0	11,350.0	11,358.0	10,974.0
Depreciation & Amort.	1,187.0	1,146.0	961.0	861.0	710.0	634.0	559.0
Operating Income	1,637.0	1,288.0	1,870.0	1,693.0	1,530.0	463.0	661.0
Net Interest Inc./(Exp.)	d271.0	d197.0	d101.0	d69.0	d113.0	d157.0	d167.0
Income Before Income Taxes	1,549.0	2,283.0	1,826.0	1,648.0	1,415.0	276.0	494.0
Income Taxes	621.0	914.0	725.0	647.0	561.0	120.0	200.0
Net Income	[5] 928.0	[4] 1,369.0	1,101.0	1,001.0	[3] 854.0	[1] 156.0	[2] 294.0
Cash Flow	2,102.0	2,503.0	2,051.0	1,851.0	1,555.0	708.0	765.0
Average Shs. Outstg. (000)	131,000	137,900	152,300	157,200	149,600	104,202	101,316
BALANCE SHEET (IN MILLIONS):							
Cash & Cash Equivalents	1,607.0	1,745.0	1,143.0	1,634.0	1,170.0	1,652.0	1,762.0
Total Current Assets	3,205.0	3,346.0	2,672.0	3,362.0	2,867.0	3,282.0	3,014.0
Net Property	14,840.0	13,491.0	11,467.0	9,321.0	8,042.0	6,795.0	6,936.0
Total Assets	21,931.0	20,566.0	16,544.0	14,603.0	12,741.0	12,226.0	12,143.0
Total Current Liabilities	5,245.0	5,940.0	5,327.0	4,577.0	4,083.0	3,638.0	3,441.0
Long-Term Obligations	5,896.0	4,525.0	1,952.0	1,782.0	1,797.0	2,175.0	3,121.0
Net Stockholders' Equity	5,577.0	5,087.0	4,643.0	4,198.0	3,163.0	2,678.0	1,947.0
Net Working Capital	d2,040.0	d2,594.0	d2,655.0	d1,215.0	d1,216.0	d356.0	d427.0
Year-end Shs. Outstg. (000)	123,013	122,640	138,600	176,000	147,400	135,556	101,632
STATISTICAL RECORD:							
Operating Profit Margin %	9.8	8.1	12.7	12.0	11.3	3.7	5.4
Net Profit Margin %	5.5	8.6	7.5	7.1	6.3	1.3	2.4
Return on Equity %	16.6	26.9	23.7	23.8	27.0	5.8	15.1
Return on Assets %	4.2	6.7	6.7	6.9	6.7	1.3	2.4
Debt/Total Assets %	26.9	22.0	11.8	12.2	14.1	17.8	25.7
Price Range	58.31-39.63	58.31-39.63	72.00-45.69	71.81-40.88	60.31-34.63	43.50-33.38	40.63-25.13
P/E Ratio	8.3-5.6	5.9-4.0	10.0-6.3	11.3-6.4	10.7-6.1	61.3-47.0	20.0-12.3
Average Yield %	0.2	0.2	0.2	0.2	0.2	0.3	0.3

Statistics are as originally reported. Adj. for 2-for-1 stk. split, 11/98. [1] Incl. $829 mil restr. chg. [2] Bef. $114 mil ($1.13/sh) acctg. cr. [3] Incl. pre-tax chgs. of $72.3 mil. [4] Bef. $66.0 mil ($0.48/sh) acctg. chg.; incl. pre-tax gain of $1.20 bil & one-time chg. of $555.0 mil. [5] Bef. $100.0 mil acctg. chg. & incl. $108.0 mil pre-tax chg. & incl. $301.0 mil pre-tax gain. [6] For 12 months to refl change in fiscal year end.

OFFICERS:
L. F. Mullin, Chmn., Pres., C.E.O.
M. M. Burns, Exec. V.P., C.F.O.

INVESTOR CONTACT: Investor Relations, (404) 715-6679

PRINCIPAL OFFICE: Hartsfield Atlanta International Airport, Atlanta, GA 30320

TELEPHONE NUMBER: (404) 715-2600
FAX: (404) 715-5042
WEB: www.delta-air.com

NO. OF EMPLOYEES: 81,000 (approx.)

SHAREHOLDERS: 21,194

ANNUAL MEETING: In Apr.

INCORPORATED: DE, Mar., 1967

INSTITUTIONAL HOLDINGS:
No. of Institutions: 318
Shares Held: 95,093,988
% Held: 77.3

INDUSTRY: Air transportation, scheduled (SIC: 4512)

TRANSFER AGENT(S): First Chicago Trust Company of New York, Jersey City, NJ

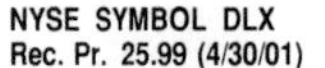

NYSE SYMBOL DLX
Rec. Pr. 25.99 (4/30/01)

DELUXE CORPORATION

YIELD 5.7%
P/E RATIO 9.8

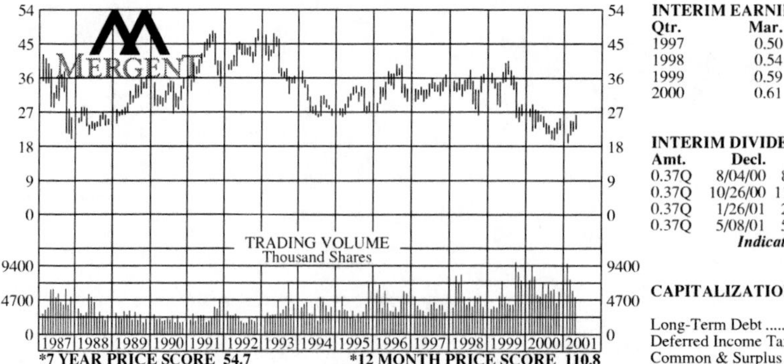

***7 YEAR PRICE SCORE 54.7** ***12 MONTH PRICE SCORE 110.8**

*NYSE COMPOSITE INDEX=100

INTERIM EARNINGS (Per Share):

Qtr.	Mar.	June	Sept.	Dec.
1997	0.50	0.46	d0.57	0.41
1998	0.54	0.52	0.04	0.70
1999	0.59	0.61	0.65	0.79
2000	0.61	0.83	0.68	0.52

INTERIM DIVIDENDS (Per Share):

Amt.	Decl.	Ex.	Rec.	Pay.
0.37Q	8/04/00	8/17/00	8/21/00	9/05/00
0.37Q	10/26/00	11/16/00	11/20/00	12/04/00
0.37Q	1/26/01	2/15/01	2/20/01	3/15/01
0.37Q	5/08/01	5/17/01	5/21/01	6/04/01

Indicated div.: $1.48

CAPITALIZATION (12/31/00):

	($000)	(%)
Long-Term Debt	10,201	3.1
Deferred Income Tax	60,712	18.2
Common & Surplus	262,808	78.8
Total	333,721	100.0

RECENT DEVELOPMENTS: For the year ended 12/31/00, income from continuing operations fell 17.1% to $169.4 million compared with $204.3 million in 1999. Results for 2000 and 1999 excluded losses from discontinued operations of $7.5 million and $1.3 million, respectively. Revenues were $1.26 billion, down 7.4% from $1.36 billion in the prior year. Revenue for 1999 included $124.1 million from a business divested at year-end. Gross profit rose to $811.5 million compared with $807.9 million in 1999.

PROSPECTS: On 1/2/01, the Company completed the separation of eFunds Corporation through the distribution of all of its 40.0 million shares of eFunds Corporation stock. Shareholders of DLX were issued 0.5514 shares of eFunds Corporation common stock for each share held. As a result of the distribution, eFunds Corporation is now an independent company. The spin-off was strategically in line with the Company's efforts to maximize shareholder value.

BUSINESS

DELUXE CORPORATION has classified its operations into three business units: Deluxe Paper Payment Systems, iDLX Technology Partners and Deluxe Government Services. Deluxe Paper Payment Systems provides check printing services to financial institutions and provides checks directly to households and small businesses. iDLX Technology Partners provides technology and technology-related services to financial institutions. Deluxe Government Services provides electronic benefits services to state governments. All segments operate primarily in the U.S. On 1/2/01, DLX completed the separation of eFunds Corporation.

ANNUAL FINANCIAL DATA

	12/31/00	12/31/99	12/31/98	12/31/97	12/31/96	12/31/95	12/31/94
Earnings Per Share	**[6] 2.34**	**2.64**	**[5] 1.80**	**[4] 0.55**	**[3] 0.80**	**[2] 1.15**	**[1] 1.71**
Cash Flow Per Share	**3.29**	**3.73**	**2.86**	**1.73**	**2.09**	**2.40**	**2.75**
Tang. Book Val. Per Share	**0.55**	**2.89**	**5.15**	**5.44**	**6.00**	**4.96**	**5.90**
Dividends Per Share	**1.48**	**1.48**	**1.48**	**1.48**	**1.48**	**1.48**	**1.46**
Dividend Payout %	**63.2**	**56.1**	**82.2**	**269.0**	**185.0**	**128.7**	**85.4**
INCOME STATEMENT (IN MILLIONS):							
Total Revenues	1,262.7	1,650.5	1,931.8	1,919.4	1,895.7	1,858.0	1,747.9
Costs & Expenses	916.8	1,264.5	1,599.4	1,666.4	1,701.9	1,570.9	1,418.4
Depreciation & Amort.	68.6	83.9	85.8	97.3	106.6	103.3	85.9
Operating Income	277.3	302.1	246.6	155.7	87.1	183.8	243.7
Net Interest Inc./(Exp.)	d10.8	d8.5	d8.3	d8.8	d10.6	d13.1	d11.3
Income Before Income Taxes	273.4	324.7	246.5	115.2	118.8	169.3	240.9
Income Taxes	104.0	121.6	101.1	70.5	53.3	74.9	100.0
Net Income	[6] 169.5	203.0	[5] 145.4	[4] 44.7	[3] 65.5	[2] 94.4	[1] 140.9
Cash Flow	238.0	286.9	231.2	141.9	172.1	197.7	226.8
Average Shs. Outstg. (000)	72,420	77,009	80,855	81,957	82,311	82,420	82,400
BALANCE SHEET (IN MILLIONS):							
Cash & Cash Equivalents	88.2	169.6	310.1	179.5	142.6	19.9	78.2
Total Current Assets	208.8	418.7	619.2	512.6	449.5	381.1	420.9
Net Property	174.0	294.8	344.6	415.0	446.9	494.2	461.8
Total Assets	649.5	992.6	1,203.0	1,148.4	1,176.4	1,295.1	1,256.3
Total Current Liabilities	305.2	404.7	451.4	381.6	341.4	368.8	290.5
Long-Term Obligations	10.2	115.5	106.3	110.0	108.9	111.0	110.9
Net Stockholders' Equity	262.8	417.3	608.9	610.2	712.9	780.4	814.4
Net Working Capital	d96.4	14.1	167.9	131.1	108.1	12.3	130.4
Year-end Shs. Outstg. (000)	72,555	72,020	80,481	81,326	82,056	82,365	82,375
STATISTICAL RECORD:							
Operating Profit Margin %	22.0	18.3	12.8	8.1	4.6	9.9	13.9
Net Profit Margin %	13.4	12.3	7.5	2.3	3.5	5.1	8.1
Return on Equity %	64.5	48.7	23.9	7.3	9.2	12.1	17.3
Return on Assets %	26.1	20.5	12.1	3.9	5.6	7.3	11.2
Debt/Total Assets %	1.6	11.6	8.8	9.6	9.3	8.6	8.8
Price Range	29.00-19.63	40.50-24.44	38.19-26.06	37.00-29.75	39.75-27.00	34.00-25.75	38.00-25.63
P/E Ratio	12.4-8.4	15.3-9.3	21.2-14.5	67.3-54.1	49.7-33.7	29.6-22.4	22.2-15.0
Average Yield %	6.1	4.6	4.6	4.4	4.4	5.0	4.6

Statistics are as originally reported. [1] Incl. $10.0 mill. pre-tax credit. [2] Bef. $7.4 mill. loss fr. disc. oper.; incl. $62.5 mill. pre-tax non-recur. chg. [3] Incl. $142.3 mill. net pre-tax chg. for goodwill impair., restr., gains & losses on sales of bus., & oth. costs. [4] Incl. $180.0 mill. net pre-tax chg. rel. to write-dwn of impaired assets & oth. bal. sheet adj. [5] Incl. $70.2 mill. pre-tax chg. [6] Excl. $7.5 mill. net income fr. disc. ops.

OFFICERS:
J. A. Blanchard III, Chmn., C.E.O.
D. Janssen, Pres., C.O.O.
D. J. Treff, Sr. V.P., C.F.O.

INVESTOR CONTACT: Stu Alexander, V.P., Inv. Rel., (651) 483-7358

PRINCIPAL OFFICE: 3680 Victoria Street North, Shoreview, MN 55126-2966

TELEPHONE NUMBER: (651) 483-7111
FAX: (651) 483-7337
WEB: www.deluxe.com

NO. OF EMPLOYEES: 7,800 (avg.)

SHAREHOLDERS: 12,770

ANNUAL MEETING: In May

INCORPORATED: MN, Mar., 1920

INSTITUTIONAL HOLDINGS:
No. of Institutions: 232
Shares Held: 37,169,367
% Held: 52.6

INDUSTRY: Blankbooks and looseleaf binders (SIC: 2782)

TRANSFER AGENT(S): Wells Fargo Shareowner Services, St. Paul, MN

NYSE SYMBOL DV
Rec. Pr. 33.40 (5/31/01)

DEVRY INC.

YIELD	...
P/E RATIO	44.5

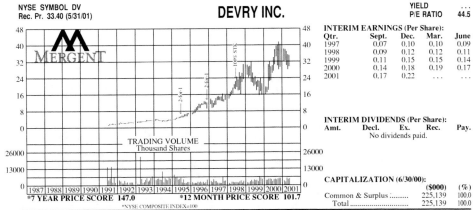

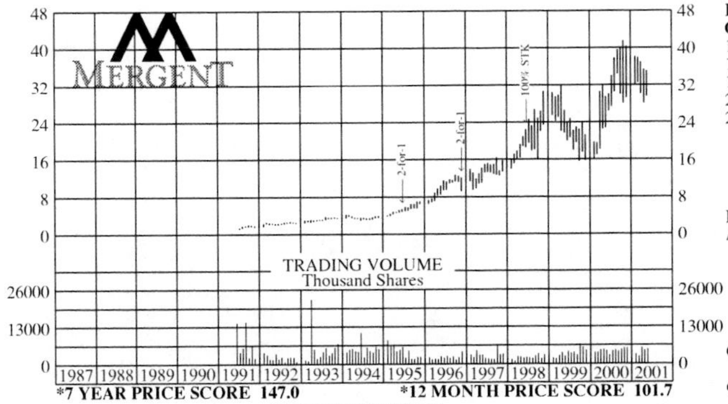

TRADING VOLUME
Thousand Shares

*7 YEAR PRICE SCORE 147.0 *12 MONTH PRICE SCORE 101.7

*NYSE COMPOSITE INDEX=100

INTERIM EARNINGS (Per Share):

Qtr.	Sept.	Dec.	Mar.	June
1997	0.07	0.10	0.10	0.09
1998	0.09	0.12	0.12	0.11
1999	0.11	0.15	0.15	0.14
2000	0.14	0.18	0.19	0.17
2001	0.17	0.22	...	...

INTERIM DIVIDENDS (Per Share):

Amt.	Decl.	Ex.	Rec.	Pay.

No dividends paid.

CAPITALIZATION (6/30/00):

	($000)	(%)
Common & Surplus	225,139	100.0
Total	225,139	100.0

RECENT DEVELOPMENTS: For the quarter ended 12/31/00, net income rose 22.9% to $15.7 million versus $12.8 million in the same period the year before. Revenues were $150.4 million, up 12.8% from $133.2 million a year earlier. Earnings were enhanced by commissions from the outsourcing of nine on-campus bookstore operations. Tuition revenues advanced 16.3% to $138.3 million, while other educational revenues declined 16.1% to $11.7 million.

PROSPECTS: On 1/9/01, Becker Conviser Professional Review, a DV subsidiary, acquired Argentum Inc., a provider of exam preparation materials for the Chartered Financial Analyst exam under the name of Stalla Seminars. The acquisition will enable Becker Conviser to expand its exam preparation services in the finance-related areas. During 2001, DV plans to pilot a new educational initiative DeVry University Centers, which will provide undergraduate and graduate degree programs to working adults.

BUSINESS

DEVRY, INC. is a holding company for DeVry University and Becker Conviser Professional Review. DeVry University includes DeVry Institutes, Denver Technical Colleges and Keller Graduate School of Management. DeVry Institutes provide career-oriented, technology-based bachelor degree programs through a system of 21 campuses in the U.S. and Canada, serving a combined enrollment of more than 47,000 full- and part-time students. Denver Technical Colleges offers undergraduate and graduate degree programs for electronics, computer technology, business and medical technology fields with campuses in Denver and Colorado Springs, Colorado. Keller Graduate School offers practitioner-oriented master's degree programs that focus on applied education. Becker Conviser Professional Review is an international training firm that offers preparatory coursework for the Certified Public Accountant, Certified Management Accountant and Chartered Financial Analyst exams.

REVENUES

(06/30/00)	($000)	(%)
Tuition	460,094	90.8
Other Educational	45,238	8.9
Interest	1,492	0.3
Total	506,824	100.0

ANNUAL FINANCIAL DATA

	6/30/00	6/30/99	6/30/98	6/30/97	6/30/96	6/30/95	6/30/94
Earnings Per Share	**0.68**	**0.55**	**0.44**	**0.36**	**0.29**	**0.22**	**0.18**
Cash Flow Per Share	**1.04**	**0.80**	**0.64**	**0.52**	**0.40**	**0.32**	**0.29**
Tang. Book Val. Per Share	**2.17**	**1.98**	**1.42**	**0.97**	**0.28**	**0.53**	**0.30**
INCOME STATEMENT (IN THOUSANDS):							
Total Revenues	506,824	420,635	353,471	308,319	260,007	228,593	211,437
Costs & Expenses	402,090	339,441	288,088	254,353	218,667	193,544	178,492
Depreciation & Amort.	25,251	17,784	13,987	11,262	7,579	6,220	7,327
Operating Income	79,483	63,410	51,396	42,704	33,761	28,829	25,618
Net Interest Inc./(Exp.)	d1,409	d300	d913	d2,848	d1,063	d3,070	d4,615
Income Before Income Taxes	78,074	63,110	50,483	39,856	32,698	25,759	21,003
Income Taxes	30,293	24,280	19,759	15,670	13,453	10,863	8,778
Net Income	47,781	38,830	30,724	24,186	19,245	14,896	12,225
Cash Flow	73,032	56,614	44,711	35,448	26,824	21,116	19,552
Average Shs. Outstg.	70,390	70,454	70,144	68,170	67,320	66,908	66,776
BALANCE SHEET (IN THOUSANDS):							
Cash & Cash Equivalents	45,246	52,614	48,756	50,969	46,538	46,431	33,753
Total Current Assets	81,964	78,941	69,720	70,516	61,567	58,019	48,856
Net Property	158,801	135,211	108,105	90,688	71,441	60,258	51,857
Total Assets	327,079	260,691	223,892	206,703	178,089	126,671	106,798
Total Current Liabilities	89,185	74,043	65,979	58,293	52,460	48,747	40,214
Long-Term Obligations	...	...	10,000	33,000	61,500	33,029	39,674
Net Stockholders' Equity	225,139	175,305	136,256	104,396	56,407	37,068	22,172
Net Working Capital	d7,221	4,898	3,741	12,223	9,107	9,272	8,642
Year-end Shs. Outstg.	69,642	69,414	69,305	69,008	66,452	66,452	66,424
STATISTICAL RECORD:							
Operating Profit Margin %	15.7	15.1	14.5	13.9	13.0	12.6	12.1
Net Profit Margin %	9.4	9.2	8.7	7.8	7.4	6.5	5.8
Return on Equity %	21.2	22.1	22.5	23.2	34.1	40.2	55.1
Return on Assets %	14.6	14.9	13.7	11.7	10.8	11.8	11.4
Debt/Total Assets %	...	...	4.5	16.0	34.5	26.1	37.1
Price Range	41.50-16.06	31.88-15.63	30.63-14.00	16.34-9.50	12.69-6.44	7.03-3.81	4.19-2.94
P/E Ratio	61.0-23.6	57.9-28.4	69.6-31.8	46.0-26.8	44.5-22.6	31.5-17.1	23.0-16.1

Statistics are as originally reported. Adj. for stk. split 100%, 6/98; 2-for-1, 12/96; 2-for-1, 6/95.

OFFICERS:
D. J. Keller, Chmn., C.E.O.
R. L. Taylor, Pres., C.O.O.
N. M. Levine, Sr. V.P., C.F.O.

INVESTOR CONTACT: Diane Salucci, Director of Communications, (630) 574-1931

PRINCIPAL OFFICE: One Tower Lane, Suite 1000, Oakbrook Terrace, IL 60181-4624

TELEPHONE NUMBER: (630) 571-7700
FAX: (630) 571-0317
WEB: www.devry.com
NO. OF EMPLOYEES: 3,600 (avg.)
SHAREHOLDERS: 709 (record); 10,000 (beneficial)
ANNUAL MEETING: In Nov.
INCORPORATED: IL, 1973; reincorp., DE, Aug., 1987

INSTITUTIONAL HOLDINGS:
No. of Institutions: 187
Shares Held: 49,277,037
% Held: 70.7

INDUSTRY: Schools & educational services, nec (SIC: 8299)

TRANSFER AGENT(S): Computershare Investor Services, LLC, Chicago, IL

NYSE SYMBOL DP
Rec. Pr. 38.86 (Adj.; 5/31/01)

DIAGNOSTIC PRODUCTS CORPORATION

YIELD 0.6%
P/E RATIO 19.4

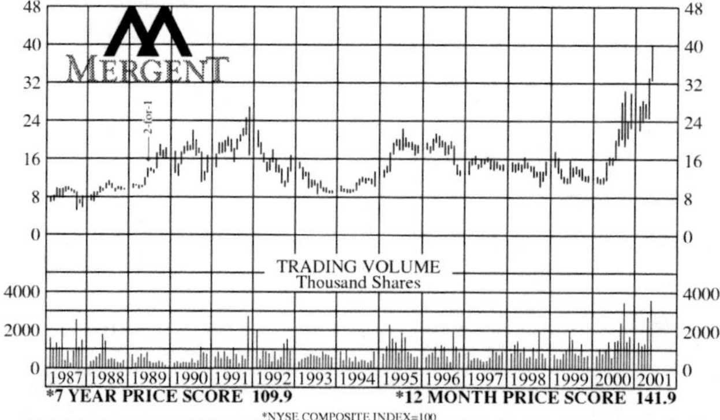

*7 YEAR PRICE SCORE 109.9 *12 MONTH PRICE SCORE 141.9

*NYSE COMPOSITE INDEX=100

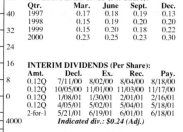

INTERIM EARNINGS (Per Share):

Qtr.	Mar.	June	Sept.	Dec.
1997	0.17	0.18	0.19	0.13
1998	0.15	0.19	0.20	0.20
1999	0.15	0.20	0.18	0.22
2000	0.23	0.25	0.23	0.30

INTERIM DIVIDENDS (Per Share):

Amt.	Decl.	Ex.	Rec.	Pay.
0.12Q	7/11/00	8/02/00	8/04/00	8/18/00
0.12Q	10/05/00	11/01/00	11/03/00	11/17/00
0.12Q	1/08/01	1/30/01	2/01/01	2/16/01
0.12Q	4/05/01	5/02/01	5/04/01	5/18/01
2-for-1	5/21/01	6/19/01	6/01/01	6/18/01

Indicated div.: $0.24 (Adj.)

CAPITALIZATION (12/31/00):

	($000)	(%)
Common & Surplus	227,024	100.0
Total	227,024	100.0

RECENT DEVELOPMENTS: For the year ended 12/31/00, net income jumped 37.9% to $28.3 million compared with $20.5 million in the previous year. Sales amounted to $247.9 million, an increase of 14.7% versus $216.2 million a year earlier. Sales of IMMULITE products rose 28.1% to $193.1 million and accounted for approximately 77.9% of the total sales for the year. Operating income jumped 40.9% to $41.9 million.

PROSPECTS: On 3/28/01, DP and Maritech, a cancer diagnosis company, entered into a product supply and marketing agreement, whereby DP will develop and market an automated version of Matritech's NMP22® test kit for bladder cancer. On 12/13/00, DP announced the release outside of the U.S. of a new diagnostic test for the quantitative measurement of L-homocysteine in plasma or serum. The IMMULITE 2000 Homocysteine is an immunassay for in vitro use with the IMMULITE 2000 Automated Analyzer.

BUSINESS

DIAGNOSTIC PRODUCTS CORPORATION develops, manufactures and markets medical immunodiagnostic test kits and related instrumentation. DP's products are used by hospitals, clinical, veterinary, and forensic laboratories and doctors' offices to obtain precise and rapid identification and measurement of hormones, drugs, viruses, bacteria, and other substances present in body fluids and tissues at infinitesimal concentrations. The Company's instrument systems include IMMULITE, a family of chemiluminescent immunoassay analyzers, ALASTAT for non-invasive allergy testing, and the MARK HSS for automated immunohistochemical staining. The principal clinical applications of the Company's more than 400 assays relate to diagnosis of various medical conditions including anemia, bone metabolism, cancer, diabetes, infectious diseases, reproductive disorders, substance abuse, thyroid disorders and veterinary applications. DP's products are sold in over 100 countries.

ANNUAL FINANCIAL DATA

	12/31/00	12/31/99	12/31/98	12/31/97	12/31/96	12/31/95	12/31/94
Earnings Per Share	**1.01**	**0.75**	**0.73**	**0.66**	**0.83**	**0.88**	**0.62**
Cash Flow Per Share	**1.67**	**1.33**	**1.43**	**1.21**	**1.34**	**1.28**	**0.92**
Tang. Book Val. Per Share	**7.70**	**7.06**	**6.81**	**6.28**	**6.16**	**5.44**	**4.68**
Dividends Per Share	**0.24**	**0.24**	**0.24**	**0.24**	**0.24**	**0.23**	**0.20**
Dividend Payout %	**23.9**	**32.2**	**32.9**	**36.4**	**29.1**	**26.3**	**32.3**
INCOME STATEMENT (IN THOUSANDS):							
Total Revenues	247,867	216,193	196,643	186,264	176,832	159,649	126,453
Costs & Expenses	188,973	171,709	150,659	147,296	133,756	119,150	97,917
Depreciation & Amort.	18,792	16,205	19,364	15,270	14,440	11,155	8,107
Operating Income	41,857	28,279	26,620	23,698	28,636	29,344	20,429
Net Interest Inc./(Exp.)	...	...	331	687	...	...	...
Income Before Income Taxes	42,523	30,143	28,213	25,748	31,727	32,579	22,640
Income Taxes	12,864	9,073	8,000	7,500	8,780	8,410	5,940
Equity Earnings/Minority Int.	346	839	1,262	1,363	1,605	1,407	1,592
Net Income	28,250	20,488	20,213	18,248	22,947	24,169	16,700
Cash Flow	47,042	36,693	39,577	33,518	37,387	35,324	24,807
Average Shs. Outstg.	28,148	27,542	27,762	27,752	27,852	27,694	27,016
BALANCE SHEET (IN THOUSANDS):							
Cash & Cash Equivalents	26,395	14,547	18,650	20,372	13,781	16,519	14,833
Total Current Assets	158,273	132,396	127,053	118,916	106,278	96,651	78,339
Net Property	93,595	88,488	87,584	73,969	67,503	60,052	45,269
Total Assets	280,484	250,494	246,224	222,180	207,002	189,462	152,735
Total Current Liabilities	53,460	43,597	46,052	35,885	24,715	26,112	17,635
Net Stockholders' Equity	227,024	206,897	200,172	186,295	182,287	163,350	135,100
Net Working Capital	104,813	88,799	81,001	83,031	81,563	70,539	60,704
Year-end Shs. Outstg.	27,837	27,346	27,324	27,434	27,194	27,048	25,906
STATISTICAL RECORD:							
Operating Profit Margin %	16.9	13.1	13.5	12.7	16.2	18.4	16.2
Net Profit Margin %	11.4	9.5	10.3	9.8	13.0	15.1	13.2
Return on Equity %	12.4	9.9	10.1	9.8	12.6	14.8	12.4
Return on Assets %	10.1	8.2	8.2	8.2	11.1	12.8	10.9
Price Range	30.38-10.84	17.66-10.94	16.44-10.19	16.75-12.75	21.44-12.50	22.44-12.13	13.31-8.88
P/E Ratio	30.2-10.8	23.7-14.7	22.5-14.0	25.4-19.3	26.0-15.2	25.6-13.9	21.5-14.3
Average Yield %	1.2	1.7	1.8	1.6	1.4	1.3	1.8

Statistics are as originally reported. Adj. for 2-for-1 stk. split.

OFFICERS:
M. Ziering, Chmn., Pres., C.E.O.
S. A. Aroesty, C.O.O.

INVESTOR CONTACT: Investor Relations, (310) 645-8200

PRINCIPAL OFFICE: 5700 West 96th Street, Los Angeles, CA 90045

TELEPHONE NUMBER: (310) 645-8200
FAX: (310) 645-9999
WEB: www.dpcweb.com

NO. OF EMPLOYEES: 1,767

SHAREHOLDERS: 308

ANNUAL MEETING: In May

INCORPORATED: CA, 1971

INSTITUTIONAL HOLDINGS:
No. of Institutions: 123
Shares Held: 14,486,208 (Adj.)
% Held: 51.8

INDUSTRY: Diagnostic substances (SIC: 2835)

TRANSFER AGENT(S): Mellon Investor Services, Los Angeles, CA

NYSE SYMBOL DL
Rec. Pr. 13.05 (4/30/01)

DIAL CORPORATION (THE)

YIELD 1.2%
P/E RATIO . . .

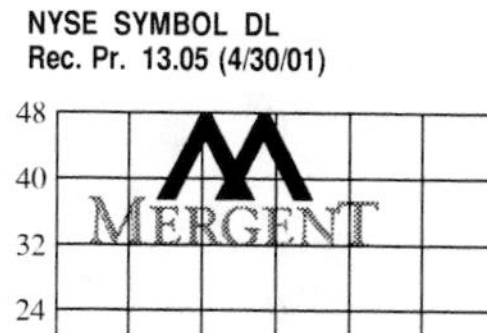

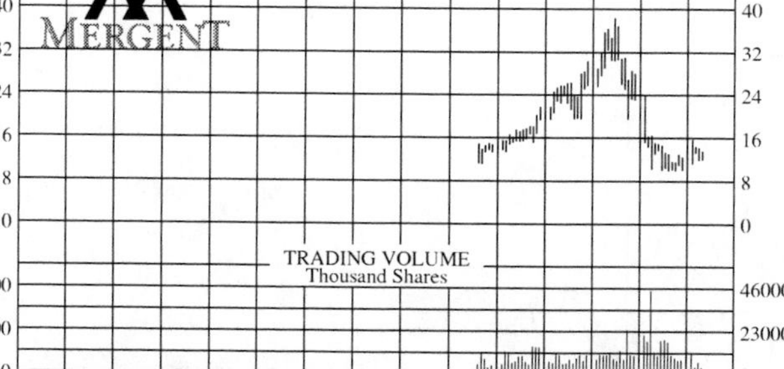

*7 YEAR PRICE SCORE N/A *12 MONTH PRICE SCORE 111.5

*NYSE COMPOSITE INDEX=100

INTERIM EARNINGS (Per Share):

Qtr.	Mar.	June	Sept.	Dec.
1997	0.20	0.22	0.24	0.23
1998	0.23	0.25	0.27	0.27
1999	0.26	0.29	0.31	0.31
2000	0.23	0.01	d0.29	d0.08

INTERIM DIVIDENDS (Per Share):

Amt.	Decl.	Ex.	Rec.	Pay.
0.08Q	6/01/00	6/13/00	6/15/00	7/17/00
0.08Q	8/03/00	9/13/00	9/15/00	10/16/00
0.04Q	10/18/00	12/13/00	12/15/00	1/15/01
0.04Q	3/07/01	3/15/01	3/19/01	4/17/01
0.04Q	6/07/01	6/14/01	6/18/01	7/17/01

Indicated div.: $0.16

CAPITALIZATION (12/31/00):

	($000)	(%)
Long-Term Debt	469,271	61.5
Common & Surplus	293,907	38.5
Total	763,178	100.0

RECENT DEVELOPMENTS: For the year ended 12/31/00, the Company reported a net loss of $11.0 million versus net income of $116.8 million in 1999. Results for 2000 included a charge of $49.2 million for asset write-downs and discontinued product inventories, restructuring charges and other asset write-downs of $18.2 million, and a gain on special items of $9.2 million. Net sales totaled $1.64 billion, a decrease of 4.8% versus $1.72 billion a year earlier.

PROSPECTS: Going forward, the Company will continue to support its strong core brands while it sorts out non-fit or weaker brands. DL's current portfolio of brands should generate sales growth of approximately 3.0% or more. Despite higher energy costs, DL will continue its aggressive efforts to reduce operating expenses and improve gross and operating margins,

BUSINESS

THE DIAL CORPORATION was created on 8/15/96 by the spin-off of the consumers products group from the former Dial Corp. The Dial Corporation is a worldwide manufacturer and marketer of consumer products. DL manufactures personal care items, household and laundry products and packaged foods under the brand names DIAL, PUREX, RENUZIT, ARMOUR STAR, SARAH MICHAELS, FREE-MAN and NATURE'S ACCENTS. In 1998, the Company acquired Free-man Cosmetics Corporation and Sarah Michaels, Inc.

ANNUAL FINANCIAL DATA

	12/31/00	12/31/99	12/31/98	1/3/98	12/28/96	[1] 12/31/95	[1] 12/31/94
Earnings Per Share	[3] d0.12	1.17	1.02	0.89	[2] 0.66	. . .	. . .
Cash Flow Per Share	0.47	1.60	1.38	1.23	0.67	. . .	. . .
Dividends Per Share	0.32	0.32	0.32	0.32	0.08	. . .	. . .
Dividend Payout %	. . .	27.3	31.4	36.0	12.1	. . .	. . .
INCOME STATEMENT (IN MILLIONS):							
Total Revenues	1,638.5	1,721.6	1,524.5	1,362.6	1,406.4	1,365.3	1,511.4
Costs & Expenses	1,525.2	1,463.3	1,304.1	1,168.7	1,305.5	1,359.8	1,316.4
Depreciation & Amort.	54.0	43.1	36.5	31.8	30.5	29.1	34.9
Operating Income	59.3	215.1	183.9	162.2	70.4	d23.7	160.0
Income Before Income Taxes	d19.3	181.1	160.6	133.9	42.4	d47.0	147.5
Income Taxes	cr8.3	64.3	58.0	50.2	12.5	cr19.5	56.5
Net Income	[3] d11.0	116.8	102.6	83.7	[2] 29.9	[2] d27.5	91.1
Cash Flow	43.0	159.9	139.1	115.5	60.4	1.6	126.0
Average Shs. Outstg. (000)	92,237	100,065	100,479	94,149	89,705	. . .	. . .
BALANCE SHEET (IN MILLIONS):							
Cash & Cash Equivalents	6.8	6.1	12.4	10.1	14.1	5.9	5.9
Total Current Assets	377.7	332.5	239.1	227.0	247.8	235.1	282.5
Net Property	301.0	306.6	281.3	260.9	226.6	201.1	261.0
Total Assets	1,382.0	1,269.7	1,175.4	883.9	866.1	798.4	887.4
Total Current Liabilities	394.9	318.0	250.6	238.8	206.7	189.4	226.3
Long-Term Obligations	469.3	301.0	280.2	84.4	269.5	2.5	2.9
Net Stockholders' Equity	293.9	411.3	390.2	320.0	140.7	496.2	555.7
Net Working Capital	d17.1	14.5	d11.5	d11.8	41.1	45.7	56.2
Year-end Shs. Outstg. (000)	94,908	100,593	103,179	102,624	95,589	. . .	. . .
STATISTICAL RECORD:							
Operating Profit Margin %	3.6	12.5	12.1	11.9	5.0	. . .	10.6
Net Profit Margin %	. . .	6.8	6.7	6.1	2.1	. . .	6.0
Return on Equity %	. . .	28.4	26.3	26.2	21.3	. . .	16.4
Return on Assets %	. . .	9.2	8.7	9.5	3.5	. . .	10.3
Debt/Total Assets %	34.0	23.7	23.8	9.5	31.1	0.3	0.3
Price Range	24.06-9.88	38.38-19.50	30.25-19.38	21.81-13.38	15.00-11.13	. . .	. . .
P/E Ratio	. . .	32.8-16.7	29.7-19.0	24.5-15.0	22.7-16.9	. . .	. . .
Average Yield %	1.9	1.1	1.3	1.8	0.6	. . .	. . .

Statistics are as originally reported. [1] Pro forma [2] Incl. non-recurr. chrg. 1996, $32.1 mill.; 1995, $135.6 mill. [3] Incl. asset write-down & disc. product inventories chrg. of $49.2 mill., a restruct. chrg. and other assets write-downs of $18.2 mill.; and a pre-tax gain of $9.2 mill.

OFFICERS:
H. M. Baum, Chmn., C.E.O.
C. A. Conrad, Sr. V.P., C.F.O.
C. J. Littlefield, Sr. V.P., Gen. Couns., Sec.

INVESTOR CONTACT: Investor Relations Dept., (480) 754-2386

PRINCIPAL OFFICE: 15501 North Dial Blvd., Scottsdale, AZ 85260-1619

TELEPHONE NUMBER: (480) 754-3425
FAX: (480) 754-1098
WEB: www.dialcorp.com

NO. OF EMPLOYEES: 3,351 (approx.)

SHAREHOLDERS: 32,644 (record)

ANNUAL MEETING: In June

INCORPORATED: DE, 1996

INSTITUTIONAL HOLDINGS:
No. of Institutions: 176
Shares Held: 63,909,145
% Held: 67.3

INDUSTRY: Soap and other detergents (SIC: 2841)

TRANSFER AGENT(S): Computershare Investor Services, Chicago, IL

NYSE SYMBOL DO
Rec. Pr. 43.92 (4/30/01)

DIAMOND OFFSHORE DRILLING, INC.

YIELD 1.1%
P/E RATIO 84.5

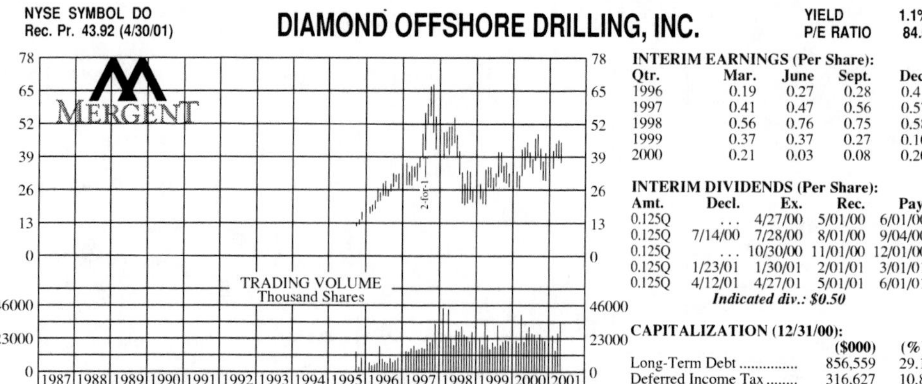

*7 YEAR PRICE SCORE N/A *12 MONTH PRICE SCORE 112.4
*NYSE COMPOSITE INDEX=100

INTERIM EARNINGS (Per Share):

Qtr.	Mar.	June	Sept.	Dec.
1996	0.19	0.27	0.28	0.41
1997	0.41	0.47	0.56	0.57
1998	0.56	0.76	0.75	0.58
1999	0.37	0.37	0.27	0.10
2000	0.21	0.03	0.08	0.20

INTERIM DIVIDENDS (Per Share):

Amt.	Decl.	Ex.	Rec.	Pay.
0.125Q	...	4/27/00	5/01/00	6/01/00
0.125Q	7/14/00	7/28/00	8/01/00	9/04/00
0.125Q	...	10/30/00	11/01/00	12/01/00
0.125Q	1/23/01	1/30/01	2/01/01	3/01/01
0.125Q	4/12/01	4/27/01	5/01/01	6/01/01

Indicated div.: $0.50

CAPITALIZATION (12/31/00):

	($000)	(%)
Long-Term Debt	856,559	29.1
Deferred Income Tax	316,627	10.8
Common & Surplus	1,767,853	60.1
Total	2,941,039	100.0

RECENT DEVELOPMENTS: For the twelve months ended 12/31/00, net income declined 53.7% to $72.3 million compared with $156.1 million in the corresponding year-earlier period. Results for 2000 and 1999 included gains on the sale of assets of $14.3 million and $231,000, respectively. Total revenues fell 19.7% to $659.4 million from $821.0 million in 1999. Operating income amounted to $56.9 million compared with $223.7 million the year before.

PROSPECTS: Near-term prospects are enhanced by strengthening utilization levels and, to a lesser degree, dayrate trends. Looking forward, DO should benefit from an expected increase in industry spending in 2001 as customers raise exploration and production spending to capitalize on historically high natural gas and crude oil prices. The higher spending levels are expected to be most evident in the offshore markets outside North America, where spending was severely curtailed in 2000, and in the gas-intensive, shallow water of the U.S. Gulf of Mexico.

BUSINESS

DIAMOND OFFSHORE DRILLING, INC., through its wholly-owned subsidiaries, is engaged principally in the operations of contract drilling of offshore oil and gas wells. Contract drilling services are conducted through DO's fleet of 45 offshore rigs. The fleet consists of 30 semisubmersibles, 14 jack-ups and one drillship. Principal markets for operation are the Gulf of Mexico, the U.K. North Sea, South America, Africa, Australia and Southeast Asia. The Company also provides a portfolio of drilling services, including project management, extended well tests, and drilling and completion operations through its wholly-owned subsidiary, Diamond Offshore Team Solutions, Inc.

REVENUES

(12/31/2000)	($000)	(%)
United States	453,837	59.9
Europe/Africa	69,495	9.2
South America	177,891	23.5
Australia/Southeast Asia	56,580	7.4
Total	757,803	100.0

ANNUAL FINANCIAL DATA

	12/31/00	12/31/99	12/31/98	12/31/97	12/31/96	12/31/95	12/31/94
Earnings Per Share	**2 0.53**	**1 1.11**	**2.66**	**1.93**	**1.18**	**d0.10**	...
Cash Flow Per Share	**1.56**	**2.06**	**3.48**	**2.63**	**1.78**	...	...
Tang. Book Val. Per Share	**12.86**	**13.02**	**11.81**	**10.17**	**7.79**	**4.93**	...
Dividends Per Share	**0.50**	**0.50**	**0.50**	**0.14**	...	...	...
Dividend Payout %	**94.3**	**45.0**	**18.8**	**7.3**	...	...	...
INCOME STATEMENT (IN MILLIONS):							
Total Revenues	659.4	821.0	1,208.8	956.1	611.4	336.6	307.9
Costs & Expenses	448.0	453.9	509.4	428.4	357.3	275.5	274.4
Depreciation & Amort.	154.5	143.5	130.8	108.8	75.8	50.8	49.9
Operating Income	56.9	223.9	569.0	419.9	213.5	11.7	d14.6
Net Interest Inc./(Exp.)	39.3	25.8	16.1	9.1	d2.3	d27.1	d31.3
Income Before Income Taxes	110.9	240.4	590.2	430.1	212.7	d13.8	d46.4
Income Taxes	38.6	84.3	206.6	151.5	66.3	cr6.8	cr11.6
Net Income	2 72.3	1 156.1	383.7	278.6	146.4	d7.0	d34.8
Cash Flow	226.8	299.6	514.5	387.4	222.2	43.8	15.1
Average Shs. Outstg. (000)	145,050	145,698	147,896	147,489	124,462	...	...
BALANCE SHEET (IN MILLIONS):							
Cash & Cash Equivalents	862.1	641.4	637.0	466.1	28.2	15.3	22.7
Total Current Assets	1,101.0	860.3	938.4	718.8	243.0	115.8	98.6
Net Property	1,902.4	1,737.9	1,551.8	1,451.7	1,198.2	502.3	488.7
Total Assets	3,079.5	2,681.0	2,609.7	2,298.6	1,574.5	618.1	587.2
Total Current Liabilities	123.0	135.4	160.4	131.1	128.0	52.3	42.0
Long-Term Obligations	856.6	400.0	400.0	400.0	63.0	...	394.8
Net Stockholders' Equity	1,767.9	1,842.2	1,755.3	1,535.5	1,194.7	492.9	124.1
Net Working Capital	977.9	724.9	778.0	587.6	115.0	63.5	56.6
Year-end Shs. Outstg. (000)	133,150	135,824	139,334	139,310	136,706	100,000	...
STATISTICAL RECORD:							
Operating Profit Margin %	8.6	27.3	47.1	43.9	34.9	3.5	...
Net Profit Margin %	11.0	19.0	31.7	29.1	23.9	...	...
Return on Equity %	4.1	8.5	21.9	18.1	12.3	...	...
Return on Assets %	2.3	5.8	14.7	12.1	9.3	...	...
Debt/Total Assets %	27.8	14.9	15.3	17.4	4.0	...	67.2
Price Range	47.94-26.50	41.00-20.25	54.63-20.06	67.50-27.69	32.50-16.63	17.25-11.69	...
P/E Ratio	90.4-50.0	36.9-18.2	20.5-7.5	35.0-14.3	27.7-14.1	...	...
Average Yield %	1.3	1.6	1.3	0.3	...	...	...

Statistics are as originally reported. Adj. for 2-for-1 stk. split, 8/97. 1 Incls. after-tax chrg. of $6.9 mill. related to a non-cash impairment of investment securities. 2 Incls. gain of $14.3 mill. on the sale of assets.

OFFICERS:
J. S. Tisch, Chmn., C.E.O.
L. R. Dickerson, Pres., C.O.O.
G. T. Krenek, V.P., C.F.O.

INVESTOR CONTACT: Caren W. Steffes, (281) 492-5393

PRINCIPAL OFFICE: 15415 Katy Freeway, Houston, TX 77094

TELEPHONE NUMBER: (281) 492-5300
FAX: (281) 492-5316
WEB: www.diamondoffshore.com
NO. OF EMPLOYEES: 4,000 (avg.)
SHAREHOLDERS: 402 (approx.)
ANNUAL MEETING: In May
INCORPORATED: DE, Apr., 1989

INSTITUTIONAL HOLDINGS:
No. of Institutions: 205
Shares Held: 129,638,906
% Held: 97.4

INDUSTRY: Drilling oil and gas wells (SIC: 1381)

TRANSFER AGENT(S): Mellon Investor Services, Ridgefield Park, NJ

NYSE SYMBOL DBD
Rec. Pr. 30.58 (5/31/01)

DIEBOLD, INC.

YIELD 2.1%
P/E RATIO 15.9

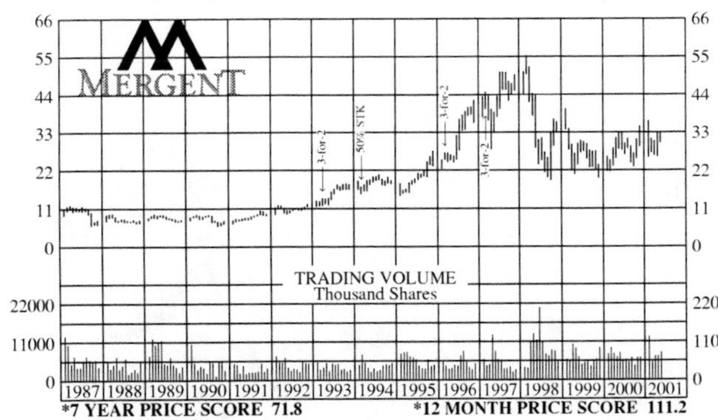

*7 YEAR PRICE SCORE 71.8 *12 MONTH PRICE SCORE 111.2

*NYSE COMPOSITE INDEX=100

INTERIM EARNINGS (Per Share):

Qtr.	Mar.	June	Sept.	Dec.
1997	0.34	0.45	0.48	0.50
1998	0.39	d0.21	0.43	0.50
1999	0.42	0.46	0.47	0.50
2000	0.44	0.50	0.49	0.49

INTERIM DIVIDENDS (Per Share):

Amt.	Decl.	Ex.	Rec.	Pay.
0.155Q	8/08/00	8/16/00	8/18/00	9/08/00
0.155Q	10/11/00	11/15/00	11/17/00	12/08/00
0.16Q	2/07/01	2/14/01	2/16/01	3/09/01
0.16Q	4/26/01	5/16/01	5/18/01	6/08/01

Indicated div.: $0.64 (Div. Reinv. Plan)

CAPITALIZATION (12/31/00):

	($000)	(%)
Long-Term Debt	20,800	2.2
Minority Interest	5,260	0.5
Common & Surplus	936,066	97.3
Total	962,126	100.0

RECENT DEVELOPMENTS: For the year ended 12/31/00, net income grew 6.3% to $136.9 million from $128.9 million the year before. Results for 1999 included one-time pre-tax realignment charges of $3.3 million. Total net sales climbed 38.5% to $1.74 billion from $1.26 billion a year earlier, due primarily to acquisitions. Product net sales jumped 41.2% to $1.07 billion, while service net sales advanced 34.3% to $674.2 million.

PROSPECTS: Results may be negatively affected by expected weak demand for bank ATMs in the U.S. during the first half of 2001. Going forward, the Company is focusing on maintaining and growing its market share in the U.S. financial industry, as well as expanding its retail operations. Moreover, the Company plans to aggressively grow its market share in Europe and the Asia-Pacific region during 2001.

BUSINESS

DIEBOLD, INC. provides card-based transaction systems, security products, and customer service solutions to the financial, education, and healthcare industries. The Company develops, manufactures, sells and services the following products: automated teller machines, electronic and physical security systems, bank facility equipment, software and integrated systems for global financial and commercial markets. The products segment accounted for 61.3% of revenues, while the services segment accounted for 38.7% for the year ended 12/31/00.

BUSINESS LINE ANALYSIS

(12/31/2000)	REV (%)	INC (%)
North American Sales & Services	55.4	79.7
International Sales & Services	41.8	20.3
Other	2.8	0.0
Total	100.0	100.0

ANNUAL FINANCIAL DATA

	12/31/00	12/31/99	12/31/98	12/31/97	12/31/96	12/31/95	12/31/94
Earnings Per Share	**1.92**	**1 1.85**	**1 1.10**	**1.76**	**1.42**	**1.11**	**0.93**
Cash Flow Per Share	**2.42**	**2.35**	**1.47**	**2.03**	**1.72**	**1.32**	**1.12**
Tang. Book Val. Per Share	**8.94**	**9.63**	**9.87**	**9.69**	**8.36**	**7.37**	**6.70**
Dividends Per Share	**0.62**	**0.60**	**0.56**	**0.50**	**0.45**	**0.43**	**0.39**
Dividend Payout %	**32.3**	**32.4**	**50.9**	**28.4**	**31.9**	**38.3**	**41.9**
INCOME STATEMENT (IN MILLIONS):							
Total Revenues	1,743.6	1,259.2	1,185.7	1,226.9	1,030.2	863.4	760.2
Costs & Expenses	1,478.8	1,038.3	1,053.8	1,024.4	868.8	742.4	656.2
Depreciation & Amort.	35.9	34.7	25.6	18.7	21.0	14.2	13.2
Operating Income	229.0	186.1	106.2	183.9	140.4	106.8	90.8
Net Interest Inc./(Exp.)	d17.7	...	...	...	...	...	...
Income Before Income Taxes	204.4	201.3	119.8	185.7	146.5	113.2	94.0
Income Taxes	67.4	72.5	43.7	63.1	49.1	37.0	30.5
Equity Earnings/Minority Int.	d3.0	d1.2	d1.8	d5.1	d4.4	d0.2	d1.9
Net Income	136.9	1 128.9	1 76.1	122.5	97.4	76.2	63.5
Cash Flow	172.8	163.6	101.8	141.2	118.4	90.4	76.8
Average Shs. Outstg. (000)	71,479	69,562	69,310	69,490	68,796	68,649	68,243
BALANCE SHEET (IN MILLIONS):							
Cash & Cash Equivalents	126.5	84.6	80.0	56.8	65.1	46.7	55.7
Total Current Assets	804.4	647.9	543.5	549.8	479.6	376.2	329.7
Net Property	174.9	160.7	147.1	143.9	95.9	84.1	64.7
Total Assets	1,585.4	1,298.8	1,004.2	991.1	859.1	745.2	666.2
Total Current Liabilities	566.8	382.4	235.5	242.1	228.2	186.0	159.8
Long-Term Obligations	20.8	20.8	20.8	20.8	...	...	...
Net Stockholders' Equity	936.1	844.4	699.1	668.6	575.6	506.2	459.2
Net Working Capital	237.6	265.5	308.0	307.8	251.4	190.2	169.9
Year-end Shs. Outstg. (000)	71,547	71,096	68,881	69,005	68,841	68,712	68,535
STATISTICAL RECORD:							
Operating Profit Margin %	13.1	14.8	9.0	15.0	13.6	12.4	11.9
Net Profit Margin %	7.9	10.2	6.4	10.0	9.5	8.8	8.4
Return on Equity %	14.6	15.3	10.9	18.3	16.9	15.1	13.8
Return on Assets %	8.6	9.9	7.6	12.4	11.3	10.2	9.5
Debt/Total Assets %	1.3	1.6	2.1	2.1	...	...	...
Price Range	34.75-21.50	39.88-19.69	55.31-19.13	50.63-28.00	42.33-22.45	27.61-14.67	20.78-15.07
P/E Ratio	18.1-11.2	21.6-10.6	50.3-17.4	28.8-15.9	29.8-15.8	24.8-13.2	22.3-16.2
Average Yield %	2.2	2.0	1.5	1.3	1.4	2.0	2.2

Statistics are as originally reported. Adj. for 3-for-2 stk. split, 2/97 & 2/96. 1 Incl. one-time pre-tax $1.2 mil chg., 1999; $41.9 mil ($0.60/sh) after-tax chg. for realignment program, 1998.

OFFICERS:
W. W. O'Dell, Chmn., Pres., C.E.O.
G. T. Geswein, Sr. V.P., C.F.O.
R. J. Warren, V.P., Treas.

INVESTOR CONTACT: Sandy K. Upperman, Mgr., Inv. Rel., (800) 766-5859

PRINCIPAL OFFICE: 5995 Mayfair Rd., P.O. Box 3077, North Canton, OH 44720-8077

TELEPHONE NUMBER: (330) 490-4000
FAX: (330) 588-3794
WEB: www.diebold.com

NO. OF EMPLOYEES: 12,544

SHAREHOLDERS: 87,684 (approx.)

ANNUAL MEETING: In Apr.

INCORPORATED: OH, Aug., 1876

INSTITUTIONAL HOLDINGS:
No. of Institutions: 248
Shares Held: 46,449,629
% Held: 64.9

INDUSTRY: Calculating and accounting equipment (SIC: 3578)

TRANSFER AGENT(S): The Bank of New York, New York, NY

NYSE SYMBOL DDS
Rec. Pr. 16.32 (5/31/01)

DILLARD'S, INC.

YIELD 1.0%
P/E RATIO 13.9

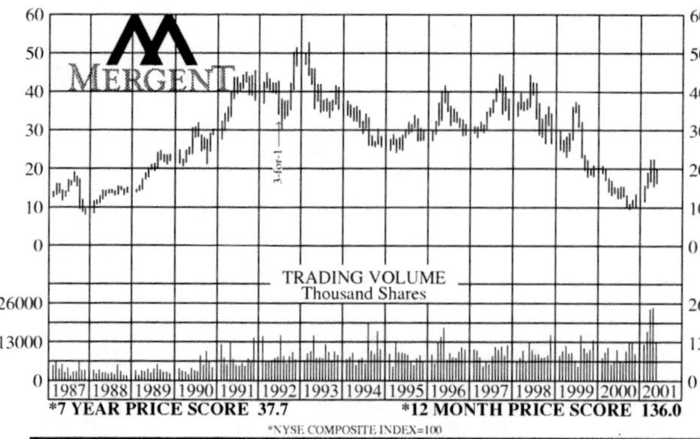

INTERIM EARNINGS (Per Share):

Qtr.	Apr.	July	Oct.	Jan.
1997-98	0.52	0.40	0.40	1.00
1998-99	0.58	0.45	d0.47	0.70
1999-00	0.63	0.34	0.33	0.26
2000-01	0.48	0.10	d0.10	0.69

INTERIM DIVIDENDS (Per Share):

Amt.	Decl.	Ex.	Rec.	Pay.
0.04Q	3/27/00	3/29/00	3/31/00	5/01/00
0.04Q	6/07/00	6/28/00	6/30/00	8/01/00
0.04Q	9/22/00	9/27/00	9/30/00	11/01/00
0.04Q	12/05/00	12/27/00	12/29/00	2/01/01
0.04Q	3/26/01	3/28/01	3/31/01	5/01/01

Indicated div.: $0.16

CAPITALIZATION (2/3/01):

	($000)	(%)
Long-Term Debt	2,374,124	41.9
Capital Lease Obligations	22,453	0.4
Deferred Income Tax	638,648	11.3
Common & Surplus	2,629,820	46.4
Total	5,665,045	100.0

RECENT DEVELOPMENTS: For the 53 weeks ended 2/3/01, DDS reported income of $96.8 million, before a $27.3 million extraordinary credit and a $130.0 million accounting charge, versus net income of $163.7 million in the corresponding 52-week period the year before. Results included pre-tax store-closing charges of $51.4 million and $69.7 million in 2001 and 2000, respectively. Total revenues slid 1.2% to $8.82 billion from $8.92 billion a year earlier. Comparable-store sales fell 3.0% year-over-year.

PROSPECTS: Long-term earnings may benefit from the Company's efforts to increase sales of private-label merchandise, coupled with the continued implementation of initiatives focused on lowering inventory levels, which should result in fewer markdowns going forward. Meanwhile, the Company anticipates capital expenditures of approximately $225.0 million in 2001. DDS plans to open seven new stores and close two under-performing locations during fiscal 2001.

BUSINESS

DILLARD'S, INC. (formerly Dillard Department Stores, Inc.) operates a chain of retail department stores located primarily in the Southwest, Southeast and Midwest. As of 2/3/01, the Company operated 337 stores in 29 states. DDS offers merchandise aimed at middle to upper-middle income consumers, with an emphasis on brand names, fashion-oriented apparel, cosmetics, accessories, and home furnishings. DDS acquired Mercantile Stores Co., Inc. in 1998, the Higbee Company in 1992 and J.B. Ivey & Co. in 1990. The 2000 sales breakdown was: Women's & Juniors' Clothing, 30.6%; Shoes, Accessories & Lingerie, 20.0%; Men's Clothing & Accessories, 19.5%; Cosmetics, 13.3%; Home, 9.2%; Children's Clothing, 6.7%; and Leased & Other, 0.7%.

QUARTERLY DATA

(2/3/01)($000)	Rev	Inc
1st Quarter	2,082,577	(74,570)
2nd Quarter	1,843,363	5,753
3rd Quarter	1,978,664	(3,633)
4th Quarter	2,661,956	66,600

ANNUAL FINANCIAL DATA

	2/3/01	1/29/00	1/30/99	1/31/98	2/1/97	2/3/96	1/28/95
Earnings Per Share	**[3] 1.06**	**[1] 1.55**	**[2] 1.26**	**2.31**	**2.09**	**[1] 1.48**	**2.23**
Cash Flow Per Share	**4.42**	**4.35**	**3.52**	**4.10**	**3.81**	**3.19**	**3.93**
Tang. Book Val. Per Share	**24.05**	**22.50**	**20.41**	**25.70**	**23.91**	**21.91**	**20.55**
Dividends Per Share	**0.16**	**0.16**	**0.16**	**0.16**	**0.13**	**0.12**	**0.09**
Dividend Payout %	**15.1**	**10.3**	**12.7**	**6.9**	**6.2**	**8.1**	**4.0**
INCOME STATEMENT (IN MILLIONS):							
Total Revenues	8,817.8	8,921.2	8,011.7	6,816.9	6,412.1	6,097.1	5,728.6
Costs & Expenses	8,019.1	7,959.9	7,286.1	6,021.5	5,661.7	5,328.7	4,941.4
Depreciation & Amort.	306.1	295.9	241.9	201.4	195.2	193.3	191.9
Operating Income	492.6	665.4	483.7	594.0	555.1	575.1	595.3
Net Interest Inc./(Exp.)	d224.3	d236.6	d196.7	d129.2	d120.6	d120.1	d124.3
Income Before Income Taxes	140.9	283.9	219.1	410.0	378.8	269.7	406.1
Income Taxes	44.0	120.2	83.8	151.7	140.1	102.5	154.3
Net Income	[3] 96.8	[1] 163.7	[2] 135.3	258.3	238.6	[1] 167.2	251.8
Cash Flow	402.9	459.6	377.2	459.7	433.8	360.5	443.6
Average Shs. Outstg. (000)	91,171	105,618	107,182	111,994	113,989	113,144	113,014
BALANCE SHEET (IN MILLIONS):							
Cash & Cash Equivalents	194.0	198.7	72.4	41.8	64.1	58.4	51.1
Total Current Assets	2,842.9	3,423.7	3,437.7	2,998.1	2,760.6	2,658.2	2,524.8
Net Property	3,508.3	3,619.2	3,684.6	2,501.5	2,191.9	2,035.5	1,984.1
Total Assets	7,199.3	7,918.2	8,177.6	5,591.8	5,059.7	4,778.5	4,577.8
Total Current Liabilities	876.7	810.6	1,093.8	1,098.9	894.7	869.7	759.0
Long-Term Obligations	2,396.6	2,919.3	3,029.6	1,377.9	1,186.7	1,178.0	1,200.8
Net Stockholders' Equity	2,629.8	2,832.8	2,841.5	2,807.9	2,717.2	2,478.3	2,323.6
Net Working Capital	1,966.3	2,613.1	2,343.9	1,899.2	1,865.9	1,788.5	1,765.8
Year-end Shs. Outstg. (000)	85,000	98,778	106,924	109,224	113,611	113,088	113,046
STATISTICAL RECORD:							
Operating Profit Margin %	5.6	7.5	6.0	8.7	8.7	9.4	10.4
Net Profit Margin %	1.1	1.8	1.7	3.8	3.7	2.7	4.4
Return on Equity %	3.7	5.8	4.8	9.2	8.8	6.7	10.8
Return on Assets %	1.3	2.1	1.7	4.6	4.7	3.5	5.5
Debt/Total Assets %	33.3	36.9	37.0	24.6	23.5	24.7	26.2
Price Range	20.81-9.44	37.44-17.75	44.50-26.50	44.75-28.00	41.75-27.13	33.88-24.00	37.63-25.50
P/E Ratio	19.6-8.9	24.2-11.5	35.3-21.0	19.4-12.1	20.0-13.0	22.9-16.2	16.9-11.4
Average Yield %	1.1	0.6	0.5	0.4	0.4	0.4	0.3

Statistics are as originally reported. [1] Incl. $55.5 mil ($0.55/sh) after-tax asset impairment chg., 2000; $78.5 mil chg., 1996. [2] Incl. $140.2 mil ($1.30/sh) after-tax chg. rel. to Mercantile Stores purchase. [3] Bef. $27.3 mil extraord. gain. from early debt repayment, $130.0 mil acctg. chg. & incl. $51.4 mil pre-tax asset impairment and store closing chg.

OFFICERS:
W. Dillard, Chmn.
W. Dillard, II, C.E.O.
A. Dillard, Pres.
J. I. Freeman, C.F.O.

INVESTOR CONTACT: Julie J. Bull, Senior Vice President, (501) 376-5965

PRINCIPAL OFFICE: 1600 Cantrell Road, Little Rock, AR 72201

TELEPHONE NUMBER: (501) 376-5200
FAX: (501) 376-5917
WEB: www.dillards.com

NO. OF EMPLOYEES: 58,796

SHAREHOLDERS: 5,127 (class A com.); 8 (class B com.)

ANNUAL MEETING: In May

INCORPORATED: DE, 1964

INSTITUTIONAL HOLDINGS:
No. of Institutions: 183
Shares Held: 65,261,634
% Held: 76.8

INDUSTRY: Department stores (SIC: 5311)

TRANSFER AGENT(S): Mellon Investor Services, Ridgefield Park, NJ

NYSE SYMBOL DME
Rec. Pr. 33.35 (4/30/01)

DIME BANCORP, INC.

YIELD 1.4%
P/E RATIO 14.1

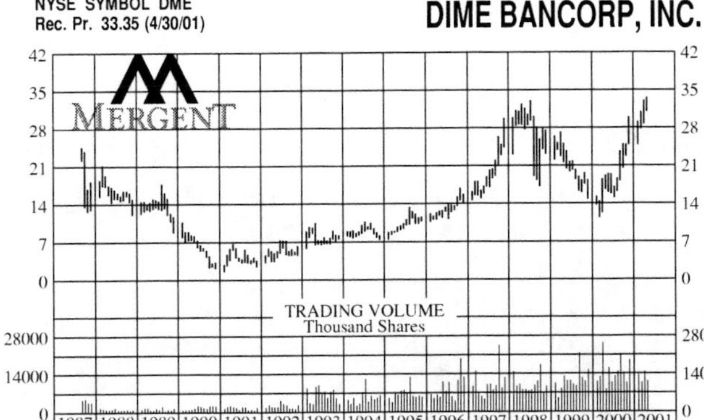

*7 YEAR PRICE SCORE 96.3 *12 MONTH PRICE SCORE 142.4

*NYSE COMPOSITE INDEX=100

INTERIM EARNINGS (Per Share):

Qtr.	Mar.	June	Sept.	Dec.
1998	0.49	0.50	0.56	0.55
1999	0.52	0.54	0.55	0.56
2000	0.59	0.60	0.59	0.59

INTERIM DIVIDENDS (Per Share):

Amt.	Decl.	Ex.	Rec.	Pay.
0.08Q	7/20/00	8/23/00	8/25/00	9/05/00
0.10Q	10/20/00	11/21/00	11/24/00	12/06/00
0.10Q	1/25/01	2/14/01	2/16/01	3/02/01
0.12Q	4/20/01	5/16/01	5/18/01	6/01/01

Indicated div.: $0.48

CAPITALIZATION (12/31/00):

	($000)	(%)
Total Deposits	13,976,941	79.5
Long-Term Debt	1,722,623	9.8
Redeemable Pfd. Stock	152,243	0.9
Common & Surplus	1,724,839	9.8
Total	17,576,646	100.0

RECENT DEVELOPMENTS: For the year ended 12/31/00, DME reported net income of $154.7 million versus income of $243.9 million, before an extraordinary charge, in 1999. Earnings for 2000 and 1999 included pre-tax net gains on sales activities of $147.8 million and $200.4 million, respectively. Earnings for 2000 also included pre-tax restructuring and other special charges of $99.3 million. Net interest income rose 7.8% to $623.3 million.

PROSPECTS: DME expects to achieve an annual earnings growth rate of 11.0% to 14.0% within three years, with earnings per share of $2.72 for 2001 and $3.02 for 2002. Also, DME anticipates return on assets to range from 1.25% to 1.40% and return on common equity to range from 17.0% to 20.0%. The Company's three-year financial performance objectives reflect DME's continuing transition to a more commercial bank-like business model.

BUSINESS

DIME BANCORP, INC., through its subsidiaries, is a unitary savings and loans bank. Its principal subsidiary is The Dime Savings Bank of New York, FSB, a federally chartered savings bank (Dime FSB). The principal subsidiary of Dime FSB is North American Mortgage Company, a mortgage banking company that was acquired in October 1997. The Company operates branches located throughout the greater New York City metropolitan area and conducts its mortgage banking activities nationwide. The Company operates four business segments: retail banking, commercial banking, mortgage banking, and investment portfolio. As of 12/31/00, the Company had assets of $25.69 billion and deposits of $13.98 billion.

LOAN DISTRIBUTION

(12/31/2000)	($000)	(%)
Residential Real Estate	7,916,035	48.6
Commercial Real Estate	4,152,874	25.5
Consumer	3,050,377	18.7
Business	1,167,878	7.2
Total	16,287,164	100.0

ANNUAL FINANCIAL DATA

	12/31/00	12/31/99	12/31/98	12/31/97	12/31/96	[6] 12/31/95	12/31/94
Earnings Per Share	[1][7] 1.35	[1][2] 2.17	[1][2] 2.09	[1][2][3] 1.13	[3][4][5] 0.95	[3][5] 0.57	[3] 1.48
Tang. Book Val. Per Share	1.71	0.03	6.21	8.36	8.78	9.13	9.98
Dividends Per Share	0.32	0.23	0.19	0.12	...	...	...
Dividend Payout %	23.7	10.6	9.1	10.6	...	...	...
INCOME STATEMENT (IN MILLIONS):							
Total Interest Income	1,701.6	1,419.1	1,420.9	1,382.8	1,350.7	1,352.8	614.3
Total Interest Expense	1,078.3	840.6	893.7	899.8	889.4	947.5	375.2
Net Interest Income	623.3	578.5	527.2	483.1	461.3	405.3	239.1
Provision for Loan Losses	28.0	29.5	32.0	49.0	41.0	39.7	41.7
Non-Interest Income	468.1	568.2	525.0	145.3	78.5	70.5	37.4
Non-Interest Expense	826.4	730.8	664.1	376.8	308.2	313.3	207.2
Income Before Taxes	237.0	386.5	354.6	198.2	154.2	109.9	d1.7
Net Income	[1][7] 154.7	[1][2] 243.9	[1][2] 241.1	[1][2][3] 123.2	[3][4][5] 104.3	[3][5] 62.2	[3] 83.8
Average Shs. Outstg. (000)	113,924	112,533	115,153	108,613	109,097	109,742	56,587
BALANCE SHEET (IN MILLIONS):							
Cash & Due from Banks	421.7	414.3	279.5	295.4	158.8	216.5	71.9
Securities Avail. for Sale	2,864.7	3,867.8	3,407.7	5,149.5	2,615.3	4,089.7	347.7
Total Loans & Leases	16,287.2	15,207.1	12,748.1	12,984.5	10,738.1	9,830.3	6,183.0
Allowance for Credit Losses	144.4	140.3	105.1	104.7	106.5	128.3	111.3
Net Loans & Leases	16,142.8	15,066.8	12,643.0	12,879.8	10,631.6	9,702.0	6,071.8
Total Assets	25,687.8	23,921.3	22,320.9	21,848.0	18,870.1	20,326.6	9,996.3
Total Deposits	13,976.9	14,261.4	13,651.5	13,847.3	12,856.7	12,572.2	5,909.2
Long-Term Obligations	1,722.6	1,165.9	4,276.0	2,929.2	1,122.7	4,800.4	3,291.6
Total Liabilities	23,963.0	22,405.2	20,935.2	20,533.1	17,847.8	19,350.1	9,429.2
Net Stockholders' Equity	1,724.8	1,516.1	1,385.7	1,314.9	1,022.3	976.5	567.0
Year-end Shs. Outstg. (000)	116,851	110,895	111,570	116,358	104,744	99,706	56,840
STATISTICAL RECORD:							
Return on Equity %	9.0	16.1	17.4	9.4	10.2	6.4	14.8
Return on Assets %	0.6	1.0	1.1	0.6	0.6	0.3	0.8
Equity/Assets %	6.7	6.3	6.2	6.0	5.4	4.8	5.7
Non-Int. Exp./Tot. Inc. %	75.7	63.7	63.1	60.0	57.1	65.9	74.9
Price Range	30.00-11.31	27.19-14.75	33.06-17.13	29.81-14.50	16.88-10.63	13.38-7.38	10.75-7.38
P/E Ratio	22.2-8.4	12.5-6.8	15.8-8.2	26.4-12.8	17.8-11.2	23.5-12.9	7.3-5.0
Average Yield %	1.5	1.1	0.8	0.5	...	...	...

Statistics are as originally reported. [1] Incl. net gains on sales activities of $147.8 mill., 2000; $200.4 mill., 1999; $244.5 mill., 1998; $12.0 mill., 1997. [2] Bef. extraord. loss of $4.1 mill., 1999; $4.1 mill., 1998; $1.5 mill., 1997. [3] Incl. pre-tax restruct. & merger-rel. exps. of $9.9 mill.,1997; $3.5 mill.,1996; $15.3 mill., 1995; $34.3 mill., 1994. [4] Incl. savings assn. ins. fund recap. assessment of $26.3 mill. [5] Incl. net loss on sales activities of $12.7 mill., 1996 and $12.4 mill., 1995. [6] Reflects the acquisition of Anchor Bancorp, Inc. on 1/13/95. [7] Incl. pre-tax restruct. & oth. special chrgs. of $99.3 mill.

OFFICERS:
T. Terracciano, Chmn.
L. J. Toal, Pres., C.E.O., C.O.O.

INVESTOR CONTACT: William S. Burns, Investor Relations, (212) 326-6170

PRINCIPAL OFFICE: 589 Fifth Ave., New York, NY 10017

TELEPHONE NUMBER: (212) 326-6170
FAX: (212) 326-6169
WEB: www.dime.com

NO. OF EMPLOYEES: 6,476

SHAREHOLDERS: 17,644 (approx.)

ANNUAL MEETING: In May

INCORPORATED: DE, May, 1994

INSTITUTIONAL HOLDINGS:
No. of Institutions: 214
Shares Held: 71,895,865
% Held: 66.3

INDUSTRY: Federal savings institutions (SIC: 6035)

TRANSFER AGENT(S): BankBoston, N.A. c/o EquiServe, Boston, MA

NYSE SYMBOL DMN
Rec. Pr. 11.15 (5/31/01)

DIMON INCORPORATED

YIELD 1.8%
P/E RATIO 18.6

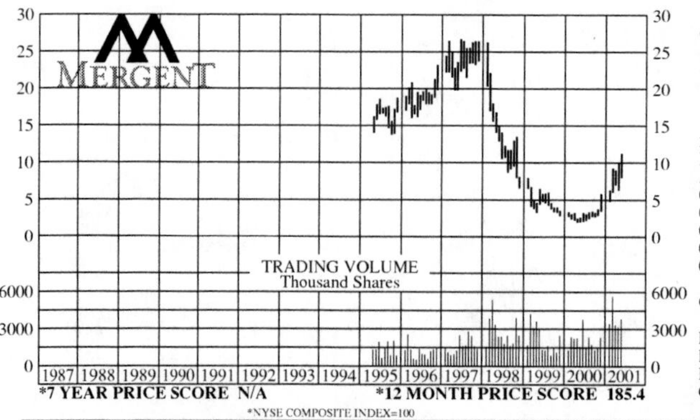

INTERIM EARNINGS (Per Share):

Qtr.	Sept.	Dec.	Mar.	June
1995-96	0.15	0.48	0.16	0.21
1996-97	0.36	0.40	0.44	0.55
1997-98	0.45	0.25	0.24	0.05
1998-99	d0.19	d0.20	d0.52	0.27
1999-00	d0.20	0.15	0.04	0.41
2000-01	d0.05	0.20	...	...

INTERIM DIVIDENDS (Per Share):

Amt.	Decl.	Ex.	Rec.	Pay.
0.05Q	5/26/00	6/01/00	6/05/00	6/15/00
0.05Q	8/29/00	9/05/00	9/07/00	9/18/00
0.05Q	10/31/00	11/29/00	12/01/00	12/13/00
0.05Q	2/20/01	3/01/01	3/05/01	3/15/01
0.05Q	5/25/01	5/31/01	6/04/01	6/15/01

Indicated div.: $0.20 (Div. Reinv. Plan)

CAPITALIZATION (6/30/00):

	($000)	(%)
Long-Term Debt	474,184	53.1
Deferred Income Tax	14,980	1.7
Minority Interest	571	0.1
Common & Surplus	403,504	45.2
Total	893,239	100.0

RECENT DEVELOPMENTS: For the quarter ended 12/31/00, net income jumped 34.4% to $8.7 million compared with $6.5 million a year earlier. Results for 2000 included a restructuring recovery credit of $367,000 and a charge of $737,000 related to derivative financial instruments. Sales and other operating revenues declined 7.2% to $512.2 million from $551.8 million in 1999. The sales decline reflected strong prior-year sales in Africa, including substantial shipments of old crop, uncommitted inventories.

PROSPECTS: Although the overall demand for leaf tobacco remains below historical levels, the Company has indicated that global trading conditions continue to improve. In addition, trading prospects for the current-year South American and African crops are encouraging. However, the Brazilian crop is somewhat later than anticipated due to local weather conditions. Separately, on 12/19/00, DMN announced the acquisition of Greece-based Austro-Hellenique S.A. from Austria Tabak Einkaufs-Und Handelsorganisation GmbH.

BUSINESS

DIMON INCORPORATED is the successor to Dibrell Brothers, Inc. and Monk-Austin Inc., which merged on 4/1/95. DMN is engaged in selecting, purchasing, processing, storing, packing and shipping leaf tobacco. The Company sells its tobacco to manufacturers of cigarettes and other consumer tobacco products located in about 60 countries around the world. DMN also provides argonomy expertise and financing for growing leaf tobacco in certain developing markets. DMN currently owns tobacco processing facilities in Virginia and North Carolina, as well as owns or has interests in processing facilities in Brazil, Malawi, Zimbabwe, Tanzania, Germany, Greece, Italy, Turkey, and Thailand. On 9/30/98, DMN completed the sale of its flower subsidiary, Florimex, to USA Floral Products, Inc.

REVENUES

(06/30/2000)	($000)	(%)
United States	416,290	28.2
Germany	210,018	14.3
Other	847,322	57.5
Total	1,473,630	100.0

ANNUAL FINANCIAL DATA

	6/30/00	6/30/99	6/30/98	6/30/97	6/30/96	6/30/95	6/30/94
Earnings Per Share	**2 0.40**	**1 d0.63**	**0.94**	**1.79**	**1.00**	**d0.79**	**0.14**
Cash Flow Per Share	**1.39**	**0.38**	**1.91**	**2.65**	**1.86**	**0.04**	**0.46**
Tang. Book Val. Per Share	**5.06**	**4.53**	**4.77**	**4.46**	**6.03**	**4.52**	**8.76**
Dividends Per Share	**0.20**	**0.24**	**0.60**	**0.62**	**0.56**	**0.41**	...
Dividend Payout %	**50.0**	...	**63.8**	**34.6**	**55.5**	...	...
INCOME STATEMENT (IN MILLIONS):							
Total Revenues	1,473.6	1,815.2	2,171.8	2,513.2	2,167.5	1,927.7	528.3
Costs & Expenses	1,348.6	1,741.2	1,988.6	2,299.1	2,019.3	1,884.4	507.2
Depreciation & Amort.	44.0	45.1	43.5	37.2	33.8	31.9	5.8
Operating Income	81.1	28.8	139.8	176.9	114.4	11.5	15.2
Net Interest Inc./(Exp.)	d57.7	d66.1	d83.8	d53.0	d46.9	d37.7	d12.4
Income Before Income Taxes	23.4	d37.3	56.0	123.9	67.5	d22.2	7.6
Income Taxes	5.4	cr8.9	14.7	47.1	27.0	6.0	3.3
Equity Earnings/Minority Int.	...	...	0.6	0.4	d0.6	d2.0	d1.7
Net Income	2 18.0	1 d28.4	41.8	77.2	39.9	d30.2	2.6
Cash Flow	62.0	16.8	85.3	114.4	73.7	1.7	8.4
Average Shs. Outstg. (000)	44,525	44,525	44,731	43,176	39,671	38,100	18,114
BALANCE SHEET (IN MILLIONS):							
Cash & Cash Equivalents	27.2	21.5	18.7	107.1	53.8	42.3	6.0
Total Current Assets	753.9	922.5	1,208.9	1,371.5	668.8	731.1	299.5
Net Property	277.2	299.7	318.1	332.8	236.8	223.0	73.0
Total Assets	1,266.7	1,471.3	1,797.5	1,987.6	1,020.0	1,093.6	414.4
Total Current Liabilities	320.1	478.9	502.5	671.5	246.4	453.5	204.2
Long-Term Obligations	474.2	531.5	797.0	826.2	390.9	337.3	39.2
Net Stockholders' Equity	403.5	396.5	421.9	408.3	315.8	238.8	158.7
Net Working Capital	433.7	443.6	706.4	700.0	422.3	277.6	95.2
Year-end Shs. Outstg. (000)	44,525	44,525	44,525	44,312	42,366	38,092	18,114
STATISTICAL RECORD:							
Operating Profit Margin %	5.5	1.6	6.4	7.0	5.3	0.6	2.9
Net Profit Margin %	1.2	...	1.9	3.1	1.8	...	0.5
Return on Equity %	4.5	...	9.9	18.9	12.6	...	1.6
Return on Assets %	1.4	...	2.3	3.9	3.9	...	0.6
Debt/Total Assets %	37.4	36.1	44.3	41.6	38.3	30.8	9.4
Price Range	5.81-1.94	7.94-2.81	26.31-6.56	26.75-19.75	23.25-16.00	18.75-13.75	...
P/E Ratio	14.5-4.8	...	28.0-7.0	14.9-11.0	23.2-16.0	...	...
Average Yield %	5.2	4.5	3.7	2.7	2.8	2.5	...

Statistics are as originally reported. 1 Incls. non-recurr. pre-tax chrg. of $23.1 mill.; bef. gain of $23.8 mill. from disc. ops. 2 Incls. restruct. recov. credit of $605,000 & chrg. of $2.0 mill. rel. to deriv. fin. instruments.

OFFICERS:
J. L. Lanier Jr., Chmn.
B. J. Harker, Pres., C.E.O.
J. A. Cooley, Sr. V.P., C.F.O.

INVESTOR CONTACT: Ritchie L. Bond, Sr. V.P. & Treas., (804) 791-6952

PRINCIPAL OFFICE: 512 Bridge Street, Danville, VA 24541

TELEPHONE NUMBER: (804) 792-7511
FAX: (804) 791-0377
WEB: www.dimon.com

NO. OF EMPLOYEES: 2,900 (approx.)

SHAREHOLDERS: 1,075 (approx. record); 3,825 (approx. beneficial)

ANNUAL MEETING: In Oct.

INCORPORATED: NC, June, 1990

INSTITUTIONAL HOLDINGS:
No. of Institutions: 68
Shares Held: 20,317,549
% Held: 45.6

INDUSTRY: Farm-product raw materials, nec (SIC: 5159)

TRANSFER AGENT(S): First Union National Bank, Charlotte, NC

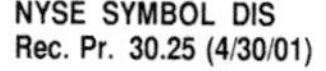

NYSE SYMBOL DIS
Rec. Pr. 30.25 (4/30/01)

DISNEY (WALT) CO. (THE)

YIELD 0.7%
P/E RATIO 54.0

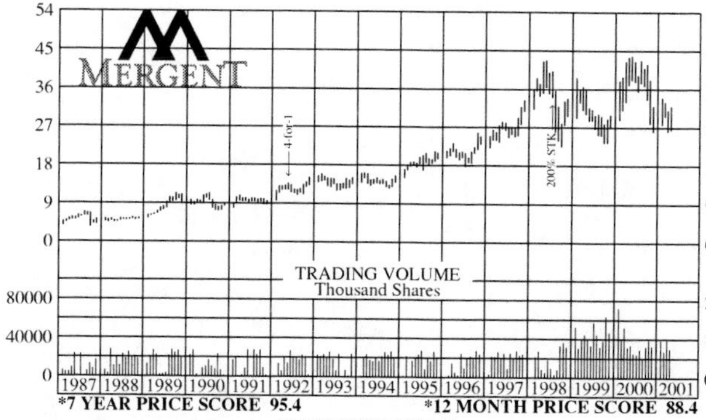

*7 YEAR PRICE SCORE 95.4 *12 MONTH PRICE SCORE 88.4

*NYSE COMPOSITE INDEX=100

INTERIM EARNINGS (Per Share):

Qtr.	Dec.	Mar.	June	Sept.
1997-98	0.37	0.55	0.20	0.14
1998-99	0.30	0.11	0.18	0.03
1999-00	0.25	0.08	0.21	0.11
2000-01	0.16	...	...	...

INTERIM DIVIDENDS (Per Share):

Amt.	Decl.	Ex.	Rec.	Pay.
0.21A	11/04/99	11/12/99	11/16/99	12/17/99
0.21A	11/28/00	12/06/00	12/08/00	12/22/00

Indicated div.: $0.21 (Div. Reinv. Plan)

CAPITALIZATION (9/30/00):

	($000)	(%)
Long-Term Debt	6,959,000	20.3
Deferred Income Tax	2,833,000	8.3
Minority Interest	356,000	1.0
Common & Surplus	24,100,000	70.4
Total	34,248,000	100.0

RECENT DEVELOPMENTS: For the quarter ended 12/31/00, income decreased 23.2% to $242.0 million, before accounting charges. Results included a nonrecurring gain of $22.0 million in 2000 and $243.0 million in 1999. Results for 2000 included nonrecurring losses of $182.0 million. Revenues rose 7.1% to $7.43 billion.

PROSPECTS: Increased guest spending and higher attendance on the Disney Cruise Line should continue to benefit DIS' Parks & Resorts segment. However, the soft advertising marketplace may continue to dampen performance in the Media Networks segment. In addition, declines at the Disney Stores may continue to pressure results in the Consumer Products segment.

BUSINESS

THE WALT DISNEY COMPANY is a diversified international entertainment company with operations in five business segments. Media Networks, which accounted for 38.4% of revenues in 2000, includes Broadcasting and Cable Networks. Parks and Resorts, 27.2%, includes Walt Disney World Resort, Disney Regional Entertainment, and Anaheim Sports, Inc. Studio Entertainment, 23.9%, includes Theatrical Films and Home Video. Consumer Products, 10.5%, includes Character Merchandise and Publications Licensing, The Disney Stores, and Books and Magazines. On 2/29/96, DIS acquired Capital Cities/ABC, Inc. for $18.90 billion.

ANNUAL FINANCIAL DATA

	9/30/00	9/30/99	9/30/98	9/30/97	9/30/96	9/30/95	9/30/94
Earnings Per Share	**[5] 0.57**	**[4] 0.62**	**[3] 0.89**	**[2] 0.95**	**[1] 0.65**	**0.87**	**0.68**
Cash Flow Per Share	**2.60**	**2.44**	**2.70**	**3.36**	**2.78**	**2.03**	**1.66**
Tang. Book Val. Per Share	**3.78**	**2.55**	**1.34**	**0.63**	**...**	**4.23**	**3.50**
Dividends Per Share	**0.21**	**0.21**	**0.20**	**0.17**	**0.14**	**0.12**	**0.10**
Dividend Payout %	**36.8**	**33.9**	**22.7**	**17.7**	**21.4**	**13.3**	**14.1**
INCOME STATEMENT (IN MILLIONS):							
Total Revenues	25,402.0	23,402.0	22,976.0	22,473.0	18,739.0	12,112.1	10,055.1
Costs & Expenses	17,890.0	16,524.0	15,207.0	13,203.0	11,762.0	7,997.0	6,643.3
Depreciation & Amort.	4,664.0	3,779.0	3,754.0	4,958.0	3,944.0	1,853.0	1,608.3
Operating Income	2,848.0	3,099.0	4,015.0	4,312.0	3,033.0	2,262.1	1,803.5
Net Interest Inc./(Exp.)	d558.0	d612.0	d622.0	d693.0	d479.0	d178.3	d119.9
Income Before Income Taxes	2,633.0	2,314.0	3,157.0	3,387.0	2,061.0	2,116.7	1,703.1
Income Taxes	1,606.0	1,014.0	1,307.0	1,421.0	847.0	736.6	592.7
Equity Earnings/Minority Int.	d107.0	...	...	...	...	d35.1	d110.4
Net Income	[5] 920.0	[4] 1,300.0	[3] 1,850.0	[2] 1,966.0	[1] 1,214.0	1,380.1	1,110.4
Cash Flow	5,584.0	5,079.0	5,604.0	6,924.0	5,158.0	3,233.1	2,718.7
Average Shs. Outstg. (000)	2,148,000	2,083,000	2,079,000	2,061,000	1,857,000	1,591,200	1,635,600
BALANCE SHEET (IN MILLIONS):							
Cash & Cash Equivalents	842.0	414.0	127.0	317.0	278.0	1,076.5	186.9
Total Current Assets	10,007.0	10,200.0	9,375.0	8,989.0	8,484.0	5,792.7	4,121.9
Net Property	12,310.0	11,346.0	10,346.0	8,951.0	8,031.0	6,190.3	5,814.5
Total Assets	45,027.0	43,679.0	41,378.0	37,379.0	37,306.0	14,605.8	12,826.3
Total Current Liabilities	8,402.0	7,707.0	7,525.0	12,149.0	13,330.0	5,885.2	5,217.0
Long-Term Obligations	6,959.0	9,278.0	9,562.0	11,068.0	12,342.0	2,984.3	2,936.9
Net Stockholders' Equity	24,100.0	20,975.0	19,388.0	17,285.0	16,086.0	6,650.8	5,508.3
Net Working Capital	1,605.0	2,493.0	1,850.0	d3,160.0	d4,846.0	d92.5	d1,095.1
Year-end Shs. Outstg. (000)	2,114,300	2,071,000	2,690,000	2,025,000	2,022,000	1,573,200	1,572,300
STATISTICAL RECORD:							
Operating Profit Margin %	11.2	13.2	17.5	19.2	16.2	18.7	17.9
Net Profit Margin %	3.6	5.6	8.1	8.7	6.5	11.4	11.0
Return on Equity %	3.8	6.2	9.5	11.4	7.5	20.8	20.2
Return on Assets %	2.0	3.0	4.5	5.3	3.3	9.4	8.7
Debt/Total Assets %	15.5	21.2	23.1	29.6	33.1	20.4	22.9
Price Range	43.88-26.00	38.69-23.38	42.79-22.50	33.42-22.13	25.75-17.75	21.42-15.00	16.21-12.58
P/E Ratio	77.0-45.6	62.4-37.7	48.1-25.3	35.1-23.2	39.4-27.2	24.7-17.3	23.8-18.5
Average Yield %	0.6	0.7	0.6	0.6	0.6	0.6	0.7

Statistics are as originally reported. Adj. for stk. split: 200%, 7/98. Results from 1996 & forward incl. Capital Cities/ABC, Inc., acq. on 2/29/96 for $18.90 bill. [1] Incl. nonrecurring costs of $525 mill. [2] Incl. $135 mill. gain. [3] Incl. $24 mill. gain. Incl. chrg. of $64.0 mill. [4] Incl. restruct. chrg. of $132.0 mill. & gain of $345.0 mill. [5] Incl. non-recurr. net chrg. of $405.0 mill.

OFFICERS:
M. D. Eisner, Chmn., C.E.O.
R. E. Disney, Vice-Chmn.
S. M. Litvak, Vice-Chmn.

INVESTOR CONTACT: Investor Relations, (818) 553-7200

PRINCIPAL OFFICE: 500 South Buena Vista Street, Burbank, CA 91521

TELEPHONE NUMBER: (818) 560-1000
FAX: (818) 560-1930
WEB: www.disney.com

NO. OF EMPLOYEES: 120,000 (avg.)

SHAREHOLDERS: 882,000 (approx. Disney); 1,000 (approx. Internet Group)

ANNUAL MEETING: In March

INCORPORATED: CA, Sept., 1938; reincorp., DE, Feb., 1987

INSTITUTIONAL HOLDINGS:
No. of Institutions: 883
Shares Held: 1,040,440,123
% Held: 49.8

INDUSTRY: Amusement parks (SIC: 7996)

TRANSFER AGENT(S): The Walt Disney Company, Glendale, CA

NYSE SYMBOL DOL
Rec. Pr. 15.48 (5/31/01)

DOLE FOOD COMPANY, INC.

YIELD 2.6%
P/E RATIO 12.8

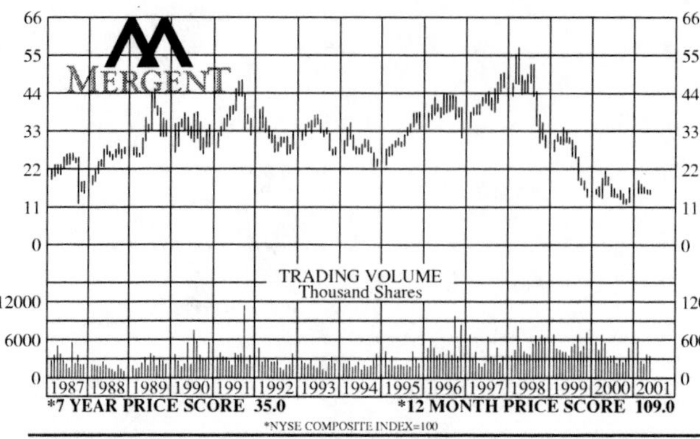

INTERIM EARNINGS (Per Share):

Qtr.	Mar.	June	Sept.	Dec.
1996	0.50	1.05	0.38	d0.46
1997	0.70	1.17	0.40	0.38
1998	0.37	1.35	0.26	d1.82
1999	0.65	0.83	d0.14	d0.51
2000	0.65	0.81	d0.13	d0.12

INTERIM DIVIDENDS (Per Share):

Amt.	Decl.	Ex.	Rec.	Pay.
0.10Q	3/24/00	5/16/00	5/18/00	6/08/00
0.10Q	7/14/00	8/30/00	9/01/00	9/21/00
0.10Q	10/04/00	11/22/00	11/27/00	12/14/00
0.10Q	2/08/01	2/22/01	2/26/01	3/22/01
0.10Q	3/22/01	5/15/01	5/17/01	6/14/01

Indicated div.: $0.40

CAPITALIZATION (12/30/00):

	($000)	(%)
Long-Term Debt	1,135,633	65.4
Minority Interest	45,565	2.6
Common & Surplus	554,788	32.0
Total	1,735,986	100.0

RECENT DEVELOPMENTS: For the year ended 12/30/00, net income was $67.7 million, up 39.4% versus $48.5 million the year before. Results in 2000 included a $42.5 million pre-tax gain from insurance proceeds from Hurricane Mitch, an $8.6 million pre-tax gain from the sale of DOL's citrus assets in California and Arizona, partially offset by a $45.8 million pre-tax downsizing charge. Earnings in 1999 included a pre-tax charge of $48.5 million and insurance proceeds of $27.9 million from Hurricane Mitch. Revenue slid to $4.76 billion from $4.79 billion in 1999.

PROSPECTS: Cost-reduction initiatives in DOL's bananas and fresh-cut flowers segments should help improve the profitability of these businesses going forward. Earnings in the Company's processed foods segment are expected to benefit from volume growth stemming from new product launches in 2000. Meanwhile, profitability growth in DOL's fresh-cut salad business is expected to continue in 2001, while earnings from the fresh vegatables segment may be diminished by a return to more normal commodity prices.

BUSINESS

DOLE FOOD COMPANY, INC. sources, processes, distributes and markets fresh fruits and vegetables, juices, flowers, and packaged foods worldwide. Operations are in North America, Europe, Latin America, and Asia. DOL's principal products are produced both directly on Company-owned or leased land and through associated producer and independent grower arrangements. DOL's products are primarily packaged and processed by Dole and sold to retail and institutional customers and other food product companies. DOL sold its juice and beverage business, excluding the canned pineapple juice business, to The Seagram Co. Ltd. On 12/28/95, DOL completed the distribution of its real estate and resorts business, Castle & Cooke, Inc., to shareholders.

REVENUES

(12/30/00)	($000)	(%)
Fresh fruit	2,764,731	58.0
Fresh vegetables	885,597	18.6
Processed foods	874,995	18.4
Fresh-cut flowers	200,562	4.2
Other	37,243	0.8
Total	4,763,128	100.0

ANNUAL FINANCIAL DATA

	12/30/00	1/1/00	1/2/99	1/3/98	12/28/96	12/31/95	12/31/94
Earnings Per Share	**[4] 1.21**	**[3] 0.85**	**[3] 0.20**	**2.65**	**[2] 1.47**	**[1] 2.00**	**1.14**
Cash Flow Per Share	**3.65**	**3.17**	**2.22**	**4.51**	**3.31**	**3.90**	**3.61**
Tang. Book Val. Per Share	**4.95**	**4.20**	**5.80**	**10.00**	**9.18**	**8.49**	**18.17**
Dividends Per Share	**0.40**	**0.40**	**0.40**	**0.40**	**0.40**	**0.40**	**0.40**
Dividend Payout %	**33.1**	**47.1**	**199.9**	**15.1**	**27.2**	**20.0**	**35.1**
INCOME STATEMENT (IN MILLIONS):							
Total Revenues	4,763.1	5,060.6	4,424.2	4,336.1	3,840.3	3,803.8	3,841.6
Costs & Expenses	4,442.3	4,522.4	4,217.2	3,980.0	3,564.9	3,497.2	3,519.9
Depreciation & Amort.	136.5	131.9	122.1	112.1	111.1	113.3	147.7
Operating Income	184.4	139.8	84.9	244.0	164.3	193.3	173.9
Net Interest Inc./(Exp.)	d82.7	d81.6	d59.6	d56.8	d60.3	d73.7	d77.0
Income Before Income Taxes	99.5	62.2	17.3	195.3	108.5	175.8	88.2
Income Taxes	31.8	13.7	5.2	35.1	19.5	56.0	20.3
Net Income	[4] 67.7	[3] 48.5	[3] 12.1	160.2	[2] 89.0	[1] 119.8	67.9
Cash Flow	204.1	180.5	134.1	272.2	200.1	233.1	215.6
Average Shs. Outstg. (000)	56,000	56,900	60,400	60,400	60,448	59,778	59,700
BALANCE SHEET (IN MILLIONS):							
Cash & Cash Equivalents	28.4	42.4	35.4	31.2	34.3	72.2	46.6
Total Current Assets	1,140.9	1,212.9	1,170.7	1,083.2	1,125.8	1,137.2	1,346.0
Net Property	1,055.2	1,125.4	1,102.3	1,024.2	1,024.1	1,017.0	1,926.5
Total Assets	2,844.7	3,034.5	2,915.1	2,463.9	2,486.8	2,442.2	3,848.7
Total Current Liabilities	785.0	832.2	804.9	676.4	661.9	656.9	705.1
Long-Term Obligations	1,135.6	1,285.7	1,116.4	754.8	903.8	896.0	1,554.5
Net Stockholders' Equity	554.8	531.9	621.8	666.5	549.6	508.4	1,080.6
Net Working Capital	355.9	380.7	365.8	406.7	463.9	480.3	640.9
Year-end Shs. Outstg. (000)	55,845	55,835	59,294	60,064	59,833	59,855	59,478
STATISTICAL RECORD:							
Operating Profit Margin %	3.9	2.8	1.9	5.6	4.3	5.1	4.5
Net Profit Margin %	1.4	1.0	0.3	3.7	2.3	3.2	1.8
Return on Equity %	12.2	9.1	1.9	24.0	16.2	23.6	6.3
Return on Assets %	2.4	1.6	0.4	6.5	3.6	4.9	1.8
Debt/Total Assets %	39.9	42.4	38.3	30.6	36.3	36.7	40.4
Price Range	21.50-11.75	34.13-13.75	57.31-28.06	50.06-33.75	43.75-30.88	38.63-23.00	35.50-22.50
P/E Ratio	17.8-9.7	40.1-16.2	286.4-140.2	18.9-12.7	29.8-21.0	19.3-11.5	31.1-19.7
Average Yield %	2.4	1.7	0.9	1.0	1.1	1.3	1.4

Statistics are as originally reported. [1] Bef. $96.5 mil gain fr discont. opers. & incl. $61.7 mil gain fr sale of bus. [2] Incl. $50 mil pre-tax restr. chg. [3] Incl. $20.6 mil pre-tax, non-recur. chg., 1999; & $120.0 mil chg., 1998. [4] Incl. $42.5 mil net insur. proceeds fr. Hurricane Mitch, $8.6 mil pre-tax gain fr. sale of assets, & $45.8 mil pre-tax business downsizing chg.

OFFICERS:
D. H. Murdock, Chmn., C.E.O.
L. A. Kern, Pres., C.O.O.
K. J. Kay, V.P., C.F.O.

INVESTOR CONTACT: Beth Potillo, Treas., (818) 879-6733

PRINCIPAL OFFICE: One Dole Drive, Westlake Village, CA 91362

TELEPHONE NUMBER: (818) 879-6600
FAX: (818) 879-6618
WEB: www.dole.com

NO. OF EMPLOYEES: 61,000 (approx.)

SHAREHOLDERS: 10,233 (approx.)

ANNUAL MEETING: In June

INCORPORATED: HI, 1894

INSTITUTIONAL HOLDINGS:
No. of Institutions: 126
Shares Held: 29,394,872
% Held: 52.6

INDUSTRY: Citrus fruits (SIC: 0174)

TRANSFER AGENT(S): American Stock Transfer & Trust Co., New York, NY

NYSE SYMBOL DG
Rec. Pr. 18.75 (5/31/01)

DOLLAR GENERAL CORPORATION

YIELD 0.7%
P/E RATIO 30.2

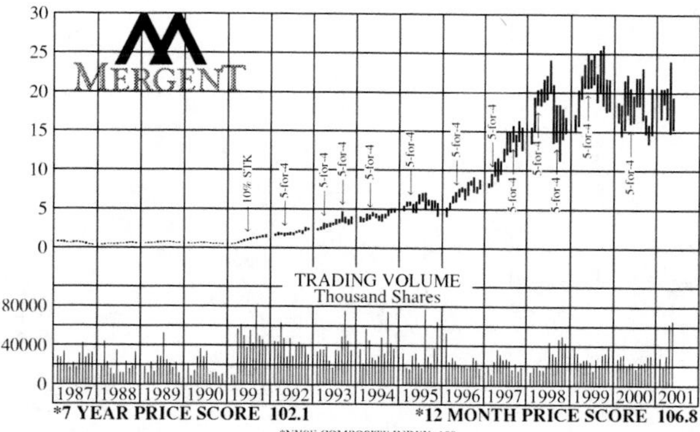

*7 YEAR PRICE SCORE 102.1 *12 MONTH PRICE SCORE 106.8

*NYSE COMPOSITE INDEX=100

INTERIM EARNINGS (Per Share):

Qtr.	Apr.	July	Oct.	Jan.
1997-98	0.06	0.08	0.10	0.19
1998-99	0.09	0.10	0.12	0.23
1999-00	0.11	0.12	0.15	0.27
2000-01	0.14	0.12	0.15	0.21

INTERIM DIVIDENDS (Per Share):

Amt.	Decl.	Ex.	Rec.	Pay.
0.032Q	4/25/00	5/04/00	5/08/00	5/22/00
0.032Q	8/07/00	8/17/00	8/21/00	9/04/00
0.032Q	11/06/00	11/16/00	11/20/00	12/04/00
0.032Q	3/01/01	3/08/01	3/12/01	3/26/01
0.032Q	4/23/01	5/03/01	5/07/01	5/21/01

Indicated div.: $0.13 (Div. Reinv. Plan)

CAPITALIZATION (1/28/00):

	($000)	(%)
Long-Term Debt	1,200	0.1
Deferred Income Tax	51,523	5.3
Common & Surplus	925,921	94.6
Total	978,644	100.0

RECENT DEVELOPMENTS: For the 53 weeks ended 2/2/01, net income slipped 6.1% to $206.0 million from $219.4 million in the corresponding 52-week period the year before. Sales climbed 17.1% to $4.55 billion from $3.89 billion a year earlier. Same-store sales, on a comparable 52-week basis, rose 0.9% year-over-year. The filing of DG's audited financial statements on Form 10-K for fiscal 2000 are being delayed due to certain accounting irregularities.

PROSPECTS: Operating profitability is being diminished by higher shrink expense and lower initial mark-up stemming from increased promotional activity. Meanwhile, the Company plans to continue to aggressively expand its store base. DG anticipates opening between 600 and 700 new stores during fiscal 2001, including 200 to 250 in the first quarter. The Company is targeting sales and earnings growth in the range of 15.0% to 18.0% in fiscal 2001.

BUSINESS

DOLLAR GENERAL CORPORATION sells general merchandise at everyday low prices through a chain of more than 5,000 stores in 27 states as of 6/7/01. The Company also operates distribution centers in Florida, Kentucky, Mississippi, Missouri, Oklahoma and Virginia. The Company offers hard goods, including health and beauty aids, cleaning supplies, housewares, stationery, and seasonal goods. DG also markets soft goods, including apparel for the whole family, shoes, and domestics. In addition to its regular hard good and soft goods inventory, the Company also sells manufacturers' overruns, closeouts, and "irregulars" at a discount from regular prices. DG emphasizes even-dollar pricing of its merchandise, most of which is priced at $1 or in increments of $1.

ANNUAL FINANCIAL DATA

	p2/2/01	1/28/00	1/29/99	1/30/98	1/31/97	1/31/96	1/31/95
Earnings Per Share	**0.62**	**0.65**	**0.54**	**0.43**	**0.34**	**0.26**	**0.22**
Cash Flow Per Share	...	**0.84**	**0.70**	**0.55**	**0.43**	**0.34**	**0.28**
Tang. Book Val. Per Share	...	**2.80**	**2.61**	**1.70**	**1.78**	**1.52**	**0.96**
Dividends Per Share	**0.12**	**0.10**	**0.08**	**0.07**	**0.05**	**0.04**	**0.03**
Dividend Payout %	**19.4**	**15.0**	**15.1**	**16.2**	**14.6**	**15.2**	**14.3**
INCOME STATEMENT (IN MILLIONS):							
Total Revenues	4,551.5	3,888.0	3,221.0	2,627.3	2,134.4	1,764.2	1,448.6
Costs & Expenses	...	3,474.7	2,878.6	2,353.0	1,913.8	1,590.0	1,310.3
Depreciation & Amort.	...	63.9	53.1	38.7	31.0	25.2	17.3
Operating Income	...	349.3	289.3	235.5	189.7	148.9	121.1
Net Interest Inc./(Exp.)	...	d5.2	d8.3	d3.8	d4.7	d7.4	d2.8
Income Before Income Taxes	...	344.1	280.9	231.8	185.0	141.5	118.3
Income Taxes	...	124.7	98.9	87.2	69.9	53.7	44.7
Net Income	206.0	219.4	182.0	144.6	115.1	87.8	73.6
Cash Flow	...	282.2	231.6	180.1	143.7	111.1	90.1
Average Shs. Outstg. (000)	...	336,963	335,499	334,943	337,582	334,888	329,060
BALANCE SHEET (IN MILLIONS):							
Cash & Cash Equivalents	...	58.8	22.3	7.1	6.6	4.3	33.0
Total Current Assets	...	1,095.5	878.9	666.7	504.6	516.2	410.2
Net Property	...	346.5	326.4	241.4	208.5	158.6	125.3
Total Assets	...	1,450.9	1,211.8	914.8	718.1	680.0	540.9
Total Current Liabilities	...	472.3	455.1	307.7	224.5	253.7	209.0
Long-Term Obligations	...	1.2	0.8	1.3	2.6	3.3	4.8
Net Stockholders' Equity	...	925.9	725.8	583.9	485.5	420.0	323.8
Net Working Capital	...	623.2	423.8	359.0	280.1	262.5	201.2
Year-end Shs. Outstg. (000)	...	330,865	277,370	343,926	272,995	275,116	336,590
STATISTICAL RECORD:							
Operating Profit Margin %	...	9.0	9.0	9.0	8.9	8.4	8.4
Net Profit Margin %	...	5.6	5.7	5.5	5.4	5.0	5.1
Return on Equity %	...	23.7	25.1	24.8	23.7	20.9	22.7
Return on Assets %	...	15.1	15.0	15.8	16.0	12.9	13.6
Debt/Total Assets %	...	0.1	0.1	0.1	0.4	0.5	0.9
Price Range	23.19-13.44	26.10-15.08	24.19-11.26	16.38-7.80	9.14-4.04	7.13-4.09	5.12-3.29
P/E Ratio	37.4-21.7	40.3-23.3	44.5-20.7	38.2-18.2	26.8-11.8	27.2-15.6	22.9-14.7
Average Yield %	0.7	0.5	0.5	0.6	0.8	0.7	0.8

Statistics are as originally reported. Adj. for all stk. splits & divs. through 5/00.

OFFICERS:
C. Turner, Jr., Chmn., C.E.O.
D. S. Shaffer, Pres., C.O.O.
J. J. Hagan, Exec. V.P., C.F.O.

INVESTOR CONTACT: Kiley Fleming, Dir., Inv. Rel., (615) 855-5525

PRINCIPAL OFFICE: 100 Mission Ridge, Goodlettsville, TN 37072

TELEPHONE NUMBER: (615) 855-4000
FAX: (615) 855-5527
WEB: www.dollargeneral.com

NO. OF EMPLOYEES: 34,600 (avg.)

SHAREHOLDERS: 10,000 (approx.)

ANNUAL MEETING: In June

INCORPORATED: KY, 1955; reincorp., TN, June, 1998

INSTITUTIONAL HOLDINGS:
No. of Institutions: 285
Shares Held: 183,688,161
% Held: 55.6

INDUSTRY: Variety stores (SIC: 5331)

TRANSFER AGENT(S): Registrar and Transfer Company, Cranford, NJ

NYSE SYMBOL D
Rec. Pr. 68.24 (4/30/01)

DOMINION RESOURCES, INC.

YIELD 3.8%
P/E RATIO 40.4

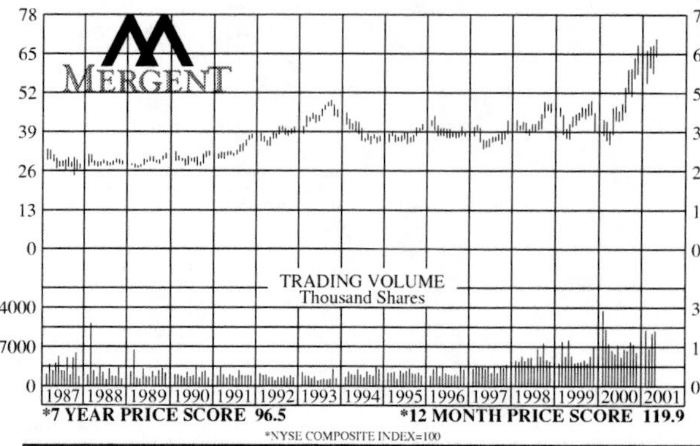

INTERIM EARNINGS (Per Share):

Qtr.	Mar.	June	Sept.	Dec.
1997	0.93	0.43	0.27	0.53
1998	0.72	d0.42	2.17	0.28
1999	d0.60	0.61	1.21	0.33
2000	0.63	d0.45	1.07	0.44

INTERIM DIVIDENDS (Per Share):

Amt.	Decl.	Ex.	Rec.	Pay.
0.645Q	7/07/00	8/23/00	8/25/00	9/20/00
0.645Q	10/20/00	11/21/00	11/24/00	12/20/00
0.645Q	2/16/01	2/28/01	3/02/01	3/20/01
0.645Q	4/27/01	5/30/01	6/01/01	6/20/01

Indicated div.: $2.58

CAPITALIZATION (12/31/00):

	($000)	(%)
Long-Term Debt	10,101,000	49.8
Deferred Income Tax	2,820,000	13.9
Minority Interest	1,000	0.0
Redeemable Pfd. Stock	385,000	1.9
Common & Surplus	6,992,000	34.4
Total	20,299,000	100.0

RECENT DEVELOPMENTS: For the year ended 12/31/00, income was $415.0 million, before an accounting credit of $21.0 million, versus $297.0 million in 1999. Results for 2000 included after-tax items totaling $392.0 million for the write-down of assets, restructuring and an accounting change. Results for 1999 included after-tax charges totaling $280.0 million. Total operating revenues advanced 67.8% to $9.26 billion from $5.52 billion in the prior year.

PROSPECTS: The Connecticut Department of Public Utility Control and the Federal Energy Regulatory Commission approved the sale of Northeast Utilities Company's Millstone Power Station to the Company for $1.28 billion. The acquisition should strengthen D's position in the Northeast region of the U.S. Separately, the Company is targeting a 23.0% increase in operating earnings to $4.10 per share in 2001.

BUSINESS

DOMINION RESOURCES, INC. is a diversified utility holding company active in regulated and unregulated electric power, natural gas and oil development and financial services. D's principal subsidiaries are Virginia Electric and Power Company, a regulated public utility engaged in the generation, transmission, distribution and sale of electric energy in Virginia and northeastern North Carolina, and Consolidated Natural Gas Company (CNG), a producer, transporter, distributor and retail marketer of natural gas serving customers in Pennsylvania, Ohio, Virginia, West Virginia, New York and other cities in the Northeast and Mid-Atlantic regions of the U.S. D's other major subsidiaries are Dominion Energy, Inc., an independent power and natural gas subsidiary, and Dominion Capital, Inc., a diversified financial services company. Dominion also owns and operates a 365-megawatt natural gas fired generating facility in the U.K. On 1/28/00, the Company acquired CNG.

ANNUAL FINANCIAL DATA

	12/31/00	12/31/99	12/31/98	12/31/97	12/31/96	12/31/95	12/31/94
Earnings Per Share	**[6] 1.76**	**[5] 2.81**	**[4] 2.75**	**[3] 2.15**	**[2] 2.65**	**[2] 2.45**	**[1] 2.81**
Cash Flow Per Share	**7.13**	**7.05**	**6.99**	**7.05**	**6.54**	**6.09**	**6.39**
Tang. Book Val. Per Share	**18.73**	**24.80**	**26.56**	**16.55**	**27.17**	**26.88**	**26.60**
Dividends Per Share	**2.58**	**2.58**	**2.58**	**2.58**	**2.58**	**2.58**	**2.55**
Dividend Payout %	**146.6**	**91.8**	**93.8**	**120.0**	**97.4**	**105.3**	**90.7**
INCOME STATEMENT (IN MILLIONS):							
Total Revenues	9,260.0	5,520.0	6,086.2	7,677.6	4,842.3	4,651.7	4,491.1
Costs & Expenses	6,463.0	3,411.0	4,168.8	5,294.9	2,792.6	2,729.7	2,579.0
Depreciation & Amort.	1,268.0	798.0	826.2	905.7	694.4	633.5	610.7
Maintenance Exp.	...	...	...	...	250.9	260.5	263.2
Operating Income	1,529.0	1,311.0	1,091.2	1,477.0	1,104.4	1,028.0	1,038.2
Net Interest Inc./(Exp.)	d958.0	d507.0	d582.7	d627.4	d387.0	d381.7	d360.3
Income Taxes	183.0	259.0	306.0	233.0	212.5	182.1	171.0
Equity Earnings/Minority Int.	d2.0	d18.0	d27.3	d46.6	...	...	...
Net Income	[6] 415.0	[5] 551.0	[4] 535.6	[3] 399.2	[2] 472.1	[2] 425.0	[1] 478.2
Cash Flow	1,683.0	1,349.0	1,361.8	1,304.9	1,166.5	1,058.5	1,088.9
Average Shs. Outstg. (000)	235,900	191,400	194,900	185,200	178,300	173,800	170,300
BALANCE SHEET (IN MILLIONS):							
Gross Property	28,011.0	18,646.0	18,106.0	19,519.2	16,815.8	15,977.4	15,415.4
Accumulated Depreciation	13,162.0	7,882.0	7,469.4	6,986.6	6,306.4	5,655.1	5,170.0
Net Property	14,849.0	10,764.0	10,636.6	12,532.6	10,509.4	10,322.3	10,245.4
Total Assets	29,348.0	17,747.0	17,517.0	20,192.7	14,905.6	13,903.3	13,562.2
Long-Term Obligations	10,101.0	6,936.0	5,070.9	7,196.0	4,727.6	4,611.9	4,710.6
Net Stockholders' Equity	6,992.0	4,752.0	5,315.9	5,040.5	4,924.4	4,742.0	4,586.1
Year-end Shs. Outstg. (000)	186,300	186,300	194,500	187,800	181,221	176,414	172,405
STATISTICAL RECORD:							
Operating Profit Margin %	16.5	23.8	17.9	19.2	22.8	22.1	23.1
Net Profit Margin %	4.5	10.0	8.8	5.2	9.7	9.1	10.6
Net Inc./Net Property %	2.8	5.1	5.0	3.2	4.5	4.1	4.7
Net Inc./Tot. Capital %	2.0	4.0	4.1	2.6	4.0	3.8	4.3
Return on Equity %	5.9	11.6	10.1	7.9	9.6	9.0	10.4
Accum. Depr./Gross Prop. %	47.0	42.3	41.3	35.8	37.5	35.4	33.5
Price Range	67.94-34.81	49.38-36.56	48.94-37.81	42.88-33.25	44.38-36.88	41.63-34.88	45.38-34.88
P/E Ratio	38.6-19.8	17.6-13.0	17.8-13.7	19.9-15.5	16.7-13.9	17.0-14.2	16.1-12.4
Average Yield %	5.0	6.0	5.9	6.8	6.4	6.7	6.4

Statistics are as originally reported. [1] Incl. $42.0 mill. chg. for employee-reduction program. [2] Incl. approx. $92.0 mill. restr. & oth. chgs., 1996; $80.0 mill., 1995. [3] Incl. $157.0 mill. one-time, pre-tax windfall profits tax. [4] Incl. $201.0 mill. after-tax non-recur. chg. & $200.7 mill. after-tax gain. [5] Bef. $255.0 mill. extraord. chg. [6] Incl. $198.0 mill. net restr. chg., $186.0 mill. net chg. for write-down of assets, $13.0 mill. net gain & excl. $21.0 mill. credit fr. acctg. change.

OFFICERS:
T. E. Capps, Chmn., Pres., C.E.O.
G. S. Hetzer, Sr. V.P., Treas.

INVESTOR CONTACT: Thomas P. Wohlfarth, Investor Relations, (804) 819-2150

PRINCIPAL OFFICE: 120 Tredegar Street, Richmond, VA 23219

TELEPHONE NUMBER: (804) 819-2000
FAX: (804) 775-5819
WEB: www.domres.com

NO. OF EMPLOYEES: 15,600 (approx.)

SHAREHOLDERS: 188,737

ANNUAL MEETING: In Apr.

INCORPORATED: VA, Feb., 1983

INSTITUTIONAL HOLDINGS:
No. of Institutions: 430
Shares Held: 115,310,267
% Held: 46.8

INDUSTRY: Electric Services (SIC: 4911)

TRANSFER AGENT(S): The Company

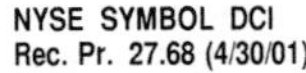

NYSE SYMBOL DCI
Rec. Pr. 27.68 (4/30/01)

DONALDSON COMPANY, INC.

YIELD	1.1%
P/E RATIO	17.9

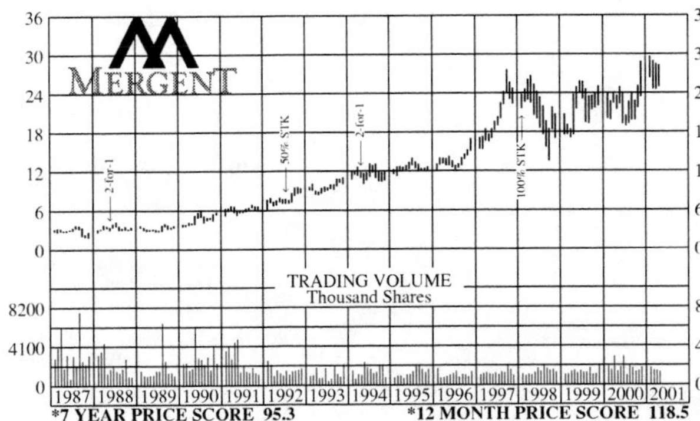

*7 YEAR PRICE SCORE 95.3 *12 MONTH PRICE SCORE 118.5
*NYSE COMPOSITE INDEX=100

INTERIM EARNINGS (Per Share):

Qtr.	Oct.	Jan.	Apr.	July
1996-97	0.23	0.22	0.28	0.27
1997-98	0.28	0.25	0.32	0.30
1998-99	0.28	0.27	0.37	0.39
1999-00	0.36	0.37	0.38	0.40
2000-01	0.37	0.40	...	...

INTERIM DIVIDENDS (Per Share):

Amt.	Decl.	Ex.	Rec.	Pay.
0.07Q	5/19/00	5/25/00	5/30/00	6/13/00
0.07Q	7/28/00	8/22/00	8/24/00	9/12/00
0.075Q	11/17/00	11/28/00	11/30/00	12/12/00
0.075Q	1/19/01	2/21/01	2/23/01	3/13/01
0.075Q	5/18/01	5/22/01	5/24/01	6/13/01

Indicated div.: $0.30 (Div. Reinv. Plan)

CAPITALIZATION (7/31/00):

	($000)	(%)
Long-Term Debt	92,645	24.9
Common & Surplus	280,165	75.1
Total	372,810	100.0

RECENT DEVELOPMENTS: For the quarter ended 1/31/01, net income advanced 4.0% to $18.1 million compared with $17.4 million in the equivalent 2000 quarter. Net sales were $279.6 million, up 7.9% from $259.3 million a year earlier. Engine Products net sales fell 13.5% to $138.6 million, while Industrial Products net sales increased 42.4% to $141.0 million. Gross margin amounted to $86.3 million compared with $79.6 million in the prior year. Operating income advanced 5.0% to $27.5 million.

PROSPECTS: DCI expects continued strength in gas turbine product sales and special application product sales within the Industrial Products segment. Within the Engine Products segment, the Company expects continued weakness in North American transportation products but expects the rate of decrease to begin to level off. DCI also expects the current difficult economic conditions to persist throughout the remainder of fiscal 2001.

BUSINESS

DONALDSON COMPANY, INC. is a worldwide manufacturer of filtration systems and replacement parts. The Company's product mix includes air and liquid filters and exhaust and emission control products for heavy duty mobile equipment; in-plant air cleaning systems; air intake systems and exhaust products for industrial gas turbines; and specialized filters for such diverse applications as computer disk drives, aircraft passenger cabins and semiconductor processing. Products are manufactured at three dozen Donaldson plants around the world and through five joint ventures.

ANNUAL FINANCIAL DATA

	7/31/00	7/31/99	7/31/98	7/31/97	7/31/96	7/31/95	7/31/94
Earnings Per Share	**1.51**	**1.31**	**1.14**	**0.99**	**0.84**	**0.73**	**1 0.59**
Cash Flow Per Share	**2.24**	**1.89**	**1.64**	**1.41**	**1.26**	**1.11**	**0.89**
Tang. Book Val. Per Share	**4.84**	**5.69**	**5.28**	**4.93**	**4.52**	**4.22**	**3.58**
Dividends Per Share	**0.28**	**0.25**	**0.21**	**0.18**	**0.17**	**0.14**	**0.14**
Dividend Payout %	**18.9**	**19.1**	**18.4**	**18.7**	**19.6**	**19.3**	**23.9**
INCOME STATEMENT (IN MILLIONS):							
Total Revenues	1,092.3	944.1	940.4	833.3	758.6	704.0	593.5
Costs & Expenses	952.4	828.1	828.3	729.1	661.3	617.9	525.1
Depreciation & Amort.	34.3	27.7	25.3	21.5	21.7	20.5	16.4
Operating Income	105.6	88.4	86.8	82.7	75.6	65.5	52.1
Net Interest Inc./(Exp.)	d9.9	d7.0	d4.7	d2.4	d2.9	d3.1	d3.4
Income Before Income Taxes	100.3	89.2	86.4	79.1	71.1	63.2	50.2
Income Taxes	30.1	26.8	29.4	28.5	27.7	24.6	18.2
Net Income	70.2	62.4	57.1	50.6	43.4	38.5	1 31.9
Cash Flow	104.6	90.1	82.3	72.1	65.1	59.1	48.3
Average Shs. Outstg. (000)	46,664	47,793	50,229	51,216	51,474	53,334	54,574
BALANCE SHEET (IN MILLIONS):							
Cash & Cash Equivalents	24.1	41.9	16.1	14.3	30.9	28.6	22.9
Total Current Assets	375.5	311.5	287.3	268.8	250.8	247.9	220.3
Net Property	204.5	182.2	178.9	154.6	124.9	110.6	99.6
Total Assets	669.7	528.4	499.3	454.4	402.9	381.0	337.4
Total Current Liabilities	235.7	151.1	167.5	176.3	138.6	123.7	115.8
Long-Term Obligations	92.6	86.7	50.3	4.2	10.0	10.2	16.0
Net Stockholders' Equity	280.2	262.8	255.7	243.9	228.9	221.2	189.7
Net Working Capital	139.8	160.3	119.8	92.5	112.2	124.2	104.6
Year-end Shs. Outstg. (000)	44,658	46,197	48,382	49,452	50,650	52,370	53,020
STATISTICAL RECORD:							
Operating Profit Margin %	9.7	9.4	9.2	9.9	10.0	9.3	8.8
Net Profit Margin %	6.4	6.6	6.1	6.1	5.7	5.5	5.4
Return on Equity %	25.1	23.8	22.3	20.8	19.0	17.4	16.8
Return on Assets %	10.5	11.8	11.4	11.1	10.8	10.1	9.5
Debt/Total Assets %	13.8	16.4	10.1	0.9	2.5	2.7	4.8
Price Range	28.88-18.81	25.94-17.06	26.75-13.50	27.69-15.31	17.00-12.00	14.00-11.25	13.13-10.00
P/E Ratio	19.1-12.5	19.8-13.0	23.5-11.8	28.0-15.5	20.2-14.3	19.3-15.5	22.4-17.1
Average Yield %	1.2	1.2	1.0	0.9	1.1	1.1	1.2

Statistics are as originally reported. Adj. for stk. splits: 2-for-1, 4/94 & 1/98. 1 Bef. a cr. of $2.2 mill. from acctg. changes.

OFFICERS:
W. G. Van Dyke, Chmn., Pres., C.E.O.
T. A. Windfeldt, V.P., Contr., Treas., C.A.O.
N. C. Linnell, V.P., Gen. Couns., Sec.

INVESTOR CONTACT: Investor Relations, (952) 887-3131

PRINCIPAL OFFICE: 1400 West 94th Street, Minneapolis, MN 55431

TELEPHONE NUMBER: (952) 887-3131
FAX: (952) 887-3155
WEB: www.donaldson.com

NO. OF EMPLOYEES: 8,478

SHAREHOLDERS: 1,870 (approx.)

ANNUAL MEETING: In Nov.

INCORPORATED: DE, Dec., 1936

INSTITUTIONAL HOLDINGS:
No. of Institutions: 148
Shares Held: 25,860,409
% Held: 58.4

INDUSTRY: Blowers and fans (SIC: 3564)

TRANSFER AGENT(S): Wells Fargo Bank Minnesota, N.A., South St.Paul, MN

NYSE SYMBOL DNY
Rec. Pr. 27.85 (4/30/01)

DONNELLEY (R.R.) & SONS CO.

YIELD 3.3%
P/E RATIO 12.8

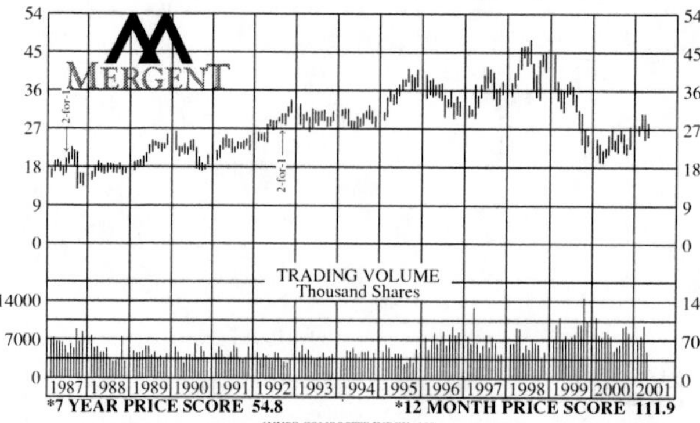

*7 YEAR PRICE SCORE 54.8 *12 MONTH PRICE SCORE 111.9

*NYSE COMPOSITE INDEX=100

INTERIM EARNINGS (Per Share):

Qtr.	Mar.	June	Sept.	Dec.
1997	0.24	0.31	0.56	0.31
1998	0.30	0.61	0.71	0.67
1999	0.33	0.40	0.67	1.01
2000	0.38	0.46	0.75	0.58

INTERIM DIVIDENDS (Per Share):

Amt.	Decl.	Ex.	Rec.	Pay.
0.23Q	7/27/00	8/09/00	8/11/00	9/01/00
0.23Q	9/28/00	11/08/00	11/10/00	12/01/00
0.23Q	1/25/01	2/05/01	2/07/01	3/01/01
0.23Q	3/22/01	5/09/01	5/11/01	6/01/01

Indicated div.: $0.92 (Div. Reinv. Plan)

CAPITALIZATION (12/31/00):

	($000)	(%)
Long-Term Debt	739,190	33.5
Deferred Income Tax	233,505	10.6
Common & Surplus	1,232,548	55.9
Total	2,205,243	100.0

RECENT DEVELOPMENTS: For the year ended 12/31/00, net income fell 14.3% to $266.9 million versus income from continuing operations of $311.5 million in 1999. Results for 2000 included a pre-tax gain of $13.0 million from the sale of shares received in the demutualization of DNY's basic life insurance carrier. Results for 1999 included a gain of $42.8 million from the sale of investments, and excluded a net loss of $3.2 million from discontinued operations. Net sales were up 6.4% to $5.76 billion.

PROSPECTS: Looking ahead, DNY plans to implement actions to improve its underperforming businesses and to better prepare for challenges posed by slowing economic conditions. The Company anticipates earnings per share for 2001 to be between $2.20 and $2.35. This range is consistent with DNY's operating plans for the year and should allow it to achieve strategic goals. Also, the Company's strong cash flow should allow it to redirect capital to existing businesses and develop new capabilities.

BUSINESS

DONNELLEY (R.R.) & SONS CO. is engaged in distributing, managing and reproducing print and digital information for the publishing, retailing, merchandising and information technology markets worldwide. Services provided to customers include presswork and binding, including on-demand customized publications; conventional and digital preproduction operations; software manufacturing, marketing and support services (through Stream International Holdings); design and related creative services (through Coris Inc.); electronic communication networks for simultaneous worldwide product releases; digital services to publishers; and the planning for and fulfillment of truck, rail, mail and air distribution for products of DNY and its customers. Sales for 2000 industry segment data were derived: commercial print, 87.7%; logistics services, 12.0%; and other, 0.3%.

ANNUAL FINANCIAL DATA

	12/31/00	12/31/99	12/31/98	12/31/97	12/31/96	12/31/95	12/31/94
Earnings Per Share	**5 2.17**	**4 2.40**	**3 2.08**	**2 1.40**	**1 d1.04**	**1.95**	**1.75**
Cash Flow Per Share	**5.34**	**5.29**	**4.67**	**3.91**	**1.53**	**4.54**	**3.78**
Tang. Book Val. Per Share	**5.88**	**6.01**	**6.85**	**8.31**	**7.49**	**7.46**	**7.13**
Dividends Per Share	**0.92**	**0.86**	**0.82**	**0.78**	**0.74**	**0.68**	**0.60**
Dividend Payout %	**42.4**	**35.8**	**39.4**	**55.7**	**...**	**34.9**	**34.3**
INCOME STATEMENT (IN MILLIONS):							
Total Revenues	5,764.3	5,183.4	5,018.4	4,850.0	6,599.0	6,511.8	4,888.8
Costs & Expenses	4,872.9	4,278.6	4,242.3	4,110.8	6,345.8	5,554.2	4,115.9
Depreciation & Amort.	390.4	374.4	367.8	370.4	389.1	398.2	313.5
Operating Income	501.0	530.4	408.4	368.8	d136.0	559.4	459.4
Net Interest Inc./(Exp.)	d89.6	d88.2	d78.2	d90.8	d95.5	d109.8	d53.5
Income Before Income Taxes	434.0	506.5	509.3	303.8	d110.5	439.5	395.0
Income Taxes	167.1	195.0	214.7	97.2	47.1	140.7	126.4
Net Income	5 266.9	4 311.5	3 294.6	2 206.5	1 d157.6	298.8	268.6
Cash Flow	657.3	685.9	662.4	577.0	231.5	697.0	582.1
Average Shs. Outstg. (000)	123,093	129,566	141,865	147,508	151,800	153,500	153,900
BALANCE SHEET (IN MILLIONS):							
Cash & Cash Equivalents	60.9	41.9	66.2	47.8	31.1	33.1	20.6
Total Current Assets	1,206.4	1,229.9	1,145.0	1,146.6	1,752.9	1,908.0	1,353.3
Net Property	1,620.6	1,710.7	1,700.9	1,788.1	1,944.7	2,009.0	1,856.8
Total Assets	3,914.2	3,853.5	3,787.8	4,134.2	4,849.0	5,384.8	4,452.1
Total Current Liabilities	1,190.6	1,203.5	898.3	812.6	1,147.5	1,130.4	801.9
Long-Term Obligations	739.2	748.5	999.0	1,153.2	1,430.7	1,561.0	1,212.3
Net Stockholders' Equity	1,232.5	1,138.3	1,300.9	1,591.5	1,631.3	2,173.2	1,978.4
Net Working Capital	15.9	26.4	246.7	333.9	605.3	777.6	551.5
Year-end Shs. Outstg. (000)	121,055	123,237	134,322	145,118	145,554	153,953	153,085
STATISTICAL RECORD:							
Operating Profit Margin %	8.7	10.2	8.1	7.6	...	8.6	9.4
Net Profit Margin %	4.6	6.0	5.9	4.3	...	4.6	5.5
Return on Equity %	21.7	27.4	22.6	13.0	...	13.7	13.6
Return on Assets %	6.8	8.1	7.8	5.0	...	5.5	6.0
Debt/Total Assets %	18.9	19.4	26.4	27.9	29.5	29.0	27.2
Price Range	27.50-19.00	44.75-21.50	48.00-33.75	41.75-29.50	39.88-29.38	41.25-28.88	32.50-26.88
P/E Ratio	12.7-8.8	18.6-9.0	23.1-16.2	29.8-21.1	...	21.2-14.8	18.6-15.4
Average Yield %	4.0	2.6	2.0	2.2	2.1	1.9	2.0

Statistics are as originally reported. 1 Incl. $560.6 mill. p-tax restr. chg. & $80.0 mill. gains from IPO's. 2 Bef. loss fr. disc. ops. of $76.9 mill. & incl. $70.7 mill. p-tax restr. chg. 3 Incl. $168.9 mill. gain fr. sale of subs. & $80.1 mill. loss fr. businesses held for sale. 4 Incl. $42.8 mill. gain fr. sale of bus. & excl. $3.2 mill. loss fr. disc. ops. 5 Excl. $13.0 mill. p-tax gain fr. sale of shares.

OFFICERS:
W. L. Davis, Chmn., Pres., C.E.O.
J. R. Donnelley, Vice-Chmn.

INVESTOR CONTACT: Sara Gopal, Director, Investor Relations, (312) 326-7754

PRINCIPAL OFFICE: 77 West Wacker Drive, Chicago, IL 60601

TELEPHONE NUMBER: (312) 326-8000
FAX: (312) 326-8543
WEB: www.rrdonnelley.com

NO. OF EMPLOYEES: 34,000 (approx.)

SHAREHOLDERS: 9,458 (record)

ANNUAL MEETING: In Mar.

INCORPORATED: DE, May, 1956

INSTITUTIONAL HOLDINGS:
No. of Institutions: 276
Shares Held: 92,801,597
% Held: 76.0

INDUSTRY: Commercial printing, lithographic (SIC: 2752)

TRANSFER AGENT(S): First Chicago Trust Company of New York, Jersey City, NJ

NYSE SYMBOL DOV
Rec. Pr. 39.07 (4/30/01)

DOVER CORPORATION

YIELD 1.3%
P/E RATIO 15.0

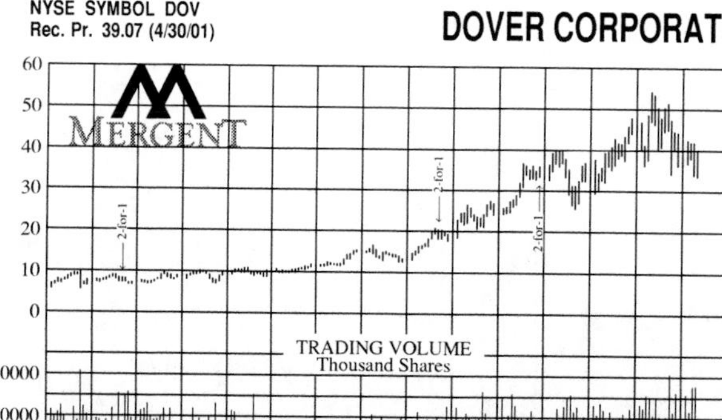

*7 YEAR PRICE SCORE 103.7 *12 MONTH PRICE SCORE 92.8

*NYSE COMPOSITE INDEX=100

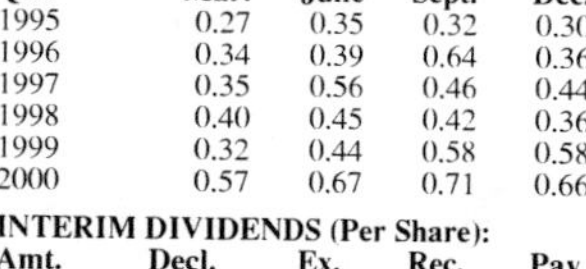

INTERIM EARNINGS (Per Share):

Qtr.	Mar.	June	Sept.	Dec.
1995	0.27	0.35	0.32	0.30
1996	0.34	0.39	0.64	0.36
1997	0.35	0.56	0.46	0.44
1998	0.40	0.45	0.42	0.36
1999	0.32	0.44	0.58	0.58
2000	0.57	0.67	0.71	0.66

INTERIM DIVIDENDS (Per Share):

Amt.	Decl.	Ex.	Rec.	Pay.
0.115Q	5/04/00	5/24/00	5/29/00	6/15/00
0.125Q	8/03/00	8/29/00	8/31/00	9/15/00
0.125Q	11/02/00	11/28/00	11/30/00	12/15/00
0.125Q	2/08/01	2/26/01	2/28/01	3/15/01
0.125Q	5/03/01	5/29/01	5/31/01	6/15/01

Indicated div.: $0.50

CAPITALIZATION (12/31/00):

	($000)	(%)
Long-Term Debt	631,846	20.1
Deferred Income Tax	67,381	2.1
Common & Surplus	2,441,575	77.7
Total	3,140,802	100.0

RECENT DEVELOPMENTS: For the year ended 12/31/00, net earnings from continuing operations totaled $533.2 million versus net earnings from continuing operations of $405.1 million a year earlier. Results for 2000 and 1999 included gains on disposition and sale of equity investments of $10.5 million and $10.3 million, respectively. Results excluded a loss of $13.6 million and a gain of $523.9 million for 2000 and 1999, respectively, on the sale of discontinued operations. Net sales rose 21.5% to $5.40 billion.

PROSPECTS: Near term earnings in Dover Technologies' Circuit Board Assembly and Test (CBAT) business are expected to continue to decline due to weak market conditions. However, CBAT expects its market conditions to improve as 2001 progresses. In the meantime, appropriate right-sizing cost reductions are underway. On a positive note, Dover Resources' Petroleum Equipment Group should continue to benefit from a strong upstream oil and gas sector.

BUSINESS

DOVER CORPORATION is a diversified industrial manufacturing corporation encompassing over 50 operating companies. DOV's businesses are divided into the following four segments: Dover Diversified (21.8% of 2000 revenues), builds packaging and printing machinery, heat transfer equipment, food refrigeration and display cases, specialized bearings and compressors, construction and agricultural cabs, as well as products for use in the defense, aerospace and automotive industries. Dover Industries (23.1%) makes products for use in the waste handling, bulk transport, automotive service, commercial food service and packaging, welding, cash dispenser and construction industries. Dover Resources Inc. (16.4%), manufactures products primarily for the automotive, fluid handling, petroleum, winch and chemical equipment industries. Dover Technologies (38.9%) builds automated assembly and testing equipment for the electronics industry, industrial printers for coding and marking, and specialized electronic components. On 1/5/99, the Company sold Dover Elevator for $1.16 billion.

ANNUAL FINANCIAL DATA

	12/31/00	12/31/99	12/31/98	12/31/97	12/31/96	12/31/95	12/31/94
Earnings Per Share	**[4] 2.61**	**[3] 1.92**	**[1] 1.45**	**[2] 1.79**	**[2] 1.73**	**[2] 1.23**	**0.89**
Cash Flow Per Share	**3.60**	**2.79**	**2.20**	**2.54**	**2.27**	**1.70**	**1.30**
Tang. Book Val. Per Share	**1.79**	**1.07**	**2.11**	**2.66**	**2.29**	**1.79**	**1.86**
Dividends Per Share	**0.48**	**0.44**	**0.40**	**0.36**	**0.32**	**0.28**	**0.24**
Dividend Payout %	**18.4**	**22.9**	**27.6**	**20.1**	**18.5**	**22.9**	**27.7**
INCOME STATEMENT (IN MILLIONS):							
Total Revenues	5,400.7	4,446.4	3,977.7	4,547.7	4,076.3	3,745.9	3,085.3
Costs & Expenses	4,354.1	3,627.8	3,278.0	3,764.3	3,412.5	3,199.6	2,664.1
Depreciation & Amort.	203.4	183.2	167.7	170.7	125.1	107.8	95.8
Operating Income	843.2	635.4	532.0	[2] 612.7	[2] 538.7	[2] 438.4	325.4
Net Interest Inc./(Exp.)	d88.5	d34.9	d46.4	d37.0	d23.5	d20.1	d17.8
Income Before Income Taxes	772.3	615.0	488.6	616.8	588.7	417.1	306.9
Income Taxes	239.1	210.0	162.2	211.4	198.5	138.8	104.5
Net Income	[4] 533.2	[3] 405.1	[1] 326.4	[2] 405.4	[2] 390.2	[2] 278.3	202.4
Cash Flow	736.6	588.3	494.1	576.1	515.3	386.1	298.2
Average Shs. Outstg. (000)	204,677	210,679	224,386	226,815	226,524	226,906	228,740
BALANCE SHEET (IN MILLIONS):							
Cash & Cash Equivalents	186.7	138.0	96.8	146.7	217.8	148.8	144.9
Total Current Assets	1,974.8	1,611.6	1,304.5	1,591.3	1,489.8	1,384.4	1,133.1
Net Property	755.5	646.5	572.0	570.6	494.9	423.9	342.7
Total Assets	4,892.1	4,131.9	3,627.3	3,277.5	2,993.4	2,666.7	2,070.6
Total Current Liabilities	1,604.6	1,334.9	989.7	1,196.6	1,139.1	1,081.0	772.2
Long-Term Obligations	631.8	608.0	610.1	262.6	253.0	255.6	253.6
Net Stockholders' Equity	2,441.6	2,038.8	1,910.9	1,703.6	1,489.7	1,227.7	995.9
Net Working Capital	370.2	276.7	314.8	394.8	350.7	303.3	360.9
Year-end Shs. Outstg. (000)	203,184	204,629	220,407	234,507	225,060	227,340	226,920
STATISTICAL RECORD:							
Operating Profit Margin %	15.6	14.3	13.4	13.5	13.2	11.7	10.5
Net Profit Margin %	9.9	9.1	8.2	8.9	9.6	7.4	6.6
Return on Equity %	21.8	19.9	17.1	23.8	26.2	22.7	20.3
Return on Assets %	10.9	9.8	9.0	12.4	13.0	10.4	9.8
Debt/Total Assets %	12.9	14.7	16.8	8.0	8.5	9.6	12.2
Price Range	54.38-34.13	47.94-29.31	39.94-25.50	36.69-24.13	27.56-18.31	20.84-12.91	16.72-12.44
P/E Ratio	20.8-13.1	25.0-15.3	27.5-17.6	20.5-13.5	16.0-10.6	17.0-10.5	18.9-14.1
Average Yield %	1.1	1.1	1.2	1.2	1.4	1.7	1.7

Statistics are as originally reported. Adj. for stk. splits: 2-for-1, 12/97; 100%, 9/95. [1] Bef. income fr. disc. ops. of $52.4 mill. [2] Incls. pre-tax credit 12/31/97: $32.2 mill.; credit 12/31/96: $75.1 mill.; chrg. 12/31/95: $31.9 mill. [3] Incls. non-recurr. gain of $10.3 mill.; bef. gain fr. disc. ops. of $523.9 mill. [4] Incls. non-recurr. gain of $10.5 mill.; bef. loss fr. disc. ops. of $13.6 mill. ($0.07/sh.)

OFFICERS:
T. L. Reece, Chmn., Pres., C.E.O.
D. S. Smith, V.P., C.F.O.
R. G. Kuhbach, V.P., Sec., Gen. Couns.

INVESTOR CONTACT: D. S. Smith, V.P., C.F.O., (212) 922-1640

PRINCIPAL OFFICE: 280 Park Avenue, New York, NY 10017-1292

TELEPHONE NUMBER: (212) 922-1640
FAX: (212) 922-1656
WEB: www.dovercorporation.com

NO. OF EMPLOYEES: 29,500 (approx.)

SHAREHOLDERS: 15,138 (approx.)

ANNUAL MEETING: In Apr.

INCORPORATED: DE, 1947

INSTITUTIONAL HOLDINGS:
No. of Institutions: 430
Shares Held: 144,090,068
% Held: 70.9

INDUSTRY: Construction machinery (SIC: 3531)

TRANSFER AGENT(S): Mellon Investor Services, Ridgefield Park, NJ

NYSE SYMBOL DOW
Rec. Pr. 34.28 (4/30/01)

DOW CHEMICAL COMPANY

YIELD 4.0%
P/E RATIO 15.4

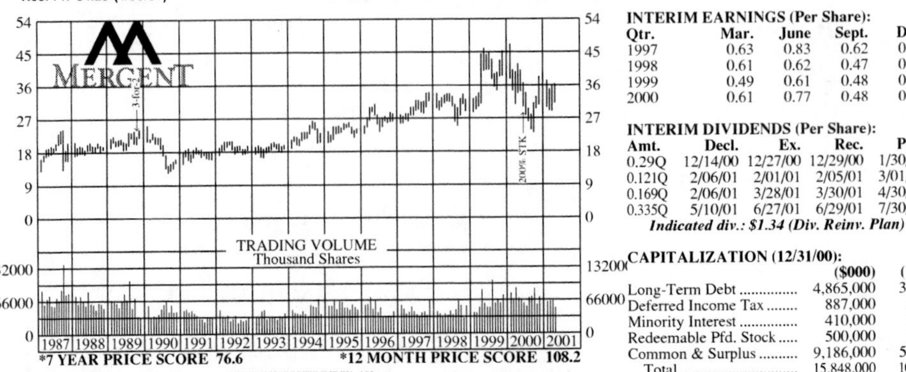

*7 YEAR PRICE SCORE 76.6 *12 MONTH PRICE SCORE 108.2

*NYSE COMPOSITE INDEX=100

INTERIM EARNINGS (Per Share):

Qtr.	Mar.	June	Sept.	Dec.
1997	0.63	0.83	0.62	0.52
1998	0.61	0.62	0.47	0.22
1999	0.49	0.61	0.48	0.40
2000	0.61	0.77	0.48	0.36

INTERIM DIVIDENDS (Per Share):

Amt.	Decl.	Ex.	Rec.	Pay.
0.29Q	12/14/00	12/27/00	12/29/00	1/30/01
0.121Q	2/06/01	2/01/01	2/05/01	3/01/01
0.169Q	2/06/01	3/28/01	3/30/01	4/30/01
0.335Q	5/10/01	6/27/01	6/29/01	7/30/01

Indicated div.: $1.34 (Div. Reinv. Plan)

CAPITALIZATION (12/31/00):

	($000)	(%)
Long-Term Debt	4,865,000	30.7
Deferred Income Tax	887,000	5.6
Minority Interest	410,000	2.6
Redeemable Pfd. Stock	500,000	3.2
Common & Surplus	9,186,000	58.0
Total	15,848,000	100.0

RECENT DEVELOPMENTS: For the year ended 12/31/00, net income rose 14.1% to $1.51 billion versus $1.33 billion in 1999. Results for 2000 and 1999 included purchased in-process research and development charges of $6.0 million. Results for 1999 also included a pre-tax special charge of $94.0 million from severance and other restructuring costs. Net sales rose 15.1% to $23.01 billion.

PROSPECTS: On 2/6/01, the Company completed its acquisition of Union Carbide Corporation. As a result, DOW improved its position in the global polyethylene business, as well as gained strength and resources to compete in the global marketplace. Separately, during the first half of 2001, DOW expects to continue to face challenging economic conditions due to volatile oil and energy prices.

BUSINESS

DOW CHEMICAL COMPANY is a diversified, worldwide manufacturer and supplier of more than 3,500 product families, which are grouped into the following industry segments: chemicals, 12.1% of 2000 net sales; performance chemicals, 13.7%; plastics, 24.9%; performance plastics, 26.6%; hydrocarbons and energy, 11.0%; agricultural products, 10.4%; and unallocated and other businesses, 1.3%. DOW supplies chemicals in 162 countries and employs about 41,000 worldwide. Geographic sales in 2000 were derived: U.S., 39%; Europe, 34%; and other countries, 27%. On 2/6/01, the Company acquired Union Carbide Corporation.

ANNUAL FINANCIAL DATA

	12/31/00	12/31/99	12/31/98	12/31/97	12/31/96	12/31/95	12/31/94
Earnings Per Share	**[7] 2.22**	**[6] 1.98**	**[5] 1.92**	**[4] 2.57**	**[1] 2.57**	**[2][3] 2.34**	**1.12**
Cash Flow Per Share	**4.14**	**3.90**	**3.83**	**4.39**	**4.33**	**4.13**	**2.50**
Tang. Book Val. Per Share	**10.77**	**9.69**	**9.80**	**9.94**	**10.76**	**9.45**	**5.42**
Dividends Per Share	**1.16**	**1.16**	**1.16**	**1.08**	**1.00**	**0.93**	**0.87**
Dividend Payout %	**52.2**	**58.6**	**60.4**	**42.1**	**38.9**	**39.8**	**77.7**
INCOME STATEMENT (IN MILLIONS):							
Total Revenues	23,008.0	19,989.0	18,441.0	20,018.0	20,053.0	20,200.0	20,015.0
Costs & Expenses	19,484.0	16,461.0	15,292.0	16,005.0	15,668.0	14,867.0	13,620.0
Depreciation & Amort.	1,315.0	1,301.0	1,305.0	1,287.0	1,298.0	1,442.0	1,302.0
Operating Income	2,209.0	2,227.0	1,386.0	2,726.0	3,087.0	3,891.0	1,820.0
Net Interest Inc./(Exp.)	d388.0	d310.0	d354.0	d277.0	d208.0	d145.0	d264.0
Income Before Income Taxes	2,401.0	2,166.0	2,012.0	2,948.0	3,288.0	3,529.0	1,626.0
Income Taxes	823.0	766.0	685.0	1,041.0	1,187.0	1,442.0	654.0
Equity Earnings/Minority Int.	206.0	13.0	47.0	d24.0	d128.0	d126.0	d171.0
Net Income	[7] 1,513.0	[6] 1,326.0	[5] 1,304.0	[4] 1,802.0	[1] 1,900.0	[2][3] 1,884.0	938.0
Cash Flow	2,828.0	2,627.0	2,603.0	3,083.0	3,191.0	3,319.0	2,060.0
Average Shs. Outstg. (000)	683,000	673,300	681,900	704,400	738,900	804,600	828,000
BALANCE SHEET (IN MILLIONS):							
Cash & Cash Equivalents	304.0	1,212.0	390.0	537.0	2,302.0	3,450.0	1,134.0
Total Current Assets	9,260.0	8,847.0	8,040.0	8,640.0	9,830.0	10,554.0	8,693.0
Net Property	9,190.0	8,490.0	8,447.0	8,052.0	8,484.0	8,113.0	8,726.0
Total Assets	27,645.0	25,499.0	23,830.0	24,040.0	24,673.0	23,582.0	26,490.0
Total Current Liabilities	7,873.0	6,295.0	6,842.0	7,011.0	6,004.0	5,601.0	6,618.0
Long-Term Obligations	4,865.0	5,022.0	4,051.0	4,196.0	4,196.0	4,705.0	5,303.0
Net Stockholders' Equity	9,186.0	8,323.0	8,123.0	8,484.0	8,680.0	8,059.0	8,872.0
Net Working Capital	1,387.0	2,552.0	1,198.0	1,629.0	3,826.0	4,953.0	2,075.0
Year-end Shs. Outstg. (000)	677,503	669,845	661,131	676,404	723,000	783,000	831,000
STATISTICAL RECORD:							
Operating Profit Margin %	9.6	11.8	7.5	13.6	15.4	19.3	9.1
Net Profit Margin %	6.6	7.0	7.1	9.0	9.5	9.3	4.6
Return on Equity %	16.5	15.9	17.6	23.6	23.9	25.6	11.4
Return on Assets %	5.5	5.2	5.5	7.5	7.7	8.0	3.5
Debt/Total Assets %	17.6	19.7	17.0	17.5	17.0	20.0	20.0
Price Range	47.16-23.00	45.00-28.50	33.81-24.89	34.00-25.46	30.83-22.75	26.00-20.46	26.41-18.83
P/E Ratio	21.2-10.4	23.2-14.4	17.6-13.0	13.2-9.9	12.0-8.9	11.1-8.7	28.6-20.4
Average Yield %	3.3	3.1	3.9	3.6	3.7	4.0	3.8

Statistics are as originally reported. Adj. for 200% stk. div., 6/00. [1] Incl. $120.0 mill. gain on sale of int. in Oasis Pipeline. [2] Bef. $187.0 mill. aft-tax gain on inc. & sale of pharm. unit. [3] Incl. $330.0 mill. chg. rel. to invest. [4] Incl. $186.0 mill. gain on sale of bus. [5] Incl. $1.00 bill. gains fr. sale of bus., $338.0 mill. chg. fr. purch. in-process R&D, cr$1.0 mill., $458.0 mill. chg. for write-dwns. [6] Incl. $6.0 mill. purch. in-process R&D chgs. & $94.0 mill. fr. sever. exps. [7] Incl. $98.0 mill. pre-tax gain fr. sale of asset & $6.0 mill. purch. in-process R&D chgs.

OFFICERS:
W. S. Stavropoulos, Chmn.
M. D. Parker, Pres., C.E.O.

INVESTOR CONTACT: Teri S. LeBea, Coporate Director, Inv. Rel., (517) 636-8193

PRINCIPAL OFFICE: 2030 Dow Center, Midland, MI 48674

TELEPHONE NUMBER: (517) 636-1000
FAX: (517) 636-3518
WEB: www.dow.com
NO. OF EMPLOYEES: 41,943 (avg.)
SHAREHOLDERS: 125,865 ; 128,000 (shareholder held in nominee names)
ANNUAL MEETING: In May
INCORPORATED: DE, June, 1947

INSTITUTIONAL HOLDINGS:
No. of Institutions: 610
Shares Held: 499,503,805
% Held: 55.6

INDUSTRY: Plastics materials and resins (SIC: 2821)

TRANSFER AGENT(S): EquiServe, L.P., Boston, MA

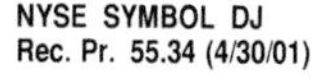
NYSE SYMBOL DJ
Rec. Pr. 55.34 (4/30/01)

DOW JONES & COMPANY, INC.

YIELD 1.8%
P/E RATIO 36.9

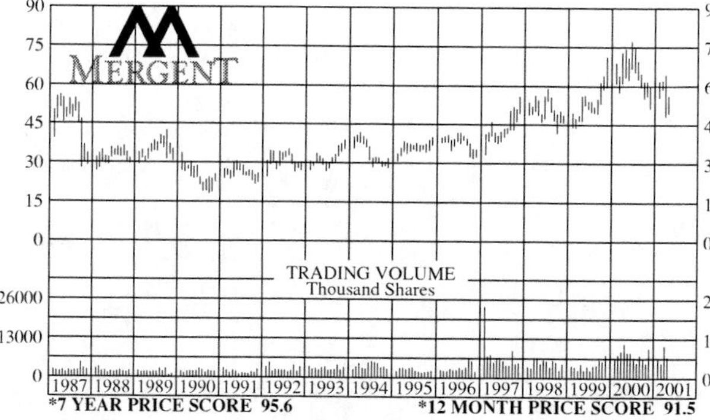

*7 YEAR PRICE SCORE 95.6 *12 MONTH PRICE SCORE 91.5
*NYSE COMPOSITE INDEX=100

INTERIM EARNINGS (Per Share):

Qtr.	Mar.	June	Sept.	Dec.
1997	0.27	0.36	0.28	d9.22
1998	0.35	d0.54	0.27	0.26
1999	0.56	0.62	1.13	0.67
2000	0.98	1.13	d0.39	d0.22

INTERIM DIVIDENDS (Per Share):

Amt.	Decl.	Ex.	Rec.	Pay.
0.25Q	6/21/00	7/28/00	8/01/00	9/01/00
0.25Q	10/18/00	10/30/00	11/01/00	12/01/00
0.25Q	1/30/01	1/30/01	2/01/01	3/01/01
0.25Q	4/12/01	4/27/01	5/01/01	6/01/01

Indicated div.: $1.00 (Div. Reinv. Plan)

CAPITALIZATION (12/31/00):

	($000)	(%)
Long-Term Debt	150,865	47.4
Minority Interest	8,593	2.7
Common & Surplus	158,768	49.9
Total	318,226	100.0

RECENT DEVELOPMENTS: For the year ended 12/31/00, the Company reported a net loss of $119.0 million. Results for 2000 included a gain of $24.1 million from the disposition of businesses and a non-cash charge of $178.5 million from the write-down of investments. Results for 1999 included a gain of $51.9 million from the disposition of businesses and a restructuring charge of $2.8 million. Total revenues rose 10.0% to $2.20 billion.

PROSPECTS: Dow Jones Newswires introduced a weekly newsletter, Dow Jones Bandwidth Intelligence Alert, which will report on issues and trading activity within the broadband market. The newsletter will cover companies and trends, and provide traders, consultants, advisors and investors with information on pending developments and deals. Going forward, the Company expects its businesses are well positioned to benefit from significant growth in 2001.

BUSINESS

DOW JONES & COMPANY, INC. is a global provider of business news and information. The print publishing segment (69.0% of 2000 revenues and 74.8% of operating income) contains the operations of DJ's print publications, which include THE WALL STREET JOURNAL, as well as its international editions in Europe and Asia; BARRONS; SMART MONEY magazines; Dow Jones interactive publishing; and DJ's television operations. The electronic publishing segment (14.8%, 7.5%) holds the operations of Dow Jones Markets and DJ's financial newswires. Community newspapers (16.2%, 17.7%) published by Ottaway Newspapers, Inc., a wholly-owned subsidiary, include 19 general interest dailies. As of 12/31/00, DJ owns a 50% interest in AmericaEconomia, a business magazine in Latin America. DJ is co-owner with Reuters Group of Factiva, and with NBC of the CNBC television operations in Asia and Europe.

ANNUAL FINANCIAL DATA

	12/31/00	12/31/99	12/31/98	12/31/97	12/31/96	12/31/95	12/31/94
Earnings Per Share	**6 d1.35**	**5 2.99**	**4 0.09**	**3 d8.36**	**1 1.96**	**1 1.96**	**2 1.82**
Cash Flow Per Share	**d0.13**	**4.13**	**1.57**	**d5.74**	**4.22**	**4.08**	**3.90**
Tang. Book Val. Per Share	**0.98**	**5.24**	**4.60**	**4.07**	**3.64**	**3.01**	**1.83**
Dividends Per Share	**1.00**	**0.96**	**0.96**	**0.96**	**0.96**	**0.92**	**0.84**
Dividend Payout %	**...**	**32.1**	**N.M.**	**...**	**49.0**	**46.9**	**46.2**
INCOME STATEMENT (IN MILLIONS):							
Total Revenues	2,202.6	2,001.8	2,158.1	2,572.5	2,481.6	2,283.8	2,091.0
Costs & Expenses	1,596.5	1,508.6	1,797.1	3,063.8	1,926.9	1,773.7	1,527.4
Depreciation & Amort.	107.9	103.7	142.4	250.7	217.8	206.1	205.3
Operating Income	498.2	389.5	218.6	d742.0	337.0	304.0	358.3
Net Interest Inc./(Exp.)	d2.0	d5.3	d7.2	d19.4	d18.8	d18.3	d16.9
Income Before Income Taxes	76.4	418.0	71.7	763.9	331.3	322.9	338.0
Income Taxes	197.0	145.5	63.1	37.8	147.7	139.9	157.6
Equity Earnings/Minority Int.	d15.6	d28.0	d22.5	d49.8	1.0	20.7	d4.6
Net Income	6 d119.0	5 272.4	4 8.8	3 d802.1	1 190.0	1 189.6	2 181.2
Cash Flow	d11.1	376.1	150.8	d551.4	407.7	395.6	386.5
Average Shs. Outstg. (000)	87,854	91,151	96,404	95,993	96,703	96,907	99,002
BALANCE SHEET (IN MILLIONS):							
Cash & Cash Equivalents	49.3	86.4	142.9	23.8	6.8	13.7	10.9
Total Current Assets	368.2	456.0	435.0	506.6	403.7	371.3	310.1
Net Property	760.9	676.4	602.1	784.0	739.4	690.0	642.1
Total Assets	1,362.1	1,530.6	1,491.3	1,919.7	2,759.6	2,598.7	2,445.8
Total Current Liabilities	587.2	578.5	592.5	672.4	601.2	581.5	531.3
Long-Term Obligations	150.9	149.9	149.9	228.8	332.3	253.9	295.6
Net Stockholders' Equity	158.8	553.5	509.3	780.8	1,644.0	1,601.8	1,481.6
Net Working Capital	d219.0	d122.5	d157.5	d165.8	d197.5	d210.3	d221.2
Year-end Shs. Outstg. (000)	86,829	89,821	91,969	96,670	102,181	97,249	96,624
STATISTICAL RECORD:							
Operating Profit Margin %	22.6	19.5	10.1	...	13.6	13.3	17.1
Net Profit Margin %	...	13.6	0.4	...	7.7	8.3	8.7
Return on Equity %	...	49.2	1.7	...	11.6	11.8	12.2
Return on Assets %	...	17.8	0.6	...	6.9	7.3	7.4
Debt/Total Assets %	11.1	9.8	10.1	11.9	12.0	9.8	12.1
Price Range	77.31-51.38	71.38-43.63	59.00-41.56	55.88-33.38	41.88-31.88	40.13-30.63	41.88-28.13
P/E Ratio	...	23.9-14.6	173.5-122.2	...	21.4-16.3	20.5-15.6	23.0-15.5
Average Yield %	1.6	1.7	1.9	2.2	2.6	2.6	2.4

Statistics are as originally reported. 1 Incl. $8.8 mill. net gain, 1996; $5.3 mill., 1995. 2 Bef. $3.0 mill. acct. adj. chg. 3 Incl. $1.0 bill. pre-tax restr. chg. & $52.6 mill. pre-tax gain on disp. of bus. 4 Incl. $24.2 mill. gain on disp. of bus. & $76.1 mill. restr. chgs. 5 Incl. $67.9 mill. after-tax gain fr. sale of interest in bus. & $1.6 mill. net restr. chg. 6 Incl. $24.1 mill. gain fr. dispost. of bus. & $178.5 mill. chg. fr. write-down of invest.

OFFICERS:
P. R. Kann, Chmn., C.E.O.
R. F. Zannino, Exec. V.P., C.F.O.

INVESTOR CONTACT: Valerie L. Gerard, Director-Investor Relations, (212) 416-2687

PRINCIPAL OFFICE: 200 Liberty Street, New York, NY 10281

TELEPHONE NUMBER: (212) 416-2000
FAX: (212) 416-2829
WEB: www.dowjones.com
NO. OF EMPLOYEES: 8,574
SHAREHOLDERS: 10,992 (approx. record); 4,053 (approx. record class B common)
ANNUAL MEETING: In Apr.
INCORPORATED: DE, Nov., 1949

INSTITUTIONAL HOLDINGS:
No. of Institutions: 264
Shares Held: 50,783,794
% Held: 58.5

INDUSTRY: Newspapers (SIC: 2711)

TRANSFER AGENT(S): Mellon Investor Services, South Hackensack, NJ

NYSE SYMBOL DPL
Rec. Pr. 28.80 (5/31/01)

DPL INC.

YIELD 3.3%
P/E RATIO 23.8

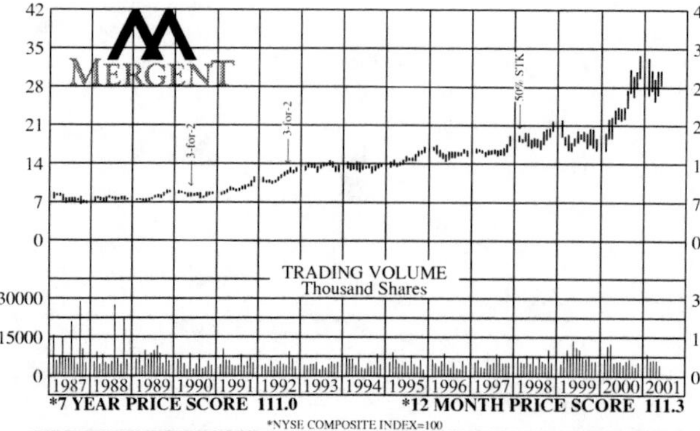

*7 YEAR PRICE SCORE 111.0 *12 MONTH PRICE SCORE 111.3
*NYSE COMPOSITE INDEX=100

INTERIM EARNINGS (Per Share):

Qtr.	Mar.	June	Sept.	Dec.
1997	0.44	0.23	0.29	0.15
1998	0.46	0.23	0.31	0.24
1999	0.47	0.25	0.36	0.27
2000	0.34	0.12	0.41	0.34

INTERIM DIVIDENDS (Per Share):

Amt.	Decl.	Ex.	Rec.	Pay.
0.235Q	4/11/00	5/11/00	5/15/00	6/01/00
0.235Q	6/20/00	8/14/00	8/16/00	9/01/00
0.235Q	9/26/00	11/15/00	11/17/00	12/01/00
0.235Q	1/30/01	2/12/01	2/14/01	3/01/01
0.235Q	4/11/01	5/11/01	5/15/01	6/01/01

Indicated div.: $0.94 (Div. Reinv. Plan)

CAPITALIZATION (12/31/00):

	($000)	(%)
Long-Term Debt	1,758,500	56.9
Deferred Income Tax	414,800	13.4
Redeemable Pfd. Stock	100	0.0
Preferred Stock	22,900	0.7
Common & Surplus	892,400	28.9
Total	3,088,700	100.0

RECENT DEVELOPMENTS: For the year ended 12/31/00, income before an extraordinary charge totaled $285.0 million, jumped 39.5% versus income of $204.2 million in 1999. Results for 2000 excluded an extraordinary charge, net of taxes of $41.4 million. Total operating revenues climbed 7.3% to $1.44 billion from $1.34 billion the year before. Utility service revenues remained flat at $1.27 billion, while other revenues more than doubled to $163.4 million. Operating income improved 9.8% to $444.7 million.

PROSPECTS: DPL continued to pursue its growth strategy based on its merchant generation expansion plan. The Company believes it is in position to profit from market needs, through its coal fired base-load units and peaking generation expansion. Meanwhile, DPL announced phase five of its regional merchant generation expansion program consisting of four Pratt & Whitney combustion turbine units. The five phases expand DPL's generation capacity by more than 1,000 megawatts and represent an investment of $350.0 million.

BUSINESS

DPL INC. is a holding company for Dayton Power and Light Company (DP&L). DP&L sells electricity and natural gas to residential, commercial and governmental customers in a 6,000 square-mile area of West Central Ohio. Electricity is generated at eight power plants in 24 counties and distributed to 500,000 retail customers. Natural gas is provided to 308,000 customers in 16 counties. Principal industries served by the Company include electrical machinery, automotive and other transportation equipment, non-electrical machinery, agriculture, paper and rubber and plastic products.

REVENUES

(12/31/00)	($000)	(%)
Electric	1,090	75.8
Gas	184	12.8
Other revenues	163	11.4
Total	1,437	100.0

ANNUAL FINANCIAL DATA

	12/31/00	12/31/99	12/31/98	12/31/97	12/31/96	12/31/95	12/31/94
Earnings Per Share	[1] **2.14**	**1.35**	**1.24**	**1.20**	**1.15**	**1.09**	**1.03**
Cash Flow Per Share	**2.14**	**2.42**	**2.29**	**2.15**	**2.08**	**1.97**	**1.86**
Tang. Book Val. Per Share	**6.98**	**9.20**	**8.58**	**8.03**	**7.55**	**7.28**	**7.03**
Dividends Per Share	**0.94**	**0.94**	**0.94**	**0.91**	**0.87**	**0.83**	**0.79**
Dividend Payout %	**43.9**	**69.6**	**75.8**	**75.5**	**75.6**	**76.0**	**76.6**
INCOME STATEMENT (IN MILLIONS):							
Total Revenues	1,436.9	1,338.9	1,379.6	1,355.8	1,282.1	1,284.8	1,218.0
Costs & Expenses	992.2	773.7	816.2	837.3	775.1	788.2	738.4
Depreciation & Amort.	...	162.3	160.1	144.4	140.7	134.3	125.6
Operating Income	444.7	402.9	403.3	374.1	366.3	362.3	354.0
Net Interest Inc./(Exp.)	d140.3	d109.5	d93.8	d87.3	d89.0	d94.3	d93.2
Income Taxes	156.6	127.9	120.4	105.4	103.5	102.4	101.2
Net Income	[1] 284.9	204.2	189.1	181.4	172.9	164.7	154.9
Cash Flow	284.9	366.5	349.2	325.8	313.6	299.0	280.5
Average Shs. Outstg. (000)	132,900	151,400	152,800	151,400	150,900	151,650	150,600
BALANCE SHEET (IN MILLIONS):							
Gross Property	3,853.4	3,900.3	3,743.3	3,642.8	3,548.7	3,394.2	3,322.7
Accumulated Depreciation	1,586.4	1,633.5	1,504.6	1,386.6	1,279.8	1,167.8	1,072.8
Net Property	2,267.0	2,266.8	2,238.7	2,256.2	2,268.9	2,281.8	2,312.2
Total Assets	4,436.0	4,340.4	3,855.9	3,585.2	3,418.7	3,322.8	3,232.7
Long-Term Obligations	1,758.5	1,336.6	1,065.9	971.0	1,014.3	1,081.5	1,093.7
Net Stockholders' Equity	915.3	1,474.5	1,406.6	1,308.9	1,223.4	1,187.7	1,151.2
Year-end Shs. Outstg. (000)	127,774	157,801	161,265	160,203	159,015	160,046	160,428
STATISTICAL RECORD:							
Operating Profit Margin %	30.9	30.1	29.2	27.6	28.6	28.2	29.1
Net Profit Margin %	19.8	15.3	13.7	13.4	13.5	12.8	12.7
Net Inc./Net Property %	12.6	9.0	8.4	8.0	7.6	7.2	6.7
Net Inc./Tot. Capital %	9.2	6.2	6.4	6.6	6.3	5.9	5.6
Return on Equity %	31.1	13.8	13.4	13.9	14.1	13.9	13.5
Accum. Depr./Gross Prop. %	41.2	41.9	40.2	38.1	36.1	34.4	32.3
Price Range	33.81-16.38	22.00-16.31	21.75-16.63	19.13-15.25	17.42-14.42	17.08-13.33	14.42-12.25
P/E Ratio	15.8-7.7	16.3-12.1	17.5-13.4	15.9-12.7	15.2-12.6	15.7-12.3	14.0-11.9
Average Yield %	3.7	4.9	4.9	5.3	5.4	5.4	5.9

Statistics are as originally reported. Adj. for stk. splits: stk. div. 50% 1/98 [1] Bef. an extraord. chrg. of $41.4 mill.

OFFICERS:
P. H. Forster, Chmn.
A. M. Hill, Pres., C.E.O.
E. McCarthy, V.P., C.F.O.

INVESTOR CONTACT: Investor Relations Dept., (800) 322-9244

PRINCIPAL OFFICE: Courthouse Plaza Southwest, Dayton, OH 45402

TELEPHONE NUMBER: (937) 224-6000
FAX: (937) 224-6500
WEB: www.waytogo.com
NO. OF EMPLOYEES: 1,778 full-time; 324 part-time
SHAREHOLDERS: 35,903
ANNUAL MEETING: In Apr.
INCORPORATED: OH, 1985

INSTITUTIONAL HOLDINGS:
No. of Institutions: 215
Shares Held: 42,323,251
% Held: 33.0

INDUSTRY: Electric and other services combined (SIC: 4931)

TRANSFER AGENT(S): EquiServe, Boston, MA

NYSE SYMBOL DQE
Rec. Pr. 23.89 (5/31/01)

DQE, INC.

YIELD 7.0%
P/E RATIO 10.3

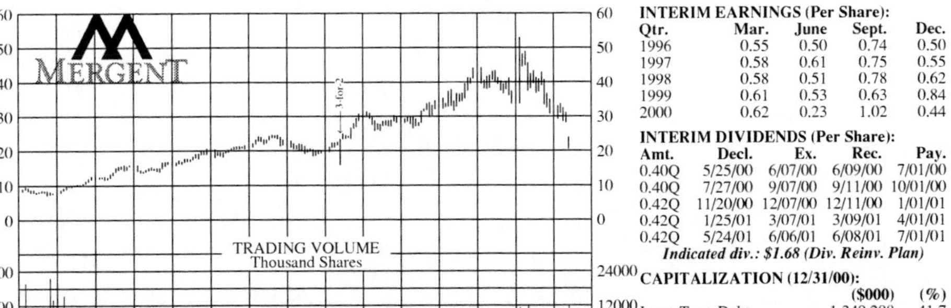

INTERIM EARNINGS (Per Share):

Qtr.	Mar.	June	Sept.	Dec.
1996	0.55	0.50	0.74	0.50
1997	0.58	0.61	0.75	0.55
1998	0.58	0.51	0.78	0.62
1999	0.61	0.53	0.63	0.84
2000	0.62	0.23	1.02	0.44

INTERIM DIVIDENDS (Per Share):

Amt.	Decl.	Ex.	Rec.	Pay.
0.40Q	5/25/00	6/07/00	6/09/00	7/01/00
0.40Q	7/27/00	9/07/00	9/11/00	10/01/00
0.42Q	11/20/00	12/07/00	12/11/00	1/01/01
0.42Q	1/25/01	3/07/01	3/09/01	4/01/01
0.42Q	5/24/01	6/06/01	6/08/01	7/01/01

Indicated div.: $1.68 (Div. Reinv. Plan)

CAPITALIZATION (12/31/00):

	($000)	(%)
Long-Term Debt	1,349,298	41.7
Deferred Income Tax	852,695	26.4
Preferred Stock	247,997	7.7
Common & Surplus	783,745	24.2
Total	3,233,735	100.0

RECENT DEVELOPMENTS: For the year ended 12/31/00, income, before an accounting change, totaled $138.1 million compared with net income of $201.4 million in the prior year. The decline in earnings was due to an increase in fuel and purchased power operating expenses. Total revenue slipped 1.8% to $1.33 billion. Electricity sales fell 5.9% to $1.03 billion, while water sales inched up 0.4% to $102.0 million.

PROSPECTS: DQE commenced a comprehensive, market-based strategic and financial review of the entire company and its component businesses, which could result in the divesture of some or all of the Company. Looking ahead, DQE expects continued earnings growth through earnings from its delivery businesses, streamlined administrative infrastructure, increased market valuations of its investments and selective asset sales.

BUSINESS

DQE, INC. is a multi-utility delivery and services company. The Company's utility services operations include an electric utility engaged in the generation, transmission, distribution, and sale of electric energy and a water resource management company that acquires, develops and manages water and wastewater utilities. DQE's expanded business lines offer a range of energy-related technologies, industrial and commercial energy services, telecommunications and other complementary services. DQE's subsidiaries are Duquesne Light Company, AquaSource, Inc., DQE Capital Corp., DQE Energy Services, Inc., DQE Energy Partners, Inc, Duquesne Enterprises, Inc., and Montauk, Inc.

REVENUES

(12/31/00)	($000)	(%)
Electricity Delivery	316,100	23.6
Electricity Supply	425,400	31.7
CTC	334,400	24.9
Water Distribution	112,200	8.4
Other Revenues	152,500	11.4
Total	1,340,600	100.0

ANNUAL FINANCIAL DATA

	12/31/00	12/31/99	12/31/98	12/31/97	12/31/96	12/31/95	12/31/94
Earnings Per Share	**2 2.39**	**2.62**	**1 2.48**	**2.54**	**2.32**	**2.20**	**1.98**
Cash Flow Per Share	**7.42**	**5.10**	**5.32**	**5.70**	**5.20**	**4.80**	**4.08**
Tang. Book Val. Per Share	**14.02**	**18.78**	**19.18**	**19.30**	**18.01**	**17.13**	**16.27**
Dividends Per Share	**1.60**	**1.52**	**1.44**	**1.36**	**1.28**	**1.19**	**1.12**
Dividend Payout %	**66.9**	**58.0**	**58.1**	**53.5**	**55.2**	**53.9**	**56.6**
INCOME STATEMENT (IN MILLIONS):							
Total Revenues	1,327.6	1,341.2	1,269.6	1,230.2	1,225.2	1,220.2	1,223.9
Costs & Expenses	829.5	750.6	705.7	623.7	621.9	613.6	661.6
Depreciation & Amort.	343.2	196.3	217.2	242.8	222.9	202.6	165.9
Maintenance Exp.	50.6	75.4	74.9	82.9	78.4	81.5	79.5
Operating Income	104.3	318.8	271.9	280.7	302.0	322.5	316.9
Net Interest Inc./(Exp.)	d123.6	d158.7	d110.2	d115.6	d110.3	d107.6	d110.0
Income Taxes	70.4	110.7	101.0	95.8	87.4	96.7	93.0
Net Income	2 138.1	201.4	1 196.7	199.1	179.1	170.6	156.8
Cash Flow	482.1	396.2	413.0	441.9	402.1	373.1	322.7
Average Shs. Outstg. (000)	65,002	77,676	77,683	77,492	77,349	77,674	79,046
BALANCE SHEET (IN MILLIONS):							
Gross Property	2,411.3	4,369.3	4,884.1	4,625.1	4,787.5	4,746.1	4,709.5
Accumulated Depreciation	704.2	2,541.2	3,167.3	1,962.8	1,969.9	1,685.9	1,570.0
Net Property	1,707.1	1,828.1	1,716.8	2,662.3	2,817.5	3,060.2	3,139.5
Total Assets	3,866.0	5,609.0	5,247.6	4,694.4	4,639.0	4,458.8	4,427.0
Long-Term Obligations	1,349.3	1,649.9	1,401.5	1,413.7	1,468.2	1,435.5	1,418.7
Net Stockholders' Equity	1,031.7	1,630.9	1,761.8	1,743.6	1,634.5	1,422.0	1,396.9
Year-end Shs. Outstg. (000)	55,886	71,766	77,373	77,680	77,273	77,556	78,459
STATISTICAL RECORD:							
Operating Profit Margin %	7.9	23.8	21.4	22.8	24.6	26.4	25.9
Net Profit Margin %	10.4	15.0	15.5	16.2	14.6	14.0	12.8
Net Inc./Net Property %	8.1	11.0	11.5	7.5	6.4	5.6	5.0
Net Inc./Tot. Capital %	4.3	4.7	5.0	5.2	4.6	4.7	4.1
Return on Equity %	13.4	12.3	11.2	11.4	11.0	12.0	11.2
Accum. Depr./Gross Prop. %	29.2	58.2	64.8	42.4	41.1	35.5	33.3
Price Range	53.00-30.75	44.25-33.63	44.13-31.56	34.63-26.50	31.50-25.75	30.75-15.83	23.00-18.42
P/E Ratio	22.2-12.9	16.9-12.8	17.8-12.7	13.6-10.4	13.6-11.1	14.0-7.2	11.6-9.3
Average Yield %	3.8	3.9	3.8	4.4	4.5	5.1	5.4

Statistics are as originally reported. Adj. for stk. splits: 3-for-2, 5/95 1 Bef. extraordinary item of $82.5 mill. 2 Excl. acct. chng. credit of $15.9 mill.

OFFICERS:
D. D. Marshall, Chmn., Pres., C.E.O.
M. K. O'Brien, C.O.O.
V. A. Roque, Exec. V.P., Sec., Gen. Couns.

INVESTOR CONTACT: Thomas E. Ross, Investor Relations, (412) 393-1238

PRINCIPAL OFFICE: Cherrington Corporate Center, Suite 100, 500 Cherrington Parkway, Coraopolis, PA 15108-3184

TELEPHONE NUMBER: (412) 393-6000
FAX: (412) 393-6065
WEB: www.dqe.com

NO. OF EMPLOYEES: 2,834

SHAREHOLDERS: 57,000 (approx.)

ANNUAL MEETING: In May

INCORPORATED: PA, 1989

INSTITUTIONAL HOLDINGS:
No. of Institutions: 172
Shares Held: 16,683,049
% Held: 29.9

INDUSTRY: Electric services (SIC: 4911)

TRANSFER AGENT(S): BankBoston, N.A., Boston, MA

NYSE SYMBOL DST
Rec. Pr. 49.12 (4/30/01)

DST SYSTEMS, INC.

YIELD	...
P/E RATIO	29.2

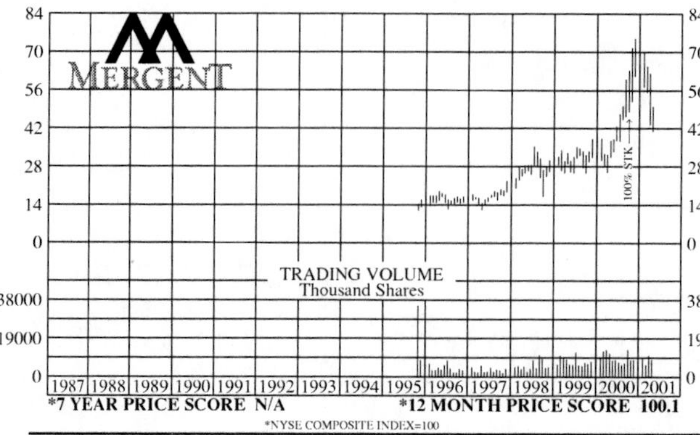

*7 YEAR PRICE SCORE N/A *12 MONTH PRICE SCORE 100.1

*NYSE COMPOSITE INDEX=100

INTERIM EARNINGS (Per Share):

Qtr.	Mar.	June	Sept.	Dec.
1996	0.05	0.13	1.39	0.12
1997	0.16	0.15	0.15	0.17
1998	0.19	0.18	0.14	0.05
1999	0.26	0.26	0.26	0.29
2000	0.44	0.37	0.35	0.52

INTERIM DIVIDENDS (Per Share):

Amt.	Decl.	Ex.	Rec.	Pay.
100% STK	9/26/00	10/20/00	10/06/00	10/19/00

CAPITALIZATION (12/31/00):

	($000)	(%)
Long-Term Debt	68,700	3.2
Deferred Income Tax	482,000	22.8
Common & Surplus	1,565,800	74.0
Total	2,116,500	100.0

RECENT DEVELOPMENTS: For the year ended 12/31/00, net income jumped 56.3% to $215.8 million versus $138.1 million in 1999. Results for 2000 included after-tax non-recurring gains totaling $19.7 million from a litigation settlement and the sale of securities. Revenues grew 11.0% to $1.36 billion. Financial services segment sales rose 14.0% to $161.7 million. Sales of the output solutions segment increased 13.9% to $151.5 million, while customer management segment sales declined 14.8% to $47.3 million.

PROSPECTS: On 3/30/01, the Company announced that it has acquired a controlling equity position in EquiServe Limited Partnership by purchasing interests held by FleetBoston Financial and Bank One Corporation. Financial terms of the transaction were not disclosed. EquiServe's financial results will be consolidated with the results of DST. Under a separate agreement with EquiServe, DST will acquire additional shares of EquiServe upon delivery of the Fairway system, a new stock transfer system.

BUSINESS

DST SYSTEMS INC. provides computer software applications and services to the financial, video/broadband, satellite TV, telecommunications and utilities industries. The financial services segment offers information processing and computer software services and products to mutual funds, investment managers, insurance companies, banks, brokers and financial planners. As of 12/31/00, DST serviced 72.1 million mutual fund accounts. The output solutions segment provides bill and statement processing services and applications to the telecommunications, utilities and other high volume industries. The customer management segment provides customer management and billing services to the video/broadband, direct broadcast satellite, wireless, wire-line and Internet-protocol telephony, Internet and utility markets.

REVENUES

(12/31/00)	($000)	(%)
Financial Services	621,000	43.1
Output Solutions	592,200	41.1
Customer Management	195,000	13.5
Investments & Other	33,200	2.3
Total	1,441,400	100.0

ANNUAL FINANCIAL DATA

	12/31/00	12/31/99	12/31/98	12/31/97	12/31/96	12/31/95	12/31/94
Earnings Per Share	**3 1.67**	**1.07**	**2 0.56**	**1 0.59**	**1 1.68**	**1 0.39**	**0.43**
Cash Flow Per Share	**2.66**	**2.01**	**1.40**	**1.40**	**2.46**	**0.98**	**0.94**
Tang. Book Val. Per Share	**12.55**	**11.46**	**9.27**	**8.52**	**7.01**	**4.66**	**2.96**
INCOME STATEMENT (IN MILLIONS):							
Total Revenues	1,362.1	1,203.3	1,096.1	650.7	580.8	484.1	401.7
Costs & Expenses	968.9	880.8	867.8	479.1	445.3	374.5	314.4
Depreciation & Amort.	128.6	122.8	108.8	79.3	78.6	68.8	52.4
Operating Income	264.6	199.7	119.5	92.2	57.0	40.8	35.0
Net Interest Inc./(Exp.)	d5.6	d5.2	d8.6	d7.7	d6.9	d22.0	d14.0
Income Before Income Taxes	336.7	214.3	115.6	88.7	273.6	73.8	46.6
Income Taxes	120.9	76.9	44.3	29.2	105.9	46.2	14.3
Equity Earnings/Minority Int.	11.4	7.3	d2.4	d1.9	d4.5	6.4	23.4
Net Income	3 215.8	138.1	2 71.6	1 59.0	1 167.2	1 27.6	33.4
Cash Flow	344.4	260.9	180.4	138.3	245.8	96.4	85.8
Average Shs. Outstg. (000)	129,400	129,600	128,600	98,616	99,742	98,564	91,738
BALANCE SHEET (IN MILLIONS):							
Cash & Cash Equivalents	116.2	89.0	28.1	15.8	8.3	13.1	4.0
Total Current Assets	590.7	464.5	375.8	231.3	201.3	188.5	134.0
Net Property	393.8	338.7	328.4	242.2	244.0	247.0	179.7
Total Assets	2,552.4	2,326.3	1,897.0	1,355.4	1,121.6	749.5	510.4
Total Current Liabilities	356.2	285.8	268.6	141.0	125.7	133.2	120.0
Long-Term Obligations	68.7	44.4	49.7	92.0	75.9	52.5	175.8
Net Stockholders' Equity	1,565.8	1,463.6	1,166.2	835.7	695.2	466.4	180.6
Net Working Capital	234.5	178.7	107.2	90.3	75.6	55.3	14.0
Year-end Shs. Outstg. (000)	124,733	127,686	125,834	98,086	99,208	100,000	61,100
STATISTICAL RECORD:							
Operating Profit Margin %	19.4	16.6	10.9	14.2	9.8	8.4	8.7
Net Profit Margin %	15.8	11.5	6.5	9.1	28.8	5.7	8.3
Return on Equity %	13.8	9.4	6.1	7.1	24.1	5.9	18.5
Return on Assets %	8.5	5.9	3.8	4.4	14.9	3.7	6.5
Debt/Total Assets %	2.7	1.9	2.6	6.8	6.8	7.0	34.4
Price Range	74.94-25.81	38.19-25.47	35.28-17.00	22.72-12.13	19.00-12.31	15.88-11.81	...
P/E Ratio	44.9-15.5	35.9-23.9	63.6-30.6	38.5-20.5	11.3-7.4	41.2-30.7	...

Statistics are as originally reported. Adj. for stk. split, 2-for-1, 10/00. 1 Incl. a pre-tax gain of $1.5 mill. fr. the sale of Continuum, 1997; $223.4 mill., 1996; $44.9 mill., 1995. 2 Incl. merger-related exp. of $33.1 mill. 3 Incl. after-tax nonrecurr. gains $19.7 mill.

OFFICERS:
T. A. McDonnell, Pres., C.E.O.
K. V. Hager, V.P., C.F.O., Treas.
R. C. Canfield, Sr. V.P., Gen. Couns., Sec.

INVESTOR CONTACT: Investor Relations, (816) 435-8684

PRINCIPAL OFFICE: 333 West 11th Street, Kansas City, MO 64105

TELEPHONE NUMBER: (816) 435-1000
FAX: (816) 435-8630
WEB: www.dstsystems.com

NO. OF EMPLOYEES: 10,100 (approx.)

SHAREHOLDERS: 29,500 (approx. beneficial)

ANNUAL MEETING: In May

INCORPORATED: DE, Aug., 1968

INSTITUTIONAL HOLDINGS:
No. of Institutions: 228
Shares Held: 55,031,455
% Held: 44.2

INDUSTRY: Information retrieval services (SIC: 7375)

TRANSFER AGENT(S): State Street Bank and Trust Company, Boston MA

NYSE SYMBOL DTE
Rec. Pr. 41.92 (4/30/01)

DTE ENERGY CO.

YIELD 4.6%
P/E RATIO 12.8

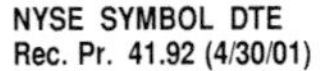

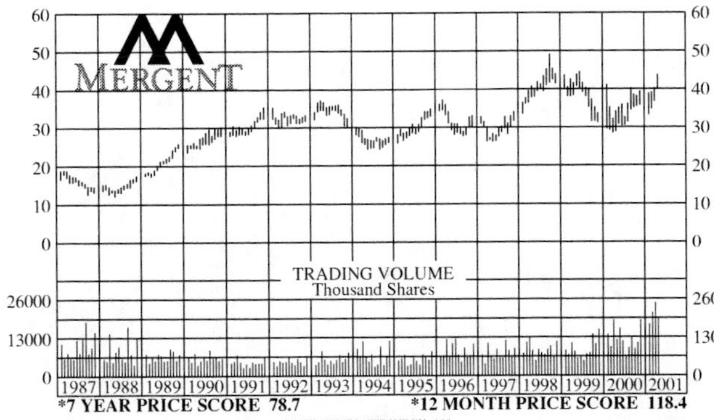

*7 YEAR PRICE SCORE 78.7 *12 MONTH PRICE SCORE 118.4

*NYSE COMPOSITE INDEX=100

INTERIM EARNINGS (Per Share):

Qtr.	Mar.	June	Sept.	Dec.
1996	0.75	0.54	0.98	0.54
1997	0.48	0.59	0.91	0.89
1998	0.72	0.69	0.91	0.73
1999	0.79	0.76	1.11	0.67
2000	0.81	0.76	0.73	0.97

INTERIM DIVIDENDS (Per Share):

Amt.	Decl.	Ex.	Rec.	Pay.
0.515Q	2/23/00	3/16/00	3/20/00	4/15/00
0.515Q	5/24/00	6/16/00	6/20/00	7/15/00
0.515Q	9/13/00	9/21/00	9/25/00	10/15/00
0.515Q	12/12/00	12/20/00	12/22/00	1/15/01
0.515Q	3/12/01	3/20/01	3/22/01	4/15/01

Indicated div.: $2.06 (Div. Reinv. Plan)

CAPITALIZATION (12/31/00):

	($000)	(%)
Long-Term Debt	3,917,000	39.7
Capital Lease Obligations	145,000	1.5
Deferred Income Tax	1,801,000	18.2
Common & Surplus	4,015,000	40.6
Total	9,878,000	100.0

RECENT DEVELOPMENTS: For the twelve months ended 12/31/00, net income slipped 3.1% to $468.0 million compared with $483.0 in the previous year. The decline in earnings was primarily due to an increase in fuel and purchased power expenses, a mild cooling season and a one-time 5.0% residential electric rate reduction required by the restructuring legislation. Operating revenues increased 18.4% to $5.60 billion. Operating income dropped 7.9% to $830.0 million from $901.0 million the year before.

PROSPECTS: DTE's subsidiaries, Detroit Edison and International Transmission Company, have assured the Michigan Public Service Commission that they are prepared to meet customer demand for electricity in the hot summer months of 2001. Meanwhile, DTE completed the purchase of four coal fines plants from MCN Energy Group Inc. The transaction was independent of DTE's pending merger with MCN. Going forward, DTE should continue to see earnings growth from its non-regulated businesses.

BUSINESS

DTE ENERGY CO. is a holding company whose principal subsidiary is Detroit Edison Co. As of 12/31/00, Detroit Edison represents approximately 87.0% and 74.0% of the Company's assets and revenues, respectively. DTE's revenues come almost entirely from the sale of electricity in Detroit and the extensive adjoining area in southeastern Michigan. The territory contains a considerable amount of industry, therefore operations are not immune to the effects of the business cycle. Seven wholly-owned subsidiaries, along with various affiliates of DTE, are engaged in non-regulated businesses, including energy-related services and products. Such services and products include the operations of a pulverized coal facility and a coke oven battery, coal sales and brokering, energy technologies, real estate development, power marketing, specialty engineering services and retail marketing of energy products.

BUSINESS LINE ANALYSIS

(12/31/00)	REV (%)	INC (%)
Electric Utility	72.7	83.0
Energy Trading	17.4	2.0
Energy Services	8.3	22.0
All Other Revenues	1.6	(7.0)
Total	100.0	100.0

ANNUAL FINANCIAL DATA

	12/31/00	12/31/99	12/31/98	12/31/97	12/31/96	12/31/95	12/31/94
Earnings Per Share	**3.27**	**3.33**	**3.05**	**2.88**	**[2] 2.13**	**[1] 2.80**	**2.67**
Cash Flow Per Share	**8.57**	**8.40**	**7.61**	**7.43**	**5.76**	**6.25**	**5.93**
Tang. Book Val. Per Share	**28.15**	**26.95**	**25.50**	**24.55**	**23.73**	**23.68**	**22.96**
Dividends Per Share	**2.06**	**2.06**	**2.06**	**2.06**	**2.06**	**2.06**	**2.06**
Dividend Payout %	**63.0**	**61.9**	**67.5**	**71.5**	**96.7**	**73.6**	**77.2**
INCOME STATEMENT (IN MILLIONS):							
Total Revenues	5,597.0	4,728.0	4,221.0	3,764.0	3,645.4	3,635.5	3,519.3
Costs & Expenses	4,009.0	3,092.0	2,623.0	2,103.0	2,004.5	1,865.8	1,790.5
Depreciation & Amort.	758.0	735.0	661.0	660.0	526.6	500.6	476.4
Maintenance Exp.	...	...	...	...	277.8	240.1	262.4
Operating Income	830.0	901.0	937.0	1,001.0	613.9	739.3	719.4
Net Interest Inc./(Exp.)	d336.0	d340.0	d319.0	d297.0	d288.2	d294.3	d293.7
Income Taxes	9.0	60.0	154.0	257.0	222.6	289.7	270.7
Net Income	468.0	483.0	443.0	417.0	[2] 309.3	[1] 405.9	390.3
Cash Flow	1,226.0	1,218.0	1,110.0	1,077.0	835.9	906.5	866.7
Average Shs. Outstg. (000)	143,000	145,000	145,000	145,000	145,120	144,940	146,152
BALANCE SHEET (IN MILLIONS):							
Gross Property	13,162.0	12,746.0	12,178.0	15,374.0	14,200.2	13,751.0	13,454.9
Accumulated Depreciation	5,775.0	5,598.0	5,235.0	6,440.0	5,367.1	4,928.3	4,529.7
Net Property	7,387.0	7,148.0	6,943.0	8,934.0	8,833.1	8,822.6	8,925.2
Total Assets	12,662.0	12,316.0	12,088.0	11,223.0	11,014.9	11,130.6	10,993.0
Long-Term Obligations	4,062.0	4,052.0	4,323.0	3,914.0	3,895.1	3,884.5	3,951.4
Net Stockholders' Equity	4,015.0	3,909.0	3,698.0	3,706.0	3,443.9	3,436.3	3,326.1
Year-end Shs. Outstg. (000)	142,651	145,041	145,000	145,098	145,120	145,120	144,864
STATISTICAL RECORD:							
Operating Profit Margin %	14.8	19.1	22.2	26.6	16.8	20.3	20.4
Net Profit Margin %	8.4	10.2	10.5	11.1	8.5	11.2	11.1
Net Inc./Net Property %	6.3	6.8	6.4	4.7	3.5	4.6	4.4
Net Inc./Tot. Capital %	4.7	4.9	4.5	4.2	3.2	4.2	4.0
Return on Equity %	11.7	12.4	12.0	11.3	9.0	11.8	11.7
Accum. Depr./Gross Prop. %	43.9	43.9	43.0	41.9	37.8	35.8	33.7
Price Range	41.31-28.44	44.69-31.06	49.25-33.44	34.13-26.13	37.25-27.63	34.88-25.75	30.25-24.25
P/E Ratio	12.6-8.7	13.4-9.3	16.1-11.0	11.8-9.1	17.5-13.0	12.5-9.2	11.3-9.1
Average Yield %	5.9	5.4	5.0	6.8	6.4	6.8	7.6

Statistics are as originally reported. [1] Incl. an after-tax write-off of $32.0 mill. [2] Incl. non-recurr. after-tax charge of $97.0 mill.

OFFICERS:
A. F. Earley Jr., Chmn., Pres., C.E.O., C.O.O.
D. E. Meador, Sr. V.P., C.F.O.
L. G. Garberding, Exec. V.P.

INVESTOR CONTACT: Investor Relations, (313) 235-8030

PRINCIPAL OFFICE: 2000 2nd Avenue, Room 2412, Detroit, MI 48226-1279

TELEPHONE NUMBER: (313) 235-4000
FAX: (313) 235-6743
WEB: www.dteenergy.com

NO. OF EMPLOYEES: 9,144

SHAREHOLDERS: 96,153

ANNUAL MEETING: In Apr.

INCORPORATED: MI, 1995

INSTITUTIONAL HOLDINGS:
No. of Institutions: 276
Shares Held: 70,497,488
% Held: 49.4

INDUSTRY: Electric services (SIC: 4911)

TRANSFER AGENT(S): The Detroit Edison Company, Detroit, MI

NYSE SYMBOL DUK
Rec. Pr. 46.76 (4/30/01)

DUKE ENERGY CORPORATION

YIELD 2.4%
P/E RATIO 19.6

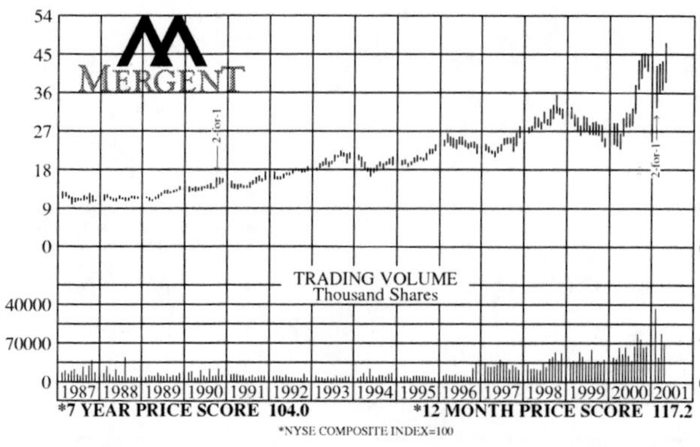

*7 YEAR PRICE SCORE 104.0 *12 MONTH PRICE SCORE 117.2

*NYSE COMPOSITE INDEX=100

INTERIM EARNINGS (Per Share):

Qtr.	Mar.	June	Sept.	Dec.
1996	0.44	0.36	0.63	0.27
1997	0.47	0.22	0.42	0.21
1998	0.45	0.38	0.59	0.30
1999	0.42	0.39	0.60	d0.27
2000	0.53	0.44	1.04	0.38

INTERIM DIVIDENDS (Per Share):

Amt.	Decl.	Ex.	Rec.	Pay.
0.55Q	6/29/00	8/09/00	8/11/00	9/18/00
0.55Q	10/31/00	11/15/00	11/17/00	12/18/00
2-for-1	12/20/00	1/29/01	1/03/01	1/26/01
0.275Q	1/04/01	2/14/01	2/16/01	3/16/01
0.275Q	4/26/01	5/09/01	5/11/01	6/18/01

Indicated div.: $1.10 (Div. Reinv. Plan)

CAPITALIZATION (12/31/00):

	($000)	(%)
Long-Term Debt	11,019,000	39.9
Deferred Income Tax	3,851,000	13.9
Minority Interest	2,435,000	8.8
Redeemable Pfd. Stock	38,000	0.1
Preferred Stock	209,000	0.8
Common & Surplus	10,056,000	36.4
Total	27,608,000	100.0

RECENT DEVELOPMENTS: For the year ended 12/31/00, net income more than doubled to $1.78 billion versus $847.0 million. Results for 1999 excluded an extraordinary gain of $660.0 million. Total operating revenues soared to $49.32 billion from $21.77 billion in 1999. Franchised electric revenues rose 5.2% to $4.95 billion, while natural gas transmission revenues fell 8.0% to $1.13 billion. Field services revenue rocketed to $9.06 billion, while North American wholesale energy revenues jumped to $33.87 billion.

PROSPECTS: The Company raised its annual earnings per share growth target to a range of 10.0% to 15.0% based on its strong performance in 2000 and favorable outlook for 2001. Going forward, DUK believes that increased expectations reflect confidence in its proven performance, solid strategy and successful expansion into key regions around the world. DUK's investment in regional growth opportunities should bolster its presence in key energy markets and its position as a wholesale energy producer and trader.

BUSINESS

DUKE ENERGY CORPORATION (formerly Duke Power Company) is a diversified energy-services corporation that conducts business through four subsidiaries. Duke Power provides electricity to 2.0 million people in North Carolina and South Carolina. The Energy Services Group offers a complete range of energy products and services to both domestic and international customers. Energy services provides electric and natural gas trading and marketing; power plant construction, operation and investment; and engineering and energy services consulting. The Diversified Businesses Group offers real estate, telecommunications and water utility services in the southeast. The Energy Transmission Group supplies access to all major U.S. natural gas supply basins through its interconnected pipeline network. PanEnergy Corporation was acquired on 5/28/97.

ANNUAL FINANCIAL DATA

	12/31/00	12/31/99	12/31/98	[5] 12/31/97	12/31/96	12/31/95	12/31/94
Earnings Per Share	**2.38**	**[4] 1.13**	**[3] 1.71**	**[2] 1.25**	**1.69**	**[1] 1.63**	**1.44**
Cash Flow Per Share	**4.20**	**2.71**	**3.17**	**2.60**	**3.32**	**3.27**	**3.02**
Tang. Book Val. Per Share	**11.49**	**11.14**	**10.54**	**9.78**	**12.13**	**11.51**	**11.06**
Dividends Per Share	**1.10**	**1.10**	**1.10**	**1.08**	**1.04**	**1.00**	**0.96**
Dividend Payout %	**46.2**	**97.8**	**64.3**	**86.4**	**61.7**	**61.5**	**66.7**
INCOME STATEMENT (IN MILLIONS):							
Total Revenues	49,318.0	21,742.0	17,610.0	16,308.9	4,758.0	4,676.7	4,488.9
Costs & Expenses	44,157.0	18,796.0	14,122.0	13,356.4	2,728.1	2,652.8	2,661.6
Depreciation & Amort.	1,348.0	1,151.0	1,055.0	982.5	667.7	674.8	647.5
Operating Income	3,813.0	1,795.0	2,433.0	1,970.0	1,362.2	1,349.1	1,179.8
Net Interest Inc./(Exp.)	d848.0	d519.0	d426.0	d362.4	d171.2	d164.3	d158.3
Income Taxes	1,020.0	453.0	777.0	638.9	475.7	466.4	397.0
Equity Earnings/Minority Int.	d307.0	d142.0	d96.0	d23.0	...	...	...
Net Income	1,776.0	[4] 847.0	[3] 1,260.0	[2] 974.4	730.0	[1] 714.5	638.9
Cash Flow	3,105.0	1,978.0	2,294.0	1,884.1	1,353.4	1,340.5	1,236.7
Average Shs. Outstg. (000)	739,400	730,000	724,000	723,400	407,106	409,718	409,718
BALANCE SHEET (IN MILLIONS):							
Gross Property	34,615.0	30,436.0	27,128.0	25,448.1	15,614.2	15,291.4	14,791.5
Accumulated Depreciation	10,146.0	9,441.0	10,253.0	9,712.2	5,801.8	5,576.1	5,225.6
Net Property	24,469.0	20,995.0	16,875.0	15,735.9	9,812.4	9,715.2	9,565.9
Total Assets	58,176.0	33,409.0	26,806.0	24,028.8	13,469.7	13,358.5	12,862.2
Long-Term Obligations	11,019.0	8,683.0	6,272.0	6,530.0	3,538.1	3,711.4	3,567.1
Net Stockholders' Equity	10,265.0	9,207.0	8,359.0	7,879.7	5,338.7	5,235.2	5,032.8
Year-end Shs. Outstg. (000)	739,000	732,000	726,000	719,600	403,180	415,718	409,718
STATISTICAL RECORD:							
Operating Profit Margin %	7.7	8.3	13.8	12.1	28.6	28.8	26.3
Net Profit Margin %	3.6	3.9	7.2	6.0	15.3	15.3	14.2
Net Inc./Net Property %	7.3	4.0	7.5	6.2	7.4	7.4	6.7
Net Inc./Tot. Capital %	6.4	3.8	6.7	5.3	6.4	6.2	5.7
Return on Equity %	17.3	9.2	15.1	12.4	13.7	13.6	12.7
Accum. Depr./Gross Prop. %	29.3	31.0	37.8	38.2	37.2	36.5	35.3
Price Range	45.22-22.88	32.66-23.38	35.50-26.56	28.28-20.94	26.50-21.69	23.94-18.69	21.50-16.44
P/E Ratio	19.0-9.6	29.0-20.8	20.8-15.5	22.6-16.7	15.7-12.9	14.7-11.5	14.9-11.4
Average Yield %	3.2	3.9	3.5	4.4	4.3	4.7	5.1

Statistics are as originally reported. Adj. for 2-for-1, 1/01 [1] Incl. non-recurr. chrg $42.0 mill. ($0.12/sh) [2] Incl. non-recurr. chrg. $46.8 mill. [3] Bef. extraord. chrg. $8.0 mill. [4] Excl. net extraord. gain of $660.0 mill. [5] Results reflect the acquisition of PanEnergy Corporation.

OFFICERS:
R. B. Priory, Chmn., Pres., C.E.O.
R. Blackburn, Exec. V.P., Gen. Couns., Sec.
R. J. Osborne, Exec. V.P., C.F.O.

INVESTOR CONTACT: Paul Mason, Inv. Rel. (704) 373-4512

PRINCIPAL OFFICE: 526 South Church Street, Charlotte, NC 28202-1904

TELEPHONE NUMBER: (704) 594-6200
FAX: (704) 382-0230
WEB: www.duke-energy.com

NO. OF EMPLOYEES: 23,000 (approx.)

SHAREHOLDERS: 148,000 (approx.)

ANNUAL MEETING: In Apr.

INCORPORATED: NC, June, 1964

INSTITUTIONAL HOLDINGS:
No. of Institutions: 648
Shares Held: 897,053,996 (Adj.)
% Held: 58.5

INDUSTRY: Electric services (SIC: 4911)

TRANSFER AGENT(S): Company

NYSE SYMBOL DRE
Rec. Pr. 23.04 (4/30/01)

DUKE-WEEKS REALTY CORP.

YIELD 7.5%
P/E RATIO 13.8

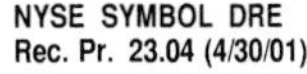

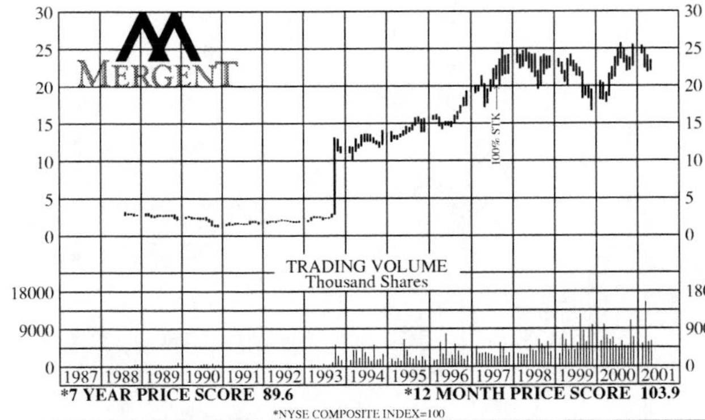

*7 YEAR PRICE SCORE 89.6 *12 MONTH PRICE SCORE 103.9

*NYSE COMPOSITE INDEX=100

INTERIM EARNINGS (Per Share):

Qtr.	Mar.	June	Sept.	Dec.
1998	0.29	0.27	0.29	0.27
1999	0.32	0.33	0.35	0.32
2000	0.39	0.36	0.35	0.57

INTERIM DIVIDENDS (Per Share):

Amt.	Decl.	Ex.	Rec.	Pay.
0.39Q	...	5/11/00	5/15/00	5/31/00
0.43Q	7/26/00	8/14/00	8/16/00	8/31/00
0.43Q	10/25/00	11/10/00	11/14/00	11/30/00
0.43Q	1/31/01	2/08/01	2/12/01	2/28/01
0.43Q	4/25/01	5/11/01	5/15/01	5/31/01

Indicated div.: $1.72

CAPITALIZATION (12/31/00):

	($000)	(%)
Long-Term Debt	1,973,215	38.5
Minority Interest	435,317	8.5
Preferred Stock	608,874	11.9
Common & Surplus	2,104,016	41.1
Total	5,121,422	100.0

RECENT DEVELOPMENTS: For the year ended 12/31/00, net income totaled $261.9 million, an increase of 43.7% from $182.4 million in the corresponding 1999 period. Total revenues jumped 34.8% to $794.6 million compared with $589.6 million in the prior year. Earnings from rental properties increased 16.0% to $229.0 million versus $197.5 million in the previous year. Earnings from service operations rose 83.3% to $32.8 million compared with $17.9 million in the equivalent year.

PROSPECTS: Looking ahead, the Company will continue to self-fund its future investments while targeting at least a two percent spread between new development yields and disposition cap rates. In addition, the Company expects to continue to post double-digit growth in funds from operations per share for 2001. Meanwhile, the Company ended 2000 with a $291.0 million portfolio of primarily build-to-suit developments that are planned for sale over the next several quarters.

BUSINESS

DUKE-WEEKS REALTY CORPORATION (formerly Duke Realty Corp.) is a self-administered and self-managed real estate investment trust company that focuses on major cities in the Midwest and the Sunbelt. As of 12/31/00, the Company owned or held an interest in 958 in-service properties totaling approximately 109 million square feet of office, industrial and retail assets. The Company also owns or controls over 4,100 acres of land that can support approximately 61 million square feet of future development. Through its service operations, the Company also provides, on a fee basis, leasing, property and asset management, development, construction, landscaping, build-to-suit, and other tenant-related services. In July 1999, Duke Realty Corporation merged with Weeks Corporation.

ANNUAL FINANCIAL DATA

	12/31/00	12/31/99	12/31/98	12/31/97	12/31/96	12/31/95	12/31/94
Earnings Per Share	**1.66**	**1.32**	**1.12**	**0.98**	**0.91**	**0.77**	**0.77**
Tang. Book Val. Per Share	**16.45**	**16.36**	**14.20**	**13.36**	**11.58**	**11.07**	**10.92**
Dividends Per Share	**1.64**	**1.46**	**1.28**	**1.10**	**1.00**	**0.96**	**0.92**
Dividend Payout %	**98.8**	**110.6**	**114.3**	**112.7**	**110.5**	**124.7**	**120.2**
INCOME STATEMENT (IN MILLIONS):							
Rental Income	697.3	524.0	337.8	221.0	156.4	112.9	87.8
Total Income	794.6	589.6	373.3	252.1	182.1	131.4	107.8
Costs & Expenses	394.1	282.1	183.0	122.9	93.6	66.8	59.0
Depreciation	159.9	110.8	68.8	44.8	32.6	24.3	18.0
Income Before Income Taxes	304.6	208.3	124.2	87.2	61.6	42.5	33.0
Equity Earnings/Minority Int.	d42.6	d26.1	d13.5	d8.7	d8.2	d7.4	d6.8
Net Income	261.9	182.2	110.7	78.5	53.4	35.0	26.2
Average Shs. Outstg. (000)	147,441	120,511	92,468	74,993	56,134	45,358	34,278
BALANCE SHEET (IN MILLIONS):							
Cash & Cash Equivalents	39.2	18.8	7.0	10.4	5.3	5.7	40.4
Total Real Estate Investments	5,074.4	5,192.4	2,682.5	2,060.5	1,208.5	907.2	685.7
Total Assets	5,460.0	5,486.2	2,853.7	2,176.2	1,361.1	1,045.6	774.9
Long-Term Obligations	1,973.2	2,113.5	1,007.3	720.1	525.8	454.8	298.6
Total Liabilities	2,747.1	2,817.6	1,283.5	941.5	606.2	510.8	329.5
Net Stockholders' Equity	2,712.9	2,668.6	1,570.1	1,234.7	754.9	534.8	445.4
Year-end Shs. Outstg. (000)	127,932	125,823	86,053	76,065	58,972	48,304	40,782
STATISTICAL RECORD:							
Net Inc.+Depr./Assets %	7.7	5.3	6.3	5.7	6.3	5.7	5.7
Return on Equity %	9.7	6.8	7.1	6.4	7.1	6.5	5.9
Return on Assets %	4.8	3.3	3.9	3.6	3.9	3.3	3.4
Price Range	25.75-17.75	24.25-16.63	25.00-19.50	25.00-17.13	19.31-14.19	15.88-12.50	14.13-10.13
P/E Ratio	15.5-10.7	18.4-12.6	22.3-17.4	25.5-17.5	21.3-15.7	20.6-16.2	18.5-13.2
Average Yield %	7.5	7.1	5.8	5.2	6.0	6.8	7.6

Statistics are as originally reported. Adj. for 100% stk. divs., 8/97

OFFICERS:
T. L. Hefner, Chmn., Pres., C.E.O.
D. E. Zink Jr., Exec. V.P., C.F.O., Asst. Sec.

INVESTOR CONTACT: Investor Relations, (317) 808-6005

PRINCIPAL OFFICE: 600 East 96th Street, Suite 100, Indianapolis, IN 46240-4640

TELEPHONE NUMBER: (317) 808-6000
WEB: www.dukereit.com

NO. OF EMPLOYEES: 1,411 (avg.)

SHAREHOLDERS: 9,946

ANNUAL MEETING: In Apr.

INCORPORATED: DE, Nov., 1985; reincorp., IN, May, 1992

INSTITUTIONAL HOLDINGS:
No. of Institutions: 215
Shares Held: 73,768,190
% Held: 57.3

INDUSTRY: Real estate investment trusts (SIC: 6798)

TRANSFER AGENT(S): American Stock Transfer & Trust Company, New York, NY

NYSE SYMBOL DNB
Rec. Pr. 26.98 (5/31/01)

DUN & BRADSTREET CORP. (THE)

YIELD ...
P/E RATIO 30.0

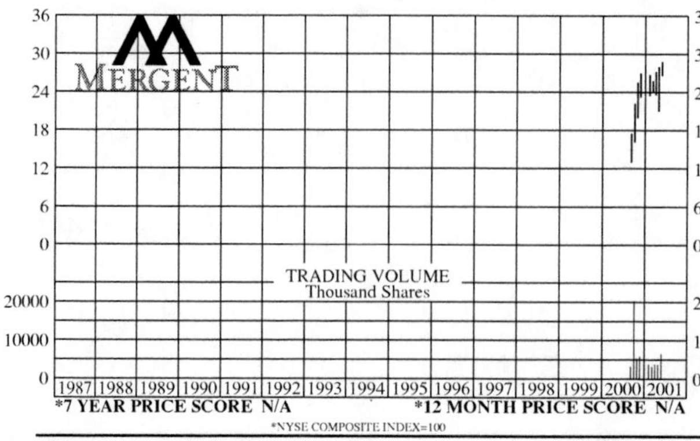

INTERIM EARNINGS (Per Share):

Qtr.	Mar.	June	Sept.	Dec.
1997		1.08		
1998		1.00		
1999		0.99		
2000	0.59		0.09	0.22

INTERIM DIVIDENDS (Per Share):

Amt.	Decl.	Ex.	Rec.	Pay.

No dividends paid.

CAPITALIZATION (12/31/00):

	($000)	(%)
Minority Interest	301,600	120.4
Common & Surplus	d51,000	-20.4
Total	250,600	100.0

RECENT DEVELOPMENTS: For the year ended 12/31/00, income from continuing operations fell 9.4% to $73.6 million versus income from continuing operation of $81.3 million in 1999. Results for 2000 and 1999 excluded income from discontinuing operations of $133.0 million and $174.7 million, respectively. Consolidated operating revenues inched up 0.7% to $1.42 billion due to growth in the North American market, despite a weaker market in Europe. Consolidated operating income rose 7.4% to $172.8 million.

PROSPECTS: The Company announced plans to complete the implementation of the first phase of its financial flexibility program that began in October 2000 as part of its growth strategy. The initiative is expected to generate approximately $100.0 million in financial flexibility for investment in 2001. The financial flexibility should enable the Company to fund its movement into the business-to-business e-commerce arena and ensure annual earnings per share growth of 10.0%.

BUSINESS

THE DUN & BRADSTREET CORPORATION is a provider of business marketing, credit and purchasing information and receivable management services. The Company, headquartered in Murray Hill, New Jersey, employs more than 10,000 people in 37 countries with majority-owned entities. In November 1996, the Company completed the spin-off of Cognizant Corporation and ACNielsen Corporation. On July 1, 1998, R. H. Donnelley became an independent publicly traded company as a result of a tax-free dividend. On September 30, 1999, the Company completed the separation of Moody's Investors Service from the Dun and Bradstreet operating company.

REVENUES

(12/31/00)	($000)	(%)
Credit Information	886,400	62.5
Marketing Information	339,400	23.9
Purchasing Information	30,600	2.2
Receivable Management	161,200	11.4
Total	1,417,600	100.0

ANNUAL FINANCIAL DATA

	12/31/00	12/31/99	12/31/98	12/31/97
Earnings Per Share	**1 0.90**	**1 0.99**	**1.00**	**1.08**
Cash Flow Per Share	**2.25**	**2.55**	**2.47**	**2.42**
INCOME STATEMENT (IN MILLIONS):				
Total Revenues	1,417.6	1,407.7	1,420.5	1,353.6
Costs & Expenses	1,133.6	1,118.9	1,106.6	1,030.6
Depreciation & Amort.	111.2	127.9	126.2	115.8
Operating Income	172.8	160.9	187.7	207.2
Net Interest Inc./(Exp.)	d4.7	d2.1	d5.7	d51.5
Income Before Income Taxes	151.7	145.4	157.3	135.7
Income Taxes	78.1	64.1	71.1	42.5
Equity Earnings/Minority Int.	d22.4	d22.4	d22.5	d16.9
Net Income	1 73.6	1 81.3	86.2	93.2
Cash Flow	184.8	209.2	212.4	209.0
Average Shs. Outstg. (000)	81,994	82,142	85,852	86,276
BALANCE SHEET (IN MILLIONS):				
Cash & Cash Equivalents	70.1	109.4	86.7	...
Total Current Assets	538.6	606.7	585.5	...
Net Property	202.8	240.3	258.2	...
Total Assets	1,423.6	1,574.8	1,574.7	...
Total Current Liabilities	743.1	1,037.0	1,008.7	...
Net Stockholders' Equity	d51.0	d416.6	d371.0	...
Net Working Capital	d204.5	d430.3	d423.2	...
Year-end Shs. Outstg. (000)	80,155	80,412	82,527	...
STATISTICAL RECORD:				
Operating Profit Margin %	12.2	11.4	13.2	15.3
Net Profit Margin %	5.2	5.8	6.1	6.9
Return on Assets %	5.2	5.2	5.5	...
Price Range	27.00-13.00	...	...	...
P/E Ratio	30.0-14.4	...	...	...

Statistics are as originally reported. 1 Excl. inc. fr. discont. opers. of $174.7 mill., 1999; $133.0 mill., 2000

OFFICERS:
A. Z. Loren, Chmn., Pres., C.E.O.
C. J. Geveda Jr., V.P., Acting C.F.O., Contr.
D. Lewinter, V.P., Corp. Sec., Acting Gen. Couns.

INVESTOR CONTACT: Sandy Parker, V.P. Inv. Rel., (908) 665-5098

PRINCIPAL OFFICE: One Diamond Hill Road, Murray Hill, NJ 07974-1218

TELEPHONE NUMBER: (908) 665-5000
FAX: (908) 665-5803
WEB: www.dnb.com

NO. OF EMPLOYEES: 10,100 (approx.)

SHAREHOLDERS: 8,115

ANNUAL MEETING: In Apr.

INCORPORATED: DE, Apr., 2000

INSTITUTIONAL HOLDINGS:
No. of Institutions: 218
Shares Held: 64,347,876
% Held: 80.1

INDUSTRY: Business services, nec (SIC: 7389)

TRANSFER AGENT(S): EquiServe Trust Company, N.A., Jersey City, NJ

NYSE SYMBOL DD
Rec. Pr. 46.22 (4/30/01)

E.I. DU PONT DE NEMOURS AND COMPANY

YIELD 3.0%
P/E RATIO 21.1

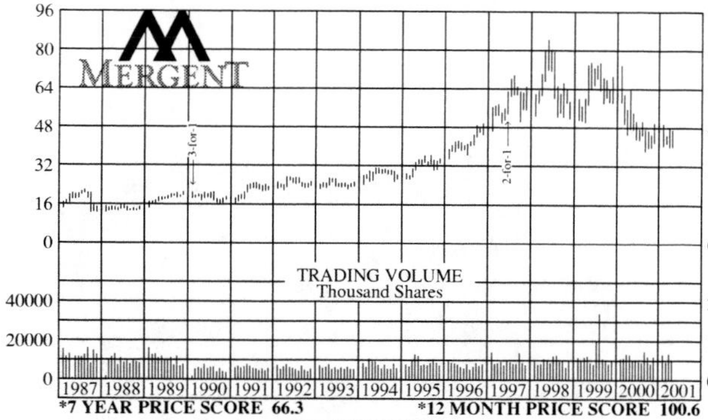

INTERIM EARNINGS (Per Share):

Qtr.	Mar.	June	Sept.	Dec.
1997	0.90	1.01	d0.02	0.23
1998	0.79	0.83	d0.50	0.68
1999	0.55	0.74	0.17	d1.38
2000	0.76	0.65	0.53	0.25

INTERIM DIVIDENDS (Per Share):

Amt.	Decl.	Ex.	Rec.	Pay.
0.35Q	7/26/00	8/11/00	8/15/00	9/12/00
0.35Q	10/25/00	11/13/00	11/15/00	12/14/00
0.35Q	1/24/01	2/13/01	2/15/01	3/14/01
0.35Q	4/25/01	5/11/01	5/15/01	6/12/01

Indicated div.: $1.40 (Div. Reinv. Plan)

CAPITALIZATION (12/31/00):

	($000)	(%)
Long-Term Debt	6,658,000	29.7
Deferred Income Tax	2,105,000	9.4
Minority Interest	380,000	1.7
Preferred Stock	237,000	1.1
Common & Surplus	13,062,000	58.2
Total	22,442,000	100.0

RECENT DEVELOPMENTS: For the year ended 12/31/00, net income soared to $2.31 billion versus income from continuing operations of $219.0 million in 1999. Results for 2000 included a charge of $101.0 million for separation costs and the write-down of assets and a gain of $29.0 million for the issuance of stock. Results for 2000 and 1999 included gains of $11.0 million and $4.70 billion, respectively. Total revenues climbed 4.7% to $29.20 billion.

PROSPECTS: The Company expects challenging economic conditions in the first half of 2001. As a result, DD will focus on improving cost management efforts to offset these conditions. DD plans to streamline logistics, production scheduling, purchasing and other processes through Six Sigma initiatives, improved pricing and product mix, and reduce working capital. Separately, DD formed a Fuel Cell business unit to pursue growth opportunities.

BUSINESS

E.I. DU PONT DE NEMOURS AND COMPANY is a leader in science and technology in a range of industries including high-performance materials, specialty chemicals, pharmaceuticals and biotechnology. DD has a portfolio of 2,000 trademarks and brands, including such consumer brands as Lycra®, Teflon®, Stainmaster®, Kevlar®, Nomex®, Tyvek®, Dacron®, Cordura®, Corian®, SilverStone® and Mylar®. DD operates in 65 countries, including an established presence in North America and Europe, and strong positions in South America and Asia Pacific. DD has been in operation since 1802. Revenues in 2000 were derived: agricultural & nutrition, 7.9%; nylon enterprises, 14.3%; performance coatings & polymers, 20.4%; pharmaceuticals, 4.7%; pigments & chemicals, 12.3%; pioneer, 6.1%; polyester enterprises, 8.0%; specialty fibers, 10.7%; specialty polymers, 14.2%; and other, 1.4%.

ANNUAL FINANCIAL DATA

	12/31/00	12/31/99	12/31/98	12/31/97	12/31/96	12/31/95	12/31/94
Earnings Per Share	**[4] 2.19**	**[3] 0.19**	**[1] [2] 1.43**	**[1] 2.08**	**3.24**	**[1] 2.81**	**[1] 2.00**
Cash Flow Per Share	**3.97**	**1.74**	**2.71**	**4.76**	**6.17**	**5.61**	**4.46**
Tang. Book Val. Per Share	**4.50**	**12.09**	**12.18**	**9.76**	**12.12**	**9.46**	**9.07**
Dividends Per Share	**1.40**	**1.40**	**1.40**	**1.23**	**1.11**	**1.01**	**0.91**
Dividend Payout %	**63.9**	**736.5**	**95.4**	**59.1**	**34.5**	**36.2**	**45.5**
INCOME STATEMENT (IN MILLIONS):							
Total Revenues	29,202.0	27,892.0	25,748.0	46,653.0	45,150.0	43,262.0	40,259.0
Costs & Expenses	23,085.0	23,977.0	21,055.0	38,946.0	35,835.0	34,392.0	32,342.0
Depreciation & Amort.	1,860.0	1,690.0	1,560.0	2,385.0	2,621.0	2,722.0	2,976.0
Operating Income	4,257.0	2,225.0	3,133.0	5,322.0	6,694.0	6,148.0	4,941.0
Net Interest Inc./(Exp.)	d810.0	d535.0	d520.0	d642.0	d713.0	d758.0	d559.0
Income Before Income Taxes	3,447.0	1,690.0	2,613.0	4,680.0	5,981.0	5,390.0	4,382.0
Income Taxes	1,072.0	1,410.0	941.0	2,275.0	2,345.0	2,097.0	1,655.0
Equity Earnings/Minority Int.	d61.0	d61.0	d24.0	...	...	...	...
Net Income	[4] 2,314.0	[3] 219.0	[1] [2] 1,648.0	[1] 3,087.0	4,305.0	[1] 3,838.0	[1] 3,088.0
Cash Flow	4,164.0	1,899.0	3,198.0	4,780.0	6,247.0	6,005.0	5,693.0
Average Shs. Outstg. (000)	1,051,043	1,097,970	1,145,000	1,150,000	1,122,000	1,170,000	1,360,000
BALANCE SHEET (IN MILLIONS):							
Cash & Cash Equivalents	1,617.0	1,582.0	1,069.0	1,146.0	1,319.0	1,455.0	1,109.0
Total Current Assets	11,656.0	12,653.0	9,236.0	11,874.0	11,103.0	10,955.0	11,108.0
Net Property	14,182.0	14,871.0	14,131.0	23,583.0	21,213.0	21,341.0	21,120.0
Total Assets	39,426.0	40,777.0	38,536.0	42,942.0	37,987.0	37,312.0	36,892.0
Total Current Liabilities	9,255.0	11,228.0	11,610.0	14,070.0	10,987.0	12,731.0	7,565.0
Long-Term Obligations	6,658.0	6,625.0	4,495.0	5,929.0	5,087.0	5,678.0	6,376.0
Net Stockholders' Equity	13,299.0	12,875.0	13,954.0	11,270.0	10,709.0	8,436.0	12,822.0
Net Working Capital	2,401.0	1,425.0	d2,374.0	d2,196.0	116.0	d1,776.0	3,543.0
Year-end Shs. Outstg. (000)	1,042,931	1,052,473	1,126,000	1,130,000	846,000	846,000	1,362,000
STATISTICAL RECORD:							
Operating Profit Margin %	14.6	8.0	12.2	11.4	14.8	14.2	12.3
Net Profit Margin %	7.9	0.8	6.4	6.6	9.5	8.9	7.7
Return on Equity %	17.4	1.7	11.8	27.4	40.2	45.5	24.1
Return on Assets %	5.9	0.5	4.3	7.2	11.3	10.3	8.4
Debt/Total Assets %	16.9	16.2	11.7	13.8	13.4	15.2	17.3
Price Range	74.00-38.19	75.19-50.06	84.44-51.69	69.75-46.38	49.69-34.81	36.50-26.31	31.19-24.13
P/E Ratio	33.8-17.4	395.5-263.4	59.0-36.1	33.5-22.3	15.4-10.8	13.0-9.4	15.6-12.1
Average Yield %	2.5	2.2	2.1	2.1	2.6	3.2	3.3

Statistics are as originally reported. Adj. for 2-for-1 split, 6/97. [1] Incl. non-recur. chgs. $2.07 bill., 1998; $1.99 bill., 1997; $96.0 mill., 1995; cr$142.0 mill., 1994. [2] Bef. disc. oper. inc. $3.03 bill. & extraord. chg. $201.0 mill. [3] Incl. $2.25 bill. in-process R&D chg., $524.0 mill. employee sep. costs & excl. $7.47 bill. net gain fr. disc. ops. [4] Incl. $101.0 mill. sep. chg., $29.0 mill. gain. fr. issuance of stock & $11.0 mill. purch. in-process R&D chg.

OFFICERS:
C. O. Holliday Jr., Chmn., C.E.O.
G. M. Pfeiffer, Sr. V.P., C.F.O.
S. J. Mobley, Sr. V.P., C.A.O., Gen. Couns.

INVESTOR CONTACT: Stockholder Relations, (302) 774-4994

PRINCIPAL OFFICE: 1007 Market Street, Wilmington, DE 19898

TELEPHONE NUMBER: (302) 774-1000
FAX: (302) 774-0748
WEB: www.dupont.com

NO. OF EMPLOYEES: 93,000 (avg.)

SHAREHOLDERS: 132,472

ANNUAL MEETING: In Apr.

INCORPORATED: DE, Sept., 1915

INSTITUTIONAL HOLDINGS:
No. of Institutions: 818
Shares Held: 543,816,479
% Held: 52.2

INDUSTRY: Plastics materials and resins (SIC: 2821)

TRANSFER AGENT(S): First Chicago Trust Company of New York, Jersey City, NJ

NYSE SYMBOL DY
Rec. Pr. 16.43 (4/30/01)

DYCOM INDUSTRIES, INC.

YIELD ...
P/E RATIO 9.8

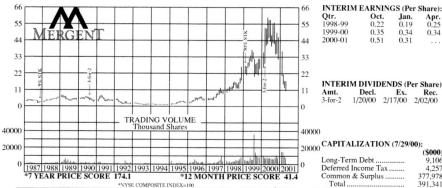

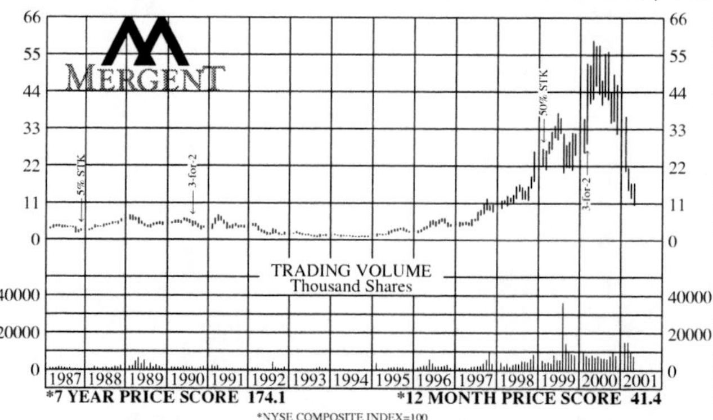

INTERIM EARNINGS (Per Share):

Qtr.	Oct.	Jan.	Apr.	July
1998-99	0.22	0.19	0.25	0.35
1999-00	0.35	0.34	0.34	0.51
2000-01	0.51	0.31	...	...

INTERIM DIVIDENDS (Per Share):

Amt.	Decl.	Ex.	Rec.	Pay.
3-for-2	1/20/00	2/17/00	2/02/00	2/16/00

CAPITALIZATION (7/29/00):

	($000)	(%)
Long-Term Debt	9,106	2.3
Deferred Income Tax	4,257	1.1
Common & Surplus	377,978	96.6
Total	391,341	100.0

RECENT DEVELOPMENTS: For the quarter ended 1/27/01, net income declined 9.1% to $13.1 million compared with $14.4 million in the previous year. Results were negatively affected by year-end budgeting issues with several customers coupled with unfavorable weather conditions. Contract revenues earned totaled $195.8 million, an increase of 10.5% from $177.2 million in the prior year. Comparisons were made with restated figures to reflect the merger with Niels Fugal Sons Company in March 2000.

PROSPECTS: Going forward, the Company is well-positioned to continue to deliver revenue growth due primarily to its robust balance sheet and strong customer relationships. On Dec. 19, 2000, the Company completed the acquisition of Point To Point Communications, Inc., a Louisiana-based Company. Point To Point Communications, Inc. offers central office equipment, engineering, installation, testing and maintenance services for telecommunications providers throughout the U.S.

BUSINESS

DYCOM INDUSTRIES, INC. is a major provider of specialty contracting services, including engineering, construction and maintenance services, to telecommunications providers throughout the United States. The Company's telecommunications infrastructure services include the engineering, placement and maintenance of aerial, underground, and buried fiber-optic, coaxial and copper cable systems owned by local and long distance communications carriers and cable television multiple system operators. Additionally, the Company provides similar services related to the installation of integrated voice, data, and video local and wide area networks within office buildings and similar structures. The Company also offers underground locating services to various utilities and provides construction and maintenance services to electrical utilities.

ANNUAL FINANCIAL DATA

	7/29/00	7/31/99	7/31/98	7/31/97	7/31/96	7/31/95	7/31/94
Earnings Per Share	**1.54**	**1.03**	**0.72**	**0.45**	**0.33**	**0.20**	**d0.40**
Cash Flow Per Share	**2.29**	**1.61**	**1.13**	**0.81**	**0.61**	**0.54**	**d0.02**
Tang. Book Val. Per Share	**6.97**	**5.93**	**3.29**	**1.19**	**0.67**	**0.32**	**0.08**
INCOME STATEMENT (IN THOUSANDS):							
Total Revenues	806,270	473,453	371,363	243,923	145,135	145,283	122,492
Costs & Expenses	665,967	392,697	321,785	216,192	130,297	131,856	122,614
Depreciation & Amort.	31,759	20,143	13,497	8,690	5,719	5,911	7,337
Operating Income	108,543	60,612	36,081	19,042	9,120	7,516	d7,459
Net Interest Inc./(Exp.)	3,448	...	...	...	...	...	...
Income Before Income Taxes	109,233	60,612	36,081	19,042	9,120	7,516	d7,459
Income Taxes	44,201	24,162	13,046	7,823	2,730	3,083	318
Net Income	65,032	36,450	23,036	11,219	6,390	4,433	d7,777
Cash Flow	96,791	56,593	36,532	19,908	12,109	10,344	d439
Average Shs. Outstg.	42,315	35,185	32,224	24,635	19,815	19,205	19,190
BALANCE SHEET (IN THOUSANDS):							
Cash & Cash Equivalents	105,702	97,955	35,927	6,646	3,835	4,307	2,626
Total Current Assets	324,429	241,129	118,193	55,199	26,788	27,643	23,154
Net Property	101,093	79,411	42,865	27,543	19,574	18,803	19,955
Total Assets	514,000	384,550	166,318	88,162	52,074	51,793	48,699
Total Current Liabilities	114,759	78,606	36,982	38,979	17,783	20,137	36,626
Long-Term Obligations	9,106	9,982	13,408	9,012	9,453	13,870	...
Net Stockholders' Equity	377,978	287,291	98,379	33,752	17,776	11,187	6,709
Net Working Capital	209,669	162,524	81,211	16,219	9,005	7,505	d13,472
Year-end Shs. Outstg.	41,901	38,442	28,503	24,453	19,353	19,224	19,190
STATISTICAL RECORD:							
Operating Profit Margin %	13.5	12.8	9.7	7.8	6.3	5.2	...
Net Profit Margin %	8.1	7.7	6.2	4.6	4.4	3.1	...
Return on Equity %	17.2	12.7	23.4	33.2	35.9	39.6	...
Return on Assets %	12.7	9.5	13.9	12.7	12.3	8.6	...
Debt/Total Assets %	1.8	2.6	8.1	10.2	18.2	26.8	...
Price Range	59.25-26.04	37.75-19.96	26.34-9.45	12.45-4.11	6.56-2.17	3.78-1.11	1.83-0.89
P/E Ratio	38.5-16.9	36.5-19.3	36.8-13.2	27.5-9.1	20.2-6.7	37,781.6-11,112.2	18,335.2-8,889.8

Statistics are as originally reported. Adj. for 3-for-2 stk. spl., 2/00; 1/99.

OFFICERS:
T. R. Pledger, Chmn.
S. E. Nielsen, Pres., C.E.O.
R. L. Dunn, Sr. V.P., C.F.O.

INVESTOR CONTACT: Investor Relations, (561) 627-7171

PRINCIPAL OFFICE: 4440 PGA Boulevard, Suite 500, Palm Beach Gardens, FL 33410-6542

TELEPHONE NUMBER: (561) 627-7171
FAX: (561) 627-7709
WEB: www.dycomind.com

NO. OF EMPLOYEES: 7,260 (approx.)

SHAREHOLDERS: 689 (approx.)

ANNUAL MEETING: In Nov.

INCORPORATED: FL, Aug., 1969

INSTITUTIONAL HOLDINGS:
No. of Institutions: 183
Shares Held: 32,740,903
% Held: 77.0

INDUSTRY: Water, sewer, and utility lines (SIC: 1623)

TRANSFER AGENT(S): First Union National Bank, Charlotte, NC

NYSE SYMBOL DYN
Rec. Pr. 49.30 (5/31/01)

DYNEGY INC.

YIELD 0.6%
P/E RATIO 33.5

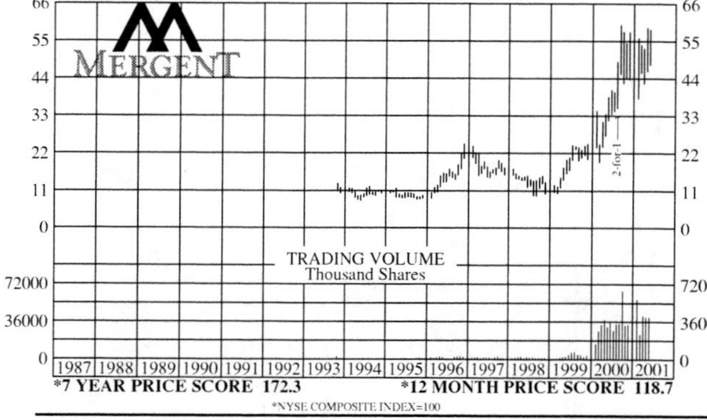

INTERIM EARNINGS (Per Share):

Qtr.	3/31	6/30	9/30	12/31
1996	0.13	0.06	0.08	0.14
1997	0.02	0.10	0.08	d0.55
1998	0.04	0.07	0.14	0.09
1999	0.09	0.09	0.15	0.13
2000	0.23	0.19	0.73	0.32

INTERIM DIVIDENDS (Per Share):

Amt.	Decl.	Ex.	Rec.	Pay.
2-for-1	7/25/00	8/22/00	8/07/00	8/21/00
0.075Q	7/25/00	8/29/00	8/31/00	9/15/00
0.075Q	11/15/00	11/29/00	12/01/00	12/15/00
0.075Q	1/19/01	2/27/01	3/01/01	3/15/01
0.075Q	3/16/01	5/29/01	5/31/01	6/15/01

Indicated div.: $0.30

CAPITALIZATION (12/31/00):

	($000)	(%)
Long-Term Debt	2,828,000	31.9
Deferred Income Tax	1,426,000	16.1
Minority Interest	1,018,000	11.5
Common & Surplus	3,598,000	40.6
Total	8,870,000	100.0

RECENT DEVELOPMENTS: For the year ended 12/31/00, net income more than tripled to $500.5 million versus $151.8 million in the prior year. Results excluded a non-recurring pre-tax gain of $83.3 million on the disposition of DYN's non-operating equity interest in Accord Energy Ltd., a U.K. gas marketing joint venture. Operating revenues soared 90.8% to $29.44 billion from $15.43 billion the year before.

PROSPECTS: On 1/31/01, DYN completed the acquisition of 1,700 megawatts of power generation facilities in the Northeast. The acquisition should significantly strengthen DYN's competitive position in the Northeast, enabling it to meet long-term demands of wholesale energy market throught the area. Going forward, the Company should continue to benefit from its solid performance across all its energy business segments.

BUSINESS

DYNEGY INC. (formerly NGC Corporation) was formed by the acquisition of Natural Gas Clearinghouse by Trident. The Company is a provider of energy products and services in North America, the United Kingdom and in continental Europe. Products marketed by the Company's wholesale marketing operations include natural gas, electricity, coal, emissions, natural gas liquids, crude oil, liquid petroleum gas and related services. The Company's wholesale marketing operations are supported by ownership or control of an extensive asset base and transportation network that includes unregulated power generation, gas and liquids storage capacity, gas, power and liquids transportation capacity and gas gathering, processing and fractionation assets. As of 12/31/00, revenues were derived: 79.6% energy convergence, and 20.4% midstream. On 2/1/00, the Company completed its acquisition of Illinova Corporation.

REVENUES

(12/31/00)	($000)	(%)
DMT	22,967,000	78.0
DMS	7,338,000	24.9
Transmission & Distrib.	1,608,000	5.4
Elimination	(2,470,000)	(8.3)
Total	29,443,000	100.0

ANNUAL FINANCIAL DATA

	12/31/00	12/31/99	12/31/98	[1] 12/31/97	12/31/96	[3] 12/31/95	12/31/94
Earnings Per Share	[5] 1.48	0.46	0.33	[2] d0.34	[2] 0.42	[4] 0.20	[2] 0.05
Cash Flow Per Share	2.72	0.78	0.63	0.85	0.67	0.59	0.69
Tang. Book Val. Per Share	6.50	3.95	3.46	3.12	3.47	2.50	4.14
Dividends Per Share	0.25	...	...	...	...	...	...
Dividend Payout %	16.7	...	...	...	...	...	...
INCOME STATEMENT (IN MILLIONS):							
Total Revenues	29,445.0	15,430.0	14,258.0	13,378.4	7,260.2	3,665.9	584.0
Costs & Expenses	28,347.0	15,108.0	14,037.9	13,149.7	6,994.1	3,542.6	507.6
Depreciation & Amort.	357.0	108.3	100.0	372.1	68.3	41.7	37.0
Operating Income	741.0	213.7	120.1	d143.4	197.8	81.7	39.5
Net Interest Inc./(Exp.)	d251.0	d78.2	d75.0	d63.5	d46.2	d32.4	d34.2
Income Before Income Taxes	762.0	226.5	158.7	d149.9	169.6	65.2	5.5
Income Taxes	261.0	74.7	50.3	62.2	56.3	cr27.5	2.7
Equity Earnings/Minority Int.	176.0	63.2	74.4	49.1	28.1	21.1	...
Net Income	[5] 501.0	151.8	108.4	[2] d87.7	[2] 113.3	[4] 92.7	[2] 2.8
Cash Flow	858.0	260.2	208.4	284.5	181.6	134.4	39.8
Average Shs. Outstg. (000)	315,000	333,950	329,210	334,018	272,198	226,352	57,502
BALANCE SHEET (IN MILLIONS):							
Cash & Cash Equivalents	86.0	45.2	28.4	23.0	50.2	16.3	1.6
Total Current Assets	10,150.0	2,805.1	2,117.2	2,018.8	1,936.7	762.9	118.1
Net Property	6,707.0	2,017.9	1,932.1	1,521.6	1,691.4	948.5	604.1
Total Assets	21,406.0	6,525.2	5,264.2	4,516.9	4,186.8	1,875.3	756.6
Total Current Liabilities	9,405.0	2,538.5	2,026.3	1,753.1	1,549.0	705.7	102.5
Long-Term Obligations	2,828.0	1,299.3	1,046.9	1,002.1	988.6	522.8	371.5
Net Stockholders' Equity	3,598.0	1,309.5	1,128.1	1,019.1	1,116.7	552.4	235.1
Net Working Capital	745.0	266.6	90.9	265.7	387.7	57.3	15.6
Year-end Shs. Outstg. (000)	322,652	312,597	304,194	302,284	299,694	220,986	56,756
STATISTICAL RECORD:							
Operating Profit Margin %	2.5	1.4	0.8	...	2.7	2.2	6.8
Net Profit Margin %	1.7	1.0	0.8	...	1.6	2.5	0.5
Return on Equity %	13.9	11.6	9.6	...	10.1	16.8	1.2
Return on Assets %	2.3	2.3	2.1	...	2.7	4.9	0.4
Debt/Total Assets %	13.2	19.9	19.9	22.2	23.6	27.9	49.1
Price Range	59.88-19.25	24.75-10.13	17.50-9.38	24.13-14.75	24.75-8.63	11.75-8.38	12.25-8.00
P/E Ratio	40.5-13.0	54.4-22.2	53.0-28.4	...	59.6-20.8	58.7-41.9	244.5-159.7
Average Yield %	0.6	...	...	...	...	...	...

Statistics are as originally reported. Adj. for 2-for-1 split, 8/22/00. [1] Refls. the acq. of Destec Energy. [2] Incls. non-recurr. chrgs. totaling 12/31/97: $289.8 mill.; 12/31/96: $2.5 mill.; pre-tax gain 12/31/94: $2.7 mill. [3] Refls. acq. of Natural Gas Clearinghouse. [4] Incls. net deferred tax benefit of $45.7 mill. & non-recurr. chrg. of $1.1 mill. [5] Excls. non-recurr. pre-tax gain of $83.3 mill.

OFFICERS:
C. L. Watson, Chmn., C.E.O.
S. W. Bergstrom, Pres., C.O.O.
J. U. Clarke, Exec. V.P., C.F.O.

INVESTOR CONTACT: Investors Relations, (713) 507-6466

PRINCIPAL OFFICE: 1000 Louisiana, Suite 5800, Houston, TX 77002

TELEPHONE NUMBER: (713) 507-6400
FAX: (713) 507-6888
WEB: www.dynegy.com

NO. OF EMPLOYEES: 5,778 (approx.)

SHAREHOLDERS: 21,968 (record)

ANNUAL MEETING: In May

INCORPORATED: DE; reincorp., IL, 2000

INSTITUTIONAL HOLDINGS:
No. of Institutions: 361
Shares Held: 183,581,653
% Held: 56.3

INDUSTRY: Crude petroleum and natural gas (SIC: 1311)

TRANSFER AGENT(S): Mellon Investor Services, L.L.C. Ridgefield Park, NJ

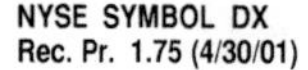

NYSE SYMBOL DX
Rec. Pr. 1.75 (4/30/01)

DYNEX CAPITAL, INC.

YIELD . . .
P/E RATIO . . .

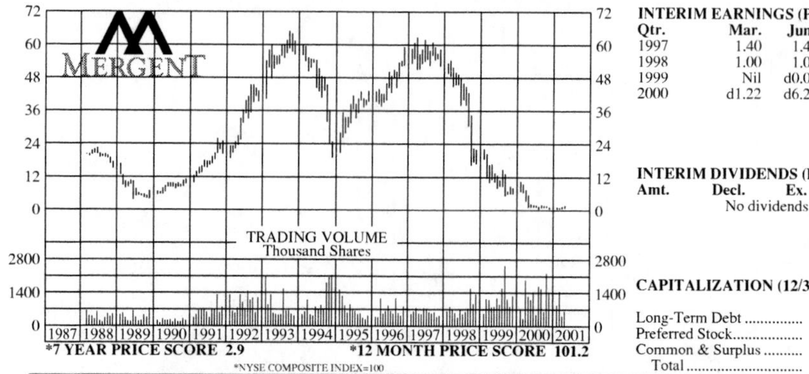

*7 YEAR PRICE SCORE 2.9 *12 MONTH PRICE SCORE 101.2

*NYSE COMPOSITE INDEX=100

INTERIM EARNINGS (Per Share):

Qtr.	Mar.	June	Sept.	Dec.
1997	1.40	1.40	1.44	1.28
1998	1.00	1.08	0.28	d0.20
1999	Nil	d0.04	d0.25	d7.30
2000	d1.22	d6.28	d0.35	d1.30

INTERIM DIVIDENDS (Per Share):

Amt.	Decl.	Ex.	Rec.	Pay.

No dividends paid.

CAPITALIZATION (12/31/00):

	($000)	(%)
Long-Term Debt	2,990,896	95.0
Preferred Stock	127,407	4.0
Common & Surplus	29,724	0.9
Total	3,148,027	100.0

RECENT DEVELOPMENTS: For the year ended 12/31/00, the Company reported a net loss of $91.9 million compared with loss of $73.6 million, before an extraordinary loss of $1.5 million, in the previous year. Results included losses on sales, write-downs, and impairment charges of $78.5 million and $96.7 million in 2000 and 1999, respectively. Total interest income fell 14.7% to $291.2 million versus $341.4 million the year before. Net interest margin amounted to a loss of $3.1 million versus a gain of $48.0 million in 1999.

PROSPECTS: On 1/26/01, the Company announced that it has exercised its right to terminate the agreement and plan of merger entered into by DX and California Investment Fund, LLC on 11/7/00, due to the failure to comply with certain terms of the agreement. In addition, DX has made claim under the escrow agreement between the parties for the escrow amount. Going forward, the Company may continue to experience a decline in net interest margin. However, the Company is taking steps to reduce general and administrative expenses.

BUSINESS

DYNEX CAPITAL, INC. (formerly Resource Mortgage Capital, Inc.) is a self-managed real estate investment trust that invests in a portfolio of residential mortgage securities. The Company also has mortgage conduit operations, which involve the purchase and securitization of mortgage loans. The primary strategy is to use the conduit operation to create investments for a portfolio that generally has higher yields than could be obtained through purchase in the market. As of 12/31/00, collateral for collateralized bonds accounted for 93% of portfolio assets; loans held for securitization, 4%; mortgage securities, 1% and other, 2%.

ANNUAL FINANCIAL DATA

	12/31/00	12/31/99	12/31/98	12/31/97	12/31/96	12/31/95	12/31/94
Earnings Per Share	**3 d9.15**	**d7.53**	**2 0.64**	**5.48**	**1 6.16**	**3.66**	**5.28**
Tang. Book Val. Per Share	**2.60**	**17.27**	**28.28**	**38.14**	**35.25**	**26.53**	**19.67**
INCOME STATEMENT (IN MILLIONS):							
Total Income	291.2	341.4	405.5	336.9	312.1	253.9	227.3
Costs & Expenses	303.4	318.1	370.3	276.8	257.9	229.6	202.1
Income Before Income Taxes	d91.2	d71.7	17.7	74.0	73.0	36.9	52.3
Equity Earnings/Minority Int.	d0.7	d1.9	2.5	. . .	. . .	. . .	. . .
Net Income	3 d91.9	d73.6	2 20.1	74.0	1 73.0	36.9	52.3
Average Shs. Outstg. (000)	11,445	11,484	11,437	12,531	. . .	10,062	9,915
BALANCE SHEET (IN MILLIONS):							
Cash & Cash Equivalents	26.8	48.6	30.1	18.3	11.4	22.2	6.3
Total Real Estate Investments	. . .	4.8	169.4	. . .	. . .	. . .	. . .
Total Assets	3,159.6	4,190.9	5,178.8	5,378.2	3,987.5	3,490.0	3,600.6
Long-Term Obligations	2,990.9	3,819.5	4,698.0	4,777.8	2,519.7	949.1	424.8
Total Liabilities	3,002.5	3,865.8	4,726.0	4,817.3	3,483.8	3,135.2	3,403.1
Net Stockholders' Equity	157.1	325.1	452.8	560.9	503.6	354.8	197.5
Year-end Shs. Outstg. (000)	11,444	11,444	11,507	11,287	10,327	10,100	10,039
STATISTICAL RECORD:							
Net Inc.+Depr./Assets %	. . .	. . .	0.4	1.4	1.8	1.1	1.5
Return on Equity %	. . .	. . .	4.4	13.2	14.5	10.4	26.5
Return on Assets %	. . .	. . .	0.4	1.4	1.8	1.1	1.5
Price Range	10.50-0.44	22.25-5.25	54.50-16.25	62.75-51.00	59.25-37.50	43.25-20.75	60.00-19.00
P/E Ratio	. . .	. . .	85.1-25.4	11.5-9.3	9.6-6.1	11.8-5.7	11.4-3.6

Statistics are as originally reported. Adj. for stk. splits: 2-for-1, 5/97 & 1-for-4 rev. spl., 8/99 1 Incl. non-recurr. chrg. $18.9 mill. 2 Incl. $1.7 mill. loss fr. sale of investments and trading activities. 3 Incl. $13.4 mill. loss on sale of investments.

OFFICERS:
T. H. Potts, Pres.
L. K. Geurin, Exec. V.P., C.F.O.
S. J. Benedetti, V.P., Treas.

INVESTOR CONTACT: Investor Relations, (804) 217-5800

PRINCIPAL OFFICE: 10900 Nuckols Road, 3rd Floor Glen Allen, VA 23060

TELEPHONE NUMBER: (804) 217-5800
FAX: (804) 217-5861
WEB: www.dynexcapital.com

NO. OF EMPLOYEES: 70

SHAREHOLDERS: 3,662 (approx.)

ANNUAL MEETING: In June

INCORPORATED: VA, Dec., 1987

INSTITUTIONAL HOLDINGS:
No. of Institutions: 16
Shares Held: 1,172,685
% Held: 10.2

INDUSTRY: Real estate investment trusts (SIC: 6798)

TRANSFER AGENT(S): First Union National Bank, Charlotte, NC

NYSE SYMBOL ET
Rec. Pr. 7.50 (5/31/01)

E*TRADE GROUP, INC.

YIELD ...
P/E RATIO 50.0

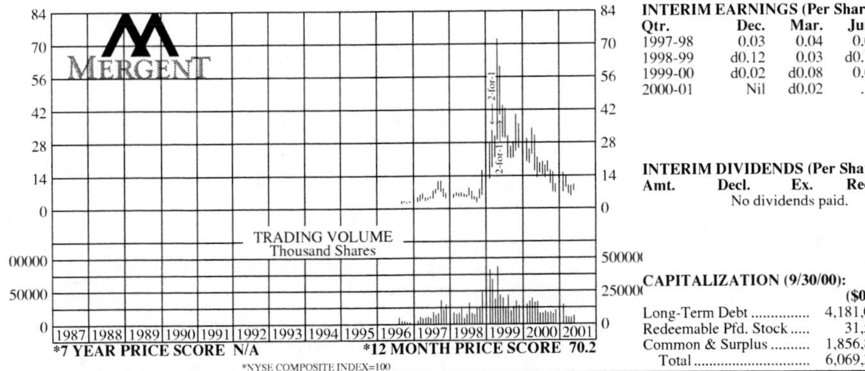

INTERIM EARNINGS (Per Share):

Qtr.	Dec.	Mar.	June	Sept.
1997-98	0.03	0.04	0.04	d0.09
1998-99	d0.12	0.03	d0.10	d0.11
1999-00	d0.02	d0.08	0.02	0.15
2000-01	Nil	d0.02	...	...

INTERIM DIVIDENDS (Per Share):

Amt.	Decl.	Ex.	Rec.	Pay.

No dividends paid.

CAPITALIZATION (9/30/00):

	($000)	(%)
Long-Term Debt	4,181,000	68.9
Redeemable Pfd. Stock	31,531	0.5
Common & Surplus	1,856,833	30.6
Total	6,069,364	100.0

RECENT DEVELOPMENTS: For the quarter ended 3/31/01, ET reported a loss of $7.2 million, before an extraordinary loss of $2.0 million, versus a net loss of $25.5 million in the previous year. Earnings for the current quarter included pre-tax merger expenses of $24.6 million. Net revenues declined 20.9% to $329.6 million from $416.7 million the year before. ET produced operating income of $2.9 million versus an operating loss of $25.3 million a year earlier, reflecting a 48.1% reduction in selling and marketing expenses to $93.7 million.

PROSPECTS: The Company continues to expand globally with the launch of E*TRADE Hong Kong and E*TRADE Israel. This marks ET's fourth E*TRADE branded Web site in the Asia-Pacific region and its first in the Middle East. Separately, ET opened E*TRADE Center, its flagship 30,000 square foot financial superstore, in New York City. Meanwhile, ET will acquire Web Street, Inc., an on-line brokerage firm, which is expected to add incremental annual revenues of about $25.0 million to ET's results.

BUSINESS

E*TRADE GROUP, INC. provides on-line personal financial services, including value-added investing, banking, research and educational tools, customer service and a proprietary Stateless Architecture® infrastructure. The Company offers automated order placement and execution, financial products and services that can be personalized, including portfolio tracking, charting and quote applications, "real-time" market commentary and analysis, news, professional research reports and other information services. ET's products also include mutual funds, proprietary mutual funds, bond trading, banking, automated teller machine services, and access to participate in initial public offerings. ET provides these services 24 hours a day, 7 days a week by means of the Internet, automated telephone service, direct modem access, Internet-enabled wireless devices, and live telephone support. On 1/12/00, ET acquired Telebanc Financial Corp., a pure-play Internet bank, for about $1.20 billion. On 5/8/00, ET acquired Card Capture Services, Inc., an independent provider of over 8,800 ATMs located in 48 states and three countries.

ANNUAL FINANCIAL DATA

	9/30/00	9/30/99	9/30/98	9/30/97	9/30/96	9/30/95	9/30/94
Earnings Per Share	**0.06**	**[1] d0.23**	**...**	**0.10**	**d0.01**	**0.03**	**0.01**
Cash Flow Per Share	**0.37**	**d0.09**	**0.07**	**0.13**	**...**	**0.03**	**0.01**
Tang. Book Val. Per Share	**4.51**	**3.81**	**3.14**	**1.82**	**0.59**	**0.19**	**...**
INCOME STATEMENT (IN MILLIONS):							
Total Revenues	1,368.3	621.4	245.3	142.7	51.6	23.3	10.9
Costs & Expenses	1,351.0	721.4	234.4	115.8	52.1	18.8	10.6
Depreciation & Amort.	97.6	32.4	12.5	3.6	0.9	0.2	0.1
Operating Income	d80.3	d132.4	d1.7	23.3	d1.4	4.3	0.2
Net Interest Inc./(Exp.)	d12.3	...	...	...	...	...	...
Income Before Income Taxes	104.4	d91.5	d1.7	23.3	d1.4	4.3	0.2
Income Taxes	85.5	cr37.1	cr1.0	9.4	cr0.6	1.7	cr0.5
Net Income	19.2	[1] d54.4	d0.7	13.9	d0.8	2.6	0.8
Cash Flow	116.8	d22.1	11.8	17.5	...	2.8	0.9
Average Shs. Outstg. (000)	319,336	235,926	169,140	138,296	114,256	105,924	104,744
BALANCE SHEET (IN MILLIONS):							
Cash & Cash Equivalents	4,489.9	378.4	529.4	228.2	85.1	9.6	0.7
Total Current Assets	15,205.1	3,332.9	1,851.2	957.5	280.6	12.0	1.9
Net Property	334.3	155.8	48.1	18.8	9.2	1.5	0.3
Total Assets	17,317.4	3,927.0	1,968.9	989.9	294.9	14.2	2.2
Total Current Liabilities	10,777.3	2,990.1	1,258.7	699.2	225.6	3.0	2.2
Long-Term Obligations	4,181.0	...	...	9.4	...	...	0.1
Net Stockholders' Equity	1,856.8	913.7	710.2	281.3	69.3	11.1	d0.1
Net Working Capital	4,427.8	342.9	592.6	258.3	55.0	9.1	d0.3
Year-end Shs. Outstg. (000)	304,505	239,823	226,413	154,629	118,157	59,564	59,816
STATISTICAL RECORD:							
Operating Profit Margin %	...	...	...	16.3	...	18.5	2.2
Net Profit Margin %	1.4	...	...	9.7	...	11.1	7.2
Return on Equity %	1.0	...	...	4.9	...	23.2	...
Return on Assets %	0.1	...	...	1.4	...	18.2	36.3
Debt/Total Assets %	24.1	...	...	0.9	...	0.3	3.0
Price Range	34.25-6.66	72.25-12.74	16.25-2.50	11.94-2.75	3.47-2.06	...	...
P/E Ratio	569.9-110.7	...	...	119.3-27.5	...	...	...

Statistics are as originally reported. Total revenues include interest income, net of interest expense; adj. for stk. splits: 2-for-1, 5/21/99; 1/29/99 [1] Incl. non-recurr. credit $34.6 mill.

OFFICERS:
C. M. Cotsakos, Chmn., C.E.O.
J. Gramaglia, Pres., C.O.O.
L. C. Purkis, C.F.O.

INVESTOR CONTACT: Erica Gessert, Sr. Mgr., Inv. Rel., (650) 331-5893

PRINCIPAL OFFICE: 4500 Bohannon Drive, Menlo Park, CA 94025

TELEPHONE NUMBER: (650) 331-6000
FAX: (650) 842-2552
WEB: www.etrade.com
NO. OF EMPLOYEES: 3,778
SHAREHOLDERS: 2,118
ANNUAL MEETING: In Dec.
INCORPORATED: CA, 1982; reincorp., DE, July, 1996

INSTITUTIONAL HOLDINGS:
No. of Institutions: 180
Shares Held: 121,140,035
% Held: 37.9

INDUSTRY: Security brokers and dealers (SIC: 6211)

TRANSFER AGENT(S): American Stock Transfer & Trust Company, New York, NY

NYSE SYMBOL EGR
Rec. Pr. 22.50 (4/30/01)

EARTHGRAINS, CO. (THE)

YIELD 1.1%
P/E RATIO 66.2

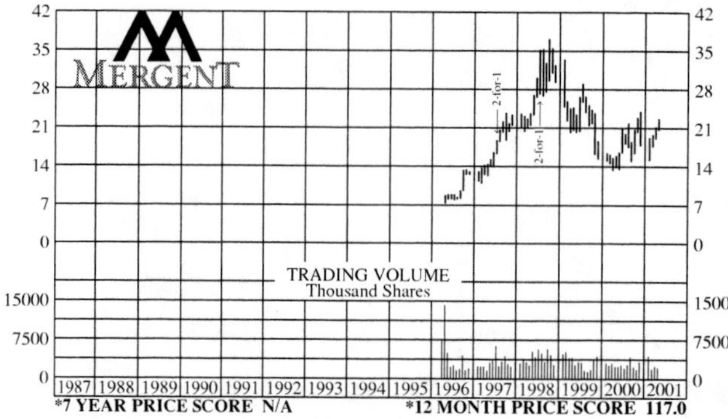

*7 YEAR PRICE SCORE N/A *12 MONTH PRICE SCORE 117.0
*NYSE COMPOSITE INDEX=100

INTERIM EARNINGS (Per Share):

Qtr.	June	Sept.	Dec.	Mar.
1997-98	0.17	0.22	0.33	0.17
1998-99	0.26	0.23	0.40	Nil
1999-00	0.30	0.37	0.45	0.18
2000-01	0.27	0.21	d0.32	...

INTERIM DIVIDENDS (Per Share):

Amt.	Decl.	Ex.	Rec.	Pay.
0.05Q	5/01/00	5/10/00	5/12/00	5/31/00
0.06Q	7/14/00	8/09/00	8/11/00	8/31/00
0.06Q	9/29/00	11/15/00	11/17/00	11/30/00
0.06Q	1/19/01	2/14/01	2/16/01	2/28/01
0.06Q	4/27/01	5/16/01	5/18/01	5/31/01

Indicated div.: $0.24

CAPITALIZATION (3/28/00):

	($000)	(%)
Long-Term Debt	562,300	41.8
Deferred Income Tax	117,600	8.7
Minority Interest	10,000	0.7
Common & Surplus	654,900	48.7
Total	1,344,800	100.0

RECENT DEVELOPMENTS: For the quarter ended 1/2/01, net loss totaled $13.0 million compared with net income of $18.7 million in previous year. Net sales improved 21.7% to $782.1 million versus $642.8 million in the prior year. Gross profit as a percentages of net sales was 44.1% compared with 44.6% in the preceding year. Operating income declined to $3.6 million from $36.7 million in the comparable period. Sales of bakery products increased 26.3% to $676.3 million, while sales of refrigerated dough products fell slightly to $105.8 million.

PROSPECTS: EGR will continue its integration of Metz Baking into its businesses. The Company expects all the bakeries acquired with Metz will be converted to its business systems by October 2001. In fiscal 2002, EGR expects to achieve a cumulative 60.0% to 70.0% of the integration's $30.0 million to $35.0 million in annual cost-reduction and improvement synergies. Meanwhile, EGR will continue to focus on rolling out new products, identifying new business, and enhancing price and product mix, while improving selling and manufacturing efficiencies.

BUSINESS

EARTHGRAINS, CO. (THE) is a manufacturer, distributor and consumer marketer of packaged fresh bread and baked goods and refrigerated dough products. The Company's operations are divided into two principal businesses: bakery products and refrigerated dough products. EGR's bakery products business manufactures and distributes fresh-baked goods such as baked breads, buns, rolls, bagels, cookies, snack cakes and other sweet goods in the South, Midwest, Southwest and West in the U.S. and fresh-baked sliced bread, buns, snack cakes, sweet buns and brioche in Spain and Portugal. EGR's refrigerated dough products business manufactures many different canned refrigerated dough products in the United States including biscuits, specialty biscuits, dinner rolls, danishes, cookie dough, crescent rolls, breadsticks, cinnamon rolls, pizza crusts, pie crusts and toaster pastries. EGR also manufactures and sells refrigerated dough products in Europe, primarily in France and Germany. EGR's brand names include EARTH GRAINS, IRON KIDS, GRANT'S FARM, COLONIAL, RAINBO, SAN LUIS SOURDOUGH, MASTER, and OLD HOME. In March 1996, the Company was spun off from Anheuser-Busch Companies, Inc. On 3/18/00, EGR acquired Metz Holdings, Inc.

ANNUAL FINANCIAL DATA

	3/28/00	3/30/99	3/31/98
Earnings Per Share	**1.30**	**0.89**	**[1] 0.89**
Cash Flow Per Share	**4.07**	**3.29**	**2.88**
Tang. Book Val. Per Share	**...**	**5.72**	**...**
Dividends Per Share	**0.18**	**0.13**	**0.07**
Dividend Payout %	**13.8**	**14.6**	**8.4**
INCOME STATEMENT (IN MILLIONS):			
Total Revenues	2,039.3	1,925.2	1,719.0
Costs & Expenses	1,813.0	1,749.6	1,567.2
Depreciation & Amort.	116.2	102.4	84.6
Operating Income	110.1	73.2	67.2
Net Interest Inc./(Exp.)	d26.5	d19.5	d8.2
Income Before Income Taxes	87.9	59.9	62.0
Income Taxes	32.8	21.9	24.2
Equity Earnings/Minority Int.	d0.6	...	...
Net Income	54.5	38.0	[1] 37.8
Cash Flow	170.7	140.4	122.4
Average Shs. Outstg. (000)	41,900	42,700	42,500
BALANCE SHEET (IN MILLIONS):			
Cash & Cash Equivalents	19.9	53.1	...
Total Current Assets	481.3	384.7	...
Net Property	915.8	761.1	...
Total Assets	2,339.5	1,591.6	...
Total Current Liabilities	828.0	282.6	...
Long-Term Obligations	562.3	369.3	...
Net Stockholders' Equity	654.9	639.4	...
Net Working Capital	d346.7	102.1	...
Year-end Shs. Outstg. (000)	42,320	41,852	...
STATISTICAL RECORD:			
Operating Profit Margin %	5.4	3.8	3.9
Net Profit Margin %	2.7	2.0	2.2
Return on Equity %	8.3	5.9	...
Return on Assets %	2.3	2.4	...
Debt/Total Assets %	24.0	23.2	...
Price Range	33.50-15.31	37.25-20.25	23.75-10.94
P/E Ratio	25.8-11.8	41.8-22.8	26.7-12.3
Average Yield %	0.7	0.5	0.4

Statistics are as originally reported. Adj. for 2-for-1 stk. spl., 7/98 & 7/97 [1] Bef. acctg. change chrg., $1.8 mill.

OFFICERS:
B. H. Beracha, Chmn., C.E.O.
M. H. Krieger, V.P., C.F.O.
M. A. Salamone, V.P., Treas.

PRINCIPAL OFFICE: 8400 Maryland Ave., St. Louis, MO 63105

TELEPHONE NUMBER: (314) 259-7000
FAX: (314) 259-7052
WEB: www.earthgrains.com

NO. OF EMPLOYEES: 26,000 (approx.)
SHAREHOLDERS: 16,400 (approx.)
ANNUAL MEETING: In July
INCORPORATED: DE, 1925

INSTITUTIONAL HOLDINGS:
No. of Institutions: 141
Shares Held: 30,366,905
% Held: 71.5

INDUSTRY: Bread, cake, and related products (SIC: 2051)

TRANSFER AGENT(S): Mellon Investor Services, Ridgefield Park, NJ

NYSE SYMBOL EMN
Rec. Pr. 54.00 (4/30/01)

EASTMAN CHEMICAL COMPANY

YIELD 3.3%
P/E RATIO 13.7

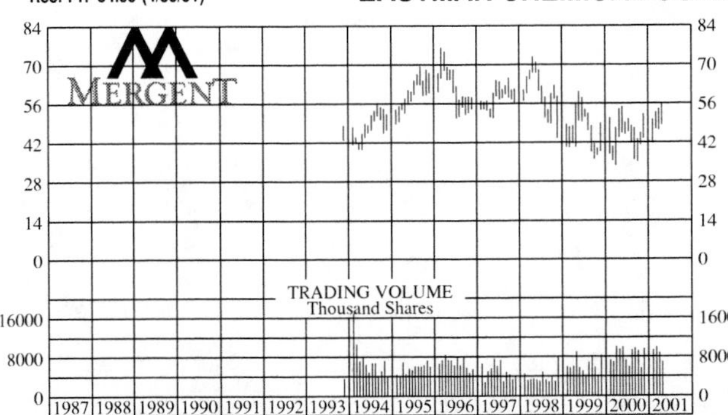

*7 YEAR PRICE SCORE 62.9 *12 MONTH PRICE SCORE 116.4
*NYSE COMPOSITE INDEX=100

INTERIM EARNINGS (Per Share):

Qtr.	Mar.	June	Sept.	Dec.
1997	0.92	1.14	1.22	0.35
1998	0.94	1.21	1.00	d0.02
1999	0.31	0.54	0.42	d0.67
2000	0.88	1.12	1.27	0.68

INTERIM DIVIDENDS (Per Share):

Amt.	Decl.	Ex.	Rec.	Pay.
0.44Q	8/03/00	9/13/00	9/15/00	10/02/00
0.44Q	12/07/00	12/13/00	12/15/00	1/02/01
0.44Q	3/01/01	3/13/01	3/15/01	4/02/01
0.44Q	5/03/01	6/13/01	6/15/01	7/02/01

Indicated div.: $1.76 (Div. Reinv. Plan)

CAPITALIZATION (12/31/00):

	($000)	(%)
Long-Term Debt	1,914,000	44.2
Deferred Income Tax	607,000	14.0
Common & Surplus	1,812,000	41.8
Total	4,333,000	100.0

RECENT DEVELOPMENTS: For the year ended 12/31/00, net earnings soared to $303.0 million versus $48.0 million in 1999. Results for 2000 included a $9.0 million charge for write-off of acquired in-process research and development related to the acquisition of McWhorter Technologies, Inc. and a $38.0 million gain from the initial public offering of an equity investment. Results for 1999 included non-recurring charges amounting to $78.0 million. Sales were $5.29 billion, up 15.3% from $4.59 billion in the prior year.

PROSPECTS: The Company announced plans to become two independent public companies, a specialty chemicals and plastics company and a PET plastics and acetate fibers company. EMN plans to launch the two new companies through a spin-off in the form of a tax-free stock dividend by the end of the fourth quarter of 2001. The transaction is subject to regulatory approvals. Separately, EMN expects 2001 to be another challenging year with higher feedstock costs and difficult economic conditions.

BUSINESS

EASTMAN CHEMICAL COMPANY manufactures and sells a broad range of plastics, chemicals and fibers. The major products in the specialty and performance segment include specialty plastics, coatings and paint raw materials, fine chemicals, performance chemicals, and fibers. The core plastics segment includes EASTPAK PET (polyethlene terephthalate) polyester packaging plastic and TENITE polyethylene, as well as cellulose acetate and polyesters. The chemical intermediates segment contains industrial intermediate chemicals that are produced based on EMN's oxo chemistry technology and chemicals-from-coal technology. Sales (and operating income) for 2000 were derived: chemicals, 47.4% (41.3%); and polymers, 52.6% (58.7%).

ANNUAL FINANCIAL DATA

	12/31/00	12/31/99	12/31/98	12/31/97	12/31/96	12/31/95	12/31/94
Earnings Per Share	**4 3.94**	**3 0.61**	**2 3.13**	**1 3.63**	**4.80**	**6.78**	**4.05**
Cash Flow Per Share	**9.36**	**5.50**	**7.55**	**7.78**	...	...	...
Tang. Book Val. Per Share	**15.64**	**16.81**	**24.42**	**22.47**	**21.01**	**18.41**	**15.60**
Dividends Per Share	**1.76**	**1.76**	**1.76**	**1.76**	**1.70**	**1.62**	**1.20**
Dividend Payout %	**44.7**	**288.5**	**56.2**	**48.5**	**35.4**	**23.9**	**29.6**
INCOME STATEMENT (IN MILLIONS):							
Total Revenues	5,292.0	4,590.0	4,481.0	4,678.0	4,782.0	5,040.0	4,329.0
Costs & Expenses	4,312.0	4,005.0	3,696.0	3,845.0	3,805.0	3,768.0	3,364.0
Depreciation & Amort.	418.0	383.0	351.0	327.0	314.0	308.0	329.0
Operating Income	562.0	202.0	434.0	506.0	663.0	964.0	636.0
Net Interest Inc./(Exp.)	d135.0	d126.0	d96.0	d87.0	d67.0	d79.0	d87.0
Income Before Income Taxes	452.0	72.0	360.0	446.0	607.0	899.0	550.0
Income Taxes	149.0	24.0	111.0	160.0	227.0	340.0	214.0
Net Income	4 303.0	3 48.0	2 249.0	1 286.0	380.0	559.0	336.0
Cash Flow	721.0	431.0	600.0	613.0	694.0	867.0	665.0
Average Shs. Outstg. (000)	77,000	78,400	79,500	78,800	...	...	...
BALANCE SHEET (IN MILLIONS):							
Cash & Cash Equivalents	101.0	186.0	29.0	29.0	24.0	100.0	90.0
Total Current Assets	1,523.0	1,489.0	1,415.0	1,490.0	1,345.0	1,469.0	1,228.0
Net Property	3,925.0	3,950.0	4,060.0	3,881.0	3,520.0	3,049.0	2,906.0
Total Assets	6,550.0	6,303.0	5,876.0	5,778.0	5,266.0	4,854.0	4,375.0
Total Current Liabilities	1,258.0	1,608.0	985.0	954.0	787.0	873.0	793.0
Long-Term Obligations	1,914.0	1,506.0	1,649.0	1,714.0	1,523.0	1,217.0	1,195.0
Net Stockholders' Equity	1,812.0	1,759.0	1,934.0	1,753.0	1,639.0	1,528.0	1,295.0
Net Working Capital	265.0	d119.0	430.0	536.0	558.0	596.0	435.0
Year-end Shs. Outstg. (000)	76,743	78,090	79,200	78,000	78,000	83,000	83,000
STATISTICAL RECORD:							
Operating Profit Margin %	10.6	4.4	9.7	10.8	13.9	19.1	14.7
Net Profit Margin %	5.7	1.0	5.6	6.1	7.9	11.1	7.8
Return on Equity %	16.7	2.7	12.9	16.3	23.2	36.6	25.9
Return on Assets %	4.6	0.8	4.2	4.9	7.2	11.5	7.7
Debt/Total Assets %	29.2	23.9	28.1	29.7	28.9	25.1	27.3
Price Range	54.75-33.63	60.31-36.00	72.94-43.50	65.38-50.75	76.25-50.75	69.50-48.50	56.00-39.50
P/E Ratio	13.9-8.5	98.9-59.0	23.3-13.9	18.0-14.0	15.9-10.6	10.3-7.2	13.8-9.8
Average Yield %	4.0	3.7	3.0	3.0	2.7	2.7	2.5

Statistics are as originally reported. 1 Incl. $62.0 mill. pre-tax chg. for early retirements. 2 Incl. $40.0 mill. non-recur. pre-tax chgs. & $15.0 mill. gain fr. tax settlement. 3 Incl. $123.0 mill. pre-tax non-recur. chg. and $29.0 mill. pre-tax gain & excl. $15.0 mill. fr. disc. ops. 4 Incl. $9.0 mill. in-process R&D write-off & $38.0 mill. gain fr. sale of equity invest.

OFFICERS:
E. W. Deavenport Jr., Chmn., C.E.O.
J. P. Rogers, Sr. V.P., C.F.O.
T. K. Lee, V.P., Sec., Gen. Couns.

INVESTOR CONTACT: Mary Ann Arico, Inv. Rel., (423) 229-8692

PRINCIPAL OFFICE: 100 N. Eastman Road, Kingsport, TN 37660

TELEPHONE NUMBER: (423) 229-2000
FAX: (423) 224-0208
WEB: www.eastman.com

NO. OF EMPLOYEES: 14,600 (approx.)

SHAREHOLDERS: 66,176 (record)

ANNUAL MEETING: In May

INCORPORATED: DE, July, 1993

INSTITUTIONAL HOLDINGS:
No. of Institutions: 265
Shares Held: 65,866,790
% Held: 85.8

INDUSTRY: Plastics materials and resins (SIC: 2821)

TRANSFER AGENT(S): First Chicago Trust Company of New York, Jersey City, NJ

NYSE SYMBOL EK
Rec. Pr. 42.23 (4/30/01)

EASTMAN KODAK COMPANY

YIELD 4.2%
P/E RATIO 9.2

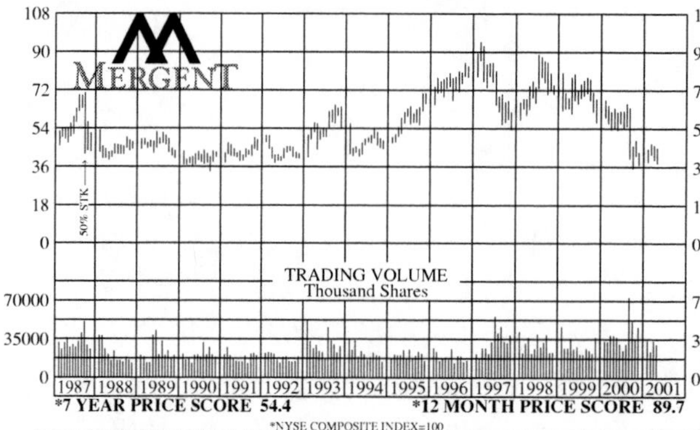

***7 YEAR PRICE SCORE 54.4** ***12 MONTH PRICE SCORE 89.7**

*NYSE COMPOSITE INDEX=100

INTERIM EARNINGS (Per Share):

Qtr.	Mar.	June	Sept.	Dec.
1997	0.45	1.12	0.71	d2.29
1998	0.69	1.51	1.21	0.83
1999	0.59	1.52	0.73	1.50
2000	0.93	1.62	1.36	0.66

INTERIM DIVIDENDS (Per Share):

Amt.	Decl.	Ex.	Rec.	Pay.
0.44Q	4/13/00	5/30/00	6/01/00	7/03/00
0.44Q	7/19/00	8/30/00	9/01/00	10/02/00
0.44Q	10/01/00	11/29/00	12/01/00	1/02/01
0.44Q	2/08/01	2/27/01	3/01/01	4/02/01
0.44Q	4/25/01	5/30/01	6/01/01	7/02/01

Indicated div.: $1.76 (Div. Reinv. Plan)

CAPITALIZATION (12/31/00):

	($000)	(%)
Long-Term Debt [4]	1,166,000	25.0
Deferred Income Tax	61,000	1.3
Common & Surplus	3,428,000	73.6
Total	4,655,000	100.0

RECENT DEVELOPMENTS: For the year ended 12/31/00, net income amounted to $1.41 billion, up 1.1% versus $1.39 billion in the prior year. The 2000 results included a pre-tax restructuring gain of $44.0 million. Sales slipped to $13.99 billion compared with $14.09 million in 1999. Gross profit declined 2.1% to $5.98 billion versus $6.10 billion a year earlier. Operating income rose 11.3% to $2.21 billion.

PROSPECTS: In an attempt to increase cash flow and offset the adverse effects associated with the industry-wide slowdown in photographic activity, EK intends to cut capital spending by $200.0 million, reduce inventories by $200.0 million, and significantly reduce stock keeping units. Meanwhile, EK should benefit from the expansion of its imaging product lines, reflecting acquisitions of Lumisys, Inc., and Bell & Howell Company.

BUSINESS

EASTMAN KODAK COMPANY is engaged primarily in developing, manufacturing and marketing consumer, professional, health and other imaging products. The consumer imaging segment supplies films, photographic papers, processing services, photofinishing equipment, photographic chemicals, cameras and projectors for traditional consumer amateur photography. The professional segment offers films, photographic papers, digital cameras, printers and scanners, chemicals, and services targeted to professional customers. Products in the health imaging segment are used to capture, store, process, print and display images and information for customers in the health care industry. Products in the other imaging segment include motion picture films, audiovisual equipment, certain digital cameras and printers, copiers, microfilm products, applications software, printers, scanners and other business equipment.

BUSINESS LINE ANALYSIS

(12/31/2000)	Rev(%)	Inc(%)
Consumer Imaging	52.9	58.2
Kodak Professional	12.2	7.5
Health Imaging	15.6	23.4
Other Imaging	19.3	10.9
Total	100.0	100.0

ANNUAL FINANCIAL DATA

	12/31/00	12/31/99	12/31/98	12/31/97	12/31/96	12/31/95	12/31/94
Earnings Per Share	**[6] 4.59**	**[5] 4.33**	**[4] 4.24**	**[3] 0.01**	**[2] 3.00**	**3.67**	**[1] 1.65**
Cash Flow Per Share	**7.49**	**7.19**	**6.84**	**2.51**	**5.68**	**6.34**	**4.34**
Tang. Book Val. Per Share	**8.54**	**9.44**	**8.54**	**8.09**	**12.51**	**13.25**	**10.00**
Dividends Per Share	**1.76**	**1.76**	**1.76**	**1.72**	**1.60**	**1.60**	**1.70**
Dividend Payout %	**38.3**	**40.6**	**41.5**	**17,029.7**	**53.3**	**43.6**	**103.0**
INCOME STATEMENT (IN MILLIONS):							
Total Revenues	13,994.0	14,089.0	13,406.0	14,538.0	15,968.0	14,980.0	13,557.0
Costs & Expenses	10,891.0	11,181.0	10,665.0	13,583.0	13,219.0	12,139.0	11,332.0
Depreciation & Amort.	889.0	918.0	853.0	828.0	903.0	916.0	903.0
Operating Income	2,214.0	1,990.0	1,888.0	127.0	1,846.0	1,925.0	1,322.0
Net Interest Inc./(Exp.)	d178.0	d142.0	d110.0	d98.0	d83.0	d78.0	d142.0
Income Before Income Taxes	2,132.0	2,109.0	2,106.0	53.0	1,556.0	1,926.0	1,002.0
Income Taxes	725.0	717.0	716.0	48.0	545.0	674.0	448.0
Equity Earnings/Minority Int.	...	...	...	175.0	276.0	289.0	130.0
Net Income	[6] 1,407.0	[5] 1,392.0	[4] 1,390.0	[3] 5.0	[2] 1,011.0	1,252.0	[1] 554.0
Cash Flow	2,296.0	2,310.0	2,243.0	833.0	1,914.0	2,168.0	1,457.0
Average Shs. Outstg. (000)	306,600	321,500	327,800	331,900	337,000	342,000	336,000
BALANCE SHEET (IN MILLIONS):							
Cash & Cash Equivalents	251.0	393.0	500.0	752.0	1,796.0	1,811.0	2,068.0
Total Current Assets	5,491.0	5,444.0	5,599.0	5,475.0	6,965.0	7,309.0	7,683.0
Net Property	5,919.0	5,947.0	5,914.0	5,509.0	5,422.0	5,377.0	5,292.0
Total Assets	14,212.0	14,370.0	14,733.0	13,145.0	14,438.0	14,477.0	14,968.0
Total Current Liabilities	6,215.0	5,769.0	6,178.0	5,177.0	5,417.0	4,643.0	5,735.0
Long-Term Obligations	1,166.0	936.0	504.0	585.0	559.0	665.0	660.0
Net Stockholders' Equity	3,428.0	3,912.0	3,988.0	3,161.0	4,734.0	5,121.0	4,017.0
Net Working Capital	d724.0	d325.0	d579.0	298.0	1,548.0	2,666.0	1,948.0
Year-end Shs. Outstg. (000)	290,484	310,421	322,798	323,067	332,000	346,000	340,000
STATISTICAL RECORD:							
Operating Profit Margin %	15.8	14.1	14.1	0.9	11.6	12.9	9.8
Net Profit Margin %	10.1	9.9	10.4	...	6.3	8.4	4.1
Return on Equity %	41.0	35.6	34.9	0.2	21.4	24.4	13.8
Return on Assets %	9.9	9.7	9.4	...	7.0	8.6	3.7
Debt/Total Assets %	8.2	6.5	3.4	4.5	3.9	4.6	4.4
Price Range	67.50-35.31	80.38-56.63	88.94-57.94	94.75-53.31	85.00-65.13	70.38-47.13	56.38-40.69
P/E Ratio	14.7-7.7	18.6-13.1	21.0-13.7	9,381.2-5,278.5	28.3-21.7	19.2-12.8	34.2-24.7
Average Yield %	3.4	2.6	2.4	2.3	2.1	2.7	3.5

Statistics are as originally reported. [1] Bef. extra. ch. of $266.0 mill. & dis. ops. of $269.0 mill. [2] Excl. inc. fr. dis. ops. of $277.0 mill. & incl. after-tax restruct. chg. of $256.0 mill. [3] Incl. pre-tax chg. of $186.0 mill., a pre-tax prov. of $46.0 mill. for litig., & an after-tax chg. of $1.29 bill. [4] Incl. chg. of $0.04 per sh., a pre-tax gain of $66.0 mill. & a pre-tax chg. of $42.0 mill. [5] Incl. pre-tax chg. of $350.0 mill. [6] Incl. pre-tax nonrecurr. gain. of $44.0 mill.

OFFICERS:
D. A. Carp, Chmn., Pres., C.E.O.
R. H. Brust, Exec. V.P., C.F.O.
G. P. Van Graafeiland, Sr. V.P., Gen. Couns.

PRINCIPAL OFFICE: 343 State Street, Rochester, NY 14650

TELEPHONE NUMBER: (716) 724-4000
FAX: (716) 724-0663
WEB: www.kodak.com

NO. OF EMPLOYEES: 78,400 (avg.)

SHAREHOLDERS: 113,308

ANNUAL MEETING: In May

INCORPORATED: NJ, Oct., 1901

INSTITUTIONAL HOLDINGS:
No. of Institutions: 460
Shares Held: 194,712,284
% Held: 67.0

INDUSTRY: Photographic equipment and supplies (SIC: 3861)

TRANSFER AGENT(S): BankBoston, NA, Boston, MA

NYSE SYMBOL ETN
Rec. Pr. 73.61 (4/30/01)

EATON CORPORATION

YIELD 2.4%
P/E RATIO 12.6

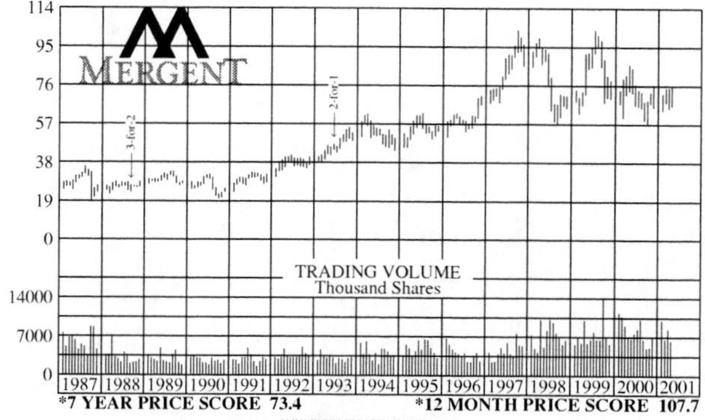

*7 YEAR PRICE SCORE 73.4 *12 MONTH PRICE SCORE 107.7
*NYSE COMPOSITE INDEX=100

INTERIM EARNINGS (Per Share):

Qtr.	Mar.	June	Sept.	Dec.
1996	1.23	1.32	1.11	0.85
1997	1.31	1.34	0.70	2.35
1998	1.42	1.57	0.80	1.01
1999	1.17	1.71	2.46	2.98
2000	1.77	1.96	1.28	0.83

INTERIM DIVIDENDS (Per Share):

Amt.	Decl.	Ex.	Rec.	Pay.
0.44Q	4/26/00	5/04/00	5/08/00	5/25/00
0.44Q	7/26/00	8/03/00	8/07/00	8/25/00
0.44Q	10/25/00	11/02/00	11/06/00	11/24/00
0.44Q	1/24/01	2/01/01	2/05/01	2/23/01
0.44Q	4/25/01	5/03/01	5/07/01	5/25/01

Indicated div.: $1.76 (Div. Reinv. Plan)

CAPITALIZATION (12/31/00):

	($000)	(%)
Long-Term Debt	2,447,000	50.4
Common & Surplus	2,410,000	49.6
Total	4,857,000	100.0

RECENT DEVELOPMENTS: For the year ended 12/31/00, income from continuing operations decreased 39.8% to $363.0 million versus income from continuing operations of $603.0 million in the previous year. The 2000 and 1999 results excluded gains from discontinued operations of $90.0 million and $14.0 million, respectively. Results for 1999 included a pre-tax gain of $340.0 million associated with the sale of a business. Total net rose 3.8% to $8.31 billion from $8.01 billion in 1999.

PROSPECTS: On 4/29/01, the Company completed the sale of its Vehicle Switch/Electronic Division to Delphi Automotive Systems for $300.0 million cash. Separately, ETN was awarded a $500.0 million contract by General Motors to supply powertrain technology. Going forward, ETN should benefit from the performance of its fluid power segment and expects profits in 2001 will also benefit from additional $0.25 per share accretion generated by the completion of its Aeroquip-Vickers integration.

BUSINESS

EATON CORPORATION is a global manufacturer of highly engineered products that serve industrial, vehicle, construction, commercial, aerospace and semiconductor markets. Principal products include hydraulic products and fluid connectors, electrical power distribution and control equipment, truck drivetrain systems, engine components, ion implanters and a wide variety of controls. The Company has manufacturing sites in 29 countries around the world. On 4/9/99, the Company acquired Aeroquip Vickers, Inc., a global manufacturer of engineered components and systems for industrial, aerospace, and automotive markets, for $1.7 billion.

BUSINESS LINE ANALYSIS

(12/31/00)	Rev (%)	Inc (%)
Automotive Components	22.0	27.5
Fluid Power & Other Components	31.4	28.7
Industrial & Commercial	29.1	30.7
Truck Components	17.5	13.1
Total	100.0	100.0

ANNUAL FINANCIAL DATA

	12/31/00	12/31/99	12/31/98	12/31/97	12/31/96	12/31/95	12/31/94
Earnings Per Share	**3 6.24**	**2 8.36**	**4.80**	**1 5.93**	**4.50**	**5.13**	**4.40**
Cash Flow Per Share	**11.36**	**14.36**	**9.35**	**10.33**	**8.69**	**...**	**0.77**
Tang. Book Val. Per Share	**...**	**1.27**	**14.33**	**14.73**	**15.48**	**...**	**10.64**
Dividends Per Share	**1.76**	**1.76**	**1.76**	**1.72**	**1.60**	**1.50**	**1.20**
Dividend Payout %	**28.2**	**21.1**	**36.7**	**29.0**	**35.6**	**29.2**	**27.3**
INCOME STATEMENT (IN MILLIONS):							
Total Revenues	8,309.0	8,402.0	6,625.0	7,563.0	6,961.0	6,822.0	6,052.0
Costs & Expenses	7,198.0	7,232.0	5,812.0	6,606.0	6,107.0	6,182.0	5,241.0
Depreciation & Amort.	462.0	441.0	331.0	342.0	320.0	...	251.0
Operating Income	649.0	729.0	482.0	615.0	534.0	640.0	560.0
Net Interest Inc./(Exp.)	d177.0	d152.0	d88.0	d79.0	d79.0	d80.0	d84.0
Income Before Income Taxes	552.0	963.0	485.0	668.0	485.0	592.0	488.0
Income Taxes	189.0	346.0	136.0	204.0	136.0	193.0	155.0
Net Income	3 363.0	2 617.0	349.0	1 464.0	349.0	399.0	333.0
Cash Flow	825.0	1,058.0	680.0	806.0	669.0	399.0	584.0
Average Shs. Outstg. (000)	72,600	73,700	72,700	78,000	77,000	...	756,000
BALANCE SHEET (IN MILLIONS):							
Cash & Cash Equivalents	126.0	165.0	122.0	90.0	60.0	...	41.0
Total Current Assets	2,571.0	2,782.0	1,982.0	2,055.0	2,017.0	...	1,846.0
Net Property	2,274.0	2,369.0	1,837.0	1,759.0	1,792.0	...	1,469.0
Total Assets	8,180.0	8,437.0	5,665.0	5,465.0	5,307.0	5,053.0	4,682.0
Total Current Liabilities	2,107.0	2,649.0	1,516.0	1,357.0	1,230.0	...	1,102.0
Long-Term Obligations	2,447.0	1,915.0	1,191.0	1,272.0	1,062.0	1,084.0	1,053.0
Net Stockholders' Equity	2,410.0	2,624.0	2,057.0	2,071.0	2,160.0	1,975.0	1,680.0
Net Working Capital	464.0	133.0	466.0	698.0	787.0	...	744.0
Year-end Shs. Outstg. (000)	68,300	74,000	72,000	75,000	77,000	...	78,000
STATISTICAL RECORD:							
Operating Profit Margin %	7.8	8.7	7.3	8.1	7.7	9.4	9.3
Net Profit Margin %	4.4	7.3	5.3	6.1	5.0	5.8	5.5
Return on Equity %	15.1	23.5	17.0	22.4	16.2	20.2	19.8
Return on Assets %	4.4	7.3	6.2	8.5	6.6	7.9	7.1
Debt/Total Assets %	29.9	22.7	21.0	23.3	20.0	21.5	22.5
Price Range	86.56-57.50	103.50-62.00	99.63-57.50	103.38-67.25	70.88-50.38	62.50-45.25	62.13-43.88
P/E Ratio	13.9-9.2	12.4-7.4	20.8-12.0	17.4-11.3	15.7-11.2	12.2-8.8	14.1-10.0
Average Yield %	2.4	2.1	2.2	2.0	2.6	2.8	2.3

Statistics are as originally reported. 1 Bef. extraord. loss $54.0 mill., but incl. $91.0 mill. gain on sale of business 2 Incl. $340.0 mill. gain from sale of businesses. 3 Bef. inc. of $90.0 mill. from disc. ops.

OFFICERS:
A. M. Cutler, Chmn., Pres., C.E.O.
A. T. Dillon, Exec. V.P., C.F.O.
R. E. Parmenter, V.P., Treas.
E. R. Franklin, Sec., Asst. Gen. Couns.

INVESTOR CONTACT: Investor Relations, (888) 328-6647

PRINCIPAL OFFICE: Eaton Center, Cleveland, OH 44114-2584

TELEPHONE NUMBER: (216) 523-5000
FAX: (216) 479-7092
WEB: www.eaton.com

NO. OF EMPLOYEES: 59,000

SHAREHOLDERS: 11,847 (record)

ANNUAL MEETING: In Apr.

INCORPORATED: OH, Aug., 1916

INSTITUTIONAL HOLDINGS:
No. of Institutions: 278
Shares Held: 45,876,822
% Held: 67.0

INDUSTRY: Electrical equipment & supplies, nec (SIC: 3699)

TRANSFER AGENT(S): First Chicago Trust Company of New York, Jersey City, NJ

NYSE SYMBOL EV
Rec. Pr. 32.30 (4/30/01)

EATON VANCE CORPORATION

YIELD 0.7%
P/E RATIO 19.7

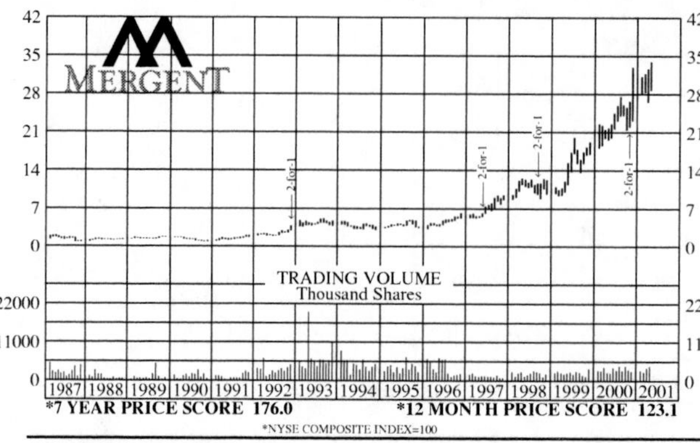

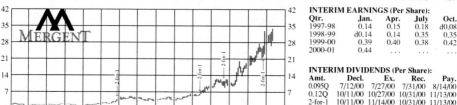

INTERIM EARNINGS (Per Share):

Qtr.	Jan.	Apr.	July	Oct.
1997-98	0.14	0.15	0.18	d0.08
1998-99	d0.14	0.14	0.35	0.35
1999-00	0.39	0.40	0.38	0.42
2000-01	0.44	...	...	...

INTERIM DIVIDENDS (Per Share):

Amt.	Decl.	Ex.	Rec.	Pay.
0.095Q	7/12/00	7/27/00	7/31/00	8/14/00
0.12Q	10/11/00	10/27/00	10/31/00	11/13/00
2-for-1	10/11/00	11/14/00	10/31/00	11/13/00
0.06Q	1/17/01	1/29/01	1/31/01	2/12/01
0.06Q	4/18/01	4/26/01	4/30/01	5/14/01

Indicated div.: $0.24

CAPITALIZATION (10/31/00):

	($000)	(%)
Long-Term Debt	21,429	5.8
Deferred Income Tax	94,817	25.5
Common & Surplus	254,950	68.7
Total	371,196	100.0

RECENT DEVELOPMENTS: For the quarter ended 1/31/01, net income increased 13.1% to $32.0 million versus $28.3 million a year earlier. Earnings for fiscal 2001 and fiscal 2000 included a loss of $255,000 and a gain of $50,000, respectively, from the sale of investments. Total revenue advanced 17.5% to $120.1 million. Revenues from investment adviser and adminstration fees and distribution income climbed 15.5% and 20.8%, respectively.

PROSPECTS: Looking ahead, EV should continue to benefit from strong growth in average assets under management. As of 1/31/01, assets under management totaled $49.30 billion, an gain of 17.9% from the previous year. Asset growth benefited from strong sales of EV's retail equity funds and taxable bond funds, and the private placements of two equity funds and two collateralized debt obligation funds.

BUSINESS

EATON VANCE CORPORATION creates, markets and manages mutual funds and provides management and counseling services to institutions and individuals. The Company conducts its investment management and counseling business through two wholly-owned subsidiaries, Eaton Vance Management and Boston Management and Research. The Company provides investment advice and administration services to over 70 funds and to over 800 separately managed individual and institutional accounts. EV's funds consist of money markets, equities, bank loans, and taxable and non-taxable fixed income. As of 1/31/00, assets under management totaled $41.80 billion.

REVENUES

(10/31/2000)	($000)	(%)
Investment Advisor Fees	226,344	52.7
Distribution Income	199,833	46.5
Income from Real Estate	54	0.0
Other income	3,335	0.8
Total	429,566	100.0

ANNUAL FINANCIAL DATA

	10/31/00	10/31/99	10/31/98	10/31/97	10/31/96	10/31/95	10/31/94
Earnings Per Share	[5] **1.58**	[3] [5] **0.71**	[4] **0.41**	**0.52**	[1] **0.47**	[2] **0.36**	[2] [3] **0.34**
Cash Flow Per Share	**2.74**	**1.58**	**1.29**	**1.26**	**1.19**	**1.07**	**1.07**
Tang. Book Val. Per Share	**3.65**	**2.73**	**2.94**	**3.03**	**2.77**	**2.59**	**2.25**
Dividends Per Share	**0.20**	**0.16**	**0.13**	**0.10**	**0.09**	**0.08**	**0.07**
Dividend Payout %	**12.8**	**22.7**	**31.5**	**20.2**	**19.0**	**22.4**	**22.1**
INCOME STATEMENT (IN THOUSANDS):							
Total Revenues	429,566	348,950	249,987	200,910	181,361	167,922	171,216
Costs & Expenses	161,959	205,380	134,591	79,941	67,335	68,175	68,220
Depreciation & Amort.	84,943	65,666	66,744	57,064	55,005	52,563	55,130
Operating Income	182,664	77,904	48,652	63,905	59,021	47,184	47,866
Net Interest Inc./(Exp.)	3,652	671	1,791	d380	d7	d2,061	d4,374
Income Before Income Taxes	187,179	85,910	50,038	67,470	59,922	43,741	43,203
Income Taxes	71,128	33,505	19,515	27,236	24,088	16,773	17,393
Net Income	[5] 116,051	[3] [5] 52,405	[4] 30,523	40,234	[1] 35,834	[2] 26,968	[2] [3] 25,810
Cash Flow	200,994	118,071	97,267	97,298	90,839	79,531	80,940
Average Shs. Outstg.	73,222	74,494	75,514	77,396	76,616	74,312	75,784
BALANCE SHEET (IN THOUSANDS):							
Cash & Cash Equivalents	102,479	77,395	96,435	140,520	116,375	79,121	34,025
Total Current Assets	120,242	90,488	130,433	164,168	130,072	98,602	38,963
Net Property	13,161	12,459	2,696	2,537	2,828	2,855	6,728
Total Assets	432,989	358,229	380,260	387,375	360,262	357,586	455,506
Total Current Liabilities	61,793	48,890	48,957	39,968	24,081	24,727	131,720
Long-Term Obligations	21,429	28,571	35,714	50,964	54,549	56,102	60,311
Net Stockholders' Equity	254,950	194,268	211,809	226,280	210,780	194,520	165,608
Net Working Capital	58,449	41,598	81,476	124,200	105,991	73,875	d92,757
Year-end Shs. Outstg.	69,544	70,520	71,332	73,876	75,072	74,528	72,720
STATISTICAL RECORD:							
Operating Profit Margin %	42.5	22.3	19.5	31.8	32.5	28.1	28.0
Net Profit Margin %	27.0	15.0	12.2	20.0	19.8	16.1	15.1
Return on Equity %	45.5	27.0	14.4	17.8	17.0	13.9	15.6
Return on Assets %	26.8	14.6	8.0	10.4	9.9	7.5	5.7
Debt/Total Assets %	4.9	8.0	9.4	13.2	15.1	15.7	13.2
Price Range	32.94-18.13	20.00-9.34	12.55-8.72	9.50-5.22	6.22-3.25	4.91-3.41	4.69-3.06
P/E Ratio	20.8-11.5	28.4-13.3	31.0-21.5	18.3-10.0	13.3-6.9	13.6-9.4	13.8-9.0
Average Yield %	0.8	1.1	1.2	1.4	1.9	2.0	1.9

Statistics are as originally reported. Adj. for 2-for-1 stk. splits: 11/00, 8/98 & 5/97 [1] Bef. extraord. credit $1.6 mill. [2] Bef. disc. oper. gain 10/31/95: $3.4 mill.; 10/31/94: $2.7 mill. [3] Bef. acct. chrg. of $36.6 mill., 10/31/99; $1.3 mill., 10/31/94. [4] Incl. impair. loss on real estate of $2.6 mill. & gain of $2.1 mill. fr. sale of invest. [5] Incl. gain on sale of invest. of $226,000, 2000; gain of $7.3 mill., 1999.

OFFICERS:
J. B. Hawkes, Chmn., Pres., C.E.O.
W. M. Steul, V.P., C.F.O., Treas.
A. R. Dynner, V.P., Sec.

INVESTOR CONTACT: William M. Steul, V.P. & C.F.O., (617) 482-8260

PRINCIPAL OFFICE: 255 State Street, Boston, MA 02109

TELEPHONE NUMBER: (617) 482-8260
FAX: (617) 482-2396
WEB: www.eatonvance.com
NO. OF EMPLOYEES: 438
SHAREHOLDERS: 950 (approx. non-voting); 11 (voting)
ANNUAL MEETING: In May
INCORPORATED: MD, May, 1959; reincorp., MD, Feb., 1981

INSTITUTIONAL HOLDINGS:
No. of Institutions: 167
Shares Held: 30,624,940
% Held: 44.2

INDUSTRY: Investment advice (SIC: 6282)

TRANSFER AGENT(S): EquiServe, L.P., Boston, MA

NYSE SYMBOL ECL
Rec. Pr. 37.83 (4/30/01)

ECOLAB, INC.

YIELD 1.4%
P/E RATIO 24.2

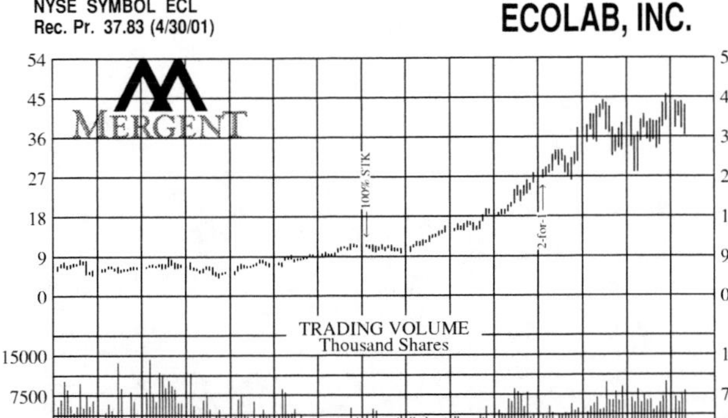

*7 YEAR PRICE SCORE 113.3 *12 MONTH PRICE SCORE 109.0
*NYSE COMPOSITE INDEX=100

INTERIM EARNINGS (Per Share):

Qtr.	Mar.	June	Sept.	Dec.
1996	0.15	0.22	0.28	0.24
1997	0.20	0.26	0.32	0.26
1998	0.23	0.28	0.35	0.29
1999	0.26	0.32	0.41	0.32
2000	0.32	0.36	0.46	0.42

INTERIM DIVIDENDS (Per Share):

Amt.	Decl.	Ex.	Rec.	Pay.
0.12Q	5/12/00	6/16/00	6/20/00	7/17/00
0.12Q	8/18/00	9/15/00	9/19/00	10/16/00
0.13Q	12/07/00	12/15/00	12/19/00	1/16/01
0.13Q	2/23/01	3/16/01	3/20/01	4/16/01
0.13Q	5/11/01	6/15/01	6/19/01	7/16/01

Indicated div.: $0.52 (Div. Reinv. Plan)

CAPITALIZATION (12/31/00):

	($000)	(%)
Long-Term Debt	234,377	23.6
Common & Surplus	757,007	76.4
Total	991,384	100.0

RECENT DEVELOPMENTS: For the year ended 12/31/00, income totaled $208.6 million, before an accounting change charge of $2.4 million, compared with net income of $175.8 million in 1999. Results for 2000 included a gain of the sale of a business of $25.9 million and restructuring and other expenses of $5.2 million. Total net sales grew 8.9% to $2.26 billion versus $2.08 billion the year before. Domestic sales climbed 8.9% to $1.78 billion, while international sales rose 10.5% to $500.3 million.

PROSPECTS: On 12/7/00, ECL agreed to combine into its operations the remaining 50.0% of the Henkel-Ecolab joint venture that it does not already own from its partner, Henkel KGaA of Dusseldorf, Germany, The transaction, which is valued between $460.0 million and $490.0 million and is expected to close on 1/2/02, should enhance ECL's ability to more rapidly and effectively grow its existing products and services in the European market and elsewhere.

BUSINESS

ECOLAB, INC. develops and markets cleaning, sanitizing, maintenance and pest elimination products and services for the hospitality, institutional and industrial markets. The Company's cleaning and sanitizing segment offers cleaners, sanitizers, detergents, lubricants, chemical cleaning, animal health, water treatment, infection control and janitorial products. The Company's other services segment provides services for the elimination and prevention of pests, and designs, manufactures, markets and repairs dishwashing and customized machines for the foodservice industry. In 1991, Ecolab and Henkel KGaH of Dusseldolf, Germany formed Henkel-Ecolab, a 50-50 joint venture comprising the parent companies' institutional and industrial cleaning and sanitizing businesses in Europe.

ANNUAL FINANCIAL DATA

	12/31/00	12/31/99	12/31/98	12/31/97	12/31/96	12/31/95	12/31/94
Earnings Per Share	**2 1.58**	**1.31**	**1 1.15**	**1.00**	**1.75**	**1.50**	**1.25**
Cash Flow Per Share	**2.71**	**2.31**	**2.06**	**1.75**	**3.14**	**2.65**	**2.24**
Tang. Book Val. Per Share	**5.95**	**5.89**	**5.33**	**4.27**	**8.02**	**7.06**	**6.82**
Dividends Per Share	**0.48**	**0.42**	**0.38**	**0.32**	**0.28**	**0.25**	**0.22**
Dividend Payout %	**30.4**	**32.1**	**33.0**	**32.0**	**16.0**	**16.7**	**17.6**
INCOME STATEMENT (IN MILLIONS):							
Total Revenues	2,264.3	2,080.0	1,888.2	1,640.4	1,490.0	1,340.9	1,207.6
Costs & Expenses	1,772.7	1,655.5	1,504.3	1,321.0	1,215.2	1,101.9	1,003.8
Depreciation & Amort.	148.4	134.5	122.0	100.9	89.5	76.3	66.9
Operating Income	343.1	290.0	262.0	218.5	185.3	162.7	137.0
Net Interest Inc./(Exp.)	d24.6	d22.7	d21.7	d12.6	d14.4	d11.5	d12.9
Income Before Income Taxes	318.5	267.2	240.2	205.9	170.9	151.2	124.1
Income Taxes	129.5	109.8	101.8	85.3	70.8	59.7	50.4
Equity Earnings/Minority Int.	19.5	18.3	16.1	13.4	13.0	7.7	11.0
Net Income	2 208.6	175.8	1 154.5	134.0	113.2	99.2	84.6
Cash Flow	357.0	310.3	276.5	234.8	202.7	175.5	151.4
Average Shs. Outstg. (000)	131,946	134,419	134,047	133,822	64,496	66,097	67,550
BALANCE SHEET (IN MILLIONS):							
Cash & Cash Equivalents	44.0	47.7	28.4	61.2	69.3	24.7	98.3
Total Current Assets	600.6	577.3	503.5	509.5	435.5	358.1	401.2
Net Property	501.6	448.1	420.2	395.6	332.3	292.9	246.2
Total Assets	1,714.0	1,585.9	1,471.0	1,416.3	1,208.4	1,060.9	1,020.4
Total Current Liabilities	532.0	470.7	399.8	404.5	327.8	310.5	253.7
Long-Term Obligations	234.4	169.0	227.0	259.4	148.7	89.4	105.4
Net Stockholders' Equity	757.0	762.0	690.5	551.7	520.0	456.7	461.8
Net Working Capital	68.5	106.6	103.7	105.0	107.7	47.5	147.5
Year-end Shs. Outstg. (000)	127,161	129,416	129,479	129,127	64,800	64,701	67,671
STATISTICAL RECORD:							
Operating Profit Margin %	15.2	13.9	13.9	13.3	12.4	12.1	11.3
Net Profit Margin %	9.2	8.5	8.2	8.2	7.6	7.4	7.0
Return on Equity %	27.5	23.1	22.4	24.3	21.8	21.7	18.3
Return on Assets %	12.2	11.1	10.5	9.5	9.4	9.3	8.3
Debt/Total Assets %	13.7	10.7	15.4	18.3	12.3	8.4	10.3
Price Range	45.69-28.00	44.44-31.69	38.00-26.13	27.81-18.13	19.75-14.56	15.88-10.00	11.75-9.63
P/E Ratio	28.9-17.7	33.9-24.2	33.0-22.7	27.8-18.1	11.3-8.3	10.6-6.7	9.4-7.7
Average Yield %	1.3	1.1	1.2	1.4	1.6	1.9	2.1

Statistics are as originally reported. Adj. for stk. splits: 2-for-1, 1/98, 1/94 1 Excl. a gain of $38.0 million from discontinued operations. 2 Bef. acctg. chrg., $2.4 mill.; incl. gain on sale of business of $25.9 mill. & restruct. exp. of $5.2 mill.

OFFICERS:
A. L. Schuman, Chmn., Pres., C.E.O.
M. E. Shannon, Chief Admin. Officer
L. W. Matthews III, Exec. V.P., C.F.O.
K. A. Iverson, V.P., Sec.

INVESTOR CONTACT: Michael J. Monahan, V.P., External Relations, (651) 293-2809

PRINCIPAL OFFICE: 370 N. Wabasha Street, St. Paul, MN 55102-1390

TELEPHONE NUMBER: (651) 293-2233
FAX: (651) 225-3080
WEB: www.ecolab.com

NO. OF EMPLOYEES: 14,250 (approx.)

SHAREHOLDERS: 5,388

ANNUAL MEETING: In May

INCORPORATED: DE, Feb., 1924

INSTITUTIONAL HOLDINGS:
No. of Institutions: 275
Shares Held: 64,082,318
% Held: 50.2

INDUSTRY: Polishes and sanitation goods (SIC: 2842)

TRANSFER AGENT(S): First ChicagoTrust Company of New York, Jersey City, NJ

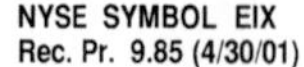

NYSE SYMBOL EIX
Rec. Pr. 9.85 (4/30/01)

EDISON INTERNATIONAL

YIELD ...
P/E RATIO ...

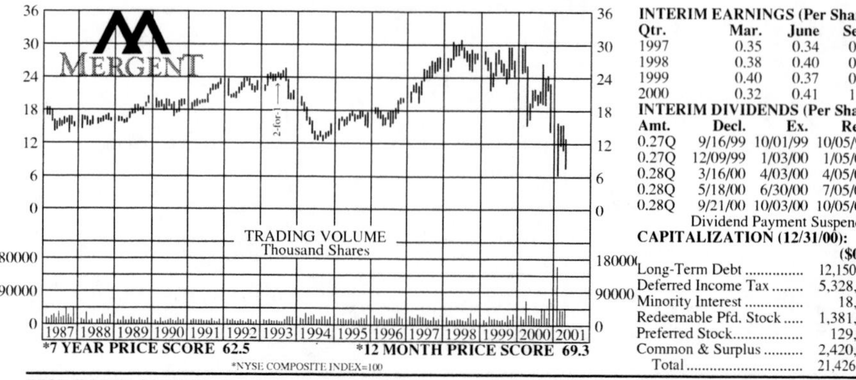

*7 YEAR PRICE SCORE 62.5 *12 MONTH PRICE SCORE 69.3

*NYSE COMPOSITE INDEX=100

INTERIM EARNINGS (Per Share):

Qtr.	Mar.	June	Sept.	Dec.
1997	0.35	0.34	0.70	0.37
1998	0.38	0.40	0.60	0.46
1999	0.40	0.37	0.73	0.28
2000	0.32	0.41	1.10	d7.83

INTERIM DIVIDENDS (Per Share):

Amt.	Decl.	Ex.	Rec.	Pay.
0.27Q	9/16/99	10/01/99	10/05/99	10/31/99
0.27Q	12/09/99	1/03/00	1/05/00	1/31/00
0.28Q	3/16/00	4/03/00	4/05/00	4/30/00
0.28Q	5/18/00	6/30/00	7/05/00	7/31/00
0.28Q	9/21/00	10/03/00	10/05/00	10/31/00

Dividend Payment Suspended

CAPITALIZATION (12/31/00):

	($000)	(%)
Long-Term Debt	12,150,000	56.7
Deferred Income Tax	5,328,000	24.9
Minority Interest	18,000	0.1
Redeemable Pfd. Stock	1,381,000	6.4
Preferred Stock	129,000	0.6
Common & Surplus	2,420,000	11.3
Total	21,426,000	100.0

RECENT DEVELOPMENTS: For the year ended 12/31/00, net loss totaled $1.94 billion compared with net income of $623.0 million in the previous year. Total operating revenues improved 20.8% to $11.72 billion versus $9.70 billion in the prior year. Electric utility revenue rose 4.3% to $7.87 billion from $7.55 billion in 1999. Nonutility power generation revenue totaled $3.25 billion, an increase of 98.1% from $1.64 billion in the prior year. Operating loss was $1.73 billion compared with operating income of $1.75 billion in 1999.

PROSPECTS: EIX is at the center of the California's power crisis. Results were dampened by a rate freeze under state deregulation laws which prevent the Company from passing on soaring wholesale power costs to customers. As a result, the Company announced that it has taken a $2.50 billion charge for 2000 due to soaring power costs. However, the California Public Utilities Commission is considering potential rate increases for 2001. In addition, the Company has agreed to sell assets to the State of California in an attempt to generate capital.

BUSINESS

EDISON INTERNATIONAL (formerly SCEcorp), through its subsidiary Southern California Edison, provides electric service to a 50,000-square-mile area of Central and Southern California, which includes some 800 cities and communities, with a population of nearly 11.0 million people. The Company's nonutility businesses are Edison Mission Energy, which is engaged in developing, acquiring, owning or leasing, and operating electric power generation facilities worldwide; Edison Capital, a provider of capital and financial services for energy and infrastructure projects; and Edison Enterprises, which provides integrated energy services, utility outsourcing, and consumer products and services.

ANNUAL FINANCIAL DATA

	12/31/00	12/31/99	12/31/98	12/31/97	12/31/96	12/31/95	12/31/94
Earnings Per Share	**d5.84**	**1.79**	**1.84**	**① 1.73**	**① 1.64**	**1.66**	**1.52**
Cash Flow Per Share	**0.47**	**7.25**	**6.87**	**5.31**	**4.54**	**4.09**	**3.93**
Tang. Book Val. Per Share	**7.43**	**15.01**	**14.55**	**14.71**	**15.12**	**14.34**	**13.72**
Dividends Per Share	**1.11**	**1.07**	**1.03**	**1.00**	**1.00**	**1.00**	**1.21**
Dividend Payout %	...	**59.8**	**56.0**	**57.8**	**61.0**	**60.2**	**79.6**
INCOME STATEMENT (IN MILLIONS):							
Total Revenues	11,717.0	9,670.0	10,208.0	9,235.0	8,545.0	8,405.0	8,345.0
Costs & Expenses	11,370.0	6,023.0	6,724.0	5,348.0	4,904.0	5,054.0	5,154.0
Depreciation & Amort.	2,101.0	1,906.0	1,831.0	1,450.0	1,269.0	1,087.0	1,079.0
Maintenance Exp.	...	...	411.0	406.0	331.0	359.0	332.0
Operating Income	d1,754.0	1,741.0	1,242.0	2,031.0	2,041.0	1,905.0	1,780.0
Net Interest Inc./(Exp.)	d996.0	d754.0	d632.0	d676.0	d576.0	d440.0	d408.0
Income Taxes	cr1,049.0	294.0	455.0	537.0	563.0	528.0	481.0
Equity Earnings/Minority Int.	...	d3.0	d3.0	d39.0	d70.0	d48.0	d46.0
Net Income	d1,943.0	623.0	668.0	① 700.0	① 717.0	739.0	681.0
Cash Flow	158.0	2,529.0	2,499.0	2,150.0	1,986.0	1,826.0	1,760.0
Average Shs. Outstg. (000)	333,000	349,000	364,000	405,000	437,000	446,000	448,000
BALANCE SHEET (IN MILLIONS):							
Gross Property	15,653.0	14,851.0	14,151.0	21,483.0	21,134.0	20,717.0	20,127.0
Accumulated Depreciation	7,834.0	7,520.0	6,897.0	10,544.0	9,431.0	8,569.0	7,710.0
Net Property	7,819.0	7,331.0	7,254.0	10,939.0	11,703.0	12,148.0	12,417.0
Total Assets	35,100.0	36,229.0	24,698.0	25,101.0	24,559.0	23,946.0	22,390.0
Long-Term Obligations	12,150.0	13,391.0	8,008.0	8,871.0	7,475.0	7,195.0	6,347.0
Net Stockholders' Equity	2,549.0	5,318.0	5,228.0	5,711.0	6,681.0	6,644.0	6,503.0
Year-end Shs. Outstg. (000)	325,811	347,207	350,553	375,764	423,000	443,608	447,799
STATISTICAL RECORD:							
Operating Profit Margin %	...	18.0	13.0	16.2	17.3	16.4	15.6
Net Profit Margin %	...	6.4	6.5	7.6	8.4	8.8	8.2
Net Inc./Net Property %	...	8.5	9.2	6.4	6.1	6.1	5.5
Net Inc./Tot. Capital %	...	2.4	3.7	3.7	3.7	3.8	3.8
Return on Equity %	...	12.0	12.8	12.3	10.7	11.1	10.5
Accum. Depr./Gross Prop. %	50.0	50.6	48.7	49.1	44.6	41.4	38.3
Price Range	30.00-14.13	29.63-21.63	31.00-25.13	27.81-19.38	20.38-15.00	18.00-14.38	20.50-12.38
P/E Ratio	...	16.5-12.1	16.8-13.7	16.1-11.2	12.4-9.1	10.8-8.7	13.5-8.1
Average Yield %	5.0	4.2	3.7	4.2	5.7	6.2	7.4

Statistics are as originally reported. ① Incl. non-recurr. chrg. 1996, $0.06/sh.; 1997, $0.04/sh. for workforce reductions.

OFFICERS:
J. E. Bryson, Chmn., Pres., C.E.O.
T. F. Craver Jr., Sr. V.P., C.F.O., Treas.

INVESTOR CONTACT: Jo Ann Goddard, V.P., Inv. Rel., (626) 302-1212

PRINCIPAL OFFICE: 2244 Walnut Grove Avenue, Rosemead, CA 91770

TELEPHONE NUMBER: (626) 302-1212
FAX: (626) 302-9935
WEB: www.edison.com

NO. OF EMPLOYEES: 18,555

SHAREHOLDERS: 80,070

ANNUAL MEETING: In May

INCORPORATED: CA, Apr., 1987

INSTITUTIONAL HOLDINGS:
No. of Institutions: 308
Shares Held: 171,762,533
% Held: 52.7

INDUSTRY: Electric services (SIC: 4911)

TRANSFER AGENT(S): Wells Fargo Bank Minnesota, N.A. South St. Paul, MN

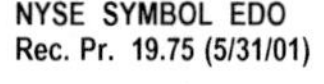

NYSE SYMBOL EDO
Rec. Pr. 19.75 (5/31/01)

EDO CORPORATION

YIELD 0.6%
P/E RATIO 493.8

*7 YEAR PRICE SCORE 99.7 *12 MONTH PRICE SCORE 182.7
*NYSE COMPOSITE INDEX=100

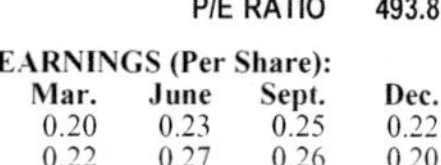

INTERIM EARNINGS (Per Share):

Qtr.	Mar.	June	Sept.	Dec.
1997	0.20	0.23	0.25	0.22
1998	0.22	0.27	0.26	0.20
1999	0.15	0.17	0.18	0.21
2000	0.24	d0.37	d0.02	0.19

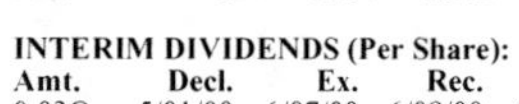

INTERIM DIVIDENDS (Per Share):

Amt.	Decl.	Ex.	Rec.	Pay.
0.03Q	5/01/00	6/07/00	6/09/00	6/30/00
0.03Q	8/02/00	9/06/00	9/08/00	9/29/00
0.03Q	12/07/00	12/13/00	12/15/00	1/05/01
0.03Q	2/07/01	3/07/01	3/09/01	3/30/01
0.03Q	5/02/01	6/06/01	6/08/01	6/29/01

Indicated div.: $0.12

CAPITALIZATION (12/31/00):

	($000)	(%)
Long-Term Debt	44,044	39.6
Deferred Income Tax	1,239	1.1
Preferred Stock	49	0.0
Common & Surplus	65,769	59.2
Total	111,101	100.0

RECENT DEVELOPMENTS: For the year ended 12/31/00, EDO reported net income of $1.3 million versus income from continuing operations of $6.1 million in 1999. Earnings for 2000 included a write-off of $11.5 million for purchased in-process research and development and merger-related costs. Earnings for 1999 excluded a loss of $4.1 million from discontinued operations. Net sales soared to $206.8 million from $97.9 million in 1999.

PROSPECTS: EDO was awarded a $4.2 million contract to provide support services to the U.S. Marine Corp's Warfighting Laboratory in Virginia. Annual options for an additional four years raise the total potential contract value to $18.2 million. Also, EDO was awarded a $4.9 million contract from the U.S. Air Force for 70 Field Test Simulator test sets, to be delivered in the next fifteen months, including options for up to 890 units through 2005.

BUSINESS

EDO CORPORATION designs, manufactures and integrates advanced electronic and mechanical systems and engineered materials for domestic and international defense, aerospace and industrial markets. The Company organizes its business into three segments: Systems and Analysis Group, which includes combat systems, technology services and analysis, electro-ceramic products, and technical services operations; Electronic Systems Group, which includes defense programs, space products, antenna products, and American nucleonics; and Integrated Systems and Structures Group, which includes marine and aircraft systems, fiber science and specialty plastics. In 1999, the Company discontinued its satellite products business, which it subsequently sold in January 2000. In November 1999, the Company acquired M. Technologies. On 4/28/00, the Company merged with AIL Technologies, Inc.

REVENUES

(12/31/2000)	($000)	(%)
Defense	147,045	71.1
Communications & Space	25,026	12.1
Engineered Materials	34,751	16.8
Total	206,822	100.0

ANNUAL FINANCIAL DATA

	12/31/00	12/31/99	12/31/98	12/31/97	12/31/96	12/31/95	12/31/94
Earnings Per Share	**4 0.05**	**3 0.65**	**0.94**	**0.81**	**2 1.95**	**0.25**	**1 d4.30**
Cash Flow Per Share	**0.93**	**1.06**	**1.51**	**1.61**	**2.82**	**1.21**	**d3.11**
Tang. Book Val. Per Share	**3.74**	**4.61**	**3.96**	**3.33**	**2.08**	**0.66**	**...**
Dividends Per Share	**0.12**	**0.12**	**0.11**	**0.07**	**...**	**...**	**0.21**
Dividend Payout %	**239.5**	**18.5**	**11.7**	**9.3**	**...**	**...**	**...**
INCOME STATEMENT (IN THOUSANDS):							
Total Revenues	206,822	97,936	96,060	94,481	94,974	91,650	90,982
Costs & Expenses	188,142	85,297	82,027	80,918	75,771	82,543	109,753
Depreciation & Amort.	9,441	3,390	4,574	6,027	5,303	5,534	6,625
Operating Income	9,239	9,249	9,459	7,536	13,900	3,573	d25,396
Net Interest Inc./(Exp.)	d2,438	d785	d428	d459	d766	d1,179	d2,109
Income Before Income Taxes	6,585	8,694	8,931	7,027	13,068	2,353	d27,170
Income Taxes	5,264	2,610	700	...	...	...	cr3,800
Equity Earnings/Minority Int.	...	...	...	...	...	307	814
Net Income	4 1,321	3 6,084	8,231	7,027	2 13,068	2,660	1 d22,556
Cash Flow	9,881	8,474	11,742	11,927	17,192	6,955	d17,264
Average Shs. Outstg.	10,662	8,032	7,785	7,395	6,086	5,768	5,551
BALANCE SHEET (IN THOUSANDS):							
Cash & Cash Equivalents	16,621	29,642	33,320	34,202	20,745	25,609	18,076
Total Current Assets	118,731	79,283	86,460	79,003	63,935	64,106	59,130
Net Property	57,485	10,218	13,964	12,865	12,968	14,133	25,845
Total Assets	214,254	124,491	126,753	108,801	94,223	103,499	102,077
Total Current Liabilities	81,179	44,173	45,742	34,526	26,553	26,434	27,980
Long-Term Obligations	44,044	34,571	36,955	39,685	40,993	42,204	43,324
Net Stockholders' Equity	65,818	40,241	38,051	28,135	19,823	14,162	10,750
Net Working Capital	37,552	35,110	40,718	44,477	37,382	37,672	31,150
Year-end Shs. Outstg.	13,637	6,760	6,632	6,399	6,045	5,808	5,644
STATISTICAL RECORD:							
Operating Profit Margin %	4.5	9.4	9.8	8.0	14.6	3.9	...
Net Profit Margin %	0.6	6.2	8.6	7.4	13.8	2.9	...
Return on Equity %	2.0	15.1	21.6	25.0	65.9	18.8	...
Return on Assets %	0.6	4.9	6.5	6.5	13.9	2.6	...
Debt/Total Assets %	20.6	27.8	29.2	36.5	43.5	40.8	42.4
Price Range	10.50-5.38	9.38-5.13	10.88-6.69	10.75-6.38	10.88-4.63	6.00-3.00	7.25-2.88
P/E Ratio	209.6-107.3	14.4-7.9	11.6-7.1	13.3-7.9	5.6-2.4	24.0-12.0	...
Average Yield %	1.5	1.7	1.3	0.9	...	...	4.1

Statistics are as originally reported. 1 Incl. chgs. of $13.4 mill. rel. to consol. 2 Incl. $7.1 mill. gain from curtail. of post-retire. benefits & bef. loss from disc. ops. of $8.6 mill. 3 Excl. disc. opers. loss of $4.1 mill. 4 Incl. a pre-tax chrg. of $11.5 mill. for write-off of purch. in-process res. & dev. and merger-rel. costs.

OFFICERS:
N. A. Armstrong, Chmn.
J. M. Smith, Pres., C.E.O.
D. L. Reed, V.P., C.F.O.

INVESTOR CONTACT: William J. Frost, V.P., Admin., Asst. Sec., (212) 716-2006

PRINCIPAL OFFICE: 60 East 42nd Street, Suite 5010, New York, NY 10165

TELEPHONE NUMBER: (212) 716-2000
FAX: (212) 716-2050
WEB: www.edocorp.com

NO. OF EMPLOYEES: 1,500 (avg.)

SHAREHOLDERS: 2,278

ANNUAL MEETING: In May

INCORPORATED: NY, Oct., 1925

INSTITUTIONAL HOLDINGS:
No. of Institutions: 27
Shares Held: 7,867,508
% Held: 53.3

INDUSTRY: Search and navigation equipment (SIC: 3812)

TRANSFER AGENT(S): American Stock Transfer & Trust Company, New York, NY

NYSE SYMBOL AGE
Rec. Pr. 42.52 (5/31/01)

EDWARDS (A.G.), INC.

YIELD 1.5%
P/E RATIO 12.4

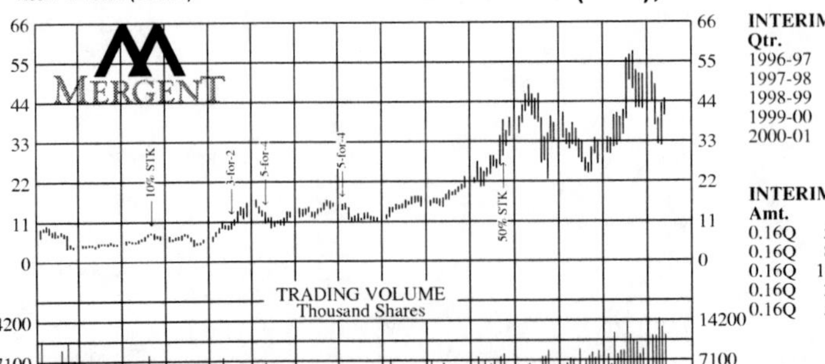

*7 YEAR PRICE SCORE 116.6 *12 MONTH PRICE SCORE 94.6

*NYSE COMPOSITE INDEX=100

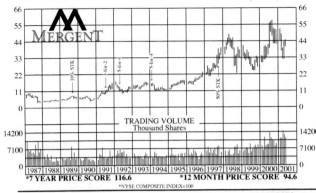

INTERIM EARNINGS (Per Share):

Qtr.	May	Aug.	Nov.	Feb.
1996-97	0.58	0.53	0.53	0.60
1997-98	0.55	0.71	0.73	0.75
1998-99	0.78	0.74	0.70	0.78
1999-00	0.88	0.86	1.23	1.11
2000-01	1.24	0.93	0.69	0.57

INTERIM DIVIDENDS (Per Share):

Amt.	Decl.	Ex.	Rec.	Pay.
0.16Q	5/19/00	5/31/00	6/02/00	7/03/00
0.16Q	8/25/00	8/31/00	9/05/00	10/02/00
0.16Q	11/17/00	12/06/00	12/08/00	1/02/01
0.16Q	2/23/01	3/07/01	3/09/01	4/02/01
0.16Q	5/25/01	6/07/01	6/11/01	7/02/01

Indicated div.: $0.64

CAPITALIZATION (2/29/00):

	($000)	(%)
Common & Surplus	1,717,122	100.0
Total	1,717,122	100.0

RECENT DEVELOPMENTS: For the year ended 2/28/01, net earnings decreased 24.9% to $287.5 million compared with $382.9 million in the previous year. Total revenues grew to $2.84 billion from $2.82 billion in the prior year. Commissions fell 6.9% to $1.33 billion from $1.43 billion the year before. Asset management and service fees grew 19.9% to $653.0 million from $544.5 million a year earlier. Revenues from principal transactions rose 2.8% to $292.3 million.

PROSPECTS: The Company will continue its efforts to control expenses, particularly expenses related to its financial consultant workstations. AGE hopes to benefit from the roll-out of its ClientOne workstations, which offer financial-planning software, Internet access and advanced investment research tools, as well as multimedia capabilities to its customers. Separately, the Company is continuing to develop enhancements for AGe connect, its on-line client access service.

BUSINESS

A.G. EDWARDS, INC. is a holding company whose subsidiaries provide securities and commodities brokerage, investment banking, trust, asset management, and insurance services. Its principal subsidiary, A.G. Edwards & Sons, Inc., operates 696 brokerage offices and 16,279 employees in 49 states, the District of Columbia and London, England. A.G. Edwards & Sons provides a full range of financial products and services to individual and institutional investors and offers investment banking services to corporate, governmental and municipal clients.

REVENUES

(02/29/00)	($000)	(%)
Commissions	1,426,426	50.6
Principal Transactions	284,218	10.1
Investment Banking...	225,719	8.0
Asset Mgt & Service Fees........................	544,531	19.3
Interest........................	248,588	8.8
Other Revenues	89,525	3.2
Total	2,819,007	100.0

ANNUAL FINANCIAL DATA

	2/29/00	2/28/99	2/28/98	2/28/97	2/29/96	2/28/95	2/28/94
Earnings Per Share	**4.08**	**3.00**	**2.75**	**2.24**	**1.77**	**1.33**	**1.71**
Cash Flow Per Share	**5.12**	**3.78**	**3.39**	**2.80**	**2.31**	**1.84**	**2.24**
Tang. Book Val. Per Share	**19.69**	**17.16**	**15.54**	**13.12**	**11.33**	**9.84**	**8.72**
Dividends Per Share	**0.59**	**0.54**	**0.48**	**0.43**	**0.37**	**0.37**	**0.31**
Dividend Payout %	**14.5**	**18.0**	**17.3**	**19.0**	**21.1**	**28.0**	**18.1**
INCOME STATEMENT (IN MILLIONS):							
Total Revenues	2,819.0	2,240.8	2,004.1	1,696.5	1,454.5	1,178.3	1,278.6
Costs & Expenses	2,075.4	1,688.7	1,501.9	1,284.2	1,122.2	924.7	986.5
Depreciation & Amort.	97.6	75.7	63.0	55.2	52.8	47.5	47.5
Operating Income	645.9	476.4	439.2	357.0	279.4	206.1	244.7
Net Interest Inc./(Exp.)	d22.8	d5.6	d1.4	d2.1	d3.2	d6.8	d1.1
Income Before Income Taxes	623.1	470.8	437.8	355.0	276.3	199.3	243.6
Income Taxes	240.2	178.7	168.5	135.9	105.7	75.2	88.7
Net Income	382.9	292.1	269.3	219.1	170.6	124.1	154.9
Cash Flow	480.5	367.8	332.3	274.3	223.4	171.6	202.4
Average Shs. Outstg. (000)	93,814	97,322	98,051	97,817	96,644	93,267	90,531
BALANCE SHEET (IN MILLIONS):							
Cash & Cash Equivalents	530.2	415.8	1,132.5	2,056.7	1,160.7	407.8	350.6
Total Current Assets	4,917.8	3,389.1	3,777.8	3,912.6	2,798.4	1,949.2	1,997.4
Net Property	312.9	240.4	230.2	189.8	178.6	167.6	145.4
Total Assets	5,347.6	3,803.1	4,193.3	4,244.3	3,102.1	2,224.3	2,236.6
Total Current Liabilities	3,547.5	2,121.9	2,672.5	2,943.1	1,973.7	1,273.4	1,409.5
Net Stockholders' Equity	1,717.1	1,627.7	1,463.1	1,261.3	1,088.7	919.3	790.4
Net Working Capital	1,370.3	1,267.2	1,105.4	969.6	824.7	675.9	587.9
Year-end Shs. Outstg. (000)	87,209	94,838	94,179	96,117	96,068	93,441	90,669
STATISTICAL RECORD:							
Operating Profit Margin %	22.9	21.3	21.9	21.0	19.2	17.5	19.1
Net Profit Margin %	13.6	13.0	13.4	12.9	11.7	10.5	12.1
Return on Equity %	22.3	17.9	18.4	17.4	15.7	13.5	19.6
Return on Assets %	7.2	7.7	6.4	5.2	5.5	5.6	6.9
Price Range	41.00-24.25	48.81-22.63	39.50-20.50	23.33-15.00	18.00-11.67	16.25-11.00	16.93-12.00
P/E Ratio	10.0-5.9	16.3-7.5	14.4-7.5	10.4-6.7	10.2-6.6	12.2-8.3	9.9-7.0
Average Yield %	1.8	1.5	1.6	2.2	2.5	2.7	2.1

Statistics are as originally reported. Adj. for all stock dividends and splits through 10/97. [1] Includes a gain of $75.2 million from an investment in a privately-held investment management company.

OFFICERS:
R. L. Bagby, Chmn., C.E.O.
B. F. Edwards IV, Vice-Chmn.
D. L. Kelly, V.P., C.F.O., Sec.

INVESTOR CONTACT: Investor Relations, (314) 955-3000

PRINCIPAL OFFICE: One North Jefferson Ave., St. Louis, MO 63103

TELEPHONE NUMBER: (314) 955-3000
FAX: (314) 955-5913
WEB: www.agedwards.com

NO. OF EMPLOYEES: 15,451

SHAREHOLDERS: 27,700 (approx.)

ANNUAL MEETING: In June

INCORPORATED: DE, 1983

INSTITUTIONAL HOLDINGS:
No. of Institutions: 244
Shares Held: 33,979,462
% Held: 42.3

INDUSTRY: Security brokers and dealers (SIC: 6211)

TRANSFER AGENT(S): The Bank of New York, New York, NY

NYSE SYMBOL EPG
Rec. Pr. 68.80 (4/30/01)

EL PASO CORPORATION

YIELD 1.2%
P/E RATIO 28.2

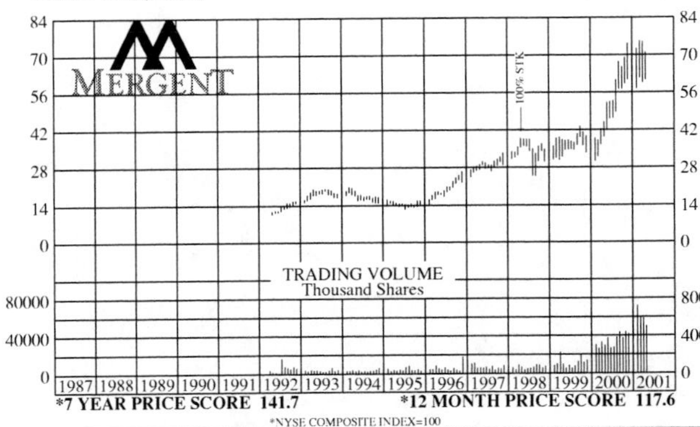

*7 YEAR PRICE SCORE 141.7 *12 MONTH PRICE SCORE 117.6
*NYSE COMPOSITE INDEX=100

INTERIM EARNINGS (Per Share):

Qtr.	Mar.	June	Sept.	Dec.
1997	0.43	0.38	0.39	0.44
1998	0.48	0.45	0.43	0.49
1999	d0.62	0.17	0.17	d0.78
2000	0.70	0.56	0.57	0.61

INTERIM DIVIDENDS (Per Share):

Amt.	Decl.	Ex.	Rec.	Pay.
0.206Q	4/28/00	5/31/00	6/02/00	7/03/00
0.206Q	7/10/00	8/30/00	9/01/00	10/02/00
0.206Q	10/26/00	11/28/00	11/30/00	1/02/01
0.212Q	1/26/01	2/28/01	3/02/01	4/02/01
0.212Q	4/17/01	5/30/01	6/01/01	7/02/01

Indicated div.: $0.85 (Div. Reinv. Plan)

CAPITALIZATION (12/31/00):

	($000)	(%)
Long-Term Debt	5,949,000	40.7
Deferred Income Tax	2,149,000	14.7
Minority Interest	2,331,000	15.9
Redeemable Pfd. Stock	625,000	4.3
Common & Surplus	3,569,000	24.4
Total	14,623,000	100.0

RECENT DEVELOPMENTS: For the year ended 12/31/00, income totaled $582.0 million, before an extraordinary gain of $70.0 million, versus a loss of $242.0 million a year earlier. Results for 2000 and 1999 included merger-related costs and assets impairment charges of $91.0 million and $557.0 million, respectively. Results for 1999 also included a ceiling test charge of $352.0 million. Operating revenues surged to $21.95 billion from $10.71 billion in 1999, mainly due to higher natural gas prices.

PROSPECTS: On 1/29/01, EPG completed its $24.00 billion acquisition of The Coastal Corporation. The combined company expects to generate cost savings in excess of $200.0 million per year and achieve earnings per share growth of 20.0% in 2001. Growth is expected to be driven by EPG's El Paso Merchant Energy segment, which is aggressively extending its merchant model to new markets in worldwide petroleum and global liquefied natural gas, including Europe and Brazil.

BUSINESS

EL PASO CORPORATION (formerly El Paso Energy Corp.) has operations in natural gas transportation, gas gathering and processing, gas and oil production, power generation, merchant energy services, international project development, and energy financing. The Pipeline Group manages approximately 58,000 miles of interstate pipelines. The Merchant Energy Group manages EPG's wholesale customer business and its extensive portfolio of natural gas, power, and petroleum assets on a worldwide basis. The Production segment has more than 6.00 trillion cubic feet equivalent of natural gas reserves and controls in excess of 3.0 million net acres. The Field Services segment provides midstream services and holds interests in 24,000 miles of intrastate pipeline and gathering systems, 35 processing and treating plants, and eight offshore platforms. On 10/25/99, EPG and Sonat Inc. completed their $6.0 billion merger. On 1/29/01, EPG completed its acquisition of The Coastal Corporation.

ANNUAL FINANCIAL DATA

	12/31/00	12/31/99	12/31/98	12/31/97	12/31/96	12/31/95	12/31/94
Earnings Per Share	[5] **2.44**	[3] **d1.06**	**1.85**	**1.59**	[2] **0.53**	**1.24**	[2] **1.23**
Cash Flow Per Share	**4.82**	**1.65**	**4.11**	**3.74**	**1.93**	**2.28**	**2.11**
Tang. Book Val. Per Share	**15.20**	**10.47**	**13.09**	**16.32**	**14.82**	**9.70**	**9.92**
Dividends Per Share	**0.82**	**0.79**	**0.76**	**0.72**	**0.69**	**0.65**	**0.59**
Dividend Payout %	**33.5**	...	**40.9**	**45.4**	**129.5**	**52.3**	**48.3**
INCOME STATEMENT (IN MILLIONS):							
Total Revenues	21,950.0	[4] 10,581.0	5,782.0	5,638.0	[1] 3,010.0	1,038.0	869.9
Costs & Expenses	20,030.0	9,999.0	4,983.0	4,862.0	2,739.0	753.5	582.5
Depreciation & Amort.	589.0	618.0	293.0	255.0	101.0	72.1	65.0
Operating Income	1,331.0	d36.0	506.0	521.0	170.0	212.4	222.3
Net Interest Inc./(Exp.)	d538.0	d405.0	d267.0	d238.0	d110.0	d86.3	d78.8
Income Taxes	286.0	cr81.0	127.0	129.0	25.0	47.6	58.5
Equity Earnings/Minority Int.	d17.0	59.0	d25.0	d25.0	d2.0	...	...
Net Income	[5] 582.0	[3] d242.0	225.0	186.0	[2] 38.0	85.4	[2] 89.6
Cash Flow	1,171.0	376.0	518.0	441.0	139.0	157.4	154.7
Average Shs. Outstg. (000)	243,000	228,000	126,000	118,000	72,000	68,990	73,264
BALANCE SHEET (IN MILLIONS):							
Gross Property	19,436.0	17,917.0	8,887.0	8,511.0	...	...	...
Accumulated Depreciation	7,777.0	7,656.0	1,546.0	1,395.0	...	...	...
Net Property	11,659.0	10,261.0	7,341.0	7,116.0	5,938.0	1,977.6	1,861.6
Total Assets	27,445.0	16,657.0	10,069.0	9,532.0	8,712.0	2,534.6	2,331.8
Long-Term Obligations	5,949.0	5,223.0	2,552.0	2,119.0	2,215.0	771.9	779.1
Net Stockholders' Equity	3,569.0	2,947.0	2,108.0	1,959.0	1,638.0	712.2	709.6
Year-end Shs. Outstg. (000)	234,780	229,597	120,000	120,000	110,550	68,448	71,104
STATISTICAL RECORD:							
Operating Profit Margin %	6.1	...	8.8	9.2	5.6	20.5	25.6
Net Profit Margin %	2.7	...	3.9	3.3	1.3	8.2	10.3
Net Inc./Net Property %	5.0	...	3.1	2.6	0.6	4.3	4.8
Net Inc./Tot. Capital %	4.0	...	3.3	3.1	0.7	4.7	5.0
Return on Equity %	16.3	...	10.7	9.5	2.3	12.0	12.6
Accum. Depr./Gross Prop. %	40.0	42.7	17.4	16.4	...	...	...
Price Range	74.25-30.31	43.44-30.69	38.94-24.69	33.38-24.44	26.63-14.31	16.25-12.38	20.94-14.81
P/E Ratio	30.4-12.4	...	21.0-13.3	21.0-15.4	50.2-27.0	13.2-10.0	17.1-12.1
Average Yield %	1.6	2.1	2.4	2.5	3.4	4.5	3.3

Statistics are as originally reported. Adj. for 100% stk. div., 4/98 [1] Refl. acq. of Tenneco [2] Incls. non-recurr. chrgs. 12/31/96, $64.6 mill.; chrg. 12/31/94, $12.0 mill. [3] Incls. one-time chrgs. of $909.0 mill.; bef. acctg. change chrg. of $13.0 mill. [4] Refl. acquis. of Sonat Inc. in 10/99. [5] Incls. merger rel. costs & asset impair. chrgs. of $91.0 mill.; bef. extraord. gain of $70.0 mill.

OFFICERS:
W. A. Wise, Chmn., Pres., C.E.O.
H. B. Austin, Exec. V.P., C.F.O.
B. White Jr., Exec. V.P., Gen. Couns.

INVESTOR CONTACT: Norma F. Dunn, Investor Relations, (888) 202-9971

PRINCIPAL OFFICE: El Paso Energy Building, 1001 Louisiana Street, Houston, TX 77002

TELEPHONE NUMBER: (713) 420-2131
WEB: www.elpaso.com

NO. OF EMPLOYEES: 15,000 (approx.)

SHAREHOLDERS: 68,070 (approx.)

ANNUAL MEETING: In May

INCORPORATED: DE, 1928

INSTITUTIONAL HOLDINGS:
No. of Institutions: 568
Shares Held: 339,791,627
% Held: 66.8

INDUSTRY: Natural gas transmission (SIC: 4922)

TRANSFER AGENT(S): Fleet National Bank, Boston, MA

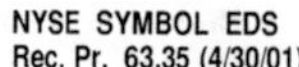
NYSE SYMBOL EDS
Rec. Pr. 63.35 (4/30/01)

ELECTRONIC DATA SYSTEMS CORPORATION

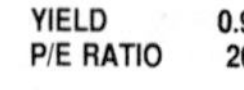
YIELD 0.9%
P/E RATIO 26.4

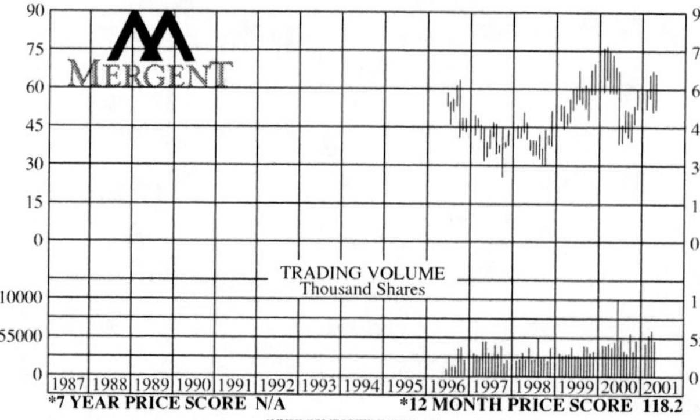

*7 YEAR PRICE SCORE N/A   *12 MONTH PRICE SCORE 118.2

*NYSE COMPOSITE INDEX=100

INTERIM EARNINGS (Per Share):

Qtr.	Mar.	June	Sept.	Dec.
1998	0.37	0.45	0.39	0.29
1999	d0.04	0.48	0.31	0.09
2000	0.60	0.53	0.59	0.68

INTERIM DIVIDENDS (Per Share):

Amt.	Decl.	Ex.	Rec.	Pay.
0.15Q	7/25/00	8/16/00	8/18/00	9/11/00
0.15Q	10/24/00	11/09/00	11/13/00	12/11/00
0.15Q	2/06/01	2/15/01	2/20/01	3/12/01
0.15Q	4/24/01	5/11/01	5/15/01	6/11/01

Indicated div.: $0.60 (Div. Reinv. Plan)

CAPITALIZATION (12/31/00):

	($000)	(%)
Long-Term Debt	2,585,600	30.8
Deferred Income Tax	129,000	1.5
Redeemable Pfd. Stock	528,700	6.3
Common & Surplus	5,138,700	61.3
Total	8,382,000	100.0

RECENT DEVELOPMENTS: For the year ended 12/31/00, net income rose to $1.14 billion versus $420.9 million in 1999. Results for 2000 included a $24.2 million acquired in-process research and development charge and a $21.7 million gain for restructuring and other items. Results for 1999 included a charge of $1.04 billion for restructuring and other charges. Results also included net pre-tax gains of $97.6 million and $199.5 million resulting from the sale of investments. Revenues climbed 2.6% to $19.23 billion.

PROSPECTS: The Company entered 2001 with a backlog of signed business of about $80.00 billion. Meanwhile, the Company's significant efforts to improve operations and productivity should enable EDS to fuel future growth via increased investments in new applications, products and services. As a result, the Company expects to achieve its operating margin target of 10.0% for 2001. Separately, the Company completed the acquisition of TransAlliance LP, a regional electronic fund transfer company.

BUSINESS

ELECTRONIC DATA SYSTEM CORPORATION is a global provider of information technology using advanced computer and communications technologies to meet the business needs of its clients. EDS offers its services to 9,000 business and government clients in about 55 countries. EDS operates in four business lines: A.T. Kearney, E.solutions, Business Process Management, and Information Solutions. A.T. Kearney provides business consulting and executive searches. E.solutions is an Internet business unit. Business Process Management is the customer services and claims processing unit. Information Solutions is the centralized outsourcing business that manages customer mainframe data. Prior to its spin-off on 7/7/96, EDS was an indirect wholly-owned subsidiary of GMC.

ANNUAL FINANCIAL DATA

	12/31/00	12/31/99	12/31/98	12/31/97	12/31/96	12/31/95	12/31/94
Earnings Per Share	**[6] 2.40**	**[5] 0.85**	**[4] 1.50**	**[3] 1.48**	**[1] 0.89**	**1.96**	**1.71**
Cash Flow Per Share	**5.40**	**3.73**	**4.31**	**3.93**	**...**	**4.11**	**...**
Tang. Book Val. Per Share	**4.53**	**3.93**	**9.02**	**7.65**	**6.93**	**6.92**	**6.15**
Dividends Per Share	**0.60**	**0.60**	**0.60**	**0.60**	**[2] 0.60**	**0.52**	**0.48**
Dividend Payout %	**25.0**	**70.6**	**40.0**	**40.5**	**67.4**	**26.5**	**28.1**
INCOME STATEMENT (IN MILLIONS):							
Total Revenues	19,226.8	18,534.2	16,891.0	15,235.6	14,441.3	12,422.1	9,960.1
Costs & Expenses	15,977.4	16,625.7	14,430.5	12,813.5	12,464.4	9,785.3	7,945.4
Depreciation & Amort.	1,431.2	1,435.8	1,393.7	1,208.5	1,180.8	1,107.8	771.1
Operating Income	1,818.2	472.7	1,066.8	1,213.6	796.1	1,529.0	1,243.6
Net Interest Inc./(Exp.)	d18.2	185.0	17.3	d72.0	d76.5	d120.8	d40.6
Income Before Income Taxes	1,800.0	657.7	1,133.7	1,141.6	674.1	1,467.0	1,284.2
Income Taxes	656.7	236.8	390.3	411.0	242.6	528.1	462.3
Net Income	[6] 1,143.3	[5] 420.9	[4] 743.4	[3] 730.6	[1] 431.5	880.1	740.7
Cash Flow	2,574.5	1,856.7	2,137.1	1,939.1	1,612.3	1,987.9	1,511.8
Average Shs. Outstg. (000)	476,400	498,000	495,500	493,900	...	483,600	...
BALANCE SHEET (IN MILLIONS):							
Cash & Cash Equivalents	692.6	728.7	1,311.7	1,024.9	962.5	638.6	757.8
Total Current Assets	6,166.7	5,877.7	5,633.3	5,169.4	5,008.3	4,381.5	3,354.1
Net Property	2,474.1	2,459.8	2,708.1	2,868.4	3,097.0	3,242.4	2,756.6
Total Assets	12,700.3	12,522.3	11,526.1	11,174.1	11,192.9	10,832.4	8,786.5
Total Current Liabilities	4,318.3	4,996.0	3,656.8	3,257.6	3,162.8	3,261.4	2,873.2
Long-Term Obligations	2,585.6	2,215.7	1,184.3	1,790.9	2,324.3	1,852.8	1,021.0
Net Stockholders' Equity	5,138.7	4,534.6	5,916.5	5,309.4	4,783.1	4,878.8	4,232.5
Net Working Capital	1,848.4	881.7	1,976.5	1,911.8	1,845.5	1,120.1	480.9
Year-end Shs. Outstg. (000)	465,299	466,193	493,124	491,567	487,151	483,700	481,700
STATISTICAL RECORD:							
Operating Profit Margin %	9.5	2.6	6.3	8.0	5.5	12.3	12.5
Net Profit Margin %	5.9	2.3	4.4	4.8	3.0	7.1	7.4
Return on Equity %	22.2	9.3	12.6	13.8	9.0	17.7	17.5
Return on Assets %	9.0	3.4	6.4	6.5	3.9	8.1	8.4
Price Range	76.69-38.38	70.00-44.13	51.31-30.44	49.63-25.50	63.38-40.75	...	...
P/E Ratio	32.0-16.0	82.3-51.9	34.2-20.3	33.5-17.2	71.2-45.8	...	...
Average Yield %	1.0	1.1	1.5	1.6	0.6	...	...

Statistics are as originally reported. [1] Incl. $850.0 mill. one-time chg. & $45.5 mill. one-time split-off costs. [2] Incl. $0.30 per sh. payable as GM class E common stk. [3] Incl. $329.6 mill. pre-tax restr. chg. & asset write-downs. [4] Incl. $70.3 mill. in-process R&D and asset write-downs chg., $49.4 mill. chg. for exec. retirements, cr$22.2 mill. restr. chgs. & $49.6 mill. gain fr. sale of stk. [5] Incl. $199.5 mill. pre-tax gain & $1.04 bill. pre-tax chgs. [6] Incl. $24.2 mill. chg. fr. acq. in-process R&D and $21.7 mill. chgs.

OFFICERS:
R. H. Brown, Chmn., C.E.O.
J. M. Heller, Vice-Chmn.

INVESTOR CONTACT: Myrna B. Vance, (888) 610-1122

PRINCIPAL OFFICE: 5400 Legacy Drive, Plano, TX 75024 -3199

TELEPHONE NUMBER: (972) 604-6000
FAX: (972) 605-6796
WEB: www.eds.com
NO. OF EMPLOYEES: 122,000 (approx.)
SHAREHOLDERS: 164,083 (approx.)
ANNUAL MEETING: In May
INCORPORATED: TX, 1962; reincorp., DE, 1994

INSTITUTIONAL HOLDINGS:
No. of Institutions: 545
Shares Held: 362,412,709
% Held: 77.5

INDUSTRY: Data processing and preparation (SIC: 7374)

TRANSFER AGENT(S): The Bank of New York, New York, NY

NYSE SYMBOL EMC
Rec. Pr. 39.18 (4/30/01)

EMC CORPORATION

YIELD ...
P/E RATIO 49.6

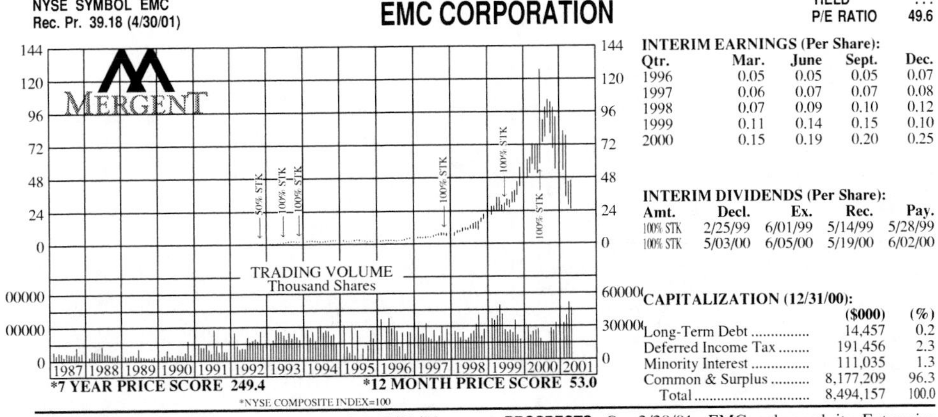

***7 YEAR PRICE SCORE 249.4** ***12 MONTH PRICE SCORE 53.0**

*NYSE COMPOSITE INDEX=100

INTERIM EARNINGS (Per Share):

Qtr.	Mar.	June	Sept.	Dec.
1996	0.05	0.05	0.05	0.07
1997	0.06	0.07	0.07	0.08
1998	0.07	0.09	0.10	0.12
1999	0.11	0.14	0.15	0.10
2000	0.15	0.19	0.20	0.25

INTERIM DIVIDENDS (Per Share):

Amt.	Decl.	Ex.	Rec.	Pay.
100% STK	2/25/99	6/01/99	5/14/99	5/28/99
100% STK	5/03/00	6/05/00	5/19/00	6/02/00

CAPITALIZATION (12/31/00):

	($000)	(%)
Long-Term Debt	14,457	0.2
Deferred Income Tax	191,456	2.3
Minority Interest	111,035	1.3
Common & Surplus	8,177,209	96.3
Total	8,494,157	100.0

RECENT DEVELOPMENTS: For the year ended 12/31/00, net income jumped 51.0% to $1.78 billion compared with $1.01 billion in 1999. Results for 1999 included a one-time after-tax restructuring and other charge of $169.9 million. Total revenues rose 32.1% to $8.87 billion from $6.72 billion in the prior year. Total storage revenue grew 44.3% to $8.29 billion due to strong performances across all major product areas, while software revenue rose 74.6% to $1.44 billion.

PROSPECTS: On 2/20/01, EMC enhanced its Enterprise Storage Network™ with new management software for mixed-vendor information storage networks. The new software, ESN Manager, unifies and streamlines management of heterogeneous information storage networks, providing a single point of management for storage area network configuration and control. In addition, EMC announced it has qualified several non-EMC storage systems for interoperability in an Enterprise Storage Network.

BUSINESS

EMC CORPORATION designs, manufactures and markets storage-related hardware, software and service products for mainframe, open systems and network attached storage systems. These products are sold as storage solutions for customers utilizing a variety of computer system platforms, including, but not limited to, IBM and IBM-compatible mainframes, Unisys, Compagnie des Machines Bull S.A., H-P, NCR and other open systems platforms. EMC's principal hardware products are based on Integrated Cached Disk Array (ICDA) technology, which combines high-speed semiconductor cache memory managed by advanced caching algorithms, with industry standard disk drives. EMC clients include: Swiss Bank Corporation, Japan Airlines, The Chicago Board Options Exchange, Toys 'R Us, ABB, GTE, Bertelsmann, and United Parcel Service. On 10/12/99, EMC acquired Data General Corporation.

ANNUAL FINANCIAL DATA

	12/31/00	[4] 12/31/99	12/31/98	12/31/97	12/31/96	[1] 12/30/95	12/31/94
Earnings Per Share	0.79	[3] 0.46	0.37	0.26	0.20	[2] 0.17	0.15
Cash Flow Per Share	1.04	0.66	0.46	0.32	0.24	0.19	0.16
Tang. Book Val. Per Share	3.72	2.38	1.65	1.20	0.84	0.61	0.46
INCOME STATEMENT (IN MILLIONS):							
Total Revenues	8,872.8	6,715.6	3,973.7	2,937.9	2,273.7	1,921.3	1,377.5
Costs & Expenses	6,072.1	5,027.4	2,788.6	2,139.7	1,690.2	1,431.9	994.2
Depreciation & Amort.	543.8	447.1	203.3	136.3	86.9	53.6	32.7
Operating Income	2,256.9	1,241.1	981.8	661.9	496.5	435.8	350.5
Net Interest Inc./(Exp.)	d14.6	d33.5	d20.2	d15.5	d12.0	d12.9	d15.3
Income Before Income Taxes	2,441.2	1,357.2	1,057.8	718.0	519.5	450.8	355.4
Income Taxes	659.1	346.6	264.5	179.5	133.2	124.0	104.7
Net Income	1,782.1	[3] 1,010.6	793.4	538.5	386.2	[2] 326.8	250.7
Cash Flow	2,325.9	1,457.7	996.7	674.8	473.2	380.5	283.4
Average Shs. Outstg. (000)	2,245,203	2,219,064	2,156,704	2,102,000	1,994,360	1,963,088	1,744,368
BALANCE SHEET (IN MILLIONS):							
Cash & Cash Equivalents	2,657.0	1,824.1	1,530.5	1,373.9	727.4	379.6	240.5
Total Current Assets	6,100.1	4,320.4	3,104.8	2,627.0	1,754.1	1,319.0	901.8
Net Property	1,510.1	1,023.2	637.5	396.5	276.4	218.9	173.0
Total Assets	10,628.3	7,173.3	4,568.6	3,490.1	2,293.5	1,745.7	1,317.5
Total Current Liabilities	2,113.6	1,397.9	653.2	505.9	417.5	359.4	301.5
Long-Term Obligations	14.5	686.6	538.9	558.5	191.2	245.8	286.1
Net Stockholders' Equity	8,177.2	4,951.8	3,325.3	2,376.3	1,636.8	1,140.3	727.6
Net Working Capital	3,986.4	2,922.5	2,451.6	2,121.2	1,336.6	959.6	600.3
Year-end Shs. Outstg. (000)	2,195,489	2,078,550	2,014,532	1,988,232	1,884,744	1,838,968	1,592,888
STATISTICAL RECORD:							
Operating Profit Margin %	25.4	18.5	24.7	22.5	21.8	22.7	25.4
Net Profit Margin %	20.1	15.0	20.0	18.3	17.0	17.0	18.2
Return on Equity %	21.8	20.4	23.9	22.7	23.6	28.7	34.4
Return on Assets %	16.8	14.1	17.4	15.4	16.8	18.7	19.0
Debt/Total Assets %	0.1	9.6	11.8	16.0	8.3	14.1	21.7
Price Range	127.00-47.50	55.50-21.00	21.66-6.00	8.14-3.97	4.55-1.89	3.42-1.63	3.00-1.56
P/E Ratio	160.7-60.1	120.6-45.6	58.2-16.1	31.3-15.3	23.2-9.6	20.1-9.6	20.4-10.6

Statistics are as originally reported. Adj. for 2-for-1 split, 11/97, 5/99 & 6/00. [1] Incl. results of McDATA Corp., acq. on 12/7/95 on a pooling-of-interests basis. [2] Excl. $38.6 mill. ($0.15/sh.) one-time after-tax chg. [3] Incl. $208.2 mill. restr. chg. [4] Refl. acq. of Data General Corp. on 10/12/99.

OFFICERS:
M. C. Ruettgers, Chmn.
J. Tucci, Pres., C.E.O.
W. J. Teuber Jr., Sr. V.P., C.F.O.

INVESTOR CONTACT: Marc Frederickson, Investor Relations, (508) 293-7137

PRINCIPAL OFFICE: 35 Parkwood Drive, Hopkinton, MA 01748-9103

TELEPHONE NUMBER: (508) 435-1000
FAX: (508) 435-5222
WEB: www.emc.com

NO. OF EMPLOYEES: 24,100 (approx.)

SHAREHOLDERS: 13,275 (approx. record)

ANNUAL MEETING: In May

INCORPORATED: MA, 1979

INSTITUTIONAL HOLDINGS:
No. of Institutions: 1,026
Shares Held: 1,422,936,498
% Held: 64.5

INDUSTRY: Computer storage devices (SIC: 3572)

TRANSFER AGENT(S): Boston EquiServe, Boston, MA

NYSE SYMBOL EME
Rec. Pr. 44.25 (5/31/01)

EMCOR GROUP, INC.

YIELD ...
P/E RATIO 15.0

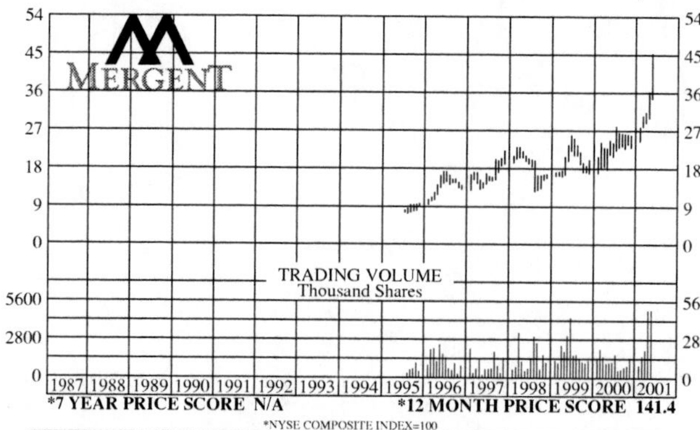

INTERIM EARNINGS (Per Share):

Qtr.	Mar.	June	Sept.	Dec.
1996	d0.37	0.93	0.19	0.20
1997	0.03	0.20	0.34	0.33
1998	0.08	0.34	0.55	0.69
1999	0.20	0.45	0.66	0.88
2000	0.40	0.68	0.83	1.04

INTERIM DIVIDENDS (Per Share):

Amt.	Decl.	Ex.	Rec.	Pay.

No dividends paid.

CAPITALIZATION (12/31/00):

	($000)	(%)
Long-Term Debt	115,878	33.2
Common & Surplus	233,503	66.8
Total	349,381	100.0

RECENT DEVELOPMENTS: For the year ended 12/31/00, net income advanced 44.1% to $40.1 million from $27.8 million in 1999. Revenues were $3.46 billion, up 19.6% from $2.89 billion a year earlier. The improvement in revenues was primarily attributed to growth in EME's operations, excluding Building Technology Engineers of North America, LLC and 1999 acquisitions. EME's backlog as of 12/31/00 was up 1.7% to $1.80 billion from a year earlier.

PROSPECTS: On 5/9/01, EME announced a number of energy and electric power generation projects awarded to its various subsidiaries, amounting to more than $300.0 million. Separately, the Company should benefit from its clients' continued trend toward outsourcing non-core operations. Meanwhile, EME is well positioned in the public and private markets, and remains committed to enhancing its presence in the emerging sectors.

BUSINESS

EMCOR GROUP, INC. is a mechanical and electrical construction and facilities services company. EME provides services to a broad range of commercial, industrial, utility and institutional customers through approximately 45 principal operating subsidiaries, including its majority interest in a limited liability company. The Company specializes in the design, integration, installation, start-up, operation and maintenance of systems for generation and distribution of electrical power; lighting systems; low-voltage systems, such as fire alarm, security, communications and process control systems; voice and data communications systems; heating, ventilation, air conditioning, refrigeration and clean-room process ventilation systems; and plumbing, process and high-purity piping systems.

REVENUES

(12/31/2000)	($000)	(%)
U.S. Electrical & Facilities	1,350,716	39.0
U.S. Mechanical & Facilities	1,253,663	36.2
U.S. Other Services	172,279	5.0
Canada Constuction	236,961	6.9
U.K. Construction	446,251	12.9
Other International Serv	334	0.0
Total	3,460,204	100.0

ANNUAL FINANCIAL DATA

	12/31/00	12/31/99	12/31/98	12/31/97	12/31/96	12/31/95	12/31/94
Earnings Per Share	**2.95**	**2.21**	**[1] 1.46**	**[1] 0.84**	**0.95**	**[2] d1.13**	**[3] d12.62**
Cash Flow Per Share	**3.76**	**2.90**	**2.03**	**1.65**	**1.74**	**d0.20**	**d10.95**
Tang. Book Val. Per Share	**17.76**	**11.00**	**13.50**	**9.94**	**8.82**	**7.49**	**8.61**
INCOME STATEMENT (IN MILLIONS):							
Total Revenues	3,460.2	2,894.0	2,210.4	1,950.9	1,669.3	1,588.7	1,764.0
Costs & Expenses	3,365.2	2,821.8	2,162.6	1,915.3	1,644.3	1,573.9	1,770.4
Depreciation & Amort.	16.1	14.1	10.6	8.2	7.9	8.9	15.7
Operating Income	78.9	58.1	37.2	27.4	17.1	5.9	d22.2
Net Interest Inc./(Exp.)	d7.3	d8.4	d7.5	d12.0	d12.6	d14.8	d2.5
Income Before Income Taxes	71.6	49.7	29.7	15.5	17.0	d9.9	d119.3
Income Taxes	31.5	21.9	12.6	6.9	7.5	1.0	cr0.3
Net Income	40.1	27.8	[1] 17.1	[1] 8.6	9.4	[2] d10.9	[3] d118.9
Cash Flow	56.2	41.9	27.7	16.8	17.3	d1.9	d103.2
Average Shs. Outstg. (000)	14,944	14,445	13,630	10,175	9,939	9,580	9,424
BALANCE SHEET (IN MILLIONS):							
Cash & Cash Equivalents	137.7	58.6	83.1	49.4	50.7	53.0	52.5
Total Current Assets	1,138.8	928.0	732.0	622.7	578.7	632.9	614.2
Net Property	39.0	36.5	32.1	27.2	27.0	27.1	33.7
Total Assets	1,261.9	1,056.5	801.0	660.7	614.7	710.9	707.5
Total Current Liabilities	852.4	717.6	511.9	456.6	421.7	525.5	522.0
Long-Term Obligations	115.9	116.0	117.3	63.2	73.1	68.2	59.8
Net Stockholders' Equity	233.5	170.2	119.8	95.3	83.9	70.6	81.1
Net Working Capital	286.4	210.4	220.1	166.1	157.0	107.4	92.2
Year-end Shs. Outstg. (000)	9,339	9,296	8,873	9,591	9,515	9,424	9,424
STATISTICAL RECORD:							
Operating Profit Margin %	2.3	2.0	1.7	1.4	1.0	0.4	...
Net Profit Margin %	1.2	1.0	0.8	0.4	0.6	...	...
Return on Equity %	17.2	16.3	14.3	9.0	11.3	...	...
Return on Assets %	3.2	2.6	2.1	1.3	1.5	...	...
Debt/Total Assets %	9.2	11.0	14.6	9.6	11.9	9.6	8.4
Price Range	28.13-16.81	26.00-16.06	23.13-12.50	22.25-12.75	17.38-9.38	9.75-7.25	...
P/E Ratio	9.5-5.7	11.8-7.3	15.8-8.6	26.5-15.2	18.3-9.9	...	...

Statistics are as originally reported. [1] Bef. extraord. chrg. 12/31/98: $4.8 mill.; chrg. 12/31/97: $1.0 mill. [2] Incls. loss of $926,000 from sale of bus. [3] Incls. net loss of $3.3 mill. & reorg. chrgs. of $91.3 mill.; Bef. inc. of $10.2 mill. from disc. ops. & acctg. chrg. of $2.1 mill.

OFFICERS:
F. T. MacInnis, Chmn., C.E.O.
J. M. Levy, Pres., C.O.O.
L. E. Chesser, Exec. V.P., C.F.O.
K. Matz, V.P., Treas.

INVESTOR CONTACT: Investor Relations, (203) 849-7800

PRINCIPAL OFFICE: 101 Merritt Seven Corporate Park, 7th Floor, Norwalk, CT 06851-1060

TELEPHONE NUMBER: (203) 849-7800
FAX: (203) 849-7870
WEB: www.emcorgroup.com

NO. OF EMPLOYEES: 22,000 (approx.)

SHAREHOLDERS: 138 (record)

ANNUAL MEETING: In July

INCORPORATED: DE, 1987

INSTITUTIONAL HOLDINGS:
No. of Institutions: 85
Shares Held: 11,285,590
% Held: 107.3

INDUSTRY: Electrical work (SIC: 1731)

TRANSFER AGENT(S): Bank of New York, New York, NY

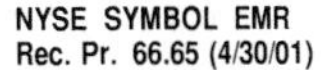

NYSE SYMBOL EMR
Rec. Pr. 66.65 (4/30/01)

EMERSON COMPANY

YIELD 2.3%
P/E RATIO 19.7

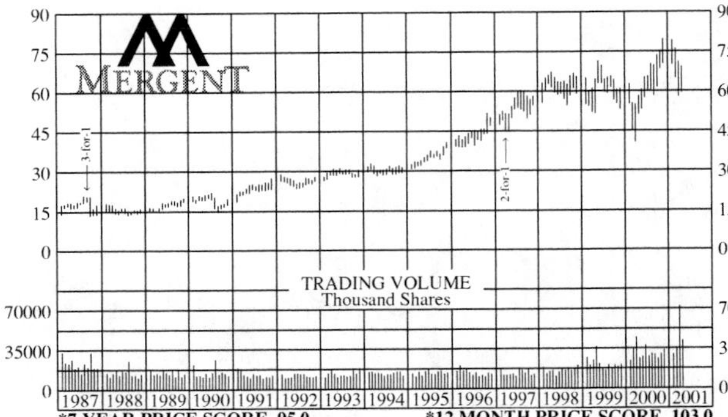

***7 YEAR PRICE SCORE 95.0** ***12 MONTH PRICE SCORE 103.0**

*NYSE COMPOSITE INDEX=100

INTERIM EARNINGS (Per Share):

Qtr.	Dec.	Mar.	June	Sept.
1996-97	0.57	0.63	0.67	0.65
1997-98	0.64	0.69	0.73	0.71
1998-99	0.69	0.74	0.79	0.78
1999-00	0.75	0.82	0.87	0.86
2000-01	0.83	...	...	...

INTERIM DIVIDENDS (Per Share):

Amt.	Decl.	Ex.	Rec.	Pay.
0.357Q	8/01/00	8/09/00	8/11/00	9/11/00
0.383Q	11/07/00	11/15/00	11/17/00	12/11/00
0.383Q	2/06/01	2/14/01	2/16/01	3/09/01
0.383Q	5/01/01	5/09/01	5/11/01	6/11/01

Indicated div.: $1.53 (Div. Reinv. Plan)

CAPITALIZATION (9/30/00):

	($000)	(%)
Long-Term Debt	2,247,700	26.0
Common & Surplus	6,402,800	74.0
Total	8,650,500	100.0

RECENT DEVELOPMENTS: For the quarter ended 12/31/00, net income rose 10.0% to $357.4 million versus $324.9 million the year before. Net sales rose 10.6% to $3.92 billion from $3.54 billion a year earlier. Process controls segment sales grew 4.3% to $761.0 million, while industrial automation segment sales slipped 2.9% to $766.1 million. Electronic and telecommunications segment sales soared to $1.09 billion, while heating, ventilating and air conditioning segment sales fell 3.9% to $519.7 million.

PROSPECTS: On 12/05/00, EMR launched a new brand identity program to reflect EMR's progression from a manufacturer of electrical products to a manufacturer of technology-driven products and services for a broad range of industries. Going forward, stronger demand for network power and process automation products should continue to more than offset weak performances at EMR's consumer and general industrial businesses. For 2001, EMR expects earnings to reach $3.66 per share.

BUSINESS

EMERSON COMPANY (formerly Emerson Electric Company) is a global manufacturer of a broad range of electrical, electromechanical and electronic products and systems sold through independent distributors and to original equipment manufacturers. The process control segment provides measurement and fluid flow instrumentation, valves and control systems as well as services for process and industrial applications. The industrial automation segment provides industrial motors, drives, controls and equipment. The electronics and telecommunications segment provides power supplies and power distribution, protection and conversion equipment, and fiber optic conduits. The heating, ventilating and air conditioning segment provides a broad range of components and systems for refrigeration and comfort control markets. The appliance and tools segment provides motors, controls and other components for appliances, refrigeration and comfort control applications as well as disposers, tools and storage products.

ANNUAL FINANCIAL DATA

	9/30/00	9/30/99	9/30/98	9/30/97	9/30/96	9/30/95	9/30/94
Earnings Per Share	**3.30**	**3.00**	**2.77**	**2.52**	**2.27**	**2.03**	**[1] 1.76**
Cash Flow Per Share	**4.87**	**4.45**	**4.03**	**3.67**	**3.31**	**2.99**	**2.83**
Tang. Book Val. Per Share	**2.53**	**4.43**	**4.79**	**5.23**	**5.75**	**5.55**	**5.54**
Dividends Per Share	**1.46**	**1.33**	**1.21**	**1.10**	**1.00**	**0.92**	**0.80**
Dividend Payout %	**44.1**	**44.4**	**43.7**	**43.8**	**44.3**	**45.3**	**45.5**
INCOME STATEMENT (IN MILLIONS):							
Total Revenues	15,544.8	14,269.5	13,447.2	12,298.6	11,149.9	10,012.9	8,607.2
Costs & Expenses	12,325.4	11,326.5	10,709.8	9,804.9	8,892.4	8,004.7	6,868.1
Depreciation & Amort.	678.5	637.5	562.5	511.6	464.6	408.9	364.5
Operating Income	2,540.9	2,305.5	2,174.9	1,982.1	1,792.9	1,599.3	1,374.6
Net Interest Inc./(Exp.)	d287.6	d189.7	d151.7	d120.9	d126.9	d110.6	d88.5
Income Before Income Taxes	2,178.3	2,020.9	1,923.5	1,783.6	1,609.0	1,459.9	1,427.8
Income Taxes	755.9	707.3	694.9	661.7	590.5	530.9	523.4
Net Income	1,422.4	1,313.6	1,228.6	1,121.9	1,018.5	929.0	[1] 904.4
Cash Flow	2,100.9	1,951.1	1,791.1	1,633.5	1,483.1	1,337.9	1,268.9
Average Shs. Outstg. (000)	431,400	438,400	444,100	445,000	448,096	447,506	448,464
BALANCE SHEET (IN MILLIONS):							
Cash & Cash Equivalents	280.8	266.1	209.7	221.1	149.0	117.3	113.3
Total Current Assets	5,482.7	5,124.4	5,001.3	4,716.8	4,187.2	3,784.1	3,338.2
Net Property	3,243.4	3,154.4	3,011.6	2,735.4	2,450.8	2,134.9	1,947.3
Total Assets	15,164.3	13,623.5	12,659.8	11,463.3	10,481.0	9,399.0	8,215.0
Total Current Liabilities	5,218.8	4,590.4	4,021.7	3,842.4	3,021.1	3,280.7	2,617.3
Long-Term Obligations	2,247.7	1,317.1	1,056.6	570.7	772.6	208.6	279.9
Net Stockholders' Equity	6,402.8	6,180.5	5,803.3	5,420.7	5,353.4	4,870.8	4,341.8
Net Working Capital	263.9	534.0	979.6	874.4	1,166.1	503.4	720.9
Year-end Shs. Outstg. (000)	427,477	433,044	438,224	440,804	447,440	447,898	447,172
STATISTICAL RECORD:							
Operating Profit Margin %	16.3	16.2	16.2	16.1	16.1	16.0	16.0
Net Profit Margin %	9.2	9.2	9.1	9.1	9.1	9.3	10.5
Return on Equity %	22.2	21.3	21.2	20.7	19.0	19.1	20.8
Return on Assets %	9.4	9.6	9.7	9.8	9.7	9.9	11.0
Debt/Total Assets %	14.8	9.7	8.3	5.0	7.4	2.2	3.4
Price Range	79.75-40.50	71.44-51.44	67.44-54.50	60.38-45.00	51.75-38.75	40.88-30.75	32.94-28.06
P/E Ratio	24.2-12.3	23.8-17.1	24.3-19.7	24.0-17.9	22.8-17.1	20.1-15.1	18.7-15.9
Average Yield %	2.4	2.2	2.0	2.1	2.2	2.6	2.6

Statistics are as originally reported. Adjusted for 2-for-1 stock split 11/96. [1] Bef. charge for cum. eff. of change in acctg. principle of $115.9 mill.

OFFICERS:
C. F. Knight, Chmn.
D. N. Farr, C.E.O.
J. G. Berges, Pres.

INVESTOR CONTACT: Robert T. Sharp, Dir., Investor Relations, (341) 553-2197

PRINCIPAL OFFICE: 8000 West Florissant Avenue, P.O. Box 4100, St. Louis, MO 63136

TELEPHONE NUMBER: (314) 553-2000
FAX: (314) 553-3527
WEB: www.gotoemerson.com

NO. OF EMPLOYEES: 123,400 (approx.)

SHAREHOLDERS: 35,000 (approx.)

ANNUAL MEETING: In Feb.

INCORPORATED: MO, Sept., 1890

INSTITUTIONAL HOLDINGS:
No. of Institutions: 835
Shares Held: 299,617,921
% Held: 69.8

INDUSTRY: Process control instruments (SIC: 3823)

TRANSFER AGENT(S): Mellon Investor Services, South Hackensack, NJ

NYSE SYMBOL EGN
Rec. Pr. 37.00 (4/30/01)

ENERGEN CORPORATION

YIELD 1.8%
P/E RATIO 19.6

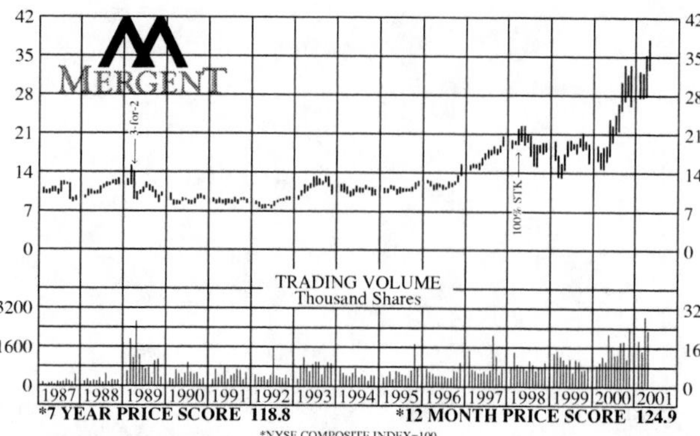

*7 YEAR PRICE SCORE 118.8 *12 MONTH PRICE SCORE 124.9

*NYSE COMPOSITE INDEX=100

INTERIM EARNINGS (Per Share):

Qtr.	Dec.	Mar.	June	Sept.
1997-98	0.21	1.37	Nil	d0.34
1998-99	0.13	1.42	0.12	d0.28
1999-00	0.30	1.36	0.15	d0.06
2000-01	0.44	...	...	...

INTERIM DIVIDENDS (Per Share):

Amt.	Decl.	Ex.	Rec.	Pay.
0.165Q	4/26/00	5/11/00	5/15/00	6/01/00
0.17Q	7/26/00	8/11/00	8/15/00	9/01/00
0.17Q	10/25/00	11/13/00	11/15/00	12/01/00
0.17Q	1/24/01	2/13/01	2/15/01	3/01/01
0.17Q	4/25/01	5/11/01	5/15/01	6/01/01

Indicated div.: $0.68 (Div. Reinv. Plan)

CAPITALIZATION (9/30/00):

	($000)	(%)
Long-Term Debt	353,932	46.9
Common & Surplus	400,860	53.1
Total	754,792	100.0

RECENT DEVELOPMENTS: For the quarter ended 12/31/00, net income soared 50.2% to $13.7 million versus $9.1 million in 1999. Operating revenues grew 36.3% to $175.9 million from $129.0 million in 1999. Revenues benefited from increases in realized prices of natural gas, oil, and natural gas liquids from Energen Resources Corporation. Natural gas distribution revenues advanced 39.4% to $119.1 million, while oil and gas revenues increased 30.3% to $56.8 million.

PROSPECTS: EGN expects to generate earnings per share growth of 25.0% to 30.0% in fiscal 2001, assuming that its unhedged gas production receives an average price of $3.00 per thousand cubic feet, unhedged oil production receives an average price of $25.00 per barrel and natural gas liquids averages $16.80 per barrel. Separately, EGN's subsidiary, Energen Resources Corporation, has entered into a strategic alliance with Southwest Energy Company to jointly explore approximately 14,200 net acres in New Mexico.

BUSINESS

ENERGEN CORPORATION is a diversified energy holding company engaged in the business of natural gas distribution and oil and gas exploration and production. EGN provides natural gas to residential, commercial and industrial customers located in Alabama. Alagasco, EGN's principal subsidiary, is the largest natural gas distribution utility in the State of Alabama. EGN's utility operations are subject to regulation by the Alabama Public Service Commission. The oil and gas exploration and production arm of Energen is Energen Resources, which conducts its activities in the Gulf of Mexico. In 2000, revenues were derived: 65.9% natural gas distribution and 34.1% oil and gas production activities.

ANNUAL FINANCIAL DATA

	9/30/00	9/30/99	9/30/98	9/30/97	9/30/96	9/30/95	9/30/94
Earnings Per Share	**[1] 1.75**	**1.38**	**1.23**	**1.16**	**0.98**	**0.89**	**1.10**
Cash Flow Per Share	**4.61**	**4.35**	**3.98**	**3.53**	**2.84**	**2.24**	**2.39**
Tang. Book Val. Per Share	**13.21**	**12.09**	**11.23**	**13.49**	**8.44**	**7.96**	**7.65**
Dividends Per Share	**0.67**	**0.65**	**0.63**	**0.61**	**0.59**	**0.57**	**0.55**
Dividend Payout %	**38.3**	**47.1**	**51.2**	**52.8**	**60.5**	**64.4**	**50.2**
INCOME STATEMENT (IN THOUSANDS):							
Total Revenues	555,595	497,517	502,627	448,230	399,442	321,204	377,073
Costs & Expenses	372,721	331,519	360,143	325,444	308,449	249,369	303,696
Depreciation & Amort.	87,073	88,615	80,999	59,688	41,118	29,577	28,000
Maintenance Exp.	...	...	...	11,112	11,078	9,849	9,469
Operating Income	95,801	77,383	61,485	51,986	38,797	32,409	35,908
Net Interest Inc./(Exp.)	d37,769	d37,173	d30,001	d22,906	d13,920	d11,818	d11,345
Income Taxes	6,789	135	cr2,221	3,097	5,048	3,681	6,611
Net Income	[1] 53,018	41,410	36,249	28,997	21,541	19,308	23,751
Cash Flow	140,091	130,025	117,248	88,685	62,659	48,885	51,751
Average Shs. Outstg.	30,359	29,921	29,438	25,126	22,046	21,812	21,668
BALANCE SHEET (IN THOUSANDS):							
Gross Property	1,422,770	1,315,581	1,148,205	1,037,840	769,112	621,710	556,948
Accumulated Depreciation	519,444	458,614	395,794	375,303	328,262	299,096	274,379
Net Property	907,829	861,107	756,344	667,003	444,916	327,264	287,182
Total Assets	1,203,041	1,184,895	993,455	919,797	570,971	459,084	411,314
Long-Term Obligations	353,932	371,824	372,782	279,602	195,545	131,600	118,302
Net Stockholders' Equity	400,860	361,504	329,249	301,143	188,405	173,924	167,026
Year-end Shs. Outstg.	30,351	29,904	29,327	22,326	22,326	21,844	21,836
STATISTICAL RECORD:							
Operating Profit Margin %	17.2	15.6	12.2	11.6	9.7	10.1	9.5
Net Profit Margin %	9.5	8.3	7.2	6.5	5.4	6.0	6.3
Net Inc./Net Property %	5.8	4.8	4.8	4.3	4.8	5.9	8.3
Net Inc./Tot. Capital %	7.0	5.6	5.2	5.0	5.6	6.3	8.3
Return on Equity %	13.2	11.5	11.0	9.6	11.4	11.1	14.2
Accum. Depr./Gross Prop. %	36.5	34.9	34.5	36.2	42.7	48.1	49.3
Price Range	33.56-14.69	21.25-13.13	22.50-15.13	20.63-14.50	15.63-10.88	12.56-10.06	11.94-9.63
P/E Ratio	19.2-8.4	15.4-9.5	18.3-12.3	17.9-12.6	16.0-11.2	14.2-11.4	10.9-8.8
Average Yield %	2.8	3.8	3.3	3.5	4.5	5.0	5.1

Statistics are as originally reported. Adjusted for 2-for-1 stock split, 3/98. [1] Incl. an after-tax gain of $1.9 mill. on the sale of offshore properties.

OFFICERS:
W. M. Warren Jr., Chmn., Pres., C.E.O.
G. C. Ketcham, Exec. V.P., C.F.O., Treas.
D. C. Reynolds, Gen. Couns., Sec.

INVESTOR CONTACT: Julie S. Ryland, Asst. V.P., Inv. Rel., (800) 654-3206

PRINCIPAL OFFICE: 605 Richard Arrington Jr. Blvd. N., Birmingham, AL 35203-2707

TELEPHONE NUMBER: (205) 326-2700
FAX: (205) 326-2704
WEB: www.energen.com

NO. OF EMPLOYEES: 1,401

SHAREHOLDERS: 8,600 (approx.)

ANNUAL MEETING: In Jan.

INCORPORATED: AL, Jan., 1978

INSTITUTIONAL HOLDINGS:
No. of Institutions: 159
Shares Held: 16,691,509
% Held: 54.3

INDUSTRY: Natural gas distribution (SIC: 4924)

TRANSFER AGENT(S): First Chicago Trust Company of New York, Jersey City, NJ

NYSE SYMBOL ENR
Rec. Pr. 23.82 (4/30/01)

ENERGIZER HOLDINGS, INC.

YIELD ...
P/E RATIO 17.4

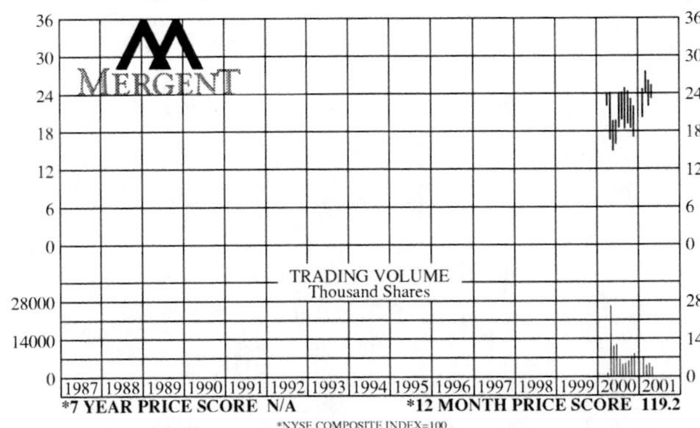

*7 YEAR PRICE SCORE N/A *12 MONTH PRICE SCORE 119.2

*NYSE COMPOSITE INDEX=100

INTERIM EARNINGS (Per Share):

Qtr.	Dec.	Mar.	June	Sept.
2000	1.07	0.18	0.24	0.38
2001	0.57	...	...	...

INTERIM DIVIDENDS (Per Share):

Amt.	Decl.	Ex.	Rec.	Pay.

No dividends paid.

CAPITALIZATION (9/30/00):

	($000)	(%)
Long-Term Debt	370,000	33.4
Common & Surplus	738,200	66.6
Total	1,108,200	100.0

RECENT DEVELOPMENTS: For the first quarter ended 12/31/00, net income fell 48.2% to $54.2 million compared with $104.7 million in the equivalent period of fiscal 2000. The decrease in earnings was primarily attributed to lower volumes. Net sales amounted to $558.7 million, a decrease of 17.1% versus $673.6 million in the comparable prior-year period. Results for 1999 reflected ENR as a wholly-owned subsidiary of Ralston Purina Company.

PROSPECTS: Revenues are pressured by lower pricing, an unfavorable product mix and inventory reductions by U.S. retail customers. Meanwhile, the Company improved its internal procedures by eliminating a one month lag in the reporting of its international operations. Separately, the Company announced an original equipment manufacturer purchase agreement with Nutek Inc. Under the terms of the agreement, ENR will supply batteries for NuLight products.

BUSINESS

ENERGIZER HOLDINGS, INC. was formed on 4/1/00, when it was spun-off from Ralston Purina Company. Energizer Holdings, Inc., through its subsidiaries, manufactures batteries, flashlights and portable lighting devices. The Company offers a full line of products in five major categories: alkaline batteries, carbon zinc batteries, miniatures and rechargeable batteries, and lighting products. The Company's line of non-rechargeable alkaline and carbon zinc batteries is sold under the brand names of ENERGIZER and EVEREADY in more than 160 countries. Although the Company sold its rechargeable battery manufacturing and assembly business in November 1999, ENR continues to market a line of rechargeable batteries for retail sale to consumers.

REVENUES

(09/30/00)	($000)	(%)
Alkaline Batteries	1,281,200	66.9
Carbon Zinc Batteries	316,400	16.5
Lighting Products	127,600	6.7
Miniature Batteries	64,500	3.4
Other revenues	124,600	6.5
Total	1,914,300	100.0

ANNUAL FINANCIAL DATA

	9/30/00	9/30/99	9/30/98	9/30/97
Earnings Per Share	2 3 1.87	...	...	...
Cash Flow Per Share	2.72	...	...	...
Tang. Book Val. Per Share	7.73	...	...	...
INCOME STATEMENT (IN MILLIONS):				
Total Revenues	1,914.3	1,872.3	1,921.8	2,005.8
Costs & Expenses	1,525.6	1,521.6	1,547.0	1,675.8
Depreciation & Amort.	82.0	94.9	101.2	112.3
Operating Income	306.7	255.8	273.6	217.7
Net Interest Inc./(Exp.)	d27.5	d7.6	d11.1	d13.8
Income Before Income Taxes	279.2	248.2	262.5	203.9
Income Taxes	99.0	85.2	54.3	44.6
Net Income	2 3 180.2	1 2 163.0	1 2 208.2	1 2 159.3
Cash Flow	262.2	257.9	309.4	271.6
Average Shs. Outstg. (000)	96,300	...	...	...
BALANCE SHEET (IN MILLIONS):				
Cash & Cash Equivalents	11.9	27.8	49.1	...
Total Current Assets	930.3	974.0	997.2	...
Net Property	485.4	472.8	476.9	...
Total Assets	1,793.5	1,833.7	2,077.6	...
Total Current Liabilities	528.6	495.9	518.7	...
Long-Term Obligations	370.0	1.9	1.3	...
Net Stockholders' Equity	738.2	1,312.9	1,531.3	...
Net Working Capital	401.7	478.1	478.5	...
Year-end Shs. Outstg. (000)	95,552	...	...	...
STATISTICAL RECORD:				
Operating Profit Margin %	16.0	13.7	14.2	10.9
Net Profit Margin %	9.4	8.7	10.8	7.9
Return on Equity %	24.4	12.4	13.6	...
Return on Assets %	10.0	8.9	10.0	...
Debt/Total Assets %	20.6	0.1	0.1	...
Price Range	24.94-14.81	...	...	...
P/E Ratio	13.3-7.9	...	...	...

Statistics are as originally reported. 1 Incl. provision for restruct. of $7.8 mill., 1999; $21.0 mill., 1998; $78.5 mill., 1997. 2 Incl. net gain fr. disc. opers. of $1.2 mill., 2000; loss $79.8 mill., 1999; loss $43.5 mill., 1998; gain $500,000, 1997. 3 Incl. net nonrecurr. gain of $10.2 mill.

OFFICERS:
W. P. Stiritz, Chmn.
J. P. Mulcahy, C.E.O.
P. C. Mannix, Pres.

INVESTOR CONTACT: Jacqueline Buritz, V.P., Investor Relations, (314) 982-2013

PRINCIPAL OFFICE: 800 Chouteau Ave., St. Louis, MO 63102

TELEPHONE NUMBER: (314) 982-2000
FAX: (314) 982-2752
WEB: www.energizer.com

NO. OF EMPLOYEES: 10,480

SHAREHOLDERS: 21,016

ANNUAL MEETING: In Jan.

INCORPORATED: MO, Sept., 1999

INSTITUTIONAL HOLDINGS:
No. of Institutions: 195
Shares Held: 54,722,303
% Held: 59.7

INDUSTRY: Primary batteries, dry and wet (SIC: 3692)

TRANSFER AGENT(S): Continental Stock Transfer & Trust Company, New York, NY

NYSE SYMBOL EAS
Rec. Pr. 19.87 (4/30/01)

ENERGY EAST CORPORATION

YIELD 4.6%
P/E RATIO 9.6

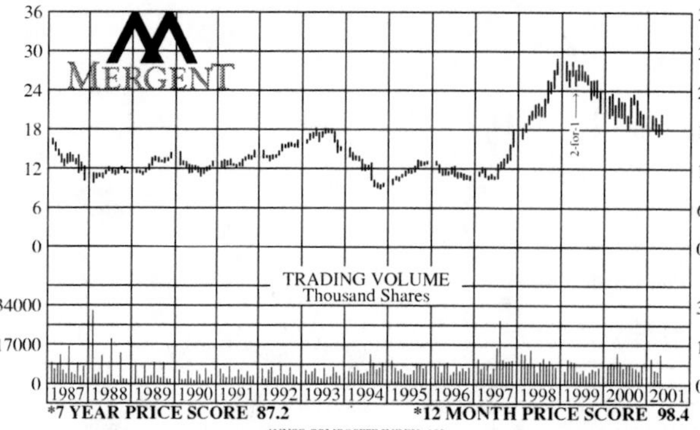

INTERIM EARNINGS (Per Share):

Qtr.	Mar.	June	Sept.	Dec.
1997	0.58	0.18	0.19	0.34
1998	0.58	0.23	0.36	0.35
1999	0.71	0.48	0.41	0.26
2000	0.83	0.50	0.30	0.45

INTERIM DIVIDENDS (Per Share):

Amt.	Decl.	Ex.	Rec.	Pay.
0.22Q	4/14/00	4/19/00	4/24/00	5/15/00
0.22Q	7/14/00	7/20/00	7/24/00	8/15/00
0.22Q	10/13/00	10/19/00	10/23/00	11/15/00
0.23Q	1/12/01	1/18/01	1/22/01	2/15/01
0.23Q	4/12/01	4/19/01	4/23/01	5/15/01

Indicated div.: $0.92 (Div. Reinv. Plan)

CAPITALIZATION (12/31/00):

	($000)	(%)
Long-Term Debt	2,346,814	49.6
Deferred Income Tax	624,389	13.2
Redeemable Pfd. Stock	43,324	0.9
Common & Surplus	1,716,522	36.3
Total	4,731,049	100.0

RECENT DEVELOPMENTS: For the year ended 12/31/00, income before an extraordinary charge climbed to $236.7 million compared with $236.3 million in 1999. Results for 2000 excluded an extraordinary charge of $1.6 million from the early retirement of debt. Results for 1999 excluded an extraordinary charge of $17.6 million partially offset by a non-recurring gain of $14.0 million from the sale of the EAS' coal-fired plants. Total operating revenues rose 29.9% to $2.96 billion.

PROSPECTS: The Company entered into a definitive agreement to acquire RGS Energy Group, Inc. in a transaction valued at about $1.40 billion, including the assumption of about $1.00 billion of RGS Energy debt. The transaction is expected to be completed within a year. Separately, as a result of higher wholesale power costs, Central Maine Power, a subsidiary of the Company, increased rates for more than 10,000 medium and large commercial customers in Maine on 3/1/01.

BUSINESS

ENERGY EAST CORPORATION (formerly New York State Electric & Gas Corporation) is a holding company that provides electricity and gas service in New York, Massachusetts, Maine, New Hampshire, Vermont, and New Jersey. EAS serves 1.4 million electric customers and 600,000 natural gas customers in New York and New England. Revenues in 2000 were divided: 68.4% electric, 26.1% gas and 5.5% other. Retail electric revenues in 2000 were derived: residential, 37.8%; commercial, 26.3%; industrial, 26.9%; and other, 9.0%. The electricity generated is fueled by 72%, coal; 24%, nuclear; and 4%, hydro. In March 1999, EAS completed the sale of its Homer City generation assets. The Company completed its merger with Connecticut Energy Corporation on 2/18/00. EAS sold XENERGY, Inc., its energy services and fuel management company, in September 2000.

ANNUAL FINANCIAL DATA

	12/31/00	12/31/99	12/31/98	12/31/97	12/31/96	12/31/95	12/31/94
Earnings Per Share	**[4] 2.06**	**[3] 1.88**	**3.02**	**[2] 1.29**	**[1] 1.19**	**1.25**	**1.19**
Cash Flow Per Share	**3.52**	**7.53**	**2.99**	**2.74**	**2.52**	**2.54**	**2.44**
Tang. Book Val. Per Share	**6.49**	**13.02**	**27.22**	**13.73**	**12.70**	**12.19**	**11.64**
Dividends Per Share	**0.88**	**0.84**	**0.78**	**0.70**	**0.70**	**0.70**	**1.00**
Dividend Payout %	**42.7**	**44.7**	**25.7**	**54.5**	**59.1**	**56.2**	**84.4**
INCOME STATEMENT (IN MILLIONS):							
Total Revenues	2,959.5	2,278.6	2,499.4	2,130.0	2,059.4	2,009.5	1,898.9
Costs & Expenses	2,172.0	1,006.5	1,722.0	1,378.4	1,304.7	1,235.8	1,175.3
Depreciation & Amort.	165.5	639.1	191.1	198.6	189.4	184.8	178.3
Maintenance Exp.	108.1	85.8	111.5	110.4	107.7	116.8	106.6
Operating Income	513.9	547.2	474.8	442.7	457.5	337.4	322.7
Net Interest Inc./(Exp.)	d152.5	d132.9	d125.6	d123.2	d122.7	d129.6	d136.1
Income Taxes	156.7	214.5	137.2	117.7	107.9	134.8	115.9
Net Income	[4] 236.7	[3] 236.3	194.2	[2] 184.6	[1] 178.2	196.7	187.6
Cash Flow	402.2	875.4	385.3	373.8	358.1	362.7	347.0
Average Shs. Outstg. (000)	114,213	116,316	128,742	136,306	142,254	143,006	142,508
BALANCE SHEET (IN MILLIONS):							
Gross Property	6,729.2	4,174.1	6,074.3	6,015.5	5,916.0	5,755.2	5,630.0
Accumulated Depreciation	3,096.3	2,034.3	2,211.6	2,093.3	1,933.6	1,791.6	1,642.7
Net Property	3,632.9	2,139.8	3,862.7	3,922.3	3,982.4	3,963.6	3,987.3
Total Assets	7,003.6	3,769.4	4,883.3	5,028.7	5,059.7	5,114.3	5,222.9
Long-Term Obligations	2,346.8	1,235.1	1,435.1	1,450.2	1,480.8	1,581.4	1,651.1
Net Stockholders' Equity	1,716.5	1,404.0	1,713.5	1,803.3	1,770.0	1,743.5	1,664.9
Year-end Shs. Outstg. (000)	117,656	109,343	125,894	131,358	139,340	143,006	143,006
STATISTICAL RECORD:							
Operating Profit Margin %	17.4	24.0	19.0	20.8	22.2	16.8	17.0
Net Profit Margin %	8.0	10.4	7.8	8.7	8.7	9.8	9.9
Net Inc./Net Property %	6.5	11.0	5.0	4.7	4.5	5.0	4.7
Net Inc./Tot. Capital %	5.0	8.1	4.7	4.2	4.1	4.5	4.7
Return on Equity %	13.8	16.8	11.3	10.2	10.1	11.3	11.3
Accum. Depr./Gross Prop. %	46.0	48.7	36.4	34.8	32.7	31.1	29.2
Price Range	23.63-17.94	28.63-20.56	29.00-16.53	17.88-10.31	13.19-10.19	13.38-9.50	15.25-8.88
P/E Ratio	11.5-8.7	15.2-10.9	19.2-10.9	13.9-8.0	11.1-8.6	10.7-7.6	12.9-7.5
Average Yield %	4.2	3.4	3.4	5.0	6.0	6.1	8.3

Statistics are as originally reported. Adj. for 2-for-1 stock split, 4/99. [1] Incl. $0.14/sh. chg. to write down an investment in EnerSoft Corp. [2] Incl. $0.24/sh. chg. for fees rel. to an unsolicited tender offer. [3] Excl. $17.6 mill. extraordinary chg. fr. early exting. of debt & incl. $0.12 per share non-recur. gain. [4] Excl. $1.6 mill. extraord. chg.

OFFICERS:
W. W. von Schack, Chmn., C.E.O.
S. Burns., Pres.
R. D. Kump, V.P., Treas.

INVESTOR CONTACT: Investor Relations, (607) 347-2561

PRINCIPAL OFFICE: P. O. Box 12904, Albany, NY 12212-2904

TELEPHONE NUMBER: (518) 434-3049
FAX: (607) 347-2560
WEB: www.energyeast.com

NO. OF EMPLOYEES: 5,721

SHAREHOLDERS: 35,918

ANNUAL MEETING: In Apr.

INCORPORATED: NY, Oct., 1852

INSTITUTIONAL HOLDINGS:
No. of Institutions: 211
Shares Held: 52,958,161
% Held: 45.2

INDUSTRY: Electric and other services combined (SIC: 4931)

TRANSFER AGENT(S): Mellon Investor Services, South Hackensack, NJ

NYSE SYMBOL ENC
Rec. Pr. 6.17 (4/30/01)

ENESCO GROUP, INC.

YIELD ...
P/E RATIO 5.7

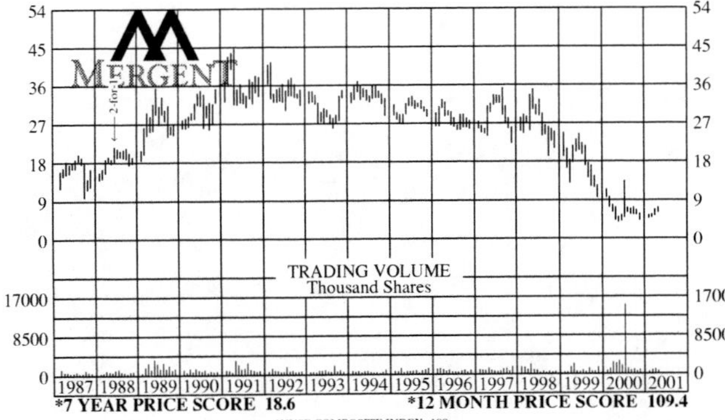

*7 YEAR PRICE SCORE 18.6 *12 MONTH PRICE SCORE 109.4

*NYSE COMPOSITE INDEX=100

INTERIM EARNINGS (Per Share):

Qtr.	Mar.	June	Sept.	Dec.
1997	0.12	0.55	d0.16	0.07
1998	0.21	0.72	0.39	d2.77
1999	0.28	0.39	0.48	0.76
2000	0.01	d0.18	0.21	1.05

INTERIM DIVIDENDS (Per Share):

Amt.	Decl.	Ex.	Rec.	Pay.
0.28Q	6/02/99	6/14/99	6/16/99	7/01/99
0.28Q	9/01/99	9/13/99	9/15/99	10/01/99
0.28Q	12/01/99	12/13/99	12/15/99	1/01/00
0.28Q	3/01/00	3/13/00	3/15/00	4/01/00

Dividend Payment Suspended

CAPITALIZATION (12/31/00):

	($000)	(%)
Deferred Income Tax	5,497	4.2
Common & Surplus	125,693	95.8
Total	131,190	100.0

RECENT DEVELOPMENTS: For the twelve months ended 12/31/00, net income decreased 43.8% to $15.1 million compared with 26.9 million in the previous year. Results for 2000 included one-time pre-tax costs of $2.2 million related to the termination of the Precious Moments acquisition, costs for executive severance, and the termination of supplemental retirement plans. Net revenues declined 17.1% to $325.0 million from $391.8 million in the prior year. Operating profit fell 61.6% to $9.1 million.

PROSPECTS: ENC initiated many strategic improvements in 2000 that should have a favorable effect on results in 2001, including the shift to an employee-based sales team in the retail specialty channel. Meanwhile, the Company should continue to benefit from the success of its HARRY POTTER product line as well as the continuing success of its Precious Moments and Mary Engelbreit lines in its core retail channels.

BUSINESS

ENESCO GROUP, INC. (formerly Stanhome Inc.) sells designed and licensed collectible figurines and ornaments, action musicals, decorative home accessories and other giftware to independent retailers, mass marketers, catalogers and other direct-response distributors through its Enesco Giftware Group subsidiaries or their licensed distributors. ENC displays the Giftware Groups products in twelve showrooms located in the U.S., as well as at periodic trade and private shows held in major U.S. and foreign cities. These products are marketed principally in the U.S. through approximately 30,000 independent retail outlets, including gift stores, greeting card and gift shops, national chains, mail order houses and department stores.

QUARTERLY DATA

(12/31/2000)($000)	REV	INC
1st Quarter	73,460	1,388
2nd Quarter................	73,296	(4,121)
3rd Quarter	88,247	6,287
4th Quarter................	89,958	5,533

ANNUAL FINANCIAL DATA

	12/31/00	12/31/99	12/31/98	12/31/97	12/31/96	12/31/95	12/31/94
Earnings Per Share	**[4] 1.11**	**[3] 1.87**	**[2] d1.38**	**[1] d0.60**	**2.12**	**2.22**	**2.26**
Cash Flow Per Share	**1.74**	**2.39**	**d0.84**	**1.12**	**2.90**	**2.92**	**2.79**
Tang. Book Val. Per Share	**6.62**	**5.64**	**6.92**	**8.10**	**8.64**	**8.02**	**7.72**
Dividends Per Share	**0.56**	**1.12**	**1.12**	**1.12**	**1.08**	**1.06**	**1.01**
Dividend Payout %	**50.4**	**59.9**	**...**	**...**	**50.7**	**47.7**	**44.9**
INCOME STATEMENT (IN THOUSANDS):							
Total Revenues	324,961	384,044	451,040	476,183	844,992	830,189	790,176
Costs & Expenses	307,268	352,884	393,088	436,385	749,545	730,555	699,185
Depreciation & Amort.	8,606	7,509	8,844	9,180	13,982	13,139	10,440
Operating Income	9,087	23,651	49,108	30,618	81,465	86,496	80,552
Net Interest Inc./(Exp.)	d3,409	d3,330	d3,575	d6,783	d8,684	d7,751	d2,019
Income Before Income Taxes	5,153	19,285	d3,295	20,830	69,279	76,339	80,739
Income Taxes	cr9,939	cr7,591	19,148	10,285	30,842	34,439	36,684
Net Income	[4] 15,092	[3] 26,876	[2] d22,443	[1] 10,545	38,437	41,900	44,056
Cash Flow	23,698	34,385	d13,599	19,725	52,419	55,039	54,495
Average Shs. Outstg.	13,636	14,371	16,258	17,661	18,092	18,851	19,525
BALANCE SHEET (IN THOUSANDS):							
Cash & Cash Equivalents	4,006	10,819	17,905	35,724	27,462	23,054	19,352
Total Current Assets	153,155	171,132	205,687	264,301	357,471	342,372	322,677
Net Property	29,249	30,993	33,613	35,578	58,655	60,847	57,959
Total Assets	231,479	277,367	319,949	431,574	554,552	534,466	512,123
Total Current Liabilities	94,224	128,698	130,831	158,852	248,598	242,445	220,218
Net Stockholders' Equity	125,693	114,432	150,581	228,914	278,828	266,790	269,396
Net Working Capital	58,931	42,434	74,856	105,449	108,873	99,927	102,460
Year-end Shs. Outstg.	13,612	13,475	15,851	17,201	17,904	18,330	19,151
STATISTICAL RECORD:							
Operating Profit Margin %	2.8	6.2	10.9	6.4	9.6	10.4	10.2
Net Profit Margin %	4.6	7.0	...	2.2	4.5	5.0	5.6
Return on Equity %	12.0	23.5	...	4.6	13.8	15.7	16.4
Return on Assets %	6.5	9.7	...	2.4	6.9	7.8	8.6
Price Range	13.44-3.81	24.75-9.50	35.00-19.19	35.31-22.25	32.63-25.38	33.38-26.88	37.00-28.75
P/E Ratio	12.1-3.4	13.2-5.1	...	...	15.4-12.0	15.0-12.1	16.4-12.7
Average Yield %	6.5	6.5	4.1	3.9	3.7	3.5	3.1

Statistics are as originally reported. [1] Excl. net losses fr. disc. opers. of $38.8 mill. & pre-tax chg. of $18.0 mill. [2] Incl. pre-tax chg. of $1.0 mill. & non-cash write-down chrg. of $46.0 mill. [3] Incl. tax ben. of $15.0 mill. & non-cash inv. write-down chrg. of $9.6 mill. [4] Incls. one-time chrgs. of $2.2 mill.

OFFICERS:
A. Verville, Chmn., C.E.O., Pres.
J. W. Lemajeur, C.F.O., Treas.
C. E. Sanders, Asst. Treas.
M. F. Durden, V.P., Sec., Gen. Couns.

INVESTOR CONTACT: Investor Relations, (630) 875-5856

PRINCIPAL OFFICE: 225 Windsor Drive, Itasca, IL 60143

TELEPHONE NUMBER: (630) 875-5300
FAX: (630) 875-5350
WEB: www.enesco.com

NO. OF EMPLOYEES: 1,670 (approx.)

SHAREHOLDERS: 2,692

ANNUAL MEETING: In Apr.

INCORPORATED: MA, July, 1931

INSTITUTIONAL HOLDINGS:
No. of Institutions: 58
Shares Held: 6,749,338
% Held: 49.7

INDUSTRY: Nondurable goods, nec (SIC: 5199)

TRANSFER AGENT(S): Mellon Investor Services, Ridgefield Park, NJ

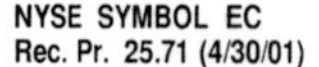

NYSE SYMBOL EC
Rec. Pr. 25.71 (4/30/01)

ENGELHARD CORP.

YIELD 1.6%
P/E RATIO 19.6

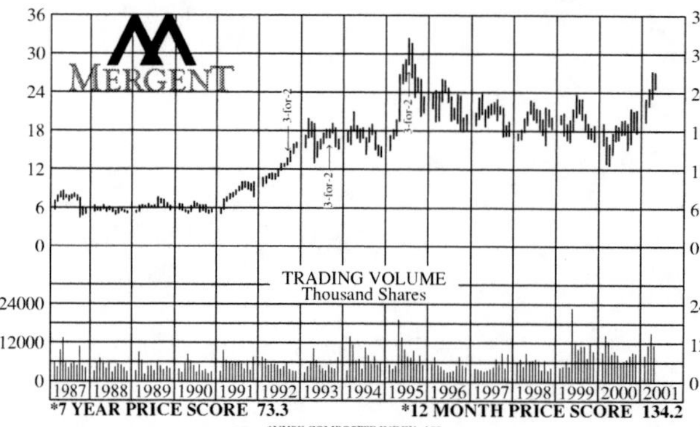

*7 YEAR PRICE SCORE 73.3 *12 MONTH PRICE SCORE 134.2
*NYSE COMPOSITE INDEX=100

INTERIM EARNINGS (Per Share):

Qtr.	Mar.	June	Sept.	Dec.
1997	0.26	0.31	0.27	d0.50
1998	0.30	0.35	0.31	0.33
1999	0.28	0.41	0.40	0.39
2000	0.45	0.47	0.40	d0.01

INTERIM DIVIDENDS (Per Share):

Amt.	Decl.	Ex.	Rec.	Pay.
0.10Q	6/01/00	6/13/00	6/15/00	6/30/00
0.10Q	8/03/00	9/13/00	9/15/00	9/30/00
0.10Q	10/05/00	12/13/00	12/15/00	12/29/00
0.10Q	3/01/01	3/13/01	3/15/01	3/30/01
0.10Q	5/03/01	6/13/01	6/15/01	6/29/01

Indicated div.: $0.40 (Div. Reinv. Plan)

CAPITALIZATION (12/31/00):

	($000)	(%)
Long-Term Debt	248,566	22.1
Common & Surplus	874,567	77.9
Total	1,123,133	100.0

RECENT DEVELOPMENTS: For the year ended 12/31/00, net earnings fell 14.8% to $168.3 million versus $197.5 million in 1999. Results for 2000 and 1999 included a gain of $18.8 and $8.6 million, respectively, from the disposal of investments and land. Results for 2000 also included a special charge of $82.5 million. Net sales were $5.54 billion, up 23.5% from $4.49 billion in 1999. Sales reflected strong performances from the materials services segment and double-digit growth from the technology segments.

PROSPECTS: Going forward, the Company expects to continue to benefit from double-digit earnings growth in its three technology segments. In addition, EC anticipates the services segment will likely return to a more sustainable level of earnings. As a result, the Company anticipates earnings per share for the full year to be between $1.70 to $1.80. However, some of the markets the Company serves may become weaker due to the ongoing rise of energy costs.

BUSINESS

ENGELHARD CORP. is a provider of environmental technologies, specialty chemical products, and engineered materials. EC operates in five business units: Environmental Technologies, Process Technologies, Paper Pigments and Additives, Specialty Pigments and Additives, and Industrial Commodities Management. The Environmental Technologies unit consists of automotive emission systems and performance systems. The Process Technologies unit is the chemical catalysts and petroleum catalysts business. The Paper Pigment and Additives segment services the global paper industry. The Specialty Pigments and Additives unit provides mineral-based additives to a range of industries. The Industrial Commodities Management unit purchases and sells metals, base metals, and related products.

ANNUAL FINANCIAL DATA

	12/31/00	12/31/99	12/31/98	12/31/97	12/31/96	12/31/95	12/31/94
Earnings Per Share	[3] **1.31**	[2] **1.47**	**1.29**	[1] **0.33**	**1.05**	**0.96**	**0.82**
Cash Flow Per Share	**2.23**	**2.30**	**1.98**	**0.93**	**1.57**	**1.41**	**1.30**
Tang. Book Val. Per Share	**4.51**	**3.49**	**4.02**	**3.95**	**5.79**	**5.13**	**4.31**
Dividends Per Share	**0.40**	**0.40**	**0.40**	**0.38**	**0.36**	**0.35**	**0.31**
Dividend Payout %	**30.5**	**27.2**	**31.0**	**115.1**	**34.3**	**36.5**	**37.4**
INCOME STATEMENT (IN MILLIONS):							
Total Revenues	5,542.6	4,404.9	4,174.6	3,630.7	3,184.4	2,840.1	2,385.8
Costs & Expenses	5,160.2	3,977.5	3,764.2	3,356.5	2,852.0	2,558.7	2,138.1
Depreciation & Amort.	117.1	111.6	100.9	88.1	74.9	65.5	69.1
Operating Income	265.4	315.8	309.4	186.1	257.6	215.9	178.6
Net Interest Inc./(Exp.)	d62.6	d56.6	d58.9	d52.8	d45.0	d31.3	d22.0
Income Before Income Taxes	245.7	284.1	260.6	85.8	210.0	185.3	157.3
Income Taxes	77.4	86.7	73.5	38.0	59.5	47.8	39.3
Equity Earnings/Minority Int.	24.2	16.3	10.1	d47.8	d5.0	0.7	0.6
Net Income	[3] 168.3	[2] 197.5	187.1	[1] 47.8	150.4	137.5	118.0
Cash Flow	285.4	309.1	288.0	135.8	225.3	203.0	187.1
Average Shs. Outstg. (000)	128,141	134,590	145,366	145,937	143,810	143,619	144,101
BALANCE SHEET (IN MILLIONS):							
Cash & Cash Equivalents	33.5	54.4	22.3	28.8	39.7	40.0	26.4
Total Current Assets	1,741.7	1,388.4	1,360.0	1,255.2	1,184.3	905.9	573.6
Net Property	767.7	871.9	876.5	788.2	744.7	609.5	540.4
Total Assets	3,166.9	2,904.0	2,866.4	2,586.3	2,494.9	1,943.3	1,440.8
Total Current Liabilities	1,826.7	1,455.8	1,270.4	1,240.1	1,069.0	792.2	499.7
Long-Term Obligations	248.6	499.5	497.4	373.6	375.1	211.5	111.8
Net Stockholders' Equity	874.6	764.4	901.6	785.3	833.2	737.7	614.7
Net Working Capital	d85.0	d67.5	89.6	15.0	115.3	113.6	73.9
Year-end Shs. Outstg. (000)	126,633	125,881	143,287	144,492	143,855	143,716	142,647
STATISTICAL RECORD:							
Operating Profit Margin %	4.8	7.2	7.4	5.1	8.1	7.6	7.5
Net Profit Margin %	3.0	4.5	4.5	1.3	4.7	4.8	4.9
Return on Equity %	19.2	25.8	20.8	6.1	18.1	18.6	19.2
Return on Assets %	5.3	6.8	6.5	1.8	6.0	7.1	8.2
Debt/Total Assets %	7.8	17.2	17.4	14.4	15.0	10.9	7.8
Price Range	21.50-12.56	23.69-16.25	22.81-15.75	23.75-17.06	26.13-17.88	32.50-14.92	21.00-13.92
P/E Ratio	16.4-9.6	16.1-11.1	17.7-12.2	71.9-51.7	24.9-17.0	33.9-15.5	25.6-17.0
Average Yield %	2.3	2.0	2.1	1.9	1.6	1.5	1.8

Statistics are as originally reported. Adj. for 3-for-2 split, 6/95. [1] Incl. $96.4 mill. after-tax chg. & $305,000 pre-tax gain fr. sale of investment. [2] Incl. $8.6 mill. gain fr. sale of investments & land. [3] Incl. gain of $18.8 mill. fr. disposal of investments & land and $82.5 mill. special chg.

OFFICERS:
B. W. Perry, Chmn., C.E.O.
A. A. Dornbusch II, V.P., Gen. Couns., Sec.

INVESTOR CONTACT: Investor Relations, (800) 458-9823

PRINCIPAL OFFICE: 101 Wood Avenue, Iselin, NJ 08830

TELEPHONE NUMBER: (732) 205-5000
FAX: (732) 632-9253
WEB: www.engelhard.com

NO. OF EMPLOYEES: 6,420 (approx.)

SHAREHOLDERS: 5,857 (record)

ANNUAL MEETING: In May

INCORPORATED: DE, Nov., 1938

INSTITUTIONAL HOLDINGS:
No. of Institutions: 235
Shares Held: 104,325,035
% Held: 82.4

INDUSTRY: Primary nonferrous metals, nec (SIC: 3339)

TRANSFER AGENT(S): Mellon Investor Services, Ridgefield Park, NJ

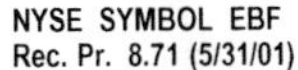
NYSE SYMBOL EBF
Rec. Pr. 8.71 (5/31/01)

ENNIS BUSINESS FORMS, INC.

YIELD 7.1%
P/E RATIO 10.8

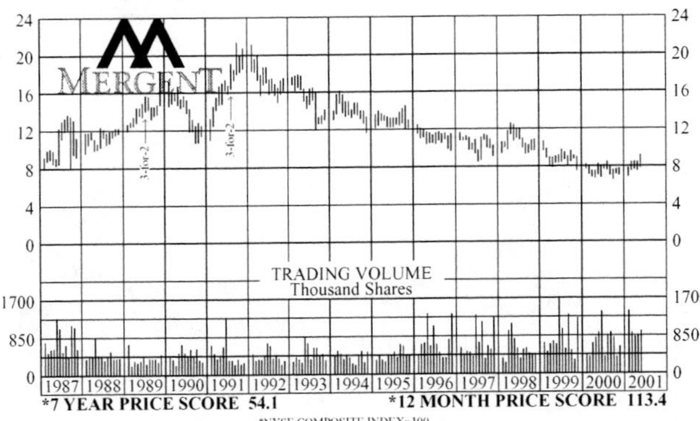

*7 YEAR PRICE SCORE 54.1 *12 MONTH PRICE SCORE 113.4

*NYSE COMPOSITE INDEX=100

INTERIM EARNINGS (Per Share):

Qtr.	May	Aug.	Nov.	Feb.
1996-97	0.26	0.22	0.19	0.15
1997-98	0.14	0.16	0.07	0.25
1998-99	0.20	0.20	0.20	0.27
1999-00	0.20	0.24	0.24	0.25
2000-01	0.24	0.23	0.25	0.09

INTERIM DIVIDENDS (Per Share):

Amt.	Decl.	Ex.	Rec.	Pay.
0.155Q	3/14/00	4/13/00	4/17/00	5/01/00
0.155Q	6/15/00	7/13/00	7/17/00	8/01/00
0.155Q	10/10/00	10/12/00	10/16/00	11/01/00
0.155Q	1/05/01	1/10/01	1/15/01	2/01/01
0.155Q	3/16/01	4/11/01	4/16/01	5/01/01

Indicated div.: $0.62

CAPITALIZATION (2/28/01):

	($000)	(%)
Long-Term Debt	23,555	20.5
Common & Surplus	91,540	79.5
Total	115,095	100.0

RECENT DEVELOPMENTS: For the fiscal year ended 2/28/01, net earnings totaled $13.2 million, down 12.9% compared with $15.1 million the previous year. The prior-year results included a fourth-quarter after-tax gain of $434,000 related to year-end inventory adjustments. Net sales jumped 29.8% to $229.2 million from $176.6 million a year earlier, due primarily to acquisitions. Earnings from operations rose 2.6% to $22.5 million from $21.9 million the year before.

PROSPECTS: The consolidation of certain manufacturing operations is expected to help increase efficiencies and boost profitability going forward. In late 2000, the Company closed a facility in Louisville, Kentucky and moved these operations into an existing plant located in Denver, Colorado. Meanwhile, sales growth is being fueled by the acquisitions of Adams McClure L.P. and American Forms, Inc. in November 1999 and Northstar Computer Forms, Inc. in June 2000.

BUSINESS

ENNIS BUSINESS FORMS, INC. is a manufacturer and marketer of business forms and other printed business products to customers primarily located in the United States. The Company operates 30 production facilities located in 14 states and distributes its products primarily through independent dealers including business forms distributors, stationers, printers, and computer software developers. In addition, the Company, through its wholly-owned subsidiary Adams McClure, is a designer, producer and distributor of printed and electronic promotional products. The Company also designs and manufactures custom tools and dies through its wholly-owned subsidiary Connolly Tool & Machine Company.

ANNUAL FINANCIAL DATA

	2/28/01	2/29/00	2/28/99	2/28/98	2/28/97	2/29/96	2/28/95
Earnings Per Share	**0.81**	**1 0.93**	**0.87**	**1 0.62**	**0.82**	**1.13**	**1.22**
Cash Flow Per Share	**1.41**	**1.29**	**1.19**	**1.00**	**1.12**	**1.41**	**1.44**
Tang. Book Val. Per Share	**4.17**	**4.92**	**4.78**	**4.69**	**4.60**	**4.52**	**3.95**
Dividends Per Share	**0.62**	**0.62**	**0.62**	**0.62**	**0.61**	**0.59**	**0.57**
Dividend Payout %	**76.5**	**66.7**	**71.3**	**100.0**	**74.4**	**52.2**	**46.7**
INCOME STATEMENT (IN THOUSANDS):							
Total Revenues	229,186	166,525	150,922	154,348	153,726	142,134	140,097
Costs & Expenses	196,966	138,722	124,135	133,326	128,617	109,179	105,724
Depreciation & Amort.	9,730	5,874	5,352	6,173	4,935	4,511	3,657
Operating Income	22,490	21,929	21,435	14,849	20,106	28,342	30,629
Net Interest Inc./(Exp.)	d2,046	d40	d57	d60	d68	d102	d87
Income Before Income Taxes	21,571	24,041	22,558	15,805	21,485	30,104	32,041
Income Taxes	8,394	8,918	8,448	5,597	7,992	11,487	12,025
Net Income	13,177	1 15,123	14,110	1 10,208	13,493	18,617	20,016
Cash Flow	22,907	20,997	19,462	16,381	18,428	23,128	23,673
Average Shs. Outstg.	16,246	16,250	16,312	16,438	16,439	16,440	16,440
BALANCE SHEET (IN THOUSANDS):							
Cash & Cash Equivalents	9,944	3,475	20,691	22,700	18,494	38,606	28,141
Total Current Assets	58,263	43,305	52,676	53,660	52,627	67,544	59,265
Net Property	57,781	41,728	33,911	34,852	33,560	21,857	19,521
Total Assets	142,854	102,934	94,335	94,474	94,957	93,662	84,991
Total Current Liabilities	17,908	10,525	8,367	10,396	10,307	13,054	12,976
Long-Term Obligations	23,555	462	7	206	195	280	360
Net Stockholders' Equity	91,540	88,267	83,499	81,672	81,586	78,195	69,338
Net Working Capital	40,355	32,780	44,309	43,264	42,320	54,490	46,289
Year-end Shs. Outstg.	16,271	16,192	16,253	16,438	16,438	16,439	16,440
STATISTICAL RECORD:							
Operating Profit Margin %	9.8	13.2	14.2	9.6	13.1	19.9	21.9
Net Profit Margin %	5.7	9.1	9.3	6.6	8.8	13.1	14.3
Return on Equity %	14.4	17.1	16.9	12.5	16.5	23.8	28.9
Return on Assets %	9.2	14.7	15.0	10.8	14.2	19.9	23.6
Debt/Total Assets %	16.5	0.4	...	0.2	0.2	0.3	0.4
Price Range	8.50-6.56	10.69-7.50	12.63-9.25	11.63-8.50	12.50-9.63	14.50-12.00	16.13-11.63
P/E Ratio	10.5-8.1	11.5-8.1	14.5-10.6	18.7-13.7	15.2-11.7	12.8-10.6	13.2-9.5
Average Yield %	8.2	6.8	5.7	6.2	5.5	4.5	4.1

Statistics are as originally reported. 1 Incl. $571,000 pre-tax gain, 2000; & $3.0 mil pre-tax special chg., 1998.

OFFICERS:
K. S. Walters, Chmn., Pres., C.E.O.
R. M. Halowec, V.P.-Fin., C.F.O.
H. Cathey, Treas.

INVESTOR CONTACT: Keith S. Walters, Chmn., Pres., C.E.O., (800) 752-5386

PRINCIPAL OFFICE: 1510 N. Hampton, Suite 300, DeSoto, TX 75115

TELEPHONE NUMBER: (972) 228-7801
FAX: (972) 872-3195
WEB: www.ennis.com

NO. OF EMPLOYEES: 2,181 (approx.)

SHAREHOLDERS: 1,507

ANNUAL MEETING: In June

INCORPORATED: TX, Dec., 1909

INSTITUTIONAL HOLDINGS:
No. of Institutions: 32
Shares Held: 6,357,281
% Held: 39.1

INDUSTRY: Manifold business forms (SIC: 2761)

TRANSFER AGENT(S): Computershare Investor Services, Chicago, IL

NYSE SYMBOL ENE
Rec. Pr. 62.72 (4/30/01)

ENRON CORP.

YIELD 0.8%
P/E RATIO 55.5

MERGENT

TRADING VOLUME
Thousand Shares

1987 1988 1989 1990 1991 1992 1993 1994 1995 1996 1997 1998 1999 2000 2001

***7 YEAR PRICE SCORE 167.0** ***12 MONTH PRICE SCORE 87.4**

*NYSE COMPOSITE INDEX=100

INTERIM EARNINGS (Per Share):

Qtr.	Mar.	June	Sept.	Dec.
1996	0.43	0.22	0.24	0.26
1997	0.44	d0.86	0.22	0.27
1998	0.33	0.21	0.24	0.25
1999	0.34	0.27	0.35	0.31
2000	0.40	0.34	0.34	0.05

INTERIM DIVIDENDS (Per Share):

Amt.	Decl.	Ex.	Rec.	Pay.
0.125Q	5/09/00	5/30/00	6/01/00	6/20/00
0.125Q	8/24/00	9/06/00	9/08/00	9/20/00
0.125Q	10/27/00	11/29/00	12/01/00	12/20/00
0.125Q	2/13/01	2/27/01	3/01/01	3/20/01
0.125Q	5/01/01	5/30/01	6/01/01	6/20/01

Indicated div.: $0.50 (Div. Reinv. Plan)

CAPITALIZATION (12/31/00):

	($000)	(%)
Long-Term Debt	8,550,000	34.2
Deferred Income Tax	1,644,000	6.6
Minority Interest	2,414,000	9.7
Redeemable Pfd. Stock	904,000	3.6
Preferred Stock	1,124,000	4.5
Common & Surplus	10,346,000	41.4
Total	24,982,001	100.0

RECENT DEVELOPMENTS: For the year ended 12/31/00, net income rose 9.6% to $979.0 million versus $893.0 million in 1999. Results for 2000 included a charge of $326.0 million to reflect impairment by Azurix Corp. and a $39.0 million gain on the issuance of stock by The New Power Company. Results for 1999 included a securities gain of $345.0 million, an impairment charge of $278.0 million and an accounting charge of $131.0 million. Total revenues jumped to $100.79 billion from $40.11 billion last year.

PROSPECTS: Results going forward should benefit from ENE's Internet-based e-commerce site, EnronOnline, which in fiscal 2000 executed 548,000 transactions on-line totaling $336.00 billion of gross value. Separately, on 1/30/01, Enron Industrial Markets, a unit of ENE, announced that it has signed a definitive agreement with Daishowa North America Corporation to purchase Daishowa Forest Products Ltd., a holding company for its Quebec City, Canada newsprint mill and related assets.

BUSINESS

ENRON CORP. is a major electricity, natural gas and communications company. ENE produces electricity and natural gas, develops, constructs and operates energy facilities worldwide, delivers physical commodities and financial and risk management services to customers around the world, and has developed an intelligent network platform to facilitate on-line business. ENE's businesses are reported as follows: Transportation and Distribution, Wholesale Services, Retail Energy Services, Broadband Services, and Corporate and Other. On 8/16/99, ENE exchanged approximately 62.3 million shares of Enron Oil & Gas Company common stock for all of the stock of EOGI-India, Inc., a subsidiary of EOG. On 7/1/97, the Company acquired Portland General Corp.

BUSINESS LINE ANALYSIS

(12/31/2000)	(%)	(%)
Transportation & Distribution	2.9	25.4
Wholesale Services	92.2	74.9
Retail Energy Services	4.5	2.6
Broadband Services	0.4	(2.9)
Total	100.0	100.0

ANNUAL FINANCIAL DATA

	[7] 12/31/00	12/31/99	12/31/98	[2] 12/31/97	12/31/96	12/31/95	12/31/94
Earnings Per Share	[6] 1.12	[5] 1.27	[1] 1.01	[3] 0.16	[3] 1.16	[4] 1.04	0.90
Cash Flow Per Share	2.55	2.95	2.17	1.24	2.03	1.83	1.72
Tang. Book Val. Per Share	8.92	7.88	7.50	5.75	7.03	6.03	5.44
Dividends Per Share	0.50	0.50	0.48	0.46	0.43	0.41	0.38
Dividend Payout %	44.6	39.4	47.6	285.0	37.3	39.2	42.4
INCOME STATEMENT (IN MILLIONS):							
Total Revenues	100,789.0	40,112.0	31,260.0	20,273.0	13,289.0	9,189.0	8,984.0
Costs & Expenses	97,655.0	37,999.0	29,055.0	19,658.0	12,168.0	8,182.0	7,870.0
Depreciation & Amort.	1,181.0	1,311.0	827.0	600.0	431.0	389.0	398.0
Operating Income	1,953.0	802.0	1,378.0	15.0	690.0	618.0	716.0
Net Interest Inc./(Exp.)	d626.0	d494.0	d550.0	d401.0	d274.0	d284.0	d273.0
Income Taxes	434.0	104.0	175.0	cr90.0	271.0	285.0	167.0
Equity Earnings/Minority Int.	d67.0	174.0	20.0	136.0	140.0	42.0	81.0
Net Income	[6] 979.0	[5] 1,024.0	[1] 703.0	[3] 105.0	[3] 584.0	[4] 520.0	453.0
Cash Flow	2,077.0	2,269.0	1,513.0	688.0	999.0	893.0	836.0
Average Shs. Outstg. (000)	814,000	769,000	696,000	554,000	492,000	488,000	486,000
BALANCE SHEET (IN MILLIONS):							
Gross Property	15,459.0	13,912.0	15,792.0	13,742.0	11,348.0	11,107.0	10,964.4
Accumulated Depreciation	3,716.0	3,231.0	5,135.0	4,572.0	4,236.0	4,239.0	4,225.7
Net Property	11,743.0	10,681.0	10,657.0	9,170.0	7,112.0	6,868.0	6,738.7
Total Assets	65,503.0	33,381.0	29,350.0	22,552.0	16,137.0	13,239.0	11,966.0
Long-Term Obligations	8,550.0	7,151.0	7,357.0	6,254.0	3,349.0	3,065.0	2,805.1
Net Stockholders' Equity	11,470.0	9,570.0	7,048.0	5,618.0	3,723.0	3,165.0	2,880.3
Year-end Shs. Outstg. (000)	751,628	715,527	662,000	622,000	510,000	502,000	504,000
STATISTICAL RECORD:							
Operating Profit Margin %	1.9	2.0	4.4	0.1	5.2	6.7	8.0
Net Profit Margin %	1.0	2.6	2.2	0.5	4.4	5.7	5.0
Net Inc./Net Property %	8.3	9.6	6.6	1.1	8.2	7.6	6.7
Net Inc./Tot. Capital %	3.9	4.6	3.5	0.7	5.5	5.6	5.5
Return on Equity %	8.5	10.7	10.0	1.9	15.7	16.4	15.7
Accum. Depr./Gross Prop. %	24.0	23.2	32.5	33.3	37.3	38.2	38.5
Price Range	90.75-41.38	44.88-28.75	29.38-19.06	22.56-17.50	23.75-17.31	19.69-14.00	17.31-13.38
P/E Ratio	81.0-36.9	35.3-22.6	29.1-18.9	140.9-109.3	20.6-15.0	19.0-13.5	19.2-14.9
Average Yield %	0.8	1.4	2.0	2.3	2.1	2.4	2.5

Statistics are as originally reported. Adj. for 2-for-1 stk. split, 8/99 [1] Incl. pre-tax cr. of $56.0 mil [2] Refl. 7/97 acq. of Portland General Corp. [3] Incl. chrg. 12/31/97: $471.0 mil; cr. 12/31/96: $90.0 mil; cr. 12/31/94: $9.8 mil [4] Incl. $43.4 mil cr. & chrg. of $19.0 mil fr. write-down of assets [5] Incl. gain of $541.0 mil & impair. chrg. of $441.0 mil; bef. acctg. chrg. of $131.0 mil [6] Incl. net chrg. of $287.0 mil [7] Refl. growth of ENE's Wholesale Services bus.

OFFICERS:
K. L. Lay, Chmn.
J. K. Skilling, Pres., C.E.O.
A. S. Fastow, Exec. V.P., C.F.O.

INVESTOR CONTACT: Vickie Nicholson, (713) 853-9864

PRINCIPAL OFFICE: 1400 Smith Street, Houston, TX 77002-7361

TELEPHONE NUMBER: (713) 853-6161
FAX: (713) 646-5801
WEB: www.enron.com

NO. OF EMPLOYEES: 20,600 (approx.)

SHAREHOLDERS: 58,920 (approx.)

ANNUAL MEETING: In May

INCORPORATED: DE, Apr., 1930

INSTITUTIONAL HOLDINGS:
No. of Institutions: 796
Shares Held: 472,052,694
% Held: 62.6

INDUSTRY: Petroleum refining (SIC: 2911)

TRANSFER AGENT(S): EquiServe, Jersey City, NJ

NYSE SYMBOL ESV
Rec. Pr. 38.90 (4/30/01)

ENSCO INTERNATIONAL INC.

YIELD 0.3%
P/E RATIO 62.4

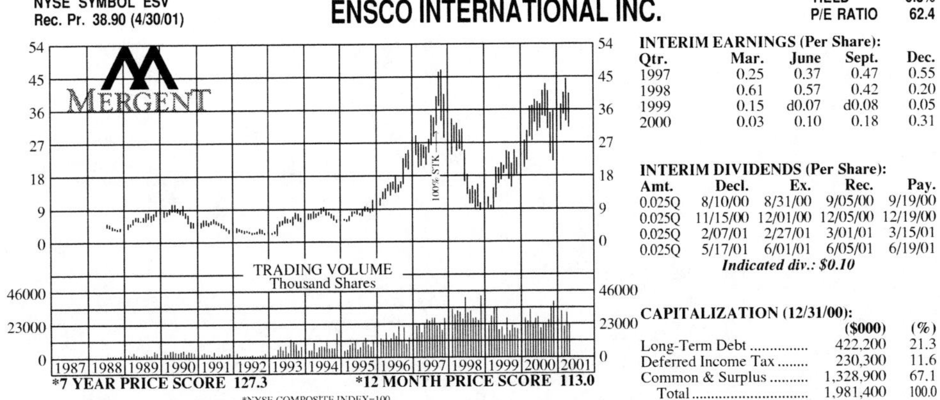

INTERIM EARNINGS (Per Share):

Qtr.	Mar.	June	Sept.	Dec.
1997	0.25	0.37	0.47	0.55
1998	0.61	0.57	0.42	0.20
1999	0.15	d0.07	d0.08	0.05
2000	0.03	0.10	0.18	0.31

INTERIM DIVIDENDS (Per Share):

Amt.	Decl.	Ex.	Rec.	Pay.
0.025Q	8/10/00	8/31/00	9/05/00	9/19/00
0.025Q	11/15/00	12/01/00	12/05/00	12/19/00
0.025Q	2/07/01	2/27/01	3/01/01	3/15/01
0.025Q	5/17/01	6/01/01	6/05/01	6/19/01

Indicated div.: $0.10

CAPITALIZATION (12/31/00):

	($000)	(%)
Long-Term Debt	422,200	21.3
Deferred Income Tax	230,300	11.6
Common & Surplus	1,328,900	67.1
Total	1,981,400	100.0

RECENT DEVELOPMENTS: For the year ended 12/31/00, net income increased to $85.4 million compared with $0.3 million in the previous year. Earnings were driven by increased activity and elevated day rates for the Company's Gulf of Mexico jackup rigs in response to the tight gas market. Operating revenues jumped 46.8% to $533.8 million from $363.7 million in the preceding year. Comparisons were made with restated results for 1999.

PROSPECTS: ESV's results should continue to benefit from rising activity and higher day rates for its Gulf of Mexico jackup rigs. Separately, on 12/11/00, ESV entered into a joint venture with Keppel FELS Limited to acquire a 25.0% ownership interest in a new harsh environment jackup rig that is currently under construction, for $30.0 million. The total cost of the rig, which ESV will have the option to purchase two years after delivery, will be about $130.0 million. The rig should be completed in early 2002.

BUSINESS

ENSCO INTERNATIONAL INC. is an international offshore contract drilling company that also provides marine transportation services in the Gulf of Mexico. The Company's contract drilling operations are conducted through its subsidiaries. These subsidiaries engage in the drilling of oil and gas wells in domestic and international markets under contracts with major international oil and gas companies, government owned oil and gas companies and independent oil and gas companies. As of 12/31/00, ESV owned 37 jackup rigs, nine barge rigs, seven platform rigs and one semisubmersible rig. The Company conducts its marine transportation operations through a wholly-owned subsidiary, ENSCO Marine Company, which is currently comprised of 28 vessels.

REVENUES

(12/31/2000)	($000)	(%)
Contract Drilling	496,100	92.9
Marine Transportation	37,700	7.1
Total	533,800	100.0

ANNUAL FINANCIAL DATA

	12/31/00	12/31/99	12/31/98	12/31/97	12/31/96	12/31/95	12/31/94
Earnings Per Share	**0.61**	**0.05**	**1.81**	**[2] 1.64**	**0.72**	**[1] 0.35**	**[3] 0.31**
Cash Flow Per Share	**1.37**	**0.83**	**2.47**	**2.44**	**1.37**	**0.86**	**0.80**
Tang. Book Val. Per Share	**9.59**	**9.05**	**9.08**	**7.57**	**5.97**	**4.38**	**3.92**
Dividends Per Share	**0.10**	**0.10**	**0.10**	**0.05**	...	...	...
Dividend Payout %	**16.4**	**199.6**	**5.5**	**3.0**	...	...	...
INCOME STATEMENT (IN MILLIONS):							
Total Revenues	533.8	363.7	813.2	815.1	468.8	279.1	262.0
Costs & Expenses	296.9	252.0	334.4	312.4	233.9	162.1	153.1
Depreciation & Amort.	105.7	108.2	93.6	113.4	86.2	61.8	57.4
Operating Income	131.2	3.5	385.2	389.3	148.7	55.2	51.5
Net Interest Inc./(Exp.)	d6.3	d5.6	d11.1	d14.0	d16.4	d10.3	d8.1
Income Before Income Taxes	125.2	5.2	382.5	375.8	142.7	47.3	43.9
Income Taxes	39.8	cr2.9	123.8	137.8	54.0	9.9	6.8
Equity Earnings/Minority Int.	...	d1.4	d4.8	d3.1	d3.3	d2.0	d2.4
Net Income	85.4	6.7	253.9	[2] 234.9	95.4	[1] 41.8	[3] 37.2
Cash Flow	191.1	114.9	347.5	348.3	181.6	103.5	92.4
Average Shs. Outstg. (000)	139,300	137,700	140,600	142,900	132,572	121,054	115,686
BALANCE SHEET (IN MILLIONS):							
Cash & Cash Equivalents	106.6	165.3	330.1	262.2	80.7	82.1	154.1
Total Current Assets	288.7	272.8	476.3	447.1	211.4	165.8	212.4
Net Property	1,685.3	1,577.1	1,389.4	1,177.1	991.6	632.9	529.0
Total Assets	2,108.0	1,978.0	1,992.8	1,772.0	1,315.4	821.5	775.4
Total Current Liabilities	117.1	134.8	159.4	130.9	103.9	86.8	88.2
Long-Term Obligations	422.2	371.2	375.5	400.8	258.6	159.2	162.5
Net Stockholders' Equity	1,328.9	1,241.0	1,245.0	1,076.7	846.0	531.2	499.0
Net Working Capital	171.6	138.0	316.9	316.2	107.5	78.9	124.2
Year-end Shs. Outstg. (000)	138,500	137,200	137,100	142,200	141,800	121,200	122,000
STATISTICAL RECORD:							
Operating Profit Margin %	24.6	1.0	47.4	47.8	31.7	19.8	19.6
Net Profit Margin %	16.0	1.8	31.2	28.8	20.3	15.0	14.2
Return on Equity %	6.4	0.5	20.4	21.8	11.3	7.9	7.4
Return on Assets %	4.1	0.3	12.7	13.3	7.3	5.1	4.8
Debt/Total Assets %	20.0	18.8	18.8	22.6	19.7	19.4	21.0
Price Range	43.13-20.25	25.00-8.75	33.56-8.69	47.00-20.25	25.06-10.00	11.50-5.63	9.63-5.38
P/E Ratio	70.7-33.2	499.0-174.7	18.5-4.8	28.7-12.3	34.8-13.9	33.3-16.3	31.5-17.6
Average Yield %	0.3	0.6	0.5	0.1	...	...	...

Statistics are as originally reported. Adj. for 2-for-1 stk. split, 9/97 [1] Bef. disc. oper. cr. of $6.3 mil. [2] Bef. extraord. chrg. of $1.0 mil. [3] Incl. subsidiary stk. sale gain of $670,000

OFFICERS:
C. F. Thorne, Chmn., Pres., C.E.O.
C. C. Gaut, Sr. V.P., C.F.O.
R. A. LeBlanc, Treas.

INVESTOR CONTACT: Investor Relations, (214) 922-1572

PRINCIPAL OFFICE: 2700 Fountain Place, 1445 Ross Avenue, Dallas, TX 75202-2792

TELEPHONE NUMBER: (214) 922-1500
FAX: (214) 855-0300
WEB: www.enscous.com

NO. OF EMPLOYEES: 3,400 (approx.)

SHAREHOLDERS: 1,800 (approx.)

ANNUAL MEETING: In May

INCORPORATED: TX, Apr., 1975; reincorp., DE, Sept., 1987

INSTITUTIONAL HOLDINGS:
No. of Institutions: 258
Shares Held: 109,135,336
% Held: 78.6

INDUSTRY: Drilling oil and gas wells (SIC: 1381)

TRANSFER AGENT(S): American Stock Transfer & Trust Company, New York, NY

NYSE SYMBOL ETM
Rec. Pr. 45.62 (4/30/01)

ENTERCOM COMMUNICATIONS CORP.

YIELD	...
P/E RATIO	43.9

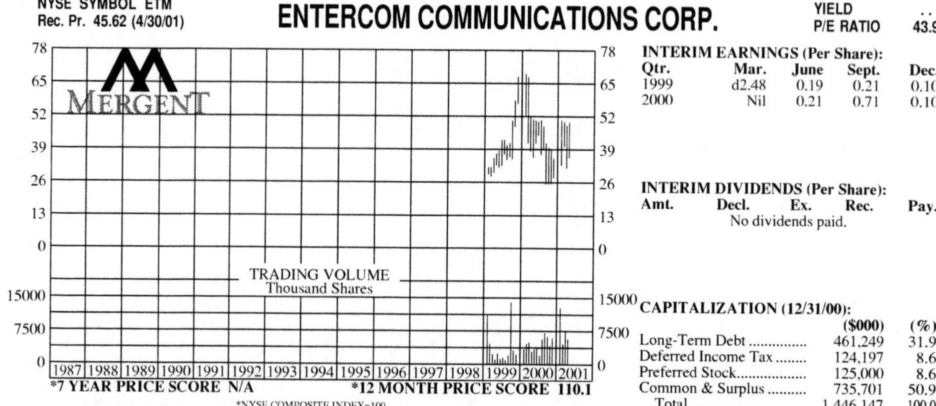

INTERIM EARNINGS (Per Share):

Qtr.	Mar.	June	Sept.	Dec.
1999	d2.48	0.19	0.21	0.10
2000	Nil	0.21	0.71	0.10

INTERIM DIVIDENDS (Per Share):

Amt.	Decl.	Ex.	Rec.	Pay.

No dividends paid.

CAPITALIZATION (12/31/00):

	($000)	(%)
Long-Term Debt	461,249	31.9
Deferred Income Tax	124,197	8.6
Preferred Stock	125,000	8.6
Common & Surplus	735,701	50.9
Total	1,446,147	100.0

RECENT DEVELOPMENTS: For the year ended 12/31/00, net income totaled $47.3 million compared with a loss of $60.0 million, before an extraordinary loss of $918,000, in the previous year. Results included gains on the sale of assets of $41.5 million and $2.0 million in the comparable year. Net revenues skyrocketed 63.7% to $352.0 million versus $215.0 million in the prior year. Operating income more than doubled to $130.9 million compared with $50.7 million in 1999.

PROSPECTS: Looking ahead, the Company expects to achieve earnings per share of $0.68 for fiscal 2001 and a loss of $0.05 for the first quarter of 2001. In addition, the Company anticipates recording $33.0 million in amortization of FCC licenses and goodwill in 2001. However, the Financial Accounting Standards Board is considering the elimination of these charges to financial statements, which should increase reported earnings per share. If adopted, this change could become effective in the second half of 2001.

BUSINESS

ENTERCOM COMMUNICATIONS CORP. is a radio broadcasting company, the fifth largest in the United States based on gross revenues. The Company has a nationwide portfolio of 95 owned or operated stations, including acquisitions that are pending. This portfolio consists of 61 FM and 34 AM stations in 18 markets, including 12 of the country's top 50 radio advertising markets. ETM's station groups rank among the three largest clusters, in 17 of its 18 markets. These markets include Boston, Seattle, Portland, Sacramento, Kansas City, Milwaukee, Norfolk, New Orleans, Greensboro, Buffalo, Memphis, Rochester, Greenville/Spartanburg, Wilkes-Barre/Scranton, Wichita, Madison, Gainesville/Ocala and Longview/Kelso, WA.

ANNUAL FINANCIAL DATA

	12/31/00	[1] 12/31/99	9/30/98	9/30/97	9/30/96
Earnings Per Share	**1.04**	**[2][3] d1.58**	**[2][4] 0.12**	**[4][5] 4.59**	**[2] 0.20**
Cash Flow Per Share	**1.99**	**d1.00**	**1.01**	**8.57**	**0.45**
INCOME STATEMENT (IN THOUSANDS):					
Total Revenues	352,025	215,001	132,998	93,862	48,675
Costs & Expenses	177,651	142,709	95,525	64,053	33,652
Depreciation & Amort.	43,475	21,564	13,066	7,685	2,960
Operating Income	130,899	50,728	24,407	22,124	12,063
Net Interest Inc./(Exp.)	d37,248	d7,929	d14,253	d10,906	d5,101
Income Before Income Taxes	79,050	40,954	9,892	177,259	7,053
Income Taxes	31,796	100,912	453	489	274
Equity Earnings/Minority Int.	d1,100	...	...	...	...
Net Income	47,254	[2][3] d59,958	[2][4] 9,439	[4][5] 176,770	[2] 6,779
Cash Flow	90,729	d38,394	22,505	184,455	9,739
Average Shs. Outstg.	45,614	38,238	22,239	21,534	21,534
BALANCE SHEET (IN THOUSANDS):					
Cash & Cash Equivalents	13,257	11,262	6,666	3,626	...
Total Current Assets	90,938	70,420	51,125	35,560	...
Net Property	93,953	90,423	43,057	29,154	...
Total Assets	1,473,928	1,396,048	522,945	364,743	...
Total Current Liabilities	27,781	27,530	16,761	10,056	...
Long-Term Obligations	461,249	465,760	321,037	173,497	...
Net Stockholders' Equity	860,701	811,611	182,970	179,019	...
Net Working Capital	63,157	42,890	34,364	25,504	...
Year-end Shs. Outstg.	45,240	45,180	21,534	21,534	...
STATISTICAL RECORD:					
Operating Profit Margin %	37.2	23.6	18.4	23.6	24.8
Net Profit Margin %	13.4	...	7.1	188.3	13.9
Return on Equity %	5.5	...	5.2	98.7	...
Return on Assets %	3.2	...	1.8	48.5	...
Debt/Total Assets %	31.3	33.4	61.4	47.6	...
Price Range	68.69-25.31	67.75-28.31	...	...	...
P/E Ratio	66.0-24.3	...	...	...	...

Statistics are as originally reported. [1] Fiscal year changed from 9/30 to 12/31. [2] Bef. extraord. chrg. 12/31/99, $918,000; 9/30/98, $2.4 mill.; 9/30/96, $539,000. [3] Incl. $2.0 mill. gain on sale of assets and non-recurr. chrg. $1.8 mill. [4] Incl. chrg. for adj. to reflect indexing of not $8.8 mill., 9/98; $29.1 mill., 9/97 [5] Incl. gain on sale of assets $197.1 mill.

OFFICERS:
J. M. Field, Chmn., C.E.O.
D. J. Field, Pres., C.O.O.
S. F. Fisher, Exec. V.P., C.F.O.

INVESTOR CONTACT: Steve Fisher, C.F.O. & Sr. V.P., (610) 660-5647

PRINCIPAL OFFICE: 401 City Avenue, Suite 409, Bala Cynwyd, PA 19004

TELEPHONE NUMBER: (610) 660-5610
FAX: (610) 660-5620
WEB: www.entercom.com

NO. OF EMPLOYEES: 1,541 full-time; 610 part-time

SHAREHOLDERS: 69 (record); 6,000 (approx. benef.); 3 (cl B com); 1 (cl C com)

ANNUAL MEETING: In May

INCORPORATED: PA, 1968

INSTITUTIONAL HOLDINGS:
No. of Institutions: 119
Shares Held: 28,279,946
% Held: 62.5

INDUSTRY: Radio broadcasting stations (SIC: 4832)

TRANSFER AGENT(S): First Union Capital Markets Corp, Philadelphia, PA

NYSE SYMBOL ETR
Rec. Pr. 40.50 (4/30/01)

ENTERGY CORPORATION

YIELD 3.1%
P/E RATIO 13.5

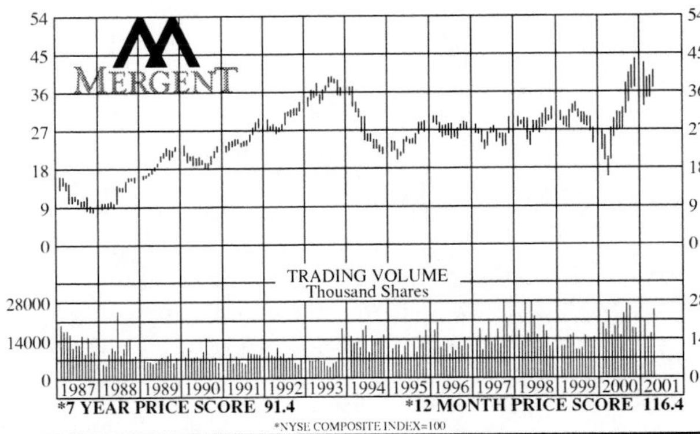

INTERIM EARNINGS (Per Share):

Qtr.	Mar.	June	Sept.	Dec.
1997	0.47	0.61	0.33	d0.36
1998	0.20	0.83	1.02	0.96
1999	0.25	0.81	1.16	0.02
2000	0.42	1.04	1.34	0.19

INTERIM DIVIDENDS (Per Share):

Amt.	Decl.	Ex.	Rec.	Pay.
0.30Q	7/28/00	8/10/00	8/14/00	9/01/00
0.315Q	10/27/00	11/08/00	11/10/00	12/01/00
0.315Q	1/26/01	2/09/01	2/13/01	3/01/01
0.315Q	4/04/01	5/11/01	5/15/01	6/01/01

Indicated div.: $1.26 (Div. Reinv. Plan)

CAPITALIZATION (12/31/00):

	($000)	(%)
Long-Term Debt	7,732,093	41.1
Capital Lease Obligations	201,873	1.1
Deferred Income Tax	3,249,083	17.3
Redeemable Pfd. Stock	280,758	1.5
Preferred Stock	334,688	1.8
Common & Surplus	7,003,665	37.2
Total	18,802,160	100.0

RECENT DEVELOPMENTS: For the year ended 12/31/00, net income increased 19.5% to $710.9 million versus $595.0 million in the prior year. Results for 2000 and 1999 included a pre-tax loss of $20.5 million and a pre-tax gain of $71.9 million on the sale of assets, respectively. Total operating revenues rose 14.2% to $10.02 billion. Domestic electric operating revenues climbed 7.22 billion, while natural gas operating reveneus grew 50.3% to $165.9 million.

PROSPECTS: The Company's 800-megawatt natural gas-fired powered plant at Damhead Creek, Southeast England, began operations on 2/5/01. Separately, Entergy Nuclear offered to buy Vermont Yankee nuclear plant for $50.0 million and offered to give each eligible plant employee a $1,000 bonus. Looking ahead, ETR raised it 2001 earnings to a range of $3.00 to $3.20 per share.

BUSINESS

ENTERGY CORPORATION is a public utility holding company engaged principally in the businesses of domestic utility, power marketing and trading, global power development, and domestic nuclear operations. The Company has five wholly-owned domestic retail electric utility subsidiaries: Entergy Arkansas, Entergy Gulf States, Entergy Louisiana, Entergy Mississippi, and Entergy New Orleans. As of 12/31/00, these utility companies provided retail electric service to approximately 2.5 million customers primarily in portions of the states of Arkansas, Louisiana, Mississippi, and Texas.

REVENUES

(12/31/00)	($000)	(%)
Domestic Electric	7,220	72.1
Natural Gas	166	1.7
Competitive Businesss	2,630	26.2
Total	10,016	100.0

ANNUAL FINANCIAL DATA

	12/31/00	12/31/99	12/31/98	12/31/97	12/31/96	12/31/95	12/31/94
Earnings Per Share	**[4] 2.97**	**[4] 2.25**	**3.00**	**[3] 1.03**	**[3] 1.83**	**[2][3] 2.13**	**[1] 1.49**
Cash Flow Per Share	**6.54**	**5.79**	**7.95**	**6.86**	**5.29**	**5.16**	**4.30**
Tang. Book Val. Per Share	**31.89**	**29.78**	**28.82**	**27.23**	**28.51**	**28.41**	**27.61**
Dividends Per Share	**1.22**	**1.20**	**1.50**	**1.80**	**1.80**	**1.80**	**1.80**
Dividend Payout %	**40.9**	**53.3**	**50.0**	**174.7**	**98.4**	**84.5**	**120.8**
INCOME STATEMENT (IN MILLIONS):							
Total Revenues	10,016.1	8,773.2	11,494.8	9,561.7	7,163.5	6,274.4	5,963.3
Costs & Expenses	7,654.6	6,654.4	8,760.7	6,302.8	4,693.9	4,014.3	4,120.3
Depreciation & Amort.	816.0	867.2	1,222.2	1,401.8	790.9	690.8	642.3
Operating Income	1,545.6	1,251.7	1,511.9	1,857.2	1,678.7	1,219.7	1,068.7
Net Interest Inc./(Exp.)	d538.6	d536.8	d789.9	d841.0	d715.2	d659.2	d678.0
Income Taxes	478.9	356.7	266.7	471.3	421.2	336.2	131.7
Net Income	[4] 710.9	[4] 595.0	785.6	[3] 300.9	[3] 420.0	[2][5] 484.6	[1] 341.8
Cash Flow	1,495.3	1,419.7	1,961.3	1,649.5	1,211.0	1,175.4	984.1
Average Shs. Outstg. (000)	228,541	245,327	246,572	240,298	229,084	227,670	228,735
BALANCE SHEET (IN MILLIONS):							
Gross Property	28,194.9	26,716.6	25,404.5	27,717.8	25,108.7	24,080.1	23,556.6
Accumulated Depreciation	11,364.0	10,898.7	10,076.0	9,585.0	8,885.6	8,259.3	7,639.5
Net Property	16,830.9	15,817.9	15,328.6	18,132.8	16,223.1	15,820.8	15,917.0
Total Assets	25,565.2	22,985.1	22,848.0	27,000.7	22,966.3	22,265.9	22,613.5
Long-Term Obligations	7,934.0	6,818.0	6,816.8	9,304.3	7,838.2	7,080.8	7,367.4
Net Stockholders' Equity	7,338.4	7,607.9	7,595.5	7,182.0	7,221.9	7,172.7	7,051.8
Year-end Shs. Outstg. (000)	219,605	239,037	246,620	245,842	232,960	227,766	230,017
STATISTICAL RECORD:							
Operating Profit Margin %	15.4	14.3	13.2	19.4	23.4	19.4	17.9
Net Profit Margin %	7.1	6.8	6.8	3.1	5.9	7.7	5.7
Net Inc./Net Property %	4.2	3.8	5.1	1.7	2.6	3.1	2.1
Net Inc./Tot. Capital %	3.8	3.3	4.3	1.4	2.2	2.7	1.8
Return on Equity %	9.7	7.8	10.3	4.2	5.8	6.8	4.8
Accum. Depr./Gross Prop. %	40.3	40.8	39.7	34.6	35.4	34.3	32.4
Price Range	43.88-15.94	33.50-23.69	32.44-23.25	30.00-22.38	30.38-24.88	29.25-20.00	37.38-21.25
P/E Ratio	14.8-5.4	14.9-10.5	10.8-7.7	29.1-21.7	16.6-13.6	13.7-9.4	25.1-14.3
Average Yield %	4.1	4.2	5.4	6.9	6.5	7.3	6.1

Statistics are as originally reported. [1] Incl. non-recurr. chrg.: 1994, $154.3 mill. ($0.67/sh) [2] Bef. acctg. change credit: 1995, $35.4 mill. [3] Incl. non-recurr chrg. 1995, $15.2 mill. ($0.07/sh);1996, $174.0 mill.;1997 $293.7 mill [4] Incl. net gain of $71.9 mill. from the sale of assets, 1999; net loss of $20.5 mill., 2000.

OFFICERS:
R. Luft, Chmn.
J. W. Leonard, C.E.O.
D. C. Hintz, Pres.
C. J. Wilder, Exec. V.P., C.F.O.

INVESTOR CONTACT: Renae Conley, (504) 576-4947

PRINCIPAL OFFICE: 639 Loyola Avenue, New Orleans, LA 70113

TELEPHONE NUMBER: (504) 576-4000
FAX: (504) 576-4428
WEB: www.entergy.com

NO. OF EMPLOYEES: 13,884 full-time; 216 part-time

SHAREHOLDERS: 67,226

ANNUAL MEETING: In May

INCORPORATED: FL, May, 1949; reincorp., DE, 1994

INSTITUTIONAL HOLDINGS:
No. of Institutions: 301
Shares Held: 165,653,088
% Held: 75.3

INDUSTRY: Electric services (SIC: 4911)

TRANSFER AGENT(S): Mellon Investor Services, LLC, Ridgefield Park, NJ

NYSE SYMBOL EOG
Rec. Pr. 46.39 (4/30/01)

EOG RESOURCES, INC.

YIELD 0.3%
P/E RATIO 14.3

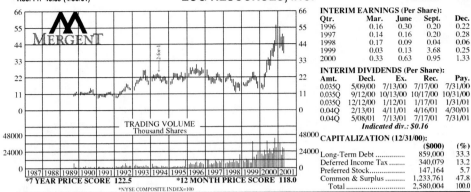

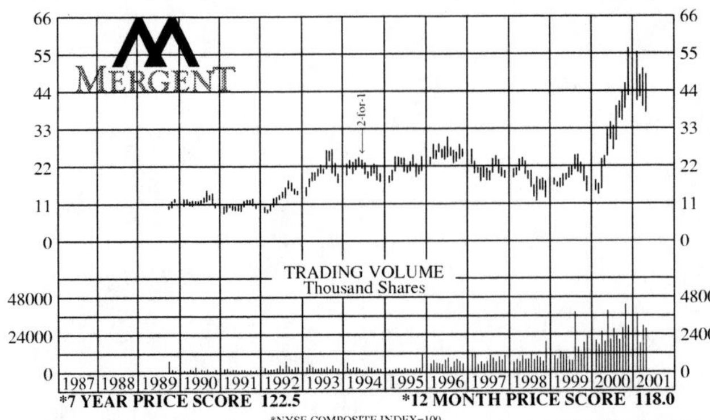

INTERIM EARNINGS (Per Share):

Qtr.	Mar.	June	Sept.	Dec.
1996	0.16	0.30	0.20	0.22
1997	0.14	0.16	0.20	0.28
1998	0.17	0.09	0.04	0.06
1999	0.03	0.13	3.68	0.25
2000	0.33	0.63	0.95	1.33

INTERIM DIVIDENDS (Per Share):

Amt.	Decl.	Ex.	Rec.	Pay.
0.035Q	5/09/00	7/13/00	7/17/00	7/31/00
0.035Q	9/12/00	10/13/00	10/17/00	10/31/00
0.035Q	12/12/00	1/12/01	1/17/01	1/31/01
0.04Q	2/13/01	4/11/01	4/16/01	4/30/01
0.04Q	5/08/01	7/13/01	7/17/01	7/31/01

Indicated div.: $0.16

CAPITALIZATION (12/31/00):

	($000)	(%)
Long-Term Debt	859,000	33.3
Deferred Income Tax	340,079	13.2
Preferred Stock	147,164	5.7
Common & Surplus	1,233,761	47.8
Total	2,580,004	100.0

RECENT DEVELOPMENTS: For the year ended 12/31/00, net income totaled $396.9 million versus $569.1 million a year earlier. Results for 1999 included nonrecurring gains of $611.3 million. Total revenues rose 76.9% to $1.49 billion. Natural gas revenues surged 69.1% to $1.16 billion as realized average natural gas prices soared to $3.49 per thousand cubic feet (Mcf) versus $2.01 Mcf in 1999. Crude oil, condensate and natural gas liquids revenues soared to $325.7 million from $159.4 million in 1999, primarily due to sharply higher average crude oil/condensate prices.

PROSPECTS: Results are being positively affected by the implementation of the Company's long-term strategy of sharpening its focus on natural gas, which is experiencing strong demand and improved pricing. Accordingly, the Company appears well-positioned to capitalize on the historically high prices of natural gas, and to a lesser extent, crude oil. Over the near term, the Company intends to further strengthen its balance sheet through long-term debt reduction and continue its aggressive drilling program.

BUSINESS

EOG RESOURCES, INC. (formerly Enron Oil & Gas Company) is engaged in the exploration for, and the development, production and marketing of, natural gas and crude oil primarily in major producing basins in the United States, as well as in Canada and Trinidad and, to a lesser extent, selected other international areas. As of 12/31/00 the Company's estimated net proved natural gas reserves were 3,381 billion cubic feet and estimated net proved crude oil, condensate and natural gas liquids reserves were 73.0 million barrels. On 8/16/99, EOG acquired 62.3 million shares of its common stock from Enron Corp. in exchange for its EOGI-India, Inc. subsidiary, which included all of the Company's assets and operations in India and China.

REVENUES

(12/31/2000)	($000)	(%)
Natural Gas	1,155,804	77.6
Crude, condensate, NGLs	325,726	21.9
Sale of reserves & assets	8,365	0.6
Total	1,489,895	0.5
		100.0

ANNUAL FINANCIAL DATA

	12/31/00	12/31/99	12/31/98	12/31/97	12/31/96	12/31/95	12/31/94
Earnings Per Share	**3.24**	**1 3.99**	**0.36**	**0.77**	**0.88**	**0.89**	**0.93**
Cash Flow Per Share	**6.35**	**7.22**	**2.11**	**2.26**	**2.18**	**1.97**	**2.44**
Tang. Book Val. Per Share	**10.55**	**8.25**	**8.33**	**8.26**	**7.92**	**7.28**	**6.52**
Dividends Per Share	**0.13**	**0.12**	**0.12**	**0.12**	**0.12**	**0.12**	**0.12**
Dividend Payout %	**4.0**	**3.0**	**33.3**	**15.6**	**13.6**	**13.5**	**12.9**
INCOME STATEMENT (IN MILLIONS):							
Total Revenues	1,489.9	801.4	769.2	783.5	730.6	648.7	625.8
Costs & Expenses	423.0	323.3	383.8	355.9	314.0	280.7	224.0
Depreciation & Amort.	370.0	459.9	271.8	234.8	207.8	172.7	242.2
Operating Income	696.9	18.2	113.7	192.8	208.8	195.3	159.6
Net Interest Inc./(Exp.)	d61.0	d61.8	d48.6	d27.7	d12.9	d11.9	d8.5
Income Before Income Taxes	633.6	567.7	60.3	163.5	191.0	184.1	153.9
Income Taxes	236.6	cr1.4	4.1	41.5	51.0	41.9	5.9
Net Income	396.9	1 569.1	56.2	122.0	140.0	142.1	148.0
Cash Flow	755.9	1,028.4	327.9	356.8	347.8	314.8	390.2
Average Shs. Outstg. (000)	119,102	142,352	155,054	158,160	159,853	159,917	159,845
BALANCE SHEET (IN MILLIONS):							
Cash & Cash Equivalents	20.2	24.8	6.3	9.3	7.6	23.0	5.8
Total Current Assets	394.4	200.5	246.4	282.0	325.9	217.8	156.4
Net Property	2,525.0	2,334.9	2,676.4	2,387.2	2,099.6	1,881.5	1,684.8
Total Assets	3,000.8	2,610.8	3,018.1	2,723.4	2,458.4	2,147.3	1,861.9
Total Current Liabilities	369.7	218.6	262.6	291.0	317.4	169.3	164.6
Long-Term Obligations	859.0	990.3	1,142.8	741.3	466.1	289.1	190.3
Net Stockholders' Equity	1,380.9	1,129.6	1,280.3	1,281.0	1,265.1	1,163.7	1,043.4
Net Working Capital	24.7	d18.1	d16.3	d9.0	8.6	48.5	d8.2
Year-end Shs. Outstg. (000)	116,904	119,105	153,724	155,064	159,757	159,850	159,991
STATISTICAL RECORD:							
Operating Profit Margin %	46.8	2.3	14.8	24.6	28.6	30.1	25.5
Net Profit Margin %	26.6	71.0	7.3	15.6	19.2	21.9	23.6
Return on Equity %	28.7	50.4	4.4	9.5	11.1	12.2	14.2
Return on Assets %	13.2	21.8	1.9	4.5	5.7	6.6	7.9
Debt/Total Assets %	28.6	37.9	37.9	27.2	19.0	13.5	10.2
Price Range	56.69-13.69	25.38-14.38	24.50-11.75	27.00-17.50	30.63-22.38	25.38-17.13	24.63-17.38
P/E Ratio	17.5-4.2	6.4-3.6	68.0-32.6	35.1-22.7	34.8-25.4	28.5-19.2	26.5-18.7
Average Yield %	0.4	0.6	0.7	0.5	0.5	0.6	0.6

Statistics are as originally reported. Adj. for 2-for-1 stk. split, 6/94. 1 Incls. gain on share exchange of $575.2 mill.

OFFICERS:
M. G. Papa, Chmn., C.E.O.
E. P. Segner III, Vice-Chmn., Pres.
W. C. Wilson, Sr. V.P., C.F.O.

INVESTOR CONTACT: Maire A. Baldwin, V.P., Inv. Rel., (713) 651-6364

PRINCIPAL OFFICE: 1200 Smith Street, Suite 300, Houston, TX 77002-7361

TELEPHONE NUMBER: (713) 651-7361
FAX: (713) 651-6992
WEB: www.eogresources.com
NO. OF EMPLOYEES: 850 (approx.)
SHAREHOLDERS: 380 (approx. holders of record); 33,630 (approx. benef. holders)
ANNUAL MEETING: In May
INCORPORATED: DE, June, 1985

INSTITUTIONAL HOLDINGS:
No. of Institutions: 321
Shares Held: 99,884,737
% Held: 85.6

INDUSTRY: Crude petroleum and natural gas (SIC: 1311)

TRANSFER AGENT(S): First Chicago Trust Company of New York, Jersey City, NJ

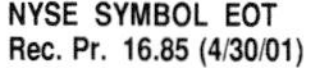

NYSE SYMBOL EOT
Rec. Pr. 16.85 (4/30/01)

EOTT ENERGY PARTNERS, L.P.

YIELD 11.3%
P/E RATIO 34.4

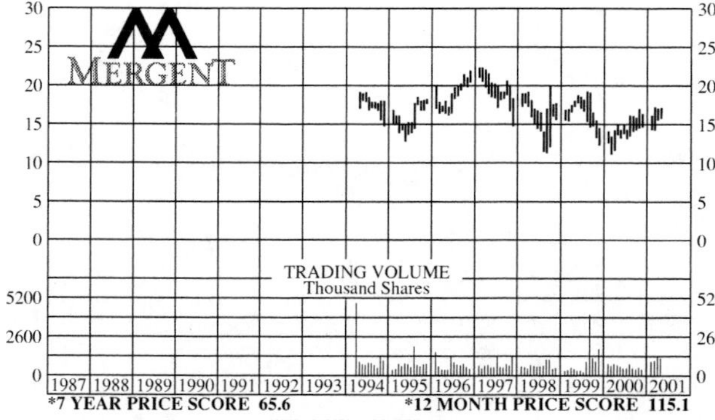

INTERIM EARNINGS (Per Share):

Qtr.	Mar.	June	Sept.	Dec.
1997	0.20	d0.32	d0.10	d0.53
1998	d0.09	d0.07	d0.09	0.03
1999	0.10	0.09	0.02	d0.27
2000	0.08	0.17	0.11	0.13

INTERIM DIVIDENDS (Per Share):

Amt.	Decl.	Ex.	Rec.	Pay.
0.475Q	4/18/00	4/26/00	4/28/00	5/15/00
0.475Q	7/20/00	7/27/00	7/31/00	8/14/00
0.475Q	10/20/00	10/27/00	10/31/00	11/14/00
0.475Q	1/19/01	1/29/01	1/31/01	2/14/01
0.475Q	4/20/01	4/26/01	4/30/01	5/15/01

Indicated div.: $1.90

CAPITALIZATION (12/31/00):

	($000)	(%)
Long-Term Debt	235,000	70.9
Common & Surplus	96,364	29.1
Total	331,364	100.0

RECENT DEVELOPMENTS: For the year ended 12/31/00, net income was $13.8 million versus a loss of $2.2 million a year earlier. Results for 2000 included a nonrecurring credit of $631,000, while results for 1999 included a one-time charge of $9.8 million. Revenues jumped 34.0% to $11.61 billion. Results for the Pipeline and North America - East of Rockies segments primarily benefited from the elimination of certain low-margin lease volumes, improved market conditions and owning assets acquired from Texas-New Mexico Pipeline Company for the entire year.

PROSPECTS: Near-term prospects are favorable. The Company's North America - East of Rockies segment results are being driven by the continued optimization of crude oil bulk sales activities and the elimination of certain low-margin crude oil lease volumes. Additionally, the Company's West Coast operations are benefiting from increased availability of crude oil blending stocks. In view of current market conditions, the Company has affirmed 2001 full-year earnings estimates of $0.59 per unit.

BUSINESS

EOTT ENERGY PARTNERS, L.P., through its affiliated limited partnerships, EOTT Energy Operating Limited Partnership, EOTT Energy Canada Limited Partnership, and EOTT Energy Pipeline Limited Partnership, is engaged in the purchasing, gathering, transporting, trading, storage and resale of crude oil, refined petroleum products, natural gas liquids and related activities. The Company's principal business segments are its North American - East of Rockies crude oil gathering and marketing operations, its Pipeline Operations and its West Coast Operations, which includes crude oil gathering and marketing, refined products marketing and a natural gas liquids business. EOTT Energy Corp., a wholly-owned subsidiary of Enron Corp., is the general partner of the Company.

QUARTERLY DATA

(12/31/2000)	Rev ($000)	Inc ($000)
First Quarter	2,681,696	2,221
Second Quarter	2,514,934	4,888
Third Quarter	3,143,529	3,011
Fourth Quarter	3,273,846	3,713

ANNUAL FINANCIAL DATA

	12/31/00	12/31/99	12/31/98	12/31/97	12/31/96	12/31/95	12/31/94
Earnings Per Share	**[4] 0.49**	**[3] d0.09**	**d0.21**	**[2] d0.75**	**1.50**	**[1] 0.33**	**0.71**
Cash Flow Per Share	**1.74**	**1.24**	**0.88**	**0.11**	...	...	...
Tang. Book Val. Per Share	**52.23**	**6.50**	**3.92**	**3.30**	**5.64**	**4.46**	**15.86**
Dividends Per Share	**1.90**	**1.90**	**1.90**	**1.90**	**1.90**	**1.80**	**0.88**
Dividend Payout %	**387.7**	...	...	...	**126.7**	**545.3**	**124.3**
INCOME STATEMENT (IN MILLIONS):							
Total Revenues	11,614.0	8,664.4	5,294.7	7,646.1	7,469.7	5,088.2	4,557.1
Costs & Expenses	11,535.2	8,605.3	5,266.5	7,637.2	7,422.1	5,069.4	4,530.0
Depreciation & Amort.	33.9	33.1	21.0	16.5	15.7	10.5	11.7
Operating Income	45.0	26.0	7.2	d7.6	31.9	8.3	15.4
Net Interest Inc./(Exp.)	d28.8	d28.9	d9.5	d6.0	d3.2	d3.5	d4.0
Income Before Income Taxes	13.8	d2.2	d4.1	d14.4	28.8	5.7	12.4
Net Income	[4] 13.8	[3] d2.2	d4.1	[2] d14.4	28.8	[1] 5.7	12.4
Cash Flow	47.7	30.9	16.9	2.1	44.5	16.2	24.1
Average Shs. Outstg. (000)	27,476	24,877	19,267	18,830	...	...	...
BALANCE SHEET (IN MILLIONS):							
Cash & Cash Equivalents	54.2	17.5	3.0	3.7	5.3	2.3	2.0
Total Current Assets	1,082.8	1,133.4	574.2	649.0	888.8	550.6	676.3
Net Property	393.9	404.5	385.2	127.3	127.8	137.6	100.5
Total Assets	1,493.0	1,558.7	965.8	782.9	1,026.2	696.1	786.3
Total Current Liabilities	1,152.3	1,197.5	868.3	707.8	910.0	609.7	614.8
Long-Term Obligations	235.0	235.0	...	...	...	...	8.5
Net Stockholders' Equity	96.4	120.1	75.6	62.1	106.2	75.8	158.6
Net Working Capital	d69.5	d64.1	d294.1	d58.8	d21.2	d59.1	61.5
Year-end Shs. Outstg. (000)	1,845	18,476	19,267	18,830	18,830	17,000	10,000
STATISTICAL RECORD:							
Operating Profit Margin %	0.4	0.3	0.1	...	0.4	0.2	0.3
Net Profit Margin %	0.1	...	...	...	0.4	0.1	0.3
Return on Equity %	14.4	...	...	...	27.1	7.5	7.8
Return on Assets %	0.9	...	...	...	2.8	0.8	1.6
Debt/Total Assets %	15.7	15.1	...	...	...	...	1.1
Price Range	17.00-11.13	19.25-12.25	20.00-11.25	22.38-14.75	22.00-16.13	18.50-12.75	20.13-14.75
P/E Ratio	34.7-22.7	...	...	...	14.7-10.7	56.0-38.6	28.3-20.8
Average Yield %	13.5	12.1	12.2	10.2	10.0	11.5	5.1

Statistics are as originally reported. [1] Bef. loss fr. disc. ops. of $65.8 mill. ($3.79/sh.) & extraord. loss of $1.3 mill. ($0.08/sh.) [2] Incls. impair. of assets chrg. of $8.0 mill. [3] Bef. acctg. change credit of $1.7 mill. ($0.07/sh.) [4] Incls. nonrecurr. credit of $631,000.

OFFICERS:
S. C. Horton, Chmn., C.E.O.
D. R. Gibbs, Pres., C.O.O.
L. Clayton Jr., Sr. V.P., C.F.O.

INVESTOR CONTACT: Scott Vonderheide, Inv. Rel., (713) 853-4863

PRINCIPAL OFFICE: 1330 Post Oak Boulevard, Suite 2700, Houston, TX 77056

TELEPHONE NUMBER: (713) 993-5200
FAX: (713) 993-5898
WEB: www.eott.com
NO. OF EMPLOYEES: 1,200 (approx.)
SHAREHOLDERS: 338 (approx.); 15,600 (beneficial holders)
ANNUAL MEETING: N/A
INCORPORATED: DE, 1993

INSTITUTIONAL HOLDINGS:
No. of Institutions: 20
Shares Held: 283,453
% Held: 1.5

INDUSTRY: Petroleum bulk stations & terminals (SIC: 5171)

TRANSFER AGENT(S): First Chicago Trust Company of New York, Jersey City, NJ

NYSE SYMBOL EFX
Rec. Pr. 33.07 (4/30/01)

EQUIFAX INC.

YIELD 1.1%
P/E RATIO 19.8

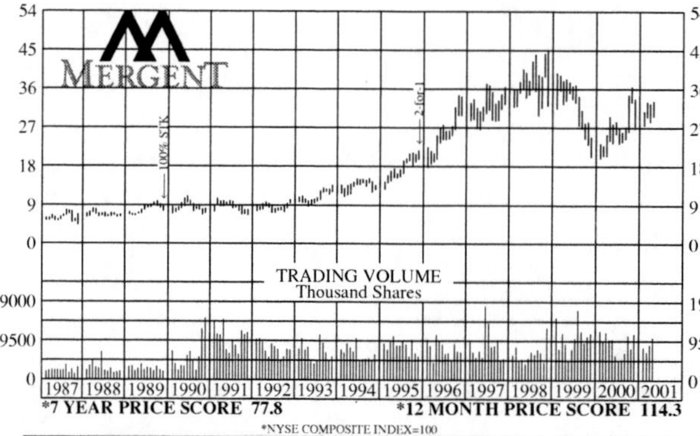

*7 YEAR PRICE SCORE 77.8 *12 MONTH PRICE SCORE 114.3

*NYSE COMPOSITE INDEX=100

INTERIM EARNINGS (Per Share):

Qtr.	Mar.	June	Sept.	Dec.
1995	0.20	0.24	0.25	0.30
1996	0.25	0.28	0.32	0.37
1997	0.31	0.42	0.33	0.26
1998	0.31	0.35	0.37	0.31
1999	0.31	0.37	0.42	0.45
2000	0.31	0.39	0.47	0.50

INTERIM DIVIDENDS (Per Share):

Amt.	Decl.	Ex.	Rec.	Pay.
0.092Q	4/27/00	5/23/00	5/25/00	6/15/00
0.092Q	7/27/00	8/23/00	8/25/00	9/15/00
0.092Q	11/07/00	11/21/00	11/24/00	12/15/00
0.092Q	2/01/01	2/20/01	2/22/01	3/15/01
0.092Q	5/02/01	5/23/01	5/25/01	6/15/01

Indicated div.: $0.37 (Div. Reinv. Plan)

CAPITALIZATION (12/31/00):

	($000)	(%)
Long-Term Debt	993,569	67.7
Deferred Income Tax	90,198	6.1
Common & Surplus	383,578	26.1
Total	1,467,345	100.0

RECENT DEVELOPMENTS: For the year ended 12/31/00, net income climbed 5.6% to $228.0 million compared with $215.9 million in the previous year. Operating revenues advanced 10.9% to $1.97 billion from $1.77 billion in the prior year. North American Information Services revenues rose 6.3% to $673.3 million, while Payment Services revenues increased 14.2% to $777.0 million. Revenues from Equifax Europe fell 3.6% to $143.4 million, while Equifax Latin America revenues dropped 4.8% to $132.5 million.

PROSPECTS: On 1/4/01, the Company sold HPI, its vehicle information business in the United Kingdom to IMVA, a vehicle mileage verification specialist for approximately $40.0 million. Separately, EFX acquired Compliance Data Center Inc. in a stock transaction worth about $10.0 million. Going forward, EFX should benefit from strategic initiatives such as the intended spinoff of Payment Services and the disposition of noncore businesses in North America and United Kingdom.

BUSINESS

EQUIFAX INC. is a provider of financial information and processing services, with global operations in consumer and commercial credit information services, payment services, software, modeling, analytics and consulting, and direct-to-consumer services. The Company serves many industries including banking, finance, retail, telecommunications, utilities, transportation and health care. Equifax was founded in 1899 in Atlanta and presently has approximately 12,000 employees located throughout North and South America, the United Kingdom and continental Europe. The Company operates in 17 countries, with sales in nearly 50 countries. In August 1997, the Company completed the spin-off of its Insurance Services Group.

BUSINESS LINE ANALYSIS

(12/31/00)	REV(%)	INC(%)
North American Info. Services	34.3	55.2
Payment Services	5.6	1.6
Equifax Europe	7.3	2.6
Equifax Latin America	6.1	5.0
Other & Divested Operations	7.2	4.6
Card Solutions	26.3	22.1
Check Solutions	13.2	8.9
Total	100.0	100.0

ANNUAL FINANCIAL DATA

	12/31/00	12/31/99	12/31/98	12/31/97	12/31/96	12/31/95	12/31/94
Earnings Per Share	**1.68**	**1.55**	**1.34**	**[2][3] 1.26**	**1.22**	**[1] 0.98**	**0.81**
Cash Flow Per Share	**2.77**	**2.44**	**2.06**	**1.78**	**1.81**	**1.48**	**1.26**
Tang. Book Val. Per Share	...	...	...	...	**0.19**	...	...
Dividends Per Share	**0.37**	**0.36**	**0.35**	**0.34**	**0.33**	**0.32**	**0.30**
Dividend Payout %	**22.0**	**23.4**	**26.3**	**27.4**	**27.0**	**32.1**	**37.3**
INCOME STATEMENT (IN MILLIONS):							
Total Revenues	1,965.9	1,772.7	1,621.0	1,366.1	1,811.2	1,623.0	1,422.0
Costs & Expenses	1,361.7	1,232.9	1,151.5	990.1	1,420.9	1,283.0	1,141.4
Depreciation & Amort.	148.8	125.3	103.8	77.1	85.9	77.0	66.5
Operating Income	455.4	414.5	365.7	298.9	304.4	262.9	214.1
Net Interest Inc./(Exp.)	d76.0	d61.0	d42.7	d20.8	d23.0	d21.2	d15.6
Income Before Income Taxes	385.4	365.9	327.2	323.1	303.6	249.2	207.5
Income Taxes	157.3	150.0	133.8	137.6	125.9	101.6	87.1
Net Income	228.0	215.9	193.4	[2][3] 185.5	177.6	[1] 147.7	120.3
Cash Flow	376.8	341.1	297.3	262.6	263.5	224.7	186.8
Average Shs. Outstg. (000)	136,016	139,603	144,403	147,818	145,518	151,357	148,608
BALANCE SHEET (IN MILLIONS):							
Cash & Cash Equivalents	89.4	136.6	90.6	52.3	48.2	26.1	79.4
Total Current Assets	604.9	609.4	520.4	400.9	345.1	366.7	375.9
Net Property	98.8	115.5	119.3	94.7	86.9	87.8	84.2
Total Assets	2,069.6	1,839.8	1,828.8	1,177.1	1,011.1	1,053.7	1,021.2
Total Current Liabilities	426.2	504.8	419.2	327.6	373.8	250.6	300.0
Long-Term Obligations	993.6	933.7	869.5	339.3	306.0	302.7	212.0
Net Stockholders' Equity	383.6	215.6	366.5	349.4	424.9	353.4	361.9
Net Working Capital	178.7	104.6	101.2	73.3	d28.6	116.1	75.8
Year-end Shs. Outstg. (000)	135,835	134,001	140,042	142,609	144,876	147,245	151,790
STATISTICAL RECORD:							
Operating Profit Margin %	23.2	23.4	22.6	21.9	16.8	16.2	15.1
Net Profit Margin %	11.6	12.2	11.9	13.6	9.8	9.1	8.5
Return on Equity %	59.4	100.1	52.8	53.1	41.8	41.8	33.3
Return on Assets %	11.0	11.7	10.6	15.8	17.6	14.0	11.8
Debt/Total Assets %	48.0	50.8	47.5	28.8	30.3	28.7	20.8
Price Range	36.50-19.88	39.88-20.13	45.00-29.75	37.19-26.50	34.50-17.75	21.75-12.63	15.25-10.94
P/E Ratio	21.7-11.8	25.7-13.0	33.6-22.2	29.5-21.0	28.3-14.5	22.2-12.9	18.8-13.5
Average Yield %	1.3	1.2	0.9	1.1	1.3	1.8	2.3

Statistics are as originally reported. Adj. for stk. splits: 2-for-1, 11/95 [1] Incl. non-recurr. credit 1995, $98,000 [2] Bef. disc. oper. gain $1.4 mill. [3] Bef. acctg. change chrg. 1997, $3.2 mill.

OFFICERS:
T. F. Chapman, Chmn., C.E.O.
L. A. Kennedy, Pres., C.O.O.
P. J. Mazzilli, Exec. V.P., C.F.O.
M. G. Schirk, V.P., Treas.

INVESTOR CONTACT: Marietta Edmunds Zakas, Investor Relations, (404) 885-8000

PRINCIPAL OFFICE: 1550 Peachtree Street, N.W., Atlanta, GA 30309

TELEPHONE NUMBER: (404) 885-8000
FAX: (404) 888-3528
WEB: www.equifax.com

NO. OF EMPLOYEES: 12,200 (approx.)

SHAREHOLDERS: 10,611 (approx.)

ANNUAL MEETING: In May

INCORPORATED: GA, Dec., 1913

INSTITUTIONAL HOLDINGS:
No. of Institutions: 299
Shares Held: 93,602,069
% Held: 65.4

INDUSTRY: Credit reporting services (SIC: 7323)

TRANSFER AGENT(S): SunTrust Bank, Atlanta, GA

NYSE SYMBOL EQT
Rec. Pr. 37.10 (Adj.; 5/31/01)

EQUITABLE RESOURCES, INC.

YIELD 1.7%
P/E RATIO 11.6

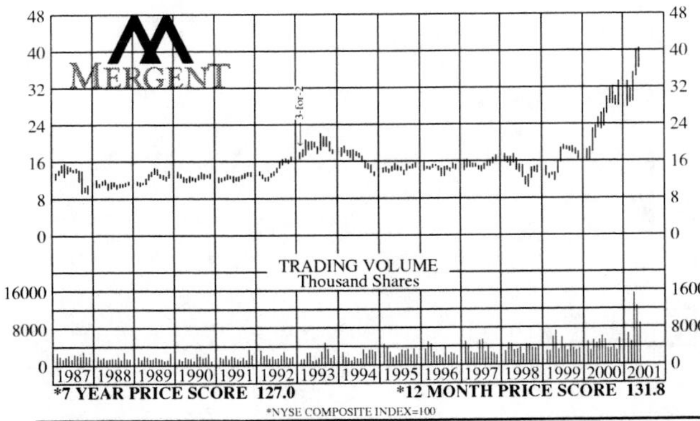

*7 YEAR PRICE SCORE 127.0 *12 MONTH PRICE SCORE 131.8
*NYSE COMPOSITE INDEX=100

INTERIM EARNINGS (Per Share):

Qtr.	Mar.	June	Sept.	Dec.
1997	0.39	d0.13	0.24	0.57
1998	0.33	0.03	0.03	d0.77
1999	0.42	0.11	0.09	0.40
2000	0.59	0.25	0.29	0.48

INTERIM DIVIDENDS (Per Share):

Amt.	Decl.	Ex.	Rec.	Pay.
0.295Q	7/19/00	8/14/00	8/16/00	9/01/00
0.295Q	10/18/00	11/13/00	11/15/00	12/01/00
0.295Q	1/18/01	2/07/01	2/09/01	3/01/01
0.32Q	4/19/01	5/09/01	5/11/01	6/01/01
2-for-1	4/19/01	6/12/01	5/11/01	6/11/01

Indicated div.: $0.64 (Adj.; Div. Reinv. Plan)

CAPITALIZATION (12/31/00):

	($000)	(%)
Long-Term Debt	287,789	23.4
Deferred Income Tax	247,833	20.2
Common & Surplus	693,695	56.4
Total	1,229,317	100.0

RECENT DEVELOPMENTS: For the year ended 12/31/00, net income surged 53.6% to $106.2 million versus $69.1 million in the previous year. Earnings for 2000 included an after-tax charge of $12.3 million for costs related to the Kentucky West labor settlement and an after-tax gain of $4.3 million for the sale of Westport Resource's stock. Operating revenues soared 58.6% to $1.65 billion from $1.04 billion the year before.

PROSPECTS: NORESCO, L.L.C. announced the creation of three new strategic business units designed to serve three key market segments including public and multi-family housing, industrial, and energy infrastructure. Separately, EQT established a capital spending plan of $175.0 million for 2001 whereby EQT has allocated $96.0 million for the Production segment, $62.0 million for the Utilities segment, and $17.0 million for NORESCO.

BUSINESS

EQUITABLE RESOURCES, INC. is an integrated energy company operating through three business segments: Equitable Production, Equitable Utilities and NORESCO. The production segment's operations include exploration and production activities in the East (Appalachian) and Gulf regions, as well as Appalachian area natural gas gathering and liquids processing. The utilities segment's activities are comprised of EQT's natural gas supply, natural gas transmission and distribution operations and energy-management services for customers throughout the U.S. EQT also has energy-service management projects in selected international markets. In December 1998, EQT sold its Gulf area midstream operations. On 2/15/00, EQT purchased the Appalachian oil and gas properties of Statoil Energy, Inc.

BUSINESS LINE ANALYSIS

(12/31/2000)	Rev (%)	Inc (%)
Equitable Utilities	74.8	41.6
Equitable Production	17.1	53.8
Noresco	8.1	4.6
Total	100.0	100.0

ANNUAL FINANCIAL DATA

	12/31/00	12/31/99	12/31/98	12/31/97	12/31/96	12/31/95	12/31/94
Earnings Per Share	**(5) 1.60**	**1.01**	**(4) d0.36**	**(3) 1.08**	**(2) 0.85**	**(1) 0.02**	**0.88**
Cash Flow Per Share	**3.09**	**2.81**	**0.85**	**2.40**	**2.01**	**1.53**	**2.23**
Tang. Book Val. Per Share	**9.73**	**8.84**	**8.93**	**10.25**	**10.38**	**10.21**	**27.48**
Dividends Per Share	**0.59**	**0.59**	**0.59**	**0.59**	**0.59**	**0.59**	**0.57**
Dividend Payout %	**36.9**	**58.7**	**...**	**54.6**	**69.8**	**2,942.6**	**65.3**
INCOME STATEMENT (IN MILLIONS):							
Total Revenues	1,652.2	1,062.7	882.6	2,151.0	1,861.8	(1) 1,426.0	1,397.3
Costs & Expenses	1,339.0	796.2	803.3	1,943.5	1,650.6	1,299.4	1,193.7
Depreciation & Amort.	99.0	123.8	89.5	95.1	82.4	104.6	93.3
Operating Income	214.2	142.8	d10.2	112.4	128.8	22.0	110.2
Net Interest Inc./(Exp.)	d75.7	d37.1	d40.3	d45.7	d41.8	d50.1	d43.9
Income Before Income Taxes	163.3	105.6	d49.4	124.2	90.0	d27.8	69.5
Income Taxes	57.2	39.4	cr22.4	46.1	30.6	cr29.3	8.8
Equity Earnings/Minority Int.	25.2	2.9	...	...	...	...	...
Net Income	(5) 106.2	69.1	(4) d27.1	(3) 78.1	(2) 59.4	(1) 1.5	60.7
Cash Flow	205.2	193.0	62.5	173.1	141.8	106.2	154.1
Average Shs. Outstg. (000)	66,332	68,674	73,666	72,232	70,376	69,586	69,018
BALANCE SHEET (IN MILLIONS):							
Cash & Cash Equivalents	52.0	18.0	102.4	69.4	14.7	30.2	23.4
Total Current Assets	614.7	326.8	445.0	684.7	485.8	377.7	307.8
Net Property	1,419.4	1,221.4	1,198.1	1,506.5	1,479.7	1,457.6	1,595.7
Total Assets	2,455.9	1,789.6	1,854.2	2,411.0	2,096.3	1,961.8	2,019.1
Total Current Liabilities	876.5	429.5	437.0	745.7	520.4	389.3	498.9
Long-Term Obligations	287.8	298.4	281.4	417.6	422.1	415.5	398.3
Net Stockholders' Equity	693.7	642.8	708.4	823.5	742.3	715.1	1,898.3
Net Working Capital	d261.8	d102.7	8.0	d61.0	d34.7	d11.5	d191.1
Year-end Shs. Outstg. (000)	65,078	65,460	71,712	73,858	70,692	70,014	69,082
STATISTICAL RECORD:							
Operating Profit Margin %	13.0	13.4	...	5.2	6.9	1.5	7.9
Net Profit Margin %	6.4	6.5	...	3.6	3.2	0.1	4.3
Return on Equity %	15.3	10.8	...	9.5	8.0	0.2	3.2
Return on Assets %	4.3	3.9	...	3.2	2.8	0.1	3.0
Debt/Total Assets %	11.7	16.7	15.2	17.3	20.1	21.2	19.7
Price Range	33.38-16.13	19.50-11.63	17.63-10.28	17.31-13.69	15.75-12.63	15.69-12.94	19.38-12.75
P/E Ratio	20.9-10.1	19.4-11.6	...	16.0-12.7	18.6-14.9	782.4-645.3	22.0-14.5
Average Yield %	2.4	3.8	4.2	3.8	4.2	4.1	3.6

Statistics are as originally reported. Adj. for 2-for-1 stk. split, 6/01. (1) Incl. net nonrecurr. chgs. of $76.1. (2) Incl. net nonrecurr. gain of $3.8 mill. (3) Incl. pretax gain of $28.3 mill. (4) Incl. net pretax chgs. of $100.5 mill. (5) Incl. aftertax chrg. of $12.3 mill. rel. to Kentucky West labor settlement & an after-tax gain of $4.3 mill. for sale of Westport Resource's stk.

OFFICERS:
M. S. Gerber, Chmn., Pres., C.E.O.
D. L. Porges, Exec. V.P., C.F.O.
J. G. O'Loughlin, V.P., Gen. Couns., Sec.

INVESTOR CONTACT: P. P. Conti, V.P. & Treas., (412) 553-5869

PRINCIPAL OFFICE: One Oxford Centre, Suite 3300, 301 Grant Street, Pittsburgh, PA 15219

TELEPHONE NUMBER: (412) 553-5700
FAX: (412) 553-5732
WEB: www.eqt.com

NO. OF EMPLOYEES: 1,614 (avg.)

SHAREHOLDERS: 4,908 (approx.)

ANNUAL MEETING: In May

INCORPORATED: PA, Mar., 1925

INSTITUTIONAL HOLDINGS:
No. of Institutions: 212
Shares Held: 46,394,510 (Adj.)
% Held: 71.1

INDUSTRY: Gas transmission and distribution (SIC: 4923)

TRANSFER AGENT(S): Mellon Investor Services, Pittsburgh, PA

NYSE SYMBOL EOP
Rec. Pr. 28.55 (4/30/01)

EQUITY OFFICE PROPERTIES TRUST

YIELD 6.3%
P/E RATIO 18.5

TRADING VOLUME
Thousand Shares

*7 YEAR PRICE SCORE N/A *12 MONTH PRICE SCORE 101.7

*NYSE COMPOSITE INDEX=100

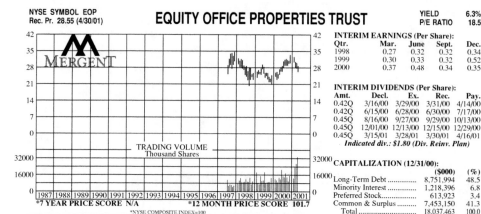

INTERIM EARNINGS (Per Share):

Qtr.	Mar.	June	Sept.	Dec.
1998	0.27	0.32	0.32	0.34
1999	0.30	0.33	0.32	0.52
2000	0.37	0.48	0.34	0.35

INTERIM DIVIDENDS (Per Share):

Amt.	Decl.	Ex.	Rec.	Pay.
0.42Q	3/16/00	3/29/00	3/31/00	4/14/00
0.42Q	6/15/00	6/28/00	6/30/00	7/17/00
0.45Q	8/16/00	9/27/00	9/29/00	10/13/00
0.45Q	12/01/00	12/13/00	12/15/00	12/29/00
0.45Q	3/15/01	3/28/01	3/30/01	4/16/01

Indicated div.: $1.80 (Div. Reinv. Plan)

CAPITALIZATION (12/31/00):

	($000)	(%)
Long-Term Debt	8,751,994	48.5
Minority Interest	1,218,396	6.8
Preferred Stock	613,923	3.4
Common & Surplus	7,453,150	41.3
Total	18,037,463	100.0

RECENT DEVELOPMENTS: For the year ended 12/31/00, net income rose 7.0% to $472.7 million, before extraordinary charges of $1.8 million, versus income of $441.9 million, before extraordinary charges of $10.5 million, in 1999. Results included gains on sales of real estate of $36.0 million and $59.7 million in 2000 and 1999, respectively. Total revenues jumped 16.6% to $2.26 billion compared with $1.94 billion in the previous year.

PROSPECTS: On 2/23/01, the Company announced that it has entered into a definitive agreement to acquire Spieker Properties, Inc. in a transaction valued at approximately $7.20 billion including transaction costs, and the assumption of about $2.10 billion in debt and $431.0 million in preferred stock. Under terms of the agreement, EOP will pay approximately $1.09 billion in cash and issue about 118.6 million shares of new common stock.

BUSINESS

EQUITY OFFICE PROPERTIES TRUST is a fully integrated real estate investment trust company and is the nation's largest publicly-held owner and manager of office properties, in terms of its property portfolio. The Company is engaged in acquiring, owning, managing and leasing office properties and parking facilities. As of 1/31/01, the Company owned or had an interest in 380 buildings comprising 98.9 million square feet in 24 states and the District of Columbia. In addition, the Company has an ownership presence in 37 Metropolitan Statistical Areas and in 104 submarkets. In June 2000, the Company acquired Cornerstone Properties Inc.

REVENUES

12/31/2000	($000)	(%)
Rental	1,732,799	76.5
Tenant reimbursement	324,193	14.3
Parking	112,107	5.0
Other revenue	48,047	2.1
Fee income	10,931	0.5
Interest/Dividends	36,166	1.6
Total	2,264,243	100.0

ANNUAL FINANCIAL DATA

	12/31/00	12/31/99	12/31/98	12/31/97	12/31/96	12/31/95	12/31/94
Earnings Per Share	**[1] 1.52**	**[1] 1.48**	**[1] 1.24**	**[1] 0.43**	...	...	...
Tang. Book Val. Per Share	**24.28**	**24.69**	**24.76**	**24.87**	...	...	...
Dividends Per Share	**1.74**	**1.58**	**1.38**	**0.56**	...	...	...
Dividend Payout %	**114.5**	**106.7**	**111.3**	**130.2**	...	...	...
INCOME STATEMENT (IN MILLIONS):							
Rental Income	1,732.8	1,493.2	1,299.0	314.2	386.5	289.3	193.0
Total Income	2,264.2	1,942.2	1,679.7	413.0	508.1	371.5	240.9
Costs & Expenses	855.4	750.7	663.9	173.4	224.2	193.7	123.0
Depreciation	436.4	359.0	306.0	70.3	96.2	74.2	46.9
Interest Expense	525.8	414.0	338.6	76.7	119.6	100.6	59.3
Income Before Income Taxes	482.6	478.2	383.6	92.7	73.4	3.0	11.6
Equity Earnings/Minority Int.	d10.0	d36.3	d27.1	d4.6	...	0.2	3.2
Net Income	[1] 472.7	[1] 441.9	[1] 356.5	[1] 88.1	73.4	[1] 3.2	[1] 14.9
Average Shs. Outstg. (000)	318,997	291,157	283,975	180,014	...	...	...
BALANCE SHEET (IN MILLIONS):							
Cash & Cash Equivalents	93.1	22.1	226.7	254.6	443.0	131.5	...
Total Real Estate Investments	16,641.3	12,572.2	13,331.6	10,976.3	3,291.8	2,393.4	...
Total Assets	18,794.3	14,046.1	14,261.3	11,751.7	3,912.6	2,650.9	...
Long-Term Obligations	8,752.0	5,398.9	4,810.5	2,243.8	1,839.8	1,359.7	...
Total Liabilities	10,727.2	7,220.0	7,210.3	5,346.5	2,185.6	1,560.9	...
Net Stockholders' Equity	8,067.1	6,826.1	7,051.0	6,405.2	1,727.0	1,090.0	...
Year-end Shs. Outstg. (000)	306,967	251,582	259,902	249,528	...	...	...
STATISTICAL RECORD:							
Net Inc.+Depr./Assets %	4.8	5.7	4.6	1.3	4.3	2.9	...
Return on Equity %	5.9	6.5	5.1	1.4	4.3	0.3	...
Return on Assets %	2.5	3.1	2.5	0.7	1.9	0.1	...
Price Range	33.50-22.88	29.38-20.81	32.00-20.19	34.69-25.25	...	...	...
P/E Ratio	22.0-15.0	19.8-14.1	25.8-16.3	80.7-58.7	...	...	...
Average Yield %	6.2	6.3	5.3	1.9	...	...	...

Statistics are as originally reported. [1] Bef. extraord. chrg. 2000, $1.8 mill.; 1999, $10.5 mill.; 1998, $7.5 mill.; 1997, $16.4 mill.; 1994, $1.7 mill.; credit, 1995, $31.3 mill.

OFFICERS:
S. Zell, Chmn.
T. H. Callahan, Pres., C.E.O.
R. D. Kincaid, Exec. V.P., C.F.O.
M. O. Fear, Sr. V.P., Treas.

INVESTOR CONTACT: Diane M. Morefield, Sr. Vice-Pres., Investor Relations, (800) 692-5304

PRINCIPAL OFFICE: Two North Riverside Plaza, Suite 2100, Chicago, IL 60606

TELEPHONE NUMBER: (312) 466-3300
FAX: (312) 454-0332
WEB: www.equityoffice.com

NO. OF EMPLOYEES: 2,061 (approx.)

SHAREHOLDERS: 942 (approx.)

ANNUAL MEETING: In May

INCORPORATED: MD, Oct., 1996

INSTITUTIONAL HOLDINGS:
No. of Institutions: 281
Shares Held: 237,134,598
% Held: 76.8

INDUSTRY: Real estate investment trusts (SIC: 6798)

TRANSFER AGENT(S): BankBoston, N.A., Boston, MA

NYSE SYMBOL EQR
Rec. Pr. 52.49 (4/30/01)

EQUITY RESIDENTIAL PROPERTIES TRUST

YIELD 6.2%
P/E RATIO 15.7

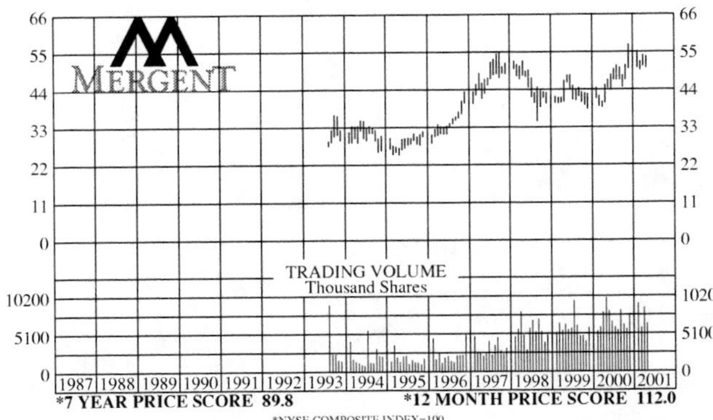

*7 YEAR PRICE SCORE 89.8 *12 MONTH PRICE SCORE 112.0
*NYSE COMPOSITE INDEX=100

INTERIM EARNINGS (Per Share):

Qtr.	Mar.	June	Sept.	Dec.
1997	0.46	0.40	0.42	0.48
1998	0.38	0.47	0.36	0.42
1999	0.54	0.57	0.55	0.63
2000	0.57	0.96	1.07	0.74

INTERIM DIVIDENDS (Per Share):

Amt.	Decl.	Ex.	Rec.	Pay.
0.76Q	5/23/00	6/16/00	6/20/00	7/14/00
0.815Q	8/21/00	9/18/00	9/20/00	10/13/00
0.815Q	11/14/00	12/15/00	12/19/00	12/29/00
0.815Q	2/12/01	3/16/01	3/20/01	4/12/01
0.815Q	5/23/01	6/18/01	6/20/01	7/13/01

Indicated div.: $3.26 (Div. Reinv. Plan)

CAPITALIZATION (12/31/00):

	($000)	(%)
Long-Term Debt	5,350,690	46.2
Minority Interest	612,618	5.3
Preferred Stock	1,183,136	10.2
Common & Surplus	4,436,411	38.3
Total	11,582,855	100.0

RECENT DEVELOPMENTS: For the year ended 12/31/00, EQR reported net income of $555.0 million versus $394.3 million in 1999. Results excluded extraordinary charges of $5.6 million and $451,000 in 2000 and 1999, respectively. Results included net gains on the sale of real estate of $198.4 million and $93.5 million in 2000 and 1999, respectively. Total revenue jumped 16.5% to $2.03 billion versus $1.74 billion in the prior-year period.

PROSPECTS: Looking ahead, EQR expects to achieve funds from operations per share of $1.30 for the first quarter of 2001 and in the range of $5.35 to $5.40 for the fiscal year 2001. In addition, the Company anticipates strong demand for apartments in the upcoming fiscal year. Meanwhile, EQR will continue to focus on expanding its business through acquisitions and new developments with emphasis on in-fill locations and high-barrier markets.

BUSINESS

EQUITY RESIDENTIAL PROPERTIES TRUST is a self-administered and self-managed equity real estate investment trust. The Company, through its subsidiaries, is engaged in the acquisition, disposition, ownership, management and operation of multifamily properties. As of December 31, 2000, the Company owned or had interests in a portfolio of 1,104 multifamily properties containing 227,704 apartment units in 36 states. On 10/31/00, the Company merged with Grove Property Trust, a Maryland real estate investment trust company, for approximately $174.7 million in cash and the issuance of approximately 344,142 operating partnership units.

QUARTERLY DATA

(12/31/00)($000)	REV	INC
1st Quarter	485,410	101,139
2nd Quarter	493,113	152,659
3rd Quarter	537,254	169,316
4th Quarter	532,196	126,337

ANNUAL FINANCIAL DATA

	12/31/00	12/31/99	12/31/98	12/31/97	12/31/96	12/31/95	12/31/94
Earnings Per Share	**[3] 3.34**	**[1] [3] 2.29**	**[1] 1.63**	**[1] 1.76**	**[1] [2] 1.70**	**[1] [3] 1.68**	**1.34**
Tang. Book Val. Per Share	**32.94**	**32.91**	**33.15**	**29.73**	**...**	**17.32**	**17.96**
Dividends Per Share	**3.15**	**2.94**	**2.72**	**3.17**	**2.36**	**2.11**	**1.96**
Dividend Payout %	**94.3**	**128.4**	**166.9**	**180.1**	**138.8**	**125.6**	**145.9**
INCOME STATEMENT (IN MILLIONS):							
Rental Income	1,959.8	1,711.7	1,293.6	707.7	454.4	372.4	220.7
Interest Income	64.0	36.4	38.3	33.9	17.2	9.4	5.6
Total Income	2,030.3	1,753.1	1,337.4	747.3	478.4	388.9	231.0
Costs & Expenses	1,192.9	1,010.0	777.8	412.1	283.9	253.3	145.8
Depreciation	456.8	412.8	304.6	159.2	97.5	75.9	39.2
Income Before Income Taxes	596.7	330.3	255.0	176.0	97.0	59.7	46.0
Equity Earnings/Minority Int.	d41.6	d29.5	d18.5	d13.3	d14.3	d15.6	d11.6
Net Income	[3] 555.0	[1] [3] 300.8	[1] 236.5	[1] 162.8	[1] [2] 82.7	[1] [3] 44.1	34.4
Average Shs. Outstg. (000)	145,633	135,655	112,578	74,251	42,586	34,358	25,621
BALANCE SHEET (IN MILLIONS):							
Cash & Cash Equivalents	255.4	140.4	73.3	69.7	167.9	31.7	28.2
Total Assets	12,264.0	11,715.7	10,700.3	7,094.6	2,986.1	2,141.3	1,847.7
Long-Term Obligations	5,350.7	5,173.9	4,390.5	2,713.3	1,254.3	910.2	832.7
Total Liabilities	6,644.4	6,210.8	5,369.8	3,404.6	1,527.3	1,256.7	1,237.7
Net Stockholders' Equity	5,619.5	5,504.9	5,330.4	3,690.0	1,458.8	884.5	609.9
Year-end Shs. Outstg. (000)	132,616	127,451	118,230	89,085	...	35,012	33,964
STATISTICAL RECORD:							
Net Inc.+Depr./Assets %	8.3	6.1	5.1	4.5	6.0	5.6	4.0
Return on Equity %	9.9	5.5	4.4	4.4	5.7	5.0	5.6
Return on Assets %	4.5	2.6	2.2	2.3	2.8	2.1	1.9
Price Range	57.25-38.69	48.38-38.13	52.56-34.69	55.00-39.75	43.50-28.25	31.88-24.88	35.13-25.75
P/E Ratio	17.1-11.6	21.1-16.6	32.2-21.3	31.2-22.6	25.6-16.6	19.0-14.8	26.2-19.2
Average Yield %	6.6	6.8	6.2	6.7	6.6	7.4	6.4

Statistics are as originally reported. [1] Bef. gain on dispos. of properties, 1999, $93.5 mill.; 1998, $21.7 mill.; 1997, $13.8 mill.; 1996, $22.4 mill.; 1995, $21.6 mill. [2] Bef. $3.5 mill. write-off of unamort. costs of refin. [3] Bef. gain on early exting. of debt., 2000, $5.6 mill.; 1999, $451,000; 1995, $2.0 mill.

OFFICERS:
S. Zell, Chmn.
D. Crocker II, Pres., C.E.O.
D. J. Neithercut, Exec. V.P., C.F.O.
M. J. McHugh, Exec. V.P., C.A.O., Treas.

INVESTOR CONTACT: Cynthia H. McHugh, V.P., Inv. Rel., (312) 466-3779

PRINCIPAL OFFICE: Two North Riverside Plaza, Suite 400, Chicago, IL 60606

TELEPHONE NUMBER: (312) 474-1300
FAX: (312) 454-8703
WEB: www.eqr.com

NO. OF EMPLOYEES: 7,400 (approx.)

SHAREHOLDERS: 61,000 (approx. bene.)

ANNUAL MEETING: In Sept.

INCORPORATED: MD, 1993

INSTITUTIONAL HOLDINGS:
No. of Institutions: 279
Shares Held: 103,017,452
% Held: 77.6

INDUSTRY: Real estate investment trusts (SIC: 6798)

TRANSFER AGENT(S): Boston EquiServe, LP, Boston, MA

NYSE SYMBOL ESE
Rec. Pr. 30.10 (5/31/01)

ESCO TECHNOLOGIES INC.

YIELD ...
P/E RATIO 24.3

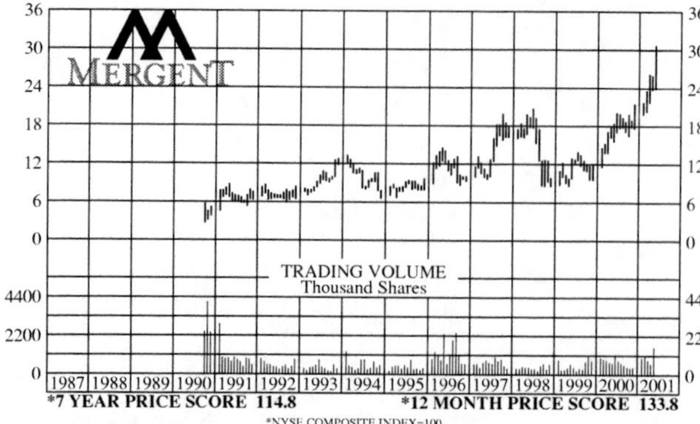

*7 YEAR PRICE SCORE 114.8 *12 MONTH PRICE SCORE 133.8
*NYSE COMPOSITE INDEX=100

INTERIM EARNINGS (Per Share):

Qtr.	Dec.	Mar.	June	Sept.
1997-98	0.21	0.26	0.31	0.12
1998-99	0.12	0.16	0.32	3.36
1999-00	0.40	0.28	0.29	0.36
2000-01	0.31	...	...	...

INTERIM DIVIDENDS (Per Share):

Amt.	Decl.	Ex.	Rec.	Pay.
No dividends paid.				

CAPITALIZATION (9/30/00):

	($000)	(%)
Long-Term Debt	610	0.2
Common & Surplus	259,422	99.8
Total	260,032	100.0

RECENT DEVELOPMENTS: For the three months ended 12/31/00, net income declined 21.3% to $4.0 million compared with $5.1 million in the corresponding quarter of 1999. Net sales increased 25.8% to $82.9 million, reflecting market acceptance of new products and favorable contributions from recent acquisitions and year-over-year sales growth in all three major business segment. Operating profit amounted to $8.5 million versus $5.9 million a year earlier.

PROSPECTS: Looking ahead, the Company anticipates sales growth in the automotive market from several new products recently designed into next generation fuel delivery, transmission and power steering systems. ESE also expects that sales to automotive system suppliers will continue to grow at a substantially higher rate than direct sales to the major car companies. Separately, ESE was awarded a follow-on contract from the Puerto Rico Electric Power Authority valued at approximately $50.0 million.

BUSINESS

ESCO TECHNOLOGIES INC. (formerly Esco Electronics Corporation) is a supplier of engineered filtration products to the Process, Health Care and Transportation markets worldwide. The Company's filtration products include depth filters, membrane based microfiltration products and precision screen filters. Major applications include semiconductor production processes, blood collection, water purification, food and beverage processing, oil production and removal of contaminants in fuel lube and hydraulic systems. Esco's filtration business contributes approximately 53.3% of the Company's total sales as of 12/31/00. The balance of Esco's sales are derived primarily from RF shielding and test products and special purpose communication systems, where the Company is positioned in niche markets based on proprietary products. In addition, Esco provides a communication system called TWACS® to the electric utility industry. The TWACS® system is currently used primarily for automatic meter reading.

QUARTERLY DATA

(09/30/00)($000)	Rev	Inc
First Quarter	65,865	5,056
Second Quarter	70,062	3,517
Third Quarter	79,235	3,708
Fourth Quarter	84,995	4,538

ANNUAL FINANCIAL DATA

	9/30/00	9/30/99	9/30/98	9/30/97	9/30/96	9/30/95	9/30/94
Earnings Per Share	**1.33**	**1 2.02**	**0.90**	**0.96**	**2.26**	**d2.76**	**0.72**
Cash Flow Per Share	**2.45**	**5.35**	**2.29**	**2.14**	**3.42**	**d1.48**	**1.90**
Tang. Book Val. Per Share	**13.73**	**12.50**	**12.22**	**12.72**	**14.41**	**14.70**	**15.27**
INCOME STATEMENT (IN THOUSANDS):							
Total Revenues	300,157	416,102	365,083	378,524	438,543	441,023	473,855
Costs & Expenses	255,897	375,089	318,198	336,509	423,697	404,901	435,917
Depreciation & Amort.	14,185	17,021	17,460	14,423	13,486	14,042	13,652
Operating Income	30,075	23,992	29,425	27,592	1,360	22,080	24,286
Net Interest Inc./(Exp.)	d359	d6,460	d7,703	d5,220	d4,781	d5,549	d3,646
Income Before Income Taxes	24,736	63,456	16,347	17,850	14,762	d29,505	12,656
Income Taxes	7,917	13,001	5,051	6,053	cr11,374	755	4,348
Net Income	16,819	1 50,455	11,296	11,797	26,136	d30,260	8,308
Cash Flow	31,004	67,476	28,756	26,220	39,622	d16,218	21,960
Average Shs. Outstg.	12,668	12,614	12,550	12,274	11,580	10,973	11,565
BALANCE SHEET (IN THOUSANDS):							
Cash & Cash Equivalents	5,620	87,709	4,241	5,818	22,209	320	2,656
Total Current Assets	118,209	173,546	167,121	156,967	162,650	211,863	189,055
Net Property	62,563	71,318	98,009	96,532	54,026	91,479	93,145
Total Assets	331,133	378,385	409,302	378,187	307,832	378,001	347,486
Total Current Liabilities	62,491	78,217	106,807	94,676	76,464	140,454	102,471
Long-Term Obligations	610	41,896	50,077	50,000	11,375	23,452	25,120
Net Stockholders' Equity	259,422	248,689	224,079	204,963	191,133	182,255	187,413
Net Working Capital	55,718	95,329	60,314	62,291	86,186	71,409	86,584
Year-end Shs. Outstg.	12,268	14,378	12,408	11,788	11,849	11,004	10,945
STATISTICAL RECORD:							
Operating Profit Margin %	10.0	5.8	8.1	7.3	0.3	5.0	5.1
Net Profit Margin %	5.6	12.1	3.1	3.1	6.0	...	1.8
Return on Equity %	6.5	20.3	5.0	5.8	13.7	...	4.4
Return on Assets %	5.1	13.3	2.8	3.1	8.5	...	2.4
Debt/Total Assets %	0.2	11.1	12.2	13.2	3.7	6.2	7.2
Price Range	21.50-11.50	13.94-8.56	20.75-8.50	19.94-9.63	14.63-8.63	9.75-6.63	13.38-6.50
P/E Ratio	16.2-8.6	6.9-4.2	23.1-9.4	20.8-10.0	6.5-3.8	...	18.6-9.0

Statistics are as originally reported. 1 Incl. pre-tax gain of $59.9 mill. from sale of SEI subsidiary and nonrecurring charges of $9.1 mill.; Excl. acctg. charge of $25.0 mill.

OFFICERS:
D. J. Moore, Chmn., Pres., C.E.O.
C. J. Kretschmer, Sr. V.P., C.F.O.
A. S. Barclay, V.P., Sec., Gen. Couns.

INVESTOR CONTACT: Patricia Moore, (314) 213-2090

PRINCIPAL OFFICE: 8888 Ladue Road, Suite 200, St. Louis, MO 63124-2056

TELEPHONE NUMBER: (314) 213-7200
FAX: (314) 213-7250
WEB: www.escotechnologies.com

NO. OF EMPLOYEES: 2,275 (approx.)

SHAREHOLDERS: 4,600 (approx. record)

ANNUAL MEETING: In Feb.

INCORPORATED: MO, Aug., 1990

INSTITUTIONAL HOLDINGS:
No. of Institutions: 87
Shares Held: 9,445,648
% Held: 76.0

INDUSTRY: Search and navigation equipment (SIC: 3812)

TRANSFER AGENT(S): Mellon Investor Services, Ridgefield Park, NJ

NYSE SYMBOL EL
Rec. Pr. 39.75 (4/30/01)

ESTEE LAUDER COMPANIES, INC. (THE)

YIELD 0.5%
P/E RATIO 30.6

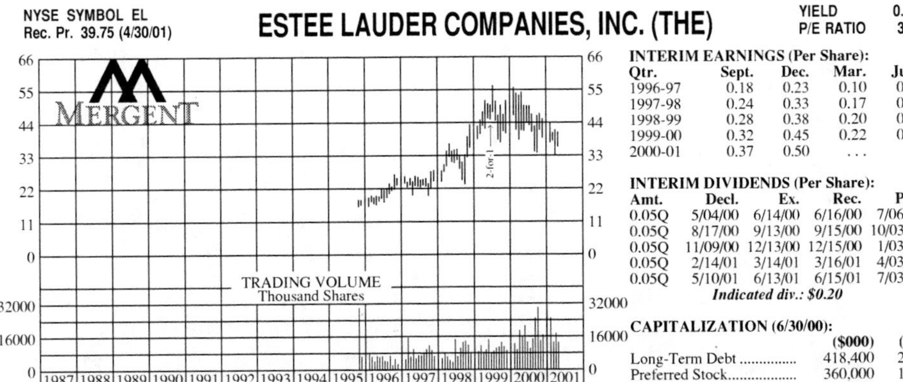

*7 YEAR PRICE SCORE N/A *12 MONTH PRICE SCORE 96.0

*NYSE COMPOSITE INDEX=100

INTERIM EARNINGS (Per Share):

Qtr.	Sept.	Dec.	Mar.	June
1996-97	0.18	0.23	0.10	0.09
1997-98	0.24	0.33	0.17	0.16
1998-99	0.28	0.38	0.20	0.18
1999-00	0.32	0.45	0.22	0.21
2000-01	0.37	0.50	...	...

INTERIM DIVIDENDS (Per Share):

Amt.	Decl.	Ex.	Rec.	Pay.
0.05Q	5/04/00	6/14/00	6/16/00	7/06/00
0.05Q	8/17/00	9/13/00	9/15/00	10/03/00
0.05Q	11/09/00	12/13/00	12/15/00	1/03/01
0.05Q	2/14/01	3/14/01	3/16/01	4/03/01
0.05Q	5/10/01	6/13/01	6/15/01	7/03/01

Indicated div.: $0.20

CAPITALIZATION (6/30/00):

	($000)	(%)
Long-Term Debt	418,400	21.6
Preferred Stock	360,000	18.6
Common & Surplus	1,160,300	59.8
Total	1,938,700	100.0

RECENT DEVELOPMENTS: For the quarter ended 12/31/00, net earnings more than doubled to $127.3 million from $113.9 million in the prior-year quarter. Net sales totaled $1.29 billion, up 4.6% versus $1.24 billion a year earlier. Skin care product sales climbed 9.0% to $423.2 million, while makeup products sales increased 13.0% to $420.5 million. Sales of hair care products advanced 44.0% to $43.0 million, while fragrance sales fell 9.0% to $396.9 million.

PROSPECTS: Replenishment orders for the second half of the Company's fiscal year may be affected by the broad economic conditions that are creating a softer retail sell-through. For the full fiscal year results, net sales growth is expected to be in the range of 8.0% to 10.0%, while earnings per share should be in the range of $1.32 to $1.35. This growth should stem from strong hair-care products sales, followed by makeup and skin care, while fragrance sales are expected to be flat.

BUSINESS

THE ESTEE LAUDER COMPANIES, INC. manufactures and markets prestige skin care, makeup and fragrance products. The Company's products are sold in approximately 120 countries and territories under the following well-recognized brand names: ESTEE LAUDER, CLINIQUE, ARAMIS, PRESCRIPTIVES, ORIGINS, MAC, BOBBI BROWN essentials, TOMMY HILFIGER, LA MER, JANE, DONNA KARAN, AVEDA, STILA, JO MALONE and BUMBLE AND BUMBLE. Each brand is distinctly positioned within the cosmetics market.

ANNUAL FINANCIAL DATA

	6/30/00	6/30/99	6/30/98	6/30/97	6/30/96	6/30/95	6/30/94
Earnings Per Share	**1 1.20**	**1.03**	**0.90**	**0.73**	**0.59**	**0.45**	...
Cash Flow Per Share	**1.80**	**1.52**	**1.30**	**1.05**	**0.69**	**0.60**	...
Tang. Book Val. Per Share	**1.77**	**1.33**	**0.56**	**1.63**	**1.06**	**1.25**	...
Dividends Per Share	**0.20**	**0.18**	**0.17**	**0.17**	**0.09**	...	...
Dividend Payout %	**16.7**	**18.0**	**19.0**	**23.3**	**14.5**	...	...
INCOME STATEMENT (IN MILLIONS):							
Total Revenues	4,366.8	3,961.5	3,618.0	3,381.6	3,194.5	2,899.1	2,576.4
Costs & Expenses	3,704.2	3,387.3	3,111.4	2,946.5	2,825.4	2,626.2	2,360.5
Depreciation & Amort.	146.8	117.3	97.5	76.0	58.8	42.0	40.1
Operating Income	515.8	456.9	409.1	359.1	310.3	230.9	175.8
Net Interest Inc./(Exp.)	d17.1	d16.7	d6.3	3.8	2.7	2.1	d2.6
Income Before Income Taxes	498.7	440.2	402.8	362.9	313.0	233.0	173.2
Income Taxes	184.6	167.3	161.1	152.4	138.3	108.0	80.2
Equity Earnings/Minority Int.	...	...	d4.9	d12.9	d14.3	d3.8	...
Net Income	1 314.1	272.9	236.8	197.6	160.4	121.2	93.0
Cash Flow	437.5	366.8	310.9	250.2	161.7	137.9	110.1
Average Shs. Outstg. (000)	242,500	241,200	239,400	238,400	233,600	229,200	...
BALANCE SHEET (IN MILLIONS):							
Cash & Cash Equivalents	320.3	347.5	277.5	255.6	254.8	281.4	182.8
Total Current Assets	1,618.5	1,570.2	1,454.6	1,311.1	1,332.6	1,282.8	1,064.3
Net Property	480.3	383.6	335.8	265.0	229.3	199.0	181.1
Total Assets	3,043.3	2,746.7	2,512.8	1,873.1	1,821.6	1,721.7	1,453.2
Total Current Liabilities	901.8	862.2	837.4	759.5	865.1	813.2	641.6
Long-Term Obligations	418.4	422.5	425.0	...	21.9	65.5	104.7
Net Stockholders' Equity	1,520.3	1,284.5	1,056.4	907.7	754.2	695.1	577.7
Net Working Capital	716.7	708.0	617.2	551.6	467.5	469.6	422.7
Year-end Shs. Outstg. (000)	237,861	237,160	236,616	236,552	234,596	234,596	...
STATISTICAL RECORD:							
Operating Profit Margin %	11.8	11.5	11.3	10.6	9.7	8.0	6.8
Net Profit Margin %	7.2	6.9	6.5	5.8	5.0	4.2	3.6
Return on Equity %	20.7	21.2	22.4	21.8	21.3	17.4	16.1
Return on Assets %	10.3	9.9	9.4	10.5	8.8	7.0	6.4
Debt/Total Assets %	13.7	15.4	16.9	...	1.2	3.8	7.2
Price Range	55.88-33.75	56.50-37.25	43.25-23.34	28.19-19.50	26.75-16.06	18.38-15.88	...
P/E Ratio	46.6-28.1	54.8-36.2	48.3-26.1	38.6-26.7	45.7-27.5	40.8-35.3	...
Average Yield %	0.4	0.4	0.5	0.7	0.4	...	...

Statistics are as originally reported. Adj. for stock split, 2-for-1, 6/99 1 Bef. acctg. change chrg. $2.2 mill.

OFFICERS:
L. A. Lauder, Chmn.
F. H. Langhammer, Pres., C.E.O.
E. M. Straw, Pres.
R. J. Bigler, Sr. V.P., C.F.O.

INVESTOR CONTACT: Investor Relations, (212) 572-4384

PRINCIPAL OFFICE: 767 Fifth Avenue, New York, NY 10153

TELEPHONE NUMBER: (212) 572-4200
FAX: (212) 572-3941
WEB: www.elcompanies.com

NO. OF EMPLOYEES: 18,000 (approx.)

SHAREHOLDERS: 3,905 (approx. record Class A); 13 (record Class B)

ANNUAL MEETING: In Nov.

INCORPORATED: DE, 1946

INSTITUTIONAL HOLDINGS:
No. of Institutions: 229
Shares Held: 91,897,391
% Held: 38.6

INDUSTRY: Toilet preparations (SIC: 2844)

TRANSFER AGENT(S): Mellon Investor Services, South Hackensack, NJ

NYSE SYMBOL ESL
Rec. Pr. 19.50 (4/30/01)

ESTERLINE TECHNOLOGIES CORPORATION

YIELD ...
P/E RATIO 10.3

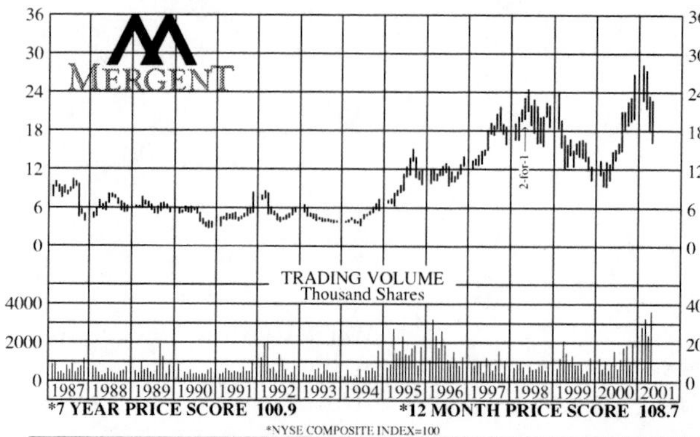

*7 YEAR PRICE SCORE 100.9 *12 MONTH PRICE SCORE 108.7

*NYSE COMPOSITE INDEX=100

INTERIM EARNINGS (Per Share):

Qtr.	Jan.	Apr.	July	Oct.
1996	0.24	0.38	0.29	0.39
1997	0.22	0.38	0.40	0.46
1998	0.28	0.45	0.45	0.53
1999	0.29	0.40	0.34	0.66
2000	0.27	0.40	0.55	0.63
2001	0.32	...	...	...

INTERIM DIVIDENDS (Per Share):

Amt.	Decl.	Ex.	Rec.	Pay.

No dividends paid.

CAPITALIZATION (10/27/00):

	($000)	(%)
Long-Term Debt	108,172	29.4
Deferred Income Tax	9,550	2.6
Common & Surplus	249,695	68.0
Total	367,417	100.0

RECENT DEVELOPMENTS: For the quarter ended 1/26/01, net earnings rose 17.1% to $5.7 million compared with net income of $4.8 million in 2000. Results for 2001 included a $791,000 loss on derivative financial instruments charge and excluded a credit from an accounting change of $384,000. Net sales were $118.0 million, up 13.2% from $104.2 million in the prior-year period. Operating earnings jumped 21.5% to $11.1 million compared with $9.1 million the year before.

PROSPECTS: ESL completed the acquisition of the Aerospace Knob and Western Indicator product lines from Dupree, Inc. These product lines will be integrated into ESL's cockpit components operations and are expected to be accretive to earnings. Separately, ESL was awarded a $12.7 million multi-year contract to produce the modular combustible case for 155mm artillery rounds. Production will begin in July 2001 at ESL's Armtec Defense Products subsidiary.

BUSINESS

ESTERLINE TECHNOLOGIES CORPORATION is a manufacturing company with operations primarily serving the aerospace and defense markets. ESL conducts its operations through three business segments: automation (25.5% of 2000 sales), aerospace (48.1%), and advanced materials (26.4%). The automation division serves electronic equipment and metal fabricating industries with printed circuit board drilling equipment and automated machine tools. The aerospace division serves jet and rocket engine manufacturers with pressure sensing devices and hydraulic controls. The advanced materials unit primarily serves the aerospace market and provides specialty clamps, seals, tubing and coverings. In 1999, the Company completed the acquisitions of Muirhead Vactric Components Limited, Norcroft Dynamics Limited and Advanced Input Devices.

ANNUAL FINANCIAL DATA

	10/27/00	10/31/99	10/31/98	10/31/97	10/31/96	10/31/95	10/31/94
Earnings Per Share	**2 1.85**	**1 1.69**	**1.70**	**1.44**	**1.31**	**1.27**	**0.58**
Cash Flow Per Share	**3.08**	**2.87**	**2.73**	**2.50**	**2.37**	**2.47**	**1.82**
Tang. Book Val. Per Share	**6.41**	**6.88**	**5.60**	**7.86**	**5.95**	**3.77**	**1.81**
INCOME STATEMENT (IN MILLIONS):							
Total Revenues	491.0	461.0	453.9	391.0	352.8	351.9	294.0
Costs & Expenses	415.9	395.9	386.4	334.3	302.2	304.4	262.8
Depreciation & Amort.	21.7	20.8	18.3	17.4	16.3	16.6	16.4
Operating Income	53.4	44.3	49.2	39.3	34.4	30.9	14.8
Net Interest Inc./(Exp.)	d5.9	d6.2	d2.2	d1.2	d2.3	d4.4	d6.0
Income Before Income Taxes	50.0	46.1	46.9	38.1	32.1	26.5	8.8
Income Taxes	17.4	16.2	16.9	12.8	10.7	9.1	1.3
Net Income	2 32.6	1 29.9	30.1	25.3	21.4	17.4	7.6
Cash Flow	54.3	50.7	48.4	42.7	37.6	34.0	24.0
Average Shs. Outstg. (000)	17,654	17,658	17,718	17,124	15,842	13,740	13,142
BALANCE SHEET (IN MILLIONS):							
Cash & Cash Equivalents	50.9	81.0	8.9	56.0	46.4	22.1	9.1
Total Current Assets	228.5	242.5	178.0	194.4	178.8	142.2	119.3
Net Property	87.4	89.3	94.1	58.4	53.8	49.2	51.6
Total Assets	474.3	453.1	387.2	289.8	276.6	225.7	216.0
Total Current Liabilities	106.9	101.6	107.9	100.9	105.3	106.5	108.8
Long-Term Obligations	108.2	117.0	74.0	23.2	29.0	35.5	41.7
Net Stockholders' Equity	249.7	224.6	196.4	172.9	145.3	84.4	68.0
Net Working Capital	121.6	140.9	70.1	93.5	73.4	35.7	10.5
Year-end Shs. Outstg. (000)	17,425	17,342	17,317	17,286	17,004	13,292	13,026
STATISTICAL RECORD:							
Operating Profit Margin %	10.9	9.6	10.8	10.0	9.8	8.8	5.0
Net Profit Margin %	6.6	6.5	6.6	6.5	6.1	4.9	2.6
Return on Equity %	13.1	13.3	15.3	14.6	14.7	20.6	11.1
Return on Assets %	6.9	6.6	7.8	8.7	7.7	7.7	3.5
Debt/Total Assets %	22.8	25.8	19.1	8.0	10.5	15.7	19.3
Price Range	26.88-9.25	24.13-10.25	24.50-15.50	21.75-11.94	14.00-9.38	15.19-6.25	7.38-3.19
P/E Ratio	14.5-5.0	14.3-6.1	14.4-9.1	15.1-8.3	10.7-7.2	12.0-4.9	12.8-5.5

Statistics are as originally reported. Adj. for 2-for-1 split, 4/98. 1 Incl. $8.0 mill. loss fr. sale of bus. 2 Incl. $2.6 mill. gain fr. sale of bus.

OFFICERS:
R. W. Cremin, Chmn., Pres., C.E.O.
R. D. George, V.P., C.F.O.

INVESTOR CONTACT: Shareholder Relations, (800) 522-6645

PRINCIPAL OFFICE: 10800 N.E. 8th Street, Bellevue, WA 98004

TELEPHONE NUMBER: (425) 453-9400
FAX: (425) 453-2916
WEB: www.esterline.com

NO. OF EMPLOYEES: 4,300 (approx.)

SHAREHOLDERS: 778 (approx.)

ANNUAL MEETING: In Mar.

INCORPORATED: DE, Aug., 1967

INSTITUTIONAL HOLDINGS:
No. of Institutions: 120
Shares Held: 15,471,354
% Held: 74.9

INDUSTRY: Special industry machinery, nec (SIC: 3559)

TRANSFER AGENT(S): Mellon Investor Services, Ridgefield Park, NJ

NYSE SYMBOL EY
Rec. Pr. 1.44 (4/30/01)

ETHYL CORP.

YIELD ...
P/E RATIO 2.0

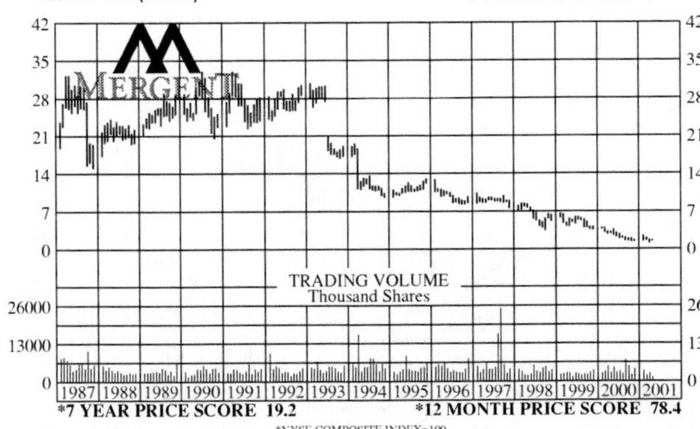

*7 YEAR PRICE SCORE 19.2 *12 MONTH PRICE SCORE 78.4

*NYSE COMPOSITE INDEX=100

INTERIM EARNINGS (Per Share):

Qtr.	Mar.	June	Sept.	Dec.
1997	0.17	0.19	0.16	0.19
1998	0.16	0.20	0.37	0.12
1999	0.18	0.16	0.20	0.12
2000	0.33	0.11	0.26	0.03

INTERIM DIVIDENDS (Per Share):

Amt.	Decl.	Ex.	Rec.	Pay.
0.063Q	7/22/99	9/13/99	9/15/99	10/01/99
0.063Q	10/28/99	12/13/99	12/15/99	1/01/00
0.063Q	2/24/00	3/13/00	3/15/00	4/01/00
0.063Q	5/25/00	6/13/00	6/15/00	7/01/00

Dividend suspended.

CAPITALIZATION (12/31/00):

	($000)	(%)
Long-Term Debt	356,053	51.0
Deferred Income Tax	82,544	11.8
Common & Surplus	259,413	37.2
Total	698,010	100.0

RECENT DEVELOPMENTS: For the year ended 12/31/00, net income climbed 10.3% to $61.0 million compared with $55.3 million in 1999. Results for 2000 included an after-tax benefit of $51.3 million, after-tax income of $2.6 million, a $4.8 million after-tax charge and a $900,000 retirement charge. Results for 1999 included after-tax income of $4.4 million. Net sales were $820.9 million, down 2.7% from $843.7 million in the previous year.

PROSPECTS: Over the last several years the Company's earnings have suffered from market deterioration in the crankcase additives segment, the high volume motor oil portion of EY's petroleum additives segment and one of its key business areas. Difficulties in this segment have resulted from overcapacity, low growth and serious price erosion. As a result, the Company plans to pursue selected growth opportunities while defending its market position.

BUSINESS

ETHYL CORP. develops, manufactures and blends performance-enhancing fuel and lubricant additives marketed worldwide to refiners and others who sell petroleum products for use in transportation and industrial equipment. EY additives increase the value of gasoline, diesel and heating fuels as well as lubricants for engines, automatic transmissions, gears and hydraulic and industrial equipment. In September of 1994, EY sold its pharmaceutical subsidiary, Whitby, Inc., to UCB, S.A. The Company acquired the operations of the worldwide lubricant additives business from Texaco on 2/29/96. Revenues and operating income for 2000 were derived: petroleum additives, (96.9%, 38.5%) and tetraethyl lead, (3.1%, 61.5%).

ANNUAL FINANCIAL DATA

	12/31/00	12/31/99	12/31/98	12/31/97	12/31/96	12/31/95	7 12/31/94
Earnings Per Share	8 0.73	6 0.66	5 0.85	2 0.71	0.78	1 0.62	3 0.83
Cash Flow Per Share	1.52	1.44	1.60	1.27	1.31	1.04	1.28
Tang. Book Val. Per Share	2.06	1.39	0.86	0.78	3.06	3.33	3.13
Dividends Per Share	0.19	0.25	0.25	0.50	0.50	0.50	4 0.53
Dividend Payout %	25.7	37.9	29.4	70.4	64.1	80.6	63.2
INCOME STATEMENT (IN MILLIONS):							
Total Revenues	820.9	843.7	974.2	1,063.6	1,149.7	960.5	1,174.1
Costs & Expenses	625.7	662.6	788.6	861.9	918.1	768.8	952.4
Depreciation & Amort.	66.3	65.1	63.3	61.8	61.9	49.2	54.0
Operating Income	129.0	116.0	122.3	139.9	169.7	142.4	167.7
Net Interest Inc./(Exp.)	d36.1	d35.5	d40.4	d25.7	d24.3	d26.8	d25.4
Income Before Income Taxes	90.1	81.1	106.4	110.0	145.8	116.2	141.1
Income Taxes	29.1	25.8	35.8	32.5	52.8	42.2	43.4
Net Income	8 61.0	6 55.3	5 70.6	2 77.5	93.0	1 74.0	3 97.8
Cash Flow	116.8	99.6	113.0	89.6	95.7	123.2	151.7
Average Shs. Outstg. (000)	83,462	83,465	83,465	109,793	118,448	118,446	118,451
BALANCE SHEET (IN MILLIONS):							
Cash & Cash Equivalents	5.7	15.8	8.4	18.2	20.1	30.0	31.2
Total Current Assets	298.2	364.9	391.4	399.1	427.2	388.5	431.5
Net Property	291.1	333.0	376.0	409.1	430.9	428.3	434.4
Total Assets	1,001.6	991.4	1,065.5	1,067.3	1,095.2	983.8	1,030.4
Total Current Liabilities	204.3	203.1	177.6	180.4	180.9	145.8	182.8
Long-Term Obligations	356.1	407.1	531.9	594.4	325.5	303.0	349.8
Net Stockholders' Equity	259.4	215.2	187.0	144.6	439.9	410.1	390.9
Net Working Capital	93.9	161.8	213.9	218.7	246.3	242.7	248.7
Year-end Shs. Outstg. (000)	83,455	83,465	83,465	83,465	118,444	118,444	118,434
STATISTICAL RECORD:							
Operating Profit Margin %	15.7	13.8	12.5	13.2	14.8	14.8	14.3
Net Profit Margin %	7.4	6.6	7.2	7.3	8.1	7.7	8.3
Return on Equity %	23.5	25.7	37.7	53.6	21.1	18.0	25.0
Return on Assets %	6.1	5.6	6.6	7.3	8.5	7.5	9.5
Debt/Total Assets %	35.5	41.1	49.9	55.7	29.7	30.8	33.9
Price Range	4.00-1.31	6.69-3.50	8.50-3.44	10.38-7.50	13.00-8.25	13.13-9.50	19.63-9.50
P/E Ratio	5.5-1.8	10.1-5.3	10.0-4.0	14.6-10.6	16.7-10.6	21.2-15.3	23.6-11.4
Average Yield %	7.1	4.9	4.2	5.6	4.7	4.4	3.6

Statistics are as originally reported. 1 Incl. $4.1 mill. net chg. 2 Incl. $3.8 mill. after-tax chg. for impairment of assets & $3.4 mill. gain fr. sale of bus. 3 Incl. $4.2 mill. after-tax gain fr. sale of Whitby, Inc. 4 0.5 shs. of Albemarle Corp. com. for each sh. held. 5 Incl. $18.7 mill. after-tax spl. item from Canadian govt. settlement, gain on sale of non-oper. assets, & tax refund fr. IRS. 6 Incl. $4.4 mill. net benefit fr. supply contract. 7 Refl. spin-off of Albemarle Corp. 8 Incl. net after-tax special gains of $48.2 mill.

OFFICERS:
B. C. Gottwald, Chmn., C.E.O.
T. E. Gottwald, Pres., C.O.O.
D. A. Fiorenza, V.P., C.F.O., Treas.

INVESTOR CONTACT: W. D. Gottwald Jr., Assistant Secretary, (804) 788-5595

PRINCIPAL OFFICE: 330 S. Fourth St., P.O. Box 2189, Richmond, VA 23218-2189

TELEPHONE NUMBER: (804) 788-5000
FAX: (804) 788-5688
WEB: www.ethyl.com

NO. OF EMPLOYEES: 1,500 (approx.)

SHAREHOLDERS: 11,654

ANNUAL MEETING: In May

INCORPORATED: VA, Feb., 1887

INSTITUTIONAL HOLDINGS:
No. of Institutions: 69
Shares Held: 16,348,755
% Held: 19.6

INDUSTRY: Industrial organic chemicals, nec (SIC: 2869)

TRANSFER AGENT(S): Computershare Investor Services, Chicago, IL

NYSE SYMBOL EXC
Rec. Pr. 67.82 (5/31/01)

EXELON CORPORATION

YIELD 2.5%
P/E RATIO 21.7

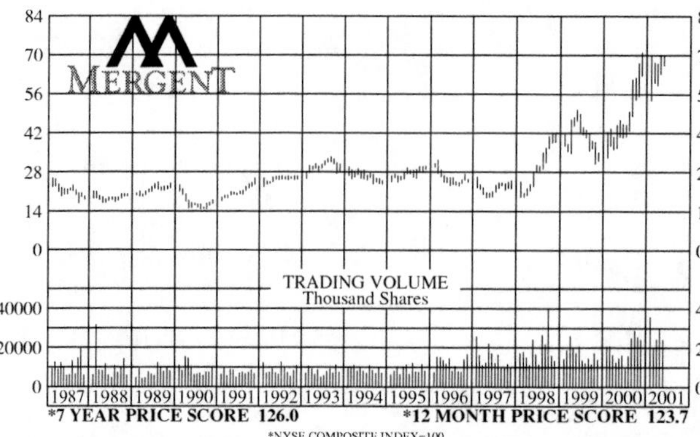

*7 YEAR PRICE SCORE 126.0 *12 MONTH PRICE SCORE 123.7
*NYSE COMPOSITE INDEX=100

INTERIM EARNINGS (Per Share):

Qtr.	Mar.	June	Sept.	Dec.
1998	0.50	0.66	1.20	d0.04
1999	0.65	0.44	1.22	0.79
2000	0.89	0.70	1.38	0.16

INTERIM DIVIDENDS (Per Share):

Amt.	Decl.	Ex.	Rec.	Pay.
0.25Q	7/25/00	8/28/00	8/30/00	9/29/00
0.158Q	10/20/00	10/23/00	10/19/00	12/20/00
0.553Q	1/30/01	2/13/01	2/15/01	3/10/01
0.422Q	4/24/01	5/11/01	5/15/01	6/10/01

Indicated div.: $1.69

CAPITALIZATION (12/31/00):

	($000)	(%)
Long-Term Debt	12,958,000	51.4
Deferred Income Tax	4,409,000	17.5
Redeemable Pfd. Stock	630,000	2.5
Common & Surplus	7,215,000	28.6
Total	25,212,000	100.0

RECENT DEVELOPMENTS: For the year ended 12/31/00, income was $566.0 million, before an extraordinary loss and an accounting credit, versus income of $607.0 million, before an extraordinary loss, in 1999. Results for 2000 included merger-related costs of $276.0 million. Total operating revenues rose 36.9% to $7.50 billion from $5.48 billion. Results for the current year included the operations of Unicom Corp. from 10/20/00, the date of acquisition. Comparisons were made with restated prior-year figures.

PROSPECTS: On 1/12/01, the Company completed the restructuring of its competitive generation and enterprises businesses. The new company structure separates EXC's regulated energy delivery business from its competitive generation and other businesses. In addition, the separation streamlines the Company's process for managing, operating and tracking the financial performances of its multiple lines of business. Separately, the Company implemented a five-year, $150.0 million strategic investment plan.

BUSINESS

EXELON CORPORATION (formerly PECO Energy Company) was formed from the acquisition by PECO Energy Company of Unicom Corporation on 10/20/00. Exelon is the holding company for ComEd, PECO Energy Company, Genco and other subsidiaries. The Company has an electric and natural gas distribution customer base of approximately five million in Illinois and Pennsylvania and is the largest nuclear operator in the U.S., with strong positions in the Midwest and Mid-Atlantic, and more than 16,500 megawatts of nuclear capacity. The Company also has holdings in the competitive businesses of energy, infrastructure services, energy services and telecommunications.

ANNUAL FINANCIAL DATA

	6 12/31/00	12/31/99	12/31/98	12/31/97	12/31/96	12/31/95	12/31/94
Earnings Per Share	5 2.77	4 3.08	3 2.32	2 1.44	2.24	2.64	1 1.76
Cash Flow Per Share	5.75	4.88	5.73	4.60	4.93	5.23	4.37
Tang. Book Val. Per Share	11.90	9.12	13.61	12.25	20.88	20.40	19.41
Dividends Per Share	0.91	1.00	1.00	1.80	1.75	1.65	1.54
Dividend Payout %	32.8	32.5	43.1	125.0	78.3	62.5	87.8
INCOME STATEMENT (IN MILLIONS):							
Total Revenues	7,499.0	5,436.8	5,210.5	4,617.9	4,283.7	4,186.2	4,040.6
Costs & Expenses	5,365.0	3,669.6	3,162.5	2,908.9	2,112.6	1,903.4	2,069.8
Depreciation & Amort.	607.0	358.0	764.6	703.4	597.8	574.2	579.6
Maintenance Exp.	...	...	...	...	324.7	307.8	327.7
Operating Income	1,527.0	1,409.2	1,283.3	1,005.6	905.4	1,003.9	829.6
Net Interest Inc./(Exp.)	d608.0	d395.7	d330.8	d372.9	d399.4	d432.0	d420.8
Income Taxes	341.0	358.0	319.7	292.8	340.1	431.7	249.3
Equity Earnings/Minority Int.	d41.0	d37.9	...	...	...	...	...
Net Income	5 566.0	4 619.0	3 532.4	2 336.6	517.2	609.7	1 426.7
Cash Flow	1,173.0	964.8	1,283.9	1,023.1	1,097.0	1,160.7	969.0
Average Shs. Outstg. (000)	204,000	197,616	223,904	222,543	222,490	221,859	221,554
BALANCE SHEET (IN MILLIONS):							
Gross Property	16,269.0	7,706.3	7,359.1	7,038.3	15,606.8	15,190.2	14,887.1
Accumulated Depreciation	6,950.0	4,367.1	2,891.3	2,690.8	5,047.0	4,623.7	4,242.6
Net Property	12,936.0	5,045.0	4,764.0	4,670.7	10,941.5	10,938.0	11,003.3
Total Assets	34,597.0	13,119.5	12,048.4	12,356.6	15,260.6	14,960.6	15,092.8
Long-Term Obligations	12,958.0	5,969.1	3,004.9	3,973.3	4,068.3	4,318.4	4,899.7
Net Stockholders' Equity	7,215.0	1,910.5	3,194.8	2,864.2	4,845.3	4,730.7	4,580.0
Year-end Shs. Outstg. (000)	170,479	181,272	224,684	222,547	222,542	222,172	221,609
STATISTICAL RECORD:							
Operating Profit Margin %	20.4	25.9	24.6	21.8	21.1	24.0	20.5
Net Profit Margin %	7.5	11.4	10.2	7.3	12.1	14.6	10.6
Net Inc./Net Property %	4.4	12.3	11.2	7.2	4.7	5.6	3.9
Net Inc./Tot. Capital %	2.2	5.9	5.9	3.5	4.0	4.8	3.3
Return on Equity %	7.8	32.4	16.7	11.8	10.7	12.9	9.3
Price Range	71.00-33.00	50.50-30.75	42.19-18.88	26.38-18.75	32.50-23.00	30.25-24.25	30.00-23.63
P/E Ratio	25.6-11.9	16.4-10.0	18.2-8.1	18.3-13.0	14.5-10.3	11.5-9.2	17.0-13.4
Average Yield %	1.7	2.5	3.3	8.0	6.3	6.1	5.8

Statistics are as originally reported. 1 Incl. $253.9 mill. pre-tax chg. for workforce reduct. 2 Incl. $214.0 mill. pre-tax non-recur. chg. & bef. $1.83 bill. extraord. chg. 3 Incl. $74.0 mill. spl. chg. rel. to sever. costs & excl. $19.0 mill. extraord. item. 4 Excl. $25.4 mill. net extraord. chg. for the early retire. of debt. 5 Incl. $276.0 mill. merger chg. and excl. $4.0 mill. net extraord. chg. & $24.0 mill. net cumul. acctg. credit 6 Results reflect the combined operations of PECO Energy Company & Unicom Corp. from 10/20/00.

OFFICERS:
C. A. McNeill Jr., Chmn., Co.-C.E.O.
J. W. Rowe, Co.-C.E.O., Pres.

INVESTOR CONTACT: Neil McDermott, (312) 394-4321

PRINCIPAL OFFICE: 37th Fl., 10 S. Dearborn St., P.O. Box A-3005, Chicago, IL 60690

TELEPHONE NUMBER: (312) 394-4321
WEB: www.exeloncorp.com

NO. OF EMPLOYEES: 29,000 (approx.)

SHAREHOLDERS: 202,312

ANNUAL MEETING: In Apr.

INCORPORATED: PA, Oct., 1929

INSTITUTIONAL HOLDINGS:
No. of Institutions: 411
Shares Held: 185,173,027
% Held: 57.8

INDUSTRY: Electric and other services combined (SIC: 4931)

TRANSFER AGENT(S): First Chicago Trust Company of New York, Jersey City, NJ

NYSE SYMBOL EX
Rec. Pr. 9.60 (4/30/01)

EXIDE CORP.

YIELD 0.8%
P/E RATIO ...

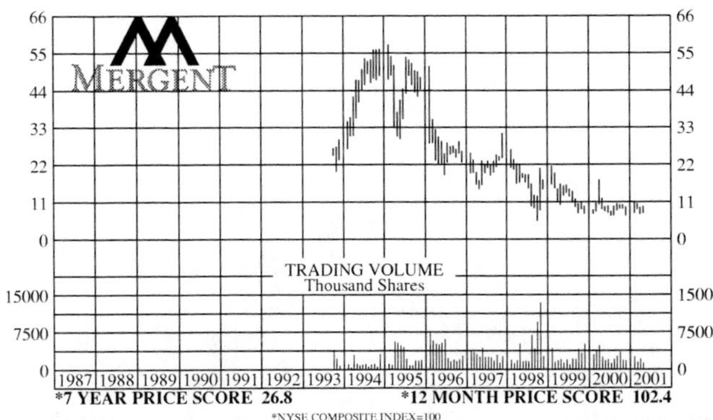

INTERIM EARNINGS (Per Share):

Qtr.	June	Sept.	Dec.	Mar.
1998-99	d0.29	0.11	d2.16	d3.76
1999-00	d0.44	0.20	d0.17	d5.99
2000-01	d0.44	d0.68	0.15	...

INTERIM DIVIDENDS (Per Share):

Amt.	Decl.	Ex.	Rec.	Pay.
0.02Q	5/17/00	5/24/00	5/27/00	6/07/00
0.02Q	8/29/00	8/31/00	9/05/00	9/15/00
0.02Q	11/08/00	11/16/00	11/20/00	11/30/00
0.02Q	2/08/01	2/16/01	2/21/01	3/02/01
0.02Q	5/15/01	5/23/01	5/25/01	6/05/01

Indicated div.: $0.08

CAPITALIZATION (3/31/00):

	($000)	(%)
Long-Term Debt	1,061,672	104.8
Minority Interest	17,993	1.8
Common & Surplus	d66,376	-6.6
Total	1,013,289	100.0

RECENT DEVELOPMENTS: For the quarter ended 12/31/00, net income totaled $4.0 million compared with a net loss of $3.6 million in the previous year. Results for 2000 included restructuring and other charges of $9.2 million. Net sales improved 23.6% to $764.4 million versus $618.5 million in the prior year. Gross profit as a percentages of net sales was 23.8% compared with 27.9% in the preceding 1999 period. Operating income declined 2.9% to $35.6 million versus $36.7 million the year before.

PROSPECTS: The Company will continue to focus on implementing its restructuring program in 2001. Accordingly, EX recently announced the closing of two additional automotive battery manufacturing plants. Also, the Company announced further restructuring actions in its European operations, including workforce reductions at two manufacturing facilities and a reorganization of its transportation business sales force. EX's restructuring plan is expected to reduce annualized costs by approximately $90.0 million.

BUSINESS

EXIDE CORP. is the largest producer of lead acid batteries in the world, with fiscal 2000 net sales of approximately $2.20 billion. The Company operates its battery business within the industrial and transportation segments. Industrial applications include network power batteries for telecommunications systems, electric utilities, railroads, photovoltaic and critical uninterruptible power supply (UPS) markets; and motive power batteries for a broad range of equipment uses including lift trucks, mining and other commercial electric vehicles. Transportation uses include automotive, heavy duty, agricultural, marine and other batteries and new technologies being developed for hybrid vehicles and new 42-volt automobile applications. On 9/29/00, EX acquired the global battery business of Australian-based Pacific Dunlop Limited, including its subsidiary GNB Technologies, Inc.

QUARTERLY DATA

(3/31/2000)($000)	Rev	Inc
1st Quarter	518,715	(9,302)
2nd Quarter	556,434	4,226
3rd Quarter	618,528	(3,643)
4th Quarter	500,770	(127,323)

ANNUAL FINANCIAL DATA

	3/31/00	3/31/99	3/31/98	3/31/97	3/31/96	3/31/95	3/31/94
Earnings Per Share	[1] **d6.40**	[2] **d6.11**	[2] **0.87**	[2] **0.90**	[2] **0.05**	[2] **0.28**	[3] **1.56**
Cash Flow Per Share	**d1.73**	**d0.08**	**5.91**	**6.33**	**5.28**	**3.27**	**4.33**
Tang. Book Val. Per Share	...	...	...	...	...	**11.41**	**6.31**
Dividends Per Share	**0.08**	**0.08**	**0.08**	**0.08**	**0.08**	**0.08**	...
Dividend Payout %	...	...	**9.2**	**8.9**	**159.7**	**28.6**	...
INCOME STATEMENT (IN MILLIONS):							
Total Revenues	2,194.4	2,374.3	2,273.1	2,333.2	2,342.6	1,198.5	679.6
Costs & Expenses	2,098.6	2,214.5	2,025.5	2,076.4	2,106.7	1,085.9	587.3
Depreciation & Amort.	99.3	127.9	109.2	115.3	106.7	48.5	30.6
Operating Income	d3.5	31.9	138.5	141.5	129.2	64.2	61.8
Net Interest Inc./(Exp.)	d104.0	d111.7	d112.3	d118.8	d120.6	d52.6	d33.1
Income Before Income Taxes	d123.5	d108.6	32.1	35.0	6.7	10.7	28.0
Income Taxes	10.8	23.0	13.5	14.7	6.3	5.2	10.8
Equity Earnings/Minority Int.	d1.7	2.0	0.1	d1.3	0.5	d1.1	...
Net Income	[1] d136.0	[2] d129.6	[2] 18.7	[2] 19.0	[2] 0.9	[2] 4.5	[3] 17.2
Cash Flow	d36.7	d1.7	127.9	134.3	107.7	53.0	47.8
Average Shs. Outstg. (000)	21,263	21,245	21,642	21,204	20,385	16,191	11,058
BALANCE SHEET (IN MILLIONS):							
Cash & Cash Equivalents	28.1	20.6	35.6	42.7	47.3	63.4	33.7
Total Current Assets	849.5	965.6	1,089.8	1,191.5	1,292.0	911.4	342.4
Net Property	443.3	498.7	535.1	521.8	578.7	423.9	181.1
Total Assets	1,901.5	2,167.8	2,348.6	2,438.5	2,717.0	1,637.6	629.1
Total Current Liabilities	636.0	526.8	550.9	561.0	687.6	515.5	188.7
Long-Term Obligations	1,061.7	1,154.5	1,195.9	1,236.1	1,301.2	518.4	246.5
Net Stockholders' Equity	d66.4	151.2	294.9	371.4	439.4	413.2	164.5
Net Working Capital	213.5	438.8	538.9	630.4	604.4	395.9	153.7
Year-end Shs. Outstg. (000)	21,359	21,359	21,328	20,894	20,894	19,992	14,800
STATISTICAL RECORD:							
Operating Profit Margin %	...	1.3	6.1	6.1	5.5	5.4	9.1
Net Profit Margin %	...	...	0.8	0.8	...	0.4	2.5
Return on Equity %	...	...	6.3	5.1	0.2	1.1	10.5
Return on Assets %	...	...	0.8	0.8	...	0.3	2.7
Debt/Total Assets %	55.8	53.3	50.9	50.7	47.9	31.7	39.2
Price Range	21.50-7.44	26.56-5.38	31.25-14.63	51.13-18.88	57.50-29.50	56.25-26.50	29.38-20.00
P/E Ratio	...	...	35.9-16.8	56.8-21.0	1,147.7-588.8	200.8-94.6	18.8-12.8
Average Yield %	0.6	0.5	0.3	0.2	0.2	0.2	...

Statistics are as originally reported. [1] Incl. restruct. chrg., $39.3 mill. & $14.3 mill. in purchased R&D. [2] Bef. extraord. chrg., 1999, $301,000; 1998, $28.5 mill.; 1997, $2.8 mill.; 1996, $9.6 mill.; 1995, $3.6 mill. [3] Bef. acctg. change chrg., $12.7 mill.

OFFICERS:
R. A. Lutz, Chmn., C.E.O.
C. H. Muhlhauser, Pres., C.O.O.
K. R. Morano, Exec. V.P., C.F.O.
J. R. Van Zile, V.P., Couns., Sec.

PRINCIPAL OFFICE: 645 Penn Street, Reading, PA 19601

TELEPHONE NUMBER: (610) 378-0500
WEB: www.exideworld.com

NO. OF EMPLOYEES: 16,100 (avg.)

SHAREHOLDERS: 600

ANNUAL MEETING: In Aug.

INCORPORATED: DE, 1966

INSTITUTIONAL HOLDINGS:
No. of Institutions: 57
Shares Held: 19,128,327
% Held: 75.2

INDUSTRY: Storage batteries (SIC: 3691)

TRANSFER AGENT(S): American Stock Transfer & Trust Co., New York, NY

NYSE SYMBOL XOM
Rec. Pr. 88.60 (4/30/01)

EXXON MOBIL CORPORATION

YIELD 2.0%
P/E RATIO 19.3

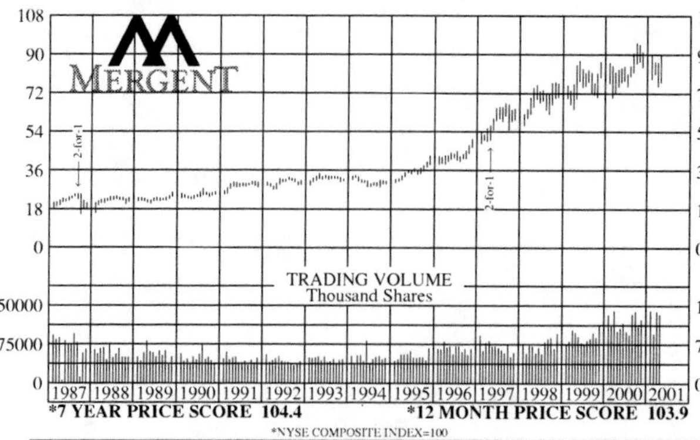

INTERIM EARNINGS (Per Share):

Qtr.	Mar.	June	Sept.	Dec.
1997	0.87	0.79	0.74	1.00
1998	0.76	0.65	0.58	0.62
1999	0.42	0.49	0.61	0.65
2000	0.87	1.15	1.17	1.41

INTERIM DIVIDENDS (Per Share):

Amt.	Decl.	Ex.	Rec.	Pay.
0.44Q	4/26/00	5/11/00	5/15/00	6/10/00
0.44Q	7/26/00	8/10/00	8/14/00	9/11/00
0.44Q	10/25/00	11/09/00	11/13/00	12/11/00
0.44Q	1/31/01	2/07/01	2/09/01	3/09/01
0.44Q	4/25/01	5/10/01	5/14/01	6/11/01

Indicated div.: $1.76 (Div. Reinv. Plan)

CAPITALIZATION (12/31/00):

	($000)	(%)
Long-Term Debt	7,280,000	7.5
Deferred Income Tax	16,442,000	16.8
Minority Interest	3,230,000	3.3
Common & Surplus	70,757,000	72.4
Total	97,709,000	100.0

RECENT DEVELOPMENTS: For the twelve months ended 12/31/00, income surged to $15.99 billion, before an extraordinary gain, versus $7.91 billion in 1999. Results for 2000 excluded a gain of $1.73 billion from asset divestitures that were required as a condition of regulatory approval of the Exxon-Mobil merger and included merger expenses of $1.41 billion. Results for 1999 included merger expenses of $625.0 million. Total revenues soared 25.4% to $232.75 billion from $185.53 billion the year before.

PROSPECTS: XOM's results are being driven by high crude oil and natural gas prices, higher refining margins and improvements in operating efficiencies, including those from the Exxon-Mobil merger synergies. Separately, the Company noted that based on the current capital spending plans and foreign exchange rates, capital spending for 2001 is projected to increase in the range of 15.0% to 20.0% over full-year 2000 spending of $11.14 billion.

BUSINESS

EXXON MOBIL CORPORATION'S principal business is energy, involving exploration for, and production of, crude oil and natural gas, manufacturing of petroleum products and transportation and sale of crude oil, natural gas and petroleum products. Exxon Mobil is a major manufacturer and marketer of basic petrochemicals, including olefins, aromatics, polyethylene and polypropylene plastics and a wide variety of specialty products. Exxon Mobil is engaged in exploration for, and mining and sale of coal, copper and other minerals. Exxon Mobil also has interests in electric power generation facilities. As of 12/31/00, XOM owned 69.6% of Imperial Oil Limited. In 2000, worldwide proved reserves were: crude oil and natural gas liquids, 11,561 million barrels; and natural gas, 55,866 billion cubic feet. On 11/30/99, Exxon Corp. acquired Mobil Corporation in a transaction valued at $81.00 billion.

ANNUAL FINANCIAL DATA

	[5] 12/31/00	12/31/99	12/31/98	12/31/97	12/31/96	12/31/95	12/31/94
Earnings Per Share	[4] 4.55	[3] 2.25	[1] 2.61	[2] 3.37	[2] 3.01	2.59	2.04
Cash Flow Per Share	6.86	4.70	4.85	5.56	5.17	4.77	4.07
Tang. Book Val. Per Share	20.42	18.24	17.98	17.69	17.41	16.10	14.84
Dividends Per Share	1.76	1.67	1.64	1.63	1.56	1.50	1.46
Dividend Payout %	38.7	74.2	62.8	48.2	51.8	57.9	71.5
INCOME STATEMENT (IN MILLIONS):							
Total Revenues	232,748.0	185,527.0	117,772.0	137,242.0	134,249.0	123,920.0	113,904.0
Costs & Expenses	196,536.0	165,233.0	103,091.0	118,149.0	116,156.0	107,306.0	100,127.0
Depreciation & Amort.	8,130.0	8,304.0	5,340.0	5,474.0	5,329.0	5,386.0	5,015.0
Operating Income	28,082.0	11,990.0	9,341.0	13,619.0	12,764.0	11,228.0	8,762.0
Net Interest Inc./(Exp.)	d589.0	d695.0	d100.0	d415.0	d464.0	d485.0	d725.0
Income Before Income Taxes	27,081.0	11,150.0	9,056.0	12,798.0	11,916.0	10,442.0	7,804.0
Income Taxes	11,091.0	3,240.0	2,616.0	4,338.0	4,406.0	3,972.0	2,704.0
Equity Earnings/Minority Int.	d412.0	d145.0	d185.0	d406.0	d384.0	d301.0	d233.0
Net Income	[4] 15,990.0	[3] 7,910.0	[1] 6,440.0	[2] 8,460.0	[2] 7,510.0	6,470.0	5,100.0
Cash Flow	24,120.0	16,214.0	11,780.0	13,934.0	12,839.0	11,856.0	10,115.0
Average Shs. Outstg. (000)	3,517,000	3,453,000	2,428,000	2,505,000	2,484,000	2,484,000	2,484,000
BALANCE SHEET (IN MILLIONS):							
Cash & Cash Equivalents	7,081.0	1,761.0	1,461.0	4,062.0	2,969.0	1,789.0	1,775.0
Total Current Assets	40,399.0	31,141.0	17,593.0	21,192.0	19,910.0	17,318.0	16,460.0
Net Property	89,829.0	94,043.0	65,199.0	66,414.0	66,607.0	65,446.0	63,425.0
Total Assets	149,000.0	144,521.0	92,630.0	96,064.0	95,527.0	91,296.0	87,862.0
Total Current Liabilities	38,191.0	38,733.0	19,412.0	19,654.0	19,505.0	18,736.0	19,493.0
Long-Term Obligations	7,280.0	8,402.0	4,530.0	7,050.0	7,236.0	7,778.0	8,831.0
Net Stockholders' Equity	70,757.0	63,466.0	43,750.0	43,660.0	43,542.0	40,436.0	37,415.0
Net Working Capital	2,208.0	d7,592.0	d1,819.0	1,538.0	405.0	d1,418.0	d3,033.0
Year-end Shs. Outstg. (000)	3,465,000	3,479,892	2,428,000	2,457,000	2,484,000	2,484,000	2,484,000
STATISTICAL RECORD:							
Operating Profit Margin %	12.1	6.5	7.9	9.9	9.5	9.1	7.7
Net Profit Margin %	6.9	4.3	5.5	6.2	5.6	5.2	4.5
Return on Equity %	22.6	12.5	14.7	19.4	17.2	16.0	13.6
Return on Assets %	10.7	5.5	7.0	8.8	7.9	7.1	5.8
Debt/Total Assets %	4.9	5.8	4.9	7.3	7.6	8.5	10.1
Price Range	95.44-69.88	87.25-64.31	77.31-56.63	67.25-48.25	50.63-38.81	43.00-30.06	33.69-28.06
P/E Ratio	21.0-15.4	38.8-28.6	29.6-21.7	20.0-14.3	16.8-12.9	16.6-11.6	16.6-13.8
Average Yield %	2.1	2.2	2.4	2.8	3.5	4.1	4.7

Statistics are as originally reported. Adj. for stk. splits: 2-for-1, 4/97 [1] Bef. acctg. chrg. of $70.0 mill. [2] Incls. non-recurr. credit 12/31/97; $305.0 mill.; credit 12/31/96: $90.0 mill. [3] Incls. non-recurr. chrg. of $625.0 mill. [4] Incls. merger rel. exp. of $1.41 bill.; bef. extraord. gain fr. required asset divest. of $1.73 bill. ($0.50/sh.) [5] Incls. results of Mobil Corporation.

OFFICERS:
L. R. Raymond, Chmn.
R. Dahan, Sr. V.P.
H. J. Longwell, Sr. V.P.

INVESTOR CONTACT: T. P. Townsend, V.P., Inv. Rel., (972) 444-1900

PRINCIPAL OFFICE: 5959 Las Colinas Blvd., Irving, TX 75039-2298

TELEPHONE NUMBER: (972) 444-1000
FAX: (972) 444-1348
WEB: www.exxon.mobil.com

NO. OF EMPLOYEES: 79,000

SHAREHOLDERS: 715,020

ANNUAL MEETING: In May

INCORPORATED: NJ, Aug., 1882

INSTITUTIONAL HOLDINGS:
No. of Institutions: 1,196
Shares Held: 1,712,882,229
% Held: 49.6

INDUSTRY: Petroleum refining (SIC: 2911)

TRANSFER AGENT(S): ExxonMobil Shareholder Services c/o EquiServe Trust Company, NA, Boston, MA

NYSE SYMBOL FCS
Rec. Pr. 18.10 (4/30/01)

FAIRCHILD SEMICONDUCTOR INTERNATIONAL, INC.

YIELD ...
P/E RATIO 6.7

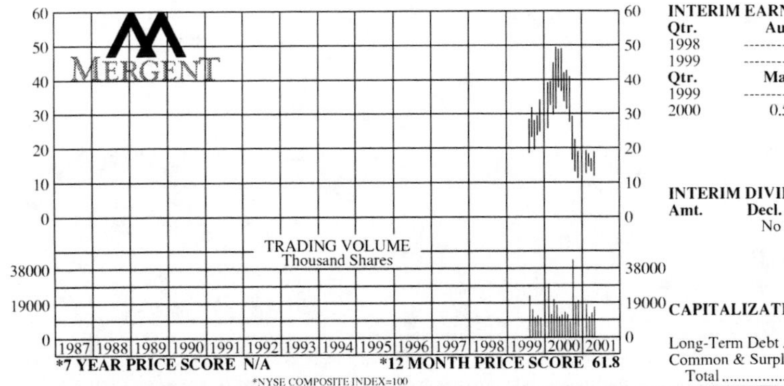

*7 YEAR PRICE SCORE N/A *12 MONTH PRICE SCORE 61.8

*NYSE COMPOSITE INDEX=100

INTERIM EARNINGS (Per Share):

Qtr.	Aug.	Nov.	Feb.	May
1998		0.20		
1999		d1.97		

Qtr.	Mar.	June	Sept.	Dec.
1999		0.23		
2000	0.51	0.59	0.68	0.92

INTERIM DIVIDENDS (Per Share):

Amt.	Decl.	Ex.	Rec.	Pay.

No dividends paid.

CAPITALIZATION (12/31/00):

	($000)	(%)
Long-Term Debt	705,200	45.7
Common & Surplus	837,700	54.3
Total	1,542,900	100.0

RECENT DEVELOPMENTS: For the year ended 12/31/00, the Company reported net income of $273.1 million compared with a net loss of $52.6 million in 1999. Results for 2000 and 1999 included restructuring and nonrecurring charges of $3.4 million and $78.1 million, respectively. Net sales amounted to $1.78 billion, an increase of 71.2% versus $1.04 billion in the previous year. Operating income more than tripled to $327.9 million compared with $113.6 million a year earlier.

PROSPECTS: FCS purchased an equity stake in Silicon Wireless Corporation, a manufacturer of silicon-based radio frequency semiconductors and power amplifier technology, enabling FCS to expand into the power transistor market. Separately, FCS competed the acquisition of the discrete power business of Intersil Corporation for about $338.0 million cash. The acquisition makes FCS the second largest supplier of metal-oxide semiconductor field-effect transistors with an overall market share of 20.0%.

BUSINESS

FAIRCHILD SEMICONDUCTOR CORPORATION is a global supplier of high-performance semiconductors used in the communications, computing, consumer, industrial, and automotive end markets. The analog, mixed signal and non-volatile memory product group consists of high-performance analog and mixed signal integrated circuits. The discrete power and signal technologies product group includes individual diodes or transistors that perform basic signal amplification and switching functions in electronic circuits. The interface and logic products group consists of high-performance interface and logic devices utilizing three water fabrication processes. The optoelectronics group supplies optocouplers, infrared components, custom optoelectronic components and light emitting diode lamps and displays.

REVENUES

(12/31/00)	($000)	%
Net sales - trade	1,681,600	94.3
Contract Manufacturing	101,600	5.7
Total	1,783,200	100.0

ANNUAL FINANCIAL DATA

	12/31/00	[2] 12/26/99	5/30/99	5/31/98	5/25/97
Earnings Per Share	[3] 2.69	0.23	[3] d1.97	[1][3] 0.20	...
Cash Flow Per Share	4.18	1.24	d0.17	1.64	...
Tang. Book Val. Per Share	5.80	...	...	...	...
INCOME STATEMENT (IN MILLIONS):					
Total Revenues	1,783.2	786.2	735.1	789.2	692.0
Costs & Expenses	1,304.2	621.4	678.8	617.1	660.1
Depreciation & Amort.	151.1	82.3	103.7	84.8	...
Operating Income	327.9	82.5	d47.4	87.3	31.9
Net Interest Inc./(Exp.)	d57.2	d56.2	d71.8	d54.5	d12.6
Income Before Income Taxes	270.7	26.3	d119.2	32.8	19.3
Income Taxes	cr2.4	5.0	cr5.1	10.7	3.8
Net Income	[3] 273.1	21.3	[3] d114.1	[1][3] 22.1	15.5
Cash Flow	424.2	103.6	d10.4	106.9	15.5
Average Shs. Outstg. (000)	101,400	83,700	62,900	65,000	...
BALANCE SHEET (IN MILLIONS):					
Cash & Cash Equivalents	401.8	138.7	62.4	6.5	...
Total Current Assets	876.4	459.0	406.4	209.5	108.0
Net Property	596.6	375.8	360.2	342.9	...
Total Assets	1,837.5	1,137.6	1,095.7	634.3	108.0
Total Current Liabilities	292.2	206.7	198.7	143.1	...
Long-Term Obligations	705.2	717.2	1,045.9	526.7	487.9
Net Stockholders' Equity	837.7	213.2	d240.4	d116.6	d133.3
Net Working Capital	584.2	252.3	207.7	66.4	108.0
Year-end Shs. Outstg. (000)	93,100	88,600	62,967	62,874	...
STATISTICAL RECORD:					
Operating Profit Margin %	18.4	10.5	...	11.1	4.6
Net Profit Margin %	15.3	2.7	...	2.8	2.2
Return on Equity %	32.6	10.0	...	...	...
Return on Assets %	14.9	1.9	...	3.5	14.4
Debt/Total Assets %	38.4	63.0	95.5	83.0	451.8
Price Range	49.50-11.19	34.13-18.50	...	...	...
P/E Ratio	18.4-4.2	148.3-80.4	...	...	...

Statistics are as originally reported. [1] Bef. acctg. chrg. $1.5 mill. [2] Results for 7 months only to reflect change in fiscal year. [3] Incl. nonrecurr. chrg. $3.4 mill., 2000; $55.3 mill., 5/99; $15.5 mill., 5/98.

OFFICERS:
K. P. Pond, Chmn., Pres., C.E.O.
J. R. Martin, Exec. V.P., C.F.O.
D. E. Boxer, Exec. V.P., Gen. Couns., Sec.
M. W. Towse, V.P., Treas.

INVESTOR CONTACT: Pete Groth, Investor Relations, (207) 775-8782

PRINCIPAL OFFICE: 82 Running Hill Road, South Portland, ME 04106

TELEPHONE NUMBER: (207) 775-8100
FAX: (207) 761-6020
WEB: www.fairchildsemi.com

NO. OF EMPLOYEES: 11,033 (avg.)

SHAREHOLDERS: 330 (approx. record class A)

ANNUAL MEETING: In Apr.

INCORPORATED: ME, Mar., 1997

INSTITUTIONAL HOLDINGS:
No. of Institutions: 108
Shares Held: 42,079,263
% Held: 42.4

INDUSTRY: Semiconductors and related devices (SIC: 3674)

TRANSFER AGENT(S): BankBoston, N.A., Canton, MA

NYSE SYMBOL FDO
Rec. Pr. 27.80 (5/31/01)

FAMILY DOLLAR STORES, INC.

YIELD 0.9%
P/E RATIO 26.2

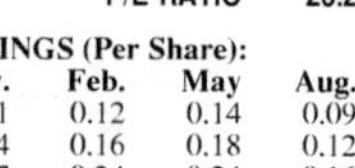

TRADING VOLUME Thousand Shares

*7 YEAR PRICE SCORE 121.0 *12 MONTH PRICE SCORE 129.5

*NYSE COMPOSITE INDEX=100

INTERIM EARNINGS (Per Share):

Qtr.	Nov.	Feb.	May	Aug.
1996-97	0.11	0.12	0.14	0.09
1997-98	0.14	0.16	0.18	0.12
1998-99	0.17	0.24	0.24	0.16
1999-00	0.21	0.32	0.29	0.18
2000-01	0.24	0.35	...	...

INTERIM DIVIDENDS (Per Share):

Amt.	Decl.	Ex.	Rec.	Pay.
0.055Q	5/15/00	6/13/00	6/15/00	7/14/00
0.055Q	8/25/00	9/13/00	9/15/00	10/16/00
0.055Q	11/06/00	12/13/00	12/15/00	1/15/01
0.06Q	1/18/01	3/13/01	3/15/01	4/16/01
0.06Q	5/15/01	6/13/01	6/15/01	7/16/01

Indicated div.: $0.24

CAPITALIZATION (8/26/00):

	($000)	(%)
Deferred Income Tax	33,733	4.1
Common & Surplus	797,964	95.9
Total	831,697	100.0

RECENT DEVELOPMENTS: For the quarter ended 3/3/01, net income rose 10.0% to $60.5 million from $55.0 million a year earlier. Net sales totaled $1.04 billion, up 20.8% versus $858.5 million the previous year. Results in the recent period benefited from an extra week, along with a 2.2% increase in existing-store sales and sales from new stores opened as part of FDO's store expansion program. Gross profit was $338.5 million, or 32.6% of net sales, versus $284.1 million, or 33.1% of net sales, in the prior year.

PROSPECTS: Strong sales and earnings growth is being fueled by continued favorable customer response to the Company's merchandising initiatives, including the introduction of more hardlines consumables in departments such as household chemicals, paper products and food. Going forward, revenue and earnings growth should continue to be driven by the Company's aggressive store expansion program. During the current fiscal year, FDO plans to open about 500 new stores and close 50 stores.

BUSINESS

FAMILY DOLLAR STORES, INC. operated 3,956 discount stores as of 4/12/01. The stores are located in a contiguous 39-state area ranging as far northwest as South Dakota, northeast to Maine, southeast to Florida and southwest to Arizona. The stores' relatively small size, generally 6,000 to 8,000 square feet, gives FDO flexibility to open them in various markets from small rural towns to large urban centers. The stores are located in strip shopping centers or as freestanding buildings convenient to FDO's low- and middle-income customer base. The merchandise, which is generally priced under $10.00, is sold in a no-frills, low overhead, self-service environment.

ANNUAL FINANCIAL DATA

	8/26/00	8/28/99	8/29/98	8/31/97	8/31/96	8/31/95	8/31/94
Earnings Per Share	**1.00**	**0.81**	**0.60**	**0.44**	**0.35**	**0.34**	**[1] 0.37**
Cash Flow Per Share	**1.31**	**1.07**	**0.80**	**0.61**	**0.50**	**0.47**	**0.48**
Tang. Book Val. Per Share	**4.66**	**4.00**	**3.36**	**2.75**	**2.61**	**2.40**	**2.06**
Dividends Per Share	**0.21**	**0.20**	**0.17**	**0.16**	**0.14**	**0.13**	**0.11**
Dividend Payout %	**21.5**	**24.1**	**29.2**	**36.0**	**40.9**	**37.4**	**30.0**
INCOME STATEMENT (IN MILLIONS):							
Total Revenues	3,132.6	2,751.2	2,361.9	1,995.0	1,714.6	1,546.9	1,428.4
Costs & Expenses	2,807.2	2,484.7	2,161.1	1,844.4	1,591.2	1,430.3	1,308.9
Depreciation & Amort.	54.5	43.8	34.8	29.1	24.6	22.2	19.5
Operating Income	270.9	222.7	166.0	121.5	98.8	94.4	100.1
Income Before Income Taxes	270.9	222.7	166.0	121.5	98.8	94.4	100.1
Income Taxes	98.9	82.6	62.7	46.8	38.2	36.3	38.2
Net Income	172.0	140.1	103.3	74.7	60.6	58.1	[1] 62.0
Cash Flow	226.5	183.9	138.1	103.8	85.2	80.3	81.4
Average Shs. Outstg. (000)	172,649	172,511	173,224	171,187	170,441	170,055	169,489
BALANCE SHEET (IN MILLIONS):							
Cash & Cash Equivalents	43.6	95.3	134.2	42.5	18.8	8.9	9.9
Total Current Assets	750.7	720.0	646.6	544.7	507.9	475.0	435.9
Net Property	487.6	371.1	291.8	231.2	184.6	156.6	151.9
Total Assets	1,243.7	1,095.3	942.2	780.3	696.8	636.2	592.8
Total Current Liabilities	412.0	378.5	343.3	261.2	234.2	210.4	205.6
Net Stockholders' Equity	798.0	690.7	578.2	500.2	445.0	407.8	370.2
Net Working Capital	338.7	341.4	303.4	283.5	273.7	264.7	230.2
Year-end Shs. Outstg. (000)	171,132	172,751	172,204	182,063	170,606	170,232	180,117
STATISTICAL RECORD:							
Operating Profit Margin %	8.6	8.1	7.0	6.1	5.8	6.1	7.0
Net Profit Margin %	5.5	5.1	4.4	3.7	3.5	3.8	4.3
Return on Equity %	21.6	20.3	17.9	14.9	13.6	14.3	16.7
Return on Assets %	13.8	12.8	11.0	9.6	8.7	9.1	10.5
Price Range	24.50-14.25	26.75-14.00	22.44-11.50	15.06-6.25	7.00-3.67	6.58-3.63	6.13-3.33
P/E Ratio	24.5-14.2	33.0-17.3	37.4-19.2	34.6-14.4	20.0-10.5	19.2-10.6	16.7-9.1
Average Yield %	1.1	1.0	1.0	1.5	2.7	2.5	2.3

Statistics are as originally reported. Adj. for 2-for-1 stk. split, 4/98 & 3-for-2 stk. split, 7/97. [1] Bef. $1.1 mil ($0.01/sh) cr. for acctg. adj.

OFFICERS:
L. Levine, Chmn.
R. J. Kelly, Vice-Chmn., C.F.O.
H. R. Levine, Pres., C.E.O.
R. D. Alexander, Exec. V.P., C.O.O.

INVESTOR CONTACT: George R. Mahoney, Jr., Exec. V.P., (704) 814-3252

PRINCIPAL OFFICE: 10401 Old Monroe Rd., Charlotte, NC 28101

TELEPHONE NUMBER: (704) 847-6961
FAX: (704) 847-5534
WEB: www.familydollar.com

NO. OF EMPLOYEES: 16,200 full-time (approx.); 15,000 part-time (approx.)

SHAREHOLDERS: 2,150 (approx.)

ANNUAL MEETING: In Jan.

INCORPORATED: DE, Nov., 1969

INSTITUTIONAL HOLDINGS:
No. of Institutions: 235
Shares Held: 139,380,561
% Held: 81.2

INDUSTRY: Variety stores (SIC: 5331)

TRANSFER AGENT(S): Mellon Investor Services, Ridgefield Park, NJ

NYSE SYMBOL FNM
Rec. Pr. 80.26 (4/30/01)

FANNIE MAE

YIELD 1.5%
P/E RATIO 18.8

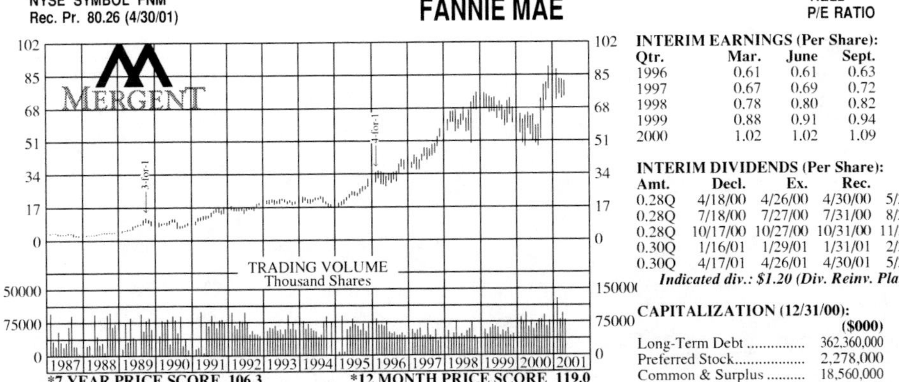

*7 YEAR PRICE SCORE 106.3 *12 MONTH PRICE SCORE 119.0

*NYSE COMPOSITE INDEX=100

INTERIM EARNINGS (Per Share):

Qtr.	Mar.	June	Sept.	Dec.
1996	0.61	0.61	0.63	0.65
1997	0.67	0.69	0.72	0.75
1998	0.78	0.80	0.82	0.85
1999	0.88	0.91	0.94	0.99
2000	1.02	1.02	1.09	1.13

INTERIM DIVIDENDS (Per Share):

Amt.	Decl.	Ex.	Rec.	Pay.
0.28Q	4/18/00	4/26/00	4/30/00	5/25/00
0.28Q	7/18/00	7/27/00	7/31/00	8/25/00
0.28Q	10/17/00	10/27/00	10/31/00	11/25/00
0.30Q	1/16/01	1/29/01	1/31/01	2/25/01
0.30Q	4/17/01	4/26/01	4/30/01	5/25/01

Indicated div.: $1.20 (Div. Reinv. Plan)

CAPITALIZATION (12/31/00):

	($000)	(%)
Long-Term Debt	362,360,000	94.6
Preferred Stock	2,278,000	0.6
Common & Surplus	18,560,000	4.8
Total	383,198,000	100.0

RECENT DEVELOPMENTS: For the year ended 12/31/00, income before an extraordinary gain totaled $4.42 billion compared with income before an extraordinary loss of $3.92 billion in the prior year. Results excluded an extraordinary gain of $31.5 million in 2000 and an extraordinary loss of $9.2 million in 1999. Net interest income rose 15.9% to $5.67 billion, while guaranty fess grew 5.4% to $1.35 billion.

PROSPECTS: Recently, FNM announced that it will begin the issuance of a regular series of large-sized subordinated debt securities known as Subordinated Benchmark Notes®. These notes are a key component of the Company's initiative to enhance its risk management, capital and disclosure practices. Going forward, the Company's expects continued strong earnings as a result of favorable credit indicators, strong momentum due to portfolio growth, and the current financial environment.

BUSINESS

FANNIE MAE (formerly Federal National Mortgage Association) is the largest investor in home mortgage loans in the U.S. The Company was established in 1938 as a U.S. government agency to provide supplemental liquidity to the mortgage market and was transformed into a stockholder-owned and privately-managed company by legislation enacted in 1968. FNM provides funds to the mortgage market by purchasing mortgage loans from lenders, thereby replenishing their funds for additional lending. FNM also issues mortgage-backed securities (MBS), primarily in exchange for pools of mortgage loans from lenders, which also increases the liquidity of residential mortgage loans. Fannie Mae receives guaranty fees for its guaranty of timely payment of principal of and interest on MBS certificates.

ANNUAL FINANCIAL DATA

	12/31/00	12/31/99	12/31/98	12/31/97	12/31/96	12/31/95	12/31/94
Earnings Per Share	**1 4.26**	**1 3.73**	**1 3.26**	**1 2.84**	**1 2.50**	**1 1.96**	**1 1.95**
Cash Flow Per Share	**13.54**	**10.45**	**8.88**	**7.59**	**6.51**	**6.56**	**4.65**
Tang. Book Val. Per Share	**18.58**	**16.02**	**13.95**	**12.34**	**11.10**	**10.04**	**8.75**
Dividends Per Share	**1.12**	**1.08**	**0.96**	**0.84**	**0.76**	**0.68**	**0.60**
Dividend Payout %	**26.3**	**29.0**	**29.4**	**29.6**	**30.4**	**34.7**	**30.8**
INCOME STATEMENT (IN MILLIONS):							
Total Revenues	44,088.0	36,968.0	31,499.0	27,777.0	25,054.0	22,250.0	18,573.0
Costs & Expenses	28,738.0	24,599.0	21,026.0	18,428.0	16,811.0	14,185.0	12,462.0
Depreciation & Amort.	9,368.0	6,929.0	5,828.0	5,012.0	4,338.0	5,070.0	2,965.0
Operating Income	5,982.0	5,440.0	4,645.0	4,337.0	3,905.0	2,995.0	3,146.0
Income Before Income Taxes	5,982.0	5,440.0	4,645.0	4,337.0	3,905.0	2,995.0	3,146.0
Income Taxes	1,566.0	1,519.0	1,201.0	1,269.0	1,151.0	840.0	1,005.0
Net Income	1 4,416.0	1 3,921.0	1 3,444.0	1 3,068.0	1 2,754.0	1 2,155.0	1 2,141.0
Cash Flow	13,663.0	10,772.0	9,206.0	8,015.0	7,050.0	7,225.0	5,106.0
Average Shs. Outstg. (000)	1,009,000	1,031,000	1,037,000	1,056,000	1,083,000	1,102,000	1,098,000
BALANCE SHEET (IN MILLIONS):							
Cash & Cash Equivalents	21,753.0	20,190.0	16,959.0	8,111.0	4,350.0	57,591.0	46,566.0
Total Current Assets	26,282.0	23,720.0	20,412.0	10,975.0	6,769.0	59,838.0	48,254.0
Total Assets	675,072.0	575,167.0	485,014.0	391,673.0	351,041.0	316,550.0	272,508.0
Total Current Liabilities	288,558.0	233,366.0	210,675.0	180,011.0	164,136.0	149,970.0	115,740.0
Long-Term Obligations	362,360.0	321,037.0	254,878.0	194,374.0	171,370.0	153,021.0	144,628.0
Net Stockholders' Equity	20,838.0	17,629.0	15,453.0	13,793.0	12,773.0	10,959.0	9,541.0
Net Working Capital	d262,276.0	d209,646.0	d190,263.0	d169,036.0	d157,367.0	d90,132.0	d67,486.0
Year-end Shs. Outstg. (000)	999,000	1,019,000	1,025,000	1,037,000	1,061,000	1,092,000	1,091,000
STATISTICAL RECORD:							
Operating Profit Margin %	13.6	14.7	14.7	15.6	15.6	13.5	16.9
Net Profit Margin %	10.0	10.6	10.9	11.0	11.0	9.7	11.5
Return on Equity %	21.2	22.2	22.3	22.2	21.6	19.7	22.4
Return on Assets %	0.7	0.7	0.7	0.8	0.8	0.7	0.8
Debt/Total Assets %	53.7	55.8	52.6	49.6	48.8	48.3	53.1
Price Range	89.38-47.88	75.88-58.56	76.19-49.56	57.31-36.13	41.63-27.50	31.50-17.19	22.59-17.03
P/E Ratio	21.0-11.2	20.3-15.7	23.4-15.2	20.2-12.7	16.6-11.0	16.1-8.8	11.6-8.7
Average Yield %	1.6	1.6	1.5	1.8	2.2	2.8	3.0

Statistics are as originally reported. Adj. for stk. splits: 4-for-1, 1/96. 1 Bef. extraord. gain $31.5 mill., 12/00; chrg., $9.2 mill.,12/99; $10.7 mill., 12/98; $12.8 mill., 12/97; $29.0 mill., 12/96; $11.4 mill., 12/95; $9.0 mill., 12/94; $169.3 mill.

OFFICERS:
F. D. Raines, Chmn., C.E.O.
D. H. Mudd, Vice-Chmn., C.O.O.
J. T. Howard, Exec. V.P., C.F.O.
L. K. Knight, Sr. V.P., Treas.

INVESTOR CONTACT: Investor Relations, (202) 752-7115

PRINCIPAL OFFICE: 3900 Wisconsin Ave., NW, Washington, DC 20016-2892

TELEPHONE NUMBER: (202) 752-7000
FAX: (202) 752-4934
WEB: www.fanniemae.com

NO. OF EMPLOYEES: 4,500 (approx.)

SHAREHOLDERS: 26,000 (approx.)

ANNUAL MEETING: In May

INCORPORATED: 1938

INSTITUTIONAL HOLDINGS:
No. of Institutions: 1,006
Shares Held: 820,803,973
% Held: 82.2

INDUSTRY: Federal & fed.-sponsored credit (SIC: 6111)

TRANSFER AGENT(S): First Chicago Trust Company of New York, Jersey City, NJ

NYSE SYMBOL FJC
Rec. Pr. 4.97 (5/31/01)

FEDDERS CORP.

YIELD 2.4%
P/E RATIO 14.2

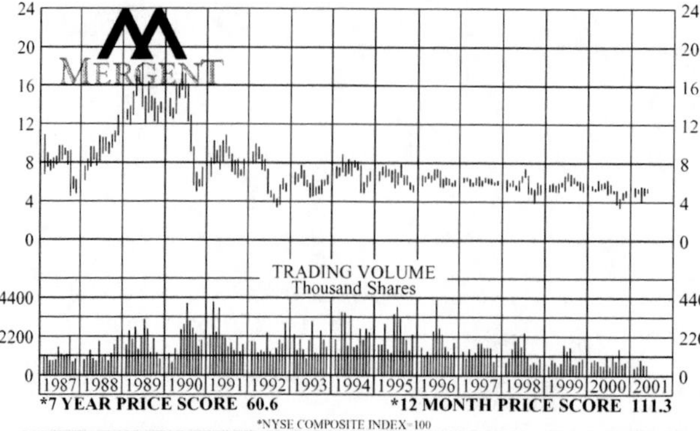

*7 YEAR PRICE SCORE 60.6 *12 MONTH PRICE SCORE 111.3
*NYSE COMPOSITE INDEX=100

INTERIM EARNINGS (Per Share):

Qtr.	Nov.	Feb.	May	Aug.
1996-97	d0.05	0.04	0.30	0.12
1997-98	d0.09	d0.32	0.37	0.11
1998-99	d0.08	0.02	0.48	0.13
1999-00	d0.06	0.04	0.47	0.12
2000-01	d0.23	d0.01	...	...

INTERIM DIVIDENDS (Per Share):

Amt.	Decl.	Ex.	Rec.	Pay.
0.03Q	2/22/00	5/10/00	5/12/00	6/01/00
0.03Q	6/27/00	8/16/00	8/18/00	9/01/00
0.03Q	10/24/00	11/08/00	11/10/00	12/01/00
0.03Q	12/19/00	2/08/01	2/12/01	3/01/01
0.03Q	4/24/01	5/09/01	5/11/01	6/01/01

Indicated div.: $0.12

CAPITALIZATION (8/31/00):

	($000)	(%)
Long-Term Debt	163,912	58.9
Minority Interest	1,979	0.7
Common & Surplus	112,260	40.4
Total	278,151	100.0

RECENT DEVELOPMENTS: For the three months ended 2/28/01, net loss totaled $220,000 compared with net income of $1.3 million a year earlier. Net sales climbed 18.4% to $83.3 million from $70.4 million the year before. Gross profit as a percentage of net sales fell to 24.5% from 31.5% in the previous year. Operating income was $5.1 million, or 6.1% of net sales, compared with $7.8 million, or 11.0% of net sales, in the prior year.

PROSPECTS: Revenue and earnings growth should benefit from FJC's focus on expanding its operations into both new and existing air treatment markets with high growth potential. In late 2000, the Company's telecommunications cooling subsidiary, Melcor Corporation, acquired Longview, Texas-based Eubank Manufacturing Enterprises, Inc., a manufacturer of cooling systems used to control the environment in cellular tower transmission equipment rooms.

BUSINESS

FEDDERS CORP. is a manufacturer of room air conditioners and dehumidifiers for residential and commercial markets. Air conditioners are manufactured in models ranging in capacity from 5,000 BTUs to 32,000 BTUs. FJC markets its products under the FEDDERS, MAYTAG, AIRTEMP, and EMERSON QUIET KOOL brand names. They are sold through distributors and retail buying groups and retail chains. These retailers represent approximately 10,000 outlets in the U.S. and 1,200 in Canada. The Company has consolidated its marketing, service, and accounting management into a Whitehouse, New Jersey headquarters location and four regional sales offices to improve its customer service and delivery capabilities.

ANNUAL FINANCIAL DATA

	8/31/00	8/31/99	8/31/98	8/31/97	8/31/96	8/31/95	8/31/94
Earnings Per Share	**0.57**	**[2] 0.56**	**[2] 0.07**	**0.40**	**0.74**	**0.72**	**[1] 0.61**
Cash Flow Per Share	**0.94**	**0.84**	**0.29**	**0.64**	**0.89**	**0.90**	**0.91**
Tang. Book Val. Per Share	**0.93**	**0.97**	**1.29**	**2.22**	**2.30**	**1.92**	**1.55**
Dividends Per Share	**0.12**	**0.11**	**0.09**	**0.08**	**0.08**	**0.04**	...
Dividend Payout %	**21.0**	**19.6**	**128.4**	**20.0**	**10.8**	**5.6**	...
INCOME STATEMENT (IN THOUSANDS):							
Total Revenues	409,809	355,956	322,121	314,100	371,772	316,494	231,572
Costs & Expenses	349,879	305,419	300,048	272,436	314,206	271,322	198,293
Depreciation & Amort.	13,076	10,279	9,263	9,935	6,578	7,519	9,374
Operating Income	46,854	40,258	12,810	31,729	50,988	37,653	23,905
Net Interest Inc./(Exp.)	d15,584	d9,684	d8,610	d3,430	d952	d1,962	d4,102
Income Before Income Taxes	31,270	30,574	4,200	28,299	50,036	35,691	19,803
Income Taxes	10,073	10,262	1,611	10,103	19,108	6,187	594
Equity Earnings/Minority Int.	d796	412	403	568	230	...	...
Net Income	20,401	[2] 20,724	[2] 2,992	18,764	31,158	29,504	[1] 19,209
Cash Flow	33,477	31,003	12,255	26,279	37,585	37,023	28,583
Average Shs. Outstg.	35,490	37,098	42,557	40,980	41,997	41,001	31,509
BALANCE SHEET (IN THOUSANDS):							
Cash & Cash Equivalents	87,193	117,509	90,986	110,393	90,295	57,707	34,869
Total Current Assets	198,137	211,808	167,977	195,327	158,666	99,421	66,431
Net Property	72,268	70,771	56,318	63,994	62,872	29,803	27,372
Total Assets	378,957	382,342	304,629	329,014	290,220	136,775	100,653
Total Current Liabilities	90,978	99,542	74,341	53,591	71,849	43,298	28,058
Long-Term Obligations	163,912	156,765	108,948	113,489	38,517	4,516	17,327
Net Stockholders' Equity	112,260	108,933	104,792	145,687	159,751	82,542	49,317
Net Working Capital	107,159	112,266	93,636	141,736	86,817	56,123	38,373
Year-end Shs. Outstg.	28,855	36,038	38,620	36,996	40,673	40,087	31,880
STATISTICAL RECORD:							
Operating Profit Margin %	11.4	11.3	4.0	10.1	13.7	11.9	10.3
Net Profit Margin %	5.0	5.8	0.9	6.0	8.4	9.3	8.3
Return on Equity %	18.2	19.0	2.9	12.9	19.5	35.7	39.0
Return on Assets %	5.4	5.4	1.0	5.7	10.7	21.6	19.1
Debt/Total Assets %	43.3	41.0	35.8	34.5	13.3	3.3	17.2
Price Range	6.25-3.38	7.06-5.00	7.44-3.88	6.63-5.63	7.38-5.50	7.88-5.00	8.88-4.88
P/E Ratio	11.0-5.9	12.6-8.9	106.1-55.3	16.6-14.1	10.0-7.4	10.9-6.9	14.5-8.0
Average Yield %	2.5	1.8	1.6	1.3	1.2	0.6	...

Statistics are as originally reported. Adj. for 25% stk. div., 6/95; & 50% class A stk. div. for ea. com. sh. or class B sh. held, 9/94. [1] Bef. $1.8 mil ($0.06/sh) gain from acctg. change. [2] Incl. $3.1 mil pre-tax restr. chg., 1999; & $16.8 mil, 1998.

OFFICERS:
S. Giordano, Chmn.
S. Giordano, Jr., Vice-Chmn., C.E.O.
M. B. Etter, Pres., C.O.O.
M. Giordano, Exec. V.P., C.F.O.

PRINCIPAL OFFICE: 505 Martinsville Road, Liberty Corner, NJ 07938-0813

TELEPHONE NUMBER: (908) 604-8686
FAX: (908) 604-0715
WEB: www.fedders.com

NO. OF EMPLOYEES: 3,250 (approx.)

SHAREHOLDERS: 2,637 (common); 2,540 (class A); 13 (class B)

ANNUAL MEETING: In Dec.

INCORPORATED: DE, 1985

INSTITUTIONAL HOLDINGS:
No. of Institutions: 60
Shares Held: 6,935,589
% Held: 22.0

INDUSTRY: Refrigeration and heating equipment (SIC: 3585)

TRANSFER AGENT(S): American Stock Transfer & Trust Co., New York, NY

NYSE SYMBOL FSS
Rec. Pr. 22.75 (4/30/01)

FEDERAL SIGNAL CORP.

YIELD 3.4%
P/E RATIO 17.9

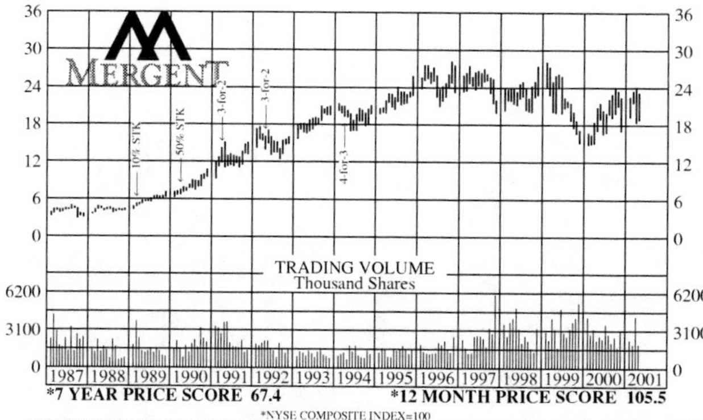

INTERIM EARNINGS (Per Share):

Qtr.	Mar.	June	Sept.	Dec.
1997	0.30	0.35	0.35	0.29
1998	0.24	0.35	0.36	0.36
1999	0.29	0.30	0.30	0.37
2000	0.30	0.36	0.32	0.29

INTERIM DIVIDENDS (Per Share):

Amt.	Decl.	Ex.	Rec.	Pay.
0.19Q	4/20/00	5/09/00	5/11/00	6/01/00
0.19Q	7/20/00	8/15/00	8/17/00	9/01/00
0.19Q	10/20/00	12/13/00	12/15/00	1/03/01
0.195Q	2/01/01	3/13/01	3/15/01	4/03/01
0.195Q	4/19/01	6/12/01	6/14/01	7/05/01

Indicated div.: $0.78 (Div. Reinv. Plan)

CAPITALIZATION (12/31/00):

	($000)	(%)
Long-Term Debt	316,932	45.1
Deferred Income Tax	27,835	4.0
Common & Surplus	357,431	50.9
Total	702,198	100.0

RECENT DEVELOPMENTS: For the twelve months ended 12/31/00, income from continuing operations climbed 6.0% to $57.7 million compared with income from continuing operations of $54.4 million the year before. Results for 2000 included a pre-tax restructuring charge of $3.7 million. Net sales increased 13.2% to $1.11 billion from $977.2 million the year before. Comparisons were made with restated prior-year figures.

PROSPECTS: Looking ahead, the Company believes that the fire rescue group will be the key earnings growth driver in 2001 due to its high backlog, good markets and steadily improving operating performance. FSS expects 2001 earnings per share from continuing operations before restructuring charges to be in the range of $1.50 to $1.60. However, the Company's performance within this range will be influenced by the strength of the industrial segment of the U.S. economy in the second half of 2001.

BUSINESS

FEDERAL SIGNAL CORP. is a manufacturer and worldwide supplier of public safety, signaling and communications equipment, fire trucks, emergency and street sweeping vehicles, parking control equipment, custom on-premise signage, carbide cutting tools, precision punches and related die components. The Safety Products Group provides warning, signal and communication products while the Sign Group produces identification signs and communication displays. Standard and special die components and precision parts are manufactured by the Tool Group. The Vehicle Group makes commercial fire apparatus and rescue vehicles.

ANNUAL FINANCIAL DATA

	12/31/00	12/31/99	12/31/98	12/31/97	12/31/96	12/31/95	12/31/94
Earnings Per Share	**3 1.27**	**1.25**	**1.30**	**1.29**	**2 1.35**	**1 1.13**	**1.02**
Cash Flow Per Share	**1.90**	**1.84**	**1.81**	**1.73**	**1.75**	**1.47**	**1.33**
Tang. Book Val. Per Share	**1.82**	**1.67**	**1.98**	**2.45**	**2.36**	**2.24**	**2.31**
Dividends Per Share	**0.76**	**0.73**	**0.70**	**0.65**	**0.56**	**0.48**	**0.41**
Dividend Payout %	**59.4**	**58.6**	**53.8**	**50.2**	**41.5**	**42.5**	**39.7**
INCOME STATEMENT (IN MILLIONS):							
Total Revenues	1,106.1	1,061.9	1,002.8	924.9	896.4	816.1	677.6
Costs & Expenses	960.4	928.2	877.5	804.7	775.1	704.3	584.7
Depreciation & Amort.	29.1	27.2	23.6	20.5	18.4	15.9	14.3
Operating Income	116.7	106.5	101.8	99.7	102.9	95.9	78.7
Net Interest Inc./(Exp.)	d31.4	d23.3	d19.3	d17.2	d15.4	d13.4	d8.5
Income Before Income Taxes	84.4	84.4	86.2	84.8	93.4	77.3	70.2
Income Taxes	26.8	26.9	26.8	25.9	31.4	25.7	23.4
Net Income	3 57.7	57.5	59.4	59.0	2 62.0	1 51.6	46.8
Cash Flow	86.7	84.8	83.0	79.5	80.4	67.5	61.0
Average Shs. Outstg. (000)	45,521	45,958	45,846	45,840	45,952	45,859	45,957
BALANCE SHEET (IN MILLIONS):							
Cash & Cash Equivalents	13.6	8.8	15.3	10.7	12.4	9.4	4.6
Total Current Assets	348.9	346.1	311.2	268.6	267.0	235.5	196.3
Net Property	112.6	115.4	97.4	84.7	82.8	78.5	72.8
Total Assets	991.1	961.0	836.0	727.9	703.9	620.0	521.6
Total Current Liabilities	288.9	269.5	195.2	227.0	374.6	314.4	252.6
Long-Term Obligations	316.9	307.0	288.8	177.5	34.3	39.7	34.9
Net Stockholders' Equity	357.4	354.0	321.8	299.8	272.8	248.1	220.3
Net Working Capital	60.0	76.7	116.0	41.6	d107.6	d78.9	d56.3
Year-end Shs. Outstg. (000)	45,304	46,114	45,329	45,606	45,318	45,290	45,372
STATISTICAL RECORD:							
Operating Profit Margin %	10.5	10.0	10.1	10.8	11.5	11.8	11.6
Net Profit Margin %	5.2	5.4	5.9	6.4	6.9	6.3	6.9
Return on Equity %	16.1	16.3	18.5	19.7	22.7	20.8	21.2
Return on Assets %	5.8	6.0	7.1	8.1	8.8	8.3	9.0
Debt/Total Assets %	32.0	31.9	34.5	24.4	4.9	6.4	6.7
Price Range	24.13-14.75	28.13-15.06	27.50-20.00	27.50-19.88	28.25-20.88	25.88-19.63	21.38-16.94
P/E Ratio	19.0-11.6	22.5-12.0	21.2-15.4	21.3-15.4	20.9-15.5	22.9-17.4	21.0-16.6
Average Yield %	3.9	3.4	2.9	2.7	2.3	2.1	2.1

Statistics are as originally reported. Adj for 4-for-3 split, 3/94. 1 Incl. $4.2 mill. ($0.09/sh) chg. for litigation. 2 Incl. $2.8 mill. after-tax gain on sale of assets. 3 Bef. inc. from disc. opers. of $726,000 and accts. change chrg. of $844,000 & incl. pre-tax restruct. chrg. of $3.7 mill.

OFFICERS:
J. J. Ross, Chmn., C.E.O.
A. E. Graves, Pres., C.O.O.
H. L. Dykema, V.P., C.F.O.
R. W. Racic, V.P., Treas.

INVESTOR CONTACT: Henry L. Dykema, V.P., C.F.O., (630) 954-2020

PRINCIPAL OFFICE: 1415 West 22nd St., Oak Brook, IL 60523-2004

TELEPHONE NUMBER: (630) 954-2000
FAX: (630) 954-2030
WEB: www.federalsignal.com

NO. OF EMPLOYEES: 6,936 (avg.)

SHAREHOLDERS: 20,000

ANNUAL MEETING: In Apr.

INCORPORATED: IL, Mar., 1901; reincorp., DE, Mar., 1969

INSTITUTIONAL HOLDINGS:
No. of Institutions: 152
Shares Held: 25,587,574
% Held: 56.5

INDUSTRY: Motor vehicles and car bodies (SIC: 3711)

TRANSFER AGENT(S): EquiServe Trust Company, Jersey City, NJ

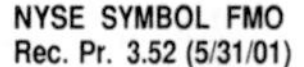

NYSE SYMBOL FMO
Rec. Pr. 3.52 (5/31/01)

FEDERAL-MOGUL CORP.

YIELD ...
P/E RATIO ...

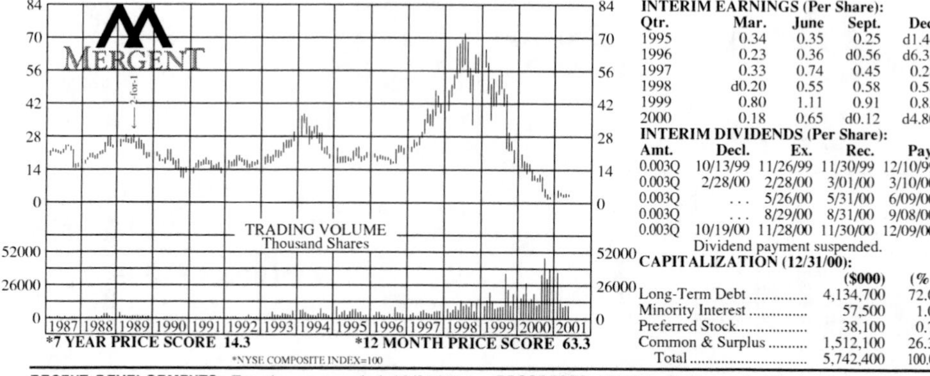

*7 YEAR PRICE SCORE 14.3 *12 MONTH PRICE SCORE 63.3
*NYSE COMPOSITE INDEX=100

INTERIM EARNINGS (Per Share):

Qtr.	Mar.	June	Sept.	Dec.
1995	0.34	0.35	0.25	d1.46
1996	0.23	0.36	d0.56	d6.32
1997	0.33	0.74	0.45	0.28
1998	d0.20	0.55	0.58	0.58
1999	0.80	1.11	0.91	0.83
2000	0.18	0.65	d0.12	d4.80

INTERIM DIVIDENDS (Per Share):

Amt.	Decl.	Ex.	Rec.	Pay.
0.003Q	10/13/99	11/26/99	11/30/99	12/10/99
0.003Q	2/28/00	2/28/00	3/01/00	3/10/00
0.003Q	...	5/26/00	5/31/00	6/09/00
0.003Q	...	8/29/00	8/31/00	9/08/00
0.003Q	10/19/00	11/28/00	11/30/00	12/09/00

Dividend payment suspended.

CAPITALIZATION (12/31/00):

	($000)	(%)
Long-Term Debt	4,134,700	72.0
Minority Interest	57,500	1.0
Preferred Stock	38,100	0.7
Common & Surplus	1,512,100	26.3
Total	5,742,400	100.0

RECENT DEVELOPMENTS: For the year ended 12/31/00, FMO reported a net loss of $281.5 million versus income from continuing operations of $279.0 million in 1999. Results for 2000 included a pre-tax restructuring charge of $135.7 million, an asbestos charge of $184.4 million and a charge of $75.4 million for adjustment of assets held of sale. The 1999 results included pre-tax integration costs of $46.9 million and a charge of $7.9 million for adjustment of assets held for sale. Net sales fell 7.3% to $6.01 billion.

PROSPECTS: FMO's Italian subsidiary, Federal-Mogul S.r.l., signed an agreement with Nagares s.a. to supply automobile manufacturers with timer/glow plug systems. The alliance should provide customers with diesel engine ignition systems with higher performance at a potentially lower cost than traditional systems. Looking ahead, FMO will focus its efforts on its six initiatives for operating improvement aimed at increasing cash flow while reducing cost structure and its asset base.

BUSINESS

FEDERAL-MOGUL CORP. is an automotive parts manufacturer providing products and systems to global customers in the automotive, small engine, heavy-duty and industrial markets. The Company manufactures engine bearings, sealing systems, fuel systems, lighting products, pistons, ignition, brake, friction and chassis products. The Company's principal customers include many of the world's original equipment manufacturers of such vehicles and industrial products. The Company also manufactures and supplies its products and related parts to the aftermarket. The Company maintains technical centers in Europe and North America to develop and provide advanced materials, products and manufacturing processes for all of its manufacturing units.

BUSINESS LINE ANALYSIS

(12/31/00)	REV(%)	INC(%)
Americas/Asia Pacific	67.5	74.3
Europe/Africa	32.2	25.5
Divested Activities	0.3	0.2
Total	100.0	100.0

ANNUAL FINANCIAL DATA

	12/31/00	12/31/99	3 12/31/98	12/31/97	12/31/96	12/31/95	12/31/94
Earnings Per Share	1 d4.02	5 3.59	4 1.67	2 1.67	1 d6.26	1 d0.53	1.55
Cash Flow Per Share	1.32	7.53	5.96	2.98	d4.20	1.47	3.39
Tang. Book Val. Per Share	...	...	...	4.39	2.89	7.48	10.09
Dividends Per Share	0.01	0.01	0.13	0.48	0.48	0.48	0.48
Dividend Payout %	...	0.3	7.6	28.7	...	...	31.0
INCOME STATEMENT (IN MILLIONS):							
Total Revenues	6,013.2	6,487.5	4,468.7	1,806.6	2,030.2	1,995.9	1,895.9
Costs & Expenses	5,400.8	5,385.1	3,854.1	1,614.9	2,169.0	1,928.1	1,717.5
Depreciation & Amort.	374.4	354.9	228.0	52.8	63.7	61.0	55.7
Operating Income	238.0	747.5	386.6	138.9	d202.5	6.8	122.7
Net Interest Inc./(Exp.)	d285.0	d268.9	d193.4	d24.9	d39.7	d27.7	d13.6
Income Before Income Taxes	d262.3	459.9	185.5	99.5	d249.3	d3.2	102.1
Income Taxes	19.2	180.9	93.6	27.5	cr38.2	6.5	38.8
Net Income	1 d281.5	5 279.0	4 91.9	2 72.0	1 d211.1	1 d9.7	63.3
Cash Flow	92.9	633.9	319.9	124.8	d147.4	51.3	119.0
Average Shs. Outstg. (000)	70,500	84,200	53,700	41,900	35,105	34,988	35,062
BALANCE SHEET (IN MILLIONS):							
Cash & Cash Equivalents	107.2	64.5	77.2	541.4	33.1	19.4	25.0
Total Current Assets	2,136.8	2,026.5	2,599.6	1,139.2	762.9	885.7	704.2
Net Property	2,388.8	2,503.7	2,477.5	313.9	350.3	434.7	437.3
Total Assets	10,255.0	9,945.2	9,940.1	1,802.1	1,455.2	1,714.4	1,496.1
Total Current Liabilities	1,703.8	1,782.6	2,029.5	329.6	663.8	418.8	335.9
Long-Term Obligations	4,134.7	3,595.0	3,705.7	848.1	209.6	481.5	319.4
Net Stockholders' Equity	1,550.2	2,075.2	1,986.2	369.3	318.5	555.1	597.2
Net Working Capital	433.0	243.9	570.1	809.6	99.1	466.9	368.3
Year-end Shs. Outstg. (000)	70,619	70,423	67,233	40,196	35,130	35,045	34,988
STATISTICAL RECORD:							
Operating Profit Margin %	4.0	11.5	8.7	7.7	...	0.3	6.5
Net Profit Margin %	...	4.3	2.1	4.0	...	...	3.3
Return on Equity %	...	13.4	4.6	19.5	...	...	10.6
Return on Assets %	...	2.8	0.9	4.0	...	...	4.2
Debt/Total Assets %	40.3	36.1	37.3	47.1	14.4	28.1	21.3
Price Range	20.63-1.69	65.25-16.88	72.00-33.00	47.63-21.63	24.50-16.13	23.75-16.75	37.63-18.63
P/E Ratio	...	18.2-4.7	43.1-19.8	28.5-12.9	...	...	24.3-12.0
Average Yield %	0.1	...	0.2	1.4	2.4	2.4	1.7

Statistics are as originally reported. 1 Incl. non-recurr. chrg. $68.6 mill., 1995: $264.0 mill., 1996; $395.5 mill., 2000 2 Incl. non-recurr. credit $1.1 mill. for restr. & Bef. extraord. chrg. $2.6 mill. 3 Incl. sales & assets fr. the integration of the auto. div. of Cooper Ind. 4 Incl. non-recurr chargs. $25.9 mill.; bef. extraord. loss $38.2 mill. 5 Bef. extraord. loss fr. early retire debt $23.1 mill. & acctg. chrg. of $12.7 mill.; incl. non-recurr. chrgs. $54.8 mill.

OFFICERS:
R. S. Miller Jr., Chmn.
F. E. Macher, C.E.O.
C. G. McClure, Pres., C.O.O.

INVESTOR CONTACT: Steve Feeny, V. P., Inv. Rel., (248) 354-8847

PRINCIPAL OFFICE: 26555 Northwestern Highway, Southfield, MI 48034

TELEPHONE NUMBER: (248) 354-7700
FAX: (248) 354-8950
WEB: www.federal-mogul.com

NO. OF EMPLOYEES: 50,000 (approx.)

SHAREHOLDERS: 6,500 (approx. record)

ANNUAL MEETING: In Apr.

INCORPORATED: MI, May, 1924

INSTITUTIONAL HOLDINGS:
No. of Institutions: 82
Shares Held: 34,045,062
% Held: 48.2

INDUSTRY: Motor vehicle parts and accessories (SIC: 3714)

TRANSFER AGENT(S): The Bank of New York, New York, NY

NYSE SYMBOL FD
Rec. Pr. 44.80 (5/31/01)

FEDERATED DEPARTMENT STORES, INC.

YIELD ...
P/E RATIO ...

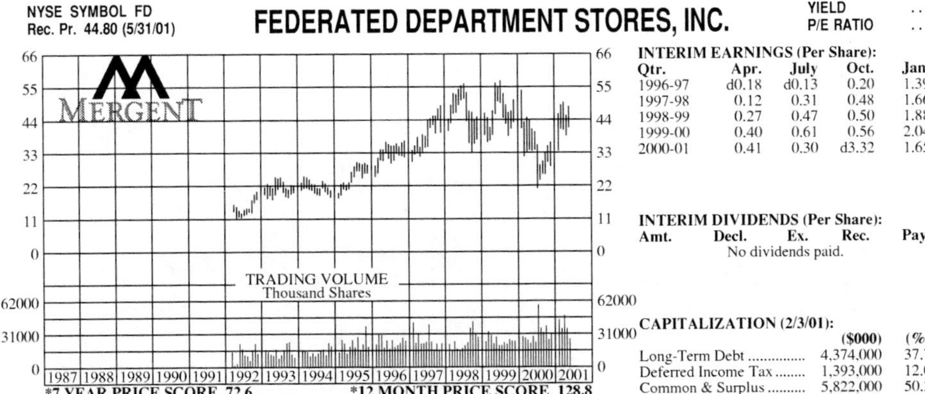

*7 YEAR PRICE SCORE 72.6 *12 MONTH PRICE SCORE 128.8

*NYSE COMPOSITE INDEX=100

INTERIM EARNINGS (Per Share):

Qtr.	Apr.	July	Oct.	Jan.
1996-97	d0.18	d0.13	0.20	1.39
1997-98	0.12	0.31	0.48	1.66
1998-99	0.27	0.47	0.50	1.88
1999-00	0.40	0.61	0.56	2.04
2000-01	0.41	0.30	d3.32	1.65

INTERIM DIVIDENDS (Per Share):

Amt.	Decl.	Ex.	Rec.	Pay.

No dividends paid.

CAPITALIZATION (2/3/01):

	($000)	(%)
Long-Term Debt	4,374,000	37.7
Deferred Income Tax	1,393,000	12.0
Common & Surplus	5,822,000	50.2
Total	11,589,000	100.0

RECENT DEVELOPMENTS: For the 53 weeks ended 2/3/01, the Company reported a net loss of $184.0 million versus net income of $795.0 million in the same 52-week period the year before. Results in the recent period included pre-tax charges totaling $962.0 million related to asset impairment, restructuring, inventory valuation adjustments, and asset write-downs. Net sales rose 3.9% to $18.41 billion from $17.72 billion the previous year. Same-store sales, on a comparable 52-week basis, were up 2.0% year-over-year.

PROSPECTS: On 2/8/01, the Company announced plans to close its New Jersey-based Stern's department store division. FD will convert 19 of Stern's 24 locations in New York and New Jersey into Macy's and Bloomingdale's stores, while the remaining five Stern's stores are expected to be closed and then sold. FD is targeting earnings of $4.00 to $4.25 per share in fiscal 2001, excluding expected one-time charges of between $130.0 million and $150.0 million from closing the Stern's division.

BUSINESS

FEDERATED DEPARTMENT STORES, INC. operates more than 400 full-line department stores in 33 states and Puerto Rico under the names of Bloomingdale's, The Bon Marche, Burdines, Goldsmith's, Lazarus, Macy's, and Rich's. FD's stores sell men's, women's and children's apparel and accessories, cosmetics, home furnishings, and other consumer goods, and are diversified by size of store, merchandising character, and character of community served. FD also operates direct-to-customer catalog and e-commerce subsidiaries under the names of Fingerhut, Bloomingdale's By Mail, bloomingdales.com, Macy's By Mail, and macys.com. FD sold its specialty store chain on 8/1/98.

REVENUES

(2/3/2001)	($000)	(%)
Department Store	16,467,000	89.5
Direct-to-Customer	1,940,000	10.5
Total	18,407,000	100.0

ANNUAL FINANCIAL DATA

	2/3/01	1/29/00	1/30/99	1/31/98	2/1/97	[3] 2/3/96	1/28/95
Earnings Per Share	**[2] d0.90**	**3.62**	**[1] 3.06**	**[1] 2.58**	**[2] 1.28**	**[2] 0.39**	**1.41**
Cash Flow Per Share	**2.71**	**7.01**	**5.83**	**5.22**	**3.98**	**3.10**	**3.87**
Tang. Book Val. Per Share	**24.93**	**19.89**	**24.35**	**21.75**	**19.00**	**18.26**	**14.42**
INCOME STATEMENT (IN MILLIONS):							
Total Revenues	18,407.0	17,716.0	15,833.0	15,668.0	15,229.0	15,048.5	8,315.9
Costs & Expenses	17,117.0	15,270.0	13,747.0	13,717.0	13,775.2	13,865.8	7,439.6
Depreciation & Amort.	740.0	745.0	631.0	610.0	560.6	519.8	326.8
Operating Income	550.0	1,701.0	1,455.0	1,341.0	893.2	662.9	549.5
Net Interest Inc./(Exp.)	d437.0	d355.0	d292.0	d383.0	d451.8	d461.0	d218.2
Income Before Income Taxes	113.0	1,346.0	1,163.0	958.0	441.4	201.9	331.3
Income Taxes	297.0	551.0	478.0	383.0	175.6	127.3	143.7
Net Income	[2] d184.0	795.0	[1] 685.0	[1] 575.0	[2] 265.9	[1] 74.6	187.6
Cash Flow	556.0	1,540.0	1,316.0	1,185.0	826.4	594.4	514.4
Average Shs. Outstg. (000)	204,800	219,600	225,900	227,100	207,537	191,800	132,862
BALANCE SHEET (IN MILLIONS):							
Cash & Cash Equivalents	322.0	218.0	307.0	142.0	148.8	172.5	206.5
Total Current Assets	8,700.0	8,522.0	5,972.0	6,194.0	6,427.3	6,360.4	5,190.5
Net Property	6,830.0	6,828.0	6,572.0	6,520.0	6,524.8	6,305.2	5,349.9
Total Assets	17,012.0	17,692.0	13,464.0	13,738.0	14,264.2	14,295.1	12,379.7
Total Current Liabilities	4,869.0	4,552.0	3,068.0	3,060.0	3,597.7	3,098.1	2,712.1
Long-Term Obligations	4,374.0	4,589.0	3,057.0	3,919.0	4,605.9	5,632.2	4,529.2
Net Stockholders' Equity	5,822.0	6,552.0	5,709.0	5,256.0	4,669.2	4,273.7	3,639.6
Net Working Capital	3,831.0	3,970.0	2,904.0	3,134.0	2,829.6	3,262.3	2,478.4
Year-end Shs. Outstg. (000)	197,600	242,200	208,500	209,900	208,000	193,300	182,600
STATISTICAL RECORD:							
Operating Profit Margin %	3.0	9.6	9.2	8.6	5.9	4.4	6.6
Net Profit Margin %	...	4.5	4.3	3.7	1.7	0.5	2.3
Return on Equity %	...	12.1	12.0	10.9	5.7	1.7	5.2
Return on Assets %	...	4.5	5.1	4.2	1.9	0.5	1.5
Debt/Total Assets %	25.7	25.9	22.7	28.5	32.3	39.4	36.6
Price Range	53.88-21.00	57.06-36.44	56.19-32.81	48.88-30.00	37.00-25.00	30.00-17.88	25.25-18.00
P/E Ratio	...	15.8-10.1	18.4-10.7	18.9-11.6	28.9-19.5	76.9-45.8	17.9-12.8

Statistics are as originally reported. [1] Bef. $23 mil ($0.10/sh) extraord. loss, 1/99; $38.7 mil ($0.18/sh) extraord. loss, 1/98. [2] Incl. $962.0 mil pre-tax chg. for Fingerhut restructuring and asset impairment, 2/01; $308.6 mil chg. for bus. integration & consol., 2/97; $293.9 mil non-recur. chg., 2/96. [3] Results include opers. of acqd. Broadway stores.

OFFICERS:
J. M. Zimmerman, Chmn., C.E.O.
T. J. Lundgren, Pres., Chief Merch. Off.
K. M. Hoguet, Sr. V.P., C.F.O.

INVESTOR CONTACT: Susan Robinson, (513) 579-7028

PRINCIPAL OFFICE: 151 West 34th Street, New York, NY 10001

TELEPHONE NUMBER: (212) 494-1602
FAX: (212) 494-1838
WEB: www.federated-fds.com

NO. OF EMPLOYEES: 129,000 (approx.)

SHAREHOLDERS: 11,700 (approx.)

ANNUAL MEETING: In May

INCORPORATED: DE, Nov., 1929

INSTITUTIONAL HOLDINGS:
No. of Institutions: 348
Shares Held: 211,024,889
% Held: 106.8

INDUSTRY: Department stores (SIC: 5311)

TRANSFER AGENT(S): The Bank of New York, New York, NY

NYSE SYMBOL FII
Rec. Pr. 29.95 (5/31/01)

FEDERATED INVESTORS INC.

YIELD 0.6%
P/E RATIO 23.6

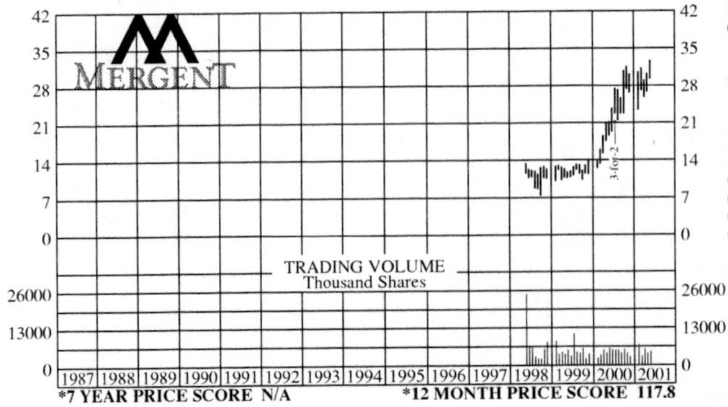

TRADING VOLUME
Thousand Shares

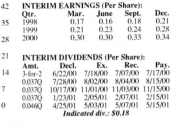

*7 YEAR PRICE SCORE N/A *12 MONTH PRICE SCORE 117.8

*NYSE COMPOSITE INDEX=100

INTERIM EARNINGS (Per Share):

Qtr.	Mar.	June	Sept.	Dec.
1998	0.17	0.16	0.18	0.21
1999	0.21	0.23	0.24	0.28
2000	0.30	0.30	0.33	0.34

INTERIM DIVIDENDS (Per Share):

Amt.	Decl.	Ex.	Rec.	Pay.
3-for-2	6/22/00	7/18/00	7/07/00	7/17/00
0.037Q	7/28/00	8/02/00	8/04/00	8/15/00
0.037Q	10/17/00	11/01/00	11/03/00	11/15/00
0.037Q	1/23/01	2/05/01	2/07/01	2/15/01
0.046Q	4/25/01	5/03/01	5/07/01	5/15/01

Indicated div.: $0.18

CAPITALIZATION (12/31/00):

	($000)	(%)
Long-Term Debt	393,992	67.6
Deferred Income Tax	40,565	7.0
Minority Interest	538	0.1
Common & Surplus	147,868	25.4
Total	582,963	100.0

RECENT DEVELOPMENTS: For the year ended 12/31/00, net income totaled $155.4 million, an increase of 25.3% from $124.0 million in 1999. Results for 1999 excluded an after-tax gain of $2.0 million from the sale of non-earnings assets. Total revenue improved 13.3% to $680.8 million compared with $601.1 million in the previous year. Operating income jumped 21.1% to $286.9 million from $236.9 million in the preceding year. Total managed assets increased to $139.60 billion at 12/31/00 from $124.80 billion the year before.

PROSPECTS: On 4/23/01, the Company acquired the assets of Edgemont Asset Management Corporation, the advisor for the $3.23 billion Kaufmann Fund. In conjunction with this transaction, shareholders of the fund approved a reorganization of the fund into the Federated Kaufmann Fund. The reorganization allows for the creation of Federated Kaufmann Fund Class A, B and C shares, as well as a K Class, which has special features designed for current shareholders. The reorganization was approved during a shareholder meeting on 4/16/01.

BUSINESS

FEDERATED INVESTORS INC. and its consolidated subsidiaries is a major provider of investment management and related financial services. The Company sponsors, markets and provides investment advisory, distribution and administrative services primarily to mutual funds. As of 3/31/01, the Company had approximately $146.00 billion in assets under management in 138 mutual funds and 60 separate accounts. These funds are offered through banks, broker/dealers and other financial intermediaries to customers including retail investors, corporations, and retirement plans. The Company also provides mutual fund administrative services to its managed funds and to funds sponsored by third parties, where FII also acts as fund distributor.

ANNUAL FINANCIAL DATA

	12/31/00	12/31/99	12/31/98	12/31/97	12/31/96	12/31/95
Earnings Per Share	**1.27**	**2 0.96**	**0.71**	**1 0.41**	**1 0.09**	**0.17**
Cash Flow Per Share	**1.88**	**1.48**	**1.18**	**0.75**	**0.35**	**0.36**
Tang. Book Val. Per Share	**0.86**	**0.70**	**0.44**	...	...	...
Dividends Per Share	**0.14**	**0.11**	**0.05**	...	...	...
Dividend Payout %	**10.9**	**11.4**	**6.9**	...	...	...
INCOME STATEMENT (IN THOUSANDS):						
Total Revenues	680,768	601,098	522,127	403,719	321,793	279,831
Costs & Expenses	319,021	297,760	283,962	250,536	236,973	191,590
Depreciation & Amort.	74,837	66,392	55,747	43,556	33,187	25,274
Operating Income	286,910	236,946	182,418	109,627	51,633	62,967
Net Interest Inc./(Exp.)	d34,180	d31,846	d27,614	d20,060	d20,287	d9,826
Income Before Income Taxes	242,522	194,881	145,934	81,983	24,535	47,340
Income Taxes	87,162	70,861	53,565	30,957	10,930	18,809
Equity Earnings/Minority Int.	d10,208	d10,219	d8,870	d7,584	d6,811	d5,801
Net Income	155,360	2 124,020	92,369	1 51,026	1 13,605	28,531
Cash Flow	230,197	190,412	26,652	94,582	43,767	47,805
Average Shs. Outstg.	122,295	129,086	125,496	125,496	124,739	133,493
BALANCE SHEET (IN THOUSANDS):						
Cash & Cash Equivalents	235,225	237,928	198,979	31,857	20,322	...
Total Current Assets	284,547	284,147	242,260	76,112	56,862	...
Net Property	36,406	31,305	21,550	22,163	29,357	...
Total Assets	704,750	673,193	580,020	337,156	247,377	...
Total Current Liabilities	115,522	115,472	86,328	64,053	70,645	...
Long-Term Obligations	393,992	394,187	371,548	284,338	244,125	...
Net Stockholders' Equity	147,868	118,812	91,730	d36,578	d86,922	...
Net Working Capital	169,025	168,675	155,932	12,059	d13,783	...
Year-end Shs. Outstg.	117,130	122,572	129,297	125,150	41,985	...
STATISTICAL RECORD:						
Operating Profit Margin %	42.1	39.4	34.9	27.2	16.0	22.5
Net Profit Margin %	22.8	20.6	17.7	12.6	4.2	10.2
Return on Equity %	105.1	104.4	100.7	...	...	...
Return on Assets %	22.0	18.4	15.9	15.1	5.5	...
Debt/Total Assets %	55.9	58.6	64.1	84.3	98.7	...
Price Range	31.69-12.46	14.13-10.04	13.46-7.33	...	...	...
P/E Ratio	24.9-9.8	14.7-10.5	18.9-10.3	...	...	...
Average Yield %	0.6	0.9	0.5	...	...	...

Statistics are as originally reported. Adj. for 3-for-2 stk. spl., 7/00 1 Results excluded extraordinary loss, 1997, $449,000; 1996, $986,000 2 Excl. after-tax gain $2.0 mill. from the sale of non-earnings assets.

OFFICERS:
J. F. Donahue, Chmn.
J. C. Donahue, Pres., C.E.O.
T. R. Donahue, V.P., C.F.O., Treas.

PRINCIPAL OFFICE: Federated Investors Twr., 5800 Corporate Dr., Pittsburgh, PA 15222-3779

TELEPHONE NUMBER: (412) 288-1900
WEB: www.federatedinvestors.com

NO. OF EMPLOYEES: 1,899 (avg.)

SHAREHOLDERS: 10,821 ; 1

ANNUAL MEETING: In April

INCORPORATED: PA,

INSTITUTIONAL HOLDINGS:
No. of Institutions: 144
Shares Held: 41,591,714
% Held: 35.5

INDUSTRY: Investment advice (SIC: 6282)

TRANSFER AGENT(S): BankBoston, N.A., c/o EquiServe, L.P., Boston, MA

NYSE SYMBOL FDX
Rec. Pr. 42.07 (4/30/01)

FEDEX CORP.

YIELD ...
P/E RATIO 17.0

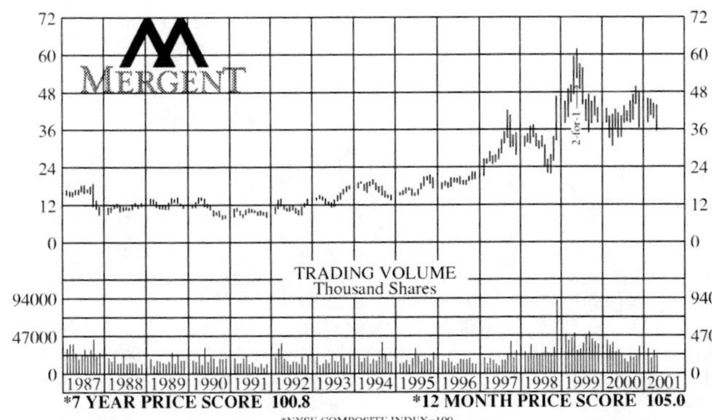

*7 YEAR PRICE SCORE 100.8 *12 MONTH PRICE SCORE 105.0

*NYSE COMPOSITE INDEX=100

INTERIM EARNINGS (Per Share):

Qtr.	Aug.	Nov.	Feb.	May
1996-97	0.25	0.36	0.21	d0.14
1997-98	0.56	0.50	0.06	0.57
1998-99	0.50	0.61	0.26	0.73
1999-00	0.52	0.57	0.39	0.85
2000-01	0.58	0.67	0.37	...

INTERIM DIVIDENDS (Per Share):

Amt. Decl. Ex. Rec. Pay.

No dividends paid.

CAPITALIZATION (5/31/00):

	($000)	(%)
Long-Term Debt	1,776,253	25.7
Deferred Income Tax	344,613	5.0
Common & Surplus	4,785,243	69.3
Total	6,906,109	100.0

RECENT DEVELOPMENTS: For the quarter ended 2/28/01, net income fell 3.5% to $109.0 million compared with $113.0 million in the corresponding period of the previous year. Total revenue increased 7.1% to $4.84 billion from $4.52 billion a year earlier. Revenue from FedEx Express grew slightly to $3.79 billion from $3.76 billion the year before. Revenue from FedEx Ground rose 8.6% to $529.0 million.

PROSPECTS: In fiscal 2001, the Company expects earnings per share to range from $2.50 to $2.65. Separately, FDX's FedEx Express subsidiary and the U.S. Postal Service approved two seven-year service agreements that should generate about $7.20 billion in revenues. Meanwhile, FDX acquired American Freightways and its sister company, Viking Freight, creating FedEx Freight, for $1.20 billion in cash, FDX common stock and assumed debt.

BUSINESS

FEDEX CORPORATION (formerly FDX Corporation) is a holding company that provides comprehensive transportation, logistics and supply chain management solutions. The Company's principal operating subsidiaries are FedEx Express, an express transportation company; FedEx Ground (formerly RPS, Inc.), a provider of small-package ground delivery service; FedEx Custom Critical, an international provider of expedited time-critical shipments; FedEx Logistics, an integrated logistics, technology and transportation-solution company; FedEx Trade Networks Inc., a provider of customs brokerage, consulting, information technology and trade facilitation solutions; and FedEx Freight, a provider of regional less-than-truckload freight services.

BUSINESS LINE ANALYSIS

(05/31/2000)	Rev(%)	Inc(%)
FedEx Express	82.6	73.8
FedEx Ground	11.1	18.4
Other revenues	6.3	7.8
Total	100.0	100.0

ANNUAL FINANCIAL DATA

	5/31/00	5/31/99	5/31/98	5/31/97	5/31/96
Earnings Per Share	**2.32**	**2.10**	**[1] 1.67**	**0.67**	**[2] 1.38**
Cash Flow Per Share	**6.22**	**5.54**	**4.90**	**3.86**	**4.35**
Tang. Book Val. Per Share	**14.35**	**14.50**	**12.23**	**10.60**	**...**
INCOME STATEMENT (IN MILLIONS):					
Total Revenues	18,256.9	16,773.5	15,872.8	14,237.9	12,721.8
Costs & Expenses	15,881.0	14,575.3	13,898.4	12,802.1	11,084.3
Depreciation & Amort.	1,154.9	1,035.1	963.7	928.8	858.0
Operating Income	1,221.1	1,163.1	1,010.7	507.0	779.6
Net Interest Inc./(Exp.)	d106.1	d98.2	d124.4	d104.2	d90.2
Income Before Income Taxes	1,137.7	1,061.1	899.5	425.9	702.1
Income Taxes	449.4	429.7	401.4	229.8	301.9
Net Income	688.3	631.3	[1] 498.2	196.1	[2] 400.2
Cash Flow	1,843.2	1,666.5	1,461.9	1,124.9	1,258.1
Average Shs. Outstg. (000)	296,326	300,643	298,408	291,426	289,390
BALANCE SHEET (IN MILLIONS):					
Cash & Cash Equivalents	68.0	325.3	229.6	160.9	...
Total Current Assets	3,284.7	3,141.0	2,880.1	2,643.7	...
Net Property	7,083.5	6,559.2	5,935.1	5,470.4	...
Total Assets	11,527.1	10,648.2	9,686.1	9,044.3	...
Total Current Liabilities	2,891.0	2,784.8	2,803.8	2,579.5	...
Long-Term Obligations	1,776.3	1,359.7	1,385.2	1,598.0	...
Net Stockholders' Equity	4,785.2	4,663.7	3,961.2	3,501.2	...
Net Working Capital	393.7	356.3	76.3	64.2	...
Year-end Shs. Outstg. (000)	298,573	297,987	294,822	295,248	...
STATISTICAL RECORD:					
Operating Profit Margin %	6.7	6.9	6.4	3.6	6.1
Net Profit Margin %	3.8	3.8	3.1	1.4	3.1
Return on Equity %	14.4	13.5	12.6	5.6	...
Return on Assets %	6.0	5.9	5.1	2.2	...
Debt/Total Assets %	15.4	12.8	14.3	17.7	...
Price Range	61.88-34.88	46.56-21.81	42.25-21.00	22.50-16.72	21.50-14.63
P/E Ratio	26.7-15.0	22.2-10.4	25.3-12.6	33.6-25.0	15.6-10.6

Statistics are as originally reported. Years prior to and including fiscal 1998 are pro forma; adj. for 2-for-1 split, 5/99. [1] Incl. merger expenses of $88.0 mill. & bef. disc. oper. gain of $4.9 mill. [2] Bef. disc. oper. loss of $119.6 mill.

OFFICERS:
F. W. Smith, Chmn., Pres., C.E.O.
A. B. Graf Jr., Exec. V.P., C.F.O.
K. R. Masterson, Exec. V.P., Gen. Couns., Sec.

INVESTOR CONTACT: Jim Clippard, (901) 818-7468

PRINCIPAL OFFICE: 942 South Shady Grove Road, Memphis, TN 38120

TELEPHONE NUMBER: (901) 369-3600
FAX: (901) 346-1013
WEB: www.fedex.com or www.fdxcorp.com

NO. OF EMPLOYEES: 96,000 full-time (approx.); 53,000 part-time (approx.)

SHAREHOLDERS: 16,293

ANNUAL MEETING: In Sept.

INCORPORATED: DE, Oct., 1997

INSTITUTIONAL HOLDINGS:
No. of Institutions: 434
Shares Held: 175,990,448
% Held: 59.2

INDUSTRY: Air transportation, scheduled (SIC: 4512)

TRANSFER AGENT(S): First Chicago Trust Company of New York, Jersey City, NJ

NYSE SYMBOL FOE
Rec. Pr. 20.87 (4/30/01)

FERRO CORP.

YIELD 2.8%
P/E RATIO 10.8

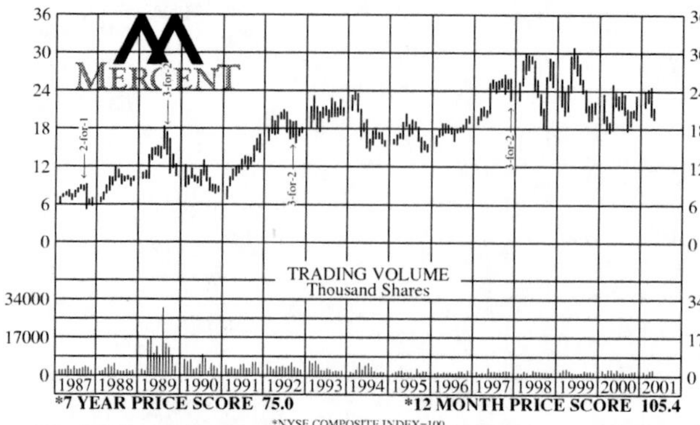

*7 YEAR PRICE SCORE 75.0 *12 MONTH PRICE SCORE 105.4

*NYSE COMPOSITE INDEX=100

INTERIM EARNINGS (Per Share):

Qtr.	Mar.	June	Sept.	Dec.
1997	0.37	d2.15	0.37	0.38
1998	0.40	0.44	0.41	0.42
1999	0.43	0.48	0.45	0.48
2000	0.48	0.53	0.48	0.44

INTERIM DIVIDENDS (Per Share):

Amt.	Decl.	Ex.	Rec.	Pay.
0.145Q	6/23/00	8/11/00	8/15/00	9/10/00
0.145Q	10/27/00	11/13/00	11/15/00	12/10/00
0.145Q	12/08/00	2/13/01	2/15/01	3/10/01
0.145Q	4/27/01	5/11/01	5/15/01	6/10/01

Indicated div.: $0.58 (Div. Reinv. Plan)

CAPITALIZATION (12/31/00):

	($000)	(%)
Long-Term Debt	350,781	53.2
Preferred Stock	70,500	10.7
Common & Surplus	238,658	36.2
Total	659,939	100.0

RECENT DEVELOPMENTS: For the year ended 12/31/00, net income climbed to $73.1 million compared with $73.0 million in 1999. Earnings were somewhat hampered by higher energy costs and increased petroleum-derived raw material costs, particularly in the Plastics segment. Total net sales were $1.45 billion, up 6.8% from $1.36 billion in the prior-year. Sales improved in all operating segments in spite of the negative effects of foreign currency translation and weakening in some U.S. markets.

PROSPECTS: In an effort to improve FOE's long-term growth profile, the Company will make strategic investments in fast-growing markets and businesses that build on FOE's core capabilities. FOE's existing core businesses will continue to seek a balance of improved organic sales and profit growth, while aggressively pursuing strategic acquisitions. In addition, FOE will continue to expand geographically in Asia, where increased living standards drive demand for durable goods that use FOE's materials.

BUSINESS

FERRO CORP. is a worldwide producer of specialty materials through organic and inorganic chemistry. FOE operates in three segments: coatings, plastics and chemicals. Specialty coatings include ceramic coatings, porcelain enamel coatings, powder coatings, pigments and colorants, electronic materials and specialty ceramics. Specialty plastics include plastic colorants, filled and reinforced plastics and liquid coatings and dispersions. Specialty chemicals include polymer additives, fuel additives and friction modifiers and industrial specialties. FOE operates globally through manufacturing facilities in 20 countries and sells products in more than 100 countries. In 2000, sales and operating income were derived: coatings, (60.7%, 64.4%); chemicals, (21.6%, 26.1%); and plastics, (17.7%, 9.5%).

ANNUAL FINANCIAL DATA

	12/31/00	12/31/99	12/31/98	12/31/97	12/31/96	12/31/95	12/31/94
Earnings Per Share	**1.92**	**1.85**	**1.67**	**[1] d1.08**	**1.28**	**1.09**	**1.01**
Cash Flow Per Share	**3.19**	**3.03**	**2.68**	**0.10**	**2.52**	**2.20**	**2.01**
Tang. Book Val. Per Share	**1.24**	**3.78**	**4.59**	**3.97**	**5.73**	**5.36**	**5.88**
Dividends Per Share	**0.58**	**0.55**	**0.54**	**0.43**	**0.39**	**0.36**	**0.36**
Dividend Payout %	**30.2**	**29.7**	**32.3**	**...**	**30.2**	**32.9**	**35.5**
INCOME STATEMENT (IN MILLIONS):							
Total Revenues	1,447.3	1,355.3	1,361.8	1,381.3	1,355.7	1,323.0	1,194.2
Costs & Expenses	1,257.5	1,170.2	1,189.6	1,369.6	1,200.3	1,180.5	1,065.9
Depreciation & Amort.	50.4	48.5	43.1	45.0	49.6	46.3	42.7
Operating Income	139.5	136.6	129.1	d33.3	105.8	96.2	85.7
Net Interest Inc./(Exp.)	d23.4	d16.8	d12.3	d9.9	d10.5	d9.7	d7.2
Income Before Income Taxes	116.6	116.1	110.5	d48.5	88.2	80.2	74.3
Income Taxes	43.5	43.1	41.2	cr11.2	33.6	30.9	26.9
Equity Earnings/Minority Int.	...	...	...	...	0.3	1.0	d1.1
Net Income	73.1	73.0	69.3	[1] d37.3	54.6	49.3	47.4
Cash Flow	120.0	117.8	108.6	3.9	100.5	91.8	86.5
Average Shs. Outstg. (000)	37,664	38,807	40,479	38,132	39,827	41,675	43,104
BALANCE SHEET (IN MILLIONS):							
Cash & Cash Equivalents	0.8	7.1	12.2	16.3	14.0	16.7	19.8
Total Current Assets	443.2	490.5	451.1	427.0	416.5	432.4	415.4
Net Property	425.7	330.4	272.7	240.2	307.4	307.3	288.6
Total Assets	1,127.0	971.8	849.2	785.7	870.5	875.9	801.4
Total Current Liabilities	365.1	337.6	282.6	277.7	252.3	257.3	228.3
Long-Term Obligations	350.8	236.8	156.3	102.0	105.3	104.9	77.6
Net Stockholders' Equity	309.2	445.9	373.1	376.7	432.8	423.3	414.8
Net Working Capital	78.1	152.9	168.6	149.3	164.2	175.1	187.1
Year-end Shs. Outstg. (000)	34,165	35,169	35,327	37,323	38,447	40,292	41,741
STATISTICAL RECORD:							
Operating Profit Margin %	9.6	10.1	9.5	...	7.8	7.3	7.2
Net Profit Margin %	5.1	5.4	5.1	...	4.0	3.7	4.0
Return on Equity %	23.7	24.6	24.5	...	14.2	12.9	12.9
Return on Assets %	6.5	7.5	8.2	...	6.3	5.6	5.9
Debt/Total Assets %	31.1	24.4	18.4	13.0	12.1	12.0	9.7
Price Range	25.13-17.31	30.94-19.19	30.13-18.00	26.67-18.67	20.08-15.25	20.42-14.25	23.92-14.42
P/E Ratio	13.1-9.0	16.7-10.4	18.0-10.8	...	15.7-11.9	18.7-13.0	23.6-14.2
Average Yield %	2.7	2.2	2.1	1.9	2.2	2.1	1.9

Statistics are as originally reported. Adj. for 3-for-2 split, 12/97. [1] Excl. $152.8 mill. pre-tax restr. chg.

OFFICERS:
H. R. Ortino, Chmn., C.E.O.
B. W. Wise, Sr. V.P., C.F.O.

INVESTOR CONTACT: Aidan Gormley, Director, Investor Relations, (216) 875-7155

PRINCIPAL OFFICE: 1000 Lakeside Ave., Cleveland, OH 44114

TELEPHONE NUMBER: (216) 641-8580
FAX: (216) 696-6930
WEB: www.ferro.com

NO. OF EMPLOYEES: 7,117 (approx.)

SHAREHOLDERS: 2,163

ANNUAL MEETING: In Apr.

INCORPORATED: OH, Oct., 1919

INSTITUTIONAL HOLDINGS:
No. of Institutions: 120
Shares Held: 24,325,696
% Held: 71.3

INDUSTRY: Paints and allied products (SIC: 2851)

TRANSFER AGENT(S): National City Bank, Cleveland, OH

NYSE SYMBOL FNF
Rec. Pr. 23.41 (4/30/01)

FIDELITY NATIONAL FINANCIAL, INC.

YIELD 1.7%
P/E RATIO 14.7

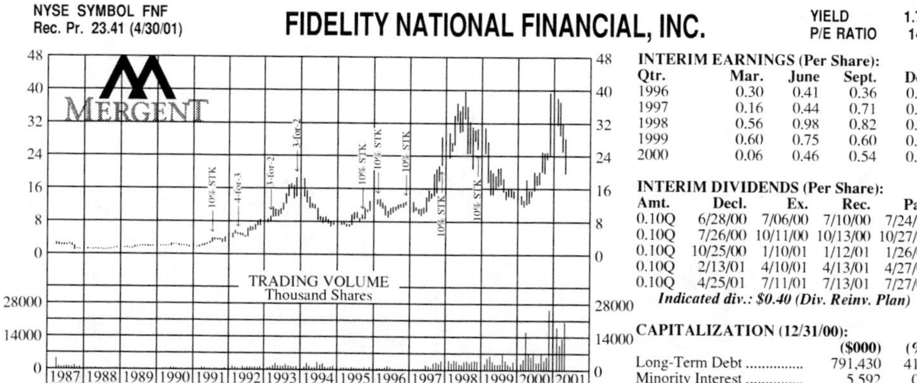

*7 YEAR PRICE SCORE 105.1 *12 MONTH PRICE SCORE 115.5

*NYSE COMPOSITE INDEX=100

INTERIM EARNINGS (Per Share):

Qtr.	Mar.	June	Sept.	Dec.
1996	0.30	0.41	0.36	0.34
1997	0.16	0.44	0.71	0.56
1998	0.56	0.98	0.82	0.87
1999	0.60	0.75	0.60	0.30
2000	0.06	0.46	0.54	0.53

INTERIM DIVIDENDS (Per Share):

Amt.	Decl.	Ex.	Rec.	Pay.
0.10Q	6/28/00	7/06/00	7/10/00	7/24/00
0.10Q	7/26/00	10/11/00	10/13/00	10/27/00
0.10Q	10/25/00	1/10/01	1/12/01	1/26/01
0.10Q	2/13/01	4/10/01	4/13/01	4/27/01
0.10Q	4/25/01	7/11/01	7/13/01	7/27/01

Indicated div.: $0.40 (Div. Reinv. Plan)

CAPITALIZATION (12/31/00):

	($000)	(%)
Long-Term Debt	791,430	41.6
Minority Interest	5,592	0.3
Common & Surplus	1,106,737	58.1
Total	1,903,759	100.0

RECENT DEVELOPMENTS: For the year ended 12/31/00, net income improved 52.9% to $108.3 million compared with $70.9 million in 1999. Total revenue more than doubled to $2.74 billion versus $1.36 billion the year before. Total title premiums surged to $1.95 billion from $939.5 million a year earlier. Escrow and other title-related fees jumped to $459.1 million. Interest and investment income soared to $87.2 million from $32.0 million in the previous year.

PROSPECTS: On 1/5/01, the Company acquired International Data Management Corporation (IDM), a provider of real estate information. On 2/14/01, FNF and VISTAinfo, a provider of real estate information products and services, signed a non-binding letter of intent to combine both companies' real estate information, technology products and assets into a jointly-owned real estate services company.

BUSINESS

FIDELITY NATIONAL FINANCIAL, INC., through its principal subsidiaries, is a major title insurance and diversified real estate-related services business. The Company's title insurance underwriters are Fidelity National Title, Chicago Title, Ticor Title, Security Union Title and Alamo Title. The Company provides title insurance in 49 states, the District of Columbia, Guam, Mexico, Puerto Rico, the U.S. Virgin Islands and Canada. In addition, the Company performs other real estate-related services such as escrow, appraisal services, collection and trust activities, real estate information and technology services, trustee's sale guarantees, credit reporting, attorney services, flood certifications, real estate tax services, reconveyances, recording, foreclosure publishing and posting services and exchange intermediary services in connection with real estate transactions. On 3/20/00, FNF acquired Chicago Title Corporation.

ANNUAL FINANCIAL DATA

	12/31/00	12/31/99	12/31/98	12/31/97	12/31/96	12/31/95	12/31/94
Earnings Per Share	**1.78**	**2.27**	**③ 3.23**	**② 1.89**	**1.41**	**① 0.44**	**① 0.45**
Tang. Book Val. Per Share	**15.92**	**15.91**	**13.73**	**9.91**	**6.55**	**4.77**	**5.58**
Dividends Per Share	**0.40**	**0.28**	**0.25**	**0.23**	**0.21**	**0.18**	**0.17**
Dividend Payout %	**22.5**	**12.3**	**7.9**	**12.2**	**14.9**	**40.7**	**39.0**
INCOME STATEMENT (IN THOUSANDS):							
Total Premium Income	1,946,159	939,452	910,278	533,220	475,961	285,552	369,275
Other Income	795,835	412,752	378,187	213,492	160,952	124,293	123,529
Total Revenues	2,741,994	1,352,204	1,288,465	746,712	636,913	409,845	492,804
Policyholder Benefits	97,322	52,713	59,294	38,661	33,302	19,031	27,838
Income Before Income Taxes	194,140	117,828	175,134	73,430	40,553	9,460	12,339
Income Taxes	85,825	46,975	69,442	31,959	16,216	1,828	2,594
Net Income	108,315	70,853	③ 105,692	② 41,471	24,337	① 7,632	① 9,745
Average Shs. Outstg.	60,937	31,336	33,474	23,631	17,261	17,263	21,930
BALANCE SHEET (IN THOUSANDS):							
Cash & Cash Equivalents	262,955	38,569	51,309	54,005	63,971	47,431	34,689
Premiums Due	936,417	79,088	86,701	61,548	73,261	58,177	48,622
Invst. Assets: Fixed-term	1,188,681	347,051	330,068	217,001	166,329	129,236	149,111
Invst. Assets: Total	1,685,331	506,916	510,515	326,277	227,674	180,082	217,648
Total Assets	3,833,985	1,029,173	969,470	600,559	509,296	405,063	418,119
Long-Term Obligations	791,430	226,359	214,624	123,023	148,922	136,047	142,129
Net Stockholders' Equity	1,106,737	432,494	396,740	196,319	110,251	77,947	73,954
Year-end Shs. Outstg.	69,499	27,188	28,895	19,815	16,844	16,331	13,258
STATISTICAL RECORD:							
Return on Revenues %	4.0	5.2	8.2	5.6	3.8	1.9	2.0
Return on Equity %	9.8	16.4	26.6	21.1	22.1	9.8	13.2
Return on Assets %	2.8	6.9	10.9	6.9	4.8	1.9	2.3
Price Range	39.38-11.63	30.75-13.44	39.66-20.85	28.58-9.50	13.52-9.02	12.98-6.74	18.36-6.66
P/E Ratio	22.1-6.5	13.5-5.9	12.3-6.5	15.1-5.0	9.6-6.4	29.6-15.4	41.1-14.9
Average Yield %	1.6	1.3	0.8	1.2	1.9	1.8	1.4

Statistics are as originally reported. Adjusted for stk. splits: 10.0% stk. div., 12/98, 12/97, 12/96, 1/96, 9/95 ① Excl. extraord. gain of $813,000, 12/95; $2.4 mill., 12/94 ② Excl. net extraord. loss of $1.7 mill. ③ Incl. $7.3 mil in pre-tax merger-related expenses.

OFFICERS:
W. P. Foley II, Chmn., C.E.O.
P. F. Stone, Pres., C.O.O.
A. L. Stinson, Exec. V.P., C.F.O., Treas.

INVESTOR CONTACT: Dan Murphy, Dir. Inv. Rel., (949) 622-4333

PRINCIPAL OFFICE: 17911 Von Karman Avenue, Suite 300, Irvine, CA 92614

TELEPHONE NUMBER: (949) 622-4333
FAX: (949) 622-4153
WEB: www.fnf.com

NO. OF EMPLOYEES: 16,000

SHAREHOLDERS: 1,897 (approx.)

ANNUAL MEETING: In June

INCORPORATED: DE, Nov., 1984

INSTITUTIONAL HOLDINGS:
No. of Institutions: 203
Shares Held: 48,894,285
% Held: 62.5

INDUSTRY: Title insurance (SIC: 6361)

TRANSFER AGENT(S): Continental Stock Transfer & Trust Company, New York, NY

NYSE SYMBOL FAF
Rec. Pr. 19.95 (4/30/01)

FIRST AMERICAN CORPORATION

YIELD 1.4%
P/E RATIO 15.8

INTERIM EARNINGS (Per Share):

Qtr.	Mar.	June	Sept.	Dec.
1996	0.17	0.38	0.27	0.23
1997	0.06	0.36	0.39	0.42
1998	0.79	0.79	0.89	0.85
1999	0.40	0.44	0.33	d0.03
2000	0.02	0.38	0.37	0.47

INTERIM DIVIDENDS (Per Share):

Amt.	Decl.	Ex.	Rec.	Pay.
0.06Q	6/23/00	6/30/00	7/05/00	7/14/00
0.06Q	8/25/00	9/27/00	9/29/00	10/13/00
0.06Q	12/15/00	12/27/00	12/29/00	1/15/01
0.06Q	2/21/01	3/28/01	3/30/01	4/13/01
0.07Q	5/10/01	7/02/01	7/05/01	7/13/01

Indicated div.: $0.28

CAPITALIZATION (12/31/00):

	($000)	(%)
Long-Term Debt	219,838	16.9
Minority Interest	114,526	8.8
Redeemable Pfd. Stock	100,000	7.7
Common & Surplus	870,237	66.7
Total	1,304,601	100.0

RECENT DEVELOPMENTS: For the year ended 12/31/00, net income totaled $82.2 million compared with income of $88.6 million, before an accounting change charge of $55.6 million, in 1999. Revenues totaled $2.93 billion, a decrease of 1.8% versus $2.99 billion the year before. Title insurance revenues fell 4.0% to $2.07 billion, while real estate information segment revenues declined 3.0% to $558.1 million. However, consumer information segment revenues grew 22.1% to $252.3 million from $206.6 million.

PROSPECTS: The Company's efforts to streamline and consolidate back office operations and provide technology enhancements across The First American Family of Companies during 2000 should position all of FAF's real estate related businesses to take advantage of the projected increase in mortgage originations that is forecasted for 2001. Meanwhile, FAF will continue to grow through strategic acquisitions, market share expansion and technology enhancements.

BUSINESS

FIRST AMERICAN CORPORATION (formerly First American Financial Corp.) is a provider of business information and related products and services. The Company's three primary business segments include: title insurance and services; real estate information and services, which includes mortgage information services and database information and services; and consumer information and services, which provides home warranties; automotive, subprime and direct-to-consumer credit reporting; property and casualty insurance; property and automotive insurance tracking services; resident screening; pre-employment screening; investment advisory; and trust and banking services. The Company currently operates more than 600 offices in the United States and abroad.

LOAN DISTRIBUTION

(12/31/2000)	($000)	(%)
Real Estate-Mortgage	97,080	99.9
Other Loans	59	0.1
Total	97,139	100.0

ANNUAL FINANCIAL DATA

	12/31/00	12/31/99	12/31/98	12/31/97	12/31/96	12/31/95	12/31/94
Earnings Per Share	**1.24**	**2 1.34**	**1 3.32**	**1.21**	**1.04**	**0.15**	**0.37**
Cash Flow Per Share	**2.55**	**2.50**	**4.32**	**1.93**	**1.47**	**0.50**	**0.75**
Tang. Book Val. Per Share	**8.20**	**8.17**	**9.28**	**5.35**	**5.10**	**4.50**	**4.50**
Dividends Per Share	**0.24**	**0.24**	**0.20**	**0.16**	**0.15**	**0.13**	**0.13**
Dividend Payout %	**19.4**	**17.9**	**6.2**	**13.6**	**14.1**	**89.4**	**36.1**
INCOME STATEMENT (IN MILLIONS):							
Total Revenues	2,934.3	2,988.2	2,877.3	1,887.5	1,597.6	1,250.2	1,376.4
Costs & Expenses	2,668.6	2,723.8	2,438.1	1,729.4	1,478.8	1,210.1	1,315.1
Depreciation & Amort.	86.3	77.0	59.8	38.1	22.2	18.0	19.8
Operating Income	179.3	187.4	379.4	119.9	96.6	22.2	41.5
Net Interest Inc./(Exp.)	d25.5	d17.4	d18.0	d10.0	d4.8	d6.2	d6.3
Income Before Income Taxes	153.9	170.0	361.4	106.2	89.2	13.8	32.2
Income Taxes	54.7	62.3	127.7	41.5	35.6	6.2	13.3
Equity Earnings/Minority Int.	d17.0	d19.0	d35.0	d3.7	d2.6	d2.1	d2.9
Net Income	82.2	2 88.6	1 198.7	64.7	53.6	7.6	18.9
Cash Flow	168.6	165.7	258.5	102.9	75.8	25.6	38.7
Average Shs. Outstg. (000)	66,050	66,351	59,822	53,355	51,530	51,314	51,512
BALANCE SHEET (IN MILLIONS):							
Cash & Cash Equivalents	332.8	382.2	408.4	210.6	195.1	164.5	172.8
Total Current Assets	556.5	571.7	599.5	338.6	284.5	239.6	227.2
Net Property	435.1	393.3	313.6	200.4	130.5	118.8	110.6
Total Assets	2,199.7	2,116.4	1,784.8	1,168.1	979.8	873.8	828.6
Total Current Liabilities	348.9	361.5	346.8	234.6	184.2	127.2	99.5
Long-Term Obligations	219.8	196.8	130.2	42.0	71.3	77.2	89.6
Net Stockholders' Equity	870.2	816.0	731.9	411.4	352.5	302.8	292.1
Net Working Capital	207.6	210.1	252.7	104.0	100.3	112.4	127.7
Year-end Shs. Outstg. (000)	63,887	65,068	60,332	52,122	51,993	51,350	51,278
STATISTICAL RECORD:							
Operating Profit Margin %	6.1	6.3	13.2	6.4	6.0	1.8	3.0
Net Profit Margin %	2.8	3.0	6.9	3.4	3.4	0.6	1.4
Return on Equity %	9.4	10.9	27.1	15.7	15.2	2.5	6.5
Return on Assets %	3.7	4.2	11.1	5.5	5.5	0.9	2.3
Debt/Total Assets %	10.0	9.3	7.3	3.6	7.3	8.8	10.8
Price Range	32.88-10.25	35.19-11.50	43.00-15.94	16.22-6.97	9.14-5.50	6.11-3.67	8.33-3.56
P/E Ratio	26.5-8.3	26.3-8.6	13.0-4.8	13.4-5.7	8.8-5.3	41.0-24.6	22.6-9.6
Average Yield %	1.1	1.0	0.7	1.4	2.0	2.7	2.2

Statistics are as originally reported. Adj. for stk. splits: 200% div., 7/98; 3-for-2, 1/98 1 Excl. investment gain of $32.4 mill. 2 Bef. acctg. chrg. $55.6 mill.

OFFICERS:
D. P. Kennedy, Chmn.
P. S. Kennedy, Pres.
T. A. Klemens, Exec. V.P., C.F.O.

INVESTOR CONTACT: Denise M. Warren, Dir., Investor Relations, (800) 854-3643

PRINCIPAL OFFICE: 1 First American Way, Santa Ana, CA 92707-5913

TELEPHONE NUMBER: (714) 800-3000
FAX: (714) 541-6372
WEB: www.firstam.com

NO. OF EMPLOYEES: 20,346 (avg.)

SHAREHOLDERS: 3,553 (approx.)

ANNUAL MEETING: In May

INCORPORATED: CA, 1894

INSTITUTIONAL HOLDINGS:
No. of Institutions: 154
Shares Held: 37,385,949
% Held: 57.4

INDUSTRY: Title insurance (SIC: 6361)

TRANSFER AGENT(S): First American Trust Company, Santa Ana, CA

NYSE SYMBOL FDC
Rec. Pr. 67.44 (4/30/01)

FIRST DATA CORPORATION

YIELD 0.1%
P/E RATIO 29.8

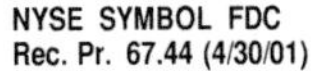

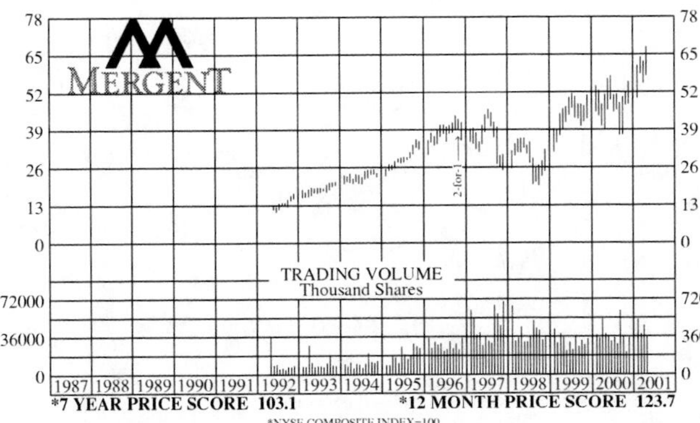

*7 YEAR PRICE SCORE 103.1 *12 MONTH PRICE SCORE 123.7

*NYSE COMPOSITE INDEX=100

INTERIM EARNINGS (Per Share):

Qtr.	Mar.	June	Sept.	Dec.
1997	0.29	d0.06	0.42	0.13
1998	0.29	0.10	0.42	0.23
1999	0.32	0.44	0.48	1.55
2000	0.39	0.52	0.75	0.60

INTERIM DIVIDENDS (Per Share):

Amt.	Decl.	Ex.	Rec.	Pay.
0.02Q	9/14/00	9/28/00	10/02/00	10/13/00
0.02Q	12/13/00	12/28/00	1/02/01	1/12/01
0.02Q	3/07/01	3/29/01	4/02/01	4/16/01
0.02Q	5/09/01	6/28/01	7/02/01	7/13/01

Indicated div.: $0.08

CAPITALIZATION (12/31/00):

	($000)	(%)
Long-Term Debt	1,830,000	32.9
Common & Surplus	3,727,700	67.1
Total	5,557,700	100.0

RECENT DEVELOPMENTS: For the year ended 12/31/00, net income fell 22.5% to $929.6 million versus $1.20 billion in 1999. Results for 2000 included a gain of $201.6 million from the sale of businesses and disposition accrual reversals, a $96.7 million restructuring charge and a charge of $33.6 million for write-down of FDC's investment in Excite@Home. Results for 1999 included an after-tax benefit of $417.6 million. Total revenues were $5.71 billion, up 4.1% from $5.48 billion in the prior year.

PROSPECTS: The Company agreed to acquire a majority equity interest in TASQ Technology, Inc., an outsource provider for the payment processing industry. Under the agreement, FDC will attain an ownership position in TASQ and combine TASQ with First Data Merchant Services' point-of-sale deployment operations. Meanwhile, FDC announced the formation of Nihon Card Processing Co. Ltd., the first company in Japan to provide third-party credit card processing outsourcing services.

BUSINESS

FIRST DATA CORPORATION is a provider of information and transaction processing services. The largest category of services involves information processing and funds transfer related to payment transactions, including credit and debit cards, checks and other types of payment instruments (such as money transfers, money orders, and official checks). These services include the authorization, processing and settlement of credit and debit card transactions, verification or guarantee of check transactions, and worldwide non-bank money transfers, as well as information processing for investment companies. FDC serves financial institutions, merchants, manufacturers, utilities, government agencies and wholesalers.

ANNUAL FINANCIAL DATA

	12/31/00	12/31/99	12/31/98	12/31/97	12/31/96	[2] 12/31/95	12/31/94
Earnings Per Share	[7] 2.25	[6] 2.76	[5] 1.04	[4] 0.79	[3] 1.42	[1] d0.20	0.94
Cash Flow Per Share	3.67	4.18	2.36	1.91	2.37	...	1.68
Tang. Book Val. Per Share	0.38	1.02	...	...	...	...	...
Dividends Per Share	0.08	0.08	0.08	0.08	0.06	0.06	0.06
Dividend Payout %	3.6	2.9	7.7	10.1	4.2	...	6.4
INCOME STATEMENT (IN MILLIONS):							
Total Revenues	5,705.2	5,539.8	5,117.6	5,234.5	4,938.1	4,186.2	1,652.2
Costs & Expenses	3,708.9	2,992.8	3,710.5	3,877.4	3,372.4	3,565.4	1,089.3
Depreciation & Amort.	588.8	617.8	591.1	534.2	423.6	346.8	165.5
Operating Income	1,407.5	1,929.2	816.0	822.9	1,142.1	274.0	397.4
Net Interest Inc./(Exp.)	d99.2	d103.8	d104.1	d116.5	d110.3	d106.4	d41.3
Income Before Income Taxes	1,308.3	1,825.4	711.9	706.4	1,031.8	167.6	356.1
Income Taxes	378.7	625.7	246.2	349.7	395.3	251.8	148.0
Net Income	[7] 929.6	[6] 1,199.7	[5] 465.7	[4] 356.7	[3] 636.5	[1] d84.2	208.1
Cash Flow	1,518.4	1,817.5	1,056.8	890.9	1,060.1	262.6	373.7
Average Shs. Outstg. (000)	414,100	435,100	448,300	466,900	447,700	...	...
BALANCE SHEET (IN MILLIONS):							
Cash & Cash Equivalents	853.3	1,044.0	459.5	410.5	271.7	231.0	363.3
Total Current Assets	1,824.0	1,952.5	1,399.6	1,394.7	1,229.8	1,066.9	3,696.8
Net Property	624.3	710.6	781.0	774.9	757.1	571.4	303.3
Total Assets	17,295.1	17,004.8	16,587.0	15,315.2	14,340.1	12,217.8	5,419.4
Total Current Liabilities	...	...	...	...	...	...	3,537.9
Long-Term Obligations	1,830.0	1,578.1	1,571.7	1,750.7	1,708.5	1,574.8	474.7
Net Stockholders' Equity	3,727.7	3,907.7	3,755.9	3,657.3	3,709.8	3,145.1	1,015.3
Net Working Capital	1,824.0	1,952.5	1,399.6	1,394.7	1,229.8	1,066.9	158.9
Year-end Shs. Outstg. (000)	417,900	417,900	435,500	446,900	448,000	446,600	215,284
STATISTICAL RECORD:							
Operating Profit Margin %	24.7	34.8	15.9	15.7	23.1	6.5	24.1
Net Profit Margin %	16.3	21.7	9.1	6.8	12.9	...	12.6
Return on Equity %	24.9	30.7	12.4	9.8	17.2	...	20.5
Return on Assets %	5.4	7.1	2.8	2.3	4.4	...	3.8
Debt/Total Assets %	10.6	9.3	9.5	11.4	11.9	12.9	8.8
Price Range	57.69-37.00	51.50-31.31	36.06-19.69	46.13-25.00	44.00-30.38	35.63-23.00	25.31-20.25
P/E Ratio	25.6-16.4	18.7-11.3	34.7-18.9	58.4-31.6	31.0-21.4	...	26.9-21.5
Average Yield %	0.2	0.2	0.3	0.2	0.2	0.2	0.3

Statistics are as originally reported. Adj. for 2-for-1 split, 11/96. [1] Incl. $539.9 mill. net chg. [2] Incl. First Financial Mgmt. Corp., acq. 10/27/95. [3] Incl. $8.3 mill. net non-recur. gain. [4] Incl. $334.0 mill. restr. chgs. [5] Incl. $231.5 mill. after-tax non-recur. chgs. [6] Incl. $429.8 mill. in net after-tax gains. [7] Incl. $201.6 mill. gain fr. sale of bus., $96.7 mill. restr. chg. & $33.6 mill. chg. for write-down of invest.

OFFICERS:
H. C. Duques, Chmn., C.E.O.
C. T. Fote, Pres., C.O.O.
K. S. Patmore, Exec. V.P., C.F.O.

INVESTOR CONTACT: Investor Relations, (770) 857-0001

PRINCIPAL OFFICE: 5660 New Northside Drive, Suite 1400, Atlanta, GA 30328

TELEPHONE NUMBER: (770) 857-0001
FAX: (770) 857-0411
WEB: www.firstdatacorp.com

NO. OF EMPLOYEES: 27,000 (approx.)

SHAREHOLDERS: 3,185

ANNUAL MEETING: In May

INCORPORATED: DE, Feb., 1992

INSTITUTIONAL HOLDINGS:
No. of Institutions: 581
Shares Held: 338,297,543
% Held: 85.7

INDUSTRY: Data processing and preparation (SIC: 7374)

TRANSFER AGENT(S): Wells Fargo Shareowner Services, South St. Paul, MN

NYSE SYMBOL FTN
Rec. Pr. 32.67 (4/30/01)

FIRST TENNESSEE NATIONAL CORPORATION

YIELD 2.7%
P/E RATIO 18.5

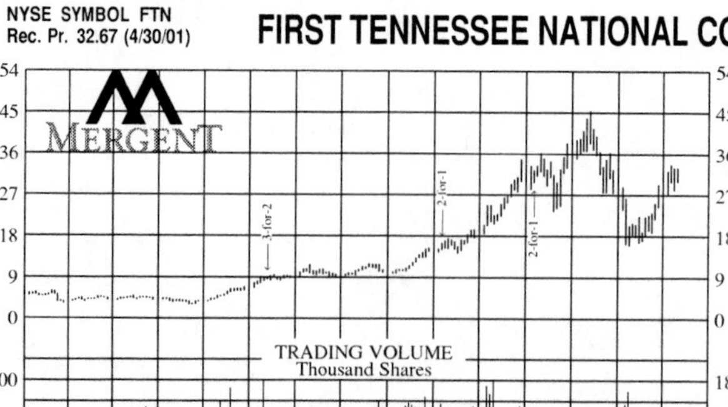

*7 YEAR PRICE SCORE 77.9 *12 MONTH PRICE SCORE 135.2

*NYSE COMPOSITE INDEX=100

INTERIM EARNINGS (Per Share):

Qtr.	Mar.	June	Sept.	Dec.
1997	0.30	0.36	0.43	0.44
1998	0.35	0.40	0.47	0.50
1999	0.40	0.45	0.52	0.48
2000	0.30	0.42	0.50	0.55

INTERIM DIVIDENDS (Per Share):

Amt.	Decl.	Ex.	Rec.	Pay.
0.22Q	4/18/00	6/07/00	6/09/00	7/01/00
0.22Q	7/18/00	9/13/00	9/15/00	10/01/00
0.22Q	10/19/00	12/13/00	12/15/00	1/01/01
0.22Q	1/16/01	3/14/01	3/16/01	4/01/01
0.22Q	4/17/01	6/13/01	6/15/01	7/01/01

Indicated div.: $0.88 (Div. Reinv. Plan)

CAPITALIZATION (12/31/00):

	($000)	(%)
Total Deposits	12,188,691	87.2
Long-Term Debt	409,676	2.9
Common & Surplus	1,384,156	9.9
Total	13,982,523	100.0

RECENT DEVELOPMENTS: For the year ended 12/31/00, net income decreased 6.0% to $232.6 million from $247.5 million in the previous year. Net interest income grew 1.5% to $598.4 million compared with $589.5 million in the prior year, primarily due to strong loan growth. Provision for loan losses increased 16.3% to $67.4 million from $57.9 million a year earlier. Total non-interest income fell 5.3% to $1.06 billion from $1.12 billion the year before. Total non-interest expense declined 1.4% to $1.26 billion from $1.28 billion in the previous year.

PROSPECTS: On 4/27/01, FTN completed the sale of its wholly-owned subsidiary, Peoples & Union Bank to First Farmers and Merchants National Bank. Separately, on 4/2/01, the Company's principal banking subsidiary, First Tennessee Bank N.A., closed on the sale of its existing porfolio of education loans to Educational Funding of the South, Inc. Also, FTN will sell its affinity, co-branded, and certain single relationship credit card accounts and assets to MBNA Corporation. The transaction is estimated to result in a pre-tax gain of about $50.0 million.

BUSINESS

FIRST TENNESSEE NATIONAL CORPORATION is one of the nation's 50 largest bank holding companies with total assets of $18.56 billion as of 12/31/00. In terms of assets, FTEN is the second largest Tennessee-headquartered bank holding company. Through its principal subsidiary, First Tennessee Bank National Association, and its other banking and banking-related subsidiaries, FTN provides a broad range of financial services. FTN is engaged in the commercial banking business. Significant operations are also conducted in the mortgage banking, capital markets, and transaction processing divisions. On 12/31/00, FTN's subsidiary banks had 432 banking locations (190 financial centers and 242 free-standing ATMs) in 23 Tennessee counties, including all of the major metropolitan areas of the state, 20 banking locations (including 13 free-standing ATMs) in Mississippi and 8 banking locations (including 4 free-standing ATMs) in Arkansas, and consumer finance offices in 10 states nationwide.

ANNUAL FINANCIAL DATA

	12/31/00	12/31/99	12/31/98	12/31/97	12/31/96	12/31/95	12/31/94
Earnings Per Share	**1.77**	**1.85**	**1.72**	**1.50**	**1.34**	**1.21**	**1.14**
Tang. Book Val. Per Share	**4.03**	**2.17**	**2.34**	**3.38**	**4.26**	**4.43**	**1.83**
Dividends Per Share	**0.88**	**0.76**	**0.66**	**0.60**	**0.53**	**0.47**	**0.42**
Dividend Payout %	**49.7**	**41.1**	**38.4**	**40.0**	**39.5**	**38.8**	**36.8**
INCOME STATEMENT (IN MILLIONS):							
Total Interest Income	1,363.0	1,207.2	1,133.8	941.3	896.5	822.5	668.7
Total Interest Expense	764.7	617.7	593.2	458.2	445.3	431.9	288.1
Net Interest Income	598.4	589.5	540.5	483.1	451.2	390.7	380.6
Provision for Loan Losses	67.4	57.9	51.4	51.1	35.7	20.6	16.7
Non-Interest Income	1,063.4	1,123.1	985.5	668.1	571.1	496.6	389.2
Non-Interest Expense	1,257.4	1,275.3	1,121.8	785.0	704.5	613.7	545.7
Income Before Taxes	337.0	379.4	352.9	315.1	282.2	253.0	207.3
Net Income	232.6	247.5	226.4	197.5	179.9	164.9	146.3
Average Shs. Outstg. (000)	131,663	133,979	131,862	131,987	134,394	136,050	128,456
BALANCE SHEET (IN MILLIONS):							
Cash & Due from Banks	838.1	956.1	811.9	775.8	959.6	710.9	691.1
Securities Avail. for Sale	2,454.5	2,479.4	2,174.8	2,386.5	2,324.0	2,219.3	1,321.3
Total Loans & Leases	10,239.5	9,363.2	8,557.1	8,311.4	7,728.2	8,122.5	6,347.5
Allowance for Credit Losses	143.7	139.6	136.0	125.9	117.7	112.6	107.0
Net Loans & Leases	10,095.8	9,223.6	8,421.1	8,185.5	7,610.5	8,009.9	6,240.5
Total Assets	18,555.1	18,373.4	18,734.0	14,387.9	13,058.9	12,076.9	10,522.4
Total Deposits	12,188.7	11,358.7	11,723.0	9,671.8	9,033.1	8,582.2	7,688.4
Long-Term Obligations	409.7	358.7	414.5	168.9	234.6	260.0	93.8
Total Liabilities	17,170.9	17,131.9	17,634.4	13,433.8	12,104.4	11,203.7	9,773.6
Net Stockholders' Equity	1,384.2	1,241.5	1,099.5	954.1	954.5	873.2	748.8
Year-end Shs. Outstg. (000)	128,745	129,878	128,974	128,209	133,716	134,356	127,412
STATISTICAL RECORD:							
Return on Equity %	16.8	19.9	20.6	20.7	18.8	18.9	19.5
Return on Assets %	1.3	1.3	1.2	1.4	1.4	1.4	1.4
Equity/Assets %	7.5	6.8	5.9	6.6	7.3	7.2	7.1
Non-Int. Exp./Tot. Inc. %	75.7	74.5	73.5	68.2	68.9	69.2	70.9
Price Range	29.31-15.94	45.38-27.38	38.38-23.38	34.81-18.38	19.44-14.25	15.44-9.81	11.94-9.25
P/E Ratio	16.6-9.0	24.5-14.8	22.3-13.6	23.2-12.2	14.5-10.6	12.8-8.1	10.5-8.1
Average Yield %	3.9	2.1	2.1	2.3	3.1	3.7	4.0

Statistics are as originally reported. Adj. for stk. splits: 2-for-1, 2/20/98; 2-for-1, 2/16/96

OFFICERS:
R. Horn, Chmn., Pres., C.E.O.
E. L. Thomas Jr., Exec. V.P., C.F.O.
H. A. Johnson III, Exec. V.P., Gen. Couns.

INVESTOR CONTACT: R. Jean Taylor, (901) 523-5620

PRINCIPAL OFFICE: 165 Madison Avenue, Memphis, TN 38103

TELEPHONE NUMBER: (901) 523-5630
FAX: (901) 523-4336
WEB: www.firsttennessee.com

NO. OF EMPLOYEES: 9,445

SHAREHOLDERS: 9,333

ANNUAL MEETING: In Apr.

INCORPORATED: TN, 1968

INSTITUTIONAL HOLDINGS:
No. of Institutions: 194
Shares Held: 48,702,960
% Held: 38.0

INDUSTRY: National commercial banks (SIC: 6021)

TRANSFER AGENT(S): Wells Fargo Shareowner Services, South St. Paul, MN

NYSE SYMBOL FTU
Rec. Pr. 29.97 (4/30/01)

FIRST UNION CORPORATION

YIELD 3.2%
P/E RATIO 333.0

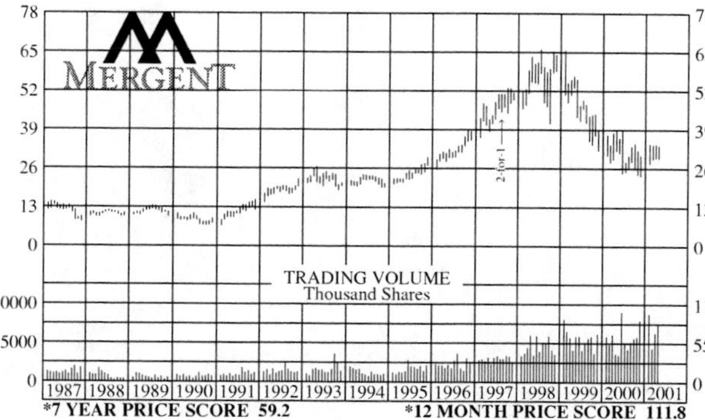

*7 YEAR PRICE SCORE 59.2 *12 MONTH PRICE SCORE 111.8

*NYSE COMPOSITE INDEX=100

INTERIM EARNINGS (Per Share):

Qtr.	Mar.	June	Sept.	Dec.
1997	0.84	0.87	0.90	0.56
1998	0.90	0.26	1.01	0.81
1999	0.73	0.90	0.84	0.86
2000	0.85	d2.27	0.86	0.65

INTERIM DIVIDENDS (Per Share):

Amt.	Decl.	Ex.	Rec.	Pay.
0.48Q	4/18/00	5/26/00	5/31/00	6/15/00
0.48Q	8/15/00	8/29/00	8/31/00	9/15/00
0.48Q	10/17/00	11/28/00	11/30/00	12/15/00
0.24Q	2/20/01	2/26/01	2/28/01	3/15/01
0.24Q	4/16/01	5/29/01	5/31/01	6/15/01

Indicated div.: $0.96 (Div. Reinv. Plan)

CAPITALIZATION (12/31/00):

	($000)	(%)
Total Deposits	142,668,000	73.6
Long-Term Debt	35,809,000	18.5
Common & Surplus	15,347,000	7.9
Total	193,824,000	100.0

RECENT DEVELOPMENTS: For the year ended 12/31/00, FTU reported income of $138.0 million, before an accounting charge of $46.0 million, versus net income of $3.22 billion in the prior year. Results for 2000 and 1999 included pre-tax merger-related and restructuring charges of $2.19 billion and $404.0 million, respectively. Net interest income fell to $7.44 billion from $7.45 billion in 1999. Total fee and other income rose 3.2% to $6.71 billion.

PROSPECTS: On 4/16/01, First Union and Wachovia Corporation signed a definitive agreement under which FTU will acquire WB in a transaction valued at approximately $13.40 billion. The combined company, which will be known as Wachovia Corporation, will have total assets of $324.00 billion and a market capitalization of $45.00 billion. The transaction is expected to close in the third quarter of 2001.

BUSINESS

FIRST UNION CORPORATION, with assets of $254.17 billion as of 12/31/00, provides a wide range of commercial and retail banking and trust services through full-service banking offices in Connecticut, Delaware, Florida, Georgia, Maryland, New Jersey, New York, North Carolina, Pennsylvania, South Carolina, Tennessee, Virginia and Washington, D.C. The Company also provides mortgage banking, credit card, investment banking, investment advisory, home equity lending, asset-based lending, leasing, insurance, international and securities brokerage services through other subsidiaries. During 1998, FTU acquired Wheat First Butcher Singer, Inc., CoreStates Financial Corp., and The Money Store, Inc. On 10/1/99, FTU acquired EVEREN Capital Corp. On 1/2/01, Co. acquired JWGenesis Financial Corp.

LOAN DISTRIBUTION

(12/31/00)	($000)	(%)
Commercial, Financial & Agricultural	54,207,000	41.6
Real Estate-Construction	3,104,000	2.3
Real Estate-Mortgage	9,218,000	7.1
Lease Financing	15,465,000	11.9
Foreign	5,453,000	4.2
Consumer	42,795,000	32.9
Total	130,242,000	100.0

ANNUAL FINANCIAL DATA

	12/31/00	12/31/99	12/31/98	12/31/97	12/31/96	12/31/95	12/31/94
Earnings Per Share	**3 4 0.12**	**3 3.33**	**3 2.95**	**3 2.99**	**2 2.68**	**1 2.52**	**2.49**
Tang. Book Val. Per Share	**11.92**	**11.22**	**12.36**	**14.71**	**12.46**	**11.30**	**11.68**
Dividends Per Share	**1.92**	**1.88**	**1.58**	**1.22**	**1.10**	**0.98**	**0.86**
Dividend Payout %	**16.0**	**56.5**	**53.6**	**40.8**	**41.1**	**38.9**	**34.5**
INCOME STATEMENT (IN MILLIONS):							
Total Interest Income	17,534.0	15,151.0	14,988.0	10,933.0	9,628.0	8,686.4	5,094.7
Total Interest Expense	10,097.0	7,699.0	7,711.0	5,190.0	4,632.0	4,051.8	2,060.9
Net Interest Income	7,437.0	7,452.0	7,277.0	5,743.0	4,996.0	4,634.6	3,033.7
Provision for Loan Losses	1,736.0	692.0	691.0	840.0	375.0	220.0	100.0
Non-Interest Income	6,712.0	6,933.0	6,555.0	3,396.0	2,357.0	1,896.5	1,159.0
Non-Interest Expense	11,710.0	8,862.0	9,176.0	5,589.0	4,668.0	4,092.5	2,677.2
Income Before Taxes	703.0	4,831.0	3,965.0	2,710.0	2,310.0	2,218.6	1,415.5
Net Income	3 4 138.0	3 3,223.0	3 2,891.0	3 1,896.0	2 1,499.0	1 1,430.2	925.4
Average Shs. Outstg. (000)	974,172	966,863	980,000	634,000	557,624	557,354	345,086
BALANCE SHEET (IN MILLIONS):							
Cash & Due from Banks	9,906.0	10,081.0	11,192.0	6,445.0	6,509.0	6,312.1	3,740.7
Securities Avail. for Sale	69,233.0	66,223.0	47,193.0	26,872.0	18,116.0	20,074.8	8,959.2
Total Loans & Leases	130,242.0	141,091.0	139,409.0	100,259.0	98,064.0	92,108.8	54,702.1
Allowance for Credit Losses	8,204.0	7,282.0	5,852.0	4,598.0	3,571.0	3,053.8	1,651.1
Net Loans & Leases	122,038.0	133,809.0	133,557.0	95,661.0	94,493.0	89,055.1	53,051.0
Total Assets	254,170.0	253,024.0	237,363.0	157,274.0	140,127.0	131,879.9	77,313.5
Total Deposits	142,668.0	250,719.0	249,320.0	184,025.0	94,815.0	92,555.2	58,958.3
Long-Term Obligations	35,809.0	31,975.0	22,949.0	9,033.0	8,155.0	7,120.9	3,428.5
Total Liabilities	238,823.0	345,987.0	327,043.0	226,378.0	130,119.0	122,836.7	71,916.0
Net Stockholders' Equity	15,347.0	16,709.0	17,173.0	12,032.0	10,008.0	9,043.1	5,397.5
Year-end Shs. Outstg. (000)	980,000	988,000	982,000	636,000	574,696	555,692	352,068
STATISTICAL RECORD:							
Return on Equity %	0.9	19.3	16.8	15.8	15.0	15.8	17.1
Return on Assets %	0.1	1.3	1.2	1.2	1.1	1.1	1.2
Equity/Assets %	5.9	6.6	7.2	7.7	7.1	6.9	7.0
Non-Int. Exp./Tot. Inc. %	82.8	61.6	66.3	61.2	63.5	62.7	63.9
Price Range	38.88-23.50	65.75-32.00	65.94-40.94	53.00-36.31	38.88-25.56	29.75-20.69	24.00-19.50
P/E Ratio	324.0-195.8	19.7-9.6	22.4-13.9	17.7-12.1	14.5-9.6	11.8-8.2	9.6-7.8
Average Yield %	6.2	3.8	3.0	2.7	3.4	3.9	4.0

Statistics are as originally reported. Adj. for 2-for-1 stk. split, 7/97. 1 Incl. merger with First Fidelity and after-tax merger-related charges of $72.8 mill. 2 Incl. pre-tax SAIF chrg. of $133.0 mill. and merger-related chrgs. of $281.0 mill. 3 Incl. pre-tax merger-related & restruct. chrgs. of $2.19 bill., 2000; $404.0 mill., 1999; $1.21 bill., 1998; $269.0 mill., 1997. 4 Bef. acctg. chrg. of $46.0 mill.

OFFICERS:
G. K. Thompson, Chmn., Pres., C.E.O.
R. Kelly, Exec. V.P., C.F.O.

INVESTOR CONTACT: Alice Lehman, Managing Dir. of Corp. Rel., (704) 374-2137

PRINCIPAL OFFICE: One First Union Center, Charlotte, NC 28288-0570

TELEPHONE NUMBER: (704) 374-6565
FAX: (704) 374-4609
WEB: www.firstunion.com

NO. OF EMPLOYEES: 71,262 (avg.)

SHAREHOLDERS: 157,524

ANNUAL MEETING: In April

INCORPORATED: NC, Dec., 1967

INSTITUTIONAL HOLDINGS:
No. of Institutions: 560
Shares Held: 474,979,527
% Held: 48.6

INDUSTRY: National commercial banks (SIC: 6021)

TRANSFER AGENT(S): First Union National Bank, Charlotte, NC

NYSE SYMBOL FVB
Rec. Pr. 43.86 (4/30/01)

FIRST VIRGINIA BANKS, INC.

YIELD 3.4%
P/E RATIO 14.6

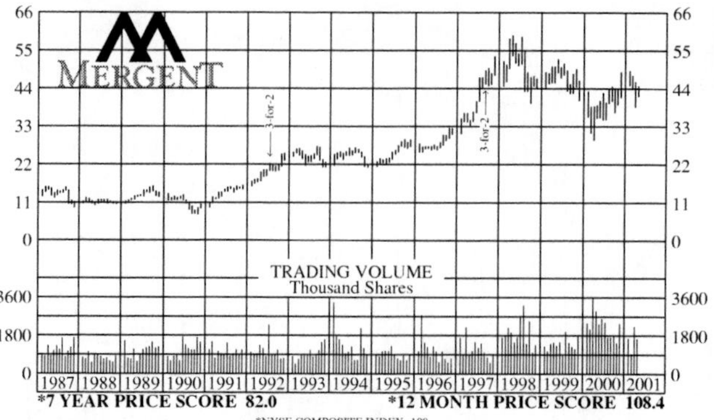

*7 YEAR PRICE SCORE 82.0 *12 MONTH PRICE SCORE 108.4

*NYSE COMPOSITE INDEX=100

INTERIM EARNINGS (Per Share):

Qtr.	Mar.	June	Sept.	Dec.
1997	0.61	0.63	0.67	0.56
1998	0.61	0.62	0.62	0.68
1999	0.88	0.68	0.75	0.70
2000	0.70	0.73	0.76	0.82

INTERIM DIVIDENDS (Per Share):

Amt.	Decl.	Ex.	Rec.	Pay.
0.37Q	5/24/00	6/28/00	6/30/00	7/17/00
0.37Q	8/23/00	9/27/00	9/29/00	10/16/00
0.38Q	11/17/00	12/27/00	12/29/00	1/10/01
0.38Q	2/28/01	3/28/01	3/30/01	4/16/01
0.39Q	5/23/01	6/27/01	6/29/01	7/16/01

Indicated div.: $1.56 (Div. Reinv. Plan)

CAPITALIZATION (12/31/00):

	($000)	(%)
Total Deposits	7,825,816	88.7
Long-Term Debt	1,116	0.0
Preferred Stock	451	0.0
Common & Surplus	992,255	11.3
Total	8,819,638	100.0

RECENT DEVELOPMENTS: For the year ended 12/31/00, net income fell 5.9% to $142.0 million from $150.9 million in 1999. Earnings for 1999 included a pre-tax gain of $17.9 million from credit card operations and pre-tax credit card fees of $5.4 million. Net interest income declined 2.1% to $424.5 million. Non-interest income, including the above gains, slipped 13.6% to $118.0 million. Non-interest expense decreased 1.6% to $322.1 million. Net loans amounted to $6.30 billion compared with $6.32 billion in 1999.

PROSPECTS: Demand for consumer loans, primarily automobile and home equity loans, continued to weaken through the first quarter of 2001. However, recent interest rate cuts bode well for the remainder of the year. Separately, FVB entered into an agreement to acquire Suffolk, Virginia-based James River Bankshares, Inc., a multi-bank holding company, with assets of $516.0 million. The transaction is valued at $107.1 million and is expected to close in the third quarter of 2001.

BUSINESS

FIRST VIRGINIA BANKS, INC., with assets of approximately $9.52 billion as of 12/31/00, provides retail, commercial, international, and mortgage banking; insurance; trust and asset management services; and personal investment services through its subsidiaries. There are nine banks in the First Virginia group with 294 offices in Virginia, 57 offices in Maryland and 25 offices in East Tennessee. In addition, FVB operates a full-service insurance agency, First Virginia Insurance Services, Inc.

LOAN DISTRIBUTION

(12/31/2000)	($000)	(%)
Consumer	4,115,200	64.6
Commercial	954,925	15.0
Construction & land development	181,575	2.9
Real estate	1,114,764	17.5
Total	6,366,464	100.0

ANNUAL FINANCIAL DATA

	12/31/00	12/31/99	12/31/98	12/31/97	12/31/96	12/31/95	12/31/94
Earnings Per Share	**3.01**	**[3] 3.00**	**2.53**	**[2] 2.45**	**[1] 2.33**	**2.19**	**2.34**
Tang. Book Val. Per Share	**18.08**	**17.49**	**16.07**	**16.13**	**15.97**	**15.19**	**14.11**
Dividends Per Share	**1.46**	**1.32**	**1.16**	**1.02**	**0.95**	**0.89**	**0.84**
Dividend Payout %	**48.5**	**44.0**	**45.8**	**41.6**	**40.6**	**40.8**	**35.9**
INCOME STATEMENT (IN MILLIONS):							
Total Interest Income	643.8	640.6	663.6	631.1	587.2	573.6	503.6
Total Interest Expense	219.3	206.9	234.3	222.9	212.3	215.5	161.6
Net Interest Income	424.5	433.7	429.3	408.2	374.9	358.1	342.0
Provision for Loan Losses	9.4	14.2	20.8	17.2	17.7	8.3	6.5
Non-Interest Income	118.0	136.6	116.8	103.6	98.5	89.9	84.7
Non-Interest Expense	322.1	327.3	325.7	303.2	279.3	271.4	252.5
Income Before Taxes	211.0	228.8	199.6	191.3	176.3	168.3	167.8
Net Income	142.0	[3] 150.9	130.2	[2] 124.8	[1] 116.3	111.6	113.2
Average Shs. Outstg. (000)	47,257	50,238	51,529	50,880	49,905	51,084	48,422
BALANCE SHEET (IN MILLIONS):							
Cash & Due from Banks	323.0	441.8	377.4	386.8	378.2	397.9	420.7
Securities Avail. for Sale	301.4	227.0	286.1	243.2	323.6	299.5	30.0
Total Loans & Leases	6,366.5	6,385.4	6,093.2	5,938.0	5,364.8	5,038.1	5,352.5
Allowance for Credit Losses	70.3	70.1	70.3	68.1	62.8	57.9	414.2
Net Loans & Leases	6,296.2	6,315.3	6,022.9	5,869.9	5,302.0	4,980.2	4,938.3
Total Assets	9,516.5	9,451.8	9,564.7	9,011.6	8,236.1	8,221.5	7,865.4
Total Deposits	7,825.8	7,863.9	8,055.1	7,619.8	7,042.7	7,056.1	6,815.8
Long-Term Obligations	1.1	2.2	3.2	2.8	3.9	2.7	3.8
Total Liabilities	8,523.8	8,421.3	8,574.4	8,000.5	7,364.8	7,351.9	7,058.5
Net Stockholders' Equity	992.7	1,030.5	990.3	1,011.2	871.3	869.6	806.9
Year-end Shs. Outstg. (000)	46,163	49,162	50,094	51,817	48,612	50,927	51,075
STATISTICAL RECORD:							
Return on Equity %	14.3	14.6	13.1	12.3	13.4	12.8	14.0
Return on Assets %	1.5	1.6	1.4	1.4	1.4	1.4	1.4
Equity/Assets %	10.4	10.9	10.4	11.2	10.6	10.6	10.3
Non-Int. Exp./Tot. Inc. %	59.4	59.3	59.8	59.3	59.2	60.6	59.3
Price Range	48.94-29.00	52.63-40.50	59.44-39.69	53.38-30.83	32.67-25.50	29.33-21.33	26.92-21.08
P/E Ratio	16.3-9.6	17.5-13.5	23.5-15.7	21.8-12.6	14.0-10.9	13.4-9.8	11.5-9.0
Average Yield %	3.7	2.8	2.3	2.4	3.3	3.5	3.5

Statistics are as originally reported. Adj. for 3-for-2 splits, 9/97. [1] Incl. one-time pre-tax SAIF chg. of $1.1 mill. [2] Incl. $2.1 mill. gain fr. the sale of seven offices. [3] Incl. a pre-tax gain of $17.9 million fr. the sale of the Co.'s credit card portfolio.

OFFICERS:
B. J. Fitzpatrick, Chmn., Pres., C.E.O.
R. F. Bowman, Exec. V.P., C.F.O., Treas.
B. J. Chapman, V.P., Sec.

INVESTOR CONTACT: Barbara J. Chapman, V.P., Sec., (800) 995-9416

PRINCIPAL OFFICE: 6400 Arlington Boulevard, Falls Church, VA 22042-2336

TELEPHONE NUMBER: (703) 241-4000
FAX: (703) 241-3360
WEB: www.firstvirginia.com
NO. OF EMPLOYEES: 4,887 full-time; 512 part-time
SHAREHOLDERS: 19,148
ANNUAL MEETING: In April
INCORPORATED: VA, Oct., 1949

INSTITUTIONAL HOLDINGS:
No. of Institutions: 172
Shares Held: 13,087,135
% Held: 28.4

INDUSTRY: State commercial banks (SIC: 6022)

TRANSFER AGENT(S): Registrar and Transfer Company, Cranford, NJ

NYSE SYMBOL FE
Rec. Pr. 30.65 (5/31/01)

FIRSTENERGY CORP.

YIELD 4.9%
P/E RATIO 11.4

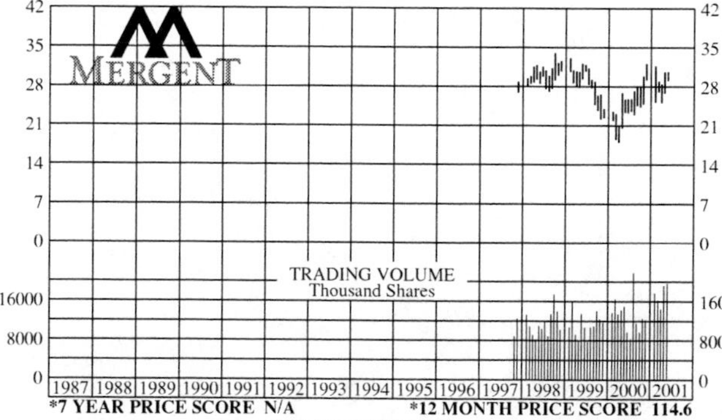

***7 YEAR PRICE SCORE N/A** ***12 MONTH PRICE SCORE 114.6**

*NYSE COMPOSITE INDEX=100

INTERIM EARNINGS (Per Share):

Qtr.	Mar.	June	Sept.	Dec.
1997		1.94		
1998	0.56	0.27	0.71	0.41
1999	0.60	0.55	0.82	0.53
2000	0.63	0.60	0.89	0.57

INTERIM DIVIDENDS (Per Share):

Amt.	Decl.	Ex.	Rec.	Pay.
0.375Q	4/18/00	5/03/00	5/05/00	6/01/00
0.375Q	7/18/00	8/03/00	8/07/00	9/01/00
0.375Q	10/17/00	11/03/00	11/07/00	12/01/00
0.375Q	1/16/01	2/05/01	2/07/01	3/01/01
0.375Q	4/17/01	5/03/01	5/07/01	6/01/01

Indicated div.: $1.50

CAPITALIZATION (12/31/00):

	($000)	(%)
Long-Term Debt	5,742,048	43.2
Deferred Income Tax	2,094,107	15.7
Redeemable Pfd. Stock	161,105	1.2
Preferred Stock	648,395	4.9
Common & Surplus	4,653,126	35.0
Total	13,298,781	100.0

RECENT DEVELOPMENTS: For the twelve months ended 12/31/00, net income rose 5.4% to $599.0 million versus $568.3 million in the previous year. Earnings growth was primarily due to increased revenues from unregulated businesses, lower fuel and financing cost. Total revenues rose 11.2% to $7.03 billion from $6.32 billion a year earlier. Sales from electric utilities slipped 0.6% to $5.42 billion, while unregulated business sales grew 85.6% to $1.61 billion. Operating income fell 2.0% to $1.50 billion.

PROSPECTS: Going forward, FE should continue to benefit from higher electric sales, economic growth in the local economy and increased power sales to customers in unregulated energy markets, including Pennsylvania, New Jersey, Maryland and Delaware. Separately, the Federal Energy Regulatory Commission approved the Company's pending acquisition of New Jersey-based GPU, Inc. Upon completion, FE will be the sixth-largest investor-owned electric system in the U.S.

BUSINESS

FIRSTENERGY CORPORATION was formed upon the merger of Ohio Edison and Centerior Energy on November 8, 1997. FE's major utility operating companies are: Ohio Edison, Pennsylvania Power, The Illuminating Company and Toledo Edison. The subsidiary companies include Roth Brothers, Inc. and RPC Mechanical, Inc., which are providers of engineered heating, ventilation, and air-conditioning equipment, and energy management and control systems. Through FirstEnergy's subsidiaries, FE serves 2.2 million customers within 13,200 square miles of northern and central Ohio and western Pennsylvania. As of 12/31/00, FE possesses nearly 12,000 megawatts of generating capacity, 8,713 miles of transmission lines, and 35 interconnections with eight electric systems.

BUSINESS LINE ANALYSIS

(12/31/00)	REV (%)	INC (%)
Regulated Services	53.4	87.5
Competitive Services	43.1	12.2
Other Business Segment	3.5	0.3
Total	100.0	100.0

ANNUAL FINANCIAL DATA

	12/31/00	12/31/99	12/31/98	12/31/97	12/31/96	12/31/95
Earnings Per Share	**2.69**	**2.50**	**[2] 1.95**	**[1] 1.94**	**2.10**	**2.05**
Cash Flow Per Share	**7.35**	**7.04**	**5.58**	**5.34**	**5.12**	**4.37**
Tang. Book Val. Per Share	**11.42**	**10.47**	**9.62**	**8.91**	**16.41**	...
Dividends Per Share	**1.50**	**1.50**	**1.50**	...	...	...
Dividend Payout %	**55.8**	**60.0**	**76.9**	...	...	...
INCOME STATEMENT (IN MILLIONS):						
Total Revenues	7,029.0	6,319.6	5,861.3	2,821.4	2,469.8	2,465.8
Costs & Expenses	4,488.7	3,752.1	3,674.9	1,545.9	1,315.8	1,374.4
Depreciation & Amort.	1,035.4	1,032.2	822.3	535.8	434.5	332.8
Operating Income	1,504.9	1,535.4	1,364.1	556.0	530.1	566.6
Net Interest Inc./(Exp.)	d493.5	d509.2	d542.8	d284.2	d240.1	d262.3
Income Taxes	376.8	394.8	321.7	183.8	189.4	192.0
Net Income	599.0	568.3	[2] 441.4	[1] 305.8	302.7	294.7
Cash Flow	1,634.3	1,600.5	1,263.7	841.6	737.2	627.6
Average Shs. Outstg. (000)	222,444	227,227	226,373	157,464	144,095	143,692
BALANCE SHEET (IN MILLIONS):						
Gross Property	12,838.6	15,012.5	15,255.3	15,209.1	8,733.2	...
Accumulated Depreciation	5,263.5	5,919.2	6,012.8	5,635.9	3,226.3	...
Net Property	7,575.1	9,093.3	9,242.6	9,573.2	5,507.0	...
Total Assets	17,941.3	18,224.0	18,063.5	18,080.8	9,054.5	...
Long-Term Obligations	5,742.0	6,001.3	6,352.4	6,969.8	2,712.8	...
Net Stockholders' Equity	5,301.5	5,212.3	5,109.4	4,819.8	2,715.2	...
Year-end Shs. Outstg. (000)	224,532	232,454	237,069	230,207	152,569	...
STATISTICAL RECORD:						
Operating Profit Margin %	21.4	24.3	23.3	19.7	21.5	23.0
Net Profit Margin %	8.5	9.0	7.5	10.8	12.3	12.0
Net Inc./Net Property %	7.9	6.2	4.8	3.2	5.5	...
Net Inc./Tot. Capital %	4.5	4.1	3.1	2.1	4.1	...
Return on Equity %	11.3	10.9	8.6	6.3	11.1	...
Accum. Depr./Gross Prop. %	41.0	39.4	39.4	37.1	36.9	...
Price Range	32.13-18.00	33.19-22.13	34.06-27.06	28.81-26.88	...	...
P/E Ratio	11.9-6.7	13.3-8.8	17.5-13.9	14.9-13.9	...	...
Average Yield %	6.0	5.4	4.9	...	...	...

Statistics are as originally reported. [1] Incl. non-recurr. chrg. $34.0 mill. ($0.17/sh) [2] Bef. extraordinary item of $30.5 mill.

OFFICERS:
H. P. Burg, Chmn., C.E.O.
A. J. Alexander, Pres.
R. H. Marsh, V.P., C.F.O.

INVESTOR CONTACT: Kurt E. Turosky, Investor Relations, (330) 384-5500

PRINCIPAL OFFICE: 76 South Main Street, Akron, OH 44308-1890

TELEPHONE NUMBER: (330) 384-5500
FAX: (330) 384-3772
WEB: www.firstenergycorp.com

NO. OF EMPLOYEES: 13,461 (avg.)

SHAREHOLDERS: 180,679

ANNUAL MEETING: In May

INCORPORATED: OH, Nov., 1997

INSTITUTIONAL HOLDINGS:
No. of Institutions: 262
Shares Held: 115,824,961
% Held: 51.7

INDUSTRY: Electric services (SIC: 4911)

TRANSFER AGENT(S): The Company

NYSE SYMBOL FSH
Rec. Pr. 29.70 (4/30/01)

FISHER SCIENTIFIC INTERNATIONAL INC.

YIELD	...
P/E RATIO	60.6

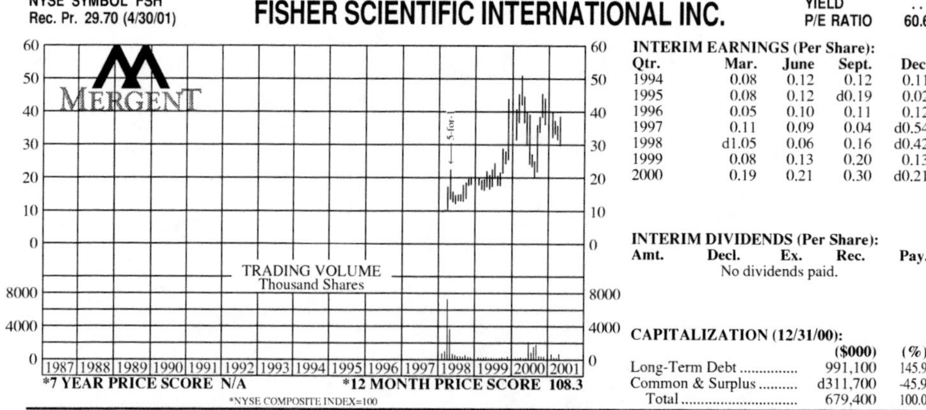

*7 YEAR PRICE SCORE N/A *12 MONTH PRICE SCORE 108.3
*NYSE COMPOSITE INDEX=100

INTERIM EARNINGS (Per Share):

Qtr.	Mar.	June	Sept.	Dec.
1994	0.08	0.12	0.12	0.11
1995	0.08	0.12	d0.19	0.02
1996	0.05	0.10	0.11	0.12
1997	0.11	0.09	0.04	d0.54
1998	d1.05	0.06	0.16	d0.42
1999	0.08	0.13	0.20	0.13
2000	0.19	0.21	0.30	d0.21

INTERIM DIVIDENDS (Per Share):

Amt.	Decl.	Ex.	Rec.	Pay.

No dividends paid.

CAPITALIZATION (12/31/00):

	($000)	(%)
Long-Term Debt	991,100	145.9
Common & Surplus	d311,700	-45.9
Total	679,400	100.0

RECENT DEVELOPMENTS: For the year ended 12/31/00, net income slipped 3.0% to $22.7 million compared with $23.4 million in 1999. Results for 2000 included a non-recurring charge of $8.4 million. Results for 1999 included a loss of $11.3 million from the disposal of operations. Sales were $2.62 billion, up 4.3% from $2.51 billion the year before. Operating income increased 6.5% to $156.3 million compared with $146.8 million in the previous year.

PROSPECTS: On 2/14/01, the Company announced that it has completed the acquisition of the pharmaceutical packaging services business of Covance Inc. for $137.5 million. The acquired business, which was renamed Fisher Clinical Services Inc., is a provider of contract packaging services for clinical trials to major pharmaceutical and biotechnology companies. The new operation should enhance FSH's current service offerings.

BUSINESS

FISHER SCIENTIFIC INTERNATIONAL is engaged principally in the supply, marketing, service and manufacture of scientific, clinical, educational, occupational health and safety products. FSH provides more than 260,000 scientific products and services to research, health care, industrial, educational and governmental markets in 145 countries. FSH serves scientists engaged in biomedical, biotechnology, pharmaceutical, chemical and other fields of R&D, and is a supplier to clinical laboratories, hospitals, health care alliances, physicians' offices, environmental testing centers, remediation companies, quality-control laboratories and many other customers. On 1/21/98, FSH acquired FSI Merger Corporation and recapitalized. FSH completed the spin-off of its ProcureNet, Inc. subsidiary on 4/15/99.

ANNUAL FINANCIAL DATA

	12/31/00	12/31/99	12/31/98	12/31/97	12/31/96	12/31/95	12/31/94
Earnings Per Share	**[5] 0.51**	**[4] 0.55**	**[3] d1.24**	**[2] d0.30**	**[1] 0.39**	**[1] 0.04**	**0.44**
Cash Flow Per Share	**1.94**	**2.00**	**0.09**	**0.16**	**0.78**	**0.39**	**...**
Tang. Book Val. Per Share	**...**	**...**	**...**	**0.94**	**0.93**	**...**	**0.87**
INCOME STATEMENT (IN MILLIONS):							
Total Revenues	2,622.3	2,469.7	2,252.3	2,175.3	2,144.4	1,435.8	1,126.7
Costs & Expenses	2,402.4	2,260.5	2,176.5	2,107.2	2,005.2	1,388.7	1,043.4
Depreciation & Amort.	63.6	62.4	53.0	47.0	44.6	28.9	19.4
Operating Income	156.3	146.8	22.8	21.1	94.6	18.2	63.9
Net Interest Inc./(Exp.)	d99.1	d104.2	d90.3	d23.0	d27.1	d15.0	d9.0
Income Before Income Taxes	37.8	57.8	d60.3	d5.1	67.6	4.3	62.7
Income Taxes	15.1	34.4	cr10.8	25.4	30.8	1.1	27.0
Net Income	[5] 22.7	[4] 23.4	[3] d49.5	[2] d30.5	[1] 36.8	[1] 3.2	35.7
Cash Flow	86.3	85.8	3.5	16.5	81.4	32.1	55.1
Average Shs. Outstg. (000)	44,400	42,800	40,000	101,500	104,000	82,000	...
BALANCE SHEET (IN MILLIONS):							
Cash & Cash Equivalents	66.0	50.3	65.6	18.2	24.7	63.7	44.5
Total Current Assets	650.6	634.8	561.1	592.4	652.8	673.6	358.2
Net Property	251.3	247.5	246.0	223.6	209.5	207.6	127.9
Total Assets	1,385.7	1,402.6	1,357.6	1,176.5	1,262.7	1,270.5	722.5
Total Current Liabilities	507.8	519.5	453.2	354.9	393.0	389.6	195.4
Long-Term Obligations	991.1	1,011.1	1,022.0	267.8	281.5	446.3	128.4
Net Stockholders' Equity	d311.7	d330.6	d324.7	347.1	386.2	226.0	218.6
Net Working Capital	142.8	115.3	107.9	237.5	259.8	284.0	162.8
Year-end Shs. Outstg. (000)	40,116	40,053	40,034	101,785	100,655	81,285	80,195
STATISTICAL RECORD:							
Operating Profit Margin %	6.0	5.9	1.0	1.0	4.4	1.3	5.7
Net Profit Margin %	0.9	0.9	...	...	1.7	0.2	3.2
Return on Equity %	...	...	...	...	9.5	1.4	16.3
Return on Assets %	1.6	1.7	...	...	2.9	0.3	4.9
Debt/Total Assets %	71.5	72.1	75.3	22.8	22.3	35.1	17.8
Price Range	51.00-19.88	44.00-16.13	22.50-9.56	...	...	...	...
P/E Ratio	100.0-39.0	80.0-29.3	...	...	...	...	...

Statistics are as originally reported. Adj. for 5-for-1 split, 4/98. [1] Incl. $11.0 mill. non-recur. chgs., 1996; $31.5 mill., 1995. [2] Incl. $76.5 mill. one-time noncash chgs. [3] Incl. $71.0 mill. trans-related costs, $23.6 mill. restr. & other chgs. & $15.1 mill. loss fr. disp. ops. [4] Incl. $11.3 mill. loss fr. disposal of ops. & $1.5 mill. non-recur. credits. [5] Incl. $8.4 mill. non-recur. expense.

OFFICERS:
P. M. Montrone, Chmn., C.E.O.
P. M. Meister, Vice-Chmn., Exec. V.P., C.F.O.
D. T. Della Penta, Pres., C.O.O.

INVESTOR CONTACT: Matthew E. Murphy, Dir. of Inv. Rel., (800) 258-0850

PRINCIPAL OFFICE: One Liberty Lane, Hampton, NH 03842

TELEPHONE NUMBER: (603) 926-5911
FAX: (603) 929-2409
WEB: www.fishersci.com

NO. OF EMPLOYEES: 7,400 (approx.)

SHAREHOLDERS: 159 (approx., record)

ANNUAL MEETING: In May

INCORPORATED: DE, Sept., 1991

INSTITUTIONAL HOLDINGS:
No. of Institutions: 52
Shares Held: 35,152,041
% Held: 87.6

INDUSTRY: Professional equipment, nec (SIC: 5049)

TRANSFER AGENT(S): Mellon Investor Services, Ridgefield Park, NJ

NYSE SYMBOL FBF
Rec. Pr. 38.37 (4/30/01)

FLEETBOSTON FINANCIAL CORPORATION

YIELD 3.4%
P/E RATIO 10.4

INTERIM EARNINGS (Per Share):

Qtr.	Mar.	June	Sept.	Dec.
1997	0.55	0.60	0.60	0.62
1998	0.53	0.65	0.66	0.69
1999	0.72	0.74	0.74	d0.05
2000	1.03	0.91	0.90	0.84

INTERIM DIVIDENDS (Per Share):

Amt.	Decl.	Ex.	Rec.	Pay.
0.30Q	4/18/00	5/31/00	6/03/00	7/01/00
0.30Q	8/16/00	8/30/00	9/03/00	10/01/00
0.33Q	10/17/00	11/29/00	12/03/00	1/01/01
0.33Q	2/21/01	2/28/01	3/03/01	4/01/01
0.33Q	4/17/01	5/30/01	6/03/01	7/01/01

Indicated div.: $1.32 (Div. Reinv. Plan)

CAPITALIZATION (12/31/00):

	($000)	(%)
Total Deposits	101,290,000	69.5
Long-Term Debt	28,357,000	19.4
Preferred Stock	566,000	0.4
Common & Surplus	15,606,000	10.7
Total	145,819,000	100.0

RECENT DEVELOPMENTS: For the year ended 12/31/00, net income grew 67.8% to $3.42 billion from $2.04 billion. Earnings for 2000 and 1999 included after-tax integration charges of $137.0 million and $760.0 million, respectively, related to the acquisition of BankBoston Corp. Earnings for 2000 included an after-tax divestiture gain of $420.0 million. Net interest income slipped 3.3% to $6.52 billion. Total non-interest income grew 29.4% to $9.02 billion.

PROSPECTS: On 3/1/01, the Company completed the acquisition of Summit Bancorp. The combined company, with assets of more than $200.00 billion, ranks as the seventh largest U.S. bank holding company. Meanwhile, FBF agreed to sell five branch offices in the Atlantic City, New Jersey area to resolve antitrust concerns over its acquisition of Summit. Separately, the FBF sold $1.00 billion of troubled commercial loans.

BUSINESS

FLEETBOSTON FINANCIAL CORPORATION (formerly Fleet Financial Group, Inc.), with assets of approximately $179.52 billion as of 12/31/00, is a diversified financial services firm with offices nationwide. FBF's products and services include: consumer banking, government banking, mortgage banking and commercial real estate lending, corporate finance, credit cards, insurance services, cash management, asset-based lending, equipment leasing, and investment management services. FBF operates one of the nation's largest discount brokerage firms through its subsidiary, Quick and Reilly, Inc. On 10/1/99, FBF acquired BankBoston Corporation. On 11/19/99, the Company changed its ticker symbol to FBF from FLT.

LOAN DISTRIBUTION

(12/31/2000)	($000)	(%)
Commercial & Industrial	46,697,000	50.6
Residential Real Estate	1,925,000	2.1
Consumer	18,085,000	19.6
Comml Rl Est-Construction	6,465,000	7.0
Comml Rl Est-Interim/Perm	6,085,000	6.6
Leasing	12,959,000	14.1
Total	92,216,000	100.0

ANNUAL FINANCIAL DATA

	12/31/00	[5] 12/31/99	12/31/98	12/31/97	12/31/96	12/31/95	12/31/94
Earnings Per Share	[4] **3.68**	[3] **2.10**	**2.52**	[2] **2.37**	**1.98**	[1] **0.79**	**1.88**
Tang. Book Val. Per Share	**9.85**	**7.78**	**7.36**	**6.54**	**6.10**	**6.79**	**6.80**
Dividends Per Share	**1.20**	**1.08**	**0.98**	**0.90**	**0.86**	**0.80**	**0.65**
Dividend Payout %	**32.6**	**51.4**	**38.9**	**38.0**	**43.5**	**101.9**	**34.7**
INCOME STATEMENT (IN MILLIONS):							
Total Interest Income	13,584.0	13,052.0	6,765.0	5,848.0	5,842.0	6,025.0	3,272.0
Total Interest Expense	7,063.0	6,310.0	2,896.0	2,221.0	2,439.0	3,005.0	1,290.0
Net Interest Income	6,521.0	6,742.0	3,869.0	3,627.0	3,403.0	3,020.0	1,982.0
Provision for Loan Losses	1,196.0	933.0	470.0	322.0	213.0	101.0	62.0
Non-Interest Income	9,024.0	6,974.0	3,237.0	2,247.0	2,201.0	1,675.0	1,173.0
Non-Interest Expense	8,633.0	9,357.0	4,129.0	3,381.0	3,460.0	3,560.0	2,070.0
Income Before Taxes	5,716.0	3,426.0	2,507.0	2,171.0	1,931.0	1,034.0	1,023.0
Equity Earnings/Minority Int.	...	...	...	...	...	...	d12.0
Net Income	[4] 3,420.0	[3] 2,038.0	1,532.0	[2] 1,303.0	1,139.0	[1] 610.0	613.0
Average Shs. Outstg. (000)	919,869	943,528	588,000	524,000	538,000	530,000	318,000
BALANCE SHEET (IN MILLIONS):							
Cash & Due from Banks	11,502.0	10,627.0	5,635.0	4,983.0	7,243.0	4,505.0	5,208.0
Securities Avail. for Sale	7,081.0	7,849.0	...	...	7,503.0	18,533.0	11,244.0
Total Loans & Leases	109,372.0	119,700.0	70,562.0	62,081.0	59,508.0	52,089.0	27,994.0
Allowance for Credit Losses	2,378.0	2,488.0	2,718.0	2,334.0	2,152.0	1,885.0	1,406.0
Net Loans & Leases	106,994.0	117,212.0	67,844.0	59,747.0	57,356.0	50,204.0	26,588.0
Total Assets	179,519.0	190,692.0	104,382.0	85,535.0	85,518.0	84,432.0	49,648.0
Total Deposits	101,290.0	114,896.0	69,678.0	63,735.0	67,071.0	57,122.0	34,806.0
Long-Term Obligations	28,357.0	25,349.0	8,820.0	4,500.0	5,114.0	6,481.0	...
Total Liabilities	163,347.0	175,385.0	94,973.0	77,501.0	78,103.0	78,067.0	45,377.0
Net Stockholders' Equity	16,172.0	15,307.0	9,409.0	8,034.0	7,415.0	6,365.0	3,380.0
Year-end Shs. Outstg. (000)	907,000	915,660	570,000	526,000	524,000	526,000	270,000
STATISTICAL RECORD:							
Return on Equity %	21.1	13.3	16.3	16.2	15.4	9.6	18.1
Return on Assets %	1.9	1.1	1.5	1.5	1.3	0.7	1.2
Equity/Assets %	9.0	8.0	9.0	9.4	8.7	7.5	6.8
Non-Int. Exp./Tot. Inc. %	55.5	68.2	58.1	57.6	61.7	73.1	65.6
Price Range	43.75-25.13	46.81-33.25	45.38-30.00	37.59-24.38	28.13-18.81	21.63-14.94	20.69-14.94
P/E Ratio	11.9-6.8	22.3-15.8	18.0-11.9	15.9-10.3	14.2-9.5	27.5-19.0	11.0-8.0
Average Yield %	3.5	2.7	2.6	2.9	3.7	4.4	3.6

Statistics are as originally reported. Adj. for 2-for-1 stk. split, 10/98. [1] Incl. after-tax merger chrgs. & loss on assets held for disposition totaling $429.0 mill. [2] Incl. pre-tax gain of $175.0 mill fr. the sale of bus. & pre-tax restr. chrg. of $155.0 mill. [3] Incl. after-tax merger & rel. charges of $760.0 mill. [4] Incl. after-tax integration chrgs. of $137.0 mill. rel. to the acq. of BankBoston Corp. & an after-tax divest. gain of $420.0 mill. [5] Incl. the acq. of BankBoston Corp. on 10/1/99.

OFFICERS:
T. Murray, Chmn., C.E.O.
E. M. McQuade, Vice-Chmn., C.F.O.

INVESTOR CONTACT: John Kahwaty, Investor Relations, (617) 434-3650

PRINCIPAL OFFICE: 100 Federal Street, Boston, MA 02110-2010

TELEPHONE NUMBER: (617) 434-2200
FAX: (617) 346-4000
WEB: www.fleet.com

NO. OF EMPLOYEES: 53,000 (approx.)

SHAREHOLDERS: 67,166 (record)

ANNUAL MEETING: In April

INCORPORATED: RI, May, 1970

INSTITUTIONAL HOLDINGS:
No. of Institutions: 674
Shares Held: 607,704,155
% Held: 56.1

INDUSTRY: National commercial banks (SIC: 6021)

TRANSFER AGENT(S): First Chicago Trust Company of New York, Jersey City, NJ

NYSE SYMBOL FLE
Rec. Pr. 12.94 (4/30/01)

FLEETWOOD ENTERPRISES, INC.

YIELD 1.2%
P/E RATIO . . .

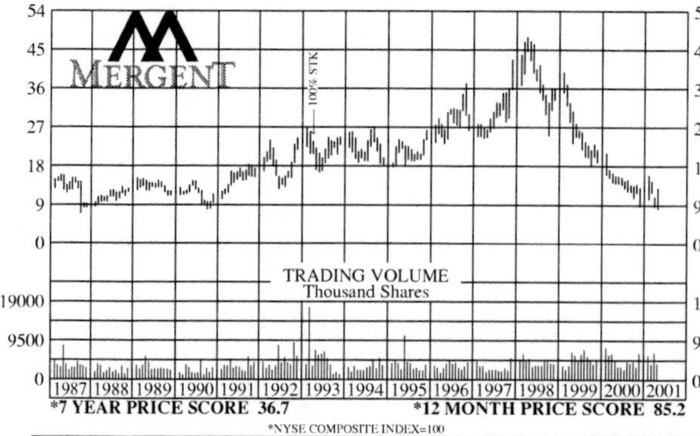

INTERIM EARNINGS (Per Share):

Qtr.	July	Oct.	Jan.	Apr.
1996-97	0.64	0.68	0.38	0.60
1997-98	0.84	0.77	0.57	0.81
1998-99	0.86	0.84	0.59	0.66
1999-00	0.72	0.84	0.48	0.37
2000-01	d0.61	d0.10	d6.26	. . .

INTERIM DIVIDENDS (Per Share):

Amt.	Decl.	Ex.	Rec.	Pay.
0.19Q	3/14/00	4/05/00	4/07/00	5/10/00
0.19Q	6/13/00	7/05/00	7/07/00	8/09/00
0.19Q	9/12/00	10/04/00	10/06/00	11/08/00
0.04Q	12/13/00	1/03/01	1/05/01	2/14/01
0.04Q	3/13/01	4/04/01	4/06/01	5/09/01

Indicated div.: $0.16

CAPITALIZATION (4/30/00):

	($000)	(%)
Long-Term Debt	80,000	7.8
Deferred Income Tax	67,750	6.6
Redeemable Pfd. Stock	287,500	28.2
Common & Surplus	584,805	57.3
Total	1,020,055	100.0

RECENT DEVELOPMENTS: For the quarter ended 1/28/01, FLE incurred a net loss of $205.0 million compared with net income of $15.9 million in the year-earlier quarter. Results for 2000 included nonrecurring charges of $174.1 million. Sales declined 40.1% to $510.2 million. Manufactured housing operating revenues decreased 38.1% to $251.7 million. Recreational vehicles operating revenues fell 42.1% to $251.3 million.

PROSPECTS: FLE has received a bank commitment for a senior credit facility of up to $260.0 million. The secured facility, led by Bank of America, will be structured as a three-year, $230.0 million syndicated revolver with an additional $30.0 million available as a one-year term loan. Approximately $80.0 million of the proceeds from the transaction will be used to retire notes payable to The Prudential Insurance Company of America.

BUSINESS

FLEETWOOD ENTERPRISES, INC. is a producer of recreational vehicles and manufactured homes. FLE's motor homes, travel trailers, folding trailers and slide-in truck campers are used for leisure-time activities, including vacation, sightseeing and fishing trips. FLE operates manufacturing plants in 10 U.S. states and in Canada. Products are marketed through independent dealers. For the fiscal year ended 4/30/00, sales were derived: RVs, 51.6%; manufactured housing, 47.1%; and supply operations, 1.3%. In May 1996, the Company sold its RV finance subsidiary, Fleetwood Credit Corp.

ANNUAL FINANCIAL DATA

	4/30/00	4/25/99	4/26/98	4/27/97	4/28/96	4/30/95	4/24/94
Earnings Per Share	**[5] 2.41**	**2.94**	**[4] 3.01**	**[3] 2.30**	**[2] 1.50**	**1.82**	**[1] 1.43**
Cash Flow Per Share	**3.03**	**3.46**	**3.69**	**3.00**	**2.09**	**2.34**	**1.90**
Tang. Book Val. Per Share	**10.08**	**9.63**	**11.96**	**12.40**	**14.22**	**13.20**	**11.88**
Dividends Per Share	**0.74**	**0.70**	**0.66**	**0.62**	**0.58**	**0.53**	**0.49**
Dividend Payout %	**30.7**	**23.8**	**21.9**	**27.0**	**38.7**	**29.1**	**34.3**
INCOME STATEMENT (IN MILLIONS):							
Total Revenues	3,713.0	3,490.2	3,050.6	2,874.4	2,809.3	2,855.7	2,369.4
Costs & Expenses	3,515.7	3,268.0	2,852.6	2,707.3	2,650.7	2,694.6	2,244.6
Depreciation & Amort.	35.1	31.8	27.8	27.6	27.1	24.1	20.4
Operating Income	162.2	190.3	170.2	139.6	131.5	136.9	104.4
Net Interest Inc./(Exp.)	d15.2	d9.8	d3.6	d4.0	d1.4	d4.0	d2.5
Income Before Income Taxes	141.5	178.9	174.9	147.1	111.0	142.1	112.0
Income Taxes	58.0	71.8	66.4	57.0	41.5	58.3	45.9
Equity Earnings/Minority Int.	. . .	. . .	. . .	. . .	0.5	0.8	1.3
Net Income	[5] 83.5	107.1	[4] 108.5	[3] 90.1	[2] 69.9	84.6	[1] 67.4
Cash Flow	118.6	139.0	136.3	117.6	97.0	108.8	87.8
Average Shs. Outstg. (000)	39,194	40,171	36,933	39,162	46,469	46,531	46,207
BALANCE SHEET (IN MILLIONS):							
Cash & Cash Equivalents	125.8	257.3	284.1	110.4	287.9	198.2	158.5
Total Current Assets	806.9	820.2	682.9	437.0	696.7	950.8	886.4
Net Property	312.1	303.9	277.2	278.3	266.6	263.1	220.8
Total Assets	1,536.7	1,531.2	1,129.5	871.5	1,108.9	1,345.1	1,224.1
Total Current Liabilities	490.4	514.7	325.8	225.8	197.6	574.8	534.9
Long-Term Obligations	80.0	55.0	55.0	55.0	80.0	. . .	. . .
Net Stockholders' Equity	584.8	586.7	376.0	443.1	649.1	608.1	546.5
Net Working Capital	316.6	305.5	357.0	211.3	499.1	376.0	351.5
Year-end Shs. Outstg. (000)	32,712	35,198	31,451	35,747	45,640	46,062	45,996
STATISTICAL RECORD:							
Operating Profit Margin %	4.4	5.5	5.6	4.9	4.7	4.8	4.4
Net Profit Margin %	2.2	3.1	3.6	3.1	2.5	3.0	2.8
Return on Equity %	14.3	18.3	28.9	20.3	10.8	13.9	12.3
Return on Assets %	5.4	7.0	9.6	10.3	6.3	6.3	5.5
Debt/Total Assets %	5.2	3.6	4.9	6.3	7.2	. . .	. . .
Price Range	39.81-18.00	48.00-25.00	42.81-24.38	37.25-23.13	26.38-17.75	27.25-17.88	26.88-16.50
P/E Ratio	16.5-7.5	16.3-8.5	14.2-8.1	16.2-10.1	17.6-11.8	15.0-9.8	18.8-11.5
Average Yield %	2.6	1.9	2.0	2.1	2.6	2.3	2.3

Statistics are as originally reported. [1] Bef. acctg. chrg. of $1.5 mill. [2] Bef. discont. oper. gain $9.7 mill. and incl. non-recurring chrg. of $16.4 mill. [3] Bef. discont. oper. gain of $34.8 mill. [4] Incl. non-recurr. pre-tax gain $16.2 mill. [5] Incl. non-recurr. pre-tax chrg. of $4.0 mill.

OFFICERS:
G. F. Kummer, Chmn.
N. W. Potter, Pres., C.E.O.
B. R. Plowman, Sr. V.P., C.F.O.

INVESTOR CONTACT: Boyd Plowman, Sr. V.P., Finance, (909) 351-3504

PRINCIPAL OFFICE: 3125 Myers Street, Riverside, CA 92513-7638

TELEPHONE NUMBER: (909) 351-3500
FAX: (909) 351-3690
WEB: www.fleetwood.com

NO. OF EMPLOYEES: 20,700 (approx.)

SHAREHOLDERS: 1,400 (approx.)

ANNUAL MEETING: In Sept.

INCORPORATED: CA, 1957; reincorp., DE, Sept., 1977

INSTITUTIONAL HOLDINGS:
No. of Institutions: 105
Shares Held: 28,228,691
% Held: 86.2

INDUSTRY: Motor homes (SIC: 3716)

TRANSFER AGENT(S): BankBoston, N.A., Boston, MA

NYSE SYMBOL FLM
Rec. Pr. 31.77 (5/31/01)

FLEMING COMPANIES, INC.

YIELD 0.3%
P/E RATIO . . .

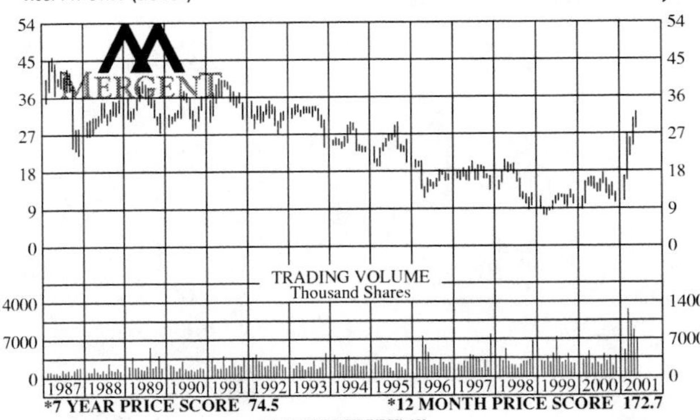

INTERIM EARNINGS (Per Share):

Qtr.	Apr.	July	Sept.	Dec.
1996	0.16	0.25	0.03	0.27
1997	0.14	0.39	0.20	0.29
1998	0.40	0.36	d0.06	d14.11
1999	d0.64	d0.06	d0.37	d0.10
2000	d0.67	d0.35	d1.17	d0.96

INTERIM DIVIDENDS (Per Share):

Amt.	Decl.	Ex.	Rec.	Pay.
0.02Q	7/19/00	8/16/00	8/18/00	9/11/00
0.02Q	9/20/00	11/16/00	11/20/00	12/08/00
0.02Q	1/23/01	2/15/01	2/20/01	3/09/01
0.02Q	2/28/01	5/16/01	5/18/01	6/08/01
0.02Q	5/15/01	8/16/01	8/20/01	9/10/01

Indicated div.: $0.08 (Div. Reinv. Plan)

CAPITALIZATION (12/30/00):

	($000)	(%)
Long-Term Debt	1,232,400	60.5
Capital Lease Obligations..	377,239	18.5
Common & Surplus	427,192	21.0
Total	2,036,831	100.0

RECENT DEVELOPMENTS: For the 53 weeks ended 12/30/00, net loss totaled $122.1 million versus a net loss of $44.7 million in the corresponding 52-week period the year before. Results included one-time pre-tax impairment/restructuring charges of $212.8 million and $103.0 million in 2000 and 1999, respectively. Net sales rose 1.2% to $14.44 billion from $14.27 billion a year earlier. Net sales for the distribution segment grew 5.8% to $11.17 billion, while net sales for the retail food segment slipped 11.9% to $3.28 billion.

PROSPECTS: On 2/7/01, the Company announced that it has entered into a supply chain agreement with Kmart Corporation, under which FLM will be the sole supplier of food and beverages to more than 2,100 Kmart and Kmart supercenter stores. The 10-year deal, which is valued at about $4.50 billion annually, includes grocery, meat, produce, frozen foods, dairy and other grocery items and is expected to boost FLM's total distribution revenue to $17.00 billion annually.

BUSINESS

FLEMING COMPANIES, INC. operates in two business segments, distribution and retail. The distribution segment (77.3% of 2000 net sales) sells food and non-food products to approximately 3,000 supermarkets, 3,000 convenience stores, and almost 1,000 supercenters, discount, limited assortment, drug, specialty, and other stores in 41 states. The retail segment (22.7%) is a major food and general merchandise retailer, including approximately 240 Company-owned supermarkets in eight states.

QUARTERLY DATA

(12/30/2000)($000)	REV	INC
1st Quarter	4,331,498	(25,873)
2nd Quarter	3,289,878	(13,349)
3rd Quarter	3,197,655	(45,559)
4th Quarter	3,624,784	(37,361)

ANNUAL FINANCIAL DATA

	12/30/00	12/25/99	12/26/98	12/27/97	12/28/96	12/31/95	12/31/94
Earnings Per Share	**[4] d3.15**	**[4] d1.17**	**[3] d13.48**	**[2] 1.02**	**[1] 0.71**	**1.12**	**1.51**
Cash Flow Per Share	**1.34**	**3.07**	**d8.58**	**5.81**	**5.67**	**5.93**	**5.42**
Tang. Book Val. Per Share	. . .	. . .	. . .	**3.31**	**2.10**	**1.65**	**2.42**
Dividends Per Share	**0.08**	**0.08**	**0.08**	**0.08**	**0.36**	**1.20**	**1.20**
Dividend Payout %	. . .	. . .	. . .	**7.8**	**50.7**	**107.1**	**79.5**
INCOME STATEMENT (IN MILLIONS):							
Total Revenues	14,443.8	14,645.6	15,069.3	15,372.7	16,486.7	17,501.6	15,753.5
Costs & Expenses	14,107.8	14,307.7	14,685.2	14,955.1	16,091.7	17,099.4	15,424.0
Depreciation & Amort.	174.1	162.4	185.4	181.4	187.6	180.8	145.9
Operating Income	161.9	175.5	198.8	236.3	207.4	221.3	183.6
Net Interest Inc./(Exp.)	d141.9	d124.9	d124.8	d115.9	d114.3	d117.2	d56.5
Income Before Income Taxes	d200.9	d62.6	d598.2	82.7	54.6	85.9	112.3
Income Taxes	cr78.7	cr17.9	cr87.6	44.0	27.9	43.9	56.2
Equity Earnings/Minority Int.	d8.0	d10.2	d11.6	d16.7	d18.5	d27.2	d14.8
Net Income	[4] d122.1	[4] d44.7	[3] d510.6	[2] 38.7	[1] 26.7	42.0	56.2
Cash Flow	52.0	117.7	d325.2	220.1	214.3	222.8	202.1
Average Shs. Outstg. (000)	38,716	38,305	37,887	37,862	37,774	37,577	37,254
BALANCE SHEET (IN MILLIONS):							
Cash & Cash Equivalents	30.4	6.7	6.0	30.3	63.7	4.4	28.4
Total Current Assets	1,623.1	1,728.8	1,587.9	1,495.0	1,563.6	1,650.8	1,820.1
Net Property	716.5	838.2	820.1	949.8	959.1	995.2	988.1
Total Assets	3,402.8	3,573.2	3,490.8	3,924.0	4,055.2	4,296.7	4,608.3
Total Current Liabilities	1,232.4	1,283.7	1,281.1	1,154.6	1,342.9	1,286.4	1,323.6
Long-Term Obligations	1,609.6	1,602.1	1,503.4	1,494.4	1,453.3	1,716.9	1,994.8
Net Stockholders' Equity	427.2	560.7	569.9	1,089.7	1,076.0	1,083.3	1,078.6
Net Working Capital	390.7	445.0	306.8	340.4	220.7	364.4	496.4
Year-end Shs. Outstg. (000)	39,618	38,856	38,542	38,264	37,798	37,716	37,480
STATISTICAL RECORD:							
Operating Profit Margin %	1.1	1.2	1.3	1.5	1.3	1.3	1.2
Net Profit Margin %	. . .	. . .	. . .	0.3	0.2	0.2	0.4
Return on Equity %	. . .	. . .	. . .	3.6	2.5	3.9	5.2
Return on Assets %	. . .	. . .	. . .	1.0	0.7	1.0	1.2
Debt/Total Assets %	47.3	44.8	43.1	38.1	35.8	40.0	43.3
Price Range	17.63-8.69	13.44-7.19	20.75-8.63	20.38-13.38	20.88-11.50	29.88-19.13	30.00-22.63
P/E Ratio	. . .	. . .	. . .	20.0-13.1	29.4-16.2	26.7-17.1	19.9-15.0
Average Yield %	0.6	0.8	0.5	0.5	2.2	4.9	4.6

Statistics are as originally reported. [1] Incl $20 mil chg. [2] Bef. $13.3 mil ($0.35/sh) extraord. chg. for early retirement of debt & incl. $21 mil chg. [3] Incl. $7.8 mil chg. for litigation & $652.7 mil restr. chg. [4] Incl. pre-tax restruc. chg. of $212.8 mil, 2000; $103.0 mil, 1999.

OFFICERS:
M. S. Hansen, Chmn., C.E.O.
W. J. Dowd, Pres., C.O.O
N. J. Rider, Exec. V.P., C.F.O.
INVESTOR CONTACT: Alan McIntyre, V.P. & Treas., (972) 906-8126
PRINCIPAL OFFICE: 1945 Lakepointe Drive, P.O. Box 299013, Lewisville, TX 75029

TELEPHONE NUMBER: (972) 906-8000
FAX: (972) 841-8149
WEB: www.fleming.com
NO. OF EMPLOYEES: 29,567 (avg.)
SHAREHOLDERS: 14,900
ANNUAL MEETING: In May
INCORPORATED: KS, Dec., 1915; reincorp., OK, Apr., 1915

INSTITUTIONAL HOLDINGS:
No. of Institutions: 110
Shares Held: 30,743,632
% Held: 77.3
INDUSTRY: Groceries, general line (SIC: 5141)
TRANSFER AGENT(S): EquiServe, Jersey City, NJ

NYSE SYMBOL FLA
Rec. Pr. 31.00 (4/30/01)

FLORIDA EAST COAST INDUSTRIES, INC.

YIELD 0.3%
P/E RATIO 43.7

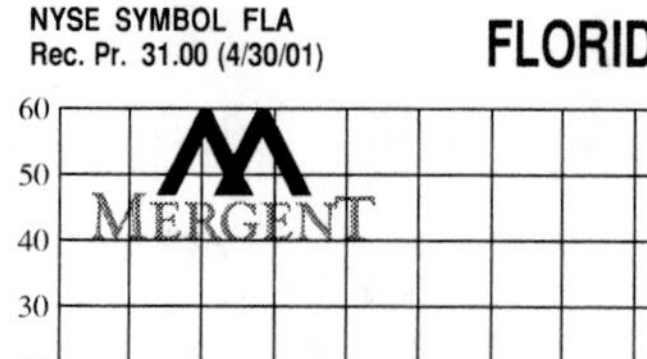

*7 YEAR PRICE SCORE 102.2 *12 MONTH PRICE SCORE 90.8

*NYSE COMPOSITE INDEX=100

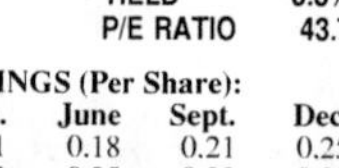

INTERIM EARNINGS (Per Share):

Qtr.	Mar.	June	Sept.	Dec.
1996	0.21	0.18	0.21	0.25
1997	0.23	0.25	0.33	0.30
1998	0.23	0.32	0.36	0.29
1999	0.46	0.10	0.23	0.33
2000	0.30	0.19	0.06	0.16

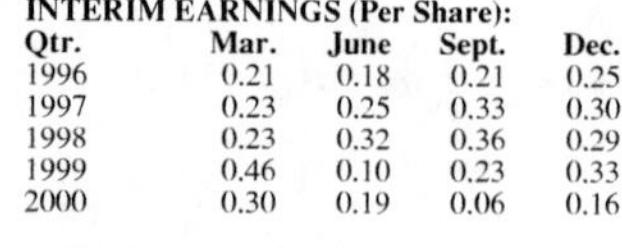

INTERIM DIVIDENDS (Per Share):

Amt.	Decl.	Ex.	Rec.	Pay.
0.025Q	5/16/00	5/31/00	6/03/00	6/14/00
0.025Q	8/31/00	9/12/00	9/14/00	9/28/00
0.025Q	12/01/00	12/12/00	12/14/00	12/28/00
0.025Q	2/22/01	3/06/01	3/08/01	3/22/01
0.025Q	5/30/01	6/12/01	6/14/01	6/28/01

Indicated div.: $0.10

CAPITALIZATION (12/31/00):

	($000)	(%)
Long-Term Debt	88,000	9.1
Deferred Income Tax	136,170	14.0
Common & Surplus	748,104	76.9
Total	972,274	100.0

RECENT DEVELOPMENTS: For the year ended 12/31/00, net income declined 36.8% to $25.8 million versus $40.8 million a year earlier. Results for 2000 included an operating loss of $14.2 million at FLA's EPIK segment versus operating income of $1.9 million in 1999. Operating revenues fell 14.7% to $276.3 million. On 2/12/01, EPIK announced an expansion of its national fiber network by executing a dark fiber transaction with El Paso Global Networks, resulting in an additional 1,600 route miles.

PROSPECTS: Near-term prospects are mixed. FLA's railway and trucking businesses face high fuel costs and softening economic conditions. However, the trucking business is expected to benefit from its refocus on providing railway-interchanged services. Also, 2001 rental revenues from commercial properties at Flagler are projected to rise about 13.0% to 17.0% versus the prior year through increases in rental rates from existing buildings and lease-up of buildings completed in 2000.

BUSINESS

FLORIDA EAST COAST INDUSTRIES, INC. conducts operations through four wholly-owned subsidiaries. Flagler Development Company owns, develops, leases and manages approximately 6.0 million square feet of office, service and warehouse space, including a number of industrial and commercial parks in Jacksonville, Orlando and Miami, and owns about 17,000 acres of land, all in Florida. Florida East Coast Railway Company is a regional freight railroad that operates 351 miles of mainline track from Jacksonville to Miami. Florida Express Carriers provides truckload service, intermodal drayage and transportation logistics and brokerage services. EPIK Communications, Incorporated provides bandwidth fiber capacity, dark fiber leases and collocation services to telecommunication providers.

BUSINESS LINE ANALYSIS

(12/31/2000)	Rev(%)	Inc($000)
Transportation-Rail	58.5	$46,663
Transportation-Trucking	11.2	(8,151)
Realty	26.6	20,957
Telecommunications	3.7	(14,240)
Total	100.0	$42,199

ANNUAL FINANCIAL DATA

	12/31/00	12/31/99	12/31/98	12/31/97	12/31/96	12/31/95	12/31/94
Earnings Per Share	**0.70**	**1.12**	**1.20**	**1.11**	**0.84**	**0.74**	**0.96**
Cash Flow Per Share	**1.84**	**1.98**	**2.00**	**1.77**	**1.49**	**1.35**	**1.57**
Tang. Book Val. Per Share	**20.50**	**19.90**	**18.91**	**17.88**	**16.81**	**16.07**	**15.34**
Dividends Per Share	**0.10**	**0.10**	**0.10**	**0.10**	**0.10**	**0.10**	**0.10**
Dividend Payout %	**14.3**	**8.9**	**8.3**	**9.0**	**11.9**	**13.5**	**10.4**
INCOME STATEMENT (IN MILLIONS):							
Total Revenues	276.3	324.3	247.8	250.5	208.0	201.1	199.5
Costs & Expenses	199.4	231.5	161.1	174.1	146.9	144.2	131.2
Depreciation & Amort.	41.7	31.4	28.9	24.1	23.5	22.3	21.7
Operating Income	35.2	61.4	57.8	52.3	37.6	34.6	46.6
Net Interest Inc./(Exp.)	...	...	...	4.7	4.2	4.7	4.6
Income Before Income Taxes	43.0	66.0	70.2	63.0	48.2	42.6	55.7
Income Taxes	17.3	25.2	26.6	22.8	17.7	15.9	21.1
Net Income	25.8	40.8	43.6	40.1	30.4	26.6	34.6
Cash Flow	67.5	72.2	72.5	64.2	53.9	48.9	56.4
Average Shs. Outstg. (000)	36,706	36,509	36,299	36,248	36,208	36,156	36,000
BALANCE SHEET (IN MILLIONS):							
Cash & Cash Equivalents	31.4	62.1	50.9	31.1	29.6	24.0	29.4
Total Current Assets	78.3	99.3	100.8	81.9	80.8	70.1	72.8
Net Property	989.3	742.2	720.9	663.7	636.0	608.6	561.6
Total Assets	1,111.5	910.9	867.8	825.5	789.7	756.2	722.5
Total Current Liabilities	94.9	41.4	36.3	34.4	39.6	32.1	33.1
Long-Term Obligations	88.0	...	...	...	...	...	...
Net Stockholders' Equity	748.1	724.4	686.8	648.9	608.8	581.9	552.3
Net Working Capital	d16.5	57.9	64.5	47.6	41.2	38.0	39.8
Year-end Shs. Outstg. (000)	36,485	36,395	36,326	36,288	36,208	36,208	36,000
STATISTICAL RECORD:							
Operating Profit Margin %	12.7	18.9	23.3	20.9	18.1	17.2	23.3
Net Profit Margin %	9.3	12.6	17.6	16.0	14.6	13.2	17.3
Return on Equity %	3.4	5.6	6.4	6.2	5.0	4.6	6.3
Return on Assets %	2.3	4.5	5.0	4.9	3.9	3.5	4.8
Debt/Total Assets %	7.9	...	...	...	...	...	...
Price Range	51.00-33.75	45.38-25.88	36.00-23.00	29.00-21.50	22.53-16.84	20.19-16.03	19.41-14.41
P/E Ratio	72.8-48.2	40.5-23.1	30.0-19.2	26.2-19.4	26.8-20.0	27.4-21.7	20.1-15.0
Average Yield %	0.2	0.3	0.3	0.4	0.5	0.6	0.6

Statistics are as originally reported. Adj. for 4-for-1 stk. split, 6/98

OFFICERS:
R. W. Anestis, Chmn., Pres., C.E.O.
R. G. Smith, Exec. V.P., C.F.O.
H. J. Eddins, Exec. V.P., Sec., Gen. Couns.

INVESTOR CONTACT: Brian J. Nicholson, (904) 819-2119

PRINCIPAL OFFICE: One Malaga Street, St. Augustine, FL 32084

TELEPHONE NUMBER: (904) 829-3421
FAX: (904) 396-4042
WEB: www.feci.com

NO. OF EMPLOYEES: 1,148 (avg.)

SHAREHOLDERS: 1,854

ANNUAL MEETING: In May

INCORPORATED: FL, Dec., 1983

INSTITUTIONAL HOLDINGS:
No. of Institutions: 61
Shares Held: 10,005,798
% Held: 27.4

INDUSTRY: Railroads, line-haul operating (SIC: 4011)

TRANSFER AGENT(S): First Union National Bank, Charlotte, NC

NYSE SYMBOL FLO
Rec. Pr. 31.85 (5/31/01)

FLOWERS FOODS, INC.

YIELD . . .
P/E RATIO 69.2

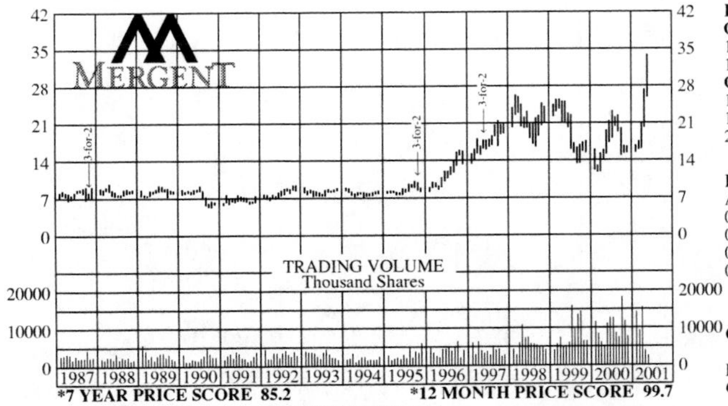

TRADING VOLUME
Thousand Shares

*7 YEAR PRICE SCORE 85.2 *12 MONTH PRICE SCORE 99.7

*NYSE COMPOSITE INDEX=100

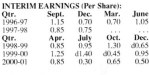

INTERIM EARNINGS (Per Share):

Qtr.	Sept.	Dec.	Mar.	June
1996-97	1.15	0.70	0.70	1.05
1997-98	0.85	0.75	. . .	. . .
Qtr.	**Apr.**	**July**	**Oct.**	**Dec.**
1998-99	0.85	0.95	1.30	d0.65
1999-00	1.25	d1.40	d0.45	0.95
2000-01	0.85	0.30	0.65	0.50

INTERIM DIVIDENDS (Per Share):

Amt.	Decl.	Ex.	Rec.	Pay.
0.133Q	2/25/00	3/08/00	3/10/00	3/24/00
0.133Q	5/31/00	6/12/00	6/14/00	6/28/00
0.133Q	9/08/00	9/13/00	9/15/00	9/29/00
0.133Q	11/17/00	11/29/00	12/01/00	12/15/00

Dividend Suspended

CAPITALIZATION (12/31/00):

	($000)	(%)
Long-Term Debt	247,847	33.0
Common & Surplus	502,460	67.0
Total	750,307	100.0

RECENT DEVELOPMENTS: For the 52 weeks ended 12/30/00, loss from continuing operations totaled $42.3 million versus a loss from continuing operations of $34.7 million a year earlier. Results in 2000 included a pre-tax gain of $17.2 million from insurance proceeds and a pre-tax one-time charge of $17.7 million. Earnings in 1999 included a pre-tax one-time credit of $6.0 million. Sales grew 3.3% to $1.62 billion from $1.57 billion the year before. Comparisons were made with restated prior-year results.

PROSPECTS: On 3/26/01, FLO shareholders received one share of Flowers Foods, Inc. common stock for every five shares of Flowers Industries, Inc. common shares, as well as $12.50 in cash in exchange for each share of Flowers Industries. In addition, FLO completed the sale of its controlling interest in Keebler Foods Company to Kellogg Company for approximately $1.25 billion in cash and the assumption of about $700,000 of debt.

BUSINESS

FLOWERS FOODS, INC. (formerly Flowers Industries, Inc.) produces and markets fresh baked breads, rolls and snack foods and frozen baked breads, desserts and snack foods. Products are distributed primarily in the Southeast, Central and Western U.S., and are sold chiefly to restaurants, fast-food chains, wholesalers, institutions, supermarkets and vending companies. Major brands include MRS SMITH'S, NATURE'S OWN, and COBBLESTONE MILL. FLO acquired Mrs. Smith's Pies in May 1996, Allied Bakery Products in September 1997, and President Baking Company, Inc. in September 1998. On 3/26/01, the Company sold its controlling interest in Keebler Foods Company and spun off its Flowers Bakeries and Mrs. Smith's businesses to its shareholders.

ANNUAL FINANCIAL DATA

	12/31/00	1/1/00	1/2/99	④ 1/3/98	6/28/97	6/29/96	7/1/95
Earnings Per Share	⑤ **d2.11**	② **0.35**	① **2.35**	③ **1.90**	② **3.55**	**1.80**	**2.49**
Cash Flow Per Share	**1.24**	**7.56**	**9.03**	**3.40**	**6.15**	**4.16**	**4.63**
Tang. Book Val. Per Share	**18.98**	. . .	. . .	**15.47**	**15.42**	**14.83**	**17.05**
Dividends Per Share	**0.53**	**0.52**	**0.47**	**0.43**	**0.43**	**0.40**	**0.37**
Dividend Payout %	. . .	**147.1**	**20.2**	**22.8**	**12.2**	**22.0**	**14.9**
INCOME STATEMENT (IN MILLIONS):							
Total Revenues	1,620.0	4,236.0	3,776.5	786.5	1,484.5	1,250.6	1,140.0
Costs & Expenses	1,543.2	3,907.4	3,415.3	722.8	1,325.6	1,143.5	1,028.2
Depreciation & Amort.	67.1	144.6	128.8	26.9	46.0	40.8	36.6
Operating Income	9.6	184.0	232.4	36.8	112.9	66.3	75.1
Net Interest Inc./(Exp.)	d68.4	d80.9	d68.7	d11.8	d25.1	d13.0	d7.1
Income Before Income Taxes	d58.7	103.1	163.7	25.0	87.8	48.3	68.0
Income Taxes	cr16.5	56.3	74.4	9.6	33.2	18.2	25.7
Net Income	⑤ d42.3	② 7.3	① 46.0	③ 33.4	② 62.3	30.8	42.3
Cash Flow	24.8	151.9	174.7	60.4	108.3	71.6	78.9
Average Shs. Outstg. (000)	20,066	20,084	19,360	17,755	17,600	17,235	17,060
BALANCE SHEET (IN MILLIONS):							
Cash & Cash Equivalents	11.8	39.4	57.0	3.9	31.1	25.0	31.8
Total Current Assets	267.3	690.5	783.2	252.9	271.5	230.2	189.0
Net Property	569.5	1,149.6	987.7	438.3	448.0	420.5	374.5
Total Assets	1,562.6	2,900.5	2,860.9	899.4	898.2	849.4	655.9
Total Current Liabilities	182.4	655.8	761.0	232.6	242.5	181.7	146.7
Long-Term Obligations	247.8	1,208.6	1,039.0	276.2	275.2	274.7	120.9
Net Stockholders' Equity	502.5	538.8	573.0	348.6	340.0	305.3	304.0
Net Working Capital	84.9	34.7	22.2	20.3	29.1	48.5	42.4
Year-end Shs. Outstg. (000)	19,866	20,059	19,964	17,686	17,615	17,575	17,284
STATISTICAL RECORD:							
Operating Profit Margin %	0.6	4.3	6.2	4.7	7.6	5.3	6.6
Net Profit Margin %	. . .	0.2	1.2	4.3	4.2	2.5	3.7
Return on Equity %	. . .	1.4	8.0	9.6	18.3	10.1	13.9
Return on Assets %	. . .	0.3	1.6	3.7	6.9	3.6	6.4
Debt/Total Assets %	15.9	41.7	36.3	30.7	30.6	32.3	18.4
Price Range	23.25-11.69	25.50-13.31	26.31-16.50	21.50-13.33	21.50-13.33	15.92-8.08	10.22-7.50
P/E Ratio	. . .	72.8-38.0	11.2-7.0	11.3-7.0	6.1-3.8	8.8-4.5	4.1-3.0
Average Yield %	3.0	2.7	2.2	2.5	2.5	3.3	4.2

Statistics are as originally reported. Adj. for 3-for-2 stk. split, 5/97 & 10/95; and a 1-for-5 sh. exch. on 3/26/01. ① Bef. $3.1 mil acctg. chg. and $938,000 extraord. chg., incl. $68.3 mil pre-tax chg. ② Incl. $60.4 mil pre-tax chg., 1/1/00; $43.0 mil pre-tax gain., 6/28/97. ③ Bef. $8.8 mil acctg. chg. ④ For six months due to fiscal year-end change. ⑤ Bef. $47.3 mil inc. fr. disc. ops., incl. $17.7 mil pre-tax chg. & $17.2 mil pre-tax gain fr insur. proceeds.

OFFICERS:
A. R. McMullian, Chmn., C.E.O.
R. P. Crozer, Vice-Chmn.
J. M. Woodward, V.P., C.F.O.

INVESTOR CONTACT: Lisa Hay, Investor Relations, (229) 227-2216

PRINCIPAL OFFICE: 1919 Flowers Circle, P.O. Box 1338, Thomasville, GA 31757

TELEPHONE NUMBER: (229) 226-9110
FAX: (229) 226-9231
WEB: www.flowersindustries.com
NO. OF EMPLOYEES: 7,300 (avg.)
SHAREHOLDERS: 6,241
ANNUAL MEETING: In May
INCORPORATED: DE, May, 1968; reincorp., GA, Mar., 2001

INSTITUTIONAL HOLDINGS:
No. of Institutions: 173
Shares Held: 46,629,816
% Held: 46.6

INDUSTRY: Bread, cake, and related products (SIC: 2051)

TRANSFER AGENT(S): First Union National Bank, Charlotte, NC

NYSE SYMBOL FLR
Rec. Pr. 58.32 (5/31/01)

FLUOR CORPORATION

YIELD 1.1%
P/E RATIO 75.7

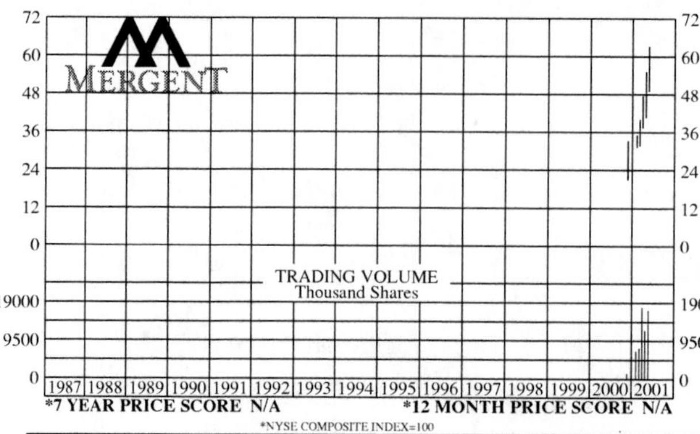

*7 YEAR PRICE SCORE N/A *12 MONTH PRICE SCORE N/A

*NYSE COMPOSITE INDEX=100

INTERIM EARNINGS (Per Share):

Qtr.	Jan.	April	July	Oct.
1999	0.40	d1.19	0.44	0.70
2000	0.49	0.48	0.12	0.22
Qtr.	**Mar.**	**June**	**Sept.**	**Dec.**
2000	...	...	...	d0.05

INTERIM DIVIDENDS (Per Share):

Amt.	Decl.	Ex.	Rec.	Pay.
0.16Q	3/05/01	3/13/01	3/15/01	3/29/01

Indicated div.: $0.64

CAPITALIZATION (10/31/00):

	($000)	(%)
Long-Term Debt	17,573	1.1
Common & Surplus	1,609,257	98.9
Total	1,626,830	100.0

RECENT DEVELOPMENTS: In connection with the reverse spin-off, FLR changed to a calendar-year basis of reporting financial results. For the two months ended 12/31/00, FLR incurred a net loss of $4.0 million compared with earnings from continuing operations of $18.6 million in the equivalent 1999 period. Revenues were $1.87 billion, up 8.3% from $1.72 billion a year earlier.

PROSPECTS: On 4/26/01, Fluor Daniel was awarded a $23.0 million contract for the engineering, procurement and construction of a hydrogen desulfurization facility in Portugal. Also on 4/26/01, FLR announced the launch of its Internet-enabled global equipment trading venture, GLOBEquip LLC. GLOBEquip offers an extensive service bundle including inspection, insurance, escrow, end-to-end logistics, currency exchange and commodity exchange.

BUSINESS

FLUOR CORPORATION is a holding company that provides services on a global basis in the fields of engineering, procurement, construction, maintenance, operations, project management and business services. These services are grouped into three operating segments. The Fluor Daniel segment provides design, engineering, procurement and construction services on a worldwide basis to an extensive range of industrial, commercial, utility, natural resources and energy clients. The Fluor Global Services segment provides outsourcing and asset management solutions to its customers. The Fluor Signature Services segment provides integrated business administration and support services to FLR and external parties. On 11/30/00, Fluor Corporation (old Fluor) completed a reverse spin-off transaction wherein two publicly-traded companies were created: Massey Energy Company and a "new" Fluor Corporation.

QUARTERLY DATA

(10/31/2000)	($000)	(%)
2nd Quarter	2,295,662	51,042
3rd Quarter	2,627,544	33,338
4th Quarter	2,308,561	(12,683)
1st Quarter	2,738,387	52,252

ANNUAL FINANCIAL DATA

	10/31/00	10/31/99	10/31/98
Earnings Per Share	[3] **1.31**	[2] **0.35**	[1] **1.72**
Cash Flow Per Share	**5.47**	**4.54**	**5.37**
Tang. Book Val. Per Share	**19.96**	**19.27**	...
INCOME STATEMENT (IN MILLIONS):			
Total Revenues	9,970.2	11,334.4	12,377.5
Costs & Expenses	9,501.5	10,937.4	11,872.0
Depreciation & Amort.	311.7	318.2	288.9
Operating Income	156.9	78.8	216.6
Net Interest Inc./(Exp.)	d14.7	d2.2	6.1
Income Before Income Taxes	142.2	76.6	222.7
Income Taxes	42.4	49.9	86.8
Net Income	[3] 99.8	[2] 26.7	[1] 135.9
Cash Flow	411.5	344.9	424.8
Average Shs. Outstg. (000)	75,256	75,929	79,135
BALANCE SHEET (IN MILLIONS):			
Cash & Cash Equivalents	69.4	209.6	...
Total Current Assets	1,447.8	1,910.2	...
Net Property	756.8	2,223.0	...
Total Assets	3,652.7	4,886.1	...
Total Current Liabilities	1,620.4	2,204.3	...
Long-Term Obligations	17.6	317.6	...
Net Stockholders' Equity	1,609.3	1,581.4	...
Net Working Capital	d172.6	d294.1	...
Year-end Shs. Outstg. (000)	75,743	76,034	75,573
STATISTICAL RECORD:			
Operating Profit Margin %	1.6	0.7	1.7
Net Profit Margin %	1.0	0.2	1.1
Return on Equity %	6.2	1.7	...
Return on Assets %	2.7	0.5	...
Debt/Total Assets %	0.5	6.5	...
Price Range	33.31-21.00	...	...
P/E Ratio	25.4-16.0	...	...

Statistics are as originally reported. [1] Bef. discont. oper. of $99.4 mill. [2] Bef. discont. oper. of $77.5 mill., but incl. a spec. prov. loss of $117.2 mill. to implement a strategic reorg. [3] Bef. inc. from discont. oper. of $49.1 mill., bef. net loss on disposal of $25.0 mill., but incl. a reverse spec. prov. credit of $17.9 mill.

OFFICERS:
P. J. Carroll, Jr., Chmn., C.E.O.
J. Stein, Vice-Chmn.
A. Boeckmann, Pres., C.O.O.
D. M. Stevert, Sr. V.P., C.F.O.

INVESTOR CONTACT: Investor Relations, (949) 349-2000

PRINCIPAL OFFICE: One Enterprise Drive, Aliso Viejo, CA 92656

TELEPHONE NUMBER: (949) 349-2000
WEB: www.fluor.com

NO. OF EMPLOYEES: 47,113 (avg.)

SHAREHOLDERS: 11,725 (record)

ANNUAL MEETING: In Apr.

INCORPORATED: DE, Sept., 2000

INSTITUTIONAL HOLDINGS:
No. of Institutions: 213
Shares Held: 59,110,326
% Held: 74.6

INDUSTRY: Holding companies, nec (SIC: 6719)

TRANSFER AGENT(S): Mellon Investor Services LLC, Los Angeles, CA

NYSE SYMBOL FMC
Rec. Pr. 71.69 (4/30/01)

FMC CORPORATION

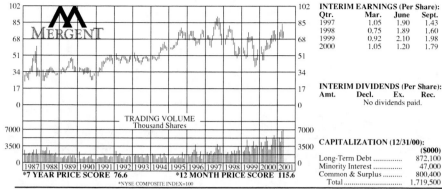

YIELD ...
P/E RATIO 12.8

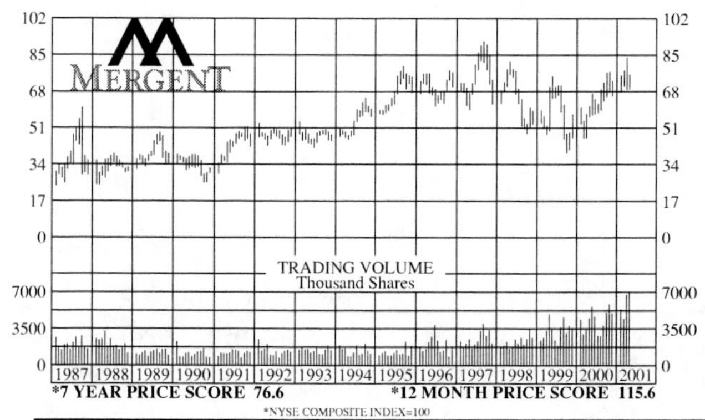

INTERIM EARNINGS (Per Share):

Qtr.	Mar.	June	Sept.	Dec.
1997	1.05	1.90	1.43	d4.50
1998	0.75	1.89	1.60	1.06
1999	0.92	2.10	1.98	1.69
2000	1.05	1.20	1.79	1.57

INTERIM DIVIDENDS (Per Share):

Amt.	Decl.	Ex.	Rec.	Pay.

No dividends paid.

CAPITALIZATION (12/31/00):

	($000)	(%)
Long-Term Debt	872,100	50.7
Minority Interest	47,000	2.7
Common & Surplus	800,400	46.5
Total	1,719,500	100.0

RECENT DEVELOPMENTS: For the year ended 12/31/00, income from continuing operations fell 17.9% to $177.3 million. Results for 2000 included an asset impairment charge of $11.6 million and a restructuring charge of $45.0 million. Earnings for 1999 included non-recurring items that resulted in a net gain of $11.7 million. Results for 2000 and 1999 excluded after-tax losses of $66.7 million and $3.4 million, respectively, from discontinued operations. Total sales fell 8.1% to $3.93 billion.

PROSPECTS: FMC anticipates earnings for 2001 to be flat to up 5.0%. In the second quarter of 2001, the Company expects to complete its planned initial public offering of about 20.0% of its machinery business, FMC Technologies, Inc. Separately, FMC Energy Systems announced a five-year frame contract with BP for the supply of subsea systems and related services for the Gulf of Mexico. The initial contract is valued at $250.0 million and is renewable for an additional five years.

BUSINESS

FMC CORPORATION manufactures and sells a broad range of machinery and chemical products. FMC's machinery products are marketed principally to industrial, agricultural and defense users. The Company's chemical products are mainly industrial and agricultural chemicals. FMC's natural resource requirements are primarily mineral-oriented and produced from mines in the U.S. FMC operates more than 90 manufacturing facilities and mines in 25 countries, and conducts its business within the following five industry segments: Energy Systems, 26.4% of 2000 sales; Food and Transportation Systems, 21.3%; Agricultural Products 16.9%; Specialty Chemicals, 12.4%; and Industrial Chemicals, 23.0%. In 1998, the Company acquired CBV and a subsea wellhead company in Brazil.

ANNUAL FINANCIAL DATA

	12/31/00	12/31/99	12/31/98	12/31/97	12/31/96	12/31/95	12/31/94
Earnings Per Share	**[6] 5.62**	**[5] 6.67**	**[4] 5.30**	**[3] d0.67**	**[2] 5.73**	**[1] 5.72**	**4.66**
Cash Flow Per Share	**11.60**	**12.56**	**11.22**	**5.81**	**12.41**	**12.31**	**10.82**
Tang. Book Val. Per Share	**9.98**	**7.84**	**10.10**	**9.74**	**9.60**	**8.38**	**8.01**
INCOME STATEMENT (IN MILLIONS):							
Total Revenues	3,925.5	4,110.6	4,378.4	4,312.6	5,080.6	4,566.6	4,051.3
Costs & Expenses	3,405.1	3,723.1	3,807.8	3,792.2	4,353.9	4,035.5	3,467.1
Depreciation & Amort.	188.9	190.8	206.6	238.4	254.2	248.9	229.0
Operating Income	331.5	359.7	364.0	282.0	472.5	282.2	355.2
Net Interest Inc./(Exp.)	d97.3	d111.8	d114.5	d117.7	d149.9	d131.6	d120.5
Income Before Income Taxes	222.6	274.3	249.5	d59.7	322.6	246.9	252.3
Income Taxes	45.3	58.3	64.2	cr35.2	104.5	31.3	78.9
Net Income	[6] 177.3	[5] 216.0	[4] 185.3	[3] d24.5	[2] 218.1	[1] 215.6	173.4
Cash Flow	366.2	406.8	391.9	213.9	472.3	464.5	402.4
Average Shs. Outstg. (000)	31,576	32,377	34,939	36,805	38,058	37,721	37,195
BALANCE SHEET (IN MILLIONS):							
Cash & Cash Equivalents	25.1	64.0	61.7	62.7	74.8	70.9	98.4
Total Current Assets	1,329.8	1,416.5	1,681.7	1,715.6	2,193.1	1,804.8	1,376.3
Net Property	1,616.1	1,691.9	1,727.5	1,679.3	1,959.3	1,829.6	1,537.4
Total Assets	3,745.9	3,995.8	4,166.4	4,113.1	4,989.8	4,301.1	3,351.5
Total Current Liabilities	1,399.9	1,576.0	1,411.9	1,464.5	2,021.4	1,792.7	1,268.9
Long-Term Obligations	872.1	945.1	1,326.4	1,140.2	1,268.4	974.4	901.2
Net Stockholders' Equity	800.4	743.6	729.4	760.6	855.8	653.4	416.5
Net Working Capital	d70.1	d159.5	269.8	251.1	171.7	12.1	107.4
Year-end Shs. Outstg. (000)	30,645	30,364	32,703	34,924	37,180	36,724	36,814
STATISTICAL RECORD:							
Operating Profit Margin %	8.4	8.8	8.3	6.5	6.3	6.2	6.2
Net Profit Margin %	4.5	5.3	4.2	...	4.3	4.7	4.3
Return on Equity %	22.2	29.0	25.4	...	25.5	33.0	41.6
Return on Assets %	4.7	5.4	4.4	...	4.4	5.0	5.2
Debt/Total Assets %	23.3	23.7	31.8	27.7	25.4	22.7	26.9
Price Range	77.19-46.06	75.25-39.25	82.19-48.25	91.44-59.38	78.00-60.88	80.00-57.13	65.13-45.50
P/E Ratio	13.7-8.2	11.3-5.9	15.5-9.1	...	13.6-10.6	14.0-10.0	14.0-9.8

Statistics are as originally reported. [1] Incl. $99.7 mill. gain & $134.5 mill. oth. chgs. [2] Bef. $7.4 mill. loss fr. disc. ops. [3] Incl. $224.0 mill. pre-tax chg. for asset impair.; $40.9 mill. pre-tax chg. for oth. chgs.; excl. $4.5 mill. net chg. for acct. chgs.; and $191.4 mill. gain fr. disc. ops. [4] Excl. d$36.1 mill. net effect of acct. chg. [5] Excl. $3.4 mill. net gain fr. disc. ops. and incl. $55.5 mill. gain fr. sale of bus., $29.1 mill. asset impair. chg., & $14.7 mill. restr. chgs. [6] Incl. $56.6 mill. asset impair. & restr. chgs. and excl. $66.7 mill. loss fr. disc. ops.

OFFICERS:
R. N. Burt, Chmn., C.E.O.
J. H. Netherland, Pres.
W. H. Schumann III, Sr. V.P., C.F.O.

INVESTOR CONTACT: Elisabeth Azzarello, Dir., Investor Relations, (312) 861-6921

PRINCIPAL OFFICE: 200 E. Randolph Dr., Chicago, IL 60601

TELEPHONE NUMBER: (312) 861-6000
FAX: (312) 861-6016
WEB: www.fmc.com

NO. OF EMPLOYEES: 14,802 (avg.)

SHAREHOLDERS: 9,055

ANNUAL MEETING: In Apr.

INCORPORATED: DE, Aug., 1928

INSTITUTIONAL HOLDINGS:
No. of Institutions: 235
Shares Held: 25,713,354
% Held: 84.4

INDUSTRY: Industrial machinery and equipment (SIC: 5084)

TRANSFER AGENT(S): Computershare Investor Services, Chicago, IL

NYSE SYMBOL F
Rec. Pr. 24.35 (5/31/01)

FORD MOTOR COMPANY

YIELD 4.9%
P/E RATIO 6.2

TRADING VOLUME
Thousand Shares

*7 YEAR PRICE SCORE 56.5 *12 MONTH PRICE SCORE 97.8
*NYSE COMPOSITE INDEX=100

INTERIM EARNINGS (Per Share):

Qtr.	Mar.	June	Sept.	Dec.
1997	1.20	2.06	0.90	1.45
1998	1.36	1.91	0.80	0.84
1999	1.60	1.89	0.90	1.47
2000	1.58	1.24	0.53	0.57

INTERIM DIVIDENDS (Per Share):

Amt.	Decl.	Ex.	Rec.	Pay.
0.30Q	10/12/00	10/30/00	11/01/00	12/01/00
0.30Q	12/14/00	1/26/01	1/30/01	3/01/01
0.30Q	4/12/01	4/30/01	5/02/01	6/01/01

Indicated div.: $1.20 (Div. Reinv. Plan)

CAPITALIZATION (12/31/00):

	($000)	(%)
Long-Term Debt	167,916,000	85.6
Deferred Income Tax	9,030,000	4.6
Redeemable Pfd. Stock	673,000	0.3
Common & Surplus	18,610,000	9.5
Total	196,229,000	100.0

RECENT DEVELOPMENTS: For the year ended 12/31/00, the Company reported income from continuing operations of $5.41 billion versus income from continuing operations of $6.50 billion in 1999. Results for 2000 and 1999 excluded a net loss of $1.94 billion and a net gain of $735,000, respectively, from discontinued operations. Total revenues rose 5.9% to $170.06 billion from $160.66 billion in 1999. Automobile sales and revenues climbed 4.6% to $141.2 million.

PROSPECTS: In an attempt to strengthen its position in the European market, the Company has launched a five-year recovery plan in which it will introduce 45 new products, including separate vehicles and engines, by 2005. In addition, the Company plans to reduce costs by 10.0% by 2004. During 2001, the Company plans to launch nine new products, including two new Focuses, a redesigned Explorer and the Maverick, a smaller sport utility vehicle.

BUSINESS

FORD MOTOR COMPANY is the world's largest producer of trucks and the second largest producer of cars and trucks combined. The Automotive segment is engaged in the design, manufacture, sale and service of cars, trucks, automotive components and systems. The Financial Services sector operates through Ford Motor Credit Company and Hertz Corporation, and is engaged in vehicle-related financing, leasing and the insurance rental of cars, trucks and industrial and construction equipment, and other activities. Ford completed the spin-off of Associates First Capital Corp. on 3/21/98 and Visteon Corp. on 6/28/00. Ford acquired AB Volvo's worldwide passenger vehicle business on 3/31/99 and the Land Rover line of products and related assembly and engineering facilities on 6/30/00. On 3/9/01, The Hertz Corporation merged with Ford.

ANNUAL FINANCIAL DATA

	12/31/00	12/31/99	12/31/98	12/31/97	12/31/96	12/31/95	12/31/94
Earnings Per Share	**4 3.59**	**5.86**	**3 17.76**	**2 5.62**	**1 3.72**	**3.58**	**4.97**
Cash Flow Per Share	**14.20**	**18.18**	**29.34**	**16.71**	**14.56**	**14.53**	**14.21**
Tang. Book Val. Per Share	**9.75**	**22.53**	**19.17**	**25.55**	**22.51**	**21.16**	**21.17**
Dividends Per Share	**1.80**	**1.88**	**1.72**	**1.645**	**1.47**	**1.23**	**0.91**
Dividend Payout %	**50.1**	**32.1**	**9.7**	**29.3**	**39.5**	**34.4**	**18.3**
INCOME STATEMENT (IN MILLIONS):							
Total Revenues	170,064.0	162,558.0	144,416.0	153,627.0	146,991.0	137,137.0	128,439.0
Costs & Expenses	145,412.0	122,655.0	106,658.0	110,051.0	109,591.0	101,996.0	96,885.0
Depreciation & Amort.	15,949.0	15,193.0	14,329.0	13,583.0	12,791.0	11,719.0	9,336.0
Operating Income	24,652.0	24,710.0	23,429.0	29,993.0	24,609.0	23,422.0	22,218.0
Net Interest Inc./(Exp.)	d9,414.0	d7,648.0	d7,534.0	d9,384.0	d9,558.0	d9,246.0	d7,079.0
Income Before Income Taxes	8,234.0	11,026.0	25,396.0	10,939.0	14,776.0	6,705.0	8,789.0
Income Taxes	2,705.0	3,670.0	3,176.0	3,741.0	2,166.0	2,379.0	3,329.0
Equity Earnings/Minority Int.	d49.0	d37.0	d187.0	d366.0	d187.0	d341.0	119.0
Net Income	4 5,410.0	7,237.0	3 22,071.0	2 6,920.0	1 4,446.0	4,139.0	5,308.0
Cash Flow	21,359.0	22,415.0	36,293.0	20,449.0	17,172.0	15,558.0	14,357.0
Average Shs. Outstg. (000)	1,504,000	1,233,000	1,237,000	1,224,000	1,179,000	1,071,000	1,010,000
BALANCE SHEET (IN MILLIONS):							
Cash & Cash Equivalents	17,967.0	25,173.0	24,956.0	22,453.0	19,103.0	15,096.0	13,822.0
Total Current Assets	39,310.0	45,679.0	39,860.0	38,465.0	35,883.0	29,971.0	28,602.0
Net Property	37,508.0	42,317.0	37,320.0	34,594.0	33,527.0	31,273.0	27,048.0
Total Assets	284,421.0	276,229.0	237,545.0	279,097.0	262,867.0	243,283.0	219,354.0
Total Current Liabilities	50,211.0	47,245.0	39,198.0	38,246.0	37,865.0	34,452.0	28,509.0
Long-Term Obligations	167,916.0	152,296.0	131,855.0	167,118.0	156,700.0	146,792.0	130,816.0
Net Stockholders' Equity	18,610.0	27,537.0	23,409.0	30,734.0	26,762.0	24,547.0	21,659.0
Net Working Capital	d10,901.0	d1,566.0	662.0	219.0	d1,982.0	d4,481.0	93.0
Year-end Shs. Outstg. (000)	1,908,000	1,222,000	1,221,000	1,203,000	1,189,000	1,160,000	1,023,000
STATISTICAL RECORD:							
Operating Profit Margin %	14.5	15.2	16.2	19.5	16.7	17.1	17.3
Net Profit Margin %	3.3	4.5	15.3	4.5	3.0	3.0	4.1
Return on Equity %	29.1	26.3	94.3	22.5	16.6	16.9	24.5
Return on Assets %	2.0	2.6	9.3	2.5	1.7	1.7	2.4
Debt/Total Assets %	59.0	55.1	55.5	59.9	59.6	60.3	59.6
Price Range	57.25-21.69 39.5	67.88-46.25 57.1	65.94-38.81 52.4	50.25-30.00 40.1	37.25-27.25 32.3	32.88-24.63 28.8	35.06-25.63 30.3
P/E Ratio	24.9-9.4	11.6-7.9	3.7-2.2	8.9-5.3	10.0-7.3	9.2-6.9	7.1-5.2
Average Yield %	4.6	3.3	3.3	4.1	4.6	4.3	3.0

Statistics are as originally reported. Adj. for stk. splits: 2-for-1, 7/94. 1 Incl. non-recurr credit $512.0 mill. & chrg. $669.0 mill. 2 Incl. non-recurr. credit $269.0 mill. from the IPO of Hertz Corp. & fr sale of Ford's heavy truck bus. 3 Incl. non-recurring gain $15.96 billion from spin-off of Associates First Capital. 4 Bef. net loss from disc. ops. of $1.94 bill.

OFFICERS:
W. C. Ford Jr., Chmn.
J. A. Nasser, Pres., C.E.O.

INVESTOR CONTACT: Mel Stephens, Investor Relations, (313) 323-8220

PRINCIPAL OFFICE: One American Road, Dearborn, MI 48126

TELEPHONE NUMBER: (313) 322-3000
FAX: (313) 222-4177
WEB: www.ford.com
NO. OF EMPLOYEES: 345,991 (avg.)
SHAREHOLDERS: 180,523 (approx.); 109 (class B)
ANNUAL MEETING: In May
INCORPORATED: DE, July, 1919

INSTITUTIONAL HOLDINGS:
No. of Institutions: 618
Shares Held: 676,658,241
% Held: 37.0

INDUSTRY: Motor vehicles and car bodies (SIC: 3711)

TRANSFER AGENT(S): First Chicago Trust Company of New York, Jersey City, NJ

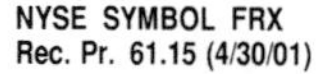

NYSE SYMBOL FRX
Rec. Pr. 61.15 (4/30/01)

FOREST LABORATORIES, INC.

YIELD ...
P/E RATIO 63.0

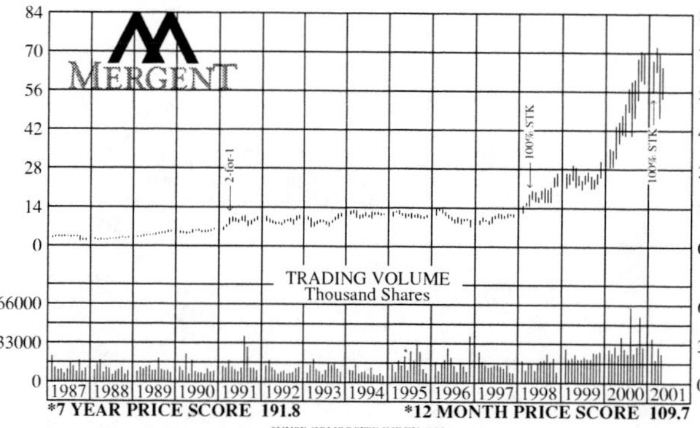

INTERIM EARNINGS (Per Share):

Qtr.	June	Sept.	Dec.	Mar.
1997-98	0.01	0.10	0.12	0.01
1998-99	0.04	0.06	0.13	0.23
1999-00	0.15	0.16	0.18	0.16
2000-01	0.16	0.29	0.36	...

INTERIM DIVIDENDS (Per Share):

Amt.	Decl.	Ex.	Rec.	Pay.
100% STK	12/18/00	1/12/01	12/26/00	1/11/01

CAPITALIZATION (3/31/00):

	($000)	(%)
Deferred Income Tax	1,862	0.2
Common & Surplus	884,690	99.8
Total	886,552	100.0

RECENT DEVELOPMENTS: For the quarter ended 12/31/00, net income more than doubled to $65.9 million versus $31.8 million in the year-earlier quarter. Net revenues increased 31.9% to $317.7 million from $240.8 million in 1999. Net sales advanced 32.3% to $310.1 million, while other income jumped 18.8% to $7.6 million. The growth in sales was primarily due to the success of CELEXA™, FRX's selective serotonin reuptake inhibitor for the treatment of depression.

PROSPECTS: Looking ahead, FRX anticipates continued strong revenue and earnings growth from its promoted products, and continued success in securing promising new compounds with favorable market potential. Meanwhile, FRX should continue to benefit from the success of CELEXA™, which has captured over 14.0% of new prescriptions in the selective serotonin reuptake inhibitor market since its launch in 1998 and its growth is continuing.

BUSINESS

FOREST LABORATORIES, INC. develops, manufactures and markets branded and generic forms of ethical drug products, which require a physician's prescription, as well as non-prescription pharmaceuticals sold over-the-counter, which are used for the treatment of a wide range of illnesses. The Company's products are marketed principally in the United States, western and eastern Europe, and in Puerto Rico and other Caribbean Islands. Marketing is conducted by FRX and through independent distributors and under exclusive marketing contracts with major pharmaceutical companies. In fiscal 1999, sales outside the U.S. contributed 9% to total sales.

QUARTERLY DATA

(03/31/00)($000)	Rev	Inc
1st Quarter	178,793	25,053
2nd Quarter	201,357	27,950
3rd Quarter	234,413	31,756
4th Quarter	258,259	27,929

ANNUAL FINANCIAL DATA

	3/31/00	3/31/99	3/31/98	3/31/97	3/31/96	3/31/95	3/31/94
Earnings Per Share	**0.64**	**0.45**	**[1] 0.22**	**[1] d0.14**	**0.56**	**0.54**	**0.44**
Cash Flow Per Share	**0.87**	**0.57**	**0.34**	**d0.03**	**0.64**	**0.61**	**0.49**
Tang. Book Val. Per Share	**3.58**	**3.20**	**2.49**	**2.45**	**3.16**	**2.86**	**2.42**
INCOME STATEMENT (IN MILLIONS):							
Total Revenues	899.3	624.0	474.7	309.1	459.9	404.8	361.3
Costs & Expenses	701.2	491.9	399.9	328.9	281.1	234.6	225.2
Depreciation & Amort.	40.6	21.3	20.1	19.2	16.5	14.1	10.7
Operating Income	157.4	110.8	54.8	d39.0	162.4	156.1	125.5
Income Before Income Taxes	157.4	110.8	54.8	d39.0	162.4	156.1	125.5
Income Taxes	44.8	33.6	18.1	cr15.5	58.1	56.0	45.3
Net Income	112.7	77.2	[1] 36.7	[1] d23.5	104.2	100.1	80.2
Cash Flow	153.3	98.4	56.8	d4.4	120.8	114.2	90.9
Average Shs. Outstg. (000)	175,890	171,912	166,850	172,036	188,212	186,728	183,828
BALANCE SHEET (IN MILLIONS):							
Cash & Cash Equivalents	337.6	241.7	181.9	172.2	123.7	142.2	181.1
Total Current Assets	645.2	502.4	371.6	359.6	470.6	349.0	347.5
Net Property	117.0	91.2	81.5	83.3	79.4	73.0	53.0
Total Assets	1,097.6	875.1	744.3	700.3	899.4	757.2	619.2
Total Current Liabilities	211.1	130.0	129.9	73.5	89.6	57.6	52.2
Net Stockholders' Equity	884.7	743.5	614.2	626.4	809.5	698.4	574.4
Net Working Capital	434.1	372.4	241.8	286.1	381.0	291.3	295.3
Year-end Shs. Outstg. (000)	169,322	166,342	160,806	164,660	181,932	180,724	174,756
STATISTICAL RECORD:							
Operating Profit Margin %	17.5	17.8	11.5	...	35.3	38.6	34.7
Net Profit Margin %	12.5	12.4	7.7	...	22.7	24.7	22.2
Return on Equity %	12.7	10.4	6.0	...	12.9	14.3	14.0
Return on Assets %	10.3	8.8	4.9	...	11.6	13.2	13.0
Price Range	30.88-20.63	26.63-12.16	12.08-7.91	13.94-7.06	13.06-10.09	13.13-10.00	11.97-6.88
P/E Ratio	48.2-32.2	59.2-27.0	54.9-35.9	...	23.5-18.2	24.4-18.6	27.3-15.7

Statistics are as originally reported. Adj. for stk. split: 2-for-1, 3/25/98 & 12/26/00 [1] Incl. non-recurr. chrg. 3/31/98: $32.3 mill.; credit 3/31/97: $19.1 mill.

OFFICERS:
H. Solomon, Chmn., C.E.O.
K. E. Goodman, Pres., C.O.O.
J. E. Eggers, V.P., C.F.O.

PRINCIPAL OFFICE: 909 Third Avenue, New York, NY 10022-4731

TELEPHONE NUMBER: (212) 421-7850
FAX: (212) 750-9152
WEB: www.forestlaboratories.com

NO. OF EMPLOYEES: 2,474

SHAREHOLDERS: 2,095

ANNUAL MEETING: In Aug.

INCORPORATED: DE, Apr., 1956

INSTITUTIONAL HOLDINGS:
No. of Institutions: 350
Shares Held: 149,867,956
% Held: 85.1

INDUSTRY: Pharmaceutical preparations (SIC: 2834)

TRANSFER AGENT(S): Mellon Investor Services, Ridgefield Park, NJ

NYSE SYMBOL FO
Rec. Pr. 31.15 (4/30/01)

FORTUNE BRANDS, INC.

YIELD 3.1%
P/E RATIO . . .

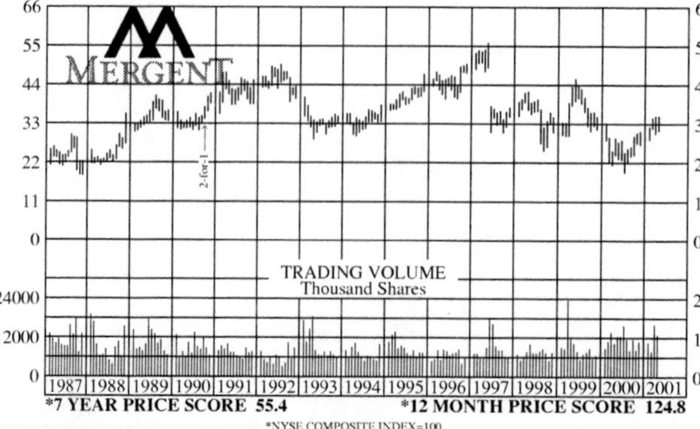

*7 YEAR PRICE SCORE 55.4 *12 MONTH PRICE SCORE 124.8

*NYSE COMPOSITE INDEX=100

INTERIM EARNINGS (Per Share):

Qtr.	Mar.	June	Sept.	Dec.
1997	0.80	0.03	0.16	d0.20
1998	0.30	0.50	0.32	0.55
1999	0.32	d7.04	0.28	0.61
2000	0.42	0.61	0.46	d2.41

INTERIM DIVIDENDS (Per Share):

Amt.	Decl.	Ex.	Rec.	Pay.
0.23Q	4/25/00	5/08/00	5/10/00	6/01/00
0.23Q	7/25/00	8/07/00	8/09/00	9/01/00
0.24Q	9/26/00	11/06/00	11/08/00	12/01/00
0.24Q	1/30/01	2/12/01	2/14/01	3/01/01
0.24Q	4/24/01	5/07/01	5/09/01	6/01/01

Indicated div.: $0.96 (Div. Reinv. Plan)

CAPITALIZATION (12/31/00):

	($000)	(%)
Long-Term Debt	1,151,800	34.5
Deferred Income Tax	54,900	1.6
Preferred Stock	9,200	0.3
Common & Surplus	2,126,700	63.6
Total	3,342,600	100.0

RECENT DEVELOPMENTS: For the year ended 12/31/00, FO incurred a net loss of $137.7 million versus a net loss of $890.6 million in 1999. Results for 2000 and 1999 included pre-tax restructuring and other nonrecurring charges of $73.0 million and $196.0 million, respectively, as well as write-downs of goodwill of $502.6 million and $1.13 billion, respectively. Net sales rose 4.8% to $5.84 billion from $5.58 billion in the prior year

PROSPECTS: The Company should continue to benefit from its restructuring program, which was designed to realign FO's cost structure, increase competitiveness, and improve supply chains. FO anticipates restructuring savings of $20.0 million in 2001. However, results for 2001 will likely continue to be affected by adverse foreign exchange translation, moderation in the housing market and a slower retail environment.

BUSINESS

FORTUNE BRANDS, INC. (formerly American Brands, Inc.) is an international consumer products holding company. FO has premier brands and leading market positions in home and office products. Home and office brands include MOEN faucets, MASTER locks and ARISTOKRAFT and SCHROCK cabinets sold by units of Masterbrand Industries, and DAY TIMER, KENSINGTON, WILSON JONES and SWINGLINE sold by units of ACCO World Corp. Acushnet Company's golf brands include TITLEIST, COBRA and FOOT-JOY. Major spirit and wine brands sold by units of Jim Beam Brands Worldwide, Inc. include JIM BEAM and KNOB CREEK Bourbons, DEKUYPER cordials, WHYTE MACKAY scotch and GEYSER PEAK and CANYON ROAD wines. In December 1994, FO sold American Tobacco. On 5/30/97, FO's international operations were spun-off. On 10/19/99, FO acquired NHB Group Ltd.

BUSINESS LINE ANALYSIS

(12/31/00)	REV (%)	INC (%)
Home Products	37.9	39.0
Office Products	24.6	9.1
Golf Products	16.5	16.6
Spirits & wine	21.0	35.3
Total	100.0	100.0

ANNUAL FINANCIAL DATA

	12/31/00	12/31/99	12/31/98	12/31/97	12/31/96	12/31/95	12/31/94
Earnings Per Share	**[1][4] d0.88**	**[1][4] d5.35**	**[2] 1.67**	**[5] 0.23**	**[1][2] 2.86**	**[1][2] 2.90**	**[1][3] 4.38**
Cash Flow Per Share	**0.63**	**d3.96**	**3.09**	**1.64**	**4.45**	**4.28**	**5.95**
Tang. Book Val. Per Share	**0.89**	**0.59**	**1.91**	**2.91**	**. . .**	**3.13**	**5.33**
Dividends Per Share	**0.93**	**0.89**	**0.85**	**1.41**	**2.00**	**2.00**	**1.99**
Dividend Payout %	. . .	. . .	**50.9**	**612.8**	**69.9**	**69.0**	**45.5**
INCOME STATEMENT (IN MILLIONS):							
Total Revenues	5,844.5	5,524.7	5,240.9	4,844.5	11,579.3	11,367.1	13,146.5
Costs & Expenses	5,429.2	5,935.3	4,370.2	4,331.3	10,305.1	10,016.6	11,519.7
Depreciation & Amort.	236.7	230.5	251.1	242.7	274.8	257.5	314.4
Operating Income	178.6	d641.1	619.6	270.5	999.4	1,093.0	1,312.4
Net Interest Inc./(Exp.)	d133.8	d106.8	d102.7	d116.7	d178.7	d159.8	d212.1
Income Before Income Taxes	38.9	d720.7	511.9	139.7	824.3	893.8	1,351.2
Income Taxes	176.6	169.9	218.3	98.2	327.5	350.7	466.1
Net Income	[1][4] d137.7	[1][4] d890.6	[2] 293.6	[5] 41.5	[1][2] 496.8	[1][2] 543.1	[1][3] 885.1
Cash Flow	99.0	d660.1	544.7	284.2	771.6	800.6	1,199.5
Average Shs. Outstg. (000)	157,600	166,600	176,200	173,300	173,300	186,900	201,600
BALANCE SHEET (IN MILLIONS):							
Cash & Cash Equivalents	20.9	71.9	40.3	54.2	119.7	139.9	110.1
Total Current Assets	2,264.5	2,312.8	2,265.3	2,095.6	3,873.4	3,164.0	4,670.9
Net Property	1,205.1	1,176.5	1,119.9	980.9	1,230.9	1,137.3	1,212.7
Total Assets	5,764.1	6,417.1	7,359.7	6,942.5	9,504.2	8,021.2	9,794.4
Total Current Liabilities	2,039.9	2,002.9	1,844.6	1,768.5	3,695.3	2,411.3	3,115.5
Long-Term Obligations	1,151.8	1,204.8	981.7	739.1	1,598.3	1,154.6	1,512.1
Net Stockholders' Equity	2,135.9	2,738.2	4,097.5	4,017.1	3,684.2	3,877.2	4,637.5
Net Working Capital	224.6	309.9	420.7	327.1	178.1	752.7	1,555.4
Year-end Shs. Outstg. (000)	153,509	229,600	170,884	114,142	170,566	178,160	201,211
STATISTICAL RECORD:							
Operating Profit Margin %	3.1	. . .	11.8	5.6	8.6	9.6	10.0
Net Profit Margin %	. . .	. . .	5.6	0.9	4.3	4.8	6.7
Return on Equity %	. . .	. . .	7.2	1.0	13.5	14.0	19.1
Return on Assets %	. . .	. . .	4.0	0.6	5.2	6.8	9.0
Debt/Total Assets %	20.0	18.8	13.3	10.6	16.8	14.4	15.4
Price Range	33.25-19.19	45.88-29.38	42.25-25.25	56.00-30.38	50.13-39.88	47.25-36.63	38.38-29.38
P/E Ratio	. . .	. . .	25.3-15.1	243.4-132.0	17.5-13.9	16.3-12.6	8.8-6.7
Average Yield %	3.5	2.4	2.5	3.3	4.4	4.8	5.9

Statistics are as originally reported. Adj. for 2-for-1 stk. split, 10/90. [1] Incl. pre-tax restruct. & oth. non-recurr. chrg.: $73.0 mill., 2000; $196.0 mill., 1999; $59.9 mill., 1996; cr$20.0 mill., 1995; cr$332.9 mill., 1994. [2] Bef. extraord. chrg.: $30.5 mill., 1998; $10.3 mill., 1996; $2.7 mill., 1995. [3] Bef. disc. oper. loss $151.0 mill. [4] Incl. a write-off of goodwill $502.6 mill., 2000; $1.13 bill., 1999. [5] Incl. pre-tax restruct. & oth. non-recurr. chrg. $209.1 mill.; bef. extraord. chrg. $8.1 mill. & disc op. gain $65.1 mill.

OFFICERS:
N. H. Wesley, Chmn., C.E.O.
C. P. Omtvedt, Sr. V.P., C.F.O.

INVESTOR CONTACT: Anthony J. Diaz, Investor Relations, (847) 484-4410

PRINCIPAL OFFICE: 300 Tower Parkway, Lincolnshire, IL 60069-3640

TELEPHONE NUMBER: (847) 484-4400
WEB: www.fortunebrands.com

NO. OF EMPLOYEES: 27,800 (avg.)

SHAREHOLDERS: 33,491 (record)

ANNUAL MEETING: In April

INCORPORATED: DE, Oct., 1985

INSTITUTIONAL HOLDINGS:
No. of Institutions: 344
Shares Held: 99,483,037
% Held: 64.7

INDUSTRY: Hardware, nec (SIC: 3429)

TRANSFER AGENT(S): Bank of New York, New York, NY

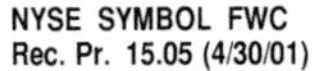

NYSE SYMBOL FWC
Rec. Pr. 15.05 (4/30/01)

FOSTER WHEELER CORPORATION

YIELD 1.6%
P/E RATIO 15.5

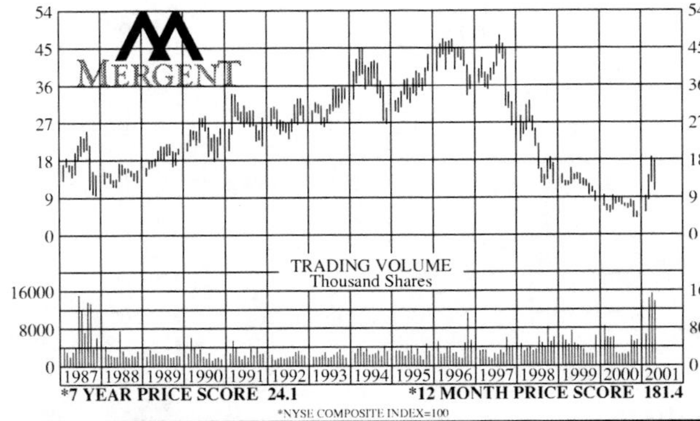

*7 YEAR PRICE SCORE 24.1 *12 MONTH PRICE SCORE 181.4

*NYSE COMPOSITE INDEX=100

INTERIM EARNINGS (Per Share):

Qtr.	Mar.	June	Sept.	Dec.
1997	0.50	d0.09	d0.72	0.06
1998	0.43	0.50	d3.80	0.41
1999	0.38	0.13	d0.56	d3.47
2000	0.21	0.21	0.25	0.30

INTERIM DIVIDENDS (Per Share):

Amt.	Decl.	Ex.	Rec.	Pay.
0.06Q	4/26/00	5/11/00	5/15/00	6/15/00
0.06Q	7/25/00	8/11/00	8/15/00	9/15/00
0.06Q	10/31/00	11/13/00	11/15/00	12/15/00
0.06Q	1/30/01	2/13/01	2/15/01	3/15/01
0.06Q	4/23/01	5/11/01	5/15/01	6/15/01

Indicated div.: $0.24 (Div. Reinv. Plan)

CAPITALIZATION (12/29/00):

	($000)	(%)
Long-Term Debt	846,645	69.1
Deferred Income Tax	15,334	1.3
Common & Surplus	364,089	29.7
Total	1,226,068	100.0

RECENT DEVELOPMENTS: For the year ended 12/31/00, net income was $39.5 million compared with a net loss of $143.6 mllion in 1999. Results for 1999 included charges for the Robbins Resource Recovery facility write-down and a third quarter cost realignment charge of $282.2 million. New orders booked increased 23.7% to $4.48 billion from $3.62 billion, while backlog was flat at $6.10 billion. Revenues were $3.97 billion, up slightly from $3.94 billion a year earlier.

PROSPECTS: On 2/1/01, the Company announced that its subsidiary, Foster Wheeler Energy Corporation, was awarded a contract by InterGen to supply 19 heat-recovery steam generators for six power projects. The contract was valued at approximately $200.0 million. On 1/25/01, Foster Wheeler Energy Corporation was awarded two contracts by PSEG Power LLC with a total value of approximately $100.0 million.

BUSINESS

FOSTER WHEELER CORPORATION provides a broad range of professional services including engineering, construction, manufacturing, management, and plant operations. The Engineering and Construction Group designs, engineers and constructs petroleum refineries, chemical, petrochemical, pharmaceutical, and industrial plants. The Energy Equipment Group designs and manufactures steam generators and auxiliary equipment for electric utilities and industrial markets. The Power Systems Group operates cogeneration and waste-to-energy facilities. FWC also provides petroleum and environmental services.

ANNUAL FINANCIAL DATA

	12/29/00	12/31/99	12/25/98	12/26/97	12/27/96	12/31/95	12/31/94
Earnings Per Share	**0.97**	[5] **d3.53**	[4] **d0.77**	[3] **0.14**	[2] **2.03**	[1] **0.79**	**1.83**
Cash Flow Per Share	**2.38**	**d2.04**	**0.74**	**1.66**	...	**2.29**	**3.07**
Tang. Book Val. Per Share	**1.87**	**1.83**	**7.05**	**8.28**	**8.79**	**9.03**	**10.83**
Dividends Per Share	**0.24**	**0.54**	**0.84**	**0.83**	**0.81**	**0.77**	**0.72**
Dividend Payout %	**24.7**	...	...	**596.0**	**39.9**	**97.5**	**39.3**
INCOME STATEMENT (IN MILLIONS):							
Total Revenues	3,969.4	3,944.1	4,597.0	4,172.0	4,040.6	3,081.9	2,271.1
Costs & Expenses	3,726.8	3,744.3	4,358.1	3,998.0	3,744.3	2,838.0	2,069.1
Depreciation & Amort.	57.7	60.4	61.6	62.0	63.6	54.6	44.3
Operating Income	184.9	139.3	177.3	112.0	232.7	189.3	157.8
Income Before Income Taxes	56.0	d190.5	47.8	19.5	126.9	69.7	106.9
Income Taxes	16.5	cr46.9	79.3	13.9	44.6	41.1	41.5
Equity Earnings/Minority Int.	d3.9	d3.0	d2.6	d2.9	d5.2	d4.5	d5.0
Net Income	39.5	[5] d143.6	[4] d31.5	[3] 5.6	[2] 82.2	[1] 28.5	65.4
Cash Flow	97.2	d83.2	30.1	67.6	145.8	83.2	109.7
Average Shs. Outstg. (000)	40,798	40,742	40,729	40,677	...	36,322	35,788
BALANCE SHEET (IN MILLIONS):							
Cash & Cash Equivalents	193.7	187.3	241.3	259.3	404.3	280.0	354.4
Total Current Assets	1,623.0	1,615.1	1,672.8	1,545.3	1,762.4	1,469.0	1,112.7
Net Property	495.0	648.2	911.1	824.5	724.8	644.8	566.2
Total Assets	3,477.5	3,438.1	3,495.0	3,357.7	3,510.3	2,975.8	2,063.3
Total Current Liabilities	1,454.6	1,471.6	1,498.7	1,412.3	1,441.9	1,270.3	890.6
Long-Term Obligations	846.6	989.5	990.7	855.7	796.3	554.4	477.0
Net Stockholders' Equity	364.1	375.9	572.1	635.5	689.0	625.9	456.5
Net Working Capital	168.4	143.5	174.2	133.0	320.6	198.7	222.1
Year-end Shs. Outstg. (000)	40,723	40,731	40,717	40,735	40,651	40,488	35,813
STATISTICAL RECORD:							
Operating Profit Margin %	4.7	3.5	3.9	2.7	5.8	6.1	6.9
Net Profit Margin %	1.0	...	...	0.1	2.0	0.9	2.9
Return on Equity %	10.8	...	...	0.9	11.9	4.6	14.3
Return on Assets %	1.1	...	...	0.2	2.3	1.0	3.2
Debt/Total Assets %	24.3	28.8	28.3	25.5	22.7	18.6	23.1
Price Range	9.50-3.94	16.06-7.88	32.25-11.75	48.13-26.13	47.25-33.50	43.50-29.38	45.13-26.63
P/E Ratio	9.8-4.1	...	...	343.5-186.5	23.3-16.5	55.1-37.2	24.7-14.5
Average Yield %	3.6	4.5	3.8	2.2	2.0	2.1	2.0

Statistics are as originally reported. [1] Incl. a net reorg. chrg. of $46.5 mill. [2] Incl. a pretax nonrecurr. chrg. of $24.0 mill. rel. to asbestos litigation. [3] Incl. pretax special chrg. and prov. of $182.1 mill.; & a pretax gain of $56.4 mill. [4] Incl. aftertax chrg. of $175.0 mill. [5] Incl. nonrecurr. pretax chrg. of $251.6 mill.

OFFICERS:
R. J. Swift, Chmn., Pres., C.E.O.
G. A. Renaud, Sr. V.P., C.F.O.
R. D. Iseman, V.P., Treas.

INVESTOR CONTACT: Scott W. Dudley, Jr., Dir., Investor Relations, (908) 730-5430

PRINCIPAL OFFICE: Perryville Corporate Park, Clinton, NJ 08809-4000

TELEPHONE NUMBER: (908) 730-4000
FAX: (908) 730-5315
WEB: www.fwc.com

NO. OF EMPLOYEES: 10,170

SHAREHOLDERS: 6,464 (record)

ANNUAL MEETING: In Apr.

INCORPORATED: NY, Feb., 1900

INSTITUTIONAL HOLDINGS:
No. of Institutions: 84
Shares Held: 18,288,499
% Held: 44.9

INDUSTRY: Heavy construction, nec (SIC: 1629)

TRANSFER AGENT(S): Mellon Investor Services, South Hakensack, NJ

NYSE SYMBOL FOX
Rec. Pr. 22.95 (4/30/01)

FOX ENTERTAINMENT GROUP, INC.

YIELD ...
P/E RATIO 327.9

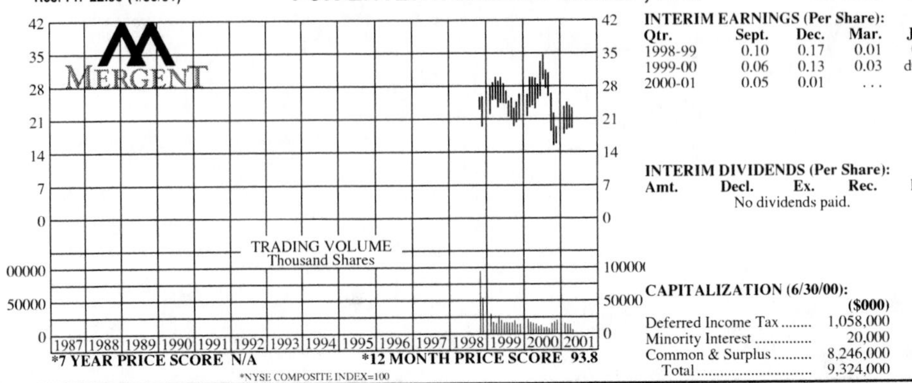

INTERIM EARNINGS (Per Share):

Qtr.	Sept.	Dec.	Mar.	June
1998-99	0.10	0.17	0.01	0.05
1999-00	0.06	0.13	0.03	d0.02
2000-01	0.05	0.01	...	...

INTERIM DIVIDENDS (Per Share):

Amt.	Decl.	Ex.	Rec.	Pay.

No dividends paid.

CAPITALIZATION (6/30/00):

	($000)	(%)
Deferred Income Tax	1,058,000	11.3
Minority Interest	20,000	0.2
Common & Surplus	8,246,000	88.4
Total	9,324,000	100.0

RECENT DEVELOPMENTS: For the quarter ended 12/31/00, net income fell 94.7% to $5.0 million from $94.0 million in 1999. Earnings included a net charge of $89.0 million related to FOX's restructuring of its Healtheon/WebMD transaction. Revenues rose 4.2% to $2.50 billion. Operating income before interest, taxes, depreciation and amortization (EBITDA) for the Filmed Entertainment segment more than tripled to $151.0 million, while EBITDA for the Television Stations fell 3.9% to $249.0 million.

PROSPECTS: The Filmed Entertainment segment is benefiting from the domestic video performance and the continuing international theatrical performance of X-MEN. In addition, several new television series delivered strong ratings, such as BOSTON PUBLIC, DARK ANGEL and YES DEAR. Separately, FOX's Television business is being negatively affected by losses at the FOX Broadcasting Company and a decline in television station contributions.

BUSINESS

FOX ENTERTAINMENT GROUP, INC. is principally engaged in the development, production and worldwide distribution of feature films and television programs, television broadcasting and cable network programming. The Company's studios, production facilities and film and television library provide content and the Company's broadcasting and cable networks provide extensive distribution platforms for the Company's programs. FOX operates in five business segments: Filmed Entertainment; Television Stations, including 23 owned and operated stations; Television Broadcast Network; Other Television Businesses; and Cable Network Programming. The News Corporation Limited owns an 82.8% equity interest in the Company.

ANNUAL FINANCIAL DATA

	6/30/00	6/30/99	6/30/98	6/30/97	6/30/96
Earnings Per Share	**0.20**	**0.33**	**0.32**	**0.05**	**0.75**
Cash Flow Per Share	**0.81**	**0.83**	**0.76**	**0.38**	**0.93**
Tang. Book Val. Per Share	**0.57**	**1.26**	...	...	...
INCOME STATEMENT (IN MILLIONS):					
Total Revenues	8,589.0	8,057.0	7,023.0	5,847.0	4,548.0
Costs & Expenses	7,493.0	7,026.0	6,117.0	5,347.0	3,970.0
Depreciation & Amort.	440.0	315.0	243.0	180.0	97.0
Operating Income	656.0	716.0	663.0	320.0	481.0
Net Interest Inc./(Exp.)	d297.0	d223.0	d271.0	d191.0	d97.0
Income Before Income Taxes	265.0	347.0	311.0	79.0	585.0
Income Taxes	120.0	142.0	135.0	49.0	174.0
Equity Earnings/Minority Int.	d94.0	d146.0	d81.0	d50.0	18.0
Net Income	145.0	205.0	176.0	30.0	411.0
Cash Flow	585.0	520.0	419.0	210.0	508.0
Average Shs. Outstg. (000)	722,000	626,000	548,000	548,000	548,000
BALANCE SHEET (IN MILLIONS):					
Cash & Cash Equivalents	114.0	121.0	101.0	256.0	...
Total Current Assets	5,743.0	4,498.0	4,121.0	3,912.0	...
Net Property	1,478.0	1,321.0	1,111.0	800.0	...
Total Assets	17,930.0	13,163.0	12,630.0	11,697.0	...
Total Current Liabilities	5,720.0	3,915.0	3,892.0	4,301.0	...
Net Stockholders' Equity	8,246.0	6,668.0	3,941.0	3,767.0	...
Net Working Capital	23.0	583.0	229.0	d389.0	...
Year-end Shs. Outstg. (000)	724,059	672,000	...	...	...
STATISTICAL RECORD:					
Operating Profit Margin %	7.6	8.9	9.4	5.5	10.6
Net Profit Margin %	1.7	2.5	2.5	0.5	9.0
Return on Equity %	1.8	3.1	4.5	0.8	...
Return on Assets %	0.8	1.6	1.4	0.3	...
Price Range	34.75-15.44	30.00-19.50	25.75-19.38	...	...
P/E Ratio	173.7-77.2	90.9-59.1	80.4-60.5	...	...

Statistics are as originally reported.

OFFICERS:
K. R. Murdoch, Chmn., C.E.O.
P. Chernin, Pres., C.O.O.
D. F. DeVoe, Sr. Exec. V.P., C.F.O.
A. M. Siskind, Sr. Exec. V.P., Gen. Couns.

INVESTOR CONTACT: Reed Nolte, V.P., Inv. Relations (212) 852-7017

PRINCIPAL OFFICE: 1211 Avenue of the Americas, New York, NY 10036

TELEPHONE NUMBER: (212) 852-7111
FAX: (212) 852-7145
WEB: www.fox.com

NO. OF EMPLOYEES: 12,000 (approx.)

SHAREHOLDERS: 815 (approx. class A)

ANNUAL MEETING: In Nov.

INCORPORATED: DE, 1985

INSTITUTIONAL HOLDINGS:
No. of Institutions: 143
Shares Held: 115,517,460
% Held: 16.0

INDUSTRY: Motion picture & video production (SIC: 7812)

TRANSFER AGENT(S): The Bank of New York, New York, NY

NYSE SYMBOL FPL
Rec. Pr. 59.90 (4/30/01)

FPL GROUP, INC.

YIELD 3.7%
P/E RATIO 14.5

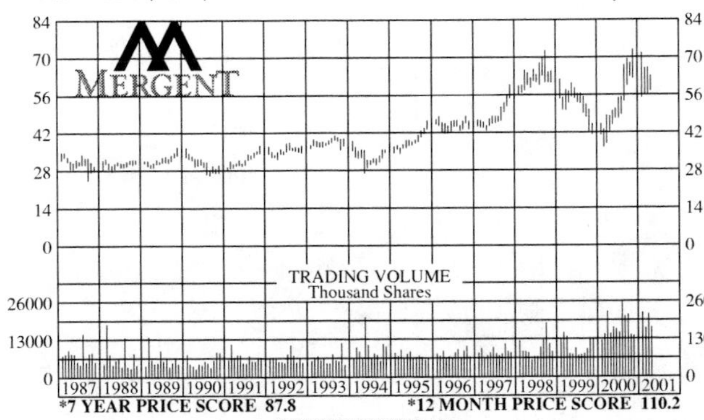

INTERIM EARNINGS (Per Share):

Qtr.	Mar.	June	Sept.	Dec.
1996	0.54	0.86	1.44	0.49
1997	0.58	0.95	1.52	0.52
1998	0.63	1.02	1.66	0.54
1999	1.22	0.45	1.70	0.71
2000	0.71	1.20	1.84	0.38

INTERIM DIVIDENDS (Per Share):

Amt.	Decl.	Ex.	Rec.	Pay.
0.54Q	5/15/00	5/24/00	5/26/00	6/15/00
0.54Q	8/14/00	8/23/00	8/25/00	9/15/00
0.54Q	11/13/00	11/21/00	11/24/00	12/15/00
0.56Q	2/12/01	2/21/01	2/23/01	3/15/01
0.56Q	5/14/01	5/23/01	5/25/01	6/15/01

Indicated div.: $2.24 (Div. Reinv. Plan)

CAPITALIZATION (12/31/00):

	($000)	(%)
Long-Term Debt	3,976,000	35.2
Deferred Income Tax	1,485,000	13.2
Preferred Stock	226,000	2.0
Common & Surplus	5,593,000	49.6
Total	11,280,000	100.0

RECENT DEVELOPMENTS: For the year ended 12/31/00, net income inched up 1.0% to $704.0 million compared with $697.0 million in the previous year. Results for 2000 and 1999 included nonrecurring charges of $67.0 million and $176.0 million, respectively. The 1999 results also included special gains of $257.0 million from the sale of cable investments. Operating revenues amounted to $7.08 billion, an increase of 10.0% versus $6.44 billion in 1999.

PROSPECTS: On 4/2/01, the Company announced that it had reached a mutual agreement with Entergy Corporation to terminate the two companies' agreement to merge. The Company's principal reason for its decision to terminate the proposed merger centered on discrepancies in Entergy's financial forecasts. Both companies agreed not to seek a termination free under the terms of the transaction unless one party agrees to a substantially comparable transaction with another party.

BUSINESS

FPL GROUP, INC. is a holding company whose principal operating subsidiary is Florida Power & Light Company, which is engaged in the generation, transmission, distribution and sale of electric energy. FPL supplies service throughout most of the east and lower west coasts of Florida. As of 5/18/01, FPL serves more than 3.9 million customer accounts. On 2/15/98, FPL formed FPL Energy, Inc., its independent power production unit, which produces electricity and clean renewable fuels. FPL Energy's project portfolio totals more than 4,100 megawatts, including natural gas, hydro, wind, solar, geothermal, and biomass generating facilities in the U.S. and abroad. FPL FiberNet LLC provides wholesale fiber-optic service to telephone and cable companies, Internet service providers and other telecommunications businesses within Florida.

QUARTERLY DATA

(12/31/00)($000)	Rev	Inc
1st Quarter	1,468,000	121,000
2nd Quarter	1,670,000	204,000
3rd Quarter	2,087,000	314,000
4th Quarter	1,857,000	65,000

ANNUAL FINANCIAL DATA

	12/31/00	12/31/99	12/31/98	12/31/97	12/31/96	12/31/95	12/31/94
Earnings Per Share	**2 4.14**	**1 4.07**	**3.85**	**3.57**	**3.33**	**3.16**	**2.91**
Cash Flow Per Share	**10.21**	**10.16**	**11.26**	**9.71**	**8.85**	**8.39**	**6.98**
Tang. Book Val. Per Share	**31.82**	**30.07**	**28.37**	**26.66**	**25.12**	**23.78**	**22.50**
Dividends Per Share	**2.16**	**2.08**	**2.00**	**1.92**	**1.84**	**1.76**	**1.88**
Dividend Payout %	**52.2**	**51.1**	**51.9**	**53.8**	**55.3**	**55.7**	**64.6**
INCOME STATEMENT (IN MILLIONS):							
Total Revenues	7,082.0	6,438.0	6,661.0	6,369.0	6,036.8	5,592.5	5,422.7
Costs & Expenses	4,810.0	4,478.0	4,125.0	4,080.0	3,905.6	3,477.4	3,550.4
Depreciation & Amort.	1,032.0	1,040.0	1,284.0	1,061.0	960.4	917.9	723.9
Operating Income	1,240.0	920.0	1,252.0	1,228.0	1,170.8	1,197.1	1,148.4
Net Interest Inc./(Exp.)	d278.0	d222.0	d322.0	d291.0	d266.5	d290.7	d319.0
Income Taxes	336.0	323.0	279.0	304.0	293.9	328.6	307.3
Net Income	2 704.0	1 697.0	664.0	618.0	579.5	553.3	518.7
Cash Flow	1,736.0	1,737.0	1,948.0	1,679.0	1,539.8	1,471.2	1,242.6
Average Shs. Outstg. (000)	170,000	171,000	173,000	173,000	174,072	175,335	178,009
BALANCE SHEET (IN MILLIONS):							
Gross Property	21,022.0	19,554.0	17,952.0	17,820.0	16,847.0	16,531.5	16,138.6
Accumulated Depreciation	11,088.0	10,290.0	9,397.0	8,466.0	7,649.7	6,873.3	6,186.7
Net Property	9,934.0	9,264.0	8,555.0	9,354.0	9,383.9	9,852.0	10,202.8
Total Assets	15,300.0	13,441.0	12,029.0	12,449.0	12,219.3	12,459.2	12,617.6
Long-Term Obligations	3,976.0	3,478.0	2,347.0	2,949.0	3,144.3	3,376.6	3,864.5
Net Stockholders' Equity	5,819.0	5,596.0	5,352.0	5,071.0	4,881.7	4,682.1	4,648.5
Year-end Shs. Outstg. (000)	175,766	178,555	180,712	181,762	182,815	184,693	186,571
STATISTICAL RECORD:							
Operating Profit Margin %	17.5	14.3	18.8	19.3	19.4	21.4	21.2
Net Profit Margin %	9.9	10.8	10.0	9.7	9.6	9.9	9.6
Net Inc./Net Property %	7.1	7.5	7.8	6.6	6.2	5.6	5.1
Net Inc./Tot. Capital %	6.2	6.8	7.3	6.4	6.0	5.6	5.0
Return on Equity %	12.1	12.5	12.4	12.2	11.9	11.8	11.2
Accum. Depr./Gross Prop. %	52.7	52.6	52.3	47.5	45.4	41.6	38.3
Price Range	73.00-36.38	61.94-41.13	72.56-56.06	60.00-42.63	48.13-41.50	46.50-34.00	39.13-26.88
P/E Ratio	17.6-8.8	15.2-10.1	18.8-14.6	16.8-11.9	14.5-12.5	14.7-10.8	13.4-9.2
Average Yield %	3.9	4.0	3.1	3.7	4.1	4.4	5.7

Statistics are as originally reported. 1 Incl. one-time net gains of $162.0 mill. & incl. one-time net charges totaling $146.0 mill. 2 Incl. nonrecurr. chrg. of $67.0 mill.

OFFICERS:
J. L. Broadhead, Chmn., C.E.O.
P. J. Evanson, Pres.
L. Hay III, Sr. V.P., C.F.O.
D. P. Coyle, Sec., Gen. Couns.

INVESTOR CONTACT: Lisa Kunzel, Dir. Inv. Rel., (516) 694-4697

PRINCIPAL OFFICE: 700 Universe Blvd., Juno Beach, FL 33408

TELEPHONE NUMBER: (561) 694-4000
FAX: (561) 694-4620
WEB: www.fplgroup.com

NO. OF EMPLOYEES: 10,852 (avg.)

SHAREHOLDERS: 44,645 approx.

ANNUAL MEETING: In May

INCORPORATED: FL, Sept., 1984

INSTITUTIONAL HOLDINGS:
No. of Institutions: 443
Shares Held: 113,550,554
% Held: 64.6

INDUSTRY: Electric services (SIC: 4911)

TRANSFER AGENT(S): EquiServe, Boston, MA

NYSE SYMBOL BEN
Rec. Pr. 44.50 (5/31/01)

FRANKLIN RESOURCES, INC.

YIELD 0.6%
P/E RATIO 18.9

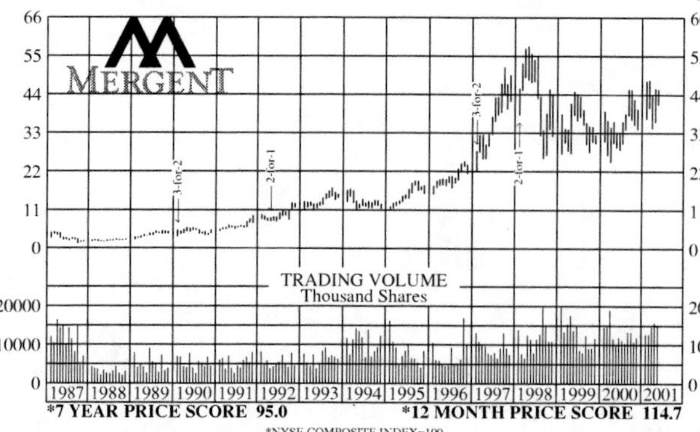

INTERIM EARNINGS (Per Share):

Qtr.	Dec.	Mar.	June	Sept.
1996-97	0.38	0.40	0.44	0.50
1997-98	0.52	0.50	0.52	0.44
1998-99	0.27	0.41	0.49	0.52
1999-00	0.55	0.58	0.58	0.58
2000-01	0.61	...	...	...

INTERIM DIVIDENDS (Per Share):

Amt.	Decl.	Ex.	Rec.	Pay.
0.06Q	3/22/00	3/29/00	3/31/00	4/14/00
0.06Q	6/27/00	6/29/00	7/03/00	7/14/00
0.06Q	9/27/00	9/29/00	10/03/00	10/16/00
0.065Q	12/15/00	12/27/00	12/29/00	1/16/01
0.065Q	3/22/01	3/29/01	4/02/01	4/16/01

Indicated div.: $0.26 (Div. Reinv. Plan)

CAPITALIZATION (9/30/00):

	($000)	(%)
Long-Term Debt	294,090	9.0
Common & Surplus	2,965,493	91.0
Total	3,259,583	100.0

RECENT DEVELOPMENTS: For the quarter ended 12/31/00, net income totaled $149.5 million, up 8.7% compared with $137.5 million in the 1999 quarter. Total operating revenues fell slightly to $564.1 million versus $565.7 million the year before. Investment management fees rose 1.0% to $345.8 million, while underwriting and distribution fees increased slightly to $164.4 million. However, shareholder servicing fees declined 6.8% to $48.2 million. Operating income decreased 11.1% to $149.0 million.

PROSPECTS: On 4/10/01, the Company completed the acquisition of Fiduciary Trust Company International of New York in a stock-for-stock transaction valued at approximately $775.0 million. The acquisition adds approximately $45.10 billion in assets under management and strengthens the Company's global investment management business for institutions and high net worth clients. In connection with the acquisition, BEN became a bank holding company and a financial holding company.

BUSINESS

FRANKLIN RESOURCES, INC., operating as Franklin Templeton Investments, is engaged in providing investment management, marketing, distribution, transfer agency and other administrative services to the open-end investment companies of the Franklin Templeton Group and to U.S. and international managed and institutional accounts. The Company also provides investment management and related services to a number of closed-end investment companies. In addition, the Company provides investment management, marketing and distribution services to certain sponsored investment companies organized in the Grand Duchy of Luxembourg. In addition, the Company also provides advisory services, variable annuity products, and sponsors and manages public and private real estate programs. As of 4/30/01, BEN's subsidiary, Franklin Templeton Investments, had approximately $269.00 billion in assets under management.

ANNUAL FINANCIAL DATA

	9/30/00	9/30/99	9/30/98	9/30/97	9/30/96	9/30/95	9/30/94
Earnings Per Share	**2.28**	**[1] 1.69**	**1.98**	**1.72**	**1.26**	**1.08**	**1.00**
Cash Flow Per Share	**3.09**	**2.48**	**2.74**	**2.20**	**1.42**	**1.27**	**1.17**
Tang. Book Val. Per Share	**7.37**	**5.79**	**4.08**	**2.50**	**3.15**	**2.06**	**1.03**
Dividends Per Share	**0.24**	**0.22**	**0.20**	**0.17**	**0.15**	**0.13**	**0.11**
Dividend Payout %	**10.5**	**13.0**	**10.1**	**9.9**	**11.6**	**12.3**	**10.7**
INCOME STATEMENT (IN MILLIONS):							
Total Revenues	2,340.1	2,262.5	2,577.3	2,163.3	1,522.6	845.8	826.9
Costs & Expenses	1,394.9	1,445.2	1,653.3	1,361.3	1,065.0	436.7	411.2
Depreciation & Amort.	199.6	200.0	191.4	123.9	40.5	40.9	36.7
Operating Income	745.6	617.3	732.6	678.1	417.1	368.1	378.9
Net Interest Inc./(Exp.)	d14.0	d21.0	d22.5	d25.3	d11.3	d11.2	d39.1
Income Before Income Taxes	739.6	574.1	676.3	615.7	456.2	386.7	362.5
Income Taxes	177.5	147.4	175.8	181.7	141.5	117.7	111.2
Net Income	562.1	[1] 426.7	500.5	434.1	314.7	268.9	251.3
Cash Flow	761.7	626.7	691.8	558.0	355.2	309.9	288.0
Average Shs. Outstg. (000)	246,624	252,757	252,941	253,430	249,939	243,729	245,796
BALANCE SHEET (IN MILLIONS):							
Cash & Cash Equivalents	746.0	819.2	556.0	442.7	502.2	261.7	210.4
Total Current Assets	1,457.3	1,395.1	1,061.1	1,196.6	1,282.3	1,170.5	966.2
Net Property	444.7	416.4	349.2	...	...	...	...
Total Assets	4,042.4	3,666.8	3,480.0	2,878.1	2,212.6	2,126.1	1,874.5
Total Current Liabilities	712.9	651.9	652.5	707.7	550.0	684.7	408.7
Long-Term Obligations	294.1	294.3	494.5	493.2	399.5	382.4	383.7
Net Stockholders' Equity	2,965.5	2,657.0	2,280.8	1,854.2	1,400.6	1,161.0	930.8
Net Working Capital	744.4	743.3	408.7	488.9	732.3	485.8	557.4
Year-end Shs. Outstg. (000)	243,730	251,007	251,742	252,064	240,816	242,820	244,791
STATISTICAL RECORD:							
Operating Profit Margin %	31.9	27.3	28.4	31.3	27.4	43.5	45.8
Net Profit Margin %	24.0	18.9	19.4	20.1	20.7	31.8	30.4
Return on Equity %	19.0	16.1	21.9	23.4	22.5	23.2	27.0
Return on Assets %	13.9	11.6	14.4	15.1	14.2	12.6	13.4
Debt/Total Assets %	7.3	8.0	14.2	17.1	18.1	18.0	20.5
Price Range	45.63-24.63	45.00-27.00	57.88-25.75	51.91-22.08	24.92-15.46	19.33-11.00	17.00-11.21
P/E Ratio	20.0-10.8	26.6-16.0	29.2-13.0	30.3-12.9	19.8-12.3	17.9-10.2	17.0-11.2
Average Yield %	0.7	0.6	0.5	0.5	0.7	0.9	0.8

Statistics are as originally reported. Adj. for stk. splits: 3-for-2, 12/96; 2-for-1, 12/97 [1] Incl. restr. chrg. $58.5 mill.

OFFICERS:
C. B. Johnson, Chmn., C.E.O.
H. E. Burns, Vice-Chmn.
R. H. Johnson Jr., Vice-Chmn.
M. L. Flanagan, Pres., C.F.O.

INVESTOR CONTACT: Alan Weinfeld, Investor Relations, (800) 632-2350-28900

PRINCIPAL OFFICE: 777 Mariners Island Blvd., San Mateo, CA 94404

TELEPHONE NUMBER: (650) 312-2000
FAX: (650) 312-3655
WEB: www.frk.com

NO. OF EMPLOYEES: 6,500 (approx.)

SHAREHOLDERS: 4,900 (approx.)

ANNUAL MEETING: In Jan.

INCORPORATED: DE, Nov., 1969

INSTITUTIONAL HOLDINGS:
No. of Institutions: 298
Shares Held: 93,981,745
% Held: 35.5

INDUSTRY: Investment advice (SIC: 6282)

TRANSFER AGENT(S): Bank of New York, New York, NY

NYSE SYMBOL FRE
Rec. Pr. 66.20 (5/31/01)

FREDDIE MAC

YIELD 1.2%
P/E RATIO 19.5

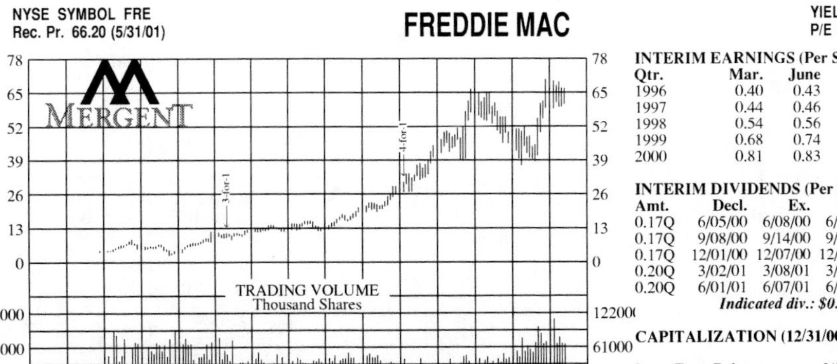

*7 YEAR PRICE SCORE 110.0 *12 MONTH PRICE SCORE 120.2

*NYSE COMPOSITE INDEX=100

INTERIM EARNINGS (Per Share):

Qtr.	Mar.	June	Sept.	Dec.
1996	0.40	0.43	0.41	0.43
1997	0.44	0.46	0.49	0.51
1998	0.54	0.56	0.58	0.62
1999	0.68	0.74	0.74	0.78
2000	0.81	0.83	0.86	0.89

INTERIM DIVIDENDS (Per Share):

Amt.	Decl.	Ex.	Rec.	Pay.
0.17Q	6/05/00	6/08/00	6/12/00	6/30/00
0.17Q	9/08/00	9/14/00	9/18/00	9/29/00
0.17Q	12/01/00	12/07/00	12/11/00	12/29/00
0.20Q	3/02/01	3/08/01	3/12/01	3/30/01
0.20Q	6/01/01	6/07/01	6/11/01	6/29/01

Indicated div.: $0.80

CAPITALIZATION (12/31/00):

	($000)	(%)
Long-Term Debt	243,323,000	94.3
Preferred Stock	3,195,000	1.2
Common & Surplus	11,642,000	4.5
Total	258,160,000	100.0

RECENT DEVELOPMENTS: For the year ended 12/31/00, net income increased 14.4% to $2.54 billion from $2.22 billion in 1999. Results benefited from portfolio growth, stable margins and continued credit strength. Revenues, net of interest expense, increased 9.9% to $4.46 billion versus $4.06 billion a year earlier. Net interest income on earning assets climbed 11.7% to $2.84 billion, while management and guarantee income improved 6.0% to $1.49 billion.

PROSPECTS: Going forward, the mortgage securities business should benefit from the Company's efforts to grow its total mortgage portfolio at a rate faster than the estimated growth in residential mortgage debt outstanding. The Company also expects the average guarantee fee rate to be generally stable in 2001. Separately, with respect to credit performance, the Company anticipates that credit expenses will increase modestly.

BUSINESS

FREDDIE MAC (formerly The Federal Home Loan Mortgage Corporation) is a federally chartered and stockholder-owned corporation. FRE purchases conventional residential mortgages from mortgage lending institutions and finances most of its purchases with sales of guaranteed mortgage securities called Mortgage Participation Certificates for which FRE ultimately assumes the risk of borrower default. FRE also maintains an investment portfolio that consists principally of federal funds sold, reverse repurchase agreements and tax-advantaged and other short-term investments. FRE's financial performance is driven primarily by the growth of its total servicing portfolio, the mix of sold versus retained portfolios, the spreads earned on the sold and retained portfolios and mortgage default costs.

ANNUAL FINANCIAL DATA

	12/31/00	12/31/99	12/31/98	12/31/97	12/31/96	12/31/95	12/31/94
Earnings Per Share	[2] **3.39**	[2] **2.95**	**2.31**	**1.88**	[1] **1.67**	**1.42**	[1] **1.27**
Tang. Book Val. Per Share	**16.81**	**11.98**	**11.55**	**8.74**	**9.62**	**8.14**	**7.08**
Dividends Per Share	**0.68**	**0.60**	**0.48**	**0.40**	**0.35**	**0.30**	**0.26**
Dividend Payout %	**20.1**	**20.3**	**20.8**	**21.3**	**21.0**	**21.1**	**20.5**
INCOME STATEMENT (IN MILLIONS):							
Total Interest Income	28,350.0	22,753.0	16,638.0	13,001.0	10,783.0	8,393.0	5,815.0
Total Interest Expense	25,512.0	20,213.0	14,711.0	11,370.0	9,241.0	6,997.0	4,703.0
Net Interest Income	2,838.0	2,540.0	1,927.0	1,631.0	1,542.0	1,396.0	1,112.0
Provision for Loan Losses	40.0	60.0	190.0	310.0	320.0	255.0	200.0
Non-Interest Income	1,489.0	1,405.0	1,307.0	1,298.0	1,249.0	1,087.0	1,108.0
Non-Interest Expense	883.0	834.0	791.0	755.0	758.0	681.0	604.0
Income Before Taxes	3,534.0	3,161.0	2,356.0	1,964.0	1,797.0	1,586.0	1,482.0
Net Income	[2] 2,539.0	[2] 2,218.0	1,700.0	1,395.0	[1] 1,258.0	1,091.0	[1] 1,027.0
Average Shs. Outstg. (000)	696,448	700,211	684,658	692,000	710,000	720,000	724,000
BALANCE SHEET (IN MILLIONS):							
Total Loans & Leases	385,451.0	322,914.0	255,670.0	164,543.0	137,826.0	107,706.0	72,585.0
Allowance for Credit Losses	334.0	345.0	322.0	293.0	306.0	295.0	290.0
Net Loans & Leases	385,117.0	322,569.0	255,348.0	164,250.0	137,520.0	107,411.0	72,295.0
Total Assets	459,297.0	386,684.0	321,421.0	194,597.0	173,866.0	137,181.0	106,199.0
Long-Term Obligations	243,323.0	185,186.0	93,525.0	87,714.0	76,876.0	57,820.0	45,972.0
Total Liabilities	444,460.0	375,159.0	310,586.0	187,076.0	167,135.0	131,318.0	101,037.0
Net Stockholders' Equity	14,837.0	11,525.0	10,835.0	7,521.0	6,731.0	5,863.0	5,162.0
Year-end Shs. Outstg. (000)	692,584	695,091	695,179	679,000	695,000	716,000	724,000
STATISTICAL RECORD:							
Return on Equity %	17.1	19.2	15.7	18.5	18.7	18.6	19.9
Return on Assets %	0.6	0.6	0.5	0.7	0.7	0.8	1.0
Equity/Assets %	3.2	3.0	3.4	3.9	3.9	4.3	4.9
Non-Int. Exp./Tot. Inc. %	20.4	21.1	24.5	25.8	27.2	27.4	27.2
Price Range	70.13-36.88	65.25-45.38	66.38-38.69	44.56-26.69	29.00-19.06	20.91-12.47	15.72-11.75
P/E Ratio	20.7-10.9	22.1-15.4	28.7-16.7	23.7-14.2	17.4-11.4	14.7-8.8	12.4-9.3
Average Yield %	1.3	1.1	0.9	1.1	1.5	1.8	1.9

Statistics are as originally reported. Adj. for stk. split: 4-for-1, 1/97 [1] Bef. extraord. chrg. $15.0 mill., 12/96; $44.0 mill., 12/94 [2] Bef. extraord. gain $8.0 mill., 12/00; $5.0 mill., 12/99

OFFICERS:
L. C. Brendsel, Chmn., C.E.O.
D. W. Glenn, Vice-Chmn., Pres.
V. A. Clarke, Sr. V.P., C.F.O.
M. Mater, Exec. V.P., Gen. Couns., Sec.

INVESTOR CONTACT: Investor Relations, (703) 903-2000

PRINCIPAL OFFICE: 8200 Jones Branch Drive, McLean, VA 22102-3110

TELEPHONE NUMBER: (703) 903-2000
FAX: (703) 903-2759
WEB: www.freddiemac.com

NO. OF EMPLOYEES: 3,500 (approx.)

SHAREHOLDERS: 5,288 (approx.)

ANNUAL MEETING: In May

INCORPORATED: July, 1970

INSTITUTIONAL HOLDINGS:
No. of Institutions: 691
Shares Held: 597,830,489
% Held: 86.3

INDUSTRY: Federal & fed.-sponsored credit (SIC: 6111)

TRANSFER AGENT(S): First Chicago Trust Company of New York, Jersey City, NJ

NYSE SYMBOL FCX
Rec. Pr. 14.16 (4/30/01)

FREEPORT-MCMORAN COPPER & GOLD INC.

YIELD . . .
P/E RATIO 50.6

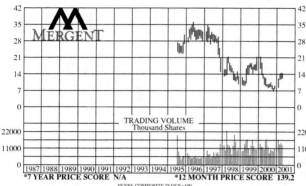

MERGENT

TRADING VOLUME
Thousand Shares

*7 YEAR PRICE SCORE N/A *12 MONTH PRICE SCORE 139.2
*NYSE COMPOSITE INDEX=100

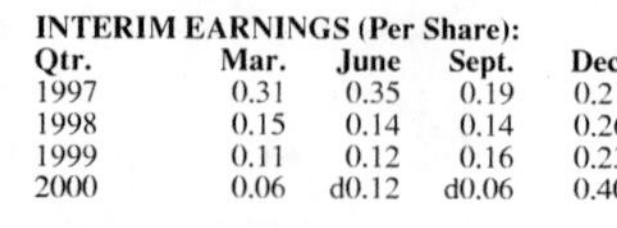

INTERIM EARNINGS (Per Share):

Qtr.	Mar.	June	Sept.	Dec.
1997	0.31	0.35	0.19	0.21
1998	0.15	0.14	0.14	0.26
1999	0.11	0.12	0.16	0.23
2000	0.06	d0.12	d0.06	0.40

INTERIM DIVIDENDS (Per Share):

Amt.	Decl.	Ex.	Rec.	Pay.

No dividends paid.

CAPITALIZATION (12/31/00):

	($000)	(%)
Long-Term Debt	1,987,731	62.0
Deferred Income Tax	599,536	18.7
Minority Interest	103,795	3.2
Redeemable Pfd. Stock	475,005	14.8
Preferred Stock	349,990	10.9
Common & Surplus	d312,059	-9.7
Total	3,203,998	100.0

RECENT DEVELOPMENTS: For the twelve months ended 12/31/00, net income declined 43.6% to $77.0 million compared with $136.5 million in the previous year. Results for 2000 included pre-tax charges of $12.4 million, partially offset by a pre-tax benefit of $4.4 million. The decrease in earnings was mainly the result of lower gold sales versus 1999 levels. Revenues slipped 1.0% to $1.87 billion from $1.89 billion the year before.

PROSPECTS: For 2001, P.T. Freeport estimates aggregate production at the Grasberg mining complex to be approximately 1.60 billion pounds of copper and in excess of 3.0 million ounces of gold. In addition, P.T. Freeport's share of sales is expected to approximate 1.40 billion of copper and 2.3 million ounces of gold. The expected improvement in gold production and sales should significantly boost the Company's profitability in 2001.

BUSINESS

FREEPORT-MCMORAN COPPER & GOLD INC. is engaged in exploring for and recovering copper, gold, and silver. The Company owns an 85.6% ownership interest in P.T. Freeport Indonesia Company, its principal operating subsidiary. The Grasberg ore mine in Indonesia contains the largest single gold reserve and the third largest open-pit copper reserve of any mine in the world. Proven reserves include approximately 50.90 billion pounds of copper, 63.7 million ounces of gold, and 139.6 million ounces of silver. The Company's operations include smelting and refining copper concentrates in Spain, as well as through a 25.0% interest in P.T. Smelting.

REVENUES

(12/31/2000)	($000)	(%)
Mining & exploration	1,413,099	75.6
Smelting & refining...	768,814	41.1
Other	(313,303)	(16.7)
Total	1,868,610	100.0

ANNUAL FINANCIAL DATA

	12/31/00	12/31/99	12/31/98	12/31/97	12/31/96	12/31/95	12/31/94
Earnings Per Share	**4 0.26**	**3 0.61**	**0.67**	**2 1.06**	**0.89**	**0.98**	**1 0.38**
Cash Flow Per Share	**2.09**	**2.39**	**2.26**	**2.14**	**1.79**	**1.58**	**0.75**
Tang. Book Val. Per Share	...	...	...	...	**1.61**	**2.59**	**2.04**
Dividends Per Share	...	...	**0.20**	**0.90**	**0.90**	**0.68**	**0.60**
Dividend Payout %	...	...	**29.8**	**84.9**	**101.1**	**68.9**	**157.9**
INCOME STATEMENT (IN MILLIONS):							
Total Revenues	1,868.6	1,887.3	1,757.1	2,000.9	1,905.0	1,834.3	1,212.3
Costs & Expenses	1,106.4	1,010.9	905.4	1,122.8	1,092.8	1,113.8	857.1
Depreciation & Amort.	283.6	293.2	277.4	213.9	174.0	124.1	75.1
Operating Income	478.7	583.2	574.3	664.2	638.3	596.4	280.1
Net Interest Inc./(Exp.)	d205.3	d194.1	d205.6	d151.7	d117.3	d50.1	...
Income Before Income Taxes	273.2	380.8	361.4	516.8	521.9	544.8	279.1
Income Taxes	159.6	195.7	170.6	231.3	247.2	234.0	123.4
Equity Earnings/Minority Int.	d36.7	d48.7	d37.0	d40.3	d48.5	d57.1	d25.4
Net Income	4 77.0	3 136.5	153.8	2 245.1	226.2	253.6	1 130.2
Cash Flow	323.1	394.0	395.7	422.4	348.7	323.5	153.5
Average Shs. Outstg. (000)	154,519	164,567	175,354	197,653	194,910	204,406	205,755
BALANCE SHEET (IN MILLIONS):							
Cash & Cash Equivalents	8.0	6.7	5.9	9.0	37.1	26.9	44.3
Total Current Assets	569.1	564.5	545.9	463.1	661.2	653.3	603.4
Net Property	3,230.6	3,363.3	3,474.5	3,521.7	3,088.6	2,845.6	2,360.5
Total Assets	3,950.7	4,082.9	4,192.6	4,152.2	3,865.5	3,581.7	3,040.2
Total Current Liabilities	633.9	515.1	518.5	475.7	597.9	526.8	431.6
Long-Term Obligations	1,987.7	2,033.5	2,329.0	2,308.1	1,426.3	1,080.3	525.6
Net Stockholders' Equity	37.9	d455.2	103.4	278.9	675.4	881.7	995.0
Net Working Capital	d64.8	49.4	27.4	d12.6	63.3	126.5	171.8
Year-end Shs. Outstg. (000)	144,041	163,497	164,308	184,255	202,120	118,620	205,950
STATISTICAL RECORD:							
Operating Profit Margin %	25.6	30.9	32.7	33.2	33.5	32.5	23.1
Net Profit Margin %	4.1	7.2	8.8	12.2	11.9	13.8	10.7
Return on Equity %	203.0	...	148.8	87.9	33.5	28.8	13.1
Return on Assets %	1.9	3.3	3.7	5.9	5.9	7.1	4.3
Debt/Total Assets %	50.3	49.8	55.5	55.6	36.9	30.2	17.3
Price Range	21.44-6.75	21.38-9.13	21.44-9.81	34.88-14.94	36.13-27.38	30.75-22.63	...
P/E Ratio	82.4-26.0	35.0-15.0	32.0-14.6	32.9-14.1	40.6-30.8	31.4-23.1	...
Average Yield %	...	...	1.3	3.6	2.8	2.5	...

Statistics are as originally reported. 1 Incl. a $32.6 mill. gain on insurance settlement. 2 Incl. a net gain of $12.3 mill. for the reversal of stock appreciation rights costs. 3 Incl. a $1.2 mill. nonrecurr. chg. for a vol. severance/early retire. program, a $500,000 chg. for costs of stock appreciation rights rel. to the incr. in FCX's stock price during the second quarter of 1999. 4 Incl. net pre-tax net chrgs. of $8.0 mill.

OFFICERS:
J. R. Moffett, Chmn., C.E.O.
B. M. Rankin Jr., Vice-Chmn.
R. C. Adkerson, Pres., C.F.O.

INVESTOR CONTACT: Investor Relations, (504) 582-4000

PRINCIPAL OFFICE: 1615 Poydras Street, New Orleans, LA 70112

TELEPHONE NUMBER: (504) 582-4000
FAX: (504) 582-1847
WEB: www.fcx.com
NO. OF EMPLOYEES: 9,777 (avg.)
SHAREHOLDERS: 6,253 (class A common); 10,457 (class B common)
ANNUAL MEETING: In May
INCORPORATED: DE, Nov., 1987

INSTITUTIONAL HOLDINGS:
No. of Institutions: 196
Shares Held: 62,622,919
% Held: 43.5

INDUSTRY: Copper ores (SIC: 1021)

TRANSFER AGENT(S): Mellon Investor Services, LLC, Ridgefield Park, NJ

NYSE SYMBOL FMT
Rec. Pr. 4.28 (4/30/01)

FREMONT GENERAL CORPORATION

YIELD 1.9%
P/E RATIO . . .

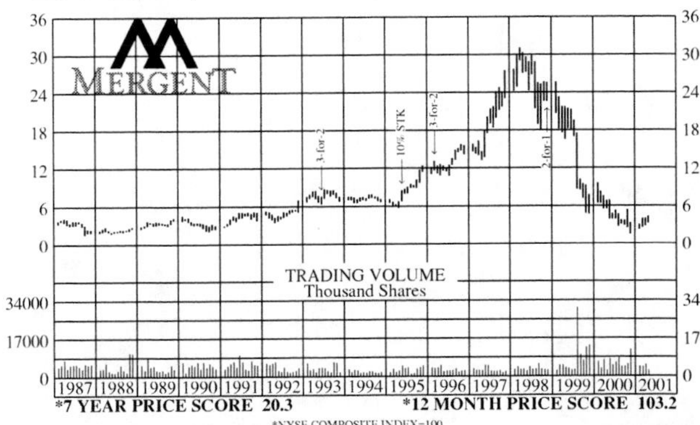

*7 YEAR PRICE SCORE 20.3 *12 MONTH PRICE SCORE 103.2
*NYSE COMPOSITE INDEX=100

INTERIM EARNINGS (Per Share):

Qtr.	Mar.	June	Sept.	Dec.
1997	0.38	0.38	0.43	0.44
1998	0.46	0.47	0.49	0.49
1999	0.49	0.50	d0.92	d0.80
2000	0.14	d4.29	0.09	d4.12

INTERIM DIVIDENDS (Per Share):

Amt.	Decl.	Ex.	Rec.	Pay.
0.08Q	2/25/00	3/29/00	3/31/00	4/28/00
0.08Q	5/16/00	6/28/00	6/30/00	7/31/00
0.04Q	8/14/00	9/27/00	9/29/00	10/31/00
0.04Q	11/09/00	12/27/00	12/29/00	1/31/01
0.02Q	3/08/01	3/28/01	3/30/01	4/30/01

Indicated div.: $0.08

CAPITALIZATION (12/31/00):

	($000)	(%)
Long-Term Debt	376,843	52.2
Redeemable Pfd. Stock	100,000	13.9
Common & Surplus	244,899	33.9
Total	721,742	100.0

RECENT DEVELOPMENTS: For the year ended 12/31/00, the Company reported a loss of $518.7 million, before an extraordinary gain of $12.4 million, compared with a loss from continuing operations of $40.4 million in 1999. Results for 2000 included a write-down of intangibles and a restructuring charge of $267.8 million. Total revenues grew 12.8% to $1.58 billion, versus $1.40 billion a year earlier. Property and casualty loss totaled $748.5 million, while financial services pre-tax income improved 27.9% to $102.2 million.

PROSPECTS: FMT announced that its workers' compensation insurance operations will be closing 16 of its 24 production and claim servicing offices. This action will result in a workforce reduction of approximately 465, or 29.0% of the insurance operations' current workforce. The Company estimates that the combined office closures, coupled with workforce reductions announced in 2000, will result in annual expense savings of approximately $55.0 million before taxes.

BUSINESS

FREMONT GENERAL CORPORATION through its subsidiaries is engaged in select insurance and financial services businesses nationwide. The Company operates select businesses in niche markets in forty-five states and the District of Columbia. FMT's insurance business includes one of the largest underwriters of workers' compensation in the nation. The financial services business includes commercial and residential real estate lending, commercial finance, syndicated loans, and insurance premium financing. The Company's workers' compensation operation currently has market positions in California, Illinois, Arizona, Wisconsin, Idaho and Alaska.

ANNUAL FINANCIAL DATA

	12/31/00	12/31/99	12/31/98	12/31/97	12/31/96	12/31/95	12/31/94
Earnings Per Share	**4 d8.23**	**2 3 d0.64**	**1 1.90**	**1.62**	**1.63**	**1.31**	**1.08**
Tang. Book Val. Per Share	**3.16**	**7.16**	**11.24**	**9.89**	**8.75**	**8.42**	**10.47**
Dividends Per Share	**0.28**	**0.32**	**0.30**	**0.30**	**0.29**	**0.25**	**0.22**
Dividend Payout %	. . .	. . .	**15.8**	**18.6**	**17.9**	**19.0**	**20.8**
INCOME STATEMENT (IN MILLIONS):							
Total Premium Income	1,016.1	831.0	552.1	601.2	486.9	606.9	433.6
Net Investment Income	540.2	536.0	427.6	344.1	287.3	282.5	190.2
Other Income	20.9	30.6	57.9	29.0	21.6	34.4	29.4
Total Revenues	1,577.2	1,397.6	1,037.6	974.3	795.8	923.8	653.1
Income Before Income Taxes	d692.9	d66.3	196.7	158.9	128.3	100.3	81.6
Income Taxes	cr174.1	cr25.9	63.7	50.6	41.0	32.3	25.8
Net Income	4 d518.7	2 3 d40.4	1 133.0	108.3	87.3	68.0	55.8
Average Shs. Outstg. (000)	63,052	63,650	70,082	68,586	53,524	52,158	51,646
BALANCE SHEET (IN MILLIONS):							
Cash & Cash Equivalents	2,165.9	2,235.9	2,449.7	2,502.3	1,534.1	1,975.7	711.9
Premiums Due	1,682.0	1,629.7	1,029.2	689.4	551.0	406.9	191.9
Invst. Assets: Fixed-term	. . .	. . .	. . .	. . .	. . .	. . .	206.4
Invst. Assets: Total	2,031.0	2,268.8	2,386.8	2,442.8	1,484.3	1,937.9	888.9
Total Assets	8,164.1	8,015.2	7,369.6	6,090.6	4,307.5	4,477.4	3,067.4
Long-Term Obligations	376.8	429.2	913.0	691.1	636.5	693.3	468.4
Net Stockholders' Equity	244.9	731.1	950.9	832.8	559.1	498.1	351.0
Year-end Shs. Outstg. (000)	70,732	80,039	69,939	69,142	56,186	50,786	30,776
STATISTICAL RECORD:							
Return on Revenues %	. . .	. . .	12.8	11.1	11.0	7.4	8.5
Return on Equity %	. . .	. . .	14.0	13.0	15.6	13.7	15.9
Return on Assets %	. . .	. . .	1.8	1.8	2.0	1.5	1.8
Price Range	9.63-1.50	25.69-4.69	31.06-18.00	27.50-13.19	15.75-10.75	12.42-5.72	7.88-6.52
P/E Ratio	. . .	. . .	16.3-9.5	17.0-8.2	9.7-6.6	9.5-4.4	7.3-6.0
Average Yield %	5.0	2.1	1.2	1.5	2.2	2.7	3.1

Statistics are as originally reported. Adj. for stk. splits: 2-for-1, 12/98; 3-for-2 spl., 2/96; 10% div., 6/95. 1 Bef. acctg. change credit $43.5 mill. 2 Bef. disc. ops. loss. $25.0 mill., 1999. 3 Incl. pre-tax chrg. $75.0 mill. & gain of $10.3 mill. 4 Bef. extraord. gain of $12.4 mill. for debt extinguishment, but incl. a write-down of intangibles and restruct. chrg. of $267.8 mill.

OFFICERS:
J. A. Mcintyre, Chmn., C.E.O.
L. J. Rampino, Pres., C.O.O.

INVESTOR CONTACT: Investor Relations, (310) 315-7442

PRINCIPAL OFFICE: 2020 Santa Monica Blvd., Suite 600, Santa Monica, CA 90404

TELEPHONE NUMBER: (310) 315-5500
FAX: (310) 315-5599
WEB: www.fmtgen.com

NO. OF EMPLOYEES: 2,316 (avg.)

SHAREHOLDERS: 1,849

ANNUAL MEETING: In May

INCORPORATED: NV, 1972

INSTITUTIONAL HOLDINGS:
No. of Institutions: 85
Shares Held: 21,428,739
% Held: 30.3

INDUSTRY: Fire, marine, and casualty insurance (SIC: 6331)

TRANSFER AGENT(S): Mellon Investor Services, Ridgefield Park, NJ

NYSE SYMBOL FTO
Rec. Pr. 13.40 (5/31/01)

FRONTIER OIL CORPORATION

YIELD ...
P/E RATIO 10.2

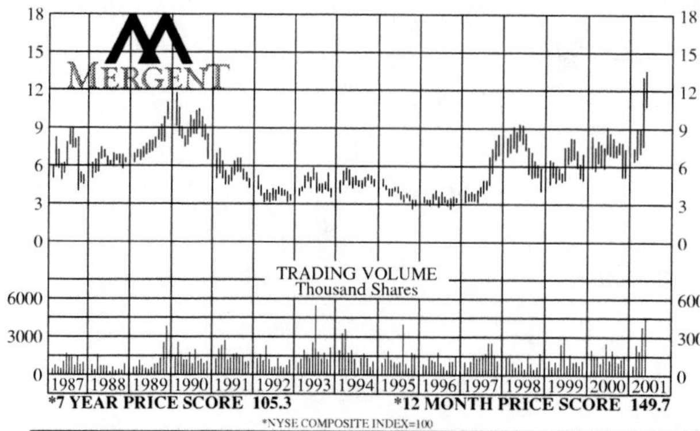

*7 YEAR PRICE SCORE 105.3 *12 MONTH PRICE SCORE 149.7
*NYSE COMPOSITE INDEX=100

INTERIM EARNINGS (Per Share):

Qtr.	Mar.	June	Sept.	Dec.
1998	d0.03	0.33	0.33	0.04
1999	d0.18	0.14	0.30	d0.90
2000	d0.22	1.13	0.36	0.05

INTERIM DIVIDENDS (Per Share):

Amt.	Decl.	Ex.	Rec.	Pay.

No dividends paid.

CAPITALIZATION (12/31/00):

	($000)	(%)
Long-Term Debt	253,108	74.8
Deferred Income Tax	3,853	1.1
Common & Surplus	81,424	24.1
Total	338,385	100.0

RECENT DEVELOPMENTS: For the twelve months ended 12/31/00, net income totaled $37.2 million compared with a net loss of $17.1 million the year before. Revenues increased to $2.05 billion from $503.6 million a year earlier. The improvement in results reflected a full year of contribution by the El Dorado refinery, which was acquired by FTO in November 1999, improved refined product margins and increased differentials in the crude oil markets. FTO reported operating income of $70.7 million versus an operating loss of $5.2 million in 1999.

PROSPECTS: The Company's results are being enhanced by the significant price differential, between light grades, which are generally lower in sulfer content, and heavy grades, which are generally higher in sulfer content, of crude oil. As of 12/31/00, the light/heavy spread amounted to $8.89 per barrel versus $2.63 per barrel in 1999. This benefits FTO as both of its refineries can process heavier, less expensive types of crude oil and still produce a higher percentage of gasoline, diesel fuel and other high margin refined products.

BUSINESS

FRONTIER OIL CORPORATION is an independent energy company engaged in crude oil refining and the wholesale marketing of refined petroleum products. FTO operates refineries in Cheyenne, WY and in El Dorado, KS with total crude oil capacity of over 150,000 barrels per day. The Company focuses its marketing efforts in the Rocky Mountain Region, which includes the states of CO, WY, MT and UT, and the Plains States, which includes KS, NE, IA, MO, ND and SD. The Cheyenne refinery has a permitted crude capacity of 41,000 barrels per day. As of 12/31/00, the Cheyenne's refinery product mix included gasoline (41.0%), diesel fuel (29.0%) and asphalt and other refined petroleum products (30.0%). The El Dorado refinery has a permitted crude capacity of more than 110,000 barrels per day. As of 12/31/00, the El Dorado refinery's product mix included gasoline (54.0%), diesel and jet fuel (35.0%) and asphalt, chemicals and other refined products (11.0%). On 11/16/99, FTO acquired the refinery located in El Dorado, KS from Equilon Enterprises LLC for total consideration of about $170.0 million.

ANNUAL FINANCIAL DATA

	12/31/00	12/31/99	12/31/98	12/31/97	12/31/96	12/31/95	12/31/94
Earnings Per Share	**1.34**	**d0.62**	**[1] 0.65**	**[2] 0.28**	**d0.25**	**d0.70**	**d0.46**
Cash Flow Per Share	**2.17**	**d0.15**	**1.03**	**0.75**	**0.38**	**0.08**	**0.52**
Tang. Book Val. Per Share	**3.06**	**1.86**	**2.53**	**1.99**	**0.93**	**1.19**	**1.81**
INCOME STATEMENT (IN THOUSANDS):							
Total Revenues	[3] 2,045,157	503,600	299,368	376,418	403,952	362,745	353,715
Costs & Expenses	1,951,495	495,801	262,958	341,697	376,110	340,326	319,620
Depreciation & Amort.	23,007	13,048	10,710	13,018	17,141	21,411	26,740
Operating Income	70,655	d5,249	25,700	21,703	10,701	1,008	7,355
Net Interest Inc./(Exp.)	d31,374	d9,947	d6,732	d13,891	d17,406	d20,000	d20,797
Income Before Income Taxes	39,281	d15,196	18,968	7,812	d6,705	d18,992	d13,442
Income Taxes	2,075	1,865	150	...	187	133	cr835
Net Income	37,206	d17,061	[1] 18,818	[2] 7,812	d6,892	d19,125	d12,607
Cash Flow	60,213	d4,013	29,528	20,830	10,249	2,286	14,133
Average Shs. Outstg.	27,789	27,373	28,746	27,951	27,257	27,254	27,335
BALANCE SHEET (IN THOUSANDS):							
Cash & Cash Equivalents	64,446	38,345	33,589	21,735	5,183	6,045	5,831
Total Current Assets	272,519	192,990	65,439	67,996	56,309	48,856	51,777
Net Property	302,993	313,308	111,873	106,659	178,606	184,321	219,999
Total Assets	588,213	521,493	182,026	177,915	239,865	238,382	277,536
Total Current Liabilities	228,909	168,158	35,314	47,068	60,061	51,341	50,245
Long-Term Obligations	253,108	277,971	70,000	70,572	145,928	145,377	170,797
Net Stockholders' Equity	81,424	50,681	70,353	55,934	25,269	32,464	49,449
Net Working Capital	43,610	24,832	30,125	20,928	d3,752	d2,485	1,532
Year-end Shs. Outstg.	26,567	27,311	27,780	28,059	27,259	27,256	27,251
STATISTICAL RECORD:							
Operating Profit Margin %	3.5	...	8.6	5.8	2.6	0.3	2.1
Net Profit Margin %	1.8	...	6.3	2.1	...	...	...
Return on Equity %	45.7	...	26.7	14.0	...	...	...
Return on Assets %	6.3	...	10.3	4.4	...	...	...
Debt/Total Assets %	43.0	53.3	38.5	39.7	60.8	61.0	61.5
Price Range	9.13-5.13	8.25-4.56	9.31-4.00	8.50-3.13	4.13-2.63	5.00-2.63	5.88-3.88
P/E Ratio	6.8-3.8	...	14.3-6.2	30.3-11.2	...	...	...

Statistics are as originally reported. [1] Bef. extraord. chrg. of $3.0 mill. [2] Bef. disc. oper. gain of $15.2 mill.; bef. extraord. chrg. of $3.9 mill. [3] Incl. results of the El Dorado refinery.

OFFICERS:
J. R. Gibbs, Chmn., Pres., C.E.O.
J. H. Edwards, Exec. V.P., C.F.O.

INVESTOR CONTACT: Gerald B. Faudel, V.P., Corporate Relations, (713) 658-9900

PRINCIPAL OFFICE: 10000 Memorial Drive, Suite 600, Houston, TX 77024-3411

TELEPHONE NUMBER: (713) 688-9600
FAX: (713) 688-0610
WEB: www.frontieroil.com

NO. OF EMPLOYEES: 700 (approx.)

SHAREHOLDERS: 1,560

ANNUAL MEETING: In Apr.

INCORPORATED: WY, Dec., 1976

INSTITUTIONAL HOLDINGS:
No. of Institutions: 49
Shares Held: 13,941,889
% Held: 52.9

INDUSTRY: Petroleum refining (SIC: 2911)

TRANSFER AGENT(S): Computershare Investor Services, Chicago, IL

NYSE SYMBOL FBN
Rec. Pr. 22.67 (4/30/01)

FURNITURE BRANDS INTERNATIONAL INC.

YIELD	...
P/E RATIO	10.5

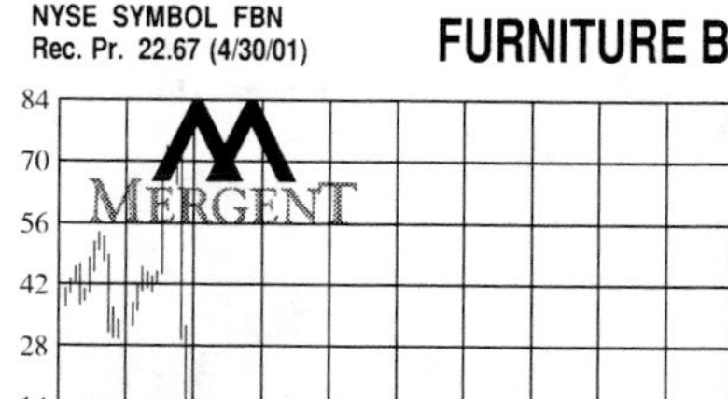

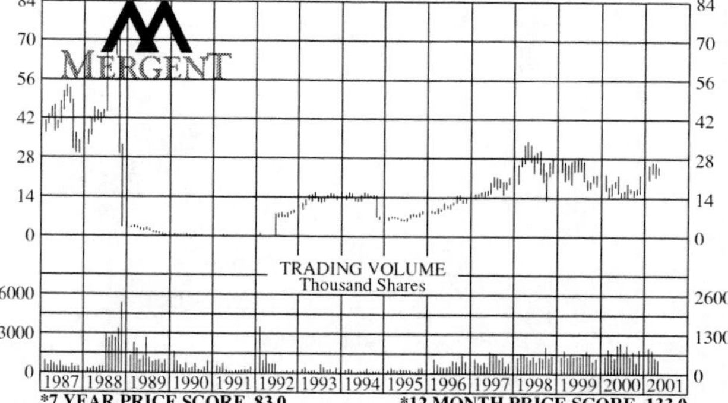

*7 YEAR PRICE SCORE 83.0 *12 MONTH PRICE SCORE 133.0
*NYSE COMPOSITE INDEX=100

INTERIM EARNINGS (Per Share):

Qtr.	Mar.	June	Sept.	Dec.
1997	0.27	0.26	0.27	0.35
1998	0.40	0.39	0.57	0.46
1999	0.52	0.52	0.52	0.58
2000	0.61	0.60	0.46	0.48

INTERIM DIVIDENDS (Per Share):

Amt.	Decl.	Ex.	Rec.	Pay.

No dividends paid.

CAPITALIZATION (12/31/00):

	($000)	(%)
Long-Term Debt	462,000	44.2
Common & Surplus	583,905	55.8
Total	1,045,905	100.0

RECENT DEVELOPMENTS: For the year ended 12/31/00, the Company reported income of $108.4 million, before an extraordinary charge of $2.5 million, versus net earnings of $111.9 million in the previous year. Net sales improved slightly to $2.12 billion compared with $2.09 billion in the prior year. The increase in net sales was due mainly to the Company's continuing efforts of introducing new products, emphasizing brand names and expanding distribution.

PROSPECTS: Going forward, the Company expects sluggish sales due to a slowdown in the economy to continue through the first half of 2001. In response, the Company plans to shut down and/or consolidate manufacturing operations at several of FBN's domestic facilities. Accordingly, the Company expects revenues in 2001 to be flat with 2000, and earnings per share for the year will be in the $2.15 to $2.25 range, versus $2.15 in 2000.

BUSINESS

FURNITURE BRANDS INTERNATIONAL INC. is one of the largest manufacturers of residential furniture in the United States. The Company, through its three operating subsidiaries: Broyhill Furniture Industries, Inc., Lane Furniture Industries, Inc., and Thomasville Furniture Industries, Inc., manufactures and distributes case goods, consisting of bedroom, dining room and living room furniture; stationary upholstery products, consisting of sofas, loveseats, sectionals and chairs; occasional furniture, consisting of wood tables, accent pieces, home entertainment centers and home office furniture; and recliners, motion furniture and sleep sofas.

QUARTERLY DATA

(12/31/2000)($000)	REV	INC
1st Quarter	519,467	24,307
2nd Quarter	499,746	23,373
3rd Quarter	533,079	27,621
4th Quarter	563,947	30,600

ANNUAL FINANCIAL DATA

	12/31/00	12/31/99	12/31/98	12/31/97	12/31/96	12/31/95	12/31/94
Earnings Per Share	**2.15**	**2.14**	**1.82**	**1.15**	**[2] 0.88**	**[2][3] 0.67**	**[1] 0.54**
Cash Flow Per Share	**3.30**	**3.22**	**2.85**	**2.10**	**1.75**	**1.39**	**1.24**
Tang. Book Val. Per Share	**5.92**	**3.46**	**1.86**	...	**1.23**	...	...
INCOME STATEMENT (IN MILLIONS):							
Total Revenues	2,116.2	2,088.1	1,960.3	1,808.3	1,696.8	1,073.9	1,072.7
Costs & Expenses	1,865.5	1,819.8	1,721.3	1,605.5	1,511.8	958.7	951.9
Depreciation & Amort.	58.2	56.5	55.5	56.0	54.1	36.1	35.8
Operating Income	192.6	211.8	183.5	146.7	130.9	79.1	85.1
Net Interest Inc./(Exp.)	d36.4	d37.6	d43.5	d42.7	d45.2	d33.8	d37.9
Income Before Income Taxes	166.0	176.8	152.1	107.3	88.3	57.0	48.8
Income Taxes	57.6	64.9	54.2	40.2	34.1	22.8	20.9
Net Income	108.4	111.9	97.9	67.1	[2] 54.2	[2][3] 34.2	[1] 27.9
Cash Flow	166.6	168.4	153.4	123.0	108.3	70.3	63.7
Average Shs. Outstg. (000)	50,443	52,335	53,809	58,473	61,946	50,639	51,495
BALANCE SHEET (IN MILLIONS):							
Cash & Cash Equivalents	14.6	7.4	13.2	12.3	19.4	26.4	32.1
Total Current Assets	691.6	671.9	675.9	618.5	607.3	590.1	404.6
Net Property	303.2	297.7	293.8	294.1	302.0	306.4	181.4
Total Assets	1,304.8	1,288.8	1,303.2	1,257.2	1,269.2	1,291.7	891.9
Total Current Liabilities	143.1	153.9	166.7	136.2	144.6	135.1	97.6
Long-Term Obligations	462.0	535.1	589.2	667.8	572.6	705.0	409.7
Net Stockholders' Equity	583.9	474.2	413.5	323.3	419.7	301.2	275.4
Net Working Capital	548.5	518.0	509.1	482.3	462.7	455.0	307.0
Year-end Shs. Outstg. (000)	49,675	49,370	51,752	52,004	61,432	50,120	50,077
STATISTICAL RECORD:							
Operating Profit Margin %	9.1	10.1	9.4	8.1	7.7	7.4	7.9
Net Profit Margin %	5.1	5.4	5.0	3.7	3.2	3.2	2.6
Return on Equity %	18.6	23.6	23.7	20.7	12.9	11.4	10.1
Return on Assets %	8.3	8.7	7.5	5.3	4.3	2.6	3.1
Debt/Total Assets %	35.4	41.5	45.2	53.1	45.1	54.6	45.9
Price Range	22.44-13.94	28.44-17.00	34.13-12.94	21.50-13.63	15.00-8.25	9.25-5.50	15.75-6.13
P/E Ratio	10.4-6.5	13.3-7.9	18.7-7.1	18.7-11.8	17.0-9.4	13.8-8.2	29.2-11.3

Statistics are as originally reported. [1] Bef. disc. oper. credit of $10.3 mill. [2] Bef. extraord. chrg., 1996, $7.4 mill.; 1995, $5.8 mill. [3] Gain on insurance settlement of $7.9 mill.

OFFICERS:
W. G. Holliman, Chmn., Pres., C.E.O.
D. P. Howard, V.P., C.F.O., Treas.
L. Chipperfield, Sr. V.P., Sec., C.A.O.

PRINCIPAL OFFICE: 101 South Hanley Road, St. Louis, MO 63105

TELEPHONE NUMBER: (314) 863-1100
FAX: (314) 863-5306
WEB: www.furniturebrands.com

NO. OF EMPLOYEES: 20,700 (avg.)

SHAREHOLDERS: 2,100 (approx.)

ANNUAL MEETING: In Apr.

INCORPORATED: DE, Mar., 1921

INSTITUTIONAL HOLDINGS:
No. of Institutions: 177
Shares Held: 44,478,933
% Held: 88.5

INDUSTRY: Household furniture, nec (SIC: 2519)

TRANSFER AGENT(S): The Bank of New York, New York, NY

NYSE SYMBOL GLC
Rec. Pr. 24.42 (4/30/01)

GALILEO INTERNATIONAL, INC.

YIELD 1.5%
P/E RATIO 14.9

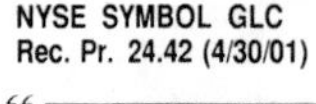

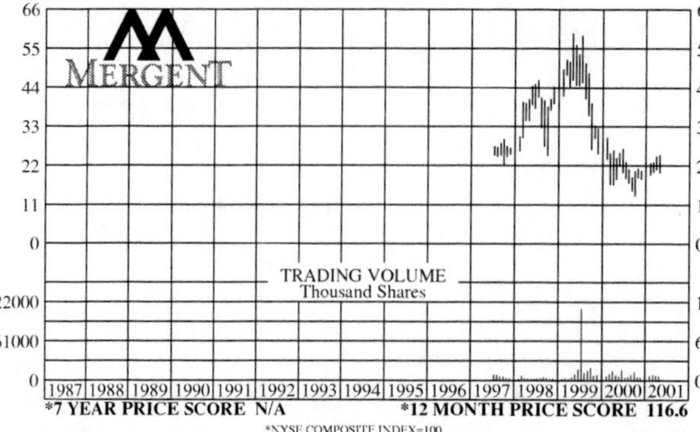

*7 YEAR PRICE SCORE N/A *12 MONTH PRICE SCORE 116.6
*NYSE COMPOSITE INDEX=100

INTERIM EARNINGS (Per Share):

Qtr.	Mar.	June	Sept.	Dec.
1997	0.44	0.36	0.29	0.21
1998	0.59	0.51	0.49	0.27
1999	0.74	0.59	0.58	0.26
2000	0.52	0.47	0.42	0.23

INTERIM DIVIDENDS (Per Share):

Amt.	Decl.	Ex.	Rec.	Pay.
0.09Q	4/21/00	5/03/00	5/05/00	5/19/00
0.09Q	7/20/00	8/02/00	8/04/00	8/18/00
0.09Q	10/19/00	11/01/00	11/03/00	11/17/00
0.09Q	1/18/01	1/31/01	2/02/01	2/16/01
0.09Q	4/20/01	5/02/01	5/04/01	5/18/01

Indicated div.: $0.36

CAPITALIZATION (12/31/00):

	($000)	(%)
Long-Term Debt	434,392	46.3
Capital Lease Obligations	2,619	0.3
Deferred Income Tax	35,398	3.8
Common & Surplus	465,236	49.6
Total	937,645	100.0

RECENT DEVELOPMENTS: For the year ended 12/31/00, net income fell 31.8% to $148.9 million versus $218.2 million in 1999. Results for 2000 included special charges of $1.7 million for restructuring, $19.7 million for services agreements with US Airways, and $7.0 million for the write-off of in-process research and development. Results for 1999 included special charges totaling $94.5 million. Revenues were up 7.7% to $1.64 billion from $1.53 billion the year before.

PROSPECTS: The Company anticipates strong revenue growth in 2001 due to increased international bookings, an airline booking fee price increase, and new revenue streams generated by the Quantitude subsidiary and Web hosting services. For the year 2001, the Company expects revenue growth to be in the range of 10.0% and 12.0% and earnings per share growth to be between 7.0% and 9.0%. In addition, GLC expects to continue to strengthen its market position in the U.S. in the traditional agency distribution channel.

BUSINESS

GALILEO INTERNATIONAL, INC. provides electronic global distribution services for the travel industry. Utilizing a computerized reservation system, the Company provides travel agencies, corporate travel managers and Internet users, with the ability to access schedule and fare information, book reservations and issue tickets for more than 500 airlines. In addition, the Company provides subscribers with information and booking capability for approximately 40 car rental companies and more than 200 hotel chains with approximately 45,000 properties throughout the world. Revenues for 2000 were derived: electronic global distribution services, 95.0%, and information services, 5.0%.

ANNUAL FINANCIAL DATA

	12/31/00	12/31/99	12/31/98	12/31/97	12/31/96	12/31/95	12/31/94
Earnings Per Share	**1.65**	**[1] 2.21**	**[1] 1.86**	**[1] 1.30**	...	...	...
Cash Flow Per Share	**4.06**	**3.90**	**3.50**	**3.11**	...	...	...
Tang. Book Val. Per Share	...	...	**0.42**	...	...	...	...
Dividends Per Share	**0.36**	**0.34**	**0.28**	**0.06**	...	...	...
Dividend Payout %	**21.8**	**15.6**	**15.3**	**4.6**	...	...	...
INCOME STATEMENT (IN MILLIONS):							
Total Revenues	1,643.3	1,526.1	1,480.8	1,256.1	1,088.3	966.4	813.8
Costs & Expenses	1,098.0	1,046.1	976.7	910.5	832.6	746.0	653.0
Depreciation & Amort.	217.7	167.1	172.5	134.1	80.4	80.2	91.5
Operating Income	327.6	312.9	331.6	211.5	175.3	140.3	69.3
Net Interest Inc./(Exp.)	d44.9	d16.0	d9.6	d8.8	d8.1	d14.4	d21.7
Income Before Income Taxes	265.9	361.3	325.5	205.6	167.1	123.7	53.2
Income Taxes	117.0	143.1	129.9	44.0	1.9	2.7	4.4
Net Income	148.9	[1] 218.2	[1] 195.6	[1] 161.6	165.2	121.1	48.8
Cash Flow	366.5	385.3	368.2	295.7	245.6	201.2	140.3
Average Shs. Outstg. (000)	90,350	98,814	105,186	95,000	...	...	...
BALANCE SHEET (IN MILLIONS):							
Cash & Cash Equivalents	2.5	1.8	9.8	19.4	78.2	8.4	...
Total Current Assets	244.7	230.5	243.5	224.3	240.8	187.3	...
Net Property	210.7	190.9	195.0	189.2	106.2	103.3	...
Total Assets	1,479.3	1,255.2	1,291.1	1,268.5	599.9	569.0	...
Total Current Liabilities	436.9	319.3	231.8	201.4	199.6	227.6	...
Long-Term Obligations	437.0	434.5	92.3	277.8	104.5	170.4	...
Net Stockholders' Equity	465.2	393.6	842.6	683.7	255.4	129.6	...
Net Working Capital	d192.2	d88.8	11.7	22.9	41.2	d40.3	...
Year-end Shs. Outstg. (000)	88,312	89,999	104,762	104,800	...	...	...
STATISTICAL RECORD:							
Operating Profit Margin %	19.9	20.5	22.4	16.8	16.1	14.5	8.5
Net Profit Margin %	9.1	14.3	13.2	12.9	15.2	12.5	6.0
Return on Equity %	32.0	55.4	23.2	23.6	64.7	93.4	...
Return on Assets %	10.1	17.4	15.2	12.7	27.5	21.3	...
Debt/Total Assets %	29.5	34.6	7.1	21.9	17.4	30.0	...
Price Range	29.94-13.44	59.31-25.31	46.13-24.75	29.38-22.00	...	...	...
P/E Ratio	18.1-8.1	26.8-11.5	24.8-13.3	22.6-16.9	...	...	...
Average Yield %	1.7	0.8	0.8	0.2	...	...	...

Statistics are as originally reported. [1] Incl. $28.4 mil one-time pre-tax chg., 2000; $71.9 mil, 1999; $26.5 mil, 1998; & $20.1 mil, 1997.

OFFICERS:
J. E. Barlett, Chmn., Pres., C.E.O.
C. M. Ballenger, Exec. V.P., C.F.O., Treas.
A. C. Swanagan, Sr. V.P., Gen Couns., Sec.

INVESTOR CONTACT: T. Bobbitt, V.P., Inv. Rel., (847) 518-4771

PRINCIPAL OFFICE: 9700 West Higgins Road, Suite 400, Rosemont, IL 60018

TELEPHONE NUMBER: (847) 518-4000
FAX: (847) 518-4085
WEB: www.galileo.com

NO. OF EMPLOYEES: 3,300 (approx.)

SHAREHOLDERS: 130 (approx. record)

ANNUAL MEETING: In May

INCORPORATED: DE, May, 1997

INSTITUTIONAL HOLDINGS:
No. of Institutions: 152
Shares Held: 59,213,073
% Held: 67.4

INDUSTRY: Data processing and preparation (SIC: 7374)

TRANSFER AGENT(S): LeSalle Bank National Assoc. of Chicago, Chicago, IL

NYSE SYMBOL AJG
Rec. Pr. 25.22 (4/30/01)

GALLAGHER (ARTHUR J.) & COMPANY

YIELD 2.1%
P/E RATIO 24.2

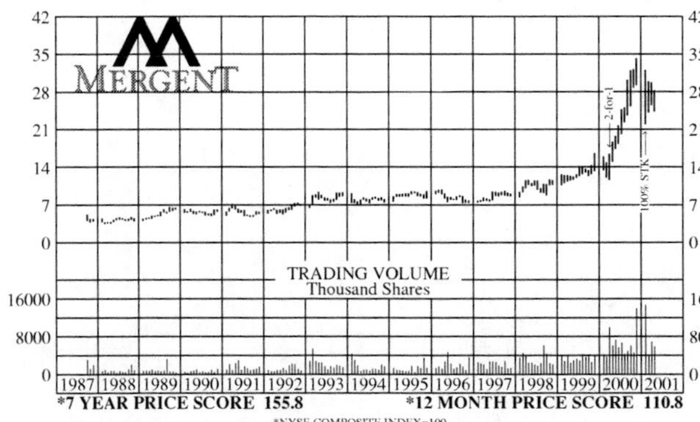

*7 YEAR PRICE SCORE 155.8 *12 MONTH PRICE SCORE 110.8
*NYSE COMPOSITE INDEX=100

INTERIM EARNINGS (Per Share):

Qtr.	Mar.	June	Sept.	Dec.
1997	0.14	0.19	0.27	0.19
1998	0.16	0.13	0.27	0.21
1999	0.18	0.17	0.30	0.24
2000	0.20	0.19	0.37	0.28

INTERIM DIVIDENDS (Per Share):

Amt.	Decl.	Ex.	Rec.	Pay.
0.23Q	7/20/00	9/27/00	9/29/00	10/13/00
0.23Q	11/16/00	12/27/00	12/29/00	1/15/01
100% STK	11/16/00	1/19/01	1/02/01	1/18/01
0.13Q	1/22/01	3/28/01	3/30/01	4/13/01
0.13Q	5/22/01	6/27/01	6/29/01	7/13/01

Indicated div.: $0.52

CAPITALIZATION (12/31/00):

	($000)	(%)
Common & Surplus	314,372	100.0
Total	314,372	100.0

RECENT DEVELOPMENTS: For the year ended 12/31/00, net income increased 24.9% to $87.8 million from $70.3 million in 1999. Total revenue amounted to $740.6 million, up 12.8% versus $656.4 million in the prior year. Commissions grew 7.1% to $418.8 million, while fees climbed 19.2% to $280.4 million from $235.3 million the year before. Investment income and other revenues improved 37.4% to $41.4 million.

PROSPECTS: The Company is benefiting from continued momentum toward higher premium rates across all lines of coverage, which is contributing to increased commissions and growth in risk management opportunities. Moreover, strong new sales from AJG's Gallagher Bassett Risk Management Division and continued emphasis on new business and renewal opportunities through the Company's niche marketing plan are also contributing to revenue growth.

BUSINESS

ARTHUR J. GALLAGHER & COMPANY is engaged in providing insurance brokerage, risk management, employee benefit and other related services to clients in the United States and abroad. The Company's principal activity is the negotiation and placement of insurance for its clients. In addition, AJG specializes in furnishing risk management services that include assisting clients in analyzing risks and determining whether proper protection is best obtained through the purchase of insurance or through retention of those risks and the adoption of corporate risk management policies and cost-effective loss control and prevention programs. Risk management also includes claims management, loss control consulting and property appraisals. The Company has offices in nine countries and does business in more than 100 countries around the world through a network of correspondent brokers and consultants.

REVENUES

(12/31/2000)	($000)	(%)
Commissions	418,807	65.6
Fees	280,369	32.1
Investment Income & Other	41,420	2.3
Total	740,596	100.0

ANNUAL FINANCIAL DATA

	12/31/00	12/31/99	12/31/98	12/31/97	12/31/96	12/31/95	12/31/94
Earnings Per Share	**1.05**	**0.88**	**0.78**	**0.78**	**0.66**	**0.64**	**0.54**
Tang. Book Val. Per Share	**3.75**	**3.14**	**2.69**	**2.31**	**1.89**	**1.79**	**1.50**
Dividends Per Share	**0.45**	**0.39**	**0.34**	**0.30**	**0.28**	**0.24**	**0.21**
Dividend Payout %	**42.4**	**44.0**	**43.9**	**39.0**	**42.6**	**38.2**	**38.7**
INCOME STATEMENT (IN MILLIONS):							
Total Revenues	740.6	605.8	540.7	488.0	456.7	412.0	356.4
Income Before Income Taxes	125.4	104.2	84.5	80.8	69.4	62.9	53.2
Income Taxes	37.6	36.5	28.0	27.5	23.6	21.4	18.7
Net Income	87.8	67.8	56.5	53.3	45.8	41.5	34.5
Average Shs. Outstg. (000)	83,924	77,132	72,824	68,152	71,100	65,260	63,608
BALANCE SHEET (IN MILLIONS):							
Cash & Cash Equivalents	258.1	170.0	148.1	148.3	144.2	121.3	108.8
Premiums Due	405.2	364.9	288.3	217.6	237.6	193.7	179.8
Invst. Assets: Total	23.3	20.3	20.1	39.2	36.9	41.7	37.8
Total Assets	1,062.3	884.1	746.0	641.8	590.4	495.8	451.1
Long-Term Obligations	...	...	...	...	...	...	3.4
Net Stockholders' Equity	314.4	242.5	202.5	163.9	134.5	118.1	96.7
Year-end Shs. Outstg. (000)	79,497	73,680	70,580	66,364	65,172	61,704	59,136
STATISTICAL RECORD:							
Return on Revenues %	11.9	11.2	10.5	10.9	10.0	10.1	9.7
Return on Equity %	27.9	27.9	27.9	32.5	34.0	35.1	35.7
Return on Assets %	8.3	7.7	7.6	8.3	7.8	8.4	7.7
Price Range	34.25-11.53	16.56-10.56	11.69-8.39	9.56-7.44	9.88-7.28	9.50-7.53	9.09-7.03
P/E Ratio	32.6-11.0	18.8-12.0	15.1-10.8	12.2-9.5	15.0-11.1	15.0-11.9	16.8-13.0
Average Yield %	1.9	2.9	3.4	3.6	3.3	2.8	2.6

Statistics are as originally reported. Adjusted for 2-for-1 stock splits: 1/01, 3/00

OFFICERS:
R. E. Gallagher, Chmn.
J. P. Gallagher Jr., Pres., C.E.O.
M. J. Cloherty, Exec. V.P., C.F.O.

INVESTOR CONTACT: Marsha J. Akin, Investor Relations, (630) 773-3800

PRINCIPAL OFFICE: Two Pierce Place, Itasca, IL 60143-3141

TELEPHONE NUMBER: (630) 773-3800
FAX: (630) 285-4000
WEB: www.ajg.com

NO. OF EMPLOYEES: 5,200 (approx.)

SHAREHOLDERS: 660 (approx.)

ANNUAL MEETING: In May

INCORPORATED: IL, 1960; reincorp., DE, 1972

INSTITUTIONAL HOLDINGS:
No. of Institutions: 186
Shares Held: 51,992,800
% Held: 65.3

INDUSTRY: Insurance agents, brokers, & service (SIC: 6411)

TRANSFER AGENT(S): Computershare Investor Services, Chicago, IL

NYSE SYMBOL GCI
Rec. Pr. 64.55 (4/30/01)

GANNETT CO., INC.

YIELD 1.4%
P/E RATIO 17.7

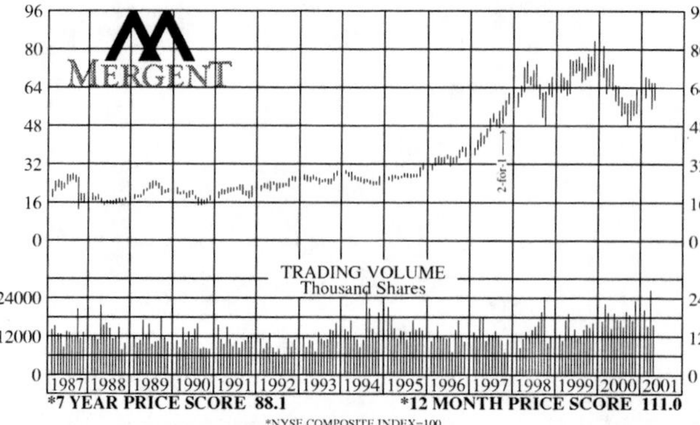

*7 YEAR PRICE SCORE 88.1 *12 MONTH PRICE SCORE 111.0

*NYSE COMPOSITE INDEX=100

INTERIM EARNINGS (Per Share):

Qtr.	Mar.	June	Sept.	Dec.
1997	0.48	0.69	0.27	0.80
1998	1.20	0.78	0.62	0.92
1999	0.64	0.98	0.74	1.01
2000	0.74	1.00	0.79	1.12

INTERIM DIVIDENDS (Per Share):

Amt.	Decl.	Ex.	Rec.	Pay.
0.21Q	5/02/00	6/07/00	6/09/00	7/03/00
0.22Q	8/29/00	9/13/00	9/15/00	10/02/00
0.22Q	10/17/00	12/13/00	12/15/00	1/02/01
0.22Q	2/21/01	3/07/01	3/09/01	4/02/01
0.22Q	5/08/01	6/06/01	6/08/01	7/02/01

Indicated div.: $0.88 (Div. Reinv. Plan)

CAPITALIZATION (12/31/00):

	($000)	(%)
Long-Term Debt	5,747,856	51.7
Deferred Income Tax	274,829	2.5
Common & Surplus	5,103,410	45.9
Total	11,126,095	100.0

RECENT DEVELOPMENTS: For the twelve months ended 12/31/00, income from continuing operations climbed 5.7% to $971.9 million compared with $919.4 million in 1999. Results excluded after-tax gains of $747.1 million and $38.5 million in 2000 and 1999, respectively, from discontinued operations. Operating revenues were $6.22 billion, up 22.1% from $5.10 billion in the previous year. Operating income rose 16.3% to $1.82 billion.

PROSPECTS: Near-term results are likely to be hampered by the absence of dot-com advertising revenue and slow advertising from automotive makers and retailers. As a result, GCI expects challenging business conditions and a less robust advertising environment. Profitability is likely to be pressured by a reduction in employment classified ads. However, ad spending appears to be strengthening.

BUSINESS

GANNETT CO., INC. is a diversified news and information company that publishes newspapers and operates broadcasting stations, cable television systems, and a television entertainment programming unit. GCI is also engaged in marketing, commercial printing, a newswire data service, data services, news programming and alarm services. GCI has operations in 45 states, the District of Columbia, Canada, Guam, and the U.S. Virgin Islands. GCI is the largest U.S. newspaper group in terms of circulation, with 99 daily newspapers, including USA TODAY, more than 300 non-daily publications and USA WEEKEND, a weekly newspaper magazine. In the U.K., GCI subsidiary Newsquest plc publishes nearly 300 titles, including 15 daily newspapers. GCI owns and operates 22 television stations in major markets. On 1/31/00, Gannett sold its cable business, Multimedia Cablevision, Inc.

REVENUES

(12/31/2000)	($000)	(%)
Newspaper advertising	3,972,936	63.8
Newspaper circulation	1,120,991	18.0
Broadcasting	788,767	12.7
All other	339,624	5.5
Total	6,222,318	100.0

ANNUAL FINANCIAL DATA

	12/31/00	12/26/99	12/27/98	12/28/97	[2] 12/31/96	12/31/95	12/25/94
Earnings Per Share	[5] 3.63	[4] 3.26	[3] 3.50	2.50	[1] 2.22	1.71	1.62
Cash Flow Per Share	5.03	4.26	4.59	3.55	3.23	2.45	2.34
Tang. Book Val. Per Share	...	...	0.66	...	...	...	1.25
Dividends Per Share	0.85	0.81	0.80	0.73	0.70	0.69	0.67
Dividend Payout %	23.4	24.8	22.9	29.2	31.8	40.2	41.2
INCOME STATEMENT (IN MILLIONS):							
Total Revenues	6,222.3	5,260.2	5,121.3	4,729.5	4,421.1	4,006.7	3,824.5
Costs & Expenses	4,029.1	3,417.0	3,367.6	3,112.2	3,067.3	2,944.9	2,802.9
Depreciation & Amort.	375.9	280.1	310.2	301.1	287.4	210.0	208.8
Operating Income	1,817.3	1,563.1	1,443.5	1,316.3	1,066.4	851.9	812.8
Net Interest Inc./(Exp.)	d192.0	d88.9	d60.1	d91.7	d128.8	d44.7	d42.4
Income Before Income Taxes	1,608.8	1,527.2	1,669.4	1,209.0	1,086.7	803.5	782.1
Income Taxes	636.9	607.8	669.5	496.3	462.7	326.2	316.7
Net Income	[5] 971.9	[4] 919.4	[3] 999.9	712.7	[1] 624.0	477.3	465.4
Cash Flow	1,347.9	1,199.5	1,310.1	1,013.8	911.3	687.2	674.2
Average Shs. Outstg. (000)	268,118	281,608	285,711	285,610	281,782	280,312	288,552
BALANCE SHEET (IN MILLIONS):							
Cash & Cash Equivalents	193.2	46.2	66.2	52.8	31.2	47.0	44.3
Total Current Assets	1,302.3	1,075.2	906.4	884.6	766.6	854.1	650.8
Net Property	2,461.4	2,223.9	2,063.8	2,192.0	1,994.1	2,070.7	1,428.1
Total Assets	12,980.4	9,006.4	6,979.5	6,890.4	6,349.6	6,503.8	3,707.1
Total Current Liabilities	1,174.0	883.8	728.0	767.5	719.0	812.8	527.1
Long-Term Obligations	5,747.9	2,463.3	1,306.9	1,740.5	1,880.3	2,767.9	767.3
Net Stockholders' Equity	5,103.4	4,629.6	3,979.8	3,479.7	2,930.8	2,145.6	1,822.2
Net Working Capital	128.3	191.4	178.4	117.1	47.6	41.3	123.8
Year-end Shs. Outstg. (000)	264,272	277,926	279,001	283,874	282,636	281,130	279,534
STATISTICAL RECORD:							
Operating Profit Margin %	29.2	29.7	28.2	27.8	24.1	21.3	21.3
Net Profit Margin %	15.6	17.5	19.5	15.1	14.1	11.9	12.2
Return on Equity %	19.0	19.9	25.1	20.5	21.3	22.2	25.5
Return on Assets %	7.5	10.2	14.3	10.3	9.8	7.3	12.6
Debt/Total Assets %	44.3	27.3	18.7	25.3	29.6	42.6	20.7
Price Range	81.56-48.38	83.63-60.63	75.13-47.63	61.69-35.69	39.38-29.50	32.44-24.75	29.50-23.06
P/E Ratio	22.5-13.3	25.7-18.6	21.5-13.6	24.7-14.3	17.8-13.3	19.0-14.5	18.3-14.3
Average Yield %	1.3	1.1	1.3	1.5	2.0	2.4	2.5

Statistics are as originally reported. Adj. for 2-for-1 spl., 10/97. [1] Excl. $294.6 mill. ($1.05/sh) aft-tx gain & $24.5 mill. ($0.09/sh) inco. fr. disc. ops; incl. $93.0 mill. ($0.66/sh) aft-tx gain. [2] Incl. ops. of Multimedia Inc., acq. on 12/9/95. [3] Incl. $184.0 mill. after-tax gain fr. disp. of five radio stations & alarm security bus. [4] Incl. $33.0 mill. net gain fr. exchange of TV stations & excl. $38.5 mill. gain fr. disc. ops. [5] Excl. $2.4 mill. net income fr. disc. ops. & $744.7 mill. net gain fr. sale of bus.

OFFICERS:
D. H. McCorkindale, Chmn., Pres., C.E.O.
L. Miller, Exec. V.P., C.F.O.

INVESTOR CONTACT: Gracia Martore, Investor Relations, (703) 284-6922

PRINCIPAL OFFICE: 1100 Wilson Blvd., 28th Floor, Arlington, VA 22234

TELEPHONE NUMBER: (703) 284-6000
FAX: (703) 364-0855
WEB: www.gannett.com

NO. OF EMPLOYEES: 45,800 (approx.)

SHAREHOLDERS: 14,000 (approx.)

ANNUAL MEETING: In May

INCORPORATED: NY, Dec., 1923; reincorp., DE, May, 1972

INSTITUTIONAL HOLDINGS:
No. of Institutions: 577
Shares Held: 208,238,290
% Held: 78.7

INDUSTRY: Newspapers (SIC: 2711)

TRANSFER AGENT(S): Wells Fargo Shareowner Services, St. Paul, MN

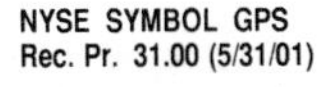

NYSE SYMBOL GPS
Rec. Pr. 31.00 (5/31/01)

GAP, INC. (THE)

YIELD 0.3%
P/E RATIO 31.0

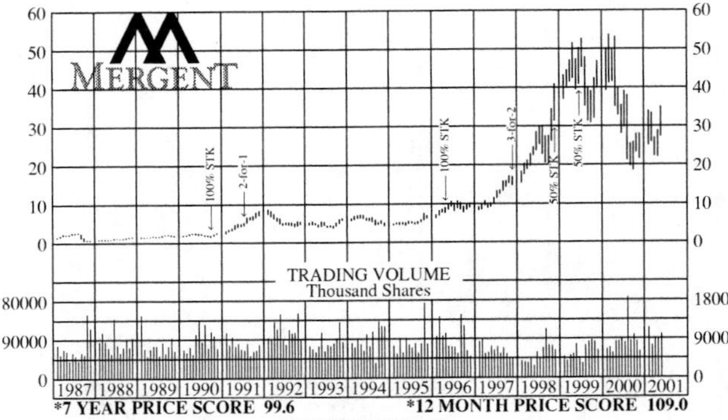

*7 YEAR PRICE SCORE 99.6 *12 MONTH PRICE SCORE 109.0
*NYSE COMPOSITE INDEX=100

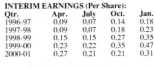

INTERIM EARNINGS (Per Share):

Qtr.	Apr.	July	Oct.	Jan.
1996-97	0.09	0.07	0.14	0.18
1997-98	0.09	0.07	0.18	0.23
1998-99	0.15	0.15	0.27	0.35
1999-00	0.23	0.22	0.35	0.47
2000-01	0.27	0.21	0.21	0.31

INTERIM DIVIDENDS (Per Share):

Amt.	Decl.	Ex.	Rec.	Pay.
0.022Q	5/16/00	5/24/00	5/26/00	6/12/00
0.022Q	9/06/00	9/14/00	9/18/00	10/03/00
0.022Q	10/24/00	11/29/00	12/01/00	12/26/00
0.022Q	1/23/01	2/21/01	2/23/01	3/12/01
0.022Q	5/23/01	5/31/01	6/04/01	6/21/01

Indicated div.: $0.09

CAPITALIZATION (2/3/01):

	($000)	(%)
Long-Term Debt	780,246	21.0
Common & Surplus	2,928,239	79.0
Total	3,708,485	100.0

RECENT DEVELOPMENTS: For the 53 weeks ended 2/3/01, net earnings slid 22.1% to $877.5 million from $1.13 billion in the corresponding 52-week period a year earlier. Net sales climbed 17.5% to $13.67 billion from $11.64 billion in the prior year. Comparable-store sales, adjusted for the extra week in the recent period, were down 5.0% year over year. Gross margin totaled $5.08 billion, or 37.1% of net sales, versus $4.86 billion, or 41.8% of net sales, the previous year.

PROSPECTS: The Company is focusing on aggressively controlling costs and improving internal management processes in an effort to boost operating performance. During the current fiscal year, the Company anticipates increasing its retail square footage between 17.0% and 20.0% through the expected opening of about 550 to 630 new stores. The Company is targeting square-footage growth of about 15.0% per year in fiscal 2002 and 2003.

BUSINESS

THE GAP, INC. is a specialty retailer that operates stores selling casual and activewear apparel for men, women, and children under five brand names: GAP, GAPKIDS and BABYGAP, which offer gender-specific contemporary clothing; BANANA REPUBLIC, which offers upscale clothing, jewelry, and small leather products; and OLD NAVY CLOTHING CO, which offers value-priced merchandise in a warehouse format. As of 2/3/01, the Company operated 3,147 stores in the U.S.: 2,079 Gap stores, 666 Old Navy stores, and 402 Banana Republics. All stores are leased and no stores are franchised or operated by others. In addition to the U.S., the Company operates 529 stores located in Canada, the United Kingdom, Japan, France, and Germany.

QUARTERLY DATA

(2/3/2001)($000)	Rev	Inc
1st Quarter	2,731,990	235,476
2nd Quarter	2,947,714	183,920
3rd Quarter	3,414,668	186,348
4th Quarter	4,579,088	271,753

ANNUAL FINANCIAL DATA

	2/3/01	1/29/00	1/30/99	1/31/98	2/1/97	2/3/96	1/28/95
Earnings Per Share	**1.00**	**1.26**	**0.91**	**0.58**	**0.47**	**0.37**	**0.33**
Cash Flow Per Share	**1.67**	**1.75**	**1.27**	**0.87**	**0.69**	**0.57**	**0.50**
Tang. Book Val. Per Share	**3.43**	**2.63**	**1.83**	**1.79**	**1.80**	**1.71**	**1.42**
Dividends Per Share	**0.09**	**0.09**	**0.09**	**0.09**	**0.09**	**0.07**	**0.07**
Dividend Payout %	**8.9**	**7.0**	**9.7**	**15.3**	**18.9**	**19.3**	**20.9**
INCOME STATEMENT (IN MILLIONS):							
Total Revenues	13,673.5	11,635.4	9,054.5	6,507.8	5,284.4	4,395.3	3,722.9
Costs & Expenses	11,638.3	9,382.5	7,395.1	5,386.9	4,340.4	3,628.4	3,036.3
Depreciation & Amort.	590.4	436.2	326.4	269.7	214.9	197.4	168.2
Operating Income	1,444.8	1,816.7	1,332.9	851.3	729.1	569.4	518.4
Net Interest Inc./(Exp.)	d62.9	d31.8	d13.6	3.0	19.5	15.8	10.9
Income Before Income Taxes	1,381.9	1,784.9	1,319.3	854.2	748.5	585.2	529.3
Income Taxes	504.4	657.9	494.7	320.3	295.7	231.2	209.1
Net Income	877.5	1,127.1	824.5	533.9	452.9	354.0	320.2
Cash Flow	1,467.9	1,563.2	1,151.0	803.6	667.8	551.5	488.5
Average Shs. Outstg. (000)	879,137	895,029	904,374	922,952	961,351	962,444	982,604
BALANCE SHEET (IN MILLIONS):							
Cash & Cash Equivalents	408.8	450.4	565.3	913.2	621.3	669.1	588.0
Total Current Assets	2,648.1	2,197.8	1,871.8	1,830.9	1,329.3	1,280.0	1,055.7
Net Property	4,007.7	2,715.3	1,876.4	1,365.2	1,135.7	957.8	828.8
Total Assets	7,012.9	5,188.8	3,963.9	3,337.5	2,626.9	2,343.1	2,004.2
Total Current Liabilities	2,799.1	1,752.9	1,553.1	991.5	774.9	551.7	499.9
Long-Term Obligations	780.2	784.9	496.5	496.0	...	...	...
Net Stockholders' Equity	2,928.2	2,233.0	1,573.7	1,584.0	1,654.5	1,640.5	1,374.5
Net Working Capital	d151.1	444.9	318.7	839.4	554.4	728.3	555.8
Year-end Shs. Outstg. (000)	853,997	850,499	857,960	884,505	926,495	971,150	977,164
STATISTICAL RECORD:							
Operating Profit Margin %	10.6	15.6	14.7	13.1	13.8	13.0	13.9
Net Profit Margin %	6.4	9.7	9.1	8.2	8.6	8.1	8.6
Return on Equity %	30.0	50.5	52.4	33.7	27.4	21.6	23.3
Return on Assets %	12.5	21.7	20.8	16.0	17.2	15.1	16.0
Debt/Total Assets %	11.1	15.1	12.5	14.9	...	...	...
Price Range	53.75-18.50	52.69-30.81	40.92-15.31	17.15-8.26	10.82-6.22	7.56-4.41	7.32-4.28
P/E Ratio	53.7-18.5	41.8-24.5	44.8-16.8	29.6-14.2	23.0-13.2	20.5-11.9	22.4-13.1
Average Yield %	0.2	0.2	0.3	0.7	1.0	1.2	1.2

Statistics are as originally reported. Adj. for 3-for-2 stk. split, 6/99, 11/98 & 12/97; 2-for-1 stk. split, 4/96.

OFFICERS:
D. G. Fisher, Chmn.
M. S. Drexler, Pres., C.E.O.
H. Kunz, Exec. V.P., C.F.O.
J. B. Wilson, Exec. V.P., C.O.O.

INVESTOR CONTACT: Leroy Barnes, (650) 874-2053

PRINCIPAL OFFICE: One Harrison Street, San Francisco, CA 94105

TELEPHONE NUMBER: (650) 952-4400
FAX: (650) 952-4407
WEB: www.gap.com

NO. OF EMPLOYEES: 166,000 (approx.)

SHAREHOLDERS: 10,086

ANNUAL MEETING: In May

INCORPORATED: CA, July, 1969; reincorp., DE, May, 1988

INSTITUTIONAL HOLDINGS:
No. of Institutions: 449
Shares Held: 371,686,505
% Held: 43.7

INDUSTRY: Family clothing stores (SIC: 5651)

TRANSFER AGENT(S): Computershare Investor Services, Chicago, IL

NYSE SYMBOL IT
Rec. Pr. 8.00 (4/30/01)

GARTNER GROUP, INC.

YIELD ...
P/E RATIO 57.1

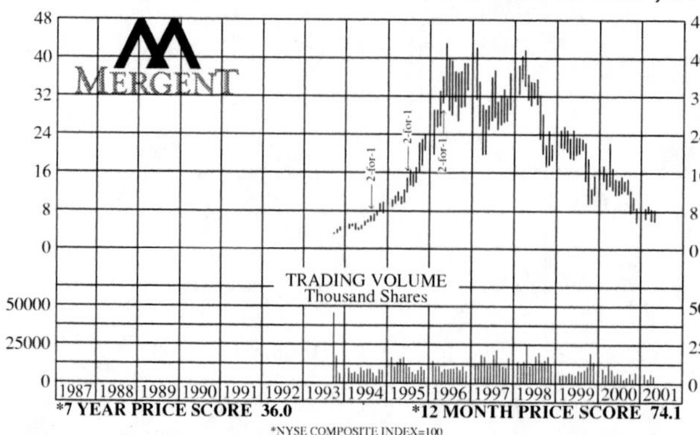

INTERIM EARNINGS (Per Share):

Qtr.	Dec.	Mar.	June	Sept.
1997-98	0.25	0.19	0.22	0.17
1998-99	0.29	0.27	0.25	0.03
1999-00	0.18	0.03	0.03	0.04
2000-01	0.04	...	...	...

INTERIM DIVIDENDS (Per Share):

Amt.	Decl.	Ex.	Rec.	Pay.
1.194Sp	...	7/19/99	7/16/99	7/22/99

CAPITALIZATION (9/30/00):

	($000)	(%)
Long-Term Debt	307,254	80.4
Common & Surplus	74,820	19.6
Total	382,074	100.0

RECENT DEVELOPMENTS: For the quarter ended 12/31/00, net income fell 76.3% to $3.9 million versus $16.5 million in 1999. Results for 2000 included a net gain of $5.3 million from the sale of investments. Results for 2000 and 1999 included a loss of $1.7 million and $1.2 million, respectively, from minority-owned investments. Results for 1999 also included charges of $6.1 million. Revenues rose 16.7% to $260.1 million from $222.9 million in the prior-year period.

PROSPECTS: The Company expects total revenue to increase about $950.0 million to $975.0 million in fiscal 2001. Research revenue is anticipated to increase about 5.0% to 7.0%, while consulting revenue should increase by 25.0% to 30.0% for the year. Diluted earnings per share for fiscal 2001 are expected to be in the range of $0.42 to $0.50. Going forward, revenues should benefit from continued growth in consulting backlog, research contract value and events deferred revenue.

BUSINESS

GARTNER GROUP, INC. is an independent provider of research and analysis on the computer hardware, software, communications and related information technology industries. IT's core business is researching and analyzing significant information technology industry trends and developments, packaging its analysis into annually renewable subscription-based products and distributing the products through print and electronic media. IT is organized into three businesses. The Research segment offers products that highlight industry developments, review products and technologies, provide market research, and analyze industry trends. The Services segment consists of consulting and measurement services that provide assessments of cost performance, efficiency and quality. The Events segment consists of vendor and user focused expositions and conferences. On 3/21/00, IT acquired TechRepublic, Inc.

ANNUAL FINANCIAL DATA

	9/30/00	9/30/99	9/30/98	9/30/97	9/30/96	9/30/95	9/30/94
Earnings Per Share	**[3] 0.30**	**[2] 0.84**	**[1] 0.84**	**0.71**	**0.17**	**0.28**	**0.17**
Cash Flow Per Share	**0.93**	**1.14**	**1.09**	**0.89**	**0.30**	**0.37**	**0.24**
Tang. Book Val. Per Share	...	...	**2.28**	**1.42**	**0.61**	**0.32**	...
Dividends Per Share	...	**1.19**	...	...	...	...	...
Dividend Payout %	...	**142.2**	...	...	...	...	...
INCOME STATEMENT (IN THOUSANDS):							
Total Revenues	858,671	734,234	641,957	511,239	394,672	229,152	169,002
Costs & Expenses	754,305	571,606	471,154	376,425	332,353	177,829	134,380
Depreciation & Amort.	56,156	31,633	27,266	18,201	12,879	8,087	7,265
Operating Income	48,210	130,995	143,537	116,613	49,440	43,236	27,357
Net Interest Inc./(Exp.)	d24,900	8,252	9,557	7,260	3,665	2,271	150
Income Before Income Taxes	56,101	139,247	151,121	123,873	53,130	45,605	27,355
Income Taxes	28,826	50,976	62,774	50,743	36,692	20,066	12,380
Equity Earnings/Minority Int.	...	...	...	...	25	98	...
Net Income	[3] 27,275	[2] 88,271	[1] 88,347	73,130	16,438	25,539	14,975
Cash Flow	83,431	119,904	115,613	91,331	29,317	33,626	22,240
Average Shs. Outstg.	89,529	104,948	105,699	102,459	98,612	91,762	92,008
BALANCE SHEET (IN THOUSANDS):							
Cash & Cash Equivalents	97,102	88,894	218,684	171,054	126,809	91,096	50,654
Total Current Assets	512,868	432,184	511,079	425,608	310,150	217,802	164,509
Net Property	91,259	63,592	50,801	44,102	32,818	19,820	9,580
Total Assets	1,002,965	803,444	832,871	645,312	444,108	300,598	232,557
Total Current Liabilities	587,339	473,621	414,835	372,183	291,408	211,799	171,333
Long-Term Obligations	307,254	250,000	...	...	...	...	6,419
Net Stockholders' Equity	74,820	74,486	414,938	269,870	150,235	85,499	49,028
Net Working Capital	d74,471	d41,437	96,244	53,425	18,742	6,003	d6,824
Year-end Shs. Outstg.	86,303	89,248	113,719	96,710	92,927	85,552	83,336
STATISTICAL RECORD:							
Operating Profit Margin %	5.6	17.8	22.4	22.8	12.5	18.9	16.2
Net Profit Margin %	3.2	12.0	13.8	14.3	4.2	11.1	8.9
Return on Equity %	36.5	118.5	21.3	27.1	10.9	29.9	30.5
Return on Assets %	2.7	11.0	10.6	11.3	3.7	8.5	6.4
Debt/Total Assets %	30.6	31.1	...	...	...	...	2.8
Price Range	22.25-5.65	25.75-9.56	41.75-17.31	42.25-19.75	43.13-19.75	24.13-8.88	9.88-4.00
P/E Ratio	74.1-18.8	30.7-11.4	49.7-20.6	59.5-27.8	253.5-116.1	86.1-31.7	59.8-24.2
Average Yield %	...	6.8	...	...	...	...	...

Statistics are as originally reported. Adj. for 2-for-1 split, 6/95 & 3/96. [1] Incl. $9.1 mill. pre-tax non-recur. chgs. & $2.0 mill. loss on sale of GartnerLearning. [2] Incl. $30.1 mill. non-recur. chg. [3] Incl. $29.6 mill. net gain fr. sale of investments & excl. $1.7 mill. net extraord. loss fr. exting. of debt.

OFFICERS:
M. A. Fernandez, Chmn.
M. D. Fleisher, C.E.O.
W. R. McDermott, Pres.

INVESTOR CONTACT: Jennifer L. Schlueter, Dir., Invest. Relations, (203) 964-0096

PRINCIPAL OFFICE: P.O. Box 10212, 56 Top Gallant Road, Stamford, CT 06904

TELEPHONE NUMBER: (203) 316-1111
FAX: (203) 316-1100
WEB: www.gartner.com
NO. OF EMPLOYEES: 4,322 (avg.)
SHAREHOLDERS: 250 (approx. class A); 4,300 (approx. class B)
ANNUAL MEETING: In Feb.
INCORPORATED: DE, 1990

INSTITUTIONAL HOLDINGS:
No. of Institutions: 94
Shares Held: 36,701,877
% Held: 42.5

INDUSTRY: Management services (SIC: 8741)

TRANSFER AGENT(S): BankBoston, NA, c/o EquiServe, Boston, MA

NYSE SYMBOL GTW
Rec. Pr. 19.00 (4/30/01)

GATEWAY INC.

YIELD ...
P/E RATIO 20.0

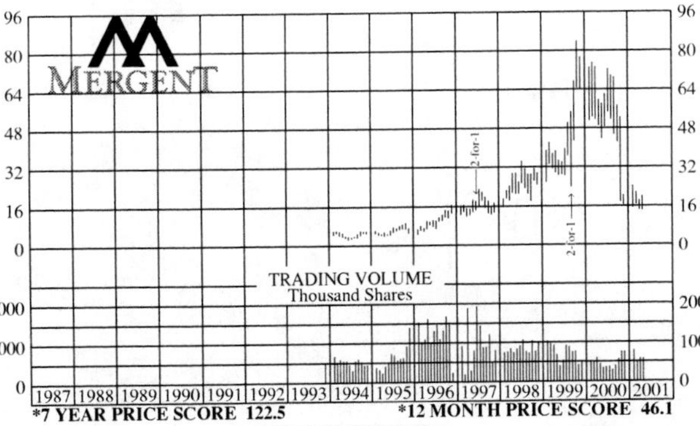

MERGENT

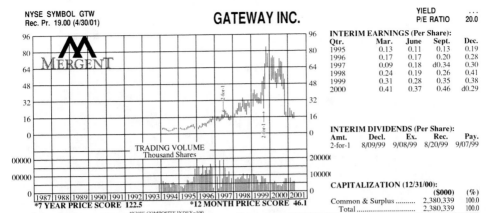

TRADING VOLUME
Thousand Shares

*7 YEAR PRICE SCORE 122.5 *12 MONTH PRICE SCORE 46.1
*NYSE COMPOSITE INDEX=100

INTERIM EARNINGS (Per Share):

Qtr.	Mar.	June	Sept.	Dec.
1995	0.13	0.11	0.13	0.19
1996	0.17	0.17	0.20	0.28
1997	0.09	0.18	d0.34	0.30
1998	0.24	0.19	0.26	0.41
1999	0.31	0.28	0.35	0.38
2000	0.41	0.37	0.46	d0.29

INTERIM DIVIDENDS (Per Share):

Amt.	Decl.	Ex.	Rec.	Pay.
2-for-1	8/09/99	9/08/99	8/20/99	9/07/99

CAPITALIZATION (12/31/00):

	($000)	(%)
Common & Surplus	2,380,339	100.0
Total	2,380,339	100.0

RECENT DEVELOPMENTS: For the year ended 12/31/00, net income fell 46.3% to $229.6 million compared with $427.9 million in 1999. Results for 2000 included a pre-tax charge of $187.0 million for the write-down of the Company's investments in technology-based companies and other assets. Net sales were $9.60 billion, up 7.1% from $8.96 billion in the prior year. Operating income decreased 9.9% to $536.6 million compared with $595.7 million in the previous year.

PROSPECTS: As a result of a decrease in consumer demand, GTW expects revenue growth of 3.0% in 2001 and earnings per share to grow 6.0% year over year. The Company anticipates that sluggish economic conditions will continue through the first half of 2001 and improvements to begin during the second half of the year. In an effort to better position the Company for future growth and profitability, GTW plans to drive revenue growth by reinvesting in its "beyond-the-box" strategy.

BUSINESS

GATEWAY INC. (formerly Gateway 2000, Inc.) is a direct marketer of personal computers and related products and services. Gateway develops, manufactures, markets, and supports a broad line of desktop and portable PCs, digital media (convergence) PCs, servers, workstations and PC-related products used by individuals, families, businesses, government agencies and educational institutions. Gateway sells its products directly to PC customers through three complementary distribution channels including phone sales, its Internet Web site, and its 327 Gateway Country® stores. Gateway began offering nationwide Internet provider service directly to its customers in November 1997.

ANNUAL FINANCIAL DATA

	12/31/00	12/31/99	12/31/98	12/31/97	12/31/96	12/31/95	12/31/94
Earnings Per Share	**2 0.76**	**1.32**	**1.09**	**1 0.35**	**0.31**	**0.55**	**0.31**
Cash Flow Per Share	**1.34**	**1.73**	**1.42**	**0.63**	**0.99**	**0.67**	**0.36**
Tang. Book Val. Per Share	**6.85**	**6.15**	**4.08**	**2.62**	**2.41**	**1.67**	**1.20**
INCOME STATEMENT (IN MILLIONS):							
Total Revenues	9,600.6	8,645.6	7,467.9	6,293.7	5,035.2	3,676.3	2,701.2
Costs & Expenses	8,900.2	7,915.8	6,868.2	5,916.6	4,617.4	3,389.2	2,542.2
Depreciation & Amort.	189.1	134.1	105.5	86.8	61.8	38.1	18.0
Operating Income	511.3	595.7	494.2	176.4	356.1	249.0	141.0
Income Before Income Taxes	408.6	663.5	541.2	203.6	382.7	262.1	146.1
Income Taxes	155.3	235.5	194.8	93.8	132.0	89.1	50.1
Net Income	2 229.6	427.9	346.4	1 109.8	250.7	173.0	96.0
Cash Flow	442.4	562.0	451.9	196.6	312.4	211.1	114.0
Average Shs. Outstg. (000)	331,320	324,421	317,858	312,402	314,624	315,976	314,624
BALANCE SHEET (IN MILLIONS):							
Cash & Cash Equivalents	614.1	1,336.4	1,328.5	632.2	516.4	169.4	243.9
Total Current Assets	2,267.1	2,696.8	2,228.2	1,544.7	1,318.3	866.2	654.2
Net Property	897.4	745.7	531.0	336.5	242.4	170.3	89.3
Total Assets	4,152.5	3,954.7	2,890.4	2,039.3	1,673.4	1,124.0	770.6
Total Current Liabilities	1,631.0	1,809.7	1,429.7	1,003.9	799.8	525.3	348.9
Long-Term Obligations	...	3.0	3.4	7.2	7.2	10.8	27.1
Net Stockholders' Equity	2,380.3	2,017.1	1,344.4	930.0	815.5	555.5	376.0
Net Working Capital	636.0	887.1	798.5	540.8	518.6	340.9	305.3
Year-end Shs. Outstg. (000)	323,403	319,286	313,138	308,256	307,024	298,212	289,584
STATISTICAL RECORD:							
Operating Profit Margin %	5.3	6.9	6.6	2.8	7.1	6.8	5.2
Net Profit Margin %	2.6	4.9	4.6	1.7	5.0	4.7	3.6
Return on Equity %	10.6	21.2	25.8	11.8	30.7	31.1	25.5
Return on Assets %	6.1	10.8	12.0	5.4	15.0	15.4	12.5
Debt/Total Assets %	...	0.1	0.1	0.4	0.4	1.0	3.5
Price Range	75.13-16.43	84.00-23.72	34.38-15.50	23.13-11.78	16.56-4.50	9.38-4.00	6.19-2.31
P/E Ratio	...	63.6-18.0	31.5-14.2	66.1-33.7	54.3-14.7	17.1-7.3	20.3-7.6

Statistics are as originally reported. Adj. for 2-for-1 split, 9/99 & 6/97. 1 Incl. $95.0 mill. after-tax non-recur. chg. 2 Incl. $187.0 mill. pre-tax chg. fr. the write-down of investments.

OFFICERS:
T. W. Waitt, Chmn., C.E.O.
J. Burke, Sr. V.P., C.F.O.
W. Elliott, Sr. V.P., Gen. Couns., Corp. Sec.

INVESTOR CONTACT: Marlys Johnson, Manager of Inv. Rel., (800) 846-4503

PRINCIPAL OFFICE: 4545 Towne Centre Court, San Diego, CA 92121

TELEPHONE NUMBER: (858) 799-3401
FAX: (858) 799-3459
WEB: www.gateway.com

NO. OF EMPLOYEES: 24,600 (approx.)

SHAREHOLDERS: 4,480

ANNUAL MEETING: In May

INCORPORATED: IA, 1986; reincorp., DE, Dec., 1991

INSTITUTIONAL HOLDINGS:
No. of Institutions: 289
Shares Held: 165,942,081
% Held: 51.4

INDUSTRY: Electronic computers (SIC: 3571)

TRANSFER AGENT(S): UMB Bank, NA, Kansas City, MO

NYSE SYMBOL GMT
Rec. Pr. 39.85 (4/30/01)

GATX CORPORATION

YIELD 3.1%
P/E RATIO 65.3

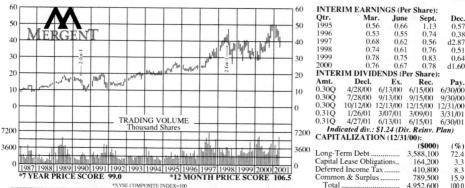

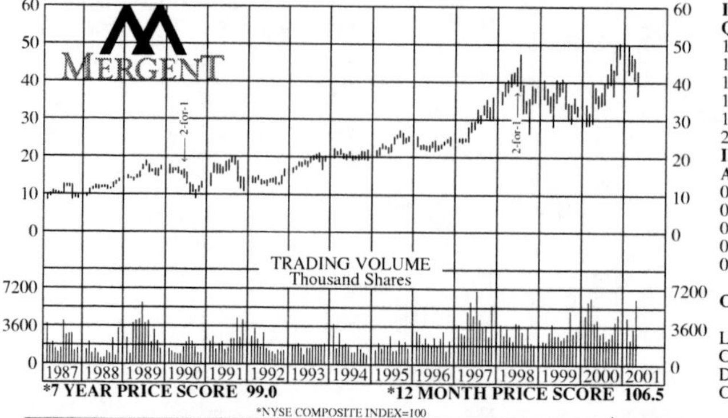

INTERIM EARNINGS (Per Share):

Qtr.	Mar.	June	Sept.	Dec.
1995	0.56	0.66	1.13	0.57
1996	0.53	0.55	0.74	0.38
1997	0.68	0.62	0.56	d2.87
1998	0.74	0.61	0.76	0.51
1999	0.78	0.75	0.83	0.64
2000	0.76	0.67	0.78	d1.60

INTERIM DIVIDENDS (Per Share):

Amt.	Decl.	Ex.	Rec.	Pay.
0.30Q	4/28/00	6/13/00	6/15/00	6/30/00
0.30Q	7/28/00	9/13/00	9/15/00	9/30/00
0.30Q	10/12/00	12/13/00	12/15/00	12/31/00
0.31Q	1/26/01	3/07/01	3/09/01	3/31/01
0.31Q	4/27/01	6/13/01	6/15/01	6/30/01

Indicated div.: $1.24 (Div. Reinv. Plan)

CAPITALIZATION (12/31/00):

	($000)	(%)
Long-Term Debt	3,588,100	72.4
Capital Lease Obligations	164,200	3.3
Deferred Income Tax	410,800	8.3
Common & Surplus	789,500	15.9
Total	4,952,600	100.0

RECENT DEVELOPMENTS: For the year ended 12/31/00, income from continuing operations totaled $30.8 million versus income from continuing operations of $126.3 million in the prior year. Results for 2000 and 1999 excluded income from discontinued operations of $35.8 million and $25.0 million, respectively. Revenues advanced 9.8% to $1.31 billion from $1.20 billion in 1999. GATX Rail revenues rose a modest 0.9% to $572.0 million, while Financial Services revenues jumped 16.4% to $736.4 million.

PROSPECTS: Several outstanding issues cloud GMT's near-term prospects. Notably, the Company's rail business is experiencing weakness, due in part to the slowing U.S. economy. Also, the timing of the sale of GATX Terminals and redeployment of the sale proceeds will influence results for 2001. GMT has indicated that it will likely use a portion of the proceeds to enhance its credit standing, thus providing it with the necessary capital to pursue future investment opportunities.

BUSINESS

GATX CORP. operates in two industry segments: Financial Services and GATX Rail. The Financial Services segment (56.1% of 2000 revenues) includes GATX Capital Corporation and its subsidiaries and affiliates, which arrange and service the financing of equipment and other capital assets on a worldwide basis, and American Steamship Company, which operates self-unloading vessels on the Great Lakes. The GATX Rail segment (43.6%) is principally engaged in leasing specialized railcars, primarily tank cars, under full service leases. As of 12/31/00, the North American fleet consisted of about 91,600 railcars, comprised of 70,000 tank cars and 21,600 specialized freight cars. GATX Rail also owns a 46.0% interest in KVG Kesselwagen Vermietgesellschaft mbH, a German and Austrian-based tank car and specialty railcar leasing company, and an 18.8% interest in Switzerland-based AAE Cargo. In December 2000, the Company completed the divestiture of GATX Logistics, Inc.

ANNUAL FINANCIAL DATA

	12/31/00	12/31/99	12/31/98	12/31/97	12/31/96	12/31/95	12/31/94
Earnings Per Share	**[2] 0.63**	**3.01**	**2.62**	**[1] d1.27**	**2.19**	**2.15**	**1.94**
Cash Flow Per Share	**10.79**	**9.14**	**7.92**	**4.32**	**7.13**	**6.37**	**6.04**
Tang. Book Val. Per Share	**16.25**	**17.20**	**14.87**	**13.39**	**16.73**	**15.60**	**14.52**
Dividends Per Share	**1.20**	**1.10**	**1.00**	**0.92**	**0.86**	**0.80**	**0.76**
Dividend Payout %	**190.4**	**36.5**	**38.2**	**...**	**39.4**	**37.2**	**39.3**
INCOME STATEMENT (IN MILLIONS):							
Total Revenues	1,311.8	1,773.0	1,763.1	1,701.9	1,414.4	1,246.4	1,155.0
Costs & Expenses	599.4	1,064.6	1,098.1	1,314.5	880.5	787.7	723.9
Depreciation & Amort.	334.8	308.2	267.5	252.3	202.4	171.6	165.1
Operating Income	377.6	400.2	397.5	[1] 135.1	331.5	287.1	266.0
Net Interest Inc./(Exp.)	d242.6	d232.2	d234.9	d222.4	d202.8	d170.1	d148.2
Income Before Income Taxes	53.5	253.9	162.6	d87.3	128.7	117.0	117.8
Income Taxes	22.7	102.6	74.3	cr5.5	54.4	47.6	48.8
Equity Earnings/Minority Int.	79.0	85.9	43.6	30.9	28.4	31.4	22.5
Net Income	[2] 30.8	151.3	131.9	[1] d50.9	102.7	100.8	91.5
Cash Flow	526.1	459.5	399.3	194.7	291.9	259.2	243.3
Average Shs. Outstg. (000)	48,753	50,301	50,426	45,084	40,966	40,718	40,306
BALANCE SHEET (IN MILLIONS):							
Cash & Cash Equivalents	173.6	102.5	94.5	77.8	46.2	34.8	27.3
Total Current Assets	1,684.5	1,144.1	1,032.4	1,168.5	1,039.1	963.9	803.9
Net Property	2,654.1	3,282.0	2,790.1	2,710.5	2,846.4	2,369.1	2,192.3
Total Assets	6,263.7	5,866.8	4,939.3	4,947.8	4,750.2	4,042.9	3,650.7
Total Current Liabilities	1,016.2	815.5	707.0	805.2	608.1	611.7	587.3
Long-Term Obligations	3,752.3	3,432.6	2,821.7	2,819.4	2,664.1	2,092.5	1,805.1
Net Stockholders' Equity	789.5	836.0	732.9	655.4	774.9	717.8	662.4
Net Working Capital	668.3	328.6	325.4	363.3	431.0	352.2	216.6
Year-end Shs. Outstg. (000)	48,599	48,599	49,284	48,942	46,128	45,792	45,372
STATISTICAL RECORD:							
Operating Profit Margin %	28.8	22.6	22.5	7.9	23.4	23.0	23.0
Net Profit Margin %	2.3	8.5	7.5	...	7.3	8.1	7.9
Return on Equity %	3.9	18.1	18.0	...	13.3	14.0	13.8
Return on Assets %	0.5	2.6	2.7	...	2.2	2.5	2.5
Debt/Total Assets %	59.9	58.5	57.1	57.0	56.1	51.8	49.4
Price Range	50.50-28.38	40.88-28.06	47.56-26.25	36.00-23.75	25.63-21.50	27.13-20.19	22.31-19.13
P/E Ratio	80.1-45.0	13.6-9.3	18.2-10.0	...	11.7-9.8	12.6-9.4	11.5-9.9
Average Yield %	3.0	3.2	2.7	3.1	3.6	3.4	3.7

Statistics are as originally reported. Adj. for 2-for-1 stk. split, 6/98 [1] Incl. non-recurr. chrg. of $163.0 mill. [2] Excl. inc. fr. disc. ops. of $35.8 mill. ($0.74/sh.)

OFFICERS:
R. H. Zech, Chmn., Pres., C.E.O.
B. A. Kenney, V.P., C.F.O.
R. J. Cinancio, V.P., Gen. Couns., Sec.

INVESTOR CONTACT: R. C. Lyons, Dir. of Inv. Rel., (312) 621-6633

PRINCIPAL OFFICE: 500 West Monroe Street, Chicago, IL 60661-3676

TELEPHONE NUMBER: (312) 621-6200
FAX: (312) 621-6665
WEB: www.gatx.com

NO. OF EMPLOYEES: 3,200 (approx.)

SHAREHOLDERS: 3,590 (approx.)

ANNUAL MEETING: In Apr.

INCORPORATED: NY, July, 1916

INSTITUTIONAL HOLDINGS:
No. of Institutions: 188
Shares Held: 39,630,371
% Held: 81.8

INDUSTRY: Rental of railroad cars (SIC: 4741)

TRANSFER AGENT(S): Mellon Investor Services, Ridgefield Park, NJ

NYSE SYMBOL GY
Rec. Pr. 11.69 (5/31/01)

GENCORP INC.

YIELD 1.0%
P/E RATIO 8.0

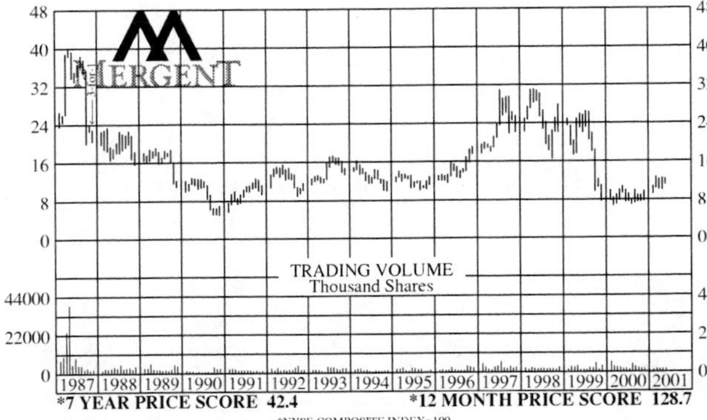

*7 YEAR PRICE SCORE 42.4 *12 MONTH PRICE SCORE 128.7
*NYSE COMPOSITE INDEX=100

INTERIM EARNINGS (Per Share):

Qtr.	Feb.	May	Aug.	Nov.
1997	0.32	2.45	0.50	0.52
1998	0.31	0.51	0.41	0.77
1999	0.41	0.77	0.48	0.26
2000	0.25	0.45	0.46	0.16
2001	0.39	...	...	...

INTERIM DIVIDENDS (Per Share):

Amt.	Decl.	Ex.	Rec.	Pay.
0.03Q	3/29/00	4/27/00	5/01/00	5/31/00
0.03Q	7/14/00	7/28/00	8/01/00	8/31/00
0.03Q	9/08/00	10/30/00	11/01/00	11/30/00
0.03Q	1/16/01	1/30/01	2/01/01	2/28/01
0.03Q	3/28/01	4/27/01	5/01/01	5/31/01

Indicated div.: $0.12 (Div. Reinv. Plan)

CAPITALIZATION (11/30/00):

	($000)	(%)
Long-Term Debt	190,000	49.4
Common & Surplus	195,000	50.6
Total	385,000	100.0

RECENT DEVELOPMENTS: For the quarter ended 2/28/01, net income totaled $16.5 million compared with income of $10.3 million, before a $74.0 million accounting credit, a year earlier. Results for 2001 included a one-time net pre-tax charge of $5.7 million and a one-time pre-tax foreign currency gain of $10.9 million. The 2000 results included a pre-tax charge of $900,000. Net sales climbed 48.0% to $353.5 million from $238.8 million in the prior year, due primarily to the acquisition of Draftex in late December 2000.

PROSPECTS: On 4/20/01, the Company announced that its Aerojet-General subsidiary has signed a definitive agreement to sell its Electronic and Information Systems (EIS) business, which had revenues of $323.0 million in fiscal 2000, to Northrop Grumman Corporation for $315.0 million in cash. Proceeds from the sale of EIS, which is expected to be completed by summer 2001 subject to government approval, will be used to pay down existing debt. Going forward, GY will focus on growing its propulsion and related defense businesses.

BUSINESS

GENCORP INC. operates in two segments: Aerospace, Defense & Fine Chemicals (53.7% of fiscal 2000 sales) and GDX Automotive (formerly Vehicle Sealing) (46.3%). Aerojet-General Corporation manufactures space electronics and smart munitions, as well as solid and liquid rocket propulsion systems and related defense products and services. Aerojet Fine Chemicals supplies special intermediates and active pharmaceutical ingredients primarily to commercial customers. GDX Automotive develops and manufactures highly-engineered extruded and molded rubber sealing systems for vehicle bodies and windows for original equipment manufacturers. On 10/1/99, GY spun off its polymer products and building products businesses under the name OMNOVA Solutions Inc. On 12/29/00, GY acquired the Draftex International Car Body Seals division of The Laird Group.

ANNUAL FINANCIAL DATA

	11/30/00	11/30/99	11/30/98	11/30/97	11/30/96	11/30/95	11/30/94
Earnings Per Share	**[3] 1.31**	**[1][2] 1.09**	**[2] 1.99**	**3.63**	**[2] 1.25**	**[2] 1.17**	**[3] d0.41**
Cash Flow Per Share	**2.50**	**2.19**	**3.31**	**5.21**	**3.18**	**3.47**	**2.01**
Tang. Book Val. Per Share	**4.64**	**1.91**	**8.29**	**6.80**	**1.67**	**1.05**	**...**
Dividends Per Share	**0.12**	**0.48**	**0.60**	**0.60**	**0.60**	**0.60**	**0.60**
Dividend Payout %	**9.2**	**44.0**	**30.1**	**16.5**	**48.0**	**51.3**	**...**
INCOME STATEMENT (IN MILLIONS):							
Total Revenues	1,047.0	1,071.0	1,737.0	1,568.0	1,515.0	1,772.0	1,740.0
Costs & Expenses	895.0	964.0	1,535.0	1,386.0	1,336.0	1,598.0	1,566.0
Depreciation & Amort.	50.0	44.0	55.0	60.0	65.0	76.0	77.0
Operating Income	102.0	63.0	147.0	122.0	114.0	98.0	97.0
Net Interest Inc./(Exp.)	d18.0	d6.0	d14.0	d16.0	d27.0	d34.0	d32.0
Income Before Income Taxes	92.0	76.0	136.0	118.0	42.0	64.0	d22.0
Income Taxes	37.0	30.0	52.0	cr19.0	...	26.0	cr9.0
Net Income	[3] 55.0	[1][2] 46.0	[2] 84.0	137.0	[2] 42.0	[2] 38.0	[3] d13.0
Cash Flow	105.0	90.0	139.0	197.0	107.0	114.0	64.0
Average Shs. Outstg. (000)	42,054	41,148	42,033	37,807	33,672	32,814	31,797
BALANCE SHEET (IN MILLIONS):							
Cash & Cash Equivalents	17.0	23.0	29.0	18.0	22.0	17.0	22.0
Total Current Assets	346.0	363.0	529.0	484.0	452.0	465.0	421.0
Net Property	365.0	335.0	500.0	410.0	413.0	543.0	566.0
Total Assets	1,324.0	1,230.0	1,743.0	1,432.0	1,330.0	1,458.0	1,455.0
Total Current Liabilities	328.0	371.0	430.0	390.0	370.0	376.0	367.0
Long-Term Obligations	190.0	149.0	356.0	84.0	263.0	383.0	378.0
Net Stockholders' Equity	195.0	80.0	344.0	281.0	56.0	35.0	d7.0
Net Working Capital	18.0	d8.0	99.0	94.0	82.0	89.0	54.0
Year-end Shs. Outstg. (000)	42,000	41,900	41,500	41,300	33,500	33,400	32,100
STATISTICAL RECORD:							
Operating Profit Margin %	9.7	5.9	8.5	7.8	7.5	5.5	5.6
Net Profit Margin %	5.3	4.3	4.8	8.7	2.8	2.1	...
Return on Equity %	28.2	57.5	24.4	48.8	75.0	108.6	...
Return on Assets %	4.2	3.7	4.8	9.6	3.2	2.6	...
Debt/Total Assets %	14.4	12.1	20.4	5.9	19.8	26.3	26.0
Price Range	10.81-6.63	26.50-7.63	31.19-16.44	31.00-17.63	19.13-11.50	14.13-10.00	16.38-9.88
P/E Ratio	8.3-5.1	24.3-7.0	15.7-8.3	8.5-4.9	15.3-9.2	12.1-8.5	...
Average Yield %	1.4	2.8	2.5	2.5	3.9	5.0	4.6

Statistics are as originally reported. [1] Bef. $26.4 mil ($0.63/sh) gain fr. discont. opers. [2] Incl. $11.8 mil non-recurr. gain, 1999; $5.0 mil gain, 1998; $42.0 mil chg., 1996; $5.0 mil chg., 1995. [3] Bef. $74.0 mil ($1.76/sh) acctg. change chg., 2000; $212.7 mil ($6.69/sh), 1994 & incl. $5.0 mil non-recur. gain, 2000; $82.8 mil chg., 1994.

OFFICERS:
R. A. Wolfe, Chmn., Pres., C.E.O.
T. L. Hall, Sr. V.P., C.F.O.
W. R. Phillips, Sr. V.P., Gen. Couns., Sec.

PRINCIPAL OFFICE: Highway 50 and Aerojet Road, Rancho Cordova, CA 95670

TELEPHONE NUMBER: (916) 355-4000
WEB: www.gencorp.com

NO. OF EMPLOYEES: 7,895 (approx.)

SHAREHOLDERS: 12,300 (approx. record)

ANNUAL MEETING: In Mar.

INCORPORATED: OH, Sept., 1915

INSTITUTIONAL HOLDINGS:
No. of Institutions: 106
Shares Held: 28,888,768
% Held: 67.7

INDUSTRY: Space propulsion units and parts (SIC: 3764)

TRANSFER AGENT(S): The Bank of New York, New York, NY

NYSE SYMBOL DNA
Rec. Pr. 50.05 (5/31/01)

GENENTECH, INC.

YIELD ...
P/E RATIO ...

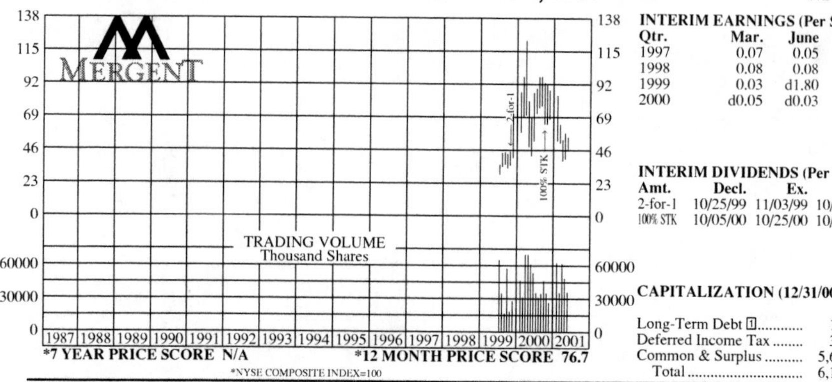

*7 YEAR PRICE SCORE N/A *12 MONTH PRICE SCORE 76.7
*NYSE COMPOSITE INDEX=100

INTERIM EARNINGS (Per Share):

Qtr.	Mar.	June	Sept.	Dec.
1997	0.07	0.05	0.07	0.09
1998	0.08	0.08	0.13	0.07
1999	0.03	d1.80	d0.13	d0.34
2000	d0.05	d0.03	0.02	0.03

INTERIM DIVIDENDS (Per Share):

Amt.	Decl.	Ex.	Rec.	Pay.
2-for-1	10/25/99	11/03/99	10/29/99	11/02/99
100% STK	10/05/00	10/25/00	10/17/00	10/24/00

CAPITALIZATION (12/31/00):

	($000)	(%)
Long-Term Debt [1]	149,692	2.4
Deferred Income Tax	349,848	5.7
Common & Surplus	5,674,203	91.9
Total	6,173,743	100.0

RECENT DEVELOPMENTS: For the year ended 12/31/00, DNA reported a loss of $16.4 million, before an accounting charge, compared with a net loss of $1.14 billion in the previous year. Results for 2000 and 1999 included pre-tax recurring charges of $375.3 million and $198.4 million, respectively. Results for 1999 also included pre-tax special charges of $1.44 billion. Revenues advanced 22.2% to $1.74 billion from $1.42 billion in 1999.

PROSPECTS: DNA's portfolio of marketed and pipeline products, along with its strategic alliances and emphasis on increasing earnings is positioning it for near-term, mid-term and long-term growth. Going forward, DNA's biooncolgy initiative should continue to benefit from the strong performance of its two lead cancer drugs, RITUXAN and HERCEPTIN.

BUSINESS

GENENTECH, INC. is a biotechnology company that uses human genetic information to discover, develop, manufacture and market human pharmaceuticals. DNA manufactures and markets nine protein-based pharmaceuticals including PROTROPIN®, used for growth hormone deficiency (GHD) in children; HERCEPTIN®, for the treatment of one type of metastic breast cancer; ACTIVASE®, which dissolves blood clots that cause strokes and heart attacks; RITUXAN®, a single-agent therapy for the treatment of a certain type of non-Hodgkins lymphoma; PULMOZYME®, used for treatment of cystic fibrosis; NUTROPIN® and NUTROPIN AQ®, used for GHD in children and adults. NUTROPIN DEPOT™, for treatment of GHD in children. As of 12/31/00, Roche Holdings, Inc. owned about 58.4% of DNA, following a recapitalization in July 1999.

REVENUES

(12/31/2000)	($000)	(%)
Product Sales	1,278,344	73.6
Royalties	207,241	11.9
Contract & Other Revenues	160,363	9.3
Interest	90,408	5.2
Total	1,736,356	100.0

ANNUAL FINANCIAL DATA

	12/31/00	12/31/99	12/31/98	12/31/97	12/31/96	12/31/95	12/31/94
Earnings Per Share	[4] **d0.03**	[3] **d2.23**	**0.35**	**0.26**	**0.24**	[2] **0.30**	**0.26**
Cash Flow Per Share	**0.86**	**d1.68**	**0.50**	**0.38**	**0.36**	**0.42**	**0.37**
Tang. Book Val. Per Share	**5.59**	**4.26**	**4.61**	**4.09**	**3.71**	**3.36**	**2.88**
INCOME STATEMENT (IN MILLIONS):							
Total Revenues	1,736.4	1,421.4	1,150.9	1,016.7	968.7	917.8	795.4
Costs & Expenses	888.8	839.5	815.6	777.8	753.6	654.2	605.3
Depreciation & Amort.	463.0	281.4	78.1	65.5	62.1	58.4	53.5
Operating Income	384.5	300.6	257.2	173.4	152.9	205.2	136.6
Net Interest Inc./(Exp.)	d5.3	d5.4	d4.6	d3.6	d5.0	d7.9	d7.1
Income Before Income Taxes	4.0	d1,340.9	252.7	169.8	147.9	172.3	129.6
Income Taxes	20.4	cr196.4	70.7	40.8	29.6	25.8	5.2
Net Income	[4] d16.4	[3] d1,144.5	181.9	129.0	118.3	[2] 146.4	124.4
Cash Flow	446.6	d863.2	260.0	194.6	180.5	204.9	177.8
Average Shs. Outstg. (000)	522,179	512,860	519,488	505,588	494,780	484,880	477,860
BALANCE SHEET (IN MILLIONS):							
Cash & Cash Equivalents	1,193.9	742.7	887.7	833.3	623.2	740.3	719.2
Total Current Assets	1,788.8	1,326.5	1,242.0	1,193.9	955.1	1,045.4	997.1
Net Property	752.9	730.1	700.2	683.3	586.2	503.7	485.3
Total Assets	6,711.8	6,554.4	2,855.4	2,507.6	2,226.4	2,011.0	1,745.1
Total Current Liabilities	448.7	484.1	291.3	289.6	250.0	233.4	220.5
Long-Term Obligations	149.7	149.7	150.0	150.0	150.0	150.0	150.4
Net Stockholders' Equity	5,674.2	5,282.8	2,343.8	2,031.2	1,801.1	1,602.0	1,348.8
Net Working Capital	1,340.1	842.4	950.6	904.4	705.1	812.0	776.6
Year-end Shs. Outstg. (000)	525,477	516,221	508,460	496,912	485,708	477,072	468,956
STATISTICAL RECORD:							
Operating Profit Margin %	22.1	21.1	22.3	17.1	15.8	22.4	17.2
Net Profit Margin %	...	...	15.8	12.7	12.2	16.0	15.6
Return on Equity %	...	...	7.8	6.4	6.6	9.1	9.2
Return on Assets %	...	...	6.4	5.1	5.3	7.3	7.1
Debt/Total Assets %	2.2	2.3	5.3	6.0	6.7	7.5	8.6
Price Range	122.50-42.25	71.50-29.13	...	...	...	...	...

Statistics are as originally reported. Adj. for 2-for-1 split, 10/00 & 11/99. [1] Incl. debs. conv. into common & capital leases. [2] Incl. a special nonrecurring pre-tax charge of $25.0 million. [3] Incl. a special pre-tax charge of $1.44 billion related to the redemption of the Company's special common stock, and pre-tax recurring charges of $198.4 million also related to the redemption. [4] Bef. acctg. chg. chrg. of $51.8 mill.; incl. recurr. chrg. of $375.3 mill.

OFFICERS:
A. D. Levinson Ph.D., Chmn., Pres., C.E.O.
L. J. Lavigne Jr., Exec. V.P., C.F.O.
S. G. Juelsgaard, Sr. V.P., Gen. Couns., Sec.

INVESTOR CONTACT: Susan Bentley, Sr. Dir., Inv. Rel., (650) 225-1260

PRINCIPAL OFFICE: 1 DNA Way, South San Francisco, CA 94080-4990

TELEPHONE NUMBER: (650) 225 1000
WEB: www.gene.com

NO. OF EMPLOYEES: 4,459 (avg.)

SHAREHOLDERS: 1,205 (approx.)

ANNUAL MEETING: In May

INCORPORATED: CA, Apr., 1976; reincorp., DE, Jan., 1987

INSTITUTIONAL HOLDINGS:
No. of Institutions: 319
Shares Held: 192,393,080
% Held: 36.5

INDUSTRY: Pharmaceutical preparations (SIC: 2834)

TRANSFER AGENT(S): EquiServe, Boston, MA

NYSE SYMBOL BGC
Rec. Pr. 11.91 (4/30/01)

GENERAL CABLE CORP.

YIELD 1.7%
P/E RATIO ...

MERGENT

TRADING VOLUME
Thousand Shares

*7 YEAR PRICE SCORE N/A *12 MONTH PRICE SCORE 136.3

*NYSE COMPOSITE INDEX=100

INTERIM EARNINGS (Per Share):

Qtr.	Mar.	June	Sept.	Dec.
1998	0.36	0.48	0.59	0.47
1999	0.22	0.36	0.50	d0.14
2000	d0.26	d0.13	d0.73	0.34

INTERIM DIVIDENDS (Per Share):

Amt.	Decl.	Ex.	Rec.	Pay.
0.05Q	4/18/00	4/26/00	4/28/00	5/12/00
0.05Q	7/20/00	7/27/00	7/31/00	8/11/00
0.05Q	10/18/00	10/26/00	10/30/00	11/13/00
0.05Q	1/29/01	2/08/01	2/12/01	3/02/01
0.05Q	4/18/01	4/26/01	4/30/01	5/16/01

Indicated div.: $0.20

CAPITALIZATION (12/31/00):

	($000)	(%)
Long-Term Debt	611,900	82.0
Deferred Income Tax	5,700	0.8
Common & Surplus	128,500	17.2
Total	746,100	100.0

RECENT DEVELOPMENTS: For the year ended 12/31/00, net loss totaled $26.4 million compared with net income of $34.2 million in the previous year. Results for 2000 included loss on sale of businesses of $31.0 million, while results for 1999 included asset impairment charges of $24.5 million. Net sales improved 29.2% to $2.70 billion from $2.09 billion in the prior year. Gross profit as a percentage of net sales was 12.0% compared with 14.4% in the preceding year. Operating income declined to $39.5 million versus $100.8 million in the prior year.

PROSPECTS: Going forward, the Company will continue to focus on growing its communications and energy cable businesses. Accordingly, on 3/9/01, the Company completed the sale of the shares of its Pyrotenax® business unit to Raychem HTS Canada Inc. for approximately $60.0 million. Meanwhile, the Company expects to achieve earnings per share of $1.55 to $1.60 for the fiscal year 2001, with further upside of approximately $0.05 per share given the current interest rate environment.

BUSINESS

GENERAL CABLE CORP. is engaged in the development, design, manufacture, marketing and distribution of copper, aluminum and fiber optic wire and cable products for the communications, energy and electrical markets. Communications wire and cable transmit low-voltage signals for voice, data, video and control applications. Energy cables include low-, medium- and high-voltage power distribution and power transmission products. Electrical wire and cable products conduct electrical current for industrial, commercial and residential power and control applications.

REVENUES

(12/31/2000)	($000)	(%)
Electrical Group	1,331,100	49.3
Communications Group	631,300	23.4
Energy Group	735,400	27.3
Total	2,697,800	100.0

ANNUAL FINANCIAL DATA

	12/31/00	12/31/99	12/31/98	12/31/97	12/31/96	12/31/95	12/31/94
Earnings Per Share	[1] d0.79	[2] 0.95	1.90	1.44	1.08	0.69	0.08
Cash Flow Per Share	0.88	1.86	2.39	1.82	1.41	1.05	0.29
Tang. Book Val. Per Share	3.94	5.21	4.79	3.33	2.95	3.38	...
Dividends Per Share	0.20	0.20	0.17	0.03	...	...	...
Dividend Payout %	...	21.1	8.8	2.3	...	...	...
INCOME STATEMENT (IN MILLIONS):							
Total Revenues	2,697.8	2,088.4	1,150.5	1,134.5	1,043.6	1,061.3	543.3
Costs & Expenses	2,602.3	1,955.2	1,002.4	1,016.1	953.0	1,003.9	515.3
Depreciation & Amort.	56.0	32.4	18.5	13.9	12.1	12.9	7.7
Operating Income	39.5	100.8	129.6	104.5	78.5	44.5	20.3
Net Interest Inc./(Exp.)	d77.1	d47.7	d15.7	d17.3	d19.6	d20.7	d11.0
Income Before Income Taxes	d40.9	53.1	113.9	87.2	58.9	23.8	9.3
Income Taxes	cr14.5	18.9	42.7	34.0	19.7	cr1.5	6.5
Net Income	[1] d26.4	[2] 34.2	71.2	53.2	39.2	25.3	2.8
Cash Flow	29.6	66.6	89.7	67.1	51.3	38.2	10.5
Average Shs. Outstg. (000)	33,600	35,900	37,500	36,900	36,450	36,450	36,450
BALANCE SHEET (IN MILLIONS):							
Cash & Cash Equivalents	21.2	38.0	3.4	4.2	1.9	13.7	...
Total Current Assets	864.3	1,017.9	390.3	361.8	335.7	369.3	...
Net Property	379.4	438.7	210.8	155.6	128.8	116.4	...
Total Assets	1,319.2	1,568.3	651.0	563.7	513.6	535.6	...
Total Current Liabilities	489.0	549.7	156.5	135.9	130.1	134.9	...
Long-Term Obligations	611.9	726.2	246.8	238.5	205.1	205.9	...
Net Stockholders' Equity	128.5	177.3	177.2	122.4	107.4	122.9	...
Net Working Capital	375.3	468.2	233.8	225.9	205.6	234.4	...
Year-end Shs. Outstg. (000)	32,649	34,000	37,000	36,773	36,375	36,375	...
STATISTICAL RECORD:							
Operating Profit Margin %	1.5	4.8	11.3	9.2	7.5	4.2	3.7
Net Profit Margin %	...	1.6	6.2	4.7	3.8	2.4	0.5
Return on Equity %	...	19.3	40.2	43.5	36.5	20.6	...
Return on Assets %	...	2.2	10.9	9.4	7.6	4.7	...
Debt/Total Assets %	46.4	46.3	37.9	42.3	39.9	38.4	...
Price Range	12.25-4.19	22.88-6.44	32.92-11.50	26.08-13.58	...	...	...
P/E Ratio	...	24.1-6.8	17.3-6.1	18.1-9.4	...	...	...
Average Yield %	2.4	1.4	0.8	0.2	...	...	...

Statistics are as originally reported. Adj. for 50% stk. div., 5/98. [1] Incl. loss on sale of businesses of $31.0 mill. [2] Incl. asset impairment charges of $24.5 mill.

OFFICERS:
S. Rabinowitz, Chmn., C.E.O.
G. B. Kenny, Pres., C.O.O.
C. F. Virgulak, Exec. V.P., C.F.O.

INVESTOR CONTACT: Investor Relations, (859) 572-8684

PRINCIPAL OFFICE: 4 Tesseneer Drive, Highland Heights, KY 41076-9753

TELEPHONE NUMBER: (859) 572-8000
FAX: (859) 572-8444
WEB: www.generalcable.com

NO. OF EMPLOYEES: 8,600 (approx.)

SHAREHOLDERS: N/A

ANNUAL MEETING: In May

INCORPORATED: DE, Apr., 1994

INSTITUTIONAL HOLDINGS:
No. of Institutions: 86
Shares Held: 26,660,931
% Held: 81.6

INDUSTRY: Nonferrous wiredrawing & insulating (SIC: 3357)

TRANSFER AGENT(S): Mellon Investor Services, New York, NY

NYSE SYMBOL GD
Rec. Pr. 77.52 (5/31/01)

GENERAL DYNAMICS CORPORATION

YIELD 1.4%
P/E RATIO 17.3

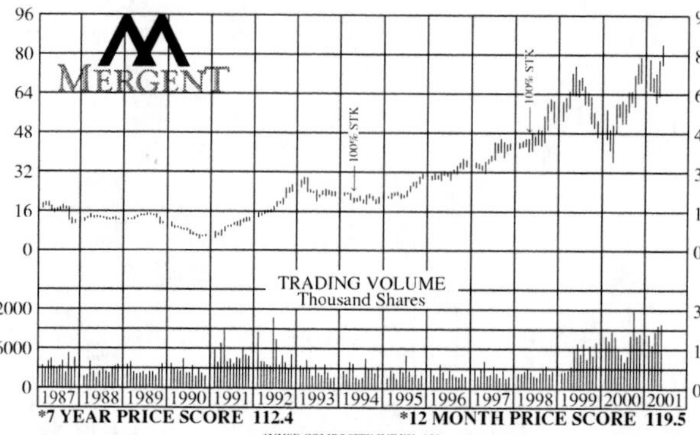

INTERIM EARNINGS (Per Share):

Qtr.	Mar.	June	Sept.	Dec.
1997	0.57	0.64	0.65	0.66
1998	0.65	0.72	0.74	0.75
1999	2.07	0.81	0.91	0.98
2000	0.91	1.01	1.47	1.09

INTERIM DIVIDENDS (Per Share):

Amt.	Decl.	Ex.	Rec.	Pay.
0.26Q	5/03/00	7/12/00	7/14/00	8/11/00
0.26Q	8/02/00	10/04/00	10/06/00	11/10/00
0.26Q	12/06/00	1/17/01	1/19/01	2/09/01
0.28Q	3/07/01	4/10/01	4/13/01	5/11/01
0.28Q	6/06/01	7/11/01	7/13/01	8/10/01

Indicated div.: $1.12 (Div. Reinv. Plan)

CAPITALIZATION (12/31/00):

	($000)	(%)
Long-Term Debt	162,000	4.1
Common & Surplus	3,820,000	95.9
Total	3,982,000	100.0

RECENT DEVELOPMENTS: For the year ended 12/31/00, net income increased 2.4% to $901.0 million from $880.0 million in 1999. Earnings for 2000 and 1999 included research and development tax credits of $90.0 million and $165.0 million, respectively. Net sales increased 15.6% to $10.36 billion. Marine Systems group sales rose 10.5% to $3.41 billion, while Aerospace group sales improved 4.1% to $3.03 billion.

PROSPECTS: GD expects earnings per share to range from $4.43 to $4.48 in 2001. Separately, GD's Combat Systems group acquired Primex Technologies, Inc., which will add about $500.0 million to the Combat Systems group revenues and nearly $1.00 billion to GD's backlog in 2001. Also, GD was awarded a $661.0 million modification to its 1998-2001 DDG 51 Class multi-year contract from the Naval Sea Systems Command in Arlington, Virginia.

BUSINESS

GENERAL DYNAMICS CORPORATION is a major defense contractor operating in four business segments. The Marine Systems Group designs, engineers, constructs, overhauls, and supports nuclear submarines. Combat Systems designs, engineers and manufactures armored vehicles and defense electronic equipment. Information Systems and Technology, created as a result of the acquisitions of Computing Devices International and Advanced Technology Systems, provides GD with broader and deeper capabilities in electronics and systems integration and information management. Other consists of coal mining, ship management, and ship financing services. On 9/1/99, GD acquired GTE Government Systems Corporation. On 1/26/01, GD acquired Primex Technologies, Inc.

BUSINESS LINE ANALYSIS

(12/31/2000)	REV (%)	INC (%)
Marine Systems	33.0	24.4
Aerospace	29.2	44.6
Info Systems & Technology	23.1	16.6
Combat Systems	12.3	11.7
Other	2.4	2.7
Total	100.0	100.0

ANNUAL FINANCIAL DATA

	12/31/00	12/31/99	12/31/98	12/31/97	12/31/96	12/31/95	12/31/94
Earnings Per Share	**3 4.48**	**4.36**	**2.86**	**2.50**	**2.14**	**2 1.96**	**1 1.76**
Cash Flow Per Share	**5.60**	**5.35**	**3.86**	**3.20**	**2.67**	**2.26**	**2.08**
Tang. Book Val. Per Share	**6.43**	**3.27**	**5.46**	**5.64**	**13.60**	**12.44**	**10.44**
Dividends Per Share	**1.02**	**0.94**	**0.86**	**0.82**	**0.80**	**0.74**	**0.68**
Dividend Payout %	**22.8**	**21.6**	**30.2**	**32.8**	**37.6**	**37.6**	**38.5**
INCOME STATEMENT (IN MILLIONS):							
Total Revenues	10,356.0	8,959.0	4,970.0	4,062.0	3,581.0	3,067.0	3,058.0
Costs & Expenses	8,801.0	7,556.0	4,302.0	3,525.0	3,161.0	2,714.0	2,698.0
Depreciation & Amort.	226.0	200.0	126.0	91.0	67.0	38.0	39.0
Operating Income	1,329.0	1,203.0	542.0	446.0	353.0	315.0	321.0
Net Interest Inc./(Exp.)	d60.0	d34.0	4.0	36.0	55.0	55.0	22.0
Income Before Income Taxes	1,262.0	1,126.0	549.0	479.0	409.0	375.0	343.0
Income Taxes	361.0	246.0	185.0	163.0	139.0	128.0	120.0
Net Income	3 901.0	880.0	364.0	316.0	270.0	2 247.0	1 223.0
Cash Flow	1,127.0	1,080.0	490.0	407.0	337.0	285.0	262.0
Average Shs. Outstg. (000)	201,262	202,057	127,000	127,000	126,000	126,000	126,000
BALANCE SHEET (IN MILLIONS):							
Cash & Cash Equivalents	177.0	270.0	220.0	441.0	894.0	1,095.0	1,059.0
Total Current Assets	3,551.0	3,491.0	1,873.0	1,689.0	1,858.0	2,013.0	1,797.0
Net Property	1,294.0	1,169.0	698.0	592.0	441.0	398.0	264.0
Total Assets	7,987.0	7,774.0	4,572.0	4,091.0	3,299.0	3,164.0	2,673.0
Total Current Liabilities	2,901.0	3,453.0	1,461.0	1,291.0	833.0	859.0	626.0
Long-Term Obligations	162.0	169.0	249.0	257.0	156.0	170.0	196.0
Net Stockholders' Equity	3,820.0	3,171.0	2,219.0	1,915.0	1,714.0	1,567.0	1,316.0
Net Working Capital	650.0	38.0	412.0	398.0	1,025.0	1,154.0	1,171.0
Year-end Shs. Outstg. (000)	200,502	201,013	127,000	126,000	126,000	126,000	126,000
STATISTICAL RECORD:							
Operating Profit Margin %	12.8	13.4	10.9	11.0	9.9	10.3	10.5
Net Profit Margin %	8.7	9.8	7.3	7.8	7.5	8.1	7.3
Return on Equity %	23.6	27.8	16.4	16.5	15.8	15.8	16.9
Return on Assets %	11.3	11.3	8.0	7.7	8.2	7.8	8.3
Debt/Total Assets %	2.0	2.2	5.4	6.3	4.7	5.4	7.3
Price Range	79.00-36.25	75.44-46.19	62.00-40.25	45.75-31.56	37.75-28.50	31.50-21.19	23.81-19.00
P/E Ratio	17.6-8.1	17.3-10.6	21.7-14.1	18.3-12.6	17.7-13.3	16.1-10.8	13.6-10.8
Average Yield %	1.8	1.5	1.7	2.1	2.4	2.8	3.2

Statistics are as originally reported. Adj. for 100% stk. div., 4/98 & 4/94. 1 Bef. inc. fr. disc. ops. of $15.0 mill. & incl. nonrecurr. gain of $62.0 mill. 2 Bef. gain on disp. of $74.0 mill. 3 Incl. research & dev. tax credit of $90.0 mill.

OFFICERS:
N. D. Chabraja, Chmn., C.E.O.
M. J. Mancuso, Sr. V.P., C.F.O.
D. H. Fogg, V.P., Treas.

INVESTOR CONTACT: R. Lewis, Inv. Rel., (703) 876-3195

PRINCIPAL OFFICE: 3190 Fairview Park Drive, Falls Church, VA 22042-4523

TELEPHONE NUMBER: (703) 876-3000
FAX: (703) 876-3125
WEB: www.generaldynamics.com

NO. OF EMPLOYEES: 43,400 (approx.)

SHAREHOLDERS: 18,500 (record)

ANNUAL MEETING: In May

INCORPORATED: DE, Feb., 1952

INSTITUTIONAL HOLDINGS:
No. of Institutions: 397
Shares Held: 142,456,479
% Held: 70.9

INDUSTRY: Guided missiles and space vehicles (SIC: 3761)

TRANSFER AGENT(S): First Chicago Trust Company of New York, Jersey City, NJ

NYSE SYMBOL GE
Rec. Pr. 48.53 (4/30/01)

GENERAL ELECTRIC COMPANY

YIELD 1.3%
P/E RATIO 37.9

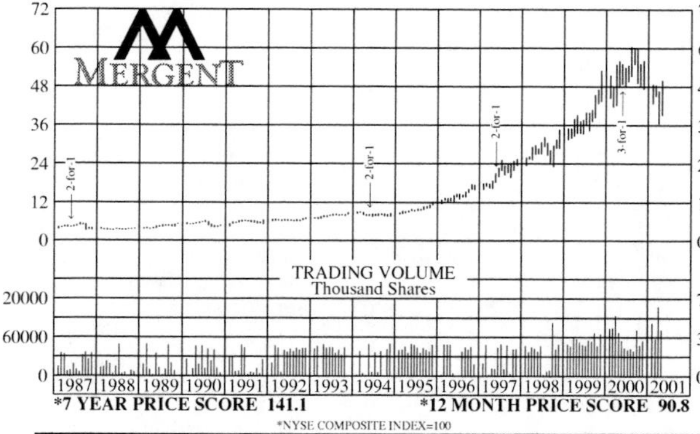

INTERIM EARNINGS (Per Share):

Qtr.	Mar.	June	Sept.	Dec.
1997	0.17	0.22	0.21	0.23
1998	0.19	0.25	0.23	0.27
1999	0.22	0.29	0.27	0.31
2000	0.26	0.34	0.32	0.36

INTERIM DIVIDENDS (Per Share):

Amt.	Decl.	Ex.	Rec.	Pay.
3-for-1	2/11/00	5/08/00	4/27/00	5/05/00
0.137Q	6/23/00	7/05/00	7/07/00	7/25/00
0.137Q	9/22/00	9/29/00	10/03/00	10/25/00
0.16Q	12/15/00	12/27/00	12/29/00	1/25/01
0.16Q	2/09/01	3/05/01	3/07/01	4/25/01

Indicated div.: $0.64 (Div. Reinv. Plan)

CAPITALIZATION (12/31/00):

	($000)	(%)
Long-Term Debt	82,132,000	56.2
Deferred Income Tax	8,690,000	5.9
Minority Interest	4,936,000	3.4
Common & Surplus	50,492,000	34.5
Total	146,250,000	100.0

RECENT DEVELOPMENTS: For the year ended 12/31/00, net income jumped 18.8% to $12.74 billion compared with $10.72 billion in the previous year. Revenues were up 16.3% to $129.85 billion. Revenues from aircraft engines inched up 0.5% to $10.78 billion, while Power Systems segment revenues surged 47.2% to $14.86 billion. GE Capital Services segment revenues jumped 18.7% to $66.18 billion.

PROSPECTS: On 2/15/01, GE Power Systems' Energy Services unit and PG&E National Energy Group signed a long-term service agreement, totaling more than $1.00 billion, which will cover more than 20 GE gas turbines at power plants to be developed by PG&E. On 1/11/01, Honeywell shareholders approved the proposed acquisition by GE. The acquisition planning continues on track with over $2.50 billion of synergies identified.

BUSINESS

GENERAL ELECTRIC COMPANY'S businesses and their contributions to 2000 revenues are as follows: Aircraft Engines (8.2%) develops and manufactures engines for commercial aircraft. Appliances (4.5%) is a supplier of kitchen appliances. The Industrial Products and Systems segment (9.0%) includes lighting, transportation systems, industrial systems, and GE Supply. Broadcasting (5.2%) operations are conducted through NBC. Financial Services (50.0%) are provided by GE Capital Services. The Plastics, Power Systems, and Technical Products and Services (23.1%) sectors are providers of medical systems, power generation, motors and transportation systems.

BUSINESS LINE ANALYSIS

(12/31/2000)	REV (%)	INC (%)
Aircraft Engines	16.4	18.1
Appliances	8.9	5.0
Industrial Products & Systems	18.0	16.1
NBC	10.3	13.2
Plastics	11.8	14.2
Power Systems	22.6	20.7
Tech Products & Services	12.0	12.7
Total	100.0	100.0

ANNUAL FINANCIAL DATA

	12/31/00	12/31/99	12/31/98	12/31/97	12/31/96	12/31/95	12/31/94
Earnings Per Share	**1.27**	**1.09**	**0.93**	**[2] 0.82**	**0.73**	**0.65**	**[1] 0.58**
Cash Flow Per Share	**2.04**	**1.77**	**1.52**	**1.34**	**1.11**	**1.01**	**0.89**
Tang. Book Val. Per Share	**2.32**	**1.68**	**1.55**	**1.56**	**1.53**	**1.63**	**1.47**
Dividends Per Share	**0.55**	**0.47**	**0.40**	**0.35**	**0.31**	**0.27**	**0.24**
Dividend Payout %	**43.0**	**42.8**	**42.9**	**42.3**	**41.8**	**42.0**	**41.6**
INCOME STATEMENT (IN MILLIONS):							
Total Revenues	129,853.0	111,630.0	100,469.0	90,840.0	79,179.0	70,028.0	60,109.0
Costs & Expenses	58,486.0	50,295.0	46,028.0	43,097.0	35,764.0	32,661.0	34,473.0
Depreciation & Amort.	7,736.0	6,691.0	5,860.0	5,269.0	3,785.0	3,594.0	3,207.0
Operating Income	63,631.0	54,644.0	48,581.0	42,474.0	39,630.0	33,773.0	22,429.0
Net Interest Inc./(Exp.)	d11,720.0	d10,013.0	d9,753.0	d8,384.0	d7,904.0	d7,286.0	d4,949.0
Income Before Income Taxes	18,446.0	15,577.0	13,477.0	11,179.0	10,806.0	9,737.0	8,661.0
Income Taxes	5,711.0	4,860.0	4,181.0	2,976.0	3,526.0	3,164.0	2,746.0
Equity Earnings/Minority Int.	d427.0	d365.0	d265.0	d240.0	d269.0	d204.0	d170.0
Net Income	12,735.0	10,717.0	9,296.0	[2] 8,203.0	7,280.0	6,573.0	[1] 5,915.0
Cash Flow	20,471.0	17,408.0	15,156.0	13,472.0	11,065.0	10,167.0	9,122.0
Average Shs. Outstg. (000)	10,057,000	9,834,000	9,990,000	10,035,000	9,924,000	10,104,000	10,254,000
BALANCE SHEET (IN MILLIONS):							
Cash & Cash Equivalents	99,534.0	90,312.0	83,034.0	76,482.0	64,080.0	43,890.0	33,556.0
Total Current Assets	116,848.0	105,850.0	97,307.0	91,301.0	77,257.0	57,020.0	44,963.0
Net Property	40,015.0	41,022.0	35,730.0	32,316.0	28,795.0	25,679.0	23,465.0
Total Assets	437,006.0	405,200.0	355,935.0	304,012.0	272,402.0	228,035.0	194,484.0
Total Current Liabilities	156,112.0	161,216.0	141,579.0	120,668.0	100,507.0	82,001.0	72,854.0
Long-Term Obligations	82,132.0	71,427.0	59,663.0	46,603.0	49,246.0	51,027.0	36,979.0
Net Stockholders' Equity	50,492.0	42,557.0	38,880.0	34,438.0	31,125.0	29,609.0	26,387.0
Net Working Capital	d39,264.0	d55,366.0	d44,272.0	d29,367.0	d23,250.0	d24,981.0	d27,891.0
Year-end Shs. Outstg. (000)	9,932,006	9,854,529	9,813,000	9,795,000	9,870,000	10,002,000	10,236,000
STATISTICAL RECORD:							
Operating Profit Margin %	49.0	49.0	48.4	46.8	50.1	48.2	37.3
Net Profit Margin %	9.8	9.6	9.3	9.0	9.2	9.4	9.8
Return on Equity %	25.2	25.2	23.9	23.8	23.4	22.2	22.4
Return on Assets %	2.9	2.6	2.6	2.7	2.7	2.9	3.0
Debt/Total Assets %	18.8	17.6	16.8	15.3	18.1	22.4	19.0
Price Range	60.50-41.64	53.16-31.35	34.64-23.00	25.52-15.98	17.69-11.58	12.19-8.31	9.15-7.50
P/E Ratio	47.6-32.8	48.8-28.8	37.1-24.6	31.1-19.5	24.1-15.8	18.7-12.8	15.8-13.0
Average Yield %	1.1	1.1	1.4	1.7	2.1	2.7	2.9

Statistics are as originally reported. Adj. for 3-for-1 stock split, 2/00; 2-for-1, 5/97 & 5/94. [1] Bef. disc. opers. of d$1.19 bill. [2] Incl. an after-tax gain of $1.50 bill. from the exchange of Lockheed Martin pfd. stk. & after-tax charges of $1.50 bill. for restruct. & oth. spec. matters.

OFFICERS:
J. F. Welch, Jr., Chmn., C.E.O.
J. R. Immelt, President, Chairman-Elect

INVESTOR CONTACT: Pauline Berardi, Shareholder Relations, (203) 373-2475

PRINCIPAL OFFICE: 3135 Easton Turnpike, Fairfield, CT 06431-0001

TELEPHONE NUMBER: (203) 373-2211
FAX: (203) 373-3131
WEB: www.ge.com

NO. OF EMPLOYEES: 313,000 (avg.)

SHAREHOLDERS: 616,000 (approx.)

ANNUAL MEETING: In Apr.

INCORPORATED: NY, Apr., 1892

INSTITUTIONAL HOLDINGS:
No. of Institutions: 1,286
Shares Held: 813,570,237
% Held: 51.4

INDUSTRY: Electrical equipment (SIC: 3600)

TRANSFER AGENT(S): The Bank of New York, New York, NY

NYSE SYMBOL GGP
Rec. Pr. 36.11 (4/30/01)

GENERAL GROWTH PROPERTIES, INC.

YIELD 5.9%
P/E RATIO 16.6

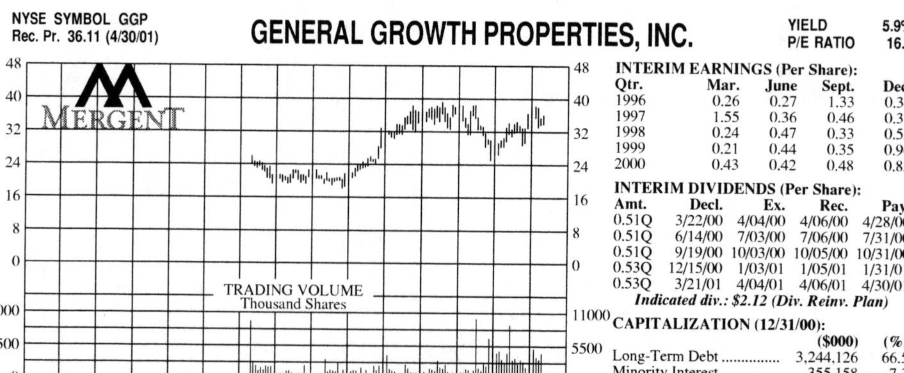

*7 YEAR PRICE SCORE 83.6 *12 MONTH PRICE SCORE 110.4
*NYSE COMPOSITE INDEX=100

INTERIM EARNINGS (Per Share):

Qtr.	Mar.	June	Sept.	Dec.
1996	0.26	0.27	1.33	0.34
1997	1.55	0.36	0.46	0.39
1998	0.24	0.47	0.33	0.55
1999	0.21	0.44	0.35	0.96
2000	0.43	0.42	0.48	0.85

INTERIM DIVIDENDS (Per Share):

Amt.	Decl.	Ex.	Rec.	Pay.
0.51Q	3/22/00	4/04/00	4/06/00	4/28/00
0.51Q	6/14/00	7/03/00	7/06/00	7/31/00
0.51Q	9/19/00	10/03/00	10/05/00	10/31/00
0.53Q	12/15/00	1/03/01	1/05/01	1/31/01
0.53Q	3/21/01	4/04/01	4/06/01	4/30/01

Indicated div.: $2.12 (Div. Reinv. Plan)

CAPITALIZATION (12/31/00):

	($000)	(%)
Long-Term Debt	3,244,126	66.5
Minority Interest	355,158	7.3
Redeemable Pfd. Stock	337,500	6.9
Common & Surplus	938,418	19.2
Total	4,875,202	100.0

RECENT DEVELOPMENTS: For the year ended 12/31/00, net income increased 20.0% to $137.9 million compared with income of $114.9 million, before an extraordinary loss, in 1999. Total revenues were $698.8 million, up 14.1% from $612.3 million a year earlier. Minimum rents increased 13.5% to $440.0 million from $387.5 million a year earlier. Tenant recoveries advanced 18.2% to $213.5 million compared with $180.6 million in 1999.

PROSPECTS: On 2/5/01, the Company announced that it has been awarded management, leasing and marketing contracts for a portfolio of 14 shopping malls owned by an institutional investor. The malls are located in 12 states, comprised of approximately 8.0 million square feet of gross leasable space area with 53 department stores. Separately, GGP has an ongoing program of renovations and expansions at several of its properties.

BUSINESS

GENERAL GROWTH PROPERTIES, INC. is the second largest self-administered regional mall real estate investment trust in the U.S., and currently owns, develops and operates regional malls in 39 states. The Company derives the majority of its income from rents received through long-term leases with retail tenants. As of 12/30/00, the Company owned: 100.0% of 53 regional mall shopping centers; 50.0% of the stock of GGP/Homart, Inc., (owner of 23 shopping centers at 9/30/00); 50.0% of the stock of GGP/ Homart II, L.L.C., (7); 51.0% of the stock of GGP Ivanhoe, Inc., (2); 51.0% of the stock of GGP Ivanhoe III, Inc., (8); 50.0% each of two regional shopping malls, Quail Springs Mall and Town East Mall; and a 100.0% non-voting preferred stock interest in General Growth Management, Inc.

REVENUES

(12/31/2000)	($000)	(%)
Minimum Rents	439,981	62.9
Tenant Recoveries	213,502	30.6
Percentage Rents	28,626	4.1
Other	9,641	1.4
Fee Income	7,017	1.0
Total	698,767	100.0

ANNUAL FINANCIAL DATA

	12/31/00	12/31/99	12/31/98	12/31/97	12/31/96	12/31/95	12/31/94
Earnings Per Share	**2.18**	**[1] 1.96**	**[1] 1.59**	**[1] 2.76**	**[1] 2.20**	**1.69**	**0.65**
Tang. Book Val. Per Share	**17.95**	**17.95**	**15.02**	**16.19**	**10.73**	**8.41**	**6.78**
Dividends Per Share	**2.04**	**1.94**	**1.86**	**1.78**	**1.72**	**1.64**	**1.54**
Dividend Payout %	**93.6**	**99.0**	**117.0**	**64.5**	**78.2**	**97.0**	**236.9**
INCOME STATEMENT (IN MILLIONS):							
Rental Income	468.6	414.6	285.2	183.8	145.9	108.7	99.2
Total Income	698.8	612.3	426.6	291.1	217.4	167.4	152.6
Costs & Expenses	226.2	206.1	151.8	109.7	76.0	64.0	63.1
Depreciation	126.7	112.9	75.2	48.5	39.8	30.9	28.2
Interest Expense	218.1	186.0	125.9	78.8	70.3	46.9	43.6
Income Before Income Taxes	140.2	123.9	89.7	62.7	35.2	26.2	18.3
Equity Earnings/Minority Int.	d2.3	d9.0	d18.5	28.0	26.8	16.8	d3.4
Net Income	137.9	[1] 114.9	[1] 71.2	[1] 90.7	[1] 62.0	43.1	14.9
Average Shs. Outstg. (000)	52,096	46,031	36,382	32,840	28,145	25,522	22,773
BALANCE SHEET (IN MILLIONS):							
Cash & Cash Equivalents	27.2	25.6	19.6	25.9	15.9	18.3	5.6
Total Real Estate Investments	4,203.1	3,949.9	3,375.0	1,630.2	1,366.3	1,095.6	695.9
Total Assets	5,284.1	4,954.9	4,027.5	2,097.7	1,757.7	1,456.0	906.5
Long-Term Obligations	3,244.1	3,119.5	2,648.8	1,275.8	1,168.5	1,027.9	607.6
Total Liabilities	4,170.7	4,027.1	3,441.8	1,599.2	1,427.5	1,226.6	752.1
Net Stockholders' Equity	938.4	927.8	585.7	498.5	330.3	229.4	154.4
Year-end Shs. Outstg. (000)	52,281	51,697	39,001	30,789	30,789	27,273	22,773
STATISTICAL RECORD:							
Net Inc.+Depr./Assets %	5.0	4.6	3.6	6.6	5.8	5.1	4.7
Return on Equity %	14.7	12.4	12.2	18.2	18.8	18.8	9.6
Return on Assets %	2.6	2.3	1.8	4.3	3.5	3.0	1.6
Price Range	36.50-26.38	38.63-25.00	39.25-32.50	38.38-30.25	32.88-20.63	22.63-18.13	22.63-19.25
P/E Ratio	16.7-12.1	19.7-12.8	24.7-20.4	13.9-11.0	14.9-9.4	13.4-10.7	34.8-29.6
Average Yield %	6.5	6.1	5.2	5.2	6.4	8.0	7.4

Statistics are as originally reported. [1] Bef. extraord. loss of $13.8 mill., 1999; $4.7 mill., 1998; $1.2 mill., 1997; $2.3 mill., 1996.

OFFICERS:
M. Bucksbaum, Chmn.
J. Bucksbaum, C.E.O.
R. Michaels, Pres.
B. Freibaum, Exec. V.P., C.F.O., Principal Acctg. Officer

PRINCIPAL OFFICE: 110 North Wacker Drive, Chicago, IL 60606

TELEPHONE NUMBER: (312) 960-5000
FAX: (312) 960-5475
WEB: www.generalgrowth.com

NO. OF EMPLOYEES: 3,506

SHAREHOLDERS: 1,388 (approx.)

ANNUAL MEETING: In May

INCORPORATED: DE, 1986

INSTITUTIONAL HOLDINGS:
No. of Institutions: 140
Shares Held: 43,766,848
% Held: 83.6

INDUSTRY: Real estate investment trusts (SIC: 6798)

TRANSFER AGENT(S): Mellon Investor Services, South Hackensack, NJ

NYSE SYMBOL GIS
Rec. Pr. 42.36 (5/31/01)

GENERAL MILLS, INC.

YIELD 2.6%
P/E RATIO 19.6

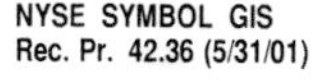

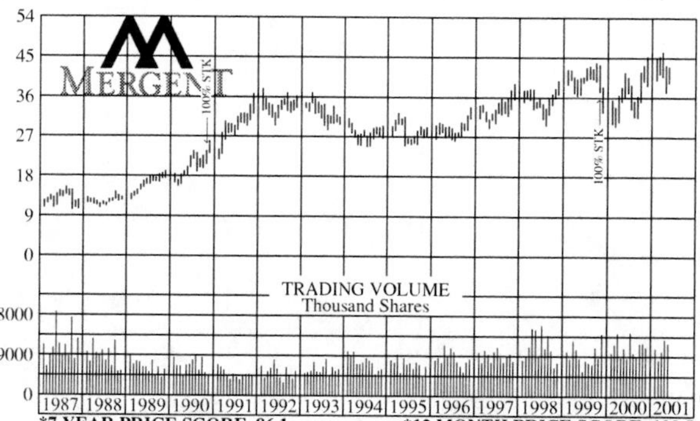

*7 YEAR PRICE SCORE 86.1 *12 MONTH PRICE SCORE 109.5

*NYSE COMPOSITE INDEX=100

INTERIM EARNINGS (Per Share):

Qtr.	Aug.	Nov.	Feb.	May
1996-97	0.31	0.50	0.39	0.21
1997-98	0.42	0.21	0.41	0.29
1998-99	0.46	0.46	0.45	0.34
1999-00	0.51	0.62	0.50	0.37
2000-01	0.55	0.70	0.54	...

INTERIM DIVIDENDS (Per Share):

Amt.	Decl.	Ex.	Rec.	Pay.
0.275Q	6/26/00	7/06/00	7/10/00	8/01/00
0.275Q	9/25/00	10/05/00	10/10/00	11/01/00
0.275Q	12/18/00	1/08/01	1/10/01	2/01/01
0.275Q	2/26/01	4/06/01	4/10/01	5/01/01

Indicated div.: $1.10 (Div. Reinv. Plan)

CAPITALIZATION (5/28/00):

	($000)	(%)
Long-Term Debt	1,760,300	94.7
Deferred Income Tax	387,000	20.8
Common & Surplus	d288,800	-15.5
Total	1,858,500	100.0

RECENT DEVELOPMENTS: For the 13 weeks ended 2/25/01, net earnings grew 2.7% to $157.5 million from $153.3 million the year before. Sales were $1.70 billion, up 5.1% versus $1.62 billion the prior year. Domestic unit volume increased 4.0%, reflecting strong volume growth from yogurt and snack products and GIS's foodservice operations. Unit volume for the Company's international operations increased 15.0%, due primarily to strong growth at Snack Ventures Europe, a joint venture with PepsiCo, Inc.

PROSPECTS: The Company is continuing to enjoy strong sales of convenience foods in the U.S. Yogurt sales are being driven by good performance by established YOPLAIT varieties, GO-GURT, and the national distribution of YOPLAIT Expresse yogurt in a tube for adults. Snacks sales are being fueled by strong demand for fruit snacks, POP SECRET microwave popcorn, NATURE VALLEY granola bars, and BUGLES. Meanwhile, GIS anticipates its acquisition of The Pillsbury Company will close in July 2001.

BUSINESS

GENERAL MILLS, INC. is a major producer of packaged consumer foods including cereals, snack products, dessert mixes, dinner and side dishes, flour, baking mix, and yogurt. Products include CHEERIOS, WHEATIES, TOTAL, and BIG G cereals, and products under the brand names BETTY CROCKER, GOLD MEDAL, BISQUICK, YOPLAIT, CHEX and COLOMBO. GIS is party to two joint ventures (% equity interest in): Cereal Partners Worldwide (50%) and Snack Ventures Europe (40.5%). On 5/28/95, GIS completed the spin-off of its restaurant operations, Darden Restaurants, Inc. The Company also sold its Gorton's frozen and canned seafood products business on 5/18/95.

ANNUAL FINANCIAL DATA

	5/28/00	5/30/99	5/31/98	5/25/97	5/26/96	[3] 5/28/95	5/29/94
Earnings Per Share	**2.00**	**[4] 1.70**	**1.30**	**[2] 1.41**	**[2] 1.50**	**[2] 0.82**	**[1] 1.48**
Cash Flow Per Share	**2.68**	**2.32**	**1.90**	**1.99**	**2.09**	**1.43**	**2.43**
Tang. Book Val. Per Share	**...**	**0.54**	**0.61**	**...**	**0.62**	**0.07**	**3.04**
Dividends Per Share	**1.10**	**1.06**	**1.04**	**0.98**	**0.94**	**0.94**	**0.89**
Dividend Payout %	**55.0**	**62.3**	**80.4**	**69.9**	**62.7**	**114.6**	**60.3**
INCOME STATEMENT (IN MILLIONS):							
Total Revenues	6,700.2	6,246.1	6,033.0	5,609.3	5,416.0	5,026.7	8,516.9
Costs & Expenses	5,392.5	5,034.2	4,887.9	4,567.6	4,369.3	4,146.3	7,213.7
Depreciation & Amort.	208.8	194.2	194.9	182.8	186.7	191.4	303.8
Operating Income	1,098.9	1,017.7	950.2	858.9	860.0	689.0	999.4
Net Interest Inc./(Exp.)	d151.9	d119.4	d117.2	d100.5	d101.4	d101.2	d99.2
Income Before Income Taxes	947.0	846.7	666.6	710.0	758.6	404.6	753.3
Income Taxes	335.9	304.0	241.9	258.3	279.4	144.9	283.6
Net Income	614.4	[4] 534.5	421.8	[2] 445.4	[2] 476.4	[2] 259.7	[1] 469.7
Cash Flow	823.2	728.7	616.7	628.2	663.1	451.1	773.5
Average Shs. Outstg. (000)	307,300	314,600	324,600	316,400	317,800	316,000	318,200
BALANCE SHEET (IN MILLIONS):							
Cash & Cash Equivalents	25.6	3.9	6.4	12.8	20.6	13.0	0.2
Total Current Assets	1,190.3	1,102.5	1,035.3	1,011.3	995.1	896.9	1,129.2
Net Property	1,404.9	1,294.7	1,186.3	1,279.4	1,312.4	1,456.6	3,092.6
Total Assets	4,573.7	4,140.7	3,861.4	3,902.4	3,294.7	3,358.2	5,198.3
Total Current Liabilities	2,529.1	1,700.3	1,443.7	1,292.5	1,191.9	1,220.9	1,832.1
Long-Term Obligations	1,760.3	1,702.4	1,640.4	1,530.4	1,220.9	1,400.9	1,417.2
Net Stockholders' Equity	d288.8	164.2	190.2	494.6	307.7	141.0	1,151.2
Net Working Capital	d1,338.8	d597.8	d408.4	d281.2	d196.8	d324.0	d702.9
Year-end Shs. Outstg. (000)	285,400	304,000	309,600	319,800	317,800	315,800	317,000
STATISTICAL RECORD:							
Operating Profit Margin %	16.4	16.3	15.8	15.3	15.9	13.7	11.7
Net Profit Margin %	9.2	8.6	7.0	7.9	8.8	5.2	5.5
Return on Equity %	...	325.5	221.8	90.1	154.8	184.2	40.8
Return on Assets %	13.4	12.9	10.9	11.4	14.5	7.7	9.0
Debt/Total Assets %	38.5	41.1	42.5	39.2	37.1	41.7	27.3
Price Range	43.94-32.50	39.84-29.59	39.13-28.88	33.75-26.00	32.31-24.88	31.13-24.69	37.06-28.44
P/E Ratio	22.0-16.2	23.4-17.4	30.1-22.2	23.9-18.4	21.5-16.6	38.0-30.1	25.1-19.3
Average Yield %	2.9	3.1	3.1	3.3	3.3	3.4	2.7

Statistics are as originally reported. Adj. for 100% stk. div., 11/99. [1] Bef. $200,000 acctg. change. [2] Incl. $400,000 pre-tax gain & $100.1 mil ($0.32/sh) after-tax restr. chg., 1997; $29.2 mil ($0.09/sh) after-tax chg., 1996; $111.6 mil ($0.36/sh) restr. chg. & $107.7 mil ($0.35/sh) after-tax inc. fr. discont. opers., 1995. [3] Refl. spin-offs of rest. & seafood bus. [4] Incl. $32.3 mil ($0.11/sh.) after-tax restr. chg.

OFFICERS:
S. W. Sanger, Chmn., C.E.O.
S. R. Demeritt, Vice-Chmn., Exec. V.P.
J. A. Lawrence, Exec. V.P., C.F.O.

INVESTOR CONTACT: Kris Wenker, V.P., Inv. Rel., (763) 764-2607

PRINCIPAL OFFICE: One General Mills Boulevard, Minneapolis, MN 55426

TELEPHONE NUMBER: (763) 764-7600
FAX: (763) 764-7384
WEB: www.generalmills.com

NO. OF EMPLOYEES: 11,077

SHAREHOLDERS: 39,712

ANNUAL MEETING: In Sept.

INCORPORATED: DE, June, 1928

INSTITUTIONAL HOLDINGS:
No. of Institutions: 482
Shares Held: 194,072,350
% Held: 68.3

INDUSTRY: Cereal breakfast foods (SIC: 2043)

TRANSFER AGENT(S): Wells Fargo Bank Minnesota, N.A., St. Paul, MN

NYSE SYMBOL GM
Rec. Pr. 56.90 (5/31/01)

GENERAL MOTORS CORP.

YIELD 3.5%
P/E RATIO 9.3

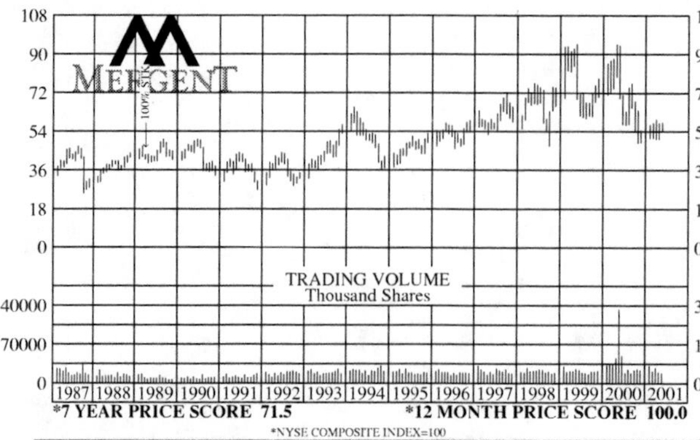

INTERIM EARNINGS (Per Share):

Qtr.	Mar.	June	Sept.	Dec.
1996	0.94	2.65	1.57	0.92
1997	2.30	2.68	1.35	2.29
1998	2.31	0.52	d1.28	2.61
1999	2.68	2.66	1.33	1.86
2000	2.80	2.93	1.55	d1.16

INTERIM DIVIDENDS (Per Share):

Amt.	Decl.	Ex.	Rec.	Pay.
0.50Q	5/02/00	5/10/00	5/12/00	6/10/00
0.50Q	8/01/00	8/09/00	8/11/00	9/09/00
0.50Q	11/06/00	11/14/00	11/16/00	12/09/00
0.50Q	2/06/01	2/14/01	2/16/01	3/10/01
0.50Q	5/01/01	5/09/01	5/11/01	6/09/01

Indicated div.: $2.00 (Div. Reinv. Plan)

CAPITALIZATION (12/31/00):

	($000)	(%)
Long-Term Debt [3]	142,447,000	82.1
Minority Interest	707,000	0.4
Redeemable Pfd. Stock	139,000	0.1
Common & Surplus	30,175,000	17.4
Total	173,468,000	100.0

RECENT DEVELOPMENTS: For the year ended 12/31/00, net income dropped 20.2% to $4.45 billion versus income of $5.58 billion, before income from discontinued operations, the year before. Results for 2000 included special charges totaling $520.0 million related to GM's restructuring initiatives, partially offset by a gain from the sale of Hughes satellite. Total net sales rose 4.6% to $184.63 billion from $176.56 billion in the previous year.

PROSPECTS: As part of the Company's restructuring initiatives, GM will phase out its Oldsmobile division, discontinue production of passenger cars in Luton, England and reduce production levels at certain North American manufacturing plants. In addition, the Company plans to reduce its workforce by 10.0% in North America and Europe. For 2001, the Company expects to reach its target of $4.25 per share.

BUSINESS

GENERAL MOTORS CORP. is the world's largest auto maker, operating through divisions including Chevrolet, Pontiac, GMC, Oldsmobile, Buick, Cadillac, Saturn, Opel, Vauxhall, Holden, Isuzu and Saab. GMAC operates the financial and insurance segment of the Company, which includes vehicle leasing, insurance and financing. Other product segments include: Hughes Electronics Corporation, a telecommunications company; Allison Transmission division, which produces medium and heavy-duty automatic transmissions for commercial trucks and buses; and GM Locomotive Group, which produces diesel-electric locomotives, diesel engines and locomotive components. GM completed the spin-off of Delphi Automotive Systems in May 1999.

ANNUAL FINANCIAL DATA

	12/31/00	12/31/99	12/31/98	12/31/97	12/31/96	12/31/95	12/31/94
Earnings Per Share	**[7] 6.68**	**[4][5] 8.53**	**[6] 4.18**	**[5] 8.62**	**[2][4] 6.06**	**[1] 7.28**	**[1] 6.20**
Cash Flow Per Share	**13.75**	**22.84**	**19.28**	**27.90**	**22.11**	**16.17**	**21.13**
Tang. Book Val. Per Share	**15.84**	**16.02**	**6.25**	**6.73**	**8.25**	**8.85**	**1.20**
Dividends Per Share	**2.00**	**2.00**	**2.00**	**2.00**	**1.60**	**1.10**	**0.80**
Dividend Payout %	**29.9**	**23.4**	**47.8**	**23.2**	**26.4**	**15.1**	**12.9**
INCOME STATEMENT (IN MILLIONS):							
Total Revenues	184,632.0	176,558.0	161,315.0	178,174.0	164,013.0	168,828.6	154,951.2
Costs & Expenses	154,505.0	145,654.0	135,303.0	146,220.0	137,775.0	139,972.4	129,382.9
Depreciation & Amort.	13,411.0	12,318.0	12,201.0	16,616.0	11,840.0	12,099.3	10,322.6
Operating Income	16,716.0	18,586.0	13,811.0	15,338.0	14,398.0	16,756.9	15,245.7
Net Interest Inc./(Exp.)	d9,552.0	d7,750.0	d6,893.0	d6,113.0	d5,695.0	d5,302.2	d5,431.9
Income Before Income Taxes	7,164.0	9,047.0	4,612.0	7,714.0	6,620.0	9,776.3	8,353.3
Income Taxes	2,393.0	3,118.0	1,463.0	1,069.0	1,723.0	2,843.8	2,694.6
Equity Earnings/Minority Int.	d319.0	d353.0	d193.0	53.0	56.0	...	...
Net Income	[7] 4,452.0	[4][5] 5,576.0	[6] 2,956.0	[5] 6,698.0	[2][4] 4,953.0	[1] 6,932.5	[1] 5,658.7
Cash Flow	17,753.0	17,814.0	15,094.0	23,216.0	16,712.0	18,668.2	15,660.6
Average Shs. Outstg. (000)	1,291,000	780,000	783,000	832,000	756,000	1,154,300	741,300
BALANCE SHEET (IN MILLIONS):							
Cash & Cash Equivalents	21,040.0	21,250.0	20,024.0	22,984.0	22,262.0	16,642.9	16,075.6
Total Current Assets	51,907.0	51,731.0	53,257.0	75,881.0	70,829.0	68,332.3	57,508.2
Net Property	33,977.0	32,779.0	37,187.0	34,567.0	37,504.0	37,739.8	34,780.6
Total Assets	303,100.0	274,730.0	257,389.0	228,888.0	222,142.0	217,123.4	198,598.7
Total Current Liabilities	63,156.0	57,362.0	54,298.0	18,705.0	17,417.0	15,130.4	14,356.0
Long-Term Obligations	142,447.0	129,697.0	112,626.0	93,027.0	85,300.0	83,323.5	73,730.2
Net Stockholders' Equity	30,175.0	20,644.0	14,984.0	17,506.0	23,418.0	23,345.5	13,275.2
Net Working Capital	d11,249.0	d5,631.0	d1,041.0	57,176.0	53,412.0	53,201.9	43,152.2
Year-end Shs. Outstg. (000)	1,423,468	756,527	761,168	897,000	1,299,507	1,292,972	754,346
STATISTICAL RECORD:							
Operating Profit Margin %	9.1	10.5	8.6	8.6	8.8	9.9	9.8
Net Profit Margin %	2.4	3.2	1.8	3.8	3.0	4.1	3.7
Return on Equity %	14.8	27.0	19.7	38.3	21.2	29.7	42.6
Return on Assets %	1.5	2.0	1.1	2.9	2.2	3.2	2.8
Debt/Total Assets %	47.0	47.2	43.8	40.6	38.4	38.4	37.1
Price Range	94.63-48.44	94.88-59.75	76.69-47.06	72.44-52.25	59.38-45.75	53.13-37.25	65.38-36.13
P/E Ratio	14.2-7.3	11.1-7.0	18.3-11.3	8.4-6.1	9.8-7.5	7.3-5.1	10.5-5.8
Average Yield %	2.8	2.6	3.2	3.2	3.0	2.4	1.6

Statistics are as originally reported. [1] Bef. acctg. change chrg. $758.0 mill., 1994; $51.8 mill., 1995. [2] Incl non-recurr chrg. $938.0 mill., 1996. [3] Incl. long-term debt from GMAC. [4] Bef. disc. opers. gain $10.0 mill., 1996; $426.0 mill., 1999. [5] Incl. non-recurr. credit $30.0 mill., 1997; $597.0 mill., 1999. [6] Bef. disc. opers. chrg. $500.0 mill. [7] Incl. spec. chrgs. totaling $520.0 mill.

OFFICERS:
J. F. Smith Jr., Chmn.
J. M. Devine, Vice-Chmn., C.F.O.
G. R. Wagoner Jr., Pres., C.E.O., C.O.O.

INVESTOR CONTACT: GM Investor Relations, (212) 418-6270

PRINCIPAL OFFICE: 300 Renaissance Center, Detroit, MI 48265-3000

TELEPHONE NUMBER: (313) 556-5000
FAX: (313) 556-5108
WEB: www.gm.com
NO. OF EMPLOYEES: 386,000 (avg.)
SHAREHOLDERS: 464,399; 192,813 (class H common)
ANNUAL MEETING: In June
INCORPORATED: DE, Oct., 1916

INSTITUTIONAL HOLDINGS:
No. of Institutions: 604
Shares Held: 300,781,766
% Held: 54.8

INDUSTRY: Motor vehicles and car bodies (SIC: 3711)

TRANSFER AGENT(S): BankBoston c/o Boston EquiServe Trust Co., Boston, MA

NYSE SYMBOL SEM
Rec. Pr. 11.54 (4/30/01)

GENERAL SEMICONDUCTOR, INC.

YIELD ...
P/E RATIO 10.6

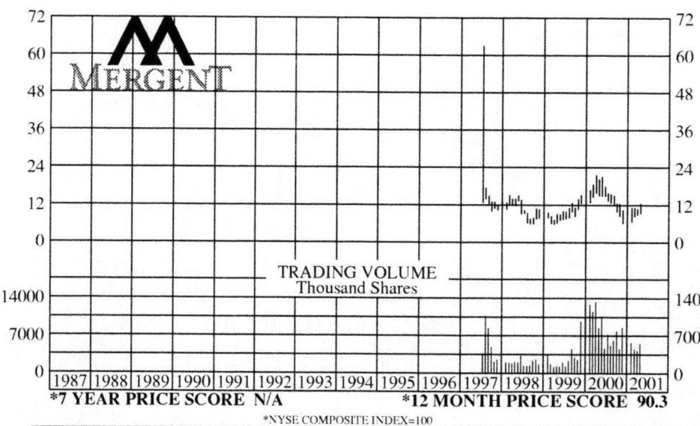

INTERIM EARNINGS (Per Share):

Qtr.	Mar.	June	Sept.	Dec.
1996	1.00	d1.80	1.24	d0.48
1997	0.52	d1.08	0.23	0.25
1998	0.26	0.19	0.16	d0.10
1999	0.12	0.14	0.17	0.23
2000	0.23	0.28	0.32	0.26

INTERIM DIVIDENDS (Per Share):

Amt.	Decl.	Ex.	Rec.	Pay.

No dividends paid.

CAPITALIZATION (12/31/00):

	($000)	(%)
Long-Term Debt	216,500	50.3
Deferred Income Tax	26,508	6.2
Common & Surplus	187,675	43.6
Total	430,683	100.0

RECENT DEVELOPMENTS: For the twelve months ended 12/31/00, net income jumped 91.6% to $46.7 million compared with $24.4 million in the previous year. Net sales advanced 18.4% to $493.7 million from $417.1 million in the prior year. The growth in sales was primarily attributed to sales from new products and an additional 24 MOSFET design wins. Gross profit surged 34.5% to $154.2 million, while operating income soared 50.4% to $84.2 million from $56.0 million in 1999.

PROSPECTS: SEM recently instituted a program to improve the cost structure on some of its mature product lines and streamline its sales and administrative functions. SEM will look to remove non-value added activities in the order through delivery process by leveraging its investment in enterprise-wide information technology. Meanwhile, in April, SEM rejected an unsolicited $563.3 million takeover proposal from Vishay Intertechnology Inc., saying the offer was not in its shareholders' best interests.

BUSINESS

GENERAL SEMICONDUCTOR, INC. (formerly General Instrument Corp.), formed 7/28/97 following the spin-off of former subsidiaries NextLevel Systems, Inc. and CommScope, Inc., designs, manufactures, and sells low-to-medium-power rectifiers and transient voltage suppression (TVS) components in axial, bridge, surface mount and array packages. Power rectifiers and TVS products are semiconductors that are essential components of most electronic devices and systems. Rectifiers convert alternating current (AC) into direct current (DC). TVS devices provide protection from electrical surges, ranging from electrostatic discharge to induced lightning. The Company's products are primarily targeted for use in the computer, automotive, telecommunications and consumer electronics industries.

QUARTERLY DATA

(12/31/00)($000)	REV	INC
1st Quarter	114,970	9,534
2nd Quarter	128,318	12,093
3rd Quarter	130,521	13,973
4th Quarter	119,912	11,140

ANNUAL FINANCIAL DATA

	12/31/00	12/31/99	12/31/98	12/31/97	[1] 12/31/96	12/31/95	12/31/94
Earnings Per Share	**1.08**	**0.66**	**0.50**	**[3] 0.25**	**[2] d0.04**	**[2] 4.00**	**0.65**
Cash Flow Per Share	**1.55**	**1.39**	**1.18**	**0.60**	**3.85**	**7.52**	**11.21**
Tang. Book Val. Per Share	**0.36**	...	...	...	**6.27**	...	...
INCOME STATEMENT (IN MILLIONS):							
Total Revenues	493.7	417.1	401.1	380.0	2,689.7	2,432.0	2,036.3
Costs & Expenses	379.6	333.3	329.0	320.9	2,509.0	2,116.6	1,622.9
Depreciation & Amort.	30.0	27.8	25.0	24.2	129.1	110.1	97.4
Operating Income	84.2	56.0	47.2	34.9	51.5	205.3	316.1
Net Interest Inc./(Exp.)	d18.8	d23.5	d20.0	d14.4	d46.4	d41.1	d53.6
Income Before Income Taxes	65.4	32.5	27.1	20.5	5.5	162.3	258.2
Income Taxes	18.6	8.1	8.6	11.6	7.4	38.6	9.7
Net Income	46.7	24.4	18.5	[3] d2.9	[2] d1.9	[2] 123.8	248.5
Cash Flow	76.7	52.2	43.5	21.3	127.3	233.9	345.8
Average Shs. Outstg. (000)	49,562	37,563	36,899	35,576	33,098	31,094	30,848
BALANCE SHEET (IN MILLIONS):							
Cash & Cash Equivalents	4.9	2.6	3.2	5.2	70.2	36.4	5.1
Total Current Assets	150.0	131.3	128.1	117.7	1,083.1	824.2	641.8
Net Property	244.9	231.2	223.7	218.8	571.1	437.2	343.9
Total Assets	595.3	573.8	563.4	550.3	2,706.9	2,300.8	2,109.0
Total Current Liabilities	99.9	66.6	76.4	101.0	534.7	462.4	428.5
Long-Term Obligations	216.5	276.5	286.0	263.8	698.8	738.6	794.7
Net Stockholders' Equity	187.7	131.4	105.3	86.4	1,173.2	915.3	677.2
Net Working Capital	50.1	64.7	51.7	16.7	548.4	361.8	213.3
Year-end Shs. Outstg. (000)	37,725	36,965	36,821	36,783	34,228	31,452	30,555
STATISTICAL RECORD:							
Operating Profit Margin %	17.1	13.4	11.8	9.2	1.9	8.4	15.5
Net Profit Margin %	9.5	5.8	4.6	...	...	5.1	12.2
Return on Equity %	24.9	18.6	17.6	...	...	13.5	36.7
Return on Assets %	7.9	4.3	3.3	...	...	5.4	11.8
Debt/Total Assets %	36.4	48.2	50.8	47.9	25.8	32.1	37.7
Price Range	21.63-6.13	15.25-5.75	15.19-5.81	63.00-9.88	...	...	...
P/E Ratio	20.0-5.7	23.1-8.7	30.4-11.6	251.9-39.5	...	...	...

Statistics are as originally reported. Adj. for stk. split: 2-for-1, 9/94; 1-for-4, 7/97 [1] Figures prior to 1997 are for General Instrument Corp. prior to spin-off. [2] Incl. non-recurr. chrg. $90.0 mill., 1995: $151.0 mill., 1996 [3] Bef. disc. opers. $19.1 mill. ($0.45/sh.)

OFFICERS:
R. A. Ostertag, Chmn., Pres., C.E.O.
R. J. Gange, Sr. V.P., C.F.O.
W. J. Nelson, C.O.O.

INVESTOR CONTACT: Tim Iris, Investor Relations, (312) 541-5000

PRINCIPAL OFFICE: 10 Melville Park Road, Suite 1300, Melville, NY 11747

TELEPHONE NUMBER: (631) 847-3000
FAX: (631) 847-3236
WEB: www.gensemi.com

NO. OF EMPLOYEES: 5,700 (approx.)

SHAREHOLDERS: 386

ANNUAL MEETING: In May

INCORPORATED: DE, 1990

INSTITUTIONAL HOLDINGS:
No. of Institutions: 106
Shares Held: 39,780,717
% Held: 105.1

INDUSTRY: Radio & TV communications equipment (SIC: 3663)

TRANSFER AGENT(S): Mellon Investor Services, LLC, South Hackensack, NJ

NYSE SYMBOL GCO
Rec. Pr. 30.35 (5/31/01)

GENESCO INC.

YIELD ...
P/E RATIO 22.6

INTERIM EARNINGS (Per Share):

Qtr.	Apr.	July	Oct.	Jan.
1996	0.04	0.08	0.23	0.31
1997	0.08	0.15	0.35	d0.28
1998	0.14	0.25	0.25	1.30
1999	0.16	0.17	0.26	0.45
2000	0.25	0.24	0.36	0.49

INTERIM DIVIDENDS (Per Share):

Amt.	Decl.	Ex.	Rec.	Pay.
No dividends paid.				

CAPITALIZATION (2/3/01):

	($000)	(%)
Long-Term Debt	103,500	42.8
Preferred Stock	7,721	3.2
Common & Surplus	130,504	54.0
Total	241,725	100.0

RECENT DEVELOPMENTS: For the year ended 2/3/01, the Company reported income of $32.6 million, before a provision for discontinued operations of $3.0 million, compared with net income of $25.9 million in 1999. Results for 2000 and 1999 included non-recurring charges of $4.4 million and $392,000, respectively. Net sales totaled $680.2 million, up 23.0% versus $553.0 million a year earlier. Sales in the Journeys' segment climbed 39.7% to $300.8 million, while Johnston & Murphy segment sales improved 12.3% to $188.1 million.

PROSPECTS: Looking ahead, the Journey's division should benefit from recent same-store sales acceleration, while Johnston & Murphy's lifestyle status continues to generate new opportunities and support long-term growth. Meanwhile, the Jarman division will concentrate on growing the Underground Station concept. Meanwhile, GCO expects sales growth for the year 2001 to be between 15.0% and 20.0% over the prior year due to better-than-expected sales of its JOURNEYS and DOCKERS brands. The Company also expects to earn $1.74 per share for the full year.

BUSINESS

GENESCO INC. is a leading retailer and wholesaler of branded footwear. The Company operates through four business segments: Journeys, Johnston & Murphy, Jarman and Licensed Brands. Genesco's owned and licensed footwear brands are sold through both wholesale and retail channels of distribution. Genesco's products are sold at wholesale to more than 2,100 retailers, including the Company's own network of 779 footwear retail stores in the U.S., operated principally under the names JOURNEYS, JOHNSTON MURPHY, JARMAN and UNDERGROUND STATION. The Company disposed of its Western Boot operations in July 1998. On 6/19/00, the Company disposed of its Volunteer Leather Company.

ANNUAL FINANCIAL DATA

	2/3/01	1/29/00	1/30/99	1/31/98	1/31/97	1/31/96	1/31/95
Earnings Per Share	**[5] 1.35**	**[4] 1.05**	**1.89**	**[1][3] 0.31**	**[1][3] 0.66**	**[1] d0.19**	**[1][2] d0.77**
Cash Flow Per Share	**1.70**	**1.30**	**2.11**	**0.66**	**1.01**	**0.13**	**d0.38**
Tang. Book Val. Per Share	**6.02**	**4.73**	**4.56**	**2.48**	**2.09**	**1.07**	**0.88**
INCOME STATEMENT (IN THOUSANDS):							
Total Revenues	680,166	573,720	549,748	536,107	461,348	434,575	462,901
Costs & Expenses	606,779	515,276	501,615	508,830	427,737	424,080	468,977
Depreciation & Amort.	13,200	10,514	9,691	8,893	7,747	7,354	9,254
Operating Income	60,187	47,930	38,442	18,384	25,864	3,141	d15,330
Net Interest Inc./(Exp.)	d7,200	d5,987	d6,611	d8,862	d8,741	d9,645	d11,955
Income Before Income Taxes	52,987	41,943	31,085	8,860	10,132	d4,256	d17,757
Income Taxes	20,156	16,021	cr23,838	40	cr422	25	757
Net Income	[5] 32,831	[4] 25,922	54,923	[1][3] 8,820	[1][3] 17,104	[1] d4,281	[1][2] d18,514
Cash Flow	45,732	36,136	63,038	17,713	18,301	3,073	d9,260
Average Shs. Outstg.	27,023	28,027	30,617	27,004	24,540	24,347	24,326
BALANCE SHEET (IN THOUSANDS):							
Cash & Cash Equivalents	60,382	57,860	58,743	49,276	43,375	35,550	10,235
Total Current Assets	243,746	214,999	228,260	194,564	174,157	156,932	183,388
Net Property	87,747	68,661	58,387	45,371	34,471	28,552	28,073
Total Assets	352,163	301,165	307,198	246,817	217,654	198,706	243,878
Total Current Liabilities	98,820	76,992	72,482	75,251	58,662	48,797	82,657
Long-Term Obligations	103,500	103,500	103,500	75,039	75,717	76,485	85,057
Net Stockholders' Equity	138,225	108,242	116,579	71,964	60,490	33,905	29,393
Net Working Capital	144,926	138,007	155,778	119,313	115,495	108,135	100,731
Year-end Shs. Outstg.	21,661	21,226	23,839	25,776	25,195	24,355	24,344
STATISTICAL RECORD:							
Operating Profit Margin %	8.8	8.4	7.0	3.4	5.6	0.7	...
Net Profit Margin %	4.8	4.5	10.0	1.6	3.7	...	...
Return on Equity %	23.8	23.9	47.1	12.3	28.3	...	...
Return on Assets %	9.3	8.6	17.9	3.6	7.9	...	...
Debt/Total Assets %	29.4	34.4	33.7	30.4	34.8	38.5	34.9
Price Range	24.94-8.25	14.63-5.38	18.88-3.94	15.44-8.50	11.13-3.38	4.88-2.00	5.63-1.63
P/E Ratio	18.5-6.1	13.9-5.1	10.0-2.1	49.8-27.4	16.9-5.1	...	...

Statistics are as originally reported. [1] Incl. non-recurr. chrg. 1998, $2.4 mill.; 1997, $17.7 mill.; 1996, $1.7 mill.; 1995, $15.1 mill.; 1994, $22.1 mill. [2] Bef. disc. oper. loss $62.7 mill. [3] Bef. extraord. chrg. 1998, $3.7 mill.; 1997, $0.2 mill. [4] Incl. non-recurr. chrg. $794,000 and a gain of $79,000. [5] Excl. provision for disc. oper. of $3.0 mill., but incl. non-recurr. chrg. of $4.4 mill.

OFFICERS:
B. T. Harris, Chmn., C.E.O.
H. N. Pennington, Pres., C.O.O.
J. S. Gulmi, Sr. V.P., C.F.O.

INVESTOR CONTACT: James S. Gulmi, Sr. V.P., C.F.O., (615) 367-8325

PRINCIPAL OFFICE: Genesco Park, 1415 Murfreesboro Rd., Nashville, TN 37217

TELEPHONE NUMBER: (615) 367-7000
FAX: (615) 367-8278
WEB: www.genesco.com

NO. OF EMPLOYEES: 4,700 (approx.)

SHAREHOLDERS: 6,200 (approx.)

ANNUAL MEETING: In June

INCORPORATED: TN, July, 1925

INSTITUTIONAL HOLDINGS:
No. of Institutions: 154
Shares Held: 21,716,140
% Held: 99.2

INDUSTRY: Shoe stores (SIC: 5661)

REGISTRAR(S): First Chicago Trust Company of New York, Jersey City, NJ

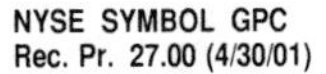
NYSE SYMBOL GPC
Rec. Pr. 27.00 (4/30/01)

GENUINE PARTS COMPANY

YIELD 4.2%
P/E RATIO 12.2

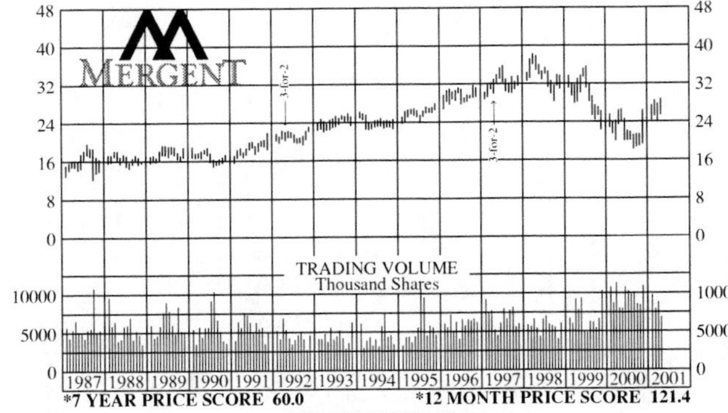

*7 YEAR PRICE SCORE 60.0 *12 MONTH PRICE SCORE 121.4
*NYSE COMPOSITE INDEX=100

INTERIM EARNINGS (Per Share):

Qtr.	Mar.	June	Sept.	Dec.
1996	0.41	0.45	0.45	0.52
1997	0.43	0.47	0.47	0.55
1998	0.45	0.48	0.48	0.58
1999	0.48	0.52	0.51	0.61
2000	0.52	0.55	0.53	0.61

INTERIM DIVIDENDS (Per Share):

Amt.	Decl.	Ex.	Rec.	Pay.
0.275Q	4/18/00	6/07/00	6/09/00	7/03/00
0.275Q	8/21/00	9/06/00	9/08/00	10/02/00
0.275Q	11/20/00	12/06/00	12/08/00	1/02/01
0.285Q	2/19/01	3/07/01	3/09/01	4/02/01
0.285Q	4/17/01	6/06/01	6/08/01	7/02/01

Indicated div.: $1.14 (Div. Reinv. Plan)

CAPITALIZATION (12/31/00):

	($000)	(%)
Long-Term Debt	770,581	24.4
Deferred Income Tax	77,814	2.5
Minority Interest	44,600	1.4
Common & Surplus	2,260,806	71.7
Total	3,153,801	100.0

RECENT DEVELOPMENTS: For the year ended 12/31/00, net income improved 2.0% to $385.3 million compared with $377.6 million in the previous year. Net sales rose 5.3% to $8.37 billion versus $7.95 billion a year earlier. Automotive segment net sales inched up 1.9% to $4.16 billion. Net sales for the Industrial segment grew 8.7% to $2.34 billion, while Office Products segment net sales increased 9.7% to $1.34 billion. Electrical and Electronic Materials segment sales climbed 6.8% to $557.9 million.

PROSPECTS: Earnings reflected revenue growth from each of GPC's four segments in their respective markets. However, sales growth in the Automotive segment may be challenged as revenues continue to be pressured by a weakening automotive market. Solid sales in GPC's Industrial Parts, Office Products, and Electrical and Electronics segments should more than offset any associated losses in the Automotive segment. Overall, the Company's outlook for 2001 is positive.

BUSINESS

GENUINE PARTS COMPANY is a service organization engaged in the distribution of automotive replacement parts, industrial replacement parts, office products and electrical and electronic materials. GPC's largest division is its Automotive Parts Group, which distributes automotive replacement parts and accessory items to NAPA auto parts stores. The Industrial Parts Group distributes replacement parts, equipment and related supplies throughout the United States, Canada and Mexico. The Office Products Group distributes products including information processing, supplies, furniture and machines. The Electrical and Electronic Materials Group distributes materials for the manufacture and repair of electrical and electronic apparatus. In January 2000, GPC purchased a 15.0% ownership interest in Mitchell Repair Information Company, LLC.

REVENUES

(12/31/00)	($000)	(%)
Automotive Parts	4,163,814	49.7
Industrial Parts	2,342,686	28.0
Office Products	1,336,500	16.0
Electrical/Electronic Materials	557,886	6.6
Other	(31,009)	(0.3)
Total	8,369,857	100.0

ANNUAL FINANCIAL DATA

	12/31/00	12/31/99	12/31/98	12/31/97	12/31/96	12/31/95	12/31/94
Earnings Per Share	**2.20**	**2.11**	**1.98**	**1.90**	**1.82**	**1.68**	**1.55**
Cash Flow Per Share	**2.72**	**2.61**	**2.36**	**2.23**	**2.10**	**1.92**	**1.75**
Tang. Book Val. Per Share	**10.50**	**9.80**	**9.52**	**10.39**	**9.62**	**9.03**	**8.30**
Dividends Per Share	**1.08**	**1.03**	**0.99**	**0.94**	**0.88**	**0.82**	**0.75**
Dividend Payout %	**49.3**	**48.8**	**50.0**	**49.6**	**48.3**	**48.9**	**48.4**
INCOME STATEMENT (IN MILLIONS):							
Total Revenues	8,369.9	7,981.7	6,614.0	6,005.2	5,720.5	5,261.9	4,858.4
Costs & Expenses	7,630.8	7,263.7	5,955.6	5,380.8	5,124.8	4,707.9	4,346.2
Depreciation & Amort.	92.3	90.0	69.3	58.9	50.4	43.2	37.4
Operating Income	646.8	628.1	589.1	565.6	545.2	510.8	474.9
Income Before Income Taxes	646.8	628.1	589.1	565.6	545.2	510.8	474.9
Income Taxes	261.4	250.4	233.3	223.2	215.2	201.6	186.3
Net Income	385.3	377.6	355.8	342.4	330.1	309.2	288.5
Cash Flow	477.6	467.6	425.1	401.3	380.5	352.4	325.9
Average Shs. Outstg. (000)	175,327	179,238	180,081	180,165	181,568	183,923	186,062
BALANCE SHEET (IN MILLIONS):							
Cash & Cash Equivalents	27.7	45.7	85.0	72.8	67.4	44.3	82.4
Total Current Assets	3,019.5	2,895.2	2,683.4	2,093.6	1,937.6	1,764.0	1,595.8
Net Property	395.3	413.5	404.0	372.5	346.0	303.2	258.0
Total Assets	4,142.1	3,929.7	3,600.4	2,754.4	2,521.6	2,274.1	2,029.5
Total Current Liabilities	988.3	916.0	818.4	556.9	568.4	475.5	422.4
Long-Term Obligations	770.6	702.4	588.6	209.5	110.2	60.6	11.4
Net Stockholders' Equity	2,260.8	2,177.5	2,053.3	1,859.5	1,732.1	1,650.9	1,526.2
Net Working Capital	2,031.2	1,979.2	1,864.9	1,536.6	1,369.3	1,288.4	1,173.4
Year-end Shs. Outstg. (000)	172,390	177,276	179,505	178,948	180,048	182,870	183,941
STATISTICAL RECORD:							
Operating Profit Margin %	7.7	7.9	8.9	9.4	9.5	9.7	9.8
Net Profit Margin %	4.6	4.7	5.4	5.7	5.8	5.9	5.9
Return on Equity %	17.0	17.3	17.3	18.4	19.1	18.7	18.9
Return on Assets %	9.3	9.6	9.9	12.4	13.1	13.6	14.2
Debt/Total Assets %	18.6	17.9	16.3	7.6	4.4	2.7	0.6
Price Range	26.69-18.25	35.75-22.25	38.25-28.25	35.88-28.67	31.67-26.67	28.00-23.67	26.25-22.42
P/E Ratio	12.1-8.3	16.9-10.5	19.3-14.3	18.9-15.1	17.4-14.7	16.7-14.1	16.9-14.4
Average Yield %	4.8	3.6	3.0	2.9	3.0	3.2	3.1

Statistics are as originally reported. Adj. for stk. splits: 3-for-2, 4/97

OFFICERS:
L. L. Prince, Chmn., C.E.O.
T. C. Gallagher, Pres., C.O.O.
J. W. Nix, Exec. V.P., C.F.O.

INVESTOR CONTACT: Jerry Nix, Exec. V.P., Finance; C.F.O., (770) 953-1700

PRINCIPAL OFFICE: 2999 Circle 75 Parkway, Atlanta, GA 30339

TELEPHONE NUMBER: (770) 953-1700
FAX: (770) 956-2211
WEB: www.genpt.com

NO. OF EMPLOYEES: 33,000 (approx.)

SHAREHOLDERS: 8,102

ANNUAL MEETING: In Apr.

INCORPORATED: GA, May, 1928

INSTITUTIONAL HOLDINGS:
No. of Institutions: 299
Shares Held: 115,007,380
% Held: 66.9

INDUSTRY: Motor vehicle supplies and new parts (SIC: 5013)

TRANSFER AGENT(S): Sun Trust Bank, Atlanta, Atlanta, GA

NYSE SYMBOL GGC
Rec. Pr. 18.37 (4/30/01)

GEORGIA GULF CORPORATION

YIELD 1.7%
P/E RATIO 9.0

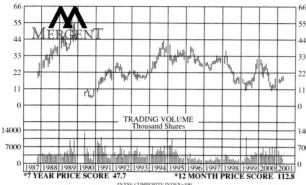

INTERIM EARNINGS (Per Share):

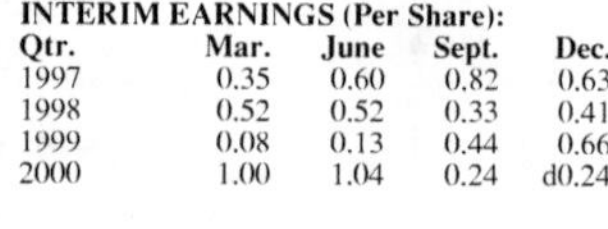

Qtr.	Mar.	June	Sept.	Dec.
1997	0.35	0.60	0.82	0.63
1998	0.52	0.52	0.33	0.41
1999	0.08	0.13	0.44	0.66
2000	1.00	1.04	0.24	d0.24

INTERIM DIVIDENDS (Per Share):

Amt.	Decl.	Ex.	Rec.	Pay.
0.08Q	5/16/00	6/15/00	6/19/00	7/10/00
0.08Q	8/15/00	9/21/00	9/25/00	10/09/00
0.08Q	12/05/00	12/18/00	12/20/00	1/10/01
0.06Q	3/06/01	3/16/01	3/20/01	4/10/01
0.08Q	5/15/01	6/15/01	6/19/01	7/13/01

Indicated div.: $0.32

CAPITALIZATION (12/31/00):

	($000)	(%)
Long-Term Debt	622,541	72.6
Deferred Income Tax	116,545	13.6
Common & Surplus	118,592	13.8
Total	857,678	100.0

TRADING VOLUME Thousand Shares

***7 YEAR PRICE SCORE 47.7** ***12 MONTH PRICE SCORE 112.8**

*NYSE COMPOSITE INDEX=100

RECENT DEVELOPMENTS: For the year ended 12/31/00, net income soared 48.7% to $64.2 million. Net income benefited from improvements in the vinyl resins profit margin and the acquisition of the CONDEA Vista vinyls business. Results for 1999 excluded a loss of $2.5 million from discontinued operations and a loss of $7.6 million from the disposal of discontinued operations. Net sales surged 74.0% to $1.58 billion.

PROSPECTS: Looking ahead, the Company expects to continue to experience overall weak demand. However, price increases in the first quarter of 2001 for phenol and vinyl resins, along with reduced natural gas prices and lower raw material costs, should improve future earnings. Based on current economic forecasts, demand for the Company's products should improve by year-end.

BUSINESS

GEORGIA GULF CORPORATION is a manufacturer and marketer of chemical and plastic products. The Company's products are manufactured through two integrated lines categorized into chlorovinyls and aromatic chemicals. Chlorovinyls products include chlorine, caustic soda, sodium chlorate, vinyl chloride monomer, vinyl resins and compounds; aromatic chemical products include cumene, phenol and acetone. Sales (and operating income) in 2000 were derived: chlorovinyls, 78.7% (114.5%); aromatics, 21.3% (d5.8%); and corporate and general plant services, 0% (d8.7%).

ANNUAL FINANCIAL DATA

	12/31/00	12/31/99	12/31/98	12/31/97	12/31/96	12/31/95	12/31/94
Earnings Per Share	**2.03**	**[3] 1.38**	**[2] 1.77**	**[1] 2.39**	**1.97**	**4.73**	**2.88**
Cash Flow Per Share	**4.36**	**2.98**	**3.21**	**3.51**	**3.06**	**5.54**	**3.53**
Tang. Book Val. Per Share	**1.21**	...	...	**1.11**	**0.54**	**1.36**	**0.74**
Dividends Per Share	**0.32**	**0.32**	**0.32**	**0.32**	**0.32**	**0.24**	...
Dividend Payout %	**15.8**	**23.2**	**18.1**	**13.4**	**16.2**	**5.1**	...
INCOME STATEMENT (IN MILLIONS):							
Total Revenues	1,581.7	857.8	875.0	965.7	896.2	1,081.6	955.3
Costs & Expenses	1,340.3	705.4	699.3	781.0	720.5	721.6	697.3
Depreciation & Amort.	73.3	49.6	45.7	37.9	39.4	32.1	27.8
Operating Income	168.0	102.8	130.0	146.8	136.3	327.9	230.2
Net Interest Inc./(Exp.)	d67.7	d34.8	d30.8	d24.6	d20.8	d24.9	d37.4
Income Before Income Taxes	100.3	68.0	89.7	130.8	115.5	303.1	192.8
Income Taxes	36.1	24.8	33.4	49.6	43.9	116.6	70.6
Net Income	64.2	[3] 43.2	[2] 56.3	[1] 81.2	71.6	186.5	122.2
Cash Flow	137.5	92.8	102.0	119.1	111.1	218.6	149.9
Average Shs. Outstg. (000)	31,540	31,107	31,787	33,947	36,288	39,428	42,445
BALANCE SHEET (IN MILLIONS):							
Cash & Cash Equivalents	2.0	4.4	1.2	1.6	0.7	2.5	1.2
Total Current Assets	283.8	293.3	153.8	176.0	170.4	187.2	249.9
Net Property	626.8	671.6	401.1	410.9	394.7	312.5	255.6
Total Assets	1,041.1	1,098.0	669.8	612.7	588.0	507.3	508.4
Total Current Liabilities	183.4	197.6	88.8	118.5	121.0	113.8	123.3
Long-Term Obligations	622.5	749.2	459.5	393.0	395.6	292.4	314.1
Net Stockholders' Equity	118.6	57.2	28.9	35.6	18.6	50.6	31.1
Net Working Capital	100.4	95.6	65.1	57.5	49.4	73.4	126.7
Year-end Shs. Outstg. (000)	31,714	31,291	30,884	32,187	34,585	37,240	42,013
STATISTICAL RECORD:							
Operating Profit Margin %	10.6	12.0	14.9	15.2	15.2	30.3	24.1
Net Profit Margin %	4.1	5.0	6.4	8.4	8.0	17.2	12.8
Return on Equity %	54.1	75.4	194.9	228.1	385.7	368.4	392.3
Return on Assets %	6.2	3.9	8.4	13.3	12.2	36.8	24.0
Debt/Total Assets %	59.8	68.2	68.6	64.1	67.3	57.6	61.8
Price Range	30.94-10.19	31.13-10.00	36.75-14.50	33.50-23.00	39.50-25.75	40.75-26.63	43.25-21.63
P/E Ratio	15.2-5.0	22.6-7.2	20.8-8.2	14.0-9.6	20.0-13.1	8.6-5.6	15.0-7.5
Average Yield %	1.6	1.6	1.2	1.1	1.0	0.7	...

Statistics are as originally reported. [1] Incl. $8.6 mill. pre-tax gain fr. sale of certain oil & gas props. [2] Incl. $6.0 mill. one-time after-tax chg. for loss on int. rate hedge agreements. [3] Excl. $10.2 mill. loss fr. disc. ops. & disposal of bus.

OFFICERS:
E. A. Schmitt, Pres., C.E.O.
R. B. Marchese, V.P., C.F.O., Treas.

INVESTOR CONTACT: Nancy O'Donnell, Director, Investor Relations, (770) 395-4587

PRINCIPAL OFFICE: 400 Perimeter Center Terrace, Suite 595, Atlanta, GA 30346

TELEPHONE NUMBER: (770) 395-4500
FAX: (770) 395-4529
WEB: www.georgiagulf.com

NO. OF EMPLOYEES: 1,329

SHAREHOLDERS: 878

ANNUAL MEETING: In May

INCORPORATED: DE, Dec., 1984

INSTITUTIONAL HOLDINGS:
No. of Institutions: 103
Shares Held: 19,415,984
% Held: 61.2

INDUSTRY: Industrial inorganic chemicals, nec (SIC: 2819)

TRANSFER AGENT(S): EquiServe, Boston, MA

NYSE SYMBOL GP
Rec. Pr. 32.51 (4/30/01)

GEORGIA-PACIFIC GROUP

YIELD 1.5%
P/E RATIO 15.6

*7 YEAR PRICE SCORE 57.3 *12 MONTH PRICE SCORE 112.2

*NYSE COMPOSITE INDEX=100

INTERIM EARNINGS (Per Share):

Qtr.	Mar.	June	Sept.	Dec.
1998	0.09	0.17	0.22	0.15
1999	0.57	1.20	1.31	1.00
2000	1.11	1.20	0.76	d0.98

INTERIM DIVIDENDS (Per Share):

Amt.	Decl.	Ex.	Rec.	Pay.
0.125Q	8/01/00	8/08/00	8/10/00	8/21/00
0.125Q	11/06/00	11/08/00	11/12/00	11/24/00
0.125Q	1/30/01	2/06/01	2/08/01	2/20/01
0.125Q	5/01/01	5/08/01	5/10/01	5/21/01

Indicated div.: $0.50 (Div. Reinv. Plan)

CAPITALIZATION (12/30/00):

	($000)	(%)
Long-Term Debt	13,490,000	62.0
Deferred Income Tax	2,561,000	11.8
Common & Surplus	5,722,000	26.3
Total	21,773,000	100.0

RECENT DEVELOPMENTS: For the year ended 12/30/00, GP reported net income of $343.0 million, up 52.1% from $716.0 million in 1999. Results included one-time unusual after-tax charges of $184.0 million resulting from the write-down of the Georgia-Pacific Tissue assets and closure of a paper mill at Kalamazoo, Michigan. Total net sales were $22.08 billion, up 19.9% from $18.42 billion a year earlier.

PROSPECTS: On 3/2/01, GP completed the sale of its commercial tissue manufacturing operations that were part of a joint venture with Chesapeake Corporation known as Georgia-Pacific Tissue LLC. The sale will result in after-tax proceeds to GP of $661.0 million. The sale satisfies an agreement between GP and the U.S. Department of Justice that resolved the department's anti-trust concerns associated with its acquisition of Fort James Corp.

BUSINESS

GEORGIA-PACIFIC GROUP (formerly Georgia-Pacific Corporation) consists of all of Georgia-Pacific Corporation's manufacturing mills and plants and its building products distribution business. These include 81 facilities in the U.S. and one in Canada manufacturing containerboard and packaging materials, communication papers, market pulp, tissue and other products; 150 facilities in the U.S. and seven in Canada that manufacture lumber, wood panels such as plywood, oriented strand board and industrial panels, gypsum products, chemicals and other products; and a distribution organization that operates a network of 73 sales centers, large distribution centers and smaller local distribution centers throughout the U.S. GP created a separate class of stock for its timber business in December 1997. In November 2000, the Company acquired Fort James Corporation.

ANNUAL FINANCIAL DATA

	12/30/00	1/1/00	12/31/98	12/31/97	12/31/96	12/31/95	12/31/94
Earnings Per Share	**3.94**	**8.80**	**[4] 1.59**	**[3] 0.70**	**[1] 0.89**	**[1] 5.65**	**[2] 1.83**
Cash Flow Per Share	**6.24**	**8.21**	**3.58**	**3.14**	**6.39**	**10.24**	**6.41**
Tang. Book Val. Per Share	**...**	**4.78**	**4.04**	**5.07**	**10.24**	**9.92**	**4.71**
Dividends Per Share	**0.50**	**0.50**	**0.50**	**1.00**	**1.00**	**0.95**	**0.80**
Dividend Payout %	**12.7**	**5.7**	**31.4**	**143.9**	**112.3**	**16.8**	**43.7**
INCOME STATEMENT (IN MILLIONS):							
Total Revenues	22,218.0	17,977.0	13,336.0	13,094.0	13,024.0	14,292.0	12,738.0
Costs & Expenses	19,663.0	14,639.0	11,392.0	11,372.0	11,287.0	11,375.0	10,898.0
Depreciation & Amort.	1,104.0	1,022.0	1,010.0	1,022.0	1,002.0	825.0	815.0
Operating Income	1,451.0	2,316.0	934.0	700.0	735.0	2,092.0	1,025.0
Net Interest Inc./(Exp.)	d639.0	d495.0	d443.0	d465.0	d439.0	d395.0	d453.0
Income Before Income Taxes	812.0	1,821.0	491.0	235.0	296.0	1,697.0	572.0
Income Taxes	307.0	705.0	202.0	106.0	135.0	679.0	246.0
Net Income	505.0	1,116.0	[4] 289.0	[3] 129.0	[1] 161.0	[1] 1,018.0	[2] 326.0
Cash Flow	1,609.0	2,138.0	1,299.0	1,151.0	1,163.0	1,843.0	1,141.0
Average Shs. Outstg. (000)	258,000	260,500	362,600	367,000	182,000	180,000	178,000
BALANCE SHEET (IN MILLIONS):							
Cash & Cash Equivalents	40.0	25.0	...	8.0	10.0	11.0	53.0
Total Current Assets	6,288.0	4,559.0	2,640.0	2,916.0	2,615.0	2,595.0	1,862.0
Net Property	13,095.0	8,268.0	7,455.0	7,490.0	7,897.0	7,387.0	6,851.0
Total Assets	30,882.0	16,897.0	12,695.0	12,950.0	12,818.0	12,335.0	10,728.0
Total Current Liabilities	6,082.0	4,191.0	2,648.0	3,020.0	2,490.0	1,762.0	2,325.0
Long-Term Obligations	13,490.0	5,484.0	4,125.0	3,713.0	4,371.0	4,704.0	3,904.0
Net Stockholders' Equity	5,722.0	3,875.0	3,124.0	3,474.0	3,521.0	3,519.0	2,620.0
Net Working Capital	206.0	368.0	d8.0	d104.0	125.0	833.0	d463.0
Year-end Shs. Outstg. (000)	305,028	246,335	358,600	369,600	182,000	182,000	180,000
STATISTICAL RECORD:							
Operating Profit Margin %	6.5	12.9	7.0	5.3	5.6	14.6	8.0
Net Profit Margin %	2.3	6.2	2.2	1.0	1.2	7.1	2.6
Return on Equity %	8.8	28.8	9.3	3.7	4.6	28.9	12.4
Return on Assets %	1.6	6.6	2.3	1.0	1.3	8.3	3.0
Debt/Total Assets %	43.7	32.5	32.5	28.7	34.1	38.1	36.4
Price Range	51.94-19.31	54.13-29.34	40.50-18.69	54.28-29.50	40.50-31.50	47.88-32.88	39.50-28.38
P/E Ratio	13.2-4.9	6.2-3.3	25.5-11.8	78.1-42.4	45.5-35.4	8.5-5.8	21.6-15.5
Average Yield %	1.4	1.2	1.7	2.4	2.8	2.4	2.4

Statistics are as originally reported. Adj. for stk. split: 100%, 6/99. Full-year results reflect the combined opers. of Georgia-Pacific Group and The Timber Co.; qtrly. earns./sh. and div./sh. subsequent to 12/97 are for Georgia-Pacific Group only. [1] Incl. nonrecurr. chrg. of $117.0 mill., 1996; chrg. $70.0 mill., 1995; & gain $3.0 mill., 1996. [2] Incl. nonrecurr. gain of $33.0 mill. Bef. chrg. of $30.0 mill. [3] Bef. acctg. chrg. of $60.0 mill.; & incl. restr. chrg. of $80.0 mill. [4] Bef. extraord. chrg. of $13.0 mill.

OFFICERS:
A. D. Correll, Chmn., Pres., C.E.O.
D. W. Huff, Exec. V.P., C.F.O.

INVESTOR CONTACT: Investor Relations, (404) 652-5555

PRINCIPAL OFFICE: 133 Peachtree Street, N.E., Atlanta, GA 30303

TELEPHONE NUMBER: (404) 652-4000
WEB: www.gp.com

NO. OF EMPLOYEES: 80,000 (avg.)

SHAREHOLDERS: 34,509 (approx. Georgia-Pacific Group common)

ANNUAL MEETING: In May

INCORPORATED: GA, Sept., 1927

INSTITUTIONAL HOLDINGS:
No. of Institutions: 341
Shares Held: 149,753,398
% Held: 66.3

INDUSTRY: Wood products, nec (SIC: 2499)

TRANSFER AGENT(S): First Chicago Trust Company of New York, Jersey City, NJ

NYSE SYMBOL GRB
Rec. Pr. 6.95 (4/30/01)

GERBER SCIENTIFIC INC.

YIELD ...
P/E RATIO ...

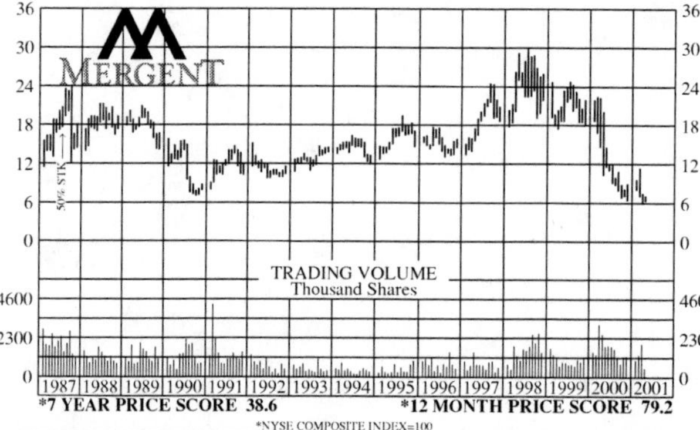

*7 YEAR PRICE SCORE 38.6 *12 MONTH PRICE SCORE 79.2

*NYSE COMPOSITE INDEX=100

INTERIM EARNINGS (Per Share):

Qtr.	July	Oct.	Jan.	Apr.
1997-98	0.19	0.24	0.27	d0.38
1998-99	0.29	0.33	0.31	0.36
1999-00	0.34	0.37	0.37	0.08
2000-01	d0.12	0.08	d0.17	...

INTERIM DIVIDENDS (Per Share):

Amt.	Decl.	Ex.	Rec.	Pay.
0.08Q	5/05/00	5/15/00	5/17/00	5/31/00
0.08Q	8/07/00	8/16/00	8/18/00	8/31/00
0.08Q	11/02/00	11/15/00	11/17/00	11/30/00
0.08Q	2/02/01	2/13/01	2/15/01	2/28/01

Dividend suspended.

CAPITALIZATION (4/30/00):

	($000)	(%)
Long-Term Debt	194,892	42.3
Deferred Income Tax	8,608	1.9
Common & Surplus	256,912	55.8
Total	460,412	100.0

RECENT DEVELOPMENTS: For the quarter ended 1/31/01, GRB reported a net loss of $3.6 million compared with net earnings of $8.3 million in the equivalent quarter of 1999. Total revenues were $134.2 million, down 13.7% from $155.5 million in the prior-year period. Operating income fell 98.8% to $179,000 compared with $14.9 million in the previous year. Net orders totaled $133.5 million compared with $148.5 million the year before. Results were hampered by slow orders in the North American market.

PROSPECTS: The Company announced a major restructuring plan for its global operations, which includes a reduction of operating costs by as much as $35.0 million on an annual basis. As a result, the Company plans to record a charge in the fourth quarter of 2001 in the range of $20.0 million to $22.0 million that will cover costs related to severance, plant closings, product line terminations and other asset write-downs. The Company plans to reduce its current workforce by about 350 to 400 employees.

BUSINESS

GERBER SCIENTIFIC INC. designs, develops, manufactures, markets, and services computer-aided design and computer-aided manufacturing (CAD/CAM) factory automation systems, software, and related aftermarket supplies for a wide range of industries, including apparel, automotive, aerospace, electronics, commercial printing, ophthalmic, graphic arts, screenprinting, and signmaking. The Company's principal CAD/CAM products consist of the following: cutting, nesting, spreading, and material handling systems; microprocessor- and PC-controlled production systems; interactive imaging and inspection systems; and ophthalmic lens manufacturing systems. GRB operates through its four wholly-owned subsidiaries: Gerber Coburn, Gerber Technology, Gerber Scientific Products, and Spandex PLC. GRB sold the operations of Gerber Systems to BARCO in March 1998.

ANNUAL FINANCIAL DATA

	4/30/00	4/30/99	4/30/98	4/30/97	4/30/96	4/30/95	4/30/94
Earnings Per Share	**4 1.16**	**1.29**	**3 0.32**	**2 0.69**	**0.84**	**0.76**	**1 0.61**
Cash Flow Per Share	**2.30**	**2.34**	**0.90**	**1.19**	**1.30**	**1.23**	**1.01**
Tang. Book Val. Per Share	**1.75**	**1.02**	**6.17**	**8.67**	**8.62**	**8.32**	**8.38**
Dividends Per Share	**0.32**	**0.32**	**0.32**	**0.32**	**0.32**	**0.28**	**0.22**
Dividend Payout %	**27.6**	**24.8**	**100.0**	**46.4**	**38.1**	**36.8**	**36.1**
INCOME STATEMENT (IN MILLIONS):							
Total Revenues	610.7	594.6	430.5	380.9	359.1	322.7	260.7
Costs & Expenses	536.6	515.0	410.5	351.2	325.0	291.7	240.1
Depreciation & Amort.	25.6	24.2	13.6	11.8	10.8	11.4	9.7
Operating Income	48.5	55.4	6.4	18.0	23.3	19.6	11.0
Net Interest Inc./(Exp.)	d10.6	d11.5	d0.7	d0.3	d0.4	d0.5	d0.3
Income Before Income Taxes	39.0	46.1	9.9	22.2	27.9	25.1	21.4
Income Taxes	13.1	16.5	2.5	6.2	8.0	7.0	6.9
Net Income	4 25.9	29.6	3 7.4	2 16.0	19.9	18.1	1 14.5
Cash Flow	51.5	53.8	21.0	27.8	30.7	29.5	24.2
Average Shs. Outstg. (000)	22,390	23,011	23,331	23,365	23,689	23,950	23,967
BALANCE SHEET (IN MILLIONS):							
Cash & Cash Equivalents	23.0	26.5	27.0	9.5	8.7	10.2	15.6
Total Current Assets	252.0	225.7	185.5	177.8	158.0	146.9	129.8
Net Property	99.2	90.6	60.0	62.6	54.7	51.1	47.5
Total Assets	572.8	542.3	338.8	325.2	313.0	324.4	286.4
Total Current Liabilities	112.4	116.0	90.7	58.9	56.3	68.4	41.9
Long-Term Obligations	194.9	173.3	7.0	7.1	7.3	7.5	7.7
Net Stockholders' Equity	256.9	243.3	230.9	248.0	239.3	237.3	224.8
Net Working Capital	139.5	109.7	94.8	118.9	101.7	78.5	87.8
Year-end Shs. Outstg. (000)	21,982	22,058	22,637	23,307	23,199	23,758	23,828
STATISTICAL RECORD:							
Operating Profit Margin %	7.9	9.3	1.5	4.7	6.5	6.1	4.2
Net Profit Margin %	4.2	5.0	1.7	4.2	5.5	5.6	5.6
Return on Equity %	10.1	12.2	3.2	6.5	8.3	7.6	6.5
Return on Assets %	4.5	5.5	2.2	4.9	6.3	5.6	5.1
Debt/Total Assets %	34.0	32.0	2.1	2.2	2.3	2.3	2.7
Price Range	24.88-17.38	29.94-17.69	24.50-13.38	17.75-13.00	19.50-12.63	16.38-11.88	14.75-10.75
P/E Ratio	21.4-15.0	23.2-13.7	76.5-41.8	25.7-18.8	23.2-15.0	21.5-15.6	24.2-17.6
Average Yield %	1.5	1.3	1.7	2.1	2.0	2.0	1.7

Statistics are as originally reported. 1 Incl. cr$3.4 mill. ($0.14/sh.) litigation settlement. 2 Incl. $1.0 mill. ($0.04/sh.) gain. 3 Incl. $1.6 mill. gain fr. litigation settlement & $16.3 mill. after-tax non-recur. special chg. from sale of Gerber Systems. 4 Incl. $6.2 mill. non-recur. chg.

OFFICERS:
M. J. Cheshire, Chmn., C.E.O.
R. F. Treacy Jr., Sr. V.P., Gen. Couns., Sec.
G. K. Bennett, Sr. V.P., Fin., C.F.O.

INVESTOR CONTACT: Investor Relations, (860) 644-1551

PRINCIPAL OFFICE: 83 Gerber Road West, South Windsor, CT 06074

TELEPHONE NUMBER: (860) 644-1551
FAX: (860) 644-5547
WEB: www.gerberscientific.com

NO. OF EMPLOYEES: 2,900 (approx.)

SHAREHOLDERS: 1,370

ANNUAL MEETING: In Sept.

INCORPORATED: CT, May, 1948

INSTITUTIONAL HOLDINGS:
No. of Institutions: 90
Shares Held: 14,673,072
% Held: 66.6

INDUSTRY: Special industry machinery, nec (SIC: 3559)

TRANSFER AGENT(S): Mellon Investor Services, East Hartford, CT

NYSE SYMBOL G
Rec. Pr. 27.81 (4/30/01)

GILLETTE COMPANY (THE)

YIELD 2.3%
P/E RATIO 36.1

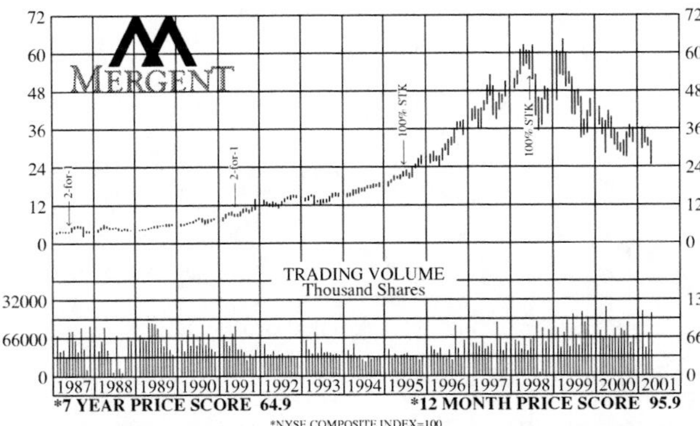

INTERIM EARNINGS (Per Share):

Qtr.	Mar.	June	Sept.	Dec.
1996	0.23	0.25	0.28	0.11
1997	0.26	0.29	0.32	0.41
1998	0.23	0.33	Nil	0.39
1999	0.24	0.26	0.32	0.32
2000	0.24	0.28	0.33	d0.08

INTERIM DIVIDENDS (Per Share):

Amt.	Decl.	Ex.	Rec.	Pay.
0.163Q	3/16/00	4/27/00	5/01/00	6/05/00
0.163Q	7/20/00	7/28/00	8/01/00	9/05/00
0.163Q	10/19/00	10/30/00	11/01/00	12/05/00
0.163Q	12/14/00	1/30/01	2/01/01	3/05/01
0.163Q	4/18/01	4/27/01	5/01/01	6/05/01

Indicated div.: $0.65 (Div. Reinv. Plan)

CAPITALIZATION (12/31/00):

	($000)	(%)
Long-Term Debt	1,650,000	40.6
Deferred Income Tax	450,000	11.1
Minority Interest	41,000	1.0
Common & Surplus	1,924,000	47.3
Total	4,065,000	100.0

RECENT DEVELOPMENTS: For the year ended 12/31/00, income from continuing operations totaled $821.0 million compared with income from continuing operations of $1.25 billion in 1999. Earnings for 2000 included a pre-tax restructuring charge of $572.0 million, and excluded a loss from discontinued operations of $429.0 million, while earnings for 1999 excluded a gain from discontinued operations of $12.0 million. Net sales grew 1.5% to $9.30 billion.

PROSPECTS: On 1/2/01, the Company and Newell Rubbermaid Inc. announced that Newell Rubbermaid acquired G's stationery products business effective 12/29/00, which includes the Paper Mate®, Parker®, Waterman® and Liquid Paper® brands. Recently, the Company approved a restructuring plan designed to increase cash flow and accelerate earnings growth. It will result in a net reduction of about 8.0% of the Company's workforce.

BUSINESS

THE GILLETTE COMPANY manufactures and sells a wide variety of consumer products throughout the world. The Company's primary businesses are: Grooming, which includes male and female wet and dry shaving franchises and related toiletries; Portable Power, including alkaline and specialty batteries and Oral Care, including toothbrushes and power-assisted plaque removers. The Company also manufactures small household appliances. G has manufacturing operations at 38 facilities in 19 countries and distributes products in over 200 countries and territories. Blades & Razors represented 36.7% of 2000 revenues; Braun Products, 17.8%; Toiletries & Cosmetics, 10.5%; Oral-B products, 7.3%; and Duracell products, 27.7%.

ANNUAL FINANCIAL DATA

	12/31/00	12/31/99	12/31/98	12/31/97	12/31/96	12/31/95	12/31/94
Earnings Per Share	**[1] [2] 0.77**	**1.14**	**[1] 0.95**	**1.25**	**[1] 0.86**	**0.93**	**0.79**
Cash Flow Per Share	**1.28**	**1.58**	**1.35**	**1.61**	**1.20**	**1.20**	**1.03**
Tang. Book Val. Per Share	**0.33**	**0.58**	**1.81**	**2.07**	**1.56**	**1.34**	**1.16**
Dividends Per Share	**0.64**	**0.57**	**0.49**	**0.41**	**0.34**	**0.29**	**0.24**
Dividend Payout %	**82.5**	**50.0**	**51.3**	**33.1**	**40.3**	**31.1**	**30.6**
INCOME STATEMENT (IN MILLIONS):							
Total Revenues	9,295.0	9,897.0	10,056.0	10,062.0	9,697.7	6,794.7	6,070.2
Costs & Expenses	7,248.0	7,292.0	7,808.0	7,316.0	7,680.3	5,175.0	4,628.1
Depreciation & Amort.	535.0	500.0	459.0	422.0	381.1	248.4	215.4
Operating Income	1,512.0	2,105.0	1,789.0	2,324.0	[2] 1,636.3	1,371.3	1,226.7
Net Interest Inc./(Exp.)	d218.0	d129.0	d86.0	d69.0	d66.9	d49.1	d42.1
Income Before Income Taxes	1,288.0	1,930.0	1,669.0	2,221.0	1,525.0	1,296.9	1,104.1
Income Taxes	467.0	670.0	588.0	794.0	576.3	473.4	405.8
Net Income	[1] [2] 821.0	1,260.0	[1] 1,081.0	1,427.0	[1] 948.7	823.5	698.3
Cash Flow	1,356.0	1,760.0	1,540.0	1,849.0	1,325.2	1,067.2	909.0
Average Shs. Outstg. (000)	1,063,000	1,111,000	1,144,000	1,148,000	1,107,000	887,000	884,800
BALANCE SHEET (IN MILLIONS):							
Cash & Cash Equivalents	62.0	80.0	102.0	105.0	83.9	49.5	46.1
Total Current Assets	4,682.0	5,132.0	5,440.0	4,690.0	4,753.2	3,104.5	2,747.4
Net Property	3,550.0	3,667.0	3,472.0	3,104.0	2,565.8	1,636.9	1,411.0
Total Assets	10,402.0	11,786.0	11,902.0	10,864.0	10,435.3	6,340.3	5,494.0
Total Current Liabilities	5,471.0	4,180.0	3,478.0	2,641.0	2,934.7	2,124.0	1,783.2
Long-Term Obligations	1,650.0	2,931.0	2,256.0	1,476.0	1,490.4	691.1	715.1
Net Stockholders' Equity	1,924.0	3,060.0	4,543.0	4,841.0	4,490.9	2,513.3	2,017.3
Net Working Capital	d789.0	952.0	1,962.0	2,049.0	1,818.5	980.5	964.2
Year-end Shs. Outstg. (000)	1,053,000	1,065,000	1,105,000	1,120,938	1,132,156	888,928	885,800
STATISTICAL RECORD:							
Operating Profit Margin %	16.3	21.3	17.8	23.1	16.9	20.2	20.2
Net Profit Margin %	8.8	12.7	10.7	14.2	9.8	12.1	11.5
Return on Equity %	42.7	41.2	23.8	29.5	21.1	32.8	34.6
Return on Assets %	7.9	10.7	9.1	13.1	9.1	13.0	12.7
Debt/Total Assets %	15.9	24.9	19.0	13.6	14.3	10.9	13.0
Price Range	43.00-27.13	64.38-33.06	62.66-35.31	53.19-36.00	38.88-24.13	27.69-17.69	19.13-14.44
P/E Ratio	55.8-35.2	56.5-29.0	65.9-37.2	42.7-28.9	45.5-28.2	29.9-19.1	24.4-18.4
Average Yield %	1.8	1.2	1.0	0.9	1.1	1.3	1.4

Statistics are as originally reported. Adj. for stk. splits: 2-for-1, 6/98, 6/95 [1] Incl. non-recurr. chrg. $572.0 mill., 12/00; $535.0 mill., 12/98; $413.0 mill., 12/96 [2] Bef. loss from disc. opers., $429.0 mill.

OFFICERS:
J. Kilts, Chmn., C.E.O.
E. F. DeGraan, Pres., C.O.O.
A. Livis, Exec. V.P.
C. W. Cramb Jr., Sr. V.P., C.F.O.

INVESTOR CONTACT: Skip Loper, V.P., Investor Relations, (617) 421-7968

PRINCIPAL OFFICE: Prudential Tower Building, Boston, MA 02199

TELEPHONE NUMBER: (617) 421-7000
FAX: (617) 421-7123
WEB: www.gillette.com

NO. OF EMPLOYEES: 35,200 (approx.)

SHAREHOLDERS: 53,027

ANNUAL MEETING: In April

INCORPORATED: DE, Sept., 1917

INSTITUTIONAL HOLDINGS:
No. of Institutions: 749
Shares Held: 664,381,094
% Held: 63.0

INDUSTRY: Hand and edge tools, nec (SIC: 3423)

TRANSFER AGENT(S): Fleet National Bank, Providence RI

NYSE SYMBOL GLT
Rec. Pr. 15.35 (5/31/01)

GLATFELTER (P.H.) COMPANY

YIELD 4.6%
P/E RATIO 14.8

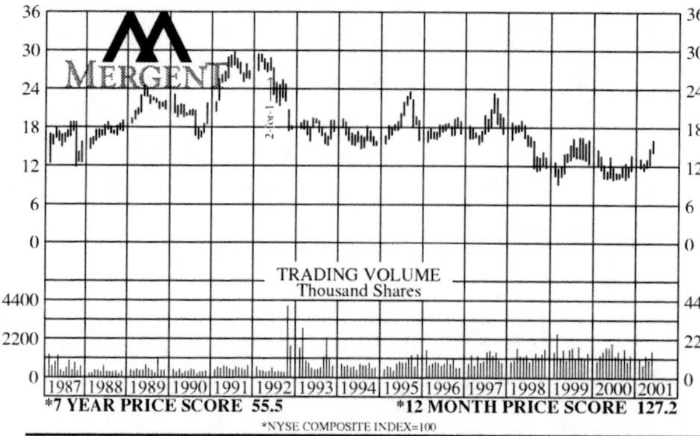

*7 YEAR PRICE SCORE 55.5 *12 MONTH PRICE SCORE 127.2

*NYSE COMPOSITE INDEX=100

INTERIM EARNINGS (Per Share):

Qtr.	Mar.	June	Sept.	Dec.
1995	0.28	0.43	0.39	0.39
1996	0.32	0.38	0.31	0.40
1997	0.30	0.27	0.17	0.33
1998	0.36	0.33	0.08	0.09
1999	0.19	0.30	0.15	0.34
2000	0.25	0.33	0.17	0.29

INTERIM DIVIDENDS (Per Share):

Amt.	Decl.	Ex.	Rec.	Pay.
0.175Q	3/16/00	4/05/00	4/07/00	5/01/00
0.175Q	6/21/00	7/05/00	7/07/00	8/01/00
0.175Q	9/21/00	10/04/00	10/06/00	11/01/00
0.175Q	12/20/00	1/03/01	1/05/01	2/01/01
0.175Q	3/14/01	4/04/01	4/06/01	5/01/01

Indicated div.: $0.70

CAPITALIZATION (12/31/00):

	($000)	(%)
Long-Term Debt	300,245	36.2
Deferred Income Tax	155,360	18.8
Common & Surplus	372,703	45.0
Total	828,308	100.0

RECENT DEVELOPMENTS: For the year ended 12/31/00, net income advanced 6.2% to $44.0 million compared with $41.4 million in 1999. Results for 2000 and 1999 included gains from property dispositions of $2.0 million and $4.1 million, respectively. Results for 2000 also included unusual charges of $3.3 million. Total revenues were $739.8 million, up 2.6% from $720.7 million. Net sales were $724.7 million, up 2.7% from $705.5 million a year earlier.

PROSPECTS: On 5/16/01, the Company announced that it reached a definitive agreement to sell its Ecusta Division to a subsidiary of privately-held PURICO (IOM) Limited of the United Kingdom for approximately $39.0 million in cash, plus the assumption of certain liabilities related to the business. The transaction will result in an after-tax charge of approximately $25.0 million once the transaction is completed.

BUSINESS

P.H. GLATFELTER COMPANY is a manufacturer of engineered and specialized printing papers. The Company's engineered papers are used in a variety of products, including tea bags, cigarette papers, cigarette tipping and plug wrap papers, metalized beverage labels, decorative laminates, food product casings, stencil papers, photo-glossy ink jet papers, greeting cards, medical dressings, highway signs and striping, billboard graphics, decorative shopping bags, playing cards, postage stamps, filters, labels and surgical gowns. Sales of these papers are generally made directly to the converter of the paper. The Company's specialized printing paper products are directed at the uncoated free-sheet portion of the industry, and are principally used for the printing of case bound and quality paperback books, commercial and financial printing and envelope converting.

QUARTERLY DATA

(12/31/2000)($000)	REV	INC
1st Quarter	187,658	10,644
2nd Quarter	184,397	14,038
3rd Quarter	187,042	7,179
4th Quarter	174,623	12,139

ANNUAL FINANCIAL DATA

	12/31/00	12/31/99	12/31/98	12/31/97	12/31/96	12/31/95	12/31/94
Earnings Per Share	**1 2 1.04**	**1 0.98**	**1 2 0.86**	**1 1.07**	**1 1.41**	**1 1.49**	**1 2 d2.67**
Cash Flow Per Share	**2.12**	**2.10**	**1.99**	**1.91**	**2.16**	**2.23**	**d1.71**
Tang. Book Val. Per Share	**8.79**	**8.48**	**8.17**	**8.08**	**7.78**	**7.26**	**6.68**
Dividends Per Share	**0.70**	**0.70**	**0.70**	**0.70**	**0.70**	**0.70**	**0.70**
Dividend Payout %	**67.3**	**71.4**	**81.4**	**65.4**	**49.6**	**47.0**	**...**
INCOME STATEMENT (IN THOUSANDS):							
Total Revenues	739,812	695,806	717,705	587,212	577,194	636,392	487,503
Costs & Expenses	605,362	564,464	579,412	459,139	436,411	485,916	422,058
Depreciation & Amort.	46,106	47,766	47,738	35,796	33,570	32,599	42,906
Operating Income	88,344	83,576	90,555	92,277	107,213	117,877	22,539
Net Interest Inc./(Exp.)	d16,405	d18,424	d22,007	d18,700	d9,308	d10,265	d6,364
Income Before Income Taxes	68,603	65,152	58,732	73,577	97,905	107,612	d192,774
Income Taxes	24,603	23,727	22,599	28,293	37,506	41,784	cr74,523
Net Income	1 2 44,000	1 41,425	1 2 36,133	1 45,284	1 60,399	1 65,828	1 2 d118,251
Cash Flow	90,106	89,191	83,871	81,080	93,969	98,427	d75,345
Average Shs. Outstg.	42,483	42,431	42,202	42,442	43,435	44,200	43,987
BALANCE SHEET (IN THOUSANDS):							
Cash & Cash Equivalents	110,552	76,035	50,907	222,093	32,613	18,975	3,244
Total Current Assets	286,624	268,127	241,908	376,479	188,069	160,423	135,369
Net Property	552,768	582,213	628,156	475,189	455,190	451,461	460,420
Total Assets	1,013,191	1,003,780	990,738	937,583	715,310	673,107	650,810
Total Current Liabilities	119,184	132,631	126,876	288,885	86,183	84,008	104,272
Long-Term Obligations	300,245	301,380	325,381	150,000	150,000	150,000	150,000
Net Stockholders' Equity	372,703	358,124	343,929	340,416	331,030	315,406	295,734
Net Working Capital	167,440	135,496	115,032	87,594	101,886	76,415	31,097
Year-end Shs. Outstg.	42,391	42,246	42,085	42,150	42,540	43,435	44,248
STATISTICAL RECORD:							
Operating Profit Margin %	11.9	12.0	12.6	15.7	18.6	18.5	4.6
Net Profit Margin %	5.9	6.0	5.0	7.7	10.5	10.3	...
Return on Equity %	11.8	11.6	10.5	13.3	18.2	20.9	...
Return on Assets %	4.3	4.1	3.6	4.8	8.4	9.8	...
Debt/Total Assets %	29.6	30.0	32.8	16.0	21.0	22.3	23.0
Price Range	14.63-9.81	16.50-9.06	19.13-11.19	23.38-15.38	19.63-15.63	23.63-15.38	19.38-14.63
P/E Ratio	14.1-9.4	16.8-9.2	22.2-13.0	21.8-14.4	13.9-11.1	15.9-10.3	...
Average Yield %	5.7	5.5	4.6	3.6	4.0	3.6	4.1

Statistics are as originally reported. 1 Incl. gain from property dispositions, etc., net of $2.0 mill., 2000; $4.1 mill., 1999; $1.0 mill., 1998; $3.2 mill., 1997; $977,000, 1996; $1.9 mill., 1995; $2.6 mill., 1994. 2 Incl. unusual items of $3.3 mill., 2000; $9.8 mill., 1998; $208.9 mill., 1994.

OFFICERS:
G. H. Glatfelter, II, Chmn., C.E.O.
R. P. Newcomer, II, Pres., C.O.O.
C. M. Smith, C.F.O.
M. R. Mueller, Couns., Sec.

INVESTOR CONTACT: Investor Relations, (717) 225-4711

PRINCIPAL OFFICE: 96 South George Street, Suite 500, York, PA 17401

TELEPHONE NUMBER: (717) 225-4711
FAX: (717) 225-6834
WEB: www.glatfelter.com

NO. OF EMPLOYEES: 3,400 (approx.)

SHAREHOLDERS: 2,826

ANNUAL MEETING: In Mar.

INCORPORATED: PA, Dec., 1905

INSTITUTIONAL HOLDINGS:
No. of Institutions: 119
Shares Held: 30,837,595
% Held: 72.7

INDUSTRY: Paper mills (SIC: 2621)

TRANSFER AGENT(S): American Stock Transfer & Trust Company, New York, NY

NYSE SYMBOL GLM
Rec. Pr. 25.65 (5/31/01)

GLOBAL MARINE INC.

YIELD ...
P/E RATIO 40.1

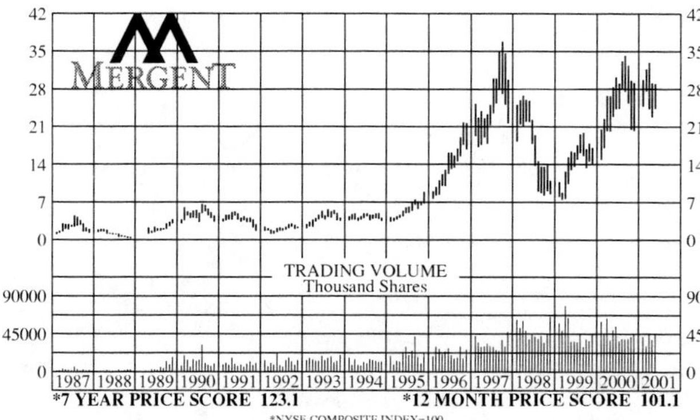

INTERIM EARNINGS (Per Share):

Qtr.	Mar.	June	Sept.	Dec.
1996	0.09	0.14	0.18	0.63
1997	0.46	0.49	0.54	0.34
1998	0.39	0.42	0.27	0.20
1999	0.21	0.16	0.08	0.06
2000	0.07	0.16	0.18	0.23

INTERIM DIVIDENDS (Per Share):

Amt.	Decl.	Ex.	Rec.	Pay.

No dividends paid.

CAPITALIZATION (12/31/00):

	($000)	(%)
Long-Term Debt	901,300	41.2
Capital Lease Obligations	17,300	0.8
Common & Surplus	1,270,900	58.0
Total	2,189,500	100.0

RECENT DEVELOPMENTS: For the year ended 12/31/00, net income advanced 27.3% to $113.9 million compared with $89.5 million in the previous year. Results for 2000 included restructuring charges of $5.2 million. Sharply higher crude oil and natural gas prices resulting in increased spending by exploration and production companies contributed to the improved outcome. Total revenues jumped 31.5% to $1.04 billion from $791.0 million in 1999.

PROSPECTS: Prospects are positive, reflecting increased exploration and production spending by customers. In addition, spending in international markets is expected to accelerate as major oil companies pursue projects that were postponed in 2000. Meanwhile, GLM's capital spending requirements for 2001 will be reduced by about 50.0% to approximately $90.0 million due to the completion in 2000 of two new drillships. GLM expects to earmark about half of its preliminary capital budget in 2001 for rig upgrades, which will result in minimal unpaid downtime.

BUSINESS

GLOBAL MARINE INC. is a holding company that provides offshore contract drilling services on a dayrate basis and offshore drilling management services on a turnkey basis. The Company's domestic offshore contract drilling operations are conducted through its subsidiary, Global Marine Drilling Company and all international offshore contract drilling operations are conducted through its subsidiary, Global Marine International Drilling Corporation. Drilling operations are conducted through the Company's active fleet of 32 mobile offshore drilling rigs and two ultra-deepwater. The Company also has one inactive concrete island drilling system designed for arctic operations. The Company's fleet is deployed in the major offshore oil and gas operating areas worldwide, with principal areas of operation including the Gulf of Mexico, offshore West Africa and the North Sea.

BUSINESS LINE ANALYSIS

(12/31/2000)	REV(%)	INC(%)
Contract Drilling	56.2	84.5
Drilling Management Services	41.9	9.9
Oil & Gas	1.9	5.6
Total	100.0	100.0

ANNUAL FINANCIAL DATA

	12/31/00	12/31/99	12/31/98	12/31/97	12/31/96	12/31/95	12/31/94
Earnings Per Share	**3 0.64**	**0.51**	**1.27**	**1 1.79**	**1.06**	**0.31**	**2 0.03**
Cash Flow Per Share	**1.23**	**1.01**	**1.86**	**2.10**	**1.30**	**0.50**	**0.26**
Tang. Book Val. Per Share	**7.22**	**6.51**	**6.00**	**4.68**	**2.71**	**1.62**	**1.29**
INCOME STATEMENT (IN MILLIONS):							
Total Revenues	1,039.8	791.0	1,162.2	1,067.1	680.7	468.0	359.0
Costs & Expenses	744.3	558.9	747.8	706.9	499.0	376.7	295.5
Depreciation & Amort.	107.0	88.8	103.9	55.1	40.9	31.0	37.4
Operating Income	188.5	143.3	310.5	305.1	140.8	60.3	26.1
Net Interest Inc./(Exp.)	d33.2	d28.0	d26.4	d11.1	d22.1	d19.9	d22.7
Income Before Income Taxes	155.3	115.3	284.1	294.0	119.7	55.1	5.4
Income Taxes	41.4	25.8	60.8	cr21.1	cr60.4	3.2	0.6
Net Income	3 113.9	89.5	223.3	1 315.1	180.1	51.9	2 4.8
Cash Flow	220.9	178.3	327.2	370.2	221.0	82.9	42.2
Average Shs. Outstg. (000)	179,343	176,775	175,785	176,162	169,495	165,142	163,829
BALANCE SHEET (IN MILLIONS):							
Cash & Cash Equivalents	144.3	83.3	56.9	78.9	120.4	86.6	57.9
Total Current Assets	404.8	213.0	269.4	327.7	246.5	168.3	149.8
Net Property	1,940.1	1,868.6	1,512.1	999.0	477.4	386.6	353.4
Total Assets	2,396.8	2,264.5	1,971.6	1,421.9	807.8	563.0	512.4
Total Current Liabilities	183.3	149.6	152.4	183.5	87.6	52.1	56.4
Long-Term Obligations	918.6	955.3	768.4	417.3	241.6	225.0	225.0
Net Stockholders' Equity	1,270.9	1,135.0	1,040.4	805.6	459.1	269.0	212.3
Net Working Capital	221.5	63.4	117.0	144.2	158.9	116.2	93.4
Year-end Shs. Outstg. (000)	176,021	174,421	173,368	172,203	169,441	166,458	164,408
STATISTICAL RECORD:							
Operating Profit Margin %	18.1	18.1	26.7	28.6	20.7	12.9	7.3
Net Profit Margin %	11.0	11.3	19.2	29.5	26.5	11.1	1.3
Return on Equity %	9.0	7.9	21.5	39.1	39.2	19.3	2.3
Return on Assets %	4.8	4.0	11.3	22.2	22.3	9.2	0.9
Debt/Total Assets %	38.3	42.2	39.0	29.3	29.9	40.0	43.9
Price Range	34.25-14.88	19.88-7.50	26.75-8.25	36.81-17.25	21.75-7.63	8.88-3.38	5.00-3.50
P/E Ratio	53.5-23.2	39.0-14.7	21.1-6.5	20.6-9.6	20.5-7.2	28.6-10.9	166.1-116.3

Statistics are as originally reported. 1 Bef. extraord. chrg. of $4.5 mill. 2 Bef. acctg. adj. chrg. of $3.5 mill. 3 Incl. non-recurr. chrg. of $5.2 mill.

OFFICERS:
R. E. Rose, Chmn., Pres., C.E.O.
J. A. Marshall, Exec. V.P., C.O.O.
W. M. Ralls, Sr. V.P., C.F.O., Treas.

INVESTOR CONTACT: Michael Dawson, Inv. Rel., (281) 596-5809

PRINCIPAL OFFICE: 777 N. Eldridge Parkway, Houston, TX 77079-4493

TELEPHONE NUMBER: (281) 596-5100
FAX: (281) 596-5163
WEB: www.glm.com

NO. OF EMPLOYEES: 2,700 (approx.)

SHAREHOLDERS: 6,027

ANNUAL MEETING: In May

INCORPORATED: DE, Oct., 1964

INSTITUTIONAL HOLDINGS:
No. of Institutions: 254
Shares Held: 137,645,967
% Held: 78.0

INDUSTRY: Drilling oil and gas wells (SIC: 1381)

TRANSFER AGENT(S): Computershare Investor Services, Chicago, IL

NYSE SYMBOL GSB
Rec. Pr. 29.80 (4/30/01)

GOLDEN STATE BANCORP, INC.

YIELD 1.3%
P/E RATIO 12.2

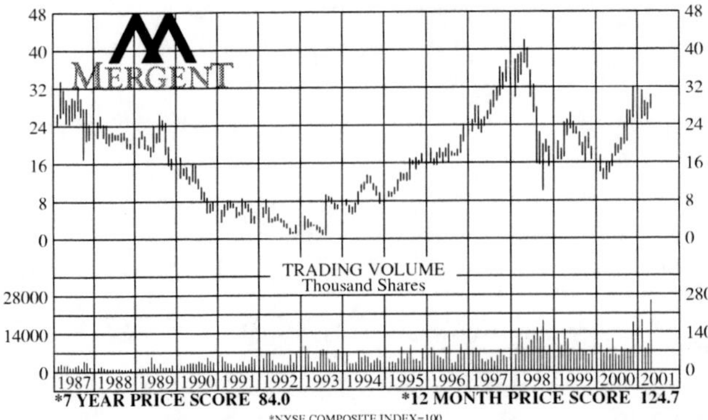

*7 YEAR PRICE SCORE 84.0 *12 MONTH PRICE SCORE 124.7
*NYSE COMPOSITE INDEX=100

INTERIM EARNINGS (Per Share):

Qtr.	Sept.	Dec.	Mar.	June
1996-97	d0.50	0.30	0.33	0.36
1997-98	0.41	0.41	0.45	0.51
Qtr.	**Mar.**	**June**	**Sept.**	**Dec.**
1998	0.84	5.07	0.65	0.11
1999	0.50	0.59	0.58	0.61
2000	0.59	0.60	0.62	0.63

INTERIM DIVIDENDS (Per Share):

Amt.	Decl.	Ex.	Rec.	Pay.
0.10Q	7/20/00	7/27/00	7/31/00	9/01/00
0.10Q	10/23/00	11/01/00	11/03/00	12/01/00
0.10Q	1/23/01	1/31/01	2/02/01	3/01/01
0.10Q	4/23/01	5/03/01	5/07/01	6/01/01

Indicated div.: $0.40

CAPITALIZATION (12/31/00):

	($000)	(%)
Total Deposits	23,429,754	42.7
Long-Term Debt	28,800,557	52.5
Minority Interest	500,000	0.9
Common & Surplus	2,150,734	3.9
Total	54,881,045	100.0

RECENT DEVELOPMENTS: For the year ended 12/31/00, GSB reported income of $347.5 million, before an extraordinary gain of $3.0 million, versus income of $320.7 million, before an extraordinary gain of $2.5 million, in the prior year. Earnings for 2000 and 1999 included pre-tax net gains of $36.3 million and $46.8 million, respectively. Net interest income declined 3.3% to $1.15 billion. Comparisons were made with restated 1999 figures.

PROSPECTS: GSB expects continued growth in 2001, despite weakened market conditions, and should continue to benefit from increased non-single family residential loans and higher core deposits. GSB will continue to implement its strategic plan targeted at achieving higher profits and revenue diversity, while maintaining credit quality. Moreover, GSB will continue to improve customer service and expand product offerings.

BUSINESS

GOLDEN STATE BANCORP, INC., with assets of $60.52 billion as of 12/31/00, is a holding company of Golden State Holdings, Inc., which owns all of the common stock of California Federal Bank, a full-service, community-oriented bank, that serves consumers and small businesses in California and Nevada. The Company's principal business consists of operating retail branches that provide deposit products such as demand, transaction and savings accounts, and investment products such as mutual funds, annuities and insurance. In 1997, GSB was formed as the holding company of Glendale Federal Bank. On 9/11/98, GSB acquired California Federal Bank.

LOAN DISTRIBUTION

12/31/2000	($000)	(%)
Real estate loans	36,914,489	92.6
Equity-line	538,524	1.4
Other consumer loans	302,559	0.8
Auto loans	1,567,257	3.9
Commercial loans	557,796	1.3
Total	39,880,625	100.0

ANNUAL FINANCIAL DATA

	12/31/00	12/31/99	3 12/31/98	4 12/31/97	6/30/97	6/30/96
Earnings Per Share	6 2.44	5 2.29	1 4.88	1.67	2 0.72	2 0.36
Tang. Book Val. Per Share	...	...	...	...	18.03	19.10
Dividends Per Share	0.20	...	...	...	...	...
Dividend Payout %	8.2	...	...	...	...	...
INCOME STATEMENT (IN MILLIONS):						
Total Interest Income	4,105.8	3,652.3	2,548.8	2,102.7	1,073.0	1,080.0
Total Interest Expense	2,959.0	2,466.4	1,819.5	1,498.4	675.3	747.0
Net Interest Income	1,146.8	1,185.9	729.3	604.3	379.0	333.1
Provision for Loan Losses	...	10.0	40.0	79.8	25.2	40.4
Non-Interest Income	440.8	418.8	477.0	364.5	97.3	34.4
Non-Interest Expense	913.2	925.5	764.0	650.6	355.9	263.7
Income Before Taxes	674.3	669.3	402.3	238.4	86.6	63.4
Equity Earnings/Minority Int.	d190.1	d162.1	d110.5	d102.1	...	...
Net Income	6 347.5	5 320.7	1 398.1	94.9	2 69.1	2 150.9
Average Shs. Outstg. (000)	142,470	130,781	81,541	56,723	49,095	47,593
BALANCE SHEET (IN MILLIONS):						
Cash & Due from Banks	697.5	509.0	855.0	350.2	221.6	153.6
Securities Avail. for Sale	85.5	84.1	60.3	25.9	4.0	...
Total Loans & Leases	39,880.6	33,953.5	30,772.3	19,924.0	12,113.2	10,952.7
Allowance for Credit Losses	287.8	...	491.4	499.6	227.1	258.1
Net Loans & Leases	39,592.8	33,953.5	30,280.9	19,424.4	11,886.1	10,694.6
Total Assets	60,516.9	57,019.1	54,869.0	31,362.2	16,218.3	14,456.6
Total Deposits	23,429.8	23,035.8	24,620.1	16,202.6	9,356.9	8,724.0
Long-Term Obligations	28,800.6	25,668.6	22,375.6	11,232.5	10.8	10.6
Total Liabilities	58,366.1	55,457.3	53,287.2	30,992.7	15,206.2	13,499.1
Net Stockholders' Equity	2,150.7	1,561.8	1,581.8	369.5	1,012.1	957.5
Year-end Shs. Outstg. (000)	134,321	122,243	128,598	56,723	50,349	46,730
STATISTICAL RECORD:						
Return on Equity %	16.2	20.5	25.2	25.7	6.8	15.8
Return on Assets %	0.6	0.6	0.7	0.3	0.4	1.0
Equity/Assets %	3.6	2.7	2.9	1.2	6.2	6.6
Non-Int. Exp./Tot. Inc. %	57.5	57.7	63.3	67.2	73.2	55.4
Price Range	31.88-12.25	26.56-16.25	42.06-10.00	37.75-22.25	37.75-22.25	23.88-15.50
P/E Ratio	13.1-5.0	11.6-7.1	8.6-2.0	22.6-13.3	52.4-30.9	66.3-43.0
Average Yield %	0.9	...	...	...	...	...

Statistics are as originally reported. 1 Bef. extraord. loss $150.3 mill.; incl. gain of $36.0 mill. fr. divs. on FHLB stk., various pre-tax gains $163.2 mill. & pre-tax merg. & integr. costs $59.2 mill. 2 Incl. various pre-tax losses of $2.1 mill., 6/97; $34.9 mill., 6/96. 3 Reflects acq. of California Federal on 9/11/98. 4 Reflects 12 mos. 5 Bef. extraord. gain $2.5 mill.; incl. various pre-tax gains $56.9 mill. & pre-tax merg. & integr. costs $7.7 mill. 6 Bef. extraord. gain $3.0 mill.; incl. various pre-tax gains $49.7 mill. & various pre-tax losses $13.4 mill.

OFFICERS:
G. J. Ford, Chmn., C.E.O.
C. B. Webb, Pres., C.O.O.
R. H. Terzian, Exec. V.P., C.F.O.

INVESTOR CONTACT: Fred Cannon, Investor Relations, (415) 904-1451

PRINCIPAL OFFICE: 135 Main Street, San Francisco, CA 94105

TELEPHONE NUMBER: (415) 904-1100
FAX: (415) 904-1157
WEB: www.goldenstatebancorp.com

NO. OF EMPLOYEES: 8,446 (avg.)

SHAREHOLDERS: 6,168

ANNUAL MEETING: In May

INCORPORATED: DE, 1997

INSTITUTIONAL HOLDINGS:
No. of Institutions: 198
Shares Held: 62,491,314
% Held: 46.3

INDUSTRY: Federal savings institutions (SIC: 6035)

TRANSFER AGENT(S): Mellon Investor Services, Ridgefield Park, NJ

NYSE SYMBOL GDW
Rec. Pr. 58.70 (4/30/01)

GOLDEN WEST FINANCIAL CORPORATION

YIELD 0.4%
P/E RATIO 17.2

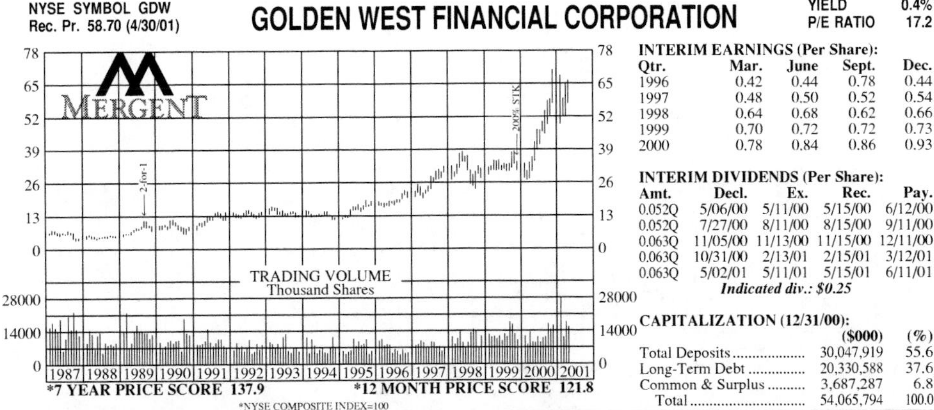

INTERIM EARNINGS (Per Share):

Qtr.	Mar.	June	Sept.	Dec.
1996	0.42	0.44	0.78	0.44
1997	0.48	0.50	0.52	0.54
1998	0.64	0.68	0.62	0.66
1999	0.70	0.72	0.72	0.73
2000	0.78	0.84	0.86	0.93

INTERIM DIVIDENDS (Per Share):

Amt.	Decl.	Ex.	Rec.	Pay.
0.052Q	5/06/00	5/11/00	5/15/00	6/12/00
0.052Q	7/27/00	8/11/00	8/15/00	9/11/00
0.063Q	11/05/00	11/13/00	11/15/00	12/11/00
0.063Q	10/31/00	2/13/01	2/15/01	3/12/01
0.063Q	5/02/01	5/11/01	5/15/01	6/11/01

Indicated div.: $0.25

CAPITALIZATION (12/31/00):

	($000)	(%)
Total Deposits	30,047,919	55.6
Long-Term Debt	20,330,588	37.6
Common & Surplus	3,687,287	6.8
Total	54,065,794	100.0

RECENT DEVELOPMENTS: For the year ended 12/31/00, net earnings grew 13.7% to $545.8 million from $480.0 million in the previous year. Results for the 2000 quarter reflected strong demand for home loans, particularly adjustable rate mortgages. Net interest income advanced 14.7% to $1.15 billion from $1.00 billion a year earlier. Non-interest income increased 12.2% to $160.8 million. Non-interest expense increased 10.0% to $424.8 million.

PROSPECTS: On 12/31/00, the Company merged two of its principal wholly-owned subsidiaries, World Savings and Loan Association and World Savings Bank, FSB. The consolidation formed a new entity named World Savings Bank, FSB. Going forward, the Company should continue to benefit from strong demand for home loans, particularly in California, the Company's largest market.

BUSINESS

GOLDEN WEST FINANCIAL CORPORATION, with assets of $55.70 billion as of 12/31/00, is a savings and loan holding company. The Company's principal subsidiary is World Savings Bank, FSB (formerly World Savings Bank, FSB and World Savings & Loan Association). As of December 31, 2000, the Company operated 120 savings branch offices in California, 37 in Florida, 36 in Colorado, 22 in Texas, 15 in Arizona, 11 in New Jersey, eight in Kansas, and four in Illinois. As of 12/31/00, GDW operated 414 offices in 32 states under the World name. The Company operates as a financial intermediary attracting deposits (primarily in the form of savings accounts) and investing funds in loans and securities backed by residential real estate.

LOAN DISTRIBUTION

(12/31/2000)	($000)	(%)
1-to-4 Family Dwelling	31,353,927	92.8
Over 4-Family Dwelling	2,444,832	7.2
Commercial Property	39,810	0.2
Land	347	0.0
Loans on Savings Accounts	21,429	0.1
Total	33,860,345	100.0

ANNUAL FINANCIAL DATA

	12/31/00	12/31/99	12/31/98	12/31/97	12/31/96	12/31/95	12/31/94
Earnings Per Share	**3.41**	**2.87**	**[2] 2.58**	**2.04**	**[1] 2.11**	**1.33**	**1.24**
Tang. Book Val. Per Share	**23.28**	**19.80**	**18.32**	**15.76**	**13.66**	**12.12**	**10.60**
Dividends Per Share	**0.22**	**0.19**	**0.17**	**0.15**	**0.13**	**0.12**	**0.10**
Dividend Payout %	**6.5**	**6.7**	**6.7**	**7.4**	**6.2**	**8.8**	**8.1**
INCOME STATEMENT (IN MILLIONS):							
Total Interest Income	3,796.5	2,825.8	2,962.6	2,832.5	2,581.6	2,427.4	1,876.5
Total Interest Expense	2,645.4	1,822.4	1,995.2	1,942.0	1,750.6	1,704.6	1,155.1
Net Interest Income	1,151.2	1,003.5	967.3	890.5	831.0	722.8	721.4
Provision for Loan Losses	9.2	cr2.1	11.3	57.6	84.3	61.2	63.0
Non-Interest Income	160.8	143.3	137.6	81.3	74.9	42.5	37.5
Non-Interest Expense	424.8	386.1	354.5	327.0	453.4	319.0	305.5
Income Before Taxes	877.9	762.7	739.2	587.2	368.2	385.2	390.4
Net Income	545.8	480.0	[2] 447.1	354.1	[1] 369.9	234.5	230.4
Average Shs. Outstg. (000)	160,278	166,951	173,462	173,319	173,967	175,971	186,387
BALANCE SHEET (IN MILLIONS):							
Securities Avail. for Sale	462.8	398.5	490.6	765.9	1,008.8	1,184.7	1,812.2
Total Loans & Leases	33,860.3	28,090.1	25,991.6	33,553.5	30,397.2	28,435.1	27,330.5
Allowance for Credit Losses	97.7	170.3	270.3	292.8	283.8	253.8	259.2
Net Loans & Leases	33,762.6	27,919.8	25,721.3	33,260.7	30,113.4	28,181.4	27,071.3
Total Assets	55,704.0	42,142.2	38,468.7	39,421.3	37,730.6	35,118.2	31,683.7
Total Deposits	30,047.9	27,714.9	26,219.1	24,109.7	22,099.9	20,847.9	19,219.4
Long-Term Obligations	20,330.6	9,728.2	7,075.2	9,627.1	10,122.4	7,769.6	7,710.0
Total Liabilities	52,016.7	38,947.4	35,344.4	36,892.2	35,380.1	32,839.8	29,683.5
Net Stockholders' Equity	3,687.3	3,194.9	3,124.3	2,698.0	2,350.5	2,278.4	2,000.3
Year-end Shs. Outstg. (000)	158,410	161,358	170,583	171,207	172,026	176,613	175,770
STATISTICAL RECORD:							
Return on Equity %	14.8	15.0	14.3	13.1	15.7	10.3	11.5
Return on Assets %	1.0	1.1	1.2	0.9	1.0	0.7	0.7
Equity/Assets %	6.6	7.6	8.1	6.8	6.2	6.5	6.3
Non-Int. Exp./Tot. Inc. %	32.4	33.7	32.1	33.6	50.1	41.7	40.3
Price Range	70.50-26.88	38.41-28.91	38.16-23.27	32.33-19.62	22.91-16.33	19.16-11.58	15.33-11.42
P/E Ratio	20.7-7.9	13.4-10.1	14.8-9.0	15.8-9.6	10.9-7.7	14.4-8.7	12.4-9.2
Average Yield %	0.5	0.6	0.6	0.6	0.7	0.8	0.7

Statistics are as originally reported. Adj. for stk. split: 3-for-1, 12/10/99. [1] Bef. acct. chg. of $205.2 mill. & incl. one-time SAIF chg. of $133.0 mill. & a tax benefit of $139.5 mill. [2] Bef. extraord. loss of $12.5 mill.

OFFICERS:
H. M. Sandler, Co-Chmn., Co-C.E.O.
M. O. Sandler, Co-Chmn., Co-C.E.O.
R. W. Kettell, Pres., C.F.O., Treas.
M. Roster, Exec. V.P., Gen. Couns., Sec.

INVESTOR CONTACT: William C. Nunan, Group Sr. V.P., (510) 446-3614

PRINCIPAL OFFICE: 1901 Harrison Street, Oakland, CA 94612

TELEPHONE NUMBER: (510) 466-3420
FAX: (510) 446-3072
WEB: www.worldsavingsjobs.com

NO. OF EMPLOYEES: 5,088 full-time; 1,015 part-time

SHAREHOLDERS: 1,262

ANNUAL MEETING: In May

INCORPORATED: DE, May, 1959

INSTITUTIONAL HOLDINGS:
No. of Institutions: 304
Shares Held: 109,042,796
% Held: 68.8

INDUSTRY: Federal savings institutions (SIC: 6035)

TRANSFER AGENT(S): Mellon Investor Services, San Francisco, CA

NYSE SYMBOL GS
Rec. Pr. 95.10 (5/31/01)

GOLDMAN SACHS GROUP, INC. (THE)

YIELD 0.5%
P/E RATIO 16.8

*7 YEAR PRICE SCORE N/A *12 MONTH PRICE SCORE 100.1

*NYSE COMPOSITE INDEX=100

INTERIM EARNINGS (Per Share):

Qtr.	Feb.	May	Aug.	Nov.
1999	Nil	0.71	1.32	1.48
2000	1.76	1.48	1.62	1.16
2001	1.40	...	...	...

INTERIM DIVIDENDS (Per Share):

Amt.	Decl.	Ex.	Rec.	Pay.
0.12Q	3/21/00	4/19/00	4/24/00	5/25/00
0.12Q	6/20/00	7/20/00	7/24/00	8/24/00
0.12Q	9/19/00	10/19/00	10/23/00	11/20/00
0.12Q	12/19/00	1/18/01	1/22/01	2/21/01
0.12Q	3/20/01	4/20/01	4/24/01	5/24/01

Indicated div.: $0.48

CAPITALIZATION (11/24/00):

	($000)	(%)
Long-Term Debt	31,395,000	48.7
Common & Surplus	33,060,000	51.3
Total	64,455,000	100.0

RECENT DEVELOPMENTS: For the quarter ended 2/23/01, net income fell 13.4% to $768.0 million from $887.0 million in the corresponding period of the previous year. Total revenues advanced 19.3% to $9.50 billion from $7.96 billion a year earlier. Global capital revenues declined 3.9% to $3.20 billion. Revenues from asset management and securities jumped 23.7% to $1.17 billion from $944.0 million in the prior-year quarter.

PROSPECTS: On 3/19/01, GS completed the acquisition of Benjamin Jacobson & Sons, L.L.C., a specialist firm on The New York Stock Exchange, for approximately $250.0 million in stock and cash. Benjamin Jacobson provides specialist services in the securities of about 90 U.S. and international corporations. Meanwhile, GS expects its earnings to continue to benefit from the acquisition of Spear, Leeds & Kellogg, L.P.

BUSINESS

THE GOLDMAN SACHS GROUP is a global investment banking and securities firm that provides a wide range of services worldwide to a substantial and diversified client base that includes corporations, financial institutions, governments and high-net-worth individuals. The Company's activities are divided into two business segments comprised of Global Capital Markets, which includes investment banking and trading and principal investments, and Asset Management and Securities Services. In November 2000, the Company completed the acquisition of Spear, Leeds & Kellogg L.P., a New York Stock Exchange specialist firm.

QUARTERLY DATA

11/24/2000(millions)	Rev	Inc
1st Quarter	7,964	887
2nd Quarter	8,196	755
3rd Quarter	8,851	824
4th Quarter	7,989	601

ANNUAL FINANCIAL DATA

	11/24/00	11/26/99	11/27/98	11/28/97	11/29/96
Earnings Per Share	**2 6.00**	**1 5.57**	...	...	...
Cash Flow Per Share	**6.95**	**6.27**	...	...	...
Tang. Book Val. Per Share	**67.47**	**45.97**	**12.57**	...	...
Dividends Per Share	**0.48**	**0.24**	...	...	...
Dividend Payout %	**8.0**	**4.3**	...	...	...
INCOME STATEMENT (IN MILLIONS):					
Total Revenues	33,000.0	25,363.0	22,478.0	20,433.0	17,289.0
Costs & Expenses	27,494.0	23,034.0	19,315.0	17,241.0	14,511.0
Depreciation & Amort.	486.0	337.0	242.0	178.0	172.0
Operating Income	5,020.0	1,992.0	2,921.0	3,014.0	2,606.0
Income Before Income Taxes	5,020.0	1,992.0	2,921.0	3,014.0	2,606.0
Income Taxes	1,953.0	cr716.0	493.0	268.0	207.0
Net Income	2 3,067.0	1 2,708.0	2,428.0	2,746.0	2,399.0
Cash Flow	3,553.0	3,045.0	2,670.0	2,924.0	2,571.0
Average Shs. Outstg. (000)	511,500	485,804	...	...	...
BALANCE SHEET (IN MILLIONS):					
Cash & Cash Equivalents	144,999.0	129,318.0	124,929.0	96,665.0	...
Total Current Assets	184,285.0	163,948.0	144,203.0	110,479.0	...
Total Assets	289,760.0	250,491.0	217,380.0	178,401.0	...
Total Current Liabilities	241,835.0	219,394.0	191,090.0	156,197.0	...
Long-Term Obligations	31,395.0	20,952.0	19,906.0	15,667.0	...
Net Stockholders' Equity	33,060.0	20,290.0	6,384.0	6,537.0	...
Net Working Capital	d57,550.0	d55,446.0	d46,887.0	d45,718.0	...
Year-end Shs. Outstg. (000)	490,000	441,422	508,000	...	...
STATISTICAL RECORD:					
Operating Profit Margin %	15.2	7.9	13.0	14.8	15.1
Net Profit Margin %	9.3	10.7	10.8	13.4	13.9
Return on Equity %	9.3	13.3	38.0	42.0	...
Return on Assets %	1.1	1.1	1.1	1.5	...
Debt/Total Assets %	10.8	8.4	9.2	8.8	...
Price Range	133.63-65.50	94.81-55.19	...	...	...
P/E Ratio	22.3-10.9	17.0-9.9	...	...	...
Average Yield %	0.5	0.3	...	...	...

Statistics are as originally reported. 1 Incl. a net non-recurr. exp. of $1.44 billion primarily related to the Co.'s conversion to a public corporation. 2 Incl. exps. of $290.0 million related to nonrecurring employee initial public offering and acquisition awards.

OFFICERS:
H. M. Paulson Jr., Chmn., C.E.O.
R. J. Hurst, Vice-Chmn.
J. A. Thain, Co-Pres., Co-C.O.O.
J. L. Thornton, Co-Pres., Co-C.O.O.

INVESTOR CONTACT: John Andrews, Investor Relations, (212) 357-2674

PRINCIPAL OFFICE: 85 Broad Street, New York, NY 10004

TELEPHONE NUMBER: (212) 902-1000
WEB: www.gs.com

NO. OF EMPLOYEES: 22,627

SHAREHOLDERS: 1,971

ANNUAL MEETING: In April

INCORPORATED: DE, 1989

INSTITUTIONAL HOLDINGS:
No. of Institutions: 369
Shares Held: 134,938,944
% Held: 28.0

INDUSTRY: Security brokers and dealers (SIC: 6211)

TRANSFER AGENT(S): Mellon Investor Services, Ridgefield, NJ

NYSE SYMBOL GR
Rec. Pr. 39.40 (4/30/01)

GOODRICH CORPORATION

YIELD 2.8%
P/E RATIO 13.2

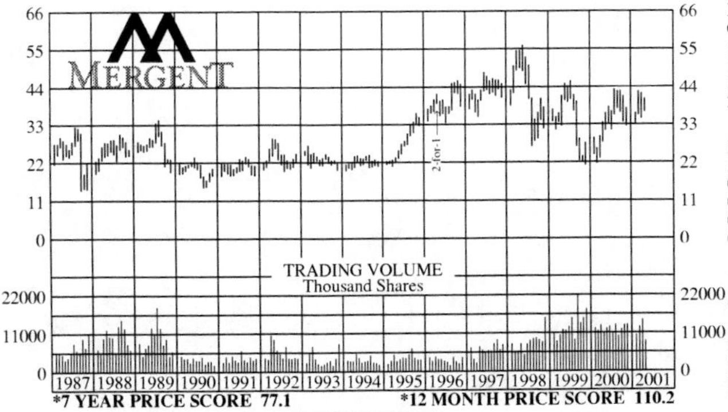

MERGENT

TRADING VOLUME
Thousand Shares

1987 1988 1989 1990 1991 1992 1993 1994 1995 1996 1997 1998 1999 2000 2001

2-for-1

***7 YEAR PRICE SCORE 77.1** ***12 MONTH PRICE SCORE 110.2**

*NYSE COMPOSITE INDEX=100

INTERIM EARNINGS (Per Share):

Qtr.	Mar.	June	Sept.	Dec.
1997	0.47	0.96	0.59	d0.26
1998	0.72	0.74	0.80	0.78
1999	0.66	0.82	d0.64	0.60
2000	0.78	0.75	0.77	0.68

INTERIM DIVIDENDS (Per Share):

Amt.	Decl.	Ex.	Rec.	Pay.
0.275Q	7/17/00	8/31/00	9/05/00	10/02/00
0.275Q	10/16/00	11/30/00	12/04/00	1/02/01
0.275Q	2/19/01	3/01/01	3/05/01	4/02/01
0.275Q	4/17/01	6/01/01	6/04/01	7/02/01

Indicated div.: $1.10 (Div. Reinv. Plan)

CAPITALIZATION (12/31/00):

	($000)	(%)
Long-Term Debt	1,316,200	46.7
Deferred Income Tax	2,300	0.1
Redeemable Pfd. Stock	273,800	9.7
Common & Surplus	1,226,600	43.5
Total	2,818,900	100.0

RECENT DEVELOPMENTS: For the year ended 12/31/00, income from continued operations more than doubled to $286.3 million compared with $138.7 million in 1999. Results for 2000 excluded a $29.5 million after-tax charge for merger-related and consolidation costs, a $1.7 million after-tax charge for an impairment loss, and after-tax income of $39.6 million from discontinued operations. Results for 1999 excluded after-tax charges totaling $136.3 million. Sales rose 1.0% to $4.36 billion.

PROSPECTS: The Company expects sales and profit growth for 2001 to be driven by the strength of the Aerospace segment due to higher deliveries of commercial transport aircraft, a strong presence in the regional and business aircraft markets. The Engineered Industrial Products segment is anticipated to report modest top-line growth due to higher shipments of engines and compressors and new products, offset by weakness in automotive, truck and trailer, and general industrial markets.

BUSINESS

GOODRICH CORPORATION (formerly The B.F. Goodrich Company) provides aircraft systems and services and manufactures a range of specialty chemicals. The Aerospace segment includes landing systems, sensors and integrated systems, safety systems, and maintenance, repair and overhauls business groups. The Engineered Industrial Products segment manufactures industrial seals, gaskets, packing products, self-lubricating bearings, diesel, gas and dual-fuel engines, air compressors, spray nozzles and vacuum pumps. Revenues for 2000 (and operating income) were derived: Aerospace, 84.2% (82.9%); and Engineered Industrial products, 15.8% (17.1%). On 7/12/99, GR acquired Coltec Industries, a manufacturer of landing gear systems. GR completed the sale of its Performance Materials segment on 2/28/01.

ANNUAL FINANCIAL DATA

	12/31/00	12/31/99	12/31/98	12/31/97	12/31/96	12/31/95	12/31/94
Earnings Per Share	**[1][5] 2.68**	**[5] 1.53**	**[4] 3.04**	**[1][3] 1.53**	**[1][3] 1.97**	**[3] 2.15**	**[2] 1.12**
Cash Flow Per Share	**4.39**	**3.62**	**5.25**	**3.38**	**4.56**	**4.32**	**3.30**
Tang. Book Val. Per Share	**3.48**	**1.41**	**9.63**	**11.35**	**8.52**	**5.74**	**4.14**
Dividends Per Share	**1.10**	**1.10**	**1.10**	**1.10**	**1.10**	**1.10**	**0.82**
Dividend Payout %	**41.0**	**71.9**	**36.2**	**71.9**	**55.8**	**51.2**	**73.7**
INCOME STATEMENT (IN MILLIONS):							
Total Revenues	4,363.8	5,537.5	3,950.8	3,373.0	2,238.8	2,408.6	2,199.2
Costs & Expenses	3,579.5	4,833.6	3,308.6	2,984.1	1,860.2	2,054.9	1,907.4
Depreciation & Amort.	192.5	230.6	165.4	138.8	139.8	113.9	112.1
Operating Income	591.8	473.3	476.8	250.1	238.8	239.8	179.7
Net Interest Inc./(Exp.)	d105.5	d133.5	d73.8	d61.0	d38.9	d41.8	d45.9
Income Before Income Taxes	461.4	334.5	384.9	217.8	178.1	198.3	108.6
Income Taxes	156.7	146.5	146.3	94.1	61.4	75.2	42.9
Equity Earnings/Minority Int.	d18.4	d18.4	d10.5	d10.5	d10.5	d5.1	...
Net Income	[1][5] 286.3	[5] 169.6	[4] 228.1	[1][3] 113.2	[1][3] 106.2	[3] 118.0	[2] 65.7
Cash Flow	478.8	400.2	393.5	252.0	246.0	226.3	169.8
Average Shs. Outstg. (000)	109,100	110,700	75,000	74,600	53,980	52,340	51,532
BALANCE SHEET (IN MILLIONS):							
Cash & Cash Equivalents	77.5	66.4	31.7	47.0	48.7	60.3	35.8
Total Current Assets	3,080.3	2,100.5	1,614.5	1,401.3	912.3	1,061.1	878.8
Net Property	1,022.0	1,577.3	1,255.9	1,065.1	946.0	859.2	873.3
Total Assets	5,717.5	5,455.6	4,192.6	3,493.9	2,663.1	2,489.6	2,468.9
Total Current Liabilities	2,147.3	1,510.9	990.8	934.9	662.5	600.7	638.0
Long-Term Obligations	1,316.2	1,516.9	995.2	564.3	400.0	422.3	427.1
Net Stockholders' Equity	1,226.6	1,293.2	1,599.6	1,422.6	1,050.2	878.6	922.6
Net Working Capital	933.0	589.6	623.7	466.4	249.8	460.4	240.8
Year-end Shs. Outstg. (000)	102,330	110,232	74,400	72,700	53,763	52,534	51,580
STATISTICAL RECORD:							
Operating Profit Margin %	13.6	8.5	12.1	7.4	10.7	10.0	8.2
Net Profit Margin %	6.6	3.1	5.8	3.4	4.7	4.9	3.0
Return on Equity %	23.3	13.1	14.3	8.0	10.1	13.4	7.1
Return on Assets %	5.0	3.1	5.4	3.2	4.0	4.5	2.7
Price Range	43.13-21.56	45.69-21.00	56.00-26.50	48.25-35.13	45.88-33.38	36.31-20.81	24.19-19.50
P/E Ratio	16.1-8.0	29.9-13.7	18.4-8.7	31.5-23.0	23.3-16.9	16.9-9.7	21.6-17.4
Average Yield %	3.4	3.3	2.7	2.6	2.8	3.9	3.8

Statistics are as originally reported. Adj. for 2-for-1 split, 4/96. [1] Excl. cr$84.3 mil. disc. ops., 1997; cr$45.5 mil. & $19.3 mil. net extra. loss, 1996; $39.6 mil., 2000. [2] Bef. $10.0 mil. non-recur. tax benefit rel. to divest. [3] Incl. $24.4 mil. net gain, 1997; $2.1 mil., 1996; $12.8 mil., 1995. [4] Incl. $6.5 mil. net restr. chg. & excl. $1.6 mil. after-tax loss fr. disc. ops. [5] Excl. $29.5 mil. net chgs., 2000; $192.1 mil., 1999 & $1.7 mil. after-tax impair. chg., 2000.

OFFICERS:
D. L. Burner, Chmn., Pres., C.E.O.
L. A. Chapman, Sr. V.P., Fin., C.F.O.

INVESTOR CONTACT: Paul S. Gifford, V.P. of Investor Relations, (704) 423-5517

PRINCIPAL OFFICE: 4 Coliseum Centre, 2730 W. Tyvola Road, Charlotte, NC 28217

TELEPHONE NUMBER: (704) 423-7000
FAX: (704) 423-7075
WEB: www.bfgoodrich.com
NO. OF EMPLOYEES: 26,322 (avg.)
SHAREHOLDERS: 11,519 (record)
ANNUAL MEETING: In Apr.
INCORPORATED: OH, May, 1880; reincorp., NY, May, 1912

INSTITUTIONAL HOLDINGS:
No. of Institutions: 272
Shares Held: 90,533,477
% Held: 88.1

INDUSTRY: Aircraft parts and equipment, nec (SIC: 3728)

TRANSFER AGENT(S): The Bank of New York, New York, NY

NYSE SYMBOL GT
Rec. Pr. 29.11 (5/31/01)

GOODYEAR TIRE & RUBBER COMPANY

YIELD 4.1%
P/E RATIO 78.7

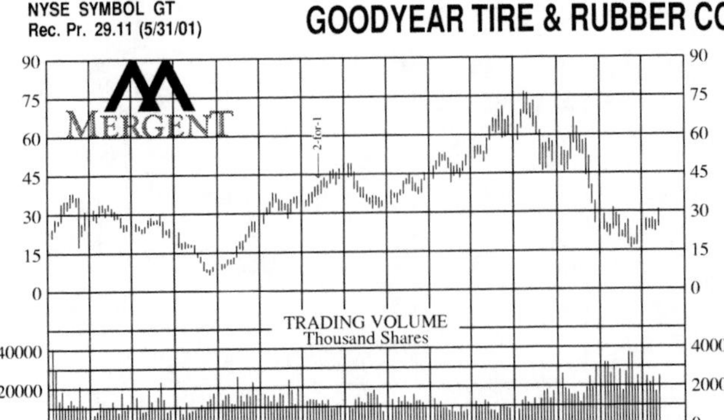

*7 YEAR PRICE SCORE 37.2 *12 MONTH PRICE SCORE 121.4

*NYSE COMPOSITE INDEX=100

INTERIM EARNINGS (Per Share):

Qtr.	Mar.	June	Sept.	Dec.
1996	0.98	1.22	1.09	d2.63
1997	1.09	1.23	1.25	0.01
1998	1.11	1.25	1.17	0.78
1999	0.16	0.41	0.69	0.26
2000	0.46	d0.08	d0.29	0.28

INTERIM DIVIDENDS (Per Share):

Amt.	Decl.	Ex.	Rec.	Pay.
0.30Q	4/10/00	5/12/00	5/16/00	6/15/00
0.30Q	8/01/00	8/11/00	8/15/00	9/15/00
0.30Q	10/03/00	11/14/00	11/16/00	12/15/00
0.30Q	2/06/01	2/13/01	2/15/01	3/15/01
0.30Q	4/02/01	5/11/01	5/15/01	6/15/01

Indicated div.: $1.20 (Div. Reinv. Plan)

CAPITALIZATION (12/31/00):

	($000)	(%)
Long-Term Debt	2,349,600	35.1
Minority Interest	844,900	12.6
Common & Surplus	3,503,000	52.3
Total	6,697,500	100.0

RECENT DEVELOPMENTS: For the year ended 12/31/00, net income fell 83.4% to $40.3 million compared with $243.2 million in the previous year. Earnings included nonrecurring items that resulted in a net after-tax charge of $158.2 million in 2000 and a net after-tax gain of $24.4 million in 1999. Net sales rose 7.9% to $14.42 billion versus $13.36 billion the year before, due to higher tire unit sales resulting from the acquisition of the Dunlop businesses. Comparisons were made with restated results for 1999.

PROSPECTS: As part of the Company's global rationalization plan, GT will reduce its worldwide work force by 6.8% in 2001. As a result, 1,600 positions will be eliminated in the European Union, 2,000 in Eastern Europe, Africa and the Middle East, 2,000 in Latin America, 600 in Asia, 500 in engineered products, a global business segment and 500 in North America. The Company anticipates savings from the workforce reduction of $150.0 million in 2001 and annual savings of $250.0 million beginning in 2002.

BUSINESS

GOODYEAR TIRE & RUBBER COMPANY's principal business is the development, manufacture, distribution and sale of tires throughout the world. In addition, GT produces and sells a broad spectrum of rubber, chemical and plastic products for the transportation industry and various industrial and consumer markets. GT also provides automotive repair and other services. In 2000, revenues (and operating income) were derived: Tire Products, 87.9% (82.1%); Engineered Products, 8.1% (7.2%); Chemical Products, 7.8% (10.7%) and Inter-Strategic Business Units, -3.9% (0.0%). On 6/14/99, GT formed a strategic global alliance with Sumitomo Rubber Industries Ltd. for tire manufacturing and sales.

ANNUAL FINANCIAL DATA

	12/31/00	12/31/99	12/31/98	12/31/97	12/31/96	12/31/95	12/31/94
Earnings Per Share	**[1] 0.25**	**[1] 1.52**	**[1][2] 4.53**	**[1] 3.53**	**[1] 0.66**	**4.02**	**3.75**
Cash Flow Per Share	**4.22**	**5.18**	**7.61**	**6.51**	**3.63**	**6.88**	**6.46**
Tang. Book Val. Per Share	**18.49**	**19.83**	**24.02**	**21.63**	**21.01**	**21.38**	**18.51**
Dividends Per Share	**1.20**	**1.20**	**1.20**	**1.14**	**1.03**	**0.95**	**0.75**
Dividend Payout %	**479.8**	**78.9**	**26.5**	**32.3**	**156.0**	**23.6**	**20.0**
INCOME STATEMENT (IN MILLIONS):							
Total Revenues	14,417.1	12,880.6	12,626.3	13,155.1	13,112.8	13,165.9	12,288.2
Costs & Expenses	13,368.4	11,958.0	10,912.7	11,731.3	12,328.0	11,595.6	10,819.3
Depreciation & Amort.	630.3	581.7	487.8	469.3	460.8	434.9	410.3
Operating Income	418.4	340.9	1,225.8	954.5	324.0	1,135.4	1,058.6
Net Interest Inc./(Exp.)	d282.6	d179.4	d147.8	d119.5	d128.6	d135.0	d53.1
Income Before Income Taxes	58.8	296.7	1,002.7	800.0	122.3	925.8	865.7
Income Taxes	18.5	55.6	285.7	241.3	20.6	314.8	298.7
Equity Earnings/Minority Int.	d55.9	d40.3	d31.5	d44.6	d43.1	d36.2	d23.8
Net Income	[1] 40.3	[1] 241.1	[1][2] 717.0	[1] 558.7	[1] 101.7	611.0	567.0
Cash Flow	670.6	822.8	1,204.8	1,028.0	562.5	1,045.9	977.3
Average Shs. Outstg. (000)	158,765	158,940	158,307	158,000	155,052	152,119	151,204
BALANCE SHEET (IN MILLIONS):							
Cash & Cash Equivalents	252.9	241.3	239.0	258.6	238.5	268.3	250.9
Total Current Assets	5,467.2	5,261.2	4,529.1	4,163.9	4,025.0	3,841.6	3,367.5
Net Property	5,521.0	5,761.0	4,358.5	4,149.7	4,067.9	4,561.2	4,382.8
Total Assets	13,568.0	13,102.6	10,589.3	9,917.4	9,671.8	9,789.6	9,123.3
Total Current Liabilities	4,225.9	3,959.9	3,276.5	3,251.0	2,766.2	2,736.3	2,572.0
Long-Term Obligations	2,349.6	2,347.9	1,186.5	844.5	1,132.2	1,320.0	1,108.7
Net Stockholders' Equity	3,503.0	3,617.1	3,745.8	3,395.5	3,279.1	3,281.7	2,803.2
Net Working Capital	1,241.3	1,301.3	1,252.6	912.9	1,258.8	1,105.3	795.5
Year-end Shs. Outstg. (000)	157,604	156,335	155,944	157,000	156,050	153,524	151,407
STATISTICAL RECORD:							
Operating Profit Margin %	2.9	2.6	9.7	7.3	2.5	8.6	8.6
Net Profit Margin %	0.3	1.9	5.7	4.2	0.8	4.6	4.6
Return on Equity %	1.2	6.7	19.1	16.5	3.1	18.6	20.2
Return on Assets %	0.3	1.8	6.8	5.6	1.1	6.2	6.2
Debt/Total Assets %	17.3	17.9	11.2	8.5	11.7	13.5	12.2
Price Range	31.63-15.60	66.75-25.50	76.75-45.88	71.25-49.25	53.00-41.50	45.38-33.00	49.25-31.63
P/E Ratio	126.4-62.4	43.9-16.8	16.9-10.1	20.2-14.0	80.3-62.9	11.3-8.2	13.1-8.4
Average Yield %	5.1	2.6	2.0	1.9	2.2	2.4	1.9

Statistics are as originally reported. [1] Incl. non-recurr. chrg. $158.2 mill., 2000; $240.1 mill., 1999; $26.8 mill., 1998; $176.5 mill., 1997; $572.2 mill., 1996. [2] Bef. disc. opers. loss of $34.7 mill.

OFFICERS:
S. G. Gibara, Chmn., C.E.O.
R. J. Keegan, Pres., C.O.O.
R. W. Tieken, Exec. V.P., C.F.O.
S. W. Bergeron, V.P., Treas.

INVESTOR CONTACT: Holly K. Ash, Dir. Investor Relations, (216) 796-8576

PRINCIPAL OFFICE: 1144 East Market Street, Akron, OH 44316-0001

TELEPHONE NUMBER: (330) 796-2121
FAX: (330) 796-4099
WEB: www.goodyear.com

NO. OF EMPLOYEES: 105,128 (approx.)

SHAREHOLDERS: 28,604 (of record)

ANNUAL MEETING: In Apr.

INCORPORATED: OH, Aug., 1898

INSTITUTIONAL HOLDINGS:
No. of Institutions: 231
Shares Held: 102,704,619
% Held: 64.7

INDUSTRY: Tires and inner tubes (SIC: 3011)

TRANSFER AGENT(S): First Chicago Trust Company of New York, Jersey City, NJ

NYSE SYMBOL GPU
Rec. Pr. 33.31 (4/30/01)

GPU, INC.

YIELD 6.5%
P/E RATIO 17.3

*7 YEAR PRICE SCORE 68.0 *12 MONTH PRICE SCORE 106.6

*NYSE COMPOSITE INDEX=100

INTERIM EARNINGS (Per Share):

Qtr.	Mar.	June	Sept.	Dec.
1997	1.28	0.58	0.14	0.77
1998	1.07	d1.54	2.65	0.65
1999	1.49	0.38	1.18	0.60
2000	1.08	d1.74	0.86	1.72

INTERIM DIVIDENDS (Per Share):

Amt.	Decl.	Ex.	Rec.	Pay.
0.545Q	7/18/00	7/26/00	7/28/00	8/30/00
0.545Q	10/05/00	10/25/00	10/27/00	11/29/00
0.545Q	12/07/00	1/24/01	1/26/01	2/28/01
0.545Q	4/04/01	4/25/01	4/27/01	5/30/01

Indicated div.: $2.18 (Div. Reinv. Plan)

CAPITALIZATION (12/31/00):

	($000)	(%)
Long-Term Debt	3,917,069	36.5
Deferred Income Tax	3,093,826	28.9
Redeemable Pfd. Stock	51,500	0.5
Preferred Stock	337,649	3.1
Common & Surplus	3,321,050	31.0
Total	10,721,094	100.0

RECENT DEVELOPMENTS: For the year ended 12/31/00, net income fell 49.1% to $233.5 million compared with $459.0 million in 1999. Results for 2000 included after-tax losses totaling $103.9 million for the sale of businesses. Earnings for 1999 included non-recurring items that resulted in a net after-tax charge of $25.1 million. Operating revenues climbed 9.2% to $5.20 billion from $4.76 billion in the previous year.

PROSPECTS: On 5/3/01, the Company announced a proposed merger agreement with FirstEnergy. The combined company will become the fourth largest electric utility in the U.S. based on a customer base of about 4.3 million. The new company will provide service across more than 37,000 square miles stretching from northern and central Ohio, through Pennsylvania to the New Jersey shore. The merger is pending regulatory approvals and is slated for completion by 6/30/01.

BUSINESS

GPU, INC. (formerly General Public Utilities) is a holding company that owns all the outstanding common stock of three electric utilities - Jersey Central Power & Light Company (JCP&L), Metropolitan Edison Company (Met-Ed) and Pennsylvania Electric Company (Penelec). Collectively, these three companies do business as GPU Energy. The subsidiaries serve areas of NJ and PA with a population of about five million. GPU owns all the common stock of GPU Capital, Inc. and GPU Electric, Inc., which operate generation facilities and gas transmission systems in foreign countries, and GPU Advanced Resources, Inc., which is involved in retail energy sales.

ANNUAL FINANCIAL DATA

	12/31/00	12/31/99	12/31/98	12/31/97	12/31/96	12/31/95	12/31/94
Earnings Per Share	**[5] 1.92**	**[4] 3.66**	**[3] 3.03**	**[1] 2.77**	**[1] 2.47**	**[2] 3.79**	**[1] 1.42**
Cash Flow Per Share	**6.84**	**8.56**	**7.77**	**6.72**	**6.43**	**9.13**	**3.91**
Tang. Book Val. Per Share	**11.17**	**6.98**	**22.81**	**20.84**	**25.27**	**24.70**	**22.33**
Dividends Per Share	**2.17**	**2.10**	**2.04**	**1.99**	**1.93**	**1.86**	**1.77**
Dividend Payout %	**112.8**	**57.5**	**67.5**	**71.7**	**77.9**	**49.1**	**125.0**
INCOME STATEMENT (IN MILLIONS):							
Total Revenues	5,196.3	4,757.1	4,248.8	4,143.4	3,918.1	3,804.7	3,649.5
Costs & Expenses	2,443.9	1,636.5	1,643.1	1,964.5	1,840.8	1,841.6	1,664.2
Depreciation & Amort.	595.3	616.4	602.7	538.1	478.1	438.9	419.9
Maintenance Exp.	1,372.4	1,495.4	1,106.9	993.7	1,090.9	963.6	1,076.9
Operating Income	784.6	1,008.8	896.1	647.1	508.3	560.6	488.5
Net Interest Inc./(Exp.)	d519.0	d438.5	d349.1	d277.9	d205.1	d209.1	d215.3
Income Taxes	176.8	239.6	240.1	...	...	...	...
Equity Earnings/Minority Int.	d2.9	d3.5	d2.2	d1.3	...	...	...
Net Income	[5] 233.5	[4] 459.0	[3] 385.9	[1] 335.1	[1] 298.6	[2] 440.1	[1] 163.7
Cash Flow	828.8	1,075.4	988.6	813.0	776.8	1,060.6	450.8
Average Shs. Outstg. (000)	121,259	125,570	127,312	121,002	120,743	116,214	115,160
BALANCE SHEET (IN MILLIONS):							
Gross Property	10,308.2	11,954.9	11,265.2	11,559.7	10,091.8	9,802.5	9,415.3
Accumulated Depreciation	3,246.2	3,930.0	4,460.3	4,050.2	3,704.0	3,433.2	3,148.7
Net Property	7,062.0	8,024.9	6,804.9	7,509.6	6,387.8	6,369.2	6,266.6
Total Assets	19,262.5	21,718.1	16,288.1	12,924.7	10,941.2	9,849.5	9,209.8
Long-Term Obligations	3,917.1	5,850.6	3,825.6	4,326.0	3,177.0	2,567.9	2,345.4
Net Stockholders' Equity	3,658.7	3,802.6	3,861.1	3,496.4	3,444.1	3,402.8	2,875.7
Year-end Shs. Outstg. (000)	119,440	121,806	127,996	120,839	120,611	120,423	115,208
STATISTICAL RECORD:							
Operating Profit Margin %	15.1	21.2	15.5	15.6	13.0	14.7	13.4
Net Profit Margin %	4.5	9.6	9.1	8.1	7.6	11.6	4.5
Net Inc./Net Property %	3.3	5.7	5.7	4.5	4.7	6.9	2.6
Net Inc./Tot. Capital %	2.2	3.5	3.6	3.5	3.6	5.8	2.4
Return on Equity %	6.4	12.1	10.0	9.6	8.7	12.9	5.7
Accum. Depr./Gross Prop. %	31.5	32.9	39.6	35.0	36.7	35.0	33.4
Price Range	37.19-23.44	45.00-28.75	47.19-35.19	42.75-30.75	35.25-30.13	34.00-26.25	31.63-23.75
P/E Ratio	19.4-12.2	12.3-7.9	15.6-11.6	15.4-11.1	14.3-12.2	9.0-6.9	22.3-16.7
Average Yield %	7.1	5.7	5.0	5.4	5.9	6.2	6.4

Statistics are as originally reported. [1] Incl. $109.3 mil. non-recur. net chg., 1997; $74.5 mil., 1996; $191.6 mil., 1994. [2] Incl. $104.9 mil. net credit & $8.4 mil. net chg. [3] Incl. $65.8 mil. net non-recur. chg. rel. to restr. orders; bef. $25.8 mil. extraord. loss. [4] Incl. $36.1 mil. net non-recur. gain fr. sale of gen. station, $68.0 mill. net chg. fr. NJ Board of PU restr. order, and $6.8 mill. net gain. [5] Incl. $295.0 mil. net non-recur. chg. & $191.1 mil. aft-tax gains.

OFFICERS:
F. D. Hafer, Chmn., Pres., C.E.O.
B. L. Levy, Sr. V.P. and C.F.O.

INVESTOR CONTACT: Ned Reynolds, (973) 401-8294

PRINCIPAL OFFICE: 300 Madison Ave., Morristown, NJ 07962-1911

TELEPHONE NUMBER: (973) 401-8200
FAX: (973) 644-4296
WEB: www.gpu.com

NO. OF EMPLOYEES: 14,100 (approx.)

SHAREHOLDERS: 32,832 (of record).

ANNUAL MEETING: In May

INCORPORATED: PA, July, 1969

INSTITUTIONAL HOLDINGS:
No. of Institutions: 260
Shares Held: 85,153,632
% Held: 71.3

INDUSTRY: Electric services (SIC: 4911)

TRANSFER AGENT(S): Mellon Investor Services, Ridgefield Park, NJ

NYSE SYMBOL GGG
Rec. Pr. 27.40 (4/30/01)

GRACO INC.

YIELD 1.5%
P/E RATIO 12.1

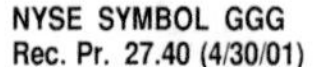

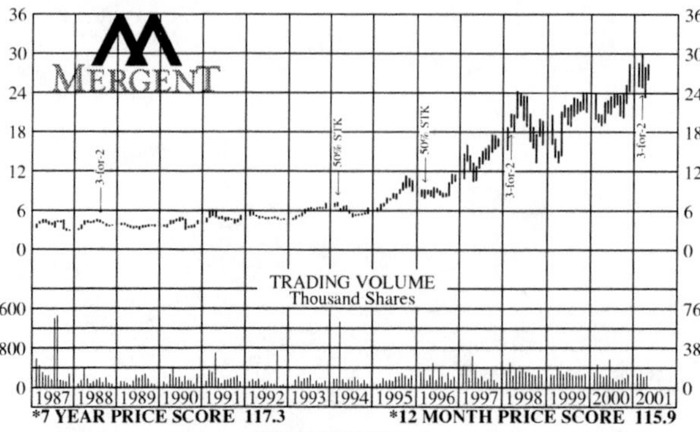

***7 YEAR PRICE SCORE 117.3** ***12 MONTH PRICE SCORE 115.9**

*NYSE COMPOSITE INDEX=100

INTERIM EARNINGS (Per Share):

Qtr.	Mar.	June	Sept.	Dec.
1997	0.15	0.27	0.33	0.39
1998	0.23	0.32	0.35	0.47
1999	0.36	0.57	0.48	0.48
2000	0.48	0.59	0.59	0.61

INTERIM DIVIDENDS (Per Share):

Amt.	Decl.	Ex.	Rec.	Pay.
0.14Q	6/16/00	7/13/00	7/17/00	8/02/00
0.14Q	9/29/00	10/12/00	10/16/00	11/01/00
3-for-2	12/08/00	2/07/01	1/15/01	2/06/01
0.10Q	12/08/00	1/10/01	1/15/01	2/07/01
0.10Q	2/23/01	4/11/01	4/16/01	5/02/01

Indicated div.: $0.40

CAPITALIZATION (12/29/00):

	($000)	(%)
Long-Term Debt	18,050	14.0
Common & Surplus	110,855	86.0
Total	128,905	100.0

RECENT DEVELOPMENTS: For the year ended 12/29/00, net earnings rose 18.1% to $70.1 million compared with $59.3 million in 1999. Net sales were $494.4 million, up 9.7% from $450.5 million in the prior year. Net sales in the Americas grew 15.0% to $359.9 million, while net sales in Europe decreased 6.0% to $84.7 million. Sales in the Asia Pacific region increased 7.0% to $49.8 million. Gross profit climbed 8.5% to $250.9 million from $231.1 million in the previous year.

PROSPECTS: The economic environment in 2001 is expected to be difficult for GGG and its industry. In response, GGG will continue to pursue its strategies of developing new products, expanding distribution, entering new markets and strategic acquisitions. Meanwhile, GGG should be well positioned to take advantage of a global economic recovery given its strong distribution channel, productive manufacturing operation, commitment to developing new products, and marketing capabilities.

BUSINESS

GRACO INC. supplies technology and expertise for the management of fluids in both industrial and commercial settings. GGG designs, manufactures and markets systems and equipment to move, measure, control, dispense and apply fluid materials. GGG manufactures a wide array of specialized pumps, applicators, regulators, valves, meters, atomizing devices, replacement parts, and accessories. These products are used in the movement, measurement, control, dispensing and application of many fluids and semi-solids. The Company offers an extensive line of portable equipment that is used in construction and maintenance businesses for the application of paint and other materials. Revenues for 2000 were derived: industrial/automotive, 46.1%; contractor, 44.8%; and lubrication, 9.1%.

ANNUAL FINANCIAL DATA

	12/29/00	12/31/99	12/25/98	12/26/97	12/27/96	12/29/95	12/30/94
Earnings Per Share	**2.27**	**1.89**	**[2] 1.34**	**1.14**	**0.92**	**0.71**	**0.39**
Cash Flow Per Share	**2.77**	**2.37**	**1.73**	**1.48**	**1.86**	**1.48**	**0.66**
Tang. Book Val. Per Share	**5.47**	**2.06**	**0.31**	**4.11**	**4.93**	**3.99**	**3.19**
Dividends Per Share	**0.37**	**0.29**	**0.29**	**0.25**	**0.21**	**0.19**	**[1] 0.97**
Dividend Payout %	**16.4**	**15.5**	**21.9**	**21.8**	**23.2**	**26.8**	**248.7**
INCOME STATEMENT (IN MILLIONS):							
Total Revenues	494.4	442.5	432.2	413.9	391.8	386.3	360.0
Costs & Expenses	367.7	334.6	341.6	334.9	326.0	330.0	323.2
Depreciation & Amort.	15.5	14.7	13.7	13.5	12.7	11.1	10.4
Operating Income	111.2	93.2	76.9	65.5	53.1	45.2	26.4
Net Interest Inc./(Exp.)	d4.1	d7.0	d5.3	d0.9	d0.8	d2.3	d1.9
Income Before Income Taxes	105.9	88.8	71.4	63.5	52.8	43.6	23.4
Income Taxes	35.8	29.5	24.1	18.8	16.6	15.9	8.1
Net Income	70.1	59.3	[2] 47.3	44.7	36.2	27.7	15.3
Cash Flow	85.6	74.0	61.0	58.2	48.8	38.8	25.8
Average Shs. Outstg. (000)	30,905	31,299	35,321	39,249	39,339	39,195	58,631
BALANCE SHEET (IN MILLIONS):							
Cash & Cash Equivalents	11.1	6.6	3.6	13.5	6.5	1.6	2.4
Total Current Assets	143.7	138.0	131.3	156.3	144.5	128.5	143.9
Net Property	84.0	86.5	96.4	100.2	94.2	76.9	70.0
Total Assets	238.0	236.0	233.7	264.5	247.8	217.8	228.4
Total Current Liabilities	81.8	78.3	83.0	69.0	80.6	71.6	89.5
Long-Term Obligations	18.1	65.7	112.6	6.2	8.1	10.1	26.8
Net Stockholders' Equity	110.9	62.9	9.3	157.5	126.1	103.6	81.9
Net Working Capital	61.9	59.7	48.4	87.3	63.9	56.9	54.4
Year-end Shs. Outstg. (000)	20,274	30,624	30,145	38,330	38,356	38,846	38,397
STATISTICAL RECORD:							
Operating Profit Margin %	22.5	21.1	17.8	15.8	13.5	11.7	7.3
Net Profit Margin %	14.2	13.4	10.9	10.8	9.2	7.2	4.3
Return on Equity %	63.2	94.3	507.5	28.4	28.7	26.8	18.7
Return on Assets %	29.5	25.1	20.2	16.9	14.6	12.7	6.7
Debt/Total Assets %	7.6	27.8	48.2	2.3	3.3	4.6	11.7
Price Range	28.50-18.96	24.13-13.25	24.33-13.25	17.64-10.45	11.56-7.89	11.33-5.85	7.30-4.96
P/E Ratio	12.6-8.4	12.7-7.0	18.2-9.9	15.5-9.2	12.6-8.6	16.0-8.3	18.7-12.7
Average Yield %	1.6	1.6	1.6	1.8	2.2	2.2	15.8

Statistics are as originally reported. Adj for 3-for-2 split, 2/01, 2/98, 2/96, & 2/94. [1] Incl. $1.20/sh special div. [2] Incl. $1.7 mill. restr. & non-recur. chgs.

OFFICERS:
D. A. Koch, Chmn.
D. D. Johnson, Pres., C.O.O.
G. Aristides, C.E.O.

INVESTOR CONTACT: Investor Relations, (612) 623-6659

PRINCIPAL OFFICE: 88 - 11th Avenue Northeast, Minneapolis, MN 55413

TELEPHONE NUMBER: (612) 623-6000
FAX: (612) 623-6703
WEB: www.graco.com

NO. OF EMPLOYEES: 1,920 (approx.)

SHAREHOLDERS: 2,500 (record); 4,600(beneficial).

ANNUAL MEETING: In May

INCORPORATED: MN, 1926

INSTITUTIONAL HOLDINGS:
No. of Institutions: 121
Shares Held: 21,786,074
% Held: 70.9

INDUSTRY: Pumps and pumping equipment (SIC: 3561)

TRANSFER AGENT(S): Wells Fargo Shareowner Services, South St. Paul, MN

NYSE SYMBOL GWW
Rec. Pr. 44.19 (5/31/01)

GRAINGER (W.W.), INC.

YIELD 1.6%
P/E RATIO 21.6

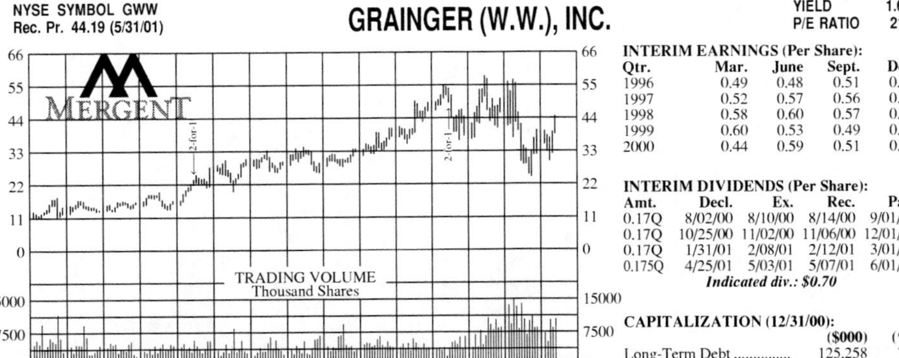

*7 YEAR PRICE SCORE 63.9 *12 MONTH PRICE SCORE 120.6
*NYSE COMPOSITE INDEX=100

INTERIM EARNINGS (Per Share):

Qtr.	Mar.	June	Sept.	Dec.
1996	0.49	0.48	0.51	0.54
1997	0.52	0.57	0.56	0.63
1998	0.58	0.60	0.57	0.69
1999	0.60	0.53	0.49	0.30
2000	0.44	0.59	0.51	0.51

INTERIM DIVIDENDS (Per Share):

Amt.	Decl.	Ex.	Rec.	Pay.
0.17Q	8/02/00	8/10/00	8/14/00	9/01/00
0.17Q	10/25/00	11/02/00	11/06/00	12/01/00
0.17Q	1/31/01	2/08/01	2/12/01	3/01/01
0.175Q	4/25/01	5/03/01	5/07/01	6/01/01

Indicated div.: $0.70

CAPITALIZATION (12/31/00):

	($000)	(%)
Long-Term Debt	125,258	7.5
Minority Interest	96	0.0
Common & Surplus	1,537,386	92.5
Total	1,662,740	100.0

RECENT DEVELOPMENTS: For the year ended 12/31/00, net earnings grew 6.7% to $192.9 million from $180.7 million the previous year. Results for 2000 included a one-time pre-tax gain of $29.8 million from the sale of an investment security. Net sales rose 7.4% to $4.98 billion from $4.64 billion a year earlier. Gross profit totaled $1.59 billion, or 31.9% of net sales, compared with $1.51 billion, or 32.6% of net sales, the year before. Operating earnings climbed 5.6% to $335.1 million from $317.2 million in 1999.

PROSPECTS: In January 2001, GWW consolidated three of its digital businesses into a separate unit called Material Logic that will provide e-procurement services in the maintenance, repair and operating supply industry. GWW expects Material Logic will become independent in 2001. GWW anticipates capital expenditures in 2001 of up to $165.0 million will be used to fund the expansion of its U.S. logistics network, the addition of 17 branches, and further enhancement of its information systems.

BUSINESS

W.W. GRAINGER, INC. is a nationwide distributor of equipment, components, and supplies to the commercial, industrial, contractor and institutional markets. Products include motors, fans, blowers, pumps, compressors, air and power tools, heating and air conditioning equipment, as well as other items offered in its Grainger Industrial Supply Catalog that features more than 85,200 products. GWW's customers have access to a much larger selection of the Company's products through Grainger.com, which has more than 220,000 products available. GWW serves its more than 1.4 million customers from regional distribution facilities in Chicago, IL, Kansas City, MO, and Greenville County, SC through a network of 574 branches in the U.S, Canada, and Mexico.

ANNUAL FINANCIAL DATA

	12/31/00	12/31/99	12/31/98	12/31/97	12/31/96	12/31/95	12/31/94
Earnings Per Share	**[1] 2.05**	**1.92**	**2.44**	**2.27**	**2.02**	**1.82**	**[1] 1.25**
Cash Flow Per Share	**3.18**	**2.96**	**3.24**	**3.05**	**2.74**	**2.51**	**1.88**
Tang. Book Val. Per Share	**14.67**	**13.47**	**11.39**	**11.13**	**11.65**	**10.87**	**9.33**
Dividends Per Share	**0.67**	**0.63**	**0.58**	**0.53**	**0.49**	**0.45**	**0.39**
Dividend Payout %	**32.7**	**32.8**	**24.0**	**23.3**	**24.3**	**24.4**	**31.2**
INCOME STATEMENT (IN MILLIONS):							
Total Revenues	4,977.0	4,533.9	4,341.3	4,136.6	3,537.2	3,276.9	3,023.1
Costs & Expenses	4,535.0	4,118.4	3,854.4	3,663.8	3,117.4	2,889.8	2,727.2
Depreciation & Amort.	106.9	98.2	78.9	79.7	74.3	70.9	64.3
Operating Income	335.1	317.2	408.0	393.2	345.5	316.3	231.5
Net Interest Inc./(Exp.)	d22.5	d14.0	d5.1	d2.6	3.3	d4.1	d1.9
Income Before Income Taxes	331.6	303.8	400.8	389.6	348.9	312.1	228.8
Income Taxes	138.7	123.0	162.3	157.8	140.4	125.5	100.9
Equity Earnings/Minority Int.	d10.9	...	...	...	...	...	...
Net Income	[1] 192.9	180.7	238.5	231.8	208.5	186.7	[1] 127.9
Cash Flow	299.8	279.0	317.4	311.5	282.8	257.5	192.2
Average Shs. Outstg. (000)	94,224	94,315	97,847	102,178	103,272	102,482	102,454
BALANCE SHEET (IN MILLIONS):							
Cash & Cash Equivalents	63.4	62.7	43.1	46.9	126.9	11.5	15.3
Total Current Assets	1,483.0	1,471.1	1,206.4	1,183.0	1,320.2	1,062.7	963.6
Net Property	676.4	697.8	660.5	592.9	551.0	518.4	469.1
Total Assets	2,459.6	2,564.8	2,103.9	1,997.8	2,119.0	1,669.2	1,534.8
Total Current Liabilities	747.3	870.5	664.5	533.9	616.1	444.1	459.1
Long-Term Obligations	125.3	124.9	122.9	131.2	6.2	8.7	1.0
Net Stockholders' Equity	1,537.4	1,480.5	1,278.7	1,294.7	1,462.7	1,179.1	1,032.8
Net Working Capital	735.7	600.6	541.9	649.1	704.2	618.5	504.6
Year-end Shs. Outstg. (000)	93,933	93,382	93,505	97,722	105,856	101,790	101,500
STATISTICAL RECORD:							
Operating Profit Margin %	6.7	7.0	9.4	9.5	9.8	9.7	7.7
Net Profit Margin %	3.9	4.0	5.5	5.6	5.9	5.7	4.2
Return on Equity %	12.5	12.2	18.7	17.9	14.3	15.8	12.4
Return on Assets %	7.8	7.0	11.3	11.6	9.8	11.2	8.3
Debt/Total Assets %	5.1	4.9	5.8	6.6	0.3	0.5	0.1
Price Range	56.88-24.31	58.13-36.88	54.72-36.44	49.88-35.25	40.75-31.31	33.81-27.75	34.56-25.75
P/E Ratio	27.7-11.9	30.3-19.2	22.4-14.9	22.0-15.5	20.2-15.5	18.6-15.2	27.6-20.6
Average Yield %	1.7	1.3	1.3	1.2	1.4	1.4	1.3

Statistics are as originally reported. Adj. for 2-for-1 stk. split, 6/98. [1] Incl. $29.8 mil ($0.19/sh) one-time gain from the sale of an investment security, 2000; $49.8 mil ($0.97/sh) non-recur. chg., 1994.

OFFICERS:
R. L. Keyser, Chmn., C.E.O.
D. E. Bielinski, Vice-Chmn.
W. M. Clark, Pres., C.O.O.
P. O. Loux, Sr. V.P., C.F.O.

INVESTOR CONTACT: William D. Chapman, Dir., Inv. Rel., (847) 535-0881

PRINCIPAL OFFICE: 100 Grainger Parkway, Lake Forest, IL 60045-5201

TELEPHONE NUMBER: (847) 535-1000
FAX: (847) 535-0878
WEB: www.grainger.com

NO. OF EMPLOYEES: 13,855 full-time; 2,337 part-time

SHAREHOLDERS: 1,600 (approx.)

ANNUAL MEETING: In Apr.

INCORPORATED: IL, Dec., 1928

INSTITUTIONAL HOLDINGS:
No. of Institutions: 262
Shares Held: 62,437,520
% Held: 65.8

INDUSTRY: Electrical apparatus and equipment (SIC: 5063)

TRANSFER AGENT(S): BankBoston, N.A., Boston, MA

NYSE SYMBOL GAP
Rec. Pr. 11.59 (5/31/01)

GREAT ATLANTIC & PACIFIC TEA COMPANY, INC. (THE)

YIELD . . .
P/E RATIO . . .

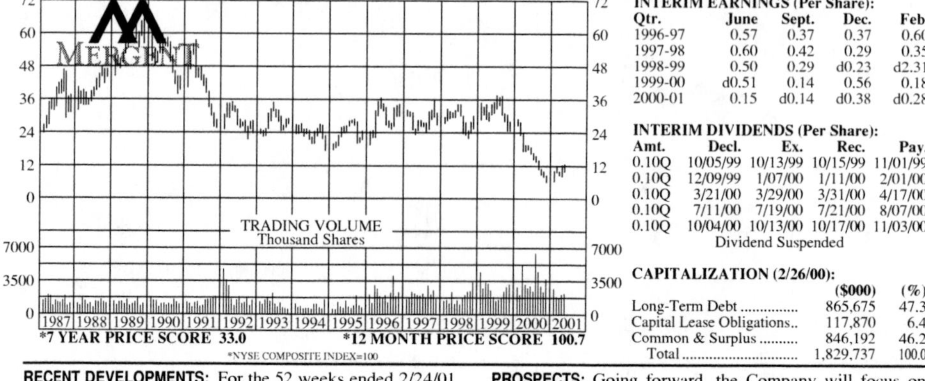

*7 YEAR PRICE SCORE 33.0 *12 MONTH PRICE SCORE 100.7

*NYSE COMPOSITE INDEX=100

INTERIM EARNINGS (Per Share):

Qtr.	June	Sept.	Dec.	Feb.
1996-97	0.57	0.37	0.37	0.60
1997-98	0.60	0.42	0.29	0.35
1998-99	0.50	0.29	d0.23	d2.31
1999-00	d0.51	0.14	0.56	0.18
2000-01	0.15	d0.14	d0.38	d0.28

INTERIM DIVIDENDS (Per Share):

Amt.	Decl.	Ex.	Rec.	Pay.
0.10Q	10/05/99	10/13/99	10/15/99	11/01/99
0.10Q	12/09/99	1/07/00	1/11/00	2/01/00
0.10Q	3/21/00	3/29/00	3/31/00	4/17/00
0.10Q	7/11/00	7/19/00	7/21/00	8/07/00
0.10Q	10/04/00	10/13/00	10/17/00	11/03/00

Dividend Suspended

CAPITALIZATION (2/26/00):

	($000)	(%)
Long-Term Debt	865,675	47.3
Capital Lease Obligations	117,870	6.4
Common & Surplus	846,192	46.2
Total	1,829,737	100.0

RECENT DEVELOPMENTS: For the 52 weeks ended 2/24/01, net loss totaled $25.1 million versus net income of $14.2 million in the corresponding period a year earlier. Results included one-time net after-tax restructuring charges of $44.1 million and $59.9 million in 2001 and 2000, respectively. Sales rose 4.6% to $10.62 billion from $10.15 billion the previous year. Gross profit increased 4.2% to $3.03 billion, or 28.5% of sales, from $2.91 billion, or 28.6% of sales, in the prior year.

PROSPECTS: Going forward, the Company will focus on further implementation of its series of strategic initiatives called Project Great Renewal. These initiatives included exiting certain markets and closing stores during fiscal 1999, along with supply chain and business process transformations in fiscal 2000. During fiscal 2001, the Company will implement new systems and processes designed to help reduce supply chain costs and improve marketing effectiveness.

BUSINESS

THE GREAT ATLANTIC & PACIFIC TEA COMPANY operates 752 stores, including 68 franchised units, located in 16 states, the District of Columbia and Ontario, Canada. Store names include A&P, Waldbaum's, Food Emporium, Super Foodmart, Super Fresh, Farmer Jack, Kohl's, Sav-A-Center, Dominion, The Barn Markets, Food Basics and Ultra Food & Drug. The stores deal in groceries, meats, fresh produce, health and beauty aids. Some have specialty food departments, including gourmet products, international cuisine and delicatessens. Through Compass Foods, GAP manufactures and distributes a line of whole-bean coffees under the Eight O'Clock, Bokar and Royale labels. The Tengelmann Group of West Germany owns 54.8% of GAP's stock.

ANNUAL FINANCIAL DATA

	2/26/00	2/27/99	2/28/98	2/22/97	2/24/96	2/25/95	2/26/94
Earnings Per Share	[3] **0.37**	[3] **d1.75**	[2] **1.66**	**1.91**	**1.50**	[1] **d4.36**	**0.10**
Cash Flow Per Share	**6.44**	**4.35**	**5.12**	**7.94**	**7.40**	**1.80**	**6.28**
Tang. Book Val. Per Share	**22.06**	**21.87**	**24.22**	**23.27**	**21.53**	**20.28**	**26.02**
Dividends Per Share	**0.40**	**0.40**	**0.35**	**0.20**	**0.20**	**0.80**	**0.80**
Dividend Payout %	**108.1**	...	**21.1**	**10.5**	**13.3**	...	**799.2**
INCOME STATEMENT (IN MILLIONS):							
Total Revenues	10,151.3	10,179.4	10,262.2	10,089.0	10,101.4	10,332.0	10,384.1
Costs & Expenses	9,813.8	10,110.1	9,872.7	9,689.0	9,724.2	10,154.0	10,079.9
Depreciation & Amort.	232.7	233.7	234.2	230.7	225.4	235.4	235.9
Operating Income	104.8	d164.4	155.3	169.3	151.7	d57.5	68.3
Net Interest Inc./(Exp.)	d77.8	d64.9	d72.4	d68.7	d70.6	d71.9	d61.7
Income Before Income Taxes	27.0	d229.3	82.9	100.6	81.1	d129.4	6.6
Income Taxes	12.8	cr162.1	19.3	27.6	23.9	37.1	2.6
Net Income	[3] 14.2	[3] d67.2	[2] 63.6	73.0	57.2	[1] d166.6	4.0
Cash Flow	246.9	166.5	297.8	303.8	282.7	68.9	239.9
Average Shs. Outstg. (000)	38,330	38,274	38,176	38,248	38,222	38,220	38,220
BALANCE SHEET (IN MILLIONS):							
Cash & Cash Equivalents	124.6	136.8	70.9	98.8	99.8	128.9	124.2
Total Current Assets	1,222.9	1,224.0	1,217.2	1,231.4	1,174.9	1,193.7	1,230.3
Net Property	1,883.8	1,686.5	1,596.9	1,590.0	1,554.5	1,573.7	1,687.5
Total Assets	3,335.5	3,141.7	2,995.3	3,002.7	2,860.8	2,894.8	3,098.7
Total Current Liabilities	1,124.6	1,134.1	955.1	1,016.0	984.0	1,096.5	1,151.1
Long-Term Obligations	983.5	844.3	816.3	839.5	780.1	758.9	707.3
Net Stockholders' Equity	846.2	837.3	926.6	890.1	822.8	774.9	994.4
Net Working Capital	98.3	90.0	262.1	215.4	191.0	97.3	79.2
Year-end Shs. Outstg. (000)	38,367	38,291	38,253	38,248	38,220	38,220	38,220
STATISTICAL RECORD:							
Operating Profit Margin %	1.0	...	1.5	1.7	1.5	...	0.7
Net Profit Margin %	0.1	...	0.6	0.7	0.6	...	...
Return on Equity %	1.7	...	6.9	8.2	7.0	...	0.4
Return on Assets %	0.4	...	2.1	2.4	2.0	...	0.1
Debt/Total Assets %	29.5	26.9	27.3	28.0	27.3	26.2	22.8
Price Range	37.69-24.50	34.38-21.88	36.00-23.13	36.75-19.50	29.00-17.63	27.38-17.38	35.00-22.50
P/E Ratio	101.8-66.2	...	21.7-13.9	19.2-10.2	19.3-11.7	...	349.7-224.8
Average Yield %	1.3	1.4	1.2	0.7	0.9	3.6	2.8

Statistics are as originally reported. [1] Bef. $5 mil ($0.13/sh) chg. for acctg. change. [2] Bef. a $544,000 ($0.01/sh) extraord. loss. [3] Incl. $59.9 mil ($1.56/sh) non-recur. after-tax chg., 2000; & $118.5 mil ($3.09/sh), 1999.

OFFICERS:
C. W. Haub, Chmn., Pres., C.E.O.
F. Corrado, Vice-Chmn., C.F.O.
E. R. Culligan, Exec. V.P., C.O.O.

INVESTOR CONTACT: Terry Galvin, V.P., Inv. Rel., (201) 571-8192

PRINCIPAL OFFICE: 2 Paragon Drive, Montvale, NJ 07645

TELEPHONE NUMBER: (201) 573-9700
FAX: (201) 930-8008
WEB: www.aptea.com

NO. OF EMPLOYEES: 80,900 (approx.)

SHAREHOLDERS: 6,890

ANNUAL MEETING: In July

INCORPORATED: MD, May, 1925

INSTITUTIONAL HOLDINGS:
No. of Institutions: 90
Shares Held: 11,292,070
% Held: 29.4

INDUSTRY: Grocery stores (SIC: 5411)

TRANSFER AGENT(S): American Stock Transfer and Trust Co., New York, NY

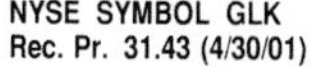

NYSE SYMBOL GLK
Rec. Pr. 31.43 (4/30/01)

GREAT LAKES CHEMICAL CORP.

YIELD 1.0%
P/E RATIO 13.0

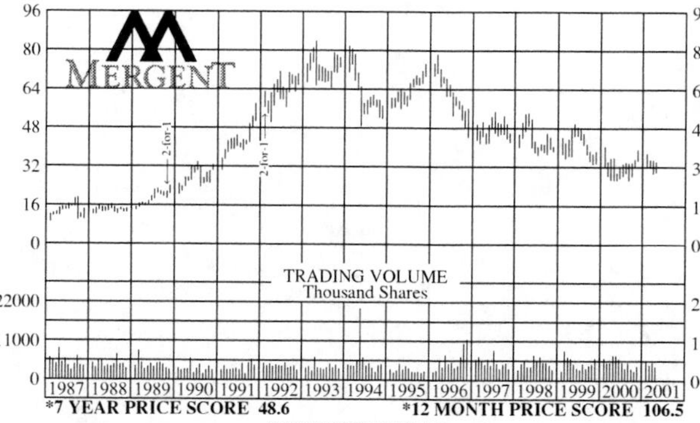

*7 YEAR PRICE SCORE 48.6 *12 MONTH PRICE SCORE 106.5

*NYSE COMPOSITE INDEX=100

INTERIM EARNINGS (Per Share):

Qtr.	Mar.	June	Sept.	Dec.
1997	0.43	0.55	0.49	d0.28
1998	0.29	0.64	0.02	d0.13
1999	0.53	0.73	0.59	0.57
2000	0.52	0.75	0.67	0.48

INTERIM DIVIDENDS (Per Share):

Amt.	Decl.	Ex.	Rec.	Pay.
0.08Q	9/12/00	9/27/00	10/01/00	10/31/00
0.08Q	12/05/00	12/27/00	1/01/01	1/31/01
0.08Q	2/12/01	3/28/01	4/01/01	4/30/01
0.08Q	5/03/01	6/27/01	7/01/01	7/31/01

Indicated div.: $0.32

CAPITALIZATION (12/31/00):

	($000)	(%)
Long-Term Debt	688,200	40.0
Deferred Income Tax	47,800	2.8
Minority Interest	34,600	2.0
Common & Surplus	949,700	55.2
Total	1,720,300	100.0

RECENT DEVELOPMENTS: For the year ended 12/31/00, net income slipped 9.0% to $127.0 million versus $139.6 million in 1999. Results for 2000 included a net special charge of $63.4 million for cost reduction efforts, a non-taxable gain of $60.4 million for the initial public offering of 43.0% stock of GLK's oil service subsidiary, OSCA, Inc. and a gain of $4.0 million for the sale of real estate. Results for 1999 included a special charge of $18.2 million. Net sales rose 11.3% to $1.67 billion.

PROSPECTS: Going forward, the Company expects to experience ongoing weakness in a number of end markets served by its polymer additives segment. As a result, the Company plans to increase productivity initiatives in its manufacturing facilities, focus on new product lines and tighten control over discretionary expenses. These initiatives should lower the Company's cost structure during a soft economic climate, while positioning GLK to increase its earnings growth as the markets recover.

BUSINESS

GREAT LAKES CHEMICAL CORP. is a producer of well-diversified specialty chemicals including flame retardants, polymer stabilizers, fire extinguishants, water treatment, and a growing line of performance and fine chemicals for the life sciences industry. Primary manufacturing operations are located in the U.S. and Europe. The principal markets include: computer and business equipment, consumer electronics, data processing, construction materials, telecommunications, pharmaceutical and pool and spa dealers and distributors. Revenues for 2000 were derived: polymer additives, 41.3%; performance chemicals, 22.1%; water treatment, 28.4%; energy services and products, 7.9%; and corporate and other, 0.3%. GLK's products are sold globally.

ANNUAL FINANCIAL DATA

	12/31/00	12/31/99	12/31/98	3 12/31/97	12/31/96	12/31/95	12/31/94
Earnings Per Share	6 2.42	5 2.42	4 0.95	2 1.19	3.94	4.52	1 4.00
Cash Flow Per Share	4.33	3.95	2.36	2.41	5.90	6.21	4.77
Tang. Book Val. Per Share	13.38	13.74	16.07	20.23	17.07	15.47	13.37
Dividends Per Share	0.32	0.32	0.48	0.62	0.54	0.42	0.38
Dividend Payout %	13.2	13.3	50.5	52.1	13.6	9.4	9.5
INCOME STATEMENT (IN MILLIONS):							
Total Revenues	1,670.5	1,453.3	1,394.3	1,311.2	2,211.7	2,361.1	2,110.7
Costs & Expenses	1,430.2	1,201.7	1,236.9	1,095.7	1,642.0	1,753.1	1,524.0
Depreciation & Amort.	100.1	89.5	83.5	73.7	124.4	110.6	102.3
Operating Income	140.2	162.1	73.9	141.8	445.4	497.3	438.7
Net Interest Inc./(Exp.)	...	...	...	...	...	...	d11.9
Income Before Income Taxes	164.9	175.4	66.2	117.2	379.2	437.9	402.7
Income Taxes	37.9	35.8	9.8	45.4	128.9	142.3	124.0
Equity Earnings/Minority Int.	...	...	...	...	30.1	d4.3	12.4
Net Income	6 127.0	5 139.6	4 56.4	2 71.8	250.3	295.6	1 278.7
Cash Flow	227.1	229.1	139.9	145.5	374.7	406.2	381.0
Average Shs. Outstg. (000)	52,500	58,000	59,200	60,298	63,539	65,364	69,659
BALANCE SHEET (IN MILLIONS):							
Cash & Cash Equivalents	222.7	478.3	411.6	73.7	202.3	181.0	144.7
Total Current Assets	1,007.8	1,167.5	995.6	668.5	1,177.2	1,125.0	979.7
Net Property	750.9	751.8	689.5	658.6	858.5	765.3	605.9
Total Assets	2,134.4	2,261.0	2,004.6	2,270.4	2,661.3	2,533.7	2,111.5
Total Current Liabilities	384.8	311.2	346.6	304.4	434.1	479.2	427.9
Long-Term Obligations	688.2	883.4	515.3	561.5	503.8	340.1	143.7
Net Stockholders' Equity	949.7	994.1	1,054.3	1,307.4	1,486.9	1,416.2	1,310.9
Net Working Capital	623.0	856.3	649.0	364.2	743.1	645.8	551.7
Year-end Shs. Outstg. (000)	50,300	54,400	58,400	58,944	61,613	64,607	67,297
STATISTICAL RECORD:							
Operating Profit Margin %	8.4	11.2	5.3	10.8	20.1	21.1	21.2
Net Profit Margin %	7.6	9.6	4.0	5.5	11.3	12.5	11.1
Return on Equity %	13.4	14.0	5.3	5.5	16.8	20.9	21.3
Return on Assets %	6.0	6.2	2.8	3.2	9.4	11.7	10.9
Price Range	40.50-26.50	50.00-33.19	54.19-36.69	54.88-41.50	78.63-44.25	74.63-55.75	82.00-48.75
P/E Ratio	16.7-10.9	20.7-13.7	57.0-38.6	46.1-34.9	20.0-11.2	16.5-12.3	20.5-12.2
Average Yield %	1.0	0.8	1.1	1.3	0.9	0.7	0.6

Statistics are as originally reported. 1 Incl. $0.15 per sh. one-time chg. to acct. adj. 2 Incl. $49.8 mill. pre-tax spl. chg. & $137.0 mill. est. loss of divest. 3 Refl. divest. of petro. add., furfural & deriv., Chemol, Four Seasons & Aquaterra businesses. 4 Incl. $129.0 mill. pre-tax restr. chgs. 5 Incl. $18.2 mill. in spl. chgs. 6 Incl. $63.4 mill. spl. chgs., $60.4 mill. non-tax gain & $4.0 mill. gain.

OFFICERS:
M. P. Bulriss, Chmn., Pres., C.E.O.
G. J. Heinlein, V.P., Treas., Asst. Sec.
S. E. Brewer, Asst. Treas.

INVESTOR CONTACT: Jeffrey Potrzebowski, Dir., Investor Relations, (317) 715-3000

PRINCIPAL OFFICE: 500 East 96th Street, Suite 500, Indianapolis, IN 46240

TELEPHONE NUMBER: (317) 715-3000
FAX: (317) 715-3050
WEB: www.greatlakeschem.com
NO. OF EMPLOYEES: 5,148 (approx.)
SHAREHOLDERS: 2,501 (approx.)
ANNUAL MEETING: In May
INCORPORATED: MI, 1933; reincorp., DE, Sept., 1933

INSTITUTIONAL HOLDINGS:
No. of Institutions: 201
Shares Held: 44,455,711
% Held: 88.4

INDUSTRY: Chemical preparations, nec (SIC: 2899)

TRANSFER AGENT(S): Computershare Investor Services, Chicago, IL

NYSE SYMBOL GMP
Rec. Pr. 15.02 (5/31/01)

GREEN MOUNTAIN POWER CORPORATION

YIELD 3.7%
P/E RATIO . . .

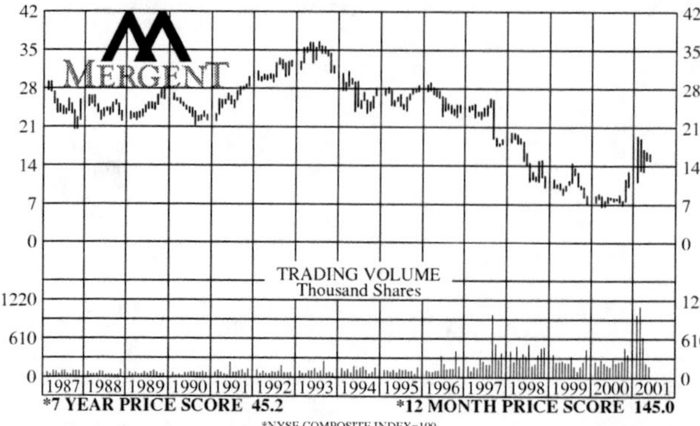

*7 YEAR PRICE SCORE 45.2 *12 MONTH PRICE SCORE 145.0
*NYSE COMPOSITE INDEX=100

INTERIM EARNINGS (Per Share):

Qtr.	Mar.	June	Sept.	Dec.
1997	0.58	0.17	0.59	0.23
1998	d0.66	0.18	0.31	d0.63
1999	0.50	d0.10	d0.02	0.07
2000	0.63	d0.80	0.36	d0.24

INTERIM DIVIDENDS (Per Share):

Amt.	Decl.	Ex.	Rec.	Pay.
0.138Q	5/17/00	6/13/00	6/15/00	6/30/00
0.138Q	8/07/00	9/12/00	9/14/00	9/30/00
0.138Q	12/04/00	12/12/00	12/14/00	12/29/00
0.138Q	2/05/01	3/13/01	3/15/01	3/30/01
0.138Q	4/09/01	6/14/01	6/18/01	6/29/01

Indicated div.: $0.55 (Div. Reinv. Plan)

CAPITALIZATION (12/31/00):

	($000)	(%)
Long-Term Debt	72,100	34.5
Capital Lease Obligations	6,449	3.1
Deferred Income Tax	25,644	12.3
Redeemable Pfd. Stock	12,560	6.0
Common & Surplus	92,044	44.1
Total	208,797	100.0

RECENT DEVELOPMENTS: For the year ended 12/31/00, GMP reported a loss from continuing operations of $709,000 versus net income of $3.1 million in 1999. Results for 2000 included a pre-tax charge of $3.2 million for disallowed regulatory litigation costs from a settlement agreement. Results for 2000 and 1999 excluded a loss of $6.5 million and $7.3 million, respectively, from the disposal of discontinued operations. Operating revenues rose 10.5% to $277.3 million.

PROSPECTS: The Vermont Public Service Board approved an agreement between GMP and the Department of Public Service to increase electric rates by 3.42% and to make permanent two earlier temporary rate increases. In addition, GMP is allowed full recovery of costs related to its long-term power and energy contract with Hydro-Quebec. As a result, GMP expects to earn its 11.25% rate of return in 2001 and 2002. Under the settlement, GMP has agreed not to seek a further rate increase.

BUSINESS

GREEN MOUNTAIN POWER CORPORATION is a Vermont-based energy services company. Serving 82,700 electric customers, GMP generates electricity and distributes it to wholesale and retail customers; GMP offers energy-efficiency programs and electrotechnology services to its customers. The Company's Mountain Energy subsidiary invests in renewable-resource projects throughout the U.S. GMP has ownership interest in facilities that supply 51% of its total power capacity of 396 megawatts. As of 12/31/00, GMP holds a 30% interest in the Vermont Electric Power Company, Inc., which owns nearly all of the transmission system that serves Vermont and that connects with the transmission system serving New England. In March 1998, the Company sold its Green Mountain Propane Gas subsidiary.

ANNUAL FINANCIAL DATA

	12/31/00	12/31/99	12/31/98	12/31/97	12/31/96	12/31/95	12/31/94
Earnings Per Share	**[2] [3] d0.06**	**[2] 0.57**	**[1] d0.80**	**1.57**	**2.22**	**2.26**	**2.23**
Cash Flow Per Share	**3.70**	**4.61**	**3.43**	**5.73**	**6.51**	**6.44**	**5.39**
Tang. Book Val. Per Share	**16.53**	**18.60**	**19.78**	**21.61**	**21.64**	**21.41**	**21.01**
Dividends Per Share	**0.55**	**0.55**	**0.96**	**1.61**	**2.12**	**2.12**	**2.12**
Dividend Payout %	**. . .**	**96.5**	**. . .**	**102.5**	**95.5**	**93.8**	**95.1**
INCOME STATEMENT (IN THOUSANDS):							
Total Revenues	277,326	251,048	184,304	179,323	179,009	161,544	148,197
Costs & Expenses	245,527	213,502	152,827	130,543	130,771	116,645	109,302
Depreciation & Amort.	20,597	21,630	22,182	21,289	21,185	19,816	14,518
Maintenance Exp.	6,633	6,728	5,190	4,785	4,463	4,210	4,465
Operating Income	4,569	9,188	4,105	22,706	22,590	20,873	19,912
Net Interest Inc./(Exp.)	d7,257	d7,183	d7,876	d7,650	d7,398	d7,426	d7,196
Income Taxes	cr691	1,242	cr1,367	7,191	6,463	5,578	5,395
Equity Earnings/Minority Int.	2,495	2,919	d28	427	2,880	3,513	3,112
Net Income	[2] [3] 709	[2] 4,216	[1] d2,877	9,438	11,959	11,503	11,002
Cash Flow	20,292	24,691	18,009	29,294	32,134	30,548	24,726
Average Shs. Outstg.	5,491	5,361	5,243	5,112	4,933	4,747	4,588
BALANCE SHEET (IN THOUSANDS):							
Gross Property	304,945	295,750	290,160	284,409	271,139	257,796	245,233
Accumulated Depreciation	110,273	102,854	94,604	87,689	81,286	75,797	69,246
Net Property	194,924	193,149	196,769	207,504	201,079	193,477	187,316
Total Assets	316,608	299,751	309,385	325,733	324,539	313,282	294,611
Long-Term Obligations	78,549	88,838	96,196	101,542	103,906	100,912	85,245
Net Stockholders' Equity	92,044	100,645	106,755	114,377	111,554	106,408	101,319
Year-end Shs. Outstg.	5,567	5,410	5,313	5,195	5,037	4,850	4,678
STATISTICAL RECORD:							
Operating Profit Margin %	1.6	3.7	2.2	12.7	12.6	12.9	13.4
Net Profit Margin %	0.3	1.7	. . .	5.3	6.7	7.1	7.4
Net Inc./Net Property %	0.4	2.2	. . .	4.5	5.9	5.9	5.9
Net Inc./Tot. Capital %	0.3	1.9	. . .	3.7	4.6	4.8	5.1
Return on Equity %	0.8	4.2	. . .	8.3	10.7	10.8	10.9
Accum. Depr./Gross Prop. %	36.2	34.8	32.6	30.8	30.0	29.4	28.2
Price Range	13.00-6.56	14.50-7.06	20.06-10.00	26.25-17.56	29.13-22.75	28.63-23.88	31.25-23.38
P/E Ratio	. . .	25.4-12.4	. . .	16.7-11.2	13.1-10.2	12.7-10.6	14.0-10.5
Average Yield %	5.6	5.1	6.4	7.3	8.2	8.1	7.8

Statistics are as originally reported. [1] Incl. $5.2 mill. pre-tax disallow. chgs. & $3.2 mill. pre-tax chg. rel. to loss on lease of HQ. & oth. restr. chgs. [2] Excl. loss on disp. of ops. of $6.7 mill., 1999; $6.5 mill., 2000. [3] Incl. $3.2 mill. pre-tax chg.

OFFICERS:
T. P. Salmon, Chmn.
C. L. Dutton, Pres., C.E.O.
N. R. Brock, V.P., C.F.O., Treas., Sec.

INVESTOR CONTACT: Gayle McKinnon-Alexander, Mgr., Inv. Rel. (802) 655-8455

PRINCIPAL OFFICE: 163 Acorn Lane, Colchester, VT 05446

TELEPHONE NUMBER: (802) 864-5731
FAX: (802) 865-9974
WEB: www.gmpvt.com

NO. OF EMPLOYEES: 197 (avg.)

SHAREHOLDERS: 6,050

ANNUAL MEETING: In May

INCORPORATED: VT, Apr., 1893

INSTITUTIONAL HOLDINGS:
No. of Institutions: 40
Shares Held: 1,439,562
% Held: 25.8

INDUSTRY: Electric services (SIC: 4911)

TRANSFER AGENT(S): Mellon Investor Services, Ridgefield Park, NJ

NYSE SYMBOL GPT
Rec. Pr. 37.99 (5/31/01)

GREENPOINT FINANCIAL CORP.

YIELD 2.6%
P/E RATIO 16.3

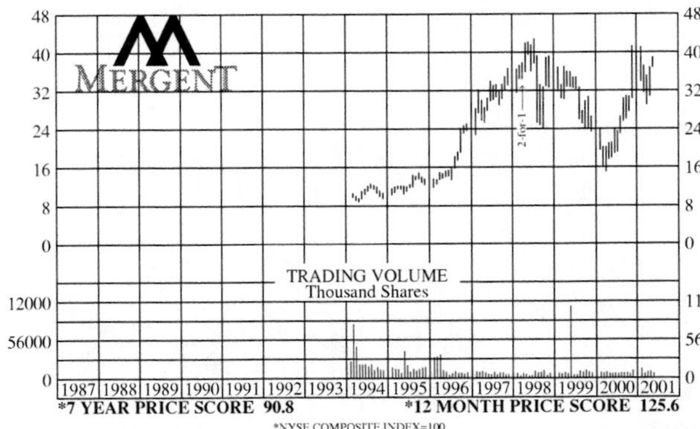

*7 YEAR PRICE SCORE 90.8 *12 MONTH PRICE SCORE 125.6
*NYSE COMPOSITE INDEX=100

INTERIM EARNINGS (Per Share):

Qtr.	Mar.	June	Sept.	Dec.
1997	0.47	0.43	0.47	0.49
1998	0.45	0.54	0.54	0.40
1999	0.36	0.61	0.63	0.62
2000	0.63	0.71	0.74	0.25

INTERIM DIVIDENDS (Per Share):

Amt.	Decl.	Ex.	Rec.	Pay.
0.25Q	5/09/00	5/17/00	5/19/00	6/06/00
0.25Q	7/11/00	7/19/00	7/21/00	9/06/00
0.25Q	11/14/00	11/21/00	11/24/00	12/06/00
0.25Q	2/13/01	2/21/01	2/23/01	3/09/01
0.25Q	5/08/01	5/16/01	5/18/01	6/05/01

Indicated div.: $1.00

CAPITALIZATION (12/31/00):

	($000)	(%)
Total Deposits	11,176,300	81.5
Long-Term Debt	287,500	2.1
Redeemable Pfd. Stock	199,700	1.5
Common & Surplus	2,049,600	14.9
Total	13,713,100	100.0

RECENT DEVELOPMENTS: For the year ended 12/31/00, net income declined to $213.1 million from $215.6 million in 1999. Results included restructuring charges of $4.9 million and $6.0 million in 2000 and 1999, respectively. Net interest income increased 6.2% to $573.4 million. Provision for loan losses more than doubled to $36.9 million from $14.2 million in 1999. Total non-interest income dropped 17.1% to $324.8 million.

PROSPECTS: Looking ahead, the Company expects the manufactured housing finance business to continue to be unstable. However, the Company is optimistic that its restructuring program, coupled with more stringent underwriting standards will help to reduce the exposure to future earnings. The Company anticipates contributions to earnings from the manufactured housing business to be smaller but more profitable going forward.

BUSINESS

GREENPOINT FINANCIAL CORPORATION is a bank holding company that conducts its business through three principal subsidiaries. GreenPoint Mortgage Funding originates adjustable and fixed-rate mortgage loans through a network of brokers, attorneys, bankers, and real estate professionals across the United States. GreenPoint Mortgage also originates commercial real estate loans in the New York metropolitan area. GreenPoint Credit originates, purchases, and services manufactured housing loans in 48 states, as of 12/31/00, and is the second largest lender nationally in the manufactured housing finance industry. GreenPoint Bank, a chartered savings bank, has over $11.00 billion in deposits in 74 full-service banking offices and over 100 ATMS serving more than 400,000 households in the Greater New York City area. In 1999, the Company acquired Headlands Mortgage Company.

LOAN DISTRIBUTION

(12/31/2000)	($000)	(%)
Mortgage Loans	8,116,200	93.3
Other Loans	580,200	6.7
Total	8,696,400	100.0

ANNUAL FINANCIAL DATA

	12/31/00	12/31/99	12/31/98	12/31/97	12/31/96	12/31/95	12/31/94
Earnings Per Share	**[3] 2.34**	**[3] 2.23**	**[1] 1.92**	**[2] 1.86**	**[2] 1.51**	**[2] 1.15**	**1.11**
Tang. Book Val. Per Share	**13.18**	**10.03**	**8.26**	**9.20**	**8.85**	**8.44**	**13.85**
Dividends Per Share	**1.00**	**0.88**	**0.64**	**0.50**	**0.40**	**0.40**	**0.30**
Dividend Payout %	**42.7**	**39.5**	**33.3**	**26.9**	**26.5**	**34.9**	**27.1**
INCOME STATEMENT (IN MILLIONS):							
Total Interest Income	1,185.9	1,090.8	986.8	972.7	974.0	696.5	563.8
Total Interest Expense	612.5	550.9	503.1	497.7	527.5	345.8	226.3
Net Interest Income	573.4	539.9	483.7	475.0	446.5	350.7	337.5
Provision for Loan Losses	36.9	14.2	13.8	18.9	15.7	9.5	32.3
Non-Interest Income	324.8	391.7	75.1	56.2	56.9	35.8	27.1
Non-Interest Expense	506.9	546.6	303.1	270.3	263.2	178.6	121.4
Income Before Taxes	354.4	370.8	241.9	242.0	224.5	198.4	210.9
Net Income	[3] 213.1	[3] 215.5	[1] 149.5	[2] 147.6	[2] 132.5	[2] 107.5	112.9
Average Shs. Outstg. (000)	91,200	96,500	77,800	79,300	...	...	...
BALANCE SHEET (IN MILLIONS):							
Cash & Due from Banks	139.9	179.5	156.0	93.2	81.9	153.7	28.3
Securities Avail. for Sale	2,774.0	2,066.5	1,337.6	2,032.7	4,355.4	5,896.5	265.0
Total Loans & Leases	8,696.4	9,308.2	9,400.3	8,935.8	7,447.5	6,022.4	5,758.4
Allowance for Credit Losses	122.0	128.0	127.2	140.2	153.2	163.8	164.3
Net Loans & Leases	8,574.4	9,180.2	9,273.1	8,795.6	7,294.3	5,858.6	5,594.1
Total Assets	15,764.8	15,401.1	13,970.3	13,083.5	13,325.6	14,670.5	6,955.0
Total Deposits	11,176.3	11,560.1	11,173.1	10,973.0	11,452.3	12,898.3	5,223.5
Long-Term Obligations	287.5	199.9	199.9	199.8	...	...	...
Total Liabilities	13,715.2	13,414.4	12,174.0	11,813.9	11,865.8	13,119.2	5,433.8
Net Stockholders' Equity	2,049.6	1,986.7	1,796.3	1,269.6	1,459.8	1,551.3	1,521.2
Year-end Shs. Outstg. (000)	89,950	104,203	94,642	75,300	94,488	104,434	109,784
STATISTICAL RECORD:							
Return on Equity %	10.4	10.8	8.3	11.6	9.1	6.9	7.4
Return on Assets %	1.4	1.4	1.1	1.1	1.0	0.7	1.6
Equity/Assets %	13.0	12.9	12.9	9.7	11.0	10.6	21.9
Non-Int. Exp./Tot. Inc. %	56.7	58.7	54.5	51.1	52.4	46.1	33.3
Price Range	41.31-15.00	37.13-23.31	42.88-24.00	36.75-22.75	25.13-11.75	14.88-10.19	12.63-8.75
P/E Ratio	17.7-6.4	16.6-10.5	22.3-12.5	19.8-12.2	16.6-7.8	13.0-8.9	11.4-7.9
Average Yield %	3.6	2.9	1.9	1.7	2.2	3.2	2.8

Statistics are as originally reported. Adj. for 2-for-1 stk. spl., 3/98. [1] Incl. non-recurr. personnel exp. $8.3 mill. [2] Incl. restruct. chrg. 1997, $2.5 mill..; 1995, $8.0 mill.; credit, 1996, $1.6 mill. [3] Incl. restruct. chrg., 2000, $4.9 mill.; 1999, $6.0 mill.

OFFICERS:
T. S. Johnson, Chmn., C.E.O.
P. T. Paul, Vice-Chmn.
B. B. Bhatt, Pres., C.O.O.
J. R. Leeds, Exec. V.P., C.F.O.

INVESTOR CONTACT: Investor Relations, (212) 834-1000

PRINCIPAL OFFICE: 90 Park Avenue, New York, NY 10016

TELEPHONE NUMBER: (212) 834-1000
FAX: (212) 834-1400
WEB: www.greenpoint.com

NO. OF EMPLOYEES: 3,817 full-time; 92 part-time

SHAREHOLDERS: 3,935 (approx.)

ANNUAL MEETING: In May

INCORPORATED: DE, Aug., 1993

INSTITUTIONAL HOLDINGS:
No. of Institutions: 205
Shares Held: 59,495,127
% Held: 58.9

INDUSTRY: Savings institutions, except federal (SIC: 6036)

TRANSFER AGENT(S): Mellon Investor Services, New York, NY

NYSE SYMBOL GPI
Rec. Pr. 25.50 (5/31/01)

GROUP 1 AUTOMOTIVE, INC.

YIELD ...
P/E RATIO 13.5

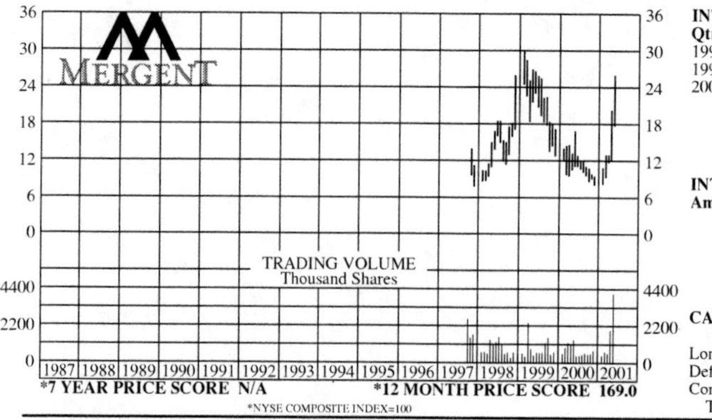

*7 YEAR PRICE SCORE N/A *12 MONTH PRICE SCORE 169.0

*NYSE COMPOSITE INDEX=100

INTERIM EARNINGS (Per Share):

Qtr.	Mar.	June	Sept.	Dec.
1998	0.20	0.31	0.35	0.29
1999	0.31	0.42	0.48	0.35
2000	0.40	0.54	0.54	0.41

INTERIM DIVIDENDS (Per Share):

Amt.	Decl.	Ex.	Rec.	Pay.

No dividends paid.

CAPITALIZATION (12/31/00):

	($000)	(%)
Long-Term Debt	140,393	35.4
Deferred Income Tax	8,668	2.2
Common & Surplus	247,416	62.4
Total	396,477	100.0

RECENT DEVELOPMENTS: For the year ended 12/31/00, net income climbed 21.8% to $40.8 million from $33.5 million the previous year. Total revenues jumped 43.0% to $3.59 billion from $2.51 billion a year earlier. New vehicle revenues surged 48.0%, while used vehicle revenues increased 34.0%. Gross profit was $527.4 million, or 14.7% of total revenues, versus $376.4 million, or 15.0% of total revenues, in the prior year. Income from operations rose 36.9% to $117.7 million from $86.0 million in 1999.

PROSPECTS: Going forward, operating profitability should benefit from the Company's focus on boosting sales of higher-margin used vehicles, parts and services, and other dealership operations. In addition, lower interest rates are expected to help fuel sales of new vehicles during the second half of 2001. Meanwhile, the Company is seeking several strategic acquisitions of dealerships in markets currently served. GPI is targeting dealerships with annual revenue of between $200.0 million and $300.0 million.

BUSINESS

GROUP 1 AUTOMOTIVE, INC. operates in the automotive retailing industry. As of 4/26/01, the Company owned 59 dealerships, comprised of 101 franchises and 22 collision service centers, located in Texas, Oklahoma, Florida, New Mexico, Georgia, Colorado, Louisiana and Massachusetts. The Company, through its dealerships and Internet sites, sells new and used cars and light trucks, provides maintenance and repair services, sells replacement parts and arranges related financing, vehicle service and insurance contracts.

REVENUES

(12/31/2000)	($000)	(%)
New Vehicle Sales	2,165,954	60.4
Used Vehicle Sales	1,003,759	28.0
Parts & Service Sales	306,089	8.5
Other Dealership Revenues	110,344	3.1
Total	3,586,146	100.0

ANNUAL FINANCIAL DATA

	12/31/00	12/31/99	12/31/98	12/31/97
Earnings Per Share	**1.88**	**1.55**	**1.16**	**0.76**
Cash Flow Per Share	**2.62**	**2.05**	**1.52**	**0.98**
Tang. Book Val. Per Share	...	...	**0.69**	**4.25**
INCOME STATEMENT (IN MILLIONS):				
Total Revenues	3,586.1	2,508.3	1,630.1	404.0
Costs & Expenses	3,452.4	2,411.8	1,571.6	392.7
Depreciation & Amort.	16.0	10.6	6.4	1.0
Operating Income	117.7	86.0	52.0	10.2
Net Interest Inc./(Exp.)	d53.0	d30.4	d16.9	4.0
Income Before Income Taxes	65.8	55.7	35.2	6.4
Income Taxes	25.0	22.2	14.5	0.6
Net Income	40.8	33.5	20.7	13.8
Cash Flow	56.9	44.1	27.1	14.8
Average Shs. Outstg. (000)	21,710	21,559	17,905	15,099
BALANCE SHEET (IN MILLIONS):				
Cash & Cash Equivalents	140.9	118.8	66.4	35.1
Total Current Assets	720.5	553.4	326.9	161.7
Net Property	70.9	46.7	22.0	21.6
Total Assets	1,099.6	842.9	477.7	213.1
Total Current Liabilities	665.8	473.3	278.7	111.5
Long-Term Obligations	140.4	113.2	42.8	7.1
Net Stockholders' Equity	247.4	232.0	136.2	89.4
Net Working Capital	54.8	80.1	48.3	50.2
Year-end Shs. Outstg. (000)	19,766	22,723	18,230	14,663
STATISTICAL RECORD:				
Operating Profit Margin %	3.3	3.4	3.2	2.5
Net Profit Margin %	1.1	1.3	1.3	3.4
Return on Equity %	16.5	14.4	15.2	15.4
Return on Assets %	3.7	4.0	4.3	6.5
Debt/Total Assets %	12.8	13.4	9.0	3.3
Price Range	16.88-8.06	30.00-12.75	26.00-8.63	13.94-7.75
P/E Ratio	9.0-4.3	19.4-8.2	22.4-7.4	18.3-10.2

Statistics are as originally reported.

OFFICERS:
B. B. Hollingsworth, Jr., Chmn., Pres., C.E.O.
S. L. Thompson, Sr. V.P., C.F.O., Treas.

PRINCIPAL OFFICE: 950 Echo Lane, Suite 100, Houston, TX 77024

TELEPHONE NUMBER: (713) 647-5700
FAX: (713) 647-5858
WEB: www.group1auto.com

NO. OF EMPLOYEES: 5,830 (approx.)

SHAREHOLDERS: 147

ANNUAL MEETING: In May

INCORPORATED: DE, Dec., 1995

INSTITUTIONAL HOLDINGS:
No. of Institutions: 67
Shares Held: 4,649,641
% Held: 23.6

INDUSTRY: New and used car dealers (SIC: 5511)

TRANSFER AGENT(S): Mellon Investor Services, Dallas, TX

NYSE SYMBOL GDT
Rec. Pr. 41.00 (4/30/01)

GUIDANT CORP.

YIELD ...
P/E RATIO 33.9

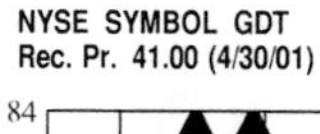

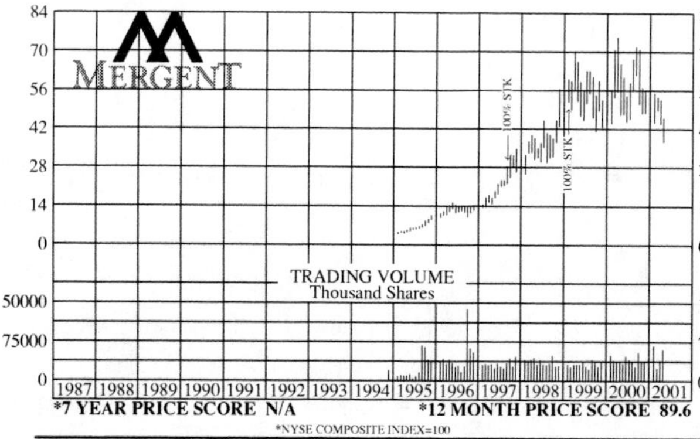

***7 YEAR PRICE SCORE N/A** ***12 MONTH PRICE SCORE 89.6**

*NYSE COMPOSITE INDEX=100

INTERIM EARNINGS (Per Share):

Qtr.	Mar.	June	Sept.	Dec.
1997	0.15	0.03	0.16	0.21
1998	0.19	0.27	d0.60	0.14
1999	0.17	0.31	0.32	0.31
2000	0.38	0.40	0.40	0.03

INTERIM DIVIDENDS (Per Share):

Amt.	Decl.	Ex.	Rec.	Pay.
	No dividends paid.			

CAPITALIZATION (12/31/00):

	($000)	(%)
Long-Term Debt	508,900	30.1
Common & Surplus	1,183,500	69.9
Total	1,692,400	100.0

RECENT DEVELOPMENTS: For the year ended 12/31/00, net income jumped 8.6% to $374.3 million versus income of $344.5 million, before the cumulative effect of a change in accounting principle, in the previous year. Results for 2000 and 1999 included non-recurring charges totaling $114.1 million and $91.0 million, respectively. Net sales climbed 8.3% to $2.55 billion from $2.35 billion the year before.

PROSPECTS: On 2/16/01, GDT launched its MULTI-LINK PLUS™ Coronary Stent System in Japan. GDT believes this product launch will add to the momentum its Vascular Intervention business is experiencing in Japan, which has been fueled by the recent launch of a full line of balloon dilation catheters. GDT expects sales growth throughout 2001 to result from contributions from its traditional product lines.

BUSINESS

GUIDANT CORPORATION is a multinational company that designs, develops, manufactures and markets a broad range of products for use in cardiac rhythm management (CRM), vascular intervention (VI), and other forms of minimally invasive systems (MIS). In CRM, GDT designs, manufactures and markets a full line of implantable pacemaker systems used in the treatment of slow or irregular arrhythmias. In VI, GDT is engaged in minimally invasive procedures for opening blocked coronary arteries. Also GDT develops, manufactures and markets products for use in MIS procedures with products for access, vision, dissection, retraction and fixation, focusing on laparoscopic market opportunities in general and cardiovascular surgeries.

QUARTERLY DATA

(12/31/2000)	REV	INC
1st Quarter	630,700	118,800
2nd Quarter	668,400	124,300
3rd Quarter	600,800	122,800
4th Quarter	648,800	8,400

ANNUAL FINANCIAL DATA

	12/31/00	12/31/99	12/31/98	12/31/97	12/31/96	12/31/95	12/31/94
Earnings Per Share	**5 1.21**	**4 1.11**	**3 d0.01**	**2 0.50**	**1 0.23**	**0.35**	...
Cash Flow Per Share	**1.64**	**1.49**	**0.24**	**0.72**	**0.46**	**0.59**	...
Tang. Book Val. Per Share	**1.75**	**0.65**	**1.02**	**1.30**	**0.84**	**0.30**	...
Dividends Per Share	...	...	**0.03**	**0.03**	**0.03**	**0.01**	...
Dividend Payout %	...	...	...	**5.0**	**11.0**	**3.6**	...
INCOME STATEMENT (IN MILLIONS):							
Total Revenues	2,548.7	2,352.3	1,897.0	1,328.2	1,048.5	931.3	862.4
Costs & Expenses	1,627.8	1,616.4	1,321.5	998.3	747.6	665.2	626.4
Depreciation & Amort.	133.1	119.7	72.9	66.0	66.2	67.8	64.7
Operating Income	787.8	616.2	521.7	279.4	255.5	221.4	191.7
Net Interest Inc./(Exp.)	d54.7	d55.6	d15.3	d19.5	d24.2	d30.2	d7.6
Income Before Income Taxes	595.8	528.0	127.6	248.8	149.5	169.8	155.9
Income Taxes	221.5	183.5	129.8	98.8	83.7	68.7	63.8
Net Income	5 374.3	4 344.5	3 d2.2	2 150.0	1 65.8	101.1	92.1
Cash Flow	507.4	464.2	70.7	216.0	132.0	168.9	156.8
Average Shs. Outstg. (000)	310,110	310,890	294,590	299,780	288,320	287,520	...
BALANCE SHEET (IN MILLIONS):							
Cash & Cash Equivalents	163.0	27.8	15.6	17.7	1.5	3.4	113.0
Total Current Assets	1,162.3	916.1	763.5	625.1	418.9	389.0	457.8
Net Property	575.5	514.5	389.2	326.1	321.0	316.4	294.8
Total Assets	2,521.4	2,250.2	1,569.5	1,225.0	1,003.9	1,057.4	1,103.6
Total Current Liabilities	709.2	738.5	587.2	541.3	308.0	278.7	341.0
Long-Term Obligations	508.9	527.7	390.0	80.0	233.5	385.0	473.0
Net Stockholders' Equity	1,183.5	867.3	553.9	581.8	448.2	384.2	264.4
Net Working Capital	453.1	177.6	176.3	83.8	110.9	110.3	116.8
Year-end Shs. Outstg. (000)	308,476	306,839	301,176	301,492	288,348	287,844	287,440
STATISTICAL RECORD:							
Operating Profit Margin %	30.9	26.2	27.5	21.0	24.4	23.8	22.2
Net Profit Margin %	14.7	14.6	...	11.3	6.3	10.9	10.7
Return on Equity %	31.6	39.7	...	25.8	14.7	26.3	34.8
Return on Assets %	14.8	15.3	...	12.2	6.6	9.6	8.3
Debt/Total Assets %	20.2	23.5	24.8	6.5	23.3	36.4	42.9
Price Range	75.38-44.00	69.88-41.00	56.50-25.50	34.75-13.41	15.34-9.88	10.66-3.88	...
P/E Ratio	62.3-36.4	62.9-36.9	...	69.5-26.8	67.3-43.3	30.3-11.0	...
Average Yield %	...	...	0.1	0.1	0.2	0.2	...

Statistics are as originally reported. Adj. for a 2-for-1 stock split 1/27/99 & 9/16/97. 1 Incl. nonrecur. pre-tax chg. of $66.9 mill. 2 Bef. acctg. chrg. $4.7 mill., incl. non-recurr. chrg. $22.6 mill. 3 Incl. a pre-tax chrg. of $309.2 mill. for litigat. settle. & the acqs. of InControl, Inc. and NeoCardia LLC. 4 Bef. acctg. chg. of $3.3 mill. but incl. pre-tax nonrecurr. chg. totaling $91.0 mill. from acqs. 5 Incl. nonrecurr. chrg. of $114.1 mill.

OFFICERS:
J. M. Cornelius, Chmn.
R. W. Dollens, Pres., C.E.O.
K. E. Brauer, V.P., C.F.O.

INVESTOR CONTACT: Andy Rieth, Inv. Rel., (317) 971-2061

PRINCIPAL OFFICE: 111 Monument Circle, 29th Floor, Indianapolis, IN 46204-0906

TELEPHONE NUMBER: (317) 971-2000
FAX: (317) 971-2040
WEB: www.guidant.com

NO. OF EMPLOYEES: 10,452

SHAREHOLDERS: 5,726 (approx. record)

ANNUAL MEETING: In May

INCORPORATED: IN, Sept., 1994

INSTITUTIONAL HOLDINGS:
No. of Institutions: 476
Shares Held: 249,953,182
% Held: 80.9

INDUSTRY: Surgical and medical instruments (SIC: 3841)

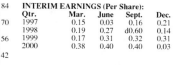

TRANSFER AGENT(S): First Chicago Trust Company of New York, a Division of EquiServe, Jersey City, NJ

NYSE SYMBOL GFD
Rec. Pr. 1.98 (5/31/01)

GUILFORD MILLS, INC.

YIELD ...
P/E RATIO ...

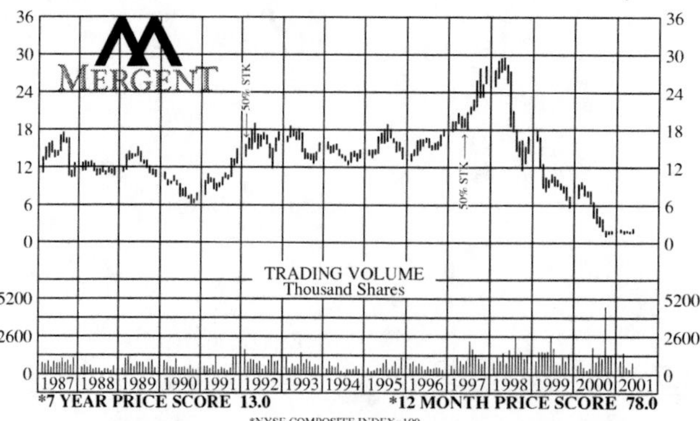

*7 YEAR PRICE SCORE 13.0 *12 MONTH PRICE SCORE 78.0
*NYSE COMPOSITE INDEX=100

INTERIM EARNINGS (Per Share):

Qtr.	Dec.	Mar.	June	Sept.
1996-97	0.25	0.34	0.66	0.66
1997-98	0.30	0.37	0.48	0.19
1998-99	0.10	0.21	0.04	0.11
1999-00	0.16	0.15	d0.14	d1.28
2000-01	d0.40	...	...	...

INTERIM DIVIDENDS (Per Share):

Amt.	Decl.	Ex.	Rec.	Pay.
0.11Q	7/26/99	8/04/99	8/06/99	8/18/99
0.11Q	11/04/99	11/10/99	11/15/99	11/29/99
0.11Q	1/24/00	2/01/00	2/03/00	2/15/00
0.11Q	4/26/00	5/02/00	5/04/00	5/16/00

CAPITALIZATION (10/1/00):

	($000)	(%)
Long-Term Debt	262,845	44.8
Deferred Income Tax	14,052	2.4
Common & Surplus	309,772	52.8
Total	586,669	100.0

RECENT DEVELOPMENTS: For the first quarter ended 12/31/00, net loss totaled $7.7 million compared with net income of $3.0 million in the 1999 quarter. Results for 2000 were reduced by plant restructuring expenses of $3.9 million. Also, earnings were negatively affected by lower sales volume and corresponding capacity underutilization. Net sales amounted to $173.6 million, a decline of 16.0% versus $206.5 million a year earlier.

PROSPECTS: The Company's sales are being negatively affected by declines in all four of its business segments due to stiff foreign competition, a poor retail market for apparel and home fashion customers and a worse-than-anticipated drop in domestic vehicle sales. Going forward, the Company expects to realize significant realignment savings in the second half of fiscal 2001.

BUSINESS

GUILFORD MILLS, INC. is a fabric producer that processes and sells warp knit, circular knit and woven velour fabric, as well as lace for apparel, home furnishings, automotive and industrial fabrics. GFD operates 17 production facilities in the United States and the United Kingdom. The Company creates its own fabric concept, then knits, dyes, prints, finishes, naps, shears, embosses, laminates, bonds and coats these fabrics for specific industries. Apparel fabric is manufactured to make robes and loungewear, sleepwear, dresswear, and swimwear. Fabrics for home furnishings include upholstery fabrics, window fashion fabrics, and fabrics for the bedding market. Fabrics supplied to the industrial markets include automotive upholstery, shoe-lining inserts, and paneling and seating fabrics.

REVENUES

(10/01/2000)	($000)	(%)
Apparel	292,467	35.9
Automotive	380,620	46.8
Home Fashions	95,529	11.7
Other	45,610	5.6
Total	814,226	100.0

ANNUAL FINANCIAL DATA

	10/1/00	10/3/99	9/27/98	9/28/97	9/29/96	10/1/95	[1] 10/2/94
Earnings Per Share	**d1.11**	**[3] 0.47**	**[2] 1.30**	**1.91**	**1.59**	**1.61**	**1.21**
Cash Flow Per Share	**2.31**	**3.41**	**3.81**	**4.54**	**4.18**	**3.83**	**3.17**
Tang. Book Val. Per Share	**16.14**	**17.76**	**16.58**	**15.88**	**13.75**	**12.64**	**11.75**
Dividends Per Share	**0.22**	**0.44**	**0.44**	**0.43**	**0.40**	**0.40**	**0.40**
Dividend Payout %	...	**93.6**	**33.8**	**22.5**	**25.2**	**24.9**	**33.0**
INCOME STATEMENT (IN THOUSANDS):							
Total Revenues	814,226	856,838	894,534	894,709	830,320	782,518	703,700
Costs & Expenses	770,026	762,297	767,471	748,539	703,305	667,992	611,528
Depreciation & Amort.	64,692	64,633	63,951	59,561	55,389	46,710	40,282
Operating Income	d20,492	29,908	63,112	86,609	71,626	67,816	51,890
Net Interest Inc./(Exp.)	d18,882	d16,598	d12,414	d16,190	d17,017	d14,122	d12,428
Income Before Income Taxes	d32,982	12,155	49,106	65,810	50,969	50,188	38,911
Income Taxes	cr12,008	1,925	15,960	22,572	16,991	16,552	13,787
Net Income	d20,974	[3] 10,230	[2] 33,146	43,238	33,978	33,636	25,124
Cash Flow	43,718	74,863	97,097	102,799	89,367	80,346	65,406
Average Shs. Outstg.	18,899	21,962	25,477	22,653	21,372	20,975	20,664
BALANCE SHEET (IN THOUSANDS):							
Cash & Cash Equivalents	23,874	22,554	30,447	24,349	31,448	17,964	6,110
Total Current Assets	322,859	338,741	361,909	348,617	351,888	285,927	263,969
Net Property	297,425	312,415	326,941	308,523	309,964	244,592	242,510
Total Assets	724,212	753,431	789,457	729,796	728,830	586,371	565,338
Total Current Liabilities	109,749	211,081	150,631	134,643	174,230	107,694	110,804
Long-Term Obligations	262,845	146,137	176,872	134,560	209,435	166,368	164,611
Net Stockholders' Equity	309,772	340,945	385,177	408,896	298,059	267,549	244,060
Net Working Capital	213,110	127,660	211,278	213,974	177,658	178,233	153,165
Year-end Shs. Outstg.	19,194	19,200	23,226	25,757	21,684	21,164	20,769
STATISTICAL RECORD:							
Operating Profit Margin %	...	3.5	7.1	9.7	8.6	8.7	7.4
Net Profit Margin %	...	1.2	3.7	4.8	4.1	4.3	3.6
Return on Equity %	...	3.0	8.6	10.6	11.4	12.6	10.3
Return on Assets %	...	1.4	4.2	5.9	4.7	5.7	4.4
Debt/Total Assets %	36.3	19.4	22.4	18.4	28.7	28.4	29.1
Price Range	9.75-1.00	18.00-5.63	29.63-11.50	28.25-17.75	18.17-13.00	18.92-13.33	16.08-12.33
P/E Ratio	...	38.3-12.0	22.8-8.8	14.8-9.3	11.4-8.2	11.8-8.3	13.3-10.2
Average Yield %	4.1	3.7	2.1	1.9	2.6	2.5	2.8

Statistics are as originally reported. Adj. for stk. split: 3-for-2, 5/97 [1] Results are for 15 months due to fiscal year change [2] Bef. extraord. chrg. of $2.9 mill., but incl. $6.5 mill. of plant restr. costs. [3] Incl. non-recurr. chrg. 10/3/99, $1.2 mill.; 6/28/92, $3.8 mill.

OFFICERS:
C. A. Hayes, Chmn.
J. A. Emrich, Pres., C.E.O.
K. A. Thompson, V.P., C.F.O.
M. E. Cook, Treas.

INVESTOR CONTACT: Jamie Vasquez, (336) 316-4462

PRINCIPAL OFFICE: 4925 West Market Street, Greensboro, NC 27407

TELEPHONE NUMBER: (336) 316-4000
FAX: (336) 316-4059
WEB: www.guilfordmills.com

NO. OF EMPLOYEES: 5,929

SHAREHOLDERS: 443

ANNUAL MEETING: In Feb.

INCORPORATED: DE, Aug., 1971

INSTITUTIONAL HOLDINGS:
No. of Institutions: 22
Shares Held: 5,851,784
% Held: 30.5

INDUSTRY: Lace & warp knit fabric mills (SIC: 2258)

TRANSFER AGENT(S): Wachovia Shareholder Service c/o EquiServe, LP, Boston, MA

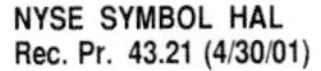

NYSE SYMBOL HAL
Rec. Pr. 43.21 (4/30/01)

HALLIBURTON COMPANY

YIELD 1.2%
P/E RATIO 102.9

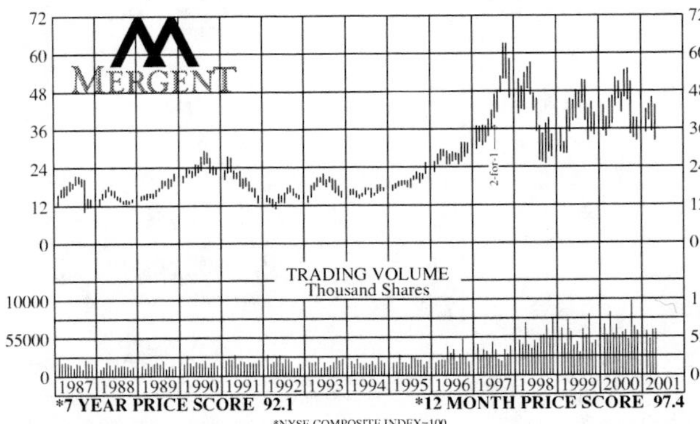

*7 YEAR PRICE SCORE 92.1 *12 MONTH PRICE SCORE 97.4

*NYSE COMPOSITE INDEX=100

INTERIM EARNINGS (Per Share):

Qtr.	Mar.	June	Sept.	Dec.
1996	0.18	0.29	0.30	0.43
1997	0.33	0.40	0.47	0.56
1998	0.44	0.51	d1.20	0.15
1999	0.18	0.19	0.13	0.17
2000	0.06	0.12	0.29	d0.05

INTERIM DIVIDENDS (Per Share):

Amt.	Decl.	Ex.	Rec.	Pay.
0.125Q	5/16/00	5/30/00	6/01/00	6/22/00
0.125Q	7/20/00	9/01/00	9/06/00	9/27/00
0.125Q	10/26/00	11/28/00	11/30/00	12/21/00
0.125Q	2/15/01	2/27/01	3/01/01	3/22/01
0.125Q	5/15/01	6/04/01	6/06/01	6/27/01

Indicated div.: $0.50

CAPITALIZATION (12/31/00):

	($000)	(%)
Long-Term Debt	1,049,000	20.9
Minority Interest	38,000	0.8
Common & Surplus	3,928,000	78.3
Total	5,015,000	100.0

RECENT DEVELOPMENTS: For the year ended 12/31/00, income from continuing operations totaled $188.0 million compared with income from continuing operations of $174.0 million a year earlier. Results for 2000 included a pre-tax charge related to the engineering and construction businesses of $193.0 million, of which $36.0 million related to severance and restructuring and $157.0 million for project losses. Results for 1999 included a special credit of $47.0 million.

PROSPECTS: On 4/10/01, HAL announced the completion of the sale of Dresser Equipment Group to an investor group consisting primarily of First Reserve Corporation and Odyssey Investment Partners, LLC in a transaction valued at $1.55 billion. Separately, HAL has initiated a reorganization of its Engineering and Construction Group segment that includes the closing of several facilities and the consolidation of all engineering and construction activities under the Engineering and Construction Group.

BUSINESS

HALLIBURTON COMPANY provides a variety of services, equipment, maintenance, and engineering and construction to energy, industrial and governmental customers. The Energy Services Group segment (66.3% of 2000 revenues) consists of Halliburton Energy Services, Brown & Root Energy Services, and Landmark Graphics. This segment provides a range of services and products to customers for the exploration, development and production of oil and gas. The segment serves independent, integrated, and national oil companies. The Engineering and Construction Group segment (33.7%), consisting of Kellogg Brown & Root and Brown & Root Services, provides a range of services to energy and industrial customers and governmental entities worldwide. On 9/29/98, HAL completed the acquisition of Dresser Industries, Inc. On 4/10/01, HAL completed the sale of Dresser Equipment Group (DEG) to an investor group consisting primarily of First Reserve Corporation and Odyssey Investment Partners, LLC in a transaction valued at $1.55 billion. HAL retained a 5.1% ownership interest in DEG as part of the transaction.

ANNUAL FINANCIAL DATA

	12/31/00	12/31/99	12/31/98	12/31/97	12/31/96	12/31/95	12/31/94
Earnings Per Share	**[5] 0.42**	**[4] 0.67**	**[1] d0.03**	**[2] 1.75**	**[2] 1.19**	**[3] 1.02**	**0.78**
Cash Flow Per Share	**1.55**	**2.02**	**1.30**	**2.94**	**2.25**	**2.15**	**1.92**
Tang. Book Val. Per Share	**7.80**	**7.96**	**7.48**	**8.62**	**7.68**	**6.74**	**7.58**
Dividends Per Share	**0.50**	**0.50**	**0.50**	**0.50**	**0.50**	**0.50**	**0.50**
Dividend Payout %	**119.0**	**74.6**	**...**	**28.6**	**42.0**	**49.0**	**64.1**
INCOME STATEMENT (IN MILLIONS):							
Total Revenues	11,944.0	14,898.0	17,353.1	8,818.6	7,385.1	5,698.7	5,740.5
Costs & Expenses	10,979.0	13,649.0	16,369.6	cr309.5	6,699.3	cr12.8	5,243.9
Depreciation & Amort.	503.0	599.0	587.0	309.5	267.9	259.1	261.6
Operating Income	462.0	650.0	396.5	798.1	417.9	383.2	235.0
Net Interest Inc./(Exp.)	d121.0	d68.0	d109.0	54.4	d9.9	d18.4	d30.9
Income Before Income Taxes	335.0	555.0	278.8	766.3	404.2	366.6	290.9
Income Taxes	129.0	214.0	244.4	300.0	103.3	131.9	112.9
Equity Earnings/Minority Int.	d18.0	d43.0	d49.1	11.9	d0.5	d0.9	d0.2
Net Income	[5] 188.0	[4] 298.0	[1] d14.7	[2] 454.4	[2] 300.4	[3] 233.8	177.8
Cash Flow	691.0	897.0	572.3	763.9	568.3	492.9	439.4
Average Shs. Outstg. (000)	446,000	443,000	438,800	259,500	252,200	229,000	228,400
BALANCE SHEET (IN MILLIONS):							
Cash & Cash Equivalents	231.0	466.0	202.6	221.3	213.6	174.9	647.1
Total Current Assets	5,568.0	6,022.0	6,083.1	2,971.6	2,398.0	2,049.9	2,375.9
Net Property	2,410.0	2,791.0	2,921.6	1,662.7	1,291.6	1,111.2	1,076.8
Total Assets	10,103.0	10,728.0	11,112.0	5,603.0	4,436.6	3,646.6	5,268.3
Total Current Liabilities	3,826.0	3,693.0	4,003.7	1,772.9	1,504.7	1,156.1	929.6
Long-Term Obligations	1,049.0	1,056.0	1,369.7	538.9	200.0	200.0	643.1
Net Stockholders' Equity	3,928.0	4,287.0	4,061.2	2,584.7	2,159.2	1,749.8	1,942.2
Net Working Capital	1,742.0	2,329.0	2,079.4	1,198.7	893.3	893.8	1,446.3
Year-end Shs. Outstg. (000)	427,000	442,000	440,000	262,300	250,600	228,950	228,200
STATISTICAL RECORD:							
Operating Profit Margin %	3.9	4.4	2.3	9.1	5.7	6.7	4.1
Net Profit Margin %	1.6	2.0	...	5.2	4.1	4.1	3.1
Return on Equity %	4.8	7.0	...	17.6	13.9	13.4	9.2
Return on Assets %	1.9	2.8	...	8.1	6.8	6.4	3.4
Debt/Total Assets %	10.4	9.8	12.3	9.6	4.5	5.5	12.2
Price Range	55.19-32.25	51.75-28.13	57.25-25.00	63.25-29.69	31.81-22.38	25.44-16.44	18.63-13.94
P/E Ratio	131.4-76.8	77.2-42.0	...	36.1-17.0	26.7-18.8	24.9-16.1	23.9-17.9
Average Yield %	1.1	1.3	1.2	1.1	1.8	2.4	3.1

Statistics are as originally reported. Adj. for 2-for-1 stk. split, 6/97 [1] Incl. pre-tax chrgs. of $980.1 mil [2] Incl. pre-tax chrg. 12/31/97, $8.6 mil; chrg. 12/31/96, $85.8 mil [3] Bef. loss fr. disc. ops. of $65.5 mil [4] Incl. gain of $47.0 mil; bef. acctg. chrg. of $19.0 mil & cr. of $159.0 mil [5] Incl. pre-tax chrg. of $193.0 mil; bef. inc. fr. disc. ops. of $313.0 mil

OFFICERS:
D. J. Lesar, Chmn., Pres., C.E.O.
D. C. Vaughn, Vice-Chmn.
G. V. Morris, Exec. V.P., C.F.O.

INVESTOR CONTACT: Guy T. Marcus, V.P., Investor Relations, (214) 978-2691

PRINCIPAL OFFICE: 3600 Lincoln Plaza, 500 North Akard Street, Dallas, TX 75201

TELEPHONE NUMBER: (214) 978-2600
FAX: (214) 978-2611
WEB: www.halliburton.com

NO. OF EMPLOYEES: 93,000 (approx.)

SHAREHOLDERS: 25,800 (approx.)

ANNUAL MEETING: In May

INCORPORATED: DE, July, 1924

INSTITUTIONAL HOLDINGS:
No. of Institutions: 573
Shares Held: 323,640,856
% Held: 75.5

INDUSTRY: Highway and street construction (SIC: 1611)

TRANSFER AGENT(S): Mellon Investor Services, Ridgefield, NJ

NYSE SYMBOL HKF
Rec. Pr. 9.14 (5/31/01)

HANCOCK FABRICS, INC.

YIELD 1.8%
P/E RATIO 14.1

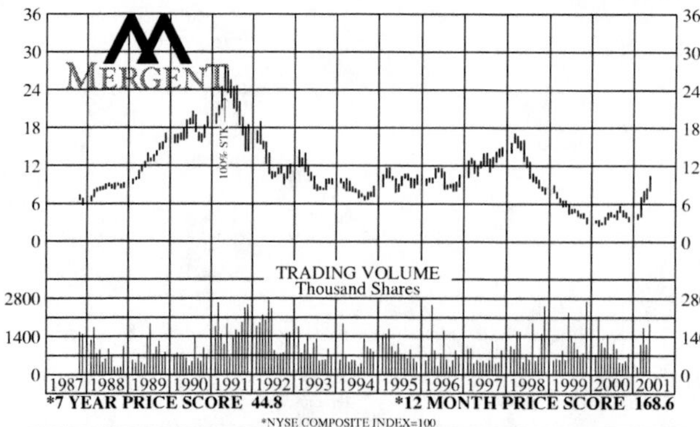

INTERIM EARNINGS (Per Share):

Qtr.	Apr.	July	Oct.	Jan.
1996-97	0.08	0.06	0.18	0.26
1997-98	0.11	0.08	0.23	0.30
1998-99	0.10	0.02	0.18	d0.14
1999-00	0.06	d0.04	0.14	0.22
2000-01	0.12	0.03	0.19	0.31

INTERIM DIVIDENDS (Per Share):

Amt.	Decl.	Ex.	Rec.	Pay.
0.025Q	3/15/00	3/29/00	4/01/00	4/15/00
0.025Q	6/15/00	6/28/00	7/01/00	7/15/00
0.025Q	9/06/00	9/27/00	10/01/00	10/15/00
0.025Q	12/08/00	12/27/00	1/01/01	1/15/01
0.04Q	3/04/01	3/28/01	4/01/01	4/15/01

Indicated div.: $0.16

CAPITALIZATION (1/28/01):

	($000)	(%)
Long-Term Debt	16,000	16.2
Common & Surplus	82,552	83.8
Total	98,552	100.0

RECENT DEVELOPMENTS: For the 52 weeks ended 1/28/01, net earnings jumped 59.4% to $10.9 million from $6.8 million in the corresponding period a year earlier. Sales rose 1.0% to $385.2 million from $381.6 million in the previous year. Comparable-store sales increased 2.0% year-over-year. Gross profit totaled $195.8 million, or 50.8% of sales, up 5.4% compared with $185.9 million, or 48.7% of sales, the year before. Earnings before taxes advanced 60.1% to $17.1 million from $10.7 million a year earlier.

PROSPECTS: HKF is aggressively expanding its store-within-a-store home-decorating alliance with Waverly Fabrics. The Company expects 150 of its stores will have these departments by the end of 2001, up from 37 stores at the end of 2000. HKF also plans to continue expanding its selection of special-occasion and quilting merchandise. Meanwhile, results may benefit from new store growth during 2001, which should boost efficiencies from HKF's existing support and distribution operations.

BUSINESS

HANCOCK FABRICS, INC. is a retail and wholesale merchant of fabrics, crafts and related home sewing accessories. As of 1/28/01, the Company operated 443 stores in 42 states under the names Hancock Fabrics, Minnesota Fabrics, Fabric Market, Fabric Warehouse and Northwest Fabrics & Crafts, and supplied more than 100 independent wholesale customers. Products include fashion piece goods, patterns, notions, crafts, home decoration items and bridal items. The Company also offers a broad selection of drapery and upholstery fabrics. As a wholesaler of fabrics, HKF also sells to independent retail fabric stores through its wholesale distribution facility. On 11/1/97, the Company acquired 48 Northwest Fabrics & Crafts stores from Silas Creek Retail, L.P.

QUARTERLY DATA

(01/28/2001) ($000)	REV	INC
1st Quarter	98,123	2,183
2nd Quarter	86,046	582
3rd Quarter	99,864	3,066
4th Quarter	101,212	5,036

ANNUAL FINANCIAL DATA

	1/28/01	1/30/00	1/31/99	2/1/98	2/2/97	1/28/96	1/29/95
Earnings Per Share	**0.65**	**0.38**	**1 0.18**	**0.72**	**0.59**	**0.42**	**0.48**
Cash Flow Per Share	**1.09**	**0.72**	**0.45**	**0.93**	**0.88**	**0.68**	**0.73**
Tang. Book Val. Per Share	**2.83**	**4.12**	**4.15**	**5.05**	**4.94**	**4.67**	**4.54**
Dividends Per Share	**0.10**	**0.40**	**0.40**	**0.34**	**0.32**	**0.32**	**0.32**
Dividend Payout %	**15.4**	**105.2**	**222.1**	**47.2**	**54.2**	**76.2**	**66.7**
INCOME STATEMENT (IN THOUSANDS):							
Total Revenues	385,245	381,572	392,303	381,910	378,218	364,192	366,816
Costs & Expenses	358,507	362,352	380,029	352,361	350,893	342,070	342,424
Depreciation & Amort.	7,462	6,190	5,411	4,545	6,086	5,464	5,336
Operating Income	19,276	13,030	6,863	25,004	21,239	16,658	19,056
Net Interest Inc./(Exp.)	d2,223	d2,380	d1,273	d162	d957	d1,937	d2,230
Income Before Income Taxes	17,053	10,650	5,590	24,842	20,282	14,721	16,826
Income Taxes	6,186	3,834	2,034	9,518	7,801	5,770	6,687
Net Income	10,867	6,816	1 3,556	15,324	12,481	8,951	10,139
Cash Flow	18,329	13,006	8,967	19,869	18,567	14,415	15,475
Average Shs. Outstg.	16,815	18,056	19,997	21,317	21,137	21,294	21,118
BALANCE SHEET (IN THOUSANDS):							
Cash & Cash Equivalents	3,891	6,904	6,959	7,057	6,870	5,026	3,855
Total Current Assets	144,814	152,721	154,578	164,797	160,786	174,386	179,836
Net Property	25,616	26,947	23,833	18,989	17,845	19,462	21,673
Total Assets	192,729	195,562	192,404	195,558	187,843	201,835	208,622
Total Current Liabilities	64,937	58,686	55,860	55,949	57,828	51,482	56,041
Long-Term Obligations	16,000	31,000	29,000	10,000	3,000	30,000	37,000
Net Stockholders' Equity	82,552	76,867	77,152	106,691	105,273	100,421	97,089
Net Working Capital	79,877	94,035	98,718	108,848	102,958	122,904	123,795
Year-end Shs. Outstg.	29,190	18,652	18,595	21,114	21,314	21,508	21,380
STATISTICAL RECORD:							
Operating Profit Margin %	5.0	3.4	1.7	6.5	5.6	4.6	5.2
Net Profit Margin %	2.8	1.8	0.9	4.0	3.3	2.5	2.8
Return on Equity %	13.2	8.9	4.6	14.4	11.9	8.9	10.4
Return on Assets %	5.6	3.5	1.8	7.8	6.6	4.4	4.9
Debt/Total Assets %	8.3	15.9	15.1	5.1	1.6	14.9	17.7
Price Range	5.69-2.44	8.94-2.88	17.13-7.50	15.00-10.13	11.75-8.00	11.75-7.75	10.00-6.50
P/E Ratio	8.7-3.8	23.5-7.6	95.1-41.6	20.8-14.1	19.9-13.6	28.0-18.4	20.8-13.5
Average Yield %	2.5	6.8	3.2	2.7	3.2	3.3	3.9

Statistics are as originally reported. 1 Incl. $6.3 mil ($0.34/sh) after-tax non-recur. chg.

OFFICERS:
L. G. Kirk, Chmn., C.E.O.
J. W. Busby Jr., Pres., C.O.O.
B. D. Smith, Sr. V.P., C.F.O., Treas.

INVESTOR CONTACT: Ellen J. Kennedy, (662) 842-2834

PRINCIPAL OFFICE: 3406 W. Main St., Tupelo, MS 38801

TELEPHONE NUMBER: (662) 842-2834
WEB: www.hancockfabrics.com

NO. OF EMPLOYEES: 6,500 (approx.)

SHAREHOLDERS: 6,919

ANNUAL MEETING: In June

INCORPORATED: DE, 1987

INSTITUTIONAL HOLDINGS:
No. of Institutions: 53
Shares Held: 8,573,657
% Held: 49.8

INDUSTRY: Sewing, needlework, and piece goods (SIC: 5949)

TRANSFER AGENT(S): Continental Stock Transfer & Trust Co., New York, NY

NYSE SYMBOL HDL
Rec. Pr. 12.15 (5/31/01)

HANDLEMAN COMPANY

YIELD ...
P/E RATIO 8.0

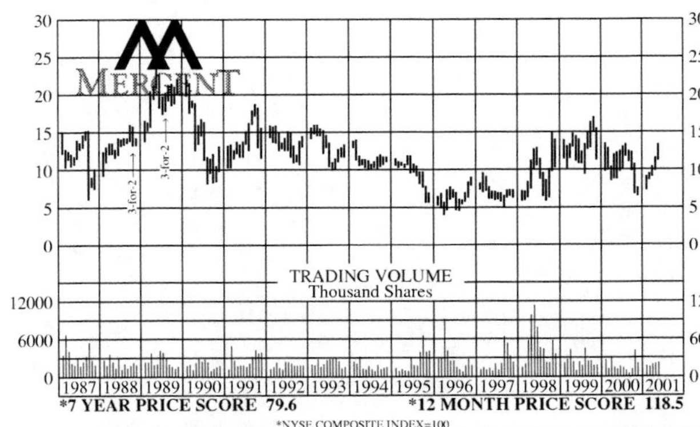

*7 YEAR PRICE SCORE 79.6 *12 MONTH PRICE SCORE 118.5
*NYSE COMPOSITE INDEX=100

INTERIM EARNINGS (Per Share):

Qtr.	July	Oct.	Jan.	Apr.
1996-97	d0.24	0.20	0.19	0.01
1997-98	d0.19	0.25	0.21	d0.26
1998-99	d1.86	0.19	0.18	0.39
1999-00	0.02	0.45	0.50	0.35
2000-01	0.06	0.51	0.60	...

INTERIM DIVIDENDS (Per Share):

Amt.	Decl.	Ex.	Rec.	Pay.

Last dist. $0.05Q, 1/10/96

CAPITALIZATION (4/29/00):

	($000)	(%)
Long-Term Debt	33,986	13.2
Common & Surplus	223,282	86.8
Total	257,268	100.0

RECENT DEVELOPMENTS: For the three months ended 1/31/01, net income grew 10.9% to $16.3 million from $14.7 million a year earlier. Revenues rose 1.7% to $349.0 million from $343.2 million the year before. Handleman Entertainment Resources' sales inched up to $314.4 million from $312.1 million in the prior year, while North Coast Entertainment's sales increased 9.6% to $38.8 million from $35.4 million in the previous year. As a percentage of sales, gross profit was essentially unchanged at 23.5% compared with the third quarter of fiscal 2000.

PROSPECTS: Long-term results are expected to benefit from the Company's international expansion efforts and the development of several strategic initiatives. On 2/1/01, the Company began category management, distribution and service to 241 ASDA stores located in the United Kingdom, which is expected to add $100.0 million in sales annually going forward. HDL is also making significant progress implementing new e-business initiatives, including the completion of a new e-fulfillment center in Reno, Nevada and the placement of test kiosks in retail stores.

BUSINESS

HANDLEMAN COMPANY operates in two business segments: Handleman Entertainment Resources (H.E.R.) and North Coast Entertainment (NCE). H.E.R. is a category manager and distributor of prerecorded music to mass merchants in the United States, Canada, United Kingdom, Mexico and Brazil. H.E.R. provides various merchandising services to retail accounts such as direct-to-store shipments, marketing and in-store merchandising. NCE is comprised of three companies. Anchor Bay Entertainment is a major independent home video label. Madacy Entertainment, a major independent record label, markets music and video products. In addition, NCE owns 75% of The itsy bitsy Entertainment Company, Inc., which licenses and markets entertainment for preschoolers, including the Teletubbies. In July, 1998, HDL sold its software publishing subsidiary, Sofsource, Inc., and its book distribution business.

ANNUAL FINANCIAL DATA

	4/29/00	5/1/99	5/2/98	5/3/97	4/27/96	4/29/95	4/30/94
Earnings Per Share	**1.30**	**1 d1.11**	**1 0.01**	**0.16**	**1 d0.67**	**1 0.84**	**0.83**
Cash Flow Per Share	**1.98**	**d0.46**	**1.01**	**1.22**	**0.43**	**1.78**	**1.78**
Tang. Book Val. Per Share	**7.52**	**7.27**	**8.56**	**8.50**	**8.35**	**9.29**	**8.96**
Dividends Per Share	...	...	...	**0.05**	**0.44**	**0.44**	**0.43**
Dividend Payout %	...	...	...	**31.2**	...	**52.4**	**51.8**
INCOME STATEMENT (IN MILLIONS):							
Total Revenues	1,137.6	1,058.6	1,104.5	1,181.0	1,132.6	1,226.1	1,066.6
Costs & Expenses	1,048.3	1,110.2	1,059.2	1,121.7	1,119.4	1,141.8	983.0
Depreciation & Amort.	20.1	20.5	32.7	35.3	36.9	31.8	31.7
Operating Income	69.2	d72.2	12.6	24.0	d23.7	52.5	51.9
Net Interest Inc./(Exp.)	d3.2	d8.1	d12.3	d11.0	d12.0	d8.0	d6.2
Income Before Income Taxes	66.0	d49.3	0.3	13.0	d35.7	44.4	45.6
Income Taxes	26.3	cr16.4	2.8	4.9	cr12.7	17.8	18.0
Equity Earnings/Minority Int.	d1.1	d2.2	2.8	d2.7	0.5	1.4	...
Net Income	38.6	1 d35.1	1 0.3	5.4	1 d22.5	1 28.0	27.7
Cash Flow	58.8	d14.6	33.0	40.7	14.4	59.8	59.4
Average Shs. Outstg. (000)	29,692	31,568	32,868	33,481	33,576	33,518	33,389
BALANCE SHEET (IN MILLIONS):							
Cash & Cash Equivalents	27.5	27.4	25.6	12.4	19.9	24.4	10.6
Total Current Assets	377.8	369.5	466.0	500.4	509.8	560.9	477.4
Net Property	51.9	53.4	78.7	95.7	111.4	124.8	112.0
Total Assets	519.7	487.9	613.1	667.9	693.9	754.1	641.0
Total Current Liabilities	248.1	216.8	219.1	239.4	264.5	290.0	261.2
Long-Term Obligations	34.0	39.9	114.8	135.5	143.6	146.2	76.4
Net Stockholders' Equity	223.3	225.7	273.8	283.7	279.6	311.7	299.5
Net Working Capital	129.7	152.7	246.9	260.9	245.3	271.0	216.1
Year-end Shs. Outstg. (000)	29,691	31,049	31,977	33,373	33,498	33,533	33,411
STATISTICAL RECORD:							
Operating Profit Margin %	6.1	...	1.1	2.0	...	4.3	4.9
Net Profit Margin %	3.4	...	...	0.5	...	2.3	2.6
Return on Equity %	17.3	...	0.1	1.9	...	9.0	9.2
Return on Assets %	7.4	...	0.1	0.8	...	3.7	4.3
Debt/Total Assets %	6.5	8.2	18.7	20.3	20.7	19.4	11.9
Price Range	17.00-9.38	15.00-5.81	9.63-5.13	9.00-4.00	11.88-5.63	14.00-10.00	16.00-9.88
P/E Ratio	13.1-7.2	...	953.0-507.4	56.2-25.0	...	16.7-11.9	19.3-11.9
Average Yield %	...	...	...	0.8	5.0	3.7	3.3

Statistics are as originally reported. 1 Incl. $127.4 mil pre-tax non-recur. chg. & $31.0 mil one-time pre-tax gain on sale of subsidiary, 1999; $11.2 mil after-tax restr. chg., 1998; $16 mil pre-tax chg., 1996; & $7.5 mil restr. chg., 1995.

OFFICERS:
S. Strome, Chmn., C.E.O.
P. J. Cline, Pres., C.O.O.
L. A. Brams, Sr. V.P., C.F.O., Sec.

INVESTOR CONTACT: Tim C. Oviatt, V.P. & Treas., (248) 362-4400

PRINCIPAL OFFICE: 500 Kirts Boulevard, Troy, MI 48084

TELEPHONE NUMBER: (248) 362-4400
FAX: (248) 362-3615
WEB: www.handleman.com

NO. OF EMPLOYEES: 2,500 (approx.)

SHAREHOLDERS: 3,240

ANNUAL MEETING: In Sept.

INCORPORATED: MI, July, 1979

INSTITUTIONAL HOLDINGS:
No. of Institutions: 79
Shares Held: 17,912,804
% Held: 66.5

INDUSTRY: Durable goods, nec (SIC: 5099)

TRANSFER AGENT(S): Fifth Third Bank, Cincinnati, OH

NYSE SYMBOL HC
Rec. Pr. 36.40 (4/30/01)

HANOVER COMPRESSOR CO.

YIELD ...
P/E RATIO 41.4

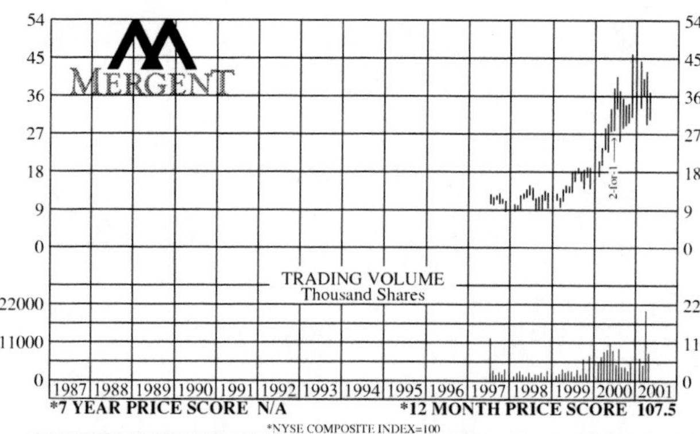

*7 YEAR PRICE SCORE N/A *12 MONTH PRICE SCORE 107.5
*NYSE COMPOSITE INDEX=100

INTERIM EARNINGS (Per Share):

Qtr.	Mar.	June	Sept.	Dec.
1997	0.14	0.14	0.17	0.20
1998	0.21	0.23	0.27	0.30
1999	0.29	0.28	0.34	0.42
2000	0.18	0.20	0.23	0.27

INTERIM DIVIDENDS (Per Share):

Amt.	Decl.	Ex.	Rec.	Pay.
2-for-1	5/18/00	6/14/00	5/30/00	6/13/00

CAPITALIZATION (12/31/00):

	($000)	(%)
Long-Term Debt	110,935	11.8
Deferred Income Tax	105,369	11.2
Redeemable Pfd. Stock	86,250	9.2
Common & Surplus	639,993	67.9
Total	942,547	100.0

RECENT DEVELOPMENTS: For the year ended 12/31/00, net income improved 45.2% to $58.7 million versus $40.4 million in the previous year. Total revenues jumped 86.8% to $603.8 million compared with $323.2 million in the prior year. Results were enhanced by continued strength of the compression outsourcing segment, a favorable operating environment for the energy industry and strong contributions from recent acquisitions. Rentals income rose 32.1% to $254.5 million.

PROSPECTS: Looking ahead, results should continue to benefit from strong growth in the compression and gas handling industries coupled with continued growth in the outsourcing business in the U.S. and international markets. In addition, the Company expects strong contributions from recent acquisitions to continue in 2001. Meanwhile, the Company completed the acquisition of OEC Compression for about $101.1 million in stock, including the assumption of about $62.1 million of debt.

BUSINESS

HANOVER COMPRESSOR CO. is a provider of a broad array of natural gas compression, gas handling and related services in the United States and across the Western Hemisphere, including Argentina, Venezuela, Mexico and Canada. The Company operates the largest compressor rental fleet, in terms of horsepower, in the gas compression industry and provides on a rental, contract compression, maintenance and acquisition leaseback services. HC's maintenance business supplies parts and services to customers who own their own compression equipment but want to outsource their compression operations. HC's compression services are complemented by the Company compressor and oil and gas production equipment fabrication operations and gas processing, gas treatment, gas measurement and power generation services. As of 12/31/00, the Company had a fleet of 4,840 compression rental units with an aggregate capacity of 2.2 million horsepower.

ANNUAL FINANCIAL DATA

	12/31/00	12/31/99	12/31/98	12/31/97	12/31/96	12/31/95	12/31/94
Earnings Per Share	**0.88**	**1 1.32**	**1 1.01**	**0.66**	**0.15**	**0.30**	**0.30**
Cash Flow Per Share	**1.58**	**2.58**	**2.27**	**1.73**	**1.09**	**1.16**	**0.89**
Tang. Book Val. Per Share	**7.49**	**12.84**	**11.08**	**10.16**	**7.72**	**6.87**	**...**
INCOME STATEMENT (IN MILLIONS):							
Total Revenues	603.8	317.0	282.0	198.8	136.0	96.0	56.1
Costs & Expenses	448.5	206.4	182.6	129.3	90.9	68.4	38.6
Depreciation & Amort.	53.4	38.2	38.0	29.3	21.3	13.9	8.5
Operating Income	98.4	72.4	61.4	40.1	23.8	13.7	9.0
Net Interest Inc./(Exp.)	d8.5	d8.8	d11.7	d10.7	d6.6	d4.6	d2.0
Income Before Income Taxes	93.5	63.6	49.6	29.4	17.2	9.1	7.0
Income Taxes	34.8	23.1	19.3	11.3	6.8	3.5	2.6
Equity Earnings/Minority Int.	3.5	...	...	...	...	...	...
Net Income	58.7	1 40.4	1 30.4	18.1	10.4	5.6	4.4
Cash Flow	112.1	78.7	68.4	47.4	24.7	18.7	12.9
Average Shs. Outstg. (000)	71,192	30,527	30,091	27,345	22,730	16,145	14,392
BALANCE SHEET (IN MILLIONS):							
Cash & Cash Equivalents	45.5	5.8	11.5	4.6	7.3	3.0	...
Total Current Assets	498.3	192.5	165.1	94.8	66.6	45.0	...
Net Property	583.6	497.5	392.5	394.1	266.4	198.1	...
Total Assets	1,289.5	756.5	614.6	506.5	341.4	252.3	...
Total Current Liabilities	188.3	84.6	51.8	36.8	25.1	21.7	...
Long-Term Obligations	110.9	69.7	156.9	158.8	122.8	50.5	...
Net Stockholders' Equity	640.0	369.2	316.7	288.3	176.9	139.3	...
Net Working Capital	309.9	108.0	113.3	58.0	41.5	23.3	...
Year-end Shs. Outstg. (000)	66,455	28,753	28,590	28,367	22,907	20,265	...
STATISTICAL RECORD:							
Operating Profit Margin %	16.4	22.8	21.8	20.2	17.5	14.2	16.1
Net Profit Margin %	9.8	12.8	10.8	9.1	7.6	5.9	7.8
Return on Equity %	9.2	11.0	9.6	6.3	5.9	4.0	...
Return on Assets %	4.6	5.3	4.9	3.6	3.0	2.2	...
Debt/Total Assets %	8.6	9.2	25.5	31.4	36.0	20.0	...
Price Range	46.06-16.91	19.19-9.63	14.81-8.66	13.00-8.56	...	...	...
P/E Ratio	52.3-19.2	14.5-7.3	14.7-8.6	19.7-13.0	...	...	...

Statistics are as originally reported. Adj. for 2-for-1 stk. spl., 6/00 1 Incl. gain on sale of prop., plt. & equip., 1999, $5.9 mill.; 1998, $2.6 mill.

OFFICERS:
M. A. O'Connor, Chmn.
M. J. McGhan, Pres., C.E.O.
W. S. Goldberg, Exec. V.P., C.F.O., Treas.

INVESTOR CONTACT: Investor Relations, (281) 447-8787

PRINCIPAL OFFICE: 12001 North Houston Rosslyn, Houston, TX 77086

TELEPHONE NUMBER: (281) 447-8787
FAX: (281) 441-0821
WEB: www.hanover.com

NO. OF EMPLOYEES: 2,700 (approx.)

SHAREHOLDERS: 321 (approx.)

ANNUAL MEETING: In May

INCORPORATED: DE, Oct., 1990

INSTITUTIONAL HOLDINGS:
No. of Institutions: 175
Shares Held: 37,577,150
% Held: 54.4

INDUSTRY: Equipment rental & leasing, nec (SIC: 7359)

TRANSFER AGENT(S): Mellon Investor Services, Dallas, TX

NYSE SYMBOL H
Rec. Pr. 58.00 (5/31/01)

HARCOURT GENERAL, INC.

YIELD 1.4%
P/E RATIO 26.0

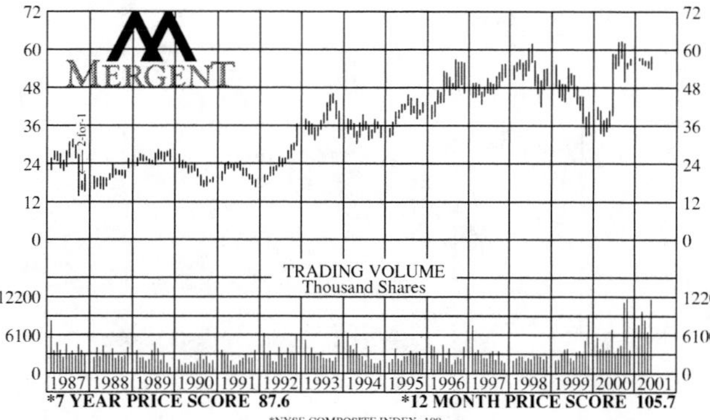

INTERIM EARNINGS (Per Share):

Qtr.	Jan.	Apr.	July	Oct.
1996-97	0.20	0.04	d2.00	0.11
1997-98	d0.21	d0.25	1.54	0.87
1998-99	d0.28	d0.33	1.95	0.97
1999-00	d0.47	d0.57	2.35	1.12
2000-01	d0.67	...	...	...

INTERIM DIVIDENDS (Per Share):

Amt.	Decl.	Ex.	Rec.	Pay.
0.21Q	6/16/00	7/12/00	7/14/00	7/31/00
0.21Q	9/29/00	10/10/00	10/12/00	10/31/00
0.21Q	12/14/00	1/10/01	1/12/01	1/31/01
0.21Q	3/14/01	4/10/01	4/13/01	4/30/01

Indicated div.: $0.84 (Div. Reinv. Plan)

CAPITALIZATION (10/31/00):

	($000)	(%)
Long-Term Debt	1,250,453	60.4
Deferred Income Tax	75,489	3.6
Preferred Stock	727	0.0
Common & Surplus	743,261	35.9
Total	2,069,930	100.0

RECENT DEVELOPMENTS: For the quarter ended 1/31/01, the Company reported a net loss of $48.6 million compared with a net loss of $33.4 million the previous year. Results in the prior-year period included an after-tax gain of $4.8 million from the sale of securities. Total revenues grew 1.0% to $407.1 million from $402.9 million the year before. Operating loss was $54.4 million versus an operating loss of $36.0 million a year earlier.

PROSPECTS: In October 2000, the Company entered into a definitive agreement to be acquired by Reed Elsevier for approximately $5.60 billion, including the assumption of about $1.20 billion of debt. On 5/7/01, Reed Elsevier announced that the U.S. Department of Justice will not challenge its acquisition of the Company. The transaction, subject to regulatory clearance from the U.K., has received clearance from authorities in Germany, Austria and Ireland.

BUSINESS

HARCOURT GENERAL, INC. (formerly General Cinema) operates through Harcourt, Inc., a publisher of textbooks and other materials for educational institutions, as well as scientific, technical, medical and professional books and journals, fiction, non-fiction, and children's books; National Education Corp., a provider of distance education in vocational, academic and professional studies, a developer of interactive media-based learning products and a publisher of supplemental education materials; and Drake Beam Morin, a provider of human resources management consulting services. On 10/22/99, the Company spun off to shareholders its controlling interest in The Neiman Marcus Group, Inc.

BUSINESS LINE ANALYSIS

(10/31/2000)	Rev(%)	Inc(%)
Education Group	31.3	41.2
Higher Education Group	15.0	12.8
Corporate & Prof. Services	22.7	10.4
Worldwide STM Group	31.0	35.6
Total	100.0	100.0

ANNUAL FINANCIAL DATA

	10/31/00	10/31/99	10/31/98	10/31/97	10/31/96	10/31/95	10/31/94
Earnings Per Share	**[1] 2.50**	**[1] [2] 1.67**	**1.96**	**[1] d1.64**	**2.62**	**[2] 2.31**	**[1] [2] 1.22**
Cash Flow Per Share	**5.96**	**5.21**	**6.21**	**3.22**	**5.10**	**4.60**	**3.27**
Tang. Book Val. Per Share	...	...	...	...	**8.10**	**6.84**	**8.00**
Dividends Per Share	**0.84**	**0.81**	**0.77**	**0.73**	**0.69**	**0.65**	**0.61**
Dividend Payout %	**33.6**	**48.5**	**39.3**	...	**26.3**	**28.1**	**50.0**
INCOME STATEMENT (IN MILLIONS):							
Total Revenues	2,408.2	2,142.6	4,235.3	3,691.6	3,289.9	3,034.7	3,154.2
Costs & Expenses	1,787.9	1,607.5	3,518.1	3,354.1	2,764.8	2,541.1	2,766.8
Depreciation & Amort.	252.7	255.5	306.2	343.2	180.4	175.7	163.1
Operating Income	367.7	279.6	410.9	d5.7	344.7	317.9	224.4
Net Interest Inc./(Exp.)	d78.9	d94.4	d103.4	d65.3	d55.6	d48.8	d72.0
Income Before Income Taxes	288.8	185.2	307.5	d71.0	289.2	269.1	152.4
Income Taxes	106.8	68.5	116.8	38.2	98.3	91.5	54.9
Equity Earnings/Minority Int.	0.9	3.7	d49.0	d5.9	...	...	...
Net Income	[1] 182.8	[1] [2] 120.3	141.6	[1] d115.1	190.9	[2] 177.6	[1] [2] 97.5
Cash Flow	435.5	375.8	447.8	228.1	371.2	353.3	260.6
Average Shs. Outstg. (000)	73,050	72,168	72,141	70,812	72,770	76,764	79,809
BALANCE SHEET (IN MILLIONS):							
Cash & Cash Equivalents	29.2	24.1	115.2	82.6	774.9	606.8	819.7
Total Current Assets	919.5	830.8	1,649.0	1,484.9	1,933.3	1,609.8	2,021.0
Net Property	125.3	128.8	645.2	593.9	574.9	540.3	521.7
Total Assets	3,079.8	2,950.1	4,449.1	3,781.4	3,326.2	2,884.3	3,242.4
Total Current Liabilities	854.9	693.6	1,124.6	993.3	948.3	745.0	875.0
Long-Term Obligations	1,250.5	1,356.8	1,729.5	1,275.1	702.0	780.7	1,123.3
Net Stockholders' Equity	744.0	641.9	925.7	845.5	1,033.5	941.1	1,047.4
Net Working Capital	64.6	137.2	524.5	491.6	984.9	864.8	1,146.0
Year-end Shs. Outstg. (000)	73,225	71,167	71,029	70,755	71,119	72,699	77,887
STATISTICAL RECORD:							
Operating Profit Margin %	15.3	13.1	9.7	...	10.5	10.5	7.1
Net Profit Margin %	7.6	5.6	3.3	...	5.8	5.9	3.1
Return on Equity %	24.6	18.7	15.3	...	18.5	18.9	9.3
Return on Assets %	5.9	4.1	3.2	...	5.7	6.2	3.0
Debt/Total Assets %	40.6	46.0	38.9	33.7	21.1	27.1	34.6
Price Range	62.81-32.63	55.50-32.81	61.94-41.88	55.69-42.63	57.00-38.00	45.75-32.38	39.50-30.25
P/E Ratio	25.1-13.0	33.2-19.6	31.6-21.4	...	21.8-14.5	19.8-14.0	32.4-24.8
Average Yield %	1.8	1.8	1.5	1.5	1.5	1.7	1.7

Statistics are as originally reported. [1] Incl. $9.8 mil ($0.13/sh) after-tax gain fr the sale of a business & $4.8 mil ($0.07/sh) after-tax gain fr the sale of securities, 2000; $3.9 mil ($0.05/sh) after-tax gain, 1999; $314.1 mil non-recur. chg., 1997; & $28.1 mil chg., 1994. [2] Bef. discont. opers. cr$63.5 mil ($0.88/sh), 1999; cr$11.7 mil, 1995; & cr$80 mil, 1994.

OFFICERS:
R. A. Smith, Chmn.
B. J. Knez, Co-C.E.O.
R. A. Smith, Co-C.E.O.
J. R. Cook, Sr. V.P., C.F.O.

INVESTOR CONTACT: Peter Farwell, V.P., Corp. Rel., (617) 232-8200

PRINCIPAL OFFICE: 27 Boylston Street, Chestnut Hill, MA 02467

TELEPHONE NUMBER: (617) 232-8200
FAX: (617) 739-0639
WEB: www.harcourtgeneral.com

NO. OF EMPLOYEES: 13,200 (approx.)

SHAREHOLDERS: 1,590 (Cl. B com.); 6,987 (com.)

ANNUAL MEETING: In Mar.

INCORPORATED: DE, 1950

INSTITUTIONAL HOLDINGS:
No. of Institutions: 227
Shares Held: 37,740,447
% Held: 51.5

INDUSTRY: Department stores (SIC: 5311)

TRANSFER AGENT(S): BankBoston, N.A., Boston, MA

NYSE SYMBOL JH
Rec. Pr. 21.72 (4/30/01)

HARLAND (JOHN H.) COMPANY

YIELD 1.4%
P/E RATIO 21.7

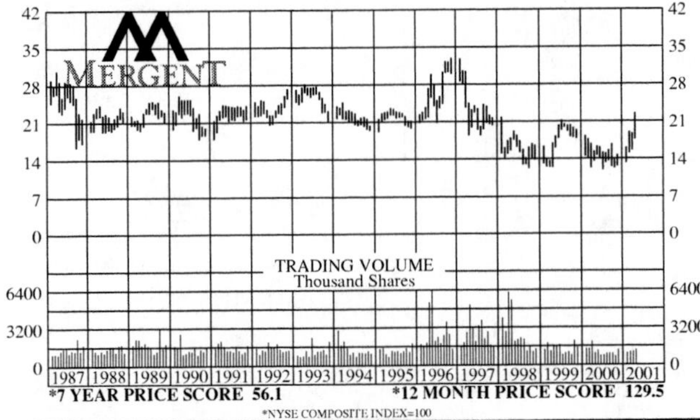

*7 YEAR PRICE SCORE 56.1 *12 MONTH PRICE SCORE 129.5

*NYSE COMPOSITE INDEX=100

INTERIM EARNINGS (Per Share):

Qtr.	Mar.	June	Sept.	Dec.
1997	0.16	0.21	0.16	0.03
1998	0.20	0.13	0.13	d1.12
1999	0.32	0.32	0.40	0.34
2000	0.40	0.43	0.16	0.01

INTERIM DIVIDENDS (Per Share):

Amt.	Decl.	Ex.	Rec.	Pay.
0.075Q	5/01/00	5/16/00	5/18/00	6/01/00
0.075Q	7/24/00	8/16/00	8/18/00	9/01/00
0.075Q	10/30/00	11/15/00	11/19/00	12/01/00
0.075Q	1/30/01	2/13/01	2/15/01	3/01/01
0.075Q	4/27/01	5/16/01	5/18/01	6/01/01

Indicated div.: $0.30 (Div. Reinv. Plan)

CAPITALIZATION (12/31/00):

	($000)	(%)
Long-Term Debt	191,617	52.8
Common & Surplus	171,365	47.2
Total	362,982	100.0

RECENT DEVELOPMENTS: For the year ended 12/31/00, net income fell 32.8% to $28.7 million compared with $42.7 million in 1999. Results for 2000 included a one-time charge of $8.2 million for acquired in-process research and development related to the acquisition of Concentrex Inc. and a restructuring charge of $14.5 million. Sales were $720.7 million, up 2.6% from $702.5 million in the prior year. Operating income decreased 17.4% to $60.4 million compared with $73.2 million in the previous year.

PROSPECTS: Results for the printed products business should benefit from ongoing technology upgrades, including the expanded use of digital technology in production facilities and improved processes. Future results should also benefit from the introduction of greater bottom-line accountability through the development of several competitive advantages in the printed products segment. Going forward, the Company plans to report earnings per share for 2001 in the range of $1.65 to $1.70.

BUSINESS

JOHN H. HARLAND COMPANY, a provider of software and printed products to the financial markets, operates in two segments. The Financial Services segment includes checks and bank forms, database marketing software, direct marketing services, and loan and deposit origination software sold primarily to financial institutions. The Scantron segment provides educational technology products and services primarily to the commercial, financial institution and education markets. Revenues (and operating income) for 2000 were derived: printed products, 78.7% (76.2%); software and services, 8.4% (8.1%); and Scantron, 12.9% (15.7%). On 8/23/00, JH acquired Concentrex Inc. for $143.0 million.

ANNUAL FINANCIAL DATA

	12/31/00	12/31/99	12/31/98	12/31/97	12/31/96	12/31/95	12/31/94
Earnings Per Share	**5 1.00**	**4 1.37**	**3 d0.66**	**2 0.56**	**1 d0.45**	**1.51**	**1.68**
Cash Flow Per Share	**2.68**	**2.66**	**0.70**	**1.80**	**0.93**	**3.11**	**3.04**
Tang. Book Val. Per Share	**1.00**	**3.76**	**3.03**	**2.49**	**1.78**	**2.91**	**3.34**
Dividends Per Share	**0.30**	**0.30**	**0.30**	**0.30**	**1.02**	**1.02**	**0.98**
Dividend Payout %	**30.0**	**21.9**	**...**	**53.6**	**...**	**67.5**	**58.3**
INCOME STATEMENT (IN MILLIONS):							
Total Revenues	720.7	702.5	566.7	562.7	609.4	561.6	521.3
Costs & Expenses	611.8	588.8	532.2	488.6	574.7	429.3	387.7
Depreciation & Amort.	48.5	40.6	42.4	39.3	42.7	48.3	41.5
Operating Income	60.4	73.2	d7.9	34.8	d8.1	83.2	92.0
Net Interest Inc./(Exp.)	d10.4	d7.2	d7.5	d8.4	d10.3	d8.7	d7.7
Income Before Income Taxes	54.3	68.5	d11.0	29.6	d15.5	76.9	85.1
Income Taxes	25.6	25.8	9.7	12.3	cr1.6	30.9	33.9
Net Income	5 28.7	4 42.7	3 d20.6	2 17.3	1 d13.9	46.8	51.2
Cash Flow	77.2	83.2	21.8	56.6	28.9	95.1	92.8
Average Shs. Outstg. (000)	28,832	31,261	31,089	31,446	30,951	30,558	30,517
BALANCE SHEET (IN MILLIONS):							
Cash & Cash Equivalents	18.5	49.8	42.5	13.0	22.8	13.3	15.3
Total Current Assets	168.0	153.0	159.4	148.4	148.4	144.2	117.2
Net Property	129.6	112.0	120.9	117.9	96.4	165.1	161.8
Total Assets	522.9	391.4	391.8	426.2	454.7	474.7	414.4
Total Current Liabilities	140.4	98.7	106.4	109.8	144.7	121.1	79.3
Long-Term Obligations	191.6	106.4	107.1	109.4	114.1	114.6	115.2
Net Stockholders' Equity	171.4	169.0	162.3	192.8	182.4	222.1	203.4
Net Working Capital	27.6	54.3	53.0	38.6	3.7	23.2	37.9
Year-end Shs. Outstg. (000)	28,524	28,644	31,093	31,058	30,924	30,655	30,439
STATISTICAL RECORD:							
Operating Profit Margin %	8.4	10.4	...	6.2	...	14.8	17.7
Net Profit Margin %	4.0	6.1	...	3.1	...	8.3	9.8
Return on Equity %	16.7	25.3	...	9.0	...	21.0	25.2
Return on Assets %	5.5	10.9	...	4.1	...	9.9	12.4
Debt/Total Assets %	36.6	27.2	27.3	25.7	25.1	24.1	27.8
Price Range	18.31-11.88	21.25-12.38	21.88-12.25	32.88-18.38	33.00-20.75	23.63-19.13	24.75-19.38
P/E Ratio	18.3-11.9	15.5-9.0	...	58.7-32.8	...	15.6-12.7	14.7-11.5
Average Yield %	2.0	1.8	1.8	1.2	3.8	4.8	4.4

Statistics are as originally reported. 1 Incl. $63.5 mill. after-tax restr. chgs. for in-process R&D. 2 Incl. $0.15/sh. for restr. & costs assoc. with develop. of printing equip. tech. & incl. $0.05/sh. gain fr. sale of bldgs. 3 Incl. $51.1 mill. loss fr. restr. chgs., $12.8 mill. loss fr. development chgs., & $10.9 mill. gain fr. sale of assets. 4 Incl. $0.03 per sh. tax benefit. 5 Incl. $8.2 mill. one-time in-process R&D chg. & $14.5 mill. restr. chg.

OFFICERS:
T. C. Tuff, Chmn., Pres., C.E.O.
C. B. Carden, V.P., Fin., C.F.O.
J. C. Walters, V.P., Sec., Gen. Couns.

INVESTOR CONTACT: Victoria P. Weyand, (770) 593-5128

PRINCIPAL OFFICE: 2939 Miller Rd., Decatur, GA 30335

TELEPHONE NUMBER: (770) 593-5127
FAX: (770) 593-5367
WEB: www.harland.net

NO. OF EMPLOYEES: 5,445 (avg.)

SHAREHOLDERS: 5,212

ANNUAL MEETING: In Apr.

INCORPORATED: GA, June, 1923

INSTITUTIONAL HOLDINGS:
No. of Institutions: 111
Shares Held: 20,350,789
% Held: 71.1

INDUSTRY: Blankbooks and looseleaf binders (SIC: 2782)

TRANSFER AGENT(S): First Chicago Trust Company of New York, Jersey City, NJ

NYSE SYMBOL HDI
Rec. Pr. 46.97 (5/31/01)

HARLEY-DAVIDSON, INC.

YIELD 0.3%
P/E RATIO 41.6

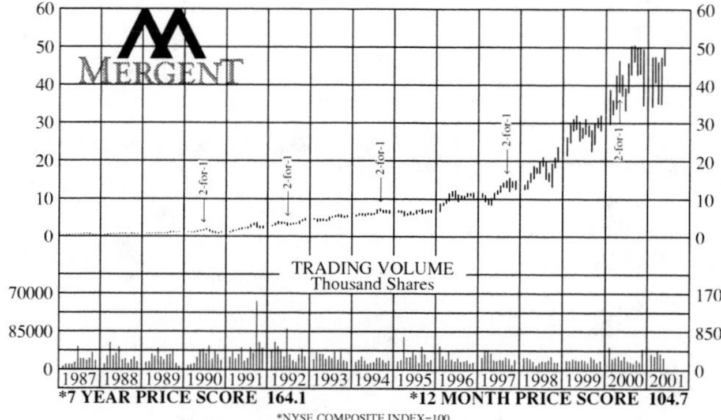

*7 YEAR PRICE SCORE 164.1 *12 MONTH PRICE SCORE 104.7

*NYSE COMPOSITE INDEX=100

INTERIM EARNINGS (Per Share):

Qtr.	Mar.	June	Sept.	Dec.
1996	0.11	0.14	0.11	0.13
1997	0.14	0.17	0.14	0.14
1998	0.18	0.18	0.17	0.20
1999	0.19	0.22	0.21	0.24
2000	0.26	0.29	0.27	0.31

INTERIM DIVIDENDS (Per Share):

Amt.	Decl.	Ex.	Rec.	Pay.
0.025Q	5/01/00	6/12/00	6/14/00	6/24/00
0.025Q	8/10/00	9/06/00	9/08/00	9/19/00
0.025Q	12/06/00	12/14/00	12/18/00	12/29/00
0.025Q	2/08/01	3/08/01	3/12/01	3/23/01
0.03Q	5/05/01	6/07/01	6/11/01	6/22/01

Indicated div.: $0.12 (Div. Reinv. Plan)

CAPITALIZATION (12/31/00):

	($000)	(%)
Long-Term Debt	355,000	20.0
Deferred Income Tax	15,633	0.9
Common & Surplus	1,405,655	79.1
Total	1,776,288	100.0

RECENT DEVELOPMENTS: For the year ended 12/31/00, net income jumped 30.1% to $347.7 million versus $267.2 million in the previous year. Results for 2000 included a pre-tax gain of $18.9 million. Net sales jumped 18.7% to $2.94 billion. Net sales of Harley-Davidson® motorcycles advanced 18.8% to $2.25 billion. Parts and accessories net sales grew 23.5% to $447.8 million, while general merchandise net sales rose 14.1% to $151.4 million. Buell® motorcycles net sales fell 8.5% to $58.1 million.

PROSPECTS: The Company increased its production target of Harley-Davidson® motorcycles by 2,000 units to 227,000 motorcycles for 2001. The Company's success in both the domestic and international markets is attributed to new products, a strong dealer network and targeted marketing programs. Going forward, the Company expects the growth rate for parts and accessories to increase at a faster pace than the motorcycle unit growth rate.

BUSINESS

HARLEY-DAVIDSON, INC. operates in two business segments. HDI's Motorcycles and Related Products segment consists primarily of the Company's wholly-owned subsidiaries, H-D Michigan, Inc., Harley-Davidson Motor Company and Buell Motorcycle Company. The Motorcycles segment designs, manufactures and sells primarily heavyweight touring, custom and sport motorcycles and a broad range of related products, which include motorcycle parts and accessories and general merchandise. The Financial Services segment, which is comprised of Harley-Davidson Financial Services, Inc., provides financing and insurance for HDI's dealers and customers.

QUARTERLY DATA

(12/31/00) ($000)	Rev	Inc
1st Quarter	681,100	80,200
2nd Quarter	755,000	90,600
3rd Quarter	714,100	83,000
4th Quarter	756,200	93,900

ANNUAL FINANCIAL DATA

	12/31/00	12/31/99	12/31/98	12/31/97	12/31/96	12/31/95	12/31/94
Earnings Per Share	**3 1.13**	**0.87**	**1 0.69**	**0.57**	**2 0.48**	**2 0.37**	**0.34**
Cash Flow Per Share	**1.56**	**1.23**	**0.97**	**0.79**	**0.66**	**0.51**	**0.46**
Tang. Book Val. Per Share	**4.47**	**3.65**	**3.20**	**2.59**	**2.05**	**1.51**	**1.42**
Dividends Per Share	**0.10**	**0.09**	**0.08**	**0.07**	**0.06**	**0.04**	**0.04**
Dividend Payout %	**8.6**	**10.1**	**11.2**	**11.9**	**11.6**	**12.2**	**10.2**
INCOME STATEMENT (IN MILLIONS):							
Total Revenues	2,943.5	2,480.6	2,084.2	1,774.9	1,539.0	1,354.1	1,541.8
Costs & Expenses	2,295.2	1,950.9	1,663.1	1,434.7	1,255.3	1,131.0	1,344.5
Depreciation & Amort.	133.3	113.8	87.4	70.2	55.3	42.3	36.9
Operating Income	515.0	415.9	333.6	270.0	228.4	180.8	160.3
Net Interest Inc./(Exp.)	17.6	8.0	3.8	7.9	3.3	0.1	. . .
Income Before Income Taxes	548.6	420.8	336.2	276.3	227.6	176.0	162.1
Income Taxes	200.8	153.6	122.7	102.2	84.2	64.9	57.8
Net Income	3 347.7	267.2	1 213.5	174.1	2 143.4	2 111.1	104.3
Cash Flow	481.1	381.0	300.9	244.2	198.7	153.4	141.2
Average Shs. Outstg. (000)	307,470	309,714	309,406	307,896	302,000	300,400	304,800
BALANCE SHEET (IN MILLIONS):							
Cash & Cash Equivalents	419.7	183.4	165.2	147.5	142.5	31.5	59.3
Total Current Assets	1,297.3	949.0	845.0	704.0	429.3	332.0	444.8
Net Property	754.1	681.7	627.8	528.9	409.4	284.8	262.8
Total Assets	2,436.4	2,112.1	1,920.2	1,598.9	1,320.0	1,000.7	778.3
Total Current Liabilities	497.7	518.2	468.5	361.7	263.6	233.2	350.3
Long-Term Obligations	355.0	280.0	280.0	280.0	258.1	164.3	9.4
Net Stockholders' Equity	1,405.7	1,161.1	1,029.9	826.7	662.7	494.6	435.0
Net Working Capital	799.5	430.8	376.4	342.3	165.7	98.8	94.5
Year-end Shs. Outstg. (000)	302,071	302,723	305,862	304,650	302,676	299,536	305,280
STATISTICAL RECORD:							
Operating Profit Margin %	17.5	16.8	16.0	15.2	14.8	13.4	10.4
Net Profit Margin %	11.8	10.8	10.2	9.8	9.3	8.2	6.8
Return on Equity %	24.7	23.0	20.7	21.1	21.6	22.5	24.0
Return on Assets %	14.3	12.7	11.1	10.9	10.9	11.1	13.4
Debt/Total Assets %	14.6	13.3	14.6	17.5	19.6	16.4	1.2
Price Range	50.63-29.53	32.03-21.38	23.75-12.47	15.63-8.34	12.38-6.59	7.53-5.50	7.47-5.41
P/E Ratio	44.8-26.1	37.0-24.7	34.4-18.1	27.6-14.8	26.0-13.9	20.3-14.9	21.8-15.8
Average Yield %	0.2	0.3	0.4	0.6	0.6	0.7	0.5

Statistics are as originally reported. Adj. for stk. splits: 2-for-1, 4/00, 9/97, 9/94. 1 Bef. extraord. loss $3.2 mill. ($0.03/sh.), 1998. 2 Bef. disc. opers. gain $1.4 mill., 1995; $22.6 mill., 1996. 3 Incl. non-recurr. gain $18.9 mill. fr. sale of Visa card bus.

OFFICERS:
J. L. Bleustein, Chmn., C.E.O.
J. L. Ziemer, V.P., C.F.O.
J. M. Brostowitz, V.P., Treas., Contr.
G. A. Lione, V.P., Sec., Gen. Couns.

INVESTOR CONTACT: Investor Relations, (877) 437-8625

PRINCIPAL OFFICE: 3700 West Juneau Avenue, Milwaukee, WI 53208

TELEPHONE NUMBER: (414) 342-4680
FAX: (414) 343-4621
WEB: www.harley-davidson.com

NO. OF EMPLOYEES: 8,180 (avg.)

SHAREHOLDERS: 70,942

ANNUAL MEETING: In May

INCORPORATED: DE, Apr., 1981; reincorp., WI, June, 1991

INSTITUTIONAL HOLDINGS:
No. of Institutions: 413
Shares Held: 203,613,354
% Held: 67.4

INDUSTRY: Motorcycles, bicycles, and parts (SIC: 3751)

TRANSFER AGENT(S): ComputerShare Investor Services, Chicago, IL

NYSE SYMBOL HAR
Rec. Pr. 31.75 (4/30/01)

HARMAN INTERNATIONAL INDUSTRIES, INC.

YIELD 0.3%
P/E RATIO 14.3

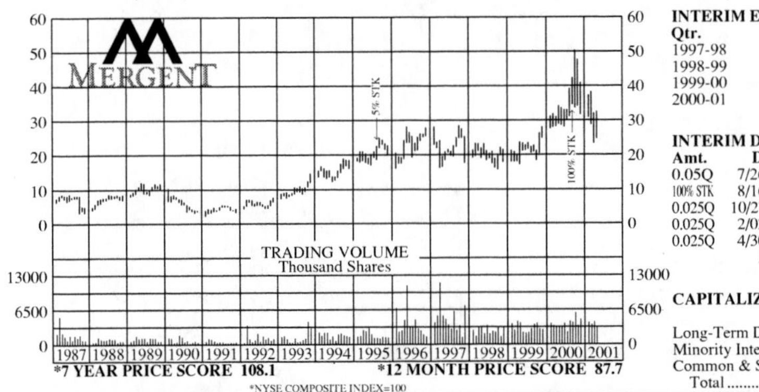

*7 YEAR PRICE SCORE 108.1 *12 MONTH PRICE SCORE 87.7

*NYSE COMPOSITE INDEX=100

INTERIM EARNINGS (Per Share):

Qtr.	Sept.	Dec.	Mar.	June
1997-98	0.23	0.42	0.40	0.39
1998-99	0.23	d0.87	0.36	0.59
1999-00	0.14	0.64	0.63	0.66
2000-01	0.21	0.72	...	...

INTERIM DIVIDENDS (Per Share):

Amt.	Decl.	Ex.	Rec.	Pay.
0.05Q	7/26/00	8/07/00	8/09/00	8/23/00
100% STK	8/16/00	9/20/00	8/28/00	9/19/00
0.025Q	10/27/00	11/06/00	11/08/00	11/22/00
0.025Q	2/02/01	2/12/01	2/14/01	2/28/01
0.025Q	4/30/01	5/07/01	5/09/01	5/23/01

Indicated div.: $0.10

CAPITALIZATION (6/30/00):

	($000)	(%)
Long-Term Debt	254,818	34.3
Minority Interest	1,055	0.1
Common & Surplus	486,333	65.5
Total	742,206	100.0

RECENT DEVELOPMENTS: For the second quarter ended 12/31/00, net income climbed 8.3% to $24.2 million compared with $22.3 million in the corresponding quarter of the prior year. Earnings for 2000 included a one-time charge of $16.6 million for the repurchase of inventory from a distributor. Net sales decreased 2.8% to $438.2 million from $450.8 million in the year-earlier period.

PROSPECTS: HAR believes growth opportunities exist within the automotive audio market by increasing product penetration in platforms currently supplied on an original equipment manufacturer basis. Also, future sales should benefit from increases in per-vehicle content through the provision of systems with additional functions and the addition of new original equipment manufacturer partners.

BUSINESS

HARMAN INTERNATIONAL INDUSTRIES, INC. designs, manufactures and markets high-quality, high-fidelity audio products, including professional and consumer loudspeakers and electronics. HAR's products are sold to worldwide consumer and professional audio markets. The Company is organized in two operating groups: Consumer Systems and Professional. Harman's brand names include JBL, HARMAN KARDON, INFINITY, AKG, CROWN, STUDER, SOUNDCRAFT, SPIRIT, DOD, DBX, DIGITECH, LEXICON, BECKER, MARK LEVINSON, PROCEED, and REVEL.

BUSINESS LINE ANALYSIS

06/30/2000	Rev(%)	Inc(%)
Consumer Sales	71.6	80.2
Professional Sales	28.4	29.7
Other Sales	0	(9.9)
Total	100.0	100.0

ANNUAL FINANCIAL DATA

	6/30/00	6/30/99	6/30/98	6/30/97	6/30/96	6/30/95	6/30/94
Earnings Per Share	**1.03**	**4 0.16**	**3 0.72**	**0.74**	**0.79**	**0.65**	**1 2 0.47**
Cash Flow Per Share	**1.95**	**1.09**	**1.54**	**1.45**	**1.56**	**1.34**	**1.04**
Tang. Book Val. Per Share	**4.69**	**4.61**	**4.70**	**4.84**	**4.12**	**2.57**	**3.12**
Dividends Per Share	**0.10**	**0.10**	**0.10**	**0.10**	**0.10**	**0.09**	**0.04**
Dividend Payout %	**9.7**	**61.5**	**14.0**	**13.5**	**12.7**	**14.3**	**8.1**
INCOME STATEMENT (IN MILLIONS):							
Total Revenues	1,677.9	1,500.1	1,513.3	1,474.1	1,361.6	1,170.2	862.1
Costs & Expenses	1,491.6	1,394.7	1,350.4	1,319.0	1,205.3	1,038.3	763.6
Depreciation & Amort.	64.6	66.8	62.5	53.1	50.9	44.5	32.3
Operating Income	121.7	38.7	100.3	102.0	105.4	87.4	66.3
Net Interest Inc./(Exp.)	d18.5	d23.6	d24.9	d23.6	d27.5	d25.3	d22.1
Income Before Income Taxes	102.8	14.4	75.7	77.9	75.0	61.2	42.7
Income Taxes	29.9	2.7	21.9	23.0	23.8	19.6	16.2
Equity Earnings/Minority Int.	d0.1	...	...	d0.1	0.8	d0.1	...
Net Income	72.8	4 11.7	3 53.8	54.8	52.0	41.4	1 2 26.4
Cash Flow	137.5	78.5	116.3	107.9	103.0	85.9	58.7
Average Shs. Outstg. (000)	70,600	72,244	75,536	74,208	65,896	63,920	56,168
BALANCE SHEET (IN MILLIONS):							
Cash & Cash Equivalents	4.4	3.0	16.2	4.2	0.3	11.3	9.7
Total Current Assets	671.0	646.6	695.2	679.3	652.0	552.7	489.8
Net Property	251.7	241.1	248.4	207.9	201.0	189.8	138.6
Total Assets	1,137.5	1,065.8	1,130.7	1,014.3	996.2	886.9	680.7
Total Current Liabilities	361.4	286.8	327.3	251.2	274.7	295.1	273.9
Long-Term Obligations	254.8	280.4	259.6	266.4	254.6	266.0	156.6
Net Stockholders' Equity	486.3	468.2	511.9	466.8	436.5	289.5	232.0
Net Working Capital	309.6	359.8	367.9	428.1	377.3	257.6	215.9
Year-end Shs. Outstg. (000)	68,125	71,028	74,532	73,828	74,472	64,940	63,284
STATISTICAL RECORD:							
Operating Profit Margin %	7.3	2.6	6.6	6.9	7.7	7.5	7.7
Net Profit Margin %	4.3	0.8	3.6	3.7	3.8	3.5	3.1
Return on Equity %	15.0	2.5	10.5	11.7	11.9	14.3	11.4
Return on Assets %	6.4	1.1	4.8	5.4	5.2	4.7	3.9
Debt/Total Assets %	22.4	26.3	23.0	26.3	25.6	30.0	23.0
Price Range	50.35-27.50	28.06-17.13	23.41-15.75	28.53-16.19	28.25-16.00	24.88-17.00	19.00-12.25
P/E Ratio	48.8-26.6	172.6-105.4	32.7-22.0	38.6-21.9	35.8-20.3	38.3-26.2	40.3-26.0
Average Yield %	0.3	0.4	0.5	0.4	0.5	0.4	0.2

Statistics are as originally reported. Adjusted for a 5% stock dividend., 8/95; 2-for-1, 9/00. 1 Bef. extraord. chg. of $748,000 ($0.03 per sh.). 2 Bef. extraord. chg. of $274,000 ($0.01 per sh.). 3 Excl. an after-tax extraord. chg. of $3.6 mill. 4 Incl. nonrecurring after-tax chgs. totaling $66.4 mill.

OFFICERS:
S. Harman, Chmn.
B. A. Girod, Vice-Chmn., C.E.O.
G. P. Stapleton, Pres., C.O.O.
F. Meredith, Exec. V.P., C.F.O.

INVESTOR CONTACT: Frank Meredith, (818) 893-5710

PRINCIPAL OFFICE: 1101 Pennsylvania Ave., NW, Suite 1010, Washington, DC 20004

TELEPHONE NUMBER: (202) 393-1101
FAX: (202) 393-3064
WEB: www.harman.com

NO. OF EMPLOYEES: 9,807

SHAREHOLDERS: 182

ANNUAL MEETING: In Nov.

INCORPORATED: DE, 1980

INSTITUTIONAL HOLDINGS:
No. of Institutions: 164
Shares Held: 29,985,729
% Held: 93.7

INDUSTRY: Household audio and video equipment (SIC: 3651)

TRANSFER AGENT(S): Mellon Investor Services, Los Angeles, CA

NYSE SYMBOL HET
Rec. Pr. 34.00 (4/30/01)

HARRAH'S ENTERTAINMENT, INC.

YIELD ...
P/E RATIO ...

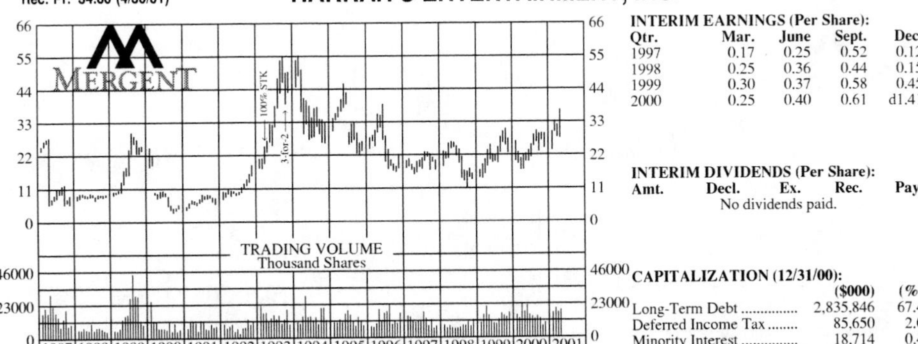

***7 YEAR PRICE SCORE 79.0** ***12 MONTH PRICE SCORE 123.3**

*NYSE COMPOSITE INDEX=100

INTERIM EARNINGS (Per Share):

Qtr.	Mar.	June	Sept.	Dec.
1997	0.17	0.25	0.52	0.12
1998	0.25	0.36	0.44	0.15
1999	0.30	0.37	0.58	0.45
2000	0.25	0.40	0.61	d1.41

INTERIM DIVIDENDS (Per Share):

Amt.	Decl.	Ex.	Rec.	Pay.
No dividends paid.				

CAPITALIZATION (12/31/00):

	($000)	(%)
Long-Term Debt	2,835,846	67.4
Deferred Income Tax	85,650	2.0
Minority Interest	18,714	0.4
Common & Surplus	1,269,718	30.2
Total	4,209,928	100.0

RECENT DEVELOPMENTS: For the year ended 12/31/00, HET reported a loss of $11.3 million, before an extraordinary loss of $716,000, versus income of $219.5 million, before an extraordinary loss of $11.0 million, in 1999. Results for 2000 and 1999 included various nonrecurring items that resulted in net losses of $355.8 million and $5.5 million, respectively. Total revenues advanced 14.8% to $3.47 billion from $3.02 billion in 1999.

PROSPECTS: HET expects to meet or exceed current consensus estimates for 2001 as the Company continues to expand its properties. In Shreveport, Louisiana, HET is developing a $150.0 million hotel and shore-side amenities. Harrah's East Chicago will complete the construction of a 292-room, $45.0 million hotel by the end of 2001. Harrah's Atlantic City will open a 450-room, $110.0 million hotel tower addition in the first quarter of 2002.

BUSINESS

HARRAH'S ENTERTAINMENT, INC. (formerly The Promus Companies Inc.) operates 21 casinos in 17 markets nationwide under the HARRAH'S, SHOWBOAT PLAYERS and RIO brand names. HET's U.S. markets include Atlantic City, Las Vegas, Reno, Shreveport, North Kansas City, Laughlin and others. HET competes in all four segments of the casino industry: traditional land-based casinos, riverboat and dockside casinos, limited stakes casinos and casinos for Indian communities. HET operates more casinos in more markets than any other casino company in North America. On 1/1/99 and 3/22/00, HET acquired Rio Hotel & Casino, Inc. and Players International, Inc., respectively.

REVENUES

(12/31/2000)	($000)	(%)
Casino	2,852,048	74.8
Food & Beverage	476,538	12.5
Rooms	270,313	7.1
Management Fees	66,398	1.7
Other	146,291	3.9
Total	3,811,588	100.0

ANNUAL FINANCIAL DATA

	12/31/00	12/31/99	12/31/98	12/31/97	12/31/96	12/31/95	12/31/94
Earnings Per Share	**[7] d0.09**	**[8] 1.71**	**[1] [7] 1.19**	**[1] [5] 1.06**	**[3] [7] 0.95**	**[4] 0.76**	**[2] 0.49**
Cash Flow Per Share	**2.31**	**3.40**	**2.77**	**2.27**	**1.94**	**1.69**	**1.33**
Tang. Book Val. Per Share	**5.04**	**7.89**	**4.58**	**6.85**	**6.99**	**5.70**	**6.09**
INCOME STATEMENT (IN MILLIONS):							
Total Revenues	3,471.2	3,024.4	2,004.0	1,619.2	1,588.1	1,550.1	1,339.4
Costs & Expenses	2,848.4	2,281.6	1,542.0	1,272.2	1,247.9	1,224.8	895.1
Depreciation & Amort.	282.1	218.3	159.2	122.4	102.3	95.4	86.6
Operating Income	282.7	481.0	287.8	213.5	237.9	229.9	269.2
Net Interest Inc./(Exp.)	d227.1	d193.4	d117.3	d79.1	d70.9	d94.4	d78.3
Income Before Income Taxes	17.8	359.6	203.3	183.6	172.1	151.6	139.3
Income Taxes	15.4	128.9	74.6	68.7	67.3	60.7	75.4
Equity Earnings/Minority Int.	d113.3	5.2	d8.8	19.0	d5.9	d12.1	d13.9
Net Income	[7] d11.3	[8] 219.5	[1] [7] 121.7	[1] [5] 107.5	[3] [7] 98.9	[4] 78.8	[2] 50.0
Cash Flow	270.8	437.8	280.9	229.9	201.2	174.2	136.6
Average Shs. Outstg. (000)	117,190	128,748	101,520	101,254	103,736	103,188	102,810
BALANCE SHEET (IN MILLIONS):							
Cash & Cash Equivalents	299.2	233.6	159.0	116.4	105.6	96.3	85.0
Total Current Assets	583.4	486.7	279.3	212.3	201.6	188.8	171.8
Net Property	3,496.4	3,061.2	1,870.2	1,478.1	1,389.9	1,204.9	1,129.8
Total Assets	5,166.1	4,766.8	3,286.3	2,005.5	1,974.1	1,636.7	1,738.0
Total Current Liabilities	778.5	371.6	232.8	211.0	204.6	201.6	295.1
Long-Term Obligations	2,835.8	2,540.3	1,999.4	924.4	889.5	753.7	727.5
Net Stockholders' Equity	1,269.7	1,486.3	851.4	735.5	719.7	585.5	623.4
Net Working Capital	d195.1	115.1	46.5	1.4	d3.1	d12.7	d123.2
Year-end Shs. Outstg. (000)	115,952	124,380	102,188	101,036	102,970	102,674	102,403
STATISTICAL RECORD:							
Operating Profit Margin %	8.1	15.9	14.4	13.2	15.0	14.8	20.1
Net Profit Margin %	...	7.3	6.1	6.6	6.2	5.1	3.7
Return on Equity %	...	14.8	14.3	14.6	13.7	13.5	8.0
Return on Assets %	...	4.6	3.7	5.4	5.0	4.8	2.9
Debt/Total Assets %	54.9	53.3	60.8	46.1	45.1	46.0	41.9
Price Range	30.06-17.00	30.75-14.19	26.38-11.06	23.06-15.50	38.88-16.38	45.88-22.13	55.25-25.88
P/E Ratio	...	18.0-8.3	22.2-9.3	21.8-14.6	40.9-17.2	60.4-29.1	112.7-52.8

Statistics are as originally reported. [1] Bef. extraord. loss of $19.7 mill., 1998; $8.1 mill., 1997. [2] Bef. disc. ops. gain of $36.3 mill. & acct. chg. of $7.9 mill. [3] Incl. pre-tax write-down & reorg. chgs. of $66.8 mill. [4] Bef. disc. oper. gain of $36,000; incl. pre-tax write-down & reorg. chrgs. of $93.3 mill. & various costs of $450,000. [5] Incl. various costs of $38.4 mill. & one-time gain of $37.4 mill. [6] Incl. various costs of $21.6 mill., 1998; $5.9 mill., 1996. [7] Bef. extraord. loss of $716,000; incl. a loss on sales of eqty. ints. in subs. of $41.6 mill. & various costs of $256.3 mill. [8] Bef. extraord. loss of $11.0 mill.; incl. a gain on sales of eqty. ints. in subs. of $59.8 mill. & various costs of $21.9 mill.

OFFICERS:
P. G. Satre, Chmn., Pres., C.E.O.
C. V. Reed, Exec. V.P., C.F.O.

INVESTOR CONTACT: Josh Hirsberg, (702) 579-2329

PRINCIPAL OFFICE: One Harrah's Court, Las Vegas, NV 89119

TELEPHONE NUMBER: (702) 407-6000
WEB: www.harrahs.com

NO. OF EMPLOYEES: 40,000 (approx.)

SHAREHOLDERS: 10,804 (approx.)

ANNUAL MEETING: In May

INCORPORATED: DE, Nov., 1989

INSTITUTIONAL HOLDINGS:
No. of Institutions: 223
Shares Held: 98,014,664
% Held: 84.3

INDUSTRY: Amusement and recreation, nec (SIC: 7999)

TRANSFER AGENT(S): The Bank of New York, New York, NY

NYSE SYMBOL HRS
Rec. Pr. 27.55 (4/30/01)

HARRIS CORPORATION

YIELD 0.7%
P/E RATIO ...

66 55 44 33 22 11 0 — MERGENT

TRADING VOLUME
Thousand Shares

26000 13000 0

1987 1988 1989 1990 1991 1992 1993 1994 1995 1996 1997 1998 1999 2000 2001

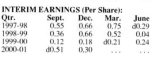

*7 YEAR PRICE SCORE 65.5 *12 MONTH PRICE SCORE 87.8

*NYSE COMPOSITE INDEX=100

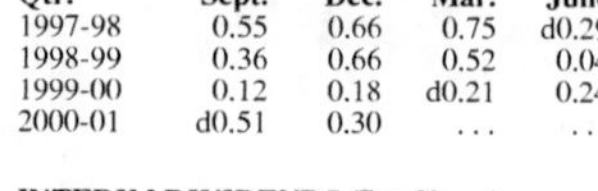

INTERIM EARNINGS (Per Share):

Qtr.	Sept.	Dec.	Mar.	June
1997-98	0.55	0.66	0.75	d0.29
1998-99	0.36	0.66	0.52	0.04
1999-00	0.12	0.18	d0.21	0.24
2000-01	d0.51	0.30	...	...

INTERIM DIVIDENDS (Per Share):

Amt.	Decl.	Ex.	Rec.	Pay.
0.05Q	4/28/00	5/26/00	5/31/00	6/14/00
0.05Q	8/28/00	9/06/00	9/08/00	9/22/00
0.05Q	10/27/00	11/15/00	11/17/00	12/01/00
0.05Q	2/23/01	3/02/01	3/06/01	3/16/01
0.05Q	4/27/01	5/25/01	5/30/01	6/13/01

Indicated div.: $0.20 (Div. Reinv. Plan)

CAPITALIZATION (6/30/00):

	($000)	(%)
Long-Term Debt	382,600	21.6
Deferred Income Tax	14,100	0.8
Common & Surplus	1,374,300	77.6
Total	1,771,000	100.0

RECENT DEVELOPMENTS: For the quarter ended 12/31/00, net income grew 1.0% to $19.7 million from $19.5 million in the prior-year period. Total revenues increased 16.7% to $486.9 million from $417.4 million in 1999. Government communications revenue rose 8.1% to $210.1 million. Commercial communications revenue advanced 24.1% to $276.8 million, reflecting continued strong demand for microwave radios and digital broadcast systems.

PROSPECTS: HRS expects continued strong growth in its point-to-point microwave business, reflecting the introduction of new point-to-multipoint products that will initially target high-speed Internet access for businesses and home offices. Also, HRS anticipates continued increased orders and strong profitability improvement in its RF Communications business, due to the successful deployment of the Falcon II data-rate multiband secure radios.

BUSINESS

HARRIS CORPORATION is an international communications equipment company focused on providing product, system, and service solutions. The Company provides a wide range of products and services for commercial and government communications markets such as wireless, broadcast, government, and network support. The Company has sales and service facilities in nearly 90 countries. On 8/16/99, the Company sold its semiconductor business. On 11/5/99, the Company completed the spin-off of its subsidiary, Lanier Worldwide, to its shareholders. The Company retained approximately 10% of the Lanier stock. On 8/31/00, the Company acquired Wavtrace, Inc.

REVENUES

(6/30/2000)	($000)	(%)
Government Communciations	815,900	45.1
Commercial Communications	991,500	54.9
Total	1,807,400	100.0

ANNUAL FINANCIAL DATA

	6/30/00	7/2/99	7/3/98	6/27/97	6/30/96	6/30/95	6/30/94
Earnings Per Share	**4 0.34**	**3 0.63**	**2 1.66**	**2.66**	**2.29**	**1.98**	**1 1.54**
Cash Flow Per Share	**1.28**	**1.42**	**4.29**	**4.96**	**4.48**	**4.08**	**3.47**
Tang. Book Val. Per Share	**17.52**	**19.04**	**17.43**	**16.96**	**14.92**	**13.92**	**13.00**
Dividends Per Share	**0.20**	**0.77**	**0.92**	**0.82**	**0.72**	**0.65**	**0.59**
Dividend Payout %	**58.8**	**122.2**	**55.4**	**30.8**	**31.4**	**32.9**	**38.4**
INCOME STATEMENT (IN MILLIONS):							
Total Revenues	1,807.4	1,743.5	3,939.1	3,834.6	3,659.3	3,480.9	3,369.4
Costs & Expenses	1,750.7	1,604.2	3,481.9	3,299.5	3,145.8	2,999.0	2,970.0
Depreciation & Amort.	68.6	63.5	210.2	183.5	170.7	165.3	153.4
Operating Income	36.3	75.8	247.0	351.6	342.8	316.6	246.0
Net Interest Inc./(Exp.)	2.2	3.5	d73.2	d59.9	d62.5	d65.4	d58.3
Income Before Income Taxes	38.5	78.0	200.0	312.0	274.4	237.6	193.5
Income Taxes	13.5	28.1	67.0	104.5	96.0	83.1	71.6
Net Income	4 25.0	3 49.9	2 133.0	207.5	178.4	154.5	1 121.9
Cash Flow	93.6	113.4	343.2	391.0	349.1	319.8	275.3
Average Shs. Outstg. (000)	73,400	79,700	80,000	78,776	77,950	78,292	79,440
BALANCE SHEET (IN MILLIONS):							
Cash & Cash Equivalents	810.7	101.2	228.8	162.0	99.4	141.6	139.1
Total Current Assets	1,629.0	1,031.4	2,099.7	2,063.5	1,940.9	1,810.7	1,698.3
Net Property	295.4	291.6	947.0	878.3	721.7	581.0	551.3
Total Assets	2,326.9	2,958.6	3,784.0	3,637.9	3,206.7	2,836.0	2,677.1
Total Current Liabilities	555.9	807.3	1,261.8	1,288.6	1,183.1	1,055.3	804.7
Long-Term Obligations	382.6	514.5	768.6	686.7	588.5	475.9	661.7
Net Stockholders' Equity	1,374.3	1,589.5	1,609.3	1,578.2	1,372.9	1,248.8	1,188.0
Net Working Capital	1,073.1	224.1	837.9	774.9	757.8	755.4	893.6
Year-end Shs. Outstg. (000)	68,958	79,651	80,013	79,626	77,744	77,754	78,596
STATISTICAL RECORD:							
Operating Profit Margin %	2.0	4.3	6.3	9.2	9.4	9.1	7.3
Net Profit Margin %	1.4	2.9	3.4	5.4	4.9	4.4	3.6
Return on Equity %	1.8	3.1	8.3	13.1	13.0	12.4	10.3
Return on Assets %	1.1	1.7	3.5	5.7	5.6	5.4	4.6
Debt/Total Assets %	16.4	17.4	20.3	18.9	18.4	16.8	24.7
Price Range	39.38-20.75	40.63-18.25	55.31-27.56	50.00-33.69	35.69-24.44	30.69-20.25	26.13-18.88
P/E Ratio	115.8-61.0	64.5-29.0	33.3-16.6	18.8-12.7	15.6-10.7	15.5-10.3	17.0-12.3
Average Yield %	0.7	2.6	2.2	2.0	2.4	2.6	2.6

Statistics are as originally reported. Adj. for 2-for-1 stk. split, 9/97. 1 Bef. acct. chrge. of $10.1 mill. 2 Incl. an $86.4 mill. aft.-tax restr. chrg. & $8.0 mill. aft.-tax prov. for costs assoc. with an intnl. contract. 3 Incl. special chrg. of $20.6 mill. for litig. costs & restruct. exps. of $5.1 mill.; excl. gain of $12.4 mill. fr. disc. opers. & extra. loss of $9.2 mill. 4 Bef. disc. opers. loss of $7.0 mill.; incl. non-recurr. chrgs. of $51.7 mill.

OFFICERS:
P. W. Farmer, Chmn., Pres., C.E.O.
B. R. Roub, Sr. V.P., C.F.O.

INVESTOR CONTACT: Pamela Padgett, V.P.-Inv. Rel., (321) 727-9383

PRINCIPAL OFFICE: 1025 West NASA Boulevard, Melbourne, FL 32919

TELEPHONE NUMBER: (321) 727-9100
FAX: (321) 724-3973
WEB: www.harris.com

NO. OF EMPLOYEES: 10,000 (approx.)

SHAREHOLDERS: 9,817 (approx.)

ANNUAL MEETING: In Oct.

INCORPORATED: DE, Dec., 1926

INSTITUTIONAL HOLDINGS:
No. of Institutions: 216
Shares Held: 52,496,202
% Held: 79.7

INDUSTRY: Radio & TV communications equipment (SIC: 3663)

TRANSFER AGENT(S): Mellon Investor Services, Ridgefield Park, NJ

NYSE SYMBOL HSC
Rec. Pr. 28.30 (4/30/01)

HARSCO CORPORATION

YIELD 3.4%
P/E RATIO 11.7

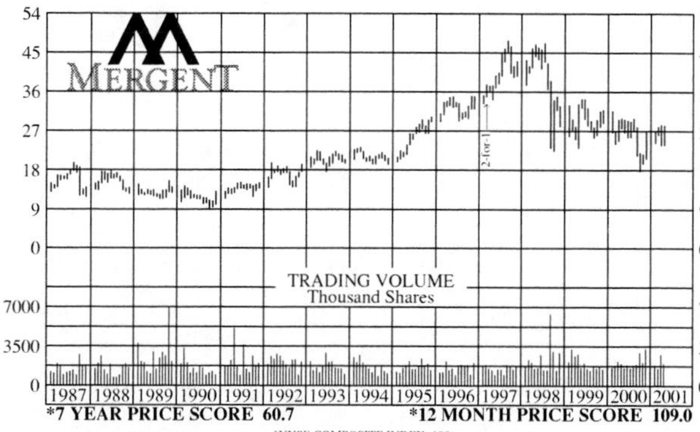

*7 YEAR PRICE SCORE 60.7 *12 MONTH PRICE SCORE 109.0

*NYSE COMPOSITE INDEX=100

INTERIM EARNINGS (Per Share):

Qtr.	March	June	Sept.	Dec.
1997	0.61	0.74	0.57	0.62
1998	0.52	0.71	0.56	0.55
1999	0.35	0.58	0.64	0.65
2000	0.50	0.70	0.56	0.65

INTERIM DIVIDENDS (Per Share):

Amt.	Decl.	Ex.	Rec.	Pay.
0.235Q	3/16/00	4/12/00	4/14/00	5/15/00
0.235Q	6/27/00	7/12/00	7/14/00	8/15/00
0.235Q	9/26/00	10/12/00	10/16/00	11/15/00
0.24Q	11/16/00	1/11/01	1/16/01	2/15/01
0.24Q	3/15/01	4/11/01	4/16/01	5/15/01

Indicated div.: $0.96 (Div. Reinv. Plan)

CAPITALIZATION (12/31/00):

	($000)	(%)
Long-Term Debt	774,450	50.4
Deferred Income Tax	88,480	5.8
Common & Surplus	674,179	43.9
Total	1,537,109	100.0

RECENT DEVELOPMENTS: For the year ended 12/31/00, net income advanced 6.7% to $96.8 million compared with $90.7 million in the equivalent 1999 quarter. Total revenues were $2.00 billion, up 14.5% from $1.75 billion a year earlier. Infrastructure segment sales soared 62.7% to $703.6 million primarily due to the inclusion of SGB Group, acquired on 6/16/00. Mill Services segment sales climbed 2.7% to $757.4 million.

PROSPECTS: Growth in the Company's international operations, coupled with reduced interest expense due to debt reduction strategies, should enable HSC to produce double-digit earnings per share increases. Meanwhile, HSC anticipates opportunities in the year ahead to improve SGB's operating position and expects its performance in 2001 to be an important contributor to full-year results.

BUSINESS

HARSCO CORPORATION is a diversified industrial services and engineered products company. The principal lines of business are: industrial mill services that are provided to steel producers in over 30 countries; scaffolding services; railway maintenance of way equipment and services; gas control and containment products; and several other lines of business, including industrial grating and bridge decking, industrial pipe fittings, process equipment, slag abrasives and roofing granules. HSC's operations fall into three Operating Groups: Mill Services, Gas and Fluid Control, and Infrastructure. HSC has over 300 locations in 38 countries. In 1997, HSC sold its 40% interest in United Defense, L.P., completing its strategic exit from the Defense business.

ANNUAL FINANCIAL DATA

	12/31/00	12/31/99	12/31/98	12/31/97	12/31/96	12/31/95	12/31/94
Earnings Per Share	**2.42**	**2.21**	[4] **2.34**	[3] **2.04**	[1] **2.39**	[1] **1.93**	[2] **1.72**
Cash Flow Per Share	**6.39**	**5.52**	**5.20**	**4.41**	**4.58**	**4.01**	**3.71**
Tang. Book Val. Per Share	**7.66**	**9.77**	**9.74**	**12.71**	**9.80**	**8.39**	**7.30**
Dividends Per Share	**0.94**	**0.90**	**0.88**	**0.80**	**0.76**	**0.74**	**0.70**
Dividend Payout %	**38.8**	**40.7**	**37.6**	**39.2**	**31.8**	**38.3**	**40.7**
INCOME STATEMENT (IN MILLIONS):							
Total Revenues	2,004.7	1,720.8	1,735.4	1,629.1	1,608.5	1,554.0	1,465.8
Costs & Expenses	1,650.9	1,415.2	1,412.1	1,332.7	1,283.7	1,264.0	1,189.7
Depreciation & Amort.	159.1	135.9	131.4	116.5	109.4	104.9	99.6
Operating Income	194.7	169.7	191.9	179.9	215.4	185.2	176.5
Net Interest Inc./(Exp.)	d44.1	d22.3	d12.1	d8.3	d14.5	d21.4	d27.6
Income Before Income Taxes	148.6	147.4	179.8	171.6	200.9	163.7	148.8
Income Taxes	46.8	51.6	67.4	65.2	76.3	63.9	59.5
Equity Earnings/Minority Int.	d7.0	d5.1	d4.9	d6.0	d5.5	d2.5	d2.8
Net Income	96.8	90.7	[4] 107.5	[3] 100.4	[1] 119.0	[1] 97.4	[2] 86.6
Cash Flow	255.9	226.6	238.9	216.9	228.4	202.2	186.1
Average Shs. Outstg. (000)	40,022	41,017	45,910	49,192	49,883	50,492	50,230
BALANCE SHEET (IN MILLIONS):							
Cash & Cash Equivalents	56.4	51.3	41.6	265.4	45.9	76.7	43.6
Total Current Assets	726.4	613.0	587.4	713.7	508.5	533.8	536.8
Net Property	896.8	671.5	626.2	511.9	513.1	459.8	435.0
Total Assets	2,180.9	1,659.8	1,623.6	1,477.2	1,324.4	1,310.7	1,314.6
Total Current Liabilities	536.2	430.5	474.8	372.5	294.0	388.5	282.4
Long-Term Obligations	774.5	418.5	309.1	198.9	227.4	179.9	340.2
Net Stockholders' Equity	674.2	650.1	685.3	781.7	681.3	626.0	581.2
Net Working Capital	190.2	182.4	112.6	341.2	214.5	145.3	254.3
Year-end Shs. Outstg. (000)	39,805	40,072	42,250	46,746	49,602	50,104	50,364
STATISTICAL RECORD:							
Operating Profit Margin %	9.7	9.9	11.1	11.0	13.4	11.9	12.0
Net Profit Margin %	4.8	5.3	6.2	6.2	7.4	6.3	5.9
Return on Equity %	14.4	14.0	15.7	12.8	17.5	15.6	14.9
Return on Assets %	4.4	5.5	6.6	6.8	9.0	7.4	6.6
Debt/Total Assets %	35.5	25.2	19.0	13.5	17.2	13.7	25.9
Price Range	31.63-17.69	34.38-23.06	47.25-22.31	47.88-33.25	35.06-29.00	30.25-19.81	23.19-19.19
P/E Ratio	13.1-7.3	15.6-10.4	20.2-9.5	23.5-16.3	14.7-12.1	15.7-10.3	13.5-11.2
Average Yield %	3.9	3.1	2.5	2.0	2.4	3.0	3.3

Statistics are as originally reported. Adj. for stk. split: 2-for-1, 2/97. [1] Incl. a pretax chrg. of $22.8 mill., 1995; and $3.3 mill., 1996. [2] Incl. results of MultiServ International, acq. on 8/31/93, and a net gain of $6.0 mill.; Bef. a $0.14 adj. per sh. gain fr. a settlement claim. [3] Bef. discont. oper. of $11.7 mill. [4] Incl. non-recur. chrg. of about $29.0 mill.

OFFICERS:
D. C. Hathaway, Chmn., Pres., C.E.O.
S. D. Fazzolari, Sr. V.P., C.F.O.
P. C. Coppock, Sr. V.P., C.A.O., Sec., Gen. Couns.

INVESTOR CONTACT: Eugene M. Truett, Dir.-Investor Relations, (717) 975-5677

PRINCIPAL OFFICE: P.O. Box 8888, Camp Hill, PA 17001-8888

TELEPHONE NUMBER: (717) 763-7064
FAX: (717) 763-6424
WEB: www.harsco.com

NO. OF EMPLOYEES: 20,000 (approx.)

SHAREHOLDERS: 21,000 (approx.)

ANNUAL MEETING: In Apr.

INCORPORATED: DE, Feb., 1956

INSTITUTIONAL HOLDINGS:
No. of Institutions: 146
Shares Held: 21,115,134
% Held: 53.0

INDUSTRY: Miscellaneous metal work (SIC: 3449)

TRANSFER AGENT(S): Mellon Investor Services, South Hackensack, NJ

NYSE SYMBOL HHS
Rec. Pr. 22.78 (4/30/01)

HARTE-HANKS, INC.

YIELD 0.5%
P/E RATIO 19.5

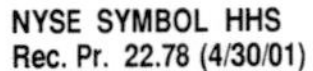

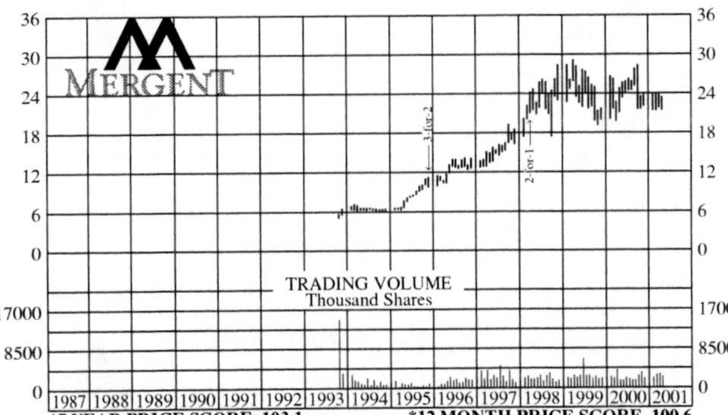

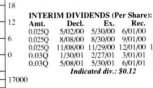

***7 YEAR PRICE SCORE 103.1** ***12 MONTH PRICE SCORE 100.6**

*NYSE COMPOSITE INDEX=100

INTERIM EARNINGS (Per Share):

Qtr.	Mar.	June	Sept.	Dec.
1998	0.28	0.22	0.22	0.18
1999	0.29	0.26	0.26	0.21
2000	0.25	0.30	0.30	0.32

INTERIM DIVIDENDS (Per Share):

Amt.	Decl.	Ex.	Rec.	Pay.
0.025Q	5/02/00	5/30/00	6/01/00	6/15/00
0.025Q	8/08/00	8/30/00	9/01/00	9/15/00
0.025Q	11/08/00	11/29/00	12/01/00	12/15/00
0.03Q	1/30/01	2/27/01	3/01/01	3/15/01
0.03Q	5/08/01	5/30/01	6/01/01	6/15/01

Indicated div.: $0.12

CAPITALIZATION (12/31/00):

	($000)	(%)
Long-Term Debt	65,370	10.6
Common & Surplus	551,003	89.4
Total	616,373	100.0

RECENT DEVELOPMENTS: For the year ended 12/31/00, net income increased 12.3% to $81.9 million from $72.9 million in 1999. Revenues grew 15.8% to $960.8 million from $829.8 million in the prior year. Revenues for direct marketing advanced 18.4% to $662.0 million, while shoppers revenues rose 10.4% to $298.7 million. Operating income amounted to $138.2 million compared with $118.2 million the year before.

PROSPECTS: In 2001, HHS expects earnings per share growth will range from 10.0% to 15.0%. As a result of the weakened economy, HHS anticipates direct marketing revenue growth will be below the double-digit range. Separately, HHS entered into an alliance with Hewlett-Packard to provide an array of e-business, customer relationship management and knowledge management applications for the pharmaceutical industry.

BUSINESS

HARTE-HANKS, INC. is a direct and interactive services company that provides end-to-end customer relationship management and related services for a host of consumer and business-to-business marketers. The Company has operations in two principal businesses: direct marketing and shoppers. The Company's direct and interactive marketing business operates both nationally and internationally, while its shopper business operates in selected local and regional markets in California and Florida. Direct and interactive marketing, which represents 68.9% of the Company's revenue as of 12/31/00, offers a complete range of specialized, coordinated and integrated direct and interactive marketing services from a single source.

BUSINESS LINE ANALYSIS

(12/31/00)($000)	Rev(%)	Inc(%)
Direct Marketing	68.9	62.1
Shoppers	31.1	37.9
Total	100.0	100.0

ANNUAL FINANCIAL DATA

	12/31/00	12/31/99	12/31/98	12/31/97	12/31/96	12/31/95	12/31/94
Earnings Per Share	**1.18**	**1.01**	**[4] 0.90**	**[3] 0.57**	**[2] 0.53**	**[1] 0.55**	**0.42**
Cash Flow Per Share	**1.81**	**1.50**	**1.29**	**0.88**	**0.93**	**1.01**	**0.88**
Tang. Book Val. Per Share	**1.73**	**2.46**	**4.02**	**4.32**	...	...	...
Dividends Per Share	**0.10**	**0.08**	**0.06**	**0.04**	**0.04**	**0.03**	...
Dividend Payout %	**8.5**	**7.9**	**6.7**	**7.0**	**6.7**	**5.5**	...
INCOME STATEMENT (IN MILLIONS):							
Total Revenues	960.8	829.8	748.5	638.3	665.9	532.9	513.6
Costs & Expenses	778.4	676.3	617.0	538.0	546.8	431.9	423.3
Depreciation & Amort.	44.2	35.2	29.6	23.2	31.1	26.9	26.3
Operating Income	138.2	118.2	102.0	77.1	88.0	74.0	64.0
Net Interest Inc./(Exp.)	0.4	5.3	13.3	d1.8	d12.1	d16.4	d17.2
Income Before Income Taxes	136.9	122.8	116.2	75.1	75.4	70.3	45.7
Income Taxes	55.0	49.9	47.8	30.8	34.7	36.3	21.8
Net Income	81.9	72.9	[4] 68.4	[3] 44.3	[2] 40.6	[1] 34.0	23.8
Cash Flow	126.0	108.2	97.9	67.5	71.7	60.9	50.1
Average Shs. Outstg. (000)	69,653	72,144	76,057	77,000	77,154	60,560	57,138
BALANCE SHEET (IN MILLIONS):							
Cash & Cash Equivalents	22.9	35.2	169.2	471.8	12.0	6.7	4.4
Total Current Assets	235.9	220.1	325.8	613.1	153.1	113.2	105.6
Net Property	112.1	106.3	92.3	89.4	112.9	87.9	91.3
Total Assets	807.1	769.4	715.2	954.9	592.3	477.7	496.9
Total Current Liabilities	150.0	154.0	116.5	371.3	97.7	70.4	71.2
Long-Term Obligations	65.4	5.0	...	...	218.0	220.0	292.9
Net Stockholders' Equity	551.0	577.6	577.1	566.2	252.7	165.1	107.6
Net Working Capital	85.9	66.1	209.3	241.8	55.4	42.8	34.5
Year-end Shs. Outstg. (000)	64,686	68,106	71,258	73,194	73,604	59,984	36,704
STATISTICAL RECORD:							
Operating Profit Margin %	14.4	14.2	13.6	12.1	13.2	13.9	12.5
Net Profit Margin %	8.5	8.8	9.1	6.9	6.1	6.4	4.6
Return on Equity %	14.9	12.6	11.8	7.8	16.1	20.6	22.1
Return on Assets %	10.1	9.5	9.6	4.6	6.9	7.1	4.8
Debt/Total Assets %	8.1	0.6	...	...	36.8	46.1	58.9
Price Range	28.44-19.63	29.25-19.06	28.50-17.34	19.34-12.69	14.25-9.81	11.31-6.19	7.19-5.88
P/E Ratio	24.1-16.6	29.0-18.9	31.7-19.3	33.9-22.3	27.1-18.7	20.6-11.3	17.1-14.0
Average Yield %	0.4	0.3	0.3	0.2	0.3	0.4	...

Statistics are as originally reported. Adj. for 2-for-1 stk. split, 3/98; 3-for-2, 12/95 [1] Incl. gain on sale of bus. $13.7 mill. [2] Incl. merger costs $12.1 mill. [3] Bef. inc. from disc. opers. $292.4 mill. & extraord. loss $875,000. [4] Incl. pension curtailment gain $2.2 mill.

OFFICERS:
L. D. Franklin, Chmn., C.E.O.
H. H. Harte, Vice-Chmn.
R. M. Hochhauser, Pres., C.O.O.

INVESTOR CONTACT: Jacques Kerrest, Sr. V.P. & C.F.O., (210) 829-9140

PRINCIPAL OFFICE: 200 Concord Plaza Drive, San Antonio, TX 78216

TELEPHONE NUMBER: (210) 829-9000
FAX: (210) 829-9403
WEB: www.harte-hanks.com

NO. OF EMPLOYEES: 7,557 full-time; 1,292 part-time

SHAREHOLDERS: 3,100 (approx.)

ANNUAL MEETING: In May

INCORPORATED: DE, Oct., 1970

INSTITUTIONAL HOLDINGS:
No. of Institutions: 133
Shares Held: 31,688,294
% Held: 47.2

INDUSTRY: Miscellaneous publishing (SIC: 2741)

TRANSFER AGENT(S): BankBoston, Boston, MA

NYSE SYMBOL HIG
Rec. Pr. 62.10 (4/30/01)

HARTFORD FINANCIAL SERVICES GROUP, INC.

YIELD 1.6%
P/E RATIO 14.3

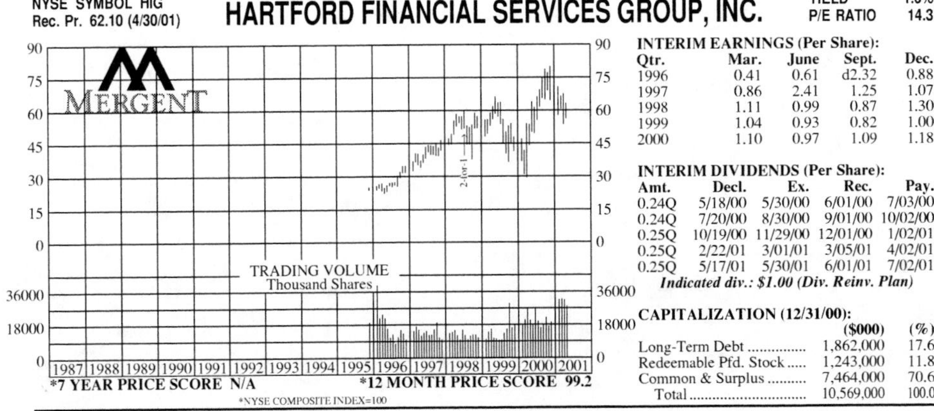

INTERIM EARNINGS (Per Share):

Qtr.	Mar.	June	Sept.	Dec.
1996	0.41	0.61	d2.32	0.88
1997	0.86	2.41	1.25	1.07
1998	1.11	0.99	0.87	1.30
1999	1.04	0.93	0.82	1.00
2000	1.10	0.97	1.09	1.18

INTERIM DIVIDENDS (Per Share):

Amt.	Decl.	Ex.	Rec.	Pay.
0.24Q	5/18/00	5/30/00	6/01/00	7/03/00
0.24Q	7/20/00	8/30/00	9/01/00	10/02/00
0.25Q	10/19/00	11/29/00	12/01/00	1/02/01
0.25Q	2/22/01	3/01/01	3/05/01	4/02/01
0.25Q	5/17/01	5/30/01	6/01/01	7/02/01

Indicated div.: $1.00 (Div. Reinv. Plan)

CAPITALIZATION (12/31/00):

	($000)	(%)
Long-Term Debt	1,862,000	17.6
Redeemable Pfd. Stock	1,243,000	11.8
Common & Surplus	7,464,000	70.6
Total	10,569,000	100.0

RECENT DEVELOPMENTS: For the year ended 12/31/00, net income amounted to $974.0 million, up 13.0% compared with $862.0 million in 1999. Results for 2000 and 1999 included after-tax catastrophe losses of $89.0 million and $131.0 million, respectively. Total revenues improved 8.7% to $14.70 billion versus $13.53 billion a year earlier. Worldwide life revenues improved 8.2% to $5.99 billion, while worldwide property and casualty revenues grew 8.9% to $8.70 billion.

PROSPECTS: On 4/2/01, the Company acquired the individual life insurance, annuity and mutual fund businesses of Fortis, Inc. (operating as Fortis Financial Group) for $1.12 billion in cash. This acquisition vaults HIG to the third-largest writer of variable life insurance in the U.S., increases HIG's mutual fund assets under management by more than 30.0%, adds a significant number of independent producers to its diversified distribution network and enhances its position in variable annuities.

BUSINESS

HARTFORD FINANCIAL SERVICES GROUP, INC. (formerly ITT Hartford Group, Inc.) is a provider of automobile and homeowners coverages, commercial property and casualty insurance, reinsurance, and a variety of life insurance, investment products, employee benefits, group retirement plans and institutional liability funding products. HIG offers its products through its Commercial, Personal, Reinsurance, Life, International segments and other operations segment. The Commercial segment provides insurance coverages to commercial accounts. The Personal segment provides insurance coverages to individuals. The Reinsurance segment offers property, casualty, marine, fidelity, surety, finite risk and specialty coverages. The Life segment offers variable annuities and mutual funds, individual and corporate owned life insurance and employee benefits products. The International segment consists primarily of Western European companies offering a variety of insurance products. The other operations segment includes operations that have ceased writing business. On 12/20/95, the Company spun off from ITT Corp.

ANNUAL FINANCIAL DATA

	12/31/00	12/31/99	12/31/98	12/31/97	12/31/96	12/31/95	12/31/94
Earnings Per Share	**4.34**	**3.79**	**4.30**	**[2] 5.58**	**d0.42**	**2.39**	...
Tang. Book Val. Per Share	**32.98**	**25.16**	**28.25**	**25.78**	**19.15**	**20.09**	...
Dividends Per Share	**0.96**	**0.90**	**0.83**	**0.80**	**0.60**	...	...
Dividend Payout %	**22.1**	**23.7**	**19.3**	**14.3**	...	...	...
INCOME STATEMENT (IN MILLIONS):							
Total Premium Income	11,434.0	10,867.0	11,616.0	10,323.0	10,076.0	9,628.0	8,728.0
Net Investment Income	2,674.0	2,627.0	3,102.0	2,655.0	2,523.0	2,420.0	2,138.0
Other Income	595.0	34.0	304.0	327.0	d126.0	102.0	91.0
Total Revenues	14,703.0	13,528.0	15,022.0	13,305.0	12,473.0	12,150.0	10,957.0
Income Before Income Taxes	1,418.0	1,235.0	1,475.0	1,703.0	d318.0	742.0	777.0
Income Taxes	390.0	287.0	388.0	334.0	cr219.0	180.0	198.0
Equity Earnings/Minority Int.	d54.0	d86.0	d72.0	331.0	...	...	...
Net Income	974.0	862.0	1,015.0	[2] 1,332.0	d99.0	562.0	[1] 579.0
Average Shs. Outstg. (000)	224,400	227,500	236,200	238,000	234,000	234,000	...
BALANCE SHEET (IN MILLIONS):							
Cash & Cash Equivalents	227.0	182.0	123.0	140.0	112.0	95.0	50.0
Premiums Due	6,874.0	6,544.0	6,811.0	12,712.0	13,026.0	13,691.0	11,760.0
Invst. Assets: Fixed-term	34,492.0	32,875.0	35,331.0	35,053.0	31,449.0	31,168.0	25,605.0
Invst. Assets: Equities	1,056.0	1,286.0	1,066.0	1,922.0	1,865.0	1,342.0	1,351.0
Invst. Assets: Loans	3,610.0	4,222.0	6,687.0	3,759.0	3,839.0	3,380.0	...
Invst. Assets: Total	40,669.0	39,141.0	43,696.0	41,122.0	37,639.0	36,675.0	30,641.0
Total Assets	171,532.0	167,051.0	150,632.0	131,743.0	108,840.0	93,855.0	72,338.0
Long-Term Obligations	1,862.0	1,548.0	1,548.0	1,482.0	1,032.0	1,022.0	596.0
Net Stockholders' Equity	7,464.0	5,466.0	6,423.0	6,085.0	4,520.0	4,702.0	2,935.0
Year-end Shs. Outstg. (000)	226,290	217,226	227,395	236,000	236,000	234,000	...
STATISTICAL RECORD:							
Return on Revenues %	6.6	6.4	6.8	10.0	...	4.6	5.3
Return on Equity %	13.0	15.8	15.8	21.9	...	12.0	19.7
Return on Assets %	0.6	0.5	0.7	1.0	...	0.6	0.8
Price Range	80.00-29.38	66.44-36.50	60.00-37.63	46.34-32.44	34.94-22.25	25.06-23.69	...
P/E Ratio	18.4-6.8	17.5-9.6	14.0-8.7	8.3-5.8	...	10.5-9.9	...
Average Yield %	1.8	1.7	1.7	2.0	2.1	...	...

Statistics are as originally reported. Adj. for stk. split: 2-for-1, 7/98 [1] Incl. non-recurr. credit $0.4 mill. [2] Bef. acctg. change credit $12.0 mill.

OFFICERS:
R. Ayer, Chmn., C.E.O.
L. A. Smith, Vice-Chmn.
D. K. Zwiener, Pres., C.O.O.
D. Johnson, Exec. V.P., C.F.O.

PRINCIPAL OFFICE: Hartford Plaza, Hartford, CT 06115-1900

TELEPHONE NUMBER: (860) 547-5000
FAX: (860) 720-6097
WEB: www.thehartford.com

NO. OF EMPLOYEES: 26,600 (approx.)

SHAREHOLDERS: 160,000 (approx.)

ANNUAL MEETING: In May

INCORPORATED: DE, Dec., 1985

INSTITUTIONAL HOLDINGS:
No. of Institutions: 446
Shares Held: 164,590,089
% Held: 69.6

INDUSTRY: Fire, marine, and casualty insurance (SIC: 6331)

TRANSFER AGENT(S): The Bank of New York, New York, NY

NYSE SYMBOL HAS
Rec. Pr. 12.25 (4/30/01)

HASBRO, INC.

YIELD 1.0%
P/E RATIO 14.4

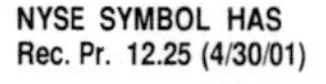

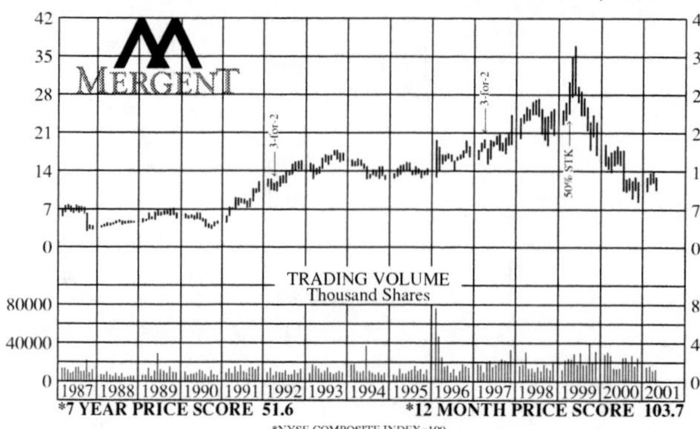

*7 YEAR PRICE SCORE 51.6 *12 MONTH PRICE SCORE 103.7

*NYSE COMPOSITE INDEX=100

INTERIM EARNINGS (Per Share):

Qtr.	Mar.	June	Sept.	Dec.
1996	0.12	0.03	0.36	0.50
1997	0.13	0.07	0.40	0.09
1998	0.04	0.03	0.30	0.65
1999	0.07	0.16	0.43	0.29
2000	0.08	0.04	0.08	d1.05

INTERIM DIVIDENDS (Per Share):

Amt.	Decl.	Ex.	Rec.	Pay.
0.06Q	5/17/00	7/28/00	8/01/00	8/15/00
0.06Q	7/14/00	10/30/00	11/01/00	11/15/00
0.03Q	12/06/00	1/30/01	2/01/01	2/15/01
0.03Q	2/15/01	4/27/01	5/01/01	5/15/01
0.03Q	5/16/01	7/30/01	8/01/01	8/15/01

Indicated div.: $0.12 (Div. Reinv. Plan)

CAPITALIZATION (12/31/00):

	($000)	(%)
Long-Term Debt	1,167,838	46.8
Common & Surplus	1,327,406	53.2
Total	2,495,244	100.0

RECENT DEVELOPMENTS: For the twelve months ended 12/31/00, the Company reported a net loss of $144.6 million compared with net income of $189.0 million in the previous year. Results for 2000 included a pre-tax charge of $44.0 million for a loss on the sale of business units. The 2000 and 1999 results included pre-tax restructuring charges of $64.0 million and $64.2 million, respectively. Net revenues declined 10.5% to $3.79 billion from $4.23 billion the year before.

PROSPECTS: The Company's international business continues to be strong, with revenues from international customers up in local currencies and U.S. dollars. In addition, the Company's worldwide core brands, including G.I. JOE, ACTION MAN, TONKA and PLAYDOH, continue to perform well. Looking ahead, HAS will concentrate on reducing its expenses, lowering its break-even and bring more focus on growing its own brands and new product development.

BUSINESS

HASBRO, INC. is a major worldwide toy manufacturer, offering a diverse line of toys, board and card games, dolls, preschool toys, boys' and girls' action toys as well as infant care products. In 1984, the Company acquired Milton Bradley Co. and in 1991, Tonka Corp., which also included Parker Bros. and Kenner. The Company's products include PLAYSKOOL®, KENNER®, TONKA®, ODDZON®, SUPER SOAKER®, MILTON BRADLEY®, PARKER BROTHERS®, TIGER™ and GALOOB®. Toys and games include MR. POTATO HEAD™, FURBY™, G.I. JOE®, TONKA® Trucks, EASY-BAKE® OVEN, PLAY-DOH®, STAR WARS™, BATMAN™, NERF®, THE GAME OF LIFE®, SCRABBLE®, MONOPOLY® KOOSH® and MICRO MACHINES®.

ANNUAL FINANCIAL DATA

	12/31/00	12/26/99	12/27/98	12/28/97	12/31/96	12/31/95	12/31/94
Earnings Per Share	**[1][3] d0.82**	**[1] 0.93**	**[1] 1.00**	**[1] 0.68**	**1.01**	**[1] 0.78**	**[1][2] 0.89**
Cash Flow Per Share	**0.68**	**2.38**	**1.83**	**1.46**	**1.71**	**1.44**	**1.50**
Tang. Book Val. Per Share	...	**0.64**	**1.92**	**4.36**	**4.28**	**3.61**	**3.15**
Dividends Per Share	**0.24**	**0.23**	**0.21**	**0.20**	**0.17**	**0.14**	**0.12**
Dividend Payout %	...	**25.1**	**21.3**	**30.1**	**16.7**	**17.6**	**13.4**
INCOME STATEMENT (IN MILLIONS):							
Total Revenues	3,787.2	4,232.3	3,304.5	3,188.6	3,002.4	2,858.2	2,670.3
Costs & Expenses	3,627.3	3,627.4	2,810.4	2,786.9	2,531.8	2,454.7	2,252.3
Depreciation & Amort.	264.2	277.3	169.2	166.6	138.3	129.9	122.3
Operating Income	d104.3	327.6	324.9	235.1	332.3	273.6	295.7
Net Interest Inc./(Exp.)	d114.4	d69.3	d36.1	d27.5	d31.5	d37.6	d30.8
Income Before Income Taxes	d226.0	273.8	303.5	204.5	306.9	252.6	291.6
Income Taxes	cr81.4	84.9	97.1	69.5	107.0	97.0	112.3
Net Income	[1][3] d144.6	[1] 189.0	[1] 206.4	[1] 135.0	199.9	[1] 155.6	[1][2] 179.3
Cash Flow	119.6	466.3	375.6	301.6	338.2	285.5	301.6
Average Shs. Outstg. (000)	176,437	196,175	205,420	206,354	197,784	198,569	200,995
BALANCE SHEET (IN MILLIONS):							
Cash & Cash Equivalents	127.1	280.2	177.7	361.8	219.0	161.0	137.0
Total Current Assets	1,580.2	2,131.7	1,790.0	1,573.9	1,486.6	1,425.5	1,252.5
Net Property	296.7	318.8	330.4	280.6	313.5	313.2	308.9
Total Assets	3,828.5	4,463.3	3,793.8	2,899.7	2,701.5	2,616.4	2,378.4
Total Current Liabilities	1,239.8	2,071.3	1,366.3	1,003.5	830.8	869.9	763.7
Long-Term Obligations	1,167.8	420.7	407.2	...	149.4	150.0	150.0
Net Stockholders' Equity	1,327.4	1,879.0	1,944.8	1,838.1	1,652.0	1,525.6	1,395.4
Net Working Capital	340.4	60.3	423.7	570.3	655.8	555.6	488.7
Year-end Shs. Outstg. (000)	172,441	192,984	209,700	200,162	193,295	196,526	196,938
STATISTICAL RECORD:							
Operating Profit Margin %	...	7.7	9.8	7.4	11.1	9.6	11.1
Net Profit Margin %	...	4.5	6.2	4.2	6.7	5.4	6.7
Return on Equity %	...	10.1	10.6	7.3	12.1	10.2	12.9
Return on Assets %	...	4.2	5.4	4.7	7.4	5.9	7.5
Debt/Total Assets %	30.5	9.4	10.7	...	5.5	5.7	6.3
Price Range	18.94-8.38	37.00-16.88	27.29-18.67	24.33-15.25	19.67-12.83	15.67-12.61	16.28-12.39
P/E Ratio	...	39.8-18.1	27.3-18.7	35.8-22.4	19.4-12.7	20.0-16.1	18.2-13.9
Average Yield %	1.8	0.9	0.9	1.0	1.0	1.0	0.8

Statistics are as originally reported. Adj. for stk. splits: 3-for-2, 3/1/99; 3-for-2, 3/97. [1] Incl. non-recurr. chrg. 12/31/00: $64.0 mill.; 12/26/99: $64.2 mill.; 12/27/98: $20.0 mill.; 12/28/97: $125.0 mill.; 12/31/95: $31.1 mill.; 12/31/94: $12.5 mill. [2] Bef. acctg. change chrg. 12/31/94: $4.3 mill. [3] Incl. pre-tax chrg. of $44.0 mill. for loss on sale of bus. units.

OFFICERS:
A. G. Hassenfeld, Chmn., C.E.O.
H. P. Gordon, Vice-Chmn.
A. J. Verrecchia, Pres., C.O.O.
D. D. Hargreaves, Sr. V.P., C.F.O.

INVESTOR CONTACT: Karen A. Warren, Inv. Rel., (401) 727-5401

PRINCIPAL OFFICE: 1027 Newport Avenue, Pawtucket, RI 02861

TELEPHONE NUMBER: (401) 431-8697
FAX: (401) 727-5544
WEB: www.hasbro.com

NO. OF EMPLOYEES: 8,900 (approx.)

SHAREHOLDERS: 8,650 (approx. record)

ANNUAL MEETING: In May

INCORPORATED: RI, Jan., 1926

INSTITUTIONAL HOLDINGS:
No. of Institutions: 232
Shares Held: 127,925,275
% Held: 74.2

INDUSTRY: Games, toys, and children's vehicles (SIC: 3944)

TRANSFER AGENT(S): Fleet National Bank, Boston, MA

NYSE SYMBOL HE
Rec. Pr. 37.07 (5/31/01)

HAWAIIAN ELECTRIC INDUSTRIES, INC.

YIELD 6.7%
P/E RATIO 26.1

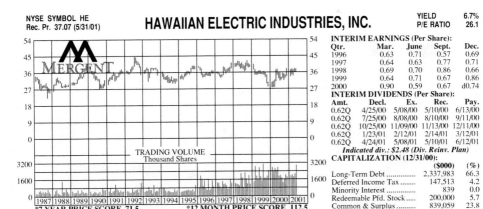

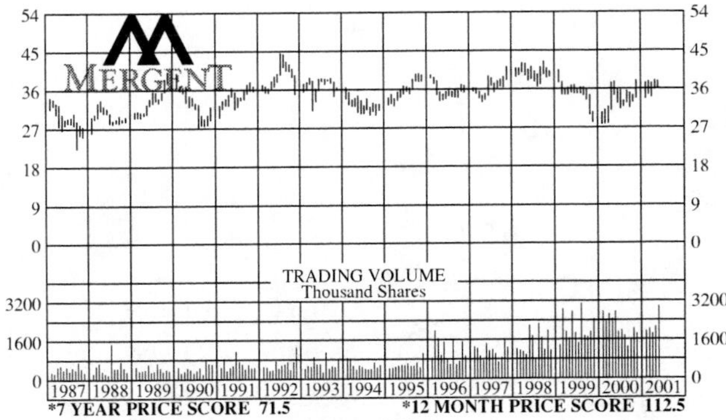

TRADING VOLUME
Thousand Shares

*7 YEAR PRICE SCORE 71.5 *12 MONTH PRICE SCORE 112.5
*NYSE COMPOSITE INDEX=100

INTERIM EARNINGS (Per Share):

Qtr.	Mar.	June	Sept.	Dec.
1996	0.63	0.71	0.57	0.69
1997	0.64	0.63	0.77	0.71
1998	0.69	0.70	0.86	0.66
1999	0.64	0.71	0.67	0.86
2000	0.90	0.59	0.67	d0.74

INTERIM DIVIDENDS (Per Share):

Amt.	Decl.	Ex.	Rec.	Pay.
0.62Q	4/25/00	5/08/00	5/10/00	6/13/00
0.62Q	7/25/00	8/08/00	8/10/00	9/11/00
0.62Q	10/25/00	11/09/00	11/13/00	12/11/00
0.62Q	1/23/01	2/12/01	2/14/01	3/12/01
0.62Q	4/24/01	5/08/01	5/10/01	6/12/01

Indicated div.: $2.48 (Div. Reinv. Plan)

CAPITALIZATION (12/31/00):

	($000)	(%)
Long-Term Debt	2,337,983	66.3
Deferred Income Tax	147,513	4.2
Minority Interest	839	0.0
Redeemable Pfd. Stock	200,000	5.7
Common & Surplus	839,059	23.8
Total	3,525,394	100.0

RECENT DEVELOPMENTS: For the year ended 12/31/00, net income totaled $45.7 million compared with income from continuing operations of $92.9 million in 1999. Results for 1999 excluded income from discontinued operations of $4.0 million. Revenues grew 12.8% to $1.72 billion versus $1.52 billion the year before. Electric utility revenues rose 21.0% to $1.28 billion, while savings bank revenues jumped 10.0% to $450.9 million. Operating income amounted to $155.3 million compared with $233.9 million the year before.

PROSPECTS: During the year, results benefited from earnings strength from the electric utilities and the savings bank, partially offset by losses from the write-off of the Company's remaining interest in East Asia Power Resources Corporation (EAPRC) in the Philippines. The decision to write off the Company's remaining interest in EARPC will limit HE's exposure in the Philippines, where civil unrest, severe devaluation of the peso and volatile fuel prices worked against the Company.

BUSINESS

HAWAIIAN ELECTRIC INDUSTRIES, INC. is a holding company with subsidiaries engaged in the electric utility, savings bank and an international power subsidiary. The Company and its subsidiaries, Maui Electric Company, Limited and Hawaii Electric Light Company, Inc., provide electricity to 95% of the state's 1.1 million residents through more than 394,355 residential, commercial and industrial accounts on Oahu, Hawaii, Maui, Lanai and Molokai. HEI Power Corp. was formed to pursue independent power and integrated energy projects in Asia and the Pacific. American Savings Bank, F.S.B., offers a full range of personal and business services to more than 600,000 accounts through a statewide network of 68 branch offices. Non-utility companies include: Malama Pacific Corporation and Hawaiian Electric Renewable Systems, Inc.

ANNUAL FINANCIAL DATA

	12/31/00	12/31/99	12/31/98	12/31/97	12/31/96	12/31/95	12/31/94
Earnings Per Share	**1.40**	**3 2.88**	**2 2.95**	**1 2.75**	**1 2.60**	**2.66**	**2.60**
Cash Flow Per Share	**5.10**	**6.69**	**6.46**	**6.09**	**5.72**	**5.56**	**5.14**
Tang. Book Val. Per Share	**22.43**	**23.00**	**22.17**	**21.70**	**23.85**	**23.12**	**22.22**
Dividends Per Share	**2.48**	**2.48**	**2.48**	**2.44**	**2.41**	**2.37**	**2.33**
Dividend Payout %	**177.1**	**86.1**	**84.1**	**88.7**	**92.7**	**89.1**	**89.6**
INCOME STATEMENT (IN MILLIONS):							
Total Revenues	1,719.0	1,523.3	1,485.2	1,464.0	1,410.6	1,295.9	1,188.5
Costs & Expenses	1,442.7	1,166.4	1,147.7	1,152.4	1,127.5	1,023.4	942.8
Depreciation & Amort.	120.9	123.0	112.8	105.3	94.8	84.9	71.6
Operating Income	155.3	233.9	224.6	206.2	188.2	187.7	174.1
Net Interest Inc./(Exp.)	d73.2	d68.4	d60.4	d53.7	d54.1	d52.7	d45.0
Income Taxes	21.2	57.0	57.0	55.3	54.8	55.7	53.0
Net Income	45.7	3 92.9	2 94.6	1 86.4	1 78.7	77.5	73.0
Cash Flow	166.7	215.9	207.4	191.8	173.5	162.4	144.6
Average Shs. Outstg. (000)	32,687	32,291	32,129	31,470	30,310	29,187	28,137
BALANCE SHEET (IN MILLIONS):							
Gross Property	3,322.0	3,195.3	3,156.4	2,994.3	2,831.8	2,623.7	2,425.3
Accumulated Depreciation	1,230.7	1,129.1	1,063.0	974.8	890.1	815.5	747.5
Net Property	2,091.3	2,066.2	2,093.4	2,019.6	1,941.8	1,808.2	1,677.8
Total Assets	8,469.3	8,291.0	8,199.3	7,953.9	5,935.8	5,603.7	5,174.5
Long-Term Obligations	2,338.0	2,166.6	1,705.2	1,539.0	1,494.4	1,259.7	1,334.6
Net Stockholders' Equity	839.1	847.6	827.0	814.7	772.9	729.6	682.1
Year-end Shs. Outstg. (000)	32,991	32,213	32,116	31,895	30,853	29,773	28,655
STATISTICAL RECORD:							
Operating Profit Margin %	9.0	15.4	15.1	14.1	13.3	14.5	14.7
Net Profit Margin %	2.7	6.1	6.4	5.9	5.6	6.0	6.1
Net Inc./Net Property %	2.2	4.5	4.5	4.3	4.1	4.3	4.4
Net Inc./Tot. Capital %	1.3	2.7	3.2	3.2	3.2	3.5	3.3
Return on Equity %	5.5	11.0	11.4	10.6	10.2	10.6	10.7
Accum. Depr./Gross Prop. %	37.0	35.3	33.7	32.6	31.4	31.1	30.8
Price Range	37.94-27.69	40.50-28.06	42.56-36.38	41.31-32.88	39.50-33.25	39.75-32.13	36.50-29.88
P/E Ratio	27.1-19.8	14.1-9.7	14.4-12.3	15.0-12.0	15.2-12.8	14.9-12.1	14.0-11.5
Average Yield %	7.6	7.2	6.3	6.6	6.6	6.6	7.0

Statistics are as originally reported. 1 Incl. non-recurr chrgs. $2.4 mill., 12/97; $13.8 mill., 12/96 2 Before loss $8.7 mill. from disc. opers. 3 Excl. a net gain of $4.0 million fr. disc. opers.

OFFICERS:
R. F. Clarke, Chmn., Pres., C.E.O.
R. F. Mougeot, V.P., C.F.O.
E. H. Kawamoto, Treas.

INVESTOR CONTACT: Edwina H. Kawamoto, Dir., Inv. Rel., (808) 543-7385

PRINCIPAL OFFICE: 900 Richards St., Honolulu, HI 96813

TELEPHONE NUMBER: (808) 543-5662
FAX: (808) 543-7966
WEB: www.hei.com

NO. OF EMPLOYEES: 3,126

SHAREHOLDERS: 17,214

ANNUAL MEETING: In April

INCORPORATED: HI, July, 1981

INSTITUTIONAL HOLDINGS:
No. of Institutions: 139
Shares Held: 8,558,873
% Held: 25.9

INDUSTRY: Electric services (SIC: 4911)

TRANSFER AGENT(S): Continental Stock Transfer & Trust Company, New York, NY

NYSE SYMBOL HAZ
Rec. Pr. 8.25 (5/31/01)

HAYES LEMMERZ INTERNATIONAL, INC.

YIELD . . .
P/E RATIO . . .

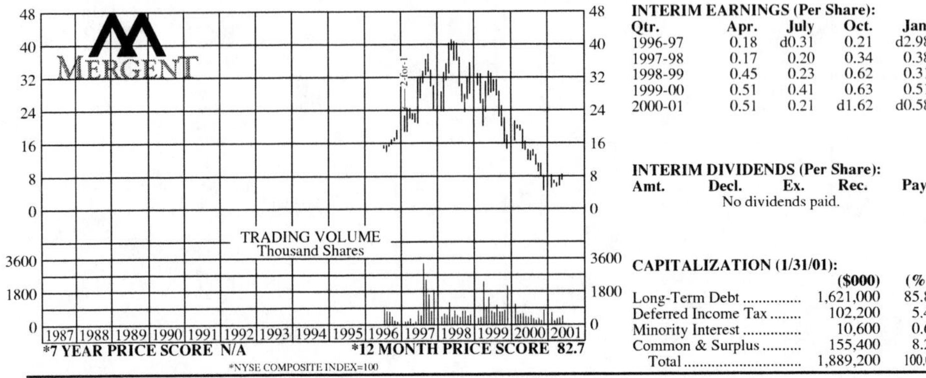

INTERIM EARNINGS (Per Share):

Qtr.	Apr.	July	Oct.	Jan.
1996-97	0.18	d0.31	0.21	d2.98
1997-98	0.17	0.20	0.34	0.38
1998-99	0.45	0.23	0.62	0.31
1999-00	0.51	0.41	0.63	0.51
2000-01	0.51	0.21	d1.62	d0.58

INTERIM DIVIDENDS (Per Share):

Amt.	Decl.	Ex.	Rec.	Pay.

No dividends paid.

CAPITALIZATION (1/31/01):

	($000)	(%)
Long-Term Debt	1,621,000	85.8
Deferred Income Tax	102,200	5.4
Minority Interest	10,600	0.6
Common & Surplus	155,400	8.2
Total	1,889,200	100.0

RECENT DEVELOPMENTS: For the year ended 1/31/01, the Company reported a net loss of $41.8 million compared with net income of $65.1 million in the previous year. Net sales decreased 5.4% to $2.17 billion versus $2.30 billion in the prior year. Revenues from the Cast Components segment fell 7.4% to $650.7 million, while other revenues declined 30.3% to $163.8 million from $235.1 million the year before. Revenues from the Automotive Wheels segement remained flat at $1.36 billion.

PROSPECTS: HAZ expects steady improvement throughout 2001, led by $150.0 million in incremental new business, and restructuring programs that are expected to contribute $20.0 million in cost savings. Initiatives for fiscal 2001 include the launch of a new aluminum components foundry in Michigan. On 3/12/01, HAZ announced that its Commercial Highway Division was awarded a $5.0 million contract to produce military wheels for the Canadian Army's medium-duty truck.

BUSINESS

HAYES LEMMERZ INTERNATIONAL, INC. (formerly Hayes Wheels International Inc.) is a supplier of suspension module components to the global automotive and commercial highway markets. The Company's products for the suspension module include wheels, wheel-end attachments, aluminum structural components and automotive brake components. The Company also designs and manufactures wheels and brake components for commercial highway vehicles, and powertrain components, engine components and aluminum non-structural components for the automotive, heating and general equipment industries. HAZ acquired Lemmerz Holdings, GmbH in 1997. The Company completed the acquisition of CMI International, Inc. on 2/3/99.

REVENUES

(01/31/01)	($000)	(%)
Automotive wheels	1,357	62.5
Cast components	651	30.0
Other revenue	164	7.5
Total	2,171	100.0

ANNUAL FINANCIAL DATA

	1/31/01	1/31/00	1/31/99	③ 1/31/98	1/31/97	1/31/96	1/31/95
Earnings Per Share	**d1.41**	**2.06**	**②⑤ 1.60**	**1.12**	**④ d2.36**	**① 0.81**	**0.85**
Cash Flow Per Share	**3.97**	**6.59**	**4.46**	**3.87**	**d0.65**	**1.74**	**1.69**
Tang. Book Val. Per Share	**6.02**	**7.21**	**7.28**	**5.37**	**. . .**	**6.98**	**6.16**
INCOME STATEMENT (IN MILLIONS):							
Total Revenues	2,171.3	2,296.4	1,672.9	1,269.8	778.2	611.1	537.6
Costs & Expenses	1,848.2	1,888.3	1,398.5	1,059.4	786.1	518.7	445.5
Depreciation & Amort.	159.4	142.6	92.4	71.2	47.6	32.7	29.6
Operating Income	95.6	272.7	188.0	145.5	d55.5	61.2	63.3
Net Interest Inc./(Exp.)	d163.3	d153.3	d94.9	d90.4	d48.5	d15.0	d13.4
Income Before Income Taxes	d67.7	119.4	93.1	55.1	d102.0	46.2	49.9
Income Taxes	cr28.5	51.3	39.1	23.2	cr36.7	17.8	20.0
Equity Earnings/Minority Int.	d4.3	d1.8	d1.4	d5.0	d2.7	. . .	. . .
Net Income	d41.8	65.1	②⑤ 52.0	31.4	④ d65.5	① 28.4	29.9
Cash Flow	117.6	207.7	144.4	102.6	d17.9	61.1	59.5
Average Shs. Outstg. (000)	29,652	31,512	32,411	26,512	27,703	35,148	35,148
BALANCE SHEET (IN MILLIONS):							
Cash & Cash Equivalents	. . .	25.9	51.3	23.1	47.5	1.8	0.5
Total Current Assets	533.4	399.6	422.3	382.4	289.5	180.2	157.6
Net Property	1,139.0	1,178.4	878.0	670.4	486.4	304.4	285.7
Total Assets	2,811.1	2,776.8	2,110.9	1,758.9	1,183.1	633.9	589.6
Total Current Liabilities	643.6	727.1	513.8	372.9	274.3	129.7	130.5
Long-Term Obligations	1,621.0	1,384.6	976.1	882.6	686.3	128.9	111.4
Net Stockholders' Equity	155.4	218.9	220.9	161.5	d41.1	245.4	216.4
Net Working Capital	d110.2	d327.5	d91.5	9.5	15.2	50.5	27.1
Year-end Shs. Outstg. (000)	25,806	30,354	30,324	30,088	22,550	35,148	35,148
STATISTICAL RECORD:							
Operating Profit Margin %	4.4	11.9	11.2	11.5	. . .	10.0	11.8
Net Profit Margin %	. . .	2.8	3.1	2.5	. . .	4.6	5.6
Return on Equity %	. . .	29.7	23.5	19.4	. . .	11.6	13.8
Return on Assets %	. . .	2.3	2.5	1.8	. . .	4.5	5.1
Debt/Total Assets %	57.7	49.9	46.2	50.2	58.0	20.3	18.9
Price Range	21.38-4.50	33.50-14.56	41.25-23.50	37.75-18.75	19.25-13.88	. . .	. . .
P/E Ratio	. . .	16.3-7.1	25.8-14.7	33.7-16.7	. . .	. . .	. . .

Statistics are as originally reported. Adj. for stk. splits: 2-for-1, 1/97. ① Bef. extraord. chrg. $7.4 mill. ($0.27/sh.) and Incl. non-recurr. chrg. $3.6 mill. ② Bef. after-tax extraordinary loss of $8.3 mill. fr. early retire. of debt. ③ Reflects combination of Hayes Wheels International Inc. and Lemmerz Holdings. ④ Incl. non-recurr. chrg. $115.4 mill. ⑤ Excl. extraord. loss of $8.3 mill.

OFFICERS:
R. Cucuz, Chmn., C.E.O.
W. D. Shovers, V.P., C.F.O.
P. B. Carey, Sec., Gen. Couns.

INVESTOR CONTACT: John A. Salvette, Dir., Inv. Rel., (313) 942-8689

PRINCIPAL OFFICE: 15300 Centennial Drive, Northville, MI 48167

TELEPHONE NUMBER: (734) 941-2000
FAX: (734) 737-4003
WEB: www.hayes-lemmerz.com

NO. OF EMPLOYEES: 15,000 (approx.)

SHAREHOLDERS: 105

ANNUAL MEETING: In June

INCORPORATED: DE, 1992

INSTITUTIONAL HOLDINGS:
No. of Institutions: 31
Shares Held: 4,119,856
% Held: 14.5

INDUSTRY: Motor vehicle parts and accessories (SIC: 3714)

TRANSFER AGENT(S): Mellon Investor Services, LLC, South Hackensack, NJ

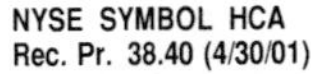

NYSE SYMBOL HCA
Rec. Pr. 38.40 (4/30/01)

HCA - THE HEALTHCARE COMPANY

YIELD 0.2%
P/E RATIO 28.4

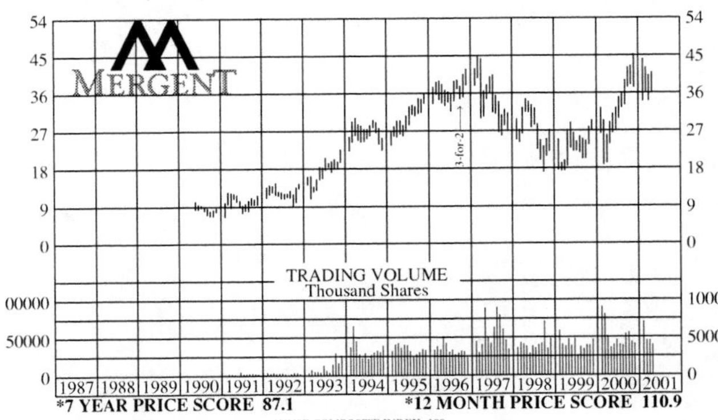

*7 YEAR PRICE SCORE 87.1 *12 MONTH PRICE SCORE 110.9

*NYSE COMPOSITE INDEX=100

INTERIM EARNINGS (Per Share):

Qtr.	Mar.	June	Sept.	Dec.
1997	0.70	0.62	0.15	d1.16
1998	0.37	0.27	0.19	0.04
1999	0.50	d0.04	0.24	0.16
2000	0.52	0.48	0.31	0.04

INTERIM DIVIDENDS (Per Share):

Amt.	Decl.	Ex.	Rec.	Pay.
0.02Q	5/25/00	7/28/00	8/01/00	9/01/00
0.02Q	9/28/00	10/30/00	11/01/00	12/01/00
0.02Q	11/30/00	1/30/01	2/01/01	3/01/01
0.02Q	1/26/01	4/27/01	5/01/01	6/01/01
0.02Q	5/24/01	7/30/01	8/01/01	9/01/01

Indicated div.: $0.08

CAPITALIZATION (12/31/00):

	($000)	(%)
Long-Term Debt	5,631,000	53.1
Minority Interest	572,000	5.4
Common & Surplus	4,405,000	41.5
Total	10,608,000	100.0

RECENT DEVELOPMENTS: For the year ended 12/31/00, net income fell 66.7% to $219.0 million. Results for 2000 included a settlement charge of $840.0 million. The 2000 and 1999 results included gains of $34.0 million and $297.0 million; impairment charges of $117.0 million and $220.0 million; and restructuring costs of $62.0 million and $116.0 million, respectively. Revenues were $16.67 billion.

PROSPECTS: The Company has signed an agreement with the Department of Justice and U.S. attorney's offices to resolve all pending federal criminal issues in the Columbia investigation. Going forward, the Company should benefit from significant investments made in 2000 to its hospitals and communities.

BUSINESS

HCA-THE HEALTHCARE COMPANY (formerly Columbia/HCA Healthcare Corporation) is a holding company whose subsidiaries own and operate hospitals and related health care entities. At 12/31/00, these affiliates owned and operated 196 hospitals, 78 ambulatory surgery centers. Affiliates of HCA are also partners in several 50/50 joint ventures that own and operate nine hospital and three ambulatory surgery centers. The Company's facilities are located in 24 U.S. states, England and Switzerland. HCA integrates fragmented providers and services (such as hospitals, physicians, outpatient centers, psychiatric facilities and home-health agencies) to create local healthcare networks. HCA typically develops networks by entering a market through the acquisition of a hospital with more than 150 beds. Additional healthcare facilities are then acquired to develop a comprehensive healthcare network in a local market.

ANNUAL FINANCIAL DATA

	12/31/00	12/31/99	12/31/98	12/31/97	12/31/96	12/31/95	12/31/94
Earnings Per Share	**5 0.39**	**5 1.11**	**4 0.82**	**3 0.27**	**2.22**	**1 2 1.58**	**1 2 1.42**
Cash Flow Per Share	**2.21**	**2.96**	**2.75**	**2.14**	**3.92**	**3.04**	**2.63**
Tang. Book Val. Per Share	**4.14**	**5.84**	**7.27**	**5.82**	**7.49**	**5.43**	**5.07**
Dividends Per Share	**0.08**	**0.08**	**0.08**	**0.08**	**0.08**	**0.08**	**0.08**
Dividend Payout %	**20.5**	**7.2**	**9.8**	**29.6**	**3.6**	**5.1**	**5.6**
INCOME STATEMENT (IN MILLIONS):							
Total Revenues	16,670.0	16,657.0	18,681.0	18,819.0	18,786.0	17,695.0	11,132.0
Costs & Expenses	13,619.0	13,859.0	15,925.0	16,036.0	14,733.0	14,075.0	8,892.0
Depreciation & Amort.	1,033.0	1,094.0	1,247.0	1,238.0	1,155.0	981.0	635.0
Operating Income	2,018.0	1,704.0	1,509.0	1,545.0	2,898.0	2,639.0	1,605.0
Net Interest Inc./(Exp.)	d559.0	d471.0	d561.0	d493.0	d488.0	d460.0	d248.0
Income Before Income Taxes	516.0	1,227.0	1,081.0	388.0	2,515.0	1,779.0	1,231.0
Income Taxes	297.0	570.0	549.0	206.0	1,010.0	715.0	486.0
Equity Earnings/Minority Int.	d84.0	d57.0	d70.0	d150.0	d141.0	d113.0	d29.0
Net Income	5 219.0	5 657.0	4 532.0	3 182.0	1,505.0	1 2 1,064.0	1 2 745.0
Cash Flow	1,252.0	1,751.0	1,779.0	1,420.0	2,660.0	2,045.0	1,380.0
Average Shs. Outstg. (000)	567,685	591,029	646,649	663,000	678,000	673,500	525,000
BALANCE SHEET (IN MILLIONS):							
Cash & Cash Equivalents	314.0	190.0	297.0	110.0	113.0	232.0	13.0
Total Current Assets	4,453.0	3,597.0	3,863.0	4,423.0	4,199.0	4,200.0	2,550.0
Net Property	8,480.0	8,490.0	9,449.0	10,230.0	10,373.0	9,751.0	6,383.0
Total Assets	17,568.0	16,885.0	19,429.0	22,002.0	21,116.0	19,892.0	12,339.0
Total Current Liabilities	4,141.0	3,332.0	3,559.0	2,773.0	2,810.0	2,738.0	1,767.0
Long-Term Obligations	5,631.0	5,284.0	5,685.0	9,276.0	6,781.0	7,137.0	3,853.0
Net Stockholders' Equity	4,405.0	5,617.0	7,581.0	7,250.0	8,609.0	7,129.0	5,022.0
Net Working Capital	312.0	265.0	304.0	1,650.0	1,389.0	1,462.0	783.0
Year-end Shs. Outstg. (000)	542,992	564,273	642,578	641,000	671,000	669,000	543,000
STATISTICAL RECORD:							
Operating Profit Margin %	12.1	10.2	8.1	8.2	15.4	14.9	14.4
Net Profit Margin %	1.3	3.9	2.8	1.0	8.0	6.0	6.7
Return on Equity %	5.0	11.7	7.0	2.5	17.5	14.9	14.8
Return on Assets %	1.2	3.9	2.7	0.8	7.1	5.3	6.0
Price Range	45.25-18.75	29.44-17.25	34.63-17.00	44.88-25.75	41.88-31.67	36.00-23.58	30.17-22.17
P/E Ratio	116.0-48.1	26.5-15.5	42.2-20.7	166.1-95.3	18.9-14.3	22.8-14.9	21.2-15.6
Average Yield %	0.3	0.3	0.3	0.2	0.2	0.3	0.3

Statistics are as originally reported. Adj. for 3-for-2 stock split 10/96. 1 Bef. an extra. chg. of $103.0 mill., 1995; $115.0 mill., 1994. 2 Incl. mgr.-rel. costs $235.0 mill., 1995; $102.0 mill., 1994. 3 Incl. chrgs. of $383.0 mill; bef. dis. opers. of $431.0 mill. & net acctg. chg. $56.0 mill. 4 Incl. a net chrg. of $58.0 mill.; bef. loss of $153.0 mill. fr. disc. opers. 5 Incl. net chrg., 2000, $985.0 mill.; 1999, $110.0 mill.

OFFICERS:
T. F. Frist Jr., Chmn.
J. O. Bovender, Pres., C.E.O.

INVESTOR CONTACT: W. Mark Kimbrough, V.P., Inv. Rel., (615) 344-1199

PRINCIPAL OFFICE: One Park Plaza, Nashville, TN 37203

TELEPHONE NUMBER: (615) 344-9551
FAX: (615) 320-2266
WEB: www.columbia-hca.com

NO. OF EMPLOYEES: 164,000 (approx.)

SHAREHOLDERS: 17,081 (approx.)

ANNUAL MEETING: In May

INCORPORATED: NV, Jan., 1990; reincorp., DE, 1993.

INSTITUTIONAL HOLDINGS:
No. of Institutions: 405
Shares Held: 409,094,456
% Held: 75.3

INDUSTRY: General medical & surgical hospitals (SIC: 8062)

TRANSFER AGENT(S): National City Bank, Cleveland, OH

NYSE SYMBOL HMA
Rec. Pr. 17.92 (4/30/01)

HEALTH MANAGEMENT ASSOCIATES, INC.

YIELD ...
P/E RATIO 25.2

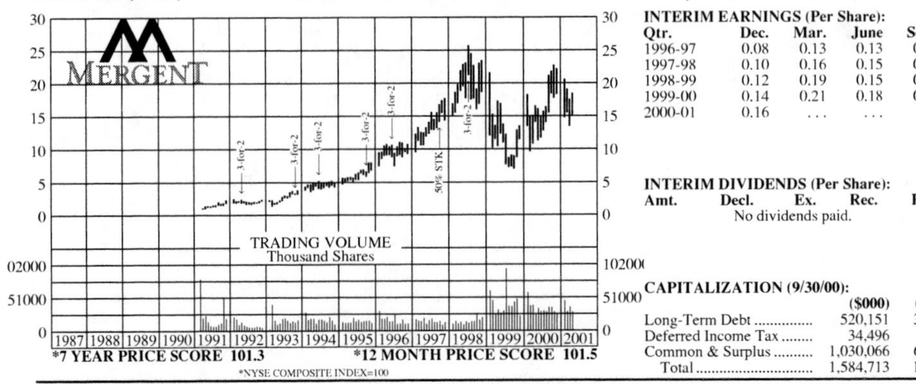

*7 YEAR PRICE SCORE 101.3 *12 MONTH PRICE SCORE 101.5

*NYSE COMPOSITE INDEX=100

INTERIM EARNINGS (Per Share):

Qtr.	Dec.	Mar.	June	Sept.
1996-97	0.08	0.13	0.13	0.10
1997-98	0.10	0.16	0.15	0.13
1998-99	0.12	0.19	0.15	0.13
1999-00	0.14	0.21	0.18	0.16
2000-01	0.16	...	...	...

INTERIM DIVIDENDS (Per Share):

Amt.	Decl.	Ex.	Rec.	Pay.

No dividends paid.

CAPITALIZATION (9/30/00):

	($000)	(%)
Long-Term Debt	520,151	32.8
Deferred Income Tax	34,496	2.2
Common & Surplus	1,030,066	65.0
Total	1,584,713	100.0

RECENT DEVELOPMENTS: For the three months ended 12/31/00, net income advanced 17.2% to $40.2 million compared with $34.3 million in the equivalent quarter of the previous year. Net patient service revenues increased 17.3% to $434.2 million from $370.1 million in the prior-year period. Revenue growth was attributed to same-hospital volume increases and previous acquisitions. Same-hospital admissions rose 3.1% to 40,235 and surgeries grew 2.5% to 37,019.

PROSPECTS: The Company should continue to benefit from its strategy of acquiring hospitals in non-urban communities located in the Southeast and Southwest, with populations of 40,000 to 400,000. The acquisitions made by HMA are all showing progress in line with its expectations. Negotiations for other potential acquisitions are underway. HMA's focus on collection efforts and the reorganization of several key regional managers are yielding positive results.

BUSINESS

HEALTH MANAGEMENT ASSOCIATES, INC. provides health care services, primarily in the Southeast and Southwest, to patients in owned and leased hospitals and also provides management services under contracts to other hospital facilities. As of 10/17/00, the Company operates 37 general acute care hospitals in 11 states with a total of 5,090 licensed beds and three psychiatric hospitals with a total of 186 licensed beds. Approximately 60.0% of gross patient service revenues for the year ended 9/30/00 were related to services rendered to patients covered by Medicare and Medicaid programs.

ANNUAL FINANCIAL DATA

	9/30/00	9/30/99	9/30/98	9/30/97	9/30/96	9/30/95	9/30/94
Earnings Per Share	**0.68**	**0.59**	**0.54**	**0.43**	**0.34**	**0.26**	**1 0.21**
Cash Flow Per Share	**0.98**	**0.83**	**0.73**	**0.58**	**0.45**	**0.34**	**0.27**
Tang. Book Val. Per Share	**3.27**	**2.89**	**2.82**	**2.30**	**1.76**	**1.36**	**1.10**
INCOME STATEMENT (IN MILLIONS):							
Total Revenues	1,577.8	1,355.7	1,138.8	895.5	714.3	531.1	438.4
Costs & Expenses	1,201.9	1,039.4	858.3	676.9	545.2	402.7	335.7
Depreciation & Amort.	74.5	61.3	50.4	36.6	27.2	20.6	16.6
Operating Income	301.4	255.0	230.0	182.0	141.9	107.9	86.0
Net Interest Inc./(Exp.)	d25.4	d8.4	d4.8	d3.7	d3.5	d3.6	d4.3
Income Before Income Taxes	276.0	246.7	225.3	178.3	138.4	104.2	81.7
Income Taxes	108.3	96.8	88.4	70.0	54.3	40.9	32.6
Net Income	167.7	149.8	136.8	108.3	84.1	63.3	1 49.1
Cash Flow	242.2	211.1	187.3	144.9	111.3	83.9	65.7
Average Shs. Outstg. (000)	247,277	255,067	255,575	251,697	248,511	243,189	239,858
BALANCE SHEET (IN MILLIONS):							
Cash & Cash Equivalents	19.0	14.7	14.1	68.6	33.4	76.8	110.4
Total Current Assets	487.0	425.5	308.7	236.1	177.8	173.4	177.6
Net Property	1,065.3	912.5	737.8	472.7	397.7	283.3	214.3
Total Assets	1,772.1	1,517.3	1,112.1	727.6	591.7	467.0	398.8
Total Current Liabilities	169.8	175.2	120.5	82.9	70.9	50.6	39.6
Long-Term Obligations	520.2	401.5	177.3	49.7	68.7	67.7	75.8
Net Stockholders' Equity	1,030.1	890.5	756.8	560.2	417.7	318.0	252.9
Net Working Capital	317.2	250.3	188.2	153.3	106.9	122.7	138.0
Year-end Shs. Outstg. (000)	255,357	253,405	251,558	244,058	237,824	233,476	230,313
STATISTICAL RECORD:							
Operating Profit Margin %	19.1	18.8	20.2	20.3	19.9	20.3	19.6
Net Profit Margin %	10.6	11.1	12.0	12.1	11.8	11.9	11.2
Return on Equity %	16.3	16.8	18.1	19.3	20.1	19.9	19.4
Return on Assets %	9.5	9.9	12.3	14.9	14.2	13.6	12.3
Debt/Total Assets %	29.4	26.5	15.9	6.8	11.6	14.5	19.0
Price Range	22.75-9.63	21.63-7.00	25.75-14.92	17.67-9.50	11.11-7.45	8.00-4.64	5.27-3.56
P/E Ratio	33.5-14.2	36.6-11.9	47.7-27.6	40.8-21.9	32.7-21.9	30.5-17.7	25.7-17.3

Statistics are as originally reported. Adjusted for 3-for-2 stock splits, 6/17/98, 10/23/97, 6/14/96, 10/2/95. 1 Excl. acctg. charge of $2.6 mill.

OFFICERS:
W. J. Schoen, Chmn., C.E.O.
E. P. Holland, Vice-Chmn., C.O.O.
J. V. Vumbacco, Pres., C.A.O.

INVESTOR CONTACT: John C. Merriwether, Dir. Inv. Rel., (941) 598-3104

PRINCIPAL OFFICE: 5811 Pelican Bay Boulevard, Suite 500, Naples, FL 34108-2710

TELEPHONE NUMBER: (941) 598-3131
FAX: (941) 913-2715
WEB: www.hma-corp.com

NO. OF EMPLOYEES: 19,000 (approx.)

SHAREHOLDERS: 1,552 (approx.)

ANNUAL MEETING: In Feb.

INCORPORATED: DE, 1979

INSTITUTIONAL HOLDINGS:
No. of Institutions: 288
Shares Held: 215,057,147
% Held: 88.3

INDUSTRY: General medical & surgical hospitals (SIC: 8062)

TRANSFER AGENT(S): First Union National Bank, Charlotte, NC

NYSE SYMBOL HNT
Rec. Pr. 21.55 (4/30/00)

HEALTH NET, INC.

YIELD ...
P/E RATIO 16.2

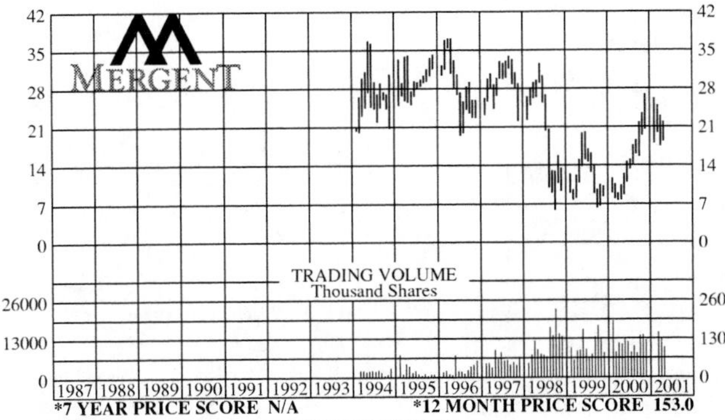

*7 YEAR PRICE SCORE N/A *12 MONTH PRICE SCORE 153.0
*NYSE COMPOSITE INDEX=100

INTERIM EARNINGS (Per Share):

Qtr.	Mar.	June	Sept.	Dec.
1996	0.54	0.51	0.52	d0.05
1997	0.38	d1.64	0.49	0.25
1998	0.22	0.01	d0.73	d0.85
1999	0.18	0.23	0.29	0.31
2000	0.28	0.32	0.36	0.37

INTERIM DIVIDENDS (Per Share):

Amt.	Decl.	Ex.	Rec.	Pay.

No dividends paid.

CAPITALIZATION (12/31/00):

	($000)	(%)
Long-Term Debt	766,450	41.7
Deferred Income Tax	8,635	0.5
Common & Surplus	1,061,131	57.8
Total	1,836,216	100.0

RECENT DEVELOPMENTS: For the year ended 12/31/00, net income increased 10.7% to $163.6 million compared with income of $147.8 million, before the cumulative effect of an accounting change charge, in the previous year. Results for 2000 and 1999 included a loss and a gain of $409,000 and $58.3 million, respectively, from the sale of businesses. The 1999 results also included pre-tax restructuring and other adjustment charges of $11.7 million. Total revenues jumped 5.0% to $9.08 billion.

PROSPECTS: Going forward, HNT expects its solid and consistent performance to continue throughout 2001. Accordingly, the Company is forcasting a range of earnings for 2001 between $1.55 and $1.58 per share. Moreover, HNT's health plan revenues are expected to grow in the low double digits, fueled by premium increases and continued enrollment growth. In addition, Government/Specialty revenues are expected to grow modestly.

BUSINESS

HEALTH NET, INC. (formerly Foundation Health Systems, Inc.) was formed upon the merger of Foundation Health Corporation and Health Systems International Inc. on 4/1/97. HNT is a managed care organization that administers the delivery of managed healthcare services. HNT's HMO, insured PPO and government contracts subsidiaries provide health benefits to approximately 5.4 million individuals in 16 states through group, individual, Medicare risk, Medicaid and TRICARE programs. HNT's subsidiaries also offer managed health care products related to behavioral health, dental, vision and prescription drugs, and offer managed health care product coordination for multi-region employers and administrative services for medical groups and self-funded benefits programs.

ANNUAL FINANCIAL DATA

	12/31/00	12/31/99	12/31/98	12/31/97	[2] 12/31/96	12/31/95	12/31/94
Earnings Per Share	[6] 1.33	[5][6] 1.21	[3][4] d1.35	[1] d0.55	1.52	1.83	1.77
Cash Flow Per Share	2.18	2.12	d0.30	0.25	2.61	2.82	2.57
Tang. Book Val. Per Share	1.61	...	...	...	1.24	...	1.74
INCOME STATEMENT (IN MILLIONS):							
Total Revenues	9,076.6	8,706.2	8,896.1	7,235.0	3,204.2	2,732.1	2,306.2
Costs & Expenses	8,707.9	8,350.2	9,022.1	7,225.3	3,040.5	2,540.8	2,121.3
Depreciation & Amort.	105.9	112.0	128.1	99.0	52.6	48.1	39.7
Operating Income	262.7	244.0	d254.2	d89.2	111.0	143.1	145.2
Net Interest Inc./(Exp.)	...	...	...	...	d24.5	d19.7	d14.6
Income Before Income Taxes	262.7	244.0	d254.2	d89.2	125.2	156.6	150.8
Income Taxes	99.1	96.2	cr89.0	cr21.4	51.7	67.3	62.8
Equity Earnings/Minority Int.	...	...	...	...	0.1	0.3	0.1
Net Income	[6] 163.6	[5][6] 147.8	[3][4] d165.2	[1] d67.8	73.6	89.6	88.1
Cash Flow	269.5	259.8	d37.1	31.2	126.2	137.7	127.8
Average Shs. Outstg. (000)	123,453	122,343	121,974	123,821	48,332	48,831	49,691
BALANCE SHEET (IN MILLIONS):							
Cash & Cash Equivalents	1,533.6	1,467.1	1,288.9	1,112.4	589.6	592.6	512.4
Total Current Assets	2,399.6	2,347.8	2,239.9	2,409.7	753.5	737.4	630.0
Net Property	296.0	280.7	345.3	427.1	71.8	84.7	75.1
Total Assets	3,670.1	3,696.5	3,929.5	4,076.4	1,211.9	1,213.7	894.4
Total Current Liabilities	1,811.1	1,730.3	1,825.4	1,764.7	478.3	568.3	478.4
Long-Term Obligations	766.5	1,039.4	1,254.3	1,309.0	362.5	354.1	158.3
Net Stockholders' Equity	1,061.1	891.2	744.0	896.0	365.0	285.5	223.6
Net Working Capital	588.5	617.5	414.5	645.0	275.1	169.1	151.7
Year-end Shs. Outstg. (000)	122,800	122,373	122,216	121,553	29,135	48,327	23,462
STATISTICAL RECORD:							
Operating Profit Margin %	2.9	2.8	...	...	3.5	5.2	6.3
Net Profit Margin %	1.8	1.7	...	...	2.3	3.3	3.8
Return on Equity %	15.4	16.6	...	...	20.2	31.4	39.4
Return on Assets %	4.5	4.0	...	...	6.1	7.4	9.8
Debt/Total Assets %	20.9	28.1	31.9	32.1	29.9	29.2	17.7
Price Range	23.50-7.63	20.06-6.25	32.63-5.88	33.94-22.06	37.13-19.38	34.25-24.88	36.75-20.00
P/E Ratio	17.7-5.7	16.6-5.2	...	...	24.4-12.7	18.7-13.6	20.8-11.3

Statistics are as originally reported. [1] Incl. after-tax restruct. & other one-time chgs. of $338.4 mill. & excl. loss fr. disc. opers. [2] Statistics for years prior to 1997 are for Health Systems International Inc. [3] Incl. a pre-tax restruct. chg. of $21.1 mill. & excl. an after-tax chg. of $5.4 mill. for the cum. eff. of a change in accg. princ. [4] Incl. a pre-tax gain of $53.6 mill. on the sale of pharmacy ben. mgmt. opers. [5] Bef. acctg. change chrg. $5.4 mill., but incl. restr. & other chrgs. of $11.7 mill. [6] Incl. a pre-tax loss on the sale of businesses of $409,000, 2000; gain of $58.3 mill., 1999.

OFFICERS:
J. M. Gellert, Pres., C.E.O.
S. P. Erwin, Exec. V.P., C.F.O.

INVESTOR CONTACT: David W. Olson, Sr. V.P., Inv. Rel., (818) 676-6978

PRINCIPAL OFFICE: 21650 Oxnard Street, Woodland Hills, CA 91367

TELEPHONE NUMBER: (818) 676-6000
FAX: (818) 676-8591
WEB: www.health.net
NO. OF EMPLOYEES: 11,000 (approx.)
SHAREHOLDERS: 1,700 (class A common, approx.)
ANNUAL MEETING: In May
INCORPORATED: DE, June, 1990

INSTITUTIONAL HOLDINGS:
No. of Institutions: 152
Shares Held: 112,217,098
% Held: 91.7

INDUSTRY: Health and allied services, nec (SIC: 8099)

TRANSFER AGENT(S): Computershare Investor Services, Chicago, IL

NYSE SYMBOL HRC
Rec. Pr. 14.05 (4/30/01)

HEALTHSOUTH CORPORATION

YIELD ...
P/E RATIO 19.8

TRADING VOLUME
Thousand Shares

*7 YEAR PRICE SCORE 53.4 *12 MONTH PRICE SCORE 132.5

*NYSE COMPOSITE INDEX=100

INTERIM EARNINGS (Per Share):

Qtr.	Mar.	June	Sept.	Dec.
1995	0.12	d0.01	0.16	0.15
1996	0.12	0.18	0.18	0.19
1997	0.19	0.23	0.24	0.25
1998	0.27	0.28	0.24	d0.46
1999	0.26	0.27	d0.01	d0.37
2000	0.17	0.17	0.18	0.19

INTERIM DIVIDENDS (Per Share):

Amt.	Decl.	Ex.	Rec.	Pay.
No dividends paid.				

CAPITALIZATION (12/31/00):

	($000)	(%)
Long-Term Debt [1]	3,168,604	45.3
Deferred Income Tax	160,365	2.3
Minority Interest	137,977	2.0
Common & Surplus	3,526,454	50.4
Total	6,993,400	100.0

RECENT DEVELOPMENTS: For the twelve months ended 12/31/00, net income more than tripled to $278.5 million compared with $76.5 million in the previous year. Net income for 2000 benefited from higher revenues and the Company's streamlined management structure. Results for 1999 included net non-recurring charges of $275.5 million. Revenues rose 3.0% to $4.20 billion from $4.07 billion in the comparable period of 1999.

PROSPECTS: On 2/6/01, the Company signed a letter of intent with HCA - The Healthcare Company to sell HEALTHSOUTH Medical Center, a 200-bed acute-care hospital in Richmond, Virginia, to HCA. Separately, HRC has partnered with Oracle Corp. to build an all digital, automated hospital. The hospital's technological features will include patient beds with display screens connected to the Internet and electronic medical records storage.

BUSINESS

HEALTHSOUTH CORPORATION (formerly HEALTHSOUTH REHABILITATION CORPORATION) is the largest provider of outpatient surgery and rehabilitation healthcare services. HRC's rehabilitation services provide inpatient services and management of rehabilitation services to acute care hospitals or organized physician groups. HRC operates more than 2,000 inpatient and outpatient locations in 50 states, the United Kingdom, Puerto Rico, Australia and Canada. The consumer base includes major insurance companies, self-insured employers, physicians, patients and communities at large.

BUSINESS LINE ANALYSIS

(12/31/00)	Rev(%)	Inc(%)
Inpatient & other clinica	2,178,060	54.6
Outpatient services	1,811,462	45.6
Total	3,989,522	100.0

ANNUAL FINANCIAL DATA

	12/31/00	12/31/99	12/31/98	12/31/97	12/31/96	12/31/95	12/31/94
Earnings Per Share	**[6] 0.71**	**[6] 0.18**	**[5] 0.11**	**[4] 0.91**	**[3] 0.68**	**[2] 0.42**	**[1] 0.35**
Cash Flow Per Share	**1.64**	**1.09**	**0.90**	**1.59**	**1.26**	**1.06**	**0.85**
Tang. Book Val. Per Share	**1.76**	**0.98**	**1.10**	**2.31**	**1.53**	**0.99**	**0.74**
INCOME STATEMENT (IN MILLIONS):							
Total Revenues	4,195.1	4,072.1	4,006.1	3,017.3	2,436.5	1,556.7	1,127.4
Costs & Expenses	3,062.4	3,180.8	2,716.9	2,042.7	1,706.9	1,161.7	893.6
Depreciation & Amort.	360.8	374.2	344.6	250.0	189.0	121.2	75.6
Operating Income	771.8	517.0	944.6	724.6	540.6	273.8	158.2
Net Interest Inc./(Exp.)	d212.5	d166.1	d136.9	d107.1	d88.6	d85.8	d53.0
Income Before Income Taxes	559.4	229.9	267.4	601.6	410.5	142.6	87.3
Income Taxes	181.8	66.9	143.3	206.2	140.2	48.1	33.8
Equity Earnings/Minority Int.	d99.1	d86.5	d77.5	d64.9	d49.4	d15.6	d0.2
Net Income	[6] 278.5	[6] 76.5	[5] 46.6	[4] 330.6	[3] 220.8	[2] 78.9	[1] 53.2
Cash Flow	639.3	450.8	391.1	580.6	409.8	200.1	128.8
Average Shs. Outstg. (000)	391,016	414,570	432,275	365,546	326,290	188,492	151,752
BALANCE SHEET (IN MILLIONS):							
Cash & Cash Equivalents	180.4	132.9	142.5	152.4	151.8	109.0	82.6
Total Current Assets	1,431.1	1,270.9	1,347.0	1,083.2	847.5	563.4	396.0
Net Property	2,871.8	2,503.0	2,288.3	1,850.8	1,390.9	1,100.2	789.5
Total Assets	7,380.4	6,832.3	6,773.0	5,401.1	3,373.5	2,460.1	1,552.3
Total Current Liabilities	382.9	418.2	401.1	516.4	303.5	236.0	177.3
Long-Term Obligations	3,168.6	3,076.8	2,780.9	1,555.3	2,936.6	1,253.4	1,874.8
Net Stockholders' Equity	3,526.5	3,206.4	3,423.0	3,157.4	1,515.9	927.7	426.1
Net Working Capital	1,048.2	852.7	945.9	566.8	544.0	327.5	218.7
Year-end Shs. Outstg. (000)	387,289	385,640	421,136	395,051	304,386	194,536	136,920
STATISTICAL RECORD:							
Operating Profit Margin %	18.4	12.7	23.6	24.0	22.2	17.6	14.0
Net Profit Margin %	6.6	1.9	1.2	11.0	9.1	5.1	4.7
Return on Equity %	7.9	2.4	1.4	10.5	14.6	8.5	12.5
Return on Assets %	3.8	1.1	0.7	6.1	6.5	3.2	3.4
Debt/Total Assets %	42.9	45.0	41.1	28.8	87.1	50.9	120.8
Price Range	17.50-4.75	17.75-4.56	30.81-7.69	28.94-17.75	19.88-13.50	16.19-8.19	9.84-5.84
P/E Ratio	24.6-6.7	98.6-25.3	279.9-69.8	31.8-19.5	29.2-19.9	38.5-19.5	28.1-16.7

Statistics are as originally reported. Adj. for 2-for-1 stk. split, 3/97, 4/95. [1] Incl. nonrecurr. pre-tax chgs. of $11.8 mill. [2] Incl. after-tax non-recurr. chgs. of $28.1 mill. [3] Incl. after-tax nonrecurr. chgs. of $28.4 mill. [4] Inc. nonrecurr. after-tax merger exps. of $11.5 mill. [5] Incl. a net nonrecurr. chg. of $427.0 mill. assoc. with the discont. of substant. all of the Company's home health opers. and other bus. [6] Incl. unusual non-recurr. charges of $352.0 mill., 2000; $275.5 mill., 1999.

OFFICERS:
R. M. Scrushy, Chmn., C.E.O.
W. T. Owens, Exec. V.P., C.F.O.
M. E. McVay, Sr. V.P., Treas.
W. W. Horton, Exec. V.P., Asst. Sec., Corp. Couns.

INVESTOR CONTACT: Investor Relations, (800) 765-4772

PRINCIPAL OFFICE: One Healthsouth Pkwy, Birmingham, AL 35243

TELEPHONE NUMBER: (205) 967-7116
FAX: (205) 969-4740
WEB: www.healthsouth.com

NO. OF EMPLOYEES: 34,427 full-time; 18,789 part-time

SHAREHOLDERS: 6,884 (approx.)

ANNUAL MEETING: In May

INCORPORATED: DE, Feb., 1984

INSTITUTIONAL HOLDINGS:
No. of Institutions: 320
Shares Held: 282,164,684
% Held: 72.4

INDUSTRY: Specialty outpatient clinics, nec (SIC: 8093)

TRANSFER AGENT(S): Mellon Investor Services, Ridgefield Park, NJ

NYSE SYMBOL HTV
Rec. Pr. 19.70 (4/30/01)

HEARST-ARGYLE TELEVISION, INC.

YIELD . . .
P/E RATIO 44.8

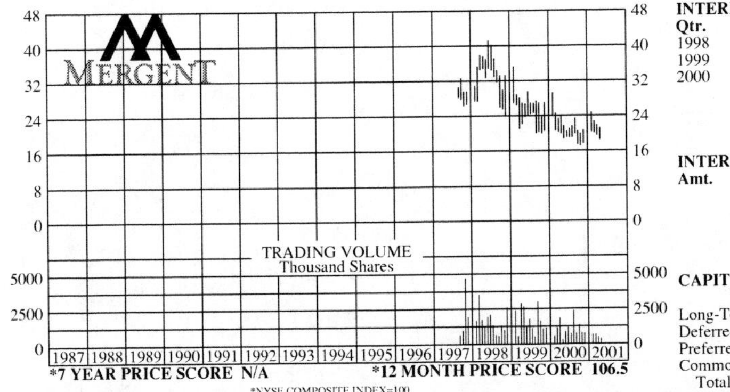

*7 YEAR PRICE SCORE N/A *12 MONTH PRICE SCORE 106.5
*NYSE COMPOSITE INDEX=100

INTERIM EARNINGS (Per Share):

Qtr.	Mar.	June	Sept.	Dec.
1998	0.10	0.39	0.20	0.40
1999	0.04	0.15	0.03	0.17
2000	0.05	0.17	0.10	0.12

INTERIM DIVIDENDS (Per Share):

Amt.	Decl.	Ex.	Rec.	Pay.

No dividends paid.

CAPITALIZATION (12/31/00):

	($000)	(%)
Long-Term Debt	1,448,492	39.5
Deferred Income Tax	777,929	21.2
Preferred Stock	2	0.0
Common & Surplus	1,444,374	39.3
Total	3,670,797	100.0

RECENT DEVELOPMENTS: For the year ended 12/31/00, HTV posted income of $42.5 million, before an extraordinary gain of $2.5 million on the early retirement of debt, compared with income of $35.4 million, before an extraordinary loss of $3.1 million, a year earlier. Results for 2000 included a one-time charge of $15.4 million resulting from the cost of the Company's early retirement program and a $5.0 million write-down of the carrying value of investments. Total revenues increased 13.0% to $747.3 million from $661.4 million in the previous year.

PROSPECTS: The soft outlook for advertising sales due to the U.S. economic slowdown clouds the Company's near-term prospects. HTV's longer-term outlook is somewhat brighter, reflecting the upcoming February 2002 Olympics and expected improvement in the advertising marketplace. Separately, on 1/24/01, HTV and NBC Enterprises announced an agreement in principle to combine their respective television production-and-distribution units into a new venture to produce and syndicate first-run and original-for-cable programming.

BUSINESS

HEARST-ARGYLE TELEVISION, INC. owns and/or manages 27 television stations and several radio stations, in geographically diverse U.S. markets. The Company's television stations reach about 17.5% of U.S. TV households, making it one of the two largest U.S. television station groups not primarily aligned with a single network, as well as one of the seven largest television groups overall as measured by audience delivered. The Company is also involved in the convergence of broadcast television and interactivity and is engaged in partnerships with several interactive-media companies. On 1/5/99, HTV acquired Kelly Broadcasting Co. for approximately $520.4 million. On 3/18/99, HTV acquired Pulitzer Broadcasting Company for approximately $1.70 billion.

ANNUAL FINANCIAL DATA

	12/31/00	12/31/99	12/31/98	12/31/97	12/31/96	12/31/95	12/31/94
Earnings Per Share	[2] **0.44**	[1] **0.41**	[1] **1.08**	[1] **0.48**	[1] **d1.37**	**d1.25**	. . .
Cash Flow Per Share	**2.41**	**2.47**	**2.60**	**1.04**	**1.26**	**1.43**	. . .
INCOME STATEMENT (IN MILLIONS):							
Total Revenues	747.3	661.4	407.3	146.4	73.3	46.9	. . .
Costs & Expenses	354.0	314.3	184.1	62.9	41.7	25.8	. . .
Depreciation & Amort.	188.1	171.2	81.2	27.4	29.6	17.1	. . .
Operating Income	205.2	175.9	142.0	56.1	2.0	4.1	. . .
Net Interest Inc./(Exp.)	d112.2	d106.9	d39.6	d15.8	d16.6	d12.1	. . .
Income Before Income Taxes	78.9	68.7	102.5	40.3	d14.6	d8.0	. . .
Income Taxes	36.4	33.3	42.8	16.4	. . .	. . .	. . .
Net Income	[2] 42.5	[1] 35.4	[1] 59.7	[1] 23.9	[1] d14.6	d8.0	. . .
Cash Flow	223.2	205.2	139.4	50.6	14.2	9.1	. . .
Average Shs. Outstg. (000)	92,457	83,229	53,699	48,752	11,246	6,388	. . .
BALANCE SHEET (IN MILLIONS):							
Cash & Cash Equivalents	5.8	5.6	381.0	12.8	0.9	2.2	. . .
Total Current Assets	232.3	237.1	515.2	227.2	27.6	24.4	. . .
Net Property	334.4	342.7	129.6	97.8	39.2	32.6	. . .
Total Assets	3,818.0	3,913.2	1,421.1	1,044.1	328.6	291.1	1.4
Total Current Liabilities	123.7	123.7	88.8	71.9	18.5	16.6	0.8
Long-Term Obligations	1,448.5	1,563.6	842.6	490.0	171.5	150.0	. . .
Net Stockholders' Equity	1,444.4	1,416.8	324.4	326.7	129.2	116.3	. . .
Net Working Capital	108.5	113.5	426.4	155.4	9.1	7.8	d0.8
Year-end Shs. Outstg. (000)	91,926	94,784	52,137	53,828	11,347	11,119	. . .
STATISTICAL RECORD:							
Operating Profit Margin %	27.5	26.6	34.9	38.3	2.7	8.7	. . .
Net Profit Margin %	5.7	5.4	14.7	16.3	. . .	. . .	. . .
Return on Equity %	4.3	2.9	18.4	7.3	. . .	. . .	. . .
Return on Assets %	1.1	0.9	4.2	2.3	. . .	. . .	. . .
Debt/Total Assets %	37.9	40.0	59.3	46.9	52.2	51.5	. . .
Price Range	29.25-17.06	35.25-19.94	41.25-24.00	32.63-26.25	. . .	. . .	. . .
P/E Ratio	66.5-38.8	86.0-48.6	38.2-22.2	68.0-54.7	. . .	. . .	. . .

Statistics are as originally reported. [1] Bef. extraord. loss of $7.8 mill. ($1.22/sh.), 1999; loss of $16.2 mill. ($0.34/sh.), 1998; loss of $10.8 mill. ($0.20/sh.), 1997; loss of $3.1 mill. ($0.04/sh.), 1996. [2] Incls. non-recurr. chrg. of $15.4 mill. & $5.0 mill. write-down of carrying value of invest.; bef. extraord. gain of $2.5 mill. ($0.03/sh.) on early retire. of debt.

OFFICERS:
B. Marbut, Chmn.
D. J. Barrett, Pres., C.E.O.
H. T. Hawks, Exec. V.P., C.F.O.

INVESTOR CONTACT: Thomas W. Campo, Investor Relations, (212) 887-6827

PRINCIPAL OFFICE: 888 Seventh Ave, Suite 700, New York, NY 10106

TELEPHONE NUMBER: (212) 887-6800
FAX: (212) 887-6875
WEB: www.hearstargyle.com
NO. OF EMPLOYEES: 3,250 (approx.)
SHAREHOLDERS: 769 (approx. series A common)
ANNUAL MEETING: In May
INCORPORATED: DE, Aug., 1994

INSTITUTIONAL HOLDINGS:
No. of Institutions: 70
Shares Held: 9,979,044
% Held: 10.9

INDUSTRY: Television broadcasting stations (SIC: 4833)

TRANSFER AGENT(S): Computershare Investor Services, Chicago, IL

NYSE SYMBOL HNZ
Rec. Pr. 43.31 (5/31/01)

HEINZ (H.J.) COMPANY

YIELD 3.6%
P/E RATIO 20.1

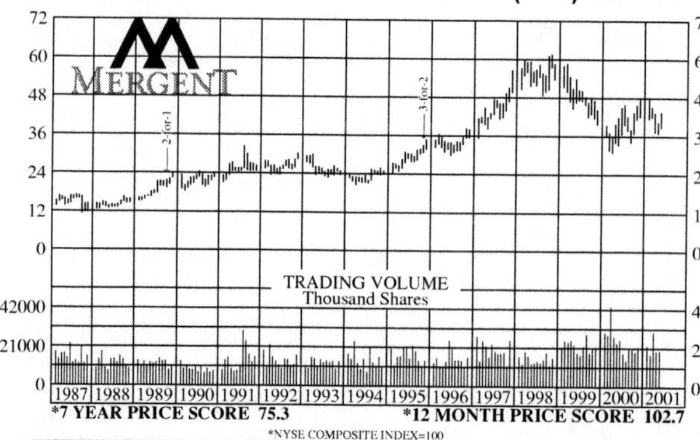

*7 YEAR PRICE SCORE 75.3 *12 MONTH PRICE SCORE 102.7

*NYSE COMPOSITE INDEX=100

INTERIM EARNINGS (Per Share):

Qtr.	July	Oct.	Jan.	Apr.
1997-98	0.65	0.51	0.50	0.49
1998-99	0.58	0.63	0.33	d0.25
1999-00	0.57	1.14	0.47	0.27
2000-01	0.57	0.54	0.77	...

INTERIM DIVIDENDS (Per Share):

Amt.	Decl.	Ex.	Rec.	Pay.
0.367Q	3/08/00	3/16/00	3/20/00	4/10/00
0.367Q	6/14/00	6/22/00	6/26/00	7/10/00
0.393Q	9/12/00	9/20/00	9/22/00	10/10/00
0.393Q	12/13/00	12/20/00	12/25/00	1/10/01
0.393Q	3/14/01	3/22/01	3/26/01	4/10/01

Indicated div.: $1.57 (Div. Reinv. Plan)

CAPITALIZATION (5/3/00):

	($000)	(%)
Long-Term Debt	3,935,826	67.8
Deferred Income Tax	271,831	4.7
Preferred Stock	139	0.0
Common & Surplus	1,595,717	27.5
Total	5,803,513	100.0

RECENT DEVELOPMENTS: For the quarter ended 1/31/01, net income was $270.5 million, up 58.1% versus $171.1 million the year before. Results in the recent period included after-tax restructuring charges of $50.1 million and a $93.2 million Italian tax gain. Prior-year earnings included a one-time after-tax restructuring charge of $56.0 million. Sales slipped 1.1% to $2.27 billion from $2.29 billion the previous year. Gross profit was $884.1 million, or 39.0% of sales, versus $902.8 million, or 39.3% of sales, a year earlier.

PROSPECTS: On 4/27/01, the Company terminated its proposed acquisition of Milnot Holding Corp., owner of the BEECH-NUT® brand of prepared baby foods, after a U.S. appeals court blocked the transaction as a threat to competition. Meanwhile, HNZ is taking steps to streamline its tuna and pet food operations and centralize its supply chain in Europe. These initiatives are expected to generate cost savings of about $25.0 million next year and about $60.0 million annually beginning in fiscal 2004.

BUSINESS

H.J. HEINZ COMPANY manufactures and markets an extensive line of processed food products throughout the world, including ketchup and other sauces/condiments, frozen dinners, pet food, baby food, frozen potato products and canned soups, vegetables and fruits. Major U.S. brands include HEINZ, WEIGHT WATCHERS, ORE-IDA, SMART ONES, STARKIST, 9-LIVES, POUNCE, BOSTON MARKET, KIBBLES 'N BITS, and BAGEL BITES. Overseas, well-known brands include PLASMON, PUDLISZKI, ABC, ORLANDO, WATTIE'S, OLIVINE, FARLEY'S, and JURAN. Fiscal 2000 sales were derived: Ketchup, Condiments & Sauces, 25.9%; Frozen Foods, 16.6%; Pet Products, 13.2%; Soups, Beans & Pasta Meals, 12.7%; Tuna, 11.2%; Infant Foods, 11.1%; and Other, 9.3%.

ANNUAL FINANCIAL DATA

	5/3/00	4/28/99	4/29/98	4/30/97	5/1/96	5/3/95	4/27/94
Earnings Per Share	[1] 2.47	[1] 1.29	[1] 2.15	[1] 0.80	1.74	1.59	[1] 1.57
Cash Flow Per Share	3.32	2.11	2.99	1.72	2.66	2.43	2.24
Tang. Book Val. Per Share	...	...	...	0.03	0.87	0.34	2.67
Dividends Per Share	1.40	1.29	1.19	1.08	0.98	0.90	0.82
Dividend Payout %	56.5	99.8	55.1	135.6	56.6	56.6	52.3
INCOME STATEMENT (IN MILLIONS):							
Total Revenues	9,407.9	9,299.6	9,209.3	9,357.0	9,112.3	8,086.8	7,046.7
Costs & Expenses	7,833.0	7,888.1	7,375.3	8,260.2	7,480.9	6,615.7	5,845.6
Depreciation & Amort.	306.5	302.2	313.6	340.5	343.8	315.3	259.8
Operating Income	1,733.1	1,109.3	1,520.3	756.3	1,287.6	1,155.8	1,068.3
Net Interest Inc./(Exp.)	d244.4	d233.7	d226.0	d235.4	d232.6	d174.0	d112.5
Income Before Income Taxes	1,463.7	835.1	1,255.0	479.1	1,023.7	938.0	922.4
Income Taxes	573.1	360.8	453.4	177.2	364.3	347.0	319.4
Net Income	[1] 890.6	[1] 474.3	[1] 801.6	[1] 301.9	659.3	591.0	[1] 602.9
Cash Flow	1,197.0	776.5	1,115.2	642.3	1,003.1	906.2	862.7
Average Shs. Outstg. (000)	360,095	367,830	372,953	373,703	377,156	372,807	385,218
BALANCE SHEET (IN MILLIONS):							
Cash & Cash Equivalents	154.1	123.1	99.4	188.4	108.4	207.0	142.4
Total Current Assets	3,169.9	2,886.8	2,686.5	3,013.1	3,046.7	2,823.0	2,291.5
Net Property	2,358.8	2,171.0	2,394.7	2,479.2	2,616.8	2,534.4	2,167.7
Total Assets	8,850.7	8,053.6	8,023.4	8,437.8	8,623.7	8,247.2	6,381.1
Total Current Liabilities	2,126.1	2,786.3	2,164.3	2,880.4	2,715.1	2,564.1	1,692.4
Long-Term Obligations	3,935.8	2,472.2	2,768.3	2,284.0	2,281.7	2,326.8	1,727.0
Net Stockholders' Equity	1,595.9	1,803.0	2,216.5	2,440.4	2,706.8	2,472.9	2,338.6
Net Working Capital	1,043.9	100.5	522.2	132.7	331.6	259.0	599.2
Year-end Shs. Outstg. (000)	347,443	359,128	363,418	367,184	368,598	365,514	373,562
STATISTICAL RECORD:							
Operating Profit Margin %	18.4	11.9	16.5	8.1	14.1	14.3	15.2
Net Profit Margin %	9.5	5.1	8.7	3.2	7.2	7.3	8.6
Return on Equity %	55.8	26.3	36.2	12.4	24.4	23.9	25.8
Return on Assets %	10.1	5.9	10.0	3.6	7.6	7.2	9.4
Debt/Total Assets %	44.5	30.7	34.5	27.1	26.5	28.2	27.1
Price Range	58.81-39.50	61.75-48.50	56.69-35.25	38.38-29.75	34.88-24.25	26.00-20.50	30.17-22.75
P/E Ratio	23.8-16.0	47.9-37.6	26.4-16.4	48.0-37.2	20.0-13.9	16.4-12.9	19.3-14.5
Average Yield %	2.8	2.3	2.6	3.2	3.3	3.9	3.1

Statistics are as originally reported. Adj. for 3-for-2 stk. split, 9/95. [1] Incl. $34.7 mil ($0.10/sh) net chg., 5/00; $408.2 mil ($1.11/sh) net chg., 4/99; $12.5 mil net gain, 4/98; $664.6 mil net chg., 4/97; & $127.0 mil gain, 4/94.

OFFICERS:
W. R. Johnson, Chmn., Pres., C.E.O.
P. F. Renne, Exec. V.P., C.F.O.
L. Stein, Sr. V.P., Gen. Couns.

INVESTOR CONTACT: Jack Runkel, V.P., Investor Relations, (412) 456-6034

PRINCIPAL OFFICE: 600 Grant Street, Pittsburgh, PA 15219

TELEPHONE NUMBER: (412) 456-5700
FAX: (412) 456-6128
WEB: www.heinz.com

NO. OF EMPLOYEES: 46,900 (approx.)

SHAREHOLDERS: 58,500 (approx.)

ANNUAL MEETING: In Sept.

INCORPORATED: PA, July, 1900

INSTITUTIONAL HOLDINGS:
No. of Institutions: 492
Shares Held: 205,626,323
% Held: 59.0

INDUSTRY: Food preparations, nec (SIC: 2099)

TRANSFER AGENT(S): Mellon Investor Services, Ridgefield Park, NJ

NYSE SYMBOL HF
Rec. Pr. 31.91 (4/30/01)

HELLER FINANCIAL, INC.

YIELD	1.3%
P/E RATIO	11.9

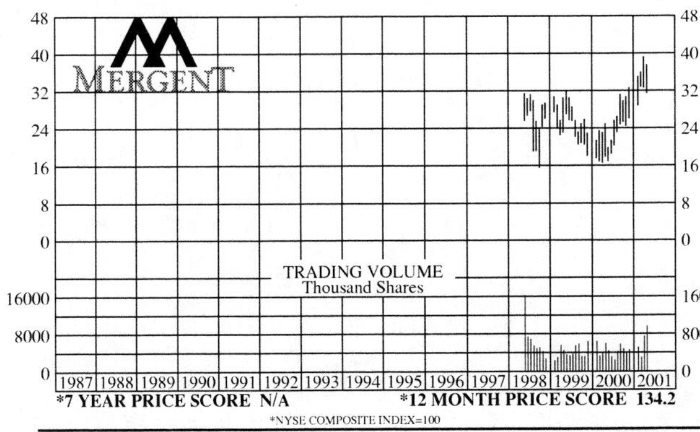

*7 YEAR PRICE SCORE N/A *12 MONTH PRICE SCORE 134.2

*NYSE COMPOSITE INDEX=100

INTERIM EARNINGS (Per Share):

Qtr.	Mar.	June	Sept.	Dec.
1997		2.82		
1998	0.84	0.60	0.47	0.32
1999	0.55	0.57	0.55	1.07
2000	0.70	0.65	0.67	0.66

INTERIM DIVIDENDS (Per Share):

Amt.	Decl.	Ex.	Rec.	Pay.
0.10Q	4/19/00	4/27/00	5/01/00	5/15/00
0.10Q	7/19/00	7/27/00	7/31/00	8/15/00
0.10Q	10/18/00	10/30/00	11/01/00	11/15/00
0.10Q	1/17/01	1/30/01	2/01/01	2/15/01
0.10Q	4/19/01	4/27/01	5/01/01	5/15/01

Indicated div.: $0.40

CAPITALIZATION (12/31/00):

	($000)	(%)
Long-Term Debt	10,525,000	80.3
Minority Interest	12,000	0.1
Preferred Stock	400,000	3.1
Common & Surplus	2,175,000	16.6
Total	13,112,000	100.0

RECENT DEVELOPMENTS: For the year ended 12/31/00, net income increased 2.1% to $290.0 million compared with $284.0 million in the previous year. Earnings for 1999 included an after-tax gain of $48.0 million on the sale of commercial services assets. Operating revenues advanced 9.0% to $1.04 billion from $952.0 million a year earlier. Net interest income grew 22.9% to $629.0 million.

PROSPECTS: Going forward, the Company expects to continue to perform well, based on the credit quality of its portfolio. On 2/20/01, the Company announced that it will discontinue its origination of U.S. Small Business Administration (SBA) loans, due to increased competition from banks that are cross-selling a range of financial products in addition to SBA loans.

BUSINESS

HELLER FINANCIAL, INC. is a worldwide commercial finance company providing a broad range of financing to middle-market and small business clients. HF offers equipment financing and leasing, sales finance programs, collateral and cash flow-based financing, financing for healthcare companies and financing for commercial real estate. The Company also offers trade finance, factoring, asset-based lending, leasing and vendor finance products and programs to clients in Europe, Asia and Latin America. The Company's business segments are Domestic Commercial Finance and International Factoring and Asset Based Finance.

LOAN DISTRIBUTION

(12/31/2000)	($000)	%
Commercial Term	4,973,000	31.1
Commercial Revolving	2,052,000	12.9
Real Estate	2,686,000	16.8
Factored Accounts Receivable	2,615,000	16.4
Equipment Loans & Leases	3,640,000	22.8
Total	15,966,000	100.0

ANNUAL FINANCIAL DATA

	12/31/00	12/31/99	12/31/98	12/31/97	12/31/96	12/31/95	12/31/94
Earnings Per Share	**2.69**	**[1] 2.74**	**[2] 2.23**	**2.82**	...	...	...
Tang. Book Val. Per Share	**17.79**	**15.06**	**17.36**	**27.51**	...	...	...
Dividends Per Share	**0.40**	**0.37**	**0.09**	...	...	...	...
Dividend Payout %	**14.9**	**13.5**	**4.0**	...	...	...	...
INCOME STATEMENT (IN MILLIONS):							
Total Interest Income	1,628.0	1,197.0	1,047.0	924.0	807.0	851.0	702.0
Total Interest Expense	999.0	685.0	624.0	516.0	452.0	464.0	336.0
Net Interest Income	629.0	512.0	423.0	408.0	355.0	387.0	366.0
Provision for Loan Losses	148.0	136.0	77.0	164.0	103.0	223.0	188.0
Non-Interest Income	409.0	519.0	360.0	346.0	178.0	233.0	191.0
Non-Interest Expense	459.0	456.0	416.0	357.0	247.0	216.0	195.0
Income Before Taxes	431.0	439.0	290.0	233.0	183.0	181.0	174.0
Equity Earnings/Minority Int.	d2.0	d1.0	d4.0	d9.0	d7.0	d7.0	d5.0
Net Income	290.0	[1] 284.0	[2] 193.0	158.0	133.0	125.0	118.0
Average Shs. Outstg. (000)	96,641	93,233	77,000	51,000	...	...	...
BALANCE SHEET (IN MILLIONS):							
Total Loans & Leases	15,966.0	14,795.0	11,854.0	10,722.0	8,529.0	8,085.0	7,585.0
Allowance for Credit Losses	342.0	316.0	271.0	261.0	225.0	229.0	227.0
Net Loans & Leases	15,624.0	14,479.0	11,583.0	10,461.0	8,304.0	7,856.0	7,358.0
Total Assets	20,061.0	17,973.0	14,366.0	12,861.0	9,926.0	9,638.0	8,476.0
Long-Term Obligations	10,525.0	8,630.0	6,768.0	6,004.0	4,761.0	5,145.0	3,930.0
Total Liabilities	17,486.0	15,626.0	12,404.0	11,183.0	8,459.0	8,254.0	7,146.0
Net Stockholders' Equity	2,575.0	2,347.0	1,962.0	1,678.0	1,467.0	1,384.0	1,330.0
Year-end Shs. Outstg. (000)	96,500	97,371	90,000	51,000	...	...	...
STATISTICAL RECORD:							
Return on Equity %	11.3	12.1	9.8	9.4	9.1	9.0	8.9
Return on Assets %	1.4	1.6	1.3	1.2	1.3	1.3	1.4
Equity/Assets %	12.8	13.1	13.7	13.0	14.8	14.4	15.7
Non-Int. Exp./Tot. Inc. %	44.2	47.9	53.1	47.3	46.3	34.8	35.0
Price Range	32.63-16.50	31.94-18.00	31.44-15.50	...	...	...	...
P/E Ratio	12.1-6.1	11.7-6.6	14.1-7.0	...	...	...	...
Average Yield %	1.6	1.5	0.4	...	...	...	...

Statistics are as originally reported. [1] Incl. $79.0 mill. gain on sale of Commercial Services assets. [2] Incl. restructuring charge of $17.0 mill.

OFFICERS:
R. J. Almeida, Chmn., C.E.O.
F. E. Wolfert, Pres., C.O.O.
L. E. Martin, Exec. V.P., C.F.O.

INVESTOR CONTACT: Investor Relations, (312) 441-7000

PRINCIPAL OFFICE: 500 West Monroe St., Chicago, IL 60661

TELEPHONE NUMBER: (312) 441-7000
FAX: (312) 441-7367
WEB: www.hellerfinancial.com

NO. OF EMPLOYEES: 2,514 (avg.)

SHAREHOLDERS: 762

ANNUAL MEETING: In May

INCORPORATED: DE, 1919

INSTITUTIONAL HOLDINGS:
No. of Institutions: 160
Shares Held: 42,224,574
% Held: 43.6

INDUSTRY: Short-term business credit (SIC: 6153)

TRANSFER AGENT(S): The Bank of New York, New York, NY

NYSE SYMBOL HP
Rec. Pr. 51.23 (4/30/01)

HELMERICH & PAYNE, INC.

YIELD 0.6%
P/E RATIO 26.8

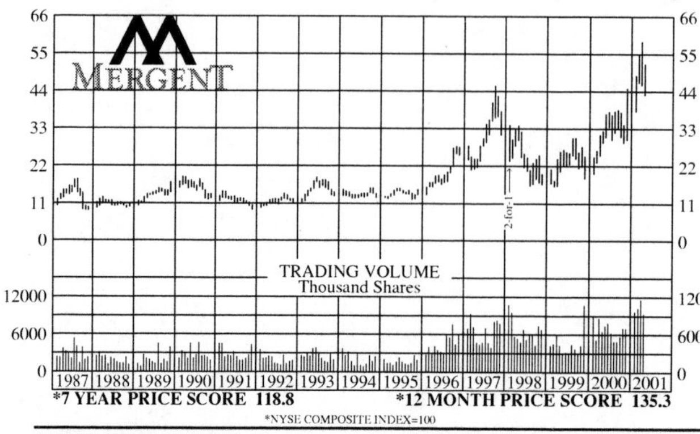

*7 YEAR PRICE SCORE 118.8 *12 MONTH PRICE SCORE 135.3

*NYSE COMPOSITE INDEX=100

INTERIM EARNINGS (Per Share):

Qtr.	Dec.	Mar.	June	Sept.
1995-96	0.23	0.23	0.26	0.27
1996-97	0.40	0.45	0.47	0.44
1997-98	0.57	0.38	0.67	0.38
1998-99	0.26	0.15	0.24	0.21
1999-00	0.41	0.39	0.37	0.48
2000-01	0.67	...	...	...

INTERIM DIVIDENDS (Per Share):

Amt.	Decl.	Ex.	Rec.	Pay.
0.07Q	3/01/00	5/11/00	5/15/00	6/01/00
0.075Q	6/07/00	8/11/00	8/15/00	9/01/00
0.075Q	9/07/00	11/13/00	11/15/00	12/01/00
0.075Q	12/06/00	2/13/01	2/15/01	3/01/01
0.075Q	3/07/01	5/11/01	5/15/01	6/01/01

Indicated div.: $0.30

CAPITALIZATION (9/30/00):

	($000)	(%)
Long-Term Debt	50,000	4.3
Deferred Income Tax	156,650	13.5
Common & Surplus	955,703	82.2
Total	1,162,353	100.0

RECENT DEVELOPMENTS: For the quarter ended 12/31/00, net income jumped 65.4% to $33.8 million versus $20.5 million a year earlier. Earnings for the prior year included non-recurring items that resulted in a net gain of $8.1 million. Revenues rose 28.7% to $192.6 million. Total contract drilling division revenues advanced 19.6% to $101.0 million and operating income surged to $24.6 million from $9.0 million the year before. Total oil and gas division revenues advanced 78.4% to $86.4 million, while operating income soared to $31.7 million from $13.6 million in 1999.

PROSPECTS: The addition of new FlexRigs and increasing day rates should give domestic results going forward a boost. However, HP is projecting only slight improvement in international operations for fiscal 2001. The Company expects to participate in the drilling of about 140 wells during the remainder of fiscal 2001, 40.0% to 50.0% of which will be development wells in the areas where HP has proven reserves. The exploration and development expenditure estimate for fiscal 2001 is $65.0 million for drilling and $21.0 million for land and seismic investments.

BUSINESS

HELMERICH & PAYNE, INC. is primarily engaged in the exploration, production, and sale of crude oil and natural gas and in contract drilling of oil and gas wells for others. HP is also engaged in the ownership, development, and operation of commercial real estate. HP is organized into three operating divisions: contract drilling, oil and gas exploration and production operations, and real estate. As of 9/30/00, proven reserves totaled 6.3 million barrels of crude oil and 262.5 billion cubic feet of natural gas. Revenues (and operating income) for 2000 were derived as follows: contract drilling, 55.6% (37.1%); oil and gas operations, 37.8% (58.5%); real estate, 1.4% (4.4%); and other, 5.2%.

QUARTERLY DATA

(9/30/2000) ($000)	Rev	Inc
1st Quarter	149,581	20,461
2nd Quarter	151,848	19,273
3rd Quarter	151,968	18,557
4th Quarter	177,698	24,009

ANNUAL FINANCIAL DATA

	9/30/00	9/30/99	9/30/98	9/30/97	9/30/96	9/30/95	9/30/94
Earnings Per Share	**1.64**	**0.86**	**2.00**	**1.69**	**[1] 0.92**	**0.20**	**[2] 0.43**
Cash Flow Per Share	**3.89**	**3.08**	**3.77**	**3.15**	**2.16**	**1.80**	**1.49**
Tang. Book Val. Per Share	**19.12**	**17.09**	**16.06**	**15.60**	**12.98**	**11.36**	**10.61**
Dividends Per Share	**0.29**	**0.28**	**0.28**	**0.26**	**0.26**	**0.25**	**0.24**
Dividend Payout %	**17.7**	**32.6**	**14.0**	**15.4**	**27.7**	**124.9**	**57.0**
INCOME STATEMENT (IN MILLIONS):							
Total Revenues	631.1	564.3	636.6	517.9	393.3	325.8	329.0
Costs & Expenses	378.9	382.2	393.8	313.7	261.9	233.1	246.4
Depreciation & Amort.	112.4	110.7	89.7	72.5	61.1	78.6	51.9
Operating Income	139.8	71.4	153.2	131.6	70.2	14.1	30.7
Net Interest Inc./(Exp.)	d3.1	d6.5	d0.9	d4.2	d0.7	d0.4	d0.4
Income Before Income Taxes	136.8	64.9	152.2	127.4	69.5	13.7	30.3
Income Taxes	57.7	25.7	56.7	45.5	25.8	5.0	10.2
Equity Earnings/Minority Int.	3.2	3.6	5.6	2.3	1.7	1.1	0.9
Net Income	82.3	42.8	101.2	84.2	[1] 45.4	9.8	[2] 21.0
Cash Flow	194.7	153.5	190.9	156.7	106.6	88.3	72.9
Average Shs. Outstg. (000)	50,035	49,817	50,565	49,779	49,380	49,072	48,832
BALANCE SHEET (IN MILLIONS):							
Cash & Cash Equivalents	108.1	21.8	24.7	29.3	17.9	28.7	38.4
Total Current Assets	265.1	160.6	184.3	158.0	114.4	115.0	122.9
Net Property	673.6	691.2	692.4	539.0	463.5	423.8	400.7
Total Assets	1,259.5	1,109.7	1,090.4	1,033.6	821.9	710.2	624.8
Total Current Liabilities	78.9	71.9	125.5	95.2	62.6	69.6	46.7
Long-Term Obligations	50.0	50.0	50.0	...	...	...	...
Net Stockholders' Equity	955.7	848.1	793.1	780.6	646.0	562.4	524.3
Net Working Capital	186.3	88.7	58.9	62.8	51.8	45.4	76.2
Year-end Shs. Outstg. (000)	49,980	49,626	49,383	50,028	49,772	49,530	49,420
STATISTICAL RECORD:							
Operating Profit Margin %	22.2	12.7	24.1	25.4	17.9	4.3	9.3
Net Profit Margin %	13.0	7.6	15.9	16.3	11.6	3.0	6.4
Return on Equity %	8.6	5.0	12.8	10.8	7.0	1.7	4.0
Return on Assets %	6.5	3.9	9.3	8.1	5.5	1.4	3.4
Debt/Total Assets %	4.0	4.5	4.6	...	...	...	...
Price Range	44.81-19.75	30.38-16.00	34.13-16.13	45.56-20.75	27.88-13.44	15.63-12.13	15.69-12.38
P/E Ratio	27.3-12.0	35.3-18.6	17.1-8.1	27.0-12.3	30.3-14.6	78.1-60.6	36.5-28.8
Average Yield %	0.9	1.2	1.1	0.8	1.2	1.8	1.7

Statistics are as originally reported. Adj. for 2-for-1 stk. split, 12/97 [1] Bef. disc. oper. gain of $27.1 mill. [2] Bef. acctg. change credit of $4.0 mill.

OFFICERS:
W. H. Helmerich III, Chmn.
H. Helmerich, Pres., C.E.O.
S. R. Mackey, V.P., Sec., General Couns.

INVESTOR CONTACT: D. E. Fears, V.P., C.F.O., (918) 742-5531

PRINCIPAL OFFICE: Utica at Twenty-First Street, Tulsa, OK 74114

TELEPHONE NUMBER: (918) 742-5531
FAX: (918) 742-0237
WEB: www.hpinc.com
NO. OF EMPLOYEES: 3,606
SHAREHOLDERS: 1,170
ANNUAL MEETING: In Mar.
INCORPORATED: DE, Feb., 1940

INSTITUTIONAL HOLDINGS:
No. of Institutions: 213
Shares Held: 39,092,142
% Held: 78.0

INDUSTRY: Drilling oil and gas wells (SIC: 1381)

TRANSFER AGENT(S): UMB Bank, Kansas City, MO

NYSE SYMBOL HPC
Rec. Pr. 11.95 (4/30/01)

HERCULES INC.

YIELD ...
P/E RATIO 13.1

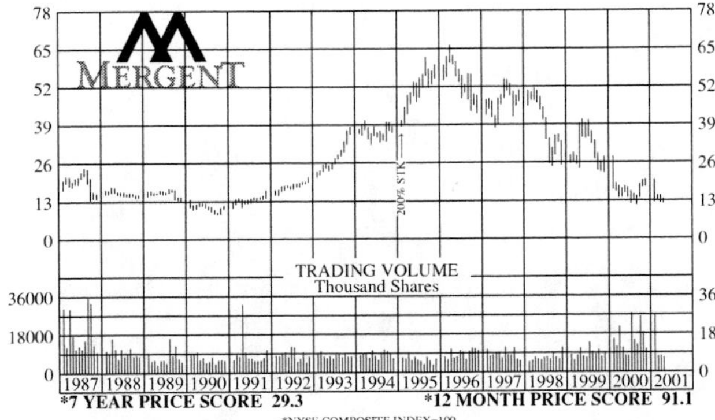

*7 YEAR PRICE SCORE 29.3 *12 MONTH PRICE SCORE 91.1
*NYSE COMPOSITE INDEX=100

INTERIM EARNINGS (Per Share):

Qtr.	Mar.	June	Sept.	Dec.
1997	1.05	0.75	0.82	0.61
1998	0.70	0.77	0.74	d1.64
1999	0.37	0.56	0.54	0.16
2000	0.34	0.15	0.70	d0.28

INTERIM DIVIDENDS (Per Share):

Amt.	Decl.	Ex.	Rec.	Pay.
0.27Q	11/03/99	12/01/99	12/03/99	12/29/99
0.27Q	2/18/00	3/01/00	3/03/00	3/29/00
0.27Q	5/02/00	5/31/00	6/02/00	6/29/00
0.08Q	8/25/00	9/01/00	9/06/00	9/29/00

Dividend suspended.

CAPITALIZATION (12/31/00):

	($000)	(%)
Long-Term Debt	2,342,000	59.0
Deferred Income Tax	187,000	4.7
Redeemable Pfd. Stock	622,000	15.7
Common & Surplus	816,000	20.6
Total	3,967,000	100.0

RECENT DEVELOPMENTS: For the year ended 12/31/00, net income fell 41.7% to $98.0 million. Results for 2000 included a gain of $168.0 million from the sale of the Food Gums business, a $25.0 million charge for the sale of the nitrocellulose business, a $66.0 million charge for asset write-downs, and a $28.0 million charge for restructuring. Results for 1999 included charges totaling $78.0 million. Net sales slipped 4.7% to $3.15 billion.

PROSPECTS: HPC completed the sale of its hydrocarbon resins business and select portions of its rosins business to Eastman Chemical Company for about $244.0 million. The proceeds will be used to reduce debt. In addition, acquired unit operations will be operated under contract by HPC at shared facilities in Savannah, GA and Franklin, VA. Going forward, the Company is reevaluating opportunities for its FiberVisions unit.

BUSINESS

HERCULES INC. is a diversified worldwide producer of chemicals. HPC operates in three industry segments: Process Chemicals and Services, Chemical Specialties and Functional Products. Principal products and markets include wet-strength and sizing aids for paper production, rosins and hydrocarbon resins for adhesives, polypropylene fiber for disposable diapers, water-soluble polymers for latex paints, and natural gums for food and beverages. On 10/15/98, HPC acquired BetzDearborn Inc. for about $2.40 billion. Sales (and operating income) for 2000 were derived: Process Chemicals and Services, 54.5% (55.8%); Functional Products, 23.5% (33.1%); and Chemical Specialties, 22.0% (11.1%).

ANNUAL FINANCIAL DATA

	12/31/00	12/31/99	12/31/98	12/31/97	12/31/96	12/31/95	12/31/94
Earnings Per Share	**4 0.91**	**3 1.62**	**2 0.10**	**1 3.18**	**3.04**	**2.93**	**2.29**
Cash Flow Per Share	**3.20**	**4.02**	**1.20**	**3.88**	**4.25**	**4.09**	**3.51**
Tang. Book Val. Per Share	...	...	...	**7.18**	**8.75**	**9.97**	**11.10**
Dividends Per Share	**0.62**	**1.08**	**1.08**	**1.00**	**0.92**	**0.84**	**0.75**
Dividend Payout %	**68.1**	**66.7**	**1,078.9**	**31.4**	**30.3**	**28.7**	**32.6**
INCOME STATEMENT (IN MILLIONS):							
Total Revenues	3,152.0	3,248.0	2,145.0	1,866.0	2,060.0	2,427.2	2,821.0
Costs & Expenses	2,462.0	2,518.0	1,845.0	1,562.0	1,513.0	1,931.7	2,254.2
Depreciation & Amort.	246.0	250.0	108.0	76.0	106.0	132.5	148.0
Operating Income	444.0	480.0	192.0	228.0	441.0	363.0	418.8
Net Interest Inc./(Exp.)	d164.0	d185.0	d103.0	d39.0	d30.0	d19.1	d19.9
Income Before Income Taxes	166.0	242.0	67.0	563.0	432.0	463.8	382.7
Income Taxes	66.0	75.0	68.0	269.0	160.0	171.9	134.1
Equity Earnings/Minority Int.	d2.0	1.0	10.0	30.0	53.0	40.8	25.6
Net Income	4 98.0	3 168.0	2 9.0	1 324.0	325.0	332.8	274.2
Cash Flow	344.0	418.0	117.0	400.0	431.0	465.3	422.1
Average Shs. Outstg. (000)	107,400	103,900	97,400	102,400	...	...	...
BALANCE SHEET (IN MILLIONS):							
Cash & Cash Equivalents	54.0	63.0	68.0	17.0	30.0	72.9	111.6
Total Current Assets	1,022.0	1,338.0	1,240.0	689.0	739.0	867.1	1,152.3
Net Property	1,104.0	1,321.0	1,438.0	687.0	865.0	999.7	1,216.1
Total Assets	5,309.0	5,896.0	5,833.0	2,411.0	2,386.0	2,493.5	2,941.3
Total Current Liabilities	922.0	1,559.0	1,317.0	799.0	694.0	686.7	767.5
Long-Term Obligations	2,342.0	1,777.0	3,096.0	419.0	345.0	297.9	307.2
Net Stockholders' Equity	816.0	863.0	559.0	690.0	887.0	1,081.9	1,294.7
Net Working Capital	100.0	d221.0	d77.0	d110.0	45.0	180.4	384.8
Year-end Shs. Outstg. (000)	107,542	106,389	100,828	96,068	101,403	108,487	116,635
STATISTICAL RECORD:							
Operating Profit Margin %	14.1	14.8	9.0	12.2	21.4	15.0	14.8
Net Profit Margin %	3.1	5.2	0.4	17.4	15.8	13.7	9.7
Return on Equity %	12.0	19.5	1.6	47.0	36.6	30.8	21.2
Return on Assets %	1.8	2.8	0.2	13.4	13.6	13.3	9.3
Price Range	28.00-11.38	40.69-22.38	51.38-24.63	54.50-37.75	66.25-42.75	62.25-38.25	40.50-32.13
P/E Ratio	30.8-12.5	25.1-13.8	513.8-246.3	17.1-11.9	21.8-14.1	21.2-13.1	17.7-14.0
Average Yield %	3.1	3.4	2.8	2.2	1.7	1.7	2.1

Statistics are as originally reported. Adj. for 3-for-1 split, 1/95. 1 Bef. $5.0 mill. acct. chg. & incl. $0.14/sh. chg. for acq. activity. 2 Incl. $197.0 mill. after-tax non-recur. chg. rel. to acq. of BetzDearborn, $40.0 mill. after-tax non-recur. chg. for legal settlement, & $59.0 mill. chg. for oth. exps. 3 Incl. $35.0 mill. non-recur. chg., $16.0 mill. gain fr. sale of subsidiary & $43.0 mill. in restr. and other chgs. 4 Incl. $25.0 mill. chgs. rel. to sale of bus., $168.0 mill. gain, $66.0 mill. asset write-down chg. & $28.0 mill. restr. chg.

OFFICERS:
T. L. Gossage, Chmn., C.E.O.
G. MacKenzie, Vice-Chmn., C.F.O.

INVESTOR CONTACT: William T. Drury, Jr., V.P., Investor Relations, (800) 441-9274

PRINCIPAL OFFICE: 1313 North Market St., Hercules Plaza, Wilmington, DE 19894

TELEPHONE NUMBER: (302) 594-5000
FAX: (302) 594-5400
WEB: www.herc.com

NO. OF EMPLOYEES: 9,789 (avg.)

SHAREHOLDERS: 16,357 (approx.)

ANNUAL MEETING: In Apr.

INCORPORATED: DE, Oct., 1912

INSTITUTIONAL HOLDINGS:
No. of Institutions: 199
Shares Held: 67,818,345
% Held: 62.7

INDUSTRY: Industrial organic chemicals, nec (SIC: 2869)

TRANSFER AGENT(S): Mellon Investor Services, Ridgefield Park, NJ

NYSE SYMBOL HSY
Rec. Pr. 60.41 (4/30/01)

HERSHEY FOODS CORPORATION

YIELD 1.9%
P/E RATIO 25.0

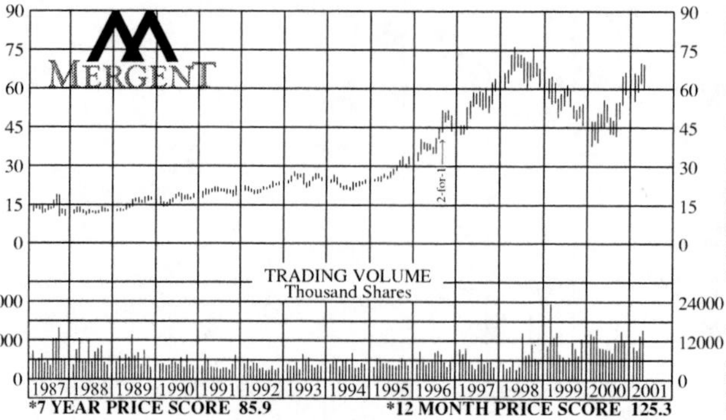

MERGENT

TRADING VOLUME
Thousand Shares

1987 1988 1989 1990 1991 1992 1993 1994 1995 1996 1997 1998 1999 2000 2001

2-for-1

***7 YEAR PRICE SCORE 85.9** ***12 MONTH PRICE SCORE 125.3**

*NYSE COMPOSITE INDEX=100

INTERIM EARNINGS (Per Share):

Qtr.	Mar.	June	Sept.	Dec.
1996	0.39	0.53	0.61	0.51
1997	0.45	0.33	0.68	0.80
1998	0.52	0.33	0.74	0.76
1999	1.57	0.35	0.62	0.70
2000	0.51	0.29	0.78	0.84

INTERIM DIVIDENDS (Per Share):

Amt.	Decl.	Ex.	Rec.	Pay.
0.26Q	4/25/00	5/23/00	5/25/00	6/15/00
0.28Q	8/01/00	8/23/00	8/25/00	9/15/00
0.28Q	11/07/00	11/20/00	11/22/00	12/15/00
0.28Q	2/07/01	2/21/01	2/23/01	3/15/01
0.28Q	4/24/01	5/23/01	5/25/01	6/15/01

Indicated div.: $1.12 (Div. Reinv. Plan)

CAPITALIZATION (12/31/00):

	($000)	(%)
Long-Term Debt	877,654	37.3
Deferred Income Tax	300,499	12.8
Common & Surplus	1,175,036	49.9
Total	2,353,189	100.0

RECENT DEVELOPMENTS: For the year ended 12/31/00, net income was $334.5 million versus $460.3 million a year earlier. Results for 1999 included a gain of $243.8 million on the sale of the Company's pasta business, as well as one month's operational results for this business. Net sales rose 6.3% to $4.22 billion from $3.97 billion in 1999. Results benefited from a strong Christmas season, which followed a successful Halloween season. In addition, HSY noted that all other business units achieved solid sales increases.

PROSPECTS: Near-term prospects are positive, reflecting improving sales trends, lower commodity and logistics costs, as well as manufacturing efficiencies. The Company should also continue to benefit from its new Eastern Distribution Center, located near Hershey, PA. Looking forward, the Company's acquisition of Nabisco Inc.'s intense and breath freshener mints and gum businesses, which was completed on 12/15/00, should strengthen its position in the overall confectionery, gum and mint category.

BUSINESS

HERSHEY FOODS CORPORATION and its subsidiaries are engaged in the manufacture, distribution and sale of consumer food products including: chocolate and non-chocolate confectionery products sold in the form of bar goods, bagged items and boxed items; and grocery products sold in the form of baking ingredients, chocolate drink mixes, peanut butter, dessert toppings and beverages. HSY's products are marketed in over 90 countries worldwide. Principal brands include: HERSHEY'S, REESE'S, MR. GOODBAR, JOLLY RANCHER, KIT KAT, MILK DUDS, WHOPPERS, YORK, TWIZZLERS, and SUPER BUBBLE. In January 1999, the Company sold 94.0% majority interest in its former U.S. pasta business to New World, LLC. On 12/15/00, HSY acquired Nabisco, Inc.'s intense and breath freshener mints and gum businesses for $135.0 million. Brands include ICE BREAKERS and BREATH SAVERS COOL BLASTS intense mints, BREATH SAVERS mints, and ICE BREAKERS, CARE*FREE, STICK*FREE, BUBBLE YUM, and FRUIT STRIPE gums.

QUARTERLY DATA

(12/31/2000)($000)	Rev	Inc
1st Quarter	993,115	71,180
2nd Quarter	836,204	39,996
3rd Quarter	1,196,755	107,405
4th Quarter	1,194,902	115,962

ANNUAL FINANCIAL DATA

	12/31/00	12/31/99	12/31/98	12/31/97	12/31/96	12/31/95	12/31/94
Earnings Per Share	**2.42**	[2] **3.26**	**2.34**	**2.23**	**1.77**	**1.70**	[1] **1.06**
Cash Flow Per Share	**3.69**	**4.41**	**3.43**	**3.24**	**2.64**	**2.50**	**1.80**
Tang. Book Val. Per Share	**5.14**	**4.68**	**3.58**	**2.11**	**3.89**	**4.23**	**5.69**
Dividends Per Share	**1.08**	**1.00**	**0.92**	**0.84**	**0.76**	**0.69**	**0.63**
Dividend Payout %	**44.6**	**30.7**	**39.3**	**37.7**	**42.9**	**40.3**	**59.0**
INCOME STATEMENT (IN MILLIONS):							
Total Revenues	4,221.0	3,970.9	4,435.6	4,302.2	3,989.3	3,690.7	3,606.3
Costs & Expenses	3,422.4	3,249.3	3,634.8	3,519.3	3,292.7	3,046.0	3,108.7
Depreciation & Amort.	176.0	163.3	158.2	152.8	133.5	133.9	129.0
Operating Income	622.7	558.4	642.7	630.2	563.1	510.8	368.5
Net Interest Inc./(Exp.)	d76.0	d74.3	d85.7	d76.3	d48.0	d44.8	d35.4
Income Before Income Taxes	546.6	727.9	557.0	554.0	479.7	466.0	333.1
Income Taxes	212.1	267.6	216.1	217.7	206.6	184.0	148.9
Net Income	334.5	[2] 460.3	340.9	336.3	273.2	281.9	[1] 184.2
Cash Flow	510.5	623.6	499.0	489.0	406.7	415.8	313.3
Average Shs. Outstg. (000)	138,365	141,300	145,563	151,016	153,995	166,036	174,367
BALANCE SHEET (IN MILLIONS):							
Cash & Cash Equivalents	32.0	118.1	39.0	54.2	61.4	32.3	26.7
Total Current Assets	1,295.3	1,280.0	1,134.0	1,034.8	986.2	922.3	948.7
Net Property	1,585.4	1,510.5	1,648.1	1,648.2	1,601.9	1,436.0	1,468.4
Total Assets	3,447.8	3,346.7	3,404.1	3,291.2	3,184.8	2,830.6	2,891.0
Total Current Liabilities	766.9	712.8	814.8	795.7	817.3	864.4	796.2
Long-Term Obligations	877.7	878.2	879.1	1,029.1	655.3	357.0	157.2
Net Stockholders' Equity	1,175.0	1,098.6	1,042.3	852.8	1,161.0	1,083.0	1,441.1
Net Working Capital	528.4	567.2	319.1	239.1	169.0	58.0	152.4
Year-end Shs. Outstg. (000)	136,282	138,460	143,147	142,932	152,942	154,532	173,470
STATISTICAL RECORD:							
Operating Profit Margin %	14.8	14.1	14.5	14.6	14.1	13.8	10.2
Net Profit Margin %	7.9	11.6	7.7	7.8	6.8	7.6	5.1
Return on Equity %	28.5	41.9	32.7	39.4	23.5	26.0	12.8
Return on Assets %	9.7	13.8	10.0	10.2	8.6	10.0	6.4
Debt/Total Assets %	25.5	26.2	25.8	31.3	20.6	12.6	5.4
Price Range	66.44-37.75	64.88-45.75	76.38-59.69	63.88-42.13	51.75-31.94	33.94-24.00	26.75-20.56
P/E Ratio	27.5-15.6	19.9-14.0	32.6-25.5	28.6-18.9	29.2-18.0	20.0-14.1	25.2-19.4
Average Yield %	2.1	1.8	1.4	1.6	1.8	2.4	2.6

Statistics are as originally reported. Adj. for 2-for-1 stk. split, 9/96 [1] Incls. non-recurr. chrg. of $80.2 mill. [2] Incls. non-recurr. credit of $165.0 mill.

OFFICERS:
K. L. Wolfe, Chmn.
R. H. Lenny, Pres., C.E.O.
F. Cerminara, V.P., C.F.O., Treas.

INVESTOR CONTACT: James A. Edris, Dir., Investor Relations, (717) 534-7556

PRINCIPAL OFFICE: 100 Crystal A Drive, Hershey, PA 17033

TELEPHONE NUMBER: (717) 534-6799
FAX: (717) 531-6161
WEB: www.hersheys.com

NO. OF EMPLOYEES: 14,300 full-time (approx.); 1,400 part-time (approx.)

SHAREHOLDERS: 41,842

ANNUAL MEETING: In Apr.

INCORPORATED: DE, Oct., 1927

INSTITUTIONAL HOLDINGS:
No. of Institutions: 355
Shares Held: 54,301,799
% Held: 39.8

INDUSTRY: Chocolate and cocoa products (SIC: 2066)

TRANSFER AGENT(S): Mellon Investor Services, Ridgefield Park, NJ

NYSE SYMBOL HWP
Rec. Pr. 28.43 (4/30/01)

HEWLETT-PACKARD COMPANY

YIELD 1.1%
P/E RATIO 18.8

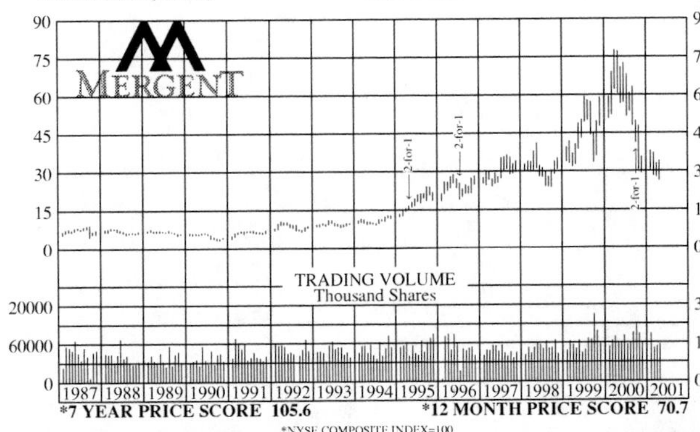

*7 YEAR PRICE SCORE 105.6 *12 MONTH PRICE SCORE 70.7

*NYSE COMPOSITE INDEX=100

INTERIM EARNINGS (Per Share):

Qtr.	Jan.	Apr.	July	Oct.
1996-97	0.44	0.38	0.29	0.38
1997-98	0.43	0.33	0.29	0.34
1998-99	0.46	0.44	0.41	0.37
1999-00	0.39	0.40	0.50	0.45
2000-01	0.16	...	...	...

INTERIM DIVIDENDS (Per Share):

Amt.	Decl.	Ex.	Rec.	Pay.
0.16Q	7/21/00	9/18/00	9/20/00	10/11/00
2-for-1	8/16/00	10/30/00	9/27/00	10/27/00
0.08Q	11/20/00	12/18/00	12/20/00	1/10/01
0.08Q	1/19/01	3/19/01	3/21/01	4/11/01
0.08Q	5/18/01	6/18/01	6/20/01	7/11/01

Indicated div.: $0.32 (Div. Reinv. Plan)

CAPITALIZATION (10/31/00):

	($000)	(%)
Long-Term Debt	3,402,000	19.3
Common & Surplus	14,209,000	80.7
Total	17,611,000	100.0

RECENT DEVELOPMENTS: For the quarter ended 1/31/01, HWP posted income of $305.0 million, before an extraordinary gain of $23.0 million, versus net income of $794.0 million in the equivalent period of the previous year. Net revenues rose 2.4% to $11.95 billion from $11.67 billion in the year-earlier quarter. Earnings from operations fell 33.1% to $637.0 million from $952.0 million the year before.

PROSPECTS: On 1/18/01, HWP completed the acquisition of Bluestone Software, Inc. in a stock-for-stock transaction. Separately, the Company and China Mobile Limited's majority-owned subsidiary, Aspire Holdings Limited, formed a strategic alliance that will include joint research and development in wireless data and the Internet, as well as the delivery of wireless platforms and services for mobile operators, on-line merchants, content providers and e-companies in China.

BUSINESS

HEWLETT-PACKARD COMPANY designs, manufactures and services electronic products and systems. The computer products, service and support unit develops hardware and software systems, networking products, printers, plotters, drives, calculators and offers support and maintenance services. The electronic test and measurement instrumentation unit provides maintenance and support for electronic equipment. The medical electronic equipment group performs monitoring, diagnostic, therapeutic and data-management applications for hospitals. The analytical and electronic components divisions offer gas and liquid chromatographs and microwave semiconductor and optoelectronic devices. On 6/2/00, HWP completed the spin off of Agilent Technologies, Inc. into an independent publicly-traded company.

ANNUAL FINANCIAL DATA

	10/31/00	10/31/99	10/31/98	10/31/97	10/31/96	10/31/95	10/31/94
Earnings Per Share	**[2] 0.87**	**[2] 0.74**	**[1] 0.69**	**0.74**	**0.62**	**0.58**	**0.38**
Cash Flow Per Share	**1.19**	**1.05**	**1.12**	**1.11**	**0.92**	**0.85**	**0.63**
Tang. Book Val. Per Share	**3.65**	**4.55**	**4.17**	**3.88**	**3.31**	**2.90**	**2.43**
Dividends Per Share	**0.32**	**0.32**	**0.30**	**0.26**	**0.22**	**0.17**	**0.14**
Dividend Payout %	**37.0**	**43.1**	**43.3**	**35.3**	**35.8**	**30.2**	**35.8**
INCOME STATEMENT (IN MILLIONS):							
Total Revenues	48,782.0	42,370.0	47,061.0	42,895.0	38,420.0	31,519.0	24,991.0
Costs & Expenses	43,525.0	37,366.0	41,351.0	37,000.0	33,397.0	26,812.0	21,436.0
Depreciation & Amort.	1,368.0	1,316.0	1,869.0	1,556.0	1,297.0	1,139.0	1,006.0
Operating Income	3,889.0	3,688.0	3,841.0	4,339.0	3,726.0	3,568.0	2,549.0
Net Interest Inc./(Exp.)	d257.0	d202.0	d235.0	d215.0	d327.0	d206.0	d155.0
Income Before Income Taxes	4,625.0	4,194.0	4,091.0	4,455.0	3,694.0	3,632.0	2,423.0
Income Taxes	1,064.0	1,090.0	1,146.0	1,336.0	1,108.0	1,199.0	796.0
Net Income	[2] 3,561.0	[2] 3,104.0	[1] 2,945.0	3,119.0	2,586.0	2,433.0	1,627.0
Cash Flow	4,929.0	4,420.0	4,814.0	4,675.0	3,883.0	3,572.0	2,633.0
Average Shs. Outstg. (000)	4,154,000	4,208,000	4,288,000	4,228,000	4,208,000	4,208,000	4,160,000
BALANCE SHEET (IN MILLIONS):							
Cash & Cash Equivalents	4,007.0	5,590.0	4,067.0	4,569.0	3,327.0	2,616.0	2,478.0
Total Current Assets	23,244.0	21,642.0	21,584.0	20,947.0	17,991.0	16,239.0	12,509.0
Net Property	4,500.0	4,333.0	6,358.0	6,312.0	5,536.0	4,711.0	4,328.0
Total Assets	34,009.0	35,297.0	33,673.0	31,749.0	27,699.0	24,427.0	19,567.0
Total Current Liabilities	15,197.0	14,321.0	13,473.0	11,219.0	10,623.0	10,944.0	8,230.0
Long-Term Obligations	3,402.0	1,764.0	2,063.0	3,158.0	2,579.0	663.0	547.0
Net Stockholders' Equity	14,209.0	18,295.0	16,919.0	16,155.0	13,438.0	11,839.0	9,926.0
Net Working Capital	8,047.0	7,321.0	8,111.0	9,728.0	7,368.0	5,295.0	4,279.0
Year-end Shs. Outstg. (000)	3,894,624	4,018,384	4,060,000	4,164,000	4,056,000	4,080,000	4,080,000
STATISTICAL RECORD:							
Operating Profit Margin %	8.0	8.7	8.2	10.1	9.7	11.3	10.2
Net Profit Margin %	7.3	7.3	6.3	7.3	6.7	7.7	6.5
Return on Equity %	25.1	17.0	17.4	19.3	19.2	20.6	16.4
Return on Assets %	10.5	8.8	8.7	9.8	9.3	10.0	8.3
Debt/Total Assets %	10.0	5.0	6.1	9.9	9.3	2.7	2.8
Price Range	77.75-29.13	59.22-31.69	41.19-23.53	36.47-24.06	28.84-18.41	24.16-12.25	12.81-8.98
P/E Ratio	89.9-33.7	79.8-42.7	59.5-34.0	49.4-32.6	46.9-29.9	41.8-21.2	33.4-23.4
Average Yield %	0.6	0.7	0.9	0.9	0.9	1.0	1.3

Statistics are as originally reported. Adj. for a 2-for-1 stock split 10/27/00, 4/13/95 & 7/15/96. [1] Incl. special pre-tax charges of approximately $170.0 million for voluntary-severance programs and fixed asset write downs. [2] Bef. inc. frm. disc. opers. of $136.0 mill., 2000; $387.0 mill., 1999.

OFFICERS:
C. S. Fiorina, Chmn., Pres., C.E.O.
R. P. Wayman, Exec. V.P., C.F.O.

INVESTOR CONTACT: Investor Relations, (800) 825-5497

PRINCIPAL OFFICE: 3000 Hanover Street, Palo Alto, CA 94304

TELEPHONE NUMBER: (650) 857-1501
FAX: (650) 857-5518
WEB: www.hp.com

NO. OF EMPLOYEES: 88,500 (approx.)

SHAREHOLDERS: 122,000 (approx.)

ANNUAL MEETING: In Feb.

INCORPORATED: CA, Aug., 1947; reincorp., DE, May, 1998

INSTITUTIONAL HOLDINGS:
No. of Institutions: 963
Shares Held: 1,041,815,608
% Held: 53.6

INDUSTRY: Electronic computers (SIC: 3571)

TRANSFER AGENT(S): Computershare Investor Services, Chicago, IL

NYSE SYMBOL HIB
Rec. Pr. 16.32 (4/30/01)

HIBERNIA CORP.

YIELD 3.2%
P/E RATIO 15.5

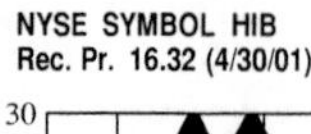

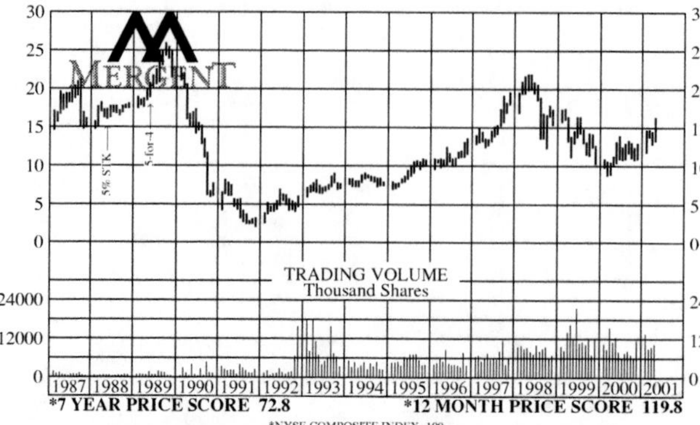

*7 YEAR PRICE SCORE 72.8 *12 MONTH PRICE SCORE 119.8

*NYSE COMPOSITE INDEX=100

INTERIM EARNINGS (Per Share):

Qtr.	Mar.	June	Sept.	Dec.
1997	0.23	0.24	0.25	0.28
1998	0.25	0.27	0.29	0.30
1999	0.18	0.29	0.30	0.30
2000	0.31	0.31	0.33	0.10

INTERIM DIVIDENDS (Per Share):

Amt.	Decl.	Ex.	Rec.	Pay.
0.12Q	4/18/00	4/26/00	4/28/00	5/22/00
0.12Q	7/26/00	8/03/00	8/07/00	8/21/00
0.13Q	10/25/00	11/02/00	11/06/00	11/20/00
0.13Q	1/24/01	2/01/01	2/05/01	2/20/01
0.13Q	4/17/01	4/25/01	4/27/01	5/21/01

Indicated div.: $0.52

CAPITALIZATION (12/31/00):

	($000)	(%)
Total Deposits	12,692,732	83.4
Long-Term Debt	1,043,996	6.9
Preferred Stock	86,950	0.6
Common & Surplus	1,392,701	9.2
Total	15,216,379	100.0

RECENT DEVELOPMENTS: For the year ended 12/31/00, net income declined 2.6% to $170.6 million compared with $175.1 million in the prior year. Net income was negatively affected in part by higher provision for loan losses, which rose 37.0% to $120.7 million compared with $87.8 million the year before. Net interest income improved 4.4% to $610.6 million versus $584.8 million in the previous year. Non-interest income totaled $248.7 million, an increase of 15.8% from $214.7 million in the prior year.

PROSPECTS: For 2001, HIB expects business conditions in its market to remain generally healthy, although additional weakening of the U.S. economy is currently forecasted. Recent projections for declining interest rates should favorably affect HIB's margin. However, growth in net interest income could be partially offset by securitizations within the indirect loan portfolio. HIB expects steady growth in non-interest income and continued improvements in non-interest expense management.

BUSINESS

HIBERNIA CORP. is a bank holding company. As of 12/31/00, the Company was the largest publicly traded bank holding company headquartered in Louisiana with assets of $16.70 billion and 265 locations in 34 Louisiana parishes, 16 Texas counties and two Mississippi counties. The Company conducts its business through its sole depository institution subsidiary, Hibernia National Bank. In addition, the Company also owns three non-bank subsidiaries: Hibernia Capital Corporation (HCC), Zachary Taylor Life Insurance Company and First National Company of Marshall, Inc. HCC is licensed as a small business investment company, which provides private equity investments to small businesses. Both Zachary Taylor and First National are currently inactive.

ANNUAL FINANCIAL DATA

	12/31/00	12/31/99	12/31/98	12/31/97	12/31/96	12/31/95	12/31/94
Earnings Per Share	**1.04**	**1.06**	**1.10**	**0.98**	**[1] 0.85**	**[1][2] 1.05**	**0.52**
Tang. Book Val. Per Share	**8.83**	**7.96**	**7.79**	**7.15**	**6.50**	**6.01**	**3.41**
Dividends Per Share	**0.49**	**0.43**	**0.38**	**0.33**	**0.29**	**0.25**	**0.19**
Dividend Payout %	**47.1**	**41.0**	**34.1**	**33.7**	**34.1**	**23.8**	**36.5**
INCOME STATEMENT (IN MILLIONS):							
Total Interest Income	1,217.3	1,055.3	953.7	750.1	625.6	523.2	414.4
Total Interest Expense	606.8	470.5	423.2	322.3	259.4	223.4	154.3
Net Interest Income	610.6	584.8	530.5	427.8	366.2	299.8	260.1
Provision for Loan Losses	120.7	87.8	26.0	0.6	cr12.6	...	cr17.2
Non-Interest Income	248.7	214.7	184.9	145.4	110.4	97.5	81.8
Non-Interest Expense	476.1	440.9	416.6	361.9	319.7	264.0	271.2
Income Before Taxes	262.5	270.8	272.9	210.6	169.5	133.3	88.0
Net Income	170.6	175.1	178.6	137.4	[1] 110.0	[1][2] 123.9	84.7
Average Shs. Outstg. (000)	158,020	158,902	156,165	133,325	126,766	117,880	162,734
BALANCE SHEET (IN MILLIONS):							
Cash & Due from Banks	...	...	555.8	529.7	558.4	377.1	353.3
Securities Avail. for Sale	2,687.0	2,660.3	3,026.4	2,541.3	2,337.0	2,183.5	537.4
Total Loans & Leases	12,124.7	10,856.7	10,006.2	7,580.3	6,043.0	4,469.4	3,375.7
Allowance for Credit Losses	178.3	156.1	128.0	107.5	127.8	146.7	148.6
Net Loans & Leases	11,946.4	10,700.6	9,878.2	7,472.7	5,915.3	4,322.7	3,227.1
Total Assets	16,698.0	15,314.2	14,011.5	11,023.0	9,306.8	7,196.2	6,335.8
Total Deposits	12,692.7	11,855.9	10,603.0	8,633.3	7,821.8	6,085.1	5,506.8
Long-Term Obligations	1,044.0	844.8	805.7	506.5	51.3	8.7	5.7
Total Liabilities	15,218.4	13,938.7	12,693.4	9,972.7	8,370.4	6,479.0	5,779.1
Net Stockholders' Equity	1,479.7	1,375.5	1,318.1	1,050.3	936.4	717.2	556.7
Year-end Shs. Outstg. (000)	157,729	160,325	156,400	133,001	128,755	119,293	163,119
STATISTICAL RECORD:							
Return on Equity %	11.5	12.7	13.6	13.1	11.7	17.3	15.2
Return on Assets %	1.0	1.1	1.3	1.2	1.2	1.7	1.3
Equity/Assets %	8.9	9.0	9.4	9.5	10.1	10.0	8.8
Non-Int. Exp./Tot. Inc. %	55.4	55.1	58.2	63.1	67.1	66.5	79.3
Price Range	13.94-8.75	17.50-10.25	22.00-12.25	19.63-12.38	13.63-9.50	11.00-6.88	9.13-7.25
P/E Ratio	13.4-8.4	16.5-9.7	20.0-11.1	20.0-12.6	16.0-11.2	10.5-6.5	17.5-13.9
Average Yield %	4.3	3.1	2.2	2.1	2.5	2.8	2.3

Statistics are as originally reported. [1] Incl. gain on sale of business lines, 1996, $517,000; 1995, $3.4 mill. [2] Incl. gain on divestiture of banking offices $2.4 mill.

OFFICERS:
R. Boh, Chmn.
E. Campbell, Vice-Chmn.
J. H. Boydstun, Pres., C.E.O.
M. M. Gassan, Sr. Exec. V.P., C.F.O.

INVESTOR CONTACT: Trisha Voltz, V.P., Mgr., Investor Relations, (504) 533-2180

PRINCIPAL OFFICE: 313 Carondelet Street, New Orleans, LA 70130

TELEPHONE NUMBER: (504) 533-5332
FAX: (504) 586-2199
WEB: www.hibernia.com

NO. OF EMPLOYEES: 5,366

SHAREHOLDERS: 16,708

ANNUAL MEETING: In Apr.

INCORPORATED: LA, Oct., 1972

INSTITUTIONAL HOLDINGS:
No. of Institutions: 199
Shares Held: 58,457,964
% Held: 37.0

INDUSTRY: National commercial banks (SIC: 6021)

TRANSFER AGENT(S): Mellon Investor Services, Ridgefield Park, NJ

NYSE SYMBOL HB
Rec. Pr. 50.50 (4/30/01)

HILLENBRAND INDUSTRIES, INC.

YIELD 1.7%
P/E RATIO 20.7

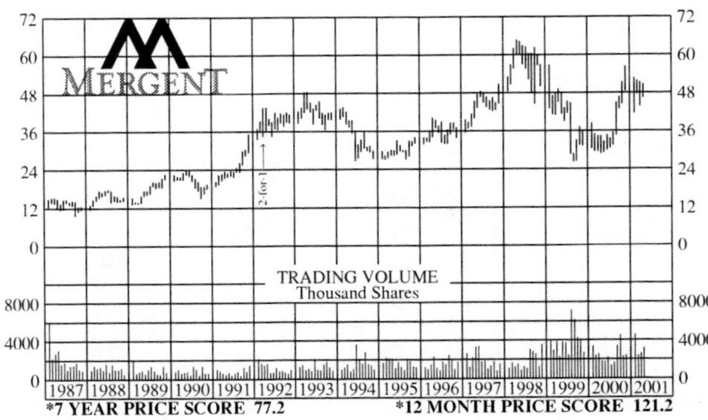

*7 YEAR PRICE SCORE 77.2 *12 MONTH PRICE SCORE 121.2
*NYSE COMPOSITE INDEX=100

INTERIM EARNINGS (Per Share):

Qtr.	Feb.	May	Aug.	Nov.
1996-97	0.56	0.54	0.51	0.67
1997-98	0.64	0.66	0.63	0.80
1998-99	0.67	0.53	0.35	0.58
1999-00	0.58	0.56	0.54	0.76

INTERIM DIVIDENDS (Per Share):

Amt.	Decl.	Ex.	Rec.	Pay.
0.20Q	4/11/00	4/18/00	4/21/00	5/26/00
0.20Q	7/11/00	7/19/00	7/21/00	8/25/00
0.20Q	10/10/00	10/18/00	10/20/00	11/24/00
0.21Q	1/16/01	2/07/01	2/09/01	2/23/01
0.21Q	4/10/01	4/18/01	4/20/01	5/25/01

Indicated div.: $0.84 (Div. Reinv. Plan)

CAPITALIZATION (12/2/00):

	($000)	(%)
Long-Term Debt	302,000	26.6
Deferred Income Tax	3,000	0.3
Common & Surplus	831,000	73.2
Total	1,136,000	100.0

RECENT DEVELOPMENTS: For the year ended 12/2/00, net income rose 24.2% to $154.0 million versus $124.0 million in the previous year. Results for 2000 and 1999 included unusual charges of $3.0 million and $38.0 million, respectively. Total net revenues advanced 2.4% to $2.10 billion. Health care group sales rose 4.4% to $800.0 million, while health care rentals sales fell 3.7% to $312.0 million. Insurance revenues grew 3.4% to $367.0 million, and funeral services sales improved 2.5% to $617.0 million.

PROSPECTS: On 1/22/01, Hill-Rom Company, Inc., a subsidiary of HB, announced plans to restructure its home care and long-term businesses due to reduced government reimbursements, changing customer needs and a transitioning health care environment. Going foward, the Company anticipates cost savings of $18.0 million to $20.0 million on an annual basis. The restructuring is part of the Company's continued focus on increasing production efficiencies by streamlining its organizational structure.

BUSINESS

HILLENBRAND INDUSTRIES, INC. is organized into two business segments. The Health Care Group consists of Hill-Rom, Inc., a manufacturer of equipment for the health care market and provider of wound care and pulmonary/trauma management services. Hill-Rom produces adjustable hospital beds, infant incubators, radiant warmers, hospital procedural stretchers, hospital patient room furniture, medical gas and vacuum systems and architectural systems designed to meet the needs of medical-surgical critical care, long-term care, home-care and perinatal providers. The Funeral Services Group consists of Batesville Casket Company, Inc., a manufacturer of caskets and other products for the funeral industry and Forethought Financial Services, Inc. a provider of funeral planning financial products.

ANNUAL FINANCIAL DATA

	12/2/00	11/27/99	11/28/98	11/29/97	11/30/96	12/2/95	12/3/94
Earnings Per Share	**3 2.44**	**2 1.87**	**1 2.73**	**2.28**	**2.02**	**1.27**	**1.26**
Cash Flow Per Share	**3.86**	**3.35**	**4.93**	**3.76**	**3.44**	**3.07**	**2.62**
Tang. Book Val. Per Share	**10.42**	**10.17**	**11.29**	**11.09**	**9.28**	**8.30**	**7.12**
Dividends Per Share	**0.80**	**0.78**	**0.72**	**0.66**	**0.62**	**0.60**	**0.57**
Dividend Payout %	**32.8**	**41.7**	**26.4**	**28.9**	**30.7**	**47.2**	**45.2**
INCOME STATEMENT (IN MILLIONS):							
Total Revenues	2,096.0	2,047.0	2,001.0	1,776.0	1,684.0	1,624.9	1,577.0
Costs & Expenses	1,763.0	1,738.0	1,624.0	1,410.0	1,349.0	1,317.8	1,320.5
Depreciation & Amort.	89.0	98.0	149.0	102.0	99.0	127.6	97.5
Operating Income	244.0	211.0	228.0	264.0	236.0	179.5	159.0
Net Interest Inc./(Exp.)	d27.0	d27.0	d27.0	d21.0	d22.0	d20.3	d23.5
Income Before Income Taxes	240.0	195.0	293.0	259.0	233.0	169.8	144.8
Income Taxes	86.0	71.0	109.0	102.0	93.0	79.9	55.3
Net Income	3 154.0	2 124.0	1 184.0	157.0	140.0	89.9	89.5
Cash Flow	243.0	222.0	333.0	259.0	239.0	217.5	187.0
Average Shs. Outstg. (000)	62,913	66,296	67,578	68,796	69,474	70,758	71,278
BALANCE SHEET (IN MILLIONS):							
Cash & Cash Equivalents	132.0	170.0	297.0	364.0	266.0	171.3	120.4
Total Current Assets	724.0	782.0	858.0	821.0	694.0	640.2	546.1
Net Property	272.0	267.0	302.0	329.0	346.0	367.1	358.6
Total Assets	4,597.0	4,433.0	4,280.0	3,828.0	3,396.0	3,070.3	2,693.8
Total Current Liabilities	282.0	371.0	375.0	359.0	320.0	300.7	238.9
Long-Term Obligations	302.0	302.0	303.0	203.0	204.0	206.8	208.7
Net Stockholders' Equity	831.0	838.0	952.0	886.0	787.0	745.8	693.5
Net Working Capital	442.0	411.0	483.0	462.0	374.0	339.4	307.3
Year-end Shs. Outstg. (000)	62,404	63,547	66,759	68,511	68,786	70,177	70,923
STATISTICAL RECORD:							
Operating Profit Margin %	11.6	10.3	11.4	14.9	14.0	11.0	10.1
Net Profit Margin %	7.3	6.1	9.2	8.8	8.3	5.5	5.7
Return on Equity %	18.5	14.8	19.3	17.7	17.8	12.0	12.9
Return on Assets %	3.4	2.8	4.3	4.1	4.1	2.9	3.3
Debt/Total Assets %	6.6	6.8	7.1	5.3	6.0	6.7	7.7
Price Range	56.38-28.75	56.81-26.13	64.69-44.38	50.88-35.50	40.25-31.88	34.13-27.00	43.63-26.63
P/E Ratio	23.1-11.8	30.4-14.0	23.7-16.3	22.3-15.6	19.9-15.8	26.9-21.3	34.6-21.1
Average Yield %	1.9	1.9	1.3	1.5	1.7	2.0	1.6

Statistics are as originally reported. 1 Incl. non-recurr. chrg. $66.0 mill. 2 Incl. unusual chrg. $38.0 mill. 3 Incl. non-recurr. chrgs. of $3.0 mill.

OFFICERS:
R. J. Hillenbrand, Chmn.
F. W. Rockwood, Pres., C.E.O.
S. K. Sorensen, V.P., C.F.O.

INVESTOR CONTACT: Mark R. Lanning, VP & Treas., (812) 934-8400

PRINCIPAL OFFICE: 700 State Route 46 East, Batesville, IN 47006-8835

TELEPHONE NUMBER: (812) 934-7000
FAX: (812) 934-7364
WEB: www.hillenbrand.com

NO. OF EMPLOYEES: 10,800 (approx.)

SHAREHOLDERS: 18,100 (approx.)

ANNUAL MEETING: In Apr.

INCORPORATED: IN, Aug., 1969

INSTITUTIONAL HOLDINGS:
No. of Institutions: 185
Shares Held: 21,562,987
% Held: 34.5

INDUSTRY: Burial caskets (SIC: 3995)

TRANSFER AGENT(S): Computershare Investor Services, Chicago, IL

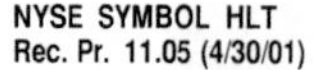

NYSE SYMBOL HLT
Rec. Pr. 11.05 (4/30/01)

HILTON HOTELS CORPORATION

YIELD 0.7%
P/E RATIO 14.9

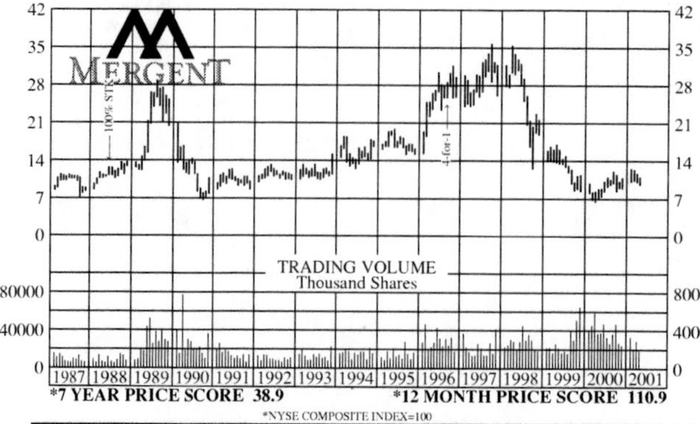

INTERIM EARNINGS (Per Share):

Qtr.	Mar.	June	Sept.	Dec.
1996	0.19	0.30	0.28	0.03
1997	0.26	0.34	0.35	d0.03
1998	0.29	0.39	0.30	0.17
1999	0.16	0.25	0.16	0.07
2000	0.16	0.25	0.16	0.17

INTERIM DIVIDENDS (Per Share):

Amt.	Decl.	Ex.	Rec.	Pay.
0.02Q	5/11/00	5/31/00	6/02/00	6/16/00
0.02Q	7/13/00	8/30/00	9/01/00	9/15/00
0.02Q	11/09/00	11/29/00	12/01/00	12/15/00
0.02Q	1/23/01	2/28/01	3/02/01	3/16/01
0.02Q	5/09/01	5/30/01	6/01/01	6/15/01

Indicated div.: $0.08

CAPITALIZATION (12/31/00):

	($000)	(%)
Long-Term Debt	5,693,000	69.1
Deferred Income Tax	902,000	11.0
Common & Surplus	1,642,000	19.9
Total	8,237,000	100.0

RECENT DEVELOPMENTS: For the year ended 12/31/00, net income advanced 25.9% to $272.0 million compared with income of $216.0 million in 1999. Results for 2000 included a pre-tax net gain of $32.0 million from the sale of certain securities and a nonrecurring credit of $8.0 million from the termination of post-retirement life insurance programs. Results for 1999 included a pre-tax net gain of $26.0 million and nonrecurring charges totaling $0.06 per share. Revenues rose 9.2% to $3.45 billion.

PROSPECTS: The Company's advance bookings are solid for 2001. Revenues should continue to benefit from an estimated 3.0% to 4.0% increase in revenue per available room at Company-owned properties. On 1/17/00, the Company signed an agreement with Hoteles Camino Real, S.A. de C.V, a luxury hotel chain, to affiliate 14 Camino Real hotels and resorts in Mexico and Texas under the Hilton® brand name.

BUSINESS

HILTON HOTELS CORPORATION is primarily engaged, together with its subsidiaries, in the ownership, management and development of hotels, resorts and vacation ownership properties and the franchising of lodging properties. The Company's hotel brands include HILTON®, HILTON GARDEN INN®, DOUBLETREE®, EMBASSY SUITES®, HAMPTON®, HOMEWOOD SUITES® by HILTON®, RED LION®, CONRAD® and HARRISON® Conference Centers. As of 12/31/00, all of these properties were located in the U.S., with the exception of ten hotels operated under the Conrad International name and 33 franchise hotels operated in Canada, Chile, Colombia, Costa Rica, Mexico and Puerto Rico. For the year ended 12/31/00, the Company owned an interest in 139 hotels, managed 191 hotels owned by others, leased 73 hotels and franchised 1,492 hotels owned and operated by third parties. In addition, the Company operates Hilton Grand Vacations Company®, a vacation ownership program and a portfolio of independent properties, including Harrison conference centers and University hotels. On 11/30/99, HLT acquired Promus Hotel Corp.

ANNUAL FINANCIAL DATA

	12/31/00	12/31/99	[3] 12/31/98	12/31/97	12/31/96	12/31/95	12/31/94
Earnings Per Share	[5] **0.73**	[4] **0.66**	[2] **0.71**	**0.94**	[1] **0.79**	**0.89**	**0.63**
Cash Flow Per Share	**1.69**	**1.75**	**1.13**	**1.97**	**1.70**	**1.62**	**1.32**
Tang. Book Val. Per Share	...	**0.39**	**0.72**	**8.25**	**7.63**	**6.50**	**5.88**
Dividends Per Share	**0.08**	**0.08**	**0.32**	**0.32**	**0.30**	**0.30**	**0.30**
Dividend Payout %	**11.0**	**12.1**	**45.1**	**34.0**	**38.6**	**33.7**	**47.6**
INCOME STATEMENT (IN MILLIONS):							
Total Revenues	3,451.0	2,150.0	1,769.0	5,316.0	3,940.0	1,589.8	1,456.1
Costs & Expenses	2,231.0	1,465.0	1,178.0	4,417.0	3,432.0	1,153.9	1,096.0
Depreciation & Amort.	390.0	190.0	127.0	303.0	179.0	141.9	133.3
Operating Income	830.0	495.0	464.0	596.0	329.0	353.6	276.9
Net Interest Inc./(Exp.)	d469.0	d239.0	d141.0	d190.0	d100.0	d110.0	d97.9
Income Before Income Taxes	479.0	313.0	336.0	448.0	267.0	280.3	200.9
Income Taxes	200.0	130.0	136.0	187.0	106.0	102.6	77.6
Equity Earnings/Minority Int.	d7.0	d7.0	d12.0	d11.0	d5.0	54.7	48.5
Net Income	[5] 272.0	[4] 176.0	[2] 188.0	250.0	[1] 156.0	172.8	121.7
Cash Flow	662.0	366.0	305.0	540.0	335.0	314.7	255.0
Average Shs. Outstg. (000)	391,633	209,195	278,000	281,231	197,000	194,000	193,136
BALANCE SHEET (IN MILLIONS):							
Cash & Cash Equivalents	47.0	104.0	47.0	373.0	438.0	408.7	393.2
Total Current Assets	840.0	763.0	469.0	1,011.0	1,151.0	717.3	673.7
Net Property	3,986.0	3,892.0	2,483.0	4,994.0	4,698.0	1,695.9	1,664.8
Total Assets	9,140.0	9,253.0	3,944.0	7,826.0	7,577.0	3,060.3	2,925.9
Total Current Liabilities	646.0	629.0	506.0	941.0	998.0	534.9	328.3
Long-Term Obligations	5,693.0	6,085.0	3,037.0	2,709.0	2,606.0	1,069.7	1,251.9
Net Stockholders' Equity	1,642.0	1,415.0	187.0	3,383.0	3,211.0	1,253.7	1,127.8
Net Working Capital	194.0	134.0	d37.0	70.0	153.0	182.4	345.4
Year-end Shs. Outstg. (000)	369,000	368,000	261,000	249,000	249,000	193,000	191,784
STATISTICAL RECORD:							
Operating Profit Margin %	24.1	23.0	26.2	11.2	8.4	22.2	19.0
Net Profit Margin %	7.9	8.2	10.6	4.7	4.0	10.9	8.4
Return on Equity %	16.6	12.4	100.5	7.4	4.9	13.8	10.8
Return on Assets %	3.0	1.9	4.8	3.2	2.1	5.6	4.2
Debt/Total Assets %	62.3	65.8	77.0	34.6	34.4	35.0	42.8
Price Range	12.13-6.38	17.13-8.38	35.50-12.50	35.81-24.00	31.75-15.28	19.94-15.09	18.50-12.44
P/E Ratio	16.6-8.7	25.9-12.7	50.0-17.6	38.1-25.5	40.2-19.3	22.4-17.0	29.4-19.7
Average Yield %	0.9	0.6	1.3	1.1	1.3	1.7	1.9

Statistics are as originally reported. Adj. for stk. split: 4-for-1, 9/96. [1] Bef. extraord. chrg. $74.0 mill. [2] Inc. a charge of $0.04 per share for the spin-off of HLT's gaming opers. & excl. a gain of $109. mill. from disc. opers. [3] Reflects the spin-off of the gaming opers. [4] Incl. an after-tax chg. of $2.0 mill. for the cum. effect of a chg. in acctg. & pre-tax chrg. of $2.0 mill. [5] Incl. pre-tax gain of $32.0 mill. & nonrecurr. cr. of $8.0 mill.

OFFICERS:
B. Hilton, Chmn.
S. F. Bollenbach, Pres., C.E.O.

INVESTOR CONTACT: (310) 278-4321

PRINCIPAL OFFICE: 9336 Civic Center Dr., Beverly Hills, CA 90210

TELEPHONE NUMBER: (310) 278-4321
FAX: (310) 205-7824
WEB: www.hilton.com
NO. OF EMPLOYEES: 77,000 (avg.)
SHAREHOLDERS: 21,100
ANNUAL MEETING: In May
INCORPORATED: DE, May, 1946

INSTITUTIONAL HOLDINGS:
No. of Institutions: 248
Shares Held: 221,646,686
% Held: 60.1

INDUSTRY: Hotels and motels (SIC: 7011)

TRANSFER AGENT(S): Mellon Investor Services, Ridgefield Park, NJ.

NYSE SYMBOL HSP
Rec. Pr. 23.97 (4/30/01)

HISPANIC BROADCASTING CORP.

YIELD ...
P/E RATIO 63.1

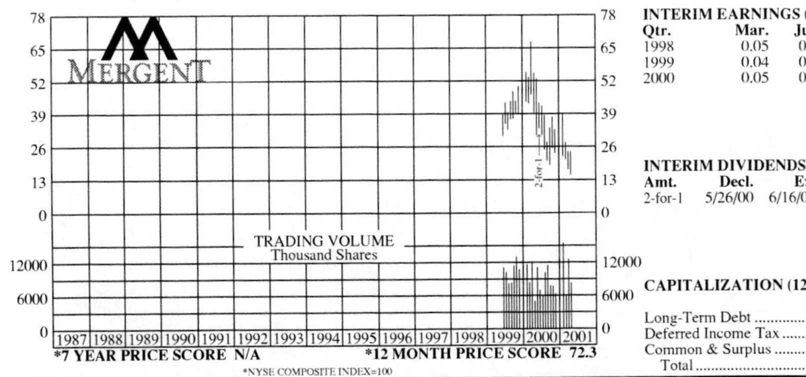

INTERIM EARNINGS (Per Share):

Qtr.	Mar.	June	Sept.	Dec.
1998	0.05	0.08	0.07	0.08
1999	0.04	0.10	0.10	0.11
2000	0.05	0.11	0.12	0.10

INTERIM DIVIDENDS (Per Share):

Amt.	Decl.	Ex.	Rec.	Pay.
2-for-1	5/26/00	6/16/00	6/05/00	6/15/00

CAPITALIZATION (12/31/00):

	($000)	(%)
Long-Term Debt	1,404	0.1
Deferred Income Tax	111,952	9.5
Common & Surplus	1,071,003	90.4
Total	1,184,359	100.0

RECENT DEVELOPMENTS: For the year ended 12/31/00, net income improved 21.5% to $41.5 million compared with $34.2 million in the corresponding year. Net revenues jumped 20.0% to $237.6 million versus $197.9 million in the previous year. Operating income increased 6.7% to $59.9 million from $56.2 million in the comparable year. During the year, HSP launched radio stations in Los Angeles, Dallas and San Antonio.

PROSPECTS: In 2001, the Company expects net revenue growth in the range of 12.0% to 14.0% if the economy remains strong, with most growth occurring in the second half of the year. Results are likely to be hampered by soft demand for advertising and higher operating costs as HSP further strengthens its sales staffs and takes actions to build its stations' ratings.

BUSINESS

HISPANIC BROADCASTING CORP. is the largest Spanish-language radio broadcasting company in the United States and currently owns and programs 47 radio stations in 15 markets. The Company's stations are located in 12 of the 15 largest Hispanic markets in the United States, including Los Angeles, New York, Miami, San Francisco/San Jose, Chicago, Houston, San Antonio, Dallas/Fort Worth, McAllen/Brownsville/Harlingen, San Diego, Phoenix and El Paso. In addition, the Company also operates the HBC Radio Network, which is one of the largest Spanish-language radio broadcast networks in the United States.

QUARTERLY DATA

(12/31/2000)($000)	REV	INC
1st Quarter	45,539	5,219
2nd Quarter	64,771	12,054
3rd Quarter	64,885	13,111
4th Quarter	61,360	11,147

ANNUAL FINANCIAL DATA

	12/31/00	12/31/99	12/31/98	12/31/97	[1] 12/31/96	9/30/96	9/30/95
Earnings Per Share	0.38	0.33	0.27	0.23	0.05	[2][3] d0.89	0.09
Cash Flow Per Share	0.69	0.61	0.49	0.40	0.08	d0.76	0.17
Tang. Book Val. Per Share	1.18	1.64	...	...	...	...	...
INCOME STATEMENT (IN MILLIONS):							
Total Revenues	237.6	197.9	164.1	136.6	18.3	71.7	68.2
Costs & Expenses	143.4	113.3	101.2	86.6	11.6	54.0	52.7
Depreciation & Amort.	34.3	28.5	21.1	14.9	1.7	5.1	3.6
Operating Income	59.9	56.2	41.7	35.0	5.0	12.6	11.9
Net Interest Inc./(Exp.)	7.1	1.8	2.6	d3.5	d2.8	d11.0	d6.4
Income Before Income Taxes	68.6	58.0	44.6	31.4	2.2	d36.6	5.0
Income Taxes	27.1	23.8	17.7	12.6	0.1	0.1	0.2
Equity Earnings/Minority Int.	...	...	...	...	...	...	d1.2
Net Income	41.5	34.2	26.9	18.8	2.1	[2][3] d36.6	3.7
Cash Flow	75.8	62.7	48.0	33.7	3.8	d31.5	4.4
Average Shs. Outstg. (000)	110,388	102,928	98,695	83,584	46,191	41,180	43,221
BALANCE SHEET (IN MILLIONS):							
Cash & Cash Equivalents	115.7	215.1	10.3	6.6	4.8	5.1	5.4
Total Current Assets	166.0	256.6	45.1	36.7	22.4	23.2	25.5
Net Property	45.1	40.9	33.8	33.3	19.7	19.8	12.2
Total Assets	1,204.6	1,157.1	746.7	512.2	163.7	165.8	151.6
Total Current Liabilities	20.3	25.4	27.9	25.7	14.0	16.0	10.5
Long-Term Obligations	1.4	1.4	1.5	14.1	135.5	136.1	95.9
Net Stockholders' Equity	1,071.0	1,026.3	622.6	390.0	14.2	12.1	43.6
Net Working Capital	145.7	231.1	17.2	11.0	8.4	7.2	15.0
Year-end Shs. Outstg. (000)	108,958	108,802	98,657	88,270	46,191	46,191	43,486
STATISTICAL RECORD:							
Operating Profit Margin %	25.2	28.4	25.4	25.6	27.2	17.6	17.5
Net Profit Margin %	17.5	17.3	16.4	13.7	11.3	...	5.4
Return on Equity %	3.9	3.3	4.3	4.8	14.6	...	8.5
Return on Assets %	3.4	3.0	3.6	3.7	1.3	...	2.4
Debt/Total Assets %	0.1	0.1	0.2	2.8	82.8	82.1	63.3
Price Range	67.50-18.69	49.81-30.06	...	...	...	...	...
P/E Ratio	177.6-49.2	150.9-91.1	...	...	...	...	...

Statistics are as originally reported. Adj. for 2-for-1 stk. spl., 6/00 [1] Fiscal year end changed from 9/30 to 12/31 [2] Incl. loss on retirement of debt, 9/96, $7.5 mill. [3] Incl. restruct. chrg. $29.0 mill. & excl. loss from discont. opers., $20.0 mill.

OFFICERS:
M. T. Tichenor Jr., Chmn., Pres., C.E.O.
J. T. Hinson, Sr. V.P., C.F.O., Treas.
D. P. Gerow, V.P., C.A.O., Contr., Sec.

INVESTOR CONTACT: Investor Relations, (214) 525-7700

PRINCIPAL OFFICE: 3102 Oak Lawn Avenue, Suite 215, Dallas, TX 75219

TELEPHONE NUMBER: (214) 525-7700
FAX: (214) 525-7750
WEB: www.heftel.com

NO. OF EMPLOYEES: 903

SHAREHOLDERS: 96 (approx. class A common)

ANNUAL MEETING: In May

INCORPORATED: HI, 1974; reincorp., DE, 1992

INSTITUTIONAL HOLDINGS:
No. of Institutions: 156
Shares Held: 64,185,576
% Held: 58.9

INDUSTRY: Radio broadcasting stations (SIC: 4832)

TRANSFER AGENT(S): Mellon Investor Services, Ridgefield Park, NJ.

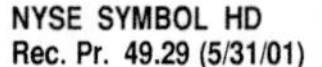

NYSE SYMBOL HD
Rec. Pr. 49.29 (5/31/01)

HOME DEPOT (THE), INC.

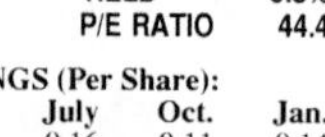

YIELD 0.3%
P/E RATIO 44.4

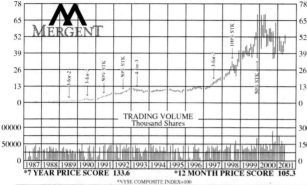

TRADING VOLUME
Thousand Shares

*7 YEAR PRICE SCORE 133.6 *12 MONTH PRICE SCORE 105.3

*NYSE COMPOSITE INDEX=100

INTERIM EARNINGS (Per Share):

Qtr.	Apr.	July	Oct.	Jan.
1997-98	0.12	0.16	0.11	0.14
1998-99	0.15	0.21	0.17	0.18
1999-00	0.21	0.29	0.25	0.25
2000-01	0.27	0.36	0.28	0.20

INTERIM DIVIDENDS (Per Share):

Amt.	Decl.	Ex.	Rec.	Pay.
0.04Q	5/31/00	6/13/00	6/15/00	6/29/00
0.04Q	8/17/00	8/29/00	8/31/00	9/14/00
0.04Q	11/16/00	11/28/00	11/30/00	12/14/00
0.04Q	2/22/01	3/06/01	3/08/01	3/22/01
0.04Q	5/30/01	6/12/01	6/14/01	6/28/01

Indicated div.: $0.16 (Div. Reinv. Plan)

CAPITALIZATION (1/28/01):

	($000)	(%)
Long-Term Debt	1,545,000	9.2
Deferred Income Tax	195,000	1.2
Minority Interest	11,000	0.1
Common & Surplus	15,004,000	89.5
Total	16,755,000	100.0

RECENT DEVELOPMENTS: For the year ended 1/28/01, net earnings grew 11.3% to $2.58 billion from $2.32 billion the previous year. Net sales climbed 19.0% to $45.74 billion from $38.43 billion a year earlier, driven by a 17.6% jump in the number of customer transactions and a 1.6% increase in the average sale per transaction. Comparable-store sales were up 4.0% year-over-year. Operating income advanced 10.1% to $4.19 billion.

PROSPECTS: The Company is focusing on launching initiatives designed to spur sales growth, including significantly expanding its selection of major appliances. In addition, HD plans to continue aggressively rolling out new services for professional contractors, such as delivery services and dedicated customer service associates. These services are expected to be available in nearly 500 stores by the end of fiscal 2001.

BUSINESS

THE HOME DEPOT, INC. operates 1,134 retail warehouse stores in the United States, Canada, Chile, Argentina and Puerto Rico that offer a wide assortment of building materials and home improvement products primarily to the "do-it-yourself" and home remodeling markets. The average Home Depot store is approximately 108,000 square feet of interior floor space and is stocked with approximately 40,000 to 50,000 separate items. Most stores have an additional approximately 24,000 square feet of outdoor selling area for landscaping supplies. HD also operates 26 EXPO Design Center stores that sell products and services primarily for design and renovation projects, four Villager's Hardware stores, and one Home Depot Floor Store outlet.

ANNUAL FINANCIAL DATA

	1/28/01	1/30/00	1/31/99	2/1/98	2/2/97	1/28/96	1/29/95
Earnings Per Share	**1.10**	**1.00**	**0.71**	**[1] 0.52**	**0.43**	**0.34**	**0.29**
Cash Flow Per Share	**1.35**	**1.19**	**0.86**	**0.63**	**0.53**	**0.42**	**0.34**
Tang. Book Val. Per Share	**6.32**	**5.22**	**3.83**	**3.17**	**2.71**	**2.28**	**1.64**
Dividends Per Share	**0.16**	**0.113**	**0.077**	**0.063**	**0.051**	**0.042**	**0.032**
Dividend Payout %	**14.5**	**11.3**	**10.8**	**12.1**	**11.9**	**12.4**	**11.4**
INCOME STATEMENT (IN MILLIONS):							
Total Revenues	45,738.0	38,434.0	30,219.0	24,156.0	19,535.5	15,470.4	12,476.7
Costs & Expenses	40,946.0	34,176.0	27,185.0	21,961.0	17,769.5	14,109.3	11,359.9
Depreciation & Amort.	601.0	463.0	373.0	283.0	232.3	181.2	129.6
Operating Income	4,191.0	3,795.0	2,661.0	1,912.0	1,533.7	1,179.8	987.2
Net Interest Inc./(Exp.)	26.0	9.0	d7.0	2.0	9.5	15.4	d7.4
Income Before Income Taxes	4,217.0	3,804.0	2,654.0	1,898.0	1,534.8	1,195.3	979.8
Income Taxes	1,636.0	1,484.0	1,040.0	738.0	597.0	463.8	375.3
Equity Earnings/Minority Int.	...	...	...	d16.0	d8.4	...	...
Net Income	2,581.0	2,320.0	1,614.0	[1] 1,160.0	937.7	731.5	604.5
Cash Flow	3,182.0	2,783.0	1,987.0	1,443.0	1,170.1	912.7	734.1
Average Shs. Outstg. (000)	2,352,000	2,342,000	2,320,000	2,286,000	2,194,884	2,150,897	2,141,762
BALANCE SHEET (IN MILLIONS):							
Cash & Cash Equivalents	177.0	170.0	62.0	174.0	558.4	108.0	57.9
Total Current Assets	7,777.0	6,390.0	4,933.0	4,460.0	3,709.4	2,672.0	2,133.0
Net Property	13,068.0	10,227.0	8,160.0	6,509.0	5,437.0	4,461.0	3,397.2
Total Assets	21,385.0	17,081.0	13,465.0	11,229.0	9,341.7	7,354.0	5,778.0
Total Current Liabilities	4,385.0	3,656.0	2,857.0	2,456.0	1,842.1	1,416.5	1,214.2
Long-Term Obligations	1,545.0	750.0	1,566.0	1,303.0	1,246.6	720.1	983.4
Net Stockholders' Equity	15,004.0	12,341.0	8,740.0	7,098.0	5,955.2	4,987.8	3,442.2
Net Working Capital	3,392.0	2,734.0	2,076.0	2,004.0	1,867.2	1,255.5	918.7
Year-end Shs. Outstg. (000)	2,323,747	2,304,317	2,213,178	2,196,324	2,162,318	2,146,977	2,040,143
STATISTICAL RECORD:							
Operating Profit Margin %	9.2	9.9	8.8	7.9	7.9	7.6	7.9
Net Profit Margin %	5.6	6.0	5.3	4.8	4.8	4.7	4.8
Return on Equity %	17.2	18.8	18.5	16.3	15.7	14.7	17.6
Return on Assets %	12.1	13.6	12.0	10.3	10.0	9.9	10.5
Debt/Total Assets %	7.2	4.4	11.6	11.6	13.3	9.8	17.0
Price Range	70.00-34.69	69.75-34.59	41.34-18.44	20.17-10.61	13.22-9.22	11.11-8.14	10.72-8.11
P/E Ratio	63.6-31.5	69.7-34.6	58.2-26.0	39.0-20.5	30.7-21.4	32.5-23.8	36.6-27.7
Average Yield %	0.3	0.2	0.3	0.4	0.5	0.4	0.4

Statistics are as originally reported. Adj. for 3-for-2 stk. split, 12/99; 100% stk. div., 7/98; & 3-for-2 stk. split, 7/97. [1] Incl. $104 mil pre-tax, non-recur. chg.

OFFICERS:
B. Marcus, Chmn.
R. L. Nardelli, Pres., C.E.O.
C. B. Tome, Exec. V.P., C.F.O.

INVESTOR CONTACT: Investor Relations, (770) 384-2666

PRINCIPAL OFFICE: 2455 Paces Ferry Road, Atlanta, GA 30339-4024

TELEPHONE NUMBER: (770) 433-8211
FAX: (770) 431-2707
WEB: www.homedepot.com

NO. OF EMPLOYEES: 227,000 (approx.)

SHAREHOLDERS: 212,010

ANNUAL MEETING: In May

INCORPORATED: DE, June, 1978

INSTITUTIONAL HOLDINGS:
No. of Institutions: 998
Shares Held: 1,330,609,902
% Held: 57.2

INDUSTRY: Lumber and other building materials (SIC: 5211)

TRANSFER AGENT(S): Fleet National Bank, Boston, MA

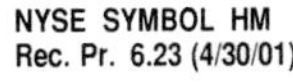
NYSE SYMBOL HM
Rec. Pr. 6.23 (4/30/01)

HOMESTAKE MINING COMPANY

YIELD 0.4%
P/E RATIO . . .

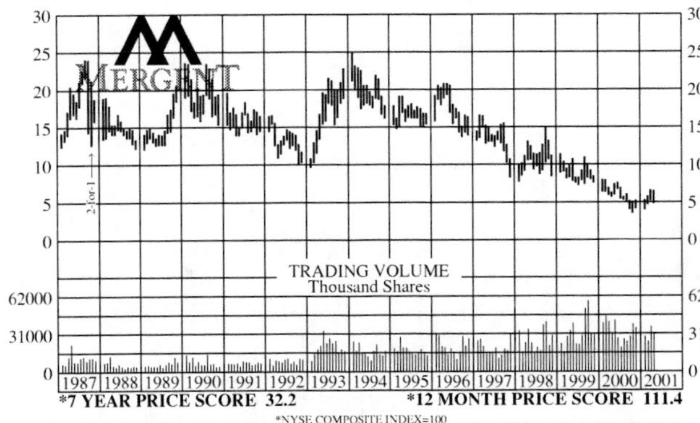

*7 YEAR PRICE SCORE 32.2 *12 MONTH PRICE SCORE 111.4

*NYSE COMPOSITE INDEX=100

INTERIM EARNINGS (Per Share):

Qtr.	Mar.	June	Sept.	Dec.
1997	0.34	d0.11	d1.12	d0.26
1998	0.03	d0.15	0.86	0.01
1999	0.01	Nil	0.01	0.02
2000	d0.06	d0.01	d0.29	0.02

INTERIM DIVIDENDS (Per Share):

Amt.	Decl.	Ex.	Rec.	Pay.
0.025S	9/24/99	10/27/99	10/29/99	11/17/99
0.025A	10/26/00	11/14/00	11/16/00	12/07/00

Indicated div.: $0.03 (Div. Reinv. Plan)

CAPITALIZATION (12/31/00):

	($000)	(%)
Long-Term Debt	224,616	21.9
Deferred Income Tax	181,961	17.7
Minority Interest	10,375	1.0
Common & Surplus	608,814	59.4
Total	1,025,766	100.0

RECENT DEVELOPMENTS: For the year ended 12/31/00, HM reported a loss from continuing operations of $89.1 million compared with income of $9.2 million in 1999. Results for 2000 and 1999 included write-downs and other unusual charges of $74.6 million and $20.4 million and excluded losses from discontinuing operations of $15.3 million and $4.4 million, respectively. Also, the 1999 results included a charge of $4.8 million for business combination and integration costs. Total revenues fell 8.6% to $666.8 million.

PROSPECTS: The Company should continue to benefit from a strong balance sheet and cash flow, increased gold production, lower expenses and changes in working capital. Meanwhile, HM will look to build its longer term gold production base with the view to further decrease operating costs and improve profitability. For 2001, the Company expects to produce 2.3 million ounces of gold and gold equivalent at an average cash cost of $168.00 per ounce.

BUSINESS

HOMESTAKE MINING COMPANY is one of the largest North American-based gold mining companies with current annual production of approximately 2.2 million gold equivalent ounces and reserves of approximately 20.8 million gold ounces and 144.3 million silver ounces at 12/31/00. HM's operations include mineral exploration, extraction, processing, refining and reclamation. Gold bullion is HM's primary product. HM is an international gold-mining company with significant gold interests in the U.S., Canada and Australia. Homestake is engaged in active exploration projects in the U.S., Canada, Australia, Argentina, Chile and the Andean region of South America. In April 1999, HM acquired Argentina Gold Corporation, whose principal asset is its 60.0% interest in the Veladero property.

ANNUAL FINANCIAL DATA

	12/31/00	12/31/99	12/31/98	12/31/97	12/31/96	12/31/95	12/31/94
Earnings Per Share 1	**7 d0.34**	**6 0.02**	**6 d1.02**	**5 d1.15**	**4 0.21**	**3 0.22**	**2 0.57**
Cash Flow Per Share	**0.21**	**0.54**	**d0.37**	**d0.39**	**0.97**	**0.94**	**1.12**
Tang. Book Val. Per Share	**2.34**	**3.02**	**3.23**	**3.62**	**5.24**	**4.52**	**4.27**
Dividends Per Share	**0.03**	**0.07**	**0.10**	**0.15**	**0.20**	**0.20**	**0.17**
Dividend Payout %	**. . .**	**373.1**	**. . .**	**. . .**	**95.2**	**90.9**	**30.7**
INCOME STATEMENT (IN MILLIONS):							
Total Revenues	666.8	748.1	797.8	723.8	765.3	744.2	702.6
Costs & Expenses	513.7	560.1	657.9	562.4	557.7	546.7	506.6
Depreciation & Amort.	144.5	134.5	139.4	112.4	112.4	99.6	76.2
Operating Income	8.7	53.6	0.5	49.0	95.3	97.9	119.8
Net Interest Inc./(Exp.)	d19.5	d17.8	d20.9	d11.3	d10.6	d11.3	d10.1
Income Before Income Taxes	d87.8	10.9	d228.2	d167.8	70.1	83.3	103.0
Income Taxes	4.4	7.4	cr13.1	cr9.2	26.3	39.1	18.9
Equity Earnings/Minority Int.	3.1	1.4	d3.2	d10.2	d13.5	d13.8	d6.1
Net Income	7 d89.1	6 4.9	6 d218.3	5 d168.9	4 30.3	3 30.3	2 78.0
Cash Flow	55.4	139.3	d79.0	d56.5	142.6	129.9	154.2
Average Shs. Outstg. (000)	261,692	259,964	213,354	146,719	146,311	138,117	137,733
BALANCE SHEET (IN MILLIONS):							
Cash & Cash Equivalents	199.7	266.6	299.4	235.9	219.8	212.4	205.2
Total Current Assets	332.2	397.1	452.1	376.0	427.0	426.8	342.8
Net Property	987.8	1,132.8	1,100.9	812.0	1,007.0	846.8	808.2
Total Assets	1,419.4	1,634.5	1,647.5	1,304.7	1,529.8	1,379.7	1,202.0
Total Current Liabilities	153.6	140.0	147.7	108.9	116.7	98.4	96.9
Long-Term Obligations	224.6	278.5	357.4	263.9	185.0	185.0	185.0
Net Stockholders' Equity	608.8	765.4	735.8	531.8	768.6	635.9	588.8
Net Working Capital	178.6	257.1	304.4	267.1	310.3	328.3	245.9
Year-end Shs. Outstg. (000)	259,846	253,808	228,012	146,735	146,672	140,541	137,785
STATISTICAL RECORD:							
Operating Profit Margin %	1.3	7.2	0.1	6.8	12.5	13.2	17.1
Net Profit Margin %	. . .	0.7	. . .	. . .	4.0	4.1	11.1
Return on Equity %	. . .	0.6	. . .	. . .	3.9	4.8	13.3
Return on Assets %	. . .	0.3	. . .	. . .	2.0	2.2	6.5
Price Range	8.00-3.50	11.44-7.19	15.00-7.69	16.63-8.25	20.88-13.63	19.13-14.75	24.88-16.13
P/E Ratio	. . .	569.1-357.6	. . .	. . .	99.4-64.9	86.9-67.0	43.6-28.3
Average Yield %	0.4	0.8	0.9	1.2	1.2	1.2	0.9

Statistics are as originally reported. 1 Bef. % depletion. 2 Incl. pre-tax gain of $26.9 mill. fr. sale of assets. 3 Incl. a gain of $5.5 mill. 4 Incl. a net lit. recov. of $4.9 mill. 5 Incl. pre-tax chgs. totaling $20.8 mill. 6 Incl. nonrecurr. chgs.. 1999, $20.4 mill.; 1998, $203.7 mill. & a pre-tax chg. 1999, $4.8 mill.; 1998, $19.1 mill. for bus. combin. & oth. integrat. exps. 7 Bef. loss from disc. oper. of $15.3 mill. & incl. non-recurr. chrg. of $74.6 mill.

OFFICERS:
J. E. Thompson, Chmn., C.E.O.
W. T. Segsworth, Pres., C.O.O.

INVESTOR CONTACT: Igor Levental, V.P. Inv. Rel., (925) 817-1369

PRINCIPAL OFFICE: 1600 Riviera Avenue, Suite 200, Walnut Creek, CA 94596-3568

TELEPHONE NUMBER: (925) 817-1300
FAX: (925) 397-5038
WEB: www.homestake.com
NO. OF EMPLOYEES: 3,309
SHAREHOLDERS: 18,713 (record); 1,460 (record HCI Exchangeable)
ANNUAL MEETING: In Apr.
INCORPORATED: DE, 1983

INSTITUTIONAL HOLDINGS:
No. of Institutions: 195
Shares Held: 102,041,127
% Held: 38.8

INDUSTRY: Gold ores (SIC: 1041)

TRANSFER AGENT(S): BankBoston, NA, Boston, MA

NYSE SYMBOL HNI
Rec. Pr. 24.96 (4/30/01)

HON INDUSTRIES INCORPORATED

YIELD 1.9%
P/E RATIO 14.1

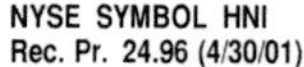

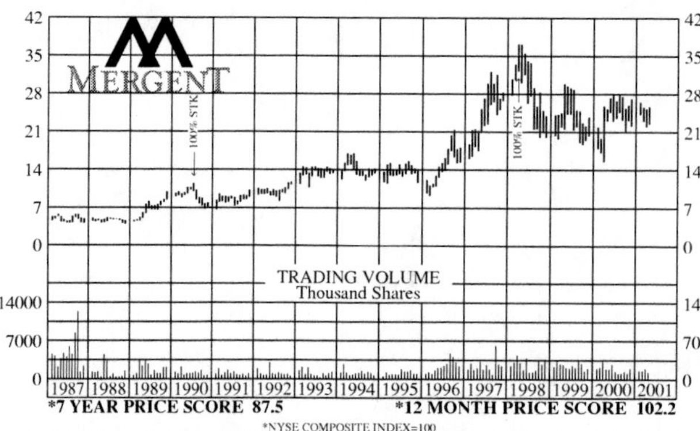

*7 YEAR PRICE SCORE 87.5 *12 MONTH PRICE SCORE 102.2
*NYSE COMPOSITE INDEX=100

INTERIM EARNINGS (Per Share):

Qtr.	Mar.	June	Sept.	Dec.
1997	0.28	0.32	0.43	0.42
1998	0.36	0.38	0.50	0.48
1999	0.19	0.37	0.47	0.41
2000	0.41	0.39	0.57	0.40

INTERIM DIVIDENDS (Per Share):

Amt.	Decl.	Ex.	Rec.	Pay.
0.11Q	5/02/00	5/10/00	5/12/00	6/01/00
0.11Q	8/07/00	8/15/00	8/17/00	9/01/00
0.11Q	11/10/00	11/16/00	11/20/00	12/01/00
0.12Q	2/14/01	2/16/01	2/21/01	3/01/01
0.12Q	5/07/01	5/15/01	5/17/01	6/01/01

Indicated div.: $0.48

CAPITALIZATION (12/30/00):

	($000)	(%)
Long-Term Debt	144,842	19.1
Capital Lease Obligations	2,192	0.3
Deferred Income Tax	37,226	4.9
Common & Surplus	573,342	75.7
Total	757,602	100.0

RECENT DEVELOPMENTS: For the year ended 12/30/00, net income increased 21.6% to $106.2 million compared with $87.4 million in the equivalent 1999 quarter. Results for 1999 included a pre-tax charge of $19.7 million for a provision for closing facilities and reorganization expenses. Net sales were $2.05 billion, up 13.6% from $1.80 billion a year earlier. Operating income was $178.0 million, or 8.7% of sales, versus $146.4 million, or 9.2% of sales, a year earlier.

PROSPECTS: Looking ahead, the Company anticipates modest growth for the retail and commercial transactional market, while growth in the convenience contract market should remain robust. HNI is continuing to focus on initiatives that are expected, in the long-term, to improve its return on equity, assets and invested capital. HNI plans to introduce a number of new products, which should enhance sales and earnings in 2001.

BUSINESS

HON INDUSTRIES INCORPORATED manufactures and markets office furniture and hearth products. Office products include filing cabinets, seating, including task chairs, executive desk chairs and side chairs, desks, tables, bookcases and credenzas. The office products are sold through mass merchandisers, warehouse clubs, a national system of dealers, retail superstores, end-user customers, and federal and state governments. The Hearth Technologies operating company products are comprised of wood-burning, pellet-burning, and gas-burning factory-built fireplaces, fireplace inserts, gas logs, and stoves. The hearth products are sold through wholesalers, a national system of dealers and large regional contractors. The Company has locations in the United States and Canada.

BUSINESS LINE ANALYSIS

(12/30/2000)	REV (%)	INC (%)
Office Furniture	80.6	85.0
Hearth Products	19.4	15.0
Total	100.0	100.0

ANNUAL FINANCIAL DATA

	12/30/00	1/1/00	1/2/99	1/3/98	12/28/96	12/31/95	12/31/94
Earnings Per Share	**1.77**	**1 1.44**	**1.72**	**1.45**	**1 1.13**	**0.67**	**0.87**
Cash Flow Per Share	**3.08**	**2.51**	**2.58**	**2.05**	**1.44**	**1.02**	**1.18**
Tang. Book Val. Per Share	**5.97**	**6.45**	**5.77**	**4.59**	**3.39**	**3.54**	**3.17**
Dividends Per Share	**0.44**	**0.38**	**0.32**	**0.28**	**0.25**	**0.24**	**0.22**
Dividend Payout %	**24.9**	**26.4**	**18.6**	**19.3**	**22.1**	**35.8**	**25.3**
INCOME STATEMENT (IN MILLIONS):							
Total Revenues	2,046.3	1,789.3	1,696.4	1,362.7	998.1	893.1	846.0
Costs & Expenses	1,789.2	1,577.4	1,464.3	1,181.9	873.1	805.0	739.8
Depreciation & Amort.	79.0	65.5	53.0	35.6	25.3	21.4	19.0
Operating Income	178.0	146.4	179.2	145.2	106.2	66.7	87.1
Net Interest Inc./(Exp.)	d12.1	d8.9	d9.1	d6.0	d0.9	d1.2	d0.8
Income Before Income Taxes	166.0	137.6	170.1	139.1	105.3	65.5	86.3
Income Taxes	59.7	50.2	63.8	52.2	37.2	24.4	31.9
Net Income	106.2	1 87.4	106.3	87.0	1 61.7	41.1	54.4
Cash Flow	185.3	152.8	159.3	122.6	86.9	62.5	73.4
Average Shs. Outstg. (000)	60,140	60,855	61,650	59,780	60,228	60,991	62,435
BALANCE SHEET (IN MILLIONS):							
Cash & Cash Equivalents	3.2	22.2	17.7	46.3	32.7	46.9	30.7
Total Current Assets	330.1	316.6	290.3	295.2	205.5	194.2	188.8
Net Property	454.3	455.6	444.2	341.0	234.6	210.0	177.8
Total Assets	1,022.5	906.7	864.5	754.7	513.5	409.5	372.6
Total Current Liabilities	264.9	225.1	217.4	200.8	152.6	128.9	111.1
Long-Term Obligations	147.0	142.2	153.6	153.1	97.8	53.6	54.7
Net Stockholders' Equity	573.3	501.3	462.0	381.7	252.4	216.2	194.6
Net Working Capital	65.3	91.4	72.9	94.4	53.0	65.3	77.7
Year-end Shs. Outstg. (000)	59,797	60,172	61,290	61,659	59,426	60,789	61,349
STATISTICAL RECORD:							
Operating Profit Margin %	8.7	8.2	10.6	10.7	10.6	7.5	10.3
Net Profit Margin %	5.2	4.9	6.3	6.4	6.2	4.6	6.4
Return on Equity %	18.5	17.4	23.0	22.8	24.4	19.0	27.9
Return on Assets %	10.4	9.6	12.3	11.5	12.0	10.0	14.6
Debt/Total Assets %	14.4	15.7	17.8	20.3	19.0	13.1	14.7
Price Range	27.88-15.56	29.88-18.75	37.19-20.00	32.13-16.00	21.38-9.25	15.63-11.50	17.00-12.00
P/E Ratio	15.7-8.8	20.7-13.0	21.6-11.6	22.2-11.0	18.9-8.2	23.3-17.2	19.5-13.8
Average Yield %	2.0	1.6	1.1	1.2	1.6	1.8	1.5

Statistics are as originally reported. Adj. for stk. split: 2-for-1, 3/27/98. 1 Incl. non-recurr. credit $3.2 mill., 1996; net chrg. $12.5 mill., 1999.

OFFICERS:
J. D. Michaels, Chmn., Pres., C.E.O.
D. C. Stuebe, V.P., C.F.O.
J. I. Johnson, V.P., Sec., Gen. Couns., Sec.

INVESTOR CONTACT: David Stuebe, V.P., C.F.O., (319) 264-7400

PRINCIPAL OFFICE: 414 East Third Street, P.O. Box 1109, Muscatine, IA 52761-7109

TELEPHONE NUMBER: (319) 264-7400
FAX: (319) 264-7217
WEB: www.honi.com

NO. OF EMPLOYEES: 11,000 (approx.)

SHAREHOLDERS: 6,563

ANNUAL MEETING: In May

INCORPORATED: IA, Jan., 1944

INSTITUTIONAL HOLDINGS:
No. of Institutions: 124
Shares Held: 26,758,741
% Held: 45.0

INDUSTRY: Office furniture, except wood (SIC: 2522)

TRANSFER AGENT(S): Computershare Investor Services, L.L.C., Chicago, IL

NYSE SYMBOL HMC
Rec. Pr. 83.65 (5/31/01)

HONDA MOTOR CO., LTD.

YIELD ...
P/E RATIO 29.5

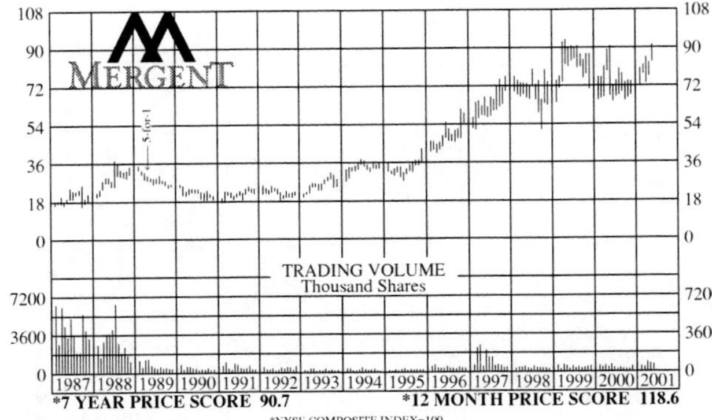

*7 YEAR PRICE SCORE 90.7 *12 MONTH PRICE SCORE 118.6

*NYSE COMPOSITE INDEX=100

INTERIM EARNINGS (Per Share):

Qtr.	June	Sept.	Dec.	Mar.
1996-97	------	3.63	------	
1997-98	------	4.12	------	
1998-99	1.14	1.22	1.34	1.22
1999-00	1.45	1.26	1.26	1.25
2000-01	0.62	0.55	0.42	...

INTERIM DIVIDENDS (Per Share):

Amt.	Decl.	Ex.	Rec.	Pay.
0.14	...	3/26/99	3/30/99	7/08/99
0.18	...	9/27/99	9/29/99	12/17/99
0.189	...	3/28/00	3/30/00	7/07/00
0.167	...	9/26/00	9/28/00	12/08/00
0.167	...	3/27/01	3/29/01	7/09/01

CAPITALIZATION (3/31/00):

	($000)	(%)
Long-Term Debt	5,573,290	22.9
Common & Surplus	18,724,618	77.1
Total	24,297,908	100.0

RECENT DEVELOPMENTS: For the third quarter ended 12/31/00, HMC reported consolidated net income of ¥47.30 billion ($412.0 million), a decrease of 25.2% from the comparable prior-year period. Consolidated net sales and other operating revenue amounted to ¥1576.10 billion ($13.74 billion), an increase of 8.8% from the year-earlier quarter. Motorcycle sales advanced 10.6% to ¥171.70 billion ($1.50 billion), while automobiles sales rose 9.4% to ¥1,304.8 billion ($11.37 billion).

PROSPECTS: Earnings were hampered by a weak performance from HMC's European operations, which continues to struggle with the devaluation of the euro. In addition, HMC's only European plant is located in Britain, which is not within the euro-zone. Therefore, production costs do not decline at the same rate as revenues. The decrease in earnings was also due to higher operating expenses due to increased advertising, which was partially offset by strong U.S. cars and motorcycles sales.

BUSINESS

HONDA MOTOR CO., LTD. develops and manufactures automobiles, power products and motorcycles that incorporate high-performance internal-combustion technology. Other products manufactured include general-purpose engines, lawn mowers and air conditioners. For the year ended 3/31/00, product revenues were as follows: automobiles, 80.1%; motorcycles, 11.9%; and other businesses, which includes power products and financial services, 6.9%. Honda's products are manufactured in 33 countries and distributed to approximately 150 countries worldwide.

ANNUAL FINANCIAL DATA

	3/31/00	3/31/99	3/31/98	3/31/97	3/31/96	3/31/95	3/31/94
Earnings Per Share 1	**5.22**	**5.20**	**4.12**	**3.63**	**1.35**	**1.46**	**0.47**
Cash Flow Per Share 1	**...**	**2.60**	**2.06**	**1.82**	**...**	**...**	**...**
Tang. Book Val. Per Share 1	**...**	**30.28**	**25.63**	**22.81**	**21.86**	**24.24**	**19.27**
Dividends Per Share 1	**0.32**	**0.28**	**0.24**	**0.21**	**0.26**	**0.24**	**0.22**
Dividend Payout %	**6.1**	**5.4**	**5.8**	**5.8**	**19.3**	**16.4**	**46.8**
INCOME STATEMENT (IN MILLIONS):							
Total Revenues	59,158.7	51,717.6	46,198.0	42,346.4	39,545.9	46,007.5	37,468.3
Costs & Expenses	55,024.3	47,163.4	42,638.2	39,134.8	38,210.1	44,755.7	36,708.6
Operating Income	4,134.4	4,554.2	3,559.8	3,211.6	1,335.8	1,251.8	759.8
Net Interest Inc./(Exp.)	d79.0	d139.1	d112.8	d116.6	d215.2	d290.4	d267.9
Income Before Income Taxes	4,035.8	4,320.2	3,413.8	3,125.8	1,070.7	1,093.7	454.8
Income Taxes	1,653.2	1,905.9	1,549.8	1,512.4	542.0	520.9	327.1
Equity Earnings/Minority Int.	162.8	117.5	142.9	155.9	129.7	140.8	102.1
Net Income	2,545.4	2,531.9	2,006.8	1,769.3	658.4	713.7	229.9
Cash Flow	2,545.4	2,531.9	2,006.8	1,769.3	658.4	713.7	229.9
Average Shs. Outstg. (000)	974,414	974,414	974,348	974,000	...	...	...
BALANCE SHEET (IN MILLIONS):							
Cash & Cash Equivalents	4,176.7	3,134.3	2,597.2	2,873.2	2,782.2	2,354.7	1,811.6
Total Current Assets	23,820.4	19,669.8	17,690.0	15,690.0	15,221.3	15,861.6	13,774.9
Net Property	10,874.1	9,523.1	8,962.6	8,291.9	8,620.7	10,285.1	8,920.2
Total Assets	47,514.8	41,784.3	37,077.5	33,530.4	32,699.9	34,967.2	28,334.5
Total Current Liabilities	21,362.4	18,801.1	17,038.5	14,469.6	14,113.1	14,642.5	12,059.0
Long-Term Obligations	5,573.3	5,586.6	5,218.7	5,874.0	6,105.1	6,838.6	5,941.4
Net Stockholders' Equity	18,724.6	14,640.0	12,380.9	11,107.4	10,644.2	11,802.6	9,383.2
Net Working Capital	2,458.0	868.7	651.5	1,220.4	1,108.2	1,219.1	1,715.9
Year-end Shs. Outstg. (000)	967,000	967,000	966,000	974,000	974,000	974,000	974,000
STATISTICAL RECORD:							
Operating Profit Margin %	7.0	8.8	7.7	7.6	3.4	2.7	2.0
Net Profit Margin %	4.3	4.9	4.3	4.2	1.7	1.6	0.6
Return on Equity %	13.6	17.3	16.2	15.9	6.2	6.0	2.4
Return on Assets %	5.4	6.1	5.4	5.3	2.0	2.0	0.8
Debt/Total Assets %	11.7	13.4	14.1	17.5	18.7	19.6	21.0
Price Range 1	94.00-64.06	80.00-51.31	76.56-51.25	61.25-40.38	42.50-27.50	37.75-27.13	31.38-19.88
P/E Ratio	18.0-12.3	15.4-9.9	18.6-12.4	16.9-11.1	31.5-20.4	25.9-18.6	66.8-42.3
Average Yield %	0.4	0.4	0.4	0.4	0.7	0.7	0.9

Statistics are as originally reported. All figures are in U.S. dollars unless otherwise noted. Exchange rates are as follows: ¥1.0=$0.0097, 3/31/00; ¥1.0=$0.0083, 3/31/99; ¥1.0=$0.0077, 3/31/98; ¥1.0=$0.0080, 3/31/97; ¥1.0=$0.0093, 3/31/96; ¥1.0=$0.0116, 3/31/95; ¥1.0=$0.0097, 3/31/94. 1 Based on ADRs. Each ADR represents two ordinary shares.

OFFICERS:
Y. Munekuni, Chmn., Rep. Dir.
H. Yoshino, Pres., Rep. Dir.
N. Kawamoto, Couns.

PRINCIPAL OFFICE: 540 Madison Ave., 32nd Floor, New York, NY 10022

TELEPHONE NUMBER: (212) 355-9191
WEB: www.world.honda.com

NO. OF EMPLOYEES: 112,400 (avg.)

SHAREHOLDERS: 37,107

ANNUAL MEETING: In June

INCORPORATED: JPN, Sept., 1948

INSTITUTIONAL HOLDINGS:
No. of Institutions: 61
Shares Held: 1,744,060
% Held: 0.4

INDUSTRY: Motor vehicles and car bodies (SIC: 3711)

TRANSFER AGENT(S): Morgan Guaranty Trust Company of New York, New York, NY

NYSE SYMBOL HRL
Rec. Pr. 23.59 (5/31/01)

HORMEL FOODS CORPORATION

YIELD 1.6%
P/E RATIO 19.5

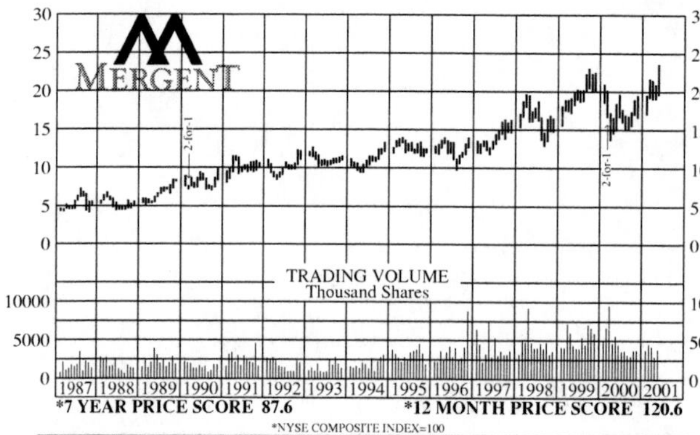

*7 YEAR PRICE SCORE 87.6 *12 MONTH PRICE SCORE 120.6

*NYSE COMPOSITE INDEX=100

INTERIM EARNINGS (Per Share):

Qtr.	Jan.	Apr.	July	Oct.
1996-97	0.14	0.17	0.12	0.30
1997-98	0.31	0.17	0.14	0.31
1998-99	0.29	0.22	0.20	0.41
1999-00	0.30	0.26	0.21	0.44
2000-01	0.30	...	...	...

INTERIM DIVIDENDS (Per Share):

Amt.	Decl.	Ex.	Rec.	Pay.
0.087Q	5/22/00	7/19/00	7/22/00	8/15/00
0.087Q	9/26/00	10/18/00	10/21/00	11/15/00
0.092Q	11/22/00	1/17/01	1/20/01	2/15/01
0.092Q	3/26/01	4/18/01	4/21/01	5/15/01
0.092Q	5/22/01	7/18/01	7/21/01	8/15/01

Indicated div.: $0.37 (Div. Reinv. Plan)

CAPITALIZATION (10/28/00):

	($000)	(%)
Long-Term Debt	145,928	14.3
Common & Surplus	873,877	85.7
Total	1,019,805	100.0

RECENT DEVELOPMENTS: For the quarter ended 1/31/01, net earnings totaled $41.5 million, down 5.3% versus $43.8 million a year earlier, due to higher-than-normal energy prices and pork raw material costs. Net sales climbed 4.8% to $947.5 million from $903.9 million the previous year. Results in the prior-year period benefited from strong sales of canned foods reflecting retail store and in-home pantry stockpiling stemming from Y2K-related concerns.

PROSPECTS: On 2/26/01, the Company completed its acquisition of The Turkey Store Company for $334.4 million in cash. The Turkey Store Company is a producer, processor and marketer of fresh and cooked turkey products, marketed under The Turkey Store brand, with annual sales of approximately $309.0 million. The acquisition is expected to accelerate revenue growth and generate significant cost savings going forward.

BUSINESS

HORMEL FOODS CORPORATION (formerly Geo. A. Hormel & Co.) and its subsidiaries produce and market a variety of processed, packaged food products. The Company's main products include: meat and meat products, including hams, sausages, wieners, sliced bacon, luncheon meats, stews, chilies, hash and meat spreads. The products are sold fresh, frozen, cured, smoked, cooked or canned. The majority of products are sold under the HORMEL name. Other trade names include: SPAM, LIGHT & LEAN, FARM FRESH, DINTY MOORE, BLACK LABEL, TOPSHELF, MARY KITCHEN, KID'S KITCHEN and OLD SMOKE HOUSE. Through its wholly-owned subsidiary, Jennie-O Foods, Inc., the Company is a producer and marketer of whole and processed turkey products.

QUARTERLY DATA

(10/28/2000)($000)	Rev	Inc
1st Quarter	903,913	43,848
2nd Quarter	879,023	36,254
3rd Quarter	886,015	29,136
4th Quarter	1,006,181	60,979

ANNUAL FINANCIAL DATA

	10/28/00	10/30/99	10/31/98	10/25/97	10/26/96	10/28/95	10/29/94
Earnings Per Share	**1.20**	**[1] 1.11**	**[1] 0.93**	**0.72**	**[1] 0.52**	**0.79**	**0.77**
Cash Flow Per Share	**1.67**	**1.55**	**1.33**	**1.06**	**0.80**	**1.03**	**1.00**
Tang. Book Val. Per Share	**5.64**	**5.20**	**4.82**	**4.55**	**4.27**	**4.24**	**3.79**
Dividends Per Share	**0.35**	**0.33**	**0.32**	**0.31**	**0.30**	**0.29**	**0.25**
Dividend Payout %	**29.2**	**29.7**	**34.6**	**43.4**	**57.7**	**36.9**	**32.5**
INCOME STATEMENT (IN MILLIONS):							
Total Revenues	3,675.1	3,357.8	3,261.0	3,256.6	3,098.7	3,046.2	3,064.8
Costs & Expenses	3,346.6	3,052.2	2,988.9	3,030.3	2,943.0	2,825.5	2,841.1
Depreciation & Amort.	65.9	64.7	60.3	52.9	42.7	37.2	36.6
Operating Income	262.6	240.9	211.9	173.3	113.0	183.4	187.1
Net Interest Inc./(Exp.)	1.3	3.6	d13.7	d15.0	d1.6	d1.5	d2.5
Income Before Income Taxes	264.4	251.5	217.3	170.9	125.5	194.7	191.1
Income Taxes	94.2	88.0	78.0	61.4	46.1	74.2	73.1
Equity Earnings/Minority Int.	0.5	7.0	4.3	3.4	...	...	...
Net Income	170.2	[1] 163.4	[1] 139.3	109.5	[1] 79.4	120.4	118.0
Cash Flow	236.1	228.1	199.6	162.4	122.1	157.7	154.6
Average Shs. Outstg. (000)	141,523	147,010	150,406	152,990	153,018	153,378	...
BALANCE SHEET (IN MILLIONS):							
Cash & Cash Equivalents	106.6	248.6	238.0	152.4	203.1	198.0	260.0
Total Current Assets	711.1	800.1	717.4	671.4	723.3	659.3	708.2
Net Property	541.5	505.6	486.9	488.7	421.5	333.1	270.9
Total Assets	1,641.9	1,685.6	1,555.9	1,528.5	1,436.1	1,223.9	1,196.7
Total Current Liabilities	342.6	385.4	267.7	260.6	266.4	217.8	264.9
Long-Term Obligations	145.9	184.7	204.9	198.2	127.0	17.0	10.3
Net Stockholders' Equity	873.9	841.1	813.3	802.2	785.6	732.0	661.1
Net Working Capital	368.5	414.7	449.7	410.8	456.9	441.5	443.3
Year-end Shs. Outstg. (000)	138,569	142,725	146,992	151,552	155,020	153,404	153,704
STATISTICAL RECORD:							
Operating Profit Margin %	7.1	7.2	6.5	5.3	3.6	6.0	6.1
Net Profit Margin %	4.6	4.9	4.3	3.4	2.6	4.0	3.8
Return on Equity %	19.5	19.4	17.1	13.6	10.1	16.5	17.8
Return on Assets %	10.4	9.7	9.0	7.2	5.5	9.8	9.9
Debt/Total Assets %	8.9	11.0	13.2	13.0	8.8	1.4	0.9
Price Range	20.97-13.63	23.09-15.50	19.69-12.84	16.38-11.75	14.00-9.69	14.00-11.44	13.38-9.38
P/E Ratio	17.5-11.4	20.8-14.0	21.3-13.9	22.9-16.4	26.9-18.6	17.8-14.6	17.4-12.2
Average Yield %	2.0	1.7	2.0	2.2	2.5	2.3	2.2

Statistics are as originally reported. Adj. for 2-for-1 stk. split, 2/15/00. [1] Incl. $3.8 mil ($0.03/sh) gain, 1999; $17.4 mil ($0.12/sh) after-tax gain, 1998; & $5.4 mil ($0.04/sh) non-recur. chg., 1996.

OFFICERS:
J. W. Johnson, Chmn., Pres., C.E.O.
M. J. McCoy, Sr. V.P., C.F.O
G. J. Ray, Exec. V.P.

INVESTOR CONTACT: Investor Relations, (507) 437-5950

PRINCIPAL OFFICE: 1 Hormel Place, Austin, MN 55912-3680

TELEPHONE NUMBER: (507) 437-5611
FAX: (507) 437-5489
WEB: www.hormel.com

NO. OF EMPLOYEES: 12,200 (avg.)

SHAREHOLDERS: 11,200 (approx.)

ANNUAL MEETING: In Jan.

INCORPORATED: DE, Sept., 1928

INSTITUTIONAL HOLDINGS:
No. of Institutions: 163
Shares Held: 36,645,880
% Held: 26.4

INDUSTRY: Meat packing plants (SIC: 2011)

TRANSFER AGENT(S): Wells Fargo Shareowner Services, South St. Paul, MN

NYSE SYMBOL DHI
Rec. Pr. 24.22 (4/30/01)

HORTON (D.R.) INC.

YIELD 0.8%
P/E RATIO 9.3

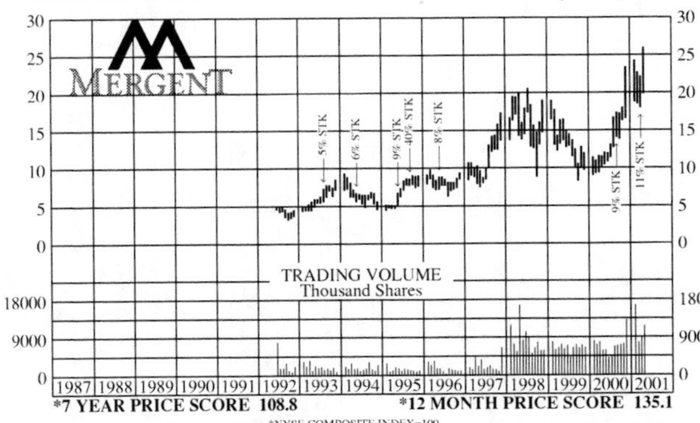

*7 YEAR PRICE SCORE 108.8 *12 MONTH PRICE SCORE 135.1
*NYSE COMPOSITE INDEX=100

INTERIM EARNINGS (Per Share):

Qtr	Dec.	Mar.	June	Sept.
1995-96		0.72		
1996-97		0.84		
1997-98	0.44	0.32	0.27	0.25
1998-99	0.64	0.56	0.43	0.43
1999-00	0.56	0.52	0.64	0.81
2000-01	0.63	...	...	...

INTERIM DIVIDENDS (Per Share):

Amt.	Decl.	Ex.	Rec.	Pay.
9% STK	9/07/00	9/14/00	9/18/00	9/29/00
0.04Q	10/09/00	10/18/00	10/20/00	10/30/00
0.05Q	1/23/01	2/01/01	2/05/01	2/15/01
11% STK	2/27/01	3/07/01	3/09/01	3/23/01
0.05Q	4/24/01	5/04/01	5/08/01	5/15/01

Indicated div.: $0.20

CAPITALIZATION (9/30/00):

	($000)	(%)
Long-Term Debt	1,245,586	56.1
Minority Interest	5,264	0.2
Common & Surplus	969,563	43.7
Total	2,220,413	100.0

RECENT DEVELOPMENTS: For the quarter 12/31/00, income advanced 12.5% to $47.8 million, before an accounting charge, compared with net income of $42.5 million in 1999. Homebuilding revenues were $873.6 million, up 9.5% from $797.6 million a year earlier. Financing revenues increased 23.7% to $14.1 million versus $11.4 million in 1999. Home closings for the current quarter decreased 4.5% to 4,290.

PROSPECTS: Going forward, sales should benefit from strong housing demand throughout the majority of DHI's markets, as well as an increase in the average selling price of homes closed. The increase in the average selling price is being driven by changes in the mix of homes closed, DHI's ability to sell more custom features with its homes and raise prices in some of its markets. Meanwhile, DHI is continuing to expand its mortgage loan and title services.

BUSINESS

D.R. HORTON, INC., a national homebuilder, builds high-quality, single-family homes designed principally for the entry-level and move-up markets. The Company currently builds and sells homes under the D.R. Horton, Arappco, Cambridge, Continental, Dobson, Mareli, Milburn, Regency, SGS Communities, Torrey and Trimark names in 23 states and 39 markets, with a geographic presence in the Midwest, Mid-Atlantic, Southeast, Southwest, and Western regions of the United States. The Company also provides mortgage financing and title services for homebuyers through its wholly-owned subsidiaries CH Mortgage, DRH Title Company, Travis County Title Company, Metro Title Company, Century Title Company and Custom Title Company.

QUARTERLY DATA

(09/30/2000) ($000)	Rev	Inc
1st Quarter	1,086,675	61,686
2nd Quarter	959,216	48,067
3rd Quarter	798,864	39,434
4th Quarter	808,940	42,532

ANNUAL FINANCIAL DATA

	9/30/00	9/30/99	9/30/98	9/30/97	9/30/96	9/30/95	9/30/94
Earnings Per Share	**2.53**	**2.07**	**1 1.29**	**0.84**	**0.72**	**0.61**	**0.62**
Cash Flow Per Share	**2.86**	**2.33**	**1.37**	**0.94**	**0.79**	**0.67**	**0.66**
Tang. Book Val. Per Share	**11.40**	**9.02**	**7.29**	**5.19**	**4.43**	**3.35**	**2.95**
Dividends Per Share	**0.14**	**0.10**	**0.07**	**0.07**	...	...	...
Dividend Payout %	**5.3**	**4.8**	**5.8**	**7.9**	...	...	...
INCOME STATEMENT (IN MILLIONS):							
Total Revenues	3,653.7	3,156.2	2,176.9	837.3	547.3	437.4	393.3
Costs & Expenses	3,312.5	2,862.0	1,987.5	770.4	500.3	402.3	364.0
Depreciation & Amort.	24.5	20.8	9.8	4.4	2.6	2.0	1.2
Operating Income	316.7	273.4	179.6	62.5	44.4	33.1	28.1
Net Interest Inc./(Exp.)	d15.8	d16.5	d16.2	d5.1	d1.5	d1.2	...
Income Before Income Taxes	309.2	263.8	159.1	59.9	44.4	32.6	28.6
Income Taxes	117.5	104.0	65.7	23.7	17.1	12.0	10.9
Net Income	191.7	159.8	1 93.4	36.2	27.4	20.5	17.7
Cash Flow	216.2	180.7	103.2	40.6	30.0	22.6	18.9
Average Shs. Outstg. (000)	75,722	77,379	75,118	43,400	38,015	33,695	28,619
BALANCE SHEET (IN MILLIONS):							
Cash & Cash Equivalents	72.5	128.6	76.8	44.0	32.5	16.7	11.2
Total Current Assets	2,263.6	1,994.7	1,434.8	648.6	377.8	299.6	215.3
Net Property	39.0	37.0	25.5	13.1	5.6	5.4	4.5
Total Assets	2,694.6	2,361.8	1,667.8	719.8	402.9	318.8	230.9
Total Current Liabilities	469.2	469.9	287.5	457.0	225.3	212.7	146.3
Long-Term Obligations	1,245.6	1,086.3	826.0	...	...	...	...
Net Stockholders' Equity	969.6	797.6	549.4	262.8	177.6	106.1	84.6
Net Working Capital	1,794.3	1,524.8	1,147.3	191.6	152.5	86.9	68.9
Year-end Shs. Outstg. (000)	74,908	75,961	67,557	45,152	39,155	30,776	28,016
STATISTICAL RECORD:							
Operating Profit Margin %	8.7	8.7	8.3	7.5	8.1	7.6	7.2
Net Profit Margin %	5.2	5.1	4.3	4.3	5.0	4.7	4.5
Return on Equity %	19.8	20.0	17.0	13.8	15.4	19.4	20.9
Return on Assets %	7.1	6.8	5.6	5.0	6.8	6.4	7.6
Debt/Total Assets %	46.2	46.0	49.5	...	...	...	...
Price Range	23.42-8.99	19.01-8.26	20.61-8.78	17.36-7.44	9.85-6.20	9.09-4.39	9.34-4.45
P/E Ratio	9.3-3.6	9.2-4.0	16.0-6.8	20.8-8.9	13.7-8.6	14.8-7.2	15.1-7.2
Average Yield %	0.8	0.7	0.5	0.5	...	...	...

Statistics are as originally reported. Adj. for all stk. splits through 3/01. 1 Incl. non-recur merger chrg. of $11.9 mill.

OFFICERS:
D. R. Horton, Chmn.
D. J. Tomnitz, Vice-Chmn., Pres., C.E.O.
S. R. Fuller, Exec. V.P., C.F.O., Treas.

INVESTOR CONTACT: Stacey Dwyer, Investor Relations, (817) 856-8200

PRINCIPAL OFFICE: 1901 Ascension Blvd., Suite 100, Arlington, TX 76006

TELEPHONE NUMBER: (817) 856-8200
FAX: (817) 856-8429
WEB: www.drhorton.com

NO. OF EMPLOYEES: 3,631

SHAREHOLDERS: 338 (approx.)

ANNUAL MEETING: In Jan.

INCORPORATED: DE, July, 1991

INSTITUTIONAL HOLDINGS:
No. of Institutions: 171
Shares Held: 47,344,182
% Held: 69.7

INDUSTRY: Operative builders (SIC: 1531)

TRANSFER AGENT(S): American Stock Transfer & Trust Co., New York, NY

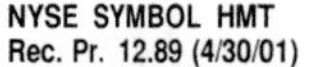

NYSE SYMBOL HMT
Rec. Pr. 12.89 (4/30/01)

HOST MARRIOTT CORPORATION

YIELD 8.1%
P/E RATIO 24.8

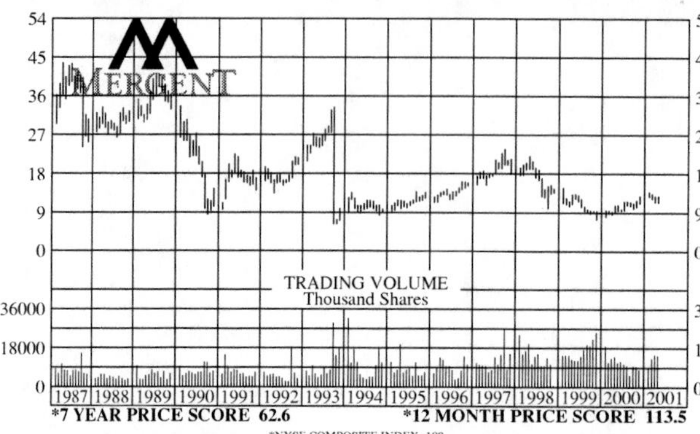

INTERIM EARNINGS (Per Share):

Qtr.	Mar.	June	Sept.	Dec.
1997	0.03	0.13	0.03	0.03
1998	0.13	0.26	0.01	0.43
1999	0.19	0.31	0.13	0.24
2000	d0.26	d0.26	d0.10	1.14

INTERIM DIVIDENDS (Per Share):

Amt.	Decl.	Ex.	Rec.	Pay.
0.21Q	3/23/00	3/29/00	3/31/00	4/14/00
0.21Q	6/21/00	6/28/00	6/30/00	7/14/00
0.23Q	9/19/00	9/27/00	9/29/00	10/16/00
0.26Q	12/18/00	12/27/00	12/29/00	1/12/01
0.26Q	3/19/01	3/28/01	3/30/01	4/13/01

Indicated div.: $1.04

CAPITALIZATION (12/31/00):

	($000)	(%)
Long-Term Debt	5,322,000	69.1
Minority Interest	485,000	6.3
Redeemable Pfd. Stock	475,000	6.2
Preferred Stock	196,000	2.5
Common & Surplus	1,225,000	15.9
Total	7,703,000	100.0

RECENT DEVELOPMENTS: For the year ended 12/31/00, the Company reported income of $159.0 million, before an extraordinary loss of $3.0 million, compared with income of $196.0 million, before an extraordinary gain of $15.0 million, in 1999. Results for 2000 included a $207.0 million lease repurchase expense. Results for 1999 included a $40.0 million loss on litigation settlement. Total revenues were $1.47 billion, an increase of 7.0% versus $1.38 billion the year before.

PROSPECTS: On 1/11/01, the Company completed the purchase of leases held by Crestline Capital Corp. on certain full-service hotels owned by HMT. The total consideration for the sale was $201.0 million. The transaction should allow HMT to simplify its corporate structure and better control the Company's full-service hotels. Separately, in 2001 the Company expects to open a 295-room golf resort and a world-class spa at the Ritz-Carlton, Naples, Florida.

BUSINESS

HOST MARRIOTT CORPORATION is a lodging real estate company operating through an umbrella partnership structure. The Company currently owns or holds controlling interests in 122 upscale and luxury full-service hotel properties operated primarily under the MARRIOTT, RITZCARLTON, HYATT, FOUR SEASONS, HILTON, and SWISSOTEL brand names. In addition, the Company operates as a self-managed and self-administered real estate investment trust and its operations are conducted solely through its subsidiaries. The Company is the sole general partner of the Operating Partnership. HMT spun off its senior living businesses and Crestline Capital Corporation in December 1998.

ANNUAL FINANCIAL DATA

	12/31/00	12/31/99	12/31/98	1/2/98	1/3/97	[3] 12/29/95	12/30/94
Earnings Per Share	**[5] 0.64**	**[1] 0.87**	**[4] 0.84**	**[1] 0.23**	**d0.07**	**[1] [2] d0.39**	**[1] [2] d0.13**
Tang. Book Val. Per Share	**5.54**	**5.80**	**5.13**	**5.89**	**7.04**	**4.22**	**4.53**
Dividends Per Share	**0.86**	**0.63**	...	...	...	...	...
Dividend Payout %	**134.4**	**72.4**	...	...	...	...	...
INCOME STATEMENT (IN MILLIONS):							
Rental Income	1,390.0	1,295.0	...	...	...	...	...
Interest Income	40.0	39.0	...	...	...	...	...
Total Income	1,473.0	1,376.0	3,513.0	1,147.0	732.0	484.0	1,501.0
Costs & Expenses	314.0	341.0	2,966.0	745.0	542.0	406.0	1,347.0
Depreciation	331.0	289.0	...	...	...	...	...
Interest Expense	433.0	430.0	335.0	302.0	237.0	178.0	206.0
Income Before Income Taxes	133.0	262.0	226.0	115.0	d2.0	d73.0	d23.0
Income Taxes	cr98.0	cr16.0	cr20.0	36.0	5.0	cr13.0	cr4.0
Equity Earnings/Minority Int.	d72.0	d82.0	d52.0	d32.0	d6.0	d2.0	...
Net Income	[5] 159.0	[1] 196.0	[4] 194.0	[1] 47.0	d13.0	[1] [2] d62.0	[1] [2] d19.0
Average Shs. Outstg. (000)	289,000	308,100	256,400	208,200	189,000	158,000	152,000
BALANCE SHEET (IN MILLIONS):							
Cash & Cash Equivalents	438.0	277.0	436.0	865.0	704.0	201.0	95.0
Total Assets	8,396.0	8,202.0	8,268.0	6,526.0	5,152.0	3,557.0	3,822.0
Long-Term Obligations	5,322.0	5,069.0	5,131.0	3,783.0	2,647.0	2,178.0	2,259.0
Total Liabilities	6,975.0	6,697.0	6,957.0	5,326.0	4,025.0	2,882.0	3,112.0
Net Stockholders' Equity	1,421.0	1,505.0	1,311.0	1,200.0	1,127.0	675.0	710.0
Year-end Shs. Outstg. (000)	221,300	225,600	255,600	203,800	160,000	160,000	154,000
STATISTICAL RECORD:							
Net Inc.+Depr./Assets %	5.8	5.9	2.3	0.7	...	...	...
Return on Equity %	11.2	13.0	14.8	3.9	...	...	...
Return on Assets %	1.9	2.4	2.3	0.7	...	...	...
Price Range	12.94-8.00	14.81-7.38	22.13-9.88	23.75-15.25	16.25-11.25	13.88-9.13	13.75-8.25
P/E Ratio	20.2-12.5	17.0-8.5	26.3-11.8	103.2-66.3	...	...	...
Average Yield %	8.2	5.7	...	...	...	...	...

Statistics are as originally reported. [1] Bef. extraord. credit 1999, $15.0 mill.; 1997, $3.0 mill.; chrg. 1995, $20.0 mill.; 1994, $6.0 mill. [2] Bef. disc. oper. loss 1995, $61.0 mill.; 1994, $6.0 mill. [3] Results exclude the opers. of Host Marriott Services which was spun-off through a special dividend distribution. [4] Incl. a pre-tax chrg. of $64.0 mill. & a pre-tax benefit of $106.0 mill.; bef. a gain of $1.0 mill. fr. disc. opers. & extraord. chrg. of $148.0 mill. [5] Bef. extraord. loss of $3.0 mill., incl. non-recurr. chrg. of $207.0 mill.

OFFICERS:
R. E. Marriott, Chmn.
C. J. Nassetts, Pres., C.E.O.
R. E. Parsons Jr., Exec. V.P., C.F.O.

INVESTOR CONTACT: Investor Relations, (301) 380-9000

PRINCIPAL OFFICE: 10400 Fernwood Road, Bethesda, MD 20817

TELEPHONE NUMBER: (301) 380-9000
FAX: (301) 380-6338
WEB: www.hostmarriott.com

NO. OF EMPLOYEES: 215 (approx.)

SHAREHOLDERS: 106,209 (approx.).

ANNUAL MEETING: In Mar.

INCORPORATED: DE, July, 1929

INSTITUTIONAL HOLDINGS:
No. of Institutions: 184
Shares Held: 152,199,783
% Held: 65.0

INDUSTRY: Real estate investment trusts (SIC: 6798)

TRANSFER AGENT(S): First Chicago Trust Company of New York, Jersey City, NJ

NYSE SYMBOL HTN
Rec. Pr. 45.51 (4/30/01)

HOUGHTON MIFFLIN COMPANY

YIELD 1.1%
P/E RATIO 25.0

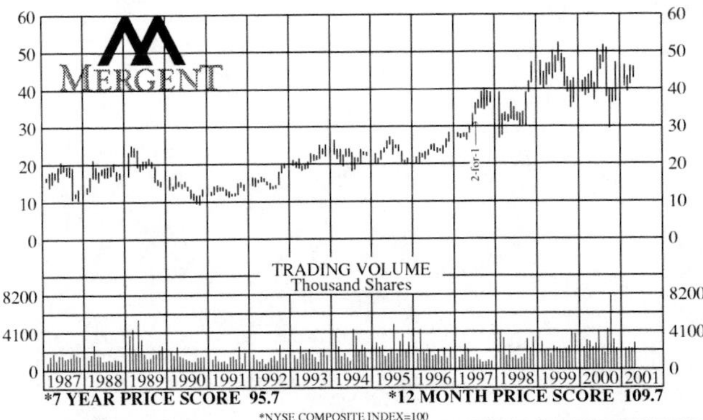

*7 YEAR PRICE SCORE 95.7 *12 MONTH PRICE SCORE 109.7

*NYSE COMPOSITE INDEX=100

INTERIM EARNINGS (Per Share):

Qtr.	Mar.	June	Sept.	Dec.
1997	d0.94	0.39	2.91	d0.59
1998	d1.26	0.24	4.43	d0.71
1999	d1.29	0.29	3.07	d0.55
2000	d1.37	0.52	3.22	d0.55

INTERIM DIVIDENDS (Per Share):

Amt.	Decl.	Ex.	Rec.	Pay.
0.13Q	4/26/00	5/08/00	5/10/00	5/24/00
0.13Q	7/26/00	8/07/00	8/09/00	8/23/00
0.13Q	10/25/00	11/06/00	11/08/00	11/22/00
0.13Q	1/31/01	2/12/01	2/14/01	2/28/01
0.13Q	4/25/01	5/07/01	5/09/01	5/23/01

Indicated div.: $0.52 (Div. Reinv. Plan)

CAPITALIZATION (12/31/00):

	($000)	(%)
Long-Term Debt	224,687	33.7
Deferred Income Tax	28,692	4.3
Common & Surplus	413,862	62.0
Total	667,241	100.0

RECENT DEVELOPMENTS: For the year ended 12/31/00, HTN reported net income of $55.8 million versus income of $46.0 million, before an extraordinary gain of $30.3 million, in the prior year. Earnings for 2000 included non-recurring after-tax charges of $4.4 million related to certain investments and impaired assets. Earnings for 1999 included a one-time after-tax charge of $3.2 million. Net sales rose 8.2% to $1.03 billion.

PROSPECTS: On 6/1/01, the Company entered into an agreement to be acquired by Vivendi Universal in a transaction valued at $2.20 billion. The acquisition is to be accomplished through a tender offer of HTN's common stock at a price of $60.00 per share. Vivendi will also assume $500 million of the Company's debt. In 2001, HTN expects net sales growth of more than 10.0% due to continued strong funding for instructional materials.

BUSINESS

HOUGHTON MIFFLIN COMPANY is a publisher of textbooks, instructional technology for the elementary, secondary, and college markets, as well as supplementary materials. The Company operates in the K-12 publishing segment through Houghton's School Division and its three principal subsidiaries: McDougal Littell Inc., Great Source Education Group, Inc. and The Riverside Publishing Company. The Company also publishes reference works, fiction, and non-fiction for adults and young readers through its Trade & Reference Division, and educational software and video through Sunburst Technology. On 12/23/98, HTN acquired Discovery Works. In May 1999, HTN acquired Sunburst Communications. On 5/3/00, HTN acquired Virtual Learning Technologies.

BUSINESS LINE ANALYSIS

(12/31/2000)	REV(%)	INC(%)
K-12 Publishing	73.0	85.3
College Publishing	17.0	17.9
Other	10.0	(3.2)
Total	100.0	100.0

ANNUAL FINANCIAL DATA

	12/31/00	12/31/99	12/31/98	12/31/97	12/31/96	12/31/95	12/31/94
Earnings Per Share	[3] **1.92**	[5] **1.57**	[4] **1.57**	[3] **1.73**	[3] **1.57**	[1] **d0.26**	[1][2] **1.90**
Cash Flow Per Share	**5.52**	**4.82**	**5.03**	**4.84**	**4.59**	**1.64**	**3.50**
Tang. Book Val. Per Share	...	...	...	...	...	...	**4.16**
Dividends Per Share	**0.52**	**0.51**	**0.50**	**0.49**	**0.48**	**0.47**	**0.43**
Dividend Payout %	**27.1**	**32.5**	**31.8**	**28.3**	**30.7**	...	**23.0**
INCOME STATEMENT (IN MILLIONS):							
Total Revenues	1,027.6	920.1	861.7	797.3	717.9	529.0	483.1
Costs & Expenses	786.7	712.8	658.8	601.0	546.1	489.7	385.2
Depreciation & Amort.	104.6	95.3	100.9	89.7	84.3	52.4	44.4
Operating Income	136.3	112.0	102.0	106.6	87.4	d13.1	53.5
Net Interest Inc./(Exp.)	d31.8	d29.8	d37.0	d38.9	d40.9	d13.0	d6.5
Income Before Income Taxes	97.2	77.1	79.3	83.5	74.0	d11.4	85.1
Income Taxes	41.4	31.1	33.6	33.7	30.3	cr4.2	32.7
Equity Earnings/Minority Int.	...	...	...	1.0	d6.8	1.6	2.0
Net Income	[3] 55.8	[5] 46.0	[4] 45.6	[3] 49.8	[3] 43.6	[1] d7.2	[1][2] 52.4
Cash Flow	160.4	141.3	146.5	139.6	128.0	45.2	96.8
Average Shs. Outstg. (000)	29,045	29,308	29,111	28,826	27,866	27,624	27,644
BALANCE SHEET (IN MILLIONS):							
Cash & Cash Equivalents	15.6	12.7	53.2	6.2	12.1	17.3	47.2
Total Current Assets	425.3	365.1	349.8	324.7	338.0	371.2	250.1
Net Property	214.8	172.2	130.3	120.4	116.4	123.1	68.9
Total Assets	1,124.0	1,038.7	975.6	981.1	1,006.4	1,046.4	497.3
Total Current Liabilities	387.2	259.2	244.3	238.7	185.9	342.4	104.7
Long-Term Obligations	224.7	254.6	274.5	371.1	501.0	426.1	99.4
Net Stockholders' Equity	413.9	433.0	398.3	317.8	270.3	233.3	244.5
Net Working Capital	38.1	105.9	105.5	86.0	152.0	28.8	145.4
Year-end Shs. Outstg. (000)	28,780	29,504	30,176	29,937	29,332	28,970	28,860
STATISTICAL RECORD:							
Operating Profit Margin %	13.3	12.2	11.8	13.4	12.2	...	11.1
Net Profit Margin %	5.4	5.0	5.3	6.2	6.1	...	10.9
Return on Equity %	13.5	10.6	11.5	15.7	16.1	...	21.4
Return on Assets %	5.0	4.4	4.7	5.1	4.3	...	10.5
Debt/Total Assets %	20.0	24.5	28.1	37.8	49.8	40.7	20.0
Price Range	51.81-29.50	52.50-34.88	47.25-26.75	40.25-26.31	28.44-20.19	27.38-19.81	26.50-18.06
P/E Ratio	27.0-15.4	33.4-22.2	30.1-17.0	23.3-15.2	18.2-12.9	...	14.0-9.5
Average Yield %	1.3	1.2	1.4	1.5	2.0	2.0	2.0

Statistics are as originally reported. Adj. for 100% stk. div., 7/97. [1] Incl. non-recurr. chrg. of $26.4 mill., 1995; gain $22.8 mill., 1994. [2] Bef. extraord. chrg. $1.2 mill., 1994. [3] Incl. net aft.-tax chrg. of $4.4 mill., 2000; gain $19.9 mill., 1996; gain $7.1 mill., 1997. [4] Bef. extraord. gain $18.0 mill. & incl. net pre-tax non-recurr. gain of $12.3 mill. [5] Bef. extraord. gain $30.3 mill. & incl. a non-recurr. loss of $3.0 mill.

OFFICERS:
N. F. Darehshori, Chmn., Pres., C.E.O.
G. Deegan, Exec. V.P., C.F.O.
P. D. Weaver, Sr. V.P., Sec., Gen. Counsel

INVESTOR CONTACT: Susan E. Hardy, V.P.-Inv. Rel., (617) 351-5114

PRINCIPAL OFFICE: 222 Berkeley Street, Boston, MA 02116-3764

TELEPHONE NUMBER: (617) 351-5000
FAX: (617) 351-1100
WEB: www.hmco.com

NO. OF EMPLOYEES: 3,500 (approx.)

SHAREHOLDERS: 5,859 (approx. record)

ANNUAL MEETING: In April

INCORPORATED: MA, 1908

INSTITUTIONAL HOLDINGS:
No. of Institutions: 159
Shares Held: 23,586,706
% Held: 81.8

INDUSTRY: Book publishing (SIC: 2731)

TRANSFER AGENT(S): BankBoston, N.A. c/o EquiServe, Boston, MA

NYSE SYMBOL HI
Rec. Pr. 65.66 (5/31/01)

HOUSEHOLD INTERNATIONAL INC.

YIELD 1.3%
P/E RATIO 18.5

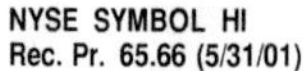

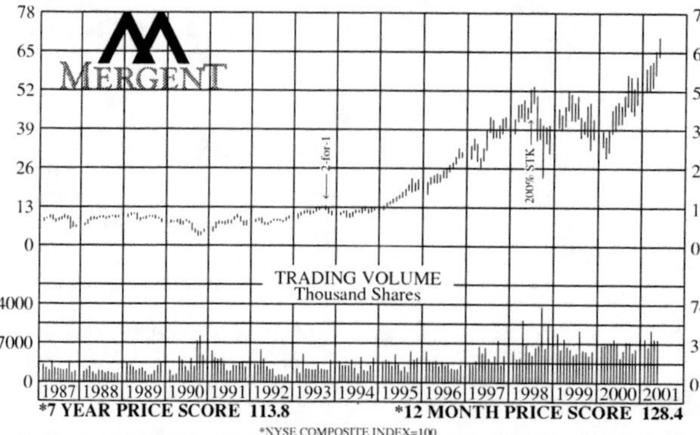

*7 YEAR PRICE SCORE 113.8 *12 MONTH PRICE SCORE 128.4

*NYSE COMPOSITE INDEX=100

INTERIM EARNINGS (Per Share):

Qtr.	Mar.	June	Sept.	Dec.
1996	0.36	0.41	0.46	0.54
1997	0.43	0.49	0.57	0.66
1998	0.51	d1.03	0.63	0.71
1999	0.65	0.67	0.83	0.92
2000	0.78	0.80	0.94	1.03

INTERIM DIVIDENDS (Per Share):

Amt.	Decl.	Ex.	Rec.	Pay.
0.19Q	5/10/00	6/28/00	6/30/00	7/15/00
0.19Q	9/12/00	9/27/00	9/29/00	10/15/00
0.19Q	11/14/00	12/27/00	12/29/00	1/15/01
0.19Q	3/13/01	3/28/01	3/30/01	4/15/01
0.22Q	5/09/01	6/27/01	6/29/01	7/15/01

Indicated div.: $0.88 (Div. Reinv. Plan)

CAPITALIZATION (12/31/00):

	($000)	(%)
Long-Term Debt	45,053,000	83.7
Redeemable Pfd. Stock	675,000	1.3
Preferred Stock	164,400	0.3
Common & Surplus	7,951,200	14.8
Total	53,843,600	100.0

RECENT DEVELOPMENTS: For the year ended 12/31/00, net income amounted to $1.70 billion, an increase of 14.4% compared with $1.49 billion in 1999. Net interest margin and other revenues grew 18.3% to $8.91 billion from $7.53 billion the year before. Provision for credit losses climbed 16.9% to $3.25 billion from $2.78 billion in the previous year. Operating expenses totaled $3.04 billion compared with $2.53 billion in the prior year.

PROSPECTS: During the year, earnings benefited from strong top-line growth and improved credit quality. Going forward, the Company expects that investments made in personnel, technology, e-commerce and marketing should support the growth of HI's franchise and enhance its ability to achieve sustainable and consistent revenue and receivables growth. As a result, HI expects to achieve annual earnings per share growth in the range of 13.0% to 15.0%.

BUSINESS

HOUSEHOLD INTERNATIONAL INC. is a major provider of consumer finance, credit card, auto finance and credit insurance products in the United States, United Kingdom and Canada. Its subsidiaries include: Household Finance Corp., a consumer finance company in the United States; Household Credit Services, an issuer of VISA and MasterCards; Household Retail Services, a private-label credit card issuer; HFC Bank Plc, a provider of secured and unsecured consumer loans; and Household Life Insurance, which offers credit life, accident, disability and unemployment insurance to its consumer finance and credit card customers. In June 1997, HI acquired the consumer finance subsidiary of Transamerica Corp. In June 1998, HI acquired Beneficial Corporation.

GEOGRAPHIC DATA

(12/31/2000)	REV (%)	INC (%)
United States	89.3	87.1
United Kingdom	8.9	10.5
Canada	1.6	1.6
Other	0.2	0.8
Total	100.0	100.0

ANNUAL FINANCIAL DATA

	12/31/00	12/31/99	12/31/98	12/31/97	12/31/96	12/31/95	12/31/94
Earnings Per Share	**3.55**	**[1] 3.07**	**1.03**	**2.17**	**1.77**	**1.44**	**1.17**
Cash Flow Per Share	**4.19**	**3.67**	**1.65**	**2.99**	**2.58**	**2.32**	**2.00**
Tang. Book Val. Per Share	**13.26**	**10.39**	**9.36**	**8.59**	**6.77**	**7.25**	**5.35**
Dividends Per Share	**0.72**	**0.66**	**0.59**	**0.53**	**0.47**	**0.43**	**0.41**
Dividend Payout %	**20.3**	**21.5**	**57.3**	**24.5**	**26.6**	**29.8**	**34.5**
INCOME STATEMENT (IN MILLIONS):							
Total Revenues	11,960.9	9,499.1	8,897.0	5,503.1	5,058.8	5,144.4	4,603.3
Costs & Expenses	9,048.7	6,986.3	7,636.2	4,217.2	3,996.0	4,127.0	3,831.7
Depreciation & Amort.	301.7	292.1	308.1	256.7	240.5	263.7	243.3
Operating Income	2,610.5	2,220.7	952.7	1,029.2	822.3	753.7	528.3
Income Before Income Taxes	2,610.5	2,220.7	952.7	1,029.2	822.3	753.7	528.3
Income Taxes	909.8	734.3	428.6	342.6	283.7	300.5	160.7
Net Income	1,700.7	[1] 1,486.4	524.1	686.6	538.6	453.2	367.6
Cash Flow	1,993.2	1,769.3	817.2	931.5	762.4	690.5	583.3
Average Shs. Outstg. (000)	476,200	481,800	496,400	311,400	295,500	297,900	291,600
BALANCE SHEET (IN MILLIONS):							
Cash & Cash Equivalents	490.2	270.6	457.4	280.4	239.2	270.4	541.2
Total Current Assets	67,651.9	52,429.0	44,405.5	24,143.1	24,484.0	22,114.5	21,319.5
Net Property	517.6	476.4	472.1	309.4	353.1	391.7	512.0
Total Assets	76,706.3	60,749.4	52,892.7	30,302.6	29,594.5	29,218.8	34,338.4
Total Current Liabilities	19,464.8	15,757.8	12,022.9	7,869.9	8,793.2	11,368.2	12,811.1
Long-Term Obligations	45,053.0	34,887.3	30,438.6	14,849.0	14,802.0	11,227.9	10,274.1
Net Stockholders' Equity	8,115.6	6,615.3	6,385.8	4,666.2	3,146.2	2,895.9	2,520.4
Net Working Capital	48,187.1	36,671.2	32,382.6	16,273.2	15,690.8	10,746.3	8,508.4
Year-end Shs. Outstg. (000)	471,020	467,911	483,100	321,474	291,195	291,486	289,809
STATISTICAL RECORD:							
Operating Profit Margin %	21.8	23.4	10.7	18.7	16.3	14.7	11.5
Net Profit Margin %	14.2	15.6	5.9	12.5	10.6	8.8	8.0
Return on Equity %	21.0	22.5	8.2	14.7	17.1	15.6	14.6
Return on Assets %	2.2	2.4	1.0	2.3	1.8	1.6	1.1
Debt/Total Assets %	58.7	57.4	57.5	49.0	50.0	38.4	29.9
Price Range	57.44-29.50	52.31-32.19	53.69-23.00	43.33-26.21	32.71-17.33	22.79-11.96	13.25-9.50
P/E Ratio	16.2-8.3	17.0-10.5	52.1-22.3	20.0-12.1	18.5-9.8	15.9-8.3	11.3-8.1
Average Yield %	1.7	1.6	1.5	1.5	1.9	2.5	3.6

Statistics are as originally reported. Adj. for stk. split: 3-for-1, 6/98 [1] Incl. chrg. of $1.00 bill. for merger costs & gain of $189.4 mill. for sale of Beneficial Canada.

OFFICERS:
W. F. Aldinger, Chmn., C.E.O.
L. N. Bangs, Vice-Chmn.
D. A. Schoenholz, Group Exec., C.F.O.

INVESTOR CONTACT: Investor Relations, (847) 564-7364

PRINCIPAL OFFICE: 2700 Sanders Road, Prospect Heights, IL 60070

TELEPHONE NUMBER: (847) 564-5000
FAX: (847) 205-7490
WEB: www.household.com

NO. OF EMPLOYEES: 28,000 (approx.)

SHAREHOLDERS: 19,468

ANNUAL MEETING: In May

INCORPORATED: DE, Feb., 1981

INSTITUTIONAL HOLDINGS:
No. of Institutions: 500
Shares Held: 385,644,454
% Held: 82.9

INDUSTRY: Personal credit institutions (SIC: 6141)

TRANSFER AGENT(S): Computershare Investor Services, Chicago, IL

NYSE SYMBOL HUBB
Rec. Pr. 27.62 (4/30/01)

HUBBELL, INC.

YIELD 4.8%
P/E RATIO 12.3

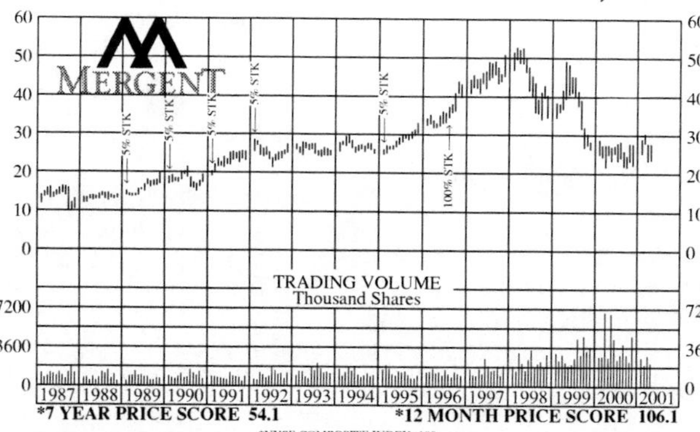

INTERIM EARNINGS (Per Share):

Qtr.	Mar.	June	Sept.	Dec.
1996	0.24	0.27	0.55	0.55
1997	0.53	0.60	0.60	0.16
1998	0.58	0.67	0.64	0.63
1999	0.60	0.65	0.54	0.42
2000	0.55	0.67	0.55	0.48

INTERIM DIVIDENDS (Per Share):

Amt.	Decl.	Ex.	Rec.	Pay.
0.32Q	3/06/00	3/16/00	3/20/00	4/11/00
0.33Q	6/08/00	6/15/00	6/19/00	7/11/00
0.33Q	9/08/00	9/14/00	9/18/00	10/11/00
0.33Q	12/06/00	12/14/00	12/18/00	1/11/01
0.33Q	3/05/01	3/15/01	3/19/01	4/11/01

Indicated div.: $1.32 (Div. Reinv. Plan)

CAPITALIZATION (12/31/00):

	($000)	(%)
Long-Term Debt	99,700	11.4
Deferred Income Tax	6,000	0.7
Common & Surplus	769,500	87.9
Total	875,200	100.0

RECENT DEVELOPMENTS: For the year ended 12/31/00, net income dropped 5.2% to $138.2 million compared with $145.8 million in the previous year. Results for 2000 included a pre-tax credit of $100,000. Also, results for 2000 and 1999 included gains of $36.2 million and $8.8 million, respectively, from the sale of assets. Net sales were $1.42 billion, down 1.9% to $1.45 billion the year before. Operating income decreased 5.1% to $184.5 million.

PROSPECTS: The Company recently completed the acquisition of Temco Electric Products Inc., a manufacturer of electrical outlet boxes, metallic wall plates, and related accessories sold primarily to Canadian customers. The acquisition of Temco should enhance HUBB's position in North American markets. Meanwhile in 2001, HUBB should continue to make progress in resolving inefficiencies at its underperforming units.

BUSINESS

HUBBELL, INC. specializes in the engineering, manufacture, and sale of electrical and electronic products for the commercial, industrial, utility, and telecommunications markets. These products may be classified into three segments: Electrical, Power Systems and Industrial Technology. The Company operates manufacturing facilities in North America, Switzerland, Puerto Rico, Mexico, and the United Kingdom and maintains sales offices in Hong Kong, the People's Republic of China, South Korea, and the Middle East. Hubbell participates in joint ventures with partners in Taiwan.

REVENUES

(12/31/2000)	($000)	(%)
Electrical	928,600	65.2
Power	372,900	26.2
Industrial Technology	122,600	8.6
Total	1,424,100	100.0

ANNUAL FINANCIAL DATA

	12/31/00	12/31/99	12/31/98	12/31/97	12/31/96	12/31/95	12/31/94
Earnings Per Share	**3 2.25**	**2 2.21**	**2.50**	**1 1.89**	**2.10**	**1.83**	**1.60**
Cash Flow Per Share	**3.15**	**3.01**	**3.21**	**2.52**	**2.74**	**2.37**	**2.11**
Tang. Book Val. Per Share	**8.64**	**9.56**	**9.27**	**9.54**	**8.79**	**8.04**	**7.09**
Dividends Per Share	**1.30**	**1.26**	**1.20**	**1.10**	**0.99**	**0.89**	**0.80**
Dividend Payout %	**57.8**	**57.0**	**48.0**	**58.2**	**47.1**	**48.8**	**50.0**
INCOME STATEMENT (IN MILLIONS):							
Total Revenues	1,424.1	1,451.8	1,424.6	1,378.8	1,297.4	1,143.1	1,013.7
Costs & Expenses	1,220.9	1,213.4	1,150.4	1,164.0	1,060.6	941.9	839.1
Depreciation & Amort.	54.9	52.8	48.1	43.2	39.3	36.2	34.0
Operating Income	184.5	194.4	226.1	171.6	197.5	165.0	140.6
Net Interest Inc./(Exp.)	d19.7	d15.9	d9.9	d7.3	d8.4	d8.5	d6.1
Income Before Income Taxes	184.3	197.0	230.5	180.2	199.3	167.0	145.9
Income Taxes	46.1	51.2	61.1	49.9	57.8	45.1	39.4
Net Income	3 138.2	2 145.8	169.4	1 130.3	141.5	121.9	106.5
Cash Flow	193.1	198.6	217.5	173.5	180.8	158.2	140.5
Average Shs. Outstg. (000)	61,300	65,900	67,700	68,843	65,938	66,744	66,582
BALANCE SHEET (IN MILLIONS):							
Cash & Cash Equivalents	74.8	24.0	30.1	75.2	134.4	87.0	38.9
Total Current Assets	620.0	552.8	564.8	596.2	591.2	500.1	444.9
Net Property	305.3	308.9	310.1	251.9	217.9	204.2	202.0
Total Assets	1,454.5	1,399.2	1,390.4	1,284.8	1,185.4	1,057.2	1,041.6
Total Current Liabilities	489.4	343.4	345.0	256.3	255.4	194.9	332.1
Long-Term Obligations	99.7	99.6	99.6	99.5	99.5	102.1	2.7
Net Stockholders' Equity	769.5	855.8	840.6	830.3	743.1	667.3	609.0
Net Working Capital	130.6	209.4	219.8	339.9	335.8	305.2	112.8
Year-end Shs. Outstg. (000)	58,758	64,252	65,600	67,027	66,059	65,852	65,904
STATISTICAL RECORD:							
Operating Profit Margin %	13.0	13.4	15.9	12.4	15.2	14.4	13.9
Net Profit Margin %	9.7	10.0	11.9	9.5	10.9	10.7	10.5
Return on Equity %	18.0	17.0	20.2	15.7	19.0	18.3	17.5
Return on Assets %	9.5	10.4	12.2	10.1	11.9	11.5	10.2
Debt/Total Assets %	6.9	7.1	7.2	7.7	8.4	9.7	0.3
Price Range	28.81-21.63	49.19-26.25	52.75-33.88	50.94-40.75	43.88-31.75	33.06-24.82	29.94-25.00
P/E Ratio	12.8-9.6	22.3-11.9	21.1-13.5	26.9-21.6	20.9-15.1	18.1-13.6	18.7-15.6
Average Yield %	5.2	3.3	2.8	2.4	2.6	3.1	2.9

Statistics are as originally reported. Adj. for 5% stock dividend, 2/95; 2-for-1 stock split, 8/96. 1 Incl. after-tax chrg. of $32.2 mill. for consolidation & reorganization. 2 Incl. a one-time gain of $8.8 mill. fr. the sale of The Kerite Company. 3 Incl. one-time credit of $100,000 & a one-time gain of $36.2 mill. fr. the sale of WavePacer DSL assets.

OFFICERS:
G. J. Ratcliffe, Chmn., Pres., C.E.O.
T. H. Powers, Sr. V.P., C.F.O.
J. H. Biggart Jr., V.P., Treas.
R. W. Davies, V.P., Sec., Gen. Couns.

INVESTOR CONTACT: Thomas R. Conlin, Dir. Pub. Affairs, (203) 799-4293

PRINCIPAL OFFICE: 584 Derby Milford Rd., Orange, CT 06477-4024

TELEPHONE NUMBER: (203) 799-4100
FAX: (203) 799-4333
WEB: www.hubbell.com

NO. OF EMPLOYEES: 10,469 (approx.)

SHAREHOLDERS: 983 (Class A); 4,442 (Class B)

ANNUAL MEETING: In May

INCORPORATED: CT, May, 1905

INSTITUTIONAL HOLDINGS:
No. of Institutions: 200
Shares Held: 33,030,345
% Held: 56.5

INDUSTRY: Commercial lighting fixtures (SIC: 3646)

TRANSFER AGENT(S): Mellon Investor Services, Ridgefield Park, NJ

NYSE SYMBOL HUF
Rec. Pr. 8.68 (4/30/01)

HUFFY CORPORATION

YIELD ...
P/E RATIO 5.8

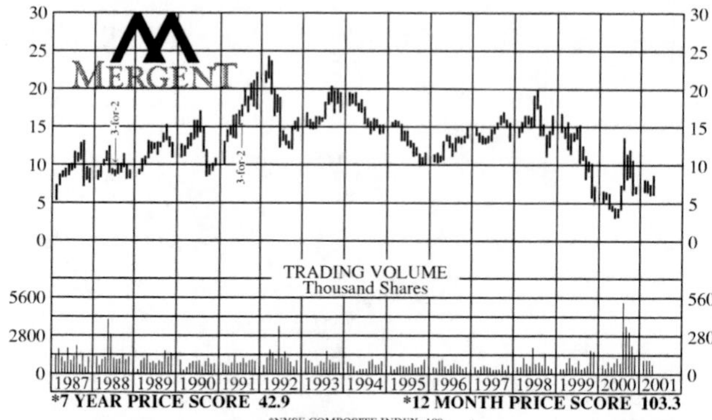

*7 YEAR PRICE SCORE 42.9 *12 MONTH PRICE SCORE 103.3

*NYSE COMPOSITE INDEX=100

INTERIM EARNINGS (Per Share):

Qtr.	Mar.	June	Sept.	Dec.
1997	0.26	0.49	0.08	0.02
1998	0.30	Nil	d0.06	d0.31
1999	d0.05	0.50	d2.80	d1.49
2000	d0.03	0.44	0.47	0.61

INTERIM DIVIDENDS (Per Share):

Amt.	Decl.	Ex.	Rec.	Pay.
0.085Q	2/11/99	4/13/99	4/15/99	5/03/99
0.085Q	4/22/99	7/13/99	7/15/99	8/02/99
0.085Q	7/22/99	10/13/99	10/15/99	...

Dividend payment suspended

CAPITALIZATION (12/31/00):

	($000)	(%)
Common & Surplus	73,131	100.0
Total	73,131	100.0

RECENT DEVELOPMENTS: For the year ended 12/31/00, income from continuing operations was $10.7 million compared with a loss from continuing operations of $39.4 million in 1999. The improvement in earnings was primarily attributed to the Huffy Bicycle Company. Net sales were $488.2 million, up 15.4% from $422.9 million a year earlier. Operating income amounted to $26.9 million compared with an operating loss of $58.0 million in 1999.

PROSPECTS: Although the Company is seeing some softness in sales of bicycles, the Huffy Micro™ scooter continues to fuel sales at the retail level. Looking ahead, the Company is well-positioned to deliver strong results in 2001 due to completion of the restructuring of the bicycle business, continued margin improvement, cost-cutting measures, and significantly lower interest expenses.

BUSINESS

HUFFY CORPORATION is engaged in the design, marketing and distribution of consumer products and the furnishing of services for retail. Huffy Bicycle Company and Huffy Sports Company comprise the consumer products segment. Huffy Service First, Inc. provides certain services to retailers, including inventory, assembly, repair and merchandising services. In 1999, Huffy Bicycle Company finalized its cessation of bicycle manufacturing in the U.S. In November 2000, the Company sold Washington Inventory Service.

ANNUAL FINANCIAL DATA

	12/31/00	12/31/99	12/31/98	12/31/97	12/31/96	12/31/95	12/31/94
Earnings Per Share	**[6] 1.03**	**[5] d3.69**	**[4] d0.05**	**[3] 0.80**	**0.48**	**[2] d0.78**	**[1] 1.20**
Cash Flow Per Share	**1.59**	**d2.51**	**1.42**	**2.15**	**2.18**	**0.89**	**2.59**
Tang. Book Val. Per Share	**6.35**	**0.61**	**5.72**	**7.19**	**6.87**	**6.78**	**7.94**
Dividends Per Share	**...**	**0.34**	**0.34**	**0.34**	**0.34**	**0.34**	**0.34**
Dividend Payout %	**...**	**...**	**...**	**42.5**	**70.8**	**...**	**28.3**
INCOME STATEMENT (IN MILLIONS):							
Total Revenues	488.2	561.0	707.6	694.5	701.9	684.8	719.5
Costs & Expenses	455.6	602.5	681.8	655.8	663.4	669.4	666.4
Depreciation & Amort.	5.7	12.5	18.1	17.7	22.9	22.4	20.2
Operating Income	26.9	d53.9	7.7	21.0	15.6	d7.1	32.8
Net Interest Inc./(Exp.)	d8.4	d6.7	d9.0	d5.5	d7.3	d7.9	d5.9
Income Before Income Taxes	17.1	d60.0	d1.1	14.5	8.9	d15.0	27.6
Income Taxes	6.4	cr20.7	cr0.4	4.1	2.4	cr4.6	10.2
Net Income	[6] 10.7	[5] d39.2	[4] d0.7	[3] 10.4	6.5	[2] d10.5	[1] 17.4
Cash Flow	16.4	d26.8	17.4	28.1	29.4	12.0	37.6
Average Shs. Outstg. (000)	10,320	10,642	12,280	13,062	13,452	13,424	14,519
BALANCE SHEET (IN MILLIONS):							
Cash & Cash Equivalents	4.3	20.2	17.9	2.1	2.1	2.6	1.6
Total Current Assets	155.8	143.8	217.2	212.9	186.2	163.4	189.3
Net Property	12.7	30.4	84.4	79.5	89.8	93.1	89.6
Total Assets	180.5	223.8	343.7	323.5	316.0	298.5	322.0
Total Current Liabilities	89.7	111.7	189.3	140.5	121.3	100.3	99.0
Long-Term Obligations	...	52.0	29.8	36.2	43.9	51.2	58.6
Net Stockholders' Equity	73.1	37.5	100.2	112.8	116.0	116.1	133.4
Net Working Capital	66.1	32.1	27.9	72.4	64.9	63.1	90.3
Year-end Shs. Outstg. (000)	10,137	10,008	11,725	12,718	13,373	13,438	13,550
STATISTICAL RECORD:							
Operating Profit Margin %	5.5	...	1.1	3.0	2.2	...	4.6
Net Profit Margin %	2.2	...	...	1.5	0.9	...	2.4
Return on Equity %	14.6	...	...	9.2	5.6	...	13.1
Return on Assets %	5.9	...	...	3.2	2.0	...	5.4
Debt/Total Assets %	...	23.2	8.7	11.2	13.9	17.2	18.2
Price Range	13.69-3.00	16.75-5.19	19.94-11.06	16.94-12.75	14.88-10.25	15.88-10.00	19.50-14.00
P/E Ratio	13.3-2.9	...	...	21.2-15.9	31.0-21.3	...	16.2-11.7
Average Yield %	...	3.1	2.2	2.3	2.7	2.6	2.0

Statistics are as originally reported. [1] Incl. nonrecurr. gain of $934,000. [2] Incl. restruct. chrg. of $3.5 mill. [3] Excl. a net loss fr. discont. oper. of $254 mill. [4] Incl. pre-tax nonrecurr. chrg. of $21.3 mill. [5] Excl. discont. oper. gain of $5.9 mill., but incl. nonrecurr. chrg. $38.8 mill. [6] Excl. extraord. chrg. of $998,000, discont. oper. inc. of $25.3 mill., incl. nonrecurr. chrg. of $714,000.

OFFICERS:
D. R. Graber, Chmn., Pres., C.E.O.
R. W. Lafferty, V.P., C.F.O., Treas.
N. A. Michaud, V.P., Sec., Gen. Couns.

INVESTOR CONTACT: Investor Relations, (937) 866-6251

PRINCIPAL OFFICE: 225 Byers Road, Miamisburg, OH 45342

TELEPHONE NUMBER: (937) 866-6251
FAX: (937) 865-5470
WEB: www.huffy.com

NO. OF EMPLOYEES: 1,606

SHAREHOLDERS: 3,271

ANNUAL MEETING: In Apr.

INCORPORATED: OH, Feb., 1928

INSTITUTIONAL HOLDINGS:
No. of Institutions: 40
Shares Held: 3,466,338
% Held: 33.9

INDUSTRY: Motorcycles, bicycles, and parts (SIC: 3751)

TRANSFER AGENT(S): LaSalle Bank NA, Chicago, IL

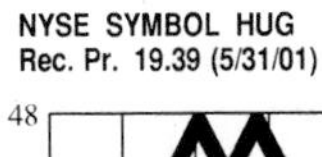
NYSE SYMBOL HUG
Rec. Pr. 19.39 (5/31/01)

HUGHES SUPPLY, INC.

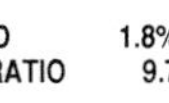
YIELD 1.8%
P/E RATIO 9.7

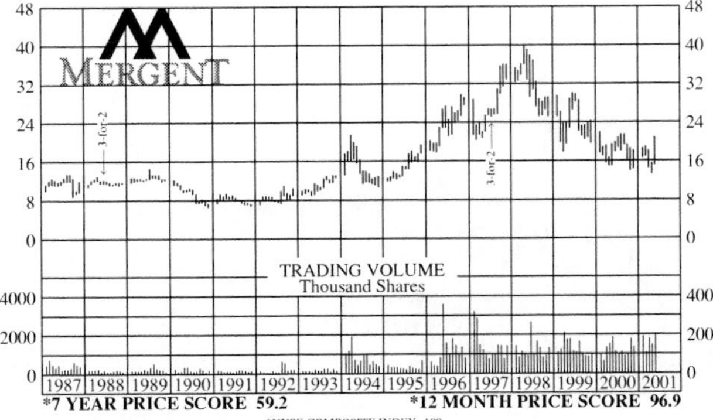

*7 YEAR PRICE SCORE 59.2 *12 MONTH PRICE SCORE 96.9

*NYSE COMPOSITE INDEX=100

INTERIM EARNINGS (Per Share):

Qtr.	Apr.	July	Oct.	Jan.
1996-97	0.38	0.60	0.61	0.42
1997-98	0.44	0.68	0.70	0.43
1998-99	0.47	0.82	0.79	0.45
1999-00	0.55	0.88	0.87	0.49
2000-01	0.62	0.96	0.80	d0.39

INTERIM DIVIDENDS (Per Share):

Amt.	Decl.	Ex.	Rec.	Pay.
0.085Q	3/16/00	4/27/00	5/01/00	5/15/00
0.085Q	7/21/00	8/03/00	8/07/00	8/21/00
0.085Q	10/03/00	11/01/00	11/03/00	11/17/00
0.085Q	1/16/01	1/31/01	2/02/01	2/16/01
0.085Q	3/14/01	5/02/01	5/04/01	5/18/01

Indicated div.: $0.34

CAPITALIZATION (1/26/01):

	($000)	(%)
Long-Term Debt	516,168	47.2
Deferred Income Tax	6,704	0.6
Common & Surplus	570,035	52.2
Total	1,092,907	100.0

RECENT DEVELOPMENTS: For the year ended 1/26/01, net income totaled $46.5 million, down 29.4% compared with $65.9 million the previous year. Results in the recent year included a one-time pre-tax charge of $15.6 million from impairment of long-lived assets and a one-time pre-tax gain of $11.0 million from the sale of HUG's pool business. Net sales rose 10.5% to $3.31 billion from $2.99 billion a year earlier. Same-store sales grew 5.0% year-over-year. Gross profit was $743.5 million, or 22.5% of net sales, versus $674.3 million, or 22.5% of net sales, the year before.

PROSPECTS: On 1/26/01, the Company sold its pool supply operations, which had approximately $120.0 million in annual sales, to SCP Pool Corporation for $48.0 million. This divestiture will help HUG sharpen its focus on its core businesses, reduce seasonality, and provide additional funds for possible acquisitions or stock repurchases. Separately, the Company has decided to discontinue the operations of bestroute.com, which specialized in supplying wholesale distributors with hard-to-find inventory products, due to lower-than-expected volume through the site.

BUSINESS

HUGHES SUPPLY, INC. is engaged in wholesale distribution of a broad range of materials, equipment and supplies primarily to the construction industry. HUG distributes more than 240,000 products from about 450 locations in 34 states and Mexico. These products are used by its customers in new construction for commercial, residential, infrastructure and industrial applications and for replacement and renovation projects. Major product lines distributed by HUG include electrical, plumbing, water and sewer, air conditioning and heating, industrial pipe, valves and fittings, building materials, electric utilities, and water systems.

ANNUAL FINANCIAL DATA

	1/26/01	1/28/00	1/29/99	1/30/98	1/31/97	1/26/96	1/27/95
Earnings Per Share	**[1] 1.97**	**2.80**	**2.55**	**2.30**	**2.05**	**1.56**	**1.19**
Cash Flow Per Share	**3.34**	**4.06**	**3.51**	**3.24**	**2.99**	**2.59**	**2.21**
Tang. Book Val. Per Share	**13.55**	**11.84**	**12.50**	**11.61**	**10.95**	**15.12**	**14.50**
Dividends Per Share	**0.34**	**0.34**	**0.33**	**0.29**	**0.25**	**0.18**	**0.14**
Dividend Payout %	**17.3**	**12.1**	**12.7**	**12.8**	**12.0**	**11.5**	**11.7**
INCOME STATEMENT (IN MILLIONS):							
Total Revenues	3,310.2	2,994.9	2,536.3	1,878.7	1,516.1	1,082.2	802.4
Costs & Expenses	3,172.4	2,832.9	2,395.8	1,776.6	1,441.9	1,041.7	774.2
Depreciation & Amort.	32.3	29.6	23.3	18.4	15.0	10.6	8.8
Operating Income	105.5	132.4	117.2	83.7	59.3	29.9	19.5
Net Interest Inc./(Exp.)	d43.3	d31.8	d25.4	d18.5	d13.5	d7.5	d2.6
Income Before Income Taxes	80.7	109.6	98.7	70.9	51.7	27.0	17.4
Income Taxes	34.2	43.7	37.2	26.1	19.2	11.0	7.1
Net Income	[1] 46.5	65.9	61.4	44.8	32.5	16.1	10.3
Cash Flow	78.8	95.5	84.7	63.3	47.5	26.6	19.1
Average Shs. Outstg. (000)	23,584	23,547	24,138	19,518	15,864	10,284	8,648
BALANCE SHEET (IN MILLIONS):							
Cash & Cash Equivalents	22.4	10.0	6.0	7.7	6.3	3.4	3.2
Total Current Assets	980.9	957.8	796.7	664.2	476.8	297.5	260.4
Net Property	152.1	144.9	127.6	105.4	73.0	57.7	53.2
Total Assets	1,400.3	1,369.0	1,123.5	942.0	649.5	379.1	328.9
Total Current Liabilities	301.8	300.3	229.3	189.8	146.4	117.0	95.1
Long-Term Obligations	516.2	535.0	402.2	335.2	222.0	106.2	100.9
Net Stockholders' Equity	570.0	522.4	484.0	414.3	278.9	154.1	131.3
Net Working Capital	679.1	657.5	567.4	474.3	330.4	180.5	165.3
Year-end Shs. Outstg. (000)	23,635	23,580	24,184	22,500	17,277	10,197	9,060
STATISTICAL RECORD:							
Operating Profit Margin %	3.2	4.4	4.6	4.5	3.9	2.8	2.4
Net Profit Margin %	1.4	2.2	2.4	2.4	2.1	1.5	1.3
Return on Equity %	8.2	12.6	12.7	10.8	11.7	10.4	7.9
Return on Assets %	3.3	4.8	5.5	4.8	5.0	4.2	3.1
Debt/Total Assets %	36.9	39.1	35.8	35.6	34.2	28.0	30.7
Price Range	21.94-13.90	30.00-17.88	39.81-25.13	36.13-20.33	29.75-17.75	19.42-11.83	21.50-10.58
P/E Ratio	11.1-7.1	10.7-6.4	15.6-9.9	15.7-8.8	14.5-8.6	12.4-7.6	18.0-8.9
Average Yield %	1.9	1.4	1.0	1.0	1.0	1.2	0.9

Statistics are as originally reported. Adj. for 3-for-2 stk. split, 7/97. [1] Incl. $15.6 mil pre-tax non-recur. chg. for impairment of long-lived assets & $11.0 mil pre-tax gain from the sale of the Company's pool business.

OFFICERS:
D. H. Hughes, Chmn., C.E.O.
T. Morgan, Pres., C.O.O.
J. S. Zepf, C.F.O., Treas.

INVESTOR CONTACT: J. Stephen Zepf, C.F.O. & Treas., (407) 841-4755

PRINCIPAL OFFICE: 20 North Orange Ave., Suite 200, Orlando, FL 32801

TELEPHONE NUMBER: (407) 841-4755
FAX: (407) 649-1670
WEB: www.hughessupply.com

NO. OF EMPLOYEES: 7,700 (approx.)

SHAREHOLDERS: 1,084 (approx. record)

ANNUAL MEETING: In May

INCORPORATED: FL, 1947

INSTITUTIONAL HOLDINGS:
No. of Institutions: 104
Shares Held: 13,879,130
% Held: 59.1

INDUSTRY: Electrical apparatus and equipment (SIC: 5063)

TRANSFER AGENT(S): American Stock Transfer & Trust Company, New York, NY

NYSE SYMBOL HUM
Rec. Pr. 9.88 (4/30/01)

HUMANA INC.

YIELD ...
P/E RATIO 18.3

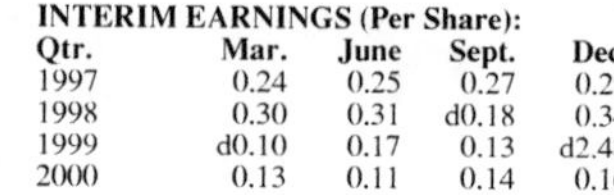

INTERIM EARNINGS (Per Share):

Qtr.	Mar.	June	Sept.	Dec.
1997	0.24	0.25	0.27	0.29
1998	0.30	0.31	d0.18	0.34
1999	d0.10	0.17	0.13	d2.48
2000	0.13	0.11	0.14	0.16

TRADING VOLUME
Thousand Shares

*7 YEAR PRICE SCORE 40.7 *12 MONTH PRICE SCORE 112.8
*NYSE COMPOSITE INDEX=100

INTERIM DIVIDENDS (Per Share):

Amt.	Decl.	Ex.	Rec.	Pay.

No dividends paid.

CAPITALIZATION (12/31/00):

	($000)	(%)
Common & Surplus	1,360,000	100.0
Total	1,360,000	100.0

RECENT DEVELOPMENTS: For the twelve months ended 12/31/00, the Company reported net income of $90.0 million compared with a net loss of $382.0 million in the previous year. Results for 1999 included pre-tax asset write-downs and other charges of $460.0 million. The improvement in earnings reflects commercial pricing discipline, favorable medical cost trends from benefit design changes and the elimination of various non-core markets and products. Total revenues rose 4.0% to $10.51 billion from $10.11 billion a year earlier.

PROSPECTS: HUM is making solid progress in its business turnaround as benefits from operational improvements are starting to emerge. Looking ahead, revenue and health plan membership growth should benefit from a new generation of products fueled by the efficiency and convenience of digital information. Meanwhile, the Company and Navigy, Inc., announced a joint business venture to create, operate and market an Internet connectivity service for physicians and other health care providers in Florida.

BUSINESS

HUMANA, INC. operates through two business divisions: the health plan division and the small group division. The health plan division includes the Company's large group commercial, Medicare, Medicaid and military or TRICARE business. The small group division is comprised of HUM's small group commercial and specialty benefit lines, including dental, life and short term disability insurance. At 12/31/00, HUM had approximately 5.3 million medical members located primarily in 15 states and Puerto Rico.

REVENUES

(12/31/2000)	($000)	(%)
Health Plan	7,386,000	70.2
Small Group	3,128,000	29.8
Total	10,514,000	100.0

ANNUAL FINANCIAL DATA

	12/31/00	12/31/99	12/31/98	12/31/97	12/31/96	[2] 12/31/95	12/31/94
Earnings Per Share	**0.54**	**[5] d2.28**	**0.77**	**[4] 1.05**	**[3] 0.07**	**1.17**	**[1] 1.10**
Cash Flow Per Share	**1.42**	**d1.54**	**1.53**	**1.69**	**1.36**	**1.60**	**1.40**
Tang. Book Val. Per Share	**3.37**	**2.76**	**3.01**	**1.69**	**4.93**	**4.64**	**5.61**
INCOME STATEMENT (IN MILLIONS):							
Total Revenues	10,514.0	10,113.0	9,781.0	8,036.0	6,899.0	4,702.0	3,654.0
Costs & Expenses	10,224.0	10,360.0	9,403.0	7,638.0	6,661.0	4,333.0	3,354.0
Depreciation & Amort.	147.0	124.0	128.0	108.0	98.0	70.0	50.0
Operating Income	143.0	d371.0	250.0	290.0	29.0	299.0	232.0
Net Interest Inc./(Exp.)	d29.0	d33.0	d47.0	d20.0	d11.0	d11.0	25.0
Income Before Income Taxes	114.0	d404.0	203.0	270.0	18.0	288.0	257.0
Income Taxes	24.0	cr22.0	74.0	97.0	6.0	98.0	81.0
Net Income	90.0	[5] d382.0	129.0	[4] 173.0	[3] 123.0	190.0	[1] 176.0
Cash Flow	237.0	d258.0	257.0	281.0	221.0	260.0	226.0
Average Shs. Outstg. (000)	166,931	167,556	168,000	165,800	163,000	162,000	161,000
BALANCE SHEET (IN MILLIONS):							
Cash & Cash Equivalents	2,067.0	2,485.0	2,507.0	2,134.0	1,584.0	1,338.0	881.0
Total Current Assets	2,499.0	3,064.0	3,119.0	2,750.0	2,002.0	1,593.0	1,038.0
Net Property	435.0	418.0	433.0	420.0	371.0	382.0	317.0
Total Assets	4,167.0	4,900.0	5,496.0	5,418.0	3,153.0	2,878.0	1,957.0
Total Current Liabilities	2,665.0	3,164.0	2,643.0	2,263.0	1,500.0	1,192.0	816.0
Long-Term Obligations	...	324.0	1,011.0	1,486.0	225.0	250.0	...
Net Stockholders' Equity	1,360.0	1,268.0	1,688.0	1,501.0	1,292.0	1,287.0	1,058.0
Net Working Capital	d166.0	d100.0	476.0	487.0	502.0	401.0	222.0
Year-end Shs. Outstg. (000)	169,066	167,515	166,000	164,100	163,000	162,000	161,000
STATISTICAL RECORD:							
Operating Profit Margin %	1.4	...	2.6	3.6	0.4	6.4	6.3
Net Profit Margin %	0.9	...	1.3	2.2	1.8	4.0	4.8
Return on Equity %	6.6	...	7.6	11.5	9.5	14.8	16.6
Return on Assets %	2.2	...	2.3	3.2	3.9	6.6	9.0
Debt/Total Assets %	...	6.6	18.4	27.4	7.1	8.7	...
Price Range	15.81-4.75	20.75-5.88	32.13-12.25	25.31-17.38	28.88-15.00	28.00-17.00	25.38-15.88
P/E Ratio	29.3-8.8	...	41.7-15.9	24.1-16.5	411.9-214.0	23.9-14.5	23.1-14.4

Statistics are as originally reported. Adj. for 3-for-2 stk. split, 7/91. [1] Incl. a nonrecur. cr$17.0 mill. [2] Incl. opers. of EMPHESYS Financial Group, Inc. [3] Incl. net chgs. of $140.0 mill. [4] Incl. a net spec. chg. of $84.0 mill. [5] Incl. net after-tax chrg. of $491.0 mill.

OFFICERS:
D. A. Jones, Chmn.
D. A. Jones Jr., Vice-Chmn.
M. B. McCallister, Pres., C.E.O.

INVESTOR CONTACT: Regina Nethery, Inv. Rel., (502) 580-3644

PRINCIPAL OFFICE: 500 West Main Street, Louisville, KY 40202

TELEPHONE NUMBER: (502) 580-1000
FAX: (502) 580-1441
WEB: www.humana.com

NO. OF EMPLOYEES: 15,600 (approx.)

SHAREHOLDERS: 7,600 (approx.)

ANNUAL MEETING: In May

INCORPORATED: DE, July, 1964

INSTITUTIONAL HOLDINGS:
No. of Institutions: 201
Shares Held: 127,034,441
% Held: 75.2

INDUSTRY: Hospital and medical service plans (SIC: 6324)

TRANSFER AGENT(S): National City Bank, Cleveland, OH

NYSE SYMBOL HUN
Rec. Pr. 5.51 (5/31/01)

HUNT CORPORATION

YIELD 7.4%
P/E RATIO 36.7

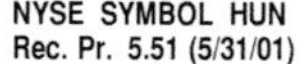

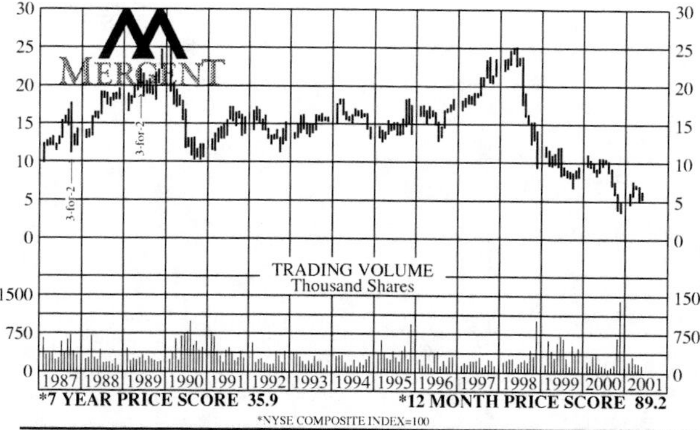

*7 YEAR PRICE SCORE 35.9 *12 MONTH PRICE SCORE 89.2

*NYSE COMPOSITE INDEX=100

INTERIM EARNINGS (Per Share):

Qtr.	Feb.	May	Aug.	Nov.
1996-97	0.22	d0.63	0.30	d0.11
1997-98	0.28	0.41	0.24	0.06
1998-99	0.22	0.22	0.22	d0.05
1999-00	0.22	0.10	d0.13	Nil
2000-01	0.18	...	...	...

INTERIM DIVIDENDS (Per Share):

Amt.	Decl.	Ex.	Rec.	Pay.
0.102Q	...	3/27/00	3/29/00	4/06/00
0.102Q	...	7/06/00	7/10/00	7/18/00
0.102Q	10/04/00	10/12/00	10/16/00	10/24/00
0.102Q	12/21/00	12/29/00	1/03/01	1/11/01
0.102Q	2/14/01	3/26/01	3/28/01	4/05/01

Indicated div.: $0.41

CAPITALIZATION (12/3/00):

	($000)	(%)
Long-Term Debt	54,682	45.9
Deferred Income Tax	2,434	2.0
Common & Surplus	61,970	52.0
Total	119,086	100.0

RECENT DEVELOPMENTS: For the quarter ended 3/4/01, net income was $1.7 million, down 23.8% versus $2.2 million the year before. Results included one-time after-tax charges of $136,000 and $164,000 in 2001 and 2000, respectively. Net sales slipped 7.9% to $55.9 million from $60.6 million the prior year. Net sales of graphics products slid 11.6% to $31.1 million, while net sales of consumer products were down 2.4% to $24.8 million. Gross profit was $21.4 million compared with $21.9 million in the previous year.

PROSPECTS: Sales are being hampered by unfavorable foreign currency exchange rates and a slowdown in economic growth in the U.S. Meanwhile, profit margins are being constrained by higher material costs, increased transportation expenses, and lower net selling prices. Restructuring initiatives implemented during 2000 in the Graphics Products segment are expected to result in annual cost savings of $5.9 million going forward. Results in 2001 should get a boost from new products introduced in 2000.

BUSINESS

HUNT CORPORATION (formerly Hunt Manufacturing Co.) is a producer and distributor of graphics products and consumer products. Graphics Products (57.3% of 2000 net sales) include a full line of mounting and finishing products, such as laminates, adhesives, and lamination, sold under the SEAL brand, as well as BIENFANG brand of foam board and project display board products. The Company's graphics products are primarily used by picture framers, graphic artists, display designers and photo laboratories. Consumer Products (42.7%) include BOSTON pencil sharpeners and staplers; RAPID staplers; and X-ACTO brand knives and blades. The Company's consumer products are sold and distributed primarily through office products superstores, drug and food chain stores, variety stores, discount chains and membership chains, and through office supply wholesalers and dealers.

BUSINESS LINE ANALYSIS

(12/03/2000)	REV (%)	INC (%)
Consumer products	42.7	74.0
Graphics products	57.3	26.0
Total	100.0	100.0

ANNUAL FINANCIAL DATA

	12/3/00	11/28/99	11/29/98	11/30/97	12/1/96	12/3/95	11/27/94
Earnings Per Share	**(1) 0.20**	**(6) 0.61**	**(5) 1.01**	**(4) d0.53**	**(3) 1.33**	**(1) 0.74**	**(2) 1.07**
Cash Flow Per Share	**1.07**	**1.43**	**1.72**	**0.26**	**2.09**	**1.49**	**1.57**
Tang. Book Val. Per Share	**3.81**	**4.20**	**4.39**	**4.04**	**3.44**	**6.89**	**6.41**
Dividends Per Share	**0.41**	**0.41**	**0.41**	**0.38**	**0.38**	**0.38**	**0.36**
Dividend Payout %	**204.9**	**67.2**	**40.6**	**...**	**28.6**	**51.3**	**33.6**
INCOME STATEMENT (IN MILLIONS):							
Total Revenues	248.6	244.8	246.6	259.5	327.5	313.9	288.2
Costs & Expenses	234.0	224.3	219.0	254.0	290.8	281.6	252.8
Depreciation & Amort.	8.6	8.5	8.3	9.1	9.2	8.8	8.0
Operating Income	6.0	12.0	19.3	d3.6	27.6	23.6	27.4
Net Interest Inc./(Exp.)	d3.1	d3.0	d1.7	d4.4	d4.3	0.5	0.3
Income Before Income Taxes	3.0	9.1	17.7	d8.8	23.3	23.6	27.1
Net Income	(1) 2.0	(6) 6.4	(5) 11.6	(4) d6.1	(3) 15.2	(1) 15.3	(2) 17.2
Cash Flow	10.6	15.0	19.9	3.0	24.4	24.1	25.2
Average Shs. Outstg. (000)	9,908	10,493	11,556	11,469	11,642	16,164	16,102
BALANCE SHEET (IN MILLIONS):							
Cash & Cash Equivalents	23.9	36.9	40.7	65.4	1.5	15.5	13.8
Total Current Assets	88.3	97.3	99.5	130.3	92.0	100.1	95.3
Net Property	41.2	45.1	49.9	43.0	52.7	52.0	49.7
Total Assets	163.5	179.6	186.9	209.5	175.7	182.8	173.4
Total Current Liabilities	31.9	35.9	35.0	64.1	33.7	31.0	30.7
Long-Term Obligations	54.7	56.6	57.7	54.1	64.6	3.6	3.6
Net Stockholders' Equity	62.0	70.5	77.9	74.7	62.7	136.2	129.2
Net Working Capital	56.4	61.4	64.6	66.2	58.3	69.1	64.6
Year-end Shs. Outstg. (000)	9,827	10,165	10,990	11,167	10,974	15,993	16,100
STATISTICAL RECORD:							
Operating Profit Margin %	2.4	4.9	7.8	...	8.4	7.5	9.5
Net Profit Margin %	0.8	2.6	4.7	...	4.6	4.9	6.0
Return on Equity %	3.2	9.1	14.9	...	24.3	11.3	13.3
Return on Assets %	1.2	3.6	6.2	...	8.7	8.4	9.9
Debt/Total Assets %	33.4	31.5	30.9	25.8	36.7	1.9	2.1
Price Range	11.13-3.50	12.19-6.63	25.19-9.25	23.94-16.75	18.38-12.75	18.38-12.63	18.25-13.00
P/E Ratio	55.6-17.5	20.0-10.9	24.9-9.2	...	13.8-9.6	24.8-17.1	17.1-12.1
Average Yield %	5.6	4.4	2.4	1.9	2.4	2.5	2.3

Statistics are as originally reported. (1) Incl. $5.7 mil ($0.57/sh) net chg., 2000; $3.5 mil net consol. chg., 1995. (2) Bef. $795,000 gain from acctg. adj. (3) Bef. $400,000 ($0.02/sh) extraord. chg. & incl. $700,000 ($0.04/sh) admin. chg. (4) Incl. $30 mil pre-tax net restr. chg., $3.7 mil gain fr. divest., & bef. $20.1 mil after-tax inc. fr. discont. opers. (5) Incl. $3.5 mil ($0.20/sh) pre-tax gain & bef. $484,000 ($0.04/sh) gain fr discont. opers. (6) Incl. $5.6 mil ($0.35/sh) pre-tax restr. chg. & $554,000 (0.03/sh) gain fr. divest.

OFFICERS:
D. L. Thompson, Chmn., Pres., C.E.O.
W. E. Chandler, Sr. V.P.-Fin., C.F.O., Sec.
D. S. Pizzica, V.P., Treas.

INVESTOR CONTACT: Dennis S. Pizzica, V.P. & Treas., (215) 841-2303

PRINCIPAL OFFICE: One Commerce Square, 2005 Market St., Philadelphia, PA 19103

TELEPHONE NUMBER: (215) 656-0300
FAX: (215) 656-3700
WEB: www.hunt-corp.com

NO. OF EMPLOYEES: 1,300 (approx.)

SHAREHOLDERS: 500 (approx.)

ANNUAL MEETING: In Apr.

INCORPORATED: PA, Nov., 1962

INSTITUTIONAL HOLDINGS:
No. of Institutions: 26
Shares Held: 3,411,022
% Held: 38.4

INDUSTRY: Stationery and office supplies (SIC: 5112)

TRANSFER AGENT(S): American Stock Transfer & Trust Company, New York, NY

NYSE SYMBOL IBP
Rec. Pr. 18.80 (5/31/01)

IBP, INC.

YIELD 0.5%
P/E RATIO 11.9

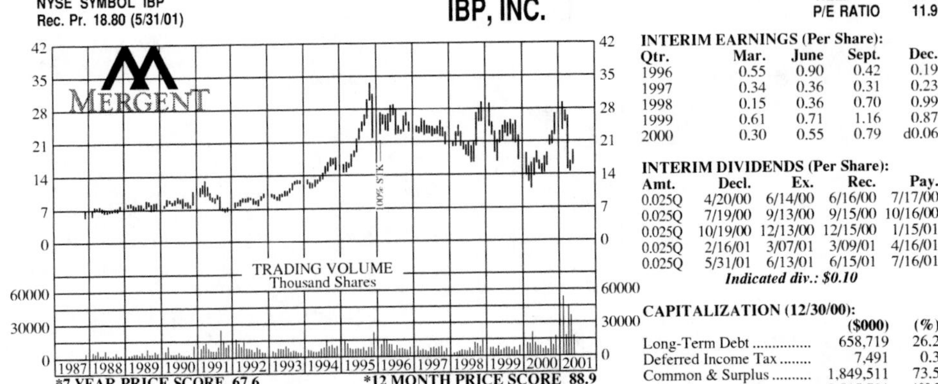

INTERIM EARNINGS (Per Share):

Qtr.	Mar.	June	Sept.	Dec.
1996	0.55	0.90	0.42	0.19
1997	0.34	0.36	0.31	0.23
1998	0.15	0.36	0.70	0.99
1999	0.61	0.71	1.16	0.87
2000	0.30	0.55	0.79	d0.06

INTERIM DIVIDENDS (Per Share):

Amt.	Decl.	Ex.	Rec.	Pay.
0.025Q	4/20/00	6/14/00	6/16/00	7/17/00
0.025Q	7/19/00	9/13/00	9/15/00	10/16/00
0.025Q	10/19/00	12/13/00	12/15/00	1/15/01
0.025Q	2/16/01	3/07/01	3/09/01	4/16/01
0.025Q	5/31/01	6/13/01	6/15/01	7/16/01

Indicated div.: $0.10

CAPITALIZATION (12/30/00):

	($000)	(%)
Long-Term Debt	658,719	26.2
Deferred Income Tax	7,491	0.3
Common & Surplus	1,849,511	73.5
Total	2,515,721	100.0

RECENT DEVELOPMENTS: For the 53 weeks ended 12/30/00, the Company reported earnings of $152.7 million, before a $15.0 million extraordinary charge and a $2.4 million accounting charge. This compares with net income of $317.9 million in the corresponding 52-week period the year before. Results for 2000 included a $60.4 million pre-tax goodwill impairment charge and a $31.3 million pre-tax merger-related charge. Net sales grew 12.1% to $16.95 billion from $15.12 billion in 1999. Comparisons were made with restated prior-year results.

PROSPECTS: On 2/28/01, Tyson Foods, Inc. announced it had decided to terminate its tender offer for 50.1% of IBP's common stock, reflecting a Securities and Exchange Commission investigation of accounting issues at the Company's DFG Foods subsidiary. Meanwhile, the Company is targeting earnings of between $1.80 and $2.20 per share for 2001. An expected increased supply of both cattle and hogs may result in lower raw material prices and increased earnings in the second and third quarters of 2001.

BUSINESS

IBP, INC. operates in two business segments, Fresh Meats and Foodbrands. IBP's Fresh Meats operation primarily involves cattle and hog slaughter, beef and pork fabrication and related allied product processing activities. This segment markets its products to food retailers, distributors, wholesalers, restaurant and hotel chains, other food processors and leather makers, as well as manufacturers of pharmaceuticals and animal feeds. The Foodbrands segment consists of three subsidiaries: Foodbrands America, Inc., The Bruss Company and IBP Foods, Inc. This segment produces, markets and distributes a variety of frozen and refrigerated products to the "away from home" food preparation market, including pizza toppings and crusts, value-added pork-based products, ethnic specialty foods, appetizers, soups, sauces and side dishes as well as deli meats and processed beef, pork and poultry products.

QUARTERLY DATA

(12/30/2000)($000)	Rev	Inc
1st Quarter	3,995,391	16,270
2nd Quarter	4,268,835	46,442
3rd Quarter	4,314,416	78,728
4th Quarter	4,410,908	(6,253)

ANNUAL FINANCIAL DATA

	12/30/00	12/25/99	12/26/98	12/27/97	12/28/96	12/30/95	12/31/94
Earnings Per Share	**3 1.40**	**2 3.36**	**1 2.19**	**1.25**	**2.06**	**1 2.90**	**1.90**
Cash Flow Per Share	**3.13**	**4.85**	**3.54**	**2.42**	**2.91**	**3.85**	**2.56**
Tang. Book Val. Per Share	**8.41**	**8.74**	**7.33**	**6.11**	**10.54**	**8.60**	**5.94**
Dividends Per Share	**0.10**	**0.10**	**0.10**	**0.10**	**0.10**	**0.10**	**0.10**
Dividend Payout %	**7.1**	**3.0**	**4.6**	**8.0**	**4.9**	**3.4**	**5.3**
INCOME STATEMENT (IN MILLIONS):							
Total Revenues	16,949.6	14,075.2	12,848.6	13,258.8	12,538.8	12,667.6	12,075.4
Costs & Expenses	16,420.6	13,406.7	12,348.7	12,922.1	12,133.2	12,094.9	11,664.6
Depreciation & Amort.	182.2	140.1	126.2	109.9	82.7	92.5	63.4
Operating Income	346.9	528.5	373.7	226.7	322.9	480.1	347.3
Net Interest Inc./(Exp.)	d88.3	d45.4	d43.2	d38.0	d3.4	d20.8	d38.4
Income Before Income Taxes	258.6	483.1	330.5	188.7	319.5	459.3	308.9
Income Taxes	106.0	169.8	125.7	71.7	120.8	179.2	126.6
Net Income	3 152.7	2 313.3	1 204.8	117.0	198.7	1 280.1	182.3
Cash Flow	334.5	453.3	331.0	226.9	281.4	372.7	245.7
Average Shs. Outstg. (000)	107,076	93,395	93,395	93,792	96,632	96,671	96,163
BALANCE SHEET (IN MILLIONS):							
Cash & Cash Equivalents	30.0	32.2	28.7	72.1	263.6	180.1	160.5
Total Current Assets	1,665.6	1,466.9	1,096.8	1,083.9	1,110.6	1,068.9	973.9
Net Property	3,810.3	1,244.9	1,072.1	1,017.1	816.2	726.9	651.4
Total Assets	6,605.8	3,713.2	3,008.1	2,838.9	2,174.5	2,027.6	1,865.5
Total Current Liabilities	1,719.4	1,260.6	865.8	876.8	604.1	641.6	614.7
Long-Term Obligations	658.7	586.5	575.5	568.3	260.0	260.8	361.8
Net Stockholders' Equity	1,849.5	1,708.8	1,400.9	1,237.1	1,203.7	1,022.9	780.5
Net Working Capital	d53.8	206.3	231.0	207.1	506.5	427.2	359.2
Year-end Shs. Outstg. (000)	105,668	93,365	92,314	92,587	94,627	94,747	94,870
STATISTICAL RECORD:							
Operating Profit Margin %	2.0	3.8	2.9	1.7	2.6	3.8	2.9
Net Profit Margin %	0.9	2.2	1.6	0.9	1.6	2.2	1.5
Return on Equity %	8.3	18.3	14.6	9.5	16.5	27.4	23.4
Return on Assets %	2.3	8.4	6.8	4.1	9.1	13.8	9.8
Debt/Total Assets %	10.0	15.8	19.1	20.0	12.0	12.9	19.4
Price Range	26.94-11.00	29.19-16.75	29.44-16.56	26.00-20.38	29.00-22.50	33.63-14.56	17.75-11.31
P/E Ratio	19.2-7.9	8.7-5.0	13.4-7.6	20.8-16.3	14.1-10.9	11.6-5.0	9.3-6.0
Average Yield %	0.5	0.4	0.4	0.4	0.4	0.4	0.7

Statistics are as originally reported. Adj. for 2-for-1 stk. split, 1/96. 1 Bef. $14.8 mil ($0.16/sh) extraord. chg., 1998; $22.2 mil extraord. chg., 1995. 2 Incl. $8.0 mil ($0.08/sh) after-tax non-recur. chg. 3 Bef. $15.0 mil ($0.14/sh) extraord. chg., $2.4 mil ($0.02/sh) acctg. chg.; incl. $31.3 mil pre-tax non-recur. merger-rel. chg. & $60.4 mil pre-tax goodwill impair. chg.

OFFICERS:
R. L. Peterson, Chmn., C.E.O.
R. L. Bond, Pres., C.O.O.
L. Shipley, C.F.O.

INVESTOR CONTACT: Dean Hanish, Dir., Inv. Rel., (605) 235-2167

PRINCIPAL OFFICE: 800 Stevens Port Drive, Dakota Dunes, SD 57049

TELEPHONE NUMBER: (605) 235-2061
FAX: (605) 235-2404
WEB: www.ibpinc.com

NO. OF EMPLOYEES: 50,000 (approx.)

SHAREHOLDERS: 4,158 (approx.)

ANNUAL MEETING: In Apr.

INCORPORATED: DE, Mar., 1960

INSTITUTIONAL HOLDINGS:
No. of Institutions: 185
Shares Held: 50,959,755
% Held: 48.3

INDUSTRY: Meat packing plants (SIC: 2011)

TRANSFER AGENT(S): Mellon Investor Services, Ridgefield Park, NJ

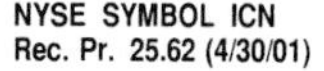

NYSE SYMBOL ICN
Rec. Pr. 25.62 (4/30/01)

ICN PHARMACEUTICALS, INC.

YIELD 1.2%
P/E RATIO 20.3

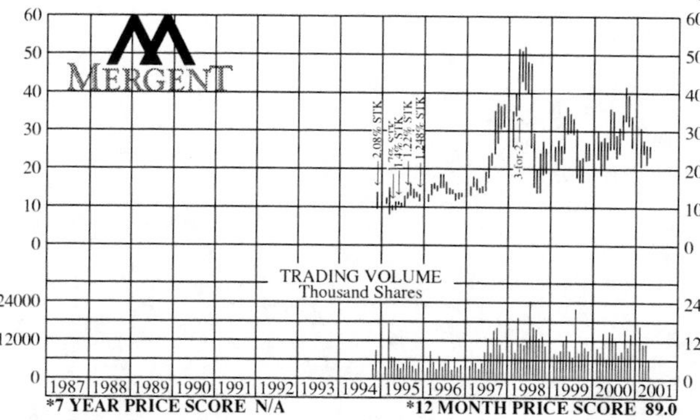

*7 YEAR PRICE SCORE N/A *12 MONTH PRICE SCORE 89.0

*NYSE COMPOSITE INDEX=100

INTERIM EARNINGS (Per Share):

Qtr.	Mar.	June	Sept.	Dec.
1998	0.44	d1.34	d0.89	d2.92
1999	0.28	0.32	0.39	0.47
2000	0.34	0.38	0.45	0.09

INTERIM DIVIDENDS (Per Share):

Amt.	Decl.	Ex.	Rec.	Pay.
0.073Q	4/11/00	4/20/00	4/25/00	5/10/00
0.073Q	7/06/00	7/18/00	7/20/00	8/03/00
0.073Q	10/02/00	10/12/00	10/16/00	10/30/00
0.073Q	1/04/01	1/10/01	1/15/01	1/29/01
0.075Q	2/23/01	4/09/01	4/11/01	4/25/01

Indicated div.: $0.30

CAPITALIZATION (12/31/00):

	($000)	(%)
Long-Term Debt	510,781	40.0
Minority Interest	9,332	0.7
Common & Surplus	757,194	59.3
Total	1,277,307	100.0

RECENT DEVELOPMENTS: For the year ended 12/31/00, the Company reported income of $93.4 million, before an extraordinary loss of $3.2 million, compared with net income of $118.6 million in the previous year. Total revenues climbed 7.1% to $800.3 million from $747.4 million the year before. Revenue growth reflected a 42.2% rise in royalties to $155.0 million for ribavarin, for the treatment of chronic hepatitis C. Product sales rose 1.1% to $645.2 million from $638.5 million.

PROSPECTS: Looking ahead, HUM expects 2001 earnings per share to be in the range of $1.50 to $1.55. ICN revenues should continue to benefit from ribavirin royalties, which are estimated to range from $180.0 million to $190.0 million in 2001. Furthermore, HUM will look to continue to expand its scientific team and research facilities by targeting research and development expense at $45.0 million in 2001, up from $19.0 million in 2000. The Company remains committed to restructuring into three publicly-traded entities in order to maximize shareholder value.

BUSINESS

ICN PHARMACEUTICALS, INC. is a global, research-based pharmaceutical company that develops, manufactures, distributes and sells pharmaceutical, research and diagnostic products. The Company distributes and sells a broad range of prescription and over-the-counter pharmaceutical and nutritional products in over 90 countries. These pharmaceutical products treat viral and bacterial infections, diseases of the skin, neuromuscular disorders, cancer, cardiovascular disease, diabetes and psychiatric disorders.

BUSINESS LINE ANALYSIS

(12/31/2000)	Rev(%)	Inc(%)
Pharmaceuticals	92.7	98.7
Biomedicals	7.3	1.3
Total	100.0	100.0

ANNUAL FINANCIAL DATA

	12/31/00	12/31/99	12/31/98	12/31/97	12/31/96	12/31/95	12/31/94
Earnings Per Share	**[1] 1.10**	**1.45**	**d4.78**	**1.69**	**1.51**	**1.47**	**d4.52**
Cash Flow Per Share	**1.92**	**2.24**	**d4.09**	**2.05**	**1.97**	**1.77**	**d4.29**
Tang. Book Val. Per Share	**3.99**	**2.88**	**1.60**	**7.98**	**5.62**	**3.43**	**1.39**
Dividends Per Share	**0.29**	**0.27**	**0.23**	**0.21**	**0.15**	**0.18**	**0.08**
Dividend Payout %	**26.1**	**18.6**	**...**	**12.5**	**10.2**	**12.4**	**...**
INCOME STATEMENT (IN MILLIONS):							
Total Revenues	800.3	747.4	838.1	752.2	614.1	507.9	366.9
Costs & Expenses	551.8	483.1	1,076.5	598.2	483.7	400.9	300.2
Depreciation & Amort.	64.5	65.5	51.1	28.8	16.3	13.8	9.2
Operating Income	184.0	198.9	d289.6	125.3	114.1	93.2	57.4
Net Interest Inc./(Exp.)	d47.8	d47.0	d25.0	d6.9	d12.8	d16.4	d4.6
Income Before Income Taxes	129.6	140.0	d395.1	105.6	99.1	86.2	d170.0
Income Taxes	37.7	29.0	2.0	cr27.7	cr6.8	3.0	10.4
Equity Earnings/Minority Int.	1.5	7.6	45.0	d19.4	d18.9	d15.9	d3.3
Net Income	[1] 93.4	118.6	d352.1	113.9	86.9	67.3	d183.6
Cash Flow	157.9	184.1	d301.0	140.8	103.2	81.2	d181.1
Average Shs. Outstg. (000)	82,264	82,089	73,637	69,650	52,379	45,935	40,611
BALANCE SHEET (IN MILLIONS):							
Cash & Cash Equivalents	155.6	178.0	120.5	210.4	39.9	52.2	43.8
Total Current Assets	565.4	564.7	440.7	786.8	444.4	283.6	240.3
Net Property	367.2	332.4	327.8	360.7	234.2	172.5	128.6
Total Assets	1,477.1	1,472.3	1,356.4	1,491.7	778.7	518.3	441.5
Total Current Liabilities	158.8	140.6	203.8	201.1	137.6	92.8	102.5
Long-Term Obligations	510.8	597.0	510.8	315.1	176.5	154.2	195.2
Net Stockholders' Equity	757.2	683.6	586.2	796.3	315.4	162.2	88.9
Net Working Capital	406.6	424.1	237.0	585.6	306.8	190.8	137.8
Year-end Shs. Outstg. (000)	80,197	78,950	76,411	71,432	50,133	45,630	51,120
STATISTICAL RECORD:							
Operating Profit Margin %	23.0	26.6	...	16.7	18.6	18.3	15.6
Net Profit Margin %	11.7	15.9	...	15.1	14.2	13.3	...
Return on Equity %	12.3	17.4	...	14.3	27.6	41.5	...
Return on Assets %	6.3	8.1	...	7.6	11.2	13.0	...
Debt/Total Assets %	34.6	40.5	37.7	21.1	22.7	29.7	44.2
Price Range	41.75-18.44	36.38-16.56	52.25-13.81	37.33-13.00	18.67-11.33	16.06-7.97	14.99-9.55
P/E Ratio	38.0-16.8	25.1-11.4	...	22.1-7.7	12.3-7.5	10.9-5.4	...
Average Yield %	1.0	1.0	0.7	0.8	1.0	1.5	0.7

Statistics are as originally reported. Adj. for all stock splits through 3/98. [1] Bef. extraord. loss of $3.2 mill.

OFFICERS:
M. Panic, Chmn., C.E.O.
A. Jerney, Pres., C.O.O.
R. A. Meier, Exec. V.P., C.F.O.

INVESTOR CONTACT: Mariann Ohanesian, Dir. Inv. Rel., (714) 545-0100 ext.3230

PRINCIPAL OFFICE: 3300 Hyland Ave., Costa Mesa, CA 92626

TELEPHONE NUMBER: (714) 545-0100
FAX: (714) 641-7215
WEB: www.icnpharm.com
NO. OF EMPLOYEES: 12,700 (avg.)
SHAREHOLDERS: 6,967
ANNUAL MEETING: In May
INCORPORATED: CA, Dec., 1960; reincorp., DE, Oct., 1986

INSTITUTIONAL HOLDINGS:
No. of Institutions: 192
Shares Held: 35,388,589
% Held: 44.1

INDUSTRY: Pharmaceutical preparations (SIC: 2834)

TRANSFER AGENT(S): American Stock Transfer & Trust Company, New York, NY

NYSE SYMBOL IDA
Rec. Pr. 38.70 (5/31/01)

IDACORP, INC.

YIELD 4.8%
P/E RATIO 10.4

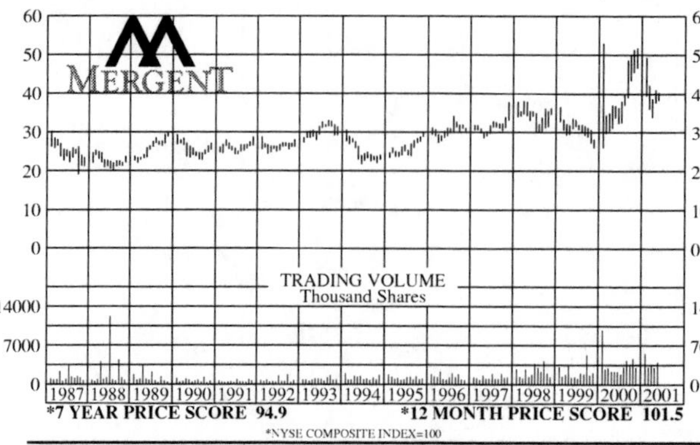

*7 YEAR PRICE SCORE 94.9 *12 MONTH PRICE SCORE 101.5

*NYSE COMPOSITE INDEX=100

INTERIM EARNINGS (Per Share):

Qtr.	Mar.	June	Sept.	Dec.
1996	0.75	0.56	0.46	0.44
1997	0.77	0.52	0.52	0.51
1998	0.75	0.54	0.59	0.49
1999	0.78	0.56	0.59	0.49
2000	1.12	0.86	1.11	0.63

INTERIM DIVIDENDS (Per Share):

Amt.	Decl.	Ex.	Rec.	Pay.
0.465Q	3/16/00	5/03/00	5/05/00	5/30/00
0.465Q	7/20/00	8/02/00	8/04/00	8/30/00
0.465Q	9/21/00	11/02/00	11/06/00	11/30/00
0.465Q	1/18/01	2/01/01	2/05/01	2/28/01
0.465Q	3/15/01	5/02/01	5/04/01	5/30/01

Indicated div.: $1.86 (Div. Reinv. Plan)

CAPITALIZATION (12/31/00):

	($000)	(%)
Long-Term Debt	864,114	38.4
Deferred Income Tax	460,464	20.5
Preferred Stock	105,066	4.7
Common & Surplus	820,811	36.5
Total	2,250,455	100.0

RECENT DEVELOPMENTS: For the year ended 12/31/00, net income totaled $139.9 million, up 53.1% compared with $91.3 million in 1999. Earnings for 2000 included a gain on the sale of an asset of $14.0 million. Total revenues grew 39.4% to $1.02 billion versus $731.2 million a year earlier. Electric utility revenues rose 26.9% to $835.7 million. Revenues from diversified operations more than doubled to $169.4 million from $60.8 million. Revenues from equity in earnings of partnership grew 19.2% to $14.3 million.

PROSPECTS: IDA is benefiting from efforts to diversify its activities outside its traditional lines of business, primarily through its non-regulated operations and subsidiaries. The Company remains on target to achieve its 8.0% to 10.0% annual five-year growth goal set in 1999. Meanwhile, IDA recently announced the sale of its former wholly-owned subsidiary, Applied Power Corp., a manufacturer, supplier and distributor of solar photovoltaic systems, to Schott Corporation of Yonkers, NY. Terms of the deal were not disclosed.

BUSINESS

IDACORP, INC. (formerly Idaho Power Corp.) is a holding company formed in 1998 as the parent of Idaho Power Company, Ida-West Energy Company and IDACORP Energy Solutions, Inc. Idaho Power Co. provides electric energy to 391,171 customers in a 20,000-square-mile area of southern Idaho, eastern Oregon and northern Nevada. IDA is a combination hydro-thermal utility with 17 hydroelectric plants and part ownership in three coal-fired generating plants. In 1997, IDA expanded operations into wholesale marketing of natural gas through trading operations in Boise, Idaho and Houston, Texas. IDA's subsidiaries include Ida-West Energy Co., which develops, finances, builds, acquires and operates energy generation facilities and projects in the U.S. and Canada; IDACORP, Inc., which invests in housing programs; Applied Power Corp., an electric utility acquired in 1996; and Stellar Dynamics, a systems integrator specializing in control systems.

ANNUAL FINANCIAL DATA

	12/31/00	12/31/99	12/31/98	12/31/97	12/31/96	12/31/95	12/31/94
Earnings Per Share	**1 3.72**	**2.43**	**2.37**	**2.32**	**2.21**	**2.10**	**1.80**
Cash Flow Per Share	**6.49**	**4.97**	**4.69**	**4.23**	**4.06**	**3.89**	**3.41**
Tang. Book Val. Per Share	**21.85**	**20.02**	**19.42**	**18.93**	**18.47**	**18.15**	**17.91**
Dividends Per Share	**1.86**	**1.86**	**1.86**	**1.86**	**1.86**	**1.86**	**1.86**
Dividend Payout %	**50.0**	**76.5**	**78.5**	**80.2**	**84.2**	**88.6**	**103.3**
INCOME STATEMENT (IN MILLIONS):							
Total Revenues	1,019.4	658.3	1,122.0	748.5	578.4	545.6	543.7
Costs & Expenses	653.7	348.4	801.7	443.1	278.8	266.3	290.3
Depreciation & Amort.	104.0	95.4	87.1	72.0	69.7	67.4	60.2
Maintenance Exp.	...	42.1	41.9	48.7	42.7	36.0	43.5
Operating Income	261.7	172.5	191.2	184.7	187.2	176.0	149.7
Net Interest Inc./(Exp.)	d61.0	d61.6	d59.8	d60.3	d57.0	d55.0	d52.7
Income Taxes	70.8	45.7	44.6	46.5	52.1	48.4	34.2
Net Income	1 139.9	91.3	89.2	92.3	90.6	86.9	74.9
Cash Flow	243.9	186.8	176.3	159.1	152.9	146.3	127.7
Average Shs. Outstg. (000)	37,556	37,612	37,612	37,612	37,612	37,612	37,499
BALANCE SHEET (IN MILLIONS):							
Gross Property	2,938.4	2,819.4	2,720.9	2,659.3	2,581.5	2,503.5	2,431.7
Accumulated Depreciation	1,142.6	1,073.7	1,009.4	942.4	886.9	830.6	775.0
Net Property	1,805.0	1,745.7	1,711.5	1,716.9	1,694.6	1,672.9	1,656.6
Total Assets	4,639.3	2,637.0	2,451.6	2,405.4	2,295.3	2,241.8	2,191.8
Long-Term Obligations	864.1	821.6	815.9	703.7	738.6	672.6	693.2
Net Stockholders' Equity	925.9	858.8	836.4	818.5	801.5	815.0	806.3
Year-end Shs. Outstg. (000)	37,568	37,612	37,612	37,612	37,612	37,612	37,612
STATISTICAL RECORD:							
Operating Profit Margin %	25.7	26.2	17.0	24.7	32.4	32.3	27.5
Net Profit Margin %	13.7	13.9	7.9	12.3	15.7	15.9	13.8
Net Inc./Net Property %	7.7	5.2	5.2	5.4	5.3	5.2	4.5
Net Inc./Tot. Capital %	6.2	4.3	4.3	4.7	4.6	4.6	4.0
Return on Equity %	15.1	10.6	10.7	11.3	11.3	10.7	9.3
Accum. Depr./Gross Prop. %	38.9	38.1	37.1	35.4	34.4	33.2	31.9
Price Range	53.00-25.94	36.50-26.00	38.06-29.88	37.75-28.50	34.25-27.25	30.00-23.38	30.63-21.75
P/E Ratio	14.2-7.0	15.0-10.7	16.1-12.6	16.3-12.3	15.5-12.3	14.3-11.1	17.0-12.1
Average Yield %	4.7	6.0	5.5	5.6	6.0	7.0	7.1

Statistics are as originally reported. 1 Incl. gain of $14.0 mill. from sale of assets.

OFFICERS:
J. H. Miller, Chmn.
J. B. Packwood, Pres., C.E.O.
J. L. Keen, Sr. V.P., C.F.O.

INVESTOR CONTACT: Lawrence F. Spencer, Dir. Inv. Rel., (208) 388-2664

PRINCIPAL OFFICE: 1221 West Idaho Street, Boise, ID 83702-5627

TELEPHONE NUMBER: (208) 388-2200
FAX: (208) 388-6903
WEB: www.idacorpinc.com
NO. OF EMPLOYEES: 2,044
SHAREHOLDERS: 21,886
ANNUAL MEETING: In May
INCORPORATED: ME, May, 1915; reincorp., ID, 1915

INSTITUTIONAL HOLDINGS:
No. of Institutions: 188
Shares Held: 12,721,792
% Held: 34.0

INDUSTRY: Electric services (SIC: 4911)

TRANSFER AGENT(S): Idaho Power Co., Boise, ID

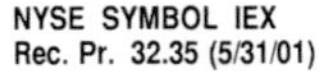

NYSE SYMBOL IEX
Rec. Pr. 32.35 (5/31/01)

IDEX CORPORATION

YIELD 1.7%
P/E RATIO 15.6

*7 YEAR PRICE SCORE 83.5 *12 MONTH PRICE SCORE 106.1

*NYSE COMPOSITE INDEX=100

INTERIM EARNINGS (Per Share):

Qtr.	Mar.	June	Sept.	Dec.
1995	0.37	0.42	0.36	0.39
1996	0.41	0.43	0.40	0.45
1997	0.45	0.50	0.48	0.48
1998	0.46	0.50	0.47	0.39
1999	0.40	0.47	0.48	0.46
2000	0.52	0.57	0.54	0.44

INTERIM DIVIDENDS (Per Share):

Amt.	Decl.	Ex.	Rec.	Pay.
0.14Q	3/28/00	4/13/00	4/17/00	4/28/00
0.14Q	6/27/00	7/13/00	7/17/00	7/31/00
0.14Q	9/26/00	10/12/00	10/16/00	10/31/00
0.14Q	12/19/00	1/11/01	1/16/01	1/31/01
0.14Q	3/27/01	4/11/01	4/16/01	4/30/01

Indicated div.: $0.56

CAPITALIZATION (12/31/00):

	($000)	(%)
Long-Term Debt	153,809	29.1
Common & Surplus	374,502	70.9
Total	528,311	100.0

RECENT DEVELOPMENTS: For the twelve months ended 12/31/00, net income increased 16.6% to $63.4 million compared with $54.4 million a year earlier. Net sales rose 7.5% to $704.3 million from $655.0 million in 1999. Pump Products sales advanced 6.1% to $395.0 million, while Dispensing Equipment sales jumped 18.0% to $166.4 million. Other Engineered Products sales rose a modest 0.9% to $145.8 million.

PROSPECTS: Near-term results could be pressured by weakening economic conditions in the U.S. manufacturing sector, specifically in the automotive, chemical processing and other industrial markets. On the other hand, the Company's diversity in products and markets, coupled with the benefits from recent acquisitions, should lead to improved results in the second half of 2001. The Company has also indicated that it will continue in its pursuit of additional acquisitions, which could lead to further gains.

BUSINESS

IDEX CORPORATION is a manufacturer of proprietary, engineered industrial products sold to customers around the world. IDEX consists of three business segments: The Pump Products Group manufactures industrial pumps, compressors and related controls for the movement of liquids, air and gases. The Dispensing Equipment Group produces engineered equipment for dispensing, metering and mixing colorants, paints, inks, dyes; refinishing equipment; and centralized lubrication systems. The Other Engineered Products Group manufactures engineered banding and clamping devices, fire fighting pumps and rescue tools.

BUSINESS LINE ANALYSIS

(12/31/2000)	Rev (%)	Inc (%)
Pump Products	55.8	55.1
Dispensing Equipment	23.5	24.3
Other Engineered Products	20.7	20.6
Total	100.0	100.0

ANNUAL FINANCIAL DATA

	12/31/00	12/31/99	12/31/98	12/31/97	12/31/96	12/31/95	12/31/94
Earnings Per Share	**2.07**	**1.81**	**1 1.81**	**2 1.78**	**1.69**	**1.53**	**1.15**
Cash Flow Per Share	**3.27**	**2.97**	**2.93**	**2.61**	**2.47**	**2.11**	**1.63**
Dividends Per Share	**0.56**	**0.56**	**0.54**	**0.48**	**0.43**	**0.37**	**...**
Dividend Payout %	**27.1**	**30.9**	**29.8**	**27.0**	**25.2**	**24.4**	**...**
INCOME STATEMENT (IN THOUSANDS):							
Total Revenues	704,276	655,041	640,131	552,163	562,551	487,336	399,502
Costs & Expenses	551,056	515,529	497,013	423,625	441,038	383,976	319,649
Depreciation & Amort.	36,704	34,835	33,575	24,943	23,208	17,122	14,315
Operating Income	116,516	104,677	109,543	103,595	98,305	86,238	65,538
Net Interest Inc./(Exp.)	d16,521	d18,020	d22,359	d18,398	d18,942	d15,948	d13,581
Income Before Income Taxes	101,026	87,225	87,663	84,504	78,854	71,043	52,516
Income Taxes	37,581	32,797	33,267	31,029	28,656	25,718	18,906
Net Income	63,445	54,428	1 54,396	2 53,475	50,198	45,325	33,610
Cash Flow	100,149	89,263	87,971	78,418	73,406	62,447	47,925
Average Shs. Outstg.	30,632	30,085	30,052	29,999	29,779	29,609	29,331
BALANCE SHEET (IN THOUSANDS):							
Cash & Cash Equivalents	8,415	2,895	2,721	11,771	5,295	5,937	6,288
Total Current Assets	232,089	213,715	195,900	197,267	201,170	185,899	151,357
Net Property	128,283	129,917	125,422	88,628	102,383	91,278	66,241
Total Assets	758,854	738,567	695,811	599,193	583,773	466,122	371,096
Total Current Liabilities	177,811	91,634	80,265	77,801	92,857	82,808	69,350
Long-Term Obligations	153,809	268,589	283,410	258,417	271,709	206,184	168,166
Net Stockholders' Equity	374,502	329,024	286,037	238,671	195,509	150,945	116,305
Net Working Capital	54,278	122,081	115,635	119,466	108,313	103,091	82,007
Year-end Shs. Outstg.	30,258	29,636	29,466	29,250	28,926	28,695	28,619
STATISTICAL RECORD:							
Operating Profit Margin %	16.5	16.0	17.1	18.8	17.5	17.7	16.4
Net Profit Margin %	9.0	8.3	8.5	9.7	8.9	9.3	8.4
Return on Equity %	16.9	16.5	19.0	22.4	25.7	30.0	28.9
Return on Assets %	8.4	7.4	7.8	8.9	8.6	9.7	9.1
Debt/Total Assets %	20.3	36.4	40.7	43.1	46.5	44.2	45.3
Price Range	36.00-22.75	34.13-21.63	38.75-19.50	36.69-23.25	27.67-19.83	29.50-18.45	19.50-15.06
P/E Ratio	17.4-11.0	18.9-11.9	21.4-10.8	20.6-13.1	16.4-11.7	19.2-12.0	17.0-13.1
Average Yield %	1.9	2.0	1.9	1.6	1.8	1.6	...

Statistics are as originally reported. Adj. for 3-for-2 stk. split, 1/97 & 1/95. 1 Bef. income from disc. ops. of $10.2 mill. & extraord. chrg. of $2.5 mill. 2 Bef. income from disc. ops. of $5.2 mill. ($0.17/sh.) 3 Bef. extraord. credit 12/31/92, $4.9 mill.; credit 12/31/91, $1.2 mill. 4 Bef. acctg. adj. chge. of $1.5 mill.

OFFICERS:
D. K. Williams, Chmn., Pres., C.E.O.
W. P. Sayatovic, Sr. V.P., Fin., C.F.O.
D. C. Lennox, V.P., Treas.

INVESTOR CONTACT: Wayne P. Sayatovic, Sr. V.P., C.F.O., (847) 498-7070

PRINCIPAL OFFICE: 630 Dundee Rd., Northbrook, IL 60062

TELEPHONE NUMBER: (847) 498-7070
FAX: (847) 498-3940
WEB: www.idexcorp.com

NO. OF EMPLOYEES: 3,900 (approx.)

SHAREHOLDERS: 4,300 (approx.)

ANNUAL MEETING: In Mar.

INCORPORATED: DE, Sept., 1987

INSTITUTIONAL HOLDINGS:
No. of Institutions: 107
Shares Held: 20,557,968
% Held: 67.7

INDUSTRY: Pumps and pumping equipment (SIC: 3561)

TRANSFER AGENT(S): Computershare Investor Services, Chicago, IL

NYSE SYMBOL IDT
Rec. Pr. 21.65 (4/30/01)

IDT CORPORATION

YIELD ...
P/E RATIO 1.0

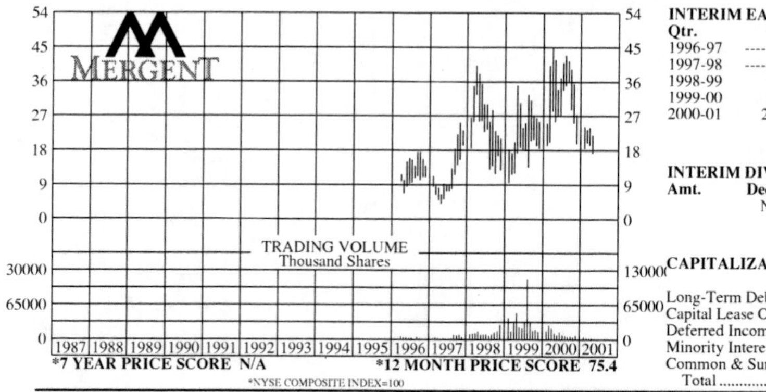

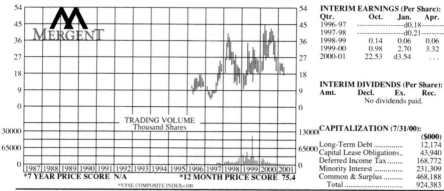

*7 YEAR PRICE SCORE N/A *12 MONTH PRICE SCORE 75.4

*NYSE COMPOSITE INDEX=100

INTERIM EARNINGS (Per Share):

Qtr.	Oct.	Jan.	Apr.	July
1996-97		d0.18		
1997-98		d0.21		
1998-99	0.14	0.06	0.06	d0.96
1999-00	0.98	2.70	3.32	d0.83
2000-01	22.53	d3.54	...	...

INTERIM DIVIDENDS (Per Share):

Amt.	Decl.	Ex.	Rec.	Pay.

No dividends paid.

CAPITALIZATION (7/31/00):

	($000)	(%)
Long-Term Debt	12,174	1.3
Capital Lease Obligations	43,940	4.8
Deferred Income Tax	168,772	18.3
Minority Interest	231,309	25.0
Common & Surplus	468,188	50.6
Total	924,383	100.0

RECENT DEVELOPMENTS: For the quarter ended 1/31/01, the Company reported a net loss of $117.1 million versus income of $101.3 million a year earlier. Results for 2000 included investment and other losses of $122.6 million, including a total of approximately $93.6 million in after-tax losses recorded in relation to the sale of Terra Networks shares, and the Company's pro-rata interest in the net loss recorded by a former subsidiary, Net2Phone. Total revenues increased 4.4% to $287.6 million from $275.5 million in the year-earlier quarter.

PROSPECTS: IDT's outlook shows promise, despite the current challenging conditions in the telecom industry. One factor is it's balance sheet, which contained cash, cash equivalents and marketable securities totaling $1.08 billion as of 1/31/01. Also, IDT is showing solid telecommunications revenue growth, due to increased prepaid calling card revenues and domestic long distance gains. IDT anticipates continued growth in its long distance business, and that this business will comprise a higher percentage of its future overall telecommunications revenues.

BUSINESS

IDT CORPORATION is a facilities-based emerging multinational carrier that provides a broad range of telecommunications services to wholesale and retail customers worldwide. IDT's telecommunications services include wholesale carrier services and retail services, including debit cards, prepaid calling cards, domestic long distance services and international retail services. In addition, IDT's Ventures division develops several innovative telecommunications and Internet-related businesses. Through its wholly-owned IDT Investments subsidiary, the Company has equity interests in other technology companies, including its former subsidiary, Net2Phone, Inc. As of 10/01/00, IDT had approximately 165 wholesale customers located in the U.S. and Europe. The Company offers long distance services to over 150,000 individual and business customers in the U.S. and worldwide. In October 2000, the Company announced plans to reconstruct into a holding company, consisting primarily of two main subsidiaries: IDT Telecom and IDT Ventures and Investments.

ANNUAL FINANCIAL DATA

	7/31/00	7/31/99	7/31/98	7/31/97	7/31/96	7/31/95	7/31/94
Earnings Per Share	**[4] 6.22**	**[3] d0.60**	**[2] d0.21**	**d0.18**	**[1] d0.85**	**d0.13**	**d0.02**
Cash Flow Per Share	**8.65**	**0.65**	**0.18**	**0.05**	**d0.78**	**d0.11**	**d0.01**
Tang. Book Val. Per Share	**8.21**	**5.11**	**4.97**	**1.10**	**1.29**	**0.06**	**0.13**
INCOME STATEMENT (IN THOUSANDS):							
Total Revenues	1,093,912	732,184	335,373	135,187	57,694	11,664	3,169
Costs & Expenses	1,219,041	687,815	327,835	133,759	72,237	13,535	3,392
Depreciation & Amort.	91,481	41,989	11,284	4,873	1,212	304	106
Operating Income	d216,611	2,380	d3,746	d3,445	d15,755	d2,175	d329
Net Interest Inc./(Exp.)	7,231	d1,229	d396	d427	345	15	23
Income Before Income Taxes	392,893	20,728	d4,038	d3,837	d15,410	d2,145	d298
Income Taxes	218,403	17,850	cr1,671	...	...	...	...
Equity Earnings/Minority Int.	53,047	3,309	d3,896	...	...	...	...
Net Income	[4] 233,826	[3] 6,186	[2] d6,263	d3,837	[1] d15,410	d2,145	d298
Cash Flow	325,307	21,878	5,021	1,036	d14,198	d1,841	d193
Average Shs. Outstg.	37,619	33,530	28,571	21,153	18,180	16,569	16,569
BALANCE SHEET (IN THOUSANDS):							
Cash & Cash Equivalents	410,799	130,773	175,592	7,674	14,894	232	1,052
Total Current Assets	641,893	292,198	227,867	29,017	30,501	2,402	2,022
Net Property	225,638	114,123	75,332	25,726	12,453	1,770	748
Total Assets	1,219,055	515,336	417,196	58,537	43,797	4,197	2,795
Total Current Liabilities	293,963	112,784	61,487	24,131	16,955	3,286	733
Long-Term Obligations	56,114	128,716	113,066	9,147	...	...	...
Net Stockholders' Equity	468,188	253,405	238,748	25,259	26,843	911	2,062
Net Working Capital	347,930	179,415	166,381	4,887	13,547	d884	1,289
Year-end Shs. Outstg.	35,929	34,013	33,105	21,812	20,841	15,666	15,666
STATISTICAL RECORD:							
Operating Profit Margin %	...	0.3	...	...	...	...	...
Net Profit Margin %	21.4	0.8	...	...	...	...	...
Return on Equity %	49.9	2.4	...	...	...	...	...
Return on Assets %	19.2	1.2	...	...	...	...	...
Debt/Total Assets %	4.6	25.0	27.1	15.6	...	...	...
Price Range	45.00-19.31	35.00-9.50	40.25-11.88	25.25-4.00	17.50-6.75	...	...
P/E Ratio	7.2-3.1	...	...	...	...	...	...

Statistics are as originally reported. [1] Excl. extraord. loss on retire. of debt of $234,000. [2] Excl. extraord. loss on retire. of debt of $132,000, but incl. non-recurr. chrgs. of $25.0 mill. related to acquired research and development. [3] Excl. extraord. loss on retire. of debt of $3.3 mill. [4] Excl. extraord. loss on retire. of debt of $3.0 mill.

OFFICERS:
H. S. Jonas, Chmn., C.E.O.
J. Courter, Vice-Chmn., Pres.
S. R. Brown, C.F.O.

INVESTOR CONTACT: Mary Jennings, Mgr., Inv. Rel., (973) 438-3124

PRINCIPAL OFFICE: 520 Broad Street, Newark, NJ 07102

TELEPHONE NUMBER: (973) 438-1000
WEB: www.idt.net

NO. OF EMPLOYEES: 1,522 (approx.)

SHAREHOLDERS: 350 (approx.)

ANNUAL MEETING: In Dec.

INCORPORATED: NY, Aug., 1990; reincorp., DE, Dec., 1995

INSTITUTIONAL HOLDINGS:
No. of Institutions: 67
Shares Held: 10,958,085
% Held: 34.0

INDUSTRY: Computer integrated systems design (SIC: 7373)

TRANSFER AGENT(S): American Stock Transfer & Trust Company, New York, NY

NYSE SYMBOL IHP
Rec. Pr. 25.50 (5/31/01)

IHOP CORP.

YIELD ...
P/E RATIO 14.6

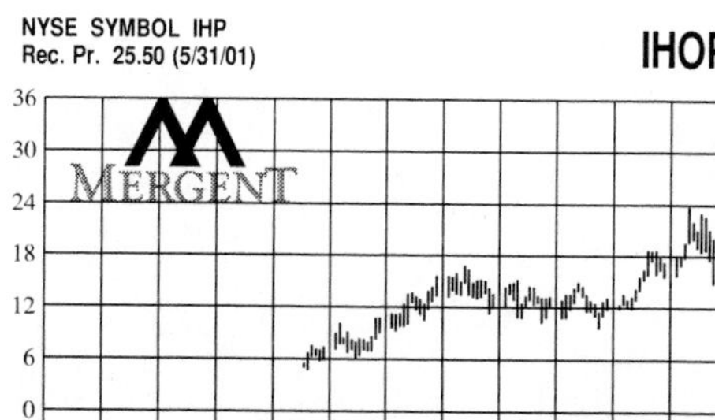

TRADING VOLUME
Thousand Shares

1987 1988 1989 1990 1991 1992 1993 1994 1995 1996 1997 1998 1999 2000 2001

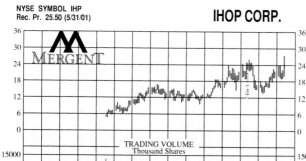

***7 YEAR PRICE SCORE 88.4** ***12 MONTH PRICE SCORE 118.0**

*NYSE COMPOSITE INDEX=100

INTERIM EARNINGS (Per Share):

Qtr.	Mar.	June	Sept.	Dec.
1996	0.16	0.23	0.28	0.31
1997	0.37	0.52	0.29	0.34
1998	0.24	0.32	0.36	0.39
1999	0.33	0.39	0.42	0.44
2000	0.36	0.41	0.50	0.48

INTERIM DIVIDENDS (Per Share):

Amt.	Decl.	Ex.	Rec.	Pay.

No dividends paid.

CAPITALIZATION (12/31/00):

	($000)	(%)
Long-Term Debt	36,363	7.1
Capital Lease Obligations	169,296	33.1
Deferred Income Tax	46,585	9.1
Common & Surplus	259,995	50.8
Total	512,239	100.0

RECENT DEVELOPMENTS: For the year ended 12/31/00, the Company reported net income of $35.3 million, up 10.0% from $32.1 million in the prior year. Total revenues advanced 11.0% to $303.2 million versus $273.2 million the year before. Sales from franchised restaurants grew 12.1% to $183.4 million. Meanwhile, Company-owned restaurant sales improved 3.7% to $72.8 million. System-wide sales increased 10.6% to $1.25 billion versus $1.13 billion a year earlier.

PROSPECTS: Revenues should benefit from new restaurant development, increased comparable-store sales and higher average sales per effective unit. During 2001, IHP plans to open as many as 75 new restaurants. IHP expects comparable store sales to grow 1.0% to 2.0% and average sales per unit to grow 2.0% to 3.0% for 2001. Separately, IHP launched the new "Any Time" advertising campaign designed to promote brand identity and showcase IHP's meals through a series of nostalgic commercials.

BUSINESS

IHOP Corp. and its subsidiaries develop, franchise and operate International House of Pancakes family restaurants. IHOP restaurants offer a diverse menu for breakfast, lunch and dinner, including 16 types of pancakes, omelettes, burgers, chicken and steak. Franchisees and area licensees are third-party operators who operate more than 90% of IHOP restaurants and actively participate in day-to-day operations. As of 12/31/00, there were 968 IHOP restaurants in the chain located in 38 states, Canada and Japan, of which 747 were operated by franchisees, 150 by licensees and 71 by the Company.

BUSINESS LINE ANALYSIS

(12/31/00)	Rev(%)	Inc(%)
Franchise Operations	60.5	71.7
Company Operations	24.0	(3.8)
Sales of Franchises & Equipment	15.5	13.9
Consolid Adjust & Other	0.0	18.2
Total	100.0	100.0

ANNUAL FINANCIAL DATA

	12/31/00	12/31/99	12/31/98	12/31/97	12/31/96	12/31/95	12/31/94
Earnings Per Share	**1.74**	**1.58**	**1.31**	**1.08**	**0.98**	[1] **0.85**	**0.80**
Cash Flow Per Share	**2.41**	**2.18**	**1.87**	**1.59**	**1.41**	**1.22**	**1.14**
Tang. Book Val. Per Share	**12.43**	**10.68**	**8.90**	**7.40**	**6.15**	**5.06**	**4.06**
INCOME STATEMENT (IN THOUSANDS):							
Total Revenues	303,244	273,235	256,208	215,458	190,096	164,323	149,994
Costs & Expenses	209,904	188,694	183,259	138,052	124,008	107,333	99,207
Depreciation & Amort.	13,562	12,310	11,271	10,029	8,279	6,918	6,382
Operating Income	79,778	72,231	61,678	67,377	57,809	50,072	44,405
Net Interest Inc./(Exp.)	d21,751	d19,391	d17,417	d14,649	d11,691	d8,873	d6,805
Income Before Income Taxes	57,460	52,236	42,805	34,286	30,751	26,701	24,984
Income Taxes	22,122	20,111	16,694	13,372	12,147	10,547	9,869
Net Income	35,338	32,125	26,111	20,914	18,604	[1] 16,154	15,115
Cash Flow	48,900	44,435	37,382	30,943	26,883	23,072	21,497
Average Shs. Outstg.	20,263	20,358	20,032	19,486	19,046	18,976	18,888
BALANCE SHEET (IN THOUSANDS):							
Cash & Cash Equivalents	7,208	4,176	8,577	5,964	8,658	3,860	2,036
Total Current Assets	51,102	47,885	40,818	40,782	41,312	27,518	21,177
Net Property	193,624	177,743	161,689	142,751	120,854	87,795	69,550
Total Assets	562,212	520,402	445,899	382,593	328,889	252,057	202,553
Total Current Liabilities	49,973	46,187	43,249	39,326	35,084	28,717	17,240
Long-Term Obligations	205,659	207,967	180,074	158,221	139,387	93,548	79,316
Net Stockholders' Equity	259,995	226,480	187,868	156,184	129,357	108,297	88,299
Net Working Capital	1,129	1,698	d2,431	1,456	6,228	d1,199	3,937
Year-end Shs. Outstg.	20,011	20,117	19,764	19,418	18,934	18,752	18,366
STATISTICAL RECORD:							
Operating Profit Margin %	26.3	26.4	24.1	31.3	30.4	30.5	29.6
Net Profit Margin %	11.7	11.8	10.2	9.7	9.8	9.8	10.1
Return on Equity %	13.6	14.2	13.9	13.4	14.4	14.9	17.1
Return on Assets %	6.3	6.2	5.9	5.5	5.7	6.4	7.5
Debt/Total Assets %	36.6	40.0	40.4	41.4	42.4	37.1	39.2
Price Range	22.63-13.63	26.00-14.94	23.75-14.75	18.69-11.81	14.94-9.63	15.25-10.25	16.88-11.25
P/E Ratio	13.0-7.8	16.5-9.5	18.2-11.3	17.4-11.0	15.3-9.9	17.9-12.1	21.1-14.1

Statistics are as originally reported. Adj. for 2-for-1 stk. split, 5/99. [1] Incl. one-time chrg. of $800,000.

OFFICERS:
R. K. Herzer, Chmn., Pres., C.E.O.
A. S. Unger, V.P., C.F.O., Treas.
D. M. Leifheit, Exec. V.P., Oper., C.O.O.

INVESTOR CONTACT: Mark D. Weisberger, V.P., Sec. & Gen. Couns., (818) 240-6055

PRINCIPAL OFFICE: 450 North Brand Boulevard, Glendale, CA 91203-2306

TELEPHONE NUMBER: (818) 240-6055
FAX: (818) 247-0694
WEB: www.ihop.com

NO. OF EMPLOYEES: 4,076 (avg.)

SHAREHOLDERS: 2,226 (approx.)

ANNUAL MEETING: In May

INCORPORATED: DE, 1976

INSTITUTIONAL HOLDINGS:
No. of Institutions: 96
Shares Held: 15,124,483
% Held: 75.1

INDUSTRY: Patent owners and lessors (SIC: 6794)

TRANSFER AGENT(S): Mellon Investor Services, South Hackensack, NJ

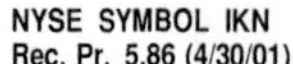
NYSE SYMBOL IKN
Rec. Pr. 5.86 (4/30/01)

IKON OFFICE SOLUTIONS, INC.

YIELD 2.7%
P/E RATIO 8.6

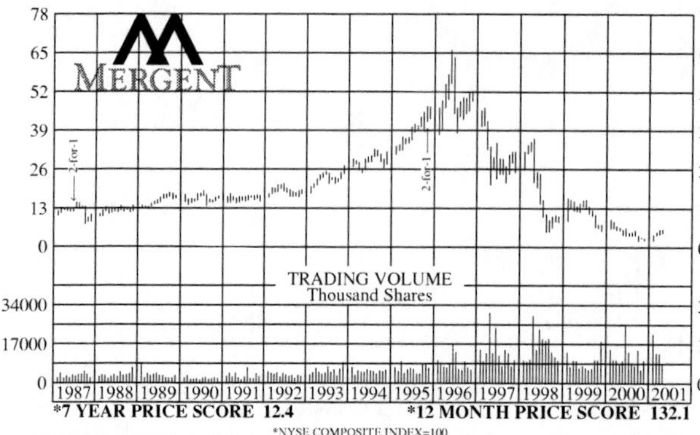

***7 YEAR PRICE SCORE 12.4** ***12 MONTH PRICE SCORE 132.1**

*NYSE COMPOSITE INDEX=100

INTERIM EARNINGS (Per Share):

Qtr.	Dec.	Mar.	June	Sept.
1997-98	0.24	0.25	d0.69	d0.49
1998-99	0.19	0.15	0.18	0.15
1999-00	d0.37	0.23	0.21	0.13
2000-01	0.11	...	...	...

INTERIM DIVIDENDS (Per Share):

Amt.	Decl.	Ex.	Rec.	Pay.
0.04Q	7/21/00	8/17/00	8/21/00	9/10/00
0.04Q	10/24/00	11/16/00	11/20/00	12/10/00
0.04Q	1/23/01	2/15/01	2/20/01	3/10/01
0.04Q	4/25/01	5/17/01	5/21/01	6/10/01

Indicated div.: $0.16 (Div. Reinv. Plan)

CAPITALIZATION (9/30/00):

	($000)	(%)
Long-Term Debt	606,861	24.6
Deferred Income Tax	415,656	16.9
Common & Surplus	1,441,092	58.5
Total	2,463,609	100.0

RECENT DEVELOPMENTS: For the quarter ended 12/31/00, IKN reported income from continuing operations of $16.2 million versus a net loss of $55.6 million in the prior-year period. Earnings for 2000 excluded a gain of $1.2 million from discontinued operations. Earnings for 1999 included a pre-tax restructuring and asset impairment charge of $105.3 million. Revenues remained relatively the same at $1.32 billion.

PROSPECTS: During 2001, IKN expects to report lower earnings compared with 2000 as it continues to focus on long-term investments. Separately, IKN announced a strategic alliance with ImageX.com®, Inc., a provider of Web-enabled design and printing services. Under the alliance, IKN's Digital Express® 2000 will be offered in conjunction with ImageX.com's customized print offering for branded office stationery and business cards.

BUSINESS

IKON OFFICE SOLUTIONS, INC. provides fully customized document-management and network solutions by offering products manufactured by a variety of vendors. IKN is comprised of three segments of product and service offerings: business services, which includes traditional analog copier and facsimile products; document services, which includes photocopying and document coding services for the legal industry, and document production; and technology services, which includes consulting and professional services for network integration and design, network support and management services, and education and training services. IKN has approximately 900 locations in the U.S., Canada, Mexico, the U.K., France, Germany, Ireland and Denmark.

ANNUAL FINANCIAL DATA

	9/30/00	9/30/99	9/30/98	9/30/97	9/30/96	[2] 9/30/95	9/30/94
Earnings Per Share	**[6] 0.18**	**[5] 0.23**	**[1] [4] d0.76**	**[3] 0.77**	**[1] 1.13**	**[1] 0.86**	**0.55**
Cash Flow Per Share	**1.49**	**1.55**	**0.74**	**1.95**	**2.07**	**1.61**	**1.45**
Tang. Book Val. Per Share	**0.87**	**0.50**	**...**	**...**	**6.67**	**5.41**	**3.85**
Dividends Per Share	**0.16**	**0.16**	**0.16**	**0.16**	**0.56**	**0.53**	**0.51**
Dividend Payout %	**88.8**	**69.5**	**...**	**20.8**	**49.6**	**61.6**	**91.8**
INCOME STATEMENT (IN MILLIONS):							
Total Revenues	5,446.9	5,522.1	5,628.7	5,128.4	4,099.8	3,091.6	7,996.1
Costs & Expenses	5,103.9	5,174.7	5,429.7	4,711.3	3,671.2	2,792.0	7,553.5
Depreciation & Amort.	195.1	196.9	202.5	156.6	118.6	87.4	96.8
Operating Income	147.9	150.6	d3.5	260.6	310.1	212.2	345.8
Net Interest Inc./(Exp.)	d69.8	d71.2	d70.7	d47.5	d37.2	d21.7	15.8
Income Before Income Taxes	81.8	79.4	d74.2	213.1	272.9	190.5	156.8
Income Taxes	55.9	45.6	8.9	90.8	108.0	75.5	86.2
Net Income	[6] 26.0	[5] 33.8	[1] [4] d83.0	[3] 122.4	[1] 164.9	[1] 115.0	70.6
Cash Flow	221.1	230.7	99.9	259.4	261.1	187.2	155.9
Average Shs. Outstg. (000)	148,327	149,003	135,145	133,261	125,856	116,474	107,458
BALANCE SHEET (IN MILLIONS):							
Cash & Cash Equivalents	170.0	33.0	1.0	21.3	46.1	66.4	53.4
Total Current Assets	2,512.5	2,233.9	2,259.4	2,125.8	1,509.2	1,132.0	1,710.5
Net Property	246.0	259.8	260.1	239.5	188.8	124.3	353.9
Total Assets	6,362.6	5,801.3	5,748.8	5,323.9	5,384.6	4,110.3	3,502.3
Total Current Liabilities	2,308.5	2,047.6	1,754.9	1,373.8	1,258.0	987.3	1,056.9
Long-Term Obligations	606.9	718.8	712.4	490.2	721.9	316.7	340.8
Net Stockholders' Equity	1,441.1	1,460.5	1,427.3	1,481.6	2,255.5	1,891.4	1,367.1
Net Working Capital	204.0	186.3	504.6	752.0	251.2	144.7	653.5
Year-end Shs. Outstg. (000)	141,698	149,218	137,015	133,304	131,556	112,064	108,896
STATISTICAL RECORD:							
Operating Profit Margin %	2.7	2.7	...	5.1	7.6	6.9	4.3
Net Profit Margin %	0.5	0.6	...	2.4	4.0	3.7	0.9
Return on Equity %	1.8	2.3	...	8.3	7.3	6.1	5.2
Return on Assets %	0.4	0.6	...	2.3	3.1	2.8	2.0
Debt/Total Assets %	9.5	12.4	12.4	9.2	13.4	7.7	9.7
Price Range	9.38-2.00	16.38-5.38	36.25-5.00	46.63-20.63	66.00-37.38	47.13-30.94	32.75-24.75
P/E Ratio	52.1-11.1	71.2-23.4	...	60.5-26.8	58.4-33.1	54.8-36.0	59.5-45.0
Average Yield %	2.8	1.5	0.8	0.5	1.1	1.4	1.8

Statistics are as originally reported. Adj. for 2-for-1 stock split, 10/95. [1] Bef. inc. from disc. ops. of $10.0 mill., 1998; d$16.5 mill., 1995; & dr$45.8 mill. reflect. spin-off of Unisource, 1996. [2] Reflects spin-off of Unisource. [3] Bef. inc. fr. disc. ops. of $20.2 mill. & $12.2 mill. extraord. chrg.; incl. transf. costs of $126.9 mill. [4] Incl. non-recurr. costs of $228.4 mill. [5] Incl. cost of $101.1 mill. fr. litigation settlement. [6] Bef. extraord. gain of $1.7 mill. & disc. oper. gain of $1.4 mill.; incl. net non-recurr. costs of $84.4 mill.

OFFICERS:
J. J. Forese, Chmn., Pres., C.E.O.
W. S. Urkiel, Sr. V.P., C.F.O.

INVESTOR CONTACT: Veronica Rosa, Investor Relations, (610) 408-7196

PRINCIPAL OFFICE: P.O. Box 834, Valley Forge, PA 19482-0834

TELEPHONE NUMBER: (610) 296-8000
FAX: (610) 644-1574
WEB: www.ikon.com

NO. OF EMPLOYEES: 39,600 (approx.)

SHAREHOLDERS: 14,440 (approx.)

ANNUAL MEETING: In Feb.

INCORPORATED: OH, Nov., 1952

INSTITUTIONAL HOLDINGS:
No. of Institutions: 106
Shares Held: 63,863,447
% Held: 45.2

INDUSTRY: Computers, peripherals & software (SIC: 5045)

TRANSFER AGENT(S): National City Bank, Cleveland, OH

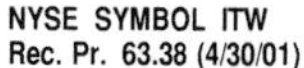

NYSE SYMBOL ITW
Rec. Pr. 63.38 (4/30/01)

ILLINOIS TOOL WORKS, INCORPORATED

YIELD 1.3%
P/E RATIO 20.1

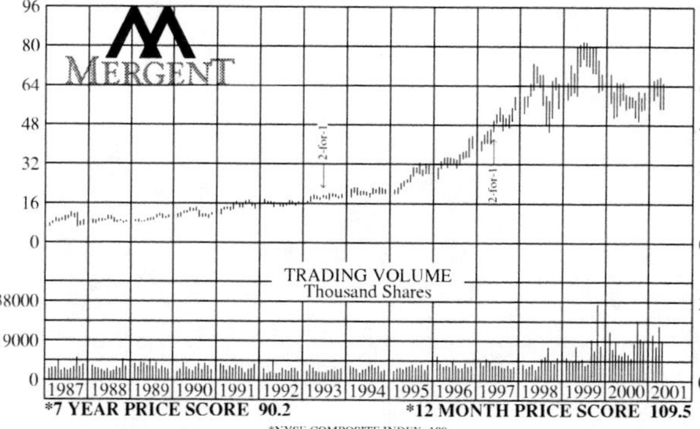

*7 YEAR PRICE SCORE 90.2 *12 MONTH PRICE SCORE 109.5
*NYSE COMPOSITE INDEX=100

INTERIM EARNINGS (Per Share):

Qtr.	Mar.	June	Sept.	Dec.
1997	0.49	0.61	0.59	0.64
1998	0.59	0.70	0.65	0.73
1999	0.65	0.79	0.74	0.59
2000	0.72	0.90	0.87	0.66

INTERIM DIVIDENDS (Per Share):

Amt.	Decl.	Ex.	Rec.	Pay.
0.18Q	5/12/00	6/28/00	6/30/00	7/21/00
0.20Q	8/11/00	9/27/00	9/30/00	10/19/00
0.20Q	10/27/00	12/27/00	12/31/00	1/26/01
0.20Q	2/16/01	3/28/01	3/31/01	4/20/01
0.20Q	5/11/01	6/27/01	6/30/01	7/20/01

Indicated div.: $0.80 (Div. Reinv. Plan)

CAPITALIZATION (12/31/00):

	($000)	(%)
Long-Term Debt	1,549,038	22.3
Common & Surplus	5,400,987	77.7
Total	6,950,025	100.0

RECENT DEVELOPMENTS: For the year ended 12/31/00, net income advanced 13.9% to $958.0 million compared with $841.1 million in 1999. Results for 1999 included Premark merger-related costs of $81.0 million. Operating revenues were $9.98 billion, up 7.0% from $9.33 billion a year earlier. The improvement in results was primarily driven by growth from acquisitions. Operating income rose 11.2% to $1.56 billion from $1.41 billion.

PROSPECTS: The Company's North American Engineered Products segment and the International Engineered Products segment should benefit from contributions from the construction and automotive businesses. Moreover, ITW's North American Specialty Systems segment and the International Specialty Systems segment should continue to benefit from contributions from the food equipment and industrial packaging businesses.

BUSINESS

ILLINOIS TOOL WORKS, INCORPORATED manufactures and markets a variety of products and systems. ITW has more than 600 operations in 43 countries. Businesses in the Engineered Products-North America segment and businesses in the Engineered Products-International segment manufacture short lead-time components and fasteners, and specialty products. Businesses in the Specialty Systems-North America segment produce longer lead-time machinery and related consumables, and specialty equipment for applications. Businesses in the Specialty Systems-International segment manufacture longer lead-time machinery and related consumables, and specialty equipment for industrial spray coating and other applications. The Leasing and Investment segment makes opportunistic investments in mortgage-related assets, leveraged and direct financing leases of equipment, properties and property developments, and affordable housing. ITW acquired Premark International, Inc. in November 1999 for $3.40 billion.

ANNUAL FINANCIAL DATA

	12/31/00	12/31/99	12/31/98	12/31/97	12/31/96	12/31/95	12/31/94
Earnings Per Share	**3.15**	**[1] 2.76**	**2.67**	**2.33**	**1.97**	**1.65**	**1.23**
Cash Flow Per Share	**4.50**	**3.89**	**3.50**	**3.07**	**2.68**	**2.29**	**1.81**
Tang. Book Val. Per Share	**9.64**	**9.27**	**8.59**	**8.14**	**6.80**	**5.94**	**5.03**
Dividends Per Share	**0.74**	**0.63**	**0.51**	**0.43**	**0.35**	**0.31**	**0.27**
Dividend Payout %	**23.5**	**22.8**	**19.1**	**18.5**	**17.8**	**18.8**	**22.0**
INCOME STATEMENT (IN MILLIONS):							
Total Revenues	9,983.6	9,333.2	5,647.9	5,220.4	4,996.7	4,152.2	3,461.3
Costs & Expenses	8,006.8	7,584.5	4,356.8	4,107.8	4,017.9	3,373.7	2,853.9
Depreciation & Amort.	413.4	343.3	211.8	185.4	178.2	151.9	132.1
Operating Income	1,563.4	1,405.4	1,079.3	927.2	800.6	626.5	475.3
Net Interest Inc./(Exp.)	d72.4	d67.5	d14.2	d19.4	d27.8	d31.6	d26.9
Income Before Income Taxes	1,478.2	1,352.7	1,059.6	924.4	770.3	623.7	450.3
Income Taxes	520.2	511.6	386.8	337.4	284.0	236.1	172.5
Net Income	958.0	[1] 841.1	672.8	587.0	486.3	387.6	277.8
Cash Flow	1,371.4	1,184.4	884.6	772.3	664.5	539.5	409.9
Average Shs. Outstg. (000)	304,414	304,649	252,443	251,760	247,556	235,978	226,774
BALANCE SHEET (IN MILLIONS):							
Cash & Cash Equivalents	151.3	233.0	93.5	185.9	137.7	116.6	76.9
Total Current Assets	3,329.1	3,272.9	1,834.5	1,858.6	1,701.1	1,532.5	1,262.9
Net Property	1,722.5	1,633.9	987.5	884.1	808.3	694.9	641.2
Total Assets	9,603.5	9,060.3	6,118.2	5,394.8	4,806.2	3,613.1	2,580.5
Total Current Liabilities	1,817.6	2,045.4	1,222.0	1,157.9	1,219.3	850.9	628.4
Long-Term Obligations	1,549.0	1,360.7	947.0	854.3	818.9	615.6	273.0
Net Stockholders' Equity	5,401.0	4,815.4	3,338.0	2,806.5	2,396.0	1,924.2	1,541.5
Net Working Capital	1,511.5	1,227.6	612.5	700.8	481.8	681.6	634.5
Year-end Shs. Outstg. (000)	302,449	300,569	250,128	249,598	247,772	236,466	227,916
STATISTICAL RECORD:							
Operating Profit Margin %	15.7	15.1	19.1	17.8	16.0	15.1	13.7
Net Profit Margin %	9.6	9.0	11.9	11.2	9.7	9.3	8.0
Return on Equity %	17.7	17.5	20.2	20.9	20.3	20.1	18.0
Return on Assets %	10.0	9.3	11.0	10.9	10.1	10.7	10.8
Debt/Total Assets %	16.1	15.0	15.5	15.8	17.0	17.0	10.6
Price Range	69.00-49.50	82.00-58.13	73.19-45.19	59.50-37.38	43.63-25.94	32.75-19.88	22.75-18.50
P/E Ratio	21.9-15.7	29.7-21.1	27.4-16.9	25.5-16.0	22.2-13.2	19.9-12.1	18.6-15.1
Average Yield %	1.2	0.9	0.9	0.9	1.0	1.2	1.3

Statistics are as originally reported. Adj. for stk. split: 2-for-1, 5/97. [1] Incl. Premark International, Inc. merger-related costs of $81.0 mill.

OFFICERS:
W. J. Farrell, Chmn., C.E.O.
F. S. Ptak, Vice-Chmn.
J. C. Kinney, Sr. V.P., C.F.O.

INVESTOR CONTACT: Investor Relations, (847) 724-7500

PRINCIPAL OFFICE: 3600 West Lake Avenue, Glenview, IL 60025-5811

TELEPHONE NUMBER: (847) 724-7500
FAX: (847) 657-4261
WEB: www.itw.com

NO. OF EMPLOYEES: 55,300 (approx.)

SHAREHOLDERS: 17,961 (approx.)

ANNUAL MEETING: In May

INCORPORATED: DE, June, 1961

INSTITUTIONAL HOLDINGS:
No. of Institutions: 515
Shares Held: 225,935,401
% Held: 74.6

INDUSTRY: Plastics products, nec (SIC: 3089)

TRANSFER AGENT(S): Computershare Investor Service, L.L.C., Chicago, IL

NYSE SYMBOL IGL
Rec. Pr. 12.00 (4/30/01)

IMC GLOBAL, INC.

YIELD 0.7%
P/E RATIO 14.3

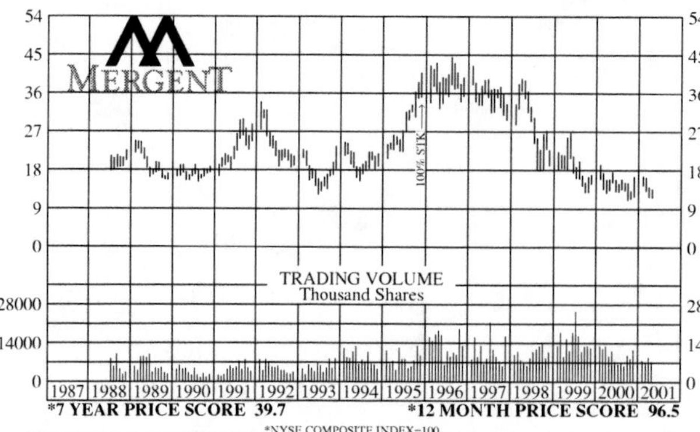

INTERIM EARNINGS (Per Share):

Qtr.	Mar.	June	Sept.	Dec.
1998	0.48	0.50	0.43	d0.90
1999	0.62	0.47	0.13	d6.54
2000	0.42	0.25	0.02	0.15

INTERIM DIVIDENDS (Per Share):

Amt.	Decl.	Ex.	Rec.	Pay.
0.08Q	4/25/00	6/13/00	6/15/00	6/30/00
0.08Q	8/22/00	9/13/00	9/15/00	9/29/00
0.08Q	10/24/00	12/13/00	12/15/00	12/31/00
0.02Q	2/28/01	3/13/01	3/15/01	3/31/01
0.02Q	5/11/01	6/13/01	6/15/01	6/30/01

Indicated div.: $0.08

CAPITALIZATION (12/31/00):

	($000)	(%)
Long-Term Debt	2,143,100	68.9
Deferred Income Tax	291,600	9.4
Common & Surplus	675,400	21.7
Total	3,110,100	100.0

RECENT DEVELOPMENTS: For the year ended 12/31/00, income from continuing operations was $84.3 million compared with a loss from continuing operations of $611.1 million in the previous year. The results for 2000 included a pre-tax restructuring credit of $1.2 million, while results for 1999 included a pre-tax restructuring charge of $175.2 million and a write-down of goodwill of $521.2 million. Net sales fell 7.9% to $2.10 billion.

PROSPECTS: IGL has made favorable progress in reshaping its operations and positioning itself to maximize the upside leverage in earnings and returns as industry fundamentals improve. Going forward, IGL's potash and phosphate businesses should continue to deliver positive margins given its low-cost producer position. IGL will look to generate several million dollars of annual savings through streamlined functions and improving productivity.

BUSINESS

IMC GLOBAL, INC. is a producer and distributor of crop nutrients to the international agricultural community and a manufacturer and distributor of animal feed ingredients to the worldwide industry. IGL mines, processes and distributes potash in the United States and Canada and is the majority joint venture partner in IMC- Agrico Company, a producer, marketer and distributor of phosphate crop nutrients and animal feed ingredients. IGL also mines, processes and distributes salt products in the United States, Canada and Europe to the following markets: water conditioning, agricultural, industrial, consumer deicing and food and road deicing salt. IGL's current operational structure consists of four continuing business units corresponding to its major product lines, as follows: IMC Phosphates, IMC Potash, IMC Salt and IMC Feed Ingredients.

ANNUAL FINANCIAL DATA

	12/31/00	12/31/99	12/31/98	[5] 12/31/97	6/30/97	6/30/96	6/30/95
Earnings Per Share	[8] 0.73	[7] d5.33	[6] 0.50	[4] 0.93	[3] 2.15	[2] 1.56	[1] 2.15
Cash Flow Per Share	2.23	d3.31	2.69	2.86	4.09	3.38	4.46
Tang. Book Val. Per Share	5.88	9.43	16.27	16.98	14.32	12.53	12.92
Dividends Per Share	0.32	0.32	0.32	0.32	0.32	0.32	0.28
Dividend Payout %	43.8	...	64.0	34.4	14.9	20.5	13.0
INCOME STATEMENT (IN MILLIONS):							
Total Revenues	2,095.9	2,369.3	2,696.2	2,988.6	2,982.0	2,981.0	1,924.0
Costs & Expenses	1,693.7	2,455.0	2,072.6	2,502.4	2,274.8	2,328.2	1,416.3
Depreciation & Amort.	171.6	232.5	251.7	183.2	184.4	168.6	134.4
Operating Income	230.6	d318.2	371.9	303.0	522.8	488.3	381.8
Net Interest Inc./(Exp.)	d112.6	d154.5	d176.0	d53.5	d51.1	d64.8	d52.2
Income Before Income Taxes	118.7	d465.8	155.7	255.7	477.4	429.9	332.7
Income Taxes	46.8	145.4	84.5	43.5	117.5	94.1	80.3
Equity Earnings/Minority Int.	12.4	0.1	d14.1	d124.4	d155.4	d191.5	d125.3
Net Income	[8] 84.3	[7] d611.1	[6] 57.1	[4] 87.8	[3] 204.5	[2] 144.3	[1] 127.1
Cash Flow	255.9	d378.6	308.8	271.0	388.9	312.9	261.5
Average Shs. Outstg. (000)	114,800	114,500	114,800	94,700	95,000	92,700	58,592
BALANCE SHEET (IN MILLIONS):							
Cash & Cash Equivalents	84.5	80.8	110.6	109.7	43.2	9.6	196.1
Total Current Assets	592.9	927.9	1,482.6	1,062.2	1,014.4	918.2	504.4
Net Property	2,345.8	3,250.7	3,697.4	2,506.0	2,409.2	2,351.3	1,868.2
Total Assets	4,261.6	5,195.9	6,456.9	4,673.9	3,611.6	3,436.8	2,693.2
Total Current Liabilities	630.5	490.9	905.1	673.1	421.8	366.4	252.0
Long-Term Obligations	2,143.1	2,518.7	2,638.7	1,235.2	694.8	736.7	515.5
Net Stockholders' Equity	675.4	1,080.1	1,860.4	1,935.7	1,339.9	1,156.3	762.9
Net Working Capital	d37.6	437.0	577.5	389.1	592.6	551.8	252.4
Year-end Shs. Outstg. (000)	114,771	114,487	114,334	113,977	93,563	92,318	59,052
STATISTICAL RECORD:							
Operating Profit Margin %	11.0	...	13.8	10.1	17.5	16.4	19.8
Net Profit Margin %	4.0	...	2.1	2.9	6.9	4.8	6.6
Return on Equity %	12.5	...	3.1	4.5	15.3	12.5	16.7
Return on Assets %	2.0	...	0.9	1.9	5.7	4.2	4.7
Price Range	19.38-11.00	27.13-12.75	39.50-17.81	42.50-29.63	42.50-29.63	44.50-32.25	40.88-20.63
P/E Ratio	26.5-15.1	...	79.0-35.6	45.7-31.9	19.8-13.8	28.5-20.7	19.0-9.6
Average Yield %	2.1	1.6	1.1	0.9	0.9	0.8	0.9

Statistics are as originally reported. [1] Bef. extraord. loss of $6.5 mill. & acctg. chrg. of $5.9 mill. [2] Incl. chrg. of $43.3 mill. [3] Bef. extraord. loss of $11.4 mill. [4] Bef. extraord. loss of $24.9 mill., but incl. chrg. of $183.7 mill. [5] For six months due to fiscal year end change [6] Bef. disc. oper. loss of $69.1 mill. and extraord. gain of $3.0 mill., but incl. chrg. of $176,100 [7] Bef. disc. oper. loss. of $155.2 mill., extraord. gain of $500,000 & acctg. chrg. of $7.5 mill. [8] Bef. disc. oper. loss of $37.6 mill., but incl. pre-tax restr. credit of $1.2 mill.

OFFICERS:
D. A. Pertz, Chmn., Pres., C.E.O.
J. B. James, Exec. V.P., C.F.O.
E. P. Dunn Jr., V.P., Treas.

INVESTOR CONTACT: David A. Prichard, V.P., Inv. Rel., (847) 205-4843

PRINCIPAL OFFICE: 100 South Saunders Road, Lake Forest, IL 60045

TELEPHONE NUMBER: (847) 739-1200
FAX: (847) 205-4805
WEB: www.imcglobal.com
NO. OF EMPLOYEES: 7,812 full-time; 21 part-time
SHAREHOLDERS: 5,957
ANNUAL MEETING: In May
INCORPORATED: DE, Jan., 1987

INSTITUTIONAL HOLDINGS:
No. of Institutions: 165
Shares Held: 91,445,605
% Held: 79.7

INDUSTRY: Phosphatic fertilizers (SIC: 2874)

TRANSFER AGENT(S): American Stock Transfer & Trust Company, New York, NY

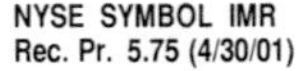

NYSE SYMBOL IMR
Rec. Pr. 5.75 (4/30/01)

IMCO RECYCLING INC.

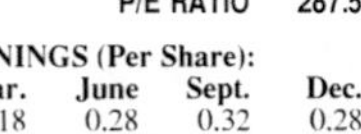

YIELD ...
P/E RATIO 287.5

MERGENT

TRADING VOLUME
Thousand Shares

1987 1988 1989 1990 1991 1992 1993 1994 1995 1996 1997 1998 1999 2000 2001

*7 YEAR PRICE SCORE 28.6 — *12 MONTH PRICE SCORE 88.2

*NYSE COMPOSITE INDEX=100

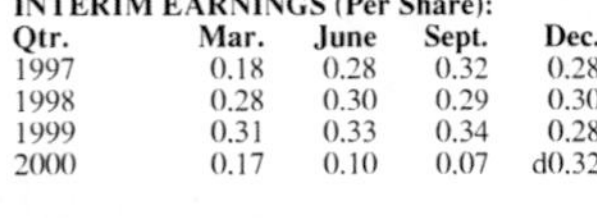

INTERIM EARNINGS (Per Share):

Qtr.	Mar.	June	Sept.	Dec.
1997	0.18	0.28	0.32	0.28
1998	0.28	0.30	0.29	0.30
1999	0.31	0.33	0.34	0.28
2000	0.17	0.10	0.07	d0.32

INTERIM DIVIDENDS (Per Share):

Amt.	Decl.	Ex.	Rec.	Pay.
0.06Q	10/21/99	12/08/99	12/10/99	12/31/99
0.06Q	2/24/00	3/15/00	3/17/00	3/31/00
0.06Q	5/11/00	6/14/00	6/16/00	6/30/00
0.06Q	8/17/00	9/13/00	9/15/00	9/29/00
0.06Q	10/19/00	12/13/00	12/15/00	12/29/00

Dividend payment suspended

CAPITALIZATION (12/31/00):

	($000)	(%)
Long-Term Debt	128,786	39.4
Deferred Income Tax	15,899	4.9
Common & Surplus	181,857	55.7
Total	326,542	100.0

RECENT DEVELOPMENTS: For the year ended 12/31/00, net income declined 98.6% to $283,000 compared with $20.8 million in 1999. Earnings for 2000 included fees on receivables sale of $1.1 million. Results for 2000 included costs of $3.8 million for the write-down of assets and related costs. Revenues were $846.9 million, up 10.7% from $764.2 million a year earlier.

PROSPECTS: IMR is making good progress in restructuring its processing network in order to raise individual plant operating rates, and in reducing costs. IMR is also recovering some of its higher natural gas costs and lowering use of that fuel through improved technology. In 2001, IMR should benefit from an 11.0% reduction in employment and lower selling, general and administrative expenses.

BUSINESS

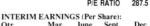

IMCO RECYCLING INC. is a recycler of aluminum and zinc, which includes used aluminum beverage can, scrap and dross (a by-product of aluminum production). IMR also processes magnesium. The Company owns and operates 21 recycling and processing plants, which have an aggregate annual melting capacity of approximately 2.9 billion pounds of aluminum and 290 million pounds of zinc, for a total annual processing capacity of more than 3.2 billion pounds. IMR also owns an aluminum recycling plant in Swansea, Wales as well as 50% of a joint venture that operates two recycling and foundry alloy plants in Germany. IMR's principal customers use aluminum recycled by the Company to produce can sheet, building construction materials or automotive products. Net sales (and operating income) for 2000 were derived from the following: aluminum, 70.7% (65.4%); and zinc, 29.3% (34.6%).

ANNUAL FINANCIAL DATA

	12/31/00	12/31/99	12/31/98	12/31/97	12/31/96	12/31/95	12/31/94
Earnings Per Share	**[3] 0.02**	**1.26**	**1.17**	**[1] 1.06**	**[2] 0.55**	**1.03**	**0.73**
Cash Flow Per Share	**1.94**	**2.89**	**2.52**	**2.30**	**1.47**	**1.80**	**1.36**
Tang. Book Val. Per Share	**4.18**	**4.85**	**4.53**	**5.72**	**6.62**	**6.13**	**5.38**
Dividends Per Share	**0.24**	**0.24**	**0.21**	**0.20**	**0.20**	**0.20**	**...**
Dividend Payout %	**N.M.**	**19.0**	**17.9**	**18.9**	**36.4**	**19.9**	**...**
INCOME STATEMENT (IN MILLIONS):							
Total Revenues	846.9	764.8	568.5	337.4	210.9	141.2	101.1
Costs & Expenses	803.5	696.7	507.9	292.6	185.8	110.9	79.2
Depreciation & Amort.	29.7	27.0	22.8	16.5	11.3	9.4	7.4
Operating Income	13.7	41.1	37.8	30.2	13.8	20.9	14.6
Net Interest Inc./(Exp.)	d16.4	d11.0	d8.4	d6.9	d2.8	d0.6	d0.9
Income Before Income Taxes	0.4	32.3	31.1	23.5	10.9	20.4	13.7
Income Taxes	cr0.4	11.2	11.3	9.1	4.1	7.9	5.2
Equity Earnings/Minority Int.	2.5	1.9	1.5	d0.1	d0.1	0.1	...
Net Income	[3] 0.3	20.8	19.6	[1] 14.1	[2] 6.7	12.5	8.5
Cash Flow	30.0	47.8	42.4	30.6	18.0	21.8	15.8
Average Shs. Outstg. (000)	15,436	16,555	16,802	13,293	12,309	12,108	11,644
BALANCE SHEET (IN MILLIONS):							
Cash & Cash Equivalents	5.0	2.6	6.1	0.4	5.1	8.7	2.9
Total Current Assets	96.7	215.3	151.8	91.7	53.3	47.9	27.9
Net Property	196.1	190.0	168.5	142.1	86.3	78.8	61.0
Total Assets	433.7	543.6	456.6	332.5	164.7	139.9	96.8
Total Current Liabilities	96.8	108.8	78.9	33.8	20.7	19.9	10.6
Long-Term Obligations	128.8	215.0	168.7	109.2	48.2	29.8	11.9
Net Stockholders' Equity	181.9	195.7	187.3	168.9	88.3	83.3	68.3
Net Working Capital	...	106.5	73.0	57.8	32.6	28.0	17.3
Year-end Shs. Outstg. (000)	15,330	16,027	16,518	16,476	11,899	11,757	11,512
STATISTICAL RECORD:							
Operating Profit Margin %	1.6	5.4	6.7	8.9	6.5	14.8	14.4
Net Profit Margin %	...	2.7	3.4	4.2	3.2	8.8	8.4
Return on Equity %	0.2	10.6	10.5	8.4	7.6	15.0	12.4
Return on Assets %	0.1	3.8	4.3	4.2	4.1	8.9	8.8
Debt/Total Assets %	29.7	39.5	37.0	32.8	29.3	21.3	12.3
Price Range	13.06-4.06	18.00-10.25	20.00-10.25	21.00-13.63	24.63-14.38	24.50-13.38	16.88-12.13
P/E Ratio	N.M.	14.3-8.1	17.1-8.8	19.8-12.9	44.8-26.1	23.8-13.0	23.1-16.6
Average Yield %	2.8	1.7	1.4	1.2	1.0	1.1	...

Statistics are as originally reported. [1] Bef. extraord. loss of $1.3 mill. recorded from early exting. of debt. [2] Incl. spec. chrg. of $2.7 mill. for the shut down of IMR's California plant. [3] Incl. $3.8 mill. chrg. for the write-down of assets and related costs & $1.1 mill. chrg. for fees on receivables sale.

OFFICERS:
D. V. Ingram, Chmn., Pres., C.E.O.
R. L. Kerr, Pres., C.O.O.
P. V. Dufour, Exec. V.P., C.F.O., Sec.
J. B. Walburg, Sr. V.P., Treas.

INVESTOR CONTACT: Paul V. Dufour, Exec. V.P., C.F.O., Sec., (972) 401-7391

PRINCIPAL OFFICE: 5215 North O'Connor Blvd., Suite 1500, Irving, TX 75039

TELEPHONE NUMBER: (972) 401-7200
FAX: (972) 401-7342
WEB: www.imcorecycle.com

NO. OF EMPLOYEES: 1,755 (avg.)

SHAREHOLDERS: 454 (record)

ANNUAL MEETING: In May

INCORPORATED: DE, Oct., 1985

INSTITUTIONAL HOLDINGS:
No. of Institutions: 50
Shares Held: 6,126,951
% Held: 39.9

INDUSTRY: Secondary nonferrous metals (SIC: 3341)

TRANSFER AGENT(S): Mellon Investor Services, L.L.C., South Hakensack, NJ

NYSE SYMBOL ICI
Rec. Pr. 25.66 (5/31/01)

IMPERIAL CHEMICAL INDUSTRIES, PLC

YIELD ...
P/E RATIO 9.6

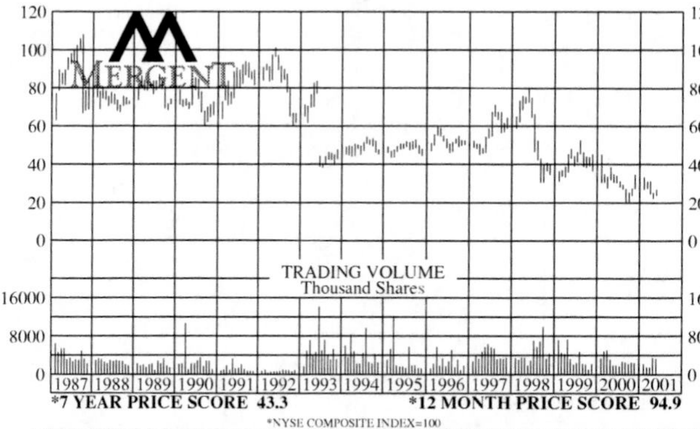

INTERIM EARNINGS (Per Share):

Qtr.	Mar.	June	Sept.	Dec.
1998	0.55	0.69	0.48	0.40
1999	0.34	0.77	0.66	0.62
2000	0.55	0.81	0.70	0.60

INTERIM DIVIDENDS (Per Share):

Amt.	Decl.	Ex.	Rec.	Pay.
0.825	...	8/18/99	8/20/99	10/12/99
1.22	...	3/08/00	3/10/00	5/02/00
0.726	...	8/16/00	8/18/00	10/12/00
1.117	...	3/07/01	3/09/01	5/02/01

CAPITALIZATION (12/31/00):

	($mill.)	(%)
Long-Term Debt	3,331.1	107.6
Minority Interest	88.1	2.8
Common & Surplus	d322.5	-10.4
Total	3,096.7	100.0

RECENT DEVELOPMENTS: For the year ended 12/31/00, income from continuing operations before goodwill and exceptional items rose 19.1% to £318.0 million ($474.8 million). Results for 2000 excluded losses totaling £518.0 million ($806.2 million) from the sale of operations and reorganization costs. Results for 1999 excluded gains totaling £314.0 million ($507.2 million). Total net sales climbed 3.8% to £6.42 billion ($9.58 billion).

PROSPECTS: ICI introduced a new strategy to focus on the requirements of industrial maintenance customers. The strategy should strengthen ICI Paints' commitment to meeting and exceeding the needs of industrial contractors and corporate customers. Separately, the sharp decrease in gross domestic product growth in the U.S. may reduce the rate of global economic activity in 2001.

BUSINESS

IMPERIAL CHEMICAL INDUSTRIES, PLC produces paints, surface coatings, and materials (acrylics, advanced materials, fibers, films and polyurethanes), explosives, industrial chemicals (basic chemicals, petrochemicals, plastics, chlorine and derivatives, fertilizers, and titanium pigments). Operations are conducted through subsidiary and associate companies located in the U.K., Europe, the Americas, Asia Pacific and a number of other countries throughout the world. Contributions to sales for 2000 were as follows: National Starch, 29.3%; Quest, 10.6%; performance specialties, 13.0%; paints, 33.3% and regional and industrial chemicals, 13.8%.

ANNUAL FINANCIAL DATA

	12/31/00	12/31/99	12/31/98	12/31/97	12/31/96	12/31/95	12/31/94
Earnings Per Share [1]	**[4] 2.63**	**[3] 2.04**	**2.12**	**[2] 2.22**	**[2] 3.29**	**[2] 4.77**	**[2] 3.96**
Cash Flow Per Share	**2.63**	**2.04**	**0.44**	**2.39**	**2.57**	**4.59**	**1.63**
Tang. Book Val. Per Share	**...**	**...**	**...**	**1.35**	**33.71**	**33.62**	**32.30**
Dividends Per Share [1]	**2.91**	**3.70**	**2.15**	**2.16**	**2.04**	**1.93**	**1.79**
Dividend Payout %	**74.1**	**181.4**	**101.4**	**97.3**	**62.0**	**40.5**	**45.2**
INCOME STATEMENT (IN MILLIONS):							
Total Revenues	9,578.2	13,444.9	15,229.0	18,570.9	17,826.1	15,947.8	14,380.8
Costs & Expenses	10,789.1	12,951.5	14,646.3	17,998.4	17,107.7	14,691.4	13,706.3
Operating Income	861.5	764.0	760.6	701.7	894.7	1,397.7	815.4
Net Interest Inc./(Exp.)	d367.3	d557.3	d545.4	d473.4	d150.8	d94.7	d137.7
Income Before Income Taxes	d129.9	812.5	481.3	869.6	843.9	1,439.6	638.5
Income Taxes	174.7	394.1	184.0	352.5	267.7	478.3	256.7
Equity Earnings/Minority Int.	113.5	87.2	24.6	d55.4	d64.4	d102.5	d175.3
Net Income	[4] 474.8	[3] 401.0	317.0	[2] 434.8	[2] 466.0	[2] 830.9	[2] 294.2
Cash Flow	d340.4	407.1	317.0	434.8	466.0	830.9	294.2
Average Shs. Outstg. (000)	722,000	723,000	726,000	727,000	725,000	724,000	723,000
BALANCE SHEET (IN MILLIONS):							
Cash & Cash Equivalents	1,000.4	1,072.6	1,350.3	2,140.5	1,526.7	2,598.2	2,752.8
Total Current Assets	5,609.6	5,794.1	7,219.7	8,479.6	7,493.1	8,089.6	7,781.2
Net Property	3,580.5	3,996.3	6,268.5	6,641.3	7,552.4	6,353.3	6,042.5
Total Assets	10,587.6	11,105.7	14,838.5	15,558.5	15,296.2	14,681.6	14,136.3
Total Current Liabilities	5,237.8	4,694.1	7,204.9	7,786.3	5,002.2	4,461.8	4,081.5
Long-Term Obligations	3,331.1	3,637.7	4,852.5	4,994.4	1,989.3	2,068.6	2,381.9
Net Stockholders' Equity	d322.5	394.1	244.8	245.1	6,110.4	6,094.0	5,846.8
Net Working Capital	371.8	1,100.0	14.8	693.3	2,490.9	3,627.8	3,699.7
Year-end Shs. Outstg. (000)	728,000	728,000	728,000	727,000	725,000	725,000	724,000
STATISTICAL RECORD:							
Operating Profit Margin %	9.0	5.6	4.9	3.8	5.0	8.7	5.6
Net Profit Margin %	5.0	3.0	2.1	2.3	2.6	5.2	2.0
Return on Equity %	...	103.3	129.5	35.6	38.0	73.9	25.9
Return on Assets %	4.5	3.6	2.1	2.8	3.0	5.6	2.1
Debt/Total Assets %	31.5	32.3	32.7	32.1	13.0	14.1	16.9
Price Range [1]	45.19-20.44	52.63-31.00	80.50-30.38	71.38-45.00	60.00-45.88	53.00-43.50	54.50-44.00
P/E Ratio	17.2-7.8	25.8-15.2	37.9-14.3	32.2-20.3	18.2-13.9	11.1-9.1	13.8-11.1
Average Yield %	8.9	8.8	3.9	3.7	3.9	4.0	3.6

Statistics are as originally reported. All figures are in U.S. dollars unless otherwise noted. Exchange rates: $1=£0.6697, 12/29/00; £0.6191, 12/31/99; £0.6088, 1/8/99; £0.5957, 12/26/97; £0.5901, 12/27/96; £0.6439, 12/29/95; £0.6390, 12/30/94. [1] Each ADR equals 4 common shares. [2] Bef. exceptional items., 1996; $140.0 mill., 1997. [3] Excl. $626.7 mill. except. gain fr. sale of bus. & disp. of assets. [4] Excl. $16.4 mill. gain fr. disp. of assets, $768.9 mill. loss fr. sale of op. & $20.9 mill. chg. fr. reorg. costs.

OFFICERS:
C. M. Smith, Chmn.
B. R. O'Neill, C.E.O.

INVESTOR CONTACT: Tim Scott, C.F.O., (202) 785-4611

PRINCIPAL OFFICE: Imperial Chemical House, Millbank, London, United Kingdom

TELEPHONE NUMBER: (212) 644-9292 (U.S. Office)
FAX: (071) 834-4444 (London)
WEB: www.ici.com
NO. OF EMPLOYEES: 45,930 (avg.)
SHAREHOLDERS: 185,805 (of record)
ANNUAL MEETING: In Apr.
INCORPORATED: GBR, Dec., 1926

INSTITUTIONAL HOLDINGS:
No. of Institutions: 66
Shares Held: 26,922,111
% Held: 14.8

INDUSTRY: Paints and allied products (SIC: 2851)

DEPOSITARY BANKS(S): J.P. Morgan Chase & Co., New York, NY

NYSE SYMBOL RX
Rec. Pr. 27.45 (4/30/01)

IMS HEALTH, INC.

YIELD 0.3%
P/E RATIO 72.2

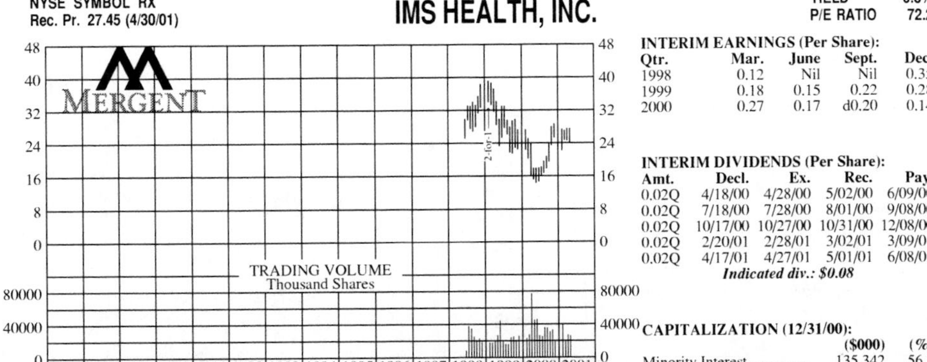

*7 YEAR PRICE SCORE N/A *12 MONTH PRICE SCORE 125.5

*NYSE COMPOSITE INDEX=100

INTERIM EARNINGS (Per Share):

Qtr.	Mar.	June	Sept.	Dec.
1998	0.12	Nil	Nil	0.35
1999	0.18	0.15	0.22	0.28
2000	0.27	0.17	d0.20	0.14

INTERIM DIVIDENDS (Per Share):

Amt.	Decl.	Ex.	Rec.	Pay.
0.02Q	4/18/00	4/28/00	5/02/00	6/09/00
0.02Q	7/18/00	7/28/00	8/01/00	9/08/00
0.02Q	10/17/00	10/27/00	10/31/00	12/08/00
0.02Q	2/20/01	2/28/01	3/02/01	3/09/01
0.02Q	4/17/01	4/27/01	5/01/01	6/08/01

Indicated div.: $0.08

CAPITALIZATION (12/31/00):

	($000)	(%)
Minority Interest	135,342	56.7
Common & Surplus	103,540	43.3
Total	238,882	100.0

RECENT DEVELOPMENTS: For the twelve months ended 12/31/00, income from continuing operations plummeted 53.6% to $116.1 million compared with income from continuing operations of $250.4 million in 1999. The 2000 and 1999 results included pre-tax non-recurring charges of $133.8 million and $34.0 million, respectively. Results for 2000 and 1999 excluded after-tax gains from discontinued operations of $4.7 million and $25.7 million, respectively. Operating revenues rose 1.9% to $1.42 billion.

PROSPECTS: Looking ahead, RX should benefit from its sharpened strategic focus, stronger demand for its core services globally and new product offerings. Moreover, the spin-off of Synavant and the divestiture of Erisco in 2000 should enable the Company to focus on its key product areas. Separately, RX announced the launch of Growth Analyser, a strategic planning tool that helps track various factors contributing to the growth or decline of a market or market share in the pharmaceutical industry.

BUSINESS

IMS HEALTH, INC. provides information applications to the pharmaceutical and healthcare industries in more than 100 countries. RX was formed as a result of its spin-off from the Cognizant Corporation on 7/1/98 and operates in three segments. The IMS segment consists of IMS, a provider of information and decision support services including market research, sales management services, sales force automation, and other professional services to pharmaceutical and healthcare industries. The CTS business segment consists of Cognizant Technology Solutions, 60.8% owned by RX as of 12/31/00, a provider of software services. The transaction business segment includes Erisco Managed Care Technologies, a supplier of software-based administrative and analytical services to the managed care industry and three small non-strategic software companies. On 7/26/99, RX completed the spin-off of the majority of its equity investment in Gartner Group Inc. On 8/31/00, RX completed the spin-off of Synavant, Inc.

ANNUAL FINANCIAL DATA

	12/31/00	12/31/99	12/31/98	12/31/97	12/31/96	12/31/95
Earnings Per Share	**[1] 0.39**	**[2] 0.78**	**[3] 0.53**	**[4] 0.70**	**[5] 0.41**	**[6] 0.12**
Cash Flow Per Share	**0.69**	**1.10**	**0.82**	**0.96**	**0.73**	**0.44**
Tang. Book Val. Per Share	...	...	**0.92**	**1.90**	**1.52**	...
Dividends Per Share	**0.08**	**0.08**	**0.03**	...	...	...
Dividend Payout %	**20.5**	**10.3**	**5.7**	...	...	...
INCOME STATEMENT (IN MILLIONS):						
Total Revenues	1,424.4	1,398.0	1,186.5	1,059.6	1,411.2	1,253.7
Costs & Expenses	1,195.2	958.5	957.7	743.3	1,058.9	1,077.9
Depreciation & Amort.	92.0	100.4	96.4	88.7	108.6	108.2
Operating Income	137.2	339.0	132.5	227.6	243.7	67.6
Net Interest Inc./(Exp.)	d13.3	0.6	18.4	10.5	8.1	9.8
Income Before Income Taxes	261.3	348.4	270.7	322.5	249.6	75.5
Income Taxes	140.4	98.1	92.2	88.4	109.8	34.2
Equity Earnings/Minority Int.	d4.8	...	...	...	...	...
Net Income	[1] 116.1	[2] 250.4	[3] 178.5	[4] 234.1	[5] 139.8	[6] 41.3
Cash Flow	208.1	350.8	274.8	322.8	248.4	149.5
Average Shs. Outstg. (000)	300,038	319,561	335,770	334,980	339,888	339,044
BALANCE SHEET (IN MILLIONS):						
Cash & Cash Equivalents	118.6	115.9	206.4	312.4	423.0	...
Total Current Assets	568.5	607.5	634.5	629.8	931.5	...
Net Property	145.4	169.2	179.2	178.5	224.6	...
Total Assets	1,243.0	1,450.8	1,731.5	1,502.1	1,793.4	...
Total Current Liabilities	827.2	723.4	550.3	397.3	634.4	...
Net Stockholders' Equity	103.5	493.7	825.3	801.6	872.6	...
Net Working Capital	d258.6	d116.0	84.2	232.5	297.1	...
Year-end Shs. Outstg. (000)	291,339	302,144	318,742	324,188	340,564	...
STATISTICAL RECORD:						
Operating Profit Margin %	9.6	24.3	11.2	21.5	17.3	5.4
Net Profit Margin %	8.2	17.9	15.0	22.1	9.9	3.3
Return on Equity %	112.2	50.7	21.6	29.2	16.0	...
Return on Assets %	9.3	17.3	10.3	15.6	7.8	...
Price Range	28.69-14.25	39.19-21.50	38.47-25.13	...	...	...
P/E Ratio	73.5-36.5	50.2-27.6	72.6-47.4	...	...	...
Average Yield %	0.4	0.3	0.1	...	...	...

Statistics are as originally reported. Adj. for stk. split: 2-for-1, 1/99 [1] Incls. one-time chrgs. of $133.8 mill., bef. inc. from disc. ops. of $4.7 mill. [2] Incls. gain of $25.3 mill.; bef. income of $25.7 mill. from disc. ops. [3] Incls. gain of $60.9 mill.; bef. income of $42.1 mill. from disc. ops. [4] Incls. gain of $24.1 mill.; bef. income of $78.2 mill. from disc. ops. [5] Incls. gain of $200,000; bef. income of $55.7 mill. from disc. ops. [6] Incls. restr. exps. of $12.8 mill. & gain from dispos. of assets of $15.1 mill., bef. disc. ops. of $47.6 mill.

OFFICERS:
D. M. Thomas, Chmn., C.E.O.
G. Pajot, Exec. V.P.
J. C. Malone, C.F.O.

INVESTOR CONTACT: Investor Relations, (203) 222-4200

PRINCIPAL OFFICE: 200 Nyala Farms, Westport, CT 06880

TELEPHONE NUMBER: (203) 222-4200
FAX: (203) 222-4201
WEB: www.imshealth.com

NO. OF EMPLOYEES: 5,000 (avg.)

SHAREHOLDERS: 6,607

ANNUAL MEETING: In May

INCORPORATED: DE, Feb., 1998

INSTITUTIONAL HOLDINGS:
No. of Institutions: 403
Shares Held: 240,993,225
% Held: 81.9

INDUSTRY: Data processing and preparation (SIC: 7374)

TRANSFER AGENT(S): Equiserve, Inc., Jersey City, NJ

NYSE SYMBOL N
Rec. Pr. 18.14 (4/30/01)

INCO LIMITED

YIELD ...
P/E RATIO 9.6

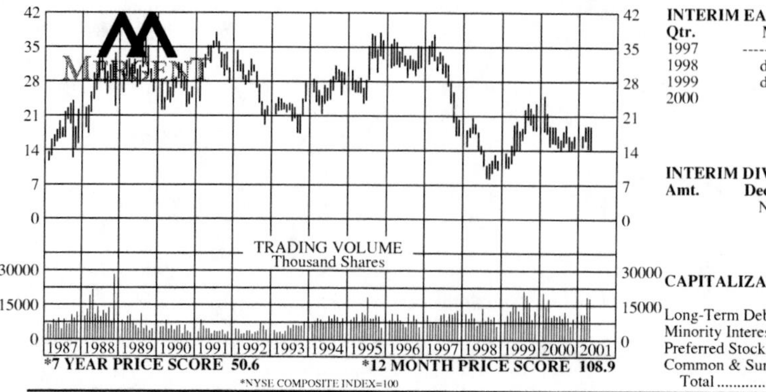

*7 YEAR PRICE SCORE 50.6 *12 MONTH PRICE SCORE 108.9
*NYSE COMPOSITE INDEX=100

INTERIM EARNINGS (Per Share):

Qtr.	Mar.	June	Sept.	Dec.
1997		d0.10		
1998	d0.32	d0.09	d0.19	d0.25
1999	d0.13	d0.05	0.04	0.12
2000	0.44	0.70	0.37	0.38

INTERIM DIVIDENDS (Per Share):

Amt.	Decl.	Ex.	Rec.	Pay.

No dividends paid.

CAPITALIZATION (12/31/00):

	($000)	(%)
Long-Term Debt	952,000	15.7
Minority Interest	334,000	5.5
Preferred Stock	472,000	7.8
Common & Surplus	4,310,000	71.0
Total	6,068,000	100.0

RECENT DEVELOPMENTS: For the year ended 12/31/00, net income skyrocketed to $400.0 million compared with income from continuing operations of $17.0 million in 1999. Net sales increased 38.1% to $2.92 billion. Sales growth was fueled by higher realized prices for and deliveries of nickel and platinum-group metals and higher realized copper prices, partially offset by higher nickel cost. Comparisons were made with restated prior-year results.

PROSPECTS: Looking ahead, the Company will strive to build upon its momentum achieved in 2000 through its strategic focus on low cost, profitable growth, aggressive cost-cutting and the expansion of its value-added specialty nickel products. The Company expects capital expenditures for 2001 to be about $300.0 million and diluted earnings to be $1.64 per share. Nickel and copper production for 2001 is estimated to be 460.0 million and 280.0 million pounds.

BUSINESS

INCO LIMITED is engaged in two principal businesses, metals and alloys and engineered products. The Company is a producer of nickel, supplying about one-third of free market demand. It is also a major producer of high-nickel and other alloys, and a manufacturer of high-performance alloy components for aerospace and other demanding industrial applications. In addition, it is an important producer of copper and cobalt, and is increasing its participation in the production of gold and other precious metals. Other business includes the Company's venture capital program, metals reclamation operations and mining equipment operations.

ANNUAL FINANCIAL DATA

	12/31/00	12/31/99	12/31/98	12/31/97	12/31/96	12/31/95	12/31/94
Earnings Per Share	**1.97**	**5 d0.02**	**4 d0.85**	**3 d0.10**	**2 1.17**	**1.82**	**1 0.15**
Cash Flow Per Share	**5.42**	**d0.22**	**d1.64**	**d0.06**	**2.09**	**3.55**	**0.28**
Tang. Book Val. Per Share	**23.71**	**22.91**	**23.41**	**24.09**	**24.29**	**13.65**	**15.08**
Dividends Per Share	...	...	**0.10**	**0.40**	**0.40**	**0.40**	**0.40**
Dividend Payout %	...	...	...	...	**34.2**	**22.0**	**266.5**
INCOME STATEMENT (IN MILLIONS):							
Total Revenues	2,917.0	2,113.0	1,766.0	2,367.0	3,139.0	3,463.0	2,502.3
Costs & Expenses	1,982.0	2,061.0	1,964.0	2,307.0	2,937.0	3,003.0	2,515.3
Depreciation & Amort.	265.0	...	...	...	...	...	...
Operating Income	670.0	52.0	d198.0	60.0	202.0	460.0	d13.0
Income Before Income Taxes	670.0	52.0	d198.0	60.0	202.0	460.0	d13.2
Income Taxes	226.0	21.0	cr94.0	30.0	...	195.0	cr48.3
Equity Earnings/Minority Int.	d44.0	d9.0	d8.0	d13.0	d34.0	d38.0	d13.4
Net Income	400.0	5 22.0	4 d112.0	3 17.0	2 168.0	227.0	1 21.7
Cash Flow	639.0	d4.0	d140.0	d17.0	146.0	215.0	17.9
Average Shs. Outstg. (000)	182,000	175,506	166,054	166,731	134,131	117,829	116,415
BALANCE SHEET (IN MILLIONS):							
Cash & Cash Equivalents	193.0	38.0	82.0	56.0	78.0	154.0	164.1
Total Current Assets	1,056.0	903.0	874.0	1,296.0	1,434.0	1,478.0	1,417.9
Net Property	8,352.0	6,250.0	6,241.0	6,252.0	6,010.0	2,507.0	2,439.4
Total Assets	9,676.0	7,369.0	7,342.0	7,772.0	7,642.0	4,693.0	4,016.2
Total Current Liabilities	691.0	580.0	560.0	606.0	629.0	712.0	498.4
Long-Term Obligations	952.0	1,154.0	1,457.0	1,495.0	1,241.0	840.0	921.5
Net Stockholders' Equity	4,782.0	4,630.0	4,358.0	4,471.0	4,514.0	1,988.0	1,822.9
Net Working Capital	365.0	323.0	314.0	690.0	805.0	766.0	919.5
Year-end Shs. Outstg. (000)	181,807	181,569	166,059	166,019	166,461	117,273	117,183
STATISTICAL RECORD:							
Operating Profit Margin %	23.0	2.5	...	2.5	6.4	13.3	...
Net Profit Margin %	13.7	1.0	...	0.7	5.4	6.6	0.9
Return on Equity %	8.4	0.5	...	0.4	3.7	11.4	1.2
Return on Assets %	4.1	0.3	...	0.2	2.2	4.8	0.5
Debt/Total Assets %	9.8	15.7	19.8	19.2	16.2	17.9	22.9
Price Range	25.13-13.94	23.69-10.38	20.69-8.25	37.63-17.00	36.75-28.75	38.00-23.50	31.25-21.38
P/E Ratio	12.8-7.1	...	...	...	31.4-24.6	20.9-12.9	208.2-142.4
Average Yield %	...	...	0.7	1.5	1.2	1.3	1.5

Statistics are as originally reported. All figures are in U.S. dollars unless otherwise noted. Div. subj. to 15% Canadian non-resident withholding tax pay. in cash or stock. 1 Incl. net chgs. of $56.0 mill. 2 Incl. a net chg. of $4.0 mill. for acctg. chg. 3 Excl. disc. opers. of $58.0 mill. & incl. a net gain of $36.0 mill. 4 Incl. a net gain of $20.0 mill. resulting fr. the sale of Inco's int. and a net chg. of $32.0 mill. assoc./w its restruct. actions; excl. inc. fr. disc. opers. of $36.0 mill. 5 Excl. disc. oper. chrge of $5.0 mill., incl. after-tax expense of $12.0 mill.

OFFICERS:
M. D. Sopko, Chmn., C.E.O.
S. M. Hand, Pres.

INVESTOR CONTACT: Sandra E. Scott, Dir., Inv. Rel., (416) 361-7758

PRINCIPAL OFFICE: 145 King Street West, Suite 1500, Toronto, Ontario, Canada

TELEPHONE NUMBER: (416) 361-7511
WEB: www.inco.com

NO. OF EMPLOYEES: 10,143

SHAREHOLDERS: 21,607

ANNUAL MEETING: In Apr.

INCORPORATED: CAN, July, 1916

INSTITUTIONAL HOLDINGS:
No. of Institutions: 195
Shares Held: 85,365,411
% Held: 46.9

INDUSTRY: Ferroalloy ores, except vanadium (SIC: 1061)

TRANSFER AGENT(S): Mellon Investor Services, New York, NY

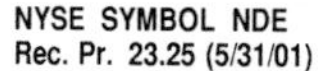

NYSE SYMBOL NDE
Rec. Pr. 23.25 (5/31/01)

INDYMAC BANCORP, INC.

YIELD ...
P/E RATIO 13.9

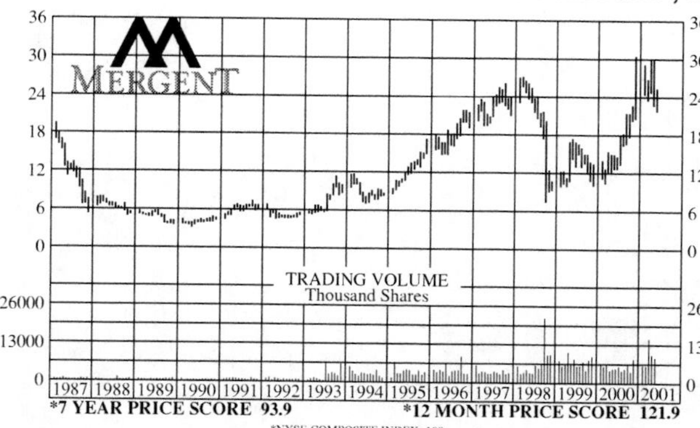

INTERIM EARNINGS (Per Share):

Qtr.	Mar.	June	Sept.	Dec.
1996	0.36	0.37	0.39	0.40
1997	0.42	0.43	d0.83	0.48
1998	0.50	0.53	0.54	d0.98
1999	0.30	0.36	0.39	0.41
2000	0.69	0.31	0.31	0.36

INTERIM DIVIDENDS (Per Share):

Amt.	Decl.	Ex.	Rec.	Pay.
0.38Q	7/21/99	7/29/99	8/02/99	9/07/99
0.60Q	10/20/99	10/28/99	11/01/99	12/06/99

Dividend Payment Suspended

CAPITALIZATION (12/31/00):

	($000)	(%)
Long-Term Debt	4,114,646	85.0
Common & Surplus	727,893	15.0
Total	4,842,539	100.0

RECENT DEVELOPMENTS: For the year ended 12/31/00, net earnings grew 74.4% to $117.9 million compared with $67.6 million in 1999. Earnings for 2000 included a non-recurring charge of $18.3 million. Total interest income rose 14.4% to 438.4 million from $383.2 million a year earlier. Net interest income declined 6.9% to $155.0 million from $166.6 million the year before. Net revenues climbed 26.3% to $337.1 million. Comparisons were made with pro forma results for 1999.

PROSPECTS: The Company made infrastructure investments in its mortgage platform to increase capacity and enhance its ability to continue to increase market share and profits in the future, particularly, as NDE moves into the current economic cycle of lower interest rates. NDE also made investments in its retail banking operation, reducing its overall funding risk and enhancing the Company's financial flexibility.

BUSINESS

INDYMAC BANCORP, INC. (formerly IndyMac Mortgage Holdings, Inc.) is an Internet bank. The Company was formed on 7/3/00 as a result of the merger of SVG Bancorp, Inc. with and into IndyMac Mortgage Holdings, Inc. This transaction created the ninth largest consumer depository institution headquartered in California. With over $5.74 billion in assets as of 12/31/00, NDE is a highly scalable consumer financial institution with an asset generation franchise predominantly over the Web. Through its branchless, technology-based infrastructure, the Company generates approximately $12.00 billion in annualized loan production.

ANNUAL FINANCIAL DATA

	12/31/00	12/31/99	12/31/98	12/31/97	12/31/96	12/31/95	12/31/94
Earnings Per Share	**1 1.69**	**1.48**	**0.48**	**1 0.43**	**1.51**	**1.25**	**0.86**
Tang. Book Val. Per Share	**11.08**	**11.02**	**10.85**	**11.11**	**9.82**	**8.56**	**7.93**
Dividends Per Share	...	**1.74**	**1.89**	**1.71**	**1.47**	**1.17**	**0.72**
Dividend Payout %	...	**117.6**	**393.7**	**397.6**	**97.3**	**93.6**	**83.7**
INCOME STATEMENT (IN MILLIONS):							
Interest Income	438.4	346.6	528.8	360.9	242.3	180.5	92.1
Total Income	636.4	350.5	512.6	369.2	244.8	181.9	93.0
Costs & Expenses	474.8	236.7	420.5	287.3	195.3	145.7	70.8
Depreciation	2.3	...	...	...	...	...	...
Income Before Income Taxes	141.1	113.8	92.0	5.9	69.0	50.0	27.8
Income Taxes	23.2	...	...	...	...	...	...
Equity Earnings/Minority Int.	...	2.1	d58.2	18.4	19.5	13.8	5.6
Net Income	1 117.9	115.9	33.8	1 24.3	69.0	50.0	27.8
Average Shs. Outstg. (000)	69,787	78,290	70,092	56,454	45,644	39,903	32,184
BALANCE SHEET (IN MILLIONS):							
Cash & Cash Equivalents	67.9	...	...	13.7	12.5	8.0	2.6
Total Real Estate Investments	...	125.4	279.7	185.7	174.4	145.5	40.0
Total Assets	5,740.2	3,726.5	4,851.2	5,849.1	3,370.5	2,643.6	1,997.6
Long-Term Obligations	4,114.6	2,864.0	200.8	281.0	323.8	224.4	202.3
Total Liabilities	5,012.3	2,899.0	4,029.0	5,145.2	2,877.6	2,280.6	1,741.6
Net Stockholders' Equity	727.9	827.5	822.1	703.9	492.9	363.0	256.0
Year-end Shs. Outstg. (000)	62,176	75,077	75,794	63,352	50,200	42,414	32,281
STATISTICAL RECORD:							
Net Inc.+Depr./Assets %	2.1	3.1	0.7	0.4	2.0	1.9	1.4
Return on Equity %	16.2	14.0	4.1	3.5	14.0	13.8	10.9
Return on Assets %	2.1	3.1	0.7	0.4	2.0	1.9	1.4
Price Range	30.44-10.38	17.44-9.81	27.19-7.38	26.13-19.38	21.88-14.75	17.25-8.50	11.75-7.00
P/E Ratio	18.0-6.1	11.8-6.6	56.6-15.4	60.7-45.0	14.5-9.8	13.8-6.8	13.7-8.1
Average Yield %	...	12.8	10.9	7.5	8.0	9.1	7.7

Statistics are as originally reported. Results through 6/30/99 reflect the operations of IndyMac Mortgage Holdings, Inc. prior to the acquisition of SVG Bancorp, Inc. on 7/3/00. 1 Incl. non-recurr. chrg. $4.6 mill., 12/00; $76.0 mill., 12/97

OFFICERS:
D. S. Loeb, Chmn.
M. W. Perry, Vice-Chmn., C.E.O.
C. L. Grahn, Exec. V.P., C.F.O.
M. K. Gerard, Sec.

INVESTOR CONTACT: Pamela Marsh, Inv. Rel., (626) 535-8465

PRINCIPAL OFFICE: 155 North Lake Avenue, Pasadena, CA 91101-7211

TELEPHONE NUMBER: (626) 535-5901
FAX: (626) 535-8203
WEB: www.indymac.com

NO. OF EMPLOYEES: 1,746

SHAREHOLDERS: 2,306

ANNUAL MEETING: In May

INCORPORATED: MD, May, 1985; reincorp., DE, March, 1987

INSTITUTIONAL HOLDINGS:
No. of Institutions: 124
Shares Held: 39,026,275
% Held: 62.8

INDUSTRY: Real estate investment trusts (SIC: 6798)

TRANSFER AGENT(S): The Bank of New York, New York, NY

NYSE SYMBOL IR
Rec. Pr. 47.00 (4/30/01)

INGERSOLL-RAND COMPANY

YIELD 1.4%
P/E RATIO 13.7

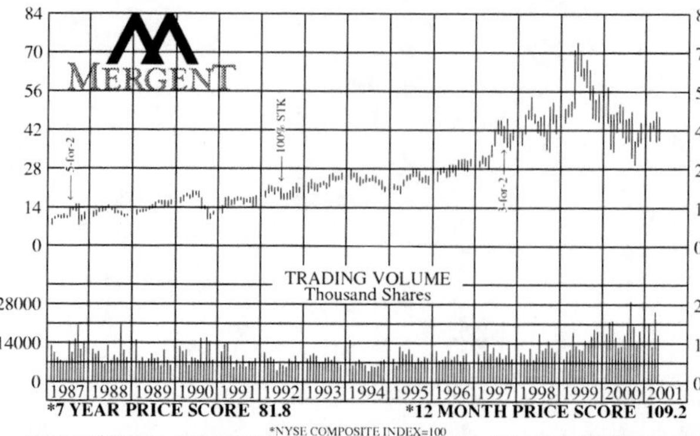

*7 YEAR PRICE SCORE 81.8 *12 MONTH PRICE SCORE 109.2

*NYSE COMPOSITE INDEX=100

INTERIM EARNINGS (Per Share):

Qtr.	Mar.	June	Sept.	Dec.
1996	0.47	0.57	0.51	0.67
1997	0.17	0.69	0.60	0.57
1998	0.60	0.85	0.72	0.91
1999	0.73	0.99	0.80	0.86
2000	0.85	1.13	0.80	0.66

INTERIM DIVIDENDS (Per Share):

Amt.	Decl.	Ex.	Rec.	Pay.
0.17Q	5/03/00	5/12/00	5/16/00	6/01/00
0.17Q	8/02/00	8/14/00	8/16/00	9/01/00
0.17Q	10/29/00	11/13/00	11/15/00	12/01/00
0.17Q	2/07/01	2/15/01	2/20/01	3/01/01
0.17Q	5/03/01	5/14/01	5/16/01	6/01/01

Indicated div.: $0.68 (Div. Reinv. Plan)

CAPITALIZATION (12/31/00):

	($000)	(%)
Long-Term Debt	1,540,100	27.8
Minority Interest	110,500	2.0
Redeemable Pfd. Stock	402,500	7.3
Common & Surplus	3,495,200	63.0
Total	5,548,300	100.0

RECENT DEVELOPMENTS: For the year ended 12/31/00, earnings from continuing operations were $546.2 million versus $563.1 million in the prior year. Results for 2000 included restructuring charges of $76.2 million. Results excluded income from discontinued operations of $123.2 million and $28.0 million for 2000 and 1999, respectively. Total revenues rose 12.4% to $8.80 billion from $7.67 billion, attributable mostly to the 6/14/00 acquisition of Hussmann International.

PROSPECTS: IR's near-term results are likely to be pressured by the negative effects of the slowing U.S. economy. Specifically, IR expects both North American auto and light-truck production declines and weaker North American heavy-duty truck and trailer markets, due to weak demand. Additionally, although full-year 2001 results should benefit from IR's corporate-wide restructuring and the acquisition of Hussmann, earnings could be negatively affected by product mix and pricing pressure in certain end markets.

BUSINESS

INGERSOLL-RAND COMPANY is a provider of security and safety, climate control, industrial productivity and infrastructure products. The climate control segment (23.0% of 2000 revenues) offers a range of temperature-control products for protecting food and other perishables. Products include Thermo King transport temperature control units and Hussmann refrigerated display cases. The industrial productivity segment (34.4%) includes a diverse group of businesses offering products and services to enhance industrial efficiency. The infrastructure segment (26.6%) supplies products and services for all types of construction projects and industrial and commercial development. The security and safety segment (16.0%) markets architectural hardware and access-control products and services for residential, commercial and institutional buildings. On 6/14/00, IR acquired Hussmann International, Inc. for about $1.70 billion. On 8/8/00, IR sold Ingersoll-Dresser Pump Company to Flowserve Corp. for $775.0 million.

ANNUAL FINANCIAL DATA

	12/31/00	12/31/99	12/31/98	12/31/97	12/31/96	12/31/95	12/31/94
Earnings Per Share	**[2] 3.36**	**[1] 3.29**	**3.08**	**2.31**	**2.22**	**1.70**	**1.33**
Cash Flow Per Share	**5.19**	**4.93**	**4.78**	**3.60**	**3.48**	**2.83**	**2.17**
Tang. Book Val. Per Share	**...**	**...**	**...**	**...**	**5.56**	**3.29**	**8.89**
Dividends Per Share	**0.68**	**0.64**	**0.60**	**0.57**	**0.52**	**0.49**	**0.48**
Dividend Payout %	**20.2**	**19.5**	**19.5**	**24.8**	**23.4**	**29.0**	**36.0**
INCOME STATEMENT (IN MILLIONS):							
Total Revenues	8,798.2	7,666.7	8,291.5	7,103.3	6,702.9	5,729.0	4,507.5
Costs & Expenses	7,386.9	6,295.0	6,964.5	6,130.7	5,816.8	5,052.6	3,997.9
Depreciation & Amort.	297.0	272.4	282.6	212.3	202.6	179.4	132.5
Operating Income	1,114.3	1,099.3	1,044.4	760.3	683.5	497.0	377.0
Net Interest Inc./(Exp.)	d253.7	d203.1	d225.8	d136.6	d119.9	d86.6	d43.8
Income Before Income Taxes	829.3	844.8	789.2	613.7	568.3	429.1	329.9
Income Taxes	283.1	299.9	280.1	233.2	210.3	158.8	118.8
Equity Earnings/Minority Int.	d39.3	d29.1	d7.4	11.5	4.1	9.3	11.4
Net Income	[2] 546.2	[1] 544.9	509.1	380.5	358.0	270.3	211.1
Cash Flow	843.2	817.3	791.7	592.8	560.6	449.7	343.7
Average Shs. Outstg. (000)	162,411	165,753	165,482	164,825	161,238	159,150	158,187
BALANCE SHEET (IN MILLIONS):							
Cash & Cash Equivalents	200.0	223.4	77.6	111.8	192.1	146.6	211.3
Total Current Assets	3,322.8	2,868.3	2,427.6	2,544.9	2,535.6	2,345.6	2,002.9
Net Property	1,528.0	1,240.2	1,347.6	1,283.2	1,145.4	1,278.4	959.3
Total Assets	10,528.5	8,400.2	8,309.5	8,415.6	5,621.6	5,563.3	3,596.9
Total Current Liabilities	3,966.6	1,738.9	1,848.8	2,327.8	1,290.2	1,329.2	1,040.1
Long-Term Obligations	1,540.1	2,113.3	2,166.0	2,528.0	1,163.8	1,304.4	315.9
Net Stockholders' Equity	3,495.2	3,083.0	2,707.5	2,341.4	2,090.8	1,795.5	1,531.3
Net Working Capital	d643.8	1,129.4	578.8	217.1	1,245.4	1,016.4	962.8
Year-end Shs. Outstg. (000)	160,567	163,129	164,389	164,825	164,223	164,558	158,244
STATISTICAL RECORD:							
Operating Profit Margin %	12.7	14.3	12.6	10.7	10.2	8.7	8.4
Net Profit Margin %	6.2	7.1	6.1	5.4	5.3	4.7	4.7
Return on Equity %	15.6	17.7	18.8	16.3	17.1	15.1	13.8
Return on Assets %	5.2	6.5	6.1	4.5	6.4	4.9	5.9
Debt/Total Assets %	14.6	25.2	26.1	30.0	20.7	23.4	8.8
Price Range	57.75-29.50	73.81-44.63	54.00-34.00	46.25-27.83	31.75-23.42	28.25-18.92	27.75-19.67
P/E Ratio	17.2-8.8	22.4-13.6	17.5-11.0	20.0-12.0	14.3-10.5	16.6-11.1	20.8-14.8
Average Yield %	1.6	1.1	1.4	1.5	1.9	2.1	2.0

Statistics are as originally reported. Adj. for 3-for-2 stk. split, 9/97 [1] Bef. inc. fr. disc. oper. of $46.2 mill. [2] Incls. restruct. chrgs. of $76.2 mill.; bef. inc. fr. disc. oper. of $123.2 mill. ($0.76/sh.)

OFFICERS:
H. L. Henkel, Chmn., Pres., C.E.O.
D. W. Devonshire, Exec. V.P., C.F.O.
P. Nachtigal, Sr. V.P., Gen. Couns.

INVESTOR CONTACT: Joseph P. Fimbianti, (201) 573-3113

PRINCIPAL OFFICE: 200 Chestnut Ridge Rd., Woodcliff Lake, NJ 07675

TELEPHONE NUMBER: (201) 573-0123
FAX: (201) 573-3168
WEB: www.ingersoll-rand.com

NO. OF EMPLOYEES: 50,855

SHAREHOLDERS: 11,066

ANNUAL MEETING: In May

INCORPORATED: NJ, 1905

INSTITUTIONAL HOLDINGS:
No. of Institutions: 398
Shares Held: 119,035,467
% Held: 74.3

INDUSTRY: General industrial machinery, nec (SIC: 3569)

TRANSFER AGENT(S): The Bank of New York, New York, NY

NYSE SYMBOL IM
Rec. Pr. 14.48 (4/30/01)

INGRAM MICRO INC.

YIELD ...
P/E RATIO 9.5

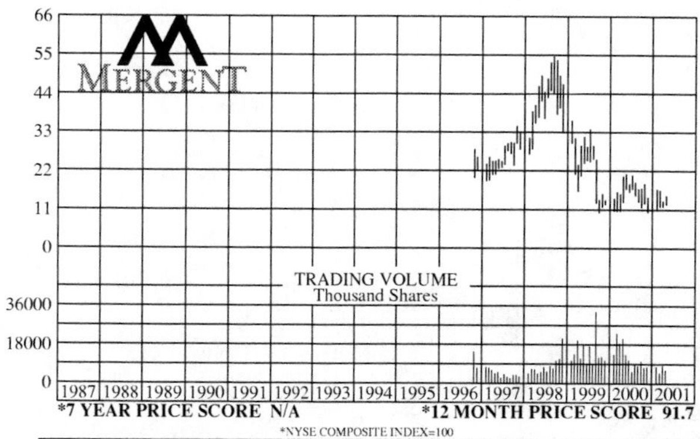

INTERIM EARNINGS (Per Share):

Qtr.	Apr.	July	Oct.	Jan.
1997-98	0.28	0.27	0.30	0.47
1998-99	0.38	0.37	0.40	0.49
1999-00	0.26	0.34	0.11	0.51
2000-01	0.65	0.22	0.26	0.39

INTERIM DIVIDENDS (Per Share):

Amt.	Decl.	Ex.	Rec.	Pay.

No dividends paid.

CAPITALIZATION (12/30/00):

	($000)	(%)
Long-Term Debt	502,844	21.2
Common & Surplus	1,874,392	78.8
Total	2,377,236	100.0

RECENT DEVELOPMENTS: For the year ended 12/30/00, income before extraordinary items rose 24.6% to $223.8 million compared with $179.6 million in the prior year. Results for fiscal 2000 and fiscal 1999 excluded after-tax extraordinary gains of $1.5 million and $2.4 million, respectively, from the repurchase of debentures. Results for fiscal 1999 also included one-time reorganization costs of $20.3 million. Net sales climbed 9.4% to $30.72 billion from $28.07 billion in the prior year.

PROSPECTS: The Company is cautious about the economic outlook and its effect on technology spending. The Company anticipates a significant slowdown in demand in the U.S. technology market and expects sales to decrease. As a result, the Company will focus on improving operating efficiencies while maintaining recent increases in gross margins. Meanwhile, the Company is targeting its product and service development efforts on emerging technology markets.

BUSINESS

INGRAM MICRO INC. is a worldwide distributor of information technology products and services. IM markets computer hardware, networking equipment, and software products to over 175,000 reseller customers in more than 100 countries. IM also provides logistics and fulfillment services to vendor and reseller customers. IM offers one-stop shopping to its reseller customers through a broad offering of 280,000 products, including desktop and notebook personal computers, servers, and workstations; mass storage devices; CD-ROM drives; monitors; printers; scanners; and modems. IM also provides a range of outsourcing programs, including tailored financing programs, channel assembly, systems configuration, and marketing programs. IM was spun off from Ingram Industries Inc. in 11/96.

ANNUAL FINANCIAL DATA

	12/30/00	1/1/00	1/2/99	1/3/98	12/28/96	12/30/95	12/31/94
Earnings Per Share	**[2] 1.51**	**[1] 1.21**	**1.64**	**1.32**	**0.88**	**0.69**	**0.52**
Cash Flow Per Share	**2.24**	**1.88**	**2.09**	**1.65**	**1.35**	**0.90**	**0.68**
Tang. Book Val. Per Share	**9.87**	**10.46**	**8.22**	**6.53**	**5.96**	**2.56**	**1.71**
INCOME STATEMENT (IN MILLIONS):							
Total Revenues	30,715.1	28,068.6	22,034.0	16,581.5	12,023.5	8,616.9	5,830.2
Costs & Expenses	30,253.2	27,771.0	21,479.5	16,157.1	11,739.8	8,404.6	5,671.2
Depreciation & Amort.	108.5	97.6	67.9	47.8	36.2	25.4	18.7
Operating Income	353.4	200.0	486.6	376.6	247.5	186.9	140.3
Net Interest Inc./(Exp.)	d80.2	d97.4	d66.5	d34.0	d47.9	d42.6	d32.0
Income Before Income Taxes	362.5	290.5	406.9	326.5	196.8	134.6	100.7
Income Taxes	138.8	110.9	161.7	131.5	84.9	53.1	39.6
Equity Earnings/Minority Int.	...	...	...	d1.4	d1.2	2.8	2.2
Net Income	[2] 223.8	[1] 179.6	245.2	193.6	110.7	84.3	63.3
Cash Flow	332.3	277.2	313.1	241.5	146.8	109.7	82.0
Average Shs. Outstg. (000)	148,641	147,785	149,538	146,308	109,044	121,407	121,407
BALANCE SHEET (IN MILLIONS):							
Cash & Cash Equivalents	203.5	270.5	96.7	92.2	48.3	56.9	58.4
Total Current Assets	5,770.1	6,968.9	6,031.6	4,446.0	3,155.3	2,799.6	1,868.9
Net Property	350.8	316.6	254.7	215.1	161.2	89.1	58.3
Total Assets	6,609.0	8,271.9	6,733.4	4,932.2	3,366.9	2,940.9	1,974.3
Total Current Liabilities	4,118.0	4,670.6	3,599.7	2,729.4	2,234.8	1,780.0	1,205.8
Long-Term Obligations	502.8	1,317.1	1,681.5	1,119.3	280.1	844.2	541.6
Net Stockholders' Equity	1,874.4	1,966.8	1,399.3	1,038.2	825.2	310.8	221.3
Net Working Capital	1,652.1	2,298.3	2,431.9	1,716.6	920.5	1,019.6	663.0
Year-end Shs. Outstg. (000)	146,208	144,493	141,980	137,081	134,091	109,814	109,814
STATISTICAL RECORD:							
Operating Profit Margin %	1.2	0.7	2.2	2.3	2.1	2.2	2.4
Net Profit Margin %	0.7	0.6	1.1	1.2	0.9	1.0	1.1
Return on Equity %	11.9	9.1	17.5	18.7	13.4	27.1	28.6
Return on Assets %	3.4	2.2	3.6	3.9	3.3	2.9	3.2
Debt/Total Assets %	7.6	15.9	25.0	22.7	8.3	28.7	27.4
Price Range	21.13-10.19	36.31-10.00	54.63-26.63	34.75-19.00	28.13-20.00	...	...
P/E Ratio	14.0-6.7	30.0-8.3	33.3-16.2	26.3-14.4	32.0-22.7	...	...

Statistics are as originally reported. [1] Excl. $13.0 mill. net tax reorg. costs and $3.8 mill. net extraord. gain. [2] Excl. $1.4 mill. net extraord. gain fr. repurchase of debentures.

OFFICERS:
K. B. Foster, Chmn., Pres., C.E.O.
M. J. Grainger, Exec. V.P., C.F.O.
J. F. Ricketts, V.P., Treas.

INVESTOR CONTACT: Investor Relations, (714) 382-8282

PRINCIPAL OFFICE: 1600 E. St. Andrew Place, Santa Ana, CA 92705

TELEPHONE NUMBER: (714) 566-1000
FAX: (714) 566-7604
WEB: www.ingrammicro.com

NO. OF EMPLOYEES: 16,500 (approx.)

SHAREHOLDERS: 639 (cl. A com.); 123 (cl. B com.); 28,000 (approx. beneficial)

ANNUAL MEETING: In May

INCORPORATED: DE, Apr., 1996

INSTITUTIONAL HOLDINGS:
No. of Institutions: 106
Shares Held: 46,012,754
% Held: 30.1

INDUSTRY: Computers, peripherals & software (SIC: 5045)

TRANSFER AGENT(S): First Chicago Trust Company of New York, Jersey City, NJ

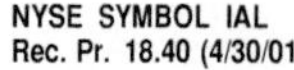

NYSE SYMBOL IAL
Rec. Pr. 18.40 (4/30/01)

INTERNATIONAL ALUMINUM CORPORATION

YIELD	6.5%
P/E RATIO	24.2

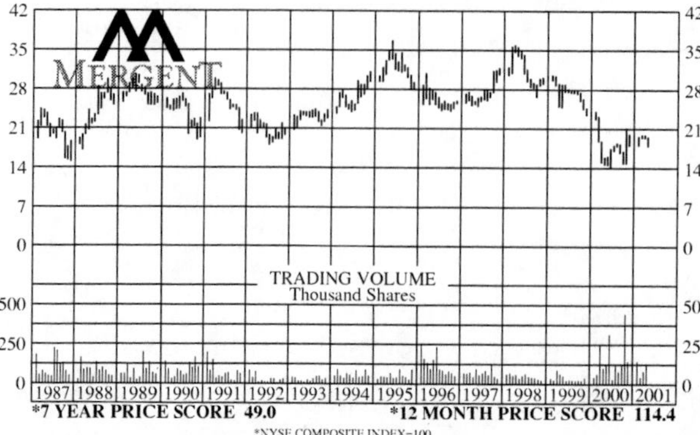

INTERIM EARNINGS (Per Share):

Qtr.	Sept.	Dec.	Mar.	June
1996-97	0.31	0.30	0.21	0.57
1997-98	0.63	0.90	0.53	0.76
1998-99	0.79	0.65	0.43	0.53
1999-00	0.46	d0.16	d0.29	0.28
2000-01	0.36	0.41	...	...

INTERIM DIVIDENDS (Per Share):

Amt.	Decl.	Ex.	Rec.	Pay.
0.30Q	5/11/00	6/16/00	6/20/00	7/10/00
0.30Q	8/22/00	9/18/00	9/20/00	10/10/00
0.30Q	10/26/00	12/18/00	12/20/00	1/10/01
0.30Q	2/13/01	3/16/01	3/20/01	4/10/01
0.30Q	5/11/01	6/18/01	6/20/01	7/10/01

Indicated div.: $1.20

CAPITALIZATION (6/30/00):

	($000)	(%)
Deferred Income Tax	4,585	3.6
Common & Surplus	124,326	96.4
Total	128,911	100.0

RECENT DEVELOPMENTS: For the quarter ended 12/31/00, net income was $1.7 million compared with a loss of $672,000 from continuing operations in the equivalent 1999 quarter. Net sales were $52.5 million, up 2.6% from $51.1 million a year earlier. The increase was mainly due to higher Commercial Products group sales, which increased 9.4% to $29.2 million. Commercial Products group operating income increased 109.2% to $3.4 million.

PROSPECTS: IAL should continue to benefit from higher sales for the Commercial Products group, which is recovering from raw material supply problems incurred in 2000. However, operating results may be impeded by the Aluminum Extrusion group, which is still in a recovery cycle as a result of severe operational problems. Results for this group should be strengthened by lower labor and overhead expenses despite of escalating energy costs.

BUSINESS

INTERNATIONAL ALUMINUM CORPORATION is an integrated building products manufacturer of diversified lines of aluminum, vinyl and wood products. Operations are conducted through fourteen North American subsidiaries. IAL produces commercial products such as curtain walls, window walls, store front framing, entrance doors and frames, interior officefronts, office partitions and interior doors and frames for the commercial building and tenant improvement markets. IAL's residential products include lines of windows and patio doors manufactured from vinyl, aluminum or wood in addition to aluminum tub and shower enclosures and wardrobe mirror doors, for the residential building and remodeling markets. Aluminum extrusions products consist of mill finish, anodized, painted and fabricated aluminum extrusions. In December 1999, the Company sold its glass operations.

REVENUES

(6/30/2000)	($000)	(%)
Commercial	108,947	40.4
Residential	61,287	22.8
Aluminum Extrusion	99,271	36.8
Total	269,505	100.0

ANNUAL FINANCIAL DATA

	6/30/00	6/30/99	6/30/98	6/30/97	6/30/96	6/30/95	6/30/94
Earnings Per Share	**0.29**	**[4] 2.41**	**[3] 2.82**	**[2] 1.39**	**1.78**	**3.18**	**[1] 1.74**
Cash Flow Per Share	**1.97**	**3.92**	**4.20**	**2.71**	**3.01**	**4.31**	**2.85**
Tang. Book Val. Per Share	**27.04**	**27.72**	**26.50**	**25.30**	**26.33**	**25.62**	**23.27**
Dividends Per Share	**1.20**	**1.20**	**1.20**	**1.00**	**1.00**	**1.00**	**1.00**
Dividend Payout %	**413.7**	**49.8**	**42.6**	**71.9**	**56.2**	**31.4**	**57.5**
INCOME STATEMENT (IN THOUSANDS):							
Total Revenues	215,547	244,606	225,789	224,026	215,573	210,906	174,773
Costs & Expenses	206,042	221,807	202,050	208,285	197,804	184,079	158,949
Depreciation & Amort.	7,156	6,503	5,956	5,596	5,204	4,793	4,696
Operating Income	2,349	16,296	17,783	10,145	12,565	22,034	11,128
Net Interest Inc./(Exp.)	d425	83	264	83	202	488	377
Income Before Income Taxes	1,924	16,379	19,282	10,228	12,767	22,522	11,505
Income Taxes	670	6,040	7,160	4,290	5,170	9,020	4,140
Net Income	1,254	[4] 10,339	[3] 12,122	[2] 5,938	7,597	13,502	[1] 7,365
Cash Flow	8,410	16,842	18,078	11,534	12,801	18,295	12,061
Average Shs. Outstg.	4,277	4,296	4,305	4,263	4,257	4,240	4,227
BALANCE SHEET (IN THOUSANDS):							
Cash & Cash Equivalents	1,678	2,269	14,320	6,485	13,230	5,763	15,700
Total Current Assets	89,260	89,617	91,653	88,259	92,195	87,291	83,117
Net Property	55,694	54,316	45,376	45,964	44,942	44,845	39,788
Total Assets	154,585	153,693	147,298	145,041	141,843	138,104	129,030
Total Current Liabilities	25,674	20,587	19,483	22,120	20,299	18,896	19,665
Long-Term Obligations	...	...	...	...	...	542	1,103
Net Stockholders' Equity	124,326	128,701	123,449	118,240	116,882	113,771	103,435
Net Working Capital	63,586	69,030	72,170	66,139	71,896	68,395	63,452
Year-end Shs. Outstg.	4,245	4,290	4,291	4,267	4,260	4,252	4,231
STATISTICAL RECORD:							
Operating Profit Margin %	1.1	6.7	7.9	4.5	5.8	10.4	6.4
Net Profit Margin %	0.6	4.2	5.4	2.7	3.5	6.4	4.2
Return on Equity %	1.0	8.0	9.8	5.0	6.5	11.9	7.1
Return on Assets %	0.8	6.7	8.2	4.1	5.4	9.8	5.7
Debt/Total Assets %	...	...	...	...	...	0.4	0.9
Price Range	24.13-14.00	30.63-23.38	36.00-26.56	31.94-24.88	31.00-24.00	36.75-27.88	31.25-23.63
P/E Ratio	83.2-48.3	12.7-9.7	12.8-9.4	23.0-17.9	17.4-13.5	11.6-8.8	18.0-13.6
Average Yield %	6.3	4.4	3.8	3.5	3.6	3.1	3.6

Statistics are as originally reported. [1] Bef. a credit of $1.4 mill. fr. acctg. changes. [2] Incl. net chrg. of $1.1 mill. for restruct. & asset write-downs. [3] Incl. $1.2 mill. gain on sale of foreign subsidiary. [4] Excl. a loss from discont. oper. of $52,000 and a gain of $377,000 on the sale of discont. oper.

OFFICERS:
C. C. Vanderstar, Chmn., C.E.O.
D. C. Treinen, Pres., C.O.O., Sec.
M. K. Fogelman, Sr. V.P., C.F.O.
M. J. Norring, Contr., C.A.O.

INVESTOR CONTACT: Investor Relations, (323) 264-1670

PRINCIPAL OFFICE: 767 Monterey Pass Rd., Monterey Park, CA 91754

TELEPHONE NUMBER: (323) 264-1670
FAX: (323) 266-3838
WEB: www.intlalum.com

NO. OF EMPLOYEES: 1,700 (approx.)

SHAREHOLDERS: 400 (approx.)

ANNUAL MEETING: In Oct.

INCORPORATED: CA, Sept., 1963

INSTITUTIONAL HOLDINGS:
No. of Institutions: 12
Shares Held: 928,760
% Held: 21.9

INDUSTRY: Metal doors, sash, and trim (SIC: 3442)

TRANSFER AGENT(S): Continental Stock Transfer & Trust Company, New York, NY

NYSE SYMBOL IBM
Rec. Pr. 115.14 (4/30/01)

INTERNATIONAL BUSINESS MACHINES CORPORATION

YIELD 0.5%
P/E RATIO 25.9

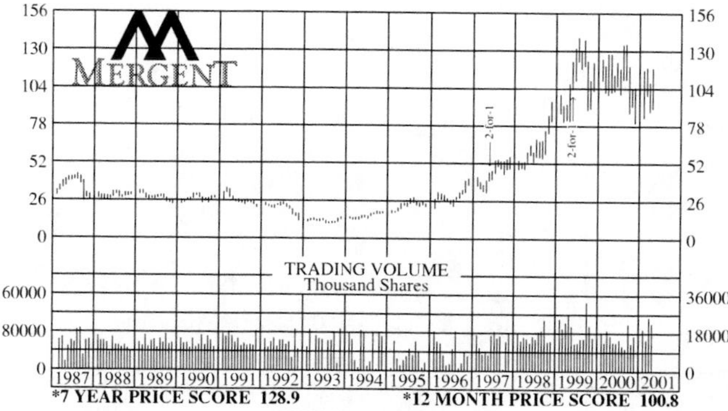

MERGENT

TRADING VOLUME
Thousand Shares

1987 1988 1989 1990 1991 1992 1993 1994 1995 1996 1997 1998 1999 2000 2001

2-for-1 2-for-1

*7 YEAR PRICE SCORE 128.9 *12 MONTH PRICE SCORE 100.8

*NYSE COMPOSITE INDEX=100

INTERIM EARNINGS (Per Share):

Qtr.	Mar.	June	Sept.	Dec.
1997	0.60	0.73	0.69	1.06
1998	0.53	0.75	0.78	1.24
1999	0.78	1.28	0.93	1.12
2000	0.83	1.06	1.08	1.48

INTERIM DIVIDENDS (Per Share):

Amt.	Decl.	Ex.	Rec.	Pay.
0.13Q	7/25/00	8/08/00	8/10/00	9/09/00
0.13Q	10/31/00	11/08/00	11/10/00	12/09/00
0.13Q	1/31/01	2/07/01	2/09/01	3/10/01
0.14Q	4/24/01	5/08/01	5/10/01	6/09/01

Indicated div.: $0.56 (Div. Reinv. Plan)

CAPITALIZATION (12/31/00):

	($000)	(%)
Long-Term Debt	18,371,000	47.1
Preferred Stock	247,000	0.6
Common & Surplus	20,377,000	52.3
Total	38,995,000	100.0

RECENT DEVELOPMENTS: For the year ended 12/31/00, net income rose 4.9% to $8.09 billion versus $7.71 billion in 1999. Results for 1999 included a net unusual after-tax gain of $750.0 million. Total revenues were $88.40 billion, up 1.0% from $87.55 billion in the prior year. Revenues from the Americas decreased 1.0% to $38.60 billion, while revenues from Europe, the Middle East and Africa fell 5.0% to $24.30 billion. Asia-Pacific revenues grew 16.0% to $17.70 billion.

PROSPECTS: Despite an uncertain economic environment, the Company's broad portfolio should position it well relative to its competitors. Moreover, the Company's large businesses in Asia and Europe should temper the effect of short-term distractions in the U.S. Separately, IBM plans to establish a consulting practice within its Global Services segment in an effort to expand into the life sciences marketplace.

BUSINESS

INTERNATIONAL BUSINESS MACHINES CORPORATION is in the business of providing customer solutions through the use of advanced information technologies. IBM operates primarily in the single industry segment that creates value by offering a variety of solutions that include, either singularly or in some combination, services, software, systems, products, financing and technologies. Products and services include servers, personal systems, storage and other peripherals, OEM hardware, services, software, maintenance, and financing. On 11/12/99, IBM acquired TheGift.com, Inc., an on-line retailer of specialty gift products. The Company completed the sale of its Floral Works, Inc. to Eaglestone Partners and the management of Floral Works on 1/12/00. Revenues for 2000 were derived: hardware, 42.7%; services, 37.5%; software, 14.3%; financing, 3.9%; and enterprise investments and other, 1.6%.

ANNUAL FINANCIAL DATA

	12/31/00	12/31/99	12/31/98	12/31/97	12/31/96	[2] 12/31/95	12/31/94
Earnings Per Share	4.44	[4] 4.12	3.29	3.01	[3] 2.56	[1] 1.81	1.26
Cash Flow Per Share	7.21	7.63	5.89	5.48	4.93	4.27	3.95
Tang. Book Val. Per Share	11.56	10.86	10.04	9.68	9.81	9.01	8.24
Dividends Per Share	0.51	0.47	0.43	0.39	0.33	0.25	0.25
Dividend Payout %	11.5	11.4	13.1	12.9	12.7	13.8	19.9
INCOME STATEMENT (IN MILLIONS):							
Total Revenues	88,396.0	87,548.0	81,667.0	78,508.0	75,947.0	71,940.0	64,052.0
Costs & Expenses	71,767.0	69,036.0	67,511.0	64,409.0	62,339.0	58,747.0	52,752.0
Depreciation & Amort.	4,995.0	6,585.0	4,992.0	5,001.0	5,012.0	5,602.0	6,295.0
Operating Income	11,634.0	11,927.0	9,164.0	9,098.0	8,596.0	7,591.0	5,005.0
Net Interest Inc./(Exp.)	d717.0	d727.0	d713.0	d728.0	d716.0	d725.0	d1,227.0
Income Before Income Taxes	11,534.0	11,757.0	9,040.0	9,027.0	8,587.0	7,813.0	5,155.0
Income Taxes	3,441.0	4,045.0	2,712.0	2,934.0	3,158.0	3,635.0	2,134.0
Net Income	8,093.0	[4] 7,712.0	6,328.0	6,093.0	[3] 5,429.0	[1] 4,178.0	3,021.0
Cash Flow	13,068.0	14,277.0	11,300.0	11,074.0	10,421.0	9,718.0	9,232.0
Average Shs. Outstg. (000)	1,812,118	1,871,074	1,920,000	2,022,000	2,112,000	2,276,000	2,340,000
BALANCE SHEET (IN MILLIONS):							
Cash & Cash Equivalents	3,722.0	5,831.0	5,768.0	7,553.0	8,137.0	7,701.0	10,554.0
Total Current Assets	43,880.0	43,155.0	42,360.0	40,418.0	40,695.0	40,691.0	41,338.0
Net Property	16,714.0	17,590.0	19,631.0	18,347.0	17,407.0	16,579.0	16,664.0
Total Assets	88,349.0	87,495.0	86,100.0	81,499.0	81,132.0	80,292.0	81,091.0
Total Current Liabilities	36,406.0	39,578.0	36,827.0	33,507.0	34,000.0	31,648.0	29,226.0
Long-Term Obligations	18,371.0	14,124.0	15,508.0	13,696.0	9,872.0	10,060.0	12,548.0
Net Stockholders' Equity	20,624.0	20,511.0	19,433.0	19,816.0	21,628.0	22,423.0	23,413.0
Net Working Capital	7,474.0	3,577.0	5,533.0	6,911.0	6,695.0	9,043.0	12,112.0
Year-end Shs. Outstg. (000)	1,762,899	1,804,216	1,852,000	1,936,000	2,032,000	2,192,000	2,352,000
STATISTICAL RECORD:							
Operating Profit Margin %	13.2	13.6	11.2	11.6	11.3	10.6	7.8
Net Profit Margin %	9.2	8.8	7.7	7.8	7.1	5.8	4.7
Return on Equity %	39.2	37.6	32.6	30.7	25.1	18.6	12.9
Return on Assets %	9.2	8.8	7.3	7.5	6.7	5.2	3.7
Debt/Total Assets %	20.8	16.1	18.0	16.8	12.2	12.5	15.5
Price Range	134.94-80.06	139.19-80.88	94.97-47.81	56.75-31.78	41.50-20.78	28.66-17.56	19.09-12.84
P/E Ratio	30.4-18.0	33.8-19.6	28.9-14.6	18.9-10.6	16.2-8.1	15.8-9.7	15.2-10.2
Average Yield %	0.5	0.4	0.6	0.9	1.0	1.1	1.6

Statistics are as originally reported. Adj. for 2-for-1 split, 5/99 & 5/97. [1] Incl. $488.0 mill. pre-tax chg. & $1.84 bill. chg. rel. to acq. of Lotus Develop. [2] Incl. Lotus Develop., acq. 7/95. [3] Incl. $435.0 mill. one-time chg. [4] Incl. $750.0 mill. net gain fr. sale of bus., restr. chgs., & acct. chg.

OFFICERS:
L. V. Gerstner Jr., Chmn., C.E.O.
J. M. Thompson, Vice-Chmn.
S. J. Palmisano, Pres., C.O.O.

INVESTOR CONTACT: IBM Investor Relations, (800) 426-4968

PRINCIPAL OFFICE: One New Orchard Road, Armonk, NY 10504

TELEPHONE NUMBER: (914) 499-1900
FAX: (914) 765-4190
WEB: www.ibm.com

NO. OF EMPLOYEES: 363,689 (avg.)

SHAREHOLDERS: 673,270 (common record)

ANNUAL MEETING: In Apr.

INCORPORATED: NY, June, 1911

INSTITUTIONAL HOLDINGS:
No. of Institutions: 1,143
Shares Held: 861,670,643
% Held: 48.9

INDUSTRY: Electronic computers (SIC: 3571)

TRANSFER AGENT(S): First Chicago Trust Company of New York, Jersey City, NJ

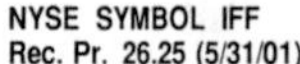
NYSE SYMBOL IFF
Rec. Pr. 26.25 (5/31/01)

INTERNATIONAL FLAVORS & FRAGRANCES, INC.

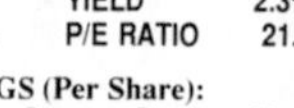

YIELD	2.3%
P/E RATIO	21.9

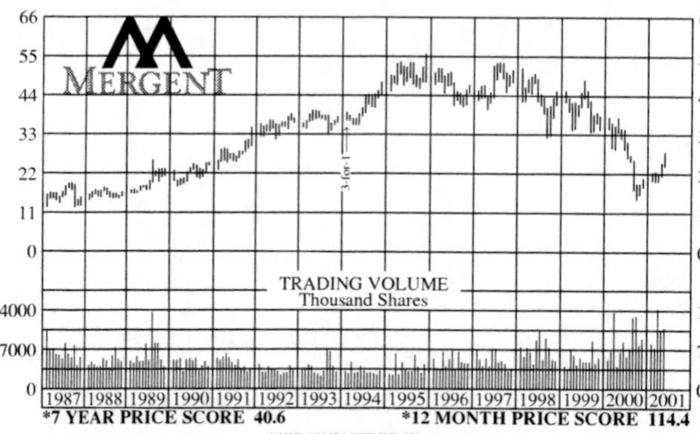

***7 YEAR PRICE SCORE 40.6 *12 MONTH PRICE SCORE 114.4**

*NYSE COMPOSITE INDEX=100

INTERIM EARNINGS (Per Share):

Qtr.	Mar.	June	Sept.	Dec.
1996	0.60	0.26	0.48	0.37
1997	0.58	0.58	0.52	0.32
1998	0.58	0.52	0.47	0.33
1999	0.46	0.26	0.46	0.35
2000	0.42	0.48	0.29	0.01

INTERIM DIVIDENDS (Per Share):

Amt.	Decl.	Ex.	Rec.	Pay.
0.38Q	6/13/00	6/22/00	6/26/00	7/10/00
0.38Q	9/12/00	9/22/00	9/26/00	10/10/00
0.15Q	12/12/00	12/20/00	12/22/00	1/09/01
0.15Q	2/13/01	3/22/01	3/26/01	4/10/01
0.15Q	...	6/22/01	6/26/01	7/10/01

Indicated div.: $0.60 (Div. Reinv. Plan)

CAPITALIZATION (12/31/00):

	($000)	(%)
Long-Term Debt	417,402	36.2
Deferred Income Tax	103,151	9.0
Common & Surplus	631,259	54.8
Total	1,151,812	100.0

RECENT DEVELOPMENTS: For the year ended 12/31/00, net income declined 24.1% to $123.0 million compared with $162.0 million in 1999. Results for 2000 and 1999 included non-recurring charges of $41.3 million and $32.9 million, respectively. Net sales grew 1.6% to $1.46 billion versus $1.44 billion the year before. Net sales were positively affected by increased fragrance sales in North America and the Asia-Pacific region, as well as in Europe, Africa and the Middle East, partially offset by a sales decline in Latin America.

PROSPECTS: The Company has identified 56 locations around the world in which there are duplicate operating facilitities and sales offices. Plans have been developed regarding the consolidation and elimination of a substantial portion of theses duplicate sites. As a result, the Company expects to achieve approximately $10.0 million of cost savings in the first half of 2001. Meanwhile, IFF's board of directors and management are currently evaluating the entire business portfolio as part of an ongoing effort to refocus IFF on its core strategic areas.

BUSINESS

INERNATIONAL FLAVORS & FRAGRANCES, INC. supplies compounds that enhance the aroma or taste of other manufacturers' products. It is one of the largest companies in its field producing and marketing on an international basis. Fragrance products (accounted for approximately 59% of 2000 total sales) are sold principally to manufacturers of perfumes, cosmetics, toiletries, hair care products, deodorants, soaps, detergents and air care products. Flavor products (accounted for approximately 41% of 2000 total sales) are sold principally to manufacturers of prepared foods, beverages, dairy foods, pharmaceuticals and confectionery products. The United States accounted for 30% of 2000 sales.

ANNUAL FINANCIAL DATA

	12/31/00	12/31/99	12/31/98	12/31/97	12/31/96	12/31/95	12/31/94
Earnings Per Share	**1 1.22**	**1 1.53**	**1.90**	**1.99**	**1 1.71**	**2.24**	**2.03**
Cash Flow Per Share	**1.90**	**2.06**	**2.35**	**2.45**	**2.15**	**2.60**	**2.35**
Tang. Book Val. Per Share	**...**	**8.19**	**8.91**	**9.17**	**9.79**	**10.06**	**9.04**
Dividends Per Share	**1.52**	**1.52**	**1.48**	**1.44**	**1.36**	**1.24**	**1.08**
Dividend Payout %	**124.6**	**99.3**	**77.9**	**72.4**	**79.5**	**55.4**	**53.2**
INCOME STATEMENT (IN MILLIONS):							
Total Revenues	1,462.8	1,439.5	1,407.3	1,426.8	1,436.1	1,439.5	1,315.2
Costs & Expenses	1,133.6	1,101.9	1,051.6	1,044.3	1,048.1	1,014.8	930.3
Depreciation & Amort.	69.3	56.4	49.0	50.3	47.8	40.7	36.4
Operating Income	259.8	281.3	306.8	332.2	340.1	384.0	348.6
Net Interest Inc./(Exp.)	d25.1	d5.2	d2.0	d2.4	d2.7	d3.2	d13.5
Income Before Income Taxes	184.1	243.5	311.1	340.2	299.1	393.7	360.4
Income Taxes	61.1	81.5	107.3	122.0	109.2	144.9	134.3
Net Income	1 123.0	1 162.0	203.8	218.2	1 189.9	248.8	226.0
Cash Flow	192.3	218.4	252.8	268.5	237.7	289.5	262.4
Average Shs. Outstg. (000)	101,093	105,943	107,430	109,625	110,773	111,262	111,527
BALANCE SHEET (IN MILLIONS):							
Cash & Cash Equivalents	129.2	63.0	116.0	260.4	318.0	296.9	301.8
Total Current Assets	1,018.9	835.4	848.0	935.5	1,006.4	1,036.0	964.5
Net Property	679.9	523.9	498.8	446.5	467.8	468.6	405.7
Total Assets	2,489.0	1,401.5	1,388.1	1,422.3	1,506.9	1,534.3	1,399.7
Total Current Liabilities	1,179.0	369.7	272.9	264.9	280.5	276.4	259.7
Long-Term Obligations	417.4	3.8	4.3	5.1	8.3	11.6	14.3
Net Stockholders' Equity	631.3	858.5	945.1	1,000.5	1,076.5	1,116.6	1,008.1
Net Working Capital	d160.1	465.7	575.1	670.6	725.9	759.6	704.8
Year-end Shs. Outstg. (000)	97,426	104,822	106,046	109,131	109,972	110,954	111,464
STATISTICAL RECORD:							
Operating Profit Margin %	17.8	19.5	21.8	23.3	23.7	26.7	26.5
Net Profit Margin %	8.4	11.3	14.5	15.3	13.2	17.3	17.2
Return on Equity %	19.5	18.9	21.6	21.8	17.6	22.3	22.4
Return on Assets %	4.9	11.6	14.7	15.3	12.6	16.2	16.1
Debt/Total Assets %	16.8	0.3	0.3	0.4	0.6	0.8	1.0
Price Range	37.94-14.69	48.50-33.63	51.88-32.06	53.44-39.88	51.88-40.75	55.88-45.13	47.88-35.63
P/E Ratio	31.1-12.0	31.7-22.0	27.3-16.9	26.9-20.0	30.3-23.8	24.9-20.1	23.6-17.5
Average Yield %	5.8	3.7	3.5	3.1	2.9	2.5	2.6

Statistics are as originally reported. Adj. for stk. split: 3-for-1, 1/94. 1 Incl. non-recurr. chrg. $41.3 mill., 12/00; $32.9 mill., 12/99; $49.7 mill., 12/96

OFFICERS:
R. A. Goldstein, Chmn., C.E.O.
D. J. Wetmore, V.P., C.F.O.
S. A. Block, Sr. V.P., Gen. Couns., Sec.

INVESTOR CONTACT: Douglas J. Wetmore, V.P., C.F.O., (212) 708-7145

PRINCIPAL OFFICE: 521 West 57th Street, New York, NY 10019-2960

TELEPHONE NUMBER: (212) 765-5500
FAX: (212) 708-7132
WEB: www.iff.com

NO. OF EMPLOYEES: 6,610

SHAREHOLDERS: 3,741 (record)

ANNUAL MEETING: In May

INCORPORATED: NY, Dec., 1909

INSTITUTIONAL HOLDINGS:
No. of Institutions: 241
Shares Held: 61,494,961
% Held: 62.9

INDUSTRY: Industrial organic chemicals, nec (SIC: 2869)

TRANSFER AGENT(S): Bank of New York, New York, NY

NYSE SYMBOL IGT
Rec. Pr. 55.93 (4/30/01)

INTERNATIONAL GAME TECHNOLOGY

YIELD ...
P/E RATIO 25.7

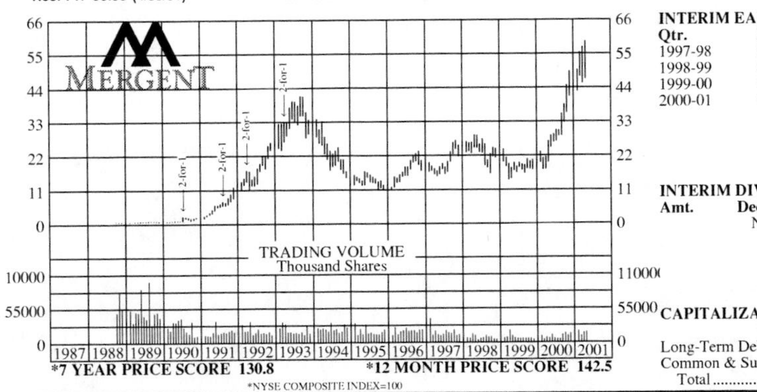

*7 YEAR PRICE SCORE 130.8 *12 MONTH PRICE SCORE 142.5
*NYSE COMPOSITE INDEX=100

INTERIM EARNINGS (Per Share):

Qtr.	Dec.	Mar.	June	Sept.
1997-98	0.26	0.31	0.40	0.37
1998-99	0.32	0.32	0.39	d0.45
1999-00	0.49	0.33	0.51	0.70
2000-01	0.64	...	...	...

INTERIM DIVIDENDS (Per Share):

Amt.	Decl.	Ex.	Rec.	Pay.

No dividends paid.

CAPITALIZATION (9/30/00):

	($000)	(%)
Long-Term Debt	991,507	91.1
Common & Surplus	96,585	8.9
Total	1,088,092	100.0

RECENT DEVELOPMENTS: For the quarter ended 12/30/00, net income rose 13.6% to $48.2 million from $42.4 million in the prior-year period. Results for fiscal 2001 included a pre-tax gain of $500,000 from the impairment of assets and restructuring. Earnings for fiscal 2000 included a one-time net after-tax gain of $16.1 million. Total revenues grew 46.1% to $301.7 million from $206.5 million the year before. Product sales advanced 75.2% to $192.4 million.

PROSPECTS: On 3/27/01, the Company announced that it completed the acquisition of Silicon Gaming, Inc., which designs and manufactures a full line of wagering products for the casino gaming industry. Separately, the Company announced a 5-year contract with Harley-Davidson Motor Co., which allows IGT to use the Harley-Davidson® name and logos in the development of a new gaming machine.

BUSINESS

INTERNATIONAL GAME TECHNOLOGY manufactures, markets and designs a broad range of gaming machines and proprietary software systems for computerized wide-area gaming machine networks throughout the world. IGT has two major divisions, IGT-North America and IGT-International. IGT's wide-area progressive games include Double Diamond; Megabucks; Player's Edge-Plus; Red, White and Blue; Five Times Pay; BonusPoker; Deuces Wild; Triple Play Poker; Elvis?; and Wheel of Fortune. In September 1999, IGT acquired Sodak Gaming, Inc.

BUSINESS LINE ANALYSIS

(9/30/2000)	Rev (%)	Inc (%)
Product Sales	60.1	33.4
Gaming Operations	39.9	66.6
Total	100.0	100.0

ANNUAL FINANCIAL DATA

	9/30/00	10/2/99	9/30/98	9/30/97	9/30/96	9/30/95	9/30/94
Earnings Per Share	**4 6 2.00**	**5 6 0.65**	**4 1.33**	**3 1.13**	**2 0.93**	**1 0.71**	**1.07**
Cash Flow Per Share	**2.73**	**1.18**	**1.69**	**1.41**	**1.17**	**0.92**	**1.23**
Tang. Book Val. Per Share	**...**	**1.03**	**3.76**	**4.57**	**4.96**	**4.30**	**3.94**
Dividends Per Share	**...**	**0.03**	**0.12**	**0.12**	**0.12**	**0.12**	**0.12**
Dividend Payout %	**...**	**4.6**	**9.0**	**10.6**	**12.9**	**16.9**	**11.2**
INCOME STATEMENT (IN MILLIONS):							
Total Revenues	1,004.4	929.7	824.1	744.0	733.5	620.8	674.5
Costs & Expenses	680.0	760.1	563.8	517.5	533.1	453.5	455.9
Depreciation & Amort.	56.8	53.2	41.5	35.0	30.5	27.9	20.6
Operating Income	267.5	116.3	218.9	191.4	169.8	139.3	197.9
Net Interest Inc./(Exp.)	d51.2	d17.2	4.3	11.3	15.6	17.2	17.7
Income Before Income Taxes	245.0	101.4	234.5	212.6	184.4	144.8	214.8
Income Taxes	88.2	36.1	82.1	75.4	66.4	52.1	74.3
Net Income	4 6 156.8	5 6 65.3	4 152.4	3 137.2	2 118.0	1 92.6	140.4
Cash Flow	213.6	118.5	193.9	172.3	148.5	120.5	161.1
Average Shs. Outstg. (000)	78,229	100,238	114,703	121,829	127,412	131,094	131,380
BALANCE SHEET (IN MILLIONS):							
Cash & Cash Equivalents	266.4	444.9	194.8	166.7	230.8	289.4	203.1
Total Current Assets	814.2	975.2	670.5	571.5	615.6	606.6	559.1
Net Property	166.9	182.1	168.8	178.5	177.8	119.3	97.2
Total Assets	1,623.7	1,765.1	1,543.6	1,215.1	1,154.2	971.7	868.0
Total Current Liabilities	259.0	212.6	200.5	164.6	127.4	97.7	78.4
Long-Term Obligations	991.5	990.4	322.5	140.7	107.2	107.5	111.5
Net Stockholders' Equity	96.6	242.2	541.3	519.8	623.2	554.1	520.9
Net Working Capital	555.2	762.7	470.0	407.0	488.1	508.9	480.7
Year-end Shs. Outstg. (000)	72,569	87,355	108,865	113,708	125,576	128,851	132,367
STATISTICAL RECORD:							
Operating Profit Margin %	26.6	12.5	26.6	25.7	23.2	22.4	29.3
Net Profit Margin %	15.6	7.0	18.5	18.4	16.1	14.9	20.8
Return on Equity %	162.3	27.0	28.2	26.4	18.9	16.7	27.0
Return on Assets %	9.7	3.7	9.9	11.3	10.2	9.5	16.2
Debt/Total Assets %	61.1	56.1	20.9	11.6	9.3	11.1	12.8
Price Range	49.38-17.44	24.13-14.13	28.69-16.13	26.94-15.25	23.50-10.75	17.00-10.75	34.00-14.88
P/E Ratio	24.7-8.7	37.1-21.7	21.6-12.1	23.8-13.5	25.3-11.6	23.9-15.1	31.8-13.9
Average Yield %	...	0.2	0.5	0.6	0.7	0.9	0.5

Statistics are as originally reported. 1 Incl one-time chg. of $14.9 mill. for decline in value of invt. in Radica Games, Inc. 2 Incl. various itmes resulting in a net loss of $1.2 mill. 3 Incl. $12.9 mill. gain from the sale of invts. 4 Incl. pre-tax gain from sale of assets of $109,000, 12/00; $3.6 mill., 9/00; $11.1 mill., 9/98. 5 Incl. a gain of $4.9 mill. on the sale of assets & bef. extraord. loss of $3.3 mill. 6 Incl. pre-tax impairment of assets & restruct. gain of $500,000, 12/00; loss of $6,000, 10/00; loss of $98.1 mill., 9/99.

OFFICERS:
C. N. Mathewson, Chmn.
A. J. Crosson, Vice-Chmn.
G. T. Baker, Pres., C.E.O., C.O.O., Treas.

INVESTOR CONTACT: Investor Relations, (775) 448-0880

PRINCIPAL OFFICE: 9295 Prototype Drive, P.O. Box 10580, Reno, NV 89510-0580

TELEPHONE NUMBER: (775) 448-7777
FAX: (775) 448-0777
WEB: www.igt.com

NO. OF EMPLOYEES: 3,600 (approx.)

SHAREHOLDERS: 3,699 (approx.)

ANNUAL MEETING: In Mar.

INCORPORATED: NV, Dec., 1980

INSTITUTIONAL HOLDINGS:
No. of Institutions: 203
Shares Held: 56,269,184
% Held: 76.7

INDUSTRY: Manufacturing industries, nec (SIC: 3999)

TRANSFER AGENT(S): The Bank of New York, New York, NY

NYSE SYMBOL IMC
Rec. Pr. 19.25 (5/31/01)

INTERNATIONAL MULTIFOODS CORP.

YIELD ...
P/E RATIO 17.2

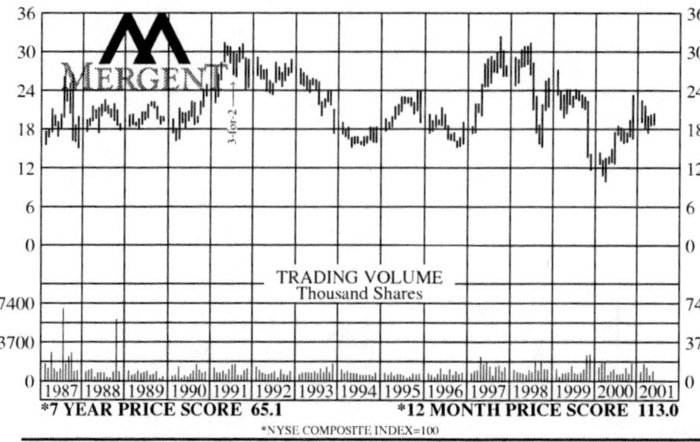

INTERIM EARNINGS (Per Share):

Qtr.	May	Aug.	Nov.	Feb.
1996-97	d0.02	0.22	0.48	d0.53
1997-98	0.11	0.25	0.51	0.21
1998-99	d1.30	0.24	0.52	0.37
1999-00	0.24	0.27	0.43	0.37
2000-01	0.25	0.28	0.45	0.14

INTERIM DIVIDENDS (Per Share):

Amt.	Decl.	Ex.	Rec.	Pay.
0.20Q	12/17/99	12/23/99	12/28/99	1/17/00
0.20Q	3/07/00	3/24/00	3/28/00	4/17/00
0.20Q	6/16/00	6/26/00	6/28/00	7/17/00
0.20Q	9/15/00	9/26/00	9/28/00	10/16/00
0.20Q	12/15/00	12/26/00	12/28/00	1/16/01

Dividend Suspended

CAPITALIZATION (2/29/00):

	($000)	(%)
Long-Term Debt	147,199	34.6
Deferred Income Tax	23,170	5.4
Common & Surplus	255,124	60.0
Total	425,493	100.0

RECENT DEVELOPMENTS: For the 53 weeks ended 3/3/01, net earnings totaled $21.2 million versus income from continuing operations of $24.7 million in the corresponding 52-week period the year before. Results included one-time pre-tax charges of $3.5 million and $500,000 in 2001 and 2000, respectively. Net sales rose 5.9% to $2.52 billion from $2.38 billion a year earlier. Gross profit was $189.0 million, or 7.5% of net sales, versus $184.0 million, or 7.7% of net sales, the prior year. Operating earnings grew 5.5% to $55.3 million from $52.4 million the previous year.

PROSPECTS: On 2/5/01, IMC entered into an agreement to acquire The Pillsbury Company's desserts and specialty products businesses, which include the HUNGRY JACK, PILLSBURY and MARTHA WHITE brands, Pillsbury's non-custom foodservice baking mix business, along with General Mills' U.S. ROBIN HOOD brand, which have combined annual net sales of about $450.0 million, for approximately $305.0 million in cash. Separately, the Company is exploring strategic alternatives for its Multifoods Distribution Group.

BUSINESS

INTERNATIONAL MULTIFOODS CORP. is a processor and distributor of food products in the U.S. and Canada. The Multifoods Distribution Group, which accounted for 80.9% of fiscal 2001 revenues (29.9% of operating profit), distributes food and other products in the United States to independent pizza restaurants and other casual-dining, limited-menu operators. Also included in the segment is IMC's vending distribution unit, which serves approximately 20,000 vending and office coffee service operators and other concessionaires. North America Foods, 19.1% (70.1%), comprises consumer and commercial products in Canada, primarily home baking products and condiments sold under the ROBIN HOOD brand, and Canadian and U.S. bakery products for foodservice, retail bakery, in-store bakery and wholesale bakery customers. On 8/19/99, IMC completed the divestiture of its Venezuelan Foods business.

ANNUAL FINANCIAL DATA

	2/29/00	2/28/99	2/28/98	2/28/97	2/29/96	2/28/95	2/28/94
Earnings Per Share	**[1][2] 1.31**	**[1][2] 0.36**	**[1] 1.08**	**[1] 0.15**	**[1] 1.33**	**[1] 3.16**	**[1] d0.72**
Cash Flow Per Share	**2.49**	**1.53**	**2.72**	**1.86**	**2.98**	**4.67**	**0.87**
Tang. Book Val. Per Share	**9.08**	**9.49**	**11.98**	**11.21**	**11.10**	**10.14**	**9.67**
Dividends Per Share	**0.80**	**0.80**	**0.80**	**0.80**	**0.80**	**0.80**	**0.80**
Dividend Payout %	**61.1**	**222.2**	**74.1**	**533.0**	**60.1**	**25.3**	**...**
INCOME STATEMENT (IN MILLIONS):							
Total Revenues	2,384.7	2,296.6	2,611.8	2,595.9	2,523.2	2,295.1	2,224.7
Costs & Expenses	2,310.6	2,222.6	2,531.3	2,522.9	2,437.6	2,207.7	2,126.0
Depreciation & Amort.	22.2	22.1	30.7	30.7	29.8	27.0	29.9
Operating Income	52.5	22.9	44.8	22.1	50.1	86.6	68.8
Net Interest Inc./(Exp.)	d11.0	d10.4	d12.4	d16.8	d17.9	d11.4	d10.7
Income Before Income Taxes	40.4	12.3	32.4	5.0	27.8	71.7	d24.9
Net Income	[1][2] 24.7	[1][2] 6.8	[1] 20.0	[1] 2.8	[1] 24.1	[1] 57.0	[1] d13.4
Cash Flow	46.9	28.9	50.7	33.5	53.6	83.9	16.3
Average Shs. Outstg. (000)	18,786	18,903	18,619	17,982	17,965	17,974	18,911
BALANCE SHEET (IN MILLIONS):							
Cash & Cash Equivalents	11.2	13.5	10.4	8.8	7.5	10.8	10.5
Total Current Assets	354.0	340.1	484.4	563.3	459.0	471.7	439.3
Net Property	204.9	165.2	220.6	225.4	226.5	228.0	245.9
Total Assets	736.2	696.9	827.4	915.3	822.3	846.7	814.8
Total Current Liabilities	277.5	264.2	312.4	372.0	272.3	316.0	301.7
Long-Term Obligations	147.2	121.2	162.9	202.3	202.9	183.1	195.1
Net Stockholders' Equity	255.1	260.3	309.4	289.6	299.6	291.1	250.0
Net Working Capital	76.5	75.8	172.0	191.3	186.7	155.7	137.6
Year-end Shs. Outstg. (000)	18,738	18,776	18,738	18,009	17,980	17,989	18,337
STATISTICAL RECORD:							
Operating Profit Margin %	2.2	1.0	1.7	0.9	2.0	3.8	3.1
Net Profit Margin %	1.0	0.3	0.8	0.1	1.0	2.5	...
Return on Equity %	9.7	2.6	6.5	1.0	8.0	19.6	...
Return on Assets %	3.4	1.0	2.4	0.3	2.9	6.7	...
Debt/Total Assets %	20.0	17.4	19.7	22.1	24.7	21.6	23.9
Price Range	27.25-11.63	31.44-15.13	32.44-17.25	21.38-15.13	23.88-17.63	19.13-15.13	27.50-17.25
P/E Ratio	20.8-8.9	87.3-42.0	30.0-16.0	142.4-100.8	17.9-13.3	6.1-4.8	...
Average Yield %	4.1	3.4	3.2	4.4	3.9	4.7	3.6

Statistics are as originally reported. [1] Incl. $500,000 pre-tax gain, 2000; $18.7 mil after-tax chg., 1999; $3.2 mil ($0.17/sh) after-tax chg., 1998; $14.8 mil ($0.83/sh) after-tax chg., 1997; $500,000 ($0.02/sh) net after-tax gain, 1996; $29 mil ($1.61/sh) after-tax gain, 1995; $48.9 mil ($2.58/sh) after-tax chg., 1994. [2] Bef. $19.6 mil ($1.04/sh) loss fr. discont. opers., 2000; $138.7 mil ($7.34/sh) loss fr. discont. opers., 1999.

OFFICERS:
G. E. Costley, Chmn., Pres., C.E.O.
J. E. Byom, V.P., C.F.O.
G. J. Keup, V.P., Treas.

INVESTOR CONTACT: Jill Schmidt, Investor Relations, (952) 594-3385

PRINCIPAL OFFICE: 200 East Lake Street, Minnetonka, MN 55391-3300

TELEPHONE NUMBER: (952) 594-3300
FAX: (952) 594-3343
WEB: www.multifoods.com

NO. OF EMPLOYEES: 4,362

SHAREHOLDERS: 4,445

ANNUAL MEETING: In June

INCORPORATED: DE, Dec., 1969

INSTITUTIONAL HOLDINGS:
No. of Institutions: 94
Shares Held: 12,640,862
% Held: 67.5

INDUSTRY: Packaged frozen foods (SIC: 5142)

TRANSFER AGENT(S): Wells Fargo Bank Minnesota, N.A., South St. Paul, MN

NYSE SYMBOL IP
Rec. Pr. 39.18 (4/30/01)

INTERNATIONAL PAPER COMPANY

YIELD 2.6%
P/E RATIO 42.6

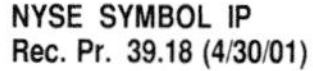

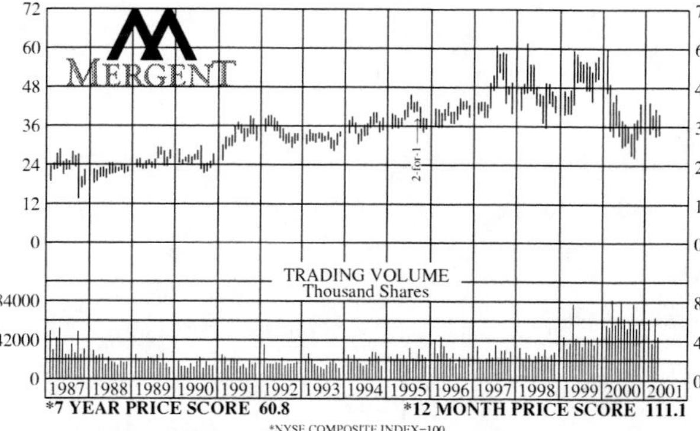

***7 YEAR PRICE SCORE 60.8** ***12 MONTH PRICE SCORE 111.1**

*NYSE COMPOSITE INDEX=100

INTERIM EARNINGS (Per Share):

Qtr.	Mar.	June	Sept.	Dec.
1997	0.11	d1.39	0.34	0.44
1998	0.25	0.28	0.07	0.10
1999	0.14	d0.14	0.35	0.19
2000	0.59	0.64	0.36	d0.67

INTERIM DIVIDENDS (Per Share):

Amt.	Decl.	Ex.	Rec.	Pay.
0.25Q	5/09/00	5/17/00	5/19/00	6/15/00
0.25Q	8/07/00	8/16/00	8/18/00	9/15/00
0.25Q	11/06/00	11/21/00	11/24/00	12/15/00
0.25Q	2/13/01	2/21/01	2/23/01	3/15/01
0.25Q	5/07/01	5/16/01	5/18/01	6/15/01

Indicated div.: $1.00 (Div. Reinv. Plan)

CAPITALIZATION (12/31/00):

	($000)	(%)
Long-Term Debt [1]	12,648,000	38.9
Deferred Income Tax	4,699,000	14.4
Minority Interest	1,355,000	4.2
Redeemable Pfd. Stock	1,805,000	5.5
Common & Surplus	12,034,000	37.0
Total	32,541,001	100.0

RECENT DEVELOPMENTS: For the year ended 12/31/00, income increased 84.9% to $368.0 million, before an extraordinary charge, versus earnings of $199.0 million, before an extraordinary charge, in 1999. Results for 2000 included a net charge of $969.0 million, while results for 1999 included net pre-tax charges of $593.0 million. Net sales rose 14.7% to $28.18 billion.

PROSPECTS: On 4/26/01, the Company announced that it has reached a definitive agreement to sell its subsidiary, Chocolate Bayou Water Company, to the North Harris County Regional Water Authority for approximately $100.0 million, subject to certain adjustments at closing. The transaction is subject to normal closing conditions, including regulatory approval.

BUSINESS

INTERNATIONAL PAPER COMPANY is a global paper and forest products company that is complemented by an extensive distribution system. IP produces printing and writing papers, pulp, tissue, paperboard and packaging and wood products. IP manufactures specialty chemicals and specialty panels and laminated products. IP's primary markets and manufacturing and distribution operations are in the U.S., Europe and the Pacific Rim. IP distributes printing, packaging, graphic arts and industrial supply products, primarily manufactured by other companies, through over 305 distribution branches located primarily in the U.S., and also engages in oil and gas and real estate activities in the U.S. IP acquired Union Camp Corp. on 4/30/99 for approximately $7.90 billion, and Champion International on 6/19/00 for approximately $7.30 billion, excluding $2.30 billion in net debt.

ANNUAL FINANCIAL DATA

	12/31/00	12/31/99	12/31/98	12/31/97	12/31/96	12/31/95	12/31/94
Earnings Per Share	**[1][5] 0.32**	**[4][5] 0.44**	**[4] 0.77**	**[4] d0.50**	**[2][3] 1.04**	**[2] 4.50**	**1.73**
Cash Flow Per Share	**5.08**	**4.13**	**4.64**	**3.68**	**1.04**	**8.74**	**5.27**
Tang. Book Val. Per Share	**11.89**	**18.65**	**20.44**	**20.36**	**22.59**	**24.68**	**22.82**
Dividends Per Share	**1.00**	**1.00**	**1.00**	**1.00**	**1.00**	**0.92**	**0.84**
Dividend Payout %	**312.4**	**227.2**	**129.9**	**. . .**	**96.1**	**20.4**	**48.6**
INCOME STATEMENT (IN MILLIONS):							
Total Revenues	28,180.0	24,573.0	19,541.0	20,096.0	20,143.0	19,797.0	14,966.0
Costs & Expenses	24,759.0	22,105.0	17,555.0	18,503.0	18,209.0	16,245.0	13,017.0
Depreciation & Amort.	1,916.0	1,520.0	1,186.0	1,258.0	1,194.0	1,031.0	885.0
Operating Income	1,539.0	989.0	888.0	506.0	1,332.0	2,521.0	1,064.0
Net Interest Inc./(Exp.)	d816.0	d541.0	d496.0	d490.0	d530.0	d493.0	d349.0
Income Before Income Taxes	723.0	448.0	392.0	16.0	802.0	2,028.0	715.0
Income Taxes	117.0	86.0	80.0	38.0	330.0	719.0	236.0
Equity Earnings/Minority Int.	d238.0	d158.0	d91.0	d128.0	d169.0	d156.0	d47.0
Net Income	[1][5] 368.0	[4][5] 199.0	[4] 236.0	[4] d151.0	[2][3] d881.0	[2] 1,153.0	432.0
Cash Flow	2,284.0	1,719.0	1,422.0	1,107.0	313.0	2,184.0	1,317.0
Average Shs. Outstg. (000)	450,000	416,100	306,300	301,000	301,000	250,000	250,000
BALANCE SHEET (IN MILLIONS):							
Cash & Cash Equivalents	1,198.0	453.0	477.0	398.0	352.0	312.0	270.0
Total Current Assets	10,455.0	7,241.0	6,010.0	5,945.0	5,998.0	5,873.0	4,830.0
Net Property	16,011.0	14,381.0	12,079.0	12,369.0	13,217.0	10,997.0	9,139.0
Total Assets	42,109.0	30,268.0	26,356.0	26,754.0	28,252.0	23,977.0	17,836.0
Total Current Liabilities	7,413.0	4,382.0	3,636.0	4,880.0	5,894.0	4,863.0	4,034.0
Long-Term Obligations	12,648.0	7,520.0	6,407.0	7,154.0	6,691.0	5,946.0	4,464.0
Net Stockholders' Equity	12,034.0	10,304.0	8,902.0	8,710.0	9,794.0	8,247.0	6,514.0
Net Working Capital	3,042.0	2,859.0	2,374.0	1,065.0	104.0	1,010.0	796.0
Year-end Shs. Outstg. (000)	481,500	413,400	307,100	302,200	292,000	261,000	252,000
STATISTICAL RECORD:							
Operating Profit Margin %	5.5	4.0	4.5	2.5	6.6	12.7	7.1
Net Profit Margin %	1.3	0.8	1.2	. . .	. . .	5.8	2.9
Return on Equity %	3.1	1.9	2.7	. . .	. . .	14.0	6.6
Return on Assets %	0.9	0.7	0.9	. . .	. . .	4.8	2.4
Debt/Total Assets %	30.0	24.8	24.3	26.7	23.7	24.8	25.0
Price Range	60.00-26.31	59.50-39.50	61.75-35.50	61.00-38.63	44.63-35.63	45.69-34.13	40.25-30.31
P/E Ratio	187.4-82.2	135.2-89.8	80.2-46.1	. . .	42.9-34.3	10.2-7.6	23.3-17.5
Average Yield %	2.3	2.0	2.1	2.0	2.5	2.3	2.4

Statistics are as originally reported. Adj. for stock split: 2-for-1, 9/95. [1] Incl. chrg. of $969.0 mill. [2] Bef. a $75 mill. acctg. chrg. of $70 mill., 1995; & $515 mill., 1996. [3] Incl. $592 mill. gain. [4] Incl. net after-tax loss for special items of $461.0 mill., 1997; $95.0 mill., 1998; & $593.0 mill., 1999. [5] Excl. extraord. chrg. of $16.0 mill., 1999; $226.0 mill., 2000.

OFFICERS:
J. T. Dillon, Chmn., C.E.O.
J. V. Faraci, Exec. V.P., C.F.O.
J. P. Melican, Exec. V.P.

INVESTOR CONTACT: Investor Relation, (914) 397-1500

PRINCIPAL OFFICE: 400 Atlantic Street, Stamford, CT 06921

TELEPHONE NUMBER: (914) 397-1500
FAX: (914) 397-1596
WEB: www.internationalpaper.com

NO. OF EMPLOYEES: 112,900 (approx.)

SHAREHOLDERS: 39,887

ANNUAL MEETING: In May

INCORPORATED: NY, June, 1941

INSTITUTIONAL HOLDINGS:
No. of Institutions: 532
Shares Held: 414,001,182
% Held: 85.7

INDUSTRY: Paper mills (SIC: 2621)

TRANSFER AGENT(S): Mellon Investor Services, L.L.C., Ridgefield Park, NJ

NYSE SYMBOL IRF
Rec. Pr. 55.50 (4/30/01)

INTERNATIONAL RECTIFIER CORP.

YIELD . . .
P/E RATIO 24.8

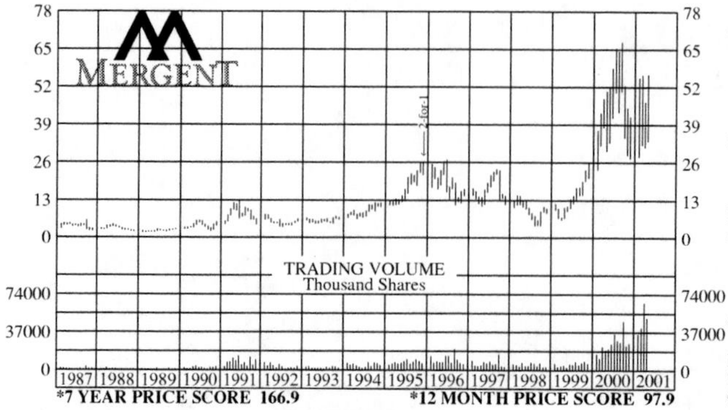

TRADING VOLUME
Thousand Shares

*7 YEAR PRICE SCORE 166.9 *12 MONTH PRICE SCORE 97.9

*NYSE COMPOSITE INDEX=100

INTERIM EARNINGS (Per Share):

Qtr.	Sept.	Dec.	Mar.	June
1995-96	0.25	0.30	0.35	0.40
1996-97	0.06	0.07	0.08	d1.04
1997-98	0.12	0.13	0.06	0.01
1998-99	Nil	0.38	0.08	d0.07
1999-00	0.10	0.23	0.38	0.52
2000-01	0.63	0.71	. . .	. . .

INTERIM DIVIDENDS (Per Share):

Amt.	Decl.	Ex.	Rec.	Pay.

No dividends paid.

CAPITALIZATION (6/30/00):

	($000)	(%)
Long-Term Debt	4,589	0.5
Deferred Income Tax	18,669	2.2
Common & Surplus	844,066	97.3
Total	867,324	100.0

RECENT DEVELOPMENTS: For the quarter ended 12/31/00, net income jumped to $46.5 million compared with $12.4 million in the equivalent quarter of 1999. Revenues soared 56.7% to $268.1 million from $171.1 million in the prior-year period. Revenue for analog power integrated circuits, advanced-circuit devices, and power systems advanced 123.0% year-to-year, and accounted for 31.0% of total revenue for the 2000 quarter. Operating profit surged to $57.7 million compared with $20.1 million the year before.

PROSPECTS: Near-term prospects remain promising despite difficult and uncertain market conditions in the U.S. IRF's focus on the faster-growing markets within its industry is yielding significant benefits, as indicated by orders for its proprietary products growing 157.0% in 2000. Sales of analog power integrated circuits, advanced-circuit devices and power systems are particularly strong. IRF expects proprietary products to account for about 40.0% of its business by the end of fiscal year 2001.

BUSINESS

INTERNATIONAL RECTIFIER CORP. is a global supplier of power semiconductors. Power semiconductors switch or condition electricity at relatively high voltage and current levels in products such as power supplies, motor controls, computers/peripherals, automobiles, portable phones, and electronic lighting ballasts. IRF's products convert electrical power to make it more usable and efficient in performing typical day-to-day operations. For the year ended 6/30/00, IRF's sales by region were derived: North America, 37%; Europe, 23%; Asia Pacific, 29%; and Japan, 11%. IRF has manufacturing facilities in North America, Europe, Asia, and uses subcontract assembly in Asia.

ANNUAL FINANCIAL DATA

	6/30/00	6/30/99	6/30/98	6/30/97	6/30/96	6/30/95	6/30/94
Earnings Per Share	**3 1.27**	**2 0.39**	**0.32**	**1 d0.84**	**1.29**	**0.84**	**0.38**
Cash Flow Per Share	**2.24**	**1.28**	**1.07**	**d0.12**	**1.88**	**1.34**	**0.83**
Tang. Book Val. Per Share	**13.70**	**7.65**	**7.78**	**7.48**	**7.97**	**6.85**	**4.99**
INCOME STATEMENT (IN MILLIONS):							
Total Revenues	753.3	545.4	551.9	486.1	576.8	429.0	328.9
Costs & Expenses	591.1	510.4	480.6	498.4	450.0	357.2	287.3
Depreciation & Amort.	55.9	46.2	38.9	37.1	30.1	23.4	18.0
Operating Income	106.2	d11.2	32.4	d49.4	96.7	48.4	23.5
Net Interest Inc./(Exp.)	d6.0	d11.1	d7.3	d4.0	d0.4	d0.4	d3.6
Income Before Income Taxes	101.5	31.2	24.6	d52.7	95.9	47.5	18.9
Income Taxes	28.4	10.8	8.1	cr9.5	29.5	8.1	3.2
Net Income	3 73.1	2 20.4	16.5	1 d43.2	66.5	39.4	15.7
Cash Flow	129.0	66.5	55.4	d6.1	96.6	62.8	33.7
Average Shs. Outstg. (000)	57,662	51,788	51,674	51,307	51,384	47,020	40,856
BALANCE SHEET (IN MILLIONS):							
Cash & Cash Equivalents	254.3	40.4	45.5	53.4	53.8	53.8	13.1
Total Current Assets	591.6	306.3	317.3	316.5	276.5	233.8	156.9
Net Property	390.8	380.5	390.9	333.6	328.0	245.2	158.6
Total Assets	1,026.0	709.1	735.8	679.8	629.1	496.2	330.6
Total Current Liabilities	150.2	140.6	153.9	113.3	124.7	106.1	89.7
Long-Term Obligations	4.6	158.4	141.5	143.2	48.0	23.9	26.8
Net Stockholders' Equity	844.1	396.3	399.7	381.7	421.2	345.2	202.9
Net Working Capital	441.5	165.6	163.3	203.2	151.8	127.8	67.2
Year-end Shs. Outstg. (000)	61,594	51,781	51,351	51,052	52,821	50,360	40,704
STATISTICAL RECORD:							
Operating Profit Margin %	14.1	. . .	5.9	. . .	16.8	11.3	7.2
Net Profit Margin %	9.7	3.7	3.0	. . .	11.5	9.2	4.8
Return on Equity %	8.7	5.1	4.1	. . .	15.8	11.4	7.7
Return on Assets %	7.1	2.9	2.2	. . .	10.6	7.9	4.8
Debt/Total Assets %	0.4	22.3	19.2	21.1	7.6	4.8	8.1
Price Range	67.44-23.50	26.00-6.25	14.75-4.25	23.75-10.88	27.00-11.25	26.00-11.06	12.19-6.50
P/E Ratio	53.1-18.5	66.6-16.0	46.1-13.3	. . .	20.9-8.7	30.9-13.2	32.1-17.1

Statistics are as originally reported. Adj. for 2-for-1 split, 12/95. 1 Incl. $58.6 mill. after-tax chg. for impairment & restr. 2 Incl. $24.5 mill. restr. chgs. & excl. $26.2 mill. cumulative effect acct. chg. 3 Excl. $4.8 mill. net extraord. chg.

OFFICERS:
E. Lidow, Chmn.
A. Lidow, C.E.O.
M. P. McGee, Exec. V.P., C.F.O.

INVESTOR CONTACT: S. Wagers, (310) 726-8512

PRINCIPAL OFFICE: 233 Kansas Street, El Segundo, CA 90245

TELEPHONE NUMBER: (310) 726-8000
FAX: (310) 322-3332
WEB: www.irf.com

NO. OF EMPLOYEES: 5,098 (approx.)

SHAREHOLDERS: 1,546

ANNUAL MEETING: In Nov.

INCORPORATED: CA, Aug., 1947; reincorp., DE, Oct., 1979

INSTITUTIONAL HOLDINGS:
No. of Institutions: 235
Shares Held: 44,725,255
% Held: 71.8

INDUSTRY: Semiconductors and related devices (SIC: 3674)

TRANSFER AGENT(S): Mellon Investor Services, Los Angeles, CA

NYSE SYMBOL IPG
Rec. Pr. 33.95 (4/30/01)

INTERPUBLIC GROUP OF COMPANIES, INC.

YIELD 1.0%
P/E RATIO 30.6

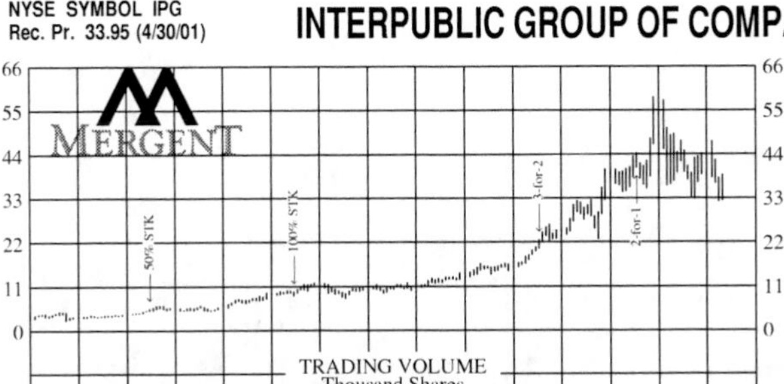

*7 YEAR PRICE SCORE 112.8 *12 MONTH PRICE SCORE 94.6

*NYSE COMPOSITE INDEX=100

INTERIM EARNINGS (Per Share):

Qtr.	Mar.	June	Sept.	Dec.
1997	0.09	0.37	0.14	0.36
1998	0.11	0.42	0.17	0.38
1999	0.16	0.49	0.21	0.27
2000	0.13	0.45	0.20	0.33

INTERIM DIVIDENDS (Per Share):

Amt.	Decl.	Ex.	Rec.	Pay.
0.095Q	5/15/00	5/25/00	5/30/00	6/15/00
0.095Q	7/27/00	8/28/00	8/30/00	9/15/00
0.095Q	10/24/00	11/27/00	11/29/00	12/15/00
0.095Q	12/15/00	2/23/01	2/27/01	3/15/01
0.095Q	5/15/01	5/25/01	5/30/01	6/15/01

Indicated div.: $0.38 (Div. Reinv. Plan)

CAPITALIZATION (12/31/00):

	($000)	(%)
Long-Term Debt	1,505,061	41.4
Minority Interest	85,806	2.4
Common & Surplus	2,046,356	56.3
Total	3,637,223	100.0

RECENT DEVELOPMENTS: For the year ended 12/31/00, net income increased 8.3% to $358.7 million from $331.3 million in the prior year. Earnings for 2000 and 1999 included pre-tax restructuring and other merger-related costs of $116.1 million and $84.2 million, respectively. Results for 2000 also included pre-tax nonrecurring transaction costs of $44.7 million. Total revenue increased 13.0% to $5.63 billion from $4.98 billion in 1999.

PROSPECTS: On 3/19/01, IPG announced that it signed a definitive agreement to acquire True North in a stock transaction valued at $2.10 billion. The combined company will have offices in more than 130 countries. The acquisition should be accretive to IPG's earnings per share in 2001 and 2002, with annualized cost savings of more than $25.0 million. Looking ahead, IPG expects double-digit earnings per share growth in 2001.

BUSINESS

INTERPUBLIC GROUP OF COMPANIES, INC. is a large organization of advertising agencies. The agencies owned include McCann-Erickson WorldGroup, the Lowe Group, DraftWorldwide, Initiative Media Worldwide, International Public Relations, NFO Worldwide, Octagon, Zentropy Partners, Allied Communications Group and other related companies. IPG also offers advertising agency services through association arrangements with local agencies in various parts of the world. Other activities conducted by the Company within the area of marketing communications include public relations, graphic design and market research. The Company also conducts business in sales promotion, interactive services, sports and event marketing, consulting and other related services.

QUARTERLY DATA

(12/31/2000)($000)	REV	INC
1st Quarter	1,225,365	42,935
2nd Quarter	1,446,538	142,461
3rd Quarter	1,353,081	70,078
4th Quarter	1,600,861	103,184

ANNUAL FINANCIAL DATA

	12/31/00	12/31/99	12/31/98	12/31/97	12/31/96	12/31/95	12/31/94
Earnings Per Share	[4][5] **1.15**	[4] **1.11**	**1.11**	**0.95**	[3] **0.85**	[2] **0.55**	[1] **0.51**
Cash Flow Per Share	**2.11**	**1.86**	**1.74**	**1.43**	**1.28**	**0.94**	**0.84**
Tang. Book Val. Per Share	...	...	...	**0.32**	**0.50**	**0.47**	**0.21**
Dividends Per Share	**0.37**	**0.33**	**0.29**	**0.25**	**0.22**	**0.20**	**0.18**
Dividend Payout %	**32.2**	**29.7**	**26.2**	**26.5**	**26.0**	**36.5**	**35.6**
INCOME STATEMENT (IN MILLIONS):							
Total Revenues	5,625.8	4,561.5	3,968.7	3,125.8	2,537.5	2,179.7	1,984.3
Costs & Expenses	4,653.6	3,694.1	3,168.0	2,504.3	2,036.2	1,796.4	1,674.9
Depreciation & Amort.	299.5	215.9	179.1	130.8	103.4	91.2	75.6
Operating Income	672.7	651.5	621.6	490.7	397.9	292.2	233.7
Net Interest Inc./(Exp.)	d109.1	d66.4	d58.7	d49.4	d40.8	d38.0	d32.9
Income Before Income Taxes	657.9	585.1	562.9	441.3	357.1	254.2	200.8
Income Taxes	273.0	236.3	232.0	184.9	150.0	122.7	86.3
Equity Earnings/Minority Int.	d26.2	d26.8	d21.0	d17.2	d1.9	d1.6	0.8
Net Income	[4][5] 358.7	[4] 321.9	309.9	239.1	[3] 205.2	[2] 129.8	[1] 115.2
Cash Flow	658.2	537.9	489.0	370.0	308.6	221.0	190.8
Average Shs. Outstg. (000)	312,653	289,548	281,050	259,088	240,879	234,540	226,710
BALANCE SHEET (IN MILLIONS):							
Cash & Cash Equivalents	748.1	1,018.2	840.5	745.9	503.9	457.4	441.6
Total Current Assets	6,026.1	5,767.8	4,776.9	4,025.7	3,353.5	2,974.4	2,675.3
Net Property	660.4	534.3	439.6	348.8	307.0	279.3	248.1
Total Assets	10,238.2	8,727.3	6,942.8	5,702.5	4,765.1	4,259.8	3,793.4
Total Current Liabilities	6,106.1	5,636.9	4,658.4	3,751.6	3,199.0	2,826.7	2,595.2
Long-Term Obligations	1,505.1	867.3	506.6	452.7	347.0	283.5	241.8
Net Stockholders' Equity	2,046.4	1,628.1	1,265.1	1,107.2	872.0	749.7	649.4
Net Working Capital	d80.0	130.9	118.6	274.0	154.4	147.7	80.1
Year-end Shs. Outstg. (000)	314,672	287,658	279,070	261,638	243,396	238,884	233,112
STATISTICAL RECORD:							
Operating Profit Margin %	12.0	14.3	15.7	15.7	15.7	13.4	11.8
Net Profit Margin %	6.4	7.1	7.8	7.7	8.1	6.0	5.8
Return on Equity %	17.5	19.8	24.5	21.6	23.5	17.3	17.7
Return on Assets %	3.5	3.7	4.5	4.2	4.3	3.0	3.0
Debt/Total Assets %	14.7	9.9	7.3	7.9	7.3	6.7	6.4
Price Range	57.69-32.69	58.38-34.41	40.31-22.56	26.50-15.67	16.75-13.21	14.46-10.58	11.96-9.17
P/E Ratio	50.2-28.4	52.6-31.0	36.5-20.4	27.9-16.5	19.6-15.5	26.1-19.1	23.4-18.0
Average Yield %	0.8	0.7	0.9	1.2	1.5	1.6	1.7

Statistics are as originally reported. Adj. for stk splits: 2-for-1, 7/99 and 3-for-2, 7/97. [1] Incl. acctg. chrg. of $21.8 mill. & restruct. chrg. of $25.7 mill. [2] Incl. aft.-tax chg. of $38.2 mill. for write-down of assets. [3] Incl. $8.1 mill. gain from sale of a portion of IPG's interest in CKS Group, Inc. [4] Incl. pre-tax restruct. & other merger-rel. chrgs. of $116.1 mill., 2000; $84.2 mill., 1999. [5] Incl. pre-tax non-recurr. transaction costs of $44.7 mill.

OFFICERS:
J. J. Dooner Jr., Chmn, C.E.O.
S. F. Orr, Exec. V.P., C.F.O.
N. J. Camera Jr., Sr. V.P., Sec., Gen. Couns.

INVESTOR CONTACT: Susan V. Watson, Sr. V.P.-Inv. Rel., (212) 399-8000

PRINCIPAL OFFICE: 1271 Avenue of the Americas, New York, NY 10020

TELEPHONE NUMBER: (212) 399-8000
FAX: (212) 399-8130
WEB: www.interpublic.com

NO. OF EMPLOYEES: 48,200 (approx.)

SHAREHOLDERS: 15,523

ANNUAL MEETING: In May

INCORPORATED: DE, Sept., 1930

INSTITUTIONAL HOLDINGS:
No. of Institutions: 480
Shares Held: 241,004,767
% Held: 77.1

INDUSTRY: Advertising agencies (SIC: 7311)

TRANSFER AGENT(S): First Chicago Trust Company of New York, Jersey City, NJ

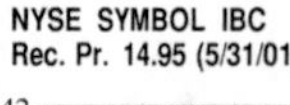

NYSE SYMBOL IBC
Rec. Pr. 14.95 (5/31/01)

INTERSTATE BAKERIES CORPORATION

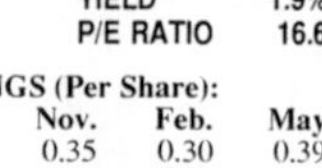

YIELD 1.9%
P/E RATIO 16.6

*7 YEAR PRICE SCORE 60.2 *12 MONTH PRICE SCORE 100.0

*NYSE COMPOSITE INDEX=100

INTERIM EARNINGS (Per Share):

Qtr.	Aug.	Nov.	Feb.	May
1996-97	0.25	0.35	0.30	0.39
1997-98	0.40	0.46	0.40	0.46
1998-99	0.47	0.44	0.41	0.42
1999-00	0.47	0.40	0.30	0.12
2000-01	0.41	0.22	0.15	...

INTERIM DIVIDENDS (Per Share):

Amt.	Decl.	Ex.	Rec.	Pay.
0.07Q	3/29/00	4/12/00	4/14/00	5/01/00
0.07Q	6/27/00	7/12/00	7/14/00	8/01/00
0.07Q	9/26/00	10/11/00	10/15/00	11/01/00
0.07Q	12/15/00	1/10/01	1/15/01	2/01/01
0.07Q	3/29/01	4/11/01	4/16/01	5/01/01

Indicated div.: $0.28 (Div. Reinv. Plan)

CAPITALIZATION (6/3/00):

	($000)	(%)
Long-Term Debt	385,000	34.7
Deferred Income Tax	131,810	11.9
Common & Surplus	591,677	53.4
Total	1,108,487	100.0

RECENT DEVELOPMENTS: For the sixteen weeks ended 3/10/01, net income fell 62.1% to $7.7 million from $20.4 million in the corresponding period the year before. Net sales totaled $1.04 billion, essentially unchanged compared with the previous year. Selling, delivery and administrative expenses rose 4.1% to $483.5 million, while interest expense grew 87.4% to $16.2 million. Operating income declined 29.9% to $29.0 million from $41.3 million in the prior year.

PROSPECTS: Earnings are being hurt by sharply higher energy and fuel costs. IBC is continuing to focus on boosting operating profitability through product quality enhancements, increased manufacturing efficiencies, and the realignment of distribution routes. Going forward, sales may benefit from the expansion of new bakery products, particularly in the Northeast and Northwest regions, along with the implementation of new promotional programs.

BUSINESS

INTERSTATE BAKERIES CORPORATION, through its wholly-owned operating subsidiary, Interstate Brands Corporation, is a baker and distributor of fresh bakery products in the United States. The Company produces, markets, distributes and sells a wide range of breads, rolls, snack cakes, donuts, sweet goods and related products. These products are sold under several national brand names, including WONDER®, HOSTESS®, ROMAN MEAL®, SUNMAID®, and HOME PRIDE®, as well as regional brand names, including BUTTERNUT®, DOLLY MADISON®, SWEETHEART®, MARIE CALLENDERS®, MERITA®, and DRAKES. In July 1995, IBC acquired Continental Baking Company from Ralston Purina Company. In March 1997, IBC acquired the assets of the San Francisco French Bread Company. At 9/1/00, Ralston Purina Company owned 29.5% of IBC's common stock.

ANNUAL FINANCIAL DATA

	6/3/00	5/29/99	5/30/98	5/31/97	6/1/96	6/3/95	5/28/94
Earnings Per Share	**[1] 1.31**	**1.74**	**1.71**	**1.28**	**0.35**	**0.53**	**0.39**
Cash Flow Per Share	**2.94**	**3.26**	**3.08**	**2.63**	**1.80**	**1.38**	**1.17**
Tang. Book Val. Per Share	**2.53**	**2.49**	**2.73**	**2.37**	**1.47**	...	...
Dividends Per Share	**0.28**	**0.28**	**0.27**	**0.26**	**0.25**	**0.25**	**0.24**
Dividend Payout %	**21.4**	**16.1**	**15.9**	**20.0**	**71.4**	**47.6**	**62.2**
INCOME STATEMENT (IN MILLIONS):							
Total Revenues	3,522.9	3,459.4	3,265.8	3,212.4	2,878.2	1,222.8	1,142.7
Costs & Expenses	3,240.9	3,124.9	2,931.5	2,918.3	2,699.3	1,131.9	1,064.2
Depreciation & Amort.	111.6	110.0	102.7	103.0	100.1	33.6	31.6
Operating Income	170.4	224.5	231.6	191.1	78.8	57.3	46.9
Net Interest Inc./(Exp.)	d27.8	d23.1	d18.6	d22.6	d29.3	d17.7	d14.7
Income Before Income Taxes	143.0	201.8	213.6	169.3	50.3	39.7	32.3
Income Taxes	53.6	75.7	85.6	72.1	25.9	19.0	16.5
Net Income	[1] 89.4	126.2	127.9	97.2	24.5	20.7	15.8
Cash Flow	201.0	236.2	230.6	200.2	124.6	54.3	47.3
Average Shs. Outstg. (000)	68,356	72,483	74,845	76,200	69,202	39,414	40,612
BALANCE SHEET (IN MILLIONS):							
Cash & Cash Equivalents	...	...	...	...	...	3.7	5.0
Total Current Assets	341.1	348.8	334.5	325.2	318.3	120.3	114.9
Net Property	886.1	902.9	848.9	807.3	817.4	223.0	215.4
Total Assets	1,651.9	1,680.8	1,550.0	1,493.1	1,486.5	598.4	574.8
Total Current Liabilities	330.5	355.2	365.1	348.5	357.2	109.2	107.3
Long-Term Obligations	385.0	369.0	261.0	251.0	303.7	212.2	201.2
Net Stockholders' Equity	591.7	603.8	565.2	538.7	460.2	198.0	187.4
Net Working Capital	10.7	d6.4	d30.6	d23.4	d38.9	11.2	7.6
Year-end Shs. Outstg. (000)	65,889	70,218	72,744	75,114	74,572	39,270	39,300
STATISTICAL RECORD:							
Operating Profit Margin %	4.8	6.5	7.1	6.0	2.7	4.7	4.1
Net Profit Margin %	2.5	3.6	3.9	3.0	0.8	1.7	1.4
Return on Equity %	15.1	20.9	22.6	18.0	5.3	10.5	8.4
Return on Assets %	5.4	7.5	8.3	6.5	1.6	3.5	2.7
Debt/Total Assets %	23.3	22.0	16.8	16.8	20.4	35.5	35.0
Price Range	27.00-16.19	38.00-23.38	36.88-21.63	24.81-10.19	11.69-6.69	7.56-5.81	10.00-6.88
P/E Ratio	20.6-12.4	21.8-13.4	21.6-12.6	19.5-8.0	33.4-19.1	14.4-11.1	25.6-17.6
Average Yield %	1.3	0.9	0.9	1.5	2.7	3.7	2.9

Statistics are as originally reported. Adj. for 2-for-1 stk. split, 11/97. [1] Incl. $23.6 mil ($0.22/sh) non-recurr. chg. related to a work stoppage, workers' comp. costs and bakery start-up costs.

OFFICERS:
C. A. Sullivan, Chmn., C.E.O.
M. D. Kafoure, Pres., C.O.O.
F. W. Coffey, Sr. V.P., C.F.O.

INVESTOR CONTACT: Frank W. Coffey, Sr. V.P. & C.F.O., (816) 502-4000

PRINCIPAL OFFICE: 12 East Armour Boulevard, Kansas City, MO 64111

TELEPHONE NUMBER: (816) 502-4000
FAX: (816) 502-4126
WEB: www.irin.com/ibc

NO. OF EMPLOYEES: 34,000 (approx.)

SHAREHOLDERS: 6,400 (approx.)

ANNUAL MEETING: In Sept.

INCORPORATED: DE, 1987

INSTITUTIONAL HOLDINGS:
No. of Institutions: 129
Shares Held: 30,316,393
% Held: 60.2

INDUSTRY: Bread, cake, and related products (SIC: 2051)

TRANSFER AGENT(S): United Missouri Bank, N.A., Kansas City, MO

NYSE SYMBOL IBI
Rec. Pr. 15.14 (5/31/01)

INTIMATE BRANDS, INC.

YIELD 1.8%
P/E RATIO 18.7

INTERIM EARNINGS (Per Share):

Qtr.	Apr.	July	Oct.	Jan.
1996-97	0.05	0.09	0.05	0.30
1997-98	0.06	0.12	0.07	0.30
1998-99	0.08	0.14	0.08	0.47
1999-00	0.09	0.17	0.08	0.55
2000-01	0.07	0.20	0.09	0.45

INTERIM DIVIDENDS (Per Share):

Amt.	Decl.	Ex.	Rec.	Pay.
0.07Q	5/15/00	6/07/00	6/09/00	6/20/00
0.07Q	8/18/00	8/30/00	9/01/00	9/12/00
0.07Q	11/10/00	11/29/00	12/01/00	12/12/00
0.07Q	1/26/01	3/07/01	3/09/01	3/20/01
0.07Q	5/21/01	6/06/01	6/08/01	6/19/01

Indicated div.: $0.28 (Div. Reinv. Plan)

CAPITALIZATION (2/3/01):

	($000)	(%)
Long-Term Debt	100,000	13.1
Common & Surplus	665,328	86.9
Total	765,328	100.0

RECENT DEVELOPMENTS: For the year ended 2/3/01, net income fell 5.8% to $432.5 million compared with $458.9 million in 1999. Earnings for 2000 included special charges of $9.9 million. Net sales grew 10.5% to $5.12 billion versus $4.63 billion a year earlier. Comparable-store sales increased 4.0% for the year. Operating income amounted to $744.5 million, a decrease of 6.2% compared with $793.5 million in the prior year.

PROSPECTS: As the fiscal year drew to a close, profitability was adversely affected by markdowns due to the clearing out of inventories. In the new year, the Company will continue to focus on enhancing its Victoria's Secret and Bath & Body Works brand positions to boost sales. However, considering the current U.S. economic environment, the Company is expecting modest profit growth in 2001. As a result, both inventory and expense management will be primary concerns for IBI.

BUSINESS

INTIMATE BRANDS, INC. is a specialty retailer of intimate apparel, beauty and personal care products through the Victoria's Secret, Bath & Body Works and White Barn Candle Company brands. As of 4/7/01, Victoria's Secret products are available through 879 lingerie and 470 beauty stores, the Victoria's Secret Catalogue and on-line. IBI offers a broad selection of personal care, home fragrance and decor products through 1,436 Bath & Body Works and 130 White Barn Candle stores, which were launched in November 1999. As of 12/31/00, the Company was approximately 84.1% owned by The Limited, Inc.

REVENUES

(02/03/2000)	($000)	(%)
Victoria's Secret Stores	2,339	56.3
Bath & Body Works	1,785	43.0
Other	31	0.7
Total	4,155	100.0

ANNUAL FINANCIAL DATA

	2/3/01	1/29/00	1/30/99	1/31/98	2/1/97	2/3/96	1/28/95
Earnings Per Share	**1 0.87**	**0.91**	**0.76**	**1 0.54**	**1 0.49**	**0.44**	**0.46**
Cash Flow Per Share	**1.11**	**1.11**	**0.94**	**0.74**	**0.65**	**0.60**	**0.62**
Tang. Book Val. Per Share	**1.36**	**1.09**	**1.29**	**1.06**	**0.76**	**0.51**	**1.30**
Dividends Per Share	**0.28**	**0.27**	**0.27**	**0.25**	**0.23**	**0.06**	...
Dividend Payout %	**32.2**	**30.2**	**35.2**	**45.6**	**47.0**	**13.0**	...
INCOME STATEMENT (IN MILLIONS):							
Total Revenues	5,117.2	4,510.8	3,885.8	3,617.9	2,997.3	2,516.6	2,108.3
Costs & Expenses	4,250.6	3,612.7	3,103.7	3,007.0	2,453.6	2,054.6	1,701.0
Depreciation & Amort.	122.2	104.6	101.2	106.2	85.6	75.7	69.3
Operating Income	744.5	793.5	680.8	504.7	458.1	386.3	338.0
Net Interest Inc./(Exp.)	d27.5	d32.0	d30.0	d30.3	d32.5	d49.5	...
Income Before Income Taxes	720.5	764.9	667.2	482.9	430.2	340.1	338.0
Income Taxes	288.0	306.0	267.0	194.0	172.0	136.0	135.0
Net Income	1 432.5	458.9	400.2	1 288.9	1 258.2	204.1	203.0
Cash Flow	554.6	563.5	501.4	395.1	343.8	279.7	272.3
Average Shs. Outstg. (000)	499,489	507,716	532,424	532,426	531,416	464,730	441,000
BALANCE SHEET (IN MILLIONS):							
Cash & Cash Equivalents	8.9	76.4	387.8	308.7	135.1	12.1	8.9
Total Current Assets	757.7	771.9	977.2	876.1	657.0	420.0	335.6
Net Property	560.5	449.0	398.5	392.5	395.6	358.0	306.2
Total Assets	1,457.3	1,345.0	1,448.1	1,347.7	1,135.2	943.4	768.6
Total Current Liabilities	636.0	653.8	537.2	412.9	323.7	247.3	139.5
Long-Term Obligations	100.0	100.0	250.0	350.0	350.0	350.0	...
Net Stockholders' Equity	665.3	544.7	644.6	560.8	402.1	268.9	573.2
Net Working Capital	121.8	118.2	440.1	463.1	333.3	172.8	196.1
Year-end Shs. Outstg. (000)	490,751	498,300	498,918	530,454	530,246	530,670	441,000
STATISTICAL RECORD:							
Operating Profit Margin %	14.5	17.6	17.5	13.9	15.3	15.4	16.0
Net Profit Margin %	8.5	10.2	10.3	8.0	8.6	8.1	9.6
Return on Equity %	65.0	84.2	62.1	51.5	64.2	75.9	35.4
Return on Assets %	29.7	34.1	27.6	21.4	22.7	21.6	26.4
Debt/Total Assets %	6.9	7.4	17.3	26.0	30.8	37.1	...
Price Range	24.31-12.31	26.19-13.66	15.18-8.57	11.91-7.86	11.73-6.37	8.81-6.55	...
P/E Ratio	27.9-14.2	28.9-15.1	20.0-11.3	21.9-14.5	24.1-13.1	20.1-14.9	...
Average Yield %	1.5	1.4	2.2	2.5	2.5	0.7	...

Statistics are as originally reported. Adj. for stk. splits: 2-for-1, 5/00; 5% div., 6/99. 1 Incl. non-recurr. chrgs. $9.9 mill., 2/01; $67.6 mill., 1/98; $12.0 mill., 2/97

OFFICERS:
L. H. Wexner, Chmn., C.E.O.
K. B. Gilman, Vice-Chmn.
T. T. Travis, V.P., C.F.O.

INVESTOR CONTACT: Investor Relations, (614) 415-8000

PRINCIPAL OFFICE: Three Limited Parkway, P.O. Box 16000, Columbus, OH 43216

TELEPHONE NUMBER: (614) 415-8000
FAX: (614) 415-7080
WEB: www.intimatebrands.com

NO. OF EMPLOYEES: 16,000 full-time (approx.); 53,000 part-time (approx.)

SHAREHOLDERS: 4,000 (approx. record)

ANNUAL MEETING: In May

INCORPORATED: DE, May, 1995

INSTITUTIONAL HOLDINGS:
No. of Institutions: 162
Shares Held: 64,077,561
% Held: 13.1

INDUSTRY: Women's accessory & specialty stores (SIC: 5632)

TRANSFER AGENT(S): First Chicago Trust Company of New York, Jersey City, NJ

NYSE SYMBOL IRM
Rec. Pr. 41.11 (5/31/01)

IRON MOUNTAIN INC.

YIELD ...
P/E RATIO ...

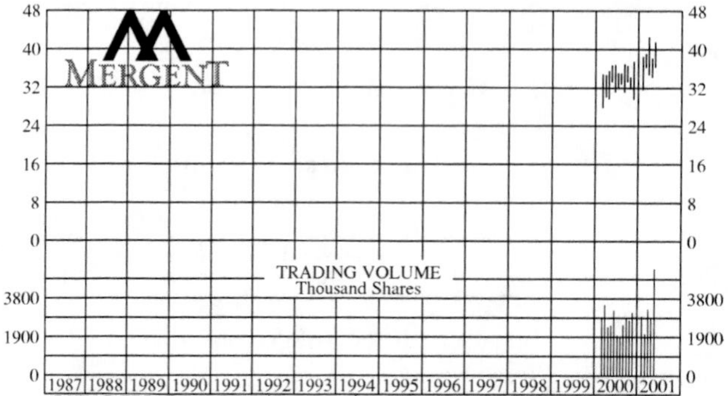

*7 YEAR PRICE SCORE N/A *12 MONTH PRICE SCORE 113.2

*NYSE COMPOSITE INDEX=100

INTERIM EARNINGS (Per Share):

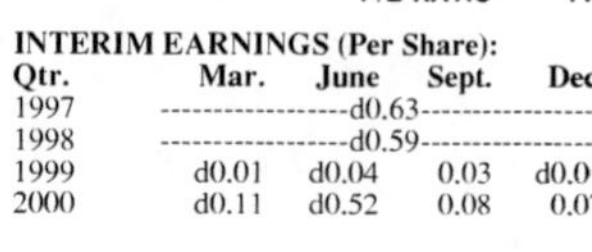

Qtr.	Mar.	June	Sept.	Dec.
1997	-------	d0.63	-------	
1998	-------	d0.59	-------	
1999	d0.01	d0.04	0.03	d0.01
2000	d0.11	d0.52	0.08	0.07

INTERIM DIVIDENDS (Per Share):

Amt.	Decl.	Ex.	Rec.	Pay.

No dividends paid.

CAPITALIZATION (12/31/00):

	($000)	(%)
Long-Term Debt	1,314,342	56.6
Deferred Income Tax	38,948	1.7
Minority Interest	43,029	1.9
Common & Surplus	924,458	39.8
Total	2,320,777	100.0

RECENT DEVELOPMENTS: For the year ended 12/31/00, the Company reported a loss of $24.9 million, before an after-tax extraordinary gain of $2.9 million, versus income from continuing operations of $1.1 million in the previous year. Results for 2000 included merger-related expenses of $9.1 million and a non-cash charge of $15.1 million. The 1999 results excluded a net loss of $13.2 million from discontinued operations. Total revenues surged 89.9% to $986.4 million from $516.5 million in 1999.

PROSPECTS: Since 2/28/01 the Company completed four acquisitions for approximately $21.0 million. Separately, the Company is expecting sales to be in the range of $1.15 billion to $1.17 billion for the year. For the year ended 12/31/00, the Company anticipates capital expenditures of $175.0 million to $200.0 million, of which $7.0 million to $10.0 million may be associated with the developmental phase of IRM's digital services.

BUSINESS

IRON MOUNTAIN INC. (formerly Pierce Leahy Inc.) is a global full-service provider of records, information management and related services to more than 125,000 customer accounts. The Company provides storage and management services for all types of media, including paper, computer disks and tapes, microfilm and microfiche, master audio and video tapes, film and optical disks, X-rays and blueprints. IRM's principal services include courier pickup and delivery, filing, retrieval and destruction of records, database management, customized reporting and disaster recovery support. In addition, the Company sells storage materials and provides consulting, facilities management and other outsourcing services. IRM operates more than 625 records management facilities located in the U.S., Canada, Europe and Latin America.

BUSINESS LINE ANALYSIS

(12/31/00)	Rev(%)	Inc(%)
Business Records Mgmt	68.4	74.0
Data Security Services	17.0	16.4
International	11.8	8.0
Corporate & Other	2.8	1.6
Total	100.0	100.0

ANNUAL FINANCIAL DATA

	12/31/00	[1] 12/31/99	12/31/98	12/31/97	12/31/96	12/31/95	12/31/94
Earnings Per Share	[6] d0.47	[5] d0.03	[4] d0.39	[3] d0.42	...	...	...
Cash Flow Per Share	1.97	1.99	0.94	0.61	...	...	...
INCOME STATEMENT (IN THOUSANDS):							
Total Revenues	986,371	519,549	270,300	183,517	129,748	95,396	82,636
Costs & Expenses	750,978	387,897	197,943	133,395	93,361	71,731	64,716
Depreciation & Amort.	129,405	67,403	37,165	22,597	13,385	8,696	9,504
Operating Income	105,988	64,249	35,192	27,525	19,748	14,969	8,416
Net Interest Inc./(Exp.)	d117,975	d54,425	d42,864	d29,262	d17,225	d9,622	d7,216
Income Before Income Taxes	d18,032	9,841	d7,672	d1,737	2,523	5,347	1,200
Income Taxes	9,125	10,579	3,318	7,424	...	...	...
Equity Earnings/Minority Int.	2,224	d322	...	...	...	...	...
Net Income	[6] d24,933	[5] d1,060	[4] d10,990	[3] d9,161	[2][4] 2,523	[2] 5,347	[2] 1,200
Cash Flow	104,472	66,343	26,175	13,436	14,347	13,154	10,688
Average Shs. Outstg.	53,125	33,345	27,728	22,085	...	...	...
BALANCE SHEET (IN THOUSANDS):							
Cash & Cash Equivalents	6,200	3,830	2,312	1,782	1,254	722	...
Total Current Assets	236,668	143,664	51,962	31,376	20,381	16,691	...
Net Property	832,394	403,739	229,694	160,481	113,134	74,427	...
Total Assets	2,659,096	1,317,212	666,458	393,900	234,820	131,328	...
Total Current Liabilities	314,053	150,348	68,109	45,095	44,314	24,830	...
Long-Term Obligations	1,314,342	603,057	514,362	277,767	209,330	116,812	...
Net Stockholders' Equity	924,458	488,754	63,095	59,323	d25,438	d18,201	...
Net Working Capital	d77,385	d6,684	d16,147	d13,719	d23,933	d8,139	...
Year-end Shs. Outstg.	55,280	35,467	28,111	27,189	16	17	...
STATISTICAL RECORD:							
Operating Profit Margin %	10.7	12.4	13.0	15.0	15.2	15.7	10.2
Net Profit Margin %	...	...	...	...	1.9	5.6	1.5
Return on Assets %	...	...	...	...	1.1	4.1	...
Debt/Total Assets %	49.4	45.8	77.2	70.5	89.1	88.9	...
Price Range	37.50-27.75	...	...	...	...	...	...

Statistics are as originally reported. [1] Financials for 1999 and prior reflect the results of Pierce Leahy. [2] Bef. extraord. loss of $2.0 mill., 1996; $3.3 mill., 1995; $6.4 mill., 1994. [3] Bef. extraord. loss of $6.0 mill. & incl. spec. chrg. of $2.5 mill. [4] Incl. non-recurr. chrg. of $7.9 mill., 1998; $3.3 mill., 1996. [5] Bef. loss from disc. opers. of $13.2 mill. [6] Incl. nonrecurr. chrg. of $9.1 mill. & a non-cash chrg. of $15.1 mill. rel. to previously granted stock options.

OFFICERS:
C. R. Reese, Chmn., Pres., C.E.O.
J. F. Kenny, Jr., Exec. V.P., C.F.O.

INVESTOR CONTACT: John Kenny, Jr., (617) 535-4799

PRINCIPAL OFFICE: 745 Atlantic Avenue, Boston, MA 02111

TELEPHONE NUMBER: (617) 535-4766
FAX: (617) 350-7881
WEB: www.pierceleahy.com

NO. OF EMPLOYEES: 8,300 (approx.)

SHAREHOLDERS: 682 (record); 6,900 (approx. beneficial)

ANNUAL MEETING: In May

INCORPORATED: PA, Mar., 1997

INSTITUTIONAL HOLDINGS:
No. of Institutions: 110
Shares Held: 35,156,508
% Held: 63.4

INDUSTRY: Special warehousing and storage, nec (SIC: 4226)

TRANSFER AGENT(S): Boston EquiServe, LLP, Canton, MA

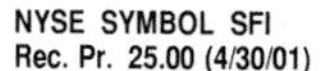

NYSE SYMBOL SFI
Rec. Pr. 25.00 (4/30/01)

ISTAR FINANCIAL INC.

YIELD 9.8%
P/E RATIO 11.9

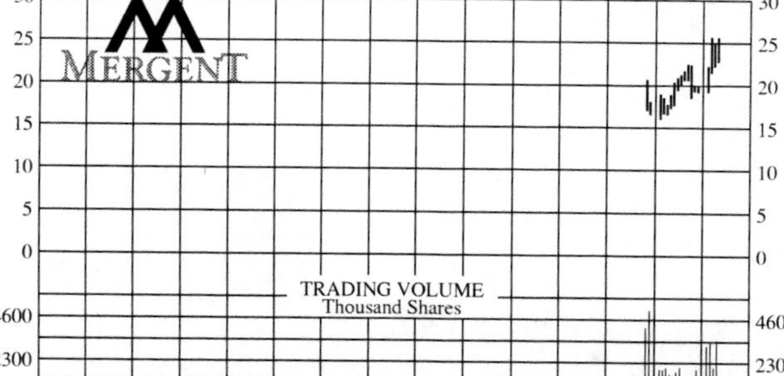

INTERIM EARNINGS (Per Share):

Qtr.	Mar.	June	Sept.	Dec.
1999		0.25		
2000	0.50	0.52	0.54	0.54

INTERIM DIVIDENDS (Per Share):

Amt.	Decl.	Ex.	Rec.	Pay.
0.60Q	4/03/00	4/12/00	4/14/00	4/28/00
0.60Q	7/03/00	7/13/00	7/17/00	7/31/00
0.60Q	10/02/00	10/12/00	10/16/00	10/30/00
0.60Q	12/15/00	12/27/00	12/29/00	1/12/01
0.613Q	4/02/01	4/11/01	4/16/01	4/30/01

Indicated div.: $2.45

CAPITALIZATION (12/31/00):

	($000)	(%)
Long-Term Debt	2,131,967	54.3
Minority Interest	6,224	0.2
Preferred Stock	11	0.0
Common & Surplus	1,787,874	45.5
Total	3,926,076	100.0

RECENT DEVELOPMENTS: For the year ended 12/31/00, income totaled $218.3 million, before an extraordinary loss of $705,000, versus net income of $38.9 million a year earlier. Results for the current year included a gain on sale of corporate tenant lease assets of $2.9 million. Total revenue jumped 78.2% to $471.8 million compared with $264.8 million in 1999. Interest income improved 27.7% to $268.0 million from $209.8 million in the prior year.

PROSPECTS: Going forward, the Company will continue to focus on its core business strategy of originating and acquiring large-balance, structured lending and corporate leasing transactions secured by high-quality commercial real estate assets in major metropolitan markets across the United States. Also, SFI expects new investment funding to occur earlier than loan repayments in the first half of 2001.

BUSINESS

ISTAR FINANCIAL INC. (formerly Starwood Financial Inc.) is a finance company that focuses on the commercial real estate industry. The Company offers structured financing to private and corporate owners of real estate nationwide, including senior and junior mortgage debt, corporate and mezzanine lending, and corporate net lease financing. The Company also provides financing solutions for a wide variety of commercial property types, including central business district and suburban office buildings, warehouse/distribution facilities, world class resorts and full service hotels, high-end multifamily properties, regional malls and mixed-use assets.

REVENUES

(12/31/2000)	($000)	(%)
Real Estate Lending	279,680	59.3
Corporate Tenant Leasing	191,821	40.6
Corporate/Other	321	0.1
Total	471,822	100.0

ANNUAL FINANCIAL DATA

	12/31/00	12/31/99	12/31/98	12/31/97	12/31/96	12/31/95	12/31/94
Earnings Per Share	**1 2.10**	**0.25**	**1.36**	...	**d0.04**	**d0.01**	**d0.02**
Tang. Book Val. Per Share	**20.86**	**21.20**	**18.52**	**0.14**	**0.10**	**0.14**	**0.15**
Dividends Per Share	**2.37**	**1.70**	**0.73**	...	...	...	...
Dividend Payout %	**112.9**	**679.7**	**53.7**	...	...	...	...
INCOME STATEMENT (IN MILLIONS):							
Interest Income	268.0	209.8	112.9	0.9	0.5	0.1	0.3
Total Income	471.8	264.8	128.1	1.9	0.5	0.1	0.3
Costs & Expenses	221.8	215.5	63.9	0.5	0.9	0.3	0.6
Depreciation	34.5	10.3	4.3	...	...	...	...
Income Before Income Taxes	218.5	38.9	60.0	1.4	d0.4	d0.1	d0.3
Equity Earnings/Minority Int.	d0.2	...	d0.1	d1.4	d0.2	...	...
Net Income	1 218.3	38.9	59.9	...	d0.6	d0.1	d0.3
Average Shs. Outstg. (000)	86,151	60,393	43,460	43,464	15,300	15,300	15,300
BALANCE SHEET (IN MILLIONS):							
Cash & Cash Equivalents	43.2	48.9	21.2	11.5	1.9	2.1	2.2
Total Assets	4,034.8	3,813.6	2,059.6	13.4	5.7	2.2	2.4
Long-Term Obligations	2,132.0	1,901.2	1,055.7	...	...	...	...
Total Liabilities	2,246.9	2,012.2	1,088.9	7.1	4.1	...	0.1
Net Stockholders' Equity	1,787.9	1,801.3	970.7	6.4	1.6	2.2	2.3
Year-end Shs. Outstg. (000)	85,726	84,985	52,408	45,300	15,300	15,300	15,300
STATISTICAL RECORD:							
Net Inc.+Depr./Assets %	6.3	1.3	3.1	0.1	...	...	...
Return on Equity %	12.2	2.2	6.2	0.2	...	...	...
Return on Assets %	5.4	1.0	2.9	0.1	...	...	...
Price Range	22.50-16.00	20.67-16.50	...	...	...	...	...
P/E Ratio	10.7-7.6	82.6-66.0	...	...	...	...	...
Average Yield %	12.3	9.1	...	...	...	...	...

Statistics are as originally reported. 1 Incl. gain on sale of corp. tenant lease assets of $2.9 mill.

OFFICERS:
J. Sugarman, Chmn., Pres., C.E.O.
S. B. Haber, Exec. V.P., C.F.O., Sec.

INVESTOR CONTACT: Investor Relations, (212) 930-9400

PRINCIPAL OFFICE: 1114 Avenue of the Americas, 27th Floor, New York, NY 10036

TELEPHONE NUMBER: (212) 930-9400
FAX: (212) 930-9494
WEB: www.istarfinancial.com

NO. OF EMPLOYEES: 126 (avg.)

SHAREHOLDERS: 1,267 (approx.)

ANNUAL MEETING: In May

INCORPORATED: CA, Apr., 1988; reincorp., MD, June, 1998

INSTITUTIONAL HOLDINGS:
No. of Institutions: 80
Shares Held: 11,773,999
% Held: 13.7

INDUSTRY: Real estate investment trusts (SIC: 6798)

TRANSFER AGENT(S): EquiServe, Inc., Jersey City, NJ

NYSE SYMBOL ITT
Rec. Pr. 46.66 (5/31/01)

ITT INDUSTRIES INC.

YIELD 1.3%
P/E RATIO 15.9

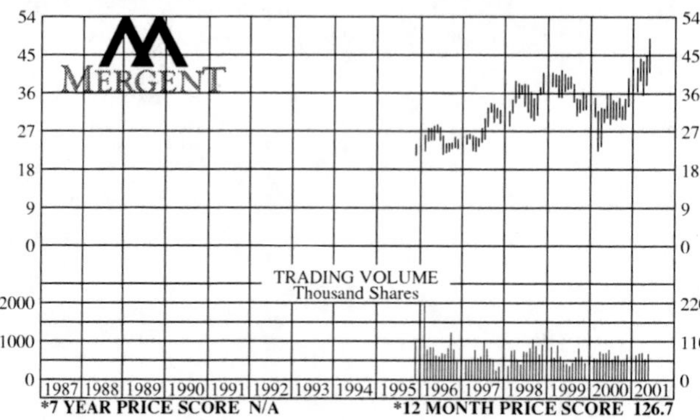

INTERIM EARNINGS (Per Share):

Qtr.	Mar.	June	Sept.	Dec.
1997	0.37	0.68	0.45	0.60
1998	0.46	0.57	0.23	0.59
1999	0.45	0.70	0.60	0.80
2000	0.57	0.78	0.72	0.87

INTERIM DIVIDENDS (Per Share):

Amt.	Decl.	Ex.	Rec.	Pay.
0.15Q	7/11/00	8/23/00	8/25/00	10/01/00
0.15Q	10/17/00	11/20/00	11/22/00	1/01/01
0.15Q	3/06/01	3/14/01	3/16/01	4/01/01
0.15Q	5/15/01	5/23/01	5/25/01	7/01/01

Indicated div.: $0.60

CAPITALIZATION (12/31/00):

	($000)	(%)
Long-Term Debt	408,400	25.2
Common & Surplus	1,211,200	74.8
Total	1,619,600	100.0

RECENT DEVELOPMENTS: For the year ended 12/31/00, net income increased 13.6% to $264.5 million compared with $232.9 million in the previous year. Results for 1999 included an after-tax net credit of $2.9 million. Earnings were driven by a 50.0% increase in revenues from the Connectors and Switches segment as well as a strong performance at the Company's water and wastewater pump operations. Revenues rose 4.6% to $4.83 billion

PROSPECTS: The Connectors and Switches segment should continue to achieve double-digit revenue growth. Defense Products and Services segment revenues are expected to decline due to reduction of defense programs. However, Defense Products and Services segment revenues are expected to rebound by the end of 2001 as new service contracts take effect. ITT expects the pumps and Complementary Products segment to perform well.

BUSINESS

ITT INDUSTRIES INC. is comprised of four major businesses: Defense Products & Services serves the military and government agencies with products such as air traffic control systems, jamming devices that guard military planes against radar-guided weapons, digital combat radios, night vision devices and satellite instruments; Pumps & Complementary Products supply mixers, heat exchangers and related products as well as name brand pumps; Connectors & Switches consist of products marketed under the Cannon® brand which include connectors, switches and cabling used in telecommunications, computing, aerospace, industrial applications and network services; Specialty Products produce engineered valves and switches, products for the marine and leisure markets, fluid handling materials and specialty shock absorbers and friction materials for the transportation industry.

ANNUAL FINANCIAL DATA

	12/31/00	12/31/99	[5] 12/31/98	12/31/97	12/31/96	12/31/95	12/31/94
Earnings Per Share	**2.94**	**[1][7] 2.53**	**[6] d0.86**	**[4] 0.94**	**1.85**	**[1][2] 0.03**	**[1][3] 7.10**
Cash Flow Per Share	**5.18**	**4.50**	**0.87**	**4.55**	**5.45**	**3.96**	**12.60**
Tang. Book Val. Per Share	...	...	**4.53**	...	**3.80**	**2.26**	**45.32**
Dividends Per Share	**0.60**	**0.60**	**0.60**	**0.60**	**0.45**	**1.49**	**1.98**
Dividend Payout %	**20.4**	**23.7**	...	**63.8**	**24.3**	**N.M.**	**27.9**
INCOME STATEMENT (IN MILLIONS):							
Total Revenues	4,829.4	4,632.2	4,492.7	8,777.1	8,718.1	8,884.0	23,620.0
Costs & Expenses	4,134.5	4,035.9	4,371.7	8,054.1	7,776.7	8,015.0	21,518.0
Depreciation & Amort.	201.8	181.1	195.6	436.4	433.0	423.0	597.0
Operating Income	493.1	415.2	d74.6	286.6	508.4	446.0	1,505.0
Net Interest Inc./(Exp.)	d75.2	d46.8	d82.4	d115.7	d136.3	d135.0	d208.0
Income Before Income Taxes	419.9	369.7	d160.0	186.4	371.0	71.0	1,259.0
Income Taxes	155.4	136.8	cr62.4	72.7	148.4	50.0	389.0
Equity Earnings/Minority Int.	...	...	...	...	...	...	d18.0
Net Income	264.5	[1][7] 232.9	[6] d97.6	[4] 113.7	222.6	[1][2] 21.0	[1][3] 852.0
Cash Flow	466.3	414.0	98.0	550.1	655.6	429.0	1,413.0
Average Shs. Outstg. (000)	90,000	92,000	113,100	121,000	120,400	112,000	115,000
BALANCE SHEET (IN MILLIONS):							
Cash & Cash Equivalents	88.7	181.7	880.9	192.2	121.9	94.0	568.0
Total Current Assets	1,506.3	1,628.3	2,382.4	2,377.4	2,289.1	2,502.0	6,396.0
Net Property	865.4	847.0	991.6	2,024.3	2,166.7	2,235.0	5,346.0
Total Assets	4,611.4	4,529.8	5,048.8	6,220.5	5,491.2	5,879.0	100,854.0
Total Current Liabilities	2,232.7	2,110.4	2,150.8	3,544.9	2,538.4	2,661.0	3,523.0
Long-Term Obligations	408.4	478.8	515.5	532.2	583.2	961.0	6,407.0
Net Stockholders' Equity	1,211.2	1,201.7	1,300.0	822.3	799.2	627.0	5,459.0
Net Working Capital	d726.4	d482.1	231.6	d1,167.5	d249.3	d159.0	2,873.0
Year-end Shs. Outstg. (000)	87,915	88,000	96,000	118,400	118,400	117,000	106,000
STATISTICAL RECORD:							
Operating Profit Margin %	10.2	9.0	...	3.3	5.8	5.0	6.4
Net Profit Margin %	5.5	5.0	...	1.3	2.6	0.2	3.6
Return on Equity %	21.8	19.4	...	13.8	27.9	3.3	15.6
Return on Assets %	5.7	5.1	...	1.8	4.1	0.4	0.8
Debt/Total Assets %	8.9	10.6	10.2	8.6	10.6	16.3	6.4
Price Range	39.63-22.38	41.50-30.50	40.88-28.13	33.69-22.13	28.63-21.50	24.00-21.25	...
P/E Ratio	13.5-7.6	16.4-12.1	...	35.8-23.5	15.5-11.6	797.3-706.0	...
Average Yield %	1.9	1.7	1.7	2.2	1.8	6.6	...

Statistics are as originally reported. Results prior to 1995 refl. ITT Corp. [1] Incl. non-recur. aft.-tax chrg. $18.0 mil, 1994; $164.0, 1995; $2.9 mil, 1999. [2] Bef. disc. ops. gain $994.0 mil & extraord. loss $307.0 mil [3] Bef. disc. ops. gain $828.0 mil & extraord. chrg. $50.0 mil [4] Inc. non-recur. aft.-tax chrg. $145.8 mil & Bef. acctg. change chrg. $5.6 mil [5] Refl. sale of ITT Auto. [6] Bef. gain of $1.63 bil fr. disc. ops. [7] Bef. non-recur. aft.-tax net cr. of $2.9 mil

OFFICERS:
L. J. Giuliano, Chmn., Pres., C.E.O.
D. J. Anderson, Sr. V.P., C.F.O.
V. A. Maffeo, Sr. V.P., Gen. Couns.

INVESTOR CONTACT: Theodore Economou, Mgr., Inv. Rel., (914) 641-2000

PRINCIPAL OFFICE: 4 West Red Oak Lane, White Plains, NY 10604

TELEPHONE NUMBER: (914) 641-2000
FAX: (914) 696-2950
WEB: www.ittind.com

NO. OF EMPLOYEES: 42,000 (approx.)

SHAREHOLDERS: 36,917

ANNUAL MEETING: In May

INCORPORATED: IN, 1995

INSTITUTIONAL HOLDINGS:
No. of Institutions: 278
Shares Held: 62,308,069
% Held: 70.9

INDUSTRY: Fluid power pumps and motors (SIC: 3594)

TRANSFER AGENT(S): The Bank of New York, New York, NY

NYSE SYMBOL JBL
Rec. Pr. 29.38 (5/31/01)

JABIL CIRCUIT, INC.

YIELD ...
P/E RATIO 32.6

MERGENT

TRADING VOLUME
Thousand Shares

1987 1988 1989 1990 1991 1992 1993 1994 1995 1996 1997 1998 1999 2000 2001

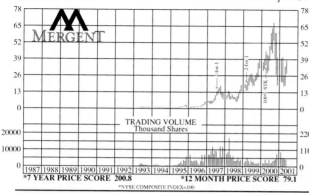

***7 YEAR PRICE SCORE 200.8** ***12 MONTH PRICE SCORE 79.1**

*NYSE COMPOSITE INDEX=100

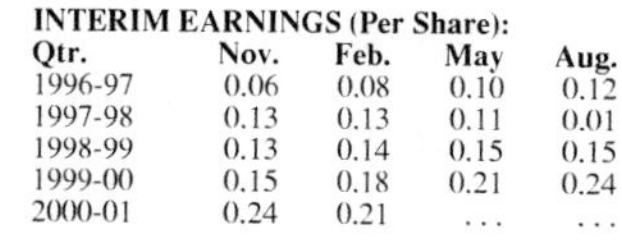

INTERIM EARNINGS (Per Share):

Qtr.	Nov.	Feb.	May	Aug.
1996-97	0.06	0.08	0.10	0.12
1997-98	0.13	0.13	0.11	0.01
1998-99	0.13	0.14	0.15	0.15
1999-00	0.15	0.18	0.21	0.24
2000-01	0.24	0.21	...	...

INTERIM DIVIDENDS (Per Share):

Amt.	Decl.	Ex.	Rec.	Pay.
100% STK	3/16/00	3/31/00	3/23/00	3/30/00

CAPITALIZATION (8/31/00):

	($000)	(%)
Long-Term Debt	25,000	1.9
Deferred Income Tax	28,112	2.1
Common & Surplus	1,270,183	96.0
Total	1,323,295	100.0

RECENT DEVELOPMENTS: For the three months ended 2/28/01, net income advanced 20.0% to $40.7 million compared with $33.9 million in the previous year. Results for 2000 included non-recurring integration costs of $843,000 related to the impending acquisition of certain manufacturing facilities of Marconi Communications. Net revenue jumped 44.6% to $1.21 billion versus $837.6 million in 1999. Gross profit rose 29.0% to $108.4 million, while operating income improved 15.2% to $58.3 million.

PROSPECTS: On 1/18/01, the Company announced the formation of Jabil Technology Services, a new technology division that includes an optic technology development lab. Separately, the Company entered into an agreement with Marconi plc, a global communications and information technology company, to acquire certain Marconi Communications manufacturing operations in the U.S., Italy, Germany and the United Kingdom, for approximately $390.0 million.

BUSINESS

JABIL CIRCUIT, INC. is a worldwide independent provider of electronic manufacturing services to original equipment manufacturers in the communications, computer peripherals, personal computer, automotive and consumer products industries. The Company's services include circuit design, board design from schematic, mechanical and production design and implementation of product testing, direct fulfillment, warranty and repair services. The Company operates 20 facilities throughout North America, Latin America, Europe and Asia. Major customers include Cisco Systems, Inc., Dell Computer Corporation, Hewlett-Packard Company, Johnson Controls, Inc. and Lucent Technologies.

GEOGRAPHIC DATA

(8/31/2000)	Rev ($000)	Inc (%)
Untied States	2,014,669	56.6
China	234,571	6.6
Mexico	561,834	15.8
Malaysia	272,999	7.7
Scotland	266,088	7.5
Other	208,160	5.8
Total	3,558,321	100.0

ANNUAL FINANCIAL DATA

	8/31/00	8/31/99	8/31/98	8/31/97	8/31/96	8/31/95	8/31/94
Earnings Per Share	**0.78**	**0.56**	**[1] 0.37**	**0.34**	**0.17**	**0.06**	**0.02**
Cash Flow Per Share	**1.30**	**0.90**	**0.60**	**0.50**	**0.29**	**0.15**	**0.10**
Tang. Book Val. Per Share	**6.68**	**3.32**	**1.67**	**1.23**	**0.87**	**0.50**	**0.45**
INCOME STATEMENT (IN MILLIONS):							
Total Revenues	3,558.3	2,000.3	1,277.4	978.1	863.3	559.5	375.8
Costs & Expenses	3,246.1	1,803.1	1,156.6	871.3	799.7	531.1	358.0
Depreciation & Amort.	99.3	56.0	35.7	24.9	18.2	12.0	9.5
Operating Income	212.9	141.2	85.1	81.9	45.4	16.4	8.4
Net Interest Inc./(Exp.)	d0.2	d1.7	d3.1	d1.6	d7.3	d6.3	d3.5
Income Before Income Taxes	212.7	139.5	82.0	80.2	38.1	10.1	4.9
Income Taxes	67.0	48.1	25.0	27.7	13.7	2.8	2.4
Net Income	145.6	91.5	[1] 56.9	52.5	24.3	7.3	2.6
Cash Flow	245.0	147.5	92.6	77.4	42.6	19.3	12.0
Average Shs. Outstg. (000)	187,448	163,656	154,302	153,360	145,336	124,400	123,576
BALANCE SHEET (IN MILLIONS):							
Cash & Cash Equivalents	337.6	140.7	23.1	45.5	73.3	5.5	1.8
Total Current Assets	1,387.3	587.9	290.4	266.0	227.3	218.2	129.2
Net Property	587.5	314.3	224.7	139.5	70.7	61.7	44.5
Total Assets	2,018.2	920.7	526.7	405.9	299.9	281.0	174.3
Total Current Liabilities	692.0	330.8	186.7	168.7	111.6	184.9	101.6
Long-Term Obligations	25.0	33.3	81.7	50.0	58.4	27.9	18.2
Net Stockholders' Equity	1,270.2	545.8	248.4	181.5	124.2	59.6	51.2
Net Working Capital	695.3	257.1	103.7	97.3	115.8	33.3	27.6
Year-end Shs. Outstg. (000)	190,251	164,454	149,072	148,000	142,384	118,200	114,872
STATISTICAL RECORD:							
Operating Profit Margin %	6.0	7.1	6.7	8.4	5.3	2.9	2.2
Net Profit Margin %	4.1	4.6	4.5	5.4	2.8	1.3	0.7
Return on Equity %	11.5	16.8	22.9	28.9	19.6	12.2	5.0
Return on Assets %	7.2	9.9	10.8	12.9	8.1	2.6	1.5
Debt/Total Assets %	1.2	3.6	15.5	12.3	19.5	9.9	10.4
Price Range	68.00-18.63	38.97-14.25	18.72-5.75	18.00-3.84	5.33-0.64	2.88-0.47	1.17-0.44
P/E Ratio	174.3-47.8	69.6-25.4	50.6-15.5	52.5-11.2	31.8-3.8	49.1-8.0	54.4-20.3

Statistics are as originally reported. Adj. for stk. split: 100.0%, 3/00; 2-for-1, 2/99; 2-for-1, 7/97. [1] Incl. nonrecurr. chrg. of $5.2 mill., 2000; $20.8 mill., 1998

OFFICERS:
W. D. Morean, Chmn.
T. A. Sansone, Vice-Chmn.
T. L. Main, Pres., C.E.O.
C. A. Lewis, C.F.O.

INVESTOR CONTACT: Investor Relations, (727) 803-3349

PRINCIPAL OFFICE: 10560 Ninth St. North, St. Petersburg, FL 33716

TELEPHONE NUMBER: (727) 803-3349
FAX: (727) 579-8529
WEB: www.jabil.com

NO. OF EMPLOYEES: 19,115

SHAREHOLDERS: 2,511 (approx.)

ANNUAL MEETING: In Jan.

INCORPORATED: MI, 1969; reincorp., DE, Feb., 1992

INSTITUTIONAL HOLDINGS:
No. of Institutions: 274
Shares Held: 113,974,530
% Held: 59.6

INDUSTRY: Printed circuit boards (SIC: 3672)

TRANSFER AGENT(S): BankBoston NA, Boston, MA

NYSE SYMBOL JEC
Rec. Pr. 65.92 (4/30/01)

JACOBS ENGINEERING GROUP INC.

YIELD ...
P/E RATIO 22.8

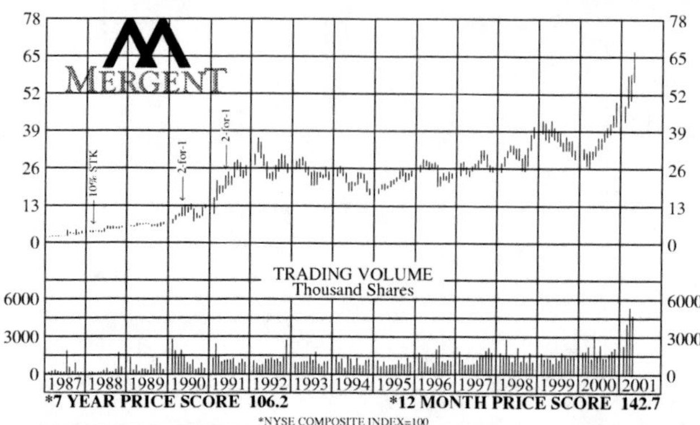

INTERIM EARNINGS (Per Share):

Qtr.	Dec.	Mar.	June	Sept.
1996-97	0.42	0.44	0.46	0.48
1997-98	0.49	0.51	0.53	0.55
1998-99	0.58	0.61	0.63	0.65
1999-00	d0.22	0.69	0.72	0.73
2000-01	0.75	...	...	...

INTERIM DIVIDENDS (Per Share):

Amt.	Decl.	Ex.	Rec.	Pay.

No dividends paid.

CAPITALIZATION (9/30/00):

	($000)	(%)
Long-Term Debt	146,820	22.7
Minority Interest	5,204	0.8
Common & Surplus	495,543	76.5
Total	647,567	100.0

RECENT DEVELOPMENTS: For the quarter ended 12/31/00, net income was $20.1 million compared with a net loss of $5.8 million in 1999. Results for 1999 included a provision for litigation settlement loss of $38.0 million. JEC's backlog at 12/31/00 totaled $5.69 billion versus $4.34 billion in 1999. Revenues were $929.2 million, up 14.8% from $809.1 million a year earlier. Operating profit increased 10.5% to $33.2 million versus $30.0 million the year before.

PROSPECTS: On 2/7/01, JEC announced that its subsidiary, Jacobs Engineering Group Inc., was selected by the Federal Aviation Administration to provide architectural and engineering design and design-build services nationwide. The eight-year, $404.0 million contract provides up to $154.0 million for design and $250.0 million for design-build. On 1/9/01, JEC announced receipt of a multimillion dollar engineering and procurement alliance contract from Chevron Products Company.

BUSINESS

JACOBS ENGINEERING GROUP INC. is a major global engineering, architecture, technology, and construction firm, specializing in the full spectrum of project delivery services including engineering, procurement, construction, and maintenance. The Company's Jacobs Facilities division, known in the government and institutional marketplace as Sverdrup CRSS, is JEC's architecture, engineering, and construction management organization for the facilities market. Jacobs Construction Management Inc. is JEC's construction organization. In January 1999, the Company acquired Sverdrup Corporation.

ANNUAL FINANCIAL DATA

	9/30/00	9/30/99	9/30/98	9/30/97	9/30/96	9/30/95	9/30/94
Earnings Per Share	**2 1.93**	**2.47**	**2.08**	**1.80**	**1.56**	**1.27**	**1 0.75**
Cash Flow Per Share	**3.44**	**2.05**	**2.96**	**2.55**	**2.25**	**1.84**	**1.19**
Tang. Book Val. Per Share	**8.58**	**12.51**	**11.48**	**9.65**	**9.44**	**7.72**	**6.45**
INCOME STATEMENT (IN MILLIONS):							
Total Revenues	3,418.9	2,875.0	2,101.1	1,780.6	1,799.0	1,723.1	1,165.8
Costs & Expenses	3,254.2	2,735.1	1,991.7	1,688.2	1,717.1	1,656.2	1,122.9
Depreciation & Amort.	40.1	31.6	23.0	18.8	17.3	14.2	11.0
Operating Income	124.6	108.3	86.5	73.6	64.6	52.7	31.8
Net Interest Inc./(Exp.)	d7.5	d5.7	2.7	3.0	1.4	0.4	0.3
Income Before Income Taxes	81.3	104.5	88.8	77.4	66.8	53.4	31.4
Income Taxes	30.3	39.1	34.4	30.6	26.5	21.1	12.6
Net Income	2 51.0	65.4	54.4	46.0	40.4	32.2	1 18.8
Cash Flow	91.1	97.0	77.4	64.8	56.9	46.1	30.5
Average Shs. Outstg. (000)	26,473	26,478	26,096	25,727	25,613	25,208	24,916
BALANCE SHEET (IN MILLIONS):							
Cash & Cash Equivalents	65.8	53.5	117.8	77.1	65.6	41.9	48.5
Total Current Assets	851.0	729.6	566.0	503.9	383.6	368.6	367.5
Net Property	150.5	139.7	100.6	93.4	79.0	80.1	60.0
Total Assets	1,384.4	1,220.2	807.5	744.2	572.5	533.9	504.4
Total Current Liabilities	683.9	585.0	368.3	325.7	228.1	255.3	261.4
Long-Term Obligations	146.8	135.4	26.2	54.1	36.3	17.8	25.0
Net Stockholders' Equity	495.5	448.7	371.4	324.3	283.4	238.8	200.4
Net Working Capital	167.2	144.6	197.7	178.2	155.6	113.3	106.1
Year-end Shs. Outstg. (000)	26,386	26,143	25,613	25,786	25,745	25,496	25,095
STATISTICAL RECORD:							
Operating Profit Margin %	3.6	3.8	4.1	4.1	3.6	3.1	2.7
Net Profit Margin %	1.5	2.3	2.6	2.6	2.2	1.9	1.7
Return on Equity %	10.3	14.6	14.6	14.5	14.2	13.5	9.4
Return on Assets %	3.7	5.4	6.7	6.3	7.0	6.0	3.7
Debt/Total Assets %	10.6	11.1	3.2	7.3	6.3	3.3	5.0
Price Range	49.19-26.19	42.75-29.25	40.75-24.75	32.56-23.25	29.38-19.63	25.75-17.25	26.88-16.88
P/E Ratio	25.5-13.6	17.3-11.8	19.6-11.9	18.1-12.9	18.8-12.6	20.3-13.6	35.8-22.5

Statistics are as originally reported. 1 Incl. a nonrecur. chrg. of $8.6 mill. rel. to wrtdwns and a chrg. of $1.6 mill. for the settlement of litigation. 2 Incl. nonrecurr. chrg. of $38.0 mill. for the settlement of litigation.

OFFICERS:
J. J. Jacobs, Chmn.
R. E. Beumer, Vice-Chmn.
N. G. Watson, Pres., C.E.O.

INVESTOR CONTACT: John W. Prosser, Jr., Sr. V.P., (626) 578-6803

PRINCIPAL OFFICE: 1111 South Arroyo Parkway, Pasadena, CA 91105

TELEPHONE NUMBER: (626) 578-3500
FAX: (626) 578-6967
WEB: www.jacobs.com

NO. OF EMPLOYEES: 18,800 (approx.)

SHAREHOLDERS: 1,115

ANNUAL MEETING: In Feb.

INCORPORATED: CA, July, 1974; reincorp., DE, Mar., 1987

INSTITUTIONAL HOLDINGS:
No. of Institutions: 150
Shares Held: 18,750,639
% Held: 70.9

INDUSTRY: Heavy construction, nec (SIC: 1629)

TRANSFER AGENT(S): Mellon Investor Services, L.L.C., South Hackensack, NJ

NYSE SYMBOL JP
Rec. Pr. 47.39 (5/31/01)

JEFFERSON-PILOT CORP.

YIELD 2.3%
P/E RATIO 14.4

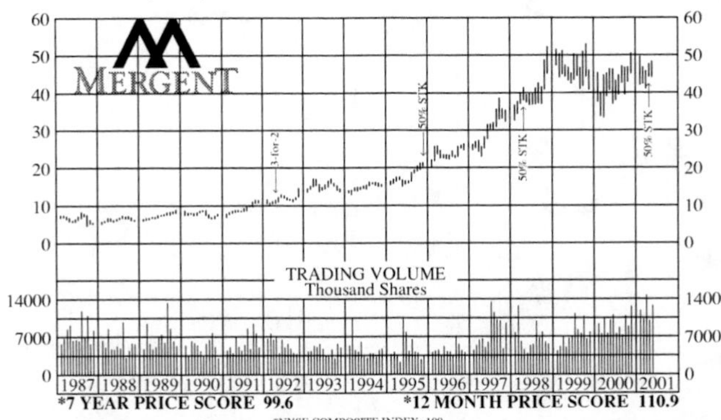

INTERIM EARNINGS (Per Share):

Qtr.	Mar.	June	Sept.	Dec.
1996	0.43	0.45	0.46	0.47
1997	0.69	0.64	0.50	0.50
1998	0.69	0.63	0.68	0.60
1999	0.79	0.73	0.73	0.69
2000	0.89	0.83	0.83	0.73

INTERIM DIVIDENDS (Per Share):

Amt.	Decl.	Ex.	Rec.	Pay.
0.37Q	8/14/00	11/08/00	11/10/00	12/05/00
0.37Q	11/06/00	2/07/01	2/09/01	3/05/01
50% STK	2/12/01	4/10/01	3/19/01	4/09/01
0.275Q	2/12/01	5/09/01	5/11/01	6/05/01
0.275Q	5/07/01	8/15/01	8/17/01	9/05/01

Indicated div.: $1.10 (Div. Reinv. Plan)

CAPITALIZATION (12/31/00):

	($000)	(%)
Long-Term Debt	139,000	4.0
Deferred Income Tax	212,000	6.0
Common & Surplus	3,159,000	90.0
Total	3,510,000	100.0

RECENT DEVELOPMENTS: For the year ended 12/31/00, net income grew 8.5% to $537.0 million from $495.0 million in 1999. Results included net realized investment gains of $66.9 million and $65.4 million in 2000 and 1999, respectively. Earnings for the Individual Products business segment improved 18.6% to $287.3 million. Earnings for Annuity and Investment Products increased 16.3% to $77.9 million, while earnings for Benfit Partners, JP's non-medical products business, grew 33.1% to $32.6 million.

PROSPECTS: Going forward, the Company is implementing new initiatives designed to accelerate growth in its core individual life insurance operations. JP will focus particularly on its relationships with the Company's more productive agents by providing a higher level of marketing support, as well as differentiated service, for those key agents. In addition, JP also will focus on selected markets in which it can tailor specific products and marketing programs for top-producing agents.

BUSINESS

JEFFERSON-PILOT CORP. is a holding company that conducts insurance, investment, broadcasting and other business through its subsidiaries. Jefferson-Pilot Life Insurance Company offers both group and individual life insurance, health insurance, annuity and pension products. Other subsidiaries provide fire and casualty insurance, title insurance and mutual fund sales and management services. Jefferson-Pilot Communications Company provides information and entertainment services through three network television and 17 radio stations, and produces and syndicates sports programming. On 12/30/99, JP acquired The Guarantee Life Companies Inc. Contributions to revenues in 2000 were as follows: Premiums & other, 42.1%; Net investment income, 44.2%; Realized investment gains, 3.2%; Communications sales, 6.5%; and Other, 4.0%.

ANNUAL FINANCIAL DATA

	12/31/00	12/31/99	12/31/98	12/31/97	12/31/96	12/31/95	12/31/94
Earnings Per Share	**3.29**	**2.95**	**2.61**	**2.31**	**1.82**	**[1] 1.58**	**[1] 1.40**
Tang. Book Val. Per Share	**18.38**	**15.80**	**17.77**	**15.73**	**13.89**	**13.02**	**10.26**
Dividends Per Share	**0.96**	**0.86**	**0.77**	**0.69**	**0.62**	**0.55**	**0.50**
Dividend Payout %	**29.2**	**29.1**	**29.4**	**30.0**	**34.2**	**35.1**	**35.6**
INCOME STATEMENT (IN MILLIONS):							
Total Premium Income	1,365.0	903.0	1,049.0	1,135.0	994.0	810.0	655.3
Net Investment Income	1,430.0	1,272.0	1,202.0	1,103.0	893.0	540.8	375.2
Other Income	1,808.0	1,289.0	1,408.0	1,475.0	1,232.0	617.5	494.5
Total Revenues	3,238.0	2,561.0	2,610.0	2,578.0	2,125.0	1,569.4	1,268.8
Policyholder Benefits	1,660.0	1,208.0	1,307.0	1,399.0	1,211.0	842.3	627.9
Income Before Income Taxes	814.0	751.0	670.0	591.0	443.0	380.8	347.6
Income Taxes	277.0	256.0	226.0	195.0	149.0	125.4	117.7
Net Income	537.0	495.0	444.0	396.0	294.0	[1] 255.3	[1] 229.9
Average Shs. Outstg. (000)	155,922	159,348	160,578	160,189	159,917	161,311	163,559
BALANCE SHEET (IN MILLIONS):							
Cash & Cash Equivalents	37.0	97.0	53.0	52.0	159.0	164.2	60.6
Premiums Due	1,450.0	1,576.0	1,342.0	1,526.0	1,260.0	1,583.7	94.2
Invst. Assets: Fixed-term	16,108.0	15,182.0	14,503.0	13,945.0	10,550.0	9,985.6	3,546.9
Invst. Assets: Equities	551.0	737.0	949.0	893.0	929.0	862.8	718.0
Invst. Assets: Loans	3,694.0	3,449.0	3,408.0	3,138.0	2,535.0	2,201.4	887.0
Invst. Assets: Total	20,499.0	19,536.0	18,978.0	18,094.0	14,143.0	13,168.1	5,220.7
Total Assets	27,321.0	26,446.0	24,338.0	23,131.0	17,562.0	16,368.1	6,039.7
Long-Term Obligations	139.0	290.0	327.0	331.0	148.0	137.1	...
Net Stockholders' Equity	3,159.0	2,753.0	3,052.0	2,732.0	2,297.0	2,156.1	1,732.5
Year-end Shs. Outstg. (000)	154,305	155,016	158,844	159,417	159,179	160,229	163,523
STATISTICAL RECORD:							
Return on Revenues %	16.6	19.3	17.0	15.4	13.8	16.3	18.1
Return on Equity %	17.0	18.0	14.5	14.5	12.8	11.8	13.3
Return on Assets %	2.0	1.9	1.8	1.7	1.7	1.6	3.8
Price Range	50.59-33.25	53.09-40.79	52.25-32.45	38.56-22.89	26.50-20.06	21.45-14.96	16.33-12.85
P/E Ratio	15.4-10.1	18.0-13.8	20.0-12.4	16.7-9.9	14.6-11.0	13.6-9.5	11.7-9.2
Average Yield %	2.3	1.8	1.8	2.3	2.7	3.0	3.4

Statistics are as originally reported. Adj. for stk. splits: 3-for-2, 4/01, 4/98 & 12/95 [1] Bef. disc. oper gain $18.5 mill, 12/95; $9.3 mill., 12/94

OFFICERS:
D. A. Stonecipher, Chmn., Pres., C.E.O.
D. R. Glass, Exec. V.P., C.F.O., Treas.
J. D. Hopkins, Exec. V.P., Gen. Couns.

INVESTOR CONTACT: Investor Relations, (336) 691-3379

PRINCIPAL OFFICE: 100 North Greene Street, Greensboro, NC 27401

TELEPHONE NUMBER: (336) 691-3000
FAX: (336) 691-3938
WEB: www.jpc.com

NO. OF EMPLOYEES: 3,000 (approx.)

SHAREHOLDERS: 9,625

ANNUAL MEETING: In May

INCORPORATED: NC, Jan., 1968

INSTITUTIONAL HOLDINGS:
No. of Institutions: 334
Shares Held: 85,607,472
% Held: 49.7

INDUSTRY: Life insurance (SIC: 6311)

TRANSFER AGENT(S): First Union National Bank, Charlotte, NC

NYSE SYMBOL JC
Rec. Pr. 1.69 (5/31/01)

JENNY CRAIG, INC.

YIELD ...
P/E RATIO ...

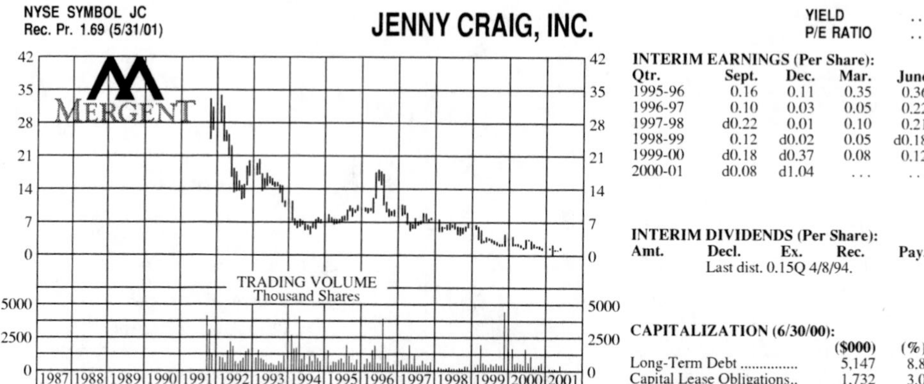

*7 YEAR PRICE SCORE 21.1 *12 MONTH PRICE SCORE 76.5
*NYSE COMPOSITE INDEX=100

INTERIM EARNINGS (Per Share):

Qtr.	Sept.	Dec.	Mar.	June
1995-96	0.16	0.11	0.35	0.36
1996-97	0.10	0.03	0.05	0.22
1997-98	d0.22	0.01	0.10	0.21
1998-99	0.12	d0.02	0.05	d0.18
1999-00	d0.18	d0.37	0.08	0.12
2000-01	d0.08	d1.04	...	...

INTERIM DIVIDENDS (Per Share):

Amt.	Decl.	Ex.	Rec.	Pay.

Last dist. 0.15Q 4/8/94.

CAPITALIZATION (6/30/00):

	($000)	(%)
Long-Term Debt	5,147	8.8
Capital Lease Obligations	1,732	3.0
Common & Surplus	51,628	88.2
Total	58,507	100.0

RECENT DEVELOPMENTS: For the quarter ended 12/31/00, the Company reported a net loss of $21.6 million versus a net loss of $7.6 million in the previous year. Results for the second quarter of fiscal 2001 included a litigation settlement charge of $219,000 and a non-cash charge of $17.7 million, while results for fiscal 2000 included a pre-tax nonrecurring charge of $7.5 million and a litigation settlement charge of $219,000. Total revenues fell 2.4% to $60.7 million from $62.2 million the year before.

PROSPECTS: Over the past several years, JC has experienced weaker demand, primarily at its U.S. centres, due to increased competition and new product introductions, including Xenical, a prescription drug for the treatment of obesity, best-selling diet books, non-prescription pills and other "do it yourself" methods of weight loss. The number of new customer enrollments was 20.0% lower in January 2001 compared with January 2000.

BUSINESS

JENNY CRAIG, INC. provides a comprehensive weight loss service program through a chain of Company-owned and franchised weight-loss centres operating under the name "Jenny Craig Weight Loss Centres." As of 2/14/01, the Company's Personal Weight Management Program was delivered through a chain of 547 Company-owned and 111 franchised centres located in the United States, Australia, New Zealand, Canada and Puerto Rico. Through these centres, the Company sells "Jenny's Cuisine," its portion and calorie-controlled food products, to participants in the program.

REVENUES

(06/30/00)	($000)	(%)
Co-owned Operations	321,687	91.3
Franchise Operations	30,562	8.7
Total	352,249	100.0

ANNUAL FINANCIAL DATA

	6/30/00	6/30/99	6/30/98	6/30/97	6/30/96	6/30/95	6/30/94
Earnings Per Share	**[3] [4] d0.34**	**[2] [3] d0.03**	**0.10**	**[1] 0.40**	**0.95**	**0.46**	**0.02**
Cash Flow Per Share	**d0.06**	**0.25**	**0.44**	**0.76**	**1.25**	**0.80**	**0.39**
Tang. Book Val. Per Share	**2.08**	**2.39**	**2.29**	**1.95**	**2.07**	**2.58**	**2.24**
Dividends Per Share	...	...	...	...	...	...	**0.30**
Dividend Payout %	...	...	...	...	...	...	**N.M.**
INCOME STATEMENT (IN THOUSANDS):							
Total Revenues	290,985	320,952	352,249	365,134	401,018	378,093	403,341
Costs & Expenses	298,087	317,882	343,108	345,833	358,092	352,190	392,776
Depreciation & Amort.	5,769	5,854	7,101	7,461	7,405	8,540	9,544
Operating Income	d12,871	d2,784	2,040	11,840	35,521	17,363	1,021
Income Before Income Taxes	d11,439	d1,084	3,414	13,425	38,481	19,766	2,610
Income Taxes	cr4,347	cr412	1,288	5,093	15,569	7,994	2,076
Net Income	[3] [4] d7,092	[2] [3] d672	2,126	[1] 8,332	22,912	11,772	534
Cash Flow	d1,323	5,182	9,227	15,793	30,317	20,312	10,078
Average Shs. Outstg.	20,689	20,689	20,953	20,767	24,195	25,534	26,147
BALANCE SHEET (IN THOUSANDS):							
Cash & Cash Equivalents	35,635	42,014	43,360	38,944	50,580	59,778	39,585
Total Current Assets	54,736	80,176	72,994	73,693	79,931	87,404	70,369
Net Property	25,797	24,360	24,832	27,554	15,474	18,254	24,743
Total Assets	106,517	112,614	106,245	112,297	104,401	115,376	104,190
Total Current Liabilities	48,010	49,781	44,933	52,663	49,939	41,229	35,842
Long-Term Obligations	6,879	5,336	5,526	5,716	...	...	...
Net Stockholders' Equity	51,628	57,497	55,786	49,894	50,696	73,317	67,420
Net Working Capital	6,726	30,395	28,061	21,030	29,992	46,175	34,527
Year-end Shs. Outstg.	20,689	20,689	20,689	20,688	20,856	25,196	26,076
STATISTICAL RECORD:							
Operating Profit Margin %	...	...	0.6	3.2	8.9	4.6	0.3
Net Profit Margin %	...	...	0.6	2.3	5.7	3.1	0.1
Return on Equity %	...	...	3.8	16.7	45.2	16.1	0.8
Return on Assets %	...	...	2.0	7.4	21.9	10.2	0.5
Debt/Total Assets %	6.5	4.7	5.2	5.1	...	...	...
Price Range	4.00-1.19	6.44-2.00	7.63-4.25	10.75-5.13	18.13-8.13	10.63-6.50	11.50-4.38
P/E Ratio	...	...	76.2-42.5	26.9-12.8	19.1-8.6	23.1-14.1	572.1-217.7
Average Yield %	...	...	...	...	...	...	3.8

Statistics are as originally reported. [1] Bef. acctg. change chrg. 1997, $7.5 mill. [2] Incl. chrg. for litigation judgement fiscal 1999, $8.2 mill. [3] Incl. restruct. chrg. of $6.9 mill., 2000; $7.5 mill., 1999. [4] Incl. chrg. for litigation judgement of $1.6 mill. & non-cash chrg. of $17.7 mill.

OFFICERS:
S. Craig, Chmn., C.E.O.
D. Weinger, Vice Chmn.
P. A. Larchet, Pres., C.O.O.
J. S. Kelly, V.P., C.F.O., Treas.

INVESTOR CONTACT: Marvin Sears, Sec., (858) 812-7000

PRINCIPAL OFFICE: 11355 North Torrey Pines Road, La Jolla, CA 92037

TELEPHONE NUMBER: (858) 812-7000
FAX: (858) 812-2700
WEB: www.jennycraig.com

NO. OF EMPLOYEES: 3,210 (approx.)

SHAREHOLDERS: 2,500 (approx.)

ANNUAL MEETING: In Nov.

INCORPORATED: DE, June, 1989

INSTITUTIONAL HOLDINGS:
No. of Institutions: 9
Shares Held: 3,060,400
% Held: 14.8

INDUSTRY: Miscellaneous personal services, nec (SIC: 7299)

TRANSFER AGENT(S): Mellon Investor Services, Los Angeles, CA

NYSE SYMBOL JASA
Rec. Pr. 4.40 (5/31/01)

JO-ANN STORES, INC.

YIELD ...
P/E RATIO ...

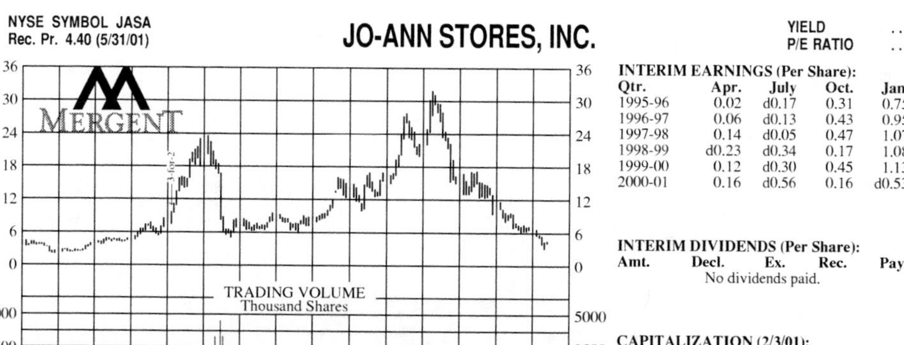

*7 YEAR PRICE SCORE 31.7 *12 MONTH PRICE SCORE 69.7

*NYSE COMPOSITE INDEX=100

INTERIM EARNINGS (Per Share):

Qtr.	Apr.	July	Oct.	Jan.
1995-96	0.02	d0.17	0.31	0.75
1996-97	0.06	d0.13	0.43	0.95
1997-98	0.14	d0.05	0.47	1.07
1998-99	d0.23	d0.34	0.17	1.08
1999-00	0.12	d0.30	0.45	1.13
2000-01	0.16	d0.56	0.16	d0.53

INTERIM DIVIDENDS (Per Share):

Amt.	Decl.	Ex.	Rec.	Pay.

No dividends paid.

CAPITALIZATION (2/3/01):

	($000)	(%)
Long-Term Debt	240,000	46.9
Deferred Income Tax	22,500	4.4
Common & Surplus	248,800	48.7
Total	511,300	100.0

RECENT DEVELOPMENTS: For the 53 weeks ended 2/3/01, net loss totaled $13.6 million compared with net income of $25.6 million in the corresponding 52-week period a year earlier. Results in the recent period included a one-time pre-tax charge of $29.7 million related to store closings and inventory writedowns, as well as a $6.5 million equity loss stemming from the Company's minority investment in IdeaForest.com. Net sales grew 7.4% to $1.48 billion from $1.38 billion the previous year. Same-store sales rose 1.3% year-over-year.

PROSPECTS: The Company is focusing on eliminating slow-selling products and closing under-performing stores in an effort to boost operating profitability and reduce debt levels. Earnings in 2001 are expected to be constrained by continued weak retail market conditions, along with higher-than-usual inventory out-of-stocks stemming from the Company's conversion to a new computer system. Several supply chain initiatives currently being implemented will likely hamper results during the first three quarters of fiscal 2001.

BUSINESS

JO-ANN STORES, INC. (formerly Fabri-Centers of America, Inc.) operates, as of 5/5/01, 991 specialty fabric stores in 49 states and the District of Columbia. The stores operate primarily under the names Jo-Ann Fabrics and Crafts and Jo-Ann etc. The stores offer a wide variety of fashion and decorator fabric, quilting and craft fabrics, related notions, craft components, patterns, seasonal merchandise, silk and dried flowers, and sewing machines and related sewing accessories. Giltex Corporation and New York Fabrics were acquired in 1992. In 1994, JAS sold its houseware stores subsidiary, Cargo Express Stores, Inc. In October 1994, JAS acquired 342 stores from Cloth World. In April 1998, the Company acquired House of Fabrics, Inc.

ANNUAL FINANCIAL DATA

	2/3/01	1/29/00	1/30/99	1/31/98	2/1/97	1/27/96	1/28/95
Earnings Per Share	**1 d0.75**	**1.38**	**1 0.69**	**2 1.60**	**1 1.30**	**0.91**	**0.63**
Cash Flow Per Share	**1.37**	**3.17**	**2.07**	**2.61**	**2.44**	**1.87**	**1.38**
Tang. Book Val. Per Share	**12.17**	**13.07**	**11.67**	**12.83**	**11.13**	**9.79**	**8.79**
INCOME STATEMENT (IN MILLIONS):							
Total Revenues	1,483.3	1,381.5	1,242.9	975.0	929.0	834.6	677.3
Costs & Expenses	1,427.4	1,281.9	1,180.3	896.3	857.4	776.2	635.8
Depreciation & Amort.	38.3	32.0	27.7	21.7	21.5	18.5	14.0
Operating Income	17.6	67.6	34.9	57.0	50.0	39.9	27.5
Net Interest Inc./(Exp.)	d29.0	d26.2	d12.5	d5.9	d10.7	d12.0	d8.4
Income Before Income Taxes	d11.4	41.4	22.4	51.2	39.4	27.9	19.1
Income Taxes	cr4.3	15.7	8.8	19.2	14.8	10.5	7.3
Net Income	1 d13.6	25.7	1 13.6	2 32.0	1 24.6	17.5	11.7
Cash Flow	24.7	57.7	41.3	53.7	46.1	36.0	25.7
Average Shs. Outstg. (000)	18,041	18,198	19,904	20,592	18,878	19,290	18,688
BALANCE SHEET (IN MILLIONS):							
Cash & Cash Equivalents	17.5	21.4	20.4	14.8	12.6	11.6	21.9
Total Current Assets	505.8	508.0	490.1	322.0	318.3	361.4	325.7
Net Property	190.2	194.7	164.0	110.0	94.6	102.0	84.1
Total Assets	742.2	757.0	701.4	447.8	429.2	479.6	427.3
Total Current Liabilities	223.5	208.1	209.2	164.8	141.2	129.2	127.5
Long-Term Obligations	240.0	245.2	182.5	24.7	72.1	155.5	127.0
Net Stockholders' Equity	248.8	269.5	259.0	240.9	199.4	181.0	161.7
Net Working Capital	282.3	299.9	280.9	157.2	177.0	232.2	198.2
Year-end Shs. Outstg. (000)	18,207	17,845	19,012	18,767	17,921	18,486	18,398
STATISTICAL RECORD:							
Operating Profit Margin %	1.2	4.9	2.8	5.9	5.4	4.8	4.1
Net Profit Margin %	...	1.9	1.1	3.3	2.6	2.1	1.7
Return on Equity %	...	9.5	5.3	13.3	12.3	9.6	7.3
Return on Assets %	...	3.4	1.9	7.1	5.7	3.6	2.7
Debt/Total Assets %	32.3	32.4	26.0	5.5	16.8	32.4	29.7
Price Range	11.69-6.00	17.25-9.38	31.88-14.94	27.81-14.88	17.00-9.88	16.13-7.88	9.31-5.81
P/E Ratio	...	12.5-6.8	46.2-21.6	17.4-9.3	13.1-7.6	17.7-8.7	14.8-9.2

Statistics are as originally reported. Adj. for 2-for-1 stk. split, 7/95. 1 Incl. $29.7 mil pre-tax chg., 2/3/01; $15.3 mil ($0.77/sh) after-tax non-recur. chg., 1/30/99; $2.1 mil ($0.11/sh) after-tax chg., 2/1/97. 2 Bef. $1.1 mil ($0.06/sh) after-tax extraord. chg.

OFFICERS:
A. Rosskamm, Chmn., Pres., C.E.O.
B. Carney, Exec. V.P., C.F.O.
B. Rosskamm, Sr. V.P., Sec.

INVESTOR CONTACT: Brian Carney, Exec. V.P. & C.F.O., (330) 656-2600

PRINCIPAL OFFICE: 5555 Darrow Road, Hudson, OH 44236

TELEPHONE NUMBER: (330) 656-2600
FAX: (330) 463-6675
WEB: www.joann.com

NO. OF EMPLOYEES: 22,300 (avg.)

SHAREHOLDERS: 710 (Cl. A); 663 (Cl. B)

ANNUAL MEETING: In June

INCORPORATED: OH, Feb., 1951

INSTITUTIONAL HOLDINGS:
No. of Institutions: 40
Shares Held: 3,670,195
% Held: 20.0

INDUSTRY: Sewing, needlework, and piece goods (SIC: 5949)

TRANSFER AGENT(S): Computershare Investor Services, Chicago, IL

NYSE SYMBOL JHF
Rec. Pr. 39.61 (5/31/01)

JOHN HANCOCK FINANCIAL SERVICES, INC.

YIELD 0.8%
P/E RATIO 15.8

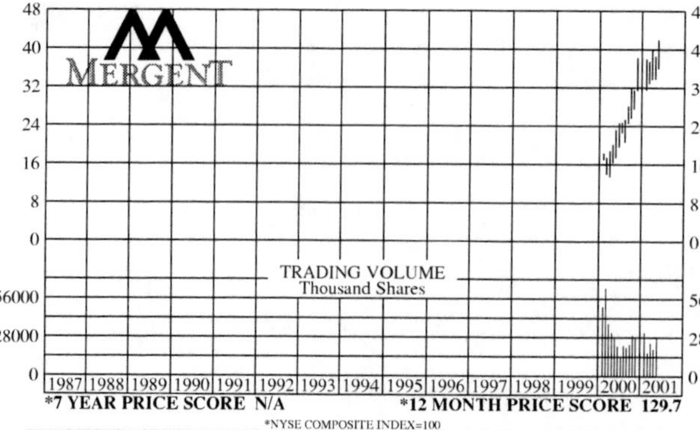

*7 YEAR PRICE SCORE N/A *12 MONTH PRICE SCORE 129.7
*NYSE COMPOSITE INDEX=100

INTERIM EARNINGS (Per Share):

Qtr.	Mar.	June	Sept.	Dec.
2000	0.47	0.72	0.58	0.73

INTERIM DIVIDENDS (Per Share):

Amt.	Decl.	Ex.	Rec.	Pay.
0.30A	11/13/00	11/16/00	11/20/00	12/14/00

Indicated div.: $0.30

CAPITALIZATION (12/31/00):

	($000)	(%)
Long-Term Debt	534,000	7.8
Deferred Income Tax	431,300	6.3
Minority Interest	93,500	1.4
Common & Surplus	5,779,200	84.5
Total	6,838,000	100.0

RECENT DEVELOPMENTS: For the year ended 12/31/00, the Company reported net income of $838.9 million compared with income of $162.9 million, before an accounting charge of $9.7 million, in the previous year. Total revenues slipped 3.3% to $7.60 billion. Premiums fell 4.8% to $2.59 billion. Net investment income declined 8.5% to $3.27 billion. Net realized investment gains were $83.2 million versus $175.1 million in 1999. Investment management revenues, commissions and other fees jumped 12.3% to $764.8 million.

PROSPECTS: In 2001, the Company expects annuity sales to be driven by continued success in the broker/dealer and bank channels, and by new private-label, market-value adjusted and Internet products. JHF is expecting earnings per share growth for 2001 in the range of 10.0% to 12.0%, driven by strong contributions from the Protection and Asset Gathering and The Guaranteed & Structured Financial Products segments.

BUSINESS

JOHN HANCOCK FINANCIAL SERVICES, INC. provides insurance and investment products and services to retail and institutional customers, primarily in North America. The Company offers variable life, universal life, whole life, term life, and individual and group long-term care insurance products, along with variable and fixed, deferred and immediate annuities, and mutual funds. In addition, the Company offers a variety of spread-based and fee-based investment products and services, most provide the customer with some form of guaranteed return, and investment management services and products marketed to institutions. As of 12/31/00, the Company and its subsidiaries had total assets under management of $125.16 billion.

REVENUES

(12/31/2000)	($000)	(%)
Premiums	2,587,100	34.0
Universal life & inv-type	749,300	9.9
Net investment income	3,271,400	43.1
Net realized invest gains	83,200	1.1
Invest mgt, commissions	764,800	10.1
Other	18,200	0.2

ANNUAL FINANCIAL DATA

	12/31/00	12/31/99	12/31/98	12/31/97	12/31/96
Earnings Per Share	**2.65**	...	...	...	...
Tang. Book Val. Per Share	**18.70**	...	...	...	...
Dividends Per Share	**0.30**	...	...	...	...
Dividend Payout %	**12.0**	...	...	...	...
INCOME STATEMENT (IN MILLIONS):					
Total Premium Income	2,587.1	2,717.5	2,197.9	2,473.6	2,922.5
Other Income	5,011.0	5,140.0	4,704.1	4,472.7	4,782.3
Total Revenues	7,598.1	7,857.5	6,902.0	6,946.3	7,704.8
Policyholder Benefits	4,457.1	5,418.4	4,152.0	4,303.1	4,676.7
Income Before Income Taxes	1,185.1	358.4	644.1	589.7	668.0
Income Taxes	346.2	101.9	183.9	106.4	247.5
Net Income	838.9	[1] 256.5	[1] 460.2	483.3	420.5
Average Shs. Outstg. (000)	316,200	...	...	...	...
BALANCE SHEET (IN MILLIONS):					
Cash & Cash Equivalents	20,322.6	20,286.5	18,374.2	16,674.7	...
Premiums Due	210.8	215.6	227.5	358.8	...
Invst. Assets: Fixed-term	11,888.6	13,800.3	12,978.2	12,712.4	...
Invst. Assets: Loans	9,398.0	12,675.2	11,495.8	11,151.9	...
Invst. Assets: Total	40,738.4	46,887.8	43,777.5	42,441.7	...
Total Assets	87,353.3	84,455.7	76,966.7	71,417.5	...
Long-Term Obligations	534.0	536.9	602.7	543.3	...
Net Stockholders' Equity	5,779.2	4,791.1	4,955.2	4,670.1	...
Year-end Shs. Outstg. (000)	309,000	...	...	...	...
STATISTICAL RECORD:					
Return on Revenues %	11.0	3.3	6.7	7.0	5.5
Return on Equity %	14.5	5.4	9.3	10.3	...
Return on Assets %	1.0	0.3	0.6	0.7	...
Price Range	38.25-13.44	...	...	...	...
P/E Ratio	15.2-5.4	...	...	...	...
Average Yield %	1.2	...	...	...	...

Statistics are as originally reported. [1] Bef. $93.6 mill. extraord. chrg. & $9.7 mil acctg. chrg., 1999; bef. $11.7 mil extraord. chg., 1998.

OFFICERS:
D. F. D'Alessandro, Chmn., Pres., C.E.O.
F. L. Aborn, Vice-Chmn.
T. E. Moloney, C.F.O.

INVESTOR CONTACT: Investor Relations, (617) 572-6000

PRINCIPAL OFFICE: John Hancock Place, 200 Clarendon Street, Boston, MA 02117

TELEPHONE NUMBER: (617) 572-6000
FAX: (617) 572-6451
WEB: www.johnhancock.com

NO. OF EMPLOYEES: 8,503 (approx.)

SHAREHOLDERS: 800,000 (approx.)

ANNUAL MEETING: In May

INCORPORATED: DE, 1999

INSTITUTIONAL HOLDINGS:
No. of Institutions: 244
Shares Held: 132,147,140
% Held: 42.9

INDUSTRY: Life insurance (SIC: 6311)

TRANSFER AGENT(S): EquiServe Trust Company, N.A., Boston, MA

NYSE SYMBOL JNJ
Rec. Pr. 48.24 (Adj.; 4/30/01)

JOHNSON & JOHNSON

YIELD 1.5%
P/E RATIO 28.2

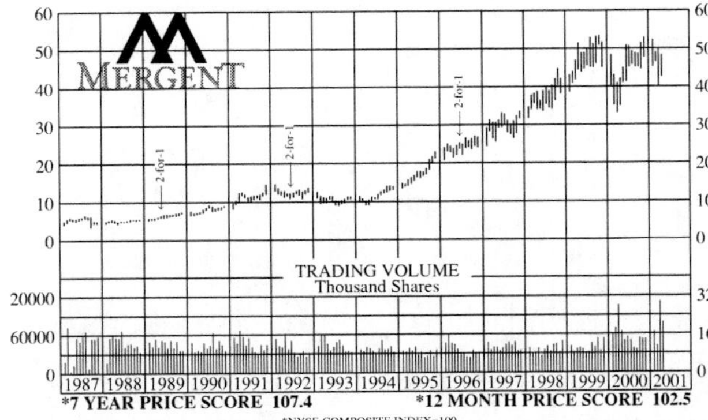

INTERIM EARNINGS (Per Share):

Qtr.	Mar.	June	Sept.	Dec.
1997	0.34	0.34	0.32	0.24
1998	0.37	0.37	0.35	0.25
1999	0.41	0.42	0.40	0.27
2000	0.47	0.47	0.45	0.32

INTERIM DIVIDENDS (Per Share):

Amt.	Decl.	Ex.	Rec.	Pay.
0.32Q	7/17/00	8/18/00	8/22/00	9/12/00
0.32Q	10/16/00	11/17/00	11/21/00	12/12/00
0.32Q	1/02/01	2/15/01	2/20/01	3/13/01
2-for-1	4/26/01	6/13/01	5/22/01	6/12/01
0.18Q	4/26/01	5/18/01	5/22/01	6/12/01

Indicated div.: $0.72 (Div. Reinv. Plan)

CAPITALIZATION (12/31/00):

	($000)	(%)
Long-Term Debt	2,037,000	9.7
Deferred Income Tax	255,000	1.2
Common & Surplus	18,808,000	89.1
Total	21,100,000	100.0

RECENT DEVELOPMENTS: For the twelve months ended 12/31/00, net earnings increased 15.2% to $4.80 billion compared with $4.17 billion in the previous year. Results for 2000 included pre-tax in-process research and development charges of $54.0 million related to the acquisition of Atrionix. Worldwide sales climbed 6.3% to $29.46 billion from $27.72 billion in the prior year.

PROSPECTS: On 3/27/01, JNJ entered into an agreement under which it will acquire Alza Corporation, a research-based pharmaceutical company, in a stock-for-stock exchange valued at more than $10.50 billion. The transaction is expected to close by the early part of the third quarter of 2001, and will be dilutive to JNJ in 2001 and 2002, and accretive in 2003 and thereafter.

BUSINESS

JOHNSON & JOHNSON is engaged in the manufacture and sale of a broad range of products in health care and other fields. The pharmaceutical segment, 41.0% of 2000 sales, consists of prescription drugs in the antifungal, anti-infective, cardiovascular, dermatology, gastrointestinal, hematology, immunology, neurology, oncology, pain management, psychotropic and women's health fields. Major pharmaceutical products include NIZORAL, SPORANOX, TERAZOL, DAKTARIN, FLOXIN, LEVAQUIN, RETAVASE, REOPRO, RETIN-A MICRO, ACIPHEX, IMODIUM, REMICADE, PROCRIT, ORTHOCLONE OKT-3, REMINYL, TOPAMAX, STUGERON, ERGAMISOL, LEUSTATIN, DURAGESIC, ULTRAM, RISPERDAL, HALDOL, ORTHO-NOVUM and TRICILEST. The consumer segment, 23.7% of 2000 sales, consists of personal care and hygienic products. Major consumer brands include BAND-AID, BENECOL, CAREFREE, CLEAN & CLEAR, IMODIUM A-D, LACTAID, MONISTAT, MOTRIN IB, MYLANTA, NEUTROGENA, STAYFREE and TYLENOL. The professional segment, 35.3% of 2000 sales, includes a broad range of products used by health care professionals, including surgical equipment and devices, infection-prevention products and diagnostic equipment and supplies.

ANNUAL FINANCIAL DATA

	12/31/00	1/2/00	1/3/99	12/28/97	12/29/96	12/31/95	1/1/95
Earnings Per Share	**[3] 1.70**	**[2] 1.47**	**[1] 1.12**	**1.21**	**1.09**	**0.93**	**0.78**
Cash Flow Per Share	**2.23**	**1.98**	**1.57**	**1.60**	**1.68**	**1.26**	**1.06**
Tang. Book Val. Per Share	**4.15**	**3.11**	**2.37**	**3.38**	**2.90**	**2.36**	**1.83**
Dividends Per Share	**0.62**	**0.55**	**0.49**	**0.43**	**0.37**	**0.32**	**0.28**
Dividend Payout %	**36.5**	**37.1**	**43.5**	**35.3**	**33.9**	**34.4**	**36.2**
INCOME STATEMENT (IN MILLIONS):							
Total Revenues	29,464.0	27,717.0	23,493.0	22,629.0	21,620.0	18,842.0	15,734.0
Costs & Expenses	21,114.0	20,101.0	17,979.0	16,940.0	16,308.0	14,474.0	12,203.0
Depreciation & Amort.	1,515.0	1,444.0	1,246.0	1,067.0	1,009.0	857.0	724.0
Operating Income	6,835.0	6,172.0	4,268.0	4,622.0	4,303.0	3,511.0	2,807.0
Net Interest Inc./(Exp.)	d146.0	d197.0	152.0	83.0	14.0	d28.0	d82.0
Income Before Income Taxes	6,622.0	5,753.0	4,269.0	4,576.0	4,033.0	3,317.0	2,681.0
Income Taxes	1,822.0	1,586.0	1,210.0	1,273.0	569.0	914.0	675.0
Net Income	[3] 4,800.0	[2] 4,167.0	[1] 3,059.0	3,303.0	3,464.0	2,403.0	2,006.0
Cash Flow	6,315.0	5,611.0	4,305.0	4,370.0	4,473.0	3,260.0	2,730.0
Average Shs. Outstg. (000)	2,834,800	2,836,400	2,743,200	2,739,800	2,666,000	2,584,000	2,572,000
BALANCE SHEET (IN MILLIONS):							
Cash & Cash Equivalents	5,744.0	3,879.0	2,578.0	2,899.0	2,136.0	1,364.0	704.0
Total Current Assets	15,450.0	13,200.0	11,132.0	10,563.0	9,370.0	7,938.0	6,680.0
Net Property	6,971.0	6,719.0	6,240.0	5,810.0	5,651.0	5,196.0	4,910.0
Total Assets	31,321.0	29,163.0	26,211.0	21,453.0	20,010.0	17,873.0	15,668.0
Total Current Liabilities	7,140.0	7,454.0	8,162.0	5,283.0	5,184.0	4,388.0	4,266.0
Long-Term Obligations	2,037.0	2,450.0	1,269.0	1,126.0	1,410.0	2,107.0	2,199.0
Net Stockholders' Equity	18,808.0	16,213.0	13,590.0	12,359.0	10,836.0	9,045.0	7,122.0
Net Working Capital	8,310.0	5,746.0	2,970.0	5,280.0	4,186.0	3,550.0	2,414.0
Year-end Shs. Outstg. (000)	2,781,874	2,779,366	2,688,000	2,690,000	2,664,000	2,588,000	2,572,000
STATISTICAL RECORD:							
Operating Profit Margin %	23.2	22.3	18.2	20.4	19.9	18.6	17.8
Net Profit Margin %	16.3	15.0	13.0	14.6	16.0	12.8	12.7
Return on Equity %	25.5	25.7	22.5	26.7	32.0	26.6	28.2
Return on Assets %	15.3	14.3	11.7	15.4	17.3	13.4	12.8
Debt/Total Assets %	6.5	8.4	4.8	5.2	7.0	11.8	14.0
Price Range	52.97-33.06	53.44-38.50	44.88-31.69	33.66-24.31	27.00-20.78	23.09-13.41	14.13-9.00
P/E Ratio	31.2-19.4	36.4-26.2	40.2-28.4	27.9-20.2	24.9-19.2	24.8-14.4	18.1-11.5
Average Yield %	1.4	1.2	1.3	1.5	1.5	1.8	2.4

Statistics are as originally reported. Adjusted for 2-for-1 stock split, 6/96 & 6/01. [1] Incl. a pre-tax in-process R&D chrg. $164.0 mill. and a pre-tax restruct. chrg. $613.0 mill. [2] Incl. nonrecurr. after-tax chrg. of $42.0 mill. [3] Incl. pre-tax chrg. of $54.0 mill. for in-process research & development.

OFFICERS:
R. S. Larsen, Chmn., C.E.O.
R. N. Wilson, Sr. Vice-Chmn.
J. T. Lenehan, Vice-Chmn.
W. C. Weldon, Vice-Chmn.

INVESTOR CONTACT: Helen E. Short, Vice President, (800) 950-5089

PRINCIPAL OFFICE: One Johnson & Johnson Plaza, New Brunswick, NJ 08933

TELEPHONE NUMBER: (732) 524-0400
FAX: (732) 214-0332
WEB: www.jnj.com

NO. OF EMPLOYEES: 98,500 (approx.)

SHAREHOLDERS: 164,158 (approx.)

ANNUAL MEETING: In April

INCORPORATED: NJ, Nov., 1887

INSTITUTIONAL HOLDINGS:
No. of Institutions: 1,171
Shares Held: 1,536,827,728 (Adj.)
% Held: 55.0

INDUSTRY: Pharmaceutical preparations (SIC: 2834)

TRANSFER AGENT(S): First Chicago Trust Company, c/o EquiServe, Jersey City, NJ

NYSE SYMBOL JCI
Rec. Pr. 72.40 (4/30/01)

JOHNSON CONTROLS, INC.

YIELD 1.7%
P/E RATIO 14.1

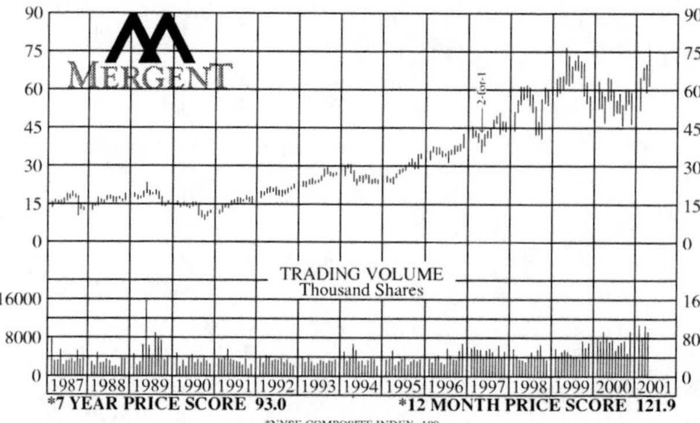

INTERIM EARNINGS (Per Share):

Qtr.	Dec.	Mar.	June	Sept.
1997-98	0.70	0.56	0.90	1.47
1998-99	0.86	1.05	1.19	1.38
1999-00	1.06	0.95	1.45	1.63
2000-01	1.10	...	...	...

INTERIM DIVIDENDS (Per Share):

Amt.	Decl.	Ex.	Rec.	Pay.
0.28Q	5/17/00	6/07/00	6/09/00	6/30/00
0.28Q	7/26/00	9/11/00	9/13/00	9/29/00
0.31Q	11/15/00	12/06/00	12/08/00	1/02/01
0.31Q	1/24/01	3/07/01	3/09/01	3/30/01
0.31Q	5/17/01	6/13/01	6/15/01	6/29/01

Indicated div.: $1.24 (Div. Reinv. Plan)

CAPITALIZATION (9/30/00):

	($000)	(%)
Long-Term Debt	1,315,300	33.8
Preferred Stock	129,000	3.3
Common & Surplus	2,447,100	62.9
Total	3,891,400	100.0

RECENT DEVELOPMENTS: For the quarter ended 12/31/00, net income climbed 3.5% to $102.5 million compared with $99.0 million in 1999. Net income benefited from increased equity and interest income and a lower tax rate. Net sales were $4.45 billion, up 3.2% from $4.32 billion in the prior-year period. Sales in the Automotive Group climbed 1.5% to $3.39 billion, while sales in the Control Group grew 8.8% to $1.07 billion due to increased levels of installed control systems and facility management activity.

PROSPECTS: The Company expects to achieve sales growth of 10.0% to 15.0% and modest operating margin improvement for its Controls Group segment in fiscal 2001. The global backlog of orders for installed control systems was substantially higher at 12/31/00 than a year ago, reflecting increased demand for JCI's systems. The outlook for the Automotive Systems Group has been reduced in light lower of North American vehicle production forecasts for 2001.

BUSINESS

JOHNSON CONTROLS, INC. operates in two business segments. The Automotive segment is engaged in the design and manufacture of complete seat systems, seating components and interior trim systems for North American and European manufacturers of cars, vans and light trucks. The Controls segment is a worldwide supplier of control systems, services and products providing energy management, temperature and ventilation control, security and fire safety for non-residential buildings. On 7/1/98, JCI acquired Becker Group, Inc., a supplier of automotive interior systems, which include door systems and instrument panels. Also, JCI completed the sale of its plastics machinery division to Milacron, Inc. for about $190.0 million on 9/30/98.

ANNUAL FINANCIAL DATA

	9/30/00	9/30/99	9/30/98	9/30/97	9/30/96	9/30/95	9/30/94
Earnings Per Share	**5.09**	**4 4.48**	**3 3.63**	**2 2.48**	**1 2.55**	**2.27**	**1.90**
Cash Flow Per Share	**10.06**	**9.25**	**7.78**	**6.67**	**6.49**	**5.76**	**5.05**
Tang. Book Val. Per Share	**3.65**	**0.45**	**...**	**...**	**9.70**	**8.04**	**6.69**
Dividends Per Share	**1.12**	**1.00**	**0.92**	**0.86**	**0.82**	**0.78**	**0.72**
Dividend Payout %	**22.0**	**22.3**	**25.3**	**34.7**	**32.2**	**34.4**	**37.9**
INCOME STATEMENT (IN MILLIONS):							
Total Revenues	17,154.6	16,139.4	12,586.8	11,145.4	9,210.0	8,330.3	6,870.5
Costs & Expenses	15,727.8	14,838.9	11,538.6	10,263.4	8,401.4	7,593.0	6,247.0
Depreciation & Amort.	461.8	445.6	384.2	354.9	329.7	288.5	258.3
Operating Income	965.0	854.9	664.0	527.1	478.9	448.8	365.2
Net Interest Inc./(Exp.)	d111.5	d136.0	d118.7	d112.8	d65.5	d4.8	10.3
Income Before Income Taxes	855.7	769.9	616.8	425.6	421.5	387.9	326.4
Income Taxes	338.9	311.7	256.0	180.9	171.8	162.9	140.3
Equity Earnings/Minority Int.	d44.4	d38.6	d23.1	d24.1	d27.0	d29.2	d20.9
Net Income	472.4	4 419.6	3 337.7	2 220.6	1 222.7	195.8	165.2
Cash Flow	924.4	852.2	712.4	565.9	542.9	474.9	414.2
Average Shs. Outstg. (000)	91,900	92,100	91,600	84,800	83,600	82,400	82,000
BALANCE SHEET (IN MILLIONS):							
Cash & Cash Equivalents	275.6	276.2	134.0	111.8	165.2	103.8	132.6
Total Current Assets	4,277.2	3,848.5	3,404.2	2,529.3	2,849.1	2,063.9	1,778.5
Net Property	2,305.0	1,996.0	1,882.9	1,533.0	1,320.2	1,518.8	1,333.4
Total Assets	9,428.0	8,614.2	7,942.1	6,048.6	4,991.2	4,320.9	3,806.9
Total Current Liabilities	4,510.0	4,266.6	4,288.4	2,972.7	2,182.6	1,909.5	1,516.4
Long-Term Obligations	1,315.3	1,283.3	997.5	706.4	752.2	630.0	670.3
Net Stockholders' Equity	2,576.1	2,270.0	1,941.4	1,687.9	1,507.8	1,340.2	1,202.8
Net Working Capital	d232.8	d418.1	d884.2	d443.4	666.5	154.4	262.1
Year-end Shs. Outstg. (000)	85,989	85,395	84,700	84,100	83,000	82,200	81,400
STATISTICAL RECORD:							
Operating Profit Margin %	5.6	5.3	5.3	4.7	5.2	5.4	5.3
Net Profit Margin %	2.8	2.6	2.7	2.0	2.4	2.4	2.4
Return on Equity %	18.3	18.5	17.4	13.1	14.8	14.6	13.7
Return on Assets %	5.0	4.9	4.3	3.6	4.5	4.5	4.3
Debt/Total Assets %	14.0	14.9	12.6	11.7	15.1	14.6	17.6
Price Range	65.13-45.81	76.69-49.00	61.88-40.50	51.00-35.38	42.69-31.25	34.88-22.88	30.88-22.44
P/E Ratio	12.8-9.0	17.1-10.9	17.0-11.2	20.6-14.3	16.7-12.3	15.4-10.1	16.2-11.8
Average Yield %	2.0	1.6	1.8	2.0	2.2	2.7	2.7

Statistics are as originally reported. Adj. for 100% stk. div., 3/97. 1 Bef. $12.0 mill. chg. fr. disc. ops. 2 Bef. $67.9 mill. disc. ops. 3 Incl. $35.0 mill. after-tax gain fr. sale of bus. 4 Incl. $32.5 mill. net one-time gain on sale of bus.

OFFICERS:
J. H. Keyes, Chmn., C.E.O.
J. M. Barth, Pres., C.O.O.
S. A. Roell, Sr. V.P., C.F.O.

INVESTOR CONTACT: Arlene Gumm, Investor Relations, (414) 228-1200

PRINCIPAL OFFICE: 5757 North Green Bay Avenue, P.O. Box 591, Milwaukee, WI 53201

TELEPHONE NUMBER: (414) 524-1200
FAX: (414) 228-2646
WEB: www.johnsoncontrols.com

NO. OF EMPLOYEES: 105,000 (approx.)

SHAREHOLDERS: 59,070

ANNUAL MEETING: In Jan.

INCORPORATED: WI, July, 1900

INSTITUTIONAL HOLDINGS:
No. of Institutions: 313
Shares Held: 55,152,369
% Held: 64.1

INDUSTRY: Building maintenance services, nec (SIC: 7349)

TRANSFER AGENT(S): Firstar Trust Company, Milwaukee, WI

NYSE SYMBOL JNY
Rec. Pr. 44.20 (5/31/01)

JONES APPAREL GROUP, INC.

YIELD ...
P/E RATIO 17.8

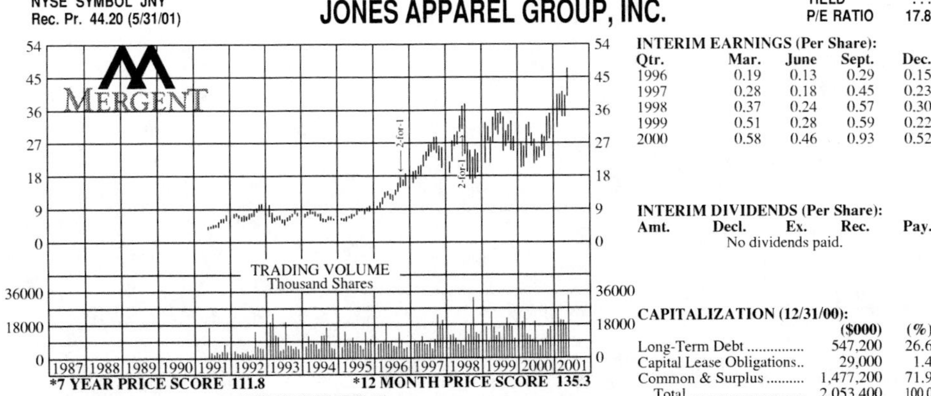

INTERIM EARNINGS (Per Share):

Qtr.	Mar.	June	Sept.	Dec.
1996	0.19	0.13	0.29	0.15
1997	0.28	0.18	0.45	0.23
1998	0.37	0.24	0.57	0.30
1999	0.51	0.28	0.59	0.22
2000	0.58	0.46	0.93	0.52

INTERIM DIVIDENDS (Per Share):

Amt.	Decl.	Ex.	Rec.	Pay.

No dividends paid.

CAPITALIZATION (12/31/00):

	($000)	(%)
Long-Term Debt	547,200	26.6
Capital Lease Obligations	29,000	1.4
Common & Surplus	1,477,200	71.9
Total	2,053,400	100.0

RECENT DEVELOPMENTS: For the year ended 12/31/00, net income totaled $301.9 million, up 96.8% compared with $153.4 million in 1999. Earnings for 2000 and 1999 included non-cash pre-tax charges of $3.1 million and $84.6 million, respectively. Total revenues improved 31.4% $4.14 billion versus $3.15 billion a year earlier. Wholesale apparal sales grew 8.7% to $2.17 billion from $1.99 billion a year earlier. Sales of wholesale footwear and accessories surged 102.4% to $940.0 million, while retail sales grew 51.0% to $1.01 billion.

PROSPECTS: On 4/16/01, the Company agreed to acquire McNaughton Apparel Group Inc. for $275.0 million in cash and stock, plus approximately $297.0 million in assumed debt. McNaughton, which sells women's and junior's moderately-priced career and casual clothing under the brand names Erika and Energie among others, markets its products nationwide to department stores, national chains, mass merchants, and specialty retailers, including JCPenney, Kohl's and Sears. The transaction is expected to be completed in the third quarter of 2001.

BUSINESS

JONES APPAREL GROUP, INC. is a designer and marketer of better priced women's sportswear, suits and dresses. JNY has pursued a multi-brand strategy by marketing its products under several nationally known brands, including its Jones New York, Evan-Picone and Rena Rowan for Saville labels and the licensed brand by Ralph Lauren Label. Each label is differentiated by its own distinctive styling and pricing strategy. JNY primarily contracts for the manufacture of its products through a worldwide network of quality manufacturers. JNY has capitalized on its nationally known brand names by entering into 32 licenses for the Jones New York brand name and 14 licenses for the Evan-Picone brand name with select manufacturers of women's and men's apparel and accessories. The Company acquired Victoria + Co. Ltd. in July 2000. On 10/2/99, JNY acquired Sun Apparel, Inc. On 6/15/99, acquired Nine West Group Inc. for approximately $1.40 billion.

QUARTERLY DATA

(12/31/2000)($000)	Rev	Inc
1st Quarter	1,082,400	70,600
2nd Quarter	906,600	55,500
3rd Quarter	1,191,500	112,300
4th Quarter	962,200	63,500

ANNUAL FINANCIAL DATA

	12/31/00	[1] 12/31/99	12/31/98	12/31/97	12/31/96	12/31/95	12/31/94
Earnings Per Share	[2] 2.48	1.60	1.47	1.13	0.76	0.60	0.52
Cash Flow Per Share	3.37	2.24	1.68	1.26	0.84	0.66	0.56
Tang. Book Val. Per Share	0.16	...	2.33	3.96	3.37	2.76	2.13
INCOME STATEMENT (IN MILLIONS):							
Total Revenues	4,142.7	3,150.7	1,685.2	1,387.5	1,021.0	776.4	633.3
Costs & Expenses	3,428.8	2,697.1	1,402.1	1,176.2	881.8	668.5	541.2
Depreciation & Amort.	109.3	75.4	21.2	14.6	8.9	6.7	4.2
Operating Income	604.6	378.2	261.9	196.6	130.3	101.1	87.9
Net Interest Inc./(Exp.)	d101.5	d63.6	d10.0	d2.0	d2.5	d1.5	d0.5
Income Before Income Taxes	503.1	314.6	251.8	194.6	127.8	99.7	87.3
Income Taxes	201.2	126.2	96.9	72.9	46.9	36.2	32.4
Net Income	[2] 301.9	188.4	154.9	121.7	80.9	63.5	54.9
Cash Flow	411.2	263.8	176.1	136.3	89.8	70.2	59.1
Average Shs. Outstg. (000)	121,900	118,000	105,128	107,810	107,330	106,092	105,848
BALANCE SHEET (IN MILLIONS):							
Cash & Cash Equivalents	60.5	47.0	129.0	40.1	30.1	16.9	21.1
Total Current Assets	1,181.7	1,130.6	631.8	440.8	389.8	331.5	258.6
Net Property	222.5	239.8	156.0	81.9	61.7	21.3	18.0
Total Assets	2,979.2	2,792.0	1,188.7	580.8	488.1	401.0	318.3
Total Current Liabilities	886.8	661.4	173.9	110.2	95.9	70.6	54.4
Long-Term Obligations	576.2	834.2	414.7	27.3	12.1	10.2	8.0
Net Stockholders' Equity	1,477.2	1,241.0	594.3	435.6	376.7	315.0	248.7
Net Working Capital	294.9	469.2	458.0	330.6	294.0	260.9	204.2
Year-end Shs. Outstg. (000)	120,100	122,600	103,494	102,188	103,990	104,604	103,596
STATISTICAL RECORD:							
Operating Profit Margin %	14.6	12.0	15.5	14.2	12.8	13.0	13.9
Net Profit Margin %	7.3	6.0	9.2	8.8	7.9	8.2	8.7
Return on Equity %	20.4	15.2	26.1	27.9	21.5	20.2	22.1
Return on Assets %	10.1	6.7	13.0	21.0	16.6	15.8	17.3
Debt/Total Assets %	19.3	29.9	34.9	4.7	2.5	2.5	2.5
Price Range	35.00-20.13	35.88-21.50	37.75-15.88	28.72-16.06	18.69-8.91	9.91-5.66	8.94-5.50
P/E Ratio	14.1-8.1	22.4-13.4	25.7-10.8	25.4-14.2	24.7-11.8	16.6-9.5	17.2-10.6

Statistics are as originally reported. Adj. for stk. splits: 2-for-1, 6/98, 10/96 [1] Incl. Nine West Group., acquired 6/15/99 [2] Incl. purchased inventory chrg. $3.1 mill.

OFFICERS:
S. Kimmel, Chmn., C.E.O.
J. Nemerov, Pres.
W. R. Card, C.F.O.

INVESTOR CONTACT: Wesley R. Card, C.F.O.

PRINCIPAL OFFICE: 250 Rittenhouse Circle, Keystone Park, Bristol, PA 19007

TELEPHONE NUMBER: (215) 785-4000
FAX: (215) 785-1228
WEB: www.jny.com

NO. OF EMPLOYEES: 18,620 (approx.)

SHAREHOLDERS: 365

ANNUAL MEETING: In June

INCORPORATED: PA, 1975

INSTITUTIONAL HOLDINGS:
No. of Institutions: 247
Shares Held: 98,161,479
% Held: 81.6

INDUSTRY: Women's & misses' blouses & shirts (SIC: 2331)

TRANSFER AGENT(S): Mellon Investor Services, Chicago, IL

NYSE SYMBOL KLU
Rec. Pr. 3.93 (4/30/01)

KAISER ALUMINUM CORP.

YIELD ...
P/E RATIO 17.9

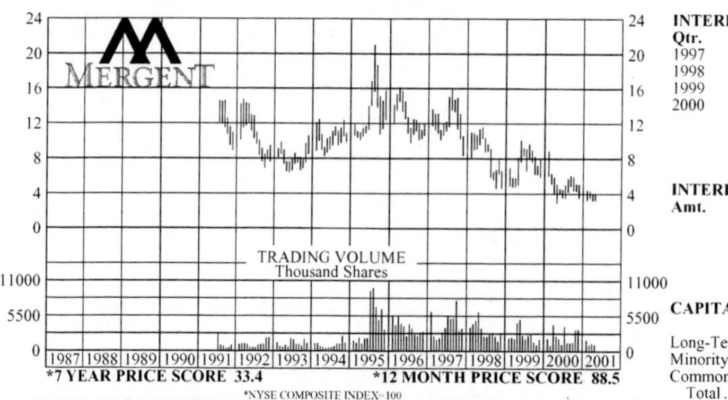

INTERIM EARNINGS (Per Share):

Qtr.	Mar.	June	Sept.	Dec.
1997	0.01	0.16	0.22	0.18
1998	0.15	0.21	0.14	d0.49
1999	d0.48	d0.20	d0.49	0.49
2000	0.15	0.14	d0.21	0.14

INTERIM DIVIDENDS (Per Share):

Amt.	Decl.	Ex.	Rec.	Pay.
No dividends paid.				

CAPITALIZATION (12/31/00):

	($000)	(%)
Long-Term Debt	957,800	83.9
Minority Interest	101,100	8.9
Common & Surplus	82,200	7.2
Total	1,141,100	100.0

RECENT DEVELOPMENTS: For the year ended 12/31/00, the Company reported net income of $16.8 million compared with a net loss of $54.1 million in the previous year. The 2000 results included a pre-tax charge of $38.5 million for a labor settlement and a net non-recurring gain of $80.4 million. Results for 1999 included a non-recurring charge of $24.1 million. Net sales grew 4.1% to $2.17 billion from $2.08 billion the year before.

PROSPECTS: KLU is encouraged by the recent strengthening of price for primary aluminum and stronger aerospace demand. However, KLU believes its alumina refineries and fabricating facilities will be negatively affected by unusual high energy prices in the near-term. In addition, KLU's engineered products are expected to be negatively affected by softness in the ground transportation and distribution markets. Going forward, KLU will look to strengthen its liquidity and near-term financial flexibility.

BUSINESS

KAISER ALUMINUM CORP. is one of the world's leading producers of alumina, primary aluminum, and fabricated products. KLU is also a major supplier of alumina and primary aluminum in domestic and international markets. KLU operates in all principal aspects of the aluminum industry: it mines bauxite, the major aluminum-bearing ore; refines bauxite into alumina, the intermediate material; and produces primary aluminum and fabricated aluminum products. KLU, through its wholly-owned subsidiary, Kaiser Aluminum & Chemical Corporation ("KACC"), operates in all principal aspects of the aluminum industry. MAXXAM Inc. (AMEX: MXM) holds an approximate 63.0% ownership interest in the Company on a fully-diluted basis as of 12/31/00.

ANNUAL FINANCIAL DATA

	12/31/00	12/31/99	12/31/98	12/31/97	12/31/96	12/31/95	12/31/94
Earnings Per Share	**[6] 0.21**	**[5] d0.68**	**[4] 0.01**	**[3] 0.57**	**Nil**	**[2] 0.69**	**[1] d2.09**
Cash Flow Per Share	**1.23**	**0.50**	**1.31**	**2.03**	**1.58**	**2.47**	**d0.34**
Tang. Book Val. Per Share	**1.03**	**0.82**	**1.51**	**1.48**	**0.96**	**0.80**	**0.29**
INCOME STATEMENT (IN MILLIONS):							
Total Revenues	2,169.8	2,044.3	2,256.4	2,373.2	2,190.5	2,237.8	1,781.5
Costs & Expenses	1,949.2	1,979.4	2,062.8	2,096.6	1,979.5	1,916.1	1,736.1
Depreciation & Amort.	81.3	93.8	103.0	108.6	113.2	111.1	101.6
Operating Income	139.3	d28.9	90.6	168.0	97.8	210.6	d56.2
Net Interest Inc./(Exp.)	d109.6	d110.1	d110.0	d110.7	d93.4	d93.9	d88.6
Income Before Income Taxes	25.4	d89.9	d15.9	60.3	1.7	102.6	d152.1
Income Taxes	11.6	cr32.7	cr16.4	8.8	cr9.3	37.2	cr53.8
Equity Earnings/Minority Int.	3.0	3.1	0.1	d3.5	d2.8	d5.1	d3.1
Net Income	[6] 16.8	[5] d54.1	[4] 0.6	[3] 48.0	8.2	[2] 60.3	[1] d101.4
Cash Flow	98.1	39.7	103.6	151.1	113.0	153.8	d19.9
Average Shs. Outstg. (000)	79,523	79,336	79,156	74,382	71,644	62,264	58,139
BALANCE SHEET (IN MILLIONS):							
Cash & Cash Equivalents	23.4	21.2	98.3	15.8	81.3	21.9	17.6
Total Current Assets	1,012.1	973.9	1,030.0	1,045.6	1,023.7	932.8	842.8
Net Property	1,176.1	1,053.7	1,108.7	1,171.8	1,168.7	1,109.6	1,133.2
Total Assets	3,343.1	3,198.8	2,990.9	3,013.9	2,934.0	2,813.2	2,698.1
Total Current Liabilities	841.4	637.9	558.4	594.1	609.4	601.1	583.1
Long-Term Obligations	957.8	972.5	962.6	962.9	953.0	749.2	751.1
Net Stockholders' Equity	82.2	65.3	119.2	117.0	69.3	57.7	17.3
Net Working Capital	170.7	336.0	471.6	451.5	414.3	331.7	259.7
Year-end Shs. Outstg. (000)	79,600	79,405	79,154	78,981	71,647	71,639	58,205
STATISTICAL RECORD:							
Operating Profit Margin %	6.4	...	4.0	7.1	4.5	9.4	...
Net Profit Margin %	0.8	...	...	2.0	0.4	2.7	...
Return on Equity %	20.4	...	0.5	41.0	11.8	104.5	...
Return on Assets %	0.5	...	...	1.6	0.3	2.1	...
Debt/Total Assets %	28.7	30.4	32.2	31.9	32.5	26.6	27.8
Price Range	8.88-2.94	10.13-4.75	11.63-4.63	16.00-8.31	16.13-9.75	21.00-10.13	12.50-8.25
P/E Ratio	42.2-14.0	...	N.M.	28.1-14.6	N.M.	30.4-14.7	...

Statistics are as originally reported. [1] Bef. $5.4 mill. chrg. [2] Incl. a pre-tax nonrecurr. charge of $17.0 mill. [3] Incl. a pre-tax charge of $19.7 mill. & $12.5 mill. [4] Incl. a pre-tax chg. of approx. $60.0 mill. & a $45.0 mill. non-cash chg. [5] Incl. a pre-tax gain of $50.5 mill. & other nonrecurr. pre-tax chgs. total. $24.1 mill. [6] Incl. pre-tax chrg. of $38.5 mill. & non-recurr. gain of $80.4 mill.

OFFICERS:
G. T. Haymaker Jr., Chmn.
R. J. Milchovich, Pres., C.E.O., C.O.O.
J. T. La Duc, Exec. V.P., C.F.O.

INVESTOR CONTACT: Investor Relations, (713) 267-3675

PRINCIPAL OFFICE: 5847 San Felipe, Suite 2600, Houston, TX 77057-3010

TELEPHONE NUMBER: (713) 267-3777
FAX: (713) 267-3701
WEB: www.kaiseral.com

NO. OF EMPLOYEES: 7,300 (approx.)

SHAREHOLDERS: 347

ANNUAL MEETING: In May

INCORPORATED: DE, Feb., 1987

INSTITUTIONAL HOLDINGS:
No. of Institutions: 41
Shares Held: 23,324,131
% Held: 29.3

INDUSTRY: Primary aluminum (SIC: 3334)

TRANSFER AGENT(S): BankBoston, N.A., Boston, MA

NYSE SYMBOL KLT
Rec. Pr. 25.11 (5/31/01)

KANSAS CITY POWER & LIGHT COMPANY

YIELD 6.6%
P/E RATIO 12.2

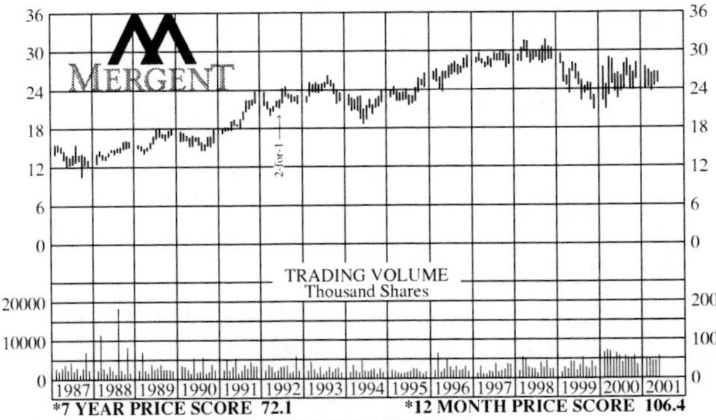

TRADING VOLUME
Thousand Shares

*7 YEAR PRICE SCORE 72.1 *12 MONTH PRICE SCORE 106.4
*NYSE COMPOSITE INDEX=100

INTERIM EARNINGS (Per Share):

Qtr.	Mar.	June	Sept.	Dec.
1996	0.38	0.43	0.57	0.31
1997	0.26	0.37	0.92	0.37
1998	0.22	0.60	0.94	0.13
1999	0.18	0.39	0.59	0.11
2000	Nil	0.43	1.31	0.31

INTERIM DIVIDENDS (Per Share):

Amt.	Decl.	Ex.	Rec.	Pay.
0.415Q	5/02/00	5/25/00	5/30/00	6/20/00
0.415Q	8/01/00	8/25/00	8/29/00	9/20/00
0.415Q	11/07/00	11/27/00	11/29/00	12/20/00
0.415Q	2/06/01	2/23/01	2/27/01	3/20/01
0.415Q	5/01/01	5/25/01	5/30/01	6/20/01

Indicated div.: $1.66 (Div. Reinv. Plan)

CAPITALIZATION (12/31/00):

	($000)	(%)
Long-Term Debt	1,041,847	38.0
Deferred Income Tax	590,220	21.5
Redeemable Pfd. Stock	150,062	5.5
Preferred Stock	39,000	1.4
Common & Surplus	921,352	33.6
Total	2,742,481	100.0

RECENT DEVELOPMENTS: For the year ended 12/31/00, the Company reported income of $128.6 million, before an accounting charge of $30.1 million, compared with net income of $81.9 million in 1999. Total operating revenues grew 21.1% to $1.12 billion versus $921.5 million a year earlier. Electric sales improved 18.5% to $1.06 billion, while gas sales surged 132.0% to $48.3 million. Operating income amounted to $292.3 million versus $185.8 million the year before.

PROSPECTS: On 2/12/01, the Company announced that its subsidiary, KLT Telecom Inc., assumed control of DTI Holdings, Inc., a St. Louis-based firm that is developing a high-capacity fiber optic network to serve 37 states. The deal was completed through the purchase of DTI Holdings from its founder, Richard D. Weinstein and through a tender offer for warrants of DTI Holdings. As a result of these transactions, KLT Telecom owns 83.6% of the outstanding shares of DTI Holdings.

BUSINESS

KANSAS CITY POWER & LIGHT COMPANY is engaged in the generation, transmission, distribution and sale of electricity to approximately 467,000 customers located in all or portions of 22 counties in western Missouri and eastern Kansas. The Company's customers include approximately 413,000 residences, 51,000 commercial firms, and 3,000 industrials, municipalities and other electric utilities. Retail electric revenues in Missouri and Kansas accounted for approximately 94% of KCPL's total electric revenues in 2000. KLT Inc. and Home Service Solutions, Inc., wholly-owned subsidiaries of KLT, pursue unregulated business ventures nationally, capturing growth opportunities in markets outside the regulated utility business.

ANNUAL FINANCIAL DATA

	12/31/00	12/31/99	12/31/98	12/31/97	12/31/96	12/31/95	12/31/94
Earnings Per Share	**3 2.05**	**2 1.26**	**1.89**	**1 1.18**	**1.69**	**1.92**	**1.64**
Cash Flow Per Share	**4.63**	**3.63**	**4.21**	**3.34**	**3.90**	**4.06**	**3.69**
Tang. Book Val. Per Share	**14.88**	**13.97**	**14.41**	**14.19**	**14.71**	**14.51**	**14.13**
Dividends Per Share	**1.66**	**1.66**	**1.64**	**1.62**	**1.59**	**1.54**	**1.50**
Dividend Payout %	**81.0**	**131.7**	**86.8**	**137.3**	**94.1**	**80.2**	**91.5**
INCOME STATEMENT (IN MILLIONS):							
Total Revenues	1,115.9	897.4	938.9	895.9	903.9	886.0	868.3
Costs & Expenses	589.6	485.8	461.3	453.9	449.3	430.7	448.0
Depreciation & Amort.	159.5	146.5	143.7	137.3	137.1	132.7	127.2
Maintenance Exp.	74.5	62.6	71.0	70.9	71.5	78.4	72.5
Operating Income	292.3	143.9	184.2	162.7	177.8	167.0	149.7
Net Interest Inc./(Exp.)	d75.7	d68.3	d71.7	d72.2	d58.1	d54.5	d47.4
Income Taxes	53.2	3.2	32.8	8.1	31.8	66.8	66.4
Net Income	3 128.6	2 81.9	120.7	1 76.6	108.2	122.6	104.8
Cash Flow	286.5	224.7	260.5	210.1	241.5	251.2	228.5
Average Shs. Outstg. (000)	61,864	61,898	61,884	62,895	61,902	61,902	61,903
BALANCE SHEET (IN MILLIONS):							
Gross Property	4,173.2	3,815.2	3,727.2	3,637.7	3,581.7	3,515.6	3,428.6
Accumulated Depreciation	1,645.5	1,516.3	1,410.8	1,314.2	1,238.2	1,156.1	1,092.4
Net Property	2,527.8	2,298.9	2,316.4	2,323.6	2,343.5	2,359.5	2,336.1
Total Assets	3,293.9	2,990.1	3,012.4	3,058.0	2,914.5	2,882.5	2,770.4
Long-Term Obligations	1,041.8	685.9	749.3	934.0	944.1	835.7	798.5
Net Stockholders' Equity	960.4	903.6	980.8	967.4	999.5	988.4	965.3
Year-end Shs. Outstg. (000)	61,909	61,909	61,909	61,909	61,902	61,902	61,909
STATISTICAL RECORD:							
Operating Profit Margin %	26.2	16.0	19.6	18.2	19.7	18.9	17.2
Net Profit Margin %	11.5	9.1	12.9	8.5	12.0	13.8	12.1
Net Inc./Net Property %	5.1	3.6	5.2	3.3	4.6	5.2	4.5
Net Inc./Tot. Capital %	4.7	3.5	5.1	2.8	4.2	5.0	4.4
Return on Equity %	13.4	9.1	12.3	7.9	10.8	12.4	10.9
Accum. Depr./Gross Prop. %	39.4	39.7	37.9	36.1	34.6	32.9	31.9
Price Range	29.00-20.88	29.63-20.81	31.81-28.00	29.94-27.38	29.38-23.63	26.63-21.50	23.88-18.63
P/E Ratio	14.1-10.2	23.5-16.5	16.8-14.8	25.4-23.2	17.4-14.0	13.9-11.2	14.6-11.4
Average Yield %	6.7	6.6	5.5	5.7	6.0	6.4	7.1

Statistics are as originally reported. 1 Incl. non-recurr. chrg. $60.0 mill. 2 Incl. net gain of $1.7 mill. and net loss of $15.0 mill. 3 Excl. acctg. credit $30.1 mill.

OFFICERS:
D. Jennings, Chmn.
B. J. Beaudoin, Pres., C.E.O.
A. F. Bielker, V.P., C.F.O., Treas.

INVESTOR CONTACT: Carol Sullivan, (816) 556-2053

PRINCIPAL OFFICE: 1201 Walnut Ave., Kansas City, MO 64106-2124

TELEPHONE NUMBER: (816) 556-2200
FAX: (816) 556-2924
WEB: www.kcpl.com

NO. OF EMPLOYEES: 2,266 (avg.)

SHAREHOLDERS: 19,110

ANNUAL MEETING: In May

INCORPORATED: MO, July, 1922

INSTITUTIONAL HOLDINGS:
No. of Institutions: 167
Shares Held: 16,578,080
% Held: 26.8

INDUSTRY: Power transmission equipment, nec (SIC: 3568)

TRANSFER AGENT(S): United Missouri Bank of Kansas City, N.A., Kansas City, MO

NYSE SYMBOL KSU
Rec. Pr. 12.81 (4/30/01)

KANSAS CITY SOUTHERN INDUSTRIES, INC.

YIELD ...
P/E RATIO 29.1

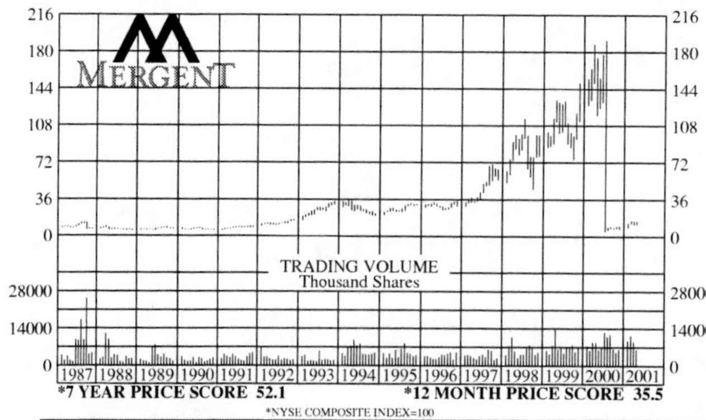

*7 YEAR PRICE SCORE 52.1 *12 MONTH PRICE SCORE 35.5

*NYSE COMPOSITE INDEX=100

INTERIM EARNINGS (Per Share):

Qtr.	June	Sept.	Dec.	Mar.
1996	0.34	0.38	1.34	0.58
1997	0.52	.058	0.76	d2.08
1998	0.82	1.02	0.98	0.50
1999	1.20	1.32	1.50	1.58
2000	0.18	0.15	0.05	0.06

INTERIM DIVIDENDS (Per Share):

Amt.	Decl.	Ex.	Rec.	Pay.

No dividends paid.

CAPITALIZATION (12/31/00):

	($000)	(%)
Long-Term Debt	638,400	39.6
Deferred Income Tax	332,200	20.6
Preferred Stock	6,100	0.4
Common & Surplus	637,300	39.5
Total	1,614,000	100.0

RECENT DEVELOPMENTS: For the year ended 12/31/00, income from continuing operations was $25.4 million versus net income of $10.2 million in 1999. Results for 2000 excluded extraordinary charges of $8.7 million related to the retirement of debt. Revenues fell 4.9% to $572.2 million, reflecting declines in coal, export grain, chemical/petroleum and haulage revenues from KSU's Kansas City Southern Railway/Gateway Western Railway Company businesses. Comparisons were made with restated prior-year results.

PROSPECTS: The effects of the U.S. economic slowdown and continued high diesel fuel prices dampen KSU's near-term prospects. However, KSU should continue to experience lower salaries and wages through the reduction of the amount of overtime hours worked and the number of relief train crews used as well as a reduction in total employee count. Looking forward, results should benefit from continued growth in Mexico through the realization of the potential of the Company's NAFTA franchise from its interests in Grupo TFM and Mexrail, Inc.

BUSINESS

KANSAS CITY SOUTHERN INDUSTRIES, INC. operates a railroad system that provides shippers with rail freight service in key commercial and industrial markets of the U.S. and Mexico. The transporation segment includes: The Kansas City Southern Railway; Gateway Western Railway Company; Grupo Transportacion Ferroviaria Mexicana, S.A. de C.V. (Grupo TFM), a 37%-owned affiliate; Mexrail, Inc., a 49%-owned affiliate; Southern Capital Corporation, LLC, a 50%-owned affiliate; and Panama Canal Railway Company, a 50%-owned affiliate. On 7/12/00, KSU completed the spin-off of its wholly-owned subsidiary, Stilwell Financial, Inc. through a special dividend of Stilwell common stock distributed to KCSI common stockholders of record on 6/28/00. Each KSU stockholder received two shares of common stock of Stilwell for each KSU share.

ANNUAL FINANCIAL DATA

	3 12/31/00	12/31/99	12/31/98	12/31/97	12/31/96	12/31/95	12/31/94
Earnings Per Share	2 0.43	5.58	3.32	1 d0.26	1 2.61	1 3.61	1.55
Cash Flow Per Share	1.40	7.29	4.66	1.14	3.94	4.75	3.31
Tang. Book Val. Per Share	10.24	19.55	10.20	7.45	8.65	8.26	6.73
INCOME STATEMENT (IN MILLIONS):							
Total Revenues	572.2	1,813.7	1,284.3	1,058.3	847.3	775.2	1,097.9
Costs & Expenses	410.2	1,139.0	816.3	876.6	567.3	541.0	776.3
Depreciation & Amort.	56.1	92.3	73.5	75.2	76.1	75.0	119.1
Operating Income	57.8	582.4	394.5	106.5	203.9	159.2	202.5
Net Interest Inc./(Exp.)	d65.8	d63.3	d66.1	d63.7	d59.6	d65.5	d53.6
Income Before Income Taxes	21.8	551.8	331.5	64.0	167.2	410.3	148.9
Income Taxes	cr3.6	223.1	130.8	68.4	70.6	192.9	63.5
Equity Earnings/Minority Int.	23.8	d5.4	d10.5	d9.7	54.3	19.3	19.5
Net Income	2 25.4	323.3	190.2	1 d14.1	1 150.9	1 236.7	104.9
Cash Flow	81.5	415.6	263.7	61.1	227.0	311.7	220.6
Average Shs. Outstg. (000)	58,390	57,025	56,529	53,801	57,641	65,606	67,591
BALANCE SHEET (IN MILLIONS):							
Cash & Cash Equivalents	21.5	360.0	176.3	133.8	22.9	31.8	12.7
Total Current Assets	216.4	733.5	469.5	373.1	292.1	281.2	380.1
Net Property	1,327.8	1,347.8	1,266.7	1,227.2	1,219.3	1,281.9	1,415.3
Total Assets	1,944.5	3,088.9	2,619.7	2,434.2	2,084.1	2,039.6	2,230.8
Total Current Liabilities	249.0	416.7	296.2	437.5	244.6	320.4	339.6
Long-Term Obligations	638.4	750.0	825.6	805.9	637.5	633.8	928.8
Net Stockholders' Equity	643.4	1,283.1	931.2	698.3	715.7	695.2	667.2
Net Working Capital	d32.6	316.8	173.3	d64.4	47.5	d39.2	40.5
Year-end Shs. Outstg. (000)	58,140	55,287	73,369	72,603	54,459	58,594	65,277
STATISTICAL RECORD:							
Operating Profit Margin %	10.1	32.1	30.7	10.1	24.1	20.5	18.4
Net Profit Margin %	4.4	17.8	14.8	...	17.8	30.5	9.6
Return on Equity %	3.9	25.2	20.4	...	21.1	34.0	15.7
Return on Assets %	1.3	10.5	7.3	...	7.2	11.6	4.7
Debt/Total Assets %	32.8	24.3	31.5	33.1	30.6	31.1	41.6
Price Range	191.50-5.13	150.00-75.00	114.88-46.00	70.25-29.17	34.50-25.67	32.42-20.67	35.08-19.92
P/E Ratio	445.2-11.9	26.9-13.4	34.6-13.9	...	13.2-9.8	9.0-5.7	22.7-12.9

Statistics are as originally reported. Adj. for 1-for-2 stk. split, 7/12/00; 3-for-1 stk. split, 9/97 1 Incls. non-recurr. pre-tax chrg. 12/31/97, $196.4 mill.; pre-tax credit 12/31/96, $47.7 mill.; net credit 12/31/95, $118.7 mill. 2 Bef. inc. fr. disc. ops. of $363.8 mill. ($6.14/sh.) & extraord. chrg. of $8.7 mill. ($0.15/sh.) 3 Refl. spin-off of Stilwell Financial, Inc.

OFFICERS:
M. R. Haverty, Chmn., Pres., C.E.O.
R. H. Berry, Sr. V.P., C.F.O.
R. P. Bruening, Sr. V.P., Sec., Gen. Couns.

INVESTOR CONTACT: William Galligan, (816) 983-1551

PRINCIPAL OFFICE: 114 West 11th Street, Kansas City, MO 64105

TELEPHONE NUMBER: (816) 983-1303
FAX: (816) 556-0297
WEB: www.kcsi.com

NO. OF EMPLOYEES: 2,862 (approx.)

SHAREHOLDERS: 5,469

ANNUAL MEETING: In May

INCORPORATED: DE, Jan., 1962

INSTITUTIONAL HOLDINGS:
No. of Institutions: 153
Shares Held: 30,549,762
% Held: 52.4

INDUSTRY: Railroads, line-haul operating (SIC: 4011)

TRANSFER AGENT(S): United Missouri Bank, N.A., Kansas City, MO

NYSE SYMBOL KDN
Rec. Pr. 25.62 (4/30/01)

KAYDON CORPORATION

YIELD 1.9%
P/E RATIO 19.4

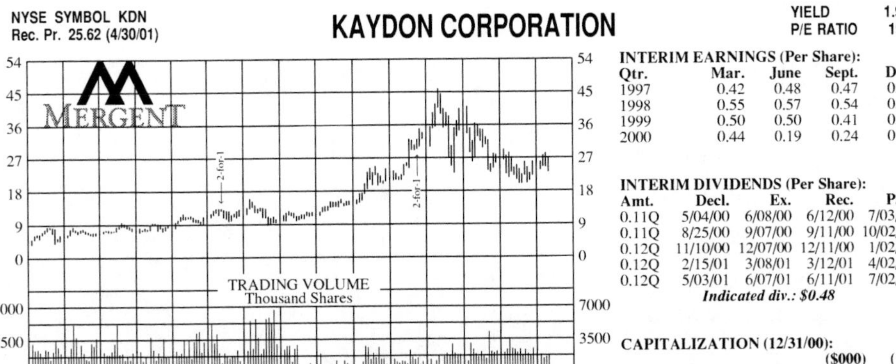

INTERIM EARNINGS (Per Share):

Qtr.	Mar.	June	Sept.	Dec.
1997	0.42	0.48	0.47	0.49
1998	0.55	0.57	0.54	0.51
1999	0.50	0.50	0.41	0.44
2000	0.44	0.19	0.24	0.45

INTERIM DIVIDENDS (Per Share):

Amt.	Decl.	Ex.	Rec.	Pay.
0.11Q	5/04/00	6/08/00	6/12/00	7/03/00
0.11Q	8/25/00	9/07/00	9/11/00	10/02/00
0.12Q	11/10/00	12/07/00	12/11/00	1/02/01
0.12Q	2/15/01	3/08/01	3/12/01	4/02/01
0.12Q	5/03/01	6/07/01	6/11/01	7/02/01

Indicated div.: $0.48

CAPITALIZATION (12/31/00):

	($000)	(%)
Long-Term Debt	47,518	12.8
Common & Surplus	322,435	87.2
Total	369,953	100.0

RECENT DEVELOPMENTS: For the year ended 12/31/00, net income declined 33.1% to $39.3 million compared with $58.8 million in 1999. Net sales were $339.2 million, up 4.2% from $325.7 million a year earlier. Results for 2000 included pre-tax special litigation-related charges of $21.7 million. Results were adversely affected by depressed conditions in certain key markets as well as by its subisidiary, Cooper Roller Bearing, in the United Kingdom.

PROSPECTS: On 3/1/01, KDN announced that it acquired all of the outstanding capital stock of ACE Controls, Inc. and its affiliated company ACE Controls International, Inc. for approximately $70.8 million. ACE Controls and ACE Controls International design, manufacture and distribute a full line of linear deceleration technology products. Going forward, KDN expects to build long-term growth using focused operating and financial strategies.

BUSINESS

KAYDON CORPORATION designs, manufactures and sells custom-engineered products for a broad and diverse customer base primarily in domestic markets. The Company's principal products include antifriction bearings, bearing systems and components, filters and filter housings, specialty retraining rings, specialty balls, custom rings, shaft seals, hydraulic cylinders, metal castings and various types of slip-rings. These products are used by customers in a wide variety of medical, instrumentation, material handling, machine tool positioning, aerospace, defense, construction and other industrial applications. The Company aims to provide cost-effective solutions for its customers through close engineering relationships with manufacturers throughout the world.

ANNUAL FINANCIAL DATA

	12/31/00	12/31/99	12/31/98	12/31/97	12/31/96	12/31/95	12/31/94
Earnings Per Share	**[2] 1.30**	**1.85**	**2.17**	**1.86**	**1.53**	**1.14**	**[1] 0.94**
Cash Flow Per Share	**1.88**	**2.34**	**2.59**	**2.24**	**1.88**	**1.47**	**1.25**
Tang. Book Val. Per Share	**7.22**	**7.78**	**7.68**	**6.57**	**5.42**	**3.91**	**3.69**
Dividends Per Share	**0.44**	**0.40**	**0.36**	**0.28**	**0.24**	**0.22**	**0.20**
Dividend Payout %	**33.8**	**21.6**	**16.6**	**15.1**	**15.7**	**19.3**	**21.4**
INCOME STATEMENT (IN THOUSANDS):							
Total Revenues	339,246	325,696	376,172	329,036	290,670	229,924	204,695
Costs & Expenses	264,833	220,894	251,748	220,599	199,967	159,462	144,295
Depreciation & Amort.	17,367	15,634	14,044	12,756	11,749	11,176	10,641
Operating Income	57,046	89,168	110,380	95,681	78,954	59,286	49,759
Net Interest Inc./(Exp.)	5,072	4,877	4,434	3,780	2,662	2,505	609
Income Before Income Taxes	62,118	94,045	114,814	99,461	81,616	61,791	50,368
Income Taxes	22,771	35,266	43,630	37,795	31,095	23,588	19,142
Net Income	[2] 39,347	58,779	71,184	61,666	50,521	38,203	[1] 31,226
Cash Flow	56,714	74,413	85,228	74,422	62,270	49,379	41,867
Average Shs. Outstg.	30,166	31,775	32,871	33,163	33,098	33,482	33,452
BALANCE SHEET (IN THOUSANDS):							
Cash & Cash Equivalents	114,965	89,749	96,203	96,802	83,267	47,159	39,667
Total Current Assets	241,185	211,553	229,800	214,778	186,056	135,454	126,788
Net Property	105,304	98,844	99,259	85,510	76,176	72,345	61,247
Total Assets	475,552	406,749	413,808	383,985	331,538	267,675	243,584
Total Current Liabilities	59,999	54,183	71,200	71,015	66,824	44,047	40,902
Long-Term Obligations	47,518	...	...	...	4,000	8,000	8,000
Net Stockholders' Equity	322,435	316,950	311,656	283,596	232,056	187,905	166,570
Net Working Capital	181,186	157,370	158,600	143,763	119,232	91,407	85,886
Year-end Shs. Outstg.	30,355	31,097	32,150	32,992	32,934	35,266	33,296
STATISTICAL RECORD:							
Operating Profit Margin %	16.8	27.4	29.3	29.1	27.2	25.8	24.3
Net Profit Margin %	11.6	18.0	18.9	18.7	17.4	16.6	15.3
Return on Equity %	12.2	18.5	22.8	21.7	21.8	20.3	18.7
Return on Assets %	8.3	14.5	17.2	16.1	15.2	14.3	12.8
Debt/Total Assets %	10.0	...	...	...	1.2	3.0	3.3
Price Range	29.31-19.94	41.06-23.00	45.94-22.81	34.94-20.88	24.75-14.44	15.81-11.38	12.63-9.88
P/E Ratio	22.5-15.3	22.2-12.4	21.2-10.5	18.8-11.2	16.2-9.5	13.9-10.0	13.5-10.6
Average Yield %	1.8	1.2	1.0	1.0	1.2	1.6	1.8

Statistics are as originally reported. Adj. for stk. split: 2-for-1, 10/97. [1] Bef. acctg. change chrg. of $2.0 mill. [2] Incl. nonrecurr. pre-tax chrg. of $21.7 mill. for special litigation-related charges.

OFFICERS:
B. P. Campbell, Chmn., Pres., C.E.O., C.F.O.
J. F. Brocci, V.P., Admin., Sec.

INVESTOR CONTACT: Brian P. Campbell, (734) 747-7025 ext. 129

PRINCIPAL OFFICE: 315 East Eisenhower Parkway, Suite 300, Ann Arbor, MI 48108-3330

TELEPHONE NUMBER: (734) 747-7025
FAX: (734) 747-6565
WEB: www.kaydon.com

NO. OF EMPLOYEES: 2,500 (approx.)

SHAREHOLDERS: 1,132 (record)

ANNUAL MEETING: In May

INCORPORATED: DE, Oct., 1983

INSTITUTIONAL HOLDINGS:
No. of Institutions: 128
Shares Held: 22,513,244
% Held: 74.1

INDUSTRY: Ball and roller bearings (SIC: 3562)

TRANSFER AGENT(S): Continental Stock Transfer and Trust Company, New York, NY

NYSE SYMBOL KBH
Rec. Pr. 25.41 (5/31/01)

KB HOME

YIELD 1.2%
P/E RATIO 5.6

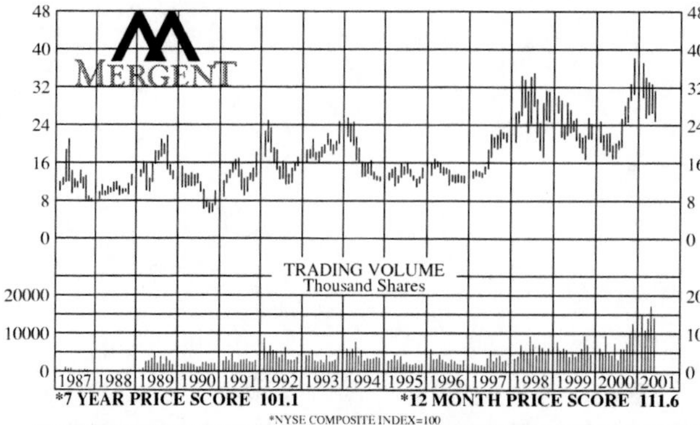

INTERIM EARNINGS (Per Share):

Qtr.	Feb.	May	Aug.	Nov.
1997	0.11	0.27	0.38	0.69
1998	0.20	0.42	0.68	1.02
1999	0.35	0.58	0.78	1.36
2000	1.47	0.68	1.14	2.00
2001	0.70	...	...	...

INTERIM DIVIDENDS (Per Share):

Amt.	Decl.	Ex.	Rec.	Pay.
0.075Q	4/06/00	5/09/00	5/11/00	5/25/00
0.075Q	7/06/00	8/15/00	8/17/00	8/31/00
0.075Q	10/05/00	11/10/00	11/14/00	11/28/00
0.075Q	12/06/00	2/06/01	2/08/01	2/22/01
0.075Q	4/05/01	5/09/01	5/11/01	5/25/01

Indicated div.: $0.30

CAPITALIZATION (11/30/00):

	($000)	(%)
Long-Term Debt	1,403,202	60.9
Minority Interest	246,616	10.7
Common & Surplus	654,759	28.4
Total	2,304,577	100.0

RECENT DEVELOPMENTS: For the quarter ended 2/28/01, net income dropped 59.8% to $25.8 million compared with $64.2 million in 2000. Results for 2000 included a non-recurring gain of $39.6 million on the issuance of French subsidiary stock. Total revenues were $821.1 million, up 2.7% from $799.6 million in 2000. Construction revenues increased 2.8% to $808.2 million, while mortgage banking revenues declined 3.7% to $12.9 million.

PROSPECTS: Looking ahead, the Company expects solid growth based on its strong backlog at the end of the first quarter of 12,375 units, representing a 30.6% increase over last year. In 2001, the Company expects to deliver approximately 24,000 homes. In addition, KBH should continue to benefit from an increase in net orders throughout its West Coast, Southwest and Central regions, demonstrating the Company's strong niche in each market.

BUSINESS

KB HOME (formerly Kaufman & Broad Home Corp.) is a builder of single-family homes with domestic operations in six western states, and international operations in France. Domestically, the Company is the largest homebuilder west of the Mississippi River, delivering more single-family homes than any other builder in the region. KBH builds innovatively designed homes which cater primarily to first-time homebuyers, generally in medium-sized developments close to major metropolitan areas. In France, the Company also builds commercial projects and high-density residential properties, such as condominium and apartment complexes. KBH provides mortgage banking services to domestic homebuyers through its wholly-owned subsidiary, Kaufman and Broad Mortgage Company.

QUARTERLY DATA

(11/30/2000)($000)	REV	INC
1st Quarter	799,585	64,214
2nd Quarter	906,182	27,700
3rd Quarter	981,024	44,639
4th Quarter	1,244,067	73,407

ANNUAL FINANCIAL DATA

	11/30/00	11/30/99	11/30/98	11/30/97	11/30/96	11/30/95	11/30/94
Earnings Per Share	**2 5.24**	**3.08**	**2.32**	**1.45**	**1 d1.54**	**0.73**	**1.16**
Cash Flow Per Share	**6.30**	**3.91**	**2.76**	**1.81**	**d1.23**	**0.93**	**1.31**
Tang. Book Val. Per Share	**10.19**	**9.79**	**10.73**	**9.02**	**7.75**	**12.37**	**12.46**
Dividends Per Share	**0.30**	**0.30**	**0.30**	**0.30**	**0.30**	**0.30**	**0.30**
Dividend Payout %	**5.7**	**9.7**	**12.9**	**20.7**	**...**	**41.1**	**25.9**
INCOME STATEMENT (IN MILLIONS):							
Total Revenues	3,930.9	3,836.3	2,449.4	1,876.3	1,787.0	1,396.5	1,336.3
Costs & Expenses	3,576.1	3,520.0	2,261.2	1,745.8	1,663.3	1,313.6	1,236.3
Depreciation & Amort.	42.3	39.8	18.1	14.2	12.3	8.0	5.7
Operating Income	312.4	276.6	170.1	116.3	111.4	74.9	94.3
Net Interest Inc./(Exp.)	d25.7	d20.5	d17.7	d24.8	d34.0	d25.4	d15.8
Income Before Income Taxes	297.7	226.9	146.6	91.0	d95.7	45.5	73.9
Income Taxes	87.7	79.4	51.3	32.8	cr34.5	16.4	27.3
Equity Earnings/Minority Int.	10.9	d29.2	d5.9	d0.5	d2.4	d4.1	d4.7
Net Income	2 210.0	147.5	95.3	58.2	1 d61.2	29.1	46.6
Cash Flow	252.3	187.2	113.3	72.4	d53.9	27.2	42.4
Average Shs. Outstg. (000)	40,069	47,831	41,033	40,058	39,763	39,757	40,026
BALANCE SHEET (IN MILLIONS):							
Cash & Cash Equivalents	33.1	28.4	63.4	68.2	9.8	43.4	54.8
Total Current Assets	2,431.5	2,188.6	1,646.5	1,308.7	1,132.1	1,493.6	1,387.0
Total Assets	2,828.9	2,664.2	1,860.2	1,419.0	1,243.5	1,574.2	1,454.5
Total Current Liabilities	322.7	338.2	220.3	170.9	159.3	165.8	156.5
Long-Term Obligations	1,403.2	1,227.3	818.5	757.8	646.0	875.3	786.8
Net Stockholders' Equity	654.8	676.6	474.5	383.1	340.4	415.5	404.7
Net Working Capital	2,108.9	1,850.4	1,426.2	1,137.8	972.8	1,327.9	1,230.6
Year-end Shs. Outstg. (000)	44,397	48,091	39,992	38,997	38,827	32,347	32,378
STATISTICAL RECORD:							
Operating Profit Margin %	7.9	7.2	6.9	6.2	6.2	5.4	7.1
Net Profit Margin %	5.3	3.8	3.9	3.1	...	2.1	3.5
Return on Equity %	32.1	21.8	20.1	15.2	...	7.0	11.5
Return on Assets %	7.4	5.5	5.1	4.1	...	1.8	3.2
Debt/Total Assets %	49.6	46.1	44.0	53.4	51.9	55.6	54.1
Price Range	38.31-16.81	30.25-16.75	35.00-17.13	23.13-12.75	16.88-11.25	16.00-10.88	25.50-12.13
P/E Ratio	7.3-3.2	9.8-5.4	15.1-7.4	15.9-8.8	...	21.9-14.9	22.0-10.5
Average Yield %	1.1	1.3	1.2	1.7	2.1	2.2	1.6

Statistics are as originally reported. 1 Incl. non-recurr. chrg. $170.8 mill. 2 Incl. non-recurr. gain $39.6 mill.

OFFICERS:
B. Karatz, Chmn., Pres., C.E.O.
B. P. Pachino, Sr. V.P., Gen. Couns.
J. T. Mezger, Exec. V.P., C.O.O.

INVESTOR CONTACT: Mary M. McAboy, V.P., Investor Relations, (310) 231-4033

PRINCIPAL OFFICE: 10990 Wilshire Boulevard, Los Angeles, CA 90024

TELEPHONE NUMBER: (310) 231-4000
FAX: (310) 231-4222
WEB: www.kbhomes.com

NO. OF EMPLOYEES: 3,500

SHAREHOLDERS: 1,357 (record)

ANNUAL MEETING: In Apr.

INCORPORATED: DE, May, 1986

INSTITUTIONAL HOLDINGS:
No. of Institutions: 62
Shares Held: 8,566,555
% Held: 25.2

INDUSTRY: Operative builders (SIC: 1531)

TRANSFER AGENT(S): Mellon Investor Services L.L.C., South Hackensack, NJ

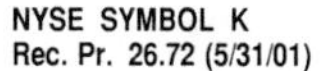

NYSE SYMBOL K
Rec. Pr. 26.72 (5/31/01)

KELLOGG COMPANY

YIELD 3.8%
P/E RATIO 18.4

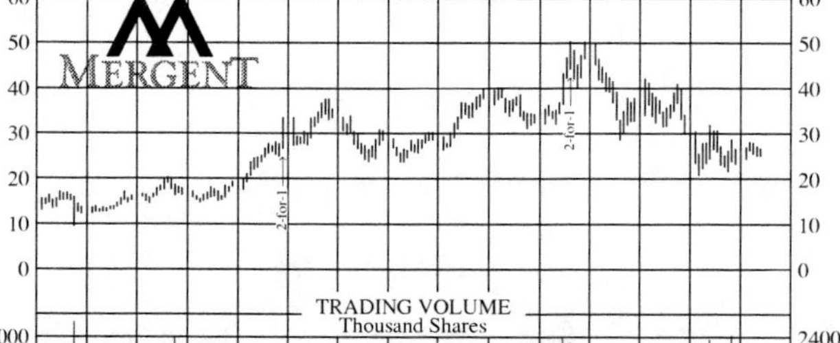

24000
12000
0

1987	1988	1989	1990	1991	1992	1993	1994	1995	1996	1997	1998	1999	2000	2001

*7 YEAR PRICE SCORE 56.2 *12 MONTH PRICE SCORE 106.2

*NYSE COMPOSITE INDEX=100

INTERIM EARNINGS (Per Share):

Qtr.	Mar.	June	Sept.	Dec.
1996	0.48	0.19	0.38	0.21
1997	0.39	0.40	0.50	0.08
1998	0.42	0.35	0.35	0.11
1999	0.29	0.38	d0.08	0.25
2000	0.40	0.37	0.45	0.23

INTERIM DIVIDENDS (Per Share):

Amt.	Decl.	Ex.	Rec.	Pay.
0.247Q	7/28/00	8/29/00	8/31/00	9/15/00
0.253Q	10/27/00	11/28/00	11/30/00	12/15/00
0.253Q	2/16/01	2/26/01	2/28/01	3/15/01
0.253Q	4/27/01	5/29/01	5/31/01	6/15/01

Indicated div.: $1.01 (Div. Reinv. Plan)

CAPITALIZATION (12/31/00):

	($000)	(%)
Long-Term Debt	709,200	44.1
Common & Surplus	897,500	55.9
Total	1,606,700	100.0

RECENT DEVELOPMENTS: For the year ended 12/31/00, net earnings totaled $587.7 million versus $338.3 million the previous year. Earnings in 2000 included a pre-tax restructuring charge of $86.5 million. Results in 1999 included a pre-tax restructuring charge of $244.6 million and pre-tax disposition-related charges of $168.5 million. Net sales were $6.95 billion, down slightly versus $6.98 billion a year earlier.

PROSPECTS: Near-term operating profit growth is expected to be limited by the combination of increased marketing spending to help spur sales of cereal in the U.S. and costs associated with the 3/26/01 acquisition of Keebler Foods Company. Meanwhile, the Company is implementing restructuring initiatives focused on streamlining its operations and offsetting the costs of the Keebler integration.

BUSINESS

KELLOGG COMPANY is a major producer of ready-to-eat cereal products and convenience foods such as frozen pies, toaster pastries, frozen waffles, cereal bars, and other snack items. Brand names include RICE KRISPIES, KELLOGG'S, SPECIAL K, EGGO, POP-TARTS, NUTRI-GRAIN, MORNINGSTAR FARMS, and KASHI. Products are manufactured in 20 countries and distributed in 160 countries, including many in Asia, Australia, Europe, Africa and Latin America. Contributions to sales (and operating profit) in 2000 were: North America, 59% (61%); Europe, 21% (19%); Latin America, 9% (13%); and Other, 11% (7%).

REVENUES

(12/31/2000)	($000)	(%)
Global Cereal	5,177,600	74.5
Global Convenience	1,771,100	25.5
Total	6,954,700	100.0

ANNUAL FINANCIAL DATA

	12/31/00	12/31/99	12/31/98	12/31/97	12/31/96	12/31/95	12/31/94
Earnings Per Share	**2 1.45**	**2 0.83**	**2 1.23**	**2 3 1.36**	**1 1.25**	**1 1.12**	**2 1.58**
Cash Flow Per Share	**2.17**	**1.54**	**1.91**	**2.06**	**1.84**	**1.71**	**2.14**
Tang. Book Val. Per Share	**2.21**	**2.01**	**2.20**	**2.43**	**3.06**	**3.67**	**4.08**
Dividends Per Share	**0.99**	**0.96**	**0.92**	**0.87**	**0.81**	**0.75**	**0.70**
Dividend Payout %	**68.3**	**115.6**	**74.8**	**64.0**	**64.8**	**67.0**	**44.4**
INCOME STATEMENT (IN MILLIONS):							
Total Revenues	6,954.7	6,984.2	6,762.1	6,830.1	6,676.6	7,003.7	6,562.0
Costs & Expenses	5,674.3	5,867.4	5,588.9	5,533.7	5,466.2	5,907.4	5,143.3
Depreciation & Amort.	290.6	288.0	278.1	287.3	251.5	258.8	256.1
Operating Income	989.8	828.8	895.1	1,009.1	958.9	837.5	1,162.6
Net Interest Inc./(Exp.)	d137.5	d118.8	d119.5	d108.3	d65.6	d62.6	d45.4
Income Before Income Taxes	867.7	536.7	782.5	904.5	859.9	796.0	1,130.0
Income Taxes	280.0	198.4	279.9	340.5	328.9	305.7	424.6
Net Income	2 587.7	2 338.3	2 502.8	2 3 564.0	1 531.0	1 490.3	2 705.4
Cash Flow	878.3	626.3	780.9	851.3	782.5	749.1	961.5
Average Shs. Outstg. (000)	405,600	405,700	408,600	414,100	424,900	438,300	448,400
BALANCE SHEET (IN MILLIONS):							
Cash & Cash Equivalents	204.4	150.6	136.4	173.2	243.8	221.9	266.3
Total Current Assets	1,606.8	1,569.2	1,496.5	1,467.7	1,528.6	1,428.8	1,433.5
Net Property	2,526.9	2,640.9	2,888.8	2,773.3	2,932.9	2,784.8	2,892.8
Total Assets	4,896.3	4,808.7	5,051.5	4,877.6	5,050.0	4,414.6	4,467.3
Total Current Liabilities	2,492.6	1,587.8	1,718.5	1,657.3	2,199.0	1,265.4	1,185.2
Long-Term Obligations	709.2	1,612.8	1,614.5	1,415.4	726.7	717.8	719.2
Net Stockholders' Equity	897.5	813.2	889.8	997.5	1,282.4	1,590.9	1,807.5
Net Working Capital	d885.8	d18.6	d222.0	d189.6	d670.4	163.4	248.3
Year-end Shs. Outstg. (000)	405,639	405,500	405,000	410,800	419,296	433,410	443,402
STATISTICAL RECORD:							
Operating Profit Margin %	14.2	11.9	13.2	14.8	14.4	12.0	17.7
Net Profit Margin %	8.5	4.8	7.4	8.3	8.0	7.0	10.7
Return on Equity %	65.5	41.6	56.5	56.5	41.4	30.8	39.0
Return on Assets %	12.0	7.0	9.9	11.6	10.5	11.1	15.8
Debt/Total Assets %	14.5	33.5	32.0	29.0	14.4	16.3	16.1
Price Range	32.00-20.75	42.25-30.00	50.19-28.50	50.50-32.00	40.31-31.00	39.75-26.25	30.38-23.69
P/E Ratio	22.1-14.3	50.9-36.1	40.8-23.2	37.1-23.5	32.2-24.8	35.5-23.4	19.3-15.0
Average Yield %	3.8	2.7	2.3	2.1	2.3	2.3	2.6

Statistics are as originally reported. Adj. for 2-for-1 stk. split, 8/97. 1 Incl. discont. opers. loss $120.1 mil, 1996; & loss $271.3 mil, 1995. 2 Incl. $64.2 mil ($0.16/sh) after-tax restr. chg., 2000; $244.6 mil pre-tax non-recur. chg. & $168.5 mil pre-tax disposition-related chgs., 1999; $46.3 mil ($0.12/sh) after-tax, 1998; $140.5 mil ($0.34/sh) chg., 1997; & net gain $200,000, 1994. 3 Bef. $18.0 mil ($0.04/sh) chg. for acctg. change.

OFFICERS:
C. M. Gutierrez, Chmn., C.E.O.
T. J. Webb, Exec. V.P., C.F.O.
J. L. Kelly, Exec. V.P., Gen. Couns., Sec.

INVESTOR CONTACT: Investor Relations, (616) 961-2767

PRINCIPAL OFFICE: One Kellogg Square, P.O. Box 3599, Battle Creek, MI 49016

TELEPHONE NUMBER: (616) 961-2000
FAX: (616) 961-2871
WEB: www.kelloggs.com

NO. OF EMPLOYEES: 15,196

SHAREHOLDERS: 46,711

ANNUAL MEETING: In Apr.

INCORPORATED: DE, Dec., 1922

INSTITUTIONAL HOLDINGS:
No. of Institutions: 320
Shares Held: 317,873,286
% Held: 78.3

INDUSTRY: Cereal breakfast foods (SIC: 2043)

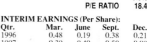

TRANSFER AGENT(S): Wells Fargo Shareowner Services, South St. Paul, MN

NYSE SYMBOL KWD
Rec. Pr. 23.51 (5/31/01)

KELLWOOD COMPANY

YIELD 2.7%
P/E RATIO 9.3

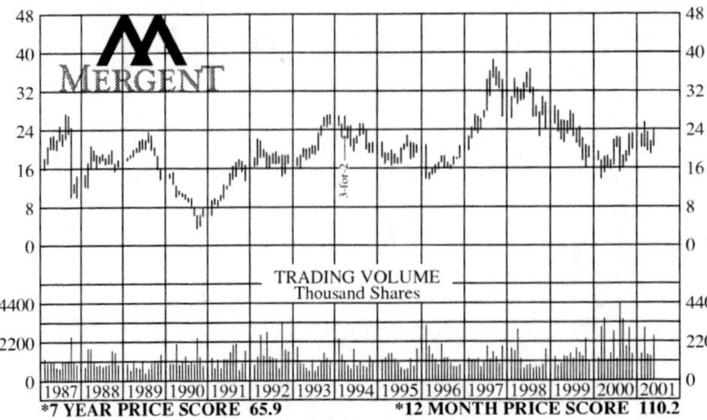

INTERIM EARNINGS (Per Share):

Qtr.	July	Oct.	Jan.	Apr.
1996-97	0.27	0.68	0.10	0.73
1997-98	0.34	0.77	0.11	0.76
1998-99	0.32	0.82	0.07	d1.13
1999-00	0.34	0.93	0.20	...
Qtr.	**Apr.**	**July**	**Oct.**	**Jan.**
2000-01	1.17	0.28	1.15	d0.07

INTERIM DIVIDENDS (Per Share):

Amt.	Decl.	Ex.	Rec.	Pay.
0.16Q	6/01/00	6/08/00	6/12/00	6/23/00
0.16Q	8/24/00	8/31/00	9/05/00	9/15/00
0.16Q	11/21/00	11/29/00	12/01/00	12/15/00
0.16Q	3/08/01	3/15/01	3/19/01	3/30/01
0.16Q	5/31/01	6/07/01	6/11/01	6/22/01

Indicated div.: $0.64 (Div. Reinv. Plan)

CAPITALIZATION (1/31/01):

	($000)	(%)
Long-Term Debt	411,331	48.8
Common & Surplus	431,096	51.2
Total	842,427	100.0

RECENT DEVELOPMENTS: For the year ended 1/31/01, net earnings surged to $60.8 million compared with $10.0 million in fiscal 1999. Earnings for fiscal 2000 included a pension termination gain of $5.9 million, while earnings for fiscal 1999 included unusual items totaling $61.0 million. Net sales totaled $2.36 billion, up 7.7% versus $2.19 billion the year before. Sales of women's sportswear grew 2.7%% to $1.64 billion, while men's sportswear sales climbed 10.5% to $362.5 million. Other soft goods sales increased 33.6% to $364.6 million.

PROSPECTS: Recently, KWD's Fritzi California division announced the launch of Jolt, a new bottoms-driven denim division for young girls. Separately, KWD's Sag Harbor division launched a new line of suits and career apparel. Going forward, given the difficult retail environment and the sharp drop in consumer confidence and activity, KWD expects earnings per share for fiscal 2002 in the range of $2.75 to $2.90. The ability of KWD to come in at the mid-to-upper end of this range will be driven by what happens in the second half of fiscal 2001.

BUSINESS

KELLWOOD COMPANY manufactures and markets apparel and other soft goods products made from cloth or fabric or knitted from yarn. These products are manufactured primarily domestically and in the Far East. The Company's products include diversified lines of men's, women's, and children's clothing, sleeping bags, and other soft goods. Operating units include: Cape Cod-Cricket Lane, Parsons Place Apparel, EZ sportswear, décorp, EnChanté, Robert Scott, David Brooks, Andrew Harvey, American Recreation products, Smart Shirts and Crowntuft Manufacturing. Clothing lines include Sag Harbor®, EMME®, and the Kathie Lee Gifford line for Wal-mart Stores Inc. Plants are operated in the United States, Hong Kong, Taiwan and Sri Lanka. Sales to Sears, Roebuck & Co. accounted for 7% of total sales in fiscal year 2000. On 4/29/99, the Company acquired Koret, Inc. On 1/4/00, KWD acquired Biflex International, Inc.

ANNUAL FINANCIAL DATA

	1/31/01	[3] 1/31/00	4/30/99	4/30/98	4/30/97	4/30/96	4/30/95
Earnings Per Share	**[4] 2.57**	**1.48**	**[2] 0.07**	**1.95**	**1.78**	**1.32**	**[1] 0.53**
Cash Flow Per Share	**3.72**	**2.17**	**1.28**	**3.30**	**3.12**	**2.66**	**1.87**
Tang. Book Val. Per Share	**17.44**	**14.43**	**15.98**	**12.96**	**11.08**	**9.65**	**8.36**
Dividends Per Share	**0.64**	**0.64**	**0.64**	**0.63**	**0.60**	**0.60**	**0.60**
Dividend Payout %	**24.9**	**43.2**	**913.0**	**32.3**	**33.7**	**45.5**	**113.2**
INCOME STATEMENT (IN MILLIONS):							
Total Revenues	2,362.2	1,565.3	2,151.1	1,781.6	1,521.0	1,466.0	1,364.8
Costs & Expenses	2,207.7	1,457.8	1,982.9	1,650.3	1,408.0	1,368.5	1,291.3
Depreciation & Amort.	27.3	19.1	33.4	29.6	28.3	28.2	28.3
Operating Income	127.2	88.4	134.9	101.6	84.7	69.4	45.1
Net Interest Inc./(Exp.)	d32.6	d22.7	d33.9	d28.9	d21.6	d22.9	d19.1
Income Before Income Taxes	99.0	68.6	39.2	73.9	64.8	48.5	28.5
Income Taxes	38.2	27.6	37.2	31.2	27.2	20.5	17.4
Net Income	[4] 60.8	41.0	[2] 2.0	42.7	37.6	28.0	[1] 11.1
Cash Flow	88.1	60.1	35.3	72.4	65.9	56.2	39.4
Average Shs. Outstg. (000)	23,700	27,748	27,605	21,946	21,131	21,170	21,080
BALANCE SHEET (IN MILLIONS):							
Cash & Cash Equivalents	10.4	54.5	25.5	31.8	22.5	25.0	11.1
Total Current Assets	907.1	824.3	797.3	759.0	621.5	544.4	511.3
Net Property	114.5	103.7	102.3	65.9	62.8	63.8	63.6
Total Assets	1,265.7	1,097.9	1,054.2	1,015.5	874.6	796.7	768.1
Total Current Liabilities	362.5	248.2	331.7	342.5	374.4	306.3	274.4
Long-Term Obligations	411.3	346.5	227.7	242.7	109.8	125.4	144.8
Net Stockholders' Equity	431.1	445.9	446.2	384.2	347.8	325.2	308.2
Net Working Capital	544.6	576.1	465.5	416.5	247.1	238.1	236.9
Year-end Shs. Outstg. (000)	17,390	26,173	24,148	21,510	21,121	21,229	21,129
STATISTICAL RECORD:							
Operating Profit Margin %	5.4	5.6	6.3	5.7	5.6	4.7	3.3
Net Profit Margin %	2.6	2.6	0.1	2.4	2.5	1.9	0.8
Return on Equity %	14.1	9.2	0.4	11.1	10.8	8.6	3.6
Return on Assets %	4.8	3.7	0.2	4.2	4.3	3.5	1.4
Debt/Total Assets %	32.5	31.6	21.6	23.9	12.6	15.7	18.8
Price Range	23.25-13.75	28.88-16.25	36.69-22.50	38.56-19.63	20.88-13.63	22.88-16.50	26.92-19.13
P/E Ratio	9.0-5.3	19.5-11.0	523.4-321.0	19.8-10.1	11.7-7.7	17.3-12.5	50.8-36.1
Average Yield %	3.5	2.8	2.2	2.2	3.5	3.0	2.6

Statistics are as originally reported. Adj. for stk. split: 3-for-2, 2/94 [1] Incl. non-recurr. chrg. 1995, $13.9 mill.; gain 1994, $3.0 mill. [2] Incl. special chrgs. totaling $62.3 mill. [3] Results for 9 months transition period due to year-end change. [4] Incl. pension termination gain of $5.9 mill.

OFFICERS:
H. J. Upbin, Chmn., Pres., C.E.O.
J. C. Jacobsen, Vice-Chmn.
W. L. Crapps III, V.P., C.F.O.
R. D. Joseph, V.P., Treas.

PRINCIPAL OFFICE: 600 Kellwood Parkway, St. Louis, MO 63178

TELEPHONE NUMBER: (314) 576-3100
FAX: (314) 576-3462
WEB: www.kellwood.com

NO. OF EMPLOYEES: 25,000 (approx.)

SHAREHOLDERS: N/A

ANNUAL MEETING: In May

INCORPORATED: DE, Aug., 1961

INSTITUTIONAL HOLDINGS:
No. of Institutions: 113
Shares Held: 18,664,727
% Held: 82.2

INDUSTRY: Men's and boys' clothing, nec (SIC: 2329)

TRANSFER AGENT(S): American Stock Transfer & Trust Company, New York, NY

NYSE SYMBOL KEM
Rec. Pr. 20.52 (4/30/01)

KEMET CORPORATION

YIELD	...
P/E RATIO	5.8

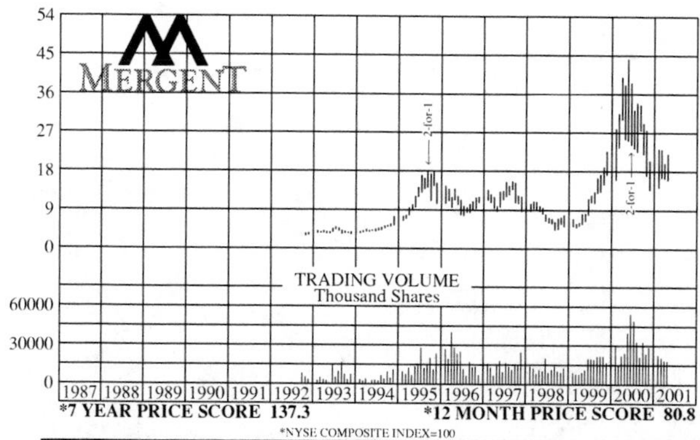

INTERIM EARNINGS (Per Share):

Qtr.	June	Sept.	Dec.	Mar.
1995-96	0.17	0.19	0.22	0.26
1996-97	0.13	0.01	0.16	0.19
1997-98	0.18	0.18	0.10	0.17
1998-99	0.02	0.01	0.02	0.03
1999-00	0.06	0.11	0.22	0.44
2000-01	0.90	1.08	1.10	...

INTERIM DIVIDENDS (Per Share):

Amt.	Decl.	Ex.	Rec.	Pay.
2-for-1	5/15/00	6/02/00	5/24/00	6/01/00

CAPITALIZATION (3/31/00):

	($000)	(%)
Long-Term Debt	100,000	14.6
Deferred Income Tax	35,902	5.3
Common & Surplus	547,456	80.1
Total	683,358	100.0

RECENT DEVELOPMENTS: For the three months ended 12/31/00, net earnings surged to $97.4 million compared with $18.2 million in the equivalent quarter of 1999. Net sales advanced 74.3% to $374.9 million from $215.1 million in the prior-year period. Export sales increased 79.3% to $199.2 million from $111.1 million the year before. Operating income jumped to $155.9 million from $32.5 million the year before. Sequential revenue growth during the quarter slowed to 3.0%.

PROSPECTS: In the near term, the Company expects unit shipments to be down about 10.0% to 15.0% due to inventory correction in the supply chain. Revenues are anticipated to be flat due to a shift in product mix to larger ceramic and tantalum capacitors and as partial material cost pass-throughs are implemented. Demand for tantalum and ceramic capacitors are expected to strengthen by mid-2001. As a result, revenue growth for fiscal 2002 is expected to grow 10.0% year over year.

BUSINESS

KEMET CORPORATION manufactures and sells solid tantalum, multilayered ceramic and organic polymer capacitors in the global market under the KEMET brand name. The Company's capacitors are used in a variety of electronic applications, including communication systems, data processing equipment, personal computers, cellular phones, automotive electronic systems and military and aerospace systems. The Company has 13 manufacturing plants in South Carolina, North Carolina and Mexico. In addition, the Company has several wholly-owned foreign subsidiaries that market KEMET's products in foreign markets. Geographic revenues for fiscal 2000 were derived: U.S., 49.7%; Asia Pacific, 23.1%; Germany, 6.0%; and other countries, 21.2%.

ANNUAL FINANCIAL DATA

	3/31/00	3/31/99	3/31/98	3/31/97	3/31/96	3/31/95	3/31/94
Earnings Per Share	**0.85**	**0.08**	**[1] 0.63**	**[2] 0.48**	**0.84**	**[3] 0.40**	**[3] 0.23**
Cash Flow Per Share	**1.53**	**0.67**	**1.12**	**0.90**	**1.32**	**0.74**	**0.56**
Tang. Book Val. Per Share	**5.76**	**3.50**	**3.31**	**2.62**	**1.92**	**0.96**	**0.66**
INCOME STATEMENT (IN THOUSANDS):							
Total Revenues	822,095	565,569	667,721	555,319	634,171	473,182	385,064
Costs & Expenses	642,081	496,092	546,576	459,184	475,855	383,732	323,755
Depreciation & Amort.	55,699	46,873	38,943	33,720	37,886	26,320	24,553
Operating Income	124,315	22,604	82,202	62,415	120,430	63,130	36,756
Net Interest Inc./(Exp.)	d7,056	d9,287	d7,305	d5,709	d4,938	d6,929	d8,937
Income Before Income Taxes	105,564	9,044	70,834	54,375	104,970	50,340	26,351
Income Taxes	35,445	2,894	21,644	17,206	39,772	19,372	9,605
Net Income	70,119	6,150	[1] 49,190	[2] 37,169	65,198	[3] 30,968	[3] 16,746
Cash Flow	125,818	53,023	88,133	70,889	103,084	57,288	41,299
Average Shs. Outstg.	82,411	78,854	78,854	78,554	78,278	77,276	73,936
BALANCE SHEET (IN THOUSANDS):							
Cash & Cash Equivalents	75,735	3,914	1,801	2,188	3,408	4,181	2,619
Total Current Assets	449,295	203,222	195,020	169,700	155,248	127,984	114,561
Net Property	423,399	406,735	393,551	319,509	267,541	191,203	176,328
Total Assets	927,256	663,690	642,109	543,244	489,828	387,459	362,083
Total Current Liabilities	189,141	112,851	146,248	106,632	122,240	97,669	71,230
Long-Term Obligations	100,000	144,000	104,000	102,900	78,072	76,542	107,400
Net Stockholders' Equity	547,456	313,674	306,260	252,123	211,940	138,776	108,467
Net Working Capital	260,154	90,371	48,772	63,068	33,008	30,315	43,331
Year-end Shs. Outstg.	87,025	76,316	78,322	77,628	77,222	76,112	61,572
STATISTICAL RECORD:							
Operating Profit Margin %	15.1	4.0	12.3	11.2	19.0	13.3	9.5
Net Profit Margin %	8.5	1.1	7.4	6.7	10.3	6.5	4.3
Return on Equity %	12.8	2.0	16.1	14.7	30.8	22.3	15.4
Return on Assets %	7.6	0.9	7.7	6.8	13.3	8.0	4.6
Debt/Total Assets %	10.8	21.7	16.2	18.9	15.9	19.8	29.7
Price Range	22.69-4.94	11.03-4.38	15.69-8.63	14.63-7.63	18.06-6.44	7.44-3.50	5.00-3.25
P/E Ratio	26.7-5.8	137.7-54.6	25.1-13.8	30.8-16.0	21.6-7.7	18.6-8.7	22.2-14.4

Statistics are as originally reported. Adj. for 2-for-1 stk. split, 9/95 & 6/00. [1] Incl. $10.5 mill. non-recurr. chg. [2] Incls. early retire. costs of $15.4 mill. [3] Bef. extraord. chg., $1.1 mill., 1995; $4.3 mill., 1994.

OFFICERS:
D. E. Maguire, Chmn., C.E.O.
C. M. Culbertson II, Pres., C.O.O.
D. R. Cash, Sr. V.P., C.F.O., Asst. Sec.
M. W. Boone, Treas.

INVESTOR CONTACT: Glenn H. Spears, Exec. V.P. and Sec., (864) 963-6674

PRINCIPAL OFFICE: 2835 Kemet Way, Simpsonville, SC 29681

TELEPHONE NUMBER: (864) 963-6300
FAX: (864) 963-6322
WEB: www.kemet.com

NO. OF EMPLOYEES: 14,200 (approx.)

SHAREHOLDERS: 895 (approx.)

ANNUAL MEETING: In July

INCORPORATED: DE, July, 1990

INSTITUTIONAL HOLDINGS:
No. of Institutions: 206
Shares Held: 60,754,869
% Held: 69.4

INDUSTRY: Electronic capacitors (SIC: 3675)

TRANSFER AGENT(S): Boston EquiServe, Boston, MA

NYSE SYMBOL KMT
Rec. Pr. 32.77 (4/30/01)

KENNAMETAL INC.

YIELD 2.1%
P/E RATIO 17.8

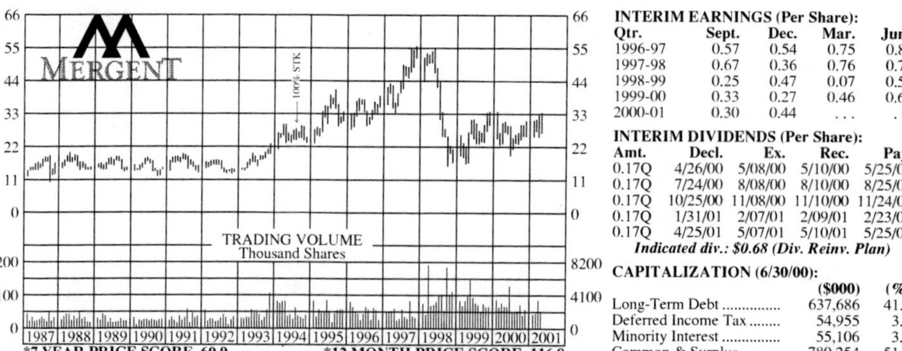

*7 YEAR PRICE SCORE 60.9 *12 MONTH PRICE SCORE 116.8

*NYSE COMPOSITE INDEX=100

INTERIM EARNINGS (Per Share):

Qtr.	Sept.	Dec.	Mar.	June
1996-97	0.57	0.54	0.75	0.85
1997-98	0.67	0.36	0.76	0.78
1998-99	0.25	0.47	0.07	0.52
1999-00	0.33	0.27	0.46	0.64
2000-01	0.30	0.44	...	...

INTERIM DIVIDENDS (Per Share):

Amt.	Decl.	Ex.	Rec.	Pay.
0.17Q	4/26/00	5/08/00	5/10/00	5/25/00
0.17Q	7/24/00	8/08/00	8/10/00	8/25/00
0.17Q	10/25/00	11/08/00	11/10/00	11/24/00
0.17Q	1/31/01	2/07/01	2/09/01	2/23/01
0.17Q	4/25/01	5/07/01	5/10/01	5/25/01

Indicated div.: $0.68 (Div. Reinv. Plan)

CAPITALIZATION (6/30/00):

	($000)	(%)
Long-Term Debt	637,686	41.7
Deferred Income Tax	54,955	3.6
Minority Interest	55,106	3.6
Common & Surplus	780,254	51.1
Total	1,528,001	100.0

RECENT DEVELOPMENTS: For the quarter ended 12/31/00, net income increased 58.9% to $13.5 million compared with income of $8.5 million, before an extraordinary loss, in the equivalent 1999 quarter. Results included charges of $812,000 in 2000 and $4.0 million in 1999 for restructuring and asset impairment charges. Net sales were $440.5 million, down 3.0% from $453.9 million a year earlier.

PROSPECTS: For the full year, sales are expected to be in line with last year's level based on softer North American markets, while earnings are anticipated to increase significantly. Meanwhile, KMT recently reacquired its subsidiary, JLK Direct Distribution Inc. Business improvement plans for JLK are expected to result in charges of $15.0 million to $20.0 million, with annual savings anticipated to be between $6.0 million and $8.0 million.

BUSINESS

KENNAMETAL INC. manufactures, purchases, and distributes a broad range of tools, tooling systems, supplies and services for the metalworking, mining and highway construction industries. KMT specializes in developing and manufacturing metalcutting tools and wear-resistant parts using a specialized type of powder metallurgy. The Company's metalcutting tools are made of cemented carbides, ceramics, cermets, high-speed steel and other hard materials. KMT manufactures a complete line of toolholders, toolholding systems and rotary cutting tools by machining and fabricating steel bars and other metal alloys. KMT also distributes a broad range of industrial supplies used in the metalworking industry. Through its 99.4%-owned subsidiary, JLK Direct Distribution Inc., the Company sells a broad range of metalworking consumables and related products. JLK markets through its direct marketing catalog, showroom programs, and integrated supply programs and distributor-based direct field sales.

ANNUAL FINANCIAL DATA

	6/30/00	6/30/99	6/30/98	6/30/97	6/30/96	6/30/95	[2] 6/30/94
Earnings Per Share	**[3][4] 1.70**	**[3] 1.31**	**2.58**	**2.71**	**2.62**	**2.58**	**[1] 0.45**
Cash Flow Per Share	**5.06**	**4.51**	**5.02**	**4.27**	**4.13**	**4.06**	**2.23**
Tang. Book Val. Per Share	**3.90**	**1.98**	**0.97**	**15.69**	**15.17**	**13.53**	**11.03**
Dividends Per Share	**0.68**	**0.68**	**0.68**	**0.68**	**0.62**	**0.60**	**0.59**
Dividend Payout %	**40.0**	**51.9**	**26.4**	**25.1**	**23.7**	**23.3**	**1.3**
INCOME STATEMENT (IN MILLIONS):							
Total Revenues	1,853.7	1,902.9	1,678.4	1,156.3	1,080.0	983.9	802.5
Costs & Expenses	1,593.0	1,659.4	1,415.5	987.9	917.9	817.6	721.3
Depreciation & Amort.	101.6	96.0	67.3	41.4	40.2	39.3	43.2
Operating Income	159.0	147.5	195.6	127.0	121.9	127.0	37.9
Net Interest Inc./(Exp.)	d55.1	d68.6	d59.5	d10.4	d11.3	d12.8	d13.8
Income Before Income Taxes	100.4	78.4	130.6	116.9	113.6	113.3	26.4
Income Taxes	43.7	32.9	53.9	44.9	43.9	45.0	15.5
Equity Earnings/Minority Int.	d4.7	d6.4	d5.5	...	...	...	...
Net Income	[3][4] 52.0	[3] 39.1	71.2	72.0	69.7	68.3	[1] 10.9
Cash Flow	153.6	135.1	138.5	113.4	110.0	107.6	54.1
Average Shs. Outstg. (000)	30,364	29,960	27,567	26,575	26,635	26,486	24,304
BALANCE SHEET (IN MILLIONS):							
Cash & Cash Equivalents	49.9	30.8	18.4	21.9	17.1	10.8	17.2
Total Current Assets	758.6	750.4	818.8	457.9	436.5	409.3	332.8
Net Property	498.8	539.8	525.9	300.4	267.1	260.3	243.1
Total Assets	1,982.9	2,043.6	2,139.0	869.3	799.5	781.6	697.5
Total Current Liabilities	361.2	376.9	377.1	282.0	218.8	225.2	202.0
Long-Term Obligations	637.7	717.9	840.9	40.4	56.1	78.7	90.2
Net Stockholders' Equity	780.3	745.1	735.5	459.6	438.9	391.9	322.8
Net Working Capital	397.4	373.6	441.8	175.9	217.7	184.1	130.8
Year-end Shs. Outstg. (000)	30,523	30,067	29,829	26,107	26,703	26,577	26,354
STATISTICAL RECORD:							
Operating Profit Margin %	8.6	7.8	11.7	11.0	11.3	12.9	4.7
Net Profit Margin %	2.8	2.1	4.2	6.2	6.5	6.9	1.4
Return on Equity %	6.7	5.2	9.7	15.7	15.9	17.4	3.4
Return on Assets %	2.6	1.9	3.3	8.3	8.7	8.7	1.6
Debt/Total Assets %	32.2	35.1	39.3	4.7	7.0	10.1	12.9
Price Range	33.81-19.13	33.88-16.38	54.75-15.63	55.69-33.13	39.00-27.75	41.13-23.00	29.56-21.06
P/E Ratio	19.9-11.4	25.9-12.5	21.2-6.1	20.5-12.2	14.9-10.6	15.9-8.9	65.7-46.8
Average Yield %	2.6	2.7	1.9	1.5	1.9	1.9	2.3

Statistics are as originally reported. Adj. for stk. split: 2-for-1, 8/94. [1] Incl. a restruct. chrg. of $24.7 mill. and bef. net acctg. chrg. of d$15.0 mill. [2] Incl. results of Hertel AG, acq. in Aug. 1993. [3] Incl. nonrecur. chrgs. of $13.9 mill., 1999; $18.5 mill., 2000. [4] Bef. extraord. loss of $267,000. [5] Bef. acctg. chrg. of $599,000, incl. nonrecurr. chrg. of $2.3 mill.

OFFICERS:
W. R. Newlin, Chmn.
M. I. Tambakeras, Pres., C.E.O.
F. N. Grasberger, III, V.P., C.F.O.
J. E. Morrison, Treas., V.P.

INVESTOR CONTACT: Charles T. Glazer, Mgr./Investor Relations, (724) 539-5638

PRINCIPAL OFFICE: 1600 Technology Way, P.O. Box 231, Latrobe, PA 15650-0231

TELEPHONE NUMBER: (724) 539-5000
FAX: (724) 539-4710
WEB: www.kennametal.com

NO. OF EMPLOYEES: 13,200 (approx.)

SHAREHOLDERS: 2,920

ANNUAL MEETING: In Oct.

INCORPORATED: PA, June, 1943

INSTITUTIONAL HOLDINGS:
No. of Institutions: 125
Shares Held: 23,711,945
% Held: 77.9

INDUSTRY: Machine tools, metal cutting types (SIC: 3541)

TRANSFER AGENT(S): Mellon Investor Services, L.L.C., Ridgefield Park, NJ

NYSE SYMBOL KMG
Rec. Pr. 71.65 (4/30/01)

KERR-MCGEE CORPORATION

YIELD 2.5%
P/E RATIO 8.6

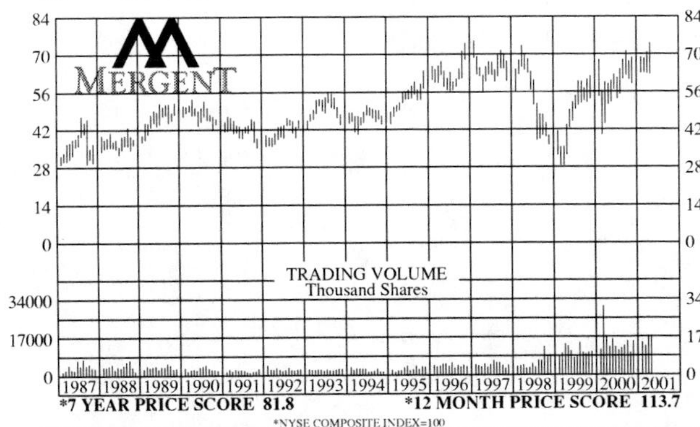

INTERIM EARNINGS (Per Share):

Qtr.	Mar.	June	Sept.	Dec.
1995	0.73	0.68	d2.56	0.70
1996	0.94	1.01	1.27	1.21
1997	1.40	0.66	0.77	0.95
1998	0.50	0.55	d0.48	d5.18
1999	d1.23	0.52	1.13	1.27
2000	1.94	1.11	2.57	2.73

INTERIM DIVIDENDS (Per Share):

Amt.	Decl.	Ex.	Rec.	Pay.
0.45Q	5/09/00	5/31/00	6/02/00	7/03/00
0.45Q	7/11/00	8/30/00	9/01/00	10/02/00
0.45Q	11/21/00	11/29/00	12/01/00	1/02/01
0.45Q	1/09/01	2/28/01	3/02/01	4/02/01
0.45Q	5/08/01	5/30/01	6/01/01	7/02/01

Indicated div.: $1.80 (Div. Reinv. Plan)

CAPITALIZATION (12/31/00):

	($000)	(%)
Long-Term Debt	2,244,000	40.2
Deferred Income Tax	704,000	12.6
Common & Surplus	2,633,000	47.2
Total	5,581,000	100.0

RECENT DEVELOPMENTS: For the year ended 12/31/00, net income soared to $842.0 million versus income of $146.2 million, before a change in accounting principle, in 1999. Results for 2000 included net non-recurring after-tax charges totaling $95.0 million related to expenses associated with the purchase of two pigment facilities. Results for 1999 included merger costs of $163.4 million. Sales jumped 50.3% to $4.12 billion. Exploration and production sales rose 60.3% to $2.86 billion, while total chemicals sales increased 31.5% to $1.26 billion.

PROSPECTS: On 5/14/01, KMG announced that it has signed a definitive agreement to acquire all of the outstanding shares of HS Resources in a transaction valued at $1.70 billion, including the assumption of approximately $450.0 million of debt. The agreement provides that KMG will pay $66.00 for each share of HS Resources' common stock, consisting of 70.0% cash and 30.0% KMG common stock. The Company expects the transaction, which is anticipated to be completed by 9/30/01, will be immediately accretive to both earnings and cash flow per share.

BUSINESS

KERR-MCGEE CORPORATION is an energy and chemical company with worldwide operations. KMG explores for, develops, produces and markets crude oil and natural gas, and its chemical operations primarily produce and market titanium dioxide pigment. The Exploration and Production division produces and explores for oil and gas in the U.S., the United Kingdom sector of the North Sea, Indonesia, China, Kazakhstan and Ecuador. Exploration efforts also extend to Australia, Benin, Brazil, Gabon, Morocco, Canada, Thailand, Yemen and the Danish sector of the North Sea. As of 12/31/00, proven developed crude-oil reserves and natural gas totaled 700.0 million barrels and 2,327.00 billion cubic feet, respectively. In 2000, revenues were derived: Exploration and Production, 69.4%; and chemicals, 30.6%. On 2/26/99, KMG acquired Oryx Energy Company.

QUARTERLY DATA

(12/31/2000)($000)	Rev	Inc
1st Quarter	886,000	328,000
2nd Quarter	1,001,000	334,000
3rd Quarter	1,106,000	459,000
4th Quarter	1,118,000	493,000

ANNUAL FINANCIAL DATA

	12/31/00	⑤ 12/31/99	12/31/98	12/31/97	12/31/96	12/31/95	12/31/94
Earnings Per Share	⑥ 8.37	④ 1.69	① d4.78	4.04	② 4.43	③ d0.47	1.74
Cash Flow Per Share	15.14	9.18	1.51	9.69	10.54	6.10	8.37
Tang. Book Val. Per Share	27.87	17.25	28.36	30.00	27.90	27.76	30.25
Dividends Per Share	1.80	1.80	1.80	1.76	1.64	1.52	1.52
Dividend Payout %	21.5	106.5	...	43.6	37.0	...	87.4
INCOME STATEMENT (IN MILLIONS):							
Total Revenues	4,121.0	2,696.0	1,396.0	1,711.0	1,931.0	1,801.0	3,353.0
Costs & Expenses	2,148.0	1,831.0	1,495.0	1,253.0	1,301.0	1,550.0	2,899.0
Depreciation & Amort.	732.0	648.0	298.0	271.0	307.0	341.0	345.0
Operating Income	1,241.0	217.0	d397.0	187.0	191.0	d90.0	109.0
Income Before Income Taxes	1,299.0	257.0	d375.0	277.0	323.0	d67.0	132.0
Income Taxes	457.0	111.0	cr148.0	83.0	103.0	cr43.0	42.0
Net Income	⑥ 842.0	④ 146.0	① d227.0	194.0	② 220.0	③ d24.0	90.0
Cash Flow	1,574.0	794.0	71.0	465.0	527.0	317.0	435.0
Average Shs. Outstg. (000)	103,987	86,497	47,000	48,000	50,000	52,000	52,000
BALANCE SHEET (IN MILLIONS):							
Cash & Cash Equivalents	144.0	267.0	114.0	183.0	121.0	87.0	82.0
Total Current Assets	1,315.0	1,161.0	751.0	689.0	805.0	766.0	963.0
Net Property	5,383.0	4,085.0	2,288.0	1,998.0	1,948.0	2,267.0	2,552.0
Total Assets	7,666.0	5,899.0	3,341.0	3,096.0	3,124.0	3,232.0	3,698.0
Total Current Liabilities	1,349.0	840.0	536.0	523.0	485.0	580.0	890.0
Long-Term Obligations	2,244.0	2,496.0	901.0	552.0	626.0	632.0	673.0
Net Stockholders' Equity	2,633.0	1,492.0	1,333.0	1,440.0	1,367.0	1,416.0	1,543.0
Net Working Capital	d34.0	321.0	215.0	166.0	320.0	186.0	73.0
Year-end Shs. Outstg. (000)	94,484	86,483	47,000	48,000	49,000	51,000	51,000
STATISTICAL RECORD:							
Operating Profit Margin %	30.1	8.0	...	10.9	9.9	...	3.3
Net Profit Margin %	20.4	5.4	...	11.3	11.4	...	2.7
Return on Equity %	32.0	9.8	...	13.5	16.1	...	5.8
Return on Assets %	11.0	2.5	...	6.3	7.0	...	2.4
Debt/Total Assets %	29.3	42.3	27.0	17.8	20.0	19.6	18.2
Price Range	71.19-39.88	62.00-28.50	73.19-36.19	75.00-55.50	74.13-55.75	64.00-44.00	51.00-40.00
P/E Ratio	8.5-4.8	36.7-16.9	...	18.6-13.7	16.7-12.6	...	29.3-23.0
Average Yield %	3.2	4.0	3.3	2.7	2.5	2.8	3.3

Statistics are as originally reported. ① Incl. pre-tax chrg. of $446.0 mil.; bef. loss fr. disc. ops. of $277.4 mil. ② Incl. non-recur. chrgs. of $9.7 mil. ③ Incl. non-recur. chrg. of $227.0 mil.; bef. disc. ops. loss of $7.1 mil. ④ Incl. non-recur. chgs. of $150.0 mil.; bef. acctg. chrg. of $4.1 mil. ⑤ Incl. rev. of Oryx Energy Co. ⑥ Incl. non-recur. aft.-tax chrgs. of $95.0 mil.

OFFICERS:
L. R. Corbett, Chmn., C.E.O.
R. M. Wohleber, Sr. V.P., C.F.O.
G. F. Pilcher, V.P., Sec., Gen. Couns.

INVESTOR CONTACT: R. C. Buterbaugh, V.P., Inv. Rel. & Comm., (866) 378-9899

PRINCIPAL OFFICE: Kerr-McGee Center, Oklahoma City, OK 73102

TELEPHONE NUMBER: (405) 270-1313
FAX: (405) 270-3123
WEB: www.kerr-mcgee.com
NO. OF EMPLOYEES: 4,426 (avg.)
SHAREHOLDERS: 30,000 (approx.)
ANNUAL MEETING: In May
INCORPORATED: DE, Nov., 1932

INSTITUTIONAL HOLDINGS:
No. of Institutions: 333
Shares Held: 80,017,570
% Held: 84.4

INDUSTRY: Crude petroleum and natural gas (SIC: 1311)

TRANSFER AGENT(S): UMB Bank, NA, Kansas City, MO

NYSE SYMBOL KEY
Rec. Pr. 23.18 (4/30/01)

KEYCORP

YIELD 5.0%
P/E RATIO 10.1

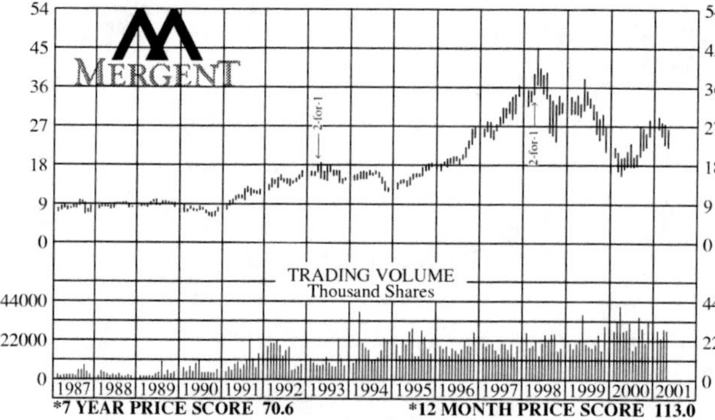

*7 YEAR PRICE SCORE 70.6 *12 MONTH PRICE SCORE 113.0

*NYSE COMPOSITE INDEX=100

INTERIM EARNINGS (Per Share):

Qtr.	Mar.	June	Sept.	Dec.
1997	0.48	0.51	0.54	0.56
1998	0.53	0.56	0.57	0.57
1999	0.65	0.62	0.60	0.59
2000	0.83	0.57	0.28	0.62

INTERIM DIVIDENDS (Per Share):

Amt.	Decl.	Ex.	Rec.	Pay.
0.28Q	5/19/00	5/25/00	5/30/00	6/15/00
0.28Q	7/20/00	8/25/00	8/29/00	9/15/00
0.28Q	11/16/00	11/24/00	11/28/00	12/15/00
0.295Q	1/18/01	2/23/01	2/27/01	3/15/01
0.295Q	5/17/01	5/24/01	5/29/01	6/15/01

Indicated div.: $1.18 (Div. Reinv. Plan)

CAPITALIZATION (12/31/00):

	($000)	(%)
Total Deposits	48,649,000	70.1
Long-Term Debt	14,161,000	20.4
Common & Surplus	6,623,000	9.5
Total	69,433,000	100.0

RECENT DEVELOPMENTS: For the year ended 12/31/00, net income fell 9.5% to $1.00 billion from $1.11 billion in 1999. Earnings for 2000 and 1999 included pre-tax restructuring charges of $102.0 million and $98.0 million, respectively, and pre-tax gains from divestitures of $332.0 million and $355.0 million, respectively. Net interest income fell 2.0% to $2.73 billion. Total non-interest income, including the above gains, slipped 5.2% to $2.19 billion.

PROSPECTS: On 2/27/01, KEY's subsidiary, KeyBank, N.A., signed a strategic marketing agreement with TD Waterhouse, the New York-based global on-line financial services firm. The agreement allows customers of TD Waterhouse to apply on-line or by phone for KeyBank's Home Equity lines of credit. The partnership will benefit KeyBank with new assets and national expansion for its home equity products.

BUSINESS

KEYCORP (formerly Society Corporation) is a multi-line financial services company, with assets of $87.27 billion as of 12/31/00. KEY provides investment management, retail and commercial banking, consumer finance, and investment banking products and services to individuals and companies throughout the U.S. and, for certain businesses, internationally. The Company operates in 46 states with a network of 2,443 ATMs, a Web site named Key.com, and telephone banking centers. In October 1998, KEY acquired McDonald & Co. Investments, Inc. On 1/31/00, KEY sold its credit card business.

LOAN DISTRIBUTION

(12/31/2000)	($000)	(%)
Commercial Loans	39,294,000	58.7
Consumer Loans	25,382,000	38.0
Loans Held for Sale	2,229,000	3.3
Total	66,905,000	100.0

ANNUAL FINANCIAL DATA

	12/31/00	12/31/99	12/31/98	12/31/97	12/31/96	12/31/95	12/31/94
Earnings Per Share	**[4] 2.30**	**[3] 2.45**	**[2] 2.23**	**[2] 2.07**	**[1] 1.69**	**1.65**	**1.73**
Tang. Book Val. Per Share	**12.42**	**11.14**	**10.30**	**9.14**	**7.97**	**8.77**	**8.20**
Dividends Per Share	**1.12**	**1.04**	**0.94**	**0.84**	**0.76**	**0.72**	**0.64**
Dividend Payout %	**48.7**	**42.4**	**42.2**	**40.6**	**45.1**	**43.6**	**37.1**
INCOME STATEMENT (IN MILLIONS):							
Total Interest Income	6,277.0	5,695.0	5,525.0	5,262.0	4,951.0	5,121.0	4,490.1
Total Interest Expense	3,547.0	2,908.0	2,841.0	2,468.0	2,234.0	2,484.3	1,796.8
Net Interest Income	2,730.0	2,787.0	2,684.0	2,794.0	2,717.0	2,636.7	2,693.2
Provision for Loan Losses	490.0	348.0	297.0	320.0	197.0	100.5	125.2
Non-Interest Income	2,194.0	2,294.0	1,575.0	1,306.0	1,087.0	933.0	882.6
Non-Interest Expense	2,917.0	3,049.0	2,483.0	2,435.0	2,464.0	2,311.6	2,167.2
Income Before Taxes	1,517.0	1,684.0	1,479.0	1,345.0	1,143.0	1,157.7	1,283.5
Net Income	[4] 1,002.0	[3] 1,107.0	[2] 996.0	[2] 919.0	[1] 783.0	789.2	853.5
Average Shs. Outstg. (000)	435,573	452,363	447,437	444,544	459,810	469,574	486,134
BALANCE SHEET (IN MILLIONS):							
Cash & Due from Banks	3,189.0	2,816.0	3,296.0	3,651.0	3,444.0	3,443.8	3,511.4
Securities Avail. for Sale	9,213.0	8,525.0	7,252.0	9,636.0	8,424.0	8,742.3	3,191.1
Total Loans & Leases	66,905.0	64,222.0	62,012.0	53,380.0	49,235.0	47,691.7	46,224.6
Allowance for Credit Losses	1,001.0	930.0	900.0	900.0	870.0	876.0	830.3
Net Loans & Leases	65,904.0	63,292.0	61,112.0	52,480.0	48,365.0	46,815.7	45,394.3
Total Assets	87,270.0	83,395.0	80,020.0	73,699.0	67,621.0	66,339.1	66,798.1
Total Deposits	48,649.0	43,233.0	42,583.0	45,073.0	45,317.0	47,281.9	48,564.2
Long-Term Obligations	14,161.0	15,881.0	12,967.0	7,446.0	4,213.0	4,003.6	3,569.8
Total Liabilities	80,647.0	77,006.0	73,853.0	68,518.0	62,740.0	61,186.5	62,099.7
Net Stockholders' Equity	6,623.0	6,389.0	6,167.0	5,181.0	4,881.0	5,152.5	4,698.5
Year-end Shs. Outstg. (000)	423,254	443,427	452,452	438,064	491,888	447,406	480,724
STATISTICAL RECORD:							
Return on Equity %	15.1	17.3	16.2	17.7	16.0	15.3	18.2
Return on Assets %	1.1	1.3	1.2	1.2	1.2	1.2	1.3
Equity/Assets %	7.6	7.7	7.7	7.0	7.2	7.8	7.0
Non-Int. Exp./Tot. Inc. %	59.2	60.0	58.3	59.4	64.8	64.8	60.6
Price Range	28.50-15.56	38.13-21.00	44.88-23.38	36.59-23.94	27.13-16.69	18.63-12.38	16.88-11.81
P/E Ratio	12.4-6.8	15.6-8.6	20.1-10.5	17.7-11.6	16.1-9.9	11.3-7.5	9.8-6.8
Average Yield %	5.1	3.5	2.8	2.8	3.5	4.6	4.5

Statistics are as originally reported. Adj. for 2-for-1 splits 3/98. [1] Incl. pre-tax SAIF chg. and restruct. chgs. totaling $17.0 mill. [2] Incl. pre-tax gain fr. sale of branch: $89.0 mill., 1998; $151.0 mill., 1997. [3] Incl. various pre-tax net gains of $355.0 mill. & restruct. chrgs. of $98.0 mill. [4] Incl. pre-tax gains from divestitures of $332.0 mill. & pre-tax restruct. chrgs. of $102.0 mill.

OFFICERS:
R. W. Gillespie, Chmn.
H. L. Meyer III, Pres, C.E.O.
K. B. Somers, Sr. Exec. V.P., C.F.O.

INVESTOR CONTACT: Bernon L. Patterson, Investor Relations, (216) 689-4520

PRINCIPAL OFFICE: 127 Public Square, Cleveland, OH 44114-1306

TELEPHONE NUMBER: (216) 689-6300
FAX: (216) 689-3595
WEB: www.key.com

NO. OF EMPLOYEES: 22,142

SHAREHOLDERS: 48,624

ANNUAL MEETING: In May

INCORPORATED: OH, Dec., 1958

INSTITUTIONAL HOLDINGS:
No. of Institutions: 388
Shares Held: 241,493,369
% Held: 56.9

INDUSTRY: National commercial banks (SIC: 6021)

TRANSFER AGENT(S): Computershare Investor Services, Chicago, IL

NYSE SYMBOL KSE
Rec. Pr. 39.70 (4/30/01)

KEYSPAN CORPORATION

YIELD 4.5%
P/E RATIO 18.9

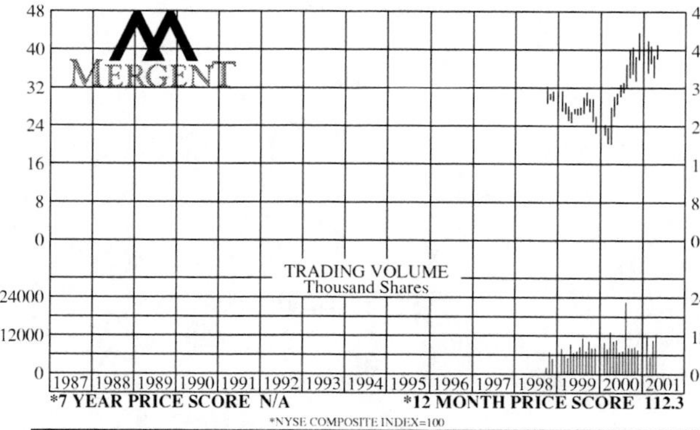

INTERIM EARNINGS (Per Share):

Qtr.	June	Sept.	Dec.	Mar.
1997-98		2.56		

Qtr.	Mar.	June	Sept.	Dec.
1998		d1.34		
1999	0.94	0.10	Nil	0.56
2000	1.22	0.35	0.10	0.44

INTERIM DIVIDENDS (Per Share):

Amt.	Decl.	Ex.	Rec.	Pay.
0.445Q	2/28/00	4/11/00	4/13/00	5/01/00
0.445Q	6/29/00	7/07/00	7/11/00	8/01/00
0.445Q	9/26/00	10/05/00	10/10/00	11/01/00
0.445Q	12/21/00	1/09/01	1/11/01	2/01/01
0.445Q	2/28/00	4/12/01	4/17/01	5/01/01

Indicated div.: $1.78 (Div. Reinv. Plan)

CAPITALIZATION (12/31/00):

	($000)	(%)
Long-Term Debt	4,274,938	29.6
Deferred Income Tax	451,721	3.1
Minority Interest	125,198	0.9
Preferred Stock	84,205	0.6
Common & Surplus	9,510,136	65.8
Total	14,446,198	100.0

RECENT DEVELOPMENTS: For the year ended 12/31/00, net income rose 16.3% to $300.8 million versus $258.6 million the year before. Results for 2000 included an after-tax nonrecurring charge of $41.1 million. Total revenues jumped 73.3% to $5.12 billion. Gas distribution revenues rose 45.8% to $2.56 billion, while revenues from electric services grew 67.7% to $1.44 billion. Revenues from gas exploration and production increased 82.1% to $274.2 million. Energy related services surged to $771.9 million.

PROSPECTS: KSE should benefit from the completion of the Islander East Pipeline. The pipeline will transport natural gas from Connecticut to Long Island and connect with KeySpan Energy Delivery Long Island. The pipeline is expected to begin operation in 2003. Islander East should strengthen KSE's position as a major energy supplier in the NorthEast by increasing and diversifying KSE's access to gas supplies, fostering competitive pricing of gas and reducing the cost of electric power production.

BUSINESS

KEYSPAN CORPORATION (formerly KeySpan Energy Corporation) is a holding company for KeySpan Energy Delivery, a natural gas distribution company with diversified businesses in gas exploration and production, propane distribution and gas-cogeneration projects. KeySpan Energy Delivery distributes natural gas to 2.4 million customers in New York City's boroughs of Brooklyn, Staten Island, Queens and on Long Island in Nassau and Suffolk counties and in Massachusetts and New Hampshire. KSE also provides electric power generation on Long Island and New York City, and provides management of the electric and distribution system and customer services to the 1.1 million customers of Long Island Power Authority (LIPA). Energy Investments owns the Company's unregulated subsidiaries and its investments in gas exploration, production and transportation businesses.

ANNUAL FINANCIAL DATA

	12/31/00	[5] 12/31/99	[3] 12/31/98	3/31/98	[1] 3/31/97	[4] 12/31/96
Earnings Per Share	**[6] 2.10**	**1.62**	**[2] d1.34**	**2.56**	**0.62**	**2.20**
Cash Flow Per Share	**4.60**	**3.45**	**0.41**	**3.87**	**1.06**	**4.22**
Tang. Book Val. Per Sh.	**55.92**	**51.85**	**60.66**	**84.40**	...	...
Dividends Per Share	**1.78**	**1.78**	**1.49**	...	...	...
Dividend Payout %	**84.8**	**109.9**	...	...	...	...
INCOME STATEMENT (IN MILLIONS):						
Total Revenues	5,121.5	2,954.6	1,721.9	3,124.1	851.2	3,150.7
Costs & Expenses	4,054.5	2,219.0	1,453.8	2,196.3	607.3	2,170.0
Depreciation & Amort.	335.1	253.4	254.9	159.5	53.9	244.1
Operating Income	731.9	482.2	13.2	768.3	190.0	736.6
Net Interest Inc./(Exp.)	d188.4	d76.1	d138.7	d404.5	d105.9	d447.6
Income Before Income Taxes	543.4	406.1	d196.1	362.2	87.7	316.5
Income Taxes	216.3	136.4	...	...	...	...
Equity Earnings/Minority Int.	d26.3	d11.1	29.1	...	...	...
Net Income	[6] 300.8	258.6	[2] d166.9	362.2	87.7	316.5
Cash Flow	617.8	477.3	59.3	469.9	128.6	508.4
Average Shs. Outstg. (000)	134,357	138,526	145,767	121,415	120,995	120,360
BALANCE SHEET (IN MILLIONS):						
Cash & Cash Equivalents	94.5	128.6	942.8	180.9	...	...
Total Current Assets	2,403.2	1,158.0	1,912.0	858.3	...	...
Net Property	6,358.3	4,240.0	3,778.3	3,814.1	...	...
Total Assets	11,550.1	6,730.7	6,895.1	11,900.7	11,849.6	12,209.7
Total Current Liabilities	2,974.1	1,388.3	1,103.0	827.8	...	...
Long-Term Obligations	4,274.9	1,682.7	1,619.1	4,381.9	4,457.0	4,456.8
Net Stockholders' Equity	9,594.3	7,281.4	8,560.8	10,832.0	7,708.2	7,682.3
Net Working Capital	d570.8	d230.3	809.0	30.5	...	...
Year-end Shs. Outstg. (000)	137,014	133,866	130,420	121,681	...	...
STATISTICAL RECORD:						
Operating Profit Margin %	14.3	16.3	0.8	24.6	22.3	23.4
Net Profit Margin %	5.9	8.8	...	11.6	10.3	10.0
Return on Equity %	3.1	3.6	...	3.3	1.1	4.1
Return on Assets %	2.6	3.8	...	3.0	0.7	2.6
Price Range	43.63-20.19	31.31-22.50	32.25-28.69	...	...	...
P/E Ratio	20.8-9.6	19.3-13.9	...	...	...	...
Average Yield %	5.6	6.6	2.4	...	...	...

Statistics are as originally reported. [1] For 3 mos. due to fiscal year-end change. [2] Incl. a net chg. of $108.0 mill. rel. to the LIPA transaction, a net chg. of $83.0 mill. assoc./with the merger with LILCO, & a non-cash net impair. chg. for the write-down of gas reserve assets. [3] For nine months due to fiscal year end change. [4] As reported from the 12/31/98 10K. [5] Reflects full-year results of LILCO. [6] Incl. after-tax nonrecurr. chrg. of $41.1 mill.

OFFICERS:
R. B. Catell, Chmn., C.E.O.
C. Matthews, Vice-Chmn

INVESTOR CONTACT: Ellen Kissler, Inv. Rel., (718) 403-6977

PRINCIPAL OFFICE: One MetroTech Center, Brooklyn, NY 11201-3850

TELEPHONE NUMBER: (631) 755-6650
FAX: (631) 545-2293
WEB: www.keyspanenergy.com

NO. OF EMPLOYEES: 13,000 (approx.)

SHAREHOLDERS: 88,640 (approx.)

ANNUAL MEETING: In May

INCORPORATED: NY, Apr., 1998

INSTITUTIONAL HOLDINGS:
No. of Institutions: 287
Shares Held: 70,796,934
% Held: 51.7

INDUSTRY: Natural gas distribution (SIC: 4924)

TRANSFER AGENT(S): EquiServe Trust Company, NA, Jersey City, NJ

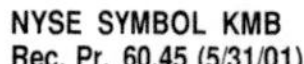

NYSE SYMBOL KMB
Rec. Pr. 60.45 (5/31/01)

KIMBERLY-CLARK CORPORATION

YIELD 1.9%
P/E RATIO 18.3

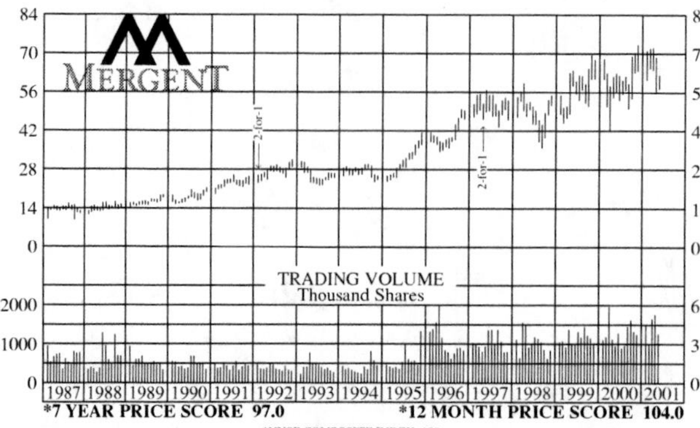

*7 YEAR PRICE SCORE 97.0 *12 MONTH PRICE SCORE 104.0
*NYSE COMPOSITE INDEX=100

INTERIM EARNINGS (Per Share):

Qtr.	Mar.	June	Sept.	Dec.
1997	0.66	0.63	0.57	d0.26
1998	0.53	0.54	0.62	0.44
1999	0.75	0.73	0.89	0.77
2000	0.86	0.79	0.81	0.85

INTERIM DIVIDENDS (Per Share):

Amt.	Decl.	Ex.	Rec.	Pay.
0.27Q	5/09/00	6/07/00	6/09/00	7/06/00
0.27Q	8/01/00	9/06/00	9/08/00	10/03/00
0.27Q	11/14/00	12/06/00	12/08/00	1/03/01
0.28Q	2/22/01	3/07/01	3/09/01	4/03/01
0.28Q	4/26/01	6/06/01	6/08/01	7/03/01

Indicated div.: $1.12 (Div. Reinv. Plan)

CAPITALIZATION (12/31/00):

	($000)	(%)
Long-Term Debt	2,000,600	22.1
Deferred Income Tax	987,500	10.9
Minority Interest	281,300	3.1
Common & Surplus	5,767,300	63.8
Total	9,036,700	100.0

RECENT DEVELOPMENTS: For the year ended 12/31/00, net income advanced 7.9% to $1.80 billion from $1.67 billion in 1999. Results for 1999 included pre-tax restructuring charges of $27.0 million. Net sales were $13.98 billion, up 7.5% from $13.01 billion in 1999. Tissue sales rose 4.8% to $7.30 billion, while sales of personal care products increased 5.8% to $5.44 billion. Sales of health care and other products advanced 37.9% to $1.29 billion.

PROSPECTS: KMB is purchasing an additional 5.0% stake in its current 50/50 Australian joint venture for approximately $39.0 million. Moreover, KMB and Amcor Limited, its joint venture partner, will exchange options for the remaining 45.0% stake for $355.0 million within the next four years. In January 2001, KMB acquired Linostar, an Italian-based diaper manufacturer that produces and markets LINES, Italy's second largest diaper brand.

BUSINESS

KIMBERLY-CLARK CORPORATION is a global manufacturer of tissue, personal care and health care products. The Company's global brands include HUGGIES, PULLUPS, KOTEX DEPEND, KLEENEX, SCOTT, KIMBERLY-CLARK, KIMWIPES, SAFES KIN, WYPALL and TECNOL. Other brands well known outside the U.S. include ANDREX, SCOTTEX, PAGE, POPEE and KIMBIES. Kimberly-Clark also is a major producer of premium business, correspondence and technical papers. The Company has manufacturing operations in 40 countries and sells its products in more than 150 countries. Net sales (and operating profit) for 2000 were derived from the following: tissue, 52.0% (49.7%); personal care, 38.8% (43.2%); and health care and other, 9.2% (7.1%).

ANNUAL FINANCIAL DATA

	12/31/00	12/31/99	12/31/98	12/31/97	12/31/96	[2] 12/31/95	12/31/94
Earnings Per Share	**3.31**	**[6] 3.09**	**[5] 2.13**	**[4] 1.58**	**[1] 2.49**	**[3] 0.06**	**[1] 1.67**
Cash Flow Per Share	**4.55**	**4.25**	**3.11**	**2.49**	**3.48**	**1.10**	**2.69**
Tang. Book Val. Per Share	**7.04**	**7.12**	**6.13**	**6.36**	**7.96**	**6.11**	**8.10**
Dividends Per Share	**1.07**	**1.03**	**0.99**	**0.95**	**0.92**	**0.90**	**0.88**
Dividend Payout %	**32.3**	**33.3**	**46.5**	**60.1**	**36.7**	**1,489.2**	**52.5**
INCOME STATEMENT (IN MILLIONS):							
Total Revenues	13,982.0	13,006.8	12,297.8	12,546.6	13,149.1	13,373.0	7,364.2
Costs & Expenses	10,674.8	9,943.4	10,079.2	10,735.7	10,534.4	12,578.3	6,215.5
Depreciation & Amort.	673.4	628.0	542.5	507.7	561.0	581.7	329.6
Operating Income	2,633.8	2,435.4	1,676.1	1,303.2	2,053.7	213.0	819.1
Net Interest Inc./(Exp.)	d197.8	d183.7	d174.4	d133.4	d158.6	d212.2	d129.4
Income Before Income Taxes	2,436.0	2,251.7	1,626.1	1,187.5	2,002.3	104.4	740.6
Income Taxes	758.5	730.2	561.9	433.1	700.8	153.5	276.4
Equity Earnings/Minority Int.	123.1	146.6	112.8	129.6	102.3	82.3	70.9
Net Income	1,800.6	[6] 1,668.1	[5] 1,177.0	[4] 884.0	[1] 1,403.8	[3] 33.2	[1] 535.1
Cash Flow	2,474.0	2,296.1	1,719.5	1,391.7	1,964.8	614.6	864.7
Average Shs. Outstg. (000)	543,800	540,100	553,100	559,300	564,000	559,000	321,800
BALANCE SHEET (IN MILLIONS):							
Cash & Cash Equivalents	206.5	322.8	144.0	90.8	83.2	221.6	23.8
Total Current Assets	3,789.9	3,561.8	3,366.9	3,489.0	3,539.2	3,813.8	1,809.9
Net Property	6,918.5	6,222.0	5,845.0	5,600.6	6,813.3	6,053.3	4,199.4
Total Assets	14,479.8	12,815.5	11,510.3	11,266.0	11,845.7	11,439.2	6,715.7
Total Current Liabilities	4,573.9	3,845.8	3,790.7	3,698.3	3,686.9	3,869.6	2,058.8
Long-Term Obligations	2,000.6	1,926.6	2,068.2	1,803.9	1,738.6	1,984.7	929.5
Net Stockholders' Equity	5,767.3	5,093.1	3,887.2	4,133.3	4,483.1	3,650.4	2,595.8
Net Working Capital	d784.0	d284.0	d423.8	d209.3	d147.7	d55.8	d248.9
Year-end Shs. Outstg. (000)	533,400	540,600	538,300	556,300	563,400	597,000	320,400
STATISTICAL RECORD:							
Operating Profit Margin %	18.8	18.7	13.6	10.4	15.6	1.6	11.1
Net Profit Margin %	12.9	12.8	9.6	7.0	10.7	0.2	7.3
Return on Equity %	31.2	32.8	30.3	21.4	31.3	0.9	20.6
Return on Assets %	12.4	13.0	10.2	7.8	11.9	0.3	8.0
Debt/Total Assets %	13.8	15.0	18.0	16.0	14.7	17.3	13.8
Price Range	73.25-42.00	69.56-44.81	59.44-35.88	56.88-43.25	49.81-34.31	41.50-23.63	30.00-23.50
P/E Ratio	22.1-12.7	22.5-14.5	27.9-16.8	36.0-27.4	20.0-13.8	690.5-393.1	18.0-14.1
Average Yield %	1.9	1.8	2.1	1.9	2.2	2.7	3.3

Statistics are as originally reported. Adj. for stk. split: 2-for-1, 4/97. [1] Incl. gain $62.5 mill., 1994; $72.6 mill., 1996. [2] Refl. acq. of Scott Paper Co. on 12/15/95. [3] Incl. $1.44 bill. chrg. for merger & incl. $40.0 mill. gain. [4] Bef. extraord. cr. $17.5 mill. & incl. restruct. chrg. $481.1 mill. [5] Bef. acctg. chrg. of $11.2 mill. [6] Incl. restruct. cr. $27.0 mill.

OFFICERS:
W. R. Sanders, Chmn., C.E.O.
T. J. Falk, Pres., C.O.O.
J. W. Donehower, Sr. V.P., C.F.O.
D. M. Crook, V.P., Sec.

INVESTOR CONTACT: Michael D. Masseth, V.P.-Investor Relations, (800) 639-1352

PRINCIPAL OFFICE: P.O. Box 619100, Dallas, TX 75261-9100

TELEPHONE NUMBER: (972) 281-1200
FAX: (972) 281-1435
WEB: www.kimberly-clark.com

NO. OF EMPLOYEES: 66,300 (avg.)

SHAREHOLDERS: 48,090

ANNUAL MEETING: In Apr.

INCORPORATED: DE, June, 1928

INSTITUTIONAL HOLDINGS:
No. of Institutions: 759
Shares Held: 376,639,435
% Held: 70.8

INDUSTRY: Paper mills (SIC: 2621)

TRANSFER AGENT(S): Bank Boston NA, Boston, MA

NYSE SYMBOL KIM
Rec. Pr. 44.00 (4/30/01)

KIMCO REALTY CORP.

YIELD 6.5%
P/E RATIO 15.4

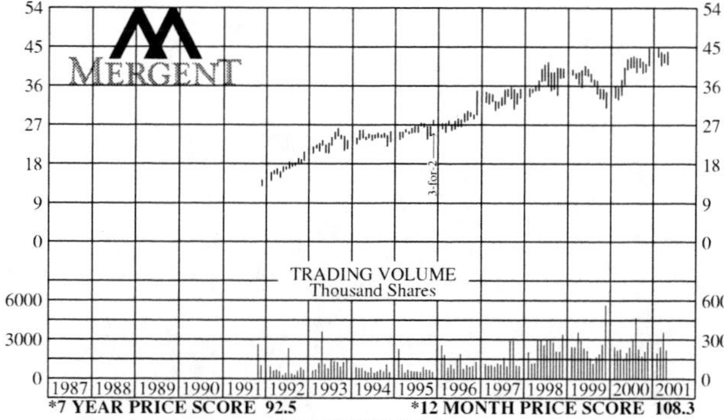

*7 YEAR PRICE SCORE 92.5 *12 MONTH PRICE SCORE 108.3

*NYSE COMPOSITE INDEX=100

INTERIM EARNINGS (Per Share):

Qtr.	Mar.	June	Sept.	Dec.
1998	0.51	0.50	0.49	0.52
1999	0.54	0.59	0.64	0.70
2000	0.69	0.72	0.71	0.74

INTERIM DIVIDENDS (Per Share):

Amt.	Decl.	Ex.	Rec.	Pay.
0.66Q	3/15/00	4/03/00	4/05/00	4/17/00
0.66Q	6/15/00	7/03/00	7/06/00	7/17/00
0.68Q	7/26/00	10/02/00	10/04/00	10/16/00
0.72Q	12/04/00	12/28/00	1/02/01	1/16/01
0.72Q	3/15/01	4/02/01	4/04/01	4/16/01

Indicated div.: $2.88

CAPITALIZATION (12/31/00):

	($000)	(%)
Long-Term Debt	245,413	12.5
Minority Interest	13,767	0.7
Preferred Stock	1,318	0.1
Common & Surplus	1,703,021	86.7
Total	1,963,519	100.0

RECENT DEVELOPMENTS: For the year ended 12/31/00, net income jumped 16.0% to $205.0 million compared with $176.8 million in 1999. Results included gains on sale of shopping center properties of $4.0 million and $1.6 million in 2000 and 1999, respectively. Revenues from rental property increased 5.9% to $459.4 million, while income from rental property totaled $184.2 million, an increase of 7.7%. Income from investment in retail store leases decreased 2.8% to $4.0 million, while management fee income jumped 20.4% to $6.1 million.

PROSPECTS: KIM formed a new wholly-owned subsidiary, Kimco Developers Inc. (KDI). This new subsidiary will develop neighborhood and community shopping centers for future sale. KDI currently has four projects underway in Texas, two projects in Ohio and one in each of the following states: Arizona, Florida, Nevada and North Carolina. Going forward, the Company will continue to focus on its strategy of acquiring assets and isolating each property with an individual, non-recourse mortgage in an attempt to deliver high risk adjusted returns.

BUSINESS

KIMCO REALTY CORP. is an owner and operator of neighborhood and community shopping centers. As of 2/15/01, the Company had interests in 495 properties, including 430 shopping center properties, two regional malls, 50 retail store leases, 12 ground-up development projects and one distribution center, totaling approximately 66.0 million square feet of leaseable space located in 41 states. The Company's portfolio includes 54 properties relating to the Kimco Income REIT, a joint venture arrangement with institutional investors established for the purpose of investing in retail properties financed primarily with individual non-recourse mortgages debt. On 1/1/01, KIM transferred nine development projects to its new wholly owned subsidiary, Kimco Developers Inc., which will be engaged in the ground-up development of neighborhood and community shopping centers and sales thereof upon completion.

QUARTERLY DATA

(12/31/2000)($000)	REV	INC
1st Quarter	112,356	48,709
2nd Quarter	114,867	50,946
3rd Quarter	115,726	51,512
4th Quarter	116,458	53,858

ANNUAL FINANCIAL DATA

	12/31/00	12/31/99	12/31/98	12/31/97	12/31/96	12/31/95	12/31/94
Earnings Per Share	**2.86**	**2.46**	**[1] 2.02**	**1.78**	**1.61**	**1.33**	**[1] 1.17**
Tang. Book Val. Per Share	**26.97**	**26.39**	**26.34**	**18.38**	**16.69**	**13.24**	**10.65**
Dividends Per Share	**2.66**	**2.37**	**1.97**	**1.72**	**1.56**	**1.44**	**1.33**
Dividend Payout %	**93.0**	**96.3**	**97.5**	**96.6**	**96.9**	**108.3**	**113.7**
INCOME STATEMENT (IN MILLIONS):							
Total Income	459.4	433.9	338.8	198.9	168.1	143.1	125.3
Costs & Expenses	229.8	219.3	174.8	96.8	80.2	71.5	65.6
Depreciation	71.1	67.4	51.3	30.1	27.1	26.2	23.5
Income Before Income Taxes	188.5	166.2	124.4	84.9	72.7	52.4	41.3
Equity Earnings/Minority Int.	16.5	10.6	2.7	0.9	1.2	d0.5	d0.2
Net Income	205.0	176.8	[1] 127.2	85.8	73.8	51.9	[1] 41.1
Average Shs. Outstg. (000)	62,435	60,978	50,641	37,850	35,906	33,388	30,072
BALANCE SHEET (IN MILLIONS):							
Cash & Cash Equivalents	19.1	28.1	43.9	31.0	37.4	16.2	10.9
Total Real Estate Investments	2,935.1	2,822.8	2,847.4	1,222.5	925.6	811.0	673.8
Total Assets	3,171.3	3,007.5	3,051.2	1,343.9	1,022.6	884.2	736.7
Long-Term Obligations	245.4	212.3	434.3	121.4	54.4	64.0	67.8
Total Liabilities	1,467.0	1,402.0	1,466.2	600.6	417.3	437.1	416.0
Net Stockholders' Equity	1,704.3	1,605.4	1,585.0	743.3	605.3	447.2	320.7
Year-end Shs. Outstg. (000)	63,145	60,796	60,134	40,395	36,215	33,731	30,098
STATISTICAL RECORD:							
Net Inc.+Depr./Assets %	8.7	8.1	5.9	8.6	9.9	8.8	8.8
Return on Equity %	12.0	11.0	8.0	11.5	12.2	11.6	12.8
Return on Assets %	6.5	5.9	4.2	6.4	7.2	5.9	5.6
Price Range	44.75-32.75	40.75-30.88	41.63-33.44	35.69-30.25	34.88-25.25	28.17-23.58	25.92-22.00
P/E Ratio	15.6-11.5	16.6-12.6	20.6-16.6	20.0-17.0	21.7-15.7	21.2-17.7	22.1-18.8
Average Yield %	6.9	6.6	5.2	5.2	5.2	5.6	5.6

Statistics are as originally reported. Adj. for 3-for-2 stk. spl., 12/95 [1] Excl. extraord. chrg., 1998, $4.9 mill.; 1994, $825,000.

OFFICERS:
M. Cooper, Chmn., C.E.O.
M. J. Flynn, Vice-Chmn., Pres., C.O.O.
M. V. Pappagallo, V.P., C.F.O.

INVESTOR CONTACT: Investor Relations, (516) 869-9000

PRINCIPAL OFFICE: 3333 New Hyde Park Road, New Hyde Park, NY 11042-0020

TELEPHONE NUMBER: (516) 869-9000
FAX: (516) 869-9001
WEB: www.kimcorealty.com
NO. OF EMPLOYEES: 260
SHAREHOLDERS: 1,552 (approx.)
ANNUAL MEETING: In May
INCORPORATED: DE, 1973; reincorp., MD, Aug., 1994

INSTITUTIONAL HOLDINGS:
No. of Institutions: 163
Shares Held: 34,460,158
% Held: 54.5

INDUSTRY: Real estate investment trusts (SIC: 6798)

TRANSFER AGENT(S): Bank Boston, Boston, MA.

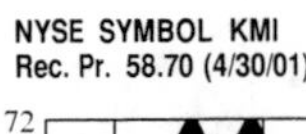

NYSE SYMBOL KMI
Rec. Pr. 58.70 (4/30/01)

KINDER MORGAN, INC.

YIELD 0.3%
P/E RATIO 36.9

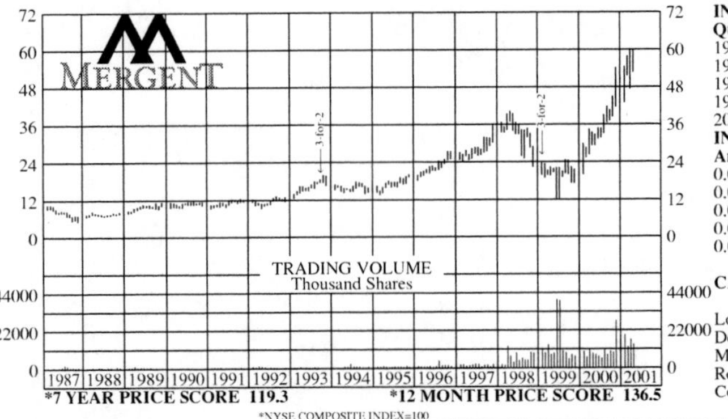

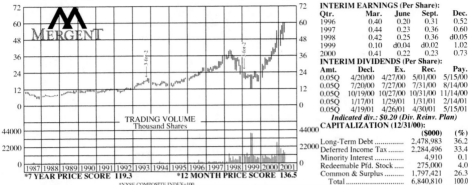

*7 YEAR PRICE SCORE 119.3 *12 MONTH PRICE SCORE 136.5

*NYSE COMPOSITE INDEX=100

INTERIM EARNINGS (Per Share):

Qtr.	Mar.	June	Sept.	Dec.
1996	0.40	0.20	0.31	0.52
1997	0.44	0.23	0.36	0.60
1998	0.42	0.25	0.36	d0.05
1999	0.10	d0.04	d0.02	1.02
2000	0.41	0.22	0.23	0.73

INTERIM DIVIDENDS (Per Share):

Amt.	Decl.	Ex.	Rec.	Pay.
0.05Q	4/20/00	4/27/00	5/01/00	5/15/00
0.05Q	7/20/00	7/27/00	7/31/00	8/14/00
0.05Q	10/19/00	10/27/00	10/31/00	11/14/00
0.05Q	1/17/01	1/29/01	1/31/01	2/14/01
0.05Q	4/19/01	4/26/01	4/30/01	5/15/01

Indicated div.: $0.20 (Div. Reinv. Plan)

CAPITALIZATION (12/31/00):

	($000)	(%)
Long-Term Debt	2,478,983	36.2
Deferred Income Tax	2,284,496	33.4
Minority Interest	4,910	0.1
Redeemable Pfd. Stock	275,000	4.0
Common & Surplus	1,797,421	26.3
Total	6,840,810	100.0

RECENT DEVELOPMENTS: For the year ended 12/31/00, income from continuing operations was $183.7 million versus $155.7 million a year earlier. Results for 1999 included merger-related charges of $37.4 million. Total operating revenues rose 47.8% to $2.71 billion. Equity in earnings from KMI's ownership of the general partner Kinder Morgan Energy Partners, L.P. totaled $140.9 million. On 3/2/01, KMI announced that it has retired $400.0 million in reset put securities due 3/1/21, resulting in a one-time extraordinary loss of about $12.0 million.

PROSPECTS: Near-term prospects are positive, reflecting expected growth across each of the Company's businesses. Accordingly, KMI anticipates 2001 earnings per share to range from $1.66 to $1.79 per share. Separately, on 2/20/01, KMI and The Williams Companies, Inc. announced a 16-year agreement under which Williams will supply and market 3,300 megawatts of capacity for six natural gas-fired, intermediate-peaking power generation facilities to be developed by Kinder Morgan Power Company over the next four years.

BUSINESS

KINDER MORGAN, INC. (formerly K N Energy, Inc.) is an integrated energy services provider. Activities include the transportation and storage of natural gas, retail distribution of natural gas and electric power generation and sales. KMI operates more than 30,000 miles of natural gas and products pipelines in 26 states and operates Kinder Morgan Energy Partners, L.P., which is a pipeline master limited partnership. KMI's consolidated businesses are segregated into Natural Gas Pipeline Company of America; MidCon Texas Pipeline Operator, Inc.; retail natural gas distribution; and electric power generation and sales. On 10/7/99, K N Energy, Inc. and Kinder Morgan completed their merger through the acquisition of Kinder by K N Energy. The combined company has been renamed Kinder Morgan, Inc. As of 12/31/00, KMI owned approximately 20.7% of the total outstanding units of Kinder Morgan Energy Partners, L.P.

ANNUAL FINANCIAL DATA

	12/31/00	[5] 12/31/99	[3] 12/31/98	12/31/97	12/31/96	12/31/95	[1] 12/31/94
Earnings Per Share	**[7] 1.60**	**[6] 1.92**	**[4] 0.92**	**1.63**	**1.43**	**1.22**	**[2] 0.35**
Cash Flow Per Share	**2.54**	**3.71**	**2.44**	**2.81**	**2.58**	**2.40**	**1.54**
Tang. Book Val. Per Share	**15.70**	**14.79**	**17.74**	**12.63**	**11.44**	**10.13**	**9.50**
Dividends Per Share	**0.20**	**0.65**	**0.76**	**0.73**	**0.70**	**0.67**	**0.65**
Dividend Payout %	**12.5**	**33.9**	**82.6**	**44.5**	**49.1**	**55.2**	**186.3**
INCOME STATEMENT (IN MILLIONS):							
Total Revenues	2,713.7	1,745.5	4,387.8	2,145.1	1,443.2	1,103.4	1,083.1
Costs & Expenses	2,210.4	1,296.2	3,945.3	1,946.9	1,257.2	939.8	978.6
Depreciation & Amort.	108.2	144.3	98.0	56.0	51.2	49.9	50.3
Operating Income	395.1	305.1	344.6	142.2	134.8	113.7	54.2
Net Interest Inc./(Exp.)	d243.2	d252.0	d247.2	d43.5	d35.9	d34.2	d31.6
Income Taxes	122.7	90.5	38.3	35.7	35.9	29.1	9.5
Equity Earnings/Minority Int.	81.9	d2.2	d16.2	d8.7	d2.9	d0.9	d0.7
Net Income	[7] 183.7	[6] 154.7	[4] 60.0	77.5	63.8	52.5	[2] 15.3
Cash Flow	291.9	298.4	157.6	133.1	114.6	101.9	65.0
Average Shs. Outstg. (000)	115,030	80,358	64,636	47,307	44,436	42,540	42,066
BALANCE SHEET (IN MILLIONS):							
Gross Property	6,137.0	6,167.3	7,767.3	1,971.6	1,547.6	1,349.0	1,312.4
Accumulated Depreciation	412.4	377.7	744.2	550.6	518.5	489.8	461.7
Net Property	5,724.6	5,789.6	7,023.2	1,421.0	1,029.2	859.2	850.6
Total Assets	8,418.1	9,540.3	9,612.2	2,305.8	1,629.7	1,257.5	1,172.4
Long-Term Obligations	2,479.0	3,293.3	3,300.0	553.8	423.7	315.6	334.6
Net Stockholders' Equity	1,797.4	1,665.8	1,223.8	613.1	526.8	433.8	400.7
Year-end Shs. Outstg. (000)	114,483	112,666	68,597	47,994	45,434	42,131	41,427
STATISTICAL RECORD:							
Operating Profit Margin %	14.6	17.5	7.9	6.6	9.3	10.3	5.0
Net Profit Margin %	6.8	8.9	1.4	3.6	4.4	4.8	1.4
Net Inc./Net Property %	3.2	2.7	0.9	5.5	6.2	6.1	1.8
Net Inc./Tot. Capital %	2.7	2.1	0.9	5.2	5.8	6.0	1.8
Return on Equity %	10.2	9.3	4.9	12.6	12.1	12.1	3.8
Accum. Depr./Gross Prop. %	6.7	6.1	9.6	27.9	33.5	36.3	35.2
Price Range	54.25-19.88	24.69-12.19	40.34-22.33	35.75-24.08	27.50-18.00	20.17-13.50	17.92-13.83
P/E Ratio	33.9-12.4	12.9-6.3	43.8-24.3	21.9-14.7	19.3-12.6	16.5-11.1	51.6-39.9
Average Yield %	0.5	3.5	2.4	2.4	3.1	4.0	4.1

Statistics are as originally reported. Adj. for 3-for-2 stk. split, 1/99 [1] Refls. acq. of American Oil and Gas Corp. [2] Incls. non-recurr. chrgs. of $19.3 mill. [3] Refls. 1/30/98 acq. of MidCon Corp. [4] Incls. non-recurr. pre-tax chrgs. of $5.8 mill. [5] Refls. 10/7/99 acq. of Kinder Morgan & disp. & discont. of non-core businesses. [6] Incls. $37.4 mill. non-recurr. chrg.; bef. $396.1 mill. loss fr. disc. ops. [7] Bef. loss on disp. of disc. ops. of $31.7 mill. ($0.28/sh.)

OFFICERS:
R. D. Kinder, Chmn., C.E.O.
W. V. Morgan, Vice-Chmn., Pres.
C. P. Shaper, V.P., C.F.O.

INVESTOR CONTACT: Investor Relations, (888) 844-5657

PRINCIPAL OFFICE: 500 Dallas, Suite 1000, Houston, TX 77002

TELEPHONE NUMBER: (713) 369-9000
FAX: (713) 844-9581
WEB: www.kindermorgan.com

NO. OF EMPLOYEES: 3,801 (avg.)

SHAREHOLDERS: 9,326

ANNUAL MEETING: In Mar.

INCORPORATED: KS, May, 1927

INSTITUTIONAL HOLDINGS:
No. of Institutions: 262
Shares Held: 67,898,328
% Held: 59.0

INDUSTRY: Gas transmission and distribution (SIC: 4923)

TRANSFER AGENT(S): EquiServe, Jersey City, NJ

NYSE SYMBOL KG
Rec. Pr. 42.13 (4/30/01)

KING PHARMACEUTICALS, INC.

YIELD ...
P/E RATIO 145.3

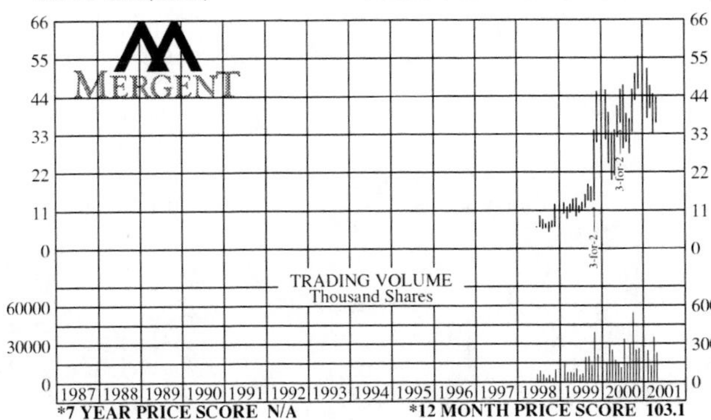

*7 YEAR PRICE SCORE N/A *12 MONTH PRICE SCORE 103.1

*NYSE COMPOSITE INDEX=100

INTERIM EARNINGS (Per Share):

Qtr.	Mar.	June	Sept.	Dec.
1997		0.11		
1998		0.37		
1999	0.08	0.14	0.21	0.19
2000	d0.10	0.19	d0.12	0.32

INTERIM DIVIDENDS (Per Share):

Amt.	Decl.	Ex.	Rec.	Pay.
3-for-2	10/04/99	11/12/99	10/28/99	11/11/99
3-for-2	6/02/00	6/22/00	6/12/00	6/21/00

CAPITALIZATION (12/31/00):

	($000)	(%)
Long-Term Debt	99,005	9.0
Deferred Income Tax	16,989	1.5
Common & Surplus	987,733	89.5
Total	1,103,727	100.0

RECENT DEVELOPMENTS: For the year ended 12/31/00, KG reported income of $104.6 million, before an extraordinary charge, compared with income of $100.6 million, before an extraordinary charge, in 1999. Results for 2000 included pre-tax non-recurring charges totaling $70.8 million. Total revenues increased 21.0% to $620.2 million from $512.5 million the year before. Results for 2000 and 1999 included the operations of Medco Research, Inc. and Jones Pharma Incorporated, which were acquired on 2/25/00 and 8/31/00, respectively.

PROSPECTS: KG received an exclusive license from Novavax, Inc. to promote, market, distribute and sell Estrasorb™, Novavax's transdermal estrogen replacement therapy. Looking ahead, KG remains very confident about the growth potential of its largest product Altace®. In addition, KG should continue to benefit from the expansion of its diversified portfolio of branded pharmaceutical products, including the addition of LEVOXL®, and CYTOMEL®/TRIOSTAT®.

BUSINESS

KING PHARMACEUTICALS, INC. is a vertically integrated pharmaceutical company that researches, develops, manufactures, markets and sells primarily branded prescription pharmaceutical products. KG markets its branded pharmaceutical products to general/family practitioners, internal medicine physicians, cardiologists, endocrinologists, pediatricians and hospitals. KG's pharmaceutical products can be divided into five therapeutic areas: cardiovascular, anti-infectives, vaccines and biologicals, thyroid-disorder drugs and women's health. KG also provides contract manufacturing for a number of pharmaceutical and biotechnology companies. In February 2000, KG acquired Medco Research, Inc., which has been renamed King Pharmaceutical Research and Development. In July 2000, KG acquired American Home Products. In August 2000, KG acquired Jones Pharma Incorporated.

ANNUAL FINANCIAL DATA

	12/31/00	12/31/99	12/31/98	12/31/97	12/31/96	12/31/95
Earnings Per Share	**2 0.63**	**1 0.63**	**1 0.37**	**0.11**	**d0.01**	**0.32**
Cash Flow Per Share	**0.91**	**1.03**	**0.52**	**0.15**	**0.02**	**0.37**
Tang. Book Val. Per Share	**1.16**	...	...	...	**0.16**	...
INCOME STATEMENT (IN THOUSANDS):						
Total Revenues	620,243	348,271	163,463	47,909	20,457	25,441
Costs & Expenses	362,924	190,352	98,042	32,157	20,888	7,633
Depreciation & Amort.	43,869	29,748	9,983	2,395	982	1,777
Operating Income	213,450	128,171	55,438	13,357	d1,413	16,031
Net Interest Inc./(Exp.)	d25,099	d55,033	d14,866	d2,749	d1,272	d2,006
Income Before Income Taxes	191,684	73,046	40,717	10,580	d347	14,392
Income Taxes	87,103	27,392	15,396	3,968	cr107	5,058
Net Income	2 104,581	1 45,654	1 25,321	6,612	d240	9,334
Cash Flow	148,450	75,402	35,304	9,007	d1,843	11,103
Average Shs. Outstg.	163,329	72,887	67,788	59,108	34,740	29,702
BALANCE SHEET (IN THOUSANDS):						
Cash & Cash Equivalents	76,395	8,451	1,159	69	1,601	...
Total Current Assets	317,243	130,673	75,610	22,812	13,885	...
Net Property	128,521	97,151	93,981	17,170	16,691	...
Total Assets	1,282,395	805,689	668,171	104,863	39,279	...
Total Current Liabilities	105,082	89,750	44,523	23,236	6,136	...
Long-Term Obligations	99,005	553,355	514,486	48,289	13,980	...
Net Stockholders' Equity	987,733	148,436	101,436	29,334	15,693	...
Net Working Capital	212,161	40,923	31,087	d424	7,749	...
Year-end Shs. Outstg.	170,841	72,308	72,236	63,000	43,801	...
STATISTICAL RECORD:						
Operating Profit Margin %	34.4	36.8	33.9	27.9	...	63.0
Net Profit Margin %	16.9	13.1	15.5	13.8	...	36.7
Return on Equity %	10.6	30.8	25.0	22.5	...	...
Return on Assets %	8.2	5.7	3.8	6.3	...	...
Debt/Total Assets %	7.7	68.7	77.0	46.0	35.6	...
Price Range	55.50-19.75	45.34-8.61	12.78-4.72	...	...	...
P/E Ratio	88.1-31.3	72.3-13.7	34.3-12.7	...	...	...

Statistics are as originally reported. Adj. for stk. splits: 3-for-2, 11/11/99; 6/21/00. 1 Bef. extraord. chrg. $705,000, 12/99; $4.4 mill., 12/98. 2 Bef. extraord. chrg. of $40.1 mill., incl. non-recurr. chrgs. of $70.7 mill.

OFFICERS:
J. M. Gregory, Chmn., C.E.O.
J. J. Gregory, Pres.

INVESTOR CONTACT: Kyle P. Macione, Exec. V.P., Inv. Rel., (423) 989-8077

PRINCIPAL OFFICE: 501 Fifth Street, Bristol, TN 37620

TELEPHONE NUMBER: (423) 989-8000
FAX: (423) 274-8677
WEB: www.kingpharm.com
NO. OF EMPLOYEES: 1,642 full-time; 14 part-time
SHAREHOLDERS: 1,300 (approx. record)
ANNUAL MEETING: In June
INCORPORATED: TN, 1993

INSTITUTIONAL HOLDINGS:
No. of Institutions: 316
Shares Held: 126,471,086
% Held: 73.8

INDUSTRY: Pharmaceutical preparations (SIC: 2834)

TRANSFER AGENT(S): Union Planters Bank, N.A., Belleville, IL

NYSE SYMBOL KM
Rec. Pr. 11.28 (5/31/01)

KMART CORPORATION

YIELD ...
P/E RATIO ...

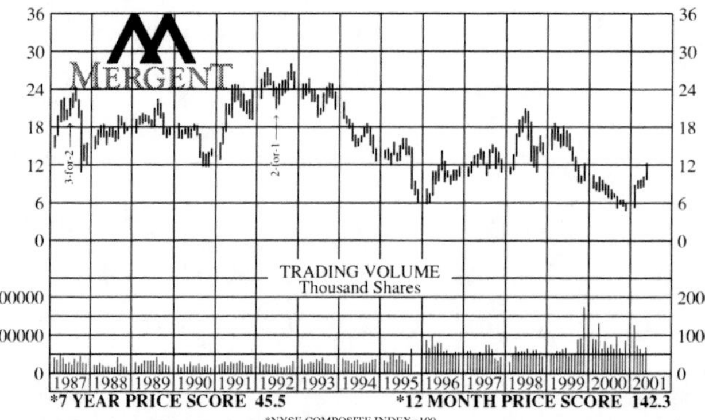

*7 YEAR PRICE SCORE 45.5 *12 MONTH PRICE SCORE 142.3

*NYSE COMPOSITE INDEX=100

INTERIM EARNINGS (Per Share):

Qtr.	Apr.	July	Oct.	Jan.
1996-97	d0.08	0.07	0.02	0.45
1997-98	0.03	0.06	0.04	0.35
1998-99	0.10	0.16	0.08	0.65
1999-00	0.14	0.26	0.09	0.77
2000-01	0.05	d0.93	d0.14	0.48

INTERIM DIVIDENDS (Per Share):

Amt.	Decl.	Ex.	Rec.	Pay.

Last dist. $0.12Q, 12/11/95

CAPITALIZATION (1/31/01):

	($000)	(%)
Long-Term Debt	2,084,000	20.8
Capital Lease Obligations..	943,000	9.4
Preferred Stock..................	887,000	8.9
Common & Surplus	6,083,000	60.8
Total	9,997,000	100.0

RECENT DEVELOPMENTS: For the 53 weeks ended 1/31/01, net loss was $244.0 million versus income from continuing operations of $633.0 million in the corresponding 52-week period the year before. Results for 2000 included a one-time after-tax charge of $463.0 million from strategic initiatives focused on productivity improvements. Sales grew 3.1% to $37.03 billion from $35.93 billion a year earlier. Comparable-store sales rose 1.1% year-over-year.

PROSPECTS: Earnings are being diminished by costs related to the implementation of strategic initiatives focused on increasing inventory levels and boosting customer service. Going forward, the Company plans to hire additional workers, increase employee training and make stores more convenient for shoppers. The Company is implementing a new "line-buster" program designed to help speed check-out times.

BUSINESS

KMART CORPORATION is a mass merchandise retailer operating more than 2,100 discount department stores in the United States, the U.S. Virgin Islands, Puerto Rico and Guam. The retail outlets include over 100 Super Kmart Centers that sell groceries in addition to general merchandise. The Company also holds a 59% interest in BlueLight.com, an e-commerce company, and a 49% interest in essentially all of the Meldisco subsidiaries of Footstar Inc., which operate the footwear departments in Kmart's stores. In 1995, the Company completed public offerings for Borders Group, Inc. and its remaining interests in OfficeMax and The Sports Authority, Inc. In June 1997, the Company sold its Canadian operations and completed the divestiture of its remaining international operations.

QUARTERLY DATA

(1/31/2001)($000)	REV	INC
1st Quarter.................	8,195,000	22,000
2nd Quarter................	8,998,000	(448,000)
3rd Quarter	8,199,000	(67,000)
4th Quarter.................	11,636,000	249,000

ANNUAL FINANCIAL DATA

	1/31/01	1/26/00	1/27/99	1/28/98	1/29/97	1/31/96	1/25/95
Earnings Per Share	**[1] d0.48**	**[5] 1.22**	**1.01**	**[1] 0.51**	**[4] 0.48**	**[3] d1.08**	**[2] 0.55**
Cash Flow Per Share	**1.10**	**2.50**	**2.10**	**1.85**	**1.82**	**0.52**	**2.15**
Tang. Book Val. Per Share	**12.50**	**13.10**	**12.12**	**11.13**	**10.51**	**10.98**	**12.24**
Dividends Per Share	...	...	...	...	...	**0.60**	**0.96**
Dividend Payout %	...	...	...	...	...	...	**174.5**
INCOME STATEMENT (IN MILLIONS):							
Total Revenues	37,028.0	35,925.0	33,674.0	32,183.0	31,437.0	34,654.0	34,313.0
Costs & Expenses	36,296.0	33,855.0	31,912.0	30,742.0	30,010.0	34,353.0	32,969.0
Depreciation & Amort.	777.0	770.0	671.0	660.0	654.0	729.0	724.0
Operating Income	d45.0	1,300.0	1,091.0	781.0	773.0	d428.0	620.0
Net Interest Inc./(Exp.)	d287.0	d280.0	d293.0	d363.0	d453.0	d446.0	d494.0
Income Before Income Taxes	d378.0	970.0	748.0	369.0	299.0	d750.0	294.0
Income Taxes	cr134.0	337.0	230.0	120.0	68.0	cr222.0	114.0
Net Income	[1] d244.0	[5] 633.0	518.0	[1] 249.0	[4] 231.0	[3] d490.0	[2] 260.0
Cash Flow	533.0	1,403.0	1,189.0	909.0	885.0	233.0	967.0
Average Shs. Outstg. (000)	482,800	561,700	564,900	491,700	486,100	460,000	457,000
BALANCE SHEET (IN MILLIONS):							
Cash & Cash Equivalents	401.0	344.0	710.0	498.0	406.0	1,095.0	480.0
Total Current Assets	7,624.0	8,160.0	7,830.0	7,476.0	7,733.0	8,822.0	9,187.0
Net Property	6,557.0	6,410.0	5,914.0	5,472.0	5,740.0	5,301.0	6,280.0
Total Assets	14,630.0	15,104.0	14,166.0	13,558.0	14,286.0	15,397.0	17,029.0
Total Current Liabilities	3,799.0	4,076.0	3,691.0	3,274.0	3,602.0	3,264.0	5,626.0
Long-Term Obligations	3,027.0	2,773.0	2,629.0	2,904.0	3,599.0	5,564.0	3,788.0
Net Stockholders' Equity	6,970.0	7,290.0	6,963.0	6,415.0	6,072.0	5,280.0	6,032.0
Net Working Capital	3,825.0	4,084.0	4,139.0	4,202.0	4,131.0	5,558.0	3,561.0
Year-end Shs. Outstg. (000)	486,509	481,384	493,359	488,200	484,700	481,000	459,000
STATISTICAL RECORD:							
Operating Profit Margin %	...	3.6	3.2	2.4	2.5	...	1.8
Net Profit Margin %	...	1.8	1.5	0.8	0.7	...	0.8
Return on Equity %	...	8.7	7.4	3.9	3.8	...	4.3
Return on Assets %	...	4.2	3.7	1.8	1.6	...	1.5
Debt/Total Assets %	20.7	18.4	18.6	21.4	25.2	36.1	22.2
Price Range	10.44-4.75	18.63-9.06	20.88-10.50	15.25-10.13	14.25-5.75	16.25-5.88	22.00-12.50
P/E Ratio	...	15.3-7.4	20.7-10.4	29.9-19.8	29.7-12.0	...	40.0-22.7
Average Yield %	...	...	...	...	...	5.4	5.6

Statistics are as originally reported. [1] Incl. $463.0 mil ($0.95/sh) after-tax chg., 1/01; $81 mil ($0.17/sh) after-tax chg., 1/98. [2] Incl. $257 pre-tax chg. & $168 mil gain; bef. $36 mil cr. from discont. opers. [3] Bef. $30 mil loss for disp. of discont. opers., bef. $51 mil extraord. chg., & incl. $390 mil impairment chg. [4] Incl. $10 mil net gain, bef. $5 mil loss from discont. opers., & bef. $446 mil loss from disp. of discont. opers. [5] Bef. $230.0 mil ($0.41/sh) loss from discont. opers.

OFFICERS:
C. Conaway, Chmn., C.E.O.
M. S. Schwartz, Pres., C.O.O.
M. E. Welch, III, Exec. V.P., C.F.O.

INVESTOR CONTACT: Investor Relations Dept., (248) 643-1040

PRINCIPAL OFFICE: 3100 West Big Beaver Road, Troy, MI 48084

TELEPHONE NUMBER: (248) 463-1000
FAX: (248) 643-5249
WEB: www.bluelight.com

NO. OF EMPLOYEES: 252,000 (approx.)

SHAREHOLDERS: 73,892 (approx.)

ANNUAL MEETING: In May

INCORPORATED: MI, Mar., 1916

INSTITUTIONAL HOLDINGS:
No. of Institutions: 238
Shares Held: 264,065,292
% Held: 54.2

INDUSTRY: Variety stores (SIC: 5331)

TRANSFER AGENT(S): Fleet National Bank, Boston, MA

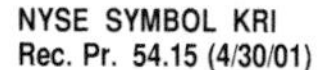

NYSE SYMBOL KRI
Rec. Pr. 54.15 (4/30/01)

KNIGHT RIDDER

YIELD 1.8%
P/E RATIO 15.9

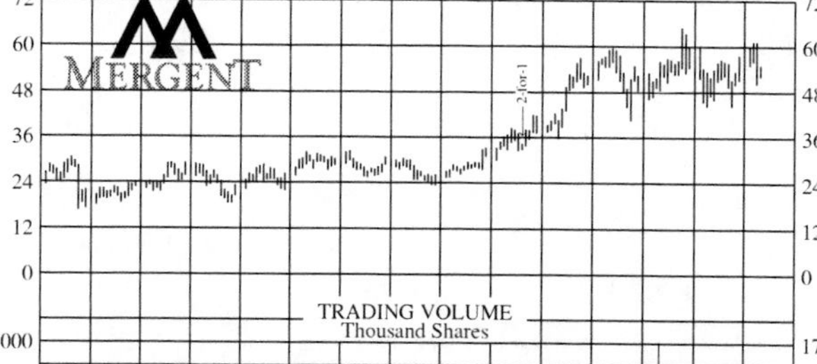

*7 YEAR PRICE SCORE 89.9 *12 MONTH PRICE SCORE 108.5
*NYSE COMPOSITE INDEX=100

INTERIM EARNINGS (Per Share):

Qtr.	Mar.	June	Sept.	Dec.
1997	1.85	0.61	0.69	1.04
1998	1.02	0.68	0.58	0.83
1999	0.65	0.88	0.78	1.18
2000	1.74	1.08	0.87	d0.29

INTERIM DIVIDENDS (Per Share):

Amt.	Decl.	Ex.	Rec.	Pay.
0.23Q	7/26/00	8/07/00	8/09/00	8/21/00
0.23Q	10/24/00	11/06/00	11/08/00	11/20/00
0.25Q	1/29/01	2/12/01	2/14/01	2/26/01
0.25Q	4/24/01	5/07/01	5/09/01	5/21/01

Indicated div.: $1.00 (Div. Reinv. Plan)

CAPITALIZATION (12/31/00):

	($000)	(%)
Long-Term Debt	1,591,910	46.7
Deferred Income Tax	269,702	7.9
Minority Interest	2,446	0.1
Preferred Stock	1,111	0.0
Common & Surplus	1,540,359	45.2
Total	3,405,528	100.0

RECENT DEVELOPMENTS: For the year ended 12/31/00, net income slipped 7.5% to $314.4 million compared with $339.9 million in 1999. Results for 2000 included a pre-tax charge of $168.0 million for the write-down of investments and a pre-tax charge of $17.2 million for severance costs. Total operating revenue was $3.21 billion, up 5.9% from $3.03 billion in the prior year. Total advertising revenue rose 6.6% to $2.51 billion.

PROSPECTS: The Company expects earnings per share growth for 2001 to be in the low double digits. Advertising revenue should increase between 3.5% and 4.5%, with revenue growth lower in the first half of 2001 and higher in the second half. The price of newsprint costs is budgeted to increase about 20.0%. Meanwhile, KnightRidder.com expanded its reach into the Pacific Northwest and the New Jersey coast with two new partners.

BUSINESS

KNIGHT RIDDER (formerly Knight-Ridder, Inc.) is the nation's second-largest newspaper publisher, with products in print and on-line. KRI publishes 32 daily newspapers in 28 U.S. markets, with a readership of 8.7 million daily and 12.9 million Sunday. KRI also has investments in a variety of Internet and technology companies and two newsprint companies. The Company's Internet operation, KnightRidder.com, creates and maintains a range of on-line services, including RealCities.com, a national network of city and regional destination sites in 40 U.S. markets. Some of the larger newspapers include THE CHARLOTTE OBSERVER, DETROIT FREE PRESS, THE MIAMI HERALD, THE PHILADELPHIA-ENQUIRER, and SAINT PAUL PIONEER PRESS.

ANNUAL FINANCIAL DATA

	12/31/00	12/26/99	12/27/98	12/28/97	12/29/96	12/31/95	12/25/94
Earnings Per Share	[7] **3.53**	[6] **3.49**	[5] **3.11**	[4] **4.08**	[3] **2.75**	[1] [2] **1.67**	**1.58**
Cash Flow Per Share	**5.63**	**5.43**	**5.03**	**5.46**	**4.45**	**3.18**	**2.95**
Tang. Book Val. Per Share	...	...	...	...	**2.29**	**1.51**	**4.88**
Dividends Per Share	**0.92**	**0.89**	**0.80**	**0.80**	**0.77**	**0.74**	**0.72**
Dividend Payout %	**26.1**	**25.5**	**25.7**	**19.6**	**28.0**	**44.3**	**45.7**
INCOME STATEMENT (IN MILLIONS):							
Total Revenues	3,211.8	3,228.2	3,091.9	2,876.8	2,774.8	2,751.8	2,649.0
Costs & Expenses	2,355.4	2,414.6	2,399.2	2,214.0	2,273.9	2,359.9	2,168.4
Depreciation & Amort.	187.6	189.4	188.1	156.7	166.1	151.6	149.3
Operating Income	668.8	624.3	504.6	506.0	334.9	240.3	331.3
Net Interest Inc./(Exp.)	d112.9	d89.8	d98.0	d93.9	d59.4	d48.5	d38.0
Income Before Income Taxes	546.6	567.4	495.4	694.6	446.2	275.5	292.3
Income Taxes	210.9	228.1	202.3	297.3	198.7	120.4	119.2
Equity Earnings/Minority Int.	d21.3	0.6	12.6	d0.7	20.4	12.3	d2.2
Net Income	[7] 314.4	[6] 339.9	[5] 305.6	[4] 396.5	[3] 267.9	[1] [2] 167.4	170.9
Cash Flow	502.0	529.3	493.7	553.2	433.9	319.0	320.2
Average Shs. Outstg. (000)	89,105	97,460	98,176	101,314	97,420	100,196	108,550
BALANCE SHEET (IN MILLIONS):							
Cash & Cash Equivalents	41.7	34.1	26.8	160.3	22.9	26.0	9.3
Total Current Assets	576.1	570.3	525.7	641.1	565.7	502.9	422.8
Net Property	1,039.4	1,059.1	1,073.0	1,046.5	902.5	931.6	832.5
Total Assets	4,243.5	4,192.3	4,257.1	4,355.1	2,900.3	3,005.7	2,447.2
Total Current Liabilities	508.4	497.1	653.8	598.7	544.6	437.6	420.6
Long-Term Obligations	1,591.9	1,260.8	1,329.0	1,599.1	771.3	1,000.7	411.5
Net Stockholders' Equity	1,541.5	1,780.7	1,662.7	1,551.7	1,131.5	1,111.0	1,224.7
Net Working Capital	67.7	73.2	d128.1	42.5	21.2	65.3	2.2
Year-end Shs. Outstg. (000)	73,995	79,612	78,328	81,598	93,341	97,196	105,786
STATISTICAL RECORD:							
Operating Profit Margin %	20.8	19.3	16.3	17.6	12.1	8.7	12.5
Net Profit Margin %	9.8	10.5	9.9	13.8	10.4	6.5	6.5
Return on Equity %	20.4	19.1	18.4	25.6	23.7	15.1	14.0
Return on Assets %	7.4	8.1	7.2	9.1	9.2	5.6	7.0
Debt/Total Assets %	37.5	30.1	31.2	36.7	26.6	33.3	16.8
Price Range	59.75-44.13	65.00-46.00	59.63-40.50	57.13-35.75	42.00-29.88	33.31-25.25	30.50-23.25
P/E Ratio	16.9-12.5	18.6-13.2	19.2-13.0	14.0-8.8	15.3-10.9	19.9-15.1	19.4-14.8
Average Yield %	1.8	1.6	1.6	1.7	2.1	2.5	2.7

Statistics are as originally reported. Adj. for 2-for-1 split, 7/96. [1] Incl. $53.8 mil aft-tax gain & $20.0 mil non-recur. chg. [2] Bef. $7.3 mil acct. adj. loss. [3] Incl. $90.9 mil gain on sale of bus. [4] Excl. $15.3 mil net gain & $1.3 mil inc. fr. sale of disc. ops. [5] Incl. $60.2 mil gain fr. disc. ops., non-recur. & reloc. costs. [6] Incl. $2.9 mil sev. chg. & $21.4 mil net gain fr. sale of stk. [7] Incl. $168.0 mil p-tax chg. fr. write-down of invest. & $17.2 mil p-tax chg. fr. sev. costs.

OFFICERS:
P. A. Ridder, Chmn., C.E.O.
J. H. Mordo, Sr. V.P., C.F.O.

INVESTOR CONTACT: Polk Laffoon IV, V.P., Corp. Rel. Manager, (408) 938-7838

PRINCIPAL OFFICE: 50 W. San Fernando Street, San Jose, CA 95113

TELEPHONE NUMBER: (408) 938-7700
FAX: (408) 938-7755
WEB: www.kri.com
NO. OF EMPLOYEES: 22,000 (avg.)
SHAREHOLDERS: 9,860
ANNUAL MEETING: In Apr.
INCORPORATED: OH, 1941; reincorp., FL, 1976

INSTITUTIONAL HOLDINGS:
No. of Institutions: 281
Shares Held: 68,462,789
% Held: 92.7

INDUSTRY: Newspapers (SIC: 2711)

TRANSFER AGENT(S): Mellon Investor Services, Ridgefield Park, NJ

NYSE SYMBOL KSS
Rec. Pr. 61.55 (5/31/01)

KOHL'S CORPORATION

YIELD ...
P/E RATIO 56.0

TRADING VOLUME
Thousand Shares

*7 YEAR PRICE SCORE 181.9 *12 MONTH PRICE SCORE 105.5
*NYSE COMPOSITE INDEX=100

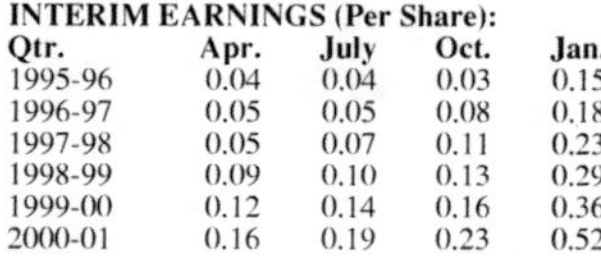

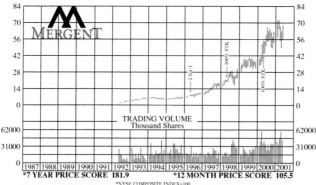

INTERIM EARNINGS (Per Share):

Qtr.	Apr.	July	Oct.	Jan.
1995-96	0.04	0.04	0.03	0.15
1996-97	0.05	0.05	0.08	0.18
1997-98	0.05	0.07	0.11	0.23
1998-99	0.09	0.10	0.13	0.29
1999-00	0.12	0.14	0.16	0.36
2000-01	0.16	0.19	0.23	0.52

INTERIM DIVIDENDS (Per Share):

Amt.	Decl.	Ex.	Rec.	Pay.
100% STK	3/06/00	4/25/00	4/07/00	4/24/00

CAPITALIZATION (2/3/01):

	($000)	(%)
Long-Term Debt	803,081	26.0
Deferred Income Tax	84,256	2.7
Common & Surplus	2,202,639	71.3
Total	3,089,976	100.0

RECENT DEVELOPMENTS: For the 53 weeks ended 2/3/01, net income advanced 44.2% to $372.1 million from $258.1 million in the corresponding 52-week period the year before. Net sales climbed 35.0% to $6.15 billion from $4.56 billion a year earlier. Results benefited from additional sales from 61 net new stores opened during the past year, along with a 9.0% increase in comparable-store sales. Gross profit was $2.10 billion, or 34.1% of net sales, versus $1.54 billion, or 33.9% of net sales, the previous year.

PROSPECTS: Long-term sales and earnings growth should benefit from the Company's focus on expanding its existing store base. KSS anticipates opening approximately 60 new stores in 2001 and about 70 new stores in 2002. During these years, the Company will continue its expansion in the Northeast, including its entry into Boston, as well as continued expansion in Texas, with a major entry in Houston and new stores in Austin and El Paso. In 2003, KSS plans to begin a major expansion into the Southwest.

BUSINESS

KOHL'S CORPORATION operates family-oriented, specialty department stores. As of 4/17/01, KSS operates 354 stores in 28 states. The Company's stores feature quality, national brand merchandise including moderately-priced apparel, shoes, accessories, soft home products and housewares targeted to middle-income customers shopping for their families and homes. In the fiscal year ended 2/3/01, sales were derived as follows: Women's, 30.1%; Men's, 20.8%; Home, 18.8%; Children's, 12.7%; Footwear, 9.4%; and Accessories, 8.2%.

ANNUAL FINANCIAL DATA

	2/3/01	1/29/00	1/30/99	1/31/98	2/1/97	2/3/96	1/28/95
Earnings Per Share	**1.10**	**0.77**	**0.59**	**0.46**	**0.35**	**[1] 0.25**	**0.23**
Cash Flow Per Share	**1.49**	**1.04**	**0.81**	**0.64**	**0.50**	**0.36**	**0.33**
Tang. Book Val. Per Share	**6.21**	**2.45**	**3.55**	**2.88**	**1.57**	**1.19**	**0.90**
INCOME STATEMENT (IN MILLIONS):							
Total Revenues	6,152.0	4,557.1	3,681.8	3,060.1	2,388.2	1,925.7	1,554.1
Costs & Expenses	5,367.4	4,020.0	3,273.5	2,743.2	2,154.8	1,755.7	1,402.7
Depreciation & Amort.	133.3	88.8	70.2	57.7	44.2	34.0	27.5
Operating Income	651.3	448.3	337.9	258.8	189.0	135.9	123.9
Net Interest Inc./(Exp.)	d46.2	d27.2	d20.9	d23.4	d17.4	d13.1	d6.4
Income Before Income Taxes	605.1	421.1	316.7	235.1	171.4	122.7	117.5
Income Taxes	233.0	163.0	124.5	93.8	68.9	50.1	48.9
Net Income	372.1	258.1	192.3	141.3	102.5	[1] 72.7	68.5
Cash Flow	505.4	347.0	262.9	199.7	147.1	106.8	96.1
Average Shs. Outstg. (000)	338,075	333,856	325,266	312,154	295,408	294,340	293,632
BALANCE SHEET (IN MILLIONS):							
Cash & Cash Equivalents	172.2	40.1	29.6	44.2	8.9	2.8	30.4
Total Current Assets	1,921.9	1,366.5	939.4	811.4	465.2	330.2	286.2
Net Property	1,726.5	1,353.0	933.0	749.6	596.2	409.2	298.7
Total Assets	3,855.2	2,914.7	1,936.1	1,619.7	1,122.4	804.9	658.7
Total Current Liabilities	723.3	634.4	380.2	286.2	235.8	154.8	171.6
Long-Term Obligations	803.1	495.0	310.9	310.4	312.0	187.7	108.8
Net Stockholders' Equity	2,202.6	1,685.5	1,162.8	954.8	517.5	410.6	334.2
Net Working Capital	1,198.6	732.1	559.2	525.3	229.3	175.4	114.6
Year-end Shs. Outstg. (000)	332,167	326,197	316,790	315,516	295,680	294,948	294,040
STATISTICAL RECORD:							
Operating Profit Margin %	10.6	9.8	9.2	8.5	7.9	7.1	8.0
Net Profit Margin %	6.0	5.7	5.2	4.6	4.3	3.8	4.4
Return on Equity %	16.9	15.3	16.6	14.9	19.9	17.7	20.5
Return on Assets %	9.7	8.9	10.0	8.8	9.2	9.0	10.4
Debt/Total Assets %	20.8	17.0	16.1	19.2	27.8	23.3	16.5
Price Range	66.50-33.50	40.63-28.63	30.75-16.20	18.84-9.06	10.50-6.33	6.89-4.75	6.91-4.89
P/E Ratio	60.4-30.5	52.8-37.2	52.1-27.5	41.4-19.9	30.3-18.2	27.9-19.2	29.5-20.9

Statistics are as originally reported. Adj. for stk. split: 2-for-1, 4/00, 4/98 & 4/96. [1] Incl. $14.1 mil non-recurr. pre-tax chrg.

OFFICERS:
W. S. Kellogg, Chmn.
R. L. Montgomery, C.E.O.
K. Mansell, Pres.

INVESTOR CONTACT: Patti Johnson, Investor Relations, (262) 703-1893

PRINCIPAL OFFICE: N56 W17000 Ridgewood Dr., Menomonee Falls, WI 53051

TELEPHONE NUMBER: (262) 703-7000
FAX: (262) 703-6373
WEB: www.kohls.com

NO. OF EMPLOYEES: 16,800 full-time; 37,200 part-time

SHAREHOLDERS: 6,128

ANNUAL MEETING: In May

INCORPORATED: DE, Oct., 1988; reincorp., WI, 1993.

INSTITUTIONAL HOLDINGS:
No. of Institutions: 386
Shares Held: 264,229,647
% Held: 79.3

INDUSTRY: Department stores (SIC: 5311)

TRANSFER AGENT(S): The Bank of New York, New York, NY

NYSE SYMBOL KKD
Rec. Pr. 36.56 (Adj.; 5/31/01)

KRISPY KREME DOUGHNUTS, INC.

YIELD ...
P/E RATIO 126.1

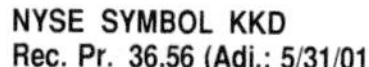

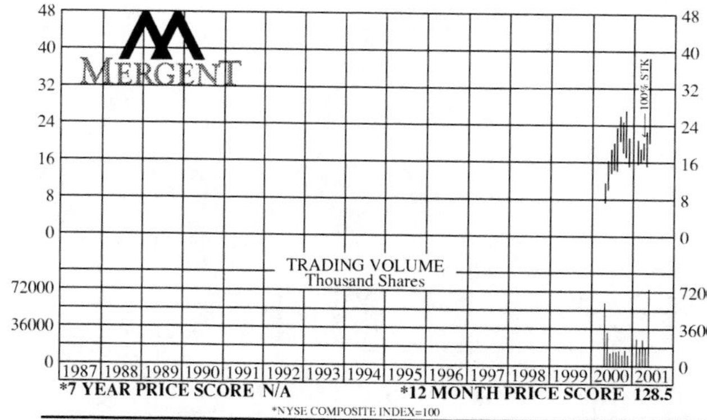

*7 YEAR PRICE SCORE N/A *12 MONTH PRICE SCORE 128.5

*NYSE COMPOSITE INDEX=100

INTERIM EARNINGS (Per Share):

Qtr.	Apr.	July	Oct.	Jan.
1999-00		3.19		
2000-01	0.07	0.07	0.07	0.08

INTERIM DIVIDENDS (Per Share):

Amt.	Decl.	Ex.	Rec.	Pay.
100% STK	2/13/01	3/20/01	3/05/01	3/19/01
100% STK	5/17/01	6/15/01	5/29/01	6/14/01

CAPITALIZATION (1/28/01):

	($000)	(%)
Long-Term Debt	1,735	1.3
Deferred Income Tax	579	0.4
Minority Interest	1,117	0.9
Common & Surplus	125,679	97.3
Total	129,110	100.0

RECENT DEVELOPMENTS: For the fiscal year ended 1/28/01, net income more than doubled to $14.7 million from $6.0 million in the previous year. Total revenues advanced 36.5% to $300.7 million from $220.2 million a year earlier. Company-owned store sales climbed 30.1% to $213.7 million, while sales at franchised stores jumped 51.6% to $234.4 million. Comparable-store sales grew 17.1%, fueled by a 22.9% increase at Company-owned stores. Income from operations totaled $23.5 million compared with $10.8 million the year before.

PROSPECTS: Sales and earnings growth should benefit from the continued expansion of the Company's store base. KKD anticipates opening approximately 36 new stores, the majority of which are expected to be franchise locations, during fiscal 2002. The Company's franchisees are contractually obligated to open over 250 new stores from fiscal 2002 through fiscal 2006. Over the long term, KKD is targeting 20.0% annual revenue growth, mid-single digit comparable-store sales growth, and 25.0% earnings per share growth annually.

BUSINESS

KRISPY KREME DOUGHNUTS, INC. is a retailer of more than 20 varieties of doughnuts, including the Company's signature HOT ORIGINAL GLAZED, as well as coffee and other beverages and bakery items. As of 5/18/01, KKD operated 182 Company-owned and franchise stores in 29 states. Each of the Company's stores has the capacity, depending on equipment size, to produce from 4,000 dozen to over 10,000 dozen doughnuts daily. In addition, KKD sells fresh doughnuts, both packaged and unpackaged, to a variety of retail customers, such as supermarkets, convenience stores and other food service and institutional accounts.

ANNUAL FINANCIAL DATA

	1/28/01	1/30/00	1/31/99	2/1/98
Earnings Per Share	**0.28**	**3.19**	**1 d1.92**	**1.86**
Cash Flow Per Share	**0.39**	**5.35**	**0.67**	**4.32**
Tang. Book Val. Per Share	**2.42**	**25.56**	**22.62**	...
INCOME STATEMENT (IN THOUSANDS):				
Total Revenues	300,715	220,243	180,880	158,743
Costs & Expenses	270,751	204,859	180,304	149,737
Depreciation & Amort.	6,457	4,546	4,278	3,586
Operating Income	23,507	10,838	d3,702	5,420
Net Interest Inc./(Exp.)	1,718	d1,232	d1,326	d1,424
Income Before Income Taxes	23,783	9,606	d5,279	4,525
Income Taxes	9,058	3,650	cr2,112	1,811
Net Income	14,725	5,956	1 d3,167	2,714
Cash Flow	21,182	10,502	1,111	6,300
Average Shs. Outstg.	53,655	1,964	1,650	1,457
BALANCE SHEET (IN THOUSANDS):				
Cash & Cash Equivalents	25,129	3,183	4,313	...
Total Current Assets	67,611	41,038	33,780	...
Net Property	78,340	60,584	53,575	...
Total Assets	171,493	104,958	93,312	...
Total Current Liabilities	38,168	29,586	25,393	...
Long-Term Obligations	1,735	22,368	20,138	...
Net Stockholders' Equity	125,679	47,755	42,247	...
Net Working Capital	29,443	11,452	8,387	...
Year-end Shs. Outstg.	51,832	1,868	1,868	1,456
STATISTICAL RECORD:				
Operating Profit Margin %	7.8	4.9	...	3.4
Net Profit Margin %	4.9	2.7	...	1.7
Return on Equity %	11.7	12.5	...	...
Return on Assets %	8.6	5.7	...	...
Debt/Total Assets %	1.0	21.3	21.6	...
Price Range	27.13-7.25	...	...	...
P/E Ratio	98.6-26.4	...	...	...

Statistics are as originally reported. Adj. for stk. splits: 100%, 6/01 & 3/01. 1 Incl. $9.5 mil pre-tax restr. chg.

OFFICERS:
S. A. Livengood, Chmn., Pres., C.E.O.
J. N. McAleer, Vice-Chmn., Exec. V.P.
J. W. Tate, C.F.O.

INVESTOR CONTACT: Michelle Parman, Sr. V.P.-Corp. Devel., (336) 733-3762

PRINCIPAL OFFICE: 370 Knollwood Street, Winston-Salem, NC 27103

TELEPHONE NUMBER: (336) 725-2981
FAX: (336) 733-3794
WEB: www.krispykreme.com
NO. OF EMPLOYEES: 2,645 full-time; 555 part-time
SHAREHOLDERS: 146 (approx.)
ANNUAL MEETING: In May
INCORPORATED: NC, Dec., 1999

INSTITUTIONAL HOLDINGS:
No. of Institutions: 103
Shares Held: 23,447,472 (Adj.)
% Held: 43.9

INDUSTRY: Retail bakeries (SIC: 5461)

TRANSFER AGENT(S): Branch Banking & Trust Company, Wilson, NC

NYSE SYMBOL KR
Rec. Pr. 24.94 (5/31/01)

KROGER COMPANY (THE)

YIELD ...
P/E RATIO 23.5

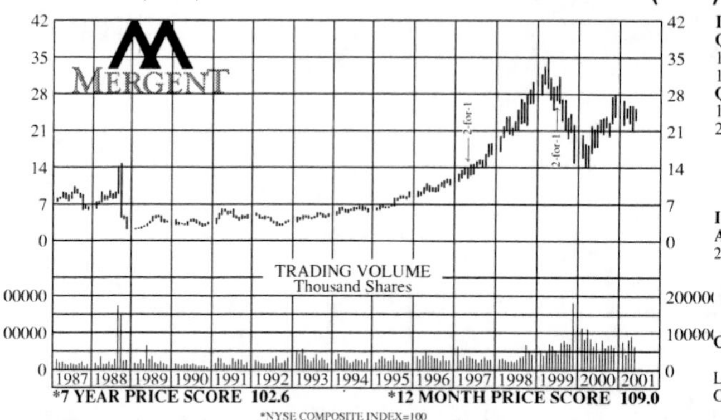

INTERIM EARNINGS (Per Share):

Qtr	Mar.	June	Sept.	Dec.
1997	0.18	0.21	0.18	0.28
1998	0.10	0.18	0.24	0.34
Qtr.	**May**	**Aug.**	**Nov.**	**Jan.**
1999-00	0.33	0.06	0.15	0.29
2000-01	0.12	0.26	0.24	0.44

INTERIM DIVIDENDS (Per Share):

Amt.	Decl.	Ex.	Rec.	Pay.
2-for-1	5/20/99	6/29/99	6/07/99	6/28/99

CAPITALIZATION (2/3/01):

	($000)	(%)
Long-Term Debt	8,210,000	72.7
Common & Surplus	3,089,000	27.3
Total	11,299,000	100.0

RECENT DEVELOPMENTS: For the 53 weeks ended 2/3/01, income before an extraordinary charge totaled $880.1 million versus net income of $623.2 million in the corresponding 52-week period the year before. Results included one-time pre-tax merger-related charges of $350.3 million and $468.4 million in 2000 and 1999, respectively. Sales grew 8.0% to $49.00 billion from $45.35 billion a year earlier. As a percentage of sales, gross profit was 26.9% versus 26.5% in the previous year.

PROSPECTS: Earnings are benefiting from increased sales of the Company's Private Selection® private-label brand products, coupled with savings stemming from new merchandising programs and technology investments, along with the integration of Fred Meyer, Inc. KR anticipates completing the integration process during the current fiscal year and realizing $380.0 million in annual synergistic savings, up from an estimated $330.0 million in fiscal 2000.

BUSINESS

THE KROGER COMPANY, the nation's largest grocery chain based on annual sales, operates 2,354 supermarkets in 31 states as of 2/3/01, principally under the Kroger, Fred Meyer, Ralphs, Smith's, King Soopers, Dillon, Fry's, City Market, Food 4 Less and Quality Food Centers banners. Most stores operate under the combination food and drug store format, which includes floral, seafood, pharmacy, bakery and other specialty departments. KR operates 789 convenience stores under the names: Kwik Shop, Quick Stop, Tom Thumb, Turkey Hill Minit Markets, Loaf 'N Jug, and Mini-Mart. KR also operates 398 fine jewelry stores, under the banners of Fred Meyer, Merksamer, Fox's, Littman, and Barclay Jewelers, 77 supermarket fuel centers, and 42 food processing plants. On 5/27/99, KR acquired Fred Meyer, Inc.

ANNUAL FINANCIAL DATA

	2/3/01	[3] 1/29/00	1/2/99	12/27/97	12/28/96	12/30/95	12/31/94
Earnings Per Share	[2] 1.04	[1][2] 0.74	[1][2] 0.85	[1] 0.85	[1] 0.67	[1] 0.66	[1] 0.59
Cash Flow Per Share	2.23	1.86	1.69	1.59	1.35	1.34	1.57
INCOME STATEMENT (IN MILLIONS):							
Total Revenues	49,000.4	45,352.0	28,203.3	26,567.3	25,170.9	23,937.8	22,959.1
Costs & Expenses	45,809.0	42,610.0	26,776.4	25,174.9	23,946.8	22,791.1	21,917.2
Depreciation & Amort.	1,008.0	961.0	447.1	394.1	356.8	324.5	293.1
Operating Income	2,183.0	1,781.0	979.9	998.3	867.3	822.2	748.9
Net Interest Inc./(Exp.)	d675.0	d652.0	d266.9	d285.9	d300.0	d312.7	d327.5
Income Before Income Taxes	1,508.0	1,129.0	713.0	712.4	567.3	509.5	421.4
Income Taxes	628.0	491.0	263.1	268.3	214.6	190.7	...
Net Income	[2] 880.1	[1][2] 638.0	[1][2] 449.9	[1] 444.0	[1] 352.7	[1] 318.9	[1] 421.4
Cash Flow	1,888.0	1,599.0	897.0	838.2	709.5	643.3	714.4
Average Shs. Outstg. (000)	846,000	858,000	530,764	525,720	525,500	481,652	454,148
BALANCE SHEET (IN MILLIONS):							
Cash & Cash Equivalents	161.0	281.0	121.4	65.5	...	...	27.2
Total Current Assets	5,416.0	5,531.0	2,673.2	2,640.6	2,352.8	2,107.0	2,152.1
Net Property	8,820.0	8,275.0	3,785.1	3,296.6	3,063.5	2,662.3	2,252.7
Total Assets	18,190.0	17,966.0	6,700.1	6,301.3	5,825.4	5,044.7	4,707.7
Total Current Liabilities	5,591.0	5,728.0	3,192.1	2,943.5	2,712.9	2,565.4	2,395.0
Long-Term Obligations	8,210.0	8,045.0	3,228.7	3,493.1	3,659.5	3,489.7	3,889.2
Net Stockholders' Equity	3,089.0	2,683.0	d387.8	d784.8	d1,181.7	d1,603.0	d2,153.7
Net Working Capital	d175.0	d197.0	d518.9	d303.0	d360.2	d458.5	d242.8
Year-end Shs. Outstg. (000)	815,000	835,000	513,916	509,942	507,520	496,808	443,988
STATISTICAL RECORD:							
Operating Profit Margin %	4.5	3.9	3.5	3.8	3.4	3.4	3.3
Net Profit Margin %	1.8	1.4	1.6	1.7	1.4	1.3	1.8
Return on Equity %	28.5	23.8	...	...	...	...	...
Return on Assets %	4.8	3.6	6.7	7.0	6.1	6.3	9.0
Debt/Total Assets %	45.1	44.8	48.2	55.4	62.8	69.2	82.6
Price Range	27.94-14.06	34.91-14.88	30.41-17.00	18.66-11.34	11.88-8.38	9.44-5.84	6.72-4.84
P/E Ratio	26.9-13.5	47.2-20.1	35.8-20.0	22.1-13.4	17.7-12.5	14.3-8.8	11.3-8.2

Statistics are as originally reported. Adj. for 2-for-1 stk. split, 6/99 & 4/97. [1] Bef. extraord. chg. $10.0 mil ($0.01/sh), 1/00; $39.1 mil ($0.08/sh), 1998; $32.4 mil ($0.07/sh), 1997; $2.8 mil ($0.01/sh), 1996; $16.1 mil ($0.04/sh), 1995; $26.7 mil ($0.06/sh), 1994. [2] Bef. $3.2 mil extraord. chg. & incl. $350.3 mil pre-tax one-time chgs., 2/01; $468.0 mil pre-tax merger-related chg., 1/00; $88.1 mil ($0.17/sh) after-tax chg., 1998. [3] Incl. results of Fred Meyer, Inc., acq. on 5/27/99.

OFFICERS:
J. A. Pichler, Chmn., C.E.O.
D. B. Dillon, Pres., C.O.O.
J. M. Schlotman, V.P., C.F.O.

INVESTOR CONTACT: Kathy Kelly, (513) 762-4969

PRINCIPAL OFFICE: 1014 Vine Street, Cincinnati, OH 45202

TELEPHONE NUMBER: (513) 762-4000
FAX: (513) 762-1400
WEB: www.kroger.com

NO. OF EMPLOYEES: 312,000 (avg.)

SHAREHOLDERS: 54,673

ANNUAL MEETING: In June

INCORPORATED: OH, Apr., 1902

INSTITUTIONAL HOLDINGS:
No. of Institutions: 473
Shares Held: 581,620,155
% Held: 71.4

INDUSTRY: Grocery stores (SIC: 5411)

TRANSFER AGENT(S): The Bank of New York, New York, NY

NYSE SYMBOL KTO
Rec. Pr. 10.30 (5/31/01)

K2 INC.

YIELD ...
P/E RATIO 11.1

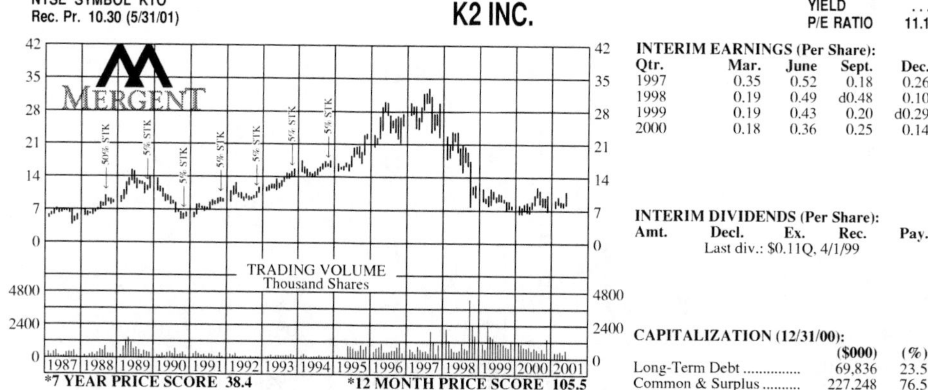

*7 YEAR PRICE SCORE 38.4 *12 MONTH PRICE SCORE 105.5
*NYSE COMPOSITE INDEX=100

INTERIM EARNINGS (Per Share):

Qtr.	Mar.	June	Sept.	Dec.
1997	0.35	0.52	0.18	0.26
1998	0.19	0.49	d0.48	0.10
1999	0.19	0.43	0.20	d0.29
2000	0.18	0.36	0.25	0.14

INTERIM DIVIDENDS (Per Share):

Amt.	Decl.	Ex.	Rec.	Pay.

Last div.: $0.11Q, 4/1/99

CAPITALIZATION (12/31/00):

	($000)	(%)
Long-Term Debt	69,836	23.5
Common & Surplus	227,248	76.5
Total	297,084	100.0

RECENT DEVELOPMENTS: For the year ended 12/31/00, income from continuing operations increased 96.2% to $16.7 million compared with income from continuing operations of $8.5 million in 1999. Results for 1999 included a nonrecurring net charge of $7.1 million. The improvement in earnings was primarily attributed to product innovation and promotion, strong demand, and global cost reduction initiatives. Net sales were $670.8 million, up 3.8% from $646.0 million a year earlier.

PROSPECTS: Although the Company is well-positioned for strong growth for 2001, the slowing domestic economy, continued softness in retail sales of in-line skates worldwide, and the possible negative effect of weather on spring business may dampen future sales growth. However, KTO is optimistic as kickboard sales continue to be strong and favorable winter weather conditions are enhancing the North American market snowboard and ski product lines.

BUSINESS

K2 INC. (formerly Anthony Industries, Inc.) designs, manufactures and markets brand name sporting goods, recreational products and industrial products. The Company's sporting goods and recreational products include names such as K2 and OLIN alpine skis, K2, RIDE and MORROW snowboards, boots and bindings, K2 in-line skates, STEARNS sports equipment, SHAKESPEARE fishing tackle, K2 bikes, DANA DESIGN backpacks. KTO's other recreational products include PLANET EARTH apparel, ADIO skateboard shoes and HILTON corporate casuals. KTO's industrial products include SHAKESPEARE extruded monofilaments, marine antennas and fiberglass light poles.

ANNUAL FINANCIAL DATA

	12/31/00	12/31/99	12/31/98	12/31/97	12/31/96	12/31/95	12/31/94
Earnings Per Share	**[1] 0.93**	**[3] [4] 0.50**	**[3] [4] 0.23**	**[2] 1.31**	**1.51**	**[1] 1.37**	**1.09**
Cash Flow Per Share	**1.72**	**1.32**	**1.00**	**2.16**	**2.17**	**2.07**	**1.82**
Tang. Book Val. Per Share	**10.42**	**10.01**	**11.02**	**11.21**	**10.43**	**9.75**	**7.02**
Dividends Per Share	**...**	**0.22**	**0.44**	**0.44**	**0.44**	**0.44**	**0.42**
Dividend Payout %	**...**	**44.0**	**191.2**	**33.6**	**29.1**	**32.1**	**38.4**
INCOME STATEMENT (IN THOUSANDS):							
Total Revenues	670,786	635,105	574,510	646,933	602,734	544,268	504,022
Costs & Expenses	617,643	596,535	545,021	591,662	547,228	496,950	467,574
Depreciation & Amort.	14,320	13,726	12,739	14,226	11,150	10,232	8,634
Operating Income	38,823	24,844	16,750	41,045	44,356	37,086	27,814
Net Interest Inc./(Exp.)	d14,814	d12,741	d12,163	d10,560	d9,294	d9,916	d7,481
Income Before Income Taxes	24,200	12,516	4,823	31,115	36,542	28,619	20,333
Income Taxes	7,502	4,005	955	9,215	11,325	8,820	7,300
Net Income	[1] 16,698	[3] [4] 8,511	[3] [4] 3,868	[2] 21,900	25,217	[1] 19,799	13,033
Cash Flow	31,018	22,237	16,607	36,126	36,367	30,031	21,667
Average Shs. Outstg.	18,040	16,883	16,637	16,713	16,734	14,498	11,919
BALANCE SHEET (IN THOUSANDS):							
Cash & Cash Equivalents	3,174	9,421	3,394	5,914	10,860	7,357	7,700
Total Current Assets	303,271	345,809	335,570	330,168	274,409	300,455	232,848
Net Property	71,995	72,595	66,591	77,788	67,523	57,107	52,364
Total Assets	419,284	487,878	452,995	428,928	367,831	384,423	304,414
Total Current Liabilities	118,777	158,623	127,138	122,553	74,250	120,533	82,602
Long-Term Obligations	69,836	107,280	110,724	88,668	89,096	75,071	109,921
Net Stockholders' Equity	227,248	218,520	202,119	202,885	188,988	175,816	98,996
Net Working Capital	184,494	187,186	208,432	207,615	200,159	179,922	150,246
Year-end Shs. Outstg.	17,935	17,940	16,567	16,536	16,556	16,583	11,842
STATISTICAL RECORD:							
Operating Profit Margin %	5.8	3.9	2.9	6.3	7.4	6.8	5.5
Net Profit Margin %	2.5	1.3	0.7	3.4	4.2	3.6	2.6
Return on Equity %	7.3	3.9	1.9	10.8	13.3	11.3	13.2
Return on Assets %	4.0	1.7	0.9	5.1	6.9	5.2	4.3
Debt/Total Assets %	16.7	22.0	24.4	20.7	24.2	19.5	36.1
Price Range	11.94-6.19	11.63-6.94	23.69-7.75	32.94-22.44	30.13-20.38	23.25-15.13	17.50-13.93
P/E Ratio	12.8-6.7	23.2-13.9	102.9-33.7	25.1-17.1	19.9-13.5	17.0-11.0	16.1-12.8
Average Yield %	...	2.4	2.8	1.6	1.7	2.3	2.7

Statistics are as originally reported. Adj. for all 5.0% stock splits thru 12/94. [1] Bef. loss fr. discont. oper. of $4.9 mill., 1995; $119,000, 2000. [2] Incl. restruct. costs of $7.0 mill. [3] Incl. non-recurring net chrg. of $9.4 mill., 1998; $7.1 mill., 1999. [4] Excl. net gain fr. discont. oper. of $975,000, 1998; $1.3 mill., 1999.

OFFICERS:
R. M. Heckmann, Chmn.
R. M. Rodstein, Pres., C.E.O.
S. E. McConnell, Sec.

INVESTOR CONTACT: John J. Rangel, Sr. V.P., (323) 890-5830

PRINCIPAL OFFICE: 4900 South Eastern Avenue, Los Angeles, CA 90040

TELEPHONE NUMBER: (323) 724-2800
FAX: (323) 724-0470
WEB: www.K2sports.com

NO. OF EMPLOYEES: 2,900 (approx.)

SHAREHOLDERS: 1,772

ANNUAL MEETING: In May

INCORPORATED: DE, Sept., 1959

INSTITUTIONAL HOLDINGS:
No. of Institutions: 60
Shares Held: 10,566,327
% Held: 58.9

INDUSTRY: Sporting and athletic goods, nec (SIC: 3949)

TRANSFER AGENT(S): Computershare Investor Services, Los Angeles, CA

NYSE SYMBOL LLL
Rec. Pr. 77.25 (4/30/01)

L-3 COMMUNICATIONS HOLDINGS, INC.

YIELD ...
P/E RATIO 32.6

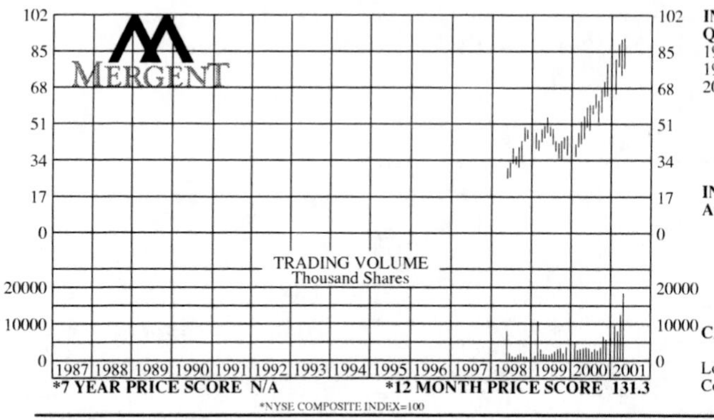

*7 YEAR PRICE SCORE N/A *12 MONTH PRICE SCORE 131.3

*NYSE COMPOSITE INDEX=100

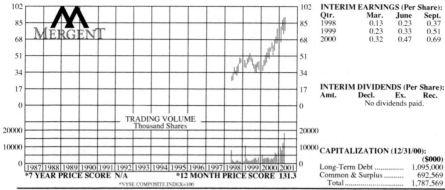

INTERIM EARNINGS (Per Share):

Qtr.	Mar.	June	Sept.	Dec.
1998	0.13	0.23	0.37	0.48
1999	0.23	0.33	0.51	0.68
2000	0.32	0.47	0.69	0.89

INTERIM DIVIDENDS (Per Share):

Amt.	Decl.	Ex.	Rec.	Pay.

No dividends paid.

CAPITALIZATION (12/31/00):

	($000)	(%)
Long-Term Debt	1,095,000	61.3
Common & Surplus	692,569	38.7
Total	1,787,569	100.0

RECENT DEVELOPMENTS: For the year ended 12/31/00, net income increased 40.9% to $82.7 million from $58.7 million in 1999. Sales totaled $1.91 billion, up 35.9% from $1.41 billion a year earlier. Operating income improved 48.0% to $222.7 million from $150.5 million in the prior year. Results benefited from strong performances from simulation and training products, data links, shipboard communications, aircraft products, ocean products and displays. Funded backlog at 12/31/00 was $1.35 billion, up 34.9% from $1.00 billion at 12/31/99.

PROSPECTS: Going forward, the Company will concentrate on growing its defense operations, mining technologies, adding businesses that fit both horizontally and vertically into LLL's operations and focusing on improving margins. On 1/3/01, the Company acquired Coleman Research Corporation, a provider of a full range of high-end services and products to military customers, for $60.0 million in cash, plus an additional $5.0 million if certain performance targets are achieved in 2001.

BUSINESS

L-3 COMMUNICATIONS HOLDINGS, INC. is a supplier of sophisticated secure communication systems and specialized communication products. LLL produces secure, high data rate communication systems, microwave components, avionics and ocean systems and telemetry, instrumentation and space products. LLL's systems and products are used to connect a variety of airborne, space, ground- and sea-based communication systems and are used in the transmission, processing, recording, monitoring and dissemination functions of these communication systems. The Company's customers include the U.S. Department of Defense, certain U.S. government intelligence agencies, major aerospace and defense contractors, foreign governments and commercial telecommunications and wireless customers. LLL acquired Aydin Corp. on 4/14/99.

ANNUAL FINANCIAL DATA

	12/31/00	12/31/99	12/31/98	12/31/97	12/31/96	12/31/95
Earnings Per Share	**2.37**	**1.75**	**1.26**	**[1] 0.61**	...	...
Cash Flow Per Share	**4.65**	**3.47**	**2.91**	**1.80**	...	...
INCOME STATEMENT (IN MILLIONS):						
Total Revenues	1,910.1	1,405.5	1,037.0	546.5	543.1	166.8
Costs & Expenses	1,607.4	1,197.4	893.8	471.4	471.3	150.6
Depreciation & Amort.	80.0	57.6	42.9	23.7	28.1	11.6
Operating Income	222.7	150.5	100.3	51.4	43.7	4.6
Net Interest Inc./(Exp.)	d93.0	d60.6	d46.9	d28.5	d24.2	d4.5
Income Before Income Taxes	134.1	95.4	53.5	23.0	19.5	0.2
Income Taxes	51.4	36.7	20.9	10.7	7.8	1.2
Net Income	82.7	58.7	32.6	[1] 12.3	11.7	d1.0
Cash Flow	162.7	116.3	75.5	36.0	39.8	10.6
Average Shs. Outstg. (000)	34,953	33,516	25,900	20,012	...	...
BALANCE SHEET (IN MILLIONS):						
Cash & Cash Equivalents	32.7	42.8	26.1	77.5	...	...
Total Current Assets	829.6	567.7	405.4	267.4	201.7	...
Net Property	156.1	141.0	123.2	83.0	91.6	...
Total Assets	2,463.5	1,633.8	1,285.4	703.4	593.3	...
Total Current Liabilities	468.7	318.3	247.5	135.6	102.9	...
Long-Term Obligations	1,095.0	605.0	605.0	392.0	...	...
Net Stockholders' Equity	692.6	583.2	300.0	113.7	473.6	...
Net Working Capital	360.9	249.4	157.8	131.8	98.8	...
Year-end Shs. Outstg. (000)	33,607	32,795	27,402	17,056	...	...
STATISTICAL RECORD:						
Operating Profit Margin %	11.7	10.7	9.7	9.4	8.0	2.8
Net Profit Margin %	4.3	4.2	3.1	2.3	2.2	...
Return on Equity %	11.9	10.1	10.9	10.8	2.5	...
Return on Assets %	3.4	3.6	2.5	1.7	2.0	...
Debt/Total Assets %	44.4	37.0	47.1	55.7	...	...
Price Range	79.31-35.69	54.25-34.25	49.50-25.56	...	...	...
P/E Ratio	33.5-15.1	31.0-19.6	39.3-20.3	...	...	...

Statistics are as originally reported. [1] Incl. $4.4 mil pre-tax non-recurr. chg.

OFFICERS:
F. C. Lanza, Chmn., C.E.O.
R. V. LaPenta, Pres., C.F.O.
L. W. O'Brien, V.P., Treas.

INVESTOR CONTACT: Cynthia Swain, V.P.-Corp. Comm., (212) 697-1111

PRINCIPAL OFFICE: 600 Third Ave., New York, NY 10016

TELEPHONE NUMBER: (212) 697-1111
FAX: (212) 805-5353
WEB: www.L-3Com.com

NO. OF EMPLOYEES: 14,000 (avg.)

SHAREHOLDERS: 152 (record)

ANNUAL MEETING: In April

INCORPORATED: DE, April, 1997

INSTITUTIONAL HOLDINGS:
No. of Institutions: 187
Shares Held: 27,570,195
% Held: 81.2

INDUSTRY: Radio & TV communications equipment (SIC: 3663)

TRANSFER AGENT(S): First Chicago Trust Company of New York, Jersey City, NJ

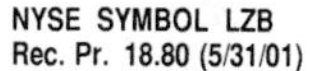

NYSE SYMBOL LZB
Rec. Pr. 18.80 (5/31/01)

LA-Z-BOY INCORPORATED

YIELD 1.9%
P/E RATIO 13.0

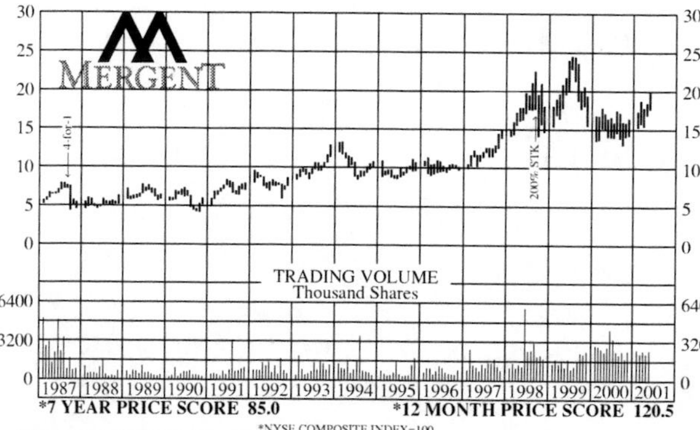

INTERIM EARNINGS (Per Share):

Qtr.	July	Oct.	Jan.	Apr.
1996-97	0.08	0.28	0.18	0.29
1997-98	0.03	0.31	0.21	0.37
1998-99	0.13	0.35	0.33	0.43
1999-00	0.25	0.44	0.41	0.49
2000-01	0.21	0.48	0.27	...

INTERIM DIVIDENDS (Per Share):

Amt.	Decl.	Ex.	Rec.	Pay.
0.08Q	5/09/00	5/24/00	5/26/00	6/09/00
0.09Q	8/01/00	8/23/00	8/25/00	9/08/00
0.09Q	11/16/00	11/22/00	11/27/00	12/08/00
0.09Q	2/12/01	2/21/01	2/23/01	3/09/01
0.09Q	5/11/01	5/23/01	5/25/01	6/08/01

Indicated div.: $0.36 (Div. Reinv. Plan)

CAPITALIZATION (4/29/00):

	($000)	(%)
Long-Term Debt	233,938	24.6
Capital Lease Obligations	2,156	0.2
Deferred Income Tax	50,280	5.3
Common & Surplus	663,092	69.8
Total	949,466	100.0

RECENT DEVELOPMENTS: For the quarter ended 1/27/01, net income decreased 24.5% to $16.1 million compared with $21.3 million in the year-earlier quarter. The decline in earnings was primarily attributed to higher interest expense, increased bad debt expense and weak demand from consumers. These declines were partially offset by growth from LZB's proprietary distribution, most notably the La-Z-Boy Furniture Galleries. Sales grew 41.0% to $531.4 million, primarily due to acquisitions.

PROSPECTS: LZB will close the Marion, Virginia plant of its Lea Industries division and the Selma, Alabama Pilliod facility as part of the restructuring of its manufacturing facilities. LZB will also eliminate the manufacturing of La-Z-Boy Contract furniture at its Lincolnton, North Carolina facility and will outsource some contract product lines. During fiscal 2002, the Company plans to add 25 to 30 new La-Z-Boy Furniture Galleries and further strengthen its in-store gallery programs at its various LZB divisions.

BUSINESS

LA-Z-BOY INCORPORATED (formerly La-Z-Boy Chair Company) is one of the largest furniture manufacturers in the U.S. The residential upholstery segment includes recliners, sofas, occasional chairs and reclining sofas. The residential casegoods segment includes dining room tables and chairs, bed frames and bed boards, dressers, coffee tables and end tables manufactured using hardwood or hardwood veneer. The contract segment manufactures and sells products to hospitality, business, government, healthcare and assisted living facilities. Brand names include LA-Z-BOY, ENGLAND, SAM MOORE, BAUHAUS, CENTURION, PENNSYLVANIA HOUSE, CLAYTON MARCUS, KINCAID, HAMMARY, ALEXVALE, AMERICAN DREW, HICKORY MARK, LA-Z-BOY CONTRACT FURNITURE, LEA, and PILLIOD. The Company operates 290 La-Z-Boy Furniture Galleries and 319 in-store galleries.

ANNUAL FINANCIAL DATA

	4/29/00	4/24/99	4/25/98	4/26/97	4/27/96	4/29/95	4/30/94
Earnings Per Share	**1.60**	**1.24**	**0.93**	**0.83**	**0.71**	**0.67**	**[1] 0.63**
Cash Flow Per Share	**2.15**	**1.66**	**1.32**	**1.21**	**1.07**	**0.95**	**0.89**
Tang. Book Val. Per Share	**6.70**	**7.03**	**6.33**	**5.97**	**5.49**	**5.06**	**4.92**
Dividends Per Share	**0.32**	**0.30**	**0.28**	**0.25**	**0.24**	**0.23**	**0.21**
Dividend Payout %	**20.0**	**24.2**	**30.1**	**30.4**	**33.9**	**33.8**	**32.6**
INCOME STATEMENT (IN MILLIONS):							
Total Revenues	1,717.4	1,287.6	1,108.0	1,005.8	947.3	850.3	804.9
Costs & Expenses	1,542.8	1,158.7	1,009.8	911.5	859.6	772.6	730.6
Depreciation & Amort.	30.3	22.1	21.0	20.4	20.1	15.2	14.0
Operating Income	144.3	106.8	77.2	73.9	67.5	62.5	60.3
Net Interest Inc./(Exp.)	d7.7	d2.3	d2.1	d2.6	d3.3	d1.7	d1.7
Income Before Income Taxes	140.3	107.2	79.3	73.8	66.2	62.0	58.2
Income Taxes	52.7	41.1	29.4	28.5	26.9	25.7	23.4
Net Income	87.6	66.1	49.9	45.3	39.3	36.3	[1] 34.7
Cash Flow	118.0	88.2	70.9	65.7	59.4	51.5	48.7
Average Shs. Outstg. (000)	54,860	53,148	53,821	54,324	55,494	54,132	54,804
BALANCE SHEET (IN MILLIONS):							
Cash & Cash Equivalents	14.4	33.6	28.7	25.4	27.1	27.0	25.9
Total Current Assets	692.4	425.6	383.0	342.8	337.1	325.4	295.6
Net Property	227.9	126.0	121.8	114.7	116.2	117.2	94.3
Total Assets	1,218.3	629.8	580.4	528.4	517.5	503.8	430.3
Total Current Liabilities	237.0	132.4	108.3	97.7	96.5	88.1	71.5
Long-Term Obligations	236.1	62.7	67.3	54.7	61.3	76.4	52.5
Net Stockholders' Equity	663.1	414.9	388.2	359.3	343.4	323.6	290.9
Net Working Capital	455.4	293.2	274.7	245.1	240.6	237.3	224.1
Year-end Shs. Outstg. (000)	61,328	52,340	53,551	53,724	55,155	55,686	54,861
STATISTICAL RECORD:							
Operating Profit Margin %	8.4	8.3	7.0	7.4	7.1	7.4	7.5
Net Profit Margin %	5.1	5.1	4.5	4.5	4.1	4.3	4.3
Return on Equity %	13.2	15.9	12.9	12.6	11.4	11.2	11.9
Return on Assets %	7.2	10.5	8.6	8.6	7.6	7.2	8.1
Debt/Total Assets %	19.4	10.0	11.6	10.3	11.8	15.2	12.2
Price Range	24.56-15.38	22.63-14.08	14.96-9.88	11.33-8.96	11.17-8.54	13.33-8.42	12.96-8.38
P/E Ratio	15.4-9.6	18.2-11.4	16.1-10.6	13.6-10.8	15.8-12.1	19.9-12.6	20.5-13.2
Average Yield %	1.6	1.6	2.3	2.5	2.4	2.1	1.9

Statistics are as originally reported. Adj. for stk split: 200%, 9/98. [1] Bef. acctg. change credit $3.4 mill.

OFFICERS:
P. H. Norton, Chmn.
G. L. Kiser, Pres., C.O.O.
D. M. Risley, Sr. V.P., C.F.O.

INVESTOR CONTACT: Gene M. Hardy, Sec., Treas., (734) 241-4414

PRINCIPAL OFFICE: 1284 North Telegraph Road, Monroe, MI 48162

TELEPHONE NUMBER: (734) 241-1444
FAX: (734) 241-4422
WEB: www.lazboy.com

NO. OF EMPLOYEES: 21,600 (approx.)

SHAREHOLDERS: 22,344

ANNUAL MEETING: In July

INCORPORATED: MI, May, 1941

INSTITUTIONAL HOLDINGS:
No. of Institutions: 110
Shares Held: 33,101,880
% Held: 54.9

INDUSTRY: Wood household furniture (SIC: 2511)

TRANSFER AGENT(S): American Stock Transfer & Trust Company, New York, NY

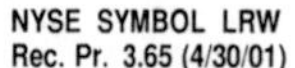

NYSE SYMBOL LRW
Rec. Pr. 3.65 (4/30/01)

LABOR READY, INC.

YIELD ...
P/E RATIO 15.2

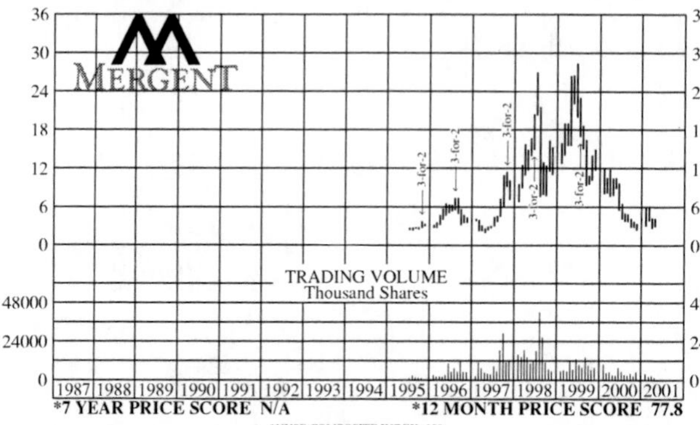

*7 YEAR PRICE SCORE N/A *12 MONTH PRICE SCORE 77.8

*NYSE COMPOSITE INDEX=100

INTERIM EARNINGS (Per Share):

Qtr.	Mar.	June	Sept.	Dec.
1996	d0.02	0.02	0.04	0.01
1997	d0.03	0.05	0.09	0.06
1998	0.01	0.08	0.20	0.18
1999	0.11	0.19	0.22	0.06
2000	d0.05	0.05	0.19	0.05

INTERIM DIVIDENDS (Per Share):

Amt.	Decl.	Ex.	Rec.	Pay.
3-for-2	6/10/99	7/13/99	6/24/99	7/12/99

CAPITALIZATION (12/31/00):

	($000)	(%)
Long-Term Debt	6,843	5.8
Common & Surplus	112,104	94.2
Total	118,947	100.0

RECENT DEVELOPMENTS: For the year ended 12/31/00, net income was $10.1 million versus income of $24.6 million, before an accounting charge, in the prior year. The decrease in earnings was attributed to higher operating expenses associated with the opening of new dispatch offices. Revenues from services advanced 14.8% to $976.6 million due to an increase in the number of high performance dispatch offices and a higher average billing rate, partially offset by lower billable hours at mature dispatch offices.

PROSPECTS: The Company continues to focus on improving the average sales per store and aligning expenses through new development projects and the closure of underperforming dispatch offices. Therefore, the Company will focus on opening new dispatch offices that will quickly reach or exceed the Company's performance standards. For 2001, the Company's development projects include the opening of at least 50 new Labor Ready and Service Ready dispatch offices.

BUSINESS

LABOR READY, INC. is a national provider of temporary workers for manual labor jobs. The Company's customers are primarily businesses in the construction, freight handling, warehousing, landscaping, light manufacturing and other light industrial markets. These businesses require workers for lifting, hauling, cleaning, assembling, digging, painting and other types of manual work. Over the past several years, LRW has been diversifying its customer base to include more customers in the retail, wholesale, sanitation, printing, and hospitality industries. The Company's dispatch offices are locations where workers as well as prospective workers report prior to being assigned jobs. As of 3/5/01, LRW operated 832 dispatch offices in 50 states, Canada, Puerto Rico and the United Kingdom.

ANNUAL FINANCIAL DATA

	12/31/00	12/31/99	12/31/98	12/31/97	12/31/96	12/31/95	12/31/94
Earnings Per Share	**0.24**	**2 0.53**	**0.46**	**0.17**	**1 0.05**	**0.07**	**0.04**
Cash Flow Per Share	**0.41**	**0.68**	**0.60**	**0.26**	**0.10**	**0.09**	**0.05**
Tang. Book Val. Per Share	**2.70**	**2.53**	**1.89**	**1.37**	**1.17**	**0.17**	**0.08**
INCOME STATEMENT (IN THOUSANDS):							
Total Revenues	976,573	850,873	606,895	335,409	163,450	94,362	38,951
Costs & Expenses	952,472	804,660	567,173	320,747	158,240	89,760	37,127
Depreciation & Amort.	7,380	4,804	6,076	4,011	1,797	522	178
Operating Income	16,721	41,409	33,646	10,651	3,413	4,080	1,645
Income Before Income Taxes	15,945	40,430	33,390	12,522	3,507	3,214	1,188
Income Taxes	5,886	15,853	13,591	5,559	1,585	1,152	336
Net Income	10,059	2 24,577	19,799	6,963	1 1,922	2,062	852
Cash Flow	17,373	29,338	25,789	10,974	3,676	2,542	980
Average Shs. Outstg.	42,508	43,456	42,999	42,251	36,649	29,674	22,089
BALANCE SHEET (IN THOUSANDS):							
Cash & Cash Equivalents	36,048	16,845	25,940	22,117	17,598	5,359	604
Total Current Assets	150,406	134,931	105,933	65,617	48,741	20,216	7,572
Net Property	43,402	30,732	20,271	10,326	7,825	2,851	827
Total Assets	205,423	174,481	130,736	80,367	64,331	26,182	8,912
Total Current Liabilities	56,247	37,197	34,842	15,788	11,505	7,956	5,631
Long-Term Obligations	6,843	6,590	5,073	76	90	9,695	319
Net Stockholders' Equity	112,104	111,136	80,497	58,041	51,592	8,531	2,962
Net Working Capital	94,159	97,734	71,091	49,828	37,236	12,260	1,941
Year-end Shs. Outstg.	40,941	42,802	41,961	41,493	41,761	44,645	25,171
STATISTICAL RECORD:							
Operating Profit Margin %	1.7	4.9	5.5	3.2	2.1	4.3	4.2
Net Profit Margin %	1.0	2.9	3.3	2.1	1.2	2.2	2.2
Return on Equity %	9.0	22.1	24.6	12.0	3.7	24.2	28.8
Return on Assets %	4.9	14.1	15.1	8.7	3.0	7.9	9.6
Debt/Total Assets %	3.3	3.8	3.9	0.1	0.1	37.0	3.6
Price Range	12.00-2.38	28.42-9.31	27.00-6.78	11.45-1.93	7.41-2.67	3.75-2.29	...
P/E Ratio	50.0-9.9	53.6-17.6	58.7-14.7	69.3-11.7	147.9-53.2	55.1-33.6	...

Statistics are as originally reported. Adj. for stk. splits: 3-for-2, 7/12/99, 6/9/98, 10/31/97, 8/9/96, 11/28/95 1 Bef. extraord. loss 12/31/96: $1.2 mill. 2 Bef. acctg. change chrg. of $1.5 mill.

OFFICERS:
R. Sullivan, Chmn.
R. King, Pres., C.E.O.
S. C. Cooper, Exec. V.P., C.F.O.
R. Junck, Exec. V.P., Sec., Gen. Couns.

INVESTOR CONTACT: Melanie DeBond, Investor Relations, (800) 640-8920

PRINCIPAL OFFICE: 1016 South 28th Street, Tacoma, WA 98409

TELEPHONE NUMBER: (253) 383-9101
FAX: (253) 383-9311
WEB: www.laborready.com

NO. OF EMPLOYEES: 3,250 (approx.)

SHAREHOLDERS: 716

ANNUAL MEETING: In Oct.

INCORPORATED: WA, Mar., 1985

INSTITUTIONAL HOLDINGS:
No. of Institutions: 66
Shares Held: 18,881,370
% Held: 46.2

INDUSTRY: Help supply services (SIC: 7363)

TRANSFER AGENT(S): American Securities Transfer & Trust, Lakewood, CO

NYSE SYMBOL LH
Rec. Pr. 63.13 (5/31/00)

LABORATORY CORPORATION OF AMERICA HOLDINGS INC.

YIELD ...
P/E RATIO 19.5

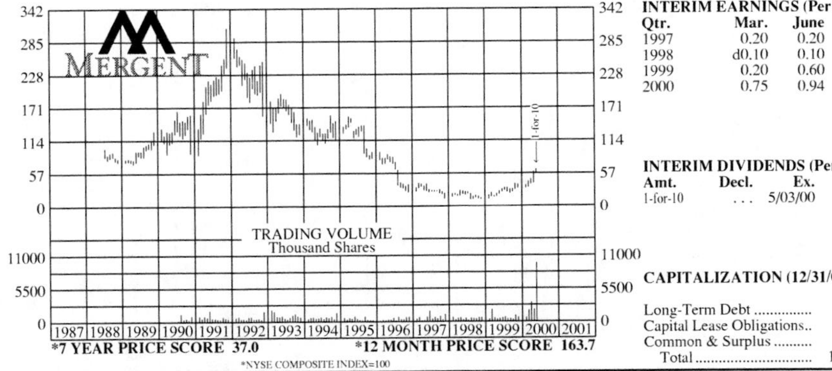

INTERIM EARNINGS (Per Share):

Qtr.	Mar.	June	Sept.	Dec.
1997	0.20	0.20	d0.50	d10.50
1998	d0.10	0.10	Nil	1.10
1999	0.20	0.60	0.30	0.10
2000	0.75	0.94	0.94	0.60

INTERIM DIVIDENDS (Per Share):

Amt.	Decl.	Ex.	Rec.	Pay.
1-for-10	...	5/03/00	...	...

CAPITALIZATION (12/31/00):

	($000)	(%)
Long-Term Debt	346,500	28.1
Capital Lease Obligations	7,200	0.6
Common & Surplus	877,400	71.3
Total	1,231,100	100.0

RECENT DEVELOPMENTS: For the year ended 12/31/00, net income amounted to $112.1 million, an increase of 71.4% from $65.4 million in the previous year. Results for 2000 included a pre-tax nonrecurring charge of $4.5 million related to the closure of a drug testing laboratory in Memphis, Tennessee. Net sales increased 13.0% to $1.92 billion compared with $1.70 billion the year before.

PROSPECTS: Revenues should benefit from increased volume and improved prices in each of the Company's business segments driven by strong demand for genomic testing. The Company will focus on the development of higher-value testing services to physicians and managed care companies, including esoteric testing services. Separately, the Company plans to complete its restructuring initiatives by the end of the second quarter of 2001.

BUSINESS

LABORATORY CORPORATION OF AMERICA HOLDINGS INC. was created by the merger of National Health Laboratories Holdings Inc. and Roche Biomedical Laboratories, Inc., a wholly-owned subsidiary of the Swiss-based Roche Holding Ltd. National Health Laboratories was the surviving corporation in the merger, which became effective on 4/28/95. The Company is a national clinical laboratory organization whose 25 major laboratories located nationwide perform a broad range of diagnostic tests for the diagnosis, monitoring and treatment of disease. Customers include physicians, managed-care organizations, hospitals, clinics, long-term care facilities, industrial companies and other clinical laboratories.

QUARTERLY DATA

(12/31/2000)($000)	Rev	Inc
1st Quarter	462,700	25,700
2nd Quarter	482,400	32,700
3rd Quarter	488,100	32,800
4th Quarter	486,100	20,900

ANNUAL FINANCIAL DATA

	12/31/00	12/31/99	12/31/98	12/31/97	12/31/96	12/31/95	[2] 12/31/94
Earnings Per Share	[7] 3.22	[6] 1.20	2.00	[5] d10.60	[4] d12.50	[3] d0.30	[1] 3.60
Cash Flow Per Share	6.94	7.73	8.70	d3.57	d5.61	6.19	8.79
Tang. Book Val. Per Share	0.34	...	...	...	...	...	...
INCOME STATEMENT (IN MILLIONS):							
Total Revenues	1,919.3	1,698.7	1,612.6	1,579.9	1,607.7	1,432.0	872.5
Costs & Expenses	1,584.1	1,464.5	1,400.8	1,585.1	1,642.0	1,292.4	739.2
Depreciation & Amort.	89.6	84.5	84.2	86.8	84.5	72.4	44.4
Operating Income	245.6	149.7	127.6	d92.0	d118.8	67.2	109.9
Net Interest Inc./(Exp.)	d38.5	d41.6	d48.7	d71.7	d71.7	d65.5	d34.5
Income Before Income Taxes	207.6	105.5	81.5	d161.3	d188.3	3.1	55.4
Income Taxes	95.5	40.1	12.7	cr54.4	cr34.8	7.1	25.3
Net Income	[7] 112.1	[6] 65.4	68.8	[5] d106.9	[4] d153.5	[3] d4.0	[1] 30.1
Cash Flow	167.1	99.5	108.6	d44.0	d69.0	68.4	74.5
Average Shs. Outstg. (000)	24,075	12,877	12,485	12,324	12,292	11,058	8,475
BALANCE SHEET (IN MILLIONS):							
Cash & Cash Equivalents	48.8	40.3	22.7	23.3	29.3	16.4	26.8
Total Current Assets	511.7	499.5	519.1	527.6	721.5	599.9	293.0
Net Property	272.8	273.2	259.1	254.9	282.9	304.8	140.1
Total Assets	1,666.9	1,590.2	1,640.9	1,658.5	1,917.0	1,837.2	1,012.7
Total Current Liabilities	311.9	245.6	251.4	196.6	252.8	350.5	202.8
Long-Term Obligations	353.7	482.8	575.5	689.6	1,261.6	940.1	563.8
Net Stockholders' Equity	877.4	175.5	154.4	129.1	258.1	411.6	166.0
Net Working Capital	199.8	253.9	267.7	331.0	468.7	249.4	90.2
Year-end Shs. Outstg. (000)	34,870	12,879	12,528	12,354	12,294	12,291	8,476
STATISTICAL RECORD:							
Operating Profit Margin %	12.8	8.8	7.9	...	...	4.7	12.6
Net Profit Margin %	5.8	3.9	4.3	...	...	...	3.4
Return on Equity %	12.8	37.3	44.6	...	...	...	18.1
Return on Assets %	6.7	4.1	4.2	...	...	...	3.0
Debt/Total Assets %	21.2	30.4	35.1	41.6	65.8	51.2	55.7
Price Range	63.75-31.25	38.75-12.50	27.50-11.25	40.00-13.13	93.75-23.75	155.00-81.25	157.50-106.25
P/E Ratio	19.8-9.7	32.3-10.4	13.7-5.6	...	...	...	43.7-29.5

Statistics are as originally reported. Adj. for 1-for-10 reverse stock split, 5/3/00 [1] Incl. one-time pre-tax chrgs. of $24.9 mill. [2] Results prior to 1995 reflect the operations of National Health Laboratories Holdings Inc. [3] Incl. pre-tax spec. chrg. of $90.0 mill. & bef. extraord. net chrg. of $8.3 mill. [4] Incl. spec. chrgs. of $218.0 mill. [5] Incl. pre-tax chrgs. of $160.0 mill. & $22.7 mill. [6] Incl. loss on sale of assets of $1.7 mill. [7] Incl. pre-tax nonrecurr. chrg. of $4.5 mill.

OFFICERS:
T. P. Mac Mahon, Chmn., Pres., C.E.O.
W. R. Elingburg, Exec. V.P., C.F.O., Treas.

INVESTOR CONTACT: Pamela J. Sherry, V.P. Inv. Rel., (336) 436-4855

PRINCIPAL OFFICE: 358 South Main Street, Burlington, NC 27215

TELEPHONE NUMBER: (336) 229-1127
FAX: (336) 229-7717
WEB: www.labcorp.com

NO. OF EMPLOYEES: 18,850 (approx.)

SHAREHOLDERS: 713

ANNUAL MEETING: In May

INCORPORATED: DE, Mar., 1991; reincorp., DE, June, 1994

INSTITUTIONAL HOLDINGS:
No. of Institutions: 77
Shares Held: 45,719,465
% Held: 35.2

INDUSTRY: Medical laboratories (SIC: 8071)

TRANSFER AGENT(S): American Stock Transfer & Trust Company, Brooklyn, NY

NYSE SYMBOL LG
Rec. Pr. 24.00 (4/30/01)

LACLEDE GAS COMPANY

YIELD 5.6%
P/E RATIO 13.0

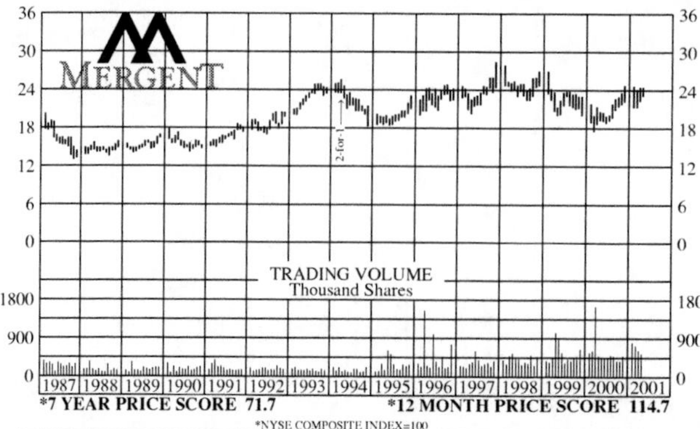

*7 YEAR PRICE SCORE 71.7 *12 MONTH PRICE SCORE 114.7

*NYSE COMPOSITE INDEX=100

INTERIM EARNINGS (Per Share):

Qtr.	Dec.	Mar.	June	Sept.
1997-98	0.78	1.04	d0.05	d0.18
1998-99	0.55	1.14	0.01	d0.21
1999-00	0.51	1.03	0.02	d0.18
2000-01	0.98	...	...	...

INTERIM DIVIDENDS (Per Share):

Amt.	Decl.	Ex.	Rec.	Pay.
0.335Q	5/25/00	6/08/00	6/12/00	7/03/00
0.335Q	8/24/00	9/07/00	9/11/00	10/02/00
0.335Q	11/16/00	12/07/00	12/11/00	1/02/01
0.335Q	2/22/01	3/08/01	3/12/01	4/02/01
0.335Q	5/24/01	6/07/01	6/11/01	7/02/01

Indicated div.: $1.34 (Div. Reinv. Plan)

CAPITALIZATION (9/30/00):

	($000)	(%)
Deferred Income Tax	134,944	32.2
Redeemable Pfd. Stock	1,763	0.4
Common & Surplus	282,985	67.4
Total	419,692	100.0

RECENT DEVELOPMENTS: For the first quarter ended 12/31/00, net income surged 93.3% to $18.5 million versus $9.6 million in the comparable prior-year period. Earnings benefited from a 45.0% increase in the amount of gas used by the Company's customers due to weather that was 28.0% colder than normal and 56.0% colder year over year. Total operating revenues more than doubled to $345.0 million compared with $151.4 million in the prior year.

PROSPECTS: On 1/25/01, LG announced that its shareholders approved the formation of Laclede Group, Inc., a parent holding company. The reorganization will allow for separation of LEA's utility operations and non-utility operations. Laclede Gas will become a wholly-owned subsidiary of the Laclede Group Inc. and will continue to operate as a regulated natural gas distribution utility.

BUSINESS

LACLEDE GAS COMPANY is a public utility engaged in the retail distribution and transportation of natural gas. The Company serves an area in eastern Missouri that includes the City of St. Louis with a population of about 2.0 million. As an adjunct to its gas distribution business, the Company operates underground natural gas storage fields and is engaged in the transportation and storage of liquid propane. LG is also involved in the exploration and development of natural gas on a utility and non-utility basis. The Company has also made investments in other non-utility businesses as part of a diversification program. In 2000, revenues were derived as follows: 65.2% residential, 23.3% commercial and industrial, and 11.5% other.

REVENUES

(9/30/2000)	($000)	(%)
Utility	531,152	93.8
Non-Utility	34,976	6.2
Total	566,128	100.0

ANNUAL FINANCIAL DATA

	9/30/00	9/30/99	9/30/98	9/30/97	9/30/96	9/30/95	9/30/94
Earnings Per Share	**1.37**	**[1] 1.43**	**1.58**	**1.84**	**1.87**	**1.27**	**1.42**
Cash Flow Per Share	**2.69**	**2.62**	**3.02**	**3.32**	**3.30**	**2.72**	**2.66**
Tang. Book Val. Per Share	**14.99**	**14.96**	**14.57**	**14.26**	**13.72**	**13.05**	**12.44**
Dividends Per Share	**1.34**	**1.34**	**1.32**	**1.30**	**1.26**	**1.24**	**1.22**
Dividend Payout %	**97.8**	**93.7**	**83.5**	**70.6**	**67.4**	**97.6**	**85.9**
INCOME STATEMENT (IN THOUSANDS):							
Total Revenues	566,128	491,588	547,229	602,832	544,816	431,917	523,866
Costs & Expenses	459,293	388,924	441,562	491,017	435,894	342,473	435,987
Depreciation & Amort.	24,875	21,592	25,403	25,923	25,037	23,728	19,393
Maintenance Exp.	18,644	19,583	18,665	18,205	18,127	17,508	18,351
Operating Income	63,316	61,489	46,666	49,725	46,395	38,330	37,618
Net Interest Inc./(Exp.)	d24,008	d20,593	d21,270	d19,088	d17,947	d18,527	d16,394
Income Taxes	14,105	14,361	14,933	17,962	17,348	9,878	12,517
Net Income	25,965	[1] 26,062	27,892	32,466	32,824	20,901	22,217
Cash Flow	50,747	47,557	53,198	58,292	57,764	44,532	41,513
Average Shs. Outstg.	18,878	18,138	17,598	17,558	17,523	16,344	15,619
BALANCE SHEET (IN THOUSANDS):							
Gross Property	921,378	876,431	833,685	792,661	780,001	745,629	709,563
Accumulated Depreciation	372,545	357,053	343,100	325,088	327,836	311,293	297,886
Net Property	548,833	519,378	490,585	467,573	452,165	434,336	411,677
Total Assets	931,740	831,619	771,147	720,710	689,395	636,694	608,295
Long-Term Obligations	...	204,323	179,238	154,413	179,346	154,279	154,211
Net Stockholders' Equity	282,985	282,324	256,785	250,387	240,843	227,253	194,939
Year-end Shs. Outstg.	18,878	18,878	17,628	17,558	17,558	17,420	15,670
STATISTICAL RECORD:							
Operating Profit Margin %	11.2	12.5	8.5	8.2	8.5	8.9	7.2
Net Profit Margin %	4.6	5.3	5.1	5.4	6.0	4.8	4.2
Net Inc./Net Property %	4.7	5.0	5.7	6.9	7.3	4.8	5.4
Net Inc./Tot. Capital %	6.2	4.2	5.2	6.6	6.6	4.5	5.2
Return on Equity %	9.2	9.2	10.9	13.0	13.6	9.2	11.4
Accum. Depr./Gross Prop. %	40.4	40.7	41.2	41.0	42.0	41.7	42.0
Price Range	24.75-17.50	27.00-20.00	27.94-22.38	28.50-20.25	24.88-20.00	23.13-18.38	25.63-18.25
P/E Ratio	18.1-12.8	18.9-14.0	17.7-14.2	15.5-11.0	13.3-10.7	18.2-14.5	18.0-12.9
Average Yield %	6.3	5.7	5.2	5.3	5.6	6.0	5.6

Statistics are as originally reported. Adj. for a 2-for-1 stock split, 3/94. [1] Incl. a non-recurr. after-tax chrg. of $2.0 mill. resulting from LG's minority participation in Clark Enterprises.

OFFICERS:
D. H. Yaeger, Chmn., Pres., C.E.O.
R. L. Krutzman, Treas., Asst. Sec.
L. D. Rawlings, Asst. Treas.

INVESTOR CONTACT: Mary C. Kullman, Sec. & Assoc. Couns., (314) 342-0500

PRINCIPAL OFFICE: 720 Olive Street, St. Louis, MO 63101

TELEPHONE NUMBER: (314) 342-0500
FAX: (314) 421-1979
WEB: www.lacledegas.com

NO. OF EMPLOYEES: 1,985 full-time; 4 part-time

SHAREHOLDERS: 8,541

ANNUAL MEETING: In Jan.

INCORPORATED: MO, Mar., 1857

INSTITUTIONAL HOLDINGS:
No. of Institutions: 89
Shares Held: 4,706,708
% Held: 24.9

INDUSTRY: Natural gas distribution (SIC: 4924)

TRANSFER AGENT(S): UMB Bank, N.A., Kansas City, MO

NYSE SYMBOL LAF
Rec. Pr. 32.77 (5/31/01)

LAFARGE CORPORATION

YIELD 1.8%
P/E RATIO 9.4

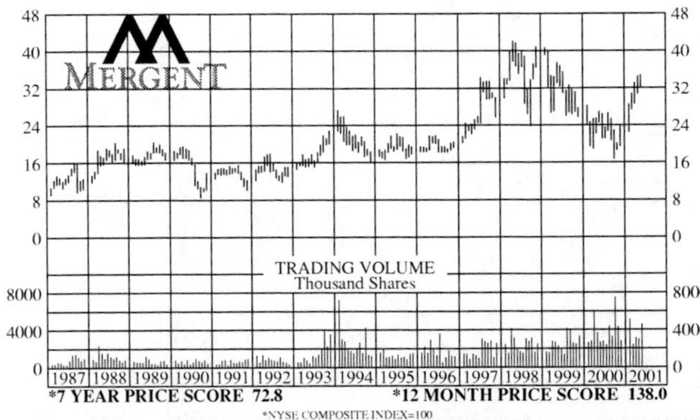

INTERIM EARNINGS (Per Share):

Qtr.	Mar.	June	Sept.	Dec.
1997	d0.48	0.84	1.35	0.82
1998	d0.39	1.17	1.70	0.91
1999	d0.40	1.22	1.90	1.05
2000	d0.34	1.30	1.72	0.81

INTERIM DIVIDENDS (Per Share):

Amt.	Decl.	Ex.	Rec.	Pay.
0.15Q	5/02/00	5/11/00	5/15/00	6/01/00
0.15Q	7/25/00	8/11/00	8/15/00	9/01/00
0.15Q	10/27/00	11/09/00	11/13/00	12/01/00
0.15Q	2/13/01	2/20/01	2/22/01	3/01/01
0.15Q	5/08/01	5/16/01	5/18/01	6/01/01

Indicated div.: $0.60 (Div. Reinv. Plan)

CAPITALIZATION (12/31/00):

	($000)	(%)
Long-Term Debt	687,448	23.7
Deferred Income Tax	206,067	7.1
Minority Interest	117,010	4.0
Preferred Stock	34,402	1.2
Common & Surplus	1,857,767	64.0
Total	2,902,694	100.0

RECENT DEVELOPMENTS: For the year ended 12/31/00, net income decreased 6.5% to $257.4 million compared with $275.4 million in 1999. The decline in earnings was primarily attributed to heavy snowfall and extremely cold weather, as well as operating losses in the gypsum drywall business. Total net sales were $2.79 billion, up 2.4% from $2.72 billion a year earlier. Comparisons were made with restated 1999 results.

PROSPECTS: LAF expects earnings to improve in 2001, as most sectors of construction in the U.S. still appear to be fairly strong. Residential construction, which is expected to weaken in 2001, should benefit from the recent reduction in interest rates. As the only nationwide supplier of construction materials in Canda, LAF also is encouraged by projections that the economy in Canada will grow faster than that of the U.S. this year, aided in part by a new round of tax cuts.

BUSINESS

LAFARGE CORPORATION is one of North America's largest diversified suppliers of cement, aggregates and concrete, gypsum wallboard and other materials for residential, commercial, institutional and public works construction. The Company operates 15 cement plants, approximately 800 construction materials operations, five gypsum wallboard manufacturing facilities and other businesses in 44 states in the U.S. and all provinces of Canada. The Company's majority shareholder is Lafarge S.A. of Paris, France.

BUSINESS LINE ANALYSIS

(12/31/2000)	Rev(%)	Inc(%)
Construction Materials	56.5	39.0
Cement	38.7	64.6
Gypsum	4.8	(3.6)
Total	100.0	100.0

ANNUAL FINANCIAL DATA

	12/31/00	12/31/99	12/31/98	12/31/97	12/31/96	12/31/95	12/31/94
Earnings Per Share	**3.51**	**3.77**	**3.24**	**2.54**	**2.02**	**1.88**	**1.18**
Cash Flow Per Share	**5.80**	**6.08**	**5.40**	**4.02**	**3.46**	**3.25**	**2.70**
Tang. Book Val. Per Share	**19.71**	**18.50**	**14.19**	**16.47**	**16.37**	**14.85**	**12.76**
Dividends Per Share	**0.60**	**0.60**	**0.51**	**0.42**	**0.40**	**0.38**	**0.30**
Dividend Payout %	**17.1**	**15.9**	**15.7**	**16.5**	**19.8**	**19.9**	**25.4**
INCOME STATEMENT (IN MILLIONS):							
Total Revenues	2,787.6	2,654.4	2,448.2	1,806.4	1,649.3	1,472.2	1,563.3
Costs & Expenses	2,217.6	2,013.0	1,876.6	1,389.9	1,305.8	1,196.0	1,314.4
Depreciation & Amort.	168.3	168.3	156.8	106.3	100.5	94.3	103.6
Operating Income	401.7	473.1	414.8	310.2	243.0	181.9	145.2
Net Interest Inc./(Exp.)	d26.9	d44.8	d27.2	d6.7	d14.0	d15.2	d28.8
Income Before Income Taxes	403.8	436.8	379.8	294.2	222.3	166.7	116.4
Income Taxes	146.5	161.4	144.3	112.3	81.5	52.3	64.5
Net Income	257.4	275.4	235.5	182.0	140.9	114.4	51.9
Cash Flow	425.7	443.6	392.3	288.3	241.4	223.9	184.2
Average Shs. Outstg. (000)	73,379	73,022	72,665	71,780	69,783	68,984	68,254
BALANCE SHEET (IN MILLIONS):							
Cash & Cash Equivalents	214.1	329.4	288.2	318.4	209.3	221.0	243.6
Total Current Assets	1,076.6	1,135.5	937.9	816.0	732.2	718.5	707.1
Net Property	2,122.4	1,618.3	1,400.8	876.7	867.7	797.0	751.9
Total Assets	3,902.6	3,304.2	2,904.8	1,899.1	1,813.0	1,713.9	1,651.4
Total Current Liabilities	740.5	510.2	415.0	295.7	337.4	269.9	304.8
Long-Term Obligations	687.4	719.8	751.2	132.3	161.9	268.6	290.7
Net Stockholders' Equity	1,892.2	1,722.9	1,415.2	1,255.7	1,110.5	981.0	841.5
Net Working Capital	336.1	625.3	522.9	520.2	394.9	448.6	402.3
Year-end Shs. Outstg. (000)	72,000	73,200	72,300	71,780	62,600	60,700	59,700
STATISTICAL RECORD:							
Operating Profit Margin %	14.4	17.8	16.9	17.2	14.7	12.4	9.3
Net Profit Margin %	9.2	10.4	9.6	10.1	8.5	8.8	5.2
Return on Equity %	13.6	16.0	16.6	14.5	12.7	13.2	9.6
Return on Assets %	6.6	8.3	8.1	9.6	7.8	7.6	4.9
Debt/Total Assets %	17.6	21.8	25.9	7.0	8.9	15.7	17.6
Price Range	28.25-16.69	40.75-25.69	42.13-23.75	34.31-20.13	21.88-18.13	22.25-16.63	27.25-16.25
P/E Ratio	8.0-4.8	10.8-6.8	13.0-7.3	13.5-7.9	10.8-9.0	11.8-8.8	23.1-13.8
Average Yield %	2.7	1.8	1.5	1.5	2.0	1.9	1.4

Statistics are as originally reported.

OFFICERS:
B. P. Collomb, Chmn.
B. L. Kasriel, Vice-Chmn.
J. M. Piecuch, Pres., C.E.O.
L. J. Waisanen, Exec. V.P., C.F.O.

INVESTOR CONTACT: Larry J. Waisanen, Exec. V.P., C.F.O., (703) 264-3670

PRINCIPAL OFFICE: 11130 Sunrise Valley Drive, Suite 300, Reston, VA 20170

TELEPHONE NUMBER: (703) 264-3600
FAX: (703) 264-1636
WEB: www.lafargecorp.com

NO. OF EMPLOYEES: 14,300 (approx.)

SHAREHOLDERS: 3,523

ANNUAL MEETING: In May

INCORPORATED: MD, Apr., 1977

INSTITUTIONAL HOLDINGS:
No. of Institutions: 119
Shares Held: 24,101,785
% Held: 33.5

INDUSTRY: Cement, hydraulic (SIC: 3241)

TRANSFER AGENT(S): Wachovia Bank of North Carolina, N.A., Boston, MA

NYSE SYMBOL LMS
Rec. Pr. 10.48 (5/31/01)

LAMSON & SESSIONS CO. (THE)

YIELD ...
P/E RATIO 6.8

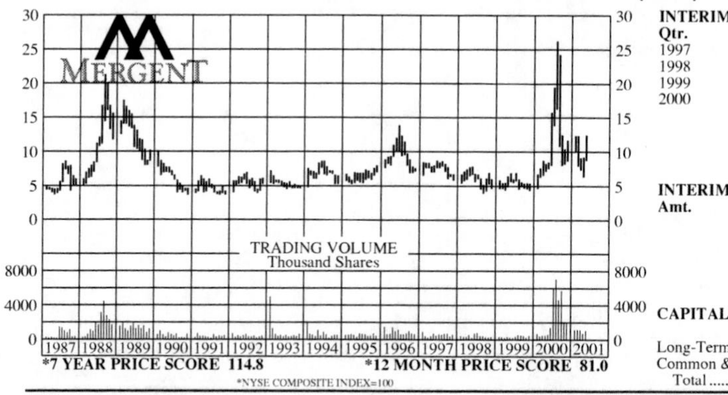

INTERIM EARNINGS (Per Share):

Qtr.	Mar.	June	Sept.	Dec.
1997	0.16	0.15	d0.42	d0.24
1998	d0.02	0.17	0.27	0.08
1999	0.20	0.13	0.28	0.78
2000	0.35	0.52	0.48	0.19

INTERIM DIVIDENDS (Per Share):

Amt.	Decl.	Ex.	Rec.	Pay.

No dividends paid.

CAPITALIZATION (12/30/00):

	($000)	(%)
Long-Term Debt	130,276	60.2
Common & Surplus	86,029	39.8
Total	216,305	100.0

RECENT DEVELOPMENTS: For the year ended 12/30/00, net income increased 14.2% to $21.4 million compared with $18.8 million in 1999. Net sales were $348.7 million, up 19.7% from $291.4 million in 1999. The improvement in sales was primarily attributed to acquisitions, the strong economy in the first nine months of the year and significant growth in the Company's key markets. Gross profit as a percentage of net sales rose significantly to 25.4% versus 21.1% in 1999.

PROSPECTS: The Company is experiencing poor market conditions, particularly in the telecommunications market. However, housing starts and housing permits indicate continued strength within the residential and commercial construction markets, which provides consistent support for LMS' electrical products. For the full-year 2001, net sales are expected to range from $460.0 million to $470.0 million, which represents a 32.0% to 35.0% rate of growth over 2000.

BUSINESS

THE LAMSON & SESSIONS CO. is a diversified manufacturer and distributor of a broad line of thermoplastic electrical, consumer, telecommunications and fluid drainage products for major domestic markets. The Carlon segment (41% of 2000 revenues), includes industrial, residential, commercial, telecommunications and utility construction. The principal products sold by this segment include electrical and wire raceway systems and a broad line of nonmetallic enclosures, outlet boxes and electrical fittings. The PVC Pipe segment (41%) supplies electrical, power and communications conduits to the electrical distribution, retail, power utility and telecommunications markets. Lamson Home Products (18%) serves home centers and mass merchandisers for the do-it-yourself home repair market. The products included in this segment are light dimmers, fan speed controls, touch controls, wireless door chimes, motion sensors and home secuity systems.

ANNUAL FINANCIAL DATA

	12/30/00	1/1/00	1/2/99	1/3/98	12/28/96	12/30/95	12/31/94
Earnings Per Share	**1.53**	**4 1.39**	**3 0.50**	**2 d0.35**	**1.02**	**0.91**	**1 0.32**
Cash Flow Per Share	**2.34**	**2.15**	**1.23**	**0.30**	**1.68**	**1.57**	**0.97**
Tang. Book Val. Per Share	**...**	**4.71**	**3.28**	**2.76**	**3.37**	**2.33**	**0.97**
INCOME STATEMENT (IN THOUSANDS):							
Total Revenues	348,733	291,381	270,914	271,780	289,052	299,166	287,645
Costs & Expenses	303,017	267,899	252,037	265,556	268,143	276,370	268,172
Depreciation & Amort.	11,229	10,136	9,957	8,719	8,770	8,758	8,544
Operating Income	34,487	13,346	8,920	d2,495	12,139	14,038	10,929
Net Interest Inc./(Exp.)	d4,539	d3,558	d4,341	d3,768	d2,611	d5,864	d6,673
Income Before Income Taxes	29,948	9,788	4,579	d6,263	9,528	8,174	4,256
Income Taxes	8,500	cr9,000	cr2,100	cr1,550	cr4,100	cr3,900	...
Net Income	21,448	4 18,788	3 6,679	2 d4,713	13,628	12,074	1 4,256
Cash Flow	32,677	28,924	16,636	4,006	22,398	20,832	12,800
Average Shs. Outstg.	13,989	13,482	13,488	13,349	13,297	13,288	13,236
BALANCE SHEET (IN THOUSANDS):							
Cash & Cash Equivalents	1,452	2,724	1,937	1,410	758	1,431	1,885
Total Current Assets	134,906	94,704	83,975	91,567	90,945	81,044	87,526
Net Property	65,297	48,093	50,735	56,329	60,473	51,747	53,979
Total Assets	320,293	183,319	160,667	162,494	161,121	135,471	147,146
Total Current Liabilities	76,656	56,223	47,278	57,580	51,906	49,584	52,032
Long-Term Obligations	130,276	36,919	40,807	44,712	36,911	24,842	46,958
Net Stockholders' Equity	86,029	63,369	44,131	36,981	44,787	30,919	12,880
Net Working Capital	58,250	38,481	36,697	33,987	39,039	31,460	35,494
Year-end Shs. Outstg.	13,697	13,453	13,445	13,414	13,301	13,292	13,279
STATISTICAL RECORD:							
Operating Profit Margin %	9.9	4.6	3.3	...	4.2	4.7	3.8
Net Profit Margin %	6.2	6.4	2.5	...	4.7	4.0	1.5
Return on Equity %	24.9	29.6	15.1	...	30.4	39.1	33.0
Return on Assets %	6.7	10.2	4.2	...	8.5	8.9	2.9
Debt/Total Assets %	40.7	20.1	25.4	27.5	22.9	18.3	31.9
Price Range	26.25-4.63	6.94-4.31	7.88-3.88	8.75-5.81	13.88-6.88	8.00-5.25	8.63-4.75
P/E Ratio	17.2-3.0	5.0-3.1	15.7-7.7	...	13.6-6.7	8.8-5.8	26.9-14.8

Statistics are as originally reported. 1 Bef. loss from discont. operations of $9.9 mill. 2 Bef. acctg. chrg. of $4.9 mill. 3 Incl. divestiture costs and a restruct. chrg. totaling $1.5 mill. 4 Incl. restruct. chrg. of $2.1 mill.

OFFICERS:
J. B. Schulze, Chmn., Pres., C.E.O.
J. J. Abel, Exec. V.P., C.F.O., Treas., Sec.

INVESTOR CONTACT: Investor Relations, (800) 321-1970

PRINCIPAL OFFICE: 25701 Science Park Drive, Cleveland, OH 44122-7313

TELEPHONE NUMBER: (216) 464-3400
FAX: (216) 464-1455
WEB: www.lamson-sessions.com

NO. OF EMPLOYEES: 1,246 (avg.)

SHAREHOLDERS: 1,377 (approx. record)

ANNUAL MEETING: In Apr.

INCORPORATED: OH, Nov., 1883

INSTITUTIONAL HOLDINGS:
No. of Institutions: 29
Shares Held: 7,131,609
% Held: 52.0

INDUSTRY: Current-carrying wiring devices (SIC: 3643)

TRANSFER AGENT(S): National City Bank, Corporate Trust Department, Cleveland, OH

NYSE SYMBOL LFG
Rec. Pr. 30.00 (4/30/01)

LANDAMERICA FINANCIAL GROUP, INC.

YIELD 0.7%
P/E RATIO ...

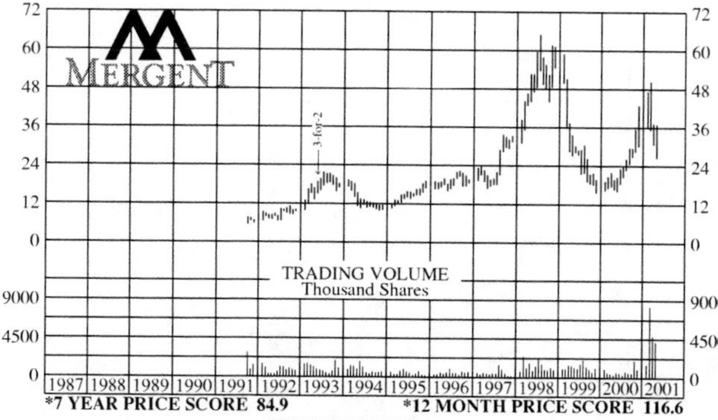

INTERIM EARNINGS (Per Share):

Qtr.	Mar.	June	Sept.	Dec.
1998	0.35	1.42	1.51	1.42
1999	0.73	0.86	0.48	0.70
2000	d0.30	0.97	0.43	d7.88

INTERIM DIVIDENDS (Per Share):

Amt.	Decl.	Ex.	Rec.	Pay.
0.05Q	5/17/00	5/30/00	6/01/00	6/15/00
0.05Q	7/28/00	8/30/00	9/01/00	9/15/00
0.05Q	10/26/00	11/29/00	12/01/00	12/15/00
0.05Q	2/22/01	2/27/01	3/01/01	3/15/01
0.05Q	4/30/01	5/30/01	6/01/01	6/15/01

Indicated div.: $0.20

CAPITALIZATION (12/31/00):

	($000)	(%)
Preferred Stock	175,700	26.5
Common & Surplus	488,400	73.5
Total	664,100	100.0

RECENT DEVELOPMENTS: For the year ended 12/31/00, net loss totaled $80.8 million versus net income of $54.3 million in 1999. Results for 2000 included write-off of intangibles costs of $177.8 million and termination costs of $3.1 million. Total revenues declined 12.0% to $1.80 billion versus $2.05 billion in 1999. Total title and other operating revenues declined 12.4% to $1.75 billion. Investment income climbed 3.7% to $51.4 million. LFG reported losses on sales of investments in 2000 and 1999 of $271,000 and $1.6 million, respectively.

PROSPECTS: Going forward, the Company will continue to focus on expanding its LandAmerica Onestop business to cover major metropolitan markets throughout the United States. On 5/15/01, LandAmerica OneStop completed the acquisition of Curry Carter & Associates, an Atlanta-based commercial appraisal firm. Separately on 5/10/01, LandAmerica OneStop announced a strategic alliance with Mortgage Information Source, Inc. to provide mortgage and equity lending clients with a complete line of residential mortgage credit reports.

BUSINESS

LANDAMERICA FINANCIAL GROUP, INC. is engaged in the business of issuing title insurance policies and performing other real estate-related services for both residential and commercial real estate transactions. The Company issues title insurance policies through its various title underwriting subsidiaries. The Company's three principal title underwriting subsidiaries are Commonwealth Land Title Insurance Company, Lawyers Title Insurance Corporation and Transnation Title Insurance Company. In addition, the Company provides escrow and closing services to a broad-based customer group that includes lenders, developers, real estate agents, attorneys and home buyers and sellers. The Company also offers a full range of residential real estate services to the national and regional mortgage lending community through its LandAmerica OneStop operation.

ANNUAL FINANCIAL DATA

	12/31/00	12/31/99	12/31/98	12/31/97	12/31/96	12/31/95	12/31/94
Earnings Per Share	**[1] d6.60**	**2.79**	**[2] 5.05**	**2.84**	**4.11**	**1.92**	**0.80**
Tang. Book Val. Per Share	**20.05**	**15.19**	**16.14**	**26.18**	**22.78**	**20.79**	**17.53**
Dividends Per Share	**0.20**	**0.20**	**0.20**	**0.20**	**0.20**	**0.18**	**0.12**
Dividend Payout %	**...**	**7.2**	**4.0**	**7.0**	**4.9**	**9.4**	**15.0**
INCOME STATEMENT (IN MILLIONS):							
Total Premium Income	1,751.3	2,000.0	1,799.5	622.8	456.4	385.9	413.9
Other Income	51.1	48.0	49.3	16.3	137.8	97.0	87.1
Total Revenues	1,802.4	2,048.0	1,848.9	639.1	594.2	482.8	501.0
Income Before Income Taxes	d128.1	84.9	146.3	40.5	55.5	23.9	9.0
Income Taxes	cr47.4	30.6	53.3	14.3	19.0	6.8	2.2
Net Income	[1] d80.8	54.3	[2] 93.0	26.2	36.5	17.1	6.8
Average Shs. Outstg. (000)	13,397	19,503	18,421	9,224	8,888	8,885	8,494
BALANCE SHEET (IN MILLIONS):							
Cash & Cash Equivalents	123.4	164.0	174.0	70.0	95.6	40.6	104.6
Premiums Due	52.3	52.5	68.5	37.0	23.1	25.1	29.5
Invst. Assets: Fixed-term	796.8	735.1	774.9	261.1	218.2	187.3	171.4
Invst. Assets: Equities	3.2	1.8	4.2	1.7	1.7	56.5	47.4
Invst. Assets: Loans	9.7	7.1	11.6	0.4	0.5	1.0	1.2
Invst. Assets: Total	890.7	853.1	895.5	297.6	292.1	266.6	308.8
Total Assets	1,619.0	1,657.9	1,692.4	554.7	521.0	475.8	525.9
Net Stockholders' Equity	664.1	730.7	771.2	292.4	262.2	238.4	203.3
Year-end Shs. Outstg. (000)	13,518	13,680	15,295	8,965	8,890	8,886	8,885
STATISTICAL RECORD:							
Return on Revenues %	...	2.7	5.0	4.1	6.1	3.5	1.4
Return on Equity %	...	7.4	12.1	8.9	13.9	7.2	3.4
Return on Assets %	...	3.3	5.5	4.7	7.0	3.6	1.3
Price Range	42.94-16.06	58.94-15.56	65.00-31.00	33.69-16.75	22.38-16.00	19.25-10.50	19.50-9.75
P/E Ratio	...	21.1-5.6	12.9-6.1	11.9-5.9	5.4-3.9	10.0-5.5	24.4-12.2
Average Yield %	0.7	0.5	0.4	0.8	1.0	1.2	0.8

Statistics are as originally reported. [1] Incl. exit and termination costs of $3.1 mill. and write-off of intangibles of $177.8 mill. [2] Incl. assimilation costs of $11.5 mill.

OFFICERS:
C. H. Foster Jr., Chmn., C.E.O.
J. A. Alpert, Pres.
G. W. Evans, Exec. V.P., C.F.O.

INVESTOR CONTACT: G. W. Evans, Exec. V.P., C.F.O., (804) 267-8114

PRINCIPAL OFFICE: 101 Gateway Centre Parkway, Richmond, VA 23235-5153

TELEPHONE NUMBER: (804) 267-8000
FAX: (804) 267-8833
WEB: www.landam.com
NO. OF EMPLOYEES: 8,100 full-time; 539 part-time
SHAREHOLDERS: 1,463 (approx.)
ANNUAL MEETING: In May
INCORPORATED: VA, June, 1991

INSTITUTIONAL HOLDINGS:
No. of Institutions: 152
Shares Held: 14,424,810
% Held: 80.2

INDUSTRY: Title insurance (SIC: 6361)

TRANSFER AGENT(S): EquiServe, L.P., Canton, MA

NYSE SYMBOL LE
Rec. Pr. 35.88 (5/31/01)

LANDS' END, INC.

YIELD ...
P/E RATIO 30.7

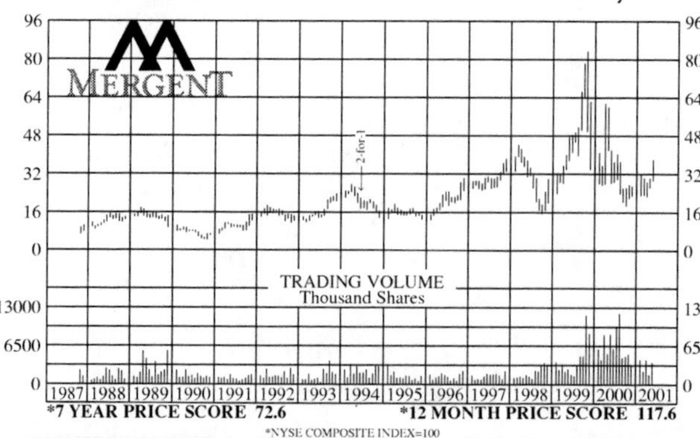

*7 YEAR PRICE SCORE 72.6 *12 MONTH PRICE SCORE 117.6
*NYSE COMPOSITE INDEX=100

INTERIM EARNINGS (Per Share):

Qtr.	Apr.	July	Oct.	Jan.
1996-97	0.13	0.09	0.19	1.15
1997-98	0.35	0.11	0.26	1.33
1998-99	0.17	Nil	0.01	0.84
1999-00	0.21	0.14	0.28	0.92
2000-01	0.01	d0.06	0.15	1.07

INTERIM DIVIDENDS (Per Share):

Amt.	Decl.	Ex.	Rec.	Pay.

Last dist. $0.20Q, 12/29/93

CAPITALIZATION (1/26/01):

	($000)	(%)
Deferred Income Tax	14,567	4.4
Common & Surplus	314,188	95.6
Total	328,755	100.0

RECENT DEVELOPMENTS: For the year ended 1/26/01, net income totaled $34.7 million, down 27.8% compared with $48.0 million in the prior year. Results in the prior year included a pre-tax non-recurring gain of $1.8 million. Total revenue grew 3.2% to $1.46 billion from $1.42 billion a year earlier. Gross profit was $621.7 million, or 42.5% of net sales, versus $589.8 million, or 41.6% of net sales, the year before. Prior-year revenue and gross profit were restated to reflect the reclassification of shipping and handling revenue and expense.

PROSPECTS: The Company anticipates sales growth in the single-digit range in the current fiscal year, due to uncertain economic conditions in the U.S. A shift in the timing of LE's end-of-season clearance catalog is helping boost sales early in the first quarter. Gross profit margin is expected to continue to improve during the year fueled by lower liquidations and improved product sourcing. In addition, the Company is targeting earnings per share growth of at least 20.0% in the fiscal year ending on 2/1/02.

BUSINESS

LANDS' END, INC. is a direct marketer of traditionally styled apparel, accessories, domestics, shoes and soft luggage for men, women and children. The Company offers its products through regular mailings of its monthly and specialty catalogs, via the Internet, and through operations in Japan, the United Kingdom and Germany. LE offers certain basic product lines including knit shirts, sweaters, dress and sport shirts, and trousers. All goods, except soft luggage, are purchased from independent manufacturers. The Company mailed about 269 million catalogs worldwide in fiscal 2001. Approximately 85% to 90% of catalog orders are placed through the Company's toll-free number, which is available 24 hours a day, seven days a week.

ANNUAL FINANCIAL DATA

	1/26/01	1/28/00	1/29/99	1/30/98	1/31/97	2/2/96	1/27/95
Earnings Per Share	**1.14**	**[1] 1.56**	**[1] 1.01**	**[1] 2.00**	**[1] 1.54**	**[1] 0.89**	**[1] 1.03**
Cash Flow Per Share	**1.91**	**2.23**	**1.62**	**2.47**	**1.95**	**1.26**	**1.32**
Tang. Book Val. Per Share	**10.71**	**9.79**	**8.07**	**7.81**	**6.80**	**5.91**	**5.36**
INCOME STATEMENT (IN MILLIONS):							
Total Revenues	1,462.3	1,319.8	1,371.4	1,263.6	1,118.7	1,031.5	992.1
Costs & Expenses	1,377.2	1,220.2	1,293.0	1,149.9	1,021.4	969.9	922.0
Depreciation & Amort.	23.4	20.7	18.7	15.1	13.6	12.5	10.3
Operating Income	61.7	78.9	59.7	98.6	83.8	49.2	59.8
Net Interest Inc./(Exp.)	0.7	d1.0	d7.7	d0.3	0.6	d2.5	d1.5
Income Before Income Taxes	55.0	76.2	49.5	101.8	84.9	50.9	59.7
Income Taxes	20.4	28.2	18.3	37.7	34.0	20.4	23.6
Net Income	34.7	[1] 48.0	[1] 31.2	[1] 64.2	[1] 51.0	[1] 30.6	[1] 36.1
Cash Flow	58.1	68.7	49.9	79.3	64.5	43.0	46.4
Average Shs. Outstg. (000)	30,422	30,854	30,763	32,132	33,100	34,200	35,200
BALANCE SHEET (IN MILLIONS):							
Cash & Cash Equivalents	75.4	76.4	6.6	6.3	92.8	17.2	5.4
Total Current Assets	321.7	289.4	294.3	299.1	272.0	222.1	198.2
Net Property	185.3	165.8	160.6	133.4	103.7	99.0	97.0
Total Assets	507.6	456.2	455.9	433.5	378.0	323.5	297.6
Total Current Liabilities	178.9	150.9	205.3	182.0	145.6	114.7	102.7
Net Stockholders' Equity	314.2	296.2	242.5	242.7	223.0	201.2	189.1
Net Working Capital	142.8	138.5	89.0	117.1	126.5	107.3	95.5
Year-end Shs. Outstg. (000)	29,276	30,150	29,904	30,940	32,443	33,660	34,826
STATISTICAL RECORD:							
Operating Profit Margin %	4.2	6.0	4.4	7.8	7.5	4.8	6.0
Net Profit Margin %	2.4	3.6	2.3	5.1	4.6	3.0	3.6
Return on Equity %	11.0	16.2	12.9	26.4	22.8	15.2	19.1
Return on Assets %	6.8	10.5	6.8	14.8	13.5	9.4	12.1
Price Range	61.50-18.70	83.50-23.75	44.25-15.44	38.50-25.13	30.25-12.75	19.50-12.88	27.75-13.63
P/E Ratio	53.9-16.4	53.5-15.2	43.8-15.3	19.2-12.6	19.6-8.3	21.9-14.5	26.9-13.2

Statistics are as originally reported. [1] Incl. $1.8 mil non-recurr. gain, 2000; $7.9 mil ($0.26/sh) net non-recurr. chg., 1999; $4.9 mil ($0.15/sh) gain, 1998; $840,000 ($0.03/sh) chg., 1997; $1.1 mil ($0.03/sh) chg. 1996; & $2.1 mil ($0.06/sh), 1995.

OFFICERS:
G. C. Comer, Chmn.
D. F. Dyer, Pres., C.E.O.
S. A. Orum, Exec. V.P., C.F.O.

INVESTOR CONTACT: Charlotte LaComb, Investor Relations, (608) 935-4835

PRINCIPAL OFFICE: Lands' End Lane, Dodgeville, WI 53595

TELEPHONE NUMBER: (608) 935-9341
FAX: (608) 935-4786
WEB: www.landsend.com
NO. OF EMPLOYEES: 4,700 (approx.)
SHAREHOLDERS: 1,927
ANNUAL MEETING: In May
INCORPORATED: IL, 1963; reincorp., DE, Aug., 1986

INSTITUTIONAL HOLDINGS:
No. of Institutions: 98
Shares Held: 8,160,892
% Held: 27.8

INDUSTRY: Catalog and mail-order houses (SIC: 5961)

TRANSFER AGENT(S): Firstar Trust Company, Milwaukee, WI

NYSE SYMBOL LEA
Rec. Pr. 34.88 (5/31/01)

LEAR CORPORATION

YIELD ...
P/E RATIO 8.4

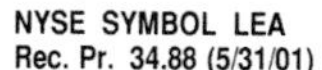

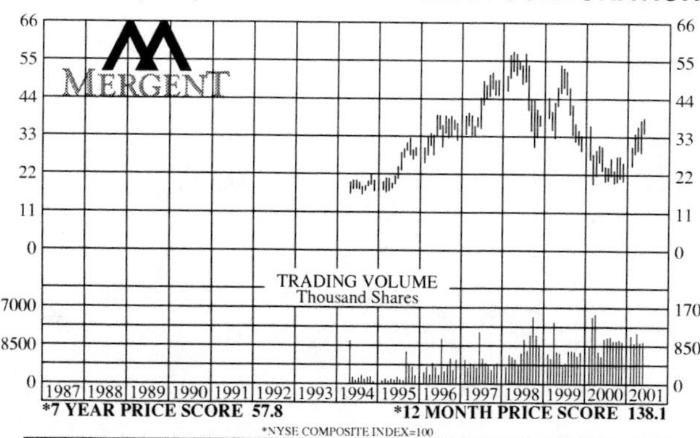

INTERIM EARNINGS (Per Share):

Qtr.	Mar.	June	Sept.	Dec.
1996	0.43	0.83	0.37	0.75
1997	0.62	0.89	0.53	1.00
1998	0.69	0.96	0.32	d0.28
1999	0.75	1.10	0.58	1.37
2000	0.93	1.53	0.59	1.12

INTERIM DIVIDENDS (Per Share):

Amt.	Decl.	Ex.	Rec.	Pay.
No dividends paid.				

CAPITALIZATION (12/31/00):

	($000)	(%)
Long-Term Debt	2,852,100	64.1
Common & Surplus	1,600,800	35.9
Total	4,452,900	100.0

RECENT DEVELOPMENTS: For the year ended 12/31/00, net income increased 6.8% to $274.7 million versus $257.1 million in the previous year. The 2000 results included a net after-tax gain of $1.9 million from the sale of assets. Results for 1999 included a $4.4 million restructuring credit. Net sales rose 13.2% to $14.07 billion due to higher volumes from new programs, partially offset by unfavorable currency exchange and divestitures. Operating income advanced 17.1% to $835.4 million.

PROSPECTS: In December 2000, the Company completed the sale of four European plastic and metal manufacturing facilities located in Italy and Sweden for approximately $30.0 million. The sale enabled the Company to repurchase approximately 3.3 million shares of its common stock. Meanwhile, revenues should benefit from the Company's $3.50 billion backlog of new business. For 2001, the Company anticipates earnings growth to be in the range of 3.0% to 5.0% per share.

BUSINESS

LEAR CORPORATION is a worldwide supplier of complete automotive interior systems. The Company engineers, develops, manufactures and markets automotive interior products including seating systems, floor and acoustic systems, door panels, headliners, and instrument panels. The Company is able to offer its customers design, engineering and project management support for the entire automotive interior. LEA's major customers include Ford, General Motors, DaimlerChrysler, Fiat, Volvo, Saab, Volkswagen and BMW. As of 5/7/01, LEA operated more than 300 manufacturing facilities in 32 countries.

QUARTERLY DATA

(12/31/00)($000)	REV	INC
1st Quarter	3,805,100	62,000
2nd Quarter	3,761,400	101,700
3rd Quarter	3,144,100	38,600
4th Quarter	3,362,200	72,400

ANNUAL FINANCIAL DATA

	12/31/00	12/31/99	12/31/98	12/31/97	12/31/96	12/31/95	12/31/94
Earnings Per Share	**[3] 4.17**	**[2] 3.80**	**1.70**	**[1] 3.05**	**2.38**	**[1] 1.79**	**1.26**
Cash Flow Per Share	**10.13**	**8.83**	**4.93**	**5.75**	**4.67**	**3.60**	**2.49**
INCOME STATEMENT (IN MILLIONS):							
Total Revenues	14,072.8	12,428.8	9,059.4	7,342.9	6,249.1	4,714.4	3,147.5
Costs & Expenses	12,845.2	11,374.6	8,497.5	6,677.4	5,727.6	4,374.9	2,919.4
Depreciation & Amort.	392.2	340.9	219.7	184.4	145.7	94.7	58.5
Operating Income	835.4	713.3	342.2	481.1	375.8	244.8	169.6
Net Interest Inc./(Exp.)	d316.2	d235.1	d110.5	d101.0	d102.8	d75.5	d46.7
Income Before Income Taxes	484.2	443.0	214.8	345.8	253.4	152.9	114.6
Income Taxes	197.3	174.0	93.9	143.1	101.5	63.1	55.0
Equity Earnings/Minority Int.	d12.2	d11.9	d5.4	5.5	...	4.4	0.2
Net Income	[3] 274.7	[2] 257.1	115.5	[1] 208.2	151.9	[1] 94.2	59.8
Cash Flow	666.9	598.0	335.2	392.6	297.6	188.9	118.3
Average Shs. Outstg. (000)	65,841	67,743	68,023	68,249	63,762	52,489	47,438
BALANCE SHEET (IN MILLIONS):							
Cash & Cash Equivalents	98.8	106.9	30.0	12.9	26.0	34.1	32.0
Total Current Assets	2,828.0	3,154.2	2,198.0	1,614.9	1,347.4	1,207.2	818.3
Net Property	1,891.3	1,970.0	1,182.3	939.1	866.3	642.8	354.2
Total Assets	8,375.5	8,717.6	5,677.3	4,459.1	3,816.8	3,061.3	1,715.1
Total Current Liabilities	3,371.6	3,487.4	2,497.5	1,854.0	1,499.3	1,276.0	981.2
Long-Term Obligations	2,852.1	3,324.8	1,463.4	1,063.1	1,054.8	1,038.0	418.7
Net Stockholders' Equity	1,600.8	1,465.3	1,300.0	1,207.0	1,018.7	580.0	213.6
Net Working Capital	d543.6	d333.2	d299.5	d239.1	d151.9	d68.8	d162.9
Year-end Shs. Outstg. (000)	63,554	66,600	66,684	56,642	65,576	56,243	46,069
STATISTICAL RECORD:							
Operating Profit Margin %	5.9	5.7	3.8	6.6	6.0	5.2	5.4
Net Profit Margin %	2.0	2.1	1.3	2.8	2.4	2.0	1.9
Return on Equity %	17.2	17.5	8.9	17.2	14.9	16.2	28.0
Return on Assets %	3.3	2.9	2.0	4.7	4.0	3.1	3.5
Debt/Total Assets %	34.1	38.1	25.8	23.8	27.6	33.9	24.4
Price Range	36.25-19.25	53.94-28.75	57.75-29.81	51.69-33.25	39.25-25.25	32.50-16.63	22.13-16.00
P/E Ratio	8.7-4.6	14.2-7.6	34.0-17.5	16.9-10.9	16.5-10.6	18.2-9.3	17.6-12.7

Statistics are as originally reported. [1] Bef. extraord. chrg. for early retire of debt. $1.0 mill., 1997; $2.6 mill., 1995. [2] Incl. restruct. credit of $4.4 mill. [3] Incl. gain of $36.6 mill. fr. sale of assets.

OFFICERS:
K. L. Way, Chmn.
J. H. Vandenberghe, Vice-Chmn.
R. E. Rossiter, Pres., C.E.O.
D. Stebbins, Sr. V.P., C.F.O.

INVESTOR CONTACT: Investor Relations, (800) 413-5327

PRINCIPAL OFFICE: 21557 Telegraph Road, Southfield, MI 48086-5008

TELEPHONE NUMBER: (248) 447-1500
FAX: (248) 447-1722
WEB: www.lear.com

NO. OF EMPLOYEES: 121,600 (approx.)

SHAREHOLDERS: 1,155 (record)

ANNUAL MEETING: In May

INCORPORATED: DE, Aug., 1988

INSTITUTIONAL HOLDINGS:
No. of Institutions: 201
Shares Held: 57,776,846
% Held: 90.7

INDUSTRY: Motor vehicle supplies and new parts (SIC: 5013)

TRANSFER AGENT(S): Bank of New York, New York, NY

NYSE SYMBOL LEE
Rec. Pr. 31.10 (4/30/01)

LEE ENTERPRISES, INC.

YIELD 2.2%
P/E RATIO 21.2

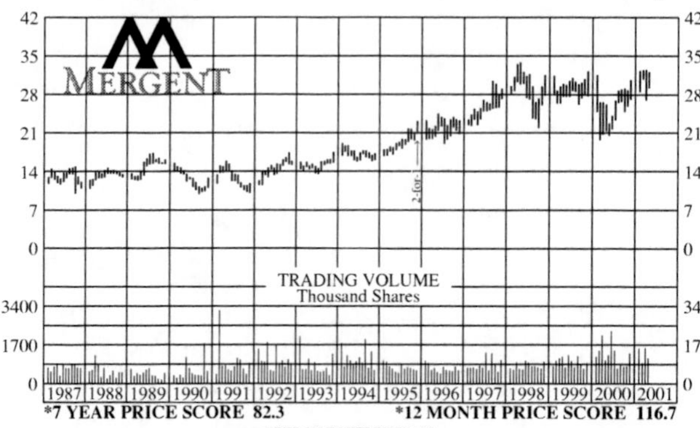

INTERIM EARNINGS (Per Share):

Qtr.	Dec.	Mar.	June	Sept.
1996-97	0.40	0.24	0.38	0.31
1997-98	0.36	0.28	0.40	0.33
1998-99	0.44	0.27	0.43	0.38
1999-00	0.68	0.27	0.36	0.36
2000-01	0.48	...	...	...

INTERIM DIVIDENDS (Per Share):

Amt.	Decl.	Ex.	Rec.	Pay.
0.16Q	7/17/00	8/30/00	9/01/00	9/29/00
0.17Q	11/15/00	11/29/00	12/01/00	1/02/01
0.17Q	1/23/01	2/27/01	3/01/01	4/02/01
0.17Q	5/17/01	5/30/01	6/01/01	7/02/01

Indicated div.: $0.68 (Div. Reinv. Plan)

CAPITALIZATION (9/30/00):

	($000)	(%)
Long-Term Debt	173,400	28.2
Deferred Income Tax	46,621	7.6
Common & Surplus	395,167	64.2
Total	615,188	100.0

RECENT DEVELOPMENTS: For the three months ended 12/31/00, income from continuing operations fell 20.4% to $21.0 million compared with $26.4 million in the equivalent quarter of 1999. Results for 2000 and 1999 excluded an after-tax gain of $250.9 million and $4.1 million, respectively, from discontinued operations. Total operating revenue was $118.6 million, up 9.1% from $108.7 million in the prior-year period.

PROSPECTS: The Company plans to sell KMAZ-TV in El Paso, Texas to Council Tree Hispanic Broadcasters, LLC of Longmont, Colorado. The sale is strategically in line with the Company's plans to exit television broadcasting and focus on newspaper publishing and related on-line services. The transaction is subject to regulatory approvals and is expected to be completed by mid-2001.

BUSINESS

LEE ENTERPRISES, INC. is a diversified media company operating primarily in the Midwest, West, Pacific Northwest and Southwestern United States. The Company's principal business is newspaper publishing. As of 12/31/00, LEE owned and operated nine full-service network affiliated television stations and seven satellite television stations and published 23 daily and more than 100 other weekly, classified, shopper or specialty publications. In fiscal 2000, revenues were as follows: advertising, 65.4%; circulation, 19.1%; and other, 15.5%. The Company acquired five classified or specialty publications and one commercial printer in 1998. Also, LEE owns a 50% interest in Madison Newspapers, Inc.

ANNUAL FINANCIAL DATA

	9/30/00	9/30/99	9/30/98	9/30/97	9/30/96	9/30/95	9/30/94
Earnings Per Share	**[3] 1.58**	**1.52**	**1.37**	**[2] 1.33**	**[1] 1.12**	**1.24**	**1.09**
Cash Flow Per Share	**2.51**	**2.40**	**2.19**	**1.95**	**1.79**	**1.80**	**1.59**
Tang. Book Val. Per Share	**1.43**	...	...	...	**1.68**	...	**0.36**
Dividends Per Share	**0.64**	**0.60**	**0.56**	**0.52**	**0.48**	**0.44**	**0.42**
Dividend Payout %	**40.5**	**39.5**	**40.9**	**39.1**	**42.9**	**35.5**	**38.5**
INCOME STATEMENT (IN THOUSANDS):							
Total Revenues	431,513	536,333	517,293	446,686	427,369	443,188	402,551
Costs & Expenses	287,783	379,845	366,870	312,954	300,469	313,782	283,578
Depreciation & Amort.	41,263	39,748	37,576	29,581	32,159	25,974	23,496
Operating Income	102,467	116,740	112,847	104,151	94,741	103,432	95,477
Net Interest Inc./(Exp.)	d9,384	d10,943	d12,715	d2,929	d7,039	d8,198	d10,592
Income Before Income Taxes	110,215	106,535	100,132	101,222	87,702	95,234	84,885
Income Taxes	40,340	38,562	37,899	38,477	34,032	36,775	34,031
Net Income	[3] 69,875	67,973	62,233	[2] 62,745	[1] 53,670	58,459	50,854
Cash Flow	111,138	107,721	99,809	92,326	85,829	84,433	74,350
Average Shs. Outstg.	44,360	44,861	45,557	47,312	47,991	46,962	46,850
BALANCE SHEET (IN THOUSANDS):							
Cash & Cash Equivalents	29,427	10,536	16,941	14,163	19,267	10,883	57,643
Total Current Assets	251,566	102,543	99,591	93,967	146,708	104,509	135,707
Net Property	127,356	139,203	128,372	120,026	104,705	108,196	82,164
Total Assets	746,233	679,513	660,585	650,963	527,416	559,929	474,701
Total Current Liabilities	117,627	79,448	98,061	248,908	97,777	116,527	99,730
Long-Term Obligations	173,400	187,005	186,028	26,174	52,290	75,511	98,641
Net Stockholders' Equity	395,167	354,329	319,759	319,390	324,954	311,042	241,930
Net Working Capital	133,939	23,095	1,530	d154,941	48,931	d12,018	35,977
Year-end Shs. Outstg.	43,810	44,259	44,350	45,508	47,022	47,366	45,520
STATISTICAL RECORD:							
Operating Profit Margin %	23.7	21.8	21.8	23.3	22.2	23.3	23.7
Net Profit Margin %	16.2	12.7	12.0	14.0	12.6	13.2	12.6
Return on Equity %	17.7	19.2	19.5	19.6	16.5	18.8	21.0
Return on Assets %	9.4	10.0	9.4	9.6	10.2	10.4	10.7
Debt/Total Assets %	23.2	27.5	28.2	4.0	9.9	13.5	20.8
Price Range	31.56-19.69	32.25-26.13	33.88-21.81	30.50-22.25	24.50-19.00	23.13-16.75	19.13-15.75
P/E Ratio	20.0-12.5	21.2-17.2	24.7-15.9	22.9-16.7	21.9-17.0	18.6-13.5	17.5-14.4
Average Yield %	2.5	2.1	2.0	2.0	2.2	2.2	2.4

Statistics are as originally reported. Adj. for 2-for-1 stock split, 12/95. [1] Excl. $7.7 mill. ($0.16/sh) income fr. disc. ops. [2] Excl. $1.0 mill. ($0.02/sh) income fr. disc. ops. [3] Excl. $13.8 mill. net income fr. disc. ops., 2000; $250.9 mill., 2001.

OFFICERS:
R. D. Gottlieb, Chmn.
M. E. Junck, Pres., C.E.O.
C. G. Schmidt, V.P., C.F.O., Treas.

INVESTOR CONTACT: Chris Wahlig, V.P., C.A.O., (319) 383-2176

PRINCIPAL OFFICE: 215 N. Main Street, Davenport, IA 52801

TELEPHONE NUMBER: (319) 383-2100
FAX: (319) 326-2972
WEB: www.lee.net

NO. OF EMPLOYEES: 4,500 full-time (approx.); 1,400 part-time (approx.)

SHAREHOLDERS: 3,185 (common); 2,064 (class B common)

ANNUAL MEETING: In Jan.

INCORPORATED: DE, Sept., 1950

INSTITUTIONAL HOLDINGS:
No. of Institutions: 132
Shares Held: 22,764,543
% Held: 51.9

INDUSTRY: Newspapers (SIC: 2711)

TRANSFER AGENT(S): EquiServe First Chicago Trust Division, Jersey City, NJ

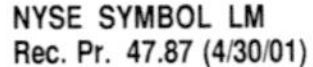

NYSE SYMBOL LM
Rec. Pr. 47.87 (4/30/01)

LEGG MASON, INC.

YIELD	0.8%
P/E RATIO	18.8

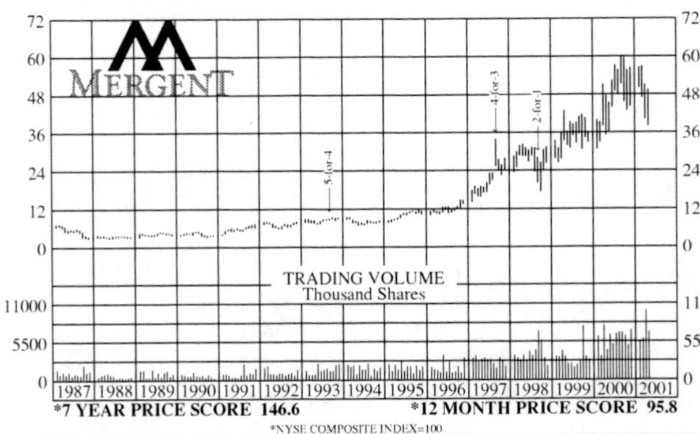

*7 YEAR PRICE SCORE 146.6 *12 MONTH PRICE SCORE 95.8

*NYSE COMPOSITE INDEX=100

INTERIM EARNINGS (Per Share):

Qtr.	June	Sept.	Dec.	Mar.
1996-97	0.30	0.30	0.31	0.28
1997-98	0.31	0.36	0.39	0.40
1998-99	0.42	0.37	0.39	0.43
1999-00	0.54	0.47	0.55	0.78
2000-01	0.60	0.55	0.61	...

INTERIM DIVIDENDS (Per Share):

Amt.	Decl.	Ex.	Rec.	Pay.
0.08Q	4/25/00	6/09/00	6/13/00	7/10/00
0.09Q	7/25/00	10/03/00	10/05/00	10/23/00
0.09Q	10/24/00	12/11/00	12/13/00	1/08/01
0.09Q	1/23/01	3/06/01	3/08/01	4/09/01
0.09Q	4/24/01	6/08/01	6/12/01	7/09/01

Indicated div.: $0.36

CAPITALIZATION (3/31/00):

	($000)	(%)
Long-Term Debt	99,723	11.7
Common & Surplus	751,929	88.3
Total	851,652	100.0

RECENT DEVELOPMENTS: For the quarter ended 12/31/00, net income grew 16.9% to $41.3 million from $35.3 million in the prior-year period. Net revenues grew 11.4% to $349.1 million from $313.3 million the year before. Investment advisory and related fees increased 15.3% to $165.6 million. Comparisons were made with restated 1999 figures to reflect the acquisition of Perigee, Inc.

PROSPECTS: On 2/5/01, LM acquired Barrett Associates, Inc. for $19.0 million. Under the terms of the agreement, LM acquired 70.0% of Barrett at closing and will acquire the remaining 30.0% over the next five years for an additional amount of up to $22.5 million. Barrett manages approximately $2.00 billion for high net worth individuals, families, endowments and foundations.

BUSINESS

LEGG MASON, INC. provides securities brokerage, investment advisory, corporate and public finance, and mortgage banking services to individuals, institutions, corporations and municipalities. The Company serves brokerage clients through 120 offices. As investment advisors, the Company manages approximately $136.90 billion in assets as of 12/31/00. LM's mortgage-banking subsidiaries have direct and master servicing responsibility for commercial mortgages.

BUSINESS LINE ANALYSIS

(03/31/00)	Rev(%)	Inc(%)
Asset Management	28.2	47.8
Private Client	55.8	46.3
Capital Markets	13.0	3.7
Other	3.0	2.1
Total	100.0	100.0

ANNUAL FINANCIAL DATA

	3/31/00	3/31/99	3/31/98	3/31/97	3/31/96	3/31/95	3/31/94
Earnings Per Share	**2.33**	**1.55**	**1.32**	**1.17**	**0.93**	**[1] 0.49**	**1.12**
Cash Flow Per Share	**2.83**	**1.92**	**1.69**	**1.53**	**1.28**	**0.80**	**1.37**
Tang. Book Val. Per Share	**10.60**	**8.83**	**7.97**	**7.33**	**5.64**	**4.71**	**6.01**
Dividends Per Share	**0.28**	**0.23**	**0.20**	**0.18**	**0.17**	**0.15**	**0.13**
Dividend Payout %	**11.8**	**14.8**	**15.3**	**15.7**	**18.1**	**31.6**	**11.4**
INCOME STATEMENT (IN MILLIONS):							
Total Revenues	1,370.8	1,046.0	889.1	639.7	516.0	371.6	397.5
Costs & Expenses	991.7	682.2	594.4	425.1	354.9	267.3	276.3
Depreciation & Amort.	29.3	21.6	22.0	17.2	14.2	10.5	8.3
Operating Income	349.7	342.2	272.7	197.3	146.9	93.8	112.9
Net Interest Inc./(Exp.)	d134.3	d94.9	d73.7	d43.4	d26.2	d17.1	d15.4
Income Before Income Taxes	239.1	148.8	128.4	95.2	63.9	27.7	59.2
Income Taxes	96.6	59.4	52.3	38.6	26.0	11.4	23.2
Net Income	142.5	89.3	76.1	56.6	37.9	[1] 16.3	36.0
Cash Flow	171.8	110.9	98.1	73.8	52.1	26.7	44.4
Average Shs. Outstg. (000)	60,787	57,657	58,006	48,157	40,728	33,411	32,293
BALANCE SHEET (IN MILLIONS):							
Cash & Cash Equivalents	2,058.1	1,740.6	1,334.3	793.1	450.1	173.9	294.9
Total Current Assets	3,813.4	2,805.9	2,129.2	1,399.4	932.7	532.7	607.8
Net Property	60.5	55.8	52.0	35.8	33.3	25.9	15.7
Total Assets	4,785.1	3,473.7	2,832.3	1,879.0	1,314.5	816.7	811.5
Total Current Liabilities	3,771.9	2,718.4	2,147.2	1,303.4	798.0	451.3	457.3
Long-Term Obligations	99.7	99.7	99.6	99.6	167.5	102.5	102.5
Net Stockholders' Equity	751.9	554.2	500.1	418.6	298.9	226.5	211.7
Net Working Capital	41.5	87.5	d18.1	96.0	134.7	81.4	150.5
Year-end Shs. Outstg. (000)	58,599	56,376	55,050	48,723	41,021	32,667	31,293
STATISTICAL RECORD:							
Operating Profit Margin %	25.5	32.7	30.7	30.8	28.5	25.2	28.4
Net Profit Margin %	10.4	8.5	8.6	8.8	7.3	4.4	9.1
Return on Equity %	19.0	16.1	15.2	13.5	12.7	7.2	17.0
Return on Assets %	3.0	2.6	2.7	3.0	2.9	2.0	4.4
Debt/Total Assets %	2.1	2.9	3.5	5.3	12.7	12.5	12.6
Price Range	42.88-26.44	32.28-17.31	33.97-14.16	14.77-9.94	11.77-7.69	9.47-6.80	9.47-7.28
P/E Ratio	18.4-11.3	20.8-11.2	25.8-10.8	12.6-8.5	12.7-8.3	19.4-14.0	8.5-6.5
Average Yield %	0.8	0.9	0.8	1.5	1.7	1.9	1.5

Statistics are as originally reported. Adj. for 2-for-1 split, 9/98; 4-for-3 split, 9/97. [1] Incl. $2.0 mill. ($0.06 sh.) pre-tax chg. for litigation.

OFFICERS:
R. A. Mason, Chmn., Pres., C.E.O.
C. J. Daley Jr., C.F.O.
T. L. Souders, Sr. V.P., Treas.
R. F. Price, Sr. V.P., Gen. Couns.

INVESTOR CONTACT: F. Barry Bilson, Investor Relations, (410) 539-0000

PRINCIPAL OFFICE: 100 Light Street, Baltimore, MD 21202

TELEPHONE NUMBER: (410) 539-0000
FAX: (410) 539-8010
WEB: www.leggmason.com

NO. OF EMPLOYEES: 4,820 (approx.)

SHAREHOLDERS: 2,202

ANNUAL MEETING: In July

INCORPORATED: MD, 1981

INSTITUTIONAL HOLDINGS:
No. of Institutions: 171
Shares Held: 39,358,740
% Held: 63.2

INDUSTRY: Security brokers and dealers (SIC: 6211)

TRANSFER AGENT(S): First Union National Bank, Charlotte, NC

NYSE SYMBOL LEG
Rec. Pr. 21.92 (5/31/01)

LEGGETT & PLATT, INCORPORATED

YIELD 2.2%
P/E RATIO 16.6

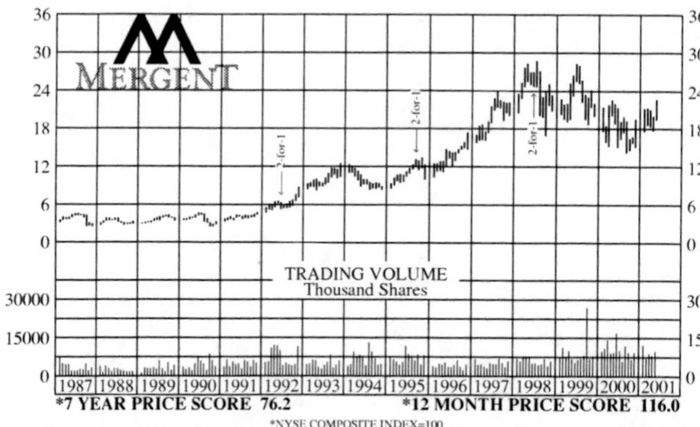

*7 YEAR PRICE SCORE 76.2 *12 MONTH PRICE SCORE 116.0

*NYSE COMPOSITE INDEX=100

INTERIM EARNINGS (Per Share):

Qtr.	Mar.	June	Sept.	Dec.
1997	0.26	0.28	0.27	0.28
1998	0.29	0.32	0.32	0.31
1999	0.33	0.36	0.39	0.37
2000	0.37	0.38	0.34	0.23

INTERIM DIVIDENDS (Per Share):

Amt.	Decl.	Ex.	Rec.	Pay.
0.10Q	5/03/00	5/17/00	5/19/00	6/15/00
0.11Q	8/09/00	8/23/00	8/25/00	9/15/00
0.11Q	11/09/00	11/21/00	11/24/00	1/02/01
0.12Q	2/14/01	2/28/01	3/02/01	3/15/01
0.12Q	5/09/01	5/23/01	5/25/01	6/15/01

Indicated div.: $0.48

CAPITALIZATION (12/31/00):

	($000)	(%)
Long-Term Debt	988,400	34.6
Deferred Income Tax	71,900	2.5
Common & Surplus	1,793,800	62.8
Total	2,854,100	100.0

RECENT DEVELOPMENTS: For the year ended 12/31/00, net income decreased 9.1% to $264.1 million compared with $290.5 million in 1999. Results for 2000 included pre-tax restructuring-related costs of $6.2 million. The decline in earnings was primarily attributed to weakened demand in the majority of LEG's business segments. Net sales were $4.28 billion, up 13.2% from $3.78 billion a year earlier due to the acquisition of 21 businesses.

PROSPECTS: LEG continues to execute its four-point performance improvement plan and is making progress toward improving future performance. However, the Company remains cautious regarding the economic outlook for 2001, expecting demand to remain soft through at least the first half of the year. As a result, LEG anticipates full year sales and margins approximately equal to 2000, with diluted earnings between $1.25 to $1.45 per share.

BUSINESS

LEGGETT & PLATT, INCORPORATED is engaged primarily in the manufacture and distribution of components used by companies that manufacture furniture and bedding for homes, offices and institutions. Also in the furnishings area, the Company produces and sells some finished products for the furnishings industry. These finished products include sleep-related finished furniture and carpet cushioning materials. In addition, a group of diversified products made principally from steel, steel wire, aluminum, plastics, textile fibers and woven and non-woven fabrics are sold in many different markets unrelated to the home furnishings industry. LEG's international division is involved primarily in the sale of machinery and equipment designed to manufacture LEG's MIRACOIL innersprings.

ANNUAL FINANCIAL DATA

	12/31/00	12/31/99	12/31/98	12/31/97	12/31/96	12/31/95	12/31/94
Earnings Per Share	**[2] 1.32**	**1.45**	**1.24**	**1.08**	**[1] 0.84**	**0.80**	**0.70**
Cash Flow Per Share	**2.18**	**2.19**	**1.87**	**1.62**	**1.34**	**1.19**	**1.04**
Tang. Book Val. Per Share	**4.58**	**4.50**	**4.59**	**3.88**	**3.37**	**3.45**	**2.90**
Dividends Per Share	**0.40**	**0.35**	**0.30**	**0.26**	**0.22**	**0.18**	**0.12**
Dividend Payout %	**30.3**	**24.1**	**24.6**	**24.1**	**26.3**	**22.6**	**16.5**
INCOME STATEMENT (IN MILLIONS):							
Total Revenues	4,276.3	3,779.0	3,370.4	2,909.2	2,466.2	2,059.3	1,858.1
Costs & Expenses	3,616.4	3,129.4	2,815.6	2,441.9	2,070.4	1,756.0	1,599.2
Depreciation & Amort.	173.3	149.3	127.9	105.6	92.2	67.1	56.9
Operating Income	486.6	500.3	426.9	361.7	303.6	236.2	202.0
Net Interest Inc./(Exp.)	d62.2	d39.9	d33.5	d31.8	d30.0	d11.5	d9.8
Income Before Income Taxes	418.6	462.6	395.6	333.3	249.7	220.7	189.5
Income Taxes	154.5	172.1	147.6	125.0	96.7	85.8	74.1
Net Income	[2] 264.1	290.5	248.0	208.3	[1] 153.0	134.9	115.4
Cash Flow	437.4	439.8	375.9	313.9	245.2	202.0	172.3
Average Shs. Outstg. (000)	200,388	200,938	200,670	193,190	183,600	170,000	166,200
BALANCE SHEET (IN MILLIONS):							
Cash & Cash Equivalents	37.3	20.6	83.5	7.7	3.7	6.7	2.7
Total Current Assets	1,405.3	1,256.2	1,137.1	944.6	763.3	571.9	799.0
Net Property	1,018.4	915.0	820.4	693.2	582.9	451.8	396.0
Total Assets	3,373.2	2,977.5	2,535.3	2,106.3	1,712.9	1,218.3	1,374.2
Total Current Liabilities	476.6	431.5	401.4	372.5	292.8	226.8	232.9
Long-Term Obligations	988.4	787.4	574.1	466.2	388.5	191.9	204.9
Net Stockholders' Equity	1,793.8	1,646.2	1,436.8	1,174.0	941.1	734.1	625.2
Net Working Capital	928.7	824.7	735.7	572.1	470.5	345.1	566.1
Year-end Shs. Outstg. (000)	196,097	196,880	197,684	192,754	184,216	167,520	166,388
STATISTICAL RECORD:							
Operating Profit Margin %	11.4	13.2	12.7	12.4	12.3	11.5	10.9
Net Profit Margin %	6.2	7.7	7.4	7.2	6.2	6.6	6.2
Return on Equity %	14.7	17.6	17.3	17.7	16.3	18.4	18.5
Return on Assets %	7.8	9.8	9.8	9.9	8.9	11.1	8.4
Debt/Total Assets %	29.3	26.4	22.6	22.1	22.7	15.8	14.9
Price Range	22.56-14.19	28.31-18.63	28.75-16.88	23.88-15.75	17.38-10.31	13.44-8.50	12.38-8.31
P/E Ratio	17.1-10.7	19.5-12.8	23.2-13.6	22.1-14.6	20.8-12.3	16.9-10.7	17.8-12.0
Average Yield %	2.2	1.5	1.3	1.3	1.6	1.6	1.1

Statistics are as originally reported. Adj. for stk. split: 2-for-1, 9/95 and 6/98. [1] Bef. extraord. chrg. $12.5 mill. [2] Incl. pre-tax chrg. of $6.2 mill. for plant closures.

OFFICERS:
H. M. Cornell, Jr., Chmn.
F. E. Wright, Vice-Chmn., Pres., C.E.O.
E. C. Jett, V.P., Sec., Gen. Couns.
D. S. Haffner, Exec. V.P., C.O.O.

INVESTOR CONTACT: Investor Relations, (417) 358-8131

PRINCIPAL OFFICE: No. 1 Leggett Road, Carthage, MO 64836

TELEPHONE NUMBER: (417) 358-8131
FAX: (417) 358-8449
WEB: www.leggett.com

NO. OF EMPLOYEES: 34,000 (approx.)

SHAREHOLDERS: 17,107 (record)

ANNUAL MEETING: In May

INCORPORATED: MO, 1901

INSTITUTIONAL HOLDINGS:
No. of Institutions: 244
Shares Held: 111,529,691
% Held: 56.8

INDUSTRY: Mattresses and bedsprings (SIC: 2515)

TRANSFER AGENT(S): Mellon Investor Services, L.L.C., Ridgefield Park, NJ

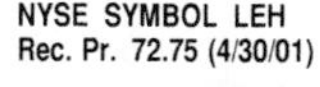

NYSE SYMBOL LEH
Rec. Pr. 72.75 (4/30/01)

LEHMAN BROTHERS HOLDINGS INC.

YIELD 0.4%
P/E RATIO 12.3

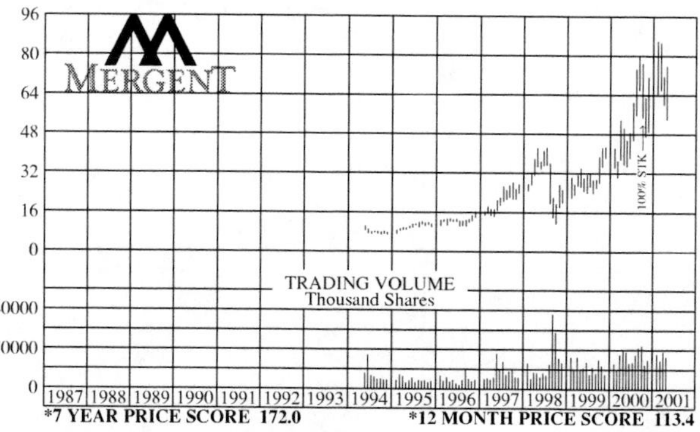

INTERIM EARNINGS (Per Share):

Qtr.	Feb.	May	Aug.	Nov.
1996-97	0.58	0.48	0.65	0.65
1997-98	0.72	1.06	0.55	0.26
1998-99	0.79	1.05	1.10	1.14
1999-00	1.85	1.39	1.69	1.46
2000-01	1.39	...	...	...

INTERIM DIVIDENDS (Per Share):

Amt.	Decl.	Ex.	Rec.	Pay.
0.11Q	8/02/00	8/11/00	8/15/00	8/31/00
100% STK	9/20/00	10/23/00	10/05/00	10/20/00
0.055Q	11/03/00	11/13/00	11/15/00	11/30/00
0.07Q	1/29/01	2/08/01	2/12/01	2/28/01
0.07Q	5/02/01	5/11/01	5/15/01	5/31/01

Indicated div.: $0.28 (Div. Reinv. Plan)

CAPITALIZATION (11/30/00):

	($000)	(%)
Long-Term Debt	35,233,000	80.3
Redeemable Pfd. Stock	860,000	2.0
Preferred Stock	700,000	1.6
Common & Surplus	7,081,000	16.1
Total	43,874,000	100.0

RECENT DEVELOPMENTS: For the quarter ended 2/28/01, net income fell 28.5% to $387.0 million from $541.0 million in the corresponding period of the previous year. Net revenues slipped 14.5% to $1.88 billion from $2.20 billion the year before. Principal transactions revenue decreased 10.4% to $998.0 million, while investment banking revenue declined 19.8% to $483.0 million. Interest and dividends increased 15.5% to $4.98 billion.

PROSPECTS: On 3/14/01, the Company and bond insurer Financial Security Assurance acquired equity stakes in TheMuniCenter, which offers Internet-based trading of municipal bonds and U.S. Treasury securities to institutional investors, financial advisors and registered representatives. Separately, the Company should continue to benefit from its overseas businesses in capital markets and merger and acquisition advisory services.

BUSINESS

LEHMAN BROTHERS HOLDINGS INC, with assets of $239.00 billion as of 2/28/01, is a holding company engaged in global investment banking. LEH provides services for institutions, corporations, governments and high-net-worth individual clients and customers. The Company provides debt and equity underwriting, merchant banking, strategic advisory services, foreign exchange trading, security trading and derivative and commodities trading. The Company derived 58.3% of its fiscal 2000 revenues from the U.S. and 41.7% from outside the U.S. On 5/31/94, LEH was spun off from American Express Company and began trading on the New York Stock Exchange.

BUSINESS LINE ANALYSIS

(11/30/2000)	REV (%)	INC (%)
Investment Banking	28.3	19.4
Capital Markets	60.8	69.8
Client Services	10.9	10.8
Total	100.0	100.0

ANNUAL FINANCIAL DATA

	11/30/00	11/30/99	11/30/98	11/30/97	11/30/96	11/30/95	① 11/30/94
Earnings Per Share	④ 6.38	4.08	2.60	2.36	③ 1.62	② 0.88	0.41
Cash Flow Per Share	7.08	4.35	2.96	2.72	2.01	1.34	0.94
Tang. Book Val. Per Share	30.21	22.75	19.04	16.51	15.97	13.38	11.90
Dividends Per Share	0.22	0.18	0.15	0.12	0.10	0.10	0.09
Dividend Payout %	3.4	4.4	5.8	5.1	6.2	11.4	21.6
INCOME STATEMENT (IN MILLIONS):							
Total Revenues	26,447.0	18,989.0	19,894.0	16,883.0	14,260.0	13,476.0	9,190.0
Costs & Expenses	23,246.0	16,907.0	18,530.0	15,860.0	13,532.0	13,002.0	8,881.0
Depreciation & Amort.	622.0	451.0	312.0	86.0	91.0	105.0	116.0
Operating Income	2,579.0	1,631.0	1,052.0	937.0	637.0	369.0	193.0
Income Before Income Taxes	2,579.0	1,631.0	1,052.0	937.0	637.0	369.0	193.0
Income Taxes	748.0	457.0	316.0	290.0	221.0	127.0	67.0
Net Income	④ 1,775.0	1,132.0	736.0	647.0	③ 416.0	② 242.0	126.0
Cash Flow	2,301.0	1,488.0	961.0	658.0	469.0	305.0	204.0
Average Shs. Outstg. (000)	264,200	258,600	250,000	242,200	232,800	226,800	216,000
BALANCE SHEET (IN MILLIONS):							
Cash & Cash Equivalents	162,949.0	142,420.0	108,285.0	115,116.0	102,030.0	91,675.0	86,641.0
Total Current Assets	173,331.0	154,780.0	120,250.0	127,954.0	111,974.0	99,845.0	97,131.0
Net Property	671.0	485.0	505.0	468.0	477.0	495.0	619.0
Total Assets	224,720.0	192,244.0	153,890.0	151,705.0	128,596.0	115,303.0	109,947.0
Total Current Liabilities	180,846.0	154,560.0	121,136.0	126,921.0	108,800.0	98,840.0	95,231.0
Long-Term Obligations	35,233.0	30,691.0	27,341.0	20,261.0	15,922.0	12,765.0	11,321.0
Net Stockholders' Equity	7,781.0	6,283.0	5,413.0	4,523.0	3,874.0	3,698.0	3,395.0
Net Working Capital	d7,515.0	220.0	d886.0	1,033.0	3,174.0	1,005.0	1,900.0
Year-end Shs. Outstg. (000)	236,395	239,826	228,000	233,200	200,000	210,000	210,000
STATISTICAL RECORD:							
Operating Profit Margin %	9.8	8.6	5.3	5.5	4.5	2.7	2.1
Net Profit Margin %	6.7	6.0	3.7	3.8	2.9	1.8	1.4
Return on Equity %	22.8	18.0	13.6	14.3	10.7	6.5	3.7
Return on Assets %	0.8	0.6	0.5	0.4	0.3	0.2	0.1
Debt/Total Assets %	15.7	16.0	17.8	13.4	12.4	11.1	10.3
Price Range	80.50-30.31	42.78-21.91	42.50-11.31	28.25-14.25	16.25-10.31	12.31-7.25	10.44-6.88
P/E Ratio	12.6-4.8	10.5-5.4	16.4-4.4	12.0-6.0	10.0-6.4	14.0-8.2	25.8-17.0
Average Yield %	0.4	0.6	0.6	0.6	0.8	1.0	1.0

Statistics are as originally reported. Adj. for 2-for-1 stk. split, 10/00. ① Results for 11 months only to reflect change in fiscal year to end 11/31. ② Incl. pre-tax restr. chgs. of $97.0 mill. & pre-tax gain of $79.9 mill. from the sale of Omnitel. ③ Incl. pre-tax $84.0 mill. severance costs. ④ Incl. a gain of $150.0 mill. fr. the sale of interest in an Internet company.

OFFICERS:
R. S. Fuld Jr., Chmn., C.E.O.
T. Russo, Vice-Chmn.
D. Goldfarb, Sr. V.P., C.F.O.

INVESTOR CONTACT: Shaun K. Butler, Investor Relations, (212) 526-8381

PRINCIPAL OFFICE: American Express Tower, 3 World Financial Center, New York, NY 10285

TELEPHONE NUMBER: (212) 526-7000
FAX: (212) 526-3738
WEB: www.lehman.com

NO. OF EMPLOYEES: 11,300 (approx.)

SHAREHOLDERS: 22,580

ANNUAL MEETING: In April

INCORPORATED: DE, Dec., 1983

INSTITUTIONAL HOLDINGS:
No. of Institutions: 462
Shares Held: 148,452,312
% Held: 60.2

INDUSTRY: Security brokers and dealers (SIC: 6211)

TRANSFER AGENT(S): The Bank of New York, New York, NY

NYSE SYMBOL LEN
Rec. Pr. 37.00 (5/31/01)

LENNAR CORPORATION

YIELD 0.1%
P/E RATIO 9.5

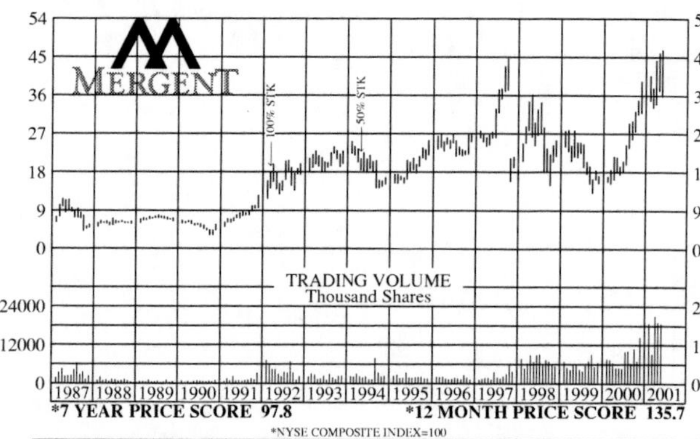

INTERIM EARNINGS (Per Share):

Qtr.	Feb.	May	Aug.	Nov.
1997	0.54	0.61	0.78	0.19
1998	0.30	0.47	0.59	1.06
1999	0.45	0.63	0.72	0.95
2000	0.40	0.64	0.90	1.59
2001	0.75	...	...	...

INTERIM DIVIDENDS (Per Share):

Amt.	Decl.	Ex.	Rec.	Pay.
0.013Q	3/23/00	5/03/00	5/05/00	5/15/00
0.013Q	6/22/00	8/03/00	8/07/00	8/17/00
0.013Q	9/21/00	11/02/00	11/06/00	11/16/00
0.013Q	1/23/01	2/01/01	2/05/01	2/15/01
0.013Q	4/03/01	5/03/01	5/07/01	5/17/01

Indicated div.: $0.05

CAPITALIZATION (11/30/00):

	($000)	(%)
Long-Term Debt	1,254,650	50.5
Common & Surplus	1,228,580	49.5
Total	2,483,230	100.0

RECENT DEVELOPMENTS: For the quarter ended 2/28/01, net income more than doubled to $51.3 million compared with $22.2 million in the equivalent 1999 quarter. Revenues soared 72.4% to $1.10 billion. Homebuilding revenues increased 75.9% to $1.02 billion, and financing revenues jumped 38.3% to $82.2 million. Total costs and expenses rose 69.0% to $1.02 billion.

PROSPECTS: Going forward, results should continue to benefit from increases in the number of home deliveries and average sales price of homes. The Company's financial services segment should continue to generate greater earnings from its mortgage and title operations, including the earnings contribution from U.S. Home Mortgage Corporation in the first quarter of 2001. The Company's backlog level as of 2/28/01 was $2.44 billion.

BUSINESS

LENNAR CORPORATION is a diversified national real estate company. LEN has homebuilding operations in 13 states and is a major builder of homes, building a variety of move-up and retirement homes. LEN builds homes under the LENNAR HOMES, U.S. HOME, GREYSTONE HOMES, VILLAGE BUILDERS, RENAISSANCE HOMES, ORRIN THOMPSON HOMES, LUNDGREN BROS., WINNCREST HOMES, and RUTENBERG HOMES brand names. LEN's financial services division provides residential mortgage services, title, closing and other ancillary services for its homebuyers and other customers. The Company's strategic technologies division provides high speed Internet access, cable television and home monitoring services for both Lennar homebuyers and other customers. In May 2000, LEN acquired U.S. Home Mortgage Corporation in a transaction valued at approximately $476.0 million.

ANNUAL FINANCIAL DATA

	11/30/00	11/30/99	11/30/98	11/30/97	11/30/96	11/30/95	11/30/94
Earnings Per Share	**3.64**	**2.74**	**2.49**	**[2] 1.34**	**2.43**	**1.95**	**[1] 1.89**
Cash Flow Per Share	**4.46**	**3.39**	**2.87**	**1.57**	**2.76**	**2.24**	**2.12**
Tang. Book Val. Per Share	**19.58**	**15.22**	**12.31**	**8.26**	**19.33**	**16.95**	**14.93**
Dividends Per Share	**0.05**	**0.05**	**0.05**	**0.09**	**0.10**	**0.10**	**0.10**
Dividend Payout %	**1.4**	**1.8**	**2.0**	**6.5**	**4.1**	**5.1**	**5.0**
INCOME STATEMENT (IN MILLIONS):							
Total Revenues	4,707.0	3,118.5	2,416.9	1,303.1	1,181.2	870.5	817.9
Costs & Expenses	4,174.2	2,736.4	2,104.7	1,183.3	993.9	725.5	682.4
Depreciation & Amort.	58.5	47.7	24.4	9.0	12.0	10.3	8.4
Operating Income	474.2	334.3	287.7	110.7	175.3	134.7	127.1
Net Interest Inc./(Exp.)	d98.6	d48.9	d47.6	d25.0	d31.0	d19.3	d15.4
Income Before Income Taxes	375.6	285.5	240.1	85.7	144.2	115.5	111.7
Income Taxes	146.5	112.8	96.0	35.1	56.3	45.0	43.6
Net Income	229.1	172.7	144.1	[2] 50.6	88.0	70.4	[1] 68.2
Cash Flow	287.7	220.4	168.4	59.6	100.0	80.7	76.6
Average Shs. Outstg. (000)	64,499	65,035	58,624	37,918	36,223	36,100	36,086
BALANCE SHEET (IN MILLIONS):							
Cash & Cash Equivalents	287.6	83.3	34.7	52.9	13.0	21.9	16.8
Total Current Assets	2,631.5	1,369.0	1,257.0	894.5	712.2	525.7	490.5
Net Property	...	...	...	8.6	221.3	189.3	193.6
Total Assets	3,777.9	2,057.6	1,917.8	1,343.3	1,703.3	1,371.6	1,242.7
Total Current Liabilities	...	...	33.4	22.6	26.0	26.7	25.5
Long-Term Obligations	1,254.7	523.7	565.5	574.8	566.2	407.3	411.9
Net Stockholders' Equity	1,228.6	881.5	715.7	439.0	695.5	607.8	534.1
Net Working Capital	2,631.5	1,369.0	1,223.6	871.9	686.2	499.0	465.0
Year-end Shs. Outstg. (000)	62,731	57,917	58,151	53,160	35,978	35,864	35,768
STATISTICAL RECORD:							
Operating Profit Margin %	10.1	10.7	11.9	8.5	14.8	15.5	15.5
Net Profit Margin %	4.9	5.5	6.0	3.9	7.4	8.1	8.3
Return on Equity %	18.7	19.6	20.1	11.5	12.7	11.6	12.8
Return on Assets %	6.1	8.4	7.5	3.8	5.2	5.1	5.5
Debt/Total Assets %	33.2	25.4	29.5	42.8	33.2	29.7	33.1
Price Range	39.38-15.25	27.88-13.06	36.19-14.88	44.69-15.81	27.25-21.63	25.50-15.25	25.17-14.25
P/E Ratio	10.8-4.2	10.2-4.8	14.5-6.0	33.3-11.8	11.2-8.9	13.1-7.8	13.3-7.5
Average Yield %	0.2	0.2	0.2	0.3	0.4	0.5	0.5

Statistics are as originally reported. Adj. for stk. split: 3-for-2, 4/94. [1] Bef. acctg. change cr. of $961,000. [2] Bef. inc. fr. discont. oper. of $33.8 mill.

OFFICERS:
L. Miller, Chmn.
R. J. Strudler, Vice-Chmn., C.O.O.
S. A. Miller, Pres., C.E.O.
B. E. Gross, C.F.O., V.P.

INVESTOR CONTACT: Kelly F. Somoza, Dir., Inv. & Media Rel., (305) 559-4000

PRINCIPAL OFFICE: 700 Northwest 107th Avenue, Miami, FL 33172

TELEPHONE NUMBER: (305) 559-4000
FAX: (305) 227-7115

NO. OF EMPLOYEES: 7,140

SHAREHOLDERS: 2,200 (approx. record)

ANNUAL MEETING: In Apr.

INCORPORATED: DE, Nov., 1969

INSTITUTIONAL HOLDINGS:
No. of Institutions: 218
Shares Held: 53,095,000
% Held: 83.6

INDUSTRY: Single-family housing construction (SIC: 1521)

TRANSFER AGENT(S): BankBoston, N.A., EquiServe, L.P., Canton, MA

NYSE SYMBOL LII
Rec. Pr. 9.15 (5/31/01)

LENNOX INTERNATIONAL INC.

YIELD 4.2%
P/E RATIO 8.7

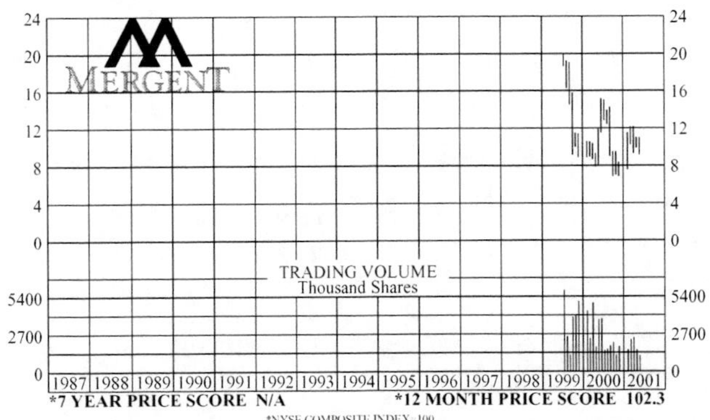

INTERIM EARNINGS (Per Share):

Qtr.	Mar.	June	Sept.	Dec.
1997		d0.99		
1998	0.24	0.48	0.68	0.07
1999	0.18	0.64	0.64	0.35
2000	0.10	0.56	0.22	0.17

INTERIM DIVIDENDS (Per Share):

Amt.	Decl.	Ex.	Rec.	Pay.
0.095Q	7/24/00	8/29/00	8/31/00	9/11/00
0.095Q	12/18/00	12/21/00	12/26/00	1/06/01
0.095Q	3/19/01	3/28/01	3/30/01	4/09/01
0.095Q	4/23/01	5/24/01	5/29/01	6/08/01

Indicated div.: $0.38

CAPITALIZATION (12/31/00):

	($000)	(%)
Long-Term Debt	627,550	45.7
Deferred Income Tax	941	0.1
Minority Interest	2,058	0.1
Common & Surplus	743,057	54.1
Total	1,373,606	100.0

RECENT DEVELOPMENTS: For the year ended 12/31/00, net income declined 19.3% to $59.1 million compared with $73.2 million in 1999. Net sales were $3.25 billion, up 37.5% from $2.36 billion a year earlier. The increase in net sales reflected a surge in North American retail sales to $1.05 billion from $218.1 million a year earlier. Income from operations was $158.6 million, up 1.7% from $155.9 million in 1999. Gross profit as a percentage of net sales was 32.0% in 2000 and 31.5% in 1999.

PROSPECTS: LII plans to realize the potential in the business portfolio it has assembled through corporate revenue growth. Revenue growth is expected to be in the low single digits and full year earnings per share, before restructuring charges, are expected to be up by more than 10.0%. Meanwhile, LII is on track to generate $80.0 million to $90.0 million in free cash flow for the year before restructuring charges.

BUSINESS

LENNOX INTERNATIONAL INC. is a global provider of climate control services. The Company designs, manufactures and markets a range of products for the heating, ventilation, air conditioning and refrigeration markets. The Company's products are sold under brand names, including LENNOX, ARMSTRONG AIR, DUCANE, BOHN, LARKIN, HEATCRAFT, ADVANCED DISTRIBUTOR PRODUCTS and others. The Company also manufactures heat transfer products, such as evaporator coils and condenser coils in North America. The Company is also in the market for hearth products, which includes pre-fabricated fireplaces and related products.

QUARTERLY DATA

(12/31/2000) ($000)	REV	INC
1st Quarter	716,324	5,740
2nd Quarter	894,200	32,277
3rd Quarter	857,618	12,386
4th Quarter	779,215	8,655

ANNUAL FINANCIAL DATA

	12/31/00	12/31/99	12/31/98	12/31/97	12/31/96
Earnings Per Share	**1.05**	**1.81**	**1.47**	**d0.99**	**1.62**
Cash Flow Per Share	**2.55**	**3.22**	**2.69**	**0.22**	**2.64**
Tang. Book Val. Per Share	**0.06**	**4.53**	**6.22**	**8.22**	...
Dividends Per Share	**0.28**	**0.18**	...	...	...
Dividend Payout %	**27.1**	**9.9**	...	...	...
INCOME STATEMENT (IN MILLIONS):					
Total Revenues	3,247.4	2,361.7	1,821.8	1,444.4	1,364.5
Costs & Expenses	3,004.3	2,148.3	1,671.7	1,438.8	1,229.8
Depreciation & Amort.	84.4	57.4	43.5	33.4	34.1
Operating Income	158.6	155.9	106.6	d35.2	100.6
Net Interest Inc./(Exp.)	d56.2	d33.1	d16.2	d8.5	d13.4
Income Before Income Taxes	101.0	123.2	89.7	d45.0	88.1
Income Taxes	41.9	50.1	37.2	cr11.5	33.4
Equity Earnings/Minority Int.	0.4	0.1	0.9	0.7	...
Net Income	59.1	73.2	52.5	d33.6	54.7
Cash Flow	143.5	130.6	96.1	7.4	88.9
Average Shs. Outstg. (000)	56,277	40,519	35,739	33,924	33,693
BALANCE SHEET (IN MILLIONS):					
Cash & Cash Equivalents	40.6	29.2	28.4	147.8	...
Total Current Assets	901.2	887.6	695.5	670.5	...
Net Property	354.2	330.0	255.1	215.3	...
Total Assets	2,055.0	1,683.7	1,151.6	970.4	...
Total Current Liabilities	589.9	463.0	432.2	334.6	...
Long-Term Obligations	627.6	520.3	242.6	183.6	...
Net Stockholders' Equity	743.1	597.9	376.4	325.5	...
Net Working Capital	311.3	424.6	263.3	335.9	...
Year-end Shs. Outstg. (000)	57,036	44,989	35,547	34,407	...
STATISTICAL RECORD:					
Operating Profit Margin %	4.9	6.6	5.9	...	7.4
Net Profit Margin %	1.8	3.1	2.9	...	4.0
Return on Equity %	7.9	12.2	14.0	...	...
Return on Assets %	2.9	4.3	4.6	...	...
Debt/Total Assets %	30.5	30.9	21.0	18.9	...
Price Range	15.13-6.81	19.88-8.88	...	...	...
P/E Ratio	14.4-6.5	11.0-4.9	...	...	...
Average Yield %	2.6	1.3	...	...	...

Statistics are as originally reported.

OFFICERS:
J. W. Norris, Jr., Chmn.
R. E. Schjerven, C.E.O.
C. E. Edwards, Jr., Exec. V.P., Gen. Couns., Sec.

INVESTOR CONTACT: Bill Moltner, Dir., Investor Relations, (972) 497-6670

PRINCIPAL OFFICE: 2140 Lake Park Blvd., Richardson, TX 75080

TELEPHONE NUMBER: (972) 497-5000
FAX: (972) 497-5292
WEB: www.lennoxinternational.com

NO. OF EMPLOYEES: 24,000 (approx.)

SHAREHOLDERS: 13,800 (approx.)

ANNUAL MEETING: In Apr.

INCORPORATED: Iowa, 1895; reincorp., DE, 1991

INSTITUTIONAL HOLDINGS:
No. of Institutions: 81
Shares Held: 12,474,944
% Held: 22.2

INDUSTRY: Refrigeration and heating equipment (SIC: 3585)

TRANSFER AGENT(S): Mellon Investor Services, L.L.C., South Hackensack, NJ

NYSE SYMBOL LXK
Rec. Pr. 61.99 (5/31/01)

LEXMARK INTERNATIONAL, INC.

YIELD ...
P/E RATIO 29.1

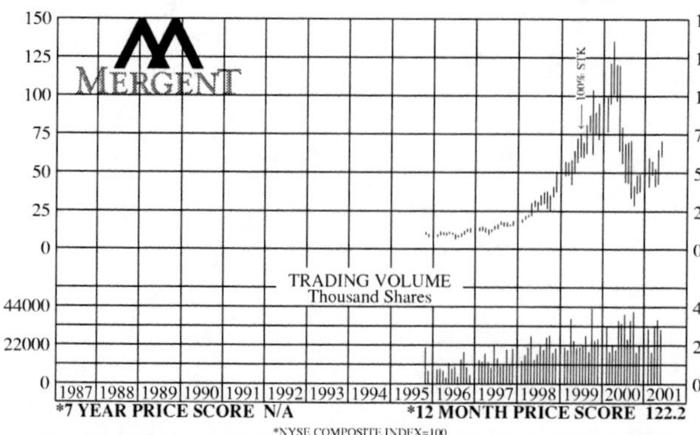

*7 YEAR PRICE SCORE N/A *12 MONTH PRICE SCORE 122.2

*NYSE COMPOSITE INDEX=100

INTERIM EARNINGS (Per Share):

Qtr.	Mar.	June	Sept.	Dec.
1996	0.15	0.20	0.20	0.30
1997	0.20	0.23	0.27	0.39
1998	0.35	0.38	0.41	0.58
1999	0.48	0.55	0.56	0.73
2000	0.59	0.62	0.50	0.42

INTERIM DIVIDENDS (Per Share):

Amt.	Decl.	Ex.	Rec.	Pay.
100% STK	4/29/99	6/11/99	5/20/99	6/10/99

CAPITALIZATION (12/31/00):

	($000)	(%)
Long-Term Debt	148,900	16.1
Common & Surplus	777,000	83.9
Total	925,900	100.0

RECENT DEVELOPMENTS: For the year ended 12/31/00, net earnings slipped 10.4% to $285.4 million from $318.5 million the year before. The 2000 results included a pre-tax restructuring charge of $41.3 million. Revenues grew 10.3% to $3.81 billion, driven by stronger sales of printer hardware and associated supplies, partially offset by unfavorable foreign currency exchange rates. Gross profit was $1.26 billion, or 33.0% of revenues, versus $1.23 billion, or 35.6% of revenues, in 1999. Operating income slid 12.8% to $415.7 million from $476.6 million the prior year.

PROSPECTS: The Company enjoyed strong printer shipment growth in 2000, especially inkjet printers, low-speed lasers and color lasers. This growth helped boost the Company's market share and may result in higher sales of supplies going forward. In 2001, the Company will focus on increasing sales outside of the U.S., which currently account for about 55.0% of LXK's sales, due to expected favorable consumer spending levels overseas. The Company is targeting earnings per share growth of between 15.0% and 20.0% in 2001.

BUSINESS

LEXMARK INTERNATIONAL, INC. (formerly Lexmark International Group, Inc.) is a global developer, manufacturer and supplier of laser and inkjet printers and associated consumable supplies for the office and home markets. The Company also sells dot matrix printers for printing single and multi-part forms by business users. In addition, LXK develops, manufactures and markets a broad line of other office imaging products, including supplies for IBM-branded printers, aftermarket supplies for original equipment manufacturer products, and typewriters and typewriter supplies that are sold under the IBM trademark. LXK acquired IBM's Information Products Division in 1991, and completed its initial public offering of common stock on 11/15/95.

ANNUAL FINANCIAL DATA

	12/31/00	12/31/99	12/31/98	12/31/97	12/31/96	12/31/95	12/31/94
Earnings Per Share	**2 2.13**	**2.32**	**1.70**	**1 1.08**	**0.84**	**1 0.32**	**d0.23**
Cash Flow Per Share	**2.80**	**2.90**	**2.23**	**1.60**	**1.29**	**0.98**	**0.80**
Tang. Book Val. Per Share	**7.89**	**6.42**	**4.41**	**3.71**	**3.72**	**2.78**	**1.90**
INCOME STATEMENT (IN MILLIONS):							
Total Revenues	3,807.0	3,452.3	3,020.6	2,493.5	2,377.6	2,157.8	1,852.3
Costs & Expenses	3,300.1	2,895.6	2,562.2	2,141.4	2,078.0	1,950.2	1,610.1
Depreciation & Amort.	91.2	80.1	75.6	77.5	69.2	99.1	127.3
Operating Income	415.7	476.6	382.8	274.6	230.4	108.5	114.9
Net Interest Inc./(Exp.)	d12.8	d10.7	d11.0	d10.8	d20.9	d35.1	d50.6
Income Before Income Taxes	396.4	458.9	365.4	254.7	201.6	63.3	50.7
Income Taxes	111.0	140.4	122.4	91.7	73.8	15.2	6.1
Net Income	2 285.4	318.5	243.0	1 163.0	127.8	1 48.1	44.6
Cash Flow	376.6	398.6	318.6	240.5	197.0	145.0	98.8
Average Shs. Outstg. (000)	134,312	137,547	142,802	150,338	152,444	149,864	122,862
BALANCE SHEET (IN MILLIONS):							
Cash & Cash Equivalents	68.5	93.9	149.0	43.0	119.3	150.5	42.0
Total Current Assets	1,243.7	1,088.7	1,020.0	776.1	765.1	715.7	557.7
Net Property	730.6	561.0	430.5	409.6	434.1	361.2	337.1
Total Assets	2,073.2	1,702.6	1,483.4	1,208.2	1,221.5	1,142.9	960.9
Total Current Liabilities	979.0	735.5	605.7	547.5	421.3	488.0	320.2
Long-Term Obligations	148.9	148.7	148.7	57.0	163.2	175.0	290.0
Net Stockholders' Equity	777.0	659.1	578.1	500.7	540.3	390.2	295.5
Net Working Capital	264.7	353.2	414.3	228.6	343.8	227.7	237.5
Year-end Shs. Outstg. (000)	98,514	102,679	130,982	135,080	145,320	140,384	137,274
STATISTICAL RECORD:							
Operating Profit Margin %	10.9	13.8	12.7	11.0	9.7	5.0	6.2
Net Profit Margin %	7.5	9.2	8.0	6.5	5.4	2.2	2.4
Return on Equity %	36.7	48.3	42.0	32.6	23.7	12.3	15.1
Return on Assets %	13.8	18.7	16.4	13.5	10.5	4.2	4.6
Debt/Total Assets %	7.2	8.7	10.0	4.7	13.4	15.3	30.2
Price Range	135.88-28.75	104.00-42.09	51.00-17.50	18.63-9.56	13.88-6.69	11.19-7.75	...
P/E Ratio	63.8-13.5	44.8-18.1	30.0-10.3	17.2-8.9	16.5-8.0	35.0-24.2	...

Statistics are as originally reported. Adj. for 2-for-1 stk. split, 6/99. 1 Bef. $14 mil ($0.10/sh) net extraord. loss, 1997; & $6.4 mil ($0.11/sh) loss, 1995. 2 Incl. $41.3 mil ($0.22/sh) pre-tax non-recur. chg. related to restructuring.

OFFICERS:
P. J. Curlander, Chmn., C.E.O.
G. E. Morin, Exec. V.P., C.F.O.
K. M. Braun, Treas.

INVESTOR CONTACT: Mark D. Sisk, (859) 232-5934

PRINCIPAL OFFICE: One Lexmark Centre Drive, Lexington, KY 40550

TELEPHONE NUMBER: (859) 232-2000
FAX: (859) 232-3120
WEB: www.lexmark.com

NO. OF EMPLOYEES: 13,000 (approx.)

SHAREHOLDERS: 1,769 (Cl. A)

ANNUAL MEETING: In Apr.

INCORPORATED: DE, 1990

INSTITUTIONAL HOLDINGS:
No. of Institutions: 287
Shares Held: 108,606,078
% Held: 85.1

INDUSTRY: Computer peripheral equipment, nec (SIC: 3577)

TRANSFER AGENT(S): Mellon Investor Services, Ridgefield Park, NJ

NYSE SYMBOL LC
Rec. Pr. 35.80 (4/30/01)

LIBERTY CORPORATION (THE)

YIELD 2.5%
P/E RATIO 28.4

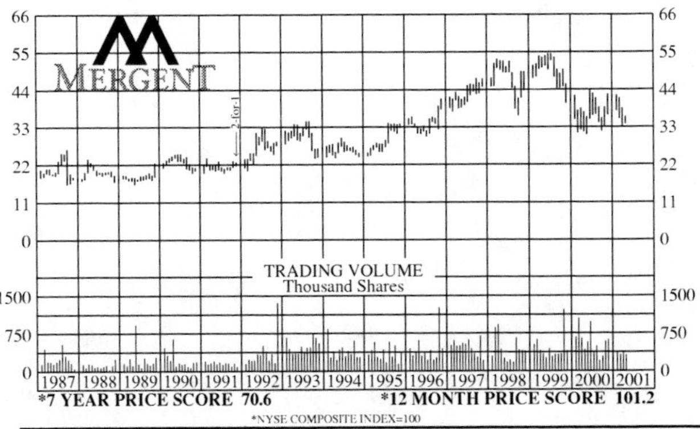

*7 YEAR PRICE SCORE 70.6 *12 MONTH PRICE SCORE 101.2

*NYSE COMPOSITE INDEX=100

INTERIM EARNINGS (Per Share):

Qtr.	Mar.	June	Sept.	Dec.
1996	0.64	0.75	d0.55	0.82
1997	0.72	0.94	0.92	0.81
1998	d0.15	0.82	0.55	d0.42
1999	0.11	0.66	0.87	0.59
2000	0.40	0.22	0.20	0.44

INTERIM DIVIDENDS (Per Share):

Amt.	Decl.	Ex.	Rec.	Pay.
0.22Q	5/02/00	6/13/00	6/15/00	7/05/00
0.22Q	8/01/00	9/13/00	9/15/00	10/03/00
0.22Q	11/07/00	12/13/00	12/15/00	1/03/01
0.22Q	2/06/01	3/13/01	3/15/01	4/03/01
0.22Q	5/08/01	6/13/01	6/15/01	7/03/01

Indicated div.: $0.88

CAPITALIZATION (12/31/00):

	($000)	(%)
Deferred Income Tax	92,797	13.8
Common & Surplus	580,993	86.2
Total	673,790	100.0

RECENT DEVELOPMENTS: For the year ended 12/31/00, LC reported income from continuing operations of $25.0 million compared with income from continuing operations of $18.8 million in 1999. Results for 2000 and 1999 excluded income from discontinued operations of $28.6 million and $25.8 million, respectively. Total revenues amounted to $173.7 million, up 12.8% versus $154.0 million a year earlier. Station revenues improved 11.9% to $161.2 million, while cable advertising and other revenues rose 25.4% to $12.5 million.

PROSPECTS: Although national advertisement business continues to be soft, the Company expects to continue to perform well by focusing on local advertisement opportunities. Going forward, the Company will look to explore different avenues of growth in broadcasting as well as other synergistic forms of media. On 12/4/00, the Company announced that its subsidiary, Cosmos Broadcasting, completed the acquisition of Civic Communications for $204.0 million, adding three television stations to the Cosmos station group.

BUSINESS

THE LIBERTY CORPORATION is a holding company with operations primarily in the television broadcasting industry. The Company's television broadcasting subsidiary, Cosmos Broadcasting Corporation, consists of fifteen network-affiliated stations located in the Southeast and Midwest. In addition, LC owns CableVantage Inc., a cable advertising sales subsidiary; Take Ten productions, a video production facility; Broadcast Merchandising Company, a professional broadcast equipment dealership, and SuperCoups USA, a direct mail coupon business serving small business owners. Eight of the Company's television stations are affiliated with NBC, five with ABC, and two with CBS. On 11/1/00, LC completed the sale of its insurance operations to Royal Bank of Canada for approximately $650.0 million in cash.

REVENUES

(12/31/2000)	($000)	(%)
Broadcasting	161,184	93.7
Cable	10,748	6.3
Total	171,932	100.0

ANNUAL FINANCIAL DATA

	12/31/00	12/31/99	12/31/98	12/31/97	12/31/96	12/31/95	12/31/94
Earnings Per Share	**2 1.27**	**2.24**	**1 0.80**	**3.34**	**1 1.66**	**2.76**	**1.22**
Cash Flow Per Share	**2.63**	**5.27**	**4.30**	**5.96**	**6.12**	**5.57**	**4.16**
Tang. Book Val. Per Share	**4.06**	**13.58**	**12.70**	**22.56**	**17.78**	**16.53**	**10.60**
Dividends Per Share	**0.88**	**0.88**	**0.84**	**0.77**	**0.71**	**0.65**	**0.60**
Dividend Payout %	**69.3**	**39.3**	**105.0**	**23.1**	**42.8**	**23.5**	**49.6**
INCOME STATEMENT (IN THOUSANDS):							
Total Revenues	173,672	556,040	584,264	660,256	619,097	605,681	541,246
Costs & Expenses	107,802	413,911	443,312	476,611	456,940	446,510	435,142
Depreciation & Amort.	26,949	60,221	63,832	58,859	90,519	55,329	56,139
Operating Income	38,921	81,908	77,120	124,786	71,638	103,842	49,965
Net Interest Inc./(Exp.)	d14,366	d15,085	d14,208	d13,209	d15,139	d15,047	d11,097
Income Before Income Taxes	41,251	66,823	49,101	111,577	56,499	88,795	38,868
Income Taxes	16,256	22,254	31,340	36,626	19,159	29,442	12,690
Net Income	2 24,995	44,569	1 17,761	74,951	1 37,340	59,353	26,178
Cash Flow	51,579	103,595	78,992	130,227	124,159	111,151	80,200
Average Shs. Outstg.	19,721	19,896	18,955	22,434	20,903	20,572	19,808
BALANCE SHEET (IN THOUSANDS):							
Cash & Cash Equivalents	149,003	874,291	952,061	1,735,924	1,554,563	1,510,780	941,693
Total Current Assets	256,428	1,224,191	1,310,707	2,105,245	1,927,133	1,862,800	1,257,249
Net Property	89,041	90,675	101,523	74,338	79,808	79,789	66,360
Total Assets	896,007	2,352,924	2,410,683	3,184,758	3,060,765	3,034,296	2,667,264
Total Current Liabilities	212,392	173,174	168,473	174,618	166,310	157,063	122,995
Long-Term Obligations	...	235,300	285,000	191,914	247,861	258,444	231,647
Net Stockholders' Equity	580,993	554,224	529,507	674,447	580,861	575,762	395,589
Net Working Capital	44,036	1,051,017	1,142,234	1,930,627	1,760,823	1,705,737	1,134,254
Year-end Shs. Outstg.	19,538	19,508	18,684	20,713	20,215	20,060	19,841
STATISTICAL RECORD:							
Operating Profit Margin %	22.4	14.7	13.2	18.9	11.6	17.1	9.2
Net Profit Margin %	14.4	8.0	3.0	11.4	6.0	9.8	4.8
Return on Equity %	4.3	8.0	3.4	11.1	6.4	10.3	6.6
Return on Assets %	2.8	1.9	0.7	2.4	1.2	2.0	1.0
Debt/Total Assets %	...	10.0	11.8	6.0	8.1	8.5	8.7
Price Range	43.88-30.75	54.56-39.81	52.94-36.25	47.31-37.38	41.25-30.13	34.25-24.38	29.88-23.88
P/E Ratio	34.5-24.2	24.4-17.8	66.2-45.3	14.2-11.2	24.8-18.1	12.4-8.8	24.5-19.6
Average Yield %	2.4	1.9	1.9	1.8	2.0	2.2	2.3

Statistics are as originally reported. 1 Incl. non-recurr. chrg. 1998, $13.8 mill.; 1996, $26.9 mill.; 1994, $20.3 mill. 2 Excl. disc. ops. of $28.6 mill.

OFFICERS:
H. Hipp, Chmn., Pres. , C.E.O.
M. G. Williams, V.P., Gen. Couns., Sec.

INVESTOR CONTACT: Shareholder Relations, (864) 609-8256

PRINCIPAL OFFICE: P.O. Box 789, Wade Hampton Blvd., Greenville, SC 29602

TELEPHONE NUMBER: (864) 609-8256
FAX: (864) 609-4390
WEB: www.libertycorp.com
NO. OF EMPLOYEES: 1,500 (approx.)
SHAREHOLDERS: 1,044
ANNUAL MEETING: In May
INCORPORATED: SC, Nov., 1967

INSTITUTIONAL HOLDINGS:
No. of Institutions: 75
Shares Held: 8,588,126
% Held: 43.5
INDUSTRY: Television broadcasting stations (SIC: 4833)
TRANSFER AGENT(S): American Stock Transfer & Trust Company, New York, NY

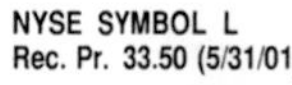

NYSE SYMBOL L
Rec. Pr. 33.50 (5/31/01)

LIBERTY FINANCIAL COMPANIES, INC.

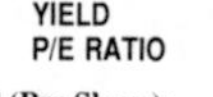

YIELD 1.2%
P/E RATIO 14.5

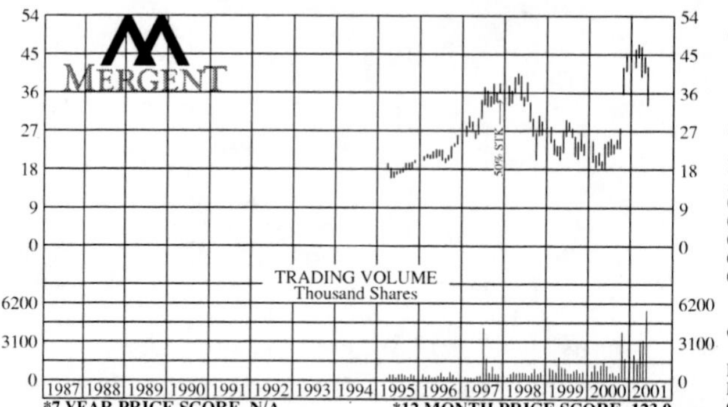

*7 YEAR PRICE SCORE N/A *12 MONTH PRICE SCORE 123.9
*NYSE COMPOSITE INDEX=100

INTERIM EARNINGS (Per Share):

Qtr.	Mar.	June	Sept.	Dec.
1996	0.54	0.51	0.55	0.64
1997	0.76	0.65	0.70	0.66
1998	0.67	0.63	0.71	0.64
1999	0.58	0.49	0.51	0.50
2000	0.62	0.50	0.45	0.74

INTERIM DIVIDENDS (Per Share):

Amt.	Decl.	Ex.	Rec.	Pay.
0.10Q	5/10/00	5/24/00	5/26/00	6/09/00
0.10Q	8/10/00	8/21/00	8/23/00	9/06/00
0.10Q	11/15/00	11/20/00	11/22/00	12/06/00
0.10Q	2/15/01	2/22/01	2/26/01	3/14/01
0.10Q	5/10/01	5/17/01	5/21/01	6/06/01

Indicated div.: $0.40

CAPITALIZATION (12/31/00):

	($000)	(%)
Long-Term Debt	763,200	34.4
Redeemable Pfd. Stock	10,700	0.5
Common & Surplus	1,447,700	65.2
Total	2,221,600	100.0

RECENT DEVELOPMENTS: For the year ended 12/31/00, net income increased 28.5% to $127.6 million from $99.3 million in 1999. Results included net realized investment losses of $47.5 million and $42.2 million in 2000 and 1999, respectively. Results for 2000 also included an unrealized gain of $31.6 million, a gain of $27.6 million and restructuring charges of $18.7 million. Investment income grew 6.4% to $862.3 million versus $810.3 million a year earlier. Total fee income rose 10.0% to $495.7 million.

PROSPECTS: Going forward, the annuity business should benefit from technology-related improvement in its customer service capabilities. Meanwhile, the asset management business should benefit from investments the Company has made in launching new products and in expanding distribution. On 1/3/01, the Company completed the sale of the Private Capital Management division of Stein Roe & Farnham, Incorporated, to the Current PCM management team and an outside investor for $40.0 million.

BUSINESS

LIBERTY FINANCIAL COMPANIES, INC. is an integrated asset accumulation and management company. The Company has two core product lines: retirement-oriented insurance products and investment management products. Retirement-oriented insurance products consist substantially of annuities. Investment management products consist of mutual funds, wealth management and institutional asset management. The Company sells its products through multiple distribution channels, including brokerage firms, banks and other depository institutions, financial planners and insurance agents, as well as directly to investors. Its operating companies include Colonial Management Associates, Crabbe Huson Group, Independent Financial Marketing Group, Keyport Life Insurance Company, Liberty Asset Management Company, Liberty Funds Group, Newport Pacific Management, Progress Investment Management Company, and Stein Roe & Farnham.

ANNUAL FINANCIAL DATA

	12/31/00	12/31/99	12/31/98	12/31/97	12/31/96	12/31/95	12/31/94
Earnings Per Share	**[2] 2.61**	**2.07**	**[1] 2.63**	**2.77**	**2.24**	**1.76**	**1.43**
Cash Flow Per Share	**5.54**	**5.35**	**5.94**	**2.77**	**3.44**	**3.41**	**2.65**
Tang. Book Val. Per Share	**18.75**	**19.04**	**21.10**	**22.82**	**19.65**	**18.40**	**17.40**
Dividends Per Share	**0.40**	**0.40**	**0.40**	**0.40**	**0.40**	**0.30**	**...**
Dividend Payout %	**15.3**	**19.3**	**15.2**	**14.4**	**17.9**	**17.0**	**...**
INCOME STATEMENT (IN MILLIONS):							
Total Revenues	1,369.7	1,218.7	1,217.0	1,247.0	1,140.3	1,030.5	887.9
Costs & Expenses	498.4	380.8	318.9	460.8	372.1	294.2	274.5
Depreciation & Amort.	143.1	156.9	157.0	...	45.2	61.3	43.1
Operating Income	728.2	681.0	741.1	786.2	723.0	675.0	570.3
Net Interest Inc./(Exp.)	d539.6	d526.6	d562.2	d594.1	d572.7	d557.2	d478.8
Income Before Income Taxes	188.6	154.4	178.9	192.1	150.3	113.9	83.3
Income Taxes	61.0	55.1	54.4	62.6	49.6	39.9	32.4
Net Income	[2] 127.6	99.3	[1] 124.5	129.5	100.7	73.9	50.8
Cash Flow	269.9	255.3	280.6	128.6	145.0	134.5	94.0
Average Shs. Outstg. (000)	48,904	47,912	47,368	46,731	42,354	39,645	35,448
BALANCE SHEET (IN MILLIONS):							
Cash & Cash Equivalents	1,891.0	1,232.6	984.1	1,290.1	875.8	875.3	726.7
Total Current Assets	1,891.0	1,232.6	984.1	1,290.1	875.8	875.3	768.5
Total Assets	20,150.7	18,372.5	16,519.1	15,851.6	14,427.7	12,749.4	10,968.8
Total Current Liabilities	13,333.0	12,864.5	12,744.5	12,808.2	11,901.2	10,463.1	9,344.0
Long-Term Obligations	763.2	552.0	486.4	229.0	229.0	229.0	75.0
Net Stockholders' Equity	1,447.7	1,185.9	1,271.3	1,198.9	1,051.4	956.4	624.7
Net Working Capital	d11,442.0	d11,631.9	d11,760.4	d11,518.1	d11,025.4	d9,587.8	d8,575.6
Year-end Shs. Outstg. (000)	48,784	47,462	46,384	43,808	43,058	41,525	34,224
STATISTICAL RECORD:							
Operating Profit Margin %	53.2	55.9	60.9	63.0	63.4	65.5	64.2
Net Profit Margin %	9.3	8.1	10.2	10.4	8.8	7.2	5.7
Return on Equity %	8.8	8.4	9.8	10.8	9.6	7.7	8.1
Return on Assets %	0.6	0.5	0.8	0.8	0.7	0.6	0.5
Debt/Total Assets %	3.8	3.0	2.9	1.4	1.6	1.8	0.7
Price Range	44.69-17.88	29.69-20.13	40.63-20.13	38.25-25.17	26.00-19.42	20.17-15.92	...
P/E Ratio	17.1-6.8	14.3-9.7	15.4-7.7	13.8-9.1	11.6-8.7	11.5-9.0	...
Average Yield %	1.3	1.6	1.3	1.3	1.8	1.7	...

Statistics are as originally reported. Adj. for 50% stk. div., 12/97 [1] Bef. extraord. loss $9.7 mill. [2] Incl. an unreal. gain of $31.6 mill., gain on sale of $27.6 mill. & a restruct. chrg. of $18.7 mill.

OFFICERS:
E. F. Kelly, Chmn.
G. L. Countryman, Pres., C.E.O.
J. A. Hilbert, Sr. V.P., C.F.O., Treas.
C. A. Merritt Jr., C.O.O.

INVESTOR CONTACT: Alicia K. Verity, Dir. of Inv. Rel., (617) 722-6000

PRINCIPAL OFFICE: 600 Atlantic Avenue, Boston, MA 02210-2214

TELEPHONE NUMBER: (617) 722-6000
FAX: (617) 742-8867
WEB: www.lib.com

NO. OF EMPLOYEES: 2,131

SHAREHOLDERS: 180 (approx.)

ANNUAL MEETING: In May

INCORPORATED: MA, Jan., 1995

INSTITUTIONAL HOLDINGS:
No. of Institutions: 90
Shares Held: 10,213,313
% Held: 20.9

INDUSTRY: Life insurance (SIC: 6311)

TRANSFER AGENT(S): BankBoston, N.A., Boston, MA

NYSE SYMBOL LRY
Rec. Pr. 28.85 (4/30/01)

LIBERTY PROPERTY TRUST

YIELD 7.9%
P/E RATIO 13.2

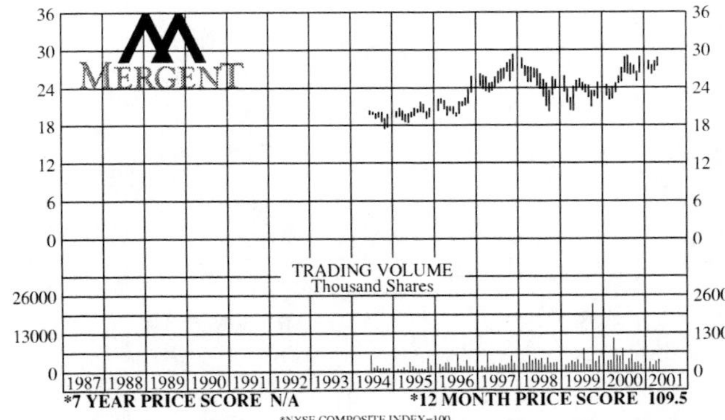

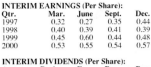

INTERIM EARNINGS (Per Share):

Qtr.	Mar.	June	Sept.	Dec.
1997	0.32	0.27	0.35	0.44
1998	0.40	0.39	0.41	0.39
1999	0.45	0.60	0.44	0.48
2000	0.53	0.55	0.54	0.57

INTERIM DIVIDENDS (Per Share):

Amt.	Decl.	Ex.	Rec.	Pay.
0.52Q	3/16/00	3/29/00	4/01/00	4/15/00
0.52Q	6/16/00	6/28/00	7/01/00	7/15/00
0.57Q	9/13/00	9/27/00	10/01/00	10/15/00
0.57Q	12/14/00	12/27/00	1/01/01	1/15/01
0.57Q	3/16/01	3/28/01	4/01/01	4/15/01

Indicated div.: $2.28

CAPITALIZATION (12/31/00):

	($000)	(%)
Long-Term Debt	1,703,896	52.9
Minority Interest	198,769	6.2
Preferred Stock	120,814	3.7
Common & Surplus	1,199,991	37.2
Total	3,223,470	100.0

RECENT DEVELOPMENTS: For the year ended 12/31/00, income was $161.4 million, before an extraordinary loss of $2.1 million, versus income of $142.5 million, before an extraordinary loss of $1.1 million, in the comparable period. Results included gains on property dispositions of $18.4 million and $13.2 million in 2000 and 1999, respectively. Total revenue jumped 12.8% to $533.0 million compared with $472.5 million in the previous year.

PROSPECTS: The Company's development pipeline should continue to increase the quality of its portfolio and help generate high yields. During the year, the Company completed 25 development properties for a total investment of $193.2 million. These properties have a current yield of 12.1% and a projected stabilized yield of 13.0%. In addition, the Company invested $105.2 million in acquisitions for the year 2000, which are currently yielding 11.1% and are expected to yield a return of 12.1% upon stabilization.

BUSINESS

LIBERTY PROPERTY TRUST is a self-administered and self-managed Maryland real estate investment trust company. The Company provides leasing, property management, development, acquisition, construction management, design management and other related services for a portfolio of industrial and office properties. The Company has properties in these geographic locations: Southeastern Pennsylvania; New Jersey; Lehigh Valley, Pennsylvania; Virginia; the Carolinas; Jacksonville, Florida; Detroit, Michigan; and all others combined (including Maryland; Tampa, Florida; South Florida; Minneapolis, Minnesota; and the United Kingdom). As of 12/31/00, the Company owned or held an interest in 650 industrial and office properties totaling approximately 48.0 million of leasable square feet.

ANNUAL FINANCIAL DATA

	12/31/00	12/31/99	12/31/98	12/31/97	12/31/96	12/31/95	12/31/94
Earnings Per Share	**[1][2] 2.20**	**[1][2] 1.97**	**1.59**	**1.38**	**1.14**	**0.89**	**[1] 0.46**
Tang. Book Val. Per Share	**17.59**	**17.53**	**17.46**	**15.84**	**11.96**	**11.84**	**10.86**
Dividends Per Share	**2.13**	**1.87**	**1.71**	**1.65**	**1.61**	**1.60**	**0.43**
Dividend Payout %	**96.8**	**94.9**	**107.5**	**119.6**	**141.2**	**179.8**	**93.5**
INCOME STATEMENT (IN MILLIONS):							
Rental Income	384.2	342.9	281.7	169.9	112.8	89.2	34.7
Total Income	533.0	472.5	387.1	232.5	154.3	117.0	46.6
Costs & Expenses	276.3	245.2	202.5	125.6	87.4	72.2	27.5
Depreciation	93.5	84.5	67.9	40.8	28.2	22.5	8.3
Income Before Income Taxes	181.6	156.0	116.7	66.1	37.6	22.3	10.9
Equity Earnings/Minority Int.	d20.2	d13.5	d8.1	d5.6	d3.9	d2.8	d7.7
Net Income	[1][2] 161.4	[1][2] 142.5	108.6	60.4	33.7	19.5	[1] 3.2
Average Shs. Outstg. (000)	68,173	66,727	61,315	40,806	29,678	21,838	20,965
BALANCE SHEET (IN MILLIONS):							
Cash & Cash Equivalents	4.6	9.1	14.4	55.1	19.6	10.6	25.2
Total Real Estate Investments	3,214.0	2,984.6	2,819.1	1,947.0	1,059.6	826.0	512.3
Total Assets	3,396.4	3,118.1	2,933.4	2,094.3	1,152.6	898.1	603.0
Long-Term Obligations	1,703.9	1,491.2	1,423.8	960.1	678.7	473.9	320.9
Total Liabilities	2,075.6	1,823.5	1,666.3	1,138.7	777.1	562.6	373.3
Net Stockholders' Equity	1,320.8	1,294.6	1,267.0	955.6	375.5	335.5	229.7
Year-end Shs. Outstg. (000)	68,213	66,971	65,645	52,693	31,400	28,348	21,143
STATISTICAL RECORD:							
Net Inc.+Depr./Assets %	7.5	7.3	6.0	4.8	5.4	4.7	1.9
Return on Equity %	12.2	11.0	8.6	6.3	9.0	5.8	1.4
Return on Assets %	4.8	4.6	3.7	2.9	2.9	2.2	0.5
Price Range	29.13-22.00	25.94-20.25	28.75-20.13	29.38-23.13	25.88-19.38	21.75-18.38	20.38-17.38
P/E Ratio	13.2-10.0	13.2-10.3	18.1-12.7	21.3-16.8	22.7-17.0	24.4-20.6	44.3-37.8
Average Yield %	8.3	8.1	7.0	6.3	7.1	8.0	2.3

Statistics are as originally reported. [1] Excl. extraord. chrg., $2.1 mill., 12/00; $1.1 mill., 12/99; credit $52.7 mill., 12/94 [2] Incl. gain on property dispositions, $18.4 mill., 12/00; $13.2 mill., 12/99

OFFICERS:
W. G. Rouse III, Chmn., Pres., C.E.O.
J. P. Denny, Vice-Chmn.
G. J. Alburger Jr., Exec. V.P., C.F.O., Treas.
J. J. Bowes, Sec., Gen. Couns.

INVESTOR CONTACT: Jeanne Leonard, Investor Relations, (610) 648-1704

PRINCIPAL OFFICE: 65 Valley Stream Parkway, Suite 100, Malvern, PA 19355

TELEPHONE NUMBER: (610) 648-1700
FAX: (610) 644-4129
WEB: www.libertyproperty.com

NO. OF EMPLOYEES: 347

SHAREHOLDERS: 1,120

ANNUAL MEETING: In May

INCORPORATED: MD, March, 1994

INSTITUTIONAL HOLDINGS:
No. of Institutions: 177
Shares Held: 54,387,301
% Held: 79.1

INDUSTRY: Real estate investment trusts (SIC: 6798)

TRANSFER AGENT(S): EquiServe, Canton, MA

NYSE SYMBOL LLY
Rec. Pr. 85.00 (4/30/01)

LILLY (ELI) & COMPANY

YIELD 1.3%
P/E RATIO 30.5

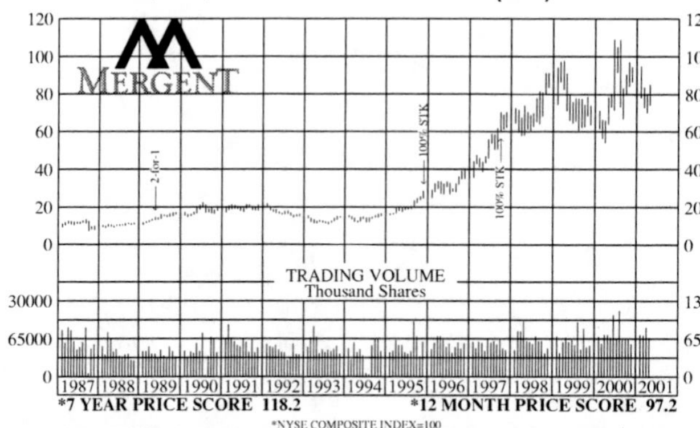

INTERIM EARNINGS (Per Share):

Qtr.	Mar.	June	Sept.	Dec.
1997	0.40	d1.57	0.41	0.40
1998	0.48	0.44	0.46	0.51
1999	0.40	0.52	0.67	0.73
2000	0.77	0.61	0.71	0.70

INTERIM DIVIDENDS (Per Share):

Amt.	Decl.	Ex.	Rec.	Pay.
0.26Q	4/17/00	5/11/00	5/15/00	6/09/00
0.26Q	6/26/00	8/11/00	8/15/00	9/11/00
0.26Q	10/16/00	11/13/00	11/15/00	12/11/00
0.28Q	12/18/00	2/13/01	2/15/01	3/09/01
0.28Q	4/16/01	5/11/01	5/15/01	6/11/01

Indicated div.: $1.12 (Div. Reinv. Plan)

CAPITALIZATION (12/31/00):

	($000)	(%)
Long-Term Debt	2,633,700	30.0
Deferred Income Tax	91,600	1.0
Common & Surplus	6,046,900	68.9
Total	8,772,200	100.0

RECENT DEVELOPMENTS: For the year ended 12/31/00, net income was $3.06 billion compared with income from continuing operations of $2.55 billion in the previous year. The 2000 results included a net one-time gain of $241.0 million from the sale of the joint venture, Kinetra. Net sales rose 8.6% to $10.86 billion versus $10.00 billion in 1999.

PROSPECTS: In 2001, LLY expects earnings per share to range from $2.75 to $2.85. Strong earnings growth in the first half of the year is likely to offset declines in the second half, when PROZAC sales are expected to decline substantially. The Company is expecting single-digit sales and earnings growth for the year.

BUSINESS

LILLY (ELI) & COMPANY discovers, develops, manufactures and markets pharmaceuticals and animal health products. Neuroscience products, (48.0%) of 2000 sales, include PROZAC®, ZYPREXA®, DARVON®, and PERMAX®. Endocrine products, (24.0%), include HUMULIN®, HUMALOG®, ILETIN®, ACTOS®, EVISTA® and HUMATROPE®. Anti-infective products, (8.0%), include CECLOR®, KEFLEX®, KEFTAB®, LORABID®, DYNABAC®, NEBCIN®, TAZIDIME®, KEFUROX®, KEFZOL®, and VANCOCIN®. Animal Health products, (5.0%), include TYLAN®, MICOTIL®, cattle feed additives, and antibodies for poultry. Cardiovascular products, (5.0%), consist primarily of REOPRO® and DOBUTREX®. Oncology products, (5.0%), include GEMZAR®, ONCOVIN®, VELBAN and ELDISINE. Gastrointestinal products, (4.0%), are entirely comprised of the ulcer treatment AXID®. Other pharmaceutical products accounted for 1.0% of sales.

ANNUAL FINANCIAL DATA

	12/31/00	12/31/99	12/31/98	12/31/97	12/31/96	12/31/95	12/31/94
Earnings Per Share	[6] **2.79**	[5] **2.30**	[4] **1.87**	[3] **d0.35**	**1.39**	[2] **1.15**	[1] [2] **1.03**
Cash Flow Per Share	**3.18**	**2.70**	**2.31**	**0.11**	**1.89**	**1.63**	**1.40**
Tang. Book Val. Per Share	**5.37**	**4.49**	**2.86**	**2.79**	**1.87**	**1.21**	**0.81**
Dividends Per Share	**1.04**	**0.92**	**0.80**	**0.74**	**0.69**	**0.66**	**0.63**
Dividend Payout %	**37.3**	**40.0**	**42.8**	**...**	**49.3**	**57.0**	**61.0**
INCOME STATEMENT (IN MILLIONS):							
Total Revenues	10,862.2	10,002.9	9,236.8	8,517.6	7,346.6	6,763.8	5,711.6
Costs & Expenses	6,866.7	6,199.5	6,049.4	5,549.5	4,756.3	4,228.3	3,608.9
Depreciation & Amort.	435.8	439.7	490.4	509.8	543.5	553.7	432.2
Operating Income	3,559.7	3,363.7	2,697.0	2,458.3	2,046.8	1,981.8	1,670.5
Net Interest Inc./(Exp.)	d182.3	d183.8	d181.3	d234.1	d288.8	d286.3	d103.8
Income Before Income Taxes	3,858.7	3,245.4	2,665.0	5,396.2	2,031.3	1,765.6	1,698.6
Income Taxes	800.9	698.7	568.7	895.3	507.8	459.0	513.5
Net Income	[6] 3,057.8	[5] 2,546.7	[4] 2,096.3	[3] d385.1	1,523.5	[2] 1,306.6	[1] [2] 1,185.1
Cash Flow	3,493.6	2,986.4	2,586.7	124.7	2,067.0	1,860.3	1,617.3
Average Shs. Outstg. (000)	1,097,725	1,106,055	1,121,486	1,101,099	1,093,654	1,138,052	1,156,756
BALANCE SHEET (IN MILLIONS):							
Cash & Cash Equivalents	4,618.2	3,836.0	1,597.1	2,024.6	955.1	1,084.1	746.7
Total Current Assets	7,943.0	7,055.5	5,406.8	5,320.7	3,891.3	4,138.6	3,962.3
Net Property	4,176.6	3,981.5	4,096.3	4,101.7	4,307.0	4,239.3	4,411.5
Total Assets	14,690.8	12,825.2	12,595.5	12,577.4	14,307.2	14,412.5	14,507.4
Total Current Liabilities	4,960.7	3,935.4	4,607.2	4,191.6	4,222.2	4,967.0	5,669.5
Long-Term Obligations	2,633.7	2,811.9	2,185.5	2,326.1	2,516.5	2,592.9	2,125.8
Net Stockholders' Equity	6,046.9	5,013.0	4,429.6	4,645.6	6,100.1	5,432.6	5,355.6
Net Working Capital	2,982.3	3,120.1	799.6	1,129.1	d330.9	d828.4	d1,707.2
Year-end Shs. Outstg. (000)	1,125,560	1,090,238	1,019,090	1,110,522	1,105,646	1,101,506	1,167,744
STATISTICAL RECORD:							
Operating Profit Margin %	32.8	33.6	29.2	28.9	27.9	29.3	29.2
Net Profit Margin %	28.2	25.5	22.7	...	20.7	19.3	20.7
Return on Equity %	50.6	50.8	47.3	...	25.0	24.1	22.1
Return on Assets %	20.8	19.9	16.6	...	10.6	9.1	8.2
Debt/Total Assets %	17.9	21.9	17.4	18.5	17.6	18.0	14.7
Price Range	109.00-54.00	97.75-60.56	91.31-57.69	70.31-35.56	40.19-24.69	28.50-15.63	16.56-11.78
P/E Ratio	39.1-19.4	42.5-26.3	48.8-30.8	...	28.9-17.8	24.8-13.6	16.2-11.5
Average Yield %	1.3	1.2	1.1	1.4	2.1	3.0	4.4

Statistics are as originally reported. Adj. for 2-for-1 stock split, 10/97 & 12/95. [1] Bef. inc. fr. dis. ops. of $984.3 mill., 1995; $1.19 bill., 1994. [2] Incl. nonrecurr. chgs. of $66.0 mill. & ref. divest. in the Medical Devices & Diagnostic Div. bus. [3] Incl. a net gain of $631.8 mill. & non-cash chg. of approx. $2.40 bill. [4] Excl. an extra. chg. of $7.2 mill. & a gain of $8.8 mill. fr. disc. opers.; incl. a pre-tax chg. of $127.5 mill. [5] Incl. a pre-tax chgs. of $237.4 mill., & a pre-tax gain of $267.8 mill.; excl. a net gain of $174.3 mill. fr. disc. opers. [6] Incl. net one-time gain of $214.4 mill. fr. the sale of Kinetra.

OFFICERS:
S. Taurel, Chmn., Pres., C.E.O.
C. E. Golden, Exec. V.P., C.F.O.
R. O. Kendall, Sr. V.P., Gen. Couns.

INVESTOR CONTACT: R.B. Graper, Dir. of Investor Relations, (317) 276-2506

PRINCIPAL OFFICE: Lilly Corporate Center, Indianapolis, IN 46285

TELEPHONE NUMBER: (317) 276-2000
FAX: (317) 276-6331
WEB: www.lilly.com

NO. OF EMPLOYEES: 35,700 (approx.)

SHAREHOLDERS: 59,190

ANNUAL MEETING: In Apr.

INCORPORATED: IN, Jan., 1901; reincorp., IN, Jan., 1936

INSTITUTIONAL HOLDINGS:
No. of Institutions: 852
Shares Held: 750,172,294
% Held: 66.7

INDUSTRY: Pharmaceutical preparations (SIC: 2834)

TRANSFER AGENT(S): Wells Fargo Shareowner Services, South St. Paul, MN

NYSE SYMBOL LTD
Rec. Pr. 16.30 (5/31/01)

LIMITED (THE), INC.

YIELD 1.8%
P/E RATIO 17.0

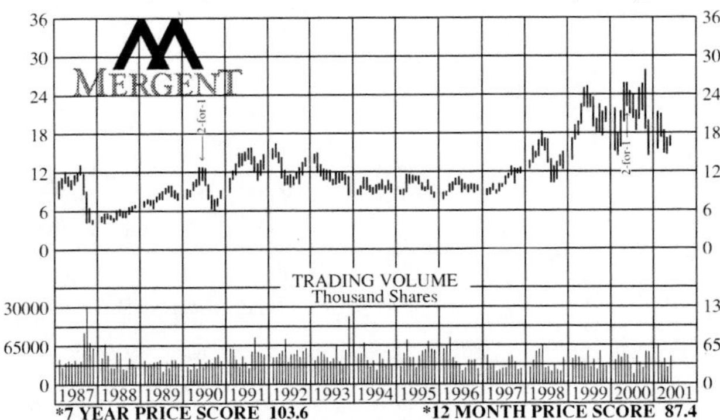

*7 YEAR PRICE SCORE 103.6 *12 MONTH PRICE SCORE 87.4
*NYSE COMPOSITE INDEX=100

INTERIM EARNINGS (Per Share):

Qtr.	Apr.	July	Oct.	Jan.
1997-98	0.05	0.05	0.08	0.16
1998-99	0.14	3.47	0.09	0.54
1999-00	0.07	0.11	0.09	0.71
2000-01	0.14	0.17	0.11	0.54

INTERIM DIVIDENDS (Per Share):

Amt.	Decl.	Ex.	Rec.	Pay.
0.075Q	8/18/00	8/30/00	9/01/00	9/12/00
0.075Q	11/10/00	11/29/00	12/01/00	12/12/00
0.075Q	1/26/01	3/07/01	3/09/01	3/20/01
0.075Q	5/21/01	6/06/01	6/08/01	6/19/01

Indicated div.: $0.30 (Div. Reinv. Plan)

CAPITALIZATION (2/3/01):

	($000)	(%)
Long-Term Debt	400,000	14.0
Minority Interest	143,085	5.0
Common & Surplus	2,316,455	81.0
Total	2,859,540	100.0

RECENT DEVELOPMENTS: For the 53 weeks ended 2/3/01, net income slipped 7.1% to $427.9 million from $460.8 million in the corresponding 52-week period the year before. Net sales rose 3.5% to $10.10 billion from $9.77 billion a year earlier. Results in the recent period included a one-time pre-tax charge of $9.9 million related to the closing of nine Bath & Body Works stores in the U.K. Prior-year results included a one-time pre-tax gain of $23.5 million. Comparable-store sales increased 5.0% year over year. Gross income rose 3.6% to $3.44 billion.

PROSPECTS: Long-term results could benefit from strategic initiatives focused on improving the Company's core operations and boosting operating profitability. On 2/28/01, LTD announced that it intends to sell its Lane Bryant division to a strategic or financial buyer. In addition, LTD plans to rebrand its Structure stores as Express Men's stores in an effort to generate synergistic savings and fuel further growth in its Express division. Meanwhile, slowing economic conditions in the U.S. are expected to constrain earnings during the first three quarters of fiscal 2001.

BUSINESS

THE LIMITED, INC. operates 2,739 specialty stores. Limited Stores, the flagship division, sells medium-priced fashion apparel. Express offers popular-priced sportswear and accessories. Lane Bryant, a subsidiary, operates stores specializing in apparel for the larger-sized woman. Lerner New York stores offer merchandise at discounted prices. Men's clothing is offered in Structure stores. Henri Bendel offers fashion apparel, cosmetics, accessories and gifts for professional women. The Company owns 40% of Galyan's Trading Co., which offers merchandise for sports enthusiasts. LTD also owns approximately 84% of Intimate Brands, Inc., which operates 2,390 Victoria's Secret, Bath & Body Works and White Barn Candle Co. stores. LTD spun off its interest in Abercrombie and Fitch Co. in May 1998, and Too, Inc., formerly named Limited Too, Inc., in August 1999.

BUSINESS LINE ANALYSIS

(2/3/2001)	Rev(%)	Inc(%)
Apparel Businesses	49.0	14.1
Intimate Brands	50.6	86.1
Other	0.4	(0.2)
Total	100.0	100.0

ANNUAL FINANCIAL DATA

	2/3/01	1/29/00	1/30/99	1/31/98	2/1/97	2/3/96	1/28/95
Earnings Per Share	**[2] 0.96**	**[1] 1.00**	**[1] 4.16**	**[2] 0.40**	**[1] [2] 0.77**	**[1] 1.34**	**0.63**
Cash Flow Per Share	**1.58**	**1.61**	**4.75**	**0.97**	**1.28**	**1.74**	**1.00**
Tang. Book Val. Per Share	**5.44**	**4.99**	**4.93**	**3.73**	**3.55**	**4.50**	**3.86**
Dividends Per Share	**0.30**	**0.30**	**0.26**	**0.24**	**0.20**	**0.20**	**0.18**
Dividend Payout %	**31.2**	**30.0**	**6.2**	**60.7**	**26.0**	**14.9**	**28.8**
INCOME STATEMENT (IN MILLIONS):							
Total Revenues	10,104.6	9,723.3	9,346.9	9,188.8	8,644.8	7,881.4	7,320.8
Costs & Expenses	8,967.3	8,530.3	6,623.4	8,395.4	7,719.1	6,982.2	6,253.9
Depreciation & Amort.	271.1	272.4	286.0	313.3	289.6	285.9	267.9
Operating Income	866.1	920.6	2,437.5	480.1	636.1	613.3	799.0
Net Interest Inc./(Exp.)	d58.2	d78.3	d68.5	d68.7	d75.4	d77.5	d65.4
Income Before Income Taxes	758.9	831.8	2,363.6	400.4	675.2	1,184.5	744.3
Income Taxes	331.0	371.0	310.0	183.0	241.0	223.0	296.0
Equity Earnings/Minority Int.	d69.3	d72.6	d64.6	d56.5	d45.6	d22.4	...
Net Income	[2] 427.9	[1] 460.8	[1] 2,053.6	[2] 217.4	[1] [2] 434.2	[1] 961.5	448.3
Cash Flow	699.1	733.2	2,339.6	530.7	723.9	1,247.4	716.2
Average Shs. Outstg. (000)	443,048	455,564	492,638	548,966	564,200	716,800	717,200
BALANCE SHEET (IN MILLIONS):							
Cash & Cash Equivalents	563.5	817.3	870.3	746.4	312.8	1,645.7	242.8
Total Current Assets	2,067.8	2,246.3	2,318.2	2,031.2	1,545.1	2,800.0	2,523.0
Net Property	1,394.6	1,229.6	1,361.8	1,415.9	1,828.9	1,741.5	1,692.1
Total Assets	4,088.1	4,087.7	4,549.7	4,300.8	4,120.0	5,266.6	4,570.1
Total Current Liabilities	1,000.2	1,238.2	1,247.9	1,093.4	906.9	716.6	797.6
Long-Term Obligations	400.0	400.0	550.0	650.0	650.0	650.0	650.0
Net Stockholders' Equity	2,316.5	2,147.1	2,233.3	2,045.0	1,922.6	3,201.0	2,761.0
Net Working Capital	1,067.6	1,008.1	1,070.2	937.7	638.2	2,083.5	1,725.4
Year-end Shs. Outstg. (000)	425,943	429,928	453,144	548,574	542,142	710,732	715,200
STATISTICAL RECORD:							
Operating Profit Margin %	8.6	9.5	26.1	5.2	7.4	7.8	10.9
Net Profit Margin %	4.2	4.7	22.0	2.4	5.0	12.2	6.1
Return on Equity %	18.5	21.5	92.0	10.6	22.6	30.0	16.2
Return on Assets %	10.5	11.3	45.1	5.1	10.5	18.3	9.8
Debt/Total Assets %	9.8	9.8	12.1	15.1	15.8	12.3	14.2
Price Range	27.88-14.44	25.31-13.75	18.25-10.25	12.88-8.25	11.25-7.63	11.63-7.94	11.19-8.38
P/E Ratio	29.0-15.0	25.3-13.7	4.4-2.5	32.6-20.9	14.6-9.9	8.7-5.9	17.9-13.4
Average Yield %	1.4	1.5	1.8	2.3	2.1	2.0	1.8

Statistics are as originally reported. Adj. for 2-for-1 stk. split, 5/00. [1] Incl. $34.5 mil pre-tax gain, 2000; $1.74 bil, 1999; $118.2 mil ($0.21/sh), 1997; $649.5 mil ($1.19/sh), 1996. [2] Incl. $9.9 mil pre-tax chg., 2001; $123.8 mil net chg., 1998; $12 mil pre-tax chg., 1997.

OFFICERS:
L. H. Wexner, Chmn., Pres., C.E.O.
L. A. Schlesinger, Exec. V.P., C.O.O.
V. A. Hailey, Exec. V.P., C.F.O.

INVESTOR CONTACT: T. J. Katzenmeyer, Vice-Pres., (614) 479-7000

PRINCIPAL OFFICE: Three Limited Parkway, P.O. Box 16000, Columbus, OH 43216

TELEPHONE NUMBER: (614) 415-7000
FAX: (614) 479-7440
WEB: www.limited.com
NO. OF EMPLOYEES: 123,700 (approx.)
SHAREHOLDERS: 77,000 (approx.)
ANNUAL MEETING: In May
INCORPORATED: OH, 1963; reincorp., DE, June, 1982

INSTITUTIONAL HOLDINGS:
No. of Institutions: 299
Shares Held: 296,986,481
% Held: 69.8

INDUSTRY: Women's clothing stores (SIC: 5621)

TRANSFER AGENT(S): First Chicago Trust Company of New York, Jersey City, NJ

NYSE SYMBOL LNC
Rec. Pr. 49.24 (5/31/01)

LINCOLN NATIONAL CORPORATION

YIELD 2.5%
P/E RATIO 15.5

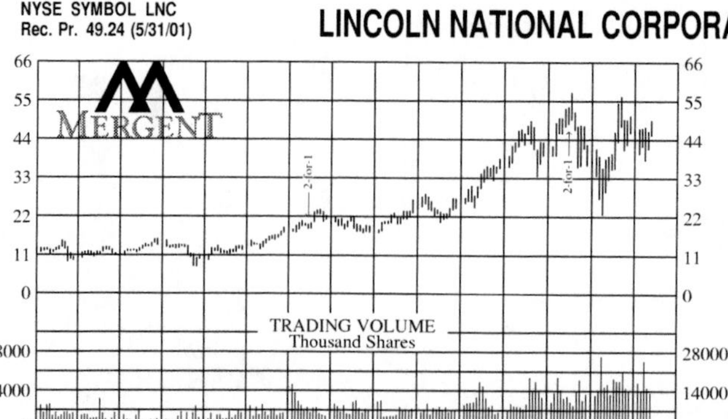

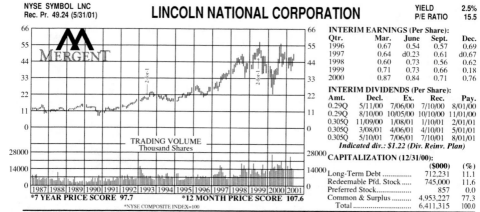

*7 YEAR PRICE SCORE 97.7 *12 MONTH PRICE SCORE 107.6

*NYSE COMPOSITE INDEX=100

INTERIM EARNINGS (Per Share):

Qtr.	Mar.	June	Sept.	Dec.
1996	0.67	0.54	0.57	0.69
1997	0.64	d0.23	0.61	d0.67
1998	0.60	0.73	0.56	0.62
1999	0.71	0.73	0.66	0.18
2000	0.87	0.84	0.71	0.76

INTERIM DIVIDENDS (Per Share):

Amt.	Decl.	Ex.	Rec.	Pay.
0.29Q	5/11/00	7/06/00	7/10/00	8/01/00
0.29Q	8/10/00	10/05/00	10/10/00	11/01/00
0.305Q	11/09/00	1/08/01	1/10/01	2/01/01
0.305Q	3/08/01	4/06/01	4/10/01	5/01/01
0.305Q	5/10/01	7/06/01	7/10/01	8/01/01

Indicated div.: $1.22 (Div. Reinv. Plan)

CAPITALIZATION (12/31/00):

	($000)	(%)
Long-Term Debt	712,231	11.1
Redeemable Pfd. Stock	745,000	11.6
Preferred Stock	857	0.0
Common & Surplus	4,953,227	77.3
Total	6,411,315	100.0

RECENT DEVELOPMENTS: For the year ended 12/31/00, net income grew 35.0% to $621.4 million compared with $460.4 million in 1999. Results for 2000 and 1999 included restructuring charges of $80.2 million and $18.9 million, respectively. Results also included a pre-tax realized loss on investments of $28.3 million in 2000 versus a pre-tax realized gain on investments of $3.0 million in 1999. Total revenues amounted to $6.85 billion, a slight increase versus $6.80 billion a year earlier.

PROSPECTS: The Company should continue to benefit from the strong performance of its Annuities, Life Insurance and Reinsurance segments. On 12/21/00, the Company announced the establishment of a strategic distribution partnership with Salomon Smith Barney. Under the partnership, LNC financial distributors will seek to increase variable life insurance sales by working closely with Salomon Smith Barney's financial consultants to serve the firm's client base.

BUSINESS

LINCOLN NATIONAL CORPORATION, a multi-line holding company, is a major diversified financial services company. Through its subsidiaries, the Company operates multiple insurance and investment management businesses. The Company's operations are divided into five business segments: Life Insurance, Annuities, Lincoln UK, Reinsurance and Investment Management. In 1994, the Company sold its employee life health benefit operations. In 1997, the Company sold its property-casualty operations. In January 1998, the Company acquired the individual life insurance and annuities business of CIGNA Corporation for $1.40 billion.

ANNUAL FINANCIAL DATA

	12/31/00	12/31/99	12/31/98	12/31/97	12/31/96	12/31/95	12/31/94
Earnings Per Share	**[1] 3.19**	**[1] 2.30**	**2.51**	**[2] 0.11**	**2.46**	**[1] 2.32**	**[1] 1.69**
Tang. Book Val. Per Share	**11.06**	**5.59**	**10.16**	**19.38**	**15.97**	**16.20**	**13.68**
Dividends Per Share	**1.16**	**1.10**	**1.04**	**0.98**	**0.92**	**0.86**	**0.82**
Dividend Payout %	**36.4**	**47.8**	**41.4**	**932.4**	**37.5**	**37.1**	**48.7**
INCOME STATEMENT (IN MILLIONS):							
Total Premium Income	1,813.1	1,881.5	1,620.6	1,328.7	3,182.0	3,253.8	4,444.1
Other Income	5,038.4	4,922.2	4,466.4	3,569.7	3,539.3	3,379.4	2,540.2
Total Revenues	6,851.5	6,803.7	6,087.1	4,898.5	6,721.3	6,633.3	6,984.4
Policyholder Benefits	3,557.2	3,805.0	3,328.9	3,191.7	3,921.3	4,113.1	4,849.2
Income Before Income Taxes	836.3	570.0	697.4	34.9	712.3	626.6	376.3
Income Taxes	214.9	109.6	187.6	12.7	179.2	144.4	26.4
Equity Earnings/Minority Int.	...	...	...	...	d19.6	...	...
Net Income	[1] 621.4	[1] 460.4	509.8	[2] 22.2	513.6	[1] 482.2	[1] 349.9
Average Shs. Outstg. (000)	194,921	200,418	203,262	207,992	209,122	208,232	207,726
BALANCE SHEET (IN MILLIONS):							
Cash & Cash Equivalents	1,927.4	1,895.9	2,433.4	3,794.7	1,231.7	1,572.9	1,041.6
Premiums Due	4,252.0	4,559.0	3,577.4	2,548.3	3,195.0	3,033.2	3,169.4
Invst. Assets: Fixed-term	27,449.8	27,688.6	30,232.9	24,066.4	27,906.4	25,834.5	21,644.2
Invst. Assets: Equities	549.7	604.0	542.8	660.4	992.7	1,164.8	1,038.6
Invst. Assets: Loans	6,623.9	6,627.8	6,233.1	4,051.3	4,031.1	3,789.4	3,406.4
Invst. Assets: Total	35,375.0	35,604.2	37,948.3	29,839.8	34,066.2	31,942.0	27,068.2
Total Assets	99,844.1	103,095.7	93,836.3	77,174.7	71,713.4	63,257.7	49,330.1
Long-Term Obligations	712.2	712.0	712.2	511.0	626.3	659.3	419.6
Net Stockholders' Equity	4,954.1	4,263.9	5,387.9	4,982.9	4,470.0	4,378.1	3,042.1
Year-end Shs. Outstg. (000)	190,748	195,495	202,112	201,718	207,318	208,370	188,956
STATISTICAL RECORD:							
Return on Revenues %	9.1	6.8	8.4	0.5	7.6	7.3	5.0
Return on Equity %	12.5	10.8	9.5	0.4	11.5	11.0	11.5
Return on Assets %	0.6	0.4	0.5	...	0.7	0.8	0.7
Price Range	56.38-22.63	57.50-36.00	49.44-33.50	38.56-24.50	28.50-20.38	26.88-17.31	22.19-17.31
P/E Ratio	17.7-7.1	25.0-15.7	19.7-13.3	366.9-233.1	11.6-8.3	11.6-7.5	13.2-10.3
Average Yield %	2.9	2.4	2.5	3.1	3.8	3.9	4.2

Statistics are as originally reported. Adj. for stk. split: 2-for-1, 6/99 [1] Incl. non-recurr. chrg. $80.2 mill. 12/00; $18.9 mill., 12/99; credit $54.2 mill., 12/95; credit $48.8 mill.12/94 [2] Bef. disc. oper. gain $911.8 mill.

OFFICERS:
J. A. Boscia, Chmn., Pres., C.E.O.
R. C. Vaughan, Exec. V.P., C.F.O.

INVESTOR CONTACT: Investor Relations, (215) 448-1422

PRINCIPAL OFFICE: 1500 Market Street, 39th Floor, Philadelphia, PA 19102-2112

TELEPHONE NUMBER: (215) 448-1400
FAX: (215) 448-3962
WEB: www.lfg.com

NO. OF EMPLOYEES: 9,240 (approx.)

SHAREHOLDERS: 11,102

ANNUAL MEETING: In May

INCORPORATED: IN, Jan., 1968

INSTITUTIONAL HOLDINGS:
No. of Institutions: 387
Shares Held: 139,874,433
% Held: 73.4

INDUSTRY: Life insurance (SIC: 6311)

TRANSFER AGENT(S): First Chicago Trust Company of New York, Jersey City, NJ

NYSE SYMBOL LAD
Rec. Pr. 19.30 (5/31/01)

LITHIA MOTORS, INC.

YIELD ...
P/E RATIO 10.8

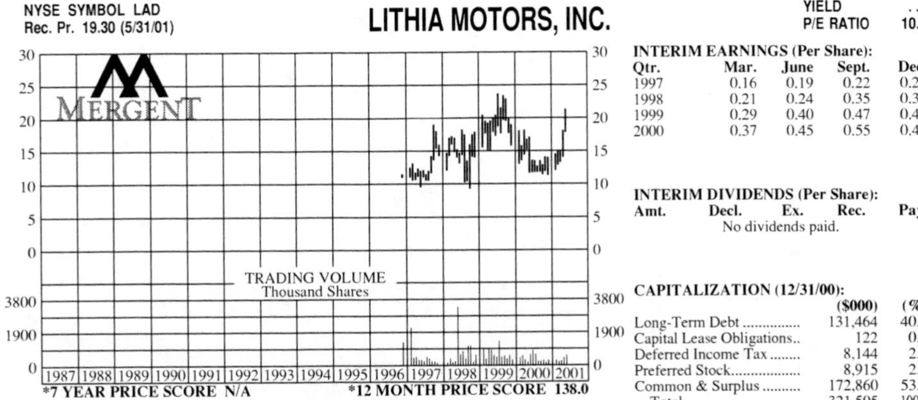

INTERIM EARNINGS (Per Share):

Qtr.	Mar.	June	Sept.	Dec.
1997	0.16	0.19	0.22	0.25
1998	0.21	0.24	0.35	0.32
1999	0.29	0.40	0.47	0.43
2000	0.37	0.45	0.55	0.41

INTERIM DIVIDENDS (Per Share):

Amt.	Decl.	Ex.	Rec.	Pay.

No dividends paid.

CAPITALIZATION (12/31/00):

	($000)	(%)
Long-Term Debt	131,464	40.9
Capital Lease Obligations	122	0.0
Deferred Income Tax	8,144	2.5
Preferred Stock	8,915	2.8
Common & Surplus	172,860	53.8
Total	321,505	100.0

RECENT DEVELOPMENTS: For the year ended 12/31/00, net income increased 26.8% to $24.3 million compared with $19.2 million in the previous year. Total revenues climbed 33.5% to $1.66 billion versus $1.24 billion in the prior year. New vehicle sales jumped 33.4% to $898.0 million, while used vehicle sales advanced 28.0% to $480.8 million. Service, body and parts sales grew 35.9% to $164.0. Gross profit amounted to $267.6 million from $199.3 million the year before.

PROSPECTS: On 3/9/01, LAD announced that it has completed the acquisition of two stores in Pocatello, Idaho. The stores have combined estimated sales of $48.0 million. LAD's net investment in the stores total about $5.5 million in cash. Separately, Lithia completed the planned alignment and disposition of its Jeep, Mitsubishi and Kia franchises in Sioux Falls, South Dakota. Separately, for the remainder of 2001, LAD expects to realize about $250.0 million to $300.0 million in annualized revenues from acquisitions.

BUSINESS

LITHIA MOTORS, INC. is an operator of automotive franchises and retailer of new and used vehicles and services. As of 3/31/01, LAD offered 26 brands of new vehicles, through 114 franchises in 56 locations in the western United States and over the Internet. The Company operates 15 stores in Oregon, 14 in California, seven in Washington, six in Colorado, six in Idaho, five in Nevada, two in South Dakota and one in Alaska. LAD sells new and used cars and light trucks, sells replacement parts, provides vehicle maintenance, warranty, paint and repair services, and arranges related financing and insurance for its automotive customers.

REVENUES

(12/31/00)	($000)	(%)
New vehicle sales	898,016	54.1
Used vehicle sales	480,846	29.0
Service, body & parts	164,002	9.9
Other revenues	115,747	7.0
Total	1,658,611	100.0

ANNUAL FINANCIAL DATA

	12/31/00	12/31/99	12/31/98	12/31/97	12/31/96	12/31/95	12/31/94
Earnings Per Share	**1.76**	**1.60**	**1.14**	**0.82**	**0.40**	**0.33**	**...**
Cash Flow Per Share	**2.31**	**2.06**	**1.51**	**1.16**	**1.17**	**1.08**	**...**
Tang. Book Val. Per Share	**3.12**	**3.25**	**4.75**	**1.96**	**3.12**	**...**	**...**
INCOME STATEMENT (IN MILLIONS):							
Total Revenues	1,658.6	1,242.7	714.7	319.8	142.8	114.2	109.4
Costs & Expenses	1,586.5	1,189.8	684.6	305.7	137.2	108.0	103.5
Depreciation & Amort.	7.6	5.6	3.5	2.5	1.8	1.9	2.0
Operating Income	64.5	47.3	26.7	11.6	3.9	4.3	3.9
Net Interest Inc./(Exp.)	d25.6	d15.4	d9.8	d2.9	d1.2	d1.2	d0.9
Income Before Income Taxes	39.5	32.1	17.8	9.5	3.2	4.1	3.5
Income Taxes	15.2	12.9	7.0	3.5	cr0.8	...	...
Equity Earnings/Minority Int.	...	...	...	0.1	d0.6	d0.7	d0.4
Net Income	24.3	19.2	10.8	6.0	4.0	3.4	3.5
Cash Flow	31.9	24.7	14.3	8.4	5.8	5.3	5.5
Average Shs. Outstg. (000)	13,804	11,998	9,470	7,303	4,973	4,893	...
BALANCE SHEET (IN MILLIONS):							
Cash & Cash Equivalents	38.8	30.4	20.9	18.5	15.4	9.4	7.0
Total Current Assets	396.5	334.6	204.2	119.9	49.1	32.8	31.1
Net Property	90.2	52.4	32.9	16.3	4.6	3.2	3.1
Total Assets	628.0	506.4	294.4	166.5	63.8	39.2	36.7
Total Current Liabilities	297.6	259.6	150.6	96.0	28.9	25.0	25.0
Long-Term Obligations	131.6	73.9	41.4	26.6	6.2	10.7	6.7
Net Stockholders' Equity	181.8	155.6	91.5	37.9	24.7	0.9	2.8
Net Working Capital	98.9	75.0	53.6	23.9	20.2	7.8	6.0
Year-end Shs. Outstg. (000)	12,499	11,911	10,215	7,036	6,610	...	...
STATISTICAL RECORD:							
Operating Profit Margin %	3.9	3.8	3.7	3.6	2.7	3.8	3.6
Net Profit Margin %	1.5	1.5	1.5	1.9	2.8	3.0	3.2
Return on Equity %	13.4	12.3	11.8	15.7	16.3	396.6	125.4
Return on Assets %	3.9	3.8	3.7	3.6	6.3	8.6	9.6
Debt/Total Assets %	21.0	14.6	14.1	15.9	9.7	27.4	18.4
Price Range	18.19-11.25	23.75-15.00	18.25-9.25	19.00-9.50	11.50-10.94	...	...
P/E Ratio	10.3-6.4	14.8-9.4	16.0-8.1	23.2-11.6	28.7-27.3	...	...

Statistics are as originally reported.

OFFICERS:
S. B. DeBoer, Chmn., C.E.O.
M. D. Heimann, Pres., C.O.O.
J. B. DeBoer, Sr. V.P., C.F.O.

INVESTOR CONTACT: Jeff DeBoer, Sr. V.P., C.F.O., (541) 776-6868

PRINCIPAL OFFICE: 360 E. Jackson Street, Medford, OR 97501

TELEPHONE NUMBER: (541) 776-6899
FAX: (541) 776-6362
WEB: www.lithia.com

NO. OF EMPLOYEES: 3,400 (approx.)

SHAREHOLDERS: 1,693 (record); (class A); 2,025 (beneficial holders); 1 (class B)

ANNUAL MEETING: In May

INCORPORATED: OR, 1946

INSTITUTIONAL HOLDINGS:
No. of Institutions: 24
Shares Held: 5,294,800
% Held: 42.2

INDUSTRY: New and used car dealers (SIC: 5511)

TRANSFER AGENT(S): Computershare Investor Services, Lakewood, CO

NYSE SYMBOL LIZ
Rec. Pr. 49.16 (4/30/01)

LIZ CLAIBORNE, INC.

YIELD 0.9%
P/E RATIO 14.3

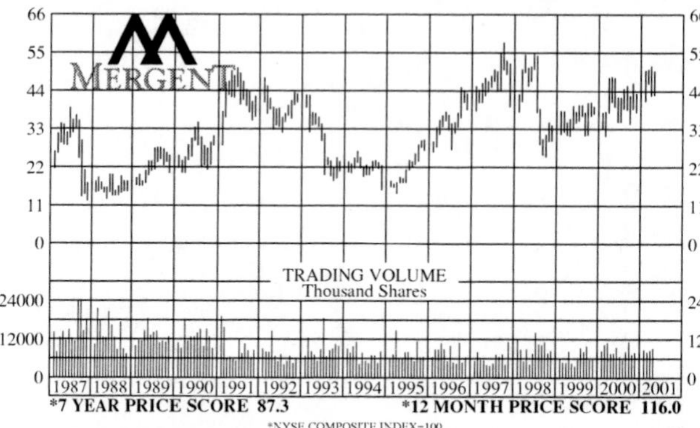

*7 YEAR PRICE SCORE 87.3 *12 MONTH PRICE SCORE 116.0
*NYSE COMPOSITE INDEX=100

INTERIM EARNINGS (Per Share):

Qtr.	Mar.	June	Sept.	Dec.
1996	0.49	0.31	0.78	0.57
1997	0.59	0.41	0.95	0.70
1998	0.69	0.47	0.96	0.46
1999	0.70	0.50	1.08	0.85
2000	0.84	0.58	1.26	0.76

INTERIM DIVIDENDS (Per Share):

Amt.	Decl.	Ex.	Rec.	Pay.
0.113Q	4/17/00	5/10/00	5/12/00	6/02/00
0.113Q	7/13/00	8/16/00	8/18/00	9/08/00
0.113Q	9/22/00	11/15/00	11/17/00	12/08/00
0.113Q	1/25/01	2/14/01	2/16/01	3/09/01
0.113Q	3/16/01	5/16/01	5/18/01	6/08/01

Indicated div.: $0.45 (Div. Reinv. Plan)

CAPITALIZATION (12/30/00):

	($000)	(%)
Long-Term Debt	269,219	23.6
Deferred Income Tax	31,019	2.7
Minority Interest	4,732	0.4
Common & Surplus	834,285	73.2
Total	1,139,255	100.0

RECENT DEVELOPMENTS: For the year ended 12/31/00, net income fell 4.1% to $184.6 million compared with $192.4 million in 1999. Results for 2000 included a restructuring charge of $21.0 million. Net sales grew 10.6% to $3.10 billion versus $2.81 billion the year before. Gross profit as a percentage of net sales increased to 39.7% compared with 39.1% in the prior year. Operating income climbed 1.3% to $303.7 million versus $299.8 million a year earlier.

PROSPECTS: The Company is planning its sales growth and taking the requisite steps to more tightly manage both expenses and inventories. The Company will also continue to pursue its diversification and share repurchase strategies. For 2001, the Company expects to achieve a 5.0% to 7.0% sales increase and an 11.0% to 13.0% increase in earnings per share, excluding any restructuring charges, special investment gains or future stock repurchases.

BUSINESS

LIZ CLAIBORNE, INC. is a designer and marketer of women's clothing—separates, dresses, suits, shoes and related accessories — with collections designed specifically for the work and leisure-time needs of career women. LIZ also designs sportswear and furnishings for men and markets fragrances and related items. Liz Claiborne Inc.'s brands include CLAIBORNE, CRAZY HORSE, CURVE, DANA BUCHMAN, ELISABETH, EMMA JAMES, FIRST ISSUE, LAUNDRY BY SHELLI SEGAL, LIZ CLAIBORNE, LUCKY BRAND, RUSS, SIGRID OLSEN, MONET, MEG ALLEN and VILLAGER. Products, which are manufactured to meet the Company's specifications in the U.S. and abroad, are marketed through leading department and specialty stores in the U.S., Canada, the United Kingdom and several other countries. Accessories include handbags and other small leather goods, shoes, jewelry and cosmetics. Stores operate under the LIZ CLAIBORNE and ELISABETH trademarks.

REVENUES

(12/30/2000)	($000)	(%)
Wholesale Apparel	2,196,125	71.1
Wholesale Non-apparel	403,924	13.1
Retail	489,566	15.8
Total	3,089,615	100.0

ANNUAL FINANCIAL DATA

	12/30/00	1/1/00	1/2/99	1/3/98	12/28/96	12/30/95	12/31/94
Earnings Per Share	**2 3.43**	**3.12**	**1 2.57**	**2.63**	**2.15**	**1.69**	**1 1.06**
Cash Flow Per Share	**4.87**	**4.22**	**3.42**	**3.29**	**2.74**	**2.21**	**1.50**
Tang. Book Val. Per Share	**10.90**	**11.89**	**14.61**	**13.94**	**14.37**	**13.41**	**12.77**
Dividends Per Share	**0.45**	**0.45**	**0.45**	**0.45**	**0.45**	**0.45**	**0.45**
Dividend Payout %	**13.1**	**14.4**	**17.5**	**17.1**	**20.9**	**26.6**	**42.4**
INCOME STATEMENT (IN MILLIONS):							
Total Revenues	3,104.1	2,806.5	2,535.3	2,412.6	2,217.5	2,081.6	2,162.9
Costs & Expenses	2,723.4	2,439.0	2,221.8	2,089.3	1,940.0	1,852.4	2,007.1
Depreciation & Amort.	77.0	67.8	55.8	46.0	42.9	39.0	35.0
Operating Income	303.7	299.8	257.7	277.3	234.7	190.2	120.8
Net Interest Inc./(Exp.)	d21.9	...	...	...	...	...	...
Income Before Income Taxes	288.4	301.6	266.7	293.1	249.1	203.1	131.4
Income Taxes	103.8	109.1	97.3	108.5	93.4	76.2	48.6
Net Income	2 184.6	192.4	1 169.4	184.6	155.7	126.9	1 82.8
Cash Flow	261.6	260.3	225.2	230.7	198.5	166.0	117.9
Average Shs. Outstg. (000)	53,747	61,720	65,847	70,191	72,396	75,003	78,527
BALANCE SHEET (IN MILLIONS):							
Cash & Cash Equivalents	54.6	37.9	230.3	359.5	528.7	437.9	330.4
Total Current Assets	910.6	858.6	1,075.3	1,057.4	1,142.1	1,065.2	1,022.5
Net Property	297.4	284.2	257.4	214.6	223.3	239.5	236.6
Total Assets	1,512.2	1,411.8	1,392.8	1,305.3	1,382.8	1,329.2	1,289.7
Total Current Liabilities	357.9	352.3	363.4	327.7	326.7	306.9	303.4
Long-Term Obligations	269.2	116.1	...	...	...	1.1	1.2
Net Stockholders' Equity	834.3	902.2	981.1	921.6	1,020.5	988.2	983.0
Net Working Capital	552.7	506.3	711.9	729.8	815.4	758.3	719.1
Year-end Shs. Outstg. (000)	51,209	56,720	63,951	66,098	71,006	73,692	77,004
STATISTICAL RECORD:							
Operating Profit Margin %	9.8	10.7	10.2	11.5	10.6	9.1	5.6
Net Profit Margin %	5.9	6.9	6.7	7.7	7.0	6.1	3.8
Return on Equity %	22.1	21.3	17.3	20.0	15.3	12.8	8.4
Return on Assets %	12.2	13.6	12.2	14.1	11.3	9.5	6.4
Debt/Total Assets %	17.8	8.2	...	...	...	0.1	0.1
Price Range	48.31-30.94	40.69-30.88	54.88-25.00	57.94-38.13	45.13-26.25	30.00-14.38	26.63-15.38
P/E Ratio	14.1-9.0	13.0-9.9	21.4-9.7	22.0-14.5	21.0-12.2	17.8-8.5	25.1-14.5
Average Yield %	1.1	1.3	1.1	0.9	1.3	2.0	2.1

Statistics are as originally reported. 1 Incl. non-recurr. chrg. $27.0 mill., 12/98; $30.0 mill., 12/94 2 Incl. restruc. chrg. of $21.0 mill.

OFFICERS:
P. R. Charron, Chmn., Pres., C.E.O.
M. Scarpa, V.P., C.F.O.
E. H. Goodell, V.P., Contr.

PRINCIPAL OFFICE: 1441 Broadway, New York, NY 10018

TELEPHONE NUMBER: (212) 354-4900
FAX: (212) 626-1800
WEB: www.lizclaiborne.com

NO. OF EMPLOYEES: 8,300 (approx.)

SHAREHOLDERS: 7,500 (approx.)

ANNUAL MEETING: In May

INCORPORATED: NY, Jan., 1976

INSTITUTIONAL HOLDINGS:
No. of Institutions: 257
Shares Held: 44,129,498
% Held: 84.1

INDUSTRY: Women's and misses' outerwear, nec (SIC: 2339)

TRANSFER AGENT(S): First Chicago Trust Company of New York, Jersey City, NJ

NYSE SYMBOL LMT
Rec. Pr. 35.16 (4/30/01)

LOCKHEED MARTIN CORPORATION

YIELD 1.3%
P/E RATIO ...

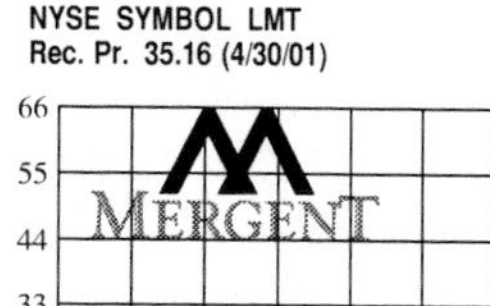

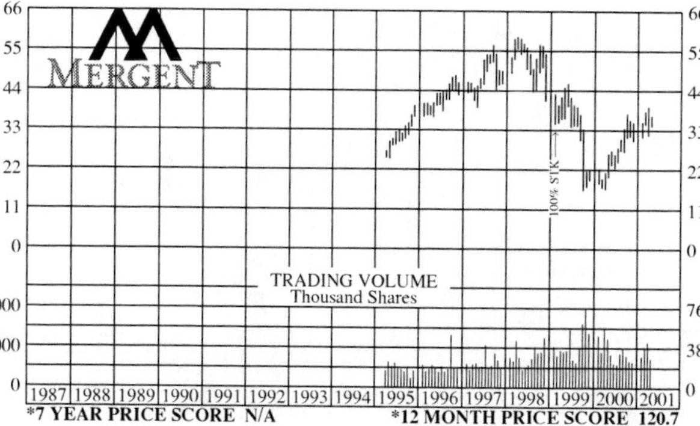

*7 YEAR PRICE SCORE N/A   *12 MONTH PRICE SCORE 120.7

*NYSE COMPOSITE INDEX=100

INTERIM EARNINGS (Per Share):

Qtr.	Mar.	June	Sept.	Dec.
1997	0.68	0.72	0.76	0.92
1998	0.72	0.76	0.84	0.34
1999	0.70	d0.11	0.57	0.76
2000	0.14	0.11	d1.74	0.44

INTERIM DIVIDENDS (Per Share):

Amt.	Decl.	Ex.	Rec.	Pay.
0.11Q	4/27/00	5/30/00	6/01/00	6/30/00
0.11Q	7/20/00	8/30/00	9/01/00	9/29/00
0.11Q	10/26/00	11/29/00	12/01/00	12/29/00
0.11Q	2/22/01	3/01/01	3/05/01	3/30/01
0.11Q	4/26/01	5/30/01	6/01/01	6/29/01

Indicated div.: $0.44 (Div. Reinv. Plan)

CAPITALIZATION (12/31/00):

	($000)	(%)
Long-Term Debt	9,065,000	55.9
Common & Surplus	7,160,000	44.1
Total	16,225,000	100.0

RECENT DEVELOPMENTS: For the year ended 12/31/00, LMT reported a loss of $424.0 million, before an extraordinary loss of $95.0 million, versus income of $737.0 million, before an accounting charge of $355.0 million, in 1999. Earnings for 2000 and 1999 included nonrecurring items that resulted in a net pre-tax charge of $539.0 million in 2000 and a net pre-tax gain of $249.0 million in 1999. Net sales decreased to $25.33 billion from $25.53 billion.

PROSPECTS: In 2001, the Company estimates earnings per share to grow 25.0% to 30.0%, excluding the effects of any nonrecurring and unusual items from the base of $1.07 per diluted share in 2000. The improved forecast reflects lower interest expense, a lower effective tax rate of 40.0%, and increased orders and backlog. For the years 2001 and 2002 combined, LMT anticipates it will generate at least $1.80 billion of free cash flow.

BUSINESS

LOCKHEED MARTIN CORPORATION was created on 3/15/95 through a merger of equals between Lockheed Corporation and Martin Marietta Corporation. LMT designs, develops, manufactures and integrates advanced technology systems, products, and services for government and commercial customers worldwide. Business areas include aeronautics, space, systems integration, and technology services. The Company is the world's largest defense, Department of Energy, and NASA contractor. In August 2000, LMT acquired the remaining 51.0% of COMSAT stock that it did not own.

REVENUES

(12/31/00)	($000)	(%)
Systems Integration	9,647,000	38.1
Space Systems	7,127,000	28.1
Aeronautical Systems	4,885,000	19.3
Technology Services	2,318,000	9.2
Global Telecommnications	766,000	3.0
Corporate & Other	586,000	2.3
Total	25,329,000	100.0

ANNUAL FINANCIAL DATA

	12/31/00	12/31/99	12/31/98	12/31/97	12/31/96	12/31/95	12/31/94
Earnings Per Share	**[5] d1.05**	**[4] 1.92**	**2.63**	**[3] 3.05**	**[2] 3.40**	**[1] 1.64**	**2.66**
Cash Flow Per Share	**1.36**	**4.44**	**5.26**	**5.51**	**6.73**	**4.24**	**5.33**
Tang. Book Val. Per Share	...	...	...	...	...	**2.03**	**0.71**
Dividends Per Share	**0.44**	**0.88**	**0.82**	**0.80**	**0.80**	**0.53**	...
Dividend Payout %	...	**45.8**	**31.2**	**26.3**	**23.5**	**32.0**	...
INCOME STATEMENT (IN MILLIONS):							
Total Revenues	25,329.0	25,530.0	26,266.0	28,069.0	26,875.0	22,853.0	22,906.0
Costs & Expenses	22,747.0	22,896.0	22,909.0	24,720.0	23,397.0	20,650.0	20,190.0
Depreciation & Amort.	968.0	969.0	1,005.0	1,052.0	1,197.0	921.0	937.0
Operating Income	1,614.0	1,665.0	2,352.0	2,297.0	2,281.0	1,282.0	1,779.0
Net Interest Inc./(Exp.)	d919.0	d809.0	d861.0	d842.0	d640.0	d288.0	d270.0
Income Before Income Taxes	286.0	1,200.0	1,661.0	1,937.0	2,033.0	1,089.0	1,675.0
Income Taxes	710.0	463.0	660.0	637.0	686.0	407.0	620.0
Net Income	[5] d424.0	[4] 737.0	1,001.0	[3] 1,300.0	[2] 1,347.0	[1] 682.0	1,055.0
Cash Flow	544.0	1,706.0	1,696.0	2,299.0	2,484.0	1,543.0	1,932.0
Average Shs. Outstg. (000)	400,800	384,100	381,100	427,000	378,200	378,000	374,000
BALANCE SHEET (IN MILLIONS):							
Cash & Cash Equivalents	1,505.0	455.0	285.0	...	...	653.0	639.0
Total Current Assets	11,259.0	10,696.0	10,611.0	10,105.0	9,940.0	8,177.0	8,143.0
Net Property	3,446.0	3,634.0	3,513.0	3,669.0	3,721.0	3,165.0	3,455.0
Total Assets	30,349.0	30,012.0	28,744.0	28,361.0	29,257.0	17,648.0	18,049.0
Total Current Liabilities	10,175.0	8,812.0	10,267.0	9,189.0	8,704.0	5,291.0	5,635.0
Long-Term Obligations	9,065.0	11,427.0	8,957.0	10,528.0	10,188.0	3,010.0	3,594.0
Net Stockholders' Equity	7,160.0	6,361.0	6,137.0	5,176.0	6,856.0	6,433.0	6,086.0
Net Working Capital	1,084.0	1,884.0	344.0	916.0	1,236.0	2,886.0	2,508.0
Year-end Shs. Outstg. (000)	432,148	398,164	393,000	388,000	394,400	398,000	398,000
STATISTICAL RECORD:							
Operating Profit Margin %	6.4	6.5	9.0	8.2	8.5	5.6	7.8
Net Profit Margin %	...	2.9	3.8	4.6	5.0	3.0	4.6
Return on Equity %	...	11.6	16.3	25.1	19.6	10.6	17.3
Return on Assets %	...	2.5	3.5	4.6	4.6	3.9	5.8
Debt/Total Assets %	29.9	37.8	31.2	37.1	34.8	17.1	19.9
Price Range	37.58-16.50	46.00-16.38	58.94-41.00	56.75-39.13	48.31-36.50	39.75-25.00	...
P/E Ratio	...	24.0-8.5	22.4-15.6	18.6-12.8	14.2-10.7	24.2-15.2	...
Average Yield %	1.6	2.8	1.6	1.7	1.9	1.6	...

Statistics are as originally reported. All financial information for 1994 is unaudited and pro forma using the pooling of interests accounting method. Adj. for 2-for-1 split, 12/98. [1] Incl. aft.-tax merg.-rel. & consol. chgs. of $436.0 mill. [2] Incl. a $365.0 mill. pre-tax gain result. from divest. & $25.0 mill. pre-tax chg. rel. to restruct. & other initiative. [3] Incl. tax-free gn. of $311.0 mill. & af.-tax chgs. of $303.0 mill. [4] Bef. acctg. chrg. $355.0 mill. & incl. various gains of $249.0 mill. [5] Bef. extraord. loss of $95.0 mill. & incl. a net nonrecurr. loss of $539.0 mill.

OFFICERS:
V. D. Coffman, Chmn., C.E.O.
R. J. Stevens, Pres., C.O.O., C.F.O.

INVESTOR CONTACT: Randa Middleton, Dir.-Inv. Rel., (301) 897-6455

PRINCIPAL OFFICE: 6801 Rockledge Drive, Bethesda, MD 20817-1877

TELEPHONE NUMBER: (301) 897-6000
FAX: (301) 897-6083
WEB: www.lockheedmartin.com
NO. OF EMPLOYEES: 126,000 (avg.)
SHAREHOLDERS: 68,000 (approx.)
ANNUAL MEETING: In April
INCORPORATED: MD, Oct., 1961; reincorp., MD, Aug., 1994

INSTITUTIONAL HOLDINGS:
No. of Institutions: 356
Shares Held: 424,326,016
% Held: 98.2

INDUSTRY: Guided missiles and space vehicles (SIC: 3761)

TRANSFER AGENT(S): First Chicago Trust Company of New York, Jersey City, NJ

NYSE SYMBOL LTR
Rec. Pr. 68.99 (5/31/01)

LOEWS CORPORATION

YIELD 0.9%
P/E RATIO 7.2

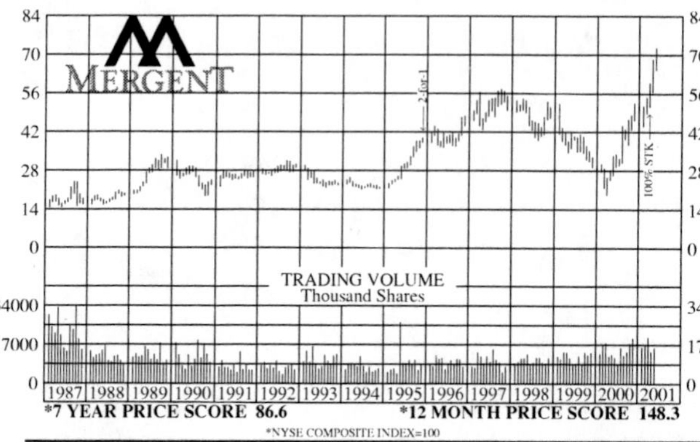

INTERIM EARNINGS (Per Share):

Qtr.	Mar.	June	Sept.	Dec.
1998	d0.38	1.08	2.70	d1.40
1999	0.92	1.18	1.26	d1.00
2000	0.92	2.60	3.46	2.56

INTERIM DIVIDENDS (Per Share):

Amt.	Decl.	Ex.	Rec.	Pay.
0.25Q	7/18/00	7/28/00	8/01/00	9/01/00
0.25Q	10/17/00	10/30/00	11/01/00	12/01/00
0.25Q	1/16/01	1/30/01	2/01/01	3/01/01
100% STK	2/20/01	3/21/01	3/06/01	3/20/01
0.15Q	2/20/01	4/27/01	5/01/01	6/01/01

Indicated div.: $0.60

CAPITALIZATION (12/31/00):

	($000)	(%)
Long-Term Debt	6,040,000	31.1
Minority Interest	2,207,900	11.4
Common & Surplus	11,191,100	57.6
Total	19,439,000	100.0

RECENT DEVELOPMENTS: For the year ended 12/31/00, the Company reported net income of $1.88 billion compared with income of $521.1 million, before an accounting charge of $157.9 million, in the previous year. Results of 2000 and 1999 included after-tax charges of $642.3 million and $637.3 related to the settlement of tobacco litigation. Total revenues fell to $21.34 billion from $21.47 billion the year before.

PROSPECTS: On 1/4/01, CNA Financial Corp. sold its Life Reinsurance business, which will result in a gain. Separately, Loews Hotels opened a second hotel at Universal Orlando in Florida and is developing a third hotel with its partners, which is scheduled to open in 2002. Meanwhile, under Diamond Offshore's five-year contract, future revenues to be generated by Ocean Confidence, a semisubmersible drilling unit, are estimated to be $311.5 million.

BUSINESS

LOEWS CORPORATION is a highly diversified company, which, through subsidiaries, operates primarily in the cigarettes and insurance businesses. The Company produces and sells cigarettes through its wholly-owned subsidiary Lorillard, Inc. Brand names include NEWPORT, KENT and TRUE. The Company owns 86.5% of CNA Financial Corporation, which has operations in property and casualty insurance. Another wholly-owned subsidiary is Loews Hotels Holding Corporation, who owns and operates 14 Loews Hotels. LTR also holds a 97% interest in Bulova Corporation. Loews owns a 52% interest in Diamond Offshore Drilling Inc., which operates 45 offshore drilling rigs.

BUSINESS LINE ANALYSIS

(12/31/2000)	Rev (%)	Inc (%)
CNA Financial	73.2	56.9
Lorillard	20.3	40.2
Loews Hotels	1.6	1.4
Diamond Offshore	3.4	1.7
Bulova	0.8	0.8
Corporate	0.7	(1.0)
Total	100.0	100.0

ANNUAL FINANCIAL DATA

	12/31/00	12/31/99	12/31/98	12/31/97	12/31/96	12/31/95	12/31/94
Earnings Per Share	[6] **9.44**	[5] **2.40**	[3] **2.03**	[3] [4] **3.45**	[3] [4] **5.96**	[2] [3] **7.49**	[1] [3] **1.11**
Cash Flow Per Share	**9.37**	**2.83**	**2.99**	**4.44**	**6.42**	**7.85**	**1.28**
Tang. Book Val. Per Share	**54.82**	**45.79**	**43.13**	**38.76**	**35.52**	**32.91**	**22.52**
Dividends Per Share	**0.50**	**0.50**	**0.50**	**0.50**	**0.50**	**0.31**	**0.25**
Dividend Payout %	**5.3**	**20.8**	**24.6**	**14.5**	**8.4**	**4.2**	**22.5**
INCOME STATEMENT (IN MILLIONS):							
Total Revenues	21,337.8	21,465.2	21,208.3	20,138.8	20,442.4	18,677.4	13,515.2
Costs & Expenses	17,788.9	20,072.6	19,542.0	17,995.7	17,609.2	15,471.2	13,033.8
Depreciation & Amort.	d13.9	94.1	219.7	226.5	107.4	84.4	40.7
Operating Income	3,562.8	1,298.5	1,446.6	1,916.6	2,725.8	3,121.8	440.7
Net Interest Inc./(Exp.)	d356.9	d354.3	d369.2	d323.4	d318.0	d282.5	d174.6
Income Before Income Taxes	3,205.9	944.2	1,077.4	1,593.2	2,407.8	2,839.3	266.1
Income Taxes	1,106.9	305.5	354.5	495.3	791.4	945.3	cr9.0
Net Income	[6] 1,876.7	[5] 521.1	[3] 464.8	[3] [4] 793.6	[3] [4] 1,383.9	[2] [3] 1,765.7	[1] [3] 267.8
Cash Flow	1,862.8	615.2	684.5	1,020.1	1,491.3	1,850.1	308.5
Average Shs. Outstg. (000)	198,733	217,067	229,078	230,000	232,322	235,670	240,766
BALANCE SHEET (IN MILLIONS):							
Cash & Cash Equivalents	9,295.5	7,501.7	8,079.5	9,252.0	8,610.6	7,378.7	8,598.2
Total Current Assets	24,597.1	21,042.6	22,145.4	23,006.9	22,788.6	21,286.2	17,085.7
Net Property	3,206.3	2,952.7	2,848.3	2,590.2	2,225.1	1,437.5	1,089.9
Total Assets	70,877.1	69,463.7	70,906.4	69,983.1	67,683.0	65,516.9	50,336.0
Total Current Liabilities	2,881.3	2,873.8	2,529.4	2,453.4	5,371.2	4,132.2	6,846.6
Long-Term Obligations	6,040.0	5,706.3	5,966.7	5,752.6	4,370.7	4,248.2	2,144.4
Net Stockholders' Equity	11,191.1	9,977.7	10,201.2	9,665.1	8,731.2	8,238.7	5,405.3
Net Working Capital	21,715.8	18,168.8	19,616.0	20,553.5	17,417.4	17,154.0	10,239.1
Year-end Shs. Outstg. (000)	197,228	208,961	225,164	230,000	230,000	235,666	235,860
STATISTICAL RECORD:							
Operating Profit Margin %	16.7	6.0	6.8	9.5	13.3	16.7	3.3
Net Profit Margin %	8.8	2.4	2.2	3.9	6.8	9.5	2.0
Return on Equity %	16.8	5.2	4.6	8.2	15.9	21.4	5.0
Return on Assets %	2.6	0.8	0.7	1.1	2.0	2.7	0.5
Debt/Total Assets %	8.5	8.2	8.4	8.2	6.5	6.5	4.3
Price Range	52.47-19.13	52.25-29.25	54.13-39.00	57.81-42.75	47.94-36.25	39.94-21.66	25.69-21.13
P/E Ratio	5.6-2.0	21.8-12.2	26.7-19.2	16.8-12.4	8.0-6.1	5.3-2.9	23.1-19.0
Average Yield %	1.4	1.2	1.1	1.0	1.2	1.0	1.1

Statistics are as originally reported. Adj. for 2-for-1 split, 3/01 & 10/95. [1] Incl. loss of $255.7 mill. [2] Incl. ops. of Continental Corp., acquired 5/95. [3] Incl. invest. gain. $149.7 mill., 1998; loss $237.9 mill., 1997; gain $491.3 mill., 1996; gain $192.9 mill., 1995; loss $447.0 mill., 1994. [4] Incl. gain on sale of sub.'s stk. of $124.3 mill., 1997; $186.6 mill., 1996. [5] Bef. an acctg. chrg. of $157.9 mill. & incl. a pre-tax invest. loss of $158.2 mill. [6] Incl. a pre-tax investment gain of $1.31 bill. & after-tax tobacco litigation chrgs. of $642.3 mill.

OFFICERS:
L. A. Tisch, Co-Chmn.
P. R. Tisch, Co-Chmn.
J. S. Tisch, Pres., C.E.O.

INVESTOR CONTACT: Barry Hirsch, Senior Vice-Pres. & Sec., (212) 521-2000

PRINCIPAL OFFICE: 667 Madison Ave., New York, NY 10021-8087

TELEPHONE NUMBER: (212) 521-2000
FAX: (212) 521-2498
WEB: www.loews.com

NO. OF EMPLOYEES: 29,700 (avg.)

SHAREHOLDERS: 2,300 (approx.)

ANNUAL MEETING: In Mar.

INCORPORATED: DE, Nov., 1969

INSTITUTIONAL HOLDINGS:
No. of Institutions: 306
Shares Held: 112,301,257
% Held: 56.9

INDUSTRY: Fire, marine, and casualty insurance (SIC: 6331)

TRANSFER AGENT(S): Mellon Investor Services, New York, NY

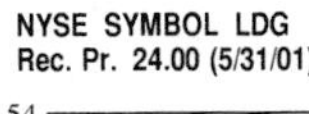

NYSE SYMBOL LDG
Rec. Pr. 24.00 (5/31/01)

LONGS DRUG STORES CORP.

YIELD 2.3%
P/E RATIO 20.0

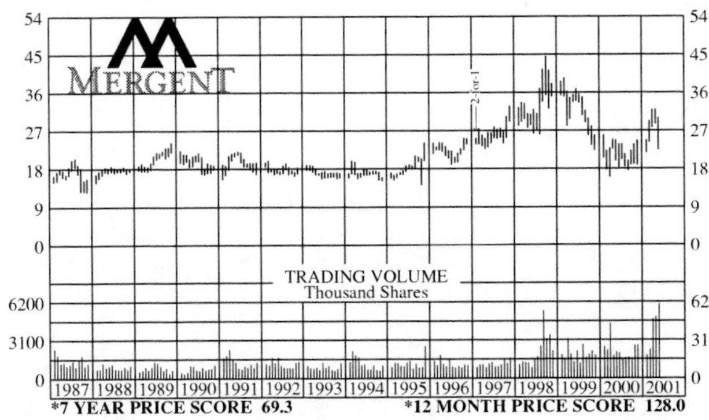

*7 YEAR PRICE SCORE 69.3 *12 MONTH PRICE SCORE 128.0

*NYSE COMPOSITE INDEX=100

INTERIM EARNINGS (Per Share):

Qtr.	Apr.	July	Oct.	Jan.
1997-98	0.36	0.31	0.26	0.56
1998-99	0.37	0.38	0.28	0.60
1999-00	0.42	0.42	0.32	0.61
2000-01	0.31	0.46	0.21	0.22

INTERIM DIVIDENDS (Per Share):

Amt.	Decl.	Ex.	Rec.	Pay.
0.14Q	5/16/00	5/25/00	5/30/00	7/10/00
0.14Q	8/18/00	8/25/00	8/29/00	10/10/00
0.14Q	11/14/00	11/24/00	11/28/00	1/10/01
0.14Q	2/27/01	3/09/01	3/13/01	4/10/01
0.14Q	5/15/01	5/24/01	5/29/01	7/10/01

Indicated div.: $0.56 (Div. Reinv. Plan)

CAPITALIZATION (1/25/01):

	($000)	(%)
Long-Term Debt	198,060	22.5
Common & Surplus	683,795	77.5
Total	881,855	100.0

RECENT DEVELOPMENTS: For the year ended 1/25/01, net income slid 34.9% to $44.9 million from $69.0 million the previous year. Results in the recent period included a $15.4 million charge to close 15 underperforming stores, a $1.0 million charge for the partial sale of a joint venture asset, and a net gain of $4.1 million from the settlement of various legal issues. Sales totaled $4.03 billion, up 9.7% versus $3.67 billion the year before. Same-store sales rose 3.3% year over year.

PROSPECTS: On 2/27/01, the Company signed an agreement with Bergen Brunswig Drug Company to jointly develop and operate a prescription fill center under which prescriptions will be filled for LDG's retail pharmacies and Bergen's chain customers and Good Neighbor Pharmacy network. The facility will be located in Sacramento, California. The facility is expected to be operational in the second quarter of 2001 and should help fuel continued growth of prescription sales.

BUSINESS

LONGS DRUG STORES CORP. operates a chain of 420 drug stores, as of 5/4/01, located in California, Hawaii, Washington, Nevada, Colorado, and Oregon. The Company's stores, which range in size from 15,000 to 30,000 square feet, sell both nationally advertised brand-name merchandise and LDG's private-label merchandise. Prescription drugs and "front end" merchandise, including over-the-counter medications, health care products, photo and photo processing, cosmetics and greeting cards are the LDG's core merchandise segments. Operations are decentralized, which allows store managers to enhance the product mix of their store based on customer preference in the communities they serve.

ANNUAL FINANCIAL DATA

	1/25/01	1/27/00	1/28/99	1/29/98	1/30/97	1/25/96	1/26/95
Earnings Per Share	**1 1.19**	**1.76**	**2 1.64**	**1.49**	**1.49**	**1 1.15**	**1.18**
Cash Flow Per Share	**3.08**	**3.20**	**2.96**	**2.66**	**2.61**	**2.15**	**2.09**
Tang. Book Val. Per Share	**14.70**	**14.37**	**16.40**	**15.12**	**14.21**	**13.19**	**12.75**
Dividends Per Share	**0.56**	**0.56**	**0.56**	**0.56**	**0.56**	**0.56**	**0.56**
Dividend Payout %	**47.1**	**31.8**	**34.1**	**37.6**	**37.6**	**48.7**	**47.5**
INCOME STATEMENT (IN MILLIONS):							
Total Revenues	4,027.1	3,672.4	3,266.9	2,952.9	2,828.3	2,644.4	2,558.3
Costs & Expenses	3,870.1	3,551.0	3,159.4	2,855.2	2,729.2	2,552.1	2,475.5
Depreciation & Amort.	71.8	56.1	51.3	45.2	43.9	40.4	37.8
Operating Income	85.3	118.5	104.8	95.6	97.5	90.8	80.8
Net Interest Inc./(Exp.)	d16.3	d4.6	d1.8	d0.6	...	...	...
Income Before Income Taxes	74.3	113.9	103.1	95.0	97.5	76.8	80.8
Income Taxes	29.4	44.9	39.7	37.3	38.9	30.6	32.1
Net Income	1 44.9	69.0	2 63.4	57.7	58.6	1 46.2	48.7
Cash Flow	116.6	125.1	114.6	103.0	102.5	86.6	86.5
Average Shs. Outstg. (000)	37,843	39,090	38,717	38,764	39,303	40,364	41,402
BALANCE SHEET (IN MILLIONS):							
Cash & Cash Equivalents	44.7	16.4	15.0	48.6	22.8	49.3	57.5
Total Current Assets	608.1	582.2	492.5	481.3	451.4	446.5	426.7
Net Property	588.4	529.0	471.9	435.1	417.4	395.3	397.8
Total Assets	1,353.7	1,270.3	1,025.1	946.3	879.6	853.6	828.0
Total Current Liabilities	448.7	351.9	339.0	312.8	286.5	287.3	257.9
Long-Term Obligations	198.1	181.2	14.3	14.2	...	...	...
Net Stockholders' Equity	683.8	702.7	638.8	584.1	553.6	522.8	524.1
Net Working Capital	159.4	230.3	153.5	168.6	164.9	159.2	168.8
Year-end Shs. Outstg. (000)	37,367	39,385	38,946	38,629	38,968	39,632	41,120
STATISTICAL RECORD:							
Operating Profit Margin %	2.1	3.2	3.2	3.2	3.4	3.4	3.2
Net Profit Margin %	1.1	1.9	1.9	2.0	2.1	1.7	1.9
Return on Equity %	6.6	9.8	9.9	9.9	10.6	8.8	9.3
Return on Assets %	3.3	5.4	6.2	6.1	6.7	5.4	5.9
Debt/Total Assets %	14.6	14.3	1.4	1.5	...	...	...
Price Range	26.00-15.94	39.50-22.25	44.50-26.00	32.75-22.63	25.19-18.94	24.13-14.13	19.94-15.13
P/E Ratio	21.8-13.4	22.4-12.6	27.1-15.9	22.0-15.2	16.9-12.7	21.0-12.3	16.9-12.8
Average Yield %	2.7	1.8	1.6	2.0	2.5	2.9	3.2

Statistics are as originally reported. Adj. for 2-for-1 stk. split, 1/97. 1 Incl. one-time after-tax chgs. totaling $12.3 mil ($0.33/sh), consisting of a $15.4 mil chg. to close 15 underperforming stores, a $1.0 mil chg. for the partial sale of a joint venture asset, & a net gain of $4.1 mil from the settlement of various legal issues, 1/01; $8.4 mil non-recur. chg., 1/96. 2 Incl. exp. of $5.5 million relating to remediation of Year 2000 issues.

OFFICERS:
R. M. Long, Chmn.
S. D. Roath, Pres., C.E.O.
S. McCann, Sr. V.P., C.F.O., Treas.

INVESTOR CONTACT: Investor Relations, (925) 937-1170

PRINCIPAL OFFICE: 141 North Civic Drive, Walnut Creek, CA 94596

TELEPHONE NUMBER: (925) 937-1170
FAX: (925) 210-6886
WEB: www.longs.com
NO. OF EMPLOYEES: 22,100 (avg.)
SHAREHOLDERS: 13,632 (approx.)
ANNUAL MEETING: In May
INCORPORATED: CA, Oct., 1946; reincorp., MD, May, 1985

INSTITUTIONAL HOLDINGS:
No. of Institutions: 135
Shares Held: 20,384,465
% Held: 54.5

INDUSTRY: Drug stores and proprietary stores (SIC: 5912)

TRANSFER AGENT(S): Mellon Investor Services, Ridgefield Park, NJ

NYSE SYMBOL LFB
Rec. Pr. 13.25 (5/31/01)

LONGVIEW FIBRE COMPANY

YIELD 3.6%
P/E RATIO 16.8

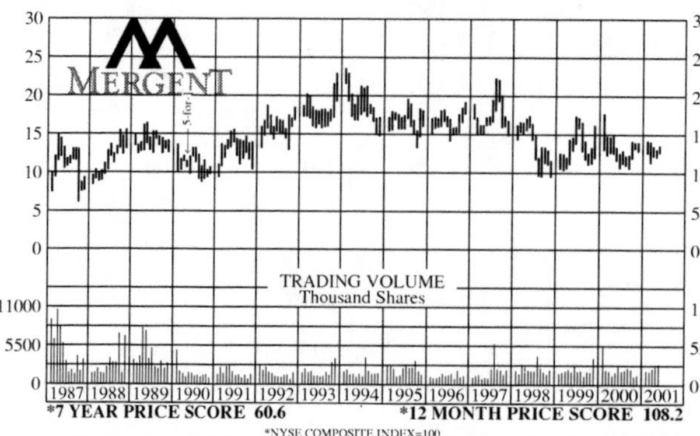

*7 YEAR PRICE SCORE 60.6 *12 MONTH PRICE SCORE 108.2
*NYSE COMPOSITE INDEX=100

INTERIM EARNINGS (Per Share):

Qtr.	Jan.	April	July	Oct.
1997	Nil	0.09	0.08	0.08
1998	d0.14	d0.09	0.08	0.02
1999	d0.02	0.10	0.08	0.23
2000	0.11	0.24	0.21	0.18
2001	0.16	...	...	...

INTERIM DIVIDENDS (Per Share):

Amt.	Decl.	Ex.	Rec.	Pay.
0.12Q	3/14/00	3/22/00	3/24/00	4/10/00
0.12Q	6/13/00	6/21/00	6/23/00	7/10/00
0.12Q	9/13/00	9/21/00	9/25/00	10/10/00
0.12Q	12/07/00	12/20/00	12/22/00	1/10/01
0.12Q	3/12/01	3/21/01	3/23/01	4/10/01

Indicated div.: $0.48

CAPITALIZATION (10/31/00):

	($000)	(%)
Long-Term Debt	490,900	44.9
Deferred Income Tax	171,518	15.7
Common & Surplus	432,042	39.5
Total	1,094,460	100.0

RECENT DEVELOPMENTS: For the quarter ended 1/31/01, net income surged 47.5% to $8.2 million compared with $5.6 million in the equivalent 2000 quarter. Net sales were $219.6 million, up 6.9% from $205.4 million a year earlier. Timber segment net sales declined 8.3% to $35.0 million. Paper and paperboard segment net sales fell 24.5% to $47.2 million. Converted products segment net sales increased 6.8% to $111.8 million. Power segment net sales were $25.6 million versus nil the year before.

PROSPECTS: The paper and paperboard segment is being negatively affected by the volatility of the energy markets. As a result, the future selling price of electrical power and energy costs are uncertain. In the converted products segment, the Company should continue to benefit from strong demand and firm prices. In addition, LFB will continue to develop its specialty products in order to improve margins in this segment.

BUSINESS

LONGVIEW FIBRE COMPANY owns and operates tree farms in Oregon and Washington which produce logs for sale in the domestic and export markets. Current holdings are 572,363 acres, as of 1/31/01. The Company owns and operates a sawmill in Leavenworth, Washington. Residual wood chips are used at the Company's pulp and paper mill in Longview, Washington, which produces pulp that is manufactured into kraft paper and containerboard. LFB's sixteen converting plants in eleven states produce shipping containers and merchandise bags. The tonnage of paper and containerboard used in the converting plants equals approximately 57.0% of the Longview mill production. The sales breakdown in 2000 was: timber, 18.0%; paper & paperboard, 30.0% and converted products, 52.0%. The Company resumed selling electrical power in fiscal 2000 as a means of mitigating the impact of higher energy costs.

ANNUAL FINANCIAL DATA

	10/31/00	10/31/99	10/31/98	10/31/97	10/31/96	10/31/95	10/31/94
Earnings Per Share	**0.73**	**0.39**	**d0.13**	**0.25**	**1.09**	**1.47**	**0.64**
Cash Flow Per Share	**2.04**	**2.02**	**1.67**	**1.92**	**2.63**	**3.00**	**2.05**
Tang. Book Val. Per Share	**8.38**	**8.14**	**8.03**	**8.70**	**9.10**	**8.65**	**7.80**
Dividends Per Share	**0.48**	**0.28**	**0.54**	**0.64**	**0.64**	**0.60**	**0.52**
Dividend Payout %	**65.7**	**71.8**	**...**	**255.9**	**58.7**	**40.8**	**81.2**
INCOME STATEMENT (IN MILLIONS):							
Total Revenues	876.3	774.3	753.2	772.8	822.7	985.5	790.9
Costs & Expenses	712.0	622.5	638.8	639.1	638.5	758.3	641.4
Depreciation & Amort.	67.4	84.2	92.9	86.4	79.5	79.4	72.7
Operating Income	97.0	67.6	21.6	47.4	104.8	147.8	76.8
Net Interest Inc./(Exp.)	d39.7	d38.2	d38.7	d30.8	d28.9	d28.9	d23.8
Income Before Income Taxes	58.9	31.5	d14.2	19.5	86.9	120.2	54.3
Income Taxes	21.3	11.5	cr7.5	6.8	30.5	44.2	20.9
Net Income	37.6	20.0	d6.7	12.7	56.4	76.0	33.4
Cash Flow	105.0	104.2	86.2	99.1	135.8	155.4	106.1
Average Shs. Outstg. (000)	51,577	51,677	51,677	51,691	51,731	51,787	51,861
BALANCE SHEET (IN MILLIONS):							
Total Current Assets	205.0	192.7	197.8	197.7	203.7	209.0	175.1
Net Property	981.9	947.4	1,004.8	1,013.4	951.1	906.6	815.5
Total Assets	1,276.7	1,212.8	1,263.3	1,260.9	1,197.3	1,153.8	1,022.0
Total Current Liabilities	162.7	124.7	142.5	157.3	152.7	166.4	139.3
Long-Term Obligations	490.9	495.9	547.0	498.1	426.3	409.4	366.5
Net Stockholders' Equity	432.0	420.5	414.9	449.5	470.4	447.9	404.3
Net Working Capital	42.4	68.0	55.3	40.4	51.0	42.6	35.8
Year-end Shs. Outstg. (000)	51,577	51,677	51,677	51,677	51,706	51,751	51,830
STATISTICAL RECORD:							
Operating Profit Margin %	11.1	8.7	2.9	6.1	12.7	15.0	9.7
Net Profit Margin %	4.3	2.6	...	1.6	6.9	7.7	4.2
Return on Equity %	8.7	4.8	...	2.8	12.0	17.0	8.3
Return on Assets %	2.9	1.6	...	1.0	4.7	6.6	3.3
Debt/Total Assets %	38.5	40.9	43.3	39.5	35.6	35.5	35.9
Price Range	17.75-10.56	17.44-10.31	17.44-9.44	22.38-14.81	19.25-14.13	19.63-13.25	23.63-14.75
P/E Ratio	24.3-14.5	44.7-26.4	...	89.5-59.2	17.7-13.0	13.3-9.0	36.9-23.0
Average Yield %	3.4	2.0	4.0	3.4	3.8	3.7	2.7

Statistics are as originally reported.

OFFICERS:
R. P. Wollenberg, Chmn., Pres., C.E.O.
L. J. Holbrook, Sr. V.P., Treas., Sec.
R. B. Arkell, V.P., Gen. Couns.

INVESTOR CONTACT: Lisa J. Holbrook, (360) 425-1550

PRINCIPAL OFFICE: 300 Fibre Way, Longview, WA 98632

TELEPHONE NUMBER: (360) 425-1550
FAX: (360) 575-5934
WEB: www.longfibre.com

NO. OF EMPLOYEES: 3,750 (approx.)
SHAREHOLDERS: 10,000 (approx.)
ANNUAL MEETING: In Jan.
INCORPORATED: DE, Aug., 1926; reincorp., WA, 1989

INSTITUTIONAL HOLDINGS:
No. of Institutions: 124
Shares Held: 26,218,496
% Held: 51.1

INDUSTRY: Paper mills (SIC: 2621)

TRANSFER AGENT(S): Mellon Investor Services, Chicago, IL

NYSE SYMBOL LPX
Rec. Pr. 11.75 (5/31/01)

LOUISIANA-PACIFIC CORPORATION

YIELD 1.7%
P/E RATIO . . .

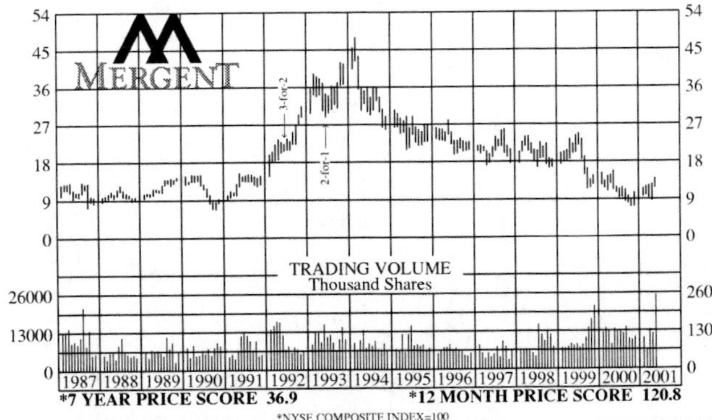

INTERIM EARNINGS (Per Share):

Qtr.	Mar.	June	Sept.	Dec.
1997	0.39	d0.10	d1.03	d0.20
1998	d0.23	1.87	d1.77	0.15
1999	0.26	0.79	0.65	0.34
2000	0.55	0.20	d0.39	d0.50

INTERIM DIVIDENDS (Per Share):

Amt.	Decl.	Ex.	Rec.	Pay.
0.14Q	5/01/00	5/15/00	5/17/00	6/01/00
0.14Q	7/31/00	8/16/00	8/18/00	9/01/00
0.14Q	11/06/00	11/15/00	11/17/00	12/01/00
0.14Q	2/05/01	2/14/01	2/16/01	3/01/01
0.05Q	5/07/01	5/15/01	5/17/01	6/01/01

Indicated div.: $0.20 (Div. Reinv. Plan)

CAPITALIZATION (12/31/00):

	($000)	(%)
Long-Term Debt	1,183,800	42.1
Deferred Income Tax	334,000	11.9
Common & Surplus	1,295,200	46.0
Total	2,813,000	100.0

RECENT DEVELOPMENTS: For the year ended 12/31/00, LPX incurred a net loss of $13.8 million compared with net income of $216.8 million in 1999. Results included non-recurring pre-tax charges of $70.5 million in 2000 and $8.2 million in 1999. The decline in earnings was primarily attributed to weak building products prices, higher energy costs and extensive downtime. Net sales climbed 1.9% to $2.93 billion from $2.88 billion a year earlier.

PROSPECTS: Looking ahead, LPX is focused on cost reduction with aggressive actions being taken at both manufacturing operations and administrative offices. Combined with restructuring at the corporate level, these actions have reduced the Company's workforce by approximately 23.0%. In addition, LPX's board recently reduced its dividend, and the Company has postponed or eliminated planned capital expenditures and will continue to streamline operations.

BUSINESS

LOUISIANA-PACIFIC CORPORATION is a building products firm with facilities throughout the U.S., Canada, and in Ireland and Chile. LPX owns almost a million acres of timberland, predominantly in the southern U.S., and has more than 66 manufacturing facilities in North America, as of 3/12/01. Structural products (62.0% of 2000 revenues), includes structural panel products, lumber, engineered wood products and wood fiber resources. Structural panel products are primarily used in new residential construction and remodeling applications such as subfloors, walls and roofs. Exterior products (11.0%) include wood and vinyl siding and accessories. LPX manufactures exterior siding and other cladding products for the residential and commercial building markets. Industrial panel products (10.0%) include particleboard, medium density fiberboard, hardboard and decorative panels. Other products (12.0%) include value-added products such as Cocoon™ cellulose insulation. Pulp (5.0%) is comprised two mills. LP recently sold a controlling interest in one and is seeking to sell the other.

ANNUAL FINANCIAL DATA

	12/31/00	12/31/99	12/31/98	12/31/97	12/31/96	12/31/95	12/31/94
Earnings Per Share	**[5] d0.13**	**[4] 2.04**	**[4] 0.02**	**[3] d0.94**	**[1] d1.87**	**[2] d0.48**	**3.15**
Cash Flow Per Share	**2.13**	**3.94**	**1.73**	**0.76**	**d0.08**	**1.41**	**4.94**
Tang. Book Val. Per Share	**9.28**	**9.64**	**10.84**	**11.02**	**12.70**	**15.12**	**16.51**
Dividends Per Share	**0.56**	**0.56**	**0.56**	**0.56**	**0.56**	**0.55**	**0.48**
Dividend Payout %	**. . .**	**27.4**	**N.M.**	**. . .**	**. . .**	**. . .**	**15.4**
INCOME STATEMENT (IN MILLIONS):							
Total Revenues	2,932.8	2,878.6	2,297.1	2,402.5	2,486.0	2,843.2	3,039.5
Costs & Expenses	2,667.8	2,307.7	2,084.9	2,339.6	2,613.2	2,738.3	2,283.6
Depreciation & Amort.	235.5	202.0	185.4	183.9	191.8	202.6	197.3
Operating Income	29.5	368.9	26.8	d121.0	d319.0	d97.7	558.6
Net Interest Inc./(Exp.)	d43.1	d11.9	d12.8	d29.0	d7.8	2.9	1.0
Income Before Income Taxes	d18.2	357.0	14.0	d150.0	d326.8	d94.8	559.6
Income Taxes	cr11.5	139.5	15.8	cr43.6	cr125.6	cr45.8	209.8
Equity Earnings/Minority Int.	d7.1	d0.7	3.8	4.6	0.5	d2.7	d2.9
Net Income	[5] d13.8	[4] 216.8	[4] 2.0	[3] d101.8	[1] d200.7	[2] d51.7	346.9
Cash Flow	221.7	418.8	187.4	82.1	d8.9	150.9	544.2
Average Shs. Outstg. (000)	104,100	106,200	108,600	108,450	107,410	107,040	110,140
BALANCE SHEET (IN MILLIONS):							
Cash & Cash Equivalents	38.1	116.0	126.5	31.9	27.8	75.4	315.9
Total Current Assets	654.1	739.4	612.1	596.8	579.2	618.5	694.4
Net Property	1,308.8	1,334.0	913.3	1,191.8	1,278.5	1,452.3	1,273.2
Total Assets	3,374.7	3,488.2	2,519.1	2,578.4	2,588.7	2,805.4	2,716.2
Total Current Liabilities	378.2	540.7	366.6	319.3	344.7	448.5	344.8
Long-Term Obligations	1,183.8	1,014.8	459.8	572.3	458.6	201.3	209.8
Net Stockholders' Equity	1,295.2	1,360.0	1,222.8	1,286.2	1,427.6	1,656.0	1,849.4
Net Working Capital	275.9	198.7	245.5	277.5	234.5	170.0	349.6
Year-end Shs. Outstg. (000)	104,361	104,968	107,273	109,628	108,766	108,349	111,992
STATISTICAL RECORD:							
Operating Profit Margin %	1.0	12.8	1.2	. . .	. . .	. . .	18.4
Net Profit Margin %	. . .	7.5	0.1	. . .	. . .	. . .	11.4
Return on Equity %	. . .	15.9	0.2	. . .	. . .	. . .	18.8
Return on Assets %	. . .	6.2	0.1	. . .	. . .	. . .	12.8
Debt/Total Assets %	35.1	29.1	18.3	22.2	17.7	7.2	7.7
Price Range	15.81-7.06	24.88-11.38	24.19-16.38	25.88-17.00	28.13-19.63	30.50-20.88	48.00-25.75
P/E Ratio	. . .	12.2-5.6	N.M.	. . .	. . .	. . .	15.2-8.2
Average Yield %	4.9	3.1	2.8	2.6	2.3	2.1	1.3

Statistics are as originally reported. [1] Incl. a net chrg. of $215 mill. [2] Incl. chrg. of $221.8 mill. related to class action settlements. [3] Incl. after-tax chrg. of $94.3 mill. for settlement & other unusual items. [4] Incl. unusual chrgs. of $36.1 mill., 1998; $5.1 mill., 1999. [5] Incl. a pre-tax nonrecurr. chrg. of $70.5 mill.

OFFICERS:
M. A. Suwyn, Chmn., C.E.O.
C. M. Stevens, V.P., C.F.O., Treas.
G. C. Wilkerson, Jr., V.P., Gen. Couns.

INVESTOR CONTACT: William L. Herbert, (503) 221-0800

PRINCIPAL OFFICE: 111 S.W. Fifth Avenue, Portland, OR 97204-3699

TELEPHONE NUMBER: (503) 221-0800
FAX: (503) 796-0204
WEB: www.lpcorp.com

NO. OF EMPLOYEES: 11,000 (approx.)

SHAREHOLDERS: 15,485 (approx.)

ANNUAL MEETING: In May

INCORPORATED: DE, July, 1972

INSTITUTIONAL HOLDINGS:
No. of Institutions: 199
Shares Held: 60,067,641
% Held: 57.6

INDUSTRY: Sawmills and planing mills, general (SIC: 2421)

TRANSFER AGENT(S): First Chicago Trust Company of New York, Jersey City, NJ

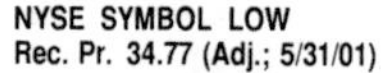
NYSE SYMBOL LOW
Rec. Pr. 34.77 (Adj.; 5/31/01)

LOWE'S COMPANIES, INC.

YIELD 0.2%
P/E RATIO 32.2

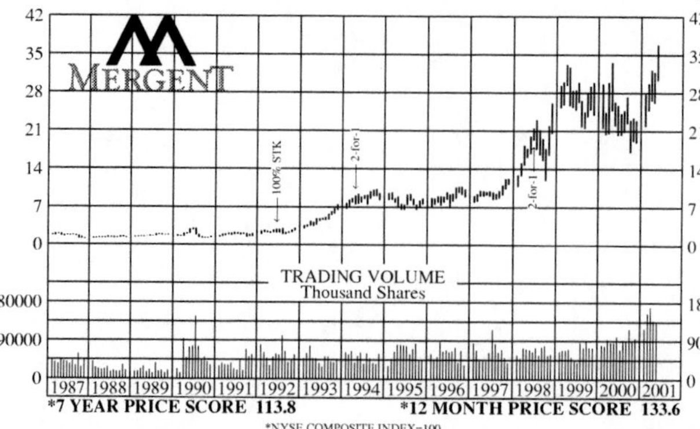

*7 YEAR PRICE SCORE 113.8 *12 MONTH PRICE SCORE 133.6

*NYSE COMPOSITE INDEX=100

INTERIM EARNINGS (Per Share):

Qtr.	Apr.	July	Oct.	Jan.
1997-98	0.11	0.19	0.13	0.11
1998-99	0.14	0.24	0.17	0.15
1999-00	0.17	0.30	0.22	0.20
2000-01	0.25	0.37	0.27	0.19

INTERIM DIVIDENDS (Per Share):

Amt.	Decl.	Ex.	Rec.	Pay.
0.035Q	9/21/00	10/11/00	10/13/00	10/27/00
0.035Q	12/06/01	1/17/01	1/19/01	2/02/01
0.035Q	4/03/01	4/18/01	4/20/01	5/04/01
2-for-1	5/25/01	7/01/01	6/08/01	6/29/01
0.02Q	5/25/01	7/18/01	7/20/01	8/03/01

Indicated div.: $0.08 (Div. Reinv. Plan)

CAPITALIZATION (2/2/01):

	($000)	(%)
Long-Term Debt	2,697,669	31.9
Deferred Income Tax	251,450	3.0
Common & Surplus	5,494,885	65.1
Total	8,444,004	100.0

RECENT DEVELOPMENTS: For the 53 weeks ended 2/2/01, net earnings advanced 20.4% to $809.9 million from $672.8 million in the corresponding 52-week period the previous year. Results in the prior-year period included a $24.4 million pre-tax charge related to the acquisition of Eagle Hardware & Garden, Inc. Net sales climbed 18.1% to $18.78 billion from $15.91 billion the year before. Comparable-store sales increased 1.2% year-over-year.

PROSPECTS: The Company anticipates it will spend about $1.30 billion to significantly expand its presence in the Northeast. LOW plans to build more than 75 new stores from Philadelphia to Maine over the next five years, including 25 superstores in the Boston area. In fiscal 2001, the Company expects to open 115 new stores, up from 100 new stores opened in fiscal 2000. Meanwhile, LOW is targeting earnings of $1.23 to $1.25 per share during fiscal 2001.

BUSINESS

LOWE'S COMPANIES, INC. is a specialty retailer that combines the merchandise, sales and service of a home improvement center, a building materials supplier and a consumer-durables retailer to serve the do-it-yourself home improvement and construction markets. As of 5/4/01, 680 retail stores were in operation in 40 states. The sales mix for 2000: Appliances, 10%; Lumber/Plywood, 9%; Outdoor Fashion, 7%; Nursery, 7%; Millwork, 6%; Building Materials, 6%; Cabinets/Furniture/Shelving, 6%; Fashion Electrical, 6%; Tools, 6%; Hardware, 6%; Fashion Plumbing, 6%; Flooring, 5%; Paint, 5%; Rough Plumbing & Electrical, 5%; Outdoor Power Equipment, 4%; Walls/Windows, 2%; and Other, 4%. On 4/2/99, LOW acquired Eagle Hardware & Garden, Inc.

ANNUAL FINANCIAL DATA

	2/2/01	1/28/00	1/29/99	1/30/98	1/31/97	1/31/96	1/31/95
Earnings Per Share	**1.06**	**[1] 0.88**	**0.68**	**0.52**	**0.44**	**0.35**	**0.36**
Cash Flow Per Share	**1.59**	**1.32**	**1.07**	**0.86**	**0.73**	**0.59**	**0.54**
Tang. Book Val. Per Share	**7.17**	**6.14**	**4.45**	**3.71**	**3.20**	**2.57**	**2.23**
Dividends Per Share	**0.07**	**0.06**	**0.06**	**0.06**	**0.05**	**0.05**	**0.04**
Dividend Payout %	**6.6**	**6.9**	**8.5**	**10.7**	**11.5**	**13.1**	**11.8**
INCOME STATEMENT (IN MILLIONS):							
Total Revenues	18,778.6	15,905.6	12,244.9	10,136.9	8,600.2	7,075.4	6,110.5
Costs & Expenses	16,966.8	14,419.8	11,139.5	9,271.7	7,897.8	6,531.7	5,626.3
Depreciation & Amort.	409.5	337.8	272.2	241.1	199.8	153.6	112.9
Operating Income	1,402.3	1,148.0	833.2	624.1	502.7	390.1	371.4
Net Interest Inc./(Exp.)	d120.8	d84.9	d74.7	d65.6	d49.1	d38.0	d27.9
Income Before Income Taxes	1,281.4	1,063.1	758.4	558.5	453.6	352.1	343.5
Income Taxes	471.6	390.3	276.0	201.1	161.5	126.1	120.0
Net Income	809.9	[1] 672.8	482.4	357.5	292.2	226.0	223.6
Cash Flow	1,219.4	1,010.6	754.6	598.6	491.9	379.6	336.4
Average Shs. Outstg. (000)	768,950	767,708	707,590	697,518	670,712	641,812	619,704
BALANCE SHEET (IN MILLIONS):							
Cash & Cash Equivalents	468.5	568.8	243.1	211.3	70.5	171.3	268.5
Total Current Assets	4,175.0	3,709.5	2,585.7	2,109.6	1,851.5	1,603.7	1,557.2
Net Property	7,035.0	5,177.2	3,636.9	3,005.2	2,494.4	1,858.3	1,397.7
Total Assets	11,375.8	9,012.3	6,344.7	5,219.3	4,435.0	3,556.4	3,106.0
Total Current Liabilities	2,928.6	2,386.0	1,765.3	1,449.3	1,348.5	949.9	945.9
Long-Term Obligations	2,697.7	1,726.6	1,283.1	1,045.6	767.3	866.2	681.2
Net Stockholders' Equity	5,494.9	4,695.5	3,136.0	2,600.6	2,217.5	1,656.7	1,419.9
Net Working Capital	1,246.4	1,323.6	820.3	660.3	502.9	653.8	611.3
Year-end Shs. Outstg. (000)	766,484	764,718	705,286	701,264	693,616	643,672	638,108
STATISTICAL RECORD:							
Operating Profit Margin %	7.5	7.2	6.8	6.2	5.8	5.5	6.1
Net Profit Margin %	4.3	4.2	3.9	3.5	3.4	3.2	3.7
Return on Equity %	14.7	14.3	15.4	13.7	13.2	13.6	15.7
Return on Assets %	7.1	7.5	7.6	6.8	6.6	6.4	7.2
Debt/Total Assets %	23.7	19.2	20.2	20.0	17.3	24.4	21.9
Price Range	33.63-17.13	33.22-21.50	26.09-10.80	12.28-7.91	10.88-7.16	9.72-6.50	10.34-6.64
P/E Ratio	31.9-16.2	38.0-24.6	38.4-15.9	23.8-15.4	25.0-16.4	27.6-18.4	28.7-18.4
Average Yield %	0.3	0.2	0.3	0.5	0.6	0.6	0.5

Statistics are as originally reported. Adj. for 2-for-1 stk. split, 6/01 & 6/98. [1] Incl. $24.4 mil pre-tax, non-recur. chg., 1999; $71.3 mil pre-tax, non-recur. chg., 1991.

OFFICERS:
R. L. Tillman, Chmn., Pres., C.E.O.
R. A. Niblock, Sr. V.P., C.F.O.
S. A. Hellrung, Sr. V.P., Gen. Couns., Sec.

INVESTOR CONTACT: Carson Anderson, Asst. Treas., (336) 658-4385

PRINCIPAL OFFICE: 1605 Curtis Bridge Road, Wilkesboro, NC 28697

TELEPHONE NUMBER: (336) 658-4000
FAX: (336) 658-4766
WEB: www.lowes.com

NO. OF EMPLOYEES: 77,000 full-time (approx.); 17,000 part-time (approx.)

SHAREHOLDERS: 16,885

ANNUAL MEETING: In May

INCORPORATED: NC, Aug., 1952

INSTITUTIONAL HOLDINGS:
No. of Institutions: 505
Shares Held: 613,255,508 (Adj.)
% Held: 79.7

INDUSTRY: Lumber and other building materials (SIC: 5211)

TRANSFER AGENT(S): EquiServe Trust Company, N.A., Boston, MA

NYSE SYMBOL LSI
Rec. Pr. 20.47 (4/30/01)

LSI LOGIC CORPORATION

YIELD	...
P/E RATIO	29.2

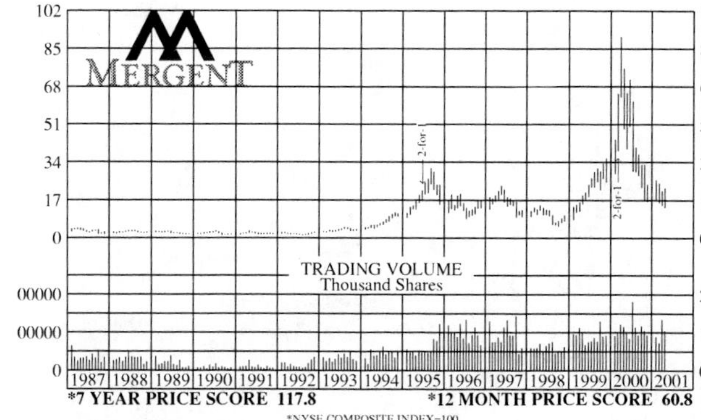

*7 YEAR PRICE SCORE 117.8 *12 MONTH PRICE SCORE 60.8

*NYSE COMPOSITE INDEX=100

INTERIM EARNINGS (Per Share):

Qtr.	Mar.	June	Sept.	Dec.
1996	0.16	0.18	0.11	0.12
1997	0.15	0.16	0.16	0.12
1998	0.11	0.12	d1.01	0.05
1999	0.02	0.03	0.17	0.32
2000	0.25	0.21	0.06	0.18

INTERIM DIVIDENDS (Per Share):

Amt.	Decl.	Ex.	Rec.	Pay.
2-for-1	1/26/00	2/17/00	2/04/00	2/16/00

CAPITALIZATION (12/31/00):

	($000)	(%)
Deferred Income Tax	130,616	5.0
Minority Interest	5,742	0.2
Common & Surplus	2,498,137	94.8
Total	2,634,495	100.0

RECENT DEVELOPMENTS: For the year ended 12/31/00, net income advanced 48.9% to $236.6 million compared with income of $158.9 million, before an accounting charge of $91.8 million, in 1999. Results for 2000 included charges totaling $194.0 million and a gain of $80.1 million. Earnings for 1999 included non-recurring items that resulted in a net charge of $769,000. Revenues jumped 31.0% to $2.74 billion from $2.09 billion in the previous year.

PROSPECTS: The Company is cautious about its outlook for 2001 as a result of adverse economic conditions and widespread inventory correction in the communications and storage markets. Meanwhile, LSI initiated a series of cost-reduction measures designed to align operating expenses, excluding goodwill amortization and special items, with current revenue projections.

BUSINESS

LSI LOGIC CORPORATION is a designer, developer, manufacturer and marketer of high performance application-specific integrated circuits (ASICs) and storage systems. The Company's integrated circuits are used in a range of communication devices, including devices used for wireless, broadband, data networking and set-top-box applications. LSI operates in two segments, the semiconductor segment and the Storage Area Network segment. The semiconductor segment uses advanced process technology and design methodology to design and develop highly complex ASICs and other integrated circuits. The Storage Area Networks segment designs and manufactures enterprise storage systems through LSI Logic Storage Systems, Inc., its wholly-owned subsidiary, under the MetaStor® brand name.

ANNUAL FINANCIAL DATA

	12/31/00	12/31/99	12/31/98	12/31/97	12/31/96	12/31/95	12/31/94
Earnings Per Share	**[4] 0.70**	**[3] 0.51**	**[2] d0.46**	**[1] 0.56**	**0.56**	**0.93**	**0.50**
Cash Flow Per Share	**1.92**	**1.62**	**0.33**	**1.14**	**1.12**	**1.46**	**0.97**
Tang. Book Val. Per Share	**5.96**	**5.21**	**4.16**	**5.59**	**5.10**	**4.70**	**2.94**
INCOME STATEMENT (IN MILLIONS):							
Total Revenues	2,737.7	2,089.4	1,490.7	1,290.3	1,238.7	1,267.7	901.8
Costs & Expenses	2,003.1	1,524.1	1,390.9	928.5	898.8	813.8	640.4
Depreciation & Amort.	445.1	367.2	225.2	166.4	147.5	135.2	103.6
Operating Income	289.5	198.2	d125.5	195.4	192.4	318.7	157.8
Net Interest Inc./(Exp.)	d41.6	d40.0	d8.5	d1.5	d13.6	d16.3	d18.5
Income Before Income Taxes	379.8	224.2	d123.6	224.2	205.1	334.9	156.2
Income Taxes	143.0	65.0	7.9	62.7	57.4	93.8	43.7
Equity Earnings/Minority Int.	d0.2	d0.2	d0.1	d0.7	d0.5	d3.0	d3.7
Net Income	[4] 236.6	[3] 158.9	[2] d131.6	[1] 160.7	147.2	238.1	108.7
Cash Flow	681.7	526.1	93.6	327.1	294.6	373.3	212.4
Average Shs. Outstg. (000)	354,337	325,088	281,598	288,054	262,492	256,044	219,812
BALANCE SHEET (IN MILLIONS):							
Cash & Cash Equivalents	1,133.2	661.3	281.3	490.9	717.3	685.5	428.5
Total Current Assets	2,072.2	1,288.3	819.5	870.5	1,051.1	1,136.7	730.9
Net Property	1,278.7	1,323.5	1,480.1	1,123.9	811.7	638.3	495.5
Total Assets	4,197.5	3,206.6	2,800.0	2,126.9	1,952.7	1,849.6	1,270.4
Total Current Liabilities	626.9	475.3	592.8	438.2	345.3	395.8	307.9
Net Stockholders' Equity	2,498.1	1,855.8	1,510.1	1,566.0	1,316.2	1,216.2	544.9
Net Working Capital	1,445.3	813.0	226.7	432.2	705.7	740.9	422.9
Year-end Shs. Outstg. (000)	321,523	299,572	282,838	280,322	258,012	258,606	228,574
STATISTICAL RECORD:							
Operating Profit Margin %	10.6	9.5	...	15.1	15.5	25.1	17.5
Net Profit Margin %	8.6	7.6	...	12.5	11.9	18.8	12.1
Return on Equity %	9.5	8.6	...	10.3	11.2	19.6	20.0
Return on Assets %	5.6	5.0	...	7.6	7.5	12.9	8.6
Price Range	90.38-16.30	35.69-8.06	14.69-5.25	23.44-9.31	19.81-8.50	31.25-9.13	11.34-3.88
P/E Ratio	129.1-23.3	70.0-15.8	...	41.8-16.6	35.4-15.2	33.6-9.8	22.9-7.8

Statistics are as originally reported. Adj. for 2-for-1 split, 2/00 & 6/95. [1] Bef. $1.4 mill. acct. chg. [2] Incl. $146.0 mill. in-process R&D chg., $75.4 mill. restr. chg., & $9.1 mill. spl. exp. chgs. [3] Incl. $2.1 mill. restr. gain, $4.6 mill. acq. in-process R&D, $48.4 mill. gain on sale of equity secs. & excl. $91.8 mill. acct. chg. [4] Incl. $2.8 mill. non-recur. chgs., $77.5 mill. in-process R&D chg., $113.8 mill. amort. chg. & $80.1 mill. gain fr. sale of sec.

OFFICERS:
W. J. Corrigan, Chmn., C.E.O.
B. Look, Exec. V.P., C.F.O.
D. G. Pursel, V.P., Gen. Couns., Sec.

INVESTOR CONTACT: Investor Relations, (408) 954-4710

PRINCIPAL OFFICE: 1551 McCarthy Blvd., Milpitas, CA 95035

TELEPHONE NUMBER: (408) 433-8000
FAX: (408) 954-3220
WEB: www.lsilogic.com

NO. OF EMPLOYEES: 7,221 (avg.)

SHAREHOLDERS: 3,883 (approx.)

ANNUAL MEETING: In May

INCORPORATED: CA, Nov., 1980; reincorp., DE, June, 1987

INSTITUTIONAL HOLDINGS:
No. of Institutions: 335
Shares Held: 166,749,836
% Held: 51.7

INDUSTRY: Semiconductors and related devices (SIC: 3674)

TRANSFER AGENT(S): Bank Boston, N.A. c/o EquiServe, Boston, MA

NYSE SYMBOL LZ
Rec. Pr. 29.29 (4/30/01)

LUBRIZOL CORPORATION

YIELD 3.6%
P/E RATIO 13.3

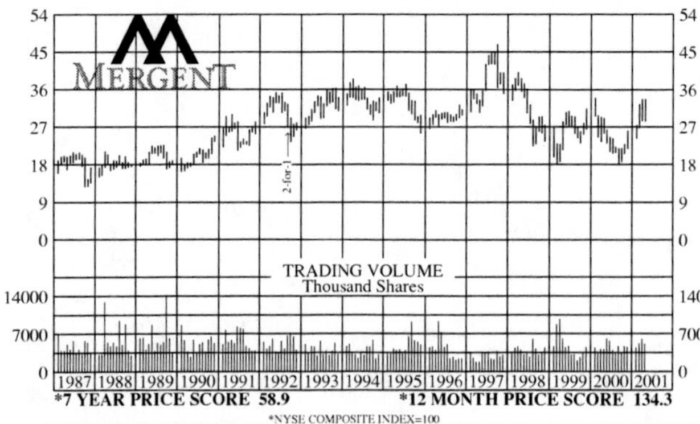

*7 YEAR PRICE SCORE 58.9 *12 MONTH PRICE SCORE 134.3
*NYSE COMPOSITE INDEX=100

INTERIM EARNINGS (Per Share):

Qtr.	Mar.	June	Sept.	Dec.
1997	0.66	0.81	0.67	0.53
1998	0.52	0.71	0.30	d0.27
1999	0.72	0.55	0.37	0.61
2000	0.55	0.59	0.44	0.63

INTERIM DIVIDENDS (Per Share):

Amt.	Decl.	Ex.	Rec.	Pay.
0.26Q	7/24/00	8/08/00	8/10/00	9/08/00
0.26Q	9/25/00	11/08/00	11/10/00	12/08/00
0.26Q	12/11/00	2/07/01	2/09/01	3/09/01
0.26Q	4/23/01	5/08/01	5/10/01	6/08/01

Indicated div.: $1.04 (Div. Reinv. Plan)

CAPITALIZATION (12/31/00):

	($000)	(%)
Long-Term Debt	378,783	30.9
Deferred Income Tax	60,614	5.0
Minority Interest	32,470	2.7
Common & Surplus	752,281	61.5
Total	1,224,148	100.0

RECENT DEVELOPMENTS: For the year ended 12/31/00, net income slipped 4.1% to $118.0 million versus $123.0 million in 1999. Results for 2000 included an after-tax litigation settlement gain of $14.9 million and a special credit of $4.5 million. Results for 1999 included a litigation settlement gain of $17.6 million and a special charge of $19.6 million. Results were hampered by difficult economic conditions and higher raw material and energy costs. Total revenues climbed 1.6% to $1.78 billion.

PROSPECTS: The Company is cautious about economic conditions in 2001. The implementation of price increases should contribute to revenues in the near term. However, the gain in revenues will likely be mitigated by higher costs related to petrochemical raw materials. LZ plans to continue to control operating expenses and anticipates some volume growth in the year through the introduction of new products. In addition, the market development of advanced fluid systems should have a positive effect on earnings.

BUSINESS

THE LUBRIZOL CORPORATION is a full service supplier of performance chemicals to diverse markets worldwide. Lubrizol develops, produces and sells specialty additive systems for gasoline and diesel engine lubrication oils, for automatic transmission fluids and for gear oils and marine and tractor lubricants. Lubrizol also supplies specialty products for industrial lubricant and functional fluids, fuel additives and diversified specialty chemical products. LZ groups its product lines into two operating segments: chemicals for transportation and chemicals for industry. Geographic revenues for 2000 were derived: U.S., 39.0%; other North American, 3.7%; Europe, 30.0%; Asia-Pacific, 19.6%; and Latin America, Middle East and other, 7.7%.

ANNUAL FINANCIAL DATA

	12/31/00	12/31/99	12/31/98	12/31/97	12/31/96	12/31/95	12/31/94
Earnings Per Share	**[6] 2.22**	**[5] 2.25**	**[4] 1.27**	**2.66**	**[1] 2.80**	**[1][3] 2.37**	**[2] 2.67**
Cash Flow Per Share	**4.11**	**4.07**	**2.84**	**4.16**	**4.13**	**3.54**	**3.67**
Tang. Book Val. Per Share	**11.34**	**11.75**	**11.04**	**14.31**	**14.00**	**13.49**	**12.83**
Dividends Per Share	**1.04**	**1.04**	**1.04**	**1.01**	**0.97**	**0.93**	**0.89**
Dividend Payout %	**46.8**	**46.2**	**81.9**	**38.0**	**34.6**	**39.2**	**33.3**
INCOME STATEMENT (IN MILLIONS):							
Total Revenues	1,775.8	1,748.0	1,617.9	1,673.8	1,597.6	1,663.6	1,599.0
Costs & Expenses	1,496.2	1,422.4	1,376.0	1,354.3	1,322.0	1,394.3	1,331.0
Depreciation & Amort.	100.8	99.7	88.0	87.2	81.0	74.2	65.9
Operating Income	178.8	225.8	153.9	232.3	194.6	195.1	202.0
Net Interest Inc./(Exp.)	d18.3	d21.8	d13.2	d6.2	d3.2	d5.6	0.9
Income Before Income Taxes	170.3	195.4	118.8	231.1	250.6	225.6	251.5
Income Taxes	52.3	72.4	47.6	76.3	80.8	74.0	75.9
Net Income	[6] 118.0	[5] 123.0	[4] 71.2	154.9	[1] 169.8	[1][3] 151.6	[2] 175.6
Cash Flow	218.8	222.7	159.2	242.1	250.8	225.9	241.5
Average Shs. Outstg. (000)	53,220	54,716	56,122	58,229	60,694	63,840	65,737
BALANCE SHEET (IN MILLIONS):							
Cash & Cash Equivalents	145.9	185.5	53.6	86.5	55.1	30.6	36.4
Total Current Assets	727.9	780.4	687.5	657.1	585.1	639.7	624.4
Net Property	677.2	670.5	718.9	692.7	707.3	693.0	558.7
Total Assets	1,659.5	1,682.4	1,643.2	1,462.3	1,402.1	1,492.0	1,394.4
Total Current Liabilities	282.2	311.3	270.0	261.9	227.1	265.6	253.5
Long-Term Obligations	378.8	365.4	390.4	182.2	157.6	194.4	114.2
Net Stockholders' Equity	752.3	790.1	769.1	815.4	819.4	849.0	832.0
Net Working Capital	445.7	469.1	417.4	395.1	358.0	374.1	370.9
Year-end Shs. Outstg. (000)	51,308	54,477	54,548	56,967	58,523	62,951	64,845
STATISTICAL RECORD:							
Operating Profit Margin %	10.1	12.9	9.5	13.9	12.2	11.7	12.6
Net Profit Margin %	6.6	7.0	4.4	9.3	10.6	9.1	11.0
Return on Equity %	15.7	15.6	9.3	19.0	20.7	17.9	21.1
Return on Assets %	7.1	7.3	4.3	10.6	12.1	10.2	12.6
Debt/Total Assets %	22.8	21.7	23.8	12.5	11.2	13.0	8.2
Price Range	33.88-18.25	31.38-18.00	40.19-22.38	46.94-30.38	32.38-26.50	37.38-25.50	38.63-28.50
P/E Ratio	15.3-8.2	13.9-8.0	31.6-17.6	17.6-11.4	11.6-9.5	15.8-10.8	14.5-10.7
Average Yield %	4.0	4.2	3.3	2.6	3.3	3.0	2.7

Statistics are as originally reported. [1] Incl. $53.3 mill. gain on sale of invest., 1996; $38.5 mill., 1995. [2] Incl. $11.5 mill. gain fr. sale of Genentech shs. [3] Incl. $9.5 mill. asset impair. chgs. [4] Incl. $10.5 mill. gain fr. settlement of litigation & $25.8 mill. after-tax spl. chgs. for restr. [5] Incl. $10.9 mill. net gain fr. litigation & $13.2 mill. net spl. chg. [6] Incl. $14.9 mill. litigation settlement gain & $4.5 mill. net spl. gain fr. adj. of prev. chgs.

OFFICERS:
W. G. Bares, Chmn., Pres., C.E.O.
C. P. Cooley, V.P., C.F.O., Treas.
K. H. Hopping, V.P., Sec.

INVESTOR CONTACT: K. H. Hopping, V.P., Sec., (440) 943-4200

PRINCIPAL OFFICE: 29400 Lakeland Blvd., Wickliffe, OH 44092-2298

TELEPHONE NUMBER: (440) 943-4200
FAX: (440) 943-5337
WEB: www.lubrizol.com
NO. OF EMPLOYEES: 4,390 (avg.)
SHAREHOLDERS: 4,628 (record)
ANNUAL MEETING: In May
INCORPORATED: OH, July, 1928; reincorp., Jan., 2000

INSTITUTIONAL HOLDINGS:
No. of Institutions: 164
Shares Held: 36,750,623
% Held: 71.7

INDUSTRY: Gum and wood chemicals (SIC: 2861)

TRANSFER AGENT(S): American Stock Transfer & Trust Company, New York, NY

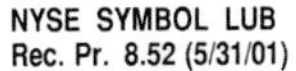
NYSE SYMBOL LUB
Rec. Pr. 8.52 (5/31/01)

LUBY'S, INC.

YIELD 4.7%
P/E RATIO ...

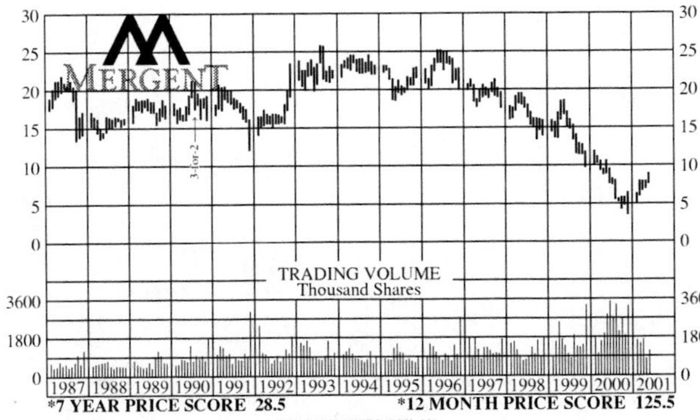

INTERIM EARNINGS (Per Share):

Qtr.	Nov.	Feb.	May	Aug.
1995-96	0.37	0.40	0.46	0.43
1996-97	0.35	0.36	0.41	0.10
1997-98	0.27	0.30	0.34	d0.70
1998-99	0.25	0.32	0.39	0.31
1999-00	0.28	0.25	0.26	d0.38
2000-01	d0.09	d0.42	...	...

INTERIM DIVIDENDS (Per Share):

Amt.	Decl.	Ex.	Rec.	Pay.
0.20Q	7/15/99	9/08/99	9/10/99	9/27/99
0.20Q	10/15/99	12/16/99	12/20/99	1/03/00
0.20Q	1/18/00	3/08/00	3/10/00	3/27/00
0.20Q	5/18/00	6/07/00	6/09/00	6/26/00
0.10Q	7/21/00	9/06/00	9/08/00	9/25/00

Indicated div.: $0.40 (Div. Reinv. Plan)

CAPITALIZATION (8/31/00):

	($000)	(%)
Long-Term Debt	116,000	37.1
Common & Surplus	196,741	62.9
Total	312,741	100.0

RECENT DEVELOPMENTS: For the three months ended 2/28/01, the Company reported a net loss of $9.4 million versus net income of $5.6 million in the prior-year quarter. Results for 2001 included a $9.4 million provision for asset impairment. Sales fell 8.0% to $112.2 million versus $121.9 million in the year-earlier quarter, reflecting the closing of three restaurants in fiscal year 2000 and 14 restaurants in fiscal year 2001. Operating loss amounted to $12.1 million versus operating income of $9.5 million.

PROSPECTS: In an attempt to reverse the Company's negative sales and earnings trend, LUB is focusing on made-from-scratch menu items, improved product offerings and effective marketing programs. The Company has reduced the percentage of outsourced products to improve customers' perceptions and managers' flexibility. Separately, LUB implemented a new manager compensation plan, including participation in store profits and offering bonuses for improved performances.

BUSINESS

LUBY'S INC. (formerly Luby's Cafeterias Inc.) owns and operates one of the nation's largest cafeteria chains in the Southern United States. As of 3/27/01, Luby's operated 218 cafeterias in ten states including New Mexico, Arizona, Arkansas, Florida, Mississippi, Louisiana, Missouri, Oklahoma, Tennessee and Texas. The cafeterias are typically located near shopping and business developments, as well as residential areas. They cater primarily to shoppers, store and office personnel at lunch and to families at dinner. Generally from 7,000 to 9,000 square feet in area, a cafeteria can typically accommodate 250 customers.

QUARTERLY DATA

(8/31/00) ($000)	Rev	Inc
1st Quarter	123,144	6,171
2nd Quarter	121,924	5,617
3rd Quarter	126,281	5,835
4th Quarter	122,035	(8,498)

ANNUAL FINANCIAL DATA

	8/31/00	8/31/99	8/31/98	8/31/97	8/31/96	8/31/95	8/31/94
Earnings Per Share	**(3) 0.41**	**1.26**	**(2) 0.22**	**(2) 1.22**	**1.66**	**1.55**	**(1) 1.45**
Cash Flow Per Share	**1.42**	**2.15**	**1.13**	**2.08**	**2.40**	**2.23**	**2.06**
Tang. Book Val. Per Share	**8.78**	**9.06**	**8.83**	**9.41**	**9.41**	**8.27**	**8.50**
Dividends Per Share	**0.70**	**0.80**	**0.80**	**0.80**	**0.74**	**0.68**	**0.61**
Dividend Payout %	**170.7**	**63.5**	**363.5**	**65.6**	**44.6**	**43.5**	**42.4**
INCOME STATEMENT (IN THOUSANDS):							
Total Revenues	493,384	501,493	508,871	495,446	450,128	419,024	390,692
Costs & Expenses	453,488	435,069	476,571	430,552	369,460	343,725	315,942
Depreciation & Amort.	22,784	20,025	21,121	20,196	17,693	16,417	15,700
Operating Income	17,112	46,399	11,179	44,698	62,975	58,882	59,050
Net Interest Inc./(Exp.)	d5,908	d4,761	d5,078	d4,037	d2,130	d1,749	...
Income Before Income Taxes	13,421	43,484	7,879	42,662	62,542	58,938	60,435
Income Taxes	4,296	14,871	2,798	14,215	23,334	21,923	22,663
Net Income	(3) 9,125	28,613	(2) 5,081	(2) 28,447	39,208	37,015	(1) 37,772
Cash Flow	31,909	48,638	26,202	48,643	56,901	53,432	53,472
Average Shs. Outstg.	22,422	22,637	23,272	23,406	23,689	23,908	25,982
BALANCE SHEET (IN THOUSANDS):							
Cash & Cash Equivalents	679	286	3,760	6,430	2,687	12,392	10,909
Total Current Assets	10,956	10,064	15,112	15,970	11,358	20,215	18,134
Net Property	338,124	314,418	298,597	334,017	311,589	279,157	257,832
Total Assets	367,094	346,025	339,041	368,778	335,290	312,380	289,668
Total Current Liabilities	42,376	49,812	47,436	45,681	46,454	99,531	56,362
Long-Term Obligations	116,000	78,000	73,000	84,000	41,000	...	...
Net Stockholders' Equity	196,741	203,204	205,414	218,840	225,673	192,704	213,526
Net Working Capital	d31,420	d39,748	d32,324	d29,711	d35,096	d79,316	d38,228
Year-end Shs. Outstg.	22,420	22,420	23,271	23,266	23,978	23,313	25,118
STATISTICAL RECORD:							
Operating Profit Margin %	3.5	9.3	2.2	9.0	14.0	14.1	15.1
Net Profit Margin %	1.8	5.7	1.0	5.7	8.7	8.8	9.7
Return on Equity %	4.6	14.1	2.5	13.0	17.4	19.2	17.7
Return on Assets %	2.5	8.3	1.5	7.7	11.7	11.8	13.0
Debt/Total Assets %	31.6	22.5	21.5	22.8	12.2	...	...
Price Range	11.94-3.50	18.63-9.69	19.50-13.38	21.38-17.50	25.25-19.88	23.25-18.50	24.63-21.63
P/E Ratio	29.1-8.5	14.8-7.7	88.6-60.8	17.5-14.3	15.2-12.0	15.0-11.9	17.0-14.9
Average Yield %	9.1	5.7	4.9	4.1	3.3	3.2	2.7

Statistics are as originally reported. (1) Bef. acctg. change credit $1.6 mill. (2) Incl. non-recurr. chrg. 1998, $23.8 mill.; 1997, $12.4 mill. (3) Incl. after-tax nonrecurr. chrg. of $9.5 mill.

OFFICERS:
R. T. Herres, Chmn.
C. J. Pappas, Pres., C.E.O.
H. J. Pappas, C.O.O.

INVESTOR CONTACT: Laura M. Bishop, Sr. V.P., (210) 654-9000

PRINCIPAL OFFICE: 2211 Northeast Loop 410, P.O. Box 33069, San Antonio, TX 78265-3069

TELEPHONE NUMBER: (210) 654-9000
FAX: (210) 654-3211
WEB: www.lubys.com

NO. OF EMPLOYEES: 14,000 (approx.)

SHAREHOLDERS: 4,280 (approx.)

ANNUAL MEETING: In Jan.

INCORPORATED: TX, 1959; reincorp., DE, Dec., 1991

INSTITUTIONAL HOLDINGS:
No. of Institutions: 70
Shares Held: 7,396,526
% Held: 33.0

INDUSTRY: Eating places (SIC: 5812)

TRANSFER AGENT(S): American Stock Transfer & Trust Company, New York, NY

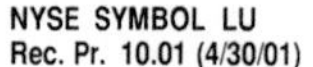

NYSE SYMBOL LU
Rec. Pr. 10.01 (4/30/01)

LUCENT TECHNOLOGIES INC.

YIELD 0.8%
P/E RATIO . . .

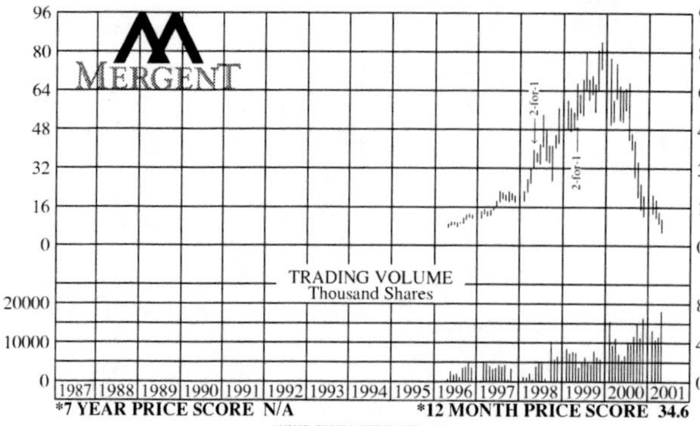

*7 YEAR PRICE SCORE N/A *12 MONTH PRICE SCORE 34.6

*NYSE COMPOSITE INDEX=100

INTERIM EARNINGS (Per Share):

Qtr.	Dec.	Mar.	June	Sept.
1996-97	0.44	0.03	0.09	d0.23
1997-98	0.31	0.01	d0.09	0.15
1998-99	1.00	0.16	0.24	0.30
1999-00	0.34	0.19	Nil	d0.01
2000-01	d0.47	. . .	. . .	. . .

INTERIM DIVIDENDS (Per Share):

Amt.	Decl.	Ex.	Rec.	Pay.
0.02Q	4/19/00	4/26/00	4/30/00	6/01/00
0.02Q	7/19/00	7/27/00	7/31/00	9/01/00
0.02Q	10/23/00	10/27/00	10/31/00	12/01/00
0.02Q	1/24/01	2/01/01	2/05/01	3/01/01
0.02Q	4/18/01	4/26/01	4/30/01	6/01/01

Indicated div.: $0.08 (Div. Reinv. Plan)

CAPITALIZATION (9/30/00):

	($000)	(%)
Long-Term Debt	3,076,000	10.1
Deferred Income Tax	1,266,000	4.1
Common & Surplus	26,172,000	85.8
Total	30,514,000	100.0

RECENT DEVELOPMENTS: For the quarter ended 12/31/00, LU reported a loss of $1.58 billion, before an extraordinary gain of $1.15 billion and an accounting change gain of $30.0 million, versus income from continuing operations of $1.12 billion a year earlier. Revenues declined 27.6% to $5.84 billion from $8.07 billion in 1999, reflecting the industry-wide slowdown in capital spending, softening of the competitive local exchange carrier market, and lower software sales.

PROSPECTS: On 1/24/01, LU announced a restructuring plan to streamline its operations, reduce its cost structure and improve working capital. Details include a business restructuring reserve and one-time charges, reduction of net headcount by about 10,000 employees, greatly expanded use of contract manufacturers, and a reduction of capital spending by $400.0 million by year end. The plan excludes Agere Systems, which includes the eptoelectronics components and integrated circuits divisions. LU intends to complete the spinoff of Agere by 9/30/01.

BUSINESS

LUCENT TECHNOLOGIES INC. is a global company with two reportable business segments. Service Provider Networks (79.2% of fiscal 2000 revenues), provides public networking systems and software to telecommunications service providers and public network operators around the world. Microelectronics and Communications Technologies (20.8%), designs and manufactures high-performance integrated circuits, power systems, optical fiber and fiber cables, and optoelectronic components for applications in the communications and computing industries. LU's research and development activities are conducted through Bell Laboratories. In April 1996, the Company, which was formed as a result of AT&T's planned restructuring, implemented an initial public offering of 112,037,037 shares of common stock. AT&T spun off its remaining 82.4% interest in Lucent Technologies to shareholders on 9/30/96. On 9/30/00, LU spun off to shareholders Avaya Inc., its enterprise networks group. On 12/29/00, LU sold its power systems business to Tyco International Ltd. for $2.50 billion in cash.

ANNUAL FINANCIAL DATA

	9/30/00	9/30/99	9/30/98	9/30/97	[2] 9/30/96	12/31/95	12/31/94
Earnings Per Share	**[4] 0.51**	**[3] 1.52**	**[1] 0.37**	**[1] 0.21**	**0.10**	**d0.41**	. . .
Cash Flow Per Share	**1.20**	**1.67**	**0.86**	**0.77**	**0.49**	**0.30**	. . .
Tang. Book Val. Per Share	**4.59**	**4.27**	**1.99**	**1.20**	**0.91**	. . .	. . .
Dividends Per Share	**0.08**	**0.08**	**0.08**	**0.07**	**0.04**	. . .	. . .
Dividend Payout %	**15.7**	**5.3**	**21.6**	**35.7**	**39.4**	. . .	. . .
INCOME STATEMENT (IN MILLIONS):							
Total Revenues	33,813.0	38,303.0	30,147.0	26,360.0	15,859.0	21,413.0	19,765.0
Costs & Expenses	28,510.0	31,091.0	26,352.0	23,279.0	14,435.0	20,920.0	17,483.0
Depreciation & Amort.	2,318.0	1,806.0	1,334.0	1,450.0	937.0	1,493.0	1,311.0
Operating Income	2,985.0	5,406.0	2,461.0	1,631.0	487.0	d1,000.0	971.0
Net Interest Inc./(Exp.)	d348.0	d406.0	d318.0	d305.0	d216.0	d302.0	d270.0
Income Before Income Taxes	3,003.0	5,443.0	2,306.0	1,467.0	367.0	d1,138.0	784.0
Income Taxes	1,322.0	1,985.0	1,336.0	926.0	143.0	cr271.0	302.0
Net Income	[4] 1,681.0	[3] 3,458.0	[1] 970.0	[1] 541.0	224.0	d867.0	482.0
Cash Flow	3,999.0	5,264.0	2,304.0	1,991.0	1,161.0	626.0	1,793.0
Average Shs. Outstg. (000)	3,325,900	3,142,700	2,666,800	2,576,000	2,384,000	2,100,000	. . .
BALANCE SHEET (IN MILLIONS):							
Cash & Cash Equivalents	1,467.0	1,816.0	685.0	1,350.0	2,241.0	448.0	580.0
Total Current Assets	21,490.0	21,931.0	14,078.0	12,501.0	12,781.0	10,679.0	8,492.0
Net Property	7,084.0	6,847.0	5,403.0	5,147.0	4,687.0	4,338.0	4,676.0
Total Assets	48,792.0	38,775.0	26,720.0	23,811.0	22,626.0	19,722.0	17,340.0
Total Current Liabilities	10,877.0	11,778.0	10,428.0	10,738.0	10,713.0	11,063.0	8,246.0
Long-Term Obligations	3,076.0	4,162.0	2,409.0	1,665.0	1,634.0	123.0	154.0
Net Stockholders' Equity	26,172.0	13,584.0	5,534.0	3,387.0	2,686.0	1,434.0	2,476.0
Net Working Capital	10,613.0	10,153.0	3,650.0	1,763.0	2,068.0	d384.0	246.0
Year-end Shs. Outstg. (000)	3,384,332	3,071,751	2,632,000	2,568,000	2,548,000	. . .	. . .
STATISTICAL RECORD:							
Operating Profit Margin %	8.8	14.1	8.2	6.2	3.1	. . .	4.9
Net Profit Margin %	5.0	9.0	3.2	2.1	1.4	. . .	2.4
Return on Equity %	6.4	25.5	17.5	16.0	8.3	. . .	19.5
Return on Assets %	3.4	8.9	3.6	2.3	1.0	. . .	2.8
Debt/Total Assets %	6.3	10.7	9.0	7.0	7.2	0.6	0.9
Price Range	77.50-12.19	84.19-47.00	56.94-18.36	22.69-11.19	13.28-7.44	. . .	. . .
P/E Ratio	151.9-23.9	55.4-30.9	156.0-50.3	108.0-53.2	139.7-78.2	. . .	. . .
Average Yield %	0.2	0.1	0.2	0.4	0.4	. . .	. . .

Statistics are as originally reported. Adj. for 2-for-1 stk. splits, 4/99 & 4/98 [1] Incls. non-recurr. pre-tax chrgs. of $1.42 bill., 9/98; $1.02 bill., 9/97 [2] Results are for the nine months ended 9/30/96 due to fiscal year changed. [3] Bef. acctg. change credit $1.31 bill., but incl. non-recurr. chrg. $375.0 mill. [4] Bef. loss of $462.0 mill. ($0.14 /sh.) fr. disc. ops.

OFFICERS:
H. Schacht, Chmn., C.E.O.
B. J. Verwaayen, Vice-Chmn.
Frank D'Amelio, C.F.O.

INVESTOR CONTACT: Mary Lou Ambrus, V.P., Ext. Comm. & Info., (908) 582-3060

PRINCIPAL OFFICE: 600 Mountain Avenue, Murray Hill, NJ 07974

TELEPHONE NUMBER: (908) 582-8500
FAX: (908) 582-7826
WEB: www.lucent.com

NO. OF EMPLOYEES: 126,000 (approx.)

SHAREHOLDERS: 1,602,553 (approx.)

ANNUAL MEETING: In Feb.

INCORPORATED: DE, Nov., 1995

INSTITUTIONAL HOLDINGS:
No. of Institutions: 948
Shares Held: 1,046,552,926
% Held: 30.7

INDUSTRY: Telephone communications, exc. radio (SIC: 4813)

TRANSFER AGENT(S): First Chicago Trust Company of New York, Jersey City, NJ

NYSE SYMBOL LYO
Rec. Pr. 15.71 (4/30/01)

LYONDELL CHEMICAL COMPANY

YIELD 5.7%
P/E RATIO 3.9

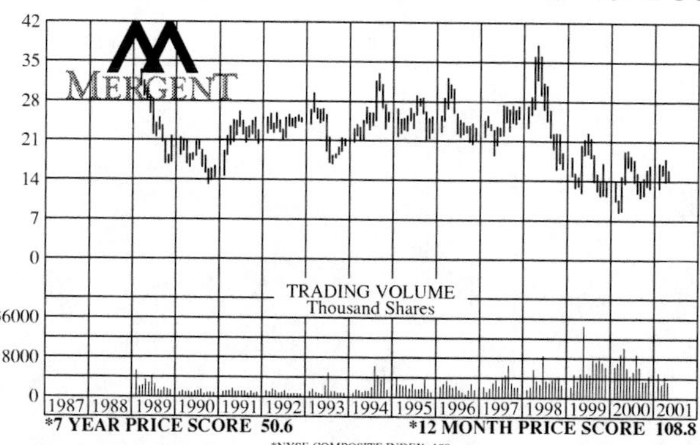

INTERIM EARNINGS (Per Share):

Qtr.	Mar.	June	Sept.	Dec.
1997	0.50	1.17	1.27	0.64
1998	0.82	0.38	d0.20	d0.35
1999	0.02	d0.11	d0.11	d0.50
2000	2.69	0.55	1.13	d0.38

INTERIM DIVIDENDS (Per Share):

Amt.	Decl.	Ex.	Rec.	Pay.
0.225Q	7/07/00	8/23/00	8/25/00	9/15/00
0.225Q	10/05/00	11/22/00	11/27/00	12/15/00
0.225Q	2/01/01	2/22/01	2/26/01	3/15/01
0.225Q	5/03/01	5/23/01	5/25/01	6/15/01

Indicated div.: $0.90 (Div. Reinv. Plan)

CAPITALIZATION (12/31/00):

	($000)	(%)
Long-Term Debt	3,844,000	65.5
Deferred Income Tax	702,000	12.0
Minority Interest	181,000	3.1
Common & Surplus	1,145,000	19.5
Total	5,872,000	100.0

RECENT DEVELOPMENTS: For the year ended 12/31/00, LYO reported income of $470.0 million versus a loss of $80.0 million in 1999. Results for 2000 included an after-tax gain of $400.0 million from the sale of LYO's polyols business. Results for 2000 and 1999 excluded net extraordinary losses of $33.0 million and $35.0 million, respectively. Sales and other operating revenues rose 9.3% to $4.04 billion from $3.69 billion the year before.

PROSPECTS: Near-term prospects remain uncertain in light of the slowing U.S. economy and elevated costs due to higher energy prices. In response, LYO is taking actions to improve its cost position, including reducing production at, and in some cases shutting down, higher-cost facilities. Separately, the joint venture formed with Bayer to build a PO-11 propylene oxide/styrene monomer facility is under construction in the Netherlands.

BUSINESS

LYONDELL CHEMICAL COMPANY (formerly Lyondell Petrochemical Co.) is a global chemical and refining company that operates in five business segments: intermediate chemicals and derivatives, petrochemicals, polymers, refining, and methanol. LYO manufactures petrochemicals, including propylene oxide and derivatives; olefins (ethylene, propylene, butadiene, and butylenes); polyolefins (polypropylene and high- and low-density polyethylene); methanol; methyl tertiary butyl ether and aromatics. As of 12/31/00, LYO holds a 58.75% participation interest in LYONDELLCITGO REFINING CO LTD, which produces refined petroleum products, including gasoline, heating oil, jet fuel, aromatics and lubricants. LYO also owns a 41% interest in Equistar Chemicals, L.P. and a 75% interest in Lyondell Methanol Company, L.P. On 8/1/98, LYO acquired ARCO Chemical Company.

ANNUAL FINANCIAL DATA

	12/31/00	12/31/99	12/31/98	12/31/97	12/31/96	12/31/95	12/31/94
Earnings Per Share	**[6] 3.99**	**[5] d0.77**	**[4] 0.67**	**[2] 3.58**	**[1] 1.58**	**4.86**	**2.78**
Cash Flow Per Share	**6.36**	**2.42**	**2.44**	**4.62**	**2.95**	**5.94**	**3.60**
Tang. Book Val. Per Share	...	...	...	**7.74**	**5.39**	**4.75**	**0.79**
Dividends Per Share	**0.90**	**0.90**	**0.90**	**0.90**	**0.90**	**0.90**	**0.90**
Dividend Payout %	**22.6**	...	**134.3**	**25.1**	**57.0**	**18.5**	**32.4**
INCOME STATEMENT (IN MILLIONS):							
Total Revenues	4,036.0	3,693.0	1,447.0	[3] 3,010.0	5,052.0	4,936.0	3,857.0
Costs & Expenses	3,418.0	2,959.0	1,144.0	2,352.0	4,694.0	4,144.0	3,368.0
Depreciation & Amort.	279.0	330.0	138.0	84.0	110.0	86.0	65.0
Operating Income	339.0	404.0	339.0	534.0	278.0	706.0	424.0
Net Interest Inc./(Exp.)	d462.0	d589.0	d262.0	d61.0	d78.0	d74.0	d69.0
Income Before Income Taxes	693.0	d104.0	89.0	456.0	196.0	618.0	349.0
Income Taxes	223.0	cr24.0	37.0	170.0	70.0	229.0	126.0
Equity Earnings/Minority Int.	199.0	76.0	...	...	...	...	...
Net Income	[6] 470.0	[5] d80.0	[4] 52.0	[2] 286.0	[1] 126.0	389.0	223.0
Cash Flow	749.0	250.0	190.0	370.0	244.0	503.0	300.0
Average Shs. Outstg. (000)	117,778	103,115	78,000	80,000	80,000	80,000	80,000
BALANCE SHEET (IN MILLIONS):							
Cash & Cash Equivalents	260.0	307.0	233.0	86.0	68.0	10.0	94.0
Total Current Assets	1,345.0	1,886.0	1,326.0	103.0	831.0	678.0	697.0
Net Property	2,429.0	4,291.0	4,511.0	46.0	2,270.0	1,814.0	880.0
Total Assets	7,047.0	9,498.0	9,225.0	1,559.0	3,276.0	2,606.0	1,663.0
Total Current Liabilities	734.0	1,021.0	2,337.0	308.0	771.0	750.0	433.0
Long-Term Obligations	3,844.0	6,046.0	5,391.0	345.0	1,194.0	807.0	707.0
Net Stockholders' Equity	1,145.0	1,007.0	574.0	619.0	431.0	380.0	63.0
Net Working Capital	611.0	865.0	d1,011.0	d205.0	60.0	d72.0	264.0
Year-end Shs. Outstg. (000)	117,560	117,571	77,000	80,000	80,000	80,000	80,000
STATISTICAL RECORD:							
Operating Profit Margin %	8.4	10.9	19.9	17.7	5.5	14.3	11.0
Net Profit Margin %	11.6	...	3.1	9.5	2.5	7.9	5.8
Return on Equity %	41.0	...	9.1	46.2	29.2	102.4	354.0
Return on Assets %	6.7	...	0.6	18.3	3.8	14.9	13.4
Debt/Total Assets %	54.5	63.7	58.4	22.1	36.4	31.0	42.5
Price Range	19.50-8.44	22.50-11.25	38.13-15.88	27.38-18.38	32.25-20.38	29.13-21.13	33.00-20.63
P/E Ratio	4.9-2.1	...	56.9-23.7	7.6-5.1	20.4-12.9	6.0-4.3	11.9-7.4
Average Yield %	6.4	5.3	3.4	3.9	3.4	3.6	3.4

Statistics are as originally reported. [1] Incl. $20.0 mill. after-tax gain on sale of assets. [2] Incl. $25.0 mill. non-recur. after-tax chg. [3] Refl. chg. in reporting of LCR fr. consol. to equity method. [4] Incl. $48.0 mill. in after-tax non-recur. chgs. & $6.0 mill. in after-tax charges rel. to formation of Equistar joint venture. [5] Excl. d$35.0 mill. net extraord. chg. [6] Incl. $400.0 mill. net gain fr. sale of bus. & excl. $33.0 mill. net extraord. chg.

OFFICERS:
W. T. Butler, Chmn.
D. F. Smith, Pres., C.E.O.
R. T. Blakely, Exec. V.P., C.F.O.

INVESTOR CONTACT: Sami Ahmad, Dir., Investor Relations, (713) 652-7245

PRINCIPAL OFFICE: 1221 McKinney St., Suite 700, Houston, TX 77010

TELEPHONE NUMBER: (713) 652-7200
FAX: (713) 652-4563
WEB: www.lyondell.com

NO. OF EMPLOYEES: 3,200 (approx.)

SHAREHOLDERS: 1,876 (approx.)

ANNUAL MEETING: In May

INCORPORATED: DE, 1985

INSTITUTIONAL HOLDINGS:
No. of Institutions: 165
Shares Held: 94,597,514
% Held: 80.5

INDUSTRY: Petroleum refining (SIC: 2911)

TRANSFER AGENT(S): The Bank of New York, New York, NY

NYSE SYMBOL MTB
Rec. Pr. 71.55 (4/30/01)

M & T BANK CORPORATION

YIELD 1.4%
P/E RATIO 20.3

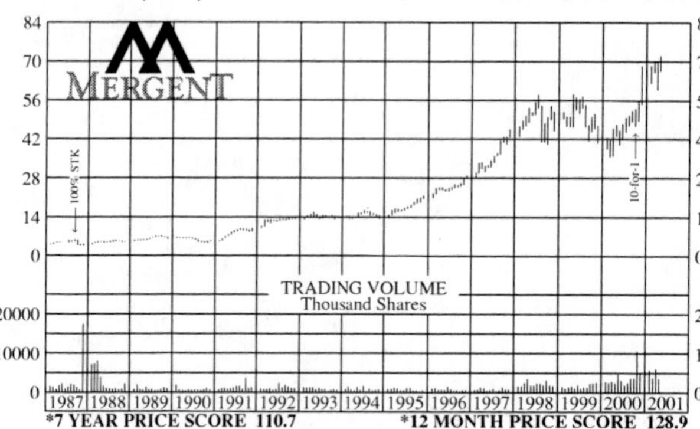

*7 YEAR PRICE SCORE 110.7 *12 MONTH PRICE SCORE 128.9

*NYSE COMPOSITE INDEX=100

INTERIM EARNINGS (Per Share):

Qtr.	Mar.	June	Sept.	Dec.
1997	0.62	0.65	0.70	0.67
1998	0.70	0.53	0.68	0.71
1999	0.83	0.80	0.83	0.82
2000	0.86	0.97	0.94	0.76

INTERIM DIVIDENDS (Per Share):

Amt.	Decl.	Ex.	Rec.	Pay.
1.25Q	7/19/00	8/30/00	9/01/00	9/29/00
10-for-1	9/21/00	10/06/00	9/29/00	10/05/00
0.25Q	10/18/00	11/29/00	12/01/00	12/29/00
0.25Q	2/21/01	2/23/01	2/27/01	3/30/01
0.25Q	4/18/01	5/30/01	6/01/01	6/29/01

Indicated div.: $1.00 (Div. Reinv. Plan)

CAPITALIZATION (12/31/00):

	($000)	(%)
Total Deposits	20,232,673	76.8
Long-Term Debt	3,414,516	13.0
Common & Surplus	2,700,485	10.2
Total	26,347,674	100.0

RECENT DEVELOPMENTS: For the year ended 12/31/00, net income increased 7.7% to $286.2 million compared with $265.6 million in the previous year. Results for 2000 and 1999 included after-tax merger-related expenses of $16.4 million and $3.0 million, respectively. Net interest income grew 12.5% to $854.2 million. Provision for credit losses declined 14.6% to $38.0 million. Total other income grew 15.0% to $324.7 million. Total other expense increased 19.9% to $694.5 million.

PROSPECTS: In 2001, MTB expects double-digit growth in earnings per share. On 2/10/01, MTB completed the acquisition of Premier National Bancorp, Inc. for $340.0 million. As a result of the acquisition, the Company has more than 470 branches in New York, Pennsylvania, Maryland, and West Virginia, and has combined assets of approximately $30.00 billion. In addition, the Company completed the merger of Premier National Bank into Manufacturers and Traders Trust Company.

BUSINESS

M&T BANK CORPORATION (formerly First Empire State Corp.), with assets of $28.95 billion as of 12/31/00, is a bank holding company. Its principal wholly-owned bank subsidiary, Manufacturers and Traders Trust Company, offers commercial banking, trust and investment services to its customers through more than 470 branches and 1,000 ATMs in New York, Pennsylvania, Maryland and West Virginia. The bank also has mortgage offices in New Jersey, Arizona, Colorado, Idaho, Massachusetts, Ohio, Oregon and Washington. On 2/10/01, the Company acquired Premier National Bancorp, Inc.

LOAN DISTRIBUTION

(12/31/00)	($000)	(%)
Comml, Finl, Agric & Other	5,007,053	22.6
Real Estate-Residential	4,427,285	20.0
Real Estate-Commercial	8,226,951	37.1
Real Estate-Construction	900,170	4.1
Consumer	3,579,515	16.2
Total	22,140,974	100.0

ANNUAL FINANCIAL DATA

	12/31/00	12/31/99	12/31/98	12/31/97	12/31/96	12/31/95	12/31/94
Earnings Per Share	**[1] 3.44**	**[1] 3.28**	**[1] 2.62**	**2.53**	**2.13**	**1.88**	**1.69**
Tang. Book Val. Per Share	**16.10**	**14.88**	**13.72**	**15.59**	**13.55**	**12.53**	**9.95**
Dividends Per Share	**0.63**	**0.45**	**0.38**	**0.32**	**0.28**	**0.25**	**0.22**
Dividend Payout %	**18.2**	**13.7**	**14.5**	**12.7**	**13.1**	**13.3**	**13.0**
INCOME STATEMENT (IN MILLIONS):							
Total Interest Income	1,772.8	1,478.6	1,351.8	1,065.0	997.4	928.2	747.3
Total Interest Expense	918.6	719.2	687.5	508.1	466.4	441.7	279.2
Net Interest Income	854.2	759.4	664.3	556.9	531.0	486.4	468.1
Provision for Loan Losses	38.0	44.5	43.2	46.0	43.3	40.4	60.5
Non-Interest Income	324.7	282.4	270.6	193.1	170.2	149.5	123.7
Non-Interest Expense	694.5	579.0	566.1	421.8	409.0	374.4	336.9
Income Before Taxes	446.4	418.3	325.6	282.2	249.0	221.2	194.5
Net Income	[1] 286.2	[1] 265.6	[1] 208.0	176.2	151.1	131.0	117.3
Average Shs. Outstg. (000)	83,171	80,900	79,500	69,770	70,480	67,810	69,520
BALANCE SHEET (IN MILLIONS):							
Cash & Due from Banks	750.3	592.8	493.8	333.8	324.7	363.1	377.8
Securities Avail. for Sale	3,071.7	2,321.9	2,756.9	1,640.6	1,434.0	1,541.6	1,519.8
Total Loans & Leases	22,970.3	17,572.9	16,005.7	11,765.5	11,120.2	9,873.7	8,447.1
Allowance for Credit Losses	602.2	482.3	520.5	543.6	668.6	580.2	473.2
Net Loans & Leases	22,368.1	17,090.6	15,485.2	11,221.9	10,451.7	9,293.5	7,974.0
Total Assets	28,949.5	22,409.1	20,583.9	14,002.9	12,943.9	11,955.9	10,528.6
Total Deposits	20,232.7	15,373.6	14,737.2	11,163.2	10,514.5	9,469.6	8,243.1
Long-Term Obligations	3,414.5	1,775.1	1,567.5	427.8	178.0	192.8	96.2
Total Liabilities	26,249.0	20,612.1	18,981.5	12,972.7	12,038.3	11,109.6	9,807.6
Net Stockholders' Equity	2,700.5	1,797.0	1,602.4	1,030.3	905.7	846.3	721.0
Year-end Shs. Outstg. (000)	93,244	77,238	76,980	66,100	66,860	64,330	66,110
STATISTICAL RECORD:							
Return on Equity %	10.6	14.8	13.0	17.1	16.7	15.5	16.3
Return on Assets %	1.0	1.2	1.0	1.3	1.2	1.1	1.1
Equity/Assets %	9.3	8.0	7.8	7.4	7.0	7.1	6.8
Non-Int. Exp./Tot. Inc. %	58.9	55.6	60.6	56.2	58.3	58.9	56.9
Price Range	68.42-35.70	58.25-40.60	58.20-40.00	45.50-28.10	28.96-20.90	21.80-13.60	16.50-13.45
P/E Ratio	19.9-10.4	17.7-12.4	22.2-15.3	18.0-11.1	13.6-9.8	11.6-7.2	9.8-8.0
Average Yield %	1.2	0.9	0.8	0.9	1.1	1.4	1.5

Statistics are as originally reported. Adj. for 10-for-1 stk. split, 10/5/00. [1] Incl. after-tax nonrecurr. merger & acquisition chrgs.: $16.4 mill., 2000; $3.0 mill., 12/31/99; $14.0 mill., 12/31/98.

OFFICERS:
R. J. Bennett, Chmn.
R. G. Wilmers, Pres. & C.E.O.
M. P. Pinto, Exec. V.P. & C.F.O.
A. C. Kugler, Exec. V.P. & Treas.

INVESTOR CONTACT: Michael S. Piemonte, (716) 842-5138

PRINCIPAL OFFICE: One M&T Plaza, Buffalo, NY 14203

TELEPHONE NUMBER: (716) 842-5445
FAX: (716) 842-5177
WEB: www.mandtbank.com

NO. OF EMPLOYEES: 7,616 full-time; 1,120 part-time

SHAREHOLDERS: 11,936

ANNUAL MEETING: In Apr.

INCORPORATED: NY, Nov., 1969

INSTITUTIONAL HOLDINGS:
No. of Institutions: 201
Shares Held: 52,491,817
% Held: 54.3

INDUSTRY: State commercial banks (SIC: 6022)

TRANSFER AGENT(S): BankBoston, N.A. c/o EquiServe, Boston, MA

NYSE SYMBOL CLI
Rec. Pr. 26.78 (4/30/01)

MACK-CALI REALTY CORP.

YIELD 9.1%
P/E RATIO 8.7

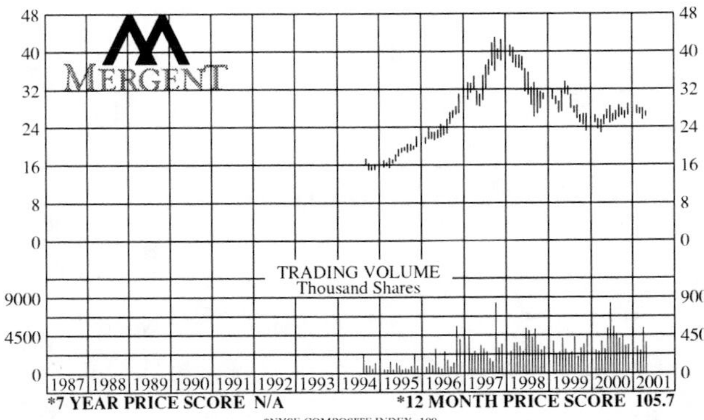

INTERIM EARNINGS (Per Share):

Qtr.	Mar.	June	Sept.	Dec.
1996	0.66	0.37	0.39	0.34
1997	0.44	0.49	0.48	d1.00
1998	0.51	0.53	0.53	0.55
1999	0.55	0.32	0.55	0.62
2000	0.62	1.52	0.34	0.59

INTERIM DIVIDENDS (Per Share):

Amt.	Decl.	Ex.	Rec.	Pay.
0.58Q	3/20/00	4/03/00	4/05/00	4/24/00
0.58Q	6/20/00	7/03/00	7/06/00	7/24/00
0.61Q	9/26/00	10/02/00	10/04/00	10/23/00
0.61Q	12/20/00	1/02/01	1/04/01	1/22/01
0.61Q	3/16/01	4/02/01	4/04/01	4/23/01

Indicated div.: $2.44 (Div. Reinv. Plan)

CAPITALIZATION (12/31/00):

	($000)	(%)
Long-Term Debt	1,628,512	46.1
Minority Interest	449,448	12.7
Common & Surplus	1,453,290	41.2
Total	3,531,250	100.0

RECENT DEVELOPMENTS: For the year ended 12/31/00, net income jumped 54.8% to $185.3 million compared with $119.7 million in the previous year. Results included non-recurring charges of $32.7 million and $14.3 million in 2000 and 1999, respectively. Results also included gains on sales of rental property of $75.0 million in 2000 and $1.7 million in 1999. Total revenues increased 4.5% to $576.2 million versus $551.5 million in the comparable period.

PROSPECTS: Looking ahead, the Company will continue to focus on its business strategy by expanding, through acquisitions and/or development, in properties with high-barrier-to-entry markets, with primary emphasis in the Northeast and in California. As a result, the Company plans to sell substantially all of its property located in the Southwestern and Western regions. Proceeds from the sales will be used for acquisitions purposes.

BUSINESS

MACK-CALI REALTY CORP. is a fully-integrated, self-administered and self-managed real estate investment trust that owns and operates a portfolio comprised predominantly of office and office/flex properties located primarily in the Northeast. The Company performs substantially all commercial real estate leasing, management, acquisition, development and construction services on an in-house basis. As of 12/31/00, the Company owned or had interests in 267 properties, totaling approximately 28.2 million square feet, plus developable land. The properties are comprised of: 155 office buildings and 87 office/flex buildings totaling approximately 26.3 million square feet, six industrial/warehouse buildings totaling approximately 387,400 square feet, two multi-family residential complexes consisting of 451 units, two stand-alone retail properties and three land leases, and eight office buildings and four office/flex buildings aggregating 1.5 million square feet, owned by unconsolidated joint ventures in which the Company has investment interests.

ANNUAL FINANCIAL DATA

	12/31/00	12/31/99	12/31/98	12/31/97	12/31/96	12/31/95	12/31/94
Earnings Per Share	[2][4] 3.10	[1][2] 2.04	[3] 2.11	[1][3] 0.12	[2][3] 1.76	1.23	0.38
Tang. Book Val. Per Share	25.50	24.67	24.86	23.22	...	12.30	10.32
Dividends Per Share	2.35	2.23	1.55	...	...	...	...
Dividend Payout %	75.8	109.3	73.5	...	...	...	...
INCOME STATEMENT (IN MILLIONS):							
Rental Income	491.2	469.9	427.5	206.2	76.9	50.8	13.8
Total Income	576.2	551.5	493.7	249.8	95.5	62.3	16.8
Costs & Expenses	195.4	194.1	175.3	91.0	35.5	24.4	6.3
Depreciation	92.1	87.2	78.9	36.8	15.8	12.1	3.8
Interest Expense	105.4	103.0	88.0	39.1	12.7	8.7	1.8
Income Before Income Taxes	231.5	152.7	151.5	36.4	37.2	17.1	5.0
Equity Earnings/Minority Int.	d46.1	d32.9	d32.5	d31.4	d4.8	d3.5	d1.1
Net Income	[2][4] 185.3	[1][2] 119.7	[3] 119.0	[1][3] 5.0	[2][3] 32.4	13.6	3.9
Average Shs. Outstg. (000)	73,070	67,133	63,893	44,156	...	11,122	10,500
BALANCE SHEET (IN MILLIONS):							
Cash & Cash Equivalents	121.2	104.9	78.3	9.5	208.0	4.2	9.4
Total Real Estate Investments	d310.0	d256.6	d177.9	d103.1	d68.6	d59.1	d50.8
Total Assets	3,677.0	3,629.6	3,452.2	2,593.4	1,026.3	363.9	225.3
Long-Term Obligations	1,628.5	1,490.2	1,420.9	972.7	268.0	135.5	77.0
Total Liabilities	2,223.7	2,187.7	2,028.3	1,436.0	324.9	178.1	117.0
Net Stockholders' Equity	1,453.3	1,441.9	1,423.9	1,157.4	701.4	185.8	108.3
Year-end Shs. Outstg. (000)	56,981	58,447	57,266	49,856	...	15,105	10,500
STATISTICAL RECORD:							
Net Inc.+Depr./Assets %	7.5	5.7	5.7	1.6	4.7	7.1	3.4
Return on Equity %	12.8	8.3	8.4	0.4	4.6	7.3	3.6
Return on Assets %	5.0	3.3	3.4	0.2	3.2	3.7	1.7
Price Range	28.88-22.75	33.63-23.13	41.38-26.13	43.00-28.38	31.00-20.50	22.00-15.38	17.38-14.88
P/E Ratio	9.3-7.3	16.5-11.3	19.6-12.4	358.0-236.3	17.6-11.6	17.9-12.5	45.7-39.1
Average Yield %	9.1	7.9	4.6	...	...	...	...

Statistics are as originally reported. [1] Incl. non-recurr. merger-related chrg., 1999, $16.5 mill.; 1997, $46.5 mill. [2] Incl. gain on sale of rental property, 2000, $75.0 mill.; 1999, $2.0 mill.; 1996, $5.7 mill. [3] Excl. extraord. chrg., 1998, $2.4 mill.; 1997, $3.6 mill.; 1996, $475,000. [4] Incl. non-recurr. chrg., $32.7 mill.

OFFICERS:
W. L. Mack, Chmn.
M. E. Hersh, C.E.O.
B. Lefkowitz, Exec. V.P., C.F.O.

INVESTOR CONTACT: Investor Relations, (908) 272-8000

PRINCIPAL OFFICE: 11 Commerce Drive, Cranford, NJ 07016-3599

TELEPHONE NUMBER: (908) 272-8000
FAX: (908) 272-6755
WEB: www.mack-cali.com

NO. OF EMPLOYEES: 400 (approx.)

SHAREHOLDERS: 396

ANNUAL MEETING: In May

INCORPORATED: MD, May, 1994

INSTITUTIONAL HOLDINGS:
No. of Institutions: 154
Shares Held: 49,477,928
% Held: 86.9

INDUSTRY: Real estate investment trusts (SIC: 6798)

TRANSFER AGENT(S): Equiserve, Inc., Jersey City, NJ

NYSE SYMBOL MAG
Rec. Pr. 9.55 (4/30/01)

MAGNETEK, INC.

YIELD ...
P/E RATIO 38.2

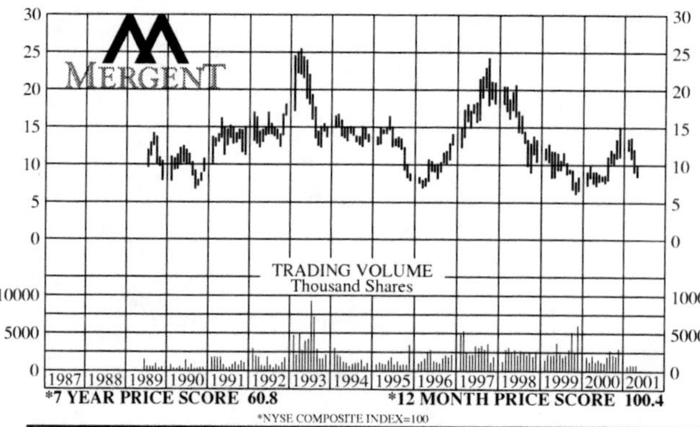

*7 YEAR PRICE SCORE 60.8 *12 MONTH PRICE SCORE 100.4
*NYSE COMPOSITE INDEX=100

INTERIM EARNINGS (Per Share):

Qtr.	Sept.	Dec.	Mar.	June
1997-98	0.25	0.28	0.32	0.35
1998-99	0.29	0.08	0.15	d1.06
1999-00	0.12	0.17	0.16	d0.04
2000-01	0.04	0.09	...	...

INTERIM DIVIDENDS (Per Share):

Amt.	Decl.	Ex.	Rec.	Pay.

No dividends paid.

CAPITALIZATION (6/30/00):

	($000)	(%)
Long-Term Debt [1]	62,308	22.3
Deferred Income Tax	32,904	11.8
Common & Surplus	184,206	65.9
Total	279,418	100.0

RECENT DEVELOPMENTS: For the quarter ended 12/31/00, income from continuing operations amounted to $2.1 million compared with income from continuing operations of $556,000 the year before. Results excluded net gains of $1.8 million in 2000 and $3.5 million in 1999 from discontinued operations. Net sales advanced 22.8% to $81.9 million versus $66.7 million in the same prior-year period.

PROSPECTS: On 3/5/01, MAG acquired ADS The Power Resource, Inc., a privately-held power systems integrator with annual revenues of about $16.0 million. The acquisition will expand MAG's capability to engineer, fabricate and install turnkey power systems. ADS specializes in power systems below 1,500 amplifiers, which complements the capabilities of the recently-acquired J-TEC Inc., a power system integrator that specializes in power plants above 1,500 amplifiers.

BUSINESS

MAGNTEK, INC. is a multi-national manufacturer of digital power products for applications that require precision power. The Company operates in a single segment called digital power products, which includes two broad product lines, power controls and motion controls. The power controls product line includes AC-to-DC switching power supplies and rectifiers/battery chargers, DC-to-DC power converters, DC-to-AC power inverters, peripheral component interconnects and voltage regulator modules. These products are used in telecommunications, data processing, data communications, data storage, networking, imaging, laser processing, power generation equipment, medical instrumentation and home appliances. The motion controls product line includes programmable power supplies that control motor speed used in industrial automation and materials handling, commercial heating, ventilating and air conditioning. In 1999, LG sold its generators business for $115.0 million and its motors business for $253.0 million.

QUARTERLY DATA

(6/30/2000) ($000)	Rev	Inc
1st Quarter	71,172	38,008
2nd Quarter	66,681	4,095
3rd Quarter	78,260	3,664
4th Quarter	77,462	(3,315)

ANNUAL FINANCIAL DATA

	6/30/00	[6] 6/30/99	6/30/98	6/30/97	6/30/96	6/30/95	6/30/94
Earnings Per Share	**[7] 0.05**	**[5] d0.74**	**1.20**	**[4] 1.09**	**[3] d3.78**	**[2] 0.87**	**d0.69**
Cash Flow Per Share	**0.59**	**0.10**	**2.38**	**2.55**	**d2.17**	**...**	**...**
Tang. Book Val. Per Share	**4.97**	**5.55**	**4.23**	**2.53**	**0.43**	**3.41**	**3.21**
INCOME STATEMENT (IN MILLIONS):							
Total Revenues	293.6	662.5	1,197.2	1,190.5	1,161.6	1,202.5	1,133.1
Costs & Expenses	273.4	663.7	1,080.4	1,072.0	1,159.1	1,088.5	1,086.8
Depreciation & Amort.	13.3	26.0	38.4	38.4	40.0	38.7	36.4
Operating Income	6.8	d27.2	78.4	80.1	d37.5	75.4	9.9
Net Interest Inc./(Exp.)	d2.9	d1.9	d16.6	d27.8	d31.6	d34.4	d32.0
Income Before Income Taxes	2.1	d33.7	59.2	48.0	d74.8	36.4	d24.4
Income Taxes	0.8	cr10.8	21.3	19.2	19.4	11.7	cr7.5
Net Income	[7] 1.3	[5] d22.9	37.9	[4] 28.8	[3] d94.2	[2] 21.5	d16.9
Cash Flow	14.6	3.1	76.3	67.2	d54.1	60.2	19.5
Average Shs. Outstg. (000)	24,947	30,953	32,005	26,378	24,922	...	...
BALANCE SHEET (IN MILLIONS):							
Cash & Cash Equivalents	0.3	6.9	6.0	6.1	0.9	0.3	7.0
Total Current Assets	119.8	269.7	417.6	407.1	432.9	490.2	453.6
Net Property	40.1	105.1	196.5	176.4	176.4	200.1	207.0
Total Assets	400.7	645.6	730.7	654.5	678.8	857.2	931.4
Total Current Liabilities	79.7	165.1	226.4	219.9	233.6	214.8	248.2
Long-Term Obligations	62.3	179.1	239.6	240.8	319.1	430.9	473.8
Net Stockholders' Equity	184.2	203.9	186.7	102.2	41.6	117.3	113.1
Net Working Capital	40.1	104.6	191.1	187.2	199.3	275.4	205.4
Year-end Shs. Outstg. (000)	23,073	29,986	31,484	28,259	25,462	24,680	24,205
STATISTICAL RECORD:							
Operating Profit Margin %	2.3	...	6.6	6.7	...	6.3	0.9
Net Profit Margin %	0.4	...	3.2	2.4	...	1.8	...
Return on Equity %	0.7	...	20.3	28.1	...	18.3	...
Return on Assets %	0.3	...	5.2	4.4	...	2.5	...
Debt/Total Assets %	15.6	27.7	32.8	36.8	47.0	50.3	50.9
Price Range	14.88-7.19	12.81-6.13	20.69-8.94	24.31-12.25	14.13-6.88	16.50-7.88	16.75-12.38
P/E Ratio	296.9-143.5	...	17.2-7.4	22.3-11.2	...	19.0-9.1	...

Statistics are as originally reported. [1] Incl. conv. subord. debt. & cap. lse. obligs. [2] Incl. $3.1 mill. gain on sale of Control Bus., bef. $4.8 mill. loss on retire. of debt & bef. $17.5 mill. loss fr. dis. opers.. [3] Incl. restruct. chgs. of $50.5 mill. & acctg. chg. of $29.2 mill. [4] Excl. net extra. chg. of $4.7 mill. [5] Incl. pre-tax chgs. of $34.4 mill. rel. to MAG's downsizing, inv. adjs., severance costs & asset write-downs & excl. net gains of $61.4 mill. fr. disc. opers. [6] Refls. the sale of the generators and motors businesses. [7] Excl. net gain fr. disc. ops. of $41.2 mill., fiscal 2000.

OFFICERS:
A. G. Galef, Chmn., Pres., C.E.O.
D. P. Reiland, Sr. V.P., C.F.O.
J. P. Colling Jr., V.P., Treas.

INVESTOR CONTACT: Investor Relations Dept., (615) 316-5261

PRINCIPAL OFFICE: 10900 Wilshire Boulevard, Suite 850, Los Angeles, CA 90024

TELEPHONE NUMBER: (615) 316-5100
FAX: (615) 316-5192
WEB: www.magnetek.com

NO. OF EMPLOYEES: 1,700 (approx.)

SHAREHOLDERS: 259

ANNUAL MEETING: In Nov.

INCORPORATED: DE, June, 1984

INSTITUTIONAL HOLDINGS:
No. of Institutions: 81
Shares Held: 18,402,238
% Held: 82.2

INDUSTRY: Transformers, except electronic (SIC: 3612)

TRANSFER AGENT(S): The Bank of New York, New York, NY

NYSE SYMBOL MBG
Rec. Pr. 25.29 (5/31/01)

MANDALAY RESORT GROUP

YIELD ...
P/E RATIO 17.1

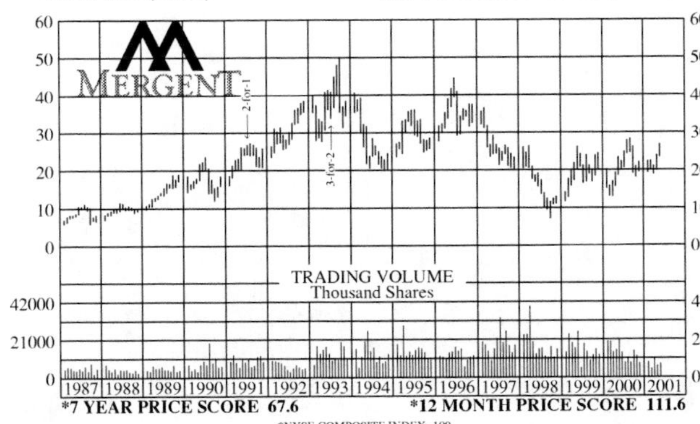

INTERIM EARNINGS (Per Share):

Qtr.	Apr.	July	Oct.	Jan.
1997-98	0.40	0.26	0.29	0.01
1998-99	0.23	0.27	0.25	0.16
1999-00	d0.05	0.26	0.31	d0.06
2000-01	0.58	0.48	0.38	0.04

INTERIM DIVIDENDS (Per Share):

Amt.	Decl.	Ex.	Rec.	Pay.

No dividends paid.

CAPITALIZATION (1/31/01):

	($000)	(%)
Long-Term Debt	2,623,597	67.1
Deferred Income Tax	235,763	6.0
Minority Interest	d18,675	-0.5
Common & Surplus	1,068,940	27.3
Total	3,909,625	100.0

RECENT DEVELOPMENTS: For the year ended 1/31/01, MBG reported net income of $119.7 million versus income of $64.2 million, before an accounting charge of $22.0 million, in 1999. Earnings for 2000 and 1999 included pre-tax pre-opening expenses of $1.8 million and $49.1 million. Results for 1999 also included a pre-tax abandonment loss of $5.4 million. Revenues increased 23.1% to $2.52 billion from $2.05 billion in the prior year.

PROSPECTS: In fiscal 2001, MBG anticipates higher earnings per share for the entire year compared with fiscal 2000. On 3/1/01, Nevada's major utilities raised electricity rates by 17.6% for most customers, with increases for major users of approximately 25.0% or higher. This will have a negative effect on earnings for large casino operators, including MBG. MBG's properties in Las Vegas will raise room rates to combat the cost increases.

BUSINESS

MANDALAY RESORT GROUP (formerly Circus Circus Enterprises, Inc.) owns and operates eleven properties in Nevada: Mandalay Bay, Luxor, Excalibur, Circus Circus, and Slots-A-Fun in Las Vegas; Circus Circus-Reno; Colorado Belle and Edgewater in Laughlin; Gold Strike and Nevada Landing in Jean and Railroad Pass in Henderson. MBG also owns and operates Gold Strike, a hotel/casino in Tunica County, Mississippi. MBG owns a 50% interest in Silver Legacy in Reno, and a 50% interest in and operates Monte Carlo in Las Vegas. In addition, MBG owns a 50% interest in and operates Grand Victoria, a riverboat casino in Elgin, Illinois, and owns a 53.5% interest in and operates MotorCity in Detroit, Michigan. MBG caters to high volume business by providing moderately-priced rooms, food and alternative entertainment in combination with gaming activity for family-oriented vacationers.

REVENUES

(01/31/2001)	($000)	(%)
Casino	1,250,035	46.4
Rooms	611,352	22.7
Food & Beverage	418,081	15.5
Other	299,753	11.1
Earnings of Unconsol Affi	114,645	4.3
Total	2,693,866	100.0

ANNUAL FINANCIAL DATA

	1/31/01	1/31/00	1/31/99	1/31/98	1/31/97	1/31/96	1/31/95
Earnings Per Share	**5 1.50**	**4 0.70**	**0.90**	**3 0.94**	**1 0.99**	**2 1.33**	**1.59**
Cash Flow Per Share	**4.24**	**2.57**	**2.40**	**2.31**	**2.01**	**2.34**	**2.55**
Tang. Book Val. Per Share	**8.98**	**8.81**	**8.72**	**7.87**	**6.23**	**7.38**	**7.88**
INCOME STATEMENT (IN MILLIONS):							
Total Revenues	2,524.2	2,050.9	1,479.8	1,354.5	1,334.3	1,299.6	1,170.2
Costs & Expenses	1,874.7	1,604.8	1,094.9	988.3	1,008.4	949.8	831.4
Depreciation & Amort.	218.0	172.4	142.1	129.7	103.7	98.4	82.8
Operating Income	431.5	273.7	242.8	236.5	222.2	251.4	256.0
Net Interest Inc./(Exp.)	d233.8	d176.8	d107.8	d104.4	d70.2	d57.2	d42.7
Income Before Income Taxes	194.4	103.1	140.8	147.9	163.9	205.8	214.5
Income Taxes	74.7	39.0	55.6	58.0	63.1	76.9	78.2
Equity Earnings/Minority Int.	d16.7	d0.3	...	...	...	...	...
Net Income	5 119.7	4 64.2	85.2	3 89.9	1 100.7	2 128.9	136.3
Cash Flow	337.7	236.6	227.3	219.6	204.5	227.3	219.0
Average Shs. Outstg. (000)	79,701	91,896	94,671	95,252	101,900	97,200	85,800
BALANCE SHEET (IN MILLIONS):							
Cash & Cash Equivalents	105.9	116.6	81.4	58.6	69.5	62.7	53.8
Total Current Assets	286.6	281.5	161.3	142.9	151.8	124.4	105.5
Net Property	3,236.8	3,335.1	3,000.8	2,466.8	1,920.0	1,474.7	1,239.1
Total Assets	4,248.3	4,329.5	3,869.7	3,263.5	2,729.1	2,211.9	1,507.1
Total Current Liabilities	296.7	244.6	231.6	167.0	129.8	93.9	82.0
Long-Term Obligations	2,623.6	2,691.3	2,259.1	1,788.8	1,405.9	715.2	632.7
Net Stockholders' Equity	1,068.9	1,187.8	1,157.6	1,123.7	971.8	1,226.8	686.1
Net Working Capital	d10.0	36.9	d70.3	d24.1	22.1	30.5	23.4
Year-end Shs. Outstg. (000)	76,276	89,870	90,663	95,113	94,059	112,795	85,852
STATISTICAL RECORD:							
Operating Profit Margin %	17.1	13.3	16.4	17.5	16.7	19.3	21.9
Net Profit Margin %	4.7	3.1	5.8	6.6	7.5	9.9	11.6
Return on Equity %	11.2	5.4	7.4	8.0	10.4	10.5	19.9
Return on Assets %	2.8	1.5	2.2	2.8	3.7	5.8	9.0
Debt/Total Assets %	61.8	62.2	58.4	54.8	51.5	32.3	42.0
Price Range	28.38-12.88	26.31-11.56	26.50-7.13	36.50-20.00	44.63-27.63	36.13-23.50	40.75-19.75
P/E Ratio	18.9-8.6	37.6-16.5	29.4-7.9	38.8-21.3	45.1-27.9	27.2-17.7	25.6-12.4

Statistics are as originally reported. 1 Incl. $48.3 mill. chrg. for write-offs rel. to construction projects. 2 Incl. $45.1 mill. chrg. for write-off of certain assets. 3 Incl. pre-open. exp. of $3.4 mill. for Gold Strike; $8.0 mill in costs assoc. with resign. of Chmn.; & a $6.0 mill. gain fr. sale of a Co. plane. 4 Bef. an acctg. chrg. of $22.0 mill.; incl. pre-tax pre-open. exp. of $49.1 mill. & a pre-tax abandonment loss of $5.4 mill. 5 Incl. a pre-tax pre-open. exp. of $1.8 mill.

OFFICERS:
M. S. Ensign, Chmn., C.E.O., C.O.O.
G. Schaeffer, Pres., C.F.O., Treas.
Y. Landau, Sec.

INVESTOR CONTACT: Investor Relations, (702) 632-6708

PRINCIPAL OFFICE: 3950 Las Vegas Blvd. South, Las Vegas, NV 89119-1000

TELEPHONE NUMBER: (702) 632-6700
FAX: (702) 634-3450
WEB: www.mandalayresortgroup.com

NO. OF EMPLOYEES: 35,000 (approx.)

SHAREHOLDERS: 3,200 (record)

ANNUAL MEETING: In June

INCORPORATED: NV, Feb., 1974

INSTITUTIONAL HOLDINGS:
No. of Institutions: 127
Shares Held: 58,889,110
% Held: 78.0

INDUSTRY: Amusement and recreation, nec (SIC: 7999)

TRANSFER AGENT(S): First Chicago Trust Company of New York, Jersey City, NJ

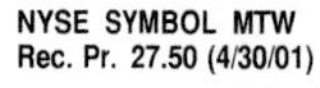

NYSE SYMBOL MTW
Rec. Pr. 27.50 (4/30/01)

MANITOWOC COMPANY, INC.

YIELD 1.1%
P/E RATIO 11.5

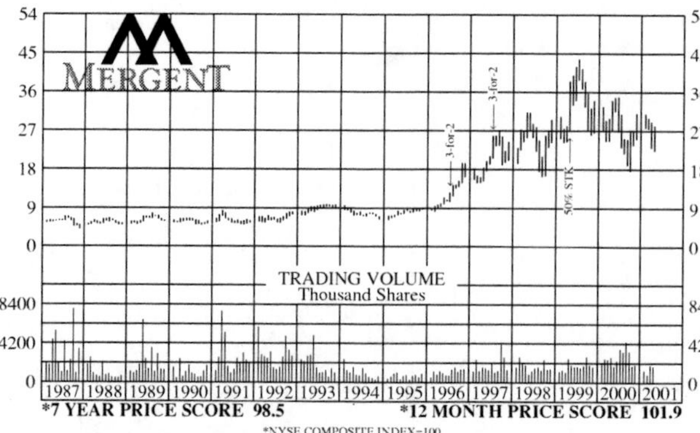

INTERIM EARNINGS (Per Share):

Qtr.	Mar.	June.	Sept.	Dec.
1995	0.07	0.21	0.14	0.15
1996	0.16	0.34	0.33	0.16
1997	0.25	0.46	0.37	0.33
1998	0.36	0.59	0.58	0.44
1999	0.47	0.80	0.74	0.53
2000	0.57	0.91	0.50	0.42

INTERIM DIVIDENDS (Per Share):

Amt.	Decl.	Ex.	Rec.	Pay.
0.075Q	2/16/00	2/28/00	3/01/00	3/10/00
0.075Q	5/03/00	5/30/00	6/01/00	6/10/00
0.075Q	7/18/00	8/30/00	9/01/00	9/07/00
0.075Q	10/17/00	11/29/00	12/01/00	12/07/00
0.075Q	2/13/01	2/27/01	3/01/01	3/08/01

Indicated div.: $0.30 (Div. Reinv. Plan)

CAPITALIZATION (12/31/00):

	($000)	(%)
Long-Term Debt	137,668	37.1
Common & Surplus	233,769	62.9
Total	371,437	100.0

RECENT DEVELOPMENTS: For the year ended 12/31/00, net earnings declined 9.8% to $60.3 million versus $66.8 million in the prior year. MTW attributed the lower results to the slower general economic and industry conditions that occurred during the second half of 2000. Net sales increased 5.9% to $873.3 million. Operating income at MTW's marine segment rose 22.0% to $8.9 million. However, foodservice operating income declined 6.1% to $61.4 million, and crane segment operating income slipped 3.0% to $62.9 million.

PROSPECTS: The potential negative effects of the slowing U.S. economy on businesses MTW serves cloud the Company's near-term prospects. Looking forward, although the Company anticipates weaker market demand in 2001 for cranes, especially for smaller capacity cranes and boom truck, rising levels of construction activity throughout the entire energy sector should result in positive demand for the Company's heavy-lift cranes. Future results should also benefit from recent acquisitions, new products, operational improvements and international opportunities.

BUSINESS

THE MANITOWOC COMPANY, INC. is a diversified capital goods manufacturer principally engaged in: the design and manufacture of commercial ice machines, ice/beverage dispensers and refrigeration products for the foodservice, lodging, convenience store, healthcare and the soft-drink bottling and dispensing industries; the design and manufacture of cranes and related products that are used by the energy, construction, mining and other industries; and ship-repair, conversion, and new construction services for the maritime industry. As of 12/31/00, revenues were derived: foodservice, 49%, cranes and related products, 43% and marine, 8%.

QUARTERLY DATA

(12/31/2000) ($000)	REV	INC
1st Quarter	205,853	14,913
2nd Quarter	243,566	22,606
3rd Quarter	214,531	12,299
4th Quarter	209,322	10,450

ANNUAL FINANCIAL DATA

	12/31/00	12/31/99	12/31/98	12/31/97	12/31/96	12/31/95	7/2/94
Earnings Per Share	**2.40**	**2.55**	**1.97**	**1.39**	**0.99**	**1 0.56**	**2 0.48**
Cash Flow Per Share	**3.14**	**3.21**	**2.54**	**1.86**	**1.44**	**0.83**	**0.69**
Tang. Book Val. Per Share	...	...	...	...	**0.24**	...	**3.26**
Dividends Per Share	**0.30**	**0.30**	**0.30**	**0.30**	**0.30**	**0.30**	**0.30**
Dividend Payout %	**12.5**	**11.8**	**15.3**	**21.4**	**29.9**	**52.6**	**62.1**
INCOME STATEMENT (IN THOUSANDS):							
Total Revenues	873,272	805,491	694,822	545,864	500,465	313,149	275,380
Costs & Expenses	741,895	669,190	587,172	468,877	437,957	283,196	247,894
Depreciation & Amort.	18,725	17,350	15,030	12,012	11,618	6,801	6,401
Operating Income	112,652	118,951	92,620	64,975	50,890	23,152	21,085
Net Interest Inc./(Exp.)	d14,508	d10,790	d9,741	d6,230	d9,097	d1,865	d263
Income Before Income Taxes	96,120	106,006	81,412	57,817	42,506	23,120	22,579
Income Taxes	35,852	39,222	30,032	21,394	16,863	8,551	8,536
Net Income	60,268	66,784	51,380	36,423	25,643	1 14,569	2 14,043
Cash Flow	78,993	84,134	66,410	48,435	37,261	21,370	20,444
Average Shs. Outstg.	25,123	26,201	26,126	26,097	25,900	25,900	29,487
BALANCE SHEET (IN THOUSANDS):							
Cash & Cash Equivalents	16,027	12,020	12,416	13,629	16,021	16,635	30,102
Total Current Assets	223,507	190,998	190,877	145,516	127,875	135,145	117,657
Net Property	99,940	92,023	93,583	91,191	84,703	87,674	63,332
Total Assets	642,530	530,240	481,014	396,368	317,710	324,915	185,848
Total Current Liabilities	239,490	189,308	198,112	170,812	110,302	110,923	63,610
Long-Term Obligations	137,668	79,223	79,834	66,359	76,501	101,180	...
Net Stockholders' Equity	233,769	232,176	172,552	128,618	100,329	81,661	93,859
Net Working Capital	d15,983	1,690	d7,235	d25,296	17,573	24,222	54,047
Year-end Shs. Outstg.	24,259	26,088	36,747	36,747	34,353	29,190	27,280
STATISTICAL RECORD:							
Operating Profit Margin %	12.9	14.8	13.3	11.9	10.2	7.4	7.7
Net Profit Margin %	6.9	8.3	7.4	6.7	5.1	4.7	5.1
Return on Equity %	25.8	28.8	29.8	28.3	25.6	17.8	15.0
Return on Assets %	9.4	12.6	10.7	9.2	8.1	4.5	7.6
Debt/Total Assets %	21.4	14.9	16.6	16.7	24.1	31.1	...
Price Range	34.88-17.63	43.75-24.21	31.33-16.33	27.13-14.83	19.56-8.19	9.07-6.22	9.59-6.37
P/E Ratio	14.5-7.3	17.2-9.5	15.9-8.3	19.5-10.6	19.7-8.3	16.1-11.1	20.1-13.4
Average Yield %	1.1	0.9	1.3	1.4	2.1	3.9	3.7

Statistics are as originally reported. Refls. 3-for-2 stk. splits, 3/99, 6/97 & 7/96. 1 Incls. non-recurr. pre-tax chrg. of $1.8 mill. 2 Incls. non-recurr. pre-tax chrg. of $14.0 mill. ($0.75/sh.)

OFFICERS:
T. D. Growcock, Pres., C.E.O.
G. E. Tellock, Sr. V.P., C.F.O.
M. D. Jones, Sec., General Counsel

INVESTOR CONTACT: Glen E. Tellock, Sr. V.P., C.F.O., (920) 683-8122

PRINCIPAL OFFICE: 500 South 16th St., Manitowoc, WI 54221-0066

TELEPHONE NUMBER: (920) 684-4410
FAX: (920) 683-8129
WEB: www.manitowoc.com
NO. OF EMPLOYEES: 4,405 (approx.)
SHAREHOLDERS: 2,787
ANNUAL MEETING: In May
INCORPORATED: WI, 1902

INSTITUTIONAL HOLDINGS:
No. of Institutions: 118
Shares Held: 15,327,124
% Held: 62.2

INDUSTRY: Construction machinery (SIC: 3531)

TRANSFER AGENT(S): First Chicago Trust Company of New York, Jersey City, NJ

NYSE SYMBOL HCR
Rec. Pr. 23.20 (4/30/01)

MANOR CARE, INC.

YIELD ...
P/E RATIO 61.1

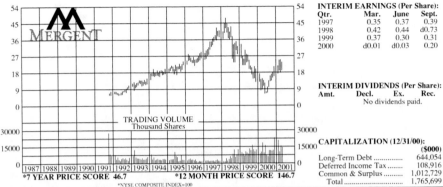

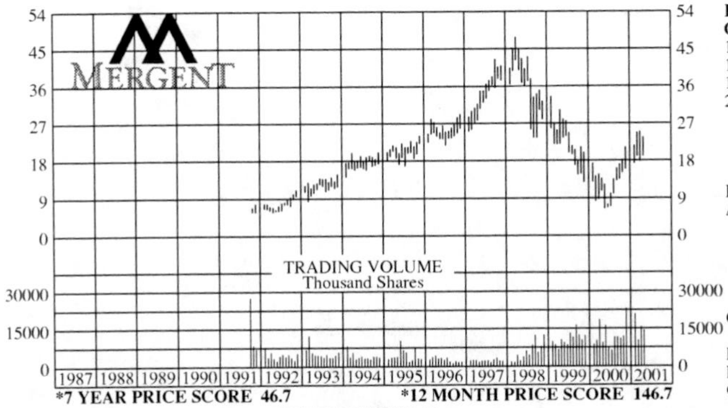

TRADING VOLUME
Thousand Shares

*7 YEAR PRICE SCORE 46.7 *12 MONTH PRICE SCORE 146.7

*NYSE COMPOSITE INDEX=100

INTERIM EARNINGS (Per Share):

Qtr.	Mar.	June	Sept.	Dec.
1997	0.35	0.37	0.39	0.40
1998	0.42	0.44	d0.73	0.25
1999	0.37	0.30	0.31	d1.59
2000	d0.01	d0.03	0.20	0.22

INTERIM DIVIDENDS (Per Share):

Amt.	Decl.	Ex.	Rec.	Pay.

No dividends paid.

CAPITALIZATION (12/31/00):

	($000)	(%)
Long-Term Debt	644,054	36.5
Deferred Income Tax	108,916	6.2
Common & Surplus	1,012,729	57.4
Total	1,765,699	100.0

RECENT DEVELOPMENTS: For the year ended 12/31/00, net income jumped to $39.1 million compared with a loss of $55.2 million, before an after-tax extraordinary gain of $11.5 million, in the previous year. Revenues climbed 11.5% to $2.38 billion from $2.14 billion a year earlier, primarily due to the acquisition of In Home Health, Inc. in December 1999.

PROSPECTS: The Company is continuing the integration of In Home Health, Inc. into its home health and hospice business, which is expected to create a $200.0 million plus unit in the coming year. Meanwhile, the Company's start-up medical transcription business is expected to start contributing to revenues in the second half of 2001.

BUSINESS

MANOR CARE, INC. (formerly HCR Manor Care, Inc.) was formed upon the merger of Manor Care, Inc. and Health Care & Retirement Corp. on 9/25/98. HCR provides a range of health care services, including long-term care, subacute medical care, rehabilitation therapy, home-health care, pharmacy services and management services for subacute care, rehabilitation therapy, vision care and eye surgery. The most significant portion of HCR's business is long-term care. The Company provides care through a network of more than 500 centers under the Manor Care, Heartland and Arden Courts names.

QUARTERLY DATA

(12/31/2000)($000)	REV	INC
1st Quarter	569,918	(783)
2nd Quarter	581,247	(3,429)
3rd Quarter	604,531	20,373
4th Quarter	624,882	22,894

ANNUAL FINANCIAL DATA

	12/31/00	12/31/99	12/31/98	12/31/97	12/31/96	12/31/95	12/31/94
Earnings Per Share	**0.38**	**2 d0.51**	**1 d0.42**	**1.51**	**1.24**	**1.03**	**0.84**
Cash Flow Per Share	**1.55**	**0.56**	**0.67**	**2.32**	**1.91**	**1.60**	**1.30**
Tang. Book Val. Per Share	**8.86**	**8.71**	**10.85**	**6.78**	**7.06**	**7.10**	**7.27**
INCOME STATEMENT (IN MILLIONS):							
Total Revenues	2,380.6	2,135.3	2,209.1	892.0	782.0	713.5	615.1
Costs & Expenses	2,120.3	1,788.3	2,089.7	740.5	656.2	604.2	521.0
Depreciation & Amort.	121.2	115.9	119.3	37.7	32.0	27.6	23.2
Operating Income	139.1	231.2	...	113.7	93.8	81.6	70.9
Net Interest Inc./(Exp.)	d60.7	d54.1	d29.5	d15.3	d10.4	d9.8	d8.7
Income Before Income Taxes	61.7	d102.4	d24.6	101.2	84.9	72.3	62.3
Income Taxes	21.5	cr47.2	21.6	31.1	25.5	21.7	20.2
Equity Earnings/Minority Int.	d0.3	1.4	4.9	2.8	1.5	0.5	...
Net Income	39.1	2 d55.2	1 d46.2	70.1	59.4	50.6	42.0
Cash Flow	160.3	60.8	73.2	107.8	91.5	78.2	65.2
Average Shs. Outstg. (000)	103,126	107,627	108,958	46,515	47,835	48,963	50,061
BALANCE SHEET (IN MILLIONS):							
Cash & Cash Equivalents	24.9	12.3	33.7	7.5	2.4	7.7	29.9
Total Current Assets	504.9	431.2	417.8	170.8	147.0	133.7	132.7
Net Property	1,577.4	1,550.5	1,740.3	553.0	533.5	505.2	496.9
Total Assets	2,358.5	2,280.9	2,715.1	936.4	802.8	729.2	657.3
Total Current Liabilities	472.5	408.6	503.7	121.3	124.5	119.3	112.6
Long-Term Obligations	644.1	687.5	693.2	293.0	202.3	159.1	149.0
Net Stockholders' Equity	1,012.7	980.0	1,199.2	434.0	393.0	374.4	344.5
Net Working Capital	32.3	22.5	d86.0	49.4	22.5	14.4	20.2
Year-end Shs. Outstg. (000)	102,667	102,365	103,100	44,223	44,861	46,430	47,390
STATISTICAL RECORD:							
Operating Profit Margin %	5.8	10.8	...	12.7	12.0	11.4	11.5
Net Profit Margin %	1.6	...	...	7.9	7.6	7.1	6.8
Return on Equity %	3.9	...	...	16.2	15.1	13.5	12.2
Return on Assets %	1.7	...	...	7.5	7.4	6.9	6.4
Debt/Total Assets %	27.3	30.1	25.5	31.3	25.2	21.8	22.7
Price Range	21.19-6.44	33.50-12.75	47.88-23.50	42.50-25.00	29.25-21.75	24.08-16.75	20.17-14.17
P/E Ratio	55.7-16.9	...	...	28.1-16.6	23.6-17.5	23.3-16.2	24.0-16.9

Statistics are as originally reported. Adj. for stk. splits 2-for-1, 3/93, 3-for-2, 6/96. Results for 12/31/97 and prior are for Health Care & Retirement Corp. prior to the merger with Manor Care, Inc. 1 Incl. a non-recurr charge of $278.3 million but excl. a gain of $67.9 million from discontinued operations, an extraord. chrg. of $19.0 mill. and an acctg. chrg. of $5.6 mill. 2 Incl. a non-recurr. chrg. totaling $14.8 mill. but excl. a net extraord. gain of $11.5 mill.

OFFICERS:
S. Bainum Jr., Chmn.
P. A. Ormond, Pres., C.E.O.
G. G. Meyers, Exec. V.P., C.F.O.

INVESTOR CONTACT: Geoffrey G. Meyers, Exec. V.P., C.F.O., (419) 252-5545

PRINCIPAL OFFICE: 333 N. Summit Street, Toledo, OH 43604-2617

TELEPHONE NUMBER: (419) 252-5500
FAX: (419) 247-1364
WEB: www.hcr–manorcare.com

NO. OF EMPLOYEES: 54,000 (avg.)

SHAREHOLDERS: 3,777 (record); 20,000 (approx. beneficial).

ANNUAL MEETING: In May

INCORPORATED: DE, Aug., 1991

INSTITUTIONAL HOLDINGS:
No. of Institutions: 226
Shares Held: 89,753,939
% Held: 87.4

INDUSTRY: Skilled nursing care facilities (SIC: 8051)

TRANSFER AGENT(S): Computershare Investor Services, Chicago, IL

NYSE SYMBOL MAN
Rec. Pr. 32.00 (5/31/01)

MANPOWER INC.

YIELD 0.6%
P/E RATIO 14.4

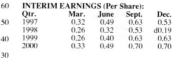

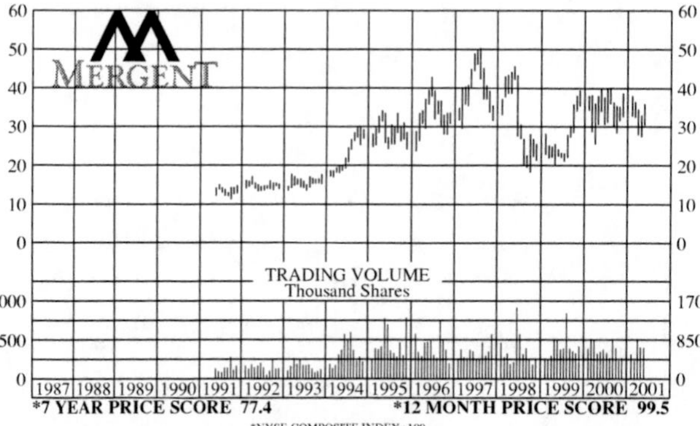

***7 YEAR PRICE SCORE 77.4** ***12 MONTH PRICE SCORE 99.5**

*NYSE COMPOSITE INDEX=100

INTERIM EARNINGS (Per Share):

Qtr.	Mar.	June	Sept.	Dec.
1997	0.32	0.49	0.63	0.53
1998	0.26	0.32	0.53	d0.19
1999	0.26	0.40	0.63	0.63
2000	0.33	0.49	0.70	0.70

INTERIM DIVIDENDS (Per Share):

Amt.	Decl.	Ex.	Rec.	Pay.
0.10S	4/26/99	5/28/99	6/02/99	6/14/99
0.10S	11/08/99	12/01/99	12/03/99	12/14/99
0.10S	5/04/00	5/31/00	6/02/00	6/14/00
0.10S	10/19/00	11/29/00	12/01/00	12/14/00
0.10S	5/02/01	5/30/01	6/01/01	6/14/01

Indicated div.: $0.20

CAPITALIZATION (12/31/00):

	($000)	(%)
Long-Term Debt	491,600	39.9
Common & Surplus	740,400	60.1
Total	1,232,000	100.0

RECENT DEVELOPMENTS: For the twelve months ended 12/31/00, net earnings increased 14.1% to $171.2 million compared with $150.0 million in the comparable period of the previous year. Systemwide sales climbed 8.1% to $12.44 billion from $11.51 billion the year before. Revenues from services advanced 11.0% to $10.84 billion from $9.77 billion a year earlier. Operating profit jumped 34.8% to $311.0 million, while gross profit improved 14.2% to $1.95 billion versus $1.70 billion in the prior year.

PROSPECTS: On 4/24/01, MAN agreed to acquire Jefferson Wells International, Inc., professional services provider of internal audit, accounting, technology and tax services, for $174.0 million. Meanwhile, the Company should continue to benefit from the solid performance and strength of its globally diversified network and recognition of the Manpower brand. In addition, MAN should benefit from the opening of almost 300 new offices and the expansion of specialty services, which took place during 2000.

BUSINESS

MANPOWER INC. is engaged primarily in temporary staffing services, contract services, and training and testing of temporary and permanent workers. The Company operates more than 3,700 offices in 59 countries. The largest operations, based on revenues, are located in the United States, France and the United Kingdom. The Company provided employment services to 400,000 customers though 2.7 million temporary workers in 2000. As of 12/31/00, the Company had 732 branch and 423 franchised offices in the United States. In France, the Company's largest market, MAN conducts operations through 879 branch offices under the name Manpower and 48 under the name Supplay. The United Kingdom operates 174 branch offices. Other European countries have 872 branch offices and 54 franchised offices, while other markets of the world have 356 branch offices and 29 franchised offices.

GEOGRAPHIC DATA

(12/31/00)	Rev (%)	Inc (%)
United States	22.3	23.3
France	36.3	35.9
United Kingdom	13.4	12.7
Other Europe	17.5	24.5
Other Countries	10.5	3.6
Total	100.0	100.0

ANNUAL FINANCIAL DATA

	12/31/00	12/31/99	12/31/98	12/31/97	12/31/96	12/31/95	12/31/94
Earnings Per Share	**2.22**	③ **1.91**	② **0.93**	**1.97**	**1.95**	**1.65**	**1.12**
Cash Flow Per Share	**3.09**	**2.72**	**1.64**	**2.46**	**2.38**	**2.01**	**1.49**
Tang. Book Val. Per Share	**6.50**	**7.39**	**8.48**	**7.69**	**7.41**	**5.61**	**2.69**
Dividends Per Share	**0.20**	**0.20**	**0.19**	**0.17**	**0.15**	**0.13**	**0.11**
Dividend Payout %	**9.0**	**10.5**	**20.4**	**8.6**	**7.7**	**7.9**	**9.8**
INCOME STATEMENT (IN MILLIONS):							
Total Revenues	10,842.8	9,770.1	8,814.3	7,258.5	6,079.9	5,484.2	4,296.4
Costs & Expenses	10,465.0	9,475.8	8,628.3	6,961.5	5,817.3	5,244.7	4,117.0
Depreciation & Amort.	66.8	63.7	55.6	41.6	35.6	27.8	27.7
Operating Income	311.0	230.6	130.4	255.4	227.0	211.7	151.7
Net Interest Inc./(Exp.)	...	...	...	...	...	...	d9.1
Income Before Income Taxes	265.2	205.8	113.8	249.2	242.3	203.8	136.5
Income Taxes	94.0	55.8	38.1	85.3	80.0	75.7	52.6
Net Income	171.2	③ 150.0	② 75.7	163.9	162.3	128.0	83.9
Cash Flow	238.0	213.7	131.2	205.5	197.9	155.9	111.6
Average Shs. Outstg. (000)	77,100	78,700	80,101	83,380	83,106	77,644	75,041
BALANCE SHEET (IN MILLIONS):							
Cash & Cash Equivalents	181.7	241.7	180.5	142.2	180.6	142.8	82.0
Total Current Assets	2,396.7	2,257.3	1,961.6	1,686.9	1,439.1	1,277.3	1,007.3
Net Property	191.6	182.4	191.3	136.4	121.4	108.0	88.5
Total Assets	3,041.6	2,718.7	2,381.1	2,047.0	1,752.3	1,517.8	1,203.7
Total Current Liabilities	1,522.2	1,418.1	1,311.1	1,004.7	811.3	776.3	668.4
Long-Term Obligations	491.6	357.5	154.6	189.8	100.8	61.8	130.9
Net Stockholders' Equity	740.4	650.6	668.9	617.6	600.7	455.0	203.5
Net Working Capital	874.5	839.2	650.5	682.2	627.8	501.0	338.9
Year-end Shs. Outstg. (000)	75,773	75,986	78,930	80,346	81,105	81,153	74,289
STATISTICAL RECORD:							
Operating Profit Margin %	2.9	2.4	1.5	3.5	3.7	3.9	3.5
Net Profit Margin %	1.6	1.5	0.9	2.3	2.7	2.3	2.0
Return on Equity %	23.1	23.1	11.3	26.5	27.0	28.1	41.2
Return on Assets %	5.6	5.5	3.2	8.0	9.3	8.4	7.0
Debt/Total Assets %	16.2	13.1	6.5	9.3	5.8	4.1	10.9
Price Range	40.25-25.50	39.50-20.25	45.75-18.25	50.38-29.50	43.00-23.63	34.25-24.13	29.88-16.88
P/E Ratio	18.1-11.5	20.7-10.6	49.2-19.6	25.6-15.0	22.1-12.1	20.8-14.6	26.7-15.1
Average Yield %	0.6	0.7	0.6	0.4	0.5	0.4	0.5

Statistics are as originally reported. ① Bef. acctg. change chrg. $7.1 mill. ② Incl. non-recurr. chrg. 1998, $92.1 mill. ③ Incl. one-time after-tax charges totaling $700,000.

OFFICERS:
J. A. Joerres, Chmn., Pres., C.E.O.
M. J. Van Handel, Sr. V.P., C.F.O., Sec.

INVESTOR CONTACT: Micheal J. Van Handel, (414) 961-1000

PRINCIPAL OFFICE: 5301 North Ironwood Road, Milwaukee, WI 53217

TELEPHONE NUMBER: (414) 961-1000
FAX: (414) 332-0796
WEB: www.manpower.com

NO. OF EMPLOYEES: 19,400 (approx.)

SHAREHOLDERS: 6,102 (record)

ANNUAL MEETING: In May

INCORPORATED: WI, Apr., 1990

INSTITUTIONAL HOLDINGS:
No. of Institutions: 204
Shares Held: 68,970,385
% Held: 90.9

INDUSTRY: Help supply services (SIC: 7363)

TRANSFER AGENT(S): Mellon Investor Services, L.L.C., New York, NY

NYSE SYMBOL MRL
Rec. Pr. 29.97 (4/30/01)

MARINE DRILLING COS., INC.

YIELD ...
P/E RATIO 37.0

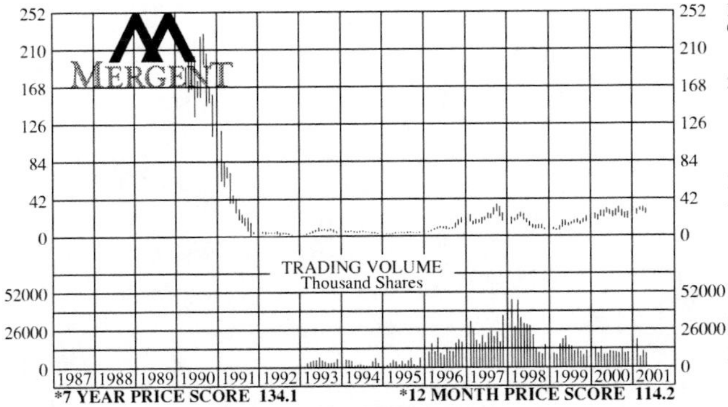

TRADING VOLUME
Thousand Shares

1987 1988 1989 1990 1991 1992 1993 1994 1995 1996 1997 1998 1999 2000 2001

*7 YEAR PRICE SCORE 134.1 *12 MONTH PRICE SCORE 114.2

*NYSE COMPOSITE INDEX=100

INTERIM EARNINGS (Per Share):

Qtr.	Mar.	June.	Sept.	Dec.
1998	0.32	0.38	0.32	0.13
1999	d0.09	d0.12	0.05	0.04
2000	0.08	0.13	0.26	0.34

INTERIM DIVIDENDS (Per Share):

Amt.	Decl.	Ex.	Rec.	Pay.

No dividends paid.

CAPITALIZATION (12/31/00):

	($000)	(%)
Long-Term Debt	75,000	11.8
Deferred Income Tax	71,748	11.3
Common & Surplus	486,336	76.8
Total	633,084	100.0

RECENT DEVELOPMENTS: For the year ended 12/31/00, the Company reported net income of $48.3 million versus a net loss of $6.1 million in the previous year. Total revenues more than doubled to $264.0 million from $115.4 million the year before. Revenues from jack-up operations more than doubled to $148.2 million from $68.4 million, while revenues from semi-submersibles operations amounted to $115.8 million from $47.0 million a year earlier. The increase in overall results was primarily attributed to higher dayrates for MRL's jackup fleet in the Gulf of Mexico.

PROSPECTS: Looking ahead, the Company believes that its presence in the Gulf of Mexico region offers logistical advantages, including reduced mobilization costs and flexibility of crew development, both of which should reduce operating costs. In addition, MRL expects drilling activity to increase, reflecting a significant upside potential for dayrates in the jack-up rig market due to both a worldwide supply of jack-up rigs that is not growing and an increasing rate of oil and natural gas depletion in the region.

BUSINESS

MARINE DRILLING COMPANIES, INC. is engaged in offshore contract drilling of oil and gas wells for independent and major oil and gas companies. Operations are conducted in the U.S. Gulf of Mexico and internationally. MRL owns and operates a fleet of 17 offshore drilling rigs consisting of five independent leg jack-up units, four of which have a cantilever feature, ten mat supported jack-up units, five of which have a cantilever feature, and two semi-submersible units. Additionally, MRL owns one independent leg jack-up rig configured as an accommodation unit.

BUSINESS LINE ANALYSIS

(12/31/2000)	REV (%)	INC (%)
Jack-Up Operations	56.1	40.9
Semi-Submersibles Operations	43.9	59.1
Total	100.0	100.0

ANNUAL FINANCIAL DATA

	12/31/00	12/31/99	12/31/98	12/31/97	12/31/96	12/31/95	12/31/94
Earnings Per Share	**0.81**	**d0.11**	**1.15**	**1.11**	**0.46**	**d0.09**	**0.14**
Cash Flow Per Share	**1.56**	**0.42**	**1.54**	**1.44**	**0.71**	**0.12**	**0.31**
Tang. Book Val. Per Share	**8.30**	**7.22**	**6.91**	**5.70**	**4.33**	**2.47**	**2.57**
INCOME STATEMENT (IN THOUSANDS):							
Total Revenues	264,031	115,406	228,015	190,257	110,329	63,067	70,597
Costs & Expenses	132,755	90,166	114,453	85,654	67,529	60,699	54,951
Depreciation & Amort.	44,315	29,569	20,191	16,995	11,315	9,229	7,733
Operating Income	86,961	d4,329	93,371	87,608	31,485	d6,861	7,913
Net Interest Inc./(Exp.)	d10,956	d5,298	1,202	1,823	366	639	1,280
Income Before Income Taxes	77,852	d8,482	95,541	89,836	32,256	d6,102	9,123
Income Taxes	29,587	cr2,352	34,720	31,456	11,586	cr2,080	3,193
Net Income	48,265	d6,130	60,821	58,380	20,670	d4,022	5,930
Cash Flow	92,580	23,439	81,012	75,375	31,985	5,207	13,663
Average Shs. Outstg.	59,246	55,275	52,726	52,452	44,918	43,812	43,819
BALANCE SHEET (IN THOUSANDS):							
Cash & Cash Equivalents	4,190	4,664	12,576	20,619	81,951	12,260	37,009
Total Current Assets	57,338	55,393	39,621	72,347	105,687	32,990	53,382
Net Property	601,242	607,840	431,629	260,487	148,737	101,352	89,421
Total Assets	660,705	666,142	475,684	334,182	254,947	134,545	143,215
Total Current Liabilities	26,346	24,577	32,922	16,875	9,016	9,674	4,969
Long-Term Obligations	75,000	180,000	50,000	...	9,000	9,000	15,000
Net Stockholders' Equity	486,336	412,745	361,588	295,742	221,733	107,572	112,731
Net Working Capital	30,992	30,816	6,699	55,472	96,671	23,316	48,413
Year-end Shs. Outstg.	58,562	57,199	52,366	51,890	51,263	43,635	43,918
STATISTICAL RECORD:							
Operating Profit Margin %	32.9	...	40.9	46.0	28.5	...	11.2
Net Profit Margin %	18.3	...	26.7	30.7	18.7	...	8.4
Return on Equity %	9.9	...	16.8	19.7	9.3	...	5.3
Return on Assets %	7.3	...	12.8	17.5	8.1	...	4.1
Debt/Total Assets %	11.4	27.0	10.5	...	3.5	6.7	10.5
Price Range	32.50-17.56	22.50-5.94	26.69-7.00	36.06-12.88	20.75-4.75	5.25-2.25	6.75-2.63
P/E Ratio	40.1-21.7	...	23.2-6.1	32.5-11.6	45.1-10.3	...	48.2-18.7

Statistics are as originally reported. Adj. for 1-for-25 rev. stk. split, 10/92 [1] Bef. extraord. gain of $104.5 mill., incl. write-down of rigs of $68.3 mill. & proceeds from settlement of litigation of $3.0 mill.

OFFICERS:
R. L. Barbanell, Chmn.
J. Rask, Pres., C.E.O.
T. S. O'Keefe, Sr. V.P., C.F.O.

PRINCIPAL OFFICE: One Sugar Creek Center Blvd, Suite 600, Sugar Land, TX 77478-3556

TELEPHONE NUMBER: (281) 243-3000
FAX: (281) 243-3090
WEB: www.mardril.com
NO. OF EMPLOYEES: 1,118
SHAREHOLDERS: 580 (approx. record)
ANNUAL MEETING: In May
INCORPORATED: TX, 1966; reincorp., TX, Jan., 1990

INSTITUTIONAL HOLDINGS:
No. of Institutions: 194
Shares Held: 52,273,890
% Held: 89.1

INDUSTRY: Drilling oil and gas wells (SIC: 1381)

TRANSFER AGENT(S): American Stock Transfer & Trust Company, New York, NY

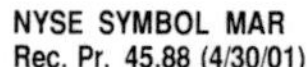

NYSE SYMBOL MAR
Rec. Pr. 45.88 (4/30/01)

MARRIOTT INTERNATIONAL, INC.

YIELD 0.6%
P/E RATIO 24.3

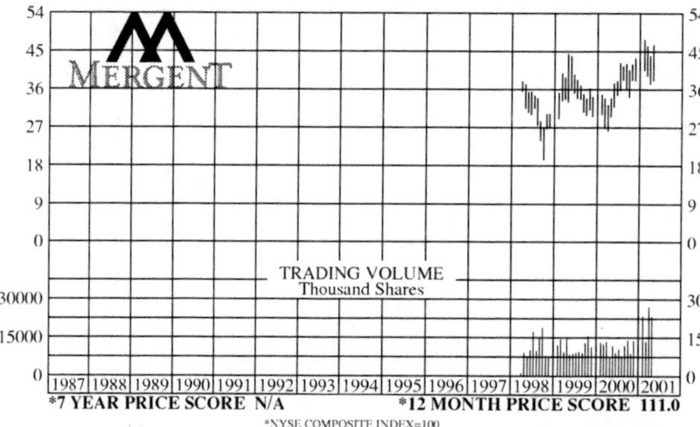

*7 YEAR PRICE SCORE N/A   *12 MONTH PRICE SCORE 111.0
*NYSE COMPOSITE INDEX=100

INTERIM EARNINGS (Per Share):

Qtr.	Mar.	June	Sept.	Dec.
1996	0.22	0.23	0.22	0.31
1997	0.26	0.31	0.27	0.36
1998	0.33	0.37	0.32	0.44
1999	0.38	0.42	0.36	0.44
2000	0.37	0.50	0.43	0.59

INTERIM DIVIDENDS (Per Share):

Amt.	Decl.	Ex.	Rec.	Pay.
0.06Q	4/28/00	6/22/00	6/26/00	7/17/00
0.06Q	8/03/00	9/21/00	9/25/00	10/16/00
0.06Q	11/02/00	12/27/00	12/29/00	1/12/01
0.06Q	2/01/01	3/28/01	3/30/01	4/20/01
0.065Q	5/04/01	6/27/01	6/29/01	7/13/01

Indicated div.: $0.26 (Div. Reinv. Plan)

CAPITALIZATION (12/29/00):

	($000)	(%)
Long-Term Debt	2,016,000	38.2
Common & Surplus	3,267,000	61.8
Total	5,283,000	100.0

RECENT DEVELOPMENTS: For the year ended 12/29/00, net income was $479.0 million, up 19.8% versus $400.0 million in 1999. Results for 2000 included a pre-tax nonrecurring charge of $15.0 million related to the write-off of an investment. The 1999 results included a pre-tax nonrecurring charge of $39.0 million. Total revenues grew 14.6% to $10.02 billion from $8.74 billion a year earlier. Lodging sales rose 11.5% to $7.85 billion, while sales for distribution services increased 31.7% to $1.50 billion.

PROSPECTS: On 2/13/01, MAR announced plans to form a joint venture with Bulgari SpA, an Italian jeweler, to establish a new luxury hotel chain of exclusive hotels and resorts under the name of Bulgari Hotels & Resorts. Both the Bulgari and the Ritz-Carlton brand hotels will be operated through MAR's new Luxury Group to be based in Atlanta. Within five years, the joint venture plans to open hotels in six locations, including Rome, Italy and Paris, France. For 2001, MAR expects to earn $2.17 per share.

BUSINESS

MARRIOTT INTERNATIONAL, INC. is a worldwide operator and franchisor of hotels and senior living communities with over 2,300 operating units in 59 countries. MAR's operations are grouped in three business segments, Lodging, Distribution Services, and Senior Living Services, which represented 78.3%, 15.0%, and 6.7%, respectively, of total sales in 2000. In its Lodging segment, MAR operates and franchises lodging facilities and develops and operates vacation timesharing resorts under the names Marriott, Ritz-Carlton, Renaissance, Residence Inn, Courtyard, TownePlace Suites, Fairfield Inn, SpringHill Suites and Ramada International brand names. In addition, the Lodging segment provides corporate housing through its ExecuStay by Marriott division and Marriott Executive Apartments as well as operates conference centers. Other Marriott businesses include senior living communities and services, wholesale food distribution and procurement services. On 3/27/98, MAR was spun off to shareholders of the former company and renamed Marriott International, Inc.

ANNUAL FINANCIAL DATA

	12/29/00	12/31/99	1/1/99	1/2/98	1/3/97	12/29/95
Earnings Per Share	**2 1.89**	**1.51**	**1.46**	**1 1.19**	**1 1.06**	**1 0.88**
Cash Flow Per Share	**2.65**	**2.27**	**1.94**	**1.62**	**1.41**	**1.14**
Tang. Book Val. Per Share	**5.95**	**4.42**	**3.36**	**4.45**	...	...
Dividends Per Share	**0.23**	**0.21**	**0.14**	...	...	...
Dividend Payout %	**12.2**	**13.9**	**9.9**	...	...	...
INCOME STATEMENT (IN MILLIONS):						
Total Revenues	10,017.0	8,739.0	7,968.0	9,046.0	7,267.0	6,255.0
Costs & Expenses	9,020.0	7,911.0	7,202.0	8,399.0	6,743.0	5,857.0
Depreciation & Amort.	195.0	162.0	140.0	126.0	89.0	67.0
Operating Income	802.0	666.0	626.0	521.0	435.0	331.0
Net Interest Inc./(Exp.)	d45.0	d29.0	6.0	10.0	...	30.0
Income Before Income Taxes	757.0	637.0	632.0	531.0	435.0	361.0
Income Taxes	278.0	237.0	242.0	207.0	165.0	142.0
Net Income	2 479.0	400.0	390.0	324.0	270.0	219.0
Cash Flow	674.0	562.0	530.0	450.0	359.0	286.0
Average Shs. Outstg. (000)	254,000	247,500	273,100	278,000	255,000	250,000
BALANCE SHEET (IN MILLIONS):						
Cash & Cash Equivalents	334.0	489.0	390.0	289.0	239.0	...
Total Current Assets	1,415.0	1,600.0	1,333.0	1,367.0	984.0	...
Net Property	3,241.0	2,845.0	2,275.0	1,537.0	1,824.0	...
Total Assets	8,237.0	7,324.0	6,233.0	5,557.0	4,198.0	...
Total Current Liabilities	1,917.0	1,743.0	1,412.0	1,639.0	1,404.0	...
Long-Term Obligations	2,016.0	1,676.0	1,267.0	422.0	681.0	...
Net Stockholders' Equity	3,267.0	2,908.0	2,570.0	2,586.0	1,444.0	...
Net Working Capital	d502.0	d143.0	d79.0	d272.0	d420.0	...
Year-end Shs. Outstg. (000)	241,000	246,300	255,600	255,600	...	...
STATISTICAL RECORD:						
Operating Profit Margin %	8.0	7.6	7.9	5.8	6.0	5.3
Net Profit Margin %	4.8	4.6	4.9	3.6	3.7	3.5
Return on Equity %	14.7	13.8	15.2	12.5	18.7	...
Return on Assets %	5.8	5.5	6.3	5.8	6.4	...
Debt/Total Assets %	24.5	22.9	20.3	7.6	16.2	...
Price Range	43.50-26.13	44.50-29.00	37.94-19.38	...	...	...
P/E Ratio	23.0-13.8	29.5-19.2	26.0-13.3	...	...	...
Average Yield %	0.7	0.6	0.5	...	...	...

Statistics are as originally reported. 1 Pro forma 2 Incl. pre-tax non-recurr. chrg. of $15.0 mill.

OFFICERS:
J. W. Marriott Jr., Chmn., C.E.O.
W. J. Shaw, Pres., C.O.O.
A. M. Sorenson, Exec. V.P., C.F.O.

INVESTOR CONTACT: Investor Relations, (301) 380-6500

PRINCIPAL OFFICE: 10400 Fernwood Road, Bethesda, MD 20817

TELEPHONE NUMBER: (301) 380-3000
FAX: (301) 380-3967
WEB: www.marriott.com

NO. OF EMPLOYEES: 153,000 (approx.)

SHAREHOLDERS: 53,053 (record)

ANNUAL MEETING: In May

INCORPORATED: DE, 1998

INSTITUTIONAL HOLDINGS:
No. of Institutions: 304
Shares Held: 134,652,660
% Held: 55.2

INDUSTRY: Hotels and motels (SIC: 7011)

TRANSFER AGENT(S): First Chicago Trust Company of New York, Jersey City, NJ

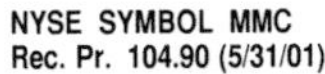
NYSE SYMBOL MMC
Rec. Pr. 104.90 (5/31/01)

MARSH & MCLENNAN COMPANIES, INC.

YIELD 2.0%
P/E RATIO 25.6

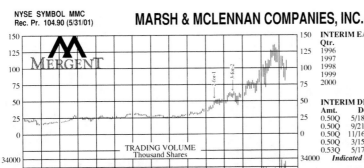

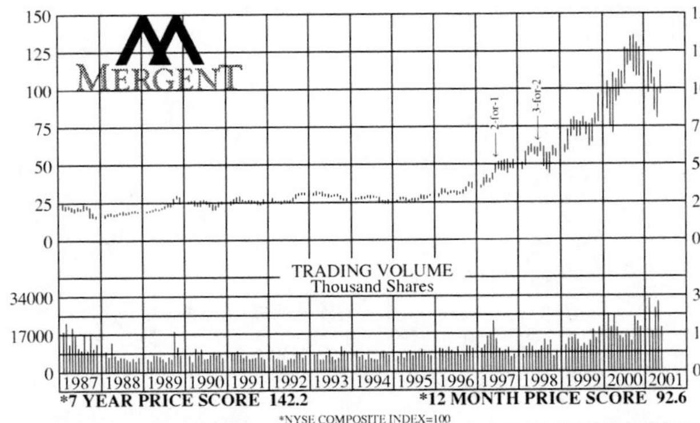

INTERIM EARNINGS (Per Share):

Qtr.	Mar.	June	Sept.	Dec.
1996	0.65	0.53	0.48	0.46
1997	0.75	0.58	0.55	d0.19
1998	0.87	0.72	0.69	0.70
1999	1.03	0.63	0.81	0.16
2000	1.19	0.96	0.97	0.98

INTERIM DIVIDENDS (Per Share):

Amt.	Decl.	Ex.	Rec.	Pay.
0.50Q	5/18/00	7/06/00	7/10/00	8/15/00
0.50Q	9/21/00	10/12/00	10/16/00	11/15/00
0.50Q	11/16/00	1/04/01	1/08/01	2/14/01
0.50Q	3/15/01	4/05/01	4/09/01	5/15/01
0.53Q	5/17/01	7/05/01	7/09/01	8/15/01

Indicated div.: $2.12 (Div. Reinv. Plan)

CAPITALIZATION (12/31/00):

	($000)	(%)
Long-Term Debt	2,347,000	31.0
Common & Surplus	5,228,000	69.0
Total	7,575,000	100.0

RECENT DEVELOPMENTS: For the year ended 12/31/00, net income totaled $1.18 billion, up 62.7% compared with $726.0 million in 1999. Total revenue improved 10.9% to $10.16 billion versus $9.16 billion a year earlier. Revenues from risk and insurance services climbed 5.7% to $4.78 billion. Investment management revenues grew 20.8% to $3.24 billion, while consulting revenues advanced 9.5% to $2.14 billion. Operating income amounted to $2.18 billion compared with $1.47 billion in the previous year.

PROSPECTS: Going forward, the Company should continue to benefit from the pricing turn in most U.S. commercial insurance lines. Premiums began to rise in the spring, and increases averaged approximately 10.0% at mid-year, with the trend continuing in early 2001. The integration of Sedgwick, which was acquired in 1999, has proceeded ahead of schedule, yielding net consolidation savings of $90.0 million in 2000 with a remaining $40.0 million anticipated in 2001.

BUSINESS

MARSH & MCLENNAN COMPANIES, INC. is engaged in the worldwide business of providing retail and wholesale insurance services, principally as a broker or consultant for insurers, insurance underwriters and other brokers. MMC subsidiaries include Marsh, a major risk and insurance services firm; Putman Investments, one of the largest investment management companies in the United States; and Mercer Consulting Group, a major global provider of consulting services. Other subsidiaries render advisory services in the area of employee benefits and compensation consulting, management consulting, economic consulting and environmental consulting. Contributions to revenues by type of service in 2000 were as follows: insurance services, 47.1%; consulting, 21.0%; and investment management, 31.9%.

ANNUAL FINANCIAL DATA

	12/31/00	12/31/99	12/31/98	12/31/97	12/31/96	12/31/95	12/31/94
Earnings Per Share	**4.10**	**[3] 2.62**	**2.98**	**[2] 1.59**	**2.11**	**1.84**	**[1] 1.73**
Tang. Book Val. Per Share	...	...	...	**3.07**	**6.19**	**4.29**	**3.46**
Dividends Per Share	**1.90**	**1.70**	**1.47**	**1.27**	**1.10**	**0.99**	**0.93**
Dividend Payout %	**46.3**	**64.9**	**49.2**	**79.5**	**52.1**	**53.8**	**53.9**
INCOME STATEMENT (IN MILLIONS):							
Total Revenues	10,157.0	9,157.0	7,190.0	6,008.6	4,149.0	3,770.3	3,435.0
Income Before Income Taxes	1,955.0	1,247.0	1,305.0	662.4	668.0	649.8	631.5
Income Taxes	753.0	521.0	509.0	263.0	208.7	246.9	249.5
Equity Earnings/Minority Int.	d21.0	...	...	...	...	...	...
Net Income	1,181.0	[3] 726.0	796.0	[2] 399.4	459.3	402.9	[1] 382.0
Average Shs. Outstg. (000)	284,000	272,000	264,000	250,800	217,200	218,700	220,800
BALANCE SHEET (IN MILLIONS):							
Cash & Cash Equivalents	240.0	428.0	610.0	424.3	299.6	328.1	294.9
Premiums Due	2,812.0	2,323.0	1,909.0	1,498.2	1,085.8	1,132.5	955.0
Invst. Assets: Total	976.0	687.0	828.0	720.2	573.3	411.8	282.8
Total Assets	13,769.0	13,021.0	11,871.0	7,914.2	4,545.2	4,329.5	3,830.6
Long-Term Obligations	2,347.0	2,357.0	1,590.0	1,239.8	458.2	410.6	409.4
Net Stockholders' Equity	5,228.0	4,170.0	3,659.0	3,198.8	1,888.6	1,665.5	1,460.6
Year-end Shs. Outstg. (000)	276,026	267,026	257,000	254,925	216,957	218,322	219,600
STATISTICAL RECORD:							
Return on Revenues %	11.6	7.9	11.1	6.6	11.1	10.7	11.1
Return on Equity %	22.6	17.4	21.8	12.5	24.3	24.2	26.2
Return on Assets %	8.6	5.6	6.7	5.0	10.1	9.3	10.0
Price Range	135.69-70.50	96.75-57.13	64.31-43.38	53.33-34.21	38.29-28.08	30.04-25.38	29.58-23.75
P/E Ratio	33.1-17.2	36.9-21.8	21.6-14.6	33.5-21.5	18.1-13.3	16.3-13.8	17.1-13.7
Average Yield %	1.8	2.2	2.7	2.9	3.3	3.6	3.5

Statistics are as originally reported. Adj. for stk. splits: 3-for-2, 6/98; 2-for-1, 6/97 [1] Bef. acctg. change chrg. $10.5 mill. [2] Incl. non-recurr. chrg. $296.8 mill. [3] Incl. special chrg. $337.0 mill.

OFFICERS:
J. W. Greenberg, Chmn., Pres., C.E.O.
M. Cabiallavetta, Vice-Chmn.
C. A. Davis, Vice-Chmn.
S. S. Wijnberg, Sr. V.P., C.F.O.

INVESTOR CONTACT: J. Michael Bischoff, V.P. Corp. Devel., (212) 345-5475

PRINCIPAL OFFICE: 1166 Avenue Of The Americas, New York, NY 10036-2774

TELEPHONE NUMBER: (212) 345-5000
FAX: (212) 345-4809
WEB: www.mmc.com

NO. OF EMPLOYEES: 57,000 (approx.)

SHAREHOLDERS: 11,245

ANNUAL MEETING: In May

INCORPORATED: DE, March, 1969

INSTITUTIONAL HOLDINGS:
No. of Institutions: 599
Shares Held: 185,687,858
% Held: 67.2

INDUSTRY: Insurance agents, brokers, & service (SIC: 6411)

TRANSFER AGENT(S): The Bank of New York, New York, NY

NYSE SYMBOL MI
Rec. Pr. 50.46 (4/30/01)

MARSHALL & ILSLEY CORPORATION

YIELD 2.3%
P/E RATIO 17.5

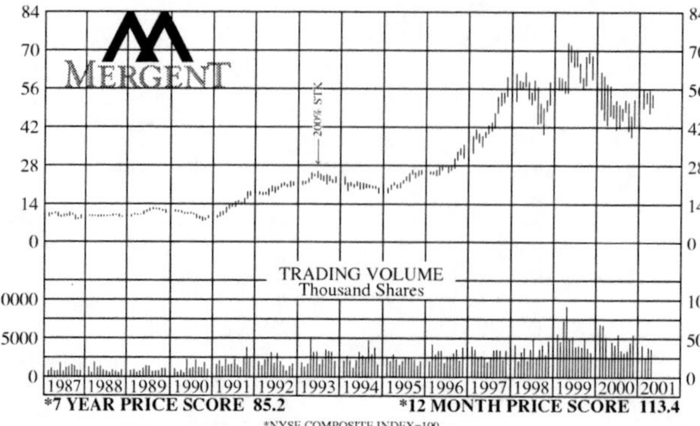

*7 YEAR PRICE SCORE 85.2 *12 MONTH PRICE SCORE 113.4

*NYSE COMPOSITE INDEX=100

INTERIM EARNINGS (Per Share):

Qtr.	Mar.	June	Sept.	Dec.
1997	0.57	0.58	0.63	0.65
1998	0.66	0.54	0.70	0.72
1999	0.75	0.77	0.81	0.81
2000	0.81	0.83	0.47	0.78

INTERIM DIVIDENDS (Per Share):

Amt.	Decl.	Ex.	Rec.	Pay.
0.265Q	4/25/00	5/26/00	5/31/00	6/14/00
0.265Q	8/23/00	8/29/00	8/31/00	9/14/00
0.265Q	10/12/00	11/28/00	11/30/00	12/14/00
0.265Q	2/22/01	3/02/01	3/06/01	3/14/01
0.29Q	4/24/01	5/29/01	5/31/01	6/14/01

Indicated div.: $1.16 (Div. Reinv. Plan)

CAPITALIZATION (12/31/00):

	($000)	(%)
Total Deposits	19,248,627	85.9
Long-Term Debt	921,276	4.1
Preferred Stock	336	0.0
Common & Surplus	2,241,853	10.0
Total	22,412,092	100.0

RECENT DEVELOPMENTS: For the year ended 12/31/00, MI reported income of $317.4 million, before an accounting charge of $2.3 million, versus net income of $354.5 million in 1999. Results for 2000 included a pre-tax nonrecurring loss of $16.7 million. Net interest income fell 4.6% to $673.0 million. Total other income rose 5.7% to $928.4 million. Total other expense, including the nonrecurring loss, increased 6.8% to $1.10 billion.

PROSPECTS: On 4/12/01, MI entered into a defintive agreement to acquire eleven Arizona locations from Fifth Third Bancorp. The transaction is expected to be closed in the third quarter of 2001. On 1/3/01, MI's subsidiary Metavante Corp. announced an eight-year outsourcing agreement with the Cape Cod Five Cents Savings Bank, under which Metavante's Financial Technology Services segment will provide technology systems.

BUSINESS

MARSHALL & ILSLEY CORPORATION, a multibank holding company with assets of $26.08 as of 12/31/00, is headquartered in Milwaukee, Wisconsin. The Company's principal subsidiary is Metavante Corporation (formerly MI's M&I Data Services Division), a provider of integrated financial transaction processing, outsourcing services, software, and consulting services. The Company has more than 200 banking offices in Wisconsin, and retail locations in Phoenix and Tucson, Arizona, Las Vegas, Nevada, and Naples, Florida. The Company also provides trust and investment management, equipment leasing, data processing, mortgage banking, financial planning, investments and insurance services from offices throughout the U.S. and on the Internet.

LOAN DISTRIBUTION

(12/31/2000)	($000)	(%)
Comm, Finl & Agricultural	5,289,537	30.0
Construction	619,281	3.5
Residential Mortgage	5,049,557	28.7
Commericial Mortgage	4,359,812	24.8
Personal	1,174,248	6.7
Lease Financing	1,094,652	6.3
Total	17,587,087	100.0

ANNUAL FINANCIAL DATA

	12/31/00	12/31/99	12/31/98	12/31/97	12/31/96	12/31/95	12/31/94
Earnings Per Share	**[2][3] 2.91**	**3.14**	**[3] 2.61**	**2.42**	**2.07**	**1.96**	**[1][3] 0.95**
Tang. Book Val. Per Share	**18.44**	**16.54**	**17.98**	**18.90**	**14.23**	**13.44**	**11.47**
Dividends Per Share	**1.03**	**0.94**	**0.86**	**0.79**	**0.72**	**0.65**	**0.59**
Dividend Payout %	**35.6**	**29.9**	**32.9**	**32.4**	**34.8**	**32.9**	**62.1**
INCOME STATEMENT (IN MILLIONS):							
Total Interest Income	1,748.0	1,496.6	1,434.0	1,143.7	971.4	924.7	817.3
Total Interest Expense	1,075.0	791.3	758.0	579.6	465.7	433.2	326.1
Net Interest Income	673.0	705.3	676.1	564.0	505.7	491.5	491.2
Provision for Loan Losses	30.4	25.4	27.1	17.3	15.2	16.2	24.9
Non-Interest Income	928.4	845.8	1,424.2	598.9	503.3	424.2	361.5
Non-Interest Expense	1,100.7	997.7	944.9	775.4	680.7	599.6	660.0
Income Before Taxes	470.4	527.9	465.3	370.3	313.1	299.9	167.8
Net Income	[2][3] 317.4	354.5	[3] 964.3	245.1	203.4	193.3	[1][3] 94.4
Average Shs. Outstg. (000)	108,883	113,005	115,240	101,510	98,482	98,757	99,420
BALANCE SHEET (IN MILLIONS):							
Cash & Due from Banks	760.1	705.3	760.4	800.1	780.6	745.9	685.9
Securities Avail. for Sale	4,801.2	4,477.0	4,247.2	4,182.2	3,213.9	2,677.8	2,005.8
Total Loans & Leases	17,587.1	16,335.1	13,996.2	12,542.3	9,301.9	8,868.9	8,792.5
Allowance for Credit Losses	235.1	225.9	226.1	202.8	155.9	161.4	154.0
Net Loans & Leases	17,352.0	16,109.2	13,770.1	12,339.5	9,146.0	8,707.5	8,638.5
Total Assets	26,077.7	24,369.7	21,566.3	19,477.5	14,763.3	13,343.1	12,612.9
Total Deposits	19,248.6	16,435.2	15,919.9	14,356.0	10,952.4	10,280.8	9,499.1
Long-Term Obligations	921.3	665.0	794.5	791.2	336.1	422.6	653.8
Total Liabilities	23,835.6	22,252.8	19,322.5	17,557.4	13,502.1	12,085.5	11,551.7
Net Stockholders' Equity	2,242.2	2,116.9	2,243.8	1,920.1	1,261.2	1,257.6	1,061.3
Year-end Shs. Outstg. (000)	102,847	105,816	106,103	101,537	88,584	93,526	92,529
STATISTICAL RECORD:							
Return on Equity %	14.2	16.7	43.0	12.8	16.1	15.4	8.9
Return on Assets %	1.2	1.5	4.5	1.3	1.4	1.4	0.7
Equity/Assets %	8.6	8.7	10.4	9.9	8.5	9.4	8.4
Non-Int. Exp./Tot. Inc. %	68.7	64.3	45.0	66.7	67.5	65.5	77.4
Price Range	62.25-38.25	72.75-54.38	62.25-39.38	60.50-32.38	35.63-24.38	26.50-18.00	24.00-17.75
P/E Ratio	21.4-13.1	23.2-17.3	23.8-15.1	25.0-13.4	17.2-11.8	13.5-9.2	25.3-18.7
Average Yield %	2.1	1.5	1.7	1.7	2.4	2.9	2.8

Statistics are as originally reported. [1] Bef. extraord. credit $11.5 mill. [2] Bef. acctg. change chrg. $2.3 mill. [3] Incl. non-recurr. chrg. of $16.7 mill., 2000; $23.4 mill., 1998; $75.2 mill.; 1994.

OFFICERS:
J. B. Wigdale, Chmn., C.E.O.
J. L. Delgadillo, Sr. V.P., C.E.O.
D. J. Kuester, Pres.
D. Wilsón, Sr. V.P., Treas.

INVESTOR CONTACT: M.A. Hatfield, Secretary, (414) 765-7801

PRINCIPAL OFFICE: 770 North Water Street, Milwaukee, WI 53202

TELEPHONE NUMBER: (414) 765-7801
FAX: (414) 765-8026
WEB: www.micorp.com

NO. OF EMPLOYEES: 11,753 (approx.)

SHAREHOLDERS: 19,660 (approx.)

ANNUAL MEETING: In April

INCORPORATED: WI, Feb., 1959

INSTITUTIONAL HOLDINGS:
No. of Institutions: 196
Shares Held: 33,639,203
% Held: 32.7

INDUSTRY: National commercial banks (SIC: 6021)

TRANSFER AGENT(S): BankBoston, N.A., Boston, MA

NYSE SYMBOL MLM
Rec. Pr. 49.37 (5/31/01)

MARTIN MARIETTA MATERIALS, INC.

YIELD 1.1%
P/E RATIO 20.6

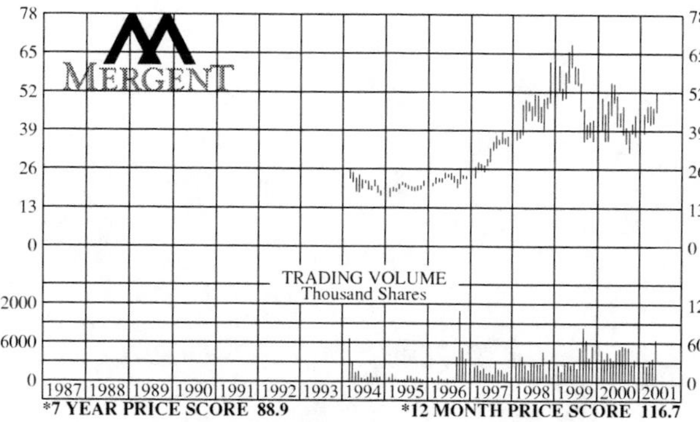

*7 YEAR PRICE SCORE 88.9 *12 MONTH PRICE SCORE 116.7
*NYSE COMPOSITE INDEX=100

INTERIM EARNINGS (Per Share):

Qtr.	Mar.	June	Sept.	Dec.
1997	0.19	0.66	0.79	0.50
1998	0.06	0.78	0.98	0.66
1999	0.17	0.88	0.94	0.70
2000	0.16	0.90	0.90	0.44

INTERIM DIVIDENDS (Per Share):

Amt.	Decl.	Ex.	Rec.	Pay.
0.13Q	5/23/00	5/30/00	6/01/00	6/30/00
0.14Q	8/18/00	8/30/00	9/01/00	9/29/00
0.14Q	11/14/00	11/29/00	12/01/00	12/29/00
0.14Q	1/23/01	2/27/01	3/01/01	3/30/01
0.14Q	5/23/01	5/30/01	6/01/01	6/29/01

Indicated div.: $0.56

CAPITALIZATION (12/31/00):

	($000)	(%)
Long-Term Debt	601,580	38.8
Deferred Income Tax	86,563	5.6
Common & Surplus	863,286	55.6
Total	1,551,429	100.0

RECENT DEVELOPMENTS: For the year ended 12/31/00, net income declined 11.0% to $112.0 million compared with $125.8 million in 1999. The decline in earnings reflected an increase in energy-related costs from the Aggregates division. Total revenues were $1.52 billion, up 5.8% from $1.43 billion a year earlier. Earnings from operations were $202.5 million, down 6.0% compared with $215.3 million in the prior year.

PROSPECTS: Looking ahead, MLM anticipates improvement in its Aggregates business based on expectations of improved pricing and higher margins at internal operations, strong infrastructure demand for roads, airports, and educational buildings, and significant new capacity ramping up at six key locations. Based on current economic forecasts, MLM expects to achieve record revenues and operating earnings for 2001, with revenue anticipated to grow 15.0% to 19.0%.

BUSINESS

MARTIN MARIETTA MATERIALS, INC. is the U.S.' second largest producer of aggregates for the construction industry, including highways, infrastructure, commercial and residential. MLM's Aggregates division processes and sells granite, sandstone, limestone, shell and other aggregates products. MLM's Magnesia Specialties division manufactures and markets magnesia-based products, including heat-resistant refractory products for the steel industry, chemicals products for industrial, agricultural and environmental uses, and dolomitic lime. MLM was spun off from Lockheed Martin Corp. in October 1996 to be the successor to substantially all of the assets and liabilities of the materials group of Martin Marietta Corporation and its subsidiaries. In 2000, MLM's Aggregates business accounted for 90.2% of total revenues and MLM's Magnesia Specialties segment accounted for 9.8%. MLM formed the MidAmerica division as a result of the American Aggregates acquisition. In 1998, MLM acquired Redland Stone Products Company.

ANNUAL FINANCIAL DATA

	12/31/00	12/31/99	12/31/98	12/31/97	12/31/96	12/31/95	12/31/94
Earnings Per Share	**2.39**	**2.68**	**[2] 2.49**	**2.13**	**1.71**	**1.47**	**[1] 1.30**
Cash Flow Per Share	**5.29**	**5.34**	**4.59**	**3.86**	**3.03**	**2.67**	**2.25**
Tang. Book Val. Per Share	**9.70**	**7.86**	**6.25**	**8.37**	**9.07**	**7.86**	**7.30**
Dividends Per Share	**0.54**	**0.52**	**0.50**	**0.48**	**0.46**	**0.44**	**0.22**
Dividend Payout %	**22.6**	**19.4**	**20.1**	**22.5**	**26.9**	**29.9**	**16.9**
INCOME STATEMENT (IN MILLIONS):							
Total Revenues	1,517.5	1,258.8	1,057.7	900.9	721.9	664.4	501.7
Costs & Expenses	1,178.7	1,094.1	762.4	658.4	540.1	501.2	366.9
Depreciation & Amort.	136.4	124.8	98.8	79.7	61.2	55.7	42.8
Operating Income	202.5	215.3	196.6	162.8	120.7	107.6	91.9
Net Interest Inc./(Exp.)	d33.7	d21.0	d22.4	d11.6	d1.7	d3.8	d1.5
Income Before Income Taxes	168.8	194.3	174.1	151.2	119.0	103.8	90.4
Income Taxes	56.8	68.5	58.5	52.7	40.3	36.2	32.1
Net Income	112.0	125.8	[2] 115.6	98.5	78.6	67.6	[1] 58.3
Cash Flow	248.4	250.5	214.4	178.2	139.8	123.2	101.2
Average Shs. Outstg. (000)	46,948	46,947	46,708	46,238	46,079	46,079	45,008
BALANCE SHEET (IN MILLIONS):							
Cash & Cash Equivalents	...	3.4	14.6	18.7	...	...	...
Total Current Assets	425.0	403.4	369.4	322.0	271.2	314.4	188.0
Net Property	914.1	847.0	777.5	591.4	408.8	392.2	291.6
Total Assets	1,841.4	1,742.6	1,588.6	1,105.7	768.9	789.4	593.9
Total Current Liabilities	189.1	182.7	152.2	108.2	88.1	173.3	55.6
Long-Term Obligations	601.6	602.0	602.1	310.7	125.9	125.0	103.7
Net Stockholders' Equity	863.3	774.0	667.7	561.8	481.0	423.5	376.3
Net Working Capital	235.9	220.7	217.2	213.8	183.0	141.0	132.4
Year-end Shs. Outstg. (000)	46,783	46,715	46,642	46,211	46,079	46,079	46,079
STATISTICAL RECORD:							
Operating Profit Margin %	13.3	17.1	18.6	18.1	16.7	16.2	18.3
Net Profit Margin %	7.4	10.0	10.9	10.9	10.9	10.2	11.6
Return on Equity %	13.0	16.3	17.3	17.5	16.3	15.9	15.5
Return on Assets %	6.1	7.2	7.3	8.9	10.2	8.6	9.8
Debt/Total Assets %	32.7	34.5	37.9	28.1	16.4	15.8	17.5
Price Range	55.25-31.65	68.13-35.25	62.19-35.81	38.50-23.00	25.75-19.50	22.13-16.50	25.88-17.00
P/E Ratio	23.1-13.2	25.4-13.2	25.0-14.4	18.1-10.8	15.1-11.4	15.0-11.2	19.9-13.1
Average Yield %	1.2	1.0	1.0	1.6	2.0	2.3	1.0

Statistics are as originally reported. [1] Bef. extraord. loss of $4.6 million (d$0.01/sh.). [2] Incl. a write-down of $1.9 mill.

OFFICERS:
S. P. Zelnak, Jr., Chmn., C.E.O.
P. J. Sipling, Exec. V.P.
J. K. Henry, Sr. V.P., C.F.O.

INVESTOR CONTACT: Investor Relations, (919) 783-4658

PRINCIPAL OFFICE: 2710 Wycliff Road, Raleigh, NC 27607-3033

TELEPHONE NUMBER: (919) 781-4550
FAX: (919) 783-4552
WEB: www.martinmarietta.com

NO. OF EMPLOYEES: 6,000 (approx.)

SHAREHOLDERS: 1,400 (approx.)

ANNUAL MEETING: In May

INCORPORATED: NC, Nov., 1993

INSTITUTIONAL HOLDINGS:
No. of Institutions: 202
Shares Held: 42,704,847
% Held: 90.3

INDUSTRY: Highway and street construction (SIC: 1611)

TRANSFER AGENT(S): First Union National Bank, Charlotte, NC

NYSE SYMBOL MAS
Rec. Pr. 23.36 (5/31/01)

MASCO CORPORATION

YIELD 2.2%
P/E RATIO 17.8

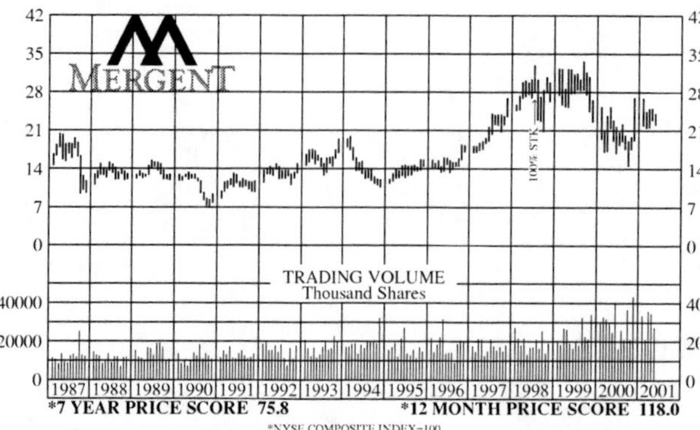

*7 YEAR PRICE SCORE 75.8 *12 MONTH PRICE SCORE 118.0

*NYSE COMPOSITE INDEX=100

INTERIM EARNINGS (Per Share):

Qtr.	Mar.	June	Sept.	Dec.
1997	0.26	0.29	0.30	0.30
1998	0.33	0.34	0.37	0.36
1999	0.36	0.41	0.15	0.40
2000	0.39	0.41	0.41	0.10

INTERIM DIVIDENDS (Per Share):

Amt.	Decl.	Ex.	Rec.	Pay.
0.12Q	3/17/00	4/05/00	4/07/00	5/08/00
0.12Q	7/05/00	7/12/00	7/14/00	8/07/00
0.13Q	9/14/00	10/11/00	10/13/00	11/13/00
0.13Q	12/07/00	1/10/01	1/12/01	2/12/01
0.13Q	3/16/01	4/04/01	4/06/01	5/08/01

Indicated div.: $0.52 (Div. Reinv. Plan)

CAPITALIZATION (12/31/00):

	($000)	(%)
Long-Term Debt	3,018,240	46.8
Common & Surplus	3,426,060	53.2
Total	6,444,300	100.0

RECENT DEVELOPMENTS: For the year ended 12/31/00, net income rose 3.9% to $591.7 million. Results for 2000 included a nonrecurring charge of $55.0 million and a charge of $90.0 million for the planned disposition of businesses within the cabinets, plumbing products, decorative architectural products, and other specialty products segments. Net sales rose 14.8% to $7.24 billion.

PROSPECTS: In April 2001, the Company acquired The Aran Group, an Italian manufacturer of kitchen cabinets, and Griffin Windows, a UK manufacturer of door and window products. The two companies have combined annual sales of approximately $70.0 million. Based on current economic conditions, MAS anticipates full-year earnings of approximately $1.20 per share.

BUSINESS

MASCO CORPORATION manufactures and sells home improvement and building products. MAS's principal product and service categories are kitchen and bathroom cabinets, faucets, other kitchen and bath products, architectural coatings, builders' hardware products and other specialty products and services. Brand-names include MERILLAT, KRAFTMAID, and QUALITY CABINETS kitchen and bathroom cabinets; DELTA and PEERLESS faucets; WEISER and BALDWIN locks; and BEHR architectural coatings. Sales in 2000 were derived as follows: cabinets and related products, 35.2%; plumbing products, 28.6%; decorative architectural products, 18.5%; other specialty products, 9.3%; insulation installation and other services, 8.4%.

ANNUAL FINANCIAL DATA

	12/31/00	12/31/99	12/31/98	12/31/97	12/31/96	12/31/95	12/31/94
Earnings Per Share	**[5] 1.31**	**[4] 1.28**	**1.39**	**1.15**	**0.92**	**[2] 0.63**	**[1] 0.61**
Cash Flow Per Share	**1.84**	**1.68**	**1.78**	**1.48**	**1.23**	**0.91**	**0.99**
Tang. Book Val. Per Share	**2.78**	**3.14**	**4.99**	**4.53**	**4.30**	**4.09**	**4.48**
Dividends Per Share	**0.49**	**0.45**	**0.43**	**0.41**	**0.39**	**0.36**	**0.34**
Dividend Payout %	**37.4**	**35.2**	**30.9**	**35.2**	**41.8**	**58.4**	**56.5**
INCOME STATEMENT (IN MILLIONS):							
Total Revenues	7,243.0	6,307.0	4,345.0	3,760.0	3,237.0	[3] 2,927.0	4,468.0
Costs & Expenses	6,038.0	5,213.8	3,528.2	3,056.9	2,656.8	2,434.6	3,837.8
Depreciation & Amort.	238.3	181.8	136.3	116.1	99.7	90.1	120.6
Operating Income	966.7	911.4	680.5	587.1	480.5	402.3	509.6
Net Interest Inc./(Exp.)	d191.4	d120.4	d85.3	d79.8	d74.7	d73.8	d104.7
Income Before Income Taxes	873.9	880.2	725.8	606.8	482.6	325.6	423.9
Income Taxes	301.7	334.5	279.0	248.5	207.5	151.7	128.9
Equity Earnings/Minority Int.	19.5	23.9	29.2	24.1	20.1	26.2	d101.3
Net Income	[5] 591.7	[4] 569.6	476.0	382.4	295.2	[2] 200.1	[1] 193.7
Cash Flow	830.0	751.4	612.3	498.5	394.9	290.1	314.3
Average Shs. Outstg. (000)	451,800	446,200	343,700	337,600	321,200	319,200	317,600
BALANCE SHEET (IN MILLIONS):							
Cash & Cash Equivalents	169.4	230.8	541.7	441.3	473.7	60.5	71.1
Total Current Assets	2,308.2	2,109.8	1,862.6	1,626.7	1,429.8	964.5	1,891.4
Net Property	1,906.8	1,624.4	1,164.3	1,037.3	940.6	856.7	1,231.8
Total Assets	7,744.0	6,634.9	5,167.4	4,333.8	3,701.7	3,778.6	4,390.0
Total Current Liabilities	1,078.1	846.4	846.6	620.0	518.4	445.9	601.3
Long-Term Obligations	3,018.2	2,431.3	1,391.4	1,321.5	1,236.3	1,577.1	1,592.6
Net Stockholders' Equity	3,426.1	3,136.5	2,728.6	2,229.0	1,839.8	1,655.4	2,112.7
Net Working Capital	1,230.1	1,263.3	1,016.0	1,006.7	911.3	518.6	1,290.2
Year-end Shs. Outstg. (000)	444,750	443,510	339,330	331,140	321,740	320,760	313,980
STATISTICAL RECORD:							
Operating Profit Margin %	13.3	14.5	15.7	15.6	14.8	13.7	11.4
Net Profit Margin %	8.2	9.0	11.0	10.2	9.1	6.8	4.3
Return on Equity %	17.3	18.2	17.4	17.2	16.0	12.1	9.2
Return on Assets %	7.6	8.6	9.2	8.8	8.0	5.3	4.4
Debt/Total Assets %	39.0	36.6	26.9	30.5	33.4	41.7	36.3
Price Range	27.00-14.50	33.69-22.50	33.00-20.75	26.91-16.88	18.44-13.25	15.75-11.25	19.94-10.63
P/E Ratio	20.6-11.1	26.3-17.6	23.7-14.9	23.4-14.7	20.0-14.4	25.2-18.0	32.7-17.4
Average Yield %	2.4	1.6	1.6	1.9	2.4	2.7	2.3

Statistics are as originally reported. Adj. for stk. split: 2-for-1, 7/98. [1] Incl. non-recurr. chrg. $79.3 mill. [2] Incl. non-recurr. chrg. $47.9 mill.; bef. discont. oper. loss $641.7 mill. [3] Reflects the sale of the Masco Home Furnishings Group businesses. [4] Incl. aftertax non-recurr. chrg. of approx. $126.0 mill. [5] Incl. pre-tax chrg. of $55.0 mill. for the write-down of assets and $90.0 mill. for the planned dispos. of assets.

OFFICERS:
R. A. Manoogian, Chmn., C.E.O.
R. F. Kennedy, Pres., C.O.O.
R. B. Rosowski, V.P., Treas., Contr.
E. A. Gargaro, Jr., V.P., Sec.

INVESTOR CONTACT: Samuel A. Cypert, Investor Contact, (313) 274-7400

PRINCIPAL OFFICE: 21001 Van Born Rd., Taylor, MI 48180

TELEPHONE NUMBER: (313) 274-7400
FAX: (313) 792-6135
WEB: www.masco.com

NO. OF EMPLOYEES: 48,600 (approx.)

SHAREHOLDERS: 6,700 (approx.)

ANNUAL MEETING: In May

INCORPORATED: MI, Dec., 1929; reincorp., DE, 1968

INSTITUTIONAL HOLDINGS:
No. of Institutions: 335
Shares Held: 316,323,838
% Held: 68.8

INDUSTRY: Plumbing fixture fittings and trim (SIC: 3432)

TRANSFER AGENT(S): Bank of New York, New York, NY

NYSE SYMBOL MTZ
Rec. Pr. 14.66 (4/30/01)

MASTEC INC.

YIELD ...
P/E RATIO 8.6

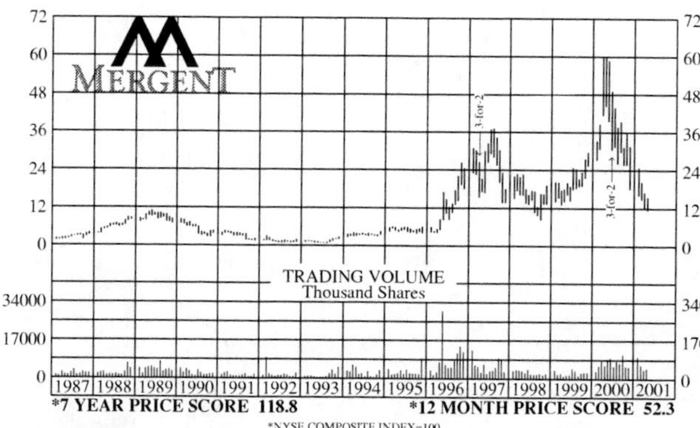

*7 YEAR PRICE SCORE 118.8 *12 MONTH PRICE SCORE 52.3

*NYSE COMPOSITE INDEX=100

INTERIM EARNINGS (Per Share):

Qtr.	Mar.	June	Sept.	Dec.
1996	0.10	0.17	0.25	0.27
1997	0.24	0.27	0.21	0.15
1998	d0.29	0.22	0.32	d0.60
1999	0.11	0.29	0.40	0.26
2000	0.25	0.44	0.51	0.50

INTERIM DIVIDENDS (Per Share):

Amt.	Decl.	Ex.	Rec.	Pay.
3-for-2	5/17/00	6/20/00	5/29/00	6/19/00

CAPITALIZATION (12/31/00):

	($000)	(%)
Long-Term Debt	206,160	29.2
Common & Surplus	500,328	70.8
Total	706,488	100.0

RECENT DEVELOPMENTS: For the year ended 12/31/00, net income jumped 45.7% to $65.1 million versus $44.7 million in 1999. Results for 2000 and 1999 included net gains of $15.9 million and $6.0 million associated with the write-down of non-core international assets. Total revenues amounted to $1.33 billion, an increase of 25.6% compared with $1.06 billion a year earlier. Datacom Network Services revenue advanced 33.4% to $1.13 billion.

PROSPECTS: During 2001, the Company plans to enhance profitability by focusing on improving operating efficiencies, building brand awareness and offering value-added services. Meanwhile, the Company anticipates revenue growth to be in the range of 17.0% to 20.0% and earnings per share growth of $2.05 to $2.15 per share for the full year 2001. Results should also benefit from the Company's efforts to strengthen its balance sheet.

BUSINESS

MASTEC, INC. (formerly Burnup & Sims, Inc.) engages in the design, manufacturing, installation and maintenance of internal and external networks that support the Internet, Internet-related applications, e-commerce and other communications and energy facilities. The Company provides comprehensive network infrastructure services to local exchange carriers, cable television operators, telecommunications providers, energy companies, facilities providers, financial institutions and other Fortune 500 companies. Major customers include BellSouth Telecommunications, Inc., Williams Communications Group, Inc., US West, Inc., Sprint Corp., Telergy, Inc., Level 3 Communications and Comcast Corp. The Company operates approximately 200 locations throughout North America.

ANNUAL FINANCIAL DATA

	12/31/00	12/31/99	12/31/98	12/31/97	12/31/96	12/31/95	1 12/31/94
Earnings Per Share	5 1.35	1.05	4 d0.34	3 0.95	3 0.80	2 0.09	3 0.16
Cash Flow Per Share	2.66	2.37	0.71	1.60	1.12	0.10	0.34
Tang. Book Val. Per Share	4.99	2.48	1.51	4.45	2.87	1.40	1.41
INCOME STATEMENT (IN MILLIONS):							
Total Revenues	1,330.3	1,059.0	1,048.9	703.4	472.8	174.6	111.3
Costs & Expenses	1,116.4	895.7	977.3	613.5	410.9	149.8	95.9
Depreciation & Amort.	63.5	56.1	43.3	24.1	12.0	6.9	5.5
Operating Income	150.4	107.2	28.3	65.8	49.9	17.8	9.9
Net Interest Inc./(Exp.)	d13.3	d17.3	d20.5	d10.0	d8.2	d1.6	d2.1
Income Before Income Taxes	111.4	79.8	2.6	64.0	42.7	d4.8	8.8
Income Taxes	45.9	33.3	12.6	21.0	15.7	cr1.8	2.3
Equity Earnings/Minority Int.	d0.4	d1.8	d4.0	d0.4	3.1	d0.1	0.2
Net Income	5 65.1	44.7	4 d13.9	3 42.5	3 30.2	2 d3.1	3 6.7
Cash Flow	128.6	100.9	29.4	66.7	42.2	3.8	12.2
Average Shs. Outstg. (000)	48,374	42,624	41,234	41,780	37,692	36,104	36,173
BALANCE SHEET (IN MILLIONS):							
Cash & Cash Equivalents	18.5	27.6	19.9	6.1	4.8	1.1	5.6
Total Current Assets	453.8	393.9	427.4	394.2	380.5	105.2	53.0
Net Property	159.7	153.5	142.9	86.1	59.6	44.6	40.1
Total Assets	964.9	728.4	735.5	587.6	483.0	170.2	142.5
Total Current Liabilities	219.9	158.5	182.9	270.4	228.8	60.6	30.8
Long-Term Obligations	206.2	267.5	310.7	94.5	117.2	44.2	36.0
Net Stockholders' Equity	500.3	256.8	204.3	180.7	103.5	50.5	50.9
Net Working Capital	233.9	235.4	244.5	123.7	151.8	44.6	22.3
Year-end Shs. Outstg. (000)	47,702	42,459	41,073	40,656	36,125	36,124	36,086
STATISTICAL RECORD:							
Operating Profit Margin %	11.3	10.1	2.7	9.4	10.6	10.2	8.9
Net Profit Margin %	4.9	4.2	...	6.0	6.4	...	6.0
Return on Equity %	13.0	17.4	...	23.5	29.2	...	13.2
Return on Assets %	6.8	6.1	...	7.2	6.2	...	4.7
Debt/Total Assets %	21.4	36.7	42.2	16.1	24.3	26.0	25.2
Price Range	60.17-18.00	29.67-13.08	22.79-8.25	37.17-13.58	26.33-4.17	6.11-3.89	4.56-2.56
P/E Ratio	44.6-13.3	28.3-12.5	...	39.0-14.3	32.9-5.2	70.2-44.6	28.5-16.0

Statistics are as originally reported. Adj. for 3-for-2 stk split, 6/00 & 3/97. 1 Reflects combined operations of Burnup & Sims, Inc. & Church Tower Group. 2 Bef. disc. ops. gain of $2.5 mill. & incl. special chrg. of $23.1 mill. 3 Bef. disc. ops. gain of $129,000, 1997; loss of $177,000, 1996; gain of $825,000, 1994. 4 Incl. pre-tax nonrecurr. chrg. of $33.8 mill. 5 Incl. net gain of $15.9 mill.

OFFICERS:
J. L. Mas, Chmn.
J. Citron, Pres., C.E.O.
C. M. Sabater, Exec. V.P., C.F.O.

INVESTOR CONTACT: Carmen M. Sabater, Sr. V.P., C.F.O., (305) 406-1866

PRINCIPAL OFFICE: 3155 N.W. 77th Ave., Miami, FL 33122-1205

TELEPHONE NUMBER: (305) 599-1800
FAX: (305) 599-1572
WEB: www.mastec.com

NO. OF EMPLOYEES: 12,400 (approx.)

SHAREHOLDERS: 4,527

ANNUAL MEETING: In Jan.

INCORPORATED: FL, 1929; reincorp., DE, July, 1968

INSTITUTIONAL HOLDINGS:
No. of Institutions: 139
Shares Held: 18,287,010
% Held: 38.3

INDUSTRY: Water, sewer, and utility lines (SIC: 1623)

TRANSFER AGENT(S): First Union National Bank of North Carolina, Charlotte, NC

NYSE SYMBOL MAT
Rec. Pr. 16.15 (4/30/01)

MATTEL, INC.

YIELD 2.2%
P/E RATIO 40.4

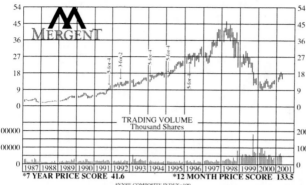

TRADING VOLUME
Thousand Shares

*7 YEAR PRICE SCORE 41.6 *12 MONTH PRICE SCORE 133.5

*NYSE COMPOSITE INDEX=100

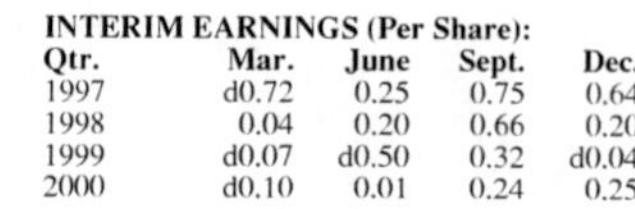

INTERIM EARNINGS (Per Share):

Qtr.	Mar.	June	Sept.	Dec.
1997	d0.72	0.25	0.75	0.64
1998	0.04	0.20	0.66	0.20
1999	d0.07	d0.50	0.32	d0.04
2000	d0.10	0.01	0.24	0.25

INTERIM DIVIDENDS (Per Share):

Amt.	Decl.	Ex.	Rec.	Pay.
0.09Q	8/13/99	9/08/99	9/10/99	10/01/99
0.09Q	11/04/99	12/08/99	12/10/99	1/04/00
0.09Q	2/10/00	3/08/00	3/10/00	4/05/00
0.09Q	6/07/00	6/16/00	6/20/00	7/06/00
0.09Q	8/17/00	9/06/00	9/08/00	10/04/00

Indicated div.: $0.36 (Div. Reinv. Plan)
Divs. payable annually as of 1/01/01.

CAPITALIZATION (12/31/00):

	($000)	(%)
Long-Term Debt [1]	1,242,396	47.0
Common & Surplus	1,403,098	53.0
Total	2,645,494	100.0

RECENT DEVELOPMENTS: For the year ended 12/31/00, income from continuing operations was $170.2 million versus income from continuing operations of $108.4 million in the previous year. Results for 2000 included pre-tax nonrecurring charges of $179.0 million, and excluded net losses from discontinued operations of $601.1 million. Net sales improved 1.6% to $4.67 billion. On 4/5/01, MAT closed its Kentucky toy factory.

PROSPECTS: MAT expects to report additional expenses of $125.0 million over the next two years and generate cost savings of $200.0 million over the next three years, due to its financial restructuring initiatives. Separately, revenues should benefit from multi-year licensing agreements with Vivendi Universal Publishing and THQ, Inc. Going forward, MAT anticipates revenue growth in the mid single-digit range over the next three to five years.

BUSINESS

MATTEL, INC. is the largest toy maker in the world in terms of revenues. MAT's four principal product lines are BARBIE fashion dolls, doll clothing and accessories; AMERICAN GIRL collection of books, dolls and accessories based on American heroines; FISHERPRICE toys and juvenile products; and HOT WHEELS. Additional principal product lines include large dolls; preschool toys, including SEE N SAY talking toys; and the UNO and SKIPBO games. MAT has offices and facilities in about 36 foreign countries and sells its products in more than 150 nations throughout the world. In November of 1993, Fisher-Price, Inc. became a wholly-owned subsidiary. MAT acquired Tyco Toys, Inc. in 3/97 and The Learning Company, a producer of educational, home and reference software, in 5/99.

REVENUES

(12/31/2000)	($000)	(%)
US Girls	1,110,390	16.1
US Boys-Entertainment	753,149	10.9
US Infant & Preschool	1,221,851	17.7
Other	364,679	5.3
International	1,531,590	22.2
Toy Manufacturing	1,924,313	27.8
Total	6,905,972	100.0

ANNUAL FINANCIAL DATA

	12/31/00	12/31/99	12/31/98	12/31/97	12/31/96	12/31/95	12/31/94
Earnings Per Share	**[7] 0.40**	**[6] d0.21**	**[5] 1.10**	**[4] 0.94**	**[3] 1.36**	**1.26**	**[2] 0.90**
Cash Flow Per Share	**1.00**	**0.51**	**1.78**	**1.59**	**1.30**	**1.19**	**0.85**
Tang. Book Val. Per Share	**0.62**	**1.35**	**1.98**	**4.38**	**3.84**	**3.09**	**2.37**
Dividends Per Share	**0.36**	**0.34**	**0.30**	**0.26**	**0.23**	**0.18**	**0.15**
Dividend Payout %	**90.0**	**...**	**27.3**	**27.7**	**16.8**	**14.5**	**16.2**
INCOME STATEMENT (IN MILLIONS):							
Total Revenues	4,669.9	5,515.0	4,781.9	4,834.6	3,786.0	3,638.8	3,205.0
Costs & Expenses	4,033.5	5,190.0	3,941.3	4,095.8	2,989.8	2,904.2	2,604.2
Depreciation & Amort.	256.4	298.6	214.9	189.9	149.1	133.0	124.3
Operating Income	380.0	26.3	625.6	548.9	647.1	601.6	476.6
Net Interest Inc./(Exp.)	d153.0	d151.6	d110.8	d90.1	d75.5	d73.6	d55.4
Income Before Income Taxes	225.4	d110.7	465.1	425.1	545.7	532.9	393.6
Income Taxes	55.2	cr28.4	132.8	135.3	334.1	328.4	274.2
Net Income	[7] 170.2	[6] d82.4	[5] 332.3	[4] 289.8	[3] 211.6	204.5	[2] 119.4
Cash Flow	426.6	212.2	539.2	469.2	360.7	334.1	239.0
Average Shs. Outstg. (000)	427,126	414,186	303,243	295,653	278,385	281,015	279,923
BALANCE SHEET (IN MILLIONS):							
Cash & Cash Equivalents	232.4	275.0	212.5	694.9	500.6	483.5	259.7
Total Current Assets	1,751.5	2,420.0	2,057.8	2,461.7	1,770.8	1,690.8	1,543.5
Net Property	647.8	749.5	736.5	601.6	579.6	499.3	415.9
Total Assets	4,313.4	5,127.0	4,262.2	3,803.8	2,893.5	2,695.5	2,459.0
Total Current Liabilities	1,502.4	1,817.5	1,317.2	1,173.4	960.4	847.7	915.9
Long-Term Obligations	1,242.4	1,183.8	983.5	664.1	364.1	464.3	355.1
Net Stockholders' Equity	1,403.1	1,962.7	1,820.2	1,822.1	1,447.8	1,275.2	1,085.7
Net Working Capital	249.1	602.5	740.6	1,288.3	810.5	843.1	627.6
Year-end Shs. Outstg. (000)	426,000	421,600	286,100	291,600	271,000	275,500	276,125
STATISTICAL RECORD:							
Operating Profit Margin %	8.1	0.5	13.1	11.4	17.1	16.5	14.9
Net Profit Margin %	3.6	...	6.9	6.0	5.6	5.6	3.7
Return on Equity %	12.1	...	18.3	15.9	14.6	16.0	11.0
Return on Assets %	3.9	...	7.8	7.6	7.3	7.6	4.9
Debt/Total Assets %	28.8	23.1	23.1	17.5	12.6	17.2	14.4
Price Range	15.13-8.94	30.31-11.69	46.56-21.25	42.25-23.38	32.50-21.63	24.90-15.76	18.88-13.25
P/E Ratio	37.8-22.3	...	42.3-19.3	44.9-24.9	23.9-15.9	19.8-12.5	21.0-14.7
Average Yield %	3.0	1.6	0.9	0.8	0.8	0.9	0.9

Statistics are as originally reported. Adj. for 5-for-4 stock split, 3/96, 1/95, 1/94 & 11/91. [1] Incl. debs. conv. into com. [2] Incl. $75.0 mill. restruct. chg. [3] Incl. after-tax spec. chg. of $15.1 mill. & after-tax refund accrual of $8.0 mill. [4] Incl. a pre-tax integrat./restruct. chg. of $275.0 mill. & excl. an after-tax extraord. chg. of $4.6 mill. [5] Incl. a net spec. chg. of $27.0 mill. & an addit. $4.0 mill. net nonreucrr. chrg. [6] Incl. net restruct. chrgs. of $265.0 mill. [7] Incl. pre-tax nonrecurr. chrgs. of $179.0 mill. & excl. loss of $601.1 mill. fr. disc. opers.

OFFICERS:
R. A. Eckert, Chmn., C.E.O.
P. Rowland, Vice-Pres.,
K. M. Farr, C.F.O.

INVESTOR CONTACT: Ned Mansour, Sr. V.P., Gen. Couns. & Sec., (310) 252-2000

PRINCIPAL OFFICE: 333 Continental Blvd., El Segundo, CA 90245-5012

TELEPHONE NUMBER: (310) 252-2000
FAX: (310) 252-3671
WEB: www.mattel.com

NO. OF EMPLOYEES: 30,000 (approx.)

SHAREHOLDERS: 51,000 (approx. record)

ANNUAL MEETING: In May

INCORPORATED: CA, Mar., 1948; reincorp., DE, Mar., 1968

INSTITUTIONAL HOLDINGS:
No. of Institutions: 353
Shares Held: 291,664,041
% Held: 67.7

INDUSTRY: Dolls and stuffed toys (SIC: 3942)

TRANSFER AGENT(S): Fleet National Bank (c/o EquiServe), Boston, MA

NYSE SYMBOL MVK
Rec. Pr. 24.15 (5/31/01)

MAVERICK TUBE CORPORATION

YIELD ...
P/E RATIO 45.6

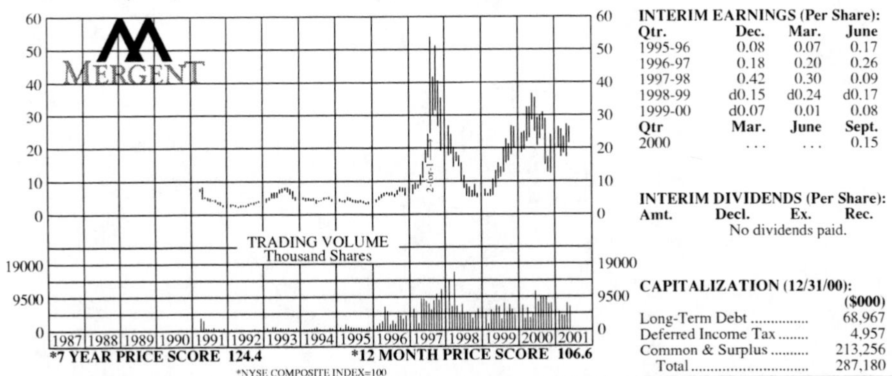

*7 YEAR PRICE SCORE 124.4 *12 MONTH PRICE SCORE 106.6

*NYSE COMPOSITE INDEX=100

INTERIM EARNINGS (Per Share):

Qtr.	Dec.	Mar.	June	Sept.
1995-96	0.08	0.07	0.17	0.19
1996-97	0.18	0.20	0.26	0.35
1997-98	0.42	0.30	0.09	d0.08
1998-99	d0.15	d0.24	d0.17	d0.11
1999-00	d0.07	0.01	0.08	...
Qtr	**Mar.**	**June**	**Sept.**	**Dec.**
2000	...	...	0.15	0.29

INTERIM DIVIDENDS (Per Share):

Amt.	Decl.	Ex.	Rec.	Pay.

No dividends paid.

CAPITALIZATION (12/31/00):

	($000)	(%)
Long-Term Debt	68,967	24.0
Deferred Income Tax	4,957	1.7
Common & Surplus	213,256	74.3
Total	287,180	100.0

RECENT DEVELOPMENTS: For the year ended 12/31/00, net income was $16.6 million compared with a net loss of $6.3 million in 1999. Results for 2000 and 1999 included start-up costs of $267,000 and $3.0 million, respectively. Results for 2000 also included transaction costs of $11.3 million related to the acquisition of Prudential Steel Ltd. on 9/22/00. Net sales surged 63.4% to $560.4 million. Comparisons were made with restated prior-year figures.

PROSPECTS: Looking ahead, should drilling move higher from the current levels of approximately 1,100 rigs in the U.S., the Company could realize drilling budget increases of over 20.0% in 2001 from 2000 levels. In addition, the Company believes many of the new drilling crews added late in 2000 should become more efficient, thereby increasing the demand for MVK's oil country tubular goods products.

BUSINESS

MAVERICK TUBE CORPORATION and its subsidiaries, Maverick Tube International, Inc., Maverick Investment Corporation and Maverick Tube, L.P., manufacture steel tubular products used in the completion and production of oil and natural gas wells. MVK also manufactures line pipe used in the transportation of oil and natural gas. For industrial applications, MVK manufactures structural tubing and standard pipe. In 1999, MVK began producing "cold drawn tubing" in its industrial products segment, which is used as a component of high quality products that require close tolerances. MVK manufactures its products at three facilities in Conroe, TX, Hickman, AR, and Beaver Falls, PA. On 9/22/00, the Company acquired Prudential Steel Ltd.

ANNUAL FINANCIAL DATA

	3 12/31/00	2 12/31/99	9/30/99	9/30/98	9/30/97	9/30/96	9/30/95
Earnings Per Share	1 0.48	0.05	1 d0.68	0.73	0.97	0.51	d0.15
Cash Flow Per Share	0.88	0.15	d0.20	1.13	1.35	0.85	0.16
Tang. Book Val. Per Share	6.33	...	5.16	5.83	5.05	3.83	3.33
INCOME STATEMENT (IN THOUSANDS):							
Total Revenues	560,382	129,616	172,417	265,389	291,060	204,182	167,896
Costs & Expenses	502,047	122,760	179,372	240,681	261,072	187,039	163,147
Depreciation & Amort.	13,819	3,327	7,355	6,172	5,697	5,201	4,691
Operating Income	44,516	3,529	d14,310	18,536	24,291	11,942	58
Net Interest Inc./(Exp.)	d3,177	d256	d1,861	d1,731	d2,067	d2,522	d3,164
Income Before Income Taxes	30,086	3,273	d16,171	16,805	22,224	9,420	d2,334
Income Taxes	13,521	1,726	cr5,722	5,420	7,339	1,882	...
Net Income	1 16,565	1,547	1 d10,449	11,385	14,885	7,538	d2,334
Cash Flow	30,384	4,874	d3,094	17,557	20,582	12,739	2,357
Average Shs. Outstg.	34,525	32,638	15,438	15,564	15,282	15,001	14,920
BALANCE SHEET (IN THOUSANDS):							
Cash & Cash Equivalents	2,193	...	1,625	748	2,886	613	491
Total Current Assets	220,677	...	82,913	86,053	105,938	73,191	54,218
Net Property	167,263	...	74,518	69,879	55,506	51,695	51,168
Total Assets	389,029	323,255	160,148	156,885	162,064	125,556	106,494
Total Current Liabilities	101,849	10,790	38,597	25,691	60,946	40,539	23,946
Long-Term Obligations	68,967	27,150	38,518	35,626	18,879	25,151	33,045
Net Stockholders' Equity	213,256	200,566	79,646	90,063	77,868	57,247	49,503
Net Working Capital	118,828	d10,790	44,316	60,362	44,992	32,652	30,272
Year-end Shs. Outstg.	33,712	...	15,440	15,437	15,411	14,944	14,880
STATISTICAL RECORD:							
Operating Profit Margin %	7.9	2.7	...	7.0	8.3	5.8	...
Net Profit Margin %	3.0	1.2	...	4.3	5.1	3.7	...
Return on Equity %	7.8	0.8	...	12.6	19.1	13.2	...
Return on Assets %	4.3	0.5	...	7.3	9.2	6.0	...
Debt/Total Assets %	17.7	8.4	24.1	22.7	11.6	20.0	31.0
Price Range	36.50-12.38	26.75-5.38	26.75-5.38	26.88-5.03	53.87-6.13	8.25-3.69	5.25-3.06
P/E Ratio	76.0-25.8	533.9-107.3	...	36.8-6.9	55.5-6.3	16.3-7.3	...

Statistics are as originally reported. Adj. for stk. splits: 2-for-1, 8/21/97. 1 Incl. non-recurr. chrg. $13.2 mill., 12/00; $3.5 mill., 9/99. 2 For three months due to fiscal year end change. 3 Refls. the acq. of Prudential Steel Ltd.

OFFICERS:
G. M. Eisenberg, Chmn., Pres., C.E.O.
P. G. Boone, Acting C.F.O., Contr.

INVESTOR CONTACT: Investor Relations, (636) 733-1600

PRINCIPAL OFFICE: 16401 Swingley Ridge Road, Suite 700, Chesterfield, MO 63017

TELEPHONE NUMBER: (636) 733-1600
FAX: (636) 537-1363
WEB: www.maverick-tube.com

NO. OF EMPLOYEES: 2,079 (approx.)

SHAREHOLDERS: 150

ANNUAL MEETING: In May

INCORPORATED: MO, 1977; reincorp., DE, 1987

INSTITUTIONAL HOLDINGS:
No. of Institutions: 109
Shares Held: 21,389,280
% Held: 63.2

INDUSTRY: Steel pipe and tubes (SIC: 3317)

TRANSFER AGENT(S): Computershare Investor Services, Chicago IL

NYSE SYMBOL MAY
Rec. Pr. 32.70 (5/31/01)

MAY DEPARTMENT STORES COMPANY (THE)

YIELD	2.9%
P/E RATIO	12.5

*7 YEAR PRICE SCORE 68.1 *12 MONTH PRICE SCORE 126.0

*NYSE COMPOSITE INDEX=100

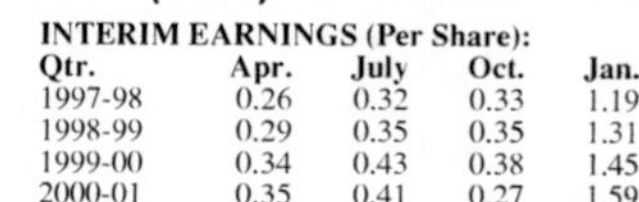

INTERIM EARNINGS (Per Share):

Qtr.	Apr.	July	Oct.	Jan.
1997-98	0.26	0.32	0.33	1.19
1998-99	0.29	0.35	0.35	1.31
1999-00	0.34	0.43	0.38	1.45
2000-01	0.35	0.41	0.27	1.59

INTERIM DIVIDENDS (Per Share):

Amt.	Decl.	Ex.	Rec.	Pay.
0.233Q	8/18/00	8/30/00	9/01/00	9/15/00
0.233Q	11/17/00	11/29/00	12/01/00	12/15/00
0.235Q	2/15/01	2/27/01	3/01/01	3/15/01
0.235Q	3/09/01	5/30/01	6/01/01	6/15/01

Indicated div.: $0.94 (Div. Reinv. Plan)

CAPITALIZATION (2/3/01):

	($000)	(%)
Long-Term Debt	4,534,000	50.5
Deferred Income Tax	586,000	6.5
Common & Surplus	3,855,000	43.0
Total	8,975,000	100.0

RECENT DEVELOPMENTS: For the 53 weeks ended 2/3/01, net earnings totaled $858.0 million, down 7.4% versus $927.0 million in the corresponding 52-week period the previous year. Revenues increased 4.7% to $14.51 billion from $13.87 billion a year earlier. Net retail sales grew 4.3% to $14.45 billion. On a 52-week basis, comparable-store sales inched up 0.5% year-over-year. Operating earnings slipped 3.5% to $1.75 billion from $1.81 billion in the prior year.

PROSPECTS: On 4/12/01, MAY acquired 13 stores formerly operated by Wards. Most of these stores will be remodeled and reopen in 2002. During 2001, MAY plans to open 21 new department stores and approximately 28 new David's Bridal stores. The August 2000 acquisition of David's Bridal, which anticipates registering more than 500,000 couples in 2001, should help provide synergies with the Company's Wedding Registry services and expand its reach to younger customers.

BUSINESS

THE MAY DEPARTMENT STORES COMPANY operated 435 department stores and 126 David's Bridal stores in 43 states, the District of Columbia and Puerto Rico as of 4/12/01. MAY's department stores are operated under the following names: Lord & Taylor, Hecht's, Strawbridge's, Foley's, Robinsons-May, Filene's, Kaufmann's, Famous-Barr, L.S. Ayers, The Jones Store and Meier & Frank. Thalhimers was acquired for $317.0 million in 1990, and was consolidated with the Hecht's division in January 1992. On 5/4/96, the Company completed its spin-off of Payless ShoeSource, Inc. On 8/11/00, MAY acquired David's Bridal, Inc.

QUARTERLY DATA

(2/3/01)($000)	Rev	Inc
1st Quarter	3,050,000	120,000
2nd Quarter	3,131,000	135,000
3rd Quarter	3,326,000	85,000
4th Quarter	5,004,000	518,000

ANNUAL FINANCIAL DATA

	2/3/01	1/29/00	1/30/99	1/31/98	2/1/97	[3] 2/3/96	1/28/95
Earnings Per Share	**2.62**	**2.60**	**2.30**	[1] **2.07**	[1] **1.96**	[2] **1.82**	**2.04**
Cash Flow Per Share	**4.18**	**3.93**	**3.51**	**3.19**	**3.01**	**2.75**	**3.10**
Tang. Book Val. Per Share	**8.53**	**9.51**	**8.67**	**8.82**	**8.09**	**10.48**	**9.50**
Dividends Per Share	**0.93**	**0.89**	**0.85**	**0.80**	**0.77**	**0.74**	**0.67**
Dividend Payout %	**35.5**	**34.2**	**36.8**	**38.6**	**39.3**	**40.8**	**33.0**
INCOME STATEMENT (IN MILLIONS):							
Total Revenues	14,511.0	13,866.0	13,413.0	12,685.0	12,000.0	10,952.0	12,223.0
Costs & Expenses	12,253.0	11,587.0	11,301.0	10,695.0	10,118.0	9,209.0	10,319.0
Depreciation & Amort.	511.0	469.0	439.0	412.0	373.0	333.0	374.0
Operating Income	1,747.0	1,810.0	1,673.0	1,578.0	1,509.0	1,410.0	1,530.0
Net Interest Inc./(Exp.)	d345.0	d287.0	d278.0	d299.0	d277.0	d250.0	d234.0
Income Before Income Taxes	1,402.0	1,523.0	1,395.0	1,279.0	1,232.0	1,160.0	1,296.0
Income Taxes	544.0	596.0	546.0	500.0	483.0	460.0	514.0
Net Income	858.0	927.0	849.0	[1] 779.0	[1] 749.0	[2] 700.0	782.0
Cash Flow	1,351.0	1,377.0	1,270.0	1,173.0	1,104.0	1,014.0	1,137.0
Average Shs. Outstg. (000)	327,700	355,600	367,400	373,600	373,050	375,000	373,500
BALANCE SHEET (IN MILLIONS):							
Cash & Cash Equivalents	156.0	41.0	112.0	199.0	102.0	159.0	55.0
Total Current Assets	5,270.0	5,115.0	4,987.0	4,878.0	5,035.0	5,097.0	4,910.0
Net Property	4,899.0	4,769.0	4,513.0	4,224.0	4,159.0	3,744.0	3,866.0
Total Assets	11,574.0	10,935.0	10,533.0	9,930.0	10,059.0	10,122.0	9,472.0
Total Current Liabilities	2,214.0	2,415.0	2,059.0	1,866.0	1,923.0	1,602.0	1,895.0
Long-Term Obligations	4,534.0	3,560.0	3,825.0	3,512.0	3,849.0	3,333.0	2,875.0
Net Stockholders' Equity	3,855.0	4,077.0	3,836.0	3,809.0	3,650.0	4,585.0	4,135.0
Net Working Capital	3,056.0	2,700.0	2,928.0	3,012.0	3,112.0	3,495.0	3,015.0
Year-end Shs. Outstg. (000)	298,200	325,500	334,700	346,500	355,350	373,500	372,000
STATISTICAL RECORD:							
Operating Profit Margin %	12.0	13.1	12.5	12.4	12.6	12.9	12.5
Net Profit Margin %	5.9	6.7	6.3	6.1	6.2	6.4	6.4
Return on Equity %	22.3	22.7	22.1	20.5	20.5	15.3	18.9
Return on Assets %	7.4	8.5	8.1	7.8	7.4	6.9	8.3
Debt/Total Assets %	39.2	32.6	36.3	35.4	38.3	32.9	30.4
Price Range	33.94-19.19	45.38-29.19	47.25-33.17	38.09-29.08	34.84-26.67	30.25-21.92	30.08-21.50
P/E Ratio	13.0-7.3	17.5-11.2	20.5-14.4	18.4-14.0	17.8-13.6	16.6-12.0	14.7-10.5
Average Yield %	3.5	2.4	2.1	2.4	2.5	2.8	2.6

Statistics are as originally reported. Adj. for 3-for-2 stk. split, 3/99. [1] Bef. $4 mil extraord. loss, 1997; & bef. $5 mil extraord. loss & cr$11 mil from discont. opers., 1996. [2] Bef. discont. opers. cr$55 mil; bef. $3 mil extraord. loss; & incl. $44 mil non-recur. chg. [3] Excl. results of spun-off PayLess ShoeSource, Inc.

OFFICERS:
J. T. Loeb, Chmn.
E. S. Kahn, Pres., C.E.O.
J. L. Dunham, Vice-Chmn., C.F.O.
A. J. Torcasio, Vice-Chmn.

INVESTOR CONTACT: Sharon L. Bateman, (314) 342-6494

PRINCIPAL OFFICE: 611 Olive Street, St. Louis, MO 63101-1799

TELEPHONE NUMBER: (314) 342-6300
FAX: (314) 342-6497
WEB: www.maycompany.com
NO. OF EMPLOYEES: 63,000 full-time (approx.); 74,000 part-time (approx.)
SHAREHOLDERS: 43,000 (approx.)
ANNUAL MEETING: In May
INCORPORATED: NY, June, 1910; reincorp., DE, May, 1996

INSTITUTIONAL HOLDINGS:
No. of Institutions: 442
Shares Held: 221,408,576
% Held: 74.1

INDUSTRY: Department stores (SIC: 5311)

TRANSFER AGENT(S): The Bank of New York, New York, NY

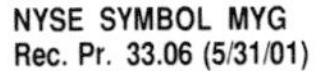

NYSE SYMBOL MYG
Rec. Pr. 33.06 (5/31/01)

MAYTAG CORPORATION

YIELD 2.2%
P/E RATIO 13.6

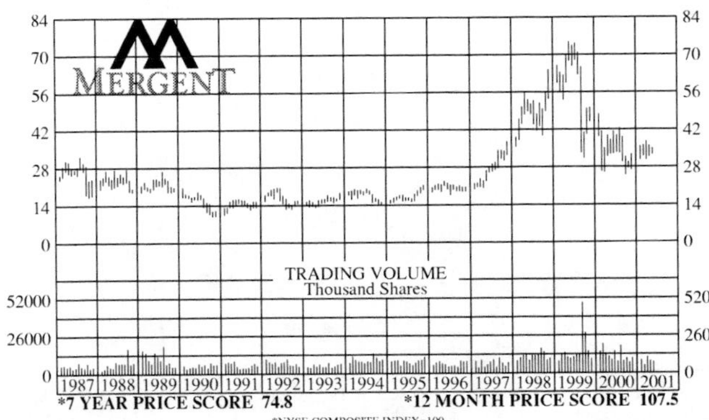

INTERIM EARNINGS (Per Share):

Qtr.	Mar.	June	Sept.	Dec.
1996	0.15	0.43	0.42	0.36
1997	0.39	0.45	0.51	0.54
1998	0.75	0.71	0.85	0.75
1999	0.95	0.97	0.92	0.82
2000	0.89	0.92	0.74	d0.12

INTERIM DIVIDENDS (Per Share):

Amt.	Decl.	Ex.	Rec.	Pay.
0.18Q	5/11/00	5/30/00	6/01/00	6/15/00
0.18Q	8/10/00	8/30/00	9/01/00	9/15/00
0.18Q	11/09/00	11/29/00	12/01/00	12/15/00
0.18Q	2/08/01	2/27/01	3/01/01	3/15/01
0.18Q	5/10/01	5/30/01	6/01/01	6/15/01

Indicated div.: $0.72 (Div. Reinv. Plan)

CAPITALIZATION (12/31/00):

	($000)	(%)
Long-Term Debt	451,336	68.4
Deferred Income Tax	21,953	3.3
Minority Interest	165,063	25.0
Common & Surplus	21,676	3.3
Total	660,028	100.0

RECENT DEVELOPMENTS: For the year ended 12/31/00, net income was $201.0 million versus $328.5 million in 1999. The 2000 results included after-tax charges totaling $31.2 million related to discontinued businesses and products, asset write-downs and severance costs. Earnings in 2000 also included an after-tax charge of $11.2 million from securities losses. Net sales slipped 1.8% to $4.25 billion, primarily due to weak sales of commercial appliances.

PROSPECTS: The Company is implementing initiatives designed to improve operating efficiencies and lower costs. Going forward, the Company is focusing its research and development spending on its core major appliance and floor care product lines, as well as on products expected to be launched in the near future. In addition, MYG plans to significantly reduce investments in Web-based businesses and e-commerce initiatives of non-core product lines.

BUSINESS

MAYTAG CORPORATION is a manufacturer of home and commercial appliances. The Company's Home Appliances segment (87.4% of 2000 net sales) includes washers, dryers, gas and electric ranges, ovens, refrigerators, dishwashers and floor care products sold under the MAYTAG, MAGIC CHEF, HOOVER, JENN-AIR, and ADMIRAL brand names to retailers in North America and Canada. The Commercial Appliances segment (9.8%) includes commercial cooking and vending equipment sold primarily under the DIXIE-NARCO, BLODGETT and PITCO FRIALATOR brands to distributors, soft drink bottlers, restaurant chains and dealers in North America and targeted international markets. The International Appliances segment (2.8%) consists of MYG's 50.5%-owned joint venture in China, Rongshida-Maytag, which manufactures and distributes laundry products and refrigerators. MYG acquired Magic Chef in 1986, Chicago Pacific Corporation in 1989, G.S. Blodgett Corp. in 1997, and Jade Range in 1999.

ANNUAL FINANCIAL DATA

	12/31/00	12/31/99	12/31/98	12/31/97	12/31/96	12/31/95	12/31/94
Earnings Per Share	**[1] 2.44**	**3.66**	**[4] 3.05**	**[4] 1.87**	**[1][4] 1.36**	**[4] d0.14**	**[2][3] 1.42**
Cash Flow Per Share	**4.38**	**5.30**	**4.63**	**3.28**	**2.45**	**0.90**	**2.53**
Tang. Book Val. Per Share	**...**	**...**	**0.23**	**1.56**	**1.85**	**2.33**	**3.14**
Dividends Per Share	**0.72**	**0.72**	**0.68**	**0.64**	**0.56**	**0.52**	**0.50**
Dividend Payout %	**29.5**	**19.7**	**22.3**	**34.2**	**41.2**	**...**	**35.2**
INCOME STATEMENT (IN MILLIONS):							
Total Revenues	4,247.5	4,323.7	4,069.3	3,407.9	3,001.7	3,039.5	3,372.5
Costs & Expenses	3,668.9	3,600.8	3,398.0	2,911.5	2,621.3	2,639.4	2,930.4
Depreciation & Amort.	160.3	147.4	148.6	138.2	111.3	111.9	119.4
Operating Income	418.3	575.5	522.7	358.3	269.1	288.2	322.8
Net Interest Inc./(Exp.)	d64.1	d59.3	d62.8	d59.0	d43.0	d52.1	d74.1
Income Before Income Taxes	332.0	530.9	470.9	300.6	228.2	59.8	241.3
Income Taxes	115.2	195.1	176.1	109.8	89.0	74.8	90.2
Net Income	[1] 201.0	328.5	[4] 286.5	[4] 183.5	[1][4] 138.0	[4] d15.0	[2][3] 151.1
Cash Flow	361.3	475.9	435.1	321.7	249.3	96.9	270.5
Average Shs. Outstg. (000)	82,425	89,731	93,973	98,055	101,727	107,062	106,795
BALANCE SHEET (IN MILLIONS):							
Cash & Cash Equivalents	27.2	28.8	28.6	28.0	27.5	141.2	110.4
Total Current Assets	1,076.6	1,021.5	968.9	934.7	905.0	910.1	1,130.1
Net Property	970.2	976.1	965.6	941.3	851.9	701.1	749.3
Total Assets	2,668.9	2,636.5	2,587.7	2,514.2	2,329.9	2,125.1	2,504.3
Total Current Liabilities	971.7	853.0	790.7	566.6	570.0	366.7	534.4
Long-Term Obligations	451.3	337.8	446.5	549.5	488.5	536.6	663.2
Net Stockholders' Equity	21.7	427.4	507.6	615.8	574.0	637.4	731.7
Net Working Capital	104.9	168.5	178.2	368.1	334.9	543.4	595.7
Year-end Shs. Outstg. (000)	76,240	82,524	89,218	95,011	98,044	105,405	107,337
STATISTICAL RECORD:							
Operating Profit Margin %	9.8	13.3	12.8	10.5	9.0	9.5	9.6
Net Profit Margin %	4.7	7.6	7.0	5.4	4.6	...	4.5
Return on Equity %	927.1	76.9	56.4	29.8	24.0	...	20.7
Return on Assets %	7.5	12.5	11.1	7.3	5.9	...	6.0
Debt/Total Assets %	16.9	12.8	17.3	21.9	21.0	25.2	26.5
Price Range	47.75-25.00	74.81-31.25	64.50-35.38	37.56-19.75	22.88-17.50	21.50-14.50	20.13-14.00
P/E Ratio	19.6-10.2	20.4-8.5	21.1-11.6	20.1-10.6	16.8-12.9	...	14.2-9.9
Average Yield %	2.0	1.4	1.4	2.2	2.8	2.9	2.9

Statistics are as originally reported. [1] Incl. $31.2 mil ($0.38/sh) non-recur. chg. & $11.2 mil ($0.13/sh) chg. fr secur. losses, 2000; $24 mil restr. chg., 1996. [2] Incl. $16.4 mil ($0.15/sh) non-recur. chg. [3] Bef. $3.2 mil ($0.03/sh) chg. for acctg. adj. & $20 mil ($0.19/sh) tax benefit. [4] Bef. $5.9 mil ($0.06/sh) extraord. chg., 1998; $3.2 mil ($0.03/sh) extraord. chg., 1997; $1.5 mil ($0.02/sh), 1996; & bef. $5.5 mil extraord. chg. & incl. $149.8 mil chg. for disp. of opers. & $9.9 mil chg. for lawsuit settlement, 1995.

OFFICERS:
L. A. Hadley, Pres., C.E.O.
S. H. Wood, Exec. V.P., C.F.O.
E. Park, Sr. V.P., Chief Info. Off.

INVESTOR CONTACT: James G. Powell, (641) 787-8392

PRINCIPAL OFFICE: 403 West Fourth Street North, Newton, IA 50208

TELEPHONE NUMBER: (641) 792-7000
FAX: (641) 787-8376
WEB: www.maytagcorp.com

NO. OF EMPLOYEES: 24,657

SHAREHOLDERS: 27,873

ANNUAL MEETING: In May

INCORPORATED: DE, Aug., 1925

INSTITUTIONAL HOLDINGS:
No. of Institutions: 247
Shares Held: 40,062,623
% Held: 52.6

INDUSTRY: Household appliances, nec (SIC: 3639)

TRANSFER AGENT(S): Computershare Investor Services, Chicago, IL

NYSE SYMBOL MBI
Rec. Pr. 52.75 (5/31/01)

MBIA INC.

YIELD 1.1%
P/E RATIO 22.3

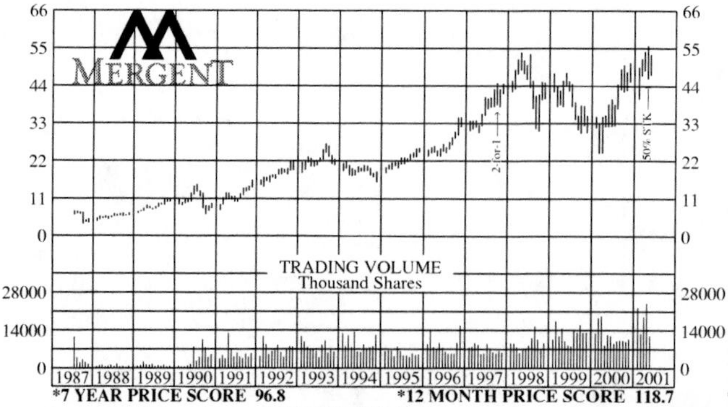

MERGENT

TRADING VOLUME
Thousand Shares

2-for-1 — 50% STK

1987 1988 1989 1990 1991 1992 1993 1994 1995 1996 1997 1998 1999 2000 2001

***7 YEAR PRICE SCORE 96.8** ***12 MONTH PRICE SCORE 118.7**

*NYSE COMPOSITE INDEX=100

INTERIM EARNINGS (Per Share):

Qtr.	Mar.	June	Sept.	Dec.
1996	0.61	0.61	0.64	0.63
1997	0.69	0.68	0.72	0.72
1998	0.67	0.78	0.72	0.69
1999	0.06	0.37	0.85	0.85
2000	0.89	0.87	0.88	0.92

INTERIM DIVIDENDS (Per Share):

Amt.	Decl.	Ex.	Rec.	Pay.
0.205Q	6/14/00	6/22/00	6/26/00	7/15/00
0.205Q	9/18/00	9/21/00	9/25/00	10/15/00
0.205Q	12/07/00	12/18/00	12/20/00	1/15/01
0.225Q	3/15/01	3/22/01	3/26/01	4/16/01
50% STK	3/15/01	4/23/01	4/02/01	4/20/01

Indicated div.: $0.60 (Adj.)

CAPITALIZATION (12/31/00):

	($000)	(%)
Long-Term Debt	795,102	15.1
Deferred Income Tax	252,463	4.8
Common & Surplus	4,223,413	80.1
Total	5,270,978	100.0

RECENT DEVELOPMENTS: For the year ended 12/31/00, net income grew 64.9% to $528.6 million from $320.5 million in 1999. Results included net realized gains of $32.9 million and $25.2 million in 2000 and 1999, respectively. Results for 1999 included one-time corporate charges of $105.0 million. Total insurance revenues climbed 4.7% to $868.6 million from $829.7 million in the prior year. Investment management services revenues rose 37.3% to $118.9 million. Municipal services revenues soared 61.8% to $37.1 million from $22.9 million the year before.

PROSPECTS: The Company's insurance operations should continue to benefit from strong growth in its structured finance and international businesses. However, the domestic municipal market may continue to experience a decline in activity. Meanwhile, the Company's investment management operations should continue to be fueled by increases in assets under management and operating earnings. Going forward, MBI should benefit from growth opportunities across all of its business lines.

BUSINESS

MBIA INC. is the holding company of MBIA Insurance Corporation, a major company in the municipal bond and structured finance insurance business. MBIA's principal business is to guarantee timely payment of principal and interest for new municipal bond issues, asset-backed securities, bonds traded in the secondary market and those held in unit investment trusts and mutual funds. In addition, it guarantees high quality obligations offered by financial institutions and provides investment management and other financial services for school districts and municipalities. MBIA serves state and local governments and other agencies, issuers of asset-backed securities, financial advisors, investment banking firms, bond traders, sponsors of unit investment trusts and mutual funds and the investing public. MBI's operations take place in North America, Europe, Asia and Australia. MBI acquired CapMAC Holdings, Inc. on 2/17/98 and 1838 Investment Advisors on 7/31/98.

ANNUAL FINANCIAL DATA

	12/31/00	12/31/99	12/31/98	12/31/97	12/31/96	12/31/95	12/31/94
Earnings Per Share	**3.55**	**3 2.13**	**2 2.88**	**2.81**	**2.48**	**2.14**	**2.06**
Tang. Book Val. Per Share	**27.86**	**22.79**	**24.59**	**21.82**	**18.28**	**16.88**	**12.76**
Dividends Per Share	**0.55**	**0.53**	**0.52**	**0.51**	**0.47**	**0.42**	**0.36**
Dividend Payout %	**15.4**	**25.1**	**18.2**	**18.1**	**19.0**	**19.8**	**17.6**
INCOME STATEMENT (IN MILLIONS):							
Total Premium Income	446.4	442.8	424.6	297.4	251.7	215.1	218.3
Net Investment Income	394.0	359.5	331.8	281.5	247.6	219.9	193.9
Other Income	184.2	162.2	164.7	75.1	46.3	27.3	27.4
Total Revenues	1,024.6	964.4	921.0	654.0	545.5	462.2	439.5
Income Before Income Taxes	714.9	387.9	565.0	479.6	408.1	345.0	329.4
Income Taxes	186.2	67.4	132.3	105.4	86.0	345.0	69.2
Net Income	528.6	3 320.5	2 432.7	374.2	322.2	...	260.2
Average Shs. Outstg. (000)	148,669	150,604	150,245	133,121	130,044	126,720	126,258
BALANCE SHEET (IN MILLIONS):							
Cash & Cash Equivalents	5,901.4	5,264.3	4,217.2	4,099.4	3,722.8	2,978.0	1,822.8
Premiums Due	487.8	459.0	402.2	266.3	217.8	207.0	187.4
Invst. Assets: Fixed-term	6,740.1	5,784.0	5,884.1	4,867.3	4,149.7	3,652.6	3,051.9
Invst. Assets: Total	12,547.6	10,954.8	10,080.5	8,943.4	7,865.2	6,607.3	4,866.8
Total Assets	13,894.3	12,263.9	11,258.3	9,810.8	8,562.0	7,267.5	5,456.4
Long-Term Obligations	795.1	689.2	689.0	473.9	374.0	373.9	298.8
Net Stockholders' Equity	4,223.4	3,513.1	3,792.2	3,048.3	2,479.7	2,234.3	1,704.7
Year-end Shs. Outstg. (000)	147,846	149,328	149,322	134,192	129,882	126,012	124,848
STATISTICAL RECORD:							
Return on Revenues %	51.6	33.2	47.0	57.2	59.1	...	59.2
Return on Equity %	12.5	9.1	11.4	12.3	13.0	...	15.3
Return on Assets %	3.8	2.6	3.8	3.8	3.8	...	4.8
Price Range	50.79-24.21	47.92-30.08	53.96-30.71	44.84-30.29	34.88-23.33	25.83-18.46	21.75-15.75
P/E Ratio	14.3-6.8	22.5-14.1	18.7-10.7	15.9-10.8	14.1-9.4	12.1-8.6	10.6-7.6
Average Yield %	1.5	1.4	1.2	1.4	1.6	1.9	1.9

Statistics are as originally reported. Adj. for stk. splits: 50% div., 4/01; 2-for-1, 10/97 1 Bef. acctg. change credit $12.9 mill. 2 Incl. non-recurr. chrg. of $36.1 mill. 3 Incl. non-recurr. chrg. of $105.0 mill.

QUARTERLY DATA

(12/31/2000)	Rev	Inc
1st Quarter	11,954	9,420
2nd Quarter	53,358	56,793
3rd Quarter	160,178	127,410
4th Quater	162,393	126,907

OFFICERS:
J. W. Brown Jr., Chmn., C.E.O.
G. C. Dunton, Pres., C.O.O.
N. G. Budnick, C.F.O., Treas.

INVESTOR CONTACT: Judith C. Radasch, Dir. Inv. Rel., (914) 765-3014

PRINCIPAL OFFICE: 113 King Street, Armonk, NY 10504

TELEPHONE NUMBER: (914) 273-4545
FAX: (914) 765-3163
WEB: www.mbia.com

NO. OF EMPLOYEES: 745 (avg.)

SHAREHOLDERS: 945

ANNUAL MEETING: In May

INCORPORATED: CT, Nov., 1986

INSTITUTIONAL HOLDINGS:
No. of Institutions: 354
Shares Held: 131,150,639
% Held: 88.5

INDUSTRY: Surety insurance (SIC: 6351)

TRANSFER AGENT(S): Mellon Investor Services, Ridgefield Park, NJ

NYSE SYMBOL KRB
Rec. Pr. 35.65 (4/30/01)

MBNA CORPORATION

YIELD 1.0%
P/E RATIO 23.3

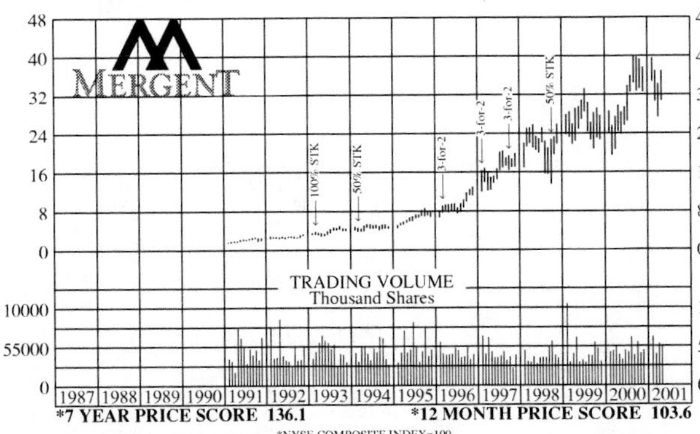

INTERIM EARNINGS (Per Share):

Qtr.	Mar.	June	Sept.	Dec.
1997	0.16	0.18	0.22	0.23
1998	0.18	0.21	0.27	0.30
1999	0.22	0.27	0.34	0.38
2000	0.28	0.34	0.43	0.48

INTERIM DIVIDENDS (Per Share):

Amt.	Decl.	Ex.	Rec.	Pay.
0.08Q	4/13/00	6/13/00	6/15/00	7/01/00
0.08Q	7/12/00	9/13/00	9/15/00	10/01/00
0.08Q	10/11/00	12/13/00	12/15/00	1/01/01
0.09Q	1/10/01	3/13/01	3/15/01	4/01/01
0.09Q	4/11/01	6/13/01	6/15/01	7/01/01

Indicated div.: $0.36

CAPITALIZATION (12/31/00):

	($000)	(%)
Total Deposits	24,343,595	66.3
Long-Term Debt	5,735,635	15.6
Preferred Stock	86	0.0
Common & Surplus	6,627,192	18.1
Total	36,706,508	100.0

RECENT DEVELOPMENTS: For the year ended 12/31/00, net income advanced 28.1% to $1.31 billion from $1.02 billion in 1999. Net interest income grew 16.1% to $1.08 billion from $933.8 million a year earlier. Provision for possible credit losses increased slightly to $409.0 million from $408.9 million the year before. Total other operating income improved 21.0% to $5.09 billion. Total other operating expense increased 18.5% to $3.65 billion.

PROSPECTS: Looking ahead, the Company should continue to benefit from the acquisition of the consumer and commercial revolving credit businesses of First Union, which was completed in the third quarter of 2000. The Company expects to continue to benefit from its on-line service, MBNA.com, which was introduced in the first quarter of 2000. Currently, MBNA.com serves more than 3.0 million customers.

BUSINESS

MBNA CORPORATION is a registered bank holding company, with assets of $38.68 billion as of 12/31/00. The Corporation is the parent company of MBNA America Bank, N.A. and has two wholly-owned foreign bank subsidiaries, MBNA International Bank Limited, located in the United Kingdom, and MBNA Canada Bank. The Corporation is an independent credit card lender and an issuer of affinity credit cards, marketed primarily to members of associations and customers of financial institutions. In addition to its credit card lending, the Corporation also makes other consumer loans and offers insurance and deposit products.

LOAN DISTRIBUTION

(12/31/2000)	($000)	(%)
Credit Card	7,798,772	66.8
Other Consumer	3,884,132	33.2
Total	11,682,904	100.0

ANNUAL FINANCIAL DATA

	12/31/00	12/31/99	12/31/98	12/31/97	12/31/96	12/31/95	12/31/94
Earnings Per Share	**1.53**	**1.21**	**0.97**	**0.77**	**[1] 0.59**	**[2] 0.46**	**[3] 0.35**
Tang. Book Val. Per Share	**4.55**	**5.24**	**3.18**	**2.62**	**2.27**	**1.68**	**1.22**
Dividends Per Share	**0.31**	**0.27**	**0.23**	**0.21**	**0.18**	**0.16**	**0.14**
Dividend Payout %	**20.3**	**22.3**	**24.1**	**27.0**	**31.1**	**35.1**	**39.5**
INCOME STATEMENT (IN MILLIONS):							
Total Interest Income	2,775.7	2,262.3	1,966.2	1,711.0	1,383.3	1,140.8	839.6
Total Interest Expense	1,691.7	1,328.5	1,223.8	1,018.6	742.8	596.6	307.5
Net Interest Income	1,084.0	933.8	742.3	692.4	640.5	544.2	532.1
Provision for Loan Losses	409.0	408.9	310.0	260.0	178.2	138.2	108.5
Non-Interest Income	5,093.2	4,207.8	3,229.0	2,812.9	1,895.9	1,424.6	1,013.6
Non-Interest Expense	3,647.7	3,077.7	2,407.2	2,223.1	1,626.9	1,246.1	996.1
Income Before Taxes	2,120.4	1,655.0	1,254.1	1,022.1	785.6	584.6	441.1
Net Income	1,312.5	1,024.4	776.3	622.5	[1] 474.5	[2] 353.1	[3] 266.6
Average Shs. Outstg. (000)	846,531	837,038	789,421	789,801	778,473	770,465	762,514
BALANCE SHEET (IN MILLIONS):							
Cash & Due from Banks	971.5	488.4	382.9	263.1	225.1	291.9	158.6
Securities Avail. for Sale	2,662.0	2,752.7	1,663.7	2,162.5	1,719.7	911.9	480.8
Total Loans & Leases	11,682.9	7,971.1	11,776.1	8,261.9	7,659.1	4,967.5	3,408.0
Allowance for Credit Losses	386.6	356.0	216.9	162.5	118.4	104.9	101.5
Net Loans & Leases	11,296.3	7,615.1	11,559.2	8,099.4	7,540.7	4,862.6	3,306.5
Total Assets	38,673.9	30,859.1	25,806.3	21,305.5	17,035.3	13,228.7	9,671.9
Total Deposits	24,343.6	18,714.8	15,407.0	12,913.2	10,151.7	8,608.9	6,632.5
Long-Term Obligations	5,735.6	5,708.9	5,939.0	5,478.9	3,950.4	2,657.6	1,687.4
Total Liabilities	32,050.8	26,659.7	23,415.2	19,335.5	15,331.0	11,963.8	8,752.3
Net Stockholders' Equity	6,627.3	4,199.4	2,391.0	1,970.1	1,704.3	1,265.1	919.6
Year-end Shs. Outstg. (000)	851,804	801,781	751,796	751,782	751,781	751,781	751,781
STATISTICAL RECORD:							
Return on Equity %	19.8	24.4	32.5	31.6	27.8	27.9	29.0
Return on Assets %	3.4	3.3	3.0	2.9	2.8	2.7	2.8
Equity/Assets %	17.1	13.6	9.3	9.2	10.0	9.6	9.5
Non-Int. Exp./Tot. Inc. %	59.1	59.9	60.6	63.4	64.1	63.3	64.4
Price Range	40.13-19.50	33.25-20.81	25.88-13.50	20.39-11.95	12.96-6.72	8.62-4.42	5.41-3.80
P/E Ratio	26.2-12.7	27.5-17.2	26.7-13.9	26.6-15.6	21.9-11.4	18.9-9.7	15.4-10.9
Average Yield %	1.0	1.0	1.2	1.3	1.9	2.5	3.0

Statistics are as originally reported. Adj. for 3-for-2 splits: 10/98, 10/97, 2/97, 2/96 & 2/94. [1] Incl. pre-tax exp. fr. termination of mktg. agreement: $54.3 mill., 1996. [2] Incl. pre-tax gain on invest. securities sold: $39,000, 1995. [3] Incl. $74,000 pre-tax loss on invest. securities sold

OFFICERS:
A. Lerner, Chmn., C.E.O.
C. M. Cawley, Pres.
M. S. Kaufman, Sr. Exec. V.P., C.F.O., Treas.

INVESTOR CONTACT: Steve Boyden, Director, Investor Relations, (800) 362-6255

PRINCIPAL OFFICE: 1100 North King Street, Wilmington, DE 19884-0141

TELEPHONE NUMBER: (302) 456-8588
FAX: (302) 456-8541
WEB: www.mbna.com

NO. OF EMPLOYEES: 22,700 (approx.)

SHAREHOLDERS: 2,770

ANNUAL MEETING: In April

INCORPORATED: MD, Dec., 1990

INSTITUTIONAL HOLDINGS:
No. of Institutions: 547
Shares Held: 629,929,252
% Held: 74.0

INDUSTRY: National commercial banks (SIC: 6021)

TRANSFER AGENT(S): The Bank of New York, New York, NY

NYSE SYMBOL MNI
Rec. Pr. 41.00 (4/30/01)

MCCLATCHY COMPANY (THE)

YIELD 1.0%
P/E RATIO 20.8

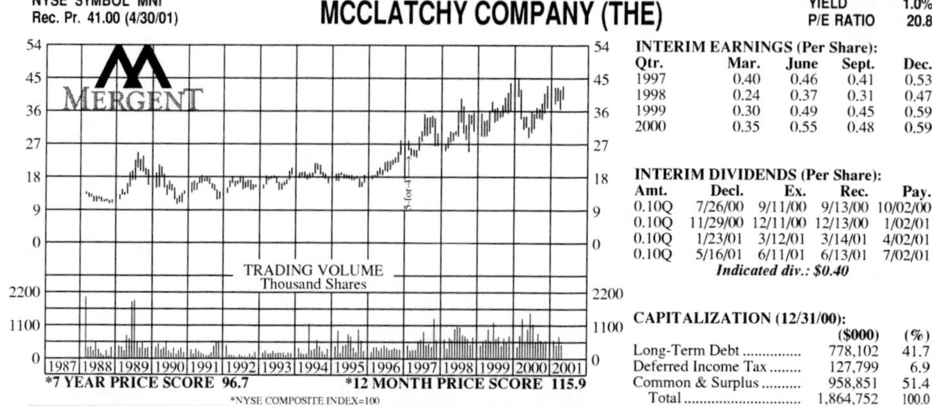

INTERIM EARNINGS (Per Share):

Qtr.	Mar.	June	Sept.	Dec.
1997	0.40	0.46	0.41	0.53
1998	0.24	0.37	0.31	0.47
1999	0.30	0.49	0.45	0.59
2000	0.35	0.55	0.48	0.59

INTERIM DIVIDENDS (Per Share):

Amt.	Decl.	Ex.	Rec.	Pay.
0.10Q	7/26/00	9/11/00	9/13/00	10/02/00
0.10Q	11/29/00	12/11/00	12/13/00	1/02/01
0.10Q	1/23/01	3/12/01	3/14/01	4/02/01
0.10Q	5/16/01	6/11/01	6/13/01	7/02/01

Indicated div.: $0.40

CAPITALIZATION (12/31/00):

	($000)	(%)
Long-Term Debt	778,102	41.7
Deferred Income Tax	127,799	6.9
Common & Surplus	958,851	51.4
Total	1,864,752	100.0

RECENT DEVELOPMENTS: For the year ended 12/31/00, net income rose 7.8% to $88.9 million compared with $82.5 million in 1999. Earnings included gains from the sales of land in the Carolinas and charges related to the Montgomery Ward bankruptcy in the last week of December 2000. Net revenues were $1.14 billion, up 5.0% from $1.09 billion in the prior year. Advertising revenues rose 5.9% to $926.7 million.

PROSPECTS: The Star Tribune Company, a subsidiary of MNI, and Vindigo, a developer of personal navigation applications for handheld devices, introduced a mobile dining, entertainment and shopping resource for the Twin Cities. The service features startribune.com® reviews on restaurants in Minneapolis-St. Paul, sorted by cuisine, neighborhood and price range.

BUSINESS

THE MCCLATCHY COMPANY (formerly McClatchy Newspapers, Inc.) owns and publishes 11 daily and 13 non-daily newspapers with a combined circulation of 1.4 million daily and 1.9 million Sunday. MNI has operations in the following regions: California, the Northwest, the Carolinas, and Minnesota. Its newspapers range from large dailies serving metropolitan areas to non-daily newspapers serving small communities. Other businesses include: Nanda.net, the Raleigh News & Observer's on-line service; The Newspaper Network, a distributor of preprinted advertising inserts and run-of-press advertising; and commercial printing operations in CA and NC. On 3/19/98, MNI acquired Cowles Media Company, publisher of the STAR TRIBUNE in Minneapolis/St. Paul, MN for $1.40 billion.

ANNUAL FINANCIAL DATA

	12/31/00	12/26/99	12/27/98	12/31/97	12/31/96	12/31/95	12/31/94
Earnings Per Share	**1.97**	**1.83**	[4] **1.41**	[3] **1.80**	**1.18**	[2] **0.90**	[1] **1.26**
Cash Flow Per Share	**4.44**	**4.28**	**3.64**	**3.20**	**2.58**	**2.07**	**2.30**
Tang. Book Val. Per Share	...	...	...	**4.50**	**2.43**	**0.97**	**8.74**
Dividends Per Share	**0.40**	**0.38**	**0.38**	**0.38**	**0.30**	**0.30**	**0.25**
Dividend Payout %	**20.0**	**20.8**	**26.9**	**21.1**	**25.8**	**32.9**	**20.1**
INCOME STATEMENT (IN MILLIONS):							
Total Revenues	1,142.1	1,087.9	968.7	642.0	624.2	540.9	471.4
Costs & Expenses	796.3	752.9	691.2	472.8	485.9	434.4	361.3
Depreciation & Amort.	112.0	110.4	96.6	53.4	53.1	44.1	38.3
Operating Income	233.8	224.7	180.9	115.8	85.2	62.4	71.9
Net Interest Inc./(Exp.)	d64.7	d65.7	d62.8	d8.7	d13.3	d7.0	...
Income Before Income Taxes	171.1	161.1	120.7	116.8	74.9	59.6	75.0
Income Taxes	82.1	77.7	61.1	47.5	33.4	25.4	22.9
Equity Earnings/Minority Int.	d0.1	d0.8	1.5	d0.5	3.0	d0.6	d5.5
Net Income	88.9	82.5	[4] 61.1	[3] 68.8	44.5	[2] 33.6	[1] 46.6
Cash Flow	200.9	192.9	157.6	122.2	97.6	77.8	84.9
Average Shs. Outstg. (000)	45,243	45,015	43,349	38,155	37,812	37,529	36,979
BALANCE SHEET (IN MILLIONS):							
Cash & Cash Equivalents	10.7	1.2	9.7	8.7	5.9	3.3	98.0
Total Current Assets	235.5	215.6	200.5	122.8	111.0	103.2	180.4
Net Property	431.7	450.1	453.4	325.2	341.8	348.4	274.6
Total Assets	2,165.7	2,204.0	[5] 2,246.7	853.8	875.7	893.0	586.6
Total Current Liabilities	227.3	233.5	220.4	98.4	92.4	94.5	79.1
Long-Term Obligations	778.1	878.2	1,004.0	94.0	190.0	243.0	...
Net Stockholders' Equity	958.9	879.7	807.0	564.7	503.1	465.7	442.2
Net Working Capital	8.2	d17.8	d19.9	24.4	18.6	8.7	101.3
Year-end Shs. Outstg. (000)	45,245	44,958	44,790	38,107	37,764	37,453	37,369
STATISTICAL RECORD:							
Operating Profit Margin %	20.5	20.7	18.7	18.0	13.7	11.5	15.2
Net Profit Margin %	7.8	7.6	6.3	10.7	7.1	6.2	9.9
Return on Equity %	9.3	9.4	7.6	12.2	8.8	7.2	10.5
Return on Assets %	4.1	3.7	2.7	8.1	5.1	3.8	8.0
Debt/Total Assets %	35.9	39.8	44.7	11.0	21.7	27.2	...
Price Range	45.13-28.75	43.75-29.00	39.56-24.94	35.19-23.38	28.10-17.40	19.30-15.30	21.80-16.30
P/E Ratio	22.9-14.6	23.9-15.8	28.1-17.7	19.5-13.0	23.8-14.7	21.4-17.0	17.2-12.9
Average Yield %	1.1	1.0	1.2	1.3	1.3	1.7	1.3

Statistics are as originally reported. Adj. for 5-for-4 split, 1/97. [1] Incl. $768,000 pre-tax restr. chg. [2] Incl. $2.7 mill. pre-tax chg. for early retirement program. [3] Incl. $6.6 mill. gain on sale of ops. [4] Incl. $1.5 mill. income fr. a partnership & $111,000 loss on the sale of certain ops. [5] Incl. amort. of goodwill of $929.0 mill. rel. to the acq. of Cowles Media Co.

OFFICERS:
E. Potts, Chmn.
G. B. Pruitt, Pres., C.E.O.
P. J. Talamantes, V.P., Fin., C.F.O.

INVESTOR CONTACT: R. Elaine Lintecum, Inv. Rel. Mgr., (916) 321-1846

PRINCIPAL OFFICE: 2100 Q Street, Sacramento, CA 95816

TELEPHONE NUMBER: (916) 321-1846
FAX: (916) 321-1964
WEB: www.mcclatchy.com
NO. OF EMPLOYEES: 9,939 (avg.)
SHAREHOLDERS: 2,022 (Class A com.); 23(Class B com.)
ANNUAL MEETING: In May
INCORPORATED: CA, June, 1930; reincorp., DE, Aug., 1987

INSTITUTIONAL HOLDINGS:
No. of Institutions: 86
Shares Held: 14,664,615
% Held: 32.3

INDUSTRY: Newspapers (SIC: 2711)

TRANSFER AGENT(S): Mellon Investor Services, Ridgefield Park, NJ

NYSE SYMBOL MKC
Rec. Pr. 40.40 (5/31/01)

MCCORMICK & COMPANY, INC.

YIELD 2.0%
P/E RATIO 20.0

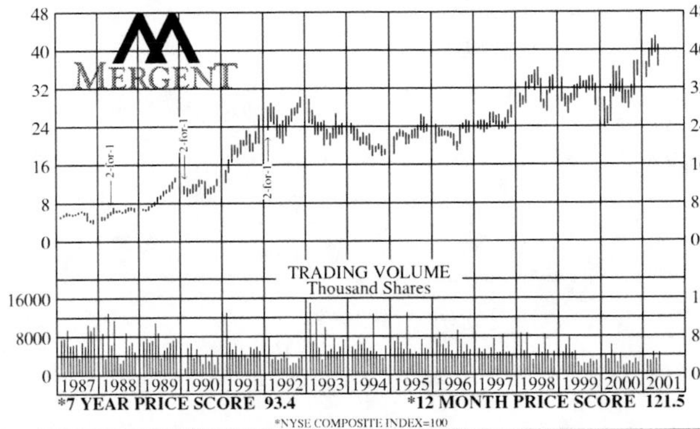

INTERIM EARNINGS (Per Share):

Qtr.	Feb.	May	Aug.	Nov.
1997-98	0.22	0.22	0.29	0.68
1998-99	0.25	0.08	0.35	0.76
1999-00	0.35	0.35	0.45	0.84
2000-01	0.38	...	...	...

INTERIM DIVIDENDS (Per Share):

Amt.	Decl.	Ex.	Rec.	Pay.
0.19Q	3/15/00	3/29/00	3/31/00	4/13/00
0.19Q	6/19/00	6/28/00	6/30/00	7/14/00
0.19Q	9/19/00	9/27/00	9/29/00	10/12/00
0.20Q	12/18/00	12/27/00	12/29/00	1/22/01
0.20Q	3/21/01	3/29/01	4/02/01	4/12/01

Indicated div.: $0.80 (Div. Reinv. Plan)

CAPITALIZATION (11/30/00):

	($000)	(%)
Long-Term Debt	160,200	30.6
Deferred Income Tax	3,200	0.6
Common & Surplus	359,300	68.7
Total	522,700	100.0

RECENT DEVELOPMENTS: For the quarter ended 2/28/01, net income was $26.6 million, up 8.9% versus $24.4 million a year earlier. Prior-year results included one-time pretax special charges of $502,000. Total net sales climbed 15.4% to $533.5 million from $462.4 million the year before. Gross profit was $208.5 million, or 39.1% of net sales, versus $163.8 million, or 35.4% of net sales, the previous year.

PROSPECTS: In 2001, MKC is targeting sales growth in the range of 12.0% to 14.0%, stemming primarily from a full year of sales from the Ducros business, which was acquired on 8/31/00. Dilution during the first half of the current fiscal year from the acquisition of Ducros is expected to result in earnings per share growth in the range of 8.0% and 10.0% in 2001. MKC expects gross profit margin will reach 40.0% in 2001 and improve to 42.0% by 2003.

BUSINESS

MCCORMICK & COMPANY, INC. is a diversified specialty food company primarily engaged in the manufacture of spices, seasonings, flavors and other specialty food products. The Company operates in three business segments: consumer, industrial, and packaging. The consumer segment sells spices, herbs, extracts, proprietary seasoning blends, sauces and marinades to the consumer food market under a variety of brands, including the McCORMICK brand, the CLUB HOUSE brand in Canada, and the SCHWARTZ brand in the U.K. The industrial segment sells spices, herbs, extracts, proprietary seasonings, condiments, coatings and compound flavors to food processors, restaurant chains, distributors, warehouse clubs and institutional operations. The packaging segment sells plastic packaging products to the food, personal care and other industries, primarily in the U.S.

ANNUAL FINANCIAL DATA

	11/30/00	11/30/99	11/30/98	11/30/97	11/30/96	11/30/95	11/30/94
Earnings Per Share	**1 1.98**	**1 1.43**	**1 1.41**	**2 1.29**	**3 0.54**	**1 1.07**	**1 0.75**
Cash Flow Per Share	**2.86**	**2.23**	**2.15**	**1.94**	**1.33**	**1.99**	**1.52**
Tang. Book Val. Per Share	**...**	**3.40**	**3.13**	**3.18**	**3.64**	**4.17**	**3.62**
Dividends Per Share	**0.76**	**0.68**	**0.64**	**0.60**	**0.56**	**0.52**	**0.48**
Dividend Payout %	**38.4**	**47.5**	**45.4**	**46.5**	**103.7**	**48.6**	**64.0**
INCOME STATEMENT (IN MILLIONS):							
Total Revenues	2,123.5	2,006.9	1,881.1	1,801.0	1,732.5	1,858.7	1,694.8
Costs & Expenses	1,837.2	1,772.6	1,643.5	1,580.8	1,575.4	1,590.0	1,504.0
Depreciation & Amort.	61.3	57.4	54.8	49.3	63.8	63.7	62.5
Operating Income	225.0	176.9	182.8	170.8	93.3	205.0	128.2
Net Interest Inc./(Exp.)	d39.7	d32.4	d36.9	d36.3	d33.8	d55.3	d38.7
Income Before Income Taxes	186.0	150.0	152.5	142.3	61.7	149.2	87.0
Income Taxes	66.6	60.1	54.9	52.7	23.9	53.7	33.8
Equity Earnings/Minority Int.	18.1	13.4	6.2	7.8	5.6	2.1	7.9
Net Income	1 137.5	1 103.3	1 103.8	2 97.4	3 43.5	1 97.5	1 61.2
Cash Flow	198.8	160.7	158.6	146.8	107.3	161.2	123.7
Average Shs. Outstg. (000)	69,600	72,000	73,800	75,658	80,641	81,181	81,240
BALANCE SHEET (IN MILLIONS):							
Cash & Cash Equivalents	23.9	12.0	17.7	13.5	22.4	12.5	15.6
Total Current Assets	620.0	490.6	503.8	506.5	534.4	670.7	657.7
Net Property	373.0	363.3	377.0	380.0	400.4	524.8	504.6
Total Assets	1,659.9	1,188.8	1,259.1	1,256.2	1,326.6	1,614.3	1,568.7
Total Current Liabilities	1,027.2	470.6	518.0	498.2	499.3	646.9	600.8
Long-Term Obligations	160.2	241.4	250.4	276.5	291.2	349.1	374.3
Net Stockholders' Equity	359.3	382.4	388.1	393.1	450.0	519.3	490.0
Net Working Capital	d407.2	20.0	d14.2	8.3	35.1	23.9	56.8
Year-end Shs. Outstg. (000)	68,300	70,400	72,500	74,024	78,205	81,218	81,206
STATISTICAL RECORD:							
Operating Profit Margin %	10.6	8.8	9.7	9.5	5.4	11.0	7.6
Net Profit Margin %	6.5	5.1	5.5	5.4	2.5	5.2	3.6
Return on Equity %	38.3	27.0	26.7	24.8	9.7	18.8	12.5
Return on Assets %	8.3	8.7	8.2	7.8	3.3	6.0	3.9
Debt/Total Assets %	9.7	20.3	19.9	22.0	22.0	21.6	23.9
Price Range	37.75-23.75	34.63-26.63	36.44-27.06	28.38-22.63	25.38-18.88	26.63-18.13	24.75-17.75
P/E Ratio	19.1-12.0	24.2-18.6	25.8-19.2	22.0-17.5	47.0-34.9	24.9-16.9	33.0-23.7
Average Yield %	2.5	2.2	2.0	2.4	2.5	2.3	2.3

Statistics are as originally reported. 1 Incl. $4.1 mil pre-tax chrg., 2000; $18.4 mill. after-tax chrg., 1999; $2.3 mill. pre-tax chrg., 1998; $3.9 mill. pre-tax credit, 1995; $70.4 mil pre-tax chrg., 1994 2 Bef. $1.0 mill. disc. oper. gain & incl. $3.2 mill. pre-tax credit. 3 Bef. $7.8 mill. extraord. chrg., $6.2 mill. disc. oper. gain & incl. $58.1 mill. pre-tax chrg.

OFFICERS:
R. J. Lawless, Chmn., Pres., C.E.O.
F. A. Contino, Exec. V.P., C.F.O.
J. A. Anderson, Sr. V.P.
C. J. Kurtzman, V.P., Treas.

INVESTOR CONTACT: Chris Kurtzman, V.P. & Treas., (410) 771-7244

PRINCIPAL OFFICE: 18 Loveton Circle, Sparks, MD 21152

TELEPHONE NUMBER: (410) 771-7301
FAX: (410) 771-7462
WEB: www.mccormick.com

NO. OF EMPLOYEES: 7,600 (avg.)

SHAREHOLDERS: 2,000 (approx. voting com.); 9,000 (approx. non-voting com.)

ANNUAL MEETING: In Mar.

INCORPORATED: MD, Nov., 1915

INSTITUTIONAL HOLDINGS:
No. of Institutions: 218
Shares Held: 44,620,475
% Held: 64.8

INDUSTRY: Food preparations, nec (SIC: 2099)

TRANSFER AGENT(S): Wells Fargo Shareowner Services, South St. Paul, MN

NYSE SYMBOL MDR
Rec. Pr. 12.21 (4/30/01)

MCDERMOTT INTERNATIONAL, INC.

YIELD ...
P/E RATIO ...

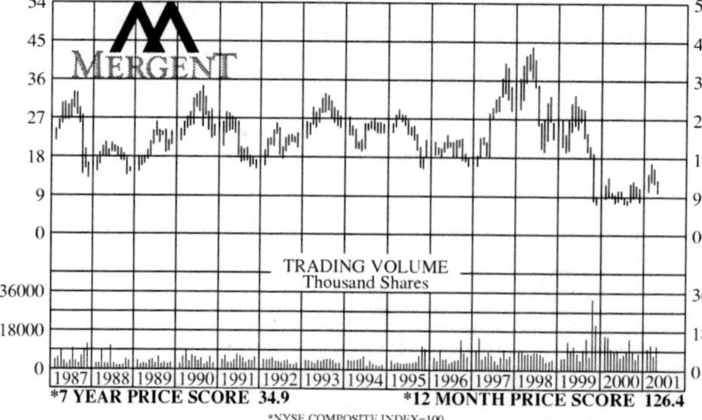

INTERIM EARNINGS (Per Share):

Qtr.	June	Sept.	Dec.	Mar.
1997-98	1.94	0.64	0.82	0.25
1998-99	1.88	0.85	0.71	d1.06
1999-2000	0.33	0.06	d0.39	...
Qtr.	**Mar.**	**June**	**Sept.**	**Dec.**
2000	0.13	d0.17	0.09	d0.42

INTERIM DIVIDENDS (Per Share):

Amt.	Decl.	Ex.	Rec.	Pay.
0.05Q	3/01/00	3/13/00	3/15/00	4/01/00
0.05Q	5/02/00	6/13/00	6/15/00	7/01/00

Dividend payment suspended.

CAPITALIZATION (12/31/00):

	($000)	(%)
Long-Term Debt	323,157	29.4
Common & Surplus	776,603	70.6
Total	1,099,760	100.0

RECENT DEVELOPMENTS: For the year ended 12/31/00, MDR posted a net loss of $22.1 million versus a loss of $22.9 million, before an extraordinary charge, in 1999. Results for 2000 and 1999 included net losses of $2.8 million and $20.8 million on asset disposals and impairments. Results for 2000 also included a restructuring charge of $4.1 million. Total revenues fell 28.9% to $1.88 billion, due to the deconsolidation of the Babcock & Wilcox Company and its subsidiaries, which are being reorganized under Chapter 11 of the U.S. Bankruptcy Code.

PROSPECTS: Near-term prospects are limited, reflecting continued low marine construction volume. However, the Company is projecting improvement in Marine Construction segment revenue as the year progresses and as the current backlog, which was $541.6 million as of 12/31/00, is realized. Furthermore, the Company should benefit from work under its agreement with BP, which is scheduled to begin in the third quarter of 2001. Meanwhile, MDR expects consolidated earnings for 2001 to range between $0.50 and $0.60 per share.

BUSINESS

MCDERMOTT INTERNATIONAL, INC. is a worldwide energy services company. The Marine Construction Services segment includes the operations of J. Ray McDermott, which supplies worldwide services to customers in the offshore oil and gas exploration and production and hydrocarbon processing industries and to other marine construction companies. The Power Generation Systems segment provides services, equipment and systems to generate steam and electric power at energy facilities worldwide, and includes the operations of the Power Generation Group, which is conducted primarily through Babcock & Wilcox. The Government Operations segment is the sole supplier of nuclear fuel assemblies and major reactor components to the U.S. Navy. The Industrial Operations segment provides project management, conceptual and process design, front-end engineering and design detailed engineering, procurement, construction management and contract maintenance services to customers in a wide range of industries.

ANNUAL FINANCIAL DATA

	12/31/00	[5] 12/31/99	3/31/99	3/31/98	3/31/97	3/31/96	3/31/95
Earnings Per Share	[4] d0.37	0.01	[3] 3.16	3.48	[3] d3.95	[2] 0.23	[1] 0.05
Cash Flow Per Share	0.70	1.14	4.76	5.48	d1.16	...	0.20
Tang. Book Val. Per Share	7.03	5.83	11.30	9.73	0.20	4.06	6.05
Dividends Per Share	0.15	0.20	0.20	0.20	1.00	1.00	1.00
Dividend Payout %	...	N.M.	6.3	5.7	...	434.6	1,996.0
INCOME STATEMENT (IN MILLIONS):							
Total Revenues	1,877.8	1,891.1	3,150.0	3,674.6	3,150.9	3,279.1	3,043.7
Costs & Expenses	1,805.9	1,737.8	2,839.6	3,262.3	3,142.4	3,253.2	3,036.9
Depreciation & Amort.	63.9	67.6	101.4	142.3	151.6	...	...
Operating Income	8.0	85.7	209.0	270.1	d143.1	25.9	6.8
Net Interest Inc./(Exp.)	d16.6	d3.6	34.7	d18.9	d48.4	d47.1	d4.4
Income Before Income Taxes	d10.0	35.1	187.3	291.8	d220.7	21.7	d9.2
Income Taxes	12.1	34.7	cr4.8	76.1	cr14.6	1.1	cr20.0
Net Income	[4] d22.1	0.4	[3] 192.1	215.7	[3] d206.1	[2] 20.6	[1] 10.9
Cash Flow	41.8	68.1	293.5	349.7	d62.8	20.6	10.9
Average Shs. Outstg. (000)	59,770	59,757	61,634	63,776	54,323	...	53,645
BALANCE SHEET (IN MILLIONS):							
Cash & Cash Equivalents	84.6	162.7	181.5	277.9	257.8	238.7	85.9
Total Current Assets	574.5	1,468.8	1,375.4	1,596.6	1,834.3	1,724.5	1,450.6
Net Property	365.4	437.8	434.0	533.7	599.7	690.7	899.7
Total Assets	2,025.1	3,874.9	4,305.5	4,501.1	4,599.5	4,387.3	4,751.7
Total Current Liabilities	659.7	1,302.4	1,266.4	1,461.1	1,608.8	1,392.6	1,491.4
Long-Term Obligations	323.2	323.0	323.8	598.2	667.2	576.3	579.1
Net Stockholders' Equity	776.6	791.9	793.7	679.8	437.0	684.5	710.6
Net Working Capital	d85.2	166.4	109.0	135.4	225.6	332.0	d40.8
Year-end Shs. Outstg. (000)	60,577	59,625	59,147	56,507	54,937	54,536	53,960
STATISTICAL RECORD:							
Operating Profit Margin %	0.4	4.5	6.6	7.3	...	0.8	0.2
Net Profit Margin %	...	...	6.1	5.9	...	0.6	0.4
Return on Equity %	...	0.1	24.2	31.7	...	3.0	1.5
Return on Assets %	...	...	4.5	4.8	...	0.5	0.2
Debt/Total Assets %	16.0	8.3	7.5	13.3	14.5	13.1	12.2
Price Range	13.56-7.19	32.50-7.25	43.94-19.25	40.13-16.00	23.25-16.00	29.13-15.38	27.50-19.38
P/E Ratio	...	N.M.	13.9-6.1	11.5-4.6	...	126.6-66.8	548.9-386.7
Average Yield %	1.4	1.0	0.6	0.7	5.1	4.5	4.3

Statistics are as originally reported. [1] Bef. acctg. adj. chrg. 3/31/95, $1.8 mill.; chrg. 3/31/94, $100.8 mill. [2] Incl. one-time cr. of $34.8 mill. & chrg. of $12.6 mill. [3] Incl. one-time cr. 3/31/97, $79.1 mill.; cr. 3/31/99, $17.9 mill. [4] Incl. net loss of $2.8 mill. fr. asset disp. & impair. and restr. chges. of $4.1 mill. [5] Results for 9 mos. only to refl. chge. in fiscal year

OFFICERS:
B. W. Wilkerson, Chmn., C.E.O.
B. F. Longaker, Exec. V.P., C.F.O.
J. T. Nesser III, Sr. V.P., Gen. Couns., Sec.

INVESTOR CONTACT: D. Washington, Inv. Rel., (504) 587-4080

PRINCIPAL OFFICE: 1450 Poydras Street, New Orleans, LA 70112-6050

TELEPHONE NUMBER: (504) 587-5400
FAX: (504) 587-6153
WEB: www.mcdermott.com

NO. OF EMPLOYEES: 11,800 (approx.)

SHAREHOLDERS: 4,110 (approx.)

ANNUAL MEETING: In May

INCORPORATED: Panama, 1959

INSTITUTIONAL HOLDINGS:
No. of Institutions: 147
Shares Held: 33,399,560
% Held: 55.0

INDUSTRY: Motors and generators (SIC: 3621)

TRANSFER AGENT(S): First Chicago Trust Company of New York, Jersey City, NJ

NYSE SYMBOL MCD
Rec. Pr. 30.28 (5/31/01)

MCDONALD'S CORPORATION

YIELD 0.7%
P/E RATIO 20.6

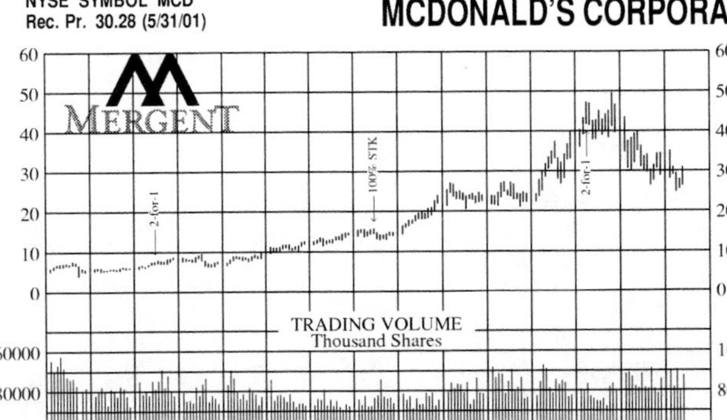

*7 YEAR PRICE SCORE 80.3 *12 MONTH PRICE SCORE 97.1

*NYSE COMPOSITE INDEX=100

INTERIM EARNINGS (Per Share):

Qtr.	Mar.	June	Sept.	Dec.
1996	0.21	0.30	0.31	0.29
1997	0.25	0.32	0.32	0.29
1998	0.26	0.25	0.35	0.25
1999	0.29	0.37	0.39	0.35
2000	0.33	0.39	0.41	0.34

INTERIM DIVIDENDS (Per Share):

Amt.	Decl.	Ex.	Rec.	Pay.
0.049Q	5/20/99	5/27/99	6/01/99	6/15/99
0.049Q	7/13/99	8/30/99	9/01/99	9/15/99
0.049Q	11/17/99	11/29/99	12/01/99	12/15/99
0.215A	9/12/00	11/13/00	11/15/00	12/01/00

Indicated div.: $0.21 (Div. Reinv. Plan)

CAPITALIZATION (12/31/00):

	($mill.)	(%)
Long-Term Debt	7,843.9	43.3
Deferred Income Tax	1,084.9	6.0
Common & Surplus	9,204.4	50.8
Total	18,133.2	100.0

RECENT DEVELOPMENTS: For the year ended 12/31/00, net income improved 1.5% to $1.98 billion versus $1.95 billion in the prior year. Total revenues grew 7.4% to $14.24 billion compared with $13.26 billion a year earlier. Sales by Company-operated restaurants advanced 10.0% to $10.47 billion. Revenues from franchised and affiliated restaurants rose slightly to $3.78 billion from $3.75 billion in 1999. Operating income was $3.33 billion versus $3.32 billion the year before.

PROSPECTS: MCD plans to pursue additional business by increasing sales at existing restaurants, improving customer service and adding approximately 1,700 restaurants. During 2001, MCD anticipates earnings-per-share growth to be in the range of 10.0% to 13.0%. Meanwhile, in an attempt to offset any losses associated with customer concern over European beef quality, MCD is educating consumers about its product specifications, safety and quality standards and is introducing additional menu items.

BUSINESS

MCDONALD'S CORPORATION develops, licenses, leases and services a worldwide system of restaurants. Units serve a standardized menu of moderately priced food consisting of hamburgers, cheeseburgers, chicken sandwiches, salads, desserts and beverages. As of 12/31/00, there were 16,795 units operated by franchisees, 7,652 units operated by the Company, and 4,262 units operated by affiliates. In addition to its McDonald's units, MCD also operates 156 Donatos Pizzas, 104 Chipotle Mexican Grills, and 41 Aroma Cafes. Revenues in 2000 were derived from: franchised restaurants, 60.9%; Company-owned units' sales, 26.0%; and affiliated restaurants, 13.1%. On 5/26/00, MCD acquired approximately 750 Boston Market restaurants from Boston Chicken, Inc.

ANNUAL FINANCIAL DATA

	12/31/00	12/31/99	12/31/98	12/31/97	12/31/96	12/31/95	12/31/94
Earnings Per Share	**1.46**	**1 1.39**	**1 1.10**	**1.15**	**1.11**	**0.99**	**0.84**
Cash Flow Per Share	**2.20**	**2.07**	**1.73**	**1.73**	**1.66**	**1.52**	**1.32**
Tang. Book Val. Per Share	**4.67**	**6.20**	**6.26**	**4.83**	**5.48**	**4.98**	**4.13**
Dividends Per Share	**0.21**	**0.20**	**0.18**	**0.16**	**0.15**	**0.13**	**0.12**
Dividend Payout %	**14.7**	**14.0**	**16.0**	**14.1**	**13.2**	**13.3**	**13.9**
INCOME STATEMENT (IN MILLIONS):							
Total Revenues	14,243.0	13,259.3	12,421.4	11,408.8	10,686.5	9,794.5	8,320.8
Costs & Expenses	9,902.6	8,983.4	8,618.4	7,806.7	7,359.9	6,595.4	5,545.1
Depreciation & Amort.	1,010.7	956.3	881.1	793.8	742.9	709.0	628.6
Operating Income	3,329.7	3,319.6	2,761.9	2,808.3	2,632.6	2,601.3	2,241.2
Net Interest Inc./(Exp.)	d429.9	d396.3	d413.8	d364.4	d342.5	d340.2	d305.7
Income Before Income Taxes	2,882.3	2,884.1	2,307.4	2,407.3	2,251.0	2,169.1	1,886.6
Income Taxes	905.0	936.2	757.3	764.8	678.4	741.8	662.2
Equity Earnings/Minority Int.	...	...	...	...	76.8	96.5	47.0
Net Income	1,977.3	1 1,947.9	1 1,550.1	1,642.5	1,572.6	1,427.3	1,224.4
Cash Flow	2,988.0	2,904.2	2,431.2	2,411.0	2,287.9	2,095.8	1,805.8
Average Shs. Outstg. (000)	1,356,500	1,404,200	1,405,700	1,410,200	1,396,400	1,403,000	1,403,600
BALANCE SHEET (IN MILLIONS):							
Cash & Cash Equivalents	421.7	419.5	299.2	341.4	329.9	334.8	179.9
Total Current Assets	1,662.4	1,572.3	1,309.4	1,142.3	1,102.5	955.8	740.7
Net Property	17,047.6	16,324.5	16,041.6	14,961.4	14,352.1	12,811.3	11,328.4
Total Assets	21,683.5	20,983.2	19,784.4	18,241.5	17,386.0	15,414.6	13,591.9
Total Current Liabilities	2,360.9	3,274.3	2,497.1	2,984.5	2,135.3	1,794.9	2,451.3
Long-Term Obligations	7,843.9	5,632.4	6,188.6	4,834.1	4,830.1	4,257.8	2,935.4
Net Stockholders' Equity	9,204.4	9,639.1	9,464.7	8,851.6	8,718.2	7,861.3	6,885.4
Net Working Capital	d698.5	d1,702.0	d1,187.7	d1,842.2	d1,032.8	d839.1	d1,710.6
Year-end Shs. Outstg. (000)	1,660,600	1,350,800	1,356,200	1,660,600	1,389,200	1,399,400	1,387,400
STATISTICAL RECORD:							
Operating Profit Margin %	23.4	25.0	22.2	24.6	24.6	26.6	26.9
Net Profit Margin %	13.9	14.7	12.5	14.4	14.7	14.6	14.7
Return on Equity %	21.5	20.2	16.4	18.6	18.0	18.2	17.8
Return on Assets %	9.1	9.3	7.8	9.0	9.0	9.3	9.0
Debt/Total Assets %	36.2	26.8	31.3	26.5	27.8	27.6	21.6
Price Range	43.63-26.38	49.56-35.94	39.75-22.31	27.44-21.06	27.13-20.50	24.00-14.31	15.69-12.78
P/E Ratio	29.9-18.1	35.7-25.9	36.1-20.3	24.0-18.4	24.5-18.6	24.4-14.5	18.7-15.2
Average Yield %	0.6	0.5	0.6	0.7	0.6	0.7	0.8

Statistics are as originally reported. Adj. for stk. splits: 2-for-1, 3/99, 5/94. 1 Incl. non-recurr. chrg. of $18.9 mill., 1999; $321.6 mill., 1998.

OFFICERS:
J. M. Greenberg, Chmn., C.E.O.
F. L. Turner, Sr. Chmn.
J. R. Cantalupo, Vice-Chmn., Pres.

INVESTOR CONTACT: Investor Relations Service Center, (630) 623-7428

PRINCIPAL OFFICE: McDonald's Plaza, Oak Brook, IL 60523

TELEPHONE NUMBER: (630) 623-3000
FAX: (630) 623-5027
WEB: www.mcdonalds.com

NO. OF EMPLOYEES: 36,400 (avg.)

SHAREHOLDERS: 954,000 (approx.)

ANNUAL MEETING: In May

INCORPORATED: DE, Mar., 1965

INSTITUTIONAL HOLDINGS:
No. of Institutions: 784
Shares Held: 786,213,550
% Held: 60.3

INDUSTRY: Eating places (SIC: 5812)

TRANSFER AGENT(S): First Chicago Trust Company of New York, Jersey City, NJ

NYSE SYMBOL MHP
Rec. Pr. 64.78 (4/30/01)

MCGRAW-HILL COMPANIES, INC. (THE)

YIELD 1.5%
P/E RATIO 26.4

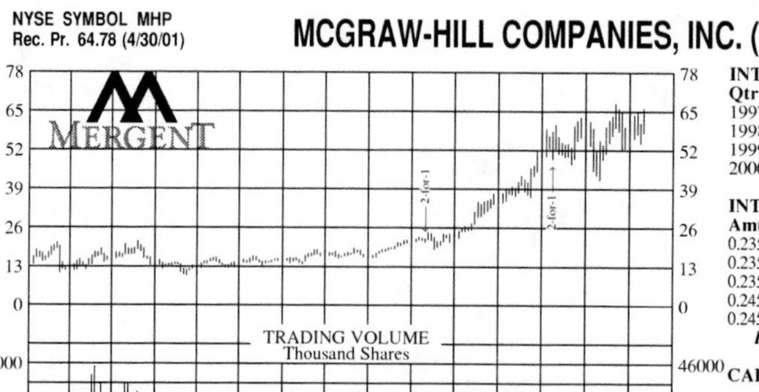

*7 YEAR PRICE SCORE 118.9 *12 MONTH PRICE SCORE 108.2
*NYSE COMPOSITE INDEX=100

INTERIM EARNINGS (Per Share):

Qtr.	Mar.	June	Sept.	Dec.
1997	0.08	0.33	0.72	0.34
1998	0.10	0.39	0.86	0.38
1999	0.12	0.45	0.96	0.61
2000	0.29	0.55	1.11	0.50

INTERIM DIVIDENDS (Per Share):

Amt.	Decl.	Ex.	Rec.	Pay.
0.235Q	4/26/00	5/24/00	5/26/00	6/12/00
0.235Q	7/26/00	8/24/00	8/28/00	9/12/00
0.235Q	10/25/00	11/24/00	11/28/00	12/12/00
0.245Q	1/31/01	2/22/01	2/26/01	3/12/01
0.245Q	4/25/01	5/24/01	5/29/01	6/12/01

Indicated div.: $0.98 (Div. Reinv. Plan)

CAPITALIZATION (12/31/00):

	($000)	(%)
Long-Term Debt	817,529	29.8
Deferred Income Tax	163,231	6.0
Preferred Stock	13	0.0
Common & Surplus	1,761,031	64.2
Total	2,741,804	100.0

RECENT DEVELOPMENTS: For the year ended 12/31/00, the Company reported income of $471.9 million, before an accounting charge of $68.1 million, compared with net income of $425.6 million in the corresponding period of the previous year. Operating revenue rose 7.2% to $4.28 billion from $3.99 billion in the prior year. Income from operations increased 10.9% to $820.2 million from $739.7 million the year before.

PROSPECTS: In 2001, the Company expects to report its ninth consecutive year of double-digit earnings growth. MHP's Financial Services segment should benefit from recent interest rate cuts and strong overseas business. The Company's Education segment will benefit from the creation of e-learning systems, and the purchase of materials by major states. On 1/11/01, MHP introduced MHLN.com, a network of interactive on-line e-textbooks.

BUSINESS

THE MCGRAW-HILL COMPANIES, INC., a multimedia publishing and information services company, serves worldwide markets in education, finance and business information. The Company has more than 400 offices in 32 countries. MHP provides information in print through books, newsletters, and magazines, including Business Week; on-line over electronic networks; over the air by television, satellite and FM sideband; and on software, videotape, facsimile and compact disks. Among the Company's business units are Standard & Poor's Financial Information Services and Standard & Poor's Ratings Services divisions.

BUSINESS LINE ANALYSIS

(12/31/2000)	REV. (%)	INC. (%)
McGraw-Hill Education	46.6	33.7
Financial Services	29.9	43.4
Info & Media Services	23.5	22.9
Total	100.0	100.0

ANNUAL FINANCIAL DATA

	12/31/00	12/31/99	12/31/98	12/31/97	12/31/96	12/31/95	12/31/94
Earnings Per Share	**[5] 2.41**	**[4] 2.14**	**[3] 1.71**	**[2] 1.46**	**[1] 2.48**	**1.14**	**1.03**
Cash Flow Per Share	**4.25**	**3.70**	**3.22**	**2.93**	**3.67**	**2.30**	**2.19**
Tang. Book Val. Per Share	**0.33**	**2.24**	**1.48**	**0.64**	**0.28**	**0.38**	**...**
Dividends Per Share	**0.94**	**0.86**	**0.78**	**0.72**	**0.66**	**0.60**	**0.58**
Dividend Payout %	**39.0**	**40.2**	**45.8**	**49.5**	**26.6**	**52.6**	**56.6**
INCOME STATEMENT (IN MILLIONS):							
Total Revenues	4,281.0	3,992.0	3,729.1	3,534.1	3,074.7	2,935.3	2,760.9
Costs & Expenses	3,098.5	2,943.7	2,821.5	2,716.8	1,973.7	2,258.8	2,133.7
Depreciation & Amort.	362.3	308.3	299.2	293.5	238.6	231.4	230.0
Operating Income	820.2	740.0	608.4	523.8	862.5	445.0	397.2
Net Interest Inc./(Exp.)	d52.8	d42.0	d48.0	d52.5	d47.7	d58.8	d51.7
Income Before Income Taxes	767.3	698.0	560.4	471.3	814.8	386.3	345.4
Income Taxes	295.4	272.2	218.6	180.6	319.1	159.1	142.3
Net Income	[5] 471.9	[4] 425.8	[3] 341.9	[2] 290.7	[1] 495.7	227.2	203.1
Cash Flow	834.2	734.1	641.1	584.2	734.3	458.6	433.1
Average Shs. Outstg. (000)	196,072	198,557	199,104	199,504	199,994	199,504	197,996
BALANCE SHEET (IN MILLIONS):							
Cash & Cash Equivalents	3.2	6.5	10.5	4.8	3.4	10.3	8.1
Total Current Assets	1,801.7	1,553.7	1,428.8	1,464.4	1,349.6	1,239.8	1,124.1
Net Property	431.9	430.4	364.0	273.6	311.5	336.1	345.8
Total Assets	4,931.4	4,088.8	3,788.1	3,724.5	3,642.2	3,104.4	3,008.5
Total Current Liabilities	1,780.8	1,525.5	1,291.5	1,206.2	1,218.7	1,046.5	1,008.0
Long-Term Obligations	817.5	354.8	452.1	607.0	556.9	557.4	657.5
Net Stockholders' Equity	1,761.0	1,691.5	1,551.8	1,434.7	1,361.1	1,035.1	913.1
Net Working Capital	20.9	28.3	137.3	258.2	130.9	193.3	116.1
Year-end Shs. Outstg. (000)	194,285	195,709	197,111	198,204	199,062	200,286	198,688
STATISTICAL RECORD:							
Operating Profit Margin %	19.2	18.5	16.3	14.8	28.1	15.2	14.4
Net Profit Margin %	11.0	10.7	9.2	8.2	16.1	7.7	7.4
Return on Equity %	26.8	25.2	22.0	20.3	36.4	21.9	22.2
Return on Assets %	9.6	10.4	9.0	7.8	13.6	7.3	6.8
Debt/Total Assets %	16.6	8.7	11.9	16.3	15.3	18.0	21.9
Price Range	67.69-41.88	63.13-47.13	51.66-34.25	37.38-22.44	24.63-18.63	21.91-15.91	19.31-15.63
P/E Ratio	28.1-17.4	29.5-22.0	30.2-20.0	25.7-15.4	9.9-7.5	19.2-14.0	18.8-15.2
Average Yield %	1.7	1.6	1.8	2.4	3.1	3.2	3.3

Statistics are as originally reported. Adj. for 2-for-1 splits 3/8/99 & 4/96. [1] Incl. $260.5 mill. net gain fr. the exchange of its legal publishing unit for Times Mirror Higher Education Group. [2] Incl. nonrecurr. gain of $40.1 mill. [3] Bef. extraord. chrg. of $8.7 mill. [4] Incl. after-tax gain of $24.2 mill. fr. the sale of the Co.'s Petrochemical publications. [5] Bef. acctg. chrg. of $68.1 mill.; incl. a gain of $10.2 mill. fr. the sale of Tower Group Int'l.

OFFICERS:
H. McGraw III, Chmn., Pres., C.E.O.
R. J. Bahash, Exec. V.P., C.F.O.
F. D. Penglase, Sr. V.P., Treasury Oper.

INVESTOR CONTACT: Steven H. Weiss, V.P.-Corp. Comm., (212) 512-2247

PRINCIPAL OFFICE: 1221 Avenue Of The Americas, New York, NY 10020-1095

TELEPHONE NUMBER: (212) 512-2000
FAX: (212) 512-2305
WEB: www.mcgraw-hill.com

NO. OF EMPLOYEES: 16,761

SHAREHOLDERS: 5,246 (approx.)

ANNUAL MEETING: In April

INCORPORATED: NY, Dec., 1925

INSTITUTIONAL HOLDINGS:
No. of Institutions: 435
Shares Held: 141,511,719
% Held: 72.6

INDUSTRY: Book publishing (SIC: 2731)

TRANSFER AGENT(S): Mellon Investor Services, New York, NY

NYSE SYMBOL MCK
Rec. Pr. 34.57 (5/31/01)

MCKESSON HBOC, INC.

YIELD 0.7%
P/E RATIO 216.1

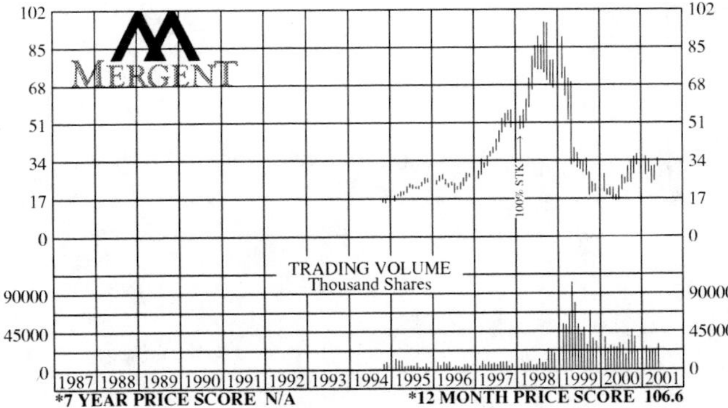

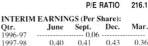

*7 YEAR PRICE SCORE N/A *12 MONTH PRICE SCORE 106.6
*NYSE COMPOSITE INDEX=100

INTERIM EARNINGS (Per Share):

Qtr.	June	Sept.	Dec.	Mar.
1996-97		0.06		
1997-98	0.40	0.41	0.43	0.36
1998-99	0.43	0.52	0.40	d0.27
1999-00	0.25	0.21	0.56	d0.31
2000-01	0.22	0.22	0.03	...

INTERIM DIVIDENDS (Per Share):

Amt.	Decl.	Ex.	Rec.	Pay.
0.06Q	7/26/00	8/30/00	9/01/00	10/02/00
0.06Q	10/25/00	11/29/00	12/01/00	1/02/01
0.06Q	1/31/01	2/27/01	3/01/01	4/02/01
0.06Q	5/25/01	5/31/01	6/04/01	7/02/01

Indicated div.: $0.24 (Div. Reinv. Plan)

CAPITALIZATION (3/31/00):

	($000)	(%)
Long-Term Debt	1,243,800	24.8
Redeemable Pfd. Stock	195,800	3.9
Common & Surplus	3,565,800	71.2
Total	5,005,400	100.0

RECENT DEVELOPMENTS: For the quarter ended 12/31/00, income from continuing operations was $7.3 million versus income from continuing operations of $160.6 million a year earlier. Earnings in 2000 included net after-tax charges of $62.0 million related primarily to equity investment impairments. Earnings in 1999 included a net one-time after-tax gain of $100.1 million from the sale of equity investments. Total revenues climbed 11.5% to $11.03 billion.

PROSPECTS: On 12/21/00, MCK expanded its existing supply agreement with Costco Corporation by signing a new four-year deal, under which the Company will serve as the primary supplier for Costco pharmacies and will supply its on-line pharmacy at www.costco.com. The new agreement is expected to generate over $2.20 billion in total revenue over the four-year term, including $600.0 million in incremental revenue.

BUSINESS

MCKESSON HBOC, INC. (formerly McKesson Corp.) is a healthcare services company providing a full range of supply management solutions and information technologies to hospitals, retail pharmacies, physicians, long-term care sites, home-care agencies, pharmaceutical manufacturers, medical surgical manufacturers, and healthcare payors. MCK acquired Automated Healthcare, Inc., a manufacturer of automated pharmacy systems, in April 1996. MCK divested its 55% interest in Armor All Products Corp. on 12/31/96. Millbrook Distribution Services, Inc., MCK's service merchandising unit, was sold on 3/31/97. On 1/12/99, MCK acquired HBO & Co.

ANNUAL FINANCIAL DATA

	3/31/00	[5] 3/31/99	3/31/98	3/31/97	3/31/96	3/31/95	3/31/94
Earnings Per Share	**[6] 0.66**	**[3] 0.31**	**[3] 1.59**	**[4] 0.06**	**[3] 1.45**	**[2] d2.25**	**[1] 1.47**
Cash Flow Per Share	**1.37**	**0.98**	**2.39**	**0.86**	**2.22**	**d1.42**	**2.37**
Tang. Book Val. Per Share	**8.47**	**5.88**	**7.02**	**5.73**	**9.80**	**9.01**	**3.35**
Dividends Per Share	**0.30**	**0.50**	**0.50**	**0.50**	**0.38**	...	...
Dividend Payout %	**46.2**	**161.2**	**31.4**	**831.9**	**25.9**	...	...
INCOME STATEMENT (IN MILLIONS):							
Total Revenues	36,734.2	30,382.3	20,857.3	12,886.7	13,716.4	13,189.1	12,251.4
Costs & Expenses	36,374.7	29,850.8	20,407.9	12,722.1	13,371.0	13,149.4	11,973.9
Depreciation & Amort.	201.3	199.3	87.2	71.8	71.3	69.8	67.2
Operating Income	158.2	332.2	362.2	92.8	274.1	d30.1	210.3
Net Interest Inc./(Exp.)	d114.2	d124.0	d102.5	d55.7	d46.7	d46.0	d41.3
Income Before Income Taxes	313.1	208.2	259.7	37.1	227.4	d70.7	224.1
Income Taxes	122.3	117.1	98.6	31.3	88.7	111.5	88.6
Net Income	[6] 184.6	[3] 84.9	[3] 154.9	[4] 5.1	[3] 135.4	[2] d193.2	[1] 126.5
Cash Flow	385.9	284.2	242.1	76.9	206.7	d128.4	183.5
Average Shs. Outstg. (000)	281,300	289,800	101,200	89,000	93,200	87,200	81,600
BALANCE SHEET (IN MILLIONS):							
Cash & Cash Equivalents	605.9	269.0	113.6	229.8	477.2	692.7	89.0
Total Current Assets	7,965.5	6,499.5	4,105.6	3,761.1	2,665.0	2,699.4	1,873.5
Net Property	555.4	694.0	430.3	373.6	379.8	366.3	396.6
Total Assets	10,372.9	9,081.6	5,607.5	5,172.8	3,503.9	3,479.2	2,835.0
Total Current Liabilities	5,121.8	4,800.1	2,577.8	2,637.2	1,722.6	1,738.2	1,428.2
Long-Term Obligations	1,243.8	945.5	1,194.2	824.9	442.5	458.8	462.3
Net Stockholders' Equity	3,565.8	2,881.8	1,638.0	1,497.4	1,309.6	1,266.3	1,008.8
Net Working Capital	2,843.7	1,699.4	1,527.8	1,123.9	942.4	961.2	445.3
Year-end Shs. Outstg. (000)	281,100	281,100	93,220	91,570	85,880	88,750	81,208
STATISTICAL RECORD:							
Operating Profit Margin %	0.4	1.1	1.7	0.7	2.0	...	1.7
Net Profit Margin %	0.5	0.3	0.7	...	1.0	...	1.0
Return on Equity %	5.2	2.9	9.5	0.3	10.3	...	12.5
Return on Assets %	1.8	0.9	2.8	0.1	3.9	...	4.5
Debt/Total Assets %	12.0	10.4	21.3	15.9	12.6	13.2	16.3
Price Range	89.75-18.56	96.25-47.00	56.88-25.88	28.50-19.50	26.63-15.94	16.75-15.06	...
P/E Ratio	136.0-28.1	310.5-151.6	35.8-16.3	475.0-325.0	18.4-11.0	...	...
Average Yield %	0.6	0.7	1.2	2.1	1.8	...	...

Statistics are as originally reported. Adj. for 100% stk. div., 1/98. [1] Bef. $4.2 mil extraord. loss & $15.8 mil acctg. chg., incl. $37.4 mil gain. [2] Bef. $21 mil cr. fr disc. ops. & $576.7 mil gain. [3] Incl. $293.9 mil chg., 1999; $20.8 mil chg., 1998; $11.2 mil gain, 1996. [4] Incl. $109.5 mil chg. & bef. $120.2 mil gain. [5] Restated to refl corrections of improper acctg practices at HBO & Co. [6] Bef. $539.1 mil gain fr. disc. ops. & incl. $80.4 mil chg.

OFFICERS:
A. Seelenfreund, Chmn.
J. H. Hammergren, Pres., C.E.O.
W. R. Graber, Sr. V.P., C.F.O.

INVESTOR CONTACT: Larry Kurtz, (415) 983-8418

PRINCIPAL OFFICE: McKesson HBOC Plaza, One Post Street, San Francisco, CA 94104

TELEPHONE NUMBER: (415) 983-8300
FAX: (415) 983-8453
WEB: www.mckhboc.com

NO. OF EMPLOYEES: 21,000 (approx.)

SHAREHOLDERS: 17,000 (approx.)

ANNUAL MEETING: In July

INCORPORATED: DE, July, 1994

INSTITUTIONAL HOLDINGS:
No. of Institutions: 297
Shares Held: 184,480,733
% Held: 64.8

INDUSTRY: Drugs, proprietaries, and sundries (SIC: 5122)

TRANSFER AGENT(S): EquiServe, Jersey City, NJ

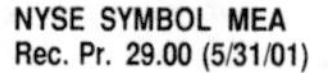

NYSE SYMBOL MEA
Rec. Pr. 29.00 (5/31/01)

MEAD CORPORATION

YIELD 2.3%
P/E RATIO 18.1

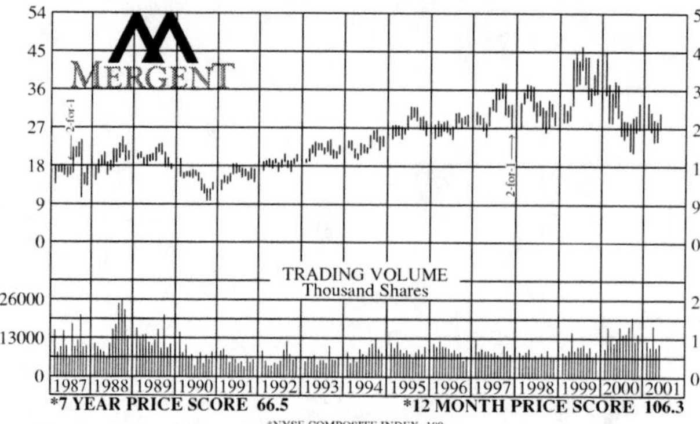

*7 YEAR PRICE SCORE 66.5 *12 MONTH PRICE SCORE 106.3

*NYSE COMPOSITE INDEX=100

INTERIM EARNINGS (Per Share):

Qtr.	Mar.	June	Sept.	Dec.
1997	0.19	0.45	0.47	0.30
1998	0.29	0.38	0.34	0.30
1999	0.22	0.43	0.48	0.87
2000	0.24	0.62	0.57	0.17

INTERIM DIVIDENDS (Per Share):

Amt.	Decl.	Ex.	Rec.	Pay.
0.17Q	4/27/00	5/04/00	5/08/00	6/01/00
0.17Q	8/03/00	8/10/00	8/14/00	9/01/00
0.17Q	10/30/00	11/06/00	11/08/00	12/01/00
0.17Q	1/25/01	2/01/01	2/05/01	3/01/01
0.17Q	4/26/01	5/03/01	5/07/01	6/01/01

Indicated div.: $0.68 (Div. Reinv. Plan)

CAPITALIZATION (12/31/00):

	($000)	(%)
Long-Term Debt [1]	1,322,800	35.6
Common & Surplus	2,397,800	64.4
Total	3,720,600	100.0

RECENT DEVELOPMENTS: For the year ended 12/31/00, income was $163.6 million, before an accounting charge, versus net income of $208.1 million the prior year. Results for 2000 included special charges of $8.5 million. Results for 1999 included a gain of $86.3 million due to the sale of MEA's share of Northwood, Inc. Net sales grew 9.3% to $4.37 billion, from $4.00 billion a year earlier.

PROSPECTS: In the near-term, the Company expects higher energy and energy-related costs to continue to dampen earnings across its businesses and unfavorable currency exchange rates to negatively affect results of its worldwide packaging systems business. Meanwhile, MEA's more cyclical businesses, coated paper and containerboard, are likely to continue to have weaker prices and sales volume as a result of the slowing economy.

BUSINESS

THE MEAD CORPORATION is a forest products company that produces coated paper, specialty paper, coated paperboard and consumer and office products in North America and multiple packaging products and corrugating medium on a worldwide basis. The Paper segment is comprised of four divisions: Mead Paper, Mead Specialty Paper, Gilbert Paper and Mead Pulp Sales. The Packaging and Paperboard segment's three divisions are Mead Packaging, Mead Coated Board and Mead Containerboard. The Consumer and Office Products segment includes AT-A-GLANCE. On 11/1/99, the Company acquired the AT-A-GLANCE Group of Cullman Ventures, Inc., a manufacturer of diaries, appointment books, calendars, posters, organizers and planners, for approximately $540.0 million in cash.

ANNUAL FINANCIAL DATA

	12/31/00	12/31/99	12/31/98	12/31/97	12/31/96	12/31/95	12/31/94
Earnings Per Share	[5] **1.60**	[2] **1.99**	[2][4] **1.34**	[4] **1.41**	[4] **1.79**	[4] **3.10**	[2][3] **0.76**
Cash Flow Per Share	**4.89**	**4.93**	**4.21**	**4.12**	**4.14**	**5.24**	**2.52**
Tang. Book Val. Per Share	**24.25**	**23.70**	**22.12**	**22.03**	**21.24**	**20.42**	**18.62**
Dividends Per Share	**0.68**	**0.65**	**0.64**	**0.61**	**0.59**	**0.55**	**0.50**
Dividend Payout %	**42.5**	**32.7**	**47.8**	**43.3**	**33.1**	**17.6**	**65.8**
INCOME STATEMENT (IN MILLIONS):							
Total Revenues	4,368.1	3,799.5	3,772.2	5,077.4	4,706.5	5,179.4	4,557.5
Costs & Expenses	3,685.8	3,211.8	3,170.0	4,478.1	4,117.5	4,419.3	4,123.4
Depreciation & Amort.	336.9	307.4	301.8	288.5	250.4	236.7	225.5
Operating Income	345.4	280.3	300.4	310.8	338.6	523.4	208.6
Net Interest Inc./(Exp.)	d121.0	d105.1	d109.0	d98.2	d57.7	d69.4	d106.8
Income Before Income Taxes	235.3	271.9	225.6	222.5	294.6	487.7	52.4
Income Taxes	82.5	98.5	83.7	81.3	109.0	184.2	22.6
Equity Earnings/Minority Int.	10.8	34.7	d1.8	8.9	4.3	39.0	59.8
Net Income	[5] 163.6	[2] 208.1	[2][4] 140.1	[4] 150.1	[4] 189.9	[4] 342.5	[2][3] 89.6
Cash Flow	500.5	515.5	441.9	438.6	440.3	579.2	315.1
Average Shs. Outstg. (000)	102,300	104,600	104,900	106,400	106,400	110,586	125,110
BALANCE SHEET (IN MILLIONS):							
Cash & Cash Equivalents	29.4	56.4	102.0	29.5	20.6	292.6	484.0
Total Current Assets	1,281.3	1,230.3	1,086.4	1,217.6	1,189.3	1,367.3	1,894.0
Net Property	3,269.9	3,357.4	3,372.7	3,309.8	3,120.4	2,364.1	2,313.9
Total Assets	5,680.0	5,661.7	5,142.2	5,229.7	4,985.9	4,372.8	4,862.6
Total Current Liabilities	1,012.3	1,000.6	679.5	714.8	757.7	821.8	1,087.5
Long-Term Obligations	1,322.8	1,333.7	1,367.4	1,428.0	1,239.7	694.8	957.7
Net Stockholders' Equity	2,397.8	2,430.8	2,252.0	2,288.5	2,246.4	2,160.2	2,182.6
Net Working Capital	269.0	229.7	406.9	502.8	431.6	545.5	806.5
Year-end Shs. Outstg. (000)	98,868	102,579	101,830	103,900	105,774	105,794	117,200
STATISTICAL RECORD:							
Operating Profit Margin %	7.9	7.4	8.0	6.1	7.2	10.1	4.6
Net Profit Margin %	3.7	5.5	3.7	3.0	4.0	6.6	2.0
Return on Equity %	6.8	8.6	6.2	6.6	8.5	15.9	4.1
Return on Assets %	2.9	3.7	2.7	2.9	3.8	7.8	1.8
Debt/Total Assets %	23.3	23.6	26.6	27.3	24.9	15.9	19.7
Price Range	45.13-21.19	46.31-28.31	37.31-25.94	37.69-24.88	30.69-24.25	32.06-24.31	26.63-19.56
P/E Ratio	28.2-13.2	23.3-14.2	27.8-19.4	26.7-17.6	17.2-13.6	10.4-7.9	35.0-25.7
Average Yield %	2.1	1.7	2.0	2.0	2.1	1.9	2.2

Statistics are as originally reported. Adj. for stk. split: 2-for-1, 12/97. [1] Incl. cap. lse. oblig. and cv. debs. [2] Incl. non-recurr. chrg. of $118.1 mill., 1994; chrg. $22.0 mill., 1998; gain of $86.3 mill., 1999. [3] Incl. gain of $628.8 mill. from sale of Mead Data Central. [4] Bef. disc. oper. of gain $7.5 mill., 1995; gain $5.4 mill., 1996; loss $12.9 mill., 1997; loss $20.4 mill., 1998. [5] Incl. pre-tax nonrecurr. chrg. of $8.5 mill., bef. acct. change chrg. of $2.4 mill.

OFFICERS:
J. F. Tatar, Chmn., Pres., C.E.O.
I. W. Millar, Exec. V.P.
T. R. McLevish, V.P., C.F.O.
P. H. Vogel Jr., V.P., Fin., Treas.

PRINCIPAL OFFICE: Mead World Headquarters, Courthouse Plaza Northeast, Dayton, OH 45463

TELEPHONE NUMBER: (937) 495-6323
FAX: (937) 461-2424
WEB: www.mead.com

NO. OF EMPLOYEES: 15,080 (approx.)

SHAREHOLDERS: 39,166 (record)

ANNUAL MEETING: In Apr.

INCORPORATED: OH, Feb., 1930

INSTITUTIONAL HOLDINGS:
No. of Institutions: 249
Shares Held: 71,903,069
% Held: 72.6

INDUSTRY: Paperboard mills (SIC: 2631)

TRANSFER AGENT(S): BankBoston, N.A., Boston, MA

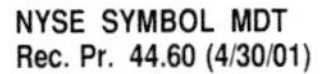

NYSE SYMBOL MDT
Rec. Pr. 44.60 (4/30/01)

MEDTRONIC, INC.

YIELD 0.4%
P/E RATIO 44.2

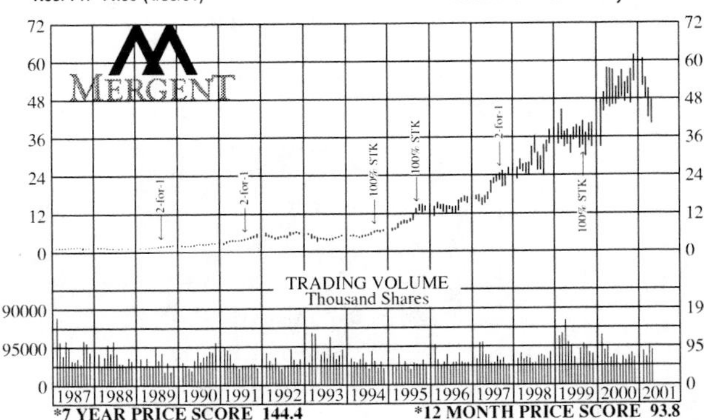

*7 YEAR PRICE SCORE 144.4   *12 MONTH PRICE SCORE 93.8

*NYSE COMPOSITE INDEX=100

INTERIM EARNINGS (Per Share):

Qtr.	July	Oct.	Jan.	Apr.
1997-98	0.32	0.16	0.01	0.17
1998-99	0.16	0.15	d0.03	0.13
1999-00	0.21	0.22	0.22	0.26
2000-01	0.24	0.26	0.25	. . .

INTERIM DIVIDENDS (Per Share):

Amt.	Decl.	Ex.	Rec.	Pay.
0.04Q	3/06/00	4/05/00	4/07/00	4/28/00
0.05Q	6/29/00	7/05/00	7/07/00	7/28/00
0.05Q	8/24/00	10/04/00	10/06/00	10/27/00
0.05Q	10/26/00	1/03/01	1/05/01	1/26/01
0.05Q	3/08/01	4/04/01	4/06/01	4/27/01

Indicated div.: $0.20 (Div. Reinv. Plan)

CAPITALIZATION (4/30/00):

	($000)	(%)
Long-Term Debt	14,100	0.3
Deferred Income Tax	15,200	0.3
Common & Surplus	4,491,500	99.4
Total	4,520,800	100.0

RECENT DEVELOPMENTS: For the quarter ended 1/26/01, net income was $302.8 million, up 16.7% from $259.5 million the year before. Results for fiscal 2001 included a one-time gain of $20.4 million from litigation settlements and an after-tax nonrecurring charge of $11.1 million related to the acquisition of PercuSurge, Inc. Net sales rose 8.1% to $1.36 billion versus $1.26 billion a year earlier.

PROSPECTS: Revenues should benefit from the U.S. launch of the Company's GEM® III AT defibrillator, which includes therapies addressing atrial fibrillation and ventricular fibrillation. Separately, MDT acquired the Contegra™ Pulmonary Valved Conduit product line from VenPro Corporation. The pulmonary valved conduit will be the first product in MDT's heart valve portfolio intended primarily for use in children.

BUSINESS

MEDTRONIC, INC. is a leading medical technology company specializing in implantable and interventional therapies. Primary products include those for bradycardia pacing, tachyarrhythmia management, atrial fibrillation management, heart failure management, coronary and peripheral vascular disease, heart valve replacement, extracorporeal cardiac support, minimally invasive cardiac surgery, malignant and non-malignant pain, movement disorders, neurosurgery and neurodegenerative disorders. MDT does business in more than 120 countries and reports on four primary product line platforms, Cardiac Rhythm Management, Cardiac Surgery, Neurological and Vascular.

ANNUAL FINANCIAL DATA

	4/30/00	4/30/99	4/30/98	4/30/97	4/30/96	4/30/95	4/30/94
Earnings Per Share	[4] **0.90**	[3] **0.40**	[2] **0.48**	**0.56**	**0.47**	**0.32**	[1] **0.25**
Cash Flow Per Share	**1.10**	**0.57**	**0.63**	**0.68**	**0.59**	**0.43**	**0.34**
Tang. Book Val. Per Share	**2.61**	**1.99**	**1.68**	**1.34**	**1.41**	**1.05**	**0.74**
Dividends Per Share	**0.15**	**0.12**	**0.10**	**0.08**	**0.06**	**0.05**	**0.04**
Dividend Payout %	**16.1**	**30.4**	**21.3**	**14.4**	**12.4**	**14.7**	**15.3**
INCOME STATEMENT (IN MILLIONS):							
Total Revenues	5,014.6	4,134.1	2,604.8	2,438.2	2,169.1	1,742.4	1,390.9
Costs & Expenses	3,157.7	3,121.2	1,744.0	1,536.9	1,410.2	1,199.6	979.7
Depreciation & Amort.	243.3	213.1	137.6	116.9	111.8	106.5	78.6
Operating Income	1,613.6	799.8	723.2	784.5	647.2	436.3	332.7
Net Interest Inc./(Exp.)	15.4	22.2	14.8	24.7	21.2	5.8	0.2
Income Before Income Taxes	1,629.0	822.0	702.0	809.1	668.4	442.1	346.8
Income Taxes	530.5	353.6	244.6	279.2	230.6	148.1	114.4
Net Income	[4] 1,098.5	[3] 468.4	[2] 457.4	530.0	437.8	294.0	[1] 232.4
Cash Flow	1,341.8	681.5	594.9	646.9	549.6	400.5	310.9
Average Shs. Outstg. (000)	1,220,800	1,185,800	951,168	954,772	932,628	921,920	918,464
BALANCE SHEET (IN MILLIONS):							
Cash & Cash Equivalents	558.1	375.9	425.9	250.6	460.8	323.6	181.4
Total Current Assets	3,013.4	2,395.2	1,551.6	1,237.9	1,343.2	1,103.9	845.9
Net Property	946.5	748.8	508.8	487.2	415.3	331.1	301.8
Total Assets	5,669.4	4,870.3	2,774.7	2,409.2	2,503.3	1,946.7	1,623.3
Total Current Liabilities	991.5	990.3	572.0	518.7	525.0	456.1	439.4
Long-Term Obligations	14.1	17.6	16.2	14.0	15.3	14.2	20.2
Net Stockholders' Equity	4,491.5	3,654.6	2,044.2	1,746.2	1,789.3	1,335.0	1,053.5
Net Working Capital	2,021.9	1,404.9	979.6	719.2	818.2	647.8	406.4
Year-end Shs. Outstg. (000)	1,197,698	1,170,452	938,090	935,256	937,272	924,072	930,064
STATISTICAL RECORD:							
Operating Profit Margin %	32.2	19.3	27.8	32.2	29.8	25.0	23.9
Net Profit Margin %	21.9	11.3	17.6	21.7	20.2	16.9	16.7
Return on Equity %	24.5	12.8	22.4	30.4	24.5	22.0	22.1
Return on Assets %	19.4	9.6	16.5	22.0	17.5	15.1	14.3
Debt/Total Assets %	0.2	0.4	0.6	0.6	0.6	0.7	1.2
Price Range	44.63-29.94	38.38-22.72	26.38-14.41	17.47-11.13	15.00-6.55	6.98-4.32	5.97-3.23
P/E Ratio	49.6-33.3	97.1-57.5	54.9-30.0	31.5-20.0	31.9-13.9	21.9-13.5	23.6-12.7
Average Yield %	0.4	0.4	0.5	0.6	0.5	0.8	0.8

Statistics are as originally reported. Adj. for 2-for-1 stk split, 9/99, 9/97, 9/95, 9/94, 8/91. [1] Incl. pre-tax gain of $14.0 mill. [2] Incl. a pre-tax chrg. of $12.9 mill., a nonrecur. pre-tax chrg. of $156.4 mill. [3] Incl. a pre-tax nonrecur. chg. of $371.3 mill. & a pre-tax chg. of $150.9 mill. for pchsd. in-process R&D. [4] Incl. a pre-tax nonrecur. chrg. of $14.7 mill. for the Xomed acquis.

OFFICERS:
W. W. George, Chmn.
G. D. Nelson M.D., Vice-Chmn.
A. D. Collins Jr., Pres., C.O.O., C.E.O.
R. L. Ryan, Sr. V.P., C.F.O.

PRINCIPAL OFFICE: 710 Medtronic Parkway N.E., Minneapolis, MN 55432

TELEPHONE NUMBER: (763) 514-4000
FAX: (763) 514-4879
WEB: www.medtronic.com

NO. OF EMPLOYEES: 21,490 full-time; 24,890 part-time

SHAREHOLDERS: 42,500

ANNUAL MEETING: In Aug.

INCORPORATED: MN, 1957

INSTITUTIONAL HOLDINGS:
No. of Institutions: 837
Shares Held: 786,154,613
% Held: 65.0

INDUSTRY: Electromedical equipment (SIC: 3845)

TRANSFER AGENT(S): Wells Fargo Bank Minnesota N.A., St. Paul, MN

NYSE SYMBOL MEL
Rec. Pr. 40.93 (4/30/01)

MELLON FINANCIAL CORPORATION

YIELD 2.3%
P/E RATIO 20.2

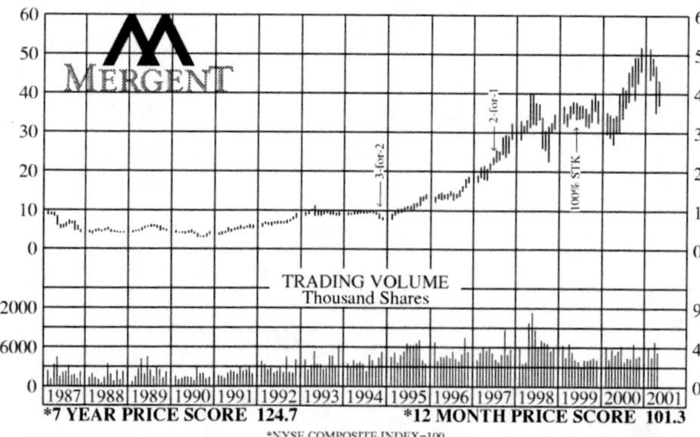

INTERIM EARNINGS (Per Share):

Qtr.	Mar.	June	Sept.	Dec.
1997	0.35	0.36	0.37	0.38
1998	0.39	0.41	0.41	0.42
1999	0.53	0.45	0.45	0.48
2000	0.50	0.50	0.51	0.52

INTERIM DIVIDENDS (Per Share):

Amt.	Decl.	Ex.	Rec.	Pay.
0.22Q	4/19/00	4/26/00	4/28/00	5/15/00
0.22Q	7/18/00	7/27/00	7/31/00	8/15/00
0.22Q	10/17/00	10/27/00	10/31/00	11/15/00
0.22Q	1/16/01	1/29/01	1/31/01	2/15/01
0.24Q	4/17/01	4/26/01	4/30/01	5/15/01

Indicated div.: $0.96 (Div. Reinv. Plan)

CAPITALIZATION (12/31/00):

	($000)	(%)
Total Deposits	36,890,000	81.0
Long-Term Debt	3,520,000	7.7
Redeemable Pfd. Stock	992,000	2.2
Common & Surplus	4,152,000	9.1
Total	45,554,000	100.0

RECENT DEVELOPMENTS: For the year ended 12/31/00, MEL reported net income of $1.01 billion versus income of $989.0 million, before an accounting charge of $26.0 million, in 1999. Results for 1999 included a pre-tax net gain of $127.0 million from divestitures. Net interest revenue fell 1.7% to $1.33 billion. Total non-interest revenue, including the above gain, decreased 2.4% to $3.15 billion. Total operating expense declined 4.0% to $2.85 billion.

PROSPECTS: On 4/26/01, MEL entered into a definitive agreement to acquire Boston-based Standish, a provider of investment management services to institutional clients and high net worth individuals. The acquisition, which is expected to close by the end of the third quarter of 2001, will increase MEL's assets under management to more than $560.00 billion. Separately, MEL expanded its asset management business internationally through the development of Mellon Global Investments.

BUSINESS

MELLON FINANCIAL CORPORATION (formerly Mellon Bank Corporation), with assets of $50.36 billion as of 12/31/00, is a provider of wealth management and global asset management for individual and institutional investors, as well as global investment services for businesses and institutions. Mellon also offers an array of banking services for individuals and small, mid-size and large businesses and institutions in selected geographies. Its asset management companies, which include The Dreyfus Corp. and Founders Asset Management, LLC in the U.S. and Newton Management Ltd. in the U.K., provide investment products in virtually every asset class or investment style. In addition, Mellon is a global provider of custody, retirement and benefits consulting services through its Mellon Trust and Buck Consultants affiliates.

LOAN DISTRIBUTION

(12/31/2000)	($000)	(%)
Commercial & financial	9,202,000	34.9
Commercial real estate	3,118,000	11.8
Consumer mortgage	5,929,000	22.5
Other consumer credit	3,912,000	14.8
Lease finance assets	3,033,000	11.5
International loans	1,175,000	4.5
Total	26,369,000	100.0

ANNUAL FINANCIAL DATA

	12/31/00	12/31/99	12/31/98	12/31/97	12/31/96	12/31/95	12/31/94
Earnings Per Share	**2.03**	**3 1.90**	**2 1.63**	**1.44**	**1.29**	**1.13**	**1 0.61**
Tang. Book Val. Per Share	**4.34**	**3.72**	**2.05**	**2.27**	**2.80**	**3.56**	**3.91**
Dividends Per Share	**0.86**	**0.78**	**0.70**	**0.65**	**0.59**	**0.50**	**0.39**
Dividend Payout %	**42.4**	**41.1**	**43.4**	**44.8**	**45.6**	**44.4**	**64.9**
INCOME STATEMENT (IN MILLIONS):							
Total Interest Income	2,829.0	2,759.0	2,892.0	2,716.0	2,739.0	2,838.0	2,310.0
Total Interest Expense	1,501.0	1,329.0	1,401.0	1,249.0	1,261.0	1,290.0	802.0
Net Interest Income	1,328.0	1,430.0	1,491.0	1,467.0	1,478.0	1,548.0	1,508.0
Provision for Loan Losses	45.0	45.0	60.0	148.0	155.0	105.0	70.0
Non-Interest Income	3,150.0	3,227.0	2,922.0	2,418.0	2,023.0	1,676.0	1,647.0
Non-Interest Expense	2,851.0	3,049.0	3,013.0	2,568.0	2,195.0	2,027.0	2,374.0
Income Before Taxes	1,582.0	1,563.0	1,340.0	1,169.0	1,151.0	1,092.0	711.0
Net Income	1,007.0	3 989.0	2 870.0	771.0	733.0	691.0	1 433.0
Average Shs. Outstg. (000)	496,825	521,986	530,000	522,000	532,000	580,000	596,000
BALANCE SHEET (IN MILLIONS):							
Cash & Due from Banks	3,506.0	3,410.0	2,926.0	3,650.0	2,846.0	2,342.0	2,285.0
Securities Avail. for Sale	8,186.0	5,303.0	5,566.0	2,842.0	4,195.0	5,383.0	5,067.0
Total Loans & Leases	26,369.0	30,248.0	32,093.0	29,142.0	27,393.0	27,690.0	26,733.0
Allowance for Credit Losses	393.0	403.0	496.0	475.0	525.0	471.0	607.0
Net Loans & Leases	25,976.0	29,845.0	31,597.0	28,667.0	26,868.0	27,219.0	26,126.0
Total Assets	50,364.0	47,946.0	50,777.0	44,892.0	42,596.0	43,165.0	41,888.0
Total Deposits	36,890.0	33,421.0	34,383.0	31,305.0	31,374.0	29,261.0	27,570.0
Long-Term Obligations	3,520.0	3,438.0	3,303.0	2,573.0	2,518.0	1,443.0	1,568.0
Total Liabilities	46,212.0	43,930.0	46,256.0	41,047.0	38,850.0	36,621.0	34,522.0
Net Stockholders' Equity	4,152.0	4,016.0	4,521.0	3,845.0	3,746.0	4,025.0	4,122.0
Year-end Shs. Outstg. (000)	486,739	500,623	524,000	508,000	516,000	548,000	588,000
STATISTICAL RECORD:							
Return on Equity %	24.3	24.6	19.2	20.1	19.6	17.2	10.5
Return on Assets %	2.0	2.1	1.7	1.7	1.7	1.6	1.0
Equity/Assets %	8.2	8.4	8.9	8.6	8.8	9.3	9.8
Non-Int. Exp./Tot. Inc. %	63.7	65.5	68.3	66.1	62.7	62.9	75.2
Price Range	51.94-26.81	40.19-31.31	40.19-22.50	32.41-17.25	18.69-12.06	14.13-7.66	10.08-7.50
P/E Ratio	25.6-13.2	21.2-16.5	24.7-13.8	22.5-12.0	14.5-9.3	12.6-6.8	16.7-12.4
Average Yield %	2.2	2.2	2.2	2.6	3.8	4.6	4.5

Statistics are as originally reported. Adj. for 2-for-1 stk. split, 5/99, 5/97 & 3-for-2 stk. split, 11/94. 1 Incl. pre-tax merger-rel. chrgs. (Dreyfus Corp.) of $104.0 mill. & one-time pre-tax chrg. of $223.0 mill. for repos. of secur. lending port. 2 Incl. gain of $35.0 mill. fr. the sale of Co.'s merchant card process. bus. 3 Bef. acctg. chrg. of $26.0 mill. & incl. pre-tax gain of $127.0 mill. fr. divestitures.

OFFICERS:
M. G. McGuinn, Chmn., C.E.O.
S. G. Elliott, Sr. Vice-Chmn., C.F.O.

INVESTOR CONTACT: Carl Krasik, Corporate Secretary, (412) 234-5601

PRINCIPAL OFFICE: One Mellon Center, Pittsburgh, PA 15258-0001

TELEPHONE NUMBER: (412) 234-5000
FAX: (412) 234-6283
WEB: www.mellon.com

NO. OF EMPLOYEES: 25,300 (approx.)

SHAREHOLDERS: 24,350

ANNUAL MEETING: In April

INCORPORATED: PA, Aug., 1971

INSTITUTIONAL HOLDINGS:
No. of Institutions: 584
Shares Held: 304,994,039
% Held: 63.9

INDUSTRY: National commercial banks (SIC: 6021)

TRANSFER AGENT(S): Mellon Investor Services, Ridgefield, NJ

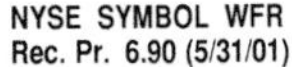

NYSE SYMBOL WFR
Rec. Pr. 6.90 (5/31/01)

MEMC ELECTRONIC MATERIALS, INC.

YIELD . . .
P/E RATIO . . .

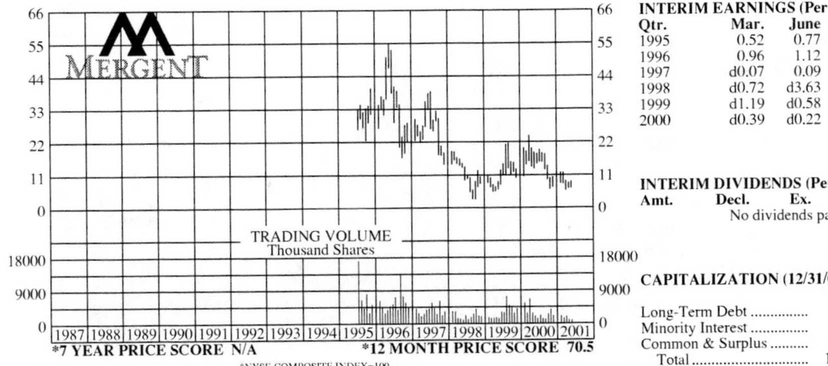

INTERIM EARNINGS (Per Share):

Qtr.	Mar.	June	Sept.	Dec.
1995	0.52	0.77	0.71	0.75
1996	0.96	1.12	0.51	d0.14
1997	d0.07	0.09	d0.10	d0.08
1998	d0.72	d3.63	d1.57	d1.74
1999	d1.19	d0.58	d0.48	d0.41
2000	d0.39	d0.22	d0.03	0.02

INTERIM DIVIDENDS (Per Share):

Amt.	Decl.	Ex.	Rec.	Pay.

No dividends paid.

CAPITALIZATION (12/31/00):

	($000)	(%)
Long-Term Debt	942,972	68.1
Minority Interest	74,413	5.4
Common & Surplus	366,419	26.5
Total	1,383,804	100.0

RECENT DEVELOPMENTS: For the year ended 12/31/00, the Company reported a net loss of $43.4 million versus a net loss of $151.5 million a year earlier. Results for 1999 included an after-tax gain from restructuring of $5.7 million. Earnings benefited primarily from the inclusion of the operating results of MEMC Korea Company. Net sales increased 25.7% to $871.6 million from $693.6 million in 1999. The Company reported gross margin of $129.0 million, while operating loss amounted to $12.4 million.

PROSPECTS: Beginning 4/1/01, MEMC Electronic Materials, Inc., a WFR subsidiary, will become a global sales representative for Ibis Technology Corporation's SIMOX-SOI wafer product line and the primary supplier to Ibis of silicon substrate material. The alliance also grants WFR the right to license Ibis' SIMOX-SOI wafer technology and to purchase oxygen implanters manufactured by Ibis. Seperately, WFR expects to report year-over-year growth.

BUSINESS

MEMC ELECTRONIC MATERIALS, INC. designs, manufactures, and markets silicon wafers for the semiconductor industry. The Company manufactures wafers with diameters ranging between 4 to 8 inches in diameter as well as a limited amount of 12-inch wafers from its pilot development lines. WFR produces wafers varying in diameter, surface features (polished or epitaxial), composition, electrical properties and method of manufacture. The Company's products are used in microelectronics applications, including computer systems, telecommunications equipment, automobiles, consumer electronic products, industrial automation and control systems, and analytic and defense systems. WFR operates manufacturing facilities directly or through joint ventures in Europe, Japan, South Korea, Taiwan, and the U.S. As of 1/29/01, the Company owned 80.0% of MEMC Korea Company.

QUARTERLY DATA

(12/31/00)($000)	REV	INC
1st Quarter	193,089	(27,339)
2nd Quarter	200,516	(15,510)
3rd Quarter	222,800	(2,281)
4th Quarter	255,232	1,740

ANNUAL FINANCIAL DATA

	12/31/00	12/31/99	12/31/98	12/31/97	12/31/96	12/31/95	12/31/94
Earnings Per Share	**d0.62**	**3 d2.43**	**2 d7.80**	**d0.16**	**2.45**	**2.78**	**1 1.43**
Cash Flow Per Share	**1.86**	**0.12**	**d3.95**	**2.91**	**4.66**	**4.92**	**3.61**
Tang. Book Val. Per Share	**4.61**	**5.55**	**8.66**	**15.67**	**16.66**	**27.45**	**9.48**
INCOME STATEMENT (IN MILLIONS):							
Total Revenues	871.6	693.6	758.9	986.7	1,119.5	886.9	660.8
Costs & Expenses	710.9	687.7	936.3	870.2	901.6	691.5	535.5
Depreciation & Amort.	173.1	159.1	155.9	126.9	91.7	67.2	50.8
Operating Income	d12.4	d153.2	d333.3	d10.4	126.2	128.2	74.5
Net Interest Inc./(Exp.)	d74.0	d64.1	d43.5	d12.2	4.9	d3.7	d9.2
Income Before Income Taxes	d77.8	d212.6	d373.2	d10.3	129.9	118.9	68.9
Income Taxes	cr21.0	cr65.9	cr89.4	2.8	51.9	43.8	26.7
Equity Earnings/Minority Int.	13.4	d4.8	d32.5	6.4	23.6	12.1	d6.8
Net Income	d43.4	3 d151.5	2 d316.3	d6.7	101.6	87.3	1 35.4
Cash Flow	129.7	7.6	d160.5	120.2	193.2	154.5	86.2
Average Shs. Outstg. (000)	69,597	62,225	40,581	41,345	41,420	31,385	23,903
BALANCE SHEET (IN MILLIONS):							
Cash & Cash Equivalents	94.8	28.6	16.2	30.1	35.1	77.2	5.1
Total Current Assets	410.4	275.9	299.1	377.0	314.3	429.2	259.0
Net Property	1,097.6	1,090.4	1,188.8	1,200.8	1,015.1	528.4	328.5
Total Assets	1,890.6	1,724.6	1,773.7	1,777.2	1,509.0	1,101.9	629.8
Total Current Liabilities	323.6	189.6	258.6	338.5	271.5	229.9	214.4
Long-Term Obligations	943.0	869.8	871.2	510.0	284.7	89.7	140.2
Net Stockholders' Equity	366.4	432.8	399.0	698.5	742.0	642.4	203.8
Net Working Capital	86.8	86.3	40.5	38.4	42.8	199.3	44.6
Year-end Shs. Outstg. (000)	69,613	69,534	40,511	41,404	41,471	21,491	21,491
STATISTICAL RECORD:							
Operating Profit Margin %	...	...	...	...	11.3	14.5	11.3
Net Profit Margin %	...	...	...	...	9.1	9.8	5.4
Return on Equity %	...	...	...	...	13.7	13.6	17.4
Return on Assets %	...	...	...	...	6.7	7.9	5.6
Debt/Total Assets %	49.9	50.4	49.1	28.7	18.9	8.1	22.3
Price Range	24.25-6.25	21.63-5.38	19.00-2.94	38.94-14.44	55.00-16.75	40.00-22.50	...
P/E Ratio	...	...	...	...	22.4-6.8	14.4-8.1	...

Statistics are as originally reported. 1 Bef. acctg. adj. chrg. $1.3 mill., 1994. 2 Incl. after-tax non-recurr. chrg. of $115.8 mill. ($2.85/sh.) from restruc. 3 Incl. net of tax restruct. chrg. reversal of $5.7 mill.

OFFICERS:
W. Simson, Chmn.
K. R. von Horde, Pres., C.E.O.
J. M. Stolze, Exec. V.P., C.F.O.
H. F. Hennelly, V.P., Sec., Gen. Couns.

INVESTOR CONTACT: Janine Orf, Dir., Investor Relations, (636) 279-5443

PRINCIPAL OFFICE: 501 Pearl Drive, (City of O'Fallon), St. Peters, MO 63376

TELEPHONE NUMBER: (636) 474-5000
FAX: (636) 474-5158
WEB: www.memc.com

NO. OF EMPLOYEES: 6,600 full-time (approx.); 370 part-time (approx.)

SHAREHOLDERS: 532 (record)

ANNUAL MEETING: In May

INCORPORATED: DE, 1984

INSTITUTIONAL HOLDINGS:
No. of Institutions: 56
Shares Held: 13,185,916
% Held: 18.9

INDUSTRY: Semiconductors and related devices (SIC: 3674)

TRANSFER AGENT(S): Wells Fargo Shareowner Services, Chicago, IL

NYSE SYMBOL MW
Rec. Pr. 26.78 (5/31/01)

MEN'S WEARHOUSE, INC. (THE)

YIELD ...
P/E RATIO 13.4

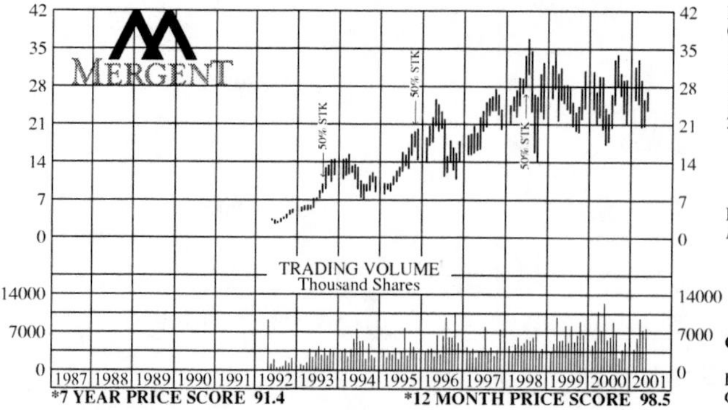

*7 YEAR PRICE SCORE 91.4 *12 MONTH PRICE SCORE 98.5
*NYSE COMPOSITE INDEX=100

INTERIM EARNINGS (Per Share):

Qtr.	Apr.	July	Oct.	Jan.
1996-97	0.15	0.19	0.18	0.49
1997-98	0.19	0.25	0.25	0.60
1998-99	0.20	0.23	0.21	0.53
1999-00	0.07	0.21	0.31	0.72
2000-01	0.32	0.38	0.40	0.90

INTERIM DIVIDENDS (Per Share):

Amt.	Decl.	Ex.	Rec.	Pay.

No dividends paid.

CAPITALIZATION (2/3/01):

	($000)	(%)
Long-Term Debt	42,645	7.9
Common & Surplus	494,987	92.1
Total	537,632	100.0

RECENT DEVELOPMENTS: For the 53 weeks ended 2/3/01, net earnings were $84.7 million versus earnings of $56.0 million, before an extraordinary charge, in the corresponding 52-week period the previous year. Prior-year results included one-time transactional costs of $7.7 million, store closing charges of $6.1 million and a litigation charge of $930,000. Net sales grew 12.4% to $1.33 billion from $1.19 billion the year before. Comparable-store sales in the U.S., on a comparable 52-week basis, increased 3.3%, while comparable-stores sales in Canada climbed 8.3%.

PROSPECTS: Strong sales growth of casual apparel is being more than offset by a decline in traditional business attire, particularly suits. Meanwhile, sales are benefiting from the Company's ongoing store expansion program. In 2001, the Company anticipates opening a total of 40 new stores, including 25 Men's Wearhouse locations and 15 K&G units, and plans to expand and/or relocate 17 Men's Wearhouse stores and 13 K&G stores. In addition, the Company plans to remodel 53 Men's Wearhouse locations during 2001.

BUSINESS

THE MEN'S WEARHOUSE, INC. is a specialty retailer of men's tailored business attire. As of 5/5/01, the Company operated 546 stores in the U.S. under the names Men's Wearhouse, K&G, and The Suit Warehouse, as well as 113 Moores, Clothing for Men stores in Canada. MW's stores offer a selection of designer, brand name and private label merchandise, including suits, sport coats, slacks, business casual, sportswear, outerwear, dress shirts, shoes and accessories, at prices typically 20.0% to 30.0% below the regular prices found at traditional department and specialty stores. On 2/10/99, MW completed the acquisition of Moores Retail Group. On 6/2/99, the Company acquired K&G Men's Center Inc.

ANNUAL FINANCIAL DATA

	2/3/01	1/29/00	1/30/99	1/31/98	2/1/97	2/3/96	1/28/95
Earnings Per Share	**2.00**	**[1] 1.32**	**[2] 1.17**	**0.87**	**0.67**	**0.55**	**0.42**
Cash Flow Per Share	**2.81**	**2.03**	**1.73**	**1.29**	**1.06**	**0.86**	**0.67**
Tang. Book Val. Per Share	**11.80**	**9.76**	**8.55**	**6.64**	**5.07**	**4.39**	**2.98**
INCOME STATEMENT (IN THOUSANDS):							
Total Revenues	1,333,501	1,186,748	767,922	631,110	483,547	406,343	317,127
Costs & Expenses	1,157,654	1,055,735	674,653	562,778	432,850	366,301	287,664
Depreciation & Amort.	34,689	30,082	21,587	16,802	12,563	9,436	7,088
Operating Income	141,158	100,931	71,682	51,530	38,134	30,606	22,375
Net Interest Inc./(Exp.)	d839	d2,580	d2,032	d2,366	d2,146	d2,518	d1,764
Income Before Income Taxes	140,319	98,351	69,650	49,164	35,988	28,088	20,611
Income Taxes	55,658	42,394	28,730	20,281	14,845	11,580	8,503
Net Income	84,661	[1] 55,957	[2] 40,920	28,883	21,143	16,508	12,108
Cash Flow	119,350	86,039	62,507	45,685	33,706	25,944	19,196
Average Shs. Outstg.	42,401	42,452	36,075	35,384	31,790	30,339	28,745
BALANCE SHEET (IN THOUSANDS):							
Cash & Cash Equivalents	84,426	77,798	19,651	59,883	34,113	2,547	1,229
Total Current Assets	469,081	423,465	270,496	277,570	208,304	145,007	114,888
Net Property	185,917	138,426	107,889	81,266	71,022	57,145	43,781
Total Assets	707,734	611,195	403,732	379,415	295,478	204,105	160,494
Total Current Liabilities	150,497	143,214	96,441	95,009	71,467	56,209	46,810
Long-Term Obligations	42,645	46,697	...	57,500	57,500	4,665	24,575
Net Stockholders' Equity	494,987	408,973	298,218	220,048	159,129	136,961	84,944
Net Working Capital	318,584	280,251	174,055	182,561	136,837	88,798	68,078
Year-end Shs. Outstg.	41,945	41,888	34,860	33,116	31,382	31,230	28,479
STATISTICAL RECORD:							
Operating Profit Margin %	10.6	8.5	9.3	8.2	7.9	7.5	7.1
Net Profit Margin %	6.3	4.7	5.3	4.6	4.4	4.1	3.8
Return on Equity %	17.1	13.7	13.7	13.1	13.3	12.1	14.3
Return on Assets %	12.0	9.2	10.1	7.6	7.2	8.1	7.5
Debt/Total Assets %	6.0	7.6	...	15.2	19.5	2.3	15.3
Price Range	34.00-17.25	34.94-19.50	36.88-14.00	27.50-15.33	25.67-10.83	20.17-8.00	15.45-7.00
P/E Ratio	17.0-8.6	26.5-14.8	31.5-12.0	31.5-17.6	38.5-16.2	36.9-14.6	36.6-16.6

Statistics are as originally reported. Adj. for stk. splits: 50% div., 6/98 & 11/95. [1] Bef. $2.9 mil ($0.07/sh) extraord. chg. & incl. $7.7 mil one-time transaction chg., $6.1 mil. store closing chg., and $930,000 litigation chg. [2] Bef. $701,000 ($0.02/sh) extraord. chg.

OFFICERS:
G. Zimmer, Chmn., C.E.O.
E. J. Lane, Pres., C.O.O.
N. P. Davis, Sr. V.P., C.F.O., V.P., Treas.

INVESTOR CONTACT: Neill Davis, (713) 592-7200

PRINCIPAL OFFICE: 5803 Glenmont Drive, Houston, TX 77081

TELEPHONE NUMBER: (713) 592-7200
FAX: (713) 657-0872
WEB: www.menswearhouse.com
NO. OF EMPLOYEES: 8,900 full-time (approx.); 3,100 part-time (approx.)
SHAREHOLDERS: 975 (approx.)
ANNUAL MEETING: In June
INCORPORATED: TX, May, 1974

INSTITUTIONAL HOLDINGS:
No. of Institutions: 153
Shares Held: 30,534,288
% Held: 74.6

INDUSTRY: Men's & boys' clothing stores (SIC: 5611)

TRANSFER AGENT(S): American Stock Transfer & Trust Company, New York, NY

NYSE SYMBOL MRK
Rec. Pr. 75.97 (4/30/01)

MERCK & CO., INC.

YIELD 1.9%
P/E RATIO 26.3

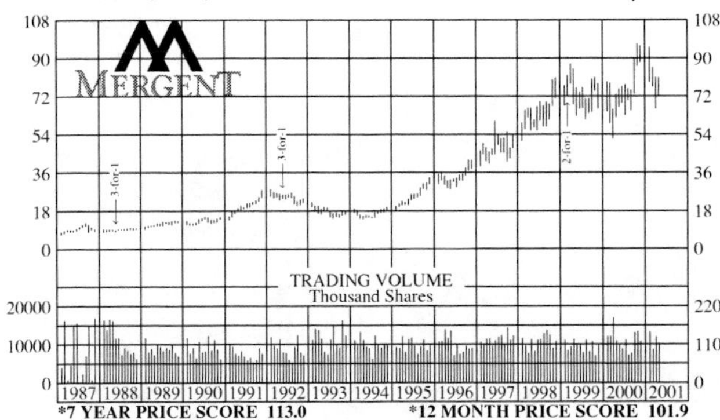

*7 YEAR PRICE SCORE 113.0 *12 MONTH PRICE SCORE 101.9

*NYSE COMPOSITE INDEX=100

INTERIM EARNINGS (Per Share):

Qtr.	Mar.	June	Sept.	Dec.
1997	0.42	0.48	0.50	0.51
1998	0.48	0.54	0.56	0.58
1999	0.54	0.61	0.64	0.66
2000	0.63	0.73	0.78	0.75

INTERIM DIVIDENDS (Per Share):

Amt.	Decl.	Ex.	Rec.	Pay.
0.29Q	5/22/00	5/31/00	6/02/00	7/03/00
0.34Q	7/25/00	8/30/00	9/01/00	10/02/00
0.34Q	11/28/00	12/06/00	12/08/00	1/02/01
0.34Q	2/27/01	3/07/01	3/09/01	4/02/01
0.34Q	5/22/01	5/31/01	6/04/01	7/02/01

Indicated div.: $1.36 (Div. Reinv. Plan)

CAPITALIZATION (12/31/00):

	($000)	(%)
Long-Term Debt	3,600,700	15.4
Minority Interest	5,021,000	21.4
Common & Surplus	14,832,400	63.2
Total	23,454,100	100.0

RECENT DEVELOPMENTS: For the year ended 12/31/00, net income increased 15.8% to $6.82 billion versus $5.89 billion in 1999. Results for 1999 included a pre-tax acquired research charge of $51.1 million. Earnings were enhanced by strong worldwide gains and manufacturing productivity improvements. Sales jumped 23.4% to $40.36 billion.

PROSPECTS: Sales should continue to benefit from strong demand for newer and established products, including VIOXX, ZOCOR, COZAAR, HYZAAR, FOSAMAX and SINGULAIR. The combined sales of these drugs accounted for 57.0% of MRK's worldwide human health sales for 2000.

BUSINESS

MERCK & CO., INC. is a pharmaceutical company that develops, manufactures and markets human and animal health products, directly and through its joint ventures, and provides pharmaceutical benefit services through Merck-Medco Managed Care LLC. The Merck Pharmaceuticals segment, (43.1% of 2000 sales), consists of therapeutic and preventive agents, generally sold by prescription, for the treatment of human disorders. Human health products include ZOCOR, a cholesterol-lowering medicine, FOSAMAX, a treatment for osteoporosis in men and women, VIOXX, a prescription arthritis medicine, SINGULAIR, for the chronic treatment of asthma, and COZAAR and HYZAAR for the treatment of high blood pressure. Animal health products include medicines used to control and alleviate disease in livestock, small animals and poultry. The Merck-Medco segment, (54.1% of 2000 sales), primarily includes sales of non-Merck products and Merck-Medco pharmaceutical benefit services, principally sales of prescription drugs through managed prescription drug programs for more than 65.0 million customers.

ANNUAL FINANCIAL DATA

	12/31/00	12/31/99	12/31/98	12/31/97	12/31/96	12/31/95	12/31/94
Earnings Per Share	**2.90**	**4 2.45**	**3 2.15**	**2 1.87**	**1.60**	**1 1.35**	**1.19**
Cash Flow Per Share	**3.44**	**2.93**	**2.57**	**2.21**	**2.00**	**1.74**	**1.56**
Tang. Book Val. Per Share	**3.23**	**2.43**	**1.91**	**2.44**	**2.17**	**2.00**	**1.57**
Dividends Per Share	**1.21**	**1.10**	**0.95**	**0.85**	**0.71**	**0.62**	**0.57**
Dividend Payout %	**41.7**	**44.9**	**44.0**	**45.2**	**44.4**	**45.9**	**47.9**
INCOME STATEMENT (IN MILLIONS):							
Total Revenues	40,363.2	32,714.0	26,898.2	23,636.9	19,828.7	16,681.1	14,969.8
Costs & Expenses	29,677.7	23,708.7	20,282.3	16,936.1	13,916.9	11,593.3	9,689.2
Depreciation & Amort.	1,277.3	1,144.8	1,015.1	837.1	730.9	667.2	681.6
Operating Income	9,408.2	7,860.5	5,600.8	5,863.7	5,180.9	4,420.6	4,599.0
Income Before Income Taxes	9,824.1	8,619.5	8,133.1	6,462.3	5,540.8	4,797.2	4,415.2
Income Taxes	3,002.4	2,729.0	2,884.9	1,848.2	1,659.5	1,462.0	1,418.2
Equity Earnings/Minority Int.	764.9	762.0	884.3	727.9	600.7	...	56.6
Net Income	6,821.7	4 5,890.5	3 5,248.2	2 4,614.1	4,122.1	1 3,641.5	3,229.8
Cash Flow	8,099.0	7,035.3	6,263.3	5,451.2	4,853.0	4,308.7	3,911.4
Average Shs. Outstg. (000)	2,353,200	2,404,600	2,441,100	2,469,400	2,427,200	2,472,200	2,514,400
BALANCE SHEET (IN MILLIONS):							
Cash & Cash Equivalents	4,254.6	3,202.4	3,355.7	2,309.3	2,181.6	3,349.8	2,269.7
Total Current Assets	13,353.4	11,259.2	10,228.5	8,213.0	7,726.6	8,617.5	6,921.7
Net Property	11,482.1	9,676.7	7,843.8	6,609.4	5,926.7	5,269.1	5,296.3
Total Assets	39,910.4	35,634.9	31,853.4	25,735.9	24,293.1	23,831.8	21,856.6
Total Current Liabilities	9,709.6	8,758.8	6,068.8	5,568.6	4,829.2	5,689.5	5,448.6
Long-Term Obligations	3,600.7	3,143.9	3,220.8	1,346.5	1,155.9	1,372.8	1,145.9
Net Stockholders' Equity	14,832.4	13,241.6	12,801.8	12,594.6	11,970.5	11,735.7	11,139.0
Net Working Capital	3,643.8	2,500.4	4,159.7	2,644.4	2,897.4	2,928.0	1,473.1
Year-end Shs. Outstg. (000)	2,307,599	2,329,078	2,360,453	2,387,296	2,413,204	2,457,698	2,495,652
STATISTICAL RECORD:							
Operating Profit Margin %	23.3	24.0	20.8	24.8	26.1	26.5	30.7
Net Profit Margin %	16.9	18.0	19.5	19.5	20.8	21.8	21.6
Return on Equity %	46.0	44.5	41.0	36.6	34.4	31.0	29.0
Return on Assets %	17.1	16.5	16.5	17.9	17.0	15.3	14.8
Debt/Total Assets %	9.0	8.8	10.1	5.2	4.8	5.8	5.2
Price Range	96.69-52.00	87.38-60.94	80.88-50.69	60.31-39.00	42.13-28.25	33.63-18.19	19.75-14.06
P/E Ratio	33.3-17.9	35.7-24.9	37.6-23.6	32.3-20.9	26.3-17.7	24.9-13.5	16.6-11.8
Average Yield %	1.6	1.5	1.4	1.7	2.0	2.4	3.4

Statistics are as originally reported. Adj. for 2-for-1 stock split, 2/99. 1 Inc. a net pre-tax gain of $169.4 mill.. 2 Inc. a nonrecurr. pre-tax gain of $213.0 mill. & non-recurr. pre-tax chgs. totaling $207.0 mill. 3 Incl. a pre-tax gain of $2.15 bill. from the sale of bus., and a pre-tax chrg. of $1.04 bill. for acq. res. and dev. 4 Incl. a pre-tax chg. of $51.1 mill. for acq. res.

OFFICERS:
R. V. Gilmartin, Chmn., Pres., C.E.O.
J. C. Lewent, Exec. V.P., C.F.O.
C. Dorsa, V.P., Treas.

INVESTOR CONTACT: Investor Relations, (908) 423-5881

PRINCIPAL OFFICE: One Merck Drive, P.O. Box 100, Whitehouse Station, NJ 08889-0100

TELEPHONE NUMBER: (908) 423-1000
FAX: (908) 735-1500
WEB: www.merck.com

NO. OF EMPLOYEES: 69,300

SHAREHOLDERS: 265,700

ANNUAL MEETING: In Apr.

INCORPORATED: NJ, June, 1927

INSTITUTIONAL HOLDINGS:
No. of Institutions: 1,225
Shares Held: 1,312,329,781
% Held: 57.0

INDUSTRY: Pharmaceutical preparations (SIC: 2834)

TRANSFER AGENT(S): Wells Fargo Bank Minnesota, N.A., South St. Paul, MN

NYSE SYMBOL MDP
Rec. Pr. 37.74 (4/30/01)

MEREDITH CORPORATION

YIELD 0.9%
P/E RATIO 28.6

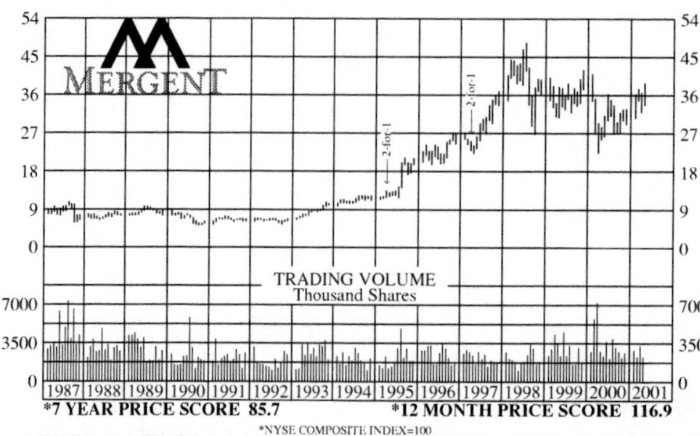

INTERIM EARNINGS (Per Share):

Qtr.	Sept.	Dec.	Mar.	June
1997-98	0.27	0.40	0.37	0.42
1998-99	0.35	0.47	0.41	0.44
1999-00	0.34	0.48	0.47	0.06
2000-01	0.32	0.47	...	...

INTERIM DIVIDENDS (Per Share):

Amt.	Decl.	Ex.	Rec.	Pay.
0.08Q	5/10/00	5/26/00	5/31/00	6/15/00
0.08Q	8/09/00	8/29/00	8/31/00	9/15/00
0.08Q	11/13/00	11/28/00	11/30/00	12/15/00
0.085Q	1/28/01	2/26/01	2/28/01	3/15/01
0.085Q	5/09/01	5/29/01	5/31/01	6/15/01

Indicated div.: $0.34 (Div. Reinv. Plan)

CAPITALIZATION (6/30/00):

	($000)	(%)
Long-Term Debt	468,480	52.3
Deferred Income Tax	48,260	5.4
Common & Surplus	379,844	42.4
Total	896,584	100.0

RECENT DEVELOPMENTS: For the quarter ended 12/31/00, net income declined 5.6% to $24.0 million from $25.5 million in the prior-year period. Total revenues fell 2.0% to $260.9 million. Publishing segment revenues decreased 4.1% to $182.3 million, while broadcasting segment revenues increased 3.2% to $78.6 million, partially due to political advertising. Segment operating profit slipped to $47.4 million from $51.6 million in 1999.

PROSPECTS: In fiscal 2001, MDP expects earnings per share to decrease about 5.0% to 10.0% compared with $1.71 in the prior year, excluding nonrecurring items. As a result, MDP announced several strategic initiatives, including the creation of a new business group, Interactive and Integrated Marketing; the expansion of Internet-related efforts; modifications in circulation; and the closing of certain operations.

BUSINESS

MEREDITH CORPORATION is a diversified media company involved in magazine and book publishing, television broadcasting, and interactive integrated marketing. The Company publishes more than twenty subscription magazines, including Ladies Home Journal, and Better Homes and Gardens, as well as more than 100 special interest publications. MDP owns twelve television stations in the U.S., and has about 300 books in print. The Company also has established marketing partnerships with companies such as The Home Depot, Kraft Foods and Nestle USA. In addition, MDP has an extensive Internet presence, including branded anchor tenant positions on America Online. On 7/1/98, MDP sold its residential real estate franchising operations.

BUSINESS LINE ANALYSIS

(06/30/2000)	Rev (%)	Inc (%)
Publishing	74.5	70.1
Broadcasting	25.5	29.9
Total	100.0	100.0

ANNUAL FINANCIAL DATA

	6/30/00	6/30/99	6/30/98	6/30/97	6/30/96	6/30/95	6/30/94
Earnings Per Share	**[6] 1.35**	**[5] 1.67**	**[5] 1.46**	**[4] 1.22**	**[3] 0.97**	**[1][2] 0.72**	**[2] 0.48**
Cash Flow Per Share	**3.01**	**3.20**	**2.64**	**1.95**	**1.75**	**1.70**	**1.48**
Tang. Book Val. Per Share	...	...	...	**1.01**	...	...	...
Dividends Per Share	**0.32**	**0.30**	**0.28**	**0.26**	**0.22**	**0.20**	**0.18**
Dividend Payout %	**23.7**	**18.0**	**19.2**	**21.3**	**22.7**	**27.8**	**37.7**
INCOME STATEMENT (IN MILLIONS):							
Total Revenues	1,097.2	1,036.1	1,009.9	855.2	867.1	884.6	799.5
Costs & Expenses	848.2	782.4	792.9	700.2	725.6	754.3	693.4
Depreciation & Amort.	87.6	82.6	64.5	40.4	44.1	54.6	56.5
Operating Income	161.3	171.1	152.5	114.7	97.5	75.7	49.6
Net Interest Inc./(Exp.)	d33.8	d21.3	d13.4	3.8	d3.3	d3.6	d9.6
Income Before Income Taxes	127.6	152.2	139.1	118.4	100.1	77.1	54.2
Income Taxes	56.6	62.5	59.3	50.8	45.4	37.2	27.1
Net Income	[6] 71.0	[5] 89.7	[5] 79.9	[4] 67.6	[3] 54.7	[1][2] 39.8	[2] 27.2
Cash Flow	158.6	172.3	144.4	108.0	98.7	94.4	83.7
Average Shs. Outstg. (000)	52,774	53,761	54,603	55,503	56,346	55,508	56,728
BALANCE SHEET (IN MILLIONS):							
Cash & Cash Equivalents	22.9	11.0	5.0	124.9	13.8	17.2	50.1
Total Current Assets	288.8	256.2	246.8	337.2	210.7	261.9	298.3
Net Property	174.2	159.8	156.1	90.2	80.0	131.8	124.7
Total Assets	1,439.8	1,423.4	1,071.5	760.9	733.8	882.3	864.5
Total Current Liabilities	358.7	344.1	346.9	278.0	279.5	287.9	280.4
Long-Term Obligations	468.5	485.0	175.0	...	35.0	166.1	126.8
Net Stockholders' Equity	379.8	360.2	349.7	326.9	261.6	248.6	263.5
Net Working Capital	d69.9	d87.9	d100.1	59.2	d68.8	d26.0	17.9
Year-end Shs. Outstg. (000)	49,209	50,284	52,276	53,257	53,898	54,970	54,884
STATISTICAL RECORD:							
Operating Profit Margin %	14.7	16.5	15.1	13.4	11.2	8.6	6.2
Net Profit Margin %	6.5	8.7	7.9	7.9	6.3	4.5	3.4
Return on Equity %	18.7	24.9	22.8	20.7	20.9	16.0	10.3
Return on Assets %	4.9	6.3	7.5	8.9	7.4	4.5	3.1
Debt/Total Assets %	32.5	34.1	16.3	...	4.8	18.8	14.7
Price Range	41.88-22.38	42.00-30.63	48.50-26.69	36.94-22.13	26.94-19.56	21.25-11.31	12.28-9.69
P/E Ratio	30.4-16.6	25.1-18.3	33.2-18.3	30.3-18.1	27.8-20.2	29.5-15.7	25.7-20.3
Average Yield %	1.0	0.8	0.7	0.9	0.9	1.2	1.6

Statistics are as originally reported. Adj. for 2-for-1 stk. split, 3/95 & 3/97. [1] Bef. acct. chrg. of $46.2 mill. [2] Incl. gain of $4.7 mill., 1995; $5.6 mill., 1994. [3] Incl. net gain of $3.4 mill. from disp. of book clubs. [4] Bef. gain of $27.7 mill. from the sale of cable ops. [5] Incl. gain on sale of BH&G Real Estate Service of $2.4 mill., 6/99; $1.4 mill., 6/98. [6] Incl. a non-recurr. chrg. of $19.1 mill.

OFFICERS:
W. T. Kerr, Chmn., C.E.O.
S. V. Radia, V.P., C.F.O.

INVESTOR CONTACT: Jennifer S. McCoy, Mgr. Inv. Commun., (800) 284-4236

PRINCIPAL OFFICE: 1716 Locust Street, Des Moines, IA 50309-3023

TELEPHONE NUMBER: (515) 284-3000
FAX: (515) 284-2700
WEB: www.meredith.com
NO. OF EMPLOYEES: 2,560 full-time; 143 part-time
SHAREHOLDERS: 1,800 (approx. common); 1,200 (class B common).
ANNUAL MEETING: In Nov.
INCORPORATED: IA, 1905

INSTITUTIONAL HOLDINGS:
No. of Institutions: 182
Shares Held: 28,934,664
% Held: 58.0

INDUSTRY: Periodicals (SIC: 2721)

TRANSFER AGENT(S): Boston EquiServe, Boston, MA

NYSE SYMBOL MER
Rec. Pr. 61.70 (4/30/01)

MERRILL LYNCH & CO., INC.

YIELD 1.0%
P/E RATIO 15.2

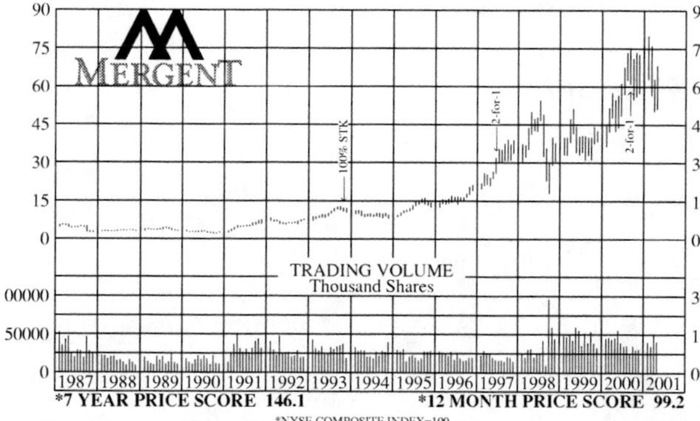

INTERIM EARNINGS (Per Share):

Qtr.	Mar.	June	Sept.	Dec.
1997	0.59	0.62	0.63	0.59
1998	0.65	0.67	d0.25	0.43
1999	0.72	0.79	0.67	0.90
2000	1.19	1.01	0.94	0.93

INTERIM DIVIDENDS (Per Share):

Amt.	Decl.	Ex.	Rec.	Pay.
0.32Q	7/18/00	8/02/00	8/04/00	8/24/00
2-for-1	7/18/00	9/01/00	8/04/00	8/31/00
0.16Q	10/23/00	11/01/00	11/03/00	11/22/00
0.16Q	1/22/01	1/31/01	2/02/01	2/28/01
0.16Q	4/27/01	5/09/01	5/11/01	5/30/01

Indicated div.: $0.64 (Div. Reinv. Plan)

CAPITALIZATION (12/29/00):

	($000)	(%)
Long-Term Debt	70,223,000	77.0
Redeemable Pfd. Stock	2,714,000	3.0
Preferred Stock	425,000	0.5
Common & Surplus	17,879,000	19.6
Total	91,241,000	100.0

RECENT DEVELOPMENTS: For the year ended 12/29/00, net income advanced 40.5% to $3.78 billion from $2.69 billion in 1999. Total net revenues rose 20.0% to $26.79 billion from $22.32 billion the year before. Commissions revenues grew 9.8% to $6.98 billion, while principal transactions revenues increased 26.2% to $6.00 billion. Total non-interest expenses rose 16.3% to $21.07 billion. Comparisons were made with restated 1999 figures.

PROSPECTS: The Company plans to pursue the expansion of its global business due to the aging of high net-worth individuals in many countries. MER anticipates the assets controlled by individuals with $1.0 million or more to invest will grow 80.0% in the next five years, with most of that growth coming from outside the U.S., particularly Europe and Japan. By 2005, MER expects non-U.S. client assets may total nearly $500.00 billion.

BUSINESS

MERRILL LYNCH & CO., Inc., with assets of $407.20 billion as of 12/29/00, provides investment, financing, insurance and related services. Merrill Lynch, Pierce, Fenner & Smith, Inc., its largest subsidiary, is one of the largest securities firms in the world. MLPF&S is a broker and a dealer in various financial instruments, and an investment banker. MER is also engaged in asset management, investment counseling, and is a dealer in U.S. government and federal agency obligations. As of 12/29/00, client assets totaled about $1.70 trillion, including $557.00 billion under management.

REVENUES

(12/29/2000)	($000)	(%)
Commissions	6,977,000	29.5
Principal Transactions	5,995,000	25.3
Investment Banking	4,049,000	17.1
Asset Management & Portfolio	5,688,000	24.0
Other Revenues	967,000	4.1
Total	23,676,000	100.0

ANNUAL FINANCIAL DATA

	12/29/00	12/31/99	12/25/98	12/26/97	12/27/96	12/29/95	12/30/94
Earnings Per Share	**4.11**	**3.09**	**1 1.50**	**2.42**	**2.05**	**1.36**	**1.19**
Cash Flow Per Share	**5.83**	**4.70**	**2.50**	**2.99**	**2.58**	**1.83**	**1.57**
Tang. Book Val. Per Share	**16.67**	**10.09**	**6.09**	**3.65**	**9.47**	**7.87**	**6.92**
Dividends Per Share	**0.61**	**0.53**	**0.46**	**0.38**	**0.29**	**0.25**	**0.22**
Dividend Payout %	**14.7**	**17.0**	**30.7**	**15.5**	**14.1**	**18.6**	**18.7**
INCOME STATEMENT (IN MILLIONS):							
Total Revenues	44,872.0	34,879.0	35,853.0	31,731.0	25,011.0	21,513.0	18,233.1
Costs & Expenses	37,582.0	29,450.0	32,946.0	28,235.0	22,034.0	19,335.0	16,178.4
Depreciation & Amort.	1,573.0	1,351.0	811.0	446.0	411.0	367.0	325.1
Operating Income	5,717.0	4,078.0	2,096.0	3,050.0	2,566.0	1,811.0	1,729.6
Income Taxes	1,738.0	1,265.0	713.0	1,097.0	947.0	697.0	712.8
Equity Earnings/Minority Int.	d195.0	d195.0	d124.0	d47.0	...	...	...
Net Income	3,784.0	2,618.0	1 1,259.0	1,906.0	1,619.0	1,114.0	1,016.8
Cash Flow	5,318.0	3,931.0	2,031.0	2,313.0	1,983.0	1,433.0	1,329.2
Average Shs. Outstg. (000)	911,416	836,262	812,600	773,498	767,344	783,988	844,964
BALANCE SHEET (IN MILLIONS):							
Cash & Cash Equivalents	78,548.0	26,852.0	23,725.0	20,725.0	11,183.0	10,868.0	9,590.3
Total Current Assets	379,028.0	300,964.0	274,679.0	171,556.0	119,835.0	101,934.0	88,793.8
Net Property	3,444.0	3,117.0	2,761.0	2,074.0	1,670.0	1,605.0	1,587.6
Total Assets	407,200.0	328,071.0	299,804.0	292,819.0	213,016.0	176,857.0	163,749.3
Total Current Liabilities	289,847.0	236,391.0	206,425.0	213,432.0	160,712.0	137,470.0	129,653.0
Long-Term Obligations	70,223.0	53,465.0	57,563.0	43,090.0	26,102.0	17,340.0	14,863.4
Net Stockholders' Equity	18,304.0	12,802.0	10,132.0	8,329.0	6,892.0	6,141.0	5,817.5
Net Working Capital	89,181.0	64,573.0	68,254.0	d41,876.0	d40,877.0	d35,536.0	d40,859.2
Year-end Shs. Outstg. (000)	807,955	735,531	712,568	670,164	662,500	701,604	751,624
STATISTICAL RECORD:							
Operating Profit Margin %	12.7	11.7	5.8	9.6	10.3	8.4	9.5
Net Profit Margin %	8.4	7.5	3.5	6.0	6.5	5.2	5.6
Return on Equity %	20.7	20.4	12.4	22.9	23.5	18.1	17.5
Return on Assets %	0.9	0.8	0.4	0.7	0.8	0.6	0.6
Debt/Total Assets %	17.2	16.3	19.2	14.7	12.3	9.8	9.1
Price Range	74.63-36.31	51.25-31.00	54.56-17.88	39.13-19.63	21.31-12.38	16.19-8.69	11.44-8.06
P/E Ratio	18.2-8.8	16.6-10.0	36.4-11.9	16.2-8.1	10.4-6.0	11.9-6.4	9.6-6.8
Average Yield %	1.1	1.3	1.3	1.3	1.7	2.0	2.3

Statistics are as originally reported. Adj. for 2-for-1 stk. split, 8/00 & 5/97. 1 Incl. after-tax provision of $430.0 million for costs related to staff reductions.

OFFICERS:
D. H. Komansky, Chmn., C.E.O.
S. L. Hammerman, Vice-Chmn., General Counsel
T. H. Patrick, Exec. V.P., , C.F.O.

INVESTOR CONTACT: Martin Wise, Investor Relations, (212) 449-7119

PRINCIPAL OFFICE: 4 World Financial Center, New York, NY 10080

TELEPHONE NUMBER: (212) 449-1000
FAX: (212) 449-7461
WEB: www.ml.com

NO. OF EMPLOYEES: 72,000 (approx.)

SHAREHOLDERS: 15,128 (approximate)

ANNUAL MEETING: In April

INCORPORATED: DE, 1973

INSTITUTIONAL HOLDINGS:
No. of Institutions: 655
Shares Held: 512,555,524
% Held: 61.7

INDUSTRY: Security brokers and dealers (SIC: 6211)

TRANSFER AGENT(S): Mellon Investor Services, New York, NY

NYSE SYMBOL MCC
Rec. Pr. 26.20 (5/31/01)

MESTEK, INC.

YIELD	...
P/E RATIO	14.0

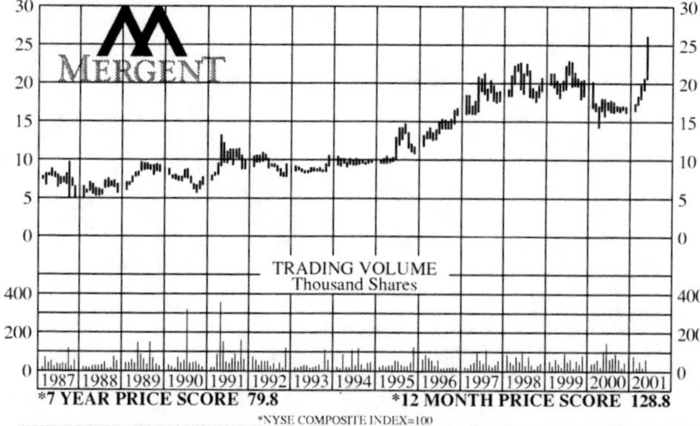

INTERIM EARNINGS (Per Share):

Qtr.	Mar.	June	Sept.	Dec.
1997	0.36	0.25	0.43	0.57
1998	0.38	0.32	0.48	0.62
1999	0.40	0.41	0.46	0.75
2000	0.42	0.29	0.44	0.72

INTERIM DIVIDENDS (Per Share):

Amt.	Decl.	Ex.	Rec.	Pay.
		No dividends paid.		

CAPITALIZATION (12/31/00):

	($000)	(%)
Long-Term Debt	240	0.1
Minority Interest	2,746	1.6
Common & Surplus	163,682	98.2
Total	166,668	100.0

RECENT DEVELOPMENTS: For the year ended 12/31/00, income from continuing operations declined 7.2% to $16.4 million compared with $17.7 million in 1999. Results for 2000 and 1999 excluded income from discontinued operations of $666,000 and $251,000, respectively. Total revenues were $376.0 million, up 14.6% from $328.1 million a year earlier. Gross profit as a percentage of total revenues was 28.9% in 2000 compared with 29.9% in 1999. Operating profit fell 7.2% to $27.1 million.

PROSPECTS: On 4/30/01, the Company entered into a letter of intent to acquire the business of Yoder Manufacturing and Mentor AGVS from SNS Properties, Inc. of Cleveland, Ohio. Yoder is a manufacturer of laser-guided automated vehicles for material handling. Yoder's and Mentor's products are complementary with other products manufactured by the Company's Metal Forming segment. The Company expects to close the transaction on or before 6/30/01.

BUSINESS

MESTEK, INC. manufactures and markets industrial products through two business segments. The Company's Heating, Ventilating, and Air Conditioning (HVAC) Equipment manufactures finned tube and baseboard radiation equipment gas-fired heating and ventilating equipment, air damper equipment and related air distribution products and commercial and residential boilers. The products are marketed under a number of franchise names, including STERLING, BEACON MORRIS, SMITH, HYDROTHERM, RBI, VULCAN, APPLIED AIR, WING, AWV, ABI, ARROW, KOLDWAVE, ANEMOSTAT, OMEGA FLEX and SPACEPAK. The Company's Metal Forming Segment designs, manufactures and sells a variety of metal forming equipment and related machinery under brand names such as COOPERWEYMOUTH, PETERSON, DAHLSTROM, LOCKFORMER, IOWA PRECISION (IPI), HILL ENGINEERING, COILMATEDICKERMAN, and ROWE. Products include roll formers, wing benders, duct forming systems, plasma and water-jet cutting equipment, coil feeds, straighteners, cradles, cut-to-length lines, specialty dies, rotary punching equipment, tube feed and cut-off and flying cut-off saws. On 1/9/01, the Company sold its 89.5%-owned subsidiary, National Northeast Corporation to Alpha Technologies Group, Inc.

ANNUAL FINANCIAL DATA

	12/31/00	12/31/99	12/31/98	12/31/97	12/31/96	12/31/95	12/31/94
Earnings Per Share	**② 1.87**	**2.02**	**1.80**	**1.61**	**① 1.49**	**1.21**	**1.02**
Cash Flow Per Share	**3.33**	**3.21**	**2.76**	**2.34**	**2.07**	**1.65**	**...**
Tang. Book Val. Per Share	**18.72**	**16.96**	**14.99**	**13.22**	**9.34**	**9.41**	**8.92**
INCOME STATEMENT (IN THOUSANDS):							
Total Revenues	375,987	375,270	338,344	327,778	299,527	245,865	224,018
Costs & Expenses	336,103	333,384	302,378	295,835	271,492	221,755	200,169
Depreciation & Amort.	12,779	10,631	8,599	6,548	5,143	3,940	4,712
Operating Income	27,105	31,255	27,367	25,395	22,892	20,170	19,137
Net Interest Inc./(Exp.)	d1,120	d1,951	d1,256	d1,434	d1,377	d718	d839
Income Before Income Taxes	26,134	28,710	25,651	23,293	21,991	18,135	16,048
Income Taxes	9,732	10,793	9,587	8,888	8,662	7,229	6,750
Net Income	② 16,402	17,917	16,064	14,405	① 13,329	10,906	9,298
Cash Flow	29,181	28,548	24,663	20,953	18,472	14,846	14,010
Average Shs. Outstg.	8,760	8,887	8,949	8,951	8,938	9,019	...
BALANCE SHEET (IN THOUSANDS):							
Cash & Cash Equivalents	2,417	4,468	3,777	2,494	11,649	1,405	4,201
Total Current Assets	148,009	132,023	117,589	112,291	108,752	89,569	76,090
Net Property	73,489	69,067	55,841	40,715	31,439	24,968	18,483
Total Assets	293,489	242,253	205,143	191,117	170,010	141,431	120,430
Total Current Liabilities	121,757	68,291	68,174	70,235	49,478	47,943	39,462
Long-Term Obligations	240	20,324	438	662	15,247	380	211
Net Stockholders' Equity	163,682	148,617	133,298	118,007	103,718	91,046	80,732
Net Working Capital	26,252	63,732	49,415	42,056	59,274	41,626	36,628
Year-end Shs. Outstg.	8,743	8,764	8,890	8,926	9,610	8,975	9,036
STATISTICAL RECORD:							
Operating Profit Margin %	7.2	8.3	8.1	7.7	7.6	8.2	8.5
Net Profit Margin %	4.4	4.8	4.7	4.4	4.5	4.4	4.2
Return on Equity %	10.0	12.1	12.1	12.2	12.9	12.0	11.5
Return on Assets %	5.6	7.4	7.8	7.5	7.8	7.7	7.7
Debt/Total Assets %	0.1	8.4	0.2	0.3	9.0	0.3	0.2
Price Range	20.25-14.19	23.00-17.88	22.75-17.50	21.38-15.88	16.75-11.75	14.75-9.50	10.50-9.00
P/E Ratio	10.8-7.6	11.4-8.8	12.6-9.7	13.3-9.9	11.2-7.9	12.2-7.9	10.3-8.8

Statistics are as originally reported. ① Incl. gain on sale of prop. of $1.4 mill. ② Excl. income from disc. oper. of $666,000.

OFFICERS:
J. E. Reed, Chmn., C.E.O.
S. M. Shea, Sr. V.P., C.F.O.
R. B. Dewey, Sr. V.P., Gen. Couns., Sec.

INVESTOR CONTACT: Investor Relations, (413) 568-9571

PRINCIPAL OFFICE: 260 North Elm Street, Westfield, MA 01085

TELEPHONE NUMBER: (413) 568-9571
FAX: (413) 568-2969
WEB: www.mestek.com

NO. OF EMPLOYEES: 3,221 (approx.)

SHAREHOLDERS: 1,248

ANNUAL MEETING: In June

INCORPORATED: PA, 1898

INSTITUTIONAL HOLDINGS:
No. of Institutions: 23
Shares Held: 2,052,392
% Held: 23.5

INDUSTRY: Refrigeration and heating equipment (SIC: 3585)

TRANSFER AGENT(S): EquiServe, LP, Canton, MA

NYSE SYMBOL MUI
Rec. Pr. 2.21 (5/31/01)

METALS USA, INC.

YIELD 5.4%
P/E RATIO 6.9

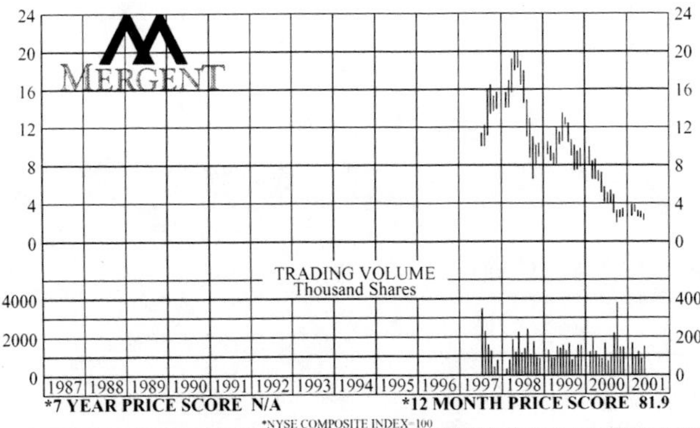

*7 YEAR PRICE SCORE N/A *12 MONTH PRICE SCORE 81.9

*NYSE COMPOSITE INDEX=100

INTERIM EARNINGS (Per Share):

Qtr.	Mar.	June	Sept.	Dec.
1998	0.21	0.32	0.27	0.27
1999	0.28	0.31	0.17	0.28
2000	0.30	0.26	0.02	d0.26

INTERIM DIVIDENDS (Per Share):

Amt.	Decl.	Ex.	Rec.	Pay.
0.03Q	2/10/00	3/15/00	3/17/00	4/10/00
0.03Q	5/24/00	6/15/00	6/19/00	7/12/00
0.03Q	7/27/00	9/14/00	9/18/00	10/11/00
0.03Q	11/13/00	11/15/00	11/17/00	1/11/01
0.03Q	3/28/01	4/04/01	4/06/01	4/17/01

Indicated div.: $0.12

CAPITALIZATION (12/31/00):

	($000)	(%)
Long-Term Debt	489,900	54.6
Deferred Income Tax	32,900	3.7
Common & Surplus	375,100	41.8
Total	897,900	100.0

RECENT DEVELOPMENTS: For the year ended 12/31/00, net income declined 70.6% to $11.7 million compared with $39.8 million in 1999. Net sales were $2.02 billion, up 15.8% from $1.75 billion a year earlier. Cost of sales as a percentage of net sales was 76.7% in 2000 compared with 73.9% in 1999. Results for 1999 included an integration charge of $9.4 million. Operating income decreased 33.0% to $71.4 million from $106.6 million in 1999.

PROSPECTS: Going forward, the Company plans to continue its concentration on providing strong customer service, cost reduction and rigorous working capital management. MUI's headcount since year-end 2000 has been reduced by approximately 5.0%. In addition, the Company's inventories have contracted by approximately $34.0 million since year-end and MUI remains aggressive at reducing inventories.

BUSINESS

METALS USA, INC. is engaged in value-added processing and distribution of steel, aluminum and specialty metals, as well as manufacturing metal components. The Company purchases metal from primary producers who focus on large volume sales of unprocessed metals in standard configurations and sizes. In most cases, the Company performs the customized, value-added processing services required to meet specifications provided by end-use customers. In addition to the Company's metals processing capabilities, the Company manufactures higher-value finished building products. The Company is organized into four business segments, Heavy Carbon, Flat Rolled, Specialty Metals and Building Products.

BUSINESS LINE ANALYSIS

(12/31/2000)	REV(%)	INC(%)
Plates and Shapes	46.6	57.0
Flat Rolled	45.2	31.4
Building Products	8.2	11.6
Total	100.0	100.0

ANNUAL FINANCIAL DATA

	12/31/00	12/31/99	12/31/98	12/31/97	12/31/96	12/31/95
Earnings Per Share	**0.32**	**[1] 1.04**	**1.07**	**0.28**	**0.31**	**0.84**
Cash Flow Per Share	**1.02**	**1.59**	**1.51**	**0.53**	...	**1.18**
Tang. Book Val. Per Share	**2.14**	**1.94**	**1.95**	**3.08**	**0.01**	...
Dividends Per Share	**0.09**	...	...	...	...	...
Dividend Payout %	**28.1**	...	...	...	...	...
INCOME STATEMENT (IN MILLIONS):						
Total Revenues	2,021.6	1,745.4	1,498.8	507.8	240.1	235.2
Costs & Expenses	1,924.2	1,617.6	1,385.6	482.3	227.4	218.7
Depreciation & Amort.	26.0	21.2	16.4	5.4	3.5	2.8
Operating Income	71.4	106.6	96.8	20.1	9.2	13.7
Net Interest Inc./(Exp.)	d50.5	d40.0	d30.9	d5.0	d1.3	d2.3
Income Before Income Taxes	22.5	67.3	67.5	15.2	7.9	11.7
Income Taxes	10.8	27.5	27.5	9.2	4.6	4.8
Net Income	11.7	[1] 39.8	40.0	6.0	3.3	6.9
Cash Flow	37.7	61.0	56.4	11.4	...	9.7
Average Shs. Outstg. (000)	37,000	38,400	37,300	21,600	...	8,200
BALANCE SHEET (IN MILLIONS):						
Cash & Cash Equivalents	3.8	4.7	9.3	7.3	1.7	...
Total Current Assets	547.4	505.9	559.0	257.9	66.3	...
Net Property	249.3	223.0	173.2	82.5	26.7	...
Total Assets	1,104.8	1,049.3	1,019.5	467.0	95.1	...
Total Current Liabilities	202.6	200.5	151.6	71.3	20.0	...
Long-Term Obligations	489.9	434.7	502.6	167.1	24.6	...
Net Stockholders' Equity	375.1	379.4	341.6	217.1	49.2	...
Net Working Capital	344.8	305.4	407.4	186.6	46.3	...
Year-end Shs. Outstg. (000)	36,510	38,055	38,156	31,461	3,768	...
STATISTICAL RECORD:						
Operating Profit Margin %	3.5	6.1	6.5	4.0	...	5.8
Net Profit Margin %	0.6	2.3	2.7	1.2	...	2.9
Return on Equity %	3.1	10.5	11.7	2.8	...	...
Return on Assets %	1.1	3.8	3.9	1.3	...	...
Debt/Total Assets %	44.3	41.4	49.3	35.8	...	...
Price Range	9.94-1.94	13.50-7.44	20.13-6.56	16.50-10.00	...	...
P/E Ratio	31.0-6.1	13.0-7.2	18.8-6.1	58.9-35.7	...	...
Average Yield %	1.5	...	...	...	...	...

Statistics are as originally reported. [1] Incl. integration chrg. of $9.4 mill.

OFFICERS:
J. M. Kirksey, Chmn., C.E.O.
R. Singer, Pres., C.O.O.
T. L. Freeman, V.P., C.A.O., Treas.
J. A. Hageman, Sr. V.P., Gen. Couns., Sec.

INVESTOR CONTACT: Terry Freeman, (713) 965-0990

PRINCIPAL OFFICE: Three Riverway, Suite 600, Houston, TX 77056

TELEPHONE NUMBER: (713) 965-0990
FAX: (713) 965-0067
WEB: www.metalsusa.com

NO. OF EMPLOYEES: 4,700 (approx.)

SHAREHOLDERS: 1,600 (approx.)

ANNUAL MEETING: In May

INCORPORATED: DE.

INSTITUTIONAL HOLDINGS:
No. of Institutions: 36
Shares Held: 12,561,971
% Held: 34.4

INDUSTRY: Metals service centers and offices (SIC: 5051)

TRANSFER AGENT(S): First Chicago Trust Company, Jersey City, NJ

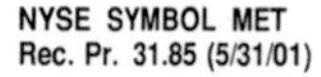

NYSE SYMBOL MET
Rec. Pr. 31.85 (5/31/01)

METLIFE, INC.

YIELD 0.6%
P/E RATIO ...

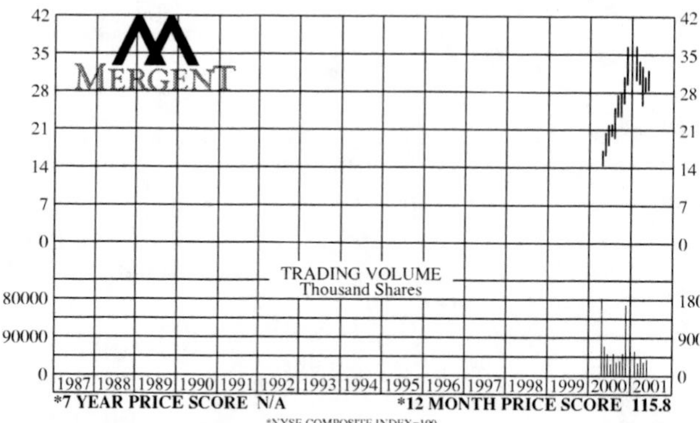

*7 YEAR PRICE SCORE N/A *12 MONTH PRICE SCORE 115.8

*NYSE COMPOSITE INDEX=100

INTERIM EARNINGS (Per Share):

Qtr.	Mar.	June	Sept.	Dec.
2000	...	0.44	0.31	0.74

INTERIM DIVIDENDS (Per Share):

Amt.	Decl.	Ex.	Rec.	Pay.
0.20A	10/24/00	11/03/00	11/07/00	12/15/00

Indicated div.: $0.20

CAPITALIZATION (12/31/00):

	($mill.)	(%)
Long-Term Debt	2,426.0	12.9
Common & Surplus	16,389.0	87.1
Total	18,815.0	100.0

RECENT DEVELOPMENTS: For the year ended 12/31/00, net income climbed 54.5% to $953.0 million from $617.0 million in 1999. Earnings for 2000 included net realized investment losses of $390.0, a one-time payout to transferred Canadian policyholders of $327.0 million and demutualization expenses of $230.0 million. Total revenues grew 25.3% to $31.95 billion from $25.49 billion a year earlier. Comparisons were made with restated prior-year figures.

PROSPECTS: On 2/13/01, the Company announced that the Federal Reserve Board approved MET's application for financial holding company status and its acquisition of Grand Bank N.A., of Kingston, New Jersey. In addition, the Board approved MET's application for bank holding company status. The acquisition of Grand Bank will allow MET to offer a wide range of integrated financial services to the Company's customers. Going forward, the Company will continue to focus on expense reduction.

BUSINESS

METLIFE, INC. is a provider of insurance and financial services to individual and group customers. MET currently provides individual insurance, annuities and investment products to approximately nine million households in the U.S. Also, MET provides group insurance and retirement and savings products and services to approximately 64,000 corporations and other institutions as of 12/31/00. The Company is organized into five major business segments: Individual Business, Institutional Business, Asset Management, Auto & Home and International. MET has international insurance operations in 12 countries with a focus on the Asia/Pacific region, Latin America and selected European countries. On 1/6/00, the Company acquired GenAmerica Corp. for about $1.20 billion. On 4/7/00, Metropolitan Life converted from a mutual life insurance company to a stock life insurance company and became a wholly-owned subsidiary of MET.

ANNUAL FINANCIAL DATA

	12/31/00	12/31/99	12/31/98
Earnings Per Share	[2] **1.49**	...	...
Tang. Book Val. Per Share	**22.31**	...	...
Dividends Per Share	**0.20**	...	...
Dividend Payout %	**13.4**	...	...
INCOME STATEMENT (IN MILLIONS):			
Total Premium Income	18,137.0	13,526.0	12,863.0
Other Income	13,810.0	11,900.0	14,243.0
Total Revenues	31,947.0	25,426.0	27,106.0
Policyholder Benefits	16,893.0	...	...
Income Before Income Taxes	1,416.0	1,435.0	2,087.0
Income Taxes	463.0	593.0	740.0
Net Income	[2] 953.0	[1] 842.0	[1] 1,347.0
Average Shs. Outstg. (000)	788,508	...	...
BALANCE SHEET (IN MILLIONS):			
Cash & Cash Equivalents	119,875.0	...	...
Premiums Due	8,343.0	...	...
Invst. Assets: Total	156,527.0	...	...
Total Assets	255,018.0	225,232.0	215,346.0
Long-Term Obligations	2,426.0	2,514.0	2,903.0
Net Stockholders' Equity	16,389.0	13,690.0	14,867.0
Year-end Shs. Outstg. (000)	734,597	...	...
STATISTICAL RECORD:			
Return on Revenues %	3.0	3.3	5.0
Return on Equity %	5.8	6.2	9.1
Return on Assets %	0.4	0.4	0.6
Price Range	36.50-14.31	...	...
P/E Ratio	24.5-9.6	...	...
Average Yield %	0.8	...	...

Statistics are as originally reported. [1] Bef. extraord. chrg. $225.0 mill, 12/99; $4.0 mill., 12/98. [2] Incls. net realized invest. losses of $236.0 mill., a one-time payout to transferred Canadian policyholders of $327.0 mill., demutualization expenses of $170.0 million and a surplus tax credit of $145.0 million.

OFFICERS:
R. H. Benmosche, Chmn., Pres., C.E.O.
G. Clark, Vice-Chmn., C.I.O.
S. G. Nagler, Vice-Chmn., C.F.O.

INVESTOR CONTACT: Investor Relations, (212) 578-2211

PRINCIPAL OFFICE: One Madison Avenue, New York, NY 10010-3690

TELEPHONE NUMBER: (212) 578-2211
FAX: (212) 578-3320
WEB: www.metlife.com

NO. OF EMPLOYEES: 46,700 (approx.)

SHAREHOLDERS: 1,073

ANNUAL MEETING: In April

INCORPORATED: DE, Aug., 1999

INSTITUTIONAL HOLDINGS:
No. of Institutions: 287
Shares Held: 228,825,147
% Held: 30.5

INDUSTRY: Insurance agents, brokers, & service (SIC: 6411)

TRANSFER AGENT(S): Mellon Investor Services, South Hackensack, NJ

NYSE SYMBOL MXT
Rec. Pr. 30.00 (4/30/01)

METRIS COMPANIES, INC.

YIELD 0.1%
P/E RATIO 13.9

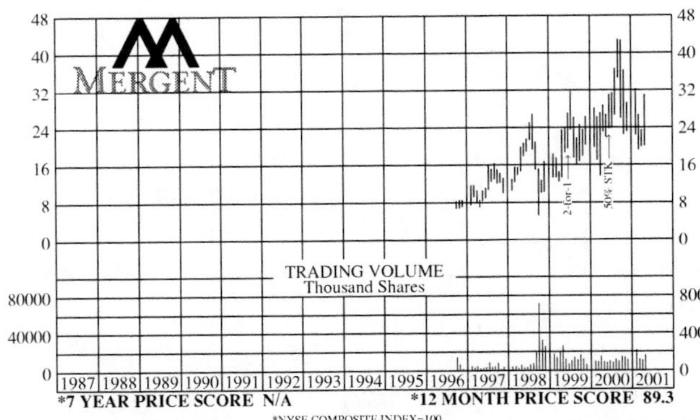

*7 YEAR PRICE SCORE N/A *12 MONTH PRICE SCORE 89.3

*NYSE COMPOSITE INDEX=100

INTERIM EARNINGS (Per Share):

Qtr.	Mar.	June	Sept.	Dec.
1996	0.08	0.11	0.12	0.11
1997	0.13	0.16	0.17	0.17
1998	0.19	0.21	0.29	0.27
1999	0.29	d1.35	0.36	0.39
2000	0.59	0.53	0.52	0.52

INTERIM DIVIDENDS (Per Share):

Amt.	Decl.	Ex.	Rec.	Pay.
50% STK	5/09/00	6/16/00	6/01/00	6/15/00
0.01Q	8/02/00	8/14/00	8/16/00	8/28/00
0.01Q	11/01/00	11/13/00	11/15/00	11/27/00
0.01Q	2/06/01	2/14/01	2/16/01	2/26/01
0.01Q	5/09/01	5/17/01	5/21/01	5/31/01

Indicated div.: $0.04

CAPITALIZATION (12/31/00):

	($000)	(%)
Long-Term Debt	356,066	28.7
Preferred Stock	360,421	29.1
Common & Surplus	523,132	42.2
Total	1,239,619	100.0

RECENT DEVELOPMENTS: For the year ended 12/31/00, the Company reported income of $198.6 million, before the cumulative effect of an accounting change of $3.4 million, compared with income of $115.4 million, before an extraordinary loss of $50.8 million, in 1999. Total interest income soared 113.7% to $504.8 million versus $236.2 million the year before. Net interest income surged 106.3% to $371.8 million from $180.3 million a year earlier.

PROSPECTS: In February, MXT and Western Union Financial Services, Inc., signed an agreement under which they will offer Western Union branded MasterCard cards to Western Union customers. Going forward, the Company should continue to benefit from solid growth in both the credit card and enhancement services businesses. The Company expects 2001 full year earnings per share should be in the range of $2.50 to $2.55.

BUSINESS

METRIS COMPANIES, INC. is a direct marketer of consumer credit products and fee-based services primarily to moderate-income consumers. The Company's consumer credit products are primarily unsecured credit cards issued by its subsidiary, Direct Merchants Credit Card Bank, N.A. Customers and prospects include individuals for whom credit bureau information is available and existing customers of a former affiliate, Fingerhut Corporation. The Company markets its fee-based services to its credit card customers and customers of third parties. The Company has operations in Champaign, Illinois; Jacksonville and Orlando, Florida; Scottsdale, Arizona; Tulsa, Oklahoma; and White Marsh, Maryland.

ANNUAL FINANCIAL DATA

	12/31/00	12/31/99	12/31/98	12/31/97	12/31/96	12/31/95	12/31/94
Earnings Per Share	[3] **2.15**	[2] **d0.19**	**0.94**	**0.63**	**0.39**	[1] **0.09**	[1] **0.05**
Cash Flow Per Share	**1.75**	**1.11**	**1.75**	**0.87**	**0.65**	...	**0.05**
Tang. Book Val. Per Share	**4.58**	**3.63**	**2.60**	**2.42**	**2.41**	**1.49**	**0.14**
Dividends Per Share	**0.03**	**0.02**	**0.02**	**0.01**	...	...	...
Dividend Payout %	**2.3**	...	**1.8**	**1.6**	...	...	...
INCOME STATEMENT (IN THOUSANDS):							
Total Revenues	1,438,565	859,941	426,169	255,871	156,416	58,699	14,725
Costs & Expenses	1,039,398	593,284	284,243	179,422	110,347	55,709	11,196
Depreciation & Amort.	76,256	75,341	48,678	14,566	13,523	d4,459	26
Operating Income	322,911	191,316	93,248	61,883	32,546	7,449	3,503
Income Before Income Taxes	322,911	191,316	93,248	61,883	32,546	7,449	3,503
Income Taxes	124,320	75,953	35,900	23,825	12,530	2,868	1,305
Net Income	[3] 198,591	[2] 115,363	57,348	38,058	20,016	4,581	2,198
Cash Flow	243,223	64,503	104,926	52,624	33,539	122	2,224
Average Shs. Outstg.	138,873	57,855	59,904	60,714	51,387	49,317	48,810
BALANCE SHEET (IN THOUSANDS):							
Cash & Cash Equivalents	521,440	194,433	37,347	48,223	32,082	34,743	23
Total Current Assets	708,134	456,115	229,291	52,533	35,024	68,563	23
Net Property	128,396	56,914	21,982	15,464	5,163	1,476	255
Total Assets	3,736,026	2,045,082	945,719	673,221	286,616	174,428	9,856
Total Current Liabilities	2,189,672	844,200	50,874	323,616	108,825	90,994	2,571
Long-Term Obligations	356,066	345,012	310,896	100,000	...	...	...
Net Stockholders' Equity	883,553	623,801	432,982	176,038	138,718	71,318	6,737
Net Working Capital	d1,481,538	d388,085	178,417	d271,083	d73,801	d22,431	d2,548
Year-end Shs. Outstg.	93,364	57,919	57,779	57,675	57,675	47,901	47,901
STATISTICAL RECORD:							
Operating Profit Margin %	22.4	22.2	21.9	24.2	20.8	12.7	23.8
Net Profit Margin %	13.8	13.4	13.5	14.9	12.8	7.8	14.9
Return on Equity %	22.5	18.5	13.2	21.6	14.4	6.4	32.6
Return on Assets %	5.3	5.6	6.1	5.7	7.0	2.6	22.3
Debt/Total Assets %	9.5	16.9	32.9	14.9	...	...	...
Price Range	42.94-13.58	31.67-12.43	26.92-5.17	16.33-7.00	8.58-6.71	...	...
P/E Ratio	30.0-9.5	...	28.6-5.5	26.1-11.2	22.0-17.2	...	...
Average Yield %	0.1	0.1	0.1	0.1	...	...	...

Statistics are as originally reported. Adj. for 3-for-2 stk. spl., 6/00; 2-for-1 stk. spl., 6/99 [1] Pro forma [2] Excl. extra. loss of $50.8 mill. [3] Excl. cum. effect of acctg. change chrg., $3.4 mill.

OFFICERS:
R. N. Zebeck, Chmn., Pres., C.E.O.
D. Wesselink, Vice Chmn.
B. Woo, C.F.O.

INVESTOR CONTACT: Mark Van Ert, V.P., Investor Relations, (952) 525-5092

PRINCIPAL OFFICE: 10900 Wayzata Blvd., Minnetonka, MN 55305-1534

TELEPHONE NUMBER: (952) 525-5020
FAX: (952) 595-0519
WEB: www.metriscompanies.com

NO. OF EMPLOYEES: 4,200 (approx.)

SHAREHOLDERS: 359 (of record); 16,000 (beneficial)

ANNUAL MEETING: In May

INCORPORATED: DE, Aug., 1996

INSTITUTIONAL HOLDINGS:
No. of Institutions: 192
Shares Held: 61,365,745
% Held: 98.2

INDUSTRY: Personal credit institutions (SIC: 6141)

TRANSFER AGENT(S): Computershare Investor Services, Chicago, IL

NYSE SYMBOL MGM
Rec. Pr. 20.43 (4/30/01)

METRO-GOLDWYN-MAYER INC.

YIELD ...
P/E RATIO 81.7

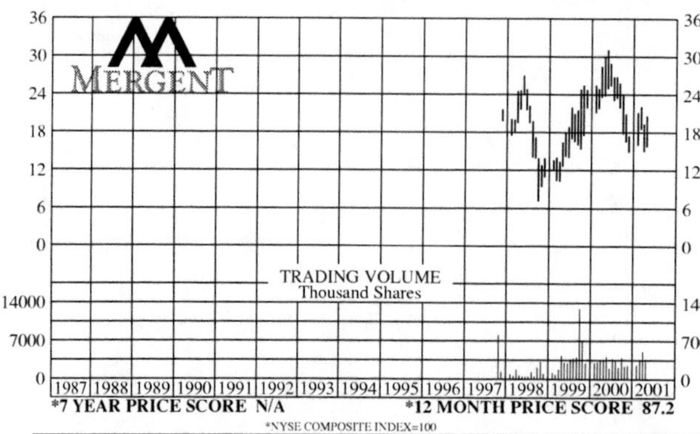

*7 YEAR PRICE SCORE N/A *12 MONTH PRICE SCORE 87.2

*NYSE COMPOSITE INDEX=100

INTERIM EARNINGS (Per Share):

Qtr.	Mar.	June	Sept.	Dec.
1998	d0.28	d0.84	d0.61	d0.30
1999	d2.03	d1.65	0.07	0.08
2000	0.03	0.03	0.13	0.06

INTERIM DIVIDENDS (Per Share):

Amt.	Decl.	Ex.	Rec.	Pay.

No dividends paid.

CAPITALIZATION (12/31/00):

	($000)	(%)
Long-Term Debt	709,952	23.5
Common & Surplus	2,309,687	76.5
Total	3,019,639	100.0

RECENT DEVELOPMENTS: For the year ended 12/31/00, the Company reported net income of $51.0 million compared with a net loss of $530.9 million in the previous year. Total revenues climbed 8.3% to $1.24 billion from $1.14 billion in the prior year. Feature film revenues increased 19.1% to $1.06 billion from $888.3 million, while television program revenues dropped 32.3% to $139.2 million from $205.7 million in 1999.

PROSPECTS: The Company and Cablevision Systems Corporation announced an agreement for MGM to acquire a 20.0% ownership interest in four of Rainbow Media's national cable networks, American Movie Classics, Bravo, The Independent Film Channel and Women's Entertainment, for $825.0 million. MGM plans to build and leverage its 4,100-title film and television library by aggressively marketing and repackaging its titles.

BUSINESS

METRO-GOLDWYN-MAYER INC. is an entertainment content company that develops, produces and distributes theatrical motion pictures and television programs, and intends to create and own branded cable and satellite programming channels. MGM's principal subsidiaries are Metro-Goldwyn-Mayer Studios Inc., United Artists Corporation, United Artists Films Inc. and Orion Pictures Corporation. MGM currently develops and produces theatrical motion picture projects through two separate production entities, MGM Pictures and UA Films. MGM Pictures concentrates on developing and producing mainstream, major studio budget level films. UA Films concentrates on developing, producing and acquiring films with a net cost investment of less than $10.0 million.

REVENUES

(12/31/2000)	($000)	(%)
Feature Films	1,058,296	85.4
Television Programs	139,229	11.3
Other	39,922	3.3
Total	1,237,447	100.0

ANNUAL FINANCIAL DATA

	12/31/00	12/31/99	12/31/98	12/31/97	12/31/96
Earnings Per Share	**0.24**	**d3.36**	**d2.08**	**d4.47**	**0.01**
Cash Flow Per Share	**3.57**	**2.24**	**8.23**	**11.32**	**5.26**
Tang. Book Val. Per Share	**8.58**	**7.80**	**9.01**	**12.22**	...
INCOME STATEMENT (IN MILLIONS):					
Total Revenues	1,237.4	1,142.4	1,240.7	831.3	228.7
Costs & Expenses	434.2	695.7	529.7	446.3	127.4
Depreciation & Amort.	700.1	885.1	781.9	452.1	87.7
Operating Income	103.2	d438.4	d70.8	d67.1	13.6
Net Interest Inc./(Exp.)	d51.4	d86.4	d80.6	d53.1	d9.9
Income Before Income Taxes	64.5	d521.1	d147.5	d117.8	4.5
Income Taxes	13.5	9.8	10.2	10.3	4.3
Net Income	51.0	d530.9	d157.6	d128.1	0.2
Cash Flow	751.1	354.2	624.3	324.0	87.9
Average Shs. Outstg. (000)	210,313	158,016	75,816	28,634	16,692
BALANCE SHEET (IN MILLIONS):					
Cash & Cash Equivalents	77.1	152.2	54.8	4.0	54.8
Total Current Assets	493.2	605.1	419.9	289.3	54.8
Net Property	47.1	48.2	38.6	32.8	...
Total Assets	3,548.2	3,424.4	3,159.0	2,822.7	2,130.5
Total Current Liabilities	419.4	458.6	367.8	395.6	...
Long-Term Obligations	710.0	719.4	715.6	890.5	715.6
Net Stockholders' Equity	2,309.7	2,116.8	1,919.7	1,378.6	1,919.7
Net Working Capital	73.8	146.5	52.1	d106.3	54.8
Year-end Shs. Outstg. (000)	207,218	201,419	150,856	65,766	...
STATISTICAL RECORD:					
Operating Profit Margin %	8.3	...	...	...	5.9
Net Profit Margin %	4.1	...	...	...	0.1
Return on Equity %	2.2	...	...	...	...
Return on Assets %	1.4	...	...	...	...
Debt/Total Assets %	20.0	21.0	22.7	31.5	33.6
Price Range	31.06-14.88	25.50-10.25	27.00-7.13	22.19-19.75	...
P/E Ratio	129.4-62.0	...	...	...	...

Statistics are as originally reported.

OFFICERS:
A. Yemenidjian, Chmn., C.E.O.
C. J. McGurk, Vice-Chmn., C.O.O.
D. J. Taylor, Sr. Exec. V.P., C.F.O.
W. A. Jones, Sr. Exec. V.P., Sec.

INVESTOR CONTACT: Craig A. Parsons, Sr. V.P. & Inv. Rel., (310) 449-3600

PRINCIPAL OFFICE: 2500 Broadway Street, Santa Monica, CA 90404

TELEPHONE NUMBER: (310) 449-3000
FAX: (310) 449-8750
WEB: www.mgm.com

NO. OF EMPLOYEES: 973 (avg.)

SHAREHOLDERS: 2,000 (approx. beneficial)

ANNUAL MEETING: In May

INCORPORATED: DE, Jul., 1996

INSTITUTIONAL HOLDINGS:
No. of Institutions: 89
Shares Held: 28,304,219
% Held: 13.0

INDUSTRY: Motion picture & video production (SIC: 7812)

TRANSFER AGENT(S): Mellon Investor Services, Ridgefield Park, NJ

NYSE SYMBOL MTG
Rec. Pr. 70.37 (5/31/01)

MGIC INVESTMENT CORPORATION

YIELD 0.1%
P/E RATIO 13.9

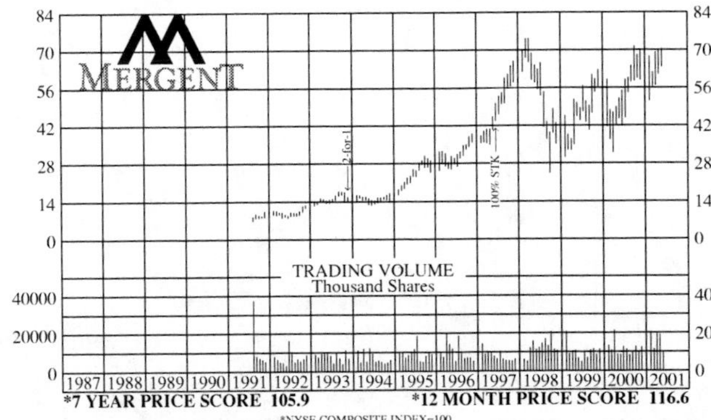

*7 YEAR PRICE SCORE 105.9 *12 MONTH PRICE SCORE 116.6

*NYSE COMPOSITE INDEX=100

INTERIM EARNINGS (Per Share):

Qtr.	Mar.	June	Sept.	Dec.
1996	0.49	0.53	0.56	0.60
1997	0.61	0.67	0.72	0.75
1998	0.81	0.82	0.86	0.91
1999	0.91	1.02	1.11	1.25
2000	1.19	1.27	1.36	1.23

INTERIM DIVIDENDS (Per Share):

Amt.	Decl.	Ex.	Rec.	Pay.
0.025Q	5/04/00	5/12/00	5/16/00	6/01/00
0.025Q	7/27/00	8/09/00	8/11/00	9/01/00
0.025Q	10/26/00	11/08/00	11/10/00	12/01/00
0.025Q	1/25/01	2/08/01	2/12/01	3/01/01
0.025Q	5/10/01	5/17/01	5/21/01	6/01/01

Indicated div.: $0.10

CAPITALIZATION (12/31/00):

	($000)	(%)
Long-Term Debt	397,364	13.9
Common & Surplus	2,464,882	86.1
Total	2,862,246	100.0

RECENT DEVELOPMENTS: For the year ended 12/31/00, net income totaled $542.0 million, up 15.3% compared with $470.2 million in 1999. Results for 2000 included a litigation settlement charge of $23.2 million. Total revenues grew 11.4% to $1.11 billion versus $996.8 million the year before. Net premiums written improved 12.0% to $887.4 million from $792.3 million a year earlier. Investment income rose 16.6% to $178.5 million from $153.1 million in the prior year. Losses incurred totaled $91.7 million compared with $97.2 million a year ago.

PROSPECTS: The Company's earnings are benefiting from strong revenue growth, lower credit losses and reduced underwriting expenses. Going forward, the Company expects the near-term housing market will remain stable to strong as it shows no signs of imminent weakness. However, while housing and real estate conditions are still favorable, it is clear overall conditions have come down a bit from the peak environment of 1998 and 1999 and that home price growth, while still solid in most markets, has slowed.

BUSINESS

MGIC INVESTMENT CORPORATION is a holding company which, through its subsidiary, Mortgage Guaranty Insurance Corp., is the provider of private mortgage insurance coverage in the United States to mortgage bankers, savings institutions, commercial banks, mortgage brokers, credit unions and other lenders. Private mortgage insurance covers residential first mortgage loans and expands home ownership opportunities. Private mortgage insurance also facilitates the sale of low down-payment mortgage loans in the secondary mortgage market, principally to the Federal Home Loan Mortgage Corporation and the Federal National Mortgage Association. In addition, MTG provides various underwriting and contract services related to home mortgage lending. MTG is licensed in all 50 states of the United States, the District of Columbia and Puerto Rico.

REVENUES

(12/31/2000)	($000)	(%)
Net Premiums Earned	890,091	80.2
Investment Income	178,535	16.1
Realized Investment Gains	1,432	0.1
Other Revenue	40,283	3.6
Total	1,110,341	100.0

ANNUAL FINANCIAL DATA

	12/31/00	12/31/99	12/31/98	12/31/97	12/31/96	12/31/95	12/31/94
Earnings Per Share	**1 5.05**	**4.30**	**3.39**	**2.75**	**2.17**	**1.75**	**1.35**
Tang. Book Val. Per Share	**23.07**	**16.79**	**15.05**	**13.07**	**11.59**	**9.89**	**7.18**
Dividends Per Share	**0.10**	**0.10**	**0.10**	**0.10**	**0.08**	**0.08**	**0.08**
Dividend Payout %	**2.0**	**2.3**	**2.9**	**3.5**	**3.7**	**4.6**	**5.9**
INCOME STATEMENT (IN MILLIONS):							
Total Premium Income	890.1	792.6	763.3	708.7	617.0	506.5	404.0
Other Income	220.3	204.2	208.4	159.5	128.6	111.4	98.2
Total Revenues	1,110.3	996.8	971.7	868.3	745.6	617.9	502.2
Income Before Income Taxes	788.8	681.0	554.6	465.4	365.0	291.4	217.1
Income Taxes	246.8	210.8	169.1	141.6	107.0	83.8	57.6
Net Income	1 542.0	470.2	385.5	323.8	258.0	207.6	159.5
Average Shs. Outstg. (000)	107,260	109,258	113,582	117,924	119,046	118,568	117,954
BALANCE SHEET (IN MILLIONS):							
Cash & Cash Equivalents	3,477.8	2,792.1	2,784.4	2,421.6	2,040.1	1,696.9	743.5
Premiums Due	41.9	42.5	54.3	35.7	41.6	49.3	52.9
Invst. Assets: Fixed-term	...	...	...	...	...	...	553.0
Invst. Assets: Total	3,611.0	2,891.3	2,855.0	2,446.1	2,036.2	1,687.2	1,293.0
Total Assets	3,857.8	3,104.4	3,050.5	2,617.7	2,222.3	1,874.7	1,476.3
Long-Term Obligations	397.4	425.0	442.0	237.5	35.4	35.8	36.1
Net Stockholders' Equity	2,464.9	1,776.0	1,640.6	1,486.8	1,366.1	1,121.4	838.1
Year-end Shs. Outstg. (000)	106,826	105,798	109,003	113,792	117,900	113,406	116,790
STATISTICAL RECORD:							
Return on Revenues %	48.8	47.2	39.7	37.3	34.6	33.6	31.8
Return on Equity %	22.0	26.5	23.5	21.8	18.9	18.5	19.0
Return on Assets %	14.0	15.1	12.6	12.4	11.6	11.1	10.8
Price Range	71.50-31.94	62.75-30.13	74.50-24.25	66.00-34.94	38.88-25.25	31.00-16.38	17.13-12.50
P/E Ratio	14.2-6.3	14.6-7.0	22.0-7.2	24.0-12.7	18.0-11.7	17.7-9.4	12.7-9.3
Average Yield %	0.2	0.2	0.2	0.2	0.2	0.3	0.5

Statistics are as originally reported. Adj. for stk. split: 2-for-1, 6/97 1 Incl. litigation settlement chrg. of $23.2 mill.

OFFICERS:
C. S. Culver, Pres., C.E.O.
J. M. Lauer, Exec. V.P., C.F.O.
J. H. Lane, Sr. V.P., Sec., Gen. Couns.

INVESTOR CONTACT: Shareholder Services, (414) 347-6596

PRINCIPAL OFFICE: 250 E. Kilbourn Ave., Milwaukee, WI 53202

TELEPHONE NUMBER: (414) 347-6480
FAX: (414) 347-6696
WEB: www.mgic.com

NO. OF EMPLOYEES: 1,093 (avg.)

SHAREHOLDERS: 238 (record)

ANNUAL MEETING: In May

INCORPORATED: WI, 1984

INSTITUTIONAL HOLDINGS:
No. of Institutions: 367
Shares Held: 106,290,072
% Held: 99.5

INDUSTRY: Surety insurance (SIC: 6351)

TRANSFER AGENT(S): Firstar Bank Milwaukee, N.A., Milwaukee, WI

NYSE SYMBOL MGG
Rec. Pr. 30.07 (4/30/01)

MGM MIRAGE

YIELD ...
P/E RATIO 26.8

MERGENT

TRADING VOLUME
Thousand Shares

*7 YEAR PRICE SCORE 116.1 *12 MONTH PRICE SCORE 90.4

*NYSE COMPOSITE INDEX=100

INTERIM EARNINGS (Per Share):

Qtr.	Mar.	June	Sept.	Dec.
1997	0.26	0.28	0.16	0.29
1998	0.14	0.13	0.16	0.21
1999	0.17	0.19	0.11	0.36
2000	0.38	d0.13	0.45	0.42

INTERIM DIVIDENDS (Per Share):

Amt.	Decl.	Ex.	Rec.	Pay.
2-for-1	12/13/99	2/28/00	2/10/00	2/25/00
0.10Q	12/13/99	2/08/00	2/10/00	3/01/00

Last div. payment on 3/1/00.

CAPITALIZATION (12/31/00):

	($000)	(%)
Long-Term Debt	5,381,701	56.6
Capital Lease Obligations	7,092	0.1
Deferred Income Tax	1,730,158	18.2
Common & Surplus	2,382,445	25.1
Total	9,501,396	100.0

RECENT DEVELOPMENTS: For the year ended 12/31/00, MGG reported income of $166.2 million, before an extraordinary loss of $5.4 million, versus income of $95.1 million, before an extraordinary loss of $898,000 and an accounting charge of $8.2 million, in 1999. Earnings for 2000 and 1999 included various special items resulting in net charges of $131.3 million and $71.5 million, respectively. Revenues soared to $3.23 billion from $1.39 billion.

PROSPECTS: MGG will begin the design phase for a world class resort in Atlantic City, adjacent to Borgata, MGG's joint venture with Boyd Gaming. Also, MGG will suspend the capitalization of interest related to its 55-acre site in Las Vegas and will expense such interest until the development process for the Las Vegas site is further advanced. This action will lower net earnings per share by $0.20 to $0.25 on an annualized basis beginning in 2001.

BUSINESS

MGM MIRAGE (formerly MGM Grand, Inc.) is an entertainment, hotel and gaming company headquartered in Las Vegas, Nevada, which owns and/or operates 18 casino properties on three continents. MGG's U.S. holdings include: the MGM Grand Hotel and Casino-The City of Entertainment, Bellagio, The Mirage, Treasure Island, New York-New York Hotel and Casino, the Boardwalk Hotel and Casino, 50% of Monte Carlo, and The Golden Nugget, all located in Las Vegas; Whiskey Pete's, Buffalo Bill's and the Primm Valley Resort in Primm, Nevada; two championship golf courses in California; the Golden Nugget in Nevada; the Beau Rivage resort in Mississippi; MGM Grand Detroit Casino; the MGM Grand Hotel and Casino in Darwin, Australia; and casinos in Nelspruit, Witbank and Johannesburg, Republic of South Africa. On 5/31/00, MGG acquired Mirage Resorts, Inc.

REVENUES

(12/31/2000)	($000)	(%)
Casino	1,913,733	54.4
Rooms	620,626	17.6
Food & Beverage	490,981	14.0
Entertainment Retail & Other	471,525	13.4
Income frm Unconsol. Affiliates	22,068	0.6
Total	3,518,933	100.0

ANNUAL FINANCIAL DATA

	12/31/00	12/31/99	12/31/98	12/31/97	12/31/96	12/31/95	12/31/94
Earnings Per Share	**[5] 1.13**	**[4] 0.80**	**0.61**	**[3] 0.98**	**[2] 0.69**	**0.48**	**[1] 0.75**
Cash Flow Per Share	**3.32**	**1.86**	**1.31**	**1.54**	**1.28**	**1.08**	**1.24**
Tang. Book Val. Per Share	**14.63**	**8.76**	**8.91**	**9.17**	**8.07**	**5.58**	**5.51**
Dividends Per Share	**0.10**	...	...	...	...	...	...
Dividend Payout %	**8.8**	...	...	...	...	...	...
INCOME STATEMENT (IN MILLIONS):							
Total Revenues	[6] 3,232.6	1,391.7	773.9	827.6	804.8	721.8	742.2
Costs & Expenses	2,370.4	1,053.1	563.7	571.3	611.0	559.3	564.2
Depreciation & Amort.	324.4	128.7	78.6	65.4	64.5	58.7	48.3
Operating Income	537.7	209.9	131.6	191.0	129.3	103.8	129.7
Net Interest Inc./(Exp.)	d261.9	d58.8	d20.0	d9.9	d29.5	d56.4	d56.4
Income Before Income Taxes	275.0	150.2	109.5	180.3	99.2	46.6	74.6
Income Taxes	108.9	55.0	40.6	65.0	24.6	...	...
Net Income	[5] 166.2	[4] 95.1	68.9	[3] 115.3	[2] 74.5	46.6	[1] 73.5
Cash Flow	490.6	223.8	147.5	180.6	139.0	105.3	121.8
Average Shs. Outstg. (000)	147,901	120,086	112,684	117,670	108,470	97,088	97,976
BALANCE SHEET (IN MILLIONS):							
Cash & Cash Equivalents	228.0	121.5	82.0	34.6	61.4	110.0	75.9
Total Current Assets	795.6	269.9	208.1	170.8	226.7	212.7	203.5
Net Property	9,064.2	2,390.5	1,327.7	1,032.7	884.8	903.9	880.0
Total Assets	10,734.6	2,760.7	1,773.8	1,398.4	1,287.7	1,282.2	1,140.8
Total Current Liabilities	1,233.2	290.1	189.4	181.5	190.8	119.4	111.4
Long-Term Obligations	5,388.8	1,323.9	537.7	51.7	78.3	561.5	485.6
Net Stockholders' Equity	2,382.4	1,033.8	964.4	1,101.6	973.4	584.5	529.4
Net Working Capital	d437.6	d20.2	18.7	d10.7	35.9	93.3	92.2
Year-end Shs. Outstg. (000)	159,130	113,880	104,066	115,970	115,768	97,550	95,850
STATISTICAL RECORD:							
Operating Profit Margin %	16.6	15.1	17.0	23.1	16.1	14.4	17.5
Net Profit Margin %	5.1	6.8	8.9	13.9	9.3	6.5	9.9
Return on Equity %	7.0	9.2	7.1	10.5	7.7	8.0	13.9
Return on Assets %	1.5	3.4	3.9	8.2	5.8	3.6	6.4
Debt/Total Assets %	50.2	48.0	30.3	3.7	6.1	43.8	42.6
Price Range	38.81-18.44	27.28-13.56	19.94-11.28	23.44-16.06	24.38-11.38	16.19-11.38	19.81-11.31
P/E Ratio	34.3-16.3	34.1-17.0	32.7-18.5	23.9-16.4	35.6-16.6	33.7-23.7	26.4-15.1
Average Yield %	0.3	...	...	...	...	...	...

Statistics are as originally reported. Adj. for 2-for-1 stk. split, 2/10/00. [1] Bef. income from disc. ops. of $1.0 mill. [2] Incl. various chrgs. of $80.2 mill. [3] Incl. $28.6 mill. chg. for asset disp. & excl. extraord. chrg. of $4.2 mill. [4] Incl. pre-open. & oth. exps. of $71.5 mill.; excl. extraord. chrg. of $898,000 & acctg. chrg. of $8.2 mill. [5] Bef. extraord. loss of $5.4 million; incl. various special items resulting in a net charge of $131.3 mill. [6] Reflects the acq. of Mirage Resorts, Inc. on 5/31/00.

OFFICERS:
J. T. Lanni, Chmn., C.E.O.
D. M. Wade, Vice-Chmn.
J. J. Murren, Pres., C.F.O.

INVESTOR CONTACT: Scott Langsner, Sr. V.P., Sec. & Treas., (702) 891-3333

PRINCIPAL OFFICE: 3600 Las Vegas Boulevard South, Las Vegas, NV 89109

TELEPHONE NUMBER: (702) 693-7120
WEB: www.mgmgrand.com

NO. OF EMPLOYEES: 39,000 full-time (approx.); 6,000 part-time (approx.)

SHAREHOLDERS: 5,300 (approx. record)

ANNUAL MEETING: In May

INCORPORATED: DE, Jan., 1986

INSTITUTIONAL HOLDINGS:
No. of Institutions: 135
Shares Held: 68,471,604
% Held: 43.0

INDUSTRY: Amusement parks (SIC: 7996)

TRANSFER AGENT(S): Mellon Investor Services, Ridgefield Park, NJ

NYSE SYMBOL MU
Rec. Pr. 45.38 (4/30/01)

MICRON TECHNOLOGY INC.

YIELD ...
P/E RATIO 17.7

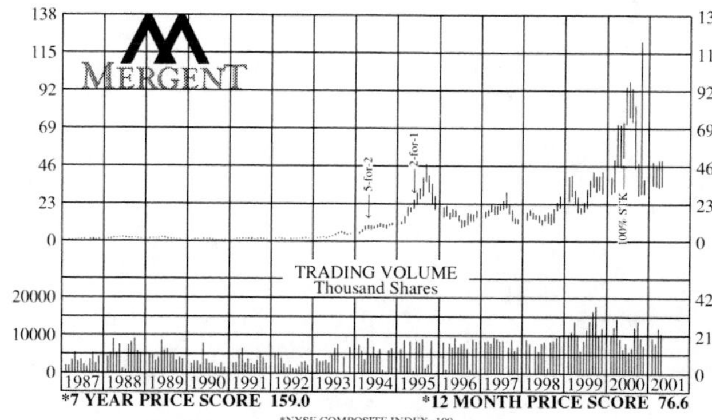

INTERIM EARNINGS (Per Share):

Qtr.	Nov.	Feb.	May.	Aug.
1997-98	0.02	d0.12	d0.25	d0.21
1998-99	d0.10	0.04	d0.05	d0.04
1999-00	0.60	0.29	0.47	1.20
2000-01	0.58	...	...	...

INTERIM DIVIDENDS (Per Share):

Amt.	Decl.	Ex.	Rec.	Pay.
100% STK	3/29/00	5/02/00	4/18/00	5/01/00

CAPITALIZATION (8/31/00):

	($000)	(%)
Long-Term Debt	933,700	11.8
Deferred Income Tax	333,500	4.2
Minority Interest	199,300	2.5
Common & Surplus	6,432,000	81.4
Total	7,898,500	100.0

RECENT DEVELOPMENTS: For the quarter ended 3/1/01, MU reported a net loss of $88.3 million versus net income of $161.3 million in the prior-year quarter. Results for 2001 and 2000 included a net loss from discontinued PC operations of $84.2 million and $7.5 million, respectively. Net sales fell 8.1% to $1.07 billion from $1.16 billion the year before. Operating loss amounted to $41.0 million versus operating income of $272.1 million in 2000.

PROSPECTS: On 2/15/01, the Company announced that it agreed to purchase of KobeSteel's 75.0% ownership interest in KMT Semiconductor, Limited, a DRAM manufacturing facility located in Nishiwaki City, Japan, for approximately $25.0 million. MU will also assume KMT's projected debt of $325.0 million. Upon completion, KMT will become a wholly-owned subsidiary of MU. Going forward, MU will focus on low-cost manufacturing.

BUSINESS

MICRON TECHNOLOGY, INC. is a holding company, which principally designs, develops, manufactures, and markets semiconductor memory products and personal computer systems. MU's semiconductor segment includes products such as Dynamic Random Access Memories (DRAMs), Static RAMs (SRAMs), and flash memory devices. The personal computer operations segment's primary products include desktop and notebook personal computer systems, multiprocessor network servers, hardware services and e-services. As of 3/1/01, Micron Electronics, Inc. is a 60.0%-owned subsidiary of MU. In 2000, sales were derived as follows: semiconductor memory products, 85.6% and personal computer systems, 14.4%.

QUARTERLY DATA

(08/31/00)($000)	Rev	Inc
1st Quarter	1,584.4	341.3
2nd Quarter	1,392.5	161.3
3rd Quarter	1,789.2	274.9
4th Quarter	2,570.2	726.7

ANNUAL FINANCIAL DATA

	8/31/00	9/2/99	9/3/98	8/28/97	8/29/96	8/31/95	9/1/94
Earnings Per Share	**5 2.56**	**4 d0.13**	**d0.55**	**3 0.77**	**2 1.38**	**1 1.98**	**0.96**
Cash Flow Per Share	**4.13**	**1.49**	**0.88**	**1.82**	**2.23**	**2.44**	**1.29**
Tang. Book Val. Per Share	**10.96**	**7.44**	**6.11**	**6.70**	**5.89**	**4.49**	**2.46**
Dividends Per Share	...	...	...	...	**0.05**	**0.09**	**0.04**
Dividend Payout %	...	...	...	...	**3.6**	**4.4**	**4.4**
INCOME STATEMENT (IN MILLIONS):							
Total Revenues	7,336.3	3,764.0	3,011.9	3,515.5	3,653.8	2,952.7	1,628.6
Costs & Expenses	4,048.7	2,967.7	2,898.9	2,657.3	2,345.6	1,457.2	869.7
Depreciation & Amort.	994.3	843.3	606.6	461.7	363.7	199.0	138.8
Operating Income	2,293.3	d47.0	d493.6	402.4	944.5	1,296.5	620.1
Net Interest Inc./(Exp.)	8.5	d46.5	0.1	0.9	14.3	25.0	5.7
Income Before Income Taxes	2,317.0	d91.5	d335.2	619.1	950.5	1,350.5	625.8
Income Taxes	796.7	cr36.0	cr118.8	267.3	357.0	506.4	225.3
Equity Earnings/Minority Int.	d16.1	d13.4	d17.3	d19.6	d8.3	...	...
Net Income	5 1,504.2	4 d68.9	d233.7	3 326.3	2 593.5	1 844.1	400.5
Cash Flow	2,498.5	774.4	372.9	788.0	957.2	1,043.1	539.3
Average Shs. Outstg. (000)	605,400	521,400	424,400	432,600	430,000	427,800	417,800
BALANCE SHEET (IN MILLIONS):							
Cash & Cash Equivalents	2,466.4	1,613.5	649.4	987.7	286.8	555.8	433.0
Total Current Assets	4,904.4	2,830.0	1,499.2	1,972.4	964.0	1,274.1	793.2
Net Property	4,257.6	3,799.6	3,030.8	2,761.2	2,708.1	1,385.6	663.5
Total Assets	9,631.5	6,965.2	4,688.3	4,851.3	3,751.5	2,774.9	1,529.7
Total Current Liabilities	1,647.5	922.0	740.3	749.9	664.5	604.8	274.2
Long-Term Obligations	933.7	1,527.5	757.3	762.3	314.6	129.4	124.7
Net Stockholders' Equity	6,432.0	3,964.1	2,693.0	2,883.1	2,502.0	1,896.2	1,049.3
Net Working Capital	3,256.9	1,908.0	758.9	1,222.5	299.5	669.3	519.0
Year-end Shs. Outstg. (000)	567,300	504,400	427,000	422,600	417,600	412,800	407,600
STATISTICAL RECORD:							
Operating Profit Margin %	31.3	...	...	11.4	25.8	43.9	38.1
Net Profit Margin %	20.5	...	...	9.3	16.2	28.6	24.6
Return on Equity %	23.4	...	...	11.3	23.7	44.5	38.2
Return on Assets %	15.6	...	...	6.7	15.8	30.4	26.2
Debt/Total Assets %	9.7	21.9	16.2	15.7	8.4	4.7	8.2
Price Range	122.06-28.00	42.50-17.13	27.81-10.03	30.03-11.00	22.00-8.31	47.38-10.63	11.47-4.46
P/E Ratio	47.7-10.9	...	...	39.0-14.3	15.9-6.0	24.0-5.4	11.9-4.6
Average Yield %	...	...	...	...	0.3	0.3	0.5

Statistics are as originally reported. Adj. for stk. splits: 100%, 5/00; 5-for-2, 4/94; 2-for-1, 5/95 1 Incl. nonrecurr pre-tax gain $29.0 mill. on merger of subs. with ZEOS. 2 Incl. nonrecurr. chrg. $29.6 mill. for restr. 3 Incl. nonrecurr. gain after-tax $211.0, 1997; pre-tax $157.7 mill., 1998. 4 Incl. nonrecurr. pre-tax loss of $47.0 mill. & pre-tax gain of $10.0 mill. 5 Incl. nonrecurr. pre-tax loss of $23.0 mill. & pre-tax gain of $56.0 mill.

OFFICERS:
S. R. Appleton, Chmn., Pres., C.E.O.
W. G. Stover Jr., V.P., C.F.O.
R. W. Lewis, V.P., Corp. Sec., Gen. Couns.

INVESTOR CONTACT: Grant Jones, (208) 368-5781

PRINCIPAL OFFICE: 8000 South Federal Way, P.O. Box 6, Boise, ID 83707-0006

TELEPHONE NUMBER: (208) 368-4000
FAX: (208) 368-4435
WEB: www.micron.com
NO. OF EMPLOYEES: 18,800 (approx.)
SHAREHOLDERS: 3,702 (record)
ANNUAL MEETING: In Nov.
INCORPORATED: ID, Oct., 1978; reincorp., DE, Apr., 1984

INSTITUTIONAL HOLDINGS:
No. of Institutions: 369
Shares Held: 375,063,396
% Held: 62.9

INDUSTRY: Semiconductors and related devices (SIC: 3674)

TRANSFER AGENT(S): Wells Fargo Shareowner Services, South St. Paul, MN

NYSE SYMBOL MME
Rec. Pr. 20.33 (4/30/01)

MID ATLANTIC MEDICAL SERVICES, INC.

YIELD ...
P/E RATIO 20.3

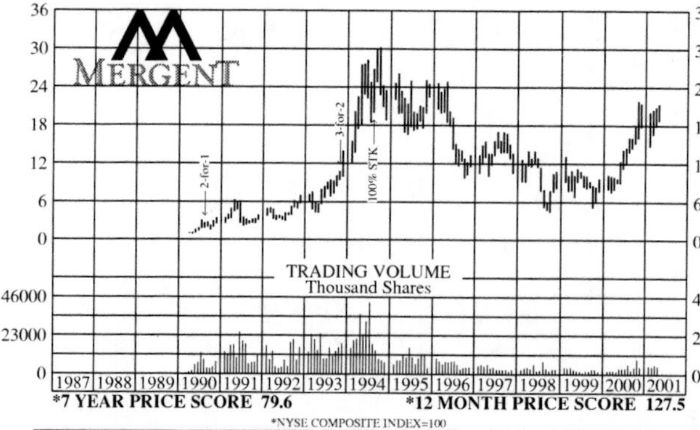

*7 YEAR PRICE SCORE 79.6 *12 MONTH PRICE SCORE 127.5

*NYSE COMPOSITE INDEX=100

INTERIM EARNINGS (Per Share):

Qtr.	Mar.	June	Sept.	Dec.
1997	0.02	0.06	0.10	0.13
1998	0.14	0.08	d0.15	0.13
1999	0.14	0.11	0.17	0.22
2000	0.22	0.19	0.28	0.31

INTERIM DIVIDENDS (Per Share):

Amt.	Decl.	Ex.	Rec.	Pay.
		No dividends paid.		

CAPITALIZATION (12/31/00):

	($000)	(%)
Deferred Income Tax........	2,174	1.0
Common & Surplus..........	225,990	99.0
Total..............................	228,164	100.0

RECENT DEVELOPMENTS: For the year ended 12/31/00, net income jumped 49.7% to $39.4 million versus $26.3 million in 1999. Results for 2000 included one-time tax adjustments totaling $1.3 million. Earnings benefited from increased premiums per member and a reduction in the medical care ratio, which is medical expenses as a percentage of health premium revenue. Total revenues increased 12.7% to $1.48 billion versus $1.32 billion the year before.

PROSPECTS: Earnings should benefit from increased commercial membership and MME's ongoing focus on disciplined pricing. During the January enrollment period, MME experienced a gain of 55,356 commercial memberships, representing the largest gain in Company history for the January enrollment period. As of 12/31/01, MME's commercial memberships totaled 762,700.

BUSINESS

MID ATLANTIC MEDICAL SERVICES, INC. is a regional holding company for healthcare organizations that provide comprehensive health-insurance products. The Company offers service coverage to Washington D.C., Virginia, Maryland, West Virginia, Delaware, North Carolina and Pennsylvania with a network of more than 14,000 providers and 300 hospitals. MME owns and operates three licensed health maintenance organizations: M.D.-Individual Practice Association, Inc., Optimum Choice, Inc. and Optimum Choice of the Carolinas, Inc. The Company also offers access to preferred provider network (PPOs) through Alliance PPO, LLC and Mid Atlantic Psychiatric Services, Inc. In addition, MAMSI Life and Health Insurance Company, a wholly-owned subsidiary, underwrites indemnity coverage of the Company's HMO point-of-service plans and offers various insurance policies. MME also operates home care companies such as HomeCall, Inc., FirstCall, Inc. and HomeCall Pharmaceutical Services, Inc. As of 12/31/00, membership totaled 1.8 million covered lives.

ANNUAL FINANCIAL DATA

	12/31/00	12/31/99	12/31/98	12/31/97	12/31/96	12/31/95	12/31/94
Earnings Per Share	**2 1.00**	**0.64**	**1 0.20**	**0.31**	**d0.06**	**1.28**	**1.15**
Cash Flow Per Share	**1.26**	**0.89**	**0.44**	**0.53**	**0.11**	**1.40**	**1.24**
Tang. Book Val. Per Share	**4.65**	**3.78**	**3.85**	**3.81**	**3.37**	**4.66**	**3.10**
INCOME STATEMENT (IN MILLIONS):							
Total Revenues	1,484.5	1,317.3	1,187.9	1,111.7	1,133.7	955.4	749.9
Costs & Expenses	1,417.5	1,267.2	1,164.9	1,080.0	1,130.8	853.0	659.1
Depreciation & Amort.	10.3	10.2	10.8	10.2	7.9	6.0	4.2
Operating Income	56.8	39.8	12.2	21.4	d4.9	96.3	86.6
Income Before Income Taxes	56.8	39.8	12.2	21.4	d4.9	96.3	86.6
Income Taxes	17.4	13.5	3.2	7.0	cr2.2	35.2	32.0
Net Income	2 39.4	26.3	1 9.0	14.5	d2.8	61.1	54.5
Cash Flow	49.7	36.6	19.8	24.7	5.1	67.2	58.8
Average Shs. Outstg. (000)	39,341	41,267	45,474	46,886	46,988	47,908	47,370
BALANCE SHEET (IN MILLIONS):							
Cash & Cash Equivalents	275.2	206.2	184.1	155.7	155.4	215.6	154.0
Total Current Assets	392.4	317.5	291.6	260.0	268.8	290.2	212.3
Net Property	47.2	43.7	45.0	57.0	45.2	38.7	33.7
Total Assets	467.0	388.6	362.8	342.8	334.7	354.2	268.5
Total Current Liabilities	238.9	198.5	168.4	131.9	150.0	136.6	120.3
Long-Term Obligations	...	...	...	0.1	0.1	0.2	5.3
Net Stockholders' Equity	226.0	186.8	191.2	208.3	184.4	217.2	141.3
Net Working Capital	153.5	119.0	123.1	128.1	118.9	153.7	92.0
Year-end Shs. Outstg. (000)	48,602	49,439	49,634	54,678	54,678	46,585	45,618
STATISTICAL RECORD:							
Operating Profit Margin %	3.8	3.0	1.0	1.9	...	10.1	11.5
Net Profit Margin %	2.7	2.0	0.8	1.3	...	6.4	7.3
Return on Equity %	17.4	14.1	4.7	7.0	...	28.1	38.6
Return on Assets %	8.4	6.8	2.5	4.2	...	17.3	20.3
Debt/Total Assets %	...	...	...	...	...	0.1	2.0
Price Range	21.88-7.50	13.13-5.13	14.00-4.44	17.06-10.00	24.88-9.75	26.13-16.50	30.25-12.06
P/E Ratio	21.9-7.5	20.5-8.0	70.0-22.2	55.0-32.2	...	20.4-12.9	26.3-10.5

Statistics are as originally reported. Adj. for 100% stk. split, 8/94. 1 Incl. nonrecurr. chgs. of $10.9 mill. 2 Incl. one-time tax adj. of $1.3 mill.

OFFICERS:
M. D. Groban, Chmn.
T. P. Barbera, Vice-Chmn., Pres., C.E.O.
R. E. Foss, Sr. Exec. V.P., C.F.O.

INVESTOR CONTACT: Diane L. King, Inv. Rel., (800) 544-2853

PRINCIPAL OFFICE: 4 Taft Court, Rockville, MD 20850

TELEPHONE NUMBER: (301) 294-5140
FAX: (301) 762-0658
WEB: www.mamsi.com

NO. OF EMPLOYEES: 2,461 full-time; 364 part-time

SHAREHOLDERS: 716 (approx.)

ANNUAL MEETING: In Apr.

INCORPORATED: DE, Oct., 1986

INSTITUTIONAL HOLDINGS:
No. of Institutions: 154
Shares Held: 31,510,728
% Held: 65.5

INDUSTRY: Hospital and medical service plans (SIC: 6324)

TRANSFER AGENT(S): Bank of New York, New York, NY

NYSE SYMBOL MZ
Rec. Pr. 16.70 (5/31/01)

MILACRON, INC.

YIELD 2.9%
P/E RATIO 8.1

MERGENT

TRADING VOLUME
Thousand Shares

*7 YEAR PRICE SCORE 55.6 *12 MONTH PRICE SCORE 114.5

*NYSE COMPOSITE INDEX=100

INTERIM EARNINGS (Per Share):

Qtr.	Mar.	June	Sept.	Dec.
1997	0.33	0.45	0.56	0.67
1998	0.44	0.52	0.47	0.62
1999	0.40	0.41	0.47	0.61
2000	0.41	0.47	0.53	0.65

INTERIM DIVIDENDS (Per Share):

Amt.	Decl.	Ex.	Rec.	Pay.
0.12Q	7/27/00	8/16/00	8/18/00	9/12/00
0.12Q	11/03/00	11/17/00	11/21/00	12/12/00
0.12Q	2/09/01	2/26/01	2/28/01	3/12/01
0.12Q	4/24/01	5/09/01	5/11/01	6/12/01

Indicated div.: $0.48 (Div. Reinv. Plan)

CAPITALIZATION (12/31/00):

	($000)	(%)
Long-Term Debt	382,600	44.1
Preferred Stock	6,000	0.7
Common & Surplus	478,400	55.2
Total	867,000	100.0

RECENT DEVELOPMENTS: For the twelve months ended 12/31/00, net earnings rose 3.1% to $72.3 million. The 2000 results included an after-tax restructuring charge of $1.9 million and an after-tax gain of $800,000 on divestitures of businesses. Results for 1999 included an after-tax restructuring charge of $10.9 million and an after-tax gain of $10.1 million on divestitures of businesses. Sales slipped 2.5% to $1.58 billion from $1.62 billion in 1999.

PROSPECTS: In the first half of 2001, the Company expects sales and orders to show continued year-over-year declines with the slowdown in automotive production and softness in other industrial sectors. Meanwhile, MZ expects earnings to remain at levels comparable to a year ago, due to restructuring efforts in 2000. Looking ahead, MZ should benefit from new product introductions, improvements in its blow molding operations, and ongoing efficiency gains.

BUSINESS

MILACRON, INC. (formerly Cincinnati Milacron) is engaged in plastics technologies and cutting process technologies for metalworking. MZ has major manufacturing facilities in North America and Europe. Milacron's plastics technologies segment includes injection molding machines, blow molding equipment, extrusion systems and wear items, mold bases, mold-making equipment and mold components, and aftermarket parts and services. The cutting process technologies segment includes carbide metalcutting inserts, insert holders, carbide and high-speed steel round tools, metalworking fluids, chemical and tool management services, precision grinding wheels, carbide wear parts and industrial magnets. MZ sold its machine tools segment on 10/2/98 for $187.0 million. On 12/31/99, MZ sold its European plastics extrusion systems business for $47.0 million.

REVENUES

(12/31/2000)	($000)	(%)
Plastics Technologies	873,800	55.2
Metalworking Technologies	710,400	44.8
Total	1,584,200	100.0

ANNUAL FINANCIAL DATA

	12/31/00	12/31/99	[3] 12/31/98	12/27/97	12/31/96	12/31/95	12/31/94
Earnings Per Share	**[5] 2.06**	**[4] 1.89**	**[2] 1.91**	**2.01**	**1.73**	**[1] 3.04**	**1.10**
Cash Flow Per Share	**3.73**	**3.47**	**3.38**	**3.36**	**3.13**	**4.39**	**1.97**
Tang. Book Val. Per Share	**1.94**	**1.77**	**1.93**	**5.93**	**5.28**	**7.72**	**4.50**
Dividends Per Share	**0.48**	**0.48**	**0.48**	**0.42**	**0.36**	**0.36**	**0.36**
Dividend Payout %	**23.3**	**25.4**	**25.1**	**20.9**	**20.8**	**11.8**	**32.7**
INCOME STATEMENT (IN MILLIONS):							
Total Revenues	1,584.2	1,624.7	1,514.7	1,896.7	1,729.7	1,649.3	1,197.1
Costs & Expenses	1,385.6	1,429.3	1,319.4	1,711.6	1,564.6	1,505.5	1,104.3
Depreciation & Amort.	58.4	58.3	57.4	53.7	50.9	43.6	28.6
Operating Income	140.2	137.1	137.9	127.1	111.1	159.1	64.2
Net Interest Inc./(Exp.)	d39.5	d38.2	d30.7	d26.5	d29.8	d24.8	d15.3
Income Before Income Taxes	100.7	98.9	107.2	100.6	81.3	134.3	48.9
Income Taxes	25.4	26.4	28.1	20.0	15.0	28.7	11.2
Equity Earnings/Minority Int.	d3.0	d2.4	d3.7	d4.3	d3.1	d2.3	...
Net Income	[5] 72.3	[4] 70.1	[2] 75.4	80.6	66.3	[1] 105.6	37.7
Cash Flow	130.5	128.2	132.6	134.1	117.0	149.0	66.1
Average Shs. Outstg. (000)	35,046	37,049	39,241	39,956	37,465	34,009	33,641
BALANCE SHEET (IN MILLIONS):							
Cash & Cash Equivalents	41.2	81.3	48.9	25.7	27.8	133.1	21.5
Total Current Assets	656.0	717.6	730.5	751.1	727.9	782.3	514.7
Net Property	305.5	323.2	350.9	343.1	319.1	265.5	198.8
Total Assets	1,464.9	1,536.7	1,557.1	1,392.5	1,336.3	1,197.1	787.6
Total Current Liabilities	406.1	556.9	550.9	425.4	409.6	389.6	363.3
Long-Term Obligations	382.6	298.1	335.7	304.2	301.9	332.2	143.0
Net Stockholders' Equity	484.4	490.9	476.6	471.9	446.2	270.7	157.8
Net Working Capital	249.9	160.7	179.6	325.7	318.3	392.7	151.4
Year-end Shs. Outstg. (000)	33,346	36,800	37,800	39,600	39,800	34,300	33,742
STATISTICAL RECORD:							
Operating Profit Margin %	8.8	8.4	9.1	6.7	6.4	9.6	5.4
Net Profit Margin %	4.6	4.3	5.0	4.2	3.8	6.4	3.1
Return on Equity %	14.9	14.3	15.8	17.1	14.9	39.0	23.9
Return on Assets %	4.9	4.6	4.8	5.8	5.0	8.8	4.8
Debt/Total Assets %	26.1	19.4	21.6	21.8	22.6	27.8	18.2
Price Range	18.25-12.06	24.50-13.50	33.75-14.63	29.88-17.88	29.25-18.38	33.63-19.88	27.63-18.63
P/E Ratio	8.9-5.9	13.0-7.1	17.7-7.7	14.9-8.9	16.9-10.6	11.1-6.5	25.1-16.9
Average Yield %	3.2	2.5	2.0	1.8	1.5	1.3	1.6

Statistics are as originally reported. [1] Incl. non-recurr. credit $56.4 mill. and Incl. non-recurr. chrg. $7.8 mill. [2] Bef. disc. opers. loss of $33.9 mill. [3] Reflects the sale of the Company's machine tools business. [4] Incl. net. non-recurr. chrg. $3.1 mill. [5] Incl. after-tax restruct. chrg. of $1.9 mill. and a gain on divest. of bus. of $800,000

OFFICERS:
D. J. Meyer, Chmn., C.E.O.
R. D. Brown, Pres., C.O.O.
R. P. Lienesch, V.P., C.F.O., Treas.

INVESTOR CONTACT: Investor Relations, (513) 487-5000

PRINCIPAL OFFICE: 2090 Florence Ave., Cincinnati, OH 45206

TELEPHONE NUMBER: (513) 487-5000
FAX: (513) 841-8991
WEB: www.milacron.com

NO. OF EMPLOYEES: 10,735 (avg.)

SHAREHOLDERS: 4,785 (approx.)

ANNUAL MEETING: In Apr.

INCORPORATED: DE, Apr., 1983

INSTITUTIONAL HOLDINGS:
No. of Institutions: 122
Shares Held: 22,426,941
% Held: 67.4

INDUSTRY: Machine tools, metal cutting types (SIC: 3541)

TRANSFER AGENT(S): Mellon Investor Services, L.L.C., Ridgefield Park, NJ

NYSE SYMBOL MCH
Rec. Pr. 16.80 (4/30/01)

MILLENNIUM CHEMICALS INC.

YIELD 3.6%
P/E RATIO 8.9

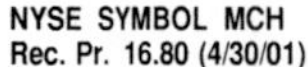

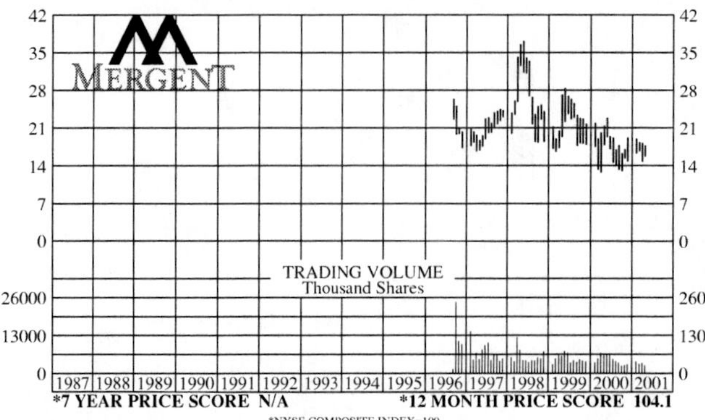

*7 YEAR PRICE SCORE N/A *12 MONTH PRICE SCORE 104.1

*NYSE COMPOSITE INDEX=100

INTERIM EARNINGS (Per Share):

Qtr.	Mar.	June	Sept.	Dec.
1998	0.66	0.57	0.42	0.52
1999	0.12	0.68	0.67	d5.86
2000	0.37	0.74	0.55	0.22

INTERIM DIVIDENDS (Per Share):

Amt.	Decl.	Ex.	Rec.	Pay.
0.15Q	7/25/00	9/11/00	9/13/00	9/29/00
0.15Q	11/07/00	11/29/00	12/01/00	12/18/00
0.15Q	1/31/01	3/12/01	3/14/01	3/30/01
0.15Q	5/02/01	6/11/01	6/13/01	6/29/01

Indicated div.: $0.60

CAPITALIZATION (12/31/00):

	($000)	(%)
Long-Term Debt	767,000	42.8
Deferred Income Tax	19,000	1.1
Minority Interest	22,000	1.2
Common & Surplus	983,000	54.9
Total	1,791,000	100.0

RECENT DEVELOPMENTS: For the year ended 12/31/00, net income was $122.0 million compared with a loss from continuing operations of $326.0 million in 1999. Results for 1999 included a charge of $639.0 million for the write-down of MCH's investment in Equistar. Net sales were $1.79 billion, up 12.8% from $1.59 billion in the prior year. Operating income jumped 26.8% to $213.0 million compared with $168.0 million in the previous year.

PROSPECTS: Results for 2001 are expected to be substantially lower than the previous year due to higher energy and raw material costs for the Company's petrochemical-based businesses, especially Equistar, and an uncertain economy. As a result, the Company plans to continue cost-reduction initiatives and focus on increasing its higher-margin businesses and product lines. MCH plans to increase its capital spending in 2001 to $130.0 million to $150.0 million.

BUSINESS

MILLENNIUM CHEMICALS INC. is an international chemicals concern with market positions in a broad range of commodity, industrial, performance and specialty chemicals. The Company conducts business through its operating subsidiaries: Millennium Inorganic Chemicals Inc., the second largest producer of titanium dioxide (TiO_2) in the world; Millennium Specialty Chemicals Inc., a major producer of terpene-based fragrance and flavor chemicals; and Millennium Petrochemicals Inc., the second largest manufacturer of acetic acid and vinyl acetate monomer in North America. As of 12/31/00, MCH also owned a 29.5% interest in Equistar Chemicals L.P., a producer of ethylene and polyethylene. In May 1999, the Company sold its 26.4% interest in Suburban Propane to Suburban Propane.

ANNUAL FINANCIAL DATA

	12/31/00	12/31/99	[5] 12/31/98	12/31/97	12/31/96	12/31/95	[1] 12/31/94
Earnings Per Share	1.89	[6] d4.71	[4] 2.17	[3] 2.47	[2] 1.84	5.10	...
Cash Flow Per Share	3.55	d3.08	3.57	5.48	4.62	7.63	...
Tang. Book Val. Per Share	9.23	8.95	14.95	12.94	...	36.30	...
Dividends Per Share	0.60	0.60	0.60	0.60	...	...	...
Dividend Payout %	31.7	...	27.6	24.3	...	...	...
INCOME STATEMENT (IN MILLIONS):							
Total Revenues	1,793.0	1,589.0	1,597.0	3,048.0	3,040.0	3,800.0	908.0
Costs & Expenses	1,473.0	1,308.0	1,284.0	2,373.0	2,556.0	2,717.0	646.0
Depreciation & Amort.	107.0	113.0	108.0	226.0	201.0	241.0	59.0
Operating Income	213.0	168.0	205.0	449.0	283.0	842.0	203.0
Net Interest Inc./(Exp.)	d77.0	d69.0	d72.0	d121.0	d177.0	d215.0	d55.0
Income Before Income Taxes	189.0	d530.0	202.0	342.0	330.0	554.0	143.0
Income Taxes	60.0	cr209.0	37.0	157.0	189.0	223.0	59.0
Net Income	122.0	[6] d326.0	[4] 163.0	[3] 185.0	[2] 141.0	331.0	84.0
Cash Flow	229.0	d213.0	271.0	411.0	342.0	572.0	143.0
Average Shs. Outstg. (000)	64,589	69,198	76,000	75,000	74,000	75,000	...
BALANCE SHEET (IN MILLIONS):							
Cash & Cash Equivalents	107.0	110.0	103.0	64.0	408.0	412.0	367.0
Total Current Assets	901.0	857.0	936.0	812.0	1,470.0	5,461.0	1,568.0
Net Property	957.0	995.0	1,044.0	851.0	2,031.0	2,262.0	2,153.0
Total Assets	3,220.0	3,250.0	4,100.0	4,326.0	5,601.0	10,043.0	10,024.0
Total Current Liabilities	783.0	495.0	379.0	441.0	767.0	877.0	835.0
Long-Term Obligations	767.0	1,023.0	1,039.0	1,327.0	2,360.0	3,304.0	3,274.0
Net Stockholders' Equity	983.0	1,015.0	1,578.0	1,464.0	1,318.0	4,801.0	4,858.0
Net Working Capital	118.0	362.0	557.0	371.0	703.0	4,584.0	733.0
Year-end Shs. Outstg. (000)	64,149	68,306	78,000	77,000	77,000	76,000	...
STATISTICAL RECORD:							
Operating Profit Margin %	11.9	10.6	12.8	14.7	9.3	22.2	22.4
Net Profit Margin %	6.8	...	10.2	6.1	4.6	8.7	9.3
Return on Equity %	12.4	...	10.3	12.6	10.7	6.9	1.7
Return on Assets %	3.8	...	4.0	4.3	2.5	3.3	0.8
Debt/Total Assets %	23.8	31.5	25.3	30.7	42.1	32.9	32.7
Price Range	22.88-12.69	28.38-16.56	37.13-18.25	24.50-16.63	26.38-17.25	...	...
P/E Ratio	12.1-6.7	...	17.1-8.4	9.9-6.7	14.3-9.4	...	...
Average Yield %	3.4	2.7	2.2	2.9	...	...	...

Statistics are as originally reported. [1] For 3 mos. due to fiscal year-end change. [2] Excl. loss fr. disc. opers. of $2.84 bill. [3] Incl. $37.0 mill. after-tax chg. rel. to formation of Equistar. [4] Incl. $10.0 mill. after-tax chg. fr. ins. settlements, $42.0 mill. tax benefit fr. prev. yrs. & $3.0 mill. chg. for trans. costs. [5] Results reflected MCH's decision to reduce prod. of TiO2. [6] Incl. $400.0 mill. net chg. fr. loss in value of Equistar invest. & excl. $38.0 mill. net gain fr. disc. ops.

OFFICERS:
W. M. Landuyt, Chmn., Pres., C.E.O.
J. E. Lushefski, Sr. V.P., C.F.O.

INVESTOR CONTACT: A. Mickey Foster, V.P., Investor Relations, (732) 933-5440

PRINCIPAL OFFICE: 230 Half Mile Road, Red Bank, NJ 07701-7015

TELEPHONE NUMBER: (732) 933-5000
FAX: (732) 933-5240
WEB: www.milleniumchem.com

NO. OF EMPLOYEES: 4,370 (approx.)

SHAREHOLDERS: 19,347

ANNUAL MEETING: In May

INCORPORATED: DE, Apr., 1996

INSTITUTIONAL HOLDINGS:
No. of Institutions: 108
Shares Held: 51,668,830
% Held: 81.4

INDUSTRY: Plastics materials and resins (SIC: 2821)

TRANSFER AGENT(S): First Chicago Trust Company of New York, Jersey City, NJ

NYSE SYMBOL MIL
Rec. Pr. 57.35 (4/30/01)

MILLIPORE CORPORATION

YIELD 0.8%
P/E RATIO 22.7

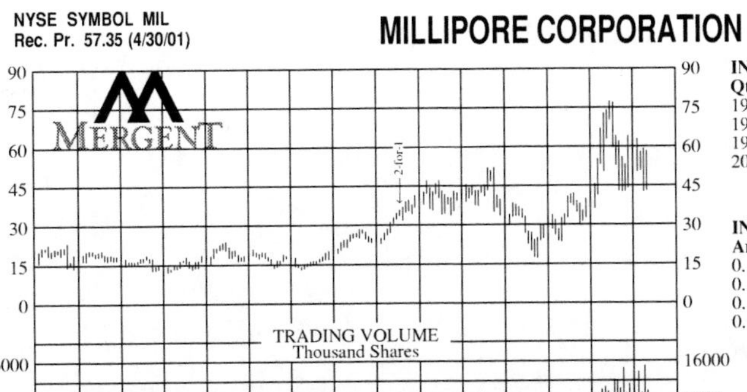

*7 YEAR PRICE SCORE 108.3 *12 MONTH PRICE SCORE 94.6
*NYSE COMPOSITE INDEX=100

INTERIM EARNINGS (Per Share):

Qtr.	Mar.	June	Sept.	Dec.
1997	d2.25	0.38	0.49	0.48
1998	0.71	0.15	d0.83	0.18
1999	0.25	0.32	0.37	0.47
2000	0.56	0.67	0.61	0.69

INTERIM DIVIDENDS (Per Share):

Amt.	Decl.	Ex.	Rec.	Pay.
0.11Q	6/15/00	6/28/00	6/30/00	7/25/00
0.11Q	9/21/00	10/04/00	10/06/00	10/24/00
0.11Q	12/07/00	12/26/00	12/28/00	1/23/01
0.11Q	2/15/01	2/28/01	3/02/01	4/24/01

Indicated div.: $0.44 (Div. Reinv. Plan)

CAPITALIZATION (12/31/00):

	($000)	(%)
Long-Term Debt	300,130	49.6
Common & Surplus	305,368	50.4
Total	605,498	100.0

RECENT DEVELOPMENTS: For the year ended 12/31/00, net income soared 85.3% to $119.2 million compared with $64.3 million in 1999. Results for 2000 included a charge of $1.5 million from a litigation settlement, a restructuring credit of $1.5 million, and a net gain of $4.2 million for the sale of securities. Results for 1999 included a restructuring credit of $5.2 million. Net sales rose 23.7% to $953.8 million from $771.2 million in the prior year. The biosciences segment benefited from revenue growth of 9.9%.

PROSPECTS: Revenues are expected to decline following the downturn in the microelectronics industry. In addition, the Company expects a negative currency effect on both near-term sales and profitability due to the lower value of the Japanese Yen compared with the U.S. dollar. As a result, the Company is implementing steps to reduce expenses consistent with the downturn. Separately, MIL announced an agreement with Proteome Systems Limited to develop and market novel kits in the field of proteomics.

BUSINESS

MILLIPORE CORPORATION develops, manufactures and sells products that are used primarily for the analysis and purification of fluids. MIL's products are based on a variety of membranes and certain other technologies that affect separations, principally through physical and chemical methods. The principal separation technologies utilized by the Company are based on membrane filters, and certain chemistries, resins and enzyme immunoassays. Membranes are used to filter either the wanted or the unwanted particulate, bacterial, molecular or viral entities from fluids, or to concentrate and retain such entities (in the fluid) for further processing. In 2000, revenues (and operating income) were derived: biosciences, 64.1% (64.8%); and microelectronics, 35.9% (35.2%).

ANNUAL FINANCIAL DATA

	12/31/00	12/31/99	12/31/98	12/31/97	12/31/96	12/31/95	12/31/94
Earnings Per Share	**4 2.53**	**3 1.42**	**2 0.22**	**d0.89**	**1 1.00**	**1.90**	**1.09**
Cash Flow Per Share	**3.51**	**2.40**	**1.23**	**0.04**	**1.70**	**2.51**	**1.59**
Tang. Book Val. Per Share	**5.25**	**2.36**	**1.37**	**1.64**	**3.66**	**4.95**	**4.67**
Dividends Per Share	**0.44**	**0.44**	**0.42**	**0.38**	**0.34**	**0.31**	**0.29**
Dividend Payout %	**17.4**	**31.0**	**190.8**	**...**	**34.0**	**16.3**	**26.6**
INCOME STATEMENT (IN THOUSANDS):							
Total Revenues	953,771	771,188	699,307	758,919	618,735	594,466	497,252
Costs & Expenses	734,685	617,416	655,564	717,151	527,736	447,912	378,989
Depreciation & Amort.	46,145	44,291	44,409	40,661	30,587	27,478	27,604
Operating Income	172,941	109,481	d666	1,107	60,412	119,076	90,659
Net Interest Inc./(Exp.)	d23,436	d27,130	d26,384	d27,547	d8,718	d8,941	d2,944
Income Before Income Taxes	153,666	82,351	8,544	d18,110	57,023	110,135	76,915
Income Taxes	34,472	18,023	cr1,320	20,674	13,401	24,781	17,306
Net Income	4 119,194	3 64,328	2 9,864	d38,784	1 43,622	85,354	59,609
Cash Flow	165,339	108,619	54,273	1,877	74,209	112,832	87,213
Average Shs. Outstg.	47,039	45,274	44,289	43,527	43,602	44,985	54,726
BALANCE SHEET (IN THOUSANDS):							
Cash & Cash Equivalents	58,398	51,060	36,022	20,269	46,870	23,758	30,236
Total Current Assets	465,483	358,947	304,752	352,408	311,912	261,759	258,804
Net Property	233,604	226,477	237,414	220,094	203,017	191,250	187,525
Total Assets	874,925	792,733	762,440	766,244	682,892	530,945	527,653
Total Current Liabilities	234,647	269,783	298,681	304,873	216,400	171,422	158,155
Long-Term Obligations	300,130	313,107	299,110	286,844	224,359	105,272	100,231
Net Stockholders' Equity	305,368	176,851	136,908	148,994	217,605	226,475	221,277
Net Working Capital	230,836	89,164	6,071	47,535	95,512	90,337	100,649
Year-end Shs. Outstg.	46,394	45,194	44,067	43,707	43,322	44,261	46,266
STATISTICAL RECORD:							
Operating Profit Margin %	18.1	14.2	...	0.1	9.8	20.0	18.2
Net Profit Margin %	12.5	8.3	1.4	...	7.1	14.4	12.0
Return on Equity %	39.0	36.4	7.2	...	20.0	37.7	26.9
Return on Assets %	13.6	8.1	1.3	...	6.4	16.1	11.3
Debt/Total Assets %	34.3	39.5	39.2	37.4	32.9	19.8	19.0
Price Range	77.38-36.25	42.13-23.44	38.44-17.25	52.00-33.50	47.13-33.63	41.50-22.88	28.50-19.19
P/E Ratio	30.6-14.3	29.7-16.5	174.6-78.4	...	47.1-33.6	21.8-12.0	26.1-17.6
Average Yield %	0.8	1.3	1.5	0.9	0.8	1.0	1.2

Statistics are as originally reported. Adj. for 2-for-1 split, 7/95. 1 Incl. $68.3 mill. ($1.21/sh. after-tax) pre-tax chg. to purch. R&D & $5.3 mill. gains fr. sale of eq. sec. 2 Incl. $33.6 mill. pre-tax restr. chg., $35.6 mill. gain fr. sale of equity secs. & excl. $5.8 mill. loss on the disp. of disc. ops. 3 Incl. cr$5.2 mill. restr. chgs. 4 Incl. $4.2 mill. net gain fr. sale of sec., $1.5 mill. chg. fr. litigation settlement & $1.5 mill. restr. credit.

OFFICERS:
C. W. Zadel, Chmn., C.E.O.
F. J. Lunger, Pres., C.O.O.
K. B. Allen, V.P., Treas., C.F.O.

INVESTOR CONTACT: Geoffrey E. Helliwell, Dir., Treasury Operations, (781) 533-2032

PRINCIPAL OFFICE: 80 Ashby Road, Bedford, MA 01730

TELEPHONE NUMBER: (781) 533-6000
FAX: (781) 533-3110
WEB: www.millipore.com

NO. OF EMPLOYEES: 5,200 (avg.)

SHAREHOLDERS: 2,751 (approx. record)

ANNUAL MEETING: In Apr.

INCORPORATED: MA, May, 1954

INSTITUTIONAL HOLDINGS:
No. of Institutions: 276
Shares Held: 43,156,673
% Held: 92.5

INDUSTRY: Analytical instruments (SIC: 3826)

TRANSFER AGENT(S): BankBoston, N.A., Boston, MA

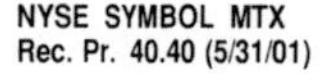

NYSE SYMBOL MTX
Rec. Pr. 40.40 (5/31/01)

MINERALS TECHNOLOGIES INC.

YIELD 0.2%
P/E RATIO 15.7

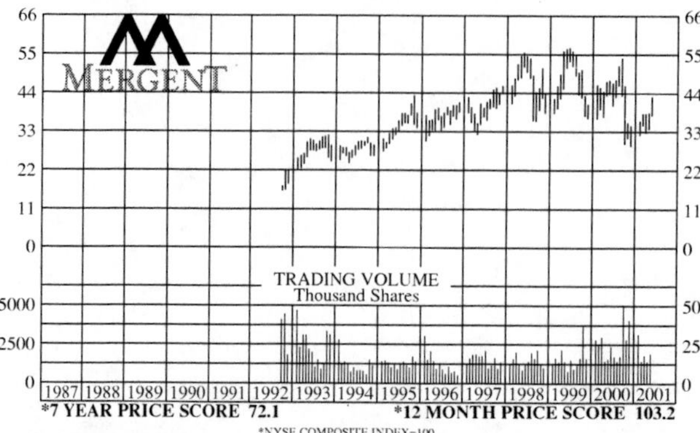

*7 YEAR PRICE SCORE 72.1 *12 MONTH PRICE SCORE 103.2
*NYSE COMPOSITE INDEX=100

INTERIM EARNINGS (Per Share):

Qtr.	Mar.	June	Sept.	Dec.
1997	0.47	0.55	0.61	0.59
1998	0.55	0.63	0.68	0.64
1999	0.62	0.70	0.71	0.78
2000	0.71	0.81	0.72	0.34

INTERIM DIVIDENDS (Per Share):

Amt.	Decl.	Ex.	Rec.	Pay.
0.025Q	4/27/00	5/24/00	5/26/00	6/16/00
0.025Q	8/24/00	9/01/00	9/06/00	9/18/00
0.025Q	10/26/00	11/01/00	11/03/00	12/18/00
0.025Q	1/25/01	3/02/01	3/06/01	3/16/01
0.025Q	4/26/01	5/23/01	5/25/01	6/15/01

Indicated div.: $0.10

CAPITALIZATION (12/31/00):

	($000)	(%)
Long-Term Debt	89,857	14.4
Deferred Income Tax	50,438	8.1
Common & Surplus	483,639	77.5
Total	623,934	100.0

RECENT DEVELOPMENTS: For the year ended 12/31/00, net income amounted to $54.2 million, down 12.7% versus $62.1 million in the previous year. Results for 2000 included special charges totaling $10.5 million due to the write-down of impaired PCC satellite assets and increased bad debt expense related to the bankruptcies of two major customers. Net sales improved 1.7% to $670.9 million compared with $662.5 million the year before.

PROSPECTS: On 1/23/01, the Company announced that MINTEQ International Inc., a MTX subsidiary, has entered into an agreement to purchase the refractories business of Martin Marietta Magnesia Specialties Inc. The acquisition should generate cost-savings for MTX through improved logistics and operating efficiencies, an expanded product line and combined sourcing of raw materials. The acquisition should be accretive to earnings within a year of operation.

BUSINESS

MINERALS TECHNOLOGIES INC. is a resource- and technology-based corporation that develops and produces performance-enhancing minerals, mineral-based and synthetic mineral products for the paper, steel, polymer and other manufacturing industries. The Company has three product lines: precipitated calcium carbonate (PCC); monolithic refractory materials, which are used to resist the effects of high temperatures; and mineral-based products including limestone, lime, talc, calcium, and metallurgical wire products.

QUARTERLY DATA

(12/31/2000)	Rev	Inc
1st Quarter	160,929	15,025
2nd Quarter	172,216	17,153
3rd Quarter	167,296	15,134
4th Quarter	170,476	6,896

ANNUAL FINANCIAL DATA

	12/31/00	12/31/99	12/31/98	12/31/97	12/31/96	12/31/95	12/31/94
Earnings Per Share	**[1] 2.58**	**2.80**	**2.50**	**2.18**	**1.91**	**1.75**	**1.48**
Cash Flow Per Share	**5.48**	**5.45**	**4.81**	**4.47**	**3.95**	**3.53**	**3.06**
Tang. Book Val. Per Share	**24.22**	**20.85**	**22.42**	**20.72**	**19.83**	**18.37**	**16.86**
Dividends Per Share	**0.10**	**0.11**	**0.10**	**0.10**	**0.10**	**0.10**	**0.10**
Dividend Payout %	**3.9**	**3.9**	**4.0**	**4.6**	**5.2**	**5.7**	**6.8**
INCOME STATEMENT (IN THOUSANDS):							
Total Revenues	670,917	637,519	609,193	602,335	555,988	524,451	472,637
Costs & Expenses	525,316	481,301	463,662	469,171	442,387	425,447	384,247
Depreciation & Amort.	60,795	58,675	53,084	52,936	46,183	40,330	35,800
Operating Income	84,806	97,543	92,447	80,228	67,418	58,674	52,590
Net Interest Inc./(Exp.)	d4,165	d3,948	d3,772	d5,443	d4,933	d1,483	d2,838
Income Before Income Taxes	79,772	92,535	86,342	72,188	62,624	58,004	49,270
Income Taxes	23,735	28,920	27,360	23,104	19,488	18,850	16,180
Equity Earnings/Minority Int.	d1,829	d1,499	d1,758	1,228	d39	375	256
Net Income	[1] 54,208	62,116	57,224	50,312	43,097	39,529	33,346
Cash Flow	115,003	120,791	110,308	103,248	89,280	79,859	69,146
Average Shs. Outstg.	21,004	22,150	22,926	23,113	22,621	22,633	22,603
BALANCE SHEET (IN THOUSANDS):							
Cash & Cash Equivalents	6,692	20,378	20,697	41,525	15,446	11,318	56,240
Total Current Assets	215,357	219,947	210,830	226,582	202,280	182,425	196,554
Net Property	548,209	521,996	524,529	500,731	501,067	455,809	382,534
Total Assets	799,832	769,131	760,912	741,407	713,861	649,144	588,124
Total Current Liabilities	133,527	117,542	97,938	94,218	86,740	95,679	60,710
Long-Term Obligations	89,857	75,238	88,167	101,571	104,900	67,927	83,031
Net Stockholders' Equity	483,639	535,920	489,163	466,997	448,250	416,153	381,098
Net Working Capital	81,830	102,405	112,892	132,364	115,540	86,746	135,844
Year-end Shs. Outstg.	19,967	25,705	21,814	22,540	22,600	22,653	22,610
STATISTICAL RECORD:							
Operating Profit Margin %	12.6	15.3	15.2	13.3	12.1	11.2	11.1
Net Profit Margin %	8.1	9.7	9.4	8.4	7.8	7.5	7.1
Return on Equity %	11.2	11.6	11.7	10.8	9.6	9.5	8.7
Return on Assets %	6.8	8.1	7.5	6.8	6.0	6.1	5.7
Debt/Total Assets %	11.2	9.8	11.6	13.7	14.7	10.5	14.1
Price Range	54.06-28.94	57.00-36.75	55.56-35.88	46.13-32.13	41.38-30.25	43.25-27.25	31.38-24.00
P/E Ratio	21.0-11.2	20.4-13.1	22.2-14.3	21.2-14.7	21.7-15.8	24.7-15.6	21.2-16.2
Average Yield %	0.2	0.2	0.2	0.3	0.3	0.3	0.4

Statistics are as originally reported. [1] Includes special charges totaling $10.5 million ($0.31/sh.)

OFFICERS:
J. P. Valles, Chmn.
P. R. Saueracker, C.E.O.
N. M. Bardach, V.P., C.F.O., Treas.

INVESTOR CONTACT: Rick B. Honey, Dir. Corp. Comm., (212) 878-1831

PRINCIPAL OFFICE: 405 Lexington Avenue, New York, NY 10174-1901

TELEPHONE NUMBER: (212) 878-1800
FAX: (212) 878-1801
WEB: www.mineralstech.com

NO. OF EMPLOYEES: 2,200 (approx.)

SHAREHOLDERS: 239 (approx.)

ANNUAL MEETING: In May

INCORPORATED: DE, Feb., 1968

INSTITUTIONAL HOLDINGS:
No. of Institutions: 126
Shares Held: 18,851,791
% Held: 95.6

INDUSTRY: Industrial organic chemicals, nec (SIC: 2869)

TRANSFER AGENT(S): State Street Bank and Trust Company, Boston, MA

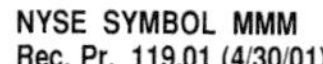

NYSE SYMBOL MMM
Rec. Pr. 119.01 (4/30/01)

MINNESOTA MINING & MANUFACTURING COMPANY

YIELD 2.0%
P/E RATIO 25.6

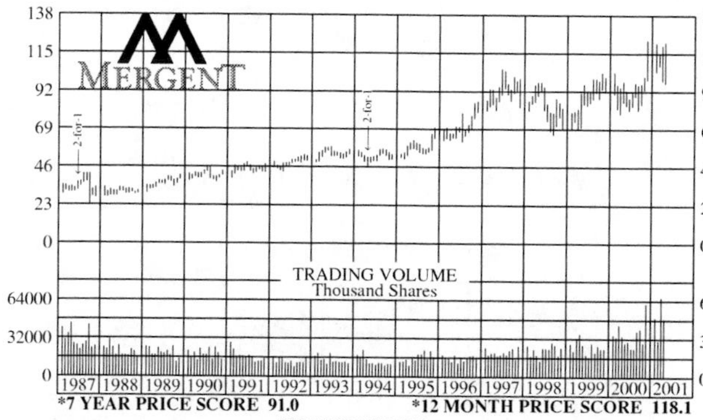

*7 YEAR PRICE SCORE 91.0 — *12 MONTH PRICE SCORE 118.1

*NYSE COMPOSITE INDEX=100

INTERIM EARNINGS (Per Share):

Qtr.	Mar.	June	Sept.	Dec.
1997	0.99	1.01	2.25	0.89
1998	0.98	0.94	0.44	0.61
1999	0.95	1.17	1.13	1.10
2000	1.21	1.18	1.25	1.00

INTERIM DIVIDENDS (Per Share):

Amt.	Decl.	Ex.	Rec.	Pay.
0.58Q	8/04/00	8/23/00	8/25/00	9/12/00
0.58Q	11/13/00	11/21/00	11/24/00	12/12/00
0.60Q	2/12/01	2/21/01	2/23/01	3/12/01
0.60Q	5/08/01	5/16/01	5/18/01	6/12/01

Indicated div.: $2.40 (Div. Reinv. Plan)

CAPITALIZATION (12/31/00):

	($000)	(%)
Long-Term Debt	971,000	12.9
Common & Surplus	6,531,000	87.1
Total	7,502,000	100.0

RECENT DEVELOPMENTS: For the year ended 12/31/00, MMM reported income of $1.86 billion, before an accounting charge of $75.0 million, compared with net income of $1.76 billion in the previous year. Earnings included non-recurring items that resulted in a net after-tax charge of $15.0 million and a net after-tax gain of $52.0 million in 2000 and 1999, respectively. Net sales grew 6.2% to $16.72 billion.

PROSPECTS: The Company announced a restructuring plan that will lower MMM's employment by about 5,000 jobs worldwide. Also, MMM launched several initiatives designed to accelerate growth, including leveraging its global size to lower costs of raw materials and other supplies, and reduce indirect costs. Morever, MMM will continue to invest in research and development, and expects to continue to benefit from its international market expansion.

BUSINESS

MINNESOTA, MINING & MANUFACTURING COMPANY (3M) is a worldwide producer of a diverse variety of industrial and consumer products. 3M operates in six business sectors: Industrial provides telecommunications products, industrial tapes, and industrial abrasives; Electro and Communications provides electronic and electrical products; Consumer and Office provides consumer and office products; Transportation, Graphics and Safety provides reflective sheeting, high-performance graphics, respirators, automotive components, and optical films; Specialty Material provides specialty materials; and Health Care provides skin health products, medical/surgical supplies and devices, infection control, cardiovascular systems, health care information systems, pharmaceuticals, and dental products.

BUSINESS LINE ANALYSIS

(12/31/2000)	REV (%)	INC (%)
Industrial	21.1	21
Transportation, Graphics	21	25.6
Health Care	18.7	22.1
Consumer & Office	17	14.2
Electro & Communications	14.8	13.2
Specialty Material	7.2	1.9
Corporate and Unallocated	0.2	2
Total	100.0	100.0

ANNUAL FINANCIAL DATA

	12/31/00	12/31/99	12/31/98	12/31/97	12/31/96	12/31/95	12/31/94
Earnings Per Share	**[6] 4.64**	**[5] 4.34**	**[4] 2.97**	**[3] 5.06**	**3.63**	**[2] 3.11**	**[1] 3.13**
Cash Flow Per Share	**7.21**	**6.55**	**5.10**	**7.14**	**5.74**	**5.15**	**5.73**
Tang. Book Val. Per Share	**16.49**	**15.77**	**14.80**	**14.63**	**15.07**	**16.43**	**16.03**
Dividends Per Share	**2.32**	**2.24**	**2.20**	**2.12**	**1.92**	**1.88**	**1.76**
Dividend Payout %	**50.0**	**51.6**	**74.1**	**41.9**	**52.9**	**60.4**	**56.2**
INCOME STATEMENT (IN MILLIONS):							
Total Revenues	16,724.0	15,659.0	15,021.0	15,070.0	14,236.0	13,460.0	15,079.0
Costs & Expenses	12,641.0	11,803.0	12,116.0	11,525.0	10,862.0	10,380.0	11,727.0
Depreciation & Amort.	1,025.0	900.0	866.0	870.0	883.0	859.0	1,101.0
Operating Income	3,058.0	2,956.0	2,039.0	2,675.0	2,491.0	2,221.0	2,251.0
Net Interest Inc./(Exp.)	d111.0	d109.0	d139.0	d94.0	d79.0	d102.0	d87.0
Income Before Income Taxes	2,974.0	2,880.0	1,952.0	3,440.0	2,479.0	2,168.0	2,154.0
Income Taxes	1,025.0	1,032.0	685.0	1,241.0	886.0	785.0	771.0
Net Income	[6] 1,857.0	[5] 1,763.0	[4] 1,213.0	[3] 2,121.0	1,516.0	[2] 1,306.0	[1] 1,322.0
Cash Flow	2,882.0	2,663.0	2,079.0	2,991.0	2,399.0	2,165.0	2,423.0
Average Shs. Outstg. (000)	399,900	406,500	408,000	419,000	418,000	420,000	423,000
BALANCE SHEET (IN MILLIONS):							
Cash & Cash Equivalents	302.0	441.0	448.0	477.0	744.0	772.0	491.0
Total Current Assets	6,379.0	6,066.0	6,318.0	6,168.0	6,486.0	6,395.0	6,928.0
Net Property	5,823.0	5,656.0	5,566.0	5,034.0	4,844.0	4,638.0	5,054.0
Total Assets	14,522.0	13,896.0	14,153.0	13,238.0	13,364.0	14,183.0	13,496.0
Total Current Liabilities	4,754.0	3,819.0	4,386.0	3,983.0	3,606.0	6,096.0	3,605.0
Long-Term Obligations	971.0	1,480.0	1,614.0	1,015.0	851.0	1,203.0	1,031.0
Net Stockholders' Equity	6,531.0	6,289.0	5,936.0	5,926.0	6,284.0	6,884.0	6,734.0
Net Working Capital	1,625.0	2,247.0	1,932.0	2,185.0	2,880.0	299.0	3,323.0
Year-end Shs. Outstg. (000)	396,085	398,700	401,000	405,000	417,000	419,000	420,000
STATISTICAL RECORD:							
Operating Profit Margin %	18.3	18.9	13.6	17.8	17.5	16.5	14.9
Net Profit Margin %	11.1	11.3	8.1	14.1	10.6	9.7	8.8
Return on Equity %	28.4	28.0	20.4	35.8	24.1	19.0	19.6
Return on Assets %	12.8	12.7	8.6	16.0	11.3	9.2	9.8
Debt/Total Assets %	6.7	10.7	11.4	7.7	6.4	8.5	7.6
Price Range	122.94-78.19	103.38-69.31	97.88-65.63	105.50-80.00	85.88-61.25	69.88-50.75	57.13-46.38
P/E Ratio	26.5-16.9	23.8-16.0	33.0-22.1	20.8-15.8	23.7-16.9	22.5-16.3	18.3-14.8
Average Yield %	2.3	2.6	2.7	2.3	2.6	3.1	3.4

Statistics are as originally reported. [1] Incl. pre-tax chg. of $35.0 mill. [2] Bef. disc. ops. loss of $330.0 mill. [3] Incl. $803.0 mill. gain fr. sale of outdoor adver. bus. [4] Bef. extraord. chrg. of $38.0 mill.; incl. pre-tax restruct. chrg. of $493.0 mill. & a gain on divestiture of $10.0 mill. [5] Incl. pre-tax chrg. of $73.0 mill. rel. to litig., a gain on divest. of $147.0 mill., & a $26.0 mill. gain. [6] Incl. a net after-tax chrg. of $15.0 mill. & excl. an acctg. chrg. of $75.0 mill.

OFFICERS:
W. J. McNerney Jr., Chmn., C.E.O.
J. J. Ursu, Sr. V.P., Gen. Couns.

INVESTOR CONTACT: Jon Greer, Director, Investor Relations, (651) 736-1915

PRINCIPAL OFFICE: 3M Center, St. Paul, MN 55144

TELEPHONE NUMBER: (651) 733-1110
FAX: (651) 733-9973
WEB: www.3m.com

NO. OF EMPLOYEES: 75,000 (approx.)

SHAREHOLDERS: 129,109 (record)

ANNUAL MEETING: In May

INCORPORATED: MN, July, 1902; reincorp., DE, June, 1929

INSTITUTIONAL HOLDINGS:
No. of Institutions: 848
Shares Held: 278,210,585
% Held: 70.0

INDUSTRY: Adhesives and sealants (SIC: 2891)

TRANSFER AGENT(S): Wells Fargo Shareowner Services, St. Paul, MN

NYSE SYMBOL MIR
Rec. Pr. 39.30 (5/31/01)

MIRANT CORP.

YIELD ...
P/E RATIO 30.2

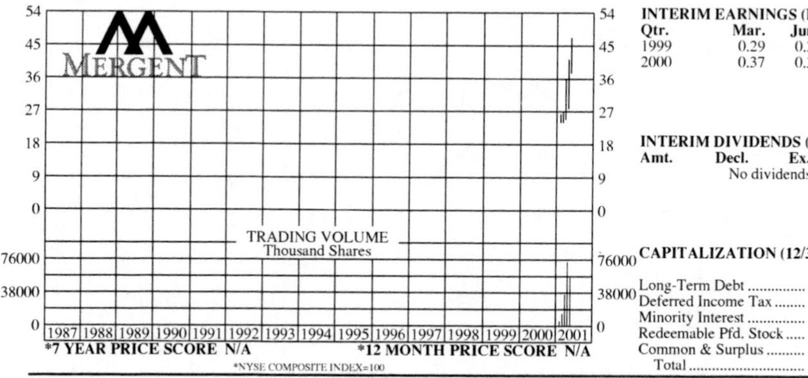

*7 YEAR PRICE SCORE N/A *12 MONTH PRICE SCORE N/A

*NYSE COMPOSITE INDEX=100

INTERIM EARNINGS (Per Share):

Qtr.	Mar.	June	Sept.	Dec.
1999	0.29	0.26	0.57	0.25
2000	0.37	0.34	0.36	0.23

INTERIM DIVIDENDS (Per Share):

Amt.	Decl.	Ex.	Rec.	Pay.

No dividends paid.

CAPITALIZATION (12/31/00):

	($000)	(%)
Long-Term Debt	390,000	7.1
Deferred Income Tax	53,000	1.0
Minority Interest	312,000	5.7
Redeemable Pfd. Stock	587,000	10.7
Common & Surplus	4,136,000	75.5
Total	5,478,001	100.0

RECENT DEVELOPMENTS: For the year ended 12/31/00, the Company reported income of $332.0 million, before income from discontinued operations of $27.0 million, versus income of $362.0 million, before discontinued operations income of $10.0 million, in the previous year. Results included write-down of assets of $18.0 million and $60.0 million in 2000 and 1999, respectively. Operating revenues skyrocketed to $13.32 billion compared with $2.27 billion in the prior year. Operating income totaled $664.0 million, an increase of 49.5% from $444.0 million in 1999.

PROSPECTS: On 3/30/01, the Company acquired an 80.0% operating stake in Jamaica Public Services Company for approximately $201.0 million. MIR expects this acquisition to increase yearly earnings by approximately $0.03 per share in 2001 and approximately $0.10 per share by 2005. Going forward, MIR anticipates strong growth from its integrated North American business unit mainly due to increases in gas marketing volumes. As a result, MIR expects to achieve earnings per share in the range of $1.55 to $1.60 for 2001.

BUSINESS

MIRANT CORP. develops, constructs, owns and operates power plants, and sells wholesale electricity, gas and other energy-related commodity products. The Company has operations in North America, Europe and Asia. As of 12/31/00, the Company owns or controls more than 20,000 megawatts of electric generating capacity around the world, with approximately another 9,000 megawatts under development. Southern Company sold 19.7% of MIR's stock through an initial public offering in September 2000, and spun off the remaining 80.3% to Southern shareholders on 4/2/01. On 8/10/00, the Company acquired Vastar Resources, Inc.'s 40% interest in Mirant Americas Energy Marketing for $250.0 million.

REVENUES

(12/31/00)	($000)	(%)
Americas	12,490	93.8
Europe	314	2.3
Asia-Pacific	502	3.8
Corporate	9	0.1
Total	13,315	100.0

ANNUAL FINANCIAL DATA

	[2] 12/31/00	12/31/99	12/31/98	12/31/97
Earnings Per Share	[1] 1.15	[1] 1.33	[1] d0.04	[1] d0.09
Cash Flow Per Share	2.30	...	...	...
Tang. Book Val. Per Share	0.31	...	...	...
INCOME STATEMENT (IN MILLIONS):				
Total Revenues	13,315.0	2,268.0	1,819.0	3,750.0
Costs & Expenses	12,318.0	1,538.0	1,595.0	3,275.0
Depreciation & Amort.	333.0	286.0	229.0	203.0
Operating Income	664.0	444.0	d5.0	272.0
Net Interest Inc./(Exp.)	d428.0	d330.0	d284.0	d207.0
Income Before Income Taxes	502.0	674.0	d55.0	180.0
Income Taxes	86.0	129.0	cr123.0	175.0
Equity Earnings/Minority Int.	d84.0	d183.0	d80.0	d29.0
Net Income	[1] 332.0	[1] 362.0	[1] d12.0	[1] d24.0
Cash Flow	265.0	483.0	217.0	179.0
Average Shs. Outstg. (000)	288,700	...	...	...
BALANCE SHEET (IN MILLIONS):				
Cash & Cash Equivalents	1,280.0	373.0	620.0	398.0
Total Current Assets	9,152.0	1,285.0	1,466.0	398.0
Net Property	5,681.0	6,025.0	4,691.0	4,255.0
Total Assets	24,136.0	13,863.0	12,054.0	5,812.0
Total Current Liabilities	9,775.0	3,215.0	3,052.0	830.0
Long-Term Obligations	390.0	397.0	420.0	...
Net Stockholders' Equity	4,136.0	3,102.0	2,642.0	2,132.0
Net Working Capital	d623.0	d1,930.0	d1,586.0	d432.0
Year-end Shs. Outstg. (000)	338,701	...	...	...
STATISTICAL RECORD:				
Operating Profit Margin %	5.0	19.6	...	7.3
Net Profit Margin %	2.5	16.0	...	...
Return on Equity %	8.0	11.7	...	...
Return on Assets %	1.4	2.6	...	...
Debt/Total Assets %	1.6	2.9	3.5	...

Statistics are as originally reported. [1] Bef. discont. oper. income, 2000, $27.0 mill.; 1999, $10.0 mill.; 1998, $12.0 mill.; 1997, $8.0 mill. [2] Incls. the acq. of Vastar's 40% int. in Mirant Americas Energy Marketing.

OFFICERS:
A. W. Dahlberg, Chmn.
S. M. Fuller, Pres., C.E.O.
F. D. Kuester, Sr. V.P.

INVESTOR CONTACT: Hank Pennington, (678) 579-7592

PRINCIPAL OFFICE: 1155 Perimeter Center West, Suite 100, Atlanta, GA 30338

TELEPHONE NUMBER: (678) 579-5000
WEB: www.mirant.com

NO. OF EMPLOYEES: 7,000 (approx.)

SHAREHOLDERS: N/A

ANNUAL MEETING: In May

INCORPORATED: DE, Apr., 1993

INSTITUTIONAL HOLDINGS:
No. of Institutions: 177
Shares Held: 80,351,540
% Held: 23.7

INDUSTRY: Electric and other services combined (SIC: 4931)

TRANSFER AGENT(S): Mellon Investor Services, Ridgefield Park, NJ

NYSE SYMBOL MND
Rec. Pr. 54.06 (5/31/01)

MITCHELL ENERGY & DEVELOPMENT CORP.

YIELD 1.0%
P/E RATIO 10.6

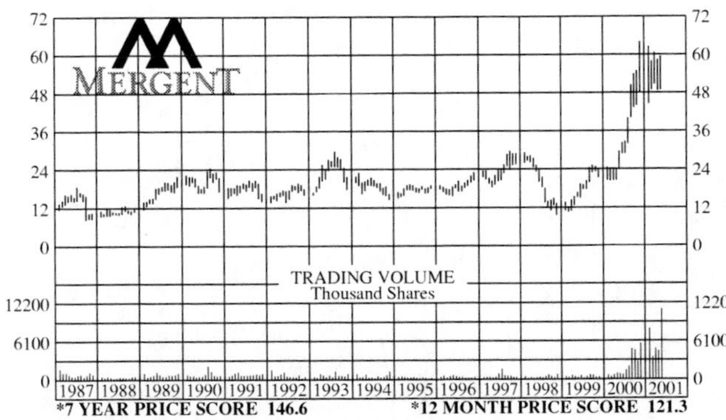

*7 YEAR PRICE SCORE 146.6 *12 MONTH PRICE SCORE 121.3
*NYSE COMPOSITE INDEX=100

INTERIM EARNINGS (Per Share):

Qtr.	Apr.	July	Oct.	Jan.
1996-97	0.45	0.40	0.36	0.78
1997-98	0.32	d0.15	0.36	0.35
1998-99	0.05	d0.09	d0.07	d0.96
1999-00	0.12	0.55	0.60	0.72
Qtr.	**Mar.**	**June**	**Sept.**	**Dec.**
2000	0.87	0.89	1.48	1.88

INTERIM DIVIDENDS (Per Share):

Amt.	Decl.	Ex.	Rec.	Pay.
0.25Sp	6/08/00	6/20/00	6/22/00	7/06/00
0.133Q	8/30/00	9/13/00	9/15/00	10/03/00
0.133Q	12/13/00	12/26/00	12/28/00	1/12/01
0.133Q	2/21/01	3/09/01	3/13/01	4/02/01
0.133Q	5/09/01	6/11/01	6/13/01	7/03/01

Indicated div.: $0.53

CAPITALIZATION (12/31/00):

	($000)	(%)
Long-Term Debt	300,342	26.7
Deferred Income Tax	203,919	18.1
Common & Surplus	620,186	55.2
Total	1,124,447	100.0

RECENT DEVELOPMENTS: For the year ended 12/31/00, net earnings soared to $257.1 million versus $67.3 million a year earlier. Results for 2000 and 1999 included net unusual credits totaling $16.1 million and $254,000, respectively. Revenues surged 87.0% to $1.67 billion, driven by increases in production volumes and energy prices. Natural gas sales rose 24.8% to 305,500 thousand cubic feet (Mcf) per day and natural gas liquids production advanced 13.2% to 49,800 barrels per day.

PROSPECTS: Near-term prospects are positive, reflecting historically high natural gas and crude oil prices and rising production. MND expects to increase gas and natural gas liquids sales over the next three years at compounded annual rates exceeding 20.0% and 10.0%, respectively. The Company's 2001 capital budget has been set at $473.0 million, a 45.5% increase versus the prior year. Of the total budget, $346.0 million is allocated to exploration and production and $124.0 million to gas services.

BUSINESS

MITCHELL ENERGY & DEVELOPMENT CORP. is an independent producer of natural gas and natural gas liquids (NGLs.) Principal energy operations include the exploration, development and production of natural gas and crude oil, the operation of natural gas gathering systems and the production of NGLs. As of 12/31/00, MND owned or had interests in more than 3,400 wells and 1.1 million acres of leases. The Company also owns and operates 6 gas processing plants and 9,100 miles of gas gathering pipeline. As of 12/31/00, proved reserves totaled 1,507.7 billion cubic feet of gas equivalent comprised of 1,436.0 billion cubic feet of natural gas and 12.0 million barrels of crude oil. On 7/31/97, MND sold its former real estate subsidiary, The Woodlands, which essentially withdrew the Company from the real estate business.

REVENUES

(12/31/00)	Rev($000)	Inc(%)
Exploration & Production	531,228	31.8
Gas Services	1,140,906	68.2
Total	1,672,134	100.0

ANNUAL FINANCIAL DATA

	5 12/31/00	1/31/00	1/31/99	1/31/98	1/31/97	1/31/96	1/31/95
Earnings Per Share	4 5.13	3 2.00	1 d1.11	2 0.71	3 1.99	3 0.71	0.87
Cash Flow Per Share	4.04	4.27	2.35	2.82	4.00	3.65	3.23
Tang. Book Val. Per Share	14.40	8.11	6.61	8.42	10.71	9.26	9.09
Dividends Per Share	0.76	0.48	0.48	0.72	0.48	0.48	0.48
Dividend Payout %	7.4	12.2	...	48.6	24.1	67.6	55.2
INCOME STATEMENT (IN MILLIONS):							
Total Revenues	1,672.1	934.0	701.4	790.5	1,104.8	1,071.7	894.6
Costs & Expenses	1,146.7	648.7	589.0	621.5	807.4	820.8	652.2
Depreciation & Amort.	144.6	112.5	168.4	105.6	104.5	152.6	124.2
Operating Income	380.8	172.8	d56.0	63.4	193.0	98.3	118.1
Net Interest Inc./(Exp.)	d28.8	d33.8	d34.2	d18.5	d29.8	d35.9	d41.2
Income Before Income Taxes	358.0	146.6	d84.6	50.7	159.6	58.3	70.6
Income Taxes	100.8	49.3	cr31.6	12.9	56.4	21.2	24.7
Net Income	4 257.1	3 97.2	1 d53.0	2 37.8	3 103.2	3 37.1	45.8
Cash Flow	401.8	209.8	115.5	143.4	207.7	189.8	170.0
Average Shs. Outstg. (000)	99,375	49,118	49,106	50,910	...	...	...
BALANCE SHEET (IN MILLIONS):							
Cash & Cash Equivalents	23.5	16.0	20.3	105.3	79.7	21.3	12.0
Total Current Assets	268.2	75.4	79.6	267.7	348.8	244.3	183.8
Net Property	1,206.0	1,055.4	1,033.7	954.7	775.9	719.5	734.1
Total Assets	1,519.8	1,168.1	1,146.5	1,252.0	1,852.7	1,835.5	1,855.9
Total Current Liabilities	304.1	152.3	241.8	198.7	382.2	221.9	170.2
Long-Term Obligations	300.3	369.3	362.5	414.3	601.3	827.9	895.0
Net Stockholders' Equity	620.2	398.5	324.8	412.9	555.3	481.9	475.0
Net Working Capital	d35.9	d76.8	d162.2	69.0	d33.5	22.4	13.6
Year-end Shs. Outstg. (000)	43,082	49,113	49,117	49,045	51,841	52,060	52,282
STATISTICAL RECORD:							
Operating Profit Margin %	22.8	18.5	...	8.0	17.5	9.2	13.2
Net Profit Margin %	15.4	10.4	...	4.8	9.3	3.5	5.1
Return on Equity %	41.5	24.4	...	9.2	18.6	7.7	9.6
Return on Assets %	16.9	8.3	...	3.0	5.6	2.0	2.5
Debt/Total Assets %	19.8	31.6	31.6	33.1	32.5	45.1	48.2
Price Range	64.00-20.25	25.25-10.50	29.25-9.63	29.75-18.25	23.00-15.50	19.38-14.88	22.88-14.50
P/E Ratio	6.2-2.0	6.4-2.7	...	20.1-12.3	11.6-7.8	27.3-20.9	26.3-16.7
Average Yield %	1.8	2.7	2.5	3.0	2.5	2.8	2.6

Statistics are as originally reported. 1 Incl. aft.-tax chrgs. of $44.5 mil.; bef. inc. of $3.3 mil. fr. disc. ops. 2 Incl. non-recur. chrgs. of $19.8 mil.; bef. loss fr. disc. ops. of $59.7 mil. & extraord. chrg. of $13.3 mil. 3 Incl. net cr. 1/31/00, $16.7 mil.; non-recur. cr. 1/31/97, $1.2 mil.; chrgs. 1/31/96, $9.1 mil. 4 Incl. net non-recur. cr. of $16.1 mil.; Company changed fiscal year fr. 1/31 to 12/31. 5 Each Cl. B com. sh. was reclass. into one Cl. A com. sh. on 6/29/00.

OFFICERS:
G. P. Mitchell, Chmn., C.E.O.
B. F. Clark, Vice-Chmn.
W. D. Stevens, Pres., C.O.O.

INVESTOR CONTACT: Daniel N. Bach, Director of Finance, (713) 377-5616

PRINCIPAL OFFICE: 2001 Timberloch Place, The Woodlands, TX 77380-4000

TELEPHONE NUMBER: (713) 377-5500
FAX: (713) 377-5802
WEB: www.mitchellenergy.com

NO. OF EMPLOYEES: 875 (approx.)

SHAREHOLDERS: 1,413

ANNUAL MEETING: In May

INCORPORATED: TX, 1946

INSTITUTIONAL HOLDINGS:
No. of Institutions: 144
Shares Held: 13,794,790
% Held: 27.7

INDUSTRY: Crude petroleum and natural gas (SIC: 1311)

TRANSFER AGENT(S): Mellon Investor Services, LLC, Ridgefield Park, NJ

NYSE SYMBOL MPS
Rec. Pr. 5.20 (4/30/01)

MODIS PROFESSIONAL SERVICES, INC.

YIELD ...
P/E RATIO 4.2

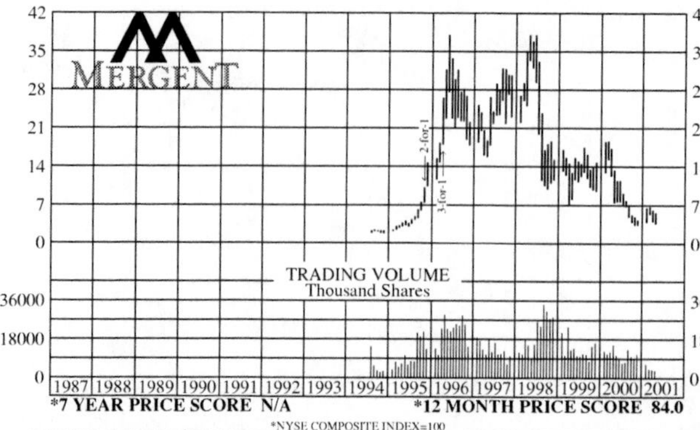

*7 YEAR PRICE SCORE N/A *12 MONTH PRICE SCORE 84.0

*NYSE COMPOSITE INDEX=100

INTERIM EARNINGS (Per Share):

Qtr.	Mar.	June	Sept.	Dec.
1997	0.21	0.23	0.27	0.25
1998	0.19	0.32	0.19	0.09
1999	0.25	0.27	0.16	0.17
2000	0.08	0.08	0.90	0.08

INTERIM DIVIDENDS (Per Share):

Amt.	Decl.	Ex.	Rec.	Pay.

No dividends paid.

CAPITALIZATION (12/31/00):

	($000)	(%)
Long-Term Debt	194,000	12.7
Deferred Income Tax	28,584	1.9
Common & Surplus	1,303,218	85.4
Total	1,525,802	100.0

RECENT DEVELOPMENTS: For the year ended 12/31/00, net income jumped 45.8% to $119.8 million compared with income from continuing operations of $82.1 million in the previous year. Results for 2000 included nonrecurring pre-tax charges of $7.3 million. Results for 2000 and 1999 included asset write-downs of $13.1 million and $25.0 million, respectively. Revenues decreased 5.9% to $1.83 billion from $1.94 billion the year before. Comparisons were made with restated prior-year results.

PROSPECTS: MPS should benefit from free cash flow in 2001 due to its debt reduction efforts over the past year. Going forward, Prolianz, MPS' Professional Business Solutions segment, should continue to benefit from demand for its services. Meanwhile, MPS plans to return its Idea Integration segment to profitability by reducing costs and improving consultant utilization, and started cost-cutting initiatives in its Information Technology Resource Management and Project Support segment.

BUSINESS

MODIS PROFESSIONAL SERVICES, INC. (formerly AccuStaff Incorporated) is a global provider of professional staffing, e-business services, IT project support and career management consulting. MPS has two main divisions: Information Technology Services and Professional Services (accounting, legal, technical/engineering, scientific, and career management and consulting). MPS acquired The McKinley Group, Inc. in June 1996 and Career Horizons, Inc. in November 1996. In October 1998, MPS sold its commercial staffing business. Modis has over 1,000 offices in the United States, United Kingdom, Canada, and continental Europe. In November 2000, MPS decided not to proceed with the previously announced spin-off of its Information Technology division.

QUARTERLY DATA

(12/31/2000) ($000)	Rev	Inc
1st Quarter	457,411	13,018
2nd Quarter	464,450	12,395
3rd Quarter	456,265	86,894
4th Quarter	449,560	7,446

ANNUAL FINANCIAL DATA

	12/31/00	[4] 12/31/99	[6] 12/31/98	12/31/97	12/31/96	12/31/95	1/1/95
Earnings Per Share	**[5] 1.23**	**[3] 0.19**	**[2] 0.61**	**[1] 0.93**	**0.31**	**0.22**	**0.12**
Cash Flow Per Share	**1.78**	**0.33**	**0.91**	**1.22**	**0.46**	**0.27**	**0.14**
Tang. Book Val. Per Share	**1.07**	**9.00**	**0.47**	**...**	**1.84**	**0.92**	**0.72**
INCOME STATEMENT (IN MILLIONS):							
Total Revenues	1,827.7	592.5	1,702.1	2,424.8	1,448.6	267.6	137.1
Costs & Expenses	1,695.5	547.1	1,533.8	2,202.2	1,334.8	251.2	131.1
Depreciation & Amort.	53.9	13.7	37.1	36.1	18.1	2.2	0.8
Operating Income	78.3	31.7	131.2	186.6	95.8	14.2	5.1
Net Interest Inc./(Exp.)	...	...	d14.0	d19.0	d2.9	d0.1	d0.2
Income Before Income Taxes	56.7	29.8	117.2	167.6	64.4	14.1	4.9
Income Taxes	cr63.1	11.2	48.3	65.5	36.5	5.4	1.9
Net Income	[5] 119.8	[3] 18.6	[2] 68.9	[1] 102.0	27.9	8.7	3.0
Cash Flow	173.6	32.3	106.0	138.1	46.0	10.9	3.8
Average Shs. Outstg. (000)	97,539	97,110	116,882	113,109	100,410	39,762	26,343
BALANCE SHEET (IN MILLIONS):							
Cash & Cash Equivalents	5.0	0.9	105.8	23.9	108.7	31.9	15.0
Total Current Assets	372.3	132.1	489.5	521.0	407.5	69.4	29.4
Net Property	55.7	14.9	37.6	48.6	25.8	6.0	1.9
Total Assets	1,653.6	1,490.3	1,571.9	1,479.5	897.1	141.7	35.4
Total Current Liabilities	123.9	69.3	473.4	195.7	136.6	25.1	7.0
Long-Term Obligations	194.0	228.0	15.5	458.9	103.5	6.8	1.9
Net Stockholders' Equity	1,303.2	1,182.5	1,070.1	812.8	654.9	109.6	26.3
Net Working Capital	248.4	62.8	16.1	325.4	270.9	44.4	22.4
Year-end Shs. Outstg. (000)	96,523	96,043	96,306	103,692	112,504	47,750	31,190
STATISTICAL RECORD:							
Operating Profit Margin %	4.3	5.4	7.7	7.7	6.6	5.3	3.7
Net Profit Margin %	6.6	3.1	4.0	4.2	1.9	3.3	2.2
Return on Equity %	9.2	1.6	6.4	12.6	4.3	7.9	11.4
Return on Assets %	7.2	1.2	4.4	6.9	3.1	6.1	8.5
Debt/Total Assets %	11.7	15.3	1.0	31.0	11.5	4.8	5.4
Price Range	18.69-3.38	17.50-7.00	38.06-9.94	32.00-15.75	38.00-11.58	14.75-2.23	2.44-1.77
P/E Ratio	15.2-2.7	92.1-36.8	62.4-16.3	34.4-16.9	122.5-37.4	67.0-10.1	20.8-15.1

Statistics are as originally reported. Adj. for stk. splits: 3-for-1, 3/96; 2-for-1, 11/95 [1] Incl. non-recurr. chrg. $5.0 mill. [2] Bef. disc. opers. gain $260.6 mill. ($2.23/sh.) & bef. extraord. loss $5.6 mill. (0.05/sh.) for debt ext. [3] Incl. asset write-down of $25.0 mill. & restructuring credit of $2.3 mill; bef. disc. oper. gain $15.0 mill. and income of $63.5 mill. [4] Excl. results of Information Technology division, which was reported as a disc. oper. Including this division, revenues and earnings totaled $1.94 bill. and $97.1 mill., respectively. [5] Incl. pre-tax canceled IPO and separation chrgs. of $7.3 mill. & asset write-down of $13.1 mill. [6] Refl. sale of commercial staffing business.

OFFICERS:
T. D. Payne, Pres., C.E.O.
R. P. Crouch, V.P., C.F.O., Treas.
G. A. Bajalia, Sr. V.P., C.O.O.

INVESTOR CONTACT: Investor Relations, (904) 360-2008

PRINCIPAL OFFICE: 1 Independent Drive, Jacksonville, FL 32202

TELEPHONE NUMBER: (904) 360-2000
FAX: (904) 360-2972
WEB: www.modispro.com

NO. OF EMPLOYEES: 18,500 (approx.)

SHAREHOLDERS: 851 (approx.)

ANNUAL MEETING: In May

INCORPORATED: FL, May, 1992

INSTITUTIONAL HOLDINGS:
No. of Institutions: 122
Shares Held: 72,925,652
% Held: 75.4

INDUSTRY: Help supply services (SIC: 7363)

TRANSFER AGENT(S): Sun Trust Bank, Atlanta, GA

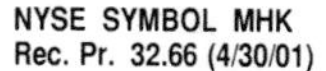

NYSE SYMBOL MHK
Rec. Pr. 32.66 (4/30/01)

MOHAWK INDUSTRIES, INC.

YIELD ...
P/E RATIO 10.9

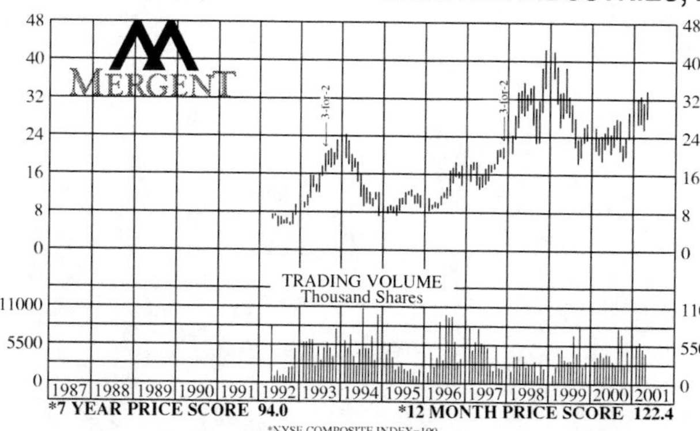

*7 YEAR PRICE SCORE 94.0 *12 MONTH PRICE SCORE 122.4

*NYSE COMPOSITE INDEX=100

INTERIM EARNINGS (Per Share):

Qtr.	Apr.	July	Oct.	Dec.
1997	0.16	0.37	0.40	0.37
1998	0.25	0.58	0.60	0.43
1999	0.46	0.72	0.74	0.70
2000	0.61	0.87	0.79	0.74

INTERIM DIVIDENDS (Per Share):

Amt.	Decl.	Ex.	Rec.	Pay.

No dividends paid.

CAPITALIZATION (12/31/00):

	($000)	(%)
Long-Term Debt	365,437	30.6
Deferred Income Tax	75,808	6.3
Common & Surplus	754,360	63.1
Total	1,195,605	100.0

RECENT DEVELOPMENTS: For the year ended 12/31/00, net income improved 3.4% to $162.6 million compared with $157.2 million in the previous year. Results for 2000 included class action legal settlement expenses of $7.0 million. Net sales jumped 5.6% to $3.26 billion versus $3.08 billion in the preceding 1999 period. Gross profit as a percentage of net sales totaled 25.3% compared with 25.2% in the prior year. Operating income increased 5.2% to $310.1 million from $294.8 million in the previous year.

PROSPECTS: In 2001, the Company will continue to focus on the roll-out of soft and hard floor covering products lines. As a result, the Company expects significant start-up costs due to sampling and personnel costs associated with the roll-out of these product lines in the first half of 2001. However, the Company announced a price increase for selected residential carpet effective March 2001, in an attempt to offset these start-up costs. Also, MHK expects lower interest rates and the consideration of potential tax reductions to favorably affect long-term results.

BUSINESS

MOHAWK INDUSTRIES, INC., through its primary operating subsidiaries Mohawk Carpet Corporation and Aladdin Manufacturing Corporation, is a major producer of woven and tufted broadloom carpet and rugs for principally residential applications. The Company is the second largest carpet and rug manufacturer in the United States. The Company designs, manufactures and markets carpet and rugs in a broad range of colors, textures and patterns. The Company's brand names include MOHAWK, LADDIN, MOHAWK HOME, AMERICAN WEAVERS, BIGELOW, CUSTOM WEAVE, DURKAN, GALAXY, HARBINGER, HELIOS, HORIZON, IMAGE, KARASTAN, MOHAWK COMMERCIAL, NEWMARK RUG, WORLD and WUNDAWEVE. MHK markets its products primarily through carpet retailers, home centers, mass merchandisers, department stores, commercial dealers and commercial end users.

ANNUAL FINANCIAL DATA

	12/31/00	12/31/99	12/31/98	12/31/97	12/31/96	12/31/95	12/31/94
Earnings Per Share	**3.00**	**2.61**	[2] **1.86**	**1.30**	[1] **0.95**	[1] **0.13**	[2] **0.66**
Cash Flow Per Share	**4.51**	**4.35**	**3.03**	**2.43**	**2.01**	**1.19**	**1.65**
Tang. Book Val. Per Share	**14.42**	**12.21**	**10.22**	**7.78**	**5.41**	**4.43**	**5.42**
INCOME STATEMENT (IN MILLIONS):							
Total Revenues	3,255.8	3,083.3	2,639.2	1,901.4	1,795.1	1,648.5	1,437.5
Costs & Expenses	2,863.4	2,683.2	2,340.1	1,700.5	1,620.2	1,547.9	1,289.6
Depreciation & Amort.	82.3	105.3	67.9	59.3	55.2	52.6	49.5
Operating Income	310.1	294.8	231.2	141.6	119.7	48.0	98.5
Net Interest Inc./(Exp.)	d38.0	d32.6	d29.3	d26.5	d31.5	d35.0	d27.1
Income Before Income Taxes	267.6	259.9	182.4	112.4	82.7	10.5	58.2
Income Taxes	105.0	102.7	74.8	44.4	33.7	4.0	25.2
Net Income	162.6	157.2	[2] 107.6	68.0	[1] 49.1	[1] 6.4	[2] 33.0
Cash Flow	244.9	262.5	175.5	127.3	104.2	59.0	82.5
Average Shs. Outstg. (000)	54,255	60,349	57,984	52,403	51,849	49,638	50,061
BALANCE SHEET (IN MILLIONS):							
Total Current Assets	1,024.1	934.4	806.9	573.3	556.2	507.4	454.2
Net Property	650.1	624.8	422.9	319.8	324.7	318.0	339.3
Total Assets	1,792.6	1,682.9	1,331.4	961.0	955.8	903.2	854.8
Total Current Liabilities	596.9	374.4	387.7	263.1	244.6	262.6	162.0
Long-Term Obligations	365.4	562.1	321.8	257.2	345.7	341.8	393.9
Net Stockholders' Equity	754.4	692.5	586.7	405.9	333.2	274.9	264.0
Net Working Capital	427.2	560.1	419.2	310.1	311.7	244.8	292.2
Year-end Shs. Outstg. (000)	52,300	56,705	57,383	52,167	51,707	49,638	48,687
STATISTICAL RECORD:							
Operating Profit Margin %	9.5	9.6	8.8	7.4	6.7	2.9	6.8
Net Profit Margin %	5.0	5.1	4.1	3.6	2.7	0.4	2.3
Return on Equity %	21.6	22.7	18.3	16.8	14.7	2.3	12.5
Return on Assets %	9.1	9.3	8.1	7.1	5.1	0.7	3.9
Debt/Total Assets %	20.4	33.4	24.2	26.8	36.2	37.8	46.1
Price Range	29.13-18.94	42.00-18.38	42.44-20.50	21.75-12.92	18.58-8.33	12.83-7.25	24.33-7.17
P/E Ratio	9.7-6.3	16.1-7.0	22.8-11.0	16.7-9.9	19.6-8.8	101.0-57.0	36.9-10.9

Statistics are as originally reported. Adj. for 3-for-2 stk. spl., 12/97 & 8/93 [1] Incl. restruct. costs, 1996, $700,000; 1995, $8.4 mill. [2] Incl. acq. costs, 1998, $17.7 mill.; 1994, $10.2 mill.

OFFICERS:
D. L. Kolb, Chmn.
J. S. Lorberbaum, Pres., C.E.O.
J. D. Swift, V.P., C.F.O., Asst. Sec.

INVESTOR CONTACT: John D. Swift, C.F.O., (706) 624-2247

PRINCIPAL OFFICE: 160 S. Industrial Blvd., P.O. Box 12069, Calhoun, GA 30701

TELEPHONE NUMBER: (706) 629-7721
WEB: www.mohawkind.com

NO. OF EMPLOYEES: 24,005 (avg.)

SHAREHOLDERS: 396 (record common)

ANNUAL MEETING: In May

INCORPORATED: DE, Dec., 1988

INSTITUTIONAL HOLDINGS:
No. of Institutions: 135
Shares Held: 43,450,993
% Held: 83.1

INDUSTRY: Carpets and rugs (SIC: 2273)

TRANSFER AGENT(S): First Union National Bank, Charlotte, NC

NYSE SYMBOL MNC
Rec. Pr. 21.96 (5/31/01)

MONACO COACH CORPORATION

YIELD ...
P/E RATIO 9.9

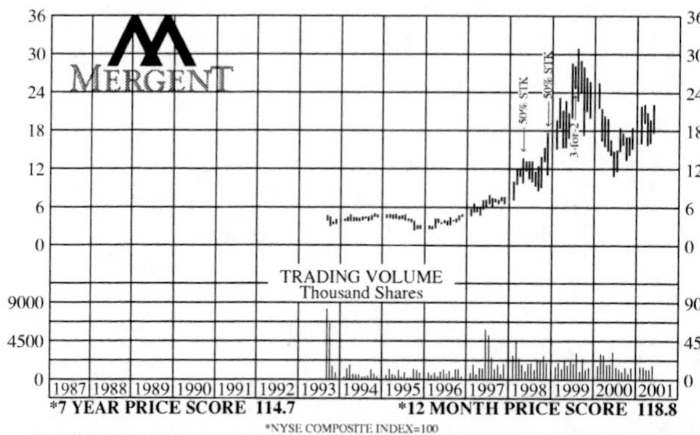

*7 YEAR PRICE SCORE 114.7 *12 MONTH PRICE SCORE 118.8

*NYSE COMPOSITE INDEX=100

INTERIM EARNINGS (Per Share):

Qtr.	Mar.	June	Sept.	Dec.
1997	0.17	0.16	0.17	0.20
1998	0.22	0.23	0.33	0.40
1999	0.51	0.59	0.58	0.58
2000	0.67	0.58	0.51	0.45

INTERIM DIVIDENDS (Per Share):

Amt.	Decl.	Ex.	Rec.	Pay.
3-for-2	6/07/99	7/08/99	6/21/99	7/07/99

CAPITALIZATION (12/30/00):

	($000)	(%)
Deferred Income Tax	7,646	3.9
Common & Surplus	186,625	96.1
Total	194,271	100.0

RECENT DEVELOPMENTS: For the year ended 12/30/00, net income declined 2.8% to $42.5 million compared with $43.8 million a year earlier. Results for 1999 included a nonrecurring gain of $1.8 million and a charge of $639,000 from the write-off of debt issuance costs. Net sales were $901.9 million, up 15.5% from $780.8 million the year before. Operating income decreased 4.1% to $69.8 million versus $72.8 million in 1999.

PROSPECTS: The Company is encouraged by the recent decision by the Federal Reserve Board to lower interest rates. The Company believes lower interest rates should have a positive effect on the recreational vehicle industry in 2001. The lower rates are expected to relieve some of the pressure that the Company's retail dealers are experiencing associated with floor-plan financing, which may encourage them to increase their current level of stock inventory.

BUSINESS

MONACO COACH CORPORATION is a manufacturer of premium Class A motor coaches and towable recreational vehicles. The Company's product line consists of sixteen models of motor coaches and eight models of towables (fifth wheel trailers and travel trailers) under the MONACO, HOLIDAY RAMBLER, ROYALE COACH and MCKENZIE TOWABLES brand names. The Company's products, which are typically priced at the high end of their respective product categories, range in suggested retail price from $70,000 to $950,000 for motor coaches and from $20,000 to $65,000 for towables. MNC's products are sold through an extensive network of 339 dealerships located primarily in the United States and Canada.

ANNUAL FINANCIAL DATA

	12/30/00	1/1/00	1/2/99	1/3/98	12/28/96	12/30/95	12/31/94
Earnings Per Share	**2.20**	[1] **2.26**	**1.19**	**0.71**	**0.38**	**0.32**	**0.39**
Cash Flow Per Share	**2.53**	**2.56**	**1.35**	**0.90**	**0.58**	**0.40**	**0.45**
Tang. Book Val. Per Share	**8.87**	**6.57**	**4.13**	**3.54**	**1.42**	**1.26**	**0.89**
INCOME STATEMENT (IN THOUSANDS):							
Total Revenues	901,890	780,815	594,802	441,895	365,638	141,611	107,300
Costs & Expenses	825,701	702,068	551,781	415,627	348,892	132,179	96,855
Depreciation & Amort.	6,359	5,904	3,005	3,641	3,005	1,077	812
Operating Income	69,830	72,843	40,016	22,627	13,741	8,355	9,633
Net Interest Inc./(Exp.)	d632	d1,143	d1,861	d2,379	d3,914	d298	d69
Income Before Income Taxes	69,380	71,842	38,762	21,255	10,071	8,017	9,717
Income Taxes	26,859	28,081	16,093	8,819	4,162	3,119	3,776
Net Income	42,521	[1] 43,761	22,669	12,436	5,909	4,898	5,941
Cash Flow	48,880	49,665	25,674	15,760	8,755	5,975	6,753
Average Shs. Outstg.	19,319	19,367	19,082	17,545	15,102	15,098	15,085
BALANCE SHEET (IN THOUSANDS):							
Cash & Cash Equivalents	...	...	...	...	...	...	234
Total Current Assets	196,638	137,946	106,901	81,432	73,889	27,684	20,129
Net Property	103,590	89,439	61,655	55,399	38,309	21,587	8,342
Total Assets	321,610	246,727	190,127	159,832	135,368	68,502	48,219
Total Current Liabilities	127,339	99,058	83,225	71,020	69,387	23,889	14,219
Long-Term Obligations	...	...	5,400	11,500	16,500	5,000	...
Net Stockholders' Equity	186,625	143,339	98,193	74,748	43,807	37,930	32,945
Net Working Capital	69,299	38,888	23,676	10,412	4,502	3,795	5,911
Year-end Shs. Outstg.	18,952	18,871	18,722	14,953	14,953	14,887	14,854
STATISTICAL RECORD:							
Operating Profit Margin %	7.7	9.3	6.7	5.1	3.8	5.9	9.0
Net Profit Margin %	4.7	5.6	3.8	2.8	1.6	3.5	5.5
Return on Equity %	22.8	30.5	23.1	16.6	13.5	12.9	18.0
Return on Assets %	13.2	17.7	11.9	7.8	4.4	7.2	12.3
Debt/Total Assets %	...	...	2.8	7.2	12.2	7.3	...
Price Range	25.56-10.81	30.94-15.13	17.67-7.11	7.91-4.59	4.89-2.52	4.96-2.37	5.00-3.78
P/E Ratio	11.6-4.9	13.7-6.7	14.9-6.0	11.2-6.5	12.9-6.6	15.4-7.3	12.7-9.6

Statistics are as originally reported. Adj. for stk. splits: 50% div., 11/30/98; 50% div., 4/16/98; 3-for-2, 7/99. [1] Incl. nonrecurr. gain of $1.2 mill. and incl. nonrecurr. loss of $639,000.

OFFICERS:
K. L. Toolson, Chmn., C.E.O.
J. Nepute, Pres.
P. M. Daley, V.P., C.F.O.

INVESTOR CONTACT: Mike Duncan, Investor Relations Mgr., (800) 634-0855

PRINCIPAL OFFICE: 91320 Industrial Way, Coburg, OR 97408

TELEPHONE NUMBER: (541) 686-8011
FAX: (541) 686-8084
WEB: www.monaco-online.com

NO. OF EMPLOYEES: 3,973 (avg.)

SHAREHOLDERS: 607 (approx.)

ANNUAL MEETING: In May

INCORPORATED: DE, Dec., 1992

INSTITUTIONAL HOLDINGS:
No. of Institutions: 85
Shares Held: 9,997,205
% Held: 52.7

INDUSTRY: Motor vehicles and car bodies (SIC: 3711)

TRANSFER AGENT(S): Wells Fargo Shareowner Services, South St. Paul, MN

NYSE SYMBOL MTP
Rec. Pr. 12.80 (5/31/01)

MONTANA POWER COMPANY

YIELD ...
P/E RATIO 6.4

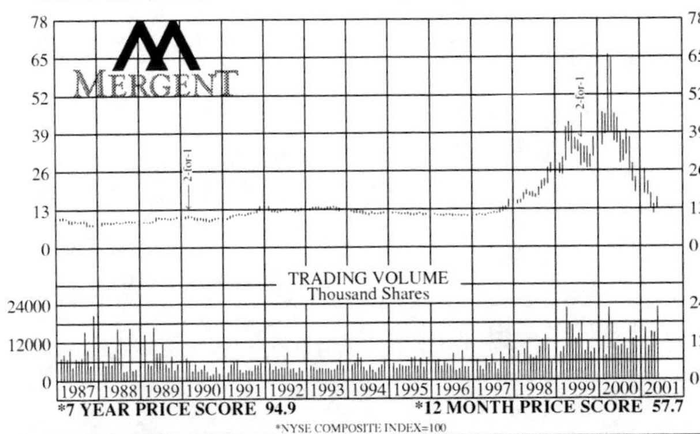

*7 YEAR PRICE SCORE 94.9 *12 MONTH PRICE SCORE 57.7

*NYSE COMPOSITE INDEX=100

INTERIM EARNINGS (Per Share):

Qtr.	Mar.	June	Sept.	Dec.
1996	0.35	0.12	0.15	d0.17
1997	0.42	0.13	0.14	0.47
1998	0.32	0.20	0.33	0.63
1999	0.30	0.22	0.26	0.56
2000	0.28	0.33	0.23	1.17

INTERIM DIVIDENDS (Per Share):

Amt.	Decl.	Ex.	Rec.	Pay.
0.20Q	9/28/99	10/06/99	10/08/99	11/01/99
0.20Q	12/14/99	1/05/00	1/07/00	2/01/00
0.20Q	3/28/00	4/05/00	4/07/00	5/01/00
0.20Q	6/27/00	7/05/00	7/07/00	8/01/00
0.20Q	9/26/00	10/04/00	10/06/00	11/01/00

Dividend Payment Suspended

CAPITALIZATION (12/31/00):

	($000)	(%)
Long-Term Debt	309,463	20.1
Redeemable Pfd. Stock	65,000	4.2
Preferred Stock	57,654	3.7
Common & Surplus	1,106,358	71.9
Total	1,538,475	100.0

RECENT DEVELOPMENTS: For the year ended 12/31/00, income from continuing operations was $76.2 million, versus income from continuing operations of $98.4 million in 1999. Results for 2000 and 1999 excluded income from discontinued operations of $123.3 million and $51.9 million, respectively. Consolidated revenues totaled $999.7 million, an increase of 28.6% from $777.2 million in the prior year. Touch America revenues surged to $237.0 million from $85.9 million in the previous year.

PROSPECTS: On 2/21/01, the Company closed on the sale of its independent power business to privately-held CES Acquisition Corp., for $84.5 million. On 4/30/01, the Company completed the sale of its coal business to Westmoreland Mining LLC for $138 million in cash. The operations, which included Western Energy Company, Colstrip, Montana and Northwestern Resources Company, produced approximately 19 million tons of coal in 2000. Going forward, the Company will focus on growing Touch America.

BUSINESS

MONTANA POWER COMPANY, mainly through Touch America, Inc., offers equipment, private lines, Internet and long distance services to customers. In addition, MTP supplies electricity and natural gas in Montana, including the cities of Butte, Great Falls and Billings. The Utility Group operates electric and natural gas utility systems serving Montana customers in a 107,600 square mile region. Entech, Inc., owns and operates non-regulated business ventures, including one of the nation's largest coal and lignite producers. The Independent Power Group is engaged in cogeneration projects and the transmission and marketing of electricity. The Company is in the process of divesting its multiple energy businesses from its telecommunications unit, Touch America.

ANNUAL FINANCIAL DATA

	[2] 12/31/00	12/31/99	12/31/98	12/31/97	12/31/96	12/31/95	12/31/94
Earnings Per Share	**[3] 1.84**	**1.33**	**1.47**	**1.14**	**1.02**	**[1] 0.46**	**1.00**
Cash Flow Per Share	**1.41**	**2.43**	**2.61**	**2.11**	**1.83**	**1.26**	**1.82**
Tang. Book Val. Per Share	**9.20**	**9.56**	**9.89**	**9.24**	**8.89**	**8.66**	**8.92**
Dividends Per Share	**0.80**	**0.80**	**0.80**	**0.80**	**0.80**	**0.80**	**0.80**
Dividend Payout %	**43.5**	**60.1**	**54.4**	**70.2**	**78.8**	**173.9**	**80.0**
INCOME STATEMENT (IN MILLIONS):							
Total Revenues	999.7	1,342.3	1,253.7	1,023.6	973.2	953.2	1,006.0
Costs & Expenses	845.1	999.3	834.2	712.4	648.2	754.8	718.2
Depreciation & Amort.	77.0	111.1	114.3	94.7	88.7	87.0	86.7
Operating Income	77.6	231.9	305.3	216.5	236.2	111.5	201.1
Net Interest Inc./(Exp.)	d39.9	d37.5	d55.4	d49.2	d48.8	d43.7	d42.8
Income Taxes	33.6	44.1	78.2	61.9	72.0	21.6	55.2
Net Income	[3] 76.2	161.3	176.6	139.6	119.4	[1] 56.9	113.6
Cash Flow	149.5	268.8	287.2	230.6	199.8	136.7	193.1
Average Shs. Outstg. (000)	106,353	110,553	110,156	109,298	109,268	108,242	106,250
BALANCE SHEET (IN MILLIONS):							
Gross Property	2,289.9	2,518.7	3,111.8	2,997.6	2,948.1	2,837.5	2,142.0
Accumulated Depreciation	593.1	813.7	1,030.3	945.5	961.6	915.8	826.7
Net Property	1,696.8	1,705.0	2,081.5	2,052.1	1,986.5	1,921.6	1,845.5
Total Assets	2,816.8	3,048.7	2,928.1	2,801.7	2,698.2	2,586.1	2,512.7
Long-Term Obligations	309.5	618.5	698.3	653.2	633.3	616.6	588.9
Net Stockholders' Equity	1,164.0	1,066.5	1,146.5	1,069.2	1,029.0	1,046.9	1,056.9
Year-end Shs. Outstg. (000)	103,743	105,537	110,122	109,458	109,262	109,228	107,158
STATISTICAL RECORD:							
Operating Profit Margin %	7.8	17.3	24.3	21.2	24.3	11.7	20.0
Net Profit Margin %	7.6	12.0	14.1	13.6	12.3	6.0	11.3
Net Inc./Net Property %	4.5	9.5	8.5	6.8	6.0	3.0	6.2
Net Inc./Tot. Capital %	5.0	9.2	7.9	6.6	5.8	2.9	5.8
Return on Equity %	6.5	15.1	15.4	13.1	11.6	5.4	10.7
Accum. Depr./Gross Prop. %	25.9	32.3	33.1	31.5	32.6	32.3	38.6
Price Range	65.75-18.50	42.63-24.56	28.56-14.53	16.13-10.50	11.50-10.31	12.06-10.56	12.94-10.88
P/E Ratio	35.7-10.1	32.0-18.5	19.4-9.9	14.1-9.2	11.3-10.2	26.2-23.0	12.9-10.9
Average Yield %	1.9	2.4	3.7	6.0	7.3	7.1	6.7

Statistics are as originally reported. Adj. for stk. split: 2-for-1, 8/99 [1] Incl. non-recurr. chrg. $74.3 for write down of assets [2] Reflects sale of oil and gas business. [3] Excl. income from disc. oper. $123.3 mill.

OFFICERS:
R. P. Gannon, Chmn., Pres., C.E.O.
J. P. Pederson, Vice-Chmn., C.F.O.
E. M. Senechal, Treas.
P. K. Merrell, V.P., Sec.

INVESTOR CONTACT: Rose Marie Ralph, Dir. Inv. Rel., (406) 497-2374

PRINCIPAL OFFICE: 40 East Broadway, Butte, MT 59701-9394

TELEPHONE NUMBER: (406) 497-3000
FAX: (406) 497-2150
WEB: www.mtpower.com

NO. OF EMPLOYEES: 2,549

SHAREHOLDERS: 29,823

ANNUAL MEETING: In May

INCORPORATED: MT, April, 1961

INSTITUTIONAL HOLDINGS:
No. of Institutions: 239
Shares Held: 46,606,496
% Held: 44.1

INDUSTRY: Electric and other services combined (SIC: 4931)

TRANSFER AGENT(S): The Company

NYSE SYMBOL MNY
Rec. Pr. 36.75 (5/31/01)

MONY GROUP, INC. (THE)

YIELD 1.2%
P/E RATIO 7.8

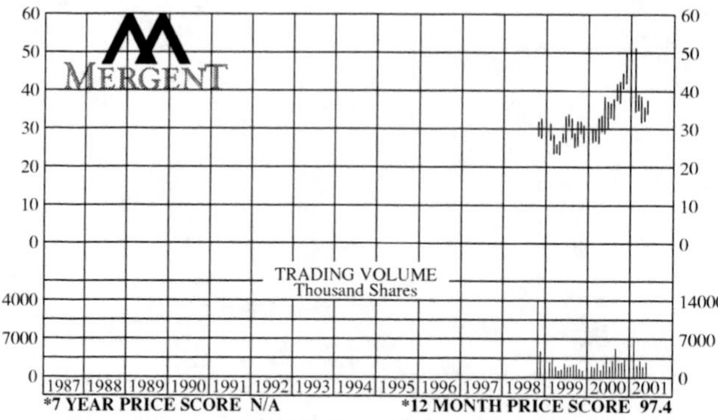

*7 YEAR PRICE SCORE N/A *12 MONTH PRICE SCORE 97.4

*NYSE COMPOSITE INDEX=100

INTERIM EARNINGS (Per Share):

Qtr.	Mar.	June	Sept.	Dec.
1998		0.18		
1999	0.97	1.29	0.58	2.36
2000	2.12	1.01	1.41	0.19

INTERIM DIVIDENDS (Per Share):

Amt.	Decl.	Ex.	Rec.	Pay.
0.10Q	5/26/99	6/04/99	6/08/99	6/29/99
0.10Q	7/29/99	9/01/99	9/03/99	9/24/99
0.10Q	11/17/99	12/01/99	12/03/99	12/24/99
0.45A	11/14/00	11/29/00	12/01/00	12/22/00

Indicated div.: $0.45

CAPITALIZATION (12/31/00):

	($000)	(%)
Long-Term Debt	571,100	21.9
Common & Surplus	2,038,900	78.1
Total	2,610,000	100.0

RECENT DEVELOPMENTS: For the year ended 12/31/00, the Company reported income of $262.3 million, before an extraordinary loss of $37.7 million, versus income of $250.6 million, before an extraordinary loss of $2.0 million, in 1999. Revenues were flat at $1.25 billion compared with the prior year. Total premium income rose 22.6% to $118.1 million from $96.3 million a year earlier.

PROSPECTS: On 2/1/01, MNY completed its acquisition of The Advest Group, a financial services company. On 2/7/01, MNY acquired Matrix Capital Markets Group, a middle-market investment bank. Going forward, MNY will continue to grow its businesses internally and pursue additional acquisitions and alliances. MNY should continue to benefit from robust life insurance sales, an expanded distribution network and a strong capital position.

BUSINESS

MONY GROUP, INC. is the parent holding company of MONY Life Insurance Company (formerly The Mutual Life Insurance Company of New York), a stock life insurance company that converted from a mutual fund structure in 1998. As of 2/8/01, MNY had $55.0 billion in assets under management. MNY provides life insurance, annuities, mutual funds, brokerage, asset management, business and estate planning, trust and investment banking products and services to individual and institutional clients. MNY focuses primarily on offering customized financial solutions through multiple distribution channels, including a career agency sales force, brokerage general agencies, financial advisors, brokers, and other compimentary channels. MNY's companies include The Advest Group, Inc., MONY Life Insurance Company, Enterprise Capital Management, Inc., U.S. Financial Life Insurance Company, MONY Securities Corporation and Trusted Securities Advisors Corp. MNY primarily sells its products in all 50 of the U.S., the District of Columbia, the U.S. Virgin Islands, Guam and the Commonwealth of Puerto Rico.

ANNUAL FINANCIAL DATA

	12/31/00	[2] 12/31/99	12/31/98	12/31/97	12/31/96	12/31/95
Earnings Per Share	**[4] 5.49**	**[1] 5.20**	**[1] 0.18**	...	...	...
Tang. Book Val.	**44.13**	**38.68**	**37.66**	...	...	...
Dividends Per Share	**0.45**	**0.40**	...	...	...	...
Dividend Payout %	**8.2**	**7.7**	...	...	...	...
INCOME STATEMENT (IN MILLIONS):						
Total Premium Income	118.1	96.3	621.7	838.6	859.8	875.9
Other Income	1,133.7	1,149.3	1,234.5	1,137.8	1,105.2	983.7
Total Revenues	1,251.8	[3] 1,245.6	1,856.2	1,976.4	1,965.0	1,859.6
Policyholder Benefits	166.9	147.0	679.8	840.1	872.2	883.6
Income Before Income Taxes	396.1	382.6	294.2	187.7	100.5	61.8
Income Taxes	133.8	132.0	103.0	57.3	44.0	21.4
Net Income	[4] 262.3	[1] 250.6	[1] 191.2	[1] 130.4	56.5	40.4
Average Shs. Outstg. (000)	47,788	47,812	47,900	...	...	...
BALANCE SHEET (IN MILLIONS):						
Cash & Cash Equivalents	701.8	265.9	329.1	313.4	315.4	...
Invst. Assets: Fixed-term	3,149.9	3,066.7	3,132.0	5,950.1	5,460.8	...
Invst. Assets: Loans	1,269.4	1,339.5	1,049.4	2,677.3	2,813.6	...
Invst. Assets: Total	4,747.9	4,926.0	4,638.6	8,965.2	8,579.6	...
Total Assets	24,575.3	24,753.4	24,956.0	23,611.3	22,143.5	...
Long-Term Obligations	571.1	245.4	375.4	423.6	269.7	...
Net Stockholders' Equity	2,038.9	1,825.5	1,777.6	1,320.6	1,170.5	...
Year-end Shs. Outstg. (000)	46,200	47,200	47,200	...	...	...
STATISTICAL RECORD:						
Return on Revenues %	21.0	20.1	10.3	6.6	2.9	2.2
Return on Equity %	12.9	13.7	10.8	9.9	4.8	...
Return on Assets %	1.1	1.0	0.8	0.6	0.3	...
Price Range	50.00-26.19	33.81-23.25	32.75-27.56	...	...	...
P/E Ratio	9.1-4.8	6.5-4.5	181.8-153.0	...	...	...
Average Yield %	1.2	1.4	...	...	...	...

Statistics are as originally reported. [1] Excl. extraord. chrgs. in connection with the plan of reorganization: $13.3 mill., 1997; $27.2 mill., 1998; $2.0 mill., 1999. [2] Includes results of Sagamore Financial Corporation, acquired on 12/31/98. [3] Reflects the conver. of MONY Life to a stk. insurance company & estab. of the Closed Block. [4] Excl. extraord. chrg. of $37.7 mill.

OFFICERS:
M. I. Roth, Chmn., C.E.O.
S. J. Foti, Pres., C.O.O.
R. Daddario, Exec. V.P., C.F.O.
D. Weigel, V.P., Treas.

INVESTOR CONTACT: John Maclane, (212) 708-2528

PRINCIPAL OFFICE: 1740 Broadway, New York, NY 10019

TELEPHONE NUMBER: (212) 708-2000
FAX: (212) 708-2056
WEB: www.mony.com

NO. OF EMPLOYEES: 2,466 (approx.)

SHAREHOLDERS: 590,717

ANNUAL MEETING: In May

INCORPORATED: DE, 1998

INSTITUTIONAL HOLDINGS:
No. of Institutions: 170
Shares Held: 16,915,437
% Held: 36.7

INDUSTRY: Life insurance (SIC: 6311)

TRANSFER AGENT(S): EquiServe Trust Company, Edison, NJ

NYSE SYMBOL MCO
Rec. Pr. 32.08 (5/31/01)

MOODY'S CORP.

YIELD	0.6%
P/E RATIO	30.6

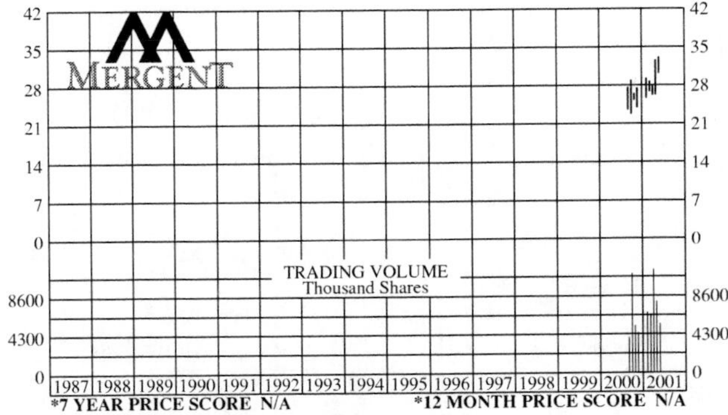

*7 YEAR PRICE SCORE N/A *12 MONTH PRICE SCORE N/A
*NYSE COMPOSITE INDEX=100

INTERIM EARNINGS (Per Share):

Qtr.	Mar.	June	Sept.	Dec.
1999	0.36	0.40	0.41	0.39
2000	0.42	0.13	0.25	0.25

INTERIM DIVIDENDS (Per Share):

Amt.	Decl.	Ex.	Rec.	Pay.
0.185Q	4/19/00	5/17/00	5/20/00	6/10/00
0.185Q	7/19/00	8/16/00	8/20/00	9/10/00
0.045Q	10/18/00	11/16/00	11/20/00	12/10/00
0.045Q	12/20/00	2/22/01	2/26/01	3/10/01
0.045Q	4/23/01	5/16/01	5/20/01	6/10/01

Indicated div.: $0.18

CAPITALIZATION (12/31/00):

	($000)	(%)
Long-Term Debt	300,000	1714.3
Common & Surplus	d282,500	-1614.3
Total	17,500	100.0

RECENT DEVELOPMENTS: For the year ended 12/31/00, net income increased slightly to $158.5 million compared with $155.6 million in the corresponding 1999 period. Revenues advanced 6.8% to $602.3 million from $564.2 million in the previous year. Results were enhanced by strong growth in ratings of international structured finance securities, especially in Europe and Japan. Comparisons were made with restated prior-year figures.

PROSPECTS: MCO expects low-teens revenue and operating income growth providing debt capital market conditions in the United States in 2001 are better than in 2000. In addition, revenue growth for MCO's U.S. operations will depend upon continued volume increases of investment grade financing, the resumption of economic growth in the U.S. and the recovery of the high-yield market. Internationally, MCO expects double-digit revenue growth.

BUSINESS

MOODY'S CORPORATION (formerly Dun & Bradstreet Corporation), through its subsidiary Moody's Investors Service, is a provider of credit ratings, research and analysis covering debt instruments and securities in the global capital markets. MCO issues ratings on more than 4,200 corporations and 68,000 public finance debt securities issued by corporations and governments in more than 100 nations. Moody's Risk Management Services, a wholly-owned subsidiary of Moody's Investors Service, is a provider of financial software, credit training and both quantitative and judgemental risk assessment models. MCO maintains offices in New York, Tokyo, London, Paris, Sydney, San Francisco, Frankfurt, Dallas, Madrid, Toronto, Hong Kong, Singapore, Limassol, Sao Paulo, Milan and Mexico City. On 9/30/00, the Company spun off its credit information and receivables management services, which were renamed The Dun & Bradstreet Corp.

ANNUAL FINANCIAL DATA

	12/31/00	12/31/99	12/31/98	12/31/97	12/31/96	12/31/95	12/31/94
Earnings Per Share	**0.97**	[3][5] **1.56**	[2][4] **1.44**	[1] **1.80**	[2][4] **d0.16**	[4] **1.89**	**3.70**
Cash Flow Per Share	**1.07**	**2.42**	**2.26**	**2.69**	**0.77**	**4.69**	**6.18**
Dividends Per Share	**0.60**	**0.74**	**0.37**	...	...	...	...
Dividend Payout %	**61.8**	**47.4**	**25.7**	...	...	...	...
INCOME STATEMENT (IN MILLIONS):							
Total Revenues	602.3	1,971.8	1,934.5	2,154.4	2,159.2	5,415.1	4,895.7
Costs & Expenses	297.2	1,392.0	1,372.2	1,452.6	1,804.2	4,418.8	3,549.1
Depreciation & Amort.	16.6	140.9	141.6	153.9	157.4	474.5	421.1
Operating Income	288.5	438.9	420.7	547.9	197.6	521.8	925.5
Net Interest Inc./(Exp.)	d3.6	d2.0	d5.7	d51.6	d32.7	d20.9	d7.8
Income Before Income Taxes	284.0	434.9	399.8	476.6	126.4	443.7	879.2
Income Taxes	125.5	178.9	153.4	165.6	153.7	122.9	249.7
Equity Earnings/Minority Int.	...	d22.4	...	...	...	...	...
Net Income	158.5	[3][5] 256.0	[2][4] 246.4	[1] 311.0	[2][4] d27.3	[4] 320.8	629.5
Cash Flow	175.1	396.9	388.0	464.9	130.1	795.3	1,050.6
Average Shs. Outstg. (000)	163,000	164,284	171,703	172,552	170,017	169,522	169,946
BALANCE SHEET (IN MILLIONS):							
Cash & Cash Equivalents	119.1	113.2	90.6	81.8	127.9	438.3	362.3
Total Current Assets	277.6	785.0	764.0	898.3	917.4	2,298.5	1,981.0
Net Property	43.4	280.0	298.3	342.7	373.1	874.4	918.5
Total Assets	398.3	1,785.7	1,789.2	2,151.9	2,294.2	5,515.8	5,463.9
Total Current Liabilities	253.1	1,414.8	1,352.7	1,561.6	2,017.6	2,833.5	2,186.6
Long-Term Obligations	300.0	...	...	...	...	...	...
Net Stockholders' Equity	d282.5	d416.6	d371.0	d490.2	d431.7	1,182.5	1,318.6
Net Working Capital	24.5	d629.8	d588.7	d663.3	d1,100.2	d535.0	d205.6
Year-end Shs. Outstg. (000)	171,451	160,824	165,054	170,567	170,508	169,389	169,761
STATISTICAL RECORD:							
Operating Profit Margin %	47.9	22.3	21.7	25.4	9.2	9.6	18.9
Net Profit Margin %	26.3	13.0	12.7	14.4	...	5.9	12.9
Return on Equity %	...	...	...	...	...	27.1	47.7
Return on Assets %	39.8	14.3	13.8	14.5	...	5.8	11.5
Debt/Total Assets %	75.3	...	...	...	...	...	...
Price Range	28.88-22.63	...	...	...	...	...	...
P/E Ratio	29.8-23.3	...	...	...	...	...	...
Average Yield %	2.3	...	...	...	...	...	...

Statistics are as originally reported. Results for 1995 and earlier include the operations of Cognizant Corp. and ACNielsen Corp. Results for 12/31/99 and prior are for the Dun & Bradstreet Corp. & subsidiaries. [1] Bef. acctg. change chrg. 1996, $150.6 mill. [2] Bef. disc. oper. gain 1998, $33.7 mill; loss 1996, $17.1 mill. [3] Incl. restruct. chrg. of $41.2 mill. [4] Incl. reorganiz. costs, 1998, $28.0 mill.; 1996, $161.2 mill.; credit, 1995, $120.3 mill. [5] Incl. after-tax gain of $5.1 mill. from the sale of financial information services business

OFFICERS:
C. L. Alexander, Chmn.
J. Rutherfurd Jr., Pres., C.E.O.
Jeanne Dering, Sr. V.P., C.F.O.

INVESTOR CONTACT: Sandy Parker, V.P., Investor Relations, (212) 553-1658

PRINCIPAL OFFICE: 99 Church Street, New York, NY 10007

TELEPHONE NUMBER: (212) 553-1658
WEB: www.moodys.com

NO. OF EMPLOYEES: 1,500 (approx.)

SHAREHOLDERS: 8,332

ANNUAL MEETING: In Apr.

INCORPORATED: DE, 1933

INSTITUTIONAL HOLDINGS:
No. of Institutions: 292
Shares Held: 128,033,115
% Held: 81.3

INDUSTRY: Credit reporting services (SIC: 7323)

TRANSFER AGENT(S): First Chicago Trust Company of New York, Jersey City, NJ

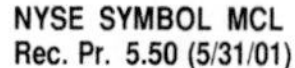

NYSE SYMBOL MCL
Rec. Pr. 5.50 (5/31/01)

MOORE CORPORATION LTD.

YIELD ...
P/E RATIO ...

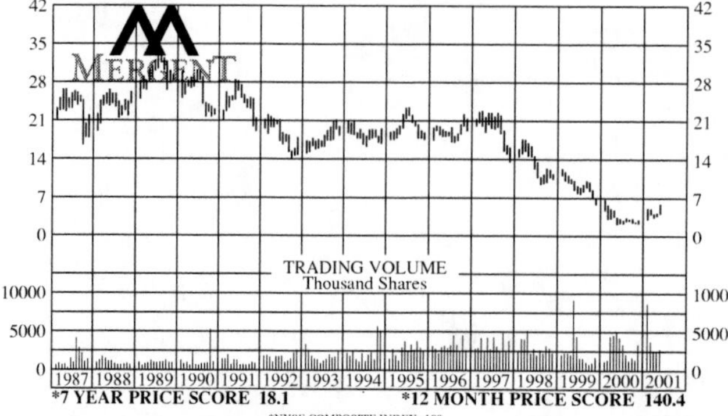

*7 YEAR PRICE SCORE 18.1   *12 MONTH PRICE SCORE 140.4

*NYSE COMPOSITE INDEX=100

INTERIM EARNINGS (Per Share):

Qtr.	Mar.	June	Sept.	Dec.
1996	0.30	0.36	0.42	0.42
1997	0.32	0.31	d0.09	0.01
1998	0.06	d0.24	d6.18	0.17
1999	0.11	0.02	0.10	0.82
2000	d0.10	d0.16	d0.09	d0.40

INTERIM DIVIDENDS (Per Share):

Amt.	Decl.	Ex.	Rec.	Pay.
0.05Q	4/28/00	5/31/00	6/02/00	7/05/00
0.05Q	7/24/00	8/30/00	9/01/00	10/03/00
0.05Q	10/27/00	11/29/00	12/01/00	1/03/01
0.05Q	2/26/01	2/28/01	3/02/01	4/02/01

Dividend Suspended

CAPITALIZATION (12/31/00):

	($000)	(%)
Long-Term Debt	272,465	24.8
Deferred Income Tax	191,121	17.4
Minority Interest	11,245	1.0
Common & Surplus	624,685	56.8
Total	1,099,516	100.0

RECENT DEVELOPMENTS: For the year ended 12/31/00, the Company reported a net loss of $66.4 million versus net earnings of $92.6 million the previous year. Results included one-time pre-tax restructuring credits of $24.0 million and $68.4 million in 2000 and 1999, respectively. Sales slipped 6.9% to $2.26 billion from $2.43 billion the year before, primarily reflecting lower sales volume from financial industry customers and MCL's strategy to exit low margin accounts.

PROSPECTS: On 1/3/01, the Company announced that it will begin implementing a series of cost-control initiatives expected to reduce annual expenses by $100.0 million over the next 12 to 18 months. MCL is taking steps to streamline its North American forms and labels operations and significantly reduced its operating costs through the elimination of 400 positions in the U.S. Meanwhile, the Company will integrate its Canadian operations with its U.S. forms and labels business in an effort to eliminate duplicate functions.

BUSINESS

MOORE CORPORATION LTD. is an international provider of products and services that help companies communicate through print and digital technologies. The Company's Forms, Print Management and Related Products segment, (69% of total revenues in 2000), includes custom business forms and equipment, print management outsourcing, facilities management, pressure seal mailing services, pressure sensitive labels, linerless labels, variable image bar codes, integrated forms/labels combinations and electronic forms. The Customer Communication Services segment (31%), includes personalized direct mail, statement printing and database management.

ANNUAL FINANCIAL DATA

	12/31/00	12/31/99	12/31/98	12/31/97	12/31/96	12/31/95	12/31/94
Earnings Per Share	**[2] d0.75**	**[2] 1.05**	**[1] d6.19**	**[1] 0.59**	**[2] 1.50**	**[2] 2.68**	**[3] 1.22**
Cash Flow Per Share	**0.96**	**2.19**	**d4.86**	**1.83**	**2.50**	**3.45**	**2.09**
Tang. Book Val. Per Share	**5.59**	**7.60**	**6.90**	**13.40**	**15.49**	**14.90**	**13.53**
Dividends Per Share	**0.20**	**0.20**	**0.57**	**0.94**	**0.94**	**0.94**	**0.94**
Dividend Payout %	**...**	**19.0**	**...**	**159.3**	**62.7**	**35.1**	**77.0**
INCOME STATEMENT (IN MILLIONS):							
Total Revenues	2,258.4	2,425.1	2,717.7	2,631.0	2,517.7	2,602.3	2,401.4
Costs & Expenses	2,153.1	2,182.1	3,230.4	2,465.8	2,275.5	2,401.7	2,181.5
Depreciation & Amort.	151.5	101.3	117.8	115.8	99.6	76.4	81.0
Operating Income	d46.2	141.7	d630.5	49.4	142.6	124.2	139.0
Net Interest Inc./(Exp.)	d25.6	d24.2	d19.1	d14.2	d11.8	d11.8	d13.1
Income Before Income Taxes	d81.6	128.6	d642.9	104.3	199.2	391.9	171.5
Income Taxes	cr17.4	35.3	cr94.3	49.2	48.6	123.7	43.9
Equity Earnings/Minority Int.	d2.2	d0.7	0.7	...	d0.7	d0.6	d1.1
Net Income	[2] d66.4	[2] 92.6	[1] d547.9	[1] 55.1	[2] 149.9	[2] 267.5	[3] 126.6
Cash Flow	85.1	193.9	d430.1	170.9	249.5	343.9	207.6
Average Shs. Outstg. (000)	88,457	88,457	88,456	93,200	99,967	99,754	99,538
BALANCE SHEET (IN MILLIONS):							
Cash & Cash Equivalents	36.5	38.2	138.6	227.1	694.3	722.0	266.9
Total Current Assets	699.6	750.9	894.3	965.1	1,369.6	1,449.7	1,009.7
Net Property	409.1	458.8	466.2	635.8	603.8	572.0	607.1
Total Assets	1,868.4	1,630.3	1,726.1	2,174.6	2,224.0	2,235.6	2,031.3
Total Current Liabilities	468.2	622.5	941.0	790.5	485.7	541.7	446.6
Long-Term Obligations	272.5	201.7	4.8	49.1	53.8	71.5	77.5
Net Stockholders' Equity	624.7	672.7	610.1	1,185.6	1,549.8	1,488.2	1,365.2
Net Working Capital	231.4	128.4	d46.7	174.6	883.8	908.0	563.1
Year-end Shs. Outstg. (000)	88,457	88,457	88,457	88,449	100,039	99,877	99,570
STATISTICAL RECORD:							
Operating Profit Margin %	...	5.8	...	1.9	5.7	4.8	5.8
Net Profit Margin %	...	3.8	...	2.1	6.0	10.3	5.3
Return on Equity %	...	13.8	...	4.6	9.7	18.0	9.3
Return on Assets %	...	5.7	...	2.5	6.7	12.0	6.2
Debt/Total Assets %	14.6	12.4	0.3	2.3	2.4	3.2	3.8
Price Range	6.75-2.19	12.38-5.81	17.69-9.44	22.88-13.50	22.25-17.00	23.50-17.50	20.88-16.25
P/E Ratio	...	11.8-5.5	...	38.8-22.9	14.8-11.3	8.8-6.5	17.1-13.3
Average Yield %	4.5	2.2	4.2	5.2	4.8	4.6	5.1

Statistics are as originally reported. All figures are in U.S. dollars unless otherwise noted. [1] Incl. $615.0 mil. pre-tax restr. chg., 1998; $32.0 mil. ($0.23/sh), 1997. [2] Incl. $24.0 mil pre-tax restr. credit, 2000; $68.4 mil., 1999; $25.0 mil. ($0.25/sh) after-tax gain fr sale of equity int., 1996; & $147.0 mill. ($1.47/sh), 1995. [3] Bef. unreal. exch. adj. $5.2 mil. chg.

OFFICERS:
R. T. Ammon, Chmn.
R. G. Burton, Pres., C.E.O.
R. B. Lewis, Exec. V.P., C.F.O.

INVESTOR CONTACT: James E. Lillie, Exec. V.P., (847) 607-7128

PRINCIPAL OFFICE: 40 King Street West, Suite 3501, Toronto, Ontario, Canada

TELEPHONE NUMBER: (416) 364-2600
FAX: (416) 364-1667
WEB: www.moore.com

NO. OF EMPLOYEES: 16,166 (approx.)

SHAREHOLDERS: 4,455

ANNUAL MEETING: In Apr.

INCORPORATED: CAN, Dec., 1938

INSTITUTIONAL HOLDINGS:
No. of Institutions: 34
Shares Held: 13,388,091
% Held: 15.1

INDUSTRY: Manifold business forms (SIC: 2761)

TRANSFER AGENT(S): Computershare Trust Company, Toronto, Ontario, Canada

NYSE SYMBOL JPM
Rec. Pr. 47.98 (4/30/01)

MORGAN (J.P.) CHASE & COMPANY

YIELD 2.8%
P/E RATIO 16.5

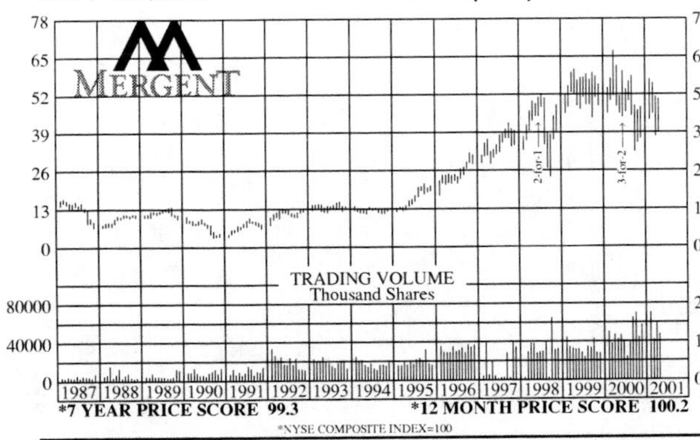

INTERIM EARNINGS (Per Share):

Qtr.	Mar.	June	Sept.	Dec.
1997	0.67	0.67	0.73	0.64
1998	0.53	0.80	0.63	0.87
1999	0.88	1.07	0.91	1.32
2000	1.06	0.85	0.66	0.34

INTERIM DIVIDENDS (Per Share):

Amt.	Decl.	Ex.	Rec.	Pay.
3-for-2	3/21/00	6/12/00	5/17/00	6/09/00
0.32Q	6/20/00	7/03/00	7/06/00	7/31/00
0.32Q	9/19/00	10/04/00	10/06/00	10/31/00
0.32Q	12/13/00	1/03/01	1/05/01	1/31/01
0.34Q	3/20/01	4/04/01	4/06/01	4/30/01

Indicated div.: $1.36 (Div. Reinv. Plan)

CAPITALIZATION (12/31/00):

	($000)	(%)
Total Deposits	279,365,000	75.6
Long-Term Debt	47,238,000	12.8
Redeemable Pfd. Stock	550,000	0.1
Preferred Stock	1,520,000	0.4
Common & Surplus	40,818,000	11.0
Total	369,491,000	100.0

RECENT DEVELOPMENTS: For the year ended 12/31/00, net income decreased 23.7% to $5.73 billion from $7.50 billion in 1999. Earnings for 2000 and 1999 included a private equity unrealized loss of $1.04 billion and an unrealized gain of $1.46 billion, respectively. Results for 2000 and 1999 also included pre-tax merger and restructuring costs of $1.43 billion and $23.0 million, respectively. Net interest income fell 7.5% to $9.51 billion. Comparisons were made with restated 1999 figures.

PROSPECTS: On 12/31/00, the Company completed the acquisition of J.P. Morgan & Co., Inc. for approximately $30.00 billion. JPM anticipates one-time, pre-tax costs of $3.20 billion related to the merger. The fourth quarter of 2000 included a pre-tax charge of $1.25 billion, with the balance of the costs expected to be incurred during 2001 and 2002. Also, JPM will eliminate 5,000 jobs, producing cost savings of $3.00 billion.

BUSINESS

J.P. MORGAN CHASE & COMPANY (formerly Chase Manhattan Corporation) is a global financial services firm with assets of $714.35 billion as of 12/31/00. On 3/31/96, Chase Manhattan Corp. merged with and into Chemical Banking Corp., which then changed its name to Chase Manhattan Corp. JPM was formed on 12/31/00 as a result of the acquisition of J.P. Morgan & Co. Inc. by Chase Manhattan Corp., subsequently adopting its present name. JPM conducts financial services businesses through various bank and non-bank subsidiaries. JPM serves 32.0 million customers throughout the U.S., and has offices in more than 60 countries. On 12/10/99, JPM acquired Hambrecht & Quist Group, Inc.

LOAN DISTRIBUTION

(12/31/2000)	($000)	(%)
Commercial	119,460,000	55.3
Consumer	96,590,000	44.7
Total	216,050,000	100.0

ANNUAL FINANCIAL DATA

	[6] 12/31/00	[5] 12/31/99	12/31/98	12/31/97	12/31/96	12/31/95	12/31/94
Earnings Per Share	[1] 2.86	[1] 4.18	[4] 2.83	[1] 2.68	[1] 1.67	[2][3] 2.26	[1] 1.55
Tang. Book Val. Per Share	12.96	18.29	17.93	15.84	14.19	14.16	12.60
Dividends Per Share	1.23	1.06	0.93	0.81	0.73	0.63	0.53
Dividend Payout %	43.1	25.4	32.8	30.1	43.4	27.8	34.0
INCOME STATEMENT (IN MILLIONS):							
Total Interest Income	36,643.0	20,237.0	22,289.0	21,756.0	19,909.0	11,118.0	9,088.0
Total Interest Expense	27,131.0	11,493.0	13,723.0	13,598.0	11,569.0	6,429.0	4,414.0
Net Interest Income	9,512.0	8,744.0	8,566.0	8,158.0	8,340.0	4,689.0	4,674.0
Provision for Loan Losses	1,377.0	1,621.0	1,554.0	804.0	897.0	478.0	550.0
Non-Interest Income	23,422.0	13,473.0	10,301.0	8,625.0	7,512.0	3,766.0	3,597.0
Non-Interest Expense	22,824.0	12,221.0	11,383.0	10,069.0	11,144.0	5,001.0	5,509.0
Income Before Taxes	8,733.0	8,375.0	5,930.0	5,910.0	3,811.0	2,976.0	2,212.0
Net Income	[1] 5,727.0	[1] 5,446.0	[4] 3,782.0	[1] 3,708.0	[1] 2,461.0	[2][3] 1,816.0	[1] 1,294.0
Average Shs. Outstg. (000)	1,969,000	1,285,500	1,303,950	1,317,600	1,339,200	759,000	747,000
BALANCE SHEET (IN MILLIONS):							
Cash & Due from Banks	23,972.0	16,229.0	17,068.0	15,704.0	14,605.0	9,077.0	8,832.0
Securities Avail. for Sale	320,099.0	123,894.0	120,495.0	122,148.0	104,647.0	66,177.0	47,233.0
Total Loans & Leases	216,050.0	176,159.0	172,754.0	170,066.0	156,465.0	82,628.0	79,227.0
Allowance for Credit Losses	3,665.0	3,457.0	3,552.0	5,236.0	4,922.0	2,864.0	2,940.0
Net Loans & Leases	212,385.0	172,702.0	169,202.0	164,830.0	151,543.0	79,764.0	76,287.0
Total Assets	715,348.0	406,105.0	365,875.0	365,521.0	336,099.0	183,890.0	171,423.0
Total Deposits	279,365.0	241,745.0	212,437.0	193,688.0	180,921.0	98,417.0	96,506.0
Long-Term Obligations	47,238.0	20,140.0	18,375.0	15,127.0	13,314.0	7,329.0	7,991.0
Total Liabilities	673,010.0	382,488.0	342,037.0	343,779.0	315,105.0	171,014.0	160,711.0
Net Stockholders' Equity	42,338.0	23,617.0	23,838.0	21,742.0	20,994.0	11,912.0	10,712.0
Year-end Shs. Outstg. (000)	1,928,490	1,240,756	1,271,850	1,262,892	1,292,433	753,000	735,000
STATISTICAL RECORD:							
Return on Equity %	13.5	23.1	15.9	17.1	11.7	15.2	12.1
Return on Assets %	0.8	1.3	1.0	1.0	0.7	1.0	0.8
Equity/Assets %	5.9	5.8	6.5	5.9	6.2	6.5	6.2
Non-Int. Exp./Tot. Inc. %	69.3	55.0	60.3	60.0	70.3	59.1	66.6
Price Range	67.17-32.38	60.75-43.88	51.71-23.71	42.19-28.21	31.96-17.38	21.58-11.92	14.04-11.21
P/E Ratio	23.5-11.3	14.5-10.5	18.3-8.4	15.8-10.5	19.1-10.4	9.6-5.3	9.1-7.2
Average Yield %	2.5	2.0	2.5	2.3	2.9	3.7	4.2

Statistics are as originally reported. Adj. for 3-for-2 split, 6/00; 2-for-1 split, 6/98. [1] Incl. restruct. chrg.: $1.43 bill., 2000; $48.0 mill., 1999; $192.0 mill., 1997; $1.81 bill., 1996; $48.0 mill., 1994. [2] Bef. acctg. chrg. of $11.0 mill. [3] Incl. $76.0 mill. gain on the sale of assets. [4] Incl. restruct. chrgs. of $529.0 mill. & prov. for risk mgmt. instrument cr. losses of $211.0 mill. [5] Results are for Chase Manhattan Corp. for 1999 and earlier. [6] Reflects merger with J.P. Morgan & Co.

OFFICERS:
D. A. Warner III, Chmn.
W. B. Harrison Jr., Pres., C.E.O.
D. Dublon, C.F.O.

INVESTOR CONTACT: Investor Relations, (212) 270-6000

PRINCIPAL OFFICE: 270 Park Ave., 39th floor, New York, NY 10017

TELEPHONE NUMBER: (212) 270-6000
FAX: (212) 682-3761
WEB: www.chase.com

NO. OF EMPLOYEES: 74,800

SHAREHOLDERS: 122,402

ANNUAL MEETING: In May

INCORPORATED: DE, 1968

INSTITUTIONAL HOLDINGS:
No. of Institutions: 198
Shares Held: 95,558,804
% Held: 4.8

INDUSTRY: National commercial banks (SIC: 6021)

TRANSFER AGENT(S): Mellon Investor Services, Ridgefield Park, NJ

NYSE SYMBOL MWD
Rec. Pr. 65.01 (5/31/01)

MORGAN STANLEY DEAN WITTER & CO.

YIELD 1.4%
P/E RATIO 13.7

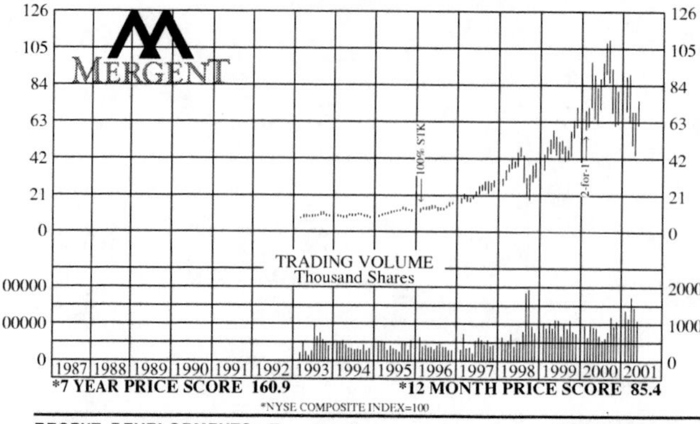

MERGENT

TRADING VOLUME
Thousand Shares

***7 YEAR PRICE SCORE 160.9** ***12 MONTH PRICE SCORE 85.4**

*NYSE COMPOSITE INDEX=100

INTERIM EARNINGS (Per Share):

Qtr.	Feb.	May	Aug.	Nov.
1997	0.47	0.43	0.56	0.67
1998	0.55	0.69	0.53	1.04
1999	0.88	0.98	0.83	1.42
2000	1.34	1.26	1.09	1.06

INTERIM DIVIDENDS (Per Share):

Amt.	Decl.	Ex.	Rec.	Pay.
0.20Q	3/23/00	4/12/00	4/14/00	4/28/00
0.20Q	06/27/00	7/05/00	7/07/00	7/28/00
0.20Q	9/22/00	10/04/00	10/06/00	10/27/00
0.23Q	12/19/00	1/10/01	1/12/01	1/30/01
0.23Q	3/21/01	4/04/01	4/06/01	4/27/01

Indicated div.: $0.92 (Div. Reinv. Plan)

CAPITALIZATION (11/30/00):

	($000)	(%)
Long-Term Debt	42,051,000	68.6
Preferred Stock	545,000	0.9
Common & Surplus	18,726,000	30.5
Total	61,322,000	100.0

RECENT DEVELOPMENTS: For the first quarter ended 2/28/01, income fell 30.4% to $1.08 billion, before an accounting charge of $59.0 million, versus $1.54 billion in the equivalent prior-year quarter. Net revenues declined 14.0% to $6.39 billion from $7.43 billion in the previous year. Net revenues for the securities segment decreased 19.4% to $4.74 billion from $5.88 billion in 1999. Credit services net sales grew 10.5% to $993.0 million, while net sales from the asset management segment rose 1.0% to $655.0 million.

PROSPECTS: The slowdown in trading revenue and equity underwriting opportunities is apparent in the Company's securities business, as net income fell 37.0% to $784.0 million during the quarter ended 2/28/01. However, these results are being partially offset by higher commission revenues, and strong performances from MWD's derivatives products, which continue to benefit from higher levels of volatility in global equity markets. Meanwhile, operating results from the credit services segment reflects higher consumer loan balances and strong transaction volume.

BUSINESS

MORGAN STANLEY DEAN WITTER & CO. (formerly Morgan Stanley, Dean Witter, Discover & Co.) was formed on June 2, 1997 resulting from a merger between Dean Witter, Discover & Co. and Morgan Stanley Group Inc., with Dean Witter, Discover & Co. as the surviving corporation. MWD is engaged in three business segments: securities, asset management and credit services. The securities business includes securities underwriting, distribution and trading; merger, acquisition, restructuring, project finance and other corporate finance advisory activities; full-service and on-line brokerage services; research services; trading of foreign exchange and commodities, derivatives, rates and indices; securities lending; and private equity activities. MWD's asset management business provides global asset management advice and services to investors. MWD's credit services business includes the issuance of the Discover® Card and the Morgan Stanley Dean Witter℠ Card and the operation of Discover Business Services.

BUSINESS LINE ANALYSIS

(11/30/2000)	Rev (%)	Inc (%)
Securities	75.6	74.2
Asset Management	9.6	12.5
Credit Services	14.8	13.3
Total	100.0	100.0

ANNUAL FINANCIAL DATA

	11/30/00	11/30/99	11/30/98	11/30/97	12/31/96	12/31/95	12/31/94
Earnings Per Share	**[2] 4.73**	**4.10**	**2.76**	**[1] 2.13**	**1.40**	**1.22**	**1.07**
Cash Flow Per Share	**5.37**	**4.56**	**3.23**	**2.40**	**1.52**	**1.32**	**1.15**
Tang. Book Val. Per Share	**16.91**	**16.38**	**11.88**	**11.00**	**8.08**	**6.92**	**5.84**
Dividends Per Share	**0.80**	**0.48**	**0.40**	**0.34**	**0.35**	**0.24**	**0.30**
Dividend Payout %	**16.9**	**11.7**	**14.5**	**16.0**	**25.1**	**19.7**	**28.1**
INCOME STATEMENT (IN MILLIONS):							
Total Revenues	45,413.0	33,928.0	31,131.0	27,132.0	9,028.6	7,934.4	6,602.6
Costs & Expenses	36,195.0	25,659.0	25,856.0	22,520.0	7,400.2	6,468.5	5,329.2
Depreciation & Amort.	727.0	541.0	575.0	338.0	83.3	70.0	58.8
Operating Income	8,491.0	7,728.0	4,700.0	4,274.0	1,545.1	1,395.9	1,214.6
Income Before Income Taxes	8,526.0	7,728.0	5,385.0	4,274.0	1,545.1	1,395.9	1,214.6
Income Taxes	3,070.0	2,937.0	1,992.0	1,688.0	593.7	539.5	473.7
Net Income	[2] 5,456.0	4,791.0	3,393.0	[1] 2,586.0	951.4	856.4	740.9
Cash Flow	6,147.0	5,288.0	3,913.0	2,858.0	1,034.7	926.4	799.7
Average Shs. Outstg. (000)	1,145,012	1,159,501	1,212,588	1,188,366	682,400	701,600	693,600
BALANCE SHEET (IN MILLIONS):							
Cash & Cash Equivalents	118,448.0	92,404.0	106,979.0	99,661.0	7,607.3	6,962.8	6,305.0
Total Current Assets	172,912.0	149,555.0	148,764.0	149,921.0	34,493.0	34,455.7	28,323.9
Net Property	2,685.0	2,204.0	1,834.0	1,705.0	379.7	341.0	280.6
Total Assets	426,794.0	366,967.0	317,590.0	302,287.0	42,413.6	38,208.2	31,859.4
Total Current Liabilities	352,271.0	309,927.0	266,014.0	253,910.0	26,056.6	23,852.7	20,114.3
Long-Term Obligations	42,051.0	28,604.0	27,435.0	24,792.0	8,144.2	6,732.4	5,292.6
Net Stockholders' Equity	19,271.0	17,014.0	14,119.0	13,956.0	5,164.4	4,833.7	4,108.0
Net Working Capital	d179,359.0	d160,372.0	d117,250.0	d103,989.0	8,436.4	10,603.0	8,209.6
Year-end Shs. Outstg. (000)	1,107,270	1,104,630	1,131,342	1,189,418	639,400	675,200	675,600
STATISTICAL RECORD:							
Operating Profit Margin %	18.7	22.8	15.1	15.8	17.1	17.6	18.4
Net Profit Margin %	12.0	14.1	10.9	9.5	10.5	10.8	11.2
Return on Equity %	28.3	28.2	24.0	18.5	18.4	17.7	18.0
Return on Assets %	1.3	1.3	1.1	0.9	2.2	2.2	2.3
Debt/Total Assets %	9.9	7.8	8.6	8.2	19.2	17.6	16.6
Price Range	110.00-58.63	71.44-35.41	48.75-18.25	29.75-16.38	17.19-11.25	14.56-8.38	10.78-7.88
P/E Ratio	23.3-12.4	17.4-8.6	17.7-6.6	14.0-7.7	12.3-8.1	11.9-6.9	10.1-7.4
Average Yield %	0.9	0.9	1.2	1.5	2.5	2.1	3.2

Statistics are as originally reported. Adj. for stk. splits: 2-for-1, 1/00 & 1/97. Figures prior to 1997 are for Dean Witter, Discover & Co. [1] Incl. non-recurr. chrg. $74.0 mill. [2] Incl. gain on the sale of a business of $35.0 mill.

OFFICERS:
P. J. Purcell, Chmn., C.E.O.
J. J. Mack, Pres.

INVESTOR CONTACT: Investor Relations, 212-762-8131

PRINCIPAL OFFICE: 1585 Broadway, 38th Floor, New York, NY 10036

TELEPHONE NUMBER: (212) 761-4000
FAX: (212) 761-0086
WEB: www.msdw.com

NO. OF EMPLOYEES: 62,679 (avg.)

SHAREHOLDERS: 130,000

ANNUAL MEETING: In March

INCORPORATED: DE, 1993

INSTITUTIONAL HOLDINGS:
No. of Institutions: 757
Shares Held: 576,705,139
% Held: 51.8

INDUSTRY: Personal credit institutions (SIC: 6141)

TRANSFER AGENT(S): Morgan Stanley Dean Witter Trust FSB, Jersey City, NJ

NYSE SYMBOL MOT
Rec. Pr. 14.70 (5/31/01)

MOTOROLA, INC.

YIELD 1.1%
P/E RATIO 25.3

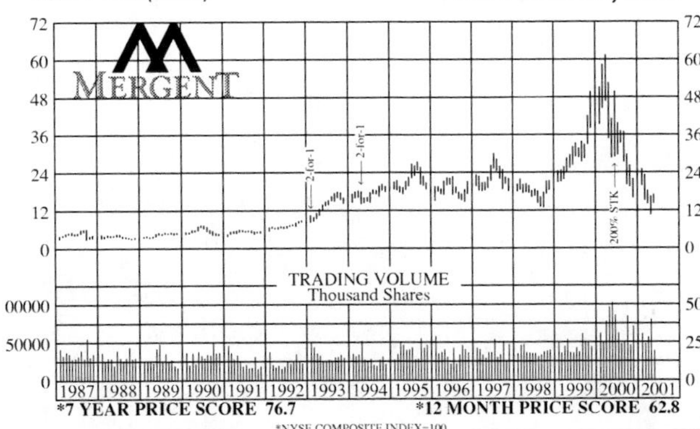

*7 YEAR PRICE SCORE 76.7 *12 MONTH PRICE SCORE 62.8
*NYSE COMPOSITE INDEX=100

INTERIM EARNINGS (Per Share):

Qtr.	Mar.	June	Sept.	Dec.
1997	0.18	0.15	0.15	0.18
1998	0.10	d0.74	0.01	0.09
1999	0.09	0.11	0.05	0.19
2000	0.20	0.09	0.23	0.06

INTERIM DIVIDENDS (Per Share):

Amt.	Decl.	Ex.	Rec.	Pay.
0.04Q	5/02/00	6/13/00	6/15/00	7/14/00
0.04Q	8/02/00	9/13/00	9/15/00	10/16/00
0.04Q	11/08/00	12/13/00	12/15/00	1/15/01
0.04Q	1/30/01	3/13/01	3/15/01	4/16/01
0.04Q	5/08/01	6/13/01	6/15/01	7/16/01

Indicated div.: $0.16 (Div. Reinv. Plan)

CAPITALIZATION (12/31/00):

	($000)	(%)
Long-Term Debt	4,293,000	17.6
Deferred Income Tax	1,504,000	6.2
Common & Surplus	18,612,000	76.3
Total	24,409,000	100.0

RECENT DEVELOPMENTS: For the year ended 12/31/00, net income soared 47.9% to $1.32 billion versus $891.0 million in the previous year. Net sales increased 13.6% to $37.58 billion from $33.08 billion the year before. Personal Communications segment sales advanced 11.2% to $13.27 billion. Global Telecom Services segment sales climbed 19.1% to $7.79 billion, while Semiconductor Products segment sales rose 6.7% to $7.88 billion.

PROSPECTS: The Company's Personal Communications Sector (PCS) will reduce its global workforce by nearly 7,000 additional positions in an effort to lower costs in its wireless handset business. This increases total PCS workforce reductions to 12,000 since December 2000. Moreover, the Company announced that it plans to sell its investments in some of its other wireless operators in the coming months.

BUSINESS

MOTOROLA, INC. provides electronic equipment, systems components and services for worldwide markets. MOT operates through four primary business segments. The Personal Communications segment includes sale of digital phones, wireless telephones and paging products. The Network Systems segment designs, manufactures, sells, installs and services wireless cellular and personal communication infrastructure equipment. The Commercial, Government and Industrial Systems segment provides integrated information and communications solutions for commercial, government and industrial customers worldwide. The Semiconductor Products segment designs and produces integrated semiconductors and software services. The Broadband Communications segment focuses on services that deliver interactive television, the Internet and cable modem business. On 1/5/00, MOT acquired General Instrument Corp.

QUARTERLY DATA

(12/31/2000)($000)	REV	INC
1st Quarter	8,768,000	448,000
2nd Quarter	9,255,000	204,000
3rd Quarter	9,493,000	531,000
4th Quarter	10,064,000	135,000

ANNUAL FINANCIAL DATA

	12/31/00	12/31/99	12/31/98	12/31/97	12/31/96	12/31/95	12/31/94
Earnings Per Share	**0.58**	**[3] 0.41**	**[2] d0.54**	**[1] 0.65**	**0.63**	**0.98**	**0.89**
Cash Flow Per Share	**1.70**	**1.43**	**0.69**	**1.92**	**1.90**	**2.03**	**1.75**
Tang. Book Val. Per Share	**8.49**	**8.74**	**6.78**	**7.41**	**6.63**	**6.20**	**5.16**
Dividends Per Share	**0.16**	**0.16**	**0.16**	**0.16**	**0.15**	**0.13**	**0.09**
Dividend Payout %	**27.6**	**39.3**	**...**	**24.7**	**23.2**	**13.6**	**10.0**
INCOME STATEMENT (IN MILLIONS):							
Total Revenues	37,580.0	33,075.0	29,398.0	29,794.0	27,973.0	27,037.0	22,245.0
Costs & Expenses	34,149.0	29,400.0	28,348.0	25,508.0	23,697.0	22,175.0	18,119.0
Depreciation & Amort.	2,522.0	2,254.0	2,208.0	2,339.0	2,316.0	1,931.0	1,547.0
Operating Income	909.0	1,421.0	d1,158.0	1,947.0	1,960.0	2,931.0	2,579.0
Net Interest Inc./(Exp.)	d248.0	d138.0	d216.0	d131.0	d185.0	d149.0	d142.0
Income Before Income Taxes	2,231.0	1,283.0	d1,374.0	1,816.0	1,775.0	2,782.0	2,437.0
Income Taxes	913.0	392.0	cr412.0	636.0	621.0	1,001.0	877.0
Net Income	1,318.0	[3] 891.0	[2] d962.0	[1] 1,180.0	1,154.0	1,781.0	1,560.0
Cash Flow	3,840.0	3,145.0	1,246.0	3,519.0	3,470.0	3,712.0	3,107.0
Average Shs. Outstg. (000)	2,256,600	2,202,000	1,795,800	1,836,600	1,830,000	1,830,000	1,776,000
BALANCE SHEET (IN MILLIONS):							
Cash & Cash Equivalents	3,655.0	4,236.0	1,624.0	1,780.0	1,811.0	1,075.0	1,059.0
Total Current Assets	19,885.0	17,585.0	13,531.0	13,236.0	11,319.0	10,510.0	8,925.0
Net Property	11,157.0	9,591.0	10,049.0	9,856.0	9,768.0	9,356.0	7,073.0
Total Assets	42,343.0	40,489.0	28,728.0	27,278.0	24,076.0	22,738.0	17,536.0
Total Current Liabilities	16,257.0	12,906.0	11,440.0	9,055.0	7,995.0	7,793.0	5,917.0
Long-Term Obligations	4,293.0	3,089.0	2,633.0	2,144.0	1,931.0	1,949.0	1,127.0
Net Stockholders' Equity	18,612.0	18,693.0	12,222.0	13,272.0	11,795.0	10,985.0	9,096.0
Net Working Capital	3,628.0	4,679.0	2,091.0	4,181.0	3,324.0	2,717.0	3,008.0
Year-end Shs. Outstg. (000)	2,191,200	2,139,300	1,803,300	1,792,200	1,779,000	1,773,000	1,764,000
STATISTICAL RECORD:							
Operating Profit Margin %	2.4	4.3	...	6.5	7.0	10.8	11.6
Net Profit Margin %	3.5	2.7	...	4.0	4.1	6.6	7.0
Return on Equity %	7.1	4.8	...	8.9	9.8	16.2	17.2
Return on Assets %	3.1	2.2	...	4.3	4.8	7.8	8.9
Debt/Total Assets %	10.1	7.6	9.2	7.9	8.0	8.6	6.4
Price Range	61.54-15.81	49.83-20.85	21.96-12.79	30.16-18.00	22.83-14.71	27.50-17.16	20.37-14.04
P/E Ratio	106.1-27.3	122.4-51.2	...	46.6-27.8	36.1-23.2	28.1-17.6	23.0-15.8
Average Yield %	0.4	0.5	0.9	0.7	0.8	0.6	0.5

Statistics are as originally reported. Adj. for stk. splits: 2-for-1, 4/94; 3-for-1, 6/00. [2] Incl. non-recurr. pre-tax chrg. $170.0 mill. for exiting DRAM business & pre-tax chrg. $95.0 mill. for exiting MacOS computer system business. [3] Incl. non-recurr. chrg. $1.98 bill. fr. restruc. [4] Incl. non-recurr. credit $236.0 million rel. to special items.

OFFICERS:
C. B. Galvin, Chmn., C.E.O.
F. T. Tucker, Exec. V.P., Deputy to the C.E.O.
R. L. Growney, Pres., C.O.O.

INVESTOR CONTACT: Investor Relations, (800) 262-8509

PRINCIPAL OFFICE: 1303 East Algonquin Road, Schaumburg, IL 60196

TELEPHONE NUMBER: (847) 576-5000
FAX: (847) 576-3477
WEB: www.motorola.com

NO. OF EMPLOYEES: 147,000 (avg.)

SHAREHOLDERS: 55,034

ANNUAL MEETING: In May

INCORPORATED: IL, Sept., 1928; reincorp., DE, May, 1973

INSTITUTIONAL HOLDINGS:
No. of Institutions: 832
Shares Held: 1,063,925,062
% Held: 48.4

INDUSTRY: Radio & TV communications equipment (SIC: 3663)

REGISTRAR(S): Computershare Investor Service, Chicago, IL

NYSE SYMBOL MOV
Rec. Pr. 17.85 (5/31/01)

MOVADO GROUP, INC.

YIELD 0.7%
P/E RATIO 10.1

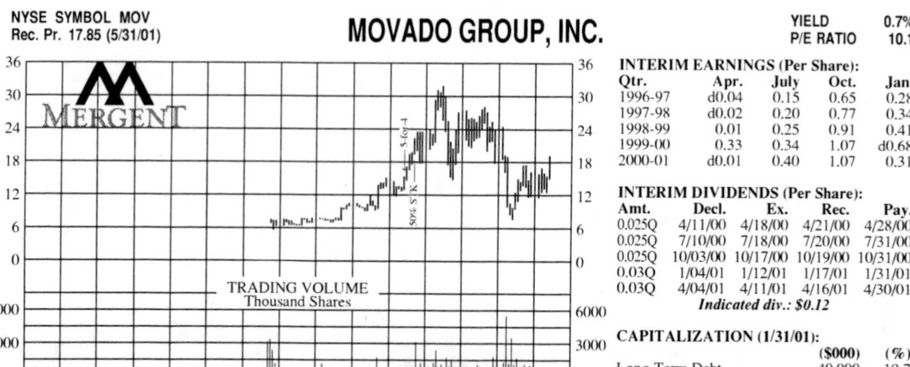

*7 YEAR PRICE SCORE 66.9 *12 MONTH PRICE SCORE 116.7
*NYSE COMPOSITE INDEX=100

INTERIM EARNINGS (Per Share):

Qtr.	Apr.	July	Oct.	Jan.
1996-97	d0.04	0.15	0.65	0.28
1997-98	d0.02	0.20	0.77	0.34
1998-99	0.01	0.25	0.91	0.41
1999-00	0.33	0.34	1.07	d0.68
2000-01	d0.01	0.40	1.07	0.31

INTERIM DIVIDENDS (Per Share):

Amt.	Decl.	Ex.	Rec.	Pay.
0.025Q	4/11/00	4/18/00	4/21/00	4/28/00
0.025Q	7/10/00	7/18/00	7/20/00	7/31/00
0.025Q	10/03/00	10/17/00	10/19/00	10/31/00
0.03Q	1/04/01	1/12/01	1/17/01	1/31/01
0.03Q	4/04/01	4/11/01	4/16/01	4/30/01

Indicated div.: $0.12

CAPITALIZATION (1/31/01):

	($000)	(%)
Long-Term Debt	40,000	19.7
Deferred Income Tax	3,517	1.7
Common & Surplus	159,470	78.6
Total	202,987	100.0

RECENT DEVELOPMENTS: For the year ended 1/31/01, net income increased 51.4% to $20.8 million compared with $13.7 million in the prior year. Results for 2001 included an after-tax gain of $3.7 million on the sale of the Piaget business, which was completed on 2/22/99, and non-recurring charges totaling $8.3 million. Results for 2001 and 2000 also included selling, general and administrative expenses of $163.3 million and $152.6 million, respectively. Net sales advanced 8.7% to $320.8 million from $295.1 million in the previous year.

PROSPECTS: Results were driven by the strength of the Company's core businesses. Domestic sales of the Company's core CONCORD, MOVADO, ESQ and COACH brands increased 7.9%, while international sales of MOV's core brands increased 6.2% and were led by the continuing international rollout of the COACH watch brand in the Far East. Separately, the Company expects significant improvements in its operating cost structure while maintaining gross margin levels.

BUSINESS

MOVADO GROUP, INC. is a designer, manufacturer and distributor of quality watches with prominent brands sold in almost every price category in the watch industry. MOVA divides the watch market into five principal categories; Exclusive ($10,000 and over), Luxury ($1,000 to $9,999), Premium ($500 to $999), Moderate ($100 to $499), and Mass Market (Less than $100). The Company currently markets four brands of watches: Movado, Concord, ESQ and Coach, which compete in the Exclusive, Luxury, Premium and Moderate categories. The Company designs and manufactures Movado and Concord watches primarily in Switzerland, as well as in the United States, for sale throughout the world. ESQ watches are manufactured to the Company's specifications by independent contractors located in the Far East and are presently sold primarily in the United States, Canada and the Caribbean. Coach watches are assembled in Switzerland by independent suppliers. On 2/22/99, the Company sold its Piaget business, and on 1/14/00, MOVA sold its Corum business.

ANNUAL FINANCIAL DATA

	1/31/01	1/31/00	1/31/99	1/31/98	1/31/97	1/31/96	1/31/95
Earnings Per Share	**2 1.75**	**1 1.06**	**1.58**	**1.29**	**1.04**	**0.86**	**1.24**
Cash Flow Per Share	**2.28**	**1.47**	**1.99**	**1.63**	**1.39**	**1.13**	**1.52**
Tang. Book Val. Per Share	**13.80**	**12.21**	**12.85**	**11.32**	**9.20**	**9.29**	**8.26**
Dividends Per Share	**0.10**	**0.10**	**0.08**	**0.07**	**0.05**	**0.05**	**0.03**
Dividend Payout %	**5.7**	**9.0**	**5.1**	**5.6**	**4.4**	**5.9**	**2.6**
INCOME STATEMENT (IN THOUSANDS):							
Total Revenues	320,841	295,067	277,836	237,005	215,107	185,867	160,853
Costs & Expenses	280,368	274,109	239,781	206,928	190,742	164,868	142,005
Depreciation & Amort.	6,341	5,189	5,380	4,121	3,946	2,949	3,109
Operating Income	34,132	15,769	32,675	25,956	20,419	18,050	15,739
Net Interest Inc./(Exp.)	d6,443	d5,372	d5,437	d5,383	d4,874	d4,450	d4,307
Income Before Income Taxes	27,689	15,149	27,238	20,573	15,545	13,600	11,432
Income Taxes	6,922	1,428	6,265	4,731	3,853	3,876	cr2,512
Net Income	2 20,767	1 13,721	20,973	15,842	11,692	9,724	13,944
Cash Flow	27,108	18,910	26,353	19,963	15,638	12,673	17,053
Average Shs. Outstg.	11,866	12,890	13,256	12,236	11,273	11,263	11,250
BALANCE SHEET (IN THOUSANDS):							
Cash & Cash Equivalents	23,059	26,615	5,626	10,874	4,885	3,829	4,896
Total Current Assets	241,220	226,826	262,431	219,649	184,664	180,786	167,662
Net Property	32,906	27,593	22,998	18,909	15,066	11,794	11,677
Total Assets	290,405	267,186	296,375	249,069	208,443	200,380	186,949
Total Current Liabilities	86,583	68,096	67,580	62,546	57,974	48,107	46,305
Long-Term Obligations	40,000	45,000	55,000	35,000	40,000	40,000	40,000
Net Stockholders' Equity	159,470	147,815	166,426	145,533	103,870	104,841	92,930
Net Working Capital	154,637	158,730	194,851	157,103	126,690	132,679	121,357
Year-end Shs. Outstg.	11,553	12,107	12,951	12,857	11,289	11,280	11,250
STATISTICAL RECORD:							
Operating Profit Margin %	10.6	5.3	11.8	11.0	9.5	9.7	9.8
Net Profit Margin %	6.5	4.7	7.5	6.7	5.4	5.2	8.7
Return on Equity %	13.0	9.3	12.6	10.9	11.3	9.3	15.0
Return on Assets %	7.2	5.1	7.1	6.4	5.6	4.9	7.5
Debt/Total Assets %	13.8	16.8	18.6	14.1	19.2	20.0	21.4
Price Range	24.50-7.56	28.13-17.75	31.88-14.75	23.50-11.73	15.20-9.07	10.53-7.00	7.80-6.27
P/E Ratio	14.0-4.3	26.5-16.7	20.2-9.3	18.2-9.1	14.7-8.8	12.2-8.1	6.3-5.1
Average Yield %	0.6	0.4	0.3	0.4	0.4	0.6	0.5

Statistics are as originally reported. Adj. for stk. splits: 50% div., 9/29/97; 5-for-4, 5/1/97
1 Incls. $4.8 mill. gain on the sale of business. 2 Incl. non-recurr. chrgs. of $4.6 mill.

OFFICERS:
G. Grinberg, Chmn.
E. Grinberg, Pres., C.E.O.
K. C. Johnson, Sr. V.P., C.F.O.

INVESTOR CONTACT: Rick Cote, Exec. V.P., C.O.O., (201) 460-4800

PRINCIPAL OFFICE: 125 Chubb Ave, Lyndhurst, NJ 07071

TELEPHONE NUMBER: (201) 460-4800
FAX: (201) 460-8891
WEB: www.movado.com
NO. OF EMPLOYEES: 838 (approx.)
SHAREHOLDERS: 46 class A; 2445 (approx. ben.) (410 common, of record)
ANNUAL MEETING: In June
INCORPORATED: NY, Nov., 1961

INSTITUTIONAL HOLDINGS:
No. of Institutions: 41
Shares Held: 6,538,446
% Held: 49.5

INDUSTRY: Watches, clocks, watchcases & parts (SIC: 3873)

TRANSFER AGENT(S): The Bank of New York, New York, NY

NYSE SYMBOL MSM
Rec. Pr. 16.84 (5/31/01)

MSC INDUSTRIAL DIRECT CO., INC.

YIELD ...
P/E RATIO 20.3

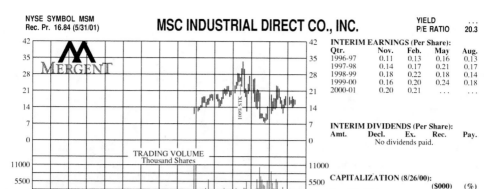

TRADING VOLUME
Thousand Shares

*7 YEAR PRICE SCORE N/A *12 MONTH PRICE SCORE 102.9

*NYSE COMPOSITE INDEX=100

INTERIM EARNINGS (Per Share):

Qtr.	Nov.	Feb.	May	Aug.
1996-97	0.11	0.13	0.16	0.13
1997-98	0.14	0.17	0.21	0.17
1998-99	0.18	0.22	0.18	0.14
1999-00	0.16	0.20	0.24	0.18
2000-01	0.20	0.21	...	...

INTERIM DIVIDENDS (Per Share):

Amt.	Decl.	Ex.	Rec.	Pay.

No dividends paid.

CAPITALIZATION (8/26/00):

	($000)	(%)
Long-Term Debt	68,398	13.6
Deferred Income Tax	12,386	2.5
Common & Surplus	421,669	83.9
Total	502,453	100.0

RECENT DEVELOPMENTS: For the quarter ended 2/24/01, net income increased 5.4% to $14.4 million compared with $13.6 million in the corresponding prior-year quarter. The increase in results was primarily attributed to higher existing customer sales and a larger number of active customers generated by an increase in the number of SKUs offered and a focused marketing effort. Net Sales were $211.5 million, up 6.7% from $198.2 million a year earlier. Income from operations grew 2.2% to $25.0 million from $24.4 million the year before.

PROSPECTS: The Company is continuing its strategy to build its market share through the addition of new customers and the securitization of several large national accounts. Going forward, the Company will develop an expanded sales force that should be instrumental in growing customer relationships. The sales force will assess customer needs while familiarizing customers with the Company's complete range of value-added services and products.

BUSINESS

MSC INDUSTRIAL DIRECT CO., INC. is a direct marketer of a broad range of industrial products to small and mid-sized industrial customers throughout the United States. The Company distributes a full line of industrial products, such as cutting tools, abrasives, measuring instruments, machine tool accessories, safety equipment, fasteners and welding and electrical supplies. The Company offers over 450,000 stock-keeping units through its 4,480 page master catalog and weekly, monthly and quarterly specialty and promotional catalogs, newspapers and brochures and services its customers from approximately 90 branch offices. Most of the Company's products are carried in stock, and orders for these products are typically fulfilled the day on which the order is received.

ANNUAL FINANCIAL DATA

	8/26/00	8/28/99	8/29/98	8/30/97	8/31/96
Earnings Per Share	**0.78**	**0.72**	**0.69**	**0.53**	**[1] 0.34**
Cash Flow Per Share	**0.99**	**0.85**	**0.80**	**0.61**	**0.52**
Tang. Book Val. Per Share	**5.25**	**4.31**	**3.88**	**3.56**	**2.54**
INCOME STATEMENT (IN THOUSANDS):					
Total Revenues	792,874	651,503	583,043	438,003	305,294
Costs & Expenses	685,169	560,582	499,086	373,332	267,298
Depreciation & Amort.	14,407	9,150	7,782	5,914	3,487
Operating Income	93,298	81,771	76,175	58,757	34,509
Net Interest Inc./(Exp.)	d4,995	d1,514	1,074	233	d887
Income Before Income Taxes	88,117	80,750	78,239	59,535	34,034
Income Taxes	35,191	31,897	30,904	23,518	5,531
Equity Earnings/Minority Int.	d465	...	...	...	...
Net Income	52,926	48,853	47,335	36,017	[1] 28,503
Cash Flow	67,333	58,003	55,117	41,931	31,990
Average Shs. Outstg.	68,203	68,317	68,964	68,218	61,392
BALANCE SHEET (IN THOUSANDS):					
Cash & Cash Equivalents	3,209	2,725	8,630	13,418	1,679
Total Current Assets	375,214	328,043	254,395	244,013	212,617
Net Property	116,378	106,750	77,493	49,658	38,989
Total Assets	580,974	514,384	401,702	334,834	265,484
Total Current Liabilities	78,521	80,795	70,645	53,669	48,832
Long-Term Obligations	68,398	69,468	2,430	2,744	42,191
Net Stockholders' Equity	421,669	355,627	321,779	274,995	172,571
Net Working Capital	296,693	247,248	183,750	190,344	163,785
Year-end Shs. Outstg.	67,956	66,900	67,825	67,696	64,622
STATISTICAL RECORD:					
Operating Profit Margin %	11.8	12.6	13.1	13.4	11.3
Net Profit Margin %	6.7	7.5	8.1	8.2	9.3
Return on Equity %	12.6	13.7	14.7	13.1	16.5
Return on Assets %	9.1	9.5	11.8	10.8	10.7
Debt/Total Assets %	11.8	13.5	0.6	0.8	15.9
Price Range	23.25-11.31	26.25-7.50	33.50-12.25	23.06-13.88	19.63-12.25
P/E Ratio	29.8-14.5	36.5-10.4	48.5-17.8	43.5-26.2	58.6-36.6

Statistics are as originally reported. Adj. for stk. splits: 100%, 5/26/98. [1] Incls. one-time chrg. of $8.6 mill.

OFFICERS:
M. Jacobson, Chmn., Pres., C.E.O.
S. Jacobson, Vice-Chmn.
C. Boehlke, Sr. V.P., C.F.O.
D. Sandler, Exec. V.P., C.O.O.

INVESTOR CONTACT: Shelley Boxer, Investor Relations

PRINCIPAL OFFICE: 75 Maxess Road, Melville, NY 11747

TELEPHONE NUMBER: (516) 812-2000
WEB: www.mscdirect.com

NO. OF EMPLOYEES: 2,651 full-time (approx.); 177 part-time (approx.)

SHAREHOLDERS: 562 (approx. Class A); 11(Class B)

ANNUAL MEETING: In Jan.

INCORPORATED: NY, Oct., 1995

INSTITUTIONAL HOLDINGS:
No. of Institutions: 90
Shares Held: 30,455,495
% Held: 43.9

INDUSTRY: Industrial machinery and equipment (SIC: 5084)

TRANSFER AGENT(S): American Stock Transfer & Trust Co., New York, NY

NYSE SYMBOL MUR
Rec. Pr. 82.00 (4/30/01)

MURPHY OIL CORPORATION

YIELD 1.8%
P/E RATIO 12.1

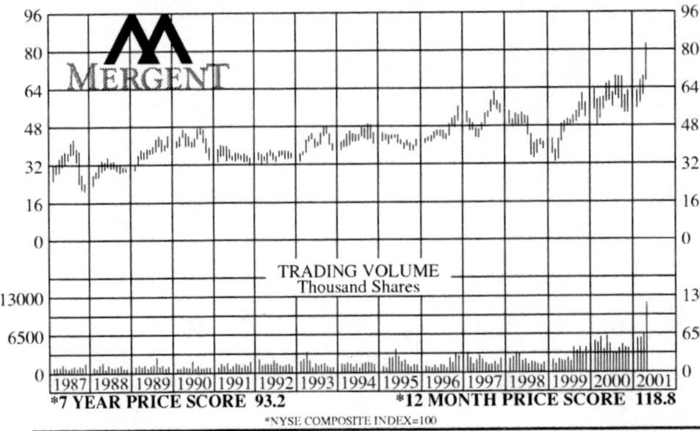

*7 YEAR PRICE SCORE 93.2 *12 MONTH PRICE SCORE 118.8

*NYSE COMPOSITE INDEX=100

INTERIM EARNINGS (Per Share):

Qtr.	Mar.	June	Sept.	Dec.
1995	0.36	0.46	0.17	d3.63
1996	0.45	0.55	0.90	0.90
1997	0.68	0.61	0.94	0.71
1998	0.35	0.49	0.20	d1.36
1999	d0.15	0.35	1.14	1.32
2000	1.09	1.61	1.99	2.06

INTERIM DIVIDENDS (Per Share):

Amt.	Decl.	Ex.	Rec.	Pay.
0.35Q	4/05/00	5/08/00	5/10/00	6/01/00
0.375Q	8/02/00	8/10/00	8/14/00	9/01/00
0.375Q	10/04/00	11/08/00	11/10/00	12/01/00
0.375Q	2/07/01	2/09/01	2/13/01	3/01/01
0.375Q	4/04/01	5/07/01	5/09/01	6/01/01

Indicated div.: $1.50

CAPITALIZATION (12/31/00):

	($000)	(%)
Long-Term Debt	524,759	26.1
Deferred Income Tax	229,968	11.4
Common & Surplus	1,259,560	62.5
Total	2,014,287	100.0

RECENT DEVELOPMENTS: For the year ended 12/31/00, income was $305.6 million, before an after-tax accounting change charge of $8.7 million, compared with net income of $119.7 million a year earlier. Results for 2000 included an impairment of properties charge of $27.9 million. Total revenues rose 68.4% to $4.64 billion from $2.76 billion the previous year. Results have been restated to conform to current presentation.

PROSPECTS: MUR's results are benefiting from strong commodity prices and improved results at its refining, marketing and transportation operations as continued expansion of the Company's Wal-Mart retail gasoline operations have led to higher gasoline sales volumes. Separately, on 3/1/01, MUR announced that it has entered into an agreement with Plains All American Pipeline, L.P. for the sale of its Canadian pipeline and trucking operation for $163.0 million, including inventory.

BUSINESS

MURPHY OIL CORPORATION is an international oil and gas company that produces oil and natural gas in the United States, Canada, the United Kingdom, and Ecuador, and conducts exploration activities worldwide. As of 12/31/00, the Company had a 5.0% interest in a Canadian synthetic oil operation, operated two oil refineries in the U.S. and owned a 30.0% interest in a U.K. refinery. MUR markets petroleum products under various brand names and to unbranded wholesale customers in the U.S. and the U.K. As of 12/31/00, net proved reserves were: crude oil, condensate and natural gas liquids, 326.1 million barrels; and natural gas, 697.4 billion cubic feet.

REVENUES

(12/31/2000)	($000)	(%)
Crude Oil & Natural Gas	751,498	16.2
Petroleum Products	2,731,988	58.9
Crude oil trading sale	1,041,524	22.5
Other operating revenue	89,331	1.9
Interest & other nonoperating revenue	24,824	0.5
Total	4,639,165	100.0

ANNUAL FINANCIAL DATA

	12/31/00	12/31/99	12/31/98	12/31/97	12/31/96	12/31/95	12/31/94
Earnings Per Share	**[6] 6.75**	**[5] 2.66**	**[1] d0.32**	**[2] 2.94**	**[3] 2.80**	**[2] d2.85**	**[4] 2.37**
Cash Flow Per Share	**11.79**	**7.44**	**4.42**	**7.84**	**7.07**	**2.33**	**7.24**
Tang. Book Val. Per Share	**26.89**	**23.49**	**21.76**	**24.04**	**22.90**	**24.56**	**28.34**
Dividends Per Share	**1.45**	**1.40**	**1.40**	**1.35**	**1.30**	**1.30**	**1.30**
Dividend Payout %	**21.5**	**52.6**	...	**45.9**	**46.4**	...	**54.9**
INCOME STATEMENT (IN MILLIONS):							
Total Revenues	4,639.2	2,041.2	1,698.8	2,137.8	2,022.2	1,631.8	1,768.5
Costs & Expenses	3,929.9	1,627.0	1,476.2	1,705.6	1,610.8	1,542.5	1,390.8
Depreciation & Amort.	227.6	215.4	213.1	219.9	192.1	232.6	218.2
Operating Income	481.7	198.8	9.5	212.3	219.3	d143.3	159.5
Net Interest Inc./(Exp.)	d16.3	d20.3	d10.5	d0.6	d2.9	d5.4	d2.6
Income Before Income Taxes	465.3	178.5	d8.3	211.7	216.4	d148.7	156.9
Income Taxes	159.8	58.8	6.1	79.2	90.4	cr20.8	50.3
Net Income	[6] 305.6	[5] 119.7	[1] d14.4	[2] 132.4	[3] 126.0	[2] d127.9	[4] 106.6
Cash Flow	533.2	335.1	198.8	352.3	318.0	104.7	324.8
Average Shs. Outstg. (000)	45,240	45,030	44,956	44,960	44,977	44,867	44,882
BALANCE SHEET (IN MILLIONS):							
Cash & Cash Equivalents	132.7	34.1	28.3	24.3	109.7	60.9	71.1
Total Current Assets	816.9	593.1	437.4	517.8	610.2	490.5	519.1
Net Property	2,184.7	1,782.7	1,662.4	1,655.8	1,556.8	1,377.5	1,722.7
Total Assets	3,134.4	2,445.5	2,164.4	2,238.3	2,243.8	2,098.5	2,312.0
Total Current Liabilities	745.2	487.6	380.8	469.4	554.0	403.1	439.5
Long-Term Obligations	524.8	393.2	333.5	205.9	201.8	193.1	172.5
Net Stockholders' Equity	1,259.6	1,057.2	978.2	1,079.4	1,027.5	1,101.1	1,270.7
Net Working Capital	71.7	105.5	56.6	48.3	56.1	87.4	79.6
Year-end Shs. Outstg. (000)	45,046	44,998	44,950	44,891	44,862	44,833	44,833
STATISTICAL RECORD:							
Operating Profit Margin %	10.4	9.7	0.6	9.9	10.8	...	9.0
Net Profit Margin %	6.6	5.9	...	6.2	6.2	...	6.0
Return on Equity %	24.3	11.3	...	12.3	12.3	...	8.4
Return on Assets %	9.7	4.9	...	5.9	5.6	...	4.6
Debt/Total Assets %	16.7	16.1	15.4	9.2	9.0	9.2	7.5
Price Range	69.06-48.19	61.63-32.88	54.44-34.50	62.56-43.00	56.50-40.63	45.38-37.50	49.13-37.88
P/E Ratio	10.2-7.1	23.2-12.4	...	21.3-14.6	20.2-14.5	...	20.7-16.0
Average Yield %	2.5	3.0	3.1	2.6	2.7	3.1	3.0

Statistics are as originally reported. [1] Incl. non-recurr. pre-tax chrg. of $87.4 mill. [2] Incl. non-recurr. net chrg. 12/31/97, $94.2 mill.; chrg. 12/31/95, $160.2 mill. [3] Bef. inc. fr. disc. ops. of $11.9 mill. [4] Bef. extraord. cr. of $20.3 mill. [5] Incl. non-recurr. chrg. of $953,000. [6] Incl. prop. impair. chrg. of $27.9 mill.; bef. acctg. chg. chrg. of $8.7 mill. ($0.19/sh.)

OFFICERS:
R. M. Murphy, Chmn.
C. P. Deming, Pres., C.E.O.
K. G. Fitzgerald, Treas.

INVESTOR CONTACT: Kevin G. Fitzgerald, Treas., (870) 864-6272

PRINCIPAL OFFICE: 200 Peach Street, P.O. Box 7000, El Dorado, AR 71730-7000

TELEPHONE NUMBER: (870) 862-6411
FAX: (870) 864-3673
WEB: www.murphyoilcorp.com

NO. OF EMPLOYEES: 1,711 full-time

SHAREHOLDERS: 3,185 (of record)

ANNUAL MEETING: In May

INCORPORATED: LA, May, 1950; reincorp., DE, May, 1963

INSTITUTIONAL HOLDINGS:
No. of Institutions: 214
Shares Held: 29,972,018
% Held: 66.5

INDUSTRY: Petroleum refining (SIC: 2911)

TRANSFER AGENT(S): Computershare Investor Services, L.L.C., Chicago, IL

NYSE SYMBOL MYE
Rec. Pr. 15.05 (5/31/01)

MYERS INDUSTRIES, INC.

YIELD 1.6%
P/E RATIO 12.6

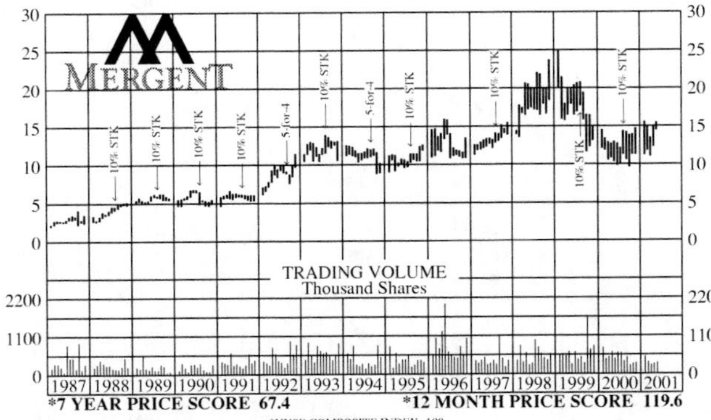

*7 YEAR PRICE SCORE 67.4 *12 MONTH PRICE SCORE 119.6

*NYSE COMPOSITE INDEX=100

INTERIM EARNINGS (Per Share):

Qtr.	Mar.	June	Sept.	Dec.
1997	0.24	0.25	0.19	0.41
1998	0.35	0.38	0.25	0.45
1999	0.41	0.45	0.20	0.49
2000	0.42	0.41	0.15	0.21

INTERIM DIVIDENDS (Per Share):

Amt.	Decl.	Ex.	Rec.	Pay.
10% STK	7/27/00	8/08/00	8/10/00	8/31/00
0.06Q	7/27/00	9/07/00	9/11/00	10/02/00
0.06Q	10/26/00	12/06/00	12/08/00	1/02/01
0.06Q	2/15/01	3/07/01	3/09/01	4/02/01
0.06Q	4/26/01	6/13/01	6/15/01	7/02/01

Indicated div.: $0.24 (Div. Reinv. Plan)

CAPITALIZATION (12/31/00):

	($000)	(%)
Long-Term Debt	284,273	55.8
Deferred Income Tax	11,038	2.2
Common & Surplus	213,903	42.0
Total	509,214	100.0

RECENT DEVELOPMENTS: For the year ended 12/31/00, net income decreased 23.0% to $24.0 million compared with $31.2 million in the prior year. The decline in earnings was attributed to higher costs of resin, mainly for high-density polyethylene, intensified competitive pressures for MYE's plastic products and softness in the U.S. automotive aftermarket. Results for 2000 included an after-tax restructuring charge of $1.9 million for closing MYE's Dayton, Ohio manufacturing facility. Net sales advanced 12.4% to $652.7 million from $580.8 million the year before.

PROSPECTS: The continued decline in the economy, including the slump in automotive, recreational vehicle, and truck markets and weakness in the automotive aftermarket, is expected to cause the Company's second half and full year performance to be below that of last year. The decline began in April and affects markets to which the Company sells plastic products. In response, the company is focusing on asset management and expense controls in an effort to reduce debt and increase profitability.

BUSINESS

MYERS INDUSTRIES, INC. is comprised of two segments: the manufacturing business and the distribution business. The manufacturing business designs, manufactures and markets reusable plastic storage systems for use in distribution and material handling, and other plastic and metal products for storage, assembly and material handling application. The Company operates in 25 facilities in Europe and North America and markets reusable plastics under the brand names NESTIER, AKROBINS and BUCKHORN. MYE also manufactures and sells molded rubber products and other materials used primarily in the tire and tire repair industries and for various other uses. The distribution business, primarily conducted by the Myers Tire Supply division through 42 branches, is engaged in the nationwide distribution of equipment, tools and supplies used for tire servicing and automotive underbody repair.

ANNUAL FINANCIAL DATA

	12/31/00	12/31/99	12/31/98	12/31/97	12/31/96	12/31/95	12/31/94
Earnings Per Share	**[1] 1.11**	**1.41**	**1.30**	**1.00**	**0.93**	**0.71**	**0.80**
Cash Flow Per Share	**3.08**	**3.10**	**2.09**	**1.59**	**1.43**	**1.18**	**1.22**
Tang. Book Val. Per Share	**0.78**	**0.38**	**7.35**	**6.95**	**6.48**	**5.57**	**5.29**
Dividends Per Share	**0.22**	**0.20**	**0.17**	**0.15**	**0.13**	**0.11**	**0.10**
Dividend Payout %	**20.1**	**14.4**	**13.4**	**15.4**	**13.7**	**15.7**	**12.6**
INCOME STATEMENT (IN THOUSANDS):							
Total Revenues	652,660	580,761	392,020	339,626	320,944	300,699	274,054
Costs & Expenses	546,563	473,711	325,129	288,098	273,733	262,408	233,907
Depreciation & Amort.	42,828	37,542	17,518	13,214	11,311	10,450	9,480
Operating Income	63,270	69,507	49,373	38,313	35,901	27,840	30,666
Net Interest Inc./(Exp.)	d22,360	d15,206	d888	d248	d285	d784	d620
Income Before Income Taxes	40,910	54,301	48,485	38,066	35,615	27,056	30,046
Income Taxes	16,909	23,125	19,806	15,727	14,612	11,087	12,215
Net Income	[1] 24,001	31,176	28,679	22,339	21,003	15,969	17,831
Cash Flow	66,828	68,719	46,197	35,553	32,314	26,419	27,312
Average Shs. Outstg.	21,693	22,184	22,149	22,350	22,529	22,456	22,401
BALANCE SHEET (IN THOUSANDS):							
Cash & Cash Equivalents	2,178	1,094	34,832	6,298	5,600	3,388	1,795
Total Current Assets	219,307	206,991	153,650	107,427	106,310	101,087	94,725
Net Property	204,198	189,496	109,443	90,551	80,660	69,430	61,378
Total Assets	624,797	600,410	306,708	224,078	207,122	193,604	172,027
Total Current Liabilities	115,583	102,244	51,234	39,644	36,853	32,372	34,094
Long-Term Obligations	284,273	280,104	48,832	4,261	4,569	13,335	4,155
Net Stockholders' Equity	213,903	207,747	202,689	176,677	162,445	145,184	130,909
Net Working Capital	103,724	104,747	102,417	67,783	69,457	68,715	60,631
Year-end Shs. Outstg.	21,590	21,986	22,189	22,117	22,433	22,502	22,401
STATISTICAL RECORD:							
Operating Profit Margin %	9.7	12.0	12.6	11.3	11.2	9.3	11.2
Net Profit Margin %	3.7	5.4	7.3	6.6	6.5	5.3	6.5
Return on Equity %	11.2	15.0	14.1	12.6	12.9	11.0	13.6
Return on Assets %	3.8	5.2	9.4	10.0	10.1	8.2	10.4
Debt/Total Assets %	45.5	46.7	15.9	1.9	2.2	6.9	2.4
Price Range	14.75-9.63	25.00-11.59	23.71-13.53	15.50-11.27	15.97-10.80	12.58-8.96	12.57-8.79
P/E Ratio	13.3-8.7	17.7-8.2	18.3-10.4	15.5-11.3	17.1-11.6	17.6-12.6	15.7-11.0
Average Yield %	1.8	1.1	0.9	1.2	1.0	1.0	0.9

Statistics are as originally reported. Adj. for stk. splits: 10% div., 8/00, 8/99, 8/97 & 8/95; 5-for-4, 8/94. [1] Incl. an after-tax restructuring chrg. of $1.9 mill.

OFFICERS:
S. E. Myers, Pres., C.E.O.
G. J. Stodnick, V.P., C.F.O.
M. I. Wiskind, Sr. V.P., Sec.

INVESTOR CONTACT: Gregory J. Stodnick, V.P., C.F.O., (330) 253-5592

PRINCIPAL OFFICE: 1293 South Main Street, Akron, OH 44301

TELEPHONE NUMBER: (330) 253-5592
FAX: (330) 761-6156
WEB: www.myersind.com

NO. OF EMPLOYEES: 4,383

SHAREHOLDERS: 2,165 (approx.)

ANNUAL MEETING: In Mar.

INCORPORATED: OH, Jan., 1955

INSTITUTIONAL HOLDINGS:
No. of Institutions: 78
Shares Held: 11,604,024
% Held: 53.8

INDUSTRY: Plastics products, nec (SIC: 3089)

TRANSFER AGENT(S): First Chicago Trust Company of New York, New York, NY

NYSE SYMBOL MYL
Rec. Pr. 26.74 (4/30/01)

MYLAN LABORATORIES, INC.

YIELD 0.6%
P/E RATIO 83.6

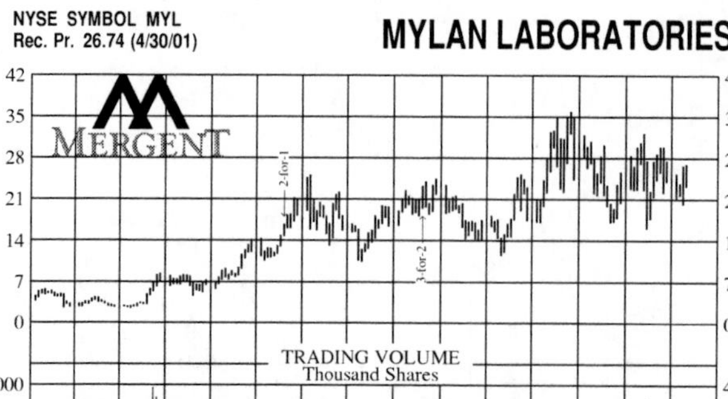

*7 YEAR PRICE SCORE 82.6 *12 MONTH PRICE SCORE 105.3

*NYSE COMPOSITE INDEX=100

INTERIM EARNINGS (Per Share):

0.30	June	Sept.	Dec.	Mar.
1997-98	0.14	0.25	0.18	0.26
1998-99	0.26	0.30	0.06	0.32
1999-00	0.25	0.28	0.31	0.34
2000-01	d0.59	0.27	0.30	...

INTERIM DIVIDENDS (Per Share):

Amt.	Decl.	Ex.	Rec.	Pay.
0.04Q	3/15/00	3/29/00	3/31/00	4/15/00
0.04Q	6/16/00	6/28/00	6/30/00	7/15/00
0.04Q	9/14/00	9/27/00	9/30/00	10/15/00
0.04Q	12/15/00	12/27/00	12/31/00	1/15/01
0.04Q	3/15/01	3/28/01	3/30/01	4/16/01

Indicated div.: $0.16

CAPITALIZATION (3/31/00):

	($000)	(%)
Long-Term Debt	30,630	2.5
Common & Surplus	1,203,722	97.5
Total	1,234,352	100.0

RECENT DEVELOPMENTS: For the quarter ended 12/31/00, net earnings fell 6.9% to $37.6 million versus $40.4 million in 1999. Net sales jumped 9.5% to $223.2 million from $203.9 million in the prior year. Net sales in the generic segment climbed 8.1% to $181.9 million due to the launch of new products, while net sales in the branded segment increased 15.7% to $41.3 million reflecting sales of new products, CLOZAPINE® and DIGITEK®, marketed by Bertek Pharmaceuticals.

PROSPECTS: On 2/7/01, the Company announced that the Food and Drug Administration has tentatively approved its abbreviated new drug application for Famotidine tablets in 20 mg and 40 mg strengths. The tablets are the generic equivalent to Merck Research Laboratories' PEPCID® tablets, which are indicated for the long-term treatment of active duodenal ulcers and the long-term treatment of gastroesophageal reflux disease.

BUSINESS

MYLAN LABORATORIES, INC. is engaged in developing, licensing, manufacturing, marketing, and distributing generic and branded pharmaceutical products. MYL's product portfolio consists of numerous prescription generic and proprietary pharmaceutical, wound care and dermatological products. These products include solid oral dosage forms as well as suspensions, liquids, injectables, transdermals and topicals, many of which are packaged in specialized systems. Revenues for fiscal 2000 were derived from the following: generic segment, 84.5%; and branded segment, 15.5%.

ANNUAL FINANCIAL DATA

	3/31/00	3/31/99	3/31/98	3/31/97	3/31/96	3/31/95	3/31/94
Earnings Per Share	**③ 1.18**	**② 0.91**	**0.82**	**0.52**	**① 0.86**	**1.02**	**0.62**
Cash Flow Per Share	**1.46**	**1.12**	**1.00**	**0.66**	**0.97**	**1.12**	**0.71**
Tang. Book Val. Per Share	**6.74**	**5.57**	**5.04**	**4.28**	**4.45**	**3.81**	**2.92**
Dividends Per Share	**0.16**	**0.16**	**0.16**	**0.16**	**0.21**	**0.11**	**0.09**
Dividend Payout %	**13.6**	**17.6**	**19.5**	**30.8**	**24.0**	**11.1**	**14.0**
INCOME STATEMENT (IN THOUSANDS):							
Total Revenues	790,145	721,123	555,423	440,192	392,860	396,120	251,773
Costs & Expenses	531,480	525,742	409,568	364,900	279,233	245,458	185,298
Depreciation & Amort.	35,706	26,911	21,708	17,347	13,450	12,700	11,154
Operating Income	222,959	168,470	124,147	57,945	100,177	137,962	55,321
Income Before Income Taxes	242,743	192,294	148,389	87,195	141,757	171,326	87,065
Income Taxes	88,497	76,885	47,612	24,068	39,432	50,457	13,998
Equity Earnings/Minority Int.	d4,193	5,482	10,282	18,814	24,968	25,406	23,596
Net Income	③ 154,246	② 115,409	100,777	63,127	① 102,325	120,869	73,067
Cash Flow	189,952	142,320	122,485	80,474	115,775	133,569	84,221
Average Shs. Outstg.	130,224	127,156	123,043	121,926	119,530	118,963	118,423
BALANCE SHEET (IN THOUSANDS):							
Cash & Cash Equivalents	303,050	259,721	145,697	140,032	189,440	179,855	88,451
Total Current Assets	686,746	582,959	451,072	379,020	379,328	331,383	209,573
Net Property	168,000	154,636	151,412	135,829	121,793	92,299	82,514
Total Assets	1,341,230	1,206,661	847,753	777,580	692,009	546,201	403,325
Total Current Liabilities	87,770	96,361	71,346	78,746	48,595	56,351	17,926
Long-Term Obligations	30,630	26,827	26,218	32,593	18,002	7,122	4,609
Net Stockholders' Equity	1,203,722	1,059,905	744,465	659,740	616,441	482,728	379,969
Net Working Capital	598,976	486,598	379,726	300,274	330,733	275,032	191,647
Year-end Shs. Outstg.	129,384	129,969	122,200	122,062	121,830	119,244	118,802
STATISTICAL RECORD:							
Operating Profit Margin %	28.2	23.4	22.4	13.2	25.5	34.8	22.0
Net Profit Margin %	19.5	16.0	18.1	14.3	26.0	30.5	29.0
Return on Equity %	12.8	10.9	13.5	9.6	16.6	25.0	19.2
Return on Assets %	11.5	9.6	11.9	8.1	14.8	22.1	18.1
Debt/Total Assets %	2.3	2.2	3.1	4.2	2.6	1.3	1.1
Price Range	32.00-17.06	35.94-17.06	25.31-11.50	23.38-14.00	24.50-16.50	19.92-10.42	25.08-13.08
P/E Ratio	27.1-14.5	39.5-18.7	30.9-14.0	44.9-26.9	28.5-19.2	19.5-10.2	40.4-21.1
Average Yield %	0.7	0.6	0.9	0.9	1.0	0.7	0.5

Statistics are as originally reported. Adjusted for 3-for-2 stock split, 8/95. ① Incl. an after-tax charge of $800,000 resulting from the sale of certain assets. ② Incl. a pre-tax charge of $29.0 million for acq. res. and dev. assoc. w/ the acq. of Penederm, Inc. ③ Incl. litig. settle. chrg. of $147.0 mill.

OFFICERS:
M. Puskar, Chmn., C.E.O.
R. F. Moldin, Pres., C.O.O.
D. C. Schilling, V.P., C.F.O.

INVESTOR CONTACT: Patricia Sunseri, V.P., (412) 232-0100

PRINCIPAL OFFICE: 1030 Century Bldg., 130 Seventh St., Pittsburgh, PA 15222

TELEPHONE NUMBER: (412) 232-0100
FAX: (412) 232-0123
WEB: www.mylan.com

NO. OF EMPLOYEES: 2,300 (approx.)

SHAREHOLDERS: 99,112 (approx.)

ANNUAL MEETING: In July

INCORPORATED: PA, 1970

INSTITUTIONAL HOLDINGS:
No. of Institutions: 247
Shares Held: 77,145,673
% Held: 61.7

INDUSTRY: Pharmaceutical preparations (SIC: 2834)

TRANSFER AGENT(S): American Stock Transfer & Trust Company, New York, NY

NYSE SYMBOL NC
Rec. Pr. 67.70 (4/30/01)

NACCO INDUSTRIES INC.

YIELD 1.4%
P/E RATIO 14.6

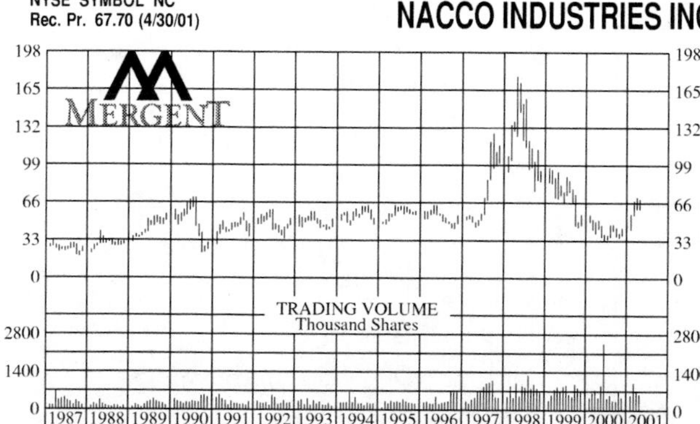

***7 YEAR PRICE SCORE 50.3** ***12 MONTH PRICE SCORE 148.8**

*NYSE COMPOSITE INDEX=100

INTERIM EARNINGS (Per Share):

Qtr.	Mar.	June	Sept.	Dec.
1997	0.35	1.82	1.78	3.62
1998	2.95	3.21	2.50	3.87
1999	1.59	2.00	0.86	2.22
2000	1.13	1.67	1.09	0.75

INTERIM DIVIDENDS (Per Share):

Amt.	Decl.	Ex.	Rec.	Pay.
0.225Q	5/10/00	5/30/00	6/01/00	6/15/00
0.225Q	8/09/00	8/30/00	9/01/00	9/15/00
0.225Q	11/08/00	11/29/00	12/01/00	12/15/00
0.225Q	2/14/01	2/27/01	3/01/01	3/15/01
0.235Q	5/09/01	5/30/01	6/01/01	6/15/01

Indicated div.: $0.94

CAPITALIZATION (12/31/00):

	($000)	(%)
Long-Term Debt	650,400	51.6
Minority Interest	4,200	0.3
Common & Surplus	606,400	48.1
Total	1,261,000	100.0

RECENT DEVELOPMENTS: For the year ended 12/31/00, NC reported income of $37.8 million, before an extraordinary gain of $29.9 million, versus income of $54.3 million, before an accounting charge of $1.2 million, in 1999. Results for 2000 included an after-tax restructuring charge of $8.3 million and an after-tax write-off of assets of $1.5 million. Total revenues rose 8.9% to $2.87 billion from $2.64 billion in the prior year.

PROSPECTS: NMHG Wholesale expects lift truck shipments in the U.S. to remain strong in 2001. Also, NMHG expects to incur after-tax restructuring costs of about $7.5 million in 2001 and $5.1 million in 2002 as part of the planned phase-out of its Danville assembly plant. These charges are expected to create after-tax cost savings of approximately $4.7 million in 2002 and about $9.3 million annually beginning in 2003.

BUSINESS

NACCO INDUSTRIES, INC., with assets of $2.19 billion as of 12/31/00, is a holding company with three operating subsidiaries: NACCO Materials Handling Group (NMHG), The North American Coal Corp., and the Housewares Group, comprised of Hamilton Beach/Proctor-Silex, Inc. (HB/PS) and the Kitchen Collection, Inc. NMHG designs and manufactures forklift trucks, marketed under the HYSTER and YALE brand names. North American Coal mines and markets lignite coal, primarily as fuel for power generation by electric utilities. HB/PS is a manufacturer of small electric appliances, and the Kitchen Collection, Inc. is a national specialty retailer of kitchenware and electric appliances.

ANNUAL FINANCIAL DATA

	12/31/00	12/31/99	12/31/98	12/31/97	12/31/96	12/31/95	12/31/94
Earnings Per Share	**1 4 4.63**	**3 6.66**	**2 12.53**	**2 7.55**	**5.67**	**1 7.31**	**1 5.06**
Cash Flow Per Share	**17.62**	**19.41**	**23.43**	**18.37**	**15.22**	**16.13**	**14.02**
Tang. Book Val. Per Share	**20.01**	**11.51**	**9.52**	...	...	...	...
Dividends Per Share	**0.89**	**0.85**	**0.81**	**0.77**	**0.74**	**0.71**	**0.68**
Dividend Payout %	**19.2**	**12.8**	**6.5**	**10.2**	**13.1**	**9.7**	**13.3**
INCOME STATEMENT (IN MILLIONS):							
Total Revenues	2,871.3	2,602.8	2,536.2	2,246.9	2,273.2	2,204.5	1,864.9
Costs & Expenses	2,647.3	2,367.5	2,249.1	2,026.3	2,056.7	1,974.2	1,649.6
Depreciation & Amort.	106.1	104.0	89.0	88.6	85.3	79.3	80.2
Operating Income	117.9	131.3	198.1	132.0	131.2	151.1	135.1
Net Interest Inc./(Exp.)	d47.1	d43.3	d34.6	d36.6	d45.9	d50.0	d58.8
Income Before Income Taxes	60.0	86.6	166.0	89.1	86.3	103.5	78.5
Income Taxes	22.3	31.7	60.7	26.4	34.3	34.7	30.7
Equity Earnings/Minority Int.	0.1	d0.6	d3.0	d0.9	d1.4	d3.3	d2.5
Net Income	1 4 37.8	3 54.3	2 102.3	2 61.8	50.6	1 65.5	1 45.3
Cash Flow	143.9	158.3	191.3	150.4	135.9	144.8	125.4
Average Shs. Outstg. (000)	8,167	8,154	8,166	8,189	8,931	8,975	8,948
BALANCE SHEET (IN MILLIONS):							
Cash & Cash Equivalents	33.7	36.2	34.7	24.1	47.8	30.9	19.5
Total Current Assets	815.7	772.2	703.2	599.6	591.8	722.0	586.6
Net Property	710.7	625.4	593.4	541.7	550.3	534.4	485.3
Total Assets	2,193.9	2,013.0	1,898.3	1,729.1	1,708.1	1,833.7	1,694.3
Total Current Liabilities	650.2	583.1	548.6	506.5	416.0	523.7	481.4
Long-Term Obligations	650.4	615.5	569.6	558.2	674.8	666.7	618.6
Net Stockholders' Equity	606.4	562.2	518.3	425.1	379.3	370.1	279.4
Net Working Capital	165.5	189.1	154.6	93.1	175.8	198.3	105.2
Year-end Shs. Outstg. (000)	8,171	9,804	8,120	8,154	8,186	8,952	8,952
STATISTICAL RECORD:							
Operating Profit Margin %	4.1	5.0	7.8	5.9	5.8	6.9	7.2
Net Profit Margin %	1.3	2.1	4.0	2.8	2.2	3.0	2.4
Return on Equity %	6.2	9.7	19.7	14.5	13.3	17.7	16.2
Return on Assets %	1.7	2.7	5.4	3.6	3.0	3.6	2.7
Debt/Total Assets %	29.6	30.6	30.0	32.3	39.5	36.4	36.5
Price Range	55.75-33.56	97.00-44.50	177.00-76.25	127.00-44.38	64.00-43.13	64.00-46.88	64.00-45.75
P/E Ratio	12.0-7.2	14.6-6.7	14.1-6.1	16.8-5.9	11.3-7.6	8.8-6.4	12.6-9.0
Average Yield %	2.0	1.2	0.6	0.9	1.4	1.3	1.2

Statistics are as originally reported. 1 Bef. extra. gain of $29.9 mill., 2000; gain $28.9 mill., 1995; chrg. $3.2 mill., 1994. 2 Incl. restruct. chrgs. $1.6 mill., 1998; $8.0 mill., 1997. 3 Bef. acctg. chrg. of $1.2 mill. & incl. chrg. of $1.9 mill. rel. to the proposed acq. of Nissan Motor Co., Ltd.'s global lift truck business. 4 Incl. an after-tax restruct. chrg. of $8.3 mill. & an after-tax write-off of assets of $1.5 mill.

OFFICERS:
A. M. Rankin Jr., Chmn., Pres., C.E.O.
J. C. Butler Jr., V.P., Treas.
C. A. Bittenbender, V.P., Gen. Couns., Sec.

INVESTOR CONTACT: Ira Gamm, Manager of Investor Relations, (440) 449-9676

PRINCIPAL OFFICE: 5875 Landerbrook Drive, Mayfield Heights, OH 44124-4017

TELEPHONE NUMBER: (440) 449-9600
FAX: (440) 449-9607
WEB: www.naccoind.com
NO. OF EMPLOYEES: 17,200 (approx.)
SHAREHOLDERS: 500 (class A com.); 400 (class B com.)
ANNUAL MEETING: In May
INCORPORATED: DE, 1986

INSTITUTIONAL HOLDINGS:
No. of Institutions: 76
Shares Held: 3,054,912
% Held: 37.4

INDUSTRY: Industrial trucks and tractors (SIC: 3537)

TRANSFER AGENT(S): First Chicago Trust Company of New York, Jersey City, NJ

NYSE SYMBOL NSH
Rec. Pr. 6.70 (5/31/01)

NASHUA CORPORATION

YIELD ...
P/E RATIO 6.9

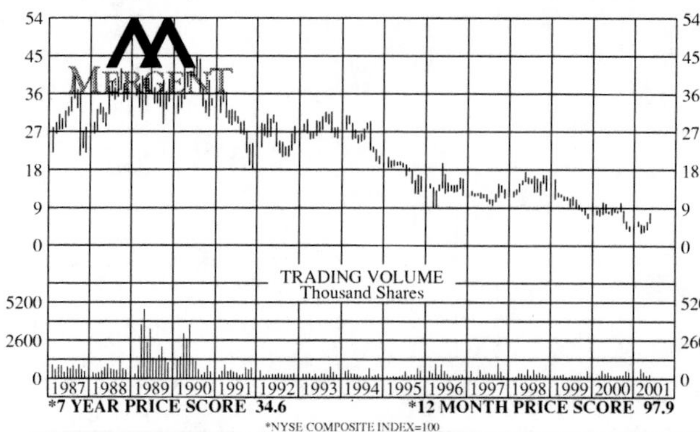

INTERIM EARNINGS (Per Share):

Qtr.	Mar.	June	Sept.	Dec.
1997	d0.22	d0.30	d0.48	d0.19
1998	d0.10	d0.35	d1.27	0.29
1999	0.04	0.09	0.12	d0.32
2000	1.75	0.04	d0.18	d0.64

INTERIM DIVIDENDS (Per Share):

Amt.	Decl.	Ex.	Rec.	Pay.
0.01RR	5/02/00	5/05/00	5/09/00	5/12/00

CAPITALIZATION (12/31/00):

	($000)	(%)
Long-Term Debt	35,905	33.2
Common & Surplus	72,337	66.8
Total	108,242	100.0

RECENT DEVELOPMENTS: For the year ended 12/31/00, net income was $5.4 million versus a loss from continuing operations of $420,000 a year earlier. Results for 2000 included an $18.6 million pre-tax gain from a pension settlement and a pre-tax restructuring and unusual charge of $966,000. Prior-year results included a pre-tax restructuring and unusual gain of $1.3 million. Net sales jumped 48.2% to $253.1 million, due to the April 2000 acquisition of Rittenhouse Paper Co.

PROSPECTS: Profits are being squeezed by higher raw material prices, underutilized toner capacity, higher-than-expected start-up costs for certain products, and increased competition. Going forward, NSH will focus on boosting sales of value-added products in growth markets and streamlining processes to help reduce costs.

BUSINESS

NASHUA CORPORATION is a multinational company providing a diverse mix of products and services, which include coated paper products, computer products and office supplies. Specific products include thermal papers, pressure-sensitive labels, cut/roll, bond, point-of-sale, ATM and wide-format papers, entertainment tickets, as well as toners and developers and ribbons used in imaging devices. Nashua products are sold internationally by wholly-owned foreign subsidiaries and approximately 80 distributors. On 4/9/98, the Company completed the sale of its photofinishing operations. On 4/6/98, NSH sold its United Kingdom-based Microsharp imaging technology operation.

QUARTERLY DATA

(12/31/2000) ($000)	Rev	Inc
1st Quarter	44,010	9,841
2nd Quarter	68,723	202
3rd Quarter	73,310	(1,035)
4th Quarter	67,079	(3,622)

ANNUAL FINANCIAL DATA

	12/31/00	12/31/99	12/31/98	[5] 12/31/97	12/31/96	12/31/95	12/31/94
Earnings Per Share	[8] 0.95	[7] d0.07	[6] d1.15	[1] d0.94	[3] 2.58	[4] d2.43	[2] 0.70
Cash Flow Per Share	2.59	1.04	d0.06	0.24	5.32	0.30	3.10
Tang. Book Val. Per Share	6.99	11.34	12.01	14.15	15.39	11.56	14.55
Dividends Per Share	0.01	...	...	...	...	0.72	0.72
Dividend Payout %	1.1	...	...	...	...	...	102.8
INCOME STATEMENT (IN THOUSANDS):							
Total Revenues	253,122	170,844	167,831	173,202	389,742	452,196	478,571
Costs & Expenses	228,906	161,938	174,125	176,181	380,785	450,099	453,968
Depreciation & Amort.	9,304	6,381	6,846	7,554	17,457	17,400	15,270
Operating Income	14,912	2,525	d13,140	d10,533	d8,500	d15,303	9,333
Net Interest Inc./(Exp.)	d1,993	678	1,190	233	d2,046	d4,846	d1,866
Income Before Income Taxes	12,914	2,883	d11,950	d9,994	28,634	d20,149	7,467
Income Taxes	7,528	3,303	cr4,721	cr3,988	12,141	cr4,679	3,025
Net Income	[8] 5,386	[7] d420	[6] d7,229	[1] d6,006	[3] 16,493	[4] d15,470	[2] 4,442
Cash Flow	14,690	5,961	d383	1,548	33,950	1,930	19,712
Average Shs. Outstg.	5,667	5,718	6,320	6,433	6,378	6,374	6,360
BALANCE SHEET (IN THOUSANDS):							
Cash & Cash Equivalents	1,035	30,056	36,965	3,736	20,018	8,390	10,219
Total Current Assets	71,543	79,567	83,347	45,770	72,165	99,192	108,162
Net Property	54,553	40,002	39,330	40,415	60,118	70,057	70,857
Total Assets	170,471	130,445	134,095	146,762	176,689	231,372	227,825
Total Current Liabilities	49,012	44,005	37,473	26,878	50,992	67,405	61,373
Long-Term Obligations	35,905	511	1,064	3,489	2,044	68,350	49,166
Net Stockholders' Equity	72,337	66,826	75,227	95,022	101,917	74,875	92,696
Net Working Capital	22,531	35,562	45,874	18,892	21,173	31,787	46,789
Year-end Shs. Outstg.	5,988	5,892	6,263	6,717	6,623	6,479	6,372
STATISTICAL RECORD:							
Operating Profit Margin %	5.9	1.5	...	...	...	...	2.0
Net Profit Margin %	2.1	...	...	...	4.2	...	0.9
Return on Equity %	7.4	...	...	...	16.2	...	4.8
Return on Assets %	3.2	...	...	...	9.3	...	1.9
Debt/Total Assets %	21.1	0.4	0.8	2.4	1.2	29.5	21.6
Price Range	10.44-3.51	15.81-6.50	17.50-11.56	14.75-9.50	19.63-9.13	21.00-12.25	30.88-19.38
P/E Ratio	11.0-3.7	...	...	...	7.6-3.5	...	44.1-27.7
Average Yield %	0.1	...	...	...	...	4.3	2.9

Statistics are as originally reported. [1] Bef. $2.8 mil loss fr. disc. ops., incl. $4.3 mil restr. chg. [2] Bef. $2.3 mil loss fr. disc. ops., incl. $3.5 mil non-recur. chg. [3] Bef. $9.0 mil net gain fr. disc. ops. & $1.3 mil extraord. chg., incl. $39.3 mil pre-tax gain & $7.2 mil chg. [4] Bef. $739,000 cr. fr. disc. ops., incl. $16.2 mil restr. chg. [5] Refl. sale of photofin. bus. [6] Bef. $5.6 mil loss fr. disc. ops., incl. $13.8 mil restr. chg. [7] Bef. $4.0 mil loss fr. disc. ops., incl. $1.3 mil pre-tax restr. gain. [8] Incl. $18.6 mil pre-tax gain & $966,000 pre-tax restr. chg.

OFFICERS:
A. Albert, Chmn., C.E.O.
J. M. Kucharski, Vice-Chmn.

INVESTOR CONTACT: William J. Manning, Assistant Treasurer, (603) 880-2736

PRINCIPAL OFFICE: 11 Trafalgar Square, Second Floor, Nashua, NH 03063

TELEPHONE NUMBER: (603) 880-2323
FAX: (603) 880-5671
WEB: www.nashua.com
NO. OF EMPLOYEES: 1,140 (approx.)
SHAREHOLDERS: 1,200
ANNUAL MEETING: In May
INCORPORATED: MA, 1904; reincorp., DE, Nov., 1957

INSTITUTIONAL HOLDINGS:
No. of Institutions: 23
Shares Held: 3,401,437
% Held: 58.3

INDUSTRY: Paper coated and laminated, nec (SIC: 2672)

TRANSFER AGENT(S): EquiServe, Boston, MA

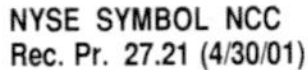

NYSE SYMBOL NCC
Rec. Pr. 27.21 (4/30/01)

NATIONAL CITY CORPORATION

YIELD 4.2%
P/E RATIO 12.8

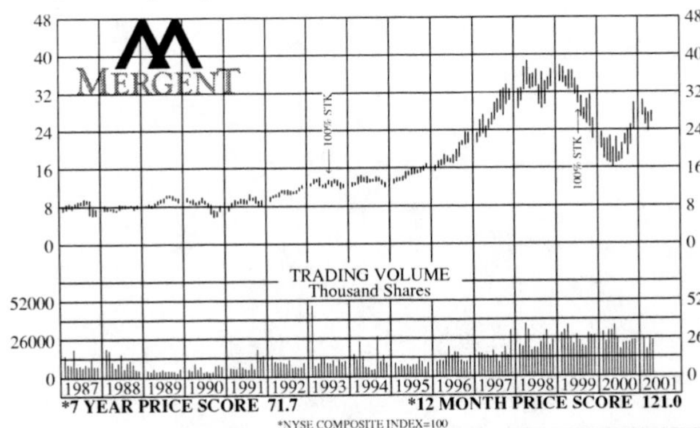

*7 YEAR PRICE SCORE 71.7 *12 MONTH PRICE SCORE 121.0

*NYSE COMPOSITE INDEX=100

INTERIM EARNINGS (Per Share):

Qtr.	Mar.	June	Sept.	Dec.
1997	0.44	0.45	0.47	0.48
1998	0.16	0.50	0.52	0.44
1999	0.54	0.56	0.57	0.55
2000	0.53	0.56	0.54	0.50

INTERIM DIVIDENDS (Per Share):

Amt.	Decl.	Ex.	Rec.	Pay.
0.285Q	7/05/00	7/13/00	7/17/00	8/01/00
0.285Q	10/02/00	10/10/00	10/12/00	11/01/00
0.285Q	10/02/00	10/10/00	10/12/00	11/01/00
0.285Q	1/02/01	1/08/01	1/10/01	2/01/01
0.285Q	4/02/01	4/10/01	4/12/01	5/01/01

Indicated div.: $1.14 (Div. Reinv. Plan)

CAPITALIZATION (12/31/00):

	($000)	(%)
Total Deposits	55,256,422	68.9
Long-Term Debt	18,144,800	22.6
Preferred Stock	29,968	0.0
Common & Surplus	6,739,853	8.4
Total	80,171,043	100.0

RECENT DEVELOPMENTS: For the year ended 12/31/00, net income declined 7.3% to $1.30 billion from $1.41 billion in the previous year. Net interest income fell 1.4% to $2.96 billion from $3.00 billion the year before. Provision for loan losses increased 14.9% to $286.8 million from $249.7 million in the prior year. Total non-interest income improved 4.3% to $2.48 billion. Total non-interest expense grew 6.8% to $3.18 billion.

PROSPECTS: Going forward, NCC expects to perform well in 2001 and to continue to benefit from its company-wide service quality improvement initiative. The Company's Retail Sales and Distribution segment intends to make increases in deposits, small business relationships and referrals to other units in the Company. NCC will also market a set of on-line banking products for small businesses.

BUSINESS

NATIONAL CITY CORPORATION is a bank holding company, with total assets of $88.53 billion as of 12/31/00, providing financial services principally in Ohio, Pennsylvania, Kentucky, Michigan, Illinois, and Indiana. Its principal banking subsidiaries are National City Bank, Cleveland; BancOhio National Bank, Columbus; First National Bank of Louisville; and Merchants National Bank & Trust Co. of Indianapolis. NCC offers financial services such as credit card, brokerage services, trust and investment management, mortgage banking, and small business and community investment services. NCC owns approximately 88.0% of National Processing Inc. In March 1998, NCC acquired Fort Wayne Corp. and First of America Bank Corp. On 9/1/99, NCC acquired First Franklin Financial Cos., Inc.

LOAN DISTRIBUTION

(12/31/2000)	($000)	(%)
Commercial	26,704,000	40.7
Real Estate-Commercial	6,511,000	9.9
Real Estate-Residential	13,357,000	20.4
Consumer	12,101,000	18.5
Credit Card	2,152,000	3.2
Home Equity	4,779,000	7.3
Total	65,604,000	100.0

ANNUAL FINANCIAL DATA

	12/31/00	12/31/99	[2] 12/31/98	12/31/97	12/31/96	12/31/95	12/31/94
Earnings Per Share	2.13	[3] 2.22	[1] 1.61	[1] 1.83	[1] 1.65	1.52	1.35
Tang. Book Val. Per Share	11.06	9.39	10.69	10.14	9.93	9.40	8.18
Dividends Per Share	1.43	1.06	0.94	0.83	0.73	0.65	0.59
Dividend Payout %	66.9	47.7	58.4	45.6	44.7	42.9	43.7
INCOME STATEMENT (IN MILLIONS):							
Total Interest Income	6,566.6	5,912.6	5,756.7	3,776.1	3,655.3	2,533.1	2,041.9
Total Interest Expense	3,608.2	2,912.6	2,845.0	1,833.3	1,712.8	1,212.0	805.1
Net Interest Income	2,958.4	3,000.0	2,911.6	1,942.8	1,942.6	1,321.1	1,236.8
Provision for Loan Losses	286.8	249.7	201.4	139.7	146.5	97.5	79.4
Non-Interest Income	2,484.2	2,380.8	2,314.1	1,375.9	1,273.0	916.8	863.4
Non-Interest Expense	3,183.9	2,982.5	3,377.1	2,010.6	2,010.7	1,470.7	1,403.1
Income Before Taxes	1,971.9	2,148.6	1,647.3	1,168.5	1,058.4	669.7	617.7
Net Income	1,302.4	[3] 1,405.5	[1] 1,070.7	[1] 807.4	[1] 736.6	465.1	429.4
Average Shs. Outstg. (000)	612,625	632,452	665,720	441,380	445,348	297,702	306,708
BALANCE SHEET (IN MILLIONS):							
Cash & Due from Banks	3,535.2	3,480.8	4,783.5	2,967.2	2,935.3	2,637.0	2,401.7
Securities Avail. for Sale	10,592.3	15,135.4	16,337.5	8,929.0	9,381.4	5,024.6	3,323.5
Total Loans & Leases	65,604.4	60,203.9	58,011.2	38,442.2	35,495.3	26,055.3	22,992.7
Allowance for Credit Losses	928.6	970.5	970.2	698.4	705.9	490.7	469.0
Net Loans & Leases	64,675.9	59,233.4	57,040.9	37,743.8	34,789.4	25,564.6	22,523.7
Total Assets	88,534.6	87,121.5	88,245.6	54,683.5	50,855.8	36,199.0	32,114.0
Total Deposits	55,256.4	50,066.3	58,246.9	36,861.1	35,999.7	25,200.5	24,471.9
Long-Term Obligations	18,144.8	15,038.0	9,689.3	4,810.4	2,994.4	1,215.4	743.7
Total Liabilities	81,764.8	81,393.8	81,232.7	50,402.2	46,423.8	33,278.0	29,513.0
Net Stockholders' Equity	6,769.8	5,727.7	7,012.9	4,281.4	4,432.1	2,921.0	2,601.1
Year-end Shs. Outstg. (000)	609,189	607,058	652,654	422,196	446,396	291,092	295,112
STATISTICAL RECORD:							
Return on Equity %	19.2	24.5	15.3	18.9	16.6	15.9	16.5
Return on Assets %	1.5	1.6	1.2	1.5	1.4	1.3	1.3
Equity/Assets %	7.6	6.6	7.9	7.8	8.7	8.1	8.1
Non-Int. Exp./Tot. Inc. %	59.1	56.9	66.3	62.1	64.7	66.4	67.1
Price Range	29.75-16.00	37.81-22.13	38.75-28.47	33.78-21.25	23.63-15.31	16.88-12.63	14.50-11.88
P/E Ratio	14.0-7.5	17.0-10.0	24.1-17.7	18.5-11.6	14.4-9.3	11.1-8.3	10.7-8.8
Average Yield %	6.2	3.5	2.8	3.0	3.8	4.4	4.5

Statistics are as originally reported. Adj. for stk. split: 2-for-1, 7/99. [1] Incl. pre-tax merger-related chgs. totaling: $379.4 mill., 1998; $65.9 mill, 1997; $74.7 mill., 1996. [2] Results reflect the consummation of the 3/31/98 merger with First of America Bank Corporation. [3] Incl. an after-tax non-recurring gain of $1.3 mill.

OFFICERS:
D. A. Daberko, Chmn., C.E.O.
William MacDonald, III, Vice-Chmn., Sr. Exec. V.P.
R. G. Siefers, Vice-Chmn.
J. D. Kelly, Exec. V.P., C.F.O.

INVESTOR CONTACT: Derek Green, Vice-Pres. of Inv. Rel., (800) 622-4204

PRINCIPAL OFFICE: 1900 East Ninth Street, Cleveland, OH 44114-3484

TELEPHONE NUMBER: (216) 575-2000
FAX: (216) 575-2353
WEB: www.national-city.com

NO. OF EMPLOYEES: 36,097

SHAREHOLDERS: 68,981

ANNUAL MEETING: In April

INCORPORATED: DE, Aug., 1972

INSTITUTIONAL HOLDINGS:
No. of Institutions: 414
Shares Held: 313,312,820
% Held: 51.4

INDUSTRY: National commercial banks (SIC: 6021)

TRANSFER AGENT(S): National City Bank Corporate Trust Operations, Cleveland, OH

NYSE SYMBOL NFG
Rec. Pr. 56.20 (4/30/01)

NATIONAL FUEL GAS COMPANY

YIELD 3.4%
P/E RATIO 16.4

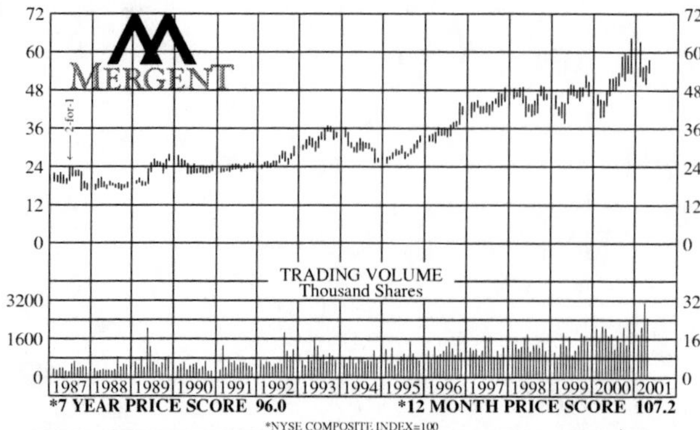

*7 YEAR PRICE SCORE 96.0 *12 MONTH PRICE SCORE 107.2
*NYSE COMPOSITE INDEX=100

INTERIM EARNINGS (Per Share):

Qtr.	Dec.	Mar.	June	Sept.
1996-97	1.02	1.50	0.50	Nil
1997-98	0.95	d0.56	0.49	d0.04
1998-99	0.97	1.57	0.30	0.11
1999-00	1.14	1.81	0.23	0.06
2000-01	1.32	...	...	...

INTERIM DIVIDENDS (Per Share):

Amt.	Decl.	Ex.	Rec.	Pay.
0.465Q	2/17/00	3/29/00	3/31/00	4/15/00
0.48Q	6/15/00	6/28/00	6/30/00	7/15/00
0.48Q	9/14/00	9/27/00	9/30/00	10/13/00
0.48Q	12/07/00	12/27/00	12/29/00	1/15/01
0.48Q	3/15/01	3/28/01	3/30/01	4/16/01

Indicated div.: $1.92 (Div. Reinv. Plan)

CAPITALIZATION (9/30/00):

	($000)	(%)
Long-Term Debt	953,622	41.6
Deferred Income Tax	326,994	14.3
Minority Interest	23,031	1.0
Common & Surplus	987,437	43.1
Total	2,291,084	100.0

RECENT DEVELOPMENTS: For the quarter ended 12/31/00, net income rose 18.1% to $53.0 million compared with $44.9 million a year earlier. Revenues advanced 48.4% to $559.5 million. Results were driven by the Exploration and Production segment, which posted operating income of $50.2 million versus $20.5 million in the prior year. Also, Energy Marketing segment operating income totaled $2.4 million versus an operating loss of $55,000 in 1999.

PROSPECTS: Results should continue to benefit from higher natural gas and crude oil prices and increased oil production, resulting mainly from Canadian properties that were acquired in June 2000. Thus, NFG has reaffirmed earnings estimates of $4.25 to $4.35 per share for fiscal 2001. However, production delays have resulted in the lowering of estimated 2001 production volumes from 95 to 100 billion cubic feet equivalent (Bcfe) to 90 to 95 Bcfe.

BUSINESS

NATIONAL FUEL GAS COMPANY is a diversified energy company consisting of six business segments. The Utility segment operations (58.1% of 2000 revenues) are carried out by National Fuel Gas Distribution Corporation, which sells natural gas or provides natural gas transportation services to approximately 735,000 customers through a local distribution system located in western New York and northwestern Pennsylvania. The Pipeline and Storage segment operations (5.7%) are carried out by National Fuel Gas Supply Corporation and Seneca Independence Pipeline Corporation. The Exploration and Production segment operations (16.7%) are carried out by Seneca Resources Corporation. The International segment operations (7.4%) are carried by Horizon Energy Development. The Energy Marketing segment operations (9.4%) are carried by National Fuel Resources, Inc. The Timber segment operations (2.7%) are carried out by Highland Forest Resources, Inc. and by a division of Seneca known as its Northeast Division.

ANNUAL FINANCIAL DATA

	9/30/00	9/30/99	9/30/98	9/30/97	9/30/96	9/30/95	9/30/94
Earnings Per Share	**3.21**	**2.95**	**0.84**	**3.01**	**2.78**	**2.03**	**[1] 2.23**
Cash Flow Per Share	**6.81**	**6.27**	**3.91**	**5.94**	**5.39**	**3.95**	**4.24**
Tang. Book Val. Per Share	**25.11**	**24.19**	**22.76**	**24.05**	**22.61**	**21.39**	**20.93**
Dividends Per Share	**1.89**	**1.83**	**1.77**	**1.71**	**1.65**	**1.60**	**1.56**
Dividend Payout %	**58.9**	**62.0**	**210.7**	**56.8**	**59.4**	**78.8**	**70.0**
INCOME STATEMENT (IN MILLIONS):							
Total Revenues	1,425.3	1,263.3	1,248.0	1,265.8	1,208.0	975.5	1,141.3
Costs & Expenses	1,041.4	917.7	1,019.4	960.2	925.9	753.6	909.7
Depreciation & Amort.	142.2	129.7	118.9	111.7	98.2	71.8	74.8
Maintenance Exp.	23.5	23.9	25.8	25.7	26.4	25.7	31.0
Operating Income	218.3	192.0	83.9	168.3	157.4	124.4	125.9
Net Interest Inc./(Exp.)	d100.1	d87.7	d85.3	d56.8	d56.6	d53.9	d47.1
Equity Earnings/Minority Int.	d1.4	d1.6	d2.2	...	...	...	...
Net Income	127.2	115.0	32.3	114.7	104.7	75.9	[1] 82.4
Cash Flow	269.4	244.7	151.2	226.3	202.9	147.7	157.2
Average Shs. Outstg. (000)	39,583	39,042	38,703	38,084	37,613	37,397	37,046
BALANCE SHEET (IN MILLIONS):							
Gross Property	3,829.6	3,383.5	3,186.9	2,668.5	2,471.1	2,322.3	2,169.1
Accumulated Depreciation	1,146.2	1,029.6	938.7	849.1	761.5	673.2	623.5
Net Property	2,683.4	2,353.9	2,248.1	1,819.4	1,709.6	1,649.2	1,545.6
Total Assets	3,236.9	2,842.6	2,684.5	2,267.3	2,149.8	2,038.3	1,981.7
Long-Term Obligations	953.6	822.7	692.7	581.6	574.0	474.0	462.5
Net Stockholders' Equity	987.4	939.3	875.6	917.9	856.0	800.6	780.3
Year-end Shs. Outstg. (000)	39,330	38,837	38,469	38,166	37,852	37,434	37,278
STATISTICAL RECORD:							
Operating Profit Margin %	15.3	15.2	6.7	13.3	13.0	12.8	11.0
Net Profit Margin %	8.9	9.1	2.6	9.1	8.7	7.8	7.2
Net Inc./Net Property %	4.7	4.9	1.4	6.3	6.1	4.6	5.3
Net Inc./Tot. Capital %	5.6	5.6	1.7	6.4	6.1	4.9	5.4
Return on Equity %	12.9	12.2	3.7	12.5	12.2	9.5	10.6
Accum. Depr./Gross Prop. %	29.9	30.4	29.5	31.8	30.8	29.0	28.7
Price Range	64.50-39.38	52.94-37.50	49.63-39.63	48.88-39.38	44.13-31.38	33.88-25.00	36.25-25.25
P/E Ratio	20.1-12.3	17.9-12.7	59.1-47.2	16.2-13.1	15.9-11.3	16.7-12.3	16.3-11.3
Average Yield %	3.6	4.0	4.0	3.9	4.4	5.4	5.1

Statistics are as originally reported. [1] Bef. acctg. change credit $3.2 mill.

OFFICERS:
B. J. Kennedy, Chmn., C.E.O.
P. C. Ackerman, Pres.
J. P. Pawlowski, Treas.

INVESTOR CONTACT: Margaret M. Suto, Director, Investor Relations, (716) 857-6987

PRINCIPAL OFFICE: 10 Lafayette Square, Buffalo, NY 14203

TELEPHONE NUMBER: (716) 857-7000
FAX: (716) 541-7841
WEB: www.nationalfuelgas.com

NO. OF EMPLOYEES: 3,597

SHAREHOLDERS: 21,164

ANNUAL MEETING: In Feb.

INCORPORATED: NJ, Dec., 1902

INSTITUTIONAL HOLDINGS:
No. of Institutions: 204
Shares Held: 17,310,306
% Held: 43.8

INDUSTRY: Natural gas distribution (SIC: 4924)

TRANSFER AGENT(S): Mellon Investor Services, South Hackensack, NJ

NYSE SYMBOL NPK
Rec. Pr. 27.50 (5/31/01)

NATIONAL PRESTO INDUSTRIES, INC.

YIELD 7.3%
P/E RATIO 12.7

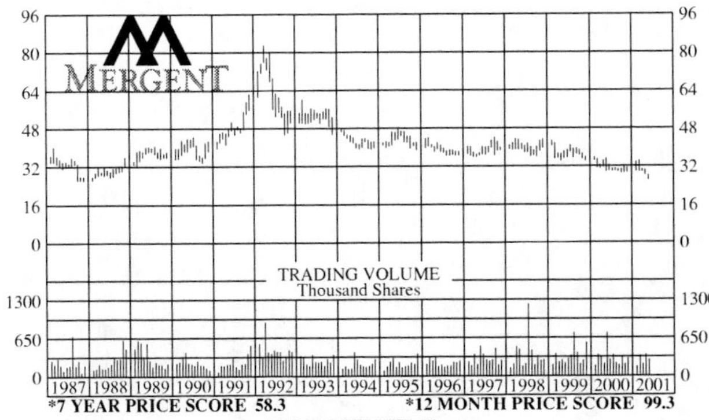

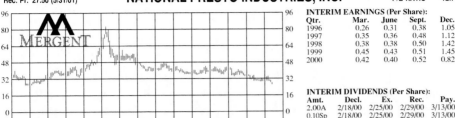

*7 YEAR PRICE SCORE 58.3 *12 MONTH PRICE SCORE 99.3
*NYSE COMPOSITE INDEX=100

INTERIM EARNINGS (Per Share):

Qtr.	Mar.	June	Sept.	Dec.
1996	0.26	0.31	0.38	1.05
1997	0.35	0.36	0.48	1.12
1998	0.38	0.38	0.50	1.42
1999	0.45	0.43	0.51	1.45
2000	0.42	0.40	0.52	0.82

INTERIM DIVIDENDS (Per Share):

Amt.	Decl.	Ex.	Rec.	Pay.
2.00A	2/18/00	2/25/00	2/29/00	3/13/00
0.10Sp	2/18/00	2/25/00	2/29/00	3/13/00
2.00A	2/16/01	2/23/01	2/27/01	3/13/01

Indicated div.: $2.00

CAPITALIZATION (12/31/00):

	($000)	(%)
Common & Surplus	245,160	100.0
Total	245,160	100.0

RECENT DEVELOPMENTS: For the year ended 12/31/00, net earnings totaled $15.2 million, down 27.2% versus $20.8 million in the previous year. Net sales rose 1.6% to $116.6 million from $114.7 million a year earlier. Results were negatively affected by lower consumer spending due to uncertain economic conditions in the U.S., coupled with lower-than expected sales of the Company's Pizzazz™ pizza oven that was introduced during the year. Gross profit slid 3.1% to $35.7 million from $36.8 million in 1999.

PROSPECTS: On 2/24/01, NPK acquired AMTEC Corporation, a manufacturer of sophisticated mechanical, electromechanical, and electronic assembly components for the U.S. Government and various government subcontractors. Going forward, NPK may acquire other defense companies as it seeks to expand its presence within the defense industry. Results in 2001 are expected to be hampered by a significant reduction in sales to Target, Inc., which plans to source more of its products from overseas manufacturers.

BUSINESS

NATIONAL PRESTO INDUSTRIES, INC. manufactures and distributes small household electric appliances and pressure cookers under the PRESTO® brand name. For the year ended 12/31/00, about 58% of consolidated revenues were generated by cast products (fry pans, griddles, grills, deep fryers and multi-cookers), about 32% by noncast/thermal appliances (stamped cookers and canners, stainless steel cookers, pizza ovens, corn poppers, coffeemakers, microwave bacon cookers, tea kettles, and heaters), and about 6% by motorized nonthermal appliances (can openers, slicer/shredders, knife sharpeners, electric knives, and bread slicing systems). The Company's largest customer, Wal-Mart Stores, Inc., accounted for 42% of 2000 revenues.

ANNUAL FINANCIAL DATA

	12/31/00	12/31/99	12/31/98	12/31/97	12/31/96	12/31/95	12/31/94
Earnings Per Share	**2.16**	**2.84**	**2.68**	**2.31**	**2.00**	**[1] 2.61**	**2.92**
Cash Flow Per Share	**2.56**	**3.15**	**2.97**	**2.59**	**2.27**	**2.79**	**3.03**
Tang. Book Val. Per Share	**35.65**	**35.42**	**34.57**	**33.88**	**33.57**	**33.57**	**33.11**
Dividends Per Share	**2.10**	**2.00**	**2.00**	**2.00**	**2.00**	**2.15**	**1.90**
Dividend Payout %	**97.2**	**70.4**	**74.6**	**86.6**	**100.0**	**82.4**	**65.1**
INCOME STATEMENT (IN MILLIONS):							
Total Revenues	116.6	114.7	107.1	109.5	106.0	120.2	128.1
Costs & Expenses	104.8	92.6	86.7	95.3	93.7	103.5	102.7
Depreciation & Amort.	2.8	2.3	2.1	2.1	2.0	1.5	1.2
Operating Income	9.0	19.8	18.3	12.2	10.4	15.1	24.2
Net Interest Inc./(Exp.)	...	...	...	...	...	d0.7	d0.5
Income Before Income Taxes	19.3	29.2	27.4	22.0	19.2	25.4	30.5
Income Taxes	4.2	8.4	7.7	5.0	4.5	6.4	9.1
Net Income	15.2	20.8	19.7	17.0	14.7	[1] 19.0	21.5
Cash Flow	17.9	23.1	21.8	19.0	16.7	20.5	22.6
Average Shs. Outstg. (000)	7,015	7,344	7,358	7,355	7,352	7,344	7,458
BALANCE SHEET (IN MILLIONS):							
Cash & Cash Equivalents	222.8	238.5	241.2	232.3	228.0	204.0	222.2
Total Current Assets	264.2	275.9	273.3	272.1	268.6	269.5	278.9
Net Property	13.3	12.3	10.6	9.0	7.3	7.3	4.3
Total Assets	288.7	299.4	294.8	291.9	285.4	284.9	291.0
Total Current Liabilities	43.5	44.1	40.4	42.7	38.5	38.2	43.0
Long-Term Obligations	...	...	...	...	...	...	5.1
Net Stockholders' Equity	245.2	255.3	254.4	249.2	246.8	246.7	242.9
Net Working Capital	220.7	231.9	232.9	229.4	230.0	231.3	235.9
Year-end Shs. Outstg. (000)	6,878	7,210	7,359	7,355	7,353	7,351	7,338
STATISTICAL RECORD:							
Operating Profit Margin %	7.7	17.2	17.1	11.1	9.8	12.6	18.9
Net Profit Margin %	13.0	18.2	18.4	15.5	13.9	15.8	16.8
Return on Equity %	6.2	8.2	7.8	6.8	6.0	7.7	8.8
Return on Assets %	5.3	7.0	6.7	5.8	5.2	6.7	7.4
Debt/Total Assets %	...	...	...	...	...	...	1.8
Price Range	35.81-29.06	42.88-34.13	43.50-36.06	44.19-35.88	44.00-36.25	48.00-38.75	48.00-39.13
P/E Ratio	16.6-13.5	15.1-12.0	16.2-13.5	19.1-15.5	22.0-18.1	18.4-14.8	16.4-13.4
Average Yield %	6.5	5.2	5.0	5.0	5.0	5.0	4.4

Statistics are as originally reported. [1] Incl. $2.9 mil gain from settlement of lawsuit.

OFFICERS:
M. S. Cohen, Chmn.
M. J. Cohen, Pres., C.E.O.
R. F. Lieble, C.F.O., Treas.
J. F. Bartl, Exec. V.P., Sec.

INVESTOR CONTACT: James F. Bartl, Exec. V.P. & Sec., (715) 839-2051

PRINCIPAL OFFICE: 3925 North Hastings Way, Eau Claire, WI 54703-3703

TELEPHONE NUMBER: (715) 839-2121
FAX: (715) 839-2148
WEB: www.presto-net.com

NO. OF EMPLOYEES: 624 (avg.)

SHAREHOLDERS: 730

ANNUAL MEETING: In May

INCORPORATED: WI, Nov., 1905

INSTITUTIONAL HOLDINGS:
No. of Institutions: 63
Shares Held: 2,682,448
% Held: 39.0

INDUSTRY: Electric housewares and fans (SIC: 3634)

TRANSFER AGENT(S): Computershare Investor Services, Chicago, IL

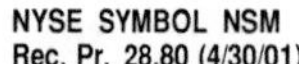

NYSE SYMBOL NSM
Rec. Pr. 28.80 (4/30/01)

NATIONAL SEMICONDUCTOR CORP.

YIELD ...
P/E RATIO 12.6

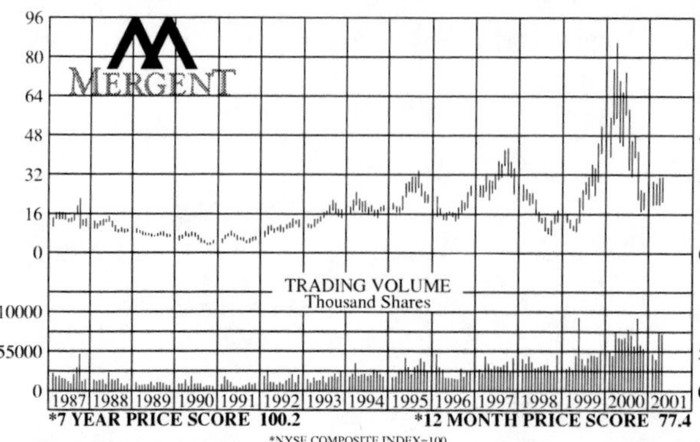

*7 YEAR PRICE SCORE 100.2 *12 MONTH PRICE SCORE 77.4
*NYSE COMPOSITE INDEX=100

INTERIM EARNINGS (Per Share):

Qtr.	Aug.	Nov.	Feb.	May
1994-95	0.44	0.49	0.42	0.62
1995-96	0.56	0.61	0.17	0.07
1996-97	d1.51	0.21	0.30	d0.10
1997-98	0.47	0.17	0.16	d1.29
1998-99	d0.63	d0.57	d0.16	d4.65
1999-00	0.25	0.49	1.68	0.78
2000-01	0.74	0.56	0.21	...

INTERIM DIVIDENDS (Per Share):

Amt.	Decl.	Ex.	Rec.	Pay.

No dividends paid.

CAPITALIZATION (5/28/00):

	($000)	(%)
Long-Term Debt	48,600	2.9
Common & Surplus	1,643,300	97.1
Total	1,691,900	100.0

RECENT DEVELOPMENTS: For the three months ended 2/25/01, net income plummeted 88.0% to $39.2 million versus $327.8 million in the previous year. Results for 2000 and 1999 included special pre-tax in-process research and development charges of $12.1 million and $4.2 million, respectively. The 1999 results also included a special pre-tax restructuring credit of $9.9 million. Net sales declined 13.4% to $475.6 million, while operating income fell 67.6% to $32.6 million.

PROSPECTS: The Company recently acquired innoCOMM wireless for about $130.0 million. The acquisition should strengthen the Company's property and market position in the wireless sector. Going forward, NSM will continue to focus on profitability and strategic investments, despite a period of slower demand and inventory corrections in the wireless handset and PC markets. In addition, NSM looks to improve its cost structure in targeted high-growth markets.

BUSINESS

NATIONAL SEMICONDUCTOR CORPORATION is engaged in the design, development, manufacture and marketing of a wide variety of semiconductor products including microprocessors, linear integrated circuits, digital integrated circuits, hybrid circuits and subsystems, electronic packaging and miscellaneous services and supplies for the semiconductor industry using both CMOS and bipolar technology. The Company is focused on two major markets: the Communications and Computing unit is composed of applications-focused businesses that cater to high-potential markets and the Standard Products group is composed of high-volume product lines.

REVENUES

(05/28/00)	($000)	(%)
Analog Segment	1,514,100	70.7
Info Appliance Seg	239,000	11.2
Cyrix Business Unit	18,600	0.9
All Others	368,100	17.2
Total	2,140,200	100.0

ANNUAL FINANCIAL DATA

	5/28/00	5/30/99	5/31/98	5/25/97	5/26/96	5/28/95	5/29/94
Earnings Per Share	**[2] 3.27**	**[1] d6.04**	**[1] d0.60**	**[1] 0.19**	**[1] 1.36**	**[1] 2.02**	**1.98**
Cash Flow Per Share	**4.65**	**d3.62**	**1.27**	**1.24**	**3.11**	**3.50**	**3.41**
Tang. Book Val. Per Share	**9.25**	**5.33**	**11.24**	**12.05**	**11.52**	**11.45**	**9.04**
INCOME STATEMENT (IN MILLIONS):							
Total Revenues	2,139.9	1,956.8	2,536.7	2,507.3	2,623.1	2,379.4	2,295.4
Costs & Expenses	1,534.2	2,637.5	2,376.9	2,325.3	2,176.4	1,879.4	1,829.0
Depreciation & Amort.	263.8	405.6	306.7	231.0	232.6	185.4	173.8
Operating Income	341.9	d1,086.3	d146.9	32.2	214.1	314.6	292.6
Net Interest Inc./(Exp.)	15.3	d2.2	22.3	15.1	13.3	14.6	10.9
Income Before Income Taxes	642.5	d1,085.4	d99.7	57.3	247.2	329.2	303.5
Income Taxes	14.9	cr75.5	cr1.1	29.8	61.8	65.0	44.4
Net Income	[2] 627.6	[1] d1,009.9	[1] d98.6	[1] d53.7	[1] 185.4	[1] 264.2	259.1
Cash Flow	891.4	d604.3	208.1	177.3	412.4	438.4	414.2
Average Shs. Outstg. (000)	191,700	167,100	163,900	142,600	132,500	125,200	121,400
BALANCE SHEET (IN MILLIONS):							
Cash & Cash Equivalents	849.9	525.9	573.2	889.7	504.3	467.4	466.8
Total Current Assets	1,467.6	989.2	1,308.2	1,552.6	1,256.0	1,178.3	1,016.4
Net Property	803.7	916.0	1,655.8	1,263.4	1,308.1	962.4	668.0
Total Assets	2,382.2	2,044.3	3,100.7	2,914.1	2,658.0	2,235.7	1,747.7
Total Current Liabilities	627.7	665.0	793.6	791.4	676.8	685.9	577.4
Long-Term Obligations	48.6	416.3	390.7	324.3	350.5	82.5	14.5
Net Stockholders' Equity	1,643.3	900.8	1,859.0	1,748.8	1,577.2	1,406.7	1,105.7
Net Working Capital	839.9	324.2	514.6	761.2	579.2	492.4	439.0
Year-end Shs. Outstg. (000)	177,561	169,053	165,461	145,181	136,923	122,800	122,300
STATISTICAL RECORD:							
Operating Profit Margin %	16.0	...	...	1.3	8.2	13.2	12.7
Net Profit Margin %	29.3	...	...	...	7.1	11.1	11.3
Return on Equity %	38.2	...	...	...	11.8	18.8	23.4
Return on Assets %	26.3	...	...	...	7.0	11.8	14.8
Debt/Total Assets %	2.0	20.4	12.6	11.1	13.2	3.7	0.8
Price Range	51.88-8.88	28.25-7.44	42.88-21.63	27.63-13.00	33.63-16.50	25.00-14.38	21.75-10.13
P/E Ratio	15.9-2.7	...	...	145.3-68.4	24.7-12.1	12.4-7.1	11.0-5.1

Statistics are as originally reported. [1] Incl. non-recurr. chrg. $700.9 mill., 1999; $196.7 mill., 1998; $134.2 mill., 1997; $166.2 mill., 1996; $30.7 mill., 1995. [2] Incl. spec. pre-tax gain of $26.8 mill. for sale of Cyrix PC bus.; excl. $6.8 mill. extraord. chrg. for debt exiting and one-time gain $270.7 mill. from the sale of Fairchild Semiconductor stock.

OFFICERS:
B. L. Halla, Chmn., Pres., C.E.O.
D. Macleod, Exec. V.P., C.F.O.
J. M. Clark III, Sr. V.P., Sec., Gen. Couns.

INVESTOR CONTACT: Jim Foltz, Investor Relations, (408) 721-5800

PRINCIPAL OFFICE: 2900 Semiconductor Drive, P.O. Box 58090, Santa Clara, CA 95052-8090

TELEPHONE NUMBER: (408) 721-5000
FAX: (408) 739-9803
WEB: www.national.com

NO. OF EMPLOYEES: 10,500 (approx.)

SHAREHOLDERS: 8,845

ANNUAL MEETING: In Sept.

INCORPORATED: DE, May, 1959

INSTITUTIONAL HOLDINGS:
No. of Institutions: 250
Shares Held: 105,109,892
% Held: 60.6

TRANSFER AGENT(S): Boston EquiServe LP, Boston, MA

NYSE SYMBOL NSI
Rec. Pr. 24.10 (4/30/01)

NATIONAL SERVICE INDUSTRIES, INC.

YIELD 5.5%
P/E RATIO 11.3

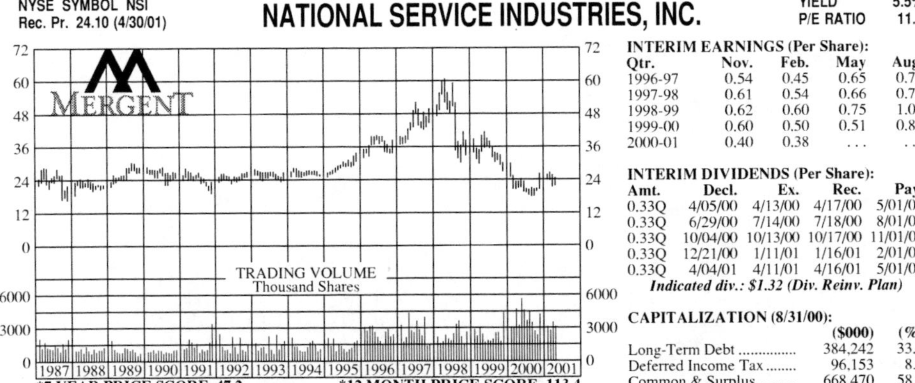

*7 YEAR PRICE SCORE 47.2 *12 MONTH PRICE SCORE 113.4

*NYSE COMPOSITE INDEX=100

INTERIM EARNINGS (Per Share):

Qtr.	Nov.	Feb.	May	Aug.
1996-97	0.54	0.45	0.65	0.71
1997-98	0.61	0.54	0.66	0.72
1998-99	0.62	0.60	0.75	1.07
1999-00	0.60	0.50	0.51	0.84
2000-01	0.40	0.38	...	...

INTERIM DIVIDENDS (Per Share):

Amt.	Decl.	Ex.	Rec.	Pay.
0.33Q	4/05/00	4/13/00	4/17/00	5/01/00
0.33Q	6/29/00	7/14/00	7/18/00	8/01/00
0.33Q	10/04/00	10/13/00	10/17/00	11/01/00
0.33Q	12/21/00	1/11/01	1/16/01	2/01/01
0.33Q	4/04/01	4/11/01	4/16/01	5/01/01

Indicated div.: $1.32 (Div. Reinv. Plan)

CAPITALIZATION (8/31/00):

	($000)	(%)
Long-Term Debt	384,242	33.4
Deferred Income Tax	96,153	8.4
Common & Surplus	668,470	58.2
Total	1,148,865	100.0

RECENT DEVELOPMENTS: For the three months ended 2/28/01, net income decreased 22.0% to $15.8 million compared with $20.3 million in the corresponding prior-year quarter. Total revenues increased slightly to $607.4 million versus $605.4 million in the previous year. Chemical revenues improved 3.1% to $123.4 million. Textile rental revenues rose 2.8% to $79.6 million, while revenues from lighting equipment dropped 1.2% to $350.0 million. Envelope segment revenues were flat at $54.5 million.

PROSPECTS: NSI continues to expect earnings to be relatively flat compared with prior-year levels, based on the current rate of activity in the general economy. Looking forward, NSI will attempt to offset the negative effects of the economic slowdown by generating higher profit from operating initiatives such as consolidating its chemical businesses, Six Sigma process improvement projects, a working capital reduction project, a major sourcing initiative, and aggressive sales efforts.

BUSINESS

NATIONAL SERVICE INDUSTRIES, INC., is a diversified manufacturing and service company with operations in four separate divisions. The lighting equipment division manufactures a wide variety of lighting equipment for commercial, industrial, institutional, and residential use. The textile rental division rents textile items to restaurants and lodging, hospitals, clinics, nursing homes and industrial concerns. The chemical division manufactures a broad line of specialty chemicals for industrial and commercial maintenance, sanitation and housekeeping. The Company also provides envelope services. Sales (and operating profit) in fiscal 2000 were derived as follows: 59% (64%), lighting equipment; 13% (12%), textile rental; 20% (22%), chemical; 8% (2%), envelopes.

ANNUAL FINANCIAL DATA

	8/31/00	8/31/99	8/31/98	8/31/97	8/31/96	8/31/95	8/31/94
Earnings Per Share	**2.45**	**[2] 3.03**	**[1] 2.53**	**[1] 2.37**	**2.11**	**1.93**	**1.67**
Cash Flow Per Share	**4.51**	**4.38**	**3.66**	**3.66**	**3.33**	**3.11**	**2.89**
Tang. Book Val. Per Share	**3.24**	**1.56**	**11.83**	**14.06**	**13.53**	**13.31**	**12.49**
Dividends Per Share	**1.32**	**1.28**	**1.24**	**1.20**	**1.16**	**1.12**	**1.08**
Dividend Payout %	**53.9**	**42.2**	**49.0**	**50.6**	**55.0**	**58.0**	**64.7**
INCOME STATEMENT (IN MILLIONS):							
Total Revenues	2,566.2	2,219.2	2,031.3	2,036.2	2,013.6	1,970.6	1,881.9
Costs & Expenses	2,276.6	1,959.9	1,812.9	1,867.7	1,795.9	1,753.2	1,678.3
Depreciation & Amort.	83.7	55.8	48.8	58.0	58.4	57.1	60.5
Operating Income	205.9	203.5	169.6	[1] 110.5	159.3	160.3	143.0
Net Interest Inc./(Exp.)	d44.9	d14.1	d0.7	d1.6	d1.6	d3.8	d3.7
Income Before Income Taxes	163.2	198.3	173.1	179.1	161.8	150.5	132.2
Income Taxes	63.3	74.0	64.4	71.8	60.7	56.4	49.5
Net Income	99.9	[2] 124.3	[1] 108.7	[1] 107.3	101.1	94.1	82.7
Cash Flow	183.6	180.2	157.6	165.3	159.6	151.2	143.2
Average Shs. Outstg. (000)	40,727	41,093	43,022	45,191	47,941	48,696	49,547
BALANCE SHEET (IN MILLIONS):							
Cash & Cash Equivalents	1.5	2.3	19.1	262.4	59.2	83.0	61.2
Total Current Assets	761.7	680.4	607.1	780.8	606.4	640.4	608.3
Net Property	427.1	382.3	271.9	236.7	357.4	349.9	348.3
Total Assets	1,820.1	1,695.8	1,010.7	1,106.4	1,094.6	1,131.3	1,106.8
Total Current Liabilities	540.7	423.9	222.0	282.0	197.4	202.6	250.8
Long-Term Obligations	384.2	435.2	78.1	26.2	24.9	26.8	26.9
Net Stockholders' Equity	668.5	615.9	578.9	671.8	718.0	744.4	727.4
Net Working Capital	221.1	256.5	385.1	498.8	409.0	437.8	357.5
Year-end Shs. Outstg. (000)	40,829	40,829	41,462	44,199	46,472	48,308	49,240
STATISTICAL RECORD:							
Operating Profit Margin %	8.0	9.2	8.3	5.4	7.9	8.1	7.6
Net Profit Margin %	3.9	5.6	5.4	5.3	5.0	4.8	4.4
Return on Equity %	14.9	20.2	18.8	16.0	14.1	12.6	11.4
Return on Assets %	5.5	7.3	10.8	9.7	9.2	8.3	7.5
Debt/Total Assets %	21.1	25.7	7.7	2.4	2.3	2.4	2.4
Price Range	30.00-17.81	41.44-26.88	60.75-30.13	52.25-36.75	40.25-31.88	33.88-24.88	28.38-24.75
P/E Ratio	12.2-7.3	13.7-8.9	24.0-11.9	22.0-15.5	19.1-15.1	17.6-12.9	17.0-14.8
Average Yield %	5.5	3.7	2.7	2.7	3.2	3.8	4.1

Statistics are as originally reported. [1] Incl. non-recurr. credit 1998, $1.8 mill.; 1997, $12.1 mill. [2] Incl. $11.2 mill. gain on sale of bus. & $9.3 mill. non-recurr. chrg.

OFFICERS:
J. S. Balloun, Chmn., Pres., C.E.O.
B. A. Hattox, Exec. V.P., C.F.O.
K. Murphy, Sr. V.P., Gen. Couns.

INVESTOR CONTACT: David Levy, Exec. V.P., (404) 853-1000

PRINCIPAL OFFICE: 1420 Peachtree Street, N.E., Atlanta, GA 30309-3002

TELEPHONE NUMBER: (404) 853-1000
FAX: (404) 853-1300
WEB: www.nationalservice.com

NO. OF EMPLOYEES: 20,000 (approx.)

SHAREHOLDERS: 5,903

ANNUAL MEETING: In Dec.

INCORPORATED: DE, Aug., 1928

INSTITUTIONAL HOLDINGS:
No. of Institutions: 182
Shares Held: 22,840,572
% Held: 55.5

INDUSTRY: Commercial lighting fixtures (SIC: 3646)

TRANSFER AGENT(S): EquiServe - First Chicago Trust Division, Jersey City, NJ

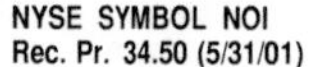

NYSE SYMBOL NOI
Rec. Pr. 34.50 (5/31/01)

NATIONAL-OILWELL, INC.

YIELD ...
P/E RATIO ...

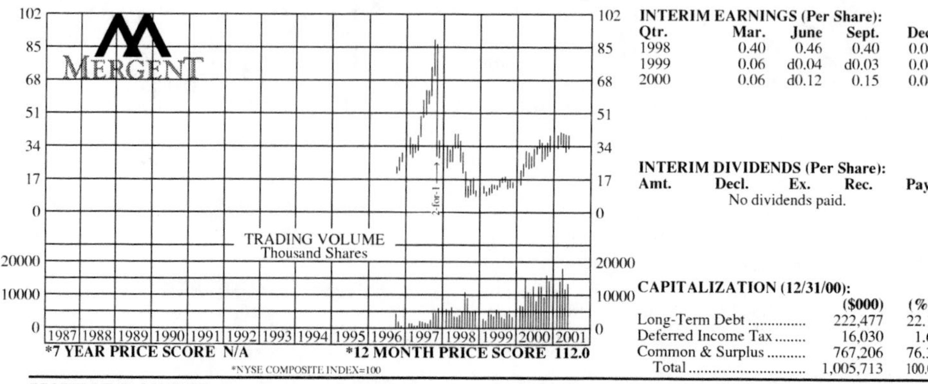

INTERIM EARNINGS (Per Share):

Qtr.	Mar.	June	Sept.	Dec.
1998	0.40	0.46	0.40	0.04
1999	0.06	d0.04	d0.03	0.04
2000	0.06	d0.12	0.15	0.08

INTERIM DIVIDENDS (Per Share):

Amt.	Decl.	Ex.	Rec.	Pay.

No dividends paid.

CAPITALIZATION (12/31/00):

	($000)	(%)
Long-Term Debt	222,477	22.1
Deferred Income Tax	16,030	1.6
Common & Surplus	767,206	76.3
Total	1,005,713	100.0

RECENT DEVELOPMENTS: For the year ended 12/31/00, net income totaled $13.1 million versus a net loss of $9.4 million in the previous year. Results included special charges of $14.1 million and $1.8 million in 2000 and 1999, respectively. Results for 2000 also included merger-related inventory write-offs of $15.7 million. Total revenues jumped 37.0% to $1.15 billion from $839.6 million in 1999.

PROSPECTS: On 1/11/01, NOI acquired Maritime Hydraulics (Canada) Ltd. for about $16.5 million. Separately, NOI has received an order from Santa Fe International Corp. for integrated drilling systems on two new high-performance jackup rigs at an aggregate value of between $35.0 million and $40.0 million. Looking ahead, NOI anticipates the strong growth in backlog for its drilling equipment to continue for 2001. As of 12/31/00, backlog stood at $282.0 million, versus $114.0 million the previous year.

BUSINESS

NATIONAL-OILWELL, INC. is a designer, manufacturer and seller of systems and components used in oil and gas drilling and production, and also provides supply chain integration services to the oil and gas industry. The Company manufactures and assembles drilling machinery, including drawworks, mud pumps and top drives, which are the major mechanical components of drilling rigs, as well as masts, derricks and substructures. The Company also provide electrical power systems, computer control systems and automation systems for drilling rigs. NOI's products and technology segment also designs and manufactures drilling motors and specialized downhole tools for rent and sale. NOI's distribution services segment offers equipment and spare parts through 130 distribution service centers.

REVENUES

(12/31/2000)	($000)	(%)
Products & Technology	683,467	59.4
Distribution Services	521,273	45.3
Corporate	(54,820)	(4.7)
Total	1,149,920	100.0

ANNUAL FINANCIAL DATA

	12/31/00	12/31/99	12/31/98	12/31/97	12/31/96	12/31/95	12/31/94
Earnings Per Share	[2] **0.16**	[2] **0.03**	[2] **1.30**	[1] [2] **0.99**	[2] **0.01**	[2] ...	[2] ...
Cash Flow Per Share	**0.60**	**0.42**	**1.66**	**1.27**	**0.13**	...	...
Tang. Book Val. Per Share	**5.44**	**3.79**	**4.31**	**4.91**	**2.88**	...	...
INCOME STATEMENT (IN MILLIONS):							
Total Revenues	1,149.9	745.2	1,172.0	1,005.6	648.6	545.8	562.1
Costs & Expenses	1,066.4	700.1	1,031.7	903.6	633.3	520.0	526.9
Depreciation & Amort.	35.0	23.2	19.2	14.7	3.6	3.6	6.0
Operating Income	48.5	21.9	121.1	87.2	11.7	22.2	29.1
Net Interest Inc./(Exp.)	d16.2	d14.8	d11.5	d4.7	d11.7	d1.3	d4.7
Income Before Income Taxes	27.0	4.5	109.3	82.5	0.4	19.6	24.9
Income Taxes	13.9	3.0	40.4	31.2	0.1	1.9	1.0
Net Income	[2] 13.1	[2] 1.5	[2] 68.9	[1] [2] 51.3	[2] 0.2	[2] 17.6	[2] 23.9
Cash Flow	48.2	24.8	88.1	66.0	3.8	21.2	29.9
Average Shs. Outstg. (000)	80,760	58,528	52,962	51,956	28,714	...	...
BALANCE SHEET (IN MILLIONS):							
Cash & Cash Equivalents	42.5	12.4	11.4	19.8	4.3	65.5	9.4
Total Current Assets	743.1	478.4	557.8	463.6	233.4	265.7	240.0
Net Property	173.6	109.1	91.8	74.3	18.7	18.9	22.4
Total Assets	1,278.9	782.3	818.0	567.5	266.7	288.6	268.3
Total Current Liabilities	262.8	176.2	211.4	211.5	103.3	88.3	88.2
Long-Term Obligations	222.5	196.0	205.6	61.6	36.4	9.1	...
Net Stockholders' Equity	767.2	395.1	386.8	277.7	109.1	178.0	161.9
Net Working Capital	480.3	302.2	346.4	252.1	130.1	177.4	151.8
Year-end Shs. Outstg. (000)	80,509	58,224	55,997	51,656	35,716	...	...
STATISTICAL RECORD:							
Operating Profit Margin %	4.2	2.9	10.3	8.7	1.8	4.1	5.2
Net Profit Margin %	1.1	0.2	5.9	5.1	...	3.2	4.2
Return on Equity %	1.7	0.4	17.8	18.5	0.2	9.9	14.8
Return on Assets %	1.0	0.2	8.4	9.0	0.1	6.1	8.9
Debt/Total Assets %	17.4	25.1	25.1	10.8	13.6	3.2	...
Price Range	39.69-14.00	18.50-8.50	40.44-7.63	88.88-27.88	30.75-20.00	...	...
P/E Ratio	247.9-87.4	614.6-282.4	31.1-5.9	89.8-28.2	N.M.	...	...

Statistics are as originally reported. Adj. for 2-for-1 stk. split, 11/97 [1] Bef. extraord. chrg. of $623,000 [2] Incl. special chrg., 2000, $29.8 mill.; 1999, $1.8 mill.; 1998, $16.4 mill.; 1997, $10.7 mill.; 1996, $23.0 mill.; income, 1995, $8.5 mill.; 1994, $13.9 mill.

OFFICERS:
J. V. Staff, Chmn., Pres., C.E.O.
S. W. Krablin, V.P., C.F.O.

INVESTOR CONTACT: M. Gay Mather, Manager, Investor Relations, (713) 346-7500

PRINCIPAL OFFICE: 10000 Richmond Avenue, 4th Floor, Houston, TX 77042-4200

TELEPHONE NUMBER: (713) 346-7500
WEB: www.natoil.com

NO. OF EMPLOYEES: 5,000 (avg.)

SHAREHOLDERS: 593

ANNUAL MEETING: In May

INCORPORATED: DE, Jan., 1996

INSTITUTIONAL HOLDINGS:
No. of Institutions: 206
Shares Held: 62,704,268
% Held: 77.8

INDUSTRY: Industrial machinery and equipment (SIC: 5084)

TRANSFER AGENT(S): American Stock Transfer & Trust Company, New York, NY

NYSE SYMBOL NFS
Rec. Pr. 44.22 (5/31/01)

NATIONWIDE FINANCIAL SERVICES INC.

YIELD 1.1%
P/E RATIO 13.0

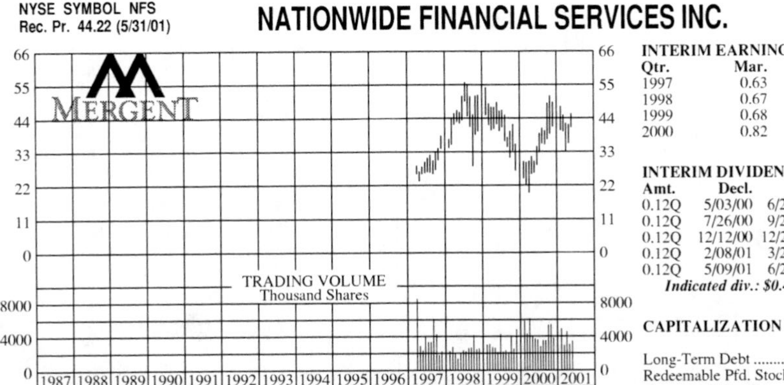

*7 YEAR PRICE SCORE N/A *12 MONTH PRICE SCORE 108.5

*NYSE COMPOSITE INDEX=100

INTERIM EARNINGS (Per Share):

Qtr.	Mar.	June	Sept.	Dec.
1997	0.63	0.43	0.51	0.59
1998	0.67	0.65	0.61	0.66
1999	0.68	0.71	0.80	0.77
2000	0.82	0.81	0.91	0.85

INTERIM DIVIDENDS (Per Share):

Amt.	Decl.	Ex.	Rec.	Pay.
0.12Q	5/03/00	6/29/00	7/03/00	7/17/00
0.12Q	7/26/00	9/28/00	10/02/00	10/16/00
0.12Q	12/12/00	12/28/00	1/02/01	1/15/01
0.12Q	2/08/01	3/29/01	4/02/01	4/16/01
0.12Q	5/09/01	6/28/01	7/02/01	7/16/01

Indicated div.: $0.48 (Div. Reinv. Plan)

CAPITALIZATION (12/31/00):

	($000)	(%)
Long-Term Debt	298,400	8.3
Redeemable Pfd. Stock	300,000	8.3
Common & Surplus	2,997,500	83.4
Total	3,595,900	100.0

RECENT DEVELOPMENTS: For the year ended 12/31/00, net income increased 14.1% to $434.9 million from $381.3 million in 1999. Earnings for 2000 and 1999 included realized investment losses of $24.9 million and $11.0 million, respectively. Total operating revenues grew 13.1% to $3.17 billion versus $2.80 billion a year earlier. Policy income rose 22.0% to $1.09 billion. Net investment income climbed 9.0% to $1.67 billion, while life insurance and immediate annuity premiums grew 8.7% to $240.0 million.

PROSPECTS: During 2000, results benefited particularly from robust individual annuity, institutional products, and life insurance sales. The Company expects revenue and operating earnings growth for the full year 2001 to be within a range of 7.0% to 10.0%. In March 2001, the Company launched its partnership with BrightLane.com, providing small business owners access to its 401(k) products and services.

BUSINESS

NATIONWIDE FINANCIAL SERVICES INC. was formed in 1996 as the holding company for Nationwide Life Insurance Company and the other companies within the Nationwide Insurance Enterprise that offer or distribute long-term savings and retirement products. NFS develops and sells a diverse range of products including individual annuities, private and public pension plans, life insurance and mutual funds as well as investment management and administrative services. NFS' life insurance segment is composed of a wide range of variable universal life insurance, whole life insurance, term life insurance and corporate-owned life insurance products. Customer funds managed totaled $111.00 billion at 12/31/00.

ANNUAL FINANCIAL DATA

	12/31/00	12/31/99	12/31/98	12/31/97	12/31/96	12/31/95	12/31/94
Earnings Per Share	[2] 3.38	2.96	[2] 2.58	[2] 2.14	[1] [2] 1.69	...	...
Cash Flow Per Share	6.10	5.15	4.20	3.48	2.82	...	...
Tang. Book Val. Per Share	23.29	19.35	19.05	16.53	20.35	...	...
Dividends Per Share	0.44	0.36	0.28	0.12	...	...	...
Dividend Payout %	13.0	12.2	10.9	5.6	...	...	...
INCOME STATEMENT (IN MILLIONS):							
Total Revenues	3,170.3	2,803.3	2,511.7	2,238.4	2,016.6	1,837.0	1,634.1
Costs & Expenses	2,195.2	1,948.9	1,798.2	1,664.8	1,547.8	1,460.0	1,302.7
Depreciation & Amort.	351.2	281.6	208.0	166.6	140.7	95.9	91.0
Operating Income	623.9	572.8	505.5	407.0	328.1	281.2	240.5
Income Before Income Taxes	623.9	572.8	505.5	407.0	328.1	281.2	240.5
Income Taxes	189.0	191.5	173.1	141.8	115.8	96.3	82.5
Net Income	[2] 434.9	381.3	[2] 332.4	[2] 265.2	[1] [2] 212.3	[1] [2] 184.9	[1] [2] 157.9
Cash Flow	786.1	662.9	540.4	431.8	353.0	280.7	248.9
Average Shs. Outstg. (000)	128,900	128,600	128,600	124,100	125,285	...	...
BALANCE SHEET (IN MILLIONS):							
Cash & Cash Equivalents	16,268.5	15,975.9	14,884.7	13,914.6	12,416.2	12,586.2	...
Total Current Assets	16,521.0	16,214.6	15,103.4	14,125.8	12,626.4	12,799.1	...
Total Assets	93,178.6	93,054.0	74,671.2	59,892.9	47,770.2	38,506.1	...
Total Current Liabilities	118.7	...	...	...	514.9	37.0	...
Long-Term Obligations	298.4	298.4	298.4	298.4	...	...	...
Net Stockholders' Equity	2,997.5	2,487.1	2,447.5	2,124.2	2,131.7	2,616.7	...
Net Working Capital	16,402.3	16,214.6	15,103.4	14,125.8	12,111.5	12,762.2	...
Year-end Shs. Outstg. (000)	128,700	128,500	128,500	128,500	104,745	...	...
STATISTICAL RECORD:							
Operating Profit Margin %	19.7	20.4	20.1	18.2	16.3	15.3	14.7
Net Profit Margin %	13.7	13.6	13.2	11.8	10.5	10.1	9.7
Return on Equity %	14.5	15.3	13.6	12.5	10.0	7.1	...
Return on Assets %	0.5	0.4	0.4	0.4	0.4	0.5	...
Debt/Total Assets %	0.3	0.3	0.4	0.5	...	...	...
Price Range	51.44-19.50	54.13-26.75	55.84-28.25	38.25-23.38	...	...	...
P/E Ratio	15.2-5.8	18.3-9.0	21.6-10.9	17.9-10.9	...	...	...
Average Yield %	1.2	0.9	0.7	0.4	...	...	...

Statistics are as originally reported. [1] Before inc. from disc. opers. of $11.3 mill, 1996; $24.7 mill., 1995; $20.5 mill., 1994. [2] Incl. realized investment gain/loss of d$16.1 mill., 2000; cr$4.0 mill., 1999; cr$17.9 mill., 1998; cr$11.1 mill., 1997; d$208,000, 1996; d$1.7 mill., 1995; d$16.5 mill., 1994.

OFFICERS:
D. R. McFerson, Chmn., C.E.O.
J. J. Gasper, Pres., C.O.O.
R. A. Oakley, Exec. V.P., C.F.O.
D. W. Click, V.P., Sec.

INVESTOR CONTACT: Kevin G. O'Brien, Dir., Inv. Rel., (614) 249-7111

PRINCIPAL OFFICE: One Nationwide Plaza, Columbus, OH 43215

TELEPHONE NUMBER: (614) 249-7111
FAX: (614) 249-9071
WEB: www.nationwide.com

NO. OF EMPLOYEES: 4,800 (approx.)

SHAREHOLDERS: 2,454 (approx. class A)

ANNUAL MEETING: In May

INCORPORATED: DE, Nov., 1996

INSTITUTIONAL HOLDINGS:
No. of Institutions: 161
Shares Held: 19,972,089
% Held: 15.5

INDUSTRY: Life insurance (SIC: 6311)

TRANSFER AGENT(S): First Chicago Trust Company of New York, Jersey City, NJ

NYSE SYMBOL NAV
Rec. Pr. 25.81 (4/30/01)

NAVISTAR INTERNATIONAL CORPORATION

YIELD ...
P/E RATIO 31.1

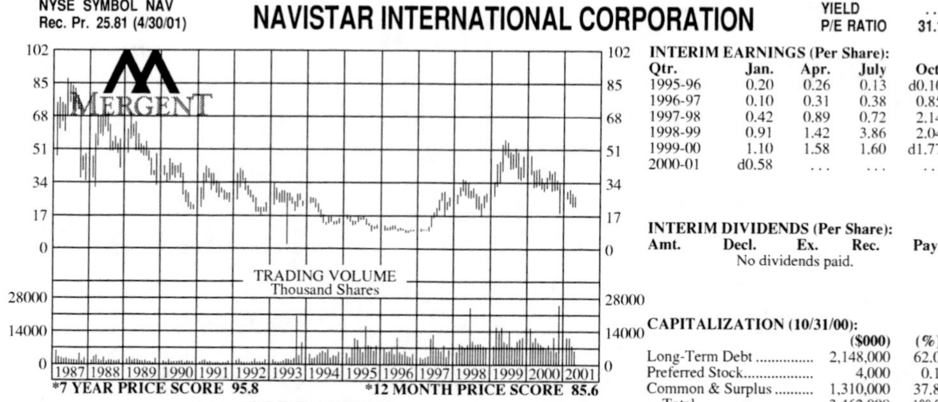

INTERIM EARNINGS (Per Share):

Qtr.	Jan.	Apr.	July	Oct.
1995-96	0.20	0.26	0.13	d0.10
1996-97	0.10	0.31	0.38	0.85
1997-98	0.42	0.89	0.72	2.14
1998-99	0.91	1.42	3.86	2.04
1999-00	1.10	1.58	1.60	d1.77
2000-01	d0.58	...	...	...

INTERIM DIVIDENDS (Per Share):

Amt.	Decl.	Ex.	Rec.	Pay.

No dividends paid.

CAPITALIZATION (10/31/00):

	($000)	(%)
Long-Term Debt	2,148,000	62.0
Preferred Stock	4,000	0.1
Common & Surplus	1,310,000	37.8
Total	3,462,000	100.0

RECENT DEVELOPMENTS: For the first quarter ended 1/31/01, the Company reported a net loss of $35.0 million versus net income of $70.0 million in 1999. Results were negatively affected by continued weak, new and used truck pricing and lower new truck shipments. Total sales and revenues fell 29.7% to $1.52 billion from $2.17 billion the year before. Sales of manufactured products decreased 31.3% to $1.43 billion, while finance and insurance revenue rose 14.5% to $79.0 million.

PROSPECTS: On 1/26/01, the Company completed the acquisition of Maxion International Motores, a Brazil-based engine company. Separately, NAV and Ford Motor Company announced that they intend to form a joint venture to build commercial trucks. Moreover, NAV and Ford intend to explore opportunities in diesel engines for potential applications in Ford's full range of truck products. The new alliance with Ford should yield positive benefits.

BUSINESS

NAVISTAR INTERNATIONAL CORPORATION operates in three principal industry segments: truck, engine and financial services. The Company's truck segment is engaged in the manufacture and marketing of medium and heavy trucks, including school buses. The Company's engine segment is engaged in the design and manufacture of mid-range diesel engines. The truck segment operates primarily in the U.S. and Canada as well as in Mexico, Brazil and other selected export markets while the engine segment operates primarily in the U.S. and Brazil. Navistar Financial is engaged in the wholesale, retail and lease financing of new and used trucks sold by Navistar and its dealers in the U.S. In fiscal 2000, manufactured sales were derived: class 5-7 medium trucks and school buses 34%, class 8 heavy trucks 32%, truck service parts 9%, OEM engines, including service parts 21%, and financial services 4%.

REVENUES

(10/31/00)	REV ($000)	INC (%)
Truck	6,365	69.3
Engine	2,430	26.5
Financial Services	387	4.2
Total	9,182	100.0

ANNUAL FINANCIAL DATA

	10/31/00	10/31/99	10/31/98	10/31/97	10/31/96	10/31/95	10/31/94
Earnings Per Share	**3 2.58**	**8.20**	**4.11**	**1.66**	**2 0.49**	**1.83**	**1 0.99**
Cash Flow Per Share	**5.82**	**10.81**	**6.39**	**3.30**	**1.91**	**2.92**	**1.93**
Tang. Book Val. Per Share	**22.05**	**20.36**	**8.55**	**7.79**	**4.90**	**4.14**	**3.57**
INCOME STATEMENT (IN MILLIONS):							
Total Revenues	8,451.0	8,647.0	7,885.0	6,371.0	5,754.0	6,342.0	5,337.0
Costs & Expenses	7,795.0	7,671.0	7,132.0	5,876.0	5,390.0	5,912.0	5,032.0
Depreciation & Amort.	199.0	174.0	159.0	120.0	105.0	81.0	72.0
Operating Income	457.0	802.0	594.0	375.0	259.0	349.0	233.0
Net Interest Inc./(Exp.)	d146.0	d135.0	d105.0	d74.0	d83.0	d87.0	d75.0
Income Before Income Taxes	224.0	591.0	410.0	242.0	105.0	262.0	158.0
Income Taxes	65.0	47.0	111.0	92.0	40.0	98.0	56.0
Net Income	3 159.0	544.0	299.0	150.0	2 65.0	164.0	1 102.0
Cash Flow	358.0	718.0	447.0	241.0	141.0	216.0	145.0
Average Shs. Outstg. (000)	61,500	66,400	70,000	73,100	73,700	74,000	75,000
BALANCE SHEET (IN MILLIONS):							
Cash & Cash Equivalents	464.0	381.0	1,064.0	965.0	881.0	1,040.0	861.0
Total Current Assets	2,467.0	2,842.0	3,715.0	3,216.0	2,999.0	3,310.0	2,870.0
Net Property	1,779.0	1,475.0	1,106.0	835.0	770.0	683.0	578.0
Total Assets	6,945.0	6,928.0	6,178.0	5,516.0	5,326.0	5,566.0	5,056.0
Total Current Liabilities	2,409.0	2,502.0	1,273.0	1,100.0	820.0	933.0	1,710.0
Long-Term Obligations	2,148.0	2,075.0	2,122.0	1,316.0	1,420.0	1,457.0	696.0
Net Stockholders' Equity	1,314.0	1,291.0	769.0	1,020.0	916.0	870.0	817.0
Net Working Capital	58.0	340.0	2,442.0	2,116.0	2,179.0	2,377.0	1,160.0
Year-end Shs. Outstg. (000)	59,400	63,200	66,200	72,400	73,000	74,000	74,000
STATISTICAL RECORD:							
Operating Profit Margin %	5.4	9.3	7.5	5.9	4.5	5.5	4.4
Net Profit Margin %	1.9	6.3	3.8	2.4	1.1	2.6	1.9
Return on Equity %	12.1	42.1	38.9	14.7	7.1	18.9	12.5
Return on Assets %	2.3	7.9	4.8	2.7	1.2	2.9	2.0
Debt/Total Assets %	30.9	30.0	34.3	23.9	26.7	26.2	13.8
Price Range	48.00-18.25	56.25-27.13	35.88-17.00	29.50-9.00	12.13-8.38	17.50-9.00	26.63-12.25
P/E Ratio	18.6-7.1	6.9-3.3	8.7-4.1	17.8-5.4	24.7-17.1	9.6-4.9	26.9-12.4

Statistics are as originally reported. 1 Bef. disc. opers. gain $20.0 mill., 1994 2 Incl. non-recurr chrg. $35.0 mill. 3 Incl. pre-tax restruct. chrg. of $286.0 mill.

OFFICERS:
J. R. Horne, Chmn., Pres., C.E.O.
R. C. Lannert, Exec. V.P., C.F.O.
T. M. Hough, V.P., Treas.
S. K. Covey, Corp. Sec.

INVESTOR CONTACT: Investor Relations, (312) 836-2143

PRINCIPAL OFFICE: 455 North Cityfront Plaza Drive, Chicago, IL 60611

TELEPHONE NUMBER: (312) 836-2000
FAX: (312) 836-2192
WEB: www.navistar.com

NO. OF EMPLOYEES: 17,000

SHAREHOLDERS: 38,700 (approx.)

ANNUAL MEETING: In Feb.

INCORPORATED: DE, Dec., 1965

INSTITUTIONAL HOLDINGS:
No. of Institutions: 196
Shares Held: 45,528,082
% Held: 76.7

INDUSTRY: Motor vehicles and car bodies (SIC: 3711)

TRANSFER AGENT(S): Mellon Investor Services, South Hackensack, NJ

NYSE SYMBOL NCH
Rec. Pr. 56.01 (4/30/01)

NCH CORPORATION

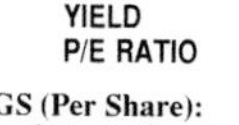

YIELD 2.5%
P/E RATIO 11.9

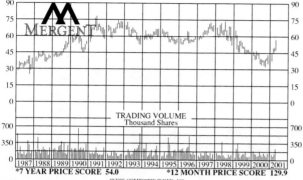

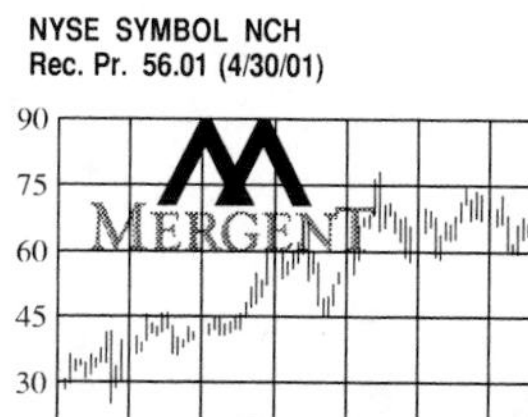

*7 YEAR PRICE SCORE 54.0 *12 MONTH PRICE SCORE 129.9

*NYSE COMPOSITE INDEX=100

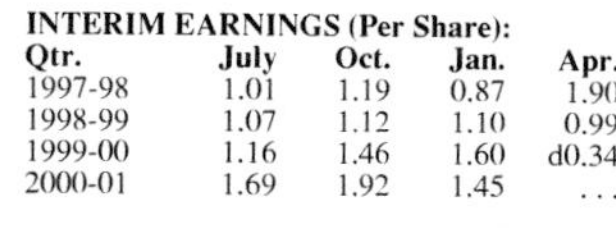

INTERIM EARNINGS (Per Share):

Qtr.	July	Oct.	Jan.	Apr.
1997-98	1.01	1.19	0.87	1.90
1998-99	1.07	1.12	1.10	0.99
1999-00	1.16	1.46	1.60	d0.34
2000-01	1.69	1.92	1.45	...

INTERIM DIVIDENDS (Per Share):

Amt.	Decl.	Ex.	Rec.	Pay.
0.35Q	7/27/00	8/30/00	9/01/00	9/15/00
0.35Q	10/30/00	11/29/00	12/01/00	12/15/00
0.35Q	1/19/01	2/27/01	3/01/01	3/15/01
0.35Q	4/19/01	5/30/01	6/01/01	6/15/01

Indicated div.: $1.40

CAPITALIZATION (4/30/00):

	($000)	(%)
Long-Term Debt	12,049	5.4
Common & Surplus	212,762	94.6
Total	224,811	100.0

RECENT DEVELOPMENTS: For the quarter ended 1/31/01, income from continuing operations slipped 6.3% to $7.7 million compared with $8.2 million in the corresponding quarter of 2000. Results for 2001 and 2000 do not include an after-tax loss of $3.3 million and income of $452,000, respectively, from discontinued operations. Net sales were $159.0 million, down 10.7% from $178.1 million in the prior-year period. Operating income decreased 33.8% to $9.2 million compared with $13.9 million the year before.

PROSPECTS: The Company closed the DBS Services Group due to weakness in the direct broadcast satellite equipment market and increased competition. Operations for the DBS Services Group ceased in January 2001 and resulted in a loss on disposition of $3.1 million. Going forward, management anticipates that operating cash flows will continue to supply enough funds to finance operating needs, capital expenditures and the payment of dividends.

BUSINESS

NCH CORPORATION markets an extensive line of maintenance, repair and supply products to customers in more than 50 countries. Products include specialty chemicals, water treatment products and services, fasteners, welding supplies, plumbing and electronic parts, and safety supplies. Products are marketed primarily through organizations directed toward specific markets. The Company has more than 500,000 maintenance clients. For the year ended 4/30/00, sales (and net income) were derived: Chemical Specialties, 56.2% (32.6%); Plumbmaster, 16.6% (18.5%); Partsmaster, 11.8% (26.4%); Landmark Direct, 4.8% (1.3%); DBS Services, 2.9% (11.1%); and other product lines, 7.7% (10.1%).

ANNUAL FINANCIAL DATA

	4/30/00	4/30/99	4/30/98	4/30/97	4/30/96	4/30/95	4/30/94
Earnings Per Share	**2 3.92**	**4.25**	**4.97**	**4.73**	**1 4.51**	**4.29**	**3.77**
Cash Flow Per Share	**6.48**	**6.71**	**7.05**	**6.79**	**6.37**	**5.96**	**5.36**
Tang. Book Val. Per Share	**39.34**	**38.72**	**41.85**	**39.45**	**39.01**	**38.04**	**35.41**
Dividends Per Share	**1.40**	**1.40**	**1.25**	**2.20**	**2.20**	**2.05**	**2.00**
Dividend Payout %	**35.7**	**32.9**	**25.2**	**46.5**	**48.8**	**47.8**	**53.0**
INCOME STATEMENT (IN MILLIONS):							
Total Revenues	728.2	786.7	784.1	766.8	772.8	735.1	680.0
Costs & Expenses	675.4	724.1	717.4	695.4	696.9	664.3	616.4
Depreciation & Amort.	13.9	14.1	15.0	15.1	15.0	13.9	13.2
Operating Income	39.0	48.5	51.7	56.3	61.0	56.9	50.4
Net Interest Inc./(Exp.)	d3.5	d2.7	d0.4	0.8	1.2	2.5	2.0
Income Before Income Taxes	32.8	44.3	60.0	58.2	61.4	59.5	52.1
Income Taxes	11.6	19.9	24.3	23.5	25.1	23.9	20.9
Net Income	2 21.2	24.4	35.7	34.7	1 36.3	35.6	31.2
Cash Flow	35.1	38.4	50.7	49.8	51.3	49.4	44.4
Average Shs. Outstg. (000)	5,413	5,728	7,186	7,326	8,052	8,294	8,278
BALANCE SHEET (IN MILLIONS):							
Cash & Cash Equivalents	52.6	23.0	118.8	91.0	103.9	128.3	124.5
Total Current Assets	299.9	308.3	396.5	367.9	382.9	404.1	363.8
Net Property	70.2	76.7	79.2	88.5	88.7	85.2	84.1
Total Assets	427.1	432.8	519.7	497.6	514.4	529.1	485.2
Total Current Liabilities	87.0	107.2	107.8	107.8	115.5	116.0	101.4
Long-Term Obligations	12.0	1.1	1.4	0.1	...	4.8	6.8
Net Stockholders' Equity	212.8	209.4	299.4	282.6	298.9	316.2	293.1
Net Working Capital	212.9	201.1	288.7	260.1	267.4	288.0	262.4
Year-end Shs. Outstg. (000)	5,408	5,408	7,154	7,163	7,664	8,311	8,277
STATISTICAL RECORD:							
Operating Profit Margin %	5.3	6.2	6.6	7.3	7.9	7.7	7.4
Net Profit Margin %	2.9	3.1	4.6	4.5	4.7	4.8	4.6
Return on Equity %	10.0	11.6	11.9	12.3	12.1	11.3	10.6
Return on Assets %	5.0	5.6	6.9	7.0	7.1	6.7	6.4
Debt/Total Assets %	2.8	0.3	0.3	...	...	0.9	1.4
Price Range	65.88-44.25	73.88-51.94	73.00-56.63	65.00-52.50	66.88-52.75	67.00-56.63	73.00-52.13
P/E Ratio	16.8-11.3	17.4-12.2	14.7-11.4	13.7-11.1	14.8-11.7	15.6-13.2	19.4-13.8
Average Yield %	2.5	2.2	1.9	3.7	3.7	3.3	3.2

Statistics are as originally reported. 1 Incl. $2.3 mill. after-tax gain on the sale of a subsidiary. 2 Excl. d$859,000 fr. disc. opers. & d$3.3 mill. fr. disp. of disc. opers.

OFFICERS:
I. L. Levy, Chmn., Pres.
G. Scivally, V.P., Treas.

INVESTOR CONTACT: Joe Cleveland, V.P. & Sec., (972) 438-0251

PRINCIPAL OFFICE: 2727 Chemsearch Boulevard, P.O. Box 152170, Irving, TX 75015

TELEPHONE NUMBER: (972) 438-0211
FAX: (972) 438-0186
WEB: www.nch.com

NO. OF EMPLOYEES: 9,330

SHAREHOLDERS: 471

ANNUAL MEETING: In July

INCORPORATED: DE, May, 1965

INSTITUTIONAL HOLDINGS:
No. of Institutions: 65
Shares Held: 1,705,829
% Held: 32.1

INDUSTRY: Polishes and sanitation goods (SIC: 2842)

TRANSFER AGENT(S): Mellon Investor Services, Ridgefield Park, NJ

NYSE SYMBOL NCR
Rec. Pr. 47.01 (4/30/01)

NCR CORPORATION

YIELD ...
P/E RATIO 26.3

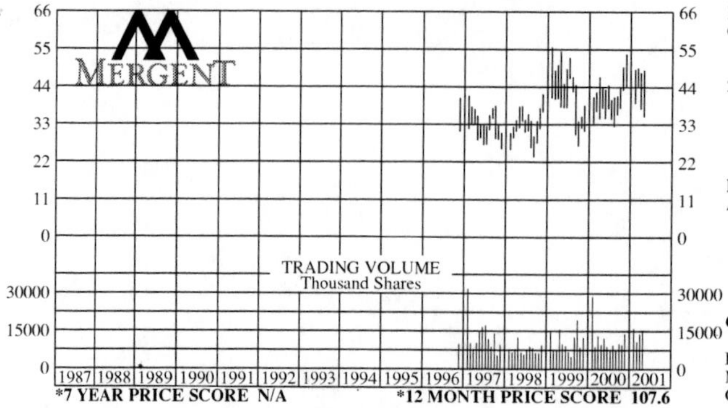

MERGENT

TRADING VOLUME
Thousand Shares

*7 YEAR PRICE SCORE N/A *12 MONTH PRICE SCORE 107.6

*NYSE COMPOSITE INDEX=100

INTERIM EARNINGS (Per Share):

Qtr.	Mar.	June	Sept.	Dec.
1998	Nil	0.46	0.25	0.49
1999	0.03	0.45	0.53	2.44
2000	d0.05	0.39	0.55	0.90

INTERIM DIVIDENDS (Per Share):

Amt.	Decl.	Ex.	Rec.	Pay.

No dividends paid.

CAPITALIZATION (12/31/00):

	($000)	(%)
Long-Term Debt	11,000	0.6
Minority Interest	27,000	1.5
Common & Surplus	1,758,000	97.9
Total	1,796,000	100.0

RECENT DEVELOPMENTS: For the year ended 12/31/00, net income fell 47.2% to $178.0 million compared with $337.0 million in 1999. Results for 2000 included a charge of $38.0 million for restructuring, a charge of $25.0 million for in-process research and development, and a one-time charge of $2.0 million for the integration of 4Front Technologies. Results for 1999 included gains totaling $205.0 million. Total revenues were $5.96 billion, down 3.8% from $6.20 billion in the previous year. Operating income more than tripled to $205.0 million.

PROSPECTS: Looking ahead, the Company will continue focusing on revenue growth initiatives and increasing profitability from its key businesses. For 2001, overall growth is anticipated to be 5.0%, including a 20.0% to 25.0% increase for data warehousing, a 5.0% increase for the financial self service and customer services maintenance businesses and a less than 1.0% increase for retail store automation. The Company's other key businesses are expected to generate revenue growth in the low single digits or higher in the first quarter.

BUSINESS

NCR CORPORATION and its subsidiaries provide applications designed to allow businesses to facilitate transactions with their clients and transform data from transactions into useful business information. The Company provides consulting services, value-added software customer support services, consumable and media products, and hardware. Its areas of focus include Teradata® warehouses, automated teller machines and retail store automation. The Company provides applications for the retail and financial industries, as well as telecommunications, transportation, insurance, utilities and electronic commerce. Revenues for 2000 were derived: store automation, 15.0%; self service/ATMs, 18.1%; data warehousing, 16.1%; customer services maintenance, 29.4%; Systemedia, 8.4%; payment and imaging, 3.1%; and other, 9.9%. NCR was acquired by AT&T in 1991 and spun off to AT&T shareholders in 1996.

ANNUAL FINANCIAL DATA

	12/31/00	12/31/99	12/31/98	12/31/97	12/31/96	12/31/95	12/31/94
Earnings Per Share	**[3] 1.82**	**[2] 3.35**	**[1] 1.20**	**0.07**	**d0.11**	**d2.26**	...
Cash Flow Per Share	**5.50**	**6.91**	**4.76**	**3.82**	**0.27**	**d2.68**	...
Tang. Book Val. Per Share	**18.47**	**17.05**	**14.66**	**13.11**	**1.38**	**0.50**	**2.35**
INCOME STATEMENT (IN MILLIONS):							
Total Revenues	5,959.0	6,196.0	6,505.0	6,589.0	6,963.0	8,162.0	8,461.0
Costs & Expenses	5,393.0	5,760.0	6,039.0	6,225.0	6,448.0	10,183.0	8,148.0
Depreciation & Amort.	361.0	358.0	364.0	383.0	385.0	350.0	415.0
Operating Income	205.0	78.0	102.0	d19.0	130.0	d2,371.0	d102.0
Net Interest Inc./(Exp.)	d13.0	d12.0	d13.0	d15.0	d56.0	d90.0	d44.0
Income Before Income Taxes	275.0	235.0	212.0	27.0	110.0	d2,416.0	d16.0
Income Taxes	97.0	cr102.0	90.0	20.0	219.0	cr136.0	187.0
Net Income	[3] 178.0	[2] 337.0	[1] 122.0	7.0	d109.0	d2,280.0	d203.0
Cash Flow	539.0	695.0	486.0	390.0	276.0	d1,930.0	212.0
Average Shs. Outstg. (000)	98,000	100,600	102,100	102,000	1,010,000	720,000	...
BALANCE SHEET (IN MILLIONS):							
Cash & Cash Equivalents	357.0	763.0	514.0	1,129.0	1,203.0	338.0	661.0
Total Current Assets	2,234.0	2,541.0	2,632.0	3,271.0	3,318.0	3,318.0	3,692.0
Net Property	742.0	793.0	872.0	858.0	930.0	957.0	1,234.0
Total Assets	5,106.0	4,895.0	4,892.0	5,293.0	5,280.0	5,256.0	5,836.0
Total Current Liabilities	1,836.0	1,662.0	1,700.0	1,964.0	1,967.0	2,921.0	1,998.0
Long-Term Obligations	11.0	40.0	33.0	35.0	48.0	330.0	642.0
Net Stockholders' Equity	1,758.0	1,596.0	1,447.0	1,353.0	1,396.0	358.0	1,690.0
Net Working Capital	398.0	879.0	932.0	1,307.0	1,351.0	397.0	1,694.0
Year-end Shs. Outstg. (000)	95,200	93,600	98,700	103,200	1,010,000	720,000	720,000
STATISTICAL RECORD:							
Operating Profit Margin %	3.4	1.3	1.6	...	1.9	...	...
Net Profit Margin %	3.0	5.4	1.9	0.1	...	...	...
Return on Equity %	10.1	21.1	8.4	0.5	...	...	...
Return on Assets %	3.5	6.9	2.5	0.1	...	...	...
Debt/Total Assets %	0.2	0.8	0.7	0.7	0.9	6.3	11.0
Price Range	53.69-32.38	55.75-26.69	41.88-23.50	41.38-25.88	40.75-30.88	...	...
P/E Ratio	29.5-17.8	16.6-8.0	34.9-19.6	590.2-369.1	...	...	...

Statistics are as originally reported. [1] Incl. $50.0 mill. non-recur. pension chg. [2] Incl. $125.0 mill. restr. chg., $98.0 mill. gain fr. dispositions & $232.0 mill. gain fr. favorable tax valuation. [3] Incl. $38.0 mill. restr. chg., $25.0 mill. R&D chg. & $2.0 mill. one-time chg.

OFFICERS:
L. Nyberg, Chmn., Pres., C.E.O.
D. Bearman, Sr. V.P., C.F.O.
J. S. Hoak, Sr. V.P., Gen. Couns.

INVESTOR CONTACT: Investor Relations, (937) 445-5905

PRINCIPAL OFFICE: 1700 South Patterson Blvd., Dayton, OH 45479

TELEPHONE NUMBER: (937) 445-5000
FAX: (937) 445-5541
WEB: www.ncr.com
NO. OF EMPLOYEES: 32,960 (approx.)
SHAREHOLDERS: 226,000 (approx.)
ANNUAL MEETING: In Apr.
INCORPORATED: OH, 1884; reincorp., MD, 1926

INSTITUTIONAL HOLDINGS:
No. of Institutions: 283
Shares Held: 64,816,274
% Held: 67.6

INDUSTRY: Data processing and preparation (SIC: 7374)

TRANSFER AGENT(S): American Stock Transfer & Trust Co., New York, NY

NYSE SYMBOL NMG
Rec. Pr. 33.25 (5/31/01)

NEIMAN-MARCUS GROUP, INC.

YIELD	...
P/E RATIO	11.1

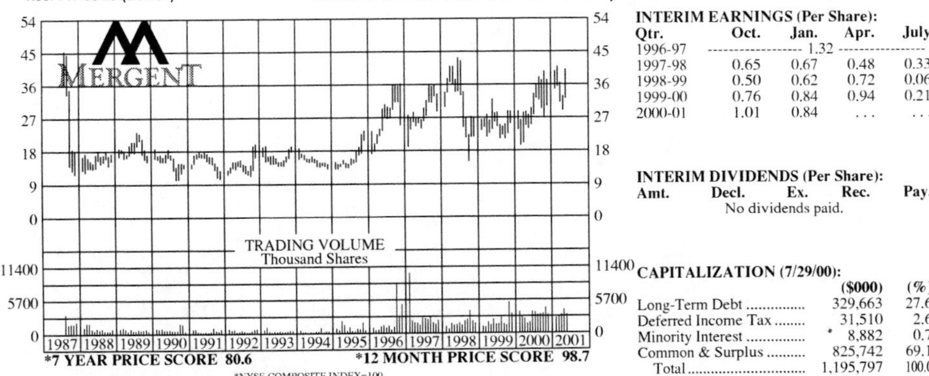

INTERIM EARNINGS (Per Share):

Qtr.	Oct.	Jan.	Apr.	July
1996-97		1.32		
1997-98	0.65	0.67	0.48	0.33
1998-99	0.50	0.62	0.72	0.06
1999-00	0.76	0.84	0.94	0.21
2000-01	1.01	0.84	...	...

INTERIM DIVIDENDS (Per Share):

Amt.	Decl.	Ex.	Rec.	Pay.

No dividends paid.

CAPITALIZATION (7/29/00):

	($000)	(%)
Long-Term Debt	329,663	27.6
Deferred Income Tax	31,510	2.6
Minority Interest	* 8,882	0.7
Common & Surplus	825,742	69.1
Total	1,195,797	100.0

RECENT DEVELOPMENTS: For the 13 weeks ended 1/27/01, net earnings slipped 3.2% to $39.9 million from $41.3 million in the prior year. Revenues grew 2.6% to $900.8 million from $878.1 million the previous year. Specialty retail store revenues inched up 0.6% to $750.9 million, while direct marketing revenues advanced 9.1% to $125.6 million. Comparable-store revenues were up 1.5% year-over-year. Operating earnings slid 6.0% to $70.1 million.

PROSPECTS: Revenue growth is being driven by strong sales of apparel sold under the Kate Spade and Laura Mercier brands, along with significantly higher e-commerce sales. However, operating margins are being squeezed by higher markdowns. Near-term earnings are expected to benefit from NMG's stepped-up marketing efforts and full-price promotions, coupled with cost-control initiatives that were implemented during 2000.

BUSINESS

NEIMAN-MARCUS GROUP, INC. operates specialty retail stores, consisting of 31 Neiman Marcus stores, two Bergdorf Goodman stores, and a direct marketing operation, NM Direct. Neiman Marcus stores offer women's, men's and children's apparel, fashion accessories, shoes, cosmetics, furs, precious and designer jewelry, decorative home accessories, fine china, crystal and silver, gourmet food products and gift items. Bergdorf Goodman stores primarily sell high-end women's apparel and unique fashion accessories. NM Direct operates an upscale direct marketing business, which primarily offers women's apparel under the Neiman Marcus name and, through its Horchow catalogue, offers quality home furnishings, tabletop, linens and decorative accessories. NM Direct also offers more modestly-priced items through its Trifles and Grand Finale catalogues and annually publishes the Neiman Marcus Christmas Book.

ANNUAL FINANCIAL DATA

	7/29/00	7/31/99	8/1/98	8/2/97	8/3/96	7/29/95	7/30/94
Earnings Per Share	**2.75**	**1.90**	**2.13**	**1.32**	**1.26**	**[1] 1.01**	**[2] d0.35**
Cash Flow Per Share	**4.16**	**3.22**	**3.33**	**2.59**	**2.74**	**2.28**	**1.26**
Tang. Book Val. Per Share	**14.69**	**15.01**	**13.20**	**9.20**	...	...	**0.10**
Dividends Per Share	...	...	...	...	...	...	**0.20**
INCOME STATEMENT (IN MILLIONS):							
Total Revenues	2,854.6	2,553.4	2,373.3	2,209.9	2,075.0	1,888.2	2,092.9
Costs & Expenses	2,537.4	2,308.1	2,114.2	1,969.1	1,859.2	1,689.8	1,972.7
Depreciation & Amort.	68.9	64.9	60.1	59.8	56.3	48.4	60.8
Operating Income	248.4	180.4	199.1	181.0	159.5	150.1	59.3
Net Interest Inc./(Exp.)	d25.4	d25.0	d21.9	d26.3	d28.2	d34.0	d31.9
Income Before Income Taxes	223.0	155.4	177.2	154.7	131.2	116.1	27.5
Income Taxes	84.7	60.6	70.9	63.4	53.8	48.8	11.5
Equity Earnings/Minority Int.	d4.2	...	...	...	...	...	...
Net Income	134.0	94.8	106.3	91.2	77.4	[1] 67.3	[2] 15.9
Cash Flow	202.9	158.4	166.4	122.5	104.6	86.6	47.7
Average Shs. Outstg. (000)	48,721	49,237	49,981	47,335	38,218	37,999	37,900
BALANCE SHEET (IN MILLIONS):							
Cash & Cash Equivalents	175.4	29.2	56.6	16.9	12.7	13.7	16.6
Total Current Assets	1,069.3	825.2	833.4	734.0	689.1	578.4	800.0
Net Property	539.7	513.4	479.3	454.1	457.6	423.6	410.9
Total Assets	1,762.1	1,502.2	1,437.8	1,287.9	1,252.4	1,108.4	1,323.1
Total Current Liabilities	492.3	380.2	388.3	331.5	374.0	334.6	434.5
Long-Term Obligations	329.7	274.6	284.6	300.0	289.6	244.4	368.7
Net Stockholders' Equity	825.7	736.2	656.7	554.7	75.6	26.5	3.7
Net Working Capital	577.0	445.0	445.1	402.6	315.0	243.8	365.5
Year-end Shs. Outstg. (000)	47,473	49,039	49,760	49,873	38,004	37,960	37,951
STATISTICAL RECORD:							
Operating Profit Margin %	8.7	7.1	8.4	8.2	7.7	7.9	2.8
Net Profit Margin %	4.7	3.7	4.5	4.1	3.7	3.6	0.8
Return on Equity %	16.2	12.9	16.2	16.4	102.4	253.6	428.6
Return on Assets %	7.6	6.3	7.4	7.1	6.2	6.1	1.2
Debt/Total Assets %	18.7	18.3	19.8	23.3	23.1	22.1	27.9
Price Range	39.63-19.38	32.00-21.19	43.44-15.00	35.88-19.00	36.25-17.13	23.50-13.00	18.75-13.00
P/E Ratio	14.4-7.0	16.8-11.2	20.4-7.0	27.2-14.4	28.8-13.6	23.3-12.9	...
Average Yield %	...	...	...	...	...	...	1.3

Statistics are as originally reported. [1] Bef. $11.7 mil ($0.31/sh) loss fr. discont. opers. [2] Incl. $48.4 mil pre-tax restr. chg.

OFFICERS:
R. A. Smith, Chmn.
B. J. Knez, Vice-Chmn.
R. A. Smith, Vice-Chmn.
B. M. Tansky, Pres., C.E.O.

INVESTOR CONTACT: Jonna Manes, Dir., Corp. Rel., (617) 232-0760

PRINCIPAL OFFICE: 27 Boylston Street, Chestnut Hill, MA 02467

TELEPHONE NUMBER: (617) 232-0760
FAX: (617) 738-4007
WEB: www.neimanmarcusgroup.com

NO. OF EMPLOYEES: 12,500 (approx.)

SHAREHOLDERS: 11,355 (Cl. A)

ANNUAL MEETING: In Jan.

INCORPORATED: DE, June, 1987

INSTITUTIONAL HOLDINGS:
No. of Institutions: 61
Shares Held: 19,940,220
% Held: 40.7

INDUSTRY: Department stores (SIC: 5311)

TRANSFER AGENT(S): EquiServe, Boston, MA

NYSE SYMBOL NEU
Rec. Pr. 71.53 (4/30/01)

NEUBERGER BERMAN INC.

YIELD 0.6%
P/E RATIO 23.6

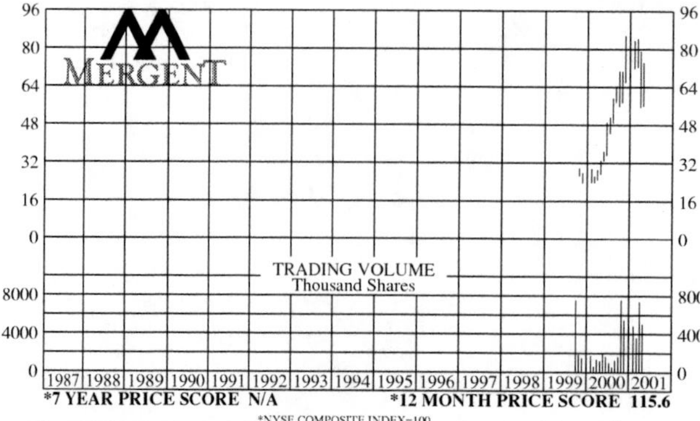

*7 YEAR PRICE SCORE N/A *12 MONTH PRICE SCORE 115.6

*NYSE COMPOSITE INDEX=100

INTERIM EARNINGS (Per Share):

Qtr.	Mar.	June	Sept.	Dec.
1998	1.67	1.84	1.68	1.49
1999	1.68	1.62	1.42	d1.33
2000	0.81	0.78	0.71	0.73

INTERIM DIVIDENDS (Per Share):

Amt.	Decl.	Ex.	Rec.	Pay.
0.10Q	4/13/00	4/28/00	5/02/00	5/16/00
0.10Q	7/19/00	7/28/00	8/01/00	8/15/00
0.10Q	10/19/00	10/27/00	10/31/00	11/14/00
0.10Q	1/19/01	1/30/01	2/01/01	2/13/01
0.10Q	4/19/01	4/27/01	5/01/01	5/15/01

Indicated div.: $0.40

CAPITALIZATION (12/31/00):

	($000)	(%)
Long-Term Debt	35,000	9.1
Common & Surplus	350,139	90.9
Total	385,139	100.0

RECENT DEVELOPMENTS: For the year ended 12/31/00, net income grew 14.1% to $150.4 million from $131.8 million in 1999. Gross revenues were $799.8 million, up 13.2% from $706.7 million in the prior year. Investment advisory and administrative fees increased 5.4% to $399.9 million from $379.4 million a year earlier. Results for 1999 were pro forma, reflecting the Company's change to a public corporation on 10/13/99.

PROSPECTS: NEU will continue its efforts to grow assets under management through growing internally, attracting experienced investment teams, and pursuing acquisition opportunities. On 2/28/01, NEU acquired New York City-based Executive Monetary Management (''EMM''). EMM, which has client assets of about $1.80 billion, provides wealth management services to high net worth individuals and families.

BUSINESS

NEUBERGER BERMAN INC. is the holding company of Neuberger Berman, LLC and Neuberger Berman Management Inc., which are investment advisory firms that provide discretionary money management for individuals, institutions and mutual funds. The Company is segregated into three business segments: private asset management, mutual fund and institutional, and professional securities services. The private asset management segment provides investment management services to high net-worth individuals, families and smaller institutions and had $22.50 billion in assets under management at 12/31/00. The mutual fund and institutional segment provides advisory services to mutual funds, and institutional clients. The professional securities services segment, formerly a partnership, markets services to third-party investment advisers and professional investors, including investor clearing services and research sales.

BUSINESS LINE ANALYSIS

(12/31/2000)	REV (%)	INC (%)
Private Asset Management	47.1	55.4
Mutual Fund & Institution	36.6	30.4
Professional Securs Servc	16.3	14.2
Total	100.0	100.0

ANNUAL FINANCIAL DATA

	12/31/00	12/31/99	12/31/98	12/31/97	12/31/96
Earnings Per Share	**2 3.03**	**1 3.05**	**6.68**	...	...
Cash Flow Per Share	**3.25**	**3.29**	...	...	...
Tang. Book Val. Per Share	**7.17**	**5.00**	**8.62**	**12.72**	...
Dividends Per Share	**0.40**	...	...	...	...
Dividend Payout %	**13.2**	...	...	...	...
INCOME STATEMENT (IN MILLIONS):					
Total Revenues	799.8	697.6	711.5	627.1	535.9
Costs & Expenses	542.2	563.7	382.6	321.9	301.2
Depreciation & Amort.	10.6	10.5	8.8	6.4	5.6
Operating Income	246.9	123.4	320.1	298.7	229.1
Income Before Income Taxes	246.9	123.4	320.1	298.7	229.1
Income Taxes	96.6	cr12.2	...	...	...
Net Income	2 150.4	1 135.6	320.1	298.7	229.1
Cash Flow	161.0	146.1	293.7	271.4	207.7
Average Shs. Outstg. (000)	49,595	44,410	...	...	...
BALANCE SHEET (IN MILLIONS):					
Cash & Cash Equivalents	1,355.7	1,422.8	1,220.2	621.7	...
Total Current Assets	4,301.5	3,752.0	3,783.4	2,360.2	...
Net Property	43.1	32.2	25.2	22.0	...
Total Assets	4,421.8	3,847.6	3,829.4	2,410.2	...
Total Current Liabilities	4,036.6	3,563.8	3,670.2	2,251.2	...
Long-Term Obligations	35.0	35.0	50.0	...	...
Net Stockholders' Equity	350.1	248.8	109.2	159.0	...
Net Working Capital	264.9	188.2	113.1	109.0	...
Year-end Shs. Outstg. (000)	48,803	49,716	12,668	12,500	...
STATISTICAL RECORD:					
Operating Profit Margin %	30.9	17.7	45.0	47.6	42.8
Net Profit Margin %	18.8	19.4	45.0	47.6	42.8
Return on Equity %	42.9	54.5	293.1	187.8	...
Return on Assets %	3.4	3.5	8.4	12.4	...
Debt/Total Assets %	0.8	0.9	1.3	...	...
Price Range	85.69-23.81	32.25-23.63	...	...	...
P/E Ratio	28.3-7.9	10.6-7.7	...	...	...
Average Yield %	0.7	...	...	...	...

Statistics are as originally reported. 1 Incl. $98.2 mill. after-tax one-time chg. fr. IPO. 2 Incl. $750,000 pre-tax chg. for sever. payments & excl. $9.6 mill. tax benefit.

OFFICERS:
L. Zicklin, Chmn.
R. A. Cantor, Vice-Chmn.
J. B. Lane, Pres., C.E.O.

INVESTOR CONTACT: Robert Matza, Exec. V.P. & CAO, (212) 476-9808

PRINCIPAL OFFICE: 605 Third Avenue, New York, NY 10158-3698

TELEPHONE NUMBER: (212) 476-9000
WEB: www.nb.com

NO. OF EMPLOYEES: 1,194 (avg.)

SHAREHOLDERS: 85 (approx.); 2,500 (approx. beneficial)

ANNUAL MEETING: In April

INCORPORATED: DE, 1998

INSTITUTIONAL HOLDINGS:
No. of Institutions: 106
Shares Held: 7,777,521
% Held: 15.9

INDUSTRY: Investment advice (SIC: 6282)

TRANSFER AGENT(S): American Stock Transfer & Trust Company, Brooklyn, NY

NYSE SYMBOL NYT
Rec. Pr. 41.03 (4/30/01)

NEW YORK TIMES COMPANY

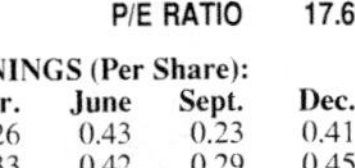

YIELD 1.2%
P/E RATIO 17.6

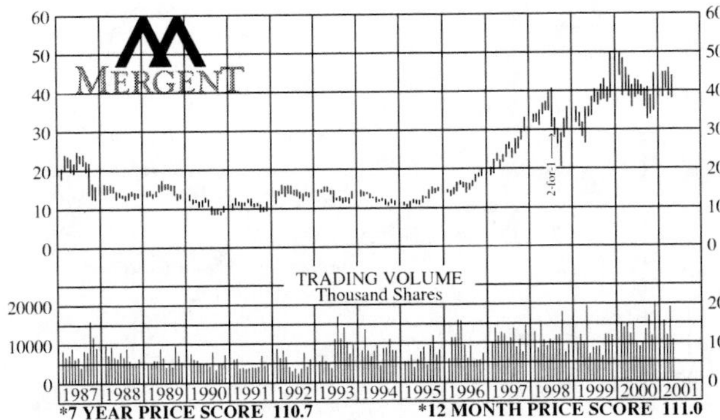

*7 YEAR PRICE SCORE 110.7 *12 MONTH PRICE SCORE 111.0

*NYSE COMPOSITE INDEX=100

INTERIM EARNINGS (Per Share):

Qtr.	Mar.	June	Sept.	Dec.
1997	0.26	0.43	0.23	0.41
1998	0.33	0.42	0.29	0.45
1999	0.34	0.47	0.34	0.59
2000	0.47	0.59	0.44	0.83

INTERIM DIVIDENDS (Per Share):

Amt.	Decl.	Ex.	Rec.	Pay.
0.115Q	6/15/00	8/30/00	9/01/00	9/18/00
0.115Q	11/16/00	11/29/00	12/01/00	12/18/00
0.115Q	2/15/01	2/27/01	3/01/01	3/19/01
0.125Q	4/17/01	5/30/01	6/01/01	6/19/01

Indicated div.: $0.50 (Div. Reinv. Plan)

CAPITALIZATION (12/31/00):

	($000)	(%)
Long-Term Debt	553,415	27.3
Capital Lease Obligations	83,451	4.1
Deferred Income Tax	106,247	5.2
Common & Surplus	1,281,163	63.3
Total	2,024,276	100.0

RECENT DEVELOPMENTS: For the year ended 12/31/00, net income rose 28.2% to $397.5 million compared with $310.2 million in 1999. Results for 2000 included a gain of $85.3 million from the disposition of assets. Total revenues were $3.49 billion, up 10.5% from $3.16 billion in the prior year. Operating profit increased 11.3% to $635.9 million. During the year, the Company sold seven of its regional newspapers and nine telephone directories.

PROSPECTS: As a result of the current slowdown in the economy, the Company has adjusted its newspaper group advertising revenue and expense guidance for 2001. Meanwhile, the Company still expects to achieve its earnings growth goal of 10.0% to 15.0% improvement in earnings per share for the full year. Accordingly, full-year advertising revenue growth for the newspaper group is expected to range between 1.0% and 3.0%.

BUSINESS

NEW YORK TIMES COMPANY is a diversified communications corporation organized into three segments. The Newspaper segment consists of THE NEW YORK TIMES, THE BOSTON GLOBE, 15 regional newspapers, newspaper distributors, a 50% interest in the INTERNATIONAL HERALD TRIBUNE S.A., a news service, a features syndicate, TimesDigest, licensing operations of THE NEW YORK TIMES databases/microfilm and new ventures, which include projects developed in electronic media. The Magazine segment publishes four magazines, including GOLF DIGEST. The Broadcasting segment is made up of eight network-affiliated television stations and two radio stations. NYT's equity interests include a newsprint company and a partnership in supercalendered paper mill. Revenues in 2000 were derived: newspapers, 90.2%; broadcasting, 4.6%; magazines, 3.3%; and New York Times Digital, 1.9%.

ANNUAL FINANCIAL DATA

	12/31/00	12/26/99	12/27/98	12/28/97	12/29/96	12/31/95	12/31/94
Earnings Per Share	[5] **2.32**	[4] **1.73**	[3] **1.49**	**1.33**	[1] [2] **0.44**	[1] **0.70**	[1] **1.03**
Cash Flow Per Share	**3.65**	**2.83**	**2.46**	**2.21**	**1.19**	**1.42**	**1.75**
Tang. Book Val. Per Share	...	**0.83**	**1.12**	**1.81**	**0.95**	**1.10**	**0.83**
Dividends Per Share	**0.45**	**0.41**	**0.37**	**0.32**	**0.28**	**0.28**	**0.28**
Dividend Payout %	**19.4**	**23.7**	**24.8**	**24.1**	**65.5**	**40.0**	**27.3**
INCOME STATEMENT (IN MILLIONS):							
Total Revenues	3,489.5	3,130.6	2,936.7	2,866.4	2,615.0	2,409.4	2,357.6
Costs & Expenses	2,625.6	2,361.9	2,233.2	2,237.4	2,293.9	2,041.9	1,996.2
Depreciation & Amort.	228.0	197.5	188.2	173.9	147.9	138.9	150.1
Operating Income	635.9	571.3	515.2	455.1	173.3	228.6	211.2
Net Interest Inc./(Exp.)	d64.1	d50.7	d43.3	d42.1	d26.4	d25.2	d28.2
Income Before Income Taxes	673.1	538.5	505.5	437.4	197.9	214.6	384.0
Income Taxes	275.6	228.3	218.9	175.1	113.4	92.8	173.9
Equity Earnings/Minority Int.	...	...	...	...	...	14.1	3.3
Net Income	[5] 397.5	[4] 310.2	[3] 286.6	262.3	[1] [2] 84.5	[1] 135.9	[1] 213.3
Cash Flow	625.5	507.7	474.9	436.1	232.3	274.7	363.3
Average Shs. Outstg. (000)	171,597	179,244	192,846	197,150	194,586	193,708	208,140
BALANCE SHEET (IN MILLIONS):							
Cash & Cash Equivalents	69.0	63.9	36.0	106.8	39.1	91.4	41.4
Total Current Assets	610.8	614.9	512.8	615.8	478.8	462.6	411.8
Net Property	1,207.2	1,218.4	1,326.2	1,366.9	1,358.0	1,276.1	1,158.8
Total Assets	3,606.7	3,495.8	3,465.1	3,639.0	3,539.9	3,376.7	3,137.6
Total Current Liabilities	877.4	673.5	624.9	697.5	653.7	516.9	451.2
Long-Term Obligations	636.9	598.3	597.8	535.4	636.6	637.9	523.2
Net Stockholders' Equity	1,281.2	1,448.7	1,531.5	1,728.1	1,625.1	1,612.1	1,545.3
Net Working Capital	d266.6	d58.6	d112.0	d81.7	d174.9	d54.3	d39.5
Year-end Shs. Outstg. (000)	161,526	173,818	181,613	193,258	195,402	195,210	196,516
STATISTICAL RECORD:							
Operating Profit Margin %	18.2	18.2	17.5	15.9	6.6	9.5	9.0
Net Profit Margin %	11.4	9.9	9.8	9.2	3.2	5.6	9.0
Return on Equity %	31.0	21.4	18.7	15.2	5.2	8.4	13.8
Return on Assets %	11.0	8.9	8.3	7.2	2.4	4.0	6.8
Debt/Total Assets %	17.7	17.1	17.3	14.7	18.0	18.9	16.7
Price Range	49.88-32.63	49.94-26.50	40.69-20.50	33.25-18.19	19.94-12.88	15.44-10.06	14.75-10.63
P/E Ratio	21.5-14.1	28.9-15.3	27.3-13.8	25.0-13.7	45.8-29.6	22.1-14.4	14.4-10.4
Average Yield %	1.1	1.1	1.2	1.2	1.7	2.2	2.2

Statistics are as originally reported. Adj. for 2-for-1 split, 7/98. [1] Incl. $32.9 mill. pre-tax gain & $31.5 mill. pre-tax chg., 1996; $11.3 mill. pre-tax gain & $10.1 mill. pre-tax chg., 1995; $205.1 mill. pre-tax gain, 1994. [2] Incl. $94.5 mill. after-tax loss impair. of assets. [3] Incl. $12.6 mill. in pre-tax gains, $5.4 mill. pre-tax chg. for sev. costs, & excl. $7.7 mill. after-tax extraord. item. [4] Incl. $3.1 mill. net chg. [5] Incl. $85.3 mill. gain fr. disp. of assets.

OFFICERS:
A. Sulzberger Jr., Chmn.
M. Golden, Vice-Chmn., Sr. V.P.
R. T. Lewis, Pres., C.E.O.

INVESTOR CONTACT: Catherine J. Mathis, Director-Investor Relations, (212) 556-1981

PRINCIPAL OFFICE: 229 West 43rd St., New York, NY 10036

TELEPHONE NUMBER: (212) 556-1234
FAX: (212) 556-4647
WEB: www.nytco.com
NO. OF EMPLOYEES: 14,000
SHAREHOLDERS: 10,664 (class A common); 37 (class B common)
ANNUAL MEETING: In May
INCORPORATED: NY, Aug., 1896

INSTITUTIONAL HOLDINGS:
No. of Institutions: 326
Shares Held: 90,018,720
% Held: 55.5

INDUSTRY: Newspapers (SIC: 2711)

TRANSFER AGENT(S): First Chicago Trust Company of New York, Jersey City, NJ

NYSE SYMBOL NWL
Rec. Pr. 25.27 (5/31/01)

NEWELL RUBBERMAID INC.

YIELD 3.3%
P/E RATIO 16.1

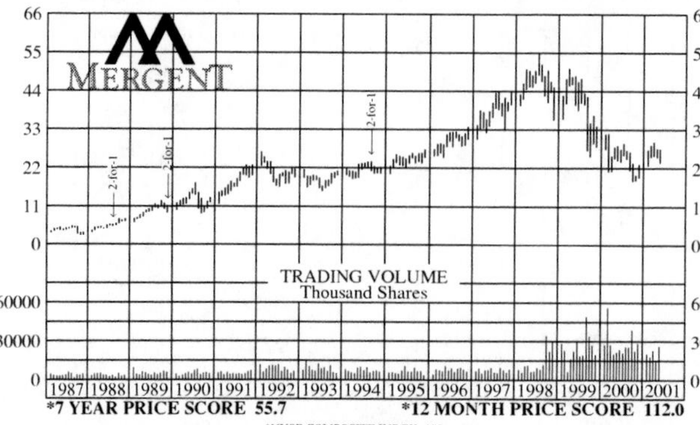

*7 YEAR PRICE SCORE 55.7 *12 MONTH PRICE SCORE 112.0
*NYSE COMPOSITE INDEX=100

INTERIM EARNINGS (Per Share):

Qtr.	Mar.	June	Sept.	Dec.
1997	0.24	0.49	0.53	0.56
1998	0.91	0.54	0.60	0.36
1999	d0.28	0.11	0.26	0.25
2000	0.28	0.48	0.46	0.35

INTERIM DIVIDENDS (Per Share):

Amt.	Decl.	Ex.	Rec.	Pay.
0.21Q	5/11/00	5/18/00	5/22/00	6/06/00
0.21Q	8/09/00	8/17/00	8/21/00	9/06/00
0.21Q	11/07/00	11/17/00	11/21/00	12/06/00
0.21Q	2/07/01	2/15/01	2/20/01	3/06/01
0.21Q	5/09/01	5/17/01	5/21/01	6/06/01

Indicated div.: $0.84 (Div. Reinv. Plan)

CAPITALIZATION (12/31/00):

	($000)	(%)
Long-Term Debt 1	2,314,774	43.2
Deferred Income Tax	93,165	1.7
Minority Interest	1,788	0.0
Redeemable Pfd. Stock	499,998	9.3
Common & Surplus	2,448,641	45.7
Total	5,358,366	100.0

RECENT DEVELOPMENTS: For the year ended 12/31/00, net income was $421.6 million compared with $95.4 million in 1999. Results included restructuring costs of $48.6 million in 2000 and $246.4 million in 1999. Net sales rose 3.3% to $6.93 billion from $6.71 billion a year earlier. Results for 2000 and 1999 were reclassified to include freight expenses as a cost of products sold.

PROSPECTS: Going forward, NWL plans to strengthen the RUBBERMAID®, SHARPIE®, CALPHALON®, LITTLE TIKES®, GRACO® and LEVELOR® brands. In addition, NWL will launch a Company-wide product development process that should yield a continuous stream of value-added innovative new products in the years to come. NWL should benefit from its new products and brand building efforts beginning in 2002 and beyond.

BUSINESS

NEWELL RUBBERMAID INC. (formerly Newell Company) is a multinational manufacturer and marketer of high-volume, long life cycle, branded, consumer products. NWL reports its results in the following six business segments: Storage, Organization & Cleaning, including RUBBERMAID® and CURVER® home products, GOODY® hair accessories and RUBBERMAID COMMERCIAL PRODUCTS™; Food Preparation, Cooking & Serving, including MIRRO® and CALPHALON® cookware; Infant/Juvenile Care & Play, including LITTLE TIKES®, GRACO® and CENTURY®; Home Decor, including LEVOLOR®, KIRSCH®, NEWELL® and GARDINIA® Window Furnishings and INTERCRAFT®, BURNES®, PANODIA®, and HOLSON® picture frames and photo albums; Hardware & Tools, including AMEROCK®, and EZ PAINTR®; and Office Products, including SANFORD®, BEROL®, SHARPIE®, ROTRING® and REYNOLDS®, PAPER MATE®, PARKER®, and WATERMAN® markers and writing instruments, ROLODEX® and ELDON office storage and organization products and LIQUID PAPER® correction fluids. In March 1999, NWL acquired Rubbermaid, Inc.

ANNUAL FINANCIAL DATA

	5 12/31/00	4 12/31/99	12/31/98	12/31/97	12/31/96	12/31/95	12/31/94
Earnings Per Share	**2 1.57**	**3 0.34**	**2 2.38**	**1.82**	**1.62**	**1.41**	**1.24**
Cash Flow Per Share	**2.57**	**1.30**	**3.14**	**2.62**	**2.35**	**2.05**	**1.70**
Tang. Book Val. Per Share	**0.92**	**2.38**	**2.06**	**2.48**	**3.68**	**2.64**	**2.76**
Dividends Per Share	**0.84**	**0.80**	**0.72**	**0.64**	**0.56**	**0.46**	**0.39**
Dividend Payout %	**53.5**	**235.2**	**30.3**	**35.2**	**34.6**	**32.6**	**31.4**
INCOME STATEMENT (IN MILLIONS):							
Total Revenues	6,934.7	6,413.1	3,720.0	3,234.3	2,872.8	2,498.4	2,074.9
Costs & Expenses	5,810.5	5,797.7	3,038.4	2,532.7	2,270.8	1,977.2	1,644.6
Depreciation & Amort.	292.6	271.7	147.5	129.9	116.4	101.7	72.5
Operating Income	831.7	343.6	534.1	571.6	485.7	419.5	357.9
Net Interest Inc./(Exp.)	d130.0	d100.0	d60.4	d73.6	d57.0	d49.8	d30.0
Income Before Income Taxes	685.5	230.9	684.8	480.8	424.6	370.8	329.3
Income Taxes	263.9	135.5	288.7	190.4	168.2	148.3	133.7
Net Income	2 421.6	3 95.4	2 396.2	290.4	256.5	222.5	195.6
Cash Flow	714.2	367.2	543.7	420.3	372.8	324.2	268.1
Average Shs. Outstg. (000)	278,365	281,806	173,041	160,214	158,764	158,212	157,774
BALANCE SHEET (IN MILLIONS):							
Cash & Cash Equivalents	22.5	102.2	57.5	36.1	4.4	58.8	14.9
Total Current Assets	2,896.7	2,738.6	1,591.0	1,381.6	1,108.1	1,132.1	917.7
Net Property	1,756.9	2,118.8	835.6	696.1	555.4	530.3	454.6
Total Assets	7,261.9	7,294.7	4,327.8	3,943.8	3,005.0	2,930.5	2,488.3
Total Current Liabilities	1,550.8	1,629.9	821.5	664.0	637.0	680.3	784.0
Long-Term Obligations	2,314.8	1,455.8	866.2	784.0	672.0	761.6	409.0
Net Stockholders' Equity	2,448.6	2,697.0	1,993.1	1,759.6	1,507.2	1,307.8	1,138.3
Net Working Capital	1,345.9	1,108.7	769.6	717.6	471.1	451.9	133.7
Year-end Shs. Outstg. (000)	282,200	282,000	162,700	159,200	158,900	158,700	157,710
STATISTICAL RECORD:							
Operating Profit Margin %	12.0	5.4	14.4	17.7	16.9	16.8	17.2
Net Profit Margin %	6.1	1.5	10.6	9.0	8.9	8.9	9.4
Return on Equity %	17.2	3.5	19.9	16.5	17.0	17.0	17.2
Return on Assets %	5.8	1.3	9.2	7.4	8.5	7.6	7.9
Debt/Total Assets %	31.9	20.0	20.0	19.9	22.4	26.0	16.4
Price Range	31.88-18.25	50.63-25.25	55.19-35.69	43.81-30.13	33.75-25.00	27.25-20.25	23.88-18.81
P/E Ratio	20.3-11.6	148.9-74.2	23.2-15.0	24.1-16.6	20.8-15.4	19.3-14.4	19.3-15.2
Average Yield %	3.4	2.1	1.6	1.7	1.9	1.9	1.8

Statistics are as originally reported. Adj. for stk. split: 2-for-1, 9/94. 1 Incl. debs. conv. into common. 2 Incl. non-recurr. chrg. of $56.5 mill., 1998; $48.6 mill., 2000. 3 Incl. non-recurr. after-tax chrg. of $369.6 mill. 4 Incl. results of Rubbermaid, Inc., acqd. 3/99. 5 Results were reclassified to incl. freight exp. as a cost of products sold.

OFFICERS:
W. P. Sovey, Chmn.
J. Galli, Jr., Pres., C.E.O.
W. T. Alldredge, C.F.O.
D. L. Matschullat, Gen. Couns.

INVESTOR CONTACT: Ross A. Parker, Jr., Investor Relations, (815) 381-8150

PRINCIPAL OFFICE: Newell Center, 29 East Stephenson Street, Freeport, IL 61032-0943

TELEPHONE NUMBER: (815) 235-4171
FAX: (815) 233-8060
WEB: www.newell.com

NO. OF EMPLOYEES: 48,800 (approx.)

SHAREHOLDERS: 26,704 (record)

ANNUAL MEETING: In May

INCORPORATED: DE, 1970

INSTITUTIONAL HOLDINGS:
No. of Institutions: 348
Shares Held: 201,112,212
% Held: 75.4

INDUSTRY: Glass containers (SIC: 3221)

TRANSFER AGENT(S): First Chicago Trust Company of New York, New York, NY

NYSE SYMBOL NFX
Rec. Pr. 36.00 (4/30/01)

NEWFIELD EXPLORATION CO.

YIELD ...
P/E RATIO 12.4

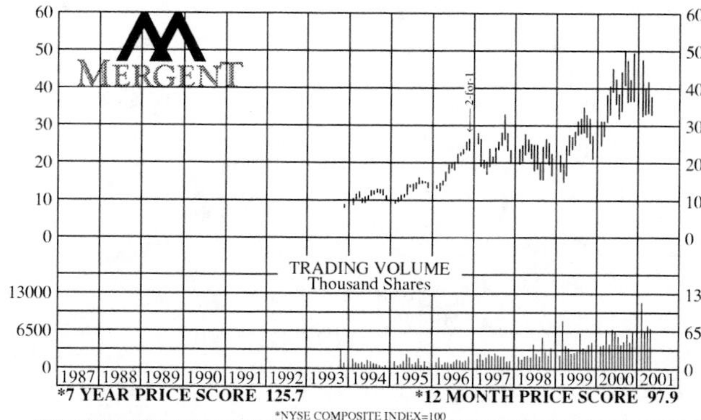

INTERIM EARNINGS (Per Share):

Qtr.	Mar.	June	Sept.	Dec.
1997	0.34	0.32	0.24	0.34
1998	0.18	0.10	0.02	d1.71
1999	Nil	0.10	0.29	0.39
2000	0.35	0.60	0.95	1.01

INTERIM DIVIDENDS (Per Share):

Amt.	Decl.	Ex.	Rec.	Pay.

No dividends paid.

CAPITALIZATION (12/31/00):

	($000)	(%)
Long-Term Debt	133,711	15.3
Deferred Income Tax	79,244	9.0
Preferred Stock	143,750	16.4
Common & Surplus	519,455	59.3
Total	876,160	100.0

RECENT DEVELOPMENTS: For the year ended 12/31/00, income totaled $134.7 million, before an accounting change charge of $2.4 million, versus net income of $33.2 million a year earlier. Results for 2000 included a ceiling test write-down charge of $503,000. Revenues surged 82.9% to $526.6 million, reflecting increased production and improved commodity prices. Net natural gas production increased 20.4% to 288.1 million cubic feet per day, while average gas prices soared 53.4% to $3.56 per thousand cubic feet.

PROSPECTS: On 1/23/01, NFX announced the closing of its acquisition of Lariat Petroleum for approximately $333.0 million, including assumption of Lariat's debt and certain other obligations. The purchase price consisted of about 1.9 million shares of NFX stock and $265.0 million in cash. The acquisition of Lariat, an exploration and production company primarily focused in the Anadarko Basin of Oklahoma, provides a new focus area for NFX. With the acquisition, about 40.0% of the Company's proved reserves are located onshore U.S.

BUSINESS

NEWFIELD EXPLORATION CO. is engaged in the exploration, development and acquisition of crude oil and natural gas properties. The Company's operations are focused in the Gulf of Mexico and the Anadarko Basin of Oklahoma, along with the U.S. onshore Gulf Coast and offshore northwest Australia. As of 12/31/00, NFX had proved reserves of 687.3 billion cubic feet equivalent. Total reserves were 76% natural gas, 24% crude oil. On 1/23/01, the Company acquired Lariat Petroleum for approximately $333.0 million.

QUARTERLY DATA

(12/31/2000)($000)	Rev	Inc
1st Quarter	97,822	30,984
2nd Quarter	114,714	45,209
3rd Quarter	150,431	68,986
4th Quarter	163,685	76,050

ANNUAL FINANCIAL DATA

	12/31/00	12/31/99	12/31/98	12/31/97	12/31/96	12/31/95	12/31/94
Earnings Per Share	**[1][2] 2.98**	**0.81**	**[1] d1.55**	**[1] 1.07**	**1.03**	**0.45**	**0.40**
Cash Flow Per Share	**6.90**	**4.39**	**1.75**	**3.54**	**2.76**	**1.83**	**1.35**
Tang. Book Val. Per Share	**12.19**	**8.99**	**8.01**	**8.12**	**6.81**	**5.63**	**5.08**
INCOME STATEMENT (IN MILLIONS):							
Total Revenues	526.6	282.0	195.7	199.4	149.3	94.6	69.7
Costs & Expenses	114.2	64.2	152.4	40.8	26.4	20.5	14.4
Depreciation & Amort.	191.2	152.6	123.1	94.0	64.0	49.9	34.1
Operating Income	221.2	65.1	d79.8	64.6	58.8	24.2	21.2
Net Interest Inc./(Exp.)	d7.2	d9.6	d8.5	d2.1	0.5	0.8	1.4
Income Before Income Taxes	204.7	52.0	d88.4	62.4	59.3	25.0	22.5
Income Taxes	70.0	18.8	cr30.7	21.8	20.8	8.7	8.1
Net Income	[1][2] 134.7	33.2	[1] d57.7	[1] 40.6	38.5	16.3	14.4
Cash Flow	325.9	185.8	65.4	134.6	102.5	66.2	48.6
Average Shs. Outstg. (000)	47,228	42,294	37,312	38,017	37,203	36,193	35,910
BALANCE SHEET (IN MILLIONS):							
Cash & Cash Equivalents	18.5	41.8	0.1	8.2	13.3	12.5	18.6
Total Current Assets	179.1	125.9	45.3	64.8	61.3	42.8	35.9
Net Property	833.3	644.8	578.4	484.0	327.5	227.7	173.4
Total Assets	1,023.3	781.6	629.3	553.6	395.9	277.4	215.6
Total Current Liabilities	141.1	90.7	54.1	64.4	49.8	31.6	24.9
Long-Term Obligations	133.7	124.7	208.7	129.6	60.0	25.2	0.6
Net Stockholders' Equity	663.2	518.8	323.9	292.0	239.9	193.6	169.5
Net Working Capital	38.1	35.2	d8.8	0.4	11.4	11.2	11.0
Year-end Shs. Outstg. (000)	42,607	41,735	40,430	35,976	35,243	34,355	33,332
STATISTICAL RECORD:							
Operating Profit Margin %	42.0	23.1	...	32.4	39.4	25.6	30.4
Net Profit Margin %	25.6	11.8	...	20.4	25.8	17.2	20.7
Return on Equity %	20.3	6.4	...	13.9	16.0	8.4	8.5
Return on Assets %	13.2	4.2	...	7.3	9.7	5.9	6.7
Debt/Total Assets %	13.1	16.0	33.2	23.4	15.2	9.1	0.3
Price Range	50.25-24.50	35.00-14.88	27.69-15.44	33.00-16.88	26.50-12.50	16.06-9.00	13.00-8.69
P/E Ratio	16.9-8.2	43.2-18.4	...	30.8-15.8	25.7-12.1	35.7-20.0	32.5-21.7

Statistics are as originally reported. Adj. for 2-for-1 split, 12/96 [1] Incls. ceiling test write-down chrg. of $4.2 mill., 1997; $105.0 mill., 1998; $503,000, 2000. [2] Bef. acctg. chrg. of $2.4 mill.

OFFICERS:
D. A. Trice, Pres., C.E.O.
T. W. Rathert, V.P., C.F.O., Sec.
S. G. Riggs, Treas.

INVESTOR CONTACT: Steve Campbell, (281) 847-6081

PRINCIPAL OFFICE: 363 N. Sam Houston Pkwy. East, Suite 2020, Houston, TX 77060

TELEPHONE NUMBER: (281) 847-6000
FAX: (281) 847-6006
WEB: www.newfld.com

NO. OF EMPLOYEES: 348 (avg.)

SHAREHOLDERS: 266

ANNUAL MEETING: In May

INCORPORATED: DE, Dec., 1988

INSTITUTIONAL HOLDINGS:
No. of Institutions: 184
Shares Held: 40,999,419
% Held: 91.8

INDUSTRY: Crude petroleum and natural gas (SIC: 1311)

TRANSFER AGENT(S): Mellon Investor Services L.L.C, Ridgefield Park, NJ

NYSE SYMBOL NHL
Rec. Pr. 27.75 (5/31/01)

NEWHALL LAND & FARMING COMPANY

YIELD 1.4%
P/E RATIO 8.8

TRADING VOLUME
Thousand Shares

*7 YEAR PRICE SCORE 86.1 *12 MONTH PRICE SCORE 109.5

*NYSE COMPOSITE INDEX=100

INTERIM EARNINGS (Per Share):

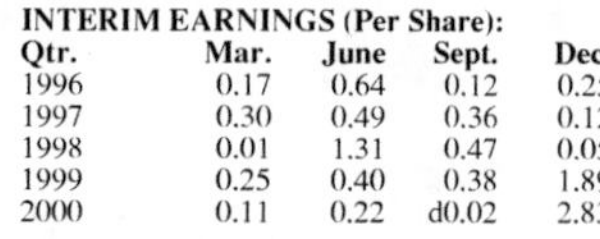

Qtr.	Mar.	June	Sept.	Dec.
1996	0.17	0.64	0.12	0.25
1997	0.30	0.49	0.36	0.12
1998	0.01	1.31	0.47	0.05
1999	0.25	0.40	0.38	1.89
2000	0.11	0.22	d0.02	2.83

INTERIM DIVIDENDS (Per Share):

Amt.	Decl.	Ex.	Rec.	Pay.
0.10Q	7/19/00	8/02/00	8/04/00	9/11/00
0.10Q	11/15/00	11/29/00	12/01/00	12/11/00
0.10Q	1/17/01	1/31/01	2/02/01	3/12/01
0.10Sp	1/17/01	1/31/01	2/02/01	3/12/01
0.10Q	5/16/01	5/30/01	6/01/01	6/11/01

Indicated div.: $0.40

CAPITALIZATION (12/31/00):

	($000)	(%)
Long-Term Debt	74,557	38.5
Common & Surplus	119,204	61.5
Total	193,761	100.0

RECENT DEVELOPMENTS: For the year ended 12/31/00, net income was $85.4 million, down 5.5% versus $90.4 million the previous year. Total revenues grew 24.3% to $401.0 million from $322.5 million the year before, driven by the sale of Castaic Shopping Center, Plaza del Rancho, four buildings in NHL's office portfolio, four apartment complexes and over 108 acres of commercial and industrial land. Operating income was $118.0 million, up 2.4% versus $115.2 million a year earlier.

PROSPECTS: In 2001, the Company expects to generate revenues from residential, commercial and industrial land sales, its portfolio of income-producing properties, and sales of the remaining two properties in its asset sale program that did not close escrow in 2000. Meanwhile, the Company is no longer marketing for sale the Valencia Town Center regional shopping mall and entertainment center and has terminated discussions with a potential buyer for its landfill.

BUSINESS

NEWHALL LAND AND FARMING COMPANY (a California limited partnership) is engaged in the development of residential, industrial and commercial real estate. NHL is also engaged in agriculture. The Company's primary activity is the development of the planned community of Valencia on the Newhall Ranch, located on 36,000 acres, 30 miles north of downtown Los Angeles. Revenues for 2000 were derived: industrial and commercial sales, 73.6%; commercial operations, 17.8%; residential home and land sales, 6.8%; and agriculture, 1.8%. NHL sold its McDowell Mountain Ranch project on 4/17/96 to Sunbelt Holdings, Inc. On 9/29/00, the Company divested its joint-venture interest in the 1,900-acre City Ranch master-planned community located in Palmdale, California.

ANNUAL FINANCIAL DATA

	12/31/00	12/31/99	12/31/98	12/31/97	12/31/96	12/31/95	12/31/94
Earnings Per Share	**3.05**	**2.85**	**1.86**	**1.28**	**1.18**	**0.75**	**1 0.42**
Cash Flow Per Share	**3.55**	**3.34**	**2.16**	**1.57**	**1.43**	**0.97**	**0.63**
Tang. Book Val. Per Share	**4.48**	**4.71**	**4.40**	**4.21**	**3.48**	**3.14**	**3.06**
Dividends Per Share	**0.75**	**0.62**	**0.52**	**0.48**	**0.40**	**0.40**	**0.40**
Dividend Payout %	**24.6**	**21.8**	**28.0**	**37.5**	**33.9**	**53.3**	**95.2**
INCOME STATEMENT (IN MILLIONS):							
Total Revenues	401.0	322.5	304.7	207.7	220.2	175.6	134.3
Costs & Expenses	269.2	192.0	210.7	133.7	150.7	121.4	92.0
Depreciation & Amort.	13.8	15.3	10.1	10.1	8.9	7.7	7.7
Operating Income	118.0	115.2	83.9	63.9	60.6	46.5	34.6
Income Before Income Taxes	85.4	90.4	64.1	44.5	41.9	27.3	15.6
Net Income	85.4	90.4	64.1	44.5	41.9	27.3	1 15.6
Cash Flow	99.2	105.7	74.2	54.6	50.7	35.0	23.3
Average Shs. Outstg. (000)	27,969	31,668	34,376	34,750	35,411	36,272	36,789
BALANCE SHEET (IN MILLIONS):							
Cash & Cash Equivalents	3.7	1.6	2.2	2.8	2.4	4.3	7.7
Total Current Assets	20.9	63.2	32.4	75.7	91.2	117.9	113.6
Net Property	67.6	61.3	58.8	54.9	239.7	186.7	184.7
Total Assets	351.7	504.8	432.2	457.8	439.7	438.2	431.2
Total Current Liabilities	100.3	91.8	82.0	61.3	52.0	48.3	54.5
Long-Term Obligations	74.6	222.8	157.6	156.9	163.3	152.3	146.0
Net Stockholders' Equity	119.2	139.7	143.8	145.3	120.7	112.9	112.4
Net Working Capital	d79.5	d28.6	d49.5	14.4	39.2	69.6	59.1
Year-end Shs. Outstg. (000)	26,590	29,668	32,676	34,527	34,701	35,910	36,761
STATISTICAL RECORD:							
Operating Profit Margin %	29.4	35.7	27.5	30.8	27.5	26.5	25.8
Net Profit Margin %	21.3	28.0	21.0	21.4	19.0	15.6	11.6
Return on Equity %	71.6	64.7	44.6	30.6	34.7	24.2	13.9
Return on Assets %	24.3	17.9	14.8	9.7	9.5	6.2	3.6
Debt/Total Assets %	21.2	44.1	36.5	34.3	37.1	34.8	33.9
Price Range	28.88-20.20	28.00-22.19	34.75-20.25	32.00-16.50	18.75-15.00	17.00-12.13	17.25-12.00
P/E Ratio	9.5-6.6	9.8-7.8	18.7-10.9	25.0-12.9	15.9-12.7	22.7-16.2	41.1-28.6
Average Yield %	3.1	2.5	1.9	2.0	2.4	2.7	2.7

Statistics are as originally reported. 1 Incl. $3.7 mil non-recur. chg.

OFFICERS:
G. M. Cusumano, Pres., C.E.O.
S. R. Mork, Sr. V.P., C.F.O.

INVESTOR CONTACT: Marcia A. Ward, Dir., Investor Relations, (661) 255-4445

PRINCIPAL OFFICE: 23823 Valencia Blvd., Valencia, CA 91355

TELEPHONE NUMBER: (661) 255-4000
FAX: (661) 255-3960
WEB: www.valencia.com

NO. OF EMPLOYEES: 195 (avg.)

SHAREHOLDERS: 1,144

ANNUAL MEETING: In Mar.

INCORPORATED: CA, June, 1883; reincorp., CA, 1985

INSTITUTIONAL HOLDINGS:
No. of Institutions: 45
Shares Held: 12,757,417
% Held: 48.0

INDUSTRY: Subdividers and developers, nec (SIC: 6552)

TRANSFER AGENT(S): Newhall Depositary Co.

NYSE SYMBOL NEM
Rec. Pr. 18.23 (4/30/01)

NEWMONT MINING CORPORATION

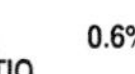

YIELD 0.6%
P/E RATIO . . .

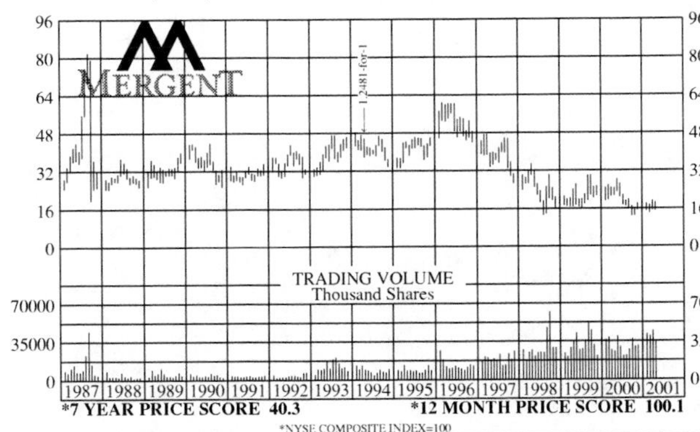

INTERIM EARNINGS (Per Share):

Qtr.	Mar.	June	Sept.	Dec.
1997	0.21	d0.41	0.28	0.25
1998	0.20	0.16	0.24	d2.53
1999	0.06	0.04	d0.23	0.28
2000	0.04	d0.10	d0.11	0.12

INTERIM DIVIDENDS (Per Share):

Amt.	Decl.	Ex.	Rec.	Pay.
0.03Q	5/17/00	6/05/00	6/07/00	6/21/00
0.03Q	7/17/00	9/05/00	9/07/00	9/20/00
0.03Q	11/15/00	12/05/00	12/07/00	12/20/00
0.03Q	1/24/01	3/02/01	3/06/01	3/21/01
0.03Q	5/16/01	6/04/01	6/06/01	6/20/01

Indicated div.: $0.12 (Div. Reinv. Plan)

CAPITALIZATION (12/31/00):

	($000)	(%)
Long-Term Debt	976,446	36.2
Deferred Income Tax	64,188	2.4
Minority Interest	188,054	7.0
Common & Surplus	1,466,388	54.4
Total	2,695,076	100.0

RECENT DEVELOPMENTS: For the year ended 12/31/00, the Company reported a loss of $10.5 million, before cumulative effect of a change in accounting principle of $8.4 million, versus net income of $24.8 million in 1999. Results for 2000 included a pre-tax charge of $42.2 million and a gain of $26.8 million, while results for 1999 included a loss of $44.8 million. Sales and other income climbed 9.4% to $1.57 billion.

PROSPECTS: On 1/10/01, the Company completed the acquisition of Battle Mountain Gold Company. As a result, NEM expects to produce approximately 5.4 million equity ounces of gold in 2001. However, total cash costs could increase 5.0% to 7.0% higher than in 2000 due to rising energy costs primarily in the U.S., lower production in Nevada and higher processing costs in Peru.

BUSINESS

NEWMONT MINING CORPORATION is engaged, directly and through its subsidiaries and affiliates, in the production of gold, the development of gold properties, the exploration for gold and the acquisition of gold properties worldwide. It produces gold from operations in Nevada and California, as well as in Peru, Indonesia, Mexico and the Central Asian Republic of Uzbekistan. In 2000, Newmont Mining produced about 4.9 million ounces of gold. On May 5, 1997, the Company acquired Santa Fe Pacific Gold Corporation.

REVENUES

(12/31/2000)	($000)	(%)
North American Operations	872,000	56.1
Yanacocha	491,800	31.6
Minahasa	120,900	7.8
Zarafshan Newmont	70,200	4.5
Total	1,554,900	100.0

ANNUAL FINANCIAL DATA

	12/31/00	12/31/99	12/31/98	[3] 12/31/97	12/31/96	12/31/95	12/31/94
Earnings Per Share	[6] d0.06	[5] 0.15	[4] d2.27	[2] 0.44	0.86	[1] 1.17	0.70
Cash Flow Per Share	2.40	1.91	d0.12	2.49	1.67	1.98	1.68
Tang. Book Val. Per Share	8.58	8.66	8.61	10.17	10.30	7.89	7.66
Dividends Per Share	0.12	0.12	0.12	0.39	0.48	0.48	0.48
Dividend Payout %	...	79.9	...	88.6	55.8	41.0	68.6
INCOME STATEMENT (IN MILLIONS):							
Total Revenues	1,566.7	1,431.6	1,474.9	1,628.0	794.9	791.6	619.7
Costs & Expenses	994.5	905.5	1,516.3	1,098.0	596.7	535.3	480.1
Depreciation & Amort.	415.3	296.4	341.7	321.0	124.8	106.8	91.1
Operating Income	77.2	167.2	d383.1	209.0	73.3	149.4	48.5
Net Interest Inc./(Exp.)	d79.6	d62.6	d78.8	d77.1	d88.0	d72.8	d19.6
Income Before Income Taxes	104.0	122.3	d461.9	131.9	d14.6	76.6	28.8
Income Taxes	11.3	14.4	cr180.9	cr7.9	cr19.4	17.0	cr29.3
Equity Earnings/Minority Int.	d103.3	d83.1	d79.4	d71.4	36.3	16.7	8.1
Net Income	[6] d10.5	[5] 24.8	[4] d360.5	[2] 68.4	41.1	[1] 76.2	66.3
Cash Flow	404.8	321.2	d18.8	389.4	165.9	171.9	141.6
Average Shs. Outstg. (000)	168,386	167,800	159,010	156,347	99,357	87,006	84,147
BALANCE SHEET (IN MILLIONS):							
Cash & Cash Equivalents	67.4	64.7	90.9	159.0	198.4	71.0	174.1
Total Current Assets	511.9	534.1	513.1	641.4	455.9	289.5	370.1
Net Property	1,949.3	1,972.3	2,048.7	2,598.8	1,302.0	1,255.3	1,119.3
Total Assets	3,510.7	3,383.4	3,186.8	3,614.0	2,081.1	1,773.8	1,656.7
Total Current Liabilities	290.7	273.9	212.3	394.5	224.1	194.4	153.2
Long-Term Obligations	976.4	1,014.2	1,201.1	1,179.4	585.0	604.3	593.6
Net Stockholders' Equity	1,466.4	1,451.6	1,439.5	1,591.1	1,024.9	742.9	673.5
Net Working Capital	221.2	260.2	300.7	246.8	231.8	95.1	216.9
Year-end Shs. Outstg. (000)	170,943	167,658	167,191	156,493	99,522	94,211	86,080
STATISTICAL RECORD:							
Operating Profit Margin %	4.9	11.7	...	12.8	9.2	18.9	7.8
Net Profit Margin %	...	1.7	...	4.2	5.2	9.6	10.7
Return on Equity %	...	1.7	...	4.3	4.0	10.3	9.8
Return on Assets %	...	0.7	...	1.9	2.0	4.3	4.0
Debt/Total Assets %	27.8	30.0	37.7	32.6	28.1	34.1	35.8
Price Range	28.38-12.75	30.06-16.38	34.88-13.25	47.50-26.56	60.75-43.88	46.25-33.13	48.08-33.88
P/E Ratio	...	200.3-109.1	...	107.9-60.4	70.6-51.0	39.5-28.3	68.7-48.4
Average Yield %	0.6	0.5	0.5	1.1	0.9	1.2	1.2

Statistics are as originally reported. [1] Incl. net nonrecurr. gain of $34.9 mill. [2] Incl. pre-tax and rel. asset write-offs of $162.7 mill. [3] Inc. results of Santa Fe Pacific Gold Corp. [4] Incl. a pre-tax chg. of $614.9 mill. & excl. a $32.9 mill. chg. for a change in acc. prin. [5] Incl. net nonrecurr. chrgs. of $41.9 mill. [6] Incl. net pre-tax chrgs. of $15.4 mill.; Bef. acctg. chrg. of $8.4 mill.

OFFICERS:
R. C. Cambre, Chmn.
W. W. Murdy, Pres., C.E.O.
B. D. Hansen, Sr. V.P., C.F.O.

INVESTOR CONTACT: James F. Hill, Vice-Pres., (303) 863-7414

PRINCIPAL OFFICE: 1700 Lincoln St., Denver, CO 80203

TELEPHONE NUMBER: (303) 863-7414
FAX: (303) 837-5928
WEB: www.newmont.com

NO. OF EMPLOYEES: 10,800 (avg.)

SHAREHOLDERS: 26,160 (record)

ANNUAL MEETING: In May

INCORPORATED: DE, May, 1921

INSTITUTIONAL HOLDINGS:
No. of Institutions: 245
Shares Held: 110,570,485
% Held: 58.8

INDUSTRY: Gold ores (SIC: 1041)

TRANSFER AGENT(S): Mellon Investor Services, South Hakensack, NJ

NYSE SYMBOL NNS
Rec. Pr. 63.93 (5/31/01)

NEWPORT NEWS SHIPBUILDING INC.

YIELD 0.3%
P/E RATIO 23.0

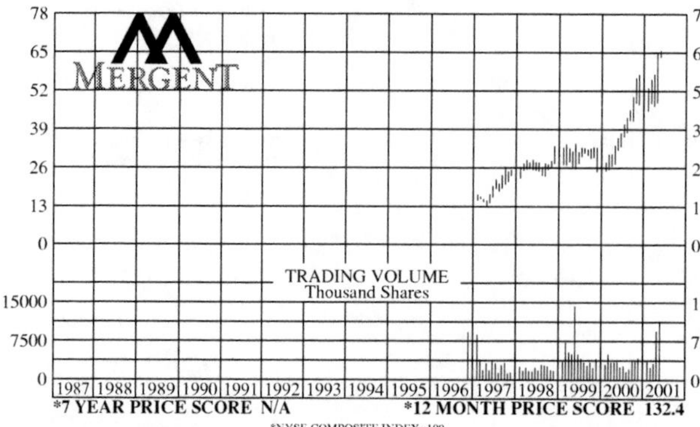

*7 YEAR PRICE SCORE N/A *12 MONTH PRICE SCORE 132.4

*NYSE COMPOSITE INDEX=100

INTERIM EARNINGS (Per Share):

Qtr.	Mar.	June	Sept.	Dec.
1997	0.38	0.39	0.05	d2.21
1998	0.44	0.45	0.46	0.50
1999	0.50	0.95	0.58	0.69
2000	0.63	0.74	0.67	0.74

INTERIM DIVIDENDS (Per Share):

Amt.	Decl.	Ex.	Rec.	Pay.
0.04Q	5/19/00	6/15/00	6/19/00	6/29/00
0.04Q	10/10/00	10/18/00	10/20/00	10/30/00
0.04Q	2/01/01	2/08/01	2/12/01	2/22/01
0.04Q	3/22/01	3/29/01	4/02/01	4/12/01
0.04Q	5/18/01	6/15/01	6/19/01	6/29/01

Indicated div.: $0.16 (Div. Reinv. Plan)

CAPITALIZATION (12/31/00):

	($000)	(%)
Long-Term Debt	498,000	49.8
Deferred Income Tax	245,000	24.5
Common & Surplus	258,000	25.8
Total	1,001,000	100.0

RECENT DEVELOPMENTS: For the year ended 12/31/00, net income increased 9.8% to $90.0 million versus $82.0 million in 1999. Revenues were $2.07 billion, up 11.2% from $1.86 billion in 1999. Construction segment revenues jumped 35.1% to $959.0 million, benefiting from a ramp-up in the Virginia-class submarine program and advance work on the aircraft carrier CVN 77. Fleet Services segment revenues fell 13.4% to $791.0 million, while Engineering segment revenues rose 33.8% to $305.0 million.

PROSPECTS: On 1/26/01, NNS was awarded a $3.80 billion contract by the U.S. Navy for construction of the tenth Nimitz-class aircraft carrier, CVN 77. CVN 77 will serve as the first transition ship to a new class of carriers and is scheduled for delivery in 2008. NNS will act as the systems integrator for the warfare system, a task previously performed by the U.S. Navy. With the addition of this contract to year-end backlog, NNS has $7.00 billion of work under contract.

BUSINESS

NEWPORT NEWS SHIPBUILDING INC. is the largest non-government-owned shipyard in the United States, measured by revenues, size of facilities and number of employees. NNS's consolidated subsidiaries include Newport News Shipbuilding and Dry Dock Company. Its principal business is designing, constructing, repairing, overhauling, and refueling nuclear-powered aircraft carriers and submarines for the United States Navy. The Company also provides ongoing fleet services for other U.S. Navy vessels through work in overhauling, lifecycle engineering, and repair. NNS's largest single customer is the United States Government. NNS is capable of building, refueling and overhauling the Navy's nuclear-powered aircraft carriers, and is one of only two shipyards capable of building nuclear-powered submarines. In 2000, revenues were derived: Construction, 47%; Fleet Services, 38%; and Engineering, 15%.

ANNUAL FINANCIAL DATA

	12/31/00	12/31/99	12/31/98	12/31/97	12/31/96	12/31/95	12/31/94
Earnings Per Share	**2.77**	[2] **2.72**	**1.85**	**d1.39**	**1.60**	...	...
Cash Flow Per Share	**4.47**	**4.60**	**3.58**	**0.58**	**3.50**	...	...
Tang. Book Val. Per Share	**7.30**	**7.74**	**6.57**	**5.24**	**6.76**	...	...
Dividends Per Share	**0.16**	**0.16**	**0.16**	**0.16**	...	...	...
Dividend Payout %	**5.8**	**5.9**	**8.6**	...	...	...	...
INCOME STATEMENT (IN MILLIONS):							
Total Revenues	2,072.0	1,863.0	1,862.0	1,707.0	1,870.0	1,756.0	1,753.0
Costs & Expenses	1,811.0	1,579.0	1,625.0	1,658.0	1,665.0	1,529.0	1,482.0
Depreciation & Amort.	55.0	66.0	62.0	68.0	65.0	67.0	70.0
Operating Income	206.0	218.0	175.0	d19.0	140.0	160.0	201.0
Net Interest Inc./(Exp.)	d53.0	d54.0	d61.0	d55.0	d38.0	d29.0	d30.0
Income Before Income Taxes	153.0	164.0	114.0	d74.0	102.0	131.0	170.0
Income Taxes	63.0	67.0	48.0	cr26.0	47.0	58.0	75.0
Net Income	90.0	[2] 97.0	66.0	d48.0	55.0	73.0	[1] 95.0
Cash Flow	145.0	163.0	128.0	20.0	120.0	140.0	165.0
Average Shs. Outstg. (000)	32,403	35,452	35,794	34,742	34,297	...	...
BALANCE SHEET (IN MILLIONS):							
Cash & Cash Equivalents	3.0	2.0	3.0	3.0	1.0	2.0	1.0
Total Current Assets	556.0	592.0	660.0	455.0	491.0	419.0	330.0
Net Property	692.0	716.0	763.0	816.0	836.0	820.0	796.0
Total Assets	1,476.0	1,512.0	1,600.0	1,476.0	1,489.0	1,380.0	1,263.0
Total Current Liabilities	437.0	446.0	518.0	356.0	256.0	438.0	405.0
Long-Term Obligations	498.0	525.0	591.0	548.0	596.0	292.0	287.0
Net Stockholders' Equity	258.0	273.0	232.0	183.0	232.0	272.0	199.0
Net Working Capital	119.0	146.0	142.0	99.0	235.0	d19.0	d75.0
Year-end Shs. Outstg. (000)	35,353	35,291	35,286	34,949	34,297	...	...
STATISTICAL RECORD:							
Operating Profit Margin %	9.9	11.7	9.4	...	7.5	9.1	11.5
Net Profit Margin %	4.3	5.2	3.5	...	2.9	4.2	5.4
Return on Equity %	34.9	35.5	28.4	...	23.7	26.8	47.7
Return on Assets %	6.1	6.4	4.1	...	3.7	5.3	7.5
Debt/Total Assets %	33.7	34.7	36.9	37.1	40.0	21.2	22.7
Price Range	57.69-24.94	34.25-24.75	33.44-22.50	26.38-13.00	...	...	...
P/E Ratio	20.8-9.0	12.6-9.1	18.1-12.2	...	...	...	...
Average Yield %	0.4	0.5	0.6	0.8	...	...	...

Statistics are as originally reported. [1] Bef. acctg. chrg. of $4.0 mill. [2] Incl. nonrecurr. gain of $25.0 mill. assoc. w/merger break-up fees and insur. settlements.

OFFICERS:
W. P. Fricks, Chmn., Pres., C.E.O.
T. C. Schievelbein, Exex. V.P., C.O.O.
S. B. Clarkson, V.P., Sec., Gen. Couns.
C. S. Ream, Sr. V.P., C.F.O.

INVESTOR CONTACT: Joe Fernandes, Dir., Investor Relations, (757) 688-6400

PRINCIPAL OFFICE: 4101 Washington Avenue, Newport News, VA 23607

TELEPHONE NUMBER: (757) 380-2000
FAX: (757) 380-3867
WEB: www.nns.com

NO. OF EMPLOYEES: 17,000 (approx.)

SHAREHOLDERS: 32,000 (approx.)

ANNUAL MEETING: In May

INCORPORATED: DE, 1996

INSTITUTIONAL HOLDINGS:
No. of Institutions: 175
Shares Held: 19,983,309
% Held: 56.5

INDUSTRY: Ship building and repairing (SIC: 3731)

TRANSFER AGENT(S): First Chicago Trust Company of New York, Jersey City, NJ

NYSE SYMBOL NMK
Rec. Pr. 17.50 (5/31/01)

NIAGARA MOHAWK HOLDINGS, INC.

YIELD ...
P/E RATIO ...

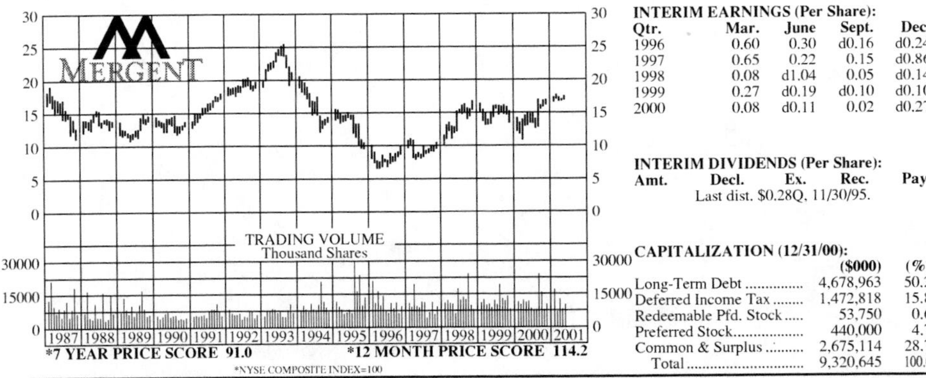

INTERIM EARNINGS (Per Share):

Qtr.	Mar.	June	Sept.	Dec.
1996	0.60	0.30	d0.16	d0.24
1997	0.65	0.22	0.15	d0.86
1998	0.08	d1.04	0.05	d0.14
1999	0.27	d0.19	d0.10	d0.10
2000	0.08	d0.11	0.02	d0.27

INTERIM DIVIDENDS (Per Share):

Amt.	Decl.	Ex.	Rec.	Pay.

Last dist. $0.28Q, 11/30/95.

CAPITALIZATION (12/31/00):

	($000)	(%)
Long-Term Debt	4,678,963	50.2
Deferred Income Tax	1,472,818	15.8
Redeemable Pfd. Stock	53,750	0.6
Preferred Stock	440,000	4.7
Common & Surplus	2,675,114	28.7
Total	9,320,645	100.0

RECENT DEVELOPMENTS: For the twelve months ended 12/31/00, loss before an extraordinary item was $45.6 million compared with a loss of $11.3 million in 1999. Results for 2000 and 1999 excluded a net extraordinary loss of $909,000 and $23.8 million, respectively, from the extinguishment of debt. Operating revenues were $4.54 billion, up 11.1% from $4.08 billion in the prior year. Electric revenues were $3.20 billion, down slightly from 1999 due to the impact of weather.

PROSPECTS: The proposed merger of the Company and National Grid Group plc received anti-trust clearance under the Hart-Scott-Rodino Act on 2/26/01. In addition, the companies received approval from the New Hampshire Public Utilities Commission. However, the companies are still awaiting approval from other regulatory agencies and expect to complete the merger by late 2001. Meanwhile, NMK completed the sale of its 25.0% ownership share of the Roseton electric generating station to Dynegy Inc.

BUSINESS

NIAGARA MOHAWK HOLDINGS, INC. (formerly Niagara Mohawk Power Corp.) is the parent company for Niagara Mohawk Power Corp. and is engaged primarily in the business of generation, purchase, transmission, distribution and sale of electricity and the purchase, distribution, sale and transportation of gas in New York State. Revenues for 2000 were 83.7% electric, 16.2% gas and 0.1% other. Electric revenues were 36.6% residential; 32.0% commercial; 15.9% industrial; and 15.5% other. Gas revenues were 76.5% residential; 22.8% commercial; and 0.7% industrial. The Company provides electric service to more than 1.5 million customers and natural gas to more than 540,000 customers.

ANNUAL FINANCIAL DATA

	12/31/00	12/31/99	12/31/98	12/31/97	12/31/96	12/31/95	12/31/94
Earnings Per Share	**[3] d0.27**	**[3] d0.06**	**[1] d0.95**	**1.01**	**[3] 0.97**	**[2] 1.44**	**[1] 1.00**
Cash Flow Per Share	**4.01**	**4.01**	**2.15**	**3.54**	**3.51**	**3.88**	**3.42**
Tang. Book Val. Per Share	**16.69**	**16.78**	**16.92**	**18.03**	**17.91**	**17.42**	**17.06**
Dividends Per Share	...	...	...	...	...	**1.12**	**1.09**
Dividend Payout %	...	...	...	...	...	**77.8**	**109.0**
INCOME STATEMENT (IN MILLIONS):							
Total Revenues	4,539.3	4,084.2	3,826.4	3,966.4	3,990.7	3,917.3	4,152.2
Costs & Expenses	3,392.2	2,797.8	3,144.3	3,042.7	3,100.4	2,881.2	3,053.1
Depreciation & Amort.	717.2	760.3	515.0	364.9	367.9	352.1	346.2
Maintenance Exp.	...	...	...	...	...	...	202.7
Operating Income	429.9	526.2	167.0	558.8	416.8	528.0	432.4
Net Interest Inc./(Exp.)	d437.3	d485.2	d397.2	d273.9	d278.0	d279.7	d279.0
Income Taxes	cr6.8	19.2	cr66.7	126.6	102.5	159.4	111.5
Net Income	[3] d45.6	[3] d11.3	[1] d120.8	183.3	[3] 177.8	[2] 248.0	[1] 177.0
Cash Flow	671.6	749.0	357.7	510.8	507.4	560.6	489.5
Average Shs. Outstg. (000)	167,383	186,689	166,186	144,404	144,350	144,329	143,261
BALANCE SHEET (IN MILLIONS):							
Gross Property	9,801.6	9,792.3	11,431.4	11,075.9	10,839.3	10,649.3	10,485.3
Accumulated Depreciation	4,019.3	3,904.0	4,553.5	4,207.8	3,881.7	3,641.4	3,449.7
Net Property	5,782.3	5,888.2	6,878.0	6,868.0	6,957.6	7,007.9	7,035.6
Total Assets	12,642.3	12,670.4	13,861.2	9,584.1	9,402.0	9,477.9	9,649.4
Long-Term Obligations	4,679.0	5,042.6	6,417.2	3,417.4	3,477.9	3,582.4	3,297.9
Net Stockholders' Equity	3,115.1	3,416.1	3,610.1	3,044.0	3,025.6	2,954.0	2,752.4
Year-end Shs. Outstg. (000)	160,240	177,365	187,365	144,419	144,365	144,332	144,311
STATISTICAL RECORD:							
Operating Profit Margin %	9.5	12.9	4.4	14.1	10.4	13.5	10.4
Net Profit Margin %	...	...	...	4.6	4.5	6.3	4.3
Net Inc./Net Property %	...	...	...	2.7	2.6	3.5	2.5
Net Inc./Tot. Capital %	...	...	...	2.3	2.2	3.1	2.3
Return on Equity %	...	...	...	6.0	5.9	8.4	6.4
Accum. Depr./Gross Prop. %	41.0	39.9	39.8	38.0	35.8	34.2	32.9
Price Range	17.00-10.81	16.44-13.06	16.81-10.13	11.13-7.88	10.13-6.50	15.63-9.50	20.63-12.00
P/E Ratio	...	...	...	11.0-7.8	10.4-6.7	10.8-6.6	20.6-12.0
Average Yield %	...	...	...	...	...	8.9	6.7

Statistics are as originally reported. [1] Incl. $263.2 mill. pre-tax chg., 1998; $196.6 mill., 1994. [2] Incl. $9.0 mill. gain from sale of subsidiary. [3] Bef. extraord. chg. of $67.4 mill., 1996; $23.8 mill., 1999; $909,000, 2000.

OFFICERS:
W. E. Davis, Chmn., C.E.O.
A. J. Budney Jr., Pres.
D. D. Kerr, Pres., C.O.O.
W. F. Edwards, Sr. V.P. & C.F.O.

INVESTOR CONTACT: Leon T Mazur, Director-Investor Relations, (315) 428-5876

PRINCIPAL OFFICE: 300 Erie Blvd. West, Syracuse, NY 13202

TELEPHONE NUMBER: (315) 474-1511
FAX: (315) 428-5101
WEB: www.niagramohawk.com

NO. OF EMPLOYEES: 7,400 (avg.)

SHAREHOLDERS: 47,500 (approx. common); 2,700 (approx. preferred)

ANNUAL MEETING: In May

INCORPORATED: NY, July, 1937

INSTITUTIONAL HOLDINGS:
No. of Institutions: 191
Shares Held: 99,565,802
% Held: 62.1

INDUSTRY: Electric and other services combined (SIC: 4931)

TRANSFER AGENT(S): The Bank of New York, New York, NY

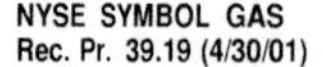

NYSE SYMBOL GAS
Rec. Pr. 39.19 (4/30/01)

NICOR INC.

YIELD 4.5%
P/E RATIO 39.6

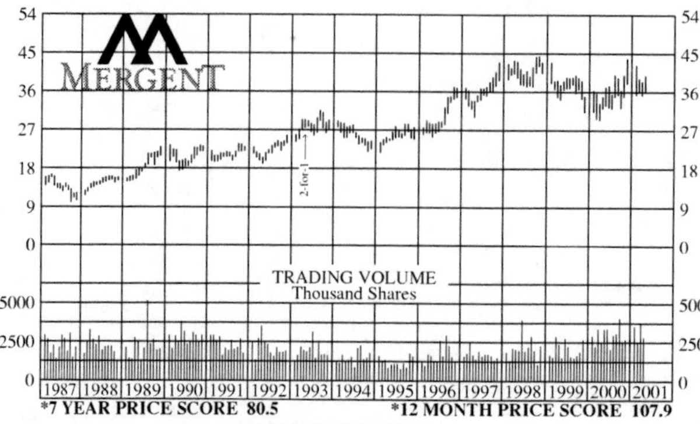

*7 YEAR PRICE SCORE 80.5 *12 MONTH PRICE SCORE 107.9

*NYSE COMPOSITE INDEX=100

INTERIM EARNINGS (Per Share):

Qtr.	Mar.	June	Sept.	Dec.
1997	0.82	0.58	0.40	0.81
1998	0.75	0.59	0.43	0.65
1999	0.82	0.56	0.42	0.83
2000	0.83	0.66	d1.37	0.87

INTERIM DIVIDENDS (Per Share):

Amt.	Decl.	Ex.	Rec.	Pay.
0.415Q	4/20/00	6/28/00	6/30/00	8/01/00
0.415Q	7/20/00	9/27/00	9/29/00	11/01/00
0.415Q	11/16/00	12/27/00	12/29/00	2/01/01
0.44Q	3/15/01	3/28/01	3/30/01	5/01/01
0.44Q	4/19/01	6/27/01	6/29/01	8/01/01

Indicated div.: $1.76 (Div. Reinv. Plan)

CAPITALIZATION (12/31/00):

	($000)	(%)
Long-Term Debt	347,100	24.3
Deferred Income Tax	367,000	25.7
Redeemable Pfd. Stock	6,300	0.4
Common & Surplus	707,800	49.6
Total	1,428,200	100.0

RECENT DEVELOPMENTS: For the year ended 12/31/00, net income fell 62.5% to $46.7 million compared with $124.4 million in the previous year. Results for 2000 included a one-time after-tax charge of $89.7 million. Operating revenues jumped 42.3% to $2.30 billion from $1.62 billion the year before, primarily due to a 43.0% increase in gas distribution revenues to $1.90 billion. Operating income decreased 55.6% to $94.1 million from $212.0 million in 1999.

PROSPECTS: On 4/5/01, Nicor Energy, the Company's 50/50 joint venture with Dynegy Inc., announced the asset acquisition of Energy Management Company (EMC) of St. Clair Shores, Michigan. EMC is an energy provider that serves schools, hospitals, municipalities as well as commercial, industrial and manufacturing businesses. Separately in 2001, excluding any nonrecurring items, GAS expects to report earnings per share in the range of $3.00 to $3.15.

BUSINESS

NICOR INC. is engaged in the purchase, storage, distribution, transportation, sale, and gathering of natural gas. The Company's natural gas unit, Northern Illinois Gas, is the largest gas distribution company in Illinois and one of the biggest in the nation. Northern Illinois serves 1.9 million customers in the northern third of the state, generally outside Chicago. NICOR also owns Tropical Shipping Co., a containerized shipping business serving 26 Caribbean ports from the Port of Palm Beach in Florida. In 2000, operating revenues were derived: 81.9% gas distribution, 10.7% shipping and 7.4% other energy ventures.

ANNUAL FINANCIAL DATA

	12/31/00	12/31/99	12/31/98	12/31/97	12/31/96	12/31/95	12/31/94
Earnings Per Share	[3] **1.00**	[2] **2.62**	**2.42**	**2.61**	[1] **2.42**	**1.96**	**2.07**
Cash Flow Per Share	**4.12**	**5.58**	**5.25**	**5.29**	**4.92**	**4.17**	**4.03**
Tang. Book Val. Per Share	**15.56**	**16.80**	**15.97**	**15.43**	**14.74**	**13.67**	**13.26**
Dividends Per Share	**1.64**	**1.54**	**1.46**	**1.37**	**1.31**	**1.27**	**1.25**
Dividend Payout %	**163.5**	**58.8**	**60.3**	**52.5**	**54.1**	**65.0**	**60.4**
INCOME STATEMENT (IN MILLIONS):							
Total Revenues	2,298.1	1,615.2	1,465.1	1,992.6	1,850.7	1,480.1	1,609.4
Costs & Expenses	2,059.7	1,262.9	1,120.0	1,631.6	1,492.3	1,178.5	1,316.8
Depreciation & Amort.	144.3	140.3	136.5	131.2	125.3	111.8	103.1
Operating Income	94.1	212.0	208.6	229.8	233.1	189.8	189.5
Net Interest Inc./(Exp.)	d48.6	d45.1	d46.6	d46.2	d46.2	d38.7	d37.8
Income Taxes	14.4	65.7	61.1	69.0	67.7	54.4	51.1
Net Income	[3] 46.7	[2] 124.4	116.4	127.9	[1] 121.2	99.8	109.5
Cash Flow	190.7	264.4	252.6	258.7	246.1	211.2	212.0
Average Shs. Outstg. (000)	46,300	47,400	48,100	48,900	50,000	50,700	52,600
BALANCE SHEET (IN MILLIONS):							
Gross Property	3,576.6	3,483.1	3,379.8	3,267.7	3,192.7	3,110.4	2,951.5
Accumulated Depreciation	1,847.0	1,747.9	1,648.0	1,531.9	1,420.8	1,331.1	1,234.5
Net Property	1,729.6	1,735.2	1,731.8	1,735.8	1,771.9	1,779.3	1,717.0
Total Assets	2,885.4	2,451.8	2,364.6	2,394.6	2,438.6	2,259.1	2,209.9
Long-Term Obligations	347.1	436.1	557.3	550.2	518.0	468.7	458.9
Net Stockholders' Equity	707.8	787.7	759.0	744.1	729.7	687.7	683.5
Year-end Shs. Outstg. (000)	45,491	46,890	47,514	48,217	49,492	50,302	51,540
STATISTICAL RECORD:							
Operating Profit Margin %	4.1	13.1	14.2	11.5	12.6	12.8	11.8
Net Profit Margin %	2.0	7.7	7.9	6.4	6.5	6.7	6.8
Net Inc./Net Property %	2.7	7.2	6.7	7.4	6.8	5.6	6.4
Net Inc./Tot. Capital %	3.3	7.9	7.1	8.0	7.8	6.8	7.8
Return on Equity %	6.6	15.8	15.3	17.2	16.6	14.5	16.0
Accum. Depr./Gross Prop. %	51.6	50.2	48.8	46.9	44.5	42.8	41.8
Price Range	43.88-29.38	42.94-31.19	44.44-37.13	42.94-30.00	37.13-25.38	28.50-21.75	29.25-21.88
P/E Ratio	43.9-29.4	16.4-11.9	18.4-15.3	16.5-11.5	15.3-10.5	14.5-11.1	14.1-10.6
Average Yield %	4.5	4.2	3.6	3.8	4.2	5.1	4.9

Statistics are as originally reported. [1] Bef. inc. fr. dis. ops. of $150.0 mill. [2] Incl. a pre-tax gain of $3.8 million on the sale of the Company's interest in QuickTrade. [3] Excls. one-time after-tax chrg. of $89.7 mill.

OFFICERS:
T. L. Fisher, Chmn., Pres., C.E.O.
K. L. Halloran, C.F.O.

INVESTOR CONTACT: Mark Knox, Asst. Sec., Dir. Inv. Rel., (630) 305-9500 ext.2529

PRINCIPAL OFFICE: 1844 Ferry Road, Naperville, IL 60563-9600

TELEPHONE NUMBER: (630) 305-9500
FAX: (630) 983-9328
WEB: www.nicorinc.com

NO. OF EMPLOYEES: 3,300 (approx.)

SHAREHOLDERS: 29,000 (approx.)

ANNUAL MEETING: In Mar.

INCORPORATED: IL, 1976

INSTITUTIONAL HOLDINGS:
No. of Institutions: 230
Shares Held: 22,967,904
% Held: 50.6

INDUSTRY: Natural gas distribution (SIC: 4924)

TRANSFER AGENT(S): Computershare Investor Services, Chicago, IL

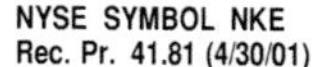

NYSE SYMBOL NKE
Rec. Pr. 41.81 (4/30/01)

NIKE, INC.

YIELD 1.1%
P/E RATIO 20.7

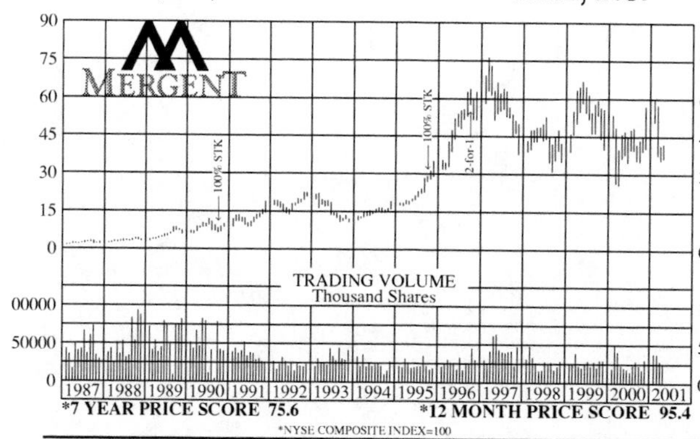

*7 YEAR PRICE SCORE 75.6 *12 MONTH PRICE SCORE 95.4
*NYSE COMPOSITE INDEX=100

INTERIM EARNINGS (Per Share):

Qtr.	Aug.	Nov.	Feb.	May
1996-97	0.77	0.60	0.80	0.52
1997-98	0.85	0.48	0.25	d0.23
1998-99	0.56	0.24	0.44	0.33
1999-00	0.70	0.39	0.53	0.46
2000-01	0.77	0.44	0.35	...

INTERIM DIVIDENDS (Per Share):

Amt.	Decl.	Ex.	Rec.	Pay.
0.12Q	5/17/00	6/14/00	6/16/00	7/05/00
0.12Q	8/14/00	9/14/00	9/18/00	10/02/00
0.12Q	11/17/00	12/14/00	12/18/00	1/03/01
0.12Q	2/16/01	3/15/01	3/19/01	4/04/01
0.12Q	5/14/01	6/13/01	6/15/01	7/03/01

Indicated div.: $0.48

CAPITALIZATION (5/31/00):

	($000)	(%)
Long-Term Debt	470,300	13.0
Redeemable Pfd. Stock	300	0.0
Common & Surplus	3,136,000	87.0
Total	3,606,600	100.0

RECENT DEVELOPMENTS: For the three months ended 2/28/01, net income fell 33.0% to $97.4 million from $145.3 million in the equivalent prior-year period. Total revenues rose slightly to $2.17 billion from $2.16 billion in 1999. Revenues in the U.S. declined 6.3% to $1.09 billion versus $1.16 billion in the previous year. Sales in Europe, Middle East and Africa increased 6.8% to $609.9 million, while total sales in the Asia Pacific region grew 8.3% to $275.0 million. Gross profit was $828.6 million, down 5.3% from $875.2 million the year before.

PROSPECTS: The Company is experiencing stronger results in all of its international regions, and in U.S. apparel and equipment. However, revenue and gross margin are being hampered by slowing sales of sneakers and athletic shoes in the U.S. Also, the Company is experiencing complications arising from the impact of implementing its new demand and supply planning system, which has resulted in supply chain disruptions and late deliveries. The Company expects that these disruptions will continue to affect revenues through the first half of fiscal year 2002.

BUSINESS

NIKE, INC. designs, manufactures and markets worldwide athletic footwear and apparel products. The Company sells its products to approximately 19,700 retail accounts, including department stores, footwear stores, sporting good stores, tennis and golf shops and other outlets. The Company's major products consist of an extensive line of athletic shoes for men, women and children for competitive and recreational use. Substantially all of the Company's footwear products are designed as athletic shoes for specific sports. However, a large percentage of the shoes are purchased and worn for casual or leisure purposes. Nike also offers active sports apparel.

ANNUAL FINANCIAL DATA

	5/31/00	5/31/99	5/31/98	5/31/97	5/31/96	5/31/95	5/31/94
Earnings Per Share	**1 2.07**	**1 1.57**	**1 1.35**	**2.68**	**1.88**	**1.36**	**0.99**
Cash Flow Per Share	**2.87**	**2.36**	**2.15**	**3.25**	**2.33**	**1.60**	**1.23**
Tang. Book Val. Per Share	**10.11**	**10.30**	**9.85**	**9.30**	**6.81**	**5.14**	**5.18**
Dividends Per Share	**0.48**	**0.48**	**0.40**	**0.30**	**0.25**	**0.20**	**0.20**
Dividend Payout %	**23.2**	**30.6**	**29.6**	**11.2**	**13.3**	**14.7**	**20.2**
INCOME STATEMENT (IN MILLIONS):							
Total Revenues	8,995.1	8,776.9	9,553.1	9,186.5	6,470.6	4,760.8	3,789.7
Costs & Expenses	7,786.6	7,691.3	8,455.8	7,638.4	5,365.5	3,989.0	3,202.9
Depreciation & Amort.	223.6	228.8	233.5	168.3	129.9	86.1	72.6
Operating Income	984.9	856.8	863.8	1,379.8	975.3	685.8	514.1
Net Interest Inc./(Exp.)	d45.0	d44.1	d60.0	d52.3	d39.5	d24.2	d15.3
Income Before Income Taxes	919.2	746.1	653.0	1,295.2	899.1	649.9	490.6
Income Taxes	340.1	294.7	253.4	499.4	345.9	250.2	191.8
Net Income	1 579.1	1 451.4	1 399.6	795.8	553.2	385.0	298.8
Cash Flow	802.7	680.2	633.1	964.1	683.0	471.0	371.4
Average Shs. Outstg. (000)	279,400	288,300	295,000	297,000	293,608	294,012	301,824
BALANCE SHEET (IN MILLIONS):							
Cash & Cash Equivalents	254.3	198.1	108.6	445.4	262.1	216.1	518.8
Total Current Assets	3,596.4	3,264.9	3,532.6	3,830.9	2,726.9	2,045.9	1,770.4
Net Property	1,583.4	1,265.8	1,153.1	922.4	643.5	554.9	405.8
Total Assets	5,856.9	5,247.7	5,397.4	5,361.2	3,951.6	3,142.7	2,373.8
Total Current Liabilities	2,140.0	1,446.9	1,703.8	1,866.9	1,467.1	1,107.5	562.0
Long-Term Obligations	470.3	386.1	379.4	296.0	9.6	10.6	12.4
Net Stockholders' Equity	3,136.0	3,334.6	3,261.6	3,155.8	2,431.4	1,964.7	1,740.9
Net Working Capital	1,456.4	1,818.0	1,828.8	1,964.0	1,259.9	938.4	1,208.4
Year-end Shs. Outstg. (000)	269,600	282,300	287,000	289,270	287,258	285,780	304,800
STATISTICAL RECORD:							
Operating Profit Margin %	10.9	9.8	9.0	15.0	15.1	14.4	13.6
Net Profit Margin %	6.4	5.1	4.2	8.7	8.5	8.1	7.9
Return on Equity %	18.5	13.5	12.3	25.2	22.8	19.6	17.2
Return on Assets %	9.9	8.6	7.4	14.8	14.0	12.2	12.6
Debt/Total Assets %	8.0	7.4	7.0	5.5	0.2	0.3	0.5
Price Range	66.94-38.75	52.69-31.00	76.38-37.75	64.00-31.75	35.19-17.19	19.13-11.56	22.31-10.78
P/E Ratio	32.3-18.7	33.6-19.7	56.6-28.0	23.9-11.8	18.7-9.1	14.1-8.5	22.5-10.9
Average Yield %	0.9	1.1	0.7	0.6	1.0	1.3	1.2

Statistics are as originally reported. Adj. for stk. splits: 2-for-1, 10/96 & 10/95 1 Incl. non-recurr. chrg. $300,000, 2000; $45.1 mill., 1999; $129.9 mill., 1998.

OFFICERS:
P. H. Knight, Chmn, C.E.O.
T. E. Clarke, Pres.
D. W. Blair, V.P., C.F.O.

INVESTOR CONTACT: Inv. Rel., (503) 671-6453

PRINCIPAL OFFICE: One Bowerman Drive, Beaverton, OR 97005-6453

TELEPHONE NUMBER: (503) 671-6453
FAX: (503) 671-6300
WEB: www.nikebiz.com
NO. OF EMPLOYEES: 21,800 (approx.)
SHAREHOLDERS: 20,000 (approx. class B); 28 (class A)
ANNUAL MEETING: In Sept.
INCORPORATED: OR, 1968

INSTITUTIONAL HOLDINGS:
No. of Institutions: 323
Shares Held: 140,117,876
% Held: 51.7

INDUSTRY: Rubber and plastics footwear (SIC: 3021)

TRANSFER AGENT(S): First Chicago Trust Company of New York, Jersey City, NJ

NYSE SYMBOL NI
Rec. Pr. 31.30 (5/31/01)

NISOURCE, INC.

YIELD 3.5%
P/E RATIO 23.7

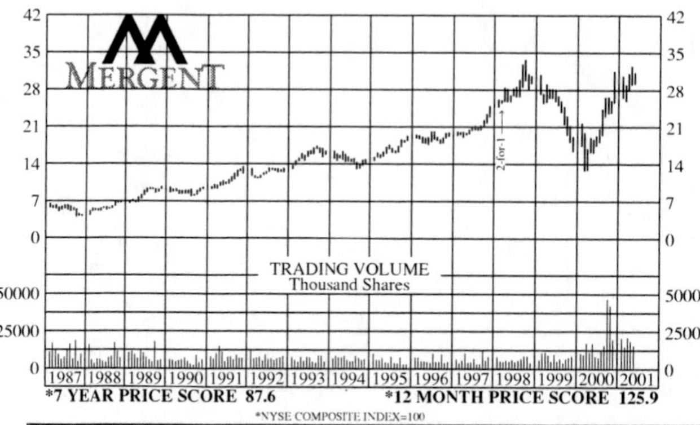

INTERIM EARNINGS (Per Share):

Qtr.	Mar.	June	Sept.	Dec.
1995	0.46	0.21	0.28	0.41
1996	0.54	0.19	0.28	0.43
1997	0.59	0.22	0.29	0.22
1998	0.48	0.24	0.35	0.51
1999	0.62	0.18	0.22	0.25
2000	0.62	0.18	0.42	Nil

INTERIM DIVIDENDS (Per Share):

Amt.	Decl.	Ex.	Rec.	Pay.
0.29Q	01/03/01	01/29/01	01/31/01	02/20/01
0.29Q	03/27/01	04/26/01	04/30/01	05/18/01
0.29Q	05/22/01	07/27/01	07/31/01	08/20/01

Indicated div.: $1.08 (Div. Reinv. Plan)

CAPITALIZATION (12/31/00):

	($000)	(%)
Long-Term Debt	5,802,700	50.5
Deferred Income Tax	1,806,200	15.7
Redeemable Pfd. Stock	394,100	3.4
Preferred Stock	83,600	0.7
Common & Surplus	3,415,200	29.7
Total	11,501,800	100.0

RECENT DEVELOPMENTS: For the year ended 12/31/00, income from continuing operations fell 4.4% to $147.1 million compared with income from continuing operations of $153.9 million in 1999. Results for 2000 included a loss on asset impairment of $65.8 million. Total revenues rocketed 84.2% to $6.03 billion from $3.27 billion a year earlier. Gas revenues more than doubled to $1.81 billion, while electric revenues rose 15.7% to $1.56 billion.

PROSPECTS: Going forward, NI is on track to realize net merger savings of approximately $100.0 million in 2001 from the elimination of duplicate corporate and administrative functions. Separately, the Company announced that its Columbia Energy Group subsidiary has signed a definitive agreement to sell the stock and assets of Columbia Propane Corporation to AmeriGas Partners L.P. for $208.0 million.

BUSINESS

NISOURCE, INC. (formerly NIPSCO Industries, Inc.) is an energy-based holding company that provides electricity, natural gas and other products and services to 3.6 million customers from the Gulf Coast through the Midwest to New England. The Company's principal subsidiaries include Columbia Energy Resources, Inc., a natural gas distribution, transmission, storage and exploration and production holding company; Northern Indiana Public Service Company, a gas and electric company providing service to customers in northern Indiana; and Bay State Gas Company, a natural gas distribution company serving customers in New England. NI provides non-regulated energy marketing and services through its wholly-owned subsidiary, EnergyUSA, Inc. and develops power projects through its subsidiary, Primary Energy, Inc. In February 1999, NI acquired Bay State Gas Company. In November 2000, NI acquired Columbia Energy Group for approximately $6.00 billion.

ANNUAL FINANCIAL DATA

	[2] 12/31/00	12/31/99	12/31/98	12/31/97	12/31/96	12/31/95	12/31/94
Earnings Per Share	[1] **1.08**	**1.27**	**1.59**	**1.53**	**1.44**	**1.36**	**1.24**
Cash Flow Per Share	**3.84**	**3.76**	**3.71**	**3.56**	**3.20**	**2.95**	**2.74**
Tang. Book Val. Per Share	...	...	**9.23**	**8.10**	**9.20**	**8.99**	**8.67**
Dividends Per Share	**1.08**	**1.02**	**0.96**	**0.90**	**0.84**	**0.78**	**0.72**
Dividend Payout %	**100.0**	**80.3**	**60.4**	**58.8**	**58.3**	**57.3**	**58.1**
INCOME STATEMENT (IN MILLIONS):							
Total Revenues	6,030.7	3,144.6	2,932.8	2,586.5	1,821.6	1,722.3	1,676.4
Costs & Expenses	5,088.7	2,289.4	2,180.2	1,849.6	1,139.3	1,049.5	1,043.1
Depreciation & Amort.	374.2	311.4	256.5	249.8	215.0	201.1	194.3
Maintenance Exp.	...	82.2	74.6	76.6	70.0	78.3	80.2
Operating Income	567.8	461.5	421.5	410.6	286.3	284.9	261.1
Net Interest Inc./(Exp.)	d304.5	d166.6	d128.8	d120.6	d106.5	d96.2	d89.5
Income Taxes	130.1	90.4	100.9	105.0	111.0	108.4	97.7
Equity Earnings/Minority Int.	d20.4	17.7	...	...	...	...	...
Net Income	[1] 147.1	160.4	193.9	190.8	176.7	175.5	164.0
Cash Flow	521.3	471.8	450.4	440.7	391.6	373.5	355.2
Average Shs. Outstg. (000)	135,811	125,339	121,335	123,849	122,382	126,562	129,640
BALANCE SHEET (IN MILLIONS):							
Gross Property	16,768.6	8,241.1	6,630.2	6,416.1	5,741.0	5,587.0	5,433.0
Accumulated Depreciation	7,308.5	3,444.3	2,968.1	2,759.9	2,546.2	2,373.7	2,202.1
Net Property	9,546.7	5,230.4	3,748.7	3,752.2	3,342.2	3,349.3	3,355.4
Total Assets	19,696.8	6,835.2	4,986.5	4,937.0	4,274.3	3,999.5	3,944.5
Long-Term Obligations	5,802.7	1,975.2	1,668.0	1,667.9	1,127.1	1,175.7	1,180.3
Net Stockholders' Equity	3,498.8	85.6	1,235.3	1,350.4	1,181.6	1,203.5	1,194.2
Year-end Shs. Outstg. (000)	205,553	124,139	117,531	147,784	119,612	124,760	147,784
STATISTICAL RECORD:							
Operating Profit Margin %	9.4	14.7	14.4	15.9	15.7	16.5	21.4
Net Profit Margin %	2.4	5.1	6.6	7.4	9.7	10.2	9.8
Net Inc./Net Property %	1.5	3.1	5.2	5.1	5.3	5.2	4.9
Net Inc./Tot. Capital %	1.3	4.6	5.3	5.1	5.9	5.7	5.4
Return on Equity %	4.2	187.4	15.7	14.1	15.0	14.6	13.7
Accum. Depr./Gross Prop. %	43.6	41.8	44.8	43.0	44.4	42.5	40.5
Price Range	31.50-12.75	30.94-16.38	33.75-24.66	24.94-19.00	20.13-17.63	19.25-14.63	16.50-13.06
P/E Ratio	29.2-11.8	24.4-12.9	21.2-15.5	16.3-12.4	14.0-12.2	14.2-10.8	13.3-10.5
Average Yield %	4.9	4.3	3.3	4.1	4.5	4.6	4.9

Statistics are as originally reported. Adj. for stk. split 2-for-1: 2/98 [1] Excl. inc. from disc. oper. of $9.8 mill., but incl. loss on asset impair. of $65.8 mill. [2] Results for 2000 reflect the acq. of Columbia Energy Group on 11/1/00.

OFFICERS:
G. L. Neale, Chmn., Pres., C.E.O.
S. P. Adik, Sr. Exec. V.P., C.F.O., Treas.

INVESTOR CONTACT: Investor Relations, (219) 853-5200

PRINCIPAL OFFICE: 801 East 86th Avenue, Merrillville, IN 46410

TELEPHONE NUMBER: (219) 853-5200
FAX: (219) 647-6061
WEB: www.nisource.com

NO. OF EMPLOYEES: 14,418

SHAREHOLDERS: 51,608

ANNUAL MEETING: In Apr.

INCORPORATED: IN, Sept., 1987

INSTITUTIONAL HOLDINGS:
No. of Institutions: 331
Shares Held: 125,828,067
% Held: 61.2

INDUSTRY: Electric and other services combined (SIC: 4931)

TRANSFER AGENT(S): Computershare Investor Services, Chicago,IL

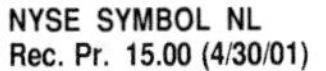

NYSE SYMBOL NL
Rec. Pr. 15.00 (4/30/01)

NL INDUSTRIES, INC.

YIELD 5.3%
P/E RATIO 4.9

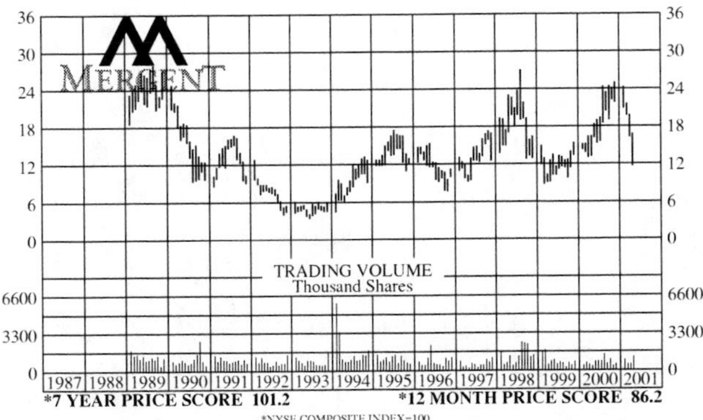

INTERIM EARNINGS (Per Share):

Qtr.	Mar.	June	Sept.	Dec.
1997	d0.79	d0.07	0.08	0.19
1998	0.31	0.45	0.60	0.36
1999	0.27	2.16	0.33	0.33
2000	0.46	1.25	0.60	0.75

INTERIM DIVIDENDS (Per Share):

Amt.	Decl.	Ex.	Rec.	Pay.
0.15Q	5/11/00	6/13/00	6/15/00	6/30/00
0.15Q	7/18/00	9/13/00	9/15/00	9/27/00
0.20Q	10/25/00	12/11/00	12/13/00	12/27/00
0.20Q	2/07/01	3/12/01	3/14/01	3/28/01
0.20Q	5/09/01	6/11/01	6/13/01	6/27/01

Indicated div.: $0.80

CAPITALIZATION (12/31/00):

	($000)	(%)
Long-Term Debt	195,363	28.2
Deferred Income Tax	145,673	21.1
Minority Interest	6,279	0.9
Common & Surplus	344,488	49.8
Total	691,803	100.0

RECENT DEVELOPMENTS: For the year ended 12/31/00, income before an extraordinary item slipped 2.8% to $155.3 million compared with net income of $159.8 million in 1999. Results for 2000 and 1999 included net gains of $73.7 million and $4.6 million, respectively, from litigation settlements and other income. Results for 2000 also excluded an extraordinary loss of $700,000. Total revenues were $1.02 billion, up 8.9% from $932.0 million in the prior year.

PROSPECTS: Results for the remainder of 2001 will greatly depend on global economic conditions. If the economy continues to soften, full year 2001 operating income will likely be below 2000 levels. However, if demand strengthens later in the year, NL should be able to realize price increases, some of which have already been announced. During 2000, the Company reduced its total debt and refinanced high fixed-rate public debt. As a result, NL anticipates its interest expense to be lower in 2001 than in 2000.

BUSINESS

NL INDUSTRIES, INC. conducts its operations through its wholly-owned subsidiary, Kronos, Inc. Kronos is the world's fifth largest producer of titanium dioxide pigments (TiO_2), with an estimated 12% share of worldwide sales volume in 2000. TiO_2 is a white pigment used to impart whiteness, brightness and opacity to a wide range of products including paints, plastics, paper, fibers and ceramics. Kronos serves more than 4,000 domestic and international customers with a majority of sales in Europe and North America. Net sales for 2000 were derived: U.S., 30.7%; Europe, 52.1%; Canada, 5.8%; Latin America, 2.9%; Asia, 5.0%; and other, 3.5%. On 1/30/98, NL sold Rhoex, its specialty chemicals business, to Elemintis PLC.

ANNUAL FINANCIAL DATA

	12/31/00	12/31/99	12/31/98	12/31/97	12/31/96	12/31/95	12/31/94
Earnings Per Share	**[4] 3.06**	**[3] 3.08**	**[2] 1.73**	**[1] d0.58**	**0.21**	**1.66**	**d0.47**
Cash Flow Per Share	**3.65**	**3.73**	**2.39**	**0.10**	**0.98**	**2.42**	**0.21**
Tang. Book Val. Per Share	**6.88**	**5.29**	**2.94**	...	...	...	...
Dividends Per Share	**0.65**	**0.14**	**0.09**	...	**0.30**	...	...
Dividend Payout %	**21.2**	**4.5**	**5.2**	...	**142.8**	...	...
INCOME STATEMENT (IN MILLIONS):							
Total Revenues	1,015.1	932.0	920.2	856.6	1,016.6	1,046.2	932.8
Costs & Expenses	717.9	762.9	717.9	783.7	876.2	826.7	827.7
Depreciation & Amort.	29.7	33.7	34.5	34.9	39.7	39.0	34.6
Operating Income	267.4	135.4	167.8	38.1	70.2	158.3	25.7
Net Interest Inc./(Exp.)	d31.2	d36.9	d58.1	d65.8	d75.0	d163.2	d167.9
Income Before Income Taxes	236.2	98.5	109.7	d27.7	25.6	98.9	d13.4
Income Taxes	78.4	cr64.6	19.8	2.2	14.8	12.7	9.7
Equity Earnings/Minority Int.	d2.4	d3.3	...	0.1	...	d0.6	d0.8
Net Income	[4] 155.3	[3] 159.8	[2] 89.9	[1] d29.9	10.8	85.6	d24.0
Cash Flow	185.1	193.5	124.4	5.0	50.5	124.6	10.6
Average Shs. Outstg. (000)	50,749	51,867	52,000	51,152	51,350	51,512	51,022
BALANCE SHEET (IN MILLIONS):							
Cash & Cash Equivalents	189.6	151.8	163.1	106.1	114.1	141.3	156.3
Total Current Assets	553.8	506.4	546.1	454.5	500.2	551.1	486.4
Net Property	324.4	348.5	382.2	411.2	466.0	459.2	407.8
Total Assets	1,120.8	1,056.2	1,155.0	1,098.2	1,221.4	1,271.7	1,162.4
Total Current Liabilities	298.0	264.8	310.0	276.4	290.3	302.4	244.9
Long-Term Obligations	195.4	244.3	292.8	666.8	737.1	740.3	746.8
Net Stockholders' Equity	344.5	271.1	152.3	d222.3	d203.5	d209.4	d293.1
Net Working Capital	255.8	241.6	236.1	178.1	209.9	248.6	241.5
Year-end Shs. Outstg. (000)	50,052	51,284	51,811	51,267	51,118	51,091	51,052
STATISTICAL RECORD:							
Operating Profit Margin %	26.3	1.5	1.9	0.5	0.7	1.5	0.3
Net Profit Margin %	15.3	17.2	9.8	...	1.1	8.2	...
Return on Equity %	45.1	58.9	59.0	...	...	...	...
Return on Assets %	13.9	15.1	7.8	...	0.9	6.7	...
Debt/Total Assets %	17.4	23.1	25.4	60.7	60.4	58.2	64.2
Price Range	25.00-13.00	15.44-8.75	27.06-12.75	17.31-9.13	15.38-7.63	17.50-10.88	13.25-4.38
P/E Ratio	8.2-4.2	5.0-2.8	15.6-7.4	...	73.2-36.3	10.5-6.6	...
Average Yield %	3.4	1.2	0.5	...	2.6	...	...

Statistics are as originally reported. [1] Incl. $30.0 mill. ($0.59/sh.) acct. chg. for environ. remediation liabs. & excl. $20.4 mill. disc. ops. fr. sale of Rheoux. [2] Excl. inc. of $287.4 mill. from disc. ops. of Rheox & d$10.6 extraord. item. [3] Incl. $64.6 mill. net income tax benefit. [4] Incl. $73.7 mill. net gain fr. litigation settlement & excl. $700,000 extraord. loss.

OFFICERS:
H. C. Simmons, Chmn.
J. L. Martin, Pres., C.E.O.
S. E. Alderton, V.P., C.F.O.

INVESTOR CONTACT: Investor Relations, (281) 423-3332

PRINCIPAL OFFICE: 16825 Northchase Drive, Suite 1200, Houston, TX 77060-2544

TELEPHONE NUMBER: (281) 423-3300
FAX: (281) 423-3216
WEB: www.nl-ind.com

NO. OF EMPLOYEES: 2,500 (approx.)

SHAREHOLDERS: 6,000 (approx.)

ANNUAL MEETING: In May

INCORPORATED: NJ, Dec., 1891

INSTITUTIONAL HOLDINGS:
No. of Institutions: 70
Shares Held: 5,842,684
% Held: 11.7

INDUSTRY: Inorganic pigments (SIC: 2816)

TRANSFER AGENT(S): First Chicago Trust Company of New York, Jersey City, NJ

NYSE SYMBOL NBL
Rec. Pr. 43.47 (4/30/01)

NOBLE AFFILIATES, INC.

YIELD 0.4%
P/E RATIO 12.8

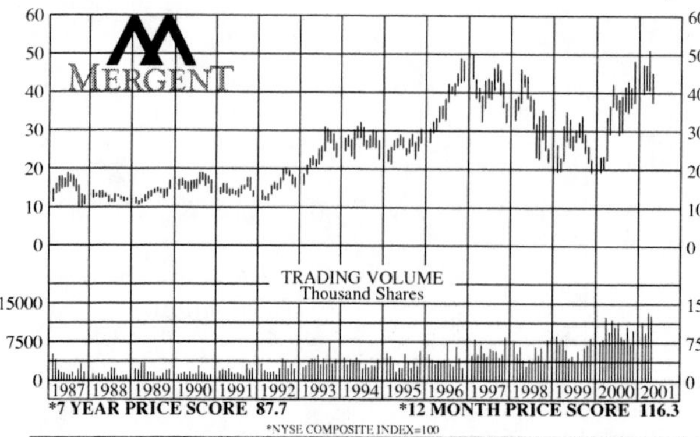

*7 YEAR PRICE SCORE 87.7 *12 MONTH PRICE SCORE 116.3
*NYSE COMPOSITE INDEX=100

INTERIM EARNINGS (Per Share):

Qtr.	Mar.	June	Sept.	Dec.
1998	0.24	0.21	d0.44	d2.89
1999	d0.16	0.16	0.48	0.38
2000	0.47	0.65	1.01	1.26

INTERIM DIVIDENDS (Per Share):

Amt.	Decl.	Ex.	Rec.	Pay.
0.04Q	4/24/00	5/04/00	5/08/00	5/22/00
0.04Q	7/25/00	8/03/00	8/07/00	8/21/00
0.04Q	10/24/00	11/02/00	11/06/00	11/20/00
0.04Q	1/30/01	2/09/01	2/13/01	2/26/01
0.04Q	4/23/01	5/03/01	5/07/01	5/21/01

Indicated div.: $0.16

CAPITALIZATION (12/31/00):

	($000)	(%)
Long-Term Debt	525,494	35.2
Deferred Income Tax	117,048	7.8
Common & Surplus	849,682	56.9
Total	1,492,224	100.0

RECENT DEVELOPMENTS: For the year ended 12/31/00, net income more than tripled to $191.6 million versus $49.5 million in the previous year. Total revenues improved 53.2% to $1.39 billion versus $909.8 million in the prior year. Oil and gas sales jumped 44.2% to $791.4 million from $548.7 million the year before. Gathering, marketing and processing revenues rose 74.5% to $589.9 million from $338.0 million in 1999. Results benefited from strong oil prices averaging $24.37 a barrel, versus $16.29 in 1999.

PROSPECTS: Looking ahead, the Company will continue to focus on investing to boost growth in production while growing the reserve base. Accordingly, NBL announced a capital investment program of about $700.0 million for the year 2001. Approximately 60.0% of the budget is allocated to developmental projects and 40.0% to exploration opportunities. Results should continue to benefit from the increased investment program coupled with higher commodity prices.

BUSINESS

NOBLE AFFILIATES, INC. is principally engaged in the exploration, production and marketing of oil and gas. NBL's wholly-owned subsidiary, Samedan Oil Corporation, investigates potential oil and gas properties, seeks to acquire exploration rights in areas of interest and conducts exploration activities. Domestically, Samedan has exploration, exploitation and production operations in the Gulf of Mexico and California, the Gulf Coast Region, the Mid-Continent Region, and the Rocky Mountain Region. International areas of operations include Argentina, China, Denmark, Ecuador, Equatorial Guinea, the Mediterranean Sea, the North Sea and the United Kingdom. NBL's wholly-owned subsidiary, Noble Gas Marketing, Inc., markets the majority of NBL's natural gas as well as third-party gas. The Company's wholly-owned subsidiary, Noble Trading, Inc., markets a portion of NBL's oil as well as third-party oil.

ANNUAL FINANCIAL DATA

	12/31/00	12/31/99	12/31/98	12/31/97	12/31/96	12/31/95	12/31/94
Earnings Per Share	**3.38**	**0.86**	**1 d2.88**	**1.73**	**1.63**	**0.08**	**0.06**
Cash Flow Per Share	**7.73**	**5.47**	**2.76**	**7.10**	**6.29**	**4.23**	**2.77**
Tang. Book Val. Per Share	**15.15**	**11.98**	**11.27**	**14.29**	**12.68**	**8.21**	**8.24**
Dividends Per Share	**0.16**	**0.16**	**0.16**	**0.16**	**0.16**	**0.16**	**0.16**
Dividend Payout %	**4.7**	**18.6**	**...**	**9.2**	**9.8**	**199.8**	**266.2**
INCOME STATEMENT (IN MILLIONS):							
Total Revenues	1,393.6	909.8	911.6	1,116.6	887.2	487.0	358.4
Costs & Expenses	815.6	525.0	793.4	603.7	475.2	252.9	200.3
Depreciation & Amort.	246.9	264.2	321.1	308.5	239.4	207.4	135.3
Operating Income	331.1	120.7	d202.9	204.5	172.6	26.7	22.8
Net Interest Inc./(Exp.)	d31.6	d43.0	d43.8	d46.8	d36.3	d18.7	d17.5
Income Before Income Taxes	299.5	77.6	d246.7	157.7	136.3	8.0	5.2
Income Taxes	107.9	28.2	cr82.7	58.4	52.4	3.9	2.1
Net Income	191.6	49.5	1 d164.0	99.3	83.9	4.1	3.2
Cash Flow	438.5	313.6	157.1	407.8	323.3	211.5	138.4
Average Shs. Outstg. (000)	56,755	57,349	56,955	57,421	51,414	50,046	49,972
BALANCE SHEET (IN MILLIONS):							
Cash & Cash Equivalents	23.2	2.9	19.1	55.1	94.8	12.4	22.2
Total Current Assets	271.3	147.9	188.3	258.6	316.8	117.5	103.9
Net Property	1,485.1	1,242.4	1,429.7	1,546.4	1,571.8	843.9	813.4
Total Assets	1,879.3	1,450.4	1,686.1	1,875.5	1,956.9	989.2	933.5
Total Current Liabilities	325.4	184.5	139.2	217.0	279.8	97.2	72.0
Long-Term Obligations	525.5	445.3	745.1	645.0	798.0	377.0	377.0
Net Stockholders' Equity	849.7	683.6	642.1	813.0	720.1	411.9	412.1
Net Working Capital	d54.2	d36.6	49.1	41.6	37.0	20.3	31.9
Year-end Shs. Outstg. (000)	56,091	57,045	56,981	56,899	56,796	50,198	50,012
STATISTICAL RECORD:							
Operating Profit Margin %	23.8	13.3	...	18.3	19.5	5.5	6.4
Net Profit Margin %	13.7	5.4	...	8.9	9.5	0.8	0.9
Return on Equity %	22.5	7.2	...	12.2	11.6	1.0	0.8
Return on Assets %	10.2	3.4	...	5.3	4.3	0.4	0.3
Debt/Total Assets %	28.0	30.7	44.2	34.4	40.8	38.1	40.4
Price Range	48.38-19.19	35.00-19.13	46.19-21.94	50.00-32.19	49.00-26.88	30.50-21.25	32.25-22.50
P/E Ratio	14.3-5.7	40.7-22.2	...	28.9-18.6	30.1-16.5	380.8-265.3	536.6-374.4
Average Yield %	0.5	0.6	0.5	0.4	0.4	0.6	0.6

Statistics are as originally reported. 1 Incl. impairm. of oper. assets, $223.3 mill.

OFFICERS:
R. Kelley, Chmn.
C. Davidson, Pres., C.E.O.
J. L. McElvany, V.P., Treas.

INVESTOR CONTACT: William R. McKown III, Assistant Treasurer, (281) 872-3140

PRINCIPAL OFFICE: 350 Glenborough Drive, Suite 100, Houston, TX 77067

TELEPHONE NUMBER: (281) 872-3100
WEB: www.nobleaff.com
FAX: (580) 221-1335

NO. OF EMPLOYEES: 576 (avg.)

SHAREHOLDERS: 1,179

ANNUAL MEETING: In Apr.

INCORPORATED: DE, Dec., 1969

INSTITUTIONAL HOLDINGS:
No. of Institutions: 239
Shares Held: 47,918,130
% Held: 85.1

INDUSTRY: Crude petroleum and natural gas (SIC: 1311)

TRANSFER AGENT(S): First Chicago Trust Company, Jersey City, NJ

NYSE SYMBOL NE
Rec. Pr. 42.70 (5/31/01)

NOBLE DRILLING CORP.

YIELD	. . .
P/E RATIO	35.0

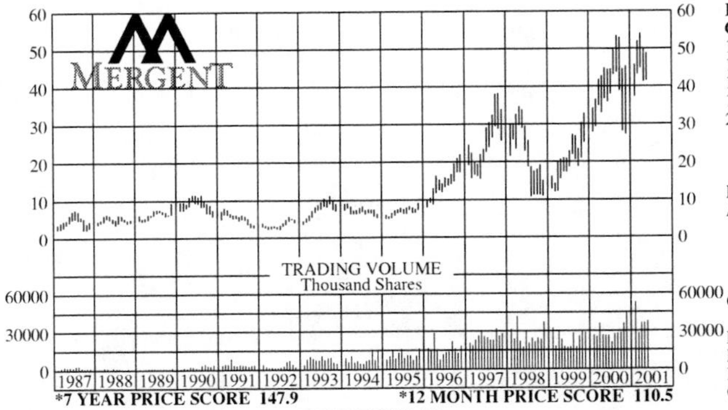

MERGENT

TRADING VOLUME
Thousand Shares

1987 1988 1989 1990 1991 1992 1993 1994 1995 1996 1997 1998 1999 2000 2001

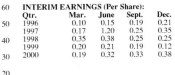

*7 YEAR PRICE SCORE 147.9 *12 MONTH PRICE SCORE 110.5

*NYSE COMPOSITE INDEX=100

INTERIM EARNINGS (Per Share):

Qtr.	Mar.	June	Sept.	Dec.
1996	0.10	0.15	0.19	0.21
1997	0.17	1.20	0.25	0.35
1998	0.35	0.38	0.25	0.25
1999	0.20	0.21	0.19	0.12
2000	0.19	0.32	0.33	0.38

INTERIM DIVIDENDS (Per Share):

Amt.	Decl.	Ex.	Rec.	Pay.

No dividends paid.

CAPITALIZATION (12/31/00):

	($000)	(%)
Long-Term Debt	650,291	27.4
Deferred Income Tax	149,084	6.3
Minority Interest	d3,737	-0.2
Common & Surplus	1,576,719	66.5
Total	2,372,357	100.0

RECENT DEVELOPMENTS: For the year ended 12/31/00, net income advanced to $165.6 million versus income before an extraordinary charge of $95.3 million a year earlier. Results for 1999 included an after-tax non-recurring charge of $4.9 million. Total operating revenues rose 25.0% to $882.6 million. Utilization of the Company's domestic jackup and submersible rigs increased to 100.0% versus 71.0% a year earlier. The average dayrate on these rigs jumped to $41,300 from $22,200 in the same quarter of the prior year.

PROSPECTS: Strong industry conditions brighten NE's near-term outlook. Looking forward, the Company is finalizing engineering on two of its idle semisubmersibles, the Noble Dave Beard and Noble Clyde Boudreaux, for deepwater applications up to a water depth of 10,000 feet. Subject to client commitments, the conversions would take approximately 20 months. Separately, on 2/20/01, NE announced that it has acquired Maurer Engineering Incorporated, a privately held engineering firm based in Houston, TX.

BUSINESS

NOBLE DRILLING CORPORATION is a provider of diversified services for the oil and gas industry. Contract drilling services are performed with a fleet of 49 offshore drilling units located in markets worldwide. The Company's fleet of floating deepwater units consists of nine semisubmersibles and three drillships, seven of which are designed to operate in water depths greater than 5,000 feet. NE's fleet of 34 independent leg, cantilever jackup rigs includes 21 units that operate in water depths of 300 feet and greater, four of which operate in water depths of 360 feet and greater. In addition, NE's fleet includes three submersible units. As of 2/20/01, over 60.0% of the fleet was deployed in international markets, principally including the North Sea, Africa, Brazil, the Middle East, and Mexico. NE also provides labor contract drilling services, well site and project management services, and engineering services.

ANNUAL FINANCIAL DATA

	12/31/00	12/31/99	12/31/98	12/31/97	12/31/96	12/31/95	12/31/94
Earnings Per Share	**1.22**	**4 0.72**	**1.23**	**3 1.98**	**2 0.66**	**d0.08**	**1 0.11**
Cash Flow Per Share	**2.04**	**1.39**	**1.77**	**2.56**	**1.19**	**0.34**	**0.63**
Tang. Book Val. Per Share	**11.80**	**10.60**	**10.00**	**8.77**	**7.01**	**5.50**	**6.69**
INCOME STATEMENT (IN MILLIONS):							
Total Revenues	882.6	705.9	788.2	713.2	514.3	328.0	352.0
Costs & Expenses	503.2	467.0	486.8	253.9	385.7	280.9	303.2
Depreciation & Amort.	110.8	89.0	71.7	77.9	52.2	36.5	39.5
Operating Income	268.6	150.0	229.8	381.3	112.6	11.4	18.2
Net Interest Inc./(Exp.)	d54.6	d23.3	1.5	d3.5	d12.3	d6.8	d6.7
Income Before Income Taxes	226.3	125.5	230.9	379.6	102.0	4.9	27.2
Income Taxes	60.8	30.2	68.9	115.7	22.7	3.3	5.7
Net Income	165.6	4 95.3	162.0	3 263.9	2 79.3	1.6	1 21.5
Cash Flow	276.3	184.3	233.7	341.8	123.9	30.9	48.3
Average Shs. Outstg. (000)	135,461	132,597	132,269	133,455	110,252	89,736	76,953
BALANCE SHEET (IN MILLIONS):							
Cash & Cash Equivalents	177.1	136.8	216.9	66.4	173.5	64.5	145.2
Total Current Assets	379.1	290.6	438.2	265.0	388.5	188.0	240.2
Net Property	2,095.1	2,049.8	1,649.1	1,200.9	957.0	543.0	493.3
Total Assets	2,595.5	2,432.3	2,178.6	1,505.8	1,367.4	741.4	739.9
Total Current Liabilities	205.4	233.3	349.5	152.9	151.5	86.4	82.3
Long-Term Obligations	650.3	730.9	460.8	138.1	239.5	129.9	126.5
Net Stockholders' Equity	1,576.7	1,398.0	1,310.5	1,149.1	925.2	523.5	527.6
Net Working Capital	173.7	57.3	88.7	112.1	237.0	101.6	157.9
Year-end Shs. Outstg. (000)	133,591	131,882	131,101	130,988	131,980	94,483	77,826
STATISTICAL RECORD:							
Operating Profit Margin %	30.4	21.2	29.1	53.5	21.9	3.5	5.2
Net Profit Margin %	18.8	13.5	20.6	37.0	15.4	0.5	6.1
Return on Equity %	10.5	6.8	12.4	23.0	8.6	0.3	4.1
Return on Assets %	6.4	3.9	7.4	17.5	5.8	0.2	2.9
Debt/Total Assets %	25.1	30.0	21.2	9.2	17.5	17.5	17.1
Price Range	53.50-27.25	32.88-12.00	34.69-10.75	38.19-15.50	22.00-8.00	9.13-5.00	9.13-5.25
P/E Ratio	43.8-22.3	45.7-16.7	28.2-8.7	19.3-7.8	33.3-12.1	. . .	82.9-47.7

Statistics are as originally reported. 1 Incls. restruct. chrgs. of $3.7 mill. & one-time gain of $8.9 mill. 2 Incls. gain of $36.1 mill.; Bef. extraord. chrg. of $660,000. 3 Incls. gain on sale of prop. & equip. of $197.7 mill.; bef. extraord. chrg. of $6.7 mill. ($0.05/sh.) 4 Incls. restruct. chrgs. of $7.5 mill.; bef. extraord. chrg. of $10.8 mill. ($0.08/sh.)

OFFICERS:
J. C. Day, Chmn., C.E.O.
R. D. Campbell, Pres.
M. A. Jackson, Sr. V.P., C.F.O.

INVESTOR CONTACT: John Rynd, V.P., Investor Relations, (218) 276-6100

PRINCIPAL OFFICE: 13135 South Dairy Ashford, Suite 800, Sugar Land, TX 77478

TELEPHONE NUMBER: (281) 276-6100
FAX: (281) 491-2091
WEB: www.noblecorp.com

NO. OF EMPLOYEES: 2,943 (avg.)

SHAREHOLDERS: 1,815

ANNUAL MEETING: In Apr.

INCORPORATED: DE, 1939

INSTITUTIONAL HOLDINGS:
No. of Institutions: 281
Shares Held: 119,323,710
% Held: 89.2

INDUSTRY: Drilling oil and gas wells (SIC: 1381)

TRANSFER AGENT(S): UMB Bank N.A., Kansas City, MO

NYSE SYMBOL JWN
Rec. Pr. 18.53 (5/31/01)

NORDSTROM, INC.

YIELD 1.9%
P/E RATIO 24.1

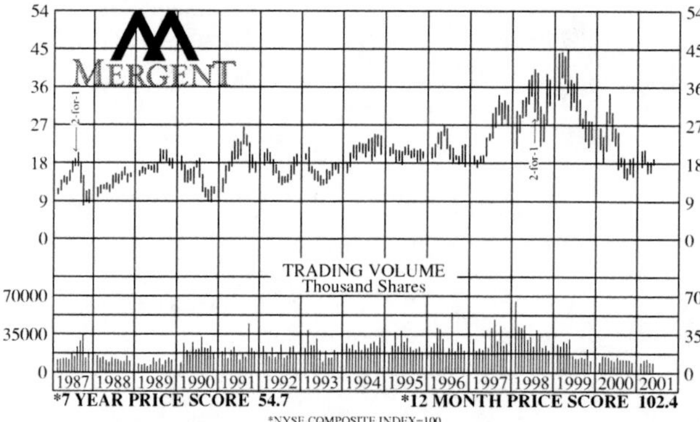

INTERIM EARNINGS (Per Share):

Qtr.	Apr.	July	Oct.	Jan.
1996-97	0.17	0.28	0.21	0.27
1997-98	0.21	0.38	0.24	0.38
1998-99	0.22	0.47	0.27	0.47
1999-00	0.22	0.51	0.25	0.50
2000-01	0.25	0.35	d0.03	0.20

INTERIM DIVIDENDS (Per Share):

Amt.	Decl.	Ex.	Rec.	Pay.
0.09Q	5/16/00	5/26/00	5/31/00	6/15/00
0.09Q	8/15/00	8/29/00	8/31/00	9/15/00
0.09Q	11/06/00	11/28/00	11/30/00	12/15/00
0.09Q	2/21/01	2/26/01	2/28/01	3/15/01
0.09Q	5/15/01	5/29/01	5/31/01	6/15/01

Indicated div.: $0.36

CAPITALIZATION (1/31/01):

	($000)	(%)
Long-Term Debt	1,099,710	47.2
Common & Surplus	1,229,568	52.8
Total	2,329,278	100.0

RECENT DEVELOPMENTS: For the year ended 1/31/01, net earnings totaled $101.9 million versus $202.6 million in the prior year. Results in the recent period included pre-tax charges totaling $56.0 million related to severance costs from restructuring and investment write-offs. Net sales grew 7.4% to $5.53 billion, while comparable-store sales inched up 0.3% year-over-year. Gross profit was $1.88 billion, or 34.0% of net sales, versus $1.79 billion, or 34.8% of net sales, in the previous year.

PROSPECTS: Going forward, the Company will focus on boosting operating profitability through better expense and inventory management. The Company is consolidating its catalog business by reducing the number of catalogs it mails to customers in an effort to accelerate Nordstrom.com's progress toward profitability. During the third quarter, the Company plans to open full-line stores in Ohio, Florida, and Arizona. In addition, the Company anticipates opening about nine new Nordstrom Rack stores in 2001.

BUSINESS

NORDSTROM, INC. operates a total of 120 stores, including large specialty stores, in 24 states, selling a wide selection of apparel, shoes and accessories for women, men and children. Included in the total number of stores are 37 Nordstrom Racks, which serve as outlets for clearance merchandise from the Company's large specialty stores. The Racks also purchase merchandise directly from manufacturers. The remaining stores include 77 full-line stores, three Faconnable boutiques, two free-standing shoe stores and one clearance store. In addition, JWN operates 20 Faconnable boutiques throughout Europe. The Company's Nordstrom.com subsidiary sells merchandise through the Internet and direct-sales catalogs.

QUARTERLY DATA

(1/31/2001)($000)	REV	INC
1st Quarter	1,153,337	32,789
2nd Quarter	1,457,035	45,401
3rd Quarter	1,262,390	(3,320)
4th Quarteer	1,655,735	27,048

ANNUAL FINANCIAL DATA

	1/31/01	1/31/00	1/31/99	1/31/98	1/31/97	1/31/96	1/31/95
Earnings Per Share	**1 0.78**	**1.46**	**1.41**	**1.20**	**0.91**	**1.01**	**1.24**
Cash Flow Per Share	**2.24**	**2.82**	**2.61**	**2.27**	**1.88**	**1.83**	**1.91**
Tang. Book Val. Per Share	**8.12**	**8.96**	**9.26**	**9.93**	**9.25**	**8.77**	**8.17**
Dividends Per Share	**0.35**	**0.32**	**0.30**	**0.27**	**0.25**	**0.25**	**0.19**
Dividend Payout %	**44.9**	**21.9**	**21.3**	**22.1**	**27.5**	**24.8**	**15.6**
INCOME STATEMENT (IN MILLIONS):							
Total Revenues	5,528.5	5,124.2	5,027.9	4,851.6	4,453.1	4,113.5	3,894.5
Costs & Expenses	5,204.6	4,663.5	4,573.1	4,459.0	4,143.5	3,792.7	3,512.1
Depreciation & Amort.	192.0	187.3	177.2	159.7	156.1	134.3	110.8
Operating Income	132.0	273.4	277.7	232.9	153.4	186.5	271.6
Net Interest Inc./(Exp.)	d62.7	d50.4	d47.1	d34.2	d39.4	d39.3	d30.7
Income Before Income Taxes	167.0	332.1	337.7	307.2	243.5	272.3	335.6
Income Taxes	65.1	129.5	131.0	121.0	96.0	107.2	132.6
Net Income	1 101.9	202.6	206.7	186.2	147.5	165.1	203.0
Cash Flow	293.9	389.9	383.9	345.9	303.6	299.5	313.7
Average Shs. Outstg. (000)	131,113	138,425	146,858	152,518	161,698	163,840	164,288
BALANCE SHEET (IN MILLIONS):							
Cash & Cash Equivalents	25.3	52.6	241.4	24.8	28.3	24.5	32.5
Total Current Assets	1,813.0	1,564.6	1,680.4	1,595.0	1,532.4	1,612.8	1,397.7
Net Property	1,599.9	1,429.5	1,362.4	1,252.5	1,152.5	1,103.3	984.2
Total Assets	3,608.5	3,062.1	3,115.4	2,865.2	2,702.5	2,732.6	2,396.8
Total Current Liabilities	950.6	866.5	768.5	942.6	787.4	832.3	690.5
Long-Term Obligations	1,099.7	746.8	804.9	319.7	329.3	365.7	297.9
Net Stockholders' Equity	1,229.6	1,185.6	1,316.7	1,475.1	1,473.2	1,423.0	1,343.8
Net Working Capital	862.4	698.1	911.9	652.4	745.0	780.5	707.3
Year-end Shs. Outstg. (000)	133,798	132,280	142,114	148,608	159,270	162,226	164,488
STATISTICAL RECORD:							
Operating Profit Margin %	2.4	5.3	5.5	4.8	3.4	4.5	7.0
Net Profit Margin %	1.8	4.0	4.1	3.8	3.3	4.0	5.2
Return on Equity %	8.3	17.1	15.7	12.6	10.0	11.6	15.1
Return on Assets %	2.8	6.6	6.6	6.5	5.5	6.0	8.5
Debt/Total Assets %	30.5	24.4	25.8	11.2	12.2	13.4	12.4
Price Range	34.50-14.13	44.81-21.69	40.38-21.43	34.09-16.94	26.75-17.13	22.63-17.50	24.88-15.50
P/E Ratio	44.2-18.1	30.7-14.9	28.6-15.2	28.4-14.1	29.4-18.8	22.4-17.3	20.1-12.5
Average Yield %	1.4	1.0	1.0	1.0	1.1	1.2	1.0

Statistics are as originally reported. Adj. for 2-for-1 stk. split, 6/98. 1 Incl. $56.0 mil. ($0.26/sh) one-time pre-tax chg. fr. an investment write-down, estimated severance costs and the write-off of certain information technology investments.

OFFICERS:
B. A. Nordstrom, Chmn.
B. W. Nordstrom, Pres.
F. R. Lennon, V.P., Pres., Chief Info. Off.
R. E. Campbell, V.P., Treas.

INVESTOR CONTACT: Rob Campbell, (206) 373-4045

PRINCIPAL OFFICE: 1617 Sixth Avenue, Suite 500, Seattle, WA 98101-1742

TELEPHONE NUMBER: (206) 628-2111
FAX: (206) 628-1795
WEB: www.nordstrom.com

NO. OF EMPLOYEES: 40,000 (approx.)

SHAREHOLDERS: 60,000 (approx.)

ANNUAL MEETING: In May

INCORPORATED: WA, 1946

INSTITUTIONAL HOLDINGS:
No. of Institutions: 204
Shares Held: 57,863,538
% Held: 43.2

INDUSTRY: Family clothing stores (SIC: 5651)

TRANSFER AGENT(S): Mellon Investor Services, Ridgefield Park, NJ

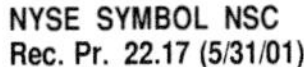

NYSE SYMBOL NSC
Rec. Pr. 22.17 (5/31/01)

NORFOLK SOUTHERN CORPORATION

YIELD 1.1%
P/E RATIO 49.3

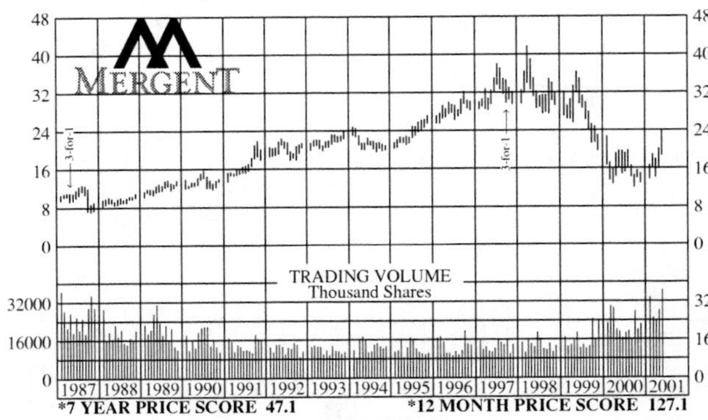

*7 YEAR PRICE SCORE 47.1 *12 MONTH PRICE SCORE 127.1

*NYSE COMPOSITE INDEX=100

INTERIM EARNINGS (Per Share):

Qtr.	Mar.	June	Sept.	Dec.
1997	0.47	0.51	0.47	0.58
1998	0.61	0.48	0.40	0.42
1999	0.30	0.20	0.05	0.08
2000	d0.12	0.30	0.26	0.01

INTERIM DIVIDENDS (Per Share):

Amt.	Decl.	Ex.	Rec.	Pay.
0.20Q	4/25/00	5/03/00	5/05/00	6/10/00
0.20Q	7/25/00	8/02/00	8/04/00	9/11/00
0.20Q	10/23/00	11/01/00	11/03/00	12/11/00
0.06Q	1/23/01	1/31/01	2/02/01	3/10/01
0.06Q	4/23/01	5/02/01	5/04/01	6/11/01

Indicated div.: $0.24 (Div. Reinv. Plan)

CAPITALIZATION (12/31/00):

	($000)	(%)
Long-Term Debt	7,339,000	46.0
Deferred Income Tax	2,745,000	17.2
Minority Interest	50,000	0.3
Common & Surplus	5,824,000	36.5
Total	15,958,000	100.0

RECENT DEVELOPMENTS: For the year ended 12/31/00, net income was $172.0 million versus $239.0 million a year earlier. Results for 2000 included after-tax workforce reduction charges of $101.0 million and an after-tax gain of $46.0 million on the sale of timber rights. Total railway operating revenues increased 17.5% to $6.16 billion, reflecting a full year of operations in the Northern Region. Coal revenues advanced 8.5% to $1.44 billion, while general merchandise revenues rose 17.4% to $3.61 billion.

PROSPECTS: On 1/23/01 NSC announced a restructuring plan designed to reduce costs and improve financial performance. The restructuring includes a workforce reduction of 1,000 to 2,000 employees over the next 12 months, disposition of 12,000 surplus freight cars; a line rationalization program targeting 3,000 to 4,000 underutilized or duplicate track miles over the next 24 months; consolidation or disposition of up to 10 underutilized or redundant facilities; and a redesign of NCS's service network.

BUSINESS

NORFOLK SOUTHERN CORPORATION is a holding company engaged principally in the transportation of freight by rail. Operations are conducted through NSC's wholly-owned subsidiary, Norfolk Southern Railway Company. NSC operates 21,800 miles of road in 22 states and in the Province of Ontario, Canada. NSC's rail freight largely consists of raw materials, intermediate products and finished goods classified in the following groups: coal; paper, clay and forest products; chemicals; automotive; agricultural, government and consumer products; metals and construction; and intermodal. On 3/28/98, NSC sold its former motor carrier business, North American Van Lines, Inc.

QUARTERLY DATA

(12/31/2000)($000)	REV	INC
First Quarter	1,508,000	(48,000)
Second Quarter	1,592,000	116,000
Third Quarter	1,535,000	99,000
Forth Quarter	1,524,000	5,000

ANNUAL FINANCIAL DATA

	12/31/00	12/31/99	12/31/98	12/31/97	12/31/96	12/31/95	12/31/94
Earnings Per Share	**5 0.45**	**4 0.63**	**1 1.65**	**2 1.84**	**2.03**	**3 1.81**	**1.63**
Cash Flow Per Share	**1.80**	**1.91**	**2.83**	**2.98**	**3.12**	**2.84**	**2.62**
Tang. Book Val. Per Share	**15.16**	**15.50**	**15.61**	**14.44**	**13.26**	**12.47**	**11.73**
Dividends Per Share	**0.80**	**0.80**	**0.80**	**0.80**	**0.75**	**0.69**	**0.64**
Dividend Payout %	**177.7**	**127.0**	**48.5**	**43.5**	**36.8**	**38.2**	**39.2**
INCOME STATEMENT (IN MILLIONS):							
Total Revenues	6,159.0	5,195.0	4,221.0	4,223.0	4,770.0	4,668.0	4,581.3
Costs & Expenses	5,009.0	3,988.0	2,719.0	2,578.0	3,143.8	3,168.2	3,112.1
Depreciation & Amort.	517.0	489.0	450.0	432.0	429.2	413.5	403.8
Operating Income	633.0	718.0	1,052.0	1,213.0	1,197.0	1,086.3	1,065.4
Net Interest Inc./(Exp.)	d551.0	d531.0	d516.0	d385.0	d115.7	d113.4	d101.6
Income Before Income Taxes	250.0	351.0	845.0	998.0	1,196.9	1,114.7	1,049.0
Income Taxes	78.0	112.0	215.0	299.0	426.5	402.0	381.2
Net Income	5 172.0	4 239.0	1 630.0	2 699.0	770.4	3 712.7	667.8
Cash Flow	689.0	728.0	1,080.0	1,131.0	1,199.6	1,126.2	1,071.6
Average Shs. Outstg. (000)	383,000	382,000	381,000	380,000	384,000	396,900	408,900
BALANCE SHEET (IN MILLIONS):							
Cash & Cash Equivalents	2.0	51.0	63.0	159.0	403.4	329.0	306.7
Total Current Assets	849.0	1,371.0	913.0	1,103.0	1,456.8	1,342.8	1,337.5
Net Property	11,105.0	10,956.0	10,477.0	9,904.0	9,529.1	9,258.8	8,987.1
Total Assets	18,976.0	19,250.0	18,180.0	17,350.0	11,416.4	10,904.8	10,587.8
Total Current Liabilities	1,887.0	1,924.0	1,117.0	1,093.0	1,190.3	1,205.8	1,131.8
Long-Term Obligations	7,339.0	7,556.0	7,483.0	7,398.0	1,800.3	1,553.3	1,547.8
Net Stockholders' Equity	5,824.0	5,932.0	5,921.0	5,445.0	4,977.6	4,829.0	4,684.8
Net Working Capital	d1,038.0	d553.0	d204.0	10.0	266.5	137.0	205.7
Year-end Shs. Outstg. (000)	384,058	382,681	379,404	377,155	375,291	387,099	399,399
STATISTICAL RECORD:							
Operating Profit Margin %	10.3	13.8	24.9	28.7	25.1	23.3	23.3
Net Profit Margin %	2.8	4.6	14.9	16.6	16.2	15.3	14.6
Return on Equity %	3.0	4.0	10.6	12.8	15.5	14.8	14.3
Return on Assets %	0.9	1.2	3.5	4.0	6.7	6.5	6.3
Debt/Total Assets %	38.7	39.3	41.2	42.6	15.8	14.2	14.6
Price Range	22.75-11.94	36.44-19.63	41.75-27.44	38.13-28.21	32.21-25.46	27.21-20.17	24.92-19.50
P/E Ratio	50.5-26.5	57.8-31.1	25.3-16.6	20.7-15.3	15.9-12.5	15.0-11.1	15.3-11.9
Average Yield %	4.6	2.9	2.3	2.4	2.6	2.9	2.9

Statistics are as originally reported. Adj. for 3-for-1 stk. split, 10/97 1 Incl. non-recurr. chrgs. of $156.0 mill.; Bef. disc. ops. credit of $104.0 mill. 2 Bef. disc. oper. gain $22.0 mill. & incls. one-time Conrail-related chrg. of $107.0 mill. 3 Incl. non-recurr. chrg. $20.4 mill. 4 Incl. special chrg. $49.0 mill. 5 Incl. net non-recurr. chrgs. of $55.0 mill.

OFFICERS:
D. R. Goode, Chmn., Pres., C.E.O.
L. I. Prillaman, Vice-Chmn., C.M.O.
S. C. Tobias, Vice-Chmn., C.O.O.
H. C. Wolf, Vice-Chmn., C.F.O.

INVESTOR CONTACT: Henry C Wolf, Vice Chmn. & C.F.O., (757) 629-2650

PRINCIPAL OFFICE: Three Commercial Place, P.O. Box 227, Norfolk, VA 23510

TELEPHONE NUMBER: (757) 629-2680
FAX: (757) 629-2345
WEB: www.nscorp.com

NO. OF EMPLOYEES: 33,738 (avg.)

SHAREHOLDERS: 53,194

ANNUAL MEETING: In May

INCORPORATED: VA, July, 1980

INSTITUTIONAL HOLDINGS:
No. of Institutions: 373
Shares Held: 269,404,605
% Held: 70.1

INDUSTRY: Railroads, line-haul operating (SIC: 4011)

TRANSFER AGENT(S): The Bank of New York, New York, NY

NYSE SYMBOL NHY
Rec. Pr. 42.29 (5/31/01)

NORSK HYDRO ASA

YIELD ...
P/E RATIO 6.9

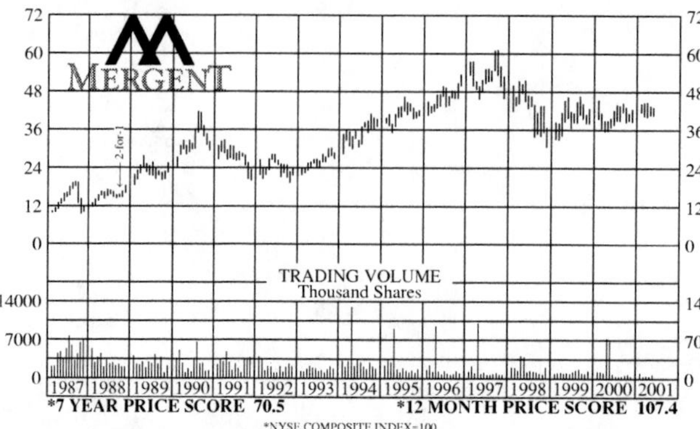

*7 YEAR PRICE SCORE 70.5 *12 MONTH PRICE SCORE 107.4

*NYSE COMPOSITE INDEX=100

INTERIM EARNINGS (Per Share):

Qtr.	Mar.	June	Sept.	Dec.
1997	1.01	0.93	0.75	0.53
1998	0.58	1.05	0.27	0.27
1999	0.40	0.70	0.31	0.19
2000	1.11	1.23	1.64	2.12

INTERIM DIVIDENDS (Per Share):

Amt.	Decl.	Ex.	Rec.	Pay.
0.742	...	4/24/00	4/26/00	5/25/00
0.888	...	4/30/01	5/02/01	5/29/01

CAPITALIZATION (12/31/00):

	($000)	(%)
Long-Term Debt	4,895,917	29.2
Deferred Income Tax	3,581,257	21.4
Minority Interest	161,908	1.0
Common & Surplus	8,127,001	48.5
Total	16,766,082	100.0

RECENT DEVELOPMENTS: For the year ended 12/31/00, net income more than quadrupled to NOK14.00 billion ($1.60 billion) versus income of NOK3.40 billion ($424.3 million) in the previous year. Operating revenues increased 40.2% to NOK157.00 billion ($17.91 billion) from NOK112.00 ($13.98 billion) in the prior year. Comparisons were made using the following exchange rates: $1=NOK8.7642 as of 12/29/00; $1=NOK8.0128 as of 12/31/99.

PROSPECTS: On 3/1/01, the Company agreed to transfer its aluminum foam process technology to Cymat, a manufacturer of stabilized aluminum foam as foam panels, foam-filled tubes and other products, in exchange for shares in the company. Going forward, the Company should continue to benefit from favorable market conditions, including high oil prices and a US dollar/Norwegian krone exchange rate favorable to NHY.

BUSINESS

NORSK HYDRO ASA is Norway's largest publicly-owned company. NHY's main products are oil and gas, nitrogen fertilizers, and aluminum and magnesium. The oil and gas segment is mainly engaged in the exploration for, and production of, oil and gas in the Norwegian sector of the North Sea and in refining and marketing in Scandinavia. The agriculture segment is engaged in the production of fertilizers, industrial gases and chemicals. Through the light metals segment, NHY is a producer of aluminum and magnesium. NHY also is a hydro-electricity producer. NHY is 44.0% owned by the Norwegian government.

ANNUAL FINANCIAL DATA

	12/31/00	12/31/99	12/31/98	12/31/97	12/31/96	12/31/95	12/31/94
Earnings Per Share 1	**6.09**	**1.87**	5 **2.21**	**3.11**	**4.21**	4 **4.93**	3 **2.65**
Tang. Book Val. Per Share 1	**31.26**	**28.37**	**25.56**	**23.86**	**24.72**	**22.45**	**17.36**
Dividends Per Share 1	**0.74**	**0.82**	**0.85**	**0.84**	**0.77**	**0.56**	**0.42**
Dividend Payout %	**6.1**	**23.7**	**38.4**	**27.0**	**18.3**	**11.4**	**15.8**
INCOME STATEMENT (IN MILLIONS):							
Total Revenues	17,897.8	13,972.0	13,109.4	13,194.4	13,167.2	12,605.6	10,554.4
Costs & Expenses	13,219.3	11,697.0	11,300.6	10,863.6	10,663.5	9,981.3	8,620.8
Depreciation & Amort.	1,430.6	1,309.7	911.8	841.2	908.2	817.4	774.1
Operating Income	3,248.0	965.3	897.1	1,489.6	1,595.5	1,806.9	1,159.5
Net Interest Inc./(Exp.)	d246.2	d193.6	...	...	...	...	...
Income Before Income Taxes	3,439.1	978.8	846.3	1,348.8	1,561.8	1,726.6	1,017.4
Income Taxes	1,845.9	541.3	292.5	692.7	626.1	587.2	395.8
Equity Earnings/Minority Int.	2.1	d11.2	d13.2	d6.6	d3.1	d12.3	d10.1
Net Income	1,595.2	426.3	5 540.6	649.5	932.6	4 1,127.1	3 611.6
Cash Flow	3,025.8	1,736.0	1,452.3	1,490.7	1,840.8	1,944.5	1,385.7
BALANCE SHEET (IN MILLIONS):							
Cash & Cash Equivalents	2,767.7	1,244.3	555.5	654.0	944.5	1,237.4	1,211.7
Total Current Assets	9,332.8	7,325.1	5,893.0	5,611.9	5,935.9	5,645.1	5,038.1
Net Property	10,842.4	12,791.8	7,482.6	6,830.9	6,901.1	6,271.7	5,892.8
Total Assets	22,404.0	22,141.9	15,292.8	14,292.0	14,864.4	14,049.2	12,522.0
Total Current Liabilities	5,103.2	4,616.7	3,791.6	4,121.5	3,982.0	3,569.3	3,529.0
Long-Term Obligations	4,895.9	5,555.5	3,485.8	2,608.9	2,922.6	2,955.0	3,031.2
Net Stockholders' Equity	8,127.0	7,425.2	5,855.1	5,466.5	5,662.3	5,143.3	3,974.7
Net Working Capital	4,229.6	2,708.4	2,101.4	1,490.4	1,954.0	2,075.9	1,509.0
Year-end Shs. Outstg. (000)	259,986	261,706	229,073	229,073	229,073	229,073	229,000
STATISTICAL RECORD:							
Operating Profit Margin %	18.1	6.9	6.8	11.3	12.1	14.3	11.0
Net Profit Margin %	8.9	3.1	4.1	4.9	7.1	8.9	5.8
Return on Equity %	19.6	5.7	9.2	11.9	16.5	21.9	15.4
Return on Assets %	7.1	1.9	3.5	4.5	6.3	8.0	4.9
Debt/Total Assets %	21.9	25.1	22.8	18.3	19.7	21.0	24.2
Price Range 1	45.44-35.50	46.63-32.75	51.75-30.56	61.25-45.63	53.63-40.50	46.38-35.00	41.00-28.38
P/E Ratio	7.5-5.8	24.9-17.5	23.5-13.9	19.7-14.6	12.7-9.6	9.4-7.1	15.5-10.7
Average Yield %	1.8	2.1	2.1	1.6	1.6	1.4	1.2

Statistics are as originally reported. All figures are in U.S. dollars unless otherwise noted. Exchange rates were as follows: US$1=NOK8.7642, 12/29/00; US$1=NOK8.0128, 12/31/99; 7.4349, 12/31/98; 7.2886, 12/31/97; 6.4433, 12/31/96; 6.3251, 12/31/95; 6.7613, 12/31/94. Based on U.S. GAAP. 1 Based on ADR shares. Each ADR represents one ordinary share at par NOK20. 2 Incl. $266.7 mill. gain on the sale of 38.3% interest in Freia Marabou AS. 3 Bef. cr$19.0 mill. acctg. adj. 4 Bef. acctg. adj. of $2.6 mill. 5 Incl. a net gain of $114.0 mill.

OFFICERS:
E. Kloster, Chmn.
E. Myklebust, Pres., C.E.O.
L. L. Nergaard, Exec. V.P., C.F.O.

INVESTOR CONTACT: Thomas Knutzen, (+47) 22 53 91 15

PRINCIPAL OFFICE: Bygdoy Alle 2, Oslo, Norway

TELEPHONE NUMBER: (212) 688-6606 (U.S. office)
FAX: (212) 750-1252
WEB: www.hydro.com

NO. OF EMPLOYEES: 38,166 (avg.)

SHAREHOLDERS: 766 (ADR holders)

ANNUAL MEETING: In May

INCORPORATED: NOR.

INSTITUTIONAL HOLDINGS:
No. of Institutions: 57
Shares Held: 14,507,318
% Held: 5.6

INDUSTRY: Nitrogenous fertilizers (SIC: 2873)

DEPOSITARY BANKS(S): Morgan ADR Service Center, Boston, MA

NYSE SYMBOL NT
Rec. Pr. 13.33 (5/31/01)

NORTEL NETWORKS CORPORATION

YIELD 0.6%
P/E RATIO ...

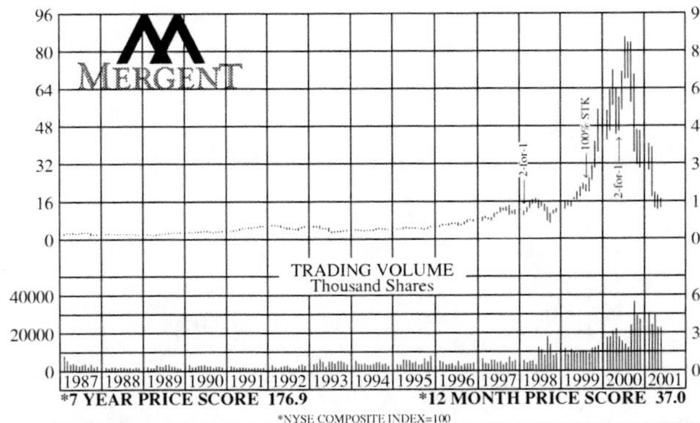

*7 YEAR PRICE SCORE 176.9 *12 MONTH PRICE SCORE 37.0

*NYSE COMPOSITE INDEX=100

INTERIM EARNINGS (Per Share):

Qtr.	Mar.	June	Sept.	Dec.
1996	0.04	0.06	0.06	0.16
1997	0.06	0.08	0.08	0.10
1998	d0.03	d0.04	0.11	d0.13
1999	d0.18	d0.06	d0.03	0.06
2000	d0.05	d0.25	d0.31	d0.38

INTERIM DIVIDENDS (Per Share):

Amt.	Decl.	Ex.	Rec.	Pay.
0.019Q	5/25/00	6/06/00	6/08/00	6/30/00
0.019Q	7/27/00	8/30/00	9/01/00	9/29/00
0.019Q	10/26/00	11/30/00	12/04/00	12/29/00
0.019Q	2/22/01	3/08/01	3/12/01	3/30/01
0.019Q	5/24/01	6/05/01	6/07/01	6/29/01

Indicated div.: $0.07

CAPITALIZATION (12/31/00):

	($000)	(%)
Long-Term Debt	1,470,000	4.6
Deferred Income Tax	993,000	3.1
Minority Interest	804,000	2.5
Common & Surplus	28,760,000	89.8
Total	32,027,000	100.0

RECENT DEVELOPMENTS: For the year ended 12/31/00, the Company reported a net loss of $2.96 billion compared with a net loss of $351.0 million in the prior year. Results for 2000 included a net after-tax charge of $5.78 billion for acquisition-related costs, stock option compensation from acquisitions and divestitures, and other one-time items. Results for 1999 included a net after-tax charge of $1.79 billion. Revenues surged 42.2% to $30.29 billion from $21.29 billion in 1999. Service provider and carrier revenues rose 53.3% to $24.93 billion.

PROSPECTS: The effects of the U.S. economic slowdown cloud near-term prospects. The Company noted that the Company is experiencing longer-than-expected delays in spending from its U.S. customers and that it expects the U.S. market slowdown to continue well into the fourth quarter of 2001. Consequently, NT will accelerate streamlining and realignment activities. Separately, the Company has completed its acquisition of JDS Uniphases's Zurich, Switzerland-based subsidiary and related assets in Poughkeepsi, NY.

BUSINESS

NORTEL NETWORKS CORPORATION (formerly Northern Telecom Limited) is a major supplier of networking solutions and services that support the Internet and other public and private data, voice, and video networks using wireless and wireline technologies. The Company operates in two segments: service provider and carrier (82.3% of 2000 revenues) and enterprise (17.6%). NT's business consists of the design, development, manufacture, assembly, marketing, sale, licensing, financing, installation, servicing, and support of networking solutions and services. In 2000, revenues were derived: U.S., 60.0%; Canada, 5.5%; and other countries, 34.5%. The Company acquired Bay Networks, Inc. on 8/31/98, in a $6.90 billion transaction.

ANNUAL FINANCIAL DATA

	12/31/00	12/31/99	12/31/98	12/31/97	12/31/96	12/31/95	12/31/94
Earnings Per Share	**4 d1.00**	**3 d0.07**	**1 d0.25**	**2 0.39**	**0.30**	**0.23**	**0.20**
Cash Flow Per Share	**1.08**	**0.68**	**0.50**	**0.41**	**0.32**	**0.25**	**0.21**
Tang. Book Val. Per Share	**3.23**	**2.68**	**2.01**	**1.90**	**1.72**	**1.45**	**1.24**
Dividends Per Share	**0.06**	...	...	...	...	...	...
INCOME STATEMENT (IN MILLIONS):							
Total Revenues	30,293.0	22,217.0	17,575.0	15,449.0	12,847.0	10,672.0	8,874.0
Costs & Expenses	27,025.0	19,816.0	16,043.0	14,067.0	11,722.0	9,881.0	8,442.0
Depreciation & Amort.	6,321.0	2,047.0	1,709.0	48.0	45.0	39.0	18.0
Operating Income	d3,053.0	354.0	d177.0	1,334.0	1,080.0	752.0	414.0
Net Interest Inc./(Exp.)	d169.0	d172.0	d232.0	d169.0	d175.0	d160.0	d188.0
Income Before Income Taxes	d2,200.0	526.0	64.0	1,267.0	944.0	706.0	569.0
Income Taxes	757.0	696.0	601.0	438.0	321.0	233.0	161.0
Net Income	4 d2,957.0	3 d170.0	1 d537.0	2 829.0	623.0	473.0	408.0
Cash Flow	3,364.0	1,850.0	1,140.0	860.0	664.0	508.0	422.0
Average Shs. Outstg. (000)	3,108,000	2,706,000	2,288,000	2,088,000	2,064,000	2,032,000	2,016,000
BALANCE SHEET (IN MILLIONS):							
Cash & Cash Equivalents	1,649.0	2,257.0	2,281.0	1,371.0	730.0	202.0	1,059.0
Total Current Assets	16,548.0	13,068.0	10,317.0	8,547.0	6,870.0	5,822.0	5,355.0
Net Property	3,421.0	2,458.0	2,263.0	2,040.0	2,035.0	1,923.0	1,705.0
Total Assets	42,227.0	22,597.0	19,732.0	12,554.0	10,903.0	9,480.0	8,785.0
Total Current Liabilities	9,064.0	7,790.0	5,893.0	4,883.0	3,771.0	3,752.0	3,195.0
Long-Term Obligations	1,470.0	1,624.0	1,648.0	1,565.0	1,663.0	1,236.0	1,507.0
Net Stockholders' Equity	28,760.0	12,518.0	11,565.0	5,410.0	4,876.0	3,871.0	3,428.0
Net Working Capital	7,484.0	5,278.0	4,424.0	3,664.0	3,099.0	2,070.0	2,160.0
Year-end Shs. Outstg. (000)	3,095,772	2,754,310	2,652,418	2,075,520	2,079,008	2,034,832	2,026,832
STATISTICAL RECORD:							
Operating Profit Margin %	...	1.6	...	8.6	8.4	7.0	4.7
Net Profit Margin %	...	...	...	5.4	4.8	4.4	4.6
Return on Equity %	...	...	...	15.3	12.8	12.2	11.9
Return on Assets %	...	...	...	6.6	5.7	5.0	4.6
Debt/Total Assets %	3.5	7.2	8.4	12.5	15.3	13.0	17.2
Price Range	86.00-30.00	55.00-12.53	17.31-6.70	14.23-7.56	8.45-5.09	5.53-3.94	4.72-3.25
P/E Ratio	...	...	...	36.5-19.4	28.2-17.0	24.0-17.1	23.6-16.2
Average Yield %	0.1	...	...	...	...	...	...

Statistics are as originally reported. All figures are in U.S. dollars unless otherwise noted. Adj. for 100% stk. div., 5/5/00; 8/99; 2-for-1, 1/98. 1 Incl. pre-tax special chrgs. of $313.0 mill. 2 Incl. non-recurr. net credit of $7.0 mill. 3 Incl. non-recurr. chrg. of $1.10 bill. 4 Incl. net after-tax chrgs. of $5.78 bill. for acq. rel. costs, stk. option comp. fr. acq. & divest., and one-time items.

OFFICERS:
L. R. Wilson, Chmn.
J. A. Roth, Pres., C.E.O.
F. A. Dunn, C.F.O.

INVESTOR CONTACT: Investor Relations, (905) 863-6049

PRINCIPAL OFFICE: 8200 Dixie Road, Suite 100, Brampton, Ontario, Canada

TELEPHONE NUMBER: (905) 863-0000
FAX: (905) 863-8496
WEB: www.nortelnetworks.com

NO. OF EMPLOYEES: 94,500 (approx.)

SHAREHOLDERS: 214,000 (approx.)

ANNUAL MEETING: In Apr.

INCORPORATED: Canada, Jan., 1914

INSTITUTIONAL HOLDINGS:
No. of Institutions: 738
Shares Held: 1,045,664,471
% Held: 32.8

INDUSTRY: Telephone and telegraph apparatus (SIC: 3661)

TRANSFER AGENT(S): Computershare Trust Company of Canada

NYSE SYMBOL NFB
Rec. Pr. 26.55 (4/30/01)

NORTH FORK BANCORPORATION, INC.

YIELD 3.2%
P/E RATIO 19.2

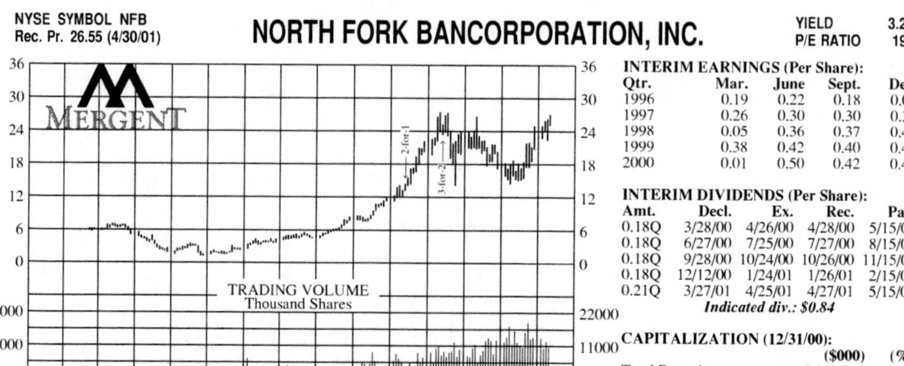

*7 YEAR PRICE SCORE 100.8 *12 MONTH PRICE SCORE 130.1

*NYSE COMPOSITE INDEX=100

INTERIM EARNINGS (Per Share):

Qtr.	Mar.	June	Sept.	Dec.
1996	0.19	0.22	0.18	0.05
1997	0.26	0.30	0.30	0.34
1998	0.05	0.36	0.37	0.40
1999	0.38	0.42	0.40	0.42
2000	0.01	0.50	0.42	0.45

INTERIM DIVIDENDS (Per Share):

Amt.	Decl.	Ex.	Rec.	Pay.
0.18Q	3/28/00	4/26/00	4/28/00	5/15/00
0.18Q	6/27/00	7/25/00	7/27/00	8/15/00
0.18Q	9/28/00	10/24/00	10/26/00	11/15/00
0.18Q	12/12/00	1/24/01	1/26/01	2/15/01
0.21Q	3/27/01	4/25/01	4/27/01	5/15/01

Indicated div.: $0.84

CAPITALIZATION (12/31/00):

	($000)	(%)
Total Deposits	9,169,195	76.2
Long-Term Debt	1,653,265	13.7
Common & Surplus	1,213,918	10.1
Total	12,036,378	100.0

RECENT DEVELOPMENTS: For the year ended 12/31/00, net income declined 5.9% to $234.8 million from $249.5 million in 1999. Results for 2000 included merger-related restructuring charges of $50.5 million and a one-time charge of $13.5 million. Net interest income improved 12.9% to $592.0 million. Provision for loan losses more than doubled to $17.0 million from $6.0 million in 1999. Total non-interest income grew 34.9% to $102.5 million.

PROSPECTS: On 2/13/01, the Company announced that it has signed a definitive agreement to acquire Commercial Bank of New York (CBNY) for approximately $175.0 million in cash. At 12/31/00, CBNY had total assets of $1.50 billion, deposits of $1.30 billion and shareholders' equity of $101.0 million. The Company estimates this acquisition to be accretive to diluted cash earnings per share in 2001 by approximately 2.0%.

BUSINESS

NORTH FORK BANCORPORATION INC. is a bank holding company, and operates through its primary subsidiary North Fork Bank and its investment management and broker/dealer subsidiaries, Compass Investment Services Corp. and Amivest Corporation, providing a variety of banking and financial services to middle market and small business organizations, local governmental units, and retail customers. North Fork Bank operates through 150 full-service retail banking facilities located in the New York metropolitan area. The Company's other bank subsidiary, Superior Savings of New England, a Connecticut chartered savings bank located in the Connecticut county of New Haven, operates from one location where it currently conducts a telebanking operation focused on gathering deposits throughout the New England region.

ANNUAL FINANCIAL DATA

	12/31/00	12/31/99	12/31/98	12/31/97	12/31/96	12/31/95	12/31/94
Earnings Per Share	**1 1.39**	**1.62**	**1 1.18**	**1.20**	**1 2 0.65**	**0.71**	**1 0.42**
Tang. Book Val. Per Share	**5.39**	**4.20**	**5.29**	**5.07**	**3.86**	**3.80**	**3.37**
Dividends Per Share	**0.72**	**0.72**	**0.47**	**0.37**	**0.25**	**0.17**	**0.08**
Dividend Payout %	**51.8**	**44.8**	**40.3**	**30.6**	**38.6**	**23.5**	**20.0**
INCOME STATEMENT (IN MILLIONS):							
Total Interest Income	1,072.6	817.7	753.1	484.5	405.3	226.4	203.7
Total Interest Expense	480.6	368.4	328.5	206.2	174.4	85.2	71.2
Net Interest Income	592.0	449.3	424.6	278.4	230.9	141.2	132.5
Provision for Loan Losses	17.0	6.0	15.5	6.0	6.8	9.0	3.3
Non-Interest Income	102.5	73.0	64.3	41.6	31.1	27.3	9.8
Non-Interest Expense	301.5	177.3	230.4	122.7	143.0	68.8	92.4
Income Before Taxes	376.0	339.0	243.1	191.2	112.3	90.7	46.6
Net Income	1 234.8	220.4	1 168.0	119.3	1 2 62.4	52.2	1 29.7
Average Shs. Outstg. (000)	168,531	135,865	141,765	99,593	96,414	73,662	71,289
BALANCE SHEET (IN MILLIONS):							
Cash & Due from Banks	292.5	299.9	151.6	153.0	150.4	106.5	67.2
Securities Avail. for Sale	17.6	...	...	...	...	814.5	141.8
Total Loans & Leases	9,409.8	6,630.5	5,731.4	3,714.7	3,194.1	1,985.0	1,831.5
Allowance for Credit Losses	104.7	82.0	88.9	70.3	76.5	68.8	67.5
Net Loans & Leases	9,305.1	6,548.5	5,642.5	3,644.3	3,117.6	1,916.2	1,764.0
Total Assets	14,841.0	12,108.1	10,679.6	6,829.4	5,750.5	3,303.3	2,717.8
Total Deposits	9,169.2	6,544.8	6,427.6	4,637.2	4,469.5	2,535.5	2,342.9
Long-Term Obligations	1,653.3	1,844.0	35.0	36.0	35.0	35.0	75.0
Total Liabilities	13,627.0	11,489.4	9,848.3	6,227.6	5,293.0	2,993.5	2,462.9
Net Stockholders' Equity	1,213.9	618.7	831.3	601.8	457.5	309.8	254.9
Year-end Shs. Outstg. (000)	160,831	128,442	141,072	99,593	97,338	74,637	69,141
STATISTICAL RECORD:							
Return on Equity %	19.3	35.6	20.2	19.8	13.6	16.9	11.6
Return on Assets %	1.6	1.8	1.6	1.7	1.1	1.6	1.1
Equity/Assets %	8.2	5.1	7.8	8.8	8.0	9.4	9.4
Non-Int. Exp./Tot. Inc. %	43.4	33.9	47.1	38.4	54.6	40.8	65.0
Price Range	25.00-14.44	26.75-17.13	27.56-14.13	22.19-11.25	12.06-7.56	8.44-4.50	5.63-4.19
P/E Ratio	18.0-10.4	16.5-10.6	23.3-12.0	18.5-9.4	18.7-11.7	11.9-6.3	13.5-10.0
Average Yield %	3.7	3.3	2.3	2.2	2.5	2.6	1.7

Statistics are as originally reported. Adj. for 2-for-1 stk. split, 5/97; 3-for-2, 5/98. 1 Incl. one-time chrgs. of $64.0 mill., 2000; $52.5 mill., 1998; $21.6 mill., 1996; $14.3 mill., 1994. 2 Incl. SAIF recapitalization chrg. $8.4 mill.

OFFICERS:
J. A. Kanas, Chmn., Pres., C.E.O.
J. Bohlsen, Vice-Chmn.
D. M. Healy, Exec. V.P., C.F.O.

INVESTOR CONTACT: Linda Bishop, Investor Relations, (631) 501-4618

PRINCIPAL OFFICE: 275 Broad Hollow Road, Melville, NY 11747

TELEPHONE NUMBER: (631) 844-1004
WEB: www.northforkbank.com

NO. OF EMPLOYEES: 2,293

SHAREHOLDERS: 8,860 (record)

ANNUAL MEETING: In May

INCORPORATED: DE, 1980

INSTITUTIONAL HOLDINGS:
No. of Institutions: 242
Shares Held: 77,103,153
% Held: 47.6

INDUSTRY: State commercial banks (SIC: 6022)

TRANSFER AGENT(S): First Chicago Trust Company of New York, Jersey City, NJ

NYSE SYMBOL NU
Rec. Pr. 17.85 (4/30/01)

NORTHEAST UTILITIES

YIELD 2.2%
P/E RATIO 11.5

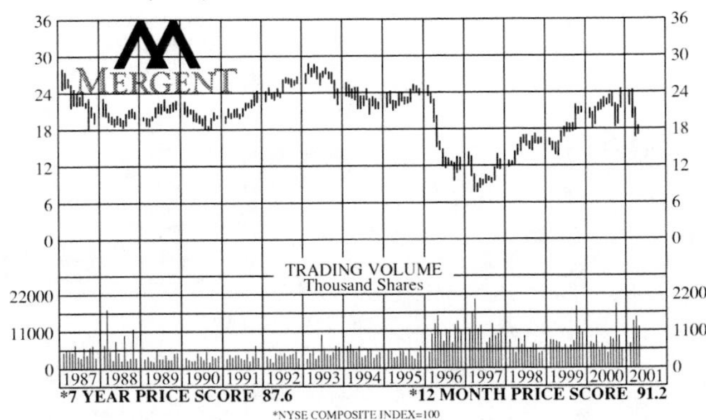

*7 YEAR PRICE SCORE 87.6 *12 MONTH PRICE SCORE 91.2

*NYSE COMPOSITE INDEX=100

INTERIM EARNINGS (Per Share):

Qtr.	Mar.	June	Sept.	Dec.
1997	0.14	d0.50	d0.40	d0.29
1998	d0.14	0.05	0.04	d1.01
1999	0.14	Nil	0.24	d0.12
2000	0.55	0.08	0.45	0.47

INTERIM DIVIDENDS (Per Share):

Amt.	Decl.	Ex.	Rec.	Pay.
0.10Q	4/12/00	5/30/00	6/01/00	6/30/00
0.10Q	7/11/00	8/30/00	9/01/00	9/29/00
0.10Q	10/11/00	11/29/00	12/01/00	12/29/00
0.10Q	1/09/01	2/27/01	3/01/01	3/30/01
0.10Q	4/10/01	5/30/01	6/01/01	6/29/01

Indicated div.: $0.40 (Div. Reinv. Plan)

CAPITALIZATION (12/31/00):

	($000)	(%)
Long-Term Debt	2,029,593	33.1
Capital Lease Obligations	47,234	0.8
Deferred Income Tax	1,585,494	25.9
Minority Interest	100,000	1.6
Redeemable Pfd. Stock	15,000	0.2
Preferred Stock	136,200	2.2
Common & Surplus	2,218,583	36.2
Total	6,132,104	100.0

RECENT DEVELOPMENTS: For the year ended 12/31/00, income before extraordinary items soared to $205.3 million compared with net income of $34.2 million in 1999. Results for 2000 excluded an after-tax write-off of $225.0 million for stranded costs, a one-time charge of $11.7 million for the settlement of certain nuclear-related issues, and a one-time after-tax gain of $10.4 million. Results for 1999 excluded write-offs totaling $83.1 million. Operating revenues rose 31.4% to $5.88 billion.

PROSPECTS: NU filed a suit against Consolidated Edison, Inc. seeking damages in excess of $1.00 billion from Con Edison's alleged breach of the merger agreement between the two companies. NU alleged that Con Edison had breached the agreement by not willing to close the merger on the previously agreed terms. The terms of the merger were agreed upon on 3/2/01 and the transaction was expected to close on 3/5/01. Separately, NU expects earnings per share for 2001 to range between $1.40 and $1.60.

BUSINESS

NORTHEAST UTILITIES is the parent company of Northeast Utilities Systems, which is comprised of the following subsidiaries: Connecticut Light and Power, Western Massachusetts Electric Co., Holyoke Water Power Co., Public Service Co. of New Hampshire, NU Enterprises, Inc., Northeast Generation Company, and Northeast Generation Services Company. In 2000, electric operating revenues were 27.5% residential; 23.5% commercial; 10.6% industrial; 35.4% other utilities; 0.9% streetlighting and railroads; 0.3% non-franchised sales; and 1.8% miscellaneous. Non-utility subsidiaries include: Charter Oak Energy, Inc., HEC Inc., Select Energy, Inc., and Mode 1 Communications, Inc. On 3/1/00, NU acquired Yankee Energy System, Inc.

ANNUAL FINANCIAL DATA

	12/31/00	12/31/99	12/31/98	12/31/97	12/31/96	12/31/95	12/31/94
Earnings Per Share	**[3] 1.45**	**[2] 0.26**	**[1] d1.12**	**d1.05**	**0.01**	**2.24**	**2.30**
Cash Flow Per Share	**4.86**	**7.44**	**3.27**	**2.38**	**3.47**	**5.05**	**5.43**
Tang. Book Val. Per Share	**15.43**	**15.91**	**15.63**	**16.34**	**17.73**	**19.08**	**18.48**
Dividends Per Share	**0.40**	**0.10**	...	**0.25**	**1.38**	**1.76**	**1.76**
Dividend Payout %	**27.6**	**38.4**	...	...	...	**78.6**	**76.5**
INCOME STATEMENT (IN MILLIONS):							
Total Revenues	5,876.6	4,471.3	3,767.7	3,834.8	3,792.1	3,750.6	3,642.7
Costs & Expenses	4,670.6	2,843.0	2,569.5	2,704.5	2,662.7	2,515.0	2,397.7
Depreciation & Amort.	485.3	943.3	574.3	443.6	442.3	354.5	390.3
Maintenance Exp.	255.9	340.4	399.2	501.7	415.5	288.9	306.4
Operating Income	464.8	344.5	224.7	185.0	271.6	592.1	548.2
Net Interest Inc./(Exp.)	d299.3	d263.7	d269.1	d272.0	d278.0	d299.2	d281.1
Income Taxes	cr68.3	cr82.3	cr76.4	cr10.7	1.7	0.7	cr13.5
Equity Earnings/Minority Int.	5.3	d4.3	3.1	2.0	3.9	4.5	14.4
Net Income	[3] 205.3	[2] 34.2	[1] d146.8	d135.7	1.8	282.4	286.9
Cash Flow	676.5	954.7	401.1	277.6	410.4	597.6	634.2
Average Shs. Outstg. (000)	141,967	131,415	130,550	129,568	127,960	126,084	124,678
BALANCE SHEET (IN MILLIONS):							
Gross Property	10,588.5	9,711.3	10,042.4	10,391.5	10,220.3	10,041.5	9,897.1
Accumulated Depreciation	7,041.3	6,088.3	4,224.4	4,330.6	3,979.9	3,629.6	3,293.7
Net Property	3,547.2	3,947.4	6,170.9	6,463.2	6,732.2	7,000.8	6,603.4
Total Assets	10,217.1	9,688.1	10,387.4	10,414.4	10,741.7	10,559.6	10,584.9
Long-Term Obligations	2,076.8	2,435.2	3,370.6	3,676.1	3,800.5	3,852.6	4,108.0
Net Stockholders' Equity	2,354.8	2,219.5	2,183.6	2,263.4	2,413.3	2,593.3	2,543.8
Year-end Shs. Outstg. (000)	143,820	130,955	130,955	130,183	128,444	127,051	124,963
STATISTICAL RECORD:							
Operating Profit Margin %	7.9	7.7	6.0	4.8	7.2	15.8	15.0
Net Profit Margin %	3.5	0.8	...	...	...	7.5	7.9
Net Inc./Net Property %	5.8	0.9	...	...	...	4.0	4.3
Net Inc./Tot. Capital %	3.3	0.5	...	...	...	3.1	3.2
Return on Equity %	8.7	1.5	...	...	0.1	10.9	11.3
Accum. Depr./Gross Prop. %	66.5	62.7	42.1	41.7	38.9	36.1	33.3
Price Range	24.56-18.00	22.00-13.56	17.25-11.69	14.25-7.63	25.25-9.50	25.38-21.00	25.75-20.38
P/E Ratio	16.9-12.4	84.6-52.1	...	...	...	11.3-9.4	11.2-8.9
Average Yield %	1.9	0.6	...	2.3	7.9	7.6	7.6

Statistics are as originally reported. [1] Incl. $163.2 mill. write-off fr. investment & Argentine power plant and $1.7 mill. gain for Mode 1 shs. [2] Incl. $308.9 mill. gain fr. sale of utility plant. [3] Bef. extraord. chg. of $225.0 mill.; incls. $11.7 mill. one-time chg. for settlement & $10.4 mill. one-time after-tax gain fr. investment.

OFFICERS:
M. G. Morris, Chmn., Pres., C.E.O.
J. H. Forsgren, Exec. V.P., C.F.O.
C. W. Grise, Sr. V.P., Sec., Gen. Couns.

INVESTOR CONTACT: Jeff Kotkin, Inv. Rel., (413) 655-5154

PRINCIPAL OFFICE: 174 Brush Hill Avenue, West Springfield, MA 01090-2010

TELEPHONE NUMBER: (413) 785-5871
FAX: (413) 665-3652
WEB: www.nu.com

NO. OF EMPLOYEES: 9,260 (approx.)

SHAREHOLDERS: 79,709

ANNUAL MEETING: In May

INCORPORATED: MA, Jan., 1927

INSTITUTIONAL HOLDINGS:
No. of Institutions: 167
Shares Held: 89,309,790
% Held: 60.0

INDUSTRY: Electric services (SIC: 4911)

TRANSFER AGENT(S): Northeast Utilities Service Company, Hartford, CT

NYSE SYMBOL NOC
Rec. Pr. 90.25 (4/30/01)

NORTHROP GRUMMAN CORPORATION

YIELD 1.8%
P/E RATIO 10.0

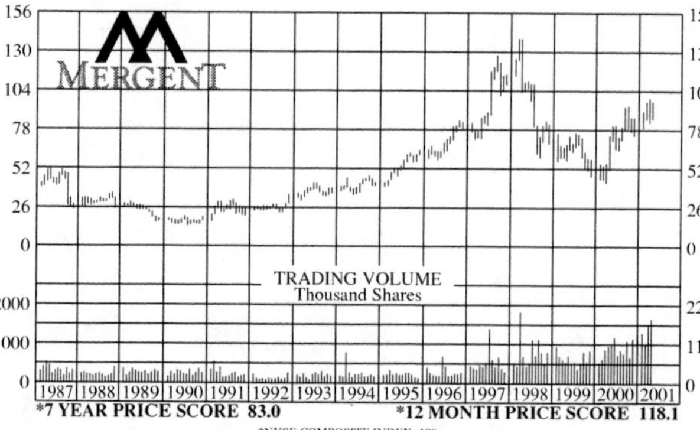

*7 YEAR PRICE SCORE 83.0 *12 MONTH PRICE SCORE 118.1
*NYSE COMPOSITE INDEX=100

INTERIM EARNINGS (Per Share):

Qtr.	Mar.	June	Sept.	Dec.
1997	1.30	1.72	1.46	1.71
1998	d0.18	1.34	1.67	0.24
1999	1.50	1.64	1.83	1.96
2000	2.47	2.50	2.11	1.99

INTERIM DIVIDENDS (Per Share):

Amt.	Decl.	Ex.	Rec.	Pay.
0.40Q	5/17/00	5/25/00	5/30/00	6/10/00
0.40Q	8/16/00	8/24/00	8/28/00	9/09/00
0.40Q	11/15/00	11/22/00	11/27/00	12/09/00
0.40Q	2/21/01	3/01/01	3/05/01	3/17/01
0.40Q	5/16/01	5/24/01	5/29/01	6/09/01

Indicated div.: $1.60 (Div. Reinv. Plan)

CAPITALIZATION (12/31/00):

	($000)	(%)
Long-Term Debt	1,605,000	27.7
Deferred Income Tax	276,000	4.8
Common & Surplus	3,919,000	67.6
Total	5,800,000	100.0

RECENT DEVELOPMENTS: For the year ended 12/31/00, NOC reported income of $625.0 million versus income of $474.0 million, before an accounting charge of $16.0 million, in 1999. Earnings for 2000 and 1999 excluded a net loss of $17.0 million and a net gain of $9.0 million, respectively, from discontinued operations. Total net sales remained relatively flat at $7.62 billion versus 1999. Comparisons were made with restated 1999 results.

PROSPECTS: On 5/30/01, NOC announced that it completed the acquisition of Litton Industries, Inc. in a transaction valued at about $5.10 billion. Under the agreement, NOC will assume Litton's $1.30 billion in debt. As a result, NOC's revenues are expected to double to $15.00 billion in 2001 and to $18.00 billion in 2003. On 5/9/01, the Company offered to acquire Newport News Shipbuilding in a transaction valued at $2.10 billion.

BUSINESS

NORTHROP GRUMMAN CORPORATION (formerly Northrop Corporation) is a technology company operating in three segments: Integrated Systems and Aerostructures, which designs, develops and manufactures aircraft and aircraft subassemblies; Electronic Sensors and Systems, which designs, develops, manufactures and integrates electronic systems and components for military and commercial use; and Logicon, Inc., which provides information technologies, systems and services to the Federal government, commercial customers and other Northrop Grumman sectors. On 5/30/01, NOC acquired Litton Industries, Inc. for $5.10 billion.

BUSINESS LINE ANALYSIS

(12/31/2000)	REV (%)	INC (%)
Integrated Systems	40.5	52.6
Electronic Sensors & Systems	37.5	30.1
Logicon	22.0	17.3
Total	100.0	100.0

ANNUAL FINANCIAL DATA

	12/31/00	12/31/99	12/31/98	12/31/97	12/31/96	12/31/95	12/31/94
Earnings Per Share	**6 8.82**	**2 6.93**	**4 5 2.79**	**5.98**	**4.33**	**5.11**	**1 0.72**
Cash Flow Per Share	**8.82**	**12.58**	**8.45**	**12.35**	**11.13**	**10.83**	**6.18**
Dividends Per Share	**1.60**	**1.60**	**1.60**	**1.60**	**1.60**	**1.60**	**1.60**
Dividend Payout %	**18.1**	**23.1**	**57.6**	**26.8**	**37.0**	**31.3**	**222.2**
INCOME STATEMENT (IN MILLIONS):							
Total Revenues	7,618.0	8,995.0	8,902.0	9,153.0	8,071.0	6,818.0	6,711.0
Costs & Expenses	6,520.0	7,637.0	6,222.0	7,855.0	7,046.0	5,999.0	6,243.0
Depreciation & Amort.	...	389.0	393.0	418.0	367.0	283.0	269.0
Operating Income	1,098.0	969.0	752.0	880.0	658.0	536.0	199.0
Net Interest Inc./(Exp.)	d146.0	d206.0	d221.0	d240.0	d261.0	d136.0	d103.0
Income Before Income Taxes	975.0	762.0	309.0	651.0	384.0	409.0	65.0
Income Taxes	350.0	279.0	116.0	244.0	150.0	157.0	30.0
Net Income	6 625.0	2 483.0	4 5 194.0	407.0	234.0	252.0	1 35.0
Cash Flow	625.0	872.0	586.0	825.0	601.0	535.0	304.0
Average Shs. Outstg. (000)	70,880	69,300	69,510	66,800	54,000	49,400	49,200
BALANCE SHEET (IN MILLIONS):							
Cash & Cash Equivalents	319.0	142.0	44.0	63.0	44.0	18.0	17.0
Total Current Assets	2,526.0	2,793.0	3,033.0	2,936.0	2,597.0	2,072.0	2,431.0
Net Property	1,015.0	1,240.0	1,274.0	1,346.0	1,402.0	1,176.0	1,378.0
Total Assets	9,622.0	9,285.0	9,536.0	9,677.0	9,422.0	5,455.0	6,047.0
Total Current Liabilities	2,688.0	2,464.0	2,367.0	2,715.0	2,600.0	1,715.0	1,964.0
Long-Term Obligations	1,605.0	2,000.0	2,562.0	2,500.0	2,950.0	1,163.0	1,633.0
Net Stockholders' Equity	3,919.0	3,257.0	2,850.0	2,623.0	2,128.0	1,459.0	1,290.0
Net Working Capital	d162.0	329.0	666.0	221.0	d3.0	357.0	467.0
Year-end Shs. Outstg. (000)	72,058	69,719	68,837	67,278	57,928	49,462	49,241
STATISTICAL RECORD:							
Operating Profit Margin %	14.4	10.8	8.5	9.6	8.2	7.9	3.0
Net Profit Margin %	8.2	5.4	2.6	4.4	2.9	3.7	0.5
Return on Equity %	15.9	14.8	6.8	15.5	11.0	17.3	2.7
Return on Assets %	6.5	5.2	2.0	4.2	2.5	4.6	0.6
Debt/Total Assets %	16.7	21.5	26.9	25.8	31.3	21.3	27.0
Price Range	93.88-42.63	75.94-47.00	139.00-59.31	127.88-71.38	84.25-57.75	64.25-39.75	47.38-34.50
P/E Ratio	10.6-4.8	11.0-6.8	50.0-21.3	21.4-11.9	19.5-13.3	12.6-7.8	65.8-47.9
Average Yield %	2.3	2.6	1.6	1.6	2.3	3.1	3.9

Statistics are as originally reported. 1 Incl. $282.0 mill. from special termination benefit. 2 Bef. acctg. chrg. $16.0 mill., 1999. 3 Incl. $87.7 mill. loss from retiree health care & life insurance benefit. 4 Incl. non-recurr. pre-tax chgs. of $186.0 mill. 5 Incl. investment loss of $30.0 mill. 6 Bef. a net loss of $17.0 mill. from disc. opers.

OFFICERS:
K. Kresa, Chmn., Pres., C.E.O.
R. B. Waugh Jr, Corp. V.P., C.F.O.
A. F. Myers, Corp. V.P., Treas.
J. H. Mullan, Corp. V.P., & Sec.

INVESTOR CONTACT: Gaston Kent, Dir., Investor Relations, (310) 201-3423

PRINCIPAL OFFICE: 1840 Century Park East, Los Angeles, CA 90067-2199

TELEPHONE NUMBER: (310) 553-6262
FAX: (310) 553-2076
WEB: www.northgrum.com

NO. OF EMPLOYEES: 80,000 (approx.)

SHAREHOLDERS: 11,750

ANNUAL MEETING: In May

INCORPORATED: CA, May, 1939; reincorp., DE, June, 1985

INSTITUTIONAL HOLDINGS:
No. of Institutions: 304
Shares Held: 60,485,680
% Held: 83.9

INDUSTRY: Search and navigation equipment (SIC: 3812)

TRANSFER AGENT(S): Equiserve, Inc., Jersey City, NJ

NYSE SYMBOL NWN
Rec. Pr. 23.90 (5/31/01)

NORTHWEST NATURAL GAS CO.

YIELD 5.2%
P/E RATIO 12.8

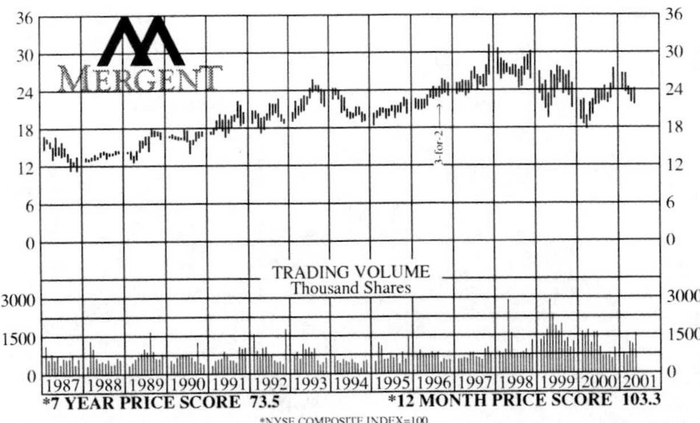

INTERIM EARNINGS (Per Share):

Qtr.	Mar.	June	Sept.	Dec.
1997	1.04	0.07	d0.14	0.76
1998	0.97	0.14	d0.26	0.21
1999	0.93	0.40	d0.17	0.53
2000	1.22	0.07	d0.22	0.80

INTERIM DIVIDENDS (Per Share):

Amt.	Decl.	Ex.	Rec.	Pay.
0.31Q	4/05/00	4/26/00	4/28/00	5/15/00
0.31Q	7/06/00	7/27/00	7/31/00	8/15/00
0.31Q	10/05/00	10/27/00	10/31/00	11/15/00
0.31Q	1/04/01	1/29/01	1/31/01	2/15/01
0.31Q	4/05/01	4/26/01	4/30/01	5/15/01

Indicated div.: $1.24 (Div. Reinv. Plan)

CAPITALIZATION (12/31/00):

	($000)	(%)
Long-Term Debt	400,790	38.9
Deferred Income Tax	141,656	13.8
Redeemable Pfd. Stock	9,750	0.9
Preferred Stock	25,000	2.4
Common & Surplus	452,309	43.9
Total	1,029,505	100.0

RECENT DEVELOPMENTS: For the year ended 12/31/00, income from continued operations was $47.8 million versus income from continued operations of $44.9 million in 1999. Earnings were positively affected by higher margins in all customer segments, aided by customer growth and weather that was 4.0% colder than in 1999 and 5.0% colder than the 20-year average. Gross operating revenues climbed 16.7% to $532.1 million from $455.8 million the year before.

PROSPECTS: Going forward, NWN will look to implement a number of strategic initiatives that should help grow earnings. These include the expansion of NWN's underground strorage facilities to meet the need of its growing customer base and serve customers in the interstate storage market. Separately, NWN submitted an application to the Oregon Energy Facility Siting Council, for a 60-mile underground transmission line that will link NWN's natural gas storage fields near Mist, Oregon to an interstate gas transmission line near Mollala.

BUSINESS

NORTHWEST NATURAL GAS CO. (doing business as NW Natural) is principally engaged in the distribution of natural gas to customers in western Oregon, including the Portland metropolitan area, most of the Willamette Valley and the coastal area from Astoria to Coos Bay. The Company also holds certificates from the Washington Utilities and Transportation Commission (WUTC) granting exclusive rights to serve portions of three Washington counties bordering the Columbia River. Gas service is provided in 96 cities, together with neighboring communities, in 17 Oregon counties, and in nine cities, together with neighboring communities, in three Washington counties. In addition, NWN operates NNG Financial Corporation, which holds financial investments as a limited partner in three solar electric generating plants, four windpower electric generation projects and a hydroelectric project, all located in California, and in two low-income housing projects in Portland. NNG Financial Corporation also holds interests in certain gas producing properties in the western United States. At 12/31/00, NWN had about 468,100 residential customers, 54,700 commercial customers and 600 industrial customers. In January 2000, the Company sold its interest in Canor Energy Ltd.

ANNUAL FINANCIAL DATA

	12/31/00	12/31/99	12/31/98	12/31/97	12/31/96	12/31/95	12/31/94
Earnings Per Share	**1 1.79**	**1 1.69**	**1.02**	**1.76**	**1.97**	**1.61**	**1.63**
Cash Flow Per Share	**3.68**	**3.67**	**3.25**	**3.66**	**3.89**	**3.47**	**3.54**
Tang. Book Val. Per Share	**17.92**	**17.12**	**16.59**	**16.02**	**15.37**	**14.55**	**13.63**
Dividends Per Share	**1.24**	**1.23**	**1.22**	**1.21**	**1.20**	**1.18**	**1.17**
Dividend Payout %	**69.3**	**72.5**	**119.6**	**68.5**	**60.9**	**73.2**	**72.1**
INCOME STATEMENT (IN MILLIONS):							
Total Revenues	532.1	455.8	416.7	361.8	380.3	356.3	368.3
Costs & Expenses	380.3	310.1	281.2	227.1	244.6	240.3	257.9
Depreciation & Amort.	47.4	51.0	55.8	44.6	43.0	40.6	38.1
Operating Income	104.3	94.8	79.6	90.0	92.7	75.4	72.3
Net Interest Inc./(Exp.)	d33.6	d30.1	d31.8	d28.5	d26.7	d25.7	d24.9
Income Taxes	26.8	24.6	12.3	21.1	27.3	22.1	20.5
Net Income	1 47.8	1 44.9	27.3	43.1	46.8	38.1	35.5
Cash Flow	92.8	93.4	80.5	85.0	87.1	75.9	70.5
Average Shs. Outstg. (000)	25,183	25,468	24,763	23,248	22,391	21,831	19,943
BALANCE SHEET (IN MILLIONS):							
Gross Property	1,407.0	1,331.4	1,239.7	1,164.5	1,055.1	969.1	908.2
Accumulated Depreciation	478.1	436.4	404.1	366.6	336.1	308.7	279.1
Net Property	928.8	895.0	835.6	797.9	719.0	660.4	629.1
Total Assets	1,278.7	1,244.4	1,191.7	1,111.6	988.9	929.3	889.3
Long-Term Obligations	400.8	396.4	366.7	344.3	271.8	279.9	291.1
Net Stockholders' Equity	477.3	454.6	437.4	391.3	371.8	348.6	300.7
Year-end Shs. Outstg. (000)	25,233	25,092	24,853	22,864	22,555	22,244	20,129
STATISTICAL RECORD:							
Operating Profit Margin %	19.6	20.8	19.1	24.9	24.4	21.2	19.6
Net Profit Margin %	9.0	9.9	6.6	11.9	12.3	10.7	9.6
Net Inc./Net Property %	5.1	5.0	3.3	5.4	6.5	5.8	5.6
Net Inc./Tot. Capital %	4.6	4.5	2.8	4.8	6.0	5.0	4.9
Return on Equity %	10.0	9.9	6.2	11.0	12.6	10.9	11.8
Accum. Depr./Gross Prop. %	34.0	32.8	32.6	31.5	31.9	31.9	30.7
Price Range	27.50-17.75	27.88-19.50	30.75-24.25	31.25-23.00	25.88-20.83	22.83-18.33	24.33-18.83
P/E Ratio	15.4-9.9	16.5-11.5	30.1-23.8	17.8-13.1	13.1-10.6	14.2-11.4	15.0-11.6
Average Yield %	5.5	5.2	4.4	4.4	5.1	5.7	5.4

Statistics are as originally reported. Adj. for stk. split: 3-for-2, 9/6/96 1 Bef. inc. from disc. opers. $2.4 mill., 2000; $355,000, 1999.

OFFICERS:
R. G. Reiten, Chmn., Pres., C.E.O.
B. R. DeBolt, Sr. V.P., C.F.O.
S. P. Feltz, Treas., Contr.

INVESTOR CONTACT: James R. Boehlke, (800) 422-4012-2451

PRINCIPAL OFFICE: 220 N.W. Second Avenue, Portland, OR 97209

TELEPHONE NUMBER: (503) 226-4211
FAX: (503) 273-4824
WEB: www.nwnatural.com

NO. OF EMPLOYEES: 1,315

SHAREHOLDERS: 10,850

ANNUAL MEETING: In May

INCORPORATED: OR, Jan., 1910

INSTITUTIONAL HOLDINGS:
No. of Institutions: 120
Shares Held: 9,070,598
% Held: 36.2

INDUSTRY: Natural gas distribution (SIC: 4924)

TRANSFER AGENT(S): The Company

NYSE SYMBOL NOR
Rec. Pr. 22.25 (5/31/01)

NORTHWESTERN CORPORATION

YIELD 5.3%
P/E RATIO 12.2

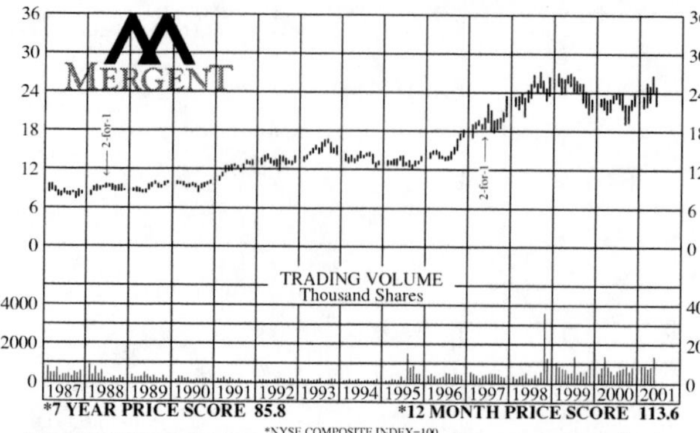

***7 YEAR PRICE SCORE 85.8** ***12 MONTH PRICE SCORE 113.6**

*NYSE COMPOSITE INDEX=100

INTERIM EARNINGS (Per Share):

Qtr.	Mar.	June	Sept.	Dec.
1997	0.55	0.14	0.17	0.45
1998	0.58	0.15	0.20	0.48
1999	0.56	0.22	0.31	0.53
2000	0.62	0.26	0.35	0.60

INTERIM DIVIDENDS (Per Share):

Amt.	Decl.	Ex.	Rec.	Pay.
0.278Q	5/03/00	5/11/00	5/15/00	6/01/00
0.278Q	8/02/00	8/11/00	8/15/00	9/01/00
0.297Q	11/01/00	11/13/00	11/15/00	12/01/00
0.297Q	2/07/01	2/13/01	2/15/01	3/01/01
0.297Q	5/03/01	5/11/01	5/15/01	6/01/01

Indicated div.: $1.19 (Div. Reinv. Plan)

CAPITALIZATION (12/31/00):

	($000)	(%)
Long-Term Debt	1,591,215	64.8
Deferred Income Tax	55,549	2.3
Minority Interest	398,004	16.2
Redeemable Pfd. Stock	89,800	3.7
Common & Surplus	319,201	13.0
Total	2,453,769	100.0

RECENT DEVELOPMENTS: For the year ended 12/31/00, income rose 13.3% to $50.6 million, before an accounting charge, from net income of $44.7 million in 1999. Operating revenues were $7.13 billion versus $3.00 billion the year before. Propane revenues more than doubled to $5.42 billion, reflecting higher wholesale commodity revenues. Communications revenues more than tripled to $1.10 billion, reflecting the purchase of Lucent Technologies' Growing and Emerging Markets business on 4/1/00.

PROSPECTS: On 2/23/01, NOR and the Montana Power Company/Touch America received the approval of the Federal Energy Regulatory Commission to sell Montana Power's utility operations to the Company. Looking ahead, NOR remains on track to achieve double-digit earnings growth by focusing on operational improvements in its energy segments and aggressive growth opportunities in its communications businesses.

BUSINESS

NORTHWESTERN CORPORATION (formerly Northwestern Public Service Company) provides energy and communications services to more than 2.0 million residential and business customers nationwide. The Company's partner entities include Expanets, Inc., a provider of integrated communication and data services to small and medium-sized businesses, with operations in 213 locations in 50 states; NorthWestern Public Service, a provider of electric, natural gas and communications services to approximately 140,000 customers in the upper Midwest; Blue Dot Services, Inc. a provider of air conditioning, heating, plumbing and related services; and CornerStone Propane Partner L.P., a publicly-held retail propane distributor for more than 480,000 residential, commercial, industrial and agricultural customers in 34 states. NorthWestern Growth Corporation, a wholly-owned subsidiary of the Company, is the development and investment capital arm of NOR.

ANNUAL FINANCIAL DATA

	12/31/00	12/31/99	12/31/98	12/31/97	12/31/96	12/31/95	12/31/94
Earnings Per Share	**2 1.87**	**1.62**	**1.44**	**1.31**	**1 1.28**	**1.11**	**1.00**
Cash Flow Per Share	**6.52**	**4.60**	**3.70**	**3.06**	**2.37**	**2.01**	**1.81**
Tang. Book Val. Per Share	...	...	...	...	...	**5.81**	**7.27**
Dividends Per Share	**1.13**	**1.05**	**0.98**	**0.93**	**0.89**	**0.86**	**0.83**
Dividend Payout %	**60.4**	**64.8**	**68.4**	**71.2**	**69.5**	**77.2**	**83.5**
INCOME STATEMENT (IN MILLIONS):							
Total Revenues	7,132.1	3,004.3	1,187.2	918.1	344.0	205.0	157.3
Costs & Expenses	6,982.5	2,856.5	1,070.6	827.8	274.2	146.2	108.3
Depreciation & Amort.	108.3	68.3	42.6	31.2	19.4	14.6	12.4
Maintenance Exp.	...	...	...	...	...	6.0	6.2
Operating Income	41.3	79.6	73.9	59.0	50.4	38.1	30.4
Net Interest Inc./(Exp.)	d77.2	d53.2	d35.7	d31.5	d18.7	d11.7	d9.7
Income Taxes	cr4.1	14.5	13.2	11.1	15.4	10.1	7.9
Equity Earnings/Minority Int.	73.4	22.9	d0.8	d1.7	...	...	...
Net Income	2 50.6	44.7	30.4	26.3	1 26.1	19.3	15.4
Cash Flow	152.1	106.2	69.7	54.6	42.3	32.6	27.8
Average Shs. Outstg. (000)	23,338	23,094	18,816	17,843	17,840	16,261	15,354
BALANCE SHEET (IN MILLIONS):							
Gross Property	980.1	918.1	825.9	720.9	682.0	487.4	389.9
Accumulated Depreciation	284.1	236.4	196.6	175.3	162.9	150.5	139.4
Net Property	696.0	681.7	629.3	545.6	519.1	336.9	250.5
Total Assets	2,898.1	1,956.8	1,736.2	1,106.1	1,113.7	558.7	359.1
Long-Term Obligations	1,591.2	783.1	588.9	850.6	424.4	212.8	127.1
Net Stockholders' Equity	319.2	300.2	282.1	166.6	163.8	152.7	114.7
Year-end Shs. Outstg. (000)	23,411	23,109	23,017	17,843	17,840	17,840	15,334
STATISTICAL RECORD:							
Operating Profit Margin %	0.6	2.6	6.2	6.4	14.7	18.6	19.3
Net Profit Margin %	0.7	1.5	2.6	2.9	7.6	9.4	9.8
Net Inc./Net Property %	7.3	6.6	4.8	4.8	5.0	5.7	6.2
Net Inc./Tot. Capital %	2.1	2.8	2.1	2.0	3.0	4.3	5.5
Return on Equity %	15.9	14.9	10.8	15.8	15.9	12.6	13.5
Accum. Depr./Gross Prop. %	29.0	25.8	23.8	24.3	23.9	30.9	35.7
Price Range	23.94-19.13	27.13-20.63	27.38-20.25	23.50-16.94	18.25-13.38	14.19-12.13	14.81-12.25
P/E Ratio	12.8-10.2	16.7-12.7	19.0-14.1	17.9-12.9	14.3-10.4	12.8-10.9	14.8-12.2
Average Yield %	5.2	4.4	4.1	4.6	5.6	6.5	6.2

Statistics are as originally reported. Adj. for 2-for-1 stock split, 5/97. 1 Incl. a non-recurr., one-time gain of $0.09 a share. 2 Excl. acctg. chrg. of $1.0 mill. ($0.04/sh.)

OFFICERS:
M. D. Lewis, Chmn., C.E.O.
R. R. Hylland, Pres., C.O.O.
K. D. Orme, V.P., C.F.O.

INVESTOR CONTACT: Investor Relations, (605) 978-2904

PRINCIPAL OFFICE: 125 South Dakota Ave., Sioux Falls, SD 57104

TELEPHONE NUMBER: (605) 978-2908
FAX: (605) 353-7631
WEB: www.northwestern.com

NO. OF EMPLOYEES: 11,000

SHAREHOLDERS: 10,475

ANNUAL MEETING: In May

INCORPORATED: DE, Nov., 1923

INSTITUTIONAL HOLDINGS:
No. of Institutions: 107
Shares Held: 8,667,281
% Held: 36.9

INDUSTRY: Electric and other services combined (SIC: 4931)

TRANSFER AGENT(S): Wells Fargo Shareowner Services, South St. Paul, MN

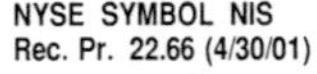

NYSE SYMBOL NIS
Rec. Pr. 22.66 (4/30/01)

NOVA CORPORATION

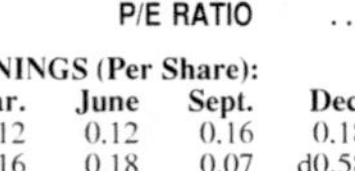

YIELD	...
P/E RATIO	...

***7 YEAR PRICE SCORE N/A** ***12 MONTH PRICE SCORE 106.2**

*NYSE COMPOSITE INDEX=100

INTERIM EARNINGS (Per Share):

Qtr.	Mar.	June	Sept.	Dec.
1997	0.12	0.12	0.16	0.18
1998	0.16	0.18	0.07	d0.58
1999	0.19	0.28	0.33	0.35
2000	0.27	d0.99	0.34	0.23

INTERIM DIVIDENDS (Per Share):

Amt.	Decl.	Ex.	Rec.	Pay.

No dividends paid.

CAPITALIZATION (12/31/00):

	($000)	(%)
Long-Term Debt	246,556	41.7
Minority Interest	8,793	1.5
Common & Surplus	335,651	56.8
Total	591,000	100.0

RECENT DEVELOPMENTS: For the year ended 12/31/00, the Company reported a loss from continuing operations of $15.4 million compared with net income of $82.5 million in 1999. Results for 2000 included a restructuring charge of $10.6 million, an asset impairment charge of $84.6 million, and excluded a net loss of $11.0 million from the discontinued operations of Econex, LLC. Revenues were $1.58 billion, up 7.6% from $1.47 billion in the prior year.

PROSPECTS: On 5/7/01, U.S. Bancorp and the Company signed a definitive agreement for U.S. Bancorp to acquire NIS in a cash and stock transaction valued at about $2.10 billion. The combined companies will have more than $100.00 billion in payment processing volume in 2001 and become the third largest merchant payment processor in the U.S. The acquisition is subject to approval by NIS shareholders and is expected to close in the third quarter of 2001.

BUSINESS

NOVA CORPORATION, through its subsidiaries, NOVA Information Systems, Inc. and PMT Services, provides integrated credit and debit card payment and information processing services, related software application products and value-added services. The Company targets small to medium-sized merchants that require a full range of processing services, as well as community banks and financial institutions that provide their merchants with payment processing. The Company is currently the fourth largest bankcard processor in the U.S. and provides transaction processing services to more than 500,000 merchant locations. The Company supports transaction processing for all major credit cards and provides access to debit card processing and check verification services.

ANNUAL FINANCIAL DATA

	12/31/00	12/31/99	12/31/98	12/31/97	12/31/96	12/31/95	2/28/95
Earnings Per Share	**[2] d0.39**	**[1] 1.14**	**[1] d0.18**	**0.58**	**0.25**	**0.24**	**d0.13**
Cash Flow Per Share	**0.78**	**1.93**	**0.46**	**0.93**	**0.62**	**0.53**	**0.20**
Tang. Book Val. Per Share	**4.91**	**5.52**	**5.88**	**3.10**	**2.49**	...	...
INCOME STATEMENT (IN MILLIONS):							
Total Revenues	1,578.4	1,466.6	1,145.7	335.6	265.8	129.0	93.6
Costs & Expenses	1,487.7	1,257.0	1,106.5	296.6	246.9	121.6	90.0
Depreciation & Amort.	68.3	57.3	44.8	10.7	7.0	4.6	3.9
Operating Income	22.4	152.3	d5.6	28.4	11.9	2.8	d0.2
Net Interest Inc./(Exp.)	d16.4	d4.1	0.6	0.7	0.1	d2.0	d1.0
Income Before Income Taxes	d12.2	131.7	d15.1	28.3	12.0	0.8	d1.2
Income Taxes	3.2	49.2	cr2.4	10.9	4.8	cr4.1	...
Equity Earnings/Minority Int.	d18.2	d16.5	d10.1	d0.8	...	...	...
Net Income	[2] d15.4	[1] 82.5	[1] d12.8	17.4	7.3	4.9	d1.2
Cash Flow	52.9	139.8	32.1	28.0	2.6	9.5	2.7
Average Shs. Outstg. (000)	67,961	72,561	70,061	30,116	22,811	18,024	13,603
BALANCE SHEET (IN MILLIONS):							
Cash & Cash Equivalents	46.8	32.6	51.1	0.7	40.3	0.6	1.0
Total Current Assets	198.7	225.5	211.1	42.6	60.5	12.7	7.4
Net Property	88.0	77.0	65.7	21.0	10.2	7.4	4.7
Total Assets	678.4	734.0	622.5	170.5	107.7	58.1	47.8
Total Current Liabilities	87.4	84.3	149.5	30.4	21.1	14.4	12.4
Long-Term Obligations	246.6	238.3	24.1	33.3	0.9	17.7	16.7
Net Stockholders' Equity	335.7	390.9	441.2	102.9	84.9	26.0	18.7
Net Working Capital	111.2	141.2	61.7	12.2	39.4	d1.7	d5.0
Year-end Shs. Outstg. (000)	65,208	68,279	72,597	29,031	28,721	11,378	1,671
STATISTICAL RECORD:							
Operating Profit Margin %	1.4	10.4	...	8.5	4.5	2.2	...
Net Profit Margin %	...	5.6	...	5.2	2.7	3.8	...
Return on Equity %	...	21.1	...	16.9	8.6	18.8	...
Return on Assets %	...	11.2	...	10.2	6.7	8.4	...
Debt/Total Assets %	36.3	32.5	3.9	19.5	0.8	30.5	34.9
Price Range	35.19-10.50	34.94-17.88	37.88-22.00	30.81-12.88	39.88-18.00	...	...
P/E Ratio	...	30.6-15.7	...	53.1-22.2	159.4-72.0	...	...

Statistics are as originally reported. [1] Incl. $180,000 pre-tax merger chgs., 1999; $90.7 mill., 1998. [2] Incl. $10.6 restr. chg., $84.6 mill. asset impairment chg. & excl. $11.0 mill. net loss fr. disc. ops.

OFFICERS:
E. Grzedzinski, Chmn., Pres., C.E.O.
G. S. Daily, Vice-Chmn.
S. M. Scheppmann, Exec. V.P., C.F.O.

INVESTOR CONTACT: Brenda Boswell, IR Coordinator, (770) 698-1052

PRINCIPAL OFFICE: One Concourse Parkway, Suite 300, Atlanta, GA 30328

TELEPHONE NUMBER: (770) 396-1456
FAX: (770) 396-2117
WEB: www.novacorp.net

NO. OF EMPLOYEES: 1,400 (approx.)

SHAREHOLDERS: 140 (approx., record)

ANNUAL MEETING: In May

INCORPORATED: GA, Dec., 1995

INSTITUTIONAL HOLDINGS:
No. of Institutions: 151
Shares Held: 57,758,226
% Held: 88.4

INDUSTRY: Business services, nec (SIC: 7389)

TRANSFER AGENT(S): First Union National Bank of North Carolina, Charlotte, NC

NYSE SYMBOL NRG
Rec. Pr. 35.75 (4/30/01)

NRG ENERGY INC.

YIELD ...
P/E RATIO 33.7

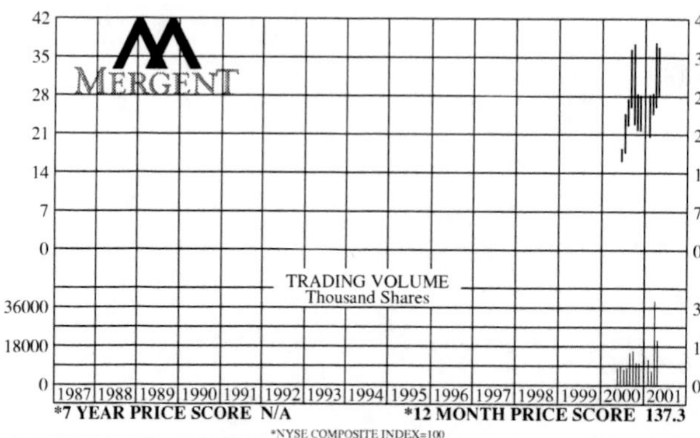

INTERIM EARNINGS (Per Share):

Qtr.	Mar.	June	Sept.	Dec.
2000	0.06	0.28	0.49	0.23

INTERIM DIVIDENDS (Per Share):

Amt.	Decl.	Ex.	Rec.	Pay.

No dividends paid.

CAPITALIZATION (12/31/00):

	($000)	(%)
Long-Term Debt	3,650,849	70.4
Deferred Income Tax	55,642	1.1
Minority Interest	14,685	0.3
Common & Surplus	1,462,088	28.2
Total	5,183,264	100.0

RECENT DEVELOPMENTS: For the year ended 12/31/00, net income more than tripled to $182.9 million compared with $57.2 million in the prior year. Results for 1999 included gain on sale of interests in projects of $11.0 million. Total operating revenues more than quadrupled to $2.16 billion versus $500.0 million in the previous year, reflecting the Company's successful execution of core business strategies and a well-positioned business platform. Operating income was $573.4 million versus $109.5 million in 1999.

PROSPECTS: The Company will continue to focus on expanding its business through a combination of acquisitions and the development of power generation facilities and related assets in the United States and abroad. For 2001, the Company expects to close six acquisitions with an aggregate capacity of 5,704 megawatts. Also, the Company will begin construction on three projects, two in Texas and one in Connecticut, with aggregate capacity of 1,395 megawatts.

BUSINESS

NRG ENERGY, INC. is a major global energy company focused on the acquisition, development, construction, ownership and operation of power generation facilities. NRG's portfolio of projects is primarily located in the U.S., Europe, the Asia-Pacific region and Latin America. As of 12/31/00, the Company owned all or a portion of 63 power generation projects and its net ownership interest in these projects was 15,007 megawatts. The Company's operating project portfolio will total approximately 30,000 megawatts once projects under construction are in operation and those in advanced development, construction and under acquisition agreements have closed. NRG's operations utilize such diverse fuel sources as natural gas, coal and coal steam methane, biomass, landfill gas, hydro and refuse-derived fuel. Formerly a subsidiary of Northern States Power Co., NRG went public in June 2000.

ANNUAL FINANCIAL DATA

	3 12/31/00	12/31/99	12/31/98	12/31/97
Earnings Per Share	**1.10**	**1 0.39**	**1 2 0.28**	**1 2 0.15**
Cash Flow Per Share	**1.83**	**0.64**	**0.39**	**0.22**
Tang. Book Val. Per Share	**7.78**	**5.68**	**3.77**	**...**
INCOME STATEMENT (IN MILLIONS):				
Total Revenues	2,158.0	500.0	182.1	118.3
Costs & Expenses	1,462.0	353.5	108.8	89.8
Depreciation & Amort.	123.0	37.0	16.3	10.3
Operating Income	573.1	109.5	57.0	18.1
Net Interest Inc./(Exp.)	d293.9	d93.4	d50.3	d31.0
Income Taxes	92.7	cr26.1	cr25.7	cr23.5
Net Income	182.9	1 57.2	1 2 41.7	1 2 22.0
Cash Flow	305.9	94.2	58.1	32.3
Average Shs. Outstg. (000)	166,989	147,605	147,605	147,605
BALANCE SHEET (IN MILLIONS):				
Gross Property	4,313.6	2,132.3	296.9	...
Accumulated Depreciation	272.0	156.8	92.2	...
Net Property	4,041.7	1,975.4	204.7	...
Total Assets	5,979.0	3,431.7	1,293.4	...
Long-Term Obligations	3,650.8	1,941.4	618.2	...
Net Stockholders' Equity	1,462.1	893.7	579.3	...
Year-end Shs. Outstg. (000)	180,001	147,605	147,605	147,605
STATISTICAL RECORD:				
Operating Profit Margin %	26.6	21.9	31.3	15.3
Net Profit Margin %	8.5	11.4	22.9	18.6
Net Inc./Net Property %	4.5	2.9	20.4	...
Net Inc./Tot. Capital %	3.5	2.0	3.4	...
Return on Equity %	12.5	6.4	7.2	...
Accum. Depr./Gross Prop. %	6.3	7.4	31.0	...
Price Range	37.50-16.06	...	...	...
P/E Ratio	34.1-14.6	...	...	...

Statistics are as originally reported. 1 Incl. gain on sale of interest in projects, 1999, $11.0 mill.; 1998, $30.0 mill.; 1997, $8.7 mill. 2 Incl. chrg. for write-off of project invest., 1998, $26.7 mill.; 1997, $9.0 mill. 3 Revenue growth reflects multiple acquisitions of power generation operating projects and facilities.

OFFICERS:
D. H. Peterson, Chmn., Pres., C.E.O.
L. A. Bluhm, Exec. V.P., C.F.O.
B. B. Bird, V.P., Treas.

INVESTOR CONTACT: R. Huckle, Inv. Rel., (612) 373-8900

PRINCIPAL OFFICE: 1221 Nicollet Mall, Suite 700, Minneapolis, MN 55403

TELEPHONE NUMBER: (612) 373-5300
FAX: (612) 373-5312
WEB: www.nrgenergy.com

NO. OF EMPLOYEES: 2,934 (approx.)

SHAREHOLDERS: 98 (approx. common, record); 1 (class A common)

ANNUAL MEETING: In June

INCORPORATED: DE, May, 1992

INSTITUTIONAL HOLDINGS:
No. of Institutions: 156
Shares Held: 37,565,344
% Held: 18.9

INDUSTRY: Electric services (SIC: 4911)

TRANSFER AGENT(S): Wells Fargo Shareowner Services, Minneapolis, MN

NYSE SYMBOL NST
Rec. Pr. 40.32 (4/30/01)

NSTAR

YIELD 5.1%
P/E RATIO 12.6

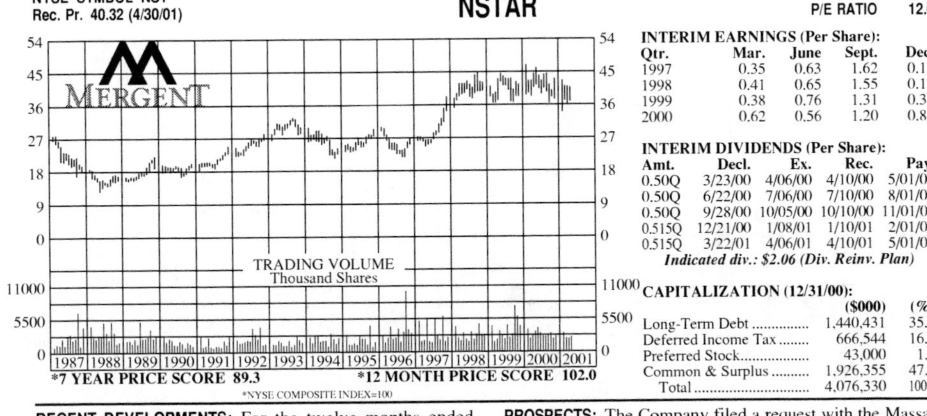

*7 YEAR PRICE SCORE 89.3 *12 MONTH PRICE SCORE 102.0
*NYSE COMPOSITE INDEX=100

INTERIM EARNINGS (Per Share):

Qtr.	Mar.	June	Sept.	Dec.
1997	0.35	0.63	1.62	0.11
1998	0.41	0.65	1.55	0.15
1999	0.38	0.76	1.31	0.35
2000	0.62	0.56	1.20	0.81

INTERIM DIVIDENDS (Per Share):

Amt.	Decl.	Ex.	Rec.	Pay.
0.50Q	3/23/00	4/06/00	4/10/00	5/01/00
0.50Q	6/22/00	7/06/00	7/10/00	8/01/00
0.50Q	9/28/00	10/05/00	10/10/00	11/01/00
0.515Q	12/21/00	1/08/01	1/10/01	2/01/01
0.515Q	3/22/01	4/06/01	4/10/01	5/01/01

Indicated div.: $2.06 (Div. Reinv. Plan)

CAPITALIZATION (12/31/00):

	($000)	(%)
Long-Term Debt	1,440,431	35.3
Deferred Income Tax	666,544	16.4
Preferred Stock	43,000	1.1
Common & Surplus	1,926,355	47.3
Total	4,076,330	100.0

RECENT DEVELOPMENTS: For the twelve months ended 12/31/00, net income rose 23.6% to $181.0 million compared with $146.5 million in 1999. Total operating revenues jumped 45.8% to $2.70 billion from $1.85 billion in the prior year. Results for 2000 reflected the merger of BEC Energy and Commonwealth Energy System, while 1999 results reflect four months of NST and eight months of BEC Energy.

PROSPECTS: The Company filed a request with the Massachusetts Department of Telecommunications and Energy to decrease its cost of gas adjustment that it charges its customers from the current $1.11 per therm to $0.94 per term, a reduction of 18.0%. The decrease reflects lower projected prices on the New York Mercantile Exchange, which would reduce the Company's cost of gas by about $20.0 million.

BUSINESS

NSTAR was formed through the merger of BEC Energy and Commonwealth Energy System on August 25, 1999. The Company provides regulated electric and gas utility services to about 1.2 million customers, including 1.0 million electric customers in 81 communities and 250,000 gas customers in 51 communities throughout Massachusetts. The Company's utility subsidiaries include Boston Edison, Cambridge Electric Light Company, Commonwealth Electric Company, and Commonwealth Gas Company. NSTAR's non-utility operations include telecommunications, district heating and cooling operations, liquefied natural gas services and five real estate trusts.

ANNUAL FINANCIAL DATA

	12/31/00	12/31/99	1 12/31/98	12/31/97
Earnings Per Share	**3.18**	**2.76**	**2.75**	**2.71**
Cash Flow Per Share	**7.28**	**6.94**	**7.52**	**7.31**
Tang. Book Val. Per Share	**27.35**	**29.35**	**22.29**	...
Dividends Per Share	**2.00**	**0.48**	...	...
Dividend Payout %	**62.9**	**17.6**	...	...
INCOME STATEMENT (IN MILLIONS):				
Total Revenues	2,699.5	1,851.4	1,622.5	1,778.5
Costs & Expenses	1,669.7	1,021.1	767.5	875.0
Depreciation & Amort.	225.5	212.9	229.7	223.5
Maintenance Exp.	414.3	353.8	382.4	423.0
Operating Income	390.1	263.7	242.9	256.9
Net Interest Inc./(Exp.)	d205.4	d126.2	d90.1	d105.9
Net Income	181.0	146.5	141.0	144.6
Cash Flow	400.5	353.4	361.9	355.0
Average Shs. Outstg. (000)	55,045	50,921	48,149	48,562
BALANCE SHEET (IN MILLIONS):				
Gross Property	3,773.3	3,854.5	2,761.6	...
Accumulated Depreciation	1,249.7	1,303.9	926.0	...
Net Property	2,629.4	2,665.9	1,857.2	...
Total Assets	5,569.5	5,482.9	3,204.0	...
Long-Term Obligations	1,440.4	986.8	955.6	...
Net Stockholders' Equity	1,969.4	2,282.5	1,143.9	...
Year-end Shs. Outstg. (000)	53,033	58,060	47,184	...
STATISTICAL RECORD:				
Operating Profit Margin %	14.4	14.2	15.0	14.4
Net Profit Margin %	6.7	7.9	8.7	8.1
Net Inc./Net Property %	6.9	5.5	7.6	...
Net Inc./Tot. Capital %	4.4	3.8	5.8	...
Return on Equity %	9.2	6.4	12.3	...
Accum. Depr./Gross Prop. %	33.1	33.8	33.5	...
Price Range	47.00-36.38	44.63-36.44	44.94-35.06	38.38-24.63
P/E Ratio	14.8-11.4	16.2-13.2	16.3-12.7	14.2-9.1
Average Yield %	4.8	1.2	...	...

Statistics are as originally reported. 1 Results for 12/98 and earlier are for BEC Energy prior to the merger with Commonwealth Energy System.

OFFICERS:
T. J. May, Chmn., C.E.O.
R. D. Wright, Pres. C.O.O.
J. J. Judge, Sr. V.P., C.F.O., Treas.

INVESTOR CONTACT: Philip Lembo, Director, Investor Relations, (617) 424-3562

PRINCIPAL OFFICE: 800 Boylston Street, Boston, MA 02199

TELEPHONE NUMBER: (617) 424-2000
FAX: (617) 424-2929
WEB: www.nstaronline.com

NO. OF EMPLOYEES: 3,300 (approx.)

SHAREHOLDERS: 32,635

ANNUAL MEETING: In May

INCORPORATED: MA, Jan., 1886; MA, Aug., 1999

INSTITUTIONAL HOLDINGS:
No. of Institutions: 178
Shares Held: 18,995,738
% Held: 35.8

INDUSTRY: Electric services (SIC: 4911)

TRANSFER AGENT(S): Boston EquiServe, Boston, MA

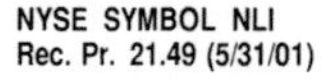

NYSE SYMBOL NLI
Rec. Pr. 21.49 (5/31/01)

NTL INC.

YIELD ...
P/E RATIO ...

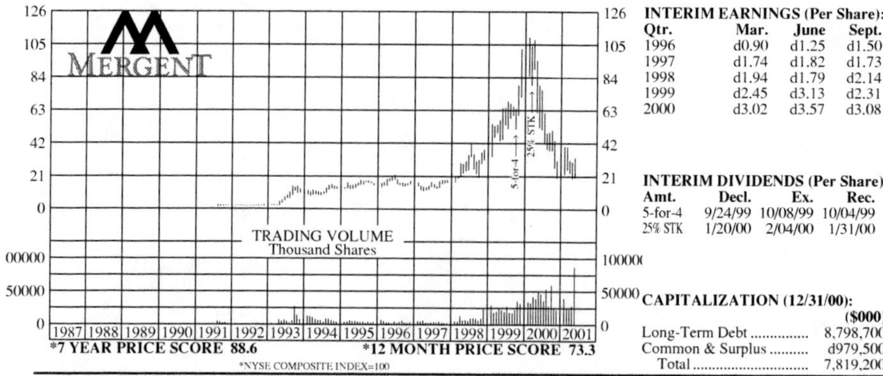

INTERIM EARNINGS (Per Share):

Qtr.	Mar.	June	Sept.	Dec.
1996	d0.90	d1.25	d1.50	d1.59
1997	d1.74	d1.82	d1.73	d1.49
1998	d1.94	d1.79	d2.14	d2.26
1999	d2.45	d3.13	d2.31	0.62
2000	d3.02	d3.57	d3.08	d4.57

INTERIM DIVIDENDS (Per Share):

Amt.	Decl.	Ex.	Rec.	Pay.
5-for-4	9/24/99	10/08/99	10/04/99	10/07/99
25% STK	1/20/00	2/04/00	1/31/00	2/03/00

CAPITALIZATION (12/31/00):

	($000)	(%)
Long-Term Debt	8,798,700	112.5
Common & Surplus	d979,500	-12.5
Total	7,819,200	100.0

RECENT DEVELOPMENTS: For the year ended 12/31/00, the Company incurred a net loss of $2.96 billion compared with a loss of $732.7 million, before an extraordinary loss of $3.0 million, in the previous year. Earnings for 2000 included a foreign currency translation loss of $120.6 million, while earnings for 1999 included foreign currency gains of $12.7 million and a gain of $493.1 million from the sale of Cable London. Total revenues climbed 79.3% to $2.84 billion from $1.58 billion a year earlier.

PROSPECTS: On 5/14/01, the Company signed an agreement with Orange SA, which has about 28.0% of the UK mobile market. Under the agreement, NTL will be able to add mobile phone services to its 3.0 million customers. Meanwhile, on 5/24/01, NLI signed a strategic information-technology (IT) outsourcing contract with IBM Corporation. Under the agreement, IBM will provide IT services for all of NLI's operations in the UK and Ireland until 2012. The contract is projected to generate cash savings for NLI in excess of $450.0 million.

BUSINESS

NTL INC. provides broadband communications and broadband services in the United Kingdom and the Republic of Ireland. The Company also provides telecommunications services in Switzerland, France and Australia and have made strategic investments in broadband cable operations in Germany and Sweden. NTL's predominant lines of business are: Consumer Services, which includes residential telephony, cable television, Internet access and interactive services, Business Services, which includes business telephony, national and international carrier telecommunications, Internet services and radio communications services; and Broadcast Transmission and Tower Services, which includes digital and analog television and radio broadcasting, wireless network management, tower and site leasing and satellite distribution services.

ANNUAL FINANCIAL DATA

	12/31/00	12/31/99	12/31/98	12/31/97	12/31/96	12/31/95	12/31/94
Earnings Per Share	**d14.24**	**3 d7.27**	**1 2 d8.12**	**1 2 d6.78**	**d5.25**	**d1.93**	**d0.63**
Cash Flow Per Share	**d3.87**	**0.49**	**d0.06**	**d1.07**	**d1.00**	**d0.60**	**0.12**
Tang. Book Val. Per Share	...	...	...	...	...	**4.27**	**8.32**
INCOME STATEMENT (IN MILLIONS):							
Total Revenues	2,840.8	1,584.1	747.0	491.8	228.3	33.7	13.7
Costs & Expenses	2,636.9	1,435.3	475.4	408.8	180.2	64.4	18.3
Depreciation & Amort.	2,122.8	791.3	500.2	275.0	205.8	62.5	35.3
Operating Income	d1,918.9	d642.5	d228.6	d192.1	d157.6	d93.1	d39.9
Net Interest Inc./(Exp.)	d1,035.2	d631.3	d328.8	d202.6	d137.0	d28.4	d11.4
Income Before Income Taxes	d3,074.7	d768.0	d507.3	d344.1	d258.6	d100.2	d30.8
Income Taxes	cr111.0	cr35.3	cr3.3	cr15.6	7.7	cr2.5	1.6
Equity Earnings/Minority Int.	...	...	...	...	11.8	7.0	2.9
Net Income	d2,963.7	1 3 d732.7	1 2 d503.9	1 2 d328.6	d254.5	d90.8	d29.6
Cash Flow	d840.9	58.6	d3.7	d53.6	d48.6	d28.3	5.7
Average Shs. Outstg. (000)	217,081	119,418	64,378	50,183	48,502	47,172	47,148
BALANCE SHEET (IN MILLIONS):							
Cash & Cash Equivalents	474.2	1,075.1	996.9	103.9	445.9	175.3	294.6
Total Current Assets	5,532.8	1,391.6	1,204.5	237.2	541.0	205.1	311.6
Net Property	7,762.0	5,597.6	3,854.4	1,757.0	1,459.5	639.7	191.7
Total Assets	18,584.7	9,502.3	6,194.1	2,421.6	2,454.6	1,010.7	664.4
Total Current Liabilities	1,884.6	950.6	604.0	289.5	298.9	129.0	60.0
Long-Term Obligations	15,044.1	8,798.0	5,043.8	2,015.1	1,732.2	513.0	143.5
Net Stockholders' Equity	1,435.6	2,136.9	355.2	d61.7	328.1	339.3	436.5
Net Working Capital	d840.0	2,261.5	600.5	d52.3	242.1	76.1	251.5
Year-end Shs. Outstg. (000)	272,100	132,416	94,139	50,328	50,103	47,191	35,367
STATISTICAL RECORD:							
Debt/Total Assets %	80.9	72.1	81.4	83.2	70.6	50.8	21.6
Price Range	109.69-20.00	102.30-33.64	41.60-17.12	18.80-11.60	21.84-13.84	18.48-12.96	15.96-8.34

Statistics are as originally reported. Adj. for stk. splits: 25% div., 2/00; 5-for-4, 10/99 1 Incl. net non-recurr. credit $4.2 mill., 12/98; chrgs. $16.2 mill., 12/99; $20.6 mill., 12/97 2 Bef. extraord. chrgs. $3.0 mill., 12/99; $30.7 mill., 12/98; $4.5 mill., 12/97 3 Incl. gain of $493.1 mill. for sale of Cable London

OFFICERS:
G. S. Blumenthal, Chmn., Treas.
B. Knapp, Pres., C.E.O.
J. F. Gregg, C.F.O.

INVESTOR CONTACT: Tamar Gerber, Investor Relations, (212) 906-8440

PRINCIPAL OFFICE: 110 East 59th Street, New York, NY 10022

TELEPHONE NUMBER: (212) 906-8440
FAX: (212) 752-1157
WEB: www.cabletel.com

NO. OF EMPLOYEES: 9,135 (approx.)

SHAREHOLDERS: 583 (approx.)

ANNUAL MEETING: In May

INCORPORATED: DE, Nov., 1990

INSTITUTIONAL HOLDINGS:
No. of Institutions: 169
Shares Held: 127,150,310
% Held: 46.0

INDUSTRY: Cable and other pay TV services (SIC: 4841)

TRANSFER AGENT(S): Continental Stock Transfer & Trust Company, New York, NY

NYSE SYMBOL NUE
Rec. Pr. 51.22 (5/31/01)

NUCOR CORPORATION

YIELD 1.3%
P/E RATIO 13.5

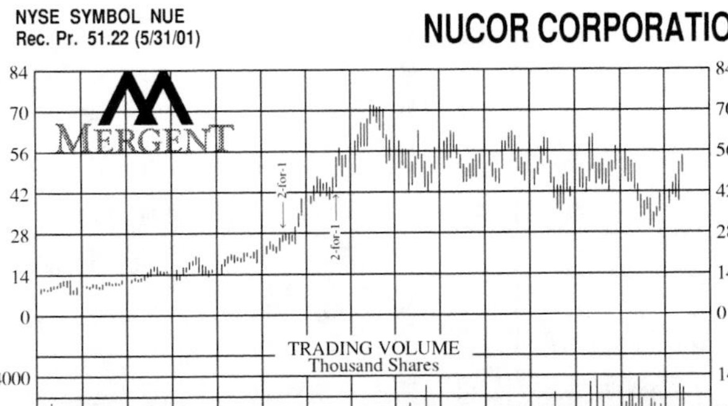

*7 YEAR PRICE SCORE 57.5 *12 MONTH PRICE SCORE 130.2

*NYSE COMPOSITE INDEX=100

INTERIM EARNINGS (Per Share):

Qtr.	Mar.	June	Sept.	Dec.
1997	0.74	0.83	0.91	0.87
1998	0.74	0.82	0.74	0.70
1999	0.32	0.58	0.78	1.12
2000	0.94	0.98	0.85	1.03

INTERIM DIVIDENDS (Per Share):

Amt.	Decl.	Ex.	Rec.	Pay.
0.15Q	3/08/00	3/29/00	3/31/00	5/12/00
0.15Q	6/06/00	6/28/00	6/30/00	8/11/00
0.15Q	9/05/00	9/27/00	9/29/00	11/10/00
0.15Q	12/05/00	12/27/00	12/29/00	2/09/01
0.17Q	3/08/01	3/28/01	3/30/01	5/11/01

Indicated div.: $0.68 (Div. Reinv. Plan)

CAPITALIZATION (12/31/00):

	($000)	(%)
Long-Term Debt	460,450	15.9
Minority Interest	312,263	10.8
Common & Surplus	2,130,952	73.4
Total	2,903,665	100.0

RECENT DEVELOPMENTS: For the year ended 12/31/00, net income increased 27.1% to $310.9 million compared with $244.6 million in 1999. Net sales were $4.59 billion, up 14.4% from $4.01 billion a year earlier. Interest income was $816,104 compared with $5.1 million in 1999. Pre-operating and start-up costs of new facilities increased 18.9% to $50.9 million versus $42.8 million a year earlier. Steel production in 2000 was 11.3 million tons, compared with 10.4 million tons produced in 1999.

PROSPECTS: On 3/31/01, the Company acquired substantially all of the assets of Auburn Steel Company, Inc.'s merchant steel bar facility in Auburn, NY for approximately $115.0 million. NUE's successful start-up is continuing at its new 1.0 million tons-per-year steel plate mill in Hertford County, North Carolina. Construction is continuing satisfactorily at the Vulcraft facility in Chemung, New York. This facility will produce steel joists, joist girders, and steel deck and should cost about $50.0 million.

BUSINESS

NUCOR CORPORATION is engaged in the manufacture and sale of steel and steel products, with facilities in eight states. The Company's principal steel products are hot-rolled steel, cold-rolled steel, cold-finished steel, steel joists and joist girders, steel deck, steel fasteners and steel-grinding balls. Hot-rolled steel products include angles, rounds, flats, channels, sheet, wide-flange beams, pilings, billets, blooms and beam blanks. The primary raw material is ferrous scrap, which is acquired from numerous sources throughout the U.S. Hot-rolled steel, cold-rolled steel, cold-finished steel, steel fasteners and steel-grinding balls are manufactured in standard sizes and inventories are maintained. Steel joists, joist girders and steel deck are sold to general contractors and fabricators throughout the U.S.

ANNUAL FINANCIAL DATA

	12/31/00	12/31/99	12/31/98	12/31/97	12/31/96	12/31/95	12/31/94
Earnings Per Share	**3.80**	**2.80**	**3.00**	**3.34**	**2.83**	**3.14**	**2.60**
Cash Flow Per Share	**6.97**	**5.74**	**5.88**	**5.84**	**4.91**	**5.13**	**4.41**
Tang. Book Val. Per Share	**27.47**	**25.93**	**23.73**	**21.32**	**18.33**	**15.78**	**12.85**
Dividends Per Share	**0.58**	**0.51**	**0.46**	**0.38**	**0.31**	**0.26**	**0.17**
Dividend Payout %	**15.3**	**18.2**	**15.3**	**11.4**	**11.0**	**8.1**	**6.7**
INCOME STATEMENT (IN MILLIONS):							
Total Revenues	4,586.1	4,009.3	4,151.2	4,184.5	3,647.0	3,462.0	2,975.6
Costs & Expenses	3,849.3	3,378.6	3,486.6	3,505.6	3,077.3	2,857.0	2,447.5
Depreciation & Amort.	259.4	256.6	253.1	218.8	182.2	173.9	157.7
Operating Income	477.5	374.1	411.5	460.1	387.5	431.2	370.4
Net Interest Inc./(Exp.)	0.8	5.1	3.8	...	0.3	1.1	d13.5
Income Before Income Taxes	478.3	379.2	415.3	460.2	387.8	432.3	356.9
Income Taxes	167.4	134.6	151.6	165.7	139.6	157.8	130.3
Net Income	310.9	244.6	263.7	294.5	248.2	274.5	226.6
Cash Flow	570.3	501.2	516.8	513.2	430.4	448.4	384.3
Average Shs. Outstg. (000)	81,777	87,287	87,878	87,922	87,686	87,430	87,166
BALANCE SHEET (IN MILLIONS):							
Cash & Cash Equivalents	490.6	572.2	308.7	283.4	104.4	201.8	101.9
Total Current Assets	1,381.4	1,538.5	1,129.5	1,125.5	828.4	830.7	638.7
Net Property	2,340.3	2,191.3	2,097.1	1,858.9	1,791.2	1,465.4	1,363.2
Total Assets	3,721.8	3,729.8	3,226.5	2,984.4	2,619.5	2,296.1	2,001.9
Total Current Liabilities	558.1	531.0	486.9	524.5	465.7	447.1	382.5
Long-Term Obligations	460.5	390.5	215.5	168.0	152.6	106.9	173.0
Net Stockholders' Equity	2,131.0	2,262.2	2,072.6	1,876.4	1,609.3	1,382.1	1,122.6
Net Working Capital	823.4	1,007.5	642.6	601.1	362.7	383.6	256.2
Year-end Shs. Outstg. (000)	77,583	87,247	87,353	87,997	87,796	87,599	87,333
STATISTICAL RECORD:							
Operating Profit Margin %	10.4	9.3	9.9	11.0	10.6	12.5	12.4
Net Profit Margin %	6.8	6.1	6.4	7.0	6.8	7.9	7.6
Return on Equity %	14.6	10.8	12.7	15.7	15.4	19.9	20.2
Return on Assets %	8.4	6.6	8.2	9.9	9.5	12.0	11.3
Debt/Total Assets %	12.4	10.5	6.7	5.6	5.8	4.7	8.6
Price Range	56.44-29.50	61.81-41.63	60.63-35.25	62.94-44.75	63.00-45.13	63.25-42.00	72.00-48.75
P/E Ratio	14.9-7.8	22.1-14.9	20.2-11.7	18.8-13.4	22.3-15.9	20.1-13.4	27.7-18.7
Average Yield %	1.3	1.0	1.0	0.7	0.6	0.5	0.3

Statistics are as originally reported.

OFFICERS:
P. C. Browning, Chmn.
D. R. DiMicco, Pres., C.E.O.
T. S. Lisenby, Exec. V.P., C.F.O., Treas.

INVESTOR CONTACT: Terry S. Lisenby, Exec. V.P., (704) 366-7000

PRINCIPAL OFFICE: 2100 Rexford Road, Charlotte, NC 28211

TELEPHONE NUMBER: (704) 366-7000
FAX: (704) 362-4208
WEB: www.nucor.com

NO. OF EMPLOYEES: 7,900

SHAREHOLDERS: 51,000

ANNUAL MEETING: In May

INCORPORATED: MI, Jan., 1940; reincorp., DE, Mar., 1958

INSTITUTIONAL HOLDINGS:
No. of Institutions: 247
Shares Held: 52,244,798
% Held: 67.3

INDUSTRY: Blast furnaces and steel mills (SIC: 3312)

TRANSFER AGENT(S): American Stock Transfer & Trust Company, New York, NY

NYSE SYMBOL OXY
Rec. Pr. 29.97 (5/31/01)

OCCIDENTAL PETROLEUM CORP.

YIELD 3.3%
P/E RATIO 7.0

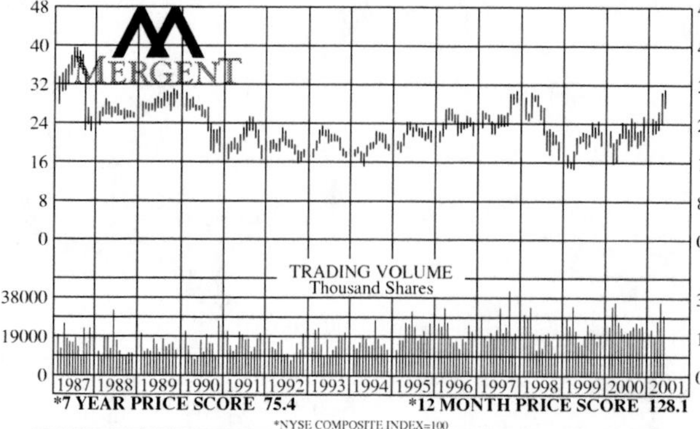

INTERIM EARNINGS (Per Share):

Qtr.	Mar.	June	Sept.	Dec.
1997	0.46	0.41	0.40	d0.58
1998	0.38	0.51	0.10	d0.12
1999	d0.17	0.03	0.35	1.33
2000	0.74	1.53	1.09	0.90

INTERIM DIVIDENDS (Per Share):

Amt.	Decl.	Ex.	Rec.	Pay.
0.25Q	4/27/00	6/07/00	6/09/00	7/15/00
0.25Q	7/20/00	9/06/00	9/08/00	10/15/00
0.25Q	11/09/00	12/06/00	12/08/00	1/15/01
0.25Q	2/08/01	3/07/01	3/09/01	4/15/01
0.25Q	4/20/01	6/06/01	6/08/01	7/15/01

Indicated div.: $1.00 (Div. Reinv. Plan)

CAPITALIZATION (12/31/00):

	($000)	(%)
Long-Term Debt	5,185,000	40.8
Minority Interest	2,265,000	17.8
Redeemable Pfd. Stock	473,000	3.7
Common & Surplus	4,774,000	37.6
Total	12,697,000	100.0

RECENT DEVELOPMENTS: For the year ended 12/31/00, net income was $1.57 billion, before an extraordinary gain of $1.0 million, versus income of $568.0 million in 1999. Results for 2000 and 1999 included a gain of $639.0 million and a loss of $13.0 million, respectively, on the disposition of assets. Results also included write-down of assets charges of $180.0 million and $212.0 million for 2000 and 1999. Net sales rose 73.6% to $13.57 billion.

PROSPECTS: The Company's near-term outlook is positive, reflecting continued strength in worldwide crude oil and natural gas prices. In addition, results going forward should benefit from rising production volumes associated with recent acquisitions, which have more than offset lower international production mainly due to asset sales. The Company also noted that it will continue with debt reduction efforts in 2001.

BUSINESS

OCCIDENTAL PETROLEUM CORPORATION explores for, develops, produces and markets crude oil and natural gas and manufactures and markets a variety of basic chemicals. The Oil & Gas segment conducts exploration and production operations in the U.S., including the Gulf of Mexico, and ten other countries. Net reserves at 12/31/00 were as follows: oil, 1.80 billion barrels, and gas, 2.20 trillion cubic feet. The Chemical segment manufactures industrial and specialty chemicals and plastics. OXY also has an interest in petrochemicals through its 29.5% interest in Equistar Chemicals, LP. On 1/31/98, OXY sold its former natural gas transmission business, MidCon, for net proceeds of $3.10 billion. On 4/18/00, OXY sold its 29.2% common stock interest in Canadian Occidental Petroleum Ltd for about $800.0 million. On 4/19/00, OXY acquired Altura Energy Ltd. in a transaction valued at approximately $3.60 billion.

REVENUES

(12/31/2000)	($000)	(%)
Oil & Gas Operations	9,779	72.0
Chemical Operations	3,795	28.0
Total	13,574	100.0

ANNUAL FINANCIAL DATA

	12/31/00	12/31/99	12/31/98	12/31/97	12/31/96	12/31/95	12/31/94
Earnings Per Share	**6 4.26**	**5 1.58**	**1 0.88**	**2 3 0.39**	**2 4 1.86**	**2 1.31**	**d0.36**
Cash Flow Per Share	**6.71**	**3.88**	**3.32**	**2.87**	**4.48**	**4.31**	**2.52**
Tang. Book Val. Per Share	**12.90**	**9.58**	**8.97**	**5.16**	**7.34**	**10.36**	**9.88**
Dividends Per Share	**1.00**	**1.00**	**1.00**	**1.00**	**1.00**	**1.00**	**1.00**
Dividend Payout %	**23.5**	**63.3**	**113.6**	**256.3**	**53.8**	**76.3**	**...**
INCOME STATEMENT (IN MILLIONS):							
Total Revenues	13,837.0	8,523.0	6,857.0	8,104.0	10,804.0	10,537.0	9,328.0
Costs & Expenses	9,741.0	5,767.0	5,277.0	6,306.0	8,334.0	8,249.0	7,828.0
Depreciation & Amort.	908.0	817.0	857.0	833.0	928.0	953.0	897.0
Operating Income	3,188.0	1,939.0	723.0	965.0	1,542.0	1,335.0	603.0
Net Interest Inc./(Exp.)	d518.0	d498.0	d559.0	d434.0	d484.0	d579.0	d584.0
Income Before Income Taxes	3,129.0	1,216.0	710.0	527.0	1,069.0	801.0	34.0
Income Taxes	1,442.0	631.0	363.0	311.0	454.0	402.0	143.0
Equity Earnings/Minority Int.	d118.0	d17.0	d22.0	1.0	83.0	112.0	73.0
Net Income	6 1,569.0	5 568.0	1 325.0	2 3 217.0	2 4 698.0	2 511.0	d36.0
Cash Flow	2,477.0	1,379.0	1,165.0	962.0	1,533.0	1,371.0	785.0
Average Shs. Outstg. (000)	369,000	355,500	350,601	335,000	342,000	318,000	311,000
BALANCE SHEET (IN MILLIONS):							
Cash & Cash Equivalents	97.0	214.0	96.0	113.0	279.0	520.0	129.0
Total Current Assets	2,067.0	1,688.0	2,795.0	1,916.0	2,190.0	2,519.0	2,258.0
Net Property	13,471.0	10,029.0	9,905.0	8,590.0	13,808.0	13,867.0	14,502.0
Total Assets	19,414.0	14,125.0	15,252.0	15,282.0	17,634.0	17,815.0	17,989.0
Total Current Liabilities	2,740.0	1,967.0	2,931.0	1,870.0	2,470.0	2,657.0	2,201.0
Long-Term Obligations	5,185.0	4,368.0	5,367.0	4,925.0	4,511.0	4,819.0	5,823.0
Net Stockholders' Equity	4,774.0	3,523.0	3,363.0	4,286.0	5,140.0	4,630.0	4,457.0
Net Working Capital	d673.0	d279.0	d136.0	46.0	d280.0	d138.0	57.0
Year-end Shs. Outstg. (000)	369,984	367,916	347,722	341,000	329,000	319,000	317,000
STATISTICAL RECORD:							
Operating Profit Margin %	23.0	22.8	10.5	11.9	14.3	12.7	6.5
Net Profit Margin %	11.3	6.7	4.7	2.7	6.5	4.8	...
Return on Equity %	32.9	16.1	9.7	5.1	13.6	11.0	...
Return on Assets %	8.1	4.0	2.1	1.4	4.0	2.9	...
Debt/Total Assets %	26.7	30.9	35.2	32.2	25.6	27.1	32.4
Price Range	25.56-15.75	24.56-14.63	30.44-16.63	30.75-21.75	27.25-20.13	24.38-18.00	22.38-15.13
P/E Ratio	6.0-3.7	15.5-9.3	34.6-18.9	78.8-55.8	14.6-10.8	18.6-13.7	...
Average Yield %	4.8	5.1	4.2	3.8	4.2	4.7	5.3

Statistics are as originally reported. 1 Bef. inc. of $38.0 mill. fr. disc. ops. 2 Incls. non-recurr. chrgs. 12/31/97, $474.0 mill.; credit 12/31/96, $11.0 mill.; chrgs. 12/31/95, $132.0 mill. 3 Bef. disc. ops. loss of $390.0 mill. 4 Bef. extraord. chrg. of $30.0 mill. 5 Bef. acctg. change chrg. of $13.0 mill. & extraord. loss of $107.0 mill. 6 Incls. net pre-tax gains of $639.0 mill. on disp. of assets & chrg. of $180.0 mill. on write-down of assets; bef. extraord. gain of $1.0 mill.

OFFICERS:
R. R. Irani, Chmn., C.E.O.
D. R. Laurance, Pres.
S. I. Chazen, Exec. V.P., C.F.O.

INVESTOR CONTACT: K. J. Huffman, Investor Relations, (212) 603-8183

PRINCIPAL OFFICE: 10889 Wilshire Boulevard, Los Angeles, CA 90024

TELEPHONE NUMBER: (310) 208-8800
FAX: (310) 443-6690
WEB: www.oxy.com

NO. OF EMPLOYEES: 8,791 (avg.)

SHAREHOLDERS: 74,175 (approx. of record)

ANNUAL MEETING: In Apr.

INCORPORATED: DE, Apr., 1986

INSTITUTIONAL HOLDINGS:
No. of Institutions: 310
Shares Held: 309,055,014
% Held: 83.5

INDUSTRY: Crude petroleum and natural gas (SIC: 1311)

TRANSFER AGENT(S): Mellon Investor Services, Ridgefield Park, NJ

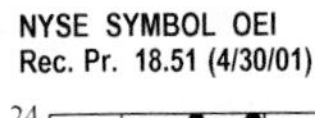

NYSE SYMBOL OEI
Rec. Pr. 18.51 (4/30/01)

OCEAN ENERGY, INC.

YIELD 0.9%
P/E RATIO 15.2

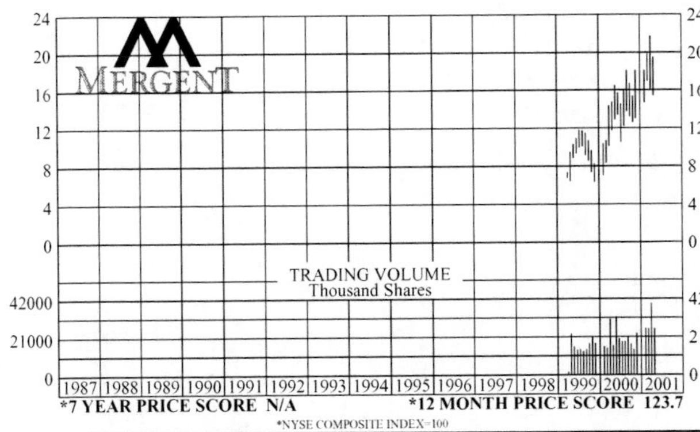

*7 YEAR PRICE SCORE N/A *12 MONTH PRICE SCORE 123.7

*NYSE COMPOSITE INDEX=100

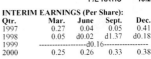

INTERIM EARNINGS (Per Share):

Qtr.	Mar.	June	Sept.	Dec.
1997	0.27	0.04	0.05	0.41
1998	0.05	d0.02	d1.37	d0.18
1999		d0.16		
2000	0.25	0.26	0.33	0.38

INTERIM DIVIDENDS (Per Share):

Amt.	Decl.	Ex.	Rec.	Pay.
0.04Q	12/18/00	1/03/01	1/05/01	1/19/01
0.04Q	3/27/01	4/04/01	4/06/01	4/20/01

Indicated div.: $0.16

CAPITALIZATION (12/31/00):

	($000)	(%)
Long-Term Debt	1,032,564	47.3
Preferred Stock	50	0.0
Common & Surplus	1,152,638	52.7
Total	2,185,252	100.0

RECENT DEVELOPMENTS: For the year ended 12/31/00, net income was $213.2 million versus a loss from continuing operations of $21.6 million in the previous year. Results included merger and integration costs of $3.3 million and $49.6 million in 2000 and 1999, respectively. Also, results for 1999 excluded income from discontinued operations of $1.1 million and an extraordinary loss of $23.4 million. Revenues improved 41.7% to $1.07 billion versus $757.6 million in 1999.

PROSPECTS: On 2/23/01, OEI announced that it has completed its tender offer for all outstanding common and Series A preferred shares of Texoil, Inc. Texoil is engaged in the acquisition of oil and gas reserves through a program that includes purchases of reserves, re-engineering, development and exploration activities currently focused in Texas and Louisiana. This acquisition should expand OEI's core operating area in South Texas as well as complement its strong position in Louisiana.

BUSINESS

OCEAN ENERGY, INC. is an independent energy company engaged in the exploration, development, production and acquisition of crude oil and natural gas, and is one of the largest independent oil and gas exploration and production companies in the United States with proved reserves of 460.0 million barrels of oil equivalent as of 12/31/00. The Company's North American operations are focused in the shelf and deepwater areas of the Gulf of Mexico, the Permian Basin, Mid-continent and Rocky Mountain regions. Internationally, the Company holds a major position among U.S. independents in West Africa with oil and gas activities in Equatorial Guinea, Cote d'Ivoire and Angola. The Company also conducts operations in the republics of Egypt, Tatarstan, Pakistan and Indonesia. On 3/30/99, the Company acquired Seagull Energy Corp.

REVENUES

(12/31/2000)	($000)	(%)
Natural Gas	526,417	49.0
Oil & Natural Gas Liquids	547,137	51.0
Total	1,073,554	100.0

ANNUAL FINANCIAL DATA

	12/31/00	12/31/99	12/31/98	12/31/97	12/31/96	12/31/95	12/31/94
Earnings Per Share	[1] 1.22	[1][2][3] d0.16	[3][4] d1.51	[4] 0.77	[1][4] 0.45	[4] 0.02	0.09
Cash Flow Per Share	2.98	1.99	1.20	3.49	2.94	3.63	4.19
Tang. Book Val. Per Share	6.89	5.69	8.68	10.27	9.53	12.35	12.22
INCOME STATEMENT (IN MILLIONS):							
Total Revenues	1,073.6	735.5	426.2	549.4	518.6	336.3	408.1
Costs & Expenses	305.6	277.1	353.1	265.3	254.2	237.3	204.7
Depreciation & Amort.	311.4	325.6	171.3	173.6	159.3	132.6	151.6
Operating Income	456.6	132.7	d98.2	110.5	105.1	d14.4	62.1
Net Interest Inc./(Exp.)	d75.1	d106.1	d39.2	d38.5	d44.8	d52.8	d51.5
Income Before Income Taxes	378.1	d21.6	d133.9	86.2	54.9	d1.7	0.9
Income Taxes	164.9	cr0.1	cr38.3	37.1	25.9	cr2.3	cr2.3
Net Income	[1] 213.2	[1][2][3] d21.6	[3][4] d95.7	[4] 49.1	[1][4] 29.0	[4] 0.6	3.2
Cash Flow	521.3	300.8	75.6	222.7	188.2	133.2	154.8
Average Shs. Outstg. (000)	174,749	151,022	63,159	63,791	64,073	36,717	36,904
BALANCE SHEET (IN MILLIONS):							
Cash & Cash Equivalents	23.0	64.9	25.7	45.7	15.3	11.2	6.4
Total Current Assets	324.6	290.0	152.8	223.0	227.6	147.4	119.4
Net Property	2,368.0	2,203.0	1,210.3	1,144.8	1,244.6	1,011.4	1,124.3
Total Assets	2,890.4	2,783.1	1,416.1	1,411.1	1,515.1	1,198.8	1,299.6
Total Current Liabilities	393.9	381.9	211.7	213.9	231.4	117.4	133.2
Long-Term Obligations	1,032.6	1,333.4	582.7	469.0	573.5	545.3	620.8
Net Stockholders' Equity	1,152.7	947.7	555.1	647.2	597.7	447.7	441.1
Net Working Capital	d69.3	d92.0	d58.9	9.1	d3.8	30.0	d13.8
Year-end Shs. Outstg. (000)	167,315	166,602	63,916	63,016	62,712	36,252	36,106
STATISTICAL RECORD:							
Operating Profit Margin %	42.5	18.0	...	20.1	20.3	...	15.2
Net Profit Margin %	19.9	...	...	8.9	5.6	0.2	0.8
Return on Equity %	18.5	...	...	7.6	4.8	0.1	0.7
Return on Assets %	7.4	...	...	3.5	1.9	0.1	0.2
Debt/Total Assets %	35.7	47.9	41.1	33.2	37.9	45.5	47.8
Price Range	18.13-7.00	11.81-6.31	...	...	...	...	...
P/E Ratio	14.9-5.7	...	...	...	...	...	...

Statistics are as originally reported. [1] Incl. merger expenses, 2000, $3.3 mill.; 1999, $49.6 mill.; 1996, $10.0 mill. [2] Bef. discontin. oper., $1.1 mill. [3] Bef. extraord. chrg., 1999, $23.4 mill.; 1998, $1.0 mill. [4] Incl. net gain on sale of assets, 1998, $127,000; 1997, $11.3 mill.; 1996, $1.1 mill.; 1995, $83.6 mill.

OFFICERS:
J. T. Hackett, Chmn., Pres., C.E.O.
W. L. Transier, Exec. V.P., C.F.O.
S. A. Thorington, Sr. V.P., Treas.

INVESTOR CONTACT: Investor Relations, (713) 265-6171

PRINCIPAL OFFICE: 1001 Fannin Street, Suite 1600, Houston, TX 77002-6714

TELEPHONE NUMBER: (713) 265-6000
FAX: (713) 265-8008
WEB: www.oceanenergy.com

NO. OF EMPLOYEES: 1,051

SHAREHOLDERS: 2,884 (record)

ANNUAL MEETING: In May

INCORPORATED: TX, 1973; reincorp., DE, May, 2001

INSTITUTIONAL HOLDINGS:
No. of Institutions: 253
Shares Held: 120,724,205
% Held: 70.9

INDUSTRY: Gas transmission and distribution (SIC: 4923)

TRANSFER AGENT(S): BankBoston, Boston, MA

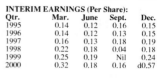

NYSE SYMBOL ODP
Rec. Pr. 9.14 (5/31/01)

OFFICE DEPOT, INC.

YIELD ...
P/E RATIO 101.6

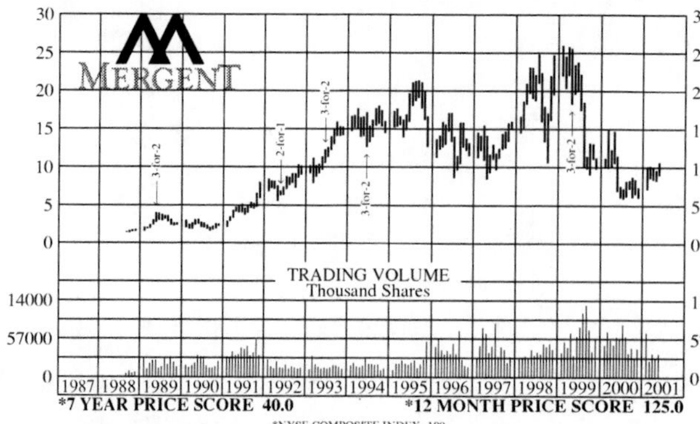

*7 YEAR PRICE SCORE 40.0 *12 MONTH PRICE SCORE 125.0

*NYSE COMPOSITE INDEX=100

INTERIM EARNINGS (Per Share):

Qtr.	Mar.	June	Sept.	Dec.
1995	0.14	0.12	0.16	0.15
1996	0.14	0.12	0.13	0.15
1997	0.16	0.13	0.18	0.19
1998	0.22	0.18	0.04	0.18
1999	0.25	0.19	Nil	0.24
2000	0.32	0.18	0.16	d0.57

INTERIM DIVIDENDS (Per Share):

Amt.	Decl.	Ex.	Rec.	Pay.

No dividends paid.

CAPITALIZATION (12/30/00):

	($000)	(%)
Long-Term Debt	598,499	27.2
Common & Surplus	1,601,251	72.8
Total	2,199,750	100.0

RECENT DEVELOPMENTS: For the 53 weeks ended 12/30/00, net earnings totaled $49.3 million compared with $257.6 million in the corresponding 52-week period the year before. Earnings for 2000 included one-time net pre-tax charges of $260.6 million related to asset disposals, store closures, severance costs and restructuring, and investment write-offs. Earnings for 1999 included one-time net pre-tax charges of $105.2 million from store closures and inventory provisions. Sales increased 12.6% to $11.57 billion from $10.27 billion a year earlier.

PROSPECTS: The Company is implementing initiatives focused on improving sales and operating performance of its retail stores in North America including closing under-performing stores and exiting certain markets completely. In addition, the Company is reducing the number of products it offers in its stores in an effort to improve inventory levels of high-demand items. Meanwhile, ODP plans to relocate warehouses in Atlanta and Baltimore in 2001 and will invest in new inventory-tracking systems to help boost efficiencies at its U.S. warehouse operations.

BUSINESS

OFFICE DEPOT, INC. operates the largest chain of high-volume retail office supply stores in the U.S. As of 2/15/01, ODP operated 820 stores in the United States and Canada, in addition to a national business-to-business delivery network supported by 25 delivery centers, more than 60 local sales offices and seven national call centers. In addition, ODP and its wholly-owned subsidiary, Viking Office Products, have operations in 16 countries outside the U.S. and Canada. ODP stores utilize a warehouse format and carry large inventories of merchandise. Products include general office supplies, business machines, business supplies, computers and accessories, and office furniture. On 8/26/98, the Company acquired Viking Office Products, Inc.

BUSINESS LINE ANALYSIS

(12/30/2000)	Rev(%)	Inc(%)
North American Retail	56.1	39.6
Business Services	31.3	31.7
International	12.6	28.7
Total	100.0	100.0

ANNUAL FINANCIAL DATA

	12/30/00	12/25/99	12/26/98	12/27/97	12/28/96	12/30/95	12/31/94
Earnings Per Share	**2 0.16**	**1 0.69**	**1 0.61**	**1 0.65**	**0.54**	**0.57**	**0.46**
Cash Flow Per Share	**0.82**	**1.08**	**0.93**	**1.07**	**0.89**	**0.85**	**0.68**
Tang. Book Val. Per Share	**4.66**	**5.06**	**4.86**	**4.82**	**4.09**	**3.46**	**2.30**
INCOME STATEMENT (IN MILLIONS):							
Total Revenues	11,569.7	10,263.3	8,997.7	6,717.5	6,068.6	5,313.2	4,266.2
Costs & Expenses	11,253.8	9,681.4	8,458.2	6,317.5	5,746.7	5,004.3	4,023.6
Depreciation & Amort.	205.7	168.6	140.9	97.0	82.5	64.8	49.6
Operating Income	110.2	413.4	398.6	303.0	239.4	244.1	193.0
Net Interest Inc./(Exp.)	d22.4	4.0	3.0	d16.4	d24.5	d21.2	d14.1
Income Before Income Taxes	92.5	413.9	388.7	263.4	212.7	221.9	178.9
Income Taxes	43.1	156.2	155.5	103.7	83.7	89.5	74.0
Net Income	2 49.3	1 257.6	1 233.2	1 159.7	129.0	132.4	105.0
Cash Flow	255.0	426.2	374.1	256.7	211.6	197.2	154.5
Average Shs. Outstg. (000)	311,231	393,657	402,320	239,514	237,983	233,327	228,855
BALANCE SHEET (IN MILLIONS):							
Cash & Cash Equivalents	151.5	218.8	715.0	199.6	51.4	62.0	32.4
Total Current Assets	2,699.1	2,631.1	2,780.4	2,020.6	1,821.6	1,731.0	1,274.2
Net Property	1,119.3	1,145.6	979.2	700.7	671.6	565.1	397.2
Total Assets	4,196.3	4,276.2	4,113.0	2,981.1	2,740.3	2,531.2	1,904.0
Total Current Liabilities	1,908.3	1,944.0	1,531.0	1,137.8	1,127.8	1,022.0	786.9
Long-Term Obligations	598.5	321.1	470.7	447.0	416.8	494.9	393.8
Net Stockholders' Equity	1,601.3	1,907.7	2,028.9	1,328.9	1,155.9	1,003.0	715.3
Net Working Capital	790.8	687.0	1,249.4	882.8	693.8	709.0	487.3
Year-end Shs. Outstg. (000)	296,498	329,442	370,572	237,455	235,881	233,697	224,060
STATISTICAL RECORD:							
Operating Profit Margin %	1.0	4.0	4.4	4.5	3.9	4.6	4.5
Net Profit Margin %	0.4	2.5	2.6	2.4	2.1	2.5	2.5
Return on Equity %	3.1	13.5	11.5	12.0	11.2	13.2	14.7
Return on Assets %	1.2	6.0	5.7	5.4	4.7	5.2	5.5
Debt/Total Assets %	14.3	7.5	11.4	15.0	15.2	19.6	20.7
Price Range	14.88-5.88	26.00-9.00	24.83-10.58	16.00-8.42	17.08-8.58	21.42-12.67	18.00-12.58
P/E Ratio	92.9-36.7	37.7-13.0	40.9-17.4	24.7-13.0	31.6-15.9	37.8-22.3	39.1-27.4

Statistics are as originally reported. Adj. for 3-for-2 stk. split, 4/99 & 6/94. 1 Incl. one-time pre-tax chgs. of $33.3 mil, 1999; $119.1 mil pre-tax merger costs, 1998; $16.1 mil, 1997. 2 Incl. $260.6 mil one-time net pre-tax chgs. fr. asset disposals, store closures, severance costs and restructuring, and investment write-off.

OFFICERS:
D. I. Fuente, Chmn.
M. B. Nelson, C.E.O.
B. J. Goldstein, Exec. V.P.-Fin., C.F.O.

INVESTOR CONTACT: Eileen H. Dunn, V.P., Inv. Rel. (561) 438-4930

PRINCIPAL OFFICE: 2200 Old Germantown Rd., Delray Beach, FL 33445

TELEPHONE NUMBER: (561) 438-4800
FAX: (561) 265-4406
WEB: www.officedepot.com
NO. OF EMPLOYEES: 48,000 (approx.)
SHAREHOLDERS: 4,062
ANNUAL MEETING: In Apr.
INCORPORATED: FL, Mar., 1986; reincorp., DE, Sept., 1986

INSTITUTIONAL HOLDINGS:
No. of Institutions: 253
Shares Held: 200,797,278
% Held: 67.6

INDUSTRY: Office equipment (SIC: 5044)

TRANSFER AGENT(S): Mellon Investor Services, Ridgefield Park, NJ

NYSE SYMBOL OMX
Rec. Pr. 3.55 (5/31/01)

OFFICEMAX, INC.

YIELD ...
P/E RATIO ...

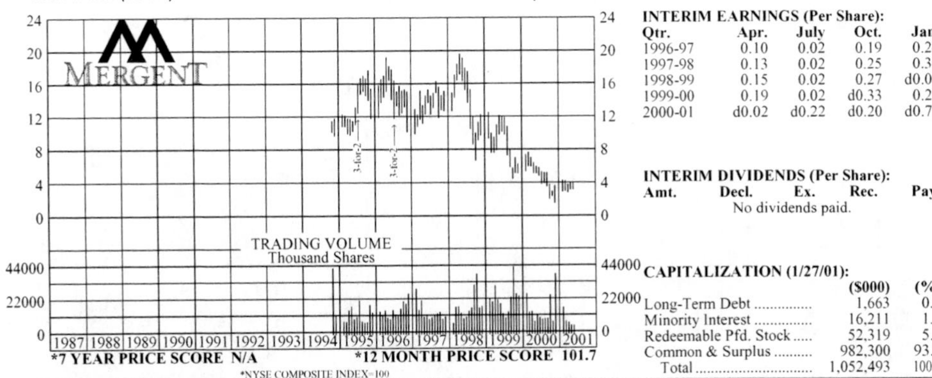

INTERIM EARNINGS (Per Share):

Qtr.	Apr.	July	Oct.	Jan.
1996-97	0.10	0.02	0.19	0.24
1997-98	0.13	0.02	0.25	0.32
1998-99	0.15	0.02	0.27	d0.06
1999-00	0.19	0.02	d0.33	0.20
2000-01	d0.02	d0.22	d0.20	d0.76

INTERIM DIVIDENDS (Per Share):

Amt.	Decl.	Ex.	Rec.	Pay.

No dividends paid.

CAPITALIZATION (1/27/01):

	($000)	(%)
Long-Term Debt	1,663	0.2
Minority Interest	16,211	1.5
Redeemable Pfd. Stock	52,319	5.0
Common & Surplus	982,300	93.3
Total	1,052,493	100.0

RECENT DEVELOPMENTS: For the 53 weeks ended 1/27/01, net loss totaled $133.2 million compared with net income of $10.0 million in the corresponding 52-week period the previous year. Results in the recent period included a $117.8 million pre-tax charge for store closings, asset impairments and inventory liquidations, as well as a pre-tax litigation charge of $19.5 million. Earnings in the prior-year period included a pre-tax inventory markdown charge of $77.4 million. Sales rose 6.4% to $5.16 billion from $4.85 billion a year earlier.

PROSPECTS: Fewer store openings, combined with significantly lower capital expenditures and aggressive cost-control efforts, are expected to boost free cash flow to more than $150.0 million in fiscal 2001, which would be an improvement of almost $300.0 million over fiscal 2000 results. Meanwhile, the implementation of a new supply-chain management network in fiscal 2000 is expected to lower inventory levels by about $200.0 million during fiscal 2001, along with an additional $200.0 million in fiscal 2002.

BUSINESS

OFFICEMAX, INC. operates 995 office product superstores in 49 states, Puerto Rico and the U.S. Virgin Islands, as well as two national call centers, 19 delivery centers and 29 OfficeMax retail joint ventures in Brazil, Mexico and Japan. The typical superstore is approximately 20,000 square feet and features CopyMax and FurnitureMax, in-store modules devoted exclusively to print-for-pay services and office furniture. The Company also operates three smaller format OfficeMax PDQ stores and OfficeMax.com on the Internet, which enables consumers and businesses to buy a wide assortment of OfficeMax merchandise using personal computers.

ANNUAL FINANCIAL DATA

	1/27/01	1/22/00	1/23/99	1/24/98	1/25/97	1/27/96	1/21/95
Earnings Per Share	[1] **d1.20**	[1] **0.09**	[1] **0.39**	**0.72**	**0.55**	[1] **1.04**	**0.27**
Cash Flow Per Share	**d0.28**	**0.87**	**0.99**	**1.25**	**0.96**	**1.38**	**0.57**
Tang. Book Val. Per Share	**5.46**	**7.18**	**7.05**	**6.73**	**5.90**	**5.25**	**3.45**
INCOME STATEMENT (IN MILLIONS):							
Total Revenues	5,156.4	4,842.7	4,337.8	3,765.4	3,179.3	2,542.5	1,841.2
Costs & Expenses	5,248.4	4,721.2	4,177.2	3,552.2	3,022.2	2,415.1	1,751.2
Depreciation & Amort.	101.5	89.1	73.9	67.3	51.6	41.2	34.4
Operating Income	d193.5	32.4	86.7	145.9	105.5	86.3	55.6
Net Interest Inc./(Exp.)	d16.5	d10.1	d5.7	0.5	7.5	7.2	0.6
Income Before Income Taxes	d210.1	22.3	81.0	146.4	112.9	213.6	56.3
Income Taxes	cr79.1	12.3	32.4	56.8	44.1	87.9	26.0
Equity Earnings/Minority Int.	d2.1	...	...	...	...	2.2	0.1
Net Income	[1] d133.2	[1] 10.0	[1] 48.6	89.6	68.8	[1] 125.8	30.4
Cash Flow	d31.6	99.1	122.5	156.9	120.4	167.0	64.8
Average Shs. Outstg. (000)	112,738	114,248	123,751	125,196	125,133	120,680	114,389
BALANCE SHEET (IN MILLIONS):							
Cash & Cash Equivalents	127.3	73.1	67.5	66.8	258.1	365.9	174.3
Total Current Assets	1,502.9	1,528.0	1,503.6	1,228.5	1,220.7	1,049.1	691.3
Net Property	434.3	402.5	353.2	311.9	292.9	180.4	132.2
Total Assets	2,293.3	2,275.0	2,231.9	1,906.0	1,867.3	1,587.9	1,257.5
Total Current Liabilities	1,099.5	1,058.9	1,002.6	667.0	731.9	549.7	479.5
Long-Term Obligations	1.7	15.1	16.4	17.7	18.7	...	...
Net Stockholders' Equity	982.3	1,116.0	1,138.1	1,160.6	1,063.6	990.9	748.6
Net Working Capital	403.4	469.1	501.1	561.5	488.8	499.4	211.9
Year-end Shs. Outstg. (000)	124,969	112,283	116,753	124,270	123,767	123,497	114,627
STATISTICAL RECORD:							
Operating Profit Margin %	...	0.7	2.0	3.9	3.3	3.4	3.0
Net Profit Margin %	...	0.2	1.1	2.4	2.2	4.9	1.6
Return on Equity %	...	0.9	4.3	7.7	6.5	12.7	4.1
Return on Assets %	...	0.4	2.2	4.7	3.7	7.9	2.4
Debt/Total Assets %	0.1	0.7	0.7	0.9	1.0	...	...
Price Range	7.63-1.50	12.50-4.44	19.63-6.63	16.31-9.88	19.25-10.13	17.67-9.72	11.78-9.61
P/E Ratio	...	138.7-49.3	50.3-17.0	22.7-13.7	35.0-18.4	17.0-9.3	44.1-36.0

Statistics are as originally reported. Adj. for 3-for-2 stk. split, 7/96 & 7/95. [1] Incl. $117.8 mil pre-tax chg. for store closings, asset impairments and inventory liquidations & a $19.5 mil pre-tax litigation chg., 1/01; $77.4 mil pre-tax inventory markdown chg., 1/00; $80.0 mil ($0.41/sh) one-time chg. from realignment of Computer Business Segment, 1/99; $69.1 mil ($0.57/sh) gain from sale of Corporate Express, Inc., 1/96.

OFFICERS:
M. Feuer, Chmn., C.E.O.
G. J. Peterson, Pres., C.O.O.
J. L. Rutherford, Sr. Exec. V.P., C.F.O.

INVESTOR CONTACT: M. W. Weisbarth, Div. V.P., Inv. Rel., (216) 295-6698

PRINCIPAL OFFICE: 3605 Warrensville Center Road, Shaker Heights, OH 44122

TELEPHONE NUMBER: (216) 471-6900
FAX: (216) 471-4040
WEB: www.officemax.com
NO. OF EMPLOYEES: 20,000 full-time (approx.); 15,000 part-time (approx.)
SHAREHOLDERS: 4,020 (approx.)
ANNUAL MEETING: In May
INCORPORATED: OH, July, 1988

INSTITUTIONAL HOLDINGS:
No. of Institutions: 88
Shares Held: 27,389,756
% Held: 24.2

INDUSTRY: Stationery stores (SIC: 5943)

TRANSFER AGENT(S): EquiServe, Jersey City, NJ

NYSE SYMBOL OGE
Rec. Pr. 22.01 (5/31/01)

OGE ENERGY CORPORATION

YIELD 6.0%
P/E RATIO 11.6

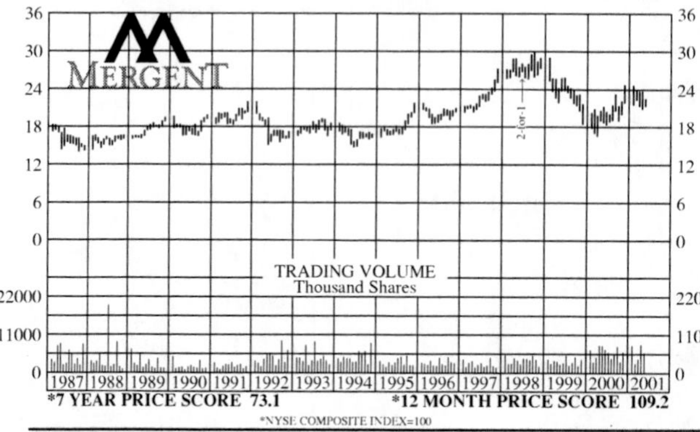

*7 YEAR PRICE SCORE 73.1 *12 MONTH PRICE SCORE 109.2

*NYSE COMPOSITE INDEX=100

INTERIM EARNINGS (Per Share):

Qtr.	Mar.	June	Sept.	Dec.
1996	Nil	0.86	2.22	0.17
1997	d0.11	0.76	2.20	0.29
1998	d0.03	0.59	1.33	0.13
1999	0.14	0.49	1.16	0.16
2000	0.01	0.41	1.38	0.09

INTERIM DIVIDENDS (Per Share):

Amt.	Decl.	Ex.	Rec.	Pay.
0.333Q	5/18/00	7/06/00	7/10/00	7/28/00
0.333Q	9/20/00	10/05/00	10/10/00	10/30/00
0.333Q	11/15/00	1/08/01	1/10/01	1/30/01
0.333Q	3/21/01	4/06/01	4/10/01	4/30/01
0.333Q	5/24/01	7/06/01	7/10/01	7/30/01

Indicated div.: $1.33 (Div. Reinv. Plan)

CAPITALIZATION (12/31/00):

	($000)	(%)
Long-Term Debt	1,648,523	49.5
Deferred Income Tax	618,360	18.6
Common & Surplus	1,064,308	31.9
Total	3,331,191	100.0

RECENT DEVELOPMENTS: For the year ended 12/31/00, net income fell 2.8% to $147.0 million from $151.3 million in 1999. Operating revenue totaled $3.30 billion, an increase of 51.8% versus $2.17 billion a year earlier. Revenues benefited from higher volumes and higher commodity prices at Egonex, reflecting the full-year impact of the Transok pipeline acquisition in mid-1999 and energy-marketing efforts. Operating income improved 3.4% to $349.8 million versus $338.2 million.

PROSPECTS: OGE's natural gas pipeline subsidiary recently signed a long-term contract with PECO Energy Company's Power Team to transport natural gas to fuel a power plant under construction in Jenks, Oklahoma. The Power Plant will be connected to the Transok pipeline system and is scheduled to begin full commercial operation in January 2002. Meanwhile, OGE will continue to pursue a convergence strategy for its electricity and natural gas business.

BUSINESS

OGE ENERGY CORPORATION (formerly Oklahoma Gas & Electric Company) is the parent company of three wholly-owned subsidiaries. OG&E Electric Services is an electric utility company with nearly 700,000 retail customers in Oklahoma and western Arkansas. Electricity comes from eight Company-owned power plants that are either coal or natural gas-fired, plus some purchased power. Power is delivered across an interconnected transmission and distribution system that spans 30,000 square miles. Enogex Inc., handles the Company's gas production, gathering, transportation, processing and energy marketing business, with interest in approximately 9,700 miles of pipeline and five gas processing plants. On 7/1/99, OGE acquired Tejas Transok Holdings, L.L.C., a gatherer, processor and transporter of natural gas in Oklahoma and Texas, for $701.3 million.

ANNUAL FINANCIAL DATA

	12/31/00	12/31/99	12/31/98	12/31/97	12/31/96	12/31/95	12/31/94
Earnings Per Share	**1.89**	**1.94**	**2.04**	**1.62**	[2] **1.42**	**1.53**	[1] **1.51**
Cash Flow Per Share	**4.16**	**4.06**	**3.90**	**3.38**	**3.11**	**3.16**	**3.07**
Tang. Book Val. Per Share	**13.66**	**12.71**	**12.91**	**12.19**	**10.41**	**11.61**	**11.41**
Dividends Per Share	**1.33**	**1.33**	**1.33**	**1.00**	...	...	...
Dividend Payout %	**70.4**	**68.6**	**65.2**	**61.6**	...	...	...
INCOME STATEMENT (IN MILLIONS):							
Total Revenues	3,298.7	2,172.4	1,617.7	1,472.3	1,200.3	1,302.0	1,355.2
Costs & Expenses	2,772.8	1,669.2	1,128.5	1,061.2	759.5	841.4	889.0
Depreciation & Amort.	176.1	165.0	149.8	142.6	136.1	132.1	126.4
Maintenance Exp.	...	...	...	...	57.2	57.6	67.2
Operating Income	349.8	338.2	230.8	194.0	177.3	202.1	200.5
Net Interest Inc./(Exp.)	d128.9	d100.3	d67.1	d62.6	d56.4	d73.3	d71.1
Income Taxes	76.5	89.9	108.6	74.5	70.2	68.8	72.1
Net Income	147.0	151.3	165.9	132.6	[2] 116.9	125.3	[1] 123.8
Cash Flow	323.2	316.3	315.0	272.9	250.7	255.1	247.8
Average Shs. Outstg. (000)	77,688	77,916	80,787	80,746	80,734	80,712	80,688
BALANCE SHEET (IN MILLIONS):							
Gross Property	5,370.6	5,266.3	4,441.3	4,151.7	3,601.0	3,928.5	3,814.2
Accumulated Depreciation	2,151.1	2,024.3	1,914.7	1,797.8	1,560.5	1,585.3	1,487.3
Net Property	3,219.5	3,242.0	2,526.6	2,353.9	2,040.5	2,343.3	2,326.9
Total Assets	4,319.6	3,921.3	2,983.9	2,765.9	2,421.2	2,754.9	2,782.6
Long-Term Obligations	1,648.5	1,140.5	935.6	841.9	709.3	843.9	730.6
Net Stockholders' Equity	1,064.3	989.4	1,043.4	1,034.2	890.4	987.5	971.2
Year-end Shs. Outstg. (000)	77,922	77,863	80,797	80,772	80,758	80,746	80,708
STATISTICAL RECORD:							
Operating Profit Margin %	10.6	15.6	14.3	13.2	14.8	15.5	14.8
Net Profit Margin %	4.5	7.0	10.3	9.0	9.7	9.6	9.1
Net Inc./Net Property %	4.6	4.7	6.6	5.6	5.7	5.3	5.3
Net Inc./Tot. Capital %	4.4	5.6	6.6	5.6	5.8	5.4	5.6
Return on Equity %	13.8	15.3	15.9	12.8	13.1	12.7	12.7
Accum. Depr./Gross Prop. %	40.1	38.4	43.1	43.3	43.3	40.4	39.0
Price Range	24.75-16.50	29.06-18.44	30.00-25.63	27.31-20.25	21.81-18.44	21.81-16.28	18.63-14.69
P/E Ratio	13.1-8.7	15.0-9.5	14.7-12.6	16.9-12.5	15.4-13.0	14.3-10.7	12.4-9.8
Average Yield %	6.4	5.6	4.8	4.2	...	...	...

Statistics are as originally reported. Adj. for stk. split: 2-for-1, 6/98. [1] Incl. restr. chrg. $21.0 mill. [2] Bef. disc. opers gain $16.5 mill.

OFFICERS:
S. E. Moore, Chmn., Pres., C.E.O.
A. M. Strecker, Exec. V.P.
J. R. Hatfield, C.F.O., Sr. V.P., Treas.
I. B. Elliot, V.P., Corp. Sec.

INVESTOR CONTACT: Jim Hatfield, Sr. V.P., C.F.O., Treas., (405) 553-3984

PRINCIPAL OFFICE: 321 North Harvey, Oklahoma City, OK 73101-0321

TELEPHONE NUMBER: (405) 553-3000
FAX: (405) 553-3760
WEB: www.oge.com

NO. OF EMPLOYEES: 3,032 (avg.)

SHAREHOLDERS: 36,236

ANNUAL MEETING: In May

INCORPORATED: OK, Feb., 1902; reincorp., OK, Aug., 1995

INSTITUTIONAL HOLDINGS:
No. of Institutions: 182
Shares Held: 28,077,707
% Held: 36.0

INDUSTRY: Natural gas transmission (SIC: 4922)

TRANSFER AGENT(S): Mellon Investor Services, South Hackensack, NJ

NYSE SYMBOL ORI
Rec. Pr. 28.89 (4/30/01)

OLD REPUBLIC INTERNATIONAL CORP.

YIELD 2.1%
P/E RATIO 11.6

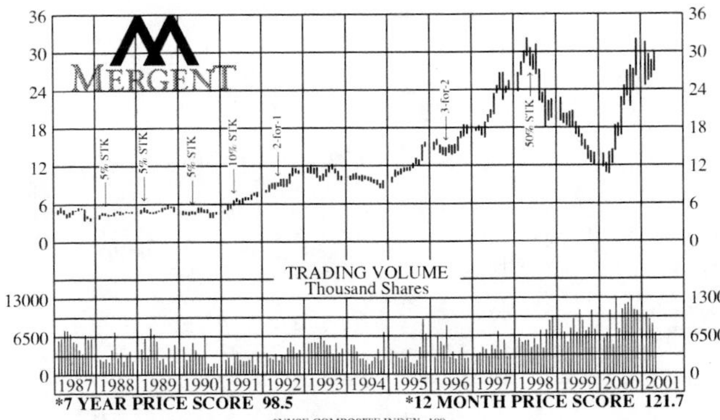

INTERIM EARNINGS (Per Share):

Qtr.	Mar.	June	Sept.	Dec.
1996	0.39	0.39	0.43	0.43
1997	0.45	0.63	0.49	0.53
1998	0.58	0.57	0.54	0.64
1999	0.55	0.48	0.31	0.39
2000	0.46	0.58	0.67	0.77

INTERIM DIVIDENDS (Per Share):

Amt.	Decl.	Ex.	Rec.	Pay.
0.14Q	5/18/00	6/01/00	6/05/00	6/15/00
0.14Q	8/17/00	8/31/00	9/05/00	9/15/00
0.14Q	11/27/00	12/01/00	12/05/00	12/15/00
0.14Q	2/26/01	3/01/01	3/05/01	3/15/01
0.15Q	3/22/01	6/01/01	6/05/01	6/15/01

Indicated div.: $0.60 (Div. Reinv. Plan)

CAPITALIZATION (12/31/00):

	($000)	(%)
Long-Term Debt	238,000	8.0
Deferred Income Tax	289,800	9.8
Preferred Stock	700	0.0
Common & Surplus	2,438,600	82.2
Total	2,967,100	100.0

RECENT DEVELOPMENTS: For the year ended 12/31/00, net income improved 31.2% to $297.4 million compared with $226.8 million in the corresponding 1999 period. Total revenues declined slightly to $2.07 billion versus $2.10 billion a year earlier. General insurance revenues fell 0.4% to $1.06 billion, while title insurance revenues decreased 13.1% to $518.7 million. Mortgage guaranty revenues climbed 11.1% to $395.3 million.

PROSPECTS: Results were enhanced by improvements in general insurance underwriting performance, lower claims and operating expenses from the mortgage guaranty insurance segment and an improving housing and mortgage lending market. Looking ahead, unabated loss-severity levels in certain coverages and inflation-driven increases in the cost of medical care and repairs are leading ORI to plan for a longer period of premium rate increases.

BUSINESS

OLD REPUBLIC INTERNATIONAL CORP. is a multiple line insurance holding company with assets of approximately $7.28 billion and total capitalization of $2.97 billion as of 12/31/00. The Company's subsidiaries market, underwrite, and manage a wide range of specialty and general insurance programs in the property & liability, title, mortgage guaranty insurance and life & disability businesses. The Company primarily serves the insurance and related needs of major financial services and industrial corporations, with an emphasis on energy services, construction and forest products, transportation and housing industries. In 2000, revenues were derived as follows: general insurance, 51.9%; title insurance, 25.5%; mortgage guaranty, 19.4%; life insurance, 3.0% and other, 0.2%.

ANNUAL FINANCIAL DATA

	12/31/00	12/31/99	12/31/98	12/31/97	12/31/96	12/31/95	12/31/94
Earnings Per Share	**2.47**	**1.75**	**2.33**	**2.10**	**[1] 1.64**	**1.61**	**1.13**
Tang. Book Val. Per Share	**20.08**	**19.65**	**17.27**	**15.59**	**14.57**	**13.58**	**11.46**
Dividends Per Share	**0.55**	**0.49**	**0.39**	**0.33**	**0.28**	**0.23**	**0.21**
Dividend Payout %	**22.3**	**28.0**	**16.6**	**15.9**	**16.9**	**14.1**	**18.4**
INCOME STATEMENT (IN MILLIONS):							
Total Premium Income	1,550.3	1,567.2	1,568.1	1,464.6	1,360.4	1,251.7	1,282.9
Net Investment Income	273.9	263.2	273.1	270.8	260.5	251.9	227.5
Other Income	246.1	271.5	330.3	227.2	182.7	192.1	168.4
Total Revenues	2,070.3	2,101.9	2,171.5	1,962.6	1,803.6	1,695.7	1,678.8
Income Before Income Taxes	426.4	317.0	466.7	426.7	342.4	316.0	225.9
Income Taxes	131.0	92.9	145.7	129.1	108.5	103.5	73.3
Equity Earnings/Minority Int.	2.2	2.7	2.7	0.6	0.9	0.2	d1.4
Net Income	297.4	226.8	323.8	297.6	[1] 234.6	212.7	151.2
Average Shs. Outstg. (000)	120,197	129,787	139,150	141,768	140,438	128,867	128,718
BALANCE SHEET (IN MILLIONS):							
Cash & Cash Equivalents	411.0	294.0	400.5	354.9	301.0	332.1	203.2
Premiums Due	1,660.4	1,626.3	1,572.2	1,634.3	1,677.9	1,714.4	1,873.1
Invst. Assets: Fixed-term	4,310.2	4,261.1	4,286.7	4,259.6	4,007.1	3,860.1	3,347.5
Invst. Assets: Equities	295.5	160.1	164.8	117.1	116.1	126.1	263.8
Invst. Assets: Total	5,038.9	4,739.4	4,854.2	4,720.1	4,414.0	4,325.8	3,810.7
Total Assets	7,280.9	6,937.7	7,018.9	6,922.8	6,655.6	6,592.8	6,262.1
Long-Term Obligations	238.0	208.3	145.1	142.9	154.0	320.5	314.7
Net Stockholders' Equity	2,439.3	3,078.7	2,305.4	2,153.0	1,901.1	1,667.8	1,387.9
Year-end Shs. Outstg. (000)	121,445	156,679	133,403	138,070	130,408	118,716	115,957
STATISTICAL RECORD:							
Return on Revenues %	14.4	10.8	14.9	15.2	13.0	12.5	9.0
Return on Equity %	12.2	7.4	14.0	13.8	12.3	12.8	10.9
Return on Assets %	4.1	3.3	4.6	4.3	3.5	3.2	2.4
Price Range	32.06-10.63	22.75-12.06	32.25-17.94	26.79-16.42	18.50-13.50	15.78-9.33	10.89-8.39
P/E Ratio	13.0-4.3	13.0-6.9	13.8-7.7	12.8-7.8	11.3-8.2	9.8-5.8	9.6-7.4
Average Yield %	2.6	2.8	1.5	1.5	1.7	1.8	2.2

Statistics are as originally reported. Adj. for stk. splits: 50% div., 5/98; 3-for-2, 5/96 [1] Bef. extraord. chrg. $4.4 mill.

OFFICERS:
A. C. Zucaro, Chmn., Pres., C.E.O.
P. D. Adams, Sr. V.P., C.F.O., Treas.
S. LeRoy III, Sr. V.P., Gen. Couns., Sec.

INVESTOR CONTACT: A.C. Zucaro, Chmn., Pres. & C.E.O., (312) 346-8100

PRINCIPAL OFFICE: 307 N. Michigan Ave., Chicago, IL 60601

TELEPHONE NUMBER: (312) 346-8100
FAX: (312) 726-0309
WEB: www.oldrepublic.com

NO. OF EMPLOYEES: 5,815 (approx.)

SHAREHOLDERS: 3,276

ANNUAL MEETING: In May

INCORPORATED: DE, 1969

INSTITUTIONAL HOLDINGS:
No. of Institutions: 254
Shares Held: 94,223,832
% Held: 79.7

INDUSTRY: Surety insurance (SIC: 6351)

TRANSFER AGENT(S): First Chicago Trust Company of New York, Jersey City, NJ

NYSE SYMBOL OLN
Rec. Pr. 18.95 (4/30/01)

OLIN CORPORATION

YIELD 4.2%
P/E RATIO 10.5

INTERIM EARNINGS (Per Share):

Qtr.	Mar.	June	Sept.	Dec.
1997	0.81	0.75	0.76	0.70
1998	0.46	0.37	d0.24	0.19
1999	0.05	0.05	0.06	0.20
2000	0.43	0.52	0.52	0.34

INTERIM DIVIDENDS (Per Share):

Amt.	Decl.	Ex.	Rec.	Pay.
0.20Q	7/28/00	8/08/00	8/10/00	9/11/00
0.20Q	10/26/00	11/08/00	11/10/00	12/11/00
0.20Q	1/25/01	2/07/01	2/09/01	3/09/01
0.20Q	4/26/01	5/08/01	5/10/01	6/11/01

Indicated div.: $0.80 (Div. Reinv. Plan)

CAPITALIZATION (12/31/00):

	($000)	(%)
Long-Term Debt	228,000	35.8
Deferred Income Tax	80,000	12.6
Common & Surplus	329,000	51.6
Total	637,000	100.0

RECENT DEVELOPMENTS: For the year ended 12/31/00, net income soared to $81.0 million versus income from continuing operations of $16.2 million in 1999. Sales rose 11.0% to $1.55 billion from $1.40 billion in 1999. Sales in the chlor alkali products segment grew 16.6% to $391.7 million due to increased selling prices, while sales in the metal division rose 13.9% to $880.3 million due to strong shipments to the ammunition and electronics markets.

PROSPECTS: Looking ahead, the Company expects earnings per share for 2001 to be approximately $1.80. The Company anticipates increased earnings from its chlor alkali products business will help offset the negative effects of the strike ended 1/23/01 at the Company's brass and Winchester operations in East Alton, IL. The Company expects the impact of the strike on full-year earnings per share for 2001 to be approximately $0.40.

BUSINESS

OLIN CORPORATION is a manufacturer concentrated in three business segments: chlor alkali products, metals, and winchester. Chlor alkali products include chlorine and caustic soda, sodium hydrosulfite and high strength bleach products. Metals products include copper and copper alloy sheet, strip, welded tube, and fabricated parts. Winchester products include sporting ammunition, canister powder, reloading components, and small caliber military ammunition. Revenues (and operating income) in 2000 were derived: chlor alkali, 25.3% (19.2%); metals, 56.8% (66.9%); and winchester, 17.9% (13.9%). On 2/8/99, the Company completed the spin-off of Arch Chemicals, Inc.

ANNUAL FINANCIAL DATA

	12/31/00	12/31/99	12/31/98	12/31/97	12/31/96	12/31/95	12/31/94
Earnings Per Share	**1.80**	**[4] 0.36**	**[3] 0.79**	**3.00**	**[1][2] 5.52**	**2.75**	**1.83**
Cash Flow Per Share	**3.60**	**2.14**	**2.43**	**5.45**	**8.30**	**5.75**	**4.87**
Tang. Book Val. Per Share	**7.48**	**6.86**	**17.21**	**18.01**	**18.12**	**12.86**	**12.52**
Dividends Per Share	**0.80**	**0.90**	**1.20**	**1.20**	**1.20**	**1.20**	**1.10**
Dividend Payout %	**44.4**	**249.9**	**151.9**	**40.0**	**21.7**	**43.6**	**60.3**
INCOME STATEMENT (IN MILLIONS):							
Total Revenues	1,549.0	1,314.8	1,426.0	2,410.0	2,638.0	3,150.0	2,658.0
Costs & Expenses	1,328.0	1,184.0	1,216.0	2,056.0	2,249.0	2,763.0	2,350.0
Depreciation & Amort.	81.0	80.0	78.0	124.0	130.0	142.0	140.0
Operating Income	140.0	51.0	132.0	230.0	259.0	245.0	168.0
Net Interest Inc./(Exp.)	d14.0	d14.0	d14.0	d14.0	d29.0	d44.0	d37.0
Income Before Income Taxes	131.0	27.0	59.0	234.0	446.0	217.0	141.0
Income Taxes	50.0	10.0	21.0	81.0	158.0	77.0	50.0
Equity Earnings/Minority Int.	2.0	d11.0	...	...	...	...	...
Net Income	81.0	[4] 16.2	[3] 38.0	153.0	[1][2] 288.0	140.0	91.0
Cash Flow	162.0	97.0	116.0	277.0	414.0	276.0	224.0
Average Shs. Outstg. (000)	45,000	45,400	47,800	50,800	49,900	48,000	46,000
BALANCE SHEET (IN MILLIONS):							
Cash & Cash Equivalents	82.0	46.0	75.0	194.0	611.0	8.0	7.0
Total Current Assets	528.0	504.0	517.0	936.0	1,336.0	1,052.0	880.0
Net Property	483.0	468.0	475.0	795.0	657.0	956.0	879.0
Total Assets	1,123.0	1,066.0	1,577.0	1,946.0	2,339.0	2,272.0	2,030.0
Total Current Liabilities	275.0	252.0	292.0	512.0	826.0	755.0	618.0
Long-Term Obligations	228.0	229.0	230.0	268.0	276.0	411.0	418.0
Net Stockholders' Equity	329.0	309.0	790.0	879.0	946.0	841.0	749.0
Net Working Capital	253.0	252.0	225.0	424.0	510.0	297.0	262.0
Year-end Shs. Outstg. (000)	43,980	45,062	45,900	48,800	52,200	50,000	44,000
STATISTICAL RECORD:							
Operating Profit Margin %	9.0	3.9	9.3	9.5	9.8	7.8	6.3
Net Profit Margin %	5.2	1.3	2.7	6.3	10.9	4.4	3.4
Return on Equity %	24.6	5.5	4.8	17.4	30.4	16.6	12.1
Return on Assets %	7.2	1.6	2.4	7.9	12.3	6.2	4.5
Debt/Total Assets %	20.3	21.5	14.6	13.8	11.8	18.1	20.6
Price Range	23.19-14.19	29.25-9.50	49.31-23.88	51.38-35.38	48.00-34.88	38.56-24.19	30.06-23.00
P/E Ratio	12.9-7.9	81.2-26.4	62.4-30.2	17.1-11.8	8.7-6.3	14.0-8.8	16.5-12.6
Average Yield %	4.3	4.6	3.3	2.8	2.9	3.8	4.1

Statistics are as originally reported. Adj. for 2-for-1 split, 10/96. [1] Incl. $115.3 mill. ($2.20/sh.) after-tax gain on sale of TDI & ADI isocyanates bus. [2] Bef. $7.9 mill. ($0.18/sh.) loss fr. disc. ops. [3] Incl. $26.2 mill. after-tax chg. on sale of bus. & restr. chgs., $15.4 mill. after-tax non-recur. chg. for spin-off of Arch Chemicals, Inc., & excl. $40.0 mill. after-tax income fr. disc. ops. [4] Excl. $4.4 mill. income fr. disc. ops.

OFFICERS:
D. W. Griffin, Chmn., Pres., C.E.O.
A. W. Ruggiero, Exec. V.P., C.F.O.
J. M. Pierpont, V.P., Treas.

INVESTOR CONTACT: Richard E. Koch, V.P., Investor Relations, (203) 750-3254

PRINCIPAL OFFICE: 501 Merritt 7, P.O. Box 4500, Norwalk, CT 06856-4500

TELEPHONE NUMBER: (203) 750-3000
FAX: (203) 750-3205
WEB: www.olin.com

NO. OF EMPLOYEES: 6,700 (avg.)

SHAREHOLDERS: 7,950 (approx.)

ANNUAL MEETING: In Apr.

INCORPORATED: VA, Aug., 1892

INSTITUTIONAL HOLDINGS:
No. of Institutions: 164
Shares Held: 26,154,554
% Held: 59.5

INDUSTRY: Alkalies and chlorine (SIC: 2812)

TRANSFER AGENT(S): Mellon Investor Services, Ridgefield Park, NJ

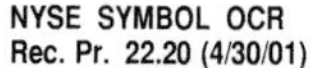

NYSE SYMBOL OCR
Rec. Pr. 22.20 (4/30/01)

OMNICARE, INC.

YIELD 0.4%
P/E RATIO 41.1

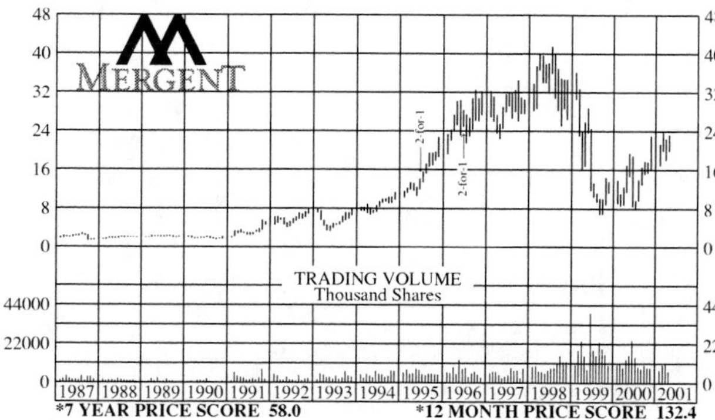

INTERIM EARNINGS (Per Share):

Qtr.	Mar.	June	Sept.	Dec.
1997	0.18	0.19	0.13	0.20
1998	0.24	0.09	0.29	0.29
1999	0.31	0.05	0.15	0.12
2000	0.16	0.12	0.15	0.11

INTERIM DIVIDENDS (Per Share):

Amt.	Decl.	Ex.	Rec.	Pay.
0.023Q	5/15/00	5/30/00	6/01/00	6/12/00
0.023Q	8/02/00	8/24/00	8/28/00	9/11/00
0.023Q	11/01/00	11/22/00	11/27/00	12/11/00
0.023Q	2/07/01	2/26/01	2/28/01	3/14/01
0.023Q	5/21/01	5/30/01	6/01/01	6/12/01

Indicated div.: $0.09 (Div. Reinv. Plan)

CAPITALIZATION (12/31/00):

	($000)	(%)
Long-Term Debt	780,706	40.8
Deferred Income Tax	63,579	3.3
Common & Surplus	1,068,423	55.9
Total	1,912,708	100.0

RECENT DEVELOPMENTS: For the year ended 12/31/00, net income totaled $48.8 million compared with $57.7 million a year earlier. Results for 2000 and 1999 included after-tax restructuring and other related charges of $17.1 million and $22.7 million, respectively. Sales advanced 5.9% to $1.97 billion from $1.86 billion in 1999. Gross profit rose modestly to $525.4 million from $523.3 million in the previous year.

PROSPECTS: OCR's prospects are mixed. On the plus side, the Company's Institutional Pharmacy business is experiencing positive new account growth and the operating environment for OCR's skilled nursing facility customers is improving gradually. OCR has also completed its 18-month productivity and consolidation initiative, which included the streamlining of operations, cost reductions, and standardization of practices.

BUSINESS

OMNICARE, INC. is a provider of pharmacy services to long-term care institutions such as skilled nursing facilities, assisted living communities and other institutional health care facilities. OCR purchases, repackages and dispenses pharmaceuticals, both prescription and non-prescription, and provides computerized medical record-keeping and third-party billing for residents in such facilities. OCR also provides consultant pharmacist services, including evaluating residents' drug therapy, monitoring the control, distribution and administration of drugs and assisting in compliance with state and federal regulations. Additionally, OCR provides ancillary services, such as infusion therapy, distributes medical supplies and offers clinical and financial software information systems to its client nursing facilities.

ANNUAL FINANCIAL DATA

	12/31/00	12/31/99	[6] 12/31/98	12/31/97	12/31/96	12/31/95	12/31/94
Earnings Per Share	[5] 0.53	[5] 0.63	[4] 0.90	[2] [3] 0.69	[2] 0.64	[2] 0.47	[1] 0.30
Cash Flow Per Share	1.33	1.39	1.43	1.01	0.87	0.68	0.47
Tang. Book Val. Per Share	...	...	...	0.99	4.87	1.08	1.21
Dividends Per Share	0.09	0.09	0.08	0.07	0.06	0.05	0.05
Dividend Payout %	17.0	14.3	8.9	10.1	9.4	10.6	14.9
INCOME STATEMENT (IN MILLIONS):							
Total Revenues	1,971.3	1,861.9	1,517.4	895.7	536.6	399.6	275.7
Costs & Expenses	1,766.7	1,656.3	1,313.6	772.7	456.7	344.9	241.5
Depreciation & Amort.	74.0	69.4	47.6	25.7	15.4	11.1	7.4
Operating Income	130.7	136.3	156.1	97.3	64.5	43.7	26.7
Net Interest Inc./(Exp.)	d55.1	d46.2	d23.6	d5.6	d3.7	d6.0	d5.8
Income Before Income Taxes	77.5	91.7	135.9	96.8	72.1	41.2	22.5
Income Taxes	28.7	34.0	55.5	41.1	28.7	16.4	9.1
Net Income	[5] 48.8	[5] 57.7	[4] 80.4	[2] [3] 55.7	[2] 43.5	[2] 24.8	[1] 13.4
Cash Flow	122.8	127.1	128.0	81.4	58.9	35.9	20.8
Average Shs. Outstg. (000)	92,012	91,238	89,786	80,303	67,388	52,396	44,152
BALANCE SHEET (IN MILLIONS):							
Cash & Cash Equivalents	113.9	97.3	54.3	131.0	216.5	40.1	79.6
Total Current Assets	817.7	752.3	603.3	472.0	390.7	161.1	162.2
Net Property	158.5	162.1	136.4	84.1	56.1	32.5	20.5
Total Assets	2,210.2	2,168.0	1,903.8	1,289.6	721.7	360.8	305.8
Total Current Liabilities	257.0	322.2	233.5	128.1	61.7	54.7	37.2
Long-Term Obligations	780.7	736.9	651.6	352.6	2.0	82.7	83.0
Net Stockholders' Equity	1,068.4	1,028.4	963.5	774.2	634.4	214.8	178.9
Net Working Capital	560.7	430.1	369.7	343.9	329.0	106.4	125.1
Year-end Shs. Outstg. (000)	92,156	91,286	90,265	82,153	77,026	52,640	50,584
STATISTICAL RECORD:							
Operating Profit Margin %	6.6	7.3	10.3	10.9	12.0	10.9	9.7
Net Profit Margin %	2.5	3.1	5.3	6.2	8.1	6.2	4.9
Return on Equity %	4.6	5.6	8.3	7.2	6.8	11.5	7.5
Return on Assets %	2.2	2.7	4.2	4.3	6.0	6.9	4.4
Debt/Total Assets %	35.3	34.0	34.2	27.3	0.3	22.9	27.1
Price Range	23.00-8.00	36.19-6.88	41.56-25.00	34.56-22.38	32.50-19.13	22.69-10.22	11.31-6.72
P/E Ratio	43.4-15.1	57.4-10.9	46.2-27.8	50.1-32.4	50.8-29.9	48.3-21.7	37.4-22.2
Average Yield %	0.6	0.4	0.2	0.2	0.2	0.3	0.5

Statistics are as originally reported. Adj. for 2-for-1 stk. split 6/95 & 6/96. [1] Incl. nonrecur. chgs. of $1.9 mill. [2] Incl. a net chg. of $989,000, 1995; $534,000, 1996; $3.1 mill., 1997. [3] Incl. a net non-recurr. chg. of $6.0 mill. [4] Incl. a net chg. of $13.9 mill. & a nonrecur. net restruct. chg. of $2.7 mill. [5] Incl. an after-tax net restruct. chg. of $17.2 mill., 1999; $17.1 mill. ($0.19/sh.), 2000. [6] Incl. the results of CompScript, Inc. and IBAH, Inc.

OFFICERS:
E. L. Hutton, Chmn.
J. F. Gemunder, Pres.
D. W. Froesel Jr., Sr. V.P., C.F.O.

INVESTOR CONTACT: Investor Relations Dept., (606) 392-3331

PRINCIPAL OFFICE: 160 East RiverCenter Boulevard, Covington, KY 41011

TELEPHONE NUMBER: (606) 392-3300
FAX: (606) 392-3333
WEB: www.omnicare.com

NO. OF EMPLOYEES: 5,600 full-time (approx.); 3,700 part-time (approx.)

SHAREHOLDERS: 2,553

ANNUAL MEETING: In May

INCORPORATED: DE, May, 1981

INSTITUTIONAL HOLDINGS:
No. of Institutions: 204
Shares Held: 80,114,052
% Held: 86.5

INDUSTRY: Drug stores and proprietary stores (SIC: 5912)

TRANSFER AGENT(S): First Chicago Trust Company of New York, Jersey City, NJ

NYSE SYMBOL OMC
Rec. Pr. 87.85 (4/30/01)

OMNICOM GROUP, INC.

YIELD 0.9%
P/E RATIO 32.1

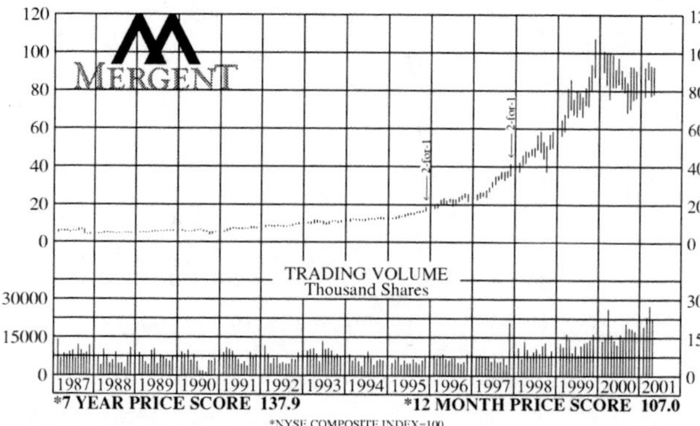

INTERIM EARNINGS (Per Share):

Qtr.	Mar.	June	Sept.	Dec.
1997	0.25	0.40	0.26	0.45
1998	0.31	0.50	0.32	0.55
1999	0.37	0.59	0.39	0.66
2000	0.78	0.70	0.48	0.78

INTERIM DIVIDENDS (Per Share):

Amt.	Decl.	Ex.	Rec.	Pay.
0.175Q	5/15/00	6/07/00	6/09/00	7/06/00
0.175Q	9/19/00	9/26/00	9/28/00	10/06/00
0.175Q	12/04/00	12/15/00	12/19/00	1/05/01
0.175Q	1/29/01	3/07/01	3/09/01	4/05/01
0.20Q	5/22/01	6/06/01	6/08/01	7/05/01

Indicated div.: $0.80

CAPITALIZATION (12/31/00):

	($000)	(%)
Long-Term Debt	1,245,387	41.9
Deferred Income Tax	37,792	1.3
Minority Interest	137,870	4.6
Common & Surplus	1,548,477	52.1
Total	2,969,526	100.0

RECENT DEVELOPMENTS: For the year ended 12/31/00, net income grew 37.5% to $498.8 million from $362.9 million in 1999. Earnings for 2001 included a pre-tax realized gain of $110.0 million on the sale of a portion of the Company's ownership position in Razorfish. Total revenues increased 20.0% to $6.15 billion. Domestic revenues grew 28.6% to $3.26 billion. International revenues rose 11.5% to $2.90 billion.

PROSPECTS: On 6/7/01, Ketchum, a unit of the Company, acquired Chicago-based Corporate Technology Communications, a business-to-business and technology communications firm. The acquisition is expected to expand Ketchum's technology business in the Midwest and nationally. Separately, the Company acquired London-based Wolff Olins, a major independent brand consultant.

BUSINESS

OMNICOM GROUP, INC. is a global provider of marketing communications and advertising services. The Omnicom Group companies service clients through worldwide, national and regional independent agency brands. These brands include BBDO Worldwide, DDB Worldwide and TBWA Worldwide. Omnicom also includes Diversified Agency Services (DAS), which operates branded independent agencies in public relations, specialty advertising, and direct response and promotional marketing; Omnicom Media Group, which includes two international media buying and planning agencies, OMD and PhD; and Communicade, which manages investments in Internet and digital media development companies. In January 1998, OMC acquired Fleishman-Hillard, Inc., GPC International Holdings, Inc., and Palmer Jarvis, Inc.

ANNUAL FINANCIAL DATA

	12/31/00	12/31/99	12/31/98	12/31/97	12/31/96	12/31/95	12/31/94
Earnings Per Share	**2 2.73**	**2.01**	**1.68**	**1.37**	**1.15**	**0.95**	**1 0.79**
Cash Flow Per Share	**3.83**	**2.94**	**2.50**	**2.02**	**1.79**	**1.51**	**1.27**
Dividends Per Share	**0.70**	**0.60**	**0.50**	**0.42**	**0.45**	**0.32**	**0.31**
Dividend Payout %	**25.6**	**29.8**	**29.8**	**31.0**	**39.3**	**33.7**	**39.2**
INCOME STATEMENT (IN MILLIONS):							
Total Revenues	6,154.2	5,130.5	4,092.0	3,124.8	2,641.7	2,257.5	1,756.2
Costs & Expenses	5,050.5	4,210.7	3,377.4	2,601.1	2,215.4	1,901.8	1,479.3
Depreciation & Amort.	225.7	195.7	154.4	120.2	99.7	84.8	72.3
Operating Income	878.1	724.1	560.2	403.5	326.6	270.9	204.6
Net Interest Inc./(Exp.)	d76.5	d50.4	d40.0	d22.3	d21.3	d28.3	d22.8
Income Before Income Taxes	911.6	673.7	520.1	381.2	305.2	242.7	181.8
Income Taxes	369.1	273.2	215.8	156.5	123.6	97.4	74.3
Equity Earnings/Minority Int.	d43.7	d37.6	d19.3	d2.3	d5.3	d5.3	0.7
Net Income	2 498.8	362.9	285.1	222.4	176.3	140.0	1 108.1
Cash Flow	724.5	558.6	439.5	342.6	276.0	224.8	180.4
Average Shs. Outstg. (000)	189,038	189,885	175,844	169,484	154,142	148,750	141,530
BALANCE SHEET (IN MILLIONS):							
Cash & Cash Equivalents	576.5	600.9	728.8	644.1	523.1	335.5	256.6
Total Current Assets	5,366.9	4,712.3	3,981.3	2,988.4	2,425.0	2,106.0	1,601.9
Net Property	483.1	444.7	326.6	239.7	221.7	200.5	172.2
Total Assets	9,891.5	9,017.6	6,910.1	4,965.7	4,055.9	3,527.7	2,852.2
Total Current Liabilities	6,625.1	6,009.1	4,796.4	3,579.0	2,863.1	2,502.4	1,986.6
Long-Term Obligations	1,245.4	711.6	715.9	341.7	409.5	580.8	187.3
Net Stockholders' Equity	1,548.5	1,552.9	1,086.5	866.7	800.7	551.5	540.7
Net Working Capital	d1,258.2	d1,296.7	d815.1	d590.6	d438.1	d396.4	d384.7
Year-end Shs. Outstg. (000)	184,079	177,488	168,593	162,115	160,858	149,316	144,528
STATISTICAL RECORD:							
Operating Profit Margin %	14.3	14.1	13.7	12.9	12.4	12.0	11.7
Net Profit Margin %	8.1	7.1	7.0	7.1	6.7	6.2	6.2
Return on Equity %	32.2	23.4	26.2	25.7	22.0	25.4	20.0
Return on Assets %	5.0	4.0	4.1	4.5	4.3	4.0	3.8
Debt/Total Assets %	12.6	7.9	10.4	6.9	10.1	16.5	6.6
Price Range	100.94-68.13	107.50-55.94	58.50-37.00	41.50-22.25	26.06-17.75	18.75-12.47	13.44-10.94
P/E Ratio	37.0-25.0	53.5-27.8	34.8-22.0	30.3-16.2	22.8-15.5	19.7-13.1	17.0-13.8
Average Yield %	0.8	0.7	1.0	1.3	2.1	2.1	2.5

Statistics are as originally reported. Adjusted for 2-for-1 stock split, 1/98 & 12/95. 1 Bef. acct. chrg. of $28.0 mill., 1994. 2 Incl. a pre-tax realized gain on the sale of an investment of $110.0 mill.

OFFICERS:
B. Crawford, Chmn.
J. D. Wren, Pres., C.E.O.
R. J. Weisenburger, Exec. V.P., C.F.O.

INVESTOR CONTACT: Randall Weisenburger, Exec. V.P., C.F.O., (212) 415-3393

PRINCIPAL OFFICE: 437 Madison Ave., New York, NY 10022

TELEPHONE NUMBER: (212) 415-3600
FAX: (212) 415-3393
WEB: www.omnicomgroup.com

NO. OF EMPLOYEES: 56,000 (approx.)

SHAREHOLDERS: 4,197

ANNUAL MEETING: In May

INCORPORATED: NY, Mar., 1944; reincorp., NY, Aug., 1986

INSTITUTIONAL HOLDINGS:
No. of Institutions: 439
Shares Held: 145,503,981
% Held: 78.9

INDUSTRY: Advertising agencies (SIC: 7311)

TRANSFER AGENT(S): Mellon Investor Services, South Hakensack, NJ

NYSE SYMBOL OCQ
Rec. Pr. 17.93 (5/31/01)

ONEIDA LTD.

YIELD 1.1%
P/E RATIO ...

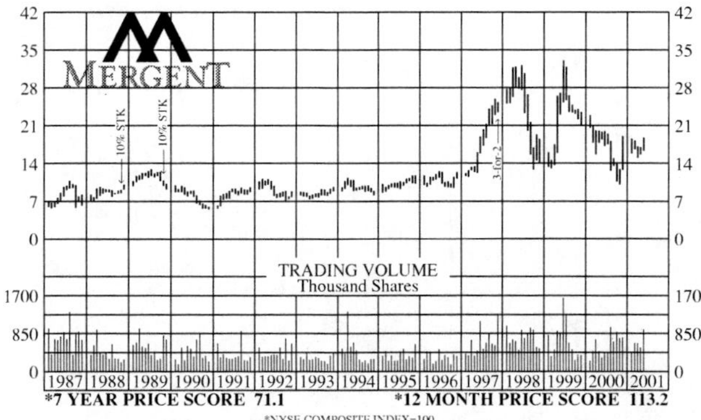

*7 YEAR PRICE SCORE 71.1 *12 MONTH PRICE SCORE 113.2

*NYSE COMPOSITE INDEX=100

INTERIM EARNINGS (Per Share):

Qtr.	Apr.	July	Oct.	Jan.
1996-97	0.15	0.19	0.31	0.37
1997-98	0.27	0.33	0.45	0.50
1998-99	0.32	0.30	0.34	0.20
1999-00	d1.11	0.46	0.29	0.69
2000-01	0.45	d1.03	0.25	0.24

INTERIM DIVIDENDS (Per Share):

Amt.	Decl.	Ex.	Rec.	Pay.
0.10Q	8/31/00	9/07/00	9/11/00	9/29/00
0.10Q	11/29/00	1/04/01	1/08/01	1/29/01
0.05Q	2/28/01	4/06/01	4/10/01	4/30/01
0.05Q	5/30/01	7/06/01	7/10/01	7/30/01

Indicated div.: $0.20 (Div. Reinv. Plan)

CAPITALIZATION (1/27/01):

	($000)	(%)
Long-Term Debt	282,815	69.5
Preferred Stock	2,167	0.5
Common & Surplus	122,141	30.0
Total	407,123	100.0

RECENT DEVELOPMENTS: For the year ended 1/27/01, net loss was $1.3 million versus net income of $5.5 million the previous year. Results in fiscal 2000 and fiscal 1999 included one-time pre-tax charges of $39.0 million and $44.3 million, respectively, primarily related to restructuring. Net sales rose 4.1% to $515.5 million from $495.1 million a year earlier. Gross profit was $161.7 million, or 31.4% of net sales, compared with $193.1 million, or 39.0% of net sales, the year before. Operating income slipped 18.0% to $20.1 million.

PROSPECTS: Earnings are being hurt by lower sales stemming from the Company's aggressive stock keeping unit (SKU) reduction program and significantly lower production levels, which are resulting in increased overhead costs and plant utilization inefficiencies. The Company has reduced its SKUs from 30,000 units at the beginning of 2000 to 12,000 units at year-end, with further reductions anticipated going forward. The elimination of this inventory is expected to significantly increase future cash flow, inventory turnover and operating efficiencies.

BUSINESS

ONEIDA LTD. operates primarily in tableware products. The Company's Tableware operations involve the manufacture and distribution of complete lines of stainless, plated and sterling flatware, and silverplated and stainless holloware for retail and institutional customers. Oneida's Buffalo China, Inc. subsidiary is a maker of china for food service customers. Oneida acquired Rego China, an importer and marketer of commercial vitreous china and porcelain for the U.S. foodservice industry, in November 1996. The Company sold its Camden Wire Co. subsidiary to International Wire Group on 2/12/97.

ANNUAL FINANCIAL DATA

	1/27/01	1/29/00	1/30/99	1/31/98	[2] 1/25/97	1/27/96	1/28/95
Earnings Per Share	[4] **d0.09**	[4] **0.32**	[4] **1.16**	[3] **1.55**	[1] **1.03**	**1.09**	**0.83**
Cash Flow Per Share	**0.87**	**1.16**	**2.11**	**2.38**	**1.72**	**2.03**	**1.72**
Tang. Book Val. Per Share	...	**6.23**	**5.95**	**5.67**	**5.11**	**6.29**	**5.68**
Dividends Per Share	**0.30**	**0.40**	**0.50**	**0.45**	**0.35**	**0.32**	**0.32**
Dividend Payout %	...	**125.0**	**43.1**	**28.8**	**33.8**	**29.4**	**38.7**
INCOME STATEMENT (IN THOUSANDS):							
Total Revenues	521,988	495,917	466,738	442,866	376,923	514,281	493,422
Costs & Expenses	486,430	457,597	410,838	378,400	329,578	459,181	447,700
Depreciation & Amort.	15,449	13,812	15,822	13,765	11,455	15,402	14,345
Operating Income	20,109	24,508	40,078	50,701	35,890	39,698	31,377
Net Interest Inc./(Exp.)	d21,602	d10,875	d8,963	d6,823	d6,503	d8,639	d7,362
Income Before Income Taxes	d2,072	13,835	31,952	42,324	28,555	29,770	22,833
Income Taxes	cr772	8,324	12,202	16,189	11,279	11,682	9,340
Net Income	[4] d1,300	[4] 5,511	[4] 19,750	[3] 26,135	[1] 17,276	18,088	13,493
Cash Flow	14,149	19,323	35,572	39,900	28,731	33,490	27,838
Average Shs. Outstg.	16,300	16,672	16,888	16,740	16,707	16,529	16,176
BALANCE SHEET (IN THOUSANDS):							
Cash & Cash Equivalents	2,163	3,899	1,913	3,095	3,183	2,847	2,207
Total Current Assets	324,788	281,743	275,938	209,844	224,775	215,233	212,124
Net Property	112,447	106,277	95,028	84,812	79,146	115,199	112,292
Total Assets	610,573	449,238	442,068	363,586	350,228	344,363	336,030
Total Current Liabilities	112,639	136,606	135,872	90,510	96,554	93,751	93,206
Long-Term Obligations	282,815	98,495	89,605	69,415	68,126	72,129	77,278
Net Stockholders' Equity	124,308	133,307	140,248	135,257	118,318	106,300	95,196
Net Working Capital	212,149	145,137	140,066	119,334	128,221	121,482	118,918
Year-end Shs. Outstg.	16,388	16,534	16,608	16,617	16,653	16,551	16,353
STATISTICAL RECORD:							
Operating Profit Margin %	3.9	4.9	8.6	11.4	9.5	7.7	6.4
Net Profit Margin %	...	1.1	4.2	5.9	4.6	3.5	2.7
Return on Equity %	...	4.1	14.1	19.3	14.6	17.0	14.2
Return on Assets %	...	1.2	4.5	7.2	4.9	5.3	4.0
Debt/Total Assets %	46.3	21.9	20.3	19.1	19.5	20.9	23.0
Price Range	22.88-10.06	33.06-13.06	32.19-12.81	25.92-11.50	12.58-9.42	11.75-8.58	11.33-8.08
P/E Ratio	...	103.3-40.8	27.7-11.0	16.7-7.4	12.3-9.2	10.8-7.9	13.7-9.8
Average Yield %	1.8	1.7	2.2	2.4	3.2	3.1	3.3

Statistics are as originally reported. Adj. for 3-for-2 stk. split, 12/97. [1] Bef. $304,000 ($0.02/sh) loss fr discont. opers. [2] Excl. results of Camden Wire subsid. [3] Excl. $2.6 mil ($0.15/sh) gain fr sale of subsid. [4] Incl. $39.0 mil ($1.50/sh) pre-tax restr. chg., 1/01; $44.3 mil ($1.83/sh) pre-tax non-recur. chg., 1/00; $5.0 mil ($0.19/sh) pre-tax restr. chg., 1/99.

OFFICERS:
P. J. Kallet, Chmn., Pres., C.E.O.
G. R. Denny, C.F.O.
C. H. Suttmeier, V.P., Gen. Couns., Sec.

INVESTOR CONTACT: Gregg Denny, C.F.O., (315) 361-3138

PRINCIPAL OFFICE: 163-181 Kenwood Avenue, Oneida, NY 13421-2899

TELEPHONE NUMBER: (315) 361-3636
FAX: (315) 361-3399
WEB: www.oneida.com

NO. OF EMPLOYEES: 4,570 (approx.)

SHAREHOLDERS: 4,011

ANNUAL MEETING: In May

INCORPORATED: NY, Nov., 1880

INSTITUTIONAL HOLDINGS:
No. of Institutions: 60
Shares Held: 9,305,943
% Held: 56.5

INDUSTRY: Silverware and plated ware (SIC: 3914)

TRANSFER AGENT(S): American Stock Transfer & Trust Co., New York, NY

NYSE SYMBOL OKE
Rec. Pr. 21.61 (Adj.; 4/30/01)

ONEOK INC.

YIELD 5.7%
P/E RATIO 15.4

INTERIM EARNINGS (Per Share):

Qtr.	Nov.	Feb.	May	Aug.
1997-98	0.27	0.72	0.26	d0.33
1998-99	0.08	0.67	0.19	d0.11
Qtr.	**Mar.**	**June**	**Sept.**	**Dec.**
1999	...	...	...	0.35
2000	0.64	0.28	0.02	0.46

INTERIM DIVIDENDS (Per Share):

Amt.	Decl.	Ex.	Rec.	Pay.
0.31Q	6/15/00	7/27/00	7/31/00	8/15/00
0.31Q	10/19/00	10/27/00	10/31/00	11/15/00
0.31Q	1/18/01	1/29/01	1/31/01	2/15/01
2-for-1	1/18/01	6/12/01	5/23/01	6/11/01
0.31Q	4/19/01	4/26/01	4/30/01	5/15/01

Indicated div.: $1.24 (Div. Reinv. Plan)

CAPITALIZATION (12/31/00):

	($000)	(%)
Long-Term Debt	1,336,082	43.4
Capital Lease Obligations	137,131	4.5
Deferred Income Tax	382,363	12.4
Preferred Stock	199	0.0
Common & Surplus	1,224,758	39.8
Total	3,080,533	100.0

RECENT DEVELOPMENTS: For the year ended 12/31/00, income rose to $143.5 million, before an accounting change credit of $2.1 million, versus net income of $106.9 million a year earlier. Operating revenues increased to $6.64 billion. Results were driven by strong gains from OKE's marketing and trading operations, primarily attributable to the marketing and trading business acquired on 4/5/00 from Kinder Morgan, Inc., and the gathering and processing segment, which benefited from both the acquisitions and strong natural gas liquids prices.

PROSPECTS: Near-term prospects are encouraging, reflecting the Company's continuing strategy of growth through unregulated acquisitions that strengthen and complement each other. Notably, results going forward should benefit from a full year of operations from the midstream assets that were acquired during 2000, the completion of OKE's 300-megawatt power plant in June 2001, improved hedges for production sales, and a full year of weather-normalized rates in Kansas.

BUSINESS

ONEOK INC. and its subsidiaries are engaged in several aspects of the energy business. The Company purchases, gathers, processes, transports, stores, and distributes natural gas. The Company drills for and produces oil and natural gas, extracts, sells and markets natural gas liquids, and is engaged in the gas marketing and trading business. The Company also engages in wholesale marketing of electricity on a limited basis and is building a 300-megawatt electric power plant in Oklahoma. In 2000, revenues (and operating income) were derived: marketing trading, 70.2% (15.4%); gathering and processing, 15.6% (33.2%); transportation and storage, 2.5% (18.6%); distribution, 19.2% (29.3%); production, 1.1% (4.6%); other and eliminations, -8.6 (-1.1). On 3/23/00, OKE acquired $307.7 million in midstream assets from Dynergy Inc. On 4/5/00, OKE acquired the natural gas gathering and processing businesses of Kinder Morgan, Inc.

ANNUAL FINANCIAL DATA

	12/31/00	1 12/31/99	8/31/99	12/31/98	8/31/98	8/31/97	8/31/96
Earnings Per Share	**2 1.48**	**1.05**	**1.03**	**1.01**	**1.12**	**1.07**	**0.97**
Cash Flow Per Share	**2.54**	**1.96**	**1.93**	**1.79**	**1.93**	**2.41**	**2.31**
Tang. Book Val. Per Share	**19.12**	**18.11**	**18.11**	**17.60**	**8.28**	**8.24**	**7.61**
Dividends Per Share	**0.62**	**0.62**	**0.62**	**0.60**	**0.60**	**0.60**	**0.59**
Dividend Payout %	**41.9**	**59.3**	**60.2**	**59.9**	**54.3**	**56.1**	**60.8**
INCOME STATEMENT (IN MILLIONS):							
Total Revenues	3 6,642.9	2,071.0	1,842.8	1,841.5	1,835.4	1,161.9	1,224.3
Costs & Expenses	6,164.9	1,701.8	1,493.5	1,531.6	1,530.3	958.6	1,030.4
Depreciation & Amort.	144.0	131.2	129.7	117.2	101.7	74.5	72.9
Operating Income	333.9	238.0	219.6	192.7	136.9	94.0	88.0
Net Interest Inc./(Exp.)	d118.6	d65.7	d52.8	d38.8	d35.1	d34.7	d35.2
Income Taxes	90.3	67.1	67.1	69.3	66.6	34.8	33.0
Net Income	2 143.5	106.9	106.4	104.2	101.8	59.3	52.8
Cash Flow	250.4	200.9	198.8	185.0	176.5	133.5	125.3
Average Shs. Outstg. (000)	98,388	102,306	103,142	103,242	91,458	55,288	54,272
BALANCE SHEET (IN MILLIONS):							
Gross Property	4,206.1	3,143.7	3,057.6	2,637.5	2,601.9	1,429.5	1,336.7
Accumulated Depreciation	1,110.6	1,021.9	988.8	931.3	915.8	586.2	541.6
Net Property	3,095.5	2,121.8	2,068.8	1,706.2	1,686.2	843.3	795.0
Total Assets	7,369.1	3,239.6	3,024.9	2,557.1	2,422.5	1,237.4	1,219.9
Long-Term Obligations	1,473.2	775.1	810.1	336.1	312.4	328.2	336.8
Net Stockholders' Equity	1,225.0	1,151.5	1,174.5	1,184.6	1,168.9	462.6	423.7
Year-end Shs. Outstg. (000)	59,177	59,109	60,338	62,709	63,152	56,160	54,522
STATISTICAL RECORD:							
Operating Profit Margin %	5.0	11.5	11.9	10.5	7.5	8.1	7.2
Net Profit Margin %	2.2	5.2	5.8	5.7	5.5	5.1	4.3
Net Inc./Net Property %	4.6	5.0	5.1	6.1	6.0	7.0	6.6
Net Inc./Tot. Capital %	4.7	4.7	4.6	5.7	5.7	6.1	5.6
Return on Equity %	11.7	9.3	9.1	8.8	8.7	12.8	12.5
Accum. Depr./Gross Prop. %	26.4	32.5	32.3	35.3	35.2	41.0	40.5
Price Range	25.31-10.88	18.59-12.25	18.59-12.25	22.13-14.88	22.13-14.88	20.34-12.94	15.19-10.00
P/E Ratio	17.1-7.3	17.8-11.7	18.1-11.9	21.9-14.7	19.8-13.3	19.1-12.1	15.7-10.4
Average Yield %	3.4	4.0	4.0	3.3	3.3	3.6	4.7

Statistics are as originally reported. Adj. for 2-for-1 stk. split, 6/01 1 Refl. change in fiscal year fr. 8/31 to 12/31 2 Bef. acctg. chge. credit of $2.1 mill. 3 Refl. acqs. of Dynergy Inc. assets & the natural gas gathering processing bus. of Kinder Morgan, Inc.

OFFICERS:
D. L. Kyle, Chmn., Pres., C.E.O.
J. C. Kneale, Sr. V.P., C.F.O., Treas.
J. A. Gaberino Jr., Sr. V.P., Gen. Couns.

INVESTOR CONTACT: Weldon Watson, V.P., Investor Relations, (918) 588-7158

PRINCIPAL OFFICE: 100 West 5th Street, Tulsa, OK 74103

TELEPHONE NUMBER: (918) 588-7000
FAX: (918) 588-7273
WEB: www.oneok.com
NO. OF EMPLOYEES: 3,664 (avg.)
SHAREHOLDERS: 14,481
ANNUAL MEETING: In May
INCORPORATED: DE, Nov., 1933; reincorp., OK, May, 1997

INSTITUTIONAL HOLDINGS:
No. of Institutions: 180
Shares Held: 24,833,066 (Adj.)
% Held: 41.9

INDUSTRY: Gas transmission and distribution (SIC: 4923)

TRANSFER AGENT(S): First Chicago Trust Company of New York, Jersey City, NJ

NYSE SYMBOL OS
Rec. Pr. 7.21 (5/31/01)

OREGON STEEL MILLS, INC.

YIELD . . .
P/E RATIO . . .

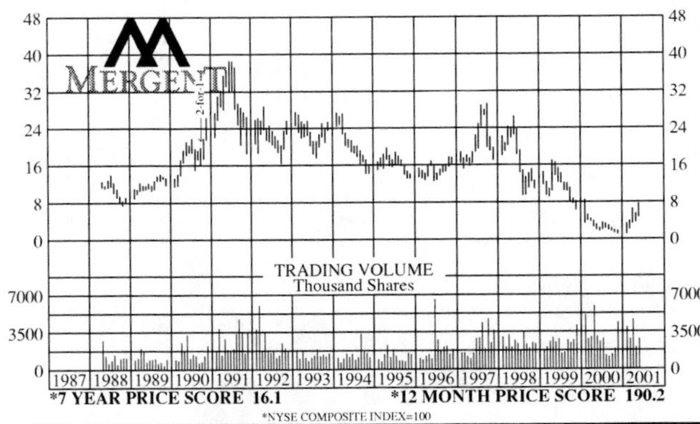

*7 YEAR PRICE SCORE 16.1 *12 MONTH PRICE SCORE 190.2

*NYSE COMPOSITE INDEX=100

INTERIM EARNINGS (Per Share):

Qtr.	Mar.	June	Sept.	Dec.
1997	0.27	0.31	0.40	d0.53
1998	0.07	0.18	0.38	d0.17
1999	0.32	0.20	0.31	d0.07
2000	d0.41	d0.11	d0.02	d0.15

INTERIM DIVIDENDS (Per Share):

Amt.	Decl.	Ex.	Rec.	Pay.
0.14Q	7/29/99	8/11/99	8/13/99	8/31/99
0.14Q	10/28/99	11/09/99	11/12/99	11/30/99
0.02Q	1/28/00	2/10/00	2/14/00	2/29/00
0.02Q	4/28/00	5/11/00	5/15/00	5/31/00
0.02Q	7/27/00	8/16/00	8/18/00	8/31/00

Dividend payment suspended.

CAPITALIZATION (12/31/00):

	($000)	(%)
Long-Term Debt	314,356	45.0
Deferred Income Tax	22,627	3.2
Minority Interest	29,771	4.3
Common & Surplus	331,645	47.5
Total	698,399	100.0

RECENT DEVELOPMENTS: For the year ended 12/31/00, OS incurred a loss $18.3 million compared with net income of $19.9 million in 1999. Results included a gain of $290,000 in 2000 and a loss of $501,000 in 1999 on the sale of assets. Results for 1999 also included a charge of $7.0 million for the settlement of litigation. Sales were $636.5 million, down 22.6% from $822.0 million a year earlier.

PROSPECTS: The Company expects pricing pressure to continue in most of its product lines into the foreseeable future. While demand for the Company's plate and large diameter pipe products is improving, pricing remains depressed. Continued low pricing for rod products is likely to result in production cutbacks during the first quarter of 2001. The Company anticipates that it will incur a net loss in the first quarter of 2001.

BUSINESS

OREGON STEEL MILLS, INC. operates two steel minimills and four finishing facilities in the western U.S. and Canada. The Company manufactures and markets a broad line of specialty and commodity steel products. OS's two business units are the Oregon Steel Division and Rocky Mountain Steel Mills (RMSM) Division (formerly the CF&I Steel Division). The Oregon Steel Division's steel pipe mill in Napa, California is a large diameter steel pipe mill and fabrication facility. Located in Pueblo, Colorado, the RMSM Division consists of the steelmaking and finishing facilities of CF&I Steel, L.P., 95.2% owned by a subsidiary of OS. In total, OS produces eight steel products that include most standard grades of steel plate and a wide range of higher-margin specialty steel plate, large diameter steel pipe, ERW pipe, long-length and standard rails, seamless pipe, wire rod, bar and wire products.

QUARTERLY DATA

(12/31/2000)($000)	Rev	Inc
1st Quarter	164,900	(10,800)
2nd Quarter	161,800	(3,000)
3rd Quarter	156,700	(400)
4th Quarter	153,100	(4,100)

ANNUAL FINANCIAL DATA

	12/31/00	12/31/99	12/31/98	12/31/97	12/31/96	12/31/95	12/31/94
Earnings Per Share	**[4] d0.69**	**[1] 0.76**	**[1] 0.45**	**[1] 0.45**	**1.02**	**[1] 0.62**	**[2] 0.60**
Cash Flow Per Share	**1.07**	**2.40**	**2.08**	**1.54**	**2.26**	**1.87**	**2.81**
Tang. Book Val. Per Share	**11.57**	**12.33**	**12.01**	**12.16**	**12.29**	**11.60**	**12.04**
Dividends Per Share	**0.06**	**0.56**	**0.56**	**0.56**	**0.56**	**0.56**	**0.56**
Dividend Payout %	**. . .**	**73.7**	**124.4**	**124.4**	**54.9**	**90.3**	**93.3**
INCOME STATEMENT (IN THOUSANDS):							
Total Revenues	636,470	821,984	892,583	[3] 768,558	772,815	710,971	838,268
Costs & Expenses	588,857	710,387	786,176	709,434	694,495	661,988	792,571
Depreciation & Amort.	46,506	43,415	42,909	28,642	29,025	24,964	44,024
Operating Income	1,107	68,182	63,498	30,482	49,295	24,019	1,673
Net Interest Inc./(Exp.)	d34,936	d35,027	d38,485	d10,216	d12,479	d10,307	d3,910
Income Before Income Taxes	d29,481	32,970	20,316	18,617	35,154	16,196	9,127
Income Taxes	cr11,216	13,056	8,387	6,662	11,407	3,762	cr2,941
Equity Earnings/Minority Int.	d7	d1,475	d4,213	d5,898	d1,204	862	d3,290
Net Income	[4] d18,265	[1] 19,914	[1] 11,929	[1] 11,955	23,747	[1] 12,434	[2] 12,068
Cash Flow	28,241	63,329	54,838	40,597	52,772	37,398	56,092
Average Shs. Outstg.	26,375	26,375	26,368	26,292	23,333	20,016	19,973
BALANCE SHEET (IN THOUSANDS):							
Cash & Cash Equivalents	3,370	9,270	9,044	570	739	644	5,039
Total Current Assets	235,501	208,205	292,765	262,818	235,725	236,780	259,466
Net Property	583,875	607,995	638,609	660,479	604,568	495,154	338,096
Total Assets	880,354	877,254	993,970	986,620	913,355	805,266	665,733
Total Current Liabilities	126,748	101,660	252,516	147,496	114,729	121,327	117,986
Long-Term Obligations	314,356	298,329	270,440	367,473	330,993	312,679	187,935
Net Stockholders' Equity	331,645	352,402	345,117	349,007	353,041	266,790	275,883
Net Working Capital	108,753	106,545	40,249	115,322	120,996	115,453	141,480
Year-end Shs. Outstg.	25,777	25,777	25,777	25,693	25,693	19,422	19,377
STATISTICAL RECORD:							
Operating Profit Margin %	0.2	8.3	7.1	4.0	6.4	3.4	0.2
Net Profit Margin %	. . .	2.4	1.3	1.6	3.1	1.7	1.4
Return on Equity %	. . .	5.7	3.5	3.4	6.7	4.7	4.4
Return on Assets %	. . .	2.3	1.2	1.2	2.6	1.5	1.8
Debt/Total Assets %	35.7	34.0	27.2	37.2	36.2	38.8	28.2
Price Range	8.50-1.00	17.00-6.25	26.50-9.44	29.25-15.13	17.75-12.50	19.75-13.13	27.38-14.13
P/E Ratio	. . .	22.4-8.2	58.9-21.0	65.0-33.6	17.4-12.3	31.8-21.2	45.6-23.5
Average Yield %	1.3	4.8	3.1	2.5	3.7	3.4	2.7

Statistics are as originally reported. [1] Incl. $6.5 mill. gain, 1999; $11.8 mill. gain, 1998; $4 mill. gain, 1997; $4 mill. gain, 1995. [2] Incl. $12.3 mil gain from sale of stk., offset by $13.7 mill. provision for shutdown of assets at the Fontana & Portland plate mills. [3] Incl. $2.5 mil insur. proceeds. [4] Incl. nonrecurr. gain of $290,000 on sale of assets.

OFFICERS:
T. B. Boklund, Chmn.
J. E. Corvin, Pres., C.E.O.
L. R. Adams, V.P., Fin., C.F.O.
L. F. Lee, V.P., Admin., Sec.

INVESTOR CONTACT: Vicki Tagliafico, Director-Investor Relations, (503) 240-5776

PRINCIPAL OFFICE: 1000 S.W. Broadway, Suite 2200, Portland, OR 97205

TELEPHONE NUMBER: (503) 223-9228
FAX: (503) 240-5232
WEB: www.osm.com

NO. OF EMPLOYEES: 1,900 (approx.)

SHAREHOLDERS: 919 (record)

ANNUAL MEETING: In Apr.

INCORPORATED: CA, 1928; reincorp., DE, 1974

INSTITUTIONAL HOLDINGS:
No. of Institutions: 40
Shares Held: 12,339,504
% Held: 47.9

INDUSTRY: Blast furnaces and steel mills (SIC: 3312)

TRANSFER AGENT(S): Mellon Investor Services, LLC, South Hackensack, NJ

NYSE SYMBOL OSM
Rec. Pr. 11.24 (5/31/01)

OSMONICS, INC.

YIELD ...
P/E RATIO 29.6

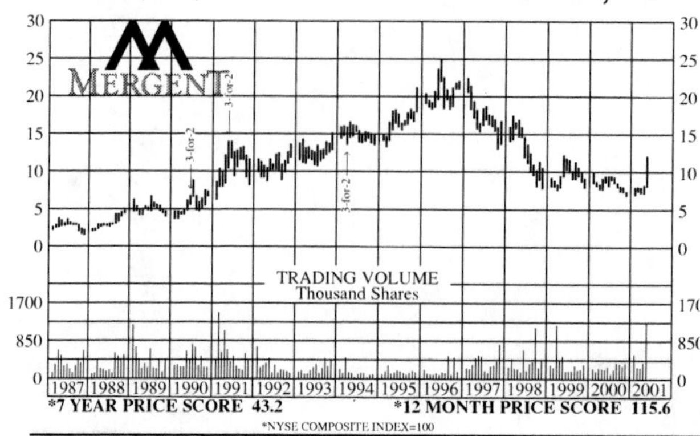

*7 YEAR PRICE SCORE 43.2   *12 MONTH PRICE SCORE 115.6

*NYSE COMPOSITE INDEX=100

INTERIM EARNINGS (Per Share):

Qtr.	Mar.	June	Sept.	Dec.
1997	0.17	0.18	0.16	0.15
1998	0.16	d1.12	0.08	0.08
1999	0.11	0.15	0.10	d0.30
2000	0.11	0.13	0.07	0.07

INTERIM DIVIDENDS (Per Share):

Amt.	Decl.	Ex.	Rec.	Pay.
No dividends paid.				

CAPITALIZATION (12/31/00):

	($000)	(%)
Long-Term Debt	24,603	17.6
Deferred Income Tax	6,335	4.5
Common & Surplus	108,945	77.9
Total	139,883	100.0

RECENT DEVELOPMENTS: For the year ended 12/31/00, net income was $5.4 million compared with $964,000 in 1999. Net sales were $200.1 million, up 7.0% from $187.0 million a year earlier. Results included special charges of $250,000 in 2000 and $2.6 million in 1999. Filtration and separations group sales inched up 1.7% to $80.0 million, well below Company expectations, as sales growth was significantly affected by the bankruptcy of Safety-Kleen.

PROSPECTS: Revenues for the Household Water Group may continue to be negatively affected by a general economic downturn. In addition, sales growth for the Filtration and Separations Group is expected to continue to suffer as a result of the bankruptcy of a significant customer, Safety-Kleen. However, strong order momentum should continue to fuel sales for the Process Water Treatment Group.

BUSINESS

OSMONICS, INC. manufactures and markets high-technology water purification and fluid filtration, fluid separation, and fluid handling equipment, as well as the replaceable components used in purification, filtration, and separation equipment. The Company's products include filtration and separation components, valves & flow control components, equipment and systems, instrumentation and controls, and laboratory products. These products are used by a broad range of industrial, commercial, and residential customers. The Company provides products and services for the industrial processing and power, potable water, health care, food and electronics manufacturing markets. OSM's three business segments are specialty filtration and separations, process water treatment and household water treatment.

ANNUAL FINANCIAL DATA

	12/31/00	12/31/99	12/31/98	12/31/97	12/31/96	12/31/95	12/31/94
Earnings Per Share	**[2] 0.38**	**[3] 0.07**	**[2] d0.08**	**[1][2] 0.59**	**0.93**	**0.83**	**0.79**
Cash Flow Per Share	**1.08**	**0.68**	**0.49**	**1.00**	**1.27**	**1.09**	**1.03**
Tang. Book Val. Per Share	**4.35**	**3.91**	**4.16**	**6.25**	**6.38**	**5.44**	**5.02**
INCOME STATEMENT (IN THOUSANDS):							
Total Revenues	200,139	184,671	177,819	164,905	155,946	130,783	96,180
Costs & Expenses	181,925	171,468	168,142	145,755	133,665	111,651	80,447
Depreciation & Amort.	10,139	8,772	7,964	5,791	4,874	3,795	3,048
Operating Income	8,075	4,431	1,713	13,359	17,407	15,337	12,685
Net Interest Inc./(Exp.)	d3,940	d3,441	d3,620	d1,313	d571	84	796
Income Before Income Taxes	8,082	3,048	d1,078	12,390	19,908	16,833	13,623
Income Taxes	2,663	2,084	cr25	3,927	6,441	4,954	3,668
Net Income	[2] 5,419	[3] 964	[2] d1,053	[1][2] 8,463	13,467	11,879	9,955
Cash Flow	15,558	9,736	6,911	14,254	18,341	15,674	13,003
Average Shs. Outstg.	14,404	14,252	13,976	14,313	14,458	14,365	12,668
BALANCE SHEET (IN THOUSANDS):							
Cash & Cash Equivalents	1,910	15,814	14,847	21,876	24,420	31,036	37,076
Total Current Assets	78,561	83,512	89,381	89,125	88,527	87,749	76,627
Net Property	56,901	58,330	56,813	55,033	51,794	42,489	22,563
Total Assets	188,692	194,366	194,049	164,483	152,176	142,419	102,035
Total Current Liabilities	48,805	51,351	55,405	43,852	34,521	34,055	20,632
Long-Term Obligations	24,603	32,201	31,665	13,792	15,900	20,919	14,050
Net Stockholders' Equity	108,945	104,542	102,155	102,375	97,943	84,273	63,751
Net Working Capital	29,756	32,161	33,976	45,273	54,006	53,694	55,995
Year-end Shs. Outstg.	14,409	14,262	13,991	13,943	14,193	14,086	12,701
STATISTICAL RECORD:							
Operating Profit Margin %	4.0	2.4	1.0	8.1	11.2	11.7	13.2
Net Profit Margin %	2.7	0.5	...	5.1	8.6	9.1	10.4
Return on Equity %	5.0	0.9	...	8.3	13.7	14.1	15.6
Return on Assets %	2.9	0.5	...	5.1	8.8	8.3	9.8
Debt/Total Assets %	13.0	16.6	16.3	8.4	10.4	14.7	13.8
Price Range	9.94-6.81	12.25-7.50	17.50-7.75	22.50-13.00	24.88-18.25	21.25-13.25	16.63-13.50
P/E Ratio	26.1-17.9	174.8-107.0	...	38.1-22.0	26.7-19.6	25.6-16.0	21.0-17.1

Statistics are as originally reported. Adj. for stk. splits: 3-for-2, 3/94 [1] Bef. disc. oper. gain $1.3 mill. [2] Incl. non-recurr. chrg. $250,000, 2000; $8.0 mill., 1998; $1.4 mill., 1997. [3] Incl. net chrg. of $2.6 mill.

OFFICERS:
D. D. Spatz, Chmn., C.E.O.
E. J. Fierko, Pres., C.O.O.
K. B. Robinson, Sr. V.P., C.F.O.
R. C. Spatz, Sec.

INVESTOR CONTACT: Keith B. Robinson, (952) 988-6627

PRINCIPAL OFFICE: 5951 Clearwater Dr., Minnetonka, MN 55343

TELEPHONE NUMBER: (952) 933-2277
FAX: (952) 933-0141
WEB: www.osmonics.com

NO. OF EMPLOYEES: 1,399

SHAREHOLDERS: 1,961

ANNUAL MEETING: In May

INCORPORATED: DE, June, 1969; reincorp., MN, June, 1992

INSTITUTIONAL HOLDINGS:
No. of Institutions: 26
Shares Held: 5,492,548
% Held: 38.0

INDUSTRY: General industrial machinery, nec (SIC: 3569)

TRANSFER AGENT(S): Wells Fargo Investor Services, St. Paul, MN

NYSE SYMBOL OSI
Rec. Pr. 28.99 (4/30/01)

OUTBACK STEAKHOUSE, INC.

YIELD ...
P/E RATIO 16.2

MERGENT

TRADING VOLUME
Thousand Shares

1987 1988 1989 1990 1991 1992 1993 1994 1995 1996 1997 1998 1999 2000 2001

***7 YEAR PRICE SCORE 86.2** ***12 MONTH PRICE SCORE 103.6**

*NYSE COMPOSITE INDEX=100

INTERIM EARNINGS (Per Share):

Qtr.	Mar.	June	Sept.	Dec.
1996	0.23	0.25	0.24	0.25
1997	0.24	0.27	0.27	0.07
1998	0.30	0.33	0.33	0.35
1999	0.37	0.40	0.40	0.38
2000	0.45	0.48	0.45	0.41

INTERIM DIVIDENDS (Per Share):

Amt.	Decl.	Ex.	Rec.	Pay.

No dividends paid.

CAPITALIZATION (12/31/00):

	($000)	(%)
Long-Term Debt	11,678	1.4
Deferred Income Tax	14,382	1.7
Minority Interest	16,840	2.0
Common & Surplus	807,590	95.0
Total	850,490	100.0

RECENT DEVELOPMENTS: For the year ended 12/31/00, net income increased 15.3% to $141.1 million versus pro forma net income of $122.4 million a year earlier. Results for 1999 included a pre-tax special charge of $5.5 million for the write-down of impaired assets and costs associated with the closure of restaurants. Total revenues rose 15.8% to $1.91 billion from $1.65 billion the year before. Restaurant sales grew 15.7% to $1.89 billion, while other revenues jumped 33.0% to $17.7 million.

PROSPECTS: Revenues should benefit from 3.0% increases in menu prices at both Outback Steakhouse and Carrabba's Italian Grills, which were implemented in December 2000. The Company expects to open 56 restaurants domestically in 2001. In addition, OSI anticipates three to six company-owned Outback Steakhouse international joint ventures. Another eight to eleven international joint venture franchises will open in 2001.

BUSINESS

OUTBACK STEAKHOUSE, INC., develops, franchises and operates 781 full-service restaurants as of 5/8/01, including 684 Outback Steakhouses, 83 Carrabba's Italian Grills, six Fleming's Prime Steakhouse and Wine Bars, six Roy's Restaurants, one Zazarac and one Lee Roy Selmon's in 49 states and 16 countries. Outback Steakhouses features steaks, prime rib, pork chops, ribs, chicken, seafood and pasta. Carrabba's features a limited menu of Italian dishes including pastas, seafood, and wood-fired pizza. Fleming's features prime cuts of beef, fresh seafood, pork, veal and chicken entrees as well as an extensive selection of wine. Roy's features Euro-Asian cuisine. Zazarac features southern Louisiana cuisine. Lee Roy's features southern cuisine. OSI's restaurants include specialty appetizers, desserts and full bar service.

QUARTERLY DATA

(12/31/00)($000)	REV	INC
1st Quarter	464,797	35,766
2nd Quarter	481,620	38,298
3rd Quarter	485,102	35,383
4th Quarter	474,487	31,683

ANNUAL FINANCIAL DATA

	12/31/00	12/31/99	12/31/98	12/31/97	12/31/96	12/31/95	12/31/94
Earnings Per Share	**1.78**	**2 1.57**	**1.29**	**1 0.84**	**0.97**	**0.77**	**0.59**
Cash Flow Per Share	**2.51**	**2.22**	**1.81**	**1.46**	**1.45**	**1.13**	**0.82**
Tang. Book Val. Per Share	**10.54**	**8.95**	**7.37**	**5.97**	**4.76**	**3.77**	**2.68**
INCOME STATEMENT (IN MILLIONS):							
Total Revenues	1,906.0	1,646.0	1,358.9	1,151.6	937.4	664.0	451.9
Costs & Expenses	1,600.0	1,367.6	1,147.2	963.3	770.9	541.3	366.0
Depreciation & Amort.	58.1	51.4	39.1	44.8	35.5	24.0	15.1
Operating Income	250.3	222.6	173.1	117.1	130.9	99.1	72.1
Net Interest Inc./(Exp.)	4.6	1.4	d1.2	d2.5	...	d0.9	0.1
Income Before Income Taxes	219.0	191.2	150.7	95.2	111.9	83.9	60.9
Income Taxes	77.9	66.9	53.5	33.7	40.3	29.2	21.6
Equity Earnings/Minority Int.	d31.4	d28.7	d20.7	d19.9	d18.0	d13.8	d10.0
Net Income	141.1	2 124.3	97.2	1 61.5	71.6	54.7	39.3
Cash Flow	199.2	175.7	136.3	106.3	107.1	78.7	54.4
Average Shs. Outstg. (000)	79,232	79,197	75,228	72,758	73,934	69,794	65,996
BALANCE SHEET (IN MILLIONS):							
Cash & Cash Equivalents	131.6	92.6	83.6	39.8	15.7	24.4	23.6
Total Current Assets	182.0	143.2	122.1	75.6	41.1	46.4	39.5
Net Property	694.0	607.0	526.8	459.1	397.8	263.9	162.3
Total Assets	1,022.5	852.3	705.2	592.8	469.8	343.8	228.5
Total Current Liabilities	168.0	130.9	108.8	80.8	74.1	56.0	41.1
Long-Term Obligations	11.7	1.5	37.5	68.3	47.6	29.0	12.3
Net Stockholders' Equity	807.6	693.0	545.0	434.7	342.4	255.1	172.3
Net Working Capital	14.0	12.3	13.2	d5.2	d33.0	d9.6	d1.6
Year-end Shs. Outstg. (000)	76,632	77,404	73,962	72,772	72,014	67,746	64,397
STATISTICAL RECORD:							
Operating Profit Margin %	13.1	13.5	12.7	10.2	14.0	14.9	16.0
Net Profit Margin %	7.4	7.6	7.2	5.3	7.6	8.2	8.7
Return on Equity %	17.5	17.9	17.8	14.1	20.9	21.4	22.8
Return on Assets %	13.8	14.6	13.8	10.4	15.2	15.9	17.2
Debt/Total Assets %	1.1	0.2	5.3	11.5	10.1	8.4	5.4
Price Range	34.44-21.50	40.13-19.81	28.08-15.58	21.58-11.92	27.17-14.25	25.25-15.25	21.33-15.08
P/E Ratio	19.3-12.1	25.6-12.6	21.8-12.1	25.7-14.2	28.1-14.7	32.9-19.9	36.0-25.4

Statistics are as originally reported. Adj. for stk. splits: 3-for-2, 3/99; 3-for-2, 2/94. 1 Incl. non-recurr. chrg. $26.0 mill. 2 Incl. spec. chrg. of $5.5 mill.

OFFICERS:
C. T. Sullivan, Chmn., C.E.O.
R. D. Basham, Pres., C.O.O.
R. S. Merritt, Sr. V.P., C.F.O., Treas.

INVESTOR CONTACT: Lisa Johnston, Inv. Rel., (813) 282-1225

PRINCIPAL OFFICE: 2202 N. Westshore Blvd., 5th Floor, Tampa, FL 33607

TELEPHONE NUMBER: (813) 282-1225
FAX: (813) 282-1209
WEB: www.outback.com

NO. OF EMPLOYEES: 49,000 (approx.)

SHAREHOLDERS: 1,824 (approx. record)

ANNUAL MEETING: In Apr.

INCORPORATED: FL, Oct., 1987; reincorp., DE, Apr., 1991

INSTITUTIONAL HOLDINGS:
No. of Institutions: 204
Shares Held: 54,557,470
% Held: 71.7

INDUSTRY: Eating places (SIC: 5812)

TRANSFER AGENT(S): Bank of New York, New York, NY

NYSE SYMBOL OSG
Rec. Pr. 30.30 (4/30/01)

OVERSEAS SHIPHOLDING GROUP, INC.

YIELD 2.0%
P/E RATIO 26.6

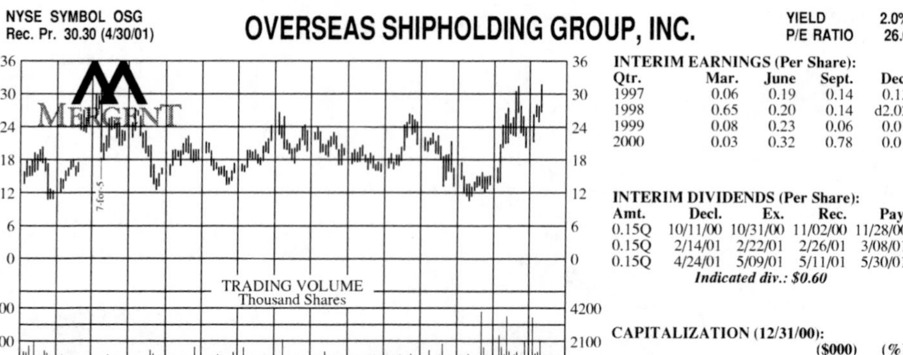

*7 YEAR PRICE SCORE 94.5 *12 MONTH PRICE SCORE 116.2
*NYSE COMPOSITE INDEX=100

INTERIM EARNINGS (Per Share):

Qtr.	Mar.	June	Sept.	Dec.
1997	0.06	0.19	0.14	0.13
1998	0.65	0.20	0.14	d2.02
1999	0.08	0.23	0.06	0.01
2000	0.03	0.32	0.78	0.01

INTERIM DIVIDENDS (Per Share):

Amt.	Decl.	Ex.	Rec.	Pay.
0.15Q	10/11/00	10/31/00	11/02/00	11/28/00
0.15Q	2/14/01	2/22/01	2/26/01	3/08/01
0.15Q	4/24/01	5/09/01	5/11/01	5/30/01

Indicated div.: $0.60

CAPITALIZATION (12/31/00):

	($000)	(%)
Long-Term Debt	770,869	48.6
Capital Lease Obligations	65,628	4.1
Common & Surplus	750,167	47.3
Total	1,586,664	100.0

RECENT DEVELOPMENTS: For the year ended 12/31/00, OSG reported income of $85.7 million, before an extraordinary gain of $573,000 and an accounting credit of $4.2 million, versus income of $13.3 million, before an extraordinary gain of $1.0 million, in 1999. Earnings for 2000 and 1999 included pre-tax gains of $21.1 million and $14.2 million from the disposal of vessels. Net revenues advanced 46.2% to $370.1 million.

PROSPECTS: In light of its $750.0 million, 16-vessel fleet renewal program, the Company should continue to benefit from the preference by major charterers for modern tonnage based on concerns about the environmental risks associated with older vessels. The newbuilding portion of the Company's fleet renewal program includes two recently ordered Aframaxes that are scheduled for delivery in late 2003 and early 2004.

BUSINESS

OVERSEAS SHIPHOLDING GROUP, INC. with assets of $1.82 billion as of 12/31/00, is one of the largest bulk shipping companies in the world. OSG is engaged in the ocean transportation of liquid and dry bulk cargoes in both the worldwide and self-contained U.S. markets. The Company owns and operates 41 vessels with an aggregate carrying capacity of approximately 5.2 million deadweight tons (dwt). Oil tankers account for 88.0% of the Company's total tonnage, while dry bulk and combination carriers account for the remaining tonnage.

REVENUES

(12/31/2000)	($000)	(%)
Very Large Crude Carriers	120,549	25.8
Aframaxes	132,006	28.2
Product Carriers	76,655	16.4
Tankers	37,486	8.0
Dry Bulk Carriers	47,490	10.2
All Other	53,432	11.4
Total	467,618	100.0

ANNUAL FINANCIAL DATA

	12/31/00	12/31/99	12/31/98	12/31/97	12/31/96	12/31/95	12/31/94
Earnings Per Share	[2][6][7] 2.49	[2][6] 0.37	[3][5] d0.66	[3][4] 0.52	[1][2] 0.07	[1][2] d0.24	[2] d0.17
Cash Flow Per Share	3.64	1.80	1.26	2.65	2.03	1.59	1.51
Tang. Book Val. Per Share	22.07	19.63	17.87	21.19	21.23	21.66	22.36
Dividends Per Share	0.60	0.60	0.60	0.60	0.60	0.60	0.60
Dividend Payout %	24.1	162.1	...	115.4	855.9	...	...
INCOME STATEMENT (IN MILLIONS):							
Total Revenues	370.1	253.2	408.8	481.1	455.9	413.9	364.1
Costs & Expenses	196.9	178.7	300.5	337.5	338.2	317.4	283.8
Depreciation & Amort.	39.2	51.2	70.8	77.9	71.0	66.1	60.0
Operating Income	134.1	23.4	37.5	65.6	46.6	30.4	20.3
Net Interest Inc./(Exp.)	d47.5	d45.3	d62.2	d83.0	d69.5	d66.4	d57.0
Income Before Income Taxes	132.2	19.5	d35.2	31.2	3.4	d13.9	d9.9
Income Taxes	46.5	6.2	cr10.9	12.2	0.9	cr5.3	cr3.7
Net Income	[2][6][7] 85.7	[2][6] 13.3	[3][5] d24.3	[3][4] 19.0	[1][2] 2.5	[1][2] d8.6	[2] d6.2
Cash Flow	124.8	64.5	46.5	97.0	73.5	57.5	53.8
Average Shs. Outstg. (000)	34,315	35,725	36,794	36,569	36,234	36,220	35,588
BALANCE SHEET (IN MILLIONS):							
Cash & Cash Equivalents	70.8	89.0	51.0	113.2	109.1	160.6	100.0
Total Current Assets	137.0	121.0	104.7	170.4	168.5	223.3	160.7
Net Property	1,294.0	1,237.5	1,229.1	1,308.1	1,293.8	1,281.6	1,183.2
Total Assets	1,823.9	1,720.9	1,695.5	2,023.2	2,037.3	2,064.8	1,905.4
Total Current Liabilities	48.8	45.2	61.8	71.0	66.2	71.3	71.2
Long-Term Obligations	836.5	827.4	833.9	1,056.3	1,093.5	1,101.8	910.1
Net Stockholders' Equity	750.2	661.1	707.6	779.8	769.4	784.8	809.8
Net Working Capital	88.2	75.8	42.9	99.3	102.3	152.0	89.5
Year-end Shs. Outstg. (000)	33,986	33,672	39,591	36,793	36,235	36,228	36,210
STATISTICAL RECORD:							
Operating Profit Margin %	36.2	9.2	9.2	13.6	10.2	7.3	5.6
Net Profit Margin %	23.1	5.3	...	4.0	0.5	...	...
Return on Equity %	11.4	2.0	...	2.4	0.3	...	...
Return on Assets %	4.7	0.8	...	0.9	0.1	...	...
Debt/Total Assets %	45.9	48.1	49.2	52.2	53.7	53.4	47.8
Price Range	31.44-13.75	17.50-10.50	22.88-13.06	26.44-16.25	20.63-15.75	23.88-17.00	26.75-17.25
P/E Ratio	12.6-5.5	47.3-28.4	...	50.8-31.2	294.2-224.7	...	...
Average Yield %	2.7	4.3	3.3	2.8	3.3	2.9	2.7

Statistics are as originally reported. [1] Incl. inc. tax credit: $2.2 mill., 1996; $5.3 mill., 1995. [2] Incl. gains from disp. of vessels: $21.1 mill., 2000; $14.2 mill., 1999; $3.8 mill., 1996; $1.8 mill., 1995; $1.6 mill., 1994; $7.3 mill. [3] Incl. pre-tax gain fr. sale of Celebrity Cruise Lines: $42.3 mill., 1998; $21.6 mill., 1997. [4] Incl. a one-time net loss of $18.7 mill. [5] Incl. prov. for loss on vessel disp. prog. of $85.1 mill. & bef. extraord. loss of $13.6 mill. [6] Bef. extraord. gain of $573,000, 2000; $1.5 mill., 1999. [7] Bef. acctg. credit of $4.2 mill.

OFFICERS:
M. P. Hyman, Chmn., Pres., C.E.O.
M. R. Itkin, Sr. V.P., C.F.O., Treas.

INVESTOR CONTACT: Corporate Relations, (212) 953-4100

PRINCIPAL OFFICE: 511 Fifth Avenue, New York, NY 10017

TELEPHONE NUMBER: (212) 935-4100
FAX: (212) 536-3776

NO. OF EMPLOYEES: 1,570 (approx.)

SHAREHOLDERS: 1,009

ANNUAL MEETING: In June

INCORPORATED: DE, July, 1969

INSTITUTIONAL HOLDINGS:
No. of Institutions: 105
Shares Held: 14,101,918
% Held: 41.4

INDUSTRY: Deep sea foreign trans. of freight (SIC: 4412)

TRANSFER AGENT(S): Mellon Investor Services, New York, NY

NYSE SYMBOL OI
Rec. Pr. 7.88 (4/30/01)

OWENS-ILLINOIS, INC.

YIELD . . .
P/E RATIO . . .

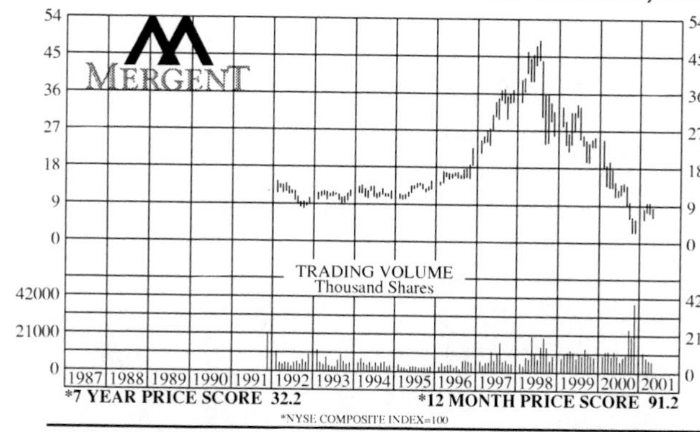

*7 YEAR PRICE SCORE 32.2 *12 MONTH PRICE SCORE 91.2

*NYSE COMPOSITE INDEX=100

INTERIM EARNINGS (Per Share):

Qtr.	Mar.	June	Sept.	Dec.
1996	0.33	0.55	0.51	0.19
1997	0.44	0.66	0.65	0.27
1998	0.56	0.75	0.69	d1.24
1999	0.41	0.67	0.46	0.24
2000	0.36	0.57	d3.12	0.18

INTERIM DIVIDENDS (Per Share):

Amt.	Decl.	Ex.	Rec.	Pay.

No dividends paid.

CAPITALIZATION (12/31/00):

	($000)	(%)
Long-Term Debt	5,729,800	71.6
Deferred Income Tax	218,200	2.7
Minority Interest	172,900	2.2
Preferred Stock	455,900	5.7
Common & Surplus	1,427,100	17.8
Total	8,003,900	100.0

RECENT DEVELOPMENTS: For the year ended 12/31/00, OI incurred a net loss of $269.7 million versus income of $299.1 million, before an extraordinary charge, in 1999. Earnings for 2000 and 1999 included unusual items, resulting in an after-tax charge of $513.1 million and an after-tax gain of $9.6 million, respectively. Results for 2000 also included a tax benefit of $9.3 million. Total revenues grew to $5.81 billion from $5.79 billion in 1999.

PROSPECTS: OI will likely continue to be negatively affected by recent natural gas price changes and unfavorable foreign currency exchange. The Company has been able to offset a portion of its increased energy costs through price adjustments. Natural gas prices in the U.S. are over twice as high as their average level during the first quarter of 2000. As a result, OI anticipates lower operating earnings in the near term.

BUSINESS

OWENS-ILLINOIS, INC. is a manufacturer of packaging products. In addition to being the largest manufacturer of glass containers in North America, South America, Australia, New Zealand, and China, and one of the largest in Europe, the Company is a leading manufacturer in North America and South America of plastic containers, plastic closures, plastic prescription containers, labels, and multipack plastic carriers for beverage bottles. The Company also has plastics packaging operations in Latin America, Australia, Europe, and Asia.

BUSINESS LINE ANALYSIS

(12/31/2000)	REV (%)	INC (%)
Glass Containers	66.6	70.1
Plastics Packaging	32.2	29.8
Other	1.2	0.1
Total	100.0	100.0

ANNUAL FINANCIAL DATA

	12/31/00	12/31/99	12/31/98	12/31/97	12/31/96	12/31/95	12/31/94
Earnings Per Share	**2 d2.00**	**1.79**	**1 0.71**	**1 2.01**	**1.58**	**1.40**	**0.64**
Cash Flow Per Share	**1.92**	**5.44**	**3.88**	**4.54**	**3.85**	**3.41**	**2.62**
Tang. Book Val. Per Share	...	...	...	**0.19**	...	...	...
INCOME STATEMENT (IN MILLIONS):							
Total Revenues	5,814.8	5,786.7	5,499.3	4,828.4	3,976.2	3,881.0	3,652.9
Costs & Expenses	5,170.2	4,317.7	4,446.4	3,729.9	3,077.9	3,033.3	2,969.8
Depreciation & Amort.	549.5	545.3	463.9	343.5	271.6	238.1	233.6
Operating Income	95.1	923.7	589.0	755.0	626.7	609.6	449.5
Net Interest Inc./(Exp.)	d486.7	d425.9	d380.0	d302.7	d302.6	d299.6	d278.2
Income Before Income Taxes	d391.6	497.8	209.0	452.3	324.1	310.0	171.3
Income Taxes	cr143.9	185.5	66.7	148.5	104.9	100.8	68.9
Equity Earnings/Minority Int.	d22.0	d13.2	d20.2	d31.4	d28.1	d40.1	d24.1
Net Income	d269.7	2 299.1	1 122.1	1 272.4	191.1	169.1	78.3
Cash Flow	258.3	822.9	575.6	615.9	462.7	407.2	311.9
Average Shs. Outstg. (000)	145,983	155,209	150,944	135,676	120,276	119,343	119,005
BALANCE SHEET (IN MILLIONS):							
Cash & Cash Equivalents	249.4	289.2	292.5	234.3	175.3	161.9	141.6
Total Current Assets	2,081.7	2,109.8	2,177.1	1,648.3	1,285.1	1,216.8	1,099.1
Net Property	3,284.9	3,444.1	3,427.0	2,405.4	1,941.6	1,784.8	1,636.5
Total Assets	10,343.2	10,756.3	11,060.7	6,845.1	6,105.3	5,439.2	5,317.6
Total Current Liabilities	1,318.0	1,273.1	1,327.1	1,043.8	904.9	888.9	928.0
Long-Term Obligations	5,729.8	5,733.1	5,667.2	3,146.7	3,253.2	2,757.7	2,624.7
Net Stockholders' Equity	1,883.0	2,349.9	2,472.0	1,341.9	729.7	531.9	375.9
Net Working Capital	763.7	836.7	850.0	604.5	380.2	327.9	171.1
Year-end Shs. Outstg. (000)	144,954	146,851	155,450	140,526	120,446	119,966	119,079
STATISTICAL RECORD:							
Operating Profit Margin %	1.6	16.0	10.7	15.6	15.8	15.7	12.3
Net Profit Margin %	...	5.2	2.2	5.6	4.8	4.4	2.1
Return on Equity %	...	12.7	4.9	20.3	26.2	31.8	20.8
Return on Assets %	...	2.8	1.1	4.0	3.1	3.1	1.5
Debt/Total Assets %	55.4	53.3	51.2	46.0	53.3	50.7	49.4
Price Range	25.19-2.50	33.44-19.31	49.00-23.75	37.13-21.50	22.75-13.63	14.75-10.13	13.63-10.25
P/E Ratio	...	18.7-10.8	69.0-33.4	18.5-10.7	14.4-8.6	10.5-7.2	21.3-16.0

Statistics are as originally reported. 1 Bef. extra. chrg. of $14.1 mill., 1998; extraord. chrg. of $104.5 mill., 1997. 2 Incl. unusual after-tax charges of $513.1 mill. & a tax benefit of $9.3 mill.

OFFICERS:
J. H. Lemieux, Chmn., C.E.O.
D. G. Van Hooser, Sr. V.P., C.F.O.
J. A. Denker, Treas.

INVESTOR CONTACT: Investor Relations, (419) 247-2400

PRINCIPAL OFFICE: One SeaGate, Toledo, OH 43666

TELEPHONE NUMBER: (419) 247-5000
FAX: (419) 247-2839
WEB: www.o-i.com

NO. OF EMPLOYEES: 34,400 (approx.)

SHAREHOLDERS: 1,279

ANNUAL MEETING: In May

INCORPORATED: DE, 1907; reincorp., DE, 1987

INSTITUTIONAL HOLDINGS:
No. of Institutions: 103
Shares Held: 99,324,590
% Held: 68.5

INDUSTRY: Glass containers (SIC: 3221)

TRANSFER AGENT(S): First Chicago Trust Co. of New York, Jersey City, NJ

NYSE SYMBOL OMI
Rec. Pr. 18.55 (5/31/01)

OWENS & MINOR, INC.

YIELD 1.5%
P/E RATIO 19.7

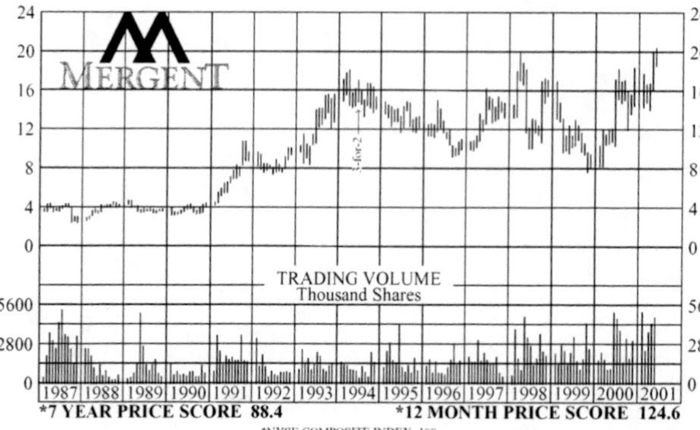

*7 YEAR PRICE SCORE 88.4 *12 MONTH PRICE SCORE 124.6

*NYSE COMPOSITE INDEX=100

INTERIM EARNINGS (Per Share):

Qtr.	Mar.	June	Sept.	Dec.
1997	0.12	0.14	0.16	0.18
1998	0.17	d0.01	0.20	0.20
1999	0.17	0.19	0.21	0.25
2000	0.20	0.23	0.24	0.27

INTERIM DIVIDENDS (Per Share):

Amt.	Decl.	Ex.	Rec.	Pay.
0.063Q	4/25/00	6/12/00	6/14/00	6/30/00
0.063Q	7/25/00	9/11/00	9/13/00	9/29/00
0.063Q	10/23/00	12/11/00	12/13/00	12/29/00
0.063Q	1/31/01	3/09/01	3/13/01	3/31/01
0.07Q	4/26/01	6/12/01	6/14/01	6/29/01

Indicated div.: $0.28 (Div. Reinv. Plan)

CAPITALIZATION (12/31/00):

	($000)	(%)
Long-Term Debt	152,872	41.8
Deferred Income Tax	371	0.1
Common & Surplus	212,772	58.1
Total	366,015	100.0

RECENT DEVELOPMENTS: For the year ended 12/31/00, net income totaled $33.1 million, up 18.3% compared with $28.0 million in the previous year. Results included pre-tax restructuring credits of $750,000 and $1.0 million in 2000 and 1999, respectively. Net sales climbed 9.7% to $3.50 billion from $3.19 billion a year earlier. Results were positively affected by the acquisition of Medix, Inc. Gross margin was $375.7 million, or 10.7% of net sales, versus $342.6 million, or 10.7% of net sales, the year before.

PROSPECTS: On 2/5/01, the Company announced the signing of a five-year distribution agreement with Baylor Health Care System, a Dallas, Texas-based not-for-profit integrated health care provider. The new agreement is expected to generate annual sales of about $30.0 million. In 2001, the Company is targeting sales growth of between 8.0% and 10.0%, driven by increased account penetration, converting direct-from-manufacturer business, and the addition of new business. OMI anticipates earnings per share growth in the range of 11.0% to 14.0% for 2001.

BUSINESS

OWENS & MINOR, INC. is a distributor of medical/surgical supplies in the U.S. OMI distributes more than 170,000 finished medical/surgical products to hospitals and alternate care facilities such as nursing homes, clinics, surgery centers, rehabilitation facilities, physicians' offices and home healthcare. Most of OMI's sales consist of disposable gloves, dressings, endoscopic products, intravenous products, needles and syringes, sterile procedure trays, surgical products and gowns, urological products and wound closure products. Owens & Minor has 45 distribution centers serving all 50 states and the District of Columbia. In May 1994, OMI acquired Stuart Medical, Inc., a medical/surgical supplies distributor. On 7/30/99, OMI acquired Medix, Inc., a distributor of medical/surgical supplies.

ANNUAL FINANCIAL DATA

	12/31/00	12/31/99	12/31/98	12/31/97	12/31/96	12/31/95	12/31/94
Earnings Per Share	**[2] 0.94**	**[2] 0.82**	**[2] 0.56**	**0.60**	**0.25**	**[2] d0.53**	**[1] 0.15**
Cash Flow Per Share	**1.38**	**1.21**	**1.12**	**1.15**	**0.75**	**d0.03**	**0.57**
Tang. Book Val. Per Share	**0.24**	...	**0.09**	...	...	...	...
Dividends Per Share	**0.25**	**0.23**	**0.20**	**0.18**	**0.18**	**0.18**	**0.17**
Dividend Payout %	**26.3**	**28.0**	**35.7**	**30.0**	**72.0**	...	**113.3**
INCOME STATEMENT (IN MILLIONS):							
Total Revenues	3,503.6	3,186.4	3,082.1	3,116.8	3,019.0	2,976.5	2,395.8
Costs & Expenses	3,396.1	3,093.8	2,994.7	3,034.9	2,954.3	2,934.6	2,327.1
Depreciation & Amort.	21.5	19.4	18.3	17.7	16.1	15.4	13.0
Operating Income	86.0	73.3	69.1	64.2	48.6	26.5	55.7
Net Interest Inc./(Exp.)	d12.6	d11.9	d14.1	d15.7	d19.0	d25.5	d12.1
Income Before Income Taxes	60.2	50.1	34.7	41.9	23.1	d16.4	14.0
Income Taxes	27.1	22.1	14.6	17.6	10.1	cr5.1	6.1
Net Income	[2] 33.1	[2] 28.0	[2] 20.1	24.3	13.0	[2] d11.3	[1] 7.9
Cash Flow	54.6	47.3	36.5	36.8	23.9	d1.1	17.6
Average Shs. Outstg. (000)	39,453	39,098	32,591	32,129	31,770	30,820	31,108
BALANCE SHEET (IN MILLIONS):							
Cash & Cash Equivalents	0.6	0.7	0.5	0.6	0.7	0.2	0.5
Total Current Assets	594.3	589.2	504.2	499.3	455.5	623.9	640.8
Net Property	24.2	25.9	25.6	26.6	29.2	39.0	38.6
Total Assets	867.5	865.0	717.8	712.6	679.5	857.8	868.6
Total Current Liabilities	360.7	369.8	269.0	265.5	262.5	292.2	359.0
Long-Term Obligations	152.9	174.6	150.0	182.6	167.5	323.3	248.4
Net Stockholders' Equity	212.8	182.4	161.1	259.3	242.4	235.3	256.2
Net Working Capital	233.6	219.4	235.2	233.8	193.0	331.7	281.8
Year-end Shs. Outstg. (000)	33,180	32,711	32,618	32,213	31,907	30,862	30,764
STATISTICAL RECORD:							
Operating Profit Margin %	2.5	2.3	2.2	2.1	1.6	0.9	2.3
Net Profit Margin %	0.9	0.9	0.7	0.8	0.4	...	0.3
Return on Equity %	15.6	15.3	12.5	9.4	5.3	...	3.1
Return on Assets %	3.8	3.2	2.8	3.4	1.9	...	0.9
Debt/Total Assets %	17.6	20.2	20.9	25.6	24.7	37.7	28.6
Price Range	18.38-8.13	17.00-7.56	19.88-10.00	16.25-9.75	15.00-9.13	14.88-11.63	18.17-13.25
P/E Ratio	19.5-8.6	20.7-9.2	35.5-17.9	27.1-16.2	60.0-36.5	...	121.0-88.3
Average Yield %	1.9	1.9	1.3	1.4	1.5	1.4	1.1

Statistics are as originally reported. [1] From recurr. opers. [2] Incl. $750,000 pre-tax restr. credit, 2000; $1.0 mil pre-tax restr. credit, 1999; $6.6 mil after-tax restr. chg., 1998; $16.7 mil restr. chg. & $3.5 mil consol. chgs., 1995.

OFFICERS:
G. G. Minor, III, Chmn., C.E.O.
C. R. Smith, Pres., C.O.O.
J. Kaczka, Sr. V.P., C.F.O.

INVESTOR CONTACT: Shareholder Relations, (800) 524-4458

PRINCIPAL OFFICE: 4800 Cox Road, Glen Allen, VA 23060

TELEPHONE NUMBER: (804) 747-9794
FAX: (804) 270-7281
WEB: www.owens-minor.com

NO. OF EMPLOYEES: 2,763 (approx.)

SHAREHOLDERS: 15,000 (approx.)

ANNUAL MEETING: In Apr.

INCORPORATED: VA, Dec., 1926

INSTITUTIONAL HOLDINGS:
No. of Institutions: 135
Shares Held: 29,882,547
% Held: 89.5

INDUSTRY: Medical and hospital equipment (SIC: 5047)

TRANSFER AGENT(S): The Bank of New York, New York, NY

NYSE SYMBOL OHP
Rec. Pr. 31.10 (4/30/01)

OXFORD HEALTH PLANS, INC.

YIELD ...
P/E RATIO 14.2

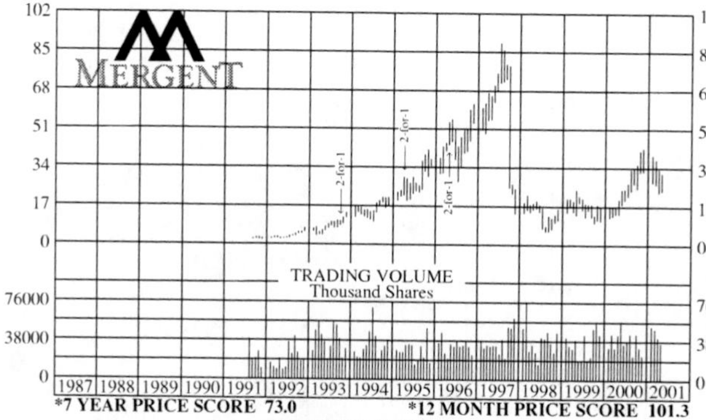

INTERIM EARNINGS (Per Share):

Qtr.	Mar.	June	Sept.	Dec.
1997	0.42	0.45	d0.99	d3.58
1998	d0.57	d6.41	d0.58	d0.23
1999	0.04	d0.16	0.34	3.05
2000	0.34	0.45	0.81	0.59

INTERIM DIVIDENDS (Per Share):

Amt.	Decl.	Ex.	Rec.	Pay.

No dividends paid.

CAPITALIZATION (12/31/00):

	($000)	(%)
Long-Term Debt	28,000	5.7
Common & Surplus	459,222	94.3
Total	487,222	100.0

RECENT DEVELOPMENTS: On 4/18/01, the Company began trading on the New York Stock Exchange with the new symbol, OHP. For the year ended 12/31/00, earnings were $285.4 million, before an extraordinary charge of $20.3 million, compared with net earnings of $319.9 million in the prior year. Results for 1999 included restructuring charges of $20.0 million. Total revenues declined 2.0% to $4.11 billion from $4.20 billion in the previous year.

PROSPECTS: On 4/24/01, the Company signed a multi-year agreement with Continuum Health Partners, Inc. of New York City, enabling Oxford-insured members to receive uninterrupted in-network medical services at facilities within this hospital network. Also, OHP signed a muti-year agreement with Lenox Hill Hospital of New York City, enabling the Company's commercial and Medicare members to receive uninterrupted in-network medical services at this facility.

BUSINESS

OXFORD HEALTH PLANS, INC. is a managed-care company that provides health-benefit plans in New York, New Jersey and Connecticut. The Company's product line includes its point-of-service plans, the Freedom Plan and the Liberty Plan, health maintenance organizations, preferred provider organizations, Medicare+Choice plans and third-party administration of employer-funded benefit plans. The Company currently offers its products through its HMO subsidiaries, Oxford Health Plans, Inc., Oxford Health Plans, Inc. and Oxford Health Plans, Inc. and through Oxford Health Insurance, Inc., the Company's health insurance subsidiary. OHP currently does business under accident and health insurance licenses granted by the Departments of Insurance of New York and Connecticut, the Department of Banking and Insurance of New Jersey and the Commonwealth of Pennsylvania.

REVENUES

(12/31/2000)	($000)	(%)
Freedom, Liberty & Other	2,839,999	69.0
HMO's	505,946	12.3
Medicare	677,452	16.5
Third Party Admin.	15,390	0.4
Total	4,111,802	100.0
Investment & Other Income	73,015	1.8

ANNUAL FINANCIAL DATA

	12/31/00	12/31/99	12/31/98	12/31/97	12/31/96	12/31/95	12/31/94
Earnings Per Share	**2 2.24**	**3.26**	**1 d7.79**	**1 d3.70**	**1.24**	**0.71**	**0.43**
Cash Flow Per Share	**2.60**	**3.91**	**d6.96**	**d2.93**	**1.78**	**1.03**	**0.54**
Tang. Book Val. Per Share	**4.67**	**1.20**	**...**	**4.39**	**7.73**	**3.20**	**2.00**
INCOME STATEMENT (IN MILLIONS):							
Total Revenues	4,111.8	4,197.8	4,719.4	4,240.1	3,075.0	1,765.4	721.0
Costs & Expenses	3,593.1	3,979.5	5,229.2	4,593.1	2,855.7	1,647.3	662.2
Depreciation & Amort.	34.2	54.5	67.1	61.0	42.9	23.0	7.1
Operating Income	484.5	163.7	d615.2	d455.6	176.5	95.1	51.5
Income Before Income Taxes	484.5	163.7	d615.2	d431.6	172.0	91.5	49.5
Income Taxes	199.1	cr156.3	cr18.4	cr140.3	72.4	39.1	21.6
Equity Earnings/Minority Int.	...	...	...	d1.1	d4.6	d3.9	d2.1
Net Income	2 285.4	319.9	1 d596.8	1 d291.3	99.6	52.4	28.2
Cash Flow	245.9	329.0	d557.3	d230.2	142.5	75.4	35.3
Average Shs. Outstg. (000)	94,573	84,231	80,120	78,635	80,019	73,454	65,410
BALANCE SHEET (IN MILLIONS):							
Cash & Cash Equivalents	1,067.0	1,161.9	1,160.7	639.9	839.5	368.6	191.1
Total Current Assets	1,255.6	1,330.7	1,360.6	1,129.6	1,200.5	492.2	255.2
Net Property	19.8	49.5	112.9	147.1	105.0	97.4	34.8
Total Assets	1,444.6	1,686.9	1,637.8	1,398.0	1,346.7	608.8	314.8
Total Current Liabilities	957.4	888.0	1,151.2	1,048.8	748.6	388.7	187.7
Long-Term Obligations	28.0	355.8	368.9	...	...	...	...
Net Stockholders' Equity	459.2	98.8	d181.1	349.2	598.2	220.0	127.1
Net Working Capital	298.2	442.7	209.4	80.8	452.0	103.4	67.5
Year-end Shs. Outstg. (000)	98,304	81,986	80,516	79,474	77,376	68,781	63,692
STATISTICAL RECORD:							
Operating Profit Margin %	11.8	3.9	...	...	5.7	5.4	7.1
Net Profit Margin %	6.9	7.6	...	...	3.2	3.0	3.9
Return on Equity %	62.2	324.0	...	...	16.7	23.8	22.2
Return on Assets %	19.8	19.0	...	...	7.4	8.6	9.0
Debt/Total Assets %	1.9	21.1	22.5	...	...	...	...
Price Range	42.75-12.06	24.25-9.75	22.00-5.81	89.00-13.75	62.25-27.69	41.88-19.25	20.88-9.88
P/E Ratio	19.1-5.4	7.4-3.0	...	...	50.2-22.3	59.0-27.1	48.5-23.0

Statistics are as originally reported. Adj. for stk. splits: 2-for-1, 4/1/96; 2-for-1, 3/27/95. 1 Incl. net non-recurr. chrgs. 12/31/98: $183.8 mill.; 12/31/97: $17.6 mill. ($0.22/sh.) 2 Bef. extraord. chrg. of $20.3 mill.

OFFICERS:
N. C. Payson M.D., Chmn., C.E.O.
C. G. Berg, Pres., C.O.O.
J. H. Boyd, Exec. V.P., Gen. Couns.

INVESTOR CONTACT: Investor Relations, (203) 459-6000

PRINCIPAL OFFICE: 48 Monroe Turnpike, Trumbull, CT 06611

TELEPHONE NUMBER: (203) 459-6000
FAX: (203) 851-2464
WEB: www.oxhp.com

NO. OF EMPLOYEES: 3,400 (approx.)

SHAREHOLDERS: 1,117 (record)

ANNUAL MEETING: In May

INCORPORATED: DE, Sept., 1984

INSTITUTIONAL HOLDINGS:
No. of Institutions: 228
Shares Held: 70,734,565
% Held: 71.9

INDUSTRY: Hospital and medical service plans (SIC: 6324)

TRANSFER AGENT(S): State Street Bank and Trust Company, Boston, MA

NYSE SYMBOL OXM
Rec. Pr. 20.00 (4/30/01)

OXFORD INDUSTRIES, INC.

YIELD 4.2%
P/E RATIO 8.8

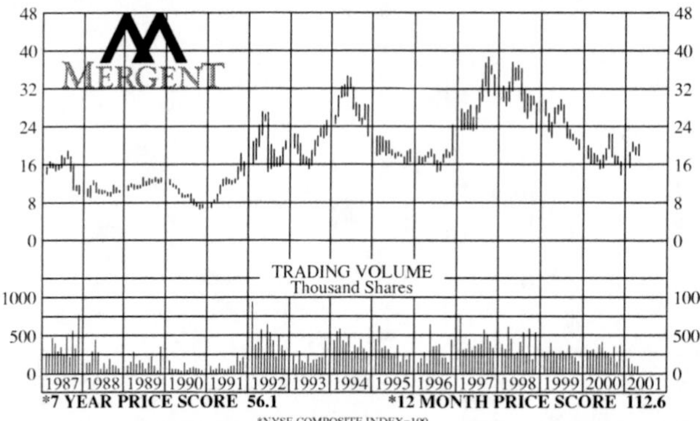

*7 YEAR PRICE SCORE 56.1 *12 MONTH PRICE SCORE 112.6

*NYSE COMPOSITE INDEX=100

INTERIM EARNINGS (Per Share):

Qtr.	Aug.	Nov.	Feb.	May
1996-97	0.40	0.75	0.51	0.59
1997-98	0.61	0.88	0.60	0.67
1998-99	0.67	0.94	0.76	0.74
1999-00	0.60	0.88	0.60	0.94
2000-01	0.45	0.36	0.53	...

INTERIM DIVIDENDS (Per Share):

Amt.	Decl.	Ex.	Rec.	Pay.
0.21Q	7/10/00	8/11/00	8/15/00	9/02/00
0.21Q	10/02/00	11/13/00	11/15/00	12/02/00
0.21Q	1/08/01	2/13/01	2/15/01	3/03/01
0.21Q	4/02/01	5/11/01	5/15/01	6/02/01

Indicated div.: $0.84

CAPITALIZATION (6/2/00):

	($000)	(%)
Long-Term Debt	40,513	19.5
Deferred Income Tax	2,619	1.3
Common & Surplus	164,314	79.2
Total	207,446	100.0

RECENT DEVELOPMENTS: For the three months ended 3/2/01, net earnings declined 14.5% to $3.9 million versus $4.6 million in the equivalent 1999 quarter. Earnings were hampered by higher operating costs required to establish and grow several new marketing initiatives. Net sales grew 5.3% to $197.4 million from $187.5 million in the prior year. Net sales for the Oxford shirt group rose 11.3% to $51.9 million, while net sales for the Oxford womenswear group increased 5.4% to $82.3 million.

PROSPECTS: Despite significant competitive pressures and increased markdown activity, operating results are benefiting from partially stabilized by improved manufacturing efficiencies and a higher proportion of branded business. Going forward, OXM expects higher operating costs associated with new marketing initiatives to continue to negatively affect short-term results; however, these new initiatives should contribute significantly to OXM's long-term sales and earnings growth.

BUSINESS

OXFORD INDUSTRIES, INC. designs, manufactures, markets and distributes a broad range of consumer apparel products. Major licensed brands include TOMMY HILFIGER®, NAUTICA®, DKNY® KIDS, GEOFFREY Beene®, SLATES®, OSCAR DE LA RENTA®, IZOD CLUB® and ROBERT STOCK®. The Company's private label brands are found in are distributed through national chains, specialty catalogs, mass merchandisers, department stores, specialty stores and Internet retailers. Revenues (and operating income) in 2000 were derived: shirts, 28.6% (32.0%); Lanier, 20.8% (27.9%); slacks, 11.9% (9.4%); womenswear, 38.6% (50.0%); and corporate and other, 0.1% (-19.3%).

ANNUAL FINANCIAL DATA

	6/2/00	5/28/99	5/29/98	5/30/97	5/31/96	6/2/95	6/3/94
Earnings Per Share	**3.02**	**3.11**	**2.75**	**2.25**	**0.25**	**1.22**	**2.23**
Cash Flow Per Share	**4.24**	**4.17**	**3.65**	**3.29**	**1.26**	**2.12**	**3.05**
Tang. Book Val. Per Share	**21.48**	**19.46**	**18.11**	**16.12**	**14.65**	**15.25**	**14.79**
Dividends Per Share	**0.84**	**0.80**	**0.80**	**0.80**	**0.80**	**0.72**	**0.66**
Dividend Payout %	**27.8**	**25.7**	**29.1**	**35.6**	**319.9**	**59.0**	**29.6**
INCOME STATEMENT (IN MILLIONS):							
Total Revenues	839.5	862.4	774.5	703.2	664.4	657.0	624.6
Costs & Expenses	788.5	805.5	722.6	657.8	645.9	627.4	583.0
Depreciation & Amort.	9.4	8.9	8.1	9.1	8.9	7.8	7.0
Operating Income	41.6	48.0	43.8	36.3	9.7	21.8	34.6
Net Interest Inc./(Exp.)	d3.8	d4.7	d3.4	d4.1	d6.1	d4.1	d2.3
Income Before Income Taxes	37.8	43.3	40.4	32.2	3.7	17.6	32.3
Income Taxes	14.4	16.9	15.7	12.6	1.5	7.1	13.1
Net Income	23.4	26.4	24.6	19.6	2.2	10.6	19.2
Cash Flow	32.8	35.3	32.7	28.7	11.0	18.4	26.2
Average Shs. Outstg. (000)	7,751	8,477	8,957	8,744	8,749	8,670	8,607
BALANCE SHEET (IN MILLIONS):							
Cash & Cash Equivalents	8.6	11.1	10.1	3.3	1.0	2.2	3.2
Total Current Assets	287.6	286.5	271.2	246.9	236.1	269.2	205.3
Net Property	37.1	37.3	35.7	34.6	36.7	38.7	33.2
Total Assets	336.6	335.3	311.5	287.1	279.1	309.0	239.9
Total Current Liabilities	124.6	131.8	101.7	96.3	98.8	125.6	96.1
Long-Term Obligations	40.5	40.7	41.4	41.8	45.1	47.0	12.4
Net Stockholders' Equity	164.3	154.4	159.8	141.5	129.0	132.6	127.7
Net Working Capital	162.9	154.7	169.5	150.6	137.3	143.6	109.2
Year-end Shs. Outstg. (000)	7,651	7,932	8,824	8,780	8,803	8,694	8,638
STATISTICAL RECORD:							
Operating Profit Margin %	5.0	5.6	5.7	5.2	1.5	3.3	5.5
Net Profit Margin %	2.8	3.1	3.2	2.8	0.3	1.6	3.1
Return on Equity %	14.3	17.1	15.4	13.9	1.7	8.0	15.0
Return on Assets %	7.0	7.9	7.9	6.8	0.8	3.4	8.0
Debt/Total Assets %	12.0	12.1	13.3	14.6	16.1	15.2	5.2
Price Range	29.75-19.00	37.69-22.50	38.75-23.00	24.38-14.38	22.00-16.00	34.75-21.88	25.38-15.00
P/E Ratio	9.9-6.3	12.1-7.2	14.1-8.4	10.8-6.4	88.0-64.0	28.5-17.9	11.4-6.7
Average Yield %	3.4	2.7	2.6	4.1	4.2	2.5	3.3

Statistics are as originally reported.

OFFICERS:
J. H. Lanier, Chmn., Pres., C.E.O.
B. B. Blount Jr., Exec. V.P., C.F.O.

INVESTOR CONTACT: J. Reese Lanier, Jr., Dir., Inv. Rel., (404) 653-1446

PRINCIPAL OFFICE: 222 Piedmont Avenue, N.E., Atlanta, GA 30308

TELEPHONE NUMBER: (404) 659-2424
FAX: (404) 653-1545
WEB: www.oxfordinc.com

NO. OF EMPLOYEES: 9,758 (avg.)

SHAREHOLDERS: 637

ANNUAL MEETING: In Oct.

INCORPORATED: GA, April, 1960

INSTITUTIONAL HOLDINGS:
No. of Institutions: 46
Shares Held: 3,831,320
% Held: 52.0

INDUSTRY: Men's and boys' shirts (SIC: 2321)

TRANSFER AGENT(S): SunTrust Bank, Atlanta, GA

NYSE SYMBOL BOH
Rec. Pr. 22.40 (4/30/01)

PACIFIC CENTURY FINANCIAL CORPORATION

YIELD 3.2%
P/E RATIO 15.7

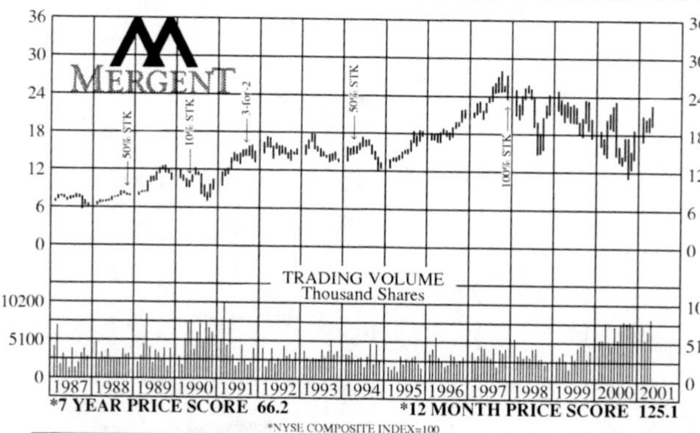

INTERIM EARNINGS (Per Share):

Qtr.	Mar.	June	Sept.	Dec.
1997	0.44	0.44	0.43	0.41
1998	0.42	0.04	0.43	0.43
1999	0.44	0.47	0.27	0.47
2000	0.50	0.08	0.44	0.41

INTERIM DIVIDENDS (Per Share):

Amt.	Decl.	Ex.	Rec.	Pay.
0.18Q	4/28/00	5/24/00	5/26/00	6/14/00
0.18Q	7/28/00	8/23/00	8/25/00	9/15/00
0.18Q	10/17/00	11/21/00	11/24/00	12/14/00
0.18Q	1/25/01	2/23/01	2/27/01	3/14/01
0.18Q	4/23/01	5/23/01	5/25/01	6/14/01

Indicated div.: $0.72 (Div. Reinv. Plan)

CAPITALIZATION (12/31/00):

	($000)	(%)
Total Deposits	9,080,581	79.8
Long-Term Debt	997,152	8.8
Minority Interest	4,536	0.0
Common & Surplus	1,301,356	11.4
Total	11,383,625	100.0

RECENT DEVELOPMENTS: For the year ended 12/31/00, net income declined 14.5% to $113.7 million from $133.0 million in 1999. Earnings for 2000 included a pre-tax gain of $11.9 million on the settlement of pension obligations. Earnings for 1999 included a pre-tax restructuring charge of $22.5 million. Net interest income fell 3.2% to $556.2 million. Total non-interest income declined to $263.4 million from $265.6 million in 1999.

PROSPECTS: On 4/2/01, the Company announced that its subsidiary, Pacific Century Bank, N.A., has completed the sale of the nine Arizona branches of Pacific Century Financial Corporation to Zions Bancorporation. As a result of this transaction, the Company expects to record a pre-tax gain of between $20.0 million and $23.0 million. Meanwhile, the Company should continue to benefit from the continuing strength of Hawaii's economy.

BUSINESS

PACIFIC CENTURY FINANCIAL CORPORATION, with assets of $14.01 billion as of 12/31/00, is a bank holding company that was initially organized as Hawaii Bancorporation, Inc. In 1979, it changed its name to Bancorp Hawaii, Inc. The present name, which was adopted in 1997, reflects the Company's strategy to expand beyond Hawaii to Asia, the West and South Pacific and the U.S. mainland. BOH provides a broad range of products and services to customers in Hawaii, the West and South Pacific, Asia, and the U.S. mainland. BOH's principal subsidiaries are the Bank of Hawaii and Pacific Century Bank, N.A.

LOAN DISTRIBUTION

(12/31/2000)	($000)	(%)
Commercial & Industrial	2,443,341	25.3
Mortgage loans	4,160,568	43.0
Installment	729,859	7.5
Construction	307,352	3.2
Foreign loans	1,301,634	13.5
Lease financing	725,536	7.5
Total	9,668,290	100.0

ANNUAL FINANCIAL DATA

	12/31/00	12/31/99	12/31/98	12/31/97	12/31/96	12/31/95	12/31/94
Earnings Per Share	**[2] 1.42**	**[1] 1.64**	**[1] 1.32**	**1.72**	**1.63**	**1.45**	**1.38**
Tang. Book Val. Per Share	**13.93**	**12.57**	**12.07**	**11.47**	**12.13**	**11.69**	**10.42**
Dividends Per Share	**0.71**	**0.68**	**0.66**	**0.63**	**0.58**	**0.54**	**0.52**
Dividend Payout %	**50.0**	**41.5**	**49.8**	**36.3**	**35.6**	**37.4**	**37.8**
INCOME STATEMENT (IN MILLIONS):							
Total Interest Income	1,057.5	1,026.5	1,099.8	1,062.6	982.1	896.7	813.0
Total Interest Expense	501.3	451.8	523.2	526.3	499.8	468.2	363.7
Net Interest Income	556.2	574.7	576.6	536.3	482.3	428.5	449.3
Provision for Loan Losses	142.9	60.9	84.0	30.3	22.2	17.0	21.9
Non-Interest Income	263.4	265.6	211.8	187.8	164.5	146.4	128.4
Non-Interest Expense	496.4	553.2	540.3	474.3	419.8	363.0	359.9
Income Before Taxes	180.0	225.7	163.6	218.0	203.3	193.8	195.4
Equity Earnings/Minority Int.	d0.4	d0.5	d0.4	d1.5	d1.4	d1.1	d0.5
Net Income	[2] 113.7	[1] 133.0	[1] 107.0	139.5	133.1	121.8	117.7
Average Shs. Outstg. (000)	79,813	80,045	81,142	80,946	81,596	84,054	85,650
BALANCE SHEET (IN MILLIONS):							
Cash & Due from Banks	524.0	639.9	564.2	795.3	581.2	469.0	508.8
Securities Avail. for Sale	2,507.1	2,542.2	3,018.4	2,651.3	2,306.6	2,194.0	1,378.6
Total Loans & Leases	9,668.3	9,717.6	9,854.0	9,498.4	8,699.3	8,152.4	7,892.0
Allowance for Credit Losses	500.2	436.7	437.2	384.1	351.4	299.4	292.5
Net Loans & Leases	9,168.1	9,280.8	9,416.8	9,114.3	8,347.9	7,853.0	7,599.5
Total Assets	14,013.8	14,440.3	15,016.6	14,995.5	14,009.2	13,206.8	12,586.4
Total Deposits	9,080.6	9,394.2	9,576.3	9,621.3	8,684.1	7,576.8	7,115.1
Long-Term Obligations	997.2	727.7	585.6	705.8	932.1	1,063.4	861.6
Total Liabilities	12,712.5	13,228.0	13,831.0	13,878.3	12,943.0	12,152.3	11,619.6
Net Stockholders' Equity	1,301.4	1,212.3	1,185.6	1,117.2	1,066.1	1,054.4	966.8
Year-end Shs. Outstg. (000)	79,612	80,036	80,326	79,685	79,918	82,682	83,702
STATISTICAL RECORD:							
Return on Equity %	8.7	11.0	9.0	12.5	12.5	11.6	12.2
Return on Assets %	0.8	0.9	0.7	0.9	1.0	0.9	0.9
Equity/Assets %	9.3	8.4	7.9	7.5	7.6	8.0	7.7
Non-Int. Exp./Tot. Inc. %	60.4	67.0	68.9	65.8	65.0	63.4	60.4
Price Range	23.19-11.06	24.94-17.38	25.88-14.75	28.06-20.31	22.00-16.56	18.56-12.44	17.38-12.06
P/E Ratio	16.3-7.8	15.2-10.6	19.6-11.2	16.3-11.8	13.5-10.2	12.8-8.6	12.6-8.8
Average Yield %	4.1	3.2	3.2	2.6	3.0	3.5	3.5

Statistics are as originally reported. Adj. for stk. split: 100% div., 12/97; 50% div., 3/94. [1] Incl. a restructuring charge of $22.5 mill., 1999; $19.4 mill., 1998. [2] Incl. a pre-tax gain of $11.9 mill. on the settlement of pension obligations.

OFFICERS:
M. E. O'Neill, Chmn., C.E.O.
A. R. Landon, Vice-Chmn., C.F.O.

INVESTOR CONTACT: Sharlene Bliss, Investor Relations, (808) 537-8037

PRINCIPAL OFFICE: 130 Merchant St., P.O. Box 2900, Honolulu, HI 96813

TELEPHONE NUMBER: (808) 537-8430
FAX: (808) 521-7602
WEB: www.boh.com

NO. OF EMPLOYEES: 3,930 full-time (approx.); 420 part-time (approx.)

SHAREHOLDERS: 8,438 (approx.)

ANNUAL MEETING: In April

INCORPORATED: HI, Aug., 1971; reincorp., DE, April, 1998

INSTITUTIONAL HOLDINGS:
No. of Institutions: 166
Shares Held: 53,871,526
% Held: 67.5

INDUSTRY: State commercial banks (SIC: 6022)

TRANSFER AGENT(S): Continental Stock Transfer & Trust Company, New York, NY

NYSE SYMBOL PTV
Rec. Pr. 13.75 (5/31/01)

PACTIV CORPORATION

YIELD ...
P/E RATIO 19.6

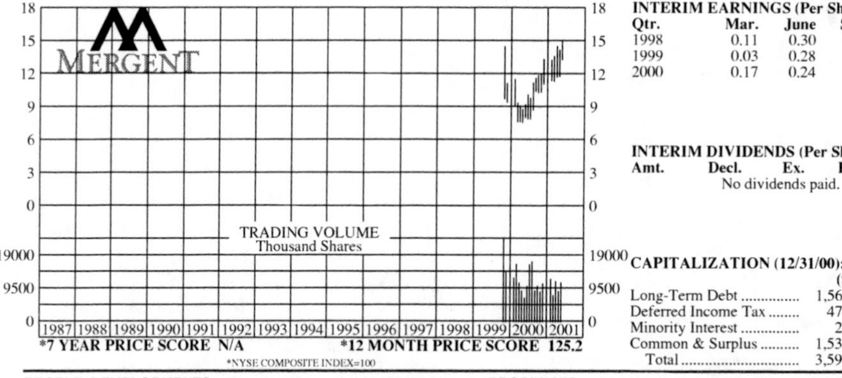

INTERIM EARNINGS (Per Share):

Qtr.	Mar.	June	Sept.	Dec.
1998	0.11	0.30	0.09	d0.01
1999	0.03	0.28	0.01	d1.00
2000	0.17	0.24	0.24	0.05

INTERIM DIVIDENDS (Per Share):

Amt.	Decl.	Ex.	Rec.	Pay.

No dividends paid.

CAPITALIZATION (12/31/00):

	($000)	(%)
Long-Term Debt	1,560,000	43.4
Deferred Income Tax	474,000	13.2
Minority Interest	22,000	0.6
Common & Surplus	1,539,000	42.8
Total	3,595,000	100.0

RECENT DEVELOPMENTS: For the year ended 12/31/00, income from continuing operations was $113.0 million versus a loss from continuing operations of $112.0 million a year earlier. The 2000 results included a $70.0 million pre-tax restructuring charge and pre-tax gains totaling $26.0 million from the sale of a business and the reversal of spin-off transaction costs, respectively. Prior-year results included pre-tax restructuring charges of $183.0 million and a $136.0 million pre-tax spin-off charge. Sales inched up to $3.13 billion from $3.11 billion in 1999.

PROSPECTS: On 4/18/01, the Company completed the sale of its remaining shares of Packaging Corporation of America. Gross proceeds from the sale of approximately $73.0 million will be used to reduce debt. Going forward, operating profitability should benefit from the Company's focus on improving productivity and adding capacity to fast-growing, high-margin product lines. In 2001, the Company is targeting sales growth in the range of 4.0% and 5.0% and earnings per share growth between 12.0% and 15.0%.

BUSINESS

PACTIV CORPORATION (formerly Tenneco Packaging Inc.) is a global supplier of consumer and specialty packaging products. The Company manufactures, markets, and sells consumer products, such as plastic storage bags for food and household items, plastic waste bags, foam and molded fiber tableware, and aluminum cookware. Well-known brands include HEFTY®, BAGGIES®, HEFTY ONEZIP®, KORDITE®, and E-Z FOIL®. The Company's protective packaging products are used to protect and cushion various commercial and industrial products from the point of manufacture to the point of delivery or pick-up, and principally serves the electronics, automotive, furniture, and e-commerce markets. The Company's flexible packaging products are mainly used in food, medical, pharmaceutical, chemical, and hygiene applications. On 11/4/99, PTV was spun off to shareholders of Tenneco Inc.

ANNUAL FINANCIAL DATA

	12/31/00	12/31/99	12/31/98	12/31/97	12/31/96
Earnings Per Share	**5 0.70**	**4 d0.67**	**3 0.49**	**2 0.63**	**1 0.38**
Cash Flow Per Share	**1.84**	**0.43**	**1.52**	**1.57**	**1.16**
Tang. Book Val. Per Share	**4.09**	**2.19**	...	...	...
INCOME STATEMENT (IN MILLIONS):					
Total Revenues	3,134.0	2,913.0	2,788.0	2,569.0	2,036.0
Costs & Expenses	2,614.0	2,742.0	2,330.0	2,100.0	1,671.0
Depreciation & Amort.	185.0	184.0	175.0	163.0	131.0
Operating Income	341.0	d13.0	283.0	306.0	234.0
Net Interest Inc./(Exp.)	d134.0	d146.0	d133.0	d124.0	d102.0
Income Before Income Taxes	207.0	d159.0	150.0	182.0	132.0
Income Taxes	91.0	cr47.0	67.0	75.0	67.0
Net Income	5 113.0	4 d112.0	3 82.0	2 106.0	1 65.0
Cash Flow	298.0	72.0	257.0	269.0	196.0
Average Shs. Outstg. (000)	161,779	167,663	168,835	170,802	169,609
BALANCE SHEET (IN MILLIONS):					
Cash & Cash Equivalents	26.0	12.0	7.0	11.0	...
Total Current Assets	900.0	866.0	917.0	924.0	...
Net Property	1,231.0	1,396.0	1,556.0	1,458.0	...
Total Assets	4,341.0	4,588.0	4,798.0	4,618.0	...
Total Current Liabilities	512.0	920.0	1,142.0	744.0	...
Long-Term Obligations	1,560.0	1,741.0	1,312.0	1,492.0	...
Net Stockholders' Equity	1,539.0	1,350.0	1,776.0	1,839.0	...
Net Working Capital	388.0	d54.0	d225.0	180.0	...
Year-end Shs. Outstg. (000)	146,416	168,373	...	...	...
STATISTICAL RECORD:					
Operating Profit Margin %	10.9	...	10.2	11.9	11.5
Net Profit Margin %	3.6	...	2.9	4.1	3.2
Return on Equity %	7.3	...	4.6	5.8	...
Return on Assets %	2.6	...	1.7	2.3	...
Debt/Total Assets %	35.9	37.9	27.3	32.3	...
Price Range	13.31-7.50	14.50-9.31	...	...	...
P/E Ratio	19.0-10.7	...	...	...	...

Statistics are as originally reported. 1 Bef. $71.0 mil ($0.42/sh) gain fr. disc. opers, $2.0 mil ($0.01/sh) extraord. chg. & incl. $15.0 mil gain fr sale of assets. 2 Bef. $21.0 mil ($0.12/sh) gain fr. disc. opers & $38.0 mil ($0.23/sh) acctg. chg. 3 Bef. $57.0 mil ($0.34/sh) inc. fr. disc. opers & incl. $9.0 mil chg. 4 Bef. $193.0 mil ($1.15/sh) loss fr. disc. opers, $7.0 mil ($0.04/sh) extraord. loss, $32.0 mil ($0.19/sh) acctg. chg. & incl. pre-tax chgs. of $195.0 mil fr. restr. and sale of assets. 5 Bef. $134.0 mil ($0.83/sh) gain fr. disc. opers. & incl. $70.0 mil pre-tax restr. chg. and a net pre-tax gain of $26.0 mil fr. the sale of a business and spin-off transaction.

OFFICERS:
R. L. Wambold, Chmn., Pres., C.E.O.
A. A. Campbell, Sr. V.P., C.F.O.
J. V. Faulkner, Jr., V.P., Gen. Couns.

INVESTOR CONTACT: Christine Hanneman, Inv. Rel., (847) 482-2429

PRINCIPAL OFFICE: 1900 West Field Court, Lake Forest, IL 60045

TELEPHONE NUMBER: (847) 482-2000
WEB: wwww.pactiv.com

NO. OF EMPLOYEES: 13,000 (approx.)

SHAREHOLDERS: 53,863 (approx.)

ANNUAL MEETING: In May

INCORPORATED: DE, 1996

INSTITUTIONAL HOLDINGS:
No. of Institutions: 236
Shares Held: 121,615,831
% Held: 76.7

INDUSTRY: Plastics products, nec (SIC: 3089)

TRANSFER AGENT(S): First Chicago Trust Company of New York, Jersey City, NJ

NYSE SYMBOL PLL
Rec. Pr. 23.47 (4/30/01)

PALL CORPORATION

YIELD 2.9%
P/E RATIO 20.2

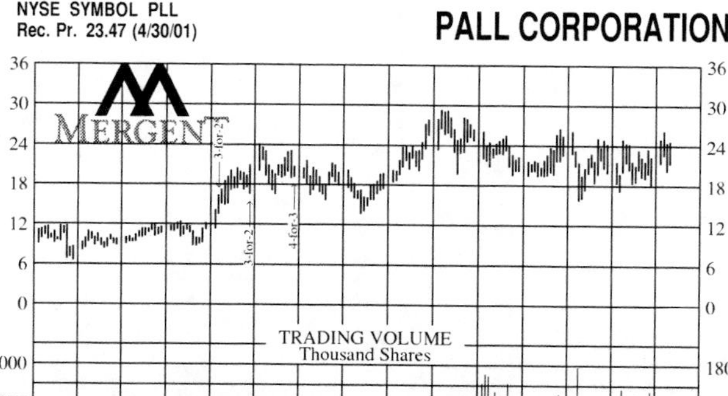

1987 1988 1989 1990 1991 1992 1993 1994 1995 1996 1997 1998 1999 2000 2001

*7 YEAR PRICE SCORE 72.0 *12 MONTH PRICE SCORE 111.4

*NYSE COMPOSITE INDEX=100

INTERIM EARNINGS (Per Share):

Qtr.	Oct.	Jan.	Apr.	July
1996-97	0.14	0.23	d0.18	0.34
1997-98	0.15	0.22	0.06	0.32
1998-99	0.12	0.15	d0.23	0.40
1999-00	0.20	0.27	0.34	0.37
2000-01	0.21	0.24	...	...

INTERIM DIVIDENDS (Per Share):

Amt.	Decl.	Ex.	Rec.	Pay.
0.165Q	4/19/00	5/02/00	5/04/00	5/19/00
0.165Q	7/12/00	7/25/00	7/27/00	8/11/00
0.165Q	10/04/00	10/26/00	10/30/00	11/17/00
0.17Q	1/17/01	1/30/01	2/01/01	2/13/01
0.17Q	4/18/01	5/07/01	5/09/01	5/23/01

Indicated div.: $0.68 (Div. Reinv. Plan)

CAPITALIZATION (7/29/00):

	($000)	(%)
Long-Term Debt	223,915	22.3
Deferred Income Tax	20,995	2.1
Common & Surplus	761,306	75.7
Total	1,006,216	100.0

RECENT DEVELOPMENTS: For the quarter ended 1/27/01, net income declined 11.6% to $29.9 million compared with $33.8 million in the equivalent 2000 quarter. Net sales were $304.7 million, up 3.4% from $294.7 million a year earlier. Medical sales slipped 2.4% to $83.2 million. Biopharmaceuticals sales increased 1.6% to $57.4 million. General Industrial sales declined slightly to $96.3 million. Aerospace sales rose 11.9% to $34.8 million.

PROSPECTS: PLL is well positioned to meet the growing filtration, separations and purification challenges of the many industries it serves. Weakness in the U.S. economy, a softening microelectronics market worldwide, and continued pressure from foreign exchange rates will likely moderate the overall rate of growth in the second half of this fiscal year. Earnings for the full year are likely to increase 6.0% to 10.0% to between $1.25 and $1.30 per share.

BUSINESS

PALL CORPORATION is a supplier of fine filters mainly made by the Company using its proprietary filter media and other fluid clarification and separations equipment for the removal of solid, liquid and gaseous contaminants from a wide variety of liquids and gases. The Company provides products for use in high-growth applications such as genomics, proteomics and biotechnology; in transfusion medicine; semiconductor; water; aerospace and a host of other industries. PLL is comprised of two operating segments: Life Sciences and Industrial. The Life Sciences segment is comprised of three sub-segments: Biosciences, BioPharmaceuticals and Medical. The Industrial sub-segments are Aerospace, Microelectronics and General Industrial.

ANNUAL FINANCIAL DATA

	7/29/00	7/31/99	8/1/98	8/2/97	8/3/96	7/29/95	7/30/94
Earnings Per Share	**1.18**	**[2] 0.41**	**[4] 0.75**	**[3] 0.53**	**1.21**	**[1] 1.04**	**[2] 0.86**
Cash Flow Per Share	**1.75**	**1.01**	**1.33**	**1.03**	**1.67**	**1.43**	**1.20**
Tang. Book Val. Per Share	**6.18**	**5.88**	**6.18**	**6.48**	**6.37**	**5.70**	**5.09**
Dividends Per Share	**0.66**	**0.64**	**0.62**	**0.56**	**0.49**	**0.42**	**0.37**
Dividend Payout %	**55.9**	**156.1**	**82.7**	**105.6**	**40.5**	**40.4**	**43.0**
INCOME STATEMENT (IN MILLIONS):							
Total Revenues	1,224.1	1,147.1	1,087.3	1,062.0	967.4	829.3	706.1
Costs & Expenses	949.7	1,000.4	871.4	910.2	706.0	606.1	524.4
Depreciation & Amort.	72.0	74.8	73.1	62.8	53.1	46.1	39.5
Operating Income	202.5	71.9	142.9	89.0	208.3	177.2	142.2
Net Interest Inc./(Exp.)	d14.1	d13.0	d7.9	d2.8	d10.4	d9.5	d7.1
Income Before Income Taxes	188.4	58.9	135.0	86.1	197.9	167.7	135.1
Income Taxes	41.8	7.4	41.4	18.8	59.4	48.5	36.2
Net Income	146.6	[2] 51.5	[4] 93.6	[3] 67.3	138.5	[1] 119.2	[2] 98.9
Cash Flow	218.6	126.3	166.7	130.1	191.6	165.3	138.5
Average Shs. Outstg. (000)	124,709	124,800	125,681	126,319	114,839	115,184	115,678
BALANCE SHEET (IN MILLIONS):							
Cash & Cash Equivalents	141.7	137.2	28.9	55.5	106.0	110.8	89.0
Total Current Assets	753.2	744.2	602.5	606.6	581.2	524.8	470.4
Net Property	503.8	507.0	520.6	504.0	463.9	427.9	397.6
Total Assets	1,507.3	1,488.3	1,346.9	1,265.6	1,185.0	1,074.9	959.6
Total Current Liabilities	437.7	558.3	394.1	301.0	330.2	287.7	256.8
Long-Term Obligations	223.9	116.8	111.5	62.1	46.7	68.8	54.1
Net Stockholders' Equity	761.3	730.7	765.6	824.8	732.3	651.8	587.2
Net Working Capital	315.5	185.9	208.4	305.6	251.0	237.0	213.6
Year-end Shs. Outstg. (000)	123,118	124,210	123,919	127,362	114,976	114,431	115,319
STATISTICAL RECORD:							
Operating Profit Margin %	16.5	6.3	13.1	8.4	21.5	21.4	20.1
Net Profit Margin %	12.0	4.5	8.6	6.3	14.3	14.4	14.0
Return on Equity %	19.3	7.0	12.2	8.2	18.9	18.3	16.8
Return on Assets %	9.7	3.5	7.0	5.3	11.7	11.1	10.3
Debt/Total Assets %	14.9	7.8	8.3	4.9	3.9	6.4	5.6
Price Range	25.00-17.13	26.19-15.75	26.63-19.38	26.13-19.50	29.38-19.63	27.88-18.38	20.25-13.63
P/E Ratio	21.2-14.5	63.9-38.4	35.5-25.8	49.3-36.8	24.3-16.2	26.8-17.7	23.5-15.8
Average Yield %	3.1	3.1	2.7	2.5	2.0	1.8	2.2

Statistics are as originally reported. [1] Bef. acctg. change chrg. $780,000. [2] Incl. restruct. chrg. $89.4 mill., 1999; $9.9 mill., 2000. [3] Incl. merger (Gelman Sciences) restruct. chrgs. & other one-time chrgs. of $95.9 mill. [4] Incl. non-recurr. income of $5.0 mill. from litigation settlement & a chrg. of $27.0 mill. acq. related Rochem chrg.

OFFICERS:
E. Krasnoff, Chmn., C.E.O.
J. Hayward-Surry, Pres.
J. Adamovich, Jr., C.F.O., Treas.
M. Barlett, Sec.

INVESTOR CONTACT: Diane Foster, Investor Relations, (516) 484-3600

PRINCIPAL OFFICE: 2200 Northern Boulevard, East Hills, NY 11548

TELEPHONE NUMBER: (516) 484-5400
FAX: (516) 484-3649
WEB: www.pall.com

NO. OF EMPLOYEES: 8,800 (avg.)

SHAREHOLDERS: 6,100 (approx. record)

ANNUAL MEETING: In Nov.

INCORPORATED: NY, July, 1946

INSTITUTIONAL HOLDINGS:
No. of Institutions: 288
Shares Held: 89,978,790
% Held: 73.3

INDUSTRY: General industrial machinery, nec (SIC: 3569)

TRANSFER AGENT(S): EquiServe Trust Co., N.A., Boston, MA

NYSE SYMBOL PPE
Rec. Pr. 11.12 (4/30/01)

PARK PLACE ENTERTAINMENT CORPORATION

YIELD ...
P/E RATIO 23.7

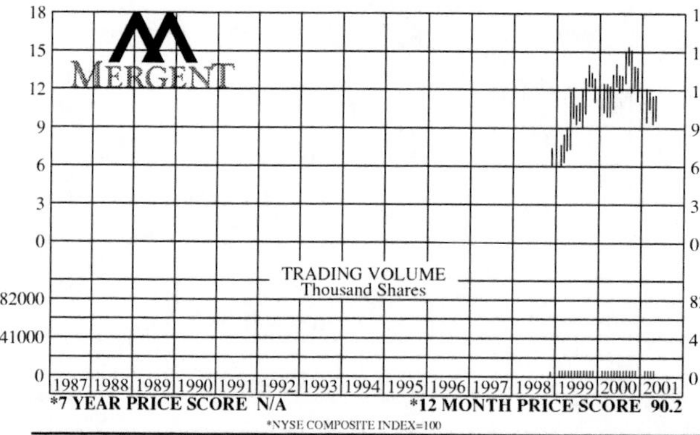

INTERIM EARNINGS (Per Share):

Qtr.	Mar.	June	Sept.	Dec.
1997	0.14	0.10	0.19	d0.17
1998	0.15	0.16	0.15	d0.03
1999	0.15	0.13	0.11	0.05
2000	0.17	0.10	0.22	d0.02

INTERIM DIVIDENDS (Per Share):

Amt.	Decl.	Ex.	Rec.	Pay.

No dividends paid.

CAPITALIZATION (12/31/00):

	($000)	(%)
Long-Term Debt	5,397,000	52.8
Deferred Income Tax	1,044,000	10.2
Common & Surplus	3,784,000	37.0
Total	10,225,000	100.0

RECENT DEVELOPMENTS: For the year ended 12/31/00, PPE reported net income of $143.0 million versus income of $138.0 million, before an accounting charge of $2.0 million, in 1999. Earnings for 2000 and 1999 included pre-tax pre-opening expenses of $3.0 million and $47.0 million, respectively, and pre-tax nonrecurring gains of $45.0 million and $26.0 million, respectively. Net revenue increased 54.2% to $4.90 billion.

PROSPECTS: On 2/22/01, PPE announced that it plans to build a 30-story, 864-room tower at its Caesars Palace resort in Las Vegas, which will bring the total number of rooms at Caesars to more than 3,300. The new tower will also include 320,000 square feet of space for restaurants, shops and meeting rooms. PPE intends to start construction of the tower in the second half of 2001, with completion in the first half of 2003.

BUSINESS

PARK PLACE ENTERTAINMENT CORPORATION is primarily engaged in the ownership, operation and development of gaming facilities, and conducts its operations under the Caesars, Bally's, Paris, Flamingo, Grand, Hilton and Conrad brands. The Company operates a total of 28 casino hotels, including 17 located in the U.S., of which nine are located in Nevada, three are located in Atlantic City, New Jersey, and five are located in Mississippi. The Company has a 49.9%-owned and managed riverboat casino in New Orleans, and an 82.0%-owned and managed riverboat casino in Harrison County, Indiana. The Company partially owns and manages two casino hotels in Australia, one casino hotel in Punta del Este, Uruguay, two casinos on cruise ships, two casinos in Nova Scotia, Canada and one casino in South Africa. The Company also provides management services to a casino in Windsor, Canada and the slot operations at the Dover Downs racetrack in Delaware.

REVENUES

(12/31/2000)	($000)	(%)
Casino	3,480,000	71.1
Rooms	568,000	11.6
Food & Beverage	460,000	9.4
Other Products & Services	388,000	7.9
Total	4,896,000	100.0

ANNUAL FINANCIAL DATA

	12/31/00	12/31/99	12/31/98	12/31/97	12/31/96	12/31/95
Earnings Per Share	**[4] 0.46**	**[2][3] 0.45**	**0.42**	**0.25**	**[1] 0.18**	**0.44**
Cash Flow Per Share	**2.16**	**1.46**	**1.28**	**1.04**	**0.74**	**0.84**
Tang. Book Val. Per Share	**6.52**	**6.01**	**7.63**	**7.22**	...	...
INCOME STATEMENT (IN MILLIONS):						
Total Revenues	4,896.0	3,176.0	2,305.0	2,572.0	1,415.0	1,284.0
Costs & Expenses	3,694.0	2,465.0	1,776.0	2,162.0	1,212.0	1,041.0
Depreciation & Amort.	506.0	312.0	227.0	209.0	111.0	78.0
Operating Income	696.0	399.0	302.0	201.0	92.0	165.0
Net Interest Inc./(Exp.)	d431.0	d146.0	d79.0	d67.0	d29.0	d34.0
Income Before Income Taxes	265.0	253.0	223.0	134.0	63.0	131.0
Income Taxes	121.0	113.0	111.0	63.0	27.0	46.0
Equity Earnings/Minority Int.	d1.0	d2.0	d3.0	d4.0	...	...
Net Income	[4] 143.0	[2][3] 138.0	109.0	67.0	[1] 36.0	85.0
Cash Flow	649.0	450.0	336.0	276.0	147.0	163.0
Average Shs. Outstg. (000)	301,000	309,000	263,000	266,000	198,000	193,000
BALANCE SHEET (IN MILLIONS):						
Cash & Cash Equivalents	321.0	346.0	382.0	224.0	252.0	...
Total Current Assets	847.0	893.0	634.0	509.0	561.0	...
Net Property	7,805.0	7,873.0	4,991.0	3,621.0	3,405.0	...
Total Assets	10,995.0	11,151.0	7,174.0	5,689.0	5,447.0	...
Total Current Liabilities	677.0	733.0	440.0	393.0	424.0	...
Long-Term Obligations	5,397.0	5,616.0	2,466.0	1,272.0	1,225.0	...
Net Stockholders' Equity	3,784.0	3,740.0	3,608.0	3,381.0	3,157.0	...
Net Working Capital	170.0	160.0	194.0	116.0	137.0	...
Year-end Shs. Outstg. (000)	297,600	304,000	303,000	288,000	...	...
STATISTICAL RECORD:						
Operating Profit Margin %	14.2	12.6	13.1	7.8	6.5	12.9
Net Profit Margin %	2.9	4.3	4.7	2.6	2.5	6.6
Return on Equity %	3.8	3.7	3.0	2.0	1.1	...
Return on Assets %	1.3	1.2	1.5	1.2	0.7	...
Debt/Total Assets %	49.1	50.4	34.4	22.4	22.5	...
Price Range	15.38-9.88	14.00-6.06	7.44-6.00	...	...	...
P/E Ratio	33.4-21.5	31.1-13.5	17.7-14.3	...	...	...

Statistics are as originally reported. [1] Bef. extraord. loss of $74.0 mill. [2] Incl. impairment losses & oth. exp. of $26.0 mill., 1999; $29.0 mill., 1998. [3] Bef. acctg. chrg. of $2.0 mill.; incl. pre-open. exp. of $47.0 mill. [4] Incl. pre-tax pre-open. exp. of $3.0 mill. & pre-tax nonrecurr. gain of $45.0 mill.

OFFICERS:
S. F. Bollenbach, Chmn.
T. E. Gallagher, Pres., C.E.O.
S. A. LaPorta, Exec. V.P., C.F.O., Treas.

INVESTOR CONTACT: Matt Maddox, Investor Relations, (702) 699-5269

PRINCIPAL OFFICE: 3930 Howard Hughes Parkway, Las Vegas, NV 89109

TELEPHONE NUMBER: (702) 699-5000
FAX: (702) 699-5121
WEB: www.parkplace.com

NO. OF EMPLOYEES: 57,000 (approx.)

SHAREHOLDERS: 13,000 (approx., record)

ANNUAL MEETING: In May

INCORPORATED: DE, Dec., 1998

INSTITUTIONAL HOLDINGS:
No. of Institutions: 182
Shares Held: 192,505,528
% Held: 64.9

INDUSTRY: Hotels and motels (SIC: 7011)

TRANSFER AGENT(S): Wells Fargo Shareowner Services, South St. Paul, MN

NYSE SYMBOL PH
Rec. Pr. 48.31 (5/31/01)

PARKER-HANNIFIN CORP.

YIELD	1.5%
P/E RATIO	13.0

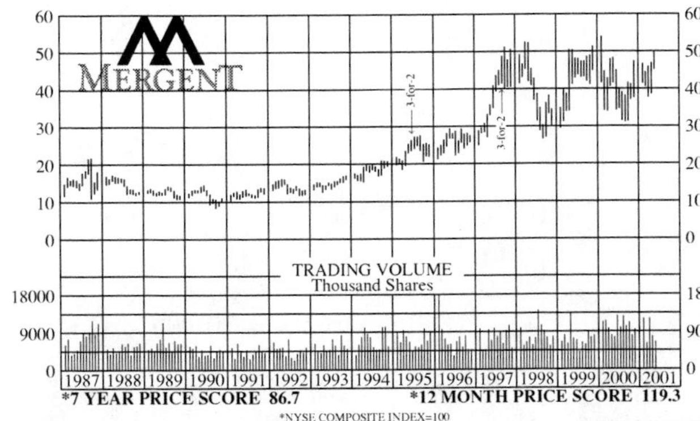

***7 YEAR PRICE SCORE 86.7** ***12 MONTH PRICE SCORE 119.3**

*NYSE COMPOSITE INDEX=100

INTERIM EARNINGS (Per Share):

Qtr.	Sept.	Dec.	Mar.	June
1996-97	0.46	0.47	0.70	0.83
1997-98	0.70	0.63	0.75	0.80
1998-99	0.71	0.58	0.70	0.84
1999-00	0.67	0.68	0.97	0.99
2000-01	1.09	0.68	...	...

INTERIM DIVIDENDS (Per Share):

Amt.	Decl.	Ex.	Rec.	Pay.
0.17Q	4/06/00	5/16/00	5/18/00	6/02/00
0.17Q	7/13/00	8/16/00	8/18/00	9/01/00
0.17Q	10/27/00	11/14/00	11/16/00	12/01/00
0.18Q	2/01/01	2/13/01	2/15/01	3/02/01
0.18Q	4/12/01	5/15/01	5/17/01	6/01/01

Indicated div.: $0.72 (Div. Reinv. Plan)

CAPITALIZATION (6/30/00):

	($000)	(%)
Long-Term Debt	701,762	22.7
Deferred Income Tax	77,939	2.5
Common & Surplus	2,309,458	74.8
Total	3,089,159	100.0

RECENT DEVELOPMENTS: For the quarter ended 12/31/00, net income rose 4.5% to $78.3 million versus $75.0 million a year earlier. Net sales advanced 17.8% to $1.46 billion. North American industrial sales grew 25.9% to $829.4 million and operating income rose 16.5% to $101.6 million, reflecting growth in the semiconductor, filtration and telecommunications markets. However, international industrial operating income fell 1.6% to $21.4 million. Aerospace operating income advanced 38.3% to $51.1 million.

PROSPECTS: The slowing North American industrial order trend clouds PH's near-term prospects. Thus, the Company has initiated spending cuts and selected workforce adjustments for the remainder of fiscal year 2001. PH also plans to record further operating realignment charges and pursue early retirement of higher-interest debt. On 1/31/01, PH acquired Stainless Connections Pty Ltd. of New South Wales, Australia and Stainless Connections Ltd. of Auckland, New Zealand, makers of stainless steel fittings. On 2/22/01, PH acquired Milan-based S.B.C. Elettronica SPA.

BUSINESS

PARKER-HANNIFIN CORP. is a worldwide manufacturer of motion control products, including fluid power systems, electromechanical controls and related components, for the industrial and aerospace markets. PH also produces fluid purification, fluid flow, process instrumentation, air conditioning, refrigeration, and electromagnetic shielding and thermal management products. The Industrial segment consists of seven groups: Fluid Connectors, Hydraulics, Automation, Climate and Industrial Controls, Seal, Filtration and Instrumentation. Principal products of The Aerospace segment are hydraulic, fuel and pneumatic systems and components that are used on commerical and military airframe and engine programs. The Company acquired Wynn's International, Inc. for approximately $497.0 million in July, 2000.

BUSINESS LINE ANALYSIS

(06/30/00)	Rev(%)	Inc(%)
Industrial	78.7	74.4
Aerospace	21.3	25.6
Total	100.0	100.0

ANNUAL FINANCIAL DATA

	6/30/00	6/30/99	6/30/98	6/30/97	6/30/96	6/30/95	6/30/94
Earnings Per Share	**3.31**	**2.83**	**[1] 2.88**	**2.46**	**2.15**	**1.97**	**[1][2] 0.48**
Cash Flow Per Share	**5.17**	**4.67**	**4.52**	**3.98**	**3.42**	**3.06**	**1.51**
Tang. Book Val. Per Share	**14.94**	**12.62**	**11.74**	**11.32**	**9.55**	**9.99**	**8.31**
Dividends Per Share	**0.68**	**0.68**	**0.60**	**0.57**	**0.48**	**0.47**	**0.44**
Dividend Payout %	**20.5**	**24.0**	**20.8**	**23.0**	**22.3**	**23.9**	**93.5**
INCOME STATEMENT (IN MILLIONS):							
Total Revenues	5,355.3	4,958.8	4,633.0	4,091.1	3,586.4	3,214.4	2,576.3
Costs & Expenses	4,526.1	4,218.0	3,900.4	3,458.3	3,040.4	2,712.9	2,297.2
Depreciation & Amort.	206.4	202.0	182.7	169.8	141.4	119.9	113.1
Operating Income	622.9	538.7	549.9	462.9	404.7	381.5	166.0
Net Interest Inc./(Exp.)	d59.2	d63.7	d52.8	d46.7	d36.7	d30.9	d37.8
Income Before Income Taxes	562.2	477.7	504.0	424.9	374.5	348.4	112.4
Income Taxes	194.0	167.2	180.8	150.8	134.8	130.2	60.3
Net Income	368.2	310.5	[1] 323.2	274.0	239.7	218.2	[1][2] 52.2
Cash Flow	574.6	512.5	505.9	443.9	381.0	338.2	165.2
Average Shs. Outstg. (000)	111,225	109,679	111,959	111,601	111,261	110,576	109,661
BALANCE SHEET (IN MILLIONS):							
Cash & Cash Equivalents	68.5	33.3	30.5	69.0	64.0	63.8	81.6
Total Current Assets	2,153.1	1,774.7	1,780.1	1,499.6	1,402.1	1,246.4	1,018.4
Net Property	1,340.9	1,200.9	1,135.2	1,020.7	991.8	815.8	717.3
Total Assets	4,646.3	3,705.9	3,524.8	2,998.9	2,887.1	2,302.2	1,912.8
Total Current Liabilities	1,186.3	754.5	988.8	716.0	766.9	652.6	504.4
Long-Term Obligations	701.8	724.8	512.9	432.9	439.8	237.2	257.3
Net Stockholders' Equity	2,309.5	1,853.9	1,683.5	1,547.3	1,384.0	1,218.5	966.4
Net Working Capital	966.8	1,020.2	791.3	783.5	635.2	593.8	513.9
Year-end Shs. Outstg. (000)	116,388	111,901	109,308	111,526	111,438	111,003	110,115
STATISTICAL RECORD:							
Operating Profit Margin %	11.6	10.9	11.9	11.3	11.3	11.9	6.4
Net Profit Margin %	6.9	6.3	7.0	6.7	6.7	6.8	2.0
Return on Equity %	15.9	16.7	19.2	17.7	17.3	17.9	5.4
Return on Assets %	7.9	8.4	9.2	9.1	8.3	9.5	2.7
Debt/Total Assets %	15.1	19.6	14.6	14.4	15.2	10.3	13.4
Price Range	54.00-31.00	51.44-29.50	52.63-26.56	51.25-24.92	29.42-21.25	27.67-18.39	20.95-15.11
P/E Ratio	16.3-9.4	18.2-10.4	18.3-9.2	20.8-10.1	13.7-9.9	14.0-9.3	44.1-31.8
Average Yield %	1.6	1.7	1.5	1.5	1.9	2.0	2.5

Statistics are as originally reported. Adj. for 3-for-2 stk. splits, 9/97 & 6/95 [1] Bef. an extraord. chrg. 6/30/98, $3.7 mill.; chrg. 6/30/94, $4.5 mill. [2] Incls. non-recurr. pre-tax chrg. of $56.5 mill.

OFFICERS:
D. E. Collins, Chmn., C.E.O.
D. E. Washkewicz, Pres., C.O.O.
M. J. Hiemstra, V.P., C.F.O.

INVESTOR CONTACT: Lorrie Paul Crum, V.P., Corp. Comm., (216) 896-2750

PRINCIPAL OFFICE: 6035 Parkland Blvd., Cleveland, OH 44124-4141

TELEPHONE NUMBER: (216) 896-3000
FAX: (216) 383-9414
WEB: www.parker.com
NO. OF EMPLOYEES: 43,895
SHAREHOLDERS: 48,650 (approx.)
ANNUAL MEETING: In Oct.
INCORPORATED: OH, Dec., 1938

INSTITUTIONAL HOLDINGS:
No. of Institutions: 286
Shares Held: 89,364,683
% Held: 76.7

INDUSTRY: Industrial valves (SIC: 3491)

TRANSFER AGENT(S): National City Bank, Cleveland, OH

NYSE SYMBOL PSS
Rec. Pr. 67.89 (5/31/01)

PAYLESS SHOESOURCE INC.

YIELD ...
P/E RATIO 13.0

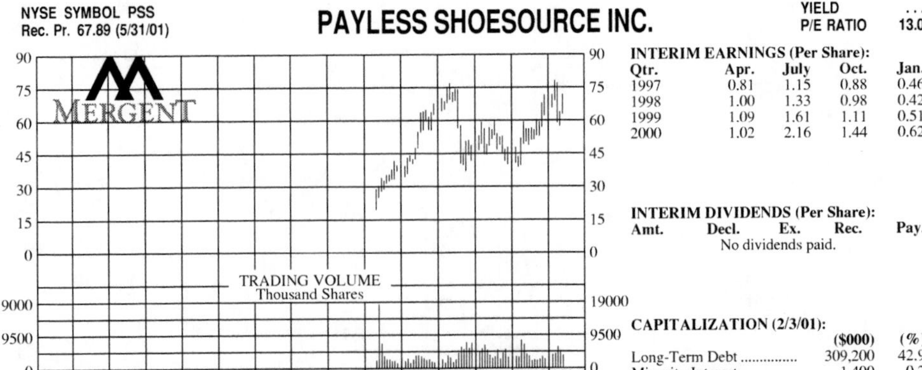

INTERIM EARNINGS (Per Share):

Qtr.	Apr.	July	Oct.	Jan.
1997	0.81	1.15	0.88	0.46
1998	1.00	1.33	0.98	0.42
1999	1.09	1.61	1.11	0.51
2000	1.02	2.16	1.44	0.62

INTERIM DIVIDENDS (Per Share):

Amt.	Decl.	Ex.	Rec.	Pay.

No dividends paid.

CAPITALIZATION (2/3/01):

	($000)	(%)
Long-Term Debt	309,200	42.9
Minority Interest	1,400	0.2
Common & Surplus	410,400	56.9
Total	721,000	100.0

RECENT DEVELOPMENTS: For the 53 weeks ended 2/3/01, earnings totaled $124.2 million, before an extraordinary loss of $3.6 million related to early extinguishment of debt, compared with net earnings of $136.5 million in the corresponding 52-week period a year earlier. Results for fiscal 2000 included a non-recurring charge of $8.0 million. Net retail sales increased 8.0% to $2.95 billion from $2.73 billion in the previous year. Gross profit was $936.9 million, or 31.8% of net retail sales, versus $861.8 million, or 31.6% of net retail sales, the prior year.

PROSPECTS: The Company's men's business should continue to benefit from the introduction of a new line of leather shoes, Hunter's Bay,™ and its new line of Stanley Footgear® work boots. Furthermore, the Company intends to continue its international expansion, including plans to open 25 to 30 stores in Central America and the Caribbean through its joint venture with PLP S.A. The Company is targeting same-store sales growth for full year fiscal 2001 in the low single-digit range and expects to achieve earnings per share growth of 15.0%.

BUSINESS

PAYLESS SHOESOURCE INC. is a retailer of family footwear. As of 3/8/01, PSS operated a total of 4,903 stores including 4,627 Payless ShoeSource® stores in 50 states, the District of Columbia, Puerto Rico, the U.S. Virgin Islands, Guam, Saipan, and Canada. Payless ShoeSource® stores, which average about 3,300 square feet, feature footwear for men, women and children, including athletic, casual, dress, sandals, work boots and slippers. In addition, the Company operates 266 Parade stores, which average about 2,400 square feet, in 16 states. Parade offers women's footwear and accessories at moderate prices. In March 1997, PSS purchased inventory, property and trademarks, and assumed leases on 186 stores of the Parade division from J. Baker, Inc. for approximately $28.0 million.

ANNUAL FINANCIAL DATA

	2/3/01	1/29/00	1/30/99	1/31/98	2/1/97	2/3/96	1/28/95
Earnings Per Share	**2 5.16**	**4.35**	**3.78**	**3.31**	**2.68**	**1 1.34**	...
Cash Flow Per Share	**9.43**	**7.54**	**6.52**	**5.75**	**5.14**	**3.70**	...
Tang. Book Val. Per Share	**18.66**	**23.75**	**21.66**	**22.40**	**21.37**	**18.80**	...
INCOME STATEMENT (IN MILLIONS):							
Total Revenues	2,948.4	2,730.1	2,615.5	2,566.9	2,333.7	2,330.3	2,116.4
Costs & Expenses	2,617.8	2,404.1	2,300.0	2,266.4	2,061.6	2,145.1	1,821.2
Depreciation & Amort.	102.6	99.9	98.1	95.1	99.2	95.3	77.0
Operating Income	228.0	226.1	217.4	205.4	172.9	89.9	218.2
Net Interest Inc./(Exp.)	...	...	...	...	...	d1.0	d1.1
Income Before Income Taxes	203.0	227.0	224.5	214.3	179.1	88.9	217.1
Income Taxes	79.0	90.5	89.5	85.4	71.4	34.9	85.6
Net Income	2 124.2	136.5	135.0	128.9	107.7	1 54.0	131.5
Cash Flow	226.8	236.4	233.1	224.0	206.9	149.3	208.5
Average Shs. Outstg. (000)	24,054	31,365	35,732	38,930	40,220	40,365	...
BALANCE SHEET (IN MILLIONS):							
Cash & Cash Equivalents	10.4	164.2	123.5	210.0	193.6	4.6	6.6
Total Current Assets	434.7	566.9	495.8	562.9	574.8	450.9	425.5
Net Property	518.7	482.9	492.8	486.7	502.5	560.0	590.6
Total Assets	1,002.8	1,075.5	1,017.9	1,073.0	1,091.8	1,014.3	1,019.8
Total Current Liabilities	228.7	197.8	194.9	178.1	182.6	218.9	182.7
Long-Term Obligations	309.2	126.1	72.0	6.5	8.2	10.3	11.6
Net Stockholders' Equity	410.4	702.9	702.8	836.4	853.0	752.9	793.9
Net Working Capital	206.0	369.1	300.9	384.8	392.2	232.0	242.8
Year-end Shs. Outstg. (000)	21,988	29,602	32,453	37,332	39,920	39,900	...
STATISTICAL RECORD:							
Operating Profit Margin %	7.7	8.3	8.3	8.0	7.4	3.9	10.3
Net Profit Margin %	4.2	5.0	5.2	5.0	4.6	2.3	6.2
Return on Equity %	30.3	19.4	19.2	15.4	12.6	7.2	16.6
Return on Assets %	12.4	12.7	13.3	12.0	9.9	5.3	12.9
Debt/Total Assets %	30.8	11.7	7.1	0.6	0.8	1.0	1.1
Price Range	71.69-38.75	59.81-40.00	77.00-37.00	67.88-34.38	41.75-19.50	...	...
P/E Ratio	13.9-7.5	13.7-9.2	20.4-9.8	20.5-10.4	15.6-7.3	...	...

Statistics are as originally reported. 1 Incl. $71.8 mill. non-recurr. chg. 2 Bef. $3.6 mill. ($0.15/sh.) extraord. chg. & incl. $8.0 mill. non-recur chg.

OFFICERS:
S. J. Douglass, Chmn., C.E.O.
K. C. Hicks, Pres.
U. E. Porzig, Sr. V.P., C.F.O., Treas.

INVESTOR CONTACT: Investor Relations, (800) 626-3204

PRINCIPAL OFFICE: 3231 S.E. Sixth Ave., Topeka, KS 66607-2207

TELEPHONE NUMBER: (785) 233-5171
WEB: www.paylessshoesource.com

NO. OF EMPLOYEES: 14,600 full-time (approx.); 13,100 part-time (approx.)

SHAREHOLDERS: 16,698 (approx.)

ANNUAL MEETING: In May

INCORPORATED: DE, June, 1998

INSTITUTIONAL HOLDINGS:
No. of Institutions: 193
Shares Held: 15,338,491
% Held: 69.2

INDUSTRY: Shoe stores (SIC: 5661)

TRANSFER AGENT(S): UMB Bank, Kansas City, MO

NYSE SYMBOL JCP
Rec. Pr. 20.91 (5/31/01)

PENNEY (J.C.) COMPANY, INC.

YIELD 2.4%
P/E RATIO ...

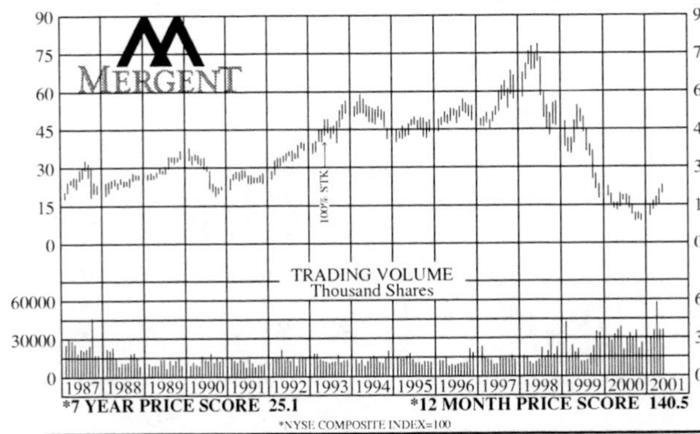

*7 YEAR PRICE SCORE 25.1 *12 MONTH PRICE SCORE 140.5

*NYSE COMPOSITE INDEX=100

INTERIM EARNINGS (Per Share):

Qtr.	Apr.	July	Oct.	Jan.
1996-97	0.58	0.37	0.98	0.36
1997-98	0.53	0.32	0.40	0.85
1998-99	0.64	0.08	0.68	0.77
1999-00	0.61	0.12	0.51	d0.08
2000-01	d0.48	0.06	d0.15	d1.11

INTERIM DIVIDENDS (Per Share):

Amt.	Decl.	Ex.	Rec.	Pay.
0.287Q	5/19/00	7/06/00	7/10/00	8/01/00
0.125Q	9/13/00	10/05/00	10/10/00	11/01/00
0.125Q	11/08/00	1/08/01	1/10/01	2/01/01
0.125Q	3/23/01	4/06/01	4/10/01	5/01/01
0.125Q	5/18/01	7/06/01	7/10/01	8/01/01

Indicated div.: $0.50 (Div. Reinv. Plan)

CAPITALIZATION (1/27/01):

	($000)	(%)
Long-Term Debt	5,448,000	42.4
Deferred Income Tax	1,136,000	8.8
Preferred Stock	399,000	3.1
Common & Surplus	5,860,000	45.6
Total	12,843,000	100.0

RECENT DEVELOPMENTS: For the year ended 1/27/01, loss from continuing operations was $568.0 million versus income from continuing operations of $174.0 million the prior year. Results included one-time pre-tax restructuring and other charges of $488.0 million and $169.0 million in fiscal 2000 and fiscal 1999, respectively. Net retail sales inched up to $31.85 billion from $31.73 billion a year earlier. Comparisons were made with restated prior-year results to reflect the Company's direct marketing services business as a discontinued operation.

PROSPECTS: On 3/8/01, the Company entered into an agreement to sell its direct marketing services business to Netherlands-based AEGON N.V. for approximately $1.30 billion in cash. The transaction is expected to be completed during the second quarter of 2001. Meanwhile, JCP plans to implement a new marketing program, improve merchandise selection at its department stores, and focus on cutting costs during 2001. The Company is targeting earnings of between $0.70 and $0.80 per share in the current fiscal year.

BUSINESS

J.C. PENNEY COMPANY, INC. is one of the largest national retailing chains operating approximately 1,075 JCPenney stores in all 50 states, Puerto Rico and Mexico. The Company also operates 50 Renner department stores in Brazil. Virtually all domestic stores feature JCPenney Catalog departments. Primarily, JCP sells family apparel, shoes, jewelry, accessories, and home furnishings. JCP also operates approximately 2,650 Eckerd drug stores. Revenues in 2000 were derived as follows: Department Stores and Catalog, 58.9% and Drugstores, 41.1%. The Company acquired Eckerd Corp. on 2/27/97. On 3/1/99, JCP acquired Genovese Drug Stores, Inc.

ANNUAL FINANCIAL DATA

	1/27/01	1/29/00	1/30/99	1/31/98	1/25/97	1/27/96	1/28/95
Earnings Per Share	**[3] d2.29**	**[2] 1.16**	**[1] 2.19**	**[2] 2.10**	**[2] 2.29**	**[1] 3.48**	**4.29**
Cash Flow Per Share	**0.48**	**3.67**	**4.54**	**4.27**	**4.11**	**5.17**	**5.84**
Tang. Book Val. Per Share	**11.37**	**14.28**	**15.04**	**15.50**	**15.73**	**23.58**	**21.96**
Dividends Per Share	**0.99**	**2.19**	**2.17**	**2.13**	**2.04**	**1.86**	**1.62**
Dividend Payout %	...	**188.3**	**99.1**	**101.2**	**89.1**	**53.4**	**37.8**
INCOME STATEMENT (IN MILLIONS):							
Total Revenues	31,846.0	32,510.0	30,678.0	30,546.0	23,649.0	21,419.0	21,082.0
Costs & Expenses	31,122.0	30,801.0	28,515.0	27,926.0	21,704.0	19,550.0	18,962.0
Depreciation & Amort.	695.0	710.0	637.0	584.0	381.0	345.0	328.0
Operating Income	29.0	999.0	1,526.0	2,036.0	1,564.0	1,524.0	1,792.0
Net Interest Inc./(Exp.)	d427.0	d299.0	d480.0	d547.0	d278.0	d183.0	d93.0
Income Before Income Taxes	d886.0	531.0	955.0	925.0	909.0	1,341.0	1,699.0
Income Taxes	cr318.0	195.0	361.0	359.0	344.0	503.0	642.0
Net Income	[3] d568.0	[2] 336.0	[1] 594.0	[2] 566.0	[2] 565.0	[1] 838.0	1,057.0
Cash Flow	127.0	1,010.0	1,230.0	1,146.0	941.0	1,154.0	1,356.0
Average Shs. Outstg. (000)	262,000	275,000	271,000	268,100	229,000	229,000	237,000
BALANCE SHEET (IN MILLIONS):							
Cash & Cash Equivalents	944.0	1,233.0	96.0	287.0	131.0	173.0	261.0
Total Current Assets	7,257.0	8,472.0	11,125.0	11,484.0	11,712.0	9,409.0	9,468.0
Net Property	5,114.0	5,312.0	5,458.0	5,329.0	5,014.0	4,281.0	3,954.0
Total Assets	19,742.0	20,888.0	23,638.0	23,493.0	22,088.0	17,102.0	16,202.0
Total Current Liabilities	4,235.0	4,465.0	5,970.0	6,137.0	4,228.0	1,616.0	2,207.0
Long-Term Obligations	5,448.0	5,844.0	7,143.0	6,986.0	4,565.0	4,080.0	3,335.0
Net Stockholders' Equity	6,259.0	7,228.0	7,169.0	7,357.0	5,952.0	5,884.0	5,615.0
Net Working Capital	3,022.0	4,007.0	5,155.0	5,347.0	7,484.0	7,793.0	7,261.0
Year-end Shs. Outstg. (000)	263,000	261,000	250,000	251,000	224,000	224,000	227,000
STATISTICAL RECORD:							
Operating Profit Margin %	0.1	3.1	5.0	6.7	6.6	7.1	8.5
Net Profit Margin %	...	1.0	1.9	1.9	2.4	3.9	5.0
Return on Equity %	...	4.6	8.3	7.7	9.5	14.2	18.8
Return on Assets %	...	1.6	2.5	2.4	2.6	4.9	6.5
Debt/Total Assets %	27.6	28.0	30.2	29.7	20.7	23.9	20.6
Price Range	22.50-8.63	54.44-17.69	78.75-42.63	68.25-44.88	57.00-44.00	50.00-39.88	59.00-41.13
P/E Ratio	...	46.9-15.2	36.0-19.5	32.5-21.4	24.9-19.2	14.4-11.5	13.8-9.6
Average Yield %	6.3	6.1	3.6	3.8	4.0	4.1	3.2

Statistics are as originally reported. [1] Incl. $22 mil ($0.05/sh) pre-tax gain, 1999; & $67 mil net gain, 1996. [2] Incl. $169 mil ($0.53/sh) non-recur. chg., 2000; $447 mil chg., 1998; $207 mil ($0.84/sh) chg., 1997. [3] Bef. $159.0 mil (0.61/sh) inc. fr. disc opers., $296.0 mil ($1.13/sh) loss on sale of disc. opers. & incl. $488.0 mil non-recur. chg.

OFFICERS:
A. I. Questrom, Chmn., C.E.O.
R. B. Cavanaugh, Exec. V.P., C.F.O.
C. R. Lotter, Exec. V.P., Sec., Gen. Couns.

INVESTOR CONTACT: W.C. Watkins, (972) 431-1488

PRINCIPAL OFFICE: 6501 Legacy Drive, Plano, TX 75024-3698

TELEPHONE NUMBER: (972) 431-1000
FAX: (972) 591-9322
WEB: www.jcpenney.com

NO. OF EMPLOYEES: 267,000 (approx.)

SHAREHOLDERS: 53,000 (approx.)

ANNUAL MEETING: In May

INCORPORATED: DE, Dec., 1924

INSTITUTIONAL HOLDINGS:
No. of Institutions: 281
Shares Held: 199,467,751
% Held: 75.8

INDUSTRY: Department stores (SIC: 5311)

TRANSFER AGENT(S): Mellon Investor Services, Ridgefield Park, NJ

NYSE SYMBOL PZL
Rec. Pr. 14.21 (4/30/01)

PENNZOIL-QUAKER STATE COMPANY

YIELD 5.3%
P/E RATIO 473.7

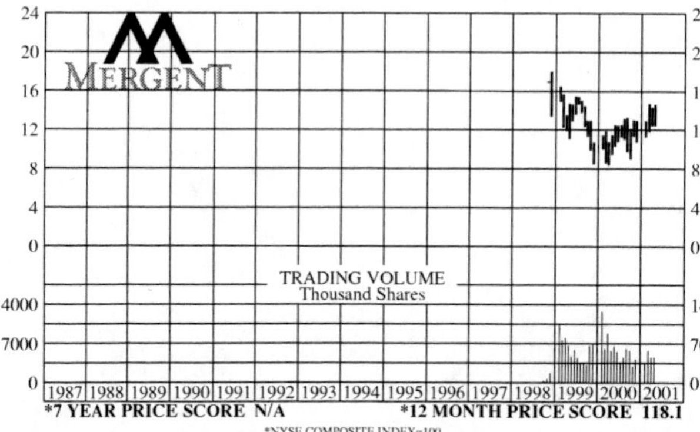

*7 YEAR PRICE SCORE N/A *12 MONTH PRICE SCORE 118.1
*NYSE COMPOSITE INDEX=100

INTERIM EARNINGS (Per Share):

Qtr.	Mar.	June	Sept.	Dec.
1998	0.01	0.13	0.01	d1.11
1999	d0.03	0.08	d0.09	d4.08
2000	d0.06	0.20	0.14	d0.25

INTERIM DIVIDENDS (Per Share):

Amt.	Decl.	Ex.	Rec.	Pay.
0.188Q	5/04/00	5/26/00	5/31/00	6/15/00
0.188Q	8/03/00	8/29/00	8/31/00	9/15/00
0.188Q	11/03/00	11/28/00	11/30/00	12/15/00
0.188Q	2/01/01	2/26/01	2/28/01	3/15/01
0.188Q	5/03/01	5/29/01	5/31/01	6/15/01

Indicated div.: $0.75 (Div. Reinv. Plan)

CAPITALIZATION (12/31/00):

	($000)	(%)
Long-Term Debt	1,194,426	57.4
Capital Lease Obligations	61,861	3.0
Common & Surplus	823,191	39.6
Total	2,079,478	100.0

RECENT DEVELOPMENTS: For the twelve months ended 12/31/00, income from continuing operations totaled $5.9 million compared with a loss from continuing operations of $10.7 million in 1999. Results included acquisition-related expenses of $34.4 million and $75.1 million for 2000 and 1999, respectively, as well as charges of $10.0 million and $13.9 million related to asset disposals. Results for 2000 and 1999 excluded losses from discontinued operations of $92.1 million and $300.5 million, respectively. Total revenues rose 1.6% to $2.32 billion from $2.28 billion in 1999.

PROSPECTS: PZL's near-term prospects are clouded by the slowdown in the U.S. economy, which could lead to lower discretionary spending on automotive products, as well as historically high gasoline prices, which have caused motorists to reduce driving, resulting in fewer oil changes. Separately, on 4/30/01, PZL announced the completion of the sale of its Shreveport, LA refinery and related assets to Calument Lubricants Company, L.P. Financial terms were not disclosed. The transaction completes the Company's program to sell non-strategic assets and businesses.

BUSINESS

PENNZOIL-QUAKER STATE COMPANY is a worldwide automotive consumer products company engaged primarily in the manufacturing and marketing of lubricants and car care products and the franchising, ownership and operation of fast oil change centers. PZL brand names include motors oils PENNZOIL®, QUAKER STATE® and WOLF'S HEAD®, fast oil change centers with JIFFY LUBE® and car care products SLICK ® RAIN-X®, BLUE CORAL®, BLACK MAGIC®, WESTLEY'S®, GUMOUT®, FIX-A-FLAT® and others. PZL's three business segments are lubricants and consumer products, Jiffy Lube and supply chain investments. The Company was formed as a result of the consolidation and spin-off on 12/30/98 of the lubricants and consumer products and fast oil change operations of Pennzoil Company.

REVENUES

12/31/2000	($000)	(%)
Lubricants	1,664,934	73.3
Consumer products	336,903	14.8
Jiffy Lube	331,899	14.6
Base oils	166,827	7.4
All other products	(2,721)	(0.1)
Intersegment sales	(227,287)	(10.0)
Total	2,270,555	100.0

ANNUAL FINANCIAL DATA

	12/31/00	12/31/99	12/31/98	12/31/97	12/31/96	12/31/95
Earnings Per Share	**3 4 0.03**	**2 d4.12**	**1 d0.96**	...	**d0.19**	...
Cash Flow Per Share	**1.30**	**d2.54**	**0.65**	...	**0.89**	...
Tang. Book Val. Per Share	...	...	**3.17**	**2.36**	**2.92**	...
Dividends Per Share	**0.75**	**0.75**	...	...	...	...
INCOME STATEMENT (IN MILLIONS):						
Total Revenues	2,319.4	2,988.9	1,850.1	2,013.2	1,968.0	1,807.7
Costs & Expenses	2,199.8	3,380.9	1,857.1	1,943.0	1,926.4	1,829.4
Depreciation & Amort.	96.1	123.4	77.2	64.5	51.9	55.5
Operating Income	23.6	d515.4	d84.2	5.7	d10.3	d77.3
Income Before Income Taxes	23.6	d515.4	d84.2	5.7	d10.3	d77.3
Income Taxes	17.7	cr194.4	cr38.3	6.2	cr1.1	cr24.0
Net Income	3 5.9	2 d320.9	1 d45.9	d0.6	d9.2	d53.2
Cash Flow	102.0	d197.6	31.3	63.9	42.7	2.3
Average Shs. Outstg. (000)	78,468	77,850	48,009	...	47,847	...
BALANCE SHEET (IN MILLIONS):						
Cash & Cash Equivalents	38.3	20.2	14.9	9.1	15.8	...
Total Current Assets	571.5	686.0	736.6	399.4	348.1	...
Net Property	476.1	502.1	1,032.1	790.2	744.1	...
Total Assets	2,774.7	2,733.2	3,145.0	1,559.6	1,370.5	...
Total Current Liabilities	293.6	369.4	413.3	731.3	548.9	...
Long-Term Obligations	1,256.3	1,094.9	1,100.5	453.1	455.2	...
Net Stockholders' Equity	823.2	949.9	1,350.2	256.4	235.7	...
Net Working Capital	277.9	316.6	323.2	d332.0	d200.8	...
Year-end Shs. Outstg. (000)	78,744	78,286	77,620	41,477	41,477	41,477
STATISTICAL RECORD:						
Operating Profit Margin %	1.0	...	...	0.3	...	...
Net Profit Margin %	0.3	...	...	...	...	...
Return on Equity %	0.7	...	...	...	...	...
Return on Assets %	0.2	...	...	...	...	...
Debt/Total Assets %	45.3	40.1	35.0	29.1	33.2	...
Price Range	13.25-8.38	16.50-8.50	18.00-13.38	...	...	...
Average Yield %	6.9	6.0	...	...	...	...

Statistics are as originally reported. 1 Incls. acq.-rel. chrgs. of $10.6 mill. 2 Incls. chrgs. rel. to asset disp. of $493.9 mill. & acq.-rel. exp. of $86.2 mill. 3 Incls. chrgs. rel. to asset disp. of $10.0 mill. & acq.-rel. exp. of $34.4 mill.; bef. loss fr. disc. ops. of $92.1 mill. ($1.17/sh.) 4 Bef. acctg. change credit

OFFICERS:
J. L. Pate, Chmn.
J. J. Postl, Pres., C.E.O.

INVESTOR CONTACT: Jay Roueche, Inv. Rel., (713) 546-4000

PRINCIPAL OFFICE: Pennzoil Place, P.O. Box 2967, Houston, TX 77252-2967

TELEPHONE NUMBER: (713) 546-4000
FAX: (713) 546-8043
WEB: www.pennzoil-quakerstate.com
NO. OF EMPLOYEES: 8,428 (approx.)
SHAREHOLDERS: 18,142 (record)
ANNUAL MEETING: In May
INCORPORATED: DE, Sept., 1998

INSTITUTIONAL HOLDINGS:
No. of Institutions: 144
Shares Held: 51,120,278
% Held: 64.7

INDUSTRY: Petroleum refining (SIC: 2911)

TRANSFER AGENT(S): Pennzoil-Quaker State Company, Houston, TX

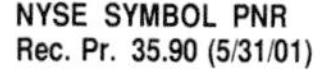

NYSE SYMBOL PNR
Rec. Pr. 35.90 (5/31/01)

PENTAIR, INC.

YIELD 1.9%
P/E RATIO 27.0

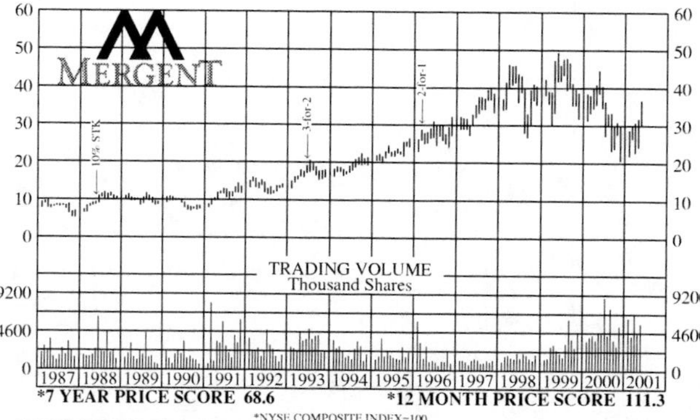

INTERIM EARNINGS (Per Share):

Qtr.	Mar.	June	Sept.	Dec.
1996	0.40	0.42	0.46	0.55
1997	0.48	0.50	0.54	0.68
1998	0.54	0.56	0.64	0.76
1999	0.05	0.66	0.69	0.90
2000	0.69	0.79	0.58	d0.38

INTERIM DIVIDENDS (Per Share):

Amt.	Decl.	Ex.	Rec.	Pay.
0.16Q	4/13/00	4/26/00	4/28/00	5/12/00
0.17Q	7/24/00	7/26/00	7/28/00	8/11/00
0.17Q	10/12/00	10/25/00	10/27/00	11/10/00
0.17Q	1/11/01	1/24/01	1/26/01	2/09/01
0.17Q	4/12/01	4/25/01	4/27/01	5/11/01

Indicated div.: $0.68 (Div. Reinv. Plan)

CAPITALIZATION (12/31/00):

	($000)	(%)
Long-Term Debt	781,834	43.5
Deferred Income Tax	5,487	0.3
Common & Surplus	1,010,591	56.2
Total	1,797,912	100.0

RECENT DEVELOPMENTS: For the year ended 12/31/00, income from continuing operations totaled $81.9 million versus $98.1 million a year earlier. Results for 2000 and 1999 included restructuring charges of $24.8 million and $23.0 million, respectively. Results for 2000 excluded a loss of $24.8 million from discontinued operations and an accounting change charge of $1.2 million. Net sales rose 29.9% to $2.75 billion from $2.12 billion in 1999, due in part from acquisitions.

PROSPECTS: Near-term results could be negatively affected by the slowdown in U.S. economic conditions, particularly the Tools segment. In response, PNR has initiated a restructuring and is cautiously optimistic that results will improve as 2001 unfolds. Future results should benefit from continued expansion of the Company's Water Technologies segment, which on 2/22/01 was reorganized into four geographic sectors to help manage its fast-growing global business.

BUSINESS

PENTAIR, INC. is a diversified manufacturer operating in three principal markets: professional tools, water and fluid technologies and electrical and electronic enclosures. The Professional Tools segment is made up of Delta International, Porter-Cable, Century Manufacturing and DeVilbiss Air Power Company, which markets products to professional users and specialized individuals. The Water and Fluid Technologies segment consists of the Pentair pump businesses, Essef businesses and Fleck Controls. Pentair's Hoffman and Schroff enclosures businesses comprise the Electrical and Electronic Enclosures segment. On 10/31/97, the Company sold its sporting ammunitions business. PNR discontinued its Equipment Group business on 12/18/00.

BUSINESS LINE ANALYSIS

(12/31/2000)	REV (%)	INC (%)
Tools	38.8	11.7
Water	32.9	59.7
Enclosures	28.3	47.8
Other	0.0	(19.1)
Total	100.0	100.0

ANNUAL FINANCIAL DATA

	12/31/00	12/31/99	12/31/98	12/31/97	12/31/96	12/31/95	12/31/94
Earnings Per Share	**3 1.68**	**2.33**	**2.46**	**1 2.11**	**1 1.83**	**2 1.48**	**1.31**
Cash Flow Per Share	**3.72**	**4.33**	**3.96**	**3.59**	**3.40**	**2.79**	**3.05**
Tang. Book Val. Per Share	**...**	**...**	**4.71**	**3.71**	**5.39**	**4.18**	**5.28**
Dividends Per Share	**0.66**	**0.64**	**0.60**	**0.54**	**0.50**	**0.40**	**0.36**
Dividend Payout %	**39.3**	**27.5**	**24.4**	**25.6**	**27.3**	**27.0**	**27.5**
INCOME STATEMENT (IN MILLIONS):							
Total Revenues	2,748.0	2,367.8	1,937.6	1,839.1	1,567.1	1,402.9	1,649.2
Costs & Expenses	2,447.0	2,064.8	1,676.0	1,601.4	1,364.6	1,237.7	1,467.6
Depreciation & Amort.	99.0	88.6	68.4	67.8	59.5	48.9	64.1
Operating Income	202.0	214.3	193.2	169.8	142.9	116.2	119.2
Net Interest Inc./(Exp.)	d74.9	d47.8	d22.2	d21.7	d18.3	d14.6	d30.1
Income Before Income Taxes	127.1	166.5	170.9	158.4	124.6	101.7	89.1
Income Taxes	45.3	63.2	64.1	66.8	50.1	41.2	35.5
Equity Earnings/Minority Int.	...	...	...	...	...	...	1.8
Net Income	3 81.9	103.3	106.8	1 91.6	1 74.5	2 60.5	53.6
Cash Flow	180.9	192.0	171.0	154.6	129.1	104.2	112.3
Average Shs. Outstg. (000)	48,645	44,287	43,149	43,067	37,949	37,300	36,844
BALANCE SHEET (IN MILLIONS):							
Cash & Cash Equivalents	34.9	66.2	32.0	34.3	23.0	36.6	32.7
Total Current Assets	1,091.8	1,150.5	748.6	705.4	614.3	647.2	569.2
Net Property	353.0	403.8	308.3	293.6	298.8	266.7	411.0
Total Assets	2,644.0	2,803.0	1,554.7	1,472.9	1,289.0	1,252.5	1,281.5
Total Current Liabilities	648.8	760.9	394.8	392.2	301.6	396.8	285.7
Long-Term Obligations	781.8	857.3	288.0	294.5	279.9	219.9	408.5
Net Stockholders' Equity	1,010.6	993.2	709.4	630.6	563.9	502.9	432.0
Net Working Capital	443.0	389.5	353.8	313.2	312.6	250.4	283.5
Year-end Shs. Outstg. (000)	48,712	48,317	38,504	38,185	37,717	37,035	36,496
STATISTICAL RECORD:							
Operating Profit Margin %	7.4	9.1	10.0	9.2	9.1	8.3	7.2
Net Profit Margin %	3.0	4.4	5.5	5.0	4.8	4.3	3.3
Return on Equity %	8.1	10.4	15.1	14.5	13.2	12.0	12.4
Return on Assets %	3.1	3.7	6.9	6.2	5.8	4.8	4.2
Debt/Total Assets %	29.6	30.6	18.5	20.0	21.7	17.6	31.9
Price Range	44.63-20.63	49.44-29.88	46.25-26.75	39.88-27.25	32.25-22.88	26.50-19.88	22.38-16.13
P/E Ratio	26.6-12.3	21.2-12.8	18.8-10.9	18.9-12.9	17.6-12.5	17.9-13.4	17.1-12.3
Average Yield %	2.0	1.6	1.6	1.6	1.8	1.7	1.9

Statistics are as originally reported. Adj. for 2-for-1 stk. split, 2/96 1 Incl. non-recurr. cr. 12/31/97: $10.3 mill.; cr. 12/31/96: $12.1 mill. 2 Bef. disc. ops. gain of $4.7 mill. 3 Incl. restruct. chrg. of $24.8 mill.; bef. loss fr. disc. ops. of $24.8 mill. & acctg. chg. chrg. of $1.2 mill.

OFFICERS:
W. H. Buxton, Chmn.
R. J. Hogan, Pres., C.E.O.
D. D. Harrison, Exec. V.P., C.F.O.

INVESTOR CONTACT: Mark Cain, Investor Relations, (651) 639-5278

PRINCIPAL OFFICE: Waters Edge Plaza, 1500 Country Road B2 West, St. Paul, MN 55113

TELEPHONE NUMBER: (651) 636-7920
FAX: (651) 639-5203
WEB: www.pentair.com

NO. OF EMPLOYEES: 13,100 (approx.)

SHAREHOLDERS: 4,271 (record)

ANNUAL MEETING: In Apr.

INCORPORATED: MN, Aug., 1966

INSTITUTIONAL HOLDINGS:
No. of Institutions: 152
Shares Held: 33,935,630
% Held: 69.3

INDUSTRY: Woodworking machinery (SIC: 3553)

TRANSFER AGENT(S): Wells Fargo Shareowner Services, St. Paul, MN

NYSE SYMBOL PGL
Rec. Pr. 39.75 (4/30/01)

PEOPLES ENERGY CORPORATION

YIELD 5.1%
P/E RATIO 15.1

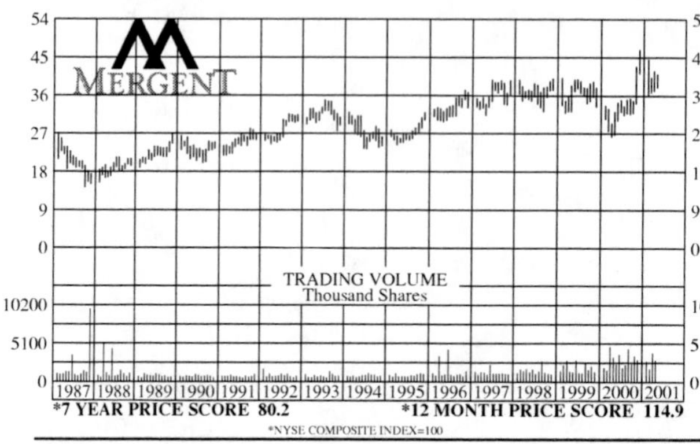

INTERIM EARNINGS (Per Share):

Qtr.	Dec.	Mar.	June	Sept.
1996-97	1.07	1.81	0.34	d0.40
1997-98	1.01	1.34	0.23	d0.32
1998-99	0.66	1.86	0.20	d0.11
1999-00	0.83	1.62	0.31	d0.32
2000-01	1.03	...	...	...

INTERIM DIVIDENDS (Per Share):

Amt.	Decl.	Ex.	Rec.	Pay.
0.50Q	5/18/00	6/20/00	6/22/00	7/14/00
0.50Q	8/02/00	9/20/00	9/22/00	10/13/00
0.50Q	12/06/00	12/20/00	12/22/00	1/15/01
0.51Q	2/07/01	3/20/01	3/22/01	4/13/01
0.51Q	5/30/01	6/20/01	6/22/01	7/13/01

Indicated div.: $2.04 (Div. Reinv. Plan)

CAPITALIZATION (9/30/00):

	($000)	(%)
Deferred Income Tax	343,359	30.6
Common & Surplus	777,082	69.4
Total	1,120,441	100.0

RECENT DEVELOPMENTS: For the three months ended 12/31/00, net income increased 22.9% to $36.4 million compared with $29.6 million in the prior period. Total operating revenues jumped 74.1% to $717.0 million from $411.9 million. Results reflected increased gas delivery volumes that were partially offset by higher gas prices. Operating income rose 31.6% to $70.6 million from $53.7 million in the year-earlier period. Operating margin slipped to 9.9% from 13.0%.

PROSPECTS: Prospects are encouraging, reflecting progress in the Company's strategic growth plan to enhance its utilities, grow its diversified energy businesses and pursue strategic alliances. For example, in the retail energy segment, PGL expects to grow its retail electricity marketing in 2001 and, under its distributed generation program, is now actively marketing Capstone MicroTurbines. Meanwhile, PGL is pursuing development of additional power generation projects.

BUSINESS

PEOPLES ENERGY CORPORATION is a holding company of two natural gas utilites: Peoples Gas Light and Coke Company and North Shore Gas Company. These utilities distribute natural and synthetic gas to 988,000 customers in Chicago and northeastern Illinois. Other operations are conducted through PGL's subsidiaries engaged in non-regulated diversified energy operations. These subsidiaries consists of: Peoples District Energy Corp., a provider of district energy services; Peoples Energy Services, a provider of nonregulated retail energy sales; Peoples Energy Resources, a provider of gas-fired electric generation; Peoples NGV, a fueling station for natural gas fueled vehicles; and Peoples Energy Ventures, which acquires investments in oil and gas production properties.

QUARTERLY DATA

(09/30/2000)($000)	Rev	Inc
1st Quarter	219,138	(11,435)
2nd Quarter	261,248	10,852
3rd Quarter	525,248	57,428
4th Quarter	412,485	29,571

ANNUAL FINANCIAL DATA

	9/30/00	9/30/99	9/30/98	9/30/97	9/30/96	9/30/95	9/30/94
Earnings Per Share	**2.44**	**2.61**	**2.25**	**2.81**	**2.96**	**1.78**	**2.13**
Cash Flow Per Share	**5.29**	**4.96**	**4.44**	**4.93**	**4.98**	**3.68**	**3.99**
Tang. Book Val. Per Share	**21.86**	**21.66**	**20.94**	**20.43**	**19.48**	**18.38**	**18.39**
Dividends Per Share	**1.99**	**1.95**	**1.91**	**1.87**	**1.83**	**1.80**	**1.79**
Dividend Payout %	**81.6**	**74.7**	**84.9**	**66.5**	**61.8**	**101.1**	**84.3**
INCOME STATEMENT (IN MILLIONS):							
Total Revenues	1,417.5	1,194.4	1,138.1	1,274.4	1,198.7	1,033.4	1,279.5
Costs & Expenses	1,157.4	954.8	858.4	964.5	893.4	788.0	1,042.9
Depreciation & Amort.	100.9	83.5	77.2	74.1	70.6	66.4	64.7
Maintenance Exp.	...	...	44.0	47.6	45.6	41.7	37.9
Operating Income	159.2	156.0	113.8	133.5	132.4	108.6	101.8
Net Interest Inc./(Exp.)	d52.9	d39.5	d35.5	d33.1	d37.5	d43.8	d41.9
Income Taxes	43.3	52.6	45.1	56.4	62.5	32.6	32.1
Net Income	86.4	92.6	79.4	98.4	103.4	62.2	74.4
Cash Flow	187.4	176.2	156.6	172.5	174.1	128.6	139.1
Average Shs. Outstg. (000)	35,413	35,490	35,276	35,000	34,942	34,901	34,854
BALANCE SHEET (IN MILLIONS):							
Gross Property	2,517.1	2,330.9	2,210.0	2,117.5	2,046.2	2,088.3	2,019.4
Accumulated Depreciation	871.8	811.1	763.3	715.3	665.1	715.2	677.4
Net Property	1,645.3	1,519.8	1,446.7	1,402.2	1,381.1	1,373.1	1,341.9
Total Assets	2,501.9	2,100.2	1,904.5	1,820.8	1,783.8	1,822.5	1,809.3
Long-Term Obligations	...	521.7	516.6	527.0	527.1	621.9	626.1
Net Stockholders' Equity	777.1	768.7	741.4	716.5	681.2	641.7	641.4
Year-end Shs. Outstg. (000)	35,544	35,489	35,402	35,070	34,960	34,913	34,868
STATISTICAL RECORD:							
Operating Profit Margin %	11.2	13.1	10.0	10.5	11.0	10.5	8.0
Net Profit Margin %	6.1	7.8	7.0	7.7	8.6	6.0	5.8
Net Inc./Net Property %	5.3	6.1	5.5	7.0	7.5	4.5	5.5
Net Inc./Tot. Capital %	7.7	5.8	5.2	6.6	7.2	4.2	5.1
Return on Equity %	11.1	12.1	10.7	13.7	15.2	9.7	11.6
Accum. Depr./Gross Prop. %	34.6	34.8	34.5	33.8	32.5	34.2	33.5
Price Range	46.94-26.19	40.25-31.75	40.13-32.13	39.88-31.25	37.38-29.63	32.00-24.25	32.13-23.31
P/E Ratio	19.2-10.7	15.4-12.2	17.8-14.3	14.2-11.1	12.6-10.0	18.0-13.6	15.1-10.9
Average Yield %	5.4	5.4	5.3	5.3	5.5	6.4	6.5

Statistics are as originally reported.

OFFICERS:
R. E. Terry, Chmn., C.E.O.
T. M. Patrick, Pres., C.O.O.
J. M. Luebbers, C.F.O., Contr.

INVESTOR CONTACT: Mary Ann Wall, Manager, Investor Relations, (312) 240-7534

PRINCIPAL OFFICE: 130 East Randolph Drive, Chicago, IL 60601

TELEPHONE NUMBER: (312) 240-4000
FAX: (312) 240-4220
WEB: www.pecorp.com

NO. OF EMPLOYEES: 2,694

SHAREHOLDERS: 23,559

ANNUAL MEETING: In Feb.

INCORPORATED: IL, 1967

INSTITUTIONAL HOLDINGS:
No. of Institutions: 194
Shares Held: 15,562,912
% Held: 44.0

INDUSTRY: Natural gas distribution (SIC: 4924)

TRANSFER AGENT(S): Computershare Investor Services, Chicago, IL

NYSE SYMBOL PBY
Rec. Pr. 8.80 (5/31/01)

PEP BOYS-MANNY, MOE & JACK

YIELD 3.1%
P/E RATIO ...

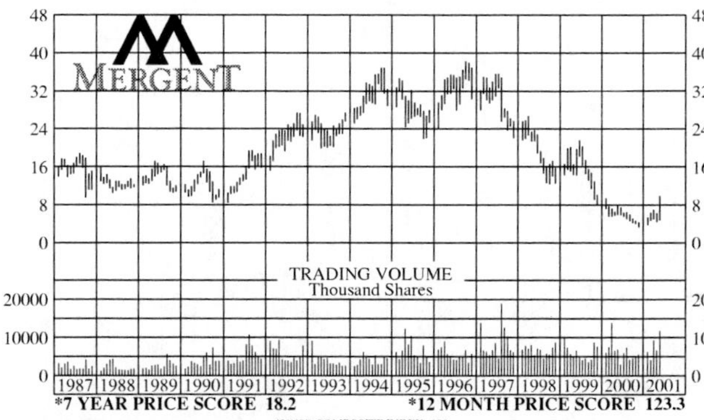

*7 YEAR PRICE SCORE 18.2 *12 MONTH PRICE SCORE 123.3
*NYSE COMPOSITE INDEX=100

INTERIM EARNINGS (Per Share):

Qtr.	Apr.	July	Oct.	Jan.
1997-98	0.37	0.47	0.38	d0.45
1998-99	0.16	0.29	d0.06	d0.31
1999-00	0.20	0.39	0.20	d0.21
2000-01	0.09	0.07	d1.24	0.03

INTERIM DIVIDENDS (Per Share):

Amt.	Decl.	Ex.	Rec.	Pay.
0.068Q	9/25/00	10/04/00	10/09/00	10/23/00
0.068Q	12/11/00	1/10/01	1/15/01	1/29/01
0.068Q	3/26/01	4/11/01	4/16/01	4/30/01
0.068Q	5/30/01	7/12/01	7/16/01	7/30/01

Indicated div.: $0.27 (Div. Reinv. Plan)

CAPITALIZATION (2/3/01):

	($000)	(%)
Long-Term Debt	654,194	49.7
Deferred Income Tax	66,192	5.0
Common & Surplus	594,766	45.2
Total	1,315,152	100.0

RECENT DEVELOPMENTS: For the 53 weeks ended 2/3/01, the Company reported a loss of $53.1 million, before an extraordinary charge of $2.1 million, compared with net earnings of $29.3 million in the corresponding 52-week period the year before. Results for 2000 included one-time pre-tax charges totaling $96.5 million, stemming primarily from PBY's profit enhancement plan. Total revenues rose 1.0% to $2.42 billion from $2.39 billion the previous year. Comparable-store sales declined 1.4% year over year.

PROSPECTS: Earnings are beginning to benefit from initiatives the Company began implementing during the third quarter of fiscal 2000 focused on lowering expenses and boosting operating profitability. However, revenues are being negatively affected by many of these initiatives, as well as by continued weakness in do-it-yourself sales and a downturn in consumer confidence in the U.S. PBY anticipates opening two Supercenters in fiscal 2001, down from five in fiscal 2000.

BUSINESS

PEP BOYS-MANNY, MOE & JACK operate a chain of 628 specialty retail stores that sell a full range of brand name and private label automotive parts and accessories at discount prices and offer automotive maintenance and service and the installation of parts. PBY's stores are located in 36 states, mainly in the middle Atlantic, Southwest and Southeast regions of the United States, the District of Columbia, and Puerto Rico. The Supercenter stores contain automotive merchandise along with a full-service maintenance center. The PartsUSA stores do not provide service bays, nor do they stock tires.

REVENUES

(2/3/2001)	($000)	(%)
Merchandise Sales	1,957,480	80.9
Service Revenues	460,988	19.1
Total	2,418,468	100.0

ANNUAL FINANCIAL DATA

	2/3/01	1/29/00	1/30/99	1/31/98	2/1/97	2/3/96	1/28/95
Earnings Per Share	**3 d1.04**	**0.58**	**2 0.08**	**2 0.80**	**1.62**	**1.34**	**1 1.32**
Cash Flow Per Share	**0.90**	**2.48**	**1.65**	**2.15**	**2.58**	**2.16**	**2.05**
Tang. Book Val. Per Share	**11.13**	**12.38**	**12.71**	**12.92**	**12.33**	**10.72**	**9.53**
Dividends Per Share	**0.27**	**0.268**	**0.26**	**0.23**	**0.21**	**0.19**	**0.17**
Dividend Payout %	**...**	**46.2**	**318.4**	**29.1**	**13.0**	**14.2**	**12.9**
INCOME STATEMENT (IN MILLIONS):							
Total Revenues	2,418.5	2,394.5	2,398.7	2,056.5	1,828.5	1,594.3	1,407.0
Costs & Expenses	2,347.2	2,203.3	2,247.8	1,862.9	1,575.7	1,381.5	1,213.7
Depreciation & Amort.	99.3	97.0	96.9	82.9	65.8	53.5	44.4
Operating Income	d28.0	94.2	54.1	110.8	187.1	159.4	148.9
Net Interest Inc./(Exp.)	d57.9	d51.6	d48.9	d39.7	d30.3	d32.1	d25.9
Income Before Income Taxes	d83.7	45.0	7.3	75.5	159.2	129.5	126.5
Income Taxes	cr30.5	15.7	2.3	25.8	58.4	48.0	46.5
Net Income	3 d53.1	29.3	2 5.0	2 49.6	100.8	81.5	1 80.0
Cash Flow	46.2	126.3	101.8	132.5	166.6	135.0	124.4
Average Shs. Outstg. (000)	51,088	50,840	61,740	61,657	64,605	62,588	60,565
BALANCE SHEET (IN MILLIONS):							
Cash & Cash Equivalents	8.0	18.5	114.5	10.8	2.6	11.5	11.7
Total Current Assets	699.7	720.7	754.1	770.2	604.9	466.5	411.3
Net Property	1,194.2	1,335.7	1,330.3	1,377.7	1,189.7	1,014.1	861.9
Total Assets	1,906.2	2,072.7	2,096.1	2,161.4	1,818.4	1,500.0	1,291.0
Total Current Liabilities	590.5	548.4	512.4	618.9	534.2	426.6	289.5
Long-Term Obligations	654.2	784.0	691.7	646.6	455.7	367.0	380.8
Net Stockholders' Equity	594.8	658.3	811.8	822.6	778.1	665.5	586.3
Net Working Capital	109.2	172.3	241.7	151.3	70.7	39.9	121.9
Year-end Shs. Outstg. (000)	53,456	53,189	63,848	63,658	63,119	62,084	61,502
STATISTICAL RECORD:							
Operating Profit Margin %	...	3.9	2.3	5.4	10.2	10.0	10.6
Net Profit Margin %	...	1.2	0.2	2.4	5.5	5.1	5.7
Return on Equity %	...	4.5	0.6	6.0	13.0	12.2	13.6
Return on Assets %	...	1.4	0.2	2.3	5.5	5.4	6.2
Debt/Total Assets %	34.3	37.8	33.0	29.9	25.1	24.5	29.5
Price Range	9.38-3.31	21.63-8.06	26.69-12.38	35.63-22.00	38.25-23.88	34.75-21.88	36.88-25.13
P/E Ratio	...	37.3-13.9	333.2-154.5	44.5-27.5	23.6-14.7	25.9-16.3	27.9-19.0
Average Yield %	4.3	1.8	1.3	0.8	0.7	0.7	0.5

Statistics are as originally reported. 1 Bef. $4.3 mil ($0.07/sh) chg. for acctg. adj. 2 Incl. $20.1 mil ($0.33/sh) net non-recur. chg., 1999; $18.4 mil ($0.30/sh) net non-recur. chg., 1998. 3 Bef. $2.1 mil ($0.04/sh) extraord. gain fr. the repurchase of a portion of the Company's Liquid Yield Option Notes & incl. one-time pre-tax chgs. of $96.5 mil fr. store closings, asset write-downs, severance payments and reserve increases.

OFFICERS:
M. G. Leibovitz, Chmn., Pres., C.E.O.
G. Babich, Jr., Exec. V.P., C.F.O.
F. A. Stampone, Exec. V.P., C.A.O., Sec.

INVESTOR CONTACT: George Babich, Exec. V.P. & C.F.O., (215) 430-9720

PRINCIPAL OFFICE: 3111 West Allegheny Avenue, Philadelphia, PA 19132

TELEPHONE NUMBER: (215) 430-9000
FAX: (215) 227-4067
WEB: www.pepboys.com
NO. OF EMPLOYEES: 17,082 full-time; 6,054 part-time
SHAREHOLDERS: 3,453
ANNUAL MEETING: In May
INCORPORATED: PA, Jan., 1925

INSTITUTIONAL HOLDINGS:
No. of Institutions: 91
Shares Held: 24,169,959
% Held: 45.2

INDUSTRY: Auto and home supply stores (SIC: 5531)

TRANSFER AGENT(S): American Stock & Transfer Company, New York, NY

NYSE SYMBOL PBG
Rec. Pr. 40.02 (4/30/01)

PEPSI BOTTLING GROUP INC.

YIELD 0.2%
P/E RATIO 26.2

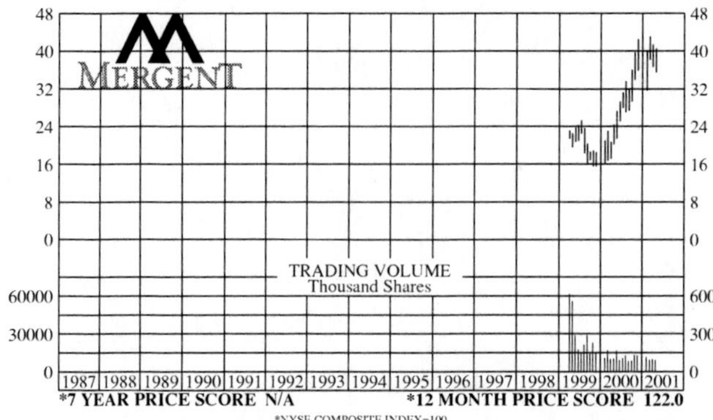

*7 YEAR PRICE SCORE N/A *12 MONTH PRICE SCORE 122.0
*NYSE COMPOSITE INDEX=100

INTERIM EARNINGS (Per Share):

Qtr.	Mar.	June	Sept.	Dec.
1999	...	0.14	0.59	0.06
2000	0.11	0.58	0.82	0.02

INTERIM DIVIDENDS (Per Share):

Amt.	Decl.	Ex.	Rec.	Pay.
0.02Q	5/09/00	6/07/00	6/09/00	6/30/00
0.02Q	8/08/00	9/06/00	9/08/00	9/29/00
0.02Q	11/16/00	12/06/00	12/08/00	1/02/01
0.02Q	2/13/01	3/07/01	3/09/01	3/30/01
0.02Q	5/08/01	6/06/01	6/08/01	6/29/01

Indicated div.: $0.08

CAPITALIZATION (12/30/00):

	($000)	(%)
Long-Term Debt	3,271,000	52.0
Deferred Income Tax	1,072,000	17.0
Minority Interest	306,000	4.9
Common & Surplus	1,646,000	26.1
Total	6,295,000	100.0

RECENT DEVELOPMENTS: For the 53 weeks ended 12/30/00, net income surged 94.1% to $229.0 million versus $118.0 million in the prior-year period, which was comprised of 52 weeks. Results for 1999 included a non-recurring credit of $16.0 million. Net revenues rose 6.4% to $7.98 billion. Worldwide net revenues per case grew 3.0%, while cost of sales per case were essentially flat due to currency translation effects, country mix, favorable effect of a depreciation accounting change and efficiencies in production and cost controls.

PROSPECTS: PBG's prospects are solid, reflecting positive worldwide volume growth that is being driven by the successful launch of SIERRA MIST and continued strength in AQUAFINA. In fiscal 2001, based on a 52-week comparison, PBG projects to achieve 3.0% volume growth and earnings per share of between $1.81 and $1.83. Separately, on 5/1/01, PBG announced that it has finalized the purchase of the general partnership interest in Pepsi-Cola Bottling of Northern California, which services 13 counties stretching from the Pacific coast to the Nevada border.

BUSINESS

PEPSI BOTTLING GROUP INC. manufactures, sells and distributes Pepsi-Cola beverages. Pepsi-Cola beverages sold by PBG include PEPSI COLA, DIET PEPSI, MOUNTAIN DEW, LIPTON BRISK, LIPTON'S ICED TEA, PEPSI ONE, SLICE, MUG, AQUAFINA, STARBUCKS FRAPPUCCINO, FRUITWORKS, SIERRA MIST, and outside the U.S., 7UP, PEPSI MAX, MIRINDA and KAS. PBG has the exclusive right to manufacture, sell and distribute Pepsi-Cola beverages in all or a portion of 41 states, the District of Columbia, eight Canadian provinces, Spain, Greece and Russia. About 20.0% of the Company's volume is sold outside the U.S. PGB was incorporated to effect the separation of most of PepsiCo's company-owned bottling businesses and became a publicly-traded company on 3/31/99. As of 2/21/01, PepsiCo's ownership represented 46.2% of the voting power of all classes of PBG's voting stock.

QUARTERLY DATA

(12/30/2000) ($000)	Rev	Inc
1st Quarter	1,545,000	17,000
2nd Quarter	1,913,000	85,000
3rd Quarter	2,125,000	123,000
4th Quarter	2,399,000	4,000

ANNUAL FINANCIAL DATA

	12/30/00	12/25/99	12/26/98	12/27/97	12/28/96
Earnings Per Share	**1.53**	**[2] 0.92**	**[1] d2.65**	**1.07**	**0.89**
Cash Flow Per Share	**4.70**	**4.87**	**5.93**	**9.05**	**8.62**
Dividends Per Share	**0.08**	**0.04**	...	...	...
Dividend Payout %	**5.2**	**4.3**	...	...	...
INCOME STATEMENT (IN MILLIONS):					
Total Revenues	7,982.0	7,505.0	7,041.0	6,592.0	6,603.0
Costs & Expenses	6,921.0	6,588.0	6,514.0	5,818.0	5,811.0
Depreciation & Amort.	471.0	505.0	472.0	439.0	425.0
Operating Income	590.0	412.0	55.0	335.0	367.0
Net Interest Inc./(Exp.)	d192.0	d202.0	d221.0	d222.0	d225.0
Income Before Income Taxes	364.0	188.0	d192.0	115.0	138.0
Income Taxes	135.0	70.0	cr46.0	56.0	89.0
Equity Earnings/Minority Int.	d33.0	d21.0	...	...	...
Net Income	229.0	[2] 118.0	[1] d146.0	59.0	49.0
Cash Flow	700.0	623.0	326.0	498.0	474.0
Average Shs. Outstg. (000)	149,000	128,000	55,000	55,000	55,000
BALANCE SHEET (IN MILLIONS):					
Cash & Cash Equivalents	318.0	190.0	36.0	86.0	...
Total Current Assets	1,584.0	1,493.0	1,318.0	1,336.0	...
Net Property	2,358.0	2,218.0	2,055.0	1,918.0	...
Total Assets	7,736.0	7,619.0	7,322.0	7,188.0	...
Total Current Liabilities	967.0	947.0	1,025.0	1,147.0	...
Long-Term Obligations	3,271.0	3,268.0	3,361.0	3,396.0	...
Net Stockholders' Equity	1,646.0	1,563.0	d238.0	d184.0	...
Net Working Capital	617.0	546.0	293.0	189.0	...
Year-end Shs. Outstg. (000)	145,088	149,000	55,000	55,000	55,000
STATISTICAL RECORD:					
Operating Profit Margin %	7.4	5.5	0.8	5.1	5.6
Net Profit Margin %	2.9	1.6	...	0.9	0.7
Return on Equity %	13.9	7.5	...	...	...
Return on Assets %	3.0	1.5	...	0.8	...
Debt/Total Assets %	42.3	42.9	45.9	47.2	...
Price Range	42.50-16.25	25.25-15.50	...	...	...
P/E Ratio	27.8-10.6	27.4-16.8	...	...	...
Average Yield %	0.3	0.2	...	...	...

Statistics are as originally reported. [1] Incls. non-recurr. impair. & oth. charges of $222.0 mill. [2] Incls. non-recurr. credit of $16.0 mill.

OFFICERS:
C. E. Weatherup, Chmn., C.E.O.
J. T. Cahill, Pres., C.O.O.
L. L. Nowell III, Exec. V.P., C.F.O.

INVESTOR CONTACT: Mary Winn Settino, Director, Inv. Rel., (914) 767-7216

PRINCIPAL OFFICE: One Pepsi Way, Somers, NY 10589

TELEPHONE NUMBER: (914) 767-6000
FAX: (914) 767-1313
WEB: www.pbg.com

NO. OF EMPLOYEES: 35,700 (approx.)

SHAREHOLDERS: 37,000 (approx.)

ANNUAL MEETING: In May

INCORPORATED: DE, Jan., 1999

INSTITUTIONAL HOLDINGS:
No. of Institutions: 178
Shares Held: 85,982,190
% Held: 59.5

INDUSTRY: Bottled and canned soft drinks (SIC: 2086)

TRANSFER AGENT(S): The Bank of New York, New York, NY

NYSE SYMBOL PAS
Rec. Pr. 15.18 (5/31/01)

PEPSIAMERICAS, INC.

YIELD 0.3%
P/E RATIO 29.8

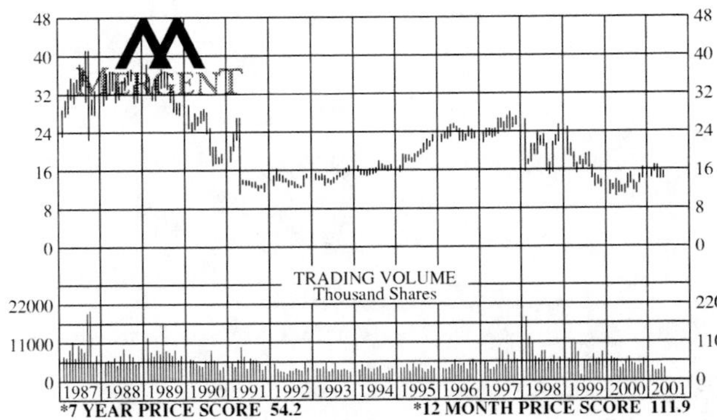

*7 YEAR PRICE SCORE 54.2 *12 MONTH PRICE SCORE 111.9

*NYSE COMPOSITE INDEX=100

INTERIM EARNINGS (Per Share):

Qtr.	Mar.	June	Sept.	Dec.
1997	0.15	0.33	d0.30	d0.15
1998	0.17	0.16	0.26	0.12
1999	0.15	d0.09	0.17	0.10
2000	0.07	0.22	0.21	0.01

INTERIM DIVIDENDS (Per Share):

Amt.	Decl.	Ex.	Rec.	Pay.
0.01Q	5/20/99	6/09/99	6/11/99	7/01/99
0.01Q	8/20/99	9/08/99	9/10/99	10/01/99
0.01Q	11/19/99	12/08/99	12/10/99	1/03/00
0.04A	2/18/00	3/02/00	3/06/00	4/03/00
0.04A	2/22/01	3/07/01	3/09/01	4/03/01

Indicated div.: $0.04 (Div. Reinv. Plan)

CAPITALIZATION (12/30/00):

	($000)	(%)
Long-Term Debt	860,100	36.4
Deferred Income Tax	47,000	2.0
Minority Interest	3,900	0.2
Common & Surplus	1,449,500	61.4
Total	2,360,500	100.0

RECENT DEVELOPMENTS: For the year ended 12/30/00, income from continuing operations was $71.5 million versus $42.9 million a year earlier. Results for 2000 included a pre-tax special charge of $21.7 million for merger-related costs and the closing of a production facility, and excluded income from discontinued operations of $8.9 million. Results for 1999 included a pre-tax special charge of $27.9 million. Sales rose 18.2% to $2.53 billion.

PROSPECTS: On 1/2/01, PAS announced the purchase of 90.0% of the shares of Pepsi-Cola Trinidad Bottling Company Limited. The purchase includes the rights to produce and market Pepsi brands along with all tangible assets. Separately, the Company has made an investment in Pepsi-Cola Bahamas Bottling Company Limited, giving it a 30.0% interest in the Bahamian bottler.

BUSINESS

PEPSIAMERICAS, INC. (formerly Whitman Corporation) is the number two anchor bottler in the Pepsi system, with operations in 18 states as well as Puerto Rico, Jamaica, Bahamas, Trinidad, Poland, Hungary, the Czech Republic, and the Republic of Slovakia. PAS manufactures, distributes and markets a broad portfolio of Pepsi-Cola, Dr. Pepper and Seven-Up brands. On 1/30/98, the Company completed the spin-off of its refrigeration systems and equipment business and its automotive services business. On 5/20/99, the Company's shareholders approved the merger with Heartland Territories Holdings, Inc., a subsidiary of Pepsico, Inc., which established a new business relationship between the Company and Pepsico. On 11/30/00, the Company completed its acquisition of PepsiAmericas, Inc. As of 2/1/01, Pepsico owned approximately 36.8% of the Company.

QUARTERLY DATA

(12/30/2000) ($000)	REV	INC
1st Quarter	548,900	10,200
2nd Quarter	682,600	39,500
3rd Quarter	655,200	28,900
4th Quarter	640,900	1,800

ANNUAL FINANCIAL DATA

	12/30/00	12/31/99	12/31/98	[3] 12/31/97	12/31/96	12/31/95	12/31/94
Earnings Per Share	[6] 0.51	[5] 0.35	[4] 0.61	[2] 0.15	1.31	1.26	[1] 1.00
Cash Flow Per Share	1.71	1.36	1.36	0.87	2.40	2.28	1.92
Tang. Book Val. Per Share	...	...	...	0.76	0.80	0.56	0.27
Dividends Per Share	0.05	0.02	...	...	...	...	...
Dividend Payout %	9.8	5.7	...	...	...	...	...
INCOME STATEMENT (IN MILLIONS):							
Total Revenues	2,527.6	2,138.2	1,635.0	1,557.5	3,111.3	2,946.5	2,658.8
Costs & Expenses	2,138.2	1,830.1	1,353.5	1,353.5	2,628.9	2,495.9	2,234.0
Depreciation & Amort.	166.4	126.6	77.7	73.8	115.8	108.3	98.0
Operating Income	223.0	181.5	203.8	130.2	366.6	342.3	326.8
Net Interest Inc./(Exp.)	d84.0	d63.9	d36.1	d42.3	d65.3	d68.2	d64.7
Income Before Income Taxes	141.1	71.6	152.2	69.9	275.7	259.7	212.7
Income Taxes	69.6	22.1	69.7	37.9	117.2	107.4	88.1
Equity Earnings/Minority Int.	...	d6.6	d20.0	d16.2	d19.1	d18.8	d18.2
Net Income	[6] 71.5	[5] 42.9	[4] 62.5	[2] 15.8	139.4	133.5	[1] 106.4
Cash Flow	237.9	169.5	140.2	89.6	255.2	241.8	204.4
Average Shs. Outstg. (000)	139,500	124,200	102,800	102,900	106,400	106,200	106,200
BALANCE SHEET (IN MILLIONS):							
Cash & Cash Equivalents	51.2	114.5	147.6	52.4	76.8	53.3	71.3
Total Current Assets	477.0	538.0	429.1	560.8	855.0	761.1	707.7
Net Property	1,004.7	831.7	499.3	406.6	734.3	697.5	613.8
Total Assets	3,335.6	2,864.3	1,569.3	2,029.7	2,409.4	2,363.3	2,135.4
Total Current Liabilities	887.0	739.1	233.2	490.0	526.0	507.6	483.1
Long-Term Obligations	860.1	809.0	603.6	604.7	837.5	828.2	723.0
Net Stockholders' Equity	1,449.5	1,142.2	326.4	539.7	642.2	627.8	552.6
Net Working Capital	d410.0	d201.1	195.9	70.8	329.0	253.5	224.6
Year-end Shs. Outstg. (000)	155,600	139,100	101,000	101,100	110,600	105,200	105,032
STATISTICAL RECORD:							
Operating Profit Margin %	8.8	8.5	12.5	8.4	11.8	11.6	12.3
Net Profit Margin %	2.8	2.0	3.8	1.0	4.5	4.5	4.0
Return on Equity %	4.9	3.8	19.1	2.9	21.7	21.3	19.3
Return on Assets %	2.1	1.5	4.0	0.8	5.8	5.6	5.0
Debt/Total Assets %	25.8	28.2	38.5	29.8	34.8	35.0	33.9
Price Range	16.44-10.38	24.94-12.19	26.63-14.88	28.13-21.63	25.75-21.75	23.38-15.63	18.00-14.75
P/E Ratio	32.2-20.3	71.2-34.8	43.6-24.4	187.4-144.1	19.7-16.6	18.6-12.4	18.0-14.7
Average Yield %	0.4	0.1	...	...	...	...	...

Statistics are as originally reported. [1] Incl. chrg. of $15.5 mil; bef. disc. oper. loss of $3.2 mil [2] Incl. pre-tax chrg. of $173.2 mil; bef. disc. oper. loss of $11.7 mil [3] Refl. divest. of Midas Inc. & Hussmann Corp. [4] Bef. extra. loss of $18.3 mil & disc. oper. loss of $500,000 [5] Incl. chrgs. of $54.9 mil & gain of $7.8 mil fr. sale of franchises; bef. disc. oper. loss of $51.7 mil [6] Incl. chrg. of $13.2 mil; bef. inc. fr. disc. ops. of $8.9 mil

OFFICERS:
R. C. Pohlad, Vice-Chmn., C.E.O.
J. F. Bierbaum, Exec. V.P.
G. M. Durkin, Jr., Sr. V.P., C.F.O.

INVESTOR CONTACT: Charles H. Connolly, Sr. V.P., Investor Relations, (800) 446-2617

PRINCIPAL OFFICE: 3501 Algonquin Road, Rolling Meadows, IL 60008

TELEPHONE NUMBER: (847) 818-5000
FAX: (847) 818-5046
WEB: www.whitmancorp.com

NO. OF EMPLOYEES: 15,400 (approx.)

SHAREHOLDERS: 13,338 (record)

ANNUAL MEETING: In May

INCORPORATED: DE, Aug., 1962

INSTITUTIONAL HOLDINGS:
No. of Institutions: 136
Shares Held: 65,704,135
% Held: 42.0

INDUSTRY: Bottled and canned soft drinks (SIC: 2086)

TRANSFER AGENT(S): EquiServe, Jersey City, NJ

NYSE SYMBOL PEP
Rec. Pr. 44.76 (5/31/01)

PEPSICO INC.

YIELD 1.3%
P/E RATIO 30.2

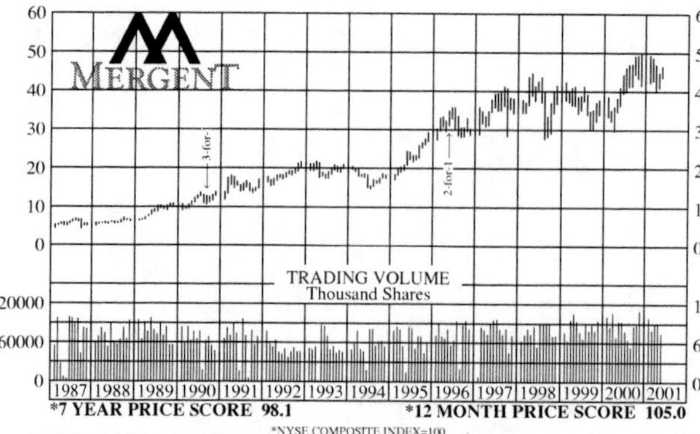

*7 YEAR PRICE SCORE 98.1 *12 MONTH PRICE SCORE 105.0
*NYSE COMPOSITE INDEX=100

INTERIM EARNINGS (Per Share):

Qtr.	Mar.	June	Sept.	Dec.
1997	0.27	0.42	0.35	0.29
1998	0.24	0.33	0.50	0.24
1999	0.22	0.49	0.32	0.33
2000	0.29	0.38	0.40	0.41

INTERIM DIVIDENDS (Per Share):

Amt.	Decl.	Ex.	Rec.	Pay.
0.14Q	5/03/00	6/07/00	6/09/00	6/30/00
0.14Q	7/20/00	9/06/00	9/08/00	9/29/00
0.14Q	11/16/00	12/06/00	12/08/00	1/02/01
0.14Q	2/01/01	3/07/01	3/09/01	3/30/01
0.145Q	5/02/01	6/06/01	6/08/01	6/29/01

Indicated div.: $0.58 (Div. Reinv. Plan)

CAPITALIZATION (12/30/00):

	($000)	(%)
Long-Term Debt	2,346,000	21.4
Deferred Income Tax	1,361,000	12.4
Common & Surplus	7,249,000	66.2
Total	10,956,000	100.0

RECENT DEVELOPMENTS: For the 53 weeks ended 12/30/00, net income totaled $2.18 billion versus $2.05 billion in the prior year, which was comprised of 52 weeks. Results for 1999 included an after-tax impairment and restructuring charge of $40.0 million and an after-tax gain of $270 million on the The Pepsi Bottling Group and Whitman bottling transactions. Net sales advanced to $20.44 billion from $20.37 billion in 1999.

PROSPECTS: PEP's near-term outlook is favorable, reflecting expected continued growth in Frito-Lay's core products, driven by new flavors and forms, new product innovation, overseas expansion, and a strong marketing calendar. Separately, on 12/4/00, PEP and The Quaker Oats Company announced an agreement for PEP to acquire Quaker in a tax-free transaction under which PEP will exchange 2.3 shares of its stock for each share of Quaker.

BUSINESS

PEPSICO INC. operates on a worldwide basis within the soft drinks, juice and snack-foods businesses. The Pepsi-Cola segment, which accounted for 25.1% of sales in 2000, manufactures concentrates, and markets PEPSI, PEPSI-COLA, DIET PEPSI, PEPSI ONE, PEPSI MAX, MOUNTAIN DEW, MUG, FRUITWORKS, SIERRA MIST, AQUAFINA, MIRINDA, SLICE and allied brands worldwide, and 7-UP internationally. The Tropicana segment, 11.9%, manufactures and sells its products under trademarks such as TROPICANA PURE PREMIUM, and TROPICANA SEASONS BEST. The Frito-Lay segment, 63.0%, manufactures, markets, sells and distributes a varied line of salty and sweet snack foods. Trademarks include LAY'S, DORITOS, CHEETOS, ROLD GOLD and WOW! On 10/6/97, PEP spun off its Restaurant unit, TRICON Global Restaurants. In August 1998, PEP acquired Tropicana Products, Inc. for $3.30 billion. On 4/6/99, The Pepsi Bottling Group (PBG) completed an initial public offering of its comon stock. As of 12/31/00, PEP maintained economic ownership of approximately 42.0% in PBG.

ANNUAL FINANCIAL DATA

	12/30/00	12/25/99	12/26/98	12/27/97	12/28/96	12/30/95	12/31/94
Earnings Per Share	**1.48**	[5] **1.37**	[4] **1.31**	[1] **0.95**	[2] **0.72**	[2] **1.00**	[3] **1.11**
Cash Flow Per Share	**2.13**	**2.06**	**2.12**	**1.65**	**1.79**	**2.08**	**2.09**
Tang. Book Val. Per Share	**1.91**	**1.47**	...	**0.72**	...	...	...
Dividends Per Share	**0.55**	**0.53**	**0.51**	**0.48**	**0.43**	**0.38**	**0.34**
Dividend Payout %	**37.2**	**38.7**	**38.9**	**50.5**	**59.7**	**38.0**	**30.6**
INCOME STATEMENT (IN MILLIONS):							
Total Revenues	20,438.0	20,367.0	22,348.0	20,917.0	31,645.0	30,421.0	28,472.4
Costs & Expenses	16,253.0	16,517.0	18,530.0	17,149.0	27,380.0	25,694.0	23,694.2
Depreciation & Amort.	960.0	1,032.0	1,234.0	1,106.0	1,719.0	1,740.0	1,577.0
Operating Income	3,225.0	2,818.0	2,584.0	2,662.0	2,546.0	2,987.0	3,201.2
Net Interest Inc./(Exp.)	d145.0	d245.0	d321.0	d353.0	d499.0	d555.0	d554.6
Income Before Income Taxes	3,210.0	3,656.0	2,263.0	2,309.0	2,047.0	2,432.0	2,664.4
Income Taxes	1,027.0	1,606.0	270.0	818.0	898.0	826.0	880.4
Equity Earnings/Minority Int.	130.0	83.0	...	...	...	...	...
Net Income	2,183.0	[5] 2,050.0	[4] 1,993.0	[1] 1,491.0	[2] 1,149.0	[2] 1,606.0	[3] 1,784.0
Cash Flow	3,143.0	3,082.0	3,227.0	2,597.0	2,868.0	3,346.0	3,361.0
Average Shs. Outstg. (000)	1,475,000	1,496,000	1,519,000	1,570,000	1,606,000	1,608,000	1,607,200
BALANCE SHEET (IN MILLIONS):							
Cash & Cash Equivalents	1,330.0	1,056.0	394.0	2,883.0	786.0	1,498.0	1,488.1
Total Current Assets	4,604.0	4,173.0	4,362.0	6,251.0	5,139.0	5,546.0	5,072.2
Net Property	5,438.0	5,266.0	7,318.0	6,261.0	10,191.0	9,870.0	9,882.8
Total Assets	18,339.0	17,551.0	22,660.0	20,101.0	24,512.0	25,432.0	24,792.0
Total Current Liabilities	3,935.0	3,788.0	7,914.0	4,257.0	5,139.0	5,230.0	5,270.4
Long-Term Obligations	2,346.0	2,812.0	4,028.0	4,946.0	8,439.0	8,509.0	8,840.5
Net Stockholders' Equity	7,249.0	6,881.0	6,401.0	6,936.0	6,623.0	7,313.0	6,856.1
Net Working Capital	669.0	385.0	d3,552.0	1,994.0	...	316.0	d198.2
Year-end Shs. Outstg. (000)	1,446,000	1,455,000	1,471,000	1,502,000	1,545,000	1,576,000	1,579,800
STATISTICAL RECORD:							
Operating Profit Margin %	15.8	13.8	11.6	12.7	8.0	9.8	11.2
Net Profit Margin %	10.7	10.1	8.9	7.1	3.6	5.3	6.3
Return on Equity %	30.1	29.8	31.1	21.5	17.3	22.0	26.0
Return on Assets %	11.9	11.7	8.8	7.4	4.7	6.3	7.2
Debt/Total Assets %	12.8	16.0	17.8	24.6	34.4	33.5	35.7
Price Range	49.94-29.69	42.56-30.13	44.81-27.56	41.31-28.25	35.88-27.25	29.38-16.94	20.56-14.63
P/E Ratio	33.7-20.1	31.1-22.0	34.2-21.0	43.5-29.7	49.8-37.8	29.4-16.9	18.5-13.2
Average Yield %	1.4	1.5	1.4	1.4	1.4	1.6	1.9

Statistics are as originally reported. Adj. for 2-for-1 stk. split, 5/96 [1] Incls. non-recurr. chrgs. of $290.0 mill.; bef. disc. oper. gain of $651.0 mill. [2] Incls. non-recurr. chrgs. 1/31/96, $716.0 mill.; non-cash chrg. 12/31/95, $520.0 mill. [3] Bef. acctg. change chrg. 12/31/94: $32.0 mill. [4] Incls. non-recurr. chrg. of $288.0 mill. [5] Incls. non-recurr. chrg. of $65.0 mill.

OFFICERS:
R. A. Enrico, Chmn., C.E.O.
S. S. Reinemund, Pres., C.O.O.
I. K. Nooyi, Sr. V.P., C.F.O.

INVESTOR CONTACT: Susan V. Watson, V.P., Inv. Rel., (914) 253-3035

PRINCIPAL OFFICE: 700 Anderson Hill Rd., Purchase, NY 10577-1444

TELEPHONE NUMBER: (914) 253-2000
FAX: (914) 253-2070
WEB: www.pepsico.com

NO. OF EMPLOYEES: 124,000 (approx.)

SHAREHOLDERS: 204,000 (approx.)

ANNUAL MEETING: In May

INCORPORATED: DE, Sept., 1919; reincorp., NC, Dec., 1986

INSTITUTIONAL HOLDINGS:
No. of Institutions: 970
Shares Held: 935,425,712
% Held: 64.5

INDUSTRY: Bottled and canned soft drinks (SIC: 2086)

TRANSFER AGENT(S): The Bank of New York, Newark, NJ

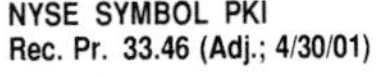

NYSE SYMBOL PKI
Rec. Pr. 33.46 (Adj.; 4/30/01)

PERKINELMER, INC.

YIELD 0.8%
P/E RATIO 38.5

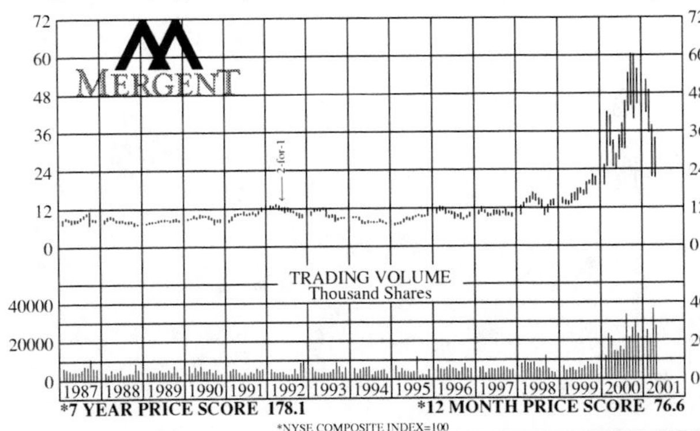

***7 YEAR PRICE SCORE 178.1** ***12 MONTH PRICE SCORE 76.6**

*NYSE COMPOSITE INDEX=100

INTERIM EARNINGS (Per Share):

Qtr.	Mar.	June	Sept.	Dec.
1997	0.11	d0.15	0.15	0.23
1998	0.38	0.34	0.17	0.23
1999	0.16	d0.03	d0.07	0.31
2000	0.16	0.31	0.02	0.38

INTERIM DIVIDENDS (Per Share):

Amt.	Decl.	Ex.	Rec.	Pay.
0.14Q	10/18/00	1/17/01	1/19/01	2/09/01
0.14Q	1/17/01	4/18/01	4/20/01	5/10/01
2-for-1	4/24/01	6/04/01	5/15/01	6/01/01
0.07Q	5/17/01	7/18/01	7/20/01	8/10/01

Indicated div.: $0.28 (Adj.; Div. Reinv. Plan)

CAPITALIZATION (12/31/00):

	($000)	(%)
Long-Term Debt	583,337	44.5
Common & Surplus	728,389	55.5
Total	1,311,726	100.0

RECENT DEVELOPMENTS: For the year ended 12/31/00, income from continuing operations soared to $86.1 million versus $28.4 million in 1999. Results for 2000 included charges totaling $13.3 million. Earnings for 1999 included net non-recurring charges totaling $48.6 million. Results for 2000 and 1999 also excluded net income of $4.5 million and $125.9 million, respectively, from discontinued operations. Sales rose 24.4% to $1.70 billion.

PROSPECTS: PKI announced plans to acquire Analytical Automation Specialists, Inc. a supplier of laboratory information management systems that integrates information across most brands of instrumentation under the brand name LABWORKS™. The acquisition is expected to enhance PKI's ability to provide integrated applications to its life sciences and analytical instruments customers. Meanwhile, PKI acquired Applied Surface Technology.

BUSINESS

PERKINELMER, INC. (formerly EG&G, Inc.) is a technology company that operates four business units. The Life Sciences segment develops bioanalytic research and diagnostic systems used in research facilities, hospitals, and clinical laboratories. The Analytical Instruments unit manufactures and markets products for detection, measurement and testing applications for the pharmaceutical, food and beverage, environmental, chemical and plastics industries. The Fluid Sciences unit specializes in the design and manufacture of advanced seals and bellows products for original equipment manufacturers and end users. The Optoelectronics segment offers a range of light products, including silicon-based sensor products, imaging technology, and specially designed component assemblies.

ANNUAL FINANCIAL DATA

	12/31/00	1/2/00	1/3/99	12/28/97	12/29/96	12/31/95	[2] 1/1/95
Earnings Per Share	**[7] 0.84**	**[6] 0.31**	**[5] 1.11**	**[3] [4] 0.34**	**[3] [4] 0.58**	**[3] 0.53**	**[1] d0.29**
Cash Flow Per Share	**1.70**	**1.01**	**1.66**	**0.82**	**1.01**	**0.91**	**0.04**
Tang. Book Val. Per Share	**...**	**...**	**0.92**	**2.75**	**2.75**	**2.56**	**2.88**
Dividends Per Share	**0.28**	**0.28**	**0.28**	**0.28**	**0.28**	**0.28**	**0.28**
Dividend Payout %	**33.3**	**91.8**	**25.2**	**83.6**	**48.7**	**54.3**	**...**
INCOME STATEMENT (IN MILLIONS):							
Total Revenues	1,695.3	1,363.1	1,407.9	1,460.8	1,427.3	1,419.6	1,332.6
Costs & Expenses	1,421.0	1,230.4	1,202.0	1,328.4	1,298.7	1,297.5	1,306.7
Depreciation & Amort.	87.7	66.1	50.4	44.6	40.9	39.4	36.8
Operating Income	186.6	66.7	155.5	59.6	87.6	82.7	d10.9
Income Before Income Taxes	144.5	44.9	156.0	54.0	80.4	86.1	d17.1
Income Taxes	58.4	16.5	54.0	23.4	25.9	31.8	15.0
Net Income	[7] 86.1	[6] 28.4	[5] 102.0	[3] [4] 30.6	[3] [4] 54.5	[3] 54.3	[1] d32.1
Cash Flow	173.8	94.5	152.4	75.3	95.4	93.7	4.7
Average Shs. Outstg. (000)	102,278	93,138	91,768	91,796	94,596	102,966	110,542
BALANCE SHEET (IN MILLIONS):							
Cash & Cash Equivalents	125.6	126.7	95.6	57.9	47.8	76.2	66.4
Total Current Assets	893.1	815.1	565.4	488.2	454.7	468.7	481.5
Net Property	274.8	228.0	221.8	181.1	192.1	147.5	121.7
Total Assets	2,260.2	1,714.6	1,184.9	832.1	822.9	803.9	793.1
Total Current Liabilities	717.6	852.5	524.1	285.6	259.8	250.5	260.3
Long-Term Obligations	583.3	114.9	129.8	114.9	115.1	115.2	0.8
Net Stockholders' Equity	728.4	550.8	399.7	328.4	365.1	366.9	445.4
Net Working Capital	175.5	d37.4	41.3	202.6	194.9	218.2	221.2
Year-end Shs. Outstg. (000)	99,548	92,732	89,494	90,666	92,620	95,220	110,248
STATISTICAL RECORD:							
Operating Profit Margin %	11.0	4.9	11.0	4.1	6.1	5.8	...
Net Profit Margin %	5.1	2.1	7.2	2.1	3.8	3.8	...
Return on Equity %	11.8	5.2	25.5	9.3	14.9	14.8	...
Return on Assets %	3.8	1.7	8.6	3.7	6.6	6.8	...
Debt/Total Assets %	25.8	6.7	11.0	13.8	14.0	14.3	0.1
Price Range	60.50-19.00	22.50-12.75	16.88-9.44	12.31-9.00	12.56-8.13	12.25-6.50	9.50-6.88
P/E Ratio	72.0-22.6	73.8-41.8	15.2-8.5	36.7-26.9	21.8-14.1	23.3-12.4	...
Average Yield %	0.7	1.6	2.1	2.6	2.7	3.0	3.4

Statistics are as originally reported. Adj. for 2-for-1 split, 6/01. [1] Incl. $40.3 mil. goodwill write-down, $30.4 mil. restr. chg. & excl. $26.5 mil. fr. disc. ops. [2] Results no longer reflect disc. DOE support segment. [3] Excl. $3.0 mil. inc. fr. disc. ops., 1997; $5.7 mil., 1996; $13.7 mil., 1995. [4] Incl. $26.7 mil. after-tax chg. for write-down, 1997; $4.2 mil. prov. rel. to infring. settlement, 1996. [5] Incl. $2.3 mil. in-process R&D chgs., $54.5 mil. restr. chgs., $7.4 mil. asset impair. chgs. & $125.8 mil. gain on dispo. [6] Incl. $42.2 mil. net chgs. & excl. $125.9 mil. net gain fr. disc. ops. [7] Incl. $13.4 mil. non-recur. chgs. & excl. $4.5 mil. gain fr. disc. ops.

OFFICERS:
G. L. Summe, Chmn., Pres., C.E.O.
R. F. Friel, Sr. V.P., C.F.O.

INVESTOR CONTACT: Diane J. Basile, Investor Relations, (781) 431-4306

PRINCIPAL OFFICE: 45 William St., Wellesley, MA 02481

TELEPHONE NUMBER: (781) 237-5100
FAX: (781) 431-4255
WEB: www.perkinelmer.com

NO. OF EMPLOYEES: 12,500 (approx.)

SHAREHOLDERS: 7,900 (approx.)

ANNUAL MEETING: In Apr.

INCORPORATED: MA, Nov., 1947

INSTITUTIONAL HOLDINGS:
No. of Institutions: 274
Shares Held: 82,223,086 (Adj.)
% Held: 81.6

INDUSTRY: Engineering services (SIC: 8711)

TRANSFER AGENT(S): BankBoston, N.A., c/o Boston EquiServe, Boston, MA

NYSE SYMBOL PFE
Rec. Pr. 43.30 (4/30/01)

PFIZER INC.

YIELD 1.0%
P/E RATIO 46.6

TRADING VOLUME
Thousand Shares

*7 YEAR PRICE SCORE 130.6 *12 MONTH PRICE SCORE 98.6

*NYSE COMPOSITE INDEX=100

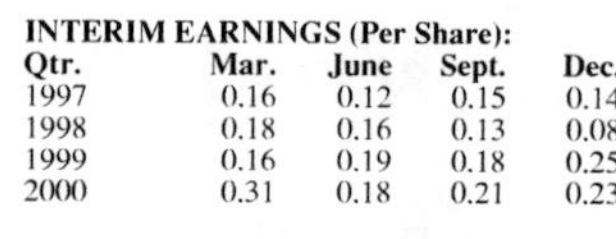

INTERIM EARNINGS (Per Share):

Qtr.	Mar.	June	Sept.	Dec.
1997	0.16	0.12	0.15	0.14
1998	0.18	0.16	0.13	0.08
1999	0.16	0.19	0.18	0.25
2000	0.31	0.18	0.21	0.23

INTERIM DIVIDENDS (Per Share):

Amt.	Decl.	Ex.	Rec.	Pay.
0.09Q	4/27/00	5/09/00	5/11/00	6/08/00
0.09Q	6/22/00	8/16/00	8/18/00	9/07/00
0.09Q	10/26/00	11/15/00	11/17/00	12/07/00
0.11Q	12/18/00	2/14/01	2/16/01	3/08/01
0.11Q	4/26/01	5/16/01	5/18/01	6/07/01

Indicated div.: $0.44 (Div. Reinv. Plan)

CAPITALIZATION (12/31/00):

	($000)	(%)
Long-Term Debt	1,123,000	6.4
Deferred Income Tax	380,000	2.2
Common & Surplus	16,076,000	91.5
Total	17,579,000	100.0

RECENT DEVELOPMENTS: For the year ended 12/31/00, income from continuing operations jumped to $3.72 billion versus a loss from continuing operations of $4.97 billion in 1999. Results in 2000 included a pre-tax merger related charge of $3.26 billion. Total revenues climbed 8.0% to $29.57 billion from $27.38 billion a year earlier. Revenue growth was due to higher sales of LIPITOR, a cholesterol-lowering agent, which climbed 32.6% to $5.03 billion.

PROSPECTS: PFE announced that the Food and Drug Administration has approved Ziprasidone HCI capsules, a novel antipsychotic medicine for the treatment of Schizophrenia. Going forward, PFE expects double-digit revenue growth in 2001, despite the continued negative effect of foreign exchange. PFE anticipates earnings in 2001 to be $1.27 per share.

BUSINESS

PFIZER INC. is a global pharmaceutical company that develops, manufactures and markets innovative medicines for humans and animals. The products include NORVASC, a once-a-day calcium channel blocker for treatment of angina and hypertension, ZYRTEC, an anti-allergy medicine, VIAGRA, an oral medication for the treatment of erectile dysfunction, ZOLOFT, a selective serotonin re-uptake inhibitor for the treatment of depression, ZITHROMAX, an oral or injectable antibiotic, DIFLUCAN, used to treat various fugal infections, as well as non-prescription self-medications. The animal health segment includes anti-parasitic, anti-infective and anti-inflammatory medicines and vaccines. Revenues for 2000 were derived as follows: 81.2% from the pharmaceutical segment and 18.8% from the consumer product segment. PFE acquired Warner-Lambert Co. on 6/19/00.

ANNUAL FINANCIAL DATA

	12/31/00	12/31/99	12/31/98	12/31/97	12/31/96	12/31/95	12/31/94
Earnings Per Share	**[4] 0.59**	**[3] 0.82**	**[2] 0.49**	**0.57**	**0.50**	**[1] 0.41**	**0.35**
Cash Flow Per Share	**0.74**	**0.96**	**0.62**	**0.69**	**0.61**	**0.51**	**0.43**
Tang. Book Val. Per Share	**2.26**	**2.11**	**2.06**	**1.71**	**1.43**	**1.12**	**1.06**
Dividends Per Share	**0.36**	**0.31**	**0.25**	**0.23**	**0.20**	**0.17**	**0.16**
Dividend Payout %	**61.0**	**37.4**	**51.7**	**40.0**	**40.2**	**42.1**	**44.9**
INCOME STATEMENT (IN MILLIONS):							
Total Revenues	29,574.0	16,204.0	13,544.0	12,504.0	11,306.0	10,021.4	8,281.3
Costs & Expenses	23,073.0	11,113.0	9,452.0	8,656.0	7,796.0	7,087.2	6,016.8
Depreciation & Amort.	968.0	542.0	489.0	502.0	430.0	374.0	292.0
Operating Income	5,533.0	4,549.0	3,603.0	3,346.0	3,080.0	2,560.2	1,972.5
Income Before Income Taxes	5,781.0	4,448.0	2,594.0	3,088.0	2,804.0	2,299.2	1,861.5
Income Taxes	2,049.0	1,244.0	642.0	865.0	869.0	738.0	558.5
Equity Earnings/Minority Int.	d14.0	d5.0	d2.0	d10.0	d6.0	d7.0	d4.6
Net Income	[4] 3,718.0	[3] 3,199.0	[2] 1,950.0	2,213.0	1,929.0	[1] 1,554.2	1,298.4
Cash Flow	4,686.0	3,741.0	2,439.0	2,715.0	2,359.0	1,928.2	1,590.4
Average Shs. Outstg. (000)	6,368,000	3,884,000	3,945,000	3,909,000	3,864,000	3,777,000	3,722,580
BALANCE SHEET (IN MILLIONS):							
Cash & Cash Equivalents	6,863.0	4,442.0	3,929.0	1,589.0	1,637.0	1,512.0	2,018.6
Total Current Assets	17,187.0	11,191.0	9,931.0	6,820.0	6,468.0	6,152.4	5,788.4
Net Property	9,425.0	5,343.0	4,415.0	4,137.0	3,850.0	3,472.6	3,073.2
Total Assets	33,510.0	20,574.0	18,302.0	15,336.0	14,667.0	12,729.3	11,098.5
Total Current Liabilities	11,981.0	9,185.0	7,192.0	5,305.0	5,640.0	5,187.2	4,825.9
Long-Term Obligations	1,123.0	525.0	527.0	729.0	687.0	833.0	604.2
Net Stockholders' Equity	16,076.0	8,887.0	8,810.0	7,933.0	6,954.0	5,506.6	4,323.9
Net Working Capital	5,206.0	2,006.0	2,739.0	1,515.0	828.0	965.2	962.5
Year-end Shs. Outstg. (000)	6,314,000	3,847,000	3,883,000	3,882,000	3,870,000	3,823,602	3,770,712
STATISTICAL RECORD:							
Operating Profit Margin %	18.7	28.1	26.6	26.8	27.2	25.5	23.8
Net Profit Margin %	12.6	19.7	14.4	17.7	17.1	15.5	15.7
Return on Equity %	23.1	36.0	22.1	27.9	27.7	28.2	30.0
Return on Assets %	11.1	15.5	10.7	14.4	13.2	12.2	11.7
Debt/Total Assets %	3.4	2.6	2.9	4.8	4.7	6.5	5.4
Price Range	49.25-30.00	50.04-31.54	42.98-23.69	26.66-13.44	15.21-10.04	11.14-6.21	6.61-4.43
P/E Ratio	83.5-50.8	61.0-38.5	87.7-48.3	47.0-23.7	30.5-20.2	27.0-15.1	18.9-12.7
Average Yield %	0.9	0.8	0.8	1.1	1.6	2.0	2.8

Statistics are as originally reported. Adj. for stock splits: 200% div., 6/30/99; 2-for-1, 9/97 & 6/95. [1] Excl. gain of $18.8 mill. for dis. ops. [2] Incl. unusual & nonrecurr. pre-tax chgs. total. $1.06 bill.; excl. a $1.40 bill. gain from disc. opers. [3] Incl. a one-time after-tax charge of $1.37 billion for TROVAN inventories. [4] Incls. merger chrgs. of $3.26 billion.

OFFICERS:
W. C. Steere Jr., Chmn.
J. F. Niblack Ph.D., Vice-Chmn.
H. A. McKinnell, Pres., C.O.O.
D. Shedlarz, Exec. V.P., C.F.O.

INVESTOR CONTACT: Investor Relation, (212) 573-2323

PRINCIPAL OFFICE: 235 East 42nd Street, New York, NY 10017-5755

TELEPHONE NUMBER: (212) 573-2323
FAX: (212) 573-2641
WEB: www.pfizer.com

NO. OF EMPLOYEES: 90,000 (approx.)

SHAREHOLDERS: 202,365 (approx.)

ANNUAL MEETING: In Apr.

INCORPORATED: DE, 1942

INSTITUTIONAL HOLDINGS:
No. of Institutions: 1,243
Shares Held: 3,782,086,000
% Held: 59.9

INDUSTRY: Pharmaceutical preparations (SIC: 2834)

TRANSFER AGENT(S): First Chicago Trust Company of New York, Jersey City, NJ

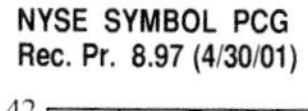

NYSE SYMBOL PCG
Rec. Pr. 8.97 (4/30/01)

PG&E CORPORATION

YIELD ...
P/E RATIO ...

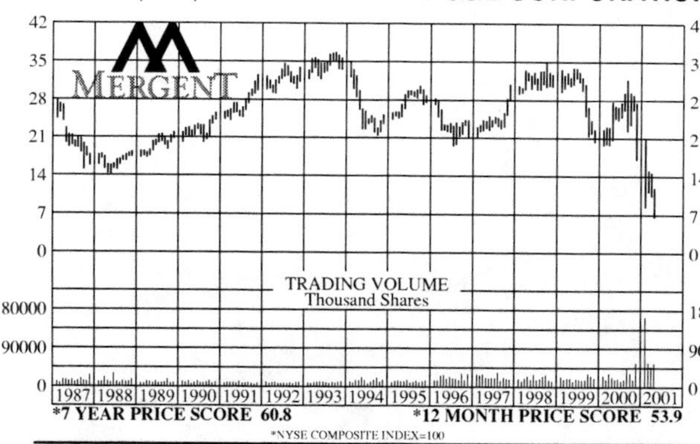

***7 YEAR PRICE SCORE 60.8** ***12 MONTH PRICE SCORE 53.9**

*NYSE COMPOSITE INDEX=100

INTERIM EARNINGS (Per Share):

Qtr.	Mar.	June	Sept.	Dec.
1996	0.61	0.25	0.55	0.34
1997	0.42	0.49	0.62	0.22
1998	0.36	0.46	0.55	0.51
1999	0.39	0.50	0.54	d1.49
2000	0.77	0.68	0.67	d11.28

INTERIM DIVIDENDS (Per Share):

Amt.	Decl.	Ex.	Rec.	Pay.
0.30Q	7/21/99	9/13/99	9/15/99	10/15/99
0.30Q	10/20/99	12/13/99	12/15/99	1/15/00
0.30Q	2/16/00	3/13/00	3/15/00	4/15/00
0.30Q	4/19/00	6/13/00	6/15/00	7/15/00
0.30Q	7/19/00	9/13/00	9/15/00	10/15/00

Dividend payment suspended

CAPITALIZATION (12/31/00):

	($000)	(%)
Long-Term Debt	6,476,000	53.6
Deferred Income Tax	1,656,000	13.7
Redeemable Pfd. Stock	780,000	6.5
Common & Surplus	3,172,000	26.2
Total	12,084,000	100.0

RECENT DEVELOPMENTS: For the year ended 12/31/01, loss from continuing operations was $3.32 billion compared with income from continuing operations of $13.0 million, before an accounting change credit of $12.0 million in the previous year. Earnings for 2000 included an after-tax charge of $4.10 billion related to uncollected wholesale power and transition costs. Results excluded losses from discontinued operations of $40.0 million and $98.0 million in 2000 and 1999, respectively. Total operating revenues grew 26.0% to $26.23 billion from $20.82 billion in 1999.

PROSPECTS: Earnings continued to be pressured by the non-reimbursement of wholesale power costs at PCG's California utility unit, Pacific Gas & Electric Co. The Company's utility unit has amassed enormous debt, estimated at nearly $9.00 billion, by purchasing wholesale power at prices well above the rates they are allowed to charge retail customers. As a result, on 4/6/01 PCG's utility unit announced that it has filed for reorganization under Chapter 11 of the U.S. Bankruptcy Code. The Company expects to file the reorganization plan before August 2001.

BUSINESS

PG&E CORPORATION is an energy-based holding company. Its subsidiary Pacific Gas and Electric Company provides electricity and natural gas distribution and transmission services throughout Northern and Central California. PG&E Corporation's National Energy Group develops, constructs, operates, owns, and manages independent power generation facilities that serve wholesale and industrial customers; owns and operates natural gas pipelines, natural gas storage facilities, and natural gas processing plants, primarily in the Pacific Northwest and Texas; and purchases and sells energy commodities and provide risk management services.

ANNUAL FINANCIAL DATA

	12/31/00	12/31/99	12/31/98	12/31/97	12/31/96	12/31/95	12/31/94
Earnings Per Share	**[2] d9.18**	**0.04**	**1.88**	**[1] 1.75**	**1.75**	**2.99**	**2.21**
Cash Flow Per Share	**0.93**	**4.87**	**6.08**	**6.66**	**4.94**	**6.42**	**5.68**
Tang. Book Val. Per Share	**8.73**	**19.10**	**21.08**	**21.28**	**20.73**	**20.77**	**20.07**
Dividends Per Share	**1.20**	**1.20**	**1.20**	**1.20**	**1.96**	**1.96**	**1.94**
Dividend Payout %	**...**	**2,992.5**	**63.8**	**68.6**	**112.0**	**65.5**	**87.8**
INCOME STATEMENT (IN MILLIONS):							
Total Revenues	26,232.0	20,820.0	19,942.0	15,400.0	9,610.0	9,621.8	10,447.4
Costs & Expenses	27,380.0	18,162.0	16,326.0	11,658.0	6,398.5	5,409.3	6,396.6
Depreciation & Amort.	3,659.0	1,780.0	1,609.0	2,014.0	1,315.9	1,449.5	1,492.8
Operating Income	d4,807.0	878.0	2,007.0	1,728.0	1,895.6	2,763.0	1,633.4
Net Interest Inc./(Exp.)	d522.0	d772.0	d782.0	d665.0	d566.9	d607.4	d636.6
Income Taxes	cr2,028.0	248.0	570.0	548.0	555.0	895.3	924.6
Net Income	[2] d3,324.0	13.0	719.0	[1] 716.0	755.2	1,338.9	1,007.5
Cash Flow	335.0	1,793.0	2,328.0	2,730.0	2,038.0	2,718.1	2,442.6
Average Shs. Outstg. (000)	362,000	368,000	383,106	410,000	412,542	423,692	429,846
BALANCE SHEET (IN MILLIONS):							
Gross Property	28,469.0	28,067.0	29,844.0	36,513.0	33,309.8	32,226.6	31,668.2
Accumulated Depreciation	11,878.0	11,291.0	12,026.0	16,041.0	14,301.9	13,308.6	12,269.4
Net Property	16,591.0	16,776.0	17,818.0	20,472.0	19,007.9	18,918.0	19,398.8
Total Assets	35,291.0	29,715.0	33,234.0	30,557.0	26,129.9	26,850.3	27,708.6
Long-Term Obligations	6,476.0	8,704.0	9,743.0	10,435.0	7,770.1	8,048.5	8,675.1
Net Stockholders' Equity	3,172.0	6,886.0	8,066.0	9,299.0	8,765.4	9,001.2	9,368.0
Year-end Shs. Outstg. (000)	363,378	360,590	382,604	418,000	403,504	414,026	430,243
STATISTICAL RECORD:							
Operating Profit Margin %	...	4.2	10.1	11.2	19.7	28.7	15.6
Net Profit Margin %	...	0.1	3.6	4.6	7.9	13.9	9.6
Net Inc./Net Property %	...	0.1	4.0	3.5	4.0	7.1	5.2
Net Inc./Tot. Capital %	...	0.1	3.2	3.0	3.6	6.3	4.6
Return on Equity %	...	0.2	8.9	7.7	8.6	14.9	10.8
Accum. Depr./Gross Prop. %	41.7	40.2	40.3	43.9	42.9	41.3	38.7
Price Range	31.81-17.00	34.00-20.25	35.06-29.06	30.94-20.88	28.38-19.50	30.63-24.25	35.00-21.38
P/E Ratio	...	847.9-505.0	18.6-15.5	17.7-11.9	16.2-11.1	10.2-8.1	15.8-9.7
Average Yield %	4.9	4.4	3.7	4.6	8.2	7.1	6.9

Statistics are as originally reported. [1] Incl. non-recurr gains of $0.28/sh. fr. sale of assets [2] Incl. after-tax chrg. of $4.10 bill.; excl. loss from disc. oper. of $40.0 mill.

OFFICERS:
R. D. Glynn Jr., Chmn., Pres., C.E.O.
P. Darbee, Sr. V.P., C.F.O., Treas.
L. H. Everett, V.P., Corp. Sec.

INVESTOR CONTACT: Gabriel B. Togneri, V.P., Inv. Rel., (415) 267-7080

PRINCIPAL OFFICE: One Mkt., Spear Twr., Suite 2400, San Francisco, CA 94105

TELEPHONE NUMBER: (415) 267-7000
FAX: (415) 267-7267
WEB: www.pgecorp.com
NO. OF EMPLOYEES: 20,850 (avg.)
SHAREHOLDERS: 132,612
ANNUAL MEETING: In May
INCORPORATED: CA, Oct., 1905; reincorp., CA, 1995

INSTITUTIONAL HOLDINGS:
No. of Institutions: 269
Shares Held: 180,696,445
% Held: 46.7

INDUSTRY: Electric and other services combined (SIC: 4931)

TRANSFER AGENT(S): Office of the Company, San Francisco, CA

NYSE SYMBOL PHA
Rec. Pr. 52.26 (4/30/01)

PHARMACIA CORPORATION

YIELD 1.0%
P/E RATIO 68.8

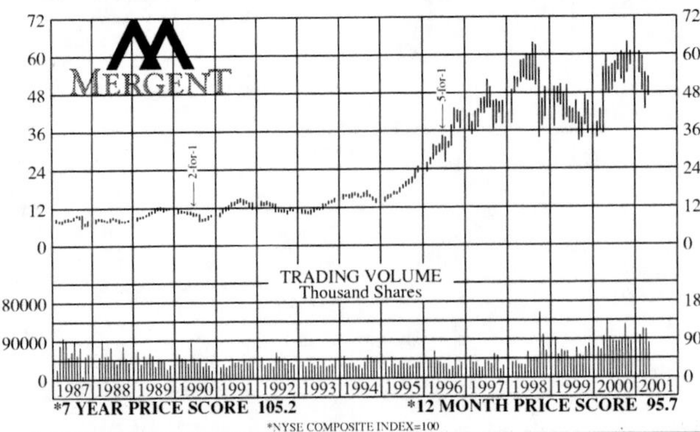

*7 YEAR PRICE SCORE 105.2 *12 MONTH PRICE SCORE 95.7

*NYSE COMPOSITE INDEX=100

INTERIM EARNINGS (Per Share):

Qtr.	Mar.	June	Sept.	Dec.
1997	0.37	0.34	0.15	d0.26
1998	0.36	0.28	0.41	0.26
1999	0.42	0.41	0.34	0.40
2000	0.07	0.33	0.21	0.15

INTERIM DIVIDENDS (Per Share):

Amt.	Decl.	Ex.	Rec.	Pay.
0.015Q	2/25/00	3/28/00	3/30/00	5/01/00
0.12Q	4/20/00	6/30/00	7/05/00	8/01/00
0.12Q	9/22/00	10/03/00	10/05/00	11/01/00
0.12Q	12/08/00	1/04/01	1/08/01	2/01/01
0.12Q	2/21/01	4/06/01	4/10/01	5/01/01

Indicated div.: $0.48 (Div. Reinv. Plan)

CAPITALIZATION (12/31/00):

	($000)	(%)
Long-Term Debt	4,586,000	25.7
Deferred Income Tax	255,000	1.4
Minority Interest	1,084,000	6.1
Preferred Stock	263,000	1.5
Common & Surplus	11,658,000	65.3
Total	17,846,000	100.0

RECENT DEVELOPMENTS: For the year ended 12/31/00, income from continuing operations decreased 24.7% to $984.0 million versus income of $1.31 billion in 1999. Results for 2000 and 1999 included a pre-tax merger charges of $1.08 billion and $55.0 million and excluded an after-tax loss of $37.0 million and an after-tax gain of $92.0 million from the sale of discontinued operations, respectively. Net sales advanced 10.5% to $18.14 billion.

PROSPECTS: On 3/7/01, PHA completed the acquisition of Sensus Drug Development Corporation, a privately-held Texas-based company focused on developing drugs to treat endocrine disorders. Separately, Pharmacia Canada Inc. acquired the Canadian Nicotine Replacement Therapy business of Aventis Pharma Inc. PHA expects double-digit sales growth in 2001 from its pharmaceutical business fueled by its prescription pharmaceutical products.

BUSINESS

PHARMACIA CORPORATION was formed through the merger of Monsanto Company and Pharmacia & Upjohn, Inc. on 3/31/00. PHA is a global pharmaceutical group engaged in the research, development, manufacture and sale of pharmaceutical and healthcare products. The Company's core business includes both prescription and non-prescription products for humans and animals, bulk pharmaceutical and contract manufacturing. The Company's major pharmaceutical brands include CELEBREX, XALATAN, DETRO, CAMPTOSAR, GENOTROPIN, AMBIEN, NICORETTE and ROGAINE. The Company has research, manufacturing, and administration and sales operations in more than 60 countries. On 10/18/00, PHA sold 16.0% of its agribusiness to the public.

REVENUES

(12/31/2000)	($000)	(%)
Pharmaceuticals-Prescription	10,824,000	59.7
Pharmaceuticals-Other	1,827,000	10.1
Agricultural-Productivity	3,855,000	21.2
Agricultural-Seeds & Genomics	1,608,000	9.0
Total	18,144,000	100.0

ANNUAL FINANCIAL DATA

	12/31/00	12/31/99	12/31/98	12/31/97	12/31/96	12/31/95	12/31/94
Earnings Per Share	**5 0.75**	**4 0.77**	**3 d0.41**	**2 0.48**	**1 0.64**	**1 1.26**	**1.06**
Cash Flow Per Share	**1.72**	**1.90**	**0.64**	**1.32**	**1.63**	**2.33**	**2.02**
Tang. Book Val. Per Share	**4.94**	**1.07**	...	**2.13**	**2.61**	**3.07**	**3.24**
Dividends Per Share	**0.28**	**0.12**	**0.12**	**0.50**	**0.59**	**0.54**	**0.49**
Dividend Payout %	**38.0**	**15.6**	...	**104.1**	**91.9**	**42.7**	**46.4**
INCOME STATEMENT (IN MILLIONS):							
Total Revenues	18,144.0	9,146.0	8,648.0	7,514.0	9,262.0	8,962.0	8,272.0
Costs & Expenses	15,262.0	7,258.0	7,897.0	6,528.0	8,075.0	7,379.0	6,788.0
Depreciation & Amort.	1,267.0	730.0	636.0	487.0	590.0	598.0	561.0
Operating Income	1,615.0	1,158.0	115.0	499.0	597.0	985.0	923.0
Net Interest Inc./(Exp.)	d242.0	d300.0	d262.0	d125.0	d120.0	d131.0	d50.0
Income Before Income Taxes	1,373.0	751.0	d243.0	366.0	540.0	1,087.0	895.0
Income Taxes	395.0	248.0	7.0	72.0	155.0	348.0	273.0
Equity Earnings/Minority Int.	6.0	...	...	...	...	...	...
Net Income	5 984.0	4 503.0	3 d250.0	2 294.0	1 385.0	1 739.0	622.0
Cash Flow	2,238.0	1,233.0	386.0	781.0	975.0	1,337.0	1,183.0
Average Shs. Outstg. (000)	1,307,000	649,800	603,500	590,200	599,000	575,000	585,000
BALANCE SHEET (IN MILLIONS):							
Cash & Cash Equivalents	2,201.0	284.0	89.0	134.0	166.0	297.0	507.0
Total Current Assets	11,567.0	5,787.0	6,190.0	4,266.0	4,340.0	4,305.0	3,883.0
Net Property	7,171.0	3,320.0	3,254.0	2,400.0	3,013.0	2,832.0	2,817.0
Total Assets	26,656.0	16,535.0	16,724.0	10,774.0	11,191.0	10,611.0	8,891.0
Total Current Liabilities	6,161.0	3,750.0	4,052.0	3,539.0	3,401.0	2,812.0	2,435.0
Long-Term Obligations	4,586.0	5,903.0	6,259.0	1,979.0	1,608.0	1,667.0	1,405.0
Net Stockholders' Equity	11,921.0	5,349.0	4,986.0	4,104.0	3,690.0	3,732.0	2,948.0
Net Working Capital	5,406.0	2,037.0	2,138.0	727.0	939.0	1,493.0	1,448.0
Year-end Shs. Outstg. (000)	1,296,300	636,233	629,295	595,000	584,000	575,000	560,000
STATISTICAL RECORD:							
Operating Profit Margin %	8.9	12.7	1.3	6.6	6.4	11.0	11.2
Net Profit Margin %	5.4	5.5	...	3.9	4.2	8.2	7.5
Return on Equity %	8.3	9.4	...	7.2	10.4	19.8	21.1
Return on Assets %	3.7	3.0	...	2.7	3.4	7.0	7.0
Debt/Total Assets %	17.2	35.7	37.4	18.4	14.4	15.7	15.8
Price Range	64.00-33.75	50.81-32.75	63.94-33.75	52.31-34.75	43.25-23.08	24.95-13.65	17.30-13.30
P/E Ratio	85.3-45.0	66.0-42.5	...	109.0-72.4	67.6-36.0	19.7-10.8	16.3-12.5
Average Yield %	0.6	0.3	0.2	1.1	1.8	2.8	3.2

Statistics are as originally reported. Stk. price, div. & fin. for 1999 & prior years refl. Monsanto Company. 1 Incl. pre-tax chg. of $241.6 mill., 1995; $436.0 mill., 1996 2 Incl. pre-tax exps. of $389.0 mill. 3 Incl. after-tax nonrecurr. chg. of $41.0 mill. 4 Incl. nonrecurr chgs. of $131.0 mill. 5 Incl. pre-tax chg. of $1.08 bill. & excl. disc. oper. of $37.0 mill.

OFFICERS:
F. Hassan, Chmn., C.E.O.
C. Coughlin, Exec. V.P., C.F.O.

INVESTOR CONTACT: A. N. Filippello, Corp. V.P., (314) 694-8148

PRINCIPAL OFFICE: 100 Route 206 North, Peapack, NJ 07977

TELEPHONE NUMBER: (908) 901-8000
FAX: (908) 901-7700
WEB: www.pharmacia.com

NO. OF EMPLOYEES: 59,000 (approx.)

SHAREHOLDERS: 76,355

ANNUAL MEETING: In Mar.

INCORPORATED: DE, Apr., 1933

INSTITUTIONAL HOLDINGS:
No. of Institutions: 752
Shares Held: 906,497,717
% Held: 69.7

INDUSTRY: Organic fibers, noncellulosic (SIC: 2824)

TRANSFER AGENT(S): First Chicago Trust Company, Jersey City, NJ

NYSE SYMBOL PD
Rec. Pr. 44.74 (4/30/01)

PHELPS DODGE CORP.

YIELD 1.1%
P/E RATIO 120.9

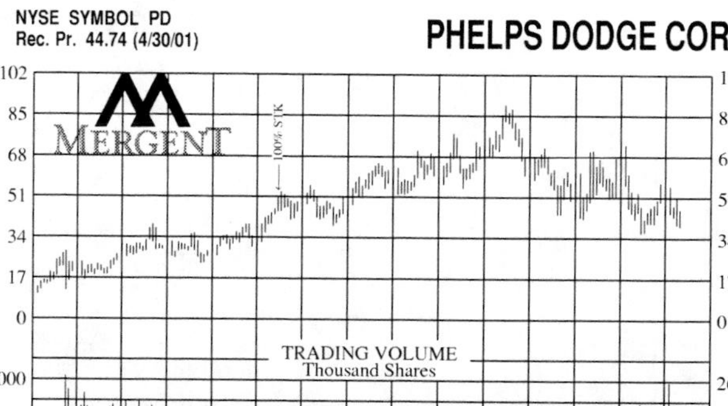

*7 YEAR PRICE SCORE 55.2 *12 MONTH PRICE SCORE 103.2

*NYSE COMPOSITE INDEX=100

INTERIM EARNINGS (Per Share):

Qtr.	Mar	June	Sept.	Dec.
1997	2.12	2.16	1.72	0.54
1998	2.80	0.69	0.49	d0.72
1999	0.01	d0.99	0.27	d2.91
2000	0.25	d0.48	0.50	0.10

INTERIM DIVIDENDS (Per Share):

Amt.	Decl.	Ex.	Rec.	Pay.
0.50Q	6/21/00	8/16/00	8/18/00	9/08/00
0.50Q	11/01/00	11/15/00	11/17/00	12/08/00
0.50Q	2/07/01	2/14/01	2/16/01	3/09/01
0.125Q	5/03/01	5/16/01	5/18/01	6/08/01

Indicated div.: $0.50 (Div. Reinv. Plan)

CAPITALIZATION (12/31/00):

	($000)	(%)
Long-Term Debt	1,963,000	35.1
Deferred Income Tax	439,000	7.8
Minority Interest	91,700	1.6
Common & Surplus	3,105,000	55.5
Total	5,598,700	100.0

RECENT DEVELOPMENTS: For the year ended 12/31/00, net income amounted to $29.0 million compared with a loss of $254.3 million, before a loss from the cumulative effect of an accounting change of $3.5 million, in 1999. Results for 2000 and 1999 included after-tax non-recurring charges and provisions of $43.3 million and $279.5 million, respectively. Total revenues jumped 45.3% to $4.53 billion from $3.11 million in the prior year.

PROSPECTS: The Company plans to build a new 50-megawatt power plant near Santa Rita, New Mexico, which is expected to yield half the energy required to run its 130,000 tons-per-year Chino mine and Hurley smelter. When construction is completed by mid-summer 2001, the natural gas fired turbine plant will aid in the production of copper by raising the self-generation capacity by 25.0%.

BUSINESS

PHELPS DODGE CORPORATION is among the world's largest producers of copper. Using copper from its own production and copper purchased from others, its Phelps Dodge Mineral subsidiary is a major producer of continuous cast copper rod, the basic feed for the electrical wire and cable industry. In the U.S., PD operates open-pit copper and molybdenum mines, concentrators, solution extraction/electrowinning (SX/EW) plants, smelters and other conversion and processing operations. Internationally, PD is majority partner in three copper mines and one concentrator in South America. In addition, it has investments in two open-pit copper mines, two concentrators, a smelter, an SX/EW facility, a refinery and a zinc mining operation in Peru. The Phelps Dodge Industries segment is comprised of a group of companies that manufacture engineered products principally for the transportation, energy and telecommunications sectors worldwide. This business segment includes PD's carbon black operations, its wheel and rim operations, and its U.S. and international wire and cable and specialty conductor operations. PD acquired Cyprus Amax Minerals Co. on 12/2/99.

ANNUAL FINANCIAL DATA

	12/31/00	12/31/99	12/31/98	12/31/97	12/31/96	12/31/95	12/31/94
Earnings Per Share	**[7] 0.37**	**[6] d4.13**	**[5] 3.26**	**[4] 6.63**	**[2] 6.97**	**[3] 10.65**	**[1] 3.81**
Cash Flow Per Share	**6.26**	**1.21**	**8.28**	**11.24**	**10.73**	**13.84**	**6.56**
Tang. Book Val. Per Share	**39.45**	**41.64**	**44.69**	**39.68**	**40.19**	**36.96**	**28.87**
Dividends Per Share	**2.00**	**2.00**	**2.00**	**2.00**	**1.95**	**1.80**	**1.69**
Dividend Payout %	**540.4**	**...**	**61.3**	**30.2**	**28.0**	**16.9**	**44.3**
INCOME STATEMENT (IN MILLIONS):							
Total Revenues	4,525.1	3,114.4	3,063.4	3,914.3	3,786.6	4,185.4	3,289.2
Costs & Expenses	3,823.9	3,100.9	2,347.4	3,019.6	2,824.2	2,861.4	2,693.5
Depreciation & Amort.	464.2	329.1	293.3	283.7	249.5	223.5	195.3
Operating Income	237.0	d315.6	422.7	611.0	712.9	1,100.5	400.4
Net Interest Inc./(Exp.)	d213.3	d120.2	d94.5	d62.5	d66.1	d62.0	d36.6
Income Before Income Taxes	53.7	d426.7	337.0	581.9	687.5	1,075.7	375.1
Income Taxes	19.2	cr165.2	134.0	180.4	220.0	322.7	104.7
Equity Earnings/Minority Int.	d5.5	7.2	d12.1	7.0	d5.7	d6.4	0.6
Net Income	[7] 29.0	[6] d254.3	[5] 190.9	[4] 408.5	[2] 461.8	[3] 746.6	[1] 271.0
Cash Flow	493.2	74.8	484.2	692.2	711.3	970.1	466.3
Average Shs. Outstg. (000)	78,800	61,600	58,500	61,600	66,300	70,100	71,100
BALANCE SHEET (IN MILLIONS):							
Cash & Cash Equivalents	250.0	234.2	221.7	157.9	470.1	608.5	286.9
Total Current Assets	1,507.6	1,693.4	980.0	1,051.1	1,421.5	1,555.2	1,207.9
Net Property	5,894.6	6,037.7	3,587.2	3,445.1	3,020.5	2,728.7	2,566.4
Total Assets	7,830.8	7,884.1	4,653.5	4,965.2	4,816.4	4,645.9	4,133.8
Total Current Liabilities	1,417.9	1,418.3	651.1	701.1	685.9	605.0	649.7
Long-Term Obligations	1,963.0	2,172.5	836.4	857.1	554.6	613.1	622.3
Net Stockholders' Equity	3,105.0	3,276.8	2,587.4	2,510.4	2,755.9	2,677.7	2,187.6
Net Working Capital	89.7	275.1	328.9	350.0	735.6	950.2	558.2
Year-end Shs. Outstg. (000)	78,700	78,700	57,900	58,634	64,711	68,593	70,672
STATISTICAL RECORD:							
Operating Profit Margin %	5.2	...	13.8	15.6	18.8	26.3	12.2
Net Profit Margin %	0.6	...	6.2	10.4	12.2	17.8	8.2
Return on Equity %	0.9	...	7.4	16.3	16.8	27.9	12.4
Return on Assets %	0.4	...	4.1	8.2	9.6	16.1	6.6
Debt/Total Assets %	25.1	26.4	16.6	17.3	11.5	13.2	15.1
Price Range	73.00-36.06	70.63-41.88	71.75-43.88	89.63-59.88	77.63-54.63	70.50-51.88	65.00-47.63
P/E Ratio	197.2-97.4	...	22.0-13.5	13.5-9.0	11.1-7.8	6.6-4.9	17.1-12.5
Average Yield %	3.7	3.6	3.5	2.7	2.9	2.9	3.0

Statistics are as originally reported. [1] Incl. a net chg. of $91.7 mill. ($1.29 a sh.). [2] Incl. an after-tax chg. of $10.0 mill. for prov. of reclaim. costs. [3] Incl. a gain of $26.8 mill. [4] Incl. after-tax chgs. of $31.6 mill. [5] Incl. $131.1 mill. after-tax gain fr. the disposal of Accuride Corp. & an after-tax loss of $32.0 mill. fr. sale & costs rel. to its mining co. [6] Incl. $455.4 mill. non-recur. chg. & excl. loss of $3.5 mill. fr. cumulative effect. [7] Incl. $51.8 mill. net non-recur. chg.

OFFICERS:
J. S. Whisler, Chmn., Pres., C.E.O.
R. G. Peru, Sr. V.P., C.F.O.
S. D. Colton, Sr. V.P., Gen. Couns.

INVESTOR CONTACT: Investor Relations, (602) 234-8100

PRINCIPAL OFFICE: 2600 North Central Avenue, Phoenix, AZ 85004-3089

TELEPHONE NUMBER: (602) 234-8100
FAX: (602) 234-8337
WEB: www.phelpsdodge.com

NO. OF EMPLOYEES: 15,500 (avg.)

SHAREHOLDERS: 29,609 (record)

ANNUAL MEETING: In May

INCORPORATED: NY, Aug., 1885

INSTITUTIONAL HOLDINGS:
No. of Institutions: 261
Shares Held: 57,158,151
% Held: 72.6

INDUSTRY: Primary copper (SIC: 3331)

TRANSFER AGENT(S): Mellon Investor Services, Ridgefield Park, NJ

NYSE SYMBOL MO
Rec. Pr. 51.41 (5/31/01)

PHILIP MORRIS COMPANIES, INC.

YIELD 4.1%
P/E RATIO 13.7

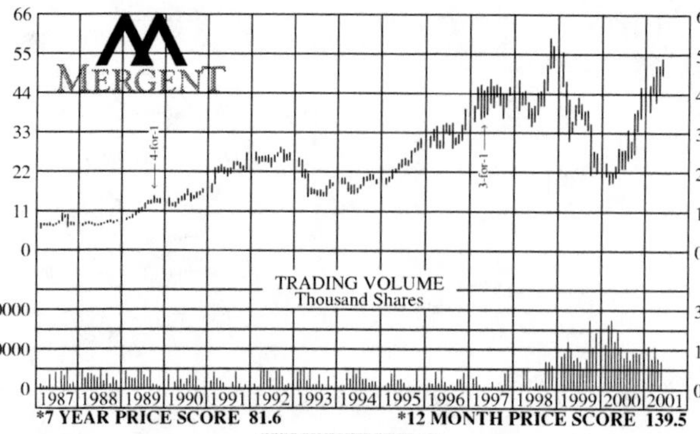

INTERIM EARNINGS (Per Share):

Qtr.	Mar.	June	Sept.	Dec.
1996	0.63	0.66	0.67	0.60
1997	0.73	0.76	0.58	0.53
1998	0.57	0.74	0.81	0.11
1999	0.73	0.84	0.84	0.79
2000	0.87	0.95	1.03	0.90

INTERIM DIVIDENDS (Per Share):

Amt.	Decl.	Ex.	Rec.	Pay.
0.48Q	6/09/00	6/16/00	6/20/00	7/10/00
0.53Q	9/30/00	9/13/00	9/15/00	10/10/00
0.53Q	11/10/00	12/13/00	12/15/00	1/10/01
0.53Q	2/28/01	3/13/01	3/15/01	4/10/01
0.53Q	5/30/01	6/13/01	6/15/01	7/10/01

Indicated div.: $2.12 (Div. Reinv. Plan)

CAPITALIZATION (12/31/00):

	($000)	(%)
Long-Term Debt	19,154,000	46.9
Deferred Income Tax	6,665,000	16.3
Common & Surplus	15,005,000	36.8
Total	40,824,000	100.0

RECENT DEVELOPMENTS: For the year ended 12/31/00, net earnings rose 10.9% to $8.51 billion versus $7.68 billion a year earlier. Results for 2000 included a gain of $139.0 million on the sale of MO's confectionery business in France and a $100.0 million gain from a transaction under which Miller sold the U.S. rights for MOLSON beer. Results for 1999 included non-recurring charges of $505.0 million. Results excluded results for Nabisco Holdings Corp., which was acquired on 12/11/00. Operating revenues rose 2.2% to $80.36 billion from $78.60 billion in 1999.

PROSPECTS: MO's prospects are favorable, reflecting its expansive worldwide tobacco business and the recent acquisition of Nabisco Holdings Corp. for a total purchase price, including assumed debt, of $18.90 billion. On 3/16/01, Kraft Foods Inc., MO's wholly-owned food and beverage subsidiary, filed with the SEC a registration statement relating to the initial public offering of Kraft Foods Inc. common stock. Meanwhile, for 2001, underlying diluted earnings per share are projected to grow in the range of 9.0% to 11.0%.

BUSINESS

PHILIP MORRIS COMPANIES, INC. is one of the world's largest consumer products companies with major operations in tobacco, food, and beer. Tobacco is manufactured and sold through Philip Morris U.S.A. and Philip Morris International Inc. Retail packaged foods are processed and marketed through Kraft Foods North America in the U.S. and Canada and Kraft Foods International in Europe and the Asia/Pacific region. Miller Brewing Co. products include MILLER LITE, MILLER GENUINE DRAFT, MILLER HIGH LIFE, ICEHOUSE and FOSTERS LAGER beers. Philip Morris Capital Corporation engages in financing and investment activities. On 12/11/00, MO acquired Nabisco Holding Corp. for total consideration of $18.90 billion.

BUSINESS LINE ANALYSIS

(12/31/2000)	Rev(%)	Inc(%)
Domestic Tobacco	28.2	33.0
International Tobacco	32.8	32.1
North American Food	23.0	21.8
International Food	10.1	7.4
Beer	5.4	4.0
Financial Services	0.5	1.7
Total	100.0	100.0

ANNUAL FINANCIAL DATA

	12/31/00	12/31/99	12/31/98	12/31/97	12/31/96	12/31/95	12/31/94
Earnings Per Share	[4] 3.75	[3] 3.19	[1] 2.20	[1] 2.58	2.56	[2] 2.17	1.82
Cash Flow Per Share	4.50	3.90	2.89	3.25	3.25	2.83	2.48
Dividends Per Share	1.97	1.80	1.64	1.60	1.40	1.16	0.95
Dividend Payout %	52.5	56.4	74.5	62.0	54.7	53.5	52.4
INCOME STATEMENT (IN MILLIONS):							
Total Revenues	80,356.0	78,596.0	74,391.0	72,055.0	69,204.0	66,071.0	65,125.0
Costs & Expenses	63,960.0	63,404.0	62,724.0	58,763.0	55,744.0	53,874.0	53,954.0
Depreciation & Amort.	1,717.0	1,702.0	1,690.0	1,629.0	1,691.0	1,671.0	1,722.0
Operating Income	14,679.0	13,490.0	9,977.0	11,663.0	11,769.0	10,526.0	9,449.0
Net Interest Inc./(Exp.)	d719.0	d795.0	d890.0	d1,052.0	d1,086.0	d1,179.0	d1,233.0
Income Before Income Taxes	13,960.0	12,695.0	9,087.0	10,611.0	10,683.0	9,347.0	8,216.0
Income Taxes	5,450.0	5,020.0	3,715.0	4,301.0	4,380.0	3,869.0	3,491.0
Net Income	[4] 8,510.0	[3] 7,675.0	[1] 5,372.0	[1] 6,310.0	6,303.0	[2] 5,478.0	4,725.0
Cash Flow	10,227.0	9,377.0	7,062.0	7,939.0	7,994.0	7,149.0	6,447.0
Average Shs. Outstg. (000)	2,272,000	2,403,000	2,446,000	2,442,000	2,463,327	2,524,674	2,597,000
BALANCE SHEET (IN MILLIONS):							
Cash & Cash Equivalents	937.0	5,100.0	4,081.0	2,282.0	240.0	1,138.0	184.0
Total Current Assets	17,238.0	20,895.0	20,230.0	17,440.0	15,190.0	14,879.0	13,908.0
Net Property	15,303.0	12,271.0	12,335.0	11,621.0	11,751.0	11,116.0	11,171.0
Total Assets	79,067.0	61,381.0	59,920.0	55,947.0	54,871.0	53,811.0	52,649.0
Total Current Liabilities	26,976.0	18,017.0	16,379.0	15,071.0	15,040.0	14,944.0	13,569.0
Long-Term Obligations	19,154.0	12,226.0	12,615.0	12,430.0	12,961.0	13,107.0	14,975.0
Net Stockholders' Equity	15,005.0	15,305.0	16,197.0	14,920.0	14,218.0	13,985.0	12,786.0
Net Working Capital	d9,738.0	2,878.0	3,851.0	2,369.0	150.0	d65.0	339.0
Year-end Shs. Outstg. (000)	2,805,961	2,338,520	2,430,535	2,425,487	2,431,347	2,493,510	2,558,577
STATISTICAL RECORD:							
Operating Profit Margin %	18.3	17.2	13.4	16.2	17.0	15.9	14.5
Net Profit Margin %	10.6	9.8	7.2	8.8	9.1	8.3	7.3
Return on Equity %	56.7	50.1	33.2	42.3	44.3	39.2	37.0
Return on Assets %	10.8	12.5	9.0	11.3	11.5	10.2	9.0
Debt/Total Assets %	24.2	19.9	21.1	22.2	23.6	24.4	28.4
Price Range	45.94-18.69	55.56-21.25	59.50-34.75	48.13-36.00	39.67-28.54	31.46-18.58	21.50-15.75
P/E Ratio	12.2-5.0	17.4-6.7	27.0-15.8	18.7-14.0	15.5-11.1	14.5-8.6	11.8-8.7
Average Yield %	6.1	4.7	3.5	3.8	4.1	4.6	5.1

Statistics are as originally reported. Adj. for 3-for-1 stk. split, 4/97 [1] Incls. pre-tax non-recurr. chrg. 12/31/98, $3.38 bill.; 12/31/97, $1.46 bill. [2] Bef. acctg. change chrg. 12/31/95, $28.0 mill. [3] Incls. one-time chrgs. of $476.0 mill. for separation programs. [4] Incls. pre-tax gain of $139.0 mill. on sale of a French confectionery business & $100.0 mill. gain on sale of beer rights.

OFFICERS:
G. C. Bible, Chmn., C.E.O.
L. C. Camilleri, Sr. V.P., C.F.O.
C. R. Wall, Sr. V.P., Gen. Counsel

INVESTOR CONTACT: Nicholas M. Rolli, (917) 663-3460

PRINCIPAL OFFICE: 120 Park Avenue, New York, NY 10017

TELEPHONE NUMBER: (917) 663-5000
WEB: www.philipmorris.com

NO. OF EMPLOYEES: 178,000 (approx.)

SHAREHOLDERS: 139,700 (approx.)

ANNUAL MEETING: In Apr.

INCORPORATED: VA, Mar., 1985

INSTITUTIONAL HOLDINGS:
No. of Institutions: 799
Shares Held: 1,324,088,497
% Held: 60.0

INDUSTRY: Cigarettes (SIC: 2111)

TRANSFER AGENT(S): First Chicago Trust Company, Jersey City, NJ

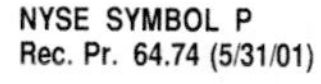
NYSE SYMBOL P
Rec. Pr. 64.74 (5/31/01)

PHILLIPS PETROLEUM COMPANY

YIELD 2.1%
P/E RATIO 8.9

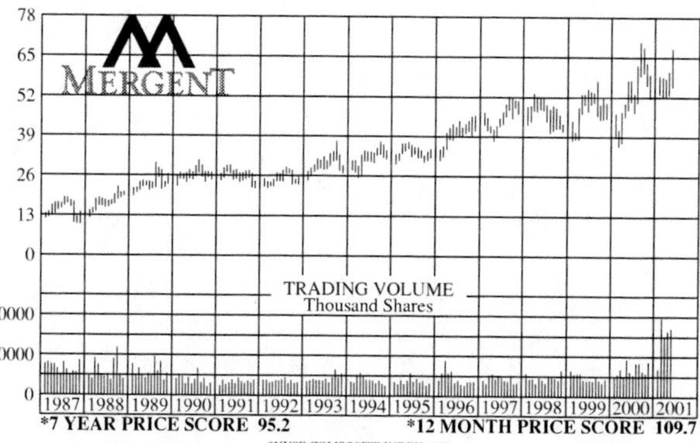

*7 YEAR PRICE SCORE 95.2 *12 MONTH PRICE SCORE 109.7

*NYSE COMPOSITE INDEX=100

INTERIM EARNINGS (Per Share):

Qtr.	Mar.	June	Sept.	Dec.
1996	2.65	0.84	0.71	0.76
1997	0.86	1.17	0.82	0.79
1998	0.92	0.58	0.18	d0.83
1999	0.28	0.27	0.87	0.98
2000	0.98	1.73	1.66	2.88

INTERIM DIVIDENDS (Per Share):

Amt.	Decl.	Ex.	Rec.	Pay.
0.34Q	4/10/00	4/27/00	5/01/00	6/01/00
0.34Q	7/10/00	7/27/00	7/31/00	9/01/00
0.34Q	10/09/00	10/26/00	10/30/00	12/01/00
0.34Q	2/12/01	2/16/01	2/21/01	3/01/01
0.34Q	4/09/01	4/26/01	4/30/01	6/01/01

Indicated div.: $1.36 (Div. Reinv. Plan)

CAPITALIZATION (12/31/00):

	($000)	(%)
Long-Term Debt	6,622,000	42.8
Deferred Income Tax	1,894,000	12.2
Redeemable Pfd. Stock	650,000	4.2
Common & Surplus	6,305,000	40.8
Total	15,471,000	100.0

RECENT DEVELOPMENTS: For the twelve months ended 12/31/00, net income soared to $1.86 billion compared with $609.0 million in the corresponding year-earlier period. Results for 2000 included a non-recurring charge of $54.0 million. Results for 1999 included a non-recurring gain of $61.0 million. Earnings were driven by higher crude oil production, improved crude oil and natural gas prices, and better margins. Revenues rose 53.2% to $21.23 billion from $13.85 billion the previous year.

PROSPECTS: On 4/11/01, P's shareholders voted to approve the proposed acquisition of Tosco Corporation, which is expected to close by 9/30/01. Going forward, P will continue to build on its worldwide strategy of expanding its exploration and production portfolio, with a focus on legacy assets, which the Company defines as very large oil and gas resources that can produce revenue for many years at competitive operating costs. On 1/2/01, P completed the sale of certain of its Canadian properties to Apache Corporation for $490.0 million.

BUSINESS

PHILLIPS PETROLEUM COMPANY, with assets of $20.51 billion at 12/31/00, is involved primarily in petroleum and chemicals operations. Through its exploration and production segment, P explores for and produces crude oil, natural gas and natural gas liquids worldwide. Gas gathering, processing and marketing operations gather and process natural gas from outside parties as well as natural gas produced from its own reserves, located primarily in Oklahoma, Texas and New Mexico. The refining, marketing and transportation segment fractionates natural gas liquids and refines, markets and transports crude oil and petroleum products primarily in the U.S. The chemical division manufactures and markets a broad range of petroleum-based chemical products worldwide. P completed the acquisition of Atlantic Richfield Company's (ARCO) Alaskan businesses on 8/1/00 for approximately $6.90 billion.

ANNUAL FINANCIAL DATA

	12/31/00	12/31/99	12/31/98	12/31/97	12/31/96	12/31/95	12/31/94
Earnings Per Share	**[4] 7.26**	**[3] 2.39**	**[2] 0.91**	**[1] 3.61**	**[1] 4.96**	**[1] 1.79**	**1.85**
Cash Flow Per Share	**11.86**	**5.94**	**5.92**	**6.88**	**8.53**	**5.11**	**4.88**
Tang. Book Val. Per Share	**22.26**	**16.13**	**16.35**	**18.30**	**16.16**	**12.17**	**11.27**
Dividends Per Share	**1.36**	**1.36**	**1.36**	**1.34**	**1.25**	**1.20**	**1.12**
Dividend Payout %	**18.7**	**56.9**	**149.4**	**37.1**	**25.2**	**66.8**	**60.5**
INCOME STATEMENT (IN MILLIONS):							
Total Revenues	21,227.0	13,852.0	11,845.0	15,424.0	15,807.0	13,521.0	12,367.0
Costs & Expenses	15,699.0	11,331.0	9,915.0	12,462.0	13,001.0	11,289.0	10,459.0
Depreciation & Amort.	1,179.0	902.0	1,302.0	863.0	941.0	871.0	794.0
Operating Income	4,349.0	1,619.0	628.0	2,099.0	1,865.0	1,361.0	1,114.0
Net Interest Inc./(Exp.)	d369.0	d279.0	d200.0	d198.0	d217.0	d265.0	d250.0
Income Before Income Taxes	3,769.0	1,185.0	421.0	1,900.0	2,172.0	1,064.0	852.0
Income Taxes	1,907.0	576.0	184.0	941.0	869.0	595.0	368.0
Net Income	[4] 1,862.0	[3] 609.0	[2] 237.0	[1] 959.0	[1] 1,303.0	[1] 469.0	484.0
Cash Flow	3,041.0	1,511.0	1,539.0	1,822.0	2,244.0	1,340.0	1,278.0
Average Shs. Outstg. (000)	256,326	254,433	260,152	265,000	263,000	262,000	262,000
BALANCE SHEET (IN MILLIONS):							
Cash & Cash Equivalents	149.0	138.0	97.0	163.0	615.0	67.0	193.0
Total Current Assets	2,606.0	2,773.0	2,349.0	2,648.0	3,306.0	2,409.0	2,465.0
Net Property	14,784.0	11,086.0	10,585.0	10,022.0	9,120.0	8,493.0	8,042.0
Total Assets	20,509.0	15,201.0	14,216.0	13,860.0	13,548.0	11,978.0	11,436.0
Total Current Liabilities	3,492.0	2,520.0	2,132.0	2,445.0	3,137.0	2,815.0	2,441.0
Long-Term Obligations	6,622.0	4,271.0	4,106.0	2,775.0	2,555.0	3,097.0	3,106.0
Net Stockholders' Equity	6,305.0	4,549.0	4,219.0	4,814.0	4,251.0	3,188.0	2,953.0
Net Working Capital	d886.0	253.0	217.0	203.0	169.0	d406.0	24.0
Year-end Shs. Outstg. (000)	283,239	281,971	258,000	263,000	263,000	262,000	262,000
STATISTICAL RECORD:							
Operating Profit Margin %	20.5	11.7	5.3	13.6	11.8	10.1	9.0
Net Profit Margin %	8.8	4.4	2.0	6.2	8.2	3.5	3.9
Return on Equity %	29.5	13.4	5.6	19.9	30.7	14.7	16.4
Return on Assets %	9.1	4.0	1.7	6.9	9.6	3.9	4.2
Debt/Total Assets %	32.3	28.1	28.9	20.0	18.9	25.9	27.2
Price Range	70.00-35.94	57.25-37.69	53.25-40.19	52.25-37.38	45.88-31.13	37.13-29.88	37.25-25.50
P/E Ratio	9.6-5.0	24.0-15.8	58.5-44.2	14.5-10.4	9.2-6.3	20.7-16.7	20.1-13.8
Average Yield %	2.6	2.9	2.9	3.0	3.2	3.6	3.6

Statistics are as originally reported. [1] Incls. non-recurr. credit 12/31/97, $412.0 mill.; chrgs. 12/31/96, $412.0 mill.; chrg. 12/31/95, $49.0 mill.; credit 12/31/90, $139.0 mill. [2] Incls. non-recurr. net chrgs. of $138.0 mill. [3] Incls. one-time gain of $61.0 mill. [4] Incl. non-recurr. chrg. of $54.0 mill.

OFFICERS:
J. J. Mulva, Chmn., C.E.O.
J. B. Whitworth, Exec. V.P., Gen. Counsel
J. A. Carrig, Sr. V.P., C.F.O., Treas.

INVESTOR CONTACT: Howard Thill, V.P., Investor Relations, (918) 661-4757

PRINCIPAL OFFICE: Phillips Building, Bartlesville, OK 74004

TELEPHONE NUMBER: (918) 661-6600
FAX: (918) 661-7636
WEB: www.phillips66.com

NO. OF EMPLOYEES: 12,400

SHAREHOLDERS: 48,200

ANNUAL MEETING: In May

INCORPORATED: DE, June, 1917

INSTITUTIONAL HOLDINGS:
No. of Institutions: 461
Shares Held: 185,120,348
% Held: 72.5

INDUSTRY: Petroleum refining (SIC: 2911)

TRANSFER AGENT(S): Mellon Investor Services, Ridgefield, NJ

NYSE SYMBOL PVH
Rec. Pr. 15.00 (4/30/01)

PHILLIPS-VAN HEUSEN CORPORATION

YIELD 1.0%
P/E RATIO 13.6

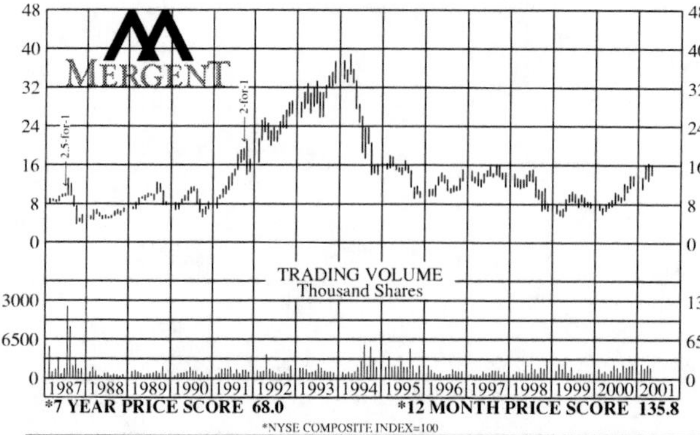

*7 YEAR PRICE SCORE 68.0 *12 MONTH PRICE SCORE 135.8

*NYSE COMPOSITE INDEX=100

INTERIM EARNINGS (Per Share):

Qtr.	Apr.	July	Oct.	Jan.
1996-97	d0.24	0.08	0.56	0.29
1997-98	d0.17	d1.23	0.54	0.20
1998-99	d0.16	0.10	0.51	0.02
1999-00	d0.17	0.13	0.56	0.10
2000-01	d0.07	0.22	0.71	0.24

INTERIM DIVIDENDS (Per Share):

Amt.	Decl.	Ex.	Rec.	Pay.
0.037Q	4/27/00	5/31/00	6/02/00	6/19/00
0.037Q	8/01/00	8/23/00	8/25/00	9/08/00
0.037Q	11/01/00	11/15/00	11/17/00	12/08/00
0.037Q	3/07/01	3/15/01	3/19/01	3/29/01
0.037Q	4/24/01	5/24/01	5/29/01	6/15/01

Indicated div.: $0.15

CAPITALIZATION (2/4/01):

	($000)	(%)
Long-Term Debt	248,851	48.1
Common & Surplus	268,561	51.9
Total	517,412	100.0

RECENT DEVELOPMENTS: For the year ended 2/4/01, net income improved 78.4% to $30.1 million from $16.9 million in the prior year. Total net sales were $1.46 billion, an increase of 14.5% versus $1.27 billion a year earlier. Apparel net sales jumped 20.9% to $1.07 billion versus $885.8 million in the previous year. Footwear and related products net sales declined slightly to $384.5 million compared with $385.7 million the year before. Gross profit as a percentage of total net sales declined to 34.7% compared with 35.5% in the previous year.

PROSPECTS: In 2001, results should continue to benefit from the acquisitions of the Arrow and Kenneth Cole licenses in July 2000. In addition, the Company anticipates continued earnings and sales increases from both the Dress Shirt and Sportswear businesses. Also, the Company believes that product and marketing initiatives currently in place should boost earnings growth. As a result, the Company expects full year revenue growth of 4.0% to 5.0% and net income per share in the range of $1.24 to $1.28.

BUSINESS

PHILLIPS-VAN HEUSEN CORPORATION is a vertically-integrated manufacturer and marketer of a broad range of men's and women's apparel and women's and children's footwear. The Company's products include shirts, sweaters and shoes and, to a lesser extent, neckwear, furnishings, bottoms, outerwear and leather and canvas accessories. PVH's brands includes Van Heusen®; Bass®, men's, women's and children's casual footwear; Geoffrey Beene®, designer dress shirt label; and three sportswear brands, IZOD®, Van Heusen® and Geoffrey Beene®. In addition, PVH licenses DKNY®, Kenneth Cole®, Arrow®, FUBU® and Regis™ by the Van Heusen Company and John Henry® for dress shirts and Arrow® for sportswear. In 2000-01, sales (operating profit) were: 74% (81%), apparel; and 26% (19%), footwear. In 2/99, PVH sold its Gant apparel brand.

REVENUES

(02/04/2001)	($000)	(%)
Apparel	1,071	73.6
Footwear & Related Prods	385	26.4
Total	1,456	100.0

ANNUAL FINANCIAL DATA

	2/4/01	1/30/00	1/31/99	2/1/98	2/2/97	1/28/96	1/29/95
Earnings Per Share	**1.10**	**1 0.62**	**1 2 0.47**	**1 d2.46**	**0.69**	**1 0.01**	**1 1.11**
Cash Flow Per Share	**1.83**	**1.33**	**1.40**	**d1.52**	**1.55**	**0.99**	**1.81**
Tang. Book Val. Per Share	**5.67**	**5.79**	**4.23**	**3.82**	**6.28**	**5.76**	**9.69**
Dividends Per Share	**0.15**	**0.15**	**0.15**	**0.15**	**0.15**	**0.19**	**0.15**
Dividend Payout %	**13.6**	**24.2**	**31.9**	**...**	**21.7**	**1,856.4**	**13.5**
INCOME STATEMENT (IN MILLIONS):							
Total Revenues	1,455.5	1,271.5	1,303.1	1,350.0	1,359.6	1,464.1	1,255.5
Costs & Expenses	1,365.0	1,203.8	1,234.2	1,411.9	1,288.6	1,417.4	1,186.7
Depreciation & Amort.	20.1	19.4	25.4	25.3	23.3	26.2	19.0
Operating Income	70.5	48.3	43.5	d87.2	47.7	20.6	49.7
Net Interest Inc./(Exp.)	d22.3	d22.4	d26.1	d20.7	d23.2	d23.2	d12.8
Income Before Income Taxes	48.2	25.9	17.4	d107.8	24.6	d2.6	36.9
Income Taxes	18.1	9.0	4.5	cr41.2	6.0	cr2.9	6.9
Net Income	30.1	1 16.9	1 2 12.9	1 d66.6	18.5	1 0.3	1 30.0
Cash Flow	50.2	36.3	38.3	d41.3	41.8	26.5	49.0
Average Shs. Outstg. (000)	27,428	27,289	27,312	27,108	27,004	26,726	27,154
BALANCE SHEET (IN MILLIONS):							
Cash & Cash Equivalents	20.2	94.8	11.0	11.7	11.6	17.5	80.5
Total Current Assets	436.4	426.0	368.0	385.0	363.0	444.7	429.7
Net Property	123.6	106.1	108.8	94.6	137.1	143.4	136.3
Total Assets	724.4	673.7	674.3	660.5	657.4	749.1	596.3
Total Current Liabilities	138.1	124.6	132.7	274.2	122.3	183.1	114.0
Long-Term Obligations	248.9	248.8	248.7	100.1	189.4	229.5	169.7
Net Stockholders' Equity	268.6	241.7	228.9	220.3	290.2	275.3	275.5
Net Working Capital	298.3	301.4	235.3	110.8	240.7	261.5	315.6
Year-end Shs. Outstg. (000)	27,403	27,290	27,288	27,179	27,046	26,979	26,610
STATISTICAL RECORD:							
Operating Profit Margin %	4.8	3.8	3.3	...	3.5	1.4	4.0
Net Profit Margin %	2.1	1.3	1.0	...	1.4	...	2.4
Return on Equity %	11.2	7.0	5.6	...	6.4	0.1	10.9
Return on Assets %	4.2	2.5	1.9	...	2.8	...	5.0
Debt/Total Assets %	34.4	36.9	36.9	15.2	28.8	30.6	28.5
Price Range	13.88-5.81	10.63-5.38	15.13-6.50	15.88-11.50	15.13-9.50	18.00-9.13	39.00-14.00
P/E Ratio	12.6-5.3	17.1-8.7	32.2-13.8	...	21.9-13.8	1,782.2-903.5	35.1-12.6
Average Yield %	1.5	1.9	1.4	1.1	1.2	1.4	0.6

Statistics are as originally reported. 1 Incl. non-recurr. chrg. 1/30/00, $8.5 mill.; 1/31/99, $8.5 mill.; 2/1/98, $86.7 mill.; 1/28/96, $27.0 mill.; 1/29/95, $7.0 mill. 2 Bef. extraord. chrg. 1/31/99, $1.1 mill.; 1/30/94, $11.4 mill.

OFFICERS:
B. J. Klatsky, Chmn., C.E.O.
A. E. Sirkin, Vice-Chmn.
M. J. Blitzer, Vice-Chmn.
M. Weber, Pres., C.O.O.

PRINCIPAL OFFICE: 200 Madison Avenue, New York, NY 10016

TELEPHONE NUMBER: (212) 381-3500
FAX: (212) 247-5309
WEB: www.pvh.com
NO. OF EMPLOYEES: 6,600 (approx.)
SHAREHOLDERS: 1,216 (approx.)
ANNUAL MEETING: In June
INCORPORATED: NY, July, 1914; reincorp., DE, April, 1976

INSTITUTIONAL HOLDINGS:
No. of Institutions: 107
Shares Held: 18,610,296
% Held: 67.7

INDUSTRY: Men's & boys' clothing stores (SIC: 5611)

TRANSFER AGENT(S): The Bank of New York, New York, NY

NYSE SYMBOL PNY
Rec. Pr. 35.55 (4/30/01)

PIEDMONT NATURAL GAS COMPANY, INC.

YIELD 4.3%
P/E RATIO 16.2

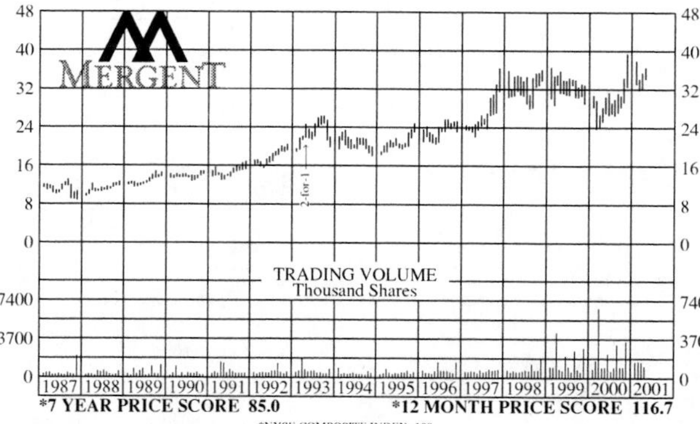

*7 YEAR PRICE SCORE 85.0 *12 MONTH PRICE SCORE 116.7

*NYSE COMPOSITE INDEX=100

INTERIM EARNINGS (Per Share):

Qtr.	Jan.	Apr.	July	Oct.
1997-98	1.36	1.17	d0.20	d0.35
1998-99	1.32	1.12	d0.26	d0.28
1999-00	1.40	1.18	d0.32	d0.23
2000-01	1.56	...	...	...

INTERIM DIVIDENDS (Per Share):

Amt.	Decl.	Ex.	Rec.	Pay.
0.365Q	6/02/00	6/21/00	6/23/00	7/14/00
0.365Q	8/25/00	9/20/00	9/22/00	10/13/00
0.365Q	12/08/00	12/20/00	12/22/00	1/12/01
0.385Q	2/23/01	3/20/01	3/22/01	4/12/01
0.385Q	6/01/01	6/20/01	6/22/01	7/13/01

Indicated div.: $1.54 (Div. Reinv. Plan)

CAPITALIZATION (10/31/00):

	($000)	(%)
Long-Term Debt	451,000	40.1
Deferred Income Tax	145,070	12.9
Common & Surplus	527,372	46.9
Total	1,123,442	100.0

RECENT DEVELOPMENTS: For the three months ended 1/31/01, net income advanced 14.1% to $50.3 million compared with $44.1 million in the corresponding period of the previous year. The increase in earnings was attributed to continued growth in the utility customer base and an increase in income from non-utility operations. Operating revenues soared 74.0% to $467.6 million from $268.6 million in 2000.

PROSPECTS: The Company filed for approval from the North Carolina Utilities Commission to lower its rates for residential natural gas service by 7.0%, as a result of decreases in its wholesale cost of gas. Separately, on 12/29/00, the Company announced it completed its purchase of the natural gas distribution system serving Gaffney, South Carolina from Atmos Energy Corporation for approximately $6.6 million.

BUSINESS

PIEDMONT NATURAL GAS COMPANY, INC. is engaged in the transportation, distribution and sale of natural gas to over 660,000 residential, commercial and industrial customers in Georgia, North Carolina, South Carolina and Tennessee. Non-utility subsidiaries and divisions are involved in the exploration, development, marketing and transportation of natural gas, oil, and propane. PNY's utility operations are subject to regulation by the North Carolina Utilities Commission, the Tennessee Public Service Commission and the Public Service Commission of South Carolina. PNY also owns Tennessee Natural Resources, Inc., and its subsidiaries. In 2000, revenues were derived as follows: 41.4% residential, 24.9% commercial, 24.3% industrial, 8.9% secondary market sales, and 0.5% other.

ANNUAL FINANCIAL DATA

	10/31/00	10/31/99	10/31/98	10/31/97	10/31/96	10/31/95	10/31/94
Earnings Per Share	**2.01**	**1.86**	**1.96**	**[1] 1.81**	**1.67**	**1.45**	**1.35**
Cash Flow Per Share	**3.65**	**3.40**	**3.46**	**3.26**	**3.04**	**2.73**	**2.42**
Tang. Book Val. Per Share	**16.52**	**15.71**	**14.91**	**13.90**	**13.07**	**12.31**	**11.36**
Dividends Per Share	**1.44**	**1.36**	**1.28**	**1.21**	**1.15**	**1.09**	**1.02**
Dividend Payout %	**71.6**	**73.1**	**65.3**	**66.6**	**68.6**	**74.8**	**75.9**
INCOME STATEMENT (IN THOUSANDS):							
Total Revenues	830,377	686,470	765,277	775,517	685,055	505,223	575,354
Costs & Expenses	637,553	492,904	576,050	599,982	526,934	365,279	456,031
Depreciation & Amort.	52,090	47,917	46,113	43,441	40,107	35,712	28,366
Maintenance Exp.	17,059	15,562	14,708	16,160	15,776	16,409	15,526
Operating Income	89,700	91,722	91,157	83,986	74,629	65,312	55,870
Net Interest Inc./(Exp.)	d40,272	d32,371	d33,187	d33,996	d31,067	d29,478	d24,541
Income Taxes	33,975	38,365	37,249	31,948	27,609	22,511	19,561
Net Income	64,031	58,207	60,313	[1] 54,074	48,562	40,310	35,506
Cash Flow	116,121	106,124	106,426	97,515	88,669	76,022	63,872
Average Shs. Outstg.	31,779	31,242	30,717	29,883	29,161	27,890	26,346
BALANCE SHEET (IN THOUSANDS):							
Gross Property	1,533,962	1,441,322	1,345,925	1,256,772	1,168,448	1,074,666	978,218
Accumulated Depreciation	462,955	420,140	381,585	342,418	306,419	273,350	243,325
Net Property	1,071,983	1,046,975	990,640	941,736	889,101	827,615	760,081
Total Assets	1,445,003	1,288,657	1,162,844	1,098,156	1,064,916	964,895	887,770
Long-Term Obligations	451,000	423,000	371,000	381,000	391,000	361,000	313,000
Net Stockholders' Equity	527,372	491,747	458,268	419,826	386,091	354,979	301,992
Year-end Shs. Outstg.	31,914	31,295	30,738	30,193	29,549	28,835	26,577
STATISTICAL RECORD:							
Operating Profit Margin %	10.8	13.4	11.9	10.8	10.9	12.9	9.7
Net Profit Margin %	7.7	8.5	7.9	7.0	7.1	8.0	6.2
Net Inc./Net Property %	6.0	5.6	6.1	5.7	5.5	4.9	4.7
Net Inc./Tot. Capital %	5.7	5.6	6.4	6.0	5.6	5.0	5.2
Return on Equity %	12.1	11.8	13.2	12.9	12.6	11.4	11.8
Accum. Depr./Gross Prop. %	30.2	29.1	28.4	27.2	26.2	25.4	24.9
Price Range	39.44-23.69	36.63-28.63	36.13-27.88	36.44-22.00	25.75-20.50	24.88-18.25	23.38-18.00
P/E Ratio	19.6-11.8	19.7-15.4	18.4-14.2	20.1-12.2	15.4-12.3	17.2-12.6	17.3-13.3
Average Yield %	4.6	4.2	4.0	4.1	5.0	5.0	5.0

Statistics are as originally reported. [1] Incl. pre-tax restruct. chg. of $1.8 mill.

OFFICERS:
J. H. Maxheim, Chmn., C.E.O.
W. F. Schiefer, Pres., C.O.O.
T. C. Coble, V.P., Treas., Asst. Sec.

INVESTOR CONTACT: Headen B. Thomas, Dir. Inv. Rel., (704) 364-3120 ext.6438

PRINCIPAL OFFICE: 1915 Rexford Road, Charlotte, NC 28211

TELEPHONE NUMBER: (704) 364-3120
FAX: (704) 365-8515
WEB: www.piedmontng.com

NO. OF EMPLOYEES: 1,603

SHAREHOLDERS: 17,176

ANNUAL MEETING: In Feb.

INCORPORATED: NY, May, 1950; reincorp., NC, Mar., 1994

INSTITUTIONAL HOLDINGS:
No. of Institutions: 143
Shares Held: 9,757,080
% Held: 30.4

INDUSTRY: Natural gas distribution (SIC: 4924)

TRANSFER AGENT(S): Wachovia Bank of North Carolina, NA, Boston, MA

NYSE SYMBOL PIR
Rec. Pr. 11.75 (5/31/01)

PIER 1 IMPORTS, INC.

YIELD 1.4%
P/E RATIO 12.1

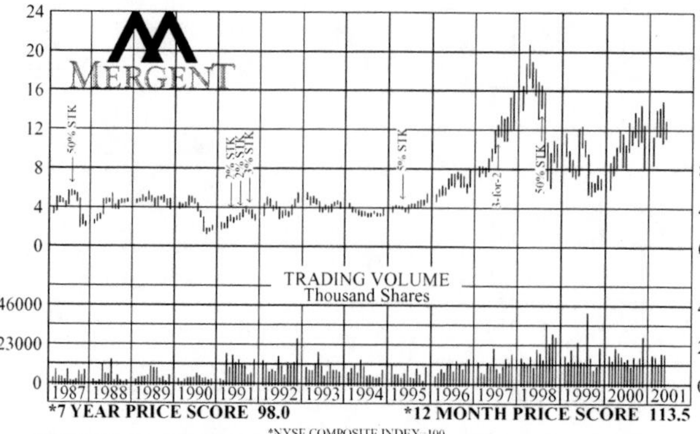

INTERIM EARNINGS (Per Share):

Qtr.	May	Aug.	Nov.	Feb.
1996-97	0.09	0.11	0.10	0.17
1997-98	0.13	0.21	0.16	0.24
1998-99	0.15	0.17	0.19	0.27
1999-00	0.13	0.12	0.16	0.34
2000-01	0.17	0.18	0.24	0.38

INTERIM DIVIDENDS (Per Share):

Amt.	Decl.	Ex.	Rec.	Pay.
0.03Q	3/16/00	5/01/00	5/03/00	5/17/00
0.04Q	6/22/00	8/14/00	8/16/00	8/30/00
0.04Q	9/26/00	10/30/00	11/01/00	11/15/00
0.04Q	12/08/00	1/29/01	1/31/01	2/14/01
0.04Q	3/29/01	4/30/01	5/02/01	5/16/01

Indicated div.: $0.16 (Div. Reinv. Plan)

CAPITALIZATION (2/26/00):

	($000)	(%)
Long-Term Debt	25,000	5.4
Common & Surplus	440,663	94.6
Total	465,663	100.0

RECENT DEVELOPMENTS: For the 53 weeks ended 3/3/01, net income advanced 26.7% to $94.7 million from $74.7 million in the corresponding 52-week period the year before. Net sales totaled $1.41 billion, up 14.7% compared with $1.23 billion a year earlier. Comparable-store sales increased 7.8% year over year. Cost of sales, including buying and store occupancy, grew 13.7% to $817.0 million from $718.5 million in the prior year. Operating income climbed 23.0% to $151.5 million from $123.2 million the previous year.

PROSPECTS: On 2/21/01, PIR completed its acquisition of Cargo Furniture, Inc. from Tandycrafts, Inc. for approximately $3.4 million. Cargo Furniture is a retailer of children's and casual-living furniture with 21 stores located in the Fort Worth/Dallas, Houston, Atlanta and Washington, D.C. markets. The Company plans to further develop the Cargo Furniture concept and open Cargo stores throughout North America. Going forward, PIR anticipates operating between 200 to 300 Cargo stores nationwide within the next ten years.

BUSINESS

PIER 1 IMPORTS, INC. is a retailer of decorative home furnishings, furniture, dining and kitchen goods, bath and bedding accessories and other specialty items for the home imported from over 60 countries. PIR operates over 850 stores in 48 states and Canada, with partnerships in Puerto Rico, Mexico and Japan. In addition, the Company owns 90% of the capital stock of The Pier Retail Group Limited, which operates 18 retail stores under the name "The Pier" in the United Kingdom. In 1993, PIR sold its 49.5% ownership interest in Sunbelt Nursery Group to General Host Corporation. In 1997, PIR acquired a national bank and its assets in Omaha, Nebraska, which operates under the name of Pier 1 National Bank and holds the credit card accounts for the Company's proprietary credit card.

ANNUAL FINANCIAL DATA

	2/26/00	2/27/99	2/28/98	3/1/97	3/2/96	2/25/95	2/26/94
Earnings Per Share	**0.75**	**0.77**	**[1] 0.72**	**[3] 0.49**	**[2] 0.11**	**[2] 0.28**	**[2] 0.07**
Cash Flow Per Share	**1.11**	**1.02**	**0.90**	**0.69**	**0.30**	**0.46**	**0.24**
Tang. Book Val. Per Share	**4.70**	**4.14**	**3.86**	**3.19**	**2.56**	**2.66**	**2.38**
Dividends Per Share	**0.12**	**0.11**	**0.08**	**0.07**	**0.05**	**0.04**	**0.04**
Dividend Payout %	**16.0**	**14.3**	**11.4**	**14.5**	**47.4**	**15.9**	**56.8**
INCOME STATEMENT (IN MILLIONS):							
Total Revenues	1,231.1	1,138.6	1,075.4	947.1	810.7	712.0	685.4
Costs & Expenses	1,067.9	972.8	929.7	837.1	720.8	640.4	642.5
Depreciation & Amort.	40.0	31.1	23.9	19.8	17.2	16.0	15.8
Operating Income	123.2	134.7	121.7	90.2	72.7	55.6	27.1
Net Interest Inc./(Exp.)	d6.9	d7.9	d8.7	d9.9	d13.8	d12.0	d16.8
Income Before Income Taxes	118.6	129.6	124.0	80.3	28.4	36.0	8.4
Income Taxes	43.9	49.3	46.0	32.1	18.4	11.2	2.4
Net Income	74.7	80.4	[1] 78.0	[3] 48.2	[2] 10.0	[2] 24.9	[2] 5.9
Cash Flow	114.7	111.5	102.0	68.0	27.3	40.8	21.7
Average Shs. Outstg. (000)	103,297	108,864	112,880	98,285	89,501	89,321	88,943
BALANCE SHEET (IN MILLIONS):							
Cash & Cash Equivalents	50.4	41.9	80.7	32.3	13.5	54.2	17.1
Total Current Assets	415.3	381.9	402.4	285.5	347.5	352.9	321.4
Net Property	213.0	226.3	216.3	216.8	144.6	105.6	111.5
Total Assets	670.7	654.0	653.4	570.3	531.1	488.7	463.3
Total Current Liabilities	176.0	129.8	121.6	110.4	100.7	85.1	92.4
Long-Term Obligations	25.0	96.0	114.9	111.3	180.1	154.4	145.2
Net Stockholders' Equity	440.7	403.9	392.7	323.0	227.9	225.2	201.1
Net Working Capital	239.3	252.1	280.8	175.1	246.8	267.8	229.0
Year-end Shs. Outstg. (000)	93,830	97,672	101,855	101,223	89,042	84,744	84,418
STATISTICAL RECORD:							
Operating Profit Margin %	10.0	11.8	11.3	9.5	9.0	7.8	4.0
Net Profit Margin %	6.1	7.1	7.3	5.1	1.2	3.5	0.9
Return on Equity %	17.0	19.9	19.9	14.9	4.4	11.0	3.0
Return on Assets %	11.1	12.3	11.9	8.5	1.9	5.1	1.3
Debt/Total Assets %	3.7	14.7	17.6	19.5	33.9	31.6	31.3
Price Range	12.38-5.25	20.75-6.06	15.96-7.22	7.95-4.61	5.50-3.45	4.50-3.02	5.56-3.49
P/E Ratio	16.5-7.0	26.9-7.9	22.2-10.0	16.2-9.4	49.5-31.0	16.1-10.8	82.8-52.0
Average Yield %	1.4	0.8	0.7	1.1	1.2	1.2	0.8

Statistics are as originally reported. Adj. for 3-for-2 stk. split, 7/98 & 7/97; & 5% stk. div., 5/95. [1] Incl. $9.1 mil ($0.08/sh) gain. [2] Incl. $9.6 mil non-recur. chg., 3/2/96; $7.5 mil non-cash chg., 2/25/95; & $21.3 mil non-recur. chg., 2/26/94. [3] Bef. $4.1 mil extraord. chg.

OFFICERS:
M. J. Girouard, Chmn., C.E.O.
C. H. Turner, Sr. V.P., C.F.O.
J. R. Lawrence, Sr. V.P., Sec.

INVESTOR CONTACT: Cary Turner, (817) 252-8400

PRINCIPAL OFFICE: 301 Commerce Street, Suite 600, Fort Worth, TX 76102

TELEPHONE NUMBER: (817) 252-8000
FAX: (817) 334-0191
WEB: www.pier1.com
NO. OF EMPLOYEES: 13,600 (approx.)
SHAREHOLDERS: 35,000 (approx.)
ANNUAL MEETING: In June
INCORPORATED: GA, May, 1978; reincorp., DE, Apr., 1979

INSTITUTIONAL HOLDINGS:
No. of Institutions: 199
Shares Held: 74,123,157
% Held: 77.3

INDUSTRY: Furniture stores (SIC: 5712)

TRANSFER AGENT(S): Mellon Investor Services, Ridgefield Park, NJ

NYSE SYMBOL PNK
Rec. Pr. 9.21 (5/31/01)

PINNACLE ENTERTAINMENT, INC.

YIELD . . .
P/E RATIO 3.2

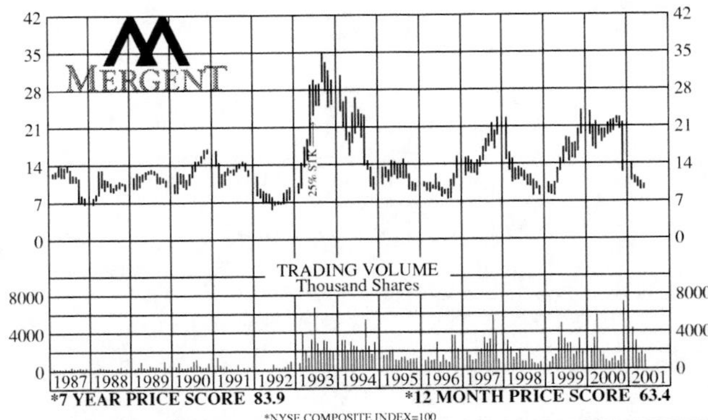

INTERIM EARNINGS (Per Share):

Qtr.	Mar.	June	Sept.	Dec.
1997	d0.07	0.27	d0.08	0.05
1998	d0.05	0.31	0.08	0.17
1999	0.16	0.37	0.98	0.15
2000	0.80	0.96	1.37	d0.23

INTERIM DIVIDENDS (Per Share):

Amt.	Decl.	Ex.	Rec.	Pay.

No dividends paid.

CAPITALIZATION (12/31/00):

	($000)	(%)
Long-Term Debt	497,162	57.3
Deferred Income Tax	9,762	1.1
Common & Surplus	361,176	41.6
Total	868,100	100.0

RECENT DEVELOPMENTS: For the year ended 12/31/00, PNK reported income of $79.5 million, before an extraordinary loss of $2.7 million, compared with net income of $44.0 million in the previous year. Results for 2000 and 1999 included net pre-tax nonrecurring income of $218.0 million and $196.1 million, respectively. Total revenues fell 17.3% to $584.6 million from $706.9 million a year earlier.

PROSPECTS: PNK remains on schedule with the sale of its remaining 97 acres of surplus land in Inglewood, California for approximately $63.0 million. Looking ahead, the Company expects total revenues in the range of $575.0 million and $600.0 million; net income between $15.00 million, or $0.55 per share, and $18.0 million, or $0.66 per share; and capital spending of about $55.0 million to $60.0 million in 2001.

BUSINESS

PINNACLE ENTERTAINMENT, INC. (formerly Hollywood Park, Inc.) is a diversified gaming company that owns and operates six casinos (three with hotels) in Nevada, Mississippi, Louisiana and Argentina, and receives lease income from two card club casinos, both in the Los Angeles metropolitan area. The Company also owns the Belterra Resort and Casino, a major hotel/casino complex in Southern Indiana, approximately 35 miles southwest of Cincinnati.

REVENUES

(12/31/2000)	($000)	(%)
Gaming	483,398	82.7
Food & Beverage	31,920	5.5
Hotel & Recreational	12,730	2.2
Truck Stop & Service Stations	21,782	3.7
Racing	9,452	1.6
Other Income	25,340	4.3
Total	584,622	100.0

ANNUAL FINANCIAL DATA

	12/31/00	12/31/99	12/31/98	12/31/97	12/31/96	12/31/95	12/31/94
Earnings Per Share	[5] **2.90**	[4] **1.67**	[3] **0.50**	[2] **0.32**	[1] **d0.33**	**d0.17**	**0.10**
Cash Flow Per Share	**4.57**	**3.65**	**1.73**	**1.13**	**0.31**	**0.53**	**0.76**
Tang. Book Val. Per Share	**8.89**	**4.92**	**3.01**	**7.18**	**7.51**	**7.48**	**8.79**
INCOME STATEMENT (IN THOUSANDS):							
Total Revenues	584,622	706,857	426,967	248,128	143,225	130,572	117,324
Costs & Expenses	485,432	552,790	348,122	208,152	133,031	116,262	95,895
Depreciation & Amort.	46,102	51,924	32,121	18,157	10,027	10,857	10,064
Operating Income	171,904	144,204	46,724	21,819	22,274	20,925	20,928
Net Interest Inc./(Exp.)	d40,016	d57,544	d22,518	d7,302	d942	d3,922	d3,061
Income Before Income Taxes	131,888	86,660	21,985	14,517	d775	d469	5,340
Income Taxes	52,396	40,926	8,442	5,850	3,459	693	1,568
Equity Earnings/Minority Int.	. . .	d1,687	d374	3	d15	. . .	. . .
Net Income	[5] 79,492	[4] 44,047	[3] 13,169	[2] 8,670	[1] d4,249	d1,162	3,772
Cash Flow	125,594	95,971	45,290	25,307	3,853	7,770	11,911
Average Shs. Outstg.	27,456	26,329	26,115	22,340	18,505	18,399	18,224
BALANCE SHEET (IN THOUSANDS):							
Cash & Cash Equivalents	172,868	246,790	47,413	24,156	21,174	31,979	37,821
Total Current Assets	224,857	437,474	100,148	60,206	40,959	48,641	65,996
Net Property	593,718	437,715	602,912	300,666	130,835	174,717	160,264
Total Assets	961,475	1,045,408	891,339	419,029	205,886	286,706	246,573
Total Current Liabilities	93,375	145,008	124,943	57,317	35,364	75,202	26,076
Long-Term Obligations	497,162	618,698	527,619	132,102	282	15,629	42,800
Net Stockholders' Equity	361,176	280,876	230,976	221,354	158,160	165,746	167,255
Net Working Capital	131,482	292,466	d24,795	2,889	5,595	d26,561	39,920
Year-end Shs. Outstg.	26,434	26,235	25,800	26,220	18,332	18,505	18,370
STATISTICAL RECORD:							
Operating Profit Margin %	29.4	20.4	10.9	8.8	15.6	16.0	17.8
Net Profit Margin %	13.6	6.2	3.1	3.5	. . .	. . .	3.2
Return on Equity %	22.0	15.7	5.7	3.9	. . .	. . .	2.3
Return on Assets %	8.3	4.2	1.5	2.1	. . .	. . .	1.5
Debt/Total Assets %	51.7	59.2	59.2	31.5	0.1	5.5	17.4
Price Range	23.81-12.38	24.06-8.00	22.63-8.00	22.75-11.75	15.50-7.50	15.00-9.00	30.75-9.25
P/E Ratio	8.2-4.3	14.4-4.8	45.2-16.0	71.1-36.7	. . .	. . .	307.2-92.4

Statistics are as originally reported. Adj. for 5-for-4 stk. split, 6/96. [1] Incl. a $2.5 mill. restr. chrg. & $11.4 mill. of HPK's investment in Sunflower Racing, Inc. [2] Incl. $609,000 on real estate investment trust restr. chrgs. [3] Incl. $2.2 mill. loss on write-off of assets & a $419,000 chrg. from the real estate investment trust restr. [4] Incl. $42.1 mill. gain on write-off of assets & pre-open. costs of $3.0 mill. [5] Bef. extraord. chrg. of $2.7 mill.; incl. a net pre-tax nonrecurr. gain of $218.0 mill.

OFFICERS:
R. D. Hubbard, Chmn.
P. R. Alanis, Pres., C.E.O.
B. C. Hinckley, Sr. V.P., C.F.O.
D. M. Robbins, Sec.

INVESTOR CONTACT: Bruce C. Hinkley, Sr. V.P. & C.F.O., (818) 662-5959

PRINCIPAL OFFICE: 330 North Brand Boulevard, Suite 1100, Glendale, CA 91203

TELEPHONE NUMBER: (818) 662-5900
FAX: (818) 662-5901
WEB: www.pinnacle-entertainment-inc.com

NO. OF EMPLOYEES: 6,748 (avg.)

SHAREHOLDERS: 3,056 (approx.)

ANNUAL MEETING: In Oct.

INCORPORATED: DE, 1981

INSTITUTIONAL HOLDINGS:
No. of Institutions: 78
Shares Held: 16,161,395
% Held: 62.0

INDUSTRY: Hotels and motels (SIC: 7011)

TRANSFER AGENT(S): Mellon Investor Services, Ridgefield Park, NJ

NYSE SYMBOL PNW
Rec. Pr. 50.19 (4/30/01)

PINNACLE WEST CAPITAL CORP.

YIELD 3.0%
P/E RATIO 14.1

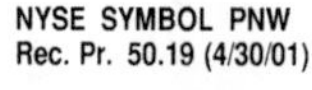

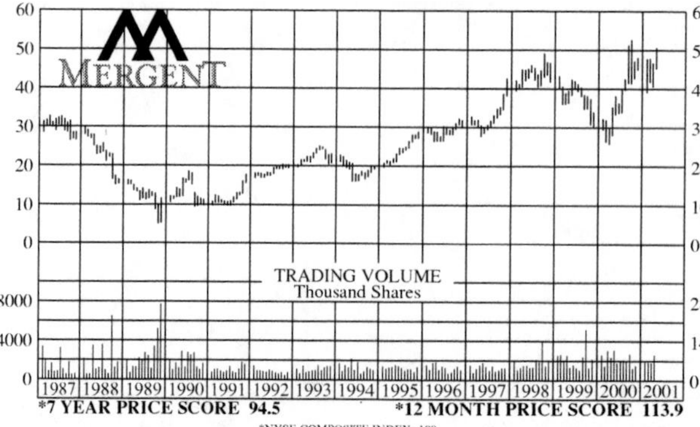

*7 YEAR PRICE SCORE 94.5 *12 MONTH PRICE SCORE 113.9

*NYSE COMPOSITE INDEX=100

INTERIM EARNINGS (Per Share):

Qtr.	Mar.	June	Sept.	Dec.
1996	0.36	0.67	0.67	0.71
1997	0.29	0.79	1.47	0.19
1998	0.36	0.57	1.49	0.42
1999	0.36	0.81	1.48	0.53
2000	0.64	1.06	1.37	0.50

INTERIM DIVIDENDS (Per Share):

Amt.	Decl.	Ex.	Rec.	Pay.
0.35Q	4/19/00	4/27/00	5/01/00	6/01/00
0.35Q	7/14/00	7/28/00	8/01/00	9/01/00
0.375Q	10/18/00	10/30/00	11/01/00	12/01/00
0.375Q	1/17/01	1/30/01	2/01/01	3/01/01
0.375Q	4/18/01	4/27/01	5/01/01	6/01/01

Indicated div.: $1.50 (Div. Reinv. Plan)

CAPITALIZATION (12/31/00):

	($000)	(%)
Long-Term Debt	1,955,083	35.7
Deferred Income Tax	1,143,040	20.9
Common & Surplus	2,382,714	43.5
Total	5,480,837	100.0

RECENT DEVELOPMENTS: For the year ended 12/31/00, the Company reported net income of $302.3 million compared with income from continuing operations of $269.8 million in the prior year. Earnings for 1999 excluded an extraordinary charge of $139.9 million and income tax benefit from discontinued operations of $38.0 million. Total operating revenues were $3.69 billion, an increase of 52.3% versus $2.42 billion a year earlier. Electric revenues climbed 54.0% to $3.53 billion, while real estate revenue rose 21.7% to $158.4 million.

PROSPECTS: Going forward, results may be dampened by volatile western energy markets and any associated market restructuring, which may affect future energy costs and prices. The Company will continue to focus on developments in the California energy markets and evaluate any potential impact on its financial position. Separately, PNW's agreements to acquire electrical generation at Palo Verde and Four Corners from Southern California Edison for $550.0 million, is pending approval from the California Public Utilities Commission.

BUSINESS

PINNACLE WEST CAPITAL CORP. is a holding company whose principal asset is Arizona Public Service (APS). APS is the state's largest utility with 827,000 customers, and provides wholesale and retail electric service to the entire state of Arizona, with the exception of Tucson and about one-half of the Phoenix area. The Company is engaged in the generation and distribution of electricity, real estate development, and venture capital investments. The Company also owns Suncor Development Company, a major real estate developer engaged in the owning, development, and sale of real estate property, including homebuilding, and El Dorado Investment, which makes equity investments in other companies.

ANNUAL FINANCIAL DATA

	12/31/00	12/31/99	12/31/98	12/31/97	12/31/96	12/31/95	12/31/94
Earnings Per Share	**3.56**	**[3] 3.17**	**2.85**	**2.74**	**[2] 2.41**	**[1] 2.28**	**2.30**
Cash Flow Per Share	**8.56**	**8.08**	**7.68**	**7.41**	**6.24**	**5.44**	**5.40**
Tang. Book Val. Per Share	**28.09**	**26.00**	**25.50**	**23.90**	**22.51**	**21.49**	**20.32**
Dividends Per Share	**1.43**	**1.32**	**1.23**	**1.13**	**1.02**	**0.93**	**0.82**
Dividend Payout %	**40.0**	**41.8**	**43.0**	**41.1**	**42.5**	**40.6**	**35.9**
INCOME STATEMENT (IN MILLIONS):							
Total Revenues	3,690.2	2,423.4	2,130.6	1,995.0	1,817.8	1,669.8	1,685.4
Costs & Expenses	2,589.7	1,427.6	1,150.9	1,035.7	939.1	831.1	880.0
Depreciation & Amort.	424.5	416.9	412.5	401.8	334.8	276.3	271.7
Operating Income	676.0	578.8	567.1	557.5	543.9	562.4	533.8
Net Interest Inc./(Exp.)	d149.6	d150.7	d150.5	d163.1	d185.7	d217.2	d239.6
Income Before Income Taxes	526.2	437.8	407.5	386.1	339.5	327.6	323.6
Income Taxes	223.9	168.1	164.6	150.3	128.5	128.0	123.0
Net Income	302.3	[3] 269.8	242.9	235.9	[2] 211.1	[1] 199.6	200.6
Cash Flow	726.8	686.7	655.4	637.7	545.9	475.9	472.3
Average Shs. Outstg. (000)	84,935	85,009	85,346	86,023	87,442	87,419	87,410
BALANCE SHEET (IN MILLIONS):							
Cash & Cash Equivalents	10.4	20.7	20.5	27.5	26.7	79.5	34.7
Total Current Assets	793.9	498.8	456.8	449.1	450.3	430.5	435.6
Net Property	5,133.2	4,778.5	4,730.6	4,677.6	4,655.1	4,647.1	4,624.1
Total Assets	7,149.2	6,608.5	6,824.5	6,850.4	6,989.3	6,997.1	6,909.8
Total Current Liabilities	1,191.3	495.5	640.2	523.7	550.6	504.5	530.8
Long-Term Obligations	1,955.1	2,206.1	2,049.0	2,244.2	2,372.1	2,510.7	2,588.5
Net Stockholders' Equity	2,382.7	2,205.7	2,163.4	2,027.4	1,970.3	1,881.1	1,776.4
Net Working Capital	d397.4	3.3	d183.4	d74.6	d100.3	d74.0	d95.3
Year-end Shs. Outstg. (000)	84,825	84,825	84,825	84,825	87,516	87,516	87,430
STATISTICAL RECORD:							
Operating Profit Margin %	18.3	23.9	26.6	27.9	29.9	33.7	31.7
Net Profit Margin %	8.2	11.1	11.4	11.8	11.6	12.0	11.9
Return on Equity %	12.7	12.2	11.2	11.6	10.7	10.6	11.3
Return on Assets %	4.2	4.1	3.6	3.4	3.0	2.9	2.9
Debt/Total Assets %	27.3	33.4	30.0	32.8	33.9	35.9	37.5
Price Range	52.69-25.69	43.38-30.19	49.25-39.38	42.75-27.63	32.25-26.25	28.88-19.63	22.88-16.00
P/E Ratio	14.8-7.2	13.7-9.5	17.3-13.8	15.6-10.1	13.4-10.9	12.7-8.6	9.9-7.0
Average Yield %	3.6	3.6	2.8	3.2	3.5	3.8	4.2

Statistics are as originally reported. [1] Bef. extraord. charge $11.6 mill. [2] Bef extraord. chrg. $31.9 mill fr. early retire. of debt & Bef. disc. opers. loss $9.5 mill. [3] Bef. income $38.0 mill. from disc. ops. & extraord. chrg. $139.9 mill.

OFFICERS:
W. J. Post, Chmn., C.E.O., Pres.
B. M. Gomez, Treas.
F. Widenmann, V.P., Sec.

PRINCIPAL OFFICE: 400 East Van Buren Street, P.O. Box 52132, Phoenix, AZ 85072-2132

TELEPHONE NUMBER: (602) 379-2500
FAX: (602) 379-2625
WEB: www.pinnaclewest.com

NO. OF EMPLOYEES: 7,534

SHAREHOLDERS: 39,847 (approx.)

ANNUAL MEETING: In May

INCORPORATED: AZ, Feb., 1985

INSTITUTIONAL HOLDINGS:
No. of Institutions: 226
Shares Held: 61,087,023
% Held: 72.1

INDUSTRY: Electric services (SIC: 4911)

TRANSFER AGENT(S): BankBoston, N.A., Boston, MA

NYSE SYMBOL PXD
Rec. Pr. 19.11 (4/30/01)

PIONEER NATURAL RESOURCES COMPANY

YIELD ...
P/E RATIO 11.6

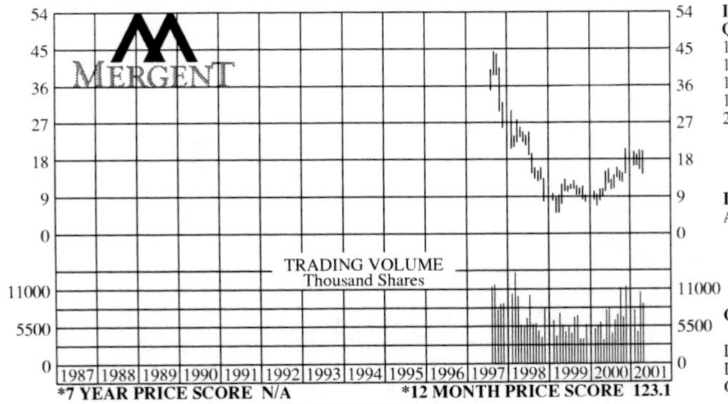

MERGENT

TRADING VOLUME
Thousand Shares

1987 1988 1989 1990 1991 1992 1993 1994 1995 1996 1997 1998 1999 2000 2001

***7 YEAR PRICE SCORE N/A** ***12 MONTH PRICE SCORE 123.1**

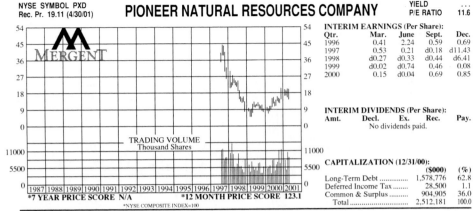

*NYSE COMPOSITE INDEX=100

INTERIM EARNINGS (Per Share):

Qtr.	Mar.	June	Sept.	Dec.
1996	0.41	2.24	0.59	0.69
1997	0.53	0.21	d0.18	d11.43
1998	d0.27	d0.33	d0.44	d6.41
1999	d0.02	d0.74	0.46	0.08
2000	0.15	d0.04	0.69	0.85

INTERIM DIVIDENDS (Per Share):

Amt.	Decl.	Ex.	Rec.	Pay.
No dividends paid.				

CAPITALIZATION (12/31/00):

	($000)	(%)
Long-Term Debt	1,578,776	62.8
Deferred Income Tax	28,500	1.1
Common & Surplus	904,905	36.0
Total	2,512,181	100.0

RECENT DEVELOPMENTS: For the year ended 12/31/00, income totaled $164.5 million, before a net extraordinary charge of $12.3 million, versus a net loss of $22.5 million in 1999. Results for 2000 included a net gain on the disposal of assets of $34.2 million. Results for 1999 included nonrecurring charges of $26.4 million. Total revenues rose 28.5% to $912.7 million from $710.1 million in 1999.

PROSPECTS: Looking forward, results should benefit from the development of the Canyon Express natural gas project in the deepwater Gulf of Mexico, with first production anticipated in mid-2002. The Company also expects to sanction the Devils Tower project and has budgeted capital to begin development during 2001 with first oil production expected in late 2002 or 2003.

BUSINESS

PIONEER NATURAL RESOURCES COMPANY is an independent oil and gas exploration and production company with principal operations located in Texas and Kansas. The Company also has exploration and development opportunities and oil and gas production activities in the U.S. Gulf Coast area, Gulf of Mexico, Argentina, Canada, South Africa and Gabon. Proved reserves as of 12/31/00 totaled 628.2 million barrels of oil equivalent, comprised of 312.3 million barrels of oil and natural gas liquids and 1.90 trillion cubic feet of natural gas. The Company was formed as a result of the 8/7/97 merger between Parker & Parsley Petroleum Company and MESA Inc.

REVENUES

(12/31/00)	($000)	(%)
Oil & Gas	852,738	93.4
Interest & Other	25,775	2.8
Disposition of Assets	34,184	3.8
Total	912,697	100.0

ANNUAL FINANCIAL DATA

	12/31/00	12/31/99	12/31/98	[1] 12/31/97	12/31/96	12/31/95	12/31/94
Earnings Per Share	[5] 1.65	[4] d0.22	[3] d7.46	[2] d16.88	3.92	[2] d2.95	d0.47
Cash Flow Per Share	3.82	2.13	d4.09	d11.86	7.06	1.56	4.37
Tang. Book Val. Per Share	8.94	7.72	7.87	15.33	15.12	11.62	...
Dividends Per Share	...	...	0.10	0.05	...	...	...
INCOME STATEMENT (IN MILLIONS):							
Total Revenues	912.7	710.1	721.5	546.0	535.3	513.7	496.2
Costs & Expenses	377.3	326.8	950.7	1,633.6	176.7	439.2	320.7
Depreciation & Amort.	214.9	236.0	337.3	212.4	112.1	159.1	145.4
Operating Income	320.5	147.3	d566.5	d1,300.0	246.5	d84.6	30.1
Net Interest Inc./(Exp.)	d162.0	d170.3	d164.3	d77.5	d46.2	d65.4	d50.6
Income Before Income Taxes	158.5	d23.1	d730.8	d1,377.6	200.3	d150.0	d20.5
Income Taxes	cr6.0	cr0.6	15.6	cr500.3	60.1	cr45.9	cr6.5
Net Income	[5] 164.5	[4] d22.5	[3] d746.4	[2] d877.3	140.2	[2] d104.1	d14.0
Cash Flow	379.4	213.6	d409.1	d664.8	252.4	55.0	131.4
Average Shs. Outstg. (000)	99,378	100,307	100,055	56,054	35,734	35,274	30,063
BALANCE SHEET (IN MILLIONS):							
Cash & Cash Equivalents	26.2	34.8	59.2	73.4	20.5	35.5	...
Total Current Assets	191.4	183.1	202.0	308.2	117.0	142.4	...
Net Property	2,540.6	2,546.0	3,089.1	3,559.9	1,068.2	1,153.5	...
Total Assets	2,954.4	2,929.5	3,481.3	3,946.6	1,199.9	1,319.2	...
Total Current Liabilities	216.5	196.8	526.8	261.6	91.0	110.9	...
Long-Term Obligations	1,578.8	1,745.1	1,868.7	1,943.7	320.9	586.5	...
Net Stockholders' Equity	904.9	774.6	789.1	1,548.8	530.3	411.0	...
Net Working Capital	d25.1	d13.7	d324.8	46.6	26.1	31.5	...
Year-end Shs. Outstg. (000)	101,269	100,340	100,296	101,037	35,066	35,383	...
STATISTICAL RECORD:							
Operating Profit Margin %	35.1	20.7	...	...	46.0	...	6.1
Net Profit Margin %	18.0	...	...	...	26.2	...	...
Return on Equity %	18.2	...	...	...	26.4	...	...
Return on Assets %	5.6	...	...	...	11.7	...	...
Debt/Total Assets %	53.4	59.6	53.7	49.3	26.7	44.5	...
Price Range	20.63-6.75	13.19-5.00	30.00-7.75	44.38-25.63	...	...	...
P/E Ratio	12.5-4.1	...	...	...	...	...	...
Average Yield %	...	...	0.5	0.1	...	...	...

Statistics are as originally reported. [1] Results prior to 12/31/97 refl. the ops. of Parker & Parsley Petroleum Company [2] Bef. extraord. chrg., 12/31/97, $13.4 mil.; cr. 12/31/95, $4.3 mil.; Incl. non-recur. pre-tax chrg. 12/31/97, $1.35 bil.; pre-tax chrg. 12/31/95, $130.5 mil. for impairmt. of oil & gas props. [3] Incl. non-recur. chrg. of $445,000 [4] Incl. non-recur. chrg. of $24.2 mil. [5] Bef. extraord. chrg. of $12.3 mil.; incl. net gain on disp. of assets of $34.2 mil.

OFFICERS:
S. D. Sheffield, Chmn., Pres., C.E.O.
T. L. Dove, Exec. V.P., C.F.O.
M. Withrow, Exec. V.P., Gen. Couns., Sec.

INVESTOR CONTACT: Susan Spratlen, Dir., Investor Relations, (972) 969-3583

PRINCIPAL OFFICE: 1400 Williams Square West, 5205 N. O'Connor Blvd., Irving, TX 75039

TELEPHONE NUMBER: (972) 444-9001
WEB: www.pioneernrc.com

NO. OF EMPLOYEES: 853

SHAREHOLDERS: 33,100 (approx.)

ANNUAL MEETING: In May

INCORPORATED: DE, Apr., 1997

INSTITUTIONAL HOLDINGS:
No. of Institutions: 162
Shares Held: 67,397,223
% Held: 68.5

INDUSTRY: Crude petroleum and natural gas (SIC: 1311)

TRANSFER AGENT(S): Continental Stock Transfer & Trust Company, New York, NY

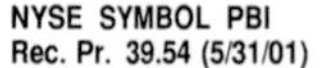

NYSE SYMBOL PBI
Rec. Pr. 39.54 (5/31/01)

PITNEY BOWES INC.

YIELD 2.9%
P/E RATIO 16.5

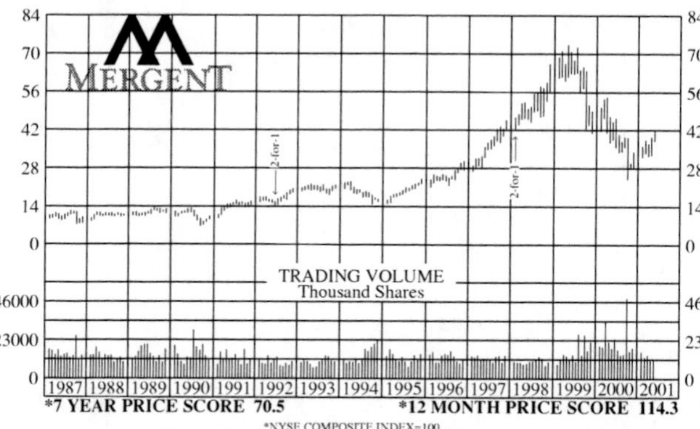

INTERIM EARNINGS (Per Share):

Qtr.	Mar.	June	Sept.	Dec.
1997	0.41	0.45	0.44	0.51
1998	0.46	0.51	0.50	0.59
1999	0.52	0.58	0.69	0.66
2000	0.57	0.64	0.63	0.55

INTERIM DIVIDENDS (Per Share):

Amt.	Decl.	Ex.	Rec.	Pay.
0.285Q	7/10/00	8/23/00	8/25/00	9/12/00
0.285Q	10/02/00	11/21/00	11/24/00	12/12/00
0.29Q	1/30/01	2/22/01	2/26/01	3/12/01
0.29Q	4/11/01	5/23/01	5/25/01	6/12/01

Indicated div.: $1.16 (Div. Reinv. Plan)

CAPITALIZATION (12/31/00):

	($000)	(%)
Long-Term Debt	1,881,947	40.0
Deferred Income Tax	1,226,597	26.1
Redeemable Pfd. Stock	310,000	6.6
Preferred Stock	1,766	0.0
Common & Surplus	1,283,209	27.3
Total	4,703,519	100.0

RECENT DEVELOPMENTS: For the year ended 12/31/00, income from continuing operations totaled $563.1 million compared with income from continuing operations of $563.0 million the year before. Total revenue rose 1.8% to $3.88 billion from $3.81 billion a year earlier. Total Messaging Solutions revenue grew 2.7% to $3.70 billion, while Capital Services revenue slid 12.9% to $183.1 million. Comparisons were made with restated prior-year results.

PROSPECTS: The Company plans to spin off its U.S. and U.K. office systems operations to shareholders as an independent, publicly-traded company. The transaction is expected to be completed by the end of the third quarter of 2001. Long-term results could benefit from the implementation of initiatives focused on streamlining the Company's operations and increasing efficiencies.

BUSINESS

PITNEY BOWES INC. and its subsidiaries operate within three industry segments: Global Mailing, Enterprise Solutions, and Capital Services. Global Mailing, 73% of 2000 revenue (86% of operating profit), includes the sale, rental, and financing of mail finishing, mail creation and shipping equipment, related supplies and services, postal payment services, and software. Enterprise Solutions, 22% (8%), includes facilities management, through Pitney Bowes Management Services, Inc., and sales, services and finances high-speed, software-enabled production mail systems, sorting equipment, incoming mail systems, electronic statement, billing and payment services, and mailing software. Capital Services, 5% (6%), includes large-ticket financing programs for a broad range of products.

ANNUAL FINANCIAL DATA

	12/31/00	12/31/99	12/31/98	12/31/97	12/31/96	12/31/95	12/31/94
Earnings Per Share	**[5] 2.18**	**[1] 2.42**	**[1] 2.03**	**1.80**	**[4] 1.56**	**[2] 1.34**	**[1][3] 1.11**
Cash Flow Per Share	**3.42**	**3.94**	**3.32**	**2.82**	**2.51**	**2.25**	**1.97**
Tang. Book Val. Per Share	**4.34**	**5.28**	**5.26**	**5.96**	**6.86**	**6.20**	**5.02**
Dividends Per Share	**1.14**	**1.02**	**0.90**	**0.80**	**0.69**	**0.60**	**0.52**
Dividend Payout %	**52.3**	**42.1**	**44.3**	**44.4**	**44.2**	**44.8**	**47.1**
INCOME STATEMENT (IN MILLIONS):							
Total Revenues	3,880.9	4,432.6	4,220.5	4,100.5	3,858.6	3,554.8	3,270.6
Costs & Expenses	2,564.5	2,906.2	2,845.8	2,796.5	2,698.8	2,445.5	2,272.0
Depreciation & Amort.	321.2	412.1	361.3	300.1	278.2	271.6	268.3
Operating Income	995.2	1,114.3	1,013.4	1,003.8	881.6	837.6	730.3
Net Interest Inc./(Exp.)	d192.4	d179.3	d149.2	d200.7	d197.2	d218.6	d189.1
Income Before Income Taxes	802.8	984.6	864.2	803.1	684.4	618.9	566.5
Income Taxes	239.7	325.4	296.2	277.1	215.0	211.2	218.1
Net Income	[5] 563.1	[1] 659.2	[1] 567.9	526.0	[4] 469.4	[2] 407.7	[1][3] 348.4
Cash Flow	884.1	1,071.1	929.1	825.9	747.4	679.1	616.5
Average Shs. Outstg. (000)	258,602	272,006	279,657	292,517	298,234	302,280	312,918
BALANCE SHEET (IN MILLIONS):							
Cash & Cash Equivalents	213.5	256.7	129.0	138.8	136.8	88.6	75.7
Total Current Assets	2,626.7	3,342.6	2,509.0	2,463.5	2,222.1	2,101.1	2,083.7
Net Property	1,114.5	1,306.1	1,287.8	1,289.7	1,307.2	1,276.2	1,286.6
Total Assets	7,901.3	8,222.7	7,661.0	7,893.4	8,155.7	7,844.6	7,399.7
Total Current Liabilities	2,881.6	2,872.8	2,721.8	3,373.2	3,305.3	3,501.6	3,978.5
Long-Term Obligations	1,881.9	1,997.9	1,712.9	1,068.4	1,300.4	1,048.5	779.2
Net Stockholders' Equity	1,285.0	1,625.6	1,648.0	1,872.6	2,239.0	2,071.1	1,745.1
Net Working Capital	d254.9	469.8	d212.8	d909.7	d1,083.2	d1,400.5	d1,894.7
Year-end Shs. Outstg. (000)	248,800	264,695	270,378	279,674	295,960	299,892	302,552
STATISTICAL RECORD:							
Operating Profit Margin %	25.6	25.1	24.0	24.5	22.8	23.6	22.3
Net Profit Margin %	14.5	14.9	13.5	12.8	12.2	11.5	10.7
Return on Equity %	43.8	40.5	34.5	28.1	21.0	19.7	20.0
Return on Assets %	7.1	8.0	7.4	6.7	5.8	5.2	4.7
Debt/Total Assets %	23.8	24.3	22.4	13.5	15.9	13.4	10.5
Price Range	54.13-24.00	73.31-40.88	66.38-42.22	45.75-26.81	30.69-20.94	24.13-15.00	23.19-14.63
P/E Ratio	24.8-11.0	30.3-16.9	32.7-20.8	25.4-14.9	19.7-13.4	18.0-11.2	21.0-13.2
Average Yield %	2.9	1.8	1.7	2.2	2.7	3.1	2.8

Statistics are as originally reported. Adj. for 2-for-1 stk. split, 1/98. [1] Bef. discont. opers. chg. $22.9 mil ($0.08/sh), 1999; $8.5 mil ($0.03/sh), 1998; & cr.$32.5 mil, 1994. [2] Bef. discont. opers. cr$175.4 mil & incl. $155 mil non-recur. gain. [3] Bef. $119.5 mil chg. for acctg. adj. [4] Incl. $30 mil restr. chg. [5] Bef. $64.1 mil ($0.25/sh) discont. oper. gain & $4.7 mil ($0.02/sh) acctg. chg.

OFFICERS:
M. J. Critelli, Chmn., C.E.O.
M. C. Breslawsky, Pres., C.O.O.
B. P. Nolop, Exec V.P., C.F.O.

INVESTOR CONTACT: Charles F. McBride, Exec. Dir., Inv. Rel., (203) 351-6349

PRINCIPAL OFFICE: One Elmcroft Road, Stamford, CT 06926-0700

TELEPHONE NUMBER: (203) 356-5000
FAX: (203) 351-7336
WEB: www.pitneybowes.com

NO. OF EMPLOYEES: 28,542 (avg.)

SHAREHOLDERS: 32,231

ANNUAL MEETING: In May

INCORPORATED: DE, Apr., 1920

INSTITUTIONAL HOLDINGS:
No. of Institutions: 427
Shares Held: 188,127,858
% Held: 76.2

INDUSTRY: Office machines, nec (SIC: 3579)

TRANSFER AGENT(S): EquiServe, Jersey City, NJ

NYSE SYMBOL PZB
Rec. Pr. 23.50 (5/31/01)

PITTSTON COMPANY (THE)

YIELD 0.4%
P/E RATIO 61.8

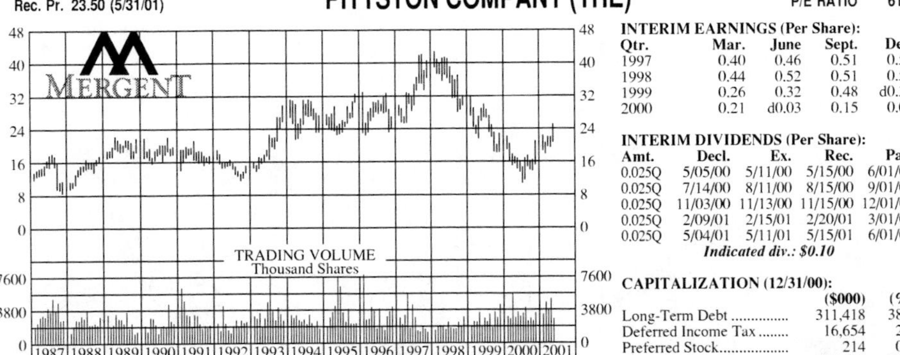

INTERIM EARNINGS (Per Share):

Qtr.	Mar.	June	Sept.	Dec.
1997	0.40	0.46	0.51	0.54
1998	0.44	0.52	0.51	0.55
1999	0.26	0.32	0.48	d0.37
2000	0.21	d0.03	0.15	0.05

INTERIM DIVIDENDS (Per Share):

Amt.	Decl.	Ex.	Rec.	Pay.
0.025Q	5/05/00	5/11/00	5/15/00	6/01/00
0.025Q	7/14/00	8/11/00	8/15/00	9/01/00
0.025Q	11/03/00	11/13/00	11/15/00	12/01/00
0.025Q	2/09/01	2/15/01	2/20/01	3/01/01
0.025Q	5/04/01	5/11/01	5/15/01	6/01/01

Indicated div.: $0.10

CAPITALIZATION (12/31/00):

	($000)	(%)
Long-Term Debt	311,418	38.7
Deferred Income Tax	16,654	2.1
Preferred Stock	214	0.0
Common & Surplus	475,609	59.2
Total	803,895	100.0

RECENT DEVELOPMENTS: For the year ended 12/31/00, income from continuing operations was $2.7 million, before an accounting charge, compared with income from continuing operations of $108.0 million in 1999. Results for 2000 included pre-tax restructuring charges of $57.5 million. Results for 1999 included a non-operating pre-tax gain of $8.3 million. Net sales and operating revenues increased 3.4% to $3.83 billion from $3.71 billion.

PROSPECTS: PZB plans to dispose of its coal business assets by year-end 2001, and expects to receive net proceeds, defined as cash received, liabilities transferred and the value of future royalties, in excess of $100.0 million. Meanwhile, BAX Global is implementing a series of actions designed to better align its resources and expenses to customer needs. These actions are expected to result in annualized cost reductions of at least $50.0 million.

BUSINESS

THE PITTSTON COMPANY (formerly Pittston Brink's Group) is comprised of five operating segments. The major activities of Brink's, Incorporated are contract-carrier armored car, ATM, air courier, coin wrapping, and currency and deposit processing services. Brink's Home Security, Inc. is engaged in marketing, selling, installing, servicing and monitoring electronic security systems primarily in owner-occupied, single-family residences. BAX Global Inc. is a transportation and supply chain management company offering multi-modal freight forwarding to business-to-business shippers through a global network. Within its other operations, Pittston Mineral Ventures mines and explores for gold and Pittston Coal's timber and gas businesses own non-coal properties. On 12/6/99, PZB announced its intention to exit the coal business through the sale of its coal mining operations and reserves. Based on progress since that date, the Company formalized its plan to dispose of those operations by the end of 2001.

ANNUAL FINANCIAL DATA

	12/31/00	2 12/31/99	12/31/98	12/31/97	12/31/96	12/31/95	12/31/94
Earnings Per Share	3 0.05	1 d4.74	0.92	3.61	4.46	4.53	d4.37
Cash Flow Per Share	3.80	2.90	3.25	3.52	3.32	3.12	1.49
Tang. Book Val. Per Share	4.69	6.28	5.49	5.48	4.10	2.73	1.65
Dividends Per Share	0.10	0.10	0.10	0.10	0.10	0.20	0.20
Dividend Payout %	N.M.	...	10.9	2.8	2.2	4.4	...
INCOME STATEMENT (IN MILLIONS):							
Total Revenues	3,834.1	4,089.2	3,746.9	3,394.4	3,106.6	2,926.1	2,667.3
Costs & Expenses	3,610.5	3,852.3	3,488.5	3,091.5	2,842.9	2,698.7	2,546.9
Depreciation & Amort.	189.0	180.3	154.4	128.8	114.6	106.4	101.9
Operating Income	34.6	56.6	104.0	174.1	149.1	121.0	18.5
Net Interest Inc./(Exp.)	d39.2	d32.6	d33.7	d22.7	d10.6	d10.9	d9.0
Income Before Income Taxes	4.6	47.4	95.2	158.3	146.7	130.3	28.3
Income Taxes	1.9	12.8	29.2	48.1	42.5	32.4	1.4
Net Income	3 2.7	1 34.7	66.1	110.2	104.2	98.0	26.9
Cash Flow	190.8	197.3	216.9	235.5	217.1	201.6	124.8
Average Shs. Outstg. (000)	50,146	68,081	66,812	66,886	65,320	64,683	83,734
BALANCE SHEET (IN MILLIONS):							
Cash & Cash Equivalents	97.8	131.2	85.7	72.1	43.1	82.2	67.5
Total Current Assets	813.6	901.9	820.6	726.8	618.7	636.7	562.0
Net Property	831.6	930.5	849.9	647.6	540.9	486.2	445.8
Total Assets	2,478.7	2,468.6	2,331.1	1,995.9	1,812.9	1,807.4	1,737.8
Total Current Liabilities	898.3	833.1	797.4	643.7	569.0	594.5	574.5
Long-Term Obligations	311.4	395.1	323.3	191.8	158.8	133.3	138.1
Net Stockholders' Equity	475.8	749.6	736.0	685.6	606.7	522.0	447.8
Net Working Capital	d84.7	68.8	23.2	83.1	49.7	42.2	d12.5
Year-end Shs. Outstg. (000)	51,778	71,772	70,972	69,914	70,413	70,767	70,676
STATISTICAL RECORD:							
Operating Profit Margin %	0.9	1.4	2.8	5.1	4.8	4.1	0.7
Net Profit Margin %	0.1	0.8	1.8	3.2	3.4	3.3	1.0
Return on Equity %	0.6	4.6	9.0	16.1	17.2	18.8	6.0
Return on Assets %	0.1	1.4	2.8	5.5	5.7	5.4	1.5
Debt/Total Assets %	12.6	16.0	13.9	9.6	8.8	7.4	7.9
Price Range	22.19-10.69	31.81-18.13	42.88-28.00	42.13-25.25	33.00-22.38	32.63-22.50	31.25-21.38
P/E Ratio	N.M.	...	46.6-30.4	11.7-7.0	7.4-5.0	7.2-5.0	...
Average Yield %	0.6	0.4	0.3	0.3	0.4	0.7	0.8

Statistics are as originally reported. Price chart reflects the The Pittston Company as a whole. 1 Incl. restruct. charge of $1.5 mill. 2 Results for 1999 and after are for The Pittston Co. as a whole, while prior years represent Pittston Brink's Group only. 3 Incl. pre-tax restruct. chrg. of $57.5 mill., but excl. loss fr. discont. oper. of $207.4 mill. & acctg. chrg. of $52.0 mill.

OFFICERS:
M. T. Dan, Chmn., Pres., C.E.O.
R. T. Ritter, V.P., C.F.O.
J. B. Hartough, V.P., Corp. Fin., Treas.
A. F. Reed, V.P., Gen. Couns., Sec.

INVESTOR CONTACT: Investor Relations, (804) 289-9600

PRINCIPAL OFFICE: 1801 Bayberry Court, P.O. Box 18100, Richmond, VA 23226-8100

TELEPHONE NUMBER: (804) 289-9600
FAX: (804) 289-9770
WEB: www.pittston.com

NO. OF EMPLOYEES: 43,800 (approx.)

SHAREHOLDERS: 5,329 (approx.)

ANNUAL MEETING: In May

INCORPORATED: DE, Jan., 1930; reincorp., VA, Dec., 1942

INSTITUTIONAL HOLDINGS:
No. of Institutions: 141
Shares Held: 43,631,567
% Held: 84.3

INDUSTRY: Minerals, ground or treated (SIC: 3295)

TRANSFER AGENT(S): Fleet National Bank, Providence, RI

NYSE SYMBOL PDG
Rec. Pr. 10.64 (5/31/01)

PLACER DOME INC.

YIELD 0.9%
P/E RATIO 56.0

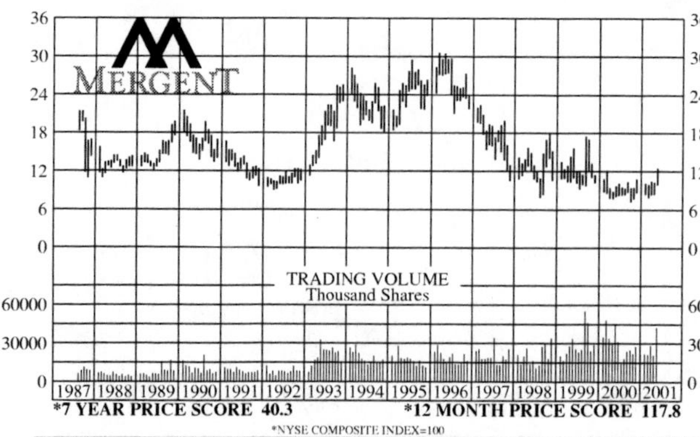

*7 YEAR PRICE SCORE 40.3 *12 MONTH PRICE SCORE 117.8
*NYSE COMPOSITE INDEX=100

INTERIM EARNINGS (Per Share):

Qtr.	Mar.	June	Sept.	Dec.
1997	0.05	0.04	0.01	d1.16
1998	0.06	0.08	0.12	0.10
1999	0.10	Nil	0.06	0.02
2000	0.13	0.23	0.10	d0.27

INTERIM DIVIDENDS (Per Share):

Amt.	Decl.	Ex.	Rec.	Pay.
0.05S	7/20/99	8/18/99	8/20/99	9/20/99
0.05S	2/24/00	3/08/00	3/10/00	3/27/00
0.05S	7/19/00	8/16/00	8/18/00	9/18/00
0.05S	2/15/01	2/28/01	3/02/01	3/19/01

Indicated div.: $0.10

CAPITALIZATION (12/31/00):

	($000)	(%)
Long-Term Debt	843,000	32.4
Deferred Income Tax	232,000	8.9
Minority Interest	12,000	0.5
Common & Surplus	1,513,000	58.2
Total	2,600,000	100.0

RECENT DEVELOPMENTS: For the year ended 12/31/00, net loss was $92.0 million versus net income of $35.0 million in 1999. Results in 2000 and 1999 included pre-tax merger and restructuring charges of $4.0 million and $49.0 million, respectively. Results for 2000 and 1999 also included write-downs of mining interests of $377.0 million and $46.0 million, respectively. Sales advanced 21.6% to $1.41 billion from $1.16 billion the year before.

PROSPECTS: Going forward, the Company will maintain a balanced program of forward selling to provide a level of downside protection to its gold earnings and cash flow. In 2001, PDG expects to produce 2.9 million ounces of gold and 430.0 million pounds of copper at cost similar to current levels. Also, PDG estimates it will incur capital expenditures of $275.0 million throughout 2001.

BUSINESS

PLACER DOME INC. is engaged in gold mining and related activities, including exploration, extraction, processing, refining and reclamation. Gold, the Company's primary product, is produced and sold in Canada, the United States, Australia, Papua New Guinea and Chile. The Company also produces and sells copper and silver. As of 12/31/00, the Company had reserves of approximately 47.0 million ounces of gold, producing over 3.0 million ounces of gold per year at a cash production cost of less than $159.00 per ounce.

ANNUAL FINANCIAL DATA

	12/31/00	12/31/99	12/31/98	12/31/97	12/31/96	12/31/95	12/31/94
Earnings Per Share	**d0.28**	**1 2 0.11**	**0.15**	**2 d1.06**	**2 d0.27**	**0.31**	**0.44**
Cash Flow Per Share	**0.59**	**0.80**	**1.44**	**0.01**	**0.56**	**0.98**	**1.01**
Tang. Book Val. Per Share	**4.62**	**5.00**	**55.97**	**5.34**	**6.00**	**6.46**	**6.41**
Dividends Per Share	**0.10**	**0.10**	**0.10**	**0.30**	**0.30**	**0.30**	**0.27**
Dividend Payout %	**. . .**	**90.8**	**66.6**	**. . .**	**. . .**	**96.7**	**61.3**
INCOME STATEMENT (IN MILLIONS):							
Total Revenues	1,413.0	1,162.0	1,313.0	1,264.0	1,223.0	1,072.0	966.0
Costs & Expenses	839.0	785.0	847.0	945.0	900.0	744.0	614.0
Depreciation & Amort.	286.0	229.0	269.0	264.0	199.0	161.0	136.0
Operating Income	d89.0	102.0	197.0	55.0	124.0	167.0	216.0
Net Interest Inc./(Exp.)	d75.0	d80.0	. . .	. . .	. . .	. . .	. . .
Income Before Income Taxes	d79.0	81.0	197.0	d263.0	34.0	167.0	216.0
Income Taxes	cr6.0	cr62.0	cr91.0	cr1.0	44.0	74.0	77.0
Equity Earnings/Minority Int.	d19.0	10.0	1.0	13.0	d55.0	d19.0	d34.0
Net Income	d92.0	1 2 35.0	. . .	2 . . .	2 d65.0	74.0	105.0
Cash Flow	194.0	264.0	269.0	264.0	134.0	235.0	241.0
Average Shs. Outstg. (000)	327,600	329,700	250,000	247,100	239,500	238,800	238,300
BALANCE SHEET (IN MILLIONS):							
Cash & Cash Equivalents	340.0	204.0	536.0	289.0	417.0	321.0	312.0
Total Current Assets	718.0	537.0	880.0	593.0	760.0	625.0	565.0
Net Property	1,975.0	2,464.0	1,697.0	1,805.0	1,719.0	1,569.0	1,276.0
Total Assets	3,040.0	3,259.0	2,750.0	2,624.0	2,979.0	2,574.0	2,246.0
Total Current Liabilities	263.0	301.0	257.0	248.0	269.0	175.0	177.0
Long-Term Obligations	843.0	905.0	600.0	600.0	656.0	541.0	225.0
Net Stockholders' Equity	1,513.0	1,639.0	1,697.0	1,631.0	1,733.0	1,541.0	1,529.0
Net Working Capital	455.0	236.0	623.0	345.0	491.0	450.0	388.0
Year-end Shs. Outstg. (000)	327,618	327,486	25,051	250,017	239,500	238,450	238,449
STATISTICAL RECORD:							
Operating Profit Margin %	. . .	8.8	15.0	4.4	10.1	15.6	22.4
Net Profit Margin %	. . .	3.0	. . .	. . .	. . .	6.9	10.9
Return on Equity %	. . .	2.1	. . .	. . .	. . .	4.8	6.9
Return on Assets %	. . .	1.1	. . .	. . .	. . .	2.9	4.7
Debt/Total Assets %	27.7	27.8	21.8	22.9	22.0	21.0	10.0
Price Range	12.19-7.25	17.50-9.19	17.88-7.88	22.38-10.50	30.63-21.00	29.50-18.38	28.25-18.13
P/E Ratio	. . .	158.9-83.5	119.1-52.5	. . .	. . .	95.1-59.3	64.2-41.2
Average Yield %	1.0	0.7	0.8	1.8	1.2	1.3	1.2

Statistics are as originally reported. 1 Incl. pre-tax restruct. chrg. of $4.0 mill., 2000; $49.0 mill., 1999 2 Incl. write-downs of mining interests of $377.0 mill., 2000; $46.0 mill, 1999; $295.0 mill., 1997; $90.0 mill., 1996.

OFFICERS:
R. Franklin, Chmn.
J. K. Taylor, Pres., C.E.O.
R. J. McLennan, Exec. V.P., C.F.O.

INVESTOR CONTACT: Ron Stewart, Mgr. Inv. Rel., (416) 363-7260

PRINCIPAL OFFICE: Suite 1600, Bentall IV, 1055 Dunsmuir Street, Vancouver, British Columbia, Canada

TELEPHONE NUMBER: (604) 682-7082
FAX: (604) 682-7092
WEB: www.placerdome.com

NO. OF EMPLOYEES: 12,000 (avg.)

SHAREHOLDERS: 18,727 (record)

ANNUAL MEETING: In Apr.

INCORPORATED: CAN, Aug., 1987

INSTITUTIONAL HOLDINGS:
No. of Institutions: 211
Shares Held: 125,280,734
% Held: 38.2

INDUSTRY: Gold ores (SIC: 1041)

TRANSFER AGENT(S): CIBC Mellon Trust Company, Toronto, Ontario, Canada

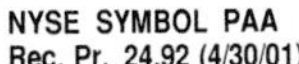
NYSE SYMBOL PAA
Rec. Pr. 24.92 (4/30/01)

PLAINS ALL AMERICAN PIPELINE, L.P.

YIELD 7.6%
P/E RATIO 9.4

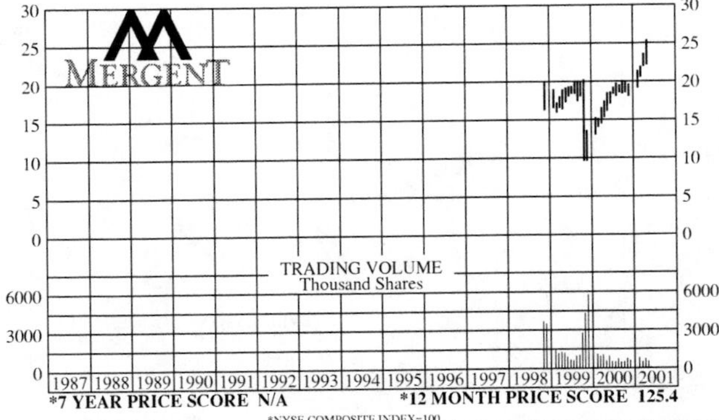

INTERIM EARNINGS (Per Share):

Qtr.	Mar.	June	Sept.	Dec.
1999	d0.33	d0.29	d1.88	d0.69
2000	1.83	0.49	0.13	0.19

INTERIM DIVIDENDS (Per Share):

Amt.	Decl.	Ex.	Rec.	Pay.
0.45Q	4/25/00	5/03/00	5/05/00	5/15/00
0.463Q	7/25/00	8/02/00	8/04/00	8/14/00
0.463Q	10/24/00	11/01/00	11/04/00	11/14/00
0.463Q	1/24/01	1/31/01	2/02/01	2/14/01
0.475Q	4/24/01	5/01/01	5/03/01	5/15/01

Indicated div.: $1.90

CAPITALIZATION (12/31/00):

	($000)	(%)
Long-Term Debt	320,000	59.9
Common & Surplus	213,999	40.1
Total	533,999	100.0

RECENT DEVELOPMENTS: For the year ended 12/31/00, income totaled $92.6 million, before an extraordinary loss of $15.2 million, compared with a loss of $101.8 million, before an extraordinary loss of $1.5 million, the year before. Results for 1999 included restructuring expenses of $1.4 million. Total revenues declined 39.1% to $6.64 billion from $10.91 billion in the prior year. Operating income totaled $62.4 million compared with an operating loss of $98.1 million in the prior year.

PROSPECTS: On 5/9/01, Plains Resources, Inc. (PLX) entered into an agreement to sell a portion of its interest in PAA to an investor group for approximately $149.3 million. The assets sold in the transaction include 50.0% of the subordinated units of PAA and an aggregate 52.0% ownership interest in Plains All American Inc., the general partner of the Company. As a result, PLX's ownership in PAA will be reduced to 39.0% from 54.0%.

BUSINESS

PLAINS ALL AMERICAN PIPELINE, L.P. is engaged in interstate and intrastate crude oil transportation, the operation of terminals and storage, as well as crude oil gathering and marketing activities, primarily in California, Texas, Oklahoma, Louisiana, the Gulf of Mexico and the Canadian provinces of Saskatchewan and Alberta. Plains All American Inc., a wholly-owned subsidiary of Plains Resources Inc., holds an effective 54.0% interest in the Company and serves as the Company's general partner.

REVENUES

(12/31/2000)	($000)	(%)
Pipeline	505,712	7.6
Marketing, Gathering, Terminals & Storage	6,135,475	92.4
Total	6,641,187	100.0

ANNUAL FINANCIAL DATA

	12/31/00	12/31/99	12/31/98	11/22/98	12/31/97	12/31/96
Earnings Per Share	1 **2.64**	1 2 **d3.16**	**0.14**	**0.40**	**0.12**	**0.07**
Cash Flow Per Share	**3.41**	**d2.67**	**0.18**	**0.66**	**0.19**	**0.14**
Tang. Book Val. Per Share	**6.22**	**5.61**	**9.23**	...	...	...
Dividends Per Share	**1.82**	**1.59**	...	...	...	...
Dividend Payout %	**69.1**	...	...	...	...	...
INCOME STATEMENT (IN MILLIONS):						
Total Revenues	6,641.2	4,701.9	176.4	953.2	752.5	531.7
Costs & Expenses	6,554.3	4,781.7	169.7	926.8	743.6	525.1
Depreciation & Amort.	24.5	17.3	1.2	4.2	1.2	1.1
Operating Income	62.4	d97.1	5.5	22.3	7.8	5.4
Net Interest Inc./(Exp.)	d17.9	d20.2	d1.4	d10.7	d4.4	d3.5
Income Before Income Taxes	92.6	d101.8	4.2	11.6	3.4	1.9
Income Taxes	...	...	...	4.6	1.3	0.7
Net Income	1 92.6	1 2 d101.8	4.2	7.0	2.1	1.2
Cash Flow	117.2	d84.5	5.4	11.2	3.3	2.4
Average Shs. Outstg. (000)	34,386	31,633	30,089	17,004	17,004	17,004
BALANCE SHEET (IN MILLIONS):						
Cash & Cash Equivalents	3.4	53.8	5.5	...	...	...
Total Current Assets	397.9	739.0	166.9	...	115.4	...
Net Property	440.6	443.3	378.0	...	32.4	...
Total Assets	885.8	1,223.0	610.2	...	149.6	...
Total Current Liabilities	350.8	637.5	157.5	...	113.4	...
Long-Term Obligations	320.0	373.5	175.0	...	28.5	...
Net Stockholders' Equity	214.0	193.0	277.6	...	6.0	...
Net Working Capital	47.1	101.5	9.3	...	2.0	...
Year-end Shs. Outstg. (000)	34,386	34,386	30,089	...	...	...
STATISTICAL RECORD:						
Operating Profit Margin %	0.9	...	3.1	2.3	1.0	1.0
Net Profit Margin %	1.4	...	2.4	0.7	0.3	0.2
Return on Equity %	43.3	...	1.5	...	35.8	...
Return on Assets %	10.5	...	0.7	...	1.4	...
Debt/Total Assets %	36.1	30.5	28.7	...	19.1	...
Price Range	20.06-13.00	20.25-9.63	20.19-16.25	20.19-16.25	...	...
P/E Ratio	7.6-4.9	...	144.1-116.0	50.5-40.6	...	...
Average Yield %	11.0	10.6	...	...	...	...

Statistics are as originally reported. 1 Bef. extraord. loss, 2000, $15.2 mill.; 1999, $1.5 mill. 2 Incl. restruct. chrg., $1.4 mill.

OFFICERS:
G. L. Armstrong, Chmn., C.E.O.
H. N. Pefanis, Pres., C.O.O.
P. D. Kramer, Exec. V.P., C.F.O.

PRINCIPAL OFFICE: 500 Dallas Street, Suite 700, Houston, TX 77002-4802

TELEPHONE NUMBER: (713) 654-1414
FAX: (713) 654-1523
WEB: www.plainsresources.com

NO. OF EMPLOYEES: 915 (approx.)

SHAREHOLDERS: 14,378 (approx. beneficial)

ANNUAL MEETING: In May

INCORPORATED: DE, Sep., 1998

INSTITUTIONAL HOLDINGS:
No. of Institutions: 38
Shares Held: 2,795,851
% Held: 8.1

INDUSTRY: Pipelines, nec (SIC: 4619)

TRANSFER AGENT(S): American Stock Transfer & Trust Company, New York, NY

NYSE SYMBOL PLA
Rec. Pr. 14.97 (5/31/01)

PLAYBOY ENTERPRISES, INC.

YIELD ...
P/E RATIO ...

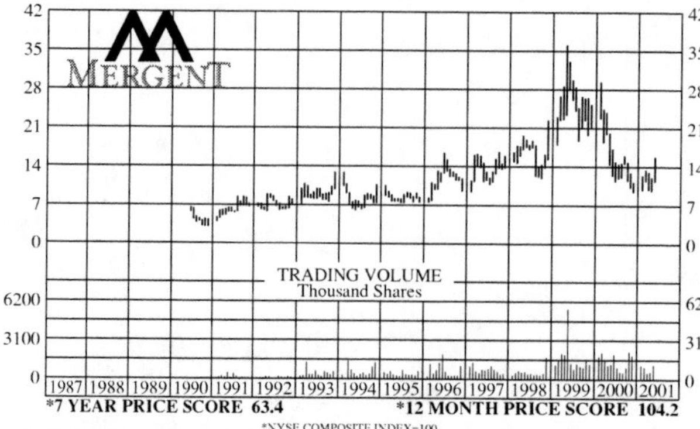

INTERIM EARNINGS (Per Share):

Qtr.	Sept.	Dec.	Mar.	June
1997-98	0.05	0.05	...	...
Qtr.	**Mar.**	**June**	**Sept.**	**Dec.**
1998	Nil	0.10	d0.13	0.24
1999	d0.05	d0.13	0.24	d0.03
2000	d0.26	d0.24	d0.27	d1.19

INTERIM DIVIDENDS (Per Share):

Amt.	Decl.	Ex.	Rec.	Pay.

No dividends paid.

CAPITALIZATION (12/31/00):

	($000)	(%)
Long-Term Debt	94,328	44.2
Deferred Income Tax	4,679	2.2
Common & Surplus	114,185	53.6
Total	213,192	100.0

RECENT DEVELOPMENTS: For the year ended 12/31/00, PLA reported a net loss of $47.6 million versus a loss from continuing operations of $5.6 million in 1999. Earnings for 2000 and 1999 included net nonrecurring items, resulting in a charge of $9.0 million and a gain of $637,000, respectively. Results for 1999 excluded an after-tax gain of $233,000 from discontinued operations. Total net revenues fell 11.5% to $307.7 million.

PROSPECTS: Going forward, PLA expects investments in its on-line business to decline to about $12.0 million from an estimated $27.0 million, and to report a profit in this business in 2002. During the first half of 2002, PLA plans to add three new sources of revenue: international sites, on-line gaming and a CyberSpice subscription site. PLA anticipates on-line revenues of $22.0 million in 2001 and $40.0 million in 2002.

BUSINESS

PLAYBOY ENTERPRISES, INC. is an international multimedia entertainment company that publishes Playboy magazine; operates Playboy and Spice television networks and distributes programming via home video and DVD; licenses the Playboy and Spice trademarks for consumer products; and is developing a Playboy-branded, location-based entertainment business, anchored by casinos. The Company also operates Playboy.com, Inc. On 10/19/00, the Company sold its Critics' Choice Video catalog and related CCVideo.com Web site.

REVENUES

(12/31/2000)	($000)	(%)
Entertainment	100,955	32.8
Publishing	139,870	45.5
Playboy Online	25,291	8.2
Catalog	32,360	10.5
Other Businesses	9,246	3.0
Total	307,722	100.0

ANNUAL FINANCIAL DATA

	12/31/00	12/31/99	12/31/98	[1] 12/31/97	6/30/97	6/30/96	6/30/95
Earnings Per Share	[4] d1.96	[3] d0.24	0.21	[2] 0.10	1.03	0.21	0.03
Cash Flow Per Share	d0.11	1.62	1.58	0.73	2.31	1.48	1.24
Tang. Book Val. Per Share	...	0.83	0.51	2.50	2.78	1.83	1.64
INCOME STATEMENT (IN THOUSANDS):							
Total Revenues	307,722	347,817	317,618	149,541	296,623	276,587	247,249
Costs & Expenses	279,751	292,238	283,638	132,077	255,420	241,665	219,941
Depreciation & Amort.	44,911	42,691	29,012	13,005	25,458	25,429	24,251
Operating Income	d16,940	12,888	4,968	4,459	15,745	9,493	3,057
Net Interest Inc./(Exp.)	d9,148	d7,977	d1,551	d289	d427	d680	d708
Income Before Income Taxes	d31,399	d6,430	7,025	4,290	14,751	8,449	2,436
Income Taxes	16,227	cr862	2,705	2,148	cr6,643	4,197	1,807
Equity Earnings/Minority Int.	d375	d13,871	...	...	...	...	...
Net Income	[4] d47,626	[3] d5,568	4,320	[2] 2,142	21,394	4,252	629
Cash Flow	d2,715	37,123	33,332	15,147	46,852	29,681	24,880
Average Shs. Outstg.	24,240	22,872	21,036	20,818	20,318	20,014	19,984
BALANCE SHEET (IN THOUSANDS):							
Cash & Cash Equivalents	5,977	26,592	846	947	1,303	2,438	1,471
Total Current Assets	155,334	188,810	152,419	125,204	120,279	108,909	96,156
Net Property	10,689	9,415	9,157	10,053	10,307	11,894	13,476
Total Assets	388,488	429,402	212,107	185,947	175,542	150,869	137,835
Total Current Liabilities	107,006	119,671	118,993	98,916	86,558	85,021	77,137
Long-Term Obligations	94,328	75,000	...	...	...	347	687
Net Stockholders' Equity	114,185	161,281	34,625	78,683	76,133	52,283	47,090
Net Working Capital	48,328	69,139	33,426	26,288	33,721	23,888	19,019
Year-end Shs. Outstg.	24,506	24,454	22,192	22,192	20,791	20,186	19,990
STATISTICAL RECORD:							
Operating Profit Margin %	...	3.7	1.6	3.0	5.3	3.4	1.2
Net Profit Margin %	...	...	1.4	1.4	7.2	1.5	0.3
Return on Equity %	...	...	12.5	2.7	28.1	8.1	1.3
Return on Assets %	...	...	2.0	1.2	12.2	2.8	0.5
Debt/Total Assets %	24.3	17.5	...	...	...	0.2	0.5
Price Range	29.50-9.44	36.13-17.94	22.44-11.88	16.69-9.38	16.69-9.38	16.50-7.50	10.63-7.38
P/E Ratio	...	...	106.8-56.5	166.7-93.7	16.2-9.1	78.5-35.7	353.0-245.0

Statistics are as originally reported. [1] 6-mth. transition period result. fr. chge. in yr.-end fr. 6/30 to 12/31. [2] Bef. acctg. change chrg. $1.1 mill. [3] Bef. acctg. change credit $233,000; incl. eqty. in loss of investments of $13.9 mill., a gain on the sale of investments of $1.7 million, restruct. exps. of $1.1 mill. [4] Incl. a net pre-tax nonrecurr. chrg. of $9.0 mill.

OFFICERS:
C. A. Hefner, Chmn., C.E.O.
L. R. Lux, Pres.
L. Havard, Exec. V.P., C.F.O.

INVESTOR CONTACT: Martha O. Linderman, V.P., Inv. Rel., (312) 751-8000

PRINCIPAL OFFICE: 680 North Lake Shore Drive, Chicago, IL 60611

TELEPHONE NUMBER: (312) 751-8000
FAX: (312) 751-2818
WEB: www.playboyenterprises.com

NO. OF EMPLOYEES: 681

SHAREHOLDERS: 7,428 (Class A common); 8,411 (Class B common)

ANNUAL MEETING: In May

INCORPORATED: IL, Oct., 1953; reincorp., DE, Feb., 1971

INSTITUTIONAL HOLDINGS:
No. of Institutions: 47
Shares Held: 10,099,872
% Held: 41.6

INDUSTRY: Periodicals (SIC: 2721)

TRANSFER AGENT(S): Computershare Investor Services, Chicago, IL

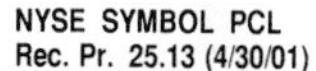

NYSE SYMBOL PCL
Rec. Pr. 25.13 (4/30/01)

PLUM CREEK TIMBER COMPANY, INC.

YIELD 9.1%
P/E RATIO 13.2

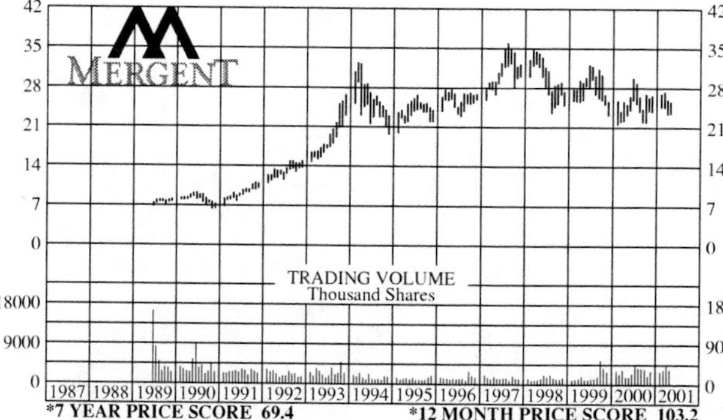

*7 YEAR PRICE SCORE 69.4 *12 MONTH PRICE SCORE 103.2

*NYSE COMPOSITE INDEX=100

INTERIM EARNINGS (Per Share):

Qtr.	Mar.	June	Sept.	Dec.
1997	0.43	0.42	0.52	0.35
1998	0.28	0.17	0.16	0.29
1999	0.20	0.30	0.72	0.38
2000	1.16	0.30	0.14	0.30

INTERIM DIVIDENDS (Per Share):

Amt.	Decl.	Ex.	Rec.	Pay.
0.57Q	4/25/00	5/15/00	5/17/00	5/30/00
0.57Q	7/18/00	8/11/00	8/15/00	8/29/00
0.57Q	10/17/00	11/13/00	11/15/00	11/29/00
0.57Q	1/25/01	2/12/01	2/14/01	2/28/01
0.57Q	4/25/01	5/15/01	5/17/01	5/31/01

Indicated div.: $2.28

CAPITALIZATION (12/31/00):

	($000)	(%)
Long-Term Debt	559,798	35.6
Common & Surplus	1,013,336	64.4
Total	1,573,134	100.0

RECENT DEVELOPMENTS: For the year ended 12/31/00, net income increased 16.3% to $131.9 million compared with income of $113.4 million, before an accounting gain, in 1999. Earnings for 2000 and 1999 included a nonrecurring gain of $49.6 million and $3.7 million, respectively. Results for 2000 and 1999 included pre-tax charges of $3.8 million and $5.1 million, respectively. Revenues were $209.1 million, down 56.4% from $479.6 million a year earlier.

PROSPECTS: During 2001, PCL should continue to enjoy good overall wood products demand. Housing starts and the repair and remodel market are at reasonably strong levels. PCL anticipates a rebound in wood products prices in the second half of the year, as lumber and plywood production curtailments begin to bring markets into better balance. Separately, PCL's upcoming acquisition of Georgia-Pacific's The Timber Company is still pending. The deal is expected to close during 2001.

BUSINESS

PLUM CREEK TIMBER COMPANY, INC. (formerly Plum Creek Timber Company, L.P.), a REIT, and its subsidiaries own, manage, and operate 3.3 million acres of timberland and eleven wood products conversion facilities in the northwest, southern and northeastern U.S. PCL owns 98% and 96% of its Plum Creek Manufacturing, L.P. and Plum Creek Marketing, Inc. subsidiaries, respectively. Segment operations include: Lumber, which produces a diverse line of lumber products; Northern Resources, which manages approximately 2.8 million acres of timberland in the northwest and northeastern U.S.; Panel, which consists of two plywood plants and a medium density fiberboard facility in western Montana; Southern Resources, which owns and manages approximately 524,000 acres of timberland and 9,000 acres of leased land in Arkansas and Louisiana; and Land Sales, which contains land with higher and better use values. On 7/1/99, PCL converted from a Master Limited Partnership to a Real Estate Investment Trust (REIT).

ANNUAL FINANCIAL DATA

	12/31/00	[4] 12/31/99	12/31/98	12/31/97	12/31/96	12/31/95	12/31/94
Earnings Per Share	**[2][3] 1.91**	**[1][2] 1.94**	**[1][2] 0.90**	**1.72**	**4.71**	**2.17**	**2.36**
Tang. Book Val. Per Share	**14.64**	**15.55**	**8.75**	**10.15**	**10.61**	**5.76**	**5.49**
Dividends Per Share	**2.28**	**1.14**	**2.26**	**2.16**	**2.00**	**1.90**	**1.62**
Dividend Payout %	**119.4**	**58.8**	**251.1**	**125.6**	**42.5**	**87.6**	**68.6**
INCOME STATEMENT (IN MILLIONS):							
Total Income	209.1	460.6	699.4	725.6	633.7	585.1	578.7
Costs & Expenses	85.5	314.2	558.3	552.3	468.8	426.1	414.5
Interest Expense	46.8	63.5	60.6	60.4	50.1	46.8	47.4
Income Before Income Taxes	131.3	82.8	76.0	111.8	225.0	111.3	113.1
Income Taxes	...	cr13.1	0.5	0.1	1.4	0.6	0.9
Equity Earnings/Minority Int.	0.6	17.5	...	111.7	...	...	...
Net Income	[2][3] 131.9	[1][2] 113.4	[1][2] 75.4	223.4	223.6	110.7	112.2
Average Shs. Outstg. (000)	69,190	55,819	46,323	46,323	41,620	40,608	40,608
BALANCE SHEET (IN MILLIONS):							
Cash & Cash Equivalents	181.4	115.4	113.8	135.4	123.9	87.6	60.9
Total Assets	1,250.1	1,250.8	1,438.2	1,300.9	413.8	358.1	327.8
Long-Term Obligations	559.8	643.0	942.6	745.0	763.4	517.3	531.4
Total Liabilities	743.4	717.7	1,032.8	830.6	844.8	592.2	600.2
Net Stockholders' Equity	1,013.3	1,066.1	405.4	470.3	491.6	233.9	223.0
Year-end Shs. Outstg. (000)	69,213	68,572	46,323	46,323	46,323	40,608	40,608
STATISTICAL RECORD:							
Net Inc.+Depr./Assets %	10.6	9.1	5.2	17.2	54.0	30.9	34.2
Return on Equity %	13.0	10.6	18.6	47.5	45.5	47.3	50.3
Return on Assets %	10.6	9.1	5.2	17.2	54.0	30.9	34.2
Price Range	29.81-21.50	32.13-23.13	34.88-23.44	36.00-25.75	27.75-22.88	26.75-19.88	32.50-19.63
P/E Ratio	15.6-11.3	16.6-11.9	38.7-26.0	20.9-15.0	5.9-4.9	12.3-9.2	13.8-8.3
Average Yield %	8.9	4.1	7.8	7.0	7.9	8.2	6.2

Statistics are as originally reported. [1] Incls. reorg. costs of $4.8 mill., 1998; $5.1 mill., 1999. [2] Incl. loss on disposition of assets of $805,000, 1998; gain of $3.7 mill., 1999; gain of $49.6 mill., 2000. [3] Incl. merger expenses of $3.8 mill. [4] Reflects conversion from an L.P. to a REIT effective 7/1/99.

OFFICERS:
D. D. Leland, Chmn.
R. R. Holley, Pres., C.E.O.
W. R. Brown, Exec. V.P., C.F.O.
J. A. Kraft, V.P., Gen. Couns., Sec.

INVESTOR CONTACT: Emilio D. Ruocco, Director, Investor Relation, (800) 858-5347

PRINCIPAL OFFICE: 999 Third Avenue, Seattle, WA 98104-4096

TELEPHONE NUMBER: (206) 467-3600
FAX: (206) 467-3795
WEB: www.plumcreek.com

NO. OF EMPLOYEES: 1,714 (avg.)

SHAREHOLDERS: 60,400 (aprox. beneficial)

ANNUAL MEETING: In May

INCORPORATED: DE, June, 1989

INSTITUTIONAL HOLDINGS:
No. of Institutions: 149
Shares Held: 9,712,139
% Held: 14.0

INDUSTRY: Logging (SIC: 2411)

TRANSFER AGENT(S): EquiServe, Boston, MA

NYSE SYMBOL PMI
Rec. Pr. 64.30 (4/30/01)

PMI GROUP, INC. (THE)

YIELD 0.2%
P/E RATIO 11.1

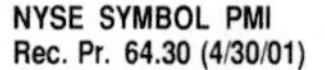

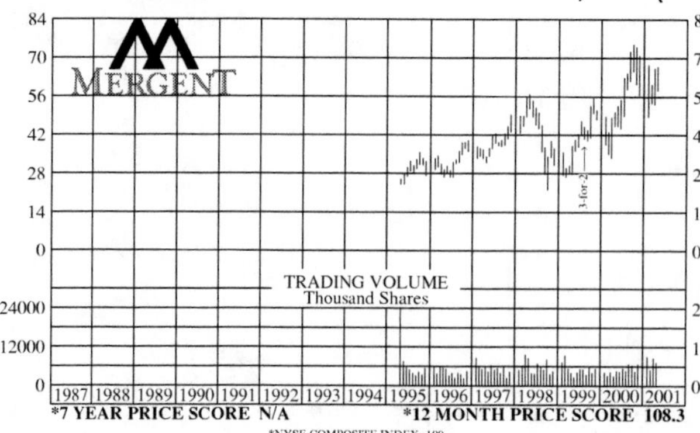

*7 YEAR PRICE SCORE N/A *12 MONTH PRICE SCORE 108.3

*NYSE COMPOSITE INDEX=100

INTERIM EARNINGS (Per Share):

Qtr.	Mar.	June	Sept.	Dec.
1998	0.93	0.97	1.15	0.97
1999	0.96	1.09	1.21	1.26
2000	1.34	1.45	1.53	1.46

INTERIM DIVIDENDS (Per Share):

Amt.	Decl.	Ex.	Rec.	Pay.
0.04Q	5/18/00	6/28/00	6/30/00	7/14/00
0.04Q	9/21/00	9/27/00	9/29/00	10/13/00
0.04Q	11/16/00	12/27/00	12/29/00	1/15/01
0.04Q	2/07/01	3/28/01	3/30/01	4/13/01
0.04Q	5/17/01	6/27/01	6/29/01	7/13/01

Indicated div.: $0.16

CAPITALIZATION (12/31/00):

	($000)	(%)
Long-Term Debt	136,819	7.6
Deferred Income Tax	74,981	4.1
Redeemable Pfd. Stock	99,109	5.5
Common & Surplus	1,499,211	82.8
Total	1,810,120	100.0

RECENT DEVELOPMENTS: For the year ended 12/31/00, net income improved 27.3% to $260.2 million compared with $204.5 million in the previous year. Results included net realized gains of $432,000 and $509,000 in 2000 and 1999, respectively. Total revenues jumped 13.8% to $762.6 million versus $670.1 million in the preceding year. Net premiums written increased 11.9% to $639.1 million compared with $571.3 million in the prior year.

PROSPECTS: In 2001, the Company anticipates operating earnings per share ranging from $6.75 to $6.95 reflecting the Company's present estimate of the impact of expected mortgage interest rates and residential mortgage originations on PMI's policy persistency, premiums earned, and contract underwriting expenses. On 2/12/01, PMI announced that it is commencing mortgage credit enhancement through a wholly-owned indirect subsidiary, PMI Mortgage Insurance Company Limited

BUSINESS

THE PMI GROUP, INC. is a holding company that conducts its residential mortgage insurance business through its direct and indirect wholly-owned subsidiaries PMI Mortgage Insurance Co., Residential Guaranty Co., Residential Insurance Co., TPG Insurance Co., PMI Mortgage Guaranty Co., TPG Segregated Portfolio Company, and PMI's wholly-owned subsidiaries, PMI Mortgage Insurance Ltd. PMI also conducts title insurance business through its wholly-owned subsidiary, American Pioneer Title Insurance Company. In addition, PMI owns all of the outstanding common stock of PMI Mortgage Services Co., which is engaged in the business of contract underwriting, and PMI Securities Co. an inactive broker-dealer. PMI also owns 50% of the outstanding shares of common stock of CMG Mortgage Insurance Company, which conducts a residential mortgage insurance business and owns 24.9% of RAM Holdings Ltd. and Ram Holdings II Ltd., a financial guaranty reinsurance company.

ANNUAL FINANCIAL DATA

	12/31/00	12/31/99	12/31/98	12/31/97	12/31/96	12/31/95	12/31/94
Earnings Per Share	**5.78**	**4.52**	**4.03**	**3.49**	**3.01**	**2.57**	**2.02**
Tang. Book Val. Per Share	**33.83**	**27.23**	**24.16**	**21.79**	**19.06**	**16.58**	**13.09**
Dividends Per Share	**0.16**	**0.14**	**0.13**	**0.13**	**0.13**	**0.07**	...
Dividend Payout %	**2.8**	**3.1**	**3.3**	**3.8**	**4.4**	**2.6**	...
INCOME STATEMENT (IN MILLIONS):							
Total Premium Income	634.4	558.6	491.2	453.9	412.7	328.8	296.3
Net Investment Income	119.2	95.1	84.7	83.1	67.4	62.0	56.8
Other Income	9.0	16.4	45.0	27.6	21.2	14.2	6.9
Total Revenues	762.6	669.6	596.3	545.1	487.1	393.1	356.9
Income Before Income Taxes	373.9	290.1	266.9	242.9	222.1	180.5	138.6
Income Taxes	113.7	85.6	76.6	67.6	64.2	45.3	32.4
Net Income	260.2	204.5	190.4	175.3	157.9	135.2	106.1
Average Shs. Outstg. (000)	45,019	45,244	47,300	50,265	52,560	52,683	52,500
BALANCE SHEET (IN MILLIONS):							
Cash & Cash Equivalents	22.0	28.1	9.8	11.1	6.6	3.7	11.4
Premiums Due	93.4	84.4	92.4	76.9	125.4	100.3	80.6
Invst. Assets: Equities	213.6	175.3	119.2	90.6	124.0	121.4	92.5
Invst. Assets: Total	2,078.2	1,817.3	1,532.2	1,490.6	1,291.7	1,133.0	960.5
Total Assets	2,392.7	2,100.8	1,777.9	1,686.6	1,509.9	1,304.4	1,116.7
Long-Term Obligations	136.8	145.4	99.5	99.4	99.3	...	...
Net Stockholders' Equity	1,499.2	1,217.3	1,097.5	1,061.2	986.9	870.5	687.2
Year-end Shs. Outstg. (000)	44,310	44,702	45,419	48,692	51,765	52,514	52,500
STATISTICAL RECORD:							
Return on Revenues %	34.1	30.5	31.9	32.2	32.4	34.4	29.7
Return on Equity %	17.4	16.8	17.3	16.5	16.0	15.5	15.4
Return on Assets %	10.9	9.7	10.7	10.4	10.5	10.4	9.5
Price Range	74.94-33.50	55.50-26.67	57.00-22.00	49.34-31.83	40.00-26.58	35.67-24.00	...
P/E Ratio	13.0-5.8	12.3-5.9	14.2-5.5	14.1-9.1	13.3-8.8	13.9-9.3	...
Average Yield %	0.3	0.3	0.3	0.3	0.4	0.2	...

Statistics are as originally reported. Adj. for 3-for-2 stk. spl., 8/99.

OFFICERS:
W. R. Haughton, Chmn., C.E.O.
L. S. Smith, Pres., C.O.O.
J. M. Lorenzen Jr., Exec. V.P., C.F.O., , Asst. Sec.

INVESTOR CONTACT: Investor Relations, (888) 641-4764

PRINCIPAL OFFICE: 601 Montgomery Street, San Francisco, CA 94111

TELEPHONE NUMBER: (415) 788-7878
FAX: (415) 291-6175
WEB: www.pmigroup.com

NO. OF EMPLOYEES: 1,117 (avg.)

SHAREHOLDERS: 43 (approx.); 8,859 (approx. beneficial)

ANNUAL MEETING: In May

INCORPORATED: DE, Dec., 1993

INSTITUTIONAL HOLDINGS:
No. of Institutions: 236
Shares Held: 42,361,660
% Held: 95.5

INDUSTRY: Surety insurance (SIC: 6351)

TRANSFER AGENT(S): Continental Stock Transfer & Trust Company, New York, NY

NYSE SYMBOL PNC
Rec. Pr. 65.07 (4/30/01)

PNC FINANCIAL SERVICES GROUP, INC.

YIELD 3.0%
P/E RATIO 15.6

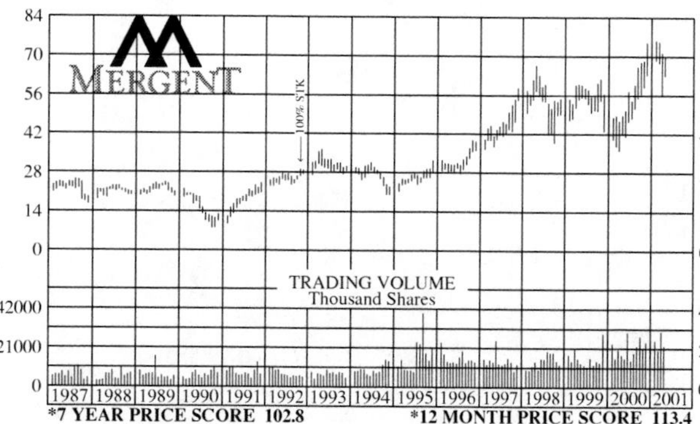

INTERIM EARNINGS (Per Share):

Qtr.	Mar.	June	Sept.	Dec.
1997	0.80	0.81	0.83	0.85
1998	0.87	0.90	0.91	0.92
1999	1.05	1.03	1.06	1.01
2000	1.03	1.06	1.01	1.06

INTERIM DIVIDENDS (Per Share):

Amt.	Decl.	Ex.	Rec.	Pay.
0.45Q	4/06/00	4/12/00	4/14/00	4/24/00
0.45Q	7/06/00	7/12/00	7/14/00	7/24/00
0.48Q	10/05/00	10/11/00	10/13/00	10/24/00
0.48Q	1/04/01	1/10/01	1/12/01	1/24/01
0.48Q	4/05/01	4/10/01	4/13/01	4/24/01

Indicated div.: $1.92 (Div. Reinv. Plan)

CAPITALIZATION (12/31/00):

	($000)	(%)
Total Deposits	47,664,000	74.5
Long-Term Debt	9,666,000	15.1
Preferred Stock	7,000	0.0
Common & Surplus	6,649,000	10.4
Total	63,986,000	100.0

RECENT DEVELOPMENTS: For the year ended 12/31/00, PNC reported income of $1.21 billion versus income of $1.20 billion in 1999. Earnings for 2000 and 1999 excluded gains of $65.0 million and $62.0 million, respectively, from discontinued operations. Earnings for 1999 included non-recurring items that resulted in a net gain of $65.0 million. Net interest income fell 7.7% to $2.16 billion. Provision for credit losses fell 16.6% to $136.0 million.

PROSPECTS: On 2/1/01, the Company sold PNC Mortgage Corporation and PNC Mortgage Securities Corporation to Washington Mutual, Inc. for $605.0 million. The transaction will result in an after-tax gain of approximately $250.0 million and should be modestly dilutive to operating earnings in 2001. PNC expects growth in diluted earnings per share from continuing operations to range from 11.0% to 13.0% in 2001.

BUSINESS

PNC FINANCIAL SERVICES GROUP, INC. (formerly PNC Bank Corporation) is one of the largest diversified financial services companies in the nation with $69.84 billion in total assets as of 12/31/00. PNC operates seven major businesses engaged in regional banking, wholesale banking and asset management activities: PNC Bank-Regional Banking; PNC Bank-Corporate Banking; PNC Secured Finance; PNC Mortgage; PNC Advisors; BlackRock; and PFPC. The Company provides products and services nationally and in PNC's primary geographic markets in Pennsylvania, New Jersey, Delaware, Ohio and Kentucky. On 12/31/95, PNC acquired Midlantic Corp. On 12/1/98, PNC acquired Hilliard-Lyons, Inc. As of 12/31/00, assets under management totaled $253.00 billion.

LOAN DISTRIBUTION

(12/31/00)	($000)	(%)
Consumer	9,133,000	17.7
Residential Mortgage	13,264,000	25.7
Commercial	21,207,000	41.1
Commercial Real Estate	2,583,000	5.0
Lease Financing	4,845,000	9.4
Other loans	568,000	1.1
Total	51,600,000	100.0

ANNUAL FINANCIAL DATA

	12/31/00	12/31/99	12/31/98	12/31/97	12/31/96	12/31/95	12/31/94
Earnings Per Share	**[5] 4.09**	**[4] 4.15**	**3.60**	**3.28**	**[3] 2.90**	**[2] 1.19**	**[1] 2.57**
Tang. Book Val. Per Share	**14.42**	**6.20**	**11.49**	**12.47**	**18.09**	**17.06**	**18.85**
Dividends Per Share	**1.80**	**1.68**	**1.58**	**1.50**	**1.42**	**1.40**	**1.31**
Dividend Payout %	**11.0**	**40.5**	**43.9**	**45.7**	**49.0**	**117.6**	**51.0**
INCOME STATEMENT (IN MILLIONS):							
Total Interest Income	4,732.0	4,921.0	5,313.0	5,051.0	4,938.0	5,149.4	3,862.0
Total Interest Expense	2,568.0	2,488.0	2,740.0	2,556.0	2,494.0	3,007.6	1,952.0
Net Interest Income	2,164.0	2,433.0	2,573.0	2,495.0	2,444.0	2,141.9	1,910.0
Provision for Loan Losses	136.0	163.0	225.0	70.0	...	6.0	60.0
Non-Interest Income	2,891.0	2,745.0	2,302.0	1,775.0	1,395.0	960.4	823.0
Non-Interest Expense	3,071.0	3,124.0	2,940.0	2,582.0	2,312.0	2,469.3	1,769.0
Income Before Taxes	1,848.0	1,891.0	1,710.0	1,618.0	1,527.0	627.0	902.0
Net Income	[5] 1,214.0	[4] 1,264.0	1,115.0	1,052.0	[3] 992.0	[2] 408.1	[1] 612.0
Average Shs. Outstg. (000)	292,800	300,000	305,100	316,200	340,246	339,134	237,000
BALANCE SHEET (IN MILLIONS):							
Cash & Due from Banks	3,662.0	3,097.0	2,534.0	4,303.0	4,016.0	3,679.0	2,592.0
Securities Avail. for Sale	7,053.0	8,759.0	8,088.0	10,048.0	12,691.0	17,450.0	4,266.0
Total Loans & Leases	51,600.0	50,770.0	58,204.0	54,657.0	52,183.0	49,056.0	35,647.0
Allowance for Credit Losses	1,674.0	1,398.0	1,307.0	1,384.0	1,551.0	1,662.0	1,242.0
Net Loans & Leases	49,926.0	49,372.0	56,897.0	53,273.0	50,632.0	47,394.0	34,405.0
Total Assets	69,844.0	75,413.0	77,207.0	75,120.0	73,260.0	73,404.0	64,145.0
Total Deposits	47,664.0	46,668.0	47,496.0	47,649.0	45,676.0	46,899.0	35,011.0
Long-Term Obligations	9,666.0	16,944.0	18,887.0	15,276.0	15,186.0	11,642.0	16,170.0
Total Liabilities	62,340.0	68,619.0	70,316.0	69,086.0	67,041.0	67,636.0	59,751.0
Net Stockholders' Equity	6,656.0	5,946.0	6,043.0	5,384.0	5,869.0	5,768.0	4,394.0
Year-end Shs. Outstg. (000)	290,000	293,000	303,700	300,430	324,118	338,048	233,000
STATISTICAL RECORD:							
Return on Equity %	18.2	21.3	18.5	19.5	16.9	7.1	13.9
Return on Assets %	1.7	1.7	1.4	1.4	1.4	0.6	1.0
Equity/Assets %	9.5	7.9	7.8	7.2	8.0	7.9	6.9
Non-Int. Exp./Tot. Inc. %	60.8	60.3	60.3	60.5	60.2	79.6	64.7
Price Range	75.00-36.00	62.00-43.00	66.75-38.75	58.75-36.50	39.75-27.50	32.38-21.13	31.63-20.00
P/E Ratio	18.3-8.8	14.9-10.4	18.5-10.8	17.9-11.1	13.7-9.5	27.2-17.8	12.3-7.8
Average Yield %	0.8	3.2	3.0	3.1	4.2	5.2	5.1

Statistics are as originally reported. [1] Incl. $79.0 mill. loss on sale of fixed incm. sec. & $31.4 mill. restr. chg. [2] Incl. after-tax merger-rel. & restr. chgs. totaling $380.2 mill. [3] Incl. pre-tax SAIF chg. of $35.1 mill. [4] Incl. various nonrecurr. after-tax net gains of $280.0 mill. [5] Excl. a gain of $65.0 mill. fr. disc. opers.

OFFICERS:
J. E. Rohr, Chmn., Pres., C.E.O.
W. E. Gregg Jr., Vice-Chmn.
R. L. Haunschild, Sr. V.P., C.F.O.

INVESTOR CONTACT: William H. Callihan, VP, Investor Relations, (412) 762-8257

PRINCIPAL OFFICE: One PNC Plaza, 249 Fifth Avenue, Pittsburgh, PA 15222-2707

TELEPHONE NUMBER: (412) 762-1553
FAX: (412) 762-5798
WEB: www.pnc.com

NO. OF EMPLOYEES: 25,300 (avg.)

SHAREHOLDERS: 56,976

ANNUAL MEETING: In April

INCORPORATED: PA, Jan., 1983

INSTITUTIONAL HOLDINGS:
No. of Institutions: 483
Shares Held: 245,400,145
% Held: 84.9

INDUSTRY: National commercial banks (SIC: 6021)

TRANSFER AGENT(S): Mellon Investor Services, Ridgefield Park, NJ

NYSE SYMBOL PII
Rec. Pr. 43.05 (5/31/01)

POLARIS INDUSTRIES INC.

YIELD 2.3%
P/E RATIO 12.3

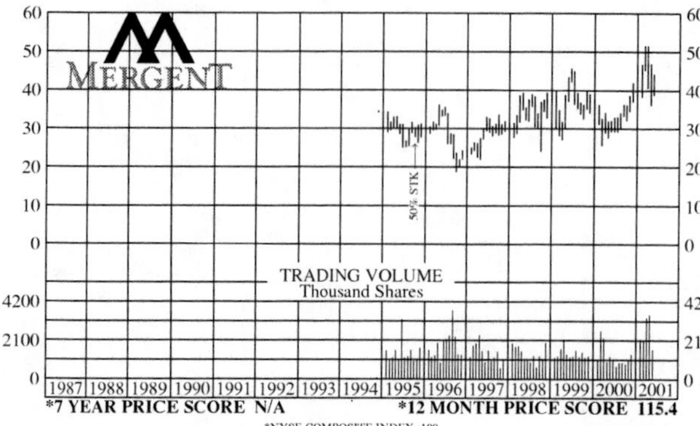

*7 YEAR PRICE SCORE N/A *12 MONTH PRICE SCORE 115.4

*NYSE COMPOSITE INDEX=100

INTERIM EARNINGS (Per Share):

Qtr.	Mar.	June	Sept.	Dec.
1997	0.44	0.49	0.81	0.71
1998	0.32	0.55	d0.56	0.88
1999	0.36	0.60	1.10	1.02
2000	0.41	0.68	1.24	1.17

INTERIM DIVIDENDS (Per Share):

Amt.	Decl.	Ex.	Rec.	Pay.
0.22Q	4/20/00	4/27/00	5/01/00	5/15/00
0.22Q	7/20/00	7/28/00	8/01/00	8/15/00
0.22Q	10/19/00	10/30/00	11/01/00	11/15/00
0.25Q	1/18/01	1/30/01	2/01/01	2/15/01
0.25Q	4/23/01	4/27/01	5/01/01	5/15/01

Indicated div.: $1.00

CAPITALIZATION (12/31/00):

	($000)	(%)
Long-Term Debt	47,068	18.7
Common & Surplus	204,734	81.3
Total	251,802	100.0

RECENT DEVELOPMENTS: For the year ended 12/31/00, net income increased 8.5% to $82.8 million compared with $76.3 million in 1999. Sales were $1.43 billion, up 7.3% from $1.33 billion a year earlier. Gross profit as a percentage of sales was 23.0% in 2000 and 22.4% in 1999. Cost of sales increased 6.5% to $1.10 billion from $1.03 billion a year earlier. Total operating expenses jumped 11.9% to $206.3 million. Operating income advanced 7.2% to $121.8 million compared with $113.6 million a year earlier.

PROSPECTS: The Company's dealers are experiencing increased orders for its new 2002 snowmobile models. Meanwhile, in March 2001, the Company initiated a new SNOW CHECK SELECT program, which allows the consumer to customize their snowmobile in a number of ways including the choice of suspension systems, colors, tracks, engines, shocks, and other features. The program is expected to contribute to PII's growth in the snowmobile business in the coming year.

BUSINESS

POLARIS INDUSTRIES INCORPORATED designs, engineers and manufactures all terrain vehicles, snowmobiles, motorcycles and personal watercraft and markets them, together with related replacement parts, garments and accessories through dealers and distributors principally located in the United States, Canada and Europe. PII produces a full line of snowmobiles, consisting of twenty-nine models, ranging from youth to utility and economy models to performance and competition models. PII produces four-wheel all terrain vehicles (ATV). PII's line of ATVs consisting of 18 models includes general purpose, sport and four-wheel drive utility models. In addition, the Company has a six-wheel off-road utility vehicle and the Polaris RANGER, a six-wheel off-road side by side utility and recreational vehicle. The Company manufactures an American-made V-twin cruiser motorcycle, the Victory V92C. PII's 2001 line of personal watercraft (PWC) consists of eight models across the touring, performance and racing segments. The Company produces or supplies a variety of replacement parts and accessories for its snowmobiles, ATVs, motorcycles and PWC.

ANNUAL FINANCIAL DATA

	12/31/00	12/31/99	12/31/98	12/31/97	12/31/96	12/31/95	12/31/94
Earnings Per Share	**3.50**	**3.07**	**② 1.19**	**2.45**	**2.24**	**2.19**	**① Nil**
Cash Flow Per Share	**5.48**	**4.64**	**7.31**	**3.69**	**3.33**	**3.00**	**3.17**
Tang. Book Val. Per Share	**7.77**	**6.03**	**5.14**	**5.60**	**4.85**	**3.42**	**5.29**
Dividends Per Share	**0.88**	**0.80**	**0.72**	**0.64**	**0.60**	**4.27**	...
Dividend Payout %	**25.1**	**26.1**	**60.5**	**26.1**	**26.8**	**195.0**	...
INCOME STATEMENT (IN MILLIONS):							
Total Revenues	1,425.7	1,321.1	1,175.5	1,048.3	1,191.9	1,113.9	826.3
Costs & Expenses	1,256.9	1,168.1	977.8	922.0	1,063.9	989.5	727.0
Depreciation & Amort.	47.0	39.3	36.2	33.2	30.6	22.7	23.7
Operating Income	121.8	113.6	100.1	93.1	97.4	101.7	75.7
Net Interest Inc./(Exp.)	d7.7	d4.3	d3.0	d2.8	d4.3	...	...
Income Before Income Taxes	128.4	118.3	48.4	102.2	97.3	98.8	75.9
Income Taxes	45.6	42.0	17.3	36.8	35.0	38.0	12.0
Equity Earnings/Minority Int.	14.4	9.7	7.8	6.7	3.1	...	...
Net Income	82.8	76.3	② 153.8	65.4	62.3	60.8	① 64.0
Cash Flow	129.8	115.6	190.0	98.6	92.9	83.5	87.6
Average Shs. Outstg. (000)	23,666	24,900	25,986	26,739	27,861	27,792	27,635
BALANCE SHEET (IN MILLIONS):							
Cash & Cash Equivalents	2.4	6.2	1.5	1.2	5.8	3.5	62.9
Total Current Assets	240.9	214.7	183.8	217.5	193.4	175.8	206.5
Net Property	167.9	150.9	124.3	98.0	93.5	78.5	53.7
Total Assets	490.2	442.0	378.7	384.7	351.7	314.4	331.2
Total Current Liabilities	238.4	233.8	205.0	191.1	161.4	195.9	161.5
Long-Term Obligations	47.1	40.0	20.5	24.4	35.0	...	...
Net Stockholders' Equity	204.7	168.2	153.2	169.2	155.3	118.5	169.7
Net Working Capital	2.5	d19.1	d21.1	26.3	32.0	d20.1	45.0
Year-end Shs. Outstg. (000)	23,542	24,226	25,355	26,014	27,011	27,324	27,167
STATISTICAL RECORD:							
Operating Profit Margin %	8.5	8.6	8.5	8.9	8.2	9.1	9.2
Net Profit Margin %	5.8	5.8	13.1	6.2	5.2	5.5	7.7
Return on Equity %	40.4	45.4	100.4	38.6	40.1	51.3	37.7
Return on Assets %	16.9	17.3	40.6	17.0	17.7	19.3	19.3
Debt/Total Assets %	9.6	9.1	5.4	6.3	10.0	...	...
Price Range	42.06-25.56	45.69-27.00	39.38-24.00	33.63-21.88	36.25-18.75	34.33-25.00	34.58-34.08
P/E Ratio	12.0-7.3	14.9-8.8	33.1-20.2	13.7-8.9	16.2-8.4	15.7-11.4	...
Average Yield %	2.6	2.2	2.3	2.3	2.2	14.4	...

Statistics are as originally reported. Adj. for stk. split: 3-for-2, 1995. ① Incl. conversion costs of $12.3 mill. ② Incl. prov. for litigation loss of $61.4 mill.

OFFICERS:
W. H. Wendel, Jr., Chmn.
T. C. Tiller, Pres., C.E.O.
M. W. Malone, V.P, C.F.O., Sec.

INVESTOR CONTACT: Investor Relations, (763) 542-0500

PRINCIPAL OFFICE: 2100 Highway 55, Medina, MN 55340

TELEPHONE NUMBER: (763) 542-0500
FAX: (763) 542-0599
WEB: www.polarisindustries.com

NO. OF EMPLOYEES: 3,560 (approx.)

SHAREHOLDERS: 2,731 (record)

ANNUAL MEETING: In May

INCORPORATED: DE, Apr., 1987; reincorp., MN, 1994

INSTITUTIONAL HOLDINGS:
No. of Institutions: 139
Shares Held: 13,418,828
% Held: 57.2

INDUSTRY: Transportation equipment, nec (SIC: 3799)

TRANSFER AGENT(S): Wells Fargo Investor Services, South St. Paul, MN

NYSE SYMBOL PRD
Rec. Pr. 3.55 (4/30/01)

POLAROID CORPORATION

YIELD ...
P/E RATIO 4.3

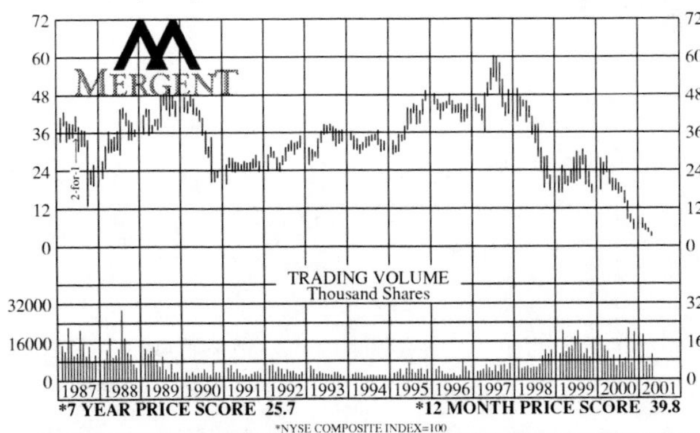

*7 YEAR PRICE SCORE 25.7 *12 MONTH PRICE SCORE 39.8

*NYSE COMPOSITE INDEX=100

INTERIM EARNINGS (Per Share):

Qtr.	Mar.	June	Sept.	Dec.
1997	0.35	0.76	0.55	d4.51
1998	d0.39	0.27	0.68	d1.72
1999	d0.39	0.27	d0.09	0.64
2000	d0.03	0.59	0.40	d0.13

INTERIM DIVIDENDS (Per Share):

Amt.	Decl.	Ex.	Rec.	Pay.
0.15Q	10/26/99	11/24/99	11/29/99	12/23/99
0.15Q	1/25/00	2/23/00	2/25/00	3/31/00
0.15Q	5/16/00	5/24/00	5/26/00	6/30/00
0.15Q	6/27/00	8/23/00	8/25/00	9/29/00
0.15Q	9/19/00	11/21/00	11/24/00	12/28/00

Dividend Payment Suspended

CAPITALIZATION (12/31/00):

	($000)	(%)
Long-Term Debt	573,500	60.5
Common & Surplus	375,200	39.5
Total	948,700	100.0

RECENT DEVELOPMENTS: For the year ended 12/31/00, net income more than quadrupled to $37.7 million compared with $8.7 million in 1999. The 2000 results included pre-tax restructuring and other charges of $5.8 million. Net sales declined 4.7% to $1.86 billion from $1.98 billion the year before. Lower revenues were attributed in part to inventory reductions in the traditional film business.

PROSPECTS: On 2/22/01, PRD announced a global restructuring plan designed to reduce overhead, realign its resources and accelerate implementation of PRD's digital strategy. The plan will result in the elimination of approximately 950 jobs, 11.0% of its global workforce, and should realize about $60.0 million in cost savings on an annual basis.

BUSINESS

POLOROID COMPANY is a major instant imaging company and is the only U.S. manufacturer of traditional silver-halide, or chemical-based, instant cameras and film. The Company's principal products, which are marketed in all of its sales and marketing segments, are instant film, instant and digital cameras, digital peripherals and secure identification systems with software and systems solutions. In addition to its principle products, PRD designs, develops, manufacturers and/or markets hardware accessories for the instant imaging market, conventional 35mm cameras and film and videotapes. The Company sells its products directly to and through mass merchandisers; food, drug, discount and department stores; specialty stores; wholesalers; original equipment manufacturers; independent agents; retail outlets; and distributors.

REVENUES

(12/31/2000)	($000)	(%)
Americas Region	1,208,700	65.1
European Region	353,900	19.1
Asia Pacific Region	293,000	15.8
Total	1,855,600	100.0

ANNUAL FINANCIAL DATA

	12/31/00	12/31/99	12/31/98	12/31/97	12/31/96	12/31/95	12/31/94
Earnings Per Share	**5 0.84**	**6 0.20**	**5 d1.15**	**4 d2.81**	**2 3 0.32**	**1 d3.09**	**2.49**
Cash Flow Per Share	**3.36**	**2.59**	**0.90**	**d0.34**	**2.90**	**d0.17**	**5.01**
Tang. Book Val. Per Share	**8.24**	**8.30**	**8.86**	**10.88**	**14.46**	**15.76**	**18.79**
Dividends Per Share	**0.60**	**0.60**	**0.60**	**0.60**	**0.60**	**0.60**	**0.60**
Dividend Payout %	**71.4**	**299.9**	**...**	**...**	**187.4**	**...**	**24.1**
INCOME STATEMENT (IN MILLIONS):							
Total Revenues	1,855.6	1,978.6	1,845.9	2,146.4	2,275.2	2,236.9	2,312.5
Costs & Expenses	1,632.6	1,765.1	1,804.2	2,194.0	2,072.1	2,262.0	1,994.0
Depreciation & Amort.	113.9	105.9	90.7	111.5	118.3	132.7	118.2
Operating Income	109.1	107.6	d49.0	d159.1	51.8	d157.8	200.3
Net Interest Inc./(Exp.)	d79.8	d74.7	d54.7	d44.1	d42.3	d43.4	d36.9
Income Before Income Taxes	57.9	13.4	d38.9	d191.9	31.2	d201.4	160.7
Income Taxes	20.2	4.7	12.1	cr65.2	16.2	cr61.2	43.5
Net Income	5 37.7	6 8.7	5 d51.0	4 d126.7	2 3 15.0	1 d140.2	117.2
Cash Flow	151.6	114.6	39.7	d15.2	133.3	d7.5	235.4
Average Shs. Outstg. (000)	45,100	44,300	44,200	45,100	45,989	45,404	46,992
BALANCE SHEET (IN MILLIONS):							
Cash & Cash Equivalents	97.2	92.0	105.0	79.0	78.3	83.1	228.9
Total Current Assets	1,118.6	1,116.9	1,293.4	1,419.3	1,386.4	1,457.5	1,488.7
Net Property	569.2	599.2	566.5	512.5	666.2	691.0	747.3
Total Assets	2,043.0	2,040.0	2,197.7	2,132.7	2,201.6	2,261.8	2,316.7
Total Current Liabilities	793.3	750.2	933.0	862.7	763.1	719.0	601.9
Long-Term Obligations	573.5	573.0	497.4	496.6	489.9	526.7	566.0
Net Stockholders' Equity	375.2	370.5	389.9	484.4	658.2	717.7	864.4
Net Working Capital	325.3	366.7	360.4	556.6	623.3	738.5	886.8
Year-end Shs. Outstg. (000)	45,532	44,616	43,990	44,536	45,533	45,533	45,998
STATISTICAL RECORD:							
Operating Profit Margin %	5.9	5.4	...	...	2.3	...	8.7
Net Profit Margin %	2.0	0.4	...	...	0.7	...	5.1
Return on Equity %	10.0	2.3	...	...	2.3	...	13.6
Return on Assets %	1.8	0.4	...	...	0.7	...	5.1
Debt/Total Assets %	28.1	28.1	22.6	23.3	22.3	23.3	24.4
Price Range	28.44-5.13	30.63-16.50	49.94-17.44	60.31-36.25	48.50-39.13	49.38-29.00	36.75-29.25
P/E Ratio	33.9-6.1	153.0-82.5	...	...	151.5-122.2	...	14.8-11.7
Average Yield %	3.6	2.5	1.8	1.2	1.4	1.5	1.8

Statistics are as originally reported. 1 Incl. $77.0 mill. restruct. chrg. 2 Incl. a $110.0 mill. restruct. & $33.0 mill. in other spec. chgs. 3 Bef. extra. chg. of $56.1 mill. 4 Incl. a gain of $19.5 mill. on the sale of real estate & a donation of real estate of $19.1 mill. 5 Incl. a pre-tax restruct. & oth. chgs. of $50.0 mill., 1998; $5.8 mill., 2000 6 Incl. net per sh. chrg. of $0.36 & a pre-tax chrg. of $40.0 mill. assoc./w the planned joint venture between PRD & Andlinger & Company, Inc.

OFFICERS:
G. T. Dicamillo, Chmn., C.E.O.
C. L. Lueders, V.P., Acting C.F.O.
N. D. Goldman, Sr. V.P., Sec., Gen. Couns.

INVESTOR CONTACT: William J. O'Neill, Jr., Exec. V.P. & C.F.O., (781) 577-4221

PRINCIPAL OFFICE: 784 Memorial Drive, Cambridge, MA 02139

TELEPHONE NUMBER: (781) 386-2000
FAX: (781) 386-3263
WEB: www.polaroid.com

NO. OF EMPLOYEES: 8,865 (avg.)

SHAREHOLDERS: 8,529

ANNUAL MEETING: In May

INCORPORATED: DE, Sept., 1937

INSTITUTIONAL HOLDINGS:
No. of Institutions: 113
Shares Held: 29,373,913
% Held: 63.9

INDUSTRY: Photographic equipment and supplies (SIC: 3861)

TRANSFER AGENT(S): First National Bank of Boston, Boston, MA

NYSE SYMBOL RL
Rec. Pr. 26.00 (4/30/01)

POLO RALPH LAUREN CORPORATION

YIELD ...
P/E RATIO 59.1

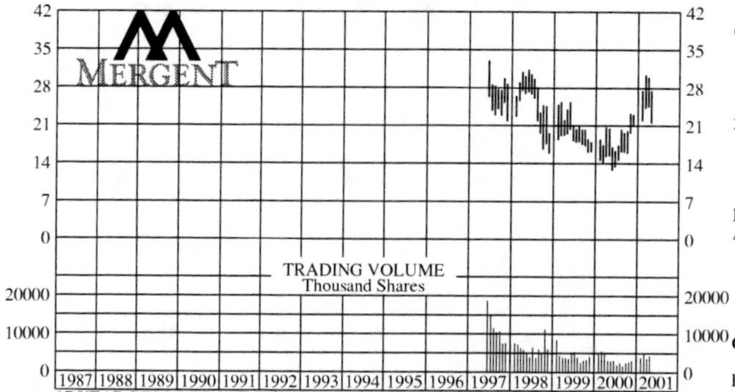

*7 YEAR PRICE SCORE N/A *12 MONTH PRICE SCORE 133.7
*NYSE COMPOSITE INDEX=100

INTERIM EARNINGS (Per Share):

Qtr.	June	Sept.	Dec.	Mar.
1996-97	0.12	0.33	0.20	0.24
1997-98	0.17	0.45	0.29	0.29
1998-99	0.23	0.50	0.25	d0.07
1999-00	0.28	0.56	0.33	0.32
2000-01	0.25	d0.65	0.52	...

INTERIM DIVIDENDS (Per Share):

Amt. Decl. Ex. Rec. Pay.

No dividends paid.

CAPITALIZATION (4/1/00):

	($000)	(%)
Long-Term Debt	342,707	30.7
Common & Surplus	772,437	69.3
Total	1,115,144	100.0

RECENT DEVELOPMENTS: For the quarter ended 12/30/00, net income increased 56.8% to $50.6 million versus $32.3 million in the equivalent prior-year quarter. Net revenues improved 20.3% to $613.7 million versus $510.3 million the year before. Net sales increased 22.4% to $554.4 million from $453.0 million a year earlier. Licensing revenue improved 4.2% to $58.1 million. Results benefited from strong holiday sales and ongoing European expansion initiatives.

PROSPECTS: The Company expects strong growth in Europe to continue given a healthy economic outlook there and a stronger Euro. For fiscal 2002, the Company anticipates earnings per share in the range of $1.93 to $1.98 due primarily to 5.0% to 7.0% revenue growth, improved gross margins and decreased operating expenses. Meanwhile, the Company will continue to focus on building its luxury-oriented retail business and its accessories business.

BUSINESS

POLO RALPH LAUREN CORPORATION is engaged in the design, marketing and distribution of premium lifestyle products. Brand names include POLO BY RALPH LAUREN, RALPH LAUREN PURPLE LABEL, RALPH LAUREN, RALPH, LAUREN, POLO JEANS CO., RL, CHAPS and CLUBMONACO, among others. RL offers broad lifestyle product collections in four categories: apparel, home, accessories and fragrance. Apparel products include extensive collections of menswear, womenswear and children's clothing. The Ralph Lauren Home Collection offers coordinated products for the home, including bedding and bath products, interior decor, furniture and tabletop and gift items. Accessories include footwear, eyewear, jewelry and leather goods. Fragrance and skin care products are sold under the Company's POLO, LAUREN, ROMANCE, SAFARI and POLO SPORT brands, among others.

ANNUAL FINANCIAL DATA

	4/1/00	4/3/99	1 3/28/98	1 3/29/97	3/30/96	4/1/95
Earnings Per Share	**1.49**	2 **0.91**	**1.20**	**0.88**	...	...
Cash Flow Per Share	**2.16**	**1.37**	**1.75**	**1.41**	...	...
Tang. Book Val. Per Share	**5.07**	**6.60**	**5.84**	...	...	...
INCOME STATEMENT (IN MILLIONS):						
Total Revenues	1,955.5	1,726.9	1,470.9	1,180.4	1,019.9	846.6
Costs & Expenses	1,625.3	1,524.9	1,243.8	1,009.3	883.0	726.6
Depreciation & Amort.	66.3	46.4	27.4	13.8	9.7	9.9
Operating Income	263.9	155.6	199.8	157.4	127.1	110.1
Net Interest Inc./(Exp.)	d15.0	d2.8	d0.2	d13.7	d16.3	d16.4
Income Before Income Taxes	248.9	152.8	199.6	140.1	109.7	93.4
Income Taxes	101.4	62.3	52.0	22.8	10.9	13.2
Equity Earnings/Minority Int.	...	...	...	d3.6	d1.1	d0.3
Net Income	147.5	2 90.6	147.6	117.3	98.8	80.2
Cash Flow	213.7	137.0	175.0	131.1	108.6	90.1
Average Shs. Outstg. (000)	98,927	99,972	100,222	92,673	...	...
BALANCE SHEET (IN MILLIONS):						
Cash & Cash Equivalents	164.6	44.5	58.8	29.6	13.6	...
Total Current Assets	852.9	679.5	556.5	436.3	459.6	...
Net Property	373.0	261.8	175.3	83.2	49.0	...
Total Assets	1,620.6	1,104.6	825.1	576.7	563.7	...
Total Current Liabilities	406.2	348.0	202.3	224.0	196.7	...
Long-Term Obligations	342.7	44.2	...	71.9	114.1	...
Net Stockholders' Equity	772.4	658.9	584.3	260.7	237.7	...
Net Working Capital	446.7	331.5	354.2	212.4	262.8	...
Year-end Shs. Outstg. (000)	97,530	99,779	100,084	...	...	...
STATISTICAL RECORD:						
Operating Profit Margin %	13.5	9.0	13.6	13.3	12.5	13.0
Net Profit Margin %	7.5	5.2	10.0	9.9	9.7	9.5
Return on Equity %	19.1	13.7	25.3	45.0	41.6	...
Return on Assets %	9.1	8.2	17.9	20.3	17.5	...
Debt/Total Assets %	21.1	4.0	...	12.5	20.3	...
Price Range	25.38-16.06	31.38-15.88	33.00-21.75	...	...	...
P/E Ratio	17.0-10.8	34.5-17.4	27.5-18.1	...	...	...

Statistics are as originally reported. 1 Pro forma 2 Incl. non-recurr. chrgs. $34.7 mill.

OFFICERS:
R. Lauren, Chmn., C.E.O.
F. L. Isham, Vice-Chmn.
R. N. Farah, Pres., C.O.O.
N. A. Platoni Poli, Sr. V.P., C.F.O.

INVESTOR CONTACT: Nancy S. Murray, Investor Relations, (212) 813-7862

PRINCIPAL OFFICE: 650 Madison Avenue, New York, NY 10022

TELEPHONE NUMBER: (212) 318-7000
FAX: (212) 888-5780
WEB: www.doublerl.com

NO. OF EMPLOYEES: 9,500 (approx.)

SHAREHOLDERS: 1,228 (class A common); 4 (class B common); 5 (class C common)

ANNUAL MEETING: In Aug.

INCORPORATED: DE, March, 1997

INSTITUTIONAL HOLDINGS:
No. of Institutions: 89
Shares Held: 26,239,955
% Held: 27.1

INDUSTRY: Men's and boys' clothing, nec (SIC: 2329)

TRANSFER AGENT(S): The Bank of New York, New York, NY

NYSE SYMBOL PGI
Rec. Pr. 1.28 (4/30/01)

POLYMER GROUP, INC.

YIELD 6.3%
P/E RATIO . . .

*7 YEAR PRICE SCORE N/A *12 MONTH PRICE SCORE 43.4

*NYSE COMPOSITE INDEX=100

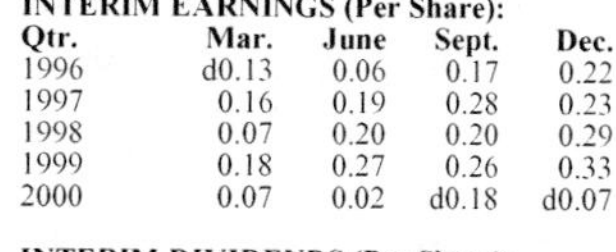

INTERIM EARNINGS (Per Share):

Qtr.	Mar.	June	Sept.	Dec.
1996	d0.13	0.06	0.17	0.22
1997	0.16	0.19	0.28	0.23
1998	0.07	0.20	0.20	0.29
1999	0.18	0.27	0.26	0.33
2000	0.07	0.02	d0.18	d0.07

INTERIM DIVIDENDS (Per Share):

Amt.	Decl.	Ex.	Rec.	Pay.
0.02Q	2/10/00	2/23/00	2/25/00	3/10/00
0.02Q	4/27/00	5/10/00	5/12/00	6/02/00
0.02Q	7/27/00	8/09/00	8/11/00	9/01/00
0.02Q	10/26/00	11/08/00	11/10/00	12/01/00
0.02Q	2/08/01	2/14/01	2/16/01	3/02/01

Indicated div.: $0.08

CAPITALIZATION (12/30/00):

	($000)	(%)
Long-Term Debt	1,023,986	76.8
Deferred Income Tax	82,574	6.2
Common & Surplus	226,235	17.0
Total	1,332,795	100.0

RECENT DEVELOPMENTS: For the year ended 12/30/00, net loss totaled $5.1 million compared with net income of $33.4 million in the previous year. Results for 2000 excluded an extraordinary gain of $741,000. Net sales fell 3.1% to $862.0 million versus $889.8 million a year earlier. Industrial and specialty sales decreased slightly to $375.7 million versus $378.6 million the year before. Consumer sales declined 4.9% to $486.3 million. Operating income dropped 29.7% to $84.6 million versus $120.2 million in the previous year.

PROSPECTS: In 2001, the Company expects continued pricing pressure and margin erosion. In addition, results may be dampened by high raw materials prices, short-term order reductions and an unfavorable shift in product mix due to adjustments of certain customers. The Company plans to cut costs and sell certain non-core assets in an attempt to reduce debt. Going forward, the Company expects revenues for fiscal 2001 to increase to between $900.0 million and $940.0 million, though it is also anticipating a net loss of $35.0 million to $45.0 million.

BUSINESS

POLYMER GROUP, INC. is a global producer of nonwoven materials. The Company's principal business lines include disposable hygiene, medical, wiping and specialized industrial materials. The Company operates 25 manufacturing facilities throughout the world. The Company is the exclusive manufacturer of Miratec® fabrics, produced using proprietary laser technologies. Miratec® is a registered trademark of the Company.

QUARTERLY DATA

(12/30/2000)($000)	REV	INC
1st Quarter	231,952	2,137
2nd Quarter	223,801	1,420
3rd Quarter	203,516	(5,646)
4th Quarter	202,766	(2,234)

ANNUAL FINANCIAL DATA

	12/30/00	1/1/00	1/2/99	1/3/98	12/28/96	12/30/95	12/31/94
Earnings Per Share	[1] **d0.16**	**1.04**	[2] **0.75**	[1] **0.86**	[1] **0.43**	**d1.39**	[1] **d0.95**
Cash Flow Per Share	**2.10**	**3.12**	**2.60**	**2.12**	**1.75**	**0.07**	**d0.55**
Tang. Book Val. Per Share	. . .	. . .	. . .	. . .	**3.09**	. . .	. . .
Dividends Per Share	**0.08**	**0.02**	. . .	. . .	. . .	. . .	. . .
Dividend Payout %	. . .	**1.9**	. . .	. . .	. . .	. . .	. . .
INCOME STATEMENT (IN MILLIONS):							
Total Revenues	862.0	889.8	802.9	535.3	521.4	437.6	165.3
Costs & Expenses	705.2	703.0	638.1	436.3	422.5	365.5	141.4
Depreciation & Amort.	72.3	66.5	59.3	40.3	36.8	29.8	8.3
Operating Income	84.6	120.2	105.6	58.6	62.1	42.3	15.6
Net Interest Inc./(Exp.)	d91.8	d71.9	d67.4	d30.5	d33.6	d37.9	d13.2
Income Before Income Taxes	d7.8	52.0	38.1	40.4	25.6	d18.4	d15.0
Income Taxes	cr2.7	18.6	14.2	13.0	10.7	5.2	3.4
Net Income	[1] d5.1	33.4	[2] 23.9	[1] 27.4	[1] 14.8	d23.6	[1] d18.3
Cash Flow	67.2	100.0	83.3	67.7	48.6	1.4	d11.2
Average Shs. Outstg. (000)	32,040	32,089	32,000	32,000	27,688	20,500	20,500
BALANCE SHEET (IN MILLIONS):							
Cash & Cash Equivalents	30.6	56.3	58.3	57.9	48.5	22.9	15.8
Total Current Assets	341.1	349.0	310.7	755.1	184.4	143.2	66.3
Net Property	858.3	823.3	685.0	606.3	406.5	380.3	113.7
Total Assets	1,508.0	1,466.2	1,283.0	1,627.8	708.1	624.7	234.9
Total Current Liabilities	150.6	160.1	98.3	535.0	91.3	81.6	35.3
Long-Term Obligations	1,024.0	963.2	863.4	741.9	362.7	439.9	190.8
Net Stockholders' Equity	226.2	242.3	220.1	199.1	195.9	13.6	2.2
Net Working Capital	190.5	188.9	212.5	220.0	93.2	61.6	31.1
Year-end Shs. Outstg. (000)	32,004	32,002	32,000	32,000	32,000	19,082	216,354
STATISTICAL RECORD:							
Operating Profit Margin %	9.8	13.5	13.1	10.9	11.9	9.7	9.4
Net Profit Margin %	. . .	3.8	3.0	5.1	2.8	. . .	. . .
Return on Equity %	. . .	13.8	10.9	13.8	7.6	. . .	. . .
Return on Assets %	. . .	2.3	1.9	1.7	2.1	. . .	. . .
Debt/Total Assets %	67.9	65.7	67.3	45.6	51.2	70.4	81.2
Price Range	19.63-4.63	20.50-8.75	13.94-7.38	16.38-9.00	20.63-10.50	. . .	. . .
P/E Ratio	. . .	19.7-8.4	18.6-9.8	19.0-10.5	48.0-24.4	. . .	. . .
Average Yield %	0.7	0.1	. . .	. . .	. . .	. . .	. . .

Statistics are as originally reported. [1] Bef. extraord. chrgs. $741,000, 12/00; $12.0 mill., 1/98; $13.9 mill., 12/96; $4.4 mill., 12/94 [2] Bef. acctg. change chrg. $1.5 mill. and extraord. chrg. $2.7 mill.

OFFICERS:
J. Zucker, Chmn., Pres., C.E.O.
J. G. Boyd, Exec. V.P., C.F.O., Treas.

INVESTOR CONTACT: Robert Johnston, Dir., Inv. Rel., (843) 566-7293

PRINCIPAL OFFICE: 4838 Jenkins Ave., North Charleston, SC 29405

TELEPHONE NUMBER: (843) 566-7293
WEB: www.polymergroupinc.com

NO. OF EMPLOYEES: 4,300 (approx.)

SHAREHOLDERS: 87 (record)

ANNUAL MEETING: In June

INCORPORATED: DE, June, 1994

INSTITUTIONAL HOLDINGS:
No. of Institutions: 43
Shares Held: 13,614,868
% Held: 42.5

INDUSTRY: Broadwoven fabric mills, manmade (SIC: 2221)

TRANSFER AGENT(S): First Union Corporation, Charlotte, NC

NYSE SYMBOL POL
Rec. Pr. 9.06 (5/31/01)

POLYONE CORPORATION

YIELD 2.8%
P/E RATIO 34.8

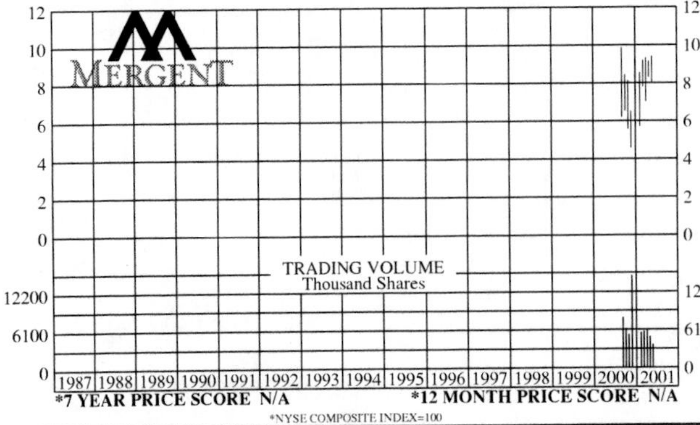

*7 YEAR PRICE SCORE N/A *12 MONTH PRICE SCORE N/A

*NYSE COMPOSITE INDEX=100

INTERIM EARNINGS (Per Share):

Qtr.	Mar.	June	Sept.	Dec.
1997	0.10	0.26	0.45	0.15
1998	0.25	0.20	0.26	d0.13
1999	0.46	2.81	0.52	0.57
2000		0.26		

INTERIM DIVIDENDS (Per Share):

Amt.	Decl.	Ex.	Rec.	Pay.
0.063Q	11/01/00	11/29/00	12/01/00	12/15/00
0.063Q	1/11/01	2/27/01	3/01/01	3/15/01
0.063Q	5/02/01	5/30/01	6/01/01	6/15/01

Indicated div.: $0.25

CAPITALIZATION (12/31/00):

	($000)	(%)
Long-Term Debt	442,400	31.2
Deferred Income Tax	132,800	9.4
Minority Interest	14,000	1.0
Common & Surplus	827,600	58.4
Total	1,416,800	100.0

RECENT DEVELOPMENTS: For the year ended 12/31/00, net income decreased 85.0% to $15.9 million compared with income of $106.2 million, before an accounting charge, in 1999. Results included employee separation and plant phase-out costs of $2.8 million in 2000 and $500,000 in 1999. Results for 1999 included a gain on formation of joint ventures of $93.5 million. Sales were $1.89 billion, up 49.7% from $1.26 billion a year earlier.

PROSPECTS: The Company plans to close four manufacturing plants by the end of the second quarter 2001 to reconfigure its manufacturing assets in North America in order to improve quality, customer response, and reduce production cost. The plant closings should yield annual pre-tax savings of $6.0 million. Savings of up to $20.0 million annually are anticipated by 2002. Meanwhile, POL is targeting earnings of $2.00 per share by 2003.

BUSINESS

POLYONE CORPORATION (formerly The Geon Company) is an international polymer services company with operations in thermoplastic compounds, specialty resins, specialty polymer formulations, engineered films, color and additive systems, elastomer compounding and thermoplastic resin distribution. The Company has 80 manufacturing sites in North America, Europe, Asia and Australia, and joint ventures in North America, South America, Europe, Asia and Australia. POL was formed on 8/31/00 as a result of the consolidation of The Geon Company and M.A. Hanna Company.

QUARTERLY DATA

(12/31/2000)($000)	Rev	Inc
1st Quarter	345,500	13,800
2nd Quarter	361,200	14,800
3rd Quarter	478,300	500
4th Quarter	702,800	(13,200)

ANNUAL FINANCIAL DATA

	12/31/00	[3] 12/31/99	12/31/98	12/31/97
Earnings Per Share	[4] **0.26**	[2] **4.37**	[1] **0.58**	[1] **0.95**
Cash Flow Per Share	**1.18**	**6.20**	**3.04**	**3.21**
Tang. Book Val. Per Share	**3.06**	**6.37**	**5.67**	**9.65**
Dividends Per Share	**0.06**	...	...	...
Dividend Payout %	**24.0**	...	...	...
INCOME STATEMENT (IN MILLIONS):				
Total Revenues	1,887.8	1,261.2	1,284.4	1,250.0
Costs & Expenses	1,765.6	1,117.1	1,185.5	1,143.7
Depreciation & Amort.	57.4	44.4	57.9	54.6
Operating Income	64.8	99.7	41.0	51.7
Net Interest Inc./(Exp.)	d35.1	d15.6	d14.8	d11.2
Income Before Income Taxes	26.1	174.0	23.6	34.6
Income Taxes	10.2	67.8	9.8	12.1
Net Income	[4] 15.9	[2] 106.2	[1] 13.8	[1] 22.5
Cash Flow	73.3	150.6	71.7	77.1
Average Shs. Outstg. (000)	62,000	24,300	23,600	23,600
BALANCE SHEET (IN MILLIONS):				
Cash & Cash Equivalents	37.9	51.2	14.4	...
Total Current Assets	796.5	357.7	234.7	...
Net Property	703.8	338.4	443.5	...
Total Assets	2,460.7	1,162.6	802.0	...
Total Current Liabilities	734.9	440.7	256.8	...
Long-Term Obligations	442.4	130.9	135.4	...
Net Stockholders' Equity	827.6	334.7	214.1	...
Net Working Capital	61.6	d83.0	d22.1	...
Year-end Shs. Outstg. (000)	93,900	23,800	23,400	...
STATISTICAL RECORD:				
Operating Profit Margin %	3.4	7.9	2.9	4.2
Net Profit Margin %	0.8	8.4	1.1	1.8
Return on Equity %	1.9	31.7	6.4	10.1
Return on Assets %	0.6	9.1	1.7	2.6
Debt/Total Assets %	18.0	11.3	16.9	...
Price Range	9.88-4.56	...	...	...
P/E Ratio	38.0-17.5	...	...	...
Average Yield %	0.8	...	...	...

Statistics are as originally reported. [1] Incl. a pretax spec. chrg. of $15.0 mill. ($0.39/sh.) related to employee separation, 1997; & $14.6 mill., 1998. [2] Bef. an acctg. adj. chrg. of $1.5 mill., but incl. gain of $93.5 mill. for formation of joint ventures and $500,000 chrg. for employee separation and plant phase-out. [3] Results for 12/31/99 and earlier represent only the operations of The Geon Company. [4] Incl. non-recurr. chrg. of $2.8 mill.

OFFICERS:
T. A. Waltermire, Chmn., Pres., C.E.O.
W. D. Wilson, V.P., C.F.O.
J. L. Rastetter, Treas.

INVESTOR CONTACT: Dennis A. Cocco, Investor Relations, (216) 589-4018

PRINCIPAL OFFICE: 200 Public Square, Suite 36-5000, Cleveland, OH 44114-2304

TELEPHONE NUMBER: (216) 589-4000
FAX: (216) 589-4077
WEB: www.polyone.com

NO. OF EMPLOYEES: 9,000 (avg.)

SHAREHOLDERS: 11,000 (approx.)

ANNUAL MEETING: In May

INCORPORATED: DE, Feb., 1993

INSTITUTIONAL HOLDINGS:
No. of Institutions: 140
Shares Held: 81,014,447
% Held: 86.3

INDUSTRY: Plastics materials and resins (SIC: 2821)

TRANSFER AGENT(S): EquiServe, Jersey City, NJ

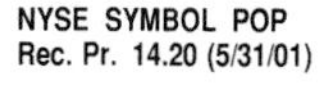

NYSE SYMBOL POP
Rec. Pr. 14.20 (5/31/01)

POPE & TALBOT, INC.

YIELD 4.2%
P/E RATIO 6.4

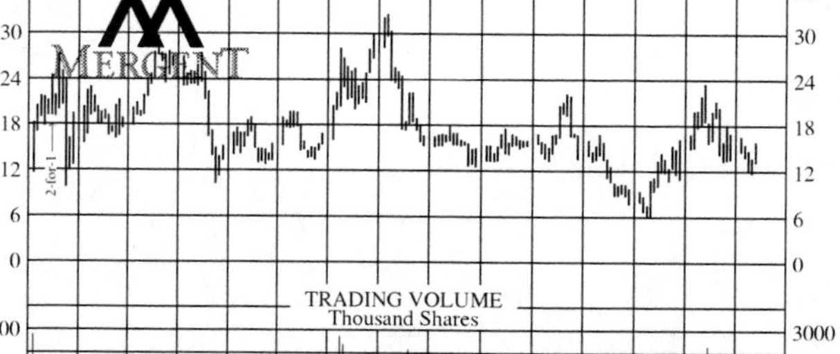

*7 YEAR PRICE SCORE 76.6 *12 MONTH PRICE SCORE 92.2

*NYSE COMPOSITE INDEX=100

INTERIM EARNINGS (Per Share):

Qtr.	Mar.	June	Sept.	Dec.
1997	0.10	0.30	0.25	0.03
1998	d0.49	d0.53	d0.50	d0.22
1999	d0.17	0.22	0.53	0.46
2000	0.64	0.66	0.64	0.29

INTERIM DIVIDENDS (Per Share):

Amt.	Decl.	Ex.	Rec.	Pay.
0.11Q	4/13/00	4/27/00	5/01/00	5/12/00
0.15Q	7/18/00	8/10/00	8/14/00	8/25/00
0.15Q	10/27/00	11/02/00	11/06/00	11/17/00
0.15Q	1/17/01	2/02/01	2/06/01	2/20/01
0.15Q	4/18/01	4/27/01	5/01/01	5/15/01

Indicated div.: $0.60

CAPITALIZATION (12/31/00):

	($000)	(%)
Long-Term Debt [5]	188,423	49.1
Common & Surplus	195,606	50.9
Total	384,029	100.0

RECENT DEVELOPMENTS: For the year ended 12/31/00, net income more than doubled to $32.6 million compared with $14.4 million in 1999. Sales were $580.1 million, up 8.2% from $536.2 million a year earlier. Wood products revenues decreased 16.3% to $232.1 million, while pulp products revenues jumped 30.8% to $348.2 million. Sales for 2000 and 1999 were reclassified to include shipping and handling costs.

PROSPECTS: Low lumber prices combined with import duties imposed under the Canadian-U.S. Softwood Lumber Agreement are resulting in significant downtime at POP's sawmills. Separately, weakness in the pulp market and escalating energy costs are hindering earnings on the pulp side. The weakness in the pulp market is primarily being felt in short fiber markets where customers have significantly reduced orders.

BUSINESS

POPE & TALBOT, INC. is engaged principally in the wood products and pulp products businesses. POP's wood products business involves the manufacture and sale of standardized and specialty lumber and wood chips. In its pulp products business, POP manufactures and sells bleached kraft pulp for newsprint, tissue and writing paper, and brokers wood chips. Separately, POP has reduced its dependency on timber from the Pacific Northwest and increased its operations in regions presently having more stable timber supplies, namely in British Columbia and the Black Hills region of South Dakota and Wyoming. In 1978, POP purchased the Halsey pulp mill. In February 1996, POP divested its disposable diaper business. In March 1998, POP divested its private label tissue business. On 11/8/99, the Company completed the acquisition of Harmac Pacific Inc.

ANNUAL FINANCIAL DATA

	12/31/00	12/31/99	[3] 12/31/98	12/31/97	12/31/96	12/31/95	12/31/94
Earnings Per Share	**2.24**	**1.05**	**[4] d1.74**	**[1] 0.33**	**[1] 0.06**	**[1] d1.03**	**[2] 1.21**
Cash Flow Per Share	**4.44**	**3.45**	**0.48**	**2.57**	**2.41**	**2.34**	**4.19**
Tang. Book Val. Per Share	**12.65**	**12.79**	**11.72**	**13.31**	**13.42**	**13.89**	**16.76**
Dividends Per Share	**0.52**	**0.52**	**0.76**	**0.76**	**0.76**	**0.76**	**0.76**
Dividend Payout %	**23.2**	**49.5**	...	**230.2**	**N.M.**	...	**62.8**
INCOME STATEMENT (IN THOUSANDS):							
Total Revenues	580,052	486,948	420,785	329,899	447,494	524,409	659,873
Costs & Expenses	484,012	421,856	423,252	285,078	406,620	486,906	598,673
Depreciation & Amort.	31,912	32,773	29,919	30,056	31,440	45,066	39,061
Operating Income	64,128	32,319	d32,386	14,765	9,434	d7,563	22,139
Net Interest Inc./(Exp.)	d8,444	d9,063	d7,973	d5,995	d8,792	d13,784	d9,322
Income Before Income Taxes	55,684	23,256	d40,359	8,770	2,494	d21,347	26,662
Income Taxes	23,118	11,422	cr13,352	4,338	1,695	cr7,551	10,765
Equity Earnings/Minority Int.	...	2,587	3,547	...	...	...	...
Net Income	32,566	14,421	[4] d23,460	[1] 4,432	[1] 799	[1] d13,796	[2] 15,897
Cash Flow	64,478	47,194	6,459	34,488	32,239	31,270	54,958
Average Shs. Outstg.	14,511	13,667	13,481	13,419	13,364	13,364	13,110
BALANCE SHEET (IN THOUSANDS):							
Cash & Cash Equivalents	11,995	33,368	37,330	31,911	32,208	13,826	6,847
Total Current Assets	182,498	202,799	188,094	210,950	164,502	207,252	223,050
Net Property	247,860	234,167	234,392	108,165	201,666	225,760	282,827
Total Assets	458,187	470,206	449,589	375,767	407,929	472,227	539,384
Total Current Liabilities	74,158	95,216	85,042	84,835	87,067	113,495	103,576
Long-Term Obligations	188,423	188,889	138,004	88,705	216,052	277,028	354,942
Net Stockholders' Equity	195,606	186,101	158,057	179,462	183,228	189,692	228,195
Net Working Capital	108,340	107,583	103,052	126,115	77,435	93,757	119,474
Year-end Shs. Outstg.	15,457	14,553	13,481	13,481	13,364	13,364	13,363
STATISTICAL RECORD:							
Operating Profit Margin %	11.1	6.6	...	4.5	2.1	...	3.4
Net Profit Margin %	5.6	3.0	...	1.3	0.2	...	2.4
Return on Equity %	16.6	7.7	...	2.5	0.4	...	7.0
Return on Assets %	7.1	3.1	...	1.2	0.2	...	2.9
Debt/Total Assets %	41.1	40.2	30.7	23.6	53.0	58.7	65.8
Price Range	23.50-13.25	16.25-6.06	16.88-7.63	22.13-13.25	17.63-13.19	17.88-12.50	32.63-15.25
P/E Ratio	10.5-5.9	15.5-5.8	...	67.0-40.1	293.3-219.4	...	27.0-12.6
Average Yield %	2.8	4.7	6.2	4.3	4.9	5.0	3.2

Statistics are as originally reported. [1] Bef. inc. from discont. oper. of $11.0 mill., 1995; $3.1 mill., 1996; & $5.6 mill., 1997. [2] Incl. nonrecur. net gain of $9.7 mill. [3] Refl. POP's tissue bus. as discont. opers. [4] Bef. inc. from disc. oper. of $23.1 mill. & acctg. gain of $743,000. [5] Incl. convert. subord. debent.

OFFICERS:
M. Flannery, Chmn., Pres., C.E.O.
M. M. Pope, V.P., C.F.O., Sec.

INVESTOR CONTACT: Investor Relations, (503) 228-9161

PRINCIPAL OFFICE: 1500 S.W. 1st Avenue, Portland, OR 97201

TELEPHONE NUMBER: (503) 228-9161
FAX: (503) 220-2722
WEB: www.poptal.com

NO. OF EMPLOYEES: 1,985

SHAREHOLDERS: 823

ANNUAL MEETING: In Apr.

INCORPORATED: DE, May, 1979

INSTITUTIONAL HOLDINGS:
No. of Institutions: 87
Shares Held: 8,935,527
% Held: 64.4

INDUSTRY: Paper mills (SIC: 2621)

TRANSFER AGENT(S): Mellon Investor Services, Ridgefield Park, NJ

NYSE SYMBOL PPS
Rec. Pr. 36.86 (4/30/01)

POST PROPERTIES, INC.

YIELD 8.5%
P/E RATIO 16.6

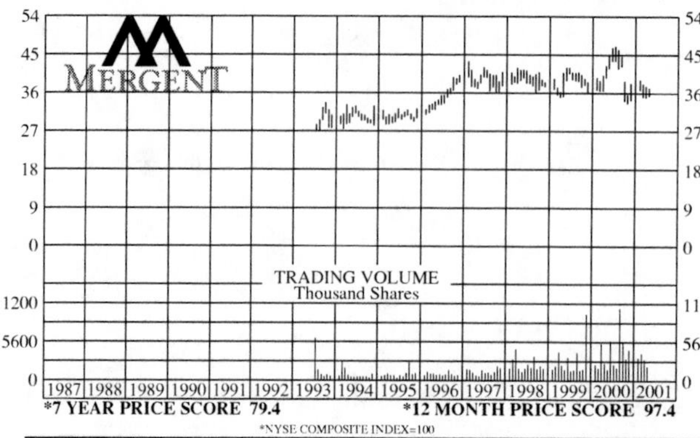

*7 YEAR PRICE SCORE 79.4 *12 MONTH PRICE SCORE 97.4

*NYSE COMPOSITE INDEX=100

INTERIM EARNINGS (Per Share):

Qtr.	Mar.	June	Sept.	Dec.
1998	0.47	0.55	0.57	0.58
1999	0.56	0.61	0.61	0.60
2000	0.63	0.65	0.60	0.34

INTERIM DIVIDENDS (Per Share):

Amt.	Decl.	Ex.	Rec.	Pay.
0.76Q	5/17/00	6/28/00	6/30/00	7/14/00
0.76Q	8/25/00	9/27/00	9/30/00	10/16/00
0.76Q	11/07/00	12/28/00	1/02/01	1/15/01
0.78Q	2/08/01	3/28/01	3/31/01	4/13/01
0.78Q	5/22/01	6/27/01	6/30/01	7/13/01

Indicated div.: $3.12

CAPITALIZATION (12/31/00):

	($000)	(%)
Long-Term Debt	1,213,309	49.9
Minority Interest	188,091	7.7
Preferred Stock	50	0.0
Common & Surplus	1,028,560	42.3
Total	2,430,010	100.0

RECENT DEVELOPMENTS: For the year ended 12/31/00, net income totaled $100.5 million versus income of $105.0 million, before an extraordinary loss of $458,000, in the previous year. Results for 2000 included non-recurring charges of $9.4 million. Also, results for 2000 included a net gain from the sale of assets of $3.2 million versus a loss of $1.5 million in 1999. Total revenue rose 15.6% to $399.8 million compared with $345.9 million a year earlier.

PROSPECTS: During 2000, PPS completed the lease-up of 2,661 units in eight communities plus the second phase of an existing community in five cities at a total investment of $283.0 million. In addition, the Company started 1,428 units in four communities and phases of two additional communities at an estimated total investment of $237.0 million. PPS' development pipeline at 12/31/00 included 4,661 units for aggregate cost of $610.0 million.

BUSINESS

POST PROPERTIES, INC. is a developer and operator of upscale multi-family apartment communities in the Southeastern and Southwestern United States. The Company operates as a real estate investment trust whose primary business consists of developing and managing Post brand name apartment communities for its own account. PPS owns approximately 36,197 apartment homes in 105 communities, primarily located in metropolitan Atlanta, Georgia, Tampa and Orlando, Florida, Northern Virginia, Nashville, Tennessee and Dallas, Texas. The Company also provides services to third-party owners through its wholly-owned operating subsidiaries: RAM Partners, Inc., Post Asset Management, Inc., and Post Landscape Group. In addition to its third party service providers, PPS offers a full-service travel agency, Post Travel.

ANNUAL FINANCIAL DATA

	12/31/00	12/31/99	12/31/98	12/31/97	12/31/96	12/31/95	12/31/94
Earnings Per Share	**[1][4] 2.22**	**[1][3] 2.39**	**[2] 2.18**	**[1][3] 2.09**	**[1] 1.95**	**[1][3] 1.63**	**[1][3] 1.32**
Tang. Book Val. Per Share	**26.47**	**27.26**	**27.64**	**24.71**	**18.20**	**19.99**	**13.97**
Dividends Per Share	**2.98**	**2.75**	**2.54**	**2.33**	**2.11**	**1.92**	**1.80**
Dividend Payout %	**134.2**	**115.1**	**116.7**	**111.2**	**108.2**	**117.8**	**136.4**
INCOME STATEMENT (IN MILLIONS):							
Rental Income	365.9	318.7	275.8	186.1	157.7	133.8	115.3
Interest Income	1.9	0.8	0.5	0.1	0.3	0.6	0.4
Total Income	399.8	345.9	298.9	200.1	170.7	144.7	124.7
Costs & Expenses	154.5	131.8	116.9	81.1	71.0	62.1	55.0
Depreciation	72.7	59.5	47.8	30.0	25.0	22.8	22.2
Interest Expense	50.3	33.2	31.3	24.7	22.1	22.7	19.2
Income Before Income Taxes	116.1	119.9	100.9	66.1	53.5	38.9	29.8
Equity Earnings/Minority Int.	d15.6	d15.0	d11.9	d11.1	d10.0	d8.9	d7.6
Net Income	[1][4] 100.5	[1][3] 105.0	[2] 89.0	[1][3] 54.9	[1] 43.5	[1][3] 30.0	[1][3] 22.2
Average Shs. Outstg. (000)	39,853	38,917	35,474	23,888	21,787	18,382	16,848
BALANCE SHEET (IN MILLIONS):							
Cash & Cash Equivalents	8.7	7.3	22.5	12.4	1.4	10.2	13.6
Total Real Estate Investments	122.0	...	...	...	...	...	d142.6
Total Assets	2,551.2	2,350.2	2,066.7	1,780.6	958.7	813.0	711.0
Long-Term Obligations	1,213.3	989.6	800.0	821.2	434.3	349.7	362.0
Total Liabilities	1,522.6	1,291.3	1,015.0	1,023.6	559.7	469.4	470.8
Net Stockholders' Equity	1,028.6	1,058.9	1,051.7	756.9	399.0	343.6	240.2
Year-end Shs. Outstg. (000)	38,854	38,834	38,052	30,627	21,922	17,194	17,194
STATISTICAL RECORD:							
Net Inc.+Depr./Assets %	6.8	7.0	6.6	4.8	7.1	6.5	6.2
Return on Equity %	9.8	9.9	8.5	7.3	10.9	8.7	9.2
Return on Assets %	3.9	4.5	4.3	3.1	4.5	3.7	3.1
Price Range	47.06-33.50	42.13-35.00	42.00-35.81	43.50-36.00	40.25-30.75	32.25-28.50	33.25-27.38
P/E Ratio	21.2-15.1	17.6-14.6	19.3-16.4	20.8-17.2	20.6-15.8	19.8-17.5	25.2-20.7
Average Yield %	7.4	7.1	6.5	5.8	5.9	6.3	5.9

Statistics are as originally reported. [1] Incl. gain on sale of assets, 2000, $3.2 mill.; loss, 1999, $1.5 mill.; gain, 1997, $3.3 mill.; 1996, $854,000; 1995, $1.7 mill.; 1994, $1.5 mill. [2] Incl. loss on unused treas. stk. of $1.9 mill. [3] Bef. extraord. loss, 1999, $458,000; 1997, $75,000; 1995, $870,000; 1994, $3.3 mill. [4] Incl. non-recurr. chrg., $9.4 mill.

OFFICERS:
J. A. Williams, Chmn., C.E.O.
J. T. Glover, Vice-Chmn.
D. P. Stockert, Pres., C.O.O.
R. G. Fox, Exec. V.P., C.F.O.

INVESTOR CONTACT: R. Byron Carlock, Jr., (404) 846-5000

PRINCIPAL OFFICE: 4401 Northside Parkway, Suite 800, Atlanta, GA 30327

TELEPHONE NUMBER: (404) 846-5000
FAX: (404) 858-1100
WEB: www.postproperties.com

NO. OF EMPLOYEES: 2,036 (approx.)

SHAREHOLDERS: 1,735

ANNUAL MEETING: In May

INCORPORATED: GA, Jan., 1984

INSTITUTIONAL HOLDINGS:
No. of Institutions: 136
Shares Held: 25,509,145
% Held: 65.8

INDUSTRY: Real estate investment trusts (SIC: 6798)

TRANSFER AGENT(S): Wachovia Shareholder Services, Boston, MA

NYSE SYMBOL PCH
Rec. Pr. 35.05 (4/30/01)

POTLATCH CORPORATION

YIELD 5.0%
P/E RATIO ...

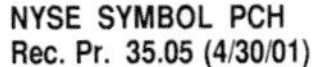

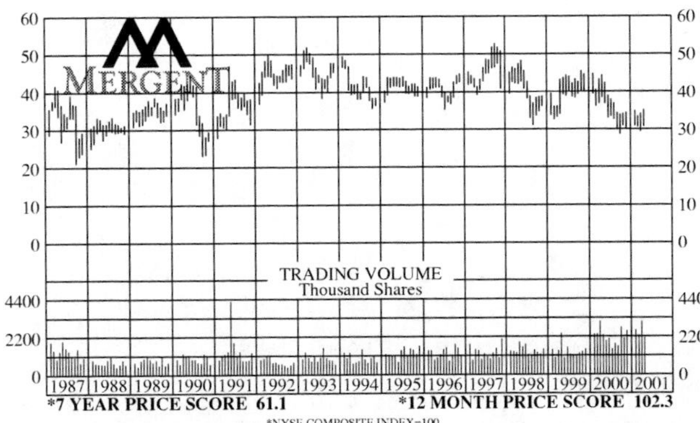

INTERIM EARNINGS (Per Share):

Qtr.	Mar.	June	Sept.	Dec.
1997	0.22	0.34	0.49	0.20
1998	0.37	0.35	0.43	0.13
1999	0.02	0.33	0.77	0.29
2000	0.08	d0.25	0.37	d0.55

INTERIM DIVIDENDS (Per Share):

Amt.	Decl.	Ex.	Rec.	Pay.
0.435Q	3/03/00	5/08/00	5/10/00	6/05/00
0.435Q	7/12/00	8/08/00	8/10/00	9/05/00
0.435Q	9/18/00	11/07/00	11/09/00	12/04/00
0.435Q	1/25/01	2/07/01	2/09/01	3/05/01
0.435Q	3/02/01	5/07/01	5/09/01	6/04/01

Indicated div.: $1.74 (Div. Reinv. Plan)

CAPITALIZATION (12/31/00):

	($000)	(%)
Long-Term Debt	801,549	42.0
Deferred Income Tax	293,961	15.4
Common & Surplus	813,236	42.6
Total	1,908,746	100.0

RECENT DEVELOPMENTS: For the year ended 12/31/00, PCH incurred a net loss of $33.2 million compared with net income of $40.9 million in 1999. Results for 2000 included pre-tax restructuring and mill closure charges of $46.4 million. The decline in earnings was primarily attributed to weakness in wood products markets and high energy costs. Net sales were flat at $1.81 billion compared with the prior year. Sales for 2000 and 1999 were reclassified to include shipping and handling costs.

PROSPECTS: PCH is meeting growing customer requirements by leasing a part of a tissue converting plant in Benton Harbor, Michigan to supply toweling products to its private label customers with mid-western and eastern outlets. In January 2001, PCH cut 124 jobs at its pulp, paperboard and consumer tissue operations in Lewiston, Idaho, as part of an on-going company-wide effort to reduce costs and increase efficiency.

BUSINESS

POTLATCH CORPORATION is an integrated forest products company with approximately 1.5 million acres of timberland in Arkansas, Idaho and Minnesota. The Company is engaged principally in the growing and harvesting of timber and the manufacture and sale of wood products. PCH's manufacturing facilities convert wood fiber into two main lines of products: wood products (lumber, plywood, oriented strand board, particleboard) and bleached fiber products (bleached kraft pulp, paperboard, coated printing papers and consumer tissue). Contributions to sales in 2000 were: pulp and paper, 34.1%; wood products, 25.9%; printing papers, 23.5%; and resource, 16.5%.

ANNUAL FINANCIAL DATA

	12/31/00	12/31/99	12/31/98	12/31/97	12/31/96	12/31/95	12/31/94
Earnings Per Share	**4 d1.16**	**3 1.41**	**1.28**	**1.24**	**2 2.13**	**3.72**	**1 1.68**
Tang. Book Val. Per Share	**28.69**	**31.79**	**32.19**	**32.82**	**33.06**	**33.23**	**31.49**
Dividends Per Share	**1.74**	**1.74**	**1.74**	**1.71**	**1.67**	**1.61**	**1.57**
Dividend Payout %	...	**123.4**	**135.9**	**137.9**	**78.4**	**43.4**	**93.4**
INCOME STATEMENT (IN MILLIONS):							
Total Revenues	1,808.8	1,676.8	1,565.9	1,568.9	1,554.4	1,605.2	1,471.3
Costs & Expenses	1,799.9	1,564.8	1,466.7	1,475.9	1,431.8	1,385.6	1,342.5
Operating Income	8.8	112.0	99.2	93.0	122.7	219.6	128.7
Net Interest Inc./(Exp.)	d59.4	d45.4	d49.7	d46.1	d43.9	d48.0	d51.1
Income Before Income Taxes	d54.4	66.0	58.2	54.6	86.3	170.9	76.0
Income Taxes	cr21.2	25.1	20.9	18.6	24.8	62.4	27.0
Net Income	4 d33.2	3 40.9	37.2	36.1	2 61.5	108.5	1 49.0
Average Shs. Outstg. (000)	28,523	28,967	29,020	28,986	28,888	29,157	29,217
BALANCE SHEET (IN MILLIONS):							
Cash & Cash Equivalents	11.7	11.7	18.1	15.5	12.3	110.2	55.8
Total Current Assets	483.8	416.5	407.9	403.8	378.1	477.2	371.3
Net Property	1,637.4	1,616.1	1,504.5	1,493.4	1,465.7	1,356.0	1,313.9
Total Assets	2,542.4	2,446.5	2,377.3	2,365.1	2,265.7	2,265.3	2,081.2
Total Current Liabilities	439.1	364.7	310.3	297.6	260.1	349.2	228.6
Long-Term Obligations	801.5	701.8	712.1	722.1	672.0	616.1	633.5
Net Stockholders' Equity	813.2	921.0	930.9	951.6	954.2	962.5	920.2
Net Working Capital	44.7	51.8	97.6	106.2	118.0	128.1	142.7
Year-end Shs. Outstg. (000)	28,346	28,972	28,919	28,995	28,866	28,961	29,224
STATISTICAL RECORD:							
Operating Profit Margin %	0.5	6.7	6.3	5.9	7.9	13.7	8.7
Net Profit Margin %	...	2.4	2.4	2.3	4.0	6.8	3.3
Return on Equity %	...	4.4	4.0	3.8	6.4	11.3	5.3
Return on Assets %	...	1.7	1.6	1.5	2.7	4.8	2.4
Debt/Total Assets %	31.5	28.7	30.0	30.5	29.7	27.2	30.4
Price Range	44.88-28.56	45.50-32.50	48.38-31.00	52.75-39.00	44.88-35.13	44.13-37.13	49.50-35.50
P/E Ratio	...	32.3-23.0	37.8-24.2	42.5-31.4	21.1-16.5	11.9-10.0	29.5-21.1
Average Yield %	4.7	4.5	4.4	3.7	4.2	4.0	3.7

Statistics are as originally reported. 1 Incl. pre-tax chrg. of $10 mill. ($0.21/sh.) for early retirement programs. 2 Bef. extraord. chrg. $3.4 mill. for loss from early exting. of debt. 3 Incl. nonrecur. pre-tax chrg. of $7.5 mill. 4 Incl. nonrecur. pre-tax chrg. of $46.4 mill.

OFFICERS:
L. P. Siegel, Chmn., C.E.O.
R. L. Paulson, Pres., C.O.O.
G. L. Zuehlke, V.P., C.F.O., Treas.
D. D. Spedden, Asst. Treas.

INVESTOR CONTACT: Michael D. Sullivan, Inv. Rel., (509) 835-1516

PRINCIPAL OFFICE: 601 West Riverside Ave., Suite 1100, Spokane, WA 99201

TELEPHONE NUMBER: (509) 835-1500
WEB: www.potlatch.com

NO. OF EMPLOYEES: 6,500 (approx.)

SHAREHOLDERS: 3,100 (approx.)

ANNUAL MEETING: In May

INCORPORATED: ME, 1931; reincorp., DE, Aug., 1931

INSTITUTIONAL HOLDINGS:
No. of Institutions: 140
Shares Held: 13,769,290
% Held: 48.6

INDUSTRY: Paper mills (SIC: 2621)

TRANSFER AGENT(S): Computershare Investor Services, Chicago, IL

NYSE SYMBOL POM
Rec. Pr. 21.86 (4/30/01)

POTOMAC ELECTRIC POWER COMPANY

YIELD 4.6%
P/E RATIO 7.3

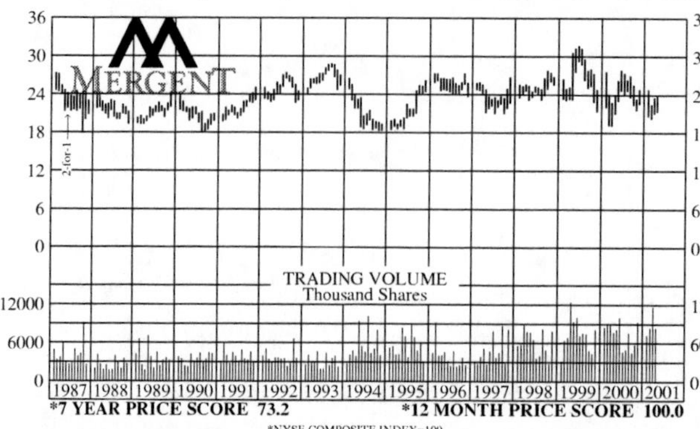

*7 YEAR PRICE SCORE 73.2 *12 MONTH PRICE SCORE 100.0
*NYSE COMPOSITE INDEX=100

INTERIM EARNINGS (Per Share):

Qtr.	Mar.	June	Sept.	Dec.
1997	0.16	0.38	1.07	d0.27
1998	0.03	0.46	1.23	d0.02
1999	0.20	0.61	1.25	d0.09
2000	0.07	0.47	1.04	1.43

INTERIM DIVIDENDS (Per Share):

Amt.	Decl.	Ex.	Rec.	Pay.
0.415Q	4/27/00	6/08/00	6/12/00	6/30/00
0.415Q	7/27/00	9/07/00	9/11/00	9/29/00
0.415Q	10/26/00	12/07/00	12/11/00	12/29/00
0.415Q	1/25/01	3/08/01	3/12/01	3/30/01
0.25Q	4/24/01	6/07/01	6/11/01	6/29/01

Indicated div.: $1.00 (Div. Reinv. Plan)

CAPITALIZATION (12/31/00):

	($000)	(%)
Long-Term Debt	1,859,600	42.7
Deferred Income Tax	418,700	9.6
Redeemable Pfd. Stock	215,300	4.9
Common & Surplus	1,862,500	42.8
Total	4,356,100	100.0

RECENT DEVELOPMENTS: For the year ended 12/31/00, net income advanced 42.5% to $352.0 million compared with $247.1 million in 1999. Results for 2000 included a gain of $423.8 million on a divestiture. Total operating revenue was $3.05 billion, up 23.1% from $2.48 billion in the prior year. Utility earnings were negatively affected by a temporary loss of $15.4 million incurred from the beginning of Customer Choice in Maryland on 7/1/00 until 12/19/00 when POM completed the sale of its generating assets.

PROSPECTS: On 2/12/01, the Company and Conectiv announced that they have approved a definitive merger agreement under which POM will acquire Conectiv for a combination of cash and stock valued at about $2.20 billion. Both companies will become subsidiaries of a new holding company to be named at a later date. The combination will create the largest electricity delivery company in the mid-Atlantic region, serving more than 1.8 million customers.

BUSINESS

POTOMAC ELECTRIC POWER COMPANY (PEPCO) is engaged in the transmission and distribution of electric energy in the Washington, DC metropolitan area. The Company is also engaged in the sale of electricity, natural gas and telecommunications in markets throughout the mid-Atlantic region through Pepco Holdings, Inc. (PHI), its wholly-owned subsidiary. PHI's wholly-owned subsidiaries include Potomac Capital Investment Corporation, Pepco Energy Services, Inc. and PepMarket.com, LLC. In addition, Potomac Electric Power Company Trust I is a wholly-owned Delaware statutory business of PEPCO, and Edison Capital Reserves Corporation is a wholly-owned Delaware investment holding company of the Company. PEPCO's telecommunication products and services are provided through Starpower.

ANNUAL FINANCIAL DATA

	12/31/00	12/31/99	12/31/98	12/31/97	12/31/96	12/31/95	12/31/94
Earnings Per Share	**4 2.96**	**3 1.98**	**2 1.73**	**1.38**	**1.86**	**1 0.65**	**1.79**
Cash Flow Per Share	**5.02**	**4.31**	**3.61**	**3.20**	**3.74**	**2.39**	**3.31**
Tang. Book Val. Per Share	**16.82**	**16.12**	**49.69**	**49.74**	**49.06**	**49.19**	**49.92**
Dividends Per Share	**1.66**	**1.66**	**1.66**	**1.66**	**1.66**	**1.66**	**1.66**
Dividend Payout %	**56.1**	**83.8**	**95.9**	**120.3**	**89.2**	**255.3**	**92.7**
INCOME STATEMENT (IN MILLIONS):							
Total Revenues	3,047.7	2,476.0	2,063.9	1,863.5	2,010.3	1,876.1	1,823.1
Costs & Expenses	1,869.1	1,627.5	1,469.8	1,306.1	1,438.9	1,322.9	1,318.6
Depreciation & Amort.	247.6	272.8	239.8	232.0	223.0	205.5	180.0
Operating Income	702.4	370.8	354.3	325.4	348.4	347.7	324.5
Net Interest Inc./(Exp.)	d220.7	d204.5	d147.6	d138.8	d139.4	d135.8	d129.6
Income Before Income Taxes	693.2	361.6	226.3	181.9	230.3	94.4	227.2
Income Taxes	341.2	114.5	...	...	...	...	...
Net Income	4 352.0	3 247.1	2 226.3	181.9	237.0	1 94.4	227.2
Cash Flow	594.1	511.0	448.1	397.4	436.7	283.0	390.7
Average Shs. Outstg. (000)	118,300	118,500	124,200	124,291	118,497	118,412	118,006
BALANCE SHEET (IN MILLIONS):							
Cash & Cash Equivalents	2,096.0	301.9	6.4	5.6	2.2	5.8	7.2
Total Current Assets	3,024.4	824.8	391.7	392.6	416.1	431.2	430.1
Net Property	2,721.8	4,524.4	4,521.2	4,486.3	4,423.2	4,400.3	4,298.3
Total Assets	7,027.3	6,910.6	6,654.8	6,707.6	6,891.9	7,118.2	6,965.8
Total Current Liabilities	2,435.4	783.5	546.7	490.1	618.7	776.9	581.3
Long-Term Obligations	1,859.6	2,867.0	2,733.5	2,892.4	2,926.8	3,029.8	3,000.6
Net Stockholders' Equity	1,862.5	1,910.3	5,888.8	5,893.8	5,813.8	5,828.5	5,903.0
Net Working Capital	589.0	41.3	d155.0	d97.5	d202.6	d345.7	d151.3
Year-end Shs. Outstg. (000)	110,752	118,531	118,500	118,501	118,500	118,495	118,248
STATISTICAL RECORD:							
Operating Profit Margin %	23.0	15.0	17.2	17.5	17.3	18.5	17.8
Net Profit Margin %	11.5	10.0	11.0	9.8	11.8	5.0	12.5
Return on Equity %	18.9	12.9	3.8	3.0	4.0	1.6	3.8
Return on Assets %	5.0	3.6	3.4	2.7	3.3	1.3	3.3
Debt/Total Assets %	26.5	41.5	41.1	43.1	42.5	42.6	43.1
Price Range	27.88-19.06	31.75-21.25	27.81-23.06	26.81-21.00	27.38-23.63	26.25-18.38	26.63-18.25
P/E Ratio	9.4-6.4	16.0-10.7	16.1-13.3	19.4-15.2	14.7-12.7	40.4-28.3	14.9-10.2
Average Yield %	7.1	6.3	6.5	6.9	6.5	7.4	7.4

Statistics are as originally reported. 1 Incl. $122.2 mill. ($1.04/sh.) after-tax non-recur. chg. 2 Incl. a net charge of $4.7 mill. associated with the Company's severance program 3 Incl. gain of $14.2 mill. contract termination fee. 4 Incl. $423.8 mill. gain fr. a divestiture.

OFFICERS:
J. M. Derrick Jr., Chmn., C.E.O.
D. R. Wraase, Pres., C.O.O.
A. W. Williams, Sr. V.P., C.F.O.

INVESTOR CONTACT: Ernest J. Bourscheid, Mgr. Investor Rel., (202) 872-2797

PRINCIPAL OFFICE: 1900 Pennsylvania Avenue Northwest, Washington, DC 20068

TELEPHONE NUMBER: (202) 872-2000
FAX: (202) 331-6874
WEB: www.pepco.com

NO. OF EMPLOYEES: 2,566

SHAREHOLDERS: 60,159

ANNUAL MEETING: In Apr.

INCORPORATED: DC, Dec., 1896; reincorp., VA, 1949

INSTITUTIONAL HOLDINGS:
No. of Institutions: 199
Shares Held: 42,686,980
% Held: 39.2

INDUSTRY: Communication services, nec (SIC: 4899)

TRANSFER AGENT(S): Mellon Investor Services, Ridgefield Park, NJ

NYSE SYMBOL PPG
Rec. Pr. 53.15 (4/30/01)

PPG INDUSTRIES, INC.

YIELD 3.2%
P/E RATIO 14.9

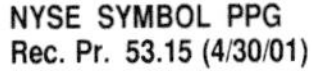

*7 YEAR PRICE SCORE 64.7 *12 MONTH PRICE SCORE 117.2

*NYSE COMPOSITE INDEX=100

INTERIM EARNINGS (Per Share):

Qtr.	Mar.	June	Sept.	Dec.
1997	0.91	1.21	0.96	0.89
1998	1.08	1.11	1.39	0.91
1999	0.70	1.05	0.56	0.92
2000	0.79	1.17	0.86	0.75

INTERIM DIVIDENDS (Per Share):

Amt.	Decl.	Ex.	Rec.	Pay.
0.40Q	7/20/00	8/08/00	8/10/00	9/12/00
0.40Q	10/19/00	11/08/00	11/10/00	12/12/00
0.42Q	1/18/01	2/15/01	2/20/01	3/12/01
0.42Q	4/19/01	5/08/01	5/10/01	6/12/01

Indicated div.: $1.68 (Div. Reinv. Plan)

CAPITALIZATION (12/31/00):

	($000)	(%)
Long-Term Debt	1,810,000	32.4
Deferred Income Tax	543,000	9.7
Minority Interest	128,000	2.3
Common & Surplus	3,097,000	55.5
Total	5,578,000	100.0

RECENT DEVELOPMENTS: For the year ended 12/31/00, net income climbed 9.2% to $620.0 million compared with $568.0 million in 1999. Results for 2000 and 1999 included one-time charges of $5.0 million and $42.0 million, respectively, from business divestitures and realignments. Results for 1999 also included an in-process research and development charge of $40.0 million and non-recurring items totaling $23.0 million. Net sales rose 7.9% to $8.63 billion.

PROSPECTS: Due to a significant downturn in the economy, the Company has begun to finalize plans to implement additional cost reductions, increase efficiencies and accelerate performance improvements. As a result, the Company expects to report a charge in the first quarter of 2001 in the range of $50.0 million to $100.0 million for facility and job consolidations. Meanwhile, PPG will focus on less cyclical, higher-margin businesses.

BUSINESS

PPG INDUSTRIES, INC. is a supplier of products for manufacturing, construction, automotive, chemical processing and numerous other industries. The diversified global manufacturer makes protective and decorative coatings, flat glass, fabricated glass products, continuous-strand fiberglass, and industrial and specialty chemicals. PPG operates 70 major manufacturing facilities in countries including Canada, China, England, France, Germany, Ireland, Italy, Mexico, the Netherlands, Portugal, Spain, Taiwan, and the U.S. In 2000, revenues (and operating income) were derived: coatings, 53.9% (55.4%); glass, 27.2% (30.5%); and chemicals, 18.9% (14.1%).

ANNUAL FINANCIAL DATA

	12/31/00	12/31/99	12/31/98	12/31/97	12/31/96	12/31/95	12/31/94
Earnings Per Share	**[6] 3.57**	**[5] 3.23**	**[4] 4.48**	**[3] 3.94**	**3.96**	**[2] 3.80**	**[1] 2.43**
Cash Flow Per Share	**6.19**	**5.62**	**6.63**	**5.99**	**5.89**	**5.54**	**4.81**
Tang. Book Val. Per Share	**8.61**	**8.30**	**13.17**	**21.29**	**13.55**	**13.21**	**12.35**
Dividends Per Share	**1.60**	**1.52**	**1.42**	**1.33**	**1.26**	**1.18**	**1.12**
Dividend Payout %	**44.8**	**47.1**	**31.7**	**33.8**	**31.8**	**31.1**	**46.1**
INCOME STATEMENT (IN MILLIONS):							
Total Revenues	[7] 8,629.0	7,757.0	7,510.0	7,379.0	7,218.1	7,057.7	6,331.2
Costs & Expenses	6,907.0	6,418.0	5,851.0	5,690.0	5,561.3	5,405.5	4,984.9
Depreciation & Amort.	447.0	419.0	383.0	373.0	362.6	351.6	335.2
Operating Income	1,275.0	1,158.0	1,276.0	1,316.0	1,294.2	1,300.6	1,011.1
Net Interest Inc./(Exp.)	d250.0	d182.0	d137.0	d105.0	d85.0	d74.0	d76.8
Income Before Income Taxes	1,017.0	973.0	1,294.0	1,175.0	1,239.6	1,262.3	855.7
Income Taxes	369.0	377.0	466.0	435.0	471.0	479.7	325.2
Equity Earnings/Minority Int.	d28.0	d28.0	d27.0	d26.0	d5.1	16.0	3.7
Net Income	[6] 620.0	[5] 568.0	[4] 801.0	[3] 714.0	744.0	[2] 767.6	[1] 684.6
Cash Flow	1,067.0	987.0	1,184.0	1,087.0	1,106.6	1,119.2	1,019.8
Average Shs. Outstg. (000)	172,300	175,500	178,700	181,500	187,800	202,000	211,900
BALANCE SHEET (IN MILLIONS):							
Cash & Cash Equivalents	111.0	158.0	128.0	129.0	69.6	105.6	62.1
Total Current Assets	3,093.0	3,062.0	2,660.0	2,584.0	2,296.4	2,275.5	2,168.2
Net Property	2,941.0	2,933.0	2,905.0	2,855.0	2,913.5	2,834.8	2,742.3
Total Assets	9,125.0	8,914.0	7,387.0	6,868.0	6,441.4	6,194.3	5,893.9
Total Current Liabilities	2,543.0	2,384.0	1,912.0	1,662.0	1,768.9	1,629.4	1,424.5
Long-Term Obligations	1,810.0	1,836.0	1,081.0	1,257.0	833.9	735.5	773.4
Net Stockholders' Equity	3,097.0	3,106.0	2,880.0	2,509.0	2,482.6	2,569.2	2,557.0
Net Working Capital	550.0	678.0	748.0	922.0	527.5	646.1	743.7
Year-end Shs. Outstg. (000)	168,222	173,988	175,000	117,826	183,215	194,450	206,988
STATISTICAL RECORD:							
Operating Profit Margin %	14.8	14.9	17.0	17.8	17.9	18.4	16.0
Net Profit Margin %	7.2	7.3	10.7	9.7	10.3	10.9	10.8
Return on Equity %	20.0	18.3	27.8	28.5	30.0	29.9	26.8
Return on Assets %	6.8	6.4	10.8	10.4	11.6	12.4	11.6
Debt/Total Assets %	19.8	20.6	14.6	18.3	12.9	11.9	13.1
Price Range	65.06-36.00	70.75-47.94	76.63-49.13	67.50-48.63	62.25-42.88	47.88-34.88	42.13-33.75
P/E Ratio	18.2-10.1	21.9-14.8	17.1-11.0	17.1-12.3	15.7-10.8	12.6-9.2	17.3-13.9
Average Yield %	3.2	2.6	2.3	2.3	2.4	2.9	3.0

Statistics are as originally reported. Adj for 2-1 split, 6/94. [1] Incl $51.9 mil a-tx chg dvst med elec bus. [2] Incl $24.2 mil a-tax nonrecur. gain. [3] Incl $102 mil nonrecur. p-tx chg & $59 mil p-tx gain dvst chem busn. [4] Incl. $85.0 mill. p-tax gain fr. sale of bus. & $27.0 mill. p-tax restr. chg. and oth. chgs. [5] Incl. $110.0 mill. in p-tax chgs. [6] Incl. $5.0 mill. one-time chg. fr. bus. divestiture & realignments. [7] Incl. outgoing freight costs.

OFFICERS:
R. W. LeBoeuf, Chmn., C.E.O.
J. C. Diggs, Sr. V.P., Gen. Couns.

INVESTOR CONTACT: Jeff Worden, (412) 434-3046

PRINCIPAL OFFICE: One PPG Place, Pittsburgh, PA 15272

TELEPHONE NUMBER: (412) 434-3131
FAX: (412) 434-2571
WEB: www.ppg.com
NO. OF EMPLOYEES: 35,600 (avg.)
SHAREHOLDERS: 30,035
ANNUAL MEETING: In Apr.
INCORPORATED: PA, Nov., 1883; reincorp., PA, Nov., 1920

INSTITUTIONAL HOLDINGS:
No. of Institutions: 376
Shares Held: 89,373,488
% Held: 53.1

INDUSTRY: Paints and allied products (SIC: 2851)

TRANSFER AGENT(S): Mellon Investor Services LLC, Ridgefield Park, NJ

NYSE SYMBOL PPL
Rec. Pr. 55.00 (4/30/01)

PPL CORPORATION

YIELD 1.9%
P/E RATIO 16.0

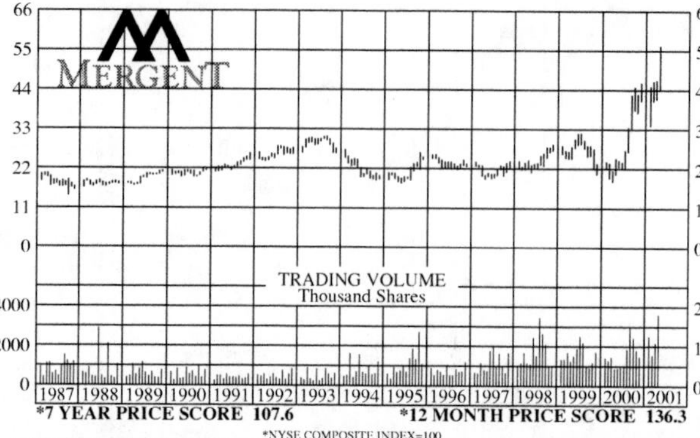

*7 YEAR PRICE SCORE 107.6 *12 MONTH PRICE SCORE 136.3
*NYSE COMPOSITE INDEX=100

INTERIM EARNINGS (Per Share):

Qtr.	Mar.	June	Sept.	Dec.
1997	0.72	0.39	0.25	0.44
1998	0.60	0.32	0.81	0.47
1999	0.70	0.40	1.07	1.02
2000	0.99	0.64	0.94	0.87

INTERIM DIVIDENDS (Per Share):

Amt.	Decl.	Ex.	Rec.	Pay.
0.265Q	5/26/00	6/07/00	6/09/00	7/01/00
0.265Q	8/25/00	9/06/00	9/08/00	10/01/00
0.265Q	11/17/00	12/06/00	12/08/00	1/01/01
0.265Q	2/23/01	3/07/01	3/09/01	4/01/01
0.265Q	5/25/01	6/06/01	6/08/01	7/01/01

Indicated div.: $1.06 (Div. Reinv. Plan)

CAPITALIZATION (12/31/00):

	($000)	(%)
Long-Term Debt	4,467,000	64.9
Minority Interest	54,000	0.8
Preferred Stock	97,000	1.4
Common & Surplus	2,262,000	32.9
Total	6,880,000	100.0

RECENT DEVELOPMENTS: For the year ended 12/31/00, income before extraordinary items climbed 1.8% to $513.0 million compared with $504.0 million in 1999. Results for 2000 and 1999 excluded a net extraordinary gain of $11.0 million and a net extraordinary charge of $46.0 million, respectively. Total operating revenues rose 23.8% to $5.68 billion from $4.59 billion in the prior year. Operating income jumped 37.8% to $1.20 billion compared with $872.0 million the year before.

PROSPECTS: PPL expects earnings to be strong due to its ability to capture value related to high forward electricity prices in both the Eastern and Western U.S. markets. As a result, PPL expects earnings per share for 2001 and 2002 to be in the ranges of $3.60 to $3.65, and $3.90 to $4.00, respectively. The major drivers for PPL's earnings forecast include increased margins on wholesale energy transactions and a higher supply of electricity to sell in the competitive wholesale markets in the West.

BUSINESS

PPL CORPORATION (formerly PP&L Resources, Inc.) delivers electricity and natural gas to more than 1.3 million customers in Pennsylvania; markets wholesale or retail energy in 42 U.S. states and Canada; provides energy services for businesses in the Mid-Atlantic and Northeastern U.S.; generates electricity at power plants in Pennsylvania, Maine and Montana; delivers electricity to 2.4 million customers in southwest Great Britain; and delivers electricity to about 1.8 million customers in Chile, Bolivia, El Salvador and Brazil. Revenues for 2000 were derived: electric 52.5%; gas and propane, 3.2%; wholesale energy marketing and trading, 36.6%; and energy-related businesses, 7.7%.

ANNUAL FINANCIAL DATA

	12/31/00	12/31/99	12/31/98	12/31/97	12/31/96	12/31/95	12/31/94
Earnings Per Share	**5 3.28**	**4 3.14**	**3 2.29**	**1.80**	**2.05**	**2 2.05**	**1 1.41**
Cash Flow Per Share	**6.00**	**4.53**	**4.71**	**4.49**	**4.76**	**4.54**	**3.76**
Tang. Book Val. Per Share	**12.96**	**12.96**	**12.96**	**18.32**	**16.88**	**16.29**	**15.79**
Dividends Per Share	**1.06**	**1.00**	**1.50**	**1.67**	**1.67**	**0.83**	...
Dividend Payout %	**32.3**	**42.6**	**65.6**	**92.8**	**81.5**	**40.7**	...
INCOME STATEMENT (IN MILLIONS):							
Total Revenues	5,683.0	4,590.0	3,786.0	3,049.0	2,910.0	2,751.8	2,725.1
Costs & Expenses	3,838.0	3,291.0	2,381.0	1,875.0	1,726.0	1,599.4	1,683.1
Depreciation & Amort.	382.0	212.0	396.0	445.0	437.0	393.1	360.8
Maintenance Exp.	261.0	215.0	182.0	184.0	191.0	185.6	180.0
Operating Income	1,202.0	872.0	827.0	545.0	556.0	835.4	501.2
Net Interest Inc./(Exp.)	d376.0	d277.0	d230.0	d215.0	d220.0	d225.9	d226.3
Income Taxes	294.0	174.0	259.0	cr9.0	...	23.9	cr38.6
Equity Earnings/Minority Int.	d4.0	d14.0	...	...	...	...	...
Net Income	5 513.0	4 504.0	3 404.0	320.0	357.0	2 350.4	1 244.3
Cash Flow	869.0	690.0	775.0	741.0	766.0	688.0	548.4
Average Shs. Outstg. (000)	144,782	152,287	164,651	165,000	161,060	157,649	153,458
BALANCE SHEET (IN MILLIONS):							
Gross Property	5,750.0	5,425.0	4,295.0	10,169.0	9,996.0	9,807.8	9,517.8
Accumulated Depreciation	...	...	...	3,570.0	3,337.0	2,904.0	2,615.1
Net Property	5,948.0	5,644.0	4,480.0	6,820.0	6,960.0	7,178.9	7,194.5
Total Assets	12,360.0	11,174.0	9,607.0	9,485.0	9,636.0	9,491.7	9,371.7
Long-Term Obligations	4,467.0	3,756.0	3,092.0	2,698.0	2,968.0	2,967.4	3,091.8
Net Stockholders' Equity	2,359.0	1,960.0	2,137.0	3,156.0	3,211.0	3,063.5	2,920.8
Year-end Shs. Outstg. (000)	145,041	143,697	157,412	167,000	162,665	159,430	155,482
STATISTICAL RECORD:							
Operating Profit Margin %	21.2	19.0	21.8	17.9	19.1	30.4	18.4
Net Profit Margin %	9.0	11.0	10.7	10.5	12.3	12.7	9.0
Net Inc./Net Property %	8.6	8.4	9.0	4.7	5.1	4.9	3.4
Net Inc./Tot. Capital %	7.5	8.2	7.7	4.1	4.4	4.4	3.1
Return on Equity %	21.5	24.3	18.9	11.4	13.0	13.5	10.0
Accum. Depr./Gross Prop. %	...	...	60.5	35.1	33.4	29.6	27.5
Price Range	46.13-18.38	32.00-20.38	28.94-20.88	24.25-19.00	26.00-21.63	26.50-17.88	27.25-18.63
P/E Ratio	13.7-5.5	10.2-6.5	12.6-9.1	13.5-10.6	12.7-10.5	12.9-8.7	19.3-13.2
Average Yield %	3.3	3.8	6.0	7.7	7.0	3.8	...

Statistics are as originally reported. 1 Incl. $83.0 mill. ($0.54 per sh.) after-tax chgs. 2 Incl. $0.21 per sh. gain fr. adjust. rel. to a rate decision, $0.12 per sh. gain fr. sale of Greene Hill reserves. & $0.11 per sh. chg. fr. employ. reductions. 3 Excl. $948.0 mill. net extraord. loss rel. to settlement of restr. cas with PA Public Utility Comm. 4 Excl. $46.0 mill. extraord. loss fr. repurchase of first mortgage bonds. 5 Excl. $11.0 mill. net extraord. gain.

OFFICERS:
W. F. Hecht, Chmn., Pres., C.E.O.
J. R. Biggar, Exec. V.P., C.F.O.
J. E. Abel, V.P., Fin., Treas.

INVESTOR CONTACT: George I. Kline, Manager, Investor Services, (800) 345-3085

PRINCIPAL OFFICE: Two North Ninth Street, Allentown, PA 18101

TELEPHONE NUMBER: (610) 774-5151
FAX: (610) 774-5106
WEB: www.pplresources.com

NO. OF EMPLOYEES: 11,893

SHAREHOLDERS: 91,777

ANNUAL MEETING: In Apr.

INCORPORATED: PA, Mar., 1994

INSTITUTIONAL HOLDINGS:
No. of Institutions: 286
Shares Held: 59,482,742
% Held: 40.9

INDUSTRY: Electric services (SIC: 4911)

TRANSFER AGENT(S): Wells Fargo Shareowner Services, South St. Paul, MN

NYSE SYMBOL PX
Rec. Pr. 47.33 (4/30/01)

PRAXAIR, INC.

YIELD 1.4%
P/E RATIO 20.9

TRADING VOLUME Thousand Shares

*7 YEAR PRICE SCORE 77.8 *12 MONTH PRICE SCORE 119.6

*NYSE COMPOSITE INDEX=100

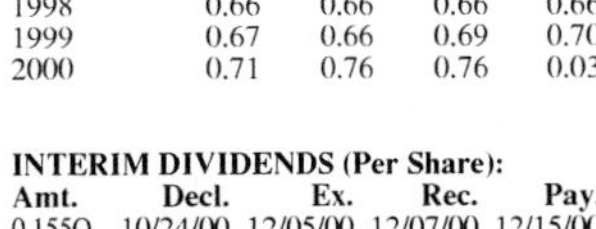

INTERIM EARNINGS (Per Share):

Qtr.	Mar.	June	Sept.	Dec.
1997	0.62	0.65	0.65	0.61
1998	0.66	0.66	0.66	0.66
1999	0.67	0.66	0.69	0.70
2000	0.71	0.76	0.76	0.03

INTERIM DIVIDENDS (Per Share):

Amt.	Decl.	Ex.	Rec.	Pay.
0.155Q	10/24/00	12/05/00	12/07/00	12/15/00
0.17Q	1/30/01	3/05/01	3/07/01	3/15/01
0.17Q	4/24/01	6/05/01	6/07/01	6/15/01

Indicated div.: $0.68 (Div. Reinv. Plan)

CAPITALIZATION (12/31/00):

	($000)	(%)
Long-Term Debt	2,641,000	51.2
Minority Interest	138,000	2.7
Redeemable Pfd. Stock	20,000	0.4
Common & Surplus	2,357,000	45.7
Total	5,156,000	100.0

RECENT DEVELOPMENTS: For the year ended 12/31/00, net income fell 17.7% to $363.0 million compared with income before an accounting change of $441.0 million in 1999. Results for 2000 included a $117.0 million after-tax charge related to a repositioning program, a $44.0 million charge for plant closures, consolidations, and project and product line termination costs, and a $67.0 million charge for the write-off of non-strategic assets. Sales rose 8.7% to $5.04 billion from $4.64 billion in the prior year.

PROSPECTS: The Company expects full-year earnings to grow from 5.0% to 10.0%, depending on economic conditions. The Company's strong position overseas and a new restructuring program are expected to offset weak U.S. market conditions, which include an uncertain economy, an ongoing downturn in the steel industry, and volatile energy markets. Separately, Praxair Distribution, a wholly-owned subsidiary of PX, agreed to acquire Interwest Home Medical for about $42.0 million, including assumption of debt.

BUSINESS

PRAXAIR, INC. is one of the largest suppliers of industrial gases worldwide, particularly in North and South America. It serves a variety of industries through the production, sale and distribution of industrial gases and high-performance surface coatings, along with related services, materials and systems. Praxair's primary products are atmospheric gases (oxygen, nitrogen, argon, and rare gases) and process gases (carbon dioxide, helium, hydrogen, electronics gases, and acetylene). PX also designs, engineers, and supervises construction of cryogenic and non-cryogenic supply systems. PX's surface technology applies metallic and ceramic coatings and powders to metal surfaces in order to resist wear, high temperatures, and corrosion.

ANNUAL FINANCIAL DATA

	12/31/00	12/31/99	12/31/98	12/31/97	12/31/96	12/31/95	12/31/94
Earnings Per Share	**5 2.25**	**4 2.72**	**3 2.60**	**2 2.53**	**1 1.77**	**1.82**	**1.45**
Cash Flow Per Share	**5.18**	**5.46**	**5.46**	**5.24**	**4.41**	**3.75**	**3.40**
Tang. Book Val. Per Share	**14.79**	**14.40**	**14.80**	**13.48**	**5.56**	**6.74**	**6.94**
Dividends Per Share	**0.62**	**0.56**	**0.50**	**0.44**	**0.38**	**0.32**	**0.28**
Dividend Payout %	**27.6**	**20.6**	**19.2**	**17.4**	**21.5**	**17.6**	**19.3**
INCOME STATEMENT (IN MILLIONS):							
Total Revenues	5,043.0	4,639.0	4,833.0	4,735.0	4,449.0	3,146.0	2,711.0
Costs & Expenses	3,823.0	3,440.0	3,552.0	3,515.0	3,409.0	2,334.0	1,974.0
Depreciation & Amort.	471.0	445.0	467.0	444.0	420.0	279.0	273.0
Operating Income	707.0	831.0	856.0	838.0	647.0	548.0	447.0
Net Interest Inc./(Exp.)	d224.0	d204.0	d260.0	d216.0	d195.0	d116.0	d108.0
Income Before Income Taxes	483.0	627.0	596.0	622.0	452.0	432.0	339.0
Income Taxes	103.0	152.0	127.0	151.0	110.0	122.0	82.0
Equity Earnings/Minority Int.	d17.0	d34.0	d44.0	d55.0	d60.0	d48.0	d54.0
Net Income	5 363.0	4 441.0	3 425.0	2 416.0	1 282.0	262.0	203.0
Cash Flow	834.0	886.0	892.0	860.0	702.0	541.0	476.0
Average Shs. Outstg. (000)	161,092	162,222	163,356	164,053	159,038	144,147	139,991
BALANCE SHEET (IN MILLIONS):							
Cash & Cash Equivalents	31.0	76.0	34.0	43.0	63.0	15.0	63.0
Total Current Assets	1,361.0	1,335.0	1,394.0	1,497.0	1,666.0	930.0	840.0
Net Property	4,771.0	4,720.0	4,875.0	4,607.0	4,269.0	2,737.0	2,350.0
Total Assets	7,762.0	7,722.0	8,096.0	7,810.0	7,161.0	4,134.0	3,520.0
Total Current Liabilities	1,439.0	1,725.0	1,289.0	1,366.0	2,550.0	1,029.0	889.0
Long-Term Obligations	2,641.0	2,111.0	2,895.0	2,874.0	1,703.0	933.0	893.0
Net Stockholders' Equity	2,357.0	2,290.0	2,332.0	2,122.0	1,924.0	1,121.0	839.0
Net Working Capital	d78.0	d390.0	105.0	131.0	d884.0	d99.0	d49.0
Year-end Shs. Outstg. (000)	159,379	159,048	157,571	157,373	157,749	140,536	137,863
STATISTICAL RECORD:							
Operating Profit Margin %	14.0	17.9	17.7	17.7	14.5	17.4	16.5
Net Profit Margin %	7.2	9.5	8.8	8.8	6.3	8.3	7.5
Return on Equity %	15.4	19.3	18.2	19.6	13.8	23.4	19.4
Return on Assets %	4.7	5.7	5.2	5.3	3.9	6.3	5.8
Price Range	54.94-30.31	58.13-32.00	53.88-30.69	58.00-39.25	50.13-31.50	34.13-19.75	24.63-16.25
P/E Ratio	24.4-13.5	21.4-11.8	20.7-11.8	22.9-15.5	28.3-17.8	18.7-10.9	17.0-11.2
Average Yield %	1.5	1.2	1.2	0.9	0.9	1.2	1.4

Statistics are as originally reported. 1 Incl. CBI integra. chg. of $53.0 mill. 2 Incl. $10.0 mill. pre-tax chg. for restr. & $11.0 mill. pre-tax profit from settlement. 3 Incl. $8.0 mill. chg. for exps. rel. to acq. & $29.0 mill. spl chgs. for impair. loss & prov. loss fr. sale of plant equip. 4 Incl. $14.0 mill. after-tax non-recur. gain & excl. d$10.0 mill. acct. chg. 5 Incl. $117.0 mill. after-tax chg., $44.0 mill. chg. for consol. costs, & $67.0 mill. write-off of assets.

OFFICERS:
D. H. Reilley, Chmn., Pres., C.E.O.
J. S. Sawyer, V.P.,C.F.O.

INVESTOR CONTACT: Scott S. Cunningham, Dir., Inv. Rel., (203) 837-2073

PRINCIPAL OFFICE: 39 Old Ridgebury Rd., Danbury, CT 06810-5113

TELEPHONE NUMBER: (203) 837-2000
FAX: (203) 837-2450
WEB: www.praxair.com

NO. OF EMPLOYEES: 23,430

SHAREHOLDERS: 28,165 (record)

ANNUAL MEETING: In Apr.
INCORPORATED: DE, Oct., 1988

INSTITUTIONAL HOLDINGS:
No. of Institutions: 343
Shares Held: 136,763,373
% Held: 85.1

INDUSTRY: Chemicals & allied products, nec (SIC: 5169)

TRANSFER AGENT(S): The Bank of New York, New York, NY

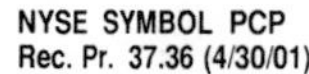

NYSE SYMBOL PCP
Rec. Pr. 37.36 (4/30/01)

PRECISION CASTPARTS CORP.

YIELD 0.3%
P/E RATIO 16.7

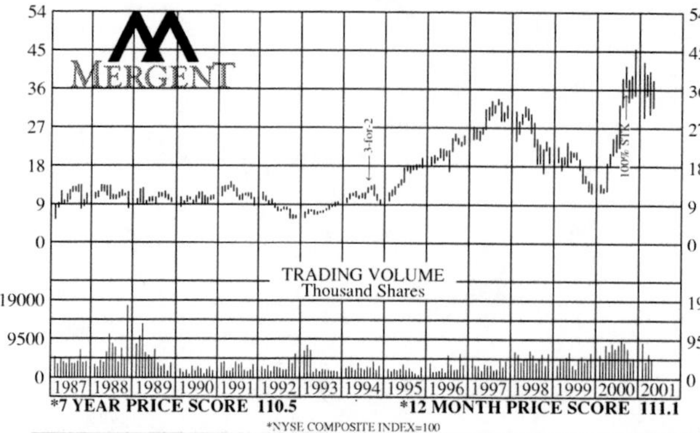

*7 YEAR PRICE SCORE 110.5 *12 MONTH PRICE SCORE 111.1

*NYSE COMPOSITE INDEX=100

INTERIM EARNINGS (Per Share):

Qtr.	June	Sept.	Dec.	Mar.
1996-97	0.28	0.32	0.35	0.35
1997-98	0.41	0.43	0.44	0.49
1998-99	0.50	0.52	0.53	0.57
1999-00	0.46	0.48	0.26	0.55
2000-01	0.57	0.61	0.51	...

INTERIM DIVIDENDS (Per Share):

Amt.	Decl.	Ex.	Rec.	Pay.
0.06Q	...	5/31/00	6/02/00	7/03/00
0.06Q	8/16/00	8/30/00	9/01/00	9/21/00
100% STK	8/16/00	9/22/00	9/01/00	9/21/00
0.03Q	11/15/00	11/29/00	12/01/00	1/02/01
0.03Q	2/14/01	2/28/01	3/02/01	4/02/01

Indicated div.: $0.12

CAPITALIZATION (4/2/00):

	($000)	(%)
Long-Term Debt	884,500	53.3
Common & Surplus	773,900	46.7
Total	1,658,400	100.0

RECENT DEVELOPMENTS: For the quarter ended 12/31/00, net income more than doubled to $26.4 million compared with $12.7 million in the corresponding quarter of 1999. Results included nonrecurring costs of $9.4 million in 2000 and $11.0 million in 1999. The improvement in earnings was primarily attributed to strong performances by certain of PCP's key non-aerospace businesses, and contributions from acquisitions. Net sales were $580.4 million, up 43.4% from $404.7 million a year earlier.

PROSPECTS: The Investment Cast Products segment should benefit from the acquisition of Drop Dies & Forgings. The Forged Products segment should benefit from strong growth in the industrial gas turbine market. The Fluid Management Products segment continues to anticipate renewed capital spending from its oil and gas customers. The Industrial Products segment should continue to experience weakness in the automotive and general industrial marketplace.

BUSINESS

PRECISION CASTPARTS CORP. is a worldwide manufacturer of complex metal components and products. PCP manufactures large, complex structural investment castings, airfoil castings and forged components used in jet aircraft engines. In addition, PCP has expanded into the industrial gas turbine, fluid management, industrial metalworking tools and machines, pulp and paper, advanced metal forming technologies, tungsten carbide, airframe components and other metal products markets. PCP's business segments are Investment Cast Products, Forged Products, Fluid Management Products and Industrial Products. Investment Cast Products includes the PCC Structurals, PCC Airfoils and Wyman-Gordon Castings businesses. Forged Products comprises all of the forging businesses of Wyman-Gordon. Fluid Management Products is the Company's PCC Flow Technologies operation. The Industrial Products segment includes PCC Specialty Products, Inc., J&L Fiber Services, Inc. and Advanced Forming Technology.

ANNUAL FINANCIAL DATA

	4/2/00	3/28/99	3/29/98	3/30/97	3/31/96	4/2/95	4/3/94
Earnings Per Share	**[1] 1.74**	**[1] 2.11**	**[1] 1.77**	**1.30**	**[1] 1.01**	**0.73**	**0.64**
Cash Flow Per Share	**3.24**	**3.21**	**2.66**	**2.10**	**1.57**	**1.32**	**1.38**
Tang. Book Val. Per Share	**...**	**3.50**	**2.96**	**2.60**	**5.41**	**4.47**	**5.67**
Dividends Per Share	**0.12**	**0.12**	**0.12**	**0.12**	**0.12**	**0.09**	**0.04**
Dividend Payout %	**6.9**	**5.7**	**6.8**	**9.3**	**11.9**	**12.4**	**6.2**
INCOME STATEMENT (IN MILLIONS):							
Total Revenues	1,673.7	1,471.9	1,316.7	972.8	556.8	436.4	420.4
Costs & Expenses	1,418.0	1,239.4	1,117.2	825.2	470.1	367.2	353.2
Depreciation & Amort.	74.2	54.1	43.5	35.2	22.9	23.9	28.7
Operating Income	181.5	178.4	156.0	112.4	63.8	45.3	38.5
Net Interest Inc./(Exp.)	d47.1	d27.6	d20.7	d16.7	d0.1	1.5	d1.1
Income Before Income Taxes	138.6	150.8	135.3	95.7	63.7	46.8	37.4
Income Taxes	53.3	47.5	49.2	39.2	22.6	17.8	12.3
Net Income	[1] 85.3	[1] 103.3	[1] 86.1	56.5	[1] 41.1	29.0	25.1
Cash Flow	159.5	157.4	129.6	91.7	64.0	52.9	53.8
Average Shs. Outstg. (000)	49,200	49,000	48,800	43,600	40,754	40,000	39,000
BALANCE SHEET (IN MILLIONS):							
Cash & Cash Equivalents	17.6	14.8	25.0	10.1	26.2	3.9	55.2
Total Current Assets	751.9	556.9	510.8	454.1	224.1	190.1	211.1
Net Property	499.3	331.4	292.7	229.1	143.8	136.2	116.5
Total Assets	2,415.7	1,449.6	1,274.6	1,070.1	450.5	406.7	342.9
Total Current Liabilities	591.5	304.6	264.8	248.9	98.3	100.2	85.4
Long-Term Obligations	884.5	369.7	347.0	261.0	8.8	13.7	10.8
Net Stockholders' Equity	773.9	697.4	595.3	504.4	303.1	258.4	222.8
Net Working Capital	160.4	252.3	246.0	205.2	125.8	89.9	125.7
Year-end Shs. Outstg. (000)	49,288	48,932	48,602	47,962	41,064	40,400	39,300
STATISTICAL RECORD:							
Operating Profit Margin %	10.8	12.1	11.8	11.6	11.5	10.4	9.2
Net Profit Margin %	5.1	7.0	6.5	5.8	7.4	6.6	6.0
Return on Equity %	11.0	14.8	14.5	11.2	13.6	11.2	11.3
Return on Assets %	3.5	7.1	6.8	5.3	9.1	7.1	7.3
Debt/Total Assets %	36.6	25.5	27.2	24.4	2.0	3.4	3.1
Price Range	23.63-11.72	32.13-16.31	33.84-24.00	25.63-16.69	20.00-9.81	13.75-9.00	9.67-5.79
P/E Ratio	13.6-6.8	15.2-7.7	19.2-13.6	19.8-12.9	19.8-9.7	19.0-12.4	15.0-9.0
Average Yield %	0.7	0.5	0.4	0.6	0.8	0.8	0.5

Statistics are as originally reported. Adj. for stk. split: 3-for-2, 8/94. [1] Incl. restruct. chrg. of $3.4 mill., 1996; $8.6 mill., 1998; $13.1 mill., 1999; $9.4 mill., 2000.

OFFICERS:
W. C. McCormick, Chmn., C.E.O.
W. D. Larsson, V.P., C.F.O.
J. A. Johnson, Treas., Asst. Sec.

INVESTOR CONTACT: Dwight E. Weber, Dir. of Comm., (503) 417-4800

PRINCIPAL OFFICE: 4650 S.W. Macadam Avenue, Suite 440, Portland, OR 97201-4254

TELEPHONE NUMBER: (503) 417-4800
FAX: (503) 417-4817
WEB: www.precast.com

NO. OF EMPLOYEES: 13,090 (avg.)

SHAREHOLDERS: 3,868

ANNUAL MEETING: In Aug.

INCORPORATED: OR, 1956

INSTITUTIONAL HOLDINGS:
No. of Institutions: 215
Shares Held: 39,770,159
% Held: 77.6

INDUSTRY: Steel investment foundries (SIC: 3324)

TRANSFER AGENT(S): The Bank of New York, New York, NY

NYSE SYMBOL PR
Rec. Pr. 18.48 (5/31/01)

PRICE COMMUNICATIONS CORP.

YIELD ...
P/E RATIO 37.0

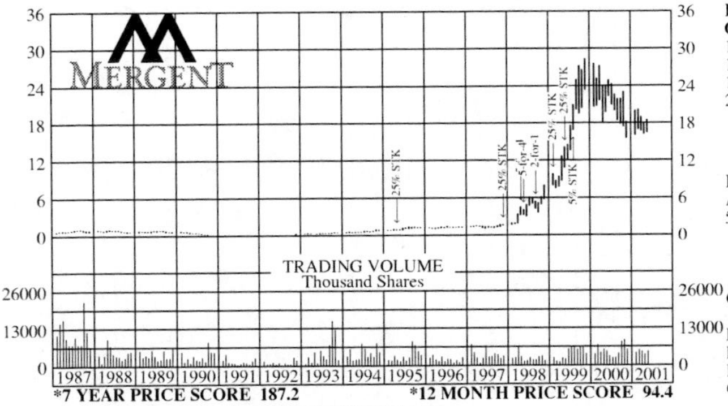

MERGENT

TRADING VOLUME
Thousand Shares

*7 YEAR PRICE SCORE 187.2 *12 MONTH PRICE SCORE 94.4
*NYSE COMPOSITE INDEX=100

INTERIM EARNINGS (Per Share):

Qtr.	Mar.	June	Sept.	Dec.
1997	Nil	0.01	d0.06	d0.16
1998	d0.19	d0.20	d0.50	d0.22
1999	d0.10	0.02	0.07	0.16
2000	0.10	0.14	0.14	0.12

INTERIM DIVIDENDS (Per Share):

Amt.	Decl.	Ex.	Rec.	Pay.
5% STK	8/05/99	8/10/99	8/12/99	8/25/99

CAPITALIZATION (12/31/00):

	($000)	(%)
Long-Term Debt	700,000	60.3
Deferred Income Tax	283,075	24.4
Minority Interest	5,279	0.5
Common & Surplus	172,612	14.9
Total	1,160,966	100.0

RECENT DEVELOPMENTS: For the twelve months ended 12/31/00, PR reported income of $28.5 million, before an accounting charge of $158,000, compared with net income of $10.2 million a year earlier. Service revenue from cellular operations totaled $252.5 million compared with $233.6 million the year before. Equipment sales and installation revenue increased 15.7% to $18.0 million in 2000. Total revenue increased 8.6% to $270.5 million from $249.1 million the previous year. Operating income advanced 23.4% to $96.9 million from $78.5 million in 1999.

PROSPECTS: On 11/14/00, PR and Verizon Wireless, Inc. entered into an agreement under which Verizon Wireless will acquire the Company's wholly-owned subsidiary, Price Communication Wireless (PCW), in a transaction valued at $2.06 billion, less PCW's net indebtedness, estimated at $550.0 million. The consummation of the transaction is subject to termination in certain events and is subject to the completion of the Verizon Wireless initial public offering. If closing of the transaction does not occur by 9/30/01, either party may terminate the agreement.

BUSINESS

PRICE COMMUNICATIONS CORP., is currently engaged through its wholly-owned subsidiary, Price Communications Wireless, in the construction, development, management and operation of cellular telephone systems in the southeastern United States. At 3/31/01, the Company provided cellular telephone service to 541,774 subscribers in Alabama, Florida, Georgia, and South Carolina in a total of 16 licensed service areas, composed of eight Metropolitan Statistical Areas and eight Rural Service Areas, with an aggregate estimated population of 3.3 million. The Company sells its cellular telephone service as well as a full line of cellular products and accessories principally through its network of retail stores. PR markets all of its products and services under the service mark CELLULARONE.

REVENUES

(12/31/2000)	($000)	(%)
Service	252,513	93.3
Equipment Sales & Installation	17,995	6.7
Total	270,508	100.0

ANNUAL FINANCIAL DATA

	12/31/00	12/31/99	12/31/98	12/31/97	12/31/96	12/31/95	12/31/94
Earnings Per Share	3 **0.49**	**0.21**	2 **d1.08**	**d0.21**	**1.12**	**0.20**	1 **0.17**
Cash Flow Per Share	**1.31**	**1.16**	**0.81**	**0.05**	**1.17**	**0.26**	**0.28**
Tang. Book Val. Per Share	...	...	...	...	**1.79**	**0.79**	**0.65**
INCOME STATEMENT (IN MILLIONS):							
Total Revenues	270.5	252.4	197.3	43.7	3.0	29.2	24.0
Costs & Expenses	124.2	126.1	110.7	28.0	4.6	19.3	18.8
Depreciation & Amort.	49.4	47.7	45.8	11.1	0.5	3.6	4.0
Operating Income	96.9	78.5	40.8	4.6	d2.1	6.3	1.3
Net Interest Inc./(Exp.)	d59.7	d72.9	d76.9	d20.1	4.4	d2.6	d1.3
Income Before Income Taxes	43.5	16.2	d23.0	d14.5	95.3	10.9	16.1
Income Taxes	15.0	6.0	cr8.5	cr5.5	24.6	cr0.2	1.7
Equity Earnings/Minority Int.	d1.4	d1.7	d2.2	d0.4	...	...	...
Net Income	3 28.5	10.2	2 d14.5	d8.9	70.7	11.1	1 14.4
Cash Flow	77.9	57.9	31.3	1.0	71.1	14.7	18.4
Average Shs. Outstg. (000)	59,358	49,870	38,523	42,261	60,823	55,986	66,618
BALANCE SHEET (IN MILLIONS):							
Cash & Cash Equivalents	204.2	196.3	210.6	52.3	96.1	1.4	1.1
Total Current Assets	255.9	229.6	239.2	79.9	96.6	10.0	9.1
Net Property	147.2	144.3	144.9	151.3	0.2	11.3	11.5
Total Assets	1,266.4	1,259.0	1,287.7	1,173.6	115.9	96.0	90.9
Total Current Liabilities	52.3	51.4	48.5	55.6	7.1	36.3	9.1
Long-Term Obligations	700.0	700.0	909.4	690.3	...	...	21.3
Net Stockholders' Equity	172.6	173.2	4.4	60.9	108.8	40.9	39.1
Net Working Capital	203.6	178.2	190.8	24.3	89.5	d26.3	...
Year-end Shs. Outstg. (000)	58,208	59,482	37,363	37,649	60,823	51,571	60,366
STATISTICAL RECORD:							
Operating Profit Margin %	35.8	31.1	20.7	10.6	...	21.7	5.4
Net Profit Margin %	10.5	4.0	...	...	2,385.8	38.2	60.0
Return on Equity %	16.5	5.9	...	...	65.0	27.2	36.9
Return on Assets %	2.3	0.8	...	...	61.0	11.6	15.9
Debt/Total Assets %	55.3	55.6	70.6	58.8	...	...	23.4
Price Range	27.63-15.50	28.38-7.43	8.00-1.58	1.74-0.99	1.48-1.03	1.40-0.76	0.94-0.44
P/E Ratio	56.9-31.9	135.4-35.4	...	...	1.3-0.9	7.1-3.9	5.4-2.5

Statistics are as originally reported. Adj. for all stock splits through 4/30/00 1 Incl. gain on sale of prop. of $17.2 mill. 2 Bef. extraord. loss of $27.1 mill. 3 Bef. acctg. chge. chrg. of $158,000

OFFICERS:
R. Price, Pres.
K. I. Pressman, Exec. V.P., C.F.O.

PRINCIPAL OFFICE: 45 Rockefeller Plaza, New York, NY 10020

TELEPHONE NUMBER: (212) 757-5600
FAX: (212) 397-3755

NO. OF EMPLOYEES: 741 (approx.)

SHAREHOLDERS: 400 (approx.)

ANNUAL MEETING: In Aug.

INCORPORATED: NY, Aug., 1979

INSTITUTIONAL HOLDINGS:
No. of Institutions: 118
Shares Held: 30,206,599
% Held: 54.8

INDUSTRY: Radiotelephone communications (SIC: 4812)

TRANSFER AGENT(S): Computershare Investor Services, LLC, Chicago, IL

NYSE SYMBOL PDE
Rec. Pr. 26.63 (5/31/01)

PRIDE INTERNATIONAL INC.

YIELD . . .
P/E RATIO 2663.0

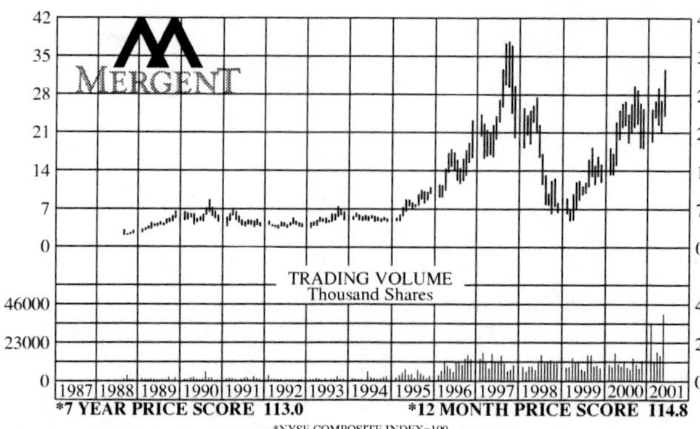

INTERIM EARNINGS (Per Share):

Qtr.	Mar.	June	Sept.	Dec.
1998	0.40	0.43	0.37	0.21
1999	d0.78	d0.13	d0.11	d0.05
2000	d0.10	d0.03	0.02	0.12

INTERIM DIVIDENDS (Per Share):

Amt.	Decl.	Ex.	Rec.	Pay.

No dividends paid.

CAPITALIZATION (12/31/00):

	($000)	(%)
Long-Term Debt	1,144,638	51.8
Capital Lease Obligations	17,682	0.8
Deferred Income Tax	40,793	1.8
Minority Interest	46,739	2.1
Common & Surplus	958,096	43.4
Total	2,207,948	100.0

RECENT DEVELOPMENTS: For the year ended 12/31/00, net income was $736,000 versus a loss of $55.8 million, before an extraordinary gain of $3.9 million, a year earlier. Results for 1999 included restructuring charges totaling $36.6 million. Revenues rose 46.8% to $909.0 million. PDE attributed the improved results to gains in utilization and day rates and the addition of two new ultra-deepwater drillships and two jackups to its international offshore operations. Operating results also benefited from contributions of the E&P services segment acquired in April 2000.

PROSPECTS: On 1/26/01, the Company entered into new five-year charter and service contracts with Petroleo Brasilerio S.A. for the operation of two recently completed deepwater, semi-submersible drilling rigs. The Company is to receive aggregate revenues of more than $500.0 million over the terms of the contracts. Going forward, the Company anticipates continued increases in utilization and day rates. Additionally, the Company expects results to improve throughout 2001, provided that commodity prices remain near their current levels.

BUSINESS

PRIDE INTERNATIONAL INC. is a major international provider of contract drilling and related services, operating both offshore and on land in more than 20 countries. As of 12/31/00, the Company operated a global fleet of 298 rigs, including two ultra-deepwater drillships, seven semisubmersible rigs, 19 jackup rigs, five tender-assisted rigs, three barge rigs, 21 offshore platform rigs and 241 land-based drilling and workover rigs. The Company, through its international company, Servicios Especiales San Antonio S.A., provides a variety of oilfield services to customers in Argentina, Venezuela, Bolivia and Peru. Services provided include integrated project management, coiled tubing drilling and completion, under-balanced drilling, directional and horizontal drilling, environmental drilling, as well as cementing, stimulation, and other related services.

REVENUES

(12/31/2000)	($000)	(%)
United States offshore	136,092	15.0
International land	364,461	40.1
International offshore	322,581	35.5
E&P Services	85,873	9.4
Total	909,007	100.0

ANNUAL FINANCIAL DATA

	12/31/00	12/31/99	12/31/98	12/31/97	12/31/96	12/31/95	12/31/94
Earnings Per Share	**0.01**	[1][2] **d1.06**	**1.39**	**2.16**	**0.81**	**0.60**	**0.30**
Cash Flow Per Share	**2.10**	**0.97**	**2.71**	**3.31**	**1.84**	**1.26**	**0.76**
Tang. Book Val. Per Share	**13.39**	**13.66**	**15.08**	**13.62**	**6.97**	**5.14**	**4.49**
INCOME STATEMENT (IN MILLIONS):							
Total Revenues	909.0	619.4	835.6	699.8	407.2	263.6	182.3
Costs & Expenses	674.7	546.4	607.3	532.7	338.0	220.7	164.8
Depreciation & Amort.	140.6	106.7	87.3	58.7	29.1	16.7	9.6
Operating Income	93.7	d33.7	141.0	108.4	40.1	26.3	8.0
Net Interest Inc./(Exp.)	d78.6	d52.4	d39.9	d30.6	d11.2	d5.5	0.4
Income Before Income Taxes	16.9	d79.0	102.2	155.6	30.8	22.4	8.1
Income Taxes	5.3	cr23.3	24.7	51.6	8.1	7.1	1.9
Equity Earnings/Minority Int.	d10.8	. . .	. . .	. . .	. . .	. . .	. . .
Net Income	0.7	[1][2] d55.8	77.5	104.0	22.7	15.4	6.2
Cash Flow	141.4	50.9	164.8	162.7	51.8	32.0	15.8
Average Shs. Outstg. (000)	67,418	52,526	60,851	49,143	28,198	25,465	20,795
BALANCE SHEET (IN MILLIONS):							
Cash & Cash Equivalents	123.5	154.5	86.5	74.4	10.8	11.9	9.0
Total Current Assets	478.1	397.5	369.8	334.2	156.4	73.2	60.3
Net Property	2,020.1	1,893.7	1,725.8	1,171.6	375.2	178.5	139.9
Total Assets	2,676.9	2,388.7	2,192.2	1,541.5	542.1	257.6	205.2
Total Current Liabilities	387.6	264.8	285.2	230.5	93.7	41.9	33.6
Long-Term Obligations	1,162.3	1,148.9	970.5	523.9	187.0	61.1	42.1
Net Stockholders' Equity	958.1	825.3	763.4	685.2	201.8	131.2	111.4
Net Working Capital	90.5	132.7	84.6	103.7	62.7	31.3	26.6
Year-end Shs. Outstg. (000)	67,689	60,416	50,383	50,043	28,518	24,809	24,028
STATISTICAL RECORD:							
Operating Profit Margin %	10.3	. . .	16.9	15.5	9.9	10.0	4.4
Net Profit Margin %	0.1	. . .	9.3	14.9	5.6	5.8	3.4
Return on Equity %	0.1	. . .	10.2	15.2	11.3	11.7	5.6
Return on Assets %	. . .	. . .	3.5	6.7	4.2	6.0	3.0
Debt/Total Assets %	43.4	48.1	44.3	34.0	34.5	23.7	20.5
Price Range	29.63-13.25	18.31-4.81	27.50-6.13	37.75-16.25	23.25-9.13	11.00-4.75	6.25-4.63
P/E Ratio	2,933.2-1,311.9	. . .	19.8-4.4	17.5-7.5	28.7-11.3	18.3-7.9	20.8-15.4

Statistics are as originally reported. [1] Incl. restruct. chrg., $36.6 mill. [2] Bef. extraord. gain, $3.9 mill.

OFFICERS:
J. B. Clement, Chmn.
P. A. Bragg, Pres., C.E.O.
E. W. McNiel, V.P., C.F.O.
R. W. Randall, V.P., Sec., Gen. Couns.

PRINCIPAL OFFICE: 5847 San Felipe, Suite 3300, Houston, TX 77057

TELEPHONE NUMBER: (713) 789-1400
FAX: (713) 789-1430
WEB: www.prde.com
NO. OF EMPLOYEES: 8,700 (approx.)
SHAREHOLDERS: 1,608 (record)
ANNUAL MEETING: In May
INCORPORATED: Dec., 1968; reincorp., LA, May, 1988

INSTITUTIONAL HOLDINGS:
No. of Institutions: 188
Shares Held: 51,327,878
% Held: 76.5

INDUSTRY: Oil and gas field services, nec (SIC: 1389)

TRANSFER AGENT(S): American Stock Transfer & Trust Company, New York, NY

NYSE SYMBOL PRM
Rec. Pr. 7.43 (4/30/01)

PRIMEDIA INC.

YIELD ...
P/E RATIO ...

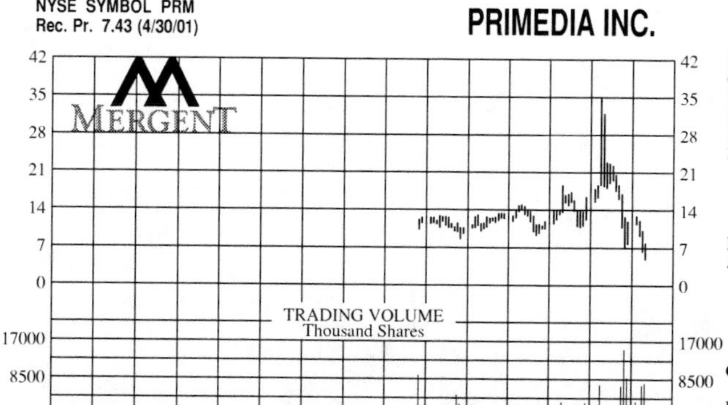

*7 YEAR PRICE SCORE N/A *12 MONTH PRICE SCORE 55.1
*NYSE COMPOSITE INDEX=100

INTERIM EARNINGS (Per Share):

Qtr.	Mar.	June	Sept.	Dec.
1997	d0.19	d0.07	d1.24	d0.22
1998	d0.25	d0.14	d0.15	d0.17
1999	d0.41	d0.12	d0.21	d0.45
2000	d0.35	d0.13	d0.34	d1.53

INTERIM DIVIDENDS (Per Share):

Amt.	Decl.	Ex.	Rec.	Pay.

No dividends paid.

CAPITALIZATION (12/31/00):

	($000)	(%)
Long-Term Debt	1,503,188	82.2
Redeemable Pfd. Stock	561,324	30.7
Common & Surplus	d236,026	-12.9
Total	1,828,486	100.0

RECENT DEVELOPMENTS: For the year ended 12/31/00, PRM incurred a net loss of $346.8 million versus a net loss of $120.1 million in 1999. Results for 2000 and 1999 included nonrecurring items that resulted in pre-tax net losses of $41.6 million and $62.2 million, respectively. Earnings for 2000 also included a pre-tax provision of $230.1 million for the impairment of securities. Net sales fell 1.5% to $1.69 billion.

PROSPECTS: On 3/1/01, PRM announced that it acquired About, Inc., an Internet media company that provides news and information. The acquisition increased PRM's ownership of Web sites to about 1,000 and is expected to reduce expenses across PRM's Internet properties by $30.0 million. Looking ahead, PRM anticipates 30.0% growth in earnings before income tax, depreciation and amortization in 2001, with 20.0% growth thereafter.

BUSINESS

PRIMEDIA INC. (formerly K-III Communications Corp.) is a media company with print, video, and Internet businesses focused on consumer and business-to-business audiences. The Company publishes more than 220 magazines, and owns and operates approximately 1,000 Web sites and other Internet properties. The Company's two business segments are consumer and business-to-business. The consumer segment includes the Primedia Consumer Magazine and Internet Group, Channel One Communications, Films for the Humanities and Sciences, the Consumer Guides and related Internet operations. The business-to-business segment includes Intertec, Bacon's, Primedia Workplace Learning, Primedia Information, QWIZ, Inc., Pictorial, Inc. and related Internet operations. On 3/1/01, PRM acquired About, Inc., an Internet media company.

BUSINESS LINE ANALYSIS

(12/31/2000)	REV (%)	INC (%)
Consumer	67.2	64.7
Business-to-Business.	30.6	35.0
Non-Core Businesses	2.2	0.3
Total	100.0	100.0

ANNUAL FINANCIAL DATA

	12/31/00	12/31/99	12/31/98	12/31/97	12/31/96	12/31/95	12/31/94
Earnings Per Share	[6] **d2.48**	[5] **d1.19**	**d0.71**	[4] **d1.72**	[3] **d0.27**	[2] **d0.91**	[1] **d0.65**
Cash Flow Per Share	**d1.33**	**0.37**	**0.85**	**d0.27**	**1.22**	**0.79**	**1.15**
INCOME STATEMENT (IN MILLIONS):							
Total Revenues	1,691.0	1,716.1	1,573.6	1,487.6	1,374.4	1,046.3	964.6
Costs & Expenses	1,472.0	1,434.5	1,233.4	1,321.2	1,094.2	877.2	794.2
Depreciation & Amort.	185.1	227.3	222.0	187.2	194.4	195.4	160.2
Operating Income	33.8	54.3	118.2	d20.8	85.9	d26.3	10.2
Net Interest Inc./(Exp.)	d144.0	d164.9	d144.4	d136.6	d125.5	d105.4	d78.2
Income Before Income Taxes	d305.6	d113.6	d37.7	d159.1	d45.3	d135.0	d83.5
Income Taxes	41.2	6.5	...	cr1.7	cr53.3	cr59.6	cr42.1
Net Income	[6] d346.8	[5] d120.1	d37.7	[4] d157.4	[3] 8.0	[2] d75.4	[1] d41.4
Cash Flow	d214.8	54.1	121.0	d35.3	158.9	91.0	107.3
Average Shs. Outstg. (000)	161,104	145,418	142,529	129,305	130,008	115,077	103,643
BALANCE SHEET (IN MILLIONS):							
Cash & Cash Equivalents	23.7	28.7	24.5	23.0	36.7	27.2	18.2
Total Current Assets	366.9	333.4	347.1	322.5	376.5	303.8	283.1
Net Property	175.6	152.3	147.7	116.4	122.8	112.0	96.8
Total Assets	2,677.5	2,714.6	3,041.1	2,486.0	2,552.2	1,881.4	1,589.7
Total Current Liabilities	713.4	533.9	581.2	468.7	421.2	360.4	281.7
Long-Term Obligations	1,503.2	1,732.9	1,957.0	1,656.5	1,565.7	1,134.9	1,034.7
Net Stockholders' Equity	d236.0	d144.2	d83.7	d162.2	81.6	92.6	27.4
Net Working Capital	d346.4	d200.5	d234.0	d146.2	d44.7	d56.6	1.3
Year-end Shs. Outstg. (000)	167,799	148,245	144,214	128,748	128,992	128,328	107,490
STATISTICAL RECORD:							
Operating Profit Margin %	2.0	3.2	7.5	...	6.2	...	1.1
Net Profit Margin %	...	...	...	...	0.6	...	...
Return on Equity %	...	...	...	...	9.9	...	...
Return on Assets %	...	...	...	...	0.3	...	...
Debt/Total Assets %	56.1	63.8	64.4	66.6	61.3	60.3	65.1
Price Range	34.88-7.00	18.69-10.75	15.00-9.25	13.44-10.00	12.88-8.50	12.63-10.25	...

Statistics are as originally reported. [1] Incl. write-off of $11.9 mill. [2] Incl. restr. & other chrgs. of $14.7 mill. [3] Incl. write-off of $8.6 mill. [4] Incl. loss of $133.6 mill.; bef. extraord. gain of $15.4 mill. [5] Incl. gain of $235.6 mill. from sale of bus. & one-time provisions totalling $297.8 mill. [6] Incl. nonrecurr. pre-tax charges of $271.7 mill.

OFFICERS:
T. S. Rogers, Chmn., C.E.O.
B. C. Chell, Vice-Chmn., Sec., Gen. Couns.
C. G. McCurdy, Pres.
L. R. Rutowski, Exec. V.P., C.F.O.

INVESTOR CONTACT: Investor Relations, (212) 745-0100

PRINCIPAL OFFICE: 745 Fifth Avenue, New York, NY 10151

TELEPHONE NUMBER: (212) 745-0100
FAX: (212) 745-0121
WEB: www.primedianic.com

NO. OF EMPLOYEES: 6,500 (approx.)

SHAREHOLDERS: 583

ANNUAL MEETING: In May

INCORPORATED: DE, Nov., 1991

INSTITUTIONAL HOLDINGS:
No. of Institutions: 107
Shares Held: 52,834,140
% Held: 24.5

INDUSTRY: Periodicals (SIC: 2721)

TRANSFER AGENT(S): The Bank of New York, New York, NY

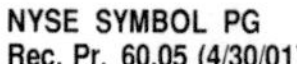

NYSE SYMBOL PG
Rec. Pr. 60.05 (4/30/01)

PROCTER & GAMBLE COMPANY (THE)

YIELD 2.3%
P/E RATIO 22.0

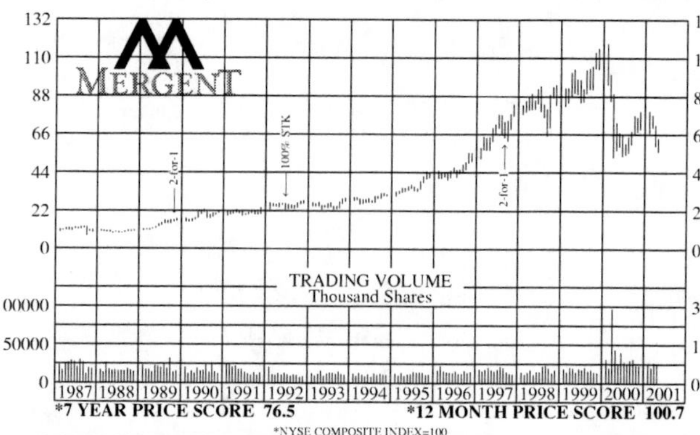

INTERIM EARNINGS (Per Share):

Qtr.	Sept.	Dec.	Mar.	June
1996-97	0.70	0.68	0.63	0.43
1997-98	0.79	0.71	0.65	0.47
1998-99	0.80	0.78	0.72	0.29
1999-00	0.80	0.78	0.52	0.55
2000-01	0.82	0.84	...	...

INTERIM DIVIDENDS (Per Share):

Amt.	Decl.	Ex.	Rec.	Pay.
0.32Q	4/12/00	4/18/00	4/20/00	5/15/00
0.35Q	7/11/00	7/19/00	7/21/00	8/15/00
0.35Q	10/10/00	10/18/00	10/20/00	11/15/00
0.35Q	1/09/01	1/17/01	1/19/01	2/15/01
0.35Q	4/10/01	4/18/01	4/20/01	5/15/01

Indicated div.: $1.40 (Div. Reinv. Plan)

CAPITALIZATION (6/30/00):

	($000)	(%)
Long-Term Debt	8,916,000	40.8
Deferred Income Tax	625,000	2.9
Preferred Stock	1,737,000	8.0
Common & Surplus	10,550,000	48.3
Total	21,828,000	100.0

RECENT DEVELOPMENTS: For the quarter ended 12/31/00, net income climbed 6.0% at $1.19 billion from $1.13 billion in the 1999 quarter. Results included a $120.0 million after-tax restructuring charge. Net sales declined slightly to $10.18 billion versus $10.59 billion in the equivalent 1999 quarter. Net sales in the fabric and home care segment declined 8.0% to $2.93 billion, while paper segment net sales fell 14.0% to $3.05 billion.

PROSPECTS: On 5/21/01, the Company announced an agreement to buy the Clairol business from Bristol-Myers Squibb Company for $4.95 billion in cash. The Company expects Clairol's hair care products, which include such brands as HERBAL ESSENCES, AUSSIE and INFUSIUM, to deliver $900.0 million in incremental sales, while the hair colorants, which include NICE 'N EASY, NATURAL INSTINCTS, and HYDRIENCE, to add another $700.0 million in sales.

BUSINESS

THE PROCTER & GAMBLE COMPANY manufactures and markets about 300 brands of consumer products including laundry, cleaning and personal-care products, pharmaceuticals, foods and beverages, and business and industrial products. Major brands include: CHEER, SPIC & SPAN and TIDE cleansing compounds; CRISCO shortenings, CREST toothpastes, IVORY soaps, HEAD AND SHOULDERS and PANTENE PROV shampoos. Other products include VICK'S cough and cold remedies, CHARMIN toilet tissue, PAMPERS diapers, OIL OF OLAY skin products, OLD SPICE fragrances, FOLGER'S coffee, HAWAIIAN PUNCH fruit drinks and PRINGLES potato chips. PG has operations in over 70 countries and markets to consumers in more than 140 countries. On 9/1/99, PG acquired The Iams Company, a global pet nutrition company.

ANNUAL FINANCIAL DATA

	6/30/00	6/30/99	6/30/98	6/30/97	6/30/96	6/30/95	6/30/94
Earnings Per Share	**2.47**	[2] **2.59**	[1] **2.56**	**2.43**	**2.15**	**1.86**	**1.55**
Cash Flow Per Share	**4.02**	**4.09**	**3.67**	**3.60**	**3.21**	**2.84**	**2.45**
Tang. Book Val. Per Share	**1.35**	**2.62**	**2.55**	**4.59**	**4.05**	**2.99**	**2.29**
Dividends Per Share	**1.34**	**1.21**	**1.07**	**0.95**	**0.85**	**0.75**	**0.66**
Dividend Payout %	**54.2**	**46.7**	**42.0**	**39.3**	**39.6**	**40.4**	**42.7**
INCOME STATEMENT (IN MILLIONS):							
Total Revenues	39,951.0	38,125.0	37,154.0	35,764.0	35,284.0	33,434.0	30,296.0
Costs & Expenses	31,806.0	29,724.0	29,501.0	28,789.0	29,111.0	28,002.0	25,582.0
Depreciation & Amort.	2,191.0	2,148.0	1,598.0	1,487.0	1,358.0	1,253.0	1,134.0
Operating Income	5,954.0	6,253.0	6,055.0	5,488.0	4,815.0	4,179.0	3,580.0
Net Interest Inc./(Exp.)	d722.0	d650.0	d548.0	d457.0	d484.0	d488.0	d482.0
Income Before Income Taxes	5,536.0	5,838.0	5,708.0	5,249.0	4,669.0	4,000.0	3,346.0
Income Taxes	1,994.0	2,075.0	1,928.0	1,834.0	1,623.0	1,355.0	1,135.0
Net Income	3,542.0	[2] 3,763.0	[1] 3,780.0	3,415.0	3,046.0	2,645.0	2,211.0
Cash Flow	5,618.0	5,802.0	5,274.0	4,798.0	4,301.0	3,796.0	3,243.0
Average Shs. Outstg. (000)	1,427,200	1,446,800	1,465,500	1,360,000	1,372,000	1,372,000	1,366,000
BALANCE SHEET (IN MILLIONS):							
Cash & Cash Equivalents	1,600.0	2,800.0	2,406.0	3,110.0	2,520.0	2,178.0	2,656.0
Total Current Assets	10,069.0	11,358.0	10,577.0	10,786.0	10,807.0	10,842.0	9,988.0
Net Property	13,692.0	12,626.0	12,180.0	11,376.0	11,118.0	11,026.0	10,024.0
Total Assets	34,194.0	32,113.0	30,966.0	27,544.0	27,730.0	28,125.0	25,535.0
Total Current Liabilities	10,065.0	10,761.0	9,250.0	7,798.0	7,825.0	8,648.0	8,040.0
Long-Term Obligations	8,916.0	6,231.0	5,765.0	4,143.0	4,670.0	5,161.0	4,980.0
Net Stockholders' Equity	12,287.0	12,058.0	12,236.0	12,046.0	11,722.0	10,589.0	8,832.0
Net Working Capital	4.0	597.0	1,327.0	2,988.0	2,982.0	2,194.0	1,948.0
Year-end Shs. Outstg. (000)	1,305,900	1,319,800	1,337,400	1,360,000	1,372,000	1,374,000	1,368,000
STATISTICAL RECORD:							
Operating Profit Margin %	14.9	16.4	16.3	15.3	13.6	12.5	11.8
Net Profit Margin %	8.9	9.9	10.2	9.5	8.6	7.9	7.3
Return on Equity %	28.8	31.2	30.9	28.3	26.0	25.0	25.0
Return on Assets %	10.4	11.7	12.2	12.4	11.0	9.4	8.7
Debt/Total Assets %	26.1	19.4	18.6	15.0	16.8	18.4	19.5
Price Range	118.38-52.75	115.63-82.00	94.81-65.13	83.44-51.81	55.50-39.69	44.75-30.31	32.31-25.63
P/E Ratio	47.9-21.4	44.6-31.7	37.0-25.4	34.3-21.3	25.9-18.5	24.1-16.3	20.9-16.6
Average Yield %	1.6	1.2	1.3	1.4	1.8	2.0	2.3

Statistics are as originally reported. Adj. for stk. split: 2-for-1, 9/97 [1] Incl. after-tax chrg. of $137.0 mill. for organization 2005 program [2] Incl. non-recurr. chrg. $385.0 mill.

OFFICERS:
J. E. Pepper, Chmn.
A. G. Lafley, Pres., C.E.O.
C. C. Daley Jr., C.F.O.

INVESTOR CONTACT: Inv. Rel., (513) 983-1100

PRINCIPAL OFFICE: One Procter & Gamble Plaza, Cincinnati, OH 45202

TELEPHONE NUMBER: (513) 983-1100
FAX: (513) 983-2062
WEB: www.pg.com

NO. OF EMPLOYEES: 110,000 (approx.)

SHAREHOLDERS: 291,965

ANNUAL MEETING: In Oct.

INCORPORATED: OH, May, 1905

INSTITUTIONAL HOLDINGS:
No. of Institutions: 978
Shares Held: 639,572,965
% Held: 49.4

INDUSTRY: Soap and other detergents (SIC: 2841)

TRANSFER AGENT(S): The Procter and Gamble Company, Cincinnati, OH

NYSE SYMBOL PGN
Rec. Pr. 42.55 (5/31/01)

PROGRESS ENERGY, INC.

YIELD 5.0%
P/E RATIO 13.6

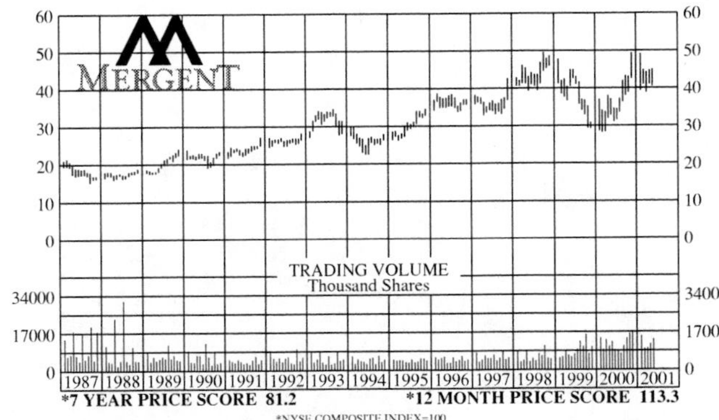

INTERIM EARNINGS (Per Share):

Qtr.	Mar.	June	Sept.	Dec.
1996	0.81	0.37	1.15	0.33
1997	0.56	0.37	1.15	0.58
1998	0.60	0.45	1.28	0.42
1999	0.63	0.43	0.97	0.51
2000	0.56	0.70	1.93	d0.07

INTERIM DIVIDENDS (Per Share):

Amt.	Decl.	Ex.	Rec.	Pay.
0.515Q	5/10/00	7/06/00	7/10/00	8/01/00
0.515Q	9/22/00	10/05/00	10/10/00	11/01/00
0.53Q	12/13/00	1/08/01	1/10/01	2/01/01
0.53Q	3/21/01	4/06/01	4/10/01	5/01/01
0.53Q	5/09/01	7/06/01	7/10/01	8/01/01

Indicated div.: $2.12 (Div. Reinv. Plan)

CAPITALIZATION (12/31/00):

	($000)	(%)
Long-Term Debt	5,890,099	44.6
Deferred Income Tax	1,807,192	13.7
Preferred Stock	92,831	0.7
Common & Surplus	5,424,201	41.0
Total	13,214,323	100.0

RECENT DEVELOPMENTS: For the year ended 12/31/00, net income advanced 26.1% to $478.4 million compared with $379.3 million in the previous year. Results for 2000 included an after-tax nonrecurring charge of $118.3 million associated with the accelerated depreciation of certain nuclear assets and an after-tax gain of $121.1 million from the sale of PGN's 10.0% interest in BellSouth PCS. Operating revenues rose 22.7% to $4.12 billion.

PROSPECTS: Revenues from electric operations should benefit from a 19.0% increase in energy usage in December 2000 due to weather that was colder than normal and high energy usage associated with the holiday season. The Company's natural gas operations continues to expand its distribution services and pipelines. PGN is expecting earnings per share to reach between $3.25 and $3.35 in 2001 with anticipated growth of 7.0% to 8.0% annually thereafter.

BUSINESS

PROGRESS ENERGY, INC. (formerly CP&L Energy, Inc.) is a full-service utility holding company. PGN's diverse portfolio includes two major electric utility companies, CP&L and Florida Power, as well as North Carolina Natural Gas (NCNG), Strategic Resource Solutions (SRS), Progress Telecom and Energy Ventures. CP&L provides electricity and energy services to 1.2 million customers in North Carolina and South Carolina. Florida Power provides electricity and energy services to 1.4 million customers in Florida. NCNG provides natural gas services to 166,000 residential, commercial and industrial customers in south-central and eastern North Carolina. SRS provides energy facility management software and Web-based services. Progress Telecom is a regional carrier whose network includes five states from Washington D.C. to southeast Florida. Energy Ventures manages wholesale energy marketing and trading, merchant generation, fuel properties, and barge and rail subsidiaries.

REVENUES

(12/31/00)	($000)	(%)
Electric	3,565,281	86.5
Natural Gas	324,499	7.9
Diversified Businesses	229,093	5.6
Total	4,118,873	100.0

ANNUAL FINANCIAL DATA

	12/31/00	12/31/99	12/31/98	12/31/97	12/31/96	12/31/95	12/31/94
Earnings Per Share	③ **3.03**	② **2.55**	**2.75**	**2.66**	**2.66**	**2.48**	① **2.03**
Cash Flow Per Share	**8.36**	**10.44**	**10.74**	**10.32**	**9.35**	**9.16**	**8.60**
Tang. Book Val. Per Share	**8.60**	**...**	**19.49**	**18.63**	**17.77**	**16.93**	**16.54**
Dividends Per Share	**2.06**	**2.00**	**1.94**	**1.88**	**1.82**	**1.76**	**1.70**
Dividend Payout %	**68.0**	**78.4**	**70.5**	**70.7**	**68.4**	**71.0**	**83.7**
INCOME STATEMENT (IN MILLIONS):							
Total Revenues	4,118.9	3,357.6	3,130.0	3,024.1	2,995.7	3,006.6	2,876.6
Costs & Expenses	2,564.4	1,928.9	1,654.2	1,663.2	1,765.4	1,767.8	1,553.5
Depreciation & Amort.	835.0	588.1	578.3	565.2	446.5	446.7	473.5
Operating Income	719.6	840.5	897.5	795.6	783.9	792.1	642.9
Net Interest Inc./(Exp.)	d235.3	d169.1	d164.7	d139.6	d167.5	d181.0	d172.6
Income Before Income Taxes	681.1	640.7	656.7	1,175.6	1,176.1	1,161.6	1,021.8
Income Taxes	202.8	258.4	257.5	253.0	269.8	259.2	198.5
Net Income	③ 478.4	② 382.3	399.2	388.3	391.3	372.6	① 313.2
Cash Flow	1,313.3	967.4	974.6	947.5	828.2	809.7	777.0
Average Shs. Outstg. (000)	157,169	148,344	143,941	143,645	143,621	146,232	149,614
BALANCE SHEET (IN MILLIONS):							
Cash & Cash Equivalents	101.3	79.9	28.9	14.4	10.9	14.5	80.2
Total Current Assets	2,656.1	1,079.3	800.9	734.8	672.0	641.7	678.4
Net Property	10,436.7	6,764.8	6,299.5	6,293.2	6,399.9	6,328.5	6,349.5
Total Assets	20,091.0	9,494.0	8,347.4	8,220.4	8,369.2	8,227.1	8,211.2
Total Current Liabilities	5,662.7	893.1	541.5	730.8	735.4	717.7	854.1
Long-Term Obligations	5,890.1	3,028.6	2,614.4	2,415.7	2,525.6	2,610.3	2,530.8
Net Stockholders' Equity	16,924.2	6,560.0	8,631.8	8,172.0	8,194.1	8,047.4	7,990.7
Net Working Capital	d3,006.5	186.2	259.4	4.0	d63.3	d76.0	d175.7
Year-end Shs. Outstg. (000)	206,089	159,600	151,338	151,340	151,416	152,103	156,382
STATISTICAL RECORD:							
Operating Profit Margin %	17.5	25.0	28.7	26.3	26.2	26.3	22.3
Net Profit Margin %	11.6	11.4	12.8	12.8	13.1	12.4	10.9
Net Inc./Net Property %	4.6	5.7	6.3	6.2	6.1	5.9	4.9
Net Inc./Tot. Capital %	3.6	20.4	13.3	13.1	12.6	12.8	12.0
Return on Equity %	8.7	9.1	13.3	13.5	13.8	13.7	11.5
Accum. Depr./Gross Prop. %	47.3	42.4	41.7	39.9	37.2	35.6	33.5
Price Range	49.38-28.25	47.88-29.25	49.63-39.19	42.69-32.75	38.75-33.75	34.63-26.13	30.00-22.50
P/E Ratio	16.3-9.3	18.8-11.5	18.0-14.2	16.0-12.3	14.6-12.7	14.0-10.5	14.8-11.1
Average Yield %	5.3	5.2	4.4	5.0	5.0	5.8	6.5

Statistics are as originally reported. ① Incl. non-recurr. chrg. $20.6 mill. ② Incl. one-time chrg. of $29.0 mill. ($0.14/sh.) related to storm damage. ③ Incl. after-tax nonrecurr. chrg. of $118.3 mill. & an after-tax gain of $121.1 mill. fr. sale of an investment.

OFFICERS:
W. Cavanaugh III, Chmn., Pres., C.E.O.
P. M. Scott III, Exec. V.P., C.F.O.
W. D. Johnson, Exec. V.P., Gen. Counc., Sec.

INVESTOR CONTACT: Investor Relations, (800) 662-7232

PRINCIPAL OFFICE: 410 South Wilmington Street, Raleigh, NC 27601-1748

TELEPHONE NUMBER: (919) 546-6111
FAX: (919) 546-7678
WEB: www.progress-energy.com

NO. OF EMPLOYEES: 16,000 (approx.)

SHAREHOLDERS: 79,058

ANNUAL MEETING: In May

INCORPORATED: NC, Apr., 1926

INSTITUTIONAL HOLDINGS:
No. of Institutions: 320
Shares Held: 96,263,235
% Held: 46.7

INDUSTRY: Electric services (SIC: 4911)

TRANSFER AGENT(S): Wachovia Bank & Trust Co., N.A., Winston-Salem, NC

NYSE SYMBOL PGR
Rec. Pr. 131.04 (5/31/01)

PROGRESSIVE CORPORATION (THE)

YIELD 0.2%
P/E RATIO 214.8

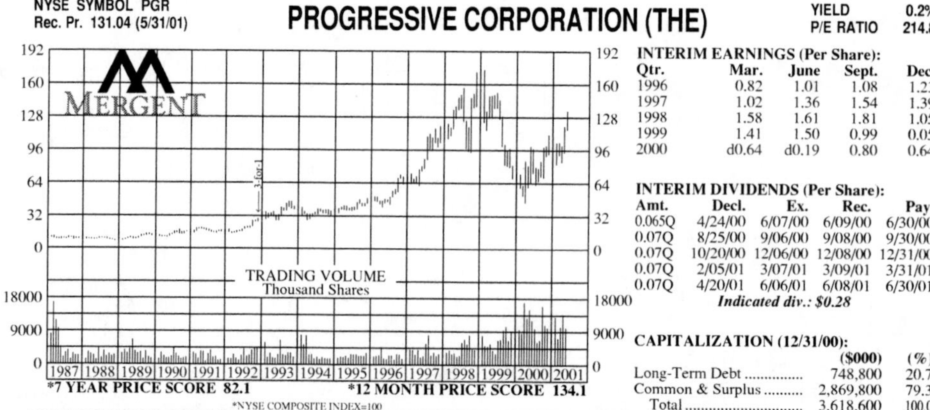

INTERIM EARNINGS (Per Share):

Qtr.	Mar.	June	Sept.	Dec.
1996	0.82	1.01	1.08	1.23
1997	1.02	1.36	1.54	1.39
1998	1.58	1.61	1.81	1.05
1999	1.41	1.50	0.99	0.05
2000	d0.64	d0.19	0.80	0.64

INTERIM DIVIDENDS (Per Share):

Amt.	Decl.	Ex.	Rec.	Pay.
0.065Q	4/24/00	6/07/00	6/09/00	6/30/00
0.07Q	8/25/00	9/06/00	9/08/00	9/30/00
0.07Q	10/20/00	12/06/00	12/08/00	12/31/00
0.07Q	2/05/01	3/07/01	3/09/01	3/31/01
0.07Q	4/20/01	6/06/01	6/08/01	6/30/01

Indicated div.: $0.28

CAPITALIZATION (12/31/00):

	($000)	(%)
Long-Term Debt	748,800	20.7
Common & Surplus	2,869,800	79.3
Total	3,618,600	100.0

RECENT DEVELOPMENTS: For the year ended 12/31/00, net income totaled $46.1 million, a decline of 84.4% compared with $295.2 million in the previous year. Results for 2000 included a non-recurring loss of $4.2 million. Total revenues grew 10.6% to $6.77 billion versus $6.12 billion the year before. Net realized gains on security sales were $16.9 million in 2000 and $47.2 million in 1999, respectively. Net premiums written rose slightly to $6.20 billion from $6.12 billion in the prior year.

PROSPECTS: On 4/30/01, the Company announced the opening of its second data center in Mayfield Village, Ohio. The data center should provide for more server capacity to accommodate increases in on-line consumer interactions and transactions. Looking ahead, the Company expects to achieve an after-tax return on shareholders' equity over a five-year period of at least 15.0% greater than the rate of inflation.

BUSINESS

THE PROGRESSIVE CORPORATION is an insurance holding company that has 76 subsidiaries and two mutual insurance company affiliates. PGR, through its subsidiaries and affiliates, provides personal automobile insurance and other specialty property-casualty insurance and related services throughout the United States. The Company's personal lines segment writes insurance for private passenger automobiles and recreation vehicles. The Company's property-casualty insurance products protect its customers against collision and physical damage to their motor vehicles and liability to others for personal injury or property damage arising out of the use of those vehicles. The Company's other lines of business include the commercial vehicle business unit, United Financial Casualty Company, Professional Liability Group and Motor Carrier business unit.

REVENUES

(12/31/2000)	($000)	(%)
Premiums earned	6,348,400	93.7
Investment income	385,200	5.7
Net real gains on securities	16,900	0.3
Service revenues	20,500	0.3
Total	6,771,000	100.0

ANNUAL FINANCIAL DATA

	12/31/00	12/31/99	12/31/98	12/31/97	12/31/96	12/31/95	12/31/94
Earnings Per Share	**[1] 0.62**	**3.96**	**6.11**	**5.31**	**4.14**	**3.26**	**3.59**
Tang. Book Val. Per Share	**34.83**	**32.96**	**31.14**	**25.95**	**20.65**	**16.79**	**12.70**
Dividends Per Share	**0.27**	**0.26**	**0.25**	**0.24**	**0.23**	**0.22**	**0.21**
Dividend Payout %	**43.5**	**6.6**	**4.1**	**4.5**	**5.6**	**6.7**	**5.8**
INCOME STATEMENT (IN MILLIONS):							
Total Premium Income	6,348.4	5,683.6	4,948.0	4,189.5	3,199.3	2,727.2	2,191.1
Other Income	422.6	440.6	344.4	418.7	279.1	284.7	224.2
Total Revenues	6,771.0	6,124.2	5,292.4	4,608.2	3,478.4	3,011.9	2,415.3
Policyholder Benefits	5,279.4	4,256.4	3,376.3	2,967.5	2,236.1	1,943.8	1,397.3
Income Before Income Taxes	31.8	412.2	661.1	578.5	441.7	345.9	379.8
Income Taxes	cr14.3	117.0	204.4	178.5	128.0	95.4	105.5
Net Income	[1] 46.1	295.2	456.7	400.0	313.7	250.5	274.3
Average Shs. Outstg. (000)	74,300	74,600	74,700	75,300	74,200	74,200	74,000
BALANCE SHEET (IN MILLIONS):							
Cash & Cash Equivalents	195.7	243.2	460.5	432.7	175.1	319.0	292.5
Premiums Due	1,804.7	2,015.5	1,737.2	1,478.3	1,130.8	988.0	922.1
Invst. Assets: Fixed-term	4,784.1	4,532.7	4,219.0	3,891.4	3,409.2	2,772.9	2,424.6
Invst. Assets: Equities	1,198.7	1,243.6	636.9	620.8	540.1	310.0	106.2
Invst. Assets: Total	6,983.3	6,427.7	5,674.3	5,270.4	4,450.6	3,768.0	3,180.0
Total Assets	10,051.6	9,704.7	8,463.1	7,559.6	6,183.9	5,352.5	4,675.1
Long-Term Obligations	748.8	1,048.6	776.6	775.9	775.7	675.9	675.6
Net Stockholders' Equity	2,869.8	2,752.8	2,557.1	2,135.9	1,676.9	1,475.8	1,151.9
Year-end Shs. Outstg. (000)	73,500	73,100	72,500	72,300	71,500	72,100	71,200
STATISTICAL RECORD:							
Return on Revenues %	0.7	4.8	8.6	8.7	9.0	8.3	11.4
Return on Equity %	1.6	10.7	17.9	18.7	18.7	17.0	23.8
Return on Assets %	0.5	3.0	5.4	5.3	5.1	4.7	5.9
Price Range	111.00-45.00	174.25-68.50	172.00-94.00	119.25-61.50	72.25-40.38	49.50-34.75	40.50-27.75
P/E Ratio	179.0-72.6	44.0-17.3	28.2-15.4	22.5-11.6	17.5-9.8	15.2-10.7	11.3-7.7
Average Yield %	0.3	0.2	0.2	0.3	0.4	0.5	0.6

Statistics are as originally reported. [2] Incl. non-recurr. chrg. $4.2 mill.

OFFICERS:
P. B. Lewis, Chmn.
G. M. Renwick, Pres., C.E.O.
W. T. Forrester, C.F.O., Treas.

INVESTOR CONTACT: Investor Relations, (440) 446-2851

PRINCIPAL OFFICE: 6300 Wilson Mills Road, Mayfield Village, OH 44143

TELEPHONE NUMBER: (440) 461-5000
FAX: (440) 446-7168
WEB: www.progressive.com

NO. OF EMPLOYEES: 19,490

SHAREHOLDERS: 3,733

ANNUAL MEETING: In April

INCORPORATED: OH, Feb., 1965

INSTITUTIONAL HOLDINGS:
No. of Institutions: 258
Shares Held: 51,557,178
% Held: 69.8

INDUSTRY: Fire, marine, and casualty insurance (SIC: 6331)

TRANSFER AGENT(S): National City Bank, Cleveland, OH

NYSE SYMBOL PLD
Rec. Pr. 20.60 (4/30/01)

PROLOGIS TRUST

YIELD 6.7%
P/E RATIO 21.5

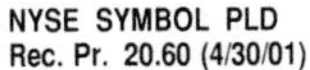

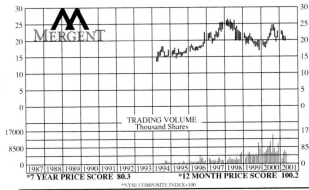

TRADING VOLUME
Thousand Shares

1987 1988 1989 1990 1991 1992 1993 1994 1995 1996 1997 1998 1999 2000 2001

*7 YEAR PRICE SCORE 80.3 *12 MONTH PRICE SCORE 100.2

*NYSE COMPOSITE INDEX=100

INTERIM EARNINGS (Per Share):

Qtr.	Mar.	June	Sept.	Dec.
1997	0.17	0.24	d0.55	0.18
1998	0.23	0.19	d0.07	0.16
1999	0.20	0.80	0.44	d0.62
2000	0.28	0.12	0.29	0.27

INTERIM DIVIDENDS (Per Share):

Amt.	Decl.	Ex.	Rec.	Pay.
0.335Q	5/01/00	5/09/00	5/11/00	5/25/00
0.335Q	8/01/00	8/08/00	8/10/00	8/24/00
0.335Q	11/01/00	11/06/00	11/08/00	11/22/00
0.345Q	12/15/00	2/07/01	2/09/01	2/23/01
0.345Q	5/01/01	5/10/01	5/14/01	5/25/01

Indicated div.: $1.38 (Div. Reinv. Plan)

CAPITALIZATION (12/31/00):

	($000)	(%)
Long-Term Debt	2,237,914	42.9
Minority Interest	46,630	0.9
Preferred Stock	691,403	13.3
Common & Surplus	2,235,968	42.9
Total	5,211,915	100.0

RECENT DEVELOPMENTS: For the year ended 12/31/00, net income increased 17.7% to $214.5 million compared with income of $182.3 million, before accounting charges of $1.4 million, in 1999. Results for 2000 and 1999 included net gains on sales of assets of $1.3 million and $39.0 million, respectively. Total revenues were $645.2 million, up 13.8% from $567.2 million a year earlier. The improvement in results was driven by expanding development business and solid internal growth.

PROSPECTS: PLD signed a 14-year lease with Schneider Electric for the first 303,000 square feet of five facilities at the new ProLogis Park Sant Boi near Barcelona. Starting in late 2001, Sant Boi will serve as Schneider Electric's distribution center in Spain. PLD eventually wants to develop facilities in secondary distribution markets such as Valencia, Bilbao, Tarragona, and Lisbon, Portugal. Separately, PLD anticipates it can achieve funds from operations of approximately $2.38 to $2.42 per share for 2001.

BUSINESS

PROLOGIS TRUST is a real estate investment trust that operates a global network of industrial distribution facilities. PLD owns 171.7 million square feet of industrial distribution facilities operating under development in North America and Europe. The Property Operations segment is engaged in long-term ownership, management and leasing of industrial distribution facilities, primarily distribution space that is adaptable for both distribution and light manufacturing or assembly uses. The Corporate Distribution Facilitaties Services segment is engaged in the development of industrial distribution facilities to be disposed of to unaffiliated customers or entities in which PLD has an ownership interest or for a development fee for unaffiliated customers. The Temperature-Controlled Distribution Operations segment provides unaffiliated customers various services associated with a temperature-controlled distribution environment.

ANNUAL FINANCIAL DATA

	12/31/00	12/31/99	12/31/98	12/31/97	12/31/96	12/31/95	12/31/94
Earnings Per Share	4 0.96	1 2 4 0.82	2 0.51	3 0.04	0.63	0.61	0.57
Tang. Book Val. Per Share	13.53	13.86	12.83	13.14	12.42	12.30	12.04
Dividends Per Share	1.34	1.30	1.24	1.07	1.01	0.94	0.64
Dividend Payout %	139.6	158.5	243.1	...	160.3	153.3	111.8
INCOME STATEMENT (IN MILLIONS):							
Rental Income	480.1	491.8	345.0	284.5	227.0	153.9	70.6
Total Income	625.6	550.6	372.8	302.5	233.5	158.5	71.7
Costs & Expenses	78.0	76.7	58.1	137.3	52.1	35.7	17.9
Depreciation	151.5	152.4	100.6	76.6	59.9	39.8	18.2
Interest Expense	172.2	171.7	103.7	52.7	38.8	32.0	7.6
Income Before Income Taxes	219.6	183.7	110.4	35.9	82.7	51.0	28.1
Income Taxes	5.1	1.5	...	...	...	...	...
Equity Earnings/Minority Int.	d4.3	34.0	0.9	3.8	d3.4	d2.3	d3.0
Net Income	4 214.5	1 2 4 182.3	2 111.3	3 39.7	79.4	48.7	25.1
Average Shs. Outstg. (000)	164,401	152,739	122,028	100,869	84,504	68,924	44,265
BALANCE SHEET (IN MILLIONS):							
Cash & Cash Equivalents	1,511.0	1,009.7	797.0	111.1	4.8	22.2	21.3
Total Real Estate Investments	4,212.5	4,608.2	3,403.2	2,834.7	2,399.6	1,771.3	1,155.5
Total Assets	5,946.3	5,848.0	4,330.7	3,034.0	2,462.3	1,834.0	1,194.9
Long-Term Obligations	2,237.9	2,456.1	1,311.4	857.1	664.1	469.8	144.3
Total Liabilities	3,019.0	2,894.3	2,074.4	1,057.2	862.9	697.8	417.2
Net Stockholders' Equity	2,927.4	2,953.7	2,256.4	1,976.7	1,599.4	1,136.2	777.8
Year-end Shs. Outstg. (000)	165,287	161,825	123,416	117,364	93,677	81,416	64,587
STATISTICAL RECORD:							
Net Inc.+Depr./Assets %	6.2	5.7	4.9	3.8	5.7	4.8	3.6
Return on Equity %	7.3	6.2	4.9	2.0	5.0	4.3	3.2
Return on Assets %	3.6	3.1	2.6	1.3	3.2	2.7	2.1
Price Range	24.69-17.56	22.19-16.75	26.50-19.75	25.50-18.88	22.50-16.50	17.75-14.50	18.25-13.50
P/E Ratio	25.7-18.3	27.1-20.4	52.0-38.7	635.9-470.7	35.7-26.2	29.1-23.8	32.0-23.7
Average Yield %	6.3	6.7	5.4	4.8	5.2	5.8	4.0

Statistics are as originally reported. 1 Bef. acctg. chrg. of $1.4 mill. 2 Incl. int. hedge expend. of $945,000, 1999; $26.1 mill., 1998. 3 Incl. a chrg. of $75.4 mill. for acq. of mgmt. companies. 4 Incl. net gains on sales of assets of $1.3 mill., 2000; $39.0 mill., 1999.

OFFICERS:
K. D. Brooksher, Chmn., C.E.O.
I. F. Lyons III, Pres., C.I.O.
W. C. Rakowich, Managing Dir., C.F.O.

INVESTOR CONTACT: Melissa Marsden, (303) 576-2622

PRINCIPAL OFFICE: 14100 East 35th Place, Aurora, CO 80011

TELEPHONE NUMBER: (303) 375-9292
FAX: (303) 375-8581
WEB: www.prologis.com

NO. OF EMPLOYEES: 640 (approx.)

SHAREHOLDERS: 10,617 (approx.)

ANNUAL MEETING: In May

INCORPORATED: MD, 1993

INSTITUTIONAL HOLDINGS:
No. of Institutions: 165
Shares Held: 97,550,278
% Held: 56.2

INDUSTRY: Real estate agents and managers (SIC: 6531)

TRANSFER AGENT(S): Boston EquiServe, Boston, MA

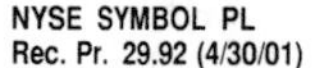
NYSE SYMBOL PL
Rec. Pr. 29.92 (4/30/01)

PROTECTIVE LIFE CORP.

YIELD 1.9%
P/E RATIO 12.9

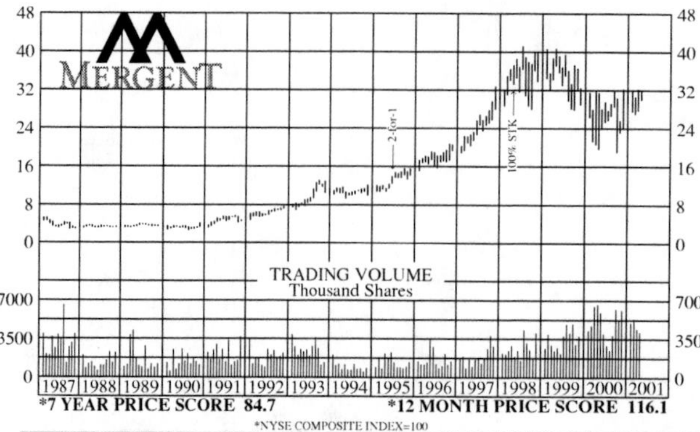

*7 YEAR PRICE SCORE 84.7 *12 MONTH PRICE SCORE 116.1

*NYSE COMPOSITE INDEX=100

INTERIM EARNINGS (Per Share):

Qtr.	Mar.	June	Sept.	Dec.
1996	0.36	0.39	0.32	0.40
1997	0.40	0.44	0.48	0.47
1998	0.47	0.52	0.52	0.53
1999	0.56	0.54	0.57	0.62
2000	0.65	0.59	0.52	0.56

INTERIM DIVIDENDS (Per Share):

Amt.	Decl.	Ex.	Rec.	Pay.
0.13Q	5/01/00	5/10/00	5/12/00	6/01/00
0.13Q	8/07/00	8/16/00	8/18/00	9/01/00
0.13Q	11/06/00	11/15/00	11/17/00	12/01/00
0.13Q	2/05/01	2/13/01	2/15/01	3/01/01
0.14Q	5/07/01	5/16/01	5/18/01	6/01/01

Indicated div.: $0.56

CAPITALIZATION (12/31/00):

	($000)	(%)
Long-Term Debt	306,125	19.4
Deferred Income Tax	79,066	5.0
Redeemable Pfd. Stock	75,000	4.8
Common & Surplus	1,114,058	70.8
Total	1,574,249	100.0

RECENT DEVELOPMENTS: For the year ended 12/31/00, net income totaled $153.5 million compared with income of $153.1 million, before an extraordinary loss of $1.8 million, in the previous year. Results for 2000 and 1999 included minority interest in net income of consolidated subsidiaries of $8.9 million and $10.5 million, respectively. Results for 1999 and 2000 also included realized investment losses of $7.0 million and $1.1 million, respectively. Total revenues rose 13.0% to $1.73 billion.

PROSPECTS: Results for the year were enhanced by strong performances in the individual life, West Coast, financial institutions and retirement savings and investment products divisions. Going forward, results should continue to benefit from lower short-term interest rates, coupled with strong contributions from PL's life insurance and specialty insurance products businesses. Also, lower short-term interest rates should lead to reduced spreads for the stable value products group.

BUSINESS

PROTECTIVE LIFE CORPORATION is a holding company that, through its subsidiaries, provides financial services through the production, distribution and administration of insurance and investment products. The Company operates seven divisions whose strategic focuses can be grouped into three segments: life insurance, specialty insurance products and retirement savings and investment products. The life insurance segment includes the individual life, West Coast and acquisitions divisions. The specialty insurance products segment includes the dental and consumer benefits and financial institutions divisions. The retirement savings and investment products segment includes the stable value products and investment products division. In addition, the Company operates a corporate and other segment.

ANNUAL FINANCIAL DATA

	12/31/00	12/31/99	12/31/98	12/31/97	12/31/96	12/31/95	12/31/94
Earnings Per Share	**2.32**	**1 2.32**	**2.04**	**1.78**	**1.47**	**1.34**	**1.28**
Tang. Book Val. Per Share	**13.38**	**10.03**	**11.51**	**12.30**	**9.99**	**9.15**	**4.93**
Dividends Per Share	**0.51**	**0.47**	**0.43**	**0.39**	**0.35**	**0.31**	**0.28**
Dividend Payout %	**22.0**	**20.3**	**21.1**	**21.9**	**23.8**	**23.1**	**21.5**
INCOME STATEMENT (IN MILLIONS):							
Total Premium Income	833.7	761.3	662.8	522.3	494.2	432.6	402.8
Net Investment Income	737.3	676.4	636.4	591.4	517.5	475.9	417.8
Other Income	163.0	96.2	67.2	33.6	26.4	13.4	27.9
Total Revenues	1,734.0	1,533.9	1,366.4	1,147.3	1,038.0	921.9	848.4
Income Before Income Taxes	253.8	255.8	220.7	179.4	139.7	121.0	106.2
Income Taxes	90.9	92.1	77.8	61.0	47.5	41.2	34.0
Equity Earnings/Minority Int.	d9.5	d10.6	d12.1	d6.4	d3.2	d3.2	d1.8
Net Income	153.5	1 153.1	130.8	112.0	89.0	76.7	70.4
Average Shs. Outstg. (000)	66,281	66,161	64,088	62,850	61,608	57,320	54,953
BALANCE SHEET (IN MILLIONS):							
Cash & Cash Equivalents	244.7	165.3	225.7	123.6	235.3	65.0	64.0
Premiums Due	1,185.4	940.3	797.2	639.4	380.0	309.7	152.6
Invst. Assets: Fixed-term	7,415.8	6,311.8	6,437.8	6,374.3	4,686.1	3,892.0	3,493.6
Invst. Assets: Equities	58.7	36.4	12.3	15.0	35.3	38.7	45.0
Invst. Assets: Total	10,241.4	8,722.0	8,606.6	8,049.4	6,552.2	6,025.1	5,301.9
Total Assets	15,145.6	12,994.2	11,989.5	10,511.6	8,263.2	7,231.3	6,130.3
Long-Term Obligations	306.1	181.0	152.3	120.0	168.2	115.5	98.0
Net Stockholders' Equity	1,114.1	865.2	944.2	758.2	615.3	526.6	270.4
Year-end Shs. Outstg. (000)	64,558	64,502	64,435	61,642	61,608	57,550	54,852
STATISTICAL RECORD:							
Return on Revenues %	8.9	10.0	9.6	9.8	8.6	8.3	8.3
Return on Equity %	13.8	17.7	13.9	14.8	14.5	14.6	26.0
Return on Assets %	1.0	1.2	1.1	1.1	1.1	1.1	1.1
Price Range	32.25-19.00	40.75-27.81	41.25-28.00	32.75-18.81	20.81-15.06	15.69-10.69	12.16-9.22
P/E Ratio	13.9-8.2	17.6-12.0	20.2-13.7	18.4-10.6	14.2-10.2	11.7-8.0	9.5-7.2
Average Yield %	2.0	1.4	1.2	1.5	2.0	2.4	2.6

Statistics are as originally reported. Adj. for 100% stk. split, 4/98, 2-for-1, 6/95. 1 Bef. extraord. loss of $1.8 mill.

OFFICERS:
D. Nabers Jr., Chmn., C.E.O.
J. D. Johns, Pres., C.O.O.
D. J. Long, Sr. V.P., Gen. Couns., Sec.

INVESTOR CONTACT: Drayton Nabers, Jr., C.E.O., (205) 868-3515

PRINCIPAL OFFICE: 2801 Highway 280 South, Birmingham, AL 35223

TELEPHONE NUMBER: (205) 879-9230
FAX: (205) 868-3541
WEB: www.protective.com

NO. OF EMPLOYEES: 2,834 (approx.)

SHAREHOLDERS: 2,700 (approx.)

ANNUAL MEETING: In May

INCORPORATED: DE, Feb., 1981

INSTITUTIONAL HOLDINGS:
No. of Institutions: 197
Shares Held: 48,675,328
% Held: 71.0

INDUSTRY: Life insurance (SIC: 6311)

TRANSFER AGENT(S): Bank of New York, New York, NY

NYSE SYMBOL PVN
Rec. Pr. 56.76 (5/31/01)

PROVIDIAN FINANCIAL CORP.

YIELD 0.1%
P/E RATIO 25.5

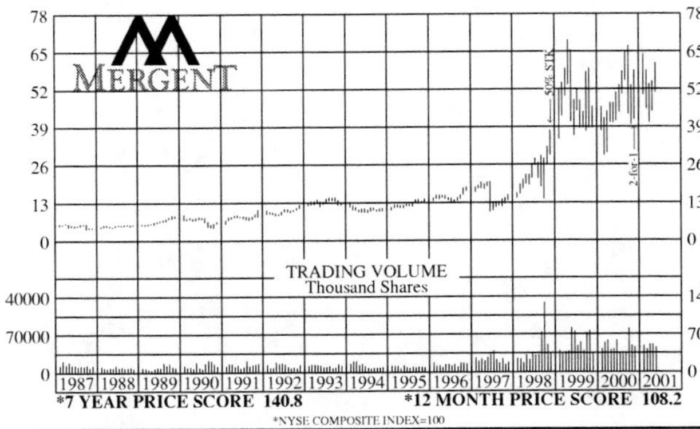

INTERIM EARNINGS (Per Share):

Qtr.	Mar.	June	Sept.	Dec.
1997	0.16	0.16	0.17	0.19
1998	0.20	0.22	0.29	0.33
1999	0.39	0.44	0.52	0.55
2000	0.60	0.22	0.68	0.73

INTERIM DIVIDENDS (Per Share):

Amt.	Decl.	Ex.	Rec.	Pay.
0.05Q	8/09/00	8/30/00	9/01/00	9/15/00
0.06Q	11/19/00	11/13/00	11/15/00	11/30/00
2-for-1	10/19/00	12/01/00	11/15/00	11/30/00
0.03Q	2/14/01	2/27/01	3/01/01	3/15/01
0.03Q	5/09/01	5/30/01	6/01/01	6/15/01

Indicated div.: $0.12 (Div. Reinv. Plan)

CAPITALIZATION (12/31/00):

	($000)	(%)
Total Deposits	13,113,416	80.5
Long-Term Debt	1,024,163	6.3
Redeemable Pfd. Stock	111,057	0.7
Common & Surplus	2,032,183	12.5
Total	16,280,819	100.0

RECENT DEVELOPMENTS: For the year ended 12/31/00, net income rose 18.4% to $651.8 million versus $550.3 million in the previous year. Total interest income increased 66.2% to $2.70 billion from $1.62 billion a year earlier. Interest income from loans grew 58.3% to $2.47 billion compared with $1.56 billion in the prior year. Non-interest income climbed 34.6% to $3.25 billion from $2.41 billion the year before. Net interest margin totaled 11.03% versus 12.92% in the previous year.

PROSPECTS: The Company will continue to focus on expanding its global e-commerce strategy. As a result on 2/6/01, the Company and PayPal, Inc. entered into a partnership agreement which will allow consumers and businesses to send and receive money from bank accounts or credit cards instantly and securely on the Internet. PVN has taken an equity stake in PayPay and will offer a co-branded credit card to PayPal's customers.

BUSINESS

PROVIDIAN FINANCIAL CORPORATION is a provider of lending and deposit products to customers throughout the United States and offers credit cards in the United Kingdom and Argentina. PVN serves a broad, diversified market with its loan products, which include credit cards, home equity loans, secured cards and membership services. The Company's lending and deposit-taking activities are conducted primarily through Providian National Bank (PNB) and Providian Bank (PB). Providian Bankcorp Services performs a variety of servicing activities in support of PNB, PB and other affiliates. PVN, formerly Providian Bancorp, was spun off from Providian Corp. in June, 1997. At 12/31/00, the Company had more than $30.00 billion in assets under management and 16.3 million customers. PVN ranks as the fifth-largest bankcard issuer in the United States.

LOAN DISTRIBUTION

(12/31/2000)	($000)	(%)
Credit Cards	13,734,789	99.7
Home Loans	13,877	0.1
Other Loans	21,491	0.2
Total	13,770,157	100.0

ANNUAL FINANCIAL DATA

	12/31/00	12/31/99	12/31/98	12/31/97	12/31/96	12/31/95	12/31/94
Earnings Per Share	**2.23**	**1.89**	**1.02**	**0.67**	**0.57**	**0.47**	**0.37**
Tang. Book Val. Per Share	**7.11**	**4.72**	**2.83**	**2.09**	...	...	...
Dividends Per Share	**0.10**	**0.10**	**0.07**	**0.03**	...	...	...
Dividend Payout %	**4.7**	**5.3**	**7.4**	**5.0**	...	...	...
INCOME STATEMENT (IN MILLIONS):							
Total Interest Income	2,699.9	1,624.3	842.6	582.5	596.0	479.6	343.7
Total Interest Expense	875.2	449.1	247.3	183.1	190.4	158.4	101.7
Net Interest Income	1,824.8	1,175.2	595.3	399.4	405.6	321.1	242.1
Provision for Loan Losses	1,515.4	1,099.1	545.9	149.3	126.6	79.9	50.3
Non-Interest Income	3,248.3	2,412.5	1,266.2	634.6	412.0	335.8	269.3
Non-Interest Expense	2,471.5	1,571.1	825.0	573.4	433.8	362.1	285.8
Income Before Taxes	1,086.2	917.4	490.6	311.3	257.3	214.9	175.2
Net Income	651.8	550.3	296.4	191.5	159.8	135.5	110.1
Average Shs. Outstg. (000)	294,042	291,094	290,368	287,184	280,992	287,583	297,957
BALANCE SHEET (IN MILLIONS):							
Securities Avail. for Sale	1,885.5	455.2	114.9	...	...	...	...
Total Loans & Leases	13,770.2	11,610.0	5,741.1	2,815.4	2,956.3	3,096.5	...
Allowance for Credit Losses	1,445.6	1,064.8	459.1	...	114.5	93.4	...
Net Loans & Leases	12,324.5	10,545.2	5,282.0	2,815.4	2,841.8	3,003.1	...
Total Assets	18,055.3	14,340.9	7,231.2	4,449.4	4,326.7	3,611.1	...
Total Deposits	13,113.4	10,538.1	4,672.3	3,212.8	3,390.1	2,157.8	...
Long-Term Obligations	1,024.2	958.1	399.8	...	50.0	...	...
Total Liabilities	16,023.1	13,008.4	6,428.0	3,854.3	3,843.6	3,261.8	...
Net Stockholders' Equity	2,032.2	1,332.5	803.2	595.1	483.1	349.3	...
Year-end Shs. Outstg. (000)	285,911	282,026	283,464	284,664	15	15	...
STATISTICAL RECORD:							
Return on Equity %	32.1	41.3	36.9	32.2	33.1	38.8	...
Return on Assets %	3.6	3.8	4.1	4.3	3.7	3.8	...
Equity/Assets %	11.3	9.3	11.1	13.4	11.2	9.7	...
Non-Int. Exp./Tot. Inc. %	48.7	43.8	44.3	55.5	53.1	55.1	55.9
Price Range	67.00-29.06	69.00-34.75	37.84-14.19	20.21-9.71	18.46-12.71	14.29-10.29	12.71-9.54
P/E Ratio	30.0-13.0	36.5-18.4	37.1-13.9	30.3-14.6	32.4-22.3	30.4-21.9	34.3-25.8
Average Yield %	0.2	0.2	0.3	0.2	...	...	...

Statistics are as originally reported. Adj. for stk. splits: 2-for-1, 11/00; 3-for-2, 12/98. Per share figures prior to 1997 are pro forma.

OFFICERS:
S. J. Mehta, Chmn., Pres., C.E.O.
E. Richey, Vice-Chmn., Gen. Couns., Sec.

INVESTOR CONTACT: Nancy Murphy, Sr. V.P., Investor Relations, (415) 278-4483

PRINCIPAL OFFICE: 201 Mission Street, 28th Floor, San Francisco, CA 94105

TELEPHONE NUMBER: (415) 543-0404
FAX: (415) 278-6498
WEB: www.providian.com

NO. OF EMPLOYEES: 12,449 (avg.)

SHAREHOLDERS: 9,711

ANNUAL MEETING: In May

INCORPORATED: DE, 1984

INSTITUTIONAL HOLDINGS:
No. of Institutions: 434
Shares Held: 227,929,263
% Held: 79.8

INDUSTRY: Short-term business credit (SIC: 6153)

REGISTRAR(S): First Chicago Trust Company of New York, Jersey City, NJ

NYSE SYMBOL PEG
Rec. Pr. 51.41 (5/31/01)

PUBLIC SERVICE ENTERPRISE GROUP INC.

YIELD 4.2%
P/E RATIO 14.5

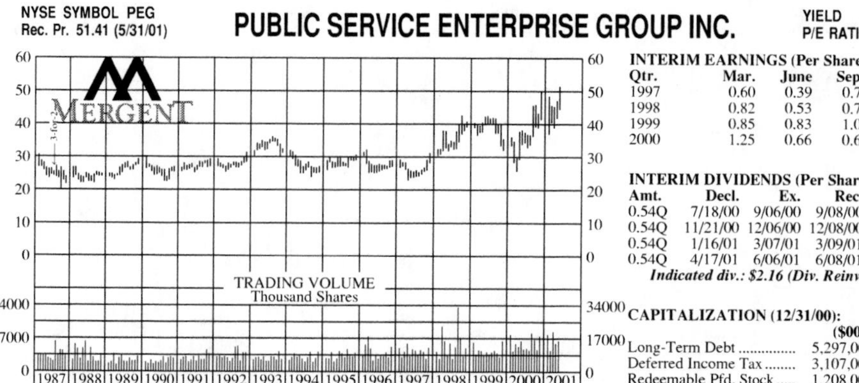

*7 YEAR PRICE SCORE 93.3 *12 MONTH PRICE SCORE 119.0

*NYSE COMPOSITE INDEX=100

INTERIM EARNINGS (Per Share):

Qtr.	Mar.	June	Sept.	Dec.
1997	0.60	0.39	0.76	0.66
1998	0.82	0.53	0.78	0.66
1999	0.85	0.83	1.01	0.53
2000	1.25	0.66	0.66	0.98

INTERIM DIVIDENDS (Per Share):

Amt.	Decl.	Ex.	Rec.	Pay.
0.54Q	7/18/00	9/06/00	9/08/00	9/29/00
0.54Q	11/21/00	12/06/00	12/08/00	12/29/00
0.54Q	1/16/01	3/07/01	3/09/01	3/31/01
0.54Q	4/17/01	6/06/01	6/08/01	6/29/01

Indicated div.: $2.16 (Div. Reinv. Plan)

CAPITALIZATION (12/31/00):

	($000)	(%)
Long-Term Debt	5,297,000	34.4
Deferred Income Tax	3,107,000	20.2
Redeemable Pfd. Stock	1,208,000	7.8
Common & Surplus	5,786,000	37.6
Total	15,398,000	100.0

RECENT DEVELOPMENTS: For the year ended 12/31/00, net income climbed 5.7% to $764.0 million compared with income of $723.0 million, before an after-tax extraordinary loss of $804.0 million, in 1999. Total operating revenues rose 6.1% to $6.84 billion from $6.45 billion in the prior year. Operating income increased 2.8% to $1.89 billion compared with $1.84 billion the year before. Results benefited from a strong fourth quarter stemming from increased gas sales by Public Service Electric and Gas Company.

PROSPECTS: The Company is targeting a 7.0% compound annual growth rate in earnings per share over the next five years. The Company estimates earnings per share for 2001 to be about $3.70. Projects currently under development by PSEG Power and PSEG Global are expected to come on line and produce earnings to support the Company's target growth. PSEG Power, which has more than 11,000 megawatts of electric generating capacity, plans to add more than 6,000 megawatts by 2005.

BUSINESS

PUBLIC SERVICE ENTERPRISE GROUP INC. is the holding company of Public Service Electric and Gas Co., the largest utility in New Jersey, serving 2,600 square miles. PSEG Energy Holdings, is the parent company for the Company's non-utility business, which includes diversified investments, oil and gas exploration and production, small power production and real estate investment. PSEG Energy Holdings consists of three primary subsidiaries: PSEG Energy Technologies, PSEG Global, and PSEG Resources. Revenues in 2000 were derived: electric, 57.2%; gas, 31.3%; and other, 11.5%.

ANNUAL FINANCIAL DATA

	12/31/00	12/31/99	12/31/98	12/31/97	12/31/96	12/31/95	12/31/94
Earnings Per Share	**3.55**	**3 3.29**	**2.79**	**2 2.41**	**1 2.42**	**2.71**	**2.78**
Cash Flow Per Share	**5.84**	**6.15**	**6.09**	**5.39**	**5.18**	**5.77**	**5.76**
Tang. Book Val. Per Share	**27.82**	**18.46**	**22.49**	**22.47**	**22.33**	**22.25**	**21.70**
Dividends Per Share	**2.16**	**2.16**	**2.16**	**2.16**	**2.16**	**2.16**	**2.16**
Dividend Payout %	**60.8**	**65.7**	**77.4**	**89.6**	**89.3**	**79.7**	**77.7**
INCOME STATEMENT (IN MILLIONS):							
Total Revenues	6,848.0	6,497.0	5,931.0	6,370.0	6,041.2	6,164.2	5,915.8
Costs & Expenses	4,467.0	4,032.0	3,982.0	4,283.0	3,998.8	3,944.6	3,714.5
Depreciation & Amort.	492.0	628.0	763.0	690.0	667.2	749.3	729.2
Maintenance Exp.	...	...	...	282.0	318.3	312.6	308.1
Operating Income	1,889.0	1,837.0	1,186.0	1,115.0	1,057.0	1,157.7	1,164.1
Net Interest Inc./(Exp.)	d574.0	d490.0	d468.0	d450.0	d435.0	d458.9	d462.1
Income Taxes	490.0	563.0	...	...	...	...	...
Net Income	764.0	3 723.0	644.0	2 560.0	1 587.4	662.3	679.0
Cash Flow	1,256.0	1,351.0	1,407.0	1,250.0	1,254.5	1,411.6	1,408.2
Average Shs. Outstg. (000)	215,121	219,814	230,974	231,986	242,401	244,698	244,471
BALANCE SHEET (IN MILLIONS):							
Gross Property	11,968.0	11,156.0	17,924.0	17,513.0	17,068.3	16,627.8	16,245.4
Accumulated Depreciation	4,266.0	4,078.0	7,048.0	6,463.0	5,889.1	5,440.4	5,147.1
Net Property	7,702.0	7,078.0	10,876.0	11,050.0	11,216.2	11,823.4	11,712.2
Total Assets	20,796.0	19,015.0	17,997.0	17,943.0	16,915.3	17,171.4	16,717.4
Long-Term Obligations	5,297.0	4,575.0	4,813.0	4,925.0	4,632.6	5,242.9	5,234.4
Net Stockholders' Equity	5,786.0	3,996.0	5,098.0	5,211.0	5,213.0	5,444.9	5,311.2
Year-end Shs. Outstg. (000)	207,971	216,417	226,643	231,958	233,470	244,698	244,698
STATISTICAL RECORD:							
Operating Profit Margin %	27.6	28.3	20.0	17.5	17.5	18.8	19.7
Net Profit Margin %	11.2	11.1	10.9	8.8	9.7	10.7	11.5
Net Inc./Net Property %	9.9	10.2	5.9	5.1	5.2	5.6	5.8
Net Inc./Tot. Capital %	5.0	5.7	4.4	3.9	4.3	4.6	4.8
Return on Equity %	13.2	17.7	12.4	10.6	11.0	11.5	11.9
Accum. Depr./Gross Prop. %	35.6	36.6	39.3	36.9	34.5	32.7	31.7
Price Range	50.00-25.69	42.63-32.00	42.75-30.31	31.25-22.88	32.13-25.13	30.63-26.00	32.00-23.88
P/E Ratio	14.1-7.2	13.0-9.7	15.3-10.9	13.0-9.5	13.3-10.4	11.3-9.6	11.5-8.6
Average Yield %	5.7	5.8	5.9	8.0	7.5	7.6	7.7

Statistics are as originally reported. 1 Excl. $10.7 mill. ($0.04/sh.) income fr. disc. ops. & $13.5 mill. ($0.06/sh.) gain on disp. of ops.; incl. $18.5 mill. pre-tax gain on pfd. stk. redemp. 2 Incl. $62.0 mill. non-recur. chg. rel. to litigation settlement. 3 Excl. a net extra. loss of $804.0 mill. resulting fr. the refinement of estimates in the impairment analysis of electric generation assets stemming from the NJ Board of Public Utilities' restr. decision in its Energy Master Plan proceedings.

OFFICERS:
E. J. Ferland, Chmn., Pres., C.E.O.
R. C. Murray, V.P., C.F.O.
V. Rado, V.P., Contr.

INVESTOR CONTACT: Investor Relations, (877) 773-4111

PRINCIPAL OFFICE: 80 Park Plaza, P.O. Box 1171, Newark, NJ 07101-1171

TELEPHONE NUMBER: (973) 430-7000
FAX: (973) 430-5983
WEB: www.pseg.com

NO. OF EMPLOYEES: 13,085 (avg.)

SHAREHOLDERS: 126,706

ANNUAL MEETING: In Apr.

INCORPORATED: NJ, July, 1985

INSTITUTIONAL HOLDINGS:
No. of Institutions: 310
Shares Held: 86,582,596
% Held: 41.6

INDUSTRY: Electric and other services combined (SIC: 4931)

TRANSFER AGENT(S): EquiServe First Chicago Trust Division, Jersey City, NJ

NYSE SYMBOL PSA
Rec. Pr. 27.23 (4/30/01)

PUBLIC STORAGE, INC.

YIELD	3.2%
P/E RATIO	19.3

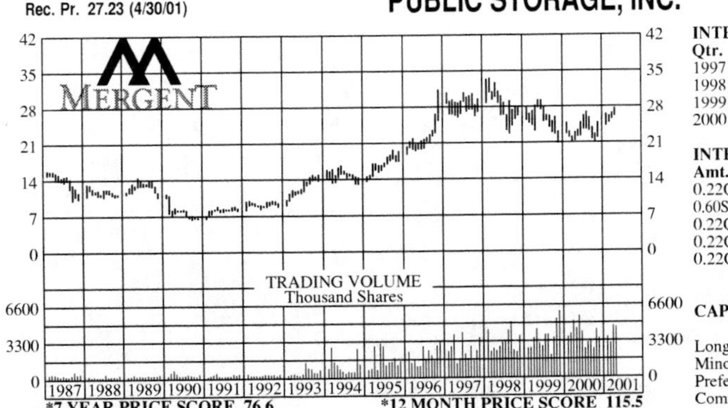

INTERIM EARNINGS (Per Share):

Qtr.	Mar.	June	Sept.	Dec.
1997	0.26	0.14	0.27	0.24
1998	0.26	0.32	0.37	0.35
1999	0.34	0.39	0.40	0.39
2000	0.34	0.35	0.37	0.35

INTERIM DIVIDENDS (Per Share):

Amt.	Decl.	Ex.	Rec.	Pay.
0.22Q	8/03/00	9/13/00	9/15/00	9/29/00
0.60Sp	8/30/00	9/13/00	9/15/00	9/29/00
0.22Q	11/02/00	12/13/00	12/15/00	12/29/00
0.22Q	3/05/01	3/13/01	3/15/01	3/30/01
0.22Q	5/10/01	6/13/01	6/15/01	6/29/01

Indicated div.: $0.88

CAPITALIZATION (12/31/00):

	($000)	(%)
Long-Term Debt	156,003	3.5
Minority Interest	532,918	12.1
Preferred Stock	1,155,150	26.2
Common & Surplus	2,568,967	58.2
Total	4,413,038	100.0

RECENT DEVELOPMENTS: For the year ended 12/31/00, income rose 2.6% to $293.3 million versus $285.7 million in the previous year. Results for 2000 and 1999 excluded after-tax gains from the disposition of real estate of $3.8 million and $2.2 million, respectively. Total revenues increasd 11.9% to $757.3 million from $676.7 million in 1999. Revenues from self-storage facilities advanced 10.3% to $653.5 million, while revenues from commercial properties jumped 38.2% to $11.3 million. Containerized storage revenue soared 40.3% to $37.9 million.

PROSPECTS: Looking ahead, PSA will continue to focus on improving the operating performance of its traditional self-storage properties, primarily through increases in revenues achieved through the telephone reservation center and associated marketing efforts. These revenue increases are expected to result mainly from higher realized rent per occupied square foot versus significant increases in occupancy levels. PSA will also focus on continuing its storage facility development program and improving the performance of its containerized storage operations.

BUSINESS

PUBLIC STORAGE, INC. is a fully integrated, self-administered and self-managed real estate investment trust that acquires, develops, owns and operates self-storage facilities. The Company owns and operates storage space in 37 states through direct and indirect equity investments in 1,361 facilities containing approximately 81.3 million square feet of net rentable space. The Company's self-storage operations are by far the largest component of its business, representing approximately 86.0% of total revenues generated in fiscal 2000. In addition, the Company has a significant ownership in PS Business Parks, Inc., which owns 140 commercial properties containing about 12.6 million rentable square feet of space.

ANNUAL FINANCIAL DATA

	12/31/00	12/31/99	12/31/98	12/31/97	12/31/96	12/31/95	12/31/94
Earnings Per Share	**[1] 1.41**	**[1] 1.52**	**1.30**	**0.91**	**1.10**	**0.95**	**1.05**
Tang. Book Val. Per Share	**18.24**	**17.50**	**16.65**	**16.31**	**14.14**	**11.04**	**12.66**
Dividends Per Share	**1.48**	**0.88**	**0.88**	**0.88**	**0.88**	**0.88**	**0.85**
Dividend Payout %	**105.0**	**57.9**	**67.7**	**96.7**	**80.0**	**92.6**	**80.9**
INCOME STATEMENT (IN MILLIONS):							
Total Income	757.3	676.7	582.2	470.8	341.1	212.7	147.2
Costs & Expenses	273.4	229.3	222.9	182.4	104.8	83.1	60.4
Depreciation	149.0	137.7	107.5	91.4	65.0	40.8	28.3
Interest Expense	3.3	8.0	4.5	6.8	8.5	8.5	6.9
Income Before Income Taxes	331.7	301.7	247.3	190.3	162.9	77.5	51.6
Equity Earnings/Minority Int.	d38.4	d16.0	d20.3	d11.7	d9.4	d7.1	d9.5
Net Income	[1] 293.3	[1] 285.7	227.0	178.6	153.5	70.4	42.1
Average Shs. Outstg. (000)	131,657	126,669	114,357	98,961	77,358	41,171	24,077
BALANCE SHEET (IN MILLIONS):							
Cash & Cash Equivalents	89.5	55.1	51.2	41.5	26.9	80.4	20.2
Total Real Estate Investments	3,915.3	3,746.6	3,001.6	2,925.2	2,273.8	1,587.4	773.8
Total Assets	4,513.9	4,214.4	3,403.9	3,311.6	2,572.2	1,937.5	820.3
Long-Term Obligations	156.0	167.3	81.4	96.6	108.4	158.1	51.8
Total Liabilities	789.8	525.3	284.6	462.7	266.7	303.0	232.5
Net Stockholders' Equity	3,724.1	3,689.1	3,119.3	2,849.0	2,305.4	1,634.5	587.8
Year-end Shs. Outstg. (000)	130,704	133,697	122,957	105,102	88,362	78,514	28,827
STATISTICAL RECORD:							
Net Inc.+Depr./Assets %	9.8	10.0	9.8	8.2	8.5	5.7	8.6
Return on Equity %	7.9	7.7	7.3	6.3	6.7	4.3	7.2
Return on Assets %	6.5	6.8	6.7	5.4	6.0	3.6	5.1
Price Range	26.94-20.88	29.38-20.81	33.63-22.63	30.88-25.88	31.38-18.75	19.75-13.50	16.75-13.00
P/E Ratio	19.1-14.8	19.3-13.7	25.9-17.4	33.9-28.4	28.5-17.0	20.8-14.2	16.0-12.4
Average Yield %	6.2	3.5	3.1	3.1	3.5	5.3	5.7

Statistics are as originally reported. [1] Bef. after-tax gain of disposition of real estate $3.8 mill., 2000; $2.2 mill., 1999.

OFFICERS:
B. W. Hughes, Chmn., C.E.O.
H. Lenkin, Pres.
J. Reyes, Sr. V.P., C.F.O.

INVESTOR CONTACT: Harvey Lenkin, (818) 244-8080

PRINCIPAL OFFICE: 701 Western Ave., Glendale, CA 91201-2349

TELEPHONE NUMBER: (818) 244-8080
FAX: (818) 244-0581
WEB: www.publicstorage.com

NO. OF EMPLOYEES: 4,600 (approx.)

SHAREHOLDERS: 21,168 (approx.)

ANNUAL MEETING: In May

INCORPORATED: CA, July, 1980

INSTITUTIONAL HOLDINGS:
No. of Institutions: 133
Shares Held: 59,747,382
% Held: 46.9

INDUSTRY: Real estate investment trusts (SIC: 6798)

TRANSFER AGENT(S): BankBoston, NA, Boston, MA

NYSE SYMBOL PSD
Rec. Pr. 23.93 (5/31/01)

PUGET ENERGY, INC.

YIELD 7.7%
P/E RATIO 11.1

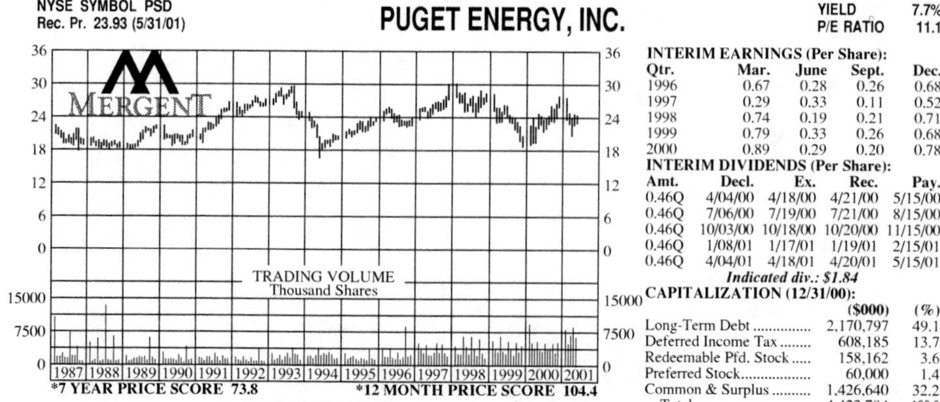

*7 YEAR PRICE SCORE 73.8 *12 MONTH PRICE SCORE 104.4

*NYSE COMPOSITE INDEX=100

INTERIM EARNINGS (Per Share):

Qtr.	Mar.	June	Sept.	Dec.
1996	0.67	0.28	0.26	0.68
1997	0.29	0.33	0.11	0.52
1998	0.74	0.19	0.21	0.71
1999	0.79	0.33	0.26	0.68
2000	0.89	0.29	0.20	0.78

INTERIM DIVIDENDS (Per Share):

Amt.	Decl.	Ex.	Rec.	Pay.
0.46Q	4/04/00	4/18/00	4/21/00	5/15/00
0.46Q	7/06/00	7/19/00	7/21/00	8/15/00
0.46Q	10/03/00	10/18/00	10/20/00	11/15/00
0.46Q	1/08/01	1/17/01	1/19/01	2/15/01
0.46Q	4/04/01	4/18/01	4/20/01	5/15/01

Indicated div.: $1.84

CAPITALIZATION (12/31/00):

	($000)	(%)
Long-Term Debt	2,170,797	49.1
Deferred Income Tax	608,185	13.7
Redeemable Pfd. Stock	158,162	3.6
Preferred Stock	60,000	1.4
Common & Surplus	1,426,640	32.2
Total	4,423,784	100.0

RECENT DEVELOPMENTS: For the year ended 12/31/00, net income increased 4.5% to $193.8 million compared with $185.6 million in the previous year. Total operating revenues jumped 66.4% to $3.44 billion versus $2.07 billion in the comparable period. Electric operating revenues advanced 77.9% to $2.77 billion compared with $1.56 billion in the prior year. Gas operating revenues climbed 26.1% to $612.3 million from $485.5 million in the prior year. Other revenues more than doubled to $57.7 million from $24.4 million the year before.

PROSPECTS: Revenues should continue to benefit from growth in wholesale and other market-priced electric sales volumes and prices and increased natural gas revenues. However, earnings growth is being tempered by an increase in operating expenses due to higher costs for purchasing natural gas and electricity, as well as fuel for electric generation. Going forward, the Company will continue to focus on improving its regulated utility distribution business while expanding its non-regulated business through its new InfrastruX subsidiary.

BUSINESS

PUGET ENERGY, INC. (formerly Puget Sound Energy Inc.) is a public utility holding company. Through its subsidiaries, the Company provides electric and gas service in a territory covering approximately 6,000 square miles, principally in the Puget Sound region of Washington. As of 12/31/00, the Company had approximately 915,900 electric customers, consisting of 811,400 residential, 98,800 commercial, 4,100 industrial and 1,600 other customers; and approximately 580,900 gas customers, consisting of 532,300 residential, 45,500 commercial, 3,000 industrial and 100 other customers. At 12/31/00, approximately 294,200 customers purchased both forms of energy from PSE. In 2000, revenues were 80.5% electric; 17.8% natural gas; and 1.7% other.

ANNUAL FINANCIAL DATA

	12/31/00	12/31/99	12/31/98	12/31/97	12/31/96	12/31/95	12/31/94
Earnings Per Share	**2.16**	**[4] 2.06**	**1.85**	**[3] 1.28**	**[2] 1.89**	**1.89**	**[1] 1.64**
Cash Flow Per Share	**4.46**	**4.14**	**3.80**	**3.19**	**4.15**	**3.58**	**3.46**
Tang. Book Val. Per Share	**16.61**	**16.24**	**16.00**	**16.06**	**18.53**	**18.48**	**18.43**
Dividends Per Share	**1.84**	**1.84**	**1.84**	**1.84**	**1.84**	**1.84**	**1.84**
Dividend Payout %	**85.2**	**89.3**	**99.5**	**143.7**	**97.3**	**97.3**	**112.2**
INCOME STATEMENT (IN MILLIONS):							
Total Revenues	3,441.7	2,066.6	1,907.3	1,676.9	1,198.8	1,179.3	1,194.1
Costs & Expenses	2,881.3	1,580.8	1,442.8	1,299.2	803.5	804.0	833.5
Depreciation & Amort.	196.5	175.7	165.6	161.9	144.2	107.6	115.7
Maintenance Exp.	...	...	...	...	50.5	53.1	51.3
Operating Income	363.9	310.1	299.0	215.9	200.6	214.6	193.5
Net Interest Inc./(Exp.)	d175.1	d150.4	d138.6	d118.2	d77.1	d86.5	d86.3
Net Income	193.8	[4] 185.6	169.6	[3] 125.7	[2] 135.4	135.7	[1] 120.1
Cash Flow	381.4	350.2	322.2	270.2	264.4	227.8	220.1
Average Shs. Outstg. (000)	85,411	84,613	84,768	84,628	63,641	63,641	63,632
BALANCE SHEET (IN MILLIONS):							
Gross Property	5,865.1	5,652.6	5,152.0	4,863.8	3,479.7	3,400.7	3,306.9
Accumulated Depreciation	2,026.7	1,901.7	1,721.1	1,613.3	1,188.6	1,118.7	1,039.9
Net Property	3,838.4	3,750.9	3,430.9	3,250.5	2,291.1	2,282.0	2,266.9
Total Assets	5,556.7	5,145.6	4,720.7	4,493.4	3,187.3	3,269.0	3,463.8
Long-Term Obligations	2,170.8	1,783.1	1,474.7	1,411.7	820.7	920.4	963.3
Net Stockholders' Equity	1,486.6	1,439.1	1,447.8	1,453.6	1,179.0	1,175.9	1,172.7
Year-end Shs. Outstg. (000)	85,904	84,922	84,561	84,561	63,641	63,641	63,641
STATISTICAL RECORD:							
Operating Profit Margin %	10.6	15.0	15.7	12.9	16.7	18.2	16.2
Net Profit Margin %	5.6	9.0	8.9	7.5	11.3	11.5	10.1
Net Inc./Net Property %	5.0	4.9	4.9	3.9	5.9	5.9	5.3
Net Inc./Tot. Capital %	4.4	4.6	4.6	3.4	5.4	5.2	4.5
Return on Equity %	13.0	12.9	11.7	8.6	11.5	11.5	10.2
Accum. Depr./Gross Prop. %	34.6	33.6	33.4	33.2	34.2	32.9	31.4
Price Range	28.00-18.94	28.38-18.63	30.25-24.06	30.19-23.50	26.00-22.13	24.00-20.13	24.88-16.50
P/E Ratio	13.0-8.8	13.8-9.0	16.4-13.0	23.6-18.4	13.8-11.7	12.7-10.6	15.2-10.1
Average Yield %	7.8	7.8	6.8	6.9	7.6	8.3	8.9

Statistics are as originally reported. [1] Inc. non-recurr. after-tax chrg. $16.3 mill. [2] Bef. disc. opers. $41.0 mill. fr. sale of invest. in conservation assets to a grantor trust in June 1995 [3] Incl. non-reucrr. pre-tax chrg. $55.8 mill. fr. merger [4] Incl. gain $7.8 mill. fr. sale of Homeguard Security Services, Inc. and investment in Cabot Oil & Gas Corp.

OFFICERS:
R. R. Sonstelie, Chmn.
W. S. Weaver, Pres., C.E.O.
R. L. Hawley, V.P., C.F.O.

INVESTOR CONTACT: Julie S. Williams, Dir. Inv. Rel., (425) 462-3808

PRINCIPAL OFFICE: 411-108th Avenue N.E., Bellevue, WA 98004-5515

TELEPHONE NUMBER: (425) 454-6363
WEB: www.pugetsoundenergy.com

NO. OF EMPLOYEES: 3,754

SHAREHOLDERS: 50,950

ANNUAL MEETING: In May

INCORPORATED: WA, Nov., 1960

INSTITUTIONAL HOLDINGS:
No. of Institutions: 171
Shares Held: 26,462,941
% Held: 30.7

INDUSTRY: Electric services (SIC: 4911)

TRANSFER AGENT(S): Mellon Investor Services, Ridgefield Park, NJ.

NYSE SYMBOL PTZ
Rec. Pr. 51.30 (5/31/01)

PULITZER INC.

YIELD 1.3%
P/E RATIO 31.9

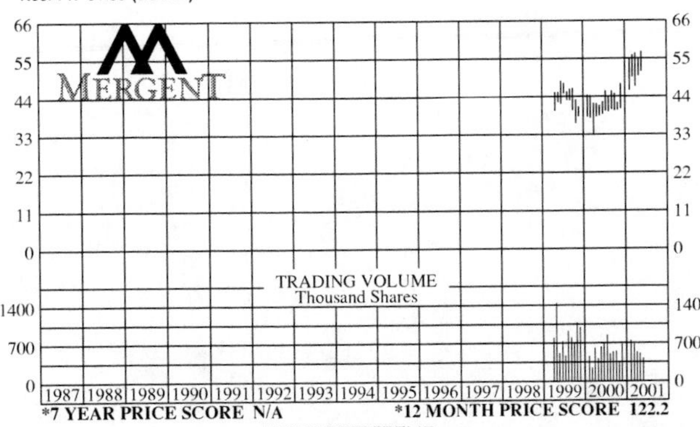

*7 YEAR PRICE SCORE N/A *12 MONTH PRICE SCORE 122.2
*NYSE COMPOSITE INDEX=100

INTERIM EARNINGS (Per Share):

Qtr.	Mar.	June	Sept.	Dec.
1997	0.28	0.32	0.26	0.29
1998	0.26	0.30	0.29	0.34
1999	d0.38	0.43	0.45	0.52
2000	0.45	0.50	0.23	0.43

INTERIM DIVIDENDS (Per Share):

Amt.	Decl.	Ex.	Rec.	Pay.
0.16Q	3/09/00	4/05/00	4/07/00	5/01/00
0.16Q	5/17/00	7/05/00	7/07/00	8/01/00
0.16Q	8/16/00	10/05/00	10/10/00	11/01/00
0.17Q	1/03/01	1/12/01	1/17/01	2/01/01
0.17Q	3/13/01	4/05/01	4/09/01	5/01/01

Indicated div.: $0.68

CAPITALIZATION (12/31/00):

	($000)	(%)
Long-Term Debt	306,000	27.7
Common & Surplus	799,701	72.3
Total	1,105,701	100.0

RECENT DEVELOPMENTS: For the year ended 12/31/00, PTZ reported net income of $34.9 million versus income from continuing operations of $23.0 million in 1999. Earnings for 2000 and 1999 included various nonrecurring items that resulted in pre-tax losses of $9.9 million and $28.6 million, respectively. Earnings for 1999 excluded an after-tax loss of $21.4 million from discontinued operations. Operating revenues rose 22.0% to $407.5 million.

PROSPECTS: PTZ is likely to continue to grow through strategic acquisitions. On 2/28/01, PTZ acquired Siebrasse Publications of DeKalb County, Illinois, a publisher of telephone directories and The MidWeek, a flagship weekly newspaper. On 2/23/01, PTZ acquired the Spanish Fork Press, a weekly newspaper, from J-Mart Publishing. Meanwhile, PTZ launched a new Web site, STLtoday.com, an on-line guide to living in St. Louis.

BUSINESS

PULITZER INC. is a diversified media company involved in newspaper operations and new media businesses. Pulitzer publishes two major metropolitan newspapers, the St. Louis Post-Dispatch and The Arizona Daily Star, and 12 other daily newspapers, primarily serving smaller markets in the West and Midwest. PTZ also owns the Suburban Journals of Greater St. Louis, a group of 39 weekly papers and various niche publications. On 3/18/99, Pulitzer Inc., consisting of publishing and new media companies, was spun off from Pulitzer Publishing Company.

REVENUES

(12/31/2000)	($000)	(%)
Advertising	314,449	77.2
Circulation	81,505	20.0
Other	11,587	2.8
Total	407,541	100.0

ANNUAL FINANCIAL DATA

	12/31/00	12/31/99	12/31/98	12/31/97	12/31/96
Earnings Per Share	**[3] 1.60**	**[2] 1.02**	**[1] 1.19**	**[1] 1.15**	**[1] 0.67**
Cash Flow Per Share	**3.15**	**1.77**	**1.81**	**1.73**	**1.07**
Tang. Book Val. Per Share	...	**28.42**	**8.35**	**5.66**	...
Dividends Per Share	**0.64**	**0.45**	...	...	...
Dividend Payout %	**40.0**	**44.1**	...	...	...
INCOME STATEMENT (IN THOUSANDS):					
Total Revenues	407,541	391,383	372,924	357,969	309,096
Costs & Expenses	334,027	355,196	315,949	303,425	273,391
Depreciation & Amort.	33,657	17,091	14,054	13,007	8,660
Operating Income	62,344	19,096	42,921	41,537	27,045
Net Interest Inc./(Exp.)	2,496	25,377	4,967	4,391	4,509
Income Before Income Taxes	59,346	41,665	47,071	44,986	25,684
Income Taxes	23,595	18,708	20,055	19,227	10,892
Equity Earnings/Minority Int.	19,910	...	...	...	...
Net Income	[3] 34,902	[2] 22,957	[1] 27,016	[1] 25,759	[1] 14,792
Cash Flow	68,559	40,048	41,070	38,766	23,452
Average Shs. Outstg.	21,786	22,601	22,753	22,452	21,926
BALANCE SHEET (IN THOUSANDS):					
Cash & Cash Equivalents	194,313	557,891	110,171	62,749	...
Total Current Assets	268,193	635,220	167,980	114,603	...
Net Property	110,807	83,604	84,151	74,797	...
Total Assets	1,282,873	978,287	546,393	464,311	...
Total Current Liabilities	49,574	39,690	43,305	38,773	...
Long-Term Obligations	306,000	...	...	...	...
Net Stockholders' Equity	799,701	813,451	385,357	310,777	...
Net Working Capital	218,619	595,530	124,675	75,830	...
Year-end Shs. Outstg.	21,152	22,092	22,536	22,198	...
STATISTICAL RECORD:					
Operating Profit Margin %	15.3	14.3	32.5	31.9	23.1
Net Profit Margin %	8.6	17.2	20.4	19.8	12.6
Return on Equity %	4.4	2.8	7.0	8.3	...
Return on Assets %	2.7	2.3	4.9	5.5	...
Debt/Total Assets %	23.9	...	...	...	...
Price Range	47.70-32.81	48.56-36.25	...	...	...
P/E Ratio	29.8-20.5	47.6-35.5	...	...	...
Average Yield %	1.6	1.1	...	...	...

Statistics are as originally reported. [1] Bef. disc oper. gain $49.3 mill., 1998; $40.3 mill., 1997; $42.7 mill., 1996. [2] Bef. disc. oper. loss $21.4 mill. & incl. exps. of $26.7 mill. from stk. option cash-outs & bonuses. [3] Incl. pre-tax loss of $8.1 mill. for newspaper transactions, a pre-tax chrg. of $607,000 for workforce reductions & a $1.2 mill. chrg. for non-oper. invest. losses.

OFFICERS:
M. E. Pulitzer, Chmn.
R. C. Woodworth, Pres., C.E.O.

INVESTOR CONTACT: James V. Maloney, Sec., (314) 340-8402

PRINCIPAL OFFICE: 900 North Tucker Boulevard, St. Louis, MO 63101

TELEPHONE NUMBER: (314) 340-8000
FAX: (314) 340-3125

NO. OF EMPLOYEES: 3,000 (approx.)

SHAREHOLDERS: 412 (approx. common); 28 (approx. class B common)

ANNUAL MEETING: In Apr.

INCORPORATED: DE, 1998

INSTITUTIONAL HOLDINGS:
No. of Institutions: 72
Shares Held: 7,854,647
% Held: 37.1

INDUSTRY: Newspapers (SIC: 2711)

TRANSFER AGENT(S): First Chicago Trust Company of New York, Jersey City, NJ

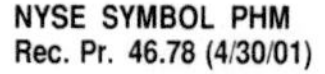

NYSE SYMBOL PHM
Rec. Pr. 46.78 (4/30/01)

PULTE HOMES, INC.

YIELD 0.3%
P/E RATIO 9.0

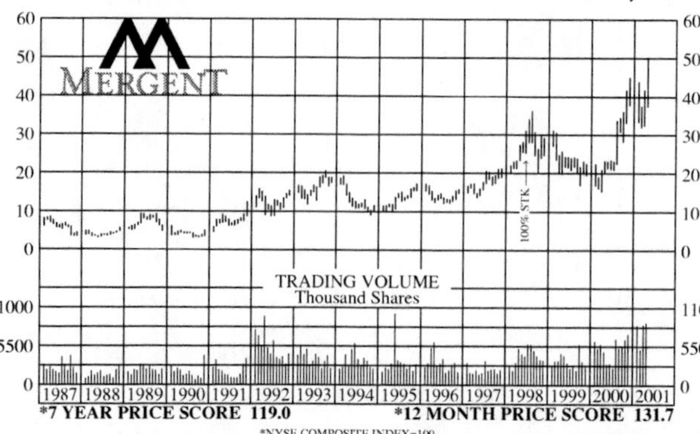

*7 YEAR PRICE SCORE 119.0 *12 MONTH PRICE SCORE 131.7
*NYSE COMPOSITE INDEX=100

INTERIM EARNINGS (Per Share):

Qtr.	Mar.	June	Sept.	Dec.
1997	0.03	0.30	0.43	0.41
1998	0.25	0.54	0.64	0.87
1999	0.54	0.85	1.08	1.60
2000	0.57	1.15	1.47	2.01

INTERIM DIVIDENDS (Per Share):

Amt.	Decl.	Ex.	Rec.	Pay.
0.04Q	5/18/00	6/14/00	6/16/00	7/05/00
0.04Q	9/13/00	9/20/00	9/22/00	10/02/00
0.04Q	12/13/00	12/20/00	12/22/00	1/02/01
0.04Q	3/08/01	3/16/01	3/20/01	4/02/01
0.04Q	5/17/01	6/13/01	6/15/01	7/02/01

Indicated div.: $0.16

CAPITALIZATION (12/31/00):

	($000)	(%)
Long-Term Debt [1]	677,602	35.2
Common & Surplus	1,247,931	64.8
Total	1,925,533	100.0

RECENT DEVELOPMENTS: For the year ended 12/31/00, income from continuing operations rose 22.5% to $218.4 million compared with income from continuing operations of $178.3 million in 1999. Revenues were $4.16 billion, up 11.5% from $3.73 billion a year earlier. Higher revenues resulted from a 9.2% increase in average selling price to $206,000, bolstered by a 4.4% increase in unit settlements to 27,781 homes.

PROSPECTS: On 5/1/01, the Company and Del Webb Corporation announced that their boards have approved a definitive merger agreement valued at $1.80 billion, under which Pulte Homes will acquire all of the outstanding shares of Del Webb in a tax-free stock-for-stock transaction. The combination of the companies will create a $6.00 billion revenue company. The companies anticipate that the transaction should be completed within three months.

BUSINESS

PULTE HOMES, INC. (formerly Pulte Corporation) is engaged in the homebuilding and financial services businesses. Pulte Home Corporation, one of the nation's largest homebuilders, has operations in 41 markets across the United States, Argentina and Puerto Rico. The Company has two operating segments: Homebuilding, which includes the domestic, international and active adult markets, and Financial Services. The Financial Services segment consists principally of mortgage banking operations. During 1994, the Company sold its banking operation, First Heights Bank.

ANNUAL FINANCIAL DATA

	12/31/00	12/31/99	12/31/98	12/31/97	12/31/96	12/31/95	12/31/94
Earnings Per Share	**[3] 5.18**	**[5] 4.07**	**[3] 2.30**	**[3][4] 1.14**	**[3] 1.26**	**[3] 0.90**	**[2] 1.12**
Cash Flow Per Share	**5.52**	**4.38**	**2.42**	**1.31**	**1.40**	**1.01**	**1.36**
Tang. Book Val. Per Share	**30.02**	**25.27**	**21.35**	**19.10**	**17.82**	**14.08**	**12.94**
Dividends Per Share	**0.16**	**0.16**	**0.14**	**0.12**	**0.12**	**0.12**	**0.12**
Dividend Payout %	**3.1**	**3.9**	**6.1**	**10.6**	**9.5**	**13.4**	**10.7**
INCOME STATEMENT (IN MILLIONS):							
Total Revenues	4,159.1	3,730.3	2,866.5	2,524.0	2,384.3	2,029.1	1,755.9
Costs & Expenses	3,795.2	3,437.3	2,695.5	2,435.2	2,275.1	1,940.8	1,639.1
Depreciation & Amort.	14.2	13.5	5.0	7.8	6.7	6.3	13.2
Operating Income	349.6	279.6	166.0	81.0	102.5	82.0	103.6
Income Before Income Taxes	355.1	286.4	165.8	81.0	102.5	82.0	103.6
Income Taxes	136.7	108.1	64.7	31.2	39.3	33.2	41.2
Equity Earnings/Minority Int.	5.5	6.8	d0.2	...	...	...	...
Net Income	[3] 218.4	[5] 178.3	[3] 101.1	[3][4] 49.8	[3] 63.2	[2] 48.8	[2] 62.4
Cash Flow	232.6	191.8	106.2	57.6	70.0	55.2	75.6
Average Shs. Outstg. (000)	42,146	43,823	43,884	43,908	50,140	54,716	55,708
BALANCE SHEET (IN MILLIONS):							
Cash & Cash Equivalents	184.0	51.7	125.2	245.2	189.6	292.2	159.6
Total Current Assets	2,147.4	1,898.0	1,629.5	1,456.9	1,280.8	1,232.1	912.0
Total Assets	2,886.5	2,596.8	2,349.8	2,150.8	1,985.1	2,048.5	1,941.4
Total Current Liabilities	961.0	920.6	802.0	673.4	606.6	567.4	667.5
Long-Term Obligations	677.6	526.0	570.1	584.3	436.5	589.2	563.3
Net Stockholders' Equity	1,247.9	1,093.3	921.4	812.8	829.3	761.0	710.6
Net Working Capital	1,186.4	977.4	827.5	783.4	674.1	664.7	244.5
Year-end Shs. Outstg. (000)	41,567	43,264	43,167	42,546	46,524	54,050	54,906
STATISTICAL RECORD:							
Operating Profit Margin %	8.4	7.5	5.8	3.2	4.3	4.0	5.9
Net Profit Margin %	5.3	4.8	3.5	2.0	2.7	2.4	3.6
Return on Equity %	17.5	16.3	11.0	6.1	7.6	6.4	8.8
Return on Assets %	7.6	6.9	4.3	2.3	3.2	2.4	3.2
Debt/Total Assets %	23.5	20.3	24.3	27.2	22.0	28.8	29.0
Price Range	45.00-15.25	31.25-16.75	36.19-19.94	21.25-13.63	17.31-12.00	17.31-10.06	19.31-9.06
P/E Ratio	8.7-2.9	7.7-4.1	15.7-8.7	18.7-12.0	13.7-9.5	19.3-11.2	17.2-8.1
Average Yield %	0.5	0.7	0.5	0.7	0.8	0.9	0.8

Statistics are as originally reported. Adj. for stk. split: 100%, 6/98. [1] Incl. sub. deb. conv. into com. [2] Excl. extraord chrg. of $2.6 mill., tax benefit of $72.0 mill. and inc. fr. discont. oper. of $103 mill. [3] Bef. inc. fr. discont. oper. of $9.5 mill., 1995; $116.4 mill., 1996; $1.0 mill., 1997; $1.0 mill., 1998; $29.9 mill., 2000. [4] Incl. restruct. costs of $20.0 mill. [5] Bef. loss fr. discont. oper. of $122,000.

OFFICERS:
R. K. Burgess, Chmn., C.E.O.
M. J. O'Brien, Pres., C.O.O.
R. A. Cregg, Sr. V.P., C.F.O.
J. R. Stoller, Sr. V.P., Gen. Couns., Sec.

INVESTOR CONTACT: James P. Zeumer, V.P., Corp. Comm., (248) 647-2750

PRINCIPAL OFFICE: 33 Bloomfield Hills Parkway, Suite 200, Bloomfield Hills, MI 48304

TELEPHONE NUMBER: (248) 647-2750
FAX: (248) 433-4598
WEB: www.pulte.com

NO. OF EMPLOYEES: 5,200 (approx.)

SHAREHOLDERS: 641

ANNUAL MEETING: In May

INCORPORATED: MI, Sept., 1987

INSTITUTIONAL HOLDINGS:
No. of Institutions: 208
Shares Held: 27,617,130
% Held: 65.9

INDUSTRY: Operative builders (SIC: 1531)

TRANSFER AGENT(S): Boston EquiServe, Canton, MA

NYSE SYMBOL OAT
Rec. Pr. 95.86 (5/31/01)

QUAKER OATS CO. (THE)

YIELD 1.2%
P/E RATIO 36.7

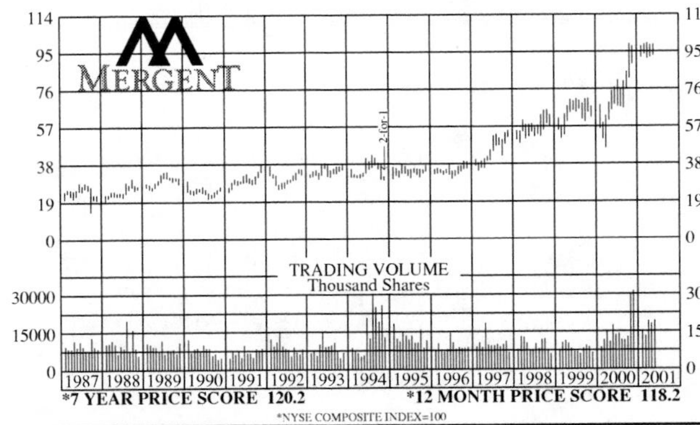

INTERIM EARNINGS (Per Share):

Qtr.	Mar.	June	Sept.	Dec.
1996	0.23	0.47	0.98	0.12
1997	d8.15	0.57	0.58	0.20
1998	0.32	0.40	0.75	0.50
1999	0.61	1.22	0.98	0.42
2000	0.01	1.10	1.15	0.35

INTERIM DIVIDENDS (Per Share):

Amt.	Decl.	Ex.	Rec.	Pay.
0.285Q	5/10/00	6/14/00	6/16/00	7/14/00
0.285Q	9/19/00	9/20/00	9/22/00	10/13/00
0.285Q	11/08/00	12/13/00	12/15/00	1/15/01
0.285Q	3/14/01	3/19/01	3/21/01	4/13/01
0.285Q	5/09/01	6/13/01	6/15/01	7/13/01

Indicated div.: $1.14 (Div. Reinv. Plan)

CAPITALIZATION (12/31/00):

	($000)	(%)
Long-Term Debt	664,100	63.8
Preferred Stock..................	100,000	9.6
Common & Surplus	276,300	26.6
Total	1,040,400	100.0

RECENT DEVELOPMENTS: For the year ended 12/31/00, net income slid 20.7% to $360.6 million from $455.0 million the year before. Results for 2000 included a one-time pre-tax restructuring charge of $182.5 million, while prior-year results included a one-time pre-tax gain of $2.3 million. Net sales rose 6.7% to $5.04 billion from $4.73 billion a year earlier. Gross profit totaled $2.75 billion, or 54.6% of net sales, versus $2.59 billion, or 54.8% of net sales, in the prior year.

PROSPECTS: The acquisition of the Company by PepsiCo, Inc. is on track to be completed by the end of June 2001, subject to approval by the U.S. Federal Trade Commission. On 5/1/01, shareholders of both companies approved the transaction. Going forward, results should benefit from the Company's cost-control initiatives and new product introductions. As an independent company in 2001, OAT is targeting mid-single-digit sales growth, high-single-digit operating income growth and low-double-digit earnings per share growth.

BUSINESS

QUAKER OATS CO. is a major international producer of foods and beverages including ready-to-eat cereals, hot cereals, grain-based snacks, fresh breakfast products, beverages, rice, pasta and institutional and food service products. Brand name products include: GATORADE thirst quencher, QUAKER cereals and grain-based snacks, RICE-A-RONI, PASTA RONI and NEAR EAST side dishes; and AUNT JEMIMA mixes and syrup. U.S. & Canadian Food and Beverage products accounted for 82% of sales in the year ended 12/31/00. International Food and Beverage products, which accounted for 18% of sales, produce and market food products in Europe, Latin America and the Pacific region. OAT divested its SNAPPLE beverage business on 5/22/97.

ANNUAL FINANCIAL DATA

	12/31/00	12/31/99	12/31/98	12/31/97	12/31/96	[3] 12/31/95	6/30/95
Earnings Per Share	[2] 2.61	[2] 3.23	[2] 1.97	[2] d6.80	[2] 1.80	0.09	[1] 6.00
Cash Flow Per Share	3.56	4.11	2.88	d5.62	3.28	0.86	7.43
Tang. Book Val. Per Share	0.36	...	...	...	...	...	...
Dividends Per Share	1.14	1.14	1.14	1.14	1.14	1.14	1.14
Dividend Payout %	43.7	35.3	57.9	...	63.3	1,265.3	19.0
INCOME STATEMENT (IN MILLIONS):							
Total Revenues	5,041.0	4,725.2	4,842.5	5,015.7	5,199.0	2,733.1	6,365.2
Costs & Expenses	4,306.6	3,914.8	4,242.9	5,828.7	4,474.5	2,545.0	4,699.0
Depreciation & Amort.	133.0	123.8	132.5	161.4	200.6	103.2	191.4
Operating Income	601.4	686.6	467.1	d974.4	523.9	84.9	1,474.8
Net Interest Inc./(Exp.)	d45.0	d50.2	d58.9	d79.1	d99.4	d54.2	d110.7
Income Before Income Taxes	551.1	618.3	396.6	d1,064.3	415.6	25.6	1,359.9
Income Taxes	190.5	163.3	112.1	cr133.4	167.7	11.9	553.8
Net Income	[2] 360.6	[2] 455.0	[2] 284.5	[2] d930.9	[2] 247.9	13.7	[1] 806.1
Cash Flow	489.4	574.4	412.5	d773.0	444.8	114.9	993.5
Average Shs. Outstg. (000)	137,491	139,920	143,197	137,460	135,466	134,355	133,763
BALANCE SHEET (IN MILLIONS):							
Cash & Cash Equivalents	174.6	283.2	354.1	84.2	110.5	93.2	101.8
Total Current Assets	1,013.7	996.7	1,115.0	1,133.0	889.7	1,080.1	1,316.6
Net Property	1,120.0	1,106.7	1,070.2	1,164.7	1,200.7	1,167.8	1,113.4
Total Assets	2,418.8	2,396.2	2,510.3	2,697.0	4,394.4	4,620.4	4,826.9
Total Current Liabilities	860.4	938.3	1,009.1	945.7	1,354.7	1,701.7	1,812.9
Long-Term Obligations	664.1	715.0	795.1	887.6	993.5	1,051.8	1,103.1
Net Stockholders' Equity	354.7	197.3	151.0	228.0	1,229.9	1,079.3	1,128.8
Net Working Capital	153.3	58.4	105.9	187.3	d465.0	d621.6	d496.3
Year-end Shs. Outstg. (000)	131,770	131,935	135,323	138,813	136,096	134,806	134,182
STATISTICAL RECORD:							
Operating Profit Margin %	11.9	14.5	9.6	...	10.1	3.1	23.2
Net Profit Margin %	7.2	9.6	5.9	...	4.8	0.5	12.7
Return on Equity %	101.7	230.6	188.4	...	20.2	1.3	71.4
Return on Assets %	14.9	19.0	11.3	...	5.6	0.3	16.7
Debt/Total Assets %	27.5	29.8	31.7	32.9	22.6	22.8	22.9
Price Range	98.94-45.81	71.00-50.88	65.56-48.50	55.13-34.38	39.50-30.38	37.50-30.38	37.50-30.38
P/E Ratio	37.9-17.6	22.0-15.8	33.3-24.6	...	21.9-16.9	416.2-337.1	6.2-5.1
Average Yield %	1.6	1.9	2.0	2.5	3.3	3.4	3.4

Statistics are as originally reported. [1] Bef. $4.1 mil acctg. chg. & incl. $1.09 bil gain and $108.6 mil. chg. [2] Incl. $182.5 mil ($0.79/sh) pre-tax restr. chg., 2000; $2.3 mil pre-tax gain, 1999; $128.5 mil ($0.36/sh) pre-tax chg., 1998; $1.49 bil ($8.70/sh) pre-tax chg., 1997; $113.4 mil gain, 1996; $40.8 mil pre-tax restr. chg., 1995. [3] For the 6 mos. ended 12/31/95.

OFFICERS:
R. S. Morrison, Chmn., Pres., C.E.O.
T. D. Martin, Sr. V.P., C.F.O.
T. L. Gettings, V.P., Treas.

INVESTOR CONTACT: Margaret M. Eichman, V.P., Inv. Rel., (312) 222-7818

PRINCIPAL OFFICE: 321 North Clark St., Chicago, IL 60610-4714

TELEPHONE NUMBER: (312) 222-7111
FAX: (312) 222-7696
WEB: www.quakeroats.com

NO. OF EMPLOYEES: 11,858 (avg.)

SHAREHOLDERS: 22,605 (record)

ANNUAL MEETING: In May

INCORPORATED: NJ, Sept., 1901

INSTITUTIONAL HOLDINGS:
No. of Institutions: 400
Shares Held: 85,793,993
% Held: 64.9

INDUSTRY: Cereal breakfast foods (SIC: 2043)

TRANSFER AGENT(S): Computershare Investor Services, Chicago, IL

NYSE SYMBOL NX
Rec. Pr. 22.35 (5/31/01)

QUANEX CORPORATION

YIELD 2.9%
P/E RATIO ...

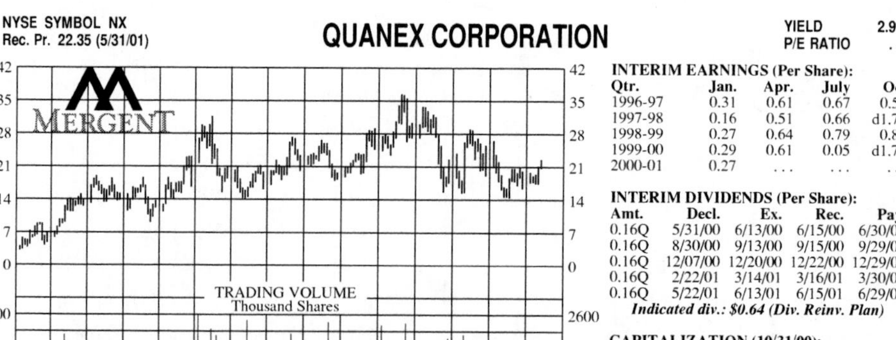

INTERIM EARNINGS (Per Share):

Qtr.	Jan.	Apr.	July	Oct
1996-97	0.31	0.61	0.67	0.59
1997-98	0.16	0.51	0.66	d1.71
1998-99	0.27	0.64	0.79	0.85
1999-00	0.29	0.61	0.05	d1.78
2000-01	0.27	...	...	...

INTERIM DIVIDENDS (Per Share):

Amt.	Decl.	Ex.	Rec.	Pay.
0.16Q	5/31/00	6/13/00	6/15/00	6/30/00
0.16Q	8/30/00	9/13/00	9/15/00	9/29/00
0.16Q	12/07/00	12/20/00	12/22/00	12/29/00
0.16Q	2/22/01	3/14/01	3/16/01	3/30/01
0.16Q	5/22/01	6/13/01	6/15/01	6/29/01

Indicated div.: $0.64 (Div. Reinv. Plan)

CAPITALIZATION (10/31/00):

	($000)	(%)
Long-Term Debt	191,657	39.5
Deferred Income Tax	27,620	5.7
Common & Surplus	266,497	54.9
Total	485,774	100.0

RECENT DEVELOPMENTS: For the quarter ended 1/31/01, income, before an after-tax extraordinary gain of $372,000, fell 11.7% to $3.7 million compared with net income of $4.2 million in the prior-year period. The decline in earnings was primarily attributed to the slow economy, particularly in the manufacturing area, and harsh winter weather. Net sales slipped 2.7% to $193.8 million compared with $199.3 million a year earlier. ce as the year progresses.

PROSPECTS: Going forward, NX's engineered steel bars segment should continue to show operating improvements due to a stronger backlog and new programs. The aluminum mill sheet products segment continues to experience reduced business activity in the building and construction markets; however, bookings and backlog continue to increase. The engineered products group should benefit from the acquisitions of Imperial Fabricated Products and Temroc Metals.

BUSINESS

QUANEX CORPORATION is a manufacturer of value-added engineered steel bars, aluminum flat-rolled products, and engineered, formed-metal products. NX operates three divisions with 14 steel and aluminum manufacturing and fabrication plants in the United States. NX emphasizes low-cost production of proprietary and customized products, including engineered hot-rolled carbon and alloy steel bars, cold-finished steel bars, finished aluminum sheet and fabricated products, and impact-extruded aluminum and steel products. Piper Impact is the Company's operating unit that uses value-added manufacturing processes to produce automotive air bag inflator parts and impact-extruded products. The Company aims for balanced market participation in the transportation, capital equipment, home building and remodeling, defense and other commercial industries. Sales in 2000 were derived as follows: engineered steel bars, 35.9%; aluminum mill sheet products, 42.1%; engineered products, 10.9%; and Piper Impact, 11.1%.

ANNUAL FINANCIAL DATA

	10/31/00	10/31/99	10/31/98	10/31/97	10/31/96	10/31/95	10/31/94
Earnings Per Share	**[1] d0.73**	**[1][4] 2.56**	**[3] d0.27**	**[2] 2.01**	**[1] 2.41**	**[1] 2.20**	**0.96**
Cash Flow Per Share	**2.80**	**5.08**	**2.72**	**4.75**	**5.22**	**4.59**	**3.07**
Tang. Book Val. Per Share	**16.17**	**17.66**	**15.50**	**12.62**	**8.12**	**10.27**	**8.45**
Dividends Per Share	**0.64**	**0.64**	**0.64**	**0.62**	**0.60**	**0.60**	**0.56**
Dividend Payout %	**...**	**25.0**	**...**	**30.8**	**24.9**	**27.3**	**58.3**
INCOME STATEMENT (IN THOUSANDS):							
Total Revenues	934,203	810,094	797,490	746,093	895,710	891,195	699,314
Costs & Expenses	889,720	692,454	752,826	653,220	790,753	792,281	629,377
Depreciation & Amort.	48,445	45,883	42,400	37,865	38,416	32,433	28,535
Operating Income	d3,962	71,757	2,264	55,008	66,541	66,481	41,402
Net Interest Inc./(Exp.)	d13,314	d12,791	d10,506	d14,002	d11,360	d8,870	d7,178
Income Before Income Taxes	d15,406	60,349	d5,964	42,643	56,707	58,380	32,503
Income Taxes	cr5,383	21,048	cr2,087	14,925	23,817	24,520	13,651
Net Income	[1] d10,023	[1][4] 39,301	[3] d3,877	[2] 27,718	[1] 32,890	[1] 33,860	18,852
Cash Flow	38,422	85,184	38,523	65,583	71,306	62,336	41,453
Average Shs. Outstg.	13,727	16,776	14,149	13,807	13,658	13,580	13,496
BALANCE SHEET (IN THOUSANDS):							
Cash & Cash Equivalents	22,409	25,874	26,279	26,851	35,985	45,213	88,111
Total Current Assets	235,946	212,387	209,812	186,896	263,338	242,375	259,396
Net Property	338,248	406,841	395,054	379,071	351,546	258,564	262,261
Total Assets	645,859	690,446	674,288	685,705	718,206	546,747	564,008
Total Current Liabilities	131,002	136,140	146,833	134,078	153,066	165,208	134,751
Long-Term Obligations	191,657	179,121	188,302	201,858	253,513	111,894	107,442
Net Stockholders' Equity	266,497	301,061	272,044	268,823	194,673	170,526	232,249
Net Working Capital	104,944	76,247	62,979	52,818	110,272	77,167	124,645
Year-end Shs. Outstg.	13,543	14,270	14,180	14,050	13,590	13,485	13,378
STATISTICAL RECORD:							
Operating Profit Margin %	...	8.9	0.3	7.4	7.4	7.5	5.9
Net Profit Margin %	...	4.9	...	3.7	3.7	3.8	2.7
Return on Equity %	...	13.1	...	10.3	16.9	19.9	8.1
Return on Assets %	...	5.7	...	4.0	4.6	6.2	3.3
Debt/Total Assets %	29.7	25.9	27.9	29.4	35.3	20.5	19.0
Price Range	26.56-14.38	29.00-15.38	33.81-15.63	36.50-23.38	29.13-18.75	26.63-18.00	27.25-17.00
P/E Ratio	...	11.3-6.0	...	18.2-11.6	12.1-7.8	12.1-8.2	28.4-17.7
Average Yield %	3.1	2.9	2.6	2.1	2.5	2.7	2.5

Statistics are as originally reported. [1] Bef. an extraord. loss of $2.0 mill., 1995; loss of $2.5 mill., 1996; gain of $415,000, 1999; gain of $358,000, 2000; gain of $372,000, 2001. [2] Bef. $41.5 mill. discont. oper. [3] Excl. gain of $13.0 mill. for sale of discont. oper., but incl. pre-tax restruct. chrg. of $58.5 mill. [4] Incl. unusual chrgs. of $70.6 mill.

OFFICERS:
V. E. Oechsle, Chmn.
R. A. Jean
Pres., C.E.O.
T. M. Murphy, V.P., C.F.O.

INVESTOR CONTACT: Geoffrey G. Galow, Dir., Inv. Rel., (800) 231-8176

PRINCIPAL OFFICE: 1900 West Loop South, Suite 1500, Houston, TX 77027

TELEPHONE NUMBER: (713) 961-4600
FAX: (713) 877-5333
WEB: www.quanex.com

NO. OF EMPLOYEES: 3,302

SHAREHOLDERS: 5,893

ANNUAL MEETING: In Feb.

INCORPORATED: MI, 1927; reincorp., DE, 1968

INSTITUTIONAL HOLDINGS:
No. of Institutions: 80
Shares Held: 9,862,614
% Held: 73.5

INDUSTRY: Blast furnaces and steel mills (SIC: 3312)

TRANSFER AGENT(S): American Stock Transfer & Trust Co., New York, NY

NYSE SYMBOL PWR
Rec. Pr. 25.69 (4/30/01)

QUANTA SERVICES, INC.

YIELD ...
P/E RATIO 18.0

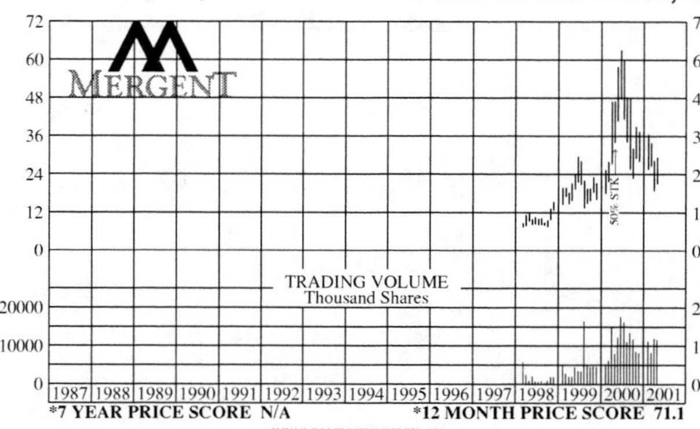

*7 YEAR PRICE SCORE N/A *12 MONTH PRICE SCORE 71.1
*NYSE COMPOSITE INDEX=100

INTERIM EARNINGS (Per Share):

Qtr.	Mar.	June	Sept.	Dec.
1996		0.20		
1997	d0.67	0.13	0.25	0.57
1998	0.27	0.11	0.20	d0.21
1999	0.09	0.11	0.35	0.45
2000	0.28	0.42	0.53	0.20

INTERIM DIVIDENDS (Per Share):

Amt.	Decl.	Ex.	Rec.	Pay.
50% STK	3/14/00	4/10/00	3/27/00	4/07/00

CAPITALIZATION (12/31/00):

	($000)	(%)
Long-Term Debt	491,102	31.5
Common & Surplus	1,068,956	68.5
Total	1,560,058	100.0

RECENT DEVELOPMENTS: For the year ended 12/31/00, net income advanced 96.0% to $105.7 million compared with $53.9 million in 1999. Results for 2000 and 1999 included merger and special charges of $28.6 million and $6.6 million, respectively. Revenues soared 93.7% to $1.79 billion from $925.7 million a year earlier primarily due to internal growth of 33.0% and strategic acquisitions.

PROSPECTS: For fiscal 2001, PWR expects internal growth in the range of 15.0% to 20.0% and earnings in the range of $2.14 to $2.18 per share, assuming no acquisitions in 2001. The Company should continue to benefit from increased demand for bandwidth as PWR's customers continue to outsource more work. PWR expects strong growth in the electric and gas utility markets for the remainder of 2001.

BUSINESS

QUANTA SERVICES, INC. is a provider of specialty electrical contracting and maintenance services primarily related to electric and telecommunications infrastructure in North America. In addition, the Company provides electrical contracting services to the commercial and industrial markets and installs transportation control and lighting systems. The Company's services include the installation, repair and maintenance of electric power transmission and distribution lines and telecommunication and cable television lines, the construction of electric substations, the erection of cellular telephone, PCS® and microwave towers, the installation of highway lighting and traffic control systems, design and engineering services and the provision of specialty contracting services for electric, video, security, fire, voice and data systems.

REVENUES

(12/31/2000)	($000)	(%)
Telecommunications	796,586	44.4
Cable Television Network	219,514	12.2
Electric Power Network	483,432	27.0
Ancillary Services	293,769	16.4
Total	1,793,301	100.0

ANNUAL FINANCIAL DATA

	12/31/00	12/31/99	12/31/98	12/31/97	12/31/96
Earnings Per Share	**[1] 1.42**	**[1] 1.00**	**[1] 0.37**	**0.28**	**0.20**
Cash Flow Per Share	**2.12**	**1.58**	**0.61**	**0.66**	**0.52**
Tang. Book Val. Per Share	**2.89**	**2.41**	**0.40**	**0.68**	...
INCOME STATEMENT (IN THOUSANDS):					
Total Revenues	1,793,301	925,654	309,209	76,204	71,294
Costs & Expenses	1,513,845	773,798	267,757	67,218	64,281
Depreciation & Amort.	57,294	35,163	10,600	3,323	2,814
Operating Income	222,162	116,693	30,852	5,663	4,199
Net Interest Inc./(Exp.)	d25,708	d15,184	d4,635	d1,219	d989
Income Before Income Taxes	199,051	102,938	26,858	4,313	3,179
Income Taxes	93,328	48,999	11,683	1,786	1,389
Net Income	[1] 105,723	[1] 53,939	[1] 15,175	2,527	1,790
Cash Flow	162,087	88,842	25,775	5,850	4,604
Average Shs. Outstg.	76,583	56,146	41,999	8,892	8,892
BALANCE SHEET (IN THOUSANDS):					
Cash & Cash Equivalents	17,306	10,775	3,246	489	...
Total Current Assets	602,407	335,063	104,729	16,702	...
Net Property	341,029	191,854	74,165	18,286	...
Total Assets	1,874,094	1,159,636	334,958	35,747	...
Total Current Liabilities	252,437	170,923	48,848	14,516	...
Long-Term Obligations	491,102	199,658	109,551	7,542	...
Net Stockholders' Equity	1,068,956	756,925	170,298	11,210	...
Net Working Capital	349,970	164,140	55,881	2,186	...
Year-end Shs. Outstg.	56,401	54,781	48,807	16,418	...
STATISTICAL RECORD:					
Operating Profit Margin %	12.4	12.6	10.0	7.4	5.9
Net Profit Margin %	5.9	5.8	4.9	3.3	2.5
Return on Equity %	9.9	7.1	8.9	22.5	...
Return on Assets %	5.6	4.7	4.5	7.1	...
Debt/Total Assets %	26.2	17.2	32.7	21.1	...
Price Range	63.13-17.92	29.58-13.42	15.33-7.33	...	...
P/E Ratio	44.5-12.6	29.6-13.4	41.1-19.7	...	...

Statistics are as originally reported. Adj. for stk. split: k50%, 4/00. [1] Incl. merger and special charges of $28.6 mill., 2000; $6.6 mill., 1999; $231,000, 1998.

OFFICERS:
V. Foster, Chmn.
J. R. Colson, C.E.O.
J. H. Haddox, C.F.O.
P. T. Dameris, C.O.O.

INVESTOR CONTACT: James H. Haddox, Investor Relations, (713) 629-7600

PRINCIPAL OFFICE: 1360 Post Oak Blvd., Suite 2100, Houston, TX 77056

TELEPHONE NUMBER: (713) 629-7600
FAX: (713) 626-7676
WEB: www.quantaservices.com

NO. OF EMPLOYEES: 13,260 (avg.)

SHAREHOLDERS: 344 (record)

ANNUAL MEETING: In May

INCORPORATED: DE, Aug., 1997

INSTITUTIONAL HOLDINGS:
No. of Institutions: 182
Shares Held: 25,009,314
% Held: 41.9

INDUSTRY: Electrical work (SIC: 1731)

TRANSFER AGENT(S): American Stock Transfer & Trust Company, New York, NY

NYSE SYMBOL DSS
Rec. Pr. 11.99 (5/31/01)

QUANTUM CORPORATION - DLT & STORAGE SYSTEMS GROUP

YIELD ...
P/E RATIO 11.9

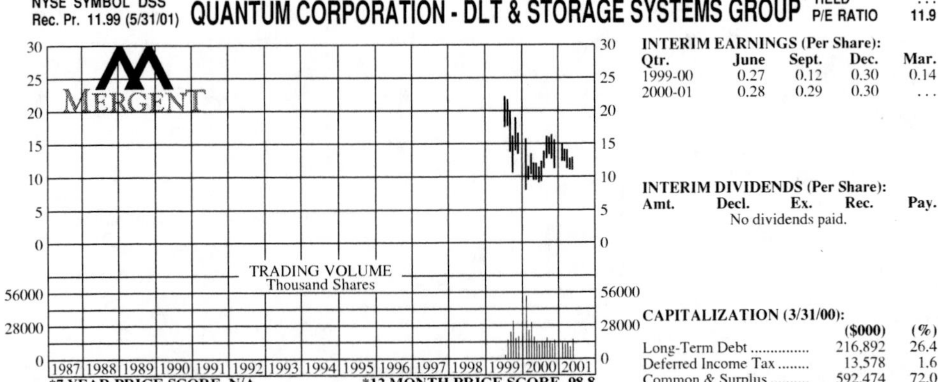

INTERIM EARNINGS (Per Share):

Qtr.	June	Sept.	Dec.	Mar.
1999-00	0.27	0.12	0.30	0.14
2000-01	0.28	0.29	0.30	...

INTERIM DIVIDENDS (Per Share):

Amt.	Decl.	Ex.	Rec.	Pay.

No dividends paid.

CAPITALIZATION (3/31/00):

	($000)	(%)
Long-Term Debt	216,892	26.4
Deferred Income Tax	13,578	1.6
Common & Surplus	592,474	72.0
Total	822,944	100.0

RECENT DEVELOPMENTS: For the quarter ended 12/31/00, net income slipped 6.4% to $47.5 million from $50.8 million the previous year. Total revenue inched up 1.0% to $369.3 million from $365.8 million in the prior year. Product revenue decreased 2.4% to $309.3 million, while royalty revenue climbed 22.9% to $60.0 million. Gross profit totaled $163.4 million, or 44.3% of total revenue, compared with $164.1 million, or 44.9% of total revenue, the year before. Income from operations slid 13.9% to $73.7 million from $85.6 million a year earlier.

PROSPECTS: Results are being negatively affected by significantly lower levels of information technology spending. Despite the current economic slowdown, the Company continues to target gross margins for its DLTtape business in the mid-40.0% range and expects that this business will generate cash from operations of more than $200.0 million annually. Going forward, results may benefit from the Company's aggressive launch of several new data protection and storage products during its fourth quarter, which ended in March 2001.

BUSINESS

QUANTUM CORPORATION - DLT & STORAGE SYSTEMS GROUP designs, develops, manufactures, licenses and markets DLTtape™ drives, DLTtape media cartridges and storage systems that are used to back up large amounts of data stored on network servers. The Company's storage systems consist of DLTtape libraries, solid state storage systems, network attached storage appliances and service. Digital Linear Tape, or DLTtape, is the Company's half-inch tape technology that is the industry standard for data back-up in the mid-range network server market.

ANNUAL FINANCIAL DATA

	3/31/00	3/31/99
Earnings Per Share	[1] **0.51**	...
Cash Flow Per Share	**1.24**	...
Tang. Book Val. Per Share	**2.19**	...
INCOME STATEMENT (IN MILLIONS):		
Total Revenues	1,418.9	1,302.7
Costs & Expenses	1,089.4	984.1
Depreciation & Amort.	62.0	41.9
Operating Income	267.5	276.7
Net Interest Inc./(Exp.)	d0.1	d12.4
Income Before Income Taxes	267.4	264.3
Income Taxes	121.7	141.3
Net Income	[1] 145.6	[1] 123.0
Cash Flow	207.6	164.9
Average Shs. Outstg. (000)	167,734	...
BALANCE SHEET (IN MILLIONS):		
Cash & Cash Equivalents	338.8	272.6
Total Current Assets	747.4	695.4
Net Property	78.1	73.1
Total Assets	1,086.0	1,013.6
Total Current Liabilities	263.1	158.1
Long-Term Obligations	216.9	229.6
Net Stockholders' Equity	592.5	598.5
Net Working Capital	484.4	537.3
Year-end Shs. Outstg. (000)	157,423	...
STATISTICAL RECORD:		
Operating Profit Margin %	18.9	21.2
Net Profit Margin %	10.3	9.4
Return on Equity %	24.6	20.5
Return on Assets %	13.4	12.1
Debt/Total Assets %	20.0	22.7
Price Range	22.25-10.63	...
P/E Ratio	43.6-20.8	...

Statistics are as originally reported. [1] Incl. $77.1 mil non-recurr. pre-tax chg., 2000; $89.0 mil, 1999.

OFFICERS:
M. A. Brown, Chmn., C.E.O.
J. Maurer, Exec. V.P.
T. Scott, Exec. V.P.

INVESTOR CONTACT: Renee Budig, Investor Relations, (408) 894-5563

PRINCIPAL OFFICE: 500 McCarthy Blvd., Milpitas, CA 95035

TELEPHONE NUMBER: (408) 894-4000
FAX: (408) 894-3218

NO. OF EMPLOYEES: 2,300 (approx.)

SHAREHOLDERS: 4,868 (approx.)

ANNUAL MEETING: In Aug.

INCORPORATED: DE, Apr., 1987

INSTITUTIONAL HOLDINGS:
No. of Institutions: 157
Shares Held: 106,454,065
% Held: 70.4

INDUSTRY: Computer storage devices (SIC: 3572)

TRANSFER AGENT(S): Computershare Investor Services, Chicago, IL

NYSE SYMBOL DGX
Rec. Pr. 61.81 (5/31/01)

QUEST DIAGNOSTICS, INC.

YIELD ...
P/E RATIO 55.2

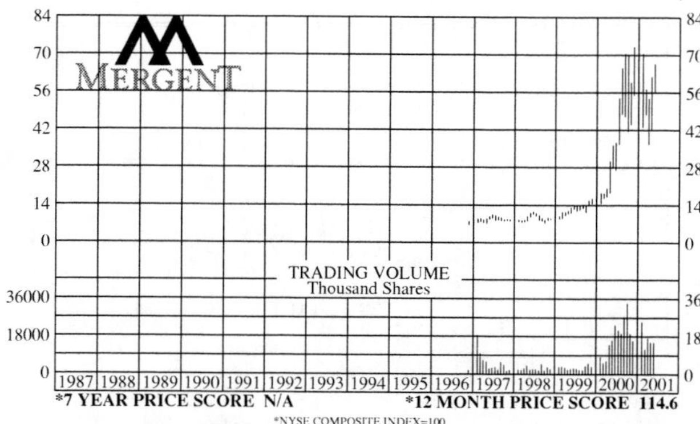

*7 YEAR PRICE SCORE N/A *12 MONTH PRICE SCORE 114.6

*NYSE COMPOSITE INDEX=100

INTERIM EARNINGS (Per Share):

Qtr.	Mar.	June	Sept.	Dec.
1997	0.07	0.14	0.05	d0.65
1998	0.11	0.15	0.10	0.09
1999	0.12	0.22	d0.10	d0.17
2000	0.20	0.32	0.30	0.30

INTERIM DIVIDENDS (Per Share):

Amt.	Decl.	Ex.	Rec.	Pay.
2-for-1	2/22/01	6/01/01	5/16/01	5/31/01

CAPITALIZATION (12/31/00):

	($000)	(%)
Long-Term Debt	760,705	42.4
Redeemable Pfd. Stock	1,000	0.1
Common & Surplus	1,030,795	57.5
Total	1,792,500	100.0

RECENT DEVELOPMENTS: For the year ended 12/31/00, income was $105.0 million, before an extraordinary loss of $2.9 million, compared with a loss of $1.3 million, before an extraordinary loss of $2.1 million in 1999. The 2000 and 1999 results included pre-tax provisions for restructuring and other special charges of $2.1 million and $73.4 million, respectively. Net revenues soared 55.1% to $3.42 billion from $2.21 billion the year before.

PROSPECTS: Looking ahead, DGX should continue to drive performance improvement through its strategic initiatives. DGX will focus on achieving Six Sigma quality as it steps up efforts to drive performance improvements. DGX's market position, demand for genomics and increased interest among consumers in managing their health should result in profitable growth.

BUSINESS

QUEST DIAGNOSTICS, INC. is a provider of diagnostic testing, information and services. DGX offers clinical laboratory testing services used by physicians in the detection, diagnosis, evaluation, monitoring and treatment of diseases and other medical conditions. DGX maintains a national network of approximately 30 full-service laboratories, 150 rapid response laboratories and mare than 1,300 patient service centers. DGX is also involved in clinical laboratory testing, and esoteric testing, as well as anatomic pathology services and testing for drugs of abuse. DGX's clinical trials business providers testing to support clinical trials of new pharmaceuticals worldwide. DGX also collects and analyzes laboratory, pharmaceutical and other data through its Quest Informatics division in order to help pharmaceutical companies with their marketing and disease management efforts, as well as help large healthcare customers better manage the health of their patients.

QUARTERLY DATA

(12/31/2000)($000)	REV	INC
First Quarter	857,479	17,809
Second Quarter	877,113	30,168
Third Quarter	850,236	28,712
Fourth Quarter	836,334	25,363

ANNUAL FINANCIAL DATA

	12/31/00	12/31/99	12/31/98	12/31/97	12/31/96	12/31/95
Earnings Per Share	[1][2] **1.11**	[1][2] **d0.02**	**0.45**	[1] **d0.38**	[1] **Nil**	[1] **Nil**
Cash Flow Per Share	**2.54**	**1.28**	**1.58**	**0.93**	...	...
Tang. Book Val. Per Share	...	...	**1.20**	**0.45**	...	...
INCOME STATEMENT (IN MILLIONS):						
Total Revenues	3,421.2	2,205.2	1,458.6	1,528.7	1,616.3	1,629.4
Costs & Expenses	2,980.5	2,041.2	1,297.5	1,427.6	2,117.3	1,497.2
Depreciation & Amort.	134.3	90.8	68.8	76.4	99.1	101.5
Operating Income	306.4	73.2	92.2	24.7	d600.1	30.7
Net Interest Inc./(Exp.)	d113.1	d61.4	d33.4	d41.0	d74.9	d82.0
Income Before Income Taxes	201.0	14.4	53.9	d19.1	d676.2	d57.6
Income Taxes	96.0	15.7	27.0	3.2	cr50.2	cr5.5
Net Income	[1][2] 104.9	[1][2] d1.3	26.9	[1] d22.3	[1] d626.0	[1] d52.1
Cash Flow	239.1	89.4	95.6	54.0	d526.9	49.5
Average Shs. Outstg. (000)	94,300	70,028	60,458	58,400	...	...
BALANCE SHEET (IN MILLIONS):						
Cash & Cash Equivalents	171.5	27.3	202.9	161.7	42.0	...
Total Current Assets	980.7	872.7	578.2	571.9	511.0	318.3
Net Property	449.9	428.0	240.4	250.2	287.7	...
Total Assets	2,864.5	2,878.5	1,360.2	1,400.9	1,395.1	318.3
Total Current Liabilities	955.0	701.2	309.5	295.1	249.4	...
Long-Term Obligations	760.7	1,171.4	413.4	482.2	515.0	1,195.6
Net Stockholders' Equity	1,030.8	862.1	566.9	540.7	537.7	295.8
Net Working Capital	25.7	171.4	268.7	276.7	261.5	318.3
Year-end Shs. Outstg. (000)	93,082	88,706	60,054	59,972	57,644	...
STATISTICAL RECORD:						
Operating Profit Margin %	9.0	3.3	6.3	1.6	...	1.9
Net Profit Margin %	3.1	...	1.8	...	...	...
Return on Equity %	10.2	...	4.7	...	...	...
Return on Assets %	3.7	...	2.0	...	...	...
Debt/Total Assets %	26.6	40.7	30.4	34.4	36.9	375.7
Price Range	73.13-14.56	16.47-8.88	11.53-7.25	10.44-7.13	7.88-6.63	...
P/E Ratio	65.9-13.1	...	25.9-16.3	...	...	...

Statistics are as originally reported. Adj. for stock split, 2-for-1, 5/31/01 [1] Incl. pre-tax provision for restruct. & other spec. chrgs. $2.1 mill, 2000; $73.4 mill., 1999; $48.7 mill., 1997; $668.5 mill., 1996; $50.6 mill., 1995 [2] Bef. extraord. loss of $2.9 mill., 2000; $2.1 mill., 1999

OFFICERS:
K. W. Freeman, Chmn., C.E.O.
S. N. Mohapatra Ph.D., Pres., C.O.O.
R. A. Hagemann, V.P., C.F.O.
M. E. Prevoznik, V.P, Gen. Couns.

INVESTOR CONTACT: Kenneth Finnegan, V.P. Inv. Rel., (201) 393-5000

PRINCIPAL OFFICE: One Malcolm Avenue, Teterboro, NJ 07608

TELEPHONE NUMBER: (201) 393-5000
FAX: (201) 462-4169
WEB: www.questdiagnostics.com

NO. OF EMPLOYEES: 25,000 full-time (approx.); 2,000 part-time (approx.)

SHAREHOLDERS: 6,800 (approx.)

ANNUAL MEETING: In May

INCORPORATED: DE, 1990

INSTITUTIONAL HOLDINGS:
No. of Institutions: 238
Shares Held: 48,245,726 (Adj.)
% Held: 51.3

INDUSTRY: Commercial physical research (SIC: 8731)

TRANSFER AGENT(S): Harris Trust and Savings Bank, Chicago, IL

NYSE SYMBOL STR
Rec. Pr. 30.99 (5/31/01)

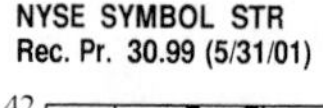

QUESTAR CORPORATION

YIELD	2.3%
P/E RATIO	16.0

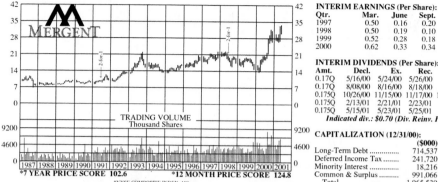

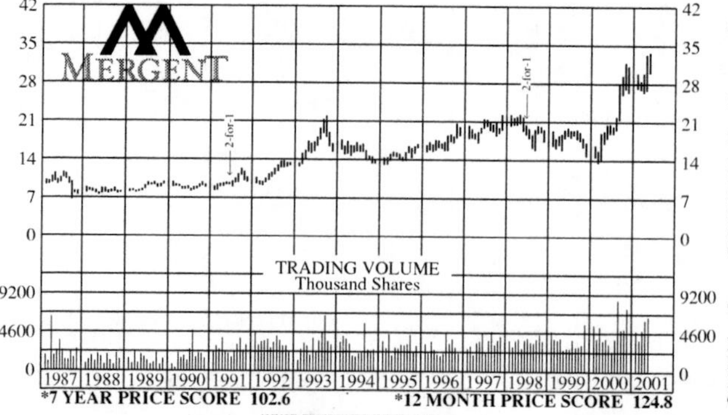

INTERIM EARNINGS (Per Share):

Qtr.	Mar.	June	Sept.	Dec.
1997	0.50	0.16	0.20	0.42
1998	0.50	0.19	0.10	0.14
1999	0.52	0.28	0.18	0.21
2000	0.62	0.33	0.34	0.65

INTERIM DIVIDENDS (Per Share):

Amt.	Decl.	Ex.	Rec.	Pay.
0.17Q	5/16/00	5/24/00	5/26/00	6/19/00
0.17Q	8/08/00	8/16/00	8/18/00	9/11/00
0.175Q	10/26/00	11/15/00	11/17/00	12/11/00
0.175Q	2/13/01	2/21/01	2/23/01	3/19/01
0.175Q	5/15/01	5/23/01	5/25/01	6/18/01

Indicated div.: $0.70 (Div. Reinv. Plan)

CAPITALIZATION (12/31/00):

	($000)	(%)
Long-Term Debt	714,537	36.4
Deferred Income Tax	241,720	12.3
Minority Interest	18,216	0.9
Common & Surplus	991,066	50.4
Total	1,965,539	100.0

RECENT DEVELOPMENTS: For the year ended 12/31/00, net income increased 58.6% to $156.7 million versus $98.8 million a year earlier. Results for 2000 and 1999 included non-recurring security gains of $16.3 million and $36.9 million, respectively. Also, results for 1999 included non-recurring after-tax charges of $33.1 million from a pipeline write-down and early retirement costs. Revenues rose 37.0% to $1.27 billion from $924.2 million a year earlier.

PROSPECTS: Results are being driven by gains from STR's exploration and production operations and improvement from its regulated interstate transmission and retail distribution businesses. Meanwhile, for fiscal 2001, STR has hedged about 55.0% of the existing gas production estimated from year-end reserves at an average net-to-the-well price of $2.90 per thousand cubic feet. Also, STR has hedged about 62.0% of its 2001 oil production at an average net-to-the-well price of $17.20 per barrel.

BUSINESS

QUESTAR CORPORATION is an integrated energy services holding company. Operations are conducted through two basic divisions: Market Resources and Regulated Services. The Market Resources division is engaged in energy development and production; gas gathering and processing; and wholesale gas, electricity and hydrocarbon liquids marketing and trading. Regulated Services conducts interstate gas transmission and storage activities and retail gas distribution services. Other operations include Questar InfoComm, a full-service provider of integrated information, communications and electronic measurement services and technologies.

REVENUES

(12/31/2000)	($000)	(%)
Market resources	742,053	50.3
Gas distribution	536,762	36.4
Gas transmission	119,076	8.1
Other	3,925	0.3
Corporate & other	73,409	4.9
Total	1,475,225	100.0

ANNUAL FINANCIAL DATA

	12/31/00	12/31/99	12/31/98	12/31/97	12/31/96	12/31/95	12/31/94
Earnings Per Share	**3 1.94**	**1.20**	**2 0.93**	**1.26**	**1.20**	**1.03**	**1 0.61**
Cash Flow Per Share	**3.76**	**2.95**	**2.48**	**2.82**	**2.55**	**2.28**	**1.82**
Tang. Book Val. Per Share	**12.01**	**11.37**	**10.62**	**10.30**	**9.41**	**8.76**	**8.08**
Dividends Per Share	**0.69**	**0.67**	**0.65**	**0.62**	**0.59**	**0.58**	**0.56**
Dividend Payout %	**35.3**	**55.8**	**70.2**	**49.2**	**49.8**	**56.6**	**93.4**
INCOME STATEMENT (IN MILLIONS):							
Total Revenues	1,266.2	924.2	906.3	933.3	818.0	649.3	670.3
Costs & Expenses	858.6	599.6	644.8	634.6	536.4	406.2	418.1
Depreciation & Amort.	147.6	144.7	128.7	128.5	110.0	101.1	97.6
Operating Income	259.9	179.9	132.8	170.2	171.6	142.0	154.7
Net Interest Inc./(Exp.)	d63.5	d53.9	d48.0	d43.8	d41.1	d42.8	d39.8
Income Taxes	85.4	47.8	29.0	45.6	45.4	32.7	8.6
Net Income	3 156.7	98.8	2 76.9	104.8	98.1	83.8	1 49.4
Cash Flow	304.4	243.5	205.6	233.1	207.8	184.4	146.4
Average Shs. Outstg. (000)	80,915	82,676	82,817	82,668	81,656	81,104	80,584
BALANCE SHEET (IN MILLIONS):							
Gross Property	3,544.3	3,258.8	3,104.5	2,741.9	2,575.0	2,330.9	2,263.2
Accumulated Depreciation	1,590.3	1,471.9	1,356.9	1,210.7	1,097.6	1,020.8	955.5
Net Property	1,954.0	1,786.9	1,747.6	1,531.2	1,477.3	1,310.1	1,307.6
Total Assets	2,539.0	2,238.0	2,161.3	1,945.0	1,816.2	1,584.6	1,585.6
Long-Term Obligations	714.5	735.0	615.8	542.0	555.5	421.7	494.7
Net Stockholders' Equity	991.1	925.8	878.0	845.8	772.1	712.7	653.6
Year-end Shs. Outstg. (000)	80,818	81,419	82,632	82,142	82,050	81,396	80,858
STATISTICAL RECORD:							
Operating Profit Margin %	20.5	19.5	14.7	18.2	21.0	21.9	23.1
Net Profit Margin %	12.4	10.7	8.5	11.2	12.0	12.9	7.4
Net Inc./Net Property %	8.0	5.5	4.4	6.8	6.6	6.4	3.8
Net Inc./Tot. Capital %	8.0	5.3	4.5	6.5	6.4	6.3	3.8
Return on Equity %	15.8	10.7	8.8	12.4	12.7	11.8	7.6
Accum. Depr./Gross Prop. %	44.9	45.2	43.7	44.2	42.6	43.8	42.2
Price Range	31.88-13.56	19.94-14.75	22.38-15.81	22.31-17.13	20.69-15.44	16.88-13.06	17.63-13.31
P/E Ratio	16.4-7.0	16.6-12.3	24.1-17.0	17.7-13.6	17.3-12.9	16.5-12.7	29.1-22.0
Average Yield %	3.0	3.9	3.4	3.1	3.3	3.9	3.7

Statistics are as originally reported. Adj. for 2-for-1 stk. split, 6/98 1 Incls. non-recurr. chrg. 12/31/94, $38.1 mill. ($0.95/sh.) 2 Incls. one-time chrg. of $20.3 mill. 3 Incls. after-tax gain of $16.3 mill. ($0.20/sh.) on sale of securities.

OFFICERS:
R. D. Cash, Chmn., C.E.O.
K. O. Rattie, Pres., C.O.O.
S. E. Parks, V.P., C.F.O., Treas.

INVESTOR CONTACT: Stephen E. Parks, V.P., Treas., C.F.O., (801) 324-5497

PRINCIPAL OFFICE: 180 East 100 South Street, P.O. Box 45433, Salt Lake City, UT 84145-0433

TELEPHONE NUMBER: (801) 324-5000
FAX: (801) 324-5483
WEB: www.questar.com

NO. OF EMPLOYEES: 2,022 (avg.)

SHAREHOLDERS: 11,279 (record)

ANNUAL MEETING: In May

INCORPORATED: UT, Oct., 1984

INSTITUTIONAL HOLDINGS:
No. of Institutions: 233
Shares Held: 51,257,210
% Held: 63.6

INDUSTRY: Gas transmission and distribution (SIC: 4923)

TRANSFER AGENT(S): Questar Corp., Salt Lake City, UT

NYSE SYMBOL Q
Rec. Pr. 40.90 (4/30/01)

QWEST COMMUNICATIONS INTERNATIONAL, INC.

YIELD . . .
P/E RATIO . . .

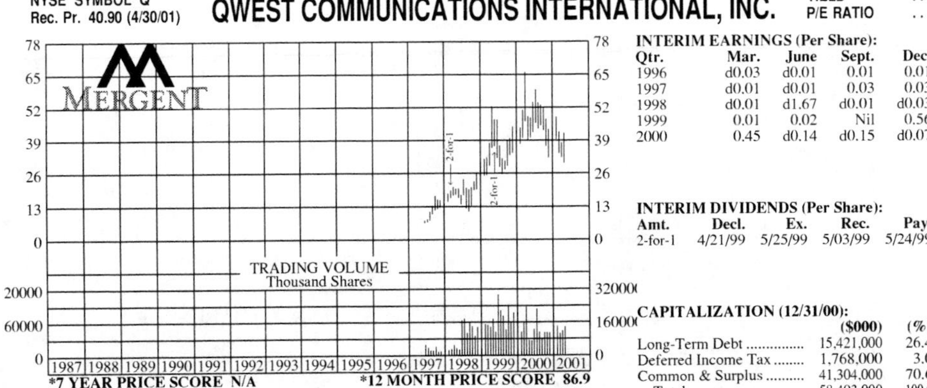

INTERIM EARNINGS (Per Share):

Qtr.	Mar.	June	Sept.	Dec.
1996	d0.03	d0.01	0.01	0.01
1997	d0.01	d0.01	0.03	0.03
1998	d0.01	d1.67	d0.01	d0.03
1999	0.01	0.02	Nil	0.56
2000	0.45	d0.14	d0.15	d0.07

INTERIM DIVIDENDS (Per Share):

Amt.	Decl.	Ex.	Rec.	Pay.
2-for-1	4/21/99	5/25/99	5/03/99	5/24/99

CAPITALIZATION (12/31/00):

	($000)	(%)
Long-Term Debt	15,421,000	26.4
Deferred Income Tax	1,768,000	3.0
Common & Surplus	41,304,000	70.6
Total	58,493,000	100.0

RECENT DEVELOPMENTS: For the year ended 12/31/00, Q posted a loss of $81.0 million versus income of $1.10 billion, before an accounting change, a year earlier. Results for 2000 included merger-related and other charges of $1.75 billion and a gain of $327.0 million from the sale of investments, while results for 1999 included a loss of $367.0 million on the sale of investments. Revenues rose 26.0% to $16.61 billion. Prior year figures have been restated to reflect the Company's acquisition of U S West, Inc.

PROSPECTS: Near-term prospects are positive, reflecting strong demand for such services as Web hosting in Qwest CyberCenters and DSL services for high-speed Internet access. Future prospects should benefit from Q's planned re-entry in the long-distance market in its 14-state local service area. The Company intends to file its first application with the Federal Communications Commission in the summer of 2001 to re-enter the long-distance business in one of the states in its local service area and to file applications for other states later in 2001 and early in 2002.

BUSINESS

QWEST COMMUNICATIONS INTERNATIONAL, INC. is a broadband Internet communications company that provides advanced communication, data, multimedia and Internet-based services on a national and global basis; and wireless, local telecommunications, and directory services in its 14-state local service area, which is located primarily in the western half of the U.S. The Qwest Macro Capacity® Fiber Network currently reaches over 25,500 miles in North America. Qwest has also built a 1,400 route-mile network in Mexico, and is part of a consortium of communications companies that is building a 13,125-mile underwater cable network connecting the U.S. to Japan. In addition, Qwest and KPN, the Dutch telecommunications company, have formed a venture to build and operate a high-capacity, pan-European fiber-optic, Internet-based network that is expected to connect over 50 cities throughout Europe when completed by the end of 2001. On 6/30/00, Qwest acquired U S West, Inc. for approximately $40.00 billion.

ANNUAL FINANCIAL DATA

	12/31/00	12/31/99	12/31/98	12/31/97	12/31/96	12/31/95	12/31/94
Earnings Per Share	**③ d0.06**	**② 0.60**	**① d1.51**	**0.04**	**d0.02**	**d0.08**	**d0.02**
Cash Flow Per Share	**2.56**	**1.13**	**d1.15**	**0.09**	**0.03**	**d0.04**	**d0.01**
Tang. Book Val. Per Share	**5.37**	**4.95**	**1.20**	**0.92**	**. . .**	**0.05**	**. . .**
INCOME STATEMENT (IN MILLIONS):							
Total Revenues	④ 16,610.0	3,927.6	2,242.7	696.7	231.0	125.1	70.9
Costs & Expenses	11,445.0	3,199.9	2,794.7	653.0	226.8	151.2	79.1
Depreciation & Amort.	3,342.0	404.1	201.7	20.3	16.2	10.0	2.4
Operating Income	1,823.0	323.6	d753.7	23.5	d12.0	d36.1	d10.6
Net Interest Inc./(Exp.)	d1,041.0	d151.0	d97.3	d7.2	d4.4	d2.5	. . .
Income Before Income Taxes	126.0	583.5	d849.8	23.6	d10.2	d38.5	d10.7
Income Taxes	207.0	125.0	cr5.8	9.1	cr3.2	cr13.3	cr3.8
Net Income	③ d81.0	② 458.5	① d844.0	14.5	d7.0	d25.1	d6.9
Cash Flow	3,261.0	862.6	d642.3	34.8	9.3	d15.1	d4.5
Average Shs. Outstg. (000)	1,272,088	764,300	558,200	388,110	346,000	352,632	352,632
BALANCE SHEET (IN MILLIONS):							
Cash & Cash Equivalents	154.0	349.2	462.8	379.8	6.9	1.5	. . .
Total Current Assets	5,376.0	1,785.2	1,439.1	723.9	56.4	52.4	. . .
Net Property	25,583.0	4,108.7	2,655.4	614.6	186.5	114.7	. . .
Total Assets	73,501.0	11,058.1	8,067.6	1,398.1	262.6	184.2	. . .
Total Current Liabilities	9,893.0	1,238.4	1,237.5	315.4	132.1	55.0	. . .
Long-Term Obligations	15,421.0	2,368.3	2,307.1	630.5	109.3	95.9	. . .
Net Stockholders' Equity	41,304.0	7,001.3	4,238.2	381.7	9.4	26.5	. . .
Net Working Capital	d4,517.0	546.8	201.6	408.5	d75.7	d2.6	. . .
Year-end Shs. Outstg. (000)	1,672,219	750,000	694,000	413,340	346,000	346,000	. . .
STATISTICAL RECORD:							
Operating Profit Margin %	11.0	8.2	. . .	3.4	. . .	. . .	. . .
Net Profit Margin %	. . .	11.7	. . .	2.1	. . .	. . .	. . .
Return on Equity %	. . .	6.5	. . .	3.8	. . .	. . .	. . .
Return on Assets %	. . .	4.1	. . .	1.0	. . .	. . .	. . .
Debt/Total Assets %	21.0	21.4	28.6	45.1	41.6	52.1	. . .
Price Range	66.00-32.13	52.38-25.03	25.66-11.00	17.22-6.59	. . .	. . .	. . .
P/E Ratio	. . .	87.3-41.7	. . .	490.6-187.9	. . .	. . .	. . .

Statistics are as originally reported. Adj. for stk. split: 2-for-1, 5/24/99 & 2/24/98 ① Incl. non-recurr. chrg. $86.5 mill. ② Incl. non-recurr. chrg. $31.5 mill. ③ Incl. merger-rel. & oth. chrgs. of $1.75 bill. and gain on sales of invest. of $327.0 mill. ④ Refls. the Company's acq. of U S West, Inc.

OFFICERS:
J. P. Nacchio, Chmn., C.E.O.
R. R. Szeliga, Sr. V.P., Interim C.F.O.
J. C. Dodd, Exec. V.P., C.I.O.

INVESTOR CONTACT: Investor Relations, (800) 567-7296

PRINCIPAL OFFICE: 1801 California Street, Denver, CO 80202

TELEPHONE NUMBER: (303) 992-1400
FAX: (303) 291-1724
WEB: www.qwest.com

NO. OF EMPLOYEES: 67,000 (avg.)

SHAREHOLDERS: 491,036 (approx.)

ANNUAL MEETING: In May

INCORPORATED: DE, 1997

INSTITUTIONAL HOLDINGS:
No. of Institutions: 777
Shares Held: 706,169,674
% Held: 42.8

INDUSTRY: Telephone communications, exc. radio (SIC: 4813)

TRANSFER AGENT(S): The Bank of New York, New York, NY

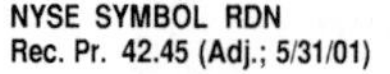

NYSE SYMBOL RDN
Rec. Pr. 42.45 (Adj.; 5/31/01)

RADIAN GROUP, INC.

YIELD	0.2%
P/E RATIO	13.1

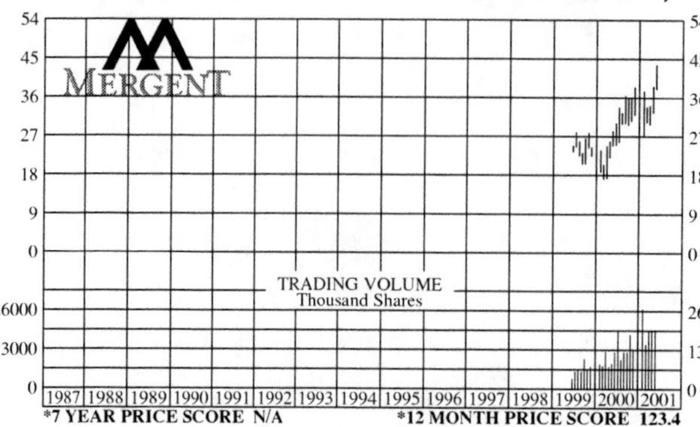

***7 YEAR PRICE SCORE N/A** ***12 MONTH PRICE SCORE 123.4**

*NYSE COMPOSITE INDEX=100

INTERIM EARNINGS (Per Share):

Qtr.	Mar.	June	Sept.	Dec.
1999	0.49	0.32	0.49	0.63
2000	0.77	0.80	0.83	0.83

INTERIM DIVIDENDS (Per Share):

Amt.	Decl.	Ex.	Rec.	Pay.
0.03Q	7/18/00	8/01/00	8/03/00	9/05/00
0.03Q	10/17/00	11/02/00	11/06/00	12/05/00
0.03Q	2/02/01	2/13/01	2/15/01	3/01/01
2-for-1	5/01/01	12/30/99	6/14/01	6/20/01
0.02Q	5/01/01	6/12/01	6/14/01	6/29/01

Indicated div.: $0.08

CAPITALIZATION (12/31/00):

	($000)	(%)
Deferred Income Tax	291,294	17.2
Redeemable Pfd. Stock	40,000	2.4
Common & Surplus	1,362,197	80.4
Total	1,693,491	100.0

RECENT DEVELOPMENTS: For the year ended 12/31/00, net income skyrocketed 68.0% to $248.9 million compared with $148.1 million in the previous year. Results for 1999 included merger expenses of $37.8 million. Total revenues improved 11.3% to $615.4 million versus $552.8 million in the prior year. Net premiums written increased 20.5% to $544.3 million from $451.8 million in 1999. Net investment income rose 22.5% to $82.4 million. Results included gains on sales of investment of $4.7 million in 2000 and $1.6 million in 1999.

PROSPECTS: On 2/28/01, RND completed the acquisition of Enhance Financial Services Group Inc., for approximately $540.0 million. Shareholders of Enhance Financial received 0.22 shares of RDN's common stock in return for each share of Enhance Financial common stock. This acquisition should expand RDN's activities into financial guaranty reinsurance of municipal and asset-backed debt obligations, direct financial guaranty insurance and other credit-based insurance businesses, as well as several asset based businesses.

BUSINESS

RADIAN GROUP INC. was formed on June 9, 1999 resulting from the acquisition by CMAC Investment Corporation of Amerin Corporation. The Company through its wholly owned subsidiaries, Radian Guaranty Inc. and Amerin Guaranty Corporation, provides private mortgage insurance coverage in the United States on residential first mortgage loans. Private mortgage insurance protects mortgage lenders and investors from default-related losses on residential first mortgage loans made primarily to home buyers who make down payments of less than 20% of the home's purchase price. RDN's customers are primarily mortgage originators, including mortgage bankers, brokers and commercial banks. As of 12/31/00, RDN had $100.90 billion primary insurance in force on 858,413 loans. On 11/9/00, RDN acquired ExpressClose.com, Inc., a provider of Internet-based mortgage processing, closing and settlement services. On 2/28/01, RDN acquired Enhance Financial Services Group Inc., a New York-based insurance holding company.

ANNUAL FINANCIAL DATA

	12/31/00	12/31/99	12/31/98	12/31/97	12/31/96	12/31/95	12/31/94
Earnings Per Share	**3.22**	**1 1.92**	**1.86**	**1.53**	**1.28**	**1.05**	**0.85**
Tang. Book Val. Per Share	**17.97**	**14.17**	**11.52**	**9.54**	**7.96**	**6.71**	**5.46**
Dividends Per Share	**0.06**	**0.06**	**0.06**	**0.06**	**0.05**	**0.05**	**0.05**
Dividend Payout %	**1.9**	**3.1**	**3.2**	**3.9**	**4.1**	**4.8**	**5.9**
INCOME STATEMENT (IN MILLIONS):							
Total Premium Income	520.9	472.6	282.2	237.7	187.9	137.1	106.1
Other Income	94.6	80.2	50.8	39.6	34.7	28.5	24.4
Total Revenues	615.4	552.8	333.0	277.3	222.6	165.6	130.5
Income Before Income Taxes	352.5	219.5	125.8	102.5	82.6	68.2	56.4
Income Taxes	103.5	71.3	34.8	27.5	20.4	17.4	15.2
Net Income	248.9	1 148.1	91.1	75.0	62.2	50.8	41.1
Average Shs. Outstg. (000)	76,298	75,712	47,148	46,832	46,220	45,440	44,408
BALANCE SHEET (IN MILLIONS):							
Cash & Cash Equivalents	1,283.3	927.6	261.0	111.4	123.1	124.6	80.0
Premiums Due	43.7	40.1	32.7	31.3	18.2	...	0.4
Invst. Assets: Fixed-term	469.6	468.5	477.5	487.9	393.3	316.6	282.6
Invst. Assets: Total	1,750.5	1,388.7	736.3	596.9	513.2	437.5	358.7
Total Assets	2,272.8	1,776.7	968.2	704.6	592.7	499.1	410.2
Net Stockholders' Equity	1,362.2	1,057.3	523.0	429.9	356.3	298.6	239.7
Year-end Shs. Outstg. (000)	75,816	74,615	45,412	45,074	44,790	44,520	43,944
STATISTICAL RECORD:							
Return on Revenues %	40.4	26.8	27.3	27.0	28.0	30.7	31.5
Return on Equity %	18.3	14.0	17.4	17.4	17.5	17.0	17.2
Return on Assets %	11.0	8.3	9.4	10.6	10.5	10.2	10.0
Price Range	38.50-17.13	27.97-20.63	...	...	...	...	...
P/E Ratio	12.0-5.3	14.6-10.8	...	...	...	...	...
Average Yield %	0.2	0.2	...	...	...	...	...

Statistics are as originally reported. Adj. for 2-for-1 stk. spl., 6/01 1 Incl. merger expenses, $37.8 mill.

OFFICERS:
F. P. Filipps, Chmn., C.E.O.
R. J. Kasmar, Pres., C.O.O.
C. R. Quint, C.F.O., Exec. V.P.

PRINCIPAL OFFICE: 1601 Market Street, Philadelphia, PA 19103

TELEPHONE NUMBER: (215) 564-6600
FAX: (215) 564-0129
WEB: www.radianmi.com

NO. OF EMPLOYEES: 835 (approx.)

SHAREHOLDERS: 8,000 (approx.)

ANNUAL MEETING: In May

INCORPORATED: DE, Dec., 1991

INSTITUTIONAL HOLDINGS:
No. of Institutions: 242
Shares Held: 39,515,447
% Held: 85.4

INDUSTRY: Surety insurance (SIC: 6351)

TRANSFER AGENT(S): Bank of New York, New York, NY

NYSE SYMBOL RSH
Rec. Pr. 27.23 (5/31/01)

RADIOSHACK CORPORATION

YIELD 0.8%
P/E RATIO 14.6

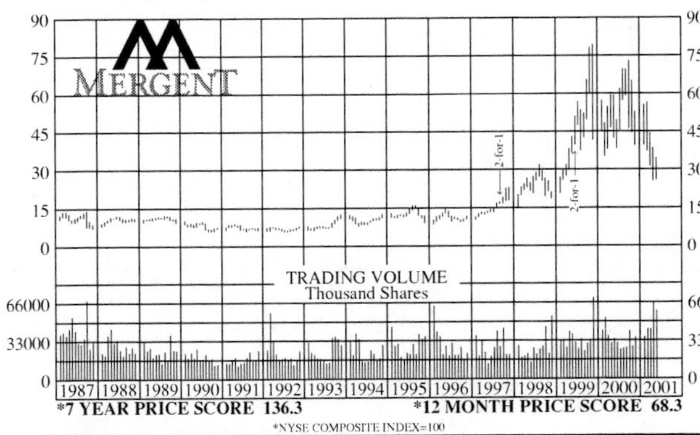

*7 YEAR PRICE SCORE 136.3 *12 MONTH PRICE SCORE 68.3

*NYSE COMPOSITE INDEX=100

INTERIM EARNINGS (Per Share):

Qtr.	Mar.	June	Sept.	Dec.
1996	0.06	0.04	0.09	d0.60
1997	0.11	0.13	0.17	0.44
1998	0.17	d0.11	d0.03	0.23
1999	0.27	0.30	0.29	0.58
2000	0.35	0.38	0.39	0.74

INTERIM DIVIDENDS (Per Share):

Amt.	Decl.	Ex.	Rec.	Pay.
0.055Q	5/19/00	6/28/00	7/01/00	7/20/00
0.055Q	8/02/00	9/27/00	10/01/00	10/19/00
0.055Q	10/24/00	12/27/00	1/01/01	1/18/01
0.055Q	3/01/01	3/28/01	4/01/01	4/20/01
0.055Q	5/21/01	6/27/01	7/01/01	7/19/01

Indicated div.: $0.22 (Div. Reinv. Plan)

CAPITALIZATION (12/31/00):

	($000)	(%)
Long-Term Debt	302,900	23.6
Minority Interest	100,000	7.8
Preferred Stock	68,800	5.4
Common & Surplus	811,500	63.2
Total	1,283,200	100.0

RECENT DEVELOPMENTS: For the year ended 12/31/00, net income advanced 23.5% to $368.0 million from $297.9 million the previous year. Net sales and operating revenues climbed 16.2% to $4.79 billion from $4.13 billion the year before. Comparable-store sales increased 11.0% year over year. Gross profit totaled $2.37 billion, or 49.4% of net sales, compared with $2.08 billion, or 50.5% of net sales, a year earlier. Operating income jumped 26.6% to $629.7 million from $497.3 million in 1999.

PROSPECTS: On 2/27/01, the Company announced a strategic alliance with Blockbuster Inc., under which RSH will create a store-within-a-store concept in Blockbuster stores that will provide a wide selection of the Company's most popular products and services. The companies plan to launch the store-within-a-store concept this summer in about 130 selected Blockbuster stores in four markets, including Las Vegas, Nevada; Norfolk, Virginia; Austin, Texas; and Tulsa, Oklahoma.

BUSINESS

RADIOSHACK CORPORATION (formerly Tandy Corporation) is one of America's largest retailers of name-brand and private label consumer electronics and personal computers. The Company's retail operations include approximately 7,100 Company-owned and dealer/franchise RadioShack® stores. The Company also designs, installs and maintains cabling systems for the transmission of video, voice and data, primarily for home use, through its wholly-owned subsidiary, AmeriLink Corporation. Private-label brands owned by RSH include Tandy®, Optimus®, Realistic®, DUoFONE, and Archer. The Company's Incredible Universe division ceased operations in 1997. On 8/31/98, RSH sold its Computer City, Inc. subsidiary.

QUARTERLY DATA

(12/31/2000)($000)	REV	INC
1st Quarter	1,047,300	69,700
2nd Quarter	1,023,300	75,400
3rd Quarter	1,140,400	77,100
4th Quarter	1,583,700	145,800

ANNUAL FINANCIAL DATA

	12/31/00	12/31/99	12/31/98	12/31/97	12/31/96	12/31/95	12/31/94
Earnings Per Share	**1.84**	**1.43**	**① 0.27**	**0.82**	**② d0.41**	**0.78**	**① 0.73**
Cash Flow Per Share	**2.38**	**1.87**	**0.73**	**1.24**	**0.04**	**1.13**	**1.01**
Tang. Book Val. Per Share	**4.37**	**4.08**	**3.86**	**4.68**	**...**	**6.03**	**5.61**
Dividends Per Share	**0.22**	**0.20**	**0.20**	**0.20**	**0.20**	**0.18**	**0.15**
Dividend Payout %	**12.0**	**14.0**	**74.0**	**24.5**	**...**	**23.1**	**20.6**
INCOME STATEMENT (IN MILLIONS):							
Total Revenues	4,794.7	4,126.2	4,787.9	5,372.2	6,285.5	5,839.1	4,943.7
Costs & Expenses	4,057.7	3,538.7	4,554.6	4,938.2	6,299.1	5,412.4	4,639.4
Depreciation & Amort.	107.3	90.2	99.0	97.2	108.6	92.0	84.8
Operating Income	629.7	497.3	134.3	336.8	d122.2	334.7	219.5
Net Interest Inc./(Exp.)	d36.1	d16.8	d34.6	d32.9	d23.4	8.6	48.6
Income Before Income Taxes	593.6	480.5	99.7	303.9	d145.6	343.3	359.5
Income Taxes	225.6	182.6	38.4	117.0	cr54.0	131.3	135.2
Net Income	368.0	297.9	① 61.3	186.9	② d91.6	212.0	① 224.3
Cash Flow	470.0	382.6	154.5	278.0	10.7	297.4	302.3
Average Shs. Outstg. (000)	197,700	205,000	211,400	224,400	239,200	263,712	299,496
BALANCE SHEET (IN MILLIONS):							
Cash & Cash Equivalents	130.7	164.6	64.5	105.9	121.5	143.5	205.6
Total Current Assets	1,818.2	1,403.3	1,298.6	1,715.5	1,939.8	2,048.2	2,556.3
Net Property	456.8	446.8	433.8	521.9	545.6	577.7	504.6
Total Assets	2,576.5	2,142.0	1,993.6	2,317.5	2,583.4	2,722.1	3,243.8
Total Current Liabilities	1,232.4	925.2	879.5	976.4	1,193.5	959.9	1,206.2
Long-Term Obligations	302.9	319.4	235.1	236.1	104.3	140.8	153.3
Net Stockholders' Equity	880.3	851.7	851.5	1,058.6	d924.1	1,601.3	1,850.2
Net Working Capital	585.8	478.1	419.1	739.1	746.3	1,088.3	1,350.1
Year-end Shs. Outstg. (000)	185,764	190,727	194,874	204,618	228,912	246,908	233,028
STATISTICAL RECORD:							
Operating Profit Margin %	13.1	12.1	2.8	6.3	...	5.7	4.4
Net Profit Margin %	7.7	7.2	1.3	3.5	...	3.6	4.5
Return on Equity %	41.8	35.0	7.2	17.7	...	13.2	12.1
Return on Assets %	14.3	13.9	3.1	8.1	...	7.8	6.9
Debt/Total Assets %	11.8	14.9	11.8	10.2	4.0	5.2	4.7
Price Range	72.94-35.06	79.50-20.59	31.94-15.19	23.00-10.16	14.78-8.53	16.09-9.13	12.66-7.69
P/E Ratio	39.6-19.1	55.6-14.4	118.2-56.2	28.2-12.5	...	20.6-11.7	17.4-10.6
Average Yield %	0.4	0.4	0.8	1.2	1.7	1.4	1.5

Statistics are as originally reported. Adj. for 2-for-1 stk. split, 6/99 & 9/97. ① Incl. $190.8 mil pre-tax, non-recur. chg., 1998; & $89.1 mil restr. chg., 1994. ② Incl. $112.8 mil pre-tax impairment chg. & $162.1 mil ($0.07/sh) restr. chg.

OFFICERS:
L. H. Roberts, Chmn., C.E.O.
D. J. Edmondson, Pres., C.O.O.
L. K. Jensen, V.P.-Fin., Acting C.F.O.

INVESTOR CONTACT: Investor Relations, (817) 415-6675

PRINCIPAL OFFICE: 100 Throckmorton Street, Suite 1800, Fort Worth, TX 76102

TELEPHONE NUMBER: (817) 415-3700
FAX: (817) 878-4887
WEB: www.radioshack.com

NO. OF EMPLOYEES: 43,600 (approx.)

SHAREHOLDERS: 31,087

ANNUAL MEETING: In May

INCORPORATED: NJ, May, 1899; reincorp., DE, Dec., 1967

INSTITUTIONAL HOLDINGS:
No. of Institutions: 323
Shares Held: 133,775,730
% Held: 72.5

INDUSTRY: Radio, TV, & electronic stores (SIC: 5731)

TRANSFER AGENT(S): BankBoston, N.A., Boston, MA

NYSE SYMBOL RAL
Rec. Pr. 30.99 (5/31/01)

RALSTON PURINA COMPANY

YIELD 0.9%
P/E RATIO 23.5

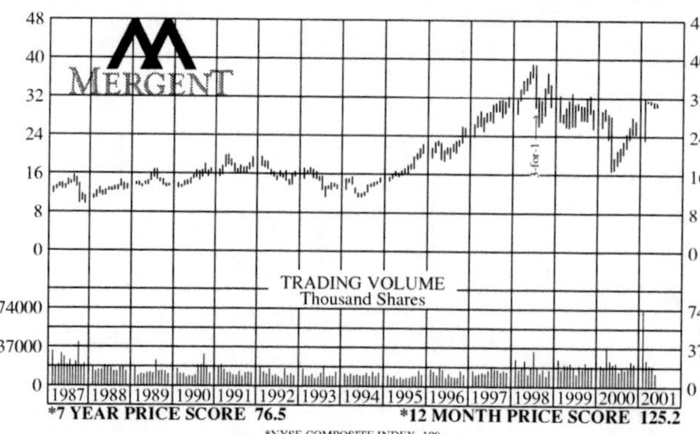

*7 YEAR PRICE SCORE 76.5 *12 MONTH PRICE SCORE 125.2
*NYSE COMPOSITE INDEX=100

INTERIM EARNINGS (Per Share):

Qtr.	Dec.	Mar.	June	Sept.
1996-97	0.44	0.24	0.32	0.35
1997-98	0.41	0.26	0.18	0.33
1998-99	0.55	0.34	0.18	0.53
1999-00	0.82	0.52	0.23	0.29
2000-01	0.28	...	...	...

INTERIM DIVIDENDS (Per Share):

Amt.	Decl.	Ex.	Rec.	Pay.
0.07Q	7/27/00	8/17/00	8/21/00	9/11/00
0.07Q	9/21/00	11/16/00	11/20/00	12/11/00
0.07Q	1/25/01	2/15/01	2/20/01	3/12/01
0.07Q	3/22/01	5/10/01	5/14/01	6/11/01

Indicated div.: $0.28 (Div. Reinv. Plan)

CAPITALIZATION (9/30/00):

	($000)	(%)
Long-Term Debt	1,245,300	63.8
Deferred Income Tax	267,800	13.7
Common & Surplus	438,600	22.5
Total	1,951,700	100.0

RECENT DEVELOPMENTS: For the quarter ended 12/31/00, net earnings were $81.4 million versus earnings from continuing operations of $135.1 million in the prior year. Results included one-time after-tax gains totaling $300,000 and $48.4 million in 2000 and 1999, respectively. Net sales inched up to $731.3 million from $728.3 million in 1999. Lower sales in the North American Pet Foods segment were more than offset by higher sales in the International Pet Foods and Golden Products segments.

PROSPECTS: On 1/16/01, the Company and Nestle S.A. announced that they have entered into a definitive merger agreement. Under the agreement, Nestle, which sells pet food under the FRISKIES, FANCY FEAST, ALPO, GOURMET, and MIGHTY DOG brand names, will acquire all of the outstanding common stock of the Company for $33.50 per share in cash. The transaction is valued at $10.30 billion, including the assumption of $1.20 billion of debt. The deal is expected to be completed by the end of 2001.

BUSINESS

RALSTON PURINA COMPANY is a major manufacturer of pet products sold primarily to grocery stores, mass merchandisers, specialty retailers and wholesalers. The Company's North American Pet Foods (74.8% of fiscal 2000 net sales) and International Pet Foods (16.2%) segments produce and market dry and moist dog foods, dry and soft-moist cat foods and pet treats, primarily under the PURINA® brand name. RAL's Golden Products (9.0%) segment manufactures TIDY CATS® cat box filler and other related products, such as cat box liners and deodorizers, in the U.S. and Canada. On 4/1/98, RAL spun off its Agribrands International Inc. animal feeds business. On 4/1/00, RAL spun off its EVEREADY and ENERGIZER batteries and flashlights business.

ANNUAL FINANCIAL DATA

	9/30/00	9/30/99	9/30/98	9/30/97	9/30/96	9/30/95	9/30/94
Earnings Per Share	**(6) 1.50**	**(1) 1.60**	**(5) 1.19**	**(5) 1.10**	**(4) 0.92**	**(3) 0.96**	**(2) 0.71**
Cash Flow Per Share	**1.85**	**2.21**	**1.76**	**1.71**	**1.56**	**1.87**	**1.40**
Tang. Book Val. Per Share	**1.43**	**4.04**	**3.49**	**2.87**	**2.17**	**1.56**	**0.95**
Dividends Per Share	**0.31**	**0.40**	**0.40**	**0.40**	**0.40**	**0.40**	**0.40**
Dividend Payout %	**20.7**	**25.0**	**33.6**	**36.4**	**43.5**	**41.5**	**56.6**
INCOME STATEMENT (IN MILLIONS):							
Total Revenues	2,763.3	4,720.5	4,653.3	4,486.8	4,301.9	7,210.3	7,705.3
Costs & Expenses	2,105.9	3,860.5	3,839.6	3,770.8	3,461.0	6,260.5	6,734.2
Depreciation & Amort.	101.9	192.6	194.7	189.0	193.8	289.5	309.4
Operating Income	555.5	667.4	619.0	527.0	647.1	660.3	661.7
Net Interest Inc./(Exp.)	d164.4	d183.4	d190.1	d173.0	d190.3	d199.8	d220.4
Income Before Income Taxes	579.2	715.8	469.4	384.9	447.7	514.2	421.7
Income Taxes	166.9	246.6	117.5	70.0	162.9	215.0	203.3
Net Income	(6) 436.5	(1) 505.1	(5) 390.6	(5) 348.9	(4) 296.4	(3) 293.3	(2) 218.4
Cash Flow	538.4	695.1	573.8	524.8	476.1	564.0	507.6
Average Shs. Outstg. (000)	290,700	314,900	326,800	306,200	305,300	302,100	363,267
BALANCE SHEET (IN MILLIONS):							
Cash & Cash Equivalents	112.2	84.7	89.8	109.1	62.3	44.3	126.0
Total Current Assets	529.9	1,472.5	1,527.5	1,505.5	1,472.7	1,763.0	1,859.2
Net Property	616.6	1,063.7	1,116.0	1,113.7	1,050.9	1,350.9	1,897.4
Total Assets	2,943.6	5,360.8	5,551.7	4,741.8	3,935.9	3,567.2	4,622.3
Total Current Liabilities	566.6	1,913.1	1,582.0	1,215.8	1,703.0	1,741.2	1,797.5
Long-Term Obligations	1,245.3	1,251.8	1,794.8	1,860.4	1,437.0	1,602.1	1,594.6
Net Stockholders' Equity	438.6	1,257.0	1,089.1	917.1	689.0	494.2	355.6
Net Working Capital	d36.7	d440.6	d54.5	289.7	d230.3	21.8	61.7
Year-end Shs. Outstg. (000)	306,819	311,406	312,428	319,500	317,844	317,568	373,959
STATISTICAL RECORD:							
Operating Profit Margin %	20.1	14.1	13.3	11.7	15.0	9.2	8.6
Net Profit Margin %	15.8	10.7	8.4	7.8	6.9	4.1	2.8
Return on Equity %	99.5	40.2	35.9	38.0	43.0	59.3	61.4
Return on Assets %	14.8	9.4	7.0	7.4	7.5	8.2	4.7
Debt/Total Assets %	42.3	23.4	32.3	39.2	36.5	44.9	34.5
Price Range	29.75-16.75	33.00-25.50	39.08-26.00	32.29-23.71	26.00-18.67	22.33-14.50	15.46-11.17
P/E Ratio	19.8-11.2	20.6-15.9	32.8-21.8	29.4-21.6	28.3-20.3	23.2-15.1	21.9-15.8
Average Yield %	1.3	1.4	1.2	1.4	1.8	2.2	3.0

Statistics are as originally reported. Adj. for 3-for-1 stk. split, 7/98. (1) Incl. $82.6 mil gain. (2) Bef. $7.9 mil extraord. loss. (3) Bef. $3.7 mil extraord. chg., incl. $90.8 mil restr. chg. & $42 mil gain. (4) Bef. $2.1 mil extraord. loss, incl. $15.5 mil restr. chg. (5) Bef. $715.1 mil inc fr disc. ops., incl. $10.3 mil net chg., 1998; & bef. $27.5 mil cr., incl. $49.8 mil gain & $36.3 mil restr. chg., 1997. (6) Bef. $93.9 mil inc. fr. disc. ops., incl. $154.3 mil pre-tax gain.

OFFICERS:
W. P. Stiritz, Chmn.
W. P. McGinnis, Pres., C.E.O.
J. R. Elsesser, V.P., C.F.O., Treas.

INVESTOR CONTACT: Michael Grabel, V.P. & Dir., Investor Rel., (314) 982-2161

PRINCIPAL OFFICE: Checkerboard Square, St. Louis, MO 63164-0001

TELEPHONE NUMBER: (314) 982-1000
FAX: (314) 982-1855
WEB: www.ralston.com

NO. OF EMPLOYEES: 6,749

SHAREHOLDERS: 22,756

ANNUAL MEETING: In Jan.

INCORPORATED: MO, Jan., 1894

INSTITUTIONAL HOLDINGS:
No. of Institutions: 336
Shares Held: 159,664,852
% Held: 51.5

INDUSTRY: Dog and cat food (SIC: 2047)

TRANSFER AGENT(S): Ralston Purina Company, St. Louis, MO and Continental Stock Transfer & Trust Co., New York, NY

NYSE SYMBOL RJF
Rec. Pr. 30.35 (4/30/01)

RAYMOND JAMES FINANCIAL, INC.

YIELD 1.2%
P/E RATIO 10.9

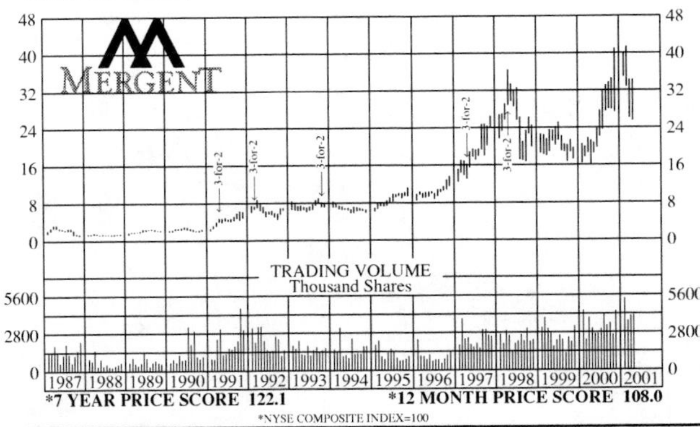

*7 YEAR PRICE SCORE 122.1 *12 MONTH PRICE SCORE 108.0
*NYSE COMPOSITE INDEX=100

INTERIM EARNINGS (Per Share):

Qtr.	Dec.	Mar.	June	Sept.
1996-97	0.37	0.79	0.35	0.53
1997-98	0.47	0.50	0.46	0.45
1998-99	0.36	0.45	0.49	0.46
1999-00	0.56	0.82	0.50	0.79
2000-01	0.67	...	...	...

INTERIM DIVIDENDS (Per Share):

Amt.	Decl.	Ex.	Rec.	Pay.
0.075Q	5/25/00	6/16/00	6/20/00	7/05/00
0.075Q	8/24/00	9/15/00	9/19/00	10/04/00
0.09Q	11/29/00	12/11/00	12/13/00	1/09/01
0.09Q	2/12/01	3/19/01	3/21/01	4/05/01
0.09Q	5/23/01	6/18/01	6/20/01	7/05/01

Indicated div.: $0.36 (Div. Reinv. Plan)

CAPITALIZATION (9/29/00):

	($000)	(%)
Common & Surplus	650,518	100.0
Total	650,518	100.0

RECENT DEVELOPMENTS: For the quarter ended 12/29/00, net income advanced 20.0% to $32.2 million from $26.8 million in the prior-year period. Total revenues increased 9.7% to $421.0 million from $383.9 million in the prior year. Total financial assets under management rose 7.6% to $16.83 billion, while investment advisory fees increased 31.7% to $33.5 million.

PROSPECTS: On 12/20/00, the Company announced that it completed the acquisition of the Canadian investment firm of Goepel McDermid, Inc. for approximately $48.0 million in cash plus 1.0 million common shares. RJF changed Goepel's name to Raymond James Ltd. The transaction will allow the Company to expand its capital market operations in Canada's growing market for investment services.

BUSINESS

RAYMOND JAMES FINANCIAL, INC., with assets totaling $7.00 billion as of 12/29/00, is a holding company primarily engaged in investment and financial planning, including securities brokerage, investment banking and asset management; banking and cash management; trust services; and life insurance. RJF's two broker/dealer subsidiaries, Raymond James & Associates and Raymond James Financial Services, serve more than 1.0 million accounts. RJF's asset management subsidiaries manage $17.60 billion in financial assets for individuals, pension plans and municipalities. RJF operates from more than 1,900 locations in the U.S., Canada and abroad. On 12/29/00, RJF acquired Vancouver-based brokerage Raymond James Ltd., formerly Goepel McDermid.

REVENUES

(09/29/2000)	($000)	(%)
Retail Distribution	1,206,775	71.0
Institutional Distrib	172,130	10.2
Investment Banking	42,848	2.5
Asset Management	124,005	7.3
Other Revenue	152,836	9.0
Total	1,698,594	100.0

ANNUAL FINANCIAL DATA

	9/29/00	9/24/99	9/25/98	9/26/97	9/27/96	9/29/95	9/30/94
Earnings Per Share	**[3] 2.67**	**1.76**	**[2] 1.86**	**[1] 2.04**	**1.40**	**0.99**	**0.88**
Cash Flow Per Share	**3.18**	**2.17**	**2.18**	**2.32**	**1.63**	**1.20**	**1.02**
Tang. Book Val. Per Share	**13.35**	**11.08**	**10.56**	**8.87**	**6.67**	**5.74**	**4.65**
Dividends Per Share	**0.30**	**0.28**	**0.24**	**0.21**	**0.17**	**0.16**	**0.14**
Dividend Payout %	**11.2**	**15.9**	**12.9**	**10.2**	**12.1**	**16.1**	**16.3**
INCOME STATEMENT (IN MILLIONS):							
Total Revenues	1,698.6	1,232.2	1,082.9	927.6	721.8	554.1	507.1
Costs & Expenses	1,470.1	1,074.6	916.4	753.8	601.9	469.9	432.9
Depreciation & Amort.	23.9	20.1	16.3	13.3	11.3	9.7	7.0
Operating Income	204.7	137.5	150.2	160.5	108.5	74.5	67.2
Income Before Income Taxes	204.7	137.5	150.2	160.5	108.5	74.5	67.2
Income Taxes	79.5	52.4	57.5	61.6	42.5	28.3	25.1
Net Income	[3] 125.2	85.1	[2] 92.7	[1] 98.9	66.0	46.1	42.1
Cash Flow	149.0	105.1	109.0	112.2	77.3	55.8	49.1
Average Shs. Outstg. (000)	46,867	48,449	49,951	48,387	47,306	46,586	48,058
BALANCE SHEET (IN MILLIONS):							
Cash & Cash Equivalents	1,119.5	1,353.8	1,243.5	888.8	735.3	454.4	295.6
Total Current Assets	5,596.5	4,259.8	3,223.7	2,769.2	2,152.1	1,739.2	1,456.3
Net Property	91.1	91.3	81.4	51.7	39.6	40.9	42.1
Total Assets	6,308.8	5,030.7	3,852.7	3,278.6	2,566.4	2,012.7	1,698.3
Total Current Liabilities	5,658.3	4,472.2	3,298.1	2,841.2	2,214.9	1,733.4	1,457.6
Long-Term Obligations	...	...	44.8	14.2	24.9	13.1	13.2
Net Stockholders' Equity	650.5	558.5	509.9	423.3	326.6	266.2	227.5
Net Working Capital	d61.8	d212.4	d74.4	d72.0	d62.7	5.8	d1.3
Year-end Shs. Outstg. (000)	46,287	47,242	48,268	47,696	48,998	46,382	48,879
STATISTICAL RECORD:							
Operating Profit Margin %	12.0	11.2	13.9	17.3	15.0	13.4	13.3
Net Profit Margin %	7.4	6.9	8.6	10.7	9.1	8.3	8.3
Return on Equity %	19.2	15.2	18.2	23.4	20.2	17.3	18.5
Return on Assets %	2.0	1.7	2.4	3.0	2.6	2.3	2.5
Debt/Total Assets %	...	...	1.2	0.4	1.0	0.7	0.8
Price Range	41.00-16.00	25.19-16.69	36.50-16.75	26.50-12.45	13.67-8.45	11.22-6.11	8.33-5.83
P/E Ratio	15.4-6.0	14.3-9.5	19.6-9.0	13.0-6.1	9.8-6.1	11.3-6.2	9.5-6.7
Average Yield %	1.1	1.3	0.9	1.1	1.5	1.8	2.0

Statistics are as originally reported. Adj for 3-for-2 stock split: 4/98 & 4/97. [1] Incl. $30.6 mill. gain fr. the sale of Liberty Investment Management, Inc. & a $2.5 mill. gin fr. the sale of the Company's former headquarters building. [2] Incl. $1.7 mill. gain related to the sale of the real estate portfolio and property management subsidiaries & $2.4 mill. gain from the sale of the Company's specialist operations on the Chicago Exchange. [3] Incl. a pre-tax chrg. of $20.0 mill. for a net incr. in litigation reserves.

OFFICERS:
T. A. James, Chmn., C.E.O.
R. F. Schuck, Vice-Chmn.
F. S. Godbold, Pres.
J. P. Julien, V.P., C.F.O.

INVESTOR CONTACT: Lawrence Silver, V.P., (727) 573-3800

PRINCIPAL OFFICE: 880 Carillon Parkway, St. Petersburg, FL 33716

TELEPHONE NUMBER: (727) 573-3800
FAX: (727) 573-8365
WEB: www.raymondjames.com

NO. OF EMPLOYEES: 4,818

SHAREHOLDERS: 11,000 (approx.)

ANNUAL MEETING: In Feb.

INCORPORATED: FL, 1974

INSTITUTIONAL HOLDINGS:
No. of Institutions: 165
Shares Held: 24,247,843
% Held: 51.0

INDUSTRY: Security brokers and dealers (SIC: 6211)

TRANSFER AGENT(S): Mellon Investor Services, Ridgefield Park, NJ

NYSE SYMBOL RTN
Rec. Pr. 29.53 (4/30/01)

RAYTHEON COMPANY

YIELD 2.7%
P/E RATIO 20.2

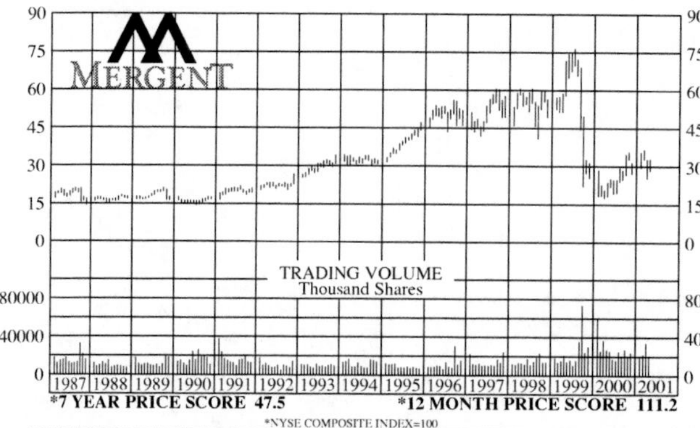

*7 YEAR PRICE SCORE 47.5 *12 MONTH PRICE SCORE 111.2
*NYSE COMPOSITE INDEX=100

INTERIM EARNINGS (Per Share):

Qtr.	Mar.	June	Sept.	Dec.
1997	0.77	0.88	0.88	d0.31
1998	0.63	0.79	0.03	1.08
1999	0.55	0.86	d0.50	0.21
2000	0.24	0.28	0.39	0.55

INTERIM DIVIDENDS (Per Share):

Amt.	Decl.	Ex.	Rec.	Pay.
0.20Q	9/27/00	10/04/00	10/09/00	11/06/00
0.20Q	12/20/00	12/28/00	1/02/01	1/30/01
0.20Q	3/28/01	4/04/01	4/06/01	4/30/01
1-for-20	4/25/01	5/14/01	...	...
20-for-1	4/25/01	5/14/01	...	...

Indicated div.: $0.80 (Div. Reinv. Plan)

CAPITALIZATION (12/31/00):

	($000)	(%)
Long-Term Debt	9,054,000	43.8
Deferred Income Tax	773,000	3.7
Common & Surplus	10,823,000	52.4
Total	20,650,000	100.0

RECENT DEVELOPMENTS: For the year ended 12/31/00, RTNB reported income from continuing operations of $498.0 million versus income of $502.0 million, before an accounting charge of $45.0 million, in 1999. Earnings for 2000 and 1999 excluded losses of $357.0 million and $45.0 million, respectively, from discontinued operations. Net sales decreased 1.8% to $16.90 billion. Comparisons were made with restated 1999 figures.

PROSPECTS: On 5/14/01, the Company reclassified its Class A and Class B common stock into a single class of new common stock. On 1/30/01, RTNA sold the recreational products division of Raytheon Marine Co. for $108.0 million to a management team backed by the venture capital firm Mercury Private Equity. The transaction also includes an ongoing supply agreement expected to provide RTNB up to $30.0 million in revenue over several years.

BUSINESS

RAYTHEON COMPANY provides products and services in the areas of defense and commercial electronics and business and special mission aircraft. Raytheon has operations throughout the United States and serves customers in more than 70 countries around the world. Electronics designs, manufactures and services electronics devices, equipment and systems for both government and commercial customers. Aircraft markets and supports piston-powered aircraft, jet props and light and medium jets for the world's commercial, regional airlines and military aircraft markets. On 12/17/97, Raytheon Company merged with HE Holdings, Inc. The operations and assets of HE Holdings consisted of the defense business of Hughes Electronics Corp. On 7/7/00, the Company sold its Raytheon Engineers and Constructors unit.

QUARTERLY DATA

(12/31/2000)($000)	REV	INC
1st Quarter	4,231	(181)
2nd Quarter	4,124	49
3rd Quarter	4,160	105
4th Quarter	4,380	168

ANNUAL FINANCIAL DATA

	12/31/00	12/31/99	12/31/98	12/31/97	12/31/96	12/31/95	12/31/94
Earnings Per Share	**7 1.46**	**6 d0.15**	**5 2.53**	**4 2.18**	**3 3.21**	**2 3.25**	**1 2.26**
Cash Flow Per Share	**3.49**	**3.47**	**4.75**	**4.07**	**4.76**	**4.77**	**3.40**
Tang. Book Val. Per Share	...	...	...	**30.76**	**12.80**	**7.25**	**12.92**
Dividends Per Share	**0.80**	**0.80**	**0.80**	...	...	...	...
Dividend Payout %	**54.8**	...	**31.6**	...	...	...	...
INCOME STATEMENT (IN MILLIONS):							
Total Revenues	16,895.0	19,841.0	19,530.0	13,673.0	12,330.5	11,715.6	10,012.9
Costs & Expenses	14,576.0	17,590.0	16,733.0	12,132.0	10,763.4	10,256.8	8,880.1
Depreciation & Amort.	694.0	724.0	761.0	457.0	368.9	371.4	304.2
Operating Income	1,625.0	1,527.0	2,036.0	1,084.0	1,198.2	1,087.4	828.6
Net Interest Inc./(Exp.)	d736.0	d713.0	d739.0	d397.0	d256.3	d196.6	d48.5
Income Before Income Taxes	877.0	828.0	1,467.0	790.0	1,083.5	1,191.7	899.9
Income Taxes	379.0	371.0	603.0	263.0	322.3	399.2	303.1
Net Income	7 498.0	6 457.0	5 864.0	4 527.0	3 761.2	2 792.5	1 596.9
Cash Flow	1,192.0	1,181.0	1,625.0	984.0	1,130.1	1,163.9	901.0
Average Shs. Outstg. (000)	341,118	340,784	341,861	242,000	237,413	243,989	264,736
BALANCE SHEET (IN MILLIONS):							
Cash & Cash Equivalents	871.0	230.0	421.0	296.0	138.8	210.3	202.2
Total Current Assets	8,013.0	8,931.0	8,637.0	9,233.0	5,603.9	5,275.2	4,985.5
Net Property	2,491.0	2,417.0	2,275.0	2,891.0	1,802.0	1,584.0	1,360.8
Total Assets	26,777.0	28,110.0	27,939.0	28,598.0	11,126.1	9,840.9	7,395.4
Total Current Liabilities	4,865.0	7,886.0	6,680.0	11,886.0	4,691.8	3,690.4	3,283.1
Long-Term Obligations	9,054.0	7,298.0	8,163.0	4,406.0	1,500.5	1,487.7	51.1
Net Stockholders' Equity	10,823.0	10,959.0	10,856.0	10,425.0	4,598.0	4,292.0	3,928.2
Net Working Capital	3,148.0	1,045.0	1,957.0	d2,653.0	912.1	1,584.8	1,702.4
Year-end Shs. Outstg. (000)	340,620	338,760	336,798	338,880	118,685	240,690	246,644
STATISTICAL RECORD:							
Operating Profit Margin %	9.6	7.7	10.4	7.9	9.7	9.3	8.3
Net Profit Margin %	2.9	2.3	4.4	3.9	6.2	6.8	6.0
Return on Equity %	4.6	4.2	8.0	5.1	16.6	18.5	15.2
Return on Assets %	1.9	1.6	3.1	1.8	6.8	8.1	8.1
Debt/Total Assets %	33.8	26.0	29.2	15.4	13.5	15.1	0.7
Price Range	35.81-17.50	76.56-22.19	60.75-40.69	60.56-41.75	56.13-43.38	47.25-31.44	34.44-30.25
P/E Ratio	24.5-12.0	...	24.0-16.1	27.8-19.2	17.5-13.5	14.5-9.7	15.3-13.4
Average Yield %	3.0	1.6	1.6	...	...	...	...

Statistics are as originally reported. Stk. prices reflect Cl. B shs. prior to the reclassif. of Cl. A & Cl. B shs. into a single class of new com. stk. on 5/14/01; adj. for 2-for-1 split, 10/95. 1 Incl. after-tax restruct. chg. of $162.3 mill. 2 Incl. non-recurr. chgs. of $202.0 mill. & gain of $210.0 mill. from sale of DC Health. 3 Incl. $34.0 mill. pre-tax chg. & $75.0 mill. tax credit. 4 Incl. after-tax restruct. chg. of $321.7 mill. 5 Incl. pre-tax restruct. & spec. chgs. of $252.0 mill. 6 Bef. acctg. chrg. of $53.0 mill. 7 Excl. disc. opers. loss of $357.0 mill.

OFFICERS:
D. P. Burnham, Chmn., C.E.O.
F. A. Caine, C.F.O., Sr. V.P.
R. A. Goglia, Treas., V.P.

INVESTOR CONTACT: Timothy C. Oliver, V.P., Investor Relations, (781) 860-2303

PRINCIPAL OFFICE: 141 Spring Street, Lexington, MA 02421

TELEPHONE NUMBER: (781) 862-6600
FAX: (781) 860-2811
WEB: www.raytheon.com

NO. OF EMPLOYEES: 93,700 (approx.)

SHAREHOLDERS: 267,164

ANNUAL MEETING: In April

INCORPORATED: DE, May, 1928

INSTITUTIONAL HOLDINGS:
No. of Institutions: 354
Shares Held: 146,705,352
% Held: 41.3

INDUSTRY: Search and navigation equipment (SIC: 3812)

TRANSFER AGENT(S): EquiServe, Canton, MA

NYSE SYMBOL RDA
Rec. Pr. 27.65 (4/30/01)

READER'S DIGEST ASSOCIATION, INC. (THE)

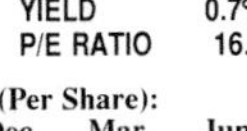

YIELD 0.7%
P/E RATIO 16.1

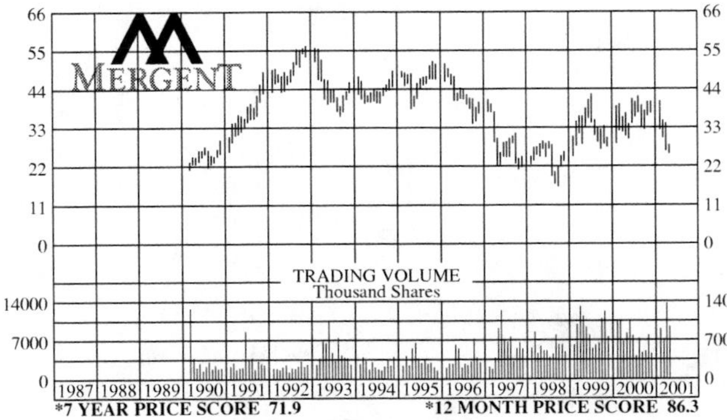

*7 YEAR PRICE SCORE 71.9 *12 MONTH PRICE SCORE 86.3
*NYSE COMPOSITE INDEX=100

INTERIM EARNINGS (Per Share):

Qtr.	Sept.	Dec.	Mar.	June
1996-97	0.32	0.78	0.35	d0.22
1997-98	d0.53	0.51	0.13	0.05
1998-99	0.02	0.80	0.23	0.11
1999-00	0.26	0.90	0.23	0.22
2000-01	0.28	0.99	...	...

INTERIM DIVIDENDS (Per Share):

Amt.	Decl.	Ex.	Rec.	Pay.
0.05Q	4/14/00	4/18/00	4/21/00	5/03/00
0.05Q	7/14/00	7/17/00	7/19/00	8/02/00
0.05Q	10/13/00	10/18/00	10/20/00	11/01/00
0.05Q	1/12/01	1/17/01	1/19/01	2/07/01
0.05Q	4/13/01	4/18/01	4/20/01	5/02/01

Indicated div.: $0.20 (Div. Reinv. Plan)

CAPITALIZATION (6/30/00):

	($000)	(%)
Common & Surplus	504,300	100.0
Total	504,300	100.0

RECENT DEVELOPMENTS: For the quarter ended 12/31/00, net income grew 20.3% to $103.8 million from $86.3 million in the prior-year period. Revenues rose 1.0% to $852.8 million from $844.0 million the year before. Global books and home entertainment revenue decreased 4.3% to $460.7 million. U.S. magazines revenue grew 14.4% to $305.4 million, while international magazines revenue slipped 6.1% to $73.6 million.

PROSPECTS: The Company announced an alliance with GE Long Term Care Insurance for the insurer to market its long-term care products to RDA customers in the U.S. The alliance is part of RDA's expansion into financial services and other affinities. Meanwhile, RDA expects continued revenue and profit growth for 2001, despite the continued effect of currency issues and unsettled economies in certain parts of the world.

BUSINESS

THE READER'S DIGEST ASSOCIATION, INC. is a global publisher and direct mail marketer of magazines, books, music, videos and other products. Reader's Digest magazine has a circulation of approximately 24.0 million and over 100.0 million readers each month. The firm also publishes Reader's Digest Condensed Books, book series, books of general interest and home entertainment products. Contributions to sales for 2000 were as follows: Global books and home entertainment, 61.2%; U.S. magazines, 25.5%; and international magazines, 11.6%.

REVENUES

(6/30/2000)	($000)	(%)
Global Books & Home Entertainment	1,562	61.1
U.S. Magazines	651	25.5
International Magazines	296	11.6
Other Businesses	45	1.8
Total	2,554	100.0

ANNUAL FINANCIAL DATA

	6/30/00	6/30/99	6/30/98	6/30/97	6/30/96	6/30/95	6/30/94
Earnings Per Share	**1.61**	**[1] 1.15**	**[3] 0.16**	**[3] 1.24**	**[2] 0.73**	**2.35**	**[1] 2.34**
Cash Flow Per Share	**2.07**	**1.58**	**0.60**	**1.69**	**1.20**	**2.76**	**2.72**
Tang. Book Val. Per Share	**0.64**	**2.22**	**1.91**	**2.70**	**3.90**	**4.94**	**6.08**
Dividends Per Share	**0.20**	**0.20**	**0.72**	**1.35**	**1.80**	**1.65**	**1.45**
Dividend Payout %	**12.4**	**17.4**	**452.8**	**108.9**	**246.5**	**70.2**	**62.0**
INCOME STATEMENT (IN MILLIONS):							
Total Revenues	2,553.7	2,532.2	2,633.7	2,839.0	3,098.1	3,068.5	2,806.4
Costs & Expenses	2,252.4	2,359.4	2,557.3	2,599.5	2,940.0	2,631.9	2,370.5
Depreciation & Amort.	47.5	43.7	46.2	46.7	48.8	44.7	42.2
Operating Income	253.8	129.1	30.2	192.8	109.3	391.9	393.7
Net Interest Inc./(Exp.)	...	...	d2.5	4.4	19.1	36.8	40.6
Income Before Income Taxes	263.8	211.7	41.5	210.2	137.7	422.5	463.2
Income Taxes	90.0	85.1	23.6	76.7	57.1	158.5	191.1
Net Income	173.8	[1] 126.6	[3] 17.9	[3] 133.5	[2] 80.6	264.0	[1] 272.1
Cash Flow	220.0	169.0	62.8	178.9	128.1	307.4	313.0
Average Shs. Outstg. (000)	107,000	108,000	106,700	106,700	107,900	112,000	115,716
BALANCE SHEET (IN MILLIONS):							
Cash & Cash Equivalents	49.7	413.4	122.8	69.1	277.0	307.6	394.7
Total Current Assets	772.5	1,146.5	972.6	925.8	1,204.1	1,215.1	1,197.2
Net Property	152.4	148.4	285.4	314.8	261.5	256.6	241.7
Total Assets	1,758.8	1,710.5	1,564.0	1,643.8	1,904.1	1,958.7	2,049.4
Total Current Liabilities	904.4	986.3	1,015.9	1,013.1	1,113.0	1,072.1	1,039.9
Net Stockholders' Equity	504.3	381.5	275.2	375.0	507.3	640.8	791.0
Net Working Capital	d131.9	160.2	d43.3	d87.3	91.1	143.0	157.3
Year-end Shs. Outstg. (000)	102,900	141,145	107,179	106,318	107,650	108,204	113,808
STATISTICAL RECORD:							
Operating Profit Margin %	9.9	5.1	1.1	6.8	3.5	12.8	14.0
Net Profit Margin %	6.8	5.0	0.7	4.7	2.6	8.6	9.7
Return on Equity %	34.5	33.2	6.5	35.6	15.9	41.2	34.4
Return on Assets %	9.9	7.4	1.1	8.1	4.2	13.5	13.3
Price Range	41.88-28.38	42.50-24.75	29.19-16.25	41.00-21.00	51.38-34.00	52.00-38.25	49.38-39.88
P/E Ratio	26.0-17.6	37.0-21.5	182.3-101.5	33.1-16.9	70.4-46.6	22.1-16.3	21.1-17.0
Average Yield %	0.6	0.6	3.2	4.4	4.2	3.7	3.2

Statistics are as originally reported. [1] Bef. acctg. change credit $25.3 mill., 6/99; chrg. $25.8 mill., 6/94. [2] Incl. after-tax restr. chg. of $169.8 mill. [3] Incl. pre-tax restr. chg.: $70.0 mill., 6/98; $35.0 mill., 6/97.

OFFICERS:
T. O. Ryder, Chmn., C.E.O.
G. S. Scimone, Sr. V.P., C.F.O.

INVESTOR CONTACT: Richard Clark, V.P.-Inv. Rel., (914) 244-5425

PRINCIPAL OFFICE: Reader's Digest Road, Pleasantville, NY 10570-7000

TELEPHONE NUMBER: (914) 238-1000
FAX: (914) 238-4559
WEB: www.readersdigest.com

NO. OF EMPLOYEES: 5,000 (approx.)

SHAREHOLDERS: 1,838 (approx. Class A); 217 (Class B)

ANNUAL MEETING: In Nov.

INCORPORATED: NY, 1926; reincorp., DE, 1951

INSTITUTIONAL HOLDINGS:
No. of Institutions: 188
Shares Held: 53,922,687
% Held: 52.6

INDUSTRY: Book publishing (SIC: 2731)

TRANSFER AGENT(S): Mellon Investor Services, Ridgefield Park, NJ

NYSE SYMBOL RBK
Rec. Pr. 25.63 (4/30/01)

REEBOK INTERNATIONAL, LTD.

YIELD ...
P/E RATIO 18.0

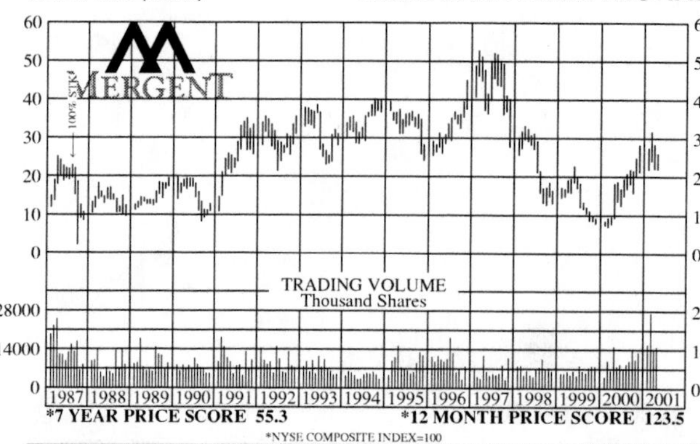

*7 YEAR PRICE SCORE 55.3 *12 MONTH PRICE SCORE 123.5
*NYSE COMPOSITE INDEX=100

INTERIM EARNINGS (Per Share):

Qtr.	Mar.	June	Sept.	Dec.
1996	0.64	0.27	0.75	0.35
1997	0.69	0.35	1.26	0.01
1998	d0.06	0.11	0.50	d0.13
1999	0.32	0.08	0.06	d0.26
2000	0.56	0.19	0.56	0.11

INTERIM DIVIDENDS (Per Share):

Amt.	Decl.	Ex.	Rec.	Pay.

No dividends paid.

CAPITALIZATION (12/31/00):

	($000)	(%)
Long-Term Debt	345,015	36.2
Common & Surplus	607,863	63.8
Total	952,878	100.0

RECENT DEVELOPMENTS: For the year ended 12/31/00, net income jumped to $80.9 million compared with $11.0 million in the prior year. Results for 1999 included an after-tax special charge of $39.4 million. Net sales declined slightly to $2.87 billion compared with $2.90 billion in the previous year. Sales of Reebok Brand footwear in the U.S. increased 1.9% to $926.4 million, while Reebok U.S. apparel sales slipped 11.3% to $233.7 million.

PROSPECTS: In 2001, the Company plans to increase its worldwide spending for advertising and other media in an attempt to generate greater consumer demand for RBK's brand and products. RBK expects sales to grow for its Rockport brand as a result of the continued introduction of new products. Separately, RBK announced an exclusive alliance with the National Football League to license, manufacture, market and sell NFL licensed merchandise.

BUSINESS

REEBOK INTERNATIONAL, LTD. is a worldwide company engaged primarily in the design and marketing of sports and fitness products, including footwear and apparel, as well as the design and marketing of footwear and apparel for casual use. The Company has four major brand groups. The Reebok Division designs, produces and markets sports, fitness and casual footwear, apparel and accessories under the REEBOK® brand. The Rockport Company designs, produces and distributes specially-engineered comfort footwear for men and women worldwide under the ROCKPORT® brand. Ralph Lauren Footwear Co., Inc., a subsidiary of the Company, is responsible for footwear and certain apparel sold under the RALPH LAUREN® and POLO SPORT® brands. The Greg Norman Division produces a range of men's apparel and accessories marketed under the GREG NORMAN name and logo. Avia Group International was sold in June 1996..

ANNUAL FINANCIAL DATA

	12/31/00	12/31/99	12/31/98	12/31/97	12/31/96	12/31/95	12/31/94
Earnings Per Share	**1.40**	**[1] 0.20**	**[1] 0.42**	**[1] 2.32**	**2.00**	**[1] 2.07**	**3.02**
Cash Flow Per Share	**2.20**	**1.06**	**1.26**	**3.13**	**2.65**	**2.57**	**3.46**
Tang. Book Val. Per Share	**9.45**	**8.17**	**8.05**	**8.27**	**5.58**	**11.11**	**11.05**
Dividends Per Share	...	...	...	...	**0.30**	**0.30**	**0.30**
Dividend Payout %	...	...	...	...	**15.0**	**14.5**	**9.9**
INCOME STATEMENT (IN MILLIONS):							
Total Revenues	2,865.2	2,891.2	3,205.4	3,637.4	3,482.9	3,484.6	3,287.6
Costs & Expenses	2,648.9	2,712.4	3,036.1	3,320.2	3,170.7	3,078.3	2,822.7
Depreciation & Amort.	46.2	48.6	48.0	47.4	42.9	39.6	37.4
Operating Income	170.2	130.2	121.3	269.8	269.3	366.7	427.5
Net Interest Inc./(Exp.)	d22.1	d40.5	d49.3	d53.6	d31.6	d18.6	d10.1
Income Before Income Taxes	135.8	28.0	37.0	158.1	237.7	276.0	417.4
Income Taxes	49.0	10.1	11.9	12.5	84.1	99.8	154.0
Equity Earnings/Minority Int.	d5.9	d6.9	d1.2	d10.5	d14.6	d11.4	d8.9
Net Income	80.9	[1] 11.0	[1] 23.9	[1] 135.1	139.0	[1] 164.8	254.5
Cash Flow	127.1	59.7	71.9	182.5	181.9	204.4	291.9
Average Shs. Outstg. (000)	57,724	56,530	57,029	58,309	68,618	79,487	84,311
BALANCE SHEET (IN MILLIONS):							
Cash & Cash Equivalents	268.7	281.7	180.1	209.8	232.4	80.4	83.9
Total Current Assets	1,225.2	1,243.1	1,361.8	1,464.8	1,463.1	1,342.9	1,337.4
Net Property	141.8	178.1	172.6	157.0	185.3	192.0	164.8
Total Assets	1,463.0	1,564.1	1,739.6	1,756.1	1,786.2	1,656.2	1,649.5
Total Current Liabilities	488.1	623.9	612.3	577.5	517.0	431.9	505.6
Long-Term Obligations	345.0	370.3	554.4	639.4	854.1	254.2	131.8
Net Stockholders' Equity	607.9	528.8	524.4	507.2	381.2	895.3	990.5
Net Working Capital	737.1	619.2	749.5	887.4	946.1	911.0	831.9
Year-end Shs. Outstg. (000)	57,492	56,270	56,590	53,375	55,840	74,804	80,945
STATISTICAL RECORD:							
Operating Profit Margin %	5.9	4.5	3.8	7.4	7.7	10.5	13.0
Net Profit Margin %	2.8	0.4	0.7	3.7	4.0	4.7	7.7
Return on Equity %	13.3	2.1	4.6	26.6	36.4	18.4	25.7
Return on Assets %	5.5	0.7	1.4	7.7	7.8	10.0	15.4
Debt/Total Assets %	23.6	23.7	31.9	36.4	47.8	15.3	8.0
Price Range	28.33-6.94	22.75-7.81	33.19-12.56	52.88-27.63	45.25-25.38	39.63-24.13	40.25-28.38
P/E Ratio	20.2-5.0	113.7-39.0	79.0-29.9	22.8-11.9	22.6-12.7	19.1-11.7	13.3-9.4
Average Yield %	...	...	...	...	0.8	0.9	0.9

Statistics are as originally reported. [1] Incl. non-recurr. chrg. $61.6 mill., 12/99; $35.0 mill., 12/98; $58.2 mill., 12/97; $72.1 mill., 12/95

OFFICERS:
P. B. Fireman, Chmn., Pres., C.E.O.
K. I. Watchmaker, Exec. V.P., C.F.O., Treas.
D. A. Pace, V.P., Gen. Couns.

INVESTOR CONTACT: Neil Kerman, V.P., Finance, (781) 401-7152

PRINCIPAL OFFICE: 1895 J.W. Foster Boulevard, Canton, MA 02021

TELEPHONE NUMBER: (781) 401-5000
FAX: (781) 401-7402
WEB: www.reebok.com

NO. OF EMPLOYEES: 6,000 (approx.)

SHAREHOLDERS: 6,335 (record)

ANNUAL MEETING: In May

INCORPORATED: MA, July, 1979

INSTITUTIONAL HOLDINGS:
No. of Institutions: 188
Shares Held: 45,210,303
% Held: 77.3

INDUSTRY: Rubber and plastics footwear (SIC: 3021)

TRANSFER AGENT(S): American Stock Transfer & Trust Company, New York, NY

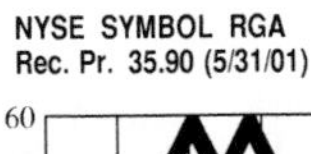

NYSE SYMBOL RGA
Rec. Pr. 35.90 (5/31/01)

REINSURANCE GROUP OF AMERICA, INC.

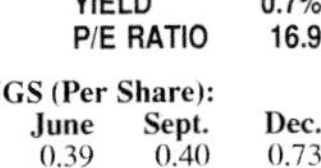

YIELD 0.7%
P/E RATIO 16.9

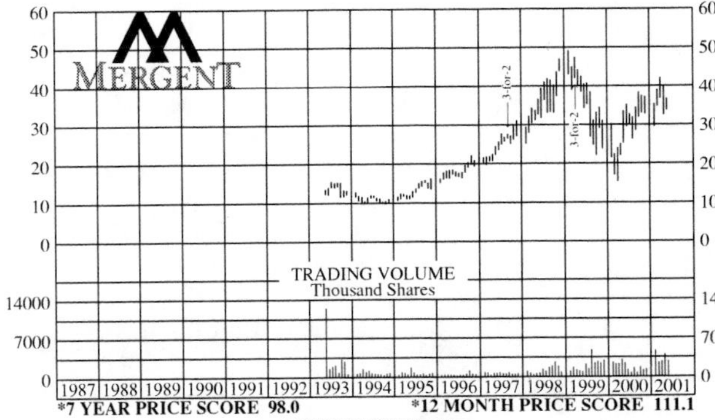

*7 YEAR PRICE SCORE 98.0 *12 MONTH PRICE SCORE 111.1

*NYSE COMPOSITE INDEX=100

INTERIM EARNINGS (Per Share):

Qtr.	Mar.	June	Sept.	Dec.
1997	0.37	0.39	0.40	0.73
1998	0.42	0.49	0.47	0.71
1999	0.48	0.56	d0.31	0.41
2000	0.48	0.43	0.63	0.58

INTERIM DIVIDENDS (Per Share):

Amt.	Decl.	Ex.	Rec.	Pay.
0.06Q	...	5/03/00	5/05/00	5/26/00
0.06Q	7/28/00	8/03/00	8/07/00	8/28/00
0.06Q	...	11/02/00	11/06/00	11/27/00
0.06Q	1/26/01	2/01/01	2/05/01	2/26/01
0.06Q	4/26/01	5/04/01	5/08/01	5/29/01

Indicated div.: $0.24

CAPITALIZATION (12/31/00):

	($000)	(%)
Long-Term Debt	272,257	20.8
Deferred Income Tax	170,905	13.1
Common & Surplus	862,923	66.1
Total	1,306,085	100.0

RECENT DEVELOPMENTS: For the year ended 12/31/00, income from continuing operations was $105.8 million compared with income from continuing operations of $53.0 million in 1999. Results for 2000 and 1999 excluded a loss from discontinued operations of $28.1 million and $12.2 million, respectively. Total revenues rose 7.4% to $1.73 billion. Results for 2000 and 1999 also included realized investment losses of $28.7 million and $75.3 million, respectively.

PROSPECTS: In 2001, the Company expects to achieve its earnings per share growth target of 15.0% over 2000. In addition, RGA anticipates continued growth in its traditional reinsurance business in the U.S. market. However, margins in the life reinsurance market may be dampened by an increasingly competitive pricing environment. Also, results may be constrained by additional losses resulting from discontinued operations.

BUSINESS

REINSURANCE GROUP OF AMERICA, INC. is an insurance holding company primarily engaged in life insurance, accident and health insurance, and international life and disability on a direct and reinsurance basis. RGA has five main operational segments segregated primarily by geographic region: U.S., Canada, Latin America, Asia Pacific, and other international operations. The U.S. operations (74.0% of 2000 net premiums) provide traditional life reinsurance and non-traditional reinsurance. The Canada operations (12.6%) provide insurers with traditional reinsurance as well as capital management. The Latin America operations (4.6%) include traditional reinsurance, reinsurance of pension products in Argentina. Asia Pacific operations (6.7%) provide life reinsurance. Other international operations (2.1%) include traditional business from Europe and South Africa. RGA's accident and health divisions has been reported as a discontinued operation since 12/31/98. Metropolitan Life Insurance Co. is the beneficial owner of approximately 58.0% of RGA's share as of 1/26/01.

ANNUAL FINANCIAL DATA

	12/31/00	12/31/99	12/31/98	12/31/97	12/31/96	12/31/95	12/31/94
Earnings Per Share	**① 2.12**	**① 1.15**	**① 2.08**	**1.42**	**1.44**	**1.24**	**1.05**
Tang. Book Val. Per Share	**17.51**	**14.68**	**16.52**	**13.21**	**11.14**	**9.96**	**7.28**
Dividends Per Share	**0.24**	**0.22**	**0.17**	**0.15**	**0.13**	**0.12**	**0.11**
Dividend Payout %	**11.3**	**19.1**	**8.3**	**10.6**	**9.3**	**9.3**	**10.2**
INCOME STATEMENT (IN MILLIONS):							
Total Premium Income	1,404.1	1,315.6	1,016.4	835.5	674.9	570.0	451.7
Other Income	321.7	291.4	328.1	236.1	155.1	98.1	74.1
Total Revenues	1,725.7	1,607.1	1,344.5	1,071.5	830.0	668.1	525.8
Policyholder Benefits	1,208.3	1,220.2	951.1	750.1	560.4	463.9	358.3
Income Before Income Taxes	175.3	93.1	138.0	84.1	87.1	74.6	64.4
Income Taxes	69.3	39.1	49.1	28.8	31.7	27.1	23.6
Equity Earnings/Minority Int.	d0.3	d1.0	0.7	d0.7	d0.3	d0.2	d0.3
Net Income	① 105.8	① 53.0	① 89.7	54.6	55.1	47.3	40.4
Average Shs. Outstg. (000)	49,920	46,246	42,559	38,406	38,259	37,987	38,592
BALANCE SHEET (IN MILLIONS):							
Cash & Cash Equivalents	3,770.7	2,936.9	4,392.3	3,008.7	1,753.9	1,059.1	601.2
Premiums Due	522.7	590.6	433.6	435.7	136.1	148.8	148.3
Invst. Assets: Loans	835.0	873.2	730.5	645.7	524.6	361.6	314.5
Invst. Assets: Total	4,560.2	3,811.9	5,129.6	3,634.0	2,272.0	1,405.5	1,016.6
Total Assets	6,061.9	5,123.7	6,318.6	4,673.6	2,893.7	1,989.9	1,394.3
Long-Term Obligations	272.3	184.0	108.0	106.8	106.5	...	...
Net Stockholders' Equity	862.9	732.9	748.5	499.3	425.6	376.9	276.8
Year-end Shs. Outstg. (000)	49,294	49,940	45,313	37,808	38,198	37,850	38,043
STATISTICAL RECORD:							
Return on Revenues %	6.1	3.3	6.7	5.1	6.6	7.1	7.7
Return on Equity %	12.3	7.2	12.0	10.9	12.9	12.5	14.6
Return on Assets %	1.7	1.0	1.4	1.2	1.9	2.4	2.9
Price Range	38.38-15.38	49.17-22.13	47.09-25.08	31.13-19.67	22.22-15.06	16.28-10.61	12.83-9.72
P/E Ratio	18.1-7.3	42.8-19.2	22.6-12.1	21.9-13.8	15.4-10.5	13.1-8.5	12.2-9.3
Average Yield %	0.9	0.6	0.5	0.6	0.7	0.9	0.9

Statistics are as originally reported. ① Excl. loss on disc. opers. $28.1 mill., 12/00; $12.2 mill., 12/99; $27.6 mill., 12/98.

OFFICERS:
R. A. Liddy, Chmn.
A. G. Woodring, Pres., C.E.O.
J. B. Lay, Exec. V.P., C.F.O.
J. E. Sherman, Gen. Couns., Sec.

INVESTOR CONTACT: Jack B. Lay, Dir., Inv. Rel., (314) 453-7300

PRINCIPAL OFFICE: 1370 Timberlake Manor Parkway, Chesterfield, MO 63017

TELEPHONE NUMBER: (314) 736-7439
FAX: (314) 453-7307
WEB: www.rgare.com

NO. OF EMPLOYEES: 601 (avg.)

SHAREHOLDERS: 116

ANNUAL MEETING: In May

INCORPORATED: MO, Dec., 1992

INSTITUTIONAL HOLDINGS:
No. of Institutions: 101
Shares Held: 21,518,086
% Held: 43.6

INDUSTRY: Accident and health insurance (SIC: 6321)

TRANSFER AGENT(S): Mellon Investor Services, Ridgefield Park, NJ

NYSE SYMBOL RS
Rec. Pr. 27.35 (5/31/01)

RELIANCE STEEL & ALUMINUM CO.

YIELD 0.9%
P/E RATIO 12.0

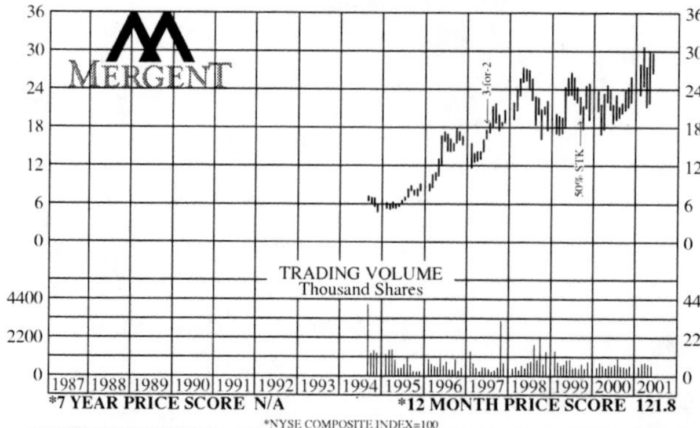

*7 YEAR PRICE SCORE N/A *12 MONTH PRICE SCORE 121.8

*NYSE COMPOSITE INDEX=100

INTERIM EARNINGS (Per Share):

Qtr.	Mar.	June	Sept.	Dec.
1997	0.30	0.37	0.37	0.39
1998	0.41	0.44	0.42	0.42
1999	0.51	0.49	0.53	0.54
2000	0.58	0.60	0.57	0.53

INTERIM DIVIDENDS (Per Share):

Amt.	Decl.	Ex.	Rec.	Pay.
0.055Q	4/25/00	5/10/00	5/12/00	6/02/00
0.055Q	7/25/00	8/03/00	8/07/00	8/28/00
0.055Q	11/14/00	12/06/00	12/08/00	1/05/01
0.06Q	2/21/01	3/07/01	3/09/01	3/30/01
0.06Q	4/25/01	5/09/01	5/11/01	6/01/01

Indicated div.: $0.24

CAPITALIZATION (12/31/00):

	($000)	(%)
Long-Term Debt	421,825	49.4
Deferred Income Tax	28,642	3.4
Common & Surplus	403,039	47.2
Total	853,506	100.0

RECENT DEVELOPMENTS: For the year ended 12/31/00, net income advanced 8.2% to $62.3 million compared with $57.6 million in 1999. Results for 1999 included a $2.3 million gain related to RS's Supplemental Executive Retirement Plan. Total revenues were $1.73 billion, up 14.0% from $1.52 billion a year earlier. American Steel, L.L.C. reported 2000 sales of $97.0 million, which were not included in total revenues.

PROSPECTS: RS's current strength, in terms of sales and profits, centers on the aerospace industry. In addition, the January 2001 acquisition of Aluminum and Stainless, Inc., which caters to the offshore oil and gas industry, represents an area of strength for RS due to the robust energy industry. Meanwhile, RS is optimistic that metal prices and customer demand will improve during the second half of 2001. RS should continue to benefit from geographic and product diversity as well as its acquisition strategy.

BUSINESS

RELIANCE STEEL & ALUMINUM CO. is a metals service center company. The Company has a network of 24 divisions and 15 subsidiaries operating metals service centers, with 82 processing and distribution facilities, excluding American Steel, L.L.C., in 23 states, France and South Korea. Through this network, RS provides value-added metals processing services and distributes a full line of more than 80,000 metal products, including carbon, alloy, stainless and specialty steel, aluminum, brass and copper products to more than 70,000 customers in a broad range of industries. Some of these metals service centers provide processing services for specialty metals only. The Company owns 50.0% and maintains operational control of American Steel, L.L.C., which operates two metals service centers in the Pacific Northwest.

QUARTERLY DATA

(12/31/2000)($000)	REV	INC
1st Quarter	430,841	16,131
2nd Quarter	440,903	16,696
3rd Quarter	443,652	15,823
4th Quarter	411,269	13,669

ANNUAL FINANCIAL DATA

	12/31/00	12/31/99	12/31/98	12/31/97	12/31/96	12/31/95	12/31/94
Earnings Per Share	**2.28**	**1 2.07**	**1.69**	**2 1.43**	**2 1.90**	**1.45**	**1.17**
Cash Flow Per Share	**3.31**	**2.98**	**2.37**	**1.99**	**2.44**	**1.79**	**1.48**
Tang. Book Val. Per Share	**6.80**	**6.66**	**6.10**	**8.71**	**11.39**	**10.64**	**9.20**
Dividends Per Share	**0.21**	**0.17**	**0.14**	**0.10**	**0.08**	**0.07**	**...**
Dividend Payout %	**9.4**	**8.2**	**8.5**	**6.9**	**4.1**	**4.6**	**...**
INCOME STATEMENT (IN MILLIONS):							
Total Revenues	1,730.1	1,517.4	1,355.8	965.1	658.4	563.7	448.7
Costs & Expenses	1,575.6	1,376.0	1,244.4	888.9	601.8	521.5	418.1
Depreciation & Amort.	28.1	25.6	19.4	13.2	8.5	5.2	4.3
Operating Income	126.3	115.8	92.0	63.0	48.2	37.0	26.3
Net Interest Inc./(Exp.)	d26.1	d23.3	d17.6	d10.9	d3.9	d1.6	d2.1
Income Before Income Taxes	102.6	96.4	80.3	58.0	49.6	38.6	24.3
Income Taxes	40.3	38.8	32.6	23.8	19.8	15.9	9.8
Equity Earnings/Minority Int.	2.3	3.9	5.9	5.8	5.3	3.2	...
Net Income	62.3	1 57.6	47.7	2 34.2	2 29.8	22.7	14.4
Cash Flow	90.4	83.2	67.1	47.3	38.3	27.9	18.7
Average Shs. Outstg. (000)	27,289	27,892	28,305	23,811	15,680	15,591	12,624
BALANCE SHEET (IN MILLIONS):							
Cash & Cash Equivalents	3.1	9.9	6.5	34.0	0.8	18.0	8.3
Total Current Assets	491.4	428.9	420.3	322.1	210.9	166.9	125.4
Net Property	245.4	227.4	213.1	161.0	133.6	66.3	58.9
Total Assets	997.2	900.0	841.4	583.9	391.2	260.5	199.4
Total Current Liabilities	143.7	155.9	129.1	108.8	74.1	66.2	40.9
Long-Term Obligations	421.8	318.1	343.3	143.4	107.5	30.4	8.5
Net Stockholders' Equity	403.0	400.3	345.8	313.2	192.6	163.9	150.0
Net Working Capital	347.7	273.0	291.2	213.3	136.8	100.7	84.5
Year-end Shs. Outstg. (000)	25,132	27,798	27,675	28,247	15,489	15,408	16,298
STATISTICAL RECORD:							
Operating Profit Margin %	7.3	7.6	6.8	6.5	7.3	6.6	5.9
Net Profit Margin %	3.6	3.8	3.5	3.5	4.5	4.0	3.2
Return on Equity %	15.5	14.4	13.8	10.9	15.5	13.8	9.6
Return on Assets %	6.2	6.4	5.7	5.9	7.6	8.7	7.2
Debt/Total Assets %	42.3	35.3	40.8	24.6	27.5	11.7	4.3
Price Range	26.06-16.88	26.75-16.83	27.50-16.08	21.79-11.56	18.06-8.00	9.22-5.06	7.28-4.67
P/E Ratio	11.4-7.4	12.9-8.1	16.3-9.5	15.2-8.1	9.5-4.2	6.3-3.5	6.2-4.0
Average Yield %	1.0	0.8	0.7	0.6	0.6	0.9	...

Statistics are as originally reported. Adj. for stk. splits: 50%, 9/24/99; 3-for-2, 6/27/97. 1 Incl. gain of $2.3 mill. from a life insur. policy in conection with RS' supplemental exec. retirement plan. 2 Incl. gain on sale of real estate of $1.0 mill., 1997; $1.5 mill., 1996.

OFFICERS:
J. D. Crider, Chmn.
D. H. Hannah, Pres., C.E.O.
G. J. Mollins, Exec. V.P., C.O.O.
K. R. McDowell, Sr. V.P., C.F.O.

INVESTOR CONTACT: Kim P. Feazle, Investor Relations, (713) 610-9937

PRINCIPAL OFFICE: 2550 East 25th Street, Los Angeles, CA 90058

TELEPHONE NUMBER: (323) 582-2272
FAX: (323) 582-2801
WEB: www.rsac.com

NO. OF EMPLOYEES: 4,400 (approx.)

SHAREHOLDERS: 300 (approx. record)

ANNUAL MEETING: In May

INCORPORATED: CA, Feb., 1939

INSTITUTIONAL HOLDINGS:
No. of Institutions: 90
Shares Held: 11,148,954
% Held: 44.2

INDUSTRY: Metals service centers and offices (SIC: 5051)

TRANSFER AGENT(S): First Chicago Trust Company, Jersey City, NJ

NYSE SYMBOL REI
Rec. Pr. 46.08 (5/31/01)

RELIANT ENERGY, INC.

YIELD 3.3%
P/E RATIO 17.7

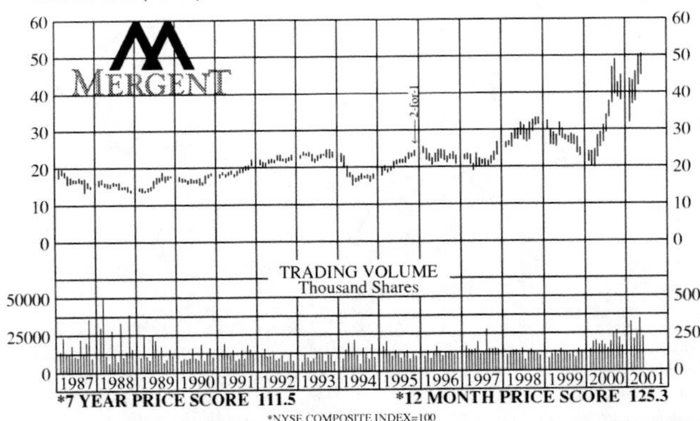

*7 YEAR PRICE SCORE 111.5 *12 MONTH PRICE SCORE 125.3
*NYSE COMPOSITE INDEX=100

INTERIM EARNINGS (Per Share):

Qtr.	Mar.	June	Sept.	Dec.
1996	0.20	0.58	0.98	0.15
1997	0.26	0.52	0.93	d0.01
1998	d0.11	0.16	0.87	d1.42
1999	d0.74	0.26	5.90	d0.26
2000	0.47	0.78	1.34	0.02

INTERIM DIVIDENDS (Per Share):

Amt.	Decl.	Ex.	Rec.	Pay.
0.375Q	3/01/00	5/12/00	5/16/00	6/10/00
0.375Q	6/08/00	8/14/00	8/16/00	9/08/00
0.375Q	9/06/00	11/14/00	11/16/00	12/08/00
0.375Q	12/06/00	2/14/01	2/16/01	3/09/01
0.375Q	3/07/01	5/14/01	5/16/01	6/08/01

Indicated div.: $1.50 (Div. Reinv. Plan)

CAPITALIZATION (12/31/00):

	($000)	(%)
Long-Term Debt	4,996,095	36.4
Deferred Income Tax	2,548,891	18.6
Redeemable Pfd. Stock	705,355	5.1
Preferred Stock	9,740	0.1
Common & Surplus	5,472,320	39.8
Total	13,732,401	100.0

RECENT DEVELOPMENTS: For the year ended 12/31/00, the Company reported income of $771.1 million versus income of $1.67 billion. Earnings for 2000 included an unrealized loss on its Time Warner investment of $205.0 million, versus a gain of $2.45 billion in 1999. Results for 2000 also included an unrealized gain on indexed securities of $101.9 million, while earnings for 1999 included an unrealized loss on indexed debt securities of $629.5 million. Total revenues improved 92.7% to $29.34 billion.

PROSPECTS: During 2000, the Company sold its investments in El Salvador, Brazil and Colombia for approximately $790.0 million. The Company will continue to focus on the sale of its remaining investments in Argentina and India during 2001. Going forward, results should continue to benefit from the strong performance of the Company's unregulated wholesale energy businesses and an increase in customer demand in its regulated electric service territories in Texas.

BUSINESS

RELIANT ENERGY, INC. (formerly Houston Industries Inc.) is an international energy services company with approximately $29.34 billion in annual revenue and assets totaling $32.08 billion at 12/31/00. The Company's retail group consists of three natural gas utilities, which serve customers located in Arkansas, Louisiana, Minnesota, Mississippi, Oklahoma and Texas. The Company's retail group also consists of one electric utility company serving 1.7 million customers in a 5,000-square-mile area on the Texas Gulf Coast, including Houston as of 12/31/00, and a retail marketing group, which provides unregulated retail energy products and services throughout North America. REI's wholesale group, which accounted for 65.6% of total revenues in 2000, invests in power generation projects and provides wholesale trading and marketing services as well as natural gas supply, gathering, transportation and storage. Reliant Energy International has operations in Mexico and India. On 3/1/00, REI acquired N.V. UNA, a Dutch power generation company.

ANNUAL FINANCIAL DATA

	12/31/00	12/31/99	[5] 12/31/98	12/31/97	12/31/96	12/31/95	12/31/94
Earnings Per Share	[7] 2.68	[6] 5.82	[4] d0.50	[3] 1.66	[3] 1.66	[2] 1.60	[1] 1.73
Cash Flow Per Share	5.89	9.36	2.77	4.33	4.05	3.65	3.44
Tang. Book Val. Per Share	8.10	7.70	7.47	9.69	15.52	15.70	12.83
Dividends Per Share	1.50	1.50	1.50	1.50	0.94	1.50	1.50
Dividend Payout %	56.0	25.8	...	90.4	56.5	93.7	87.0
INCOME STATEMENT (IN MILLIONS):							
Total Revenues	29,339.4	15,302.8	11,488.5	6,873.4	4,095.3	3,730.2	3,746.1
Costs & Expenses	26,553.9	13,151.2	9,152.6	5,128.8	2,520.9	2,318.7	2,328.5
Depreciation & Amort.	906.3	911.1	870.1	680.1	583.9	506.6	420.8
Operating Income	1,879.1	1,240.5	1,465.8	1,064.5	990.5	904.9	996.8
Net Interest Inc./(Exp.)	d700.1	d511.5	d509.6	d332.2	d301.1	d286.6	d279.4
Income Taxes	377.1	899.1	cr30.4	206.4	200.2	199.6	230.4
Equity Earnings/Minority Int.	42.9	...	...	...	...	...	...
Net Income	[7] 771.1	[6] 1,665.7	[4] d141.1	[3] 421.1	[3] 404.9	[2] 397.4	[1] 424.0
Cash Flow	1,677.1	2,678.9	787.0	1,101.1	988.9	904.0	844.7
Average Shs. Outstg. (000)	284,652	286,164	284,095	254,198	244,443	247,706	245,706
BALANCE SHEET (IN MILLIONS):							
Gross Property	...	20,133.7	17,002.6	16,039.2	13,015.5	12,781.4	12,579.5
Accumulated Depreciation	...	6,866.3	5,499.4	4,770.2	4,259.1	3,916.5	3,527.6
Net Property	15,260.2	13,267.4	11,503.1	11,269.0	8,756.4	8,864.8	9,051.9
Total Assets	32,076.7	26,220.9	19,138.5	18,414.6	12,287.9	11,819.6	11,453.2
Long-Term Obligations	4,996.1	4,961.3	6,800.7	5,218.0	3,025.7	3,338.4	3,734.1
Net Stockholders' Equity	5,482.1	5,306.3	4,321.9	4,896.5	3,963.1	4,474.9	3,720.6
Year-end Shs. Outstg. (000)	295,103	293,987	296,168	295,264	246,706	262,672	262,594
STATISTICAL RECORD:							
Operating Profit Margin %	6.4	8.1	12.8	15.5	24.2	24.3	26.6
Net Profit Margin %	2.6	11.6	...	6.1	9.9	10.7	11.3
Net Inc./Net Property %	5.1	13.3	...	3.7	4.6	4.5	4.7
Net Inc./Tot. Capital %	5.6	13.2	...	3.2	4.3	3.8	4.3
Return on Equity %	14.1	33.3	...	8.6	10.2	8.9	11.4
Accum. Depr./Gross Prop. %	...	34.1	32.3	29.7	32.7	30.6	28.0
Price Range	49.00-19.75	32.50-22.75	33.38-25.00	26.75-18.88	25.63-20.50	24.50-17.69	23.88-15.00
P/E Ratio	18.3-7.4	5.6-3.9	...	16.1-11.4	15.4-12.3	15.3-11.1	13.8-8.7
Average Yield %	4.4	5.4	5.1	6.6	4.1	7.1	7.7

Statistics are as originally reported. Adj. for 2-for-1 split, 12/95. [1] Incl. non-recurr. after-tax chrg. $46.1 mill. [2] Bef. acctg. chrg. $8.2 mill. and disc. opers. gain of $691.6 mill. [3] Incl. non-recurr. chrg. 1997, $42.3 mill.; 1996, $66.9 mill. [4] Incl. unrealized acctg. loss of $1.18 bill. [5] Refl. first full year of results since the acq. of Reliant Energy Resources Corp. on 8/6/97. [6] Incl. one-time unrealized gain of $2.45 bill. on Time Warner investments, but bef. extraord. loss of $183.3 mill. [7] Bef. disc. opers. chrg., $331.1 and extraord. gain, $7.4 mill.; incl. one-time unrealized loss of $205.0 mill. from Time Warner investments

OFFICERS:
R. S. Letbetter, Chmn., Pres., C.E.O.
R. W. Harvey, Vice-Chmn.
S. W. Naeve, Vice-Chmn., C.F.O.

PRINCIPAL OFFICE: 1111 Louisiana Street, Houston, TX 77002

TELEPHONE NUMBER: (713) 207-3000
FAX: (713) 207-0206
WEB: www.reliantenergy.com
NO. OF EMPLOYEES: 15,633
SHAREHOLDERS: 75,089
ANNUAL MEETING: In May
INCORPORATED: TX, Oct., 1976

INSTITUTIONAL HOLDINGS:
No. of Institutions: 395
Shares Held: 143,791,472
% Held: 48.6

INDUSTRY: Electric services (SIC: 4911)

TRANSFER AGENT(S): The Company

NYSE SYMBOL RSG
Rec. Pr. 18.00 (4/30/01)

REPUBLIC SERVICES, INC.

YIELD ...
P/E RATIO 14.2

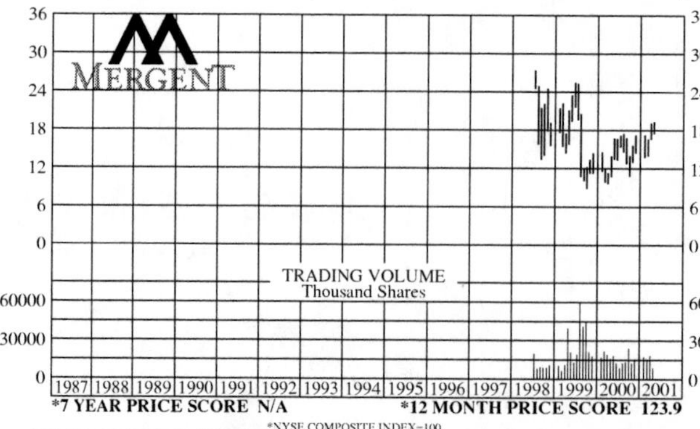

*7 YEAR PRICE SCORE N/A *12 MONTH PRICE SCORE 123.9

*NYSE COMPOSITE INDEX=100

INTERIM EARNINGS (Per Share):

Qtr.	Mar.	June	Sept.	Dec.
1998	0.36	0.26	0.26	0.25
1999	0.25	0.31	0.31	0.29
2000	0.29	0.34	0.31	0.33

INTERIM DIVIDENDS (Per Share):

Amt.	Decl.	Ex.	Rec.	Pay.

No dividends paid.

CAPITALIZATION (12/31/00):

	($000)	(%)
Long-Term Debt	1,200,200	40.0
Deferred Income Tax	126,600	4.2
Common & Surplus	1,674,900	55.8
Total	3,001,700	100.0

RECENT DEVELOPMENTS: For the year ended 12/31/00, net income increased 10.1% to $221.0 million compared with $200.8 million in 1999. Results for 2000 and 1999 included pre-tax special charges of $6.7 million and $6.9 million, respectively. Results for 1999 included $5.3 million for AutoNation overhead charges. Revenues were $2.10 billion, up 12.5% from $1.87 billion a year earlier. Operating income advanced 11.1% to $434.0 million compared with $390.6 million a year earlier.

PROSPECTS: In 2001, the Company anticipates achieving $145.0 million in free cash flow, an increase of 17.9% from $123.0 million in the prior year. In addition, earnings per share are expected to grow 7.9% to $1.36. Meanwhile, RSG is targeting internal growth of approximately 5.0%, with 2.0% from price increases and 3.0% from volume growth. Revenue growth for 2001 is estimated at 7.0%, with approximately 5.0% from internal growth and 2.0% from acquisition rollover.

BUSINESS

REPUBLIC SERVICES, INC. is a provider of services in the domestic non-hazardous solid waste industry. The company provides solid waste collection services for commercial, industrial, municipal and residential customers through 139 collection companies in 22 states. RSG also owns or operates 79 transfer stations, 53 solid waste landfills and 21 recycling facilities. RSG's internal growth strategy is supported by its presence in high growth markets throughout the Sunbelt, including Florida, Georgia, Nevada, Southern California and Texas, and other domestic markets that have experienced higher than average population growth during the past several years. RSG was formerly a subsidiary of AutoNation, Inc. The Company completed its initial public offering of common stock in June, 1998, and secondary offering in May, 1999.

QUARTERLY DATA

(12/31/2000)($000)	REV	INC
1st Quarter	501,500	50,200
2nd Quarter	533,500	59,200
3rd Quarter	539,100	55,000
4th Quarter	529,200	56,600

ANNUAL FINANCIAL DATA

	12/31/00	12/31/99	12/31/98	12/31/97	12/31/96	12/31/95
Earnings Per Share	3 1.26	1 1.14	2 1.13	...	...	...
Cash Flow Per Share	2.39	2.07	1.92	...	...	...
Tang. Book Val. Per Share	1.37	1.17	7.41	...	...	...
INCOME STATEMENT (IN MILLIONS):						
Total Revenues	2,103.3	1,838.5	1,369.1	1,127.7	953.3	805.0
Costs & Expenses	1,471.9	1,284.7	978.5	840.3	772.4	648.1
Depreciation & Amort.	197.4	163.2	106.3	86.1	75.3	63.0
Operating Income	434.0	390.6	284.3	201.3	105.6	93.9
Net Interest Inc./(Exp.)	d79.9	d60.7	d43.2	d25.9	d29.7	d19.1
Income Before Income Taxes	356.4	326.5	240.2	182.1	89.8	81.0
Income Taxes	135.4	125.7	86.5	65.9	38.0	31.6
Net Income	3 221.0	1 200.8	2 153.7	116.2	51.8	49.4
Cash Flow	418.4	364.0	260.0	202.3	127.1	112.4
Average Shs. Outstg. (000)	175,000	175,700	135,600	...	...	...
BALANCE SHEET (IN MILLIONS):						
Cash & Cash Equivalents	86.3	23.4	563.7	18.8	43.9	...
Total Current Assets	405.8	332.0	784.0	175.9	192.8	...
Net Property	1,667.8	1,605.5	1,096.1	801.8	661.3	...
Total Assets	3,561.5	3,288.3	2,812.1	1,348.0	1,090.3	...
Total Current Liabilities	381.8	385.3	783.8	436.1	422.7	...
Long-Term Obligations	1,200.2	1,152.1	557.2	110.3	148.8	...
Net Stockholders' Equity	1,674.9	1,502.7	1,299.1	750.8	494.5	...
Net Working Capital	24.0	d53.3	0.2	d260.2	d229.9	...
Year-end Shs. Outstg. (000)	175,658	175,482	175,413	...	...	...
STATISTICAL RECORD:						
Operating Profit Margin %	20.6	21.2	20.8	17.9	11.1	11.7
Net Profit Margin %	10.5	10.9	11.2	10.3	5.4	6.1
Return on Equity %	13.2	13.4	11.8	15.5	10.5	...
Return on Assets %	6.2	6.1	5.5	8.6	4.8	...
Debt/Total Assets %	33.7	35.0	19.8	8.2	13.6	...
Price Range	17.50-9.63	25.50-8.88	27.44-13.38	...	...	...
P/E Ratio	13.9-7.6	22.4-7.8	24.3-11.8	...	...	...

Statistics are as originally reported. 1 Incl. pre-tax chrg. of $6.4 mill. for costs related to the Company's separation from its former parent company, AutoNation, Inc. 2 Incl. pre-tax charges of $15.0 mill. for AutoNation overhead charges. 3 Incl. pre-tax nonrec. chrg. of $6.7 mill.

OFFICERS:
H. W. Huizenga, Chmn.
H. W. Hudson, Vice-Chmn., Sec.
J. E. O'Connor, C.E.O., Pres., C.O.O.
T. C. Holmes, Sr. V.P., C.F.O.

PRINCIPAL OFFICE: 110 S.E. 6th Street, 28th Floor, Ft. Lauderdale, FL 33301

TELEPHONE NUMBER: (954) 769-2400
FAX: (954) 769-6416

NO. OF EMPLOYEES: 12,700 (approx.)

SHAREHOLDERS: 97 (approx.)

ANNUAL MEETING: In May

INCORPORATED: DE, 1998

INSTITUTIONAL HOLDINGS:
No. of Institutions: 156
Shares Held: 173,949,202
% Held: 101.9

INDUSTRY: Refuse systems (SIC: 4953)

TRANSFER AGENT(S): First Union National Bank, Charlotte, NC

NYSE SYMBOL RMD
Rec. Pr. 44.80 (4/30/01)

RESMED INC.

YIELD ...
P/E RATIO 57.4

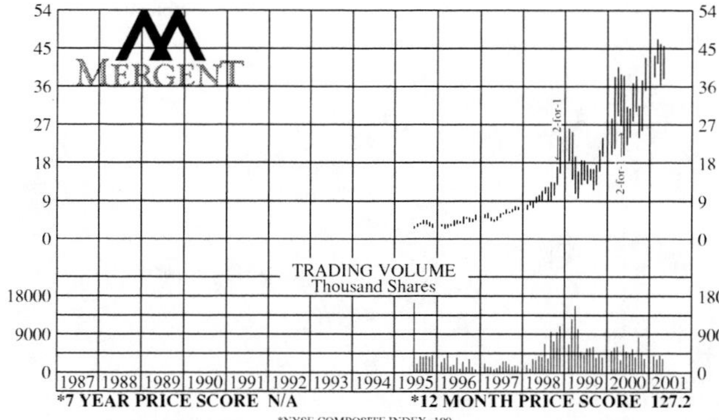

*7 YEAR PRICE SCORE N/A *12 MONTH PRICE SCORE 127.2

*NYSE COMPOSITE INDEX=100

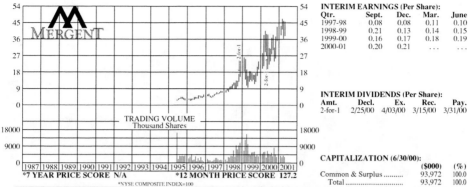

INTERIM EARNINGS (Per Share):

Qtr.	Sept.	Dec.	Mar.	June
1997-98	0.08	0.08	0.11	0.10
1998-99	0.21	0.13	0.14	0.15
1999-00	0.16	0.17	0.18	0.19
2000-01	0.20	0.21	...	...

INTERIM DIVIDENDS (Per Share):

Amt.	Decl.	Ex.	Rec.	Pay.
2-for-1	2/25/00	4/03/00	3/15/00	3/31/00

CAPITALIZATION (6/30/00):

	($000)	(%)
Common & Surplus	93,972	100.0
Total	93,972	100.0

RECENT DEVELOPMENTS: For the three months ended 12/31/00, net income advanced 28.6% to $6.9 million compared with $5.4 million in the corresponding period of the previous year. The increase in earnings was primarily due to higher sales in all global markets. Net revenues increased 22.1% to $34.4 million from $28.1 million in the year-earlier period. Gross profit climbed 17.9% to $23.0 million from $19.5 million the year before.

PROSPECTS: On 2/19/01, the Company announced it has acquired all of the outstanding shares of MAP Medizin-Technologie GmbH, Munich, Germany. The transaction is valued at approximately $69.0 million. MAP designs, manufacturers and distributes medical devices for the diagnosis and treatment of sleep-disordered breathing with a particular focus on obstructive sleep apnea.

BUSINESS

RESMED INC. is a designer, manufacturer and distributor of medical equipment for treating, diagnosing and managing sleep-disordered breathing. Sleep-disordered breathing includes sleep apnea and related respiratory conditions. The Company currently sells a comprehensive range of diagnostic and treatment devices in over 50 countries through a combination of wholly owned subsidiaries and independent distributors.

QUARTERLY DATA

(06/30/00)($000)	REV	INC
1st Quarter.................	25,945	4,835
2nd Quarter................	28,135	5,362
3rd Quarter	29,971	5,838
4th Quarter.................	31,564	6,191

ANNUAL FINANCIAL DATA

	6/30/00	6/30/99	6/30/98	6/30/97	6/30/96	6/30/95	6/30/94
Earnings Per Share	**0.69**	**0.52**	**0.36**	**0.26**	**0.16**	**0.16**	**0.09**
Cash Flow Per Share	**0.90**	**0.67**	**0.48**	**0.34**	**0.20**	**0.19**	**0.10**
Tang. Book Val. Per Share	**2.84**	**2.17**	**1.54**	**1.38**	**1.20**	**1.10**	...
INCOME STATEMENT (IN THOUSANDS):							
Total Revenues	115,615	88,627	66,519	49,180	34,562	23,501	13,857
Costs & Expenses	75,539	58,766	45,441	38,243	29,690	20,124	12,313
Depreciation & Amort.	6,938	4,606	3,715	2,610	1,277	590	255
Operating Income	33,138	25,255	17,363	8,327	3,595	2,787	1,289
Net Interest Inc./(Exp.)	801	779	1,011	1,205	1,072	205	98
Income Before Income Taxes	34,166	24,577	16,112	11,087	6,561	3,781	1,831
Income Taxes	11,940	8,475	5,501	3,622	2,058	948	599
Net Income	22,226	16,102	10,611	7,465	4,503	2,833	1,232
Cash Flow	29,164	20,708	14,326	10,075	5,780	3,423	1,487
Average Shs. Outstg.	32,303	31,068	30,044	29,268	28,796	17,800	14,556
BALANCE SHEET (IN THOUSANDS):							
Cash & Cash Equivalents	21,963	16,734	20,746	27,985	23,531	23,766	3,739
Total Current Assets	69,172	50,771	46,604	44,391	38,226	33,013	8,524
Net Property	36,576	29,322	11,111	4,916	3,284	1,981	776
Total Assets	115,594	89,889	64,618	54,895	47,299	35,313	9,608
Total Current Liabilities	21,622	18,242	13,845	9,996	7,382	5,659	3,514
Long-Term Obligations	...	...	...	274	578	787	386
Net Stockholders' Equity	93,972	71,647	50,773	44,625	38,986	28,867	5,630
Net Working Capital	47,550	32,529	32,759	34,395	30,844	27,354	5,010
Year-end Shs. Outstg.	30,594	29,616	29,104	28,808	28,688	26,136	...
STATISTICAL RECORD:							
Operating Profit Margin %	28.7	28.5	26.1	16.9	10.4	11.9	9.3
Net Profit Margin %	19.2	18.2	16.0	15.2	13.0	12.1	8.9
Return on Equity %	23.7	22.5	20.9	16.7	11.6	9.8	21.9
Return on Assets %	19.2	17.9	16.4	13.6	9.5	8.0	12.8
Debt/Total Assets %	...	...	...	0.5	1.2	2.2	4.0
Price Range	42.88-19.75	26.06-9.59	24.13-6.94	7.75-4.13	5.75-2.50	4.50-2.44	...
P/E Ratio	62.1-28.6	50.1-18.4	67.9-19.5	30.4-16.2	36.4-15.8	28.5-15.4	...

Statistics are as originally reported. Adj. for stk. split: 2-for-1, 3/00 & 11/98.

OFFICERS:
P. C. Farrell, Chmn., Pres., C.E.O.
A. M. Smith, V.P., C.F.O.
W. Flicker, V.P., Sec.

INVESTOR CONTACT: Inv. Rel., (858) 746-2400

PRINCIPAL OFFICE: 14040 Danielson Street, Poway, CA 92064-6857

TELEPHONE NUMBER: (858) 746-2400
FAX: (858) 746-2900
WEB: www.resmed.com

NO. OF EMPLOYEES: 605 (avg.)

SHAREHOLDERS: 5,000 (approx.)

ANNUAL MEETING: In Nov.

INCORPORATED: DE, Mar., 1994

INSTITUTIONAL HOLDINGS:
No. of Institutions: 105
Shares Held: 10,453,568
% Held: 33.5

INDUSTRY: Surgical and medical instruments (SIC: 3841)

TRANSFER AGENT(S): American Stock Transfer and Trust Company, New York, NY

NYSE SYMBOL REY
Rec. Pr. 22.45 (5/31/01)

REYNOLDS & REYNOLDS COMPANY

YIELD 2.0%
P/E RATIO 18.3

MERGENT

TRADING VOLUME
Thousand Shares

*7 YEAR PRICE SCORE 72.7 *12 MONTH PRICE SCORE 112.0

*NYSE COMPOSITE INDEX=100

INTERIM EARNINGS (Per Share):

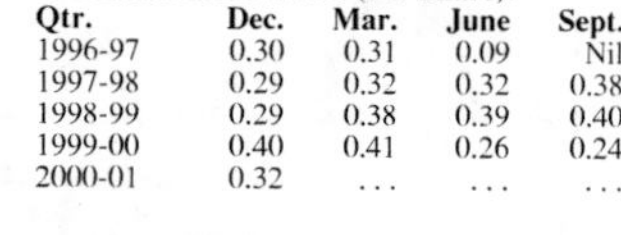

Qtr.	Dec.	Mar.	June	Sept.
1996-97	0.30	0.31	0.09	Nil
1997-98	0.29	0.32	0.32	0.38
1998-99	0.29	0.38	0.39	0.40
1999-00	0.40	0.41	0.26	0.24
2000-01	0.32	...	...	...

INTERIM DIVIDENDS (Per Share):

Amt.	Decl.	Ex.	Rec.	Pay.
0.11Q	8/09/00	8/18/00	8/22/00	9/08/00
0.11Q	11/14/00	12/14/00	12/18/00	1/11/01
0.11Q	2/15/01	3/19/01	3/21/01	4/12/01
0.11Q	5/08/01	5/21/01	5/23/01	6/12/01

Indicated div.: $0.44 (Div. Reinv. Plan)

CAPITALIZATION (9/30/00):

	($000)	(%)
Long-Term Debt	323,300	34.9
Deferred Income Tax	103,591	11.2
Common & Surplus	498,494	53.9
Total	925,385	100.0

RECENT DEVELOPMENTS: For the quarter ended 12/31/00, net income was $23.9 million versus income from continuing operations of $25.1 million a year earlier. Total revenues rose 10.1% to $243.5 million from $221.1 million in 1999. Gross profit was $135.5 million, or 55.7% of net sales, versus $120.1 million, or 54.3% of net sales, in 1999. Comparisons were made with restated prior-year results.

PROSPECTS: The Company is aggressively investing in research and development in an effort to fuel growth of new customer relationship management and retail management systems. Going forward, earnings are expected to be in line with the consensus analyst estimates of $1.31 per share for the current fiscal year.

BUSINESS

REYNOLDS & REYNOLDS COMPANY operates in two business segments: the Automotive Group and Financial Services. The Automotive Group provides integrated computer systems products and services, customer relationship networking software, paper-based and electronic business forms for automotive retailers and manufacturers. Through its wholly-owned subsidiary, Reyna Capital Corporation, REY provides financing services to automotive retailers across North America who wish to invest in the acquisition of one of the Automotive Group's retail management systems. On 8/4/00, the Company sold its document outsourcing and customer relationship management business to The Carlyle Group for $360.0 million.

REVENUES

(9/30/2000)	($000)	(%)
Automotive services	521,032	56.4
Automotive products	363,143	39.3
Financial Services	40,206	4.3
Total	924,381	100.0

ANNUAL FINANCIAL DATA

	9/30/00	9/30/99	9/30/98	9/30/97	9/30/96	9/30/95	9/30/94
Earnings Per Share	**2 1.11**	**2 1.46**	**2 1.40**	**1 0.70**	**1.10**	**0.92**	**0.76**
Cash Flow Per Share	**1.60**	**2.04**	**2.13**	**1.43**	**1.62**	**1.36**	**1.16**
Tang. Book Val. Per Share	**3.30**	**3.88**	**3.12**	**2.50**	**2.50**	**1.99**	**1.83**
Dividends Per Share	**0.44**	**0.40**	**0.36**	**0.32**	**0.25**	**0.20**	**0.17**
Dividend Payout %	**39.6**	**27.4**	**25.7**	**45.7**	**22.7**	**21.7**	**21.9**
INCOME STATEMENT (IN MILLIONS):							
Total Revenues	924.4	1,563.0	1,486.0	1,385.7	1,100.4	910.9	808.8
Costs & Expenses	730.5	1,310.4	1,223.0	1,199.0	891.3	736.5	675.8
Depreciation & Amort.	38.7	47.3	59.6	60.6	44.3	37.3	34.9
Operating Income	155.2	205.3	203.4	126.0	164.8	137.0	98.1
Net Interest Inc./(Exp.)	d0.7	d6.2	d12.7	d8.1	d4.1	d2.1	d2.4
Income Before Income Taxes	150.1	199.3	188.0	115.7	162.2	136.8	97.3
Income Taxes	61.7	82.3	74.5	56.5	68.5	58.2	31.1
Equity Earnings/Minority Int.	d4.4	...	...	...	...	...	...
Net Income	2 88.4	2 116.9	2 113.6	1 59.2	93.7	78.6	66.2
Cash Flow	127.1	164.3	173.1	119.9	138.1	115.9	101.1
Average Shs. Outstg. (000)	79,499	80,340	81,146	84,012	85,228	85,032	87,562
BALANCE SHEET (IN MILLIONS):							
Cash & Cash Equivalents	205.5	103.6	40.0	7.6	11.1	18.4	20.2
Total Current Assets	383.5	467.6	372.0	327.9	271.1	188.2	175.5
Net Property	138.1	187.8	174.2	188.5	167.7	128.5	117.5
Total Assets	1,217.3	1,262.1	1,157.7	1,102.5	923.6	755.5	634.7
Total Current Liabilities	194.7	212.0	198.2	208.6	167.3	125.8	90.0
Long-Term Obligations	323.3	383.4	372.1	368.5	246.5	173.1	145.4
Net Stockholders' Equity	498.5	463.4	404.5	364.2	373.0	332.6	293.0
Net Working Capital	188.9	255.6	173.8	119.3	103.8	62.4	85.5
Year-end Shs. Outstg. (000)	93,622	96,532	97,757	98,986	100,961	102,012	103,414
STATISTICAL RECORD:							
Operating Profit Margin %	16.8	13.1	13.7	9.1	15.0	15.0	12.1
Net Profit Margin %	9.6	7.5	7.6	4.3	8.5	8.6	8.2
Return on Equity %	17.7	25.2	28.1	16.3	25.1	23.6	22.6
Return on Assets %	7.3	9.3	9.8	5.4	10.1	10.4	10.4
Debt/Total Assets %	26.6	30.4	32.1	33.4	26.7	22.9	22.9
Price Range	33.00-15.94	25.31-17.31	24.00-12.63	30.63-14.38	28.25-18.19	19.81-11.44	13.31-9.88
P/E Ratio	29.7-14.4	17.3-11.9	17.1-9.0	43.7-20.5	25.7-16.5	21.5-12.4	17.6-13.1
Average Yield %	1.8	1.9	2.0	1.4	1.1	1.3	1.4

Statistics are as originally reported. Adj. for 2-for-1 stk. split, 9/96. 1 Incl. $34.1 mil ($0.41/sh) non-recur. after-tax chg. 2 Bef. disc. oper. gain of $28.2 mil ($0.36/sh) & incl. $10.6 mil ($0.08/sh) restr. chg., 2000; $5.8 mil ($0.07/sh), 1999; loss $10.4 mil ($0.13/sh.), 1998.

OFFICERS:
D. R. Holmes, Chmn.
L. G. Waterhouse, Pres., C.E.O.
D. L. Medford, V.P.-Fin., C.F.O.
M. J. Gapinski, Treas., Asst. Sec.

INVESTOR CONTACT: Mitch Haws, Director of Investor Relations, (937) 485-4460

PRINCIPAL OFFICE: 115 South Ludlow Street, Dayton, OH 45402

TELEPHONE NUMBER: (937) 485-2000
FAX: (937) 449-4213
WEB: www.reyrey.com

NO. OF EMPLOYEES: 4,945

SHAREHOLDERS: 3,444 (Cl. A); 1 (Cl. B)

ANNUAL MEETING: In Feb.

INCORPORATED: OH, 1889

INSTITUTIONAL HOLDINGS:
No. of Institutions: 189
Shares Held: 56,668,443
% Held: 77.3

INDUSTRY: Manifold business forms (SIC: 2761)

TRANSFER AGENT(S): Wells Fargo Shareowner Services, South St. Paul, MN

NYSE SYMBOL RJR
Rec. Pr. 59.48 (5/31/01)

REYNOLDS (R.J.) TOBACCO HOLDINGS, INC.

YIELD 5.2%
P/E RATIO 17.2

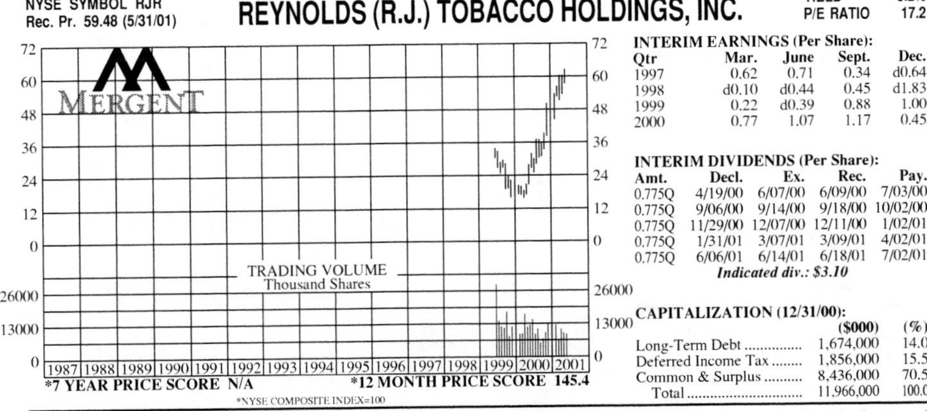

*7 YEAR PRICE SCORE N/A *12 MONTH PRICE SCORE 145.4

*NYSE COMPOSITE INDEX=100

INTERIM EARNINGS (Per Share):

Qtr	Mar.	June	Sept.	Dec.
1997	0.62	0.71	0.34	d0.64
1998	d0.10	d0.44	0.45	d1.83
1999	0.22	d0.39	0.88	1.00
2000	0.77	1.07	1.17	0.45

INTERIM DIVIDENDS (Per Share):

Amt.	Decl.	Ex.	Rec.	Pay.
0.775Q	4/19/00	6/07/00	6/09/00	7/03/00
0.775Q	9/06/00	9/14/00	9/18/00	10/02/00
0.775Q	11/29/00	12/07/00	12/11/00	1/02/01
0.775Q	1/31/01	3/07/01	3/09/01	4/02/01
0.775Q	6/06/01	6/14/01	6/18/01	7/02/01

Indicated div.: $3.10

CAPITALIZATION (12/31/00):

	($000)	(%)
Long-Term Debt	1,674,000	14.0
Deferred Income Tax	1,856,000	15.5
Common & Surplus	8,436,000	70.5
Total	11,966,000	100.0

RECENT DEVELOPMENTS: For the year ended 12/31/00, income was $352.0 million, before an extraordinary gain, versus income from continuing operations of $195.0 million a year earlier. Results for 2000 included ongoing tobacco settlement and related expenses of $2.33 billion and impairment charges of $89.0 million. Results for 1999 included ongoing tobacco settlement charges of $2.18 billion and headquarters closedown and related charges of $141.0 million. Net sales rose 7.9% to $8.17 billion.

PROSPECTS: RJR's prospects are mixed. Despite increased promotional activity and more competitive in-store pricing in support of its brands, RJR is projecting shipment volumes in 2001 to decline approximately 3.0% to 5.0%. However, net income is expected to rise between 25.0% and 30.7% to $440.0 million and $460.0 million, due in part to higher selling prices. RJR projects diluted earnings per share to range from $4.50 to $4.70, up from 30.1% to 35.8% from 2000.

BUSINESS

R. J. REYNOLDS TOBACCO HOLDINGS, INC. (formerly RJR Nabisco, Inc.) was formed through a reorganization and spun off from its parent, Nabisco Group Holdings Corp. (formerly RJR Nabsico Holdings Corp.) on 6/15/99. As a part of the spin-off, RJR transferred its 80.5% interest in Nabisco Holdings Corp. and nearly $1.60 billion in net proceeds from the sale of its international tobacco business to Nabisco Group Holdings. The Company is presently the holding company of R.J. Reynolds Tobacco Company, the second-largest manufacturer of cigarettes in the United States. Major cigarette brands include DORAL, WINSTON, CAMEL, and SALEM.

QUARTERLY DATA

(12/31/2000)	Rev	Inc
First Quarter	1,922,000	80,000
Second Quarter	2,085,000	109,000
Third Quarter	2,119,000	117,000
Fourth Quarter	2,041,000	46,000

ANNUAL FINANCIAL DATA

	12/31/00	12/31/99	12/31/98	12/31/97	12/31/96	12/31/95	12/31/94
Earnings Per Share	**[6] 3.46**	**[5] 1.80**	...	...	...	...	...
Cash Flow Per Share	**8.22**	**6.24**	...	...	...	...	...
Dividends Per Share	**3.10**	**0.78**	...	...	...	...	...
Dividend Payout %	**89.6**	**43.1**	...	...	...	...	...
INCOME STATEMENT (IN MILLIONS):							
Total Revenues	8,167.0	7,567.0	17,037.0	17,057.0	17,063.0	16,008.0	15,366.0
Costs & Expenses	6,854.0	6,363.0	15,506.0	13,891.0	13,642.0	12,499.0	11,652.0
Depreciation & Amort.	485.0	482.0	1,135.0	1,138.0	1,174.0	1,171.0	1,152.0
Operating Income	828.0	722.0	396.0	2,028.0	2,247.0	2,338.0	2,562.0
Net Interest Inc./(Exp.)	d49.0	d154.0	d775.0	d817.0	d832.0	d872.0	d1,065.0
Income Before Income Taxes	748.0	510.0	d511.0	1,104.0	1,288.0	1,291.0	1,376.0
Income Taxes	396.0	315.0	19.0	566.0	619.0	594.0	614.0
Equity Earnings/Minority Int.	...	...	14.0	d84.0	d3.0	d59.0	...
Net Income	[6] 352.0	[5] 195.0	[1] d516.0	[2] 454.0	[1] 666.0	[3] 638.0	[4] 762.0
Cash Flow	837.0	677.0	619.0	1,592.0	1,840.0	1,809.0	1,914.0
Average Shs. Outstg. (000)	101,857	108,570	...	...	...	...	...
BALANCE SHEET (IN MILLIONS):							
Cash & Cash Equivalents	2,543.0	1,287.0	299.0	348.0	251.0	232.0	409.0
Total Current Assets	3,871.0	2,468.0	4,427.0	4,621.0	4,745.0	4,551.0	4,349.0
Net Property	1,048.0	1,080.0	5,298.0	5,939.0	5,835.0	5,690.0	5,434.0
Total Assets	15,554.0	14,377.0	28,863.0	30,657.0	31,260.0	31,508.0	31,393.0
Total Current Liabilities	2,776.0	3,068.0	4,505.0	3,942.0	4,124.0	3,965.0	5,550.0
Long-Term Obligations	1,674.0	1,653.0	8,655.0	9,456.0	9,256.0	9,429.0	8,883.0
Net Stockholders' Equity	8,436.0	7,064.0	9,886.0	11,079.0	11,669.0	12,153.0	11,410.0
Net Working Capital	1,095.0	d600.0	d78.0	679.0	621.0	586.0	d1,201.0
Year-end Shs. Outstg. (000)	101,265	106,903	...	...	...	...	...
STATISTICAL RECORD:							
Operating Profit Margin %	10.1	9.5	2.3	11.9	13.2	14.6	16.7
Net Profit Margin %	4.3	2.6	...	2.7	3.9	4.0	5.0
Return on Equity %	4.2	2.8	...	4.1	5.7	5.2	6.7
Return on Assets %	2.3	1.4	...	1.5	2.1	2.0	2.4
Debt/Total Assets %	10.8	11.5	30.0	30.8	29.6	29.9	28.3
Price Range	50.25-15.75	34.00-16.00	...	...	...	...	...
P/E Ratio	14.5-4.6	18.9-8.9	...	...	...	...	...
Average Yield %	9.4	3.1	...	...	...	...	...

Statistics are as originally reported. Results prior to 1999 refl. ops. of RJR Nabisco, Inc. [1] Incl. chrg. of $2.03 bil., 1998; $428.0 mil., 1996 [2] Incl. chrg. of $660.0 mil.; bef. extraord. chrg. of $21.0 mil. [3] Incl. chrgs. of $154.0 mil.; bef. extraord. chrg. of $16.0 mil. [4] Bef. extraord. chrg. of $245.0 mil. [5] Incl. tobc. setlmt. chrgs. of $2.20 bil.; bef. gain of $2.40 bil. fr. disc. ops. & extraord. chrg. of $250.0 mil. [6] Incl. tobc. setlmt. chrgs. of $2.33 bil. & impair. chrg. of $89.0 mil.; bef. extraord. gain of $1.48 bil.

OFFICERS:
A. J. Schindler, Chmn., Pres., C.E.O.
K. J. Lapiejko, Exec. V.P., C.F.O.

INVESTOR CONTACT: Office of Investor Relations, (336) 741-5165

PRINCIPAL OFFICE: 401 North Main Street, Winston-Salem, NC 27102-2866

TELEPHONE NUMBER: (336) 741-5500
FAX: (336) 741-5511
WEB: www.rjrt.com
NO. OF EMPLOYEES: 8,100 (approx.)
SHAREHOLDERS: 38,000 (approx.)
ANNUAL MEETING: In Apr.
INCORPORATED: DE, Mar., 1970

INSTITUTIONAL HOLDINGS:
No. of Institutions: 179
Shares Held: 71,635,484
% Held: 70.2

INDUSTRY: Cigarettes (SIC: 2111)

TRANSFER AGENT(S): The Bank of New York, New York, NY

NYSE SYMBOL RGS
Rec. Pr. 37.34 (5/31/01)

RGS ENERGY GROUP, INC.

YIELD	4.8%
P/E RATIO	14.4

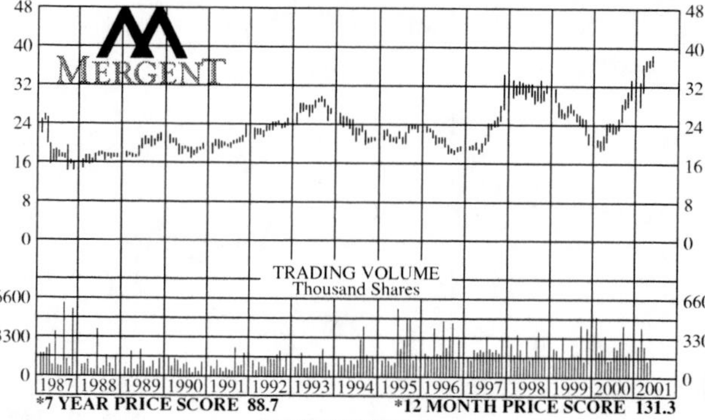

INTERIM EARNINGS (Per Share):

Qtr.	Mar.	June	Sept.	Dec.
1997	1.02	0.42	0.52	0.32
1998	0.95	0.37	0.62	0.37
1999	0.97	0.37	0.44	0.65
2000	1.07	0.49	0.38	0.66

INTERIM DIVIDENDS (Per Share):

Amt.	Decl.	Ex.	Rec.	Pay.
0.45Q	6/21/00	6/29/00	7/03/00	7/25/00
0.45Q	9/20/00	9/29/00	10/03/00	10/25/00
0.45Q	12/20/00	12/28/00	1/02/01	1/25/01
0.45Q	3/21/01	3/29/01	4/02/01	4/25/01

Indicated div.: $1.80 (Div. Reinv. Plan)

CAPITALIZATION (12/31/00):

	($000)	(%)
Long-Term Debt	823,860	42.5
Deferred Income Tax	277,787	14.3
Redeemable Pfd. Stock	72,000	3.7
Common & Surplus	767,115	39.5
Total	1,940,762	100.0

RECENT DEVELOPMENTS: For the year ended 12/31/00, net income slipped 2.1% to $95.6 million versus $93.6 million in 1999. Earnings benefited from increased electric and gas sales, a profitable unregulated business, the recognition of non-cash pension income and reduced operating expenses and taxes. Total operating revenues were $1.45 billion, up 19.9% from $1.21 billion in the prior year, reflecting higher revenues from sales in the wholesale market and higher gas space heating sales.

PROSPECTS: On 2/20/01, the Company and Energy East Corporation announced that their boards of directors have approved a definitive merger agreement in which all of the outstanding shares of RGS will be acquired for a combination of cash and Energy East stock totaling about $1.40 billion. In addition, Energy East will assume approximately $1.00 billion of RGS' debt. The combined company will serve about 3.0 million customers in the Northeast. The merger is expected to be completed within a year.

BUSINESS

RGS ENERGY GROUP, INC. (formerly Rochester Gas & Electric Corporation) is a holding company for Rochester Gas & Electric, RGS Development and Energetix. Rochester Gas & Electric is an electric and gas company operating in a nine-county area centering around the City of Rochester, NY, which has a population of about 1,000,000. Revenue breakdown in 2000 was: 50.5% electric, 23.5% gas, and 26.0% other. Electric revenue in 2000 was: 24.7% residential, 19.2% commercial, 18.2% industrial, 4.5% municipal and other, and 33.4% other electric. Gas revenues were: 47.4% residential; 7.0% commercial; 0.7% industrial; 0.7% municipal; and 44.2% other. In 2000, sources of generated energy were 17.0% fossil fuel, 54.1% nuclear, 2.3% hydro, and 26.6% purchased. Energetix, an unregulated subsidiary of RGS, owns Griffith Oil Co., a liquid fuels business with over 200,000 customers.

ANNUAL FINANCIAL DATA

	12/31/00	12/31/99	12/31/98	12/31/97	12/31/96	12/31/95	12/31/94
Earnings Per Share	**2.60**	**2.44**	**2.31**	**2.30**	**2.32**	**2 1.69**	**1 1.79**
Cash Flow Per Share	**6.36**	**6.11**	**5.79**	**5.74**	**5.47**	**4.89**	**4.62**
Tang. Book Val. Per Share	**20.72**	**20.84**	**20.38**	**20.80**	**20.25**	**19.71**	**19.78**
Dividends Per Share	**1.80**	**1.80**	**1.80**	**1.80**	**1.80**	**1.80**	**1.76**
Dividend Payout %	**69.2**	**73.8**	**77.9**	**78.3**	**77.6**	**106.5**	**98.3**
INCOME STATEMENT (IN MILLIONS):							
Total Revenues	1,448.1	1,207.5	1,034.4	1,036.6	1,054.0	1,016.3	1,000.8
Costs & Expenses	1,166.6	931.4	772.9	757.4	779.8	739.0	740.3
Depreciation & Amort.	132.4	135.1	134.3	133.9	121.8	122.0	105.5
Operating Income	149.1	141.0	127.2	145.3	152.5	155.4	155.0
Net Interest Inc./(Exp.)	d62.7	d57.4	d46.1	d50.7	d56.5	d59.2	d58.2
Income Taxes	1.1	cr1.1	0.5	cr3.7	cr3.4	cr16.9	cr16.3
Net Income	95.6	93.6	94.1	95.4	97.5	2 71.9	1 74.4
Cash Flow	224.3	224.6	223.6	223.5	211.9	186.4	172.5
Average Shs. Outstg. (000)	35,281	36,757	38,600	38,909	38,762	38,113	37,327
BALANCE SHEET (IN MILLIONS):							
Gross Property	3,507.3	3,349.6	3,425.5	3,308.1	3,229.5	3,189.8	3,110.0
Accumulated Depreciation	2,004.9	1,876.2	1,863.5	1,714.4	1,569.1	1,518.9	1,423.1
Net Property	1,502.4	1,473.4	1,562.1	1,593.7	1,660.4	1,671.0	1,686.9
Total Assets	2,565.8	2,462.9	2,452.9	2,268.3	2,361.5	2,475.4	2,466.2
Long-Term Obligations	823.9	815.5	758.2	587.3	647.0	716.2	735.2
Net Stockholders' Equity	767.1	770.2	782.8	808.3	786.6	757.8	745.1
Year-end Shs. Outstg. (000)	34,577	35,943	37,379	38,862	38,851	38,453	37,670
STATISTICAL RECORD:							
Operating Profit Margin %	10.3	11.7	12.3	14.0	14.5	15.3	15.5
Net Profit Margin %	6.6	7.7	9.1	9.2	9.3	7.1	7.4
Net Inc./Net Property %	6.4	6.4	6.0	6.0	5.9	4.3	4.4
Net Inc./Tot. Capital %	4.9	4.7	4.9	5.2	5.1	3.6	3.7
Return on Equity %	12.5	12.2	12.0	11.8	12.4	9.5	10.0
Accum. Depr./Gross Prop. %	57.2	56.0	54.4	51.8	48.6	47.6	45.8
Price Range	33.31-18.69	31.56-20.00	33.25-28.38	34.50-18.00	23.75-17.88	24.13-20.00	26.38-19.75
P/E Ratio	12.8-7.2	12.9-8.2	14.4-12.3	15.0-7.8	10.2-7.7	14.3-11.8	14.7-11.0
Average Yield %	6.9	1.7	...	...	...	...	...

Statistics are as originally reported. 1 Incl. $33.7 mill. ($0.59/sh.) net one-time chg. 2 Incl. $44.2 mill. ($0.75/sh.) chg. rel. to gas costs with negotiated settlement.

OFFICERS:
T. S. Richards, Chmn., Pres., C.E.O.
J. B. Stokes, Sr. V.P., C.F.O.
M. T. Tomaino, Sr. V.P., Gen. Couns.

INVESTOR CONTACT: Mark J. Graham, Mgr. of Investor Relations, (716) 724-8176

PRINCIPAL OFFICE: 89 East Ave., Rochester, NY 14649-0001

TELEPHONE NUMBER: (716) 771-4444
FAX: (716) 771-2895
WEB: www.rgs-energy.com

NO. OF EMPLOYEES: 2,673

SHAREHOLDERS: 25,518

ANNUAL MEETING: In Apr.

INCORPORATED: NY, June, 1904

INSTITUTIONAL HOLDINGS:
No. of Institutions: 145
Shares Held: 15,026,684
% Held: 43.5

INDUSTRY: Electric and other services combined (SIC: 4931)

TRANSFER AGENT(S): BankBoston, NA, c/o Boston EquiServe, Boston, MA

NYSE SYMBOL RAD
Rec. Pr. 8.37 (5/31/01)

RITE AID CORPORATION

YIELD ...
P/E RATIO ...

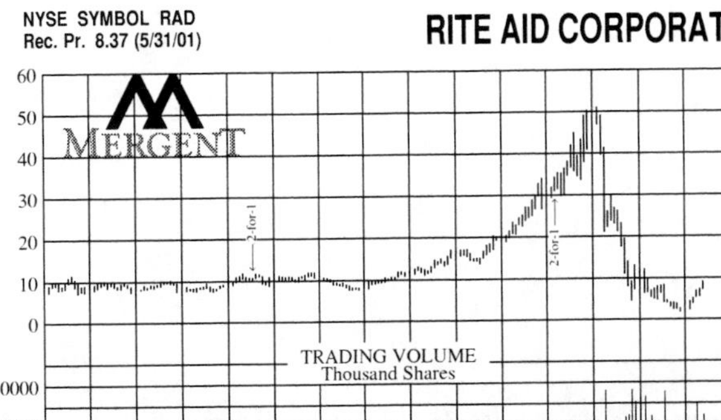

*7 YEAR PRICE SCORE 19.4 *12 MONTH PRICE SCORE 156.9

*NYSE COMPOSITE INDEX=100

INTERIM EARNINGS (Per Share):

Qtr.	May	Aug.	Nov.	Feb.
1996-97	0.20	0.21	0.23	0.24
1997-98	0.28	0.25	0.27	0.44
1998-99	0.34	d0.31	0.33	0.28
1999-00	0.31	d0.06	d0.98	d2.68
2000-01	d0.92	d1.87	d0.74	d1.07

INTERIM DIVIDENDS (Per Share):

Amt.	Decl.	Ex.	Rec.	Pay.

Last dist. $0.115Q, 10/25/99

CAPITALIZATION (2/26/00):

	($000)	(%)
Long-Term Debt	5,388,647	76.6
Capital Lease Obligations	1,118,204	15.9
Deferred Income Tax	79,220	1.1
Redeemable Pfd. Stock	19,457	0.3
Preferred Stock	308,250	4.4
Common & Surplus	123,258	1.8
Total	7,037,036	100.0

RECENT DEVELOPMENTS: For the 53 weeks ended 3/3/01, loss from continuing operations was $1.43 billion versus a loss from continuing operations of $1.11 billion in the corresponding 52-week period a year earlier. Results included one-time pre-tax charges of $519.3 million and $74.5 million in 2001 and 2000, respectively. Revenues grew 8.8% to $14.52 billion, while same-store sales rose 9.1%, reflecting prescription same-store sales growth of 10.9% and a 6.5% increase in front-end same-store sales. Comparisons were made with restated prior-year figures.

PROSPECTS: The Company is focusing on reducing its debt levels. During the fourth quarter, RAD reduced debt by about $157.6 million and has contracted to complete exchanges of its stock for $219.4 million of debt since the end of the fiscal year. These are in addition to debt reductions of about $763.5 million related to proceeds from the sale of shares in a drug benefits company, a note repayment, and by exchanging some debt for stock in March 2001. These actions are expected to reduce annual cash interest payments by about $85.0 million.

BUSINESS

RITE AID CORPORATION operates the second largest retail drugstore chain in the U.S. based on store count. As of 4/28/01, RAD operates 3,636 drugstores in 30 states and the District of Columbia. The Company's stores sell prescription drugs and a wide assortment of general merchandise including prescription health and personal care items, cosmetics, household items, beverages, convenience foods, greeting cards, one-hour photo development and seasonal and other convenience products. On 10/2/00, RAD completed the sale of its pharmacy benefits management subsidiary, PCS Health Systems, Inc.

ANNUAL FINANCIAL DATA

	2/26/00	2/27/99	2/28/98	3/1/97	3/2/96	3/4/95	2/26/94
Earnings Per Share	**4 d4.34**	**3 0.54**	**1.22**	**2 0.87**	**0.95**	**0.84**	**1 0.15**
Cash Flow Per Share	**d2.37**	**1.69**	**2.17**	**1.78**	**1.66**	**1.41**	**0.75**
Tang. Book Val. Per Share	**...**	**...**	**3.68**	**3.44**	**4.56**	**4.50**	**4.82**
Dividends Per Share	**0.46**	**0.43**	**0.40**	**0.38**	**0.34**	**0.30**	**0.30**
Dividend Payout %	**...**	**79.6**	**32.8**	**43.1**	**35.8**	**35.9**	**199.9**
INCOME STATEMENT (IN MILLIONS):							
Total Revenues	14,681.4	12,731.9	11,375.1	6,970.2	5,446.0	4,533.9	4,058.7
Costs & Expenses	14,844.1	12,035.0	10,411.1	6,446.7	5,002.8	4,161.5	3,878.5
Depreciation & Amort.	501.0	302.6	274.2	168.1	118.7	98.6	105.8
Operating Income	d663.6	394.3	689.8	355.4	324.5	273.8	74.4
Net Interest Inc./(Exp.)	d520.3	d194.7	d159.8	d96.5	d68.3	d42.3	d28.7
Income Before Income Taxes	d1,115.8	199.6	530.0	258.9	256.2	231.5	45.7
Income Taxes	...	55.9	213.6	98.4	97.3	90.2	19.5
Net Income	4 d1,115.8	3 143.7	316.4	2 160.5	158.9	141.3	1 26.2
Cash Flow	d614.8	445.7	590.6	328.6	277.6	239.8	132.0
Average Shs. Outstg. (000)	259,139	263,354	271,634	184,422	167,616	169,542	175,944
BALANCE SHEET (IN MILLIONS):							
Cash & Cash Equivalents	184.6	82.9	91.0	7.0	3.1	7.1	17.4
Total Current Assets	3,805.5	3,802.4	3,378.3	2,771.5	1,465.0	1,373.2	1,125.4
Net Property	3,629.9	2,868.1	2,171.1	1,896.1	979.5	778.5	638.7
Total Assets	10,807.9	10,421.7	7,655.3	6,417.0	2,842.0	2,472.6	1,989.1
Total Current Liabilities	2,912.4	3,690.5	1,770.9	1,172.0	630.0	577.2	362.2
Long-Term Obligations	6,506.9	3,304.2	2,551.4	2,415.7	994.3	806.0	613.4
Net Stockholders' Equity	431.5	2,953.7	2,916.5	2,488.7	1,103.6	1,011.8	954.7
Net Working Capital	893.1	111.9	1,607.4	1,599.5	835.0	796.0	763.2
Year-end Shs. Outstg. (000)	259,927	258,862	258,215	245,620	167,696	168,330	172,022
STATISTICAL RECORD:							
Operating Profit Margin %	...	1.6	4.7	3.7	4.7	5.1	1.1
Net Profit Margin %	...	1.1	2.8	2.3	2.9	3.1	0.6
Return on Equity %	...	4.9	10.8	6.5	14.4	14.0	2.7
Return on Assets %	...	1.4	4.1	2.5	5.6	5.7	1.3
Debt/Total Assets %	60.2	31.7	33.3	37.6	35.0	32.6	30.8
Price Range	51.13-4.50	50.38-29.22	34.19-18.81	20.44-13.63	17.19-11.00	12.00-7.88	10.75-7.63
P/E Ratio	...	93.3-54.1	28.0-15.4	23.5-15.7	18.1-11.6	14.4-9.4	71.6-50.8
Average Yield %	1.7	1.1	1.5	2.2	2.4	3.0	3.3

Statistics are as originally reported. Adj. for 2-for-1 stk. split, 2/98. 1 Bef. $16.9 mil loss fr disc. opers. & incl. $90.6 mil restr. chg. 2 Bef. $45.2 mil ($0.25/sh) extraord. loss & incl. $42.4 mil ($0.20/sh) non-recur. chg. 3 Incl. $176.9 mil ($0.67/sh) after-tax, non-recur. chg. 4 Bef. $27.3 mil ($0.11/sh) acctg. chg. & incl. $80.1 mil pre-tax gain fr. sale of stores.

OFFICERS:
R. G. Miller, Chmn., C.E.O.
M. F. Sammons, Pres., C.O.O.
J. T. Standley, Sr. Exec. V.P., C.F.O.

INVESTOR CONTACT: Dave Jessick, (717) 975-5750

PRINCIPAL OFFICE: 30 Hunter Lane, Camp Hill, PA 17011

TELEPHONE NUMBER: (717) 761-2633
FAX: (717) 975-5905
WEB: www.riteaid.com
NO. OF EMPLOYEES: 77,258
SHAREHOLDERS: 11,660 (approx.)
ANNUAL MEETING: In June
INCORPORATED: PA, 1958; reincorp., DE, Apr., 1968

INSTITUTIONAL HOLDINGS:
No. of Institutions: 149
Shares Held: 107,354,049
% Held: 31.5

INDUSTRY: Drug stores and proprietary stores (SIC: 5912)

TRANSFER AGENT(S): Computershare Investor Services, Chicago, IL

NYSE SYMBOL RHI
Rec. Pr. 28.20 (5/31/01)

ROBERT HALF INTERNATIONAL, INC.

YIELD ...
P/E RATIO 27.9

TRADING VOLUME
Thousand Shares

*7 YEAR PRICE SCORE 134.4 *12 MONTH PRICE SCORE 98.1

*NYSE COMPOSITE INDEX=100

INTERIM EARNINGS (Per Share):

Qtr.	Mar.	June	Sept.	Dec.
1996	0.08	0.08	0.09	0.10
1997	0.11	0.12	0.13	0.15
1998	0.16	0.17	0.19	0.19
1999	0.19	0.19	0.19	0.21
2000	0.24	0.25	0.26	0.26

INTERIM DIVIDENDS (Per Share):

Amt.	Decl.	Ex.	Rec.	Pay.
2-for-1	5/04/00	6/13/00	5/19/00	6/12/00

CAPITALIZATION (12/31/00):

	($000)	(%)
Long-Term Debt	2,541	0.3
Deferred Income Tax	12,793	1.7
Common & Surplus	718,539	97.9
Total	733,873	100.0

RECENT DEVELOPMENTS: For the year ended 12/31/00, net income jumped 31.6% to $186.1 million versus $141.4 million in 1999. Net service revenues increased 29.7% to $2.70 billion versus $2.08 billion the year before. ACCOUNTEMPS, OFFICETEAM and RHI CONSULTING revenues rose 22.6%, 30.0% and 19.7% to $1.17 billion, $644.4 million and $382.6 million, respectively. RHI MANAGEMENT RESOURCES revenues leapt 63.2% to $254.3 million. ROBERT HALF revenues grew 58.6% to $252.5 million.

PROSPECTS: The Company continues to benefit from technology investments, primarily on-line candidate recruiting initiatives. During January 2001, RHI launched enhanced Web sites for three operating divisions to increase functionality, improve user experience and provide greater efficiencies for RHI's staff. Separately, the Company anticipates its ongoing investments in technology along with on-line and off-line recruitment proposals will contribute to higher revenues in the long-term.

BUSINESS

ROBERT HALF INTERNATIONAL, INC. provides financial staffing services through separate divisions serving distinct markets including, ACCOUNTEMPS, ROBERT HALF, and RHI MANAGEMENT RESOURCES, for temporary, full-time and project professionals, respectively, in the fields of accounting and finance; OFFICETEAM, for highly skilled temporary administrative support personnel; RHI CONSULTING, for contract information technology professionals; THE AFFILIATES, for legal personnel; and THE CREATIVE GROUP, for advertising, marketing and web design professionals. As of 4/18/01, the Company owned and operated more than 330 offices throughout North America, Europe and Australia.

BUSINESS LINE ANALYSIS

(12/31/00)	REV(%)	INC(%)
Temporary and consultant	90.6	78.4
Permanent placement staff	9.4	21.6
Total	100.0	100.0

ANNUAL FINANCIAL DATA

	12/31/00	12/31/99	12/31/98	12/31/97	12/31/96	12/31/95	12/31/94
Earnings Per Share	**1.00**	**0.77**	**0.70**	**0.50**	**0.35**	**0.24**	**0.15**
Cash Flow Per Share	**1.30**	**0.98**	**0.82**	**0.59**	**0.41**	**0.28**	**0.20**
Tang. Book Val. Per Share	**3.13**	**2.27**	**1.89**	**1.32**	**0.75**	**0.42**	**0.14**
INCOME STATEMENT (IN MILLIONS):							
Total Revenues	2,699.3	2,081.3	1,793.0	1,302.9	898.6	628.5	446.3
Costs & Expenses	2,351.5	1,813.6	1,552.8	1,130.6	785.4	551.6	392.3
Depreciation & Amort.	56.6	39.1	24.6	17.7	11.9	8.3	7.3
Operating Income	291.2	228.7	215.6	154.6	101.4	68.6	46.8
Net Interest Inc./(Exp.)	10.4	6.0	5.6	4.2	2.2	0.5	d1.6
Income Before Income Taxes	301.6	234.7	221.2	158.8	103.6	69.1	45.2
Income Taxes	115.5	93.3	89.6	65.1	42.5	28.8	19.1
Net Income	186.1	141.4	131.6	93.7	61.1	40.3	26.1
Cash Flow	242.7	180.6	156.2	111.3	73.0	48.6	33.4
Average Shs. Outstg. (000)	186,068	184,588	189,644	187,998	176,534	170,958	164,190
BALANCE SHEET (IN MILLIONS):							
Cash & Cash Equivalents	239.2	151.1	166.1	131.3	80.2	41.3	2.6
Total Current Assets	671.6	490.5	430.4	334.0	214.6	133.7	67.7
Net Property	131.4	110.9	95.0	49.9	26.7	12.0	7.2
Total Assets	971.0	777.2	703.7	561.4	416.0	301.1	227.8
Total Current Liabilities	237.2	176.2	152.8	122.1	86.6	55.9	29.6
Long-Term Obligations	2.5	2.6	3.4	4.5	5.1	1.5	3.1
Net Stockholders' Equity	718.5	576.1	522.5	418.8	308.4	227.9	177.0
Net Working Capital	434.5	314.3	277.6	211.9	128.1	77.8	38.1
Year-end Shs. Outstg. (000)	176,050	176,148	182,451	183,292	179,244	173,352	168,912
STATISTICAL RECORD:							
Operating Profit Margin %	10.8	11.0	12.0	11.9	11.3	10.9	10.5
Net Profit Margin %	6.9	6.8	7.3	7.2	6.8	6.4	5.9
Return on Equity %	25.9	24.6	25.2	22.4	19.8	17.7	14.8
Return on Assets %	19.2	18.2	18.7	16.7	14.7	13.4	11.5
Debt/Total Assets %	0.3	0.3	0.5	0.8	1.2	0.5	1.4
Price Range	38.63-12.34	24.19-10.22	30.13-14.50	21.53-11.13	13.83-6.50	7.44-3.27	4.46-2.13
P/E Ratio	38.6-12.3	31.6-13.4	43.3-20.9	43.1-22.2	40.1-18.8	31.6-13.9	29.1-13.9

Statistics are as originally reported. Adj. for stk. splits: 2-for-1, 6/00, 6/96 & 8/94; and 3-for-2, 9/97

OFFICERS:
H. M. Messmer Jr., Chmn., Pres., C.E.O.
M. K. Waddell, Vice-Chmn., C.F.O., Treas.
Steven Karel, V.P., Sec., Gen. Couns.

INVESTOR CONTACT: M. Keith Waddell, C.F.O., (650) 234-6000

PRINCIPAL OFFICE: 2884 Sand Hill Road, Suite 200, Menlo Park, CA 94025

TELEPHONE NUMBER: (650) 234-6000
FAX: (650) 234-6999
WEB: www.rhii.com

NO. OF EMPLOYEES: 8,300 (approx.)

SHAREHOLDERS: 2,400 (approx. record)

ANNUAL MEETING: In May

INCORPORATED: DE, June, 1987

INSTITUTIONAL HOLDINGS:
No. of Institutions: 250
Shares Held: 135,860,111
% Held: 77.5

INDUSTRY: Help supply services (SIC: 7363)

TRANSFER AGENT(S): Mellon Investor Services, San Francisco, CA

NYSE SYMBOL ROK
Rec. Pr. 47.00 (5/31/01)

ROCKWELL INTERNATIONAL CORP.

YIELD 2.2%
P/E RATIO 16.2

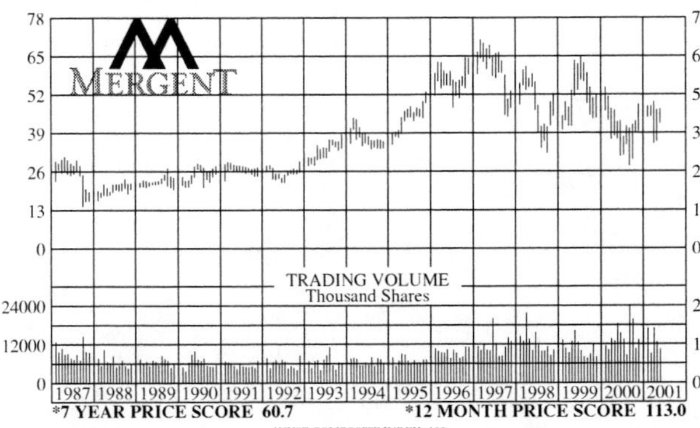

*7 YEAR PRICE SCORE 60.7 *12 MONTH PRICE SCORE 113.0

*NYSE COMPOSITE INDEX=100

INTERIM EARNINGS (Per Share):

Qtr.	Dec.	Mar.	June	Sept.
1996-97	0.82	0.72	0.62	0.70
1997-98	0.43	0.53	d2.15	0.67
1998-99	0.70	0.74	0.77	0.80
1999-00	0.81	0.85	0.90	0.78
2000-01	0.38	...	...	...

INTERIM DIVIDENDS (Per Share):

Amt.	Decl.	Ex.	Rec.	Pay.
0.255Q	4/07/00	5/11/00	5/15/00	6/05/00
0.255Q	6/07/00	8/10/00	8/14/00	9/05/00
0.255Q	11/01/00	11/09/00	11/13/00	12/04/00
0.255Q	2/07/01	2/08/01	2/12/01	3/05/01
0.255Q	4/09/01	5/10/01	5/14/01	6/04/01

Indicated div.: $1.02 (Div. Reinv. Plan)

CAPITALIZATION (9/30/00):

	($000)	(%)
Long-Term Debt	924,000	25.7
Common & Surplus	2,669,000	74.3
Total	3,593,000	100.0

RECENT DEVELOPMENTS: For the quarter ended 12/31/00, income from continuing operations declined 20.7% to $69.0 million versus income from continuing operations of $87.0 million in 1999. Results for 2000 and 1999 excluded after-tax gains from discontinued operations of $65.0 million and $70.0 million, respectively. Total revenues rose 1.3% to $1.12 billion from $1.11 billion the year before. Control systems sales grew 1.3% to $883.0 million, while power systems sales inched up 0.6% to $172.0 million.

PROSPECTS: On 2/19/01, the Company announced that it will change its name to Rockwell Automation to better reflect its business focus after the completion of the planned spin-off of Rockwell Collins, ROK's avionics business, as an independent publicly-traded company. ROK remains on track to complete the spin-off in June of 2001. ROK also announced that it will establish the Rockwell Science Center as an independent company owned jointly by Rockwell Collins and Rockwell Automation.

BUSINESS

ROCKWELL INTERNATIONAL CORP. is engaged in the research and development, manufacture, sale and service of electronic controls and communication products through two main business segments. Rockwell Automation, which supplies industrial automation equipment and systems, contributed 61.8% of total sales in 2000. The Company's other business segment includes the Electric Commerce business and the Science Center. On 12/6/96, ROK sold its Aerospace and Defense units to The Boeing Company for approximately $3.20 billion. On 9/30/97, ROK completed the spin-off of its Automotive Component Systems business. On 12/31/98, ROK spun off of its semiconductor business, Conexant Systems, Inc. The Company plans to spin-off its Avionics & Communications business, which includes Rockwell Collins, in June 2001.

REVENUES

(09/30/00)	($000)	(%)
Automation	4,419,000	61.8
Avionics & Communications	2,515,000	35.2
Other Businesses	217,000	3.0
Total	7,151,000	100.0

ANNUAL FINANCIAL DATA

	9/30/00	9/30/99	9/30/98	9/30/97	9/30/96	9/30/95	9/30/94
Earnings Per Share	**3.35**	**4 3.01**	**3 d0.55**	**2 2.74**	**1 2.55**	**3.42**	**2.87**
Cash Flow Per Share	**5.29**	**4.75**	**1.00**	**5.00**	**5.04**	**6.05**	**5.12**
Tang. Book Val. Per Share	**6.90**	**5.76**	**8.85**	**14.61**	**19.48**	**8.13**	**11.79**
Dividends Per Share	**1.02**	**1.02**	**1.02**	**1.13**	...	...	...
Dividend Payout %	**30.4**	**33.9**	...	**41.1**	...	...	...
INCOME STATEMENT (IN MILLIONS):							
Total Revenues	7,220.0	7,151.0	6,840.0	7,882.0	10,542.0	13,099.0	11,204.7
Costs & Expenses	5,835.0	5,840.0	6,451.0	6,448.0	9,072.0	11,132.0	9,592.9
Depreciation & Amort.	369.0	337.0	306.0	484.0	542.0	571.0	493.9
Operating Income	1,016.0	974.0	83.0	950.0	928.0	1,396.0	1,117.9
Net Interest Inc./(Exp.)	d73.0	d84.0	d58.0	d27.0	d32.0	d170.0	d96.6
Income Before Income Taxes	943.0	890.0	25.0	923.0	896.0	1,226.0	1,021.3
Income Taxes	307.0	308.0	134.0	337.0	341.0	484.0	387.2
Net Income	636.0	4 582.0	3 d109.0	2 586.0	1 555.0	742.0	634.1
Cash Flow	1,005.0	919.0	197.0	1,070.0	1,097.0	1,078.0	1,127.7
Average Shs. Outstg. (000)	189,900	193,600	197,900	213,800	217,600	217,200	220,500
BALANCE SHEET (IN MILLIONS):							
Cash & Cash Equivalents	190.0	356.0	103.0	283.0	715.0	665.0	628.3
Total Current Assets	3,206.0	3,582.0	4,096.0	3,684.0	5,358.0	8,315.0	7,195.0
Net Property	1,616.0	1,581.0	1,535.0	2,245.0	2,662.0	3,026.0	2,383.4
Total Assets	6,390.0	6,704.0	7,170.0	7,971.0	10,065.0	15,015.0	12,128.0
Total Current Liabilities	1,820.0	2,108.0	1,983.0	1,970.0	4,281.0	4,111.0	2,238.1
Long-Term Obligations	924.0	911.0	908.0	156.0	161.0	1,776.0	831.0
Net Stockholders' Equity	2,669.0	2,637.0	3,245.0	4,811.0	4,256.0	3,782.0	3,355.6
Net Working Capital	1,386.0	1,474.0	2,113.0	1,714.0	1,077.0	4,204.0	4,956.9
Year-end Shs. Outstg. (000)	183,500	216,400	216,400	206,800	218,500	217,000	218,600
STATISTICAL RECORD:							
Operating Profit Margin %	14.1	13.6	1.2	12.1	8.8	10.7	10.0
Net Profit Margin %	8.8	8.1	...	7.4	5.3	5.7	5.7
Return on Equity %	23.8	22.1	...	12.2	13.0	19.6	18.9
Return on Assets %	10.0	8.7	...	7.4	5.5	4.9	5.2
Debt/Total Assets %	14.5	13.6	12.7	2.0	1.6	11.8	6.9
Price Range	54.50-27.69	64.94-39.94	61.63-32.13	70.63-44.31	64.63-47.50	53.00-35.00	44.13-33.50
P/E Ratio	16.3-8.3	21.6-13.3	...	25.8-16.2	25.3-18.6	15.5-10.2	15.4-11.7
Average Yield %	2.5	1.9	2.2	2.0	...	...	...

Statistics are as originally reported. 1 Bef. disc. oper. credit $171.0 mill., but incl. non-recurr. chrg. $122.0 mill. 2 Bef. disc. oper. credit $58.0 mill. 3 Bef. disc. oper. loss $301.0 mill. & acctg. change chrg. $17.0 mill. 4 Bef. disc. oper. loss $20.0 mill.

OFFICERS:
D. H. Davis Jr, Chmn., C.E.O.
W. M. Barnes, Sr. V.P., C.F.O.
William Calise, Jr., Sr. VP, Gen. Couns., Sec.

INVESTOR CONTACT: Thomas J. Mullany, Investor Relations, (414) 212-5210

PRINCIPAL OFFICE: 777 East Wisconsin Avenue, Suite 1400, Milwaukee, WI 53202

TELEPHONE NUMBER: (414) 212-5299
FAX: (414) 212-5212
WEB: www.rockwell.com

NO. OF EMPLOYEES: 41,200 (approx.)

SHAREHOLDERS: 49,529

ANNUAL MEETING: In Feb.

INCORPORATED: DE, Dec., 1928

INSTITUTIONAL HOLDINGS:
No. of Institutions: 322
Shares Held: 89,653,801
% Held: 49.0

INDUSTRY: Process control instruments (SIC: 3823)

TRANSFER AGENT(S): Mellon Investor Services, LLC, South Hackensack, NJ

NYSE SYMBOL ROH
Rec. Pr. 34.37 (4/30/01)

ROHM & HAAS COMPANY

YIELD 2.3%
P/E RATIO 21.3

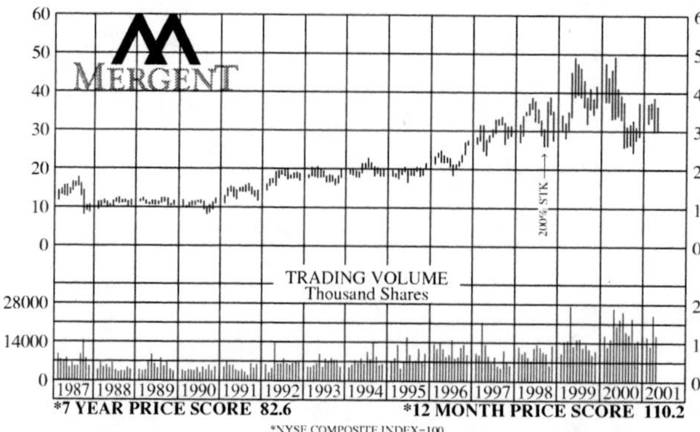

*7 YEAR PRICE SCORE 82.6 *12 MONTH PRICE SCORE 110.2

*NYSE COMPOSITE INDEX=100

INTERIM EARNINGS (Per Share):

Qtr.	Mar.	June	Sept.	Dec.
1998	0.58	0.96	0.50	0.44
1999	0.64	d0.06	0.26	0.41
2000	0.56	0.35	0.38	0.32

INTERIM DIVIDENDS (Per Share):

Amt.	Decl.	Ex.	Rec.	Pay.
0.20Q	10/19/00	11/01/00	11/03/00	12/01/00
0.20Q	2/05/01	2/14/01	2/16/01	3/01/01
0.20Q	5/08/01	5/16/01	5/18/01	6/01/01

Indicated div.: $0.80 (Div. Reinv. Plan)

CAPITALIZATION (12/31/00):

	($000)	(%)
Long-Term Debt	3,225,000	39.4
Deferred Income Tax	1,287,000	15.7
Minority Interest	23,000	0.3
Common & Surplus	3,653,000	44.6
Total	8,188,000	100.0

RECENT DEVELOPMENTS: For the year ended 12/31/00, net earnings rose 42.2% to $354.0 million versus $249.0 million in 1999. Results for 2000 and 1999 included purchased in-process research and development charges of $13.0 million and $105.0 million, respectively, and a provision for restructuring charge of $13.0 million and $36.0 million, respectively. Results for 1999 were restated and included a non-recurring loss of $22.0 million. Net sales rose 28.0% to $6.88 billion from $5.37 billion in 1999.

PROSPECTS: If the economic situation remains uncertain and ore prices continue to rise, ROH expects its earnings in the first half of 2001 to be below levels from the first half of 2000. If global conditions improve by mid-year, then full-year 2001 earnings may improve over 2000. ROH plans to streamline its organizational structure, work processes, manufacturing and non-manufacturing resources. Meanwhile, Dow AgroSciences LLC agreed to purchase ROH's agricultural chemicals business.

BUSINESS

ROHM & HAAS COMPANY is a multinational producer of specialty polymers and biologically active compounds. Products range from basic petrochemicals such as propylene, acetone and styrene to differentiated specialty products. ROH has developed acrylic plastics, a field which it pioneered with its development of Plexiglas (used in outdoor signs, industrial lighting, skylights, and boat windshields). Other products include polymers, resins and monomers geared toward a wide variety of industrial applications. The Company also manufactures agricultural and industrial chemicals. Contributions to sales in 2000 were as follows: performance polymers, 49.4%; chemical specialties, 20.5%; electronic materials, 17.4%; and salt, 12.7%. In January 1999, ROH acquired LeaRonal, an electronic materials firm. In June 1999, ROH acquired Morton International, a manufacturer of specialty chemicals and salt.

ANNUAL FINANCIAL DATA

	12/31/00	12/31/99	12/31/98	12/31/97	12/31/96	12/31/95	12/31/94
Earnings Per Share	[5] **1.61**	[4] **1.27**	[3] **2.52**	**2.13**	[1] **1.82**	[2] **1.41**	**1.26**
Cash Flow Per Share	**4.39**	**3.19**	**4.02**	**3.55**	**3.15**	**2.60**	**2.40**
Tang. Book Val. Per Share	...	...	**9.66**	**9.15**	**8.44**	**8.16**	**7.32**
Dividends Per Share	**0.78**	**0.74**	**0.69**	**0.63**	**0.57**	**0.52**	**0.48**
Dividend Payout %	**48.4**	**58.3**	**27.5**	**29.7**	**31.6**	**37.0**	**38.0**
INCOME STATEMENT (IN MILLIONS):							
Total Revenues	6,879.0	5,339.0	3,720.0	3,999.0	3,982.0	3,884.0	3,534.0
Costs & Expenses	5,510.0	4,260.0	2,822.0	3,103.0	3,153.0	3,129.0	2,836.0
Depreciation & Amort.	613.0	451.0	276.0	279.0	262.0	242.0	231.0
Operating Income	756.0	628.0	622.0	617.0	567.0	513.0	467.0
Net Interest Inc./(Exp.)	d241.0	d159.0	d34.0	d39.0	d32.0	d32.0	d39.0
Income Before Income Taxes	581.0	464.0	700.0	611.0	530.0	441.0	407.0
Income Taxes	227.0	215.0	247.0	201.0	167.0	149.0	143.0
Equity Earnings/Minority Int.	19.0	7.0	2.0	11.0	d17.0	d3.0	...
Net Income	[5] 354.0	[4] 249.0	[3] 453.0	410.0	[1] 363.0	[2] 292.0	264.0
Cash Flow	967.0	698.0	723.0	682.0	618.0	527.0	488.0
Average Shs. Outstg. (000)	220,500	218,981	179,700	192,300	196,200	202,500	203,100
BALANCE SHEET (IN MILLIONS):							
Cash & Cash Equivalents	92.0	57.0	16.0	40.0	11.0	43.0	127.0
Total Current Assets	2,781.0	2,497.0	1,287.0	1,397.0	1,456.0	1,421.0	1,440.0
Net Property	3,339.0	3,496.0	1,908.0	2,008.0	2,066.0	2,048.0	1,960.0
Total Assets	11,267.0	11,256.0	3,648.0	3,900.0	3,933.0	3,916.0	3,861.0
Total Current Liabilities	2,194.0	2,510.0	875.0	850.0	886.0	828.0	932.0
Long-Term Obligations	3,225.0	3,122.0	409.0	509.0	562.0	606.0	629.0
Net Stockholders' Equity	3,653.0	3,475.0	1,561.0	1,797.0	1,728.0	1,781.0	1,620.0
Net Working Capital	587.0	d13.0	412.0	547.0	570.0	593.0	508.0
Year-end Shs. Outstg. (000)	219,937	218,981	154,000	182,700	189,300	201,900	203,100
STATISTICAL RECORD:							
Operating Profit Margin %	11.0	11.8	16.7	15.4	14.2	13.2	13.2
Net Profit Margin %	5.1	4.7	12.2	10.3	9.1	7.5	7.5
Return on Equity %	9.7	7.2	29.0	22.8	21.0	16.4	16.3
Return on Assets %	3.1	2.2	12.4	10.5	9.2	7.5	6.8
Debt/Total Assets %	28.6	27.7	11.2	13.1	14.3	15.5	16.3
Price Range	49.44-24.38	49.25-28.13	38.88-26.00	33.75-23.54	27.50-18.29	21.63-16.50	22.83-17.75
P/E Ratio	30.7-15.1	38.8-22.1	15.4-10.3	15.8-11.1	15.1-10.1	15.4-11.7	18.1-14.1
Average Yield %	2.1	1.9	2.1	2.2	2.5	2.7	2.4

Statistics are as originally reported. Adj. for 3-for-1 split, 9/98. [1] Incl. $6.0 mill. aft-tax non-recur. chgs. [2] Incl. $17.0 mill. chg. for environ. cleanup. [3] Excl. $13.0 mill. after-tax extraord. loss fr. early exting. of debt. [4] Incl. $105.0 mill. in-process R&D chg., $22.0 mill. loss fr. disp. of joint vent. & $36.0 mill. restr. chg. [5] Incl. $26.0 mill. purch. R&D chg. & restr. chgs.

OFFICERS:
R. L. Gupta, Chmn., C.E.O.
J. M. Fitzpatrick, Pres., C.O.O.
B. J. Bell, Sr. V.P., C.F.O.

INVESTOR CONTACT: Laura L. Hadden, Mgr. Bus. & Fin. Comm., (215) 592-3052

PRINCIPAL OFFICE: 100 Independence Mall West, Philadelphia, PA 19106-2399

TELEPHONE NUMBER: (215) 592-3000
FAX: (215) 592-3377
WEB: www.rohmhaas.com

NO. OF EMPLOYEES: 18,474 (avg.)

SHAREHOLDERS: 9,226

ANNUAL MEETING: In May

INCORPORATED: DE, Apr., 1917

INSTITUTIONAL HOLDINGS:
No. of Institutions: 298
Shares Held: 161,843,255
% Held: 73.5

INDUSTRY: Plastics materials and resins (SIC: 2821)

TRANSFER AGENT(S): EquiServe, LP, Boston, MA

NYSE SYMBOL ROL
Rec. Pr. 18.66 (4/30/01)

ROLLINS, INC.

YIELD 1.1%
P/E RATIO 58.3

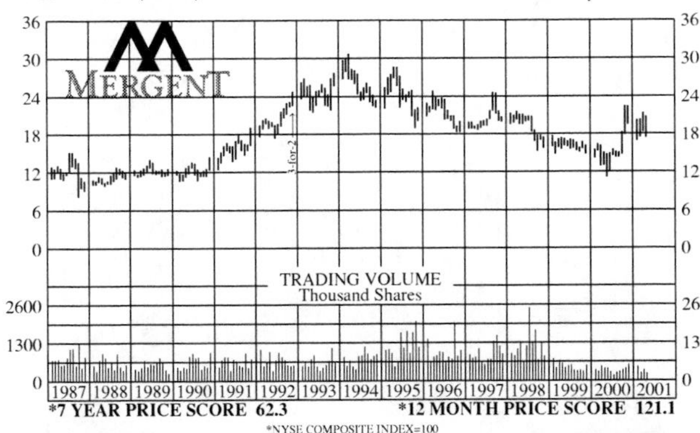

INTERIM EARNINGS (Per Share):

Qtr.	Mar.	June	Sept.	Dec.
1996	0.18	0.36	0.09	0.01
1997	0.15	0.19	d0.08	d3.07
1998	d0.05	0.21	0.03	d0.09
1999	0.02	0.25	0.05	d0.08
2000	0.03	0.27	0.08	d0.06

INTERIM DIVIDENDS (Per Share):

Amt.	Decl.	Ex.	Rec.	Pay.
0.05Q	4/26/00	5/08/00	5/10/00	6/12/00
0.05Q	7/25/00	8/08/00	8/10/00	9/11/00
0.05Q	10/24/00	11/08/00	11/10/00	12/11/00
0.05Q	1/23/01	2/07/01	2/09/01	3/09/01
0.05Q	4/23/01	5/08/01	5/10/01	6/11/01

Indicated div.: $0.20 (Div. Reinv. Plan)

CAPITALIZATION (12/31/00):

	($000)	(%)
Capital Lease Obligations..	256	0.3
Common & Surplus	78,599	99.7
Total	78,855	100.0

RECENT DEVELOPMENTS: For the twelve months ended 12/31/00, net income jumped 33.6% to $9.6 million versus $7.2 million in the comparable period of 1999. Revenues rose 10.7% to $649.6 million from $586.6 million in the previous year. Revenue growth was fueled by increases in termite and pest control revenue. Termite revenue was favorably affected by a new termite baiting method combined with directed liquid treatments. Pest control revenue was positively affected by a new alternate service offering.

PROSPECTS: In 2001, the Company should look for positive results to carry over from 2000 as a result of the successful integration of strategic acquisitions, the effectiveness of new sales and service programs and efforts to make operations more efficient. Financial results are expected to continue to improve as new sales and service programs mature. On 2/12/01, ROL's wholly-owned subsidiary, Orkin Exterminating Company, Inc., launched Acurid[SM], a customized approach to pest control service.

BUSINESS

ROLLINS, INC. provides termite and pest control services to both residential and commercial customers. Orkin Exterminating Company, Inc., the Company's wholly-owned subsidiary, was founded in 1901, and is one of the world's largest termite, rodent and pest control companies. It provides customized services to approximately 1.6 million customers through a network of over 400 Company-owned and franchised branch locations serving customers in the U.S., Canada, and Mexico. It provides customized pest control services to homes and businesses, including hotels, food service establishments, dairy farms and transportation companies.

QUARTERLY DATA

(12/31/00)($000)	REV	INC
1st Quarter................	149,550	794
2nd Quarter................	180,528	8,102
3rd Quarter	172,373	2,363
4th Quarter................	147,107	(1,709)

ANNUAL FINANCIAL DATA

	12/31/00	12/31/99	12/31/98	12/31/97	12/31/96	12/31/95	12/31/94
Earnings Per Share	**0.32**	**0.24**	**② 0.10**	**② d3.09**	**0.64**	**① 1.10**	**1.39**
Cash Flow Per Share	**0.93**	**0.68**	**0.38**	**d2.83**	**0.89**	**1.32**	**1.61**
Tang. Book Val. Per Share	**...**	**...**	**1.30**	**3.19**	**4.29**	**4.81**	**4.23**
Dividends Per Share	**0.20**	**0.20**	**0.50**	**0.60**	**0.58**	**0.56**	**0.50**
Dividend Payout %	**62.5**	**83.3**	**499.5**	**...**	**90.6**	**50.9**	**36.0**
INCOME STATEMENT (IN THOUSANDS):							
Total Revenues	649,558	586,639	549,136	538,639	627,431	620,435	605,327
Costs & Expenses	616,184	564,722	544,059	706,847	588,020	542,123	519,604
Depreciation & Amort.	18,421	13,433	8,934	8,382	8,612	7,950	8,130
Operating Income	14,953	8,484	d3,857	d176,590	30,799	70,362	77,593
Net Interest Inc./(Exp.)	450	3,048	8,981	7,588	5,967	4,988	2,994
Income Before Income Taxes	15,403	11,532	5,124	d169,002	36,766	63,350	80,587
Income Taxes	5,853	4,382	1,947	cr64,221	13,971	24,073	31,026
Net Income	9,550	7,150	② 3,177	② d104,781	22,795	① 39,277	49,561
Cash Flow	27,971	20,583	12,111	d96,399	31,407	47,227	57,691
Average Shs. Outstg.	30,046	30,332	32,003	34,033	35,478	35,849	35,770
BALANCE SHEET (IN THOUSANDS):							
Cash & Cash Equivalents	399	18,656	111,473	200,879	96,935	99,366	83,737
Total Current Assets	88,969	107,749	199,108	301,618	205,736	222,765	214,899
Net Property	49,349	46,245	35,466	34,639	41,042	37,799	27,989
Total Assets	298,819	312,940	327,265	432,680	308,783	314,925	295,265
Total Current Liabilities	110,806	111,441	115,093	130,718	79,519	71,009	66,889
Long-Term Obligations	256	2,450	6,090	9,239	12,163	7,422	...
Net Stockholders' Equity	78,599	71,790	80,235	145,644	190,290	214,318	193,633
Net Working Capital	d21,837	d3,692	84,015	170,900	126,217	151,756	148,010
Year-end Shs. Outstg.	30,036	29,881	30,489	33,279	34,594	35,858	35,826
STATISTICAL RECORD:							
Operating Profit Margin %	2.3	1.4	...	...	4.9	11.3	12.8
Net Profit Margin %	1.5	1.2	0.6	...	3.6	6.3	8.2
Return on Equity %	12.2	10.0	4.0	...	12.0	18.3	25.6
Return on Assets %	3.2	2.3	1.0	...	7.4	12.5	16.8
Debt/Total Assets %	0.1	0.8	1.9	2.1	3.9	2.4	...
Price Range	22.38-11.13	17.75-14.75	21.56-15.25	24.63-18.63	24.88-18.25	28.63-18.88	30.75-22.13
P/E Ratio	69.9-34.8	73.9-61.4	215.4-152.3	...	38.9-28.5	26.0-17.2	22.1-15.9
Average Yield %	1.2	1.2	2.7	2.8	2.7	2.4	1.9

Statistics are as originally reported. ① Incl. non-recurr. chrg. $7.4 mill. ② Bef. disc. oper. gain $3.4 mill., 1998: $106.3 mill., 1997

OFFICERS:
R. R. Rollins, Chmn., C.E.O.
G. W. Rollins, Pres., C.O.O.
H. J. Cynkus, C.F.O., Treas.
M. W. Knottek, V.P., Sec.

INVESTOR CONTACT: Harry J. Cynkus, C.F.O., Treas., (404) 888-2000

PRINCIPAL OFFICE: 2170 Piedmont Road, N.E., Atlanta, GA 30324

TELEPHONE NUMBER: (404) 888-2000
FAX: (404) 888-2670

NO. OF EMPLOYEES: 9,000 (approx.)

SHAREHOLDERS: 1,927 (record)

ANNUAL MEETING: In Apr.

INCORPORATED: DE, Feb., 1948

INSTITUTIONAL HOLDINGS:
No. of Institutions: 70
Shares Held: 10,776,843
% Held: 35.8

INDUSTRY: Disinfecting & pest control services (SIC: 7342)

TRANSFER AGENT(S): Sun Trust Bank, Atlanta, GA

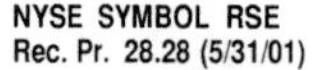

NYSE SYMBOL RSE
Rec. Pr. 28.28 (5/31/01)

ROUSE COMPANY (THE)

YIELD 5.0%
P/E RATIO 12.8

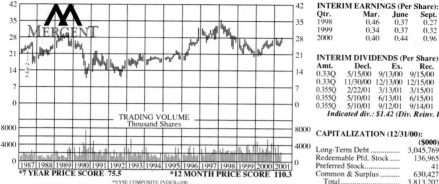

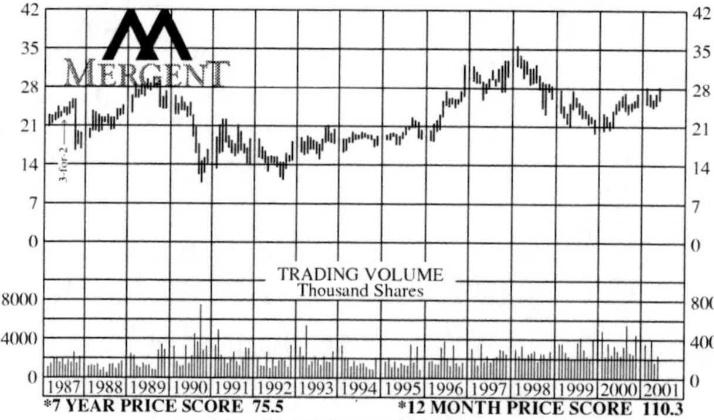

*7 YEAR PRICE SCORE 75.5 *12 MONTH PRICE SCORE 110.3
*NYSE COMPOSITE INDEX=100

INTERIM EARNINGS (Per Share):

Qtr.	Mar.	June	Sept.	Dec.
1998	0.46	0.37	0.27	0.24
1999	0.34	0.37	0.32	0.73
2000	0.40	0.44	0.96	0.41

INTERIM DIVIDENDS (Per Share):

Amt.	Decl.	Ex.	Rec.	Pay.
0.33Q	5/15/00	9/13/00	9/15/00	9/29/00
0.33Q	11/30/00	12/13/00	12/15/00	12/21/00
0.355Q	2/22/01	3/13/01	3/15/01	3/30/01
0.355Q	5/10/01	6/13/01	6/15/01	6/29/01
0.355Q	5/10/01	9/12/01	9/14/01	9/28/01

Indicated div.: $1.42 (Div. Reinv. Plan)

CAPITALIZATION (12/31/00):

	($000)	(%)
Long-Term Debt	3,045,769	79.9
Redeemable Pfd. Stock	136,965	3.6
Preferred Stock	41	0.0
Common & Surplus	630,427	16.5
Total	3,813,202	100.0

RECENT DEVELOPMENTS: For the year ended 12/31/00, net earnings were $168.3 million, excluding a $2.2 million extraordinary gain, versus net earnings of $141.2 million, excluding a $5.9 million extraordinary charge, the previous year. Results included net one-time gains on dispositions of operating property assets of $33.2 million and $44.0 million in 2000 and 1999, respectively. Total revenues fell slightly to $633.7 million from $635.9 million the year before.

PROSPECTS: High occupancy levels, strong sales productivity, and improved re-leasing results are fueling earnings growth at the Company's retail centers. Meanwhile, improved operating profitability from RSE's office and other properties portfolio is being driven by increased rents, high occupancy levels, improved parking revenues and new buildings in Las Vegas, NV and Summerlin, MD. Going forward, results should benefit from an accelerated pace of development.

BUSINESS

THE ROUSE COMPANY operates more than 250 properties encompassing retail, office, research and development, hotel and industrial space in 22 states. RSE owns and/or operates 45 regional retail centers and 14 community centers, with more than 41.0 million square feet and including approximately 135 nationally known department stores and 7,000 small merchants. RSE also owns and/or operates five mixed-use projects and an additional 10.0 million square feet of office/industrial space, primarily located either in the Baltimore-Washington corridor or in Las Vegas, Nevada. RSE, through its affiliates, is the developer of the cities of Columbia, Maryland and Summerlin, Nevada.

ANNUAL FINANCIAL DATA

	12/31/00	12/31/99	12/31/98	12/31/97	12/31/96	12/31/95	12/31/94
Earnings Per Share	**[7] 2.21**	**[6] 1.77**	**[5] 1.34**	**[4] 2.59**	**[3] 0.14**	**[2] d0.18**	**[1] d0.14**
Cash Flow Per Share	**3.72**	**3.37**	**2.61**	**3.45**	**1.57**	**1.34**	**1.42**
Tang. Book Val. Per Share	**9.29**	**9.03**	**8.71**	**6.96**	**2.65**	**0.89**	**2.00**
Dividends Per Share	**1.32**	**1.20**	**1.12**	**1.00**	**0.88**	**0.80**	**0.68**
Dividend Payout %	**59.7**	**67.8**	**83.6**	**38.6**	**628.1**	**. . .**	**. . .**
INCOME STATEMENT (IN MILLIONS):							
Total Revenues	633.7	715.7	692.6	916.8	831.9	672.8	671.2
Costs & Expenses	300.7	338.4	358.4	535.8	472.1	350.9	362.1
Depreciation & Amort.	90.3	100.3	84.1	82.9	80.0	73.1	74.2
Operating Income	242.7	276.9	250.1	298.0	279.9	248.9	234.8
Net Interest Inc./(Exp.)	d236.7	d244.5	d209.6	d207.5	d220.4	d213.0	d213.6
Income Before Income Taxes	39.0	141.5	105.2	73.8	43.6	10.2	13.3
Income Taxes	0.3	0.3	. . .	cr116.1	25.7	4.3	6.7
Equity Earnings/Minority Int.	129.6	76.5	75.8	6.8	. . .	. . .	. . .
Net Income	[7] 168.3	[6] 141.2	[5] 105.2	[4] 189.9	[3] 17.9	[2] 5.9	[1] 6.6
Cash Flow	246.4	229.4	177.1	262.5	87.3	64.3	67.7
Average Shs. Outstg. (000)	69,475	71,705	67,874	76,005	55,572	47,814	47,565
BALANCE SHEET (IN MILLIONS):							
Cash & Cash Equivalents	37.6	49.2	42.0	90.7	47.4	97.8	79.5
Total Current Assets	82.2	110.4	117.9	205.0	139.7	134.6	110.8
Total Assets	4,175.5	4,427.2	5,154.6	3,589.8	3,643.5	2,985.6	2,915.9
Long-Term Obligations	3,045.8	3,334.4	4,068.5	2,684.1	2,895.4	2,538.3	2,532.9
Net Stockholders' Equity	630.5	638.6	628.9	465.5	177.1	42.6	95.0
Net Working Capital	82.2	110.4	117.9	205.0	139.7	134.6	110.8
Year-end Shs. Outstg. (000)	67,880	70,694	72,225	66,911	66,743	47,923	47,571
STATISTICAL RECORD:							
Operating Profit Margin %	38.3	38.7	36.1	32.5	33.6	37.0	35.0
Net Profit Margin %	26.6	19.7	15.2	20.7	2.1	0.9	1.0
Return on Equity %	26.7	22.1	16.7	40.8	10.1	13.7	7.0
Return on Assets %	4.0	3.2	2.0	5.3	0.5	0.2	0.2
Debt/Total Assets %	72.9	75.3	78.9	74.8	79.5	85.0	86.9
Price Range	27.13-20.13	27.75-19.75	35.69-23.13	33.00-25.75	32.25-18.25	22.63-17.63	20.00-16.25
P/E Ratio	12.3-9.1	15.7-11.2	26.6-17.3	12.7-9.9	230.2-130.3	. . .	. . .
Average Yield %	5.6	5.1	3.8	3.4	3.5	4.0	3.8

Statistics are as originally reported. [1] Bef. $4.4 mil extraord. chg. & incl. $7.9 mil non-recurr. chg. [2] Bef. $8.6 mil extraord. chg. & incl. $25.7 mil non-recurr. chg. [3] Bef. $1.5 mil extraord. chg. & incl. $15.9 mil non-recurr. chg. [4] Bef. $21.3 mil extraord. chg. and $1.2 mil acctg. chg. & incl. $23.5 mil non-recurr. chg. [5] Bef. $4.4 mil extraord. gain and $4.6 mil acctg. chg. & incl. $11.2 mil non-recurr. chg. [6] Bef. $5.9 mil extraord. chg. & incl. $32.6 mil non-recurr. gain [7] Bef. $2.2 mil extraord. gain & incl. $33.2 mil non-recurr. gain.

OFFICERS:
A. W. Deering, Chmn., Pres., C.E.O.
D. A. McGregor, Vice-Chmn., C.O.O.
J. H. Donahue, Exec. V.P., C.F.O.

INVESTOR CONTACT: David L. Tripp, (410) 992-6326

PRINCIPAL OFFICE: 10275 Little Patuxent Pkwy., Columbia, MD 21044-3456

TELEPHONE NUMBER: (410) 992-6000
FAX: (410) 992-6363
WEB: www.therousecompany.com

NO. OF EMPLOYEES: 3,749 (avg.)

SHAREHOLDERS: 2,409

ANNUAL MEETING: In May

INCORPORATED: MD, Oct., 1956

INSTITUTIONAL HOLDINGS:
No. of Institutions: 126
Shares Held: 50,223,059
% Held: 73.0

INDUSTRY: Nonresidential building operators (SIC: 6512)

TRANSFER AGENT(S): The Bank of New York, New York, NY

NYSE SYMBOL RDC
Rec. Pr. 29.93 (5/31/01)

ROWAN COMPANIES, INC.

YIELD	. . .
P/E RATIO	39.9

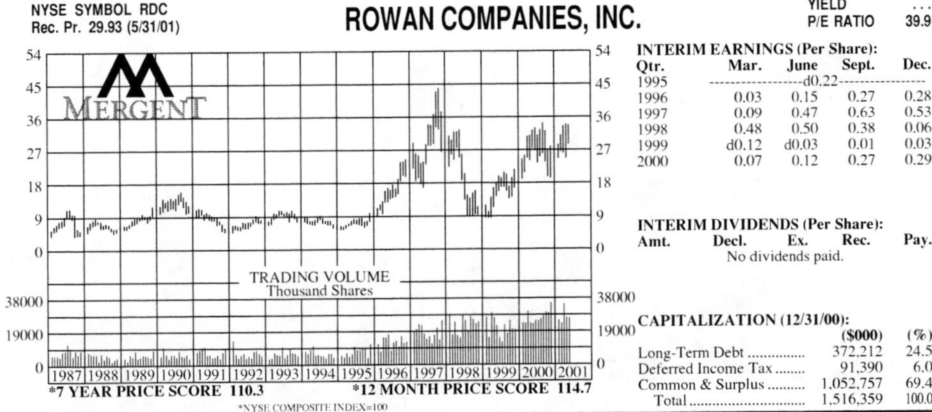

*7 YEAR PRICE SCORE 110.3 *12 MONTH PRICE SCORE 114.7
*NYSE COMPOSITE INDEX=100

INTERIM EARNINGS (Per Share):

Qtr.	Mar.	June	Sept.	Dec.
1995		d0.22		
1996	0.03	0.15	0.27	0.28
1997	0.09	0.47	0.63	0.53
1998	0.48	0.50	0.38	0.06
1999	d0.12	d0.03	0.01	0.03
2000	0.07	0.12	0.27	0.29

INTERIM DIVIDENDS (Per Share):

Amt.	Decl.	Ex.	Rec.	Pay.

No dividends paid.

CAPITALIZATION (12/31/00):

	($000)	(%)
Long-Term Debt	372,212	24.5
Deferred Income Tax	91,390	6.0
Common & Surplus	1,052,757	69.4
Total	1,516,359	100.0

RECENT DEVELOPMENTS: For the twelve months ended 12/31/00, net income was $70.2 million compared with a net loss of $9.7 million in the corresponding year-earlier period. Total revenues jumped 40.3% to $646.0 million from $460.6 million in 1999. Drilling services revenues surged 60.6% to $418.9 million, while manufacturing sales and services revenues advanced 8.3% to $103.5 million. Aviation services increased 18.7% to $123.5 million.

PROSPECTS: RDC's near-term outlook remains favorable, reflecting reactivation of the Company's land rig fleet and expectations of continued improvement in average day rates. Future results should benefit from the anticipated increase in worldwide exploration and production spending by oil and gas companies that is being driven by sharply higher natural gas prices and, to a lesser extent, improved crude oil prices.

BUSINESS

ROWAN COMPANIES, INC. provides international and domestic contract drilling and aviation services. Drilling operations are conducted through RDC's offshore mobile fleet of 21 self-elevating deep-water drilling platforms and 14 deep-well land rigs and one mobile offshore floating platform. Other operations are conducted through RDC's wholly-owned subsidiaries, LeTourneau, Inc., and Era Aviation, Inc. LeTourneau operates a mini-steel mill, a manufacturing facility that produces heavy equipment for mining, timber, and transportation industries, and a marine group that designs and builds mobile offshore jack-up drilling rigs. Era Aviation provides charter and contract helicopter and fixed-wing aircraft services, in Alaska, the coastal areas of Louisiana and Texas, and the western U.S.

REVENUES

(12/31/2000)	($000)	(%)
Drilling Services	418,948	64.9
Manufacturing & Services	103,465	16.0
Aviation Services	123,546	19.1
Total	645,959	100.0

ANNUAL FINANCIAL DATA

	12/31/00	12/31/99	12/31/98	12/31/97	12/31/96	12/31/95	12/31/94
Earnings Per Share	**0.74**	**d0.12**	**1.43**	**[1] 1.76**	**0.70**	**d0.22**	**d0.27**
Cash Flow Per Share	**1.33**	**0.50**	**1.96**	**2.24**	. . .	. . .	. . .
Tang. Book Val. Per Share	**11.17**	**8.69**	**8.77**	**7.53**	**5.80**	**4.97**	**5.25**
INCOME STATEMENT (IN MILLIONS):							
Total Revenues	646.0	460.6	706.4	695.3	571.2	471.3	438.2
Costs & Expenses	478.3	418.7	477.6	468.9	447.8	426.2	392.0
Depreciation & Amort.	56.1	51.5	46.5	43.9	44.7	47.4	47.6
Operating Income	111.6	d9.6	182.2	182.5	78.7	d2.3	d1.4
Net Interest Inc./(Exp.)	d1.2	d6.9	6.0	d11.1	d20.9	d22.5	d22.7
Income Before Income Taxes	110.9	d14.5	193.7	173.3	60.5	d17.7	d22.5
Income Taxes	40.7	cr4.9	69.2	16.9	cr0.8	0.8	0.5
Net Income	70.2	d9.7	124.5	[1] 156.4	61.3	d18.4	d23.0
Cash Flow	126.3	41.8	171.0	200.3	106.0	28.9	24.6
Average Shs. Outstg. (000)	94,637	83,176	87,289	89,223	. . .	. . .	. . .
BALANCE SHEET (IN MILLIONS):							
Cash & Cash Equivalents	192.8	87.1	148.8	108.3	97.2	90.3	111.1
Total Current Assets	483.4	325.1	365.7	412.4	317.3	273.5	253.7
Net Property	1,182.8	1,025.7	877.2	677.2	546.2	487.0	506.1
Total Assets	1,678.4	1,356.1	1,249.1	1,122.1	899.3	802.5	805.2
Total Current Liabilities	104.4	202.3	79.6	81.5	85.3	72.9	57.8
Long-Term Obligations	372.2	296.7	310.3	256.2	267.3	247.7	248.5
Net Stockholders' Equity	1,052.8	723.7	730.0	653.1	496.2	429.2	442.3
Net Working Capital	379.0	122.8	286.1	330.9	232.0	200.6	195.9
Year-end Shs. Outstg. (000)	94,235	83,302	83,247	86,704	85,597	86,354	84,280
STATISTICAL RECORD:							
Operating Profit Margin %	17.3	. . .	25.8	26.2	13.8	. . .	. . .
Net Profit Margin %	10.9	. . .	17.6	22.5	10.7	. . .	. . .
Return on Equity %	6.7	. . .	17.0	24.0	12.4	. . .	. . .
Return on Assets %	4.2	. . .	10.0	13.9	6.8	. . .	. . .
Debt/Total Assets %	22.2	21.9	24.8	22.8	29.7	30.9	30.9
Price Range	34.25-19.06	21.69-8.50	32.50-9.00	43.94-16.75	24.50-8.88	10.00-5.38	9.25-5.75
P/E Ratio	46.3-25.8	. . .	22.7-6.3	25.0-9.5	35.0-12.7	. . .	. . .

Statistics are as originally reported. [1] Bef. extraord. chrg. 12/31/97, $9.8 mill.

OFFICERS:
C. R. Palmer, Chmn., Pres., C.E.O.
E. E. Thiele, Sr. V.P., Treas.
M. H. Hay, Sec., Asst. Treas.

INVESTOR CONTACT: William C. Provine, Vice President, (713) 960-7575

PRINCIPAL OFFICE: 2800 Post Oak Blvd., Suite 5450, Houston, TX 77056-6127

TELEPHONE NUMBER: (713) 621-7800
FAX: (713) 960-7660
WEB: www.rowancompanies.com

NO. OF EMPLOYEES: 4,862

SHAREHOLDERS: 2,400 (approx.)

ANNUAL MEETING: In Apr.

INCORPORATED: DE, Dec., 1947

INSTITUTIONAL HOLDINGS:
No. of Institutions: 246
Shares Held: 70,431,242
% Held: 74.7

INDUSTRY: Drilling oil and gas wells (SIC: 1381)

TRANSFER AGENT(S): Computershare Investor Services LLC, Chicago, IL

NYSE SYMBOL RD
Rec. Pr. 60.98 (5/31/01)

ROYAL DUTCH PETROLEUM COMPANY

YIELD ...
P/E RATIO 17.1

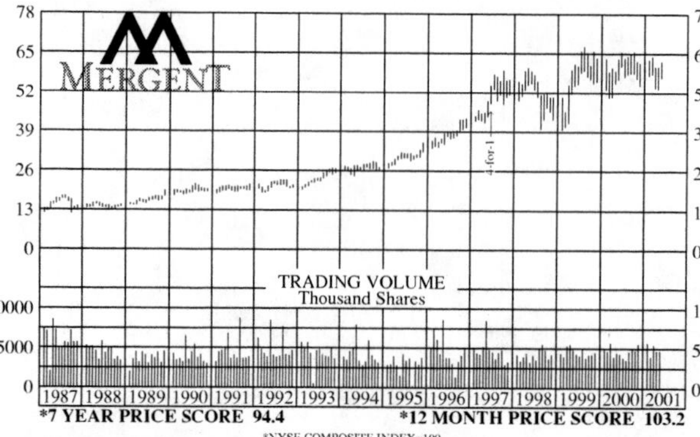

*7 YEAR PRICE SCORE 94.4 *12 MONTH PRICE SCORE 103.2

*NYSE COMPOSITE INDEX=100

INTERIM EARNINGS (Per Share):

Qtr.	Mar.	June	Sept.	Dec.
1996	0.79	0.54	0.62	0.74
1997	0.68	0.51	0.61	0.51
1998	0.47	0.42	0.25	d1.01
1999	0.47	0.54	0.67	0.72
2000	0.93	0.90	0.86	0.87

INTERIM DIVIDENDS (Per Share):

Amt.	Decl.	Ex.	Rec.	Pay.
0.70	...	8/06/99	8/10/99	9/29/99
0.77	...	5/10/00	5/12/00	5/26/00
0.60	...	8/04/00	8/08/00	9/20/00
0.81	...	5/18/01	5/22/01	6/06/01

CAPITALIZATION (12/31/00):

	($000)	(%)
Long-Term Debt	4,070,000	6.4
Minority Interest	2,881,000	4.5
Common & Surplus	57,086,000	89.1
Total	64,037,000	100.0

RECENT DEVELOPMENTS: For the year ended 12/31/00, the Group's net income increased 48.2% to $12.72 billion versus $8.58 billion a year earlier. Sales advanced 27.9% to $191.51 billion. Results were driven by the exploration and production segment, where operating earnings soared to $9.88 billion from $4.52 billion a year ago, due to higher oil and gas prices, higher gas volumes and lower operating expenses.

PROSPECTS: Prospects appear positive, supported by the Group's aggressive cost improvement goals. According to the Group, the cost improvement target for 2001 (relative to a 1998 baseline), which was increased to $4.00 billion in December 1999, has been attained a full year ahead of schedule. The new cost improvement target of $5.00 billion for 2001 was announced in December 2000.

BUSINESS

ROYAL DUTCH PETROLEUM COMPANY holds a 60.0% interest in the investments of numerous companies collectively known as the Royal Dutch/Shell Group. The companies engage in the exploration, production and marketing of oil and natural gas through five business segments: Exploration and Production, Oil Products, Chemicals, Downstream Gas and Power, and Renewables. The Group operates in more than 135 countries through a network of 46,000 service stations, which serve approximately 20.0 million customers daily. Sales in 2000 were derived as follows: oil and gas, 91.5%; chemicals, 8.2%; and other, 0.3%.

ANNUAL FINANCIAL DATA

	12/31/00	12/31/99	12/31/98	12/31/97	12/31/96	12/31/95	12/31/94
Earnings Per Share	**3.56**	**2.41**	**0.13**	**2.30**	**2.66**	**2.04**	**1.84**
Tang. Book Val. Per Share	**15.50**	**14.98**	**14.65**	**10.20**	**10.40**	**10.63**	**10.07**
Dividends Per Share	**1.37**	**1.60**	**1.61**	**1.35**	**1.23**	**1.16**	**1.03**
Dividend Payout %	**38.5**	**66.4**	**N.M.**	**58.7**	**46.2**	**56.9**	**56.0**
INCOME STATEMENT (IN MILLIONS):							
Total Revenues	191,511.0	149,706.0	138,274.0	175,891.2	186,452.6	148,232.3	131,956.1
Costs & Expenses	170,870.0	136,795.0	134,414.0	161,727.2	169,961.7	137,813.2	123,782.1
Operating Income	20,641.0	12,911.0	3,860.0	14,164.0	16,490.9	10,419.1	8,174.0
Net Interest Inc./(Exp.)	d1,324.0	d1,253.0	d1,333.0	d371.0	d308.4	d310.6	d424.1
Income Before Income Taxes	24,036.0	14,521.0	2,405.0	15,609.5	18,414.1	12,386.7	10,371.3
Income Taxes	11,273.0	5,696.0	1,913.0	7,613.4	8,481.0	5,412.2	3,884.3
Equity Earnings/Minority Int.	d44.0	d241.0	d142.0	d45.3	d289.8	d180.1	d117.4
Net Income	12,719.0	8,584.0	350.0	7,950.8	9,643.4	6,794.4	6,369.6
BALANCE SHEET (IN MILLIONS):							
Cash & Cash Equivalents	11,435.0	4,051.0	2,736.0	5,242.9	12,339.3	11,391.3	11,637.3
Total Current Assets	45,930.0	30,392.0	22,599.0	33,889.9	43,128.4	39,070.4	36,004.4
Net Property	47,314.0	59,239.0	60,777.0	66,446.9	71,309.6	69,454.8	63,329.3
Total Assets	122,498.0	116,524.0	110,068.0	116,084.0	124,117.0	117,973.6	108,196.3
Total Current Liabilities	42,698.0	33,463.0	31,140.0	30,134.5	33,085.1	31,657.9	28,193.5
Long-Term Obligations	4,070.0	6,009.0	6,032.0	5,889.2	6,123.9	7,372.1	5,972.0
Net Stockholders' Equity	57,086.0	56,171.0	54,962.0	61,195.6	62,996.4	58,967.4	56,321.2
Net Working Capital	3,232.0	d3,071.0	d8,541.0	3,755.5	10,043.3	7,412.5	7,810.9
Year-end Shs. Outstg. (000)	2,114,296	2,144,296	2,144,000	2,144,000	2,144,000	2,144,000	2,144,000
STATISTICAL RECORD:							
Operating Profit Margin %	10.8	8.6	2.8	8.1	8.8	7.0	6.2
Net Profit Margin %	6.6	5.7	0.3	4.5	5.2	4.6	4.8
Return on Equity %	22.3	15.3	0.6	13.0	15.3	11.5	11.3
Return on Assets %	10.4	7.4	0.3	6.8	7.8	5.8	5.9
Debt/Total Assets %	3.3	5.2	5.5	5.1	4.9	6.2	5.5
Price Range	65.69-50.44	67.38-39.56	60.38-39.75	59.44-42.00	43.47-33.41	35.44-26.81	29.19-24.22
P/E Ratio	18.5-14.2	28.0-16.4	464.1-305.5	25.8-18.3	16.3-12.6	17.4-13.1	15.9-13.2
Average Yield %	2.4	3.0	3.2	2.7	3.2	3.7	3.9

Statistics are as originally reported. US$; Figures are for the Royal Dutch/Shell Group of Companies (60.0% owned by the Company) except per sh. figs., which refl. Royal Dutch Petroleum Co. Adj. for 4-for-1 stk. split, 6/97.

OFFICERS:
L. van Wachem, Chmn.
J. van der Veer, Pres.

INVESTOR CONTACT: D. Sexton, (212) 218-3113

PRINCIPAL OFFICE: GSDF Division, 630 Fifth Avenue, Suite 1970 New York, NY 10111

TELEPHONE NUMBER: (212) 218-3113
WEB: www.shell.com

NO. OF EMPLOYEES: 90,000 (avg.)

SHAREHOLDERS: 740,000

ANNUAL MEETING: In May

INCORPORATED: NLD, June, 1890

INSTITUTIONAL HOLDINGS:
No. of Institutions: 787
Shares Held: 559,518,854
% Held: 26.1

INDUSTRY: Crude petroleum and natural gas (SIC: 1311)

TRANSFER AGENT(S): J.P. Morgan Service Center, Boston, MA

NYSE SYMBOL RPM
Rec. Pr. 8.26 (5/31/01)

RPM, INC.

YIELD 6.1%
P/E RATIO 17.6

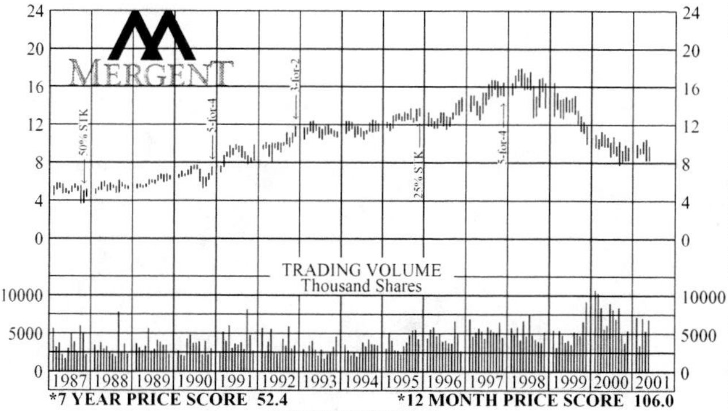

*7 YEAR PRICE SCORE 52.4 *12 MONTH PRICE SCORE 106.0

*NYSE COMPOSITE INDEX=100

INTERIM EARNINGS (Per Share):

Qtr.	Aug.	Nov.	Feb.	May
1996-97	0.25	0.19	0.08	0.29
1997-98	0.29	0.22	0.06	0.33
1998-99	0.29	0.20	0.06	0.32
1999-00	0.07	0.19	0.04	0.09
2000-01	0.28	0.17	d0.07	...

INTERIM DIVIDENDS (Per Share):

Amt.	Decl.	Ex.	Rec.	Pay.
0.122Q	4/03/00	4/12/00	4/14/00	4/28/00
0.122Q	7/05/00	7/13/00	7/17/00	7/28/00
0.125Q	10/12/00	10/19/00	10/23/00	10/31/00
0.125Q	1/05/01	1/10/01	1/15/01	1/31/01
0.125Q	4/02/01	4/10/01	4/13/01	4/30/01

Indicated div.: $0.50 (Div. Reinv. Plan)

CAPITALIZATION (5/31/00):

	($000)	(%)
Long-Term Debt	959,330	57.6
Deferred Income Tax	60,566	3.6
Common & Surplus	645,724	38.8
Total	1,665,620	100.0

RECENT DEVELOPMENTS: For the quarter ended 2/28/01, RPM reported a net loss of $7.0 million compared with net income of $3.7 million in the equivalent 2000 quarter. Earnings were adversely affected by the generally soft retail environment and high costs involved with the restructuring of RPM's Wood Finishes Group. Net sales were $403.7 million, down 1.9% from $411.4 million a year earlier. The decline in sales was primarily attributed to extremely cold temperatures.

PROSPECTS: RPM anticipates fiscal year results will be in the range of the consensus of earnings estimates. However, the weak economy has caused many project delays. The Company anticipates that the overall fiscal year earnings will likely fall below the $0.73 per diluted share pre-restructuring charges reported last year. In addition, RPM continues to encounter difficulties in the last major component of its restructuring program, which is the consolidation of RPM's Wood Finishes Group.

BUSINESS

RPM, INC. is a widely-diversified manufacturer of protective coatings, with manufacturing facilities in the United States, Argentina, Belgium, Brazil, Canada, China, Colombia, Germany, Italy, Malaysia, Mexico, New Zealand, the Netherlands, Poland, South Africa, the United Arab Emirates and the United Kingdom. RPM participates in two broad market categories worldwide: industrial and consumer. As of 5/31/00, approximately 55.0% of RPM's sales were derived from the industrial market sectors, with the remainder in consumer products. RPM industrial division consists of the StonCor Group, Tremco Group and RPM II Group product lines. The major product line groupings comprising RPM's consumer division include the Rust-Oleum Group, Zinsser Group, Wood Finishes Group, DAP/Bondex Group and Testor Hobby and Leisure Group. On 8/31/99, RPM acquired DAP Products Inc. and DAP Canada Corp.

ANNUAL FINANCIAL DATA

	5/31/00	5/31/99	5/31/98	5/31/97	5/31/96	5/31/95	5/31/94
Earnings Per Share	**[1] 0.38**	**0.86**	**0.84**	**0.80**	**0.72**	**0.86**	**0.74**
Cash Flow Per Share	**1.12**	**1.41**	**1.30**	**1.32**	**1.17**	**1.37**	**1.11**
Tang. Book Val. Per Share	**...**	**0.77**	**...**	**...**	**0.18**	**0.71**	**2.50**
Dividends Per Share	**0.47**	**0.45**	**0.42**	**0.39**	**0.36**	**0.34**	**0.31**
Dividend Payout %	**125.0**	**52.7**	**50.5**	**49.0**	**50.7**	**39.6**	**42.1**
INCOME STATEMENT (IN MILLIONS):							
Total Revenues	1,954.1	1,712.2	1,615.3	1,350.5	1,136.4	1,017.0	815.6
Costs & Expenses	1,699.5	1,457.6	1,372.0	1,131.1	948.1	849.7	688.2
Depreciation & Amort.	79.2	62.1	57.0	51.1	42.6	36.9	25.9
Operating Income	175.5	192.4	186.3	168.3	145.7	130.3	101.5
Net Interest Inc./(Exp.)	d51.8	d32.8	d36.7	d32.6	d25.8	d23.4	d13.4
Income Before Income Taxes	71.8	159.6	149.6	135.7	119.9	106.9	88.1
Income Taxes	30.8	65.1	61.7	57.4	51.0	45.8	35.5
Net Income	[1] 41.0	94.5	87.8	78.3	68.9	61.1	52.6
Cash Flow	120.1	156.7	144.8	129.5	111.5	98.0	78.5
Average Shs. Outstg. (000)	107,384	111,376	111,663	97,894	95,685	71,554	70,896
BALANCE SHEET (IN MILLIONS):							
Cash & Cash Equivalents	31.3	19.7	40.8	37.4	34.3	28.0	25.4
Total Current Assets	785.1	705.4	672.5	720.3	465.1	421.3	334.5
Net Property	366.2	339.7	305.9	270.3	224.7	204.0	151.0
Total Assets	2,099.2	1,737.2	1,683.3	1,633.2	1,155.1	959.1	660.8
Total Current Liabilities	376.2	302.5	285.8	241.8	189.4	151.1	104.0
Long-Term Obligations	959.3	582.1	715.7	784.4	447.7	406.4	233.0
Net Stockholders' Equity	645.7	742.9	567.1	493.3	445.8	347.6	314.5
Net Working Capital	408.9	402.9	386.7	478.5	275.7	270.2	230.5
Year-end Shs. Outstg. (000)	103,134	109,443	100,254	98,029	96,811	71,196	70,939
STATISTICAL RECORD:							
Operating Profit Margin %	9.0	11.2	11.5	12.5	12.8	12.8	12.4
Net Profit Margin %	2.1	5.5	5.4	5.8	6.1	6.0	6.5
Return on Equity %	6.3	12.7	15.5	15.9	15.5	17.6	16.7
Return on Assets %	2.0	5.4	5.2	4.8	6.0	6.4	8.0
Debt/Total Assets %	45.7	33.5	42.5	48.0	38.8	42.4	35.3
Price Range	16.50-9.94	18.00-12.75	16.80-12.50	14.90-11.50	13.80-11.36	12.56-10.40	12.40-10.40
P/E Ratio	43.4-26.1	20.9-14.8	20.0-14.9	18.6-14.4	19.2-15.8	14.7-12.1	16.7-14.0
Average Yield %	3.6	2.9	2.9	3.0	2.9	3.0	2.8

Statistics are as originally reported. Adj. for stk. splits: 5-for-4, 12/8/97; 25% div., 12/8/95. [1] Incl. restruct. chrg. of $45.0 mill.

OFFICERS:
T. C. Sullivan, Chmn., C.E.O.
J. A. Karman, Vice-Chmn., C.F.O.
F. C. Sullivan, Pres.

INVESTOR CONTACT: Investor Relations, (330) 273-5090

PRINCIPAL OFFICE: 2628 Pearl Road, P.O. Box 777, Medina, OH 44258

TELEPHONE NUMBER: (330) 273-5090
FAX: (330) 225-8743
WEB: www.rpminc.com

NO. OF EMPLOYEES: 7,960 (avg.)

SHAREHOLDERS: 44,163 (approx. record)

ANNUAL MEETING: In Oct.

INCORPORATED: OH, May, 1947

INSTITUTIONAL HOLDINGS:
No. of Institutions: 185
Shares Held: 53,459,161
% Held: 52.3

INDUSTRY: Paints and allied products (SIC: 2851)

TRANSFER AGENT(S): Computershare Investor Services, Chicago, IL

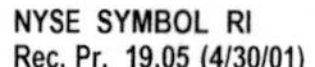

NYSE SYMBOL RI
Rec. Pr. 19.05 (4/30/01)

RUBY TUESDAY, INC.

YIELD 0.2%
P/E RATIO 28.9

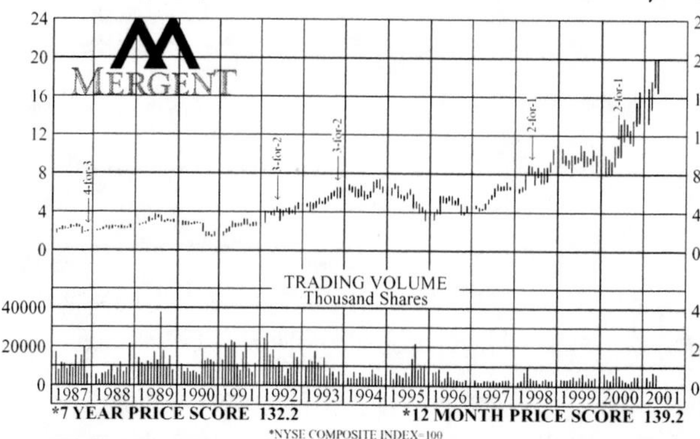

*7 YEAR PRICE SCORE 132.2 *12 MONTH PRICE SCORE 139.2
*NYSE COMPOSITE INDEX=100

INTERIM EARNINGS (Per Share):

Qtr.	Aug.	Nov.	Feb.	May
1996-97	0.08	0.06	0.12	0.11
1997-98	0.09	0.07	0.07	0.07
1998-99	0.12	0.10	0.18	0.16
1999-00	0.16	0.13	0.22	0.07
2000-01	0.20	0.17	...	...

INTERIM DIVIDENDS (Per Share):

Amt.	Decl.	Ex.	Rec.	Pay.
0.045S	7/01/99	7/14/99	7/16/99	7/30/99
0.045S	1/12/00	1/26/00	1/28/00	2/11/00
2-for-1	4/11/00	5/22/00	4/28/00	5/19/00
0.022S	7/10/00	7/20/00	7/24/00	8/07/00
0.022S	1/08/01	1/24/01	1/26/01	2/09/01

Indicated div.: $0.04

CAPITALIZATION (6/4/00):

	($000)	(%)
Long-Term Debt	636	0.3
Common & Surplus	229,824	99.7
Total	230,460	100.0

RECENT DEVELOPMENTS: For the thirteen weeks ended 12/3/00, net income rose 30.2% to $11.0 million versus $8.4 million in the comparable prior-year period. Total operating costs and expenses as a percentage of total operating revenues declined to 91.3% from 93.0% in fiscal 2000. Total operating revenues improved 1.5% to $196.7 million versus $193.8 million a year earlier. Company restaurant revenues inched up 1.0% to $193.9 million, while franchise income jumped 65.2% to $66.1 million.

PROSPECTS: The Company is benefiting from investments made over the last four years in its teams, training and facilities, including the managing partner program and domestic franchise program. The managing partner program, which has been implemented in more than 55.0% of RI's restaurants, continues to produce strong revenues and profits. RI plans to open 20 Company-owned Ruby Tuesday® restaurants and 15 domestic and international franchisees restaurants in fiscal 2001.

BUSINESS

RUBY TUESDAY INC. (formerly Morrison Restaurants Inc.) owns and operates 350 full-service, casual restaurants under the name Ruby Tuesday®. The restaurants are located primarily in the southeast, northeast, mid-Atlantic and midwest regions of the United States. Ruby Tuesday® restaurants offer a variety of entrees and sandwiches in the price range of $5.49 to $15.99. In addition, the Company franchises Ruby Tuesday® restaurants to domestic and international franchise partners. On 11/20/00, the Company sold its American Cafe® and Tia's® restaurant divisions for about $59.0 million.

QUARTERLY DATA

(06/04/00) ($000)	Rev	Inc
1st Quarter	195,285	10,300
2nd Quarter	193,779	8,432
3rd Quarter	209,222	13,730
4th Quarter	199,209	4,708

ANNUAL FINANCIAL DATA

	6/4/00	6/6/99	6/6/98	5/31/97	[2] 6/1/96	6/3/95	6/4/94
Earnings Per Share	[3] **0.57**	**0.54**	**0.42**	**0.35**	[1] **d0.01**	**0.87**	**0.60**
Cash Flow Per Share	**1.22**	**1.13**	**1.00**	**0.90**	**0.48**	**0.77**	**1.14**
Tang. Book Val. Per Share	**3.59**	**3.17**	**2.93**	**2.89**	**2.52**	**3.16**	**2.81**
Dividends Per Share	**0.04**	**0.04**	...	**0.02**	**0.09**	**0.08**	**0.08**
Dividend Payout %	**7.9**	**8.3**	...	**6.6**	...	**9.8**	**13.5**
INCOME STATEMENT (IN MILLIONS):							
Total Revenues	797.5	722.3	711.4	655.4	620.1	1,035.1	1,213.4
Costs & Expenses	680.7	622.2	622.4	573.4	557.1	916.6	1,101.4
Depreciation & Amort.	42.6	40.1	40.2	39.3	34.8	39.9	40.8
Operating Income	74.2	60.1	48.8	42.7	28.2	78.6	71.2
Net Interest Inc./(Exp.)	d1.4	d2.9	d3.8	d3.9	d4.6	d0.9	d0.1
Income Before Income Taxes	62.8	57.2	45.0	38.8	d2.3	104.7	71.2
Income Taxes	26.2	20.7	16.0	13.8	cr1.7	42.5	26.5
Net Income	[3] 36.5	36.5	29.1	25.0	[1] d0.7	15.4	44.7
Cash Flow	79.1	76.6	69.3	64.3	34.2	55.3	85.5
Average Shs. Outstg. (000)	64,576	67,528	69,140	71,500	70,756	71,844	74,736
BALANCE SHEET (IN MILLIONS):							
Cash & Cash Equivalents	10.2	9.1	8.3	7.6	7.1	8.3	5.0
Total Current Assets	94.5	52.2	46.9	35.5	33.3	80.2	79.6
Net Property	281.9	317.5	310.4	346.8	313.5	345.2	267.7
Total Assets	439.2	430.8	409.6	418.9	381.1	484.1	408.5
Total Current Liabilities	151.8	84.2	84.4	69.1	66.6	125.0	122.6
Long-Term Obligations	0.6	76.8	65.9	78.0	76.1	52.1	9.5
Net Stockholders' Equity	229.8	221.8	212.2	223.6	197.3	245.5	221.1
Net Working Capital	d57.3	d31.9	d37.6	d33.6	d33.3	d44.8	d43.0
Year-end Shs. Outstg. (000)	61,719	64,034	65,574	70,372	69,856	69,052	70,620
STATISTICAL RECORD:							
Operating Profit Margin %	9.3	8.3	6.9	6.5	4.5	7.6	5.9
Net Profit Margin %	4.6	5.1	4.1	3.8	...	1.5	3.7
Return on Equity %	15.9	16.5	13.7	11.2	...	6.3	20.2
Return on Assets %	8.3	8.5	7.1	6.0	...	3.2	10.9
Debt/Total Assets %	0.1	17.8	16.1	18.6	20.0	10.8	2.3
Price Range	11.03-8.16	10.63-6.03	7.16-4.16	5.75-3.19	6.97-3.13	7.44-5.22	6.56-3.96
P/E Ratio	19.4-14.3	19.7-11.2	17.0-9.9	16.4-9.1	...	8.6-6.0	10.9-6.6
Average Yield %	0.5	0.5	...	0.5	1.8	1.3	1.5

Statistics are as originally reported. Adj. for stk. splits: 2-for-1, 5/00, 5/98. [1] Bef. disc. oper. loss, $2.2 mill. & incl. non-recurr. chrg. $5.3 mill. [2] On 3/9/96, the Company was spun off from Morrisons Restaurants Inc. [3] Incl. a net loss of $10.1 mill. ($0.15/sh.) related to the sale of American Cafe® and Tia's® Tex Mex restaurants.

OFFICERS:
S. E. Beall III, Chmn., C.E.O.
R. D. McClenagan, Pres.
J. R. Mothershed, Sr. V.P., C.F.O.

INVESTOR CONTACT: Price Cooper, Dir., Inv. Rel. & Planning, (865) 379-5700

PRINCIPAL OFFICE: 150 West Church Ave., Maryville, TN 37801

TELEPHONE NUMBER: (865) 379-5700
FAX: (865) 379-6817
WEB: www.ruby-tuesday.com
NO. OF EMPLOYEES: 8,500 full-time (approx.); 19,900 part-time (approx.)
SHAREHOLDERS: 5,600 (approx. record)
ANNUAL MEETING: In Oct.
INCORPORATED: LA, July, 1928; reincorp., GA, Mar., 1996

INSTITUTIONAL HOLDINGS:
No. of Institutions: 171
Shares Held: 50,484,265
% Held: 78.7

INDUSTRY: Eating places (SIC: 5812)

TRANSFER AGENT(S): AmSouth Bank of Alabama, Birmingham, AL

NYSE SYMBOL RDK
Rec. Pr. 15.08 (5/31/01)

RUDDICK CORPORATION

YIELD 2.4%
P/E RATIO 14.2

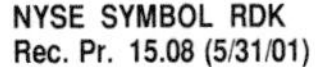

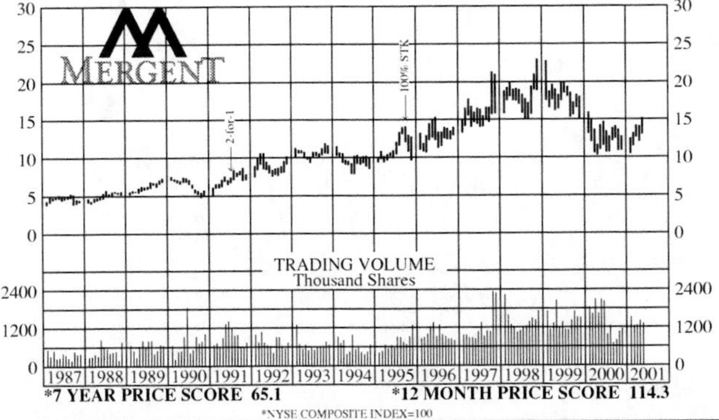

*7 YEAR PRICE SCORE 65.1 *12 MONTH PRICE SCORE 114.3

*NYSE COMPOSITE INDEX=100

INTERIM EARNINGS (Per Share):

Qtr.	Dec.	Mar.	June	Sept.
1996-97	0.25	0.24	0.28	0.25
1997-98	0.26	0.24	0.22	0.28
1998-99	0.27	0.27	0.26	0.28
1999-00	0.29	0.29	0.27	0.26
2000-01	0.24	...	...	...

INTERIM DIVIDENDS (Per Share):

Amt.	Decl.	Ex.	Rec.	Pay.
0.09Q	8/17/00	9/06/00	9/08/00	10/01/00
0.09Q	11/16/00	12/06/00	12/08/00	1/01/01
0.09Q	2/15/01	3/07/01	3/09/01	4/01/01
0.09Q	5/17/01	6/06/01	6/08/01	7/01/01

Indicated div.: $0.36 (Div. Reinv. Plan)

CAPITALIZATION (10/1/00):

	($000)	(%)
Long-Term Debt	224,996	29.5
Deferred Income Tax	56,544	7.4
Minority Interest	8,458	1.1
Common & Surplus	473,005	62.0
Total	763,003	100.0

RECENT DEVELOPMENTS: For the quarter ended 12/31/00, net income slipped 16.2% to $11.2 million from $13.4 million in 1999. Net sales rose 7.4% to $715.0 million from $665.5 million a year earlier. Harris Teeter's net sales grew 8.5% to $632.9 million, while comparable-store sales increased 2.5% year over year. American & Efird's net sales fell slightly to $82.0 million from $82.2 million in 1999. Gross profit was $193.9 million, or 27.1% of net sales, versus $188.3 million, or 28.3% of net sales, the previous year. Operating profit slid 10.1% to $24.7 million.

PROSPECTS: Going forward, earnings may benefit from an expanded selection of higher-margin, private-label products at RDK's Harris Teeter grocery stores. In addition, Harris Teeter plans to reduce capital expenditures going forward and sharpen its focus on new store growth opportunities in its core markets. Meanwhile, operating profitability at American & Efird is being dampened by competitive pricing pressures, reduced manufacturing schedules, a lower sales mix of higher-margin products, and increased expenses for utilities, freight, labor and health benefits.

BUSINESS

RUDDICK CORPORATION is a diversified holding company that is engaged in two primary businesses. Harris Teeter, Inc. operates a chain of 160 supermarkets in North Carolina, South Carolina, Virginia, Georgia, Tennessee, and Florida. American & Efird, Inc. manufactures and distributes industrial and consumer sewing thread and sales yarn. The Company was created through the consolidation of the predecessor companies of American & Efird and Ruddick Investment Company. In 1969, Ruddick acquired Harris Teeter. Sales (and operating profit) in fiscal 2000 were derived as follows: Harris Teeter, 87.0% (55.5%) and American & Efird, 13.0% (44.5%).

ANNUAL FINANCIAL DATA

	10/1/00	10/3/99	9/27/98	9/28/97	9/29/96	10/1/95	10/2/94
Earnings Per Share	**1.10**	**1.08**	**1.00**	**1.02**	**[1] 0.92**	**0.84**	**0.67**
Cash Flow Per Share	**2.76**	**2.60**	**2.41**	**2.29**	**2.03**	**1.78**	**1.52**
Tang. Book Val. Per Share	**10.23**	**9.55**	**8.82**	**8.17**	**7.47**	**6.82**	**6.28**
Dividends Per Share	**0.36**	**0.33**	**0.32**	**0.32**	**0.26**	**0.25**	**0.22**
Dividend Payout %	**32.7**	**30.6**	**32.0**	**31.4**	**28.3**	**29.8**	**32.8**
INCOME STATEMENT (IN MILLIONS):							
Total Revenues	2,682.8	2,624.8	2,487.4	2,300.1	2,142.5	2,070.8	1,908.4
Costs & Expenses	2,499.2	2,450.1	2,327.0	2,146.5	2,008.1	1,949.5	1,804.5
Depreciation & Amort.	77.0	70.6	66.2	58.7	51.2	43.4	40.0
Operating Income	106.6	104.1	94.2	94.8	83.1	77.9	64.0
Net Interest Inc./(Exp.)	d15.5	d14.7	d16.0	d14.6	d12.2	d10.5	d8.3
Income Before Income Taxes	84.4	81.4	70.7	71.3	62.0	59.3	50.1
Income Taxes	33.4	30.7	23.9	23.6	19.2	20.0	18.3
Net Income	51.0	50.7	46.8	47.7	[1] 42.8	39.3	31.8
Cash Flow	128.0	121.3	113.0	106.5	94.0	82.7	71.7
Average Shs. Outstg. (000)	46,350	46,747	46,964	46,549	46,420	46,536	47,193
BALANCE SHEET (IN MILLIONS):							
Cash & Cash Equivalents	9.5	14.5	16.7	17.2	21.0	19.0	14.5
Total Current Assets	363.2	358.9	332.8	323.3	298.5	299.1	276.6
Net Property	580.5	539.6	513.8	466.6	410.6	351.3	299.7
Total Assets	1,021.0	970.1	931.6	885.2	801.7	721.9	640.8
Total Current Liabilities	230.4	238.9	245.4	234.4	233.3	231.2	190.4
Long-Term Obligations	225.0	198.5	191.4	189.9	159.2	120.0	104.2
Net Stockholders' Equity	473.0	443.7	410.7	380.5	346.9	316.2	291.2
Net Working Capital	132.9	120.0	87.3	88.9	65.1	67.9	86.2
Year-end Shs. Outstg. (000)	46,221	46,451	46,555	46,599	46,461	46,374	46,352
STATISTICAL RECORD:							
Operating Profit Margin %	4.0	4.0	3.8	4.1	3.9	3.8	3.4
Net Profit Margin %	1.9	1.9	1.9	2.1	2.0	1.9	1.7
Return on Equity %	10.8	11.4	11.4	12.5	12.3	12.4	10.9
Return on Assets %	5.0	5.2	5.0	5.4	5.3	5.4	5.0
Debt/Total Assets %	22.0	20.5	20.5	21.5	19.9	16.6	16.3
Price Range	15.94-10.25	22.75-15.13	23.00-15.00	21.38-13.25	15.38-10.63	14.13-9.38	11.50-7.81
P/E Ratio	14.5-9.3	21.1-14.0	23.0-15.0	21.0-13.0	16.7-11.5	16.8-11.2	17.2-11.7
Average Yield %	2.7	1.7	1.7	1.8	2.0	2.1	2.2

Statistics are as originally reported. Adj. for 100% stk. div., 10/95. [1] Bef. $76,000 of income from discont. opers.

OFFICERS:
A. T. Dickson, Chmn.
T. W. Dickson, Pres.
D. A. Stephenson, V.P., Treas.

INVESTOR CONTACT: Katherine W. Kenny, V.P., Inv. Rel., (704) 372-5404

PRINCIPAL OFFICE: 301 S. Tryon St., Suite 1800, Charlotte, NC 28202

TELEPHONE NUMBER: (704) 372-5404
FAX: (704) 372-6409
WEB: www.ruddickcorp.com

NO. OF EMPLOYEES: 20,025 (avg.)

SHAREHOLDERS: 6,235

ANNUAL MEETING: In Feb.

INCORPORATED: NC, Oct., 1968

INSTITUTIONAL HOLDINGS:
No. of Institutions: 105
Shares Held: 18,824,369
% Held: 40.7

INDUSTRY: Grocery stores (SIC: 5411)

TRANSFER AGENT(S): First Union National Bank, Charlotte, NC

NYSE SYMBOL RUS
Rec. Pr. 26.75 (5/31/01)

RUSS BERRIE & COMPANY, INC.

YIELD 3.6%
P/E RATIO 11.3

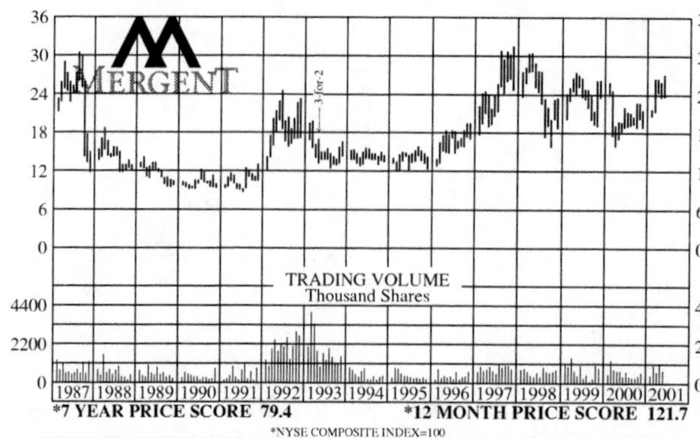

*7 YEAR PRICE SCORE 79.4 *12 MONTH PRICE SCORE 121.7
*NYSE COMPOSITE INDEX=100

INTERIM EARNINGS (Per Share):

Qtr.	Mar.	June	Sept.	Dec.
1997	0.29	0.22	0.73	0.45
1998	0.44	0.18	0.73	0.46
1999	0.53	0.19	0.88	0.11
2000	0.57	0.24	1.02	0.53

INTERIM DIVIDENDS (Per Share):

Amt.	Decl.	Ex.	Rec.	Pay.
0.22Q	5/09/00	5/22/00	5/24/00	6/07/00
0.22Q	7/26/00	8/16/00	8/18/00	9/01/00
0.22Q	10/24/00	11/15/00	11/17/00	12/01/00
0.24Q	2/08/01	3/07/01	3/09/01	3/23/01
0.24Q	4/26/01	5/23/01	5/25/01	6/08/01

Indicated div.: $0.96

CAPITALIZATION (12/31/00):

	($000)	(%)
Common & Surplus	334,591	100.0
Total	334,591	100.0

RECENT DEVELOPMENTS: For the year ended 12/31/00, net income jumped 31.6% to $47.9 million compared with $36.4 million in 1999. Results in 2000 included an after-tax gain of $591,000 for the reversal of certain contingency reserves related to RUS' sale of its toy business segment. The 1999 results included an after-tax information system write-off of $6.6 million. Net sales rose 4.8% to $300.8 million from $287.0 million the year before.

PROSPECTS: The Company announced the grand opening of a showroom in Miami, Florida that encompasses 2,500 square feet at the Miami International Merchandise Mart. The new show room is expected to further more growth both for RUS and for the mart in 2001 and beyond. Going forward, the Company believes that its 2001 results will reflect low double-digit revenue and net income growth.

BUSINESS

RUSS BERRIE & COMPANY, INC. designs, manufactures through third parties, and markets a wide variety of gift products to retail stores throughout the U.S. and most countries throughout the world. RUS's product line of approximately 6,000 items are marketed under the trade name and trademark RUSS®. Products include heirloom bears, stuffed animals, candles, figurines and home decor gifts based on current fashions and trends. The Company maintains product depth in categories such as Birthday, Anniversaries, Over-The-Hill, Fun 'N Games, Gifted Moments, Inspirational Gifts, Lifestyles, Home Styles, Gentlemen's Gifts, Collectibles and Baby Products. Extensive seasonal lines include products for all the major holidays.

QUARTERLY DATA

(12/31/2000) ($000)	REV	INC
First Quarter	78,279	11,839
Second Quarter	57,574	4,963
Third Quarter	97,251	20,546
Fourth Quarter	67,697	10,593

ANNUAL FINANCIAL DATA

	12/31/00	12/31/99	12/31/98	12/31/97	12/31/96	12/31/95	12/31/94
Earnings Per Share	[5] **2.37**	[4] **1.72**	[3] **1.81**	[2] **1.67**	[1] **1.23**	**0.77**	**0.25**
Cash Flow Per Share	**2.56**	**1.95**	**1.93**	**1.80**	**1.39**	**1.10**	**0.57**
Tang. Book Val. Per Share	**16.85**	**15.53**	**15.46**	**14.35**	**11.37**	**8.77**	**8.49**
Dividends Per Share	**0.88**	**0.80**	**0.76**	**0.68**	**0.60**	**0.60**	**0.60**
Dividend Payout %	**37.1**	**46.5**	**42.0**	**40.7**	**48.8**	**77.9**	**239.9**
INCOME STATEMENT (IN THOUSANDS):							
Total Revenues	300,801	277,516	270,511	271,336	226,243	348,474	278,105
Costs & Expenses	235,901	227,128	218,492	220,926	191,470	317,498	266,527
Depreciation & Amort.	3,998	5,008	2,631	2,995	3,375	7,208	6,985
Operating Income	60,902	45,380	49,388	47,415	31,398	23,768	4,593
Income Before Income Taxes	71,104	53,967	59,584	53,664	42,555	25,573	7,024
Income Taxes	23,163	17,531	18,988	16,399	15,856	9,033	1,697
Net Income	[5] 47,941	[4] 36,436	[3] 40,596	[2] 37,265	[1] 26,699	16,540	5,327
Cash Flow	51,939	41,444	43,227	40,260	30,074	23,748	12,312
Average Shs. Outstg.	20,256	21,202	22,387	22,377	21,698	21,533	21,458
BALANCE SHEET (IN THOUSANDS):							
Cash & Cash Equivalents	218,826	202,051	225,823	202,001	52,257	36,836	47,961
Total Current Assets	337,065	324,051	334,216	323,017	215,613	200,629	188,892
Net Property	26,745	28,297	35,340	21,287	21,765	24,797	25,298
Total Assets	367,009	355,420	378,456	353,445	276,966	265,163	254,826
Total Current Liabilities	32,418	35,822	34,521	36,659	28,240	42,167	36,438
Net Stockholders' Equity	334,591	319,598	343,935	316,786	248,726	222,996	218,388
Net Working Capital	304,647	288,229	299,695	286,358	187,373	158,462	152,454
Year-end Shs. Outstg.	19,856	20,573	22,245	22,073	21,879	21,556	21,499
STATISTICAL RECORD:							
Operating Profit Margin %	20.2	16.4	18.3	17.5	13.9	6.8	1.7
Net Profit Margin %	15.9	13.1	15.0	13.7	11.8	4.7	1.9
Return on Equity %	14.3	11.4	11.8	11.8	10.7	7.4	2.4
Return on Assets %	13.1	10.3	10.7	10.5	9.6	6.2	2.1
Price Range	25.94-15.88	27.50-18.94	30.50-15.75	31.56-17.63	19.50-12.75	15.88-12.00	15.63-12.75
P/E Ratio	10.9-6.7	16.0-11.0	16.8-8.7	18.9-10.6	15.9-10.4	20.6-15.6	62.5-51.0
Average Yield %	4.2	3.4	3.3	2.8	3.7	4.3	4.2

Statistics are as originally reported. [1] Bef. inc. from disc. opers. of $5.0 mill., incl. a $3.0 mill. after-tax gain on the sale of Papel/Freelance and $2.8 mill. for the reversal of a litig. prov. [2] Excl. pre-tax gain of $46.7 mill. from the sale of assets and a pre-tax loss of $1.3 mill. fr. disc. opers. & incl. a net prov. to close all remaining retail opers. of $945,000. [3] Incl. after-tax charge of $1.2 million for a transaction agreement related to the sale of Papel/Freelance, Inc. [4] Incl. after-tax chrg. of $6.5 mill. [5] Incl. after-tax gain $591,000.

OFFICERS:
R. Berrie, Chmn., C.E.O.
B. J. Sottile, Vice-Chmn.
J. D. Wille, V.P., C.F.O.

PRINCIPAL OFFICE: 111 Bauer Drive, Oakland, NJ 07436

TELEPHONE NUMBER: (201) 337-9000
FAX: (201) 337-7909
WEB: www.russberrie.com

NO. OF EMPLOYEES: 1,500 (approx.)

SHAREHOLDERS: 546

ANNUAL MEETING: In Apr.

INCORPORATED: NJ, 1966

INSTITUTIONAL HOLDINGS:
No. of Institutions: 88
Shares Held: 13,138,367
% Held: 65.5

INDUSTRY: Dolls and stuffed toys (SIC: 3942)

TRANSFER AGENT(S): First City Transfer Company, Iselin, NJ

NYSE SYMBOL RML
Rec. Pr. 17.95 (5/31/01)

RUSSELL CORPORATION

YIELD 3.1%
P/E RATIO 40.8

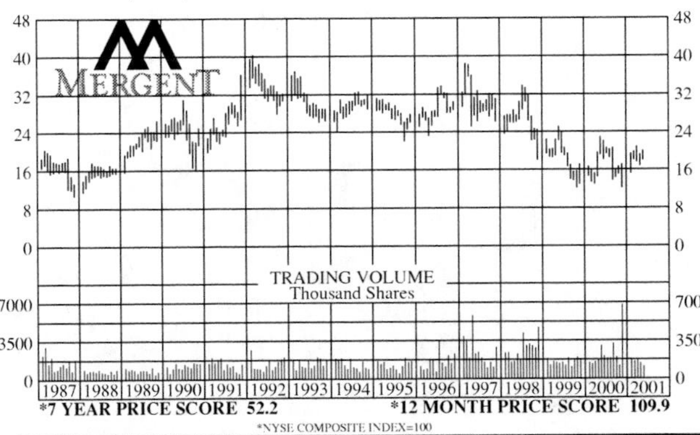

*7 YEAR PRICE SCORE 52.2 *12 MONTH PRICE SCORE 109.9

*NYSE COMPOSITE INDEX=100

INTERIM EARNINGS (Per Share):

Qtr.	Mar.	June	Sept.	Dec.
1996	0.30	0.42	0.63	0.76
1997	0.30	0.22	0.64	0.32
1998	0.05	0.18	d0.39	d0.13
1999	d0.41	0.04	0.60	0.04
2000	0.01	0.07	0.02	0.34

INTERIM DIVIDENDS (Per Share):

Amt.	Decl.	Ex.	Rec.	Pay.
0.14Q	4/19/00	5/01/00	5/03/00	5/18/00
0.14Q	7/26/00	8/03/00	8/07/00	8/17/00
0.14Q	9/27/00	11/02/00	11/06/00	11/20/00
0.14Q	12/06/00	2/01/01	2/05/01	2/19/01
0.14Q	4/25/01	5/08/01	5/10/01	5/24/01

Indicated div.: $0.56 (Div. Reinv. Plan)

CAPITALIZATION (12/30/00):

	($000)	(%)
Long-Term Debt	384,211	40.2
Deferred Income Tax	45,928	4.8
Common & Surplus	525,940	55.0
Total	956,079	100.0

RECENT DEVELOPMENTS: For the year ended 12/30/00, net income totaled $14.5 million, an increase of 73.0% compared with $8.4 million in the previous year. Results for 2000 and 1999 included non-recurring charges totaling $47.6 million and $46.6 million, respectively. Net sales improved 6.6% to $1.22 billion versus $1.14 billion in the prior year. Cost of goods sold rose 3.8% to $876.7 million from $845.0 million a year earlier. Operating income amounted to $65.5 million, up 35.3% from $48.4 million the year before.

PROSPECTS: Looking ahead, the Company expects continued growth in the JERZEES® and Russell Athletic® brands. Also, the Company anticipates strong contribution from past acquisitions. Meanwhile, the Company announced that it will restructure its Russell Athletic® operations in Europe. As part of this restructuring, the Company is pursuing alternative business models, including licensing, a joint venture or exports from the U.S. and other markets. The restructuring is expected to be completed in the second quarter of 2001.

BUSINESS

RUSSELL CORPORATION is an international branded apparel company specializing in activewear, casualwear and athletic uniforms. RML's major brands include Russell Athletic®, JERZEES® and Cross Creek®. RML designs and merchandises a variety of leisure and sports apparel marketed to sporting goods dealers, department and specialty stores, mass merchandisers, golf pro shops, college bookstores, screen printers and embroiderers, distributors, mail order houses and other apparel manufacturers. Products are derived from a combination of internally produced products, contractors and third-party sources. More than 95% of the Company's total revenues were derived from the sale of completed apparel, with the balance from woven fabrics. Foreign and export sales for 2000 were 9.1%. Wal-Mart Stores, Inc. and affiliates, accounted for 17.9% of total revenues in 2000.

REVENUES

(12/31/2000)	Rev	(%)
Activewear	967,835	79.5
International	110,393	9.1
All other	139,350	11.4
Total	1,217,578	100.0

ANNUAL FINANCIAL DATA

	12/30/00	1/1/00	1/2/99	1/3/98	1/4/97	12/30/95	1 12/31/94
Earnings Per Share	**2 0.44**	**2 0.25**	**d0.29**	**1.47**	**2.11**	**1.38**	**1.96**
Cash Flow Per Share	**2.12**	**2.13**	**1.77**	**3.48**	**3.98**	**3.11**	**3.63**
Tang. Book Val. Per Share	**16.49**	**16.74**	**17.31**	**18.25**	**17.87**	**16.34**	**15.84**
Dividends Per Share	**0.56**	**0.56**	**0.56**	**0.53**	**0.50**	**0.48**	**0.42**
Dividend Payout %	**127.2**	**223.9**	**...**	**36.1**	**23.7**	**34.8**	**21.4**
INCOME STATEMENT (IN MILLIONS):							
Total Revenues	1,217.6	1,142.2	1,180.1	1,228.2	1,244.2	1,152.6	1,098.3
Costs & Expenses	1,097.5	1,030.0	1,088.2	1,037.3	1,016.7	975.2	884.2
Depreciation & Amort.	54.6	63.9	74.4	74.4	72.2	68.0	67.0
Operating Income	65.5	48.4	17.6	116.5	154.3	106.5	145.5
Net Interest Inc./(Exp.)	d32.4	d28.1	d27.8	d28.2	d25.7	d21.7	d19.4
Income Before Income Taxes	33.1	20.3	d10.3	88.4	129.5	87.7	127.6
Income Taxes	18.6	11.9	0.1	33.9	48.0	33.6	48.8
Net Income	2 14.5	2 8.4	d10.4	54.4	81.6	54.1	78.8
Cash Flow	69.2	72.3	64.0	128.9	153.8	122.1	145.9
Average Shs. Outstg. (000)	32,686	33,867	36,217	37,047	38,653	39,307	40,228
BALANCE SHEET (IN MILLIONS):							
Cash & Cash Equivalents	4.2	9.1	13.9	8.6	7.4	4.5	4.1
Total Current Assets	640.1	615.1	584.7	647.0	600.0	564.9	510.9
Net Property	453.0	482.6	520.0	526.1	526.8	481.7	467.0
Total Assets	1,153.2	1,153.1	1,153.6	1,248.0	1,195.2	1,118.2	1,046.6
Total Current Liabilities	168.7	155.1	148.9	145.6	187.4	126.8	200.5
Long-Term Obligations	384.2	377.9	323.0	360.6	255.9	287.9	144.2
Net Stockholders' Equity	525.9	549.3	614.8	665.6	679.8	632.6	628.7
Net Working Capital	471.4	460.0	435.8	501.4	412.6	438.1	310.3
Year-end Shs. Outstg. (000)	31,896	32,814	35,519	36,463	38,049	38,715	39,689
STATISTICAL RECORD:							
Operating Profit Margin %	5.4	4.2	1.5	9.5	12.4	9.2	13.3
Net Profit Margin %	1.2	0.7	...	4.4	6.6	4.7	7.2
Return on Equity %	2.8	1.5	...	8.2	12.0	8.6	12.5
Return on Assets %	1.3	0.7	...	4.4	6.8	4.8	7.5
Debt/Total Assets %	33.3	32.8	28.0	28.9	21.4	25.7	13.8
Price Range	22.94-12.13	25.13-12.13	33.88-18.00	38.50-25.00	33.75-23.13	31.25-22.00	32.63-24.00
P/E Ratio	52.1-27.6	100.5-48.5	...	26.2-17.0	16.0-11.0	22.6-15.9	16.6-12.2
Average Yield %	3.2	3.0	2.2	1.7	1.8	1.8	1.5

Statistics are as originally reported. 1 Incl. results of The Game Inc., acquired in Dec. 1993. 2 Incl. restruct., asset impairment and other chrg. $47.6 mill., 12/00; $46.6 mill., 1/00

OFFICERS:
J. F. Ward, Chmn., Pres., C.E.O.
R. D. Martin, Sr. V.P., C.F.O.
K. R. Holliday, V.P., Treas.

INVESTOR CONTACT: Roger Holliday, V.P., Treas., (678) 742-8117

PRINCIPAL OFFICE: 755 Lee Street, Alexander City, AL 35011-0272

TELEPHONE NUMBER: (256) 500-4000
WEB: www.russellcorp.com

NO. OF EMPLOYEES: 16,540 (avg.)

SHAREHOLDERS: 8,000 (approx.)

ANNUAL MEETING: In April

INCORPORATED: AL, 1902

INSTITUTIONAL HOLDINGS:
No. of Institutions: 104
Shares Held: 17,290,494
% Held: 54.2

INDUSTRY: Knit outerwear mills (SIC: 2253)

TRANSFER AGENT(S): SunTrust Bank, Atlanta, Atlanta, GA

NYSE SYMBOL R
Rec. Pr. 19.81 (4/30/01)

RYDER SYSTEM, INC.

YIELD 3.0%
P/E RATIO 13.3

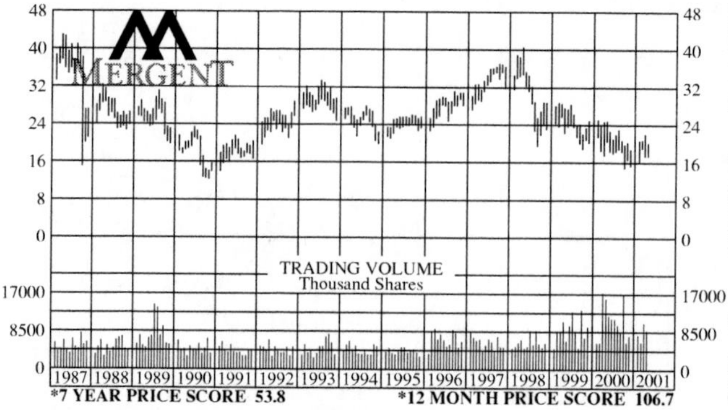

TRADING VOLUME
Thousand Shares

*7 YEAR PRICE SCORE 53.8 *12 MONTH PRICE SCORE 106.7
*NYSE COMPOSITE INDEX=100

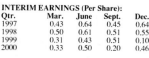

INTERIM EARNINGS (Per Share):

Qtr.	Mar.	June	Sept.	Dec.
1997	0.43	0.64	0.45	0.64
1998	0.50	0.61	0.51	0.55
1999	0.31	0.43	0.51	0.10
2000	0.33	0.50	0.20	0.46

INTERIM DIVIDENDS (Per Share):

Amt.	Decl.	Ex.	Rec.	Pay.
0.15Q	7/27/00	8/30/00	9/01/00	9/20/00
0.15Q	10/03/00	11/15/00	11/17/00	12/20/00
0.15Q	2/16/01	2/28/01	3/02/01	3/20/01
0.15Q	5/04/01	5/23/01	5/26/01	6/20/01

Indicated div.: $0.60 (Div. Reinv. Plan)

CAPITALIZATION (12/31/00):

	($000)	(%)
Long-Term Debt	1,604,242	41.4
Deferred Income Tax	1,017,304	26.3
Common & Surplus	1,252,708	32.3
Total	3,874,254	100.0

RECENT DEVELOPMENTS: For the year ended 12/31/00, net earnings rose 22.1% to $89.0 million compared with income from continuing operations of $72.9 million in 1999. Results for 2000 included restructuring and other charges of $42.0 million. Results for 1999 included non-recurring charges totaling $76.1 million, and excluded income totaling $346.7 million from discontinued operations. Total revenue grew 7.8% to $5.34 billion from $4.95 billion a year earlier.

PROSPECTS: The economic slowdown in the U.S. has resulted in production cutbacks in certain key customer industries, particularly in the automotive industry. These factors are expected to negatively affect the Company throughout 2001. In addition, the Company is experiencing a continued slowdown in its commercial rental business segment, as well as the effects of a depressed used truck market. As a result, the Company anticipates revenue growth to be modest.

BUSINESS

RYDER SYSTEM, INC. provides logistics, supply chain and transportation management services worldwide. R's product offerings range from full-service leasing, commercial rental and programmed maintenance of vehicles to integrated services such as dedicated contract carriage and carrier management. In addition, R offers comprehensive supply chain services, lead logistics management services and e-commerce services that support clients' entire supply chains. Revenues for 2000 were derived as follows: fleet management solutions, 62.3%; supply chain solutions, 28.2%; and dedicated contract carriage, 9.5%. As of 12/31/00, Ryder and its subsidiaries had a fleet of 176,345 vehicles. On 9/13/99, R sold its public transportation subsidiary.

ANNUAL FINANCIAL DATA

	12/31/00	12/31/99	12/31/98	12/31/97	12/31/96	12/31/95	12/31/94
Earnings Per Share	**[6] 1.49**	**[1] [5] 1.06**	**[1] 2.16**	**[2] 2.05**	**[4] d0.39**	**[3] 1.96**	**1.95**
Cash Flow Per Share	**11.75**	**9.69**	**10.40**	**9.74**	**8.39**	**10.33**	**9.46**
Tang. Book Val. Per Share	**20.86**	**20.29**	**15.37**	**14.39**	**14.19**	**15.64**	**14.33**
Dividends Per Share	**0.60**	**0.60**	**0.60**	**0.60**	**0.60**	**0.60**	**0.60**
Dividend Payout %	**40.3**	**56.6**	**27.8**	**29.3**	**...**	**30.6**	**30.8**
INCOME STATEMENT (IN MILLIONS):							
Total Revenues	5,336.8	4,952.2	5,188.7	4,893.9	5,519.4	5,167.4	4,685.6
Costs & Expenses	4,378.6	3,984.6	4,095.0	3,845.3	4,641.5	4,049.3	3,686.1
Depreciation & Amort.	613.3	593.0	606.5	601.5	713.3	664.1	591.7
Operating Income	337.3	377.3	494.0	456.8	164.5	454.0	407.9
Net Interest Inc./(Exp.)	d154.0	d183.7	d198.9	d189.4	d206.6	d191.2	d144.7
Income Before Income Taxes	141.3	117.5	257.0	264.0	d17.6	264.4	260.5
Income Taxes	52.3	44.6	97.9	103.7	13.7	109.0	107.0
Net Income	[6] 89.0	[1] [5] 72.9	[1] 159.1	[2] 160.2	[4] d31.3	[3] 155.4	153.5
Cash Flow	702.3	665.9	765.6	761.7	682.1	819.5	745.2
Average Shs. Outstg. (000)	59,759	68,732	73,645	78,192	81,263	79,370	78,768
BALANCE SHEET (IN MILLIONS):							
Cash & Cash Equivalents	122.0	113.0	138.4	78.4	191.4	92.9	75.9
Total Current Assets	928.3	1,209.4	1,109.7	1,092.0	1,147.8	884.1	758.8
Net Property	3,625.4	581.1	782.4	760.8	907.8	933.5	836.4
Total Assets	5,474.9	5,770.5	5,708.6	5,509.1	5,645.4	5,893.8	5,014.5
Total Current Liabilities	1,302.3	1,449.5	1,362.7	1,089.5	1,155.0	1,120.2	1,093.2
Long-Term Obligations	1,604.2	1,819.1	2,099.7	2,267.6	2,237.0	2,411.0	1,794.8
Net Stockholders' Equity	1,252.7	1,204.9	1,095.6	1,060.7	1,106.0	1,240.0	1,129.0
Net Working Capital	d374.0	d240.1	d253.0	2.5	d7.2	d236.1	d334.3
Year-end Shs. Outstg. (000)	60,044	59,395	71,280	73,692	77,961	79,281	78,761
STATISTICAL RECORD:							
Operating Profit Margin %	6.3	8.0	8.8	9.1	3.0	8.8	8.7
Net Profit Margin %	1.7	1.5	3.1	3.3	...	3.0	3.3
Return on Equity %	7.1	6.1	14.5	15.1	...	12.5	13.6
Return on Assets %	1.7	1.3	2.8	2.9	...	2.6	3.1
Debt/Total Assets %	29.3	68.0	78.3	89.2	84.4	100.9	84.6
Price Range	25.13-14.81	28.75-18.81	40.56-19.44	37.13-27.13	31.13-22.63	26.13-21.00	28.00-19.88
P/E Ratio	16.9-9.9	27.1-17.7	18.8-9.0	18.1-13.2	...	13.3-10.7	14.4-10.2
Average Yield %	3.0	2.5	2.0	1.9	2.2	2.5	2.5

Statistics are as originally reported. [1] Incl. $23.6 mill. after-tax chg. for Year 2000 costs, 1998; $24.0 mill. chg. for Year 2000 costs, 1999. [2] Bef. $15.5 mill. inc. fr. disc. op. [3] Bef. $7.8 mill. chg. fr. change in acct. [4] Bef. $10.0 mill. extraord. loss, incl. $163.9 mill. restr. chgs. & $15.1 mill. gain on Consumer Truck sale. [5] Bef. gain of $351.0 mill. fr. disc. opers. and extra. loss of $4.4 mill. & incl. non-recur. chgs. of $76.1 mill. [6] Incl. $42.0 mill. restr. & other chgs.

OFFICERS:
M. A. Burns, Chmn.
G. T. Swienton, Pres., C.E.O.
C. J. Nelson, Sr. Exec. V.P., C.F.O.

INVESTOR CONTACT: Investor Relations, (305) 500-4053

PRINCIPAL OFFICE: 3600 N.W. 82nd Avenue, Miami, FL 33166

TELEPHONE NUMBER: (305) 500-3726
FAX: (305) 500-4129
WEB: www.ryder.com

NO. OF EMPLOYEES: 33,089 (avg.)

SHAREHOLDERS: 14,492

ANNUAL MEETING: In May

INCORPORATED: FL, Mar., 1955

INSTITUTIONAL HOLDINGS:
No. of Institutions: 183
Shares Held: 47,452,207
% Held: 78.6

INDUSTRY: Transportation services, nec (SIC: 4789)

TRANSFER AGENT(S): Boston EquiServe, Boston, MA

NYSE SYMBOL RT
Rec. Pr. 13.10 (5/31/01)

RYERSON TULL, INC.

YIELD 1.5%
P/E RATIO . . .

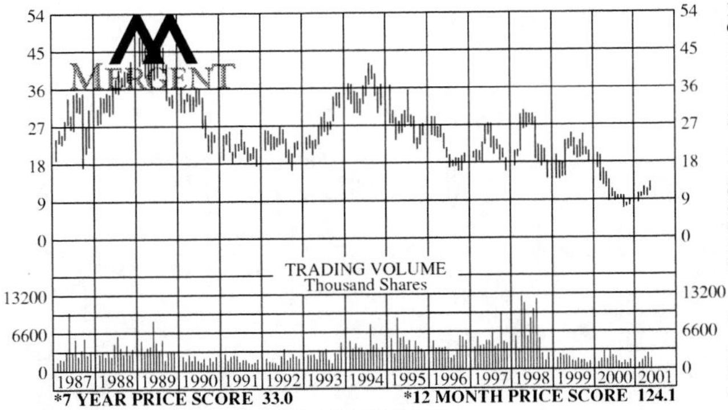

TRADING VOLUME
Thousand Shares

*7 YEAR PRICE SCORE 33.0 *12 MONTH PRICE SCORE 124.1
*NYSE COMPOSITE INDEX=100

INTERIM EARNINGS (Per Share):

Qtr.	Mar.	June	Sept.	Dec.
1996	0.31	0.65	0.13	d0.03
1997	0.59	0.77	0.57	0.30
1998	0.38	0.51	0.21	0.46
1999	0.42	0.41	0.38	0.34
2000	0.44	d0.55	d0.15	d0.77

INTERIM DIVIDENDS (Per Share):

Amt.	Decl.	Ex.	Rec.	Pay.
0.05Q	1/27/00	4/05/00	4/07/00	5/01/00
0.05Q	6/28/00	7/07/00	7/11/00	8/01/00
0.05Q	9/27/00	10/04/00	10/06/00	11/01/00
0.05Q	11/22/00	1/04/01	1/08/01	2/01/01
0.05Q	1/24/01	4/05/01	4/09/01	5/01/01

Indicated div.: $0.20 (Div. Reinv. Plan)

CAPITALIZATION (12/31/00):

	($000)	(%)
Long-Term Debt [1]	100,700	13.2
Preferred Stock	100	0.0
Common & Surplus	661,600	86.8
Total	762,400	100.0

RECENT DEVELOPMENTS: For the year ended 12/31/00, RT incurred a loss from continuing operations of $25.1 million compared with income from continuing operations of $38.4 million in 1999. Results for 2000 and 1999 included pre-tax net nonrecurring charges of $39.6 million and $3.6 million, respectively. Results for 1999 also included a pre-tax gain of $1.8 million. Net sales rose 3.6% to $2.86 billion.

PROSPECTS: RT's performance continues to be adversely affected by deteriorating market conditions and pricing as a result of the economic slowdown. Separately, RT is in the process of negotiating revised terms regarding its revolving credit line with its banks. Meanwhile, the Company's balance sheet remains strong, with a debt to total capitalization ratio of 34.0% at year-end 2000.

BUSINESS

RYERSON TULL, INC. (formerly Inland Steel Industries, Inc.) is a holding company. RT conducts its materials distribution operations in the U.S. through its operating subsidiaries, Ryerson and Tull; in Canada through Washington Specialty Metals; in Mexico through Ryerson de Mexico, S.A. de C.V.; in China through Shanghai Ryerson Limited; and in India through Tata Ryerson Limited. RT is organized into five business units along regional and product lines. The Company is the largest metals service center in the U.S. The Company distributes and processes metals and other materials throughout the continental U.S., and is among the largest purchasers of steel in the U.S. On 7/16/98, RT completed the sale of its subsidiary, Inland Steel Company. On 2/1/99, the Company acquired Washington Specialty Metals, an eight-location metals service center specializing in stainless steel. On 2/25/99, Ryerson Tull (old) was merged into Inland Steel Industries. Following the merger, the Company's name was changed to Ryerson Tull,Inc.

ANNUAL FINANCIAL DATA

	12/31/00	12/31/99	[5] 12/31/98	12/31/97	12/31/96	12/31/95	12/31/94
Earnings Per Share	[7] d1.03	[6] 1.56	[4] 0.99	[3] 2.13	[2] 1.23	2.69	1.81
Cash Flow Per Share	0.26	2.86	1.77	5.17	4.36	5.72	5.00
Tang. Book Val. Per Share	21.92	23.80	22.10	17.20	14.71	13.41	11.65
Dividends Per Share	0.20	0.20	0.20	0.20	0.20	0.15	. . .
Dividend Payout %	. . .	12.8	20.2	9.4	16.3	5.6	. . .
INCOME STATEMENT (IN MILLIONS):							
Total Revenues	2,862.4	2,763.5	2,782.7	5,046.8	4,584.1	4,781.5	4,497.0
Costs & Expenses	2,834.7	2,634.3	2,653.5	4,603.1	4,271.4	4,309.9	4,108.9
Depreciation & Amort.	31.8	32.1	33.2	157.9	147.0	143.1	138.7
Operating Income	d4.1	97.1	96.0	285.8	165.7	328.5	249.4
Net Interest Inc./(Exp.)	d29.7	. . .	d33.6	d62.6	d77.1	d71.9	d71.4
Income Before Income Taxes	d33.5	73.9	83.0	208.0	115.8	237.1	169.5
Income Taxes	cr8.4	34.8	30.6	80.3	43.8	90.3	62.1
Equity Earnings/Minority Int.	. . .	d0.7	d4.7	d8.4	d3.0	. . .	. . .
Net Income	[7] d25.1	[6] 38.4	[4] 47.7	[3] 119.3	[2] 69.0	146.8	107.4
Cash Flow	6.5	70.3	74.0	268.1	206.9	270.9	217.7
Average Shs. Outstg. (000)	24,800	24,600	41,700	51,900	47,400	47,400	43,545
BALANCE SHEET (IN MILLIONS):							
Cash & Cash Equivalents	23.8	39.5	52.5	97.0	238.0	267.4	107.1
Total Current Assets	877.0	890.1	843.0	1,275.1	1,227.8	1,262.3	1,081.5
Net Property	274.7	273.2	293.6	1,641.8	1,637.0	1,600.4	1,610.3
Total Assets	1,372.1	1,387.2	1,343.9	3,646.5	3,541.6	3,558.3	3,353.4
Total Current Liabilities	458.7	279.6	271.0	614.9	536.8	644.2	564.8
Long-Term Obligations	100.7	258.8	257.0	704.9	773.2	784.5	705.9
Net Stockholders' Equity	661.7	697.8	563.6	928.2	821.1	783.1	547.1
Net Working Capital	418.3	610.5	572.0	660.2	691.0	618.1	516.7
Year-end Shs. Outstg. (000)	25,782	24,773	21,757	48,999	48,908	48,742	44,550
STATISTICAL RECORD:							
Operating Profit Margin %	. . .	3.5	3.4	5.7	3.6	6.9	5.5
Net Profit Margin %	. . .	1.4	1.7	2.4	1.5	3.1	2.4
Return on Equity %	. . .	5.5	8.5	12.9	8.4	18.7	19.6
Return on Assets %	. . .	2.8	3.5	3.3	1.9	4.1	3.2
Debt/Total Assets %	7.3	18.7	19.1	19.3	21.8	22.0	21.1
Price Range	20.19-6.94	25.06-14.00	30.50-14.13	27.50-15.88	29.00-16.00	36.75-21.25	42.00-29.38
P/E Ratio	. . .	16.1-9.0	30.8-14.3	12.9-7.5	23.6-13.0	13.7-7.9	23.2-16.2
Average Yield %	1.5	1.0	0.9	0.9	0.9	0.5	. . .

Statistics are as originally reported. [1] Incl. cap. lease oblig. [2] Excl. extraord. chrg. $23.3 mill. & incl. nonrecurr. $31.4 mill. pretax gain & pretax loss $26.3 mill. [3] Incl. nonrecur. gain $17.2 mill. [4] Bef. discont. oper. inc. $524.6 mill. & extraord. loss $21.4 mill. [5] Figures for 1998 & prior are for Inland Steel Industries, Inc. [6] Incl. pretax gain $1.8 mill. & excl. net gain $17.3 mill fr. disc. oper. [7] Incl. pretax chrg. $39.5 mill. & gain $27.8 mill. & excl. disc. oper. loss $4.8 mill.

OFFICERS:
N. S. Novich, Chmn., Pres., C.E.O.
J. M. Gratz, Exec. V.P., C.F.O.
T. R. Rogers, Treas.
J. E. Mims, V.P., Gen. Couns., Sec.

INVESTOR CONTACT: Terence R. Rogers, Treas., (773) 788-3206

PRINCIPAL OFFICE: 2621 West 15th Place, Chicago, IL 60608

TELEPHONE NUMBER: (773) 762-2121
FAX: (773) 762-3311
WEB: www.ryersontull.com

NO. OF EMPLOYEES: 4,500 (approx.)

SHAREHOLDERS: 11,145

ANNUAL MEETING: In Apr.

INCORPORATED: DC, Feb., 1917; reincorp., DE, Feb., 1986

INSTITUTIONAL HOLDINGS:
No. of Institutions: 86
Shares Held: 17,265,131
% Held: 69.7

INDUSTRY: Blast furnaces and steel mills (SIC: 3312)

TRANSFER AGENT(S): Computershare Investor Services, Chicago, IL

NYSE SYMBOL RYL
Rec. Pr. 45.30 (5/31/01)

RYLAND GROUP, INC. (THE)

YIELD 0.4%
P/E RATIO 7.7

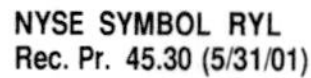

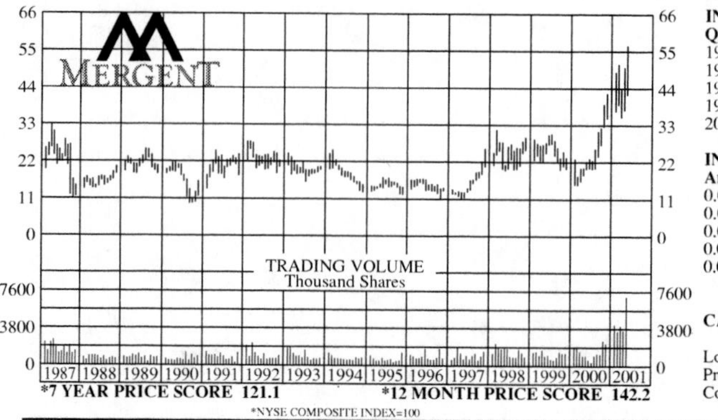

INTERIM EARNINGS (Per Share):

Qtr.	Mar.	June	Sept.	Dec.
1996	0.03	0.31	0.25	0.29
1997	0.08	0.22	0.42	0.62
1998	0.29	0.57	0.81	1.12
1999	0.65	1.12	1.15	1.40
2000	0.78	1.24	1.67	2.22

INTERIM DIVIDENDS (Per Share):

Amt.	Decl.	Ex.	Rec.	Pay.
0.04Q	6/29/00	7/12/00	7/15/00	7/30/00
0.04Q	8/22/00	10/11/00	10/13/00	10/30/00
0.04Q	12/13/00	1/10/01	1/15/01	1/30/01
0.04Q	2/21/01	4/10/01	4/15/01	4/30/01
0.04Q	4/27/01	7/11/01	7/15/01	7/30/01

Indicated div.: $0.16 (Div. Reinv. Plan)

CAPITALIZATION (12/31/00):

	($000)	(%)
Long-Term Debt	450,000	49.8
Preferred Stock	295	0.0
Common & Surplus	453,334	50.2
Total	903,629	100.0

RECENT DEVELOPMENTS: For the year ended 12/31/00, net income advanced 23.3% to $82.3 million compared with $66.7 million in 1999. The improvement in earnings was primarily attributed to improved operating efficiencies and strategic land acquisitions. Total revenues were $2.33 billion, up 16.0% from $2.01 billion a year earlier. Homebuilding segment revenues rose 16.7% to $2.29 billion, driven by 12.0% higher closing volume of 11,418 homes.

PROSPECTS: During March 2001, RYL invested $1.0 million in iBidCo, a new home industry provider of on-line sales systems. RYL's strategic investment in iBidCo should enhance RYL's on-line sales and marketing initiatives to deliver increased sales and dynamic pricing. RYL continues to increase its presence and profitability in its key growth markets. If current market conditions prevail, RYL anticipates earnings for fiscal 2001 to be in the range of $6.10 to $6.37 per share.

BUSINESS

THE RYLAND GROUP, INC. is a national homebuilder and mortgage-related financial services firm. The Company builds homes in 19 markets across the country. The Company's current average price home is $190,000. RYL's homebuilding segment specializes in the sale and construction of single-family attached and detached housing. The financial services segment, whose business is conducted through Ryland Mortgage Company and its subsidiaries (RMC), complements the Company's homebuilding activities by providing various mortgage-related products and services for retail customers including loan origination, title and escrow services, and by conducting investment activities. In the second quarter of 1995, RYL sold its mortgage securities administration business to Norwest Bank Minnesota. Contributions to 2000 revenues were as follows: homebuilding, 98%; and financial services, 2%.

ANNUAL FINANCIAL DATA

	12/31/00	12/31/99	12/31/98	12/31/97	12/31/96	12/31/95	12/31/94
Earnings Per Share	**5.92**	**4.30**	**[1] 2.79**	**1.32**	**0.88**	**[3] d1.78**	**[2] 1.29**
Cash Flow Per Share	**7.92**	**132.39**	**112.97**	**104.44**	**96.18**	**0.44**	**2.94**
Tang. Book Val. Per Share	**32.71**	**26.31**	**21.55**	**19.07**	**17.61**	**21.35**	**17.86**
Dividends Per Share	**0.16**	**0.16**	**0.16**	**0.38**	**0.60**	**0.60**	**0.60**
Dividend Payout %	**2.7**	**3.7**	**5.7**	**28.8**	**68.2**	**...**	**46.5**
INCOME STATEMENT (IN MILLIONS):							
Total Revenues	2,331.6	2,009.3	1,765.5	1,649.8	1,580.2	1,585.1	1,642.8
Costs & Expenses	2,111.8	1,827.0	1,613.8	1,525.8	1,463.9	1,526.5	1,457.5
Depreciation & Amort.	28.5	28.0	25.6	31.4	31.4	34.5	25.6
Operating Income	191.3	154.3	126.1	92.6	84.9	24.1	159.6
Net Interest Inc./(Exp.)	d28.5	d21.6	d34.3	d41.9	d46.5	d53.6	d105.0
Income Before Income Taxes	134.8	109.3	75.2	36.5	26.4	d8.5	37.5
Income Taxes	52.6	42.6	31.6	14.6	10.6	cr17.0	14.9
Net Income	82.3	66.7	[1] 43.6	21.9	15.8	[3] d25.5	[2] 22.5
Cash Flow	110.0	2,052.7	1,762.7	1,609.0	1,518.5	6.8	45.7
Average Shs. Outstg. (000)	13,893	15,505	15,603	15,405	15,789	15,585	15,561
BALANCE SHEET (IN MILLIONS):							
Cash & Cash Equivalents	142.2	69.9	49.8	36.1	28.7	56.0	26.8
Total Current Assets	1,030.6	892.6	691.5	591.0	603.3	593.9	621.6
Net Property	35.6	26.6	26.8	26.5	31.6	34.7	24.0
Total Assets	1,361.3	1,248.3	1,215.4	1,283.4	1,338.5	1,580.8	1,704.5
Total Current Liabilities	381.4	410.1	500.9	612.2	635.9	838.2	955.3
Long-Term Obligations	450.0	378.0	308.2	310.2	354.3	396.6	408.7
Net Stockholders' Equity	453.6	386.5	346.3	305.1	310.4	301.1	312.1
Net Working Capital	649.2	482.5	190.7	d21.2	d32.6	d244.3	d333.7
Year-end Shs. Outstg. (000)	13,249	13,851	14,752	14,522	15,855	12,682	15,475
STATISTICAL RECORD:							
Operating Profit Margin %	8.2	7.7	7.1	5.6	5.4	1.5	9.7
Net Profit Margin %	3.5	3.3	2.5	1.3	1.0	...	1.4
Return on Equity %	18.1	17.3	12.6	7.2	5.1	...	7.2
Return on Assets %	6.0	5.3	3.6	1.7	1.2	...	1.3
Debt/Total Assets %	33.1	30.3	25.4	24.2	26.5	25.1	24.0
Price Range	42.38-15.19	30.44-19.75	31.63-19.44	26.00-11.13	17.13-11.25	17.50-12.25	25.63-12.88
P/E Ratio	7.2-2.6	7.1-4.6	11.3-7.0	19.7-8.4	19.5-12.8	...	19.9-10.0
Average Yield %	0.6	0.6	0.6	2.0	4.2	4.0	3.1

Statistics are as originally reported. [1] Bef. extraord. loss of $3.3 mill. [2] Bef. an acctg. chrg. of $2.1 mill. [3] Incl. net chrg. of $27.0 mill. from write-down of inventories, bef. gain from discont. oper. of $22.9 mill.

OFFICERS:
C. Dreier, Chmn., Pres., C.E.O.
G. A. Milne, Sr. V.P., C.F.O.
T. J. Geckle, Sr. V.P., Sec., Gen. Couns.

INVESTOR CONTACT: Cathey Lowe, V.P., Treas. & Inv. Rel., (818) 223-7500

PRINCIPAL OFFICE: 24025 Park Sorrento, Suite 400, Calabasas, CA 91302

TELEPHONE NUMBER: (818) 223-7500
FAX: (818) 223-7667
WEB: www.ryland.com

NO. OF EMPLOYEES: 2,130

SHAREHOLDERS: 3,114

ANNUAL MEETING: In Apr.

INCORPORATED: MD, Mar., 1967

INSTITUTIONAL HOLDINGS:
No. of Institutions: 127
Shares Held: 11,861,427
% Held: 88.6

INDUSTRY: Operative builders (SIC: 1531)

TRANSFER AGENT(S): Mellon Investor Services L.L.C., Ridgefield Park, NJ

NYSE SYMBOL TSG
Rec. Pr. 49.86 (4/30/01)

SABRE HOLDING CORPORATION

YIELD . . .
P/E RATIO 47.5

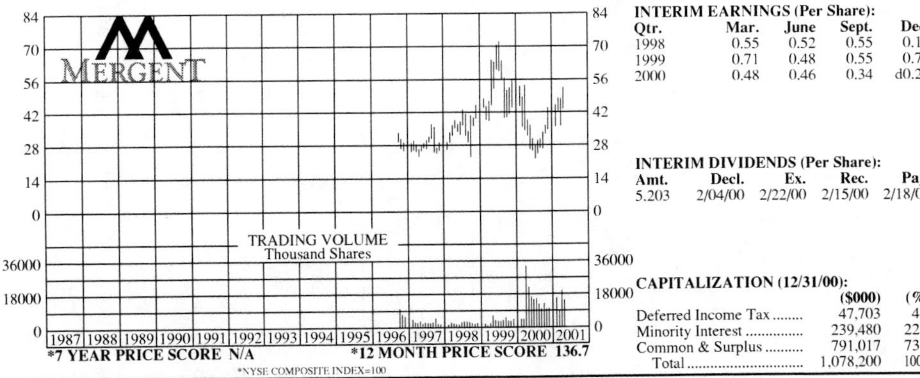

INTERIM EARNINGS (Per Share):

Qtr.	Mar.	June	Sept.	Dec.
1998	0.55	0.52	0.55	0.16
1999	0.71	0.48	0.55	0.75
2000	0.48	0.46	0.34	d0.23

INTERIM DIVIDENDS (Per Share):

Amt.	Decl.	Ex.	Rec.	Pay.
5.203	2/04/00	2/22/00	2/15/00	2/18/00

CAPITALIZATION (12/31/00):

	($000)	(%)
Deferred Income Tax	47,703	4.4
Minority Interest	239,480	22.2
Common & Surplus	791,017	73.4
Total	1,078,200	100.0

RECENT DEVELOPMENTS: For the year ended 12/31/00, net earnings fell 56.6% to $144.1 million versus $331.9 million in 1999. Results for 2000 included special charges totaling $158.4 million for severance costs, expenses incurred from a spin-off, and amortization of goodwill and other intangibles related to the options issued to US Airways, Inc. and acquisition-related expenses. Results for 1999 included special charges totaling $26.5 million. Total revenues rose 7.5% to $2.62 billion.

PROSPECTS: Electronic Data Systems Corporation agreed to purchase the Company's airline data centers and other technology assets for $670.0 million. Consequently, TSG awarded Electronic Data a ten-year service contract worth $2.20 billion. The sale of these assets is strategically in line with TSG's plans to divest a slower-growing and lower-margin business. The travel marketing and distribution group should continue to benefit from growth in global travel bookings.

BUSINESS

SABRE HOLDING CORPORATION, through its Sabre computer reservations system, is a major processor of travel reservations booked through travel agents. TSG also engages in consumer direct Internet travel distribution through its Travelocity.com subsidiary and Web site. More than 435 million reservations are made through the Sabre system annually. Revenues for 2000 were derived: travel marketing and distribution, 67.4%; and outsourcing and software solutions, 32.6%. On 3/1/00, AMR Corp., parent of American Airlines, spun off its 83.0% stake in TSG to shareholders. On 3/7/00, the Company completed the acquisition of Preview Travel, Inc.

ANNUAL FINANCIAL DATA

	12/31/00	12/31/99	12/31/98	12/31/97	12/31/96	12/31/95	12/31/94
Earnings Per Share	**1 1.11**	**2.54**	**1.78**	**1.53**	**1.43**	**1.73**	**. . .**
Cash Flow Per Share	**3.77**	**4.52**	**3.68**	**2.94**	**2.69**	**3.84**	**. . .**
Tang. Book Val. Per Share	**. . .**	**9.72**	**7.35**	**5.79**	**4.36**	**. . .**	**. . .**
Dividends Per Share	**5.20**	**. . .**	**. . .**	**. . .**	**. . .**	**. . .**	**. . .**
Dividend Payout %	**468.7**	**. . .**	**. . .**	**. . .**	**. . .**	**. . .**	**. . .**
INCOME STATEMENT (IN MILLIONS):							
Total Revenues	2,617.4	2,434.6	2,306.4	1,783.5	1,622.0	1,529.6	1,406.7
Costs & Expenses	2,021.2	1,803.9	1,708.3	1,290.7	1,130.1	977.7	881.6
Depreciation & Amort.	345.8	258.2	247.7	185.2	165.1	171.5	175.0
Operating Income	250.4	372.5	350.4	307.7	326.8	380.4	350.2
Net Interest Inc./(Exp.)	d15.4	17.7	6.5	8.3	d14.1	1.3	d8.9
Income Before Income Taxes	267.2	527.9	371.5	323.6	305.9	370.1	324.1
Income Taxes	123.2	196.0	139.5	123.8	119.3	144.2	126.9
Equity Earnings/Minority Int.	30.8	. . .	. . .	. . .	. . .	. . .	. . .
Net Income	1 144.1	331.9	231.9	199.9	186.6	225.9	197.2
Cash Flow	489.8	590.2	479.7	385.0	351.6	397.3	372.1
Average Shs. Outstg. (000)	129,841	130,655	130,521	130,988	130,758	103,604	. . .
BALANCE SHEET (IN MILLIONS):							
Cash & Cash Equivalents	145.0	611.1	537.7	584.9	442.9	94.9	263.0
Total Current Assets	693.0	976.4	944.4	874.2	694.5	271.2	404.3
Net Property	556.0	572.6	643.8	581.6	559.7	380.7	401.4
Total Assets	2,650.4	1,951.2	1,926.8	1,524.0	1,287.1	729.4	873.5
Total Current Liabilities	1,266.4	525.1	400.8	316.5	289.8	218.6	503.2
Long-Term Obligations	. . .	. . .	317.9	317.9	317.9	. . .	. . .
Net Stockholders' Equity	791.0	1,262.0	953.7	757.3	569.6	432.1	289.5
Net Working Capital	d573.4	451.3	543.6	557.6	404.7	52.6	d98.9
Year-end Shs. Outstg. (000)	130,007	129,796	129,813	130,854	130,770	. . .	. . .
STATISTICAL RECORD:							
Operating Profit Margin %	9.6	15.3	15.2	17.3	20.1	24.9	24.9
Net Profit Margin %	5.5	13.6	10.1	11.2	11.5	14.8	14.0
Return on Equity %	18.2	26.3	24.3	26.4	32.8	52.3	68.1
Return on Assets %	5.4	17.0	12.0	13.1	14.5	31.0	22.6
Debt/Total Assets %	. . .	. . .	16.5	20.9	24.7	. . .	. . .
Price Range	53.50-22.31	72.00-38.25	44.88-23.00	37.00-23.25	33.38-25.63	. . .	. . .
P/E Ratio	48.2-20.1	28.3-15.1	25.2-12.9	24.2-15.2	23.3-17.9	. . .	. . .
Average Yield %	13.7	. . .	. . .	. . .	. . .	. . .	. . .

Statistics are as originally reported. 1 Incl. $158.4 mill. special chgs.

OFFICERS:
W. J. Hannigan, Chmn., Pres., C.E.O.
J. M. Jackson, Exec. V.P., C.F.O., Treas.
D. A. Schwarte, Exec. V.P., Gen. Couns.

INVESTOR CONTACT: Investor Relations, (817) 963-6400

PRINCIPAL OFFICE: 4255 Amon Carter Boulevard, Fort Worth, TX 76155

TELEPHONE NUMBER: (817) 963-6400
FAX: (817) 967-5582
WEB: www.sabre.com

NO. OF EMPLOYEES: 10,000 (approx.)

SHAREHOLDERS: 11,080 (class A)

ANNUAL MEETING: In May

INCORPORATED: DE, June, 1996

INSTITUTIONAL HOLDINGS:
No. of Institutions: 270
Shares Held: 123,271,740
% Held: 93.6

INDUSTRY: Data processing and preparation (SIC: 7374)

TRANSFER AGENT(S): First Chicago Trust Company of New York, Jersey City, NJ

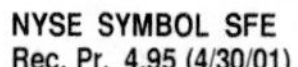

NYSE SYMBOL SFE
Rec. Pr. 4.95 (4/30/01)

SAFEGUARD SCIENTIFICS, INC.

YIELD ...
P/E RATIO ...

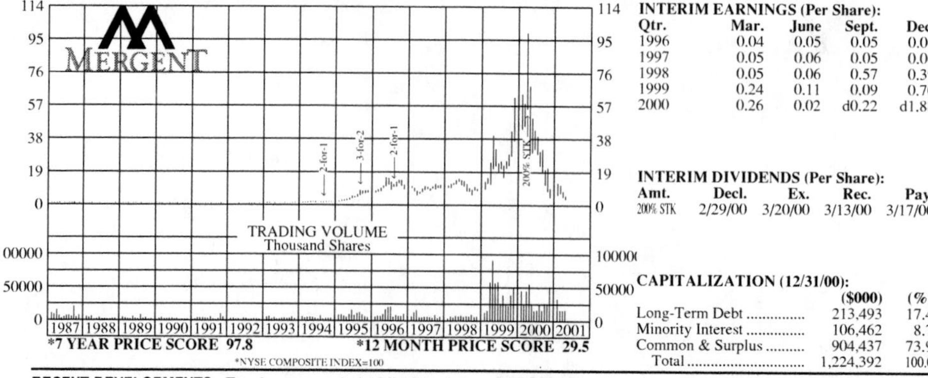

INTERIM EARNINGS (Per Share):

Qtr.	Mar.	June	Sept.	Dec.
1996	0.04	0.05	0.05	0.06
1997	0.05	0.06	0.05	0.06
1998	0.05	0.06	0.57	0.39
1999	0.24	0.11	0.09	0.70
2000	0.26	0.02	d0.22	d1.88

INTERIM DIVIDENDS (Per Share):

Amt.	Decl.	Ex.	Rec.	Pay.
200% STK	2/29/00	3/20/00	3/13/00	3/17/00

CAPITALIZATION (12/31/00):

	($000)	(%)
Long-Term Debt	213,493	17.4
Minority Interest	106,462	8.7
Common & Surplus	904,437	73.9
Total	1,224,392	100.0

RECENT DEVELOPMENTS: For the year ended 12/31/00, the Company reported a net loss of $212.4 million compared with net income of $123.5 million in the comparable period of 1999. Results for 2000 were unfavorably affected by a tremendously volatile technology market. Total revenue decreased 7.5% to $2.77 billion from $3.00 billion a year earlier. Total operating expenses declined to $2.83 billion from $2.99 billion in the prior year.

PROSPECTS: The Company believes its experience developing technology companies, its focus on infrastructure technology and breadth of its network will enable it to identify and attract companies with significant potential in the infrastructure technology market. In addition, SFE will remain focused on its core strategy of identifying emerging technology trends, acquiring positions in technology companies and managing these companies.

BUSINESS

SAFEGUARD SCIENTIFICS, INC. is a holding company that identifies, acquires, operates, and manages companies in the Internet infrastructure market with a focus on three sectors: software, communications and eServices. SFE also has interests in, participates in, and in some cases is involved in the management of, several private equity funds. SFE's main business segments are CompuCom and Tangram. CompuCom's operations include sales of distributed desktop computer products and configuration, network integration and technology support. Tangram's operations include the design, development, sale, and implementation of enterprise-wide asset tracking and software management services. In September 1998, the Company acquired Pac-West Telecomm.

REVENUES

(12/31/00)	($000)	(%)
Product Sales	2,457,572	88.7
Service Sales	290,510	10.5
Other revenue	22,299	0.8
Total	2,770,381	100.0

ANNUAL FINANCIAL DATA

	12/31/00	12/31/99	12/31/98	12/31/97	12/31/96	12/31/95	12/31/94
Earnings Per Share	[4] **d1.86**	[2] [3] **1.16**	[3] **1.07**	**0.22**	**0.20**	**0.19**	[1] **0.17**
Cash Flow Per Share	**d1.57**	**1.45**	**1.26**	**0.41**	**0.43**	**0.38**	**0.37**
Tang. Book Val. Per Share	**6.69**	**4.35**	**2.93**	**1.93**	**1.51**	**1.42**	**1.04**
INCOME STATEMENT (IN MILLIONS):							
Total Revenues	2,770.4	2,953.3	2,483.5	2,025.0	2,101.8	1,545.8	1,438.4
Costs & Expenses	2,796.8	2,917.8	2,258.4	1,923.4	2,005.7	1,467.8	1,378.2
Depreciation & Amort.	33.5	36.8	21.7	18.1	20.6	16.9	17.3
Operating Income	d59.9	d1.3	203.4	83.5	75.5	61.0	42.9
Net Interest Inc./(Exp.)	69.3	76.6	d29.7	d22.4	d23.9	d19.5	d17.5
Income Before Income Taxes	9.4	251.0	171.5	35.8	33.2	30.4	23.7
Income Taxes	cr100.3	66.5	61.4	14.3	13.3	12.1	7.9
Equity Earnings/Minority Int.	d322.1	d60.9	d2.1	d25.3	d18.4	d11.1	d1.8
Net Income	[4] d212.4	[2] [3] 123.5	[3] 110.1	21.5	19.9	18.3	[1] 15.7
Cash Flow	d178.9	160.3	131.9	39.6	40.6	35.2	33.1
Average Shs. Outstg. (000)	114,068	110,910	104,742	95,988	94,044	92,202	88,320
BALANCE SHEET (IN MILLIONS):							
Cash & Cash Equivalents	219.4	49.8	149.4	5.4	12.9	7.3	7.9
Total Current Assets	572.9	455.5	589.0	397.3	654.1	498.3	450.1
Net Property	53.0	56.2	96.8	77.0	78.9	43.3	43.6
Total Assets	1,648.3	1,499.9	1,068.7	714.5	936.1	742.9	617.2
Total Current Liabilities	259.1	321.7	337.0	169.3	308.5	271.6	249.3
Long-Term Obligations	213.5	325.1	276.4	218.0	354.9	221.8	219.0
Net Stockholders' Equity	904.4	574.7	342.9	207.1	169.0	154.3	110.5
Net Working Capital	313.8	133.8	252.0	228.0	345.5	226.7	200.9
Year-end Shs. Outstg. (000)	116,887	104,749	94,639	93,708	91,704	88,092	85,356
STATISTICAL RECORD:							
Operating Profit Margin %	...	...	8.2	4.1	3.6	3.9	3.0
Net Profit Margin %	...	4.2	4.4	1.1	0.9	1.2	1.1
Return on Equity %	...	21.5	32.1	10.4	11.8	11.8	14.2
Return on Assets %	...	8.2	10.3	3.0	2.1	2.5	2.6
Debt/Total Assets %	13.0	21.7	25.9	30.5	37.9	29.9	35.5
Price Range	98.99-4.50	61.81-9.17	15.12-5.71	12.17-5.62	15.81-7.02	8.58-1.89	1.99-1.27
P/E Ratio	...	53.3-7.9	14.1-5.3	55.3-25.6	77.8-34.6	45.1-9.9	11.6-7.4

Statistics are as originally reported. Adj. for stk. splits: 200% div., 3/17/00; 2-for-1, 9/94 & 7/96; 3-for-2, 9/95. [1] Incl. $2.7 mill. gain fr. sale of int. in Micro Decisionware. [2] Incl. $175.7 mill. fr. sale of stk. by Internet Capital Group. [3] Incl. non-recurr. chrg. $387,000, 12/99; $16.4 mill., 12/98. [4] Incl. restructure chrg. of $5.2 mill.

OFFICERS:
W. V. Musser, Chmn.
V. Bell, Jr., Acting C.E.O.
H. Wallaesa, Pres., C.O.O.
G. Blitstein, Exec. V.P., C.F.O.

INVESTOR CONTACT: Mona Zeehandelaar, Inv. Rel. Coord., (610) 293-0600

PRINCIPAL OFFICE: 800 The Safeguard Building, 435 Devon Park Drive, Wayne, PA 19087

TELEPHONE NUMBER: (610) 293-0600
FAX: (610) 293-0601
WEB: www.safeguard.com

NO. OF EMPLOYEES: 4,628 (approx.)

SHAREHOLDERS: 105,000 (approx.)

ANNUAL MEETING: In May

INCORPORATED: PA, Sept., 1953

INSTITUTIONAL HOLDINGS:
No. of Institutions: 130
Shares Held: 23,458,780
% Held: 20.0

INDUSTRY: Investors, nec (SIC: 6799)

TRANSFER AGENT(S): Mellon Investor Services, L.L.C., S. Hackensack, NJ

NYSE SYMBOL SWY
Rec. Pr. 50.65 (5/31/01)

SAFEWAY INC.

YIELD ...
P/E RATIO 23.7

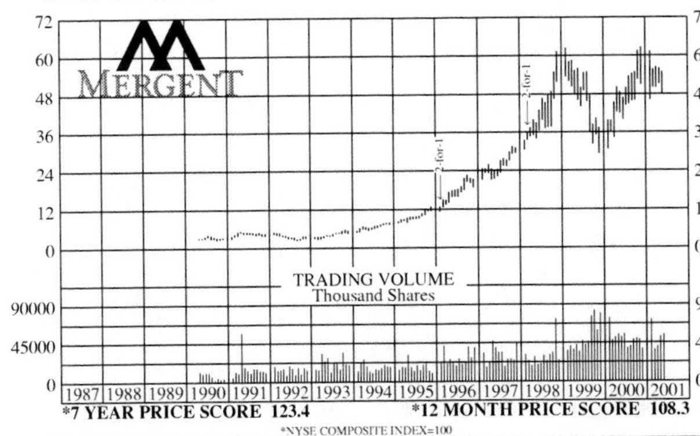

*7 YEAR PRICE SCORE 123.4 *12 MONTH PRICE SCORE 108.3
*NYSE COMPOSITE INDEX=100

INTERIM EARNINGS (Per Share):

Qtr.	Mar.	June	Sept.	Dec.
1996	0.20	0.22	0.22	0.32
1997	0.26	0.27	0.30	0.43
1998	0.33	0.38	0.38	0.50
1999	0.40	0.46	0.44	0.59
2000	0.48	0.55	0.53	0.58

INTERIM DIVIDENDS (Per Share):

Amt.	Decl.	Ex.	Rec.	Pay.
		No dividends paid.		

CAPITALIZATION (12/30/00):

	($000)	(%)
Long-Term Debt	5,406,300	46.1
Capital Lease Obligations	415,800	3.5
Deferred Income Tax	508,700	4.3
Common & Surplus	5,389,800	46.0
Total	11,720,600	100.0

RECENT DEVELOPMENTS: For the 52 weeks ended 12/30/00, net income rose 12.5% to $1.09 billion from $970.9 million the year before. Sales increased 10.8% to $31.98 billion from $28.86 billion a year earlier. Gross profit was $9.49 billion, or 29.7% of sales, versus $8.51 billion, or 29.5% of sales, in 1999. Operating profit grew 14.2% to $2.28 billion from $2.00 billion in the prior year. Results were hampered by a 47-day strike during the fourth quarter at Summit Logistics, the operator of the Company's northern California distribution center.

PROSPECTS: On 2/5/01, the Company completed its acquisition of Genuardi's Family Markets, Inc., a privately-owned supermarket chain based in Norristown, Pennsylvania. Genuardi's operates 39 stores in Pennsylvania, Delaware and New Jersey and has annual sales of about $1.00 billion. The acquisition, expected to be accretive to earnings in 2001, will help expand SWY's operations in the fast-growing Mid-Atlantic region. Meanwhile, SWY plans to spend more than $2.10 billion to open between 85 and 90 new stores and remodel 275 existing locations during 2001.

BUSINESS

SAFEWAY INC. operates 1,688 grocery stores in the United States and Canada that offer a wide selection of both food and general merchandise and feature a variety of specialty departments. U.S. retail operations are located in northern California, Oregon, Washington, and the Rocky Mountain, Southwest, and Mid-Atlantic regions. Canadian retail operations are located principally in British Columbia, Alberta, Saskatchewan, and Manitoba. The Vons Companies, Inc., which operated 336 grocery stores located mainly in southern California, became a wholly-owned subsidiary on 4/8/97. In November, 1998, SWY acquired Dominick's Supermarkets, Inc., which operated 114 grocery stores in the Chicago area. In April 1999, SWY acquired Carr-Gottstein Foods Co., which operated 49 food stores in Alaska. As of 12/30/00, SWY holds a 49% interest in Casa Ley, S.A. de C.V., which operated 97 stores in western Mexico.

GEOGRAPHIC DATA

(12/30/00)	REV (%)	INC (%)
United States	89.2	91.2
Canada	10.8	8.8
Total	100.0	100.0

ANNUAL FINANCIAL DATA

	12/30/00	1/1/00	1/2/99	1/3/98	12/28/96	12/30/95	12/31/94
Earnings Per Share	**2.13**	**1.88**	**1.59**	**① 1.25**	**0.97**	**① 0.68**	**① 0.63**
Cash Flow Per Share	**3.77**	**3.24**	**2.63**	**2.17**	**1.68**	**1.38**	**1.19**
Tang. Book Val. Per Share	**1.35**	**...**	**...**	**0.68**	**1.97**	**1.10**	**0.75**
INCOME STATEMENT (IN MILLIONS):							
Total Revenues	31,976.9	28,859.9	24,484.2	22,483.8	17,269.0	16,397.5	15,626.6
Costs & Expenses	28,857.5	26,161.6	22,349.5	20,746.6	16,037.0	15,336.4	14,685.1
Depreciation & Amort.	837.7	700.4	533.0	457.5	340.3	333.7	329.4
Operating Income	2,281.7	1,997.9	1,601.7	1,279.7	891.7	727.4	612.1
Net Interest Inc./(Exp.)	d457.2	d362.2	d235.0	d241.2	d178.5	d199.8	d221.7
Income Before Income Taxes	1,866.5	1,674.0	1,396.9	1,076.3	767.6	556.5	424.1
Income Taxes	774.6	703.1	590.2	454.8	307.0	228.2	173.9
Equity Earnings/Minority Int.	31.2	34.5	28.5	34.9	50.0	26.9	27.3
Net Income	1,091.9	970.9	806.7	① 621.5	460.6	① 328.3	① 250.2
Cash Flow	1,929.6	1,671.3	1,339.7	1,079.0	800.9	662.0	579.6
Average Shs. Outstg. (000)	511,600	515,400	508,800	497,700	475,600	481,200	488,000
BALANCE SHEET (IN MILLIONS):							
Cash & Cash Equivalents	91.7	106.2	45.7	77.2	79.7	74.8	60.7
Total Current Assets	3,223.5	3,052.1	2,319.9	2,029.7	1,654.4	1,514.8	1,437.6
Net Property	7,146.1	6,444.7	5,182.6	4,115.3	2,756.4	2,592.9	2,506.4
Total Assets	15,965.3	14,900.3	11,389.6	8,493.9	5,545.2	5,194.3	5,022.1
Total Current Liabilities	3,779.5	3,582.6	2,893.6	2,538.6	2,030.0	1,939.0	1,823.6
Long-Term Obligations	5,822.1	6,357.4	4,650.6	3,040.9	1,728.5	1,949.8	2,024.3
Net Stockholders' Equity	5,389.8	4,085.8	3,082.1	2,149.0	1,186.8	795.5	643.8
Net Working Capital	d556.0	d530.5	d573.7	d508.9	d375.6	d424.2	d386.0
Year-end Shs. Outstg. (000)	504,100	493,600	550,900	476,200	442,800	427,400	419,200
STATISTICAL RECORD:							
Operating Profit Margin %	7.1	6.9	6.5	5.7	5.2	4.4	3.9
Net Profit Margin %	3.4	3.4	3.3	2.8	2.7	2.0	1.6
Return on Equity %	20.3	23.8	26.2	28.9	38.8	41.3	38.9
Return on Assets %	6.8	6.5	7.1	7.3	8.3	6.3	5.0
Debt/Total Assets %	36.5	42.7	40.8	35.8	31.2	37.5	40.3
Price Range	62.69-30.75	62.44-29.31	61.38-30.50	31.66-21.06	22.69-11.22	12.88-7.66	7.97-4.81
P/E Ratio	29.4-14.4	33.2-15.6	38.6-19.2	25.3-16.8	23.4-11.6	18.9-11.3	12.7-7.7

Statistics are as originally reported. Adj. for 2-for-1 stk. split, 2/98 & 1/96. ① Bef. $64.1 mil ($0.13/sh) extraord. loss, 1997; $2 mil loss, 1995; $10.5 mil loss, 1994.

OFFICERS:
S. A. Burd, Chmn., Pres., C.E.O.
V. M. Prabhu, Exec. V.P., C.F.O.
R. A. Gordon, Sr. V.P., Gen. Couns.

INVESTOR CONTACT: Michelle McPhee, (925) 467-3723

PRINCIPAL OFFICE: 5918 Stoneridge Mall Rd., Pleasanton, CA 94588-3229

TELEPHONE NUMBER: (925) 467-3000
FAX: (925) 467-3323
WEB: www.safeway.com
NO. OF EMPLOYEES: 192,000 (approx.)
SHAREHOLDERS: 13,740
ANNUAL MEETING: In May
INCORPORATED: DE, July, 1986

INSTITUTIONAL HOLDINGS:
No. of Institutions: 546
Shares Held: 389,460,902
% Held: 77.1

INDUSTRY: Grocery stores (SIC: 5411)

TRANSFER AGENT(S): First Chicago Trust Company of New York, Jersey City, NJ

NYSE SYMBOL JOE
Rec. Pr. 25.89 (5/31/01)

ST. JOE COMPANY (THE)

YIELD 0.3%
P/E RATIO 24.2

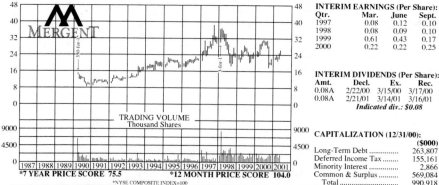

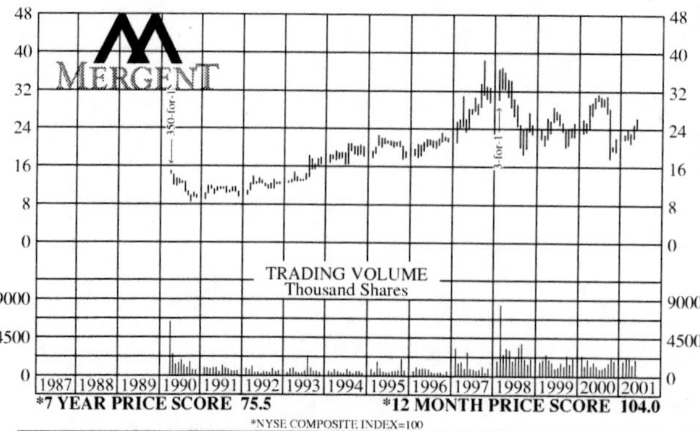

INTERIM EARNINGS (Per Share):

Qtr.	Mar.	June	Sept.	Dec.
1997	0.08	0.12	0.10	0.09
1998	0.08	0.09	0.10	0.05
1999	0.61	0.43	0.17	0.19
2000	0.22	0.22	0.25	0.47

INTERIM DIVIDENDS (Per Share):

Amt.	Decl.	Ex.	Rec.	Pay.
0.08A	2/22/00	3/15/00	3/17/00	3/31/00
0.08A	2/21/01	3/14/01	3/16/01	3/30/01

Indicated div.: $0.08

CAPITALIZATION (12/31/00):

	($000)	(%)
Long-Term Debt	263,807	26.6
Deferred Income Tax	155,161	15.7
Minority Interest	2,866	0.3
Common & Surplus	569,084	57.4
Total	990,918	100.0

RECENT DEVELOPMENTS: For the fiscal year ended 12/31/00, the Company reported net income of $100.3 million compared with net income of $77.6 million in the previous year. Results for 1999 excluded income from discontinued operations of $5.4 million and a gain on the disposition of assets of $41.4 million. Revenues increased 17.4% to $880.8 million versus $750.4 million in 1999. Operating profit totaled $158.9 million compared with $87.9 million in a year earlier.

PROSPECTS: On 4/16/01, the Company announced the sale of a 310,000 square-foot office building in Boca Raton, FL, to the National Council on Compensation Insurance Holdings, Inc. for $52.5 million. Sales of land for conservation purposes is also expected to progress, as the Company expects to close a sale of over 10,000 acres known as the Big Bend Coast and Snipe Island by 7/31/01. Meanwhile, community residential development sales are benefiting from increased activity in northwest Florida.

BUSINESS

THE ST. JOE COMPANY develops large-scale, mixed-use communities primarily on the Company's land and through Arvida Realty Services, and engages in residential real estate sales, relocation services, asset and property management, title and mortgage services, rentals and international real estate marketing. JOE, through St. Joe Land Company, is also engaged in the sale of certain timberlands owned by the Company. JOE develops and manages office, industrial and retail properties and oversees the management and harvesting of the Company's timberland holdings. The Company conducts business in the following operating segments: community residential development, residential real estate, land sales, commercial real estate development and services, forestry and transportation. The Company owns the Northern Railroad Company a short-line railroad between Port St. Joe and Chattahoochee, FL.

ANNUAL FINANCIAL DATA

	12/31/00	12/31/99	12/31/98	12/31/97	12/31/96	12/31/95	12/31/94
Earnings Per Share	**1.15**	**1.34**	**0.28**	**0.38**	**1.00**	**0.32**	**0.46**
Cash Flow Per Share	**1.75**	**1.43**	**0.70**	**0.73**	**1.30**	**0.63**	**0.72**
Tang. Book Val. Per Share	**5.20**	**9.28**	**8.52**	**9.89**	**13.08**	**11.10**	**10.24**
Dividends Per Share	**0.08**	**0.02**	**0.08**	**3.74**	**0.07**	**0.07**	**0.07**
Dividend Payout %	**7.0**	**1.5**	**28.6**	**984.0**	**6.6**	**20.8**	**14.5**
INCOME STATEMENT (IN MILLIONS):							
Total Revenues	880.8	750.4	392.2	346.3	431.2	334.9	330.9
Costs & Expenses	670.2	613.1	303.8	261.0	254.3	259.1	243.3
Depreciation & Amort.	51.8	49.4	38.9	32.5	28.8	28.6	27.6
Operating Income	158.9	87.9	49.5	52.8	148.2	47.3	60.0
Net Interest Inc./(Exp.)	d12.4	...	...	d0.4	d0.6	d2.2	d2.0
Income Before Income Taxes	166.9	120.8	81.4	94.4	189.0	66.1	85.1
Income Taxes	56.6	24.0	36.2	40.5	83.1	24.5	31.4
Equity Earnings/Minority Int.	d10.0	d19.2	d19.1	d18.4	d14.0	d12.2	d15.8
Net Income	100.3	77.6	26.1	35.5	91.9	29.4	37.9
Cash Flow	152.1	127.0	65.0	68.0	120.7	57.9	65.5
Average Shs. Outstg. (000)	86,867	88,553	92,285	93,074	91,496	91,497	91,497
BALANCE SHEET (IN MILLIONS):							
Cash & Cash Equivalents	81.7	141.2	104.4	209.6	537.0	113.7	105.5
Total Current Assets	140.9	197.5	167.3	302.4	630.7	497.2	485.3
Net Property	56.1	384.4	358.9	859.1	834.2	805.0	757.0
Total Assets	1,115.0	1,821.6	1,604.3	1,546.6	1,806.2	1,531.0	1,449.4
Total Current Liabilities	114.4	131.6	93.4	50.7	57.0	44.5	68.5
Long-Term Obligations	263.8	116.0	9.9	...	...	...	16.7
Net Stockholders' Equity	569.1	940.9	883.3	906.8	1,196.9	1,016.1	937.0
Net Working Capital	26.5	65.9	73.9	251.7	573.7	452.7	416.7
Year-end Shs. Outstg. (000)	82,926	86,432	89,154	91,698	91,497	91,497	91,497
STATISTICAL RECORD:							
Operating Profit Margin %	18.0	11.7	12.6	15.2	34.4	14.1	18.1
Net Profit Margin %	11.4	10.3	6.7	10.2	21.3	8.8	11.4
Return on Equity %	17.6	8.3	3.0	3.9	7.7	2.9	4.0
Return on Assets %	9.0	4.3	1.6	2.3	5.1	1.9	2.6
Debt/Total Assets %	23.7	6.4	0.6	...	...	...	1.2
Price Range	31.38-17.69	28.56-20.06	37.00-18.50	38.50-21.04	23.17-17.88	22.67-17.50	20.88-16.38
P/E Ratio	27.3-15.4	21.3-15.0	132.1-66.1	101.3-55.4	23.1-17.8	70.8-54.7	45.4-35.6
Average Yield %	0.3	0.1	0.3	12.6	0.3	0.3	0.4

Statistics are as originally reported. Adj. for stk. split: 3-for-1, 1/98.

OFFICERS:
P. S. Rummell, Chmn., C.E.O.
K. Twomey, Pres., C.F.O., C.O.O.
M. F. Bayer, Sr. V.P., Gen. Couns., Human Res.
R. M. Rhodes, Sr. V.P., Gen. Counsel

PRINCIPAL OFFICE: 1650 Prudential Drive, Suite 400, Jacksonville, FL 32207

TELEPHONE NUMBER: (904) 396-6600
FAX: (904) 396-4042
WEB: www.joe.com

NO. OF EMPLOYEES: 1,666 (approx.)

SHAREHOLDERS: 19,000 (approx. beneficial)

ANNUAL MEETING: In May

INCORPORATED: FL, 1936

INSTITUTIONAL HOLDINGS:
No. of Institutions: 115
Shares Held: 18,899,356
% Held: 23.3

INDUSTRY: Paperboard mills (SIC: 2631)

TRANSFER AGENT(S): First Union National Bank, Charlotte, NC

NYSE SYMBOL STJ
Rec. Pr. 57.25 (4/30/01)

ST. JUDE MEDICAL, INC.

YIELD ...
P/E RATIO 38.2

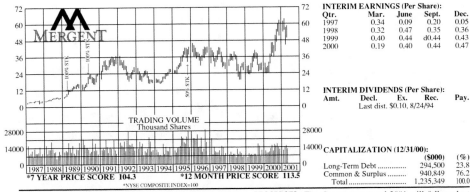

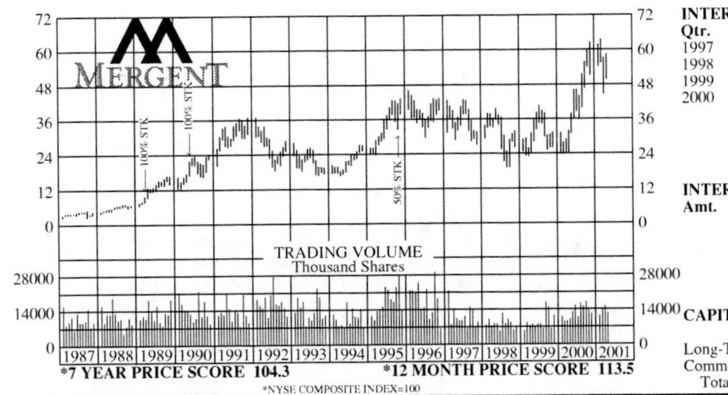

INTERIM EARNINGS (Per Share):

Qtr.	Mar.	June	Sept.	Dec.
1997	0.34	0.09	0.20	0.05
1998	0.32	0.47	0.35	0.36
1999	0.40	0.44	d0.44	0.43
2000	0.19	0.40	0.44	0.47

INTERIM DIVIDENDS (Per Share):

Amt.	Decl.	Ex.	Rec.	Pay.

Last dist. $0.10, 8/24/94

CAPITALIZATION (12/31/00):

	($000)	(%)
Long-Term Debt	294,500	23.8
Common & Surplus	940,849	76.2
Total	1,235,349	100.0

RECENT DEVELOPMENTS: For the twelve months ended 12/31/00, net income skyrocketed to $129.1 million compared with $24.2 million in the previous year. The 2000 results included pre-tax special charges and purchased research and development expenses totaling $31.1 million. Results for 1999 included pre-tax special charges and purchased research and development expenses totaling $125.0 million. Net sales rose 5.8% to $1.18 billion from $1.11 billion the year before.

PROSPECTS: The Company entered 2001 will full product lines in all of its businesses, strong new product flow and expectations for accelerating growth. The Photon family is expected to drive the growth of St. Jude Medical's tachycardia business in 2001. STJ expects to bring to market two additional implantable cardioverter defibrillator (ICD) models this year and to achieve 2001 ICD sales in the range of $180.0 million to $200.0 million.

BUSINESS

ST. JUDE MEDICAL, INC. develops, manufactures and distributes medical devices and provides services for the cardiovascular segment of the medical device industry. STJ operates through a heart valve division and a cardiac rhythm management division. The Company's products are distributed worldwide through a combination of direct sales personnel, independent manufacturers' representatives and distribution organizations. The main markets for the Company's products are the U.S., Western Europe and Japan. On 3/16/99, STJ acquired the Angio-Seal business of Tyco International Ltd. On 9/27/99, STJ acquired Vascular Science, Inc.

REVENUES

(12/31/2000)	($000)	(%)
Cardiac Rhythm Management	921,857	78.2
Cardiac Surgery	256,949	21.8
Total	1,178,806	100.0

ANNUAL FINANCIAL DATA

	12/31/00	12/31/99	12/31/98	12/31/97	12/31/96	12/31/95	12/31/94
Earnings Per Share	**5 1.51**	**4 0.29**	**1.50**	**2 3 0.59**	**1 2 1.12**	**1.82**	**1 1.13**
Cash Flow Per Share	**2.58**	**1.30**	**2.30**	**1.31**	**1.67**	**2.39**	**1.36**
Tang. Book Val. Per Share	**5.98**	**4.08**	**9.58**	**10.74**	**10.32**	**10.05**	**7.92**
Dividends Per Share	...	...	...	...	...	...	**0.20**
Dividend Payout %	...	...	...	...	...	...	**17.7**
INCOME STATEMENT (IN MILLIONS):							
Total Revenues	1,178.8	1,114.5	1,016.0	994.4	808.8	723.5	359.6
Costs & Expenses	858.0	929.9	753.2	782.8	589.3	489.0	244.2
Depreciation & Amort.	92.3	85.7	68.9	66.1	44.9	40.3	16.1
Operating Income	202.4	89.2	194.0	86.8	126.8	194.2	99.3
Net Interest Inc./(Exp.)	...	...	...	...	3.5	...	...
Income Before Income Taxes	177.3	67.0	185.7	88.2	141.8	187.6	106.4
Income Taxes	48.2	42.8	56.6	33.5	49.6	58.1	27.1
Net Income	5 129.1	4 24.2	129.1	2 3 54.7	1 2 92.2	129.4	1 79.2
Cash Flow	221.4	109.9	197.9	120.8	137.1	169.7	95.4
Average Shs. Outstg. (000)	85,817	84,735	86,145	92,052	81,953	71,067	70,169
BALANCE SHEET (IN MILLIONS):							
Cash & Cash Equivalents	107.9	88.9	88.0	184.5	184.6	166.1	137.0
Total Current Assets	704.6	690.3	682.5	743.3	664.6	520.2	434.1
Net Property	317.2	342.8	328.3	307.6	267.7	156.2	132.2
Total Assets	1,532.7	1,554.0	1,384.6	1,458.6	1,301.4	1,015.9	919.9
Total Current Liabilities	297.4	282.5	203.4	251.6	293.3	192.6	112.7
Long-Term Obligations	294.5	477.5	375.0	220.0	172.0	120.0	255.0
Net Stockholders' Equity	940.8	794.0	806.2	987.0	836.0	703.3	552.2
Net Working Capital	407.3	407.8	479.1	491.7	371.3	327.5	321.4
Year-end Shs. Outstg. (000)	85,336	83,781	84,175	91,911	81,010	69,992	69,719
STATISTICAL RECORD:							
Operating Profit Margin %	17.2	8.0	19.1	8.7	15.7	26.8	27.6
Net Profit Margin %	11.0	2.2	12.7	5.5	11.4	17.9	22.0
Return on Equity %	13.7	3.1	16.0	5.5	11.0	18.4	14.3
Return on Assets %	8.4	1.6	9.3	3.8	7.1	12.7	8.6
Debt/Total Assets %	19.2	30.7	27.1	15.1	13.2	11.8	27.7
Price Range	62.50-23.63	40.75-22.94	39.69-19.19	42.94-27.00	46.00-29.63	43.25-23.67	27.33-16.50
P/E Ratio	41.4-15.6	140.5-79.1	26.5-12.8	72.8-45.8	41.1-26.4	23.8-13.0	24.2-14.6
Average Yield %	...	...	...	...	...	...	0.9

Statistics are as originally reported. Adj. for stk splits: 50% div., 11/95. 1 Incl. pre-tax chg. of $40.4 mill., 1996; $40.8 mill., 1994. 2 Incl. pre-tax spec. chg. of $58.7 mill., 12/97; $47.8 mill., 12/96. 3 Bef. acctg. chrg. of $1.6 mill. 4 Incl. pre-tax chrgs. totaling $125.0 mill. 5 Incl. pre-tax exp. of $5.0 mill. & spec. chrgs. of $26.1 mill.

OFFICERS:
R. Matricaria, Chmn.
T. L. Shepherd, C.E.O.
D. J. Starks, Pres., C.E.O.

INVESTOR CONTACT: Laura Merriam, Dir., Inv. Rel., (800) 552-7664

PRINCIPAL OFFICE: One Lillehei Plaza, St. Paul, MN 55117

TELEPHONE NUMBER: (651) 483-2000
FAX: (651) 482-8318
WEB: www.sjm.com

NO. OF EMPLOYEES: 4,951

SHAREHOLDERS: 3,573 (record)

ANNUAL MEETING: In May

INCORPORATED: MN, May, 1976

INSTITUTIONAL HOLDINGS:
No. of Institutions: 248
Shares Held: 60,994,788
% Held: 71.2

INDUSTRY: Electromedical equipment (SIC: 3845)

TRANSFER AGENT(S): First Chicago Trust Company of New York, Jersey City, NJ

NYSE SYMBOL SPC
Rec. Pr. 50.60 (5/31/01)

ST. PAUL COMPANIES, INC. (THE)

YIELD 2.2%
P/E RATIO 11.7

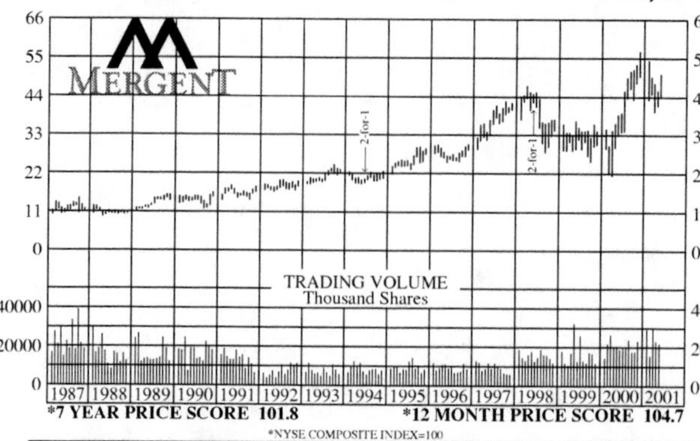

*7 YEAR PRICE SCORE 101.8 *12 MONTH PRICE SCORE 104.7
*NYSE COMPOSITE INDEX=100

INTERIM EARNINGS (Per Share):

Qtr.	Mar.	June	Sept.	Dec.
1996	0.75	0.76	0.75	0.93
1997	1.13	1.25	0.94	1.01
1998	0.76	d1.18	0.27	0.40
1999	0.68	0.90	0.56	0.93
2000	1.53	0.95	0.98	0.86

INTERIM DIVIDENDS (Per Share):

Amt.	Decl.	Ex.	Rec.	Pay.
0.27Q	5/02/00	6/28/00	6/30/00	7/17/00
0.27Q	8/01/00	9/27/00	9/29/00	10/17/00
0.27Q	11/09/00	12/27/00	12/29/00	1/17/01
0.28Q	2/06/01	3/28/01	3/30/01	4/17/01
0.28Q	5/01/01	6/27/01	6/29/01	7/17/01

Indicated div.: $1.12 (Div. Reinv. Plan)

CAPITALIZATION (12/31/00):

	($000)	(%)
Long-Term Debt	1,647,000	17.9
Redeemable Pfd. Stock	337,000	3.7
Preferred Stock	49,000	0.5
Common & Surplus	7,178,000	77.9
Total	9,211,000	100.0

RECENT DEVELOPMENTS: For the year ended 12/31/00, income from continuing operations was $1.01 billion versus income from continuing operations of $779.0 million in the previous year. Results excluded a discontinued operations charge of $19.3 million in 2000 and a credit of $85.1 million in 1999. Results for 1999 also excluded an accounting charge of $29.9 million. Total revenues improved 13.7% to $8.61 billion versus $7.57 billion the year before.

PROSPECTS: Looking ahead, the Company expects to achieve 2001 operating earnings per share in the range of $3.00 to $3.25, resulting from a continuation of low-double-digit premium rate increases and growth in net premiums written. On 1/29/01, the Company purchased the municipality book of business of PENCO, a program administrator, for an undisclosed amount. PENCO is one of the largest program administrators of public insurance in the U.S.

BUSINESS

THE ST. PAUL COMPANIES, INC. is a management company principally engaged, through its subsidiaries, in two industry segments: property-liability insurance and investment banking/asset management. As a management company, SPC oversees the operations of its subsidiaries and provides those subsidiaries with capital, management and administrative services. The primary business of the Company is underwriting, which produced 65.0% of consolidated revenues in 2000. The Company's investment banking-asset management operations accounted for 35.0% of consolidated revenues in 2000. In May 1997, the Company sold its insurance brokerage operation, The Minet Group. In April 1998, SPC acquired USF&G Corporation.

ANNUAL FINANCIAL DATA

	12/31/00	12/31/99	[3] 12/31/98	12/31/97	12/31/96	12/31/95	12/31/94
Earnings Per Share	[5] 4.32	[4] 3.19	[2] 0.32	[1] 4.20	[1] 3.25	3.00	2.56
Tang. Book Val. Per Share	30.54	26.42	25.79	25.09	22.87	20.76	14.57
Dividends Per Share	1.07	1.03	0.98	0.93	0.86	0.79	0.74
Dividend Payout %	24.8	32.3	307.7	22.0	26.5	26.3	28.8
INCOME STATEMENT (IN MILLIONS):							
Total Premium Income	5,898.0	5,290.0	6,944.6	4,616.5	4,448.2	3,971.3	3,412.1
Net Investment Income	1,616.0	1,557.0	1,585.0	886.2	807.3	771.6	694.6
Other Income	1,094.0	722.0	578.8	716.6	478.6	666.7	594.6
Total Revenues	8,608.0	7,569.0	9,108.4	6,219.3	5,734.2	5,409.6	4,701.3
Policyholder Benefits	3,913.0	3,720.0	5,603.6	3,345.2	3,318.3	2,864.3	2,461.7
Income Before Income Taxes	1,453.0	1,017.0	d46.3	1,018.7	699.1	656.2	563.6
Income Taxes	440.0	238.0	cr135.6	245.5	141.3	135.0	120.8
Net Income	[5] 1,013.0	[4] 779.0	[2] 89.3	[1] 773.2	[1] 557.9	521.2	442.8
Average Shs. Outstg. (000)	233,000	246,000	238,682	184,522	168,838	170,798	169,632
BALANCE SHEET (IN MILLIONS):							
Cash & Cash Equivalents	1,347.0	1,583.0	1,209.2	552.9	470.6	1,223.6	1,092.8
Premiums Due	8,661.0	7,185.0	6,404.5	3,544.7	3,622.6	3,979.6	3,710.4
Invst. Assets: Fixed-term	20,470.0	19,329.0	21,056.3	12,449.8	11,944.1	10,372.9	8,828.7
Invst. Assets: Equities	1,466.0	1,618.0	1,258.5	1,033.9	808.3	711.5	531.0
Invst. Assets: Total	27,099.0	26,252.0	27,222.7	15,166.3	14,509.2	13,316.6	11,310.6
Total Assets	41,075.0	38,873.0	38,322.7	21,500.7	20,681.0	19,557.2	17,495.8
Long-Term Obligations	1,647.0	1,466.0	1,260.4	782.8	689.1	704.0	622.6
Net Stockholders' Equity	7,227.0	6,472.0	6,636.4	4,626.7	4,003.8	3,811.7	2,737.5
Year-end Shs. Outstg. (000)	218,308	224,830	233,750	167,456	167,032	167,952	168,404
STATISTICAL RECORD:							
Return on Revenues %	11.8	10.3	1.0	12.4	9.7	9.6	9.4
Return on Equity %	14.0	12.0	1.3	16.7	13.9	13.7	16.2
Return on Assets %	2.5	2.0	0.2	3.6	2.7	2.7	2.5
Price Range	57.00-21.31	37.06-25.38	47.19-28.06	42.75-28.81	30.38-25.06	29.69-21.75	22.75-18.84
P/E Ratio	13.2-4.9	11.6-8.0	147.4-87.7	10.2-6.9	9.4-7.7	9.9-7.3	8.9-7.4
Average Yield %	2.7	3.3	2.6	2.6	3.1	3.1	3.5

Statistics are as originally reported. Adj. for stk. splits: 2-for-1, 5/98 & 6/94 [1] Bef. disc. oper. loss 97: $67.8 mill.; 96: $107.8 mill. [2] Incl. non-recurr. chrg. $221.0 mill. [3] Incl. the oper. of USF&G Corp., from the acquisition date. [4] Bef. acctg. change chrg. $29.9 mill. and excl. from disc. oper. $85.1 mill. [5] Bef. disc. ops. chrg., $19.3 mill.

OFFICERS:
D. W. Leatherdale, Chmn., C.E.O.
T. E. Bergmann, V.P., Treas.
T. A. Bradley, C.F.O.

INVESTOR CONTACT: Christine Hagen, Investor Relations, (651) 310-7788

PRINCIPAL OFFICE: 385 Washington St., St. Paul, MN 55102

TELEPHONE NUMBER: (651) 310-7788
FAX: (651) 310-3386
WEB: www.stpaul.com

NO. OF EMPLOYEES: 10,500 (avg.)

SHAREHOLDERS: 18,409

ANNUAL MEETING: In May

INCORPORATED: MN, May, 1853

INSTITUTIONAL HOLDINGS:
No. of Institutions: 410
Shares Held: 193,685,100
% Held: 89.3

INDUSTRY: Fire, marine, and casualty insurance (SIC: 6331)

TRANSFER AGENT(S): Wells Fargo Shareowner Services, South St. Paul, MN

NYSE SYMBOL SKS
Rec. Pr. 11.54 (5/31/01)

SAKS INCORPORATED

YIELD ...
P/E RATIO 21.8

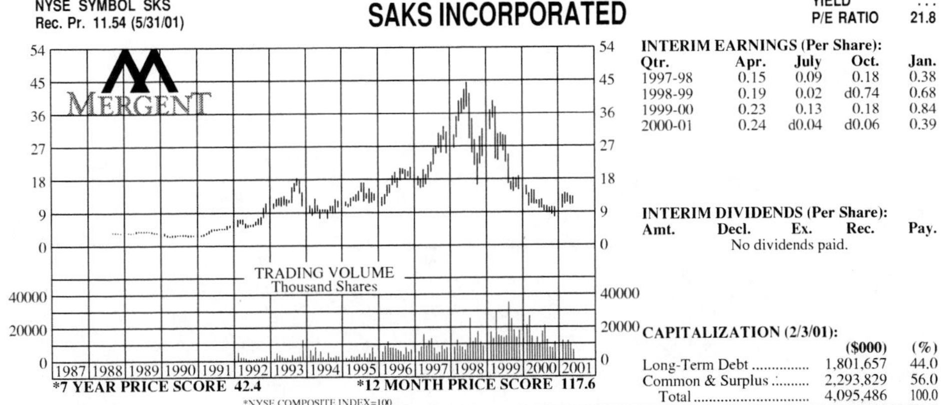

INTERIM EARNINGS (Per Share):

Qtr.	Apr.	July	Oct.	Jan.
1997-98	0.15	0.09	0.18	0.38
1998-99	0.19	0.02	d0.74	0.68
1999-00	0.23	0.13	0.18	0.84
2000-01	0.24	d0.04	d0.06	0.39

INTERIM DIVIDENDS (Per Share):

Amt.	Decl.	Ex.	Rec.	Pay.

No dividends paid.

CAPITALIZATION (2/3/01):

	($000)	(%)
Long-Term Debt	1,801,657	44.0
Common & Surplus	2,293,829	56.0
Total	4,095,486	100.0

RECENT DEVELOPMENTS: For the 53 weeks ended 2/3/01, net income totaled $75.2 million compared with earnings of $198.9 million, before an extraordinary charge of $9.3 million, in the corresponding 52-week period the year before. Results included one-time after-tax charges totaling $57.5 million and $49.4 million in 2000 and 1999, respectively. Net sales rose 2.3% to $6.58 billion from $6.43 billion a year earlier. Gross margin was $2.37 billion, or 36.0% of net sales, versus $2.41 billion, or 37.4% of net sales, the previous year.

PROSPECTS: On 2/8/01, the Company terminated its plans to spin off its Saks Fifth Avenue, Saks Direct, and Saks Off 5th operations into a separate, publicly-owned company, due to unfavorable market conditions. Going forward, SKS will operate in two principal business segments, Saks Fifth Avenue Enterprises and the Department Store Group. On 3/16/01, SKS completed the sale of nine department stores to The May Department Stores Company for approximately $308.0 million. The Company plans to use the proceeds primarily to reduce debt.

BUSINESS

SAKS INCORPORATED (formerly Proffitt's, Inc.) operates in two business segments. The Saks Department Store Group segment includes 243 stores in 24 states operating under the names Proffitt's, McRae's, Younkers, Parisian, Herberger's, Carson Pirie Scott, Bergner's and Boston Store. These stores are principally anchor stores in malls and sell a broad selection of fashion apparel, shoes, accessories, jewelry, cosmetics, and decorative home furnishings, as well as furniture in selected locations. The Saks Fifth Avenue Enterprises segment includes 62 Saks Fifth Avenue stores in 23 states and 50 Off 5th Saks Fifth Avenue Outlet stores in 23 states, along with the Company's direct response business called Saks Direct, which includes the Folio and Bullock & Jones catalogs and saks.com.

ANNUAL FINANCIAL DATA

	2/3/01	1/29/00	1/30/99	1/31/98	2/1/97	2/3/96	1/28/95
Earnings Per Share	**[2] 0.53**	**[1][2] 1.36**	**[1][2] 0.17**	**[1][2] 0.81**	**[2] 0.66**	**[1][2] d0.21**	**0.73**
Cash Flow Per Share	**2.03**	**2.59**	**1.23**	**1.51**	**1.49**	**0.72**	**1.69**
Tang. Book Val. Per Share	**12.56**	**11.40**	**9.95**	**9.19**	**4.68**	**7.20**	**5.38**
INCOME STATEMENT (IN MILLIONS):							
Total Revenues	6,581.2	6,423.8	6,219.9	3,544.7	1,889.8	1,333.5	617.4
Costs & Expenses	6,105.3	5,788.8	5,909.6	3,381.4	1,785.2	1,309.7	570.8
Depreciation & Amort.	214.1	178.8	155.4	65.3	42.7	36.3	19.1
Operating Income	261.9	456.2	154.9	98.0	61.9	d12.5	27.5
Net Interest Inc./(Exp.)	d150.0	d139.0	d111.0	37.6	5.5	5.2	d2.0
Income Before Income Taxes	115.6	317.4	66.2	137.9	69.0	d4.5	26.6
Income Taxes	40.4	118.5	41.2	65.8	31.6	1.9	10.5
Net Income	[2] 75.2	[1][2] 198.9	[1][2] 25.0	[1][2] 72.1	[2] 37.4	[1][2] d6.4	16.1
Cash Flow	289.3	377.7	180.3	137.4	76.3	28.0	33.5
Average Shs. Outstg. (000)	142,718	146,056	146,383	91,086	51,128	38,744	19,824
BALANCE SHEET (IN MILLIONS):							
Cash & Cash Equivalents	64.7	19.6	32.8	39.4	3.4	26.2	1.1
Total Current Assets	1,916.2	1,894.7	1,792.9	1,151.9	596.0	378.8	179.6
Net Property	2,390.9	2,350.5	2,118.6	765.9	510.5	381.8	300.3
Total Assets	5,050.6	5,099.0	5,189.0	2,224.9	1,403.8	815.7	540.1
Total Current Liabilities	830.3	783.9	905.0	454.0	251.6	166.6	76.4
Long-Term Obligations	1,801.7	1,966.8	2,110.4	552.6	502.6	245.6	225.7
Net Stockholders' Equity	2,293.8	2,208.3	2,007.6	1,094.6	539.9	356.9	180.7
Net Working Capital	1,086.0	1,110.8	887.9	697.9	344.4	212.1	103.1
Year-end Shs. Outstg. (000)	141,897	143,043	142,856	89,256	56,032	38,240	19,942
STATISTICAL RECORD:							
Operating Profit Margin %	4.0	7.1	2.5	2.8	3.3	...	4.5
Net Profit Margin %	1.1	3.1	0.4	2.0	2.0	...	2.6
Return on Equity %	3.3	9.0	1.2	6.6	6.9	...	8.9
Return on Assets %	1.5	3.9	0.5	3.2	2.7	...	3.0
Debt/Total Assets %	35.7	38.6	40.7	24.8	35.8	30.1	41.8
Price Range	16.25-7.63	39.50-14.63	44.44-16.38	32.44-15.63	21.38-10.75	17.13-10.38	12.88-7.38
P/E Ratio	30.7-14.4	29.0-10.8	261.2-96.3	40.0-19.3	32.6-16.4	...	17.6-10.1

Statistics are as originally reported. Adj. for 2-for-1 stk. split, 10/28/97. [1] Bef. $9.3 mil ($0.06/sh) extraord. chg., 1/00; $25.9 mil ($0.18/sh), 1/99; $9.3 mil ($0.10/sh), 1/98; $2.1 mil ($0.06/sh), 2/96; [2] Incl. $57.5 mil ($0.40/sh) after-tax non-recurr. chg., 2/01; $35.7 mil pre-tax chg., 1/00; $111.3 mil, 1/99; $43.5 mil, 1/98; $15.9 mil, 2/97; $20.8 mil, 2/96.

OFFICERS:
R. B. Martin, Chmn., C.E.O.
J. A. Coggin, Pres., Chief Admin. Off.
D. A. Coltharp, Exec. V.P., C.F.O.

INVESTOR CONTACT: Julia Bentley, Sr. V.P., Inv. Rel., (865) 981-6243

PRINCIPAL OFFICE: 750 Lakeshore Parkway, Birmingham, AL 35211

TELEPHONE NUMBER: (205) 940-4000
WEB: www.saksincorporated.com

NO. OF EMPLOYEES: 33,000 full-time (approx.); 22,000 part-time (approx.)

SHAREHOLDERS: 2,600 (approx.)

ANNUAL MEETING: In June

INCORPORATED: TN, 1919

INSTITUTIONAL HOLDINGS:
No. of Institutions: 157
Shares Held: 75,794,427
% Held: 53.4

INDUSTRY: Department stores (SIC: 5311)

TRANSFER AGENT(S): Union Planters Bank, N.A., Belleville, IL

NYSE SYMBOL SLE
Rec. Pr. 18.84 (5/31/01)

SARA LEE CORPORATION

YIELD 3.1%
P/E RATIO 17.4

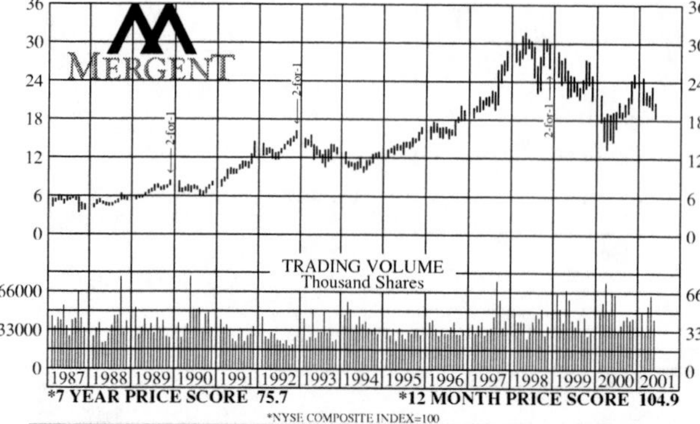

*7 YEAR PRICE SCORE 75.7 *12 MONTH PRICE SCORE 104.9

*NYSE COMPOSITE INDEX=100

INTERIM EARNINGS (Per Share):

Qtr.	Sept.	Dec.	Mar.	June
1997-98	0.23	d1.36	0.23	0.31
1998-99	0.35	0.34	0.26	0.31
1999-00	0.28	0.42	0.29	0.35
2000-01	0.27	0.17	...	...

INTERIM DIVIDENDS (Per Share):

Amt.	Decl.	Ex.	Rec.	Pay.
0.135Q	6/29/00	8/30/00	9/01/00	10/02/00
0.145Q	10/26/00	11/29/00	12/01/00	1/02/01
0.145Q	1/25/01	2/27/01	3/01/01	4/03/01
0.145Q	4/26/01	5/30/01	6/01/01	7/02/01

Indicated div.: $0.58 (Div. Reinv. Plan)

CAPITALIZATION (7/1/00):

	($000)	(%)
Long-Term Debt	2,248,000	50.0
Deferred Income Tax	148,000	3.3
Minority Interest	616,000	13.7
Redeemable Pfd. Stock	252,000	5.6
Common & Surplus	1,234,000	27.4
Total	4,498,000	100.0

RECENT DEVELOPMENTS: For the quarter ended 12/30/00, income from continuing operations was $151.0 million versus income from continuing operations of $375.0 million in 1999. The 2000 results included a pre-tax one-time charge of $344.0 million from business dispositions and restructuring and a $105.0 million gain from the initial public offering of its Coach leather goods subsidiary. Net sales rose 2.6% to $4.76 billion from $4.63 billion the year before.

PROSPECTS: The Company is taking steps to sharpen its focus on a smaller number of brand-name consumer products through the divestiture of several non-core businesses. On 3/22/01, SLE entered into an agreement to sell its Champion Europe operations, which has annual revenues of about $210.0 million. In February, SLE reached an agreement to sell its Australia-based apparel operations and completed the sale of its Artal Spanish meat business.

BUSINESS

SARA LEE CORPORATION is a global manufacturer and marketer of brand-name foods and consumer products. Intimates & Underwear (37% of fiscal 2000 sales) is comprised of SLE's intimates, knit products, legwear and accessories businesses. Well-known brands include BALI, HANES HER WAY, and PLAYTEX. Sara Lee Foods (25%) is comprised of the packaged meats segment, which includes such brands as HILLSHIRE FARM, JIMMY DEAN, BALL PARK, and BRYAN, and the bakery segment. Beverage (13%) includes such brands as HILLS BROS., CHOCK FULL O'NUTS, DOUWE EGBERTS, MARCILLA and PICKWICK. Household Products (10%) is comprised of shoe care, body care, insecticides, air fresheners, and SLE's direct sales operations. On 12/4/00, SLE sold PYA/Monarch (14%), its U.S. foodservice distributor.

ANNUAL FINANCIAL DATA

	7/1/00	7/3/99	6/27/98	6/28/97	6/29/96	7/1/95	7/2/94
Earnings Per Share	[4] **1.27**	[2] **1.26**	[3] **d0.57**	**1.02**	**0.92**	**0.81**	[1] **0.22**
Cash Flow Per Share	**1.92**	**1.83**	**0.09**	**1.71**	**1.57**	**1.44**	**0.81**
Tang. Book Val. Per Share	...	...	...	**0.35**	**0.46**	**0.02**	...
Dividends Per Share	**0.54**	**0.50**	**0.46**	**0.42**	**0.38**	**0.34**	**0.32**
Dividend Payout %	**42.5**	**39.7**	...	**41.4**	**41.5**	**42.0**	**145.4**
INCOME STATEMENT (IN MILLIONS):							
Total Revenues	17,511.0	20,012.0	20,011.0	19,734.0	18,624.0	17,719.0	15,536.0
Costs & Expenses	15,166.0	17,708.0	17,620.0	17,411.0	16,439.0	15,709.0	13,702.0
Depreciation & Amort.	602.0	553.0	618.0	680.0	634.0	606.0	568.0
Operating Income	1,743.0	1,751.0	1,773.0	1,643.0	1,551.0	1,404.0	1,266.0
Net Interest Inc./(Exp.)	d176.0	d141.0	d176.0	d159.0	d173.0	d185.0	d145.0
Income Before Income Taxes	1,567.0	1,671.0	d443.0	1,484.0	1,378.0	1,219.0	389.0
Income Taxes	409.0	480.0	80.0	475.0	462.0	415.0	155.0
Net Income	[4] 1,158.0	[2] 1,191.0	[3] d523.0	1,009.0	916.0	804.0	[1] 234.0
Cash Flow	1,748.0	1,732.0	81.0	1,663.0	1,523.0	1,382.0	778.0
Average Shs. Outstg. (000)	912,000	944,000	939,000	970,000	970,000	960,000	960,000
BALANCE SHEET (IN MILLIONS):							
Cash & Cash Equivalents	314.0	279.0	273.0	272.0	243.0	202.0	189.0
Total Current Assets	5,974.0	4,987.0	5,220.0	5,391.0	5,081.0	4,928.0	4,469.0
Net Property	2,319.0	2,169.0	2,090.0	3,079.0	3,007.0	2,964.0	2,900.0
Total Assets	11,611.0	10,521.0	10,989.0	12,953.0	12,602.0	12,431.0	11,665.0
Total Current Liabilities	6,759.0	5,953.0	5,733.0	5,016.0	4,642.0	4,844.0	4,919.0
Long-Term Obligations	2,248.0	1,892.0	2,270.0	1,933.0	1,842.0	1,817.0	1,496.0
Net Stockholders' Equity	1,234.0	1,266.0	1,816.0	4,280.0	4,320.0	3,939.0	3,326.0
Net Working Capital	d785.0	d966.0	d513.0	375.0	439.0	84.0	d450.0
Year-end Shs. Outstg. (000)	846,332	883,783	921,328	960,554	970,110	961,312	961,530
STATISTICAL RECORD:							
Operating Profit Margin %	10.0	8.7	8.9	8.3	8.3	7.9	8.1
Net Profit Margin %	6.6	6.0	...	5.1	4.9	4.5	1.5
Return on Equity %	93.8	94.1	...	23.6	21.2	20.4	7.0
Return on Assets %	10.0	11.3	...	7.8	7.3	6.5	2.0
Debt/Total Assets %	19.4	18.0	20.7	14.9	14.6	14.6	12.8
Price Range	25.31-13.38	28.75-21.06	31.81-22.16	28.91-18.25	20.25-14.94	16.88-12.13	13.00-9.69
P/E Ratio	19.9-10.5	22.8-16.7	...	28.5-18.0	22.1-16.3	20.8-15.0	59.1-44.0
Average Yield %	2.8	2.0	1.7	1.8	2.2	2.3	2.8

Statistics are as originally reported. Adj. for 2-for-1 stk. split, 12/98. [1] Bef. $35 mil ($0.04/sh) chg. for acctg. adj. & incl. $495 mil ($0.52/sh) net non-recur. chg. [2] Incl. $50 mil ($0.05/sh) net chg. from product recall & incl. $97 mil ($0.10/sh) net gain on sale of int'l tobacco opers. [3] Incl. $1.60 bil ($1.72/sh) after-tax restr. chg. [4] Bef. $64.0 mil ($0.07/sh) income fr. disc. oper.

OFFICERS:
J. H. Bryan, Chmn.
C. S. McMillan, Pres., C.E.O.
C. D. McMillan, C.F.O., Chief Admin. Off.

INVESTOR CONTACT: Janet Bergman, V.P., Inv. Rel. & Corp. Affairs, (312) 558-8651

PRINCIPAL OFFICE: Three First National Plaza, Chicago, IL 60602-4260

TELEPHONE NUMBER: (312) 726-2600
FAX: (312) 558-4913
WEB: www.saralee.com

NO. OF EMPLOYEES: 154,000 (approx.)

SHAREHOLDERS: 82,500 (approx.)

ANNUAL MEETING: In Oct.

INCORPORATED: MD, Sept., 1941

INSTITUTIONAL HOLDINGS:
No. of Institutions: 540
Shares Held: 471,330,641
% Held: 56.9

INDUSTRY: Sausages and other prepared meats (SIC: 2013)

TRANSFER AGENT(S): Sara Lee Corp., Chicago, IL

NYSE SYMBOL SBC
Rec. Pr. 43.05 (5/31/01)

SBC COMMUNICATIONS, INC.

YIELD 2.4%
P/E RATIO 18.5

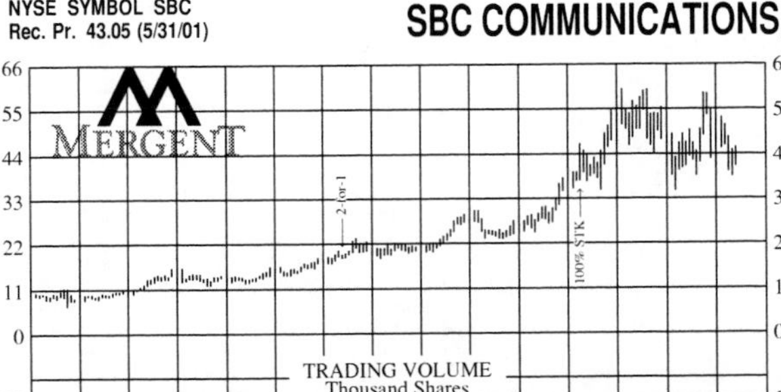

1987 1988 1989 1990 1991 1992 1993 1994 1995 1996 1997 1998 1999 2000 2001

*7 YEAR PRICE SCORE 96.0 *12 MONTH PRICE SCORE 96.2

*NYSE COMPOSITE INDEX=100

INTERIM EARNINGS (Per Share):

Qtr.	Mar.	June	Sept.	Dec.
1997	0.43	d0.43	0.45	0.32
1998	0.49	0.52	0.65	2.05
1999	0.56	0.59	0.64	0.50
2000	0.53	0.54	0.88	0.38

INTERIM DIVIDENDS (Per Share):

Amt.	Decl.	Ex.	Rec.	Pay.
0.254Q	3/31/00	4/06/00	4/10/00	5/01/00
0.254Q	6/30/00	7/06/00	7/10/00	8/01/00
0.254Q	10/02/00	10/05/00	10/10/00	11/01/00
0.254Q	12/15/00	1/08/01	1/10/01	2/01/01
0.256Q	3/30/01	4/06/01	4/10/01	5/01/01

Indicated div.: $1.02 (Div. Reinv. Plan)

CAPITALIZATION (12/31/00):

	($000)	(%)
Long-Term Debt	15,492,000	28.8
Deferred Income Tax	6,806,000	12.7
Redeemable Pfd. Stock	1,000,000	1.9
Common & Surplus	30,463,000	56.7
Total	53,761,000	100.0

RECENT DEVELOPMENTS: For the twelve months ended 12/31/00, net income was $7.97 billion versus income of $6.57 billion a year earlier. Results for 2000 included a non-recurring charge of $204.0 million related to the acquisition of Ameritech, an impairment charge of $677.0 million, and non-recurring gains of $222.0 million. Results for 1999 excluded a $1.38 billion extraordinary gain and an after-tax accounting credit of $207.0 million. Revenues rose 3.9% to $51.48 billion from $49.53 billion in 1999.

PROSPECTS: Results are being driven by strong growth in data services, the Company's entry into the long-distance market in Texas, and contributions from Cingular Wireless, its nationwide wireless joint venture with BellSouth. Future prospects should benefit from SBC's entry into the Kansas and Oklahoma long-distance markets, which commenced on 3/7/01. The Company also plans to enter 30 metropolitan-area markets outside its traditional region, with marketing activities under way in 12 of those 30 markets.

BUSINESS

SBC COMMUNICATIONS, INC. (formerly Southwestern Bell) is one of seven regional holding companies divested by AT&T in 1984. SBC has 94.1 million voice grade equivalent lines and 11.7 million wireless customers across the U.S., as well as investments in telecommunications businesses in 22 foreign countries. SBC offers a variety of products and services under the Southwestern Bell, Ameritech, Pacific Bell, SBC Telecom, SNET, Nevada Bell and Cellular One brands including local exchange services, wireless communications, long distance services, Internet services, cable and wireless television services, security monitoring, telecommunications equipment, messaging, paging, and directory advertising and publishing. On 4/1/97, SBC acquired Pacific Telesis Group. On 10/26/98, SBC acquired Southern New England Telecommunications Corporation. On 10/8/99, SBC acquired Ameritech Corp. As of 12/31/00, SBC owned 60.0% of Cingular Wireless, a joint venture with BellSouth that was formed in April 2000.

ANNUAL FINANCIAL DATA

	12/31/00	12/31/99	12/31/98	[1] 12/31/97	12/31/96	12/31/95	12/31/94
Earnings Per Share	[6] 2.32	[5] 1.90	[4] 2.05	[2][3] 0.80	1.73	1.55	1.37
Cash Flow Per Share	5.14	4.35	4.62	3.42	3.55	3.30	3.01
Tang. Book Val. Per Share	7.38	5.87	4.95	3.61	3.62	2.94	4.68
Dividends Per Share	1.00	0.96	0.93	0.89	0.85	0.82	0.78
Dividend Payout %	43.3	50.8	45.1	110.8	49.2	52.7	57.0
INCOME STATEMENT (IN MILLIONS):							
Total Revenues	51,476.0	49,489.0	28,777.0	24,856.0	13,898.0	12,670.0	11,618.5
Costs & Expenses	31,056.0	29,423.0	16,786.0	16,845.0	8,134.0	7,505.0	6,851.0
Depreciation & Amort.	9,677.0	8,468.0	5,105.0	4,841.0	2,208.0	2,128.0	1,977.2
Operating Income	10,743.0	11,598.0	6,886.0	3,170.0	3,556.0	3,037.0	2,790.3
Net Interest Inc./(Exp.)	d1,313.0	d1,430.0	d993.0	d947.0	d472.0	d515.0	d480.2
Income Before Income Taxes	12,888.0	10,853.0	6,374.0	2,337.0	3,267.0	2,792.0	2,433.8
Income Taxes	4,921.0	4,280.0	2,306.0	863.0	1,166.0	903.0	785.1
Net Income	[6] 7,967.0	[5] 6,573.0	[4] 4,068.0	[2][3] 1,474.0	2,101.0	1,889.0	1,648.7
Cash Flow	17,644.0	15,041.0	9,173.0	6,315.0	4,309.0	4,017.0	3,625.9
Average Shs. Outstg. (000)	3,433,000	3,458,000	1,984,000	1,844,000	1,214,000	1,218,000	1,202,800
BALANCE SHEET (IN MILLIONS):							
Cash & Cash Equivalents	643.0	495.0	460.0	398.0	242.0	490.0	364.6
Total Current Assets	23,216.0	11,930.0	7,538.0	7,062.0	3,912.0	3,679.0	3,493.3
Net Property	47,195.0	46,571.0	29,920.0	27,339.0	14,007.0	12,988.0	17,316.6
Total Assets	98,651.0	83,215.0	45,066.0	42,132.0	23,449.0	22,002.0	26,005.3
Total Current Liabilities	30,357.0	19,313.0	9,989.0	10,252.0	5,820.0	5,056.0	5,190.8
Long-Term Obligations	15,492.0	17,475.0	11,612.0	12,019.0	5,505.0	5,672.0	5,848.3
Net Stockholders' Equity	30,463.0	26,726.0	12,780.0	9,892.0	6,835.0	6,256.0	8,355.6
Net Working Capital	d7,141.0	d7,383.0	d2,451.0	d3,190.0	d1,908.0	d1,377.0	d1,697.5
Year-end Shs. Outstg. (000)	3,386,709	3,395,272	1,959,000	1,837,000	1,200,000	1,218,000	1,218,164
STATISTICAL RECORD:							
Operating Profit Margin %	20.9	23.4	23.9	12.8	25.6	24.0	24.0
Net Profit Margin %	15.5	13.3	14.1	5.9	15.1	14.9	14.2
Return on Equity %	26.2	24.6	31.8	14.9	30.7	30.2	19.7
Return on Assets %	8.1	7.9	9.0	3.5	9.0	8.6	6.3
Debt/Total Assets %	15.7	21.0	25.8	28.5	23.5	25.8	22.5
Price Range	59.00-34.81	59.94-44.06	54.88-35.00	38.06-24.63	30.13-23.00	29.25-19.81	22.19-18.38
P/E Ratio	25.4-15.0	31.5-23.2	26.8-17.1	47.6-30.8	17.4-13.3	18.9-12.8	16.2-13.4
Average Yield %	2.1	1.9	2.1	2.8	3.2	3.3	3.9

Statistics are as originally reported. Adj. for 100% stk. split, 3/98 [1] Incls. ops. of Pacific Telesis Group, acq. 4/97. [2] Incls. non-recurr. chrgs. $1.89 bill. [3] Bef. extraord. chrg. 12/31/97: $2.82 bill. [4] Bef. extraord. loss of $60.0 mill.; bef. acctg. change credit of $15.0 mill. [5] Bef. extraord. gain of $1.38 bill.; bef. acctg. change credit of $207.0 mill.; incl. non-recurr. chrgs. of $866.0 mill. [6] Incls. non-recurr. net chrg. of $659.0 mill.

OFFICERS:
E. E. Whitacre, Jr., Chmn., C.E.O.
R. S. Caldwell, Vice-Chmn.
D. E. Kiernan, Sr. Exec. V.P., C.F.O., Treas.

INVESTOR CONTACT: Larry L. Solomon, (210) 351-3990

PRINCIPAL OFFICE: 175 E. Houston, P.O. Box 2933, San Antonio, TX 78205-2933

TELEPHONE NUMBER: (210) 821-4105
FAX: (210) 351-3553
WEB: www.sbc.com

NO. OF EMPLOYEES: 215,088

SHAREHOLDERS: 1,148,570

ANNUAL MEETING: In Apr.

INCORPORATED: DE, Oct., 1983

INSTITUTIONAL HOLDINGS:
No. of Institutions: 1,067
Shares Held: 1,539,679,229
% Held: 45.6

INDUSTRY: Telephone communications, exc. radio (SIC: 4813)

TRANSFER AGENT(S): First Chicago Trust Company of New York, Jersey City, NJ

NYSE SYMBOL SCG
Rec. Pr. 28.70 (5/31/01)

SCANA CORPORATION

YIELD 4.2%
P/E RATIO 12.0

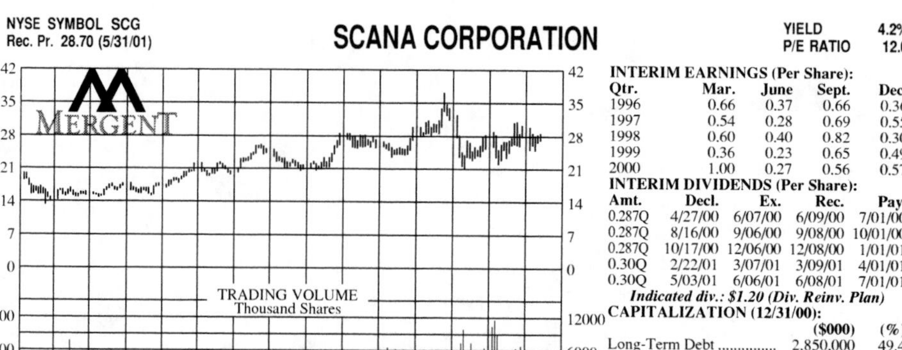

*7 YEAR PRICE SCORE 76.8 *12 MONTH PRICE SCORE 107.8

*NYSE COMPOSITE INDEX=100

INTERIM EARNINGS (Per Share):

Qtr.	Mar.	June	Sept.	Dec.
1996	0.66	0.37	0.66	0.36
1997	0.54	0.28	0.69	0.55
1998	0.60	0.40	0.82	0.30
1999	0.36	0.23	0.65	0.49
2000	1.00	0.27	0.56	0.57

INTERIM DIVIDENDS (Per Share):

Amt.	Decl.	Ex.	Rec.	Pay.
0.287Q	4/27/00	6/07/00	6/09/00	7/01/00
0.287Q	8/16/00	9/06/00	9/08/00	10/01/00
0.287Q	10/17/00	12/06/00	12/08/00	1/01/01
0.30Q	2/22/01	3/07/01	3/09/01	4/01/01
0.30Q	5/03/01	6/06/01	6/08/01	7/01/01

Indicated div.: $1.20 (Div. Reinv. Plan)

CAPITALIZATION (12/31/00):

	($000)	(%)
Long-Term Debt	2,850,000	49.4
Deferred Income Tax	721,000	12.5
Redeemable Pfd. Stock	60,000	1.0
Preferred Stock	106,000	1.8
Common & Surplus	2,032,000	35.2
Total	5,769,000	100.0

RECENT DEVELOPMENTS: For the year ended 12/31/00, income was $232.0 million, before an accounting credit of $29.0 million, versus net income of $179.0 million in the previous year. Operating revenues soared 65.2% to $3.43 billion. Revenues from electric operations rose 9.6% to $1.34 billion, while revenues from regulated gas operations more than doubled to $998.0 million. Nonregulated gas operations revenues rocketed to $1.09 billion from $430.0 million in the prior year.

PROSPECTS: Operating results should continue to benefit from SCG's completed transaction from start-up to ongoing operations in the new Georgia market. Meanwhile, SCG expects earnings from contributing operations for fiscal 2001 to range from $2.15 to $2.25 per share. Separately, on 1/30/01, SCG's subsidiary, South Carolina Electric & Gas Company, announced that the V.C. Summer Nuclear Station was scheduled to return to service in March following repairs.

BUSINESS

SCANA CORPORATION is a public utility holding company. Through its wholly-owned subsidiaries, SCG is engaged mainly in the generation and sale of electricity and in the purchase, sale and transportation of natural gas to wholesale and retail customers in South Carolina. Regulated utilities include South Carolina Electric & Gas Co. (SCE&G), South Carolina Fuel Co., Inc. South Carolina Generating Co., Inc. (GENCO), and South Carolina Pipeline Corp. SCANA is also engaged in other energy-related businesses, including natural gas marketing, oil and natural gas production and power plant operations maintenance. In addition, the Company has investments in telecommunications companies and provides fiber optic communications in South Carolina.

REVENUES

(12/31/00)	($000)	(%)
Electric Operations	1,344,000	39.2
Gas - Regulated	998,000	29.0
Gas -Nonregulated	1,091,000	31.8
Total	3,433,000	100.0

ANNUAL FINANCIAL DATA

	12/31/00	12/31/99	12/31/98	12/31/97	12/31/96	12/31/95	12/31/94
Earnings Per Share	**2 2.12**	**1 1.73**	**2.12**	**1 2.06**	**2.05**	**1.70**	**1.60**
Cash Flow Per Share	**7.26**	**6.36**	**6.24**	**6.20**	**6.34**	**6.19**	**6.44**
Tang. Book Val. Per Share	**19.40**	**20.27**	**16.86**	**16.68**	**15.86**	**15.00**	**14.69**
Dividends Per Share	**0.86**	...	...	...	...	...	...
Dividend Payout %	**40.7**	...	...	...	...	...	...
INCOME STATEMENT (IN MILLIONS):							
Total Revenues	3,433.0	1,650.0	1,632.0	1,523.0	1,512.8	1,353.0	1,322.1
Costs & Expenses	2,341.0	770.0	769.0	694.0	678.9	561.9	539.3
Depreciation & Amort.	243.0	195.0	172.0	195.0	201.2	217.8	224.4
Maintenance Exp.	...	90.0	84.0	72.0	68.4	58.4	63.7
Operating Income	554.0	310.0	345.0	314.0	313.9	287.5	259.6
Net Interest Inc./(Exp.)	d225.0	d142.0	d123.0	d121.0	d122.2	d121.5	d108.4
Income Taxes	141.0	...	...	...	...	...	...
Net Income	2 232.0	1 190.0	235.0	1 231.0	220.7	174.0	157.2
Cash Flow	475.0	385.0	407.0	426.0	421.9	391.8	381.6
Average Shs. Outstg. (000)	104,500	103,600	105,300	107,100	105,123	99,044	94,762
BALANCE SHEET (IN MILLIONS):							
Gross Property	6,630.0	5,615.0	5,436.0	5,190.0	4,980.7	4,763.9	4,556.3
Accumulated Depreciation	2,212.0	1,829.0	1,728.0	1,619.0	1,517.8	1,367.5	1,333.4
Net Property	4,949.0	3,851.0	3,787.0	3,648.0	3,529.0	3,469.0	3,293.7
Total Assets	7,420.0	6,011.0	5,281.0	4,932.0	4,759.3	4,534.4	4,393.1
Long-Term Obligations	2,850.0	1,563.0	1,623.0	1,566.0	1,581.6	1,588.9	1,537.6
Net Stockholders' Equity	2,138.0	2,205.0	1,852.0	1,894.0	1,709.5	1,580.7	1,436.5
Year-end Shs. Outstg. (000)	104,729	103,573	103,573	107,200	106,175	103,624	96,036
STATISTICAL RECORD:							
Operating Profit Margin %	16.1	18.8	21.1	20.6	20.7	21.3	19.6
Net Profit Margin %	6.8	11.5	14.4	15.2	14.6	12.9	11.9
Net Inc./Net Property %	4.7	4.9	6.2	6.3	6.3	5.0	4.7
Net Inc./Tot. Capital %	4.0	5.0	6.6	6.6	6.6	5.9	5.2
Return on Equity %	10.8	8.6	12.7	12.2	12.9	11.0	10.9
Accum. Depr./Gross Prop. %	33.4	32.6	31.8	31.2	30.5	28.7	29.3
Price Range	31.13-22.00	32.56-21.13	37.25-27.88	29.94-23.38	28.63-25.25	28.63-20.56	25.06-20.50
P/E Ratio	14.7-10.4	18.8-12.2	17.6-13.1	14.5-11.3	14.0-12.3	16.8-12.1	15.7-12.9
Average Yield %	3.2	...	...	...	...	...	...

Statistics are as originally reported. Adj. for stk. splits: 2-for-1, 5/95 1 Incl. non-recur. gain $39.0 mill, 1999; incl. non-recurr. gain $18.0 mill. ($0.16/sh.), 1997. 2 Excl. acctg. credit of $29.0 mill.

OFFICERS:
W. B. Timmerman, Chmn., Pres., C.E.O.
K. B. Marsh, Sr. V.P., Fin., C.F.O.
H. T. Arthur II, Sr. V.P., General Couns.

INVESTOR CONTACT: H. John Winn, III, Inv. Rel. & Shareholder Services, (803) 217-9240

PRINCIPAL OFFICE: 1426 Main Street, Columbia, SC 29201

TELEPHONE NUMBER: (803) 217-9000
FAX: (803) 343-2389
WEB: www.scana.com

NO. OF EMPLOYEES: 5,426

SHAREHOLDERS: 43,245

ANNUAL MEETING: In Apr.

INCORPORATED: SC, Oct., 1984

INSTITUTIONAL HOLDINGS:
No. of Institutions: 197
Shares Held: 35,687,112
% Held: 34.1

INDUSTRY: Electric and other services combined (SIC: 4931)

TRANSFER AGENT(S): The Company

NYSE SYMBOL SGP
Rec. Pr. 38.54 (4/30/01)

SCHERING-PLOUGH CORPORATION

YIELD	1.7%
P/E RATIO	23.5

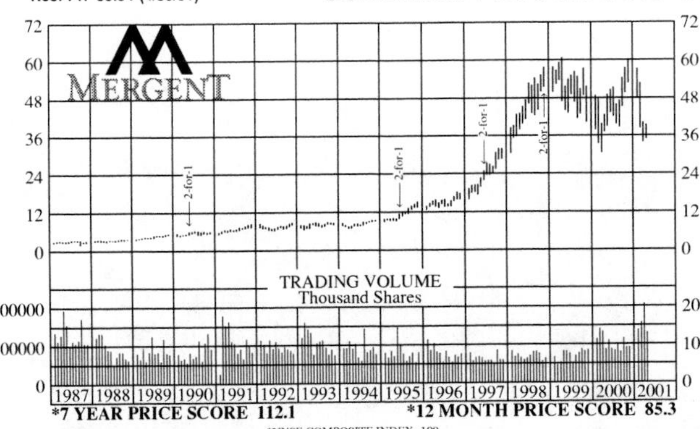

INTERIM EARNINGS (Per Share):

Qtr.	Mar.	June	Sept.	Dec.
1997	0.26	0.26	0.24	0.24
1998	0.31	0.31	0.29	0.28
1999	0.36	0.37	0.35	0.34
2000	0.42	0.43	0.40	0.39

INTERIM DIVIDENDS (Per Share):

Amt.	Decl.	Ex.	Rec.	Pay.
0.14Q	4/25/00	5/03/00	5/05/00	5/30/00
0.14Q	6/19/00	8/02/00	8/04/00	8/29/00
0.14Q	10/24/00	11/01/00	11/03/00	11/28/00
0.14Q	1/23/01	1/31/01	2/02/01	2/27/01
0.16Q	4/24/01	5/02/01	5/04/01	5/29/01

Indicated div.: $0.64 (Div. Reinv. Plan)

CAPITALIZATION (12/31/00):

	($000)	(%)
Deferred Income Tax	214,000	3.4
Common & Surplus	6,119,000	96.6
Total	6,333,000	100.0

RECENT DEVELOPMENTS: For the twelve months ended 12/31/00, net income increased 14.8% to $2.42 billion compared with $2.11 billion in the previous year. Net sales climbed 7.7% to $9.82 from $9.12 billion in the prior year. Revenue growth was primarily due to higher worldwide pharmaceutical product sales such as CLARITIN®, a prescribed antihistamine, and INTRON®, an antiviral/anticancer agent.

PROSPECTS: Schering Canada Inc. announced that CAELYX® has been approved by the Therapeutic Products Program of Health Canada for the treatment of advanced ovarian carcinoma in women who have failed standard first-line therapy. In 2001, SGP's results should continue to be led by growth in its three largest therapeutic product categories which are allergy/respiratory, anti-infective/anticancer and cardiovasculars.

BUSINESS

SCHERING-PLOUGH CORPORATION is a global company primarily engaged in the discovery, development, manufacturing and marketing of pharmaceutical and consumer products. Pharmaceutical products include prescription drugs, over-the-counter medicines, vision-care products and animal health products promoted to the medical and allied professions. Prescription products include: CLARITIN, CLARITIN-D, NASONEX, PROVENTIL, VANCENASE and VANCERIL. The healthcare product segment consists of over-the-counter foot care products, including DR. SHOLLS, and sun care products, including COPPERTONE and BAIN DE SOLEIL. Healthcare products are sold primarily in the United States. In 2000, contributions to sales were pharmaceutical products, 85.0%; and healthcare products, 15.0%.

REVENUES

(12/31/2000)	($000)	(%)
Allergy & Respiratory	4,189,000	42.7
Anti-Infective & Anti-Cancer	2,015,000	20.5
Cardiovasculars	746,000	7.6
Dermatologicals	680,000	6.9
Other Pharmaceuticals	716,000	7.3
Foot Care, Over-The-Counter, Sun Care	749,000	7.6
Animal Health	720,000	7.4

ANNUAL FINANCIAL DATA

	12/31/00	12/31/99	12/31/98	12/31/97	12/31/96	12/31/95	12/31/94
Earnings Per Share	**1.64**	**1.42**	**1.18**	**0.97**	**0.83**	**[1] 0.71**	**0.60**
Cash Flow Per Share	**1.84**	**1.60**	**1.34**	**1.11**	**0.94**	**0.82**	**0.71**
Tang. Book Val. Per Share	**3.75**	**3.11**	**2.33**	**1.60**	**1.41**	**1.11**	**1.06**
Dividends Per Share	**0.55**	**0.49**	**0.43**	**0.37**	**0.32**	**0.28**	**0.25**
Dividend Payout %	**33.2**	**34.2**	**36.0**	**37.9**	**38.8**	**39.4**	**41.0**
INCOME STATEMENT (IN MILLIONS):							
Total Revenues	9,815.0	9,176.0	8,077.0	6,778.0	5,656.0	5,104.0	4,657.1
Costs & Expenses	6,328.0	6,117.0	5,513.0	4,665.0	3,836.8	3,495.0	3,249.9
Depreciation & Amort.	299.0	264.0	238.0	200.0	173.2	157.0	157.6
Operating Income	3,188.0	2,795.0	2,326.0	1,913.0	1,646.0	1,452.0	1,249.6
Net Interest Inc./(Exp.)	...	...	...	...	...	...	d27.6
Income Before Income Taxes	3,188.0	2,795.0	2,326.0	1,913.0	1,606.0	1,395.0	1,213.2
Income Taxes	765.0	685.0	570.0	469.0	393.0	342.0	291.2
Net Income	2,423.0	2,110.0	1,756.0	1,444.0	1,213.0	[1] 1,053.0	922.0
Cash Flow	2,722.0	2,374.0	1,994.0	1,644.0	1,386.2	1,210.0	1,079.6
Average Shs. Outstg. (000)	1,476,000	1,486,000	1,488,000	1,480,000	1,470,800	1,478,800	1,530,400
BALANCE SHEET (IN MILLIONS):							
Cash & Cash Equivalents	2,397.0	1,876.0	1,259.0	714.0	535.1	321.4	160.6
Total Current Assets	5,720.0	4,909.0	3,958.0	2,920.0	2,364.6	1,956.3	1,739.1
Net Property	3,362.0	2,939.0	2,675.0	2,526.0	2,246.3	2,098.9	2,082.3
Total Assets	10,805.0	9,375.0	7,840.0	6,507.0	5,398.1	4,664.6	4,325.7
Total Current Liabilities	3,645.0	3,209.0	3,032.0	2,891.0	3,454.2	3,203.4	2,811.1
Long-Term Obligations	...	...	...	46.0	46.4	87.1	185.8
Net Stockholders' Equity	6,119.0	5,165.0	4,002.0	2,821.0	2,059.9	1,622.9	1,574.4
Net Working Capital	2,075.0	1,700.0	926.0	29.0	d1,089.6	d1,247.1	d1,072.0
Year-end Shs. Outstg. (000)	1,463,000	1,472,000	1,472,000	1,466,000	1,461,468	1,456,800	1,488,112
STATISTICAL RECORD:							
Operating Profit Margin %	32.5	30.5	28.8	28.2	29.1	28.4	26.8
Net Profit Margin %	24.7	23.0	21.7	21.3	21.4	20.6	19.8
Return on Equity %	39.6	40.9	43.9	51.2	58.9	64.9	58.6
Return on Assets %	22.4	22.5	22.4	22.2	22.5	22.6	21.3
Debt/Total Assets %	...	...	...	0.7	0.9	1.9	4.3
Price Range	60.00-30.50	60.81-40.25	57.75-30.34	32.00-15.88	18.28-12.63	15.19-8.88	9.48-6.81
P/E Ratio	36.6-18.6	42.8-28.3	48.9-25.7	33.0-16.4	22.2-15.3	21.3-12.4	15.7-11.3
Average Yield %	1.2	1.0	1.0	1.5	2.1	2.3	3.0

Statistics are as originally reported. Adjusted for 2-for-1 stock split, 12/98, 8/97 & 6/95.
[1] Bef. dis. opers. loss of $166.4 mill.

OFFICERS:
R. J. Kogan, Chmn., C.E.O.
R. E. Cesan, Pres., C.O.O.
J. L. Wyszomierski, Exec. V.P., C.F.O.
E. K. Moore, V.P., Treas.

INVESTOR CONTACT: Geraldine U. Foster, Sr. V.P., (908)298-4000

PRINCIPAL OFFICE: 2000 Galloping Hill Road, Kenilworth, NJ 07033

TELEPHONE NUMBER: (908) 298-4000
FAX: (908) 822-7048
WEB: www.sch-plough.com

NO. OF EMPLOYEES: 28,100 (approx.)

SHAREHOLDERS: 49,200 (approx.)

ANNUAL MEETING: In Apr.

INCORPORATED: NJ, July, 1970

INSTITUTIONAL HOLDINGS:
No. of Institutions: 981
Shares Held: 996,514,119
% Held: 68.1

INDUSTRY: Pharmaceutical preparations (SIC: 2834)

TRANSFER AGENT(S): The Bank of New York, New York, NY

NYSE SYMBOL SLB
Rec. Pr. 63.03 (5/31/01)

SCHLUMBERGER LIMITED

YIELD 1.2%
P/E RATIO 49.6

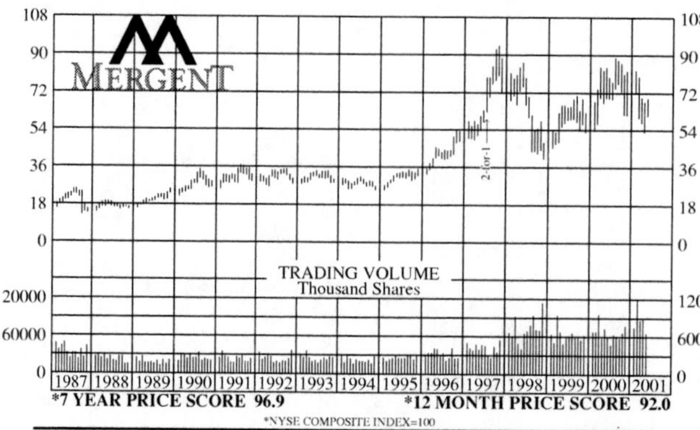

*7 YEAR PRICE SCORE 96.9 *12 MONTH PRICE SCORE 92.0

*NYSE COMPOSITE INDEX=100

INTERIM EARNINGS (Per Share):

Qtr.	Mar.	June	Sept.	Dec.
1996	0.35	0.40	0.47	0.52
1997	0.53	0.62	0.72	0.72
1998	0.68	0.69	d0.05	0.50
1999	0.12	0.16	0.20	0.10
2000	0.24	0.27	0.35	0.41

INTERIM DIVIDENDS (Per Share):

Amt.	Decl.	Ex.	Rec.	Pay.
0.188Q	4/20/00	6/05/00	6/07/00	7/07/00
0.188Q	7/20/00	9/01/00	9/06/00	10/06/00
0.188Q	10/19/00	12/21/00	12/26/00	1/05/01
0.188Q	1/18/01	2/20/01	2/22/01	4/06/01
0.188Q	4/19/01	6/04/01	6/06/01	7/06/01

Indicated div.: $0.75

CAPITALIZATION (12/31/00):

	($000)	(%)
Long-Term Debt	3,573,047	28.6
Minority Interest	605,313	4.9
Common & Surplus	8,295,216	66.5
Total	12,473,576	100.0

RECENT DEVELOPMENTS: For the year ended 12/31/00, net income advanced to $734.6 million versus income from continuing operations of $329.3 million a year earlier. Total revenues jumped 14.7% to $10.03 billion. Results were led by the oilfield services segment which posted operating income of $997.0 million, an increase of 73.1% versus the prior year. SLB attributed the gains at the oilfield services segment to increased activity, improved pricing levels and productivity gains from the use of advanced technologies.

PROSPECTS: On 4/6/01, SLB completed the acquisition of Sema plc, an information technology and technical services company, in a transaction valued approximately $5.20 billion. Also, in March 2001, SLB acquired Bull CP8, whose operations include microprocessor-based smart cards and associated systems applications for the banking, mobile communications and network security industries, for $313.0 million.

BUSINESS

SCHLUMBERGER LIMITED is engaged in the oilfield services, resource management services and test & transactions businesses. The oilfield services segment (72.6% of 2000 operating revenues) supplies services and technology to the international petroleum industry. The resource management services segment (12.8%) provides professional business services such as consulting, meter deployment and management, data collection and processing for electricity, gas and water resource industry clients worldwide. The test & transactions segment (14.6%) provides consulting, integration and products for testing and measurement of semiconductor devices, smart card-based transactions, Internet protocol network security and wireless services. On 12/31/99, SLB completed the spin-off of its offshore contract drilling business, Sedco Forex, to its stockholders. As of 12/31/00, SLB owned 70.0% of WesternGeco, a seismic joint venture that was formed with Baker Hughes on 11/30/00.

ANNUAL FINANCIAL DATA

	12/31/00	12/31/99	12/31/98	12/31/97	12/31/96	12/31/95	12/31/94
Earnings Per Share	**1.27**	**2 0.58**	**1 1.81**	**2.52**	**3 1.74**	**1.35**	**1.11**
Cash Flow Per Share	**1.27**	**0.58**	**1.81**	**2.52**	**2.42**	**1.33**	**1.10**
Tang. Book Val. Per Share	**17.34**	**13.64**	**14.87**	**13.44**	**9.11**	**10.21**	**9.46**
Dividends Per Share	**0.75**	**0.75**	**0.75**	**0.75**	**0.75**	**0.68**	**0.60**
Dividend Payout %	**59.1**	**115.4**	**41.4**	**29.8**	**433.3**	**50.2**	**54.3**
INCOME STATEMENT (IN MILLIONS):							
Total Revenues	10,034.7	8,751.7	11,997.3	10,754.4	9,025.7	7,713.2	6,780.7
Costs & Expenses	9,074.0	8,281.6	10,674.4	9,086.1	8,016.8	6,942.9	6,163.3
Income Before Income Taxes	960.7	470.1	1,322.9	1,668.3	1,008.9	770.4	617.5
Income Taxes	228.2	140.8	308.7	372.7	cr175.7	121.2	81.4
Equity Earnings/Minority Int.	2.2	...	...	...	...	...	...
Net Income	734.6	2 329.3	1 1,014.2	1,295.7	3 851.5	649.2	536.1
Average Shs. Outstg. (000)	580,076	563,789	561,855	514,345	490,042	486,276	486,846
BALANCE SHEET (IN MILLIONS):							
Cash & Cash Equivalents	3,040.2	4,389.8	3,956.7	1,761.1	1,358.9	1,120.5	1,231.9
Total Current Assets	7,493.2	8,606.0	8,805.2	6,071.2	5,042.6	4,023.7	3,823.8
Net Property	4,394.5	3,560.7	4,694.5	3,768.6	3,358.6	3,118.5	2,857.5
Total Assets	17,172.7	15,081.2	16,077.9	12,096.7	10,325.1	8,910.1	8,322.1
Total Current Liabilities	3,990.9	3,474.5	3,918.7	3,629.9	3,474.4	2,764.3	2,786.7
Long-Term Obligations	3,573.0	3,183.2	3,285.4	1,069.1	637.2	613.4	394.2
Net Stockholders' Equity	8,295.2	7,721.0	8,119.1	6,694.9	5,626.4	4,964.0	4,583.0
Net Working Capital	3,502.3	5,131.5	4,886.6	2,441.3	1,568.2	1,259.4	1,037.1
Year-end Shs. Outstg. (000)	478,364	565,931	546,134	498,036	617,734	486,276	484,464
STATISTICAL RECORD:							
Operating Profit Margin %	9.6	5.4	11.0	15.5	11.2	10.0	9.1
Net Profit Margin %	7.3	3.8	8.5	12.0	9.4	8.4	7.9
Return on Equity %	8.9	4.3	12.5	19.4	15.1	13.1	11.7
Return on Assets %	4.3	2.2	6.3	10.7	11.5	7.3	6.4
Debt/Total Assets %	20.8	21.1	20.4	8.8	6.2	6.9	4.7
Price Range	88.88-53.50	70.69-45.44	86.44-40.06	94.44-49.00	54.13-32.69	35.25-25.06	31.50-25.00
P/E Ratio	70.0-42.1	121.8-78.3	47.8-22.1	37.5-19.4	31.1-18.8	26.2-18.6	28.5-22.6
Average Yield %	1.1	1.3	1.2	1.0	1.7	2.2	2.1

Statistics are as originally reported. All figures are in U.S. dollars unless otherwise noted. Adj. for 2-for-1 stk. split, 7/97. 1 Bef. disc. oper. gain of $396.2 mill. 2 Bef. disc. oper. gain of $37.4 mill. ($0.07/sh.); incl. non-recurr. chrgs. $129.0 mill. 3 Incl. unusual chrg. of $333.0 mill.

OFFICERS:
E. Baird, Chmn., C.E.O.
V. E. Grijalva, Vice-Chmn.
J. Lui, Exec. V.P., C.F.O., C.A.O.

INVESTOR CONTACT: Rex Ross, V.P., Communications, (212) 350-9432

PRINCIPAL OFFICE: 153 East 53 Street, 57 Floor, New York, NY 10022

TELEPHONE NUMBER: (212) 350-9400
FAX: (212) 350-8129
WEB: www.slb.com

NO. OF EMPLOYEES: 60,000 (avg.)

SHAREHOLDERS: 23,000 (approx.)

ANNUAL MEETING: In Apr.

INCORPORATED: Nov. 6, 1956, Netherlands

INSTITUTIONAL HOLDINGS:
No. of Institutions: 840
Shares Held: 380,662,986
% Held: 66.4

INDUSTRY: Crude petroleum and natural gas (SIC: 1311)

TRANSFER AGENT(S): Fleet National Bank c/o EquiServe, Providence, RI

NYSE SYMBOL SCH
Rec. Pr. 19.80 (4/30/01)

SCHWAB (CHARLES) CORPORATION

YIELD 0.2%
P/E RATIO 31.9

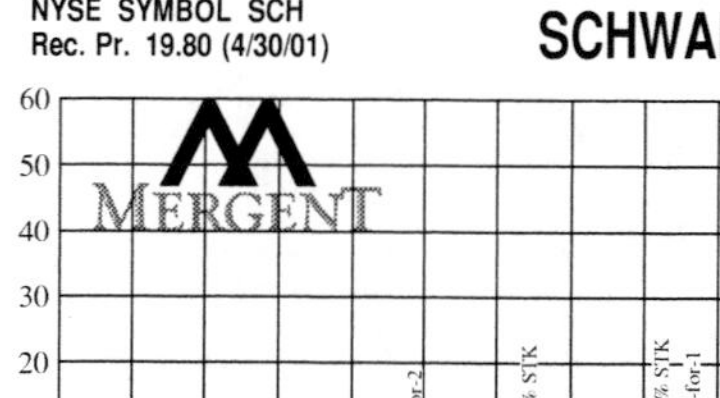

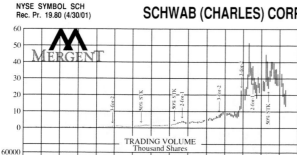

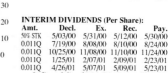

*7 YEAR PRICE SCORE 163.4 *12 MONTH PRICE SCORE 65.9

*NYSE COMPOSITE INDEX=100

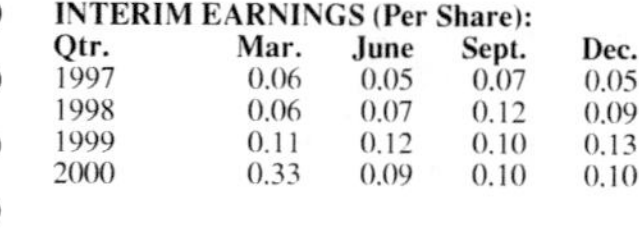

INTERIM EARNINGS (Per Share):

Qtr.	Mar.	June	Sept.	Dec.
1997	0.06	0.05	0.07	0.05
1998	0.06	0.07	0.12	0.09
1999	0.11	0.12	0.10	0.13
2000	0.33	0.09	0.10	0.10

INTERIM DIVIDENDS (Per Share):

Amt.	Decl.	Ex.	Rec.	Pay.
50% STK	5/03/00	5/31/00	5/12/00	5/30/00
0.011Q	7/19/00	8/08/00	8/10/00	8/24/00
0.011Q	10/25/00	11/08/00	11/10/00	11/24/00
0.011Q	1/25/01	2/07/01	2/09/01	2/23/01
0.011Q	4/26/01	5/07/01	5/09/01	5/23/01

Indicated div.: $0.04 (Div. Reinv. Plan)

CAPITALIZATION (12/31/00):

	($000)	(%)
Long-Term Debt	770,229	15.4
Common & Surplus	4,229,712	84.6
Total	4,999,941	100.0

RECENT DEVELOPMENTS: For the year ended 12/31/00, net income increased 7.8% to $718.1 million from $666.4 million in 1999. Earnings for 2000 included various net after-tax charges of $131.0 million. Total revenues advanced 29.0% to $5.79 billion. Commissions revenue grew 22.4% to $2.29 billion. Asset management and administration fees rose 29.7% to $1.58 billion. Results for 1999 have been restated to reflect the acquisition of U.S. Trust Corporation.

PROSPECTS: On 3/22/01, SCH announced that it will reduce its workforce by 2,750 to 3,400, or 11.0% to 13.0%, as part of a plan to lower operating expenses. SCH expects to record a pre-tax restructuring charge of $70.0 million to $100.0 million in the second quarter of 2001. The restructuring should lower pre-tax operating expenses by as much as $45.0 million per quarter, beginning in the third quarter of 2001.

BUSINESS

THE CHARLES SCHWAB CORPORATION provides brokerage and related investment services to 7.5 million active investor accounts, with $871.70 billion in client assets as of 12/31/00. The Company's principal subsidiary, Charles Schwab & Co. Inc., is a securities broker-dealer. Mayer & Schweitzer, Inc., a market-maker in Nasdaq securities, provides trade-execution services to institutional clients and broker-dealers. As of 12/31/00, SCH operated 384 domestic branch offices in 48 states, Puerto Rico, and the U.S. Virgin Islands. SCH also has offices in Australia, Brazil, Canada, the Cayman Islands, Hong Kong, Japan and the U.K. On 5/31/00, SCH acquired U.S. Trust Corporation.

REVENUES

(12/31/2000)	($000)	(%)
Commissions	2,294,145	39.6
Asset management & adminstrative	1,583,089	27.4
Interest revenue	1,237,100	21.4
Principal transactions	570,207	10.0
Other	103,101	1.6
Total	5,787,651	100.0

ANNUAL FINANCIAL DATA

	12/31/00	12/31/99	12/31/98	12/31/97	12/31/96	12/31/95	12/31/94
Earnings Per Share	2 0.51	0.47	0.28	1 0.22	0.19	0.14	0.11
Cash Flow Per Share	0.73	0.59	0.39	0.32	0.28	0.20	0.16
Tang. Book Val. Per Share	2.69	1.81	1.15	0.90	0.66	0.47	0.38
Dividends Per Share	0.041	0.037	0.035	0.031	0.027	0.021	0.014
Dividend Payout %	8.0	8.0	12.7	14.1	13.8	14.4	12.1
INCOME STATEMENT (IN MILLIONS):							
Total Revenues	5,787.7	3,944.8	2,736.2	2,298.8	1,850.9	1,419.9	1,064.6
Costs & Expenses	4,245.3	2,816.9	2,021.2	1,726.8	1,358.5	1,074.0	785.7
Depreciation & Amort.	310.9	156.7	138.5	124.7	98.3	68.8	54.6
Operating Income	1,231.5	971.2	576.5	447.2	394.1	277.1	224.3
Income Before Income Taxes	1,231.5	971.2	576.5	447.2	394.1	277.1	224.3
Income Taxes	513.3	382.4	228.1	177.0	160.3	104.5	89.0
Net Income	2 718.1	588.9	348.5	1 270.3	233.8	172.6	135.3
Cash Flow	1,029.0	745.6	486.9	395.0	332.1	241.4	189.9
Average Shs. Outstg. (000)	1,403,763	1,264,635	1,234,515	1,226,589	1,169,591	1,204,713	1,182,641
BALANCE SHEET (IN MILLIONS):							
Cash & Cash Equivalents	14,300.6	10,544.7	11,398.9	7,571.5	7,869.3	5,855.9	4,587.1
Total Current Assets	34,128.4	28,087.5	21,379.3	15,590.1	13,113.0	9,944.1	7,597.0
Net Property	1,132.6	597.8	396.2	342.3	315.4	243.5	129.1
Total Assets	38,154.0	29,299.1	22,264.4	16,481.7	13,778.8	10,552.0	7,917.9
Total Current Liabilities	33,154.0	26,570.1	20,484.8	14,975.5	12,640.4	9,673.0	7,279.5
Long-Term Obligations	770.2	455.0	351.0	361.0	283.8	246.1	171.4
Net Stockholders' Equity	4,229.7	2,273.9	1,428.6	1,145.1	854.6	632.9	467.0
Net Working Capital	974.3	1,517.4	894.6	614.5	472.6	271.2	317.5
Year-end Shs. Outstg. (000)	1,385,625	1,233,374	1,205,649	1,204,599	1,181,709	1,174,716	1,153,548
STATISTICAL RECORD:							
Operating Profit Margin %	21.3	24.6	21.1	19.5	21.3	19.5	21.1
Net Profit Margin %	12.4	14.9	12.7	11.8	12.6	12.2	12.7
Return on Equity %	17.0	25.9	24.4	23.6	27.4	27.3	29.0
Return on Assets %	1.9	2.0	1.6	1.6	1.7	1.6	1.7
Debt/Total Assets %	2.0	1.6	1.6	2.2	2.1	2.3	2.2
Price Range	44.75-22.46	51.67-16.96	22.83-6.17	9.83-4.50	4.87-2.67	4.30-1.64	1.83-1.17
P/E Ratio	87.7-44.0	110.6-36.3	80.7-21.8	44.7-20.4	25.2-13.8	29.8-11.4	16.0-10.3
Average Yield %	0.1	0.1	0.2	0.4	0.7	0.7	0.9

Statistics are as originally reported. Total revenues include interest income, net of interest expense; adj. for 3-for-2 split: 5/00, 12/98, 9/97 & 3/95; 2-for-1 split: 7/99 & 9/95. 1 Incl. $23.6 mill. chg. for litigation settlement. 2 Incl. an after-tax chrg. of $22.0 mill. for merger retention programs, after-tax merger-rel. costs of $63.0 mill. & an after-tax chrg. of $46.0 mill. for amort. of goodwill & other intangibles assoc. with acquistions.

OFFICERS:
C. R. Schwab, Chmn., Co-C.E.O.
D. S. Pottruck, Pres., Co-C.E.O.
S. L. Scheid, Exec. V.P., C.F.O.

INVESTOR CONTACT: Barb Novak, Investor Relations, (651) 450-4053

PRINCIPAL OFFICE: 120 Kearny Street, San Francisco, CA 94108

TELEPHONE NUMBER: (415) 627-7000
FAX: (415) 627-8894
WEB: www.schwab.com

NO. OF EMPLOYEES: 26,300

SHAREHOLDERS: 12,449

ANNUAL MEETING: In May

INCORPORATED: DE, Nov., 1986

INSTITUTIONAL HOLDINGS:
No. of Institutions: 558
Shares Held: 673,156,265
% Held: 48.5

INDUSTRY: Security brokers and dealers (SIC: 6211)

TRANSFER AGENT(S): Wells Fargo Shareowner Services, South St. Paul, MN

NYSE SYMBOL SCI
Rec. Pr. 25.55 (4/30/01)

SCI SYSTEMS, INC.

YIELD ...
P/E RATIO 17.9

INTERIM EARNINGS (Per Share):

Qtr.	Sept.	Dec.	Mar.	June
1996-97	0.21	0.25	0.22	0.24
1997-98	0.31	0.28	0.25	0.27
1998-99	0.23	0.24	0.24	0.30
1999-00	0.28	0.34	0.34	0.38
2000-01	0.34	0.37	...	...

INTERIM DIVIDENDS (Per Share):

Amt.	Decl.	Ex.	Rec.	Pay.
2-for-1	1/28/00	2/22/00	2/04/00	2/18/00

CAPITALIZATION (6/30/00):

	($000)	(%)
Long-Term Debt	748,402	33.8
Deferred Income Tax	97,607	4.4
Common & Surplus	1,367,922	61.8
Total	2,213,931	100.0

RECENT DEVELOPMENTS: For the three months ended 12/24/00, net income rose 13.6% to $56.0 million compared with $49.3 million in the equivalent quarter of 1999. Sales were $2.60 billion, up 20.4% from $2.16 billion in the prior-year period. The top-line benefited from increased demand for telecom/datacom products. The Company reported sales growth in Europe, Asia and particularly, Canada and Latin America. Operating income jumped 28.0% to $102.0 million.

PROSPECTS: The Company agreed to acquire Nokia Networks' manufacturing business in Haukipudas, Finland and in Camberley, U.K. Under the agreement, the Company will manufacture for Nokia Networks units for mobile communication base stations and narrowband products. Upon closing of the acquisition, the Company and Nokia will enter into a worldwide multi-year manufacturing and engineering services agreement. Separately, the Company is implementing a realignment program.

BUSINESS

SCI SYSTEMS, INC. is a designer, manufacturer, marketer, distributor, and service provider for the global electronics industry. SCI provides products and services for the computer, computer peripheral, telecommunication, medical, industrial, consumer, and military and aerospace markets. The Company operates 40 manufacturing facilities in 17 countries. The Company's geographical markets include North America, South America, Western Europe, Central Europe, and East Asia. The plants design and manufacture both subassemblies and finished products, primarily for original equipment manufacturers. Sales in fiscal 2000 were derived: domestic, 49.5% and foreign, 50.5%.

ANNUAL FINANCIAL DATA

	6/30/00	6/30/99	6/30/98	6/30/97	6/30/96	6/30/95	6/30/94
Earnings Per Share	**1.34**	**1.01**	**1.07**	**0.84**	**0.67**	**0.39**	**1 d0.08**
Cash Flow Per Share	**2.33**	**1.80**	**1.71**	**1.56**	**1.18**	**0.85**	**0.71**
Tang. Book Val. Per Share	**7.26**	**8.10**	**6.23**	**4.98**	**3.99**	**3.19**	**2.79**
INCOME STATEMENT (IN MILLIONS):							
Total Revenues	8,342.6	6,710.8	6,805.9	5,762.7	4,544.8	2,673.8	1,852.5
Costs & Expenses	7,869.4	6,352.1	6,445.3	5,479.6	4,324.3	2,532.9	1,743.1
Depreciation & Amort.	151.5	123.9	103.5	76.8	61.0	49.8	48.6
Operating Income	321.7	234.8	257.1	206.2	159.5	91.0	60.7
Net Interest Inc./(Exp.)	d30.9	d16.9	d21.3	d18.0	d24.2	d16.9	d15.4
Income Before Income Taxes	293.6	217.1	235.9	189.4	136.1	75.7	46.9
Income Taxes	96.9	79.2	90.8	76.7	55.1	30.4	17.0
Net Income	196.7	137.8	145.1	112.7	81.0	45.2	1 29.9
Cash Flow	348.3	261.8	248.6	189.6	141.9	95.1	78.6
Average Shs. Outstg. (000)	149,657	145,224	145,156	121,746	120,562	111,284	110,812
BALANCE SHEET (IN MILLIONS):							
Cash & Cash Equivalents	166.8	216.1	184.3	290.8	46.5	10.3	35.8
Total Current Assets	2,390.8	1,831.7	1,486.0	1,548.1	1,004.4	745.1	721.5
Net Property	589.2	448.0	436.1	301.0	264.1	214.0	182.8
Total Assets	3,351.3	2,322.7	1,944.7	1,869.9	1,283.2	981.3	920.2
Total Current Liabilities	1,102.0	955.3	726.5	793.8	454.7	464.9	325.9
Long-Term Obligations	748.4	140.9	440.5	454.3	338.8	156.4	278.4
Net Stockholders' Equity	1,367.9	1,164.8	748.0	594.7	472.3	349.8	304.6
Net Working Capital	1,288.8	876.4	759.4	754.2	549.6	280.1	395.6
Year-end Shs. Outstg. (000)	144,878	143,886	120,090	119,430	118,368	109,744	109,224
STATISTICAL RECORD:							
Operating Profit Margin %	3.9	3.5	3.8	3.6	3.5	3.4	3.3
Net Profit Margin %	2.4	2.1	2.1	2.0	1.8	1.7	1.6
Return on Equity %	14.4	11.8	19.4	19.0	17.1	12.9	9.8
Return on Assets %	5.9	5.9	7.5	6.0	6.3	4.6	3.3
Debt/Total Assets %	22.3	6.1	22.7	24.3	26.4	15.9	30.3
Price Range	65.13-22.56	43.16-12.63	28.97-10.38	26.69-10.81	15.75-6.44	9.50-4.25	5.56-3.16
P/E Ratio	48.6-16.8	42.9-12.6	27.2-9.7	31.8-12.9	23.5-9.6	24.4-10.9	...

Statistics are as originally reported. Adj. for 2-for-1 stock split 2/18/00 and 8/22/97. 1 Excl. d$8.8 mill. fr. disc. ops.

OFFICERS:
A. E. Sapp Jr., Chmn., C.E.O.
R. C. Bradshaw, Pres., C.O.O.
J. E. Moylan Jr., Sr. V.P., C.F.O.
R. G. Sibold, Treas.

INVESTOR CONTACT: Jim Moylan, Sr. V.P., C.F.O., (256) 882-4116

PRINCIPAL OFFICE: 2101 West Clinton Avenue, Huntsville, AL 35805

TELEPHONE NUMBER: (256) 882-4800
FAX: (256) 882-4804
WEB: www.sci.com

NO. OF EMPLOYEES: 34,000 (avg.)

SHAREHOLDERS: 1,800

ANNUAL MEETING: In Oct.

INCORPORATED: DE, June, 1961

INSTITUTIONAL HOLDINGS:
No. of Institutions: 237
Shares Held: 122,268,017
% Held: 83.2

INDUSTRY: Printed circuit boards (SIC: 3672)

TRANSFER AGENT(S): Mellon Investor Services, Ridgefield Park, NJ

NYSE SYMBOL SFA
Rec. Pr. 57.73 (4/30/01)

SCIENTIFIC-ATLANTA INC.

YIELD 0.1%
P/E RATIO 34.6

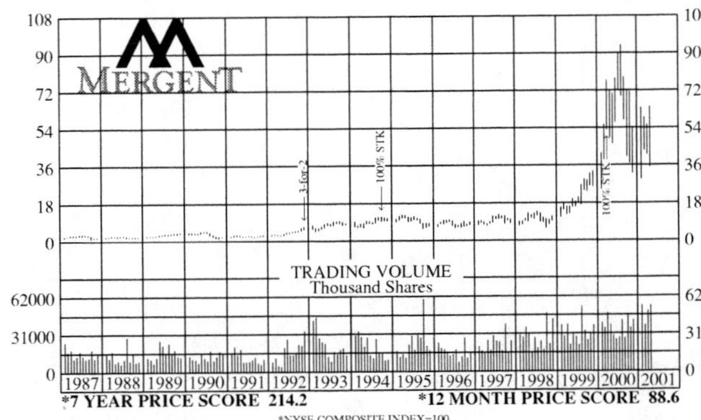

*7 YEAR PRICE SCORE 214.2 *12 MONTH PRICE SCORE 88.6
*NYSE COMPOSITE INDEX=100

INTERIM EARNINGS (Per Share):

Qtr.	Sept.	Dec.	Mar.	June
1996-97	0.07	0.09	0.11	0.13
1997-98	0.11	0.10	0.11	0.20
1998-99	0.10	0.13	0.14	0.30
1999-00	0.16	0.21	0.23	0.35
2000-01	0.67	0.42	...	...

INTERIM DIVIDENDS (Per Share):

Amt.	Decl.	Ex.	Rec.	Pay.
0.01Q	5/22/00	5/30/00	6/01/00	6/16/00
0.01Q	8/22/00	8/29/00	8/31/00	9/18/00
0.01Q	11/10/00	11/28/00	11/30/00	12/15/00
0.01Q	2/20/01	2/28/01	3/02/01	3/16/01
0.01Q	5/17/01	5/30/01	6/01/01	6/15/01

Indicated div.: $0.04 (Div. Reinv. Plan)

CAPITALIZATION (6/30/00):

	($000)	(%)
Long-Term Debt	102	0.0
Deferred Income Tax	114,428	8.6
Common & Surplus	1,214,960	91.4
Total	1,329,490	100.0

RECENT DEVELOPMENTS: For the three months ended 12/29/00, net income more than doubled to $70.8 million compared with $33.4 million in the corresponding period of the previous year. Sales soared 69.4% to $631.4 million from $372.7 million in the year-earlier quarter. Subscriber sales surged 162.0% to $423.7 million, and transmission sales grew 10.0% to $184.1 million. Subscriber bookings leapt 118.0% to $506.4 million, while transmission bookings rose 9.0% to $184.9 million.

PROSPECTS: On 4/10/01, the Company announced that it has completed its tender offer for the outstanding shares of PowerTV, Inc. not already owned by SFA, for $66.8 million. Meanwhile, SFA announced plans to increase production capacity of the Explorer® digital interactive set-tops to 6.0 million per year. In 2001, SFA believes that funds generated from operations and existing cash balances will be sufficient to support growth and planned expansion of manufacturing capacity.

BUSINESS

SCIENTIFIC-ATLANTA, INC. provides its customers with content distribution networks, broadband transmission networks, digital interactive subscriber systems and worldwide customer service and support. The Company's Broadband segment includes modulators, demodulators and signal processors for video and audio receiving stations, products for distributing communications signals by coaxial cable and fiber optics from headend systems to subscribers and analog channels transmitted by cable television system operators. The products also include receivers, transmitters, distribution amplifiers, taps and passives, signal encoders and decoders, controllers, optical amplifiers, source lasers, digital video compression and transmission equipment and fiber optic distribution equipment. On 4/25/00, SFA sold its satelite network business to ViaSat, Inc.

REVENUES

(06/30/00)	($000)	(%)
Broadband	1,550,122	90.4
Satellite	164,049	9.6
Total	1,715,410	100.0

ANNUAL FINANCIAL DATA

	6/30/00	7/2/99	6/26/98	6/27/97	6/28/96	6/30/95	7/1/94
Earnings Per Share	**0.94**	**0.65**	**[3] 0.51**	**[2] 0.39**	**[1] 0.05**	**0.42**	**0.23**
Cash Flow Per Share	**1.25**	**0.94**	**0.81**	**0.66**	**0.29**	**0.61**	**0.37**
Tang. Book Val. Per Share	**7.58**	**4.72**	**3.94**	**3.35**	**2.97**	**3.04**	**2.57**
Dividends Per Share	**0.04**	**0.03**	**0.03**	**0.03**	**0.03**	**0.03**	**0.03**
Dividend Payout %	**4.3**	**4.6**	**5.9**	**7.7**	**66.5**	**7.2**	**13.0**
INCOME STATEMENT (IN MILLIONS):							
Total Revenues	1,715.4	1,243.5	1,181.4	1,168.2	1,047.9	1,146.5	811.6
Costs & Expenses	1,461.9	1,121.4	1,103.1	1,040.9	973.5	1,026.9	723.8
Depreciation & Amort.	50.7	46.1	48.3	43.2	36.6	29.8	20.9
Operating Income	202.8	76.0	30.1	84.2	37.8	89.9	66.8
Net Interest Inc./(Exp.)	19.1	7.9	5.5	3.5	1.1	2.1	2.1
Income Before Income Taxes	222.6	146.2	115.4	89.2	10.6	93.4	51.5
Income Taxes	66.8	43.9	34.6	28.5	3.4	29.9	16.5
Net Income	155.8	102.3	[3] 80.8	[2] 60.6	[1] 7.2	63.5	35.0
Cash Flow	206.5	148.4	129.1	103.8	43.8	93.3	56.0
Average Shs. Outstg. (000)	164,895	157,130	160,006	156,396	153,332	152,388	153,276
BALANCE SHEET (IN MILLIONS):							
Cash & Cash Equivalents	523.1	302.9	271.3	107.1	20.9	80.3	123.4
Total Current Assets	1,150.6	831.5	716.5	597.1	563.0	615.4	505.0
Net Property	179.2	157.5	160.0	166.4	150.6	124.6	85.8
Total Assets	1,779.5	1,062.3	940.1	823.6	763.3	785.3	640.2
Total Current Liabilities	380.2	267.8	258.7	249.8	261.9	275.7	202.3
Long-Term Obligations	0.1	0.4	1.0	1.8	0.4	0.8	1.1
Net Stockholders' Equity	1,215.0	738.2	632.0	532.7	463.7	474.2	395.6
Net Working Capital	770.5	563.6	457.8	347.3	301.1	339.7	302.8
Year-end Shs. Outstg. (000)	159,319	154,694	158,170	155,766	153,980	153,900	150,990
STATISTICAL RECORD:							
Operating Profit Margin %	11.8	6.1	2.5	7.2	3.6	7.8	8.2
Net Profit Margin %	9.1	8.2	6.8	5.2	0.7	5.5	4.3
Return on Equity %	12.8	13.9	12.8	11.4	1.5	13.4	8.9
Return on Assets %	8.8	9.6	8.6	7.4	0.9	8.1	5.5
Debt/Total Assets %	...	...	0.1	0.2	0.1	0.1	0.2
Price Range	94.00-24.41	33.25-11.06	13.97-5.88	12.47-7.13	10.19-6.00	12.44-5.69	11.63-6.22
P/E Ratio	100.0-26.0	51.1-17.0	27.4-11.5	32.0-18.3	225.9-133.0	30.0-13.7	50.5-27.0
Average Yield %	0.1	0.1	0.3	0.3	0.4	0.3	0.3

Statistics are as originally reported. Adj. for stk. splits: 2-for-1, 10/94; 100%, 3/00. [1] Bef. disc. opers. loss $13.2 mill. ($0.17/sh.) & Incl. chrg. $14.6 mill. [2] Bef. disc. opers. gain $3.4 mill. [3] Incl. non-recurr. chrg. $23.4 mill. fr. restruc.

OFFICERS:
J. F. McDonald, Chmn., Pres., C.E.O.
W. G. Haislip, Sr. V.P., C.F.O., Treas.
W. E. Eason Jr., Sr. V.P., Sec., Gen. Couns.
C. Wredberg Jr., Sr. V.P., C.O.O.

INVESTOR CONTACT: Thomas B. Robey, V.P., Inv. Rel., (770) 903-4608

PRINCIPAL OFFICE: 5030 Sugarloaf Parkway, Lawrenceville, GA 30042-5447

TELEPHONE NUMBER: (770) 903-5000
FAX: (770) 903-4775
WEB: www.scientificatlanta.com

NO. OF EMPLOYEES: 10,634 (avg.)

SHAREHOLDERS: 5,901 (approx.)

ANNUAL MEETING: In Nov.

INCORPORATED: GA, Oct., 1951

INSTITUTIONAL HOLDINGS:
No. of Institutions: 350
Shares Held: 106,566,154
% Held: 65.4

INDUSTRY: Radio & TV communications equipment (SIC: 3663)

TRANSFER AGENT(S): The Bank of New York, New York, NY

NYSE SYMBOL SMG
Rec. Pr. 45.70 (5/31/01)

SCOTTS COMPANY (THE)

YIELD ...
P/E RATIO 27.7

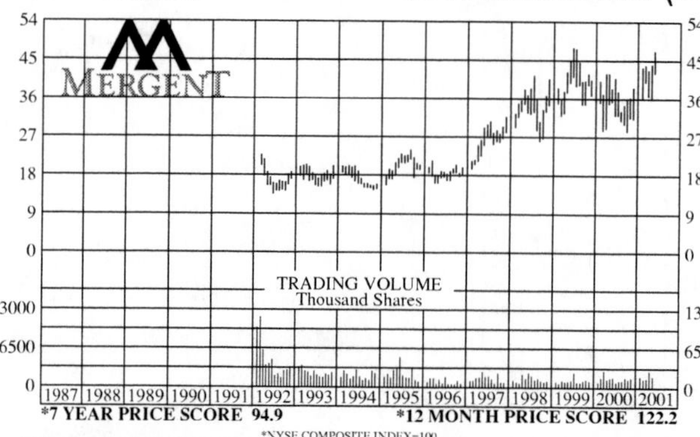

*7 YEAR PRICE SCORE 94.9 *12 MONTH PRICE SCORE 122.2

*NYSE COMPOSITE INDEX=100

INTERIM EARNINGS (Per Share):

Qtr.	Dec.	Mar.	June	Sept.
1996-97	d0.45	0.95	0.70	d0.32
1997-98	d0.42	1.08	0.80	d0.96
1998-99	d0.70	1.63	1.35	d1.08
1999-00	d1.32	2.15	1.77	d0.44
2000-01	d1.83	...	...	...

INTERIM DIVIDENDS (Per Share):

Amt.	Decl.	Ex.	Rec.	Pay.

No dividends paid.

CAPITALIZATION (9/30/00):

	($000)	(%)
Long-Term Debt	813,400	63.0
Common & Surplus	477,900	37.0
Total	1,291,300	100.0

RECENT DEVELOPMENTS: For the quarter ended 12/30/00, the Company reported a net loss of $51.2 million compared with a net loss of $30.8 million in the corresponding period of the previous year. Net sales declined 20.3% to $152.6 million from $191.5 million in the year-earlier period. Gross profit as a percentage of sales declined to 25.1% from 38.6% the year before. Operating loss was $64.0 million versus an operating loss of $28.1 million in 1999.

PROSPECTS: The Company anticipates annual sales growth of 6.0% to 8.0% in its core businesses and annual earnings growth of at least 15.0% in fiscal 2001. to achieve these earnings targets, SMG will continue to emphasize consumer marketing to grow market share. Also, the Company plans to pursue opportunities to recover raw material and fuel costs through increased manufacturing and distribution efficiencies, consolidate its North American sales force, and reduce the rate of increases in selling, general and administrative costs.

BUSINESS

THE SCOTTS COMPANY manufactures and markets products for lawns, gardens, professional turf and horticulture. Products include: lawn fertilizers, lawn fertilizer combination products and lawn control products, garden tools, walk-behind and riding mowers, grass seed, lawn spreaders and lawn and garden carts; garden and indoor plant care products; potting soils and other growing media products; and pesticides (including herbicides, insecticides and fungicides). SMG operates in three principle business segments: the North American Consumer Business Group (72.0% of fiscal 2000 consolidated sales), includes products of the Consumer Lawns, Consumer Gardens, Consumer Growing Media and Consumer Ortho groups, sold in the United States and Canada; the North American Professional Business Group (7.0%), includes primarily horticultural products sold in the United States and Canada; and the International Business Group (21.0%). The Company's major customers include mass merchandisers, home improvement centers, large hardware chains, independent hardware stores, nurseries, garden centers, food and drug stores, lawn and landscape service companies, commercial nurseries and greenhouses, and specialty crop growers.

ANNUAL FINANCIAL DATA

	9/30/00	9/30/99	9/30/98	9/30/97	9/30/96	9/30/95	9/30/94
Earnings Per Share	**2.25**	**[1][3] 2.27**	**[1][3] 1.22**	**1.35**	**[2] d0.65**	**1.11**	**[1] 1.27**
Cash Flow Per Share	**4.49**	**3.92**	**2.15**	**2.05**	**0.91**	**2.24**	**2.44**
Tang. Book Val. Per Share	...	...	...	...	...	...	**1.86**
INCOME STATEMENT (IN MILLIONS):							
Total Revenues	1,764.3	1,648.3	1,113.0	900.8	751.9	732.8	606.3
Costs & Expenses	1,523.1	1,425.9	981.1	774.1	677.7	640.2	525.1
Depreciation & Amort.	66.3	60.2	37.8	30.4	29.3	25.7	21.9
Operating Income	174.9	162.2	94.1	96.3	44.9	67.0	59.3
Net Interest Inc./(Exp.)	d93.9	d79.1	d32.2	d26.7	d26.5	d26.3	d17.4
Income Before Income Taxes	116.3	117.0	61.9	69.6	1.3	40.7	41.8
Income Taxes	43.2	47.9	24.9	30.1	3.8	15.6	17.9
Net Income	73.1	[1][3] 69.1	[1][3] 37.0	39.5	[2] d2.5	25.1	[1] 23.9
Cash Flow	133.0	119.6	65.0	60.1	17.0	49.6	45.8
Average Shs. Outstg. (000)	29,600	30,500	30,300	29,300	18,786	22,617	18,785
BALANCE SHEET (IN MILLIONS):							
Cash & Cash Equivalents	33.0	30.3	10.6	13.0	10.6	7.0	10.7
Total Current Assets	643.9	641.7	367.2	285.8	292.0	349.2	250.3
Net Property	290.5	259.4	197.0	146.1	139.5	148.8	140.1
Total Assets	1,761.4	1,769.6	1,035.2	787.6	731.7	807.4	528.6
Total Current Liabilities	409.8	366.9	231.9	139.3	110.8	119.4	109.7
Long-Term Obligations	813.4	893.6	359.2	219.8	223.1	272.0	220.1
Net Stockholders' Equity	477.9	443.3	403.9	389.2	364.3	383.5	168.2
Net Working Capital	234.1	274.8	135.3	146.5	181.2	229.7	140.6
Year-end Shs. Outstg. (000)	27,900	18,400	18,300	18,700	18,575	18,694	18,667
STATISTICAL RECORD:							
Operating Profit Margin %	9.9	9.8	8.5	10.7	6.0	9.1	9.8
Net Profit Margin %	4.1	4.2	3.3	4.4	...	3.4	3.9
Return on Equity %	15.3	15.6	9.2	10.1	...	6.5	14.2
Return on Assets %	4.2	3.9	3.6	5.0	...	3.1	4.5
Debt/Total Assets %	46.2	50.5	34.7	27.9	30.5	33.7	41.6
Price Range	42.00-28.25	48.00-31.94	41.63-26.00	31.75-19.50	21.50-16.13	24.00-15.63	20.25-14.50
P/E Ratio	18.7-12.6	21.1-14.1	34.1-21.3	23.5-14.4	...	21.6-14.1	15.9-11.4

Statistics are as originally reported. [1] Bef. loss on early extinguish. of debt of $992,000, 1994; $700,000, 1998; $5.9 mill., 1999; [2] Incl. pre-tax unusual chrgs. of $17.7 mill. [3] Incl. pre-tax restruct. & other chrgs. of $15.4 mill., 1998; $1.4 mill., 1999.

OFFICERS:
C. M. Berger, Chmn., C.E.O.
J. Hagedorn, Pres., C.O.O.
P. J. Norton, Exec. V.P., C.F.O.

INVESTOR CONTACT: Kristen L. Bibby, Mgr. Inv. Rel., (614) 719-5500

PRINCIPAL OFFICE: 41 South High Street, Suite 3500, Columbus, OH 43215

TELEPHONE NUMBER: (614) 719-5500
FAX: (614) 644-7244
WEB: www.scotts.com
NO. OF EMPLOYEES: 4,068 (approx.)
SHAREHOLDERS: 8,200 (approx.)
ANNUAL MEETING: In Jan.
INCORPORATED: DE, Jan., 1992; reincorp., OH

INSTITUTIONAL HOLDINGS:
No. of Institutions: 141
Shares Held: 15,899,510
% Held: 55.6

INDUSTRY: Agricultural chemicals, nec (SIC: 2879)

TRANSFER AGENT(S): National City Bank, Cleveland, OH

NYSE SYMBOL SSP
Rec. Pr. 64.22 (4/30/01)

SCRIPPS (E.W.) COMPANY (THE)

YIELD 0.9%
P/E RATIO 29.9

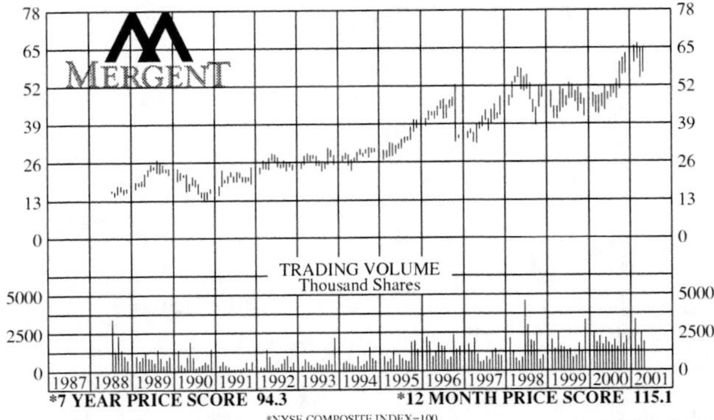

*7 YEAR PRICE SCORE 94.3 *12 MONTH PRICE SCORE 115.1
*NYSE COMPOSITE INDEX=100

INTERIM EARNINGS (Per Share):

Qtr.	Mar.	June	Sept.	Dec.
1998		1.62		
1999	0.40	0.56	0.32	0.58
2000	0.43	0.58	0.45	0.69

INTERIM DIVIDENDS (Per Share):

Amt.	Decl.	Ex.	Rec.	Pay.
0.14Q	8/17/00	8/29/00	8/31/00	9/08/00
0.14Q	11/16/00	11/28/00	11/30/00	12/08/00
0.15Q	2/13/01	2/26/01	2/28/01	3/09/01
0.15Q	5/17/01	5/29/01	5/31/01	6/08/01

Indicated div.: $0.60

CAPITALIZATION (12/31/00):

	($000)	(%)
Long-Term Debt	501,781	26.3
Deferred Income Tax	129,932	6.8
Common & Surplus	1,277,810	66.9
Total	1,909,523	100.0

RECENT DEVELOPMENTS: For the year ended 12/31/00, net income rose 11.9% to $163.5 million compared with $146.1 million in 1999. Results for 2000 included a net investment charge of $24.8 million and a net gain of $6.2 million from divested operations. Results for 1999 included a net investment charge of $544,000. Total operating revenues grew 9.4% to $1.72 billion from $1.57 billion in the previous year. Operating income increased 16.8% to $345.1 million.

PROSPECTS: Both Home & Garden Television and The Television Food Network are expected to perform well in 2001. In addition, SSP anticipates significantly improved results for the newspaper segment in the second half of the year. Meanwhile, SSP will continue with its plans to establish the Do It Yourself brand and launch Fine Living, the Company's fourth cable network brand. Separately, the Company entered into a joint operating agreement with MediaNews Group.

BUSINESS

THE E.W. SCRIPPS COMPANY is a diversified media company operating in four business segments: newspapers, broadcast television, category television and licensing and other media. The newspaper segment includes 21 daily newspapers and is the tenth largest newspaper publisher in the U.S. The broadcast television segment includes 10 network-affiliated stations and is the largest independent operator of ABC affiliates in the nation. Category television includes Home & Garden Television, The Television Food Network, the Do It Yourself Network and the Company's 12.0% interest in FOX Sports South, a regional cable television network. The licensing and other media segment includes syndication and licensing of news features and comics, publication of independent telephone directories, and investments in businesses focusing on new media technology.

ANNUAL FINANCIAL DATA

	12/31/00	12/31/99	12/31/98	12/31/97	12/31/96	12/31/95	12/31/94
Earnings Per Share	4 2.06	1.86	1.62	1 1.93	1 2 3 1.62	2 1.17	1 2 1.22
Cash Flow Per Share	3.44	3.18	2.90	2.88	2.48	2.00	1.99
Tang. Book Val. Per Share	0.87	...	...	...	4.38	8.69	...
Dividends Per Share	0.56	0.56	0.54	0.52	0.13	...	...
Dividend Payout %	27.2	30.1	33.3	26.9	8.0	...	...
INCOME STATEMENT (IN MILLIONS):							
Total Revenues	1,719.4	1,571.3	1,454.6	1,242.0	1,121.9	1,030.4	964.6
Costs & Expenses	1,265.1	1,170.8	1,074.7	913.5	846.6	782.6	722.0
Depreciation & Amort.	109.2	103.9	103.8	77.6	69.4	66.6	58.9
Operating Income	345.1	296.6	276.0	250.8	205.9	181.2	183.6
Net Interest Inc./(Exp.)	d51.9	d45.2	d47.1	d18.5	d9.6	d11.2	d16.3
Income Before Income Taxes	276.0	255.5	229.2	280.3	219.6	171.5	181.1
Income Taxes	108.1	104.1	93.1	117.5	86.0	74.5	80.4
Equity Earnings/Minority Int.	d4.5	d4.4	d4.9	d5.1	d3.4	d3.3	d7.8
Net Income	4 163.5	146.9	131.2	1 157.7	1 2 3 130.1	2 93.6	1 2 92.8
Cash Flow	272.6	250.8	235.1	235.3	199.5	160.2	151.7
Average Shs. Outstg. (000)	79,161	78,951	80,921	81,645	80,401	79,956	76,246
BALANCE SHEET (IN MILLIONS):							
Cash & Cash Equivalents	14.1	10.5	35.0	17.4	12.8	55.0	...
Total Current Assets	524.0	477.3	407.3	379.1	309.0	334.2	...
Net Property	502.0	485.6	478.7	480.0	430.7	426.0	...
Total Assets	2,572.9	2,520.2	2,345.1	2,280.8	1,463.6	1,655.6	...
Total Current Liabilities	533.0	577.5	532.5	430.0	323.4	266.1	...
Long-Term Obligations	501.8	501.8	501.8	601.9	31.8	2.2	...
Net Stockholders' Equity	1,277.8	1,164.3	1,068.7	1,049.0	944.6	1,191.4	...
Net Working Capital	d9.0	d100.2	d125.2	d50.8	d14.4	68.1	...
Year-end Shs. Outstg. (000)	78,739	78,142	78,544	80,630	80,764	80,064	...
STATISTICAL RECORD:							
Operating Profit Margin %	20.1	18.9	19.0	20.2	18.3	17.6	19.0
Net Profit Margin %	9.5	9.4	9.0	12.7	11.6	9.1	9.6
Return on Equity %	12.8	12.6	12.3	15.0	13.8	7.9	...
Return on Assets %	6.4	5.8	5.6	6.9	8.9	5.7	...
Price Range	63.25-42.38	53.00-40.50	58.50-38.50	48.50-32.25	52.38-32.75	40.63-26.75	31.00-23.00
P/E Ratio	30.7-20.6	28.5-21.8	36.1-23.8	25.1-16.7	32.3-20.2	34.7-22.9	25.4-18.9
Average Yield %	1.1	1.2	1.1	1.3	0.3	...	...

Statistics are as originally reported. 1 Incl. non-recur. gain of $44.9 mill., 1997; $21.5 mill., 1996; and $14.7 mill., 1994. 2 Excl. gain fr. disc. opers. of $39.5 mill., 1996; $39.8 mill., 1995; and $29.9 mill., 1994. 3 Excl. loss of $12.3 mill. fr. cost of cable transaction. 4 Incl. net gain on divested opers. of $6.2 mill.

OFFICERS:
W. R. Burleigh, Chmn.
K. W. Lowe, Pres., C.E.O., C.O.O.

INVESTOR CONTACT: Investor Relations, (513) 977-3825

PRINCIPAL OFFICE: 312 Walnut Street, Cincinnati, OH 45202

TELEPHONE NUMBER: (513) 977-3000
FAX: (513) 977-3721
WEB: www.scripps.com
NO. OF EMPLOYEES: 8,400 (approx.)
SHAREHOLDERS: 8,000 (approx. class A); 18 (common voting)
ANNUAL MEETING: In May
INCORPORATED: OH, 1878, reincorp., DE, 1994

INSTITUTIONAL HOLDINGS:
No. of Institutions: 138
Shares Held: 26,371,295
% Held: 33.3

INDUSTRY: Newspapers (SIC: 2711)

TRANSFER AGENT(S): The Fifth Third Bank, Cincinnati, OH

NYSE SYMBOL SEE
Rec. Pr. 38.80 (4/30/01)

SEALED AIR CORPORATION

YIELD ...
P/E RATIO 20.3

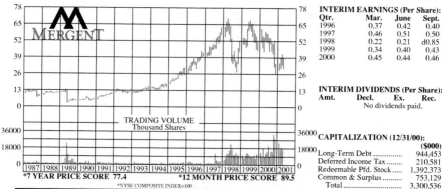

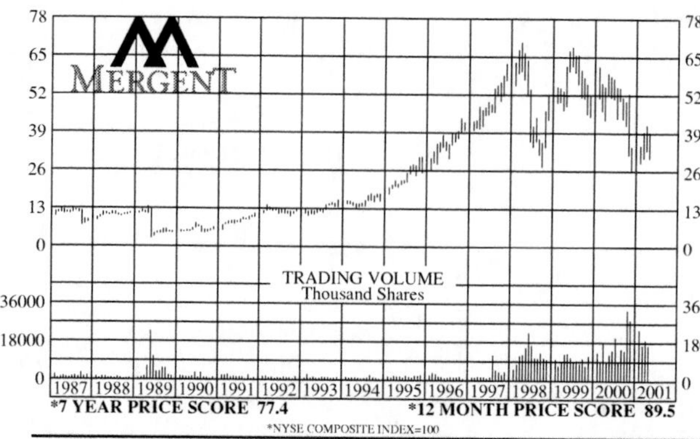

INTERIM EARNINGS (Per Share):

Qtr.	Mar.	June	Sept.	Dec.
1996	0.37	0.42	0.40	0.44
1997	0.46	0.51	0.50	0.41
1998	0.22	0.21	d0.85	0.56
1999	0.34	0.40	0.43	0.50
2000	0.45	0.44	0.46	0.56

INTERIM DIVIDENDS (Per Share):

Amt.	Decl.	Ex.	Rec.	Pay.

No dividends paid.

CAPITALIZATION (12/31/00):

	($000)	(%)
Long-Term Debt	944,453	28.6
Deferred Income Tax	210,581	6.4
Redeemable Pfd. Stock	1,392,373	42.2
Common & Surplus	753,129	22.8
Total	3,300,536	100.0

RECENT DEVELOPMENTS: For the year ended 12/31/00, net income increased 6.6% to $225.3 million compared with $211.5 million in 1999. Results for 2000 included a restructuring credit of $1.2 million. Total net sales rose 4.6% to $3.07 billion from $2.93 billion a year earlier. Food packaging net sales increased 3.1% to $1.84 billion, while protective and specialty packaging net sales advanced 7.0% to $1.23 billion.

PROSPECTS: Looking ahead, SEE expects the continuing disruption in meat supply and consumption, the sluggish global economy and sustained higher energy costs will continue for the remainder of 2001. As a result, SEE will exercise strict cost controls over selling, general and administrative expenses and review its business processes and organizational structure in an attempt to better serve its customers and reach its sales growth objective.

BUSINESS

SEALED AIR CORPORATION is engaged in the manufacture and sale of a wide range of food, protective and specialty packaging materials and systems throughout the world. SEE's principal food and specialty packaging products are its flexible materials and related systems marketed primarily under Cryovac™ for a broad range of perishable food applications. This segment also includes SEE's foam trays used by supermarkets and food processors, absorbent pads used for the retail packaging of meat, fish and poultry, and rigid plastic containers for dairy and other food products. SEE's protective packaging products include its cushioning and surface protection products and certain other products, which are used by manufacturing, distribution and retail customers. In April 1998, after W.R. Grace spun off its specialty chemical business (which became the "new" W.R. Grace) it acquired the "old" Sealed Air Corporation. The "old" W.R. Grace, consisting of the Cryovac business and the "old" Sealed Air then changed its name to Sealed Air Corporation.

ANNUAL FINANCIAL DATA

	12/31/00	12/31/99	12/31/98	12/31/97	12/31/96	12/31/95	12/31/94
Earnings Per Share	**4 1.93**	**1.68**	**3 0.02**	**2 1.88**	**1.63**	**1.25**	**1 0.94**
Cash Flow Per Share	**4.85**	**4.34**	**2.71**	**2.41**	**2.57**	**2.09**	**1.52**
Tang. Book Val. Per Share	...	...	...	**4.80**	**2.98**	**1.24**	...
INCOME STATEMENT (IN MILLIONS):							
Total Revenues	3,067.7	2,839.6	2,506.8	842.8	789.6	723.1	519.2
Costs & Expenses	2,379.3	2,163.9	2,051.5	682.1	619.6	579.0	411.8
Depreciation & Amort.	220.0	223.6	196.0	22.6	39.9	35.3	23.5
Operating Income	468.5	452.2	259.3	138.1	130.1	108.9	83.9
Net Interest Inc./(Exp.)	d64.5	d58.1	d53.6	d5.3	d11.9	d17.9	d18.2
Income Before Income Taxes	413.4	395.7	198.9	133.5	114.6	87.2	61.2
Income Taxes	188.1	184.2	125.9	53.6	45.3	34.4	24.0
Net Income	4 225.3	211.5	3 73.0	2 79.9	69.3	52.7	1 37.2
Cash Flow	426.3	365.2	198.8	102.5	109.2	88.0	60.7
Average Shs. Outstg. (000)	87,951	84,128	73,273	42,613	42,459	42,057	39,884
BALANCE SHEET (IN MILLIONS):							
Cash & Cash Equivalents	11.2	13.7	45.0	35.5	3.0	7.7	11.2
Total Current Assets	877.1	803.2	844.6	250.8	207.0	196.2	151.8
Net Property	1,032.1	1,023.4	1,116.6	171.1	174.6	169.9	136.2
Total Assets	4,048.1	3,855.2	4,039.9	498.4	467.1	443.5	331.1
Total Current Liabilities	674.6	582.1	535.0	163.6	148.1	154.2	136.1
Long-Term Obligations	944.5	665.1	996.5	48.5	99.9	149.8	155.3
Net Stockholders' Equity	753.1	551.0	437.0	257.3	186.6	106.3	11.0
Net Working Capital	202.5	221.1	309.6	87.2	58.9	41.9	15.8
Year-end Shs. Outstg. (000)	83,646	83,600	83,312	42,624	42,521	42,282	19,989
STATISTICAL RECORD:							
Operating Profit Margin %	15.3	15.9	10.3	16.4	16.5	15.1	16.2
Net Profit Margin %	7.3	7.4	2.9	9.5	8.8	7.3	7.2
Return on Equity %	29.9	38.4	16.7	31.1	37.1	49.6	338.0
Return on Assets %	5.6	5.5	1.8	16.0	14.8	11.9	11.2
Debt/Total Assets %	23.3	17.3	24.7	9.7	21.4	33.8	46.9
Price Range	61.88-26.38	68.44-44.50	70.00-27.38	62.75-39.75	44.13-26.00	30.75-17.94	18.13-13.31
P/E Ratio	32.1-13.7	40.7-26.5	3,482.6-1,361.9	33.4-21.1	27.1-15.9	24.6-14.3	19.3-14.2

Statistics are as originally reported. Adj. for stk. split: 100% stk. div., 9/95. Figures are for the "old" Sealed Air Corp. prior to 3/31/98 acquisition of Sealed Air Corp. 1 Bef. $5.6 mill. chrg. for early retirement of debt. 2 Incl. transaction exp. of $8.4 mill. rel. to pending merger with the packaging business of W.R. Grace & Co. 3 Incl. restruct. chrg. of $87.5 million. 4 Incl. restruct. credit of $1.2 mill.

OFFICERS:
W. V. Hickey, Pres., C.E.O.
D. S. Van Riper, Sr. V.P., C.F.O.
T. S. Christie, Treas.

INVESTOR CONTACT: Mary A. Conventry, V.P.-Corp. Dev., (201) 791-7600

PRINCIPAL OFFICE: Park 80 East, Saddle Brook, NJ 07663-5291

TELEPHONE NUMBER: (201) 791-7600
FAX: (201) 703-4205
WEB: www.sealedair.com

NO. OF EMPLOYEES: 17,750 (approx.)

SHAREHOLDERS: 10,078 (approx. common); 8,274 (approx. preferred)

ANNUAL MEETING: In May

INCORPORATED: DE, Feb., 1960; reincorp., DE, Feb., 1969

INSTITUTIONAL HOLDINGS:
No. of Institutions: 283
Shares Held: 70,783,502
% Held: 84.6

INDUSTRY: Unsupported plastics film & sheet (SIC: 3081)

TRANSFER AGENT(S): First Chicago Trust Company, Jersey City, NJ

NYSE SYMBOL S
Rec. Pr. 39.88 (5/31/01)

SEARS, ROEBUCK & CO.

YIELD 2.3%
P/E RATIO 10.3

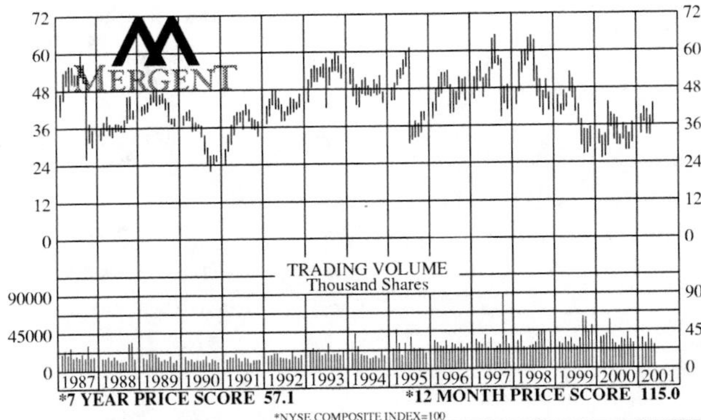

INTERIM EARNINGS (Per Share):

Qtr.	Mar.	June	Sept.	Dec.
1996	0.36	0.67	0.68	1.42
1997	0.46	0.29	0.89	1.35
1998	0.34	0.85	0.17	1.39
1999	0.38	0.86	0.62	1.98
2000	0.65	1.11	0.81	1.32

INTERIM DIVIDENDS (Per Share):

Amt.	Decl.	Ex.	Rec.	Pay.
0.23Q	5/10/00	5/26/00	5/31/00	7/03/00
0.23Q	8/09/00	8/28/00	8/30/00	10/02/00
0.23Q	10/11/00	11/28/00	11/30/00	1/02/01
0.23Q	2/14/01	2/28/01	3/02/01	4/02/01
0.23Q	5/10/01	5/30/01	6/01/01	7/02/01

Indicated div.: $0.92 (Div. Reinv. Plan)

CAPITALIZATION (12/30/00):

	($000)	(%)
Long-Term Debt	11,020,000	57.5
Minority Interest	1,363,000	7.1
Common & Surplus	6,769,000	35.3
Total	19,152,000	100.0

RECENT DEVELOPMENTS: For the year ended 12/30/00, net income slid 7.6% to $1.34 billion from $1.45 billion the year before. Results included one-time pre-tax restructuring charges of $251.0 million and $41.0 million in 2000 and 1999, respectively. Total revenues rose 3.7% to $40.94 billion from $39.48 billion the previous year. Operating income was $2.19 billion, down 9.4% versus $2.41 billion in 1999. Comparisons were made with restated prior-year results reflecting a change in the classification of revenue and related costs of licensed businesses.

PROSPECTS: Results may be negatively affected by continued sluggish consumer spending due to weakening economic conditions in the U.S. In 2001, the Company is targeting mid-single digit operating income growth, which along with the Company's ongoing stock repurchase program, is expected to result in high-single to low-double digit earnings per share growth. Meanwhile, the Company is evaluating strategic alternatives, including the possible sale, for its termite and pest control business.

BUSINESS

SEARS, ROEBUCK AND CO. is a retailer of apparel, home and automotive products and related services, serving nearly 60 million households in North America through approximately 860 full-line department stores and about 2,100 specialty format stores, including National Tire & Battery automotive stores and neighborhood hardware stores operating under the Sears Hardware and Orchard Supply Hardware names. Sears Merchandise Group sells goods and services and provides credit services. In 1993, the Company sold Dean Witter, Discover & Co. and Coldwell Banker Residential services. In 1995, the Company spun off The Allstate Corporation and divested its real estate concern, Homart Development Co. Sears sold PRODIGY, its joint venture on-line service, in May 1996. On 11/2/98, the Company sold its Western Auto subsidiary.

REVENUES

(12/30/2000)	($000)	(%)
Merchandise Sales & Services	36,548,000	89.4
Credit Revenues	4,389,000	10.6
Total	40,937,000	100.0

ANNUAL FINANCIAL DATA

	12/30/00	1/1/00	1/2/99	1/3/98	12/28/96	5 12/30/95	12/31/94
Earnings Per Share	1 3.88	1 3.81	4 2.74	3 2.99	1 3.12	2 2.53	3 3.12
Cash Flow Per Share	3.88	3.81	2.74	2.99	3.18	2.60	3.20
Tang. Book Val. Per Share	20.32	18.53	15.82	15.00	12.63	10.40	26.27
Dividends Per Share	0.92	0.92	0.92	0.92	0.92	1.43	1.60
Dividend Payout %	23.7	24.1	33.6	30.8	29.5	56.5	51.3
INCOME STATEMENT (IN MILLIONS):							
Total Revenues	40,937.0	41,071.0	41,322.0	41,296.0	38,236.0	34,925.0	54,559.0
Costs & Expenses	38,750.0	38,658.0	39,467.0	38,827.0	36,153.0	33,220.0	52,883.0
Operating Income	2,187.0	2,413.0	1,855.0	1,994.0	2,083.0	1,705.0	1,676.0
Net Interest Inc./(Exp.)	...	...	...	...	d1,365.0	d1,373.0	d1,339.0
Income Before Income Taxes	2,223.0	2,419.0	1,883.0	2,100.0	2,105.0	1,728.0	1,712.0
Income Taxes	831.0	904.0	766.0	912.0	834.0	703.0	358.0
Equity Earnings/Minority Int.	d49.0	d62.0	d45.0	...	d8.0	...	d91.0
Net Income	1 1,343.0	1 1,453.0	4 1,072.0	3 1,188.0	1 1,271.0	2 1,025.0	3 1,244.0
Cash Flow	1,343.0	1,453.0	1,072.0	1,188.0	1,246.0	972.0	1,107.0
Average Shs. Outstg. (000)	346,300	381,000	391,700	397,800	399,100	394,000	388,900
BALANCE SHEET (IN MILLIONS):							
Cash & Cash Equivalents	842.0	729.0	495.0	358.0	660.0	606.0	1,421.0
Total Current Assets	28,794.0	28,667.0	29,271.0	30,682.0	28,447.0	26,441.0	27,434.0
Net Property	6,653.0	6,450.0	6,380.0	6,414.0	5,878.0	5,077.0	5,041.0
Total Assets	36,899.0	36,954.0	37,675.0	38,700.0	36,167.0	33,130.0	91,896.0
Total Current Liabilities	15,796.0	13,701.0	14,109.0	15,790.0	14,950.0	14,607.0	14,699.0
Long-Term Obligations	11,020.0	12,884.0	13,631.0	13,071.0	12,170.0	10,044.0	10,854.0
Net Stockholders' Equity	6,769.0	6,839.0	6,066.0	5,862.0	4,945.0	4,385.0	10,801.0
Net Working Capital	12,998.0	14,966.0	15,162.0	14,892.0	13,497.0	11,834.0	12,735.0
Year-end Shs. Outstg. (000)	333,200	369,100	383,500	390,900	391,400	390,500	351,740
STATISTICAL RECORD:							
Operating Profit Margin %	5.3	5.9	4.5	4.8	5.4	4.9	3.1
Net Profit Margin %	3.3	3.5	2.6	2.9	3.3	2.9	2.3
Return on Equity %	19.8	21.2	17.7	20.3	25.7	23.4	11.5
Return on Assets %	3.6	3.9	2.8	3.1	3.5	3.1	1.4
Debt/Total Assets %	29.9	34.9	36.2	33.8	33.6	30.3	11.8
Price Range	43.50-25.25	53.19-26.69	65.00-39.06	65.25-38.75	53.88-38.25	61.25-30.38	55.13-42.13
P/E Ratio	11.2-6.5	14.0-7.0	23.7-14.3	21.8-13.0	17.3-12.3	24.2-12.0	17.7-13.5
Average Yield %	2.7	2.3	1.8	1.8	2.0	3.1	3.3

Statistics are as originally reported. 1 Incl. $251.0 mil pre-tax restr. chg., 2000; $41.0 mil, 1999; & $10.0 mil, 1996. 2 Bef. cr$776 mil from discont. opers. 3 Incl. $115.0 mil ($0.28/sh) net chg., 1997; & $1.42 bil non-recur. chg., 1994. 4 Bef. extraord. chg. of $24.0 mil ($0.06/sh.) & incl. $228.0 mil ($0.58/sh) net chg. 5 Results reflect the spin-off of Allstate Corp.

OFFICERS:
A. J. Lacy, Chmn., C.E.O.
J. N. Boyer, C.F.O.
A. D. Kelly, Exec. V.P., Gen. Couns.

INVESTOR CONTACT: Investor Relations, (847) 286-7385

PRINCIPAL OFFICE: 3333 Beverly Road, Hoffman Estates, IL 60179

TELEPHONE NUMBER: (847) 286-2500
FAX: (847) 875-0658
WEB: www.sears.com

NO. OF EMPLOYEES: 323,000 (approx.)

SHAREHOLDERS: 209,101

ANNUAL MEETING: In May

INCORPORATED: NY, June, 1906

INSTITUTIONAL HOLDINGS:
No. of Institutions: 390
Shares Held: 293,828,035
% Held: 88.2

INDUSTRY: Department stores (SIC: 5311)

TRANSFER AGENT(S): First Chicago Trust Company of New York, Jersey City, NJ

NYSE SYMBOL SRE
Rec. Pr. 27.67 (4/30/01)

SEMPRA ENERGY

YIELD 3.6%
P/E RATIO 13.4

MERGENT

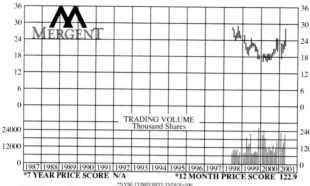

TRADING VOLUME
Thousand Shares

1987 1988 1989 1990 1991 1992 1993 1994 1995 1996 1997 1998 1999 2000 2001

*7 YEAR PRICE SCORE N/A *12 MONTH PRICE SCORE 122.9

*NYSE COMPOSITE INDEX=100

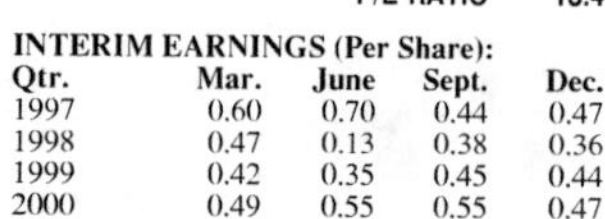

INTERIM EARNINGS (Per Share):

Qtr.	Mar.	June	Sept.	Dec.
1997	0.60	0.70	0.44	0.47
1998	0.47	0.13	0.38	0.36
1999	0.42	0.35	0.45	0.44
2000	0.49	0.55	0.55	0.47

INTERIM DIVIDENDS (Per Share):

Amt.	Decl.	Ex.	Rec.	Pay.
0.25Q	3/08/00	3/16/00	3/20/00	4/15/00
0.25Q	6/06/00	6/19/00	6/21/00	7/15/00
0.25Q	9/05/00	9/18/00	9/20/00	10/15/00
0.25Q	12/05/00	12/19/00	12/21/00	1/15/01
0.25Q	3/06/01	3/16/01	3/20/01	4/15/01

Indicated div.: $1.00 (Div. Reinv. Plan)

CAPITALIZATION (12/31/00):

	($000)	(%)
Long-Term Debt	3,268,000	46.7
Deferred Income Tax	826,000	11.8
Redeemable Pfd. Stock	404,000	5.8
Common & Surplus	2,494,000	35.7
Total	6,992,000	100.0

RECENT DEVELOPMENTS: For the year ended 12/31/00, net income climbed 8.9% to $429.0 million compared with $394.0 million in the previous year. The higher earnings for the year were primarily due to improved results in the Company's energy trading, generation and international operations. Total revenues increased 32.0% to $7.14 billion from $5.41 billion in 1999. The increase in revenues was attributed to growth in the unregulated energy-service businesses.

PROSPECTS: On 1/22/01, SRE completed the sale of its 72.5% stake in Energy America, the U.S.-based energy marketing firm, to Centrica plc, the British energy and home services company for $56.0 million. Separately, SRE's subsidiary, Sempra Energy Resources broke ground on the Mesquite Power Generating Station, a $500.0 million, 1,200-megawatt facility intended to provide clean, efficient and reliable electricity to growing wholesale energy markets in Arizona and the Southwest.

BUSINESS

SEMPRA ENERGY is an energy services holding company formed upon the merger of Pacific Enterprises and Enova Corporation on 6/26/98. Through its eight principal subsidiaries, Southern California Gas Company, San Diego Gas & Electric, Sempra Energy Solutions, Sempra Energy Trading, Sempra Energy International, Sempra Energy Resources, Sempra Communications and Sempra Energy Financial, Sempra Energy serves more than 9.0 million customers in the United States, Europe, Canada, Mexico, South America and Asia.

REVENUES

(12/31/2000)	($000)	(%)
Natural Gas	3,305,000	47.0
Electric	2,184,000	31.0
Other Operating Revenues	1,548,000	22.0
Total	7,037,000	100.0

ANNUAL FINANCIAL DATA

	12/31/00	12/31/99	12/31/98	12/31/97	12/31/96	12/31/95
Earnings Per Share	**[3] 2.06**	**[2] 1.66**	**[1] 1.24**	**1.82**	**1.77**	**1.67**
Cash Flow Per Share	**4.76**	**4.08**	**5.16**	**4.37**	**4.21**	**3.84**
Tang. Book Val. Per Share	**12.35**	**12.58**	**12.14**	**12.54**	**12.21**	...
Dividends Per Share	**1.14**	**1.56**	**0.39**	...	...	...
Dividend Payout %	**55.3**	**94.0**	**31.4**	...	...	...
INCOME STATEMENT (IN MILLIONS):						
Total Revenues	7,143.0	5,435.0	5,525.0	5,127.0	4,524.0	4,201.0
Costs & Expenses	5,569.0	4,046.0	3,945.0	3,566.0	2,988.0	2,764.0
Depreciation & Amort.	563.0	576.0	929.0	604.0	587.0	521.0
Operating Income	1,011.0	813.0	651.0	957.0	949.0	916.0
Net Interest Inc./(Exp.)	d286.0	d229.0	d207.0	d206.0	d200.0	d221.0
Income Taxes	270.0	179.0	138.0	301.0	300.0	264.0
Net Income	[3] 429.0	[2] 394.0	[1] 294.0	432.0	427.0	401.0
Cash Flow	992.0	970.0	1,223.0	1,036.0	1,014.0	922.0
Average Shs. Outstg. (000)	208,345	237,553	237,000	237,000	241,000	240,000
BALANCE SHEET (IN MILLIONS):						
Gross Property	11,889.0	11,127.0	11,235.0	12,040.0	11,835.0	...
Accumulated Depreciation	6,163.0	5,733.0	5,794.0	5,921.0	5,492.0	...
Net Property	5,726.0	5,394.0	5,441.0	6,119.0	6,343.0	...
Total Assets	15,612.0	11,270.0	10,456.0	10,751.0	9,762.0	...
Long-Term Obligations	3,268.0	2,902.0	2,795.0	3,175.0	2,704.0	...
Net Stockholders' Equity	2,494.0	2,986.0	2,913.0	2,959.0	2,930.0	...
Year-end Shs. Outstg. (000)	201,928	237,408	240,000	236,000	240,000	...
STATISTICAL RECORD:						
Operating Profit Margin %	14.2	15.0	11.8	18.7	21.0	21.8
Net Profit Margin %	6.0	7.2	5.3	8.4	9.4	9.5
Net Inc./Net Property %	7.5	7.3	5.4	7.1	6.7	...
Net Inc./Tot. Capital %	6.1	5.9	4.5	6.0	6.3	...
Return on Equity %	17.2	13.2	10.1	14.6	14.6	...
Accum. Depr./Gross Prop. %	51.8	51.5	51.6	49.2	46.4	...
Price Range	24.88-16.19	26.00-17.13	29.31-23.75	...	...	...
P/E Ratio	12.1-7.9	15.7-10.3	23.6-19.2	...	...	...
Average Yield %	5.6	7.2	1.5	...	...	...

Statistics are as originally reported. [1] Incl. after-tax business combination charges of $85.0 million. [2] Incl. net busines combination costs of $13.0 million related to the proposed merger with KN Energy, which was terminated by both companies 6/20/99. [3] Incl. non-recurr. chrgs. total. $40.0 mill.

OFFICERS:
S. L. Baum, Chmn., Pres., C.E.O.
N. E. Schmale, Exec. V.P., C.F.O.

INVESTOR CONTACT: Clem Teng, Dir. Inv. Rel., (619) 696-2901

PRINCIPAL OFFICE: 101 Ash Street, San Diego, CA 92101

TELEPHONE NUMBER: (619) 696-2000
FAX: (619) 696-2374
WEB: www.sempra.com

NO. OF EMPLOYEES: 11,232 (avg.)

SHAREHOLDERS: 75,000 (approx.)

ANNUAL MEETING: In May

INCORPORATED: CA, June, 1998

INSTITUTIONAL HOLDINGS:
No. of Institutions: 252
Shares Held: 78,979,604
% Held: 38.3

INDUSTRY: Gas and other services combined (SIC: 4932)

TRANSFER AGENT(S): First Chicago Trust Company of New York, Jersey City, NJ

NYSE SYMBOL SXT
Rec. Pr. 19.02 (5/31/01)

SENSIENT TECHNOLOGIES CORP.

YIELD 2.8%
P/E RATIO 16.3

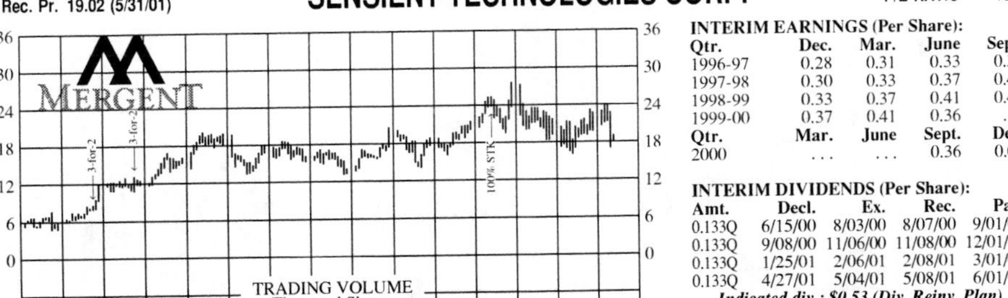

*7 YEAR PRICE SCORE 78.2 *12 MONTH PRICE SCORE 99.5

*NYSE COMPOSITE INDEX=100

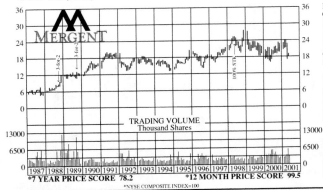

INTERIM EARNINGS (Per Share):

Qtr.	Dec.	Mar.	June	Sept.
1996-97	0.28	0.31	0.33	0.36
1997-98	0.30	0.33	0.37	0.41
1998-99	0.33	0.37	0.41	0.46
1999-00	0.37	0.41	0.36	...
Qtr.	Mar.	June	Sept.	Dec.
2000	...	...	0.36	0.04

INTERIM DIVIDENDS (Per Share):

Amt.	Decl.	Ex.	Rec.	Pay.
0.133Q	6/15/00	8/03/00	8/07/00	9/01/00
0.133Q	9/08/00	11/06/00	11/08/00	12/01/00
0.133Q	1/25/01	2/06/01	2/08/01	3/01/01
0.133Q	4/27/01	5/04/01	5/08/01	6/01/01

Indicated div.: $0.53 (Div. Reinv. Plan)

CAPITALIZATION (12/31/00):

	($000)	(%)
Long-Term Debt	417,141	48.0
Deferred Income Tax	35,707	4.1
Common & Surplus	417,058	47.9
Total	869,906	100.0

RECENT DEVELOPMENTS: For the twelve months ended 12/31/00, earnings from continuing operations were $56.3 million, down 15.3% versus earnings from continuing operations of $66.5 million in 1999. Results for 2000 included a one-time pre-tax charge of $19.0 million for the consolidation of manufacturing facilities in the U.S. and in Europe. Revenue grew 1.6% to $809.2 million from $796.3 million the year before. Flavors and Fragrances segment revenue slipped 3.0% to $511.1 million, while Color segment revenue increased 13.8% to $283.7 million.

PROSPECTS: On 2/26/01, the Company completed the sale of its Red Star Yeast business to Paris-based Lesaffre et Compagnie for $109.0 million. In an effort to gain government approval for the sale, SXT agreed to maintain its 20.0% stake in Minn-Dak Yeast Company, a small domestic yeast producer. Meanwhile, SXT is consolidating the plants in its European flavor and synthetic color operations and in its domestic dairy flavors business. These actions are expected to generate annual cost savings of more than $10.0 million after the consolidations are complete in 2001.

BUSINESS

SENSIENT TECHNOLOGIES CORPORATION (formerly Universal Foods Corporation) is an international manufacturer and marketer of value-added food products and ingredients. The Company's major customers are food processors and the food service industry. SXT's Flavors and Fragrances segment manufactures flavors, flavor enhancers and dehydrated vegetables for the food, beverage and dairy industries. The Color segment produces synthetic color products used in food, beverages, cosmetics, pharmaceuticals, specialty inks and a variety of other applications. The Company also develops and markets products in the Pacific Rim that appeal to regional preferences. In August 1994, the Company sold its frozen foods business to Conagra, Inc.

ANNUAL FINANCIAL DATA

	[3] 12/31/00	9/30/99	9/30/98	9/30/97	9/30/96	9/30/95	9/30/94
Earnings Per Share	[4] 1.15	1.57	1.40	[1] 1.27	[1] 0.86	[2] 1.27	[1] 0.98
Cash Flow Per Share	2.07	2.53	2.25	2.00	1.51	1.93	1.67
Tang. Book Val. Per Share	2.54	3.04	3.69	3.89	4.12	4.08	3.45
Dividends Per Share	0.53	0.53	0.53	0.52	0.51	0.48	0.47
Dividend Payout %	46.1	33.8	37.9	41.1	58.7	38.2	47.7
INCOME STATEMENT (IN MILLIONS):							
Total Revenues	809.2	920.2	856.8	825.7	806.4	793.0	929.9
Costs & Expenses	632.4	726.2	683.7	681.2	663.9	655.5	784.3
Depreciation & Amort.	45.6	48.9	44.2	37.3	33.5	34.6	36.4
Operating Income	112.2	145.1	128.9	107.2	83.9	129.7	97.0
Net Interest Inc./(Exp.)	d34.2	d26.0	d21.2	d16.8	d15.3	d15.1	d15.9
Income Before Income Taxes	78.0	119.1	107.7	90.4	68.6	114.6	81.1
Income Taxes	21.7	38.9	35.0	25.7	24.4	48.5	30.2
Net Income	[4] 56.3	80.1	72.6	[1] 64.7	[1] 44.2	[2] 66.1	[1] 50.9
Cash Flow	101.9	129.1	116.9	102.0	77.7	100.7	87.3
Average Shs. Outstg. (000)	49,166	51,109	51,837	51,026	51,597	52,122	52,262
BALANCE SHEET (IN MILLIONS):							
Cash & Cash Equivalents	3.2	4.6	1.6	1.3	3.4	8.7	43.4
Total Current Assets	491.4	404.6	357.8	342.2	324.6	326.4	327.8
Net Property	315.5	390.3	355.6	309.0	268.5	259.7	255.7
Total Assets	1,164.2	1,142.7	991.2	887.7	779.5	776.9	763.7
Total Current Liabilities	252.1	241.7	209.8	178.5	162.2	182.6	192.2
Long-Term Obligations	417.1	385.4	291.6	252.5	196.9	160.7	172.2
Net Stockholders' Equity	417.1	431.6	405.6	380.5	351.0	361.8	327.4
Net Working Capital	239.3	162.9	147.9	163.7	162.5	143.8	135.7
Year-end Shs. Outstg. (000)	48,552	50,340	51,157	51,182	50,840	52,198	52,122
STATISTICAL RECORD:							
Operating Profit Margin %	13.9	15.8	15.0	13.0	10.4	16.4	10.4
Net Profit Margin %	7.0	8.7	8.5	7.8	5.5	8.3	5.5
Return on Equity %	13.5	18.6	17.9	17.0	12.6	18.3	15.6
Return on Assets %	4.8	7.0	7.3	7.3	5.7	8.5	6.7
Debt/Total Assets %	35.8	33.7	29.4	28.4	25.3	20.7	22.6
Price Range	23.19-16.00	27.38-18.25	27.75-19.44	21.47-16.00	20.19-14.00	20.63-13.63	17.19-13.06
P/E Ratio	20.2-13.9	17.4-11.6	19.8-13.9	16.9-12.6	23.5-16.3	16.2-10.7	17.6-13.4
Average Yield %	2.7	2.3	2.2	2.8	3.0	2.8	3.1

Statistics are as originally reported. Adj. for 100% stk. div., 5/98. [1] Incl. non-recur. chg. $4.6 mil, 1997; $16.7 mil, 1996; $12.1 mil, 1994. [2] Incl. non-recur. $49.6 mil gain & $22.8 mil chg. [3] For 12 mos. to refl. a change in fiscal year end. [4] Bef. $3.3 mil gain fr. disc. ops. & $2.4 mil acctg. chg.; Incls. a $19.0 mil pre-tax special chg.

OFFICERS:
K. P. Manning, Chmn., Pres., C.E.O.
R. S. Manning, Exec. V.P.
R. F. Hobbs, V.P., C.F.O.

INVESTOR CONTACT: Steven O. Cordier, V.P.-Admin., (414) 347-3868

PRINCIPAL OFFICE: 777 East Wisconsin Avenue, Milwaukee, WI 53202-5304

TELEPHONE NUMBER: (414) 271-6755
FAX: (414) 347-4794
WEB: www.sensient-tech.com

NO. OF EMPLOYEES: 3,722 (avg.)

SHAREHOLDERS: 4,782

ANNUAL MEETING: In Apr.

INCORPORATED: WI, Dec., 1882

INSTITUTIONAL HOLDINGS:
No. of Institutions: 161
Shares Held: 33,218,031
% Held: 68.8

INDUSTRY: Flavoring extracts and syrups, nec (SIC: 2087)

TRANSFER AGENT(S): Firstar Trust Company, Milwaukee, WI

NYSE SYMBOL SQAA
Rec. Pr. 46.60 (4/30/01)

SEQUA CORPORATION

YIELD ...
P/E RATIO 22.0

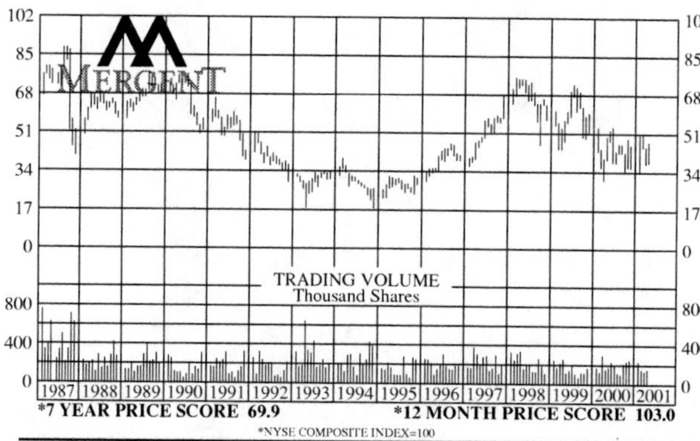

INTERIM EARNINGS (Per Share):

Qtr.	Mar.	June	Sept.	Dec.
1997	0.08	0.38	0.58	0.60
1998	0.41	1.10	0.97	3.35
1999	0.53	1.00	0.57	0.38
2000	0.36	0.47	0.44	0.85

INTERIM DIVIDENDS (Per Share):

Amt.	Decl.	Ex.	Rec.	Pay.

No dividends paid.

CAPITALIZATION (12/31/00):

	($000)	(%)
Long-Term Debt	590,607	45.2
Deferred Income Tax	45,396	3.5
Preferred Stock	797	0.1
Common & Surplus	669,010	51.2
Total	1,305,810	100.0

RECENT DEVELOPMENTS: For the year ended 12/31/00, SQAA reported net income of $24.0 million versus income of $27.8 million, before an extraordinary loss of $5.7 million, in 1999. Earnings for 2000 included net other expense of $9.8 million, while earnings for 1999 included net other income of $6.5 million. Sales advanced 3.6% to $1.77 billion. Sales in the Aerospace segment increased 2.5% to $764.7 million.

PROSPECTS: During 2001, the Company reported a pre-tax gain of about $4.0 million related to the divestiture of Chromalloy Gas Turbine's Caval Tool division. Moreover, SQAA anticipates an improvement in its sales and operating income due to the current conditions in the building products and domestic automobile markets, as well as the generally favorable outlook for jet engine component repair.

BUSINESS

SEQUA CORPORATION has operations in the following segments: Aerospace (43.1% of 2000 sales) consists of Chromalloy Gas Turbine, which repairs and manufactures components for jet aircraft engines; Propulsion (15.4%) consists of Atlantic Research Corporation, a supplier of solid rocket fuel; Metal Coatings (12.8%) consists of Precoat Metals, which is engaged in the application of protective and decorative coatings to continuous steel and aluminum coils; The Specialty Chemicals group (8.2%) consists of Warwick International, which produces detergent additives; Other Products (20.5%) includes group professional consulting services, automotive products, food cans and men's apparel.

BUSINESS LINE ANALYSIS

(12/31/2000)	REV (%)	INC (%)
Aerospace	43.1	51.1
Propulsion	15.4	7.5
Metal Coating	12.8	14.4
Specialty Chemical	8.2	12.6
Other Products	20.5	14.4
Total	100.0	100.0

ANNUAL FINANCIAL DATA

	12/31/00	12/31/99	12/31/98	12/31/97	12/31/96	12/31/95	12/31/94
Earnings Per Share	**[4] 2.12**	**[1] 2.48**	**[3] 5.87**	**[2] 1.66**	**[1] 0.65**	**0.57**	**[1] d2.87**
Cash Flow Per Share	**10.66**	**10.89**	**13.86**	**10.22**	**9.92**	**10.35**	**7.79**
Tang. Book Val. Per Share	**35.02**	**32.14**	**32.51**	**28.79**	**28.47**	**26.15**	**24.58**
INCOME STATEMENT (IN MILLIONS):							
Total Revenues	1,773.1	1,699.5	1,802.4	1,595.1	1,459.0	1,414.1	1,419.6
Costs & Expenses	1,581.3	1,517.9	1,607.6	1,424.6	1,302.3	1,249.7	1,275.8
Depreciation & Amort.	88.6	87.2	89.3	85.8	91.6	96.5	104.0
Operating Income	103.2	94.5	105.5	84.7	65.2	67.9	39.8
Net Interest Inc./(Exp.)	d51.3	d51.5	d45.9	d44.2	d47.5	d49.4	d56.3
Income Before Income Taxes	42.0	49.4	108.0	41.8	26.0	27.5	d27.9
Income Taxes	18.0	21.6	44.1	22.2	16.4	18.7	cr3.2
Equity Earnings/Minority Int.	d2.0	d2.9	d4.9	0.2	4.0	d1.8	d2.2
Net Income	[4] 24.0	[1] 27.8	[3] 63.9	[2] 19.6	[1] 9.6	8.8	[1] d24.7
Cash Flow	110.6	112.9	151.0	102.4	98.0	102.1	76.1
Average Shs. Outstg. (000)	10,374	10,371	10,894	10,014	9,880	9,867	9,772
BALANCE SHEET (IN MILLIONS):							
Cash & Cash Equivalents	50.0	68.2	96.4	118.7	92.1	62.7	18.7
Total Current Assets	723.3	680.3	715.9	695.8	612.2	621.2	604.3
Net Property	482.8	474.6	451.4	435.5	457.5	496.6	524.2
Total Assets	1,731.1	1,671.7	1,624.1	1,591.7	1,548.2	1,622.0	1,648.2
Total Current Liabilities	337.4	300.7	337.9	366.7	302.7	324.7	321.3
Long-Term Obligations	590.6	569.9	500.7	508.7	531.9	563.2	586.6
Net Stockholders' Equity	669.8	668.9	667.5	608.0	569.8	571.9	570.3
Net Working Capital	386.0	379.6	377.9	329.1	309.4	296.6	283.0
Year-end Shs. Outstg. (000)	10,377	11,008	11,000	10,005	9,905	9,772	9,772
STATISTICAL RECORD:							
Operating Profit Margin %	5.8	5.6	5.9	5.3	4.5	4.8	2.8
Net Profit Margin %	1.4	1.6	3.5	1.2	0.7	0.6	...
Return on Equity %	3.6	4.2	9.6	3.3	1.6	1.5	...
Return on Assets %	1.4	1.7	3.9	1.2	0.6	0.5	...
Debt/Total Assets %	34.1	34.1	30.8	32.0	34.4	34.7	35.6
Price Range	54.06-30.25	72.75-44.00	75.88-45.75	67.94-36.25	46.50-29.50	32.13-21.88	39.75-17.63
P/E Ratio	25.5-14.3	29.3-17.7	12.9-7.8	40.9-21.8	71.5-45.4	56.3-38.4	...

Statistics are as originally reported. [1] Bef. an extraord. loss of $5.7 mill., 1999; $369,000, 1996; $1.1 mill., 1994. [2] Incl. restruct. charges of $7.2 mill. and a $6.5 mill. gain from the sale of Kollsman operations. [3] Incl. a pre-tax gain of $56.5 mill. fr. the sale of businesses. [4] Incl. a provision of $3.2 million to cover the cost of an early retirement program.

OFFICERS:
N. E. Alexander, Chmn., C.E.O.
J. J. Quicke, Pres., C.O.O.
S. Z. Krinsly, Sr. Exec. V.P., Gen. Couns.

INVESTOR CONTACT: Linda G. Kyriakou, Vice-Pres. Corp. Comm., (212) 986-5500

PRINCIPAL OFFICE: 200 Park Avenue, New York, NY 10166

TELEPHONE NUMBER: (212) 986-5500
FAX: (212) 370-1969; 983-2774
WEB: www.sequa.com

NO. OF EMPLOYEES: 11,550 (approx.)

SHAREHOLDERS: 2,150 (approx. class A); 450 (approx. class B)

ANNUAL MEETING: In May

INCORPORATED: DE, Mar., 1929

INSTITUTIONAL HOLDINGS:
No. of Institutions: 64
Shares Held: 3,467,485
% Held: 33.4

INDUSTRY: Aircraft engines and engine parts (SIC: 3724)

TRANSFER AGENT(S): Bank of New York, New York, NY

NYSE SYMBOL SRV
Rec. Pr. 7.06 (5/31/01)

SERVICE CORPORATION INTERNATIONAL

YIELD ...
P/E RATIO ...

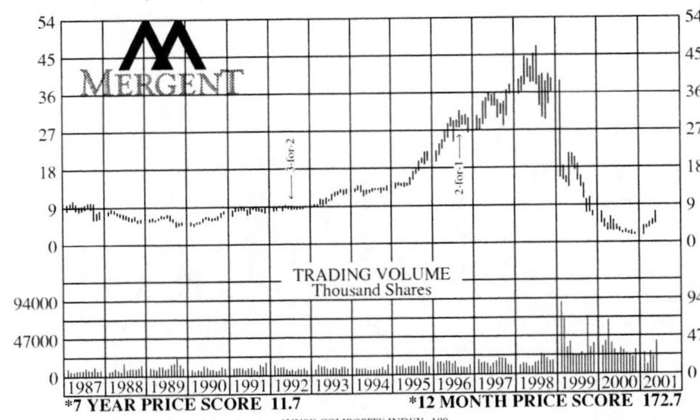

INTERIM EARNINGS (Per Share):

Qtr.	Mar.	June	Sept.	Dec.
1996	0.30	0.26	0.24	0.30
1997	0.54	0.32	0.28	0.36
1998	0.42	0.35	0.32	0.23
1999	0.15	0.28	0.12	d0.68
2000	0.25	0.07	0.05	d1.55

INTERIM DIVIDENDS (Per Share):

Amt.	Decl.	Ex.	Rec.	Pay.
0.09Q	5/13/99	7/13/99	7/15/99	7/30/99
0.09Q	8/12/99	10/13/99	10/15/99	10/29/99

Dividend payment suspended.

CAPITALIZATION (12/31/00):

	($000)	(%)
Long-Term Debt	4,929,672	66.5
Deferred Income Tax	503,292	6.8
Common & Surplus	1,975,821	26.7
Total	7,408,785	100.0

RECENT DEVELOPMENTS: For the year ended 12/31/00, SRV reported a loss from continuing operations of $425.5 million versus $210.7 million a year earlier. Results for 2000 included nonrecurring items that resulted in a pre-tax charge totaling $517.8 million. The 1999 results included nonrecurring charges of $362.4 million. Revenues declined 6.6% to $2.56 billion. Funeral division revenues slipped 4.9% to $1.91 billion, while Cemetery division revenues fell 10.2% to $641.3 million.

PROSPECTS: Following a comprehensive review of its funeral and cemetery operations in North America, the Company announced plans to sell 431 funeral locations and 105 cemeteries due to a lack of geographic proximity to major population areas. The proceeds from these sales will be used to pay down debt. Over the next two years, the Company plans to reduce its debt to within the range of $2.00 billion to $2.50 billion.

BUSINESS

SERVICE CORPORATION INTERNATIONAL is a major provider of funeral and cemetery services. As of 12/31/00, SRV operated 3,611 funeral service locations, 569 cemeteries, 200 crematoria in 18 countries on five continents. The Funeral division, 75.0% of 2000 revenues, performs all personal and professional services, including the preparation and embalming processes, and preparing death certificates and related documents. The Cemetery division, 25.0%, offers a wide range of property, merchandise, and services. On 1/19/99, SRV acquired Equity Corporation International.

REVENUES

(12/31/00)	($000)	(%)
Funeral	1,911,969	74.5
Cemetery	641,267	25.0
Other Services	11,494	0.5
Total	2,564,730	100.0

ANNUAL FINANCIAL DATA

	12/31/00	12/31/99	12/31/98	12/31/97	12/31/96	12/31/95	12/31/94
Earnings Per Share	**3 d1.56**	**2 d0.13**	**1.31**	**1 1.47**	**1.10**	**0.90**	**0.76**
Cash Flow Per Share	**d0.74**	**0.80**	**2.07**	**2.06**	**1.64**	**1.38**	**1.19**
Tang. Book Val. Per Share	...	**3.75**	**5.17**	**4.85**	**3.64**	**3.51**	**2.03**
Dividends Per Share	...	**0.36**	**0.34**	**0.28**	**0.23**	**0.22**	**0.21**
Dividend Payout %	...	...	**26.3**	**19.4**	**21.4**	**24.2**	**27.8**
INCOME STATEMENT (IN MILLIONS):							
Total Revenues	2,564.7	3,321.8	2,875.1	2,468.4	2,294.2	1,652.1	1,117.2
Costs & Expenses	2,554.1	2,900.9	2,020.9	1,690.0	1,623.1	1,142.1	751.6
Depreciation & Amort.	224.0	252.1	202.3	157.6	129.8	98.4	76.1
Operating Income	d213.4	168.7	651.9	620.8	541.2	411.6	289.5
Net Interest Inc./(Exp.)	d281.5	d238.2	d177.1	d136.7	d138.6	d118.1	d80.1
Income Before Income Taxes	d517.0	d37.7	518.5	580.0	413.9	294.2	219.0
Income Taxes	cr91.5	cr3.4	176.4	205.4	148.6	110.6	88.0
Net Income	3 d425.5	2 d34.3	342.1	1 374.6	265.3	183.6	131.0
Cash Flow	d201.5	217.8	544.4	532.1	395.1	282.0	207.1
Average Shs. Outstg. (000)	272,544	273,792	262,520	257,781	241,178	204,148	173,852
BALANCE SHEET (IN MILLIONS):							
Cash & Cash Equivalents	47.9	88.2	358.2	46.9	44.1	29.7	218.3
Total Current Assets	907.3	996.2	1,209.1	811.4	714.0	629.5	591.8
Net Property	1,675.3	1,881.5	1,825.0	1,644.1	1,457.1	1,273.7	832.4
Total Assets	12,898.5	14,601.6	13,266.2	10,306.9	8,869.8	7,663.8	5,161.9
Total Current Liabilities	684.3	1,057.9	630.3	535.4	607.5	584.0	471.6
Long-Term Obligations	4,929.7	3,636.1	3,764.6	2,634.7	2,048.7	1,732.0	1,330.2
Net Stockholders' Equity	1,975.8	3,495.3	3,154.1	2,726.0	2,235.3	1,975.3	1,196.6
Net Working Capital	223.0	d61.7	578.8	276.0	106.5	45.5	120.2
Year-end Shs. Outstg. (000)	272,507	272,065	259,201	252,924	236,193	234,542	189,714
STATISTICAL RECORD:							
Operating Profit Margin %	...	5.1	22.7	25.2	23.6	24.9	25.9
Net Profit Margin %	...	...	11.9	15.2	11.6	11.1	11.7
Return on Equity %	...	...	10.8	13.7	11.9	9.3	11.0
Return on Assets %	...	...	2.6	3.6	3.0	2.4	2.5
Debt/Total Assets %	38.2	24.9	28.4	25.6	23.1	22.6	25.8
Price Range	7.44-1.69	38.88-6.19	47.13-29.50	38.00-26.88	31.75-19.44	22.00-13.13	14.00-11.25
P/E Ratio	...	...	36.0-22.5	25.8-18.3	28.9-17.7	24.4-14.6	18.5-14.9
Average Yield %	...	1.6	0.9	0.9	0.9	1.2	1.7

Statistics are as originally reported. Adj. for stk. splits: 2-for-1, 8/96. 1 Bef. extraord. chrg. $40.8 mill., 1997. 2 Bef. extraord. gain $1.9 mill. & incl. non-recurr. chrg. $362.4 mill. 3 Bef. disc. opers. net loss of $43.7 mill., extraord. gain of $22.0 mill., net acctg. chrg. of $909.3 mill. & incl. pre-tax nonrecurr. chrg. of $517.8 mill.

OFFICERS:
R. L. Waltrip, Chmn., C.E.O.
B. D. Hunter, Vice-Chmn.
J. L. Pullins, Pres., C.O.O.
J. E. Curtis, Sr. V.P., C.F.O.

INVESTOR CONTACT: Investor Relations, (800) 716-2104

PRINCIPAL OFFICE: 1929 Allen Parkway, Houston, TX 77019

TELEPHONE NUMBER: (713) 522-5141
FAX: (713) 525-5586
WEB: www.sci-corp.com

NO. OF EMPLOYEES: 29,326 full-time; 10,690 part-time

SHAREHOLDERS: 7,457

ANNUAL MEETING: In May

INCORPORATED: TX, July, 1962

INSTITUTIONAL HOLDINGS:
No. of Institutions: 147
Shares Held: 136,593,319
% Held: 48.1

INDUSTRY: Funeral service and crematories (SIC: 7261)

TRANSFER AGENT(S): The Bank of New York, New York, NY

NYSE SYMBOL SVM
Rec. Pr. 10.93 (4/30/01)

SERVICEMASTER COMPANY (THE)

YIELD 3.7%
P/E RATIO 16.1

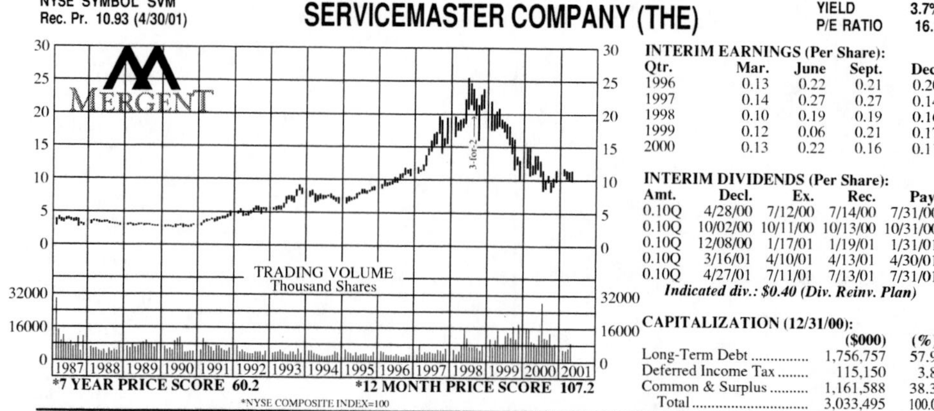

INTERIM EARNINGS (Per Share):

Qtr.	Mar.	June	Sept.	Dec.
1996	0.13	0.22	0.21	0.20
1997	0.14	0.27	0.27	0.14
1998	0.10	0.19	0.19	0.16
1999	0.12	0.06	0.21	0.17
2000	0.13	0.22	0.16	0.11

INTERIM DIVIDENDS (Per Share):

Amt.	Decl.	Ex.	Rec.	Pay.
0.10Q	4/28/00	7/12/00	7/14/00	7/31/00
0.10Q	10/02/00	10/11/00	10/13/00	10/31/00
0.10Q	12/08/00	1/17/01	1/19/01	1/31/01
0.10Q	3/16/01	4/10/01	4/13/01	4/30/01
0.10Q	4/27/01	7/11/01	7/13/01	7/31/01

Indicated div.: $0.40 (Div. Reinv. Plan)

CAPITALIZATION (12/31/00):

	($000)	(%)
Long-Term Debt	1,756,757	57.9
Deferred Income Tax	115,150	3.8
Common & Surplus	1,161,588	38.3
Total	3,033,495	100.0

RECENT DEVELOPMENTS: For the year ended 12/31/00, income was $185.0 million, before an accounting charge of $11.2 million, versus net income of $173.6 million in the previous year. Results for 1999 included an after-tax gain of $30.0 million from the sale of assets and an after-tax nonrecurring charge of $81.0 million. Operating revenues rose 4.7% to $5.97 billion versus $5.70 billion a year earlier. Operating income rose 8.8% to $416.9 million.

PROSPECTS: Earnings for 2001 may be hampered by higher operating costs and weaker operating margins. However, SVM expects to return to double-digit growth in 2002. On 1/2/01, the Company announced that Terminix, an SVM subsidiary, acquired the assets of Allied Bruce Terminix Companies, Inc., the largest Terminix franchise with 76 locations in eight states and estimated 2000 revenues in excess of $66.0 million.

BUSINESS

THE SERVICEMASTER COMPANY (formerly ServiceMaster Limited Partnership), as of 5/24/01, provides outsourcing services to more than 12.0 million customers in the United States and in 45 other countries. The core services of the Company include lawn care and landscaping, termite and pest control, plumbing, heating and air conditioning maintenance and repair, appliance maintenance and repair, cleaning, plant maintenance and supportive management. These services are provided through a network of over 5,500 Company-owned and franchised service centers and business units, operating under brands including TruGreen-ChemLawn, TruGreen-LandCare, Terminix, American Home Shield, Rescue Rooter, American Residential Services, ServiceMaster Clean, Merry Maids, AmeriSpec, Furniture Medic, WeServeHomes.com and ServiceMaster Management Services.

ANNUAL FINANCIAL DATA

	12/31/00	12/31/99	12/31/98	[3] 12/31/97	12/31/96	12/31/95	12/31/94
Earnings Per Share	[1] 0.61	[2] 0.55	0.64	0.55	0.76	0.64	0.33
Cash Flow Per Share	1.12	0.99	1.42	1.19	0.99	0.88	0.76
Dividends Per Share	0.38	0.36	0.33	0.31	0.29	0.28	0.27
Dividend Payout %	62.3	65.4	51.6	56.4	38.2	43.8	81.8
INCOME STATEMENT (IN MILLIONS):							
Total Revenues	5,970.6	5,703.5	4,724.1	3,961.5	3,458.3	3,202.5	2,985.2
Costs & Expenses	5,396.0	5,181.9	4,223.1	3,524.5	3,084.1	2,884.6	2,717.0
Depreciation & Amort.	157.7	138.4	104.6	93.1	79.0	66.0	54.2
Operating Income	416.9	383.2	396.4	343.9	295.2	251.9	214.0
Net Interest Inc./(Exp.)	d136.8	d109.0	d92.9	d76.4	d38.3	d35.9	d31.5
Income Before Income Taxes	318.3	296.2	318.8	274.3	252.4	177.6	142.6
Income Taxes	133.3	122.6	128.8	10.2	7.3	5.6	2.8
Equity Earnings/Minority Int.	13.2	...	...	d7.5	d14.7	d45.7	d45.2
Net Income	[1] 185.0	[2] 173.6	190.0	329.1	245.1	172.0	139.9
Cash Flow	342.7	312.0	423.4	357.1	324.1	238.0	194.1
Average Shs. Outstg. (000)	305,518	314,406	298,887	299,640	326,403	270,275	255,650
BALANCE SHEET (IN MILLIONS):							
Cash & Cash Equivalents	100.9	114.2	120.4	124.1	114.4	49.4	34.4
Total Current Assets	984.8	959.2	670.2	594.1	499.3	393.2	331.0
Net Property	306.0	318.1	212.2	158.3	146.4	145.9	128.4
Total Assets	3,967.7	3,870.2	2,914.9	2,475.2	1,846.8	1,649.9	1,230.8
Total Current Liabilities	833.4	845.8	753.7	558.2	425.6	372.9	304.4
Long-Term Obligations	1,756.8	1,697.6	1,076.2	1,247.8	482.3	411.9	386.5
Net Stockholders' Equity	1,161.6	1,205.7	956.5	524.4	796.8	746.7	307.3
Net Working Capital	151.3	113.4	d83.5	35.9	73.8	20.3	26.6
Year-end Shs. Outstg. (000)	298,474	307,530	298,030	279,944	331,196	275,144	256,574
STATISTICAL RECORD:							
Operating Profit Margin %	7.0	6.7	8.4	8.7	8.5	7.9	7.2
Net Profit Margin %	3.1	3.0	4.0	8.3	7.1	5.4	4.7
Return on Equity %	15.9	14.4	19.9	62.7	30.8	23.0	45.5
Return on Assets %	4.7	4.5	6.5	13.3	13.3	10.4	11.4
Debt/Total Assets %	44.3	43.9	36.9	50.4	26.1	25.0	31.4
Price Range	14.94-8.25	22.00-10.13	25.50-16.00	19.67-10.95	11.83-8.63	9.00-6.37	8.41-6.37
P/E Ratio	24.5-13.5	40.0-18.4	39.8-25.0	35.9-20.0	15.7-11.4	14.0-9.9	25.5-19.3
Average Yield %	3.3	2.2	1.6	2.0	2.9	3.6	3.7

Statistics are as originally reported. Adj. for stk. splits: 3-for-2, 6/98, 6/97, 6/96. [1] Bef. acctg. change chrg. $11.2 mill., 2000. [2] Incl. non-recurr. chrg. $85.5 mill., 1999. [3] On 12/26/97, SVM converted from a publicly traded partnership to a taxable corporation. Prior to that date, net income was not subject to federal and state taxes.

OFFICERS:
C. W. Pollard, Chmn., C.E.O.
J. P. Ward, Pres., C.E.O.
S. C. Preston, Exec. V.P., C.F.O.

INVESTOR CONTACT: Bruce J. Byots, V.P., Inv. Rel., (630) 271-2906

PRINCIPAL OFFICE: One Servicemaster Way, Downers Grove, IL 60515-1700

TELEPHONE NUMBER: (630) 271-1300
FAX: (630) 271-2710
WEB: www. servicemaster.com

NO. OF EMPLOYEES: 72,000 (avg.)

SHAREHOLDERS: 41,000 (approx.)

ANNUAL MEETING: In Apr.

INCORPORATED: DE, Oct., 1986

INSTITUTIONAL HOLDINGS:
No. of Institutions: 226
Shares Held: 125,105,084
% Held: 41.8

INDUSTRY: Management services (SIC: 8741)

TRANSFER AGENT(S): Computershare Investor Services, Chicago, IL

NYSE SYMBOL SE
Rec. Pr. 12.60 (5/31/01)

7-ELEVEN, INC.

YIELD	. . .
P/E RATIO	13.3

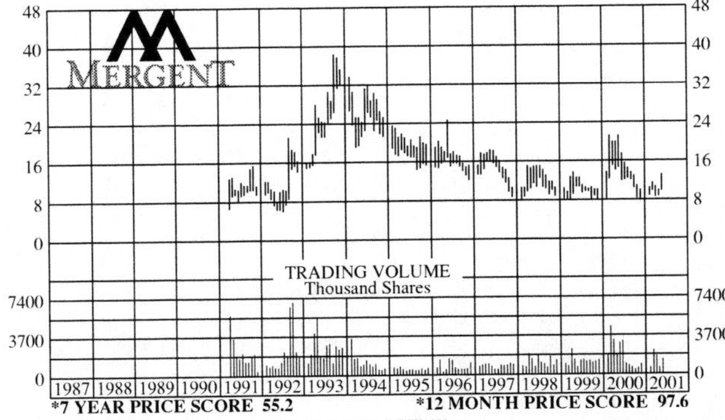

*7 YEAR PRICE SCORE 55.2 *12 MONTH PRICE SCORE 97.6

*NYSE COMPOSITE INDEX=100

INTERIM EARNINGS (Per Share):

Qtr.	Mar.	June	Sept.	Dec.
1996	0.10	0.35	0.40	0.20
1997	0.05	0.30	0.35	0.05
1998	d0.15	0.30	0.35	0.05
1999	0.05	0.30	0.40	0.15
2000	0.16	0.32	0.35	0.12

INTERIM DIVIDENDS (Per Share):

Amt.	Decl.	Ex.	Rec.	Pay.
1-for-5	12/30/99	5/1/00	12/30/99	5/1/00

CAPITALIZATION (12/31/00):

	($000)	(%)
Long-Term Debt	1,641,322	95.2
Common & Surplus	82,106	4.8
Total	1,723,428	100.0

RECENT DEVELOPMENTS: For the year ended 12/31/00, earnings were $106.5 million, before an extraordinary gain of $1.8 million, versus earnings of $78.8 million, before an extraordinary gain of $4.3 million, a year earlier. Total revenues grew 13.2% to $9.45 billion from $8.35 billion in the prior year. Merchandise sales rose 6.7% to $6.63 billion from $6.22 billion the year before. Gasoline sales were up 33.3% to $2.71 billion from $2.04 billion the previous year. Total gross profit was $2.54 billion, up 7.5% versus $2.37 billion in 1999.

PROSPECTS: Sales are benefiting from U.S. same-store merchandise sales growth, reflecting increases in pre-paid cards, tobacco, beer and wine, non-carbonated beverages, fresh foods and bakery items. In addition, the operation of additional stores is helping boost sales and will be a major initiative going forward. During 2000, the Company opened 120 new stores in the U.S. and Canada. In 2001, the Company plans to open approximately 150 to 200 new stores, primarily in existing markets.

BUSINESS

7-ELEVEN, INC. (formerly The Southland Corporation) is a major specialty retailer, with more than 21,000 Company-owned, franchised and licensed convenience stores, operating principally under the name 7-Eleven. As of 3/30/01, the Company operated or franchised over 5,700 convenience stores in the United States and Canada. Another 15,400 7-Eleven stores are operated by area licensees and affiliates in the United States, Guam, Puerto Rico, and 15 other countries. IYG Holding Company, a wholly-owned subsidiary of Ito-Yokado Co., Ltd., and Seven-Eleven Japan Co., Ltd. has had a majority interest in the Company since 1991. Seven-Eleven Japan operates more than 8,500 7-Eleven stores under an area license agreement.

REVENUES

(12/31/2000)	($000)	(%)
Merchandise Sales	6,632,211	71.0
Gasoline Sales	2,713,770	29.0
Total	9,346,981	100.0

ANNUAL FINANCIAL DATA

	12/31/00	12/31/99	12/31/98	12/31/97	12/31/96	12/31/95	12/31/94
Earnings Per Share	**[1] 0.97**	**[1] 0.85**	**[1] 0.60**	**0.80**	**1.00**	**[1] 2.00**	**1.10**
Cash Flow Per Share	**2.85**	**2.76**	**2.41**	**2.76**	**2.85**	**4.01**	**3.11**
Tang. Book Val. Per Share	**0.78**	. . .	. . .	. . .	. . .	. . .	. . .
INCOME STATEMENT (IN MILLIONS):							
Total Revenues	9,451.0	8,349.5	7,349.8	7,060.6	6,955.3	6,816.8	6,759.8
Costs & Expenses	8,978.8	7,914.5	6,981.2	6,658.9	6,548.9	6,463.2	6,415.0
Depreciation & Amort.	239.3	205.5	194.7	196.2	185.4	166.4	162.7
Operating Income	233.0	229.6	173.9	205.4	221.0	187.1	182.1
Net Interest Inc./(Exp.)	d79.3	d102.2	d91.3	d90.1	d90.2	d85.6	d108.6
Income Before Income Taxes	153.7	127.3	82.6	115.3	130.8	101.5	73.5
Income Taxes	47.2	48.5	31.9	45.3	41.3	cr66.1	cr18.5
Net Income	[1] 106.5	[1] 78.8	[1] 50.7	70.0	89.5	[1] 167.6	92.0
Cash Flow	345.8	284.3	245.4	266.2	274.8	334.0	254.7
Average Shs. Outstg. (000)	121,439	102,960	101,926	96,441	96,422	83,347	81,985
BALANCE SHEET (IN MILLIONS):							
Cash & Cash Equivalents	133.2	76.9	26.9	38.6	36.5	43.0	59.3
Total Current Assets	540.4	505.3	438.6	386.6	350.9	356.1	303.4
Net Property	1,926.8	1,880.5	1,652.9	1,416.7	1,349.8	1,335.8	1,314.5
Total Assets	2,742.3	2,685.7	2,415.8	2,090.1	2,039.1	2,081.1	2,000.6
Total Current Liabilities	753.3	811.3	668.6	729.6	674.9	720.1	684.8
Long-Term Obligations	1,641.3	2,182.8	2,168.8	1,894.5	1,938.8	2,005.2	2,227.2
Net Stockholders' Equity	82.1	d559.6	d642.2	d721.5	d789.0	d880.8	d1,157.2
Net Working Capital	d213.0	d306.1	d230.0	d343.0	d324.0	d364.0	d381.4
Year-end Shs. Outstg. (000)	104,768	82,000	81,985	81,985	81,985	81,985	81,985
STATISTICAL RECORD:							
Operating Profit Margin %	2.5	2.7	2.4	2.9	3.2	2.7	2.7
Net Profit Margin %	1.1	0.9	0.7	1.0	1.3	2.5	1.4
Return on Equity %	129.7	. . .	. . .	. . .	. . .	. . .	. . .
Return on Assets %	3.9	2.9	2.1	3.4	4.4	8.1	4.6
Debt/Total Assets %	59.9	81.3	89.8	90.6	95.1	96.4	111.3
Price Range	21.25-8.00	13.75-7.97	15.16-7.82	18.44-8.60	24.69-12.19	23.60-14.38	33.75-19.07
P/E Ratio	21.9-8.2	16.2-9.4	25.3-13.0	23.0-10.7	24.7-12.2	11.8-7.2	30.7-17.3

Statistics are as originally reported. Adj. for stk. split: 1-for-5, 5/1/00. [1] Bef. extraord. credit $1.8 mill., 2000; $4.3 mill., 1999; $23.3 mill., 1998; $103.2 mill., 1995; $99.0 mill., 1993. [2] Bef. acctg. change chrg. $16.5 mill.

OFFICERS:
M. Ito, Chmn.
J. W. Keyes, Pres., C.E.O.
B. F. Smith, Jr., Sr. V.P., Gen. Couns., Sec.

INVESTOR CONTACT: Carole Davidson, (214) 828-7021

PRINCIPAL OFFICE: 2711 North Haskell Ave., Dallas, TX 75204-2906

TELEPHONE NUMBER: (214) 828-7011
FAX: (214) 841-6799
WEB: www.7-Eleven.com
NO. OF EMPLOYEES: 33,400 (avg.)
SHAREHOLDERS: 2,385
ANNUAL MEETING: In Apr.
INCORPORATED: DE, 1934; reincorp., TX, Nov., 1961

INSTITUTIONAL HOLDINGS:
No. of Institutions: 37
Shares Held: 3,697,897
% Held: 3.5

INDUSTRY: Grocery stores (SIC: 5411)

TRANSFER AGENT(S): Computershare Investor Services, Chicago, IL

NYSE SYMBOL SHW
Rec. Pr. 20.98 (4/30/01)

SHERWIN-WILLIAMS COMPANY

YIELD 2.8%
P/E RATIO 299.7

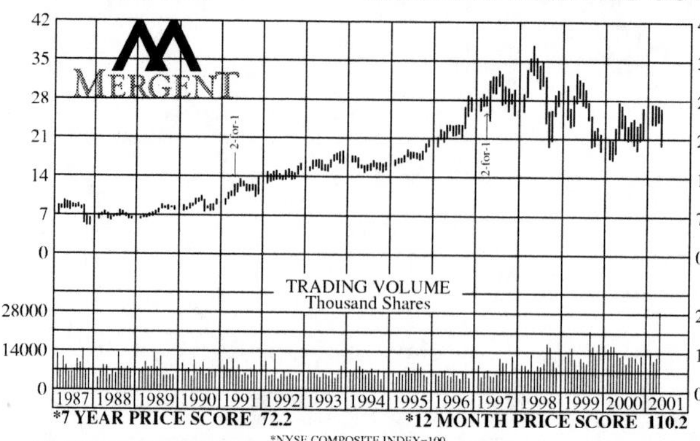

*7 YEAR PRICE SCORE 72.2 *12 MONTH PRICE SCORE 110.2

*NYSE COMPOSITE INDEX=100

INTERIM EARNINGS (Per Share):

Qtr.	Mar.	June	Sept.	Dec.
1997	0.13	0.54	0.57	0.26
1998	0.14	0.57	0.58	0.28
1999	0.17	0.63	0.66	0.34
2000	0.25	0.71	0.66	d1.55

INTERIM DIVIDENDS (Per Share):

Amt.	Decl.	Ex.	Rec.	Pay.
0.135Q	4/26/00	5/24/00	5/26/00	6/09/00
0.135Q	7/26/00	8/16/00	8/18/00	9/01/00
0.135Q	10/19/00	10/30/00	11/01/00	11/17/00
0.145Q	2/07/01	2/22/01	2/26/01	3/12/01
0.145Q	4/25/01	5/23/01	5/25/01	6/08/01

Indicated div.: $0.58 (Div. Reinv. Plan)

CAPITALIZATION (12/31/00):

	($000)	(%)
Long-Term Debt 1	623,587	29.8
Common & Surplus	1,471,864	70.2
Total	2,095,451	100.0

RECENT DEVELOPMENTS: For the year ended 12/31/00, net income was $16.0 million, down 94.7% from $303.9 million in 1999. Results for 2000 included an impairment of long-lived assets charge of $352.0 million. Net sales rose 4.1% to $5.21 billion. Net sales in the Paint Stores segment increased 6.1% to $3.20 billion. Consumer segment net sales decreased slightly to $1.20 billion. The Automotive Finishes segment's net sales advanced 4.8% to $493.4 million.

PROSPECTS: Due to raw material cost increases and cautious consumer spending, SHW expects that comparisons of its year-over-year sales and profits will be challenging through the first half of 2001. However, the Company plans to continue launching new products, improving the focus of its sales efforts, opening new stores and improving its profitability. SHW plans to explore the sale of its Cleaning Solutions and Graphic Arts business units.

BUSINESS

SHERWIN-WILLIAMS COMPANY is engaged in the manufacture, distribution and sale of coatings and related products. SHW has a network of 115 company-owned facilities, supported by an additional 2,300 SHW outlets throughout North America. The Paint Stores' division sells products through company-operated specialty paint stores located in the U.S., Canada, the Virgin Islands and Puerto Rico. The Consumer segment develops, manufactures and distributes architectural paints, stains, varnishes, industrial maintenance products, wood finishing products, paint applicators, corrosion inhibitors, and paint-related products in the U.S. and Canada. The Automotive Finishes segment develops, manufactures and distributes motor vehicle finish, refinish and touch-up products primarily throughout North and South America and the Caribbean Islands. The International Coatings segment develops, licenses, manufactures and distributes architectural paints, stains, varnishes, industrial maintenance products, product finishes, wood finishing, and paint-related products worldwide. The Company's brands include SHERWIN WILLIAMS®, DUTCH BOY®, KRYLON®, and MINWAX®.

ANNUAL FINANCIAL DATA

	12/31/00	12/31/99	12/31/98	12/31/97	12/31/96	12/31/95	12/31/94
Earnings Per Share	**2 0.10**	**1.80**	**1.57**	**1.50**	**1.34**	**1.18**	**1.08**
Cash Flow Per Share	**1.08**	**2.72**	**2.42**	**2.30**	**1.92**	**1.62**	**1.51**
Tang. Book Val. Per Share	**3.18**	**2.32**	**1.76**	**0.70**	**3.65**	**5.85**	**5.39**
Dividends Per Share	**0.54**	**0.48**	**0.45**	**0.40**	**0.35**	**0.32**	**0.28**
Dividend Payout %	**539.5**	**26.7**	**28.7**	**26.8**	**26.1**	**27.1**	**25.9**
INCOME STATEMENT (IN MILLIONS):							
Total Revenues	5,211.6	5,003.8	4,934.4	4,881.1	4,132.9	3,273.8	3,100.1
Costs & Expenses	4,836.4	4,273.0	4,254.9	4,218.7	3,610.6	2,874.6	2,717.4
Depreciation & Amort.	160.0	155.7	147.9	139.2	103.6	77.9	73.7
Operating Income	215.2	575.1	531.6	523.2	418.6	321.3	308.9
Net Interest Inc./(Exp.)	d62.0	d61.2	d72.0	d80.8	d24.5	d2.5	d3.2
Income Before Income Taxes	143.4	490.1	440.1	427.3	371.1	318.5	298.5
Income Taxes	127.4	186.3	167.2	166.7	146.2	117.8	111.9
Net Income	2 16.0	303.9	272.9	260.6	224.9	200.7	186.6
Cash Flow	176.1	459.6	420.8	399.9	328.5	278.6	260.3
Average Shs. Outstg. (000)	162,695	169,026	173,536	174,032	171,117	171,487	172,151
BALANCE SHEET (IN MILLIONS):							
Cash & Cash Equivalents	2.9	18.6	19.1	3.5	1.9	269.5	251.4
Total Current Assets	1,551.5	1,597.4	1,547.3	1,532.3	1,416.2	1,238.9	1,188.6
Net Property	722.4	711.7	718.9	692.3	549.4	456.4	409.2
Total Assets	3,750.7	4,052.1	4,065.5	4,035.8	2,994.6	2,141.1	1,962.0
Total Current Liabilities	1,115.2	1,189.9	1,112.0	1,115.7	1,051.0	618.9	597.0
Long-Term Obligations	623.6	624.4	730.3	843.9	142.7	24.0	20.5
Net Stockholders' Equity	1,471.9	1,698.5	1,715.9	1,592.2	1,401.2	1,212.1	1,053.3
Net Working Capital	436.3	407.5	435.3	416.6	365.2	620.0	591.6
Year-end Shs. Outstg. (000)	159,558	165,664	171,033	172,907	171,831	170,910	169,652
STATISTICAL RECORD:							
Operating Profit Margin %	4.1	11.5	10.8	10.7	10.1	9.8	10.0
Net Profit Margin %	0.3	6.1	5.5	5.3	5.4	6.1	6.0
Return on Equity %	1.1	17.9	15.9	16.4	16.1	16.6	17.7
Return on Assets %	0.4	7.5	6.7	6.5	7.5	9.4	9.5
Debt/Total Assets %	16.6	15.4	18.0	20.9	4.8	1.1	1.0
Price Range	27.63-17.13	32.88-18.75	37.88-19.44	33.38-24.13	28.88-19.50	20.75-16.00	17.88-14.75
P/E Ratio	276.0-171.1	18.3-10.4	24.1-12.4	22.2-16.1	21.5-14.6	17.6-13.6	16.5-13.7
Average Yield %	2.4	1.9	1.6	1.4	1.4	1.7	1.7

Statistics are as originally reported. Adj. for stk. split: 2-for-1, 3/97. 1 Incl. debentures conv. into common. 2 Incl. impairment of long-lived assets chrg. of $352.0 mill.

OFFICERS:
C. M. Connor, Chmn., C.E.O.
J. M. Scaminace, Pres., C.O.O.
L. J. Pitorak, Sr. V.P., C.F.O., Treas.
L. E. Stellato, V.P., Gen. Couns., Sec.

INVESTOR CONTACT: Conway G. Ivy, Investor Relations, (216) 566-2102

PRINCIPAL OFFICE: 101 Prospect Avenue N.W., Cleveland, OH 44115-1075

TELEPHONE NUMBER: (216) 566-2000
FAX: (216) 566-3310
WEB: www.sherwin.com

NO. OF EMPLOYEES: 26,095

SHAREHOLDERS: 10,708

ANNUAL MEETING: In Apr.

INCORPORATED: OH, July, 1884

INSTITUTIONAL HOLDINGS:
No. of Institutions: 323
Shares Held: 95,401,114
% Held: 59.7

INDUSTRY: Paints and allied products (SIC: 2851)

TRANSFER AGENT(S): The Bank of New York, New York, NY

NYSE SYMBOL SKO
Rec. Pr. 7.50 (5/31/01)

SHOPKO STORES, INC.

YIELD	...
P/E RATIO	...

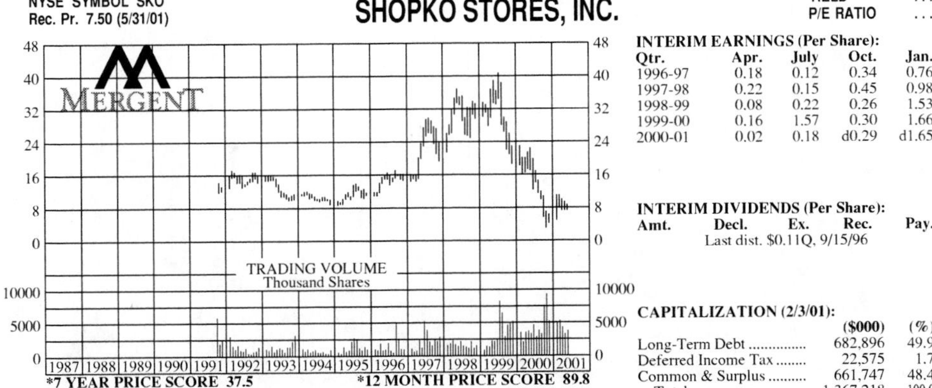

INTERIM EARNINGS (Per Share):

Qtr.	Apr.	July	Oct.	Jan.
1996-97	0.18	0.12	0.34	0.76
1997-98	0.22	0.15	0.45	0.98
1998-99	0.08	0.22	0.26	1.53
1999-00	0.16	1.57	0.30	1.66
2000-01	0.02	0.18	d0.29	d1.65

INTERIM DIVIDENDS (Per Share):

Amt.	Decl.	Ex.	Rec.	Pay.

Last dist. $0.11Q, 9/15/96

CAPITALIZATION (2/3/01):

	($000)	(%)
Long-Term Debt	682,896	49.9
Deferred Income Tax	22,575	1.7
Common & Surplus	661,747	48.4
Total	1,367,218	100.0

RECENT DEVELOPMENTS: For the 53 weeks ended 2/3/01, loss from continuing operations totaled $50.0 million compared with income from continuing operations of $62.7 million in the corresponding 52-week period the year before. Results included pre-tax non-recurring charges of $123.8 million and $8.1 million in 2000 and 1999, respectively. Total revenues climbed 15.3% to $3.53 billion from $3.06 billion a year earlier. Comparisons were made with restated prior-year figures.

PROSPECTS: Going forward, results are expected to benefit from SKO's strategic restructuring initiatives focused on boosting operating profitability and lowering debt levels. During the first quarter of fiscal 2001, the Company closed 23 ShopKo stores located in Illinois, Indiana, Iowa, Kansas, Kentucky, Missouri and Nebraska, along with a distribution center in Quincy, IL. As part of the restructuring, SKO reduced its total workforce by approximately 2,500 employees.

BUSINESS

SHOPKO STORES, INC. operates, as of 5/24/01, 370 retail stores in 23 states, primarily in the Midwest, Western Mountain and Pacific Northwest regions of the U.S. Retail operations include 141 specialty discount stores operating under the ShopKo name in mid-sized and larger cities, and 229 Pamida discount stores in smaller, rural communities. On 7/6/99, the Company acquired Pamida Holdings Corporation. On 6/16/00, the Company sold its healthcare benefits management subsidiary, ProVantage Health Services, Inc.

QUARTERLY DATA

(2/3/2001)($000)	REV	INC
1st Quarter	749,591	1,796
2nd Quarter	819,543	38,078
3rd Quarter	814,191	(8,424)
4th Quarter	1,133,787	(47,268)

ANNUAL FINANCIAL DATA

	2/3/01	1/29/00	1/30/99	[3] 1/31/98	2/22/97	2/24/96	2/25/95
Earnings Per Share	**[4] d1.72**	**[1][2] 3.70**	**[2] 2.10**	**[2] 1.71**	**1.40**	**1.20**	**1.18**
Cash Flow Per Share	**1.52**	**6.66**	**4.65**	**3.75**	**3.26**	**2.96**	**2.85**
Tang. Book Val. Per Share	**15.60**	**14.27**	**14.72**	**12.59**	**12.45**	**12.55**	**12.41**
Dividends Per Share	...	...	...	...	**0.33**	**0.44**	**0.44**
Dividend Payout %	...	...	...	...	**23.6**	**36.7**	**37.3**
INCOME STATEMENT (IN MILLIONS):							
Total Revenues	3,530.5	3,911.9	2,993.8	2,459.6	2,346.5	1,981.9	1,865.4
Costs & Expenses	3,440.3	3,649.1	2,790.5	2,287.5	2,180.8	1,828.1	1,720.4
Depreciation & Amort.	94.1	84.4	67.6	58.3	59.8	56.4	53.5
Operating Income	d13.0	170.4	129.9	111.0	105.8	97.4	91.5
Net Interest Inc./(Exp.)	d66.0	d46.9	d38.3	d30.6	d31.8	d34.3	d29.0
Income Before Income Taxes	d79.0	180.2	91.6	80.4	74.0	63.1	62.4
Income Taxes	cr29.0	71.8	36.0	31.6	29.1	24.7	24.6
Net Income	[4] d50.0	[1][2] 106.0	[2] 55.6	[2] 48.8	44.9	38.4	37.8
Cash Flow	44.1	190.4	123.2	107.1	104.8	94.8	91.3
Average Shs. Outstg. (000)	29,014	28,595	26,517	28,569	32,092	32,005	32,014
BALANCE SHEET (IN MILLIONS):							
Cash & Cash Equivalents	2.8	26.9	30.2	54.3	124.6	89.5	12.6
Total Current Assets	791.3	885.3	588.0	542.2	565.2	476.2	468.7
Net Property	976.8	909.4	703.8	629.7	602.8	617.1	618.1
Total Assets	1,996.7	2,083.3	1,373.5	1,250.8	1,233.9	1,118.0	1,109.8
Total Current Liabilities	617.3	814.3	420.8	397.8	333.3	260.8	281.5
Long-Term Obligations	682.9	453.1	467.2	436.1	418.7	415.1	413.6
Net Stockholders' Equity	661.7	694.5	459.2	396.0	460.9	421.6	397.3
Net Working Capital	174.1	71.0	167.2	144.4	231.9	215.4	187.3
Year-end Shs. Outstg. (000)	28,699	29,584	26,129	25,767	32,167	32,005	32,005
STATISTICAL RECORD:							
Operating Profit Margin %	...	4.4	4.3	4.5	4.5	4.9	4.9
Net Profit Margin %	...	2.7	1.9	2.0	1.9	1.9	2.0
Return on Equity %	...	15.3	12.1	12.3	9.8	9.1	9.5
Return on Assets %	...	5.1	4.1	3.9	3.6	3.4	3.4
Debt/Total Assets %	34.2	21.7	34.0	34.9	33.9	37.1	37.3
Price Range	23.00-3.00	40.75-18.50	37.00-21.38	29.94-14.38	17.13-10.88	14.00-8.63	12.13-8.75
P/E Ratio	...	11.0-5.0	17.6-10.2	17.5-8.4	12.2-7.8	11.7-7.2	10.3-7.4
Average Yield %	...	...	...	...	2.4	3.9	4.2

Statistics are as originally reported. [1] Bef. $3.8 mil extraord. chg. [2] Incl. $48.7 mil pre-tax gain, 10/99; $5.7 mil chg., 1/99; $2.8 mil chg., 1/98. [3] For 49 weeks due to fiscal year-end change. [4] Bef. $34.2 mil gain fr. disc. opers. & incl. $75.9 mil after-tax restr. chg.

OFFICERS:
J. W. Eugster, Chmn.
W. J. Podany, Pres., C.E.O.
B. W. Bender, Sr. V.P., C.F.O.

INVESTOR CONTACT: Vicki Shamion, (920) 429-7039

PRINCIPAL OFFICE: 700 Pilgrim Way, Green Bay, WI 54304

TELEPHONE NUMBER: (920) 429-2211
FAX: (920) 496-4225
WEB: www.shopko.com

NO. OF EMPLOYEES: 17,200 full-time (approx.); 10,000 part-time (approx.)

SHAREHOLDERS: 1,045

ANNUAL MEETING: In June

INCORPORATED: MN, 1961; reincorp., WI, May, 1998

INSTITUTIONAL HOLDINGS:
No. of Institutions: 94
Shares Held: 22,910,917
% Held: 79.8

INDUSTRY: Variety stores (SIC: 5331)

TRANSFER AGENT(S): Wells Fargo Shareowner Services, St. Paul, MN

NYSE SYMBOL SRP
Rec. Pr. 15.40 (5/31/01)

SIERRA PACIFIC RESOURCES

YIELD ...
P/E RATIO ...

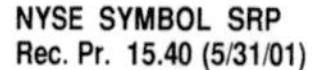

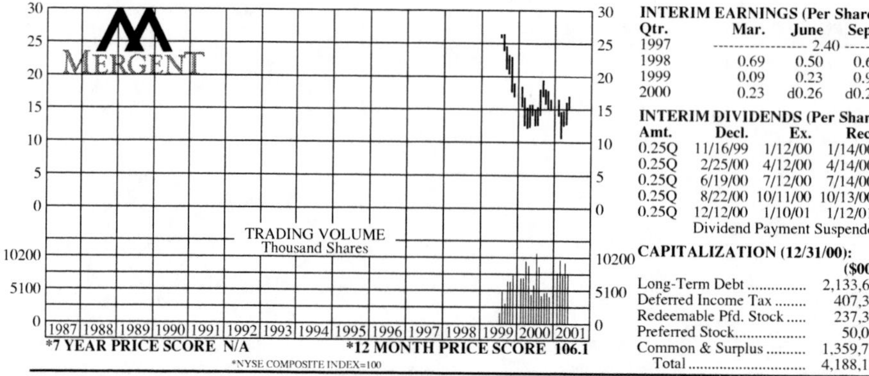

INTERIM EARNINGS (Per Share):

Qtr.	Mar.	June	Sept.	Dec.
1997		2.40		
1998	0.69	0.50	0.68	0.62
1999	0.09	0.23	0.93	d0.42
2000	0.23	d0.26	d0.29	d0.23

INTERIM DIVIDENDS (Per Share):

Amt.	Decl.	Ex.	Rec.	Pay.
0.25Q	11/16/99	1/12/00	1/14/00	2/01/00
0.25Q	2/25/00	4/12/00	4/14/00	5/01/00
0.25Q	6/19/00	7/12/00	7/14/00	8/01/00
0.25Q	8/22/00	10/11/00	10/13/00	11/01/00
0.25Q	12/12/00	1/10/01	1/12/01	2/01/01

Dividend Payment Suspended

CAPITALIZATION (12/31/00):

	($000)	(%)
Long-Term Debt	2,133,679	50.9
Deferred Income Tax	407,370	9.7
Redeemable Pfd. Stock	237,372	5.7
Preferred Stock	50,000	1.2
Common & Surplus	1,359,712	32.5
Total	4,188,133	100.0

RECENT DEVELOPMENTS: For the year ended 12/31/00, the Company reported a loss of $49.4 million, before discontinued operations, compared with income of $48.2 million in the previous year. Earnings were dampened by unanticipated fuel and purchased power costs and an increase in operating expenses, which rose 96.7% to $2.21 billion. Operating revenues improved 81.7% to $2.33 billion compared with $1.28 billion a year earlier. Figures for 1999 include five months of Sierra Pacific results due to the merger.

PROSPECTS: The Public Utilities Commission of Nevada recently approved rate increases for both Nevada Power Company and Sierra Pacific Power Company to help the utilities recover from the surge in costs. While these rate changes should help, the Company notes that the adjustment mechanism for rate increases lags changes in actual energy costs and is capped. Therefore, SRP does not expect any substantial relief from the rise in costs until the Comprehensive Energy Plan is implemented or energy costs decline.

BUSINESS

SIERRA PACIFFIC RESOURCES is a holding company whose principal subsidiaries are Sierra Pacific Power Company and Nevada Power Company. The Company was created from the merger between Sierra Pacific Resources (old) and Nevada Power Company. As of 12/31/01, the Company serves 843,000 electric customers in southern and northern Nevada and the Lake Tahoe area of California, along with 105,000 natural gas and 67,000 water customers in Reno and Sparks, Nevada. Nevada Power Company is engaged in the electricity utility business in the City of Las Vegas and the vicinity in Southern Nevada. Sierra Pacific Power Company provides electricity to customers in a 54,531 square mile region in Northern Nevada and the Lake Tahoe area in California. Other subsidiaries include the Tuscarora Gas Pipeline Company, which owns 50% interest in an interstate natural gas transmission partnership, and Sierra Pacific Communications, a telecommunications company.

ANNUAL FINANCIAL DATA

	12/31/00	12/31/99	[1] 12/31/98	12/31/97	12/31/96
Earnings Per Share	[3] **d0.63**	[2] **0.83**	**2.49**	**2.40**	**2.19**
Cash Flow Per Share	**1.45**	**5.93**	**8.45**	**7.75**	**7.46**
Tang. Book Val. Per Share	**13.25**	**14.66**	**21.72**	**20.49**	...
Dividends Per Share	**1.00**	**0.50**	...	...	...
Dividend Payout %	...	**60.2**	...	...	...
INCOME STATEMENT (IN MILLIONS):					
Total Revenues	2,334.3	1,309.1	741.8	663.2	627.7
Costs & Expenses	1,517.0	818.6	433.5	379.6	358.1
Depreciation & Amort.	163.4	113.2	69.4	64.1	58.1
Operating Income	127.4	171.2	124.1	118.6	108.9
Net Interest Inc./(Exp.)	d159.8	d100.0	d41.6	d41.5	d40.5
Net Income	[3] d49.4	[2] 51.8	77.3	74.4	66.9
Cash Flow	110.1	368.4	256.1	234.0	221.7
Average Shs. Outstg. (000)	78,435	62,577	30,955	30,880	30,495
BALANCE SHEET (IN MILLIONS):					
Gross Property	5,617.8	5,644.6	2,404.7	2,265.3	...
Accumulated Depreciation	1,636.7	1,571.1	727.6	664.5	...
Net Property	3,981.1	4,073.5	1,677.0	1,600.8	...
Total Assets	5,639.5	5,247.7	2,041.4	1,935.9	...
Long-Term Obligations	2,133.7	1,556.3	616.8	627.2	...
Net Stockholders' Equity	1,409.7	1,527.1	746.5	706.5	...
Year-end Shs. Outstg. (000)	78,475	78,428	31,009	30,915	...
STATISTICAL RECORD:					
Operating Profit Margin %	5.5	13.1	16.7	17.9	17.3
Net Profit Margin %	...	4.0	10.4	11.2	10.7
Net Inc./Net Property %	...	1.3	4.6	4.7	...
Net Inc./Tot. Capital %	...	1.4	4.9	4.8	...
Return on Equity %	...	3.4	10.4	10.5	...
Accum. Depr./Gross Prop. %	29.1	27.8	30.3	29.3	...
Price Range	19.44-12.13	26.44-16.88	...	...	...
P/E Ratio	...	31.8-20.3	...	...	...
Average Yield %	6.3	2.3	...	...	...

Statistics are as originally reported. [1] Results for 1998 and prior are for Sierra Pacific Resources (old). [2] Incl. pre-tax chrg. $56.0 mill. for the disallowance of energy expenses. [3] Bef. inc. from disc. opers. of $9.6 mill.

OFFICERS:
W. M. Higgins, Chmn., Pres., C.E.O.
M. A. Ruelle, Sr. V.P., C.F.O., Treas.
W. E. Peterson, Sr. V.P., Gen. Couns., Sec.

INVESTOR CONTACT: Shareholder Relations, (775) 834-3616

PRINCIPAL OFFICE: 6100 Neil Road, P.O. Box 30150, Reno, NV 89520-0400

TELEPHONE NUMBER: (775) 834-4011
WEB: www.sierrapacific.com

NO. OF EMPLOYEES: 3,232

SHAREHOLDERS: 28,126

ANNUAL MEETING: In May

INCORPORATED: NV, Dec., 1983

INSTITUTIONAL HOLDINGS:
No. of Institutions: 145
Shares Held: 34,341,751
% Held: 43.8

INDUSTRY: Electric and other services combined (SIC: 4931)

TRANSFER AGENT(S): Computershare Investor Services, Chicago, IL

NYSE SYMBOL SGI
Rec. Pr. 2.62 (4/30/01)

SILICON GRAPHICS, INC.

YIELD . . .
P/E RATIO . . .

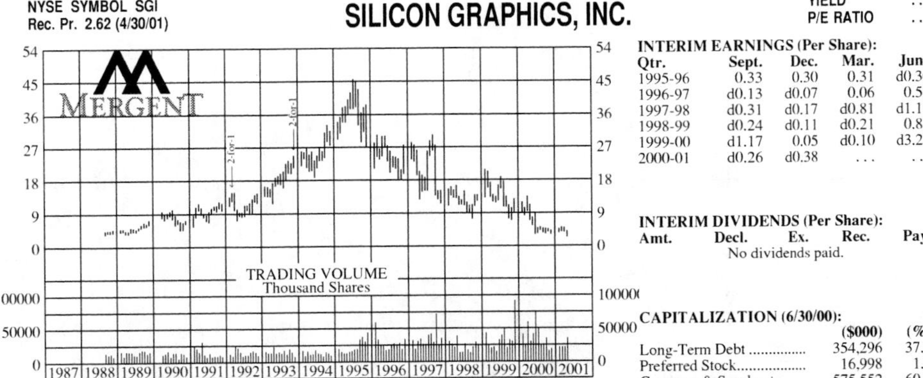

*7 YEAR PRICE SCORE 17.3 *12 MONTH PRICE SCORE 89.6

*NYSE COMPOSITE INDEX=100

INTERIM EARNINGS (Per Share):

Qtr.	Sept.	Dec.	Mar.	June
1995-96	0.33	0.30	0.31	d0.30
1996-97	d0.13	d0.07	0.06	0.56
1997-98	d0.31	d0.17	d0.81	d1.17
1998-99	d0.24	d0.11	d0.21	0.81
1999-00	d1.17	0.05	d0.10	d3.27
2000-01	d0.26	d0.38	. . .	. . .

INTERIM DIVIDENDS (Per Share):

Amt.	Decl.	Ex.	Rec.	Pay.

No dividends paid.

CAPITALIZATION (6/30/00):

	($000)	(%)
Long-Term Debt	354,296	37.4
Preferred Stock	16,998	1.8
Common & Surplus	575,552	60.8
Total	946,846	100.0

RECENT DEVELOPMENTS: For the three months ended 12/31/00, the Company reported a net loss of $71.1 million compared with net income of $9.1 million in 1999. Results for fiscal 2001 included a gain of $10.8 million from the sale of marketable investments. Total revenues were $486.9 million, down 24.9% from $648.2 million in the prior-year period. Operating loss was $93.3 million compared with an operating loss of $12.4 million in the previous year.

PROSPECTS: The Company enters the second half of fiscal 2001 with strong product momentum and expects to be profitable in its fiscal fourth quarter. The Company has delivered more than 10,000 processors of its new-generation SGI Origin family systems. Separately, Alias/Wavefront™, an SGI company, announced it has ported its entire suite of Maya® 3D software products to the Red Hat™ Linux® operating system.

BUSINESS

SILICON GRAPHICS, INC. is a provider of high-performance computing systems and software to customers throughout the world. SGI delivers three-dimensional graphics, digital media and symmetric multiprocessing technologies for a wide range of technical, scientific, corporate and entertainment applications. The Company's product portfolio ranges from desktop workstations to database and computer servers through multi-million dollar, high-performance, supercomputing systems. SGI's products are primarily manufactured in Wisconsin and Switzerland. Revenues in 2000 were derived: U.S., 56.4%; Europe, 23.6%; and other, 20.0%.

ANNUAL FINANCIAL DATA

	6/30/00	6/30/99	6/30/98	6/30/97	[3] 6/30/96	6/30/95	6/30/94
Earnings Per Share	[6] **d4.52**	[5] **0.28**	[4] **d2.47**	**0.43**	[1] **0.65**	[2] **1.28**	**0.91**
Cash Flow Per Share	**d3.60**	**1.45**	**d0.78**	**2.37**	**1.78**	**1.89**	**1.46**
Tang. Book Val. Per Share	**3.09**	**7.71**	**7.72**	**10.18**	**9.62**	**8.28**	**6.37**
INCOME STATEMENT (IN MILLIONS):							
Total Revenues	2,331.1	2,749.0	3,100.6	3,662.6	2,921.3	2,228.3	1,481.6
Costs & Expenses	2,524.3	2,654.6	3,382.1	3,196.4	2,549.1	1,814.1	1,204.3
Depreciation & Amort.	168.5	221.5	314.6	354.3	197.8	106.9	84.2
Operating Income	d361.7	d127.1	d596.1	111.9	174.4	307.3	193.1
Net Interest Inc./(Exp.)	d19.0	d22.6	d24.7	d24.8	d22.4	d18.2	d8.3
Income Before Income Taxes	d381.9	125.7	d596.9	98.2	188.8	316.7	197.7
Income Taxes	447.7	71.9	cr137.3	19.6	73.8	91.9	57.0
Equity Earnings/Minority Int.	. . .	. . .	. . .	. . .	4.0	. . .	. . .
Net Income	[6] d829.5	[5] 53.8	[4] d459.6	78.6	[1] 115.0	[2] 224.9	140.7
Cash Flow	d661.5	274.8	d145.6	432.3	312.3	331.7	223.8
Average Shs. Outstg. (000)	183,528	189,427	186,149	182,637	175,790	175,435	154,486
BALANCE SHEET (IN MILLIONS):							
Cash & Cash Equivalents	258.1	688.1	736.7	287.3	295.4	516.0	400.9
Total Current Assets	920.3	1,847.0	2,065.4	2,315.6	2,096.3	1,508.9	1,024.4
Net Property	466.7	380.8	445.4	525.5	464.9	254.4	183.3
Total Assets	1,839.2	2,788.3	2,964.7	3,344.6	3,158.2	2,206.6	1,518.8
Total Current Liabilities	861.5	977.1	1,096.7	1,086.2	1,101.4	573.2	356.3
Long-Term Obligations	354.3	. . .	. . .	. . .	. . .	287.3	230.0
Net Stockholders' Equity	592.6	1,424.2	1,464.5	1,839.2	1,675.3	1,346.2	921.3
Net Working Capital	58.8	870.0	968.7	1,229.4	994.8	935.7	668.1
Year-end Shs. Outstg. (000)	186,476	182,545	187,523	179,033	172,374	160,479	139,212
STATISTICAL RECORD:							
Operating Profit Margin %	. . .	. . .	. . .	3.1	6.0	13.8	13.0
Net Profit Margin %	. . .	2.0	. . .	2.1	3.9	10.1	9.5
Return on Equity %	. . .	3.8	. . .	4.3	6.9	16.7	15.3
Return on Assets %	. . .	1.9	. . .	2.3	3.6	10.2	9.3
Debt/Total Assets %	19.3	. . .	. . .	. . .	. . .	13.0	15.1
Price Range	13.50-3.06	20.88-6.88	16.50-7.38	30.31-11.56	30.38-17.88	45.63-26.88	33.13-18.75
P/E Ratio	. . .	74.5-24.5	. . .	70.5-26.9	46.7-27.5	35.6-21.0	36.4-20.6

Statistics are as originally reported. [1] Incl. $5.2 mill. non-recur. chg. [2] Incl. $22.0 mill. chg. rel. to merger exp. [3] Incl. results of Cray Research, Inc. fr. 4/2/96. [4] Incl. $144.0 mill. restr. chg., $47.0 mill. chg. for asset impairment, & $15.0 mill. chg. rel. to merger exp. [5] Incl. $272.5 mill. gain fr. sale of partial int. in MIPS & about $14.0 mill. chg. for restr. costs. [6] Incl. $103.0 mill. pre-tax restr. chg.

OFFICERS:
R. Bishop, Chmn., C.E.O.
H. L. Covert, Exec. V.P., C.F.O., C.A.O.
S. M. Escher, V.P., Gen. Couns.

INVESTOR CONTACT: Investor Relations, (650) 933-2607

PRINCIPAL OFFICE: 1600 Amphitheatre Parkway, Mountain View, CA 94043-1351

TELEPHONE NUMBER: (650) 960-1980
FAX: (650) 932-0661
WEB: www.sgi.com

NO. OF EMPLOYEES: 6,726

SHAREHOLDERS: 7,549

ANNUAL MEETING: In Oct.

INCORPORATED: CA, Nov., 1981; reincorp., DE, Jan., 1990

INSTITUTIONAL HOLDINGS:
No. of Institutions: 106
Shares Held: 92,296,313
% Held: 48.2

INDUSTRY: Electronic computers (SIC: 3571)

TRANSFER AGENT(S): BankBoston, N.A. c/o EquiServe, L.P., Boston, MA

NYSE SYMBOL SPG
Rec. Pr. 26.47 (4/30/01)

SIMON PROPERTY GROUP, INC.

YIELD 7.7%
P/E RATIO 23.4

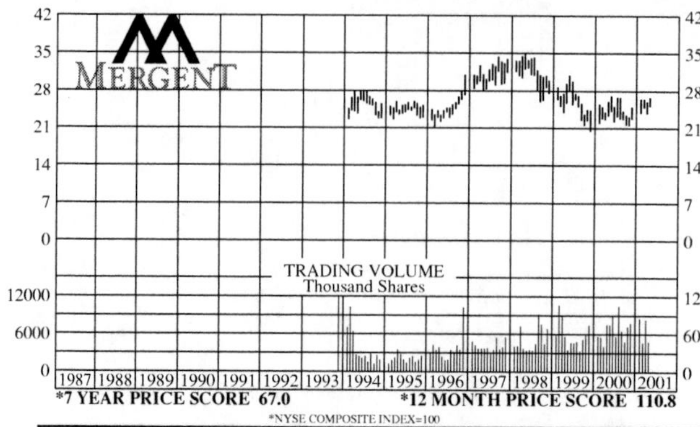

*7 YEAR PRICE SCORE 67.0 *12 MONTH PRICE SCORE 110.8

*NYSE COMPOSITE INDEX=100

INTERIM EARNINGS (Per Share):

Qtr.	Mar.	June	Sept.	Dec.
1998	0.22	0.21	0.25	0.32
1999	0.21	0.22	0.25	0.32
2000	0.21	0.24	0.24	0.44

INTERIM DIVIDENDS (Per Share):

Amt.	Decl.	Ex.	Rec.	Pay.
0.505Q	1/20/00	2/02/00	2/04/00	2/18/00
0.505Q	4/19/00	5/03/00	5/05/00	5/19/00
0.505Q	7/21/00	8/02/00	8/04/00	8/18/00
0.505Q	10/18/00	11/01/00	11/03/00	11/17/00
0.505Q	2/06/01	2/14/01	2/16/01	2/28/01
0.525Q	5/08/01	5/16/01	5/18/01	5/31/01

Indicated div.: $2.04

CAPITALIZATION (12/31/00):

	($000)	(%)
Long-Term Debt	8,728,582	66.2
Minority Interest	1,059,376	8.0
Redeemable Pfd. Stock	339,866	2.6
Preferred Stock	538,684	4.1
Common & Surplus	2,515,328	19.1
Total	13,181,836	100.0

RECENT DEVELOPMENTS: For the year ended 12/31/00, income from continuing operations totaled $241.9 million versus $221.7 million in 1999. Results for 2000 excluded an accounting charge of $12.3 million and an extraordinary charge of $649,000. Results for 1999 excluded a charge of $12.0 million for unusual items and an extraordinary charge of $6.7 million for debt-related transactions. Total revenue improved 6.2% to $2.01 billion.

PROSPECTS: Going forward, operating results should continue to benefit from SPG's strong portfolio of assets, coupled with the relative health of its core in-line retailers. Meanwhile, SPG will continue to focus on revenue enhancement opportunities through the redevelopment and acquisition of strategic assets. Accordingly, SPG plans to open a 560,000 square foot open-air regional shopping center in Annapolis, Maryland in October 2001.

BUSINESS

SIMON PROPERTY GROUP, INC. is a self-administered and self-managed, real estate investment trust company. The Company, through its subsidiary operating partnerships, is engaged in the ownership, operation, management, leasing, acquisition, expansion and development of real estate properties, primarily regional malls, community shopping centers and specialty retail centers. As of 2/23/01, SPG owned or held an interest in 251 income-producing properties containing an aggregate 186.0 million square feet of gross leasable space in 36 states, and five additional retail real estate properties operating in Europe. The Company also owned an interest in two properties currently under construction and 11 parcels of land held for future development.

ANNUAL FINANCIAL DATA

	12/31/00	12/31/99	12/31/98	12/31/97	12/31/96	12/31/95	12/31/94
Earnings Per Share	**2 4 1.16**	**1 2 0.99**	**2 1.01**	**2 1.08**	**2 1.02**	**2 1.08**	**2 3 0.71**
Tang. Book Val. Per Share	**14.23**	**15.95**	**15.70**	**11.11**	**10.45**	**2.28**	**1.18**
Dividends Per Share	**2.02**	**2.02**	**2.02**	**2.01**	**2.12**	**1.95**	**1.43**
Dividend Payout %	**174.1**	**204.0**	**200.0**	**185.9**	**208.0**	**180.8**	**200.7**
INCOME STATEMENT (IN MILLIONS):							
Rental Income	1,284.3	1,207.1	900.0	680.2	468.9	331.1	281.2
Total Income	2,012.7	1,895.0	1,405.1	1,054.2	747.7	553.7	473.7
Costs & Expenses	1,320.4	1,234.6	914.9	664.1	482.6	360.0	333.6
Depreciation	419.9	381.8	267.9	200.9	135.8	92.7	75.9
Income Before Income Taxes	240.9	244.3	207.2	189.2	129.4	102.8	64.1
Equity Earnings/Minority Int.	1.0	d22.6	d47.4	d52.0	d40.6	d40.2	d22.8
Net Income	2 4 241.9	1 2 221.7	2 159.8	2 137.2	2 88.8	2 62.6	2 3 41.4
Average Shs. Outstg. (000)	172,994	172,226	126,879	100,304	73,586	55,312	47,012
BALANCE SHEET (IN MILLIONS):							
Cash & Cash Equivalents	214.4	154.9	127.6	118.3	70.4	62.7	105.1
Total Real Estate Investments	11,558.1	11,696.9	11,106.3	6,405.6	5,021.9	2,009.3	1,829.1
Total Assets	13,911.4	14,199.3	13,269.1	7,662.7	5,895.9	2,556.4	2,316.9
Long-Term Obligations	8,728.6	8,768.8	7,972.4	5,078.0	3,682.0	1,980.8	1,938.1
Total Liabilities	10,857.4	10,961.8	9,875.0	6,105.8	4,591.0	2,323.5	2,259.6
Net Stockholders' Equity	3,054.0	3,237.5	3,394.1	1,556.9	1,304.9	232.9	57.3
Year-end Shs. Outstg. (000)	174,044	166,460	166,775	109,639	96,876	58,360	48,412
STATISTICAL RECORD:							
Net Inc.+Depr./Assets %	4.8	4.3	3.2	4.4	3.8	6.1	5.1
Return on Equity %	7.9	6.8	4.7	8.8	6.8	26.9	72.2
Return on Assets %	1.7	1.6	1.2	1.8	1.5	2.4	1.8
Price Range	27.13-21.50	30.94-20.44	34.88-25.81	34.38-27.88	31.00-21.13	26.00-22.50	28.00-22.50
P/E Ratio	23.4-18.5	31.2-20.6	34.5-25.6	31.8-25.8	30.4-20.7	24.1-20.8	39.4-31.7
Average Yield %	8.3	7.9	6.7	6.4	8.1	8.1	5.6

Statistics are as originally reported. 1 Excl. unusual chrg. $12.0 mill. 2 Excl. extraord. chrg., 2000, $649,000; chrg., 1999, $6.7 mill.; credit, 1998, $7.2 mill.; credit, 1997, $58,000.; chrg., 1996, $3.5 mill.; chrg., 1995, $3.3 mill.; chrg., 1994, $18.0 mill. 3 Incl. non-recurr. interest exp., $27.2 mill. 4 Bef. acctg. change chrg., $12.3 mill.

OFFICERS:
M. Simon, Co-Chmn.
H. Simon, Co-Chmn.
H. C. Mautner, Vice-Chmn.
D. Simon, C.E.O.

INVESTOR CONTACT: Shelly J. Doran, Dir., Inv. Rel., (317) 685-7330

PRINCIPAL OFFICE: National City Center, 115 West Washington Sreet, Suite 15 East, Indianapolis, IN 46204

TELEPHONE NUMBER: (317) 636-1600
FAX: (317) 685-7336
WEB: www.simon.com

NO. OF EMPLOYEES: 2,780 full-time (approx.); 2,590 part-time (approx.)

SHAREHOLDERS: 2,390

ANNUAL MEETING: In May

INCORPORATED: MD; reincorp., DE

INSTITUTIONAL HOLDINGS:
No. of Institutions: 197
Shares Held: 119,103,700
% Held: 69.3

INDUSTRY: Real estate investment trusts (SIC: 6798)

TRANSFER AGENT(S): First Chicago Trust Company, Jersey City, NJ

NYSE SYMBOL SSD
Rec. Pr. 48.55 (4/30/01)

SIMPSON MANUFACTURING CO., INC.

YIELD	...
P/E RATIO	15.6

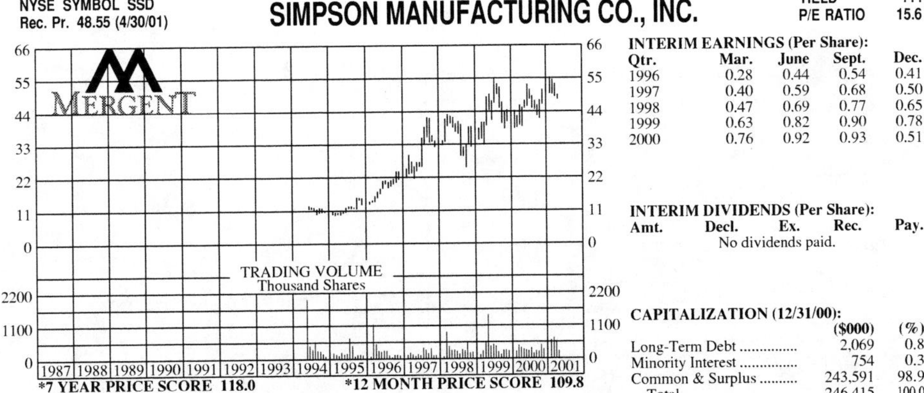

*7 YEAR PRICE SCORE 118.0 *12 MONTH PRICE SCORE 109.8

*NYSE COMPOSITE INDEX=100

INTERIM EARNINGS (Per Share):

Qtr.	Mar.	June	Sept.	Dec.
1996	0.28	0.44	0.54	0.41
1997	0.40	0.59	0.68	0.50
1998	0.47	0.69	0.77	0.65
1999	0.63	0.82	0.90	0.78
2000	0.76	0.92	0.93	0.51

INTERIM DIVIDENDS (Per Share):

Amt.	Decl.	Ex.	Rec.	Pay.
	No dividends paid.			

CAPITALIZATION (12/31/00):

	($000)	(%)
Long-Term Debt	2,069	0.8
Minority Interest	754	0.3
Common & Surplus	243,591	98.9
Total	246,415	100.0

RECENT DEVELOPMENTS: For the year ended 12/31/00, net income declined slightly to $38.4 million compared with $38.5 million in 1999. Net sales were $369.1 million, up 12.4% from $328.4 million a year earlier. Most of the sales growth occurred domestically, particularly in California. Income from operations was $59.7 million, down 4.5% from $62.6 million in 1999. Gross margins decreased from 40.4% in 1999 to 38.4% in 2000

PROSPECTS: In January 2001, SSD acquired 100.0% of the shares of BMF Bygningsbeslag A/S of Denmark for $12.8 million in cash with an additional amount of approximately $2.6 million contingent on operating performance. BMF is a connector manufacturer in northern and central Europe. In December 2000, SSD purchased the assets of Masterset Fastening Systems, Inc. for approximately $2.3 million in cash plus an earn-out of up to $300,000.

BUSINESS

SIMPSON MANUFACTURING CO., INC., through its subsidiary, Simpson Strong-Tie Company Inc., designs, engineers and is a major manufacturer of wood-to-wood, wood-to-concrete and wood-to-masonry connectors and shearwalls. Simpson Strong-Tie also offers a full line of adhesives, mechanical anchors and powder actuated tools for concrete, masonry and steel. Through its subsidiary Simpson Dura-Vent Company, Inc., the Company designs, engineers and manufactures venting systems for gas and wood-burning appliances. SSD markets its products to the residential construction, light industrial and commercial construction, remodeling and do-it-yourself markets. The Company has continuously manufactured structural connectors since 1956. SSD's two product segments are construction connector products and venting products. Keybuilder.com is a joint venture 60.0% owned by SSD and 40.0% owned by Keymark Enterprises, Inc., a software developer based in Boulder, Colorado.

ANNUAL FINANCIAL DATA

	12/31/00	12/31/99	12/31/98	12/31/97	12/31/96	12/31/95	12/31/94
Earnings Per Share	**3.12**	**3.14**	**2.58**	**2.17**	**1.68**	**1.23**	**0.51**
Cash Flow Per Share	**4.19**	**4.03**	**3.27**	**2.73**	**2.29**	**1.69**	**0.89**
Tang. Book Val. Per Share	**20.36**	**17.52**	**13.93**	**11.20**	**8.93**	**7.18**	**5.90**
INCOME STATEMENT (IN THOUSANDS):							
Total Revenues	369,088	328,440	279,081	246,074	202,409	167,958	151,290
Costs & Expenses	296,214	255,027	219,594	196,039	162,517	139,759	133,242
Depreciation & Amort.	13,136	10,862	8,258	6,712	7,198	5,291	3,973
Operating Income	59,737	62,551	51,230	43,324	32,694	22,907	14,075
Net Interest Inc./(Exp.)	3,010	1,669	940	429	595	142	d559
Income Before Income Taxes	62,747	64,220	52,170	43,753	33,290	23,049	13,516
Income Taxes	25,639	25,753	21,028	17,767	13,569	8,927	8,098
Equity Earnings/Minority Int.	1,246	...	...	...	...	...	33
Net Income	38,354	38,467	31,142	25,986	19,721	14,122	5,451
Cash Flow	51,490	49,329	39,399	32,698	26,918	19,413	9,424
Average Shs. Outstg.	12,295	12,234	12,048	11,966	11,755	11,461	10,562
BALANCE SHEET (IN THOUSANDS):							
Cash & Cash Equivalents	59,418	54,510	37,402	19,419	23,712	6,956	5,811
Total Current Assets	200,642	175,750	132,864	104,288	91,875	67,828	59,152
Net Property	63,823	61,144	54,965	42,925	28,688	26,420	20,843
Total Assets	279,480	247,254	191,600	150,765	123,630	97,573	81,581
Total Current Liabilities	32,724	33,693	27,221	20,991	20,090	14,913	13,755
Long-Term Obligations	2,069	2,415	2,565	...	...	...	...
Net Stockholders' Equity	243,591	210,589	161,282	128,951	102,297	81,553	66,522
Net Working Capital	167,918	142,056	105,643	83,297	71,785	52,916	45,397
Year-end Shs. Outstg.	11,967	12,019	11,579	11,517	11,451	11,358	11,275
STATISTICAL RECORD:							
Operating Profit Margin %	16.2	19.0	18.4	17.6	16.2	13.6	9.3
Net Profit Margin %	10.4	11.7	11.2	10.6	9.7	8.4	3.6
Return on Equity %	15.7	18.3	19.3	20.2	19.3	17.3	8.2
Return on Assets %	13.7	15.6	16.3	17.2	16.0	14.5	6.7
Debt/Total Assets %	0.7	1.0	1.3	...	...	...	...
Price Range	53.00-38.19	54.94-32.75	43.00-25.25	42.00-21.50	24.00-13.00	15.38-9.38	12.75-9.75
P/E Ratio	17.0-12.2	17.5-10.4	16.7-9.8	19.4-9.9	14.3-7.7	12.5-7.6	25.0-19.1

Statistics are as originally reported.

OFFICERS:
B. Simpson, Chmn.
T. J. Fitzmyers, Pres., C.E.O.
M. J. Herbert, C.F.O., Treas., Sec.

INVESTOR CONTACT: Investor Relations, (925) 738-9097

PRINCIPAL OFFICE: 4120 Dublin Blvd, Suite 400, Dublin, CA 94568

TELEPHONE NUMBER: (925) 560-9000
FAX: (925) 833-1496
WEB: www.simpsonmfg.com

NO. OF EMPLOYEES: 1,892

SHAREHOLDERS: 3,158 (approx. beneficial)

ANNUAL MEETING: In May

INCORPORATED: CA, 1994; reincorp., DE, June, 1999

INSTITUTIONAL HOLDINGS:
No. of Institutions: 83
Shares Held: 5,660,044
% Held: 46.9

INDUSTRY: Hardware, nec (SIC: 3429)

TRANSFER AGENT(S): Fleet National Bank c/o Boston EquiServe, Boston, MA

NYSE SYMBOL PKS
Rec. Pr. 22.50 (5/31/01)

SIX FLAGS, INC.

YIELD ...
P/E RATIO ...

MERGENT

TRADING VOLUME
Thousand Shares

1987	1988	1989	1990	1991	1992	1993	1994	1995	1996	1997	1998	1999	2000	2001

2-for-1

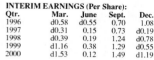

*7 YEAR PRICE SCORE 79.2 *12 MONTH PRICE SCORE 122.1
*NYSE COMPOSITE INDEX=100

INTERIM EARNINGS (Per Share):

Qtr.	Mar.	June	Sept.	Dec.
1996	d0.58	d0.55	0.70	1.08
1997	d0.31	0.15	0.73	d0.19
1998	d0.39	0.19	1.24	d0.78
1999	d1.16	0.38	1.29	d0.55
2000	d1.53	0.12	1.49	d1.19

INTERIM DIVIDENDS (Per Share):

Amt. Decl. Ex. Rec. Pay.

No dividends paid.

CAPITALIZATION (12/31/00):

	($000)	(%)
Long-Term Debt	2,319,912	57.9
Deferred Income Tax	144,919	3.6
Preferred Stock	12	0.0
Common & Surplus	1,544,975	38.5
Total	4,009,818	100.0

RECENT DEVELOPMENTS: For the year ended 12/31/00, the Company incurred a net loss of $52.0 million compared with a loss of $19.2 million, before an extraordinary loss, in 1999. During 2000, PKS faced challenging business conditions, including extremely adverse weather conditions and the negative effect of the relative decline in the value of the Euro. Revenues were $1.01 billion, up 8.6% from $927.0 million a year earlier. Income from operations rose 16.2% to $176.7 million.

PROSPECTS: PKS is implementing its capital and marketing programs for 2001. PKS is rebranding its park in the Brussels market, which will become Six Flags Belgium. In addition, PKS is adding major rides and attractions to a number of other parks, including its Six Flags Over Texas park as part of its fortieth anniversary season. PKS is also devoting a portion of its capital investment program to in-park spending opportunities at several of its major market parks.

BUSINESS

SIX FLAGS, INC. (formerly Premier Park, Inc.) is the largest regional theme park operator in the world. The 38 parks it now operates, such as Six Flags Darien Lake and Six Flags America, had attendance of approximately 46.4 million in 2000. These parks include 16 of the 50 highest attendance theme parks in North America, the largest paid admission theme park in Mexico and seven theme parks in Europe. PKS is also managing the development and construction of a new theme park in Spain. Each of PKS' theme parks is individually themed and provides a complete family-oriented entertainment experience. The theme parks generally offer a broad selection of state-of-the-art and traditional thrill rides, water attractions, themed areas, concerts and shows, restaurants, game venues and merchandise outlets.

REVENUES

(12/31/2000)	($000)	(%)
Theme Park Admissions	544,809	54.1
Theme Park Food, Merchandise, and Other	462,172	45.9
Total	1,006,981	100.0

ANNUAL FINANCIAL DATA

	12/31/00	12/31/99	12/31/98	12/31/97	12/31/96	12/31/95	12/31/94
Earnings Per Share	**d0.96**	**[1] d0.55**	**[1] 0.26**	**0.38**	**0.07**	**[1] d0.08**	**0.03**
Cash Flow Per Share	**1.73**	**1.53**	**1.95**	**0.97**	**0.62**	**d0.02**	**0.39**
Tang. Book Val. Per Share	**4.23**	**4.54**	**4.55**	**7.36**	**3.63**	**1.89**	**2.69**
INCOME STATEMENT (IN MILLIONS):							
Total Revenues	1,007.0	927.0	792.7	193.9	93.4	41.5	24.9
Costs & Expenses	641.7	613.9	507.4	139.0	69.6	33.7	20.3
Depreciation & Amort.	188.6	161.0	115.2	21.7	9.3	3.9	2.1
Operating Income	176.7	152.0	170.1	33.2	14.5	3.9	2.5
Net Interest Inc./(Exp.)	d224.8	d169.4	d115.8	d17.8	d11.1	d5.8	d2.3
Income Before Income Taxes	d46.3	5.2	76.3	23.7	3.3	d1.8	0.2
Income Taxes	5.6	24.5	40.7	9.6	1.5	d0.8	0.1
Equity Earnings/Minority Int.	11.8	26.2	24.1	...	...	...	d0.1
Net Income	d52.0	[1] d19.2	[1] 35.6	14.1	1.8	[1] d1.0	0.1
Cash Flow	113.3	118.5	133.4	35.8	11.1	...	2.2
Average Shs. Outstg. (000)	78,735	77,656	68,518	36,876	17,944	19,689	5,621
BALANCE SHEET (IN MILLIONS):							
Cash & Cash Equivalents	43.0	138.1	400.6	84.3	4.0	28.8	1.4
Total Current Assets	161.0	248.2	689.0	101.1	12.8	35.0	4.0
Net Property	2,257.9	2,064.7	1,571.2	443.8	245.3	116.0	38.6
Total Assets	4,191.3	4,161.6	4,052.5	611.3	304.8	173.3	45.5
Total Current Liabilities	143.6	159.3	357.2	33.8	16.9	11.6	3.3
Long-Term Obligations	2,319.9	2,202.9	1,866.2	216.2	149.3	93.2	22.2
Net Stockholders' Equity	1,545.0	1,615.6	1,626.6	323.7	113.2	45.9	18.1
Net Working Capital	17.4	88.8	331.8	67.3	d4.0	23.4	0.7
Year-end Shs. Outstg. (000)	80,069	78,351	76,489	37,746	22,680	24,288	6,744
STATISTICAL RECORD:							
Operating Profit Margin %	17.5	16.4	21.5	17.1	15.5	9.5	10.2
Net Profit Margin %	...	...	4.5	7.3	1.9	...	0.4
Return on Equity %	...	...	2.2	4.4	1.6	...	0.6
Return on Assets %	...	...	0.9	2.3	0.6	...	0.2
Debt/Total Assets %	55.4	52.9	46.0	35.4	49.0		48.8
Price Range	28.88-13.38	41.63-23.38	33.69-14.00	21.75-12.50	16.44-5.63	10.00-1.25	...
P/E Ratio	...	...	129.5-53.8	57.2-32.9	252.5-86.4	...	...

Statistics are as originally reported. Adj. for stk. split: 1-for-5, 5/6/96; 2-for-1, 8/10/98. [1] Bef. extraord. loss of $140,000, 1995; $788,000, 1998; $11.3 mill., 1999.

OFFICERS:
K. E. Burke, Chmn., C.E.O.
G. Story, Pres., C.O.O.
J. F. Dannhauser, C.F.O.
R. A. Kipf, V.P., Sec., Treas.

INVESTOR CONTACT: Jim Dannhauser, (212) 599-4693

PRINCIPAL OFFICE: 11501 Northeast Expressway, Oklahoma City, OK 73131

TELEPHONE NUMBER: (405) 475-2500
WEB: www.sixflags.com

NO. OF EMPLOYEES: 3,081 full-time; 40,000 part-time (approx.)

SHAREHOLDERS: 780 (record)

ANNUAL MEETING: In Jun.

INCORPORATED: DE, 1981

INSTITUTIONAL HOLDINGS:
No. of Institutions: 157
Shares Held: 79,373,332
% Held: 86.4

INDUSTRY: Amusement parks (SIC: 7996)

TRANSFER AGENT(S): The Bank of New York, New York, NY

NYSE SYMBOL SKY
Rec. Pr. 24.30 (5/31/01)

SKYLINE CORPORATION

YIELD 3.0%
P/E RATIO 19.3

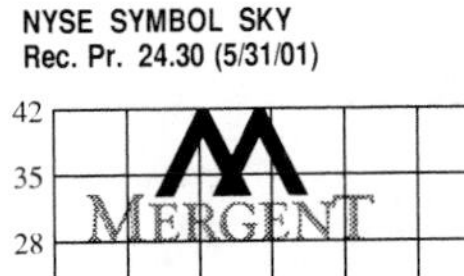

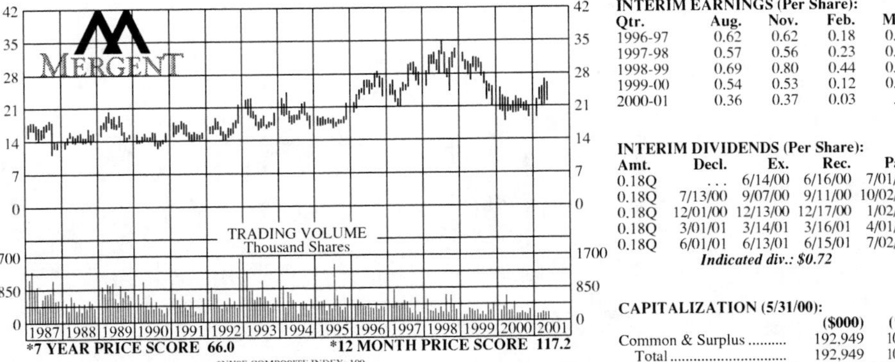

INTERIM EARNINGS (Per Share):

Qtr.	Aug.	Nov.	Feb.	May
1996-97	0.62	0.62	0.18	0.64
1997-98	0.57	0.56	0.23	0.74
1998-99	0.69	0.80	0.44	0.87
1999-00	0.54	0.53	0.12	0.50
2000-01	0.36	0.37	0.03	...

INTERIM DIVIDENDS (Per Share):

Amt.	Decl.	Ex.	Rec.	Pay.
0.18Q	...	6/14/00	6/16/00	7/01/00
0.18Q	7/13/00	9/07/00	9/11/00	10/02/00
0.18Q	12/01/00	12/13/00	12/17/00	1/02/01
0.18Q	3/01/01	3/14/01	3/16/01	4/01/01
0.18Q	6/01/01	6/13/01	6/15/01	7/02/01

Indicated div.: $0.72

CAPITALIZATION (5/31/00):

	($000)	(%)
Common & Surplus	192,949	100.0
Total	192,949	100.0

RECENT DEVELOPMENTS: For the third quarter ended 2/28/01, net income declined 74.1% to $262,000 compared with $1.0 million in the equivalent 2000 quarter. Sales were $90.8 million, down 22.6% from $117.3 million a year earlier. Results for 2001 included a gain of $666,000 on the sale of property, plant and equipment. Manufactured housing unit sales decreased 25.3% to $66.9 million. Recreational vehicle sales fell 13.9% to $23.9 million.

PROSPECTS: Looking ahead, manufactured housing sales should continue to be adversely affected by difficult market conditions, high inventories at the retail level and a restrictive retail financing environment. These conditions emerged in early fiscal 2000. In addition, recreational vehicle sales may continue to be negatively affected by declining demand for fifth wheels and travel trailers as a result of difficult market conditions.

BUSINESS

SKYLINE CORPORATION designs, produces and distributes manufactured housing, which includes mobile homes and multi-sectional homes, and recreational vehicles, which include travel trailers, including park models and fifth wheels, and truck campers. SKY's manufactured homes are marketed under a number of trademarks. They are available in lengths ranging from 36' to 80' and in single wide widths from 12' to 18', double wide widths from 20' to 32', and triple wide widths from 36' to 42'. SKYs recreational vehicles are sold under the NOMAD, LAYTON, and ALJO trademarks for travel trailers, fifth wheel travel trailers and park models, and the WEEKENDER trademark for truck campers. Manufactured housing contributed 77.9% of sales at 5/31/00. Recreational vehicles accounted for 22.1% of sales.

ANNUAL FINANCIAL DATA

	5/31/00	5/31/99	5/31/98	5/31/97	5/30/96	5/31/95	5/31/94
Earnings Per Share	**1.70**	**2.80**	**2.10**	**2.07**	**1.84**	**1.38**	**1.34**
Cash Flow Per Share	**2.16**	**3.22**	**2.49**	**2.44**	**2.16**	**1.68**	**1.59**
Tang. Book Val. Per Share	**22.22**	**21.30**	**19.46**	**18.23**	**17.43**	**16.16**	**15.27**
Dividends Per Share	**0.72**	**0.60**	**0.60**	**0.57**	**0.48**	**0.48**	**0.48**
Dividend Payout %	**42.4**	**21.4**	**28.6**	**27.5**	**26.1**	**34.8**	**35.8**
INCOME STATEMENT (IN THOUSANDS):							
Total Revenues	589,242	664,791	623,395	613,191	645,956	642,118	580,144
Costs & Expenses	566,646	624,600	592,401	582,364	614,914	618,834	558,025
Depreciation & Amort.	4,083	3,838	3,724	3,704	3,489	3,399	2,892
Operating Income	18,513	36,353	27,270	27,123	27,553	19,885	19,227
Net Interest Inc./(Exp.)	6,572	6,264	6,233	6,047	6,192	5,827	5,741
Income Before Income Taxes	25,085	42,601	33,339	34,702	32,952	25,700	24,975
Income Taxes	10,057	17,040	13,393	13,871	13,269	10,358	9,984
Net Income	15,028	25,561	19,946	20,831	19,683	15,342	14,991
Cash Flow	19,111	29,399	23,670	24,535	23,172	18,741	17,883
Average Shs. Outstg.	8,859	9,136	9,511	10,070	10,711	11,147	11,217
BALANCE SHEET (IN THOUSANDS):							
Cash & Cash Equivalents	108,938	133,042	128,783	110,497	55,093	39,911	17,128
Total Current Assets	162,436	193,058	188,482	172,528	123,867	107,336	83,578
Net Property	44,188	44,102	40,951	41,952	43,400	45,256	32,330
Total Assets	235,666	240,982	233,004	217,867	230,336	215,464	208,531
Total Current Liabilities	39,035	45,660	46,297	38,586	43,106	33,246	35,819
Net Stockholders' Equity	192,949	191,692	183,523	176,221	184,267	179,732	170,383
Net Working Capital	123,401	147,398	142,185	133,942	80,761	74,090	47,759
Year-end Shs. Outstg.	8,683	9,000	9,433	9,666	10,573	11,121	11,157
STATISTICAL RECORD:							
Operating Profit Margin %	3.1	5.5	4.4	4.4	4.3	3.1	3.3
Net Profit Margin %	2.6	3.8	3.2	3.4	3.0	2.4	2.6
Return on Equity %	7.8	13.3	10.9	11.8	10.7	8.5	8.8
Return on Assets %	6.4	10.6	8.6	9.6	8.5	7.1	7.2
Price Range	32.50-21.13	34.88-24.19	30.50-21.00	28.63-19.75	21.88-16.50	24.13-16.38	23.00-16.13
P/E Ratio	19.1-12.4	12.5-8.6	14.5-10.0	13.8-9.5	11.9-9.0	17.5-11.9	17.2-12.0
Average Yield %	2.7	2.0	2.3	2.4	2.5	2.4	2.5

Statistics are as originally reported.

OFFICERS:
A. J. Decio, Chmn.
R. F. Kloska, Vice-Chmn., C.E.O., C.A.O.
W. H. Murschel, Pres., C.O.O.
J. R. Weigand, V.P., C.F.O., Treas.

INVESTOR CONTACT: Invesotr Relations, (219) 294-6521

PRINCIPAL OFFICE: 2520 Bypass Road, Elkhart, IN 46514

TELEPHONE NUMBER: (219) 294-6521
FAX: (219) 293-0693
WEB: www.skylinecorp.com

NO. OF EMPLOYEES: 3,200 (approx.)

SHAREHOLDERS: 1,500 (approx.)

ANNUAL MEETING: In Sept.

INCORPORATED: IN, May, 1959

INSTITUTIONAL HOLDINGS:
No. of Institutions: 62
Shares Held: 5,088,624
% Held: 60.6

INDUSTRY: Mobile homes (SIC: 2451)

TRANSFER AGENT(S): Computershare Investor Services, Chicago, IL

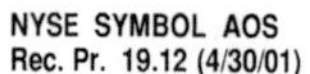

NYSE SYMBOL AOS
Rec. Pr. 19.12 (4/30/01)

SMITH (A.O.) CORPORATION

YIELD 2.7%
P/E RATIO 10.9

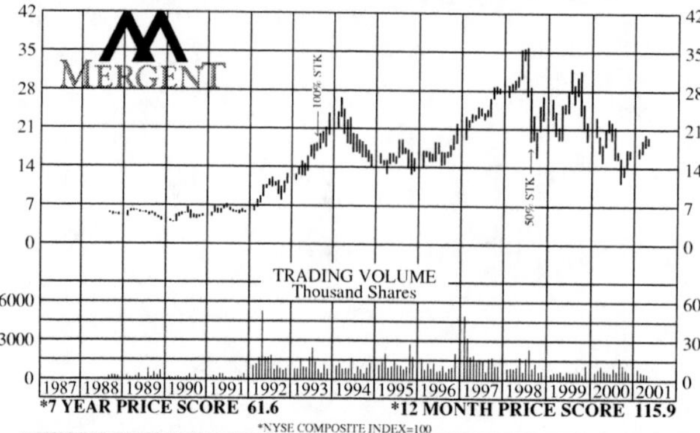

*7 YEAR PRICE SCORE 61.6 *12 MONTH PRICE SCORE 115.9

*NYSE COMPOSITE INDEX=100

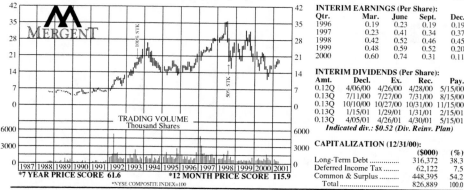

INTERIM EARNINGS (Per Share):

Qtr.	Mar.	June	Sept.	Dec.
1996	0.19	0.23	0.19	0.19
1997	0.23	0.41	0.34	0.37
1998	0.42	0.52	0.46	0.45
1999	0.48	0.59	0.52	0.20
2000	0.60	0.74	0.31	0.11

INTERIM DIVIDENDS (Per Share):

Amt.	Decl.	Ex.	Rec.	Pay.
0.12Q	4/06/00	4/26/00	4/28/00	5/15/00
0.13Q	7/11/00	7/27/00	7/31/00	8/15/00
0.13Q	10/10/00	10/27/00	10/31/00	11/15/00
0.13Q	1/15/01	1/29/01	1/31/01	2/15/01
0.13Q	4/05/01	4/26/01	4/30/01	5/15/01

Indicated div.: $0.52 (Div. Reinv. Plan)

CAPITALIZATION (12/31/00):

	($000)	(%)
Long-Term Debt	316,372	38.3
Deferred Income Tax	62,122	7.5
Common & Surplus	448,395	54.2
Total	826,889	100.0

RECENT DEVELOPMENTS: For the year ended 12/31/00, income from continuing operations was $41.7 million versus income from continuing operations of $50.3 million a year earlier. Results excluded net losses from discontinued operations of $11.9 million and $7.8 million, respectively. Net sales rose 16.6% to $1.25 billion from $1.07 billion in 1999. Sales for the Electric Motor Technologies segment jumped 22.8% to $902.4 million, while Water Systems Technologies segment sales grew 3.0% to $345.5 million.

PROSPECTS: AOS sold its engineered storage products business to CST Industries, Inc. on 1/10/01, and its fiberglass products business to Varco International Corporation on 12/8/00 for combined cash proceeds of about $63.0 million. The sale of these two businesses completed the divestiture of AOS' Storage and Fluid Handling business segment. Going forward, sales to the ventilation and appliance markets may be adversely affected by diminished consumer confidence and a slowing domestic economy.

BUSINESS

A.O. SMITH CORPORATION consists of two divisions, Electric Motor Technologies (72.3% of total 2000 revenues) and Water Systems Technologies (27.7%). The Electric Motor Technologies segment consists of A.O. Smith Electrical Products Company, which manufactures hermetic motors directly to original equipment manufacturers and through a distributor network. The Water Systems Technologies segment consists of A.O. Smith Water Products Company, which manufactures residential and commercial gas and electric water heating systems and copper tube boilers. The Company markets its gas and water heaters through a network of plumbing wholesalers in the United States and Canada.

REVENUES

(12/31/00)	($000)	(%)
Electric Motor Technologies	902,400,000	72.3
Water Systems Technologies	345,500,000	27.7
Total	1,247,900,000	100.0

ANNUAL FINANCIAL DATA

	12/31/00	12/31/99	12/31/98	12/31/97	12/31/96	12/31/95	12/31/94
Earnings Per Share	**3 1.76**	**2 2.11**	**1.84**	**1 1.33**	**1 0.81**	**1.96**	**1.83**
Cash Flow Per Share	**3.66**	**3.68**	**3.13**	**2.26**	**1.52**	**3.73**	**3.40**
Tang. Book Val. Per Share	**8.64**	**7.69**	**10.93**	**10.69**	**13.52**	**11.87**	**9.61**
Dividends Per Share	**0.50**	**0.48**	**0.47**	**0.45**	**0.44**	**0.39**	**0.33**
Dividend Payout %	**28.4**	**22.7**	**25.4**	**34.0**	**54.5**	**19.7**	**18.2**
INCOME STATEMENT (IN MILLIONS):							
Total Revenues	1,247.9	1,039.3	917.6	832.9	781.2	1,544.8	1,373.5
Costs & Expenses	1,108.5	905.7	806.0	742.9	699.0	1,378.9	1,221.2
Depreciation & Amort.	45.1	37.3	31.2	26.3	22.6	55.7	49.2
Operating Income	94.4	96.3	80.4	63.7	59.6	110.2	103.2
Net Interest Inc./(Exp.)	d22.1	d11.4	d3.1	1.3	d8.1	d13.1	d12.1
Income Before Income Taxes	65.1	77.1	73.0	61.7	46.2	93.5	90.5
Income Taxes	23.4	26.8	25.3	21.4	17.1	35.5	34.7
Equity Earnings/Minority Int.	...	...	d3.2	d2.7	d3.9	3.4	1.6
Net Income	3 41.7	2 50.3	44.5	1 37.6	1 25.2	61.4	57.3
Cash Flow	86.7	87.6	75.7	63.8	47.8	117.1	106.5
Average Shs. Outstg. (000)	23,691	23,787	24,184	28,191	31,383	31,370	31,299
BALANCE SHEET (IN MILLIONS):							
Cash & Cash Equivalents	15.3	14.8	37.7	145.9	6.4	5.7	8.5
Total Current Assets	406.1	388.6	287.4	365.7	239.2	352.5	329.5
Net Property	282.8	283.5	248.8	207.8	182.6	447.4	401.8
Total Assets	1,059.2	1,064.0	767.4	716.5	885.0	952.9	847.9
Total Current Liabilities	170.4	168.4	132.2	127.9	138.4	213.6	215.9
Long-Term Obligations	316.4	351.3	131.2	101.0	238.4	190.9	166.1
Net Stockholders' Equity	448.4	431.1	401.1	399.7	424.6	372.4	312.7
Net Working Capital	235.7	220.2	155.2	237.8	100.8	138.8	113.6
Year-end Shs. Outstg. (000)	23,549	23,394	23,252	32,550	31,412	31,379	32,550
STATISTICAL RECORD:							
Operating Profit Margin %	7.6	9.3	8.8	7.6	7.6	7.1	7.5
Net Profit Margin %	3.3	4.8	4.8	4.5	3.2	4.0	4.2
Return on Equity %	9.3	11.7	11.1	9.4	5.9	16.5	18.3
Return on Assets %	3.9	4.7	5.8	5.2	2.9	6.4	6.8
Debt/Total Assets %	29.9	33.0	17.1	14.1	26.9	20.0	19.6
Price Range	23.13-11.19	32.00-18.81	35.88-15.81	28.92-19.08	22.00-13.92	19.08-12.75	26.67-14.08
P/E Ratio	13.1-6.4	15.2-8.9	19.5-8.6	21.7-14.3	27.3-17.2	9.7-6.5	14.5-7.7
Average Yield %	2.9	1.9	1.8	1.9	2.5	2.4	1.6

Statistics are as originally reported. Adj. for stk. splits: 3-for-2, 8/98. 1 Bef. disc. opers. gain $15.2 mill. & gain of $101.0 mill. on disposition, 1997; $109.8 mill. ($5.80/sh.), 1996. 2 Bef. loss from disc. opers. of $890,000 & loss of $7.0 mill. ($0.29/sh.) on disposition. 3 Bef. net loss of $11.9 mill. fr. disc. opers.

OFFICERS:
R. J. O'Toole, Chmn., Pres., C.E.O.
K. W. Krueger, Sr. V.P., C.F.O.
W. D. Romoser, V.P., Sec., Gen. Couns.

INVESTOR CONTACT: Craig Watson, Dir., Investor Relations, (414) 359-4009

PRINCIPAL OFFICE: P.O. Box 245008, Milwaukee, WI 53224-9508

TELEPHONE NUMBER: (414) 359-4000
FAX: (414) 351-4180
WEB: www.aosmith.com
NO. OF EMPLOYEES: 13,800 (approx.)
SHAREHOLDERS: 1,205 (common); 522 (class A common)
ANNUAL MEETING: In Apr.
INCORPORATED: DE, Oct., 1986

INSTITUTIONAL HOLDINGS:
No. of Institutions: 90
Shares Held: 12,009,211
% Held: 50.9

INDUSTRY: Motors and generators (SIC: 3621)

TRANSFER AGENT(S): Firstar Trust Company, Milwaukee, WI

NYSE SYMBOL SII
Rec. Pr. 81.19 (4/30/01)

SMITH INTERNATIONAL, INC.

YIELD	...
P/E RATIO	55.6

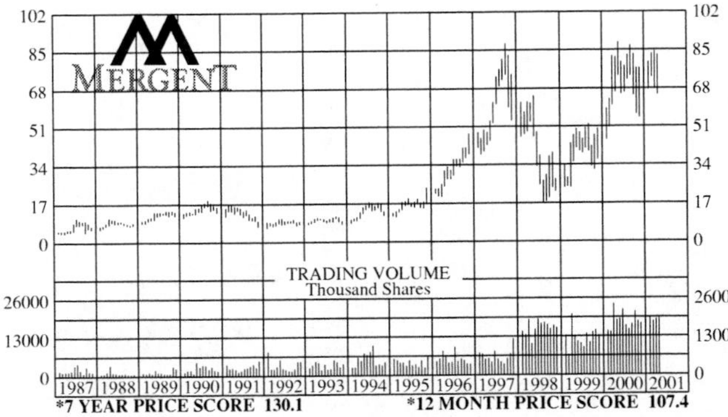

MERGENT

TRADING VOLUME
Thousand Shares

*7 YEAR PRICE SCORE 130.1 — *12 MONTH PRICE SCORE 107.4

*NYSE COMPOSITE INDEX=100

INTERIM EARNINGS (Per Share):

Qtr.	Mar.	June	Sept.	Dec.
1996	0.33	0.38	0.42	0.51
1997	0.53	0.60	0.69	0.76
1998	0.75	d0.16	0.50	d0.33
1999	0.14	d0.06	0.95	0.13
2000	0.23	0.30	0.41	0.52

INTERIM DIVIDENDS (Per Share):

Amt.	Decl.	Ex.	Rec.	Pay.

No dividends paid.

CAPITALIZATION (12/31/00):

	($000)	(%)
Long-Term Debt	374,176	23.2
Deferred Income Tax	44,659	2.8
Minority Interest	377,682	23.4
Common & Surplus	817,481	50.6
Total	1,613,998	100.0

RECENT DEVELOPMENTS: For the year ended 12/31/00, net income rose 28.3% to $72.8 million versus $56.7 million a year earlier. Results for 1999 included a non-recurring gain of $84.0 million. Revenues advanced 52.9% to $2.76 billion from $1.81 billion in 1999, reflecting gains in the U.S., Europe/Africa and Latin America and improved activity levels. M-I revenues advanced 46.9% to $1.24 billion, Smith Bits revenues increased 36.7% to $328.2 million, Smith Services' revenues rose 27.6% to $289.9 million, and Wilson revenues leapt 82.4% to $232.7 million.

PROSPECTS: Near-term prospects are positive. The strong revenue growth experienced across SII's segments is being driven by increased levels of offshore-directed spending, higher exploration and production spending in North America, recent acquisitions, and improved pricing. Separately, SII's Wilson Industries, Inc. subsidiary completed the acquisition of substantially all of the net assets of Van Leeuwen Pipe and Tube Corporation, a distribution company providing pipe, valves and fittings to new construction and maintenance, repair and operating projects.

BUSINESS

SMITH INTERNATIONAL, INC. is a worldwide supplier of products and services to the oil and natural gas exploration and production industry, the petrochemical industry and other industrial markets. SII provides a comprehensive line of products and engineering services, including drilling and completion fluid systems, solids-control services, waste management services, three-cone drill bits, diamond drill bits, fishing services, drilling tools, underreamers and liner hangers. The Company also offers supply-chain management services through a branch network providing pipevalves, fittings, mill, safety and other maintenance products. Operations are conducted through SII's four business units, which consists of M-I (44.8% of 2000 revenues), Smith Bits (11.9%), Smith Services (10.5%), and Wilson Industries (32.8%). On 4/30/98, the Company completed its acquisition of Wilson Industries, Inc.

QUARTERLY DATA

(12/31/00) ($000)	REV	INC
1st Quarter	625,432	11,323
2nd Quarter	657,229	14,974
3rd Quarter	718,470	20,474
4th Quarter	759,883	26,029

ANNUAL FINANCIAL DATA

	12/31/00	12/31/99	12/31/98	12/31/97	12/31/96	12/31/95	12/31/94
Earnings Per Share	**1.45**	**[2] 1.15**	**[1] 0.70**	**2.55**	**1.62**	**1.16**	**0.92**
Cash Flow Per Share	**3.05**	**2.70**	**2.16**	**3.71**	**2.41**	**1.81**	**1.48**
Tang. Book Val. Per Share	**7.31**	**7.57**	**7.16**	**6.56**	**5.17**	**6.56**	**5.52**
INCOME STATEMENT (IN MILLIONS):							
Total Revenues	2,761.0	1,806.2	2,118.7	1,563.1	1,156.7	874.5	653.9
Costs & Expenses	2,481.3	1,580.6	1,923.1	1,298.9	992.5	762.8	572.0
Depreciation & Amort.	80.7	76.0	70.3	46.7	31.6	25.5	21.8
Operating Income	199.0	149.5	125.3	217.5	132.5	86.2	60.1
Net Interest Inc./(Exp.)	d34.9	d38.8	d43.4	d25.0	d16.4	d12.2	d8.6
Income Before Income Taxes	164.1	110.8	81.9	192.5	116.1	74.0	51.5
Income Taxes	55.0	47.9	26.3	50.7	26.8	12.6	6.8
Equity Earnings/Minority Int.	d36.3	d6.2	d21.6	d39.5	d24.8	d15.8	d8.8
Net Income	72.8	[2] 56.7	[1] 34.1	102.4	64.4	45.6	35.9
Cash Flow	153.5	132.8	104.4	149.1	96.0	71.1	57.7
Average Shs. Outstg. (000)	50,302	49,190	48,341	40,183	39,880	39,383	39,065
BALANCE SHEET (IN MILLIONS):							
Cash & Cash Equivalents	36.5	24.1	22.7	29.0	25.5	14.8	8.1
Total Current Assets	1,310.0	1,054.8	997.2	851.0	665.3	485.3	421.6
Net Property	409.0	381.1	375.2	270.9	205.3	132.5	117.7
Total Assets	2,295.3	1,894.6	1,759.0	1,396.0	1,074.6	702.8	619.8
Total Current Liabilities	642.8	457.3	693.3	372.9	300.5	185.3	164.2
Long-Term Obligations	374.2	346.6	368.8	306.3	228.4	117.2	115.0
Net Stockholders' Equity	817.5	720.2	634.0	469.5	368.5	300.9	253.1
Net Working Capital	667.2	597.5	303.9	478.0	364.8	300.0	257.3
Year-end Shs. Outstg. (000)	49,763	48,930	48,137	39,660	40,157	39,178	38,804
STATISTICAL RECORD:							
Operating Profit Margin %	7.2	8.3	5.9	13.9	11.5	9.9	9.2
Net Profit Margin %	2.6	3.1	1.6	6.5	5.6	5.2	5.5
Return on Equity %	8.9	7.9	5.4	21.8	17.5	15.2	14.2
Return on Assets %	3.2	3.0	1.9	7.3	6.0	6.5	5.8
Debt/Total Assets %	16.3	18.3	21.0	21.9	21.3	16.7	18.6
Price Range	88.50-45.00	52.06-24.00	64.50-17.25	87.88-38.50	48.00-19.88	23.88-11.00	17.63-8.38
P/E Ratio	61.0-31.0	45.3-20.9	92.1-24.6	34.5-15.1	29.6-12.3	20.6-9.5	19.2-9.1

Statistics are as originally reported. [1] Incls. one-time pre-tax chrgs. of $82.5 mill. [2] Incls. one-time pre-tax credit of $84.0 mill.

OFFICERS:
D. L. Rock, Chmn., C.E.O.
M. K. Dorman, Sr. V.P., C.F.O., Treas.
N. S. Sutton, Sr. V.P., Sec., Gen. Couns.

INVESTOR CONTACT: Margaret K. Dorman, Sr. V.P., C.F.O., Treas., (800) 877-6424

PRINCIPAL OFFICE: 411 North Sam Houston Parkway, Suite 600, Houston, TX 77060

TELEPHONE NUMBER: (281) 443-3370
FAX: (281) 233-5199
WEB: www.smith.com
NO. OF EMPLOYEES: 9,892
SHAREHOLDERS: 2,403
ANNUAL MEETING: In Apr.
INCORPORATED: CA, Jan., 1937; reincorp., DE, May, 1983

INSTITUTIONAL HOLDINGS:
No. of Institutions: 225
Shares Held: 45,722,992
% Held: 90.4

INDUSTRY: Chemical preparations, nec (SIC: 2899)

TRANSFER AGENT(S): First Chicago Trust Company of New York, Jersey City, NJ

NYSE SYMBOL SJM
Rec. Pr. 25.02 (5/31/01)

SMUCKER (J.M.) COMPANY

YIELD 2.6%
P/E RATIO 27.8

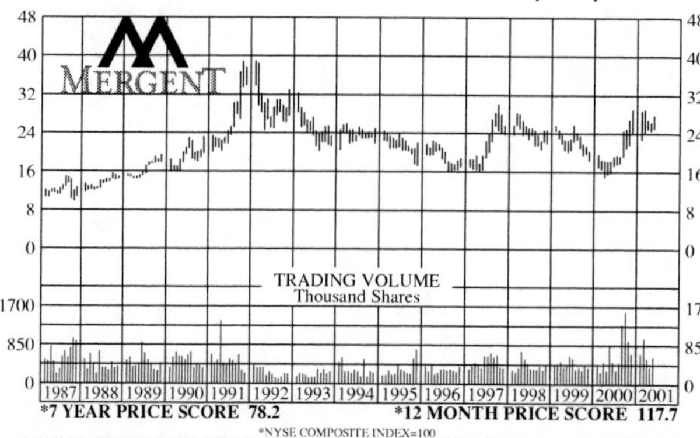

INTERIM EARNINGS (Per Share):

Qtr.	July	Oct.	Jan.	Apr.
1995-96	0.33	0.32	0.22	0.19
1996-97	0.26	0.26	0.23	0.31
1997-98	0.34	0.30	0.27	0.33
1998-99	0.36	0.31	0.28	0.34
1999-00	0.38	0.32	0.17	0.03
2000-01	0.35	0.24	0.28	...

INTERIM DIVIDENDS (Per Share):

Amt.	Decl.	Ex.	Rec.	Pay.
0.16Q	10/24/00	11/15/00	11/17/00	12/01/00
0.16Q	1/24/01	2/13/01	2/15/01	3/01/01
0.16Q	4/18/01	5/16/01	5/18/01	6/01/01

Indicated div.: $0.64 (Div. Reinv. Plan)

CAPITALIZATION (4/30/00):

	($000)	(%)
Long-Term Debt	75,000	19.1
Deferred Income Tax	3,221	0.8
Common & Surplus	313,473	80.0
Total	391,694	100.0

RECENT DEVELOPMENTS: For the three months ended 1/31/01, net income climbed 38.9% to $6.9 million from $5.0 million the year before. Results in the prior-year period included a one-time pre-tax charge of $4.8 million. Net sales inched up to $151.0 million from $150.4 million a year earlier. Gross profit was $54.5 million, or 36.1% of net sales, compared with $54.5 million, or 36.2% of net sales, the previous year. Operating income advanced 54.6% to $12.8 million.

PROSPECTS: Domestic sales are benefiting from strong sales to warehouse clubs and mass retailers, expanded distribution of SMUCKER'S UNCRUSTABLES, a line of thaw-and-serve peanut butter and jelly sandwiches, and increased sales of bakery ingredient products to industrial customers. Going forward, earnings are expected to benefit from continued lower fruit costs through 2001 and SJM's efforts to improve operating efficiencies.

BUSINESS

THE J.M. SMUCKER COMPANY manufactures and markets food products, including fruit spreads, dessert toppings, peanut butter, industrial fruit products, fruit and vegetable juices, juice beverages, syrups, condiments and gift packages. Well-recognized brand names include: SMUCKER'S, DICKINSON'S, GOOBER and MAGIC SHELL. Products are sold primarily through brokers to chain, wholesale, cooperative, independent grocery accounts, as well as through food service distributors and chains including hotels, restaurants, and institutions, and to other food manufacturers. Distribution outside of the U.S. is principally in Canada, Australia, Mexico, Latin America, the Pacific Rim, and Greater Europe, although products are exported to other countries as well. During fiscal 2000, international sales represented approximately 14.0% of SJM's consolidated sales.

ANNUAL FINANCIAL DATA

	4/30/00	4/30/99	4/30/98	4/30/97	[2] 4/30/96	4/30/95	4/30/94
Earnings Per Share	**[4] 0.92**	**1.29**	**[1] 1.24**	**1.06**	**[3] 1.01**	**1.25**	**1.05**
Cash Flow Per Share	**1.83**	**2.09**	**2.01**	**1.81**	**1.61**	...	...
Tang. Book Val. Per Share	**9.29**	**9.04**	**8.91**	**8.44**	**7.96**	**6.08**	**5.99**
Dividends Per Share	**0.59**	**0.55**	**0.52**	**0.52**	**0.52**	**0.49**	**0.45**
Dividend Payout %	**64.1**	**42.6**	**41.9**	**49.1**	**51.0**	**39.2**	**42.9**
INCOME STATEMENT (IN THOUSANDS):							
Total Revenues	632,486	602,457	565,476	542,602	528,576	628,279	511,525
Costs & Expenses	565,053	520,088	485,873	467,559	457,109	545,623	445,365
Depreciation & Amort.	26,198	23,394	22,539	21,839	17,473	20,157	15,378
Operating Income	41,235	58,975	57,064	53,204	53,994	62,499	50,782
Net Interest Inc./(Exp.)	d405	1,769	2,380	300	d1,220	d3,745	627
Income Before Income Taxes	41,531	61,631	60,759	53,166	44,795	61,380	52,723
Income Taxes	15,174	23,868	24,411	22,231	15,342	25,077	22,225
Net Income	[4] 26,357	37,763	[1] 36,348	30,935	[3] 29,453	36,303	30,498
Cash Flow	52,555	61,157	58,887	52,774	46,926	56,460	45,876
Average Shs. Outstg.	28,750	29,275	29,345	29,105	29,105	...	...
BALANCE SHEET (IN THOUSANDS):							
Cash & Cash Equivalents	33,103	8,683	36,484	24,091	17,647	11,244	14,059
Total Current Assets	229,132	186,142	201,506	178,472	214,462	191,836	171,685
Net Property	174,648	166,543	143,714	139,635	143,084	140,125	137,506
Total Assets	475,384	433,883	407,973	384,773	424,952	421,017	378,641
Total Current Liabilities	68,189	87,631	84,900	72,016	67,510	79,843	83,195
Long-Term Obligations	75,000	...	...	...	60,800	67,100	48,558
Net Stockholders' Equity	313,473	324,329	302,177	291,891	276,341	257,992	234,402
Net Working Capital	160,943	98,511	116,606	106,456	146,952	111,993	88,490
Year-end Shs. Outstg.	28,325	29,159	29,142	29,208	29,170	29,164	29,110
STATISTICAL RECORD:							
Operating Profit Margin %	6.5	9.8	10.1	9.8	10.2	9.9	9.9
Net Profit Margin %	4.2	6.3	6.4	5.7	5.6	5.8	6.0
Return on Equity %	8.4	11.6	12.0	10.6	10.7	14.1	13.0
Return on Assets %	5.5	8.7	8.9	8.0	6.9	8.6	8.1
Debt/Total Assets %	15.8	...	...	...	14.3	15.9	12.8
Price Range	25.75-18.38	28.19-20.63	30.00-16.00	22.50-16.13	24.50-17.25	26.00-20.50	32.38-20.25
P/E Ratio	28.0-20.0	21.8-16.0	24.2-12.9	21.2-15.2	24.3-17.1	20.8-16.4	30.8-19.3
Average Yield %	2.7	2.3	2.3	2.7	2.5	2.1	1.7

Statistics are as originally reported. On 8/29/00, the Company combined its Cl. A and Cl. B shs. into a new class of com. stk. [1] Bef. $3.0 mil ($0.10/sh) chg. for acctg. adj. [2] Reflects disposition of Mrs. Smith's frozen pie business. [3] Bef. $140,000 loss from discont. opers. [4] Incl. $9.6 mil ($0.34/sh) after-tax non-recur. chg. related to the impairment of certain long-lived assets.

OFFICERS:
T. P. Smucker, Chmn.
R. K. Smucker, Pres.
S. J. Ellcessor, V.P.-Fin. & Admin., Sec., Treas., Gen. Couns.

PRINCIPAL OFFICE: One Strawberry Lane, Orrville, OH 44667-0280

TELEPHONE NUMBER: (330) 682-3000
FAX: (330) 682-3370
WEB: www.smucker.com

NO. OF EMPLOYEES: 2,250 (approx.)

SHAREHOLDERS: 5,403 Cl A; 3,457 Cl. B

ANNUAL MEETING: In Aug.

INCORPORATED: OH, Sept., 1921

INSTITUTIONAL HOLDINGS:
No. of Institutions: 106
Shares Held: 10,083,098
% Held: 41.6

INDUSTRY: Canned fruits and vegetables (SIC: 2033)

TRANSFER AGENT(S): Computershare Investor Services, Chicago, IL

NYSE SYMBOL SNA
Rec. Pr. 28.80 (5/31/01)

SNAP-ON INCORPORATED

YIELD	3.3%
P/E RATIO	14.2

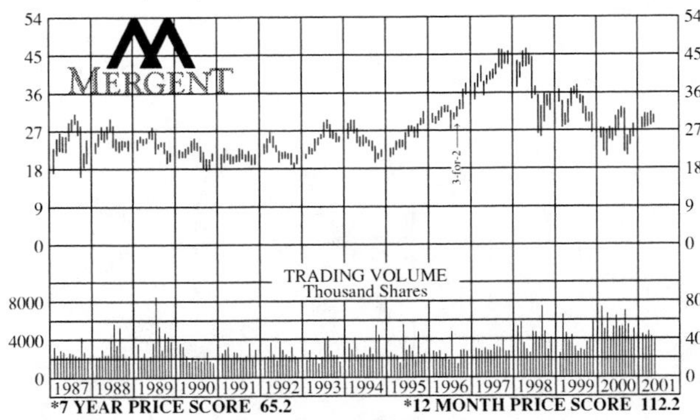

*7 YEAR PRICE SCORE 65.2 *12 MONTH PRICE SCORE 112.2
*NYSE COMPOSITE INDEX=100

INTERIM EARNINGS (Per Share):

Qtr.	Mar.	June	Sept.	Dec.
1997	0.56	0.64	0.58	0.68
1998	0.56	0.38	d1.24	0.21
1999	0.55	0.42	0.72	0.47
2000	0.58	0.75	0.46	0.24

INTERIM DIVIDENDS (Per Share):

Amt.	Decl.	Ex.	Rec.	Pay.
0.23Q	5/01/00	5/17/00	5/19/00	6/09/00
0.24Q	6/23/00	8/17/00	8/21/00	9/11/00
0.24Q	10/27/00	11/16/00	11/20/00	12/11/00
0.24Q	1/26/01	2/14/01	2/16/01	3/09/01
0.24Q	4/27/01	5/16/01	5/18/01	6/08/01

Indicated div.: $0.96 (Div. Reinv. Plan)

CAPITALIZATION (12/30/00):

	($000)	(%)
Long-Term Debt	473,000	35.3
Deferred Income Tax	24,700	1.8
Common & Surplus	844,000	62.9
Total	1,341,700	100.0

RECENT DEVELOPMENTS: For the year ended 12/30/00, income declined 3.2% to $123.1 million, before an accounting gain, compared with net income of $127.2 million in 1999. Results included nonrecurring charges that amounted $21.8 million in 2000 and $37.2 million in 1999. Net sales advanced 11.8% to $2.18 billion, due to a 5.0% increase in internal sales, and 11.0% contribution from the Bahco acquisition.

PROSPECTS: Looking ahead, SNA believes that it will achieve strong sales, operating profit and earnings per share based on its solid core business and product portfolio. Going forward, SNA is focused on growing its dealer network in 2001 and on strengthening its market positions worldwide. In addition, SNA will focus on improving working capital management in order to produce strong cash flow.

BUSINESS

SNAP-ON INCORPORATED is a global developer, manufacturer and marketer of tools and equipment for professional technicians, motor service shop owners, franchised service centers, national accounts, original equipment manufacturers, and commercial industrial tool and equipment users worldwide. Product lines include hand and power tools, diagnostics and shop equipment, tool storage products, diagnostics software and other tools for the transportation service, industrial, government, education, agricultural and other commercial applications. Products are sold through the Company's franchised dealer van, company direct sales and distributor channels. On 9/30/99, the Company completed the acquisition of the Sandvik Saws and Tools business, which was renamed Bahco Group AB.

ANNUAL FINANCIAL DATA

	12/30/00	1/1/00	1/2/99	1/3/98	12/28/96	12/30/95	12/31/94
Earnings Per Share	**[4] 2.10**	**[3] 2.16**	**[2] d0.08**	**2.44**	**2.16**	**1.84**	**[1] 1.53**
Cash Flow Per Share	**3.23**	**3.10**	**0.68**	**3.06**	**2.68**	**2.36**	**1.99**
Tang. Book Val. Per Share	**13.13**	**12.65**	**11.61**	**14.74**	**13.62**	**12.35**	**11.92**
Dividends Per Share	**0.94**	**0.90**	**0.86**	**0.82**	**0.76**	**0.72**	**0.72**
Dividend Payout %	**44.8**	**41.7**	**...**	**33.6**	**35.2**	**39.1**	**47.0**
INCOME STATEMENT (IN MILLIONS):							
Total Revenues	2,175.7	1,945.6	1,772.6	1,672.2	1,485.3	1,292.1	1,194.3
Costs & Expenses	1,879.5	1,677.8	1,693.5	1,368.3	1,232.9	1,071.9	1,005.7
Depreciation & Amort.	66.2	55.4	45.0	38.4	31.9	31.5	29.6
Operating Income	230.0	212.4	34.1	265.5	220.5	188.6	158.9
Net Interest Inc./(Exp.)	d40.7	d27.4	d21.3	d17.7	d12.6	d13.3	d10.8
Income Before Income Taxes	192.6	197.9	10.8	238.7	208.7	179.9	153.7
Income Taxes	69.5	70.7	15.6	88.3	77.2	66.6	55.4
Net Income	[4] 123.1	[3] 127.2	[2] d4.8	150.4	131.5	113.3	[1] 98.3
Cash Flow	189.3	182.6	40.2	188.7	163.3	144.9	127.9
Average Shs. Outstg. (000)	58,600	58,877	59,220	61,686	60,968	61,511	64,188
BALANCE SHEET (IN MILLIONS):							
Cash & Cash Equivalents	6.1	17.6	15.0	25.7	15.4	16.2	9.0
Total Current Assets	1,186.4	1,206.3	1,079.8	1,021.7	1,017.3	946.7	873.0
Net Property	345.1	362.6	272.0	265.8	245.3	220.1	209.1
Total Assets	2,050.4	2,149.8	1,674.9	1,641.4	1,520.8	1,361.0	1,234.9
Total Current Liabilities	538.0	452.7	458.1	352.5	341.4	336.1	237.9
Long-Term Obligations	473.0	607.5	246.6	151.0	149.8	143.8	109.0
Net Stockholders' Equity	844.0	825.3	762.3	892.1	828.2	750.7	766.4
Net Working Capital	648.4	753.6	621.8	669.2	676.0	610.6	635.2
Year-end Shs. Outstg. (000)	64,300	65,224	65,669	60,516	60,785	60,786	64,319
STATISTICAL RECORD:							
Operating Profit Margin %	10.6	10.9	1.9	15.9	14.8	14.6	13.3
Net Profit Margin %	5.7	6.5	...	9.0	8.9	8.8	8.2
Return on Equity %	14.6	15.4	...	16.9	15.9	15.1	12.8
Return on Assets %	6.0	5.9	...	9.2	8.6	8.3	8.0
Debt/Total Assets %	23.1	28.3	14.7	9.2	9.9	10.6	8.8
Price Range	32.44-20.88	37.81-26.44	46.44-25.50	46.31-34.25	38.25-27.33	31.50-20.67	29.58-19.33
P/E Ratio	15.4-9.9	17.5-12.2	...	19.0-14.0	17.7-12.7	17.1-11.2	19.3-12.6
Average Yield %	3.5	2.8	2.4	2.0	2.3	2.8	2.9

Statistics are as originally reported. Adj. for stk. split: 3-for-2, 9/96. [1] Incl. net gain of $2.2 mill. from sale of Systems Control, Inc. [2] Incl. pre-tax chrgs. of $149.9 mill. [3] Incl. nonrecurr. chrgs. of $20.6 mill. [4] Incl. nonrecurr. chrg. of $21.8 mill., excl. acctg. chrg. of $25.4 mill.

OFFICERS:
R. A. Cornog, Chmn., Pres., C.E.O.
D. S. Huml, Sr. V.P., C.F.O.
S. F. Marrinan, V.P., Sec., Gen. Couns.

INVESTOR CONTACT: Bill Pfund, (262) 656-6488

PRINCIPAL OFFICE: P.O. Box 1430, Kenosha, WI 53141-1430

TELEPHONE NUMBER: (262) 656-5200
FAX: (262) 656-5577
WEB: www.snapon.com

NO. OF EMPLOYEES: 14,000 (approx.)

SHAREHOLDERS: 10,931

ANNUAL MEETING: In Apr.

INCORPORATED: WI, Apr., 1920; reincorp., DE, Apr., 1930

INSTITUTIONAL HOLDINGS:
No. of Institutions: 205
Shares Held: 39,944,956
% Held: 69.1

INDUSTRY: Instruments to measure electricity (SIC: 3825)

TRANSFER AGENT(S): First Chicago Trust Company of New York, Jersey City, NJ

NYSE SYMBOL SDH
Rec. Pr. 31.86 (5/31/01)

SODEXHO MARRIOTT SERVICES, INC.

YIELD ...
P/E RATIO 27.5

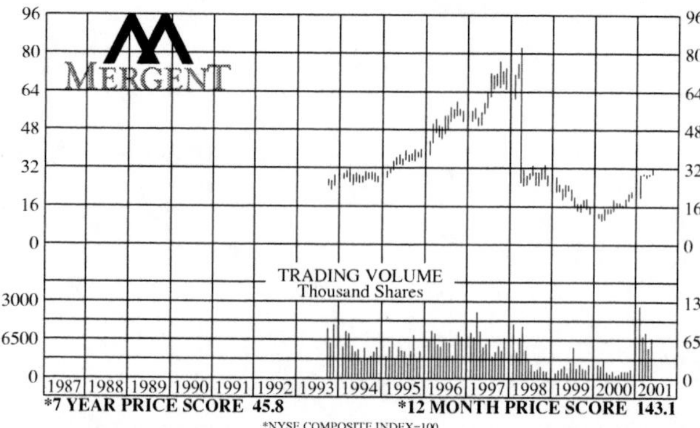

*7 YEAR PRICE SCORE 45.8 *12 MONTH PRICE SCORE 143.1
*NYSE COMPOSITE INDEX=100

INTERIM EARNINGS (Per Share):

Qtr.	Nov.	Feb.	May	Aug.
1997-98		d0.36		
1998-99	0.45	0.18	0.24	d0.07
1999-00	0.44	0.23	0.32	0.01
2000-01	0.56	0.27	...	...

INTERIM DIVIDENDS (Per Share):

Amt.	Decl.	Ex.	Rec.	Pay.
0.08	10/14/99	11/18/99	11/22/99	12/10/99

CAPITALIZATION (9/1/00):

	($000)	(%)
Long-Term Debt	900,000	184.8
Common & Surplus	d413,000	-84.8
Total	487,000	100.0

RECENT DEVELOPMENTS: For the 13 weeks ended 3/2/01, net income totaled $17.0 million, up 21.4% compared with $14.0 million in the corresponding period a year earlier. Total sales rose 4.9% to $1.24 billion from $1.18 billion the year before, reflecting increased sales across all operating divisions. Operating profit grew 2.6% to $80.0 million from $78.0 million the previous year, stemming from strong improvement in the Education and Health Care segments, partially offset by underperformance in the Corporate Services and Schools segments.

PROSPECTS: On 5/2/01, SDH announced that it entered into an agreement under which Sodexho Alliance, S.A. will acquire the remaining 52% of the Company's outstanding stock it does not already own for $32.00 per share in cash, or approximately $1.08 billion. The transaction, which is subject to customary closing conditions, has been approved by the Company's Board of Directors. Upon completion, the two companies combined would create the largest caterer, based on revenues, with more than $11.80 billion in annual sales.

BUSINESS

SODEXHO MARRIOTT SERVICES, INC. (formerly Marriott International, Inc.) is a provider in North America of outsourced food and facilities management services to businesses, health care facilities, colleges and universities, and primary and secondary schools. Food services include food and beverage procurement, preparation and menu planning, as well as the operation and maintenance of food service and catering facilities, generally on a client's premises. Facilities management services include plant maintenance, energy management, groundkeeping, and housekeeping and custodial services. The Company was formed on 3/27/98 when Marriott International, Inc. spun off its lodging, senior living and distribution businesses to its stockholders. The remaining food and facilities management services business merged with the North American operations of Sodexho Alliance, S.A., which owns 48% of the Company, to form SDH.

ANNUAL FINANCIAL DATA

	9/1/00	9/3/99	[1] 8/28/98	1/2/98	1/3/97	12/29/95	12/30/94
Earnings Per Share	**1.00**	[3] **0.81**	[2] **d0.36**	**9.84**	**8.96**	**7.48**	**6.04**
Cash Flow Per Share	**2.31**	**2.13**	**0.73**	**15.03**	**13.29**	**11.39**	**9.61**
Tang. Book Val. Per Share	...	...	...	...	**20.95**	**20.70**	**12.03**
Dividends Per Share	...	**0.08**	...	...	...	...	...
Dividend Payout %	...	**9.9**	...	...	...	...	...
INCOME STATEMENT (IN MILLIONS):							
Total Revenues	4,734.0	4,502.0	2,828.0	12,034.0	10,172.0	8,961.0	8,415.0
Costs & Expenses	4,331.0	4,113.0	2,652.0	11,120.0	9,387.0	8,342.0	7,885.0
Depreciation & Amort.	84.0	85.0	57.0	188.0	156.0	129.0	117.0
Operating Income	319.0	304.0	119.0	726.0	629.0	490.0	413.0
Net Interest Inc./(Exp.)	d84.0	d87.0	d54.0	d78.0	d48.0	d14.0	d3.0
Income Before Income Taxes	112.0	92.0	d32.0	554.0	502.0	412.0	342.0
Income Taxes	49.0	41.0	cr13.0	219.0	196.0	165.0	142.0
Net Income	63.0	[3] 51.0	[2] d19.0	335.0	306.0	247.0	200.0
Cash Flow	147.0	136.0	38.0	523.0	462.0	376.0	317.0
Average Shs. Outstg. (000)	63,500	63,900	52,000	34,800	34,750	33,000	33,000
BALANCE SHEET (IN MILLIONS):							
Cash & Cash Equivalents	54.0	48.0	79.0	312.0	268.0	219.0	204.0
Total Current Assets	682.0	642.0	605.0	1,789.0	1,432.0	1,376.0	1,232.0
Net Property	96.0	85.0	82.0	1,597.0	1,894.0	1,049.0	802.0
Total Assets	1,364.0	1,347.0	1,341.0	6,322.0	5,075.0	4,018.0	3,207.0
Total Current Liabilities	765.0	718.0	695.0	2,024.0	1,759.0	1,526.0	1,398.0
Long-Term Obligations	900.0	1,010.0	1,091.0	1,844.0	1,307.0	806.0	506.0
Net Stockholders' Equity	d413.0	d494.0	d555.0	1,463.0	1,260.0	1,054.0	767.0
Net Working Capital	d83.0	d76.0	d90.0	d235.0	d327.0	d150.0	d166.0
Year-end Shs. Outstg. (000)	63,200	62,300	61,900	32,150	31,500	31,500	32,250
STATISTICAL RECORD:							
Operating Profit Margin %	6.7	6.8	4.2	6.0	6.2	5.5	4.9
Net Profit Margin %	1.3	1.1	...	2.8	3.0	2.8	2.4
Return on Equity %	...	...	...	22.9	24.3	23.4	26.1
Return on Assets %	4.6	3.8	...	5.3	6.0	6.1	6.2
Debt/Total Assets %	66.0	75.0	81.4	29.2	25.8	20.1	15.8
Price Range	22.31-10.13	28.38-12.88	82.63-24.31	76.75-49.63	59.88-37.25	39.88-27.75	32.13-24.63
P/E Ratio	22.3-10.1	35.0-15.9	...	7.8-5.0	6.7-4.2	5.3-3.7	5.3-4.1
Average Yield %	...	0.4	...	...	...	...	...

Statistics are as originally reported. Adj. for 1-for-4 reverse split, 3/98. [1] For the eight-month period from 1/3/98 to 8/28/98. Reflects spin-off of lodging, senior living and distribution businesses. [2] Bef. disc. oper. gain $77.0 mill. & extraord. chrg. $44.0 mill. [3] Incl. $8.3 mil. pre-tax gain from the sale of an investment.

OFFICERS:
W. J. Shaw, Chmn.
M. Landel, Pres., C.E.O.
J. Bush, Sr. V.P., C.F.O.

INVESTOR CONTACT: Jim Duke, (301) 987-4333

PRINCIPAL OFFICE: 9801 Washingtonian Boulevard, Gaithersburg, MD 20878

TELEPHONE NUMBER: (301) 987-4500
FAX: (301) 380-3967
WEB: www.sodexhomarriott.com

NO. OF EMPLOYEES: 111,000 (approx.)

SHAREHOLDERS: 36,000 (approx.)

ANNUAL MEETING: In Jan.

INCORPORATED: DE, July, 1971

INSTITUTIONAL HOLDINGS:
No. of Institutions: 77
Shares Held: 16,057,630
% Held: 25.4

INDUSTRY: Eating places (SIC: 5812)

TRANSFER AGENT(S): First Chicago Trust Company of New York, Jersey City, NJ

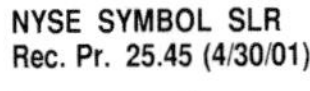

NYSE SYMBOL SLR
Rec. Pr. 25.45 (4/30/01)

SOLECTRON CORPORATION

YIELD	...
P/E RATIO	27.1

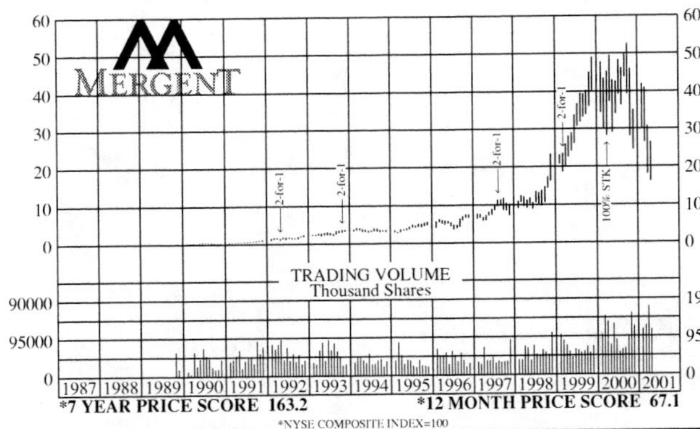

*7 YEAR PRICE SCORE 163.2 *12 MONTH PRICE SCORE 67.1

*NYSE COMPOSITE INDEX=100

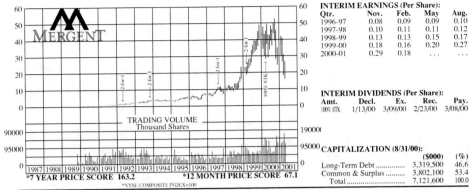

INTERIM EARNINGS (Per Share):

Qtr.	Nov.	Feb.	May	Aug.
1996-97	0.08	0.09	0.09	0.10
1997-98	0.10	0.11	0.11	0.12
1998-99	0.13	0.13	0.15	0.17
1999-00	0.18	0.16	0.20	0.27
2000-01	0.29	0.18	...	...

INTERIM DIVIDENDS (Per Share):

Amt.	Decl.	Ex.	Rec.	Pay.
100% STK	1/13/00	3/09/00	2/23/00	3/08/00

CAPITALIZATION (8/31/00):

	($000)	(%)
Long-Term Debt	3,319,500	46.6
Common & Surplus	3,802,100	53.4
Total	7,121,600	100.0

RECENT DEVELOPMENTS: For the second quarter ended 3/2/01, net income rose 26.1% to $121.9 million versus $96.7 million in the prior year. Results for 2000 included pre-tax nonrecurring charges totaling $54.5 million mainly due to the consolidation of recently-acquired NatSteel Electronic sites in Guadalajara, Mexico and Budapest, Hungary. The 1999 results included pre-tax nonrecurring charges totaling $26.2 million. Revenues jumped 85.5% to $5.42 billion compared with $2.92 billion in 1999.

PROSPECTS: SLR plans to restructure facilities, relocate certain capabilities and change the focus of several sites in 2001. In addition, SLR announced plans to reduce its workforce by more than 10.0%, or 8,200 jobs, worldwide. On 4/30/01, SLR announced that it has completed its acquisition of Centennial Technologies, Inc., a supplier of personal computer cards to original equipment manufacturers and end users. This acquisition is expected to enable SLR to strengthen its Technology Solutions Business Unit.

BUSINESS

SOLECTRON CORPORATION is a global, independent provider of customized, integrated manufacturing services to electronic original equipment manufacturers. The Company furnishes integrated supply-chain services that span the entire product life cycle from technology to manufacturing to global services. SLR's manufacturing services include advanced building block design services, product design and manufacturing, new product introduction management, materials purchasing and management, prototyping, printed circuit board assembly, systems assembly, distribution, product repair and warranty services. As of 12/18/00, SLR operated 60 locations worldwide.

REVENUES

(08/31/00)	($000)	(%)
Manufacturing and Operations	12,419	87.8
Technology Solutions	1,487	10.5
Global Services	233	1.6
Total	14,138	100.0

ANNUAL FINANCIAL DATA

	[3] 8/31/00	8/31/99	8/31/98	8/31/97	8/31/96	8/31/95	8/31/94
Earnings Per Share	**[2] 0.80**	**0.57**	**0.41**	**[1] 0.34**	**0.27**	**0.23**	**0.17**
Cash Flow Per Share	**1.21**	**0.91**	**0.64**	**0.57**	**0.48**	**0.40**	**0.30**
Tang. Book Val. Per Share	**6.28**	**5.15**	**2.51**	**2.01**	**1.67**	**1.36**	**1.00**
INCOME STATEMENT (IN MILLIONS):							
Total Revenues	14,137.5	8,391.4	5,288.3	3,694.4	2,817.2	2,065.6	1,456.8
Costs & Expenses	13,181.9	7,769.3	4,865.1	3,353.4	2,557.0	1,880.7	1,322.7
Depreciation & Amort.	251.4	183.2	124.2	104.6	84.8	61.4	45.7
Operating Income	704.2	438.9	299.0	236.4	175.4	123.4	88.4
Net Interest Inc./(Exp.)	35.3	d6.6	...	2.0	d2.3	d2.9	d4.2
Income Before Income Taxes	739.5	432.3	299.0	238.4	173.1	120.5	84.2
Income Taxes	238.8	138.4	100.2	80.3	58.8	41.0	28.6
Net Income	[2] 500.7	293.9	198.8	[1] 158.1	114.2	79.5	55.5
Cash Flow	752.1	477.1	323.0	262.6	199.0	140.9	101.3
Average Shs. Outstg. (000)	623,500	527,000	506,268	461,284	417,016	350,184	337,640
BALANCE SHEET (IN MILLIONS):							
Cash & Cash Equivalents	2,434.1	1,688.4	308.8	482.9	410.4	148.6	162.0
Total Current Assets	8,628.2	3,994.1	1,887.6	1,475.6	1,144.7	726.4	602.1
Net Property	1,080.4	653.6	448.0	326.4	249.6	203.6	147.8
Total Assets	10,375.6	4,834.7	2,410.6	1,852.4	1,452.2	940.9	766.4
Total Current Liabilities	3,216.8	1,113.2	840.8	543.9	358.4	370.8	292.9
Long-Term Obligations	3,319.5	922.6	385.5	385.9	386.9	30.0	140.7
Net Stockholders' Equity	3,802.1	2,793.1	1,181.3	919.1	700.6	538.1	330.8
Net Working Capital	5,411.4	2,880.9	1,046.7	931.7	786.4	355.6	309.2
Year-end Shs. Outstg. (000)	605,000	542,800	470,668	458,184	420,088	396,672	330,416
STATISTICAL RECORD:							
Operating Profit Margin %	5.0	5.2	5.7	6.4	6.2	6.0	6.1
Net Profit Margin %	3.5	3.5	3.8	4.3	4.1	3.9	3.8
Return on Equity %	13.2	10.5	16.8	17.2	16.3	14.8	16.8
Return on Assets %	4.8	6.1	8.2	8.5	7.9	8.5	7.2
Debt/Total Assets %	32.0	19.1	16.0	20.8	26.6	3.2	18.4
Price Range	52.63-24.54	49.00-18.64	23.38-8.86	11.86-5.89	7.52-3.63	5.64-2.77	4.25-2.92
P/E Ratio	65.8-30.7	86.7-33.0	56.7-21.5	34.6-17.2	27.4-13.2	24.7-12.1	25.7-17.7

Statistics are as originally reported. Adj. for stk. split: 2-for-1, 3/00; 2/99; 8/97. [1] Incl. non-recurr. pre-tax chrg. $54.5 mill., 2001; $4.0 mill., 8/97. [2] Excl. acctg. chrg. of $3.5 mill. and incl. non-recurr. chrgs. of $37.9 mill. [3] Revs. reflected strategic acqs. & robust global demand.

OFFICERS:
K. Nishimura, Chmn., Pres., C.E.O.
S. S. Wang, Sr. V.P., C.F.O., Sec.
S. Zohouri, Sr. V.P., C.O.O.

INVESTOR CONTACT: Sylvia Chou, Investor Relations Manager, (408) 956-6542

PRINCIPAL OFFICE: 777 Gibraltar Drive, Milpitas, CA 95035

TELEPHONE NUMBER: (408) 957-8500
FAX: (408) 956-6077
WEB: www.solectron.com
NO. OF EMPLOYEES: 48,206 full-time; 17,067 part-time
SHAREHOLDERS: 1,726 (approx.)
ANNUAL MEETING: In Jan.
INCORPORATED: CA, Aug., 1977; reincorp., DE, Feb., 1997

INSTITUTIONAL HOLDINGS:
No. of Institutions: 539
Shares Held: 532,491,789
% Held: 81.5

INDUSTRY: Printed circuit boards (SIC: 3672)

TRANSFER AGENT(S): EquiServe Limited Partnership, Canton, MA

NYSE SYMBOL SOI
Rec. Pr. 14.28 (5/31/01)

SOLUTIA, INC.

YIELD 0.3%
P/E RATIO 33.2

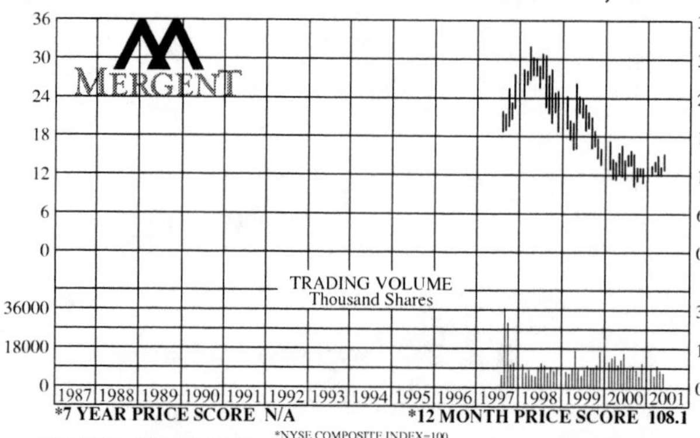

*7 YEAR PRICE SCORE N/A *12 MONTH PRICE SCORE 108.1

*NYSE COMPOSITE INDEX=100

INTERIM EARNINGS (Per Share):

Qtr.	Mar.	June	Sept.	Dec.
1995	0.47	0.35	0.35	0.10
1996	0.30	0.39	0.51	d0.93
1997	0.54	0.51	0.44	0.06
1998	0.51	0.58	0.47	0.46
1999	0.20	0.61	0.53	0.46
2000	0.46	0.04	0.74	d0.81

INTERIM DIVIDENDS (Per Share):

Amt.	Decl.	Ex.	Rec.	Pay.
0.04A	10/27/99	11/10/99	11/15/99	12/10/99
0.04A	...	11/13/00	11/15/00	12/12/00

Indicated div.: $0.04 (Div. Reinv. Plan)

CAPITALIZATION (12/31/00):

	($000)	(%)
Long-Term Debt	784,000	104.5
Common & Surplus	d34,000	-4.5
Total	750,000	100.0

RECENT DEVELOPMENTS: For the year ended 12/31/00, net income fell 76.2% to $49.0 million versus $206.0 million in 1999. Results for 2000 included after-tax charges totaling $125.0 million and after-tax gains totaling $82.0 million from the sales of the polymer modifiers business and a minority interest. Results for 1999 included after-tax charges totaling $40.0 million. Net sales were $3.19 billion, up 12.5% from $2.83 billion the year before.

PROSPECTS: The Company announced several new plant manufacturing expansions and quality improvements, which should strengthen SOI's performance films segment. These improvements were needed to meet the anticipated growth in both the architectural and automotive markets. In addition, these increases should enable SOI to increase its global production capacity by about 20.0% over the next five years.

BUSINESS

SOLUTIA INC. is an international producer and marketer of a range of high performance chemical-based materials that are used to make consumer, household, automotive and industrial products. The Company operates in three business segments: chemicals, which is comprised of the intermediates, phosphorus derivatives and industrial products; fibers, which is comprised of carpet fibers, nylon industrial fibers, and Acrilan acrylic fibers; and polymers & resins, which include Saflex™ plastic interlayer, nylon plastics and polymers, resins and polymer modifier. Revenues (and operating profit) in 2000 were derived: performance films, 23.0% (35.1%); specialty products, 27.3% (34.5%); and integrated nylons, 49.7% (30.4%). On 9/1/97, the Company was spun off from Monsanto Company.

ANNUAL FINANCIAL DATA

	12/31/00	12/31/99	12/31/98	12/31/97	12/31/96	12/31/95	12/31/94
Earnings Per Share	**[4] 0.46**	**[2] 1.80**	**[1] 2.03**	**1.55**	**[3] 0.27**	**[3] 1.27**	...
Cash Flow Per Share	**2.12**	**3.03**	**3.17**	**2.70**	**1.71**	**2.82**	...
Dividends Per Share	**0.04**	**0.04**	**0.04**	**0.01**	...	...	...
Dividend Payout %	**8.7**	**2.2**	**2.0**	**0.6**	...	...	...
INCOME STATEMENT (IN MILLIONS):							
Total Revenues	3,185.0	2,830.0	2,835.0	2,969.0	2,977.0	2,964.0	3,097.0
Costs & Expenses	2,982.0	2,395.0	2,308.0	2,537.0	2,778.0	2,544.0	2,622.0
Depreciation & Amort.	179.0	141.0	141.0	142.0	166.0	162.0	219.0
Operating Income	24.0	294.0	386.0	290.0	33.0	258.0	256.0
Net Interest Inc./(Exp.)	d83.0	d40.0	d43.0	d41.0	d36.0	d36.0	d29.0
Income Before Income Taxes	41.0	303.0	375.0	290.0	33.0	231.0	228.0
Income Taxes	cr8.0	97.0	126.0	98.0	1.0	84.0	79.0
Equity Earnings/Minority Int.	35.0	36.0	25.0	31.0	21.0	15.0	...
Net Income	[4] 49.0	[2] 206.0	[1] 249.0	192.0	[3] 32.0	[3] 147.0	[3] 149.0
Cash Flow	228.0	347.0	390.0	334.0	198.0	321.0	368.0
Average Shs. Outstg. (000)	107,500	114,600	123,000	123,700	116,000	114,000	...
BALANCE SHEET (IN MILLIONS):							
Cash & Cash Equivalents	19.0	28.0	89.0	24.0	...	...	...
Total Current Assets	1,015.0	1,114.0	991.0	1,001.0	891.0	885.0	...
Net Property	1,205.0	1,316.0	944.0	923.0	911.0	912.0	...
Total Assets	3,581.0	3,770.0	2,765.0	2,768.0	2,483.0	2,462.0	2,435.0
Total Current Liabilities	1,349.0	1,327.0	732.0	895.0	770.0	654.0	...
Long-Term Obligations	784.0	802.0	597.0	597.0	...	...	...
Net Stockholders' Equity	d34.0	82.0	d7.0	d131.0	656.0	755.0	...
Net Working Capital	d334.0	d213.0	259.0	106.0	121.0	231.0	...
Year-end Shs. Outstg. (000)	102,916	109,541	113,000	117,000	...	...	...
STATISTICAL RECORD:							
Operating Profit Margin %	0.8	10.4	13.6	9.8	1.1	8.7	8.3
Net Profit Margin %	1.5	7.3	8.8	6.5	1.1	5.4	4.8
Return on Equity %	...	251.2	...	...	4.9	21.1	...
Return on Assets %	1.4	5.5	9.0	6.9	1.3	6.5	6.1
Debt/Total Assets %	21.9	21.3	21.6	21.6	...	...	...
Price Range	17.25-10.19	26.31-13.50	32.00-18.69	27.75-18.69	...	...	...
P/E Ratio	37.5-22.1	14.6-7.5	15.8-9.2	17.9-12.1	...	...	...
Average Yield %	0.3	0.2	0.2	...	...	...	...

Statistics are as originally reported. [1] Incl. reversal of $6.0 mill. after-tax chg. rel. to the closing of some facilities & a reduction plan. [2] Incl. $40.0 mill. net special chgs. [3] Incl. restr. chgs. $192.0 mill., 1996; $53.0 mill., 1995; $34.0 mill., 1994. [4] Incl. $90.0 mill. net closing & sev. costs, $4.0 mill. net impair. chg., $15.0 mill. net chg. fr. jt. ventures, $16.0 mill. net write-down of equity invest. & $82.0 mill. net gain fr. sale of assets.

OFFICERS:
J. C. Hunter III, Chmn., Pres., C.E.O.
M. E. Miller, Vice-Chmn., C.O.O.
R. A. Clausen, Sr. V.P., C.F.O.

INVESTOR CONTACT: Liesl Livingston, Director, Inv. Rel., (314) 674-7777

PRINCIPAL OFFICE: 575 Maryville Centre Dr., P.O. Box 66760, St. Louis, MO 63166

TELEPHONE NUMBER: (314) 674-1000
FAX: (314) 674-7625
WEB: www.solutia.com

NO. OF EMPLOYEES: 10,200 (avg.)

SHAREHOLDERS: 36,703

ANNUAL MEETING: In Apr.

INCORPORATED: DE, Apr., 1997

INSTITUTIONAL HOLDINGS:
No. of Institutions: 200
Shares Held: 63,767,645
% Held: 61.6

INDUSTRY: Chemical preparations, nec (SIC: 2899)

TRANSFER AGENT(S): EquiServe, First Chicago Trust Division, Jersey City, NJ

NYSE SYMBOL SAH
Rec. Pr. 13.30 (5/31/01)

SONIC AUTOMOTIVE, INC.

YIELD ...
P/E RATIO 7.8

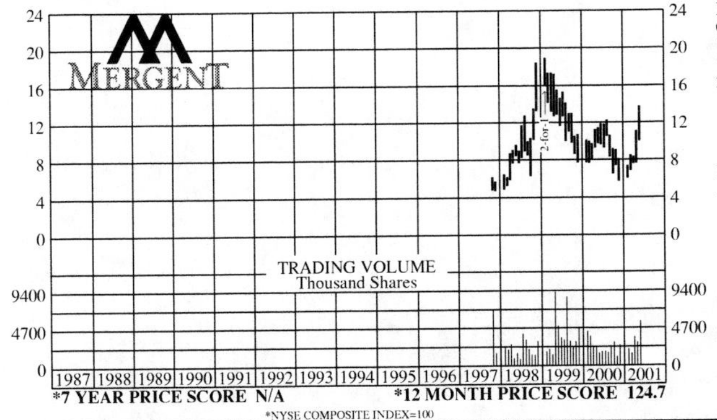

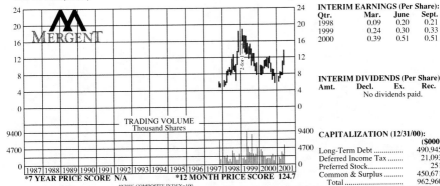

*7 YEAR PRICE SCORE N/A *12 MONTH PRICE SCORE 124.7

*NYSE COMPOSITE INDEX=100

INTERIM EARNINGS (Per Share):

Qtr.	Mar.	June	Sept.	Dec.
1998	0.09	0.20	0.21	0.24
1999	0.24	0.30	0.33	0.38
2000	0.39	0.51	0.51	0.29

INTERIM DIVIDENDS (Per Share):

Amt.	Decl.	Ex.	Rec.	Pay.

No dividends paid.

CAPITALIZATION (12/31/00):

	($000)	(%)
Long-Term Debt	490,945	51.0
Deferred Income Tax	21,093	2.2
Preferred Stock	251	0.0
Common & Surplus	450,671	46.8
Total	962,960	100.0

RECENT DEVELOPMENTS: For the year ended 12/31/00, net income advanced 66.1% to $74.2 million from $44.6 million a year earlier. Total revenues jumped 80.6% to $6.05 billion from $3.35 billion the year before, fueled primarily by acquisitions. Same-store sales rose 2.5% year-over-year. Gross profit was $865.2 million, or 14.3% of total revenue, compared with $454.4 million, or 13.6% of total revenue, a year earlier.

PROSPECTS: Uncertain economic conditions in the U.S. are hampering sales of new vehicles made by domestic manufacturers. This rapid slowdown in sales has left many of the Company's dealerships with excess new-vehicle inventory. Going forward, the Company is focusing on aggressively reducing inventory levels and lowering operating expenses. Full-year 2001 earnings are anticipated to be in the range of $1.43 to $1.47 per share.

BUSINESS

SONIC AUTOMOTIVE, INC., the second largest automotive retailer in the United States based on total revenue, operates 167 dealership franchises and 31 collision repair centers in 13 states. The Company's franchises provide comprehensive services including sales of both new and used cars and light trucks, replacement parts and vehicle maintenance, warranty, paint and repair services. The Company also offers extended warranty contracts and financing and insurance for its customers.

REVENUES

(12/31/00)	($000)	(%)
New Vehicles	3,522,049	58.2
Used Vehicles	1,249,188	20.6
Wholesale vehicles	430,513	7.1
Parts, Service & Collision Repair	687,975	11.4
Finance, Insurance & Other	162,751	2.7
Total	6,052,476	100.0

ANNUAL FINANCIAL DATA

	12/31/00	12/31/99	12/31/98	12/31/97	12/31/96	12/31/95	12/31/94
Earnings Per Share	**1.69**	**1.27**	**0.74**	**0.27**	**0.24**	...	...
Cash Flow Per Share	**2.21**	**1.60**	**0.93**	**0.36**	**0.32**	...	...
Tang. Book Val. Per Share	...	...	...	**0.44**	**1.76**	...	...
INCOME STATEMENT (IN MILLIONS):							
Total Revenues	[1] 6,052.5	3,350.8	1,603.7	536.0	376.6	311.0	267.1
Costs & Expenses	5,820.6	3,223.3	1,546.4	519.8	364.7	300.2	257.6
Depreciation & Amort.	22.7	11.7	4.6	1.3	1.1	0.8	0.8
Operating Income	209.1	115.8	52.7	14.9	10.8	9.9	8.6
Net Interest Inc./(Exp.)	d89.4	d44.1	d23.5	d9.2	d6.4	d4.9	d3.4
Income Before Income Taxes	119.9	73.0	29.6	6.0	5.0	5.4	5.8
Income Taxes	45.7	28.3	11.1	2.2	1.9	2.2	2.1
Equity Earnings/Minority Int.	...	...	...	...	d0.1	...	...
Net Income	74.2	44.6	18.6	3.7	3.0	3.2	3.7
Cash Flow	96.9	56.3	23.2	5.0	4.1	4.1	4.5
Average Shs. Outstg. (000)	43,826	35,248	24,970	13,898	12,500	...	...
BALANCE SHEET (IN MILLIONS):							
Cash & Cash Equivalents	109.3	83.1	51.8	18.6	7.3	9.7	...
Total Current Assets	1,037.4	835.6	364.8	197.4	91.4	70.6	...
Net Property	73.0	63.7	26.3	19.1	12.5	8.5	...
Total Assets	1,789.2	1,501.1	576.1	291.5	111.0	79.5	...
Total Current Liabilities	818.3	657.9	285.7	152.7	71.6	52.4	...
Long-Term Obligations	490.9	421.9	135.0	43.0	6.2	4.8	...
Net Stockholders' Equity	450.9	402.6	142.4	84.4	26.3	16.3	...
Net Working Capital	219.1	177.7	79.2	44.7	19.8	18.1	...
Year-end Shs. Outstg. (000)	41,966	40,602	24,359	22,500	12,500	...	...
STATISTICAL RECORD:							
Operating Profit Margin %	3.5	3.5	3.3	2.8	2.9	3.2	3.2
Net Profit Margin %	1.2	1.3	1.2	0.7	0.8	1.0	1.4
Return on Equity %	16.4	11.1	13.0	4.4	11.3	19.9	...
Return on Assets %	4.1	3.0	3.2	1.3	2.7	4.1	...
Debt/Total Assets %	27.4	28.1	23.4	14.8	5.6	6.0	...
Price Range	12.25-5.69	18.94-7.69	18.44-4.84	6.19-4.69	...	...	...
P/E Ratio	7.2-3.4	14.9-6.1	24.9-6.5	23.3-17.7	...	...	...

Statistics are as originally reported. Adj. for 2-for-1 stk. split, 1/99. [1] Revenue growth reflects multiple acquisitions of dealerships.

OFFICERS:
O. B. Smith, Chmn., C.E.O.
T. A. Price, Vice-Chmn.
B. S. Smith, Pres., C.O.O.
T. M. Wright, V.P., C.F.O., Treas.

INVESTOR CONTACT: Todd Atenhan, (888) 766-4218

PRINCIPAL OFFICE: 5401 East Independence Blvd., P.O. Box 18747, Charlotte, NC 28212

TELEPHONE NUMBER: (704) 532-3320
FAX: (704) 536-5116
WEB: www.sonicautomotive.com

NO. OF EMPLOYEES: 9,400 (approx.)

SHAREHOLDERS: 155 (class A common); 4 (class B common)

ANNUAL MEETING: In May

INCORPORATED: DE, Feb., 1997

INSTITUTIONAL HOLDINGS:
No. of Institutions: 63
Shares Held: 17,048,505
% Held: 40.3

INDUSTRY: New and used car dealers (SIC: 5511)

TRANSFER AGENT(S): First Union National Bank of North Carolina, Charlotte, NC

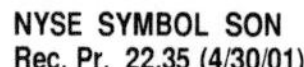
NYSE SYMBOL SON
Rec. Pr. 22.35 (4/30/01)

SONOCO PRODUCTS COMPANY

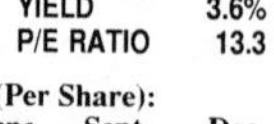
YIELD 3.6%
P/E RATIO 13.3

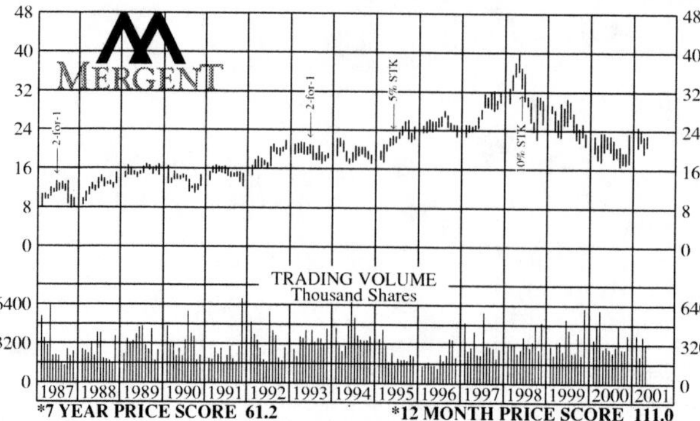

*7 YEAR PRICE SCORE 61.2 *12 MONTH PRICE SCORE 111.0

*NYSE COMPOSITE INDEX=100

INTERIM EARNINGS (Per Share):

Qtr.	Mar.	June	Sept.	Dec.
1996	0.41	0.45	0.38	0.40
1997	0.39	0.43	0.39	d1.20
1998	0.48	0.70	0.39	0.31
1999	0.43	0.46	0.44	0.50
2000	0.45	0.47	0.39	0.37

INTERIM DIVIDENDS (Per Share):

Amt.	Decl.	Ex.	Rec.	Pay.
0.20Q	4/19/00	5/17/00	5/19/00	6/09/00
0.20Q	7/19/00	8/16/00	8/18/00	9/08/00
0.20Q	10/18/00	11/15/00	11/17/00	12/08/00
0.20Q	2/07/01	2/21/01	2/23/01	3/09/01
0.20Q	4/18/01	5/16/01	5/18/01	6/08/01

Indicated div.: $0.80 (Div. Reinv. Plan)

CAPITALIZATION (12/31/00):

	($000)	(%)
Long-Term Debt	812,085	50.3
Common & Surplus	801,471	49.7
Total	1,613,556	100.0

RECENT DEVELOPMENTS: For the year ended 12/31/00, net income declined 11.5% to $166.3 million compared with $187.8 million in 1999. Results for 2000 included a one-time non-operational charge of $5.5 million, while results for 1999 included a one-time credit of $3.5 million. Sales were $2.71 billion, up 6.5% from $2.55 billion a year earlier.

PROSPECTS: The Company recently announced details of a restructuring program that is expected to permanently reduce annual costs by $25.0 million to $30.0 million. The restructuring will be primarily implemented in the first quarter of 2001, with an expected global reduction of 235 salaried positions and 252 hourly positions.

BUSINESS

SONOCO PRODUCTS COMPANY is a multinational manufacturer of industrial and consumer packaging products. SON is also vertically integrated into paperboard production and recovered-paper collection. The paperboard utilized in SON's packaging products is produced substantially from recovered paper. SON operates 275 facilities in 33 countries. The industrial packaging segment (53.5% of 2000 sales) includes engineered carriers (paper and plastic tubes and cores, paper manufacturing and recovered paper operations) and protective packaging (designed interior packaging and protective reels). The consumer packaging segment (46.5%) includes composite cans, flexible packaging (printing flexibles and high density bag and film products) and packaging services and specialty products (e-marketplace/supply chain management, graphics management, folding cartons, and paper glass covers and coasters).

ANNUAL FINANCIAL DATA

	12/31/00	12/31/99	12/31/98	12/31/97	12/31/96	12/31/95	12/31/94
Earnings Per Share	**3 1.66**	**1.83**	**2 1.84**	**1 Nil**	**1.64**	**1.56**	**1.22**
Cash Flow Per Share	**3.17**	**3.25**	**3.24**	**1.43**	**3.08**	**2.82**	**2.34**
Tang. Book Val. Per Share	**5.94**	**6.37**	**6.40**	**6.69**	**3.49**	**3.34**	**3.00**
Dividends Per Share	**0.79**	**0.75**	**0.70**	**0.64**	**0.59**	**0.53**	**0.48**
Dividend Payout %	**47.6**	**41.0**	**38.2**	**N.M.**	**35.8**	**33.9**	**39.4**
INCOME STATEMENT (IN MILLIONS):							
Total Revenues	2,711.5	2,546.7	2,557.9	2,847.8	2,788.1	2,706.2	2,300.1
Costs & Expenses	2,234.3	2,064.2	2,023.8	2,578.4	2,315.8	2,270.4	1,942.9
Depreciation & Amort.	150.8	145.8	145.7	153.5	142.9	125.8	112.8
Operating Income	326.4	336.7	388.5	115.9	329.4	309.9	244.4
Net Interest Inc./(Exp.)	d55.8	d47.2	d48.9	d52.2	d49.3	d39.1	d33.5
Income Before Income Taxes	270.6	289.6	339.6	63.7	280.1	270.8	210.9
Income Taxes	112.0	108.6	154.0	60.1	107.4	106.6	82.5
Equity Earnings/Minority Int.	7.7	6.8	6.4	d1.0	d1.8	0.4	1.4
Net Income	3 166.3	187.8	2 192.0	1 2.6	170.9	164.5	129.8
Cash Flow	317.1	333.7	337.7	153.1	306.6	282.6	234.9
Average Shs. Outstg. (000)	99,900	102,780	104,275	107,350	99,564	100,253	100,590
BALANCE SHEET (IN MILLIONS):							
Cash & Cash Equivalents	35.2	36.5	57.2	53.6	71.3	61.6	28.4
Total Current Assets	695.8	723.1	661.4	873.0	737.6	661.8	570.7
Net Property	973.5	1,032.5	1,013.8	939.5	995.4	865.6	763.1
Total Assets	2,212.6	2,297.0	2,083.0	2,176.9	2,387.5	2,115.4	1,835.1
Total Current Liabilities	437.1	416.6	436.1	434.1	475.1	432.5	348.6
Long-Term Obligations	812.1	819.5	686.8	696.7	791.0	591.9	488.0
Net Stockholders' Equity	801.5	901.2	821.6	848.8	920.6	918.7	832.2
Net Working Capital	258.7	306.4	225.3	438.9	262.5	229.3	222.1
Year-end Shs. Outstg. (000)	95,006	101,448	101,683	105,417	98,850	100,229	100,378
STATISTICAL RECORD:							
Operating Profit Margin %	12.0	13.2	15.2	4.1	11.8	11.5	10.6
Net Profit Margin %	6.1	7.4	7.5	0.1	6.1	6.1	5.6
Return on Equity %	20.7	20.8	23.4	0.3	18.6	17.9	15.6
Return on Assets %	7.5	8.2	9.2	0.1	7.2	7.8	7.1
Debt/Total Assets %	36.7	35.7	33.0	32.0	33.1	28.0	26.6
Price Range	23.50-16.56	30.50-20.69	40.00-22.13	32.27-22.61	28.07-22.61	26.14-17.37	22.30-17.10
P/E Ratio	14.2-10.0	16.7-11.3	21.7-12.0	N.M.	17.1-13.8	16.7-11.1	18.3-14.0
Average Yield %	3.9	2.9	2.3	2.3	2.3	2.4	2.4

Statistics are as originally reported. Adj. for stk. splits: 5% div., 6/95; 10%, 6/98. 1 Incl. non-recurr. after-tax chrg. $174.5 mill. for asset write-down. 2 Bef. exraord. loss of $11.8 mill. and net gain on sale of divested assets of $85.4 mill. 3 Incl. nonrecurr. chrg. of $5.5 mill.

OFFICERS:
C. W. Coker, Chmn.
H. E. DeLoach, Jr., Pres., C.E.O.
F. T. Hill, Jr., V.P., C.F.O.
C. J. Hupfer, V.P., Treas., Corp. Sec.

INVESTOR CONTACT: Allan V. Cecil, V.P. Inv. Rel. & Corp. Affairs, (843) 383-7524

PRINCIPAL OFFICE: North Second Street, Hartsville, SC 29550

TELEPHONE NUMBER: (843) 383-7000
FAX: (843) 383-7008
WEB: www.sonoco.com

NO. OF EMPLOYEES: 17,450 (approx.)

SHAREHOLDERS: 45,200 (approx.)

ANNUAL MEETING: In Apr.

INCORPORATED: SC, May, 1899

INSTITUTIONAL HOLDINGS:
No. of Institutions: 186
Shares Held: 44,003,859
% Held: 46.2

INDUSTRY: Paperboard mills (SIC: 2631)

TRANSFER AGENT(S): EquiServe, Providence, RI

NYSE SYMBOL SNE
Rec. Pr. 78.10 (5/31/01)

SONY CORPORATION

YIELD 0.2%
P/E RATIO 137.0

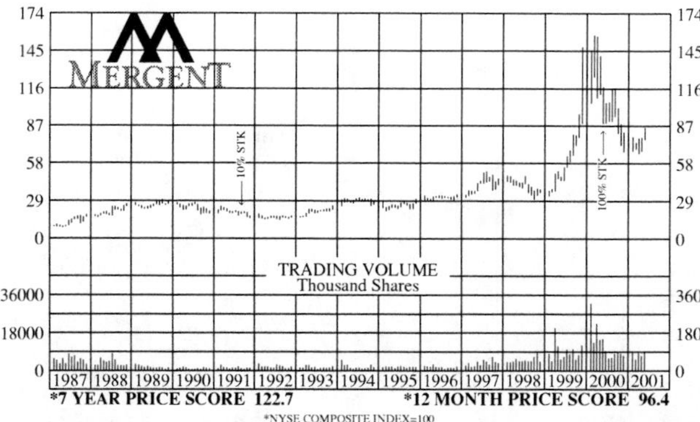

*7 YEAR PRICE SCORE 122.7 *12 MONTH PRICE SCORE 96.4

*NYSE COMPOSITE INDEX=100

INTERIM EARNINGS (Per Share):

Qtr.	June	Sept.	Dec.	Mar.
1997-98	----------	1.86	----------	
1998-99	----------	1.62	----------	
1999-00	0.17	0.48	1.00	d0.39
2000-01	0.13	0.19	0.64	...

INTERIM DIVIDENDS (Per Share):

Amt.	Decl.	Ex.	Rec.	Pay.
0.204S	...	9/27/99	9/29/99	12/06/99
100% STK	...	5/25/00	3/30/00	5/24/00
0.197S	...	3/28/00	3/30/00	7/07/00
0.095S	...	9/26/00	9/28/00	12/08/00
0.088S	...	3/27/01	3/29/01	...

Indicated div.: $0.18

CAPITALIZATION (3/31/00):

	($000)	(%)
Long-Term Debt	7,894,132	25.3
Deferred Income Tax	1,784,994	5.7
Minority Interest	335,281	1.1
Common & Surplus	21,174,188	67.9
Total	31,188,594	100.0

RECENT DEVELOPMENTS: For the third quarter ended 12/31/00, net income decreased to ¥72.24 billion ($628.0 million) compared with ¥93.63 billion ($917.6 million) in the previous year. Sales and operating revenues were ¥2,110.39 billion ($18.35 billion) versus ¥1,916.01 billion ($18.78 million) the year before. Revenues growth was due to favorable sales in the game business, offset by unfavorable foreign currency translation.

PROSPECTS: SNE plans to transform itself into a Personal Broadband Network Solutions Company. SNE will continue to focus on and consolidate its resources in brand recognition, electronics hardware, entertainment and venture business development both within and outside the company. In enhancing group corporate value, SNE will pursue "soft alliance" with outside companies that should complement its existing internal resources.

BUSINESS

SONY CORPORATION is a maker of electronics and audio equipment such as still-image video cameras, CD players, mini-component stereos, digital audio tape decks and televisions. Sony also manufactures semiconductors, computers, information-related equipment and telecommunications equipment. Sony Music Entertainment and Sony Pictures Entertainment serve the music and imaged-based software markets. Sales for the year ended 3/31/00 were derived: electronics, 64.5%; games, 8.9%; music, 9.7%; pictures, 6.7%; insurance, 5.2% and other, 4.0%. Global revenues were: Japan, 31.7%; U.S., 30.3%; Europe, 22.0%; and other, 16.0%.

ANNUAL FINANCIAL DATA

	3/31/00	3/31/99	3/31/98	3/31/97	3/31/96	3/31/95	3/31/94
Earnings Per Share	**1.28**	**2 1.62**	**1.86**	**1.24**	**0.62**	**d4.04**	**1 0.20**
Tang. Book Val. Per Share	**17.86**	**15.80**	**14.48**	**12.35**	**11.39**	**12.47**	**10.43**
Dividends Per Share	**0.19**	**0.19**	**0.19**	**0.19**	**0.23**	**0.21**	**0.20**
Dividend Payout %	**14.8**	**11.7**	**10.4**	**15.4**	**36.8**	**...**	**95.8**
INCOME STATEMENT (IN MILLIONS):							
Total Revenues	64,860.6	56,395.3	52,017.3	45,305.1	42,710.9	46,290.8	36,217.1
Costs & Expenses	62,526.5	53,584.6	48,011.7	42,342.4	40,522.3	48,223.8	35,250.3
Operating Income	2,334.1	2,810.8	4,005.6	2,962.6	2,188.5	d1,933.0	966.8
Net Interest Inc./(Exp.)	d407.7	d400.7	d481.4	d567.1	d624.0	d758.1	d671.4
Income Before Income Taxes	2,563.8	3,055.5	3,493.9	2,499.4	1,284.9	d2,563.0	991.0
Income Taxes	918.0	1,468.9	1,654.5	1,308.6	717.6	756.0	762.5
Equity Earnings/Minority Int.	d464.0	d100.9	d129.5	d75.2	d62.8	d83.9	d80.0
Net Income	1,181.8	2 1,485.7	1,709.9	1,115.7	504.5	d3,402.9	1 148.4
Average Shs. Outstg. (000)	944,353	927,661	928,243	917,984	843,946	835,330	834,908
BALANCE SHEET (IN MILLIONS):							
Cash & Cash Equivalents	7,175.1	6,095.3	5,387.2	4,809.0	4,839.4	6,476.8	5,481.3
Total Current Assets	30,406.0	25,476.0	25,159.6	22,363.7	23,473.1	24,901.7	19,630.2
Net Property	12,179.0	10,372.9	10,372.9	9,911.3	10,423.1	11,939.9	10,179.4
Total Assets	66,029.8	52,282.1	49,303.4	45,442.7	46,925.2	48,997.5	41,417.9
Total Current Liabilities	20,955.3	16,123.1	16,295.7	15,614.9	15,880.7	18,663.9	13,654.1
Long-Term Obligations	7,894.1	8,610.9	8,504.0	8,798.1	11,193.4	10,515.2	9,542.0
Net Stockholders' Equity	21,174.2	15,136.4	13,979.8	11,675.4	10,873.3	11,690.6	12,896.8
Net Working Capital	9,450.7	9,352.8	8,863.9	6,748.8	7,592.4	6,237.8	5,976.1
Year-end Shs. Outstg. (000)	907,270	820,000	814,000	768,000	748,000	748,000	748,000
STATISTICAL RECORD:							
Operating Profit Margin %	3.6	5.0	7.7	6.5	5.1	...	2.7
Net Profit Margin %	1.8	2.6	3.3	2.5	1.2	...	0.4
Return on Equity %	5.6	9.8	12.2	9.6	4.6	...	1.2
Return on Assets %	1.8	2.8	3.5	2.5	1.1	...	0.4
Debt/Total Assets %	12.0	16.5	17.2	19.4	23.9	21.5	23.0
Price Range	147.94-32.75	48.59-30.13	51.84-31.69	33.94-28.69	30.75-21.25	31.63-24.69	25.31-16.00
P/E Ratio	115.8-25.6	29.9-18.6	27.9-17.0	27.4-23.2	49.3-34.1	...	124.0-78.4
Average Yield %	0.2	0.5	0.5	0.6	0.9	0.8	0.9

Statistics are as originally reported. All figures are in U.S. dollars unless otherwise noted. Conv. into U.S. dollars at the following rates: $1= 2000, ¥103.09; 1999, ¥120.48; 1998, ¥129.87; 1997, ¥125.00; 1996, ¥107.53; 1995, ¥86.21; 1994. Adj. for stk. split 2-for-1, 5/00. All per share figures and ratios are calculated using ADR's. One ADR is equal to one Ordinary share. 1 Incl. a $30.0 mill. write-off of goodwill in the Pictures Group. 2 Incl. pre-tax gain of $506.0 mill. & one-time net gain of $256.0 mill. & tax ben. of about $112.0 mill.

OFFICERS:
N. Idei, Chmn., C.E.O.
K. Ando, Pres., C.O.O.
T. Tokunaka, Exec. Dep. Pres., C.F.O.

INVESTOR CONTACT: Investor Relations, (212) 448-2180

PRINCIPAL OFFICE: 550 Madison Avenue, 9th Floor New York, NY

TELEPHONE NUMBER: (212) 833-6849
FAX: (212) 833-6938
WEB: www.world.sony.com

NO. OF EMPLOYEES: 189,700 (avg.)

SHAREHOLDERS: 291,844

ANNUAL MEETING: In June

INCORPORATED: JPN, May, 1946

INSTITUTIONAL HOLDINGS:
No. of Institutions: 210
Shares Held: 37,480,562
% Held: 4.1

INDUSTRY: Household audio and video equipment (SIC: 3651)

TRANSFER AGENT(S): The Toyo Trust & Banking Co., Ltd., Tokyo.

NYSE SYMBOL SJI
Rec. Pr. 30.40 (5/31/01)

SOUTH JERSEY INDUSTRIES, INC.

YIELD 4.9%
P/E RATIO 14.1

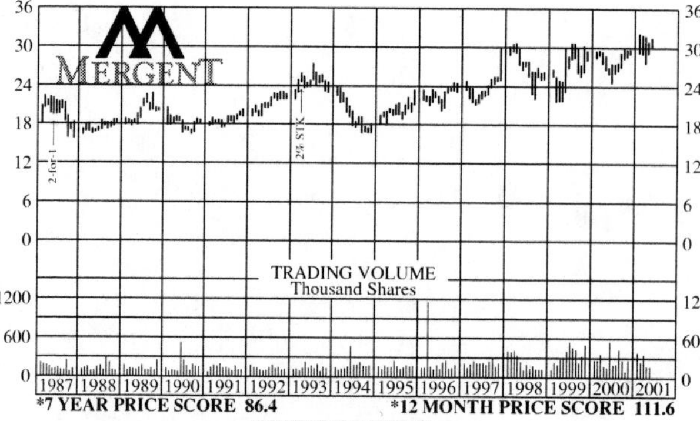

*7 YEAR PRICE SCORE 86.4 *12 MONTH PRICE SCORE 111.6

*NYSE COMPOSITE INDEX=100

INTERIM EARNINGS (Per Share):

Qtr.	Mar.	June	Sept.	Dec.
1997	1.39	d0.01	d0.42	0.73
1998	1.15	d0.14	d0.27	0.55
1999	1.66	Nil	d0.38	0.74
2000	1.69	Nil	d0.36	0.83

INTERIM DIVIDENDS (Per Share):

Amt.	Decl.	Ex.	Rec.	Pay.
0.365Q	5/18/00	6/07/00	6/09/00	7/03/00
0.365Q	8/24/00	9/07/00	9/11/00	10/02/00
0.365Q	11/17/00	12/07/00	12/11/00	1/04/01
0.37Q	1/30/01	3/07/01	3/09/01	4/03/01
0.37Q	5/18/01	6/07/01	6/11/01	7/03/01

Indicated div.: $1.48 (Div. Reinv. Plan)

CAPITALIZATION (12/31/00):

	($000)	(%)
Long-Term Debt	204,981	37.4
Deferred Income Tax	105,037	19.1
Redeemable Pfd. Stock	36,804	6.7
Common & Surplus	201,739	36.8
Total	548,561	100.0

RECENT DEVELOPMENTS: For the year ended 12/31/00, the Company reported income from continuing operations of $24.7 million versus income from continuing operations of $22.0 million in the prior year. Results for 2000 and 1999 excluded net losses of $481,000 and $289,000, respectively, from discontinued operations. Total operating revenues amounted to $515.9 million, up 31.4% from $392.5 million a year earlier.

PROSPECTS: On 1/16/01, the Company's subsidiary, Marina Energy LLC, received a 20-year contract from Marina District Development Corporation to provide energy services to the Borgata Resort, which is scheduled to open in July 2003 in Atlantic City, New Jersey. Marina Energy will provide heat, hot water and cooling services via a new $40.0 million thermal energy plant that will be constructed adjacent to the resort.

BUSINESS

SOUTH JERSEY INDUSTRIES, INC. is a diversified holding company with two operating subsidiaries, South Jersey Gas Co. (SJG) and South Jersey Energy Co. (SJE). SJG is engaged in the purchase, transmission and sale of natural gas for residential, commercial and industrial use in an area of about 2,500 square miles in southern New Jersey. SJE provides services for the acquisition and transportation of natural gas for retail and end users and markets total energy management services. SJE has one subsidiary, SJEnerTrade, which provides services for the sale of natural gas to energy marketers, electric and gas utilities and other wholesale users in the mid-Atlantic and southern regions.

BUSINESS LINE ANALYSIS

(12/31/2000)	REV(%)	INC(%)
Gas Utility	84.0	93.5
Non-Utility	16.0	6.5
Total	100.0	100.0

ANNUAL FINANCIAL DATA

	12/31/00	12/31/99	12/31/98	12/31/97	12/31/96	12/31/95	12/31/94
Earnings Per Share	**[2] 2.16**	**[2] 2.01**	**[2] 1.28**	**[2] 1.71**	**[2] 1.70**	**1.65**	**[1] 1.21**
Cash Flow Per Share	**4.19**	**4.00**	**3.05**	**3.40**	**3.70**	**3.58**	**3.07**
Tang. Book Val. Per Share	**17.54**	**16.01**	**15.70**	**16.11**	**16.06**	**14.67**	**14.46**
Dividends Per Share	**1.46**	**1.44**	**1.44**	**1.44**	**1.44**	**1.44**	**1.44**
Dividend Payout %	**67.4**	**71.6**	**112.5**	**84.2**	**84.7**	**87.3**	**119.0**
INCOME STATEMENT (IN THOUSANDS):							
Total Revenues	515,928	392,477	450,246	348,567	355,458	353,808	373,959
Costs & Expenses	417,315	302,320	383,238	275,574	285,282	284,855	317,143
Depreciation & Amort.	23,104	21,765	19,063	18,112	21,462	20,722	19,142
Maintenance Exp.	7,820	6,077	...	5,500	...	...	...
Operating Income	49,031	45,887	36,085	38,642	38,559	38,857	30,865
Net Interest Inc./(Exp.)	d21,292	d20,826	d19,181	d18,111	d20,294	d21,214	d16,211
Income Taxes	18,658	16,428	11,860	10,739	10,155	9,374	6,809
Net Income	[2] 24,665	[2] 21,977	[2] 13,816	[2] 18,429	[2] 18,265	17,645	[1] 12,379
Cash Flow	47,769	43,742	32,879	36,541	39,727	38,365	31,521
Average Shs. Outstg.	11,401	10,922	10,776	10,763	10,732	10,720	10,258
BALANCE SHEET (IN THOUSANDS):							
Gross Property	771,603	726,537	684,829	624,747	582,646	603,389	570,022
Accumulated Depreciation	209,280	193,191	180,570	168,209	158,742	180,690	167,922
Net Property	562,323	533,346	504,259	456,538	423,904	422,699	402,100
Total Assets	869,979	766,925	748,095	670,601	658,381	604,309	571,095
Long-Term Obligations	204,981	183,561	194,710	176,360	149,736	168,721	153,086
Net Stockholders' Equity	201,739	185,275	169,234	173,499	172,731	157,297	154,972
Year-end Shs. Outstg.	11,500	11,572	10,779	10,771	10,757	10,722	10,715
STATISTICAL RECORD:							
Operating Profit Margin %	9.5	11.7	8.0	11.1	10.8	11.0	8.3
Net Profit Margin %	4.8	5.6	3.1	5.3	5.1	5.0	3.3
Net Inc./Net Property %	4.4	4.1	2.7	4.0	4.3	4.2	3.1
Net Inc./Tot. Capital %	4.5	4.4	2.8	4.0	4.6	4.4	3.3
Return on Equity %	12.2	11.9	8.2	10.6	10.6	11.2	8.0
Accum. Depr./Gross Prop. %	27.1	26.6	26.4	26.9	27.2	29.9	29.5
Price Range	30.13-24.50	30.75-21.50	30.75-22.00	29.88-21.00	24.63-20.13	23.50-17.88	24.00-16.63
P/E Ratio	13.9-11.3	15.3-10.7	24.0-17.2	17.5-12.3	14.5-11.8	14.2-10.8	19.8-13.7
Average Yield %	5.3	5.5	5.5	5.7	6.4	7.0	7.1

Statistics are as originally reported. [1] Incl. net charges of $2.3 mill. [2] Excl. disc. opers. loss of $481,000, 2000; loss $289,000, 1999; loss $2.8 mill., 1998; loss $2.6 mill., 1997; inc. $12.2 mill., 1996.

OFFICERS:
C. Biscieglia, Chmn., Pres., C.E.O.
W. J. Smethurst Jr., Treas.
G. L. Baulig, V.P., Corp. Sec.

INVESTOR CONTACT: Stephen H. Clark, Dir. Inv. Rel., (609) 561-9000 ext. 4260

PRINCIPAL OFFICE: 1 South Jersey Plaza, Folsom, NJ 08037-9917

TELEPHONE NUMBER: (609) 561-9000
FAX: (609) 561-8225
WEB: www.sjindustries.com

NO. OF EMPLOYEES: 643 (avg.)

SHAREHOLDERS: 9,076

ANNUAL MEETING: In Apr.

INCORPORATED: NJ, Nov., 1969

INSTITUTIONAL HOLDINGS:
No. of Institutions: 58
Shares Held: 3,800,574
% Held: 32.8

INDUSTRY: Natural gas distribution (SIC: 4924)

TRANSFER AGENT(S): First Union National Bank, Charlotte, NC

NYSE SYMBOL SO
Rec. Pr. 23.39 (4/30/01)

SOUTHERN COMPANY (THE)

YIELD 5.7%
P/E RATIO 11.6

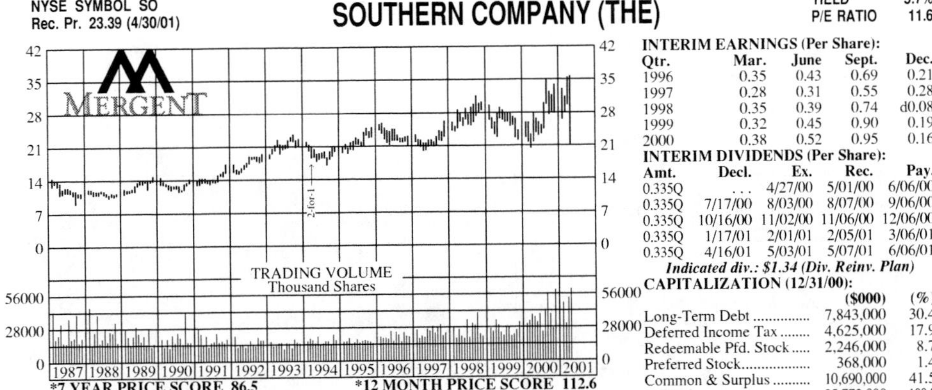

*7 YEAR PRICE SCORE 86.5 *12 MONTH PRICE SCORE 112.6

*NYSE COMPOSITE INDEX=100

INTERIM EARNINGS (Per Share):

Qtr.	Mar.	June	Sept.	Dec.
1996	0.35	0.43	0.69	0.21
1997	0.28	0.31	0.55	0.28
1998	0.35	0.39	0.74	d0.08
1999	0.32	0.45	0.90	0.19
2000	0.38	0.52	0.95	0.16

INTERIM DIVIDENDS (Per Share):

Amt.	Decl.	Ex.	Rec.	Pay.
0.335Q	...	4/27/00	5/01/00	6/06/00
0.335Q	7/17/00	8/03/00	8/07/00	9/06/00
0.335Q	10/16/00	11/02/00	11/06/00	12/06/00
0.335Q	1/17/01	2/01/01	2/05/01	3/06/01
0.335Q	4/16/01	5/03/01	5/07/01	6/06/01

Indicated div.: $1.34 (Div. Reinv. Plan)

CAPITALIZATION (12/31/00):

	($000)	(%)
Long-Term Debt	7,843,000	30.4
Deferred Income Tax	4,625,000	17.9
Redeemable Pfd. Stock	2,246,000	8.7
Preferred Stock	368,000	1.4
Common & Surplus	10,690,000	41.5
Total	25,772,000	100.0

RECENT DEVELOPMENTS: For the year ended 12/31/00, income from continuing operations decreased 8.6% to $994.0 million versus income from continuing operations of $915.0 million in the previous year. Total operating revenues dropped 8.0% to $10.07 billion from $9.32 billion the year before. Retail sales increased 6.5% to $8.61 billion versus $8.09 billion in the prior year. Sales for resale jumped 18.7% to $977.0 million, while other operating revenues advanced 16.7% to $476.0 million.

PROSPECTS: On 4/2/01, the Company completed the spin-off of its 80.3% ownership interest in Mirant Corporation, formerly Southern Energy, Inc., to SO's shareholders in the form of a special dividend. By 2004, SO plans to increase generating capacity by 6,600 megawatts in the Southeast. On 1/10/01, SO received approval from the Securities and Exchange Commission to form Southern Power Company, a new subsidiary that will own, manage and finance wholesale generating assets in the Southeast.

BUSINESS

THE SOUTHERN COMPANY is an energy company with more than 32,000 megawatts of electric generating capacity in the Southeast. The Company is one of the largest producers of electricity in the U.S. The Southern Company is the parent firm of Alabama Power, Georgia Power, Mississippi Power, Savannah Electric, Southern Nuclear, Southern Company Energy Solutions, Southern LINC and Southern Telecom. On 4/2/01, the Company completed the spin-off of its 80.3% ownership interest in Mirant Corporation.

REVENUES

(12/31/00)	($000)	(%)
Retail Sales	8,613,000	85.6
Sales For Resale	977,000	9.7
Other Revenues	476,000	4.7
Total	10,066,000	100.0

ANNUAL FINANCIAL DATA

	12/31/00	12/31/99	12/31/98	12/31/97	12/31/96	12/31/95	12/31/94
Earnings Per Share	**[5][6] 1.52**	**[4] 1.86**	**[3] 1.40**	**[2] 1.42**	**1.68**	**1.66**	**[1] 1.52**
Cash Flow Per Share	**3.56**	**4.08**	**3.95**	**3.57**	**3.46**	**3.36**	**3.14**
Tang. Book Val. Per Share	**15.67**	**13.82**	**14.14**	**13.92**	**13.59**	**13.09**	**12.46**
Dividends Per Share	**1.34**	**1.34**	**1.34**	**1.30**	**1.26**	**1.22**	**1.18**
Dividend Payout %	**88.2**	**72.0**	**95.7**	**91.5**	**75.0**	**73.5**	**77.6**
INCOME STATEMENT (IN MILLIONS):							
Total Revenues	10,066.0	11,585.0	11,403.0	12,611.0	10,358.0	9,180.0	8,297.0
Costs & Expenses	5,473.0	6,339.0	6,990.0	8,437.0	6,521.0	5,477.0	4,872.0
Depreciation & Amort.	1,337.0	1,522.0	1,773.0	1,471.0	1,201.0	1,134.0	1,050.0
Maintenance Exp.	852.0	945.0	887.0	763.0	782.0	683.0	660.0
Operating Income	2,404.0	2,779.0	1,753.0	1,940.0	1,854.0	1,886.0	1,715.0
Net Interest Inc./(Exp.)	d608.0	d895.0	d710.0	d721.0	d643.0	d658.0	d628.0
Income Taxes	588.0	726.0	cr8.0	114.0	10.0	cr36.0	cr26.0
Equity Earnings/Minority Int.	...	d183.0	d80.0	d29.0	d13.0	d13.0	d20.0
Net Income	[5][6] 994.0	[4] 1,276.0	[3] 977.0	[2] 972.0	1,127.0	1,103.0	[1] 989.0
Cash Flow	2,331.0	2,798.0	2,750.0	2,443.0	2,328.0	2,237.0	2,039.0
Average Shs. Outstg. (000)	654,194	685,000	697,000	685,000	673,000	665,000	650,000
BALANCE SHEET (IN MILLIONS):							
Gross Property	35,972.0	38,620.0	37,363.0	35,586.0	34,190.0	33,093.0	30,694.0
Accumulated Depreciation	14,350.0	14,076.0	13,239.0	11,934.0	10,921.0	10,067.0	9,577.0
Net Property	21,622.0	24,544.0	24,124.0	23,652.0	23,269.0	23,026.0	21,117.0
Total Assets	31,362.0	38,396.0	36,192.0	35,271.0	30,292.0	30,554.0	27,042.0
Long-Term Obligations	7,843.0	11,747.0	10,472.0	10,274.0	7,935.0	8,306.0	7,593.0
Net Stockholders' Equity	11,058.0	9,573.0	10,166.0	10,140.0	10,196.0	10,204.0	9,618.0
Year-end Shs. Outstg. (000)	682,000	666,000	693,000	693,000	678,000	670,000	657,000
STATISTICAL RECORD:							
Operating Profit Margin %	23.9	24.0	15.4	15.4	17.9	20.5	20.7
Net Profit Margin %	9.9	11.0	8.6	7.7	10.9	12.0	11.9
Net Inc./Net Property %	4.6	5.2	4.0	4.1	4.8	4.8	4.7
Net Inc./Tot. Capital %	3.9	4.3	3.4	3.5	4.6	4.5	4.4
Return on Equity %	9.0	13.3	9.6	9.6	11.1	10.8	10.3
Accum. Depr./Gross Prop. %	39.9	36.4	35.4	33.5	31.9	30.4	31.2
Price Range	35.00-20.38	29.63-22.06	31.56-23.94	26.25-19.88	25.88-21.13	25.00-19.38	22.06-17.00
P/E Ratio	23.0-13.4	15.9-11.9	22.5-17.1	18.5-14.0	15.4-12.6	15.1-11.7	14.5-11.2
Average Yield %	4.8	5.2	4.8	5.6	5.4	5.5	6.0

Statistics are as originally reported. Adj. for stk. splits: 2-for-1, 3/94. [1] Incl. a $61.0 mill. chrg. for workforce reduction programs [2] Incl. non-recurr. chrg. $111.0 mill. ($0.16/sh.) for UK windfall profit tax [3] Incl. non-recurr. chrg. of $342.0 mill. for the write-down of assets and a gain of $59.0 mill. on assets sales. [4] Incl. non-recurr. chrg. of $69.0 mill. and a gain of $315.0 mill. on asset sales. [5] Incl. non-recurr. chrg. of $90.0 mill. & a gain of $8.0 mill. fr. a litigation settlement. [6] Excl. income from disc. opers. of $319.0 mill.

OFFICERS:
H. A. Franklin, Pres., C.E.O.
G. Klappa, V.P., C.F.O., Treas.

INVESTOR CONTACT: Tommy Chisholm, Sec. & Asst. Treas., (404) 393-0650

PRINCIPAL OFFICE: 270 Peachtree St., N.W., Atlanta, GA 30303

TELEPHONE NUMBER: (404) 506-5000
FAX: (404) 506-0455
WEB: www.southernco.com
NO. OF EMPLOYEES: 26,021
SHAREHOLDERS: 160,116
ANNUAL MEETING: In May
INCORPORATED: DE, Nov., 1945

INSTITUTIONAL HOLDINGS:
No. of Institutions: 480
Shares Held: 224,750,835
% Held: 32.8

INDUSTRY: Electric services (SIC: 4911)

TRANSFER AGENT(S): SCS Stockholder Services, Atlanta, GA

NYSE SYMBOL LUV
Rec. Pr. 20.00 (5/31/01)

SOUTHWEST AIRLINES CO.

YIELD 0.1%
P/E RATIO 25.6

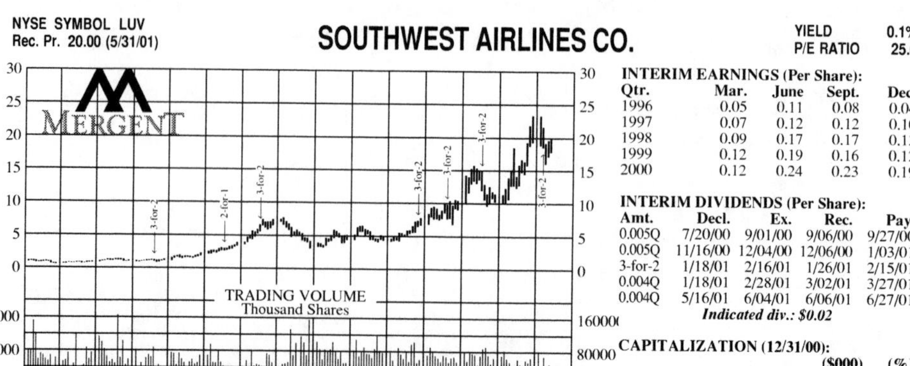

*7 YEAR PRICE SCORE 146.2 *12 MONTH PRICE SCORE 111.3
*NYSE COMPOSITE INDEX=100

INTERIM EARNINGS (Per Share):

Qtr.	Mar.	June	Sept.	Dec.
1996	0.05	0.11	0.08	0.04
1997	0.07	0.12	0.12	0.10
1998	0.09	0.17	0.17	0.13
1999	0.12	0.19	0.16	0.12
2000	0.12	0.24	0.23	0.19

INTERIM DIVIDENDS (Per Share):

Amt.	Decl.	Ex.	Rec.	Pay.
0.005Q	7/20/00	9/01/00	9/06/00	9/27/00
0.005Q	11/16/00	12/04/00	12/06/00	1/03/01
3-for-2	1/18/01	2/16/01	1/26/01	2/15/01
0.004Q	1/18/01	2/28/01	3/02/01	3/27/01
0.004Q	5/16/01	6/04/01	6/06/01	6/27/01

Indicated div.: $0.02

CAPITALIZATION (12/31/00):

	($000)	(%)
Long-Term Debt	760,992	15.0
Deferred Income Tax	852,865	16.8
Common & Surplus	3,451,320	68.1
Total	5,065,177	100.0

RECENT DEVELOPMENTS: For the year ended 12/31/00, income before an accounting charge was $625.2 million versus net income of $474.4 million the year before. Total operating revenues climbed 19.3% to $5.65 billion from $4.74 billion in 1999. Operating income totaled $1.02 billion, up 30.7% compared with $781.6 million a year earlier. Revenue passenger miles increased 15.7% and available seat miles were up 13.3%, resulting in a passenger load factor, or percentage of seats filled, of 70.5% versus 69.0% the year before.

PROSPECTS: The Company is continuing to offset higher energy costs with its fuel hedging program, which saved LUV $64.1 million during the fourth quarter of 2000 and $113.5 million over the entire year. The Company has hedged 80.0% of its expected fuel needs for 2001 at crude oil prices averaging $22.00 per barrel. Separately, LUV has accelerated the delivery of four new 737 aircraft from the first half of 2002 to the fourth quarter of 2001. This brings the Company's total planned aircraft deliveries to 25 and 27 in 2001 and 2002, respectively.

BUSINESS

SOUTHWEST AIRLINES CO. provides single-class, high-frequency, point-to-point, air transport service to 57 cities in 29 states. Southwest principally concentrates on short-haul markets and emphasizes high aircraft utilization and high employee productivity. Primary hubs include Dallas Love Field, Houston Hobby Airport and Phoenix Sky Harbor International. Southwest acquired Morris Air Corporation on 12/31/93 and completed the integration of Morris' operations with its own by March 1995. At 12/31/00, Southwest operated 344 Boeing 737 aircraft.

REVENUES

(12/31/2000)	($000)	(%)
Passenger	5,468	96.8
Freight	111	2.0
Other	71	1.2
Total	5,650	100.0

ANNUAL FINANCIAL DATA

	12/31/00	12/31/99	12/31/98	12/31/97	12/31/96	12/31/95	12/31/94
Earnings Per Share	**1 0.79**	**0.59**	**0.55**	**0.42**	**0.27**	**0.24**	**0.24**
Cash Flow Per Share	**1.16**	**0.92**	**0.84**	**0.68**	**0.51**	**0.44**	**0.41**
Tang. Book Val. Per Share	**4.56**	**4.21**	**3.21**	**2.69**	**2.24**	**1.96**	**1.71**
Dividends Per Share	**0.01**	**0.01**	**0.01**	**0.01**	**0.01**	**0.01**	**0.01**
Dividend Payout %	**1.9**	**2.4**	**2.2**	**2.2**	**3.1**	**3.3**	**2.5**
INCOME STATEMENT (IN MILLIONS):							
Total Revenues	5,649.6	4,735.6	4,164.0	3,816.8	3,406.2	2,872.8	2,591.9
Costs & Expenses	4,326.0	3,691.6	3,247.6	3,091.9	2,869.6	2,409.4	2,152.3
Depreciation & Amort.	302.4	262.4	232.7	200.7	185.7	149.8	122.9
Operating Income	1,021.1	781.6	683.6	524.2	350.8	313.5	316.7
Net Interest Inc./(Exp.)	d2.3	2.3	0.4	d7.1	d11.2	d7.3	d17.9
Income Before Income Taxes	1,017.4	773.6	705.1	517.0	341.4	305.1	299.5
Income Taxes	392.1	299.2	271.7	199.2	134.0	122.5	120.2
Net Income	1 625.2	474.4	433.4	317.8	207.3	182.6	179.3
Cash Flow	927.7	736.8	666.2	518.5	393.1	332.4	302.3
Average Shs. Outstg. (000)	796,317	803,891	794,624	767,674	768,452	753,558	745,732
BALANCE SHEET (IN MILLIONS):							
Cash & Cash Equivalents	523.0	418.8	378.5	623.3	581.8	317.4	174.5
Total Current Assets	831.5	631.0	574.2	806.4	751.0	473.1	314.9
Net Property	5,819.7	5,008.2	4,137.6	3,435.7	2,969.2	2,779.3	2,505.0
Total Assets	6,669.6	5,652.1	4,716.0	4,246.2	3,723.5	3,256.1	2,823.1
Total Current Liabilities	1,298.4	960.5	850.7	868.5	765.4	610.6	522.3
Long-Term Obligations	761.0	871.7	623.3	628.1	650.2	661.0	583.1
Net Stockholders' Equity	3,451.3	2,835.8	2,397.9	2,009.0	1,648.3	1,427.3	1,238.7
Net Working Capital	d466.9	d329.5	d276.5	d62.1	d14.4	d137.5	d207.4
Year-end Shs. Outstg. (000)	756,243	674,139	747,682	746,574	734,630	729,167	725,234
STATISTICAL RECORD:							
Operating Profit Margin %	18.1	16.5	16.4	13.7	10.3	10.9	12.2
Net Profit Margin %	11.1	10.0	10.4	8.3	6.1	6.4	6.9
Return on Equity %	18.1	16.7	18.1	15.8	12.6	12.8	14.5
Return on Assets %	9.4	8.4	9.2	7.5	5.6	5.6	6.4
Debt/Total Assets %	11.4	15.4	13.2	14.8	17.5	20.3	20.7
Price Range	23.33-10.00	15.72-9.58	10.56-6.81	7.78-4.20	6.57-4.07	5.90-3.23	7.70-3.06
P/E Ratio	29.6-12.7	26.5-16.2	19.3-12.4	18.7-10.1	24.2-15.0	24.3-13.3	32.0-12.7
Average Yield %	0.1	0.1	0.1	0.2	0.2	0.2	0.1

Statistics are as originally reported. Adj. for all stk. div. & splits through 2/01. 1 Bef. $22.1 mil ($0.03/sh.) acctg. chrg.

OFFICERS:
H. D. Kelleher, Chmn.
J. F. Parker, Vice-Chmn., C.E.O.
C. C. Barrett, Pres., C.O.O.

INVESTOR CONTACT: Investor Relations, (214) 792-4908

PRINCIPAL OFFICE: 2702 Love Field Drive, P.O. Box 36611, Dallas, TX 75235-1611

TELEPHONE NUMBER: (214) 792-4000
FAX: (214) 792-5015
WEB: www.southwest.com

NO. OF EMPLOYEES: 29,274 (avg.)

SHAREHOLDERS: 10,223

ANNUAL MEETING: In May

INCORPORATED: TX, Mar., 1967

INSTITUTIONAL HOLDINGS:
No. of Institutions: 409
Shares Held: 567,362,793
% Held: 74.9

INDUSTRY: Air transportation, scheduled (SIC: 4512)

TRANSFER AGENT(S): Continental Stock Transfer & Trust Co., New York, NY

NYSE SYMBOL SWN
Rec. Pr. 13.15 (4/30/01)

SOUTHWESTERN ENERGY COMPANY

YIELD 1.8%
P/E RATIO ...

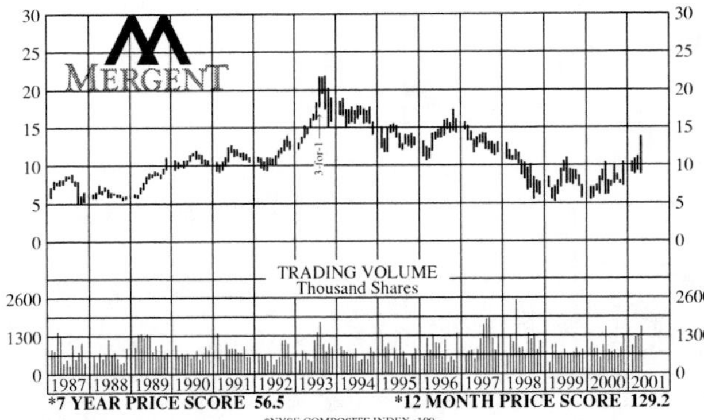

INTERIM EARNINGS (Per Share):

Qtr.	Mar.	June	Sept.	Dec.
1996	0.38	0.11	0.01	0.28
1997	0.50	Nil	d0.05	0.31
1998	0.37	d1.70	d0.05	0.15
1999	0.37	d0.07	d0.08	0.18
2000	0.37	d2.53	d0.03	0.36

INTERIM DIVIDENDS (Per Share):

Amt.	Decl.	Ex.	Rec.	Pay.
0.06Q	4/07/99	4/16/99	4/20/99	5/05/99
0.06Q	7/07/99	7/16/99	7/20/99	8/05/99
0.06Q	10/07/99	10/18/99	10/20/99	11/05/99
0.06Q	1/05/00	1/18/00	1/20/00	2/04/00
0.06Q	4/05/00	4/18/00	4/20/00	5/05/00

Indicated div.: $0.24 (Div. Reinv. Plan)

CAPITALIZATION (12/31/00):

	($000)	(%)
Long-Term Debt	225,000	48.5
Deferred Income Tax	97,431	21.0
Common & Surplus	141,291	30.5
Total	463,722	100.0

RECENT DEVELOPMENTS: For the year ended 12/31/00, SWN reported a loss of $45.8 million, before an extraordinary loss of $890,000, versus net income of $9.9 million a year earlier. Results for 2000 included an unusual charge of $111.3 million related to the judgment in the Hales lawsuit and a $3.2 million gain from the sale of the Company's Missouri utility properties. Operating revenues increased 29.8% to $363.9 million, reflecting increased production and higher natural gas and oil prices.

PROSPECTS: Near-term results should benefit from higher average realizations for natural gas and oil production, as lower fixed-price hedges that were put in place in 1999 and the first part of 2000 expired in the fourth quarter of 2000. Meanwhile, SWN indicated that while there is no further activity on the sale of its utility assets, it is comfortable holding these assets at this time. On 1/9/01, SWN and Energen Resources Corporation announced a strategic exploration alliance in the southeast New Mexico portion of the Permian Basin.

BUSINESS

SOUTHWESTERN ENERGY COMPANY is an energy company primarily focused on natural gas. The Company operates in three business segments. The Exploration and Production segment is engaged in natural gas and oil exploration, development and production, with operations principally located in Arkansas, Oklahoma, Texas, New Mexico and Louisiana. The Natural Gas Distribution segment is engaged in the gathering, distribution and transmission of natural gas to approximately 131,000 customers in northern Arkansas. The Marketing and Transportation segment provides marketing and transportation services in SWN's core operations and owns a 25.0% interest in the NOARK Pipeline System, Limited Partnership.

REVENUES

(12/31/2000)	($000)	(%)
Gas sales	200,269	55.0
Gas marketing	137,234	37.7
Oil sales	15,537	4.3
Gas transport & other	10,843	3.0
Total	363,883	100.0

ANNUAL FINANCIAL DATA

	12/31/00	12/31/99	12/31/98	12/31/97	12/31/96	12/31/95	12/31/94
Earnings Per Share	**3 d1.82**	**0.40**	**1 d1.23**	**0.76**	**0.78**	**2 0.46**	**0.98**
Cash Flow Per Share	**0.06**	**2.12**	**0.71**	**2.71**	**2.50**	**1.90**	**2.37**
Tang. Book Val. Per Share	**5.61**	**7.66**	**7.45**	**8.92**	**8.41**	**7.87**	**7.92**
Dividends Per Share	**0.12**	**0.24**	**0.24**	**0.24**	**0.24**	**0.24**	**0.24**
Dividend Payout %	**...**	**60.0**	**...**	**31.6**	**30.8**	**52.2**	**24.5**
INCOME STATEMENT (IN MILLIONS):							
Total Revenues	363.9	280.4	266.3	276.2	189.2	153.1	170.2
Costs & Expenses	370.1	201.4	247.0	175.8	98.6	85.7	82.3
Depreciation & Amort.	47.2	43.0	48.3	48.5	42.7	36.3	35.8
Operating Income	d53.5	36.1	d29.0	51.9	48.0	31.2	52.1
Net Interest Inc./(Exp.)	d23.2	d17.4	d17.2	d16.4	d13.0	d11.2	d8.9
Income Taxes	cr28.9	6.4	cr19.5	11.8	11.8	7.3	15.7
Net Income	3 d45.8	9.9	1 d30.6	18.7	19.2	2 11.5	25.1
Cash Flow	1.4	52.9	17.7	67.2	61.9	47.8	60.9
Average Shs. Outstg. (000)	25,044	24,947	24,822	24,778	24,705	25,131	25,684
BALANCE SHEET (IN MILLIONS):							
Gross Property	1,118.7	1,095.9	1,028.5	969.9	887.8	763.6	667.5
Accumulated Depreciation	554.6	519.9	478.8	366.6	319.1	277.8	242.0
Net Property	564.1	576.0	549.7	603.3	568.7	485.8	425.5
Total Assets	705.4	671.4	647.6	710.9	660.2	569.1	484.6
Long-Term Obligations	225.0	294.7	281.9	296.5	275.2	207.8	136.2
Net Stockholders' Equity	141.3	190.4	185.9	221.6	207.9	194.5	203.5
Year-end Shs. Outstg. (000)	25,181	24,849	24,935	24,834	24,719	24,701	25,684
STATISTICAL RECORD:							
Operating Profit Margin %	...	12.9	...	18.8	25.4	20.4	30.6
Net Profit Margin %	...	3.5	...	6.8	10.1	7.5	14.8
Net Inc./Net Property %	...	1.7	...	3.1	3.4	2.4	5.9
Net Inc./Tot. Capital %	...	1.6	...	2.8	3.1	2.2	5.7
Return on Equity %	...	5.2	...	8.4	9.2	5.9	12.3
Accum. Depr./Gross Prop. %	49.6	47.4	46.6	37.8	35.9	36.4	36.3
Price Range	10.44-5.44	11.00-5.19	12.94-5.50	15.75-11.25	17.38-10.63	15.50-11.75	18.88-14.00
P/E Ratio	...	27.5-13.0	...	20.7-14.8	22.3-13.6	33.7-25.5	19.3-14.3
Average Yield %	1.5	3.0	2.6	1.8	1.7	1.8	1.5

Statistics are as originally reported. 1 Incls. non-recurr. pre-tax chrg. of $66.4 mill. 2 Bef. extraord. chrg. of $295,000. 3 Incls. non-recurr. charges of $111.3 mill. & pre-tax gain on sale of assets of $3.2 mill.; bef. extraord. loss of $890,000 ($0.04/sh.)

OFFICERS:
C. E. Scharlau, Chmn.
H. M. Korell, Pres., C.E.O.
G. D. Kerley, Exec. V.P., C.F.O.
INVESTOR CONTACT: Greg D. Kerley, Exec. V.P., C.F.O., (501) 521-1141
PRINCIPAL OFFICE: 1083 Sain Street, Fayetteville, AR 72702-1408

TELEPHONE NUMBER: (501) 521-1141
FAX: (501) 521-0328
WEB: www.swn.com
NO. OF EMPLOYEES: 536
SHAREHOLDERS: 2,192
ANNUAL MEETING: In May
INCORPORATED: AR, July, 1929

INSTITUTIONAL HOLDINGS:
No. of Institutions: 86
Shares Held: 18,849,572
% Held: 74.8
INDUSTRY: Gas transmission and distribution (SIC: 4923)
TRANSFER AGENT(S): EquiServe, Jersey City, NJ

NYSE SYMBOL SFN
Rec. Pr. 8.17 (4/30/01)

SPHERION CORPORATION

YIELD ...
P/E RATIO 7.1

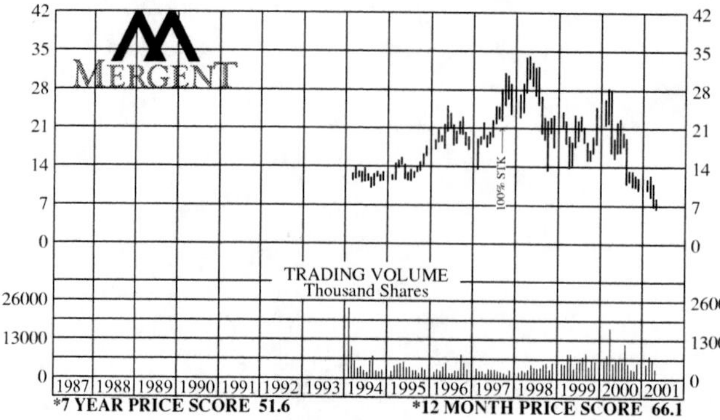

TRADING VOLUME
Thousand Shares

*7 YEAR PRICE SCORE 51.6   *12 MONTH PRICE SCORE 66.1

*NYSE COMPOSITE INDEX=100

INTERIM EARNINGS (Per Share):

Qtr.	Mar.	June	Sept.	Dec.
1996	0.18	d0.01	0.25	0.27
1997	0.22	0.13	0.15	0.29
1998	0.26	0.31	0.35	0.36
1999	0.33	0.40	0.21	0.35
2000	0.37	0.42	0.37	d0.01

INTERIM DIVIDENDS (Per Share):

Amt.	Decl.	Ex.	Rec.	Pay.

No dividends paid.

CAPITALIZATION (12/29/00):

	($000)	(%)
Long-Term Debt	489,911	29.2
Common & Surplus	1,190,550	70.8
Total	1,680,461	100.0

RECENT DEVELOPMENTS: For the year ended 12/29/00, net income advanced 5.2% to $74.5 million versus $70.8 million a year earlier. Results for 2000 and 1999 included nonrecurring charges of $24.8 million and $34.0 million, respectively. Revenues rose 18.1% to $3.74 billion versus $3.17 billion in 1999. Information Technology segment revenues fell 3.3% to $755.6 million, while Professional Services segment revenues rose 37.3% to $1.31 billion. Commercial Staffing revenues jumped 17.0% to $1.68 billion.

PROSPECTS: On 4/2/01, SFN completed the sale of Michael Page International plc, a wholly-owned subsidiary, through an initial public offering on the London Stock Exchange. SFN received approximately $710.0 million of cash proceeds. Separately, SFN was selected by the Society of the Plastics Industry, Inc. to provide automated prescreening services for its 1,700 members. For 2001, SFN plans to grow revenues through the development of higher-margin professional services and acquisitions.

BUSINESS

SPHERION CORPORATION (formerly Interim Services Inc.) provides customized staffing and personnel management to businesses, professional and service organizations, governmental agencies and individuals. SFN operates through a network of more than 1,000 offices in North America, Europe, Australia, and Asia. SFN provides five types of services through its three operating segments, Information Technology, Professional Services and Commercial Staffing. Consulting Services provides information technology consulting, outplacement and executive coaching. Managed Staffing Services offers on-premise workforce management and vendor management. Outsourcing Services offers various outsourced functions for clients. Search/Recruitment Services focuses on full-time placement for entry-level professionals to senior executives. Flexible Staffing Services place SFN employees at the client's facility for various assignments.

REVENUES

(12/29/00)	($000)	(%)
Information Technology	755,551	20.2
Professional Services	1,306,579	34.9
Commercial Staffing	1,678,693	44.9
Total	3,740,823	100.0

ANNUAL FINANCIAL DATA

	12/29/00	12/31/99	12/25/98	12/26/97	12/27/96	12/29/95	12/30/94
Earnings Per Share	**[4] 1.16**	**[4] 1.27**	**[3] 1.29**	**[2] 1.05**	**[1] 0.69**	**0.75**	**0.62**
Cash Flow Per Share	**2.23**	**2.24**	**2.13**	**1.92**	**1.25**	**1.34**	**1.12**
Tang. Book Val. Per Share	...	...	...	...	**6.16**	**1.08**	**3.78**
INCOME STATEMENT (IN MILLIONS):							
Total Revenues	3,740.8	3,168.0	1,890.1	1,608.3	1,147.2	780.9	634.4
Costs & Expenses	3,483.2	2,938.2	1,716.6	1,473.0	1,068.8	734.0	595.9
Depreciation & Amort.	80.9	65.2	44.4	34.9	18.9	13.7	11.5
Operating Income	176.7	164.6	129.2	100.4	59.4	33.2	27.0
Net Interest Inc./(Exp.)	d50.4	d36.3	d23.8	d24.3	d5.7	d1.8	d0.5
Income Before Income Taxes	126.3	123.9	105.4	81.4	45.1	31.4	26.5
Income Taxes	51.8	53.0	46.8	38.9	22.1	13.9	12.3
Net Income	[4] 74.5	[4] 70.8	[3] 58.6	[2] 42.5	[1] 23.0	17.5	14.2
Cash Flow	155.4	136.0	102.9	77.4	41.9	31.2	25.6
Average Shs. Outstg. (000)	69,757	60,837	48,244	40,407	33,418	23,304	22,854
BALANCE SHEET (IN MILLIONS):							
Cash & Cash Equivalents	38.5	37.5	153.3	15.6	26.4	2.1	0.8
Total Current Assets	725.1	708.4	544.8	308.1	264.3	191.0	140.5
Net Property	149.1	136.0	90.6	65.5	49.8	24.2	18.0
Total Assets	2,483.2	2,438.9	1,613.4	1,091.7	512.5	406.6	260.7
Total Current Liabilities	717.5	657.9	418.5	234.9	95.0	150.2	82.1
Long-Term Obligations	489.9	513.6	426.9	379.2	...	60.0	...
Net Stockholders' Equity	1,190.6	1,159.3	737.9	473.6	414.7	196.4	178.6
Net Working Capital	7.6	50.5	126.3	73.2	169.3	40.7	58.4
Year-end Shs. Outstg. (000)	61,754	63,590	47,336	39,476	38,954	23,040	23,000
STATISTICAL RECORD:							
Operating Profit Margin %	4.7	5.2	6.8	6.2	5.2	4.3	4.3
Net Profit Margin %	2.0	2.2	3.1	2.6	2.0	2.2	2.2
Return on Equity %	6.3	6.1	7.9	9.0	5.5	8.9	7.9
Return on Assets %	3.0	2.9	3.6	3.9	4.5	4.3	5.4
Debt/Total Assets %	19.7	21.1	26.5	34.7	...	14.8	...
Price Range	28.38-9.69	24.81-13.75	34.25-13.25	31.13-13.50	25.13-17.00	17.75-11.31	14.13-10.06
P/E Ratio	24.5-8.4	19.5-10.8	26.5-10.3	29.6-12.9	36.4-24.6	23.7-15.1	22.8-16.2

Statistics are as originally reported. Adj. for stk. splits: 2-for-1, 9/97. [1] Incl. $8.6 mill. merger exp. [2] Incl. $5.3 mill. gain on sale of HealthCare business. [3] Bef. extraord. chrg. $2.8 mill. [4] Incl. non-recurr. chrg. $24.8 mill., 2000; $33.9 mill., 1999.

OFFICERS:
S. S. Elbaum, Chmn.
C. A. Hallman, Pres., C.E.O.
R. G. Krause, Exec. V.P., C.F.O.

INVESTOR CONTACT: Tabitha N. Zane, Investor Relations Director, (954) 489-6334

PRINCIPAL OFFICE: 2050 Spectrum Blvd., Ft. Lauderdale, FL 33309-3008

TELEPHONE NUMBER: (954) 938-7600
FAX: (954) 351-8117
WEB: www.interim.com
NO. OF EMPLOYEES: 9,000 full-time (approx.); 538,000 part-time (approx.)
SHAREHOLDERS: 2,344 (approx.)
ANNUAL MEETING: In May
INCORPORATED: DE, 1946

INSTITUTIONAL HOLDINGS:
No. of Institutions: 128
Shares Held: 48,155,349
% Held: 79.1

INDUSTRY: Help supply services (SIC: 7363)

TRANSFER AGENT(S): The Bank of New York, New York, NY

NYSE SYMBOL SPK
Rec. Pr. 56.80 (5/31/01)

SPIEKER PROPERTIES, INC.

YIELD 4.9%
P/E RATIO 12.8

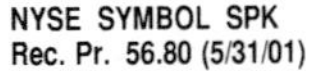

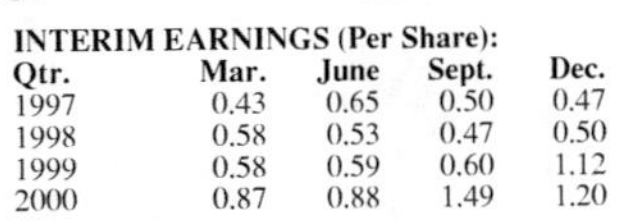

TRADING VOLUME
Thousand Shares

*7 YEAR PRICE SCORE 111.3 *12 MONTH PRICE SCORE 108.8
*NYSE COMPOSITE INDEX=100

INTERIM EARNINGS (Per Share):

Qtr.	Mar.	June	Sept.	Dec.
1997	0.43	0.65	0.50	0.47
1998	0.58	0.53	0.47	0.50
1999	0.58	0.59	0.60	1.12
2000	0.87	0.88	1.49	1.20

INTERIM DIVIDENDS (Per Share):

Amt.	Decl.	Ex.	Rec.	Pay.
0.70Q	3/08/00	3/29/00	3/31/00	4/20/00
0.70Q	6/07/00	6/28/00	6/30/00	7/20/00
0.70Q	9/06/00	9/27/00	9/29/00	10/20/00
0.70Q	12/06/00	12/27/00	12/29/00	2/02/01
0.70Q	3/07/01	3/28/01	3/30/01	4/20/01

Indicated div.: $2.80 (Div. Reinv. Plan)

CAPITALIZATION (12/31/00):

	($000)	(%)
Long-Term Debt	2,054,857	48.0
Minority Interest	284,148	6.6
Preferred Stock	368,373	8.6
Common & Surplus	1,571,684	36.7
Total	4,279,062	100.0

RECENT DEVELOPMENTS: For the year ended 12/31/00, net income jumped 51.5% to $333.5 million compared with $220.2 million in the previous year. Results included gain on disposition of property of $140.1 million and $58.5 million in 2000 and 1999, respectively. Total revenue improved 17.1% to $753.8 million from $643.8 million in the comparable year. Rental income increased 16.7% to $744.5 million versus $637.8 million in the preceding year. Interest and other income totaled $9.3 million, an increase of 56.0% from $6.0 million in the prior year.

PROSPECTS: On 2/23/01, the Company entered into an agreement to be acquired by Equity Office Properties Trust (EOP), in a transaction valued at approximately $7.20 billion. Under terms of the agreement, EOP will pay approximately $1.09 billion in cash and issue about 118.6 million shares of new EOP common stock. The transaction includes a $160.0 million break-up fee to EOP if the deal is not completed. The acquisition is subject to regulatory approval by the shareholders of both companies.

BUSINESS

SPIEKER PROPERTIES, INC. owns and operates office and industrial properties located in Seattle, Washington; Portland, Oregon; Northern California and Southern California. The Company is a self-managed and self-administrated real estate investment trust. The Company was formed to continue and expand the real estate activities, including the acquisition, development, management and leasing of the properties of its predecessor firm, Spieker Partners. Substantially all of the Company's business activities are conducted through Spieker Properties, L.P. in which SPK owns an approximate 88.2% general partnership interest. As of 12/31/00, the Company owned 37.7 million square feet of commercial real estate, which was 97.4% occupied. The portfolio mix consists of 24.9 million square feet of office property and 12.8 million square feet of industrial property.

ANNUAL FINANCIAL DATA

	12/31/00	12/31/99	12/31/98	12/31/97	12/31/96	12/31/95	12/31/94
Earnings Per Share	**4.45**	**2.89**	**2.07**	**2.04**	**1.51**	**[1] 0.84**	**0.46**
Cash Flow Per Share	**6.46**	**4.63**	**3.62**	**4.50**	**2.63**	**2.42**	**2.37**
Tang. Book Val. Per Share	**23.89**	**21.94**	**21.48**	**21.91**	**13.76**	**11.00**	**8.93**
Dividends Per Share	**2.71**	**2.40**	**2.28**	**1.84**	**1.71**	**1.66**	**1.39**
Dividend Payout %	**60.9**	**83.0**	**110.1**	**90.2**	**113.2**	**197.6**	**302.1**
INCOME STATEMENT (IN MILLIONS):							
Total Revenues	753.8	643.8	561.1	331.3	200.7	153.4	121.0
Costs & Expenses	373.9	334.7	300.3	166.1	95.8	81.7	68.7
Depreciation & Amort.	140.1	113.7	96.9	55.1	39.1	41.3	39.0
Operating Income	239.9	195.5	163.9	110.1	65.8	30.3	13.4
Income Before Income Taxes	379.9	254.0	185.9	130.4	74.1	30.3	13.4
Equity Earnings/Minority Int.	d46.4	d33.8	d26.3	d15.4	d9.9	d5.7	d2.8
Net Income	333.5	220.2	159.7	115.0	64.2	[1] 24.7	10.5
Cash Flow	440.3	301.0	227.3	155.0	91.2	63.4	48.3
Average Shs. Outstg. (000)	68,166	64,983	62,878	34,438	34,691	26,141	20,418
BALANCE SHEET (IN MILLIONS):							
Cash & Cash Equivalents	13.0	17.1	4.9	22.6	29.3	7.6	9.7
Total Current Assets	83.2	92.6	52.8	119.5	49.2	17.0	18.0
Net Property	5.9	5.1	4.5	3.4	2.4	1.7	1.2
Total Assets	4,528.3	4,268.5	4,056.9	3,242.9	1,390.3	1,011.5	809.9
Total Current Liabilities	242.4	201.2	176.5	118.9	55.9	41.6	30.0
Long-Term Obligations	2,054.9	1,996.8	1,847.2	1,431.5	720.0	490.4	514.1
Net Stockholders' Equity	1,940.1	1,793.4	1,723.5	1,493.8	563.9	419.8	206.3
Net Working Capital	d159.1	d108.6	d123.7	0.6	d6.6	d24.6	d12.0
Year-end Shs. Outstg. (000)	65,783	64,961	63,093	55,773	31,822	26,724	20,418
STATISTICAL RECORD:							
Operating Profit Margin %	31.8	30.4	29.2	33.2	32.8	19.8	11.0
Net Profit Margin %	44.2	34.2	28.5	34.7	32.0	16.1	8.7
Return on Equity %	17.2	12.3	9.3	7.7	11.4	5.9	5.1
Return on Assets %	7.4	5.2	3.9	3.5	4.6	2.4	1.3
Debt/Total Assets %	45.4	46.8	45.5	44.1	51.8	48.5	63.5
Price Range	59.13-35.75	41.56-32.25	43.94-31.00	43.00-32.63	36.00-23.75	25.88-19.38	23.25-18.63
P/E Ratio	13.3-8.0	14.4-11.2	21.2-15.0	21.1-16.0	23.8-15.7	30.8-23.1	50.5-40.5
Average Yield %	5.7	6.5	6.1	4.9	5.7	7.3	6.6

Statistics are as originally reported. [1] Bef. extraord. chrg., $33.5 mill.

OFFICERS:
W. E. Spieker Jr., Chmn.
J. A. Foster, Co-C.E.O.
C. G. Vought, Co-C.E.O.

INVESTOR CONTACT: Karen Morris, Mgr., Inv. Rel., (650) 854-5600

PRINCIPAL OFFICE: 2180 Sand Hill Rd., Suite 200, Menlo Park, CA 94025

TELEPHONE NUMBER: (650) 854-5600
FAX: (650) 233-3838
WEB: www.spieker.com

NO. OF EMPLOYEES: 607 (avg.)

SHAREHOLDERS: 504 (approx.)

ANNUAL MEETING: In June

INCORPORATED: MD, Aug., 1993

INSTITUTIONAL HOLDINGS:
No. of Institutions: 215
Shares Held: 44,712,422
% Held: 66.4

INDUSTRY: Real estate investment trusts (SIC: 6798)

TRANSFER AGENT(S): The Bank of New York, New York, NY

NYSE SYMBOL SMI
Rec. Pr. 45.20 (5/31/01)

SPRINGS INDUSTRIES, INC.

YIELD 2.9%
P/E RATIO 12.3

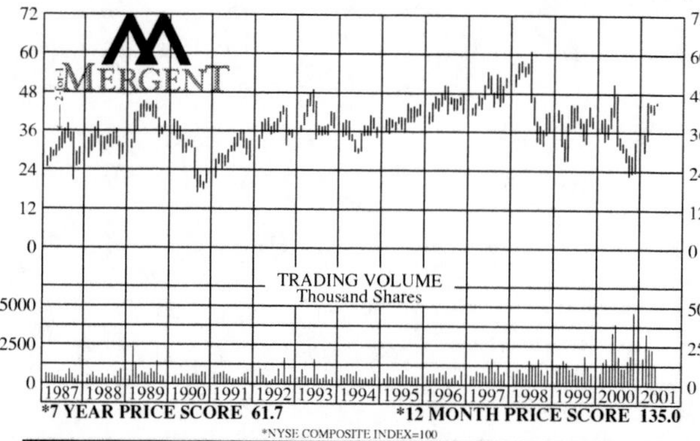

***7 YEAR PRICE SCORE 61.7** ***12 MONTH PRICE SCORE 135.0**

*NYSE COMPOSITE INDEX=100

INTERIM EARNINGS (Per Share):

Qtr.	Mar.	June	Sept.	Dec.
1996	0.60	2.10	1.11	0.51
1997	0.55	0.73	1.34	0.74
1998	d0.16	0.28	1.19	0.72
1999	0.84	0.73	0.99	1.23
2000	1.10	1.06	1.00	0.52

INTERIM DIVIDENDS (Per Share):

Amt.	Decl.	Ex.	Rec.	Pay.
0.33Q	5/08/00	6/14/00	6/16/00	6/30/00
0.33Q	7/13/00	9/13/00	9/15/00	9/29/00
0.33Q	10/05/00	12/20/00	12/22/00	1/02/01
0.33Q	2/21/01	3/14/01	3/16/01	3/30/01
0.33Q	6/07/01	6/14/01	6/18/01	6/29/01

Indicated div.: $1.32

CAPITALIZATION (12/30/00):

	($000)	(%)
Long-Term Debt	283,280	25.7
Common & Surplus	819,787	74.3
Total	1,103,067	100.0

RECENT DEVELOPMENTS: For the year ended 12/30/00, net income declined slightly to $67.1 million compared with $69.0 million in the previous year. Results for 2000 included restructuring and realignment expenses of $5.3 million and results for 1999 included Year 2000 expenses of $1.0 million. Net sales totaled $2.28 billion, an increase of 2.5% versus $2.22 billion the year before. Cost of goods sold grew 7.4% to $447.6 million. Operating income amounted to $139.2 million, up 4.7% from $133.0 million a year earlier.

PROSPECTS: On 4/27.01, SMI entered into a definitive recapitalization agreement with Heartland Springs Investment Company, an affiliate of Heartland Industrial Partners, L.P., a private equity firm. Upon completion of the recapitalization, which would be accomplished through a merger between SMI and the Heartland affiliate, each shareholder of SMI would receive $46.00 per share in cash and SMI would become privately hald by the close family. SMI expects to hold a shareholders meeting to vote on the transaction by late July or early August, 2001.

BUSINESS

SPRINGS INDUSTRIES, INC. is a manufacturer and marketer of home furnishings products. The home furnishings products unit produces sheets, pillowcases, bedspreads, comforters, infant and toddler bedding, shower curtains, accent and bath rugs, towels, other bath fashion accessories, home-sewing fabrics, draperies, drapery hardware, and decorative window furnishings. Trademarks include SPRINGMAID, WAMSUTTA, PERFORMANCE, NANIK, DUNDEE, GRABER, BALI. Licenses include Bill Blass, Liz Claiborne and Walt Disney. SMI operates facilities in 13 U.S. states and owns marketing and distribution subsidiaries in Canada and Mexico. On 1/5/99, the Company acquired the remaining 50.0% interest in American Fiber Industries. On 1/23/99, SMI acquired Regal Rugs, Inc., a manufacturer of bath and accent rugs for sale to department and specialty stores, national chain stores, and catalog retailers.

ANNUAL FINANCIAL DATA

	12/30/00	1/1/00	1/2/99	1/3/98	12/28/96	12/30/95	12/31/94
Earnings Per Share	**4 3.70**	**3 3.80**	**1.97**	**2 3.34**	**1 2 4.32**	**3.71**	**3.50**
Cash Flow Per Share	**9.72**	**9.37**	**6.56**	**7.43**	**8.69**	**8.82**	**8.57**
Tang. Book Val. Per Share	**38.48**	**36.24**	**40.62**	**40.69**	**38.75**	**36.48**	**33.20**
Dividends Per Share	**1.32**	**1.32**	**1.32**	**1.32**	**1.32**	**1.23**	**1.20**
Dividend Payout %	**35.7**	**34.7**	**67.0**	**39.5**	**30.6**	**33.2**	**34.3**
INCOME STATEMENT (IN MILLIONS):							
Total Revenues	2,275.1	2,220.4	2,180.5	2,226.1	2,243.3	2,233.1	2,068.9
Costs & Expenses	2,026.5	1,986.1	2,020.8	2,026.4	2,074.1	2,001.0	1,842.8
Depreciation & Amort.	109.4	101.3	87.0	84.6	89.4	98.5	90.3
Operating Income	139.2	133.0	72.7	115.1	79.8	...	135.8
Net Interest Inc./(Exp.)	d32.0	d26.5	d25.1	d18.6	d22.1	d32.0	d29.3
Income Before Income Taxes	106.6	111.2	58.8	102.9	104.5	110.9	106.7
Income Taxes	39.5	42.3	21.5	34.0	16.1	39.3	44.5
Net Income	4 67.1	3 69.0	37.3	2 69.0	1 2 88.4	71.6	62.2
Cash Flow	176.5	170.3	124.3	153.5	177.9	170.1	152.5
Average Shs. Outstg. (000)	18,160	18,168	18,938	20,668	20,460	19,300	17,793
BALANCE SHEET (IN MILLIONS):							
Cash & Cash Equivalents	2.9	4.2	48.1	0.4	30.7	2.6	0.8
Total Current Assets	836.4	823.4	787.2	786.7	789.6	769.3	617.0
Net Property	617.9	625.6	555.4	540.5	534.6	614.0	555.3
Total Assets	1,584.1	1,575.0	1,435.3	1,408.7	1,398.0	1,527.5	1,289.0
Total Current Liabilities	271.0	300.4	232.3	240.1	252.5	263.0	244.0
Long-Term Obligations	283.3	283.5	268.0	164.3	177.6	326.9	265.4
Net Stockholders' Equity	819.8	774.9	724.1	804.6	780.8	734.5	584.1
Net Working Capital	565.4	523.0	554.9	546.6	537.1	506.3	373.0
Year-end Shs. Outstg. (000)	17,932	17,905	17,827	19,772	20,148	20,137	17,595
STATISTICAL RECORD:							
Operating Profit Margin %	6.1	6.0	3.3	5.2	3.6	...	6.6
Net Profit Margin %	3.0	3.1	1.7	3.1	3.9	3.2	3.0
Return on Equity %	8.2	8.9	5.2	8.6	11.3	9.8	10.7
Return on Assets %	4.2	4.4	2.6	4.9	6.3	4.7	4.8
Debt/Total Assets %	17.9	18.0	18.7	11.7	12.7	21.4	20.6
Price Range	51.00-22.50	44.50-27.06	61.00-31.75	54.75-41.00	50.50-38.38	44.75-35.25	41.00-29.25
P/E Ratio	13.8-6.1	11.7-7.1	31.0-16.1	16.4-12.3	11.7-8.9	12.1-9.5	11.7-8.4
Average Yield %	3.6	3.7	2.8	2.8	3.0	3.1	3.4

Statistics are as originally reported. 1 Bef. extraord. chrg. $3.6 mill. 2 Incl. non-recurr. chrg. 1998, $24.7 mill.; 1997, $11.1 mill.; 1996, $33.9 mill. 3 Incl. Year 2000 exp., $1.0 mill. 4 Incl. restruct. & realign. chrg., $5.3 mill.

OFFICERS:
C. C. Bowles, Chmn., Pres., C.E.O.
J. A. Atkins, Exec. V.P., C.F.O.
S. J. Ilardo, V.P., Treas.

INVESTOR CONTACT: Jeffry A. Atkins, Exec. V.P. & C.F.O., (803) 547-3757

PRINCIPAL OFFICE: 205 North White Street, Fort Mill, SC 29715

TELEPHONE NUMBER: (803) 547-1500
FAX: (803) 547-3786
WEB: www.springs.com
NO. OF EMPLOYEES: 18,200 (approx.)
SHAREHOLDERS: 2,350 (approx. class A); 70 (approx. class B)
ANNUAL MEETING: In May
INCORPORATED: SC, July, 1966

INSTITUTIONAL HOLDINGS:
No. of Institutions: 114
Shares Held: 7,364,815
% Held: 41.0

INDUSTRY: Broadwoven fabric mills, cotton (SIC: 2211)

TRANSFER AGENT(S): Wachovia Bank of North Carolina, N.A., Winston-Salem, NC

NYSE SYMBOL FON
Rec. Pr. 20.31 (5/31/01)

SPRINT CORPORATION FON GROUP

YIELD 2.5%
P/E RATIO 14.0

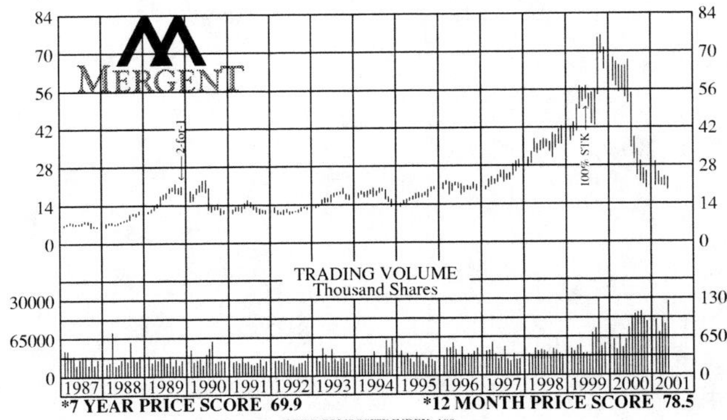

*7 YEAR PRICE SCORE 69.9 *12 MONTH PRICE SCORE 78.5

*NYSE COMPOSITE INDEX=100

INTERIM EARNINGS (Per Share):

Qtr.	Mar.	June	Sept.	Dec.
1997	0.34	0.30	0.25	0.23
1998	----------------	1.78	----------------	
1999	0.47	0.44	0.41	0.49
2000	0.50	0.41	0.43	0.11

INTERIM DIVIDENDS (Per Share):

Amt.	Decl.	Ex.	Rec.	Pay.
0.125Q	4/18/00	6/07/00	6/09/00	6/30/00
0.125Q	8/07/00	9/06/00	9/08/00	9/29/00
0.125Q	10/10/00	12/05/00	12/07/00	12/28/00
0.125Q	2/13/01	3/07/01	3/09/01	3/30/01
0.125Q	4/17/01	6/06/01	6/08/01	6/29/01

Indicated div.: $0.50 (Div. Reinv. Plan)

CAPITALIZATION (12/31/00):

	($000)	(%)
Long-Term Debt	17,514,000	55.6
Preferred Stock	247,000	0.8
Common & Surplus	13,716,000	43.6
Total	31,477,000	100.0

RECENT DEVELOPMENTS: For the year ended 12/31/00, income from continuing operations was $1.29 billion compared with $1.74 billion a year earlier. Results for 2000 included asset write-down and merger-related costs of $401.0 million associated with the proposed WorldCom merger, which has been terminated. Net operating revenues rose 3.1% to $17.69 billion from $17.16 billion in 1999.

PROSPECTS: FON's near-term prospects are likely to be restrained by higher bad debt expense due to bankruptcies by wholesale customers and less-than-anticipated results from the Company's recently launched Web hosting and related professional services business, which FON attributed to a near-term deceleration in overall market demand.

BUSINESS

SPRINT CORPORATION is a global telecommunications company that provides long distance, local, wireless, internet and other communications-related services. Its principal businesses are divided into two groups: The FON Group, comprised of Sprint's wireline telecommunications operations, including long distance and local telephone, and its product distribution and directory publishing businesses; and the PCS Group, which consists of Sprint's wireless personal communications services operations. The Company has more than $23.00 billion combined annual revenues and serves more than 20.0 million business and residential customers worldwide.

REVENUES

(12/31/2000)	($000)	(%)
FON Group	17,688	74.9
PCS Group	6,341	26.9
Inter Group Eliminations	(416)	(1.8)
Total	23,613	100.0

ANNUAL FINANCIAL DATA

	12/31/00	12/31/99	12/31/98	12/31/97	12/31/96	12/31/95	12/31/94
Earnings Per Share	**6 1.45**	**5 1.97**	**4 1.78**	**1 1.09**	**2 1.40**	**3 1.35**	**1 1.27**
Cash Flow Per Share	**4.04**	**4.36**	**4.14**	**3.07**	**3.26**	**3.44**	**3.38**
Tang. Book Val. Per Share	**12.65**	**11.59**	**12.59**	**10.49**	**9.90**	**6.65**	**5.48**
Dividends Per Share	**0.50**	**0.50**	**0.50**	**0.50**	**0.50**	**0.50**	**0.50**
Dividend Payout %	**34.5**	**25.4**	**28.1**	**46.1**	**35.8**	**37.2**	**39.5**
INCOME STATEMENT (IN MILLIONS):							
Total Revenues	17,688.0	17,016.0	16,016.9	14,873.9	14,044.7	12,765.1	12,661.8
Costs & Expenses	12,988.0	11,957.0	11,342.0	10,696.2	10,186.5	9,464.4	9,395.6
Depreciation & Amort.	2,267.0	2,129.0	1,915.1	1,726.3	1,591.0	1,466.4	1,478.4
Operating Income	2,433.0	2,930.0	2,759.8	2,451.4	2,267.2	1,834.3	1,787.8
Net Interest Inc./(Exp.)	d76.0	d182.0	d317.8	d187.2	d196.7	d260.7	d398.0
Income Before Income Taxes	2,170.0	2,797.0	2,474.1	1,583.0	1,911.9	1,480.4	1,382.1
Income Taxes	878.0	1,061.0	934.0	630.5	721.0	534.3	498.4
Equity Earnings/Minority Int.	...	...	...	d821.7	...	...	...
Net Income	6 1,292.0	5 1,736.0	4 1,540.1	1 952.5	2 1,190.9	3 946.1	1 883.7
Cash Flow	3,559.0	3,865.0	3,450.4	2,677.8	2,780.6	2,409.9	2,359.4
Average Shs. Outstg. (000)	880,900	887,000	868,900	873,000	852,000	700,200	697,400
BALANCE SHEET (IN MILLIONS):							
Cash & Cash Equivalents	122.0	104.0	432.5	101.7	1,150.6	124.2	123.3
Total Current Assets	4,512.0	4,282.0	4,042.1	3,772.6	4,352.8	3,619.4	2,188.5
Net Property	15,833.0	14,002.0	12,464.0	11,494.1	10,464.1	9,715.8	10,878.6
Total Assets	23,649.0	21,803.0	19,274.8	18,184.8	16,953.0	15,195.9	14,936.3
Total Current Liabilities	5,004.0	4,301.0	3,293.4	3,076.8	3,314.2	5,142.1	3,054.6
Long-Term Obligations	3,482.0	4,531.0	4,682.8	3,748.6	2,981.5	3,253.0	4,604.8
Net Stockholders' Equity	12,343.0	10,514.0	9,024.5	9,025.2	8,519.9	4,642.6	4,524.8
Net Working Capital	d492.0	d19.0	748.7	695.8	1,038.6	d1,522.7	d866.1
Year-end Shs. Outstg. (000)	880,900	868,000	854,000	860,000	860,200	698,400	696,600
STATISTICAL RECORD:							
Operating Profit Margin %	13.8	17.2	17.2	16.5	16.1	14.4	14.1
Net Profit Margin %	7.3	10.2	9.6	6.4	8.5	7.4	7.0
Return on Equity %	10.5	16.5	17.2	10.6	14.0	20.4	19.5
Return on Assets %	5.5	8.0	8.0	5.2	7.0	6.2	5.9
Debt/Total Assets %	14.7	20.8	24.3	20.6	17.6	21.4	30.8
Price Range	67.81-19.63	75.94-36.88	42.66-27.63	30.31-19.19	22.75-17.25	20.56-12.94	20.06-13.06
P/E Ratio	46.8-13.5	38.5-18.7	24.0-15.5	27.8-17.6	16.3-12.4	15.3-9.6	15.9-10.3
Average Yield %	1.1	0.9	1.4	2.0	2.5	3.0	3.0

Statistics are as originally reported. Refls. ops. of FON Group only as of 12/31/98. Adj. for 2-for-1 stk. split, 5/13/99 1 Incl. non-recur. cr. 12/31/97, $31.0 mil.; cr. 12/31/94, $22.0 mil. 2 Incl. non-recur. chrg. of $36.0 mil.; bef. disc. ops. cr. of $2.6 mil. & extraord. chrg. of $4.5 mil. 3 Bef. acctg. adj. chg. of $565.3 mil. & disc. ops. cr. of $14.5 mil. 4 Bef. extraord. chrg. of $5.0 mil. 5 Bef. extraord. chrg. of $39.0 mil. 6 Incl. merger-rel. costs of $401.0 mil.; bef. inc. fr. disc. ops. of $675.0 mil., extraord. loss of $1.0 mil. & acctg. chge. chrg. of $2.0 mil.

OFFICERS:
W. T. Esrey, Chmn., C.E.O.
R. T. LeMay, Pres., C.O.O.
A. B. Krause, Exec. V.P., C.F.O.

INVESTOR CONTACT: Don A. Jensen, V.P. & Sec., (913) 624-2541

PRINCIPAL OFFICE: P.O. Box 11315, Kansas City, MO 64112

TELEPHONE NUMBER: (913) 624-3000
FAX: (913) 624-3496
WEB: www.sprint.com

NO. OF EMPLOYEES: 84,100 (avg.)

SHAREHOLDERS: 71,000 (FON)

ANNUAL MEETING: In Apr.

INCORPORATED: KS, 1938

INSTITUTIONAL HOLDINGS:
No. of Institutions: 547
Shares Held: 464,911,911
% Held: 52.5

INDUSTRY: Telephone communications, exc. radio (SIC: 4813)

TRANSFER AGENT(S): UMB Bank, Kansas City, MO

NYSE SYMBOL ST
Rec. Pr. 50.30 (5/31/01)

SPS TECHNOLOGIES, INC.

YIELD	...
P/E RATIO	14.7

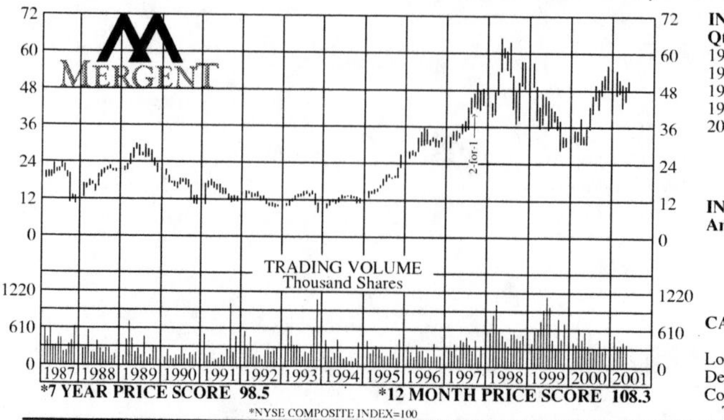

INTERIM EARNINGS (Per Share):

Qtr.	Mar.	June	Sept.	Dec.
1996	0.41	0.48	0.48	0.41
1997	0.56	0.66	0.66	0.66
1998	0.85	0.90	0.84	0.83
1999	1.02	1.00	0.95	0.98
2000	0.81	0.77	0.89	0.95

INTERIM DIVIDENDS (Per Share):

Amt.	Decl.	Ex.	Rec.	Pay.
		No dividends paid.		

CAPITALIZATION (12/31/00):

	($000)	(%)
Long-Term Debt	243,586	39.3
Deferred Income Tax	31,619	5.1
Common & Surplus	344,867	55.6
Total	620,072	100.0

RECENT DEVELOPMENTS: For the year ended 12/31/00, net income decreased 13.4% to $44.4 million compared with $51.2 million in 1999. Results for 2000 included a non-recurring after-tax charge of $3.0 million. Net sales were $872.8 million, up 10.8% from $787.7 million a year earlier. Precision Fasteners and Components net sales were up 11.9% to $606.9 million, while Specialty Materials and Alloys net sales advanced 18.9% to $127.4 million.

PROSPECTS: On 3/29/01, the Company announced that it has approved the purchase of an additional vacuum induction melting furnace to expand the production capacity of its Cannon-Muskegon subsidiary. The new furnace will add 5.0 million pounds of alloy production capacity, an increase of 56.0%. The capacity expansion is in response to continued growth in the aerospace and industrial gas turbine markets in North America, Europe and Asia.

BUSINESS

SPS TECHNOLOGIES INC. designs, manufactures and markets fasteners, specialty materials, magnetic products, aerospace structures and precision tools. The Company is multinational in operation. In addition to 24 manufacturing plants in the U.S. as of 12/31/00, ST operates 18 manufacturing facilities in seven different countries: England, Ireland, Canada, Brazil, Australia, Italy and France. The Company also has a 55.0% interest in a manufacturing operation in China and a minority interest in a manufacturing operation in India. Marketing operations are carried on by subsidiaries in four other countries.

ANNUAL FINANCIAL DATA

	12/31/00	12/31/99	12/31/98	12/31/97	12/31/96	12/31/95	12/31/94
Earnings Per Share	**2 3.42**	**3.95**	**3.42**	**2.54**	**1.77**	**1.25**	**1 0.31**
Cash Flow Per Share	**6.25**	**6.55**	**5.68**	**4.34**	**3.27**	**2.48**	**1.58**
Tang. Book Val. Per Share	**26.98**	**24.17**	**21.02**	**17.36**	**14.80**	**12.44**	**11.01**
INCOME STATEMENT (IN THOUSANDS):							
Total Revenues	872,752	787,661	716,605	588,616	485,903	409,814	348,905
Costs & Expenses	752,628	663,211	607,942	507,455	428,823	369,074	327,864
Depreciation & Amort.	36,736	33,615	29,329	23,083	18,902	14,730	13,063
Operating Income	83,388	90,835	79,334	58,078	38,178	26,010	7,978
Net Interest Inc./(Exp.)	d19,813	d13,593	d9,913	d7,996	d7,368	d5,963	d6,484
Income Before Income Taxes	64,079	74,820	66,570	49,300	31,050	21,275	6,120
Income Taxes	19,700	23,600	22,000	16,800	8,750	6,400	2,920
Equity Earnings/Minority Int.	...	d2,128	d2,965	6	753	1,701	1,726
Net Income	2 44,379	51,220	44,570	32,500	22,300	14,875	1 3,200
Cash Flow	81,115	84,835	73,899	55,583	41,202	29,605	16,263
Average Shs. Outstg.	12,971	12,955	13,019	12,796	12,596	11,916	10,264
BALANCE SHEET (IN THOUSANDS):							
Cash & Cash Equivalents	31,933	50,479	8,414	18,659	33,310	8,093	9,472
Total Current Assets	349,611	333,149	271,940	226,888	231,776	179,338	160,351
Net Property	228,632	221,147	207,800	172,599	148,616	112,738	87,764
Total Assets	810,522	700,964	607,235	472,048	428,000	322,087	289,246
Total Current Liabilities	162,654	142,770	137,913	120,503	105,457	77,431	71,860
Long-Term Obligations	243,586	201,895	154,010	95,507	98,838	58,119	56,426
Net Stockholders' Equity	344,867	305,039	266,800	214,790	177,596	145,649	124,104
Net Working Capital	186,957	190,379	134,027	106,385	126,319	101,907	88,491
Year-end Shs. Outstg.	12,783	12,620	12,693	12,372	12,002	11,704	11,272
STATISTICAL RECORD:							
Operating Profit Margin %	9.6	11.5	11.1	9.9	7.9	6.3	2.3
Net Profit Margin %	5.1	6.5	6.2	5.5	4.6	3.6	0.9
Return on Equity %	12.9	16.8	16.7	15.1	12.6	10.2	2.6
Return on Assets %	5.5	7.3	7.3	6.9	5.2	4.6	1.1
Debt/Total Assets %	30.1	28.8	25.4	20.2	23.1	18.0	19.5
Price Range	56.19-30.38	57.00-28.38	65.00-37.00	50.56-29.19	35.63-25.63	26.88-12.69	13.69-9.38
P/E Ratio	16.4-8.9	14.4-7.2	19.0-10.8	19.9-11.5	20.1-14.5	21.5-10.1	44.1-30.2

Statistics are as originally reported. Adj. for stk. split: 2-for-1, 8/97. 1 Incl. one-time chrg. of $3.5 mill. 2 Incl. nonrecurr. after-tax chrg. of $3.0 mill.

OFFICERS:
C. W. Grigg, Chmn., C.E.O., Pres.
J. S. Thompson, Pres., C.O.O.
W. M. Shockley, V.P., C.F.O.
J. D. Dee, V.P., Gen. Couns., Sec.

INVESTOR CONTACT: Investor Relations, (215) 517-2000

PRINCIPAL OFFICE: Two Pitcairn Place, Ste. 200, 165 Township Line Road, Jenkintown, PA 19046

TELEPHONE NUMBER: (215) 517-2000
FAX: (215) 517-2032
WEB: www.spstech.com

NO. OF EMPLOYEES: 6,740 (approx.)

SHAREHOLDERS: 884 (approx.)

ANNUAL MEETING: In Apr.

INCORPORATED: PA, 1903

INSTITUTIONAL HOLDINGS:
No. of Institutions: 97
Shares Held: 8,057,870
% Held: 61.6

INDUSTRY: Bolts, nuts, rivets, and washers (SIC: 3452)

TRANSFER AGENT(S): Mellon Investor Services, L.L.C., Ridgefield Park, NJ

NYSE SYMBOL SPW
Rec. Pr. 112.61 (4/30/01)

SPX CORPORATION

YIELD	...
P/E RATIO	18.1

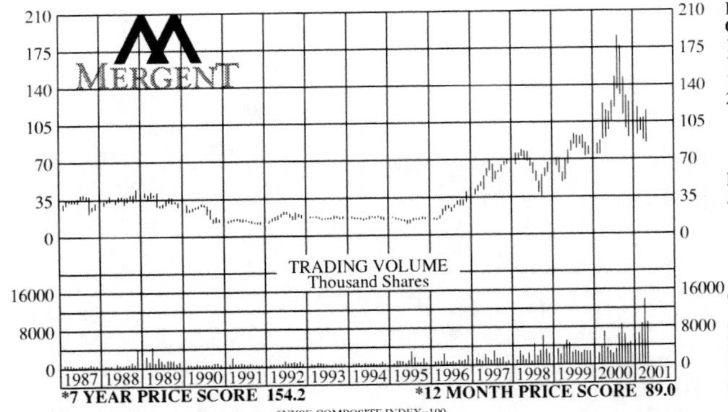

*7 YEAR PRICE SCORE 154.2 *12 MONTH PRICE SCORE 89.0
*NYSE COMPOSITE INDEX=100

INTERIM EARNINGS (Per Share):

Qtr.	Mar.	June	Sept.	Dec.
1997	2.39	0.88	0.80	d4.77
1998	1.54	0.78	0.94	d3.99
1999	1.01	1.34	1.40	d0.49
2000	1.20	1.53	1.94	1.56

INTERIM DIVIDENDS (Per Share):

Amt.	Decl.	Ex.	Rec.	Pay.

No dividends paid.

CAPITALIZATION (12/31/00):

	($000)	(%)
Long-Term Debt	1,295,600	55.5
Deferred Income Tax	403,400	17.3
Minority Interest	28,200	1.2
Common & Surplus	608,200	26.0
Total	2,335,400	100.0

RECENT DEVELOPMENTS: For the year ended 12/31/00, income was $198.3 million versus $107.5 million in 1999. Results for 2000 included after-tax gains totaling $71.6 million mainly due to an initial public offering. The 2000 results also included after-tax restructuring and special charges of $61.0 million. The 1999 results included pre-tax special charges of $38.4 million. Total revenues slipped 1.2% to $2.68 billion.

PROSPECTS: On 4/24/01, the Company announced that it completed the acquisition of United Dominion Industries Limited, a manufacturer of proprietary engineered products. The all-stock transaction was valued at $1.83 billion, including the assumption of United Dominion's debt. Separately, SPW announced that it sold the assets of its GS Electric business to AMETEK, Inc. for approximately $32.0 million in cash.

BUSINESS

SPX CORPORATION is a provider of industrial products and services, technical products and systems, service applications and vehicle components. The Industrial Products and Services segment designs, manufactures and markets industrial valves, mixers, power transformers, electric motors, laboratory and industrial freezers and ovens, material handling systems and electric motors. The Technical Products and Systems segment designs, manufactures and markets fire detection and building life-safety systems, networking and switching products, broadcast transmission systems and fare collection systems. The Service Solutions segment designs, manufactures and markets a wide range of specialty service tools, equipment and services. The Vehicle Components segment designs, manufactures and markets transmission and steering and suspension components. SPW acquired General Signal Corp. on 10/6/98 and United Dominion Industries Ltd. on 4/24/01.

ANNUAL FINANCIAL DATA

	12/31/00	12/31/99	12/31/98	12/31/97	12/31/96	12/31/95	12/31/94
Earnings Per Share	[7] 6.25	[6] 3.46	[5] d1.94	[4] d0.27	[3] d3.98	[1] d0.10	[2] 1.10
Cash Flow Per Share	9.74	6.86	1.29	1.69	d1.06	3.20	4.11
Tang. Book Val. Per Share	...	...	...	...	3.20	...	...
Dividends Per Share	...	...	...	0.10	0.40	0.40	0.40
Dividend Payout %	...	...	...	...	...	...	36.4
INCOME STATEMENT (IN MILLIONS):							
Total Revenues	2,678.9	2,712.3	[6] 1,825.4	922.3	1,109.4	1,098.1	1,092.7
Costs & Expenses	2,201.0	2,255.1	1,693.8	822.8	1,003.1	1,013.3	994.3
Depreciation & Amort.	110.9	105.4	69.4	25.0	40.8	43.5	38.5
Operating Income	276.1	313.4	d39.5	d42.4	d17.0	31.1	64.8
Net Interest Inc./(Exp.)	d95.0	d117.6	d45.1	d14.0	d31.8	d35.7	d40.9
Income Before Income Taxes	335.6	294.8	d44.9	17.9	d48.0	d1.6	23.9
Income Taxes	137.3	187.3	cr3.2	21.3	7.6	cr0.2	9.8
Equity Earnings/Minority Int.	34.3	34.7	40.2	d0.4	5.3	0.6	4.9
Net Income	[7] 198.3	[6] 107.5	[5] d41.7	[4] d3.4	[3] d55.6	[1] d1.4	[2] 14.1
Cash Flow	309.2	212.9	27.7	21.6	d14.9	42.2	52.6
Average Shs. Outstg. (000)	31,751	31,055	21,546	12,754	13,998	13,174	12,805
BALANCE SHEET (IN MILLIONS):							
Cash & Cash Equivalents	73.7	78.8	70.3	12.1	12.3	17.1	9.9
Total Current Assets	1,062.9	976.5	975.7	383.5	408.1	363.5	406.3
Net Property	492.0	444.7	433.1	122.1	123.9	213.0	214.9
Total Assets	3,164.6	2,846.0	2,968.3	583.8	616.0	831.4	931.7
Total Current Liabilities	637.1	754.9	679.4	240.7	174.4	211.0	221.9
Long-Term Obligations	1,295.6	1,017.0	1,466.5	202.5	227.9	318.9	414.1
Net Stockholders' Equity	608.2	552.3	390.5	d43.3	105.9	162.2	162.0
Net Working Capital	425.8	221.6	296.3	142.8	233.7	152.5	184.4
Year-end Shs. Outstg. (000)	30,322	31,473	30,075	12,531	14,764	14,315	14,015
STATISTICAL RECORD:							
Operating Profit Margin %	10.3	11.6	...	...	...	2.8	5.9
Net Profit Margin %	7.4	4.0	...	...	...	...	1.3
Return on Equity %	32.6	19.5	...	...	...	...	8.7
Return on Assets %	6.3	3.8	...	...	...	...	1.5
Price Range	186.00-74.00	94.00-48.75	79.25-36.06	70.63-37.38	40.50-13.63	17.38-10.75	18.50-13.88
P/E Ratio	29.8-11.8	27.2-14.1	...	...	...	...	16.8-12.6
Average Yield %	...	...	...	0.2	1.5	2.8	2.5

Statistics are as originally reported. [1] Bef. disc. opers. loss $4.2 mil; non-recurr. chg. $7.0 mil & bef. extraord. chg. $1.1 mil [2] Incl. non-recurr gain $1.3 mil [3] Inc. after-tax restr. chg. & writeoff $87.9 mil & bef. extraord. loss $6.63 mil [4] Bef. after-tax extraord. chrg $10.3 mil & incl. spl. chg. & write-off $116.5 mil [5] Incl. spl. chgs. of $101.7 mil [6] Bef. net extraord. chg. of $6.0 mil & incl. spl. chgs. of $38.4 mil [7] Bef. extraord. chg. of $8.8 mil & incl. net gain of $71.6 mil & spl. chg. $61.0 mil

OFFICERS:
J. B. Blystone, Chmn., Pres., C.E.O.
P. J. O'Leary, V.P., Fin., C.F.O., Treas.

INVESTOR CONTACT: Charles Bowman, Dir. of Corp. Fin., (231) 724-5194

PRINCIPAL OFFICE: 700 Terrace Point Drive, Muskegon, MI 49443-3301

TELEPHONE NUMBER: (231) 724-5000
FAX: (231) 724-5720
WEB: www.spx.com
NO. OF EMPLOYEES: 14,000 (approx.)
SHAREHOLDERS: 5,664 (approx. record)
ANNUAL MEETING: In Apr.
INCORPORATED: MI, Jan., 1911; reincorp., DE, Apr., 1968

INSTITUTIONAL HOLDINGS:
No. of Institutions: 237
Shares Held: 27,327,398
% Held: 89.7

INDUSTRY: Machine tools, metal cutting types (SIC: 3541)

TRANSFER AGENT(S): First Chicago Trust Company, c/o EquiServe, Jersey City, NJ

NYSE SYMBOL STW
Rec. Pr. 14.75 (4/30/01)

STANDARD COMMERCIAL CORP.

YIELD 1.4%
P/E RATIO 11.6

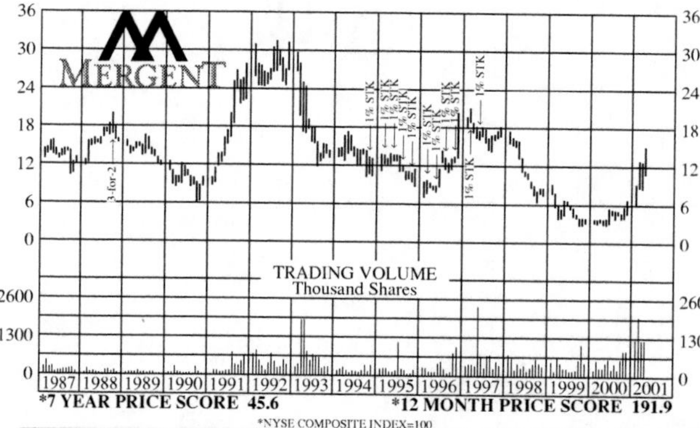

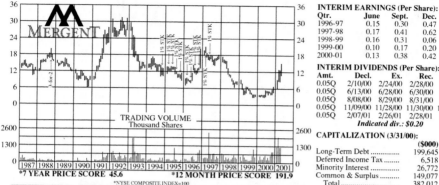

INTERIM EARNINGS (Per Share):

Qtr.	June	Sept.	Dec.	Mar.
1996-97	0.15	0.30	0.47	0.85
1997-98	0.17	0.41	0.62	0.79
1998-99	0.16	0.31	0.06	0.13
1999-00	0.10	0.17	0.20	0.34
2000-01	0.13	0.38	0.42	...

INTERIM DIVIDENDS (Per Share):

Amt.	Decl.	Ex.	Rec.	Pay.
0.05Q	2/10/00	2/24/00	2/28/00	3/15/00
0.05Q	6/13/00	6/28/00	6/30/00	6/17/00
0.05Q	8/08/00	8/29/00	8/31/00	9/15/00
0.05Q	11/09/00	11/28/00	11/30/00	12/15/00
0.05Q	2/07/01	2/26/01	2/28/01	3/15/01

Indicated div.: $0.20

CAPITALIZATION (3/31/00):

	($000)	(%)
Long-Term Debt	199,645	52.3
Deferred Income Tax	6,518	1.7
Minority Interest	26,772	7.0
Common & Surplus	149,077	39.0
Total	382,012	100.0

RECENT DEVELOPMENTS: For the quarter ended 12/31/00, STW posted income of $5.7 million, before an extraordinary gain of $1.4 million, versus net income of $2.5 million in 1999. Results for 2000 included after-tax write-downs of $5.5 million related to the termination of STW's Tanzania operations. Total sales gained 37.0% to $380.8 million. Tobacco sales rose 43.4% to $317.9 million due to volume gains in tobacco processed in the U.S., Brazil, Russia and Thailand. Nontobacco sales rose 12.0% to $62.9 million.

PROSPECTS: Near-term prospects are positive. According to the Company, its facility in Russia continues to operate at near capacity and STW had a very strong flue-cured season in the U.S. market. Additionally, the installation of the second processing line in the Company's Brazilian factory is on schedule and should help it meet increased customer demand. Meanwhile, the Company's wool business should continue to recover, helped by improving supply/demand conditions.

BUSINESS

STANDARD COMMERCIAL CORP. is primarily engaged in the purchasing, processing and selling of leaf tobacco and wool. STW's tobacco operations consist of purchasing and processing tobacco of all types and origins, and selling to domestic and international manufacturers of cigarettes, cigars and other tobacco products. The Company's nontobacco operations is comprised of STW's wool operations, which consists of an integrated group of wool companies that purchase, process, and sell wool to topmakers and spinners of yarn for use in the manufacture of worsted and woolen products.

REVENUES

(03/31/00)	($000)	(%)
Tobacco	882,648	79.8
Non-tobacco	223,078	20.8
Total	1,105,726	100.0

ANNUAL FINANCIAL DATA

	3/31/00	3/31/99	3/31/98	3/31/97	[1] 3/31/96	[3] 3/31/95	3/31/94
Earnings Per Share	**0.80**	**0.66**	**2.05**	**1.76**	[2] **d1.06**	[4] **d3.08**	[4] [5] **d3.95**
Cash Flow Per Share	**2.07**	**2.09**	**3.22**	**3.98**	**1.54**	**d1.85**	**d2.22**
Tang. Book Val. Per Share	**11.48**	**11.69**	**11.68**	**9.34**	**6.69**	**7.78**	**10.96**
Dividends Per Share	**0.20**	**0.10**	...	...	...	**0.27**	**0.49**
Dividend Payout %	**25.0**	**15.1**	...	...	...	...	...
INCOME STATEMENT (IN MILLIONS):							
Total Revenues	1,105.7	1,102.8	1,492.8	1,354.3	1,359.5	773.5	1,042.0
Costs & Expenses	1,058.0	1,063.5	1,429.4	1,301.5	1,334.7	771.0	1,053.8
Depreciation & Amort.	21.3	23.3	20.5	20.9	24.4	11.3	16.3
Operating Income	26.4	16.0	42.9	31.9	0.4	d8.8	d28.0
Net Interest Inc./(Exp.)	d11.0	d13.6	d15.2	d9.9	d9.6	...	...
Income Before Income Taxes	20.4	15.1	37.1	32.2	2.3	...	d24.4
Income Taxes	10.7	7.3	8.8	12.8	6.8	13.6	5.1
Equity Earnings/Minority Int.	0.6	0.6	d1.4	d2.5	d4.9	d14.3	d7.0
Net Income	10.3	8.4	26.9	16.9	[2] d9.4	[4] d27.9	[4] [5] d36.5
Cash Flow	31.7	31.7	47.4	37.5	14.5	d17.1	d20.7
Average Shs. Outstg. (000)	15,305	15,191	14,726	9,407	9,400	9,236	9,349
BALANCE SHEET (IN MILLIONS):							
Cash & Cash Equivalents	38.9	44.4	34.8	42.0	84.0	47.2	70.6
Total Current Assets	611.9	655.6	659.3	571.3	599.6	456.4	710.5
Net Property	146.6	155.4	113.6	122.0	134.5	99.1	128.0
Total Assets	820.8	878.4	839.5	735.7	782.8	608.4	890.8
Total Current Liabilities	418.3	456.8	440.2	451.2	543.8	383.5	640.0
Long-Term Obligations	199.6	213.2	197.1	139.3	100.8	95.9	98.2
Net Stockholders' Equity	149.1	151.0	149.6	90.0	80.2	73.1	102.6
Net Working Capital	193.6	198.8	219.1	120.1	55.8	72.9	70.5
Year-end Shs. Outstg. (000)	12,988	12,922	12,807	9,629	11,976	9,394	9,365
STATISTICAL RECORD:							
Operating Profit Margin %	2.4	1.5	2.9	2.4	...	...	...
Net Profit Margin %	0.9	0.8	1.8	1.3	...	...	...
Return on Equity %	6.9	5.6	18.0	18.8	...	...	...
Return on Assets %	1.3	1.0	3.2	2.3	...	...	...
Debt/Total Assets %	24.3	24.3	23.5	18.9	12.9	15.8	11.0
Price Range	9.25-2.75	17.50-6.38	21.08-14.25	20.34-7.07	13.97-8.71	17.31-10.19	29.76-11.77
P/E Ratio	11.6-3.4	26.5-9.7	10.3-7.0	11.5-4.0	...	...	...
Average Yield %	3.3	0.8	...	...	...	2.0	2.4

Statistics are as originally reported. Adj. for all stk. splits & divs. thru 6/97. [1] Refls. reinstat. of wool bus. as cont. ops. [2] Incls. non-recurr. chrg. of $12.5 mill.; bef. revers. of $10.1 mill. in provs. [3] Refls. wool. bus. as disc. ops. [4] Bef. disc. ops. loss 3/31/95, $10.1 mill.; income 3/31/94, $689,000 [5] Bef. acctg. adj. credit of $23,000

OFFICERS:
J. A. Murray, Chmn.
R. E. Harrison, Pres., C.E.O.
R. A. Sheets, V.P., C.F.O.

INVESTOR CONTACT: Henry C. Babb, V.P., Gen. Couns. & Sec., (252) 291-5507

PRINCIPAL OFFICE: 2201 Miller Road, Wilson, NC 27893

TELEPHONE NUMBER: (252) 291-5507
FAX: (252) 237-0018
WEB: www.sccgroup.com
NO. OF EMPLOYEES: 2,768 (approx.)
SHAREHOLDERS: 628
ANNUAL MEETING: In Aug.
INCORPORATED: NY, 1913; reincorp., NC, Mar., 1913

INSTITUTIONAL HOLDINGS:
No. of Institutions: 28
Shares Held: 7,738,924
% Held: 58.4

INDUSTRY: Farm-product raw materials, nec (SIC: 5159)

TRANSFER AGENT(S): First Union National Bank, Charlotte, NC

NYSE SYMBOL SMP
Rec. Pr. 13.50 (5/31/01)

STANDARD MOTOR PRODUCTS, INC.

YIELD 2.7%
P/E RATIO 17.1

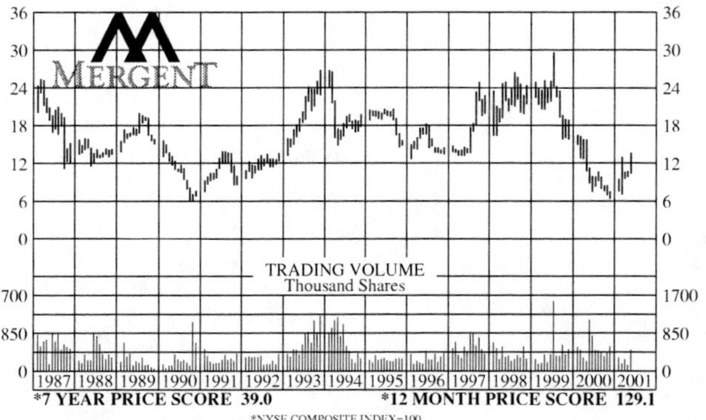

*7 YEAR PRICE SCORE 39.0 *12 MONTH PRICE SCORE 129.1

*NYSE COMPOSITE INDEX=100

INTERIM EARNINGS (Per Share):

Qtr.	Mar.	June	Sept.	Dec.
1996	0.33	0.46	0.27	0.06
1997	d0.07	0.50	0.60	d1.07
1998	0.20	0.65	0.72	0.11
1999	0.28	0.91	0.74	d1.36
2000	0.03	0.54	0.40	d0.18

INTERIM DIVIDENDS (Per Share):

Amt.	Decl.	Ex.	Rec.	Pay.
0.09Q	4/14/00	5/11/00	5/15/00	6/01/00
0.09Q	7/20/00	8/11/00	8/15/00	9/01/00
0.09Q	10/19/00	11/13/00	11/15/00	12/01/00
0.09Q	12/22/00	2/13/01	2/15/01	3/01/01
0.09Q	4/26/01	5/11/01	5/15/01	6/01/01

Indicated div.: $0.36

CAPITALIZATION (12/31/00):

	($000)	(%)
Long-Term Debt	150,018	43.6
Common & Surplus	194,305	56.4
Total	344,323	100.0

RECENT DEVELOPMENTS: For the year ended 12/31/00, the Company reported income from continuing operations of $10.2 million, versus income from continuing operations of $8.7 million in the previous year. Net sales declined 7.9% to $606.5 million compared with $658.2 million in the prior year. The decrease in net sales was attributed to weak performance from the temperature control segment. Operating income was $30.7 million, up 3.8% versus $29.5 million in 1999.

PROSPECTS: SMP's main objective for 2001 is to significantly reduce inventory levels, which during 2000 increased about $46.0 million over 1999 levels, due to the sales shortfall in the temperature control segment and the build-up in the engine management segment for a major new account. Separately, net sales in 2001 should benefit from the recovery of a lost account and the completion of customer inventory reductions. However, net sales may continue to be hampered by poor weather conditions.

BUSINESS

STANDARD MOTOR PRODUCTS, INC. manufactures and distributes replacement parts for motor vehicles. The engine management division manufactures replacement parts for automotive ignition and emission control systems including distributor caps and rotors, electric ignition modules, voltage regulators, coils, switches, sensors and EGR valves. The temperature control division manufactures, re-manufactures and markets replacement parts for temperature control systems including compressors, small motors, fan clutches, dryers, evaporators, accumulators and hoses, heating cores and valves. The Company distributes parts under the brand names STANDARD, BLUE STREAK, HYGRADE, CHAMP, FOUR SEASONS, EIS, and GPSORENSEN throughout the U.S. and foreign countries. SPW operates more than 20 distribution and manufacturing facilities throughout the U.S., Puerto Rico, Canada, Europe, and the Far East.

REVENUES

(12/31/00)	($000)	(%)
Engine Management	297,386	49.0
Temperature Control	267,145	44.1
All Other	41,919	6.9
Total	606,450	100.0

ANNUAL FINANCIAL DATA

	12/31/00	12/31/99	12/31/98	12/31/97	12/31/96	12/31/95	12/31/94
Earnings Per Share	[3] **0.85**	[2] **0.66**	**1.69**	[1] **d0.12**	**1.12**	**1.23**	**1.80**
Cash Flow Per Share	**2.43**	**1.97**	**3.00**	**1.32**	**2.36**	**2.27**	**2.73**
Tang. Book Val. Per Share	**13.14**	**12.72**	**12.70**	**11.71**	**13.89**	**15.33**	**14.34**
Dividends Per Share	**0.36**	**0.34**	**0.16**	**0.32**	**0.32**	**0.32**	**0.32**
Dividend Payout %	**42.3**	**51.5**	**9.5**	**...**	**28.6**	**26.0**	**17.8**
INCOME STATEMENT (IN THOUSANDS):							
Total Revenues	606,450	658,241	649,420	559,823	721,805	663,485	640,810
Costs & Expenses	556,864	611,467	588,215	531,388	668,650	617,325	582,083
Depreciation & Amort.	18,922	17,230	17,274	18,980	16,326	13,680	12,278
Operating Income	30,664	29,544	43,931	9,455	36,829	32,480	46,449
Net Interest Inc./(Exp.)	d18,045	d15,951	d16,419	d14,158	d18,795	d14,618	d12,288
Income Before Income Taxes	13,116	12,386	26,090	d3,705	19,845	20,291	35,397
Income Taxes	2,886	3,344	3,577	cr2,417	5,100	4,159	11,732
Equity Earnings/Minority Int.	...	d357	d256	d332	1,249	1,700	828
Net Income	[3] 10,230	[2] 8,685	22,257	[1] d1,620	14,658	16,132	23,665
Cash Flow	29,152	25,915	39,531	17,360	30,984	29,812	35,943
Average Shs. Outstg.	11,974	13,146	13,168	13,119	13,131	13,126	13,165
BALANCE SHEET (IN THOUSANDS):							
Cash & Cash Equivalents	7,699	40,380	23,457	16,809	4,666	17,528	8,814
Total Current Assets	372,759	374,693	342,511	390,476	418,470	374,539	328,877
Net Property	104,536	106,578	109,404	126,024	126,919	109,537	104,126
Total Assets	549,396	556,021	521,556	577,137	624,806	521,230	462,351
Total Current Liabilities	184,668	168,887	164,187	213,050	206,744	142,366	139,670
Long-Term Obligations	150,018	163,868	133,749	159,109	172,387	148,665	109,927
Net Stockholders' Equity	194,305	203,518	205,025	183,782	223,340	210,400	195,089
Net Working Capital	188,091	205,806	178,324	177,426	211,726	232,173	189,207
Year-end Shs. Outstg.	11,695	12,726	13,056	13,077	13,130	13,128	13,121
STATISTICAL RECORD:							
Operating Profit Margin %	5.1	4.5	6.8	1.7	5.1	4.9	7.2
Net Profit Margin %	1.7	1.3	3.4	...	2.0	2.4	3.7
Return on Equity %	5.3	4.3	10.9	...	6.6	7.7	12.1
Return on Assets %	1.9	1.6	4.3	...	2.3	3.1	5.1
Debt/Total Assets %	27.3	29.5	25.6	27.6	27.6	28.5	23.8
Price Range	16.50-6.38	29.63-15.75	26.50-16.31	25.00-13.13	18.25-12.63	20.63-14.50	26.88-14.75
P/E Ratio	19.4-7.5	44.9-23.9	15.7-9.7	...	16.3-11.3	16.8-11.8	14.9-8.2
Average Yield %	3.1	1.5	0.7	1.7	2.1	1.8	1.5

Statistics are as originally reported. [1] Bef. $15.1 mill. loss on disc. opers of brake group and $17.8 mill. on disc. opers. of line group. [2] Bef. after-tax extraord. chrg. of $707,000 & incl. non-recurr. chrgs. of $9.1 mill. [3] Bef. after-tax extraord. chrg. of $501,000.

OFFICERS:
L. I. Sills, Chmn., C.E.O.
J. Gethin, Pres., C.O.O.
J. J. Burke, V.P., C.F.O.

INVESTOR CONTACT: J. J. Burke, (718) 392-0200

PRINCIPAL OFFICE: 37-18 Northern Blvd., Long Island City, NY 11101

TELEPHONE NUMBER: (718) 392-0200
FAX: (718) 472-0122
WEB: www.smpcorp.com

NO. OF EMPLOYEES: 3,400 (approx.)

SHAREHOLDERS: 583 (approx. record)

ANNUAL MEETING: In May

INCORPORATED: NY, Dec., 1926

INSTITUTIONAL HOLDINGS:
No. of Institutions: 41
Shares Held: 5,871,784
% Held: 47.2

INDUSTRY: Engine electrical equipment (SIC: 3694)

TRANSFER AGENT(S): Registrar and Transfer Co., Cranford, NJ

NYSE SYMBOL SXI
Rec. Pr. 22.10 (5/31/01)

STANDEX INTERNATIONAL CORPORATION

YIELD 3.8%
P/E RATIO 10.9

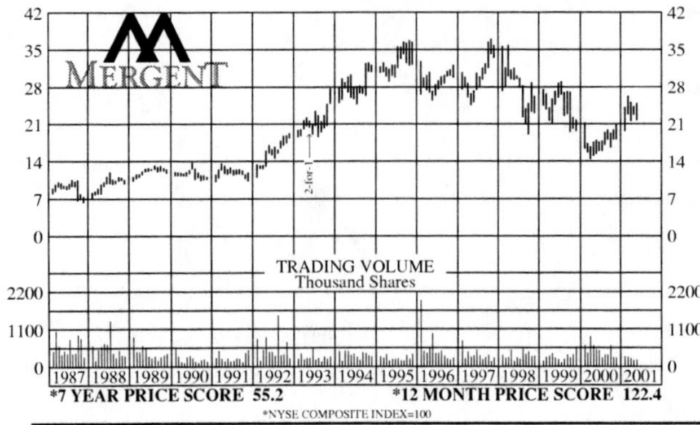

*7 YEAR PRICE SCORE 55.2 *12 MONTH PRICE SCORE 122.4

*NYSE COMPOSITE INDEX=100

INTERIM EARNINGS (Per Share):

Qtr.	Sept.	Dec.	Mar.	June
1996-97	0.56	0.60	0.31	0.53
1997-98	0.58	0.63	0.38	d0.07
1998-99	0.61	0.72	0.51	0.57
1999-00	0.74	0.59	0.51	0.33
2000-01	0.57	0.61	...	...

INTERIM DIVIDENDS (Per Share):

Amt.	Decl.	Ex.	Rec.	Pay.
0.20Q	4/26/00	5/04/00	5/08/00	5/25/00
0.20Q	7/26/00	8/03/00	8/07/00	8/25/00
0.21Q	10/31/00	11/08/00	11/10/00	11/25/00
0.21Q	1/31/01	2/08/01	2/12/01	2/24/01
0.21Q	4/25/01	5/03/01	5/07/01	5/25/01

Indicated div.: $0.84 (Div. Reinv. Plan)

CAPITALIZATION (6/30/00):

	($000)	(%)
Long-Term Debt	153,436	45.8
Deferred Income Tax	16,610	5.0
Common & Surplus	164,815	49.2
Total	334,861	100.0

RECENT DEVELOPMENTS: For the quarter ended 12/31/00, net income was essentially flat at $7.6 million compared with the corresponding period of the previous year. Net sales decreased 2.7% to $158.7 million from $163.1 million the year before. Industrial revenues fell 7.3% to $61.7 million. Consumer revenues slipped 3.8% to $60.1 million, while food service revenues improved 8.2% to $36.9 million.

PROSPECTS: In 2001, the Company anticipates sales declines across most of its business units, reflecting the slowdown in the world economic markets, as well as shipment delays from its customers. As a result, the Company will take the necessary actions to mitigate these effects. Meanwhile, SXI will focus on investing in its technology, improving productivity, maintaining its strong backlog position, and pursuing strategic acquisitions.

BUSINESS

STANDEX INTERNATIONAL CORPORATION is a diversified manufacturing and marketing company, with operations in the U.S., Western Europe, Canada, Australia, Singapore and Mexico. SXI also operates retail stores in various sections of the U.S. SXI operates in three business segments: Industrial Products, which include rotary pumps, hydraulic equipment, texturization and engraving operations; Consumer Products, which targets consumers in niche markets through publishing, retailing, direct marketing and products used in home construction; and Food Service Products, which include ready-to-eat meals-to-go from BKI in the U.S. and Barbecue King in the U.K., as well as commercial food preparation equipment.

BUSINESS LINE ANALYSIS

(06/30/2000)	Rev(%)	Inc(%)
Food Service	22.7	17.5
Consumer	34.6	36.7
Industrial	42.7	45.8
Total	100.0	100.0

ANNUAL FINANCIAL DATA

	6/30/00	6/30/99	6/30/98	6/30/97	6/30/96	6/30/95	6/30/94
Earnings Per Share	**[2][4] 2.17**	**[2][3] 2.41**	**[1] 1.52**	**[1] 2.00**	**2.21**	**[1] 2.64**	**1.78**
Cash Flow Per Share	**3.24**	**3.46**	**2.57**	**2.94**	**3.10**	**3.49**	**2.59**
Tang. Book Val. Per Share	**10.84**	**10.10**	**8.67**	**9.60**	**8.92**	**8.35**	**7.04**
Dividends Per Share	**0.81**	**0.77**	**0.76**	**0.76**	**0.73**	**0.68**	**0.57**
Dividend Payout %	**37.3**	**31.9**	**50.0**	**38.0**	**33.0**	**25.8**	**32.0**
INCOME STATEMENT (IN THOUSANDS):							
Total Revenues	637,049	641,400	618,174	565,530	563,558	570,400	531,242
Costs & Expenses	568,698	565,685	560,129	501,774	493,889	497,300	470,604
Depreciation & Amort.	13,622	13,770	13,852	12,777	12,497	12,356	12,478
Operating Income	54,729	61,944	44,193	50,978	57,171	60,744	48,160
Net Interest Inc./(Exp.)	d11,336	d11,155	d10,779	d8,497	d9,048	d8,367	d5,938
Income Before Income Taxes	46,853	51,491	33,064	43,516	48,124	57,803	42,222
Income Taxes	19,150	20,130	12,915	16,597	17,410	19,483	15,075
Net Income	[2][4] 27,703	[2][3] 31,361	[1] 20,149	[1] 26,919	30,714	[1] 38,320	27,147
Cash Flow	41,325	45,131	34,001	39,696	43,211	50,676	39,625
Average Shs. Outstg.	12,763	13,037	13,219	13,491	13,927	14,540	15,293
BALANCE SHEET (IN THOUSANDS):							
Cash & Cash Equivalents	10,438	5,909	9,256	6,149	5,147	9,543	5,023
Total Current Assets	231,386	228,509	235,230	207,086	207,392	220,347	196,953
Net Property	112,137	104,783	102,973	85,598	86,616	84,528	89,697
Total Assets	424,200	410,396	411,243	341,038	335,333	342,702	323,721
Total Current Liabilities	86,376	81,995	86,287	70,140	68,532	77,211	70,150
Long-Term Obligations	153,436	148,111	163,448	112,347	113,822	111,845	112,854
Net Stockholders' Equity	164,815	162,301	146,197	141,185	134,691	132,352	118,932
Net Working Capital	145,009	146,513	148,944	136,946	138,860	143,136	126,803
Year-end Shs. Outstg.	12,325	12,896	13,042	13,130	13,449	14,012	14,583
STATISTICAL RECORD:							
Operating Profit Margin %	8.6	9.7	7.1	9.0	10.1	10.6	9.1
Net Profit Margin %	4.3	4.9	3.3	4.8	5.4	6.7	5.1
Return on Equity %	16.8	19.3	13.8	19.1	22.8	29.0	22.8
Return on Assets %	6.5	7.6	4.9	7.9	9.2	11.2	8.4
Debt/Total Assets %	36.2	36.1	39.7	32.9	33.9	32.6	34.9
Price Range	21.25-14.34	29.00-19.50	35.88-19.00	37.00-24.50	32.88-25.38	36.75-29.00	32.63-24.63
P/E Ratio	9.8-6.6	12.0-8.1	23.6-12.5	18.5-12.2	14.9-11.5	13.9-11.0	18.3-13.8
Average Yield %	4.6	3.2	2.8	2.5	2.5	2.1	2.0

Statistics are as originally reported. Adj. for 2-for-1 split, 5/93. [1] Incl. net gain/loss on disposition of bus. & prod.: d$350,000, 6/98; cr$1.0 mill., 6/97; cr$5.4 mill., 6/95. [2] Incl. restruct. chrg. of $4.4 mill., 6/00; $12.8 mill., 6/99. [3] Incl. after-tax restruct. credit $589,000. [4] Incl. an after-tax unusual gain of $1.7 mill.

OFFICERS:
T. L. King, Chmn.
E. J. Trainor, Pres., C.E.O.
E. F. Paquette, V.P., C.F.O.

INVESTOR CONTACT: Edward F. Paquette, V.P., C.F.O, (603) 893-9701

PRINCIPAL OFFICE: 6 Manor Parkway, Salem, NH 03079

TELEPHONE NUMBER: (603) 893-9701
FAX: (603) 893-7324
WEB: www.standex.com

NO. OF EMPLOYEES: 5,600 (approx.)

SHAREHOLDERS: 3,200 (approx.)

ANNUAL MEETING: In Oct.

INCORPORATED: OH, Jan., 1955; reincorp., DE, May, 1975

INSTITUTIONAL HOLDINGS:
No. of Institutions: 75
Shares Held: 6,977,472
% Held: 57.4

INDUSTRY: Service industry machinery, nec (SIC: 3589)

TRANSFER AGENT(S): Fleet National Bank c/o EquiServe, Boston, MA

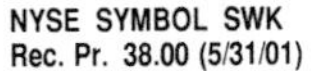

NYSE SYMBOL SWK
Rec. Pr. 38.00 (5/31/01)

STANLEY WORKS

YIELD 2.4%
P/E RATIO 17.1

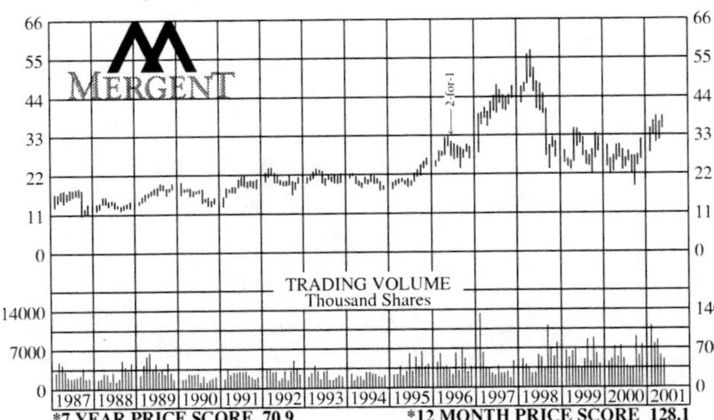

*7 YEAR PRICE SCORE 70.9 *12 MONTH PRICE SCORE 128.1

*NYSE COMPOSITE INDEX=100

INTERIM EARNINGS (Per Share):

Qtr.	Mar.	June	Sept.	Dec.
1997	0.41	d0.72	d0.46	0.29
1998	0.40	0.47	0.37	0.29
1999	0.34	0.28	0.56	0.49
2000	0.54	0.58	0.56	0.54

INTERIM DIVIDENDS (Per Share):

Amt.	Decl.	Ex.	Rec.	Pay.
0.22Q	5/30/00	6/01/00	6/05/00	6/30/00
0.23Q	7/12/00	8/31/00	9/05/00	9/26/00
0.23Q	10/18/00	11/21/00	11/24/00	12/26/00
0.23Q	1/25/01	3/01/01	3/05/01	3/23/01
0.23Q	5/24/01	5/31/01	6/04/01	6/29/01

Indicated div.: $0.92

CAPITALIZATION (12/30/00):

	($000)	(%)
Long-Term Debt	248,700	25.2
Common & Surplus	736,500	74.8
Total	985,200	100.0

RECENT DEVELOPMENTS: For the year ended 12/30/00, net income increased 29.6% to $194.4 million compared with $150.0 million in 1999. Net sales were essentially flat at $2.75 billion compared with 1999. SWK's sales growth was constrained by a weakening U.S. economy and inventory corrections by major U.S. retailers. Results for 1999 included a restructuring gain of $21.3 million. Tools segment net sales increased 1.2% to $2.14 billion. Doors segment net sales declined 4.6% to $606.4 million.

PROSPECTS: The first half of fiscal 2001 will be difficult due to the slowing economy, but if the economy rebounds in the second half and the Euro stays at its current level, SWK is predicting double-digit percentage earnings per share gains. On 1/24/01, SWK announced that it formed a strategic alliance with Wal-Mart Stores, Inc. that will significantly expand the mega-retailer's offerings of Stanley tool and toolbox products. In April 2001, SWK completed the acquisition of Contact East, a business-to-business distributor of mission-critical tools and supplies.

BUSINESS

STANLEY WORKS is a worldwide producer of tools and door products for professional, industrial and consumer use. The Tools segment manufactures and markets carpenters', mechanics', pneumatic and hydraulic tools as well as tool sets. SWK markets its carpenters' tools under the Stanley®, IntelliTools™, Contractor Grade™, and Goldblatt® brands. The Doors segment manufactures and markets commercial and residential doors as well as closet doors and systems, home decor and door and consumer hardware. Products in the Doors segment include residential insulated steel, reinforced fiberglass and wood entrance door systems. Door products are marketed under the Stanley®, Magic-Door®, Stanley-Acmetrack™, Monarch™ and Acme® brands. A substantial portion of SWK's products are sold through home centers and mass merchant distribution channels in the U.S.

ANNUAL FINANCIAL DATA

	12/30/00	1/1/00	1/2/99	1/3/98	12/28/96	12/30/95	12/31/94
Earnings Per Share	**2.22**	**3 1.67**	**2 1.53**	**1 d0.47**	**1 1.09**	**1 0.67**	**1.40**
Cash Flow Per Share	**3.17**	**2.62**	**2.41**	**0.34**	**1.93**	**1.58**	**2.31**
Tang. Book Val. Per Share	**6.58**	**6.19**	**5.32**	**5.67**	**7.68**	**6.79**	**6.52**
Dividends Per Share	**0.90**	**0.87**	**0.83**	**0.77**	**0.73**	**0.71**	**0.69**
Dividend Payout %	**40.5**	**52.1**	**54.2**	**...**	**67.0**	**106.8**	**49.3**
INCOME STATEMENT (IN MILLIONS):							
Total Revenues	2,748.9	2,751.8	2,729.1	2,669.5	2,670.8	2,624.3	2,510.9
Costs & Expenses	2,324.8	2,410.0	2,397.8	2,577.2	2,377.1	2,385.7	2,162.6
Depreciation & Amort.	83.3	85.6	79.7	72.4	74.7	81.2	81.8
Operating Income	340.8	256.2	251.6	19.9	219.0	157.4	266.5
Net Interest Inc./(Exp.)	d27.1	d27.9	d23.1	d16.6	d22.5	d30.3	d29.0
Income Before Income Taxes	293.7	230.8	215.4	d18.6	174.2	112.8	201.8
Income Taxes	99.3	80.8	77.6	23.3	77.3	53.7	76.5
Net Income	194.4	3 150.0	2 137.8	1 d41.9	1 96.9	1 59.1	125.3
Cash Flow	277.7	235.6	217.5	30.5	171.6	140.3	207.1
Average Shs. Outstg. (000)	87,668	89,887	90,193	89,469	88,824	88,720	89,550
BALANCE SHEET (IN MILLIONS):							
Cash & Cash Equivalents	93.6	88.0	110.1	152.2	84.0	75.4	69.3
Total Current Assets	1,094.3	1,091.0	1,086.4	1,005.3	910.9	915.1	888.5
Net Property	503.7	520.6	511.4	513.2	570.4	556.5	559.8
Total Assets	1,884.8	1,890.6	1,932.9	1,758.7	1,659.6	1,670.0	1,701.1
Total Current Liabilities	707.3	693.0	702.1	622.7	381.6	387.7	421.5
Long-Term Obligations	248.7	290.0	344.8	283.7	342.6	391.1	387.1
Net Stockholders' Equity	736.5	735.4	669.4	607.8	780.1	734.6	744.2
Net Working Capital	387.0	398.0	384.3	382.6	529.3	527.4	467.0
Year-end Shs. Outstg. (000)	85,188	88,945	88,772	88,788	88,720	88,758	88,898
STATISTICAL RECORD:							
Operating Profit Margin %	12.4	9.3	9.2	0.7	8.2	6.0	10.6
Net Profit Margin %	7.1	5.5	5.0	...	3.6	2.3	5.0
Return on Equity %	26.4	20.4	20.6	...	12.4	8.0	16.8
Return on Assets %	10.3	7.9	7.1	...	5.8	3.5	7.4
Debt/Total Assets %	13.2	15.3	17.8	16.1	20.6	23.4	22.8
Price Range	31.88-18.44	35.00-22.00	57.25-23.50	47.38-28.00	32.81-23.63	26.69-17.81	22.44-17.44
P/E Ratio	14.4-8.3	21.0-13.2	37.4-15.4	...	30.1-21.7	40.1-26.8	16.0-12.5
Average Yield %	3.6	3.1	2.1	2.0	2.6	3.2	3.5

Statistics are as originally reported. Adj. for stk. split: 2-for-1, 6/96. 1 Incl. pretax restruct chrgs. of $238.5 mill., 1997; $47.8 mill., 1996; & $85.8 mill., 1995. 2 Incl. restruct. chrg. of $27.8 mill. 3 Incl. restruct. credit of $21.3 mill.

OFFICERS:
J. M. Trani, Chmn., C.E.O.
J. M. Loree, V.P., C.F.O.
S.. S. Weddle, V.P., Gen. Couns.

INVESTOR CONTACT: Gerard J. Gould, Dir., Investor Relations, (860) 827-3833

PRINCIPAL OFFICE: 1000 Stanley Dr., P.O. Box 7000, New Britain, CT 06053

TELEPHONE NUMBER: (860) 225-5111
FAX: (860) 827-3895
WEB: www.stanleyworks.com

NO. OF EMPLOYEES: 15,500 (approx.)

SHAREHOLDERS: 16,014

ANNUAL MEETING: In Apr.

INCORPORATED: CT, July, 1852

INSTITUTIONAL HOLDINGS:
No. of Institutions: 207
Shares Held: 52,427,711
% Held: 61.2

INDUSTRY: Hardware, nec (SIC: 3429)

TRANSFER AGENT(S): EquiServe, Boston, MA

NYSE SYMBOL SCX
Rec. Pr. 22.15 (5/31/01)

STARRETT (L.S.) COMPANY

YIELD 3.6%
P/E RATIO 14.0

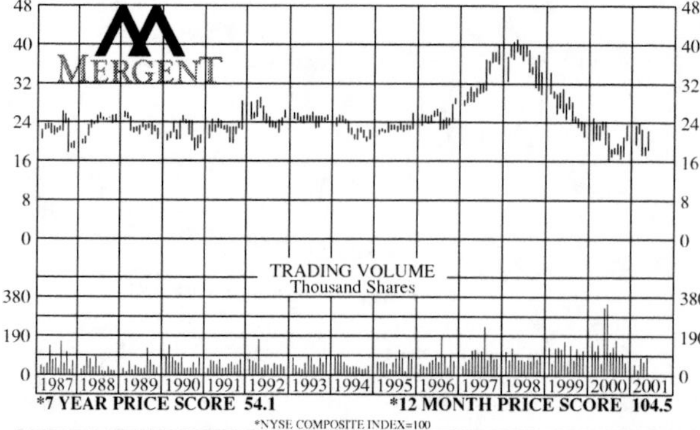

*7 YEAR PRICE SCORE 54.1 *12 MONTH PRICE SCORE 104.5

*NYSE COMPOSITE INDEX=100

INTERIM EARNINGS (Per Share):

Qtr.	Sept.	Dec.	Mar.	June
1997-98	0.78	0.93	0.72	0.90
1998-99	0.57	0.65	0.53	0.69
1999-00	0.43	0.57	0.37	0.36
2000-01	0.45	0.40	...	...

INTERIM DIVIDENDS (Per Share):

Amt.	Decl.	Ex.	Rec.	Pay.
0.20Q	9/06/00	9/13/00	9/15/00	9/29/00
0.20Q	12/07/00	12/14/00	12/18/00	1/04/01
0.20Q	3/07/01	3/15/01	3/19/01	3/30/01
0.20Q	6/07/01	6/13/01	6/15/01	6/29/01

Indicated div.: $0.80

CAPITALIZATION (6/24/00):

	($000)	(%)
Long-Term Debt	3,000	1.5
Deferred Income Tax	13,969	6.8
Common & Surplus	188,022	91.7
Total	204,991	100.0

RECENT DEVELOPMENTS: For the three months ended 12/23/00, net earnings fell 32.3% to $2.6 million compared with $3.8 million in the corresponding quarter of 1999. Net sales were $60.7 million, down 1.0% from $61.2 million in the prior-year period. Foreign sales increased slightly for the quarter, but were offset by a 4.0% decrease in domestic sales which were down during the holiday season. For the first half of fiscal 2001, sales at the Company's Brazil subsidiary increased.

PROSPECTS: Approximately 30.0% of the Company's sales and net assets relate to foreign operations. The Company's Brazilian operations, which contribute more than half of SCX's revenues from foreign operations, can be volatile due to changes in global political situations and economies. Looking ahead, the global economic weakness, particularly in the industrial manufacturing sector, may adversely affect demand for SCX's products and future results.

BUSINESS

L.S. STARRETT COMPANY manufactures industrial, professional and consumer products. The total number of different items made and sold by the Company exceeds 5,000. Among the items produced are precision tools, tape measures, levels, steel tapes, electronic gages, dial indicators, gage blocks, digital readout measuring tools, granite surface plates, optical measuring projectors, coordinate measuring machines, vises, M1 lubricant, hacksaw blades, hole saws, band saw blades, jig saw blades, reciprocating saw blades, and precision ground flat stock. By far the largest consumer of these products is the metalworking industry. Other important consumers are automotive, aviation, marine, farm equipment shops, do-it-yourselfers and tradesmen such as builders, carpenters, plumbers, and electricians. Geographical sales for 2000 were derived: North America, 69.7%; U.K., 13.4%; and Brazil, 16.9%.

ANNUAL FINANCIAL DATA

	6/24/00	6/26/99	6/27/98	6/28/97	6/29/96	6/24/95	6/25/94
Earnings Per Share	**1.73**	**2.44**	**3.33**	**2.84**	**2.45**	**1.91**	**1.28**
Cash Flow Per Share	**3.44**	**4.08**	**4.89**	**4.23**	**3.76**	**3.19**	**2.51**
Tang. Book Val. Per Share	**28.01**	**27.28**	**27.23**	**24.87**	**22.56**	**20.84**	**19.39**
Dividends Per Share	**0.80**	**0.80**	**0.78**	**0.73**	**0.72**	**0.70**	**0.68**
Dividend Payout %	**46.2**	**32.8**	**23.4**	**25.7**	**29.4**	**36.6**	**53.1**
INCOME STATEMENT (IN THOUSANDS):							
Total Revenues	235,169	232,385	262,340	250,503	235,467	214,215	180,178
Costs & Expenses	207,056	199,170	219,297	212,177	201,537	184,253	158,636
Depreciation & Amort.	11,380	11,207	10,727	9,799	9,268	9,098	8,681
Operating Income	16,733	22,008	32,316	28,527	24,662	20,864	12,861
Income Before Income Taxes	17,229	23,626	34,122	30,059	26,152	22,512	10,854
Income Taxes	5,740	6,930	11,113	10,200	8,821	9,025	1,813
Net Income	11,489	16,696	23,009	19,859	17,331	13,487	9,041
Cash Flow	22,869	27,903	33,736	29,658	26,599	22,585	17,722
Average Shs. Outstg.	6,653	6,846	6,903	7,003	7,069	7,078	7,071
BALANCE SHEET (IN THOUSANDS):							
Cash & Cash Equivalents	14,051	17,204	30,820	30,442	29,211	31,100	29,433
Total Current Assets	137,719	137,422	150,696	147,595	141,998	130,638	116,463
Net Property	75,683	73,854	68,818	64,101	59,602	58,135	57,386
Total Assets	250,418	245,728	250,263	238,746	227,312	213,940	198,032
Total Current Liabilities	29,398	24,322	25,434	27,804	29,853	26,165	20,009
Long-Term Obligations	3,000	3,300	3,900	6,500	7,100	8,700	10,843
Net Stockholders' Equity	188,022	190,036	195,294	180,465	167,285	156,829	146,648
Net Working Capital	108,321	113,100	125,262	119,791	112,145	104,473	96,454
Year-end Shs. Outstg.	6,474	6,706	6,897	6,944	7,055	7,118	7,107
STATISTICAL RECORD:							
Operating Profit Margin %	7.1	9.5	12.3	11.4	10.5	9.7	7.1
Net Profit Margin %	4.9	7.2	8.8	7.9	7.4	6.3	5.0
Return on Equity %	6.1	8.8	11.8	11.0	10.4	8.6	6.2
Return on Assets %	4.6	6.8	9.2	8.3	7.6	6.3	4.6
Debt/Total Assets %	1.2	1.3	1.6	2.7	3.1	4.1	5.5
Price Range	25.00-16.13	34.44-21.00	41.13-29.81	40.00-27.38	29.00-22.38	25.88-21.50	25.50-20.00
P/E Ratio	14.5-9.3	14.1-8.6	12.3-9.0	14.1-9.6	11.8-9.1	13.5-11.3	19.9-15.6

Statistics are as originally reported. Fiscal year ends last Saturday in June.

OFFICERS:
D. R. Starrett, Chmn., C.E.O.
D. A. Starrett, Pres.
R. U. Wellington Jr., C.F.O., Treas.

INVESTOR CONTACT: Roger U. Wellington, Jr., C.F.O. & Treas., (978) 249-3551

PRINCIPAL OFFICE: 121 Crescent Street, Athol, MA 01331

TELEPHONE NUMBER: (978) 249-3551
FAX: (978) 249-8495
WEB: www.lsstarrett.com

NO. OF EMPLOYEES: 2,776 (avg.)

SHAREHOLDERS: 2,160 (class A common); 1,712 (class B common)

ANNUAL MEETING: In Sept.

INCORPORATED: MA, July, 1920

INSTITUTIONAL HOLDINGS:
No. of Institutions: 21
Shares Held: 2,021,447
% Held: 31.4

INDUSTRY: Saw blades and handsaws (SIC: 3425)

TRANSFER AGENT(S): Fleet National Bank, c/o EquiServe, Boston, MA

NYSE SYMBOL HOT
Rec. Pr. 36.09 (4/30/01)

STARWOOD HOTELS & RESORTS WORLDWIDE, INC.

YIELD 2.1%
P/E RATIO 18.4

MERGENT

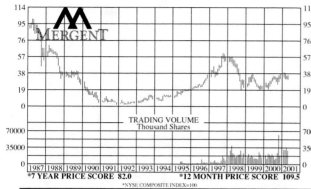

TRADING VOLUME
Thousand Shares

*7 YEAR PRICE SCORE 82.0 *12 MONTH PRICE SCORE 109.5

*NYSE COMPOSITE INDEX=100

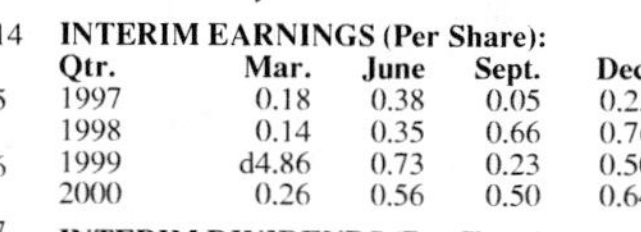

INTERIM EARNINGS (Per Share):

Qtr.	Mar.	June	Sept.	Dec.
1997	0.18	0.38	0.05	0.25
1998	0.14	0.35	0.66	0.76
1999	d4.86	0.73	0.23	0.50
2000	0.26	0.56	0.50	0.64

INTERIM DIVIDENDS (Per Share):

Amt.	Decl.	Ex.	Rec.	Pay.
0.173Q	6/28/00	6/28/00	6/30/00	7/21/00
0.173Q	9/07/00	9/27/00	9/30/00	10/23/00
0.173Q	12/07/00	12/27/00	12/31/00	1/22/01
0.20Q	2/26/01	3/28/01	3/31/01	4/23/01
0.20Q	5/21/01	6/27/01	6/30/01	7/20/01

Indicated div.: $0.80

CAPITALIZATION (12/31/00):

	($000)	(%)
Long-Term Debt	4,957,000	47.6
Deferred Income Tax	1,444,000	13.9
Minority Interest	48,000	0.5
Redeemable Pfd. Stock	117,000	1.1
Common & Surplus	3,851,000	37.0
Total	10,417,000	100.0

RECENT DEVELOPMENTS: For the year ended 12/31/00, income from continuing operations was $401.0 million versus net income of $303.0 million in 1999. Results for 2000 included a net gain of $2.0 million from the sale of investments. Total revenues advanced 13.5% to $4.35 billion from $3.83 billion a year earlier. Operating income grew 20.8% to $1.03 billion from $851.0 million in 1999.

PROSPECTS: In 2001, HOT will focus on renovating and repositioning and converting its independent properties to its major brands. The conversion of one underperforming hotel to a W hotel is expected to generate greater bottom line growth than 50 new franchise agreements. In addition, HOT plans to reduce costs through the implementation of a new yield management system, SIX SIGMA.

BUSINESS

STARWOOD HOTELS & RESORTS WORLDWIDE, INC., (formerly Starwood Lodging), is a hotel and leisure company that operates directly and through its subsidiaries, ITT Sheraton Corporation and Ciga, S.p.A. The Company offers luxury and upscale full-service hotels under the following brand names: Sheraton, Westin, The Luxury Collection, St. Regis, W brands, Ciga and Four Points by Sheraton. As of 3/12/01, the Company's portfolio of owned, managed and franchised hotels totaled more than 725 hotels in 80 countries. In addition, the Company's subsidiary, Starwood Vacation Ownership, Inc., offers vacation ownership interest in twelve resorts located in Florida, South Carolina, Arizona, Colorado, the Bahamas and the U.S. Virgin Islands.

QUARTERLY DATA

(12/31/2000)	REV	INC
1st Quarter	996,000	50,000
2nd Quarter	1,142,000	119,000
3rd Quarter	1,102,000	103,000
4th Quarter	1,105,000	131,000

ANNUAL FINANCIAL DATA

	12/31/00	12/31/99	[3] 12/31/98	12/31/97	12/31/96	12/31/95	12/31/94
Earnings Per Share	[5] 1.96	[4] d3.41	[2] d1.37	[1] 0.85	[1] 0.86	[1] 0.95	d1.54
Cash Flow Per Share	4.36	d0.77	1.04	3.43	2.73	2.28	1.15
Tang. Book Val. Per Share	4.99	4.32	...	9.95	7.39	5.20	2.87
Dividends Per Share	0.67	0.45	...	1.65	1.28	0.31	...
Dividend Payout %	34.1	...	...	194.1	148.8	32.6	...
INCOME STATEMENT (IN MILLIONS):							
Total Revenues	4,345.0	3,862.0	4,700.0	933.6	428.5	161.7	114.0
Costs & Expenses	2,825.0	2,520.0	4,099.0	682.9	313.3	115.0	92.9
Depreciation & Amort.	492.0	492.0	447.0	125.4	55.7	15.5	8.2
Operating Income	1,028.0	850.0	154.0	125.2	59.4	31.3	12.9
Net Interest Inc./(Exp.)	d420.0	d493.0	d589.0	d65.0	d23.3	d13.1	d17.6
Income Before Income Taxes	610.0	533.0	d380.0	873.4	392.4	143.6	118.7
Income Taxes	201.0	1,076.0	cr109.0	...	...	...	...
Equity Earnings/Minority Int.	d8.0	d95.0	17.0	...	...	...	...
Net Income	[5] 401.0	[4] d638.0	[2] d254.0	[1] 41.5	[1] 25.9	[1] 11.1	d4.7
Cash Flow	893.0	d146.0	193.0	185.7	91.9	33.6	3.5
Average Shs. Outstg. (000)	205,000	189,000	185,000	48,663	29,884	11,657	3,033
BALANCE SHEET (IN MILLIONS):							
Cash & Cash Equivalents	189.0	436.0	278.0	23.5	25.4	9.3	5.1
Total Current Assets	1,048.0	1,176.0	1,038.0	291.9	96.4	39.1	16.8
Net Property	7,889.0	7,777.0	5,439.0	...	...	...	...
Total Assets	12,660.0	12,923.0	11,214.0	3,009.5	1,312.7	460.0	184.0
Total Current Liabilities	1,805.0	2,303.0	2,041.0	495.8	133.8	32.7	61.4
Long-Term Obligations	4,957.0	4,643.0	9,957.0	1,221.7	422.3	119.1	113.9
Net Stockholders' Equity	3,851.0	3,690.0	d3,025.0	1,021.6	592.7	215.5	8.7
Net Working Capital	d757.0	d1,127.0	d1,003.0	d204.0	d37.3	6.4	d44.5
Year-end Shs. Outstg. (000)	194,272	189,272	175,574	102,692	80,156	41,475	3,033
STATISTICAL RECORD:							
Operating Profit Margin %	23.7	22.0	3.3	13.4	13.9	19.3	11.4
Net Profit Margin %	9.2	...	...	4.4	6.0	6.9	...
Return on Equity %	10.4	...	...	4.1	4.4	5.2	...
Return on Assets %	3.2	...	...	1.4	2.0	2.4	...
Debt/Total Assets %	39.2	35.9	88.8	40.6	32.2	25.9	61.9
Price Range	37.50-19.75	37.75-19.50	57.88-18.75	61.50-33.50	36.92-19.67	20.08-9.98	13.47-5.99
P/E Ratio	19.1-10.1	...	...	72.3-39.4	42.9-22.9	21.1-10.5	...
Average Yield %	2.3	1.6	...	...	...	...	...

Statistics are as originally reported. Adj. for stk. splits: 3-for-2, 1/97; 1-for-6, 6/95. [1] Bef. extra. chg. 2000, $3.0 mill., 1997, $3.5 mil.; cr. 1996, $1.1 mil.; chg. 1995, $2.2 mil. [2] Incl. net nonrecurr chrg. $149.0 mill.; excl. net gain $1.11 bill. [3] Results of ITT Corp. for yr. end 12/31/98 & results of Starwood Hotels & Resorts, Starwood Hotels & Resorts Worldwide, Inc., incl. of Westin, from closing of ITT merger 2/23/98-12/31/98. [4] Incl. net nonrecurr. gain $188.0 mill.; bef. net losses $103.0 mill. [5] Bef. extra. chrg. $3.0 mill. & net gains $2.0 mill.

OFFICERS:
B. S. Sternlicht, Chmn., C.E.O.
R. C. Brown, Exec. V.P., C.F.O.
R. F. Cotter, C.O.O.

INVESTOR CONTACT: Dan Gibson, V.P., Inv. Rel., (914) 640-8175

PRINCIPAL OFFICE: 777 Westchester Ave., White Plains, NY 10604

TELEPHONE NUMBER: (914) 640-8100
FAX: (914) 640-8310
WEB: www.starwoodlodging.com

NO. OF EMPLOYEES: 129,000 (approx.)

SHAREHOLDERS: 21,000 (approx. com of record); 1 (cl A exchble pref of record)

ANNUAL MEETING: In May

INCORPORATED: MD, 1969

INSTITUTIONAL HOLDINGS:
No. of Institutions: 278
Shares Held: 171,290,609
% Held: 86.6

INDUSTRY: Hotels and motels (SIC: 7011)

TRANSFER AGENT(S): Mellon Investor Services, Los Angeles, CA

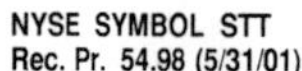
NYSE SYMBOL STT
Rec. Pr. 54.98 (5/31/01)

STATE STREET CORPORATION

YIELD 0.7%
P/E RATIO 15.1

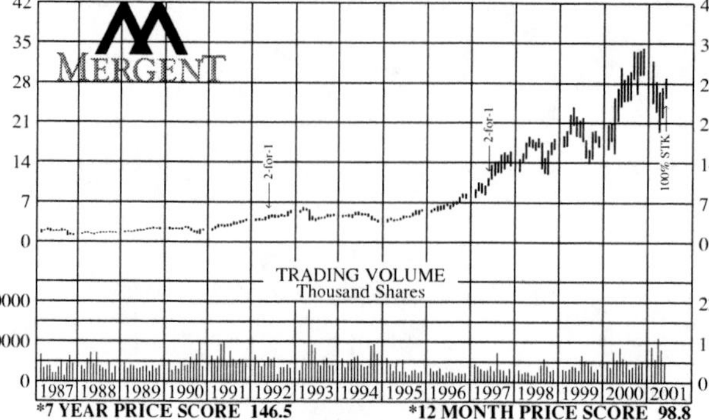

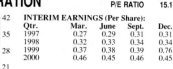

*7 YEAR PRICE SCORE 146.5 *12 MONTH PRICE SCORE 98.8

*NYSE COMPOSITE INDEX=100

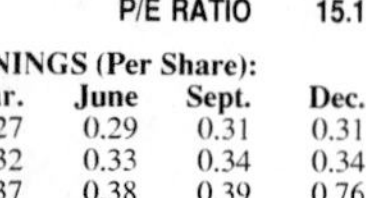

INTERIM EARNINGS (Per Share):

Qtr.	Mar.	June	Sept.	Dec.
1997	0.27	0.29	0.31	0.31
1998	0.32	0.33	0.34	0.34
1999	0.37	0.38	0.39	0.76
2000	0.46	0.45	0.46	0.45

INTERIM DIVIDENDS (Per Share):

Amt.	Decl.	Ex.	Rec.	Pay.
0.17Q	6/15/00	6/29/00	7/03/00	7/17/00
0.17Q	9/21/00	9/28/00	10/02/00	10/16/00
0.19Q	12/21/00	12/28/00	1/02/01	1/16/01
0.19Q	3/15/01	3/29/01	4/02/01	4/16/01
100% STK	12/21/00	5/31/01	4/30/01	5/30/01

Indicated div.: $0.38 (Adj.; Div. Reinv. Plan)

CAPITALIZATION (12/31/00):

	($000)	(%)
Total Deposits	37,937,000	89.4
Long-Term Debt	1,219,000	2.9
Common & Surplus	3,262,000	7.7
Total	42,418,000	100.0

RECENT DEVELOPMENTS: For the year ended 12/31/00, net income declined 3.9% to $595.0 million compared with $619.0 million in the previous year. Earnings for 1999 included nonrecurring items that resulted in a net after-tax gain of $130.0 million. Net interest revenue increased 14.5% to $894.0 million from $781.0 million the year before. Total fee revenue climbed 18.2% to $2.67 billion. Total revenue grew 7.4% to $3.55 billion from $3.30 billion in the prior year.

PROSPECTS: On 2/8/01, STT completed the acquisition of a majority interest in Bel Air Investment Advisors LLC, a Los-Angeles-based independent investment management firm. The acquisition should enable the Company to significantly enhance its position as a provider of wealth management services to high net worth individuals. Meanwhile, STT expects earnings per share to range from $3.95 to $4.20 in 2001.

BUSINESS

STATE STREET CORPORATION (formerly State Street Boston Corporation) as of 12/31/00, is a $69.30 billion bank holding company that conducts business worldwide principally through its subsidiary, State Street Bank and Trust Company. The Company has two lines of business: services for institutional investors and investment management. Services for institutional investors are primarily accounting, custody and other services for large pools of assets. Investment management offers index and active equity strategies, short-term investment funds and fixed income products. On 10/1/99, the Company sold its commercial lending business.

ANNUAL FINANCIAL DATA

	12/31/00	12/31/99	12/31/98	12/31/97	12/31/96	12/31/95	12/31/94
Earnings Per Share	**1.82**	**[1] 1.89**	**1.33**	**1.16**	**0.90**	**0.75**	**0.68**
Tang. Book Val. Per Share	**10.09**	**8.31**	**7.19**	**5.97**	**5.47**	**4.82**	**4.03**
Dividends Per Share	**0.33**	**0.29**	**0.25**	**0.21**	**0.18**	**0.17**	**0.14**
Dividend Payout %	**18.2**	**15.3**	**18.8**	**18.1**	**20.6**	**22.1**	**21.5**
INCOME STATEMENT (IN MILLIONS):							
Total Interest Income	3,256.0	2,437.0	2,237.0	1,755.0	1,443.0	1,336.6	904.7
Total Interest Expense	2,362.0	1,656.0	1,492.0	1,114.0	892.0	907.2	537.5
Net Interest Income	894.0	781.0	745.0	641.0	551.0	429.4	367.2
Provision for Loan Losses	9.0	14.0	17.0	16.0	8.0	8.0	11.6
Non-Interest Income	2,665.0	2,537.0	1,997.0	1,673.0	1,302.0	1,119.1	981.0
Non-Interest Expense	2,644.0	2,336.0	2,068.0	1,734.0	1,398.0	1,174.0	1,016.4
Income Before Taxes	906.0	968.0	657.0	564.0	447.0	366.5	320.3
Net Income	595.0	[1] 619.0	436.0	380.0	293.0	247.1	207.4
Average Shs. Outstg. (000)	328,088	327,502	327,854	327,578	326,532	332,232	307,404
BALANCE SHEET (IN MILLIONS):							
Cash & Due from Banks	1,618.0	2,930.0	1,365.0	2,411.0	1,623.0	1,421.9	1,004.9
Securities Avail. for Sale	14,744.0	15,489.0	10,072.0	10,580.0	9,642.0	6,039.2	3,754.2
Total Loans & Leases	5,273.0	4,293.0	6,309.0	5,562.0	4,713.0	3,986.1	3,233.2
Allowance for Credit Losses	57.0	48.0	84.0	83.0	73.0	63.5	58.2
Net Loans & Leases	5,216.0	4,245.0	6,225.0	5,479.0	4,640.0	3,922.7	3,175.0
Total Assets	69,298.0	60,896.0	47,082.0	37,975.0	31,524.0	25,785.2	21,729.5
Total Deposits	37,937.0	34,145.0	27,539.0	24,878.0	19,519.0	16,647.2	13,902.7
Long-Term Obligations	1,219.0	921.0	922.0	774.0	476.0	126.6	127.5
Total Liabilities	66,036.0	58,244.0	44,771.0	35,980.0	29,749.0	24,197.7	20,498.2
Net Stockholders' Equity	3,262.0	2,652.0	2,311.0	1,995.0	1,775.0	1,587.5	1,231.3
Year-end Shs. Outstg. (000)	323,422	319,180	321,390	334,446	324,616	329,552	305,900
STATISTICAL RECORD:							
Return on Equity %	18.2	23.3	18.9	19.0	16.5	15.6	16.8
Return on Assets %	0.9	1.0	0.9	1.0	0.9	1.0	1.0
Equity/Assets %	4.7	4.4	4.9	5.3	5.6	6.2	5.7
Non-Int. Exp./Tot. Inc. %	74.3	70.4	75.4	74.9	75.4	75.8	75.4
Price Range	68.40-31.22	47.63-27.75	37.16-23.94	31.84-15.66	17.13-10.44	11.56-7.00	10.78-6.91
P/E Ratio	37.7-17.2	25.2-14.7	27.9-18.0	27.5-13.5	19.1-11.6	15.5-9.4	16.0-10.2
Average Yield %	0.7	0.8	0.8	0.9	1.3	1.8	1.6

Statistics are as originally reported. Adj. for 2-for-1 stock splits, 5/01 & 5/97. [1] Incl. pre-tax net gain on the sale of Co.'s commercial banking business of $282.0 mill.

OFFICERS:
D. A. Spina, Chmn., Pres., C.E.O.
N. A. Lopardo, Vice-Chmn.
R. E. Logue, Vice-Chmn., C.O.O.

INVESTOR CONTACT: Karen A. Warren, Inv. Rel., (617) 664-3477

PRINCIPAL OFFICE: 225 Franklin Street, Boston, MA 02110

TELEPHONE NUMBER: (617) 786-3000
FAX: (617) 985-8055
WEB: www.statestreet.com

NO. OF EMPLOYEES: 17,022 full-time; 582 part-time

SHAREHOLDERS: 5,623

ANNUAL MEETING: In Apr.

INCORPORATED: MA, Oct., 1969

INSTITUTIONAL HOLDINGS:
No. of Institutions: 567
Shares Held: 241,362,034 (Adj.)
% Held: 74.0

INDUSTRY: State commercial banks (SIC: 6022)

TRANSFER AGENT(S): State Street Bank and Trust Company, Boston, MA

NYSE SYMBOL SCS
Rec. Pr. 12.39 (4/30/01)

STEELCASE INC.

YIELD	3.3%
P/E RATIO	9.6

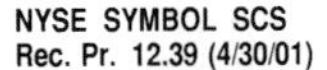

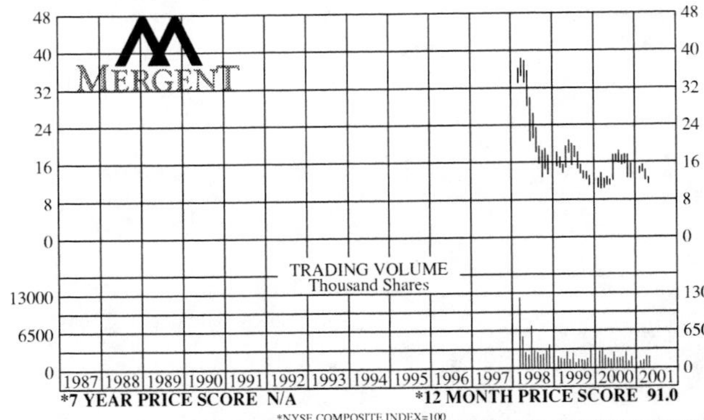

*7 YEAR PRICE SCORE N/A *12 MONTH PRICE SCORE 91.0

*NYSE COMPOSITE INDEX=100

INTERIM EARNINGS (Per Share):

Qtr.	May	Aug.	Nov.	Feb.
1997-98	0.30	0.43	0.32	0.35
1998-99	0.35	0.41	0.37	0.31
1999-00	0.37	0.25	0.30	0.29
2000-01	0.41	0.36	0.35	0.17

INTERIM DIVIDENDS (Per Share):

Amt.	Decl.	Ex.	Rec.	Pay.
0.11Q	3/28/00	3/29/00	4/01/00	4/14/00
0.11Q	6/19/00	6/28/00	7/01/00	7/15/00
0.11Q	9/20/00	9/27/00	10/01/00	10/16/00
0.11Q	12/14/00	12/27/00	1/01/01	1/16/01
0.11Q	3/21/01	3/28/01	4/01/01	4/16/01

Indicated div.: $0.44

CAPITALIZATION (2/25/00):

	($000)	(%)
Long-Term Debt	257,800	13.9
Deferred Income Tax	29,500	1.6
Common & Surplus	1,562,200	84.5
Total	1,849,500	100.0

RECENT DEVELOPMENTS: For the year ended 2/23/01, net income advanced 5.2% to $193.7 million compared with $184.2 million in 2000. Results included net non-recurring after-tax charges totaling $9.9 million in 2001 and $5.7 million in 2000. Net sales were $3.89 billion, up 16.2% from $3.34 billion a year earlier due to acquisitions as well as the continued growth of new and established products across most business and customer segments.

PROSPECTS: Looking ahead, the Company expects a continuation of negative factors into fiscal year 2002, including a shift in sales mix to newer products with lower margins and competitive pricing pressures. However, SCS expects an improved business climate in the second half of fiscal year 2002. Meanwhile, the Company anticipates earnings for fiscal year 2002 in the range of $1.00 to $1.15 per share.

BUSINESS

STEELCASE INC. provides products and services designed to create work environments that integrate architecture, furniture and technology. SCS's product portfolio includes interior architectural products, furniture systems, technology products, seating, lighting, storage and related products and services. SCS operates on a worldwide basis within three business segments. The North America business segment (79.7% of 2001 revenues) includes SCS's furniture operations in the U.S. and Canada, including the Steelcase Design Partnership (a group of seven wholly owned Steelcase subisidiaries that serve specialty markets), and the Company's Attwood and IDEO subsidiaries. The International furniture segment (18.3%) includes the rest of the world, with the major portion of operations in Europe. The Financial Services business segment (2.0%) includes customer leasing and dealer financing services. The Company and its subsidiaries have dealers in more than 800 locations and manufacturing facilities in more than 30 locations. Founded in 1912, Steelcase launched its initial public offering on 2/18/98.

ANNUAL FINANCIAL DATA

	2/25/00	2/26/99	2/27/98	2/28/97	2/23/96	2/28/95
Earnings Per Share	**[1] 1.21**	**1.44**	**1.40**	**d2.29**	...	...
Cash Flow Per Share	**2.13**	**2.14**	**2.02**	**0.78**	...	...
Tang. Book Val. Per Share	**7.54**	**9.12**	**8.26**	...	...	...
Dividends Per Share	**0.44**	**0.30**	...	...	...	...
Dividend Payout %	**36.4**	**20.8**	...	...	...	...
INCOME STATEMENT (IN MILLIONS):						
Total Revenues	3,316.1	2,742.5	2,760.0	2,408.4	2,155.9	2,048.7
Costs & Expenses	2,902.5	2,318.3	2,347.3	2,173.4	1,899.8	1,873.5
Depreciation & Amort.	141.8	107.0	95.3	93.4	92.5	97.0
Operating Income	271.8	317.2	317.4	141.6	163.6	78.2
Net Interest Inc./(Exp.)	d15.9	...	...	d111.7	...	...
Income Before Income Taxes	296.4	337.4	340.0	51.3	187.6	105.3
Income Taxes	115.5	124.9	130.9	23.6	68.1	40.9
Equity Earnings/Minority Int.	3.3	8.9	7.9	...	4.0	d0.2
Net Income	[1] 184.2	221.4	217.0	27.7	123.5	64.2
Cash Flow	326.0	328.4	312.3	101.4	196.3	141.5
Average Shs. Outstg. (000)	152,800	153,800	154,800	155,100	...	...
BALANCE SHEET (IN MILLIONS):						
Cash & Cash Equivalents	88.6	76.1	116.1	187.6	224.3	...
Total Current Assets	1,127.3	737.4	825.0	824.6	791.3	...
Net Property	939.1	739.0	671.2	644.7	624.3	...
Total Assets	3,037.6	2,182.5	2,007.2	1,922.1	1,884.5	...
Total Current Liabilities	927.2	446.8	469.9	350.0	315.7	...
Long-Term Obligations	257.8	...	...	...	...	...
Net Stockholders' Equity	1,562.2	1,500.0	1,332.4	1,380.0	1,393.6	...
Net Working Capital	200.1	290.6	355.1	474.6	475.6	...
Year-end Shs. Outstg. (000)	151,158	153,619	153,368	201	...	...
STATISTICAL RECORD:						
Operating Profit Margin %	8.2	11.6	11.5	5.9	7.6	3.8
Net Profit Margin %	5.6	8.1	7.9	1.2	5.7	3.1
Return on Equity %	11.8	14.8	16.3	2.0	8.9	...
Return on Assets %	6.1	10.1	10.8	1.4	6.6	...
Debt/Total Assets %	8.5	...	...	...	...	...
Price Range	20.75-11.00	38.38-12.75	...	...	...	...
P/E Ratio	17.1-9.1	26.6-8.9	...	...	...	...
Average Yield %	2.8	1.2	...	...	...	...

Statistics are as originally reported. [1] Incl. net nonrecur. after-tax chrg. of $5.7 mill.

OFFICERS:
E. D. Holton, Chmn.
P. M. Wege, Vice-Chmn.
J. P. Hackett, Pres., C.E.O.
J. Keane, Sr. V.P., C.F.O.

INVESTOR CONTACT: Gary Malburg, (616) 247-2200

PRINCIPAL OFFICE: 901 44th St., Grand Rapids, MI 49508

TELEPHONE NUMBER: (616) 247-2710
FAX: (616) 475-2270
WEB: www.steelcase.com

NO. OF EMPLOYEES: 20,900 (approx.)

SHAREHOLDERS: 14,221 (class A); 243 (class B)

ANNUAL MEETING: In June

INCORPORATED: MI, 1912

INSTITUTIONAL HOLDINGS:
No. of Institutions: 89
Shares Held: 13,441,007
% Held: 9.1

INDUSTRY: Office furniture, except wood (SIC: 2522)

TRANSFER AGENT(S): Bank of Boston, NA, Boston, MA

NYSE SYMBOL STE
Rec. Pr. 18.18 (4/30/01)

STERIS CORPORATION

YIELD ...
P/E RATIO ...

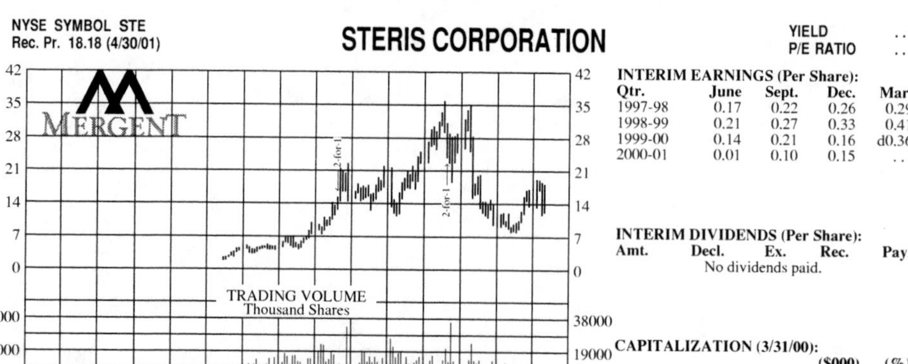

*7 YEAR PRICE SCORE 58.0 *12 MONTH PRICE SCORE 123.5

*NYSE COMPOSITE INDEX=100

INTERIM EARNINGS (Per Share):

Qtr.	June	Sept.	Dec.	Mar.
1997-98	0.17	0.22	0.26	0.29
1998-99	0.21	0.27	0.33	0.41
1999-00	0.14	0.21	0.16	d0.36
2000-01	0.01	0.10	0.15	...

INTERIM DIVIDENDS (Per Share):

Amt.	Decl.	Ex.	Rec.	Pay.

No dividends paid.

CAPITALIZATION (3/31/00):

	($000)	(%)
Long-Term Debt	268,700	38.5
Deferred Income Tax	8,880	1.3
Common & Surplus	421,094	60.3
Total	698,674	100.0

RECENT DEVELOPMENTS: For the three months ended 12/31/00, net income fell 5.0% to $10.4 million compared with $10.9 million in the corresponding quarter of the previous year. Net revenues grew 4.8% to $204.5 million from $195.1 million in the prior-year period. The increase in revenues for the quarter was due to significant growth in scientific and industrial group revenues.

PROSPECTS: The Company plans to take a pre-tax charge of approximately $40.0 million in its fiscal year 2001 fourth quarter ending 3/31/01. The charge will cover costs and asset write-downs related to manufacturing consolidations, upgrading of the Company's service and distribution organization, support function restructuring and related workforce reductions.

BUSINESS

STERIS CORPORATION develops, manufactures, and markets infection prevention systems and related consumables, accessories, and services for the worldwide health care market. The Company's systems support cost containment, productivity, and risk reduction in health care institutions through process standardization, automatic monitoring and documentation, decentralization, and reduced processing time. STERIS SYSTEM 1™, the Company's site-of-care sterile processing system, enables health care professionals to safely and economically sterilize immersible surgical and diagnostic devices between patient procedures in less than thirty minutes. On 5/13/96, the Company acquired Amsco International, Inc. in a pooling-of-interest transaction.

ANNUAL FINANCIAL DATA

	3/31/00	3/31/99	3/31/98	3/31/97	3/31/96	3/31/95	3/31/94
Earnings Per Share	**3 0.15**	**1.20**	**0.94**	**1 d0.45**	**0.33**	**0.23**	**2 0.14**
Cash Flow Per Share	**0.73**	**1.67**	**1.28**	**d0.21**	**0.37**	**0.26**	**0.16**
Tang. Book Val. Per Share	**3.21**	**3.35**	**2.72**	**2.58**	**1.42**	**1.18**	**1.00**
Dividends Per Share	...	**2.00**	...	...	...	...	...
Dividend Payout %	...	**166.7**	...	...	...	...	...
INCOME STATEMENT (IN THOUSANDS):							
Total Revenues	760,626	797,611	719,656	587,852	91,192	64,272	45,822
Costs & Expenses	691,248	627,953	582,840	577,811	69,148	49,893	37,140
Depreciation & Amort.	39,672	33,279	24,202	16,528	1,765	1,153	699
Operating Income	29,706	136,379	112,614	d6,487	20,279	13,226	7,983
Net Interest Inc./(Exp.)	d16,166	d10,736	d6,239	d2,919	756	634	570
Income Before Income Taxes	16,912	127,196	107,355	d4,862	21,035	13,860	8,553
Income Taxes	6,427	42,342	41,859	25,744	8,241	5,124	3,407
Net Income	3 10,485	84,854	65,496	1 d30,606	12,794	8,736	2 5,146
Cash Flow	50,157	118,133	89,698	d14,078	14,559	9,889	5,845
Average Shs. Outstg.	68,567	70,592	70,224	67,356	39,008	38,016	37,388
BALANCE SHEET (IN THOUSANDS):							
Cash & Cash Equivalents	35,476	23,680	17,172	23,553	9,351	14,717	20,458
Total Current Assets	389,119	393,397	344,332	300,042	52,455	39,029	37,527
Net Property	305,005	261,281	205,292	102,852	19,237	11,230	3,666
Total Assets	903,574	865,996	732,325	539,455	85,367	54,893	42,715
Total Current Liabilities	155,902	157,137	169,654	158,688	19,367	9,540	7,239
Long-Term Obligations	268,700	221,500	152,879	35,879	...	...	...
Net Stockholders' Equity	421,094	435,937	358,952	294,716	62,394	44,595	35,158
Net Working Capital	233,217	236,260	174,678	141,354	33,088	29,489	30,288
Year-end Shs. Outstg.	67,517	67,956	68,020	67,968	35,888	35,044	34,740
STATISTICAL RECORD:							
Operating Profit Margin %	3.9	17.1	15.6	...	22.2	20.6	17.4
Net Profit Margin %	1.4	10.6	9.1	...	14.0	13.6	11.2
Return on Equity %	2.5	19.5	18.2	...	20.5	19.6	14.6
Return on Assets %	1.2	9.8	8.9	...	15.0	15.9	12.0
Debt/Total Assets %	29.7	25.6	20.9	6.7	...	...	...
Price Range	35.06-9.44	35.94-18.50	25.13-11.31	22.00-12.50	22.50-7.44	10.00-4.19	5.31-3.19
P/E Ratio	233.6-62.9	29.9-15.4	26.9-12.1	...	68.2-22.5	43.5-18.2	37.9-22.8
Average Yield %	...	7.3	...	...	...	...	...

Statistics are as originally reported. Adj. for stk. splits: 2-for-1, 8/24/98; 2-for-1, 8/24/95 1 Incl. non-recurr. after-tax chrg. $81.3 mill. 2 Bef. acctg. change credit $1.2 mill. 3 Incl. pre-tax non-recurr. chrg. of $39.7 mill.

OFFICERS:
J. E. Robertson, Chmn.
L. C. Vinney, Pres., C.E.O.
L. Brlas, Sr. V.P., C.F.O.

INVESTOR CONTACT: Investor Relations, (440) 354-2600

PRINCIPAL OFFICE: 5960 Heisley Rd., Mentor, OH 44060-1834

TELEPHONE NUMBER: (440) 354-2600
FAX: (440) 639-4457
WEB: www.steris.com

NO. OF EMPLOYEES: 4,810

SHAREHOLDERS: 2,085 (approx.)

ANNUAL MEETING: In July

INCORPORATED: OH, 1985

INSTITUTIONAL HOLDINGS:
No. of Institutions: 158
Shares Held: 47,124,875
% Held: 68.7

INDUSTRY: Surgical appliances and supplies (SIC: 3842)

TRANSFER AGENT(S): National City Bank, Cleveland, OH

NYSE SYMBOL STC
Rec. Pr. 17.15 (5/31/01)

STEWART INFORMATION SERVICES CORPORATION

YIELD ...
P/E RATIO 428.7

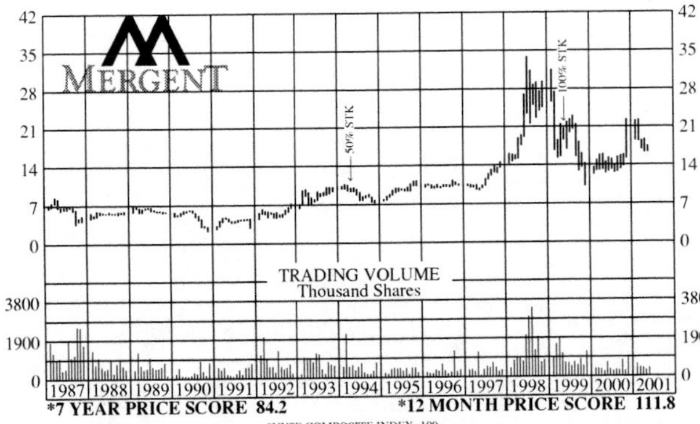

INTERIM EARNINGS (Per Share):

Qtr.	Mar.	June	Sept.	Dec.
1996	0.17	0.43	0.33	0.16
1997	0.01	0.41	0.40	0.30
1998	0.62	0.80	0.99	0.92
1999	0.67	0.80	0.41	0.07
2000	d0.23	0.13	0.12	0.02

INTERIM DIVIDENDS (Per Share):

Amt.	Decl.	Ex.	Rec.	Pay.
0.04Q	6/21/99	6/28/99	6/30/99	7/30/99
0.04Q	9/20/99	9/28/99	9/30/99	10/29/99
0.04Q	12/13/99	12/29/99	12/31/99	1/31/00

Dividend Payment Suspended

CAPITALIZATION (12/31/00):

	($000)	(%)
Long-Term Debt	32,543	9.7
Minority Interest	6,901	2.1
Common & Surplus	295,089	88.2
Total	334,533	100.0

RECENT DEVELOPMENTS: For the year ended 12/31/00, net income dropped to $606,000 compared with $28.4 million in the prior year. Total revenues declined 12.7% to $935.5 million versus $1.07 billion the year before. Title, premiums, fees and other revenues decreased 15.1% to $861.2 million, while real estate information revenues dropped 11.1% to $52.5 million. However, investment income improved 7.5% to $21.8 million from $20.3 million in the prior year.

PROSPECTS: STC's goal going forward is to reduce expenses in the real estate information group while increasing productivity within the Company. Meanwhile, the favorable outlook for lower interest rates bodes well going into 2001; however, a slowing economy could offset gains in real estate sales and construction activity. Separately, in March, STC acquired Western Colorado Title Co., and agreed to acquire a majority share of stock in Cuesta Title Co.

BUSINESS

STEWART INFORMATION SERVICES CORPORATION engages in the title insurance and real estate information businesses. The title segment includes the functions of searching, examining, closing and insuring the condition of the title to real property. The real estate information segment offers services to the real estate and mortgage industries primarily through the electronic delivery of services needed for settlement, which include title reports, flood determinations, property appraisals, document preparation, credit reports and other real estate information. The Company issues policies through over 5,300 locations on homes and other real property in all 50 states, Washington, D.C., Canada, Belize (reinsurance), Mexico, Guam, the Bahamas and the Commonwealth of the Northern Marianas. The Company also sells computer-related services and information, as well as mapping products and geographic information systems to government and private entities, both domestic and foreign.

ANNUAL FINANCIAL DATA

	12/31/00	12/31/99	12/31/98	12/31/97	12/31/96	12/31/95	12/31/94
Earnings Per Share	**0.04**	**1.95**	**3.33**	**[1] 1.11**	**1.08**	**0.56**	**0.78**
Tang. Book Val. Per Share	**18.45**	**18.56**	**16.76**	**13.83**	**12.94**	**12.82**	**13.31**
Dividends Per Share	**0.04**	**0.15**	**0.14**	**0.13**	**0.12**	**0.10**	**0.10**
Dividend Payout %	**99.8**	**7.9**	**4.2**	**11.3**	**11.2**	**18.0**	**12.4**
INCOME STATEMENT (IN THOUSANDS):							
Total Premium Income	861,185	991,649	899,673	657,298	328,296	266,728	289,265
Net Investment Income	21,814	20,300	18,515	15,929	14,451	13,564	12,382
Other Income	52,486	59,305	50,573	35,683	1,334	2,213	508
Total Revenues	935,485	1,071,254	968,761	708,910	344,081	282,505	302,155
Income Before Income Taxes	1,146	46,565	76,327	23,679	22,878	10,729	13,840
Income Taxes	540	18,143	29,289	8,391	8,441	3,722	4,162
Equity Earnings/Minority Int.	d5,048	d4,887	d5,070	d2,614	d1,514	d933	d687
Net Income	606	28,422	47,038	[1] 15,378	14,437	7,007	9,678
Average Shs. Outstg.	14,980	14,606	14,154	13,794	13,414	12,584	12,492
BALANCE SHEET (IN THOUSANDS):							
Cash & Cash Equivalents	89,476	104,258	104,329	66,152	50,430	44,936	42,954
Premiums Due	57,039	48,580	46,732	31,868	31,616	30,240	32,749
Invst. Assets: Total	326,116	316,045	296,328	254,081	239,964	223,420	200,553
Total Assets	563,448	535,741	498,481	417,691	383,372	351,359	325,176
Long-Term Obligations	32,543	19,054	16,194	19,087	12,324	12,589	7,865
Net Stockholders' Equity	295,089	284,924	260,443	209,504	190,990	174,852	156,353
Year-end Shs. Outstg.	14,002	13,646	14,130	13,812	13,482	12,780	11,374
STATISTICAL RECORD:							
Return on Revenues %	0.1	2.7	4.9	2.2	4.2	2.5	3.2
Return on Equity %	0.2	10.0	18.1	7.3	7.6	4.0	6.2
Return on Assets %	0.1	5.3	9.4	3.7	3.8	2.0	3.0
Price Range	22.31-12.25	31.50-10.13	33.88-14.25	14.63-9.38	11.31-9.81	11.25-7.56	10.71-7.19
P/E Ratio	556.4-305.5	16.2-5.2	10.2-4.3	13.2-8.4	10.5-9.1	20.3-13.6	13.7-9.2
Average Yield %	0.2	0.7	0.6	1.0	1.1	1.1	1.1

Statistics are as originally reported. Adj. for stk. split: 2-for-1, 5/99; 3-for-2, 4/94. Title revenues include amounts retained by agents. [1] Incl. non-recurr. chrg. $1.9 mill.

OFFICERS:
M. S. Morris, Chmn., Co-C.E.O.
S. Morris Jr., Pres., Co-C.E.O.
M. Crisp, V.P., Treas., Sec.

INVESTOR CONTACT: Ted C. Jones, Inv. Rel., (800) 729-1900

PRINCIPAL OFFICE: 1980 Post Oak Blvd., Houston, TX 77056

TELEPHONE NUMBER: (713) 625-8100
FAX: (713) 629-2244
WEB: www.stewart.com

NO. OF EMPLOYEES: 5,627 (approx.)

SHAREHOLDERS: 2,684

ANNUAL MEETING: In April

INCORPORATED: DE, 1970

INSTITUTIONAL HOLDINGS:
No. of Institutions: 49
Shares Held: 10,115,584
% Held: 66.4

INDUSTRY: Title insurance (SIC: 6361)

TRANSFER AGENT(S): Mellon Investor Services, LLC, Ridgefield Park, NJ

NYSE SYMBOL SV
Rec. Pr. 29.47 (4/30/01)

STILWELL FINANCIAL, INC.

YIELD 0.1%
P/E RATIO 10.2

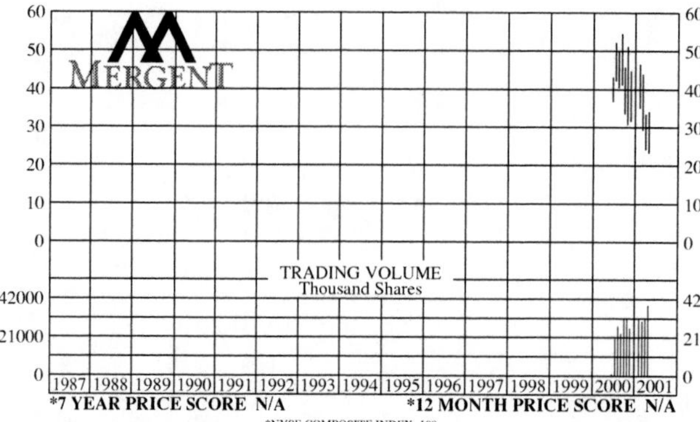

*7 YEAR PRICE SCORE N/A *12 MONTH PRICE SCORE N/A

*NYSE COMPOSITE INDEX=100

INTERIM EARNINGS (Per Share):

Qtr.	Mar.	June	Sept.	Dec.
2000	0.83	0.67	0.73	0.66

INTERIM DIVIDENDS (Per Share):

Amt.	Decl.	Ex.	Rec.	Pay.
0.01Q	10/04/00	10/12/00	10/16/00	10/31/00
0.01Q	12/07/00	1/10/01	1/15/01	1/31/01
0.01Q	4/10/01	4/11/01	4/16/01	4/30/01
0.01Q	5/10/01	7/12/01	7/16/01	7/31/01

Indicated div.: $0.04

CAPITALIZATION (12/31/00):

	($mill.)	(%)
Deferred Income Tax	211.1	15.7
Minority Interest	73.3	5.5
Common & Surplus	1,057.8	78.8
Total	1,342.2	100.0

RECENT DEVELOPMENTS: For the year ended 12/31/00, net income more than doubled to $663.7 million versus $313.1 million in 1999. Earnings for 2000 included a net after-tax nonrecurring gain of $52.9 million. Total revenues advanced 85.4% to $2.25 billion from $1.21 billion in 1999. Revenues from investment management fees increased 86.4% to $1.85 billion. Revenues from shareowner servicing fees grew 76.7% to $338.2 million.

PROSPECTS: On 1/26/01, SV announced that it will acquire 600,000 shares of Janus Capital Corp. common stock from Thomas H. Bailey, the Chairman, President, Chief Executive Officer of Janus, increasing SV's ownership of Janus to 88.7%. Meanwhile, Janus closed five funds during 2000 with the objective of ensuring ongoing success for existing fund shareowners. These funds totaled nearly 50.0% of Janus's total assets under management.

BUSINESS

STILWELL FINANCIAL, INC. was spun off from Kansas City Southern Industries Inc. on 7/12/00. As of 12/31/00, SV primarily operates through 81.9%-owned Janus Capital Corporation, 86.0%-owned Berger LLC, 80.0%-owned Nelson Money Managers Plc. Janus Capital is the investment adviser of the Janus Investment Fund, Janus Aspen Series, Janus World Funds Plc, Janus Universal Funds, other investment companies and institutional and private accounts. Berger is the investment adviser of the Berger Advised Funds. Nelson provides investment management services in the U.K. to retirees. The Company also owns a 33.0% interest in DST Systems, which provides information processing and software to the mutual fund industry.

REVENUES

12/31/2000	($000)	(%)
Investment management fees	1,850,700	82.3
Shareowner servicing fees	338,200	15.0
Other	59,200	2.7
Total	2,248,100	100.0

ANNUAL FINANCIAL DATA

	12/31/00	12/31/99	12/31/98	12/31/97
Earnings Per Share	**1 2.90**	**1.23**	**0.60**	**0.47**
Cash Flow Per Share	**3.30**	**1.56**	**0.76**	**0.59**
Tang. Book Val. Per Share	**3.50**	**2.93**	**1.76**	...
Dividends Per Share	**0.01**	...	...	...
Dividend Payout %	**0.3**	...	...	...
INCOME STATEMENT (IN MILLIONS):				
Total Revenues	2,248.1	1,212.3	670.8	485.1
Costs & Expenses	1,130.6	658.6	373.4	272.8
Depreciation & Amort.	81.2	35.4	16.8	13.1
Operating Income	1,036.3	518.3	280.6	199.2
Net Interest Inc./(Exp.)	d7.7	d5.9	d6.5	d10.4
Income Before Income Taxes	1,202.4	586.5	289.3	229.9
Income Taxes	427.0	216.1	103.7	87.0
Equity Earnings/Minority Int.	d111.7	d57.3	d33.4	d24.9
Net Income	1 663.7	313.1	152.2	118.0
Cash Flow	744.9	348.5	169.0	131.1
Average Shs. Outstg. (000)	225,423	223,000	223,000	223,000
BALANCE SHEET (IN MILLIONS):				
Cash & Cash Equivalents	394.5	348.0	170.7	...
Total Current Assets	641.1	525.0	259.3	...
Net Property	137.7	70.4	37.4	...
Total Assets	1,581.0	1,231.5	822.9	...
Total Current Liabilities	196.1	162.5	71.1	...
Long-Term Obligations	...	...	16.6	...
Net Stockholders' Equity	1,057.8	814.6	540.2	...
Net Working Capital	445.0	362.5	188.2	...
Year-end Shs. Outstg. (000)	218,909	223,000	223,000	223,000
STATISTICAL RECORD:				
Operating Profit Margin %	46.1	42.8	41.8	41.1
Net Profit Margin %	29.5	25.8	22.7	24.3
Return on Equity %	62.7	38.4	28.2	...
Return on Assets %	42.0	25.4	18.5	...
Debt/Total Assets %	...	...	2.0	...
Price Range	54.50-30.75	...	...	...
P/E Ratio	18.8-10.6	...	...	...

Statistics are as originally reported. 1 Incl. a net after-tax nonrecurring gain of $52.9 mill.

OFFICERS:
L. H. Rowland, Chmn., Pres., C.E.O.
G. E. Royle, V.P., Legal, Corporate Sec.

INVESTOR CONTACT: Douglas E. Pittman, Mgr. of Inv. Rel., (816) 218-2415

PRINCIPAL OFFICE: 920 Main Street, 21st Floor, Kansas City, MO 64105

TELEPHONE NUMBER: (816) 218-2400
FAX: (816) 218-2452
WEB: www.stilwellfinancial.com

NO. OF EMPLOYEES: 3,100 (approx.)

SHAREHOLDERS: 4,971

ANNUAL MEETING: In May

INCORPORATED: DE, Jan., 1998

INSTITUTIONAL HOLDINGS:
No. of Institutions: 310
Shares Held: 171,756,712
% Held: 78.3

INDUSTRY: Investment advice (SIC: 6282)

TRANSFER AGENT(S): UMB Bank, N.A.

NYSE SYMBOL STK
Rec. Pr. 12.79 (4/30/01)

STORAGE TECHNOLOGY CORPORATION

YIELD ...
P/E RATIO ...

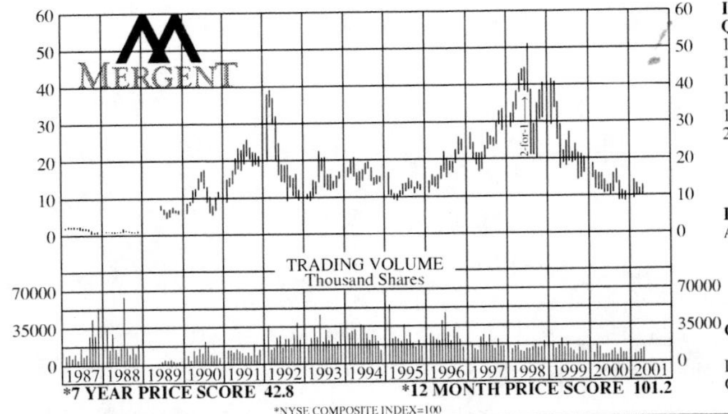

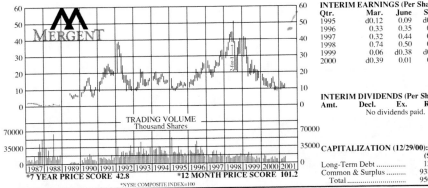

*7 YEAR PRICE SCORE 42.8 *12 MONTH PRICE SCORE 101.2
*NYSE COMPOSITE INDEX=100

INTERIM EARNINGS (Per Share):

Qtr.	Mar.	June	Sept.	Dec.
1995	d0.12	0.09	d0.10	d1.33
1996	0.33	0.35	0.33	0.58
1997	0.32	0.44	0.44	0.75
1998	0.74	0.50	0.48	0.52
1999	0.06	d0.38	d0.16	d0.26
2000	d0.39	0.01	0.06	0.30

INTERIM DIVIDENDS (Per Share):

Amt.	Decl.	Ex.	Rec.	Pay.

No dividends paid.

CAPITALIZATION (12/29/00):

	($000)	(%)
Long-Term Debt	12,083	1.3
Common & Surplus	938,635	98.7
Total	950,718	100.0

RECENT DEVELOPMENTS: For the year ended 12/29/00, the Company reported a net loss of $1.8 million compared with a net loss of $74.6 million in 1999. Results for 2000 and 1999 included restructuring charges of $27.2 million and $43.3 million, respectively. Results for 1999 also included a litigation expense of $103.6 million. Total revenues fell 13.0% to $2.06 billion from $2.37 billion in the prior year. Gross profit decreased 11.8% to $831.5 million from $943.0 million in 1999.

PROSPECTS: STK is looking to gain momentum through improvements to its business model and product portfolio. Recent strength in STK's gross margin and a stronger balance sheet bode well for the Company. Moreover, STK's cash position is much stronger, as the Company generated cash in excess of $300.0 million from operations for fiscal 2000 and ended the year with a cash balance of $280.0 million. STK has also managed to lower its debt-to-capital ratio to 9.0%.

BUSINESS

STORAGE TECHNOLOGY CORPORATION designs, develops, manufactures, and markets a range of information storage products and provides maintenance and consulting services. The Company is organized into two business segments: storage products and storage services. The Company's storage product offerings include tape, disk and network products. The storage services segment is divided into two categories: maintenance services and consulting services. The Company provides maintenance services for both StorageTek products and third-party products. The storage consulting services segment primarily supports sales of STK's hardware and software products, particularly for the Virtual Storage Manager®, a software-driven data storage management application, and its storage networking products. Revenues for 2000 were derived: storage products, 68.5%; and storage services, 31.5%.

ANNUAL FINANCIAL DATA

	12/29/00	12/31/99	12/25/98	12/26/97	12/27/96	12/29/95	12/30/94
Earnings Per Share	**3 d0.02**	**2 d0.75**	**1.86**	**1.90**	**1.50**	**1 d1.45**	**0.33**
Cash Flow Per Share	**1.37**	**0.69**	**3.02**	**2.81**	**3.03**	**0.52**	**2.65**
Tang. Book Val. Per Share	**9.11**	**9.13**	**9.97**	**10.39**	**10.16**	**9.03**	**12.07**
INCOME STATEMENT (IN MILLIONS):							
Total Revenues	2,060.2	2,368.2	2,258.2	2,144.7	2,039.6	1,929.5	1,625.0
Costs & Expenses	1,916.5	2,322.5	1,822.6	1,741.6	1,639.3	1,854.0	1,362.5
Depreciation & Amort.	139.7	143.0	122.9	112.3	174.8	209.0	206.3
Operating Income	4.0	d97.2	312.8	290.8	225.5	d133.5	56.2
Net Interest Inc./(Exp.)	d6.8	d19.2	6.9	25.4	1.2	9.0	2.3
Income Before Income Taxes	d2.7	d116.4	319.7	316.1	226.7	d124.5	58.4
Income Taxes	cr1.0	cr41.9	121.5	84.3	55.9	17.8	17.0
Net Income	3 d1.8	2 d74.5	198.2	231.8	170.8	1 d142.3	41.4
Cash Flow	137.9	68.5	321.1	344.1	345.6	55.1	235.7
Average Shs. Outstg. (000)	100,859	99,900	106,497	122,513	113,886	105,596	89,026
BALANCE SHEET (IN MILLIONS):							
Cash & Cash Equivalents	279.7	215.4	232.0	333.6	417.6	264.5	205.9
Total Current Assets	1,173.4	1,228.1	1,364.4	1,269.6	1,260.4	975.0	922.7
Net Property	267.1	322.1	320.9	305.1	327.5	472.7	470.0
Total Assets	1,653.6	1,735.5	1,842.9	1,740.0	1,884.3	1,888.6	1,890.0
Total Current Liabilities	702.8	787.3	826.1	608.4	536.2	549.6	448.5
Long-Term Obligations	12.1	29.0	17.3	19.1	150.8	364.0	356.9
Net Stockholders' Equity	938.6	919.2	999.6	1,112.5	1,181.0	962.8	1,074.5
Net Working Capital	470.6	440.8	538.3	661.2	724.2	425.4	474.2
Year-end Shs. Outstg. (000)	103,058	100,712	100,221	107,090	116,226	106,616	89,050
STATISTICAL RECORD:							
Operating Profit Margin %	0.2	...	13.9	13.6	11.1	...	3.5
Net Profit Margin %	...	...	8.8	10.8	8.4	...	2.6
Return on Equity %	...	...	19.8	20.8	14.5	...	3.9
Return on Assets %	...	...	10.8	13.3	9.1	...	2.2
Debt/Total Assets %	0.7	1.7	0.9	1.1	8.0	19.3	18.9
Price Range	18.75-8.50	41.63-14.25	51.13-20.13	33.50-16.63	26.00-11.00	16.63-8.94	20.75-12.50
P/E Ratio	...	...	27.5-10.8	17.7-8.8	17.3-7.3	...	62.9-37.9

Statistics are as originally reported. Adj. for 2-for-1 split, 6/98. 1 Incl. $74.8 mill. restr. chg. & excl. $40.0 mill. acct. credit. 2 Incl. $43.3 mill. restr. chg. & $103.6 mill. litigation expense. 3 Incl. $27.2 mill. restr. chgs.

OFFICERS:
P. J. Martin, Chmn., Pres., C.E.O.
R. S. Kocol, V.P., C.F.O.
J. M. Dumas, V.P., Sec., Gen. Couns.

INVESTOR CONTACT: Bill Watts, (303) 673-5020

PRINCIPAL OFFICE: One StorageTek Drive, Louisville, CO 80028-4309

TELEPHONE NUMBER: (303) 673-5151
FAX: (303) 673-5019
WEB: www.storagetek.com

NO. OF EMPLOYEES: 7,600 (approx.)

SHAREHOLDERS: 11,287 (record)

ANNUAL MEETING: In May

INCORPORATED: DE, Aug., 1969

INSTITUTIONAL HOLDINGS:
No. of Institutions: 130
Shares Held: 88,590,170
% Held: 86.1

INDUSTRY: Computer storage devices (SIC: 3572)

TRANSFER AGENT(S): American Stock Transfer & Trust Company, New York, NY

NYSE SYMBOL SRR
Rec. Pr. 8.10 (5/31/01)

STRIDE RITE CORPORATION

YIELD 2.5%
P/E RATIO 14.2

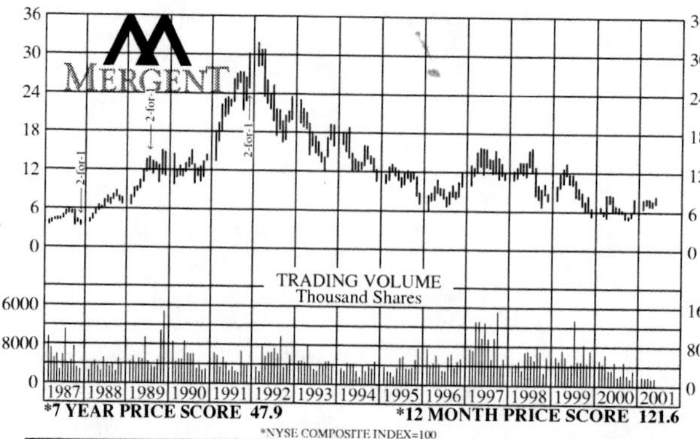

*7 YEAR PRICE SCORE 47.9 *12 MONTH PRICE SCORE 121.6

*NYSE COMPOSITE INDEX=100

INTERIM EARNINGS (Per Share):

Qtr.	Feb.	May	Aug.	Nov.
1996-97	0.08	0.14	0.17	0.01
1997-98	0.09	0.20	0.27	d0.12
1998-99	0.13	0.21	0.22	0.01
1999-00	0.17	0.24	0.18	d0.02

INTERIM DIVIDENDS (Per Share):

Amt.	Decl.	Ex.	Rec.	Pay.
0.05Q	4/13/00	5/25/00	5/30/00	6/15/00
0.05Q	8/03/00	8/25/00	8/29/00	9/15/00
0.05Q	11/09/01	11/28/00	11/30/00	12/15/00
0.05Q	2/08/01	2/22/01	2/26/01	3/15/01
0.05Q	4/12/01	5/24/01	5/29/01	6/15/01

Indicated div.: $0.20 (Div. Reinv. Plan)

CAPITALIZATION (12/1/00):

	($000)	(%)
Deferred Income Tax	5,929	2.3
Common & Surplus	249,592	97.7
Total	255,521	100.0

RECENT DEVELOPMENTS: For the year ended 12/1/00, net income totaled $25.2 million, a decline of 4.7% compared with $26.4 million in the previous year. Results included a nonrecurring charge of $396,000 in 2000 and a credit of $3.3 million in 1999. Net sales fell 4.3% to $548.3 million versus $572.7 million the year before. Gross profit as a percentage of net sales slipped to 36.2% compared with 36.8% in the previous year.

PROSPECTS: The Company will continue to focus on expanding and improving its two key brands, Stride Rite and Keds. Hence, SRR introduced the Natural Motion System™ baby product line, a new store design, improvements in retail execution and the launching of the Munchkin® product line during Spring 2001. Also, SRR introduced the Keds Original™ product line, which features an update of Keds classic Champion® oxford style. In addition, SRR anticipates the opening of approximately 24 stores in 2001.

BUSINESS

STRIDE RITE CORPORATION markets children's footwear in the U.S. as well as athletic and casual footwear for adults. The Company is also engaged in the manufacture of boating and outdoor recreational shoes and adult workboots. Products are sold to independent retail shoe stores, department stores, sporting goods stores and marinas. As of 12/31/00, SRR owned 117 Stride Rite children's shoe stores, 46 leased children's shoe departments in department stores and 38 manufacturers' outlet stores under the name Stride Rite Family footwear. Trademarks include: STRIDE RITE, KEDS, SPERRY TOP-SIDER, TOMMY HILFIGER, STREET HOT, NINE WEST KIDS and GRASSHOPPERS.

QUARTERLY DATA

(12/01/2000)($000)	REV	INC
1st Quarter	151,663	7,487
2nd Quarter	156,533	10,609
3rd Quarter	144,760	7,782
4th Quarter	95,378	(685)

ANNUAL FINANCIAL DATA

	12/1/00	12/3/99	11/27/98	11/28/97	11/29/96	12/1/95	12/2/94
Earnings Per Share	[1] 0.58	[1] 0.57	0.45	0.40	0.05	[1] d0.17	0.40
Cash Flow Per Share	0.87	0.79	0.64	0.60	0.24	0.05	0.57
Tang. Book Val. Per Share	5.98	5.59	5.25	5.09	5.24	5.37	5.88
Dividends Per Share	0.20	0.20	0.20	0.20	0.20	0.34	0.38
Dividend Payout %	34.5	35.1	44.4	50.0	399.2	...	95.0
INCOME STATEMENT (IN THOUSANDS):							
Total Revenues	548,334	572,696	539,413	515,728	448,297	496,432	523,877
Costs & Expenses	498,097	521,990	500,482	474,872	437,236	501,980	483,507
Depreciation & Amort.	12,252	10,061	9,384	9,833	9,698	10,860	8,486
Operating Income	37,985	40,645	29,547	31,023	1,363	d16,408	31,884
Net Interest Inc./(Exp.)	d1,881	d1,760	d1,730	d188	d701	d1,034	d538
Income Before Income Taxes	40,102	42,656	33,222	31,928	3,027	d18,065	32,542
Income Taxes	14,909	16,232	12,170	12,148	528	cr9,635	12,744
Net Income	[1] 25,193	[1] 26,424	21,052	19,780	2,499	[1] d8,430	19,798
Cash Flow	37,445	36,485	30,436	29,613	12,197	2,430	28,284
Average Shs. Outstg.	43,154	46,414	47,335	48,949	49,909	49,780	49,904
BALANCE SHEET (IN THOUSANDS):							
Cash & Cash Equivalents	62,976	57,186	42,427	51,080	91,880	54,341	75,947
Total Current Assets	255,127	257,029	258,229	271,651	296,128	292,363	330,943
Net Property	76,240	67,425	58,350	55,395	52,894	60,434	48,267
Total Assets	352,473	346,192	335,496	343,918	364,330	366,616	396,620
Total Current Liabilities	96,952	90,478	84,727	95,388	94,531	87,578	94,315
Long-Term Obligations	...	...	...	...	...	833	1,667
Net Stockholders' Equity	249,592	250,495	244,727	242,026	261,524	267,456	292,506
Net Working Capital	158,175	166,551	173,502	176,263	201,597	204,785	236,628
Year-end Shs. Outstg.	41,591	44,634	46,381	47,337	49,668	49,531	49,518
STATISTICAL RECORD:							
Operating Profit Margin %	6.9	7.1	5.5	6.0	0.3	...	6.1
Net Profit Margin %	4.6	4.6	3.9	3.8	0.6	...	3.8
Return on Equity %	10.1	10.5	8.6	8.2	1.0	...	6.8
Return on Assets %	7.1	7.6	6.3	5.8	0.7	...	5.0
Debt/Total Assets %	...	...	...	...	...	0.2	0.4
Price Range	8.69-4.81	13.44-5.19	15.75-6.63	15.88-9.88	11.88-6.00	13.25-7.00	18.88-10.50
P/E Ratio	15.0-8.3	23.6-9.1	35.0-14.7	39.7-24.7	237.0-119.8	...	47.2-26.2
Average Yield %	3.0	2.1	1.8	1.6	2.2	3.3	2.6

Statistics are as originally reported. [1] Incl. non-recurr. credit 1999, $3.3 mill.; 1998, $3.8 mill.; chrg. 2000, $396,000; 1995, $16.6 mill.

OFFICERS:
D. M. Chamberlain, Chmn., C.E.O.
D. M. Sullivan, Pres., C.O.O.
J. M. Kelliher, V.P., C.F.O., Treas.

INVESTOR CONTACT: John M. Kelliher, C.F.O., V.P., Treas., (617) 824-6028

PRINCIPAL OFFICE: 191 Spring Street, P.O. Box 9191, Lexington, MA 02420

TELEPHONE NUMBER: (617) 824-6000
FAX: (617) 824-6969
WEB: www.striderite.com

NO. OF EMPLOYEES: 2,200 (avg.)

SHAREHOLDERS: 4,200 (approx. record)

ANNUAL MEETING: In April

INCORPORATED: MA, Nov., 1919

INSTITUTIONAL HOLDINGS:
No. of Institutions: 100
Shares Held: 26,908,298
% Held: 64.5

INDUSTRY: Footwear, except rubber, nec (SIC: 3149)

TRANSFER AGENT(S): BankBoston, NA, Boston, MA

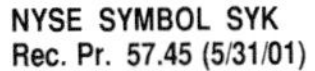
NYSE SYMBOL SYK
Rec. Pr. 57.45 (5/31/01)

STRYKER CORPORATION

YIELD 0.1%
P/E RATIO 52.2

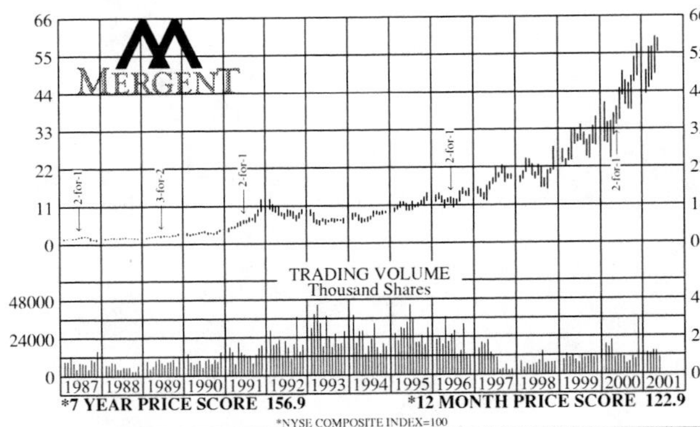

*7 YEAR PRICE SCORE 156.9 *12 MONTH PRICE SCORE 122.9

*NYSE COMPOSITE INDEX=100

INTERIM EARNINGS (Per Share):

Qtr.	Mar.	June	Sept.	Dec.
1997	0.16	0.16	0.15	0.19
1998	0.19	0.18	0.18	d0.34
1999	d0.11	d0.02	Nil	0.22
2000	0.26	0.26	0.25	0.33

INTERIM DIVIDENDS (Per Share):

Amt.	Decl.	Ex.	Rec.	Pay.
0.13A	12/08/99	12/29/99	12/31/99	1/31/00
2-for-1	4/19/00	5/15/00	5/01/00	5/12/00
0.08A	12/15/00	12/27/00	12/29/00	1/31/01

Indicated div.: $0.08

CAPITALIZATION (12/31/00):

	($000)	(%)
Long-Term Debt	876,500	50.6
Common & Surplus	854,900	49.4
Total	1,731,400	100.0

RECENT DEVELOPMENTS: For the year ended 12/31/00, net income soared to $221.0 million compared with $19.4 million in the previous year. Results for 2000 included a net, non-recurring after-tax gain of $700,000. The 1999 results included after-tax non-recurring charges of $141.1 million. Net sales amounted to $2.29 billion, up 8.8% versus $2.10 billion a year earlier.

PROSPECTS: On 5/17/01, the Company announced the European Commission has granted marketing authorization for Osteogenic Protein 1 (OP-1), a recombinant human protein that induces bone formation, in the 15 member-countries of the European Union. On 5/4/01, the Company also was granted marketing registration of OP-1 in Australia by the Therapeutic Goods Administration.

BUSINESS

STRYKER CORPORATION and its subsidiaries develop, manufacture and market specialty surgical and medical products, including orthopaedic implants, bone cement, trauma systems used in bone repair, powered surgical instruments, craniomaxillofacial fixation devices, endoscopic systems and patient care and handling equipment for the global market and provides physical and occupational therapy services in the U.S. The Company, through its subsidiary, develops, builds, and markets video communications hardware and software for medical education. Revenues for 2000 were derived as follows: 57.4% from orthopaedic implants, 36.2% from MedSurg equipment, and 6.4% from physical therapy services. On 12/4/98, SYK acquired Howmedica, Inc., which was the orthopaedic division of Pfizer Inc.

REVENUES

(12/31/00)	($000)	(%)
Orthopaedic Implants	1,313,000	57.3
Medical & Surgical Equipment	829,100	36.2
Other..........................	147,300	6.4
Total	2,289,400	100.0

ANNUAL FINANCIAL DATA

	12/31/00	12/31/99	12/31/98	12/31/97	12/31/96	12/31/95	12/31/94
Earnings Per Share	**4 1.10**	**3 0.10**	**2 0.20**	**0.64**	**1 0.54**	**0.45**	**0.38**
Cash Flow Per Share	**1.94**	**0.92**	**0.39**	**0.81**	**0.09**	**0.60**	**0.48**
Tang. Book Val. Per Share	**0.08**	**...**	**...**	**2.95**	**2.51**	**2.25**	**1.76**
Dividends Per Share	**0.07**	**0.06**	**0.06**	**0.05**	**0.02**	**0.02**	**0.02**
Dividend Payout %	**5.9**	**60.0**	**27.5**	**7.8**	**4.2**	**4.4**	**4.7**
INCOME STATEMENT (IN MILLIONS):							
Total Revenues	2,289.4	2,103.7	1,103.2	980.1	910.1	872.0	681.9
Costs & Expenses	1,653.4	1,759.4	1,010.0	762.9	802.3	686.0	540.5
Depreciation & Amort.	168.6	162.8	37.6	33.3	34.7	28.7	20.9
Operating Income	467.4	181.5	55.6	184.0	153.5	157.3	120.5
Net Interest Inc./(Exp.)	d96.6	d122.6	...	...	...	...	...
Income Before Income Taxes	334.9	29.8	60.0	194.5	160.4	163.1	127.6
Income Taxes	113.9	10.4	20.4	70.0	61.7	66.9	50.8
Equity Earnings/Minority Int.	...	...	...	0.9	5.7	d9.2	d4.4
Net Income	4 221.0	3 19.4	2 39.6	125.3	1 d17.7	87.0	72.4
Cash Flow	389.6	182.2	77.2	158.6	16.9	115.7	93.3
Average Shs. Outstg. (000)	201,100	198,600	196,260	196,264	193,676	193,872	193,468
BALANCE SHEET (IN MILLIONS):							
Cash & Cash Equivalents	54.0	83.5	142.2	351.1	367.6	264.6	202.0
Total Current Assets	997.0	1,110.4	1,311.8	756.6	753.5	623.3	540.5
Net Property	378.1	391.5	429.5	163.9	172.3	182.6	180.7
Total Assets	2,430.8	2,580.5	2,885.9	985.1	993.5	854.9	768.0
Total Current Liabilities	617.4	669.6	699.5	303.0	251.7	174.4	179.2
Long-Term Obligations	876.5	1,181.1	1,488.0	4.4	89.5	97.0	95.3
Net Stockholders' Equity	854.9	671.5	652.1	612.8	530.4	454.3	358.3
Net Working Capital	379.6	440.8	612.4	453.6	501.8	448.8	361.3
Year-end Shs. Outstg. (000)	195,900	194,400	193,080	192,118	193,574	194,216	193,476
STATISTICAL RECORD:							
Operating Profit Margin %	20.4	8.6	5.0	18.8	16.9	18.0	17.7
Net Profit Margin %	9.7	0.9	3.6	12.8	...	10.0	10.6
Return on Equity %	25.9	2.9	6.1	20.5	...	19.2	20.2
Return on Assets %	9.1	0.8	1.4	12.7	...	10.2	9.4
Debt/Total Assets %	36.1	45.8	51.6	0.5	9.0	11.3	12.4
Price Range	57.75-24.44	36.63-22.22	27.88-15.50	22.66-12.13	16.06-9.94	14.63-9.03	9.38-5.94
P/E Ratio	52.5-22.2	366.1-222.1	139.3-77.5	35.4-18.9	29.7-18.4	32.5-20.1	25.0-15.8
Average Yield %	0.2	0.2	0.3	0.3	0.2	0.2	0.2

Statistics are as originally reported. Adjusted for a 2-for-1 stock split 6/10/96 & 5/12/00. 1 Incl. a pre-tax charge of $41.8 mill. & a pre-tax gain of $61.1 mill. on a patent. 2 Incl. a pre-tax chg. of $83.3 mill. for purchased research and development & a pre-tax chg. of $49.9 mill. for acquisition-related expenses. 3 Incl. net nonrecurr. chrgs. of $141.1 mill. 4 Incl. net nonrecur. after-tax gain of $700,000.

OFFICERS:
J. W. Brown, Chmn., Pres., C.E.O.
J. P. Anderson, V.P., Business Devel., Asst. Chmn.
D. J. Simpson, V.P., C.F.O., Sec.
C. F. Homrich, Treas.

INVESTOR CONTACT: David J. Simpson, VP, CFO, & Sec., (616) 385-2600

PRINCIPAL OFFICE: P.O. Box 4085, Kalamazoo, MI 49002

TELEPHONE NUMBER: (616) 385-2600
FAX: (616) 385-1062
WEB: www.strykercorp.com

NO. OF EMPLOYEES: 12,084

SHAREHOLDERS: 3,035

ANNUAL MEETING: In Apr.

INCORPORATED: MI, Feb., 1946

INSTITUTIONAL HOLDINGS:
No. of Institutions: 360
Shares Held: 86,757,161
% Held: 44.2

INDUSTRY: Surgical and medical instruments (SIC: 3841)

TRANSFER AGENT(S): First Chicago Trust, Jersey City, NJ

NYSE SYMBOL SZA
Rec. Pr. 51.95 (5/31/01)

SUIZA FOODS CORPORATION

YIELD ...
P/E RATIO 13.6

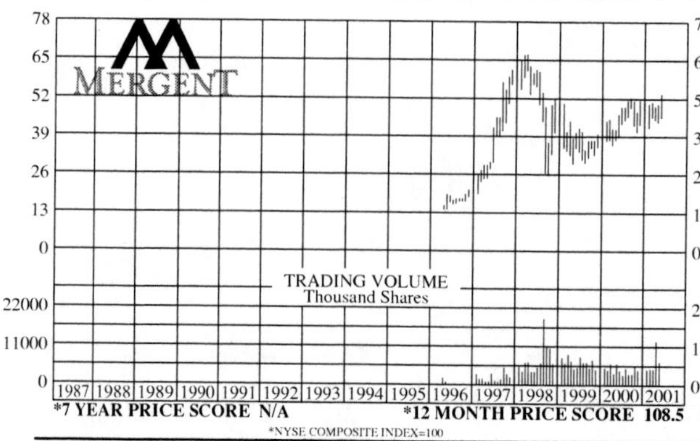

INTERIM EARNINGS (Per Share):

Qtr.	Mar.	June	Sept.	Dec.
1997	0.70	0.56	0.61	d0.60
1998	0.45	0.82	0.76	0.76
1999	0.60	0.87	0.83	0.78
2000	0.69	1.04	1.01	1.09

INTERIM DIVIDENDS (Per Share):

Amt.	Decl.	Ex.	Rec.	Pay.
No dividends paid.				

CAPITALIZATION (12/31/00):

	($000)	(%)
Long-Term Debt	1,225,045	40.2
Deferred Income Tax	123,614	4.1
Minority Interest	514,845	16.9
Redeemable Pfd. Stock	584,032	19.2
Common & Surplus	598,832	19.7
Total	3,046,368	100.0

RECENT DEVELOPMENTS: For the year ended 12/31/00, the Company reported earnings of $113.8 million, before an extraordinary gain of $5.0 million, versus earnings of $108.8 million, before an extraordinary gain of $904,000, the year before. Results included one-time pre-tax charges of $3.4 million and $12.6 million in 2000 and 1999, respectively, related to plant closings and administrative restructuring. Net sales grew 28.4% to $5.76 billion from $4.48 billion the previous year. As a percentage of net sales, gross profit was 24.8% versus 22.2% in 1999.

PROSPECTS: On 4/5/01, the Company announced that it signed a definitive agreement to acquire Dean Foods Company, a major processor and distributor of dairy products and other specialty foods, for approximately $2.50 billion, including the assumption of about $1.00 billion of debt. Upon completion of the transaction, which is expected during the third quarter of 2001 subject to shareholder and regulatory approvals, SZA will change its name to Dean Foods. The combination is expected to generate $60.0 million of synergistic savings during the first year.

BUSINESS

SUIZA FOODS CORPORATION is a manufacturer and distributor of dairy products including fluid milk, ice cream and novelties, dairy and non-dairy coffee creamers, half-and-half and whipping cream, sour cream, cottage cheese, yogurt, and dairy and non-dairy frozen whipped toppings. SZA also manufactures and distributes fruit juices and other flavored drinks, bottled water and coffee. The Company sells its products to retail and food service customers including grocery stores, club stores, convenience stores, institutional food service, gas stores, schools, restaurants and hotels. National brand names include INTERNATIONAL DELIGHT®, SUN SOY™, SECOND NATURE®, MOCHA MIX®, NATURALLY YOURS®, KIDSMILK™, FITMILK™ and LIFEMILK™.

ANNUAL FINANCIAL DATA

	12/31/00	12/31/99	12/31/98	12/31/97	12/31/96	12/31/95	12/31/94
Earnings Per Share	[1][2] 3.68	[1][2] 3.11	[1][3] 2.90	[1][2][3] 1.25	[1][2] 2.81	[1][2] d0.26	[1][2] 0.69
Cash Flow Per Share	7.06	5.26	4.64	2.68	4.48	5.38	3.36
Tang. Book Val. Per Share	21.95	19.94	19.52	11.67	8.71	1.50	...
INCOME STATEMENT (IN MILLIONS):							
Total Revenues	5,756.3	4,482.0	3,320.9	1,794.9	520.9	430.5	341.1
Costs & Expenses	5,243.3	4,088.5	2,986.7	1,655.0	469.8	375.7	300.6
Depreciation & Amort.	145.0	116.6	91.8	44.6	15.4	13.9	13.1
Operating Income	368.1	276.9	242.5	95.3	35.1	30.6	25.8
Net Interest Inc./(Exp.)	d112.6	d49.2	d52.1	d36.7	d17.5	d19.9	d19.3
Income Before Income Taxes	234.0	193.1	164.5	82.7	21.1	0.9	5.1
Income Taxes	90.3	75.5	59.8	43.4	cr6.8	2.5	0.8
Net Income	[1][2] 113.8	[1][2] 108.8	[1][3] 103.1	[1][2][3] 39.3	[1][2] 29.1	[1][2] 18.9	[1][2] 7.6
Cash Flow	258.7	225.5	194.6	83.6	44.5	32.8	20.7
Average Shs. Outstg. (000)	36,671	42,858	41,966	31,349	9,922	6,109	6,156
BALANCE SHEET (IN MILLIONS):							
Cash & Cash Equivalents	31.1	25.2	64.1	24.4	9.0	3.2	5.4
Total Current Assets	817.9	639.4	813.9	396.1	87.5	48.4	48.0
Net Property	1,003.8	758.5	847.0	363.6	123.3	92.7	90.9
Total Assets	3,780.5	2,658.9	3,013.8	1,403.5	384.1	232.5	239.0
Total Current Liabilities	699.9	479.1	559.1	232.9	60.6	50.0	45.9
Long-Term Obligations	1,225.0	689.4	893.1	777.8	226.7	171.7	173.3
Net Stockholders' Equity	598.8	584.0	655.8	359.3	93.5	9.5	9.9
Net Working Capital	118.0	160.3	254.8	163.2	26.9	d1.6	2.1
Year-end Shs. Outstg. (000)	27,286	29,288	33,598	30,463	10,742	6,314	...
STATISTICAL RECORD:							
Operating Profit Margin %	6.4	6.2	7.3	5.3	6.7	7.1	7.6
Net Profit Margin %	2.0	2.4	3.1	2.2	5.6	4.4	2.2
Return on Equity %	19.0	18.6	15.7	10.9	31.1	199.8	76.5
Return on Assets %	3.0	4.1	3.4	2.8	7.6	8.1	3.2
Debt/Total Assets %	32.4	25.9	29.6	55.4	59.0	73.9	72.5
Price Range	52.44-36.00	50.25-29.63	67.00-25.69	61.75-19.25	20.75-14.00	...	...
P/E Ratio	14.2-9.8	16.2-9.5	23.1-8.9	49.4-15.4	7.4-5.0	...	...

Statistics are as originally reported. [1] Bef. $5.0 mil ($0.13/sh) extraord. gain, 2000; $904,000 ($0.02/sh) gain, 1999; $31.7 mil ($0.76/sh) gain, 1998; $11.3 mil ($0.36/sh) chg., 1997; $2.2 mil chg., 1996; $8.5 mil chg., 1995; $197,000 chg., 1994. [2] Incl. $3.4 mil non-recur. pre-tax chg., 2000; $17.5 mil, 1999; $37.0 mil, 1997; $571,000, 1996; $10.2 mil, 1995; & $1.7 mil 1994. [3] Bef. $3.2 mil ($0.08/sh) disc. oper. chg., 1998; $717,000 ($0.02/sh) gain, 1997.

OFFICERS:
G. L. Engles, Chmn., C.E.O.
B. A. Fromberg, Exec. V.P., C.F.O.

INVESTOR CONTACT: Cory M. Olson, (214) 303-3645

PRINCIPAL OFFICE: 2515 McKinney Avenue, Suite 1200, Dallas, TX 75201

TELEPHONE NUMBER: (214) 303-3400
FAX: (214) 303-3499
WEB: www.suizafoods.com

NO. OF EMPLOYEES: 18,000 (approx.)

SHAREHOLDERS: 375 (approx.)

ANNUAL MEETING: In May

INCORPORATED: DE, Sept., 1994

INSTITUTIONAL HOLDINGS:
No. of Institutions: 201
Shares Held: 25,747,036
% Held: 94.8

INDUSTRY: Ice cream and frozen desserts (SIC: 2024)

TRANSFER AGENT(S): Computershare Investor Services, Dallas, TX

NYSE SYMBOL SDS
Rec. Pr. 29.74 (Adj.; 5/31/01)

SUNGARD DATA SYSTEMS INC.

YIELD ...
P/E RATIO 37.2

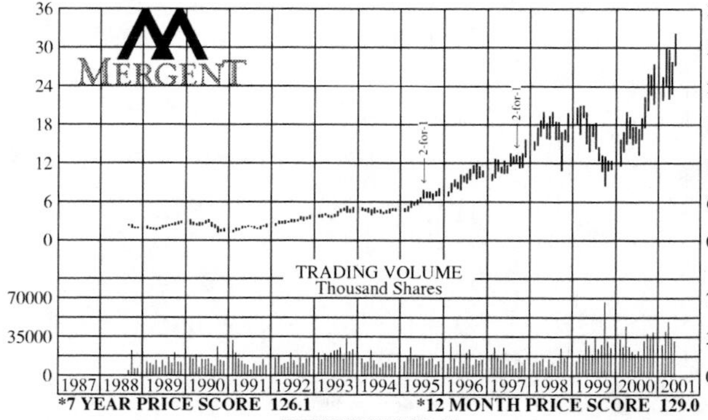

INTERIM EARNINGS (Per Share):

Qtr.	Mar.	June	Sept.	Dec.
1998	0.10	0.14	0.15	0.17
1999	d0.08	0.16	0.14	0.17
2000	0.16	0.20	0.21	0.23

INTERIM DIVIDENDS (Per Share):

Amt.	Decl.	Ex.	Rec.	Pay.
2-for-1	5/14/01	6/19/01	5/25/01	6/18/01

CAPITALIZATION (12/31/00):

	($000)	(%)
Long-Term Debt	7,939	0.5
Common & Surplus	1,442,476	99.5
Total	1,450,415	100.0

RECENT DEVELOPMENTS: For the year ended 12/31/00, net income totaled $213.0 million compared with income of $73.2 million, before an extraordinary gain of $10.7 million, in the previous year. Results included merger costs of $13.2 million and $99.2 million in 2000 and 1999, respectively. Revenues improved 15.0% to $1.66 billion versus $1.44 billion in the prior year. Results benefited from strong growth within all of the Company's core businesses.

PROSPECTS: Going forward, the Company is well-positioned to deliver strong revenues and earnings growth. As a result, the Company expects to achieve diluted net income per share in the range of $1.91 to $1.96 for 2001. In addition, the Company anticipates that long-term internal revenue growth, excluding new acquisitions, will average 12.0% to 15.0% per year.

BUSINESS

SUNGARD DATA SYSTEMS INC. is engaged in integrated information technology and "eProcessing" for financial services. The Company serves more than 10,000 clients in over 50 countries, including 47 of the world's 50 largest financial services institutions. The Company offers integrated, Web-enabled services and software for the management, trading, processing and accounting of financial assets and offers high-availability infrastructure, outsourcing and hosting for online and other operations. The Company's products and services generally are delivered and supported through individual business units that offer product-specific development and customer support.

ANNUAL FINANCIAL DATA

	12/31/00	12/31/99	12/31/98	12/31/97	12/31/96	12/31/95	12/31/94
Earnings Per Share	**② 0.31**	**①② 0.40**	**0.55**	**0.44**	**0.20**	**0.31**	**0.28**
Cash Flow Per Share	**1.32**	**0.75**	**1.05**	**0.96**	**0.62**	**0.65**	**0.58**
Tang. Book Val. Per Share	**3.25**	**3.09**	**2.52**	**1.82**	**1.40**	**1.61**	**1.60**
INCOME STATEMENT (IN MILLIONS):							
Total Revenues	1,660.7	1,444.5	1,159.7	862.2	670.3	532.6	437.2
Costs & Expenses	1,179.4	1,146.5	849.1	633.3	539.5	397.8	321.2
Depreciation & Amort.	146.1	122.0	107.8	94.8	71.0	54.7	45.7
Operating Income	335.3	175.9	202.8	134.0	59.8	80.1	70.3
Net Interest Inc./(Exp.)	21.5	14.5	5.4	d0.3	3.8	5.0	2.2
Income Before Income Taxes	356.8	190.5	208.2	133.7	63.6	85.1	72.5
Income Taxes	143.8	117.3	89.3	56.2	28.7	36.4	29.4
Net Income	② 213.0	①② 73.2	118.9	77.5	34.9	48.7	43.1
Cash Flow	357.6	189.0	226.7	172.3	105.9	103.4	88.8
Average Shs. Outstg. (000)	271,404	260,390	216,146	178,670	172,032	158,544	153,992
BALANCE SHEET (IN MILLIONS):							
Cash & Cash Equivalents	436.1	391.2	258.0	64.9	46.1	115.2	102.6
Total Current Assets	911.7	786.8	584.3	310.1	236.5	281.2	222.3
Net Property	208.6	182.7	132.5	120.0	109.5	95.7	90.4
Total Assets	1,845.2	1,564.8	1,075.3	786.3	679.3	579.7	485.7
Total Current Liabilities	394.8	348.5	311.6	224.5	210.3	147.6	113.4
Long-Term Obligations	7.9	5.5	2.8	2.8	4.4	3.2	4.9
Net Stockholders' Equity	1,442.5	1,210.8	760.9	559.0	465.2	422.3	359.3
Net Working Capital	517.0	438.3	272.7	85.6	26.2	133.6	108.9
Year-end Shs. Outstg. (000)	266,658	257,010	211,424	177,724	169,028	167,688	150,136
STATISTICAL RECORD:							
Operating Profit Margin %	20.2	12.2	17.5	15.5	8.9	15.0	16.1
Net Profit Margin %	12.8	5.1	10.3	9.0	5.2	9.1	9.9
Return on Equity %	14.8	6.0	15.6	13.9	7.5	11.5	12.0
Return on Assets %	11.5	4.7	11.1	9.9	5.1	8.4	8.9
Debt/Total Assets %	0.4	0.4	0.3	0.4	0.6	0.6	1.0
Price Range	27.50-11.50	20.97-8.44	20.00-10.84	15.72-9.25	11.88-6.88	8.13-4.44	5.13-3.94
P/E Ratio	90.1-37.7	52.4-21.1	36.4-19.7	36.1-21.3	58.6-33.9	26.4-14.4	18.3-14.1

Statistics are as originally reported. Adj. for 2-for-1 stk. spl., 6/01, 9/97 & 7/95. ① Bef. extraord. gain, $10.7 mill. ② Incl. $13.2 mill. in merger costs, 2000; $99.2 mill., 1999.

OFFICERS:
J. L. Mann, Chmn., C.E.O.
C. I. Conde, Pres., C.O.O.
M. J. Ruane, Sr. V.P., Fin., C.F.O.

INVESTOR CONTACT: Investor Relations, (610) 341-8700

PRINCIPAL OFFICE: 1285 Drummers Lane, Wayne, PA 19087

TELEPHONE NUMBER: (610) 341-8700
FAX: (610) 341-8739
WEB: www.sungard.com

NO. OF EMPLOYEES: 7,800 (approx.)

SHAREHOLDERS: 5,900 (approx. record)

ANNUAL MEETING: In May

INCORPORATED: DE, 1982

INSTITUTIONAL HOLDINGS:
No. of Institutions: 331
Shares Held: 224,763,002 (Adj.)
% Held: 83.7

INDUSTRY: Data processing and preparation (SIC: 7374)

TRANSFER AGENT(S): Wells Fargo Shareowner Services, South St. Paul, MN

NYSE SYMBOL SUN
Rec. Pr. 38.02 (4/30/01)

SUNOCO, INC.

YIELD 2.6%
P/E RATIO 8.1

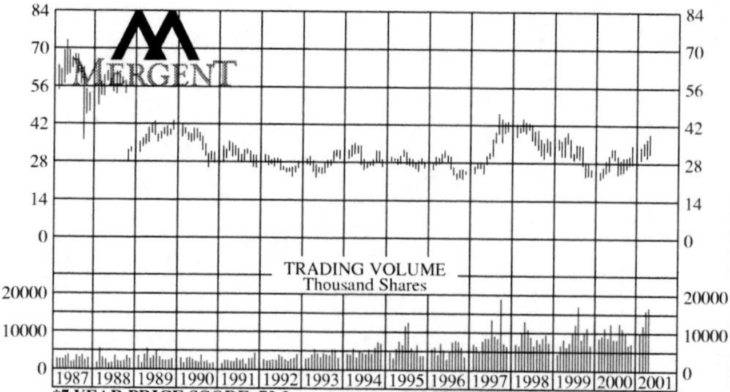

TRADING VOLUME
Thousand Shares

*7 YEAR PRICE SCORE 72.2 *12 MONTH PRICE SCORE 119.6
*NYSE COMPOSITE INDEX=100

INTERIM EARNINGS (Per Share):

Qtr.	Mar.	June	Sept.	Dec.
1996	d0.22	d0.19	d0.30	d3.22
1997	0.10	1.29	1.38	0.25
1998	0.58	0.97	0.85	0.55
1999	0.21	0.28	0.15	0.42
2000	0.75	2.44	d0.29	1.80

INTERIM DIVIDENDS (Per Share):

Amt.	Decl.	Ex.	Rec.	Pay.
0.25Q	4/06/00	5/08/00	5/10/00	6/09/00
0.25Q	7/06/00	8/08/00	8/10/00	9/08/00
0.25Q	10/05/00	11/08/00	11/10/00	12/08/00
0.25Q	1/04/01	2/07/01	2/09/01	3/09/01
0.25Q	4/05/01	5/08/01	5/10/01	6/08/01

Indicated div.: $1.00 (Div. Reinv. Plan)

CAPITALIZATION (12/31/00):

	($000)	(%)
Long-Term Debt	933,000	32.3
Deferred Income Tax	250,000	8.7
Common & Surplus	1,702,000	59.0
Total	2,885,000	100.0

RECENT DEVELOPMENTS: For the twelve months ended 12/31/00, income from continuing operations surged to $411.0 million compared with net income of $97.0 million a year earlier. Results for 2000 and 1999 included a net non-recurring after-tax charge of $16.0 million and a net non-recurring after-tax gain of $47.0 million, respectively. Total revenues rose 42.0% to $14.30 billion from $10.07 billion in 1999.

PROSPECTS: Results are being driven by higher wholesale fuels margins at SUN's refining centers, coupled with improved margins for base oils, propylene and retail gasoline and increased gasoline sales volumes and non-gasoline income at its retail marketing operations. In January 2001, SUN signed a letter of intent to sell its Kendall® motor oil brand, and the customer lists and other related assets for both the Sunoco® and Kendall® brand labels to Tosco Corporation. The Sunoco trademark is not part of the sale.

BUSINESS

SUNOCO, INC. (formerly Sun Company, Inc.) is principally a petroleum refiner and marketer and chemicals manufacturer with interests in cokemaking. SUN operates five domestic refineries with 730,000 barrels per day and markets gasoline under the SUNOCO brand through approximately 3,600 service stations in 17 states from Maine to Virginia and west to Indiana. Sunoco Logistics operates all of SUN's transportation functions, including its crude oil and product terminals, rail and tank car transport and marine operations. SUN also sells lubricants and petrochemicals worldwide, and operates domestic pipelines and terminals. Effective 1/1/01, SUN acquired Aristech Chemical Corporation for $695.0 million.

REVENUES

(12/31/2000)	($000)	(%)
Northeast Refining	4,572,000	32.5
Northeast Marketing	4,512,000	32.1
Chemicals	730,000	5.2
Lubricants	1,567,000	11.1
Midamerica Marketing & Refining	2,403,000	17.1
Logistics	56,000	0.4
Coke	222,000	1.6
Total	14,062,000	100.0

ANNUAL FINANCIAL DATA

	12/31/00	12/31/99	12/31/98	12/31/97	12/31/96	12/31/95	12/31/94
Earnings Per Share	**[6] 4.70**	**[5] 1.07**	**[4] 2.95**	**2.70**	**[1] d4.43**	**[2] 2.24**	**[3] 0.91**
Cash Flow Per Share	**8.10**	**4.10**	**5.44**	**4.91**	**d0.80**	**6.67**	**4.26**
Tang. Book Val. Per Share	**20.07**	**16.77**	**16.82**	**10.41**	**9.45**	**12.82**	**17.41**
Dividends Per Share	**1.00**	**1.00**	**1.00**	**1.00**	**1.00**	**1.40**	**1.80**
Dividend Payout %	**21.3**	**93.4**	**33.9**	**37.0**	**...**	**62.5**	**197.8**
INCOME STATEMENT (IN MILLIONS):							
Total Revenues	14,300.0	10,068.0	8,583.0	10,531.0	11,300.0	10,441.0	9,919.0
Costs & Expenses	13,328.0	9,560.0	7,866.0	9,816.0	11,364.0	9,639.0	9,310.0
Depreciation & Amort.	298.0	276.0	257.0	259.0	267.0	341.0	359.0
Operating Income	674.0	232.0	460.0	456.0	d331.0	461.0	250.0
Net Interest Inc./(Exp.)	d78.0	d82.0	d71.0	d71.0	d77.0	d101.0	d84.0
Income Before Income Taxes	596.0	150.0	389.0	385.0	d408.0	319.0	120.0
Income Taxes	185.0	53.0	109.0	122.0	cr127.0	92.0	23.0
Equity Earnings/Minority Int.	...	...	...	...	...	d2.0	d22.0
Net Income	[6] 411.0	[5] 97.0	[4] 280.0	263.0	[1] d281.0	[2] 266.0	[3] 97.0
Cash Flow	709.0	373.0	517.0	478.0	d59.0	584.0	456.0
Average Shs. Outstg. (000)	87,500	91,000	95,000	97,400	73,600	91,000	107,000
BALANCE SHEET (IN MILLIONS):							
Cash & Cash Equivalents	239.0	87.0	38.0	33.0	67.0	14.0	117.0
Total Current Assets	1,683.0	1,456.0	1,180.0	1,248.0	1,535.0	1,460.0	1,508.0
Net Property	3,390.0	3,415.0	3,346.0	3,064.0	3,044.0	3,262.0	4,348.0
Total Assets	5,426.0	5,196.0	4,849.0	4,667.0	5,025.0	5,375.0	6,485.0
Total Current Liabilities	1,646.0	1,766.0	1,384.0	1,464.0	1,817.0	1,530.0	1,915.0
Long-Term Obligations	933.0	878.0	823.0	824.0	835.0	888.0	1,073.0
Net Stockholders' Equity	1,702.0	1,506.0	1,514.0	1,462.0	1,438.0	1,699.0	1,863.0
Net Working Capital	37.0	d310.0	d204.0	d216.0	d282.0	d70.0	d407.0
Year-end Shs. Outstg. (000)	84,800	89,800	90,000	71,000	73,000	74,000	107,000
STATISTICAL RECORD:							
Operating Profit Margin %	4.7	2.3	5.4	4.3	...	4.4	2.5
Net Profit Margin %	2.9	1.0	3.3	2.5	...	2.5	1.0
Return on Equity %	24.1	6.4	18.5	18.0	...	15.7	5.2
Return on Assets %	7.6	1.9	5.8	5.6	...	4.9	1.5
Debt/Total Assets %	17.2	16.9	17.0	17.7	16.6	16.5	16.5
Price Range	34.56-21.94	39.44-22.88	44.31-29.50	46.38-24.00	32.63-21.88	32.88-24.75	35.25-25.13
P/E Ratio	7.4-4.7	36.9-21.4	15.0-10.0	17.2-8.9	...	14.7-11.0	38.7-27.6
Average Yield %	3.5	3.2	2.7	2.8	3.7	4.9	6.0

Statistics are as originally reported. [1] Bef. disc. ops. credit of $166.0 mill. [2] Incl. non-recurr. chrg. of $96.0 mill.; bef. acctg. adj. chrg. of $87.0 mill. [3] Bef. acctg. adj. chrg. of $7.0 mill. [4] Incl. aft.-tax benefit of $13.0 mill. [5] Incl. aft.-tax credit of $46.0 mill. [6] Incl. aft.-tax chrg. of $147.0 mill. & non-recurr. gain of $131.0 mill.; bef. disc. ops. of $11.0 mill. ($0.12/sh.)

OFFICERS:
J. G. Drosdick, Chmn., Pres., C.E.O.
T. W. Hofmann, V.P., C.F.O.
M. S. Kuritzkes, V.P., Gen. Couns.

INVESTOR CONTACT: T. P. Delaney, Mgr., Investor Relations (215) 977-6106

PRINCIPAL OFFICE: Ten Penn Center, 1801 Market Street, Philadelphia, PA 19103-1699

TELEPHONE NUMBER: (215) 977-3000
FAX: (215) 977-3409
WEB: www.sunocoInc.com

NO. OF EMPLOYEES: 12,300 (approx.)

SHAREHOLDERS: 29,000 (approx.)

ANNUAL MEETING: In May

INCORPORATED: PA, 1971

INSTITUTIONAL HOLDINGS:
No. of Institutions: 257
Shares Held: 61,209,266
% Held: 72.2

INDUSTRY: Petroleum refining (SIC: 2911)

TRANSFER AGENT(S): First Chicago Trust Co. of New York, Jersey City, NJ

NYSE SYMBOL SDP
Rec. Pr. 5.20 (5/31/01)

SUNSOURCE INC.

YIELD	...
P/E RATIO	1.3

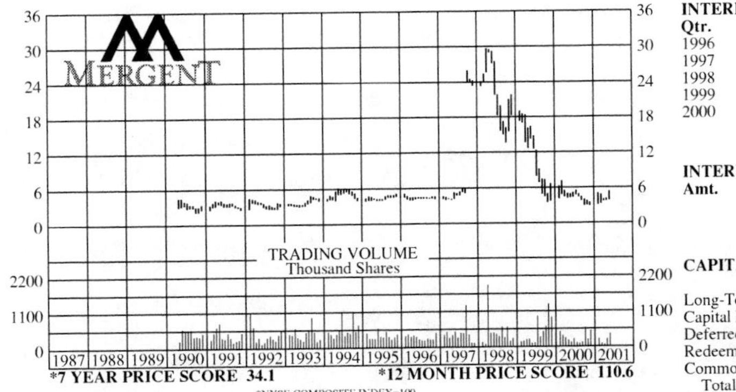

INTERIM EARNINGS (Per Share):

Qtr.	Mar.	June	Sept.	Dec.
1996	0.04	0.24	0.24	d0.20
1997	0.07	0.28	0.56	0.48
1998	0.25	0.64	0.64	0.44
1999	0.13	d1.44	0.01	d0.36
2000	6.11	d0.07	d0.07	d1.87

INTERIM DIVIDENDS (Per Share):

Amt.	Decl.	Ex.	Rec.	Pay.

Last dist. $0.10Q, 4/19/99

CAPITALIZATION (12/31/00):

	($000)	(%)
Long-Term Debt	98,196	43.1
Capital Lease Obligations	627	0.3
Deferred Income Tax	1,629	0.7
Redeemable Pfd. Stock	114,848	50.4
Common & Surplus	12,604	5.5
Total	227,904	100.0

RECENT DEVELOPMENTS: For the year ended 12/31/00, income from continuing operations was $27.3 million versus a loss from continuing operations of $11.3 million the year before. The 2000 results included a $49.1 million gain from the sale of its majority interest in its Kar Products affiliate and a $4.3 million charge related to pension plans. Results in 1999 included restructuring charges of $10.2 million. Net sales slid 15.0% to $459.8 million. Comparisons were made with restated prior-year results.

PROSPECTS: In December 2000, the Company's board of directors approved a plan to discontinue SunSource Integrated Services de Mexico, which provides inventory management services of maintenance, repair, and operating materials to large manufacturing plants in Mexico. The discontinuation of SDP's Mexican operations is expected to be completed during the first half of 2001 and will help sharpen the Company's focus on growing its core Hillman Group and Technology Services businesses.

BUSINESS

SUNSOURCE INC. (formerly SunSource L.P.) operates in two business segments. The Company's Hillman Group, which includes its Axxess Technologies, Inc. subsidiary, provides small hardware items and merchandising services to retail outlets, primarily hardware stores, home centers, pet suppliers, and mass merchants, in the U.S., Canada, Mexico and South America. The Technology Services segment provides engineering, repair, and fabrication services, as well as parts and equipment, to manufacturers throughout the U.S. and Canada. Also included in the Technology Services segment is Kar Products, the Company's 44.0%-owned affiliate that distributes maintenance and repair parts and provides customized inventory management services in the U.S. and Canada. On 9/30/97, SDP was converted to a corporation from a limited partnership.

REVENUES

(12/31/2000)	($000)	(%)
Technology Services	224,538	51.4
Hillman Group	212,118	48.6
Total	436,656	100.0

ANNUAL FINANCIAL DATA

	12/31/00	12/31/99	12/31/98	12/31/97	12/31/96	12/31/95	12/31/94
Earnings Per Share	**[5] 3.97**	**[4] d1.65**	**[3] 2.00**	**[1] 1.88**	**[3] 1.42**	**[1][2] 2.58**	**1.89**
Cash Flow Per Share	**5.83**	**d0.74**	**3.06**	**5.99**	**0.76**	**1.54**	**1.12**
Tang. Book Val. Per Share	...	...	...	...	**1.55**	**1.51**	**0.86**
Dividends Per Share	...	**0.20**	**0.40**	...	...	...	...
Dividend Payout %	...	...	**20.0**	...	...	...	...
INCOME STATEMENT (IN MILLIONS):							
Total Revenues	459.8	555.7	712.5	698.1	649.3	628.9	735.9
Costs & Expenses	442.8	548.8	664.0	656.2	619.3	592.0	691.0
Depreciation & Amort.	12.8	6.1	7.3	5.9	5.5	5.7	7.1
Operating Income	4.2	0.7	41.2	36.1	24.5	31.3	37.7
Net Interest Inc./(Exp.)	d11.3	d9.7	d6.8	d7.2	d6.9	d6.9	d10.1
Income Before Income Taxes	32.2	d21.2	22.1	25.9	18.1	45.3	29.6
Income Taxes	4.9	cr10.1	8.3	cr6.7	cr1.1	0.5	0.1
Net Income	[5] 27.3	[4] d11.1	[3] 13.8	[1] 32.5	[3] 19.3	[1][2] 44.7	29.5
Cash Flow	40.1	d5.0	21.1	38.4	24.8	50.4	36.7
Average Shs. Outstg. (000)	6,881	6,747	6,907	6,419	32,776	32,776	32,776
BALANCE SHEET (IN MILLIONS):							
Cash & Cash Equivalents	13.8	5.2	2.8	5.6	1.7	5.9	4.9
Total Current Assets	161.8	222.3	219.2	206.9	187.3	182.5	181.8
Net Property	58.3	17.3	26.8	21.9	21.4	20.2	27.5
Total Assets	322.1	323.0	341.6	306.1	262.6	254.6	266.2
Total Current Liabilities	84.8	86.7	97.6	85.9	86.5	86.6	105.7
Long-Term Obligations	98.8	122.1	95.6	93.6	69.0	63.9	74.8
Net Stockholders' Equity	12.6	d17.2	20.7	d0.5	94.6	94.9	79.2
Net Working Capital	77.0	135.6	121.6	120.9	100.8	95.8	76.1
Year-end Shs. Outstg. (000)	7,229	6,749	6,756	6,419	32,776	32,776	32,775
STATISTICAL RECORD:							
Operating Profit Margin %	0.9	0.1	5.8	5.2	3.8	5.0	5.1
Net Profit Margin %	5.9	...	1.9	4.7	3.0	7.1	4.0
Return on Equity %	216.5	...	66.7	...	20.4	47.1	37.3
Return on Assets %	8.5	...	4.0	10.6	7.3	17.6	11.1
Debt/Total Assets %	30.7	37.8	28.0	30.6	26.3	25.1	28.1
Price Range	7.13-2.88	19.00-3.44	29.69-13.63	26.00-4.00	5.13-4.00	5.13-3.88	6.13-4.00
P/E Ratio	1.8-0.7	...	14.8-6.8	13.8-2.1	3.6-2.8	2.0-1.5	3.2-2.1
Average Yield %	...	1.8	1.8	...	...	...	...

Statistics are as originally reported. Earn. per sh. figs. prior to 9/97 represent Cl. B ltd. part. int. [1] Bef. $3.4 mil extraord loss, 1997; $629,000 loss, 1995. [2] Incl. $20.6 mil gain fr. sale of business. [3] Incl. $1.6 mil chg., 1998; $8.1 mil restr. chg., 1996. [4] Bef. loss fr. disc. opers $26.0 mil, $235,000 extraord. chg. & incl. $8.1 mil. restr. chg and $5.6 mil gain. [5] Bef. $2.6 mil loss fr. disc. opers. & incl. $49.1 mil one-time gain fr sale of maj. int. in Kar Products and $4.3 mil loss fr. term. of pension plans.

OFFICERS:
D. T. Marshall, Chmn.
M. P. Andrien, Jr., Pres., C.E.O.
J. M. Corvino, V.P., C.F.O., Treas. & Sec.

PRINCIPAL OFFICE: 3000 One Logan Square, Philadelphia, PA 19103

TELEPHONE NUMBER: (215) 282-1290
FAX: (215) 665-3662
WEB: www.sun-source.com
NO. OF EMPLOYEES: 2,100 (approx.)
SHAREHOLDERS: 433 (approx.)
ANNUAL MEETING: In May
INCORPORATED: DE, 1975

INSTITUTIONAL HOLDINGS:
No. of Institutions: 12
Shares Held: 1,896,376
% Held: 27.6

INDUSTRY: Industrial supplies (SIC: 5085)

TRANSFER AGENT(S): Registrar & Transfer Company, Cranford, NJ

NYSE SYMBOL STI
Rec. Pr. 63.50 (4/30/01)

SUNTRUST BANKS, INC.

YIELD 2.5%
P/E RATIO 14.8

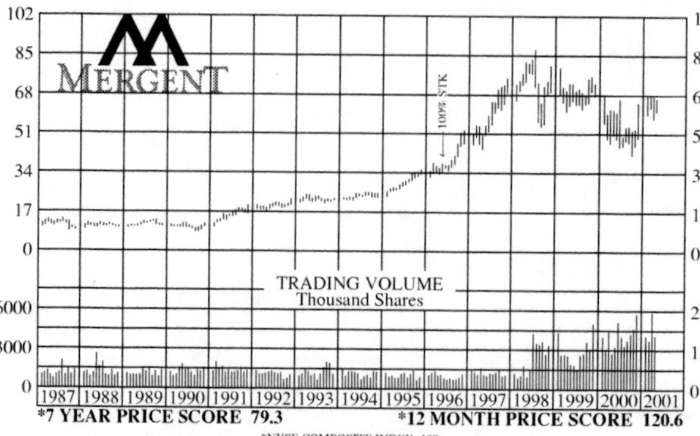

*7 YEAR PRICE SCORE 79.3 *12 MONTH PRICE SCORE 120.6

*NYSE COMPOSITE INDEX=100

INTERIM EARNINGS (Per Share):

Qtr.	Mar.	June	Sept.	Dec.
1997	0.74	0.77	0.80	0.82
1998	0.85	0.88	0.91	0.49
1999	0.87	0.91	1.00	0.71
2000	1.04	1.05	1.10	1.11

INTERIM DIVIDENDS (Per Share):

Amt.	Decl.	Ex.	Rec.	Pay.
0.37Q	4/18/00	5/30/00	6/01/00	6/15/00
0.37Q	8/08/00	8/30/00	9/01/00	9/15/00
0.37Q	11/15/00	11/29/00	12/01/00	12/15/00
0.40Q	2/13/01	2/27/01	3/01/01	3/15/01
0.40Q	4/17/01	5/30/01	6/01/01	6/15/01

Indicated div.: $1.60 (Div. Reinv. Plan)

CAPITALIZATION (12/31/00):

	($000)	(%)
Total Deposits	69,533,337	81.2
Long-Term Debt	7,895,430	9.2
Common & Surplus	8,239,208	9.6
Total	85,667,975	100.0

RECENT DEVELOPMENTS: For the year ended 12/31/00, STI reported net income of $1.29 billion versus income of $1.12 billion, before an extraordinary gain of $202.6 million, in 1999. Earnings for 2000 and 1999 included pre-tax merger-related expenses of $42.4 million and $45.6 million, respectively. Net interest income fell 1.2% to $3.11 billion. Total non-interest income grew 9.1% to $1.77 billion. Total non-interest expense, including the merger-related charges, declined 2.6% to $2.83 billion.

PROSPECTS: Over the next several years, the Company expects low-double-digit growth in fee income, reflecting an increase in trust profits. STI also anticipates mid-single-digit growth in net interest income, resulting from loan growth. Earnings per share are expected to grow in the high-single-digit to low-double-digit range, while operating expense is expected to increase in the mid-single-digit range. On 5/14/01, STI made a hostile bid to acquire Wachovia Corporation for approximately $14.70 billion.

BUSINESS

SUNTRUST BANKS, INC. offers a full line of consumer and commercial banking services to more than 5.5 million customers through 1,100 branches and 1,900 ATMs across six states, including Alabama, Florida, Georgia, Maryland, Tennessee and Virginia, as well as the District of Columbia. STI's banking network also includes telephone and computer-based banking alternatives. At 12/31/00, SunTrust had total assets of $103.50 billion. The Company's primary businesses include traditional deposit and credit services as well as trust and investment services. Through various subsidiaries, SunTrust provides credit cards, mortgage banking, credit-related insurance, data processing and information services, discount brokerage and investment banking services.

LOAN DISTRIBUTION

(12/31/2000)	($000)	(%)
Commercial	30,781,090	42.6
Construction	2,966,087	4.1
Residential Mortgages	19,953,027	27.6
Other Real Estate	8,121,441	11.3
Credit Card	76,747	0.1
Other Consumer Loans	10,341,428	14.3
Total	72,239,820	100.0

ANNUAL FINANCIAL DATA

	12/31/00	12/31/99	12/31/98	12/31/97	12/31/96	12/31/95	12/31/94
Earnings Per Share	**[3] 4.35**	**[1] [2] 3.50**	**[1] 3.04**	**3.13**	**2.76**	**2.47**	**2.25**
Tang. Book Val. Per Share	**27.58**	**23.24**	**22.99**	**23.38**	**20.87**	**17.71**	**13.90**
Dividends Per Share	**1.48**	**1.38**	**1.00**	**0.93**	**0.82**	**0.74**	**0.66**
Dividend Payout %	**34.0**	**39.4**	**32.9**	**29.6**	**29.9**	**30.0**	**29.3**
INCOME STATEMENT (IN MILLIONS):							
Total Interest Income	6,845.4	5,960.2	5,675.9	3,650.7	3,246.0	3,027.2	2,552.4
Total Interest Expense	3,737.0	2,814.8	2,746.8	1,756.4	1,461.8	1,350.8	932.5
Net Interest Income	3,108.4	3,145.5	2,929.1	1,894.4	1,784.2	1,676.4	1,619.9
Provision for Loan Losses	134.0	170.4	214.6	117.0	115.9	112.1	137.8
Non-Interest Income	1,773.6	1,660.0	1,716.2	934.2	818.0	713.1	699.9
Non-Interest Expense	2,828.5	2,939.4	2,932.4	1,685.6	1,583.1	1,451.5	1,400.0
Income Before Taxes	1,919.6	1,695.7	1,498.3	1,026.0	903.2	825.9	782.0
Net Income	[3] 1,294.1	[1] [2] 1,124.0	[1] 971.0	667.3	616.6	565.5	522.7
Average Shs. Outstg. (000)	297,834	317,079	319,711	213,480	223,486	229,544	232,078
BALANCE SHEET (IN MILLIONS):							
Cash & Due from Banks	4,110.5	3,909.7	4,289.9	2,991.3	3,037.3	2,641.4	2,595.1
Securities Avail. for Sale	941.9	259.5	239.7	178.4	80.4	96.6	98.1
Total Loans & Leases	73,999.1	67,534.6	65,089.2	40,135.5	35,404.2	31,301.4	28,548.9
Allowance for Credit Losses	874.5	871.3	944.6	751.8	725.8	698.9	647.0
Net Loans & Leases	73,124.6	66,663.3	64,144.6	39,383.7	34,678.3	30,602.5	27,901.9
Total Assets	103,496.4	95,390.0	93,169.9	57,982.7	52,468.2	46,471.5	42,709.1
Total Deposits	69,533.3	60,100.5	59,033.3	38,197.5	36,890.4	33,183.2	32,218.4
Long-Term Obligations	7,895.4	4,967.3	4,757.9	3,171.8	1,565.3	1,002.4	930.4
Total Liabilities	95,257.2	87,763.1	84,991.3	52,783.4	47,588.3	42,201.9	39,255.8
Net Stockholders' Equity	8,239.2	7,626.9	8,178.6	5,199.4	4,880.0	4,269.6	3,453.3
Year-end Shs. Outstg. (000)	269,370	293,544	321,124	209,909	220,469	225,726	231,358
STATISTICAL RECORD:							
Return on Equity %	15.7	14.7	11.9	12.8	12.6	13.2	15.1
Return on Assets %	1.3	1.2	1.0	1.2	1.2	1.2	1.2
Equity/Assets %	8.0	8.0	8.8	9.0	9.3	9.2	8.1
Non-Int. Exp./Tot. Inc. %	57.9	61.2	63.1	59.6	60.8	60.7	60.3
Price Range	68.06-41.63	79.81-60.44	87.75-54.00	75.25-44.13	52.50-32.00	35.44-23.63	25.69-21.75
P/E Ratio	15.6-9.6	22.8-17.3	28.9-17.8	24.0-14.1	19.0-11.6	14.3-9.6	11.4-9.7
Average Yield %	2.7	2.0	1.4	1.5	2.0	2.5	2.8

Statistics are as originally reported. Adj. for 2-for-1 stk. split, 5/96. [1] Incl. pre-tax merger-related chrg.: $45.6 mill., 1999; $119.4 mill., 1998. [2] Bef. extraord. gain of $202.6 mill., 1999. [3] Incl. pre-tax merger-related charges of $42.4 mill.

OFFICERS:
L. P. Humann, Chmn., Pres., C.E.O.
T. J. Hoepner, Vice-Chmn.
J. W. Clay Jr., Vice-Chmn.

INVESTOR CONTACT: Gary Peacock, Jr., Dir., Inv. Rel. & Corp. Commun., (404) 588-7711

PRINCIPAL OFFICE: 303 Peachtree Street N.E., Atlanta, GA 30308

TELEPHONE NUMBER: (404) 588-7711
FAX: (404) 827-6173
WEB: www.suntrust.com

NO. OF EMPLOYEES: 28,268

SHAREHOLDERS: 39,886

ANNUAL MEETING: In Apr.

INCORPORATED: GA, July, 1985

INSTITUTIONAL HOLDINGS:
No. of Institutions: 429
Shares Held: 132,997,300
% Held: 44.7

INDUSTRY: National commercial banks (SIC: 6021)

TRANSFER AGENT(S): SunTrust Bank Atlanta, Atlanta, GA

NYSE SYMBOL SUP
Rec. Pr. 40.25 (4/30/01)

SUPERIOR INDUSTRIES INTERNATIONAL, INC.

YIELD 1.1%
P/E RATIO 13.2

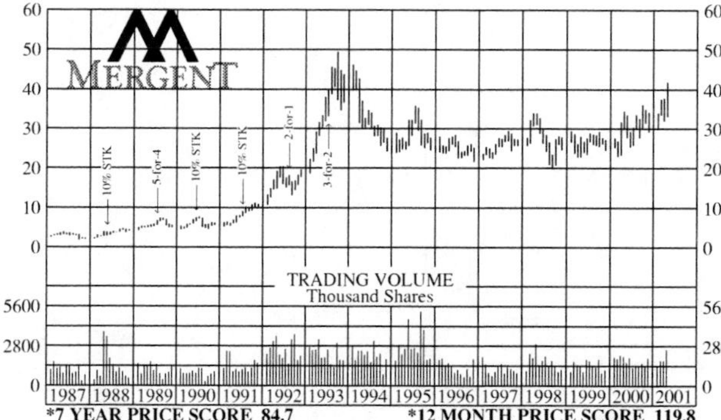

***7 YEAR PRICE SCORE 84.7** ***12 MONTH PRICE SCORE 119.8**

*NYSE COMPOSITE INDEX=100

INTERIM EARNINGS (Per Share):

Qtr.	Mar.	June	Sept.	Dec.
1996	0.30	0.48	0.40	0.45
1997	0.41	0.54	0.47	0.56
1998	0.46	0.44	0.28	0.71
1999	0.57	0.71	0.54	0.81
2000	0.70	0.83	0.66	0.85

INTERIM DIVIDENDS (Per Share):

Amt.	Decl.	Ex.	Rec.	Pay.
0.10Q	5/12/00	6/28/00	6/30/00	7/14/00
0.10Q	8/01/00	10/04/00	10/06/00	10/20/00
0.10Q	10/20/00	1/10/01	1/12/01	1/26/01
0.10Q	3/21/01	4/04/01	4/06/01	4/20/01
0.11Q	5/11/01	6/27/01	6/29/01	7/13/01

Indicated div.: $0.44 (Div. Reinv. Plan)

CAPITALIZATION (12/31/00):

	($000)	(%)
Deferred Income Tax	4,768	1.2
Common & Surplus	399,319	98.8
Total	404,087	100.0

RECENT DEVELOPMENTS: For the year ended 12/31/00, net income amounted to $79.9 million, an increase of 12.9% compared with $70.8 million in the previous year. Results for 2000 included nonrecurring start-up costs of $2.5 million associated with SUP's new aluminum components business and capacity expansions. Net sales increased 12.8% to $644.9 million versus $571.8 million in 1999.

PROSPECTS: Revenues should benefit from more than $400.0 million in new and replacement aluminum wheel supply contracts from both existing and new customers, including Ford Motor Company, DaimlerChrysler, Mitsubishi Motor Manufacturing and Toyota Motor Manufacturing of North America. As a result, the Company's manufacturing facilities operated at peak efficiency.

BUSINESS

SUPERIOR INDUSTRIES INTERNATIONAL, INC. designs and manufactures automotive parts and accessories for original equipment manufacturers (OEMs) and for the automotive aftermarket. The OEM cast aluminum road wheels, the Company's primary product, are sold to Ford, Mazda, BMW, Volkswagen, Audi, Rover, Toyota, Nissan, Isuzu, Mitsubishi, DaimlerChrysler and General Motors for factory installation as optional or standard equipment on selected vehicle models. In addition, the Company manufactures and distributes aftermarket accessories including bed mats, exhaust extensions, license frames, lug nuts, springs and suspension products, steering wheel covers and other miscellaneous accessories. Aftermarket products are sold to customers including Sears, Pep Boys, Wal-Mart and Western Auto. The Company operates 12 manufacturing facilities within the U.S., Mexico and Europe.

ANNUAL FINANCIAL DATA

	12/31/00	12/31/99	12/31/98	12/31/97	12/31/96	12/31/95	12/31/94
Earnings Per Share	**1 3.04**	**2.62**	**1.88**	**1.96**	**1.63**	**1.78**	**1.85**
Cash Flow Per Share	**4.07**	**3.67**	**2.84**	**2.92**	**2.58**	**2.70**	**2.73**
Tang. Book Val. Per Share	**15.45**	**13.35**	**11.42**	**10.30**	**8.87**	**7.89**	**6.76**
Dividends Per Share	**0.38**	**0.34**	**0.30**	**0.26**	**0.22**	**0.19**	**0.15**
Dividend Payout %	**12.5**	**13.0**	**16.0**	**13.3**	**13.5**	**10.7**	**8.1**
INCOME STATEMENT (IN THOUSANDS):							
Total Revenues	644,899	571,782	539,431	549,131	504,241	521,997	456,638
Costs & Expenses	496,474	438,051	432,387	434,030	395,129	400,449	337,869
Depreciation & Amort.	26,920	28,523	26,698	26,917	27,330	27,716	26,604
Operating Income	121,505	105,208	80,346	88,184	81,782	93,832	92,165
Net Interest Inc./(Exp.)	7,323	5,451	4,287	2,170	d326	d2,182	d1,022
Income Before Income Taxes	122,510	108,518	80,801	86,208	74,071	84,918	90,304
Income Taxes	42,573	37,710	28,482	30,819	27,221	31,854	33,989
Net Income	1 79,937	70,808	52,319	55,389	46,850	53,064	56,315
Cash Flow	106,857	99,331	79,017	82,306	74,180	80,780	82,919
Average Shs. Outstg.	26,255	27,056	27,818	28,221	28,798	29,895	30,376
BALANCE SHEET (IN THOUSANDS):							
Cash & Cash Equivalents	93,503	108,081	86,566	73,693	42,103	11,179	27,042
Total Current Assets	245,579	263,740	235,886	199,846	164,080	142,659	160,771
Net Property	218,713	163,113	158,194	147,989	161,670	177,538	185,853
Total Assets	491,664	460,468	427,430	382,679	357,590	341,770	357,683
Total Current Liabilities	75,022	86,847	91,111	65,415	76,369	81,746	106,923
Long-Term Obligations	...	340	673	1,344	1,940	5,814	23,075
Net Stockholders' Equity	399,319	353,086	312,034	287,416	251,111	229,153	200,182
Net Working Capital	170,557	176,893	144,775	134,431	87,711	60,913	53,848
Year-end Shs. Outstg.	25,840	26,454	27,312	27,902	28,324	29,029	29,612
STATISTICAL RECORD:							
Operating Profit Margin %	18.8	18.4	14.9	16.1	16.2	18.0	20.2
Net Profit Margin %	12.4	12.4	9.7	10.1	9.3	10.2	12.3
Return on Equity %	20.0	20.1	16.8	19.3	18.7	23.2	28.1
Return on Assets %	16.3	15.4	12.2	14.5	13.1	15.5	15.7
Debt/Total Assets %	...	0.1	0.2	0.4	0.5	1.7	6.5
Price Range	36.00-22.94	29.38-22.75	33.88-20.06	29.50-22.13	28.38-21.63	35.75-23.88	46.25-24.25
P/E Ratio	11.8-7.5	11.2-8.7	18.0-10.7	15.1-11.3	17.4-13.3	20.1-13.4	25.0-13.1
Average Yield %	1.3	1.3	1.1	1.0	0.9	0.6	0.4

Statistics are as originally reported. 1 Incl. non-recurr. chrg. $2.5 mill.

OFFICERS:
L. L. Borick, Chmn., Pres.
R. J. Ornstein, V.P., C.F.O.
D. L. Levine, Corp. Sec., Treas.

INVESTOR CONTACT: Cathy Buccieri, Shareholder Rel., (818) 902-2701

PRINCIPAL OFFICE: 7800 Woodley Avenue, Van Nuys, CA 91406

TELEPHONE NUMBER: (818) 781-4973
FAX: (818) 780-3500
WEB: www.supind.com

NO. OF EMPLOYEES: 6,000 (approx.)

SHAREHOLDERS: 990 (approx.)

ANNUAL MEETING: In May

INCORPORATED: DE, June, 1969; reincorp., CA, June, 1994

INSTITUTIONAL HOLDINGS:
No. of Institutions: 140
Shares Held: 14,430,971
% Held: 55.7

INDUSTRY: Motor vehicle parts and accessories (SIC: 3714)

TRANSFER AGENT(S): Mellon Investor Services, Los Angeles, CA

NYSE SYMBOL SUT
Rec. Pr. 3.10 (5/31/01)

SUPERIOR TELECOM, INC.

YIELD ...
P/E RATIO ...

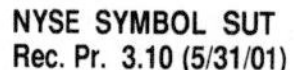

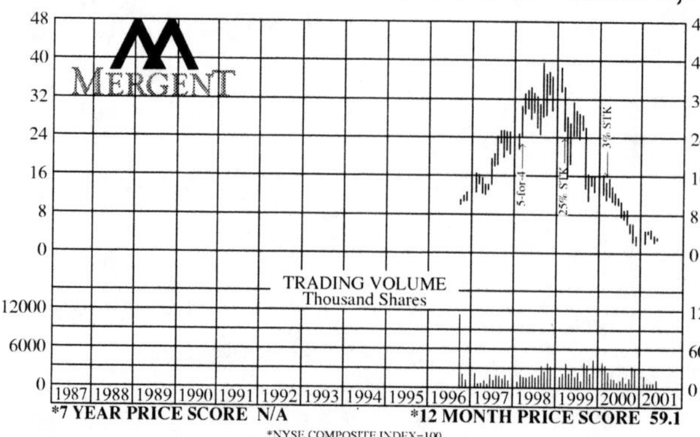

*7 YEAR PRICE SCORE N/A *12 MONTH PRICE SCORE 59.1

*NYSE COMPOSITE INDEX=100

INTERIM EARNINGS (Per Share):

Qtr.	July	Oct.	Jan.	Apr.
1997-98	0.46	0.50	0.39	0.56
1998	---------------- 1.04 ----------------			
Qtr.	**Mar.**	**June**	**Sept.**	**Dec.**
1999	0.49	0.68	0.52	0.14
2000	0.02	0.42	d0.08	d0.46

INTERIM DIVIDENDS (Per Share):

Amt.	Decl.	Ex.	Rec.	Pay.
0.063Q	7/20/99	7/28/99	7/30/99	8/05/99
0.063Q	10/19/99	10/27/99	10/29/99	11/05/99
3% STK	1/25/00	2/01/00	2/03/00	2/11/00

Dividend payment suspended

CAPITALIZATION (12/31/00):

	($000)	(%)
Long-Term Debt	1,217,802	82.8
Minority Interest	8,429	0.6
Redeemable Pfd. Stock	134,941	9.2
Common & Surplus	110,003	7.5
Total	1,471,175	100.0

RECENT DEVELOPMENTS: For the year ended 12/31/00, the Company posted a net loss of $2.1 million versus income of $38.8 million, before an extraordinary loss on the early retirement of debt, a year earlier. Results included non-recurring charges of $15.0 million and $8.4 million, respectively. Results were negatively effected by general industrial sector weakness and difficult pricing conditions in SUT's electrical wire market. Net sales rose less than 1.0% to $2.05 billion from $2.04 billion the previous year.

PROSPECTS: Near-term results will likely remain sluggish; however, SUT appears well positioned for long term growth. For example, SUT recently completed a $40.0 million expansion project of its art magnet wire facility in Mexico, which is expected to provide growth opportunities outside the U.S. Also, reduced capital expenditures in 2001 and 2002 should allow for long-term debt reduction. Further, sales of the Company's copper outside plant (OSP) cable products should remain positive.

BUSINESS

SUPERIOR TELECOM, INC. manufactures wire and cable products for the communications, original equipment manufacturer (OEM), and electrical markets. SUT is a manufacturer and supplier of communications wire and cable products; magnet wire and insulation materials for motors, transformers and electrical controls; and building and industrial wire for applications in commercial and residential construction and industrial facilities. The Company operates manufacturing and distribution facilities in the U.S., Canada, the U.K., Israel and Mexico. On 11/27/98, SUT acquired approximately 81.0% of Essex International Inc. for about $770.0 million and, on 3/31/99, acquired the remaining 19.0% in a transaction valued at $167.0 million. As of 12/31/00, The Alpine Group, Inc.'s ownership interest in the Company totaled 51.5%.

BUSINESS LINE ANALYSIS

(12/31/2000)	Rev(%)	Inc(%)
Communications	41.4	88.4
OEM	29.9	5.4
Electrical	28.7	6.1
Total	100.0	100.0

ANNUAL FINANCIAL DATA

	12/31/00	12/31/99	[2] 12/31/98	4/30/98	4/30/97	4/28/96	4/30/95
Earnings Per Share	[5] d0.11	[4] 1.86	[3] 1.04	1.91	1.08	...	...
Cash Flow Per Share	3.28	4.90	1.65	2.43	1.47	...	...
Tang. Book Val. Per Share	...	...	...	1.81	...	...	...
Dividends Per Share	...	0.24	0.19	...	...	...	...
Dividend Payout %	...	13.0	18.7	...	...	...	...
INCOME STATEMENT (IN MILLIONS):							
Total Revenues	2,049.0	2,027.5	486.1	516.6	252.8	410.4	164.5
Costs & Expenses	1,832.7	1,758.9	418.4	430.2	211.4	369.8	150.0
Depreciation & Amort.	68.6	63.6	13.0	11.1	6.2	8.8	4.8
Operating Income	147.8	205.0	54.7	75.3	35.2	31.8	9.6
Net Interest Inc./(Exp.)	d129.9	d120.1	d16.7	d8.1	d5.9	d17.4	d3.7
Income Before Income Taxes	18.8	87.4	37.7	67.5	29.0	14.8	6.1
Income Taxes	10.9	36.7	15.5	26.8	11.6	6.7	2.2
Equity Earnings/Minority Int.	5.1	d0.6	0.1	...	...	...	0.2
Net Income	[5] d2.1	[4] 38.8	[3] 22.3	40.7	17.4	[1] 8.1	4.1
Cash Flow	66.4	102.4	35.2	51.8	23.6	16.9	8.9
Average Shs. Outstg. (000)	20,238	20,908	21,348	21,303	16,058	...	...
BALANCE SHEET (IN MILLIONS):							
Cash & Cash Equivalents	13.0	14.3	16.1	9.9	1.1	0.4	0.3
Total Current Assets	596.7	627.5	630.0	100.8	110.0	117.9	51.0
Net Property	539.1	513.9	513.4	83.1	77.0	76.5	30.0
Total Assets	1,991.7	2,000.4	1,886.6	232.2	238.1	244.1	120.1
Total Current Liabilities	520.5	465.9	397.6	62.3	62.4	59.2	28.2
Long-Term Obligations	1,217.8	1,274.3	1,333.0	87.7	131.7	133.2	42.1
Net Stockholders' Equity	110.0	113.0	91.4	82.2	44.0	51.7	49.9
Net Working Capital	76.2	161.5	232.4	38.5	47.6	58.7	22.8
Year-end Shs. Outstg. (000)	21,133	20,980	20,722	20,820	16,644	3	3
STATISTICAL RECORD:							
Operating Profit Margin %	7.2	10.1	11.3	14.6	13.9	7.7	5.8
Net Profit Margin %	...	1.9	4.6	7.9	6.9	2.0	2.5
Return on Equity %	...	34.3	24.4	49.5	39.5	15.7	8.2
Return on Assets %	...	1.9	1.2	17.5	7.3	3.3	3.4
Debt/Total Assets %	61.1	63.7	70.7	37.8	55.3	54.6	35.0
Price Range	16.32-1.69	38.59-10.80	39.52-21.48	25.48-12.04	12.66-9.94	...	...
P/E Ratio	...	20.7-5.8	38.0-20.7	13.3-6.3	11.7-9.2	...	...
Average Yield %	...	1.0	0.6	...	...	...	...

Statistics are as originally reported. Adj. for 3% stk. div., 2/00; 25% stk. div., 2/99; 5-for-4 stk. split, 2/98 [1] Bef. extraord. loss of $2.6 mill. [2] Eight mos. only due to fiscal year end chge. [3] Incl. non-recurr. chrg. of $13.5 mill.; bef. extraord. loss of $1.2 mill. [4] Incl. non-recurr. chrg. of $8.4 mill.; bef. extraord. loss of $1.6 mill. [5] Incl. non-recurr. chrg. of $15.0 mill.

OFFICERS:
S. S. Elbaum, Chmn., C.E.O.
S. C. Knup, Pres., C.O.O.
D. S. Aldridge, C.F.O., Treas.

INVESTOR CONTACT: Melanie T. Hall, V.P., Corp. Comm., (800) 257-6585

PRINCIPAL OFFICE: 1790 Broadway, New York, NY 10019-1412

TELEPHONE NUMBER: (212) 757-3333
FAX: (212) 757-3423
WEB: www.superioressex.com

NO. OF EMPLOYEES: 5,900 (approx.)

SHAREHOLDERS: 55 (approx.)

ANNUAL MEETING: In June

INCORPORATED: DE, July, 1996

INSTITUTIONAL HOLDINGS:
No. of Institutions: 29
Shares Held: 5,956,180
% Held: 29.1

INDUSTRY: Nonferrous wiredrawing & insulating (SIC: 3357)

TRANSFER AGENT(S): American Stock Transfer & Trust Company, New York, NY

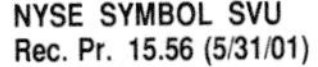

NYSE SYMBOL SVU
Rec. Pr. 15.56 (5/31/01)

SUPERVALU INC.

YIELD	3.5%
P/E RATIO	25.1

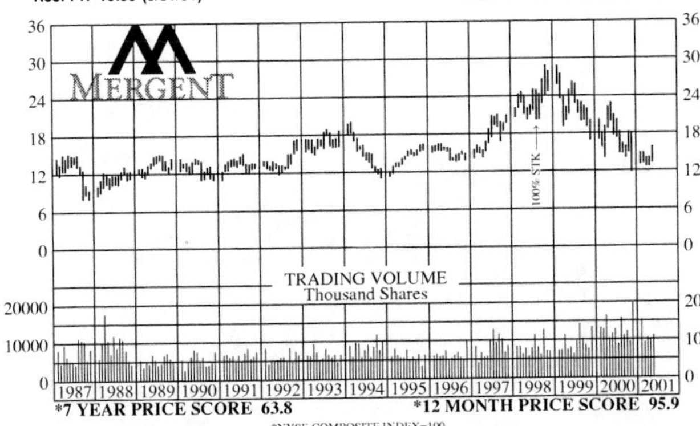

INTERIM EARNINGS (Per Share):

Qtr.	May	Aug.	Nov.	Feb.
1997-98	0.37	0.72	0.34	0.43
1998-99	0.43	0.33	0.37	0.45
1999-00	0.55	0.37	0.42	0.52
2000-01	0.53	0.43	0.36	d0.70

INTERIM DIVIDENDS (Per Share):

Amt.	Decl.	Ex.	Rec.	Pay.
0.135Q	4/12/00	5/30/00	6/01/00	6/15/00
0.138Q	6/29/00	8/30/00	9/01/00	9/15/00
0.138Q	10/05/00	11/29/00	12/01/00	12/15/00
0.138Q	12/13/00	2/27/01	3/01/01	3/15/01
0.138Q	4/11/01	5/30/01	6/01/01	6/15/01

Indicated div.: $0.55 (Div. Reinv. Plan)

CAPITALIZATION (2/24/01):

	($000)	(%)
Long-Term Debt	1,444,376	37.7
Capital Lease Obligations	564,098	14.7
Deferred Income Tax	29,656	0.8
Common & Surplus	1,793,495	46.8
Total	3,831,625	100.0

RECENT DEVELOPMENTS: For the fiscal year ended 2/24/01, net earnings totaled $82.0 million versus $242.9 million the year before. Results in the recent fiscal year included pre-tax restructuring and other charges of $240.1 million. Results in the prior year included a pre-tax gain of $163.7 million from the sale of Hazelwood Farms Bakeries, partially offset by restructuring and other charges totaling $103.6 million. Net sales rose 14.0% to $23.19 billion from $20.34 billion a year earlier.

PROSPECTS: Near-term results will likely be hurt by the early termination of a supply agreement with Kmart Corporation, which generates annual revenues of approximately $2.50 billion. Earnings for the fiscal year ending February 2002 are expected to be diminished by $0.18 to $0.22 per share, reflecting the 6/30/01 contract termination. Meanwhile, SVU is implementing restructuring initiatives focused on eliminating low-return assets and increasing efficiencies.

BUSINESS

SUPERVALU INC. is a major food retailer and distributor to independently-owned retail food stores. The Company operates three principal store formats at retail and sells food and non-food products at wholesale. SVU operates 207 price superstores under the Cub Foods, Shop 'n Save, Shoppers Food Warehouse, Metro and bigg's banners and 905 limited assortment stores including 727 licensed locations under the Save-A-Lot banner, and 82 other supermarkets, under the names Farm Fresh, Laneco, Scott's Foods, and Hornbachers. Additionally, the Company is the primary supplier to approximately 3,200 supermarkets and 55 Cub Foods franchised locations, while serving as a secondary supplier to approximately 2,250 stores.

REVENUES

(2/24/2001)	($000)	(%)
Retail Food	9,354	40.3
Food Distribution	13,840	59.7
Total	23,194	100.0

ANNUAL FINANCIAL DATA

	2/24/01	2/26/00	2/27/99	2/28/98	2/22/97	2/24/96	2/25/95
Earnings Per Share	**4 0.62**	**3 1.87**	**1.57**	**2 1.83**	**1.30**	**1.22**	**1 0.31**
Cash Flow Per Share	**3.24**	**4.06**	**3.45**	**3.64**	**3.03**	**2.82**	**1.70**
Tang. Book Val. Per Share	**1.64**	**1.58**	**6.09**	**5.80**	**6.06**	**5.27**	**4.79**
Dividends Per Share	**0.55**	**0.54**	**0.53**	**0.51**	**0.49**	**0.48**	**0.46**
Dividend Payout %	**87.9**	**28.9**	**33.4**	**27.9**	**38.1**	**39.3**	**149.1**
INCOME STATEMENT (IN MILLIONS):							
Total Revenues	23,194.3	20,339.1	17,420.5	17,201.4	16,551.9	16,486.3	16,563.8
Costs & Expenses	22,500.3	19,470.9	16,772.7	16,565.9	15,939.3	15,900.5	16,255.2
Depreciation & Amort.	348.8	285.3	229.6	230.1	232.1	219.1	198.7
Operating Income	345.2	582.8	418.2	405.4	380.5	366.8	109.8
Net Interest Inc./(Exp.)	d190.8	d135.4	d101.9	d114.0	d120.7	d116.7	d111.3
Income Before Income Taxes	154.4	447.5	316.3	384.8	280.5	267.7	15.9
Income Taxes	72.4	204.5	124.9	154.0	105.5	101.3	cr27.4
Equity Earnings/Minority Int.	...	...	...	93.4	20.7	17.6	17.4
Net Income	4 82.0	3 242.9	191.3	2 230.8	175.0	166.4	1 43.3
Cash Flow	430.7	528.3	421.0	460.8	407.1	385.5	242.1
Average Shs. Outstg. (000)	132,829	130,090	121,961	126,550	134,510	136,554	142,776
BALANCE SHEET (IN MILLIONS):							
Cash & Cash Equivalents	10.4	10.9	7.6	6.1	6.5	5.2	4.8
Total Current Assets	2,091.7	2,177.6	1,582.5	1,612.1	1,600.8	1,553.7	1,646.3
Net Property	2,232.8	2,168.2	1,699.0	1,589.6	1,648.5	1,600.2	1,571.3
Total Assets	6,407.2	6,495.4	4,265.9	4,093.0	4,283.3	4,183.5	4,305.1
Total Current Liabilities	2,341.2	2,509.6	1,521.9	1,457.2	1,369.1	1,326.7	1,447.1
Long-Term Obligations	2,008.5	1,953.7	1,246.3	1,260.7	1,420.6	1,445.6	1,459.8
Net Stockholders' Equity	1,793.5	1,821.5	1,305.6	1,201.9	1,307.4	1,216.2	1,193.2
Net Working Capital	d249.5	d332.0	60.6	154.9	231.7	227.0	199.2
Year-end Shs. Outstg. (000)	132,374	134,662	120,109	120,368	133,764	134,886	140,348
STATISTICAL RECORD:							
Operating Profit Margin %	1.5	2.9	2.4	2.4	2.3	2.2	0.7
Net Profit Margin %	0.4	1.2	1.1	1.3	1.1	1.0	0.3
Return on Equity %	4.6	13.3	14.7	19.2	13.4	13.7	3.6
Return on Assets %	1.3	3.7	4.5	5.6	4.1	4.0	1.0
Debt/Total Assets %	31.3	30.1	29.2	30.8	33.2	34.6	33.9
Price Range	22.88-11.75	28.88-16.81	28.94-20.19	21.09-14.06	16.50-13.56	16.44-11.25	20.06-11.00
P/E Ratio	36.9-18.9	15.4-9.0	18.4-12.9	11.6-7.7	12.7-10.4	13.5-9.2	65.8-36.1
Average Yield %	3.1	2.3	2.1	2.9	3.3	3.5	2.9

Statistics are as originally reported. Adj. for 100% stk. div., 8/98. 1 Incl. $244 mil total non-recur. chg. 2 Incl. $53.7 mil ($0.43/sh.) non-recur net gain from sale of int. in ShopKo Stores, Inc. 3 Incl. $163.7 pre-tax gain on sale of Hazelwood Farms Bakeries & incl. $103.6 pre-tax restructuring chg. 4 Incl. $153.9 mil ($1.16/sh.) after-tax restr. & other chgs.

OFFICERS:
M. W. Wright, Chmn.
J. Noddle, Pres., C.E.O.
P. K. Knous, Exec. V.P., C.F.O.

INVESTOR CONTACT: Yolanda Scharton, (612) 828-4540

PRINCIPAL OFFICE: 11840 Valley View Road, Eden Prairie, MN 55344

TELEPHONE NUMBER: (612) 828-4000
FAX: (612) 828-8998
WEB: www.supervalu.com

NO. OF EMPLOYEES: 62,100 (approx.)

SHAREHOLDERS: 7,265

ANNUAL MEETING: In June

INCORPORATED: DE, Dec., 1925

INSTITUTIONAL HOLDINGS:
No. of Institutions: 267
Shares Held: 85,468,695
% Held: 64.6

INDUSTRY: Groceries, general line (SIC: 5141)

TRANSFER AGENT(S): Wells Fargo Shareowner Services, St. Paul, MN

NYSE SYMBOL SY
Rec. Pr. 15.55 (5/31/01)

SYBASE, INC.

YIELD ...
P/E RATIO 19.9

*7 YEAR PRICE SCORE 71.5 *12 MONTH PRICE SCORE 79.5
*NYSE COMPOSITE INDEX=100

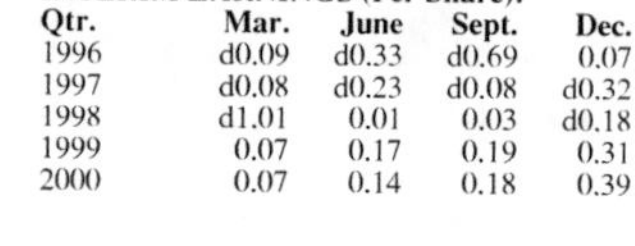

INTERIM EARNINGS (Per Share):

Qtr.	Mar.	June	Sept.	Dec.
1996	d0.09	d0.33	d0.69	0.07
1997	d0.08	d0.23	d0.08	d0.32
1998	d1.01	0.01	0.03	d0.18
1999	0.07	0.17	0.19	0.31
2000	0.07	0.14	0.18	0.39

INTERIM DIVIDENDS (Per Share):

Amt.	Decl.	Ex.	Rec.	Pay.

No dividends paid.

CAPITALIZATION (12/31/00):

	($000)	(%)
Minority Interest	1,866	0.4
Common & Surplus	490,752	99.6
Total	492,618	100.0

RECENT DEVELOPMENTS: For the year ended 12/31/00, net income jumped 15.4% to $72.1 million compared with income of $62.5 million the year before. Earnings for 2000 and 1999 included amortization of goodwill and other intangibles of $32.7 million and $13.9 million, respectively. Also, results for 2000 included in-process research and development of $8.0 million. Total revenue increased 10.2% to $960.5 million from $871.6 million in the previous year.

PROSPECTS: The Company announced a marketing alliance with Document Sciences Corporation, a developer of software that enables companies to communicate with their customers via the Web. Under the agreement, Document Sciences will offer SYBS's Enterprise Portal customers rapid application development tools for Web and print content automation. Separately, the Company signed an agreement to acquire New Era of Networks, Inc. in a stock-for-stock transaction valued at about $373.0 million.

BUSINESS

SYBASE, INC. develops, markets and supports a full line of relational database management software products and services for on-line applications in networked computing environments. The Company offers a broad range of relational database management system servers, application development tools and connectivity software and complements this product portfolio by providing consulting and integration services required to support enterprise-wide on-line applications. Sybase's business is organized into five principal operating divisions: Enterprise Solutions, iAnywhere Solutions, Inc., Business Intelligence, Internet Applications and Financial Fusion, Inc. iAnywhere Solutions, Inc. and Financial Fusion, Inc. are wholly-owned subsidiaries. The Company markets its products and services worldwide through a direct sales force, distributors, value-added remarketers, systems integrators and original equipment manufacturers.

ANNUAL FINANCIAL DATA

	12/31/00	12/31/99	12/31/98	12/31/97	12/31/96	12/31/95	12/31/94
Earnings Per Share	**0.78**	**2 0.74**	**1 d1.15**	**d0.70**	**1 d1.05**	**1 d0.27**	**1.38**
Cash Flow Per Share	**1.95**	**1.81**	**0.18**	**0.63**	**0.25**	**0.78**	**2.11**
Tang. Book Val. Per Share	**3.53**	**3.71**	**3.27**	**4.09**	**4.25**	**4.95**	**6.30**
INCOME STATEMENT (IN THOUSANDS):							
Total Revenues	960,458	871,633	867,469	903,937	1,011,545	956,586	693,806
Costs & Expenses	762,122	694,599	846,484	845,600	987,925	904,753	537,754
Depreciation & Amort.	107,879	90,009	107,798	104,739	97,835	75,178	39,611
Operating Income	90,457	87,025	d86,813	d46,402	d74,215	d23,345	116,441
Net Interest Inc./(Exp.)	17,857	13,626	10,077	9,184	9,243	8,936	5,570
Income Before Income Taxes	107,586	100,798	d79,065	d40,756	d66,708	d14,742	121,301
Income Taxes	35,461	38,303	14,063	14,668	12,298	4,760	46,094
Equity Earnings/Minority Int.	94	...	...	...	...	...	...
Net Income	72,125	2 62,495	1 d93,128	d55,424	1 d79,006	1 d19,502	75,207
Cash Flow	180,004	152,504	14,670	49,315	18,829	55,676	114,818
Average Shs. Outstg.	92,150	84,156	80,893	78,794	75,160	71,292	54,422
BALANCE SHEET (IN THOUSANDS):							
Cash & Cash Equivalents	313,974	309,197	248,632	236,003	174,522	223,721	197,123
Total Current Assets	574,113	522,655	477,700	475,661	445,268	461,497	384,011
Net Property	59,296	67,587	101,433	149,661	191,328	194,916	110,891
Total Assets	915,040	737,335	696,604	781,625	751,891	766,292	575,597
Total Current Liabilities	416,627	395,426	393,521	408,151	352,212	321,191	232,385
Net Stockholders' Equity	490,752	336,110	301,072	371,515	396,808	439,649	337,180
Net Working Capital	157,486	127,229	84,179	67,510	93,056	140,306	151,626
Year-end Shs. Outstg.	87,656	80,921	81,169	79,998	76,609	72,646	51,647
STATISTICAL RECORD:							
Operating Profit Margin %	9.4	10.0	...	...	...	...	16.8
Net Profit Margin %	7.5	7.2	...	...	...	...	10.8
Return on Equity %	14.7	18.6	...	...	...	...	22.3
Return on Assets %	7.9	8.5	...	...	...	...	13.1
Price Range	31.00-15.44	19.81-5.31	11.25-4.50	23.63-11.50	37.38-13.50	55.00-19.88	57.00-35.25
P/E Ratio	39.7-19.8	26.8-7.2	...	...	...	...	41.3-25.5

Statistics are as originally reported. 1 Incl. non-recurr. chrg. $74.2 mill., 12/31/98, $49.2 mill., 12/31/96; $44.0 mill., 12/31/95. 2 Incl. restr. credit of $8.5 mill.

OFFICERS:
J. Chen, Chmn., Pres., C.E.O.
P. Van der Vorst, V.P., C.F.O.
D. R. Carl, V.P., Gen. Couns.

INVESTOR CONTACT: Scott Irey, Treas., (510) 922-3500

PRINCIPAL OFFICE: 6475 Christie Avenue, Emeryville, CA 94608

TELEPHONE NUMBER: (510) 922-3500
FAX: (510) 922-3210
WEB: www.sybase.com

NO. OF EMPLOYEES: 4,864

SHAREHOLDERS: 1,503

ANNUAL MEETING: In May

INCORPORATED: CA, Nov., 1984; reincorp., DE, July, 1991

INSTITUTIONAL HOLDINGS:
No. of Institutions: 186
Shares Held: 69,640,920
% Held: 68.3

INDUSTRY: Prepackaged software (SIC: 7372)

TRANSFER AGENT(S): EquiServe, Boston, MA

NYSE SYMBOL SBL
Rec. Pr. 31.50 (4/30/01)

SYMBOL TECHNOLOGIES, INC.

YIELD 0.1%
P/E RATIO ...

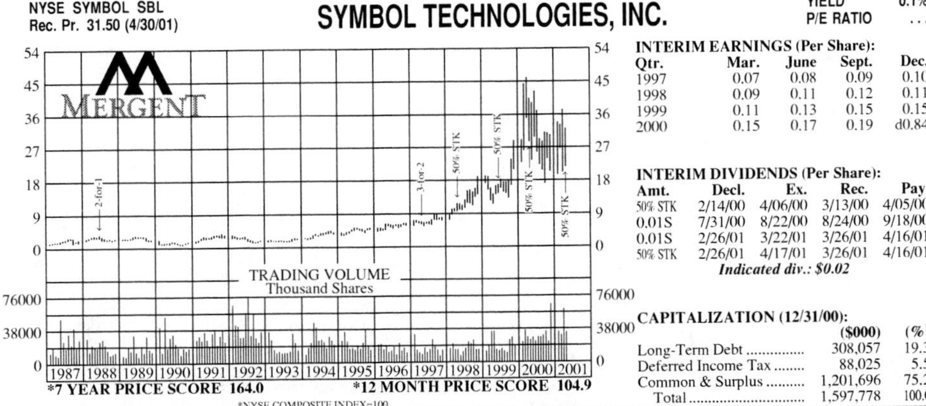

INTERIM EARNINGS (Per Share):

Qtr.	Mar.	June	Sept.	Dec.
1997	0.07	0.08	0.09	0.10
1998	0.09	0.11	0.12	0.11
1999	0.11	0.13	0.15	0.15
2000	0.15	0.17	0.19	d0.84

INTERIM DIVIDENDS (Per Share):

Amt.	Decl.	Ex.	Rec.	Pay.
50% STK	2/14/00	4/06/00	3/13/00	4/05/00
0.01S	7/31/00	8/22/00	8/24/00	9/18/00
0.01S	2/26/01	3/22/01	3/26/01	4/16/01
50% STK	2/26/01	4/17/01	3/26/01	4/16/01

Indicated div.: $0.02

CAPITALIZATION (12/31/00):

	($000)	(%)
Long-Term Debt	308,057	19.3
Deferred Income Tax	88,025	5.5
Common & Surplus	1,201,696	75.2
Total	1,597,778	100.0

RECENT DEVELOPMENTS: For the twelve months ended 12/31/00, the Company reported a net loss of $68.9 million compared with net earnings of $116.4 million in 1999. Results for 2000 included a $87.6 million in-process research and development charge, a $146.7 million restructuring and impairment charge, and a $39.2 million merger integration charge. Net revenues were $1.45 billion, up 27.2% from $1.14 billion in the prior year. Gross profit slipped 5.0% to $460.4 million versus $484.7 million.

PROSPECTS: Long-term prospects are promising. The Company's integration of Telxon Corporation, which was acquired on 12/1/00, is proceeding well and SBL is on track to achieve synergies targeted from the acquisition. Moreover, recent momentum in bookings has continued into 2001 as demand for the Company's products is being driven by customers looking for ways to cut costs, improve operating efficiency and create new revenue streams, coupled with increasing use of mobile devices.

BUSINESS

SYMBOL TECHNOLOGIES, INC. develops, manufactures, sells and services bar code scanning products that employ laser technology to read data encoded in bar code symbols, and data collection systems incorporating application specific hand-held computers. The Company's bar code scanning equipment is compatible with a variety of data collection systems, including computers, electronic cash registers and portable data collection devices. Bar code scanners are used to enhance accurate data entry and productivity in retail, transportation, parcel delivery and postal service, warehousing and distribution, factory automation and many other applications.

ANNUAL FINANCIAL DATA

	12/31/00	12/31/99	12/31/98	12/31/97	12/31/96	12/31/95	12/31/94
Earnings Per Share	**4 d0.33**	**0.55**	**3 0.44**	**0.34**	**2 0.25**	**1 0.23**	**0.18**
Cash Flow Per Share	**0.06**	**0.86**	**0.70**	**0.56**	**0.44**	**1.06**	**0.32**
Tang. Book Val. Per Share	**3.49**	**2.23**	**1.87**	**1.57**	**1.32**	**1.21**	**1.02**
Dividends Per Share	**0.01**	**0.01**	**0.01**	**0.01**	...	...	...
Dividend Payout %	...	**2.3**	**2.2**	**2.3**	...	...	...
INCOME STATEMENT (IN MILLIONS):							
Total Revenues	1,449.5	1,139.3	977.9	774.3	656.7	555.2	465.3
Costs & Expenses	1,434.7	896.2	781.0	616.1	533.0	306.9	374.2
Depreciation & Amort.	82.1	66.2	55.2	45.3	39.5	34.3	27.8
Operating Income	d67.3	176.9	141.7	113.0	84.2	76.4	63.3
Net Interest Inc./(Exp.)	d12.2	d5.8	d3.4	d3.3	d3.1	d1.4	d5.0
Income Before Income Taxes	d79.6	171.1	138.8	109.7	81.1	75.0	58.3
Income Taxes	cr10.6	54.8	45.8	39.5	30.8	28.5	23.3
Net Income	4 d69.0	116.4	3 93.0	70.2	2 50.3	1 184.1	35.0
Cash Flow	13.1	182.5	148.1	115.5	89.8	218.4	62.8
Average Shs. Outstg. (000)	206,444	212,357	210,722	206,672	205,631	205,426	198,668
BALANCE SHEET (IN MILLIONS):							
Cash & Cash Equivalents	63.4	30.1	16.3	60.0	34.3	63.7	31.4
Total Current Assets	1,078.3	584.2	479.6	400.0	352.4	316.6	266.1
Net Property	234.5	206.1	174.9	118.7	101.3	88.3	71.7
Total Assets	2,093.2	1,047.9	838.4	679.2	614.2	544.3	474.2
Total Current Liabilities	458.0	232.6	184.3	158.1	130.7	106.7	74.3
Long-Term Obligations	308.1	99.6	64.6	40.3	50.5	60.8	59.9
Net Stockholders' Equity	1,201.7	640.5	530.9	453.7	399.7	352.9	316.2
Net Working Capital	620.2	351.6	295.3	241.8	221.7	209.9	191.8
Year-end Shs. Outstg. (000)	224,136	199,512	198,302	198,248	198,217	194,559	195,319
STATISTICAL RECORD:							
Operating Profit Margin %	...	15.5	14.5	14.6	12.8	13.8	13.6
Net Profit Margin %	...	10.2	9.5	9.1	7.7	33.2	7.5
Return on Equity %	...	18.2	17.5	15.5	12.6	52.2	11.1
Return on Assets %	...	11.1	11.1	10.3	8.2	33.8	7.4
Debt/Total Assets %	14.7	9.5	7.7	5.9	8.2	11.2	12.6
Price Range	46.03-17.08	28.89-11.56	19.08-7.25	8.88-5.63	6.52-4.20	5.35-3.21	4.53-2.06
P/E Ratio	...	52.8-21.1	43.3-16.5	26.1-16.6	26.6-17.1	23.6-14.1	25.7-11.7
Average Yield %	...	0.1	0.1	0.1	...	...	...

Statistics are as originally reported. Adj. for 3-for-2 split, 4/97, 9/98, & 6/99. Adj. for 50% stk. div., 4/98, 9/98, 6/99, 4/00 & 4/01. 1 Incl. $2.5 mill. pre-tax chg. on mgmt. change. 2 Incl. $12.3 mill. pre-tax chg. rel. to acq. costs & merger integr. costs. 3 Incl. a pre-tax charge of $3.6 million rel. to a term. acq. & a pre-tax gain of $500,000 on the sale of a bus. 4 Incl. $146.7 mill. restr. chg., $87.6 mill. in-process R&D chg., & $39.2 mill. merger integr. chg.

OFFICERS:
J. Swartz, Chmn., Chief Scientist
T. Razmilovic, Pres., C.E.O.
K. V. Jaeggi, Sr. V.P., Fin., C.F.O.

INVESTOR CONTACT: Ken Jaeggi, Sr. V.P., C.F.O., (631) 738-4191

PRINCIPAL OFFICE: One Symbol Plaza, Holtsville, NY 11742-1300

TELEPHONE NUMBER: (631) 738-2400
FAX: (631) 738-5990
WEB: www.symbol.com
NO. OF EMPLOYEES: 6,000 (approx.)
SHAREHOLDERS: 1,196
ANNUAL MEETING: In May
INCORPORATED: NY, 1973; reincorp., DE, Nov., 1987

INSTITUTIONAL HOLDINGS:
No. of Institutions: 280
Shares Held: 194,259,525
% Held: 85.8

INDUSTRY: Computer peripheral equipment, nec (SIC: 3577)

TRANSFER AGENT(S): Continental Stock & Transfer Company, New York, NY

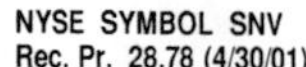

NYSE SYMBOL SNV
Rec. Pr. 28.78 (4/30/01)

SYNOVUS FINANCIAL CORPORATION

YIELD 1.7%
P/E RATIO 30.9

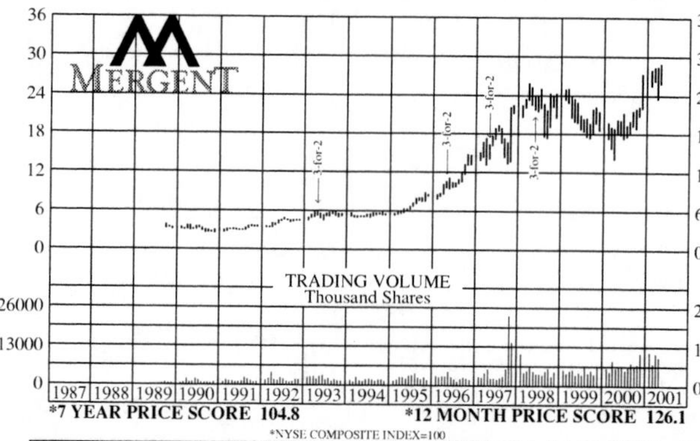

INTERIM EARNINGS (Per Share):

Qtr.	Mar.	June	Sept.	Dec.
1997	0.13	0.15	0.16	0.17
1998	0.15	0.17	0.18	0.20
1999	0.18	0.19	0.21	0.22
2000	0.22	0.22	0.23	0.26

INTERIM DIVIDENDS (Per Share):

Amt.	Decl.	Ex.	Rec.	Pay.
0.11Q	5/15/00	6/20/00	6/22/00	7/01/00
0.11Q	9/11/00	9/19/00	9/21/00	10/02/00
0.11Q	12/11/00	12/19/00	12/21/00	1/02/01
0.128Q	2/28/01	3/20/01	3/22/01	4/02/01
0.128Q	5/15/01	6/19/01	6/21/01	7/02/01

Indicated div.: $0.51

CAPITALIZATION (12/31/00):

	($000)	(%)
Total Deposits	11,161,710	82.7
Long-Term Debt	840,859	6.2
Minority Interest	80,890	0.6
Common & Surplus	1,417,171	10.5
Total	13,500,630	100.0

RECENT DEVELOPMENTS: For the year ended 12/31/00, net income increased 16.5% to $262.6 million from $225.3 million in the prior year. Net interest income rose 9.6% to $562.3 million from $513.3 million in 1999. Provision for losses on loans advanced 30.4% to $44.3 million. Total non-interest income grew 12.7% to $833.5 million. Total non-interest expense climbed 8.1% to $939.8 million.

PROSPECTS: On 2/28/01, SNV completed the acquisition of Atlanta, Georgia-based Creative Financial Group, Ltd. in a stock transaction. The units of Creative Financial will operate as wholly-owned subsidiaries and divisions of Synovus Wealth Management. Going forward, SNV expects growth in earnings per share of at least 15.0% in 2001, and in the range of 15.0% to 18.0% by 2003.

BUSINESS

SYNOVUS FINANCIAL CORPORATION, with assets of $15.18 billion as of 3/31/01, is a registered bank holding company engaged in two principal business segments: banking, which encompasses commercial banking, trust services, mortgage banking, credit card banking and certain securities brokerage operations, and bankcard data processing. The Company currently has 39 wholly-owned subsidiaries located in Georgia, Alabama, Florida and South Carolina, and holds an 80.8% stake in Total System Services, Inc. a payment services provider. SNV and its subsidiaries offer a wide range of commercial banking services, including accepting customary types of demand and savings deposits; making individual, consumer, commercial, installment, first and second mortgage loans; offering money transfers, safe deposit services, trust, investment, IRA, and other fiduciary services.

LOAN DISTRIBUTION

(12/31/2000)	($000)	(%)
Commercial	8,494,770	78.9
Retail	2,273,507	21.1
Total	10,768,277	100.0

ANNUAL FINANCIAL DATA

	12/31/00	12/31/99	12/31/98	12/31/97	12/31/96	12/31/95	12/31/94
Earnings Per Share	**0.92**	**0.80**	**0.70**	**0.62**	**0.53**	**0.45**	**0.38**
Tang. Book Val. Per Share	**4.98**	**4.35**	**3.96**	**3.44**	**2.99**	**2.66**	**2.22**
Dividends Per Share	**0.42**	**0.34**	**0.28**	**0.23**	**0.19**	**0.15**	**0.13**
Dividend Payout %	**45.6**	**42.9**	**40.0**	**36.9**	**35.0**	**34.4**	**33.4**
INCOME STATEMENT (IN MILLIONS):							
Total Interest Income	1,097.8	888.0	769.2	725.7	663.3	615.8	429.4
Total Interest Expense	535.5	374.7	328.7	313.3	288.4	273.9	169.9
Net Interest Income	562.3	513.3	440.5	412.4	374.9	341.9	259.5
Provision for Loan Losses	44.3	34.0	26.7	32.3	31.8	25.8	22.1
Non-Interest Income	833.5	739.8	562.0	489.2	425.4	340.8	263.9
Non-Interest Expense	939.8	869.7	684.2	610.4	549.2	477.5	366.9
Income Before Taxes	411.7	349.3	291.6	258.9	219.3	179.5	134.5
Net Income	262.6	225.3	187.1	165.2	139.6	114.6	86.4
Average Shs. Outstg. (000)	286,882	283,355	269,151	265,665	261,299	258,647	226,942
BALANCE SHEET (IN MILLIONS):							
Cash & Due from Banks	558.1	466.5	348.4	388.1	405.0	...	290.8
Securities Avail. for Sale	1,807.0	1,716.7	1,514.1	1,325.0	1,276.1	1,106.3	763.1
Total Loans & Leases	10,768.3	9,077.5	7,420.5	6,615.6	6,075.5	5,528.8	4,330.5
Allowance for Credit Losses	164.3	136.8	119.4	108.8	104.9	96.2	81.0
Net Loans & Leases	10,604.0	8,940.7	7,301.2	6,506.8	5,970.5	5,432.6	4,249.5
Total Assets	14,908.1	12,547.0	10,498.0	9,260.3	8,612.3	7,545.8	6,115.4
Total Deposits	11,161.7	9,440.1	8,542.8	7,707.9	7,203.0	6,727.9	5,027.5
Long-Term Obligations	840.9	318.6	127.0	7.2	97.3	106.8	119.8
Total Liabilities	13,490.9	11,320.3	9,426.4	8,237.7	7,828.6	7,234.0	5,607.3
Net Stockholders' Equity	1,417.2	1,226.7	1,070.6	903.7	783.8	693.6	508.1
Year-end Shs. Outstg. (000)	284,643	282,014	270,218	262,808	261,779	260,665	228,499
STATISTICAL RECORD:							
Return on Equity %	18.5	18.4	17.5	18.3	17.8	16.5	17.0
Return on Assets %	1.8	1.8	1.8	1.8	1.6	1.5	1.4
Equity/Assets %	9.5	9.8	10.2	9.8	9.1	9.2	8.3
Non-Int. Exp./Tot. Inc. %	67.4	69.5	68.3	67.7	68.6	70.0	70.1
Price Range	27.38-14.00	25.13-17.25	25.92-17.25	22.42-13.11	14.83-7.78	8.89-5.26	5.89-4.93
P/E Ratio	29.8-15.2	31.4-21.6	37.0-24.6	36.2-21.1	27.8-14.6	20.0-11.8	15.4-12.9
Average Yield %	2.0	1.6	1.3	1.3	1.7	2.2	2.4

Statistics are as originally reported. Adj. for stk. splits: 3-for-2, 5/98; 4/97; 4/96 & 4/93
[1] Bef. acctg. change chrg. $2.9 mill.

OFFICERS:
J. H. Blanchard, Chmn., C.E.O.
R. E. Anthony, Vice-Chmn.
W. M. Deriso Jr., Vice-Chmn.
J. D. Yancey, Pres.

INVESTOR CONTACT: Patrick A. Reynolds, Dir.-Inv. Rel., (706) 649-5220

PRINCIPAL OFFICE: One Arsenal Place, 901 Front Avenue, Suite 301, Columbus, GA 31901

TELEPHONE NUMBER: (706) 649-2387
FAX: (706) 649-2342
WEB: www.synovus.com

NO. OF EMPLOYEES: 9,672

SHAREHOLDERS: 32,597 (approx.)

ANNUAL MEETING: In Apr.

INCORPORATED: GA, June, 1972

INSTITUTIONAL HOLDINGS:
No. of Institutions: 213
Shares Held: 100,204,464
% Held: 35.1

INDUSTRY: National commercial banks (SIC: 6021)

TRANSFER AGENT(S): State Street Bank and Trust Company, Boston, MA

NYSE SYMBOL SYY
Rec. Pr. 29.73 (5/31/01)

SYSCO CORPORATION

YIELD 0.9%
P/E RATIO 37.2

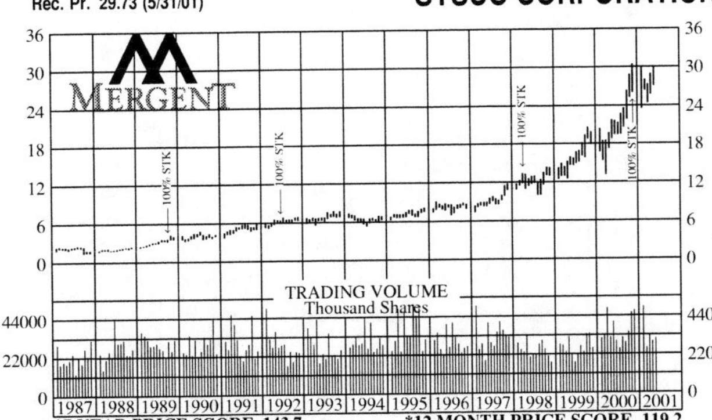

*7 YEAR PRICE SCORE 143.7 *12 MONTH PRICE SCORE 119.2
*NYSE COMPOSITE INDEX=100

INTERIM EARNINGS (Per Share):

Qtr.	Sept.	Dec.	Mar.	June
1997-98	0.12	0.13	0.10	0.15
1998-99	0.13	0.13	0.11	0.18
1999-00	0.16	0.16	0.16	0.22
2000-01	0.21	0.21	...	...

INTERIM DIVIDENDS (Per Share):

Amt.	Decl.	Ex.	Rec.	Pay.
0.12Q	9/08/00	10/04/00	10/06/00	10/27/00
100% STK	11/03/00	12/18/00	11/15/00	12/15/00
0.07Q	11/03/00	1/03/01	1/05/01	1/26/01
0.07Q	2/09/01	4/04/01	4/06/01	4/27/01
0.07Q	5/11/01	7/03/01	7/06/01	7/27/01

Indicated div.: $0.28 (Div. Reinv. Plan)

CAPITALIZATION (7/1/00):

	($000)	(%)
Long-Term Debt	1,023,642	33.8
Deferred Income Tax	245,810	8.1
Common & Surplus	1,761,568	58.1
Total	3,031,020	100.0

RECENT DEVELOPMENTS: For the 13 weeks ended 12/30/00, net earnings jumped 36.8% to $139.4 million from $101.9 million in the corresponding period a year earlier. Total sales increased 13.7% to $5.29 billion from $4.65 billion the year before. Sales benefited from recent acquisitions, partially offset by higher costs for paper and disposables and produce. Earnings before income taxes advanced 36.3% to $225.8 million from $165.7 million the previous year.

PROSPECTS: In March 2001, the Company completed its acquisition of Guest Supply, Inc., a specialty distributor to the lodging industry with annual sales of about $366.0 million, for approximately $161.0 million in SYY common stock. The acquisition will help increase the number of products the Company sells by enabling SYY to expand into the distribution of housekeeping supplies, health and beauty products, and room accessories to hotels.

BUSINESS

SYSCO CORPORATION is a major marketer and distributor of foodservice products. Included among its customers are about 356,000 restaurants, hotels, hospitals, schools and other institutions. The Company distributes entree items, dry and canned foods, fresh produce, beverages, dairy products and certain nonfood products, including paper products and cleaning supplies. Through its SYGMA Network, Inc. subsidiary, the Company serves pizza, chicken, steak and hamburgers to fast-food chains and other limited menu chain restaurants. SYY has three Canadian facilities located in Vancouver, Edmonton and Toronto. In fiscal 2000, the foodservice sales breakdown was: 65% restaurants; 10% hospitals and nursing homes; 6% schools and colleges; 5% hotels and motels; and 14% other.

ANNUAL FINANCIAL DATA

	7/1/00	7/3/99	6/27/98	6/28/97	6/29/96	7/1/95	7/2/94
Earnings Per Share	**[1] 0.68**	**0.54**	**[1] 0.48**	**0.43**	**0.38**	**0.35**	**0.30**
Cash Flow Per Share	**1.01**	**0.84**	**0.74**	**0.65**	**0.58**	**0.52**	**0.46**
Tang. Book Val. Per Share	**1.90**	**1.71**	**1.57**	**1.67**	**1.70**	**1.57**	**1.33**
Dividends Per Share	**0.24**	**0.20**	**0.18**	**0.15**	**0.13**	**0.11**	**0.09**
Dividend Payout %	**35.3**	**37.0**	**37.4**	**35.3**	**34.2**	**31.9**	**30.5**
INCOME STATEMENT (IN MILLIONS):							
Total Revenues	19,303.3	17,422.8	15,327.5	14,454.6	13,395.1	12,118.0	10,942.5
Costs & Expenses	18,272.6	16,550.1	14,555.3	13,752.0	12,756.5	11,533.3	10,420.4
Depreciation & Amort.	220.7	205.0	181.2	160.3	144.7	130.8	120.0
Operating Income	810.0	667.7	591.0	542.3	494.0	454.0	402.1
Net Interest Inc./(Exp.)	d70.8	d72.8	d58.4	d46.5	d41.0	d38.6	d36.3
Income Before Income Taxes	737.6	593.9	532.5	496.0	453.9	417.6	367.6
Income Taxes	284.0	231.6	207.7	193.4	177.0	165.8	150.8
Net Income	[1] 453.6	362.3	[1] 324.8	302.5	276.9	251.8	216.8
Cash Flow	674.3	567.3	506.1	462.8	421.6	382.6	336.7
Average Shs. Outstg. (000)	669,556	673,594	686,880	708,940	730,396	731,120	737,356
BALANCE SHEET (IN MILLIONS):							
Cash & Cash Equivalents	159.1	149.3	110.3	117.7	107.8	133.9	86.7
Total Current Assets	2,733.2	2,408.8	2,180.1	1,964.4	1,922.3	1,789.4	1,599.6
Net Property	1,344.7	1,227.7	1,151.1	1,058.4	990.6	896.1	817.2
Total Assets	4,814.0	4,096.6	3,780.2	3,436.6	3,325.4	3,097.2	2,811.7
Total Current Liabilities	1,782.9	1,427.5	1,324.2	1,113.8	1,037.5	932.6	846.6
Long-Term Obligations	1,023.6	997.7	867.0	685.6	581.7	541.6	538.7
Net Stockholders' Equity	1,761.6	1,427.2	1,356.8	1,400.5	1,474.7	1,403.6	1,240.9
Net Working Capital	950.3	981.2	855.9	850.6	884.8	856.7	753.1
Year-end Shs. Outstg. (000)	662,970	659,344	670,018	689,752	721,652	731,460	732,276
STATISTICAL RECORD:							
Operating Profit Margin %	4.2	3.8	3.9	3.8	3.7	3.7	3.7
Net Profit Margin %	2.4	2.1	2.1	2.1	2.1	2.1	2.0
Return on Equity %	25.8	25.4	23.9	21.6	18.8	17.9	17.5
Return on Assets %	9.4	8.8	8.6	8.8	8.3	8.1	7.7
Debt/Total Assets %	21.3	24.4	22.9	20.0	17.5	17.5	19.2
Price Range	30.44-13.06	20.56-12.47	14.34-9.97	11.81-7.31	9.06-6.91	8.16-6.22	7.31-5.28
P/E Ratio	44.8-19.2	38.1-23.1	30.2-21.0	27.8-17.2	23.8-18.2	23.6-18.0	24.8-17.9
Average Yield %	1.1	1.2	1.5	1.6	1.6	1.5	1.4

Statistics are as originally reported. Adj. for 2-for-1 stk. split, 12/00, & 3/98. [1] Bef. $8.0 mil ($0.01/sh) chg. for acctg. adj., 2000; $28.1 mil ($0.04/sh), 1998.

OFFICERS:
C. H. Cotros, Chmn. & C.E.O.
R. J. Schnieders, Pres. & C.O.O.
J. K. Stubblefield, Exec. V.P. & C.F.O.

INVESTOR CONTACT: Toni R. Spigelmyer, Asst. V.P., (281) 584-1458

PRINCIPAL OFFICE: 1390 Enclave Pkwy., Houston, TX 77077-2099

TELEPHONE NUMBER: (281) 584-1390
FAX: (281) 584-2880
WEB: www.sysco.com

NO. OF EMPLOYEES: 40,400 (approx.)

SHAREHOLDERS: 15,207

ANNUAL MEETING: In Nov.

INCORPORATED: DE, May, 1969

INSTITUTIONAL HOLDINGS:
No. of Institutions: 559
Shares Held: 460,850,658
% Held: 68.5

INDUSTRY: Groceries, general line (SIC: 5141)

TRANSFER AGENT(S): Fleet National Bank, Boston, MA

NYSE SYMBOL SYX
Rec. Pr. 2.85 (5/31/01)

SYSTEMAX INC.

YIELD ...
P/E RATIO ...

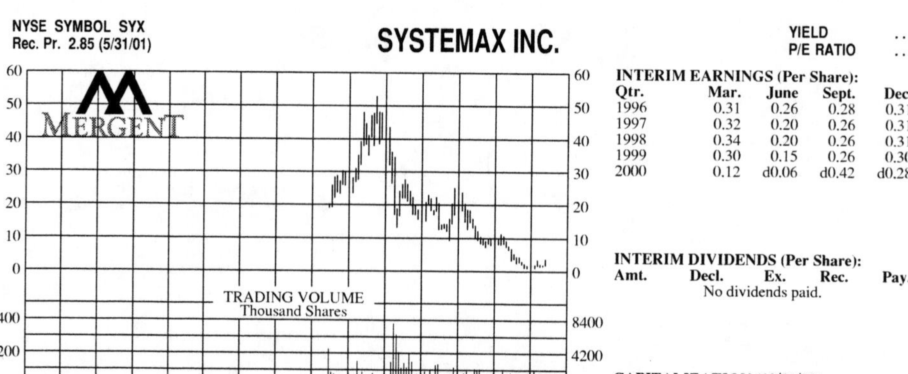

*7 YEAR PRICE SCORE N/A *12 MONTH PRICE SCORE 88.7

*NYSE COMPOSITE INDEX=100

INTERIM EARNINGS (Per Share):

Qtr.	Mar.	June	Sept.	Dec.
1996	0.31	0.26	0.28	0.31
1997	0.32	0.20	0.26	0.31
1998	0.34	0.20	0.26	0.31
1999	0.30	0.15	0.26	0.30
2000	0.12	d0.06	d0.42	d0.28

INTERIM DIVIDENDS (Per Share):

Amt.	Decl.	Ex.	Rec.	Pay.

No dividends paid.

CAPITALIZATION (12/31/00):

	($000)	(%)
Common & Surplus	255,671	100.0
Total	255,671	100.0

RECENT DEVELOPMENTS: For the year ended 12/31/00, SYX reported a net loss of $40.8 million compared with net income of $36.0 million in the previous year. Net sales slipped 3.9% to $1.69 billion from $1.75 billion a year earlier. Gross profit totaled $209.9 million, or 12.4% of net sales, compared with $314.5 million, or 17.9% of net sales, the year before. Loss from operations was $61.0 million versus income from operations of $59.8 million in the prior year.

PROSPECTS: The Company is reducing inventory levels and reconfiguring certain assembly operations to help boost manufacturing efficiencies. SYX plans to implement additional cost-reduction initiatives in the near future. Going forward, results could benefit from the Company's efforts to develop marketing partnerships with other established companies to sell and distribute Systemax computers, along with its plans to implement a new internal information system.

BUSINESS

SYSTEMAX INC. (formerly Global DirectMail Corp.) is a direct marketer of brand-name and private-label personal desktop computers, notebook computers, computer-related products and supplies, and industrial products, in North America and Europe. The Company also assembles build-to-order personal computers under the SYSTEMAX™, TIGER®, and ULTRA™ brand names. The Company markets its products to businesses through mailings of its full-line and specialty catalogs, e-commerce Web sites, and through outbound telemarketing. Catalog brand names include GLOBAL COMPUTER SUPPLIES™, MISCO®, HCS MISCO™, GLOBALDIRECT™, ARROWSTAR™, DARTEK.COM™, TIGERDIRECT.COM™, 06™, MIDWEST MICRO™ and INFOTEL™.

QUARTERLY DATA

(12/31/2000)($000)	REV	INC
1st Quarter.................	448,870	(2,552)
2nd Quarter................	405,972	(14,531)
3rd Quarter	409,795	(14,236)
4th Quarter.................	421,466	(9,452)

ANNUAL FINANCIAL DATA

	12/31/00	12/31/99	12/31/98	12/31/97	12/31/96	12/31/95	12/31/94
Earnings Per Share	**d1.19**	**1.01**	**1.11**	**1.02**	**1.15**	**[1] 0.93**	**[1] 0.65**
Cash Flow Per Share	**d0.79**	**1.32**	**1.31**	**1.17**	**1.25**	**1.07**	**0.56**
Tang. Book Val. Per Share	**5.42**	**6.66**	**6.37**	**5.73**	**5.68**	**3.64**	...
INCOME STATEMENT (IN MILLIONS):							
Total Revenues	1,686.1	1,754.5	1,435.7	1,145.4	911.9	634.5	484.2
Costs & Expenses	1,733.5	1,683.5	1,363.8	1,080.4	838.6	578.1	445.8
Depreciation & Amort.	13.6	11.2	7.5	5.7	3.8	2.1	1.8
Operating Income	d61.0	59.8	64.3	59.3	69.5	54.3	36.5
Net Interest Inc./(Exp.)	d4.2	0.7	2.7	2.8	1.9	d1.1	d0.7
Income Before Income Taxes	d65.3	60.5	67.1	62.1	71.4	48.4	18.0
Income Taxes	cr24.5	24.5	25.8	23.3	27.7	12.7	0.9
Net Income	d40.8	36.0	41.3	38.8	43.7	35.7	17.1
Cash Flow	d27.2	47.2	48.7	44.5	47.5	37.8	18.9
Average Shs. Outstg. (000)	34,300	35,800	37,300	38,200	38,129	35,499	33,807
BALANCE SHEET (IN MILLIONS):							
Cash & Cash Equivalents	14.5	17.5	47.1	52.4	66.2	28.5	8.8
Total Current Assets	389.0	426.8	359.9	313.3	294.0	212.8	151.3
Net Property	74.7	46.8	34.0	29.4	21.9	17.3	11.8
Total Assets	538.0	550.0	454.4	399.7	331.4	247.5	164.2
Total Current Liabilities	282.3	239.9	165.3	125.6	99.5	90.6	77.1
Long-Term Obligations	...	1.7	2.5	2.0	2.0	2.9	11.5
Net Stockholders' Equity	255.7	308.3	286.6	272.2	228.6	154.0	69.1
Net Working Capital	106.7	186.9	194.6	187.8	194.4	122.2	74.2
Year-end Shs. Outstg. (000)	34,104	35,238	36,128	38,232	37,857	37,857	...
STATISTICAL RECORD:							
Operating Profit Margin %	...	3.4	4.5	5.2	7.6	8.6	7.5
Net Profit Margin %	...	2.1	2.9	3.4	4.8	5.6	3.5
Return on Equity %	...	11.7	14.4	14.3	19.1	23.2	24.8
Return on Assets %	...	6.5	9.1	9.7	13.2	14.4	10.4
Debt/Total Assets %	...	0.3	0.5	0.5	0.6	1.2	7.0
Price Range	11.38-0.88	23.81-7.19	25.25-9.25	43.63-13.13	53.00-23.50	30.38-19.00	...
P/E Ratio	...	23.6-7.1	22.7-8.3	42.8-12.9	46.1-20.4	32.7-20.4	...

Statistics are as originally reported. [1] Pro-forma until the third quarter of 1995.

OFFICERS:
Richard Leeds, Chmn., C.E.O.
B. Leeds, Vice-Chmn.
Robert Leeds, Vice-Chmn.
S. Goldschein, Sr. V.P., C.F.O.

INVESTOR CONTACT: Jennifer Saccone, Inv. Rel. Coordinator, (516) 608-7000

PRINCIPAL OFFICE: 22 Harbor Park Drive, Port Washington, NY 11050

TELEPHONE NUMBER: (516) 608-7000
FAX: (516) 625-0038
WEB: www.systemax.com

NO. OF EMPLOYEES: 3,865 full-time; 154 part-time

SHAREHOLDERS: 246

ANNUAL MEETING: In May

INCORPORATED: DE, May, 1995

INSTITUTIONAL HOLDINGS:
No. of Institutions: 32
Shares Held: 3,516,737
% Held: 10.3

INDUSTRY: Catalog and mail-order houses (SIC: 5961)

TRANSFER AGENT(S): The Bank of New York, New York, NY

NYSE SYMBOL TLB
Rec. Pr. 36.00 (5/31/01)

TALBOTS (THE), INC.

YIELD 0.9%
P/E RATIO 20.0

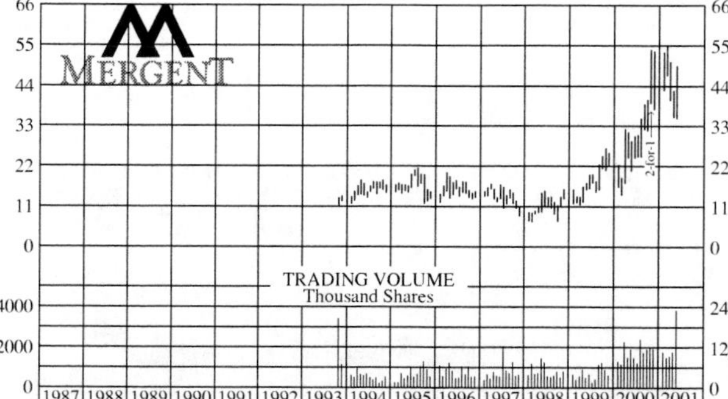

*7 YEAR PRICE SCORE 152.3 *12 MONTH PRICE SCORE 109.6

*NYSE COMPOSITE INDEX=100

INTERIM EARNINGS (Per Share):

Qtr.	Apr.	July	Oct.	Jan.
1997-98	0.25	d0.18	0.18	d0.16
1998-99	0.23	0.02	0.20	0.13
1999-00	0.31	0.06	0.32	0.24
2000-01	0.52	0.23	0.54	0.51

INTERIM DIVIDENDS (Per Share):

Amt.	Decl.	Ex.	Rec.	Pay.
0.14Q	8/15/00	8/31/00	9/05/00	9/18/00
2-for-1	10/11/00	11/08/00	10/25/00	11/07/00
0.07Q	11/09/00	11/30/00	12/04/00	12/18/00
0.07Q	3/01/01	3/08/01	3/12/01	3/26/01
0.08Q	5/24/01	5/31/01	6/04/01	6/18/01

Indicated div.: $0.32

CAPITALIZATION (2/3/01):

	($000)	(%)
Long-Term Debt	100,000	15.4
Common & Surplus	550,771	84.6
Total	650,771	100.0

RECENT DEVELOPMENTS: For the 53 weeks ended 2/3/01, net income more than doubled to $115.2 million from $58.5 million in the corresponding 52-week period the year before. Net sales climbed 21.9% to $1.59 billion from $1.31 billion a year earlier. Retail store sales rose 20.6% to $1.33 billion from $1.10 billion the prior year, driven by a 16.3% increase in comparable-store sales. Catalog sales totaled $269.0 million, up 28.8% compared with $208.8 million the previous year. Operating income jumped 88.6% to $191.6 million from $101.6 million the year before.

PROSPECTS: In 2001, the Company plans to accelerate its store expansion program to about 78 new store openings, up from 55 new stores opened in 2000. Meanwhile, TLB is enjoying consistently robust regular price sales across all sales channels, including stores, catalogs and the Internet, and geographic regions. In addition, strong demand for the Company's classic-styled merchandise is helping boost comparable-store sales growth. Going forward, TLB is focusing on broadening its customer base through increased marketing and a balanced merchandise selection.

BUSINESS

THE TALBOTS, INC. is a national specialty retailer and cataloger of women's and children's classic apparel, accessories and shoes. As of 5/22/01, the Company operated 748 stores in the U.S., Canada and the United Kingdom. The Company's stores and catalogs offer sportswear, casual wear, dresses, coats, sweaters, accessories and shoes, consisting primarily of the Company's own private-label merchandise in misses and petites sizes. Talbots Kids & Babies stores and catalogs sell an assortment of clothing and accessories for infants, toddlers, boys and girls. During 2000, the Company circulated approximately 58.0 million catalogs worldwide. At 4/5/01, Jusco (U.S.A.), Inc. owned approximately 58.1% of TLB's common stock.

REVENUES

(2/3/2001)	($000)	(%)
Store sales	1,325,961	83.1
Catalog sales	269,035	16.9
Total	1,594,996	100.0

ANNUAL FINANCIAL DATA

	2/3/01	1/29/00	1/30/99	1/31/98	2/1/97	2/3/96	1/28/95
Earnings Per Share	**1.80**	**0.93**	**0.58**	**0.09**	**0.96**	**0.91**	**0.78**
Cash Flow Per Share	**2.52**	**1.61**	**1.20**	**0.71**	**1.49**	**1.40**	**1.22**
Tang. Book Val. Per Share	**6.90**	**5.05**	**4.47**	**4.24**	**4.55**	**3.87**	**3.44**
Dividends Per Share	**0.27**	**0.23**	**0.22**	**0.21**	**0.17**	**0.13**	**0.09**
Dividend Payout %	**15.0**	**24.9**	**38.3**	**233.1**	**17.7**	**14.3**	**11.5**
INCOME STATEMENT (IN MILLIONS):							
Total Revenues	1,595.0	1,290.9	1,142.2	1,053.8	1,018.8	981.0	879.6
Costs & Expenses	1,357.6	1,146.0	1,035.3	996.4	874.9	838.9	754.6
Depreciation & Amort.	45.8	43.4	40.0	40.4	35.1	33.6	31.0
Operating Income	191.6	101.6	66.9	17.1	108.8	108.6	94.0
Net Interest Inc./(Exp.)	d4.3	d6.5	d7.3	d7.6	d5.3	d4.2	d2.8
Income Before Income Taxes	187.3	95.1	59.6	9.5	103.4	104.3	91.2
Income Taxes	72.1	36.6	23.0	3.7	39.8	41.7	36.8
Net Income	115.2	58.5	36.7	5.8	63.6	62.6	54.5
Cash Flow	161.0	101.8	76.7	46.2	98.7	96.2	85.4
Average Shs. Outstg. (000)	63,995	63,368	63,866	64,872	66,370	68,790	69,816
BALANCE SHEET (IN MILLIONS):							
Cash & Cash Equivalents	70.0	22.0	20.2	10.7	12.3	14.9	19.0
Total Current Assets	506.4	369.8	339.9	360.4	311.8	275.3	240.8
Net Property	234.8	203.2	189.5	182.6	170.8	154.2	141.1
Total Assets	858.6	693.9	657.1	676.4	621.8	572.1	532.5
Total Current Liabilities	188.0	143.9	138.4	215.3	127.4	113.9	102.9
Long-Term Obligations	100.0	100.0	100.0	50.0	50.0	50.0	35.0
Net Stockholders' Equity	550.8	431.3	402.1	396.5	431.5	398.0	385.6
Net Working Capital	318.4	225.9	201.5	145.1	184.4	161.4	137.9
Year-end Shs. Outstg. (000)	63,107	61,885	62,518	63,610	65,832	67,276	69,816
STATISTICAL RECORD:							
Operating Profit Margin %	12.0	7.9	5.9	1.6	10.7	11.1	10.7
Net Profit Margin %	7.2	4.5	3.2	0.6	6.2	6.4	6.2
Return on Equity %	20.9	13.6	9.1	1.5	14.7	15.7	14.1
Return on Assets %	13.4	8.4	5.6	0.9	10.2	10.9	10.2
Debt/Total Assets %	11.6	14.4	15.2	7.4	8.0	8.7	6.6
Price Range	54.00-14.13	26.97-11.28	15.78-6.75	17.19-8.38	20.25-11.94	21.50-11.75	18.25-11.63
P/E Ratio	30.0-7.8	29.2-12.2	27.4-11.7	190.8-93.0	21.1-12.4	23.6-12.9	23.4-14.9
Average Yield %	0.8	1.2	2.0	1.6	1.1	0.8	0.6

Statistics are as originally reported. Adj. for 2-for-1 stk. split, 11/00.

OFFICERS:
A. B. Zetcher, Chmn., Pres., C.E.O.
H. J. Metscher, Exec. V.P., Ch. Merch. Off.
E. L. Larsen, Sr. V.P., Fin., C.F.O., Treas.

INVESTOR CONTACT: Julie Lorigan, Dir., Inv. Rel., (781) 741-7775

PRINCIPAL OFFICE: One Talbots Drive, Hingham, MA 02043-9982

TELEPHONE NUMBER: (781) 749-7600
FAX: (781) 741-4369
WEB: www.talbots.com
NO. OF EMPLOYEES: 4,300 full-time (approx.); 6,800 part-time (approx.)
SHAREHOLDERS: 417
ANNUAL MEETING: In May
INCORPORATED: MA; reincorp., DE, 1989

INSTITUTIONAL HOLDINGS:
No. of Institutions: 160
Shares Held: 28,294,595
% Held: 44.8

INDUSTRY: Women's clothing stores (SIC: 5621)

TRANSFER AGENT(S): EquiServe Shareholder Services, Boston, MA

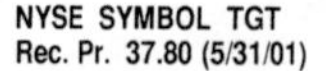

NYSE SYMBOL TGT
Rec. Pr. 37.80 (5/31/01)

TARGET CORPORATION

YIELD 0.6%
P/E RATIO 27.2

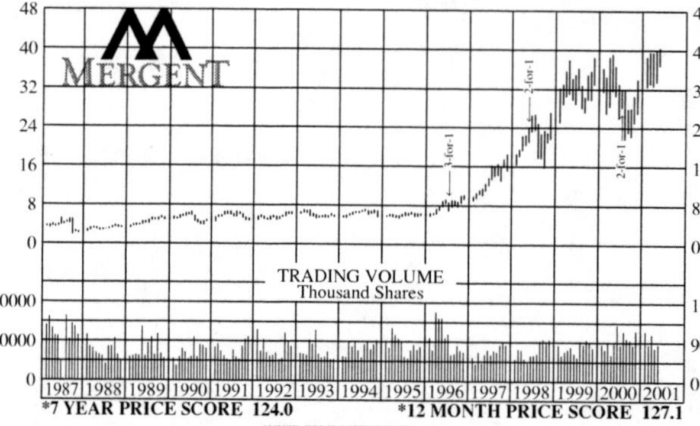

***7 YEAR PRICE SCORE 124.0** ***12 MONTH PRICE SCORE 127.1**

*NYSE COMPOSITE INDEX=100

INTERIM EARNINGS (Per Share):

Qtr.	Apr.	July	Oct.	Jan.
1997-98	0.14	0.16	0.20	0.38
1998-99	0.17	0.18	0.20	0.48
1999-00	0.21	0.25	0.26	0.53
2000-01	0.26	0.28	0.24	0.61

INTERIM DIVIDENDS (Per Share):

Amt.	Decl.	Ex.	Rec.	Pay.
0.055Q	6/15/00	8/16/00	8/20/00	9/10/00
0.055Q	11/09/00	11/16/00	11/20/00	12/10/00
0.055Q	1/11/01	2/15/01	2/20/01	3/10/01
0.055Q	3/15/01	5/16/01	5/20/01	6/10/01

Indicated div.: $0.22 (Div. Reinv. Plan)

CAPITALIZATION (2/3/01):

	($000)	(%)
Long-Term Debt	5,634,000	46.4
Common & Surplus	6,519,000	53.6
Total	12,153,000	100.0

RECENT DEVELOPMENTS: For the 53 weeks ended 2/3/01, net earnings totaled $1.26 billion, up 6.7% versus earnings of $1.19 billion, before an extraordinary charge, in the corresponding 52-week period the year before. Total revenues climbed 9.5% to $36.90 billion from $33.70 billion the year before. Comparable-store sales, on a comparable 52-week basis, rose 2.4% year-over-year, primarily reflecting a 3.4% comparable-store sales increase at Target stores.

PROSPECTS: The Company is continuing to aggressively expand its base of Target stores. On 7/29/01, TGT plans to open 36 new Target stores in twenty states and anticipates opening an additional 36 new Target stores, including its first store in Maine, on 10/14/01. Separately, the Company has agreed to acquire the rights to 35 former Wards stores. TGT expects to open 30 or more of these locations as Target stores in 2002 after extensive remodeling has been completed.

BUSINESS

TARGET CORPORATION (formerly Dayton Hudson Corporation) is a diversified general merchandise retailer. As of 2/3/01, the Company operated 1,307 stores in 46 states including 977 Target stores, 266 Mervyn's stores and 64 Marshall Field's stores. Target is a national discount store chain offering low prices with stores selling hardlines and fashion softgoods; Mervyn's is a moderate-priced department store chain specializing in active and casual apparel and home softlines. Marshall Field's is a full-service, full-line department store chain offering moderate to better merchandise.

QUARTERLY DATA

(2/3/2001)	REV	INC
1st Quarter	7,746,000	239,000
2nd Quarter	8,251,000	258,000
3rd Quarter	8,582,000	215,000
4th Quarter	12,324,000	552,000

ANNUAL FINANCIAL DATA

	2/3/01	1/29/00	1/30/99	1/31/98	2/3/97	2/3/96	1/28/95
Earnings Per Share	**1.38**	**1 1.27**	**1 1.02**	**1 0.85**	**1 0.52**	**0.33**	**0.48**
Cash Flow Per Share	**2.41**	**2.19**	**1.86**	**1.61**	**1.28**	**1.04**	**1.14**
Tang. Book Val. Per Share	**7.15**	**6.43**	**6.12**	**4.77**	**4.05**	**3.64**	**3.37**
Dividends Per Share	**0.21**	**0.20**	**0.18**	**0.17**	**0.15**	**0.145**	**0.14**
Dividend Payout %	**15.2**	**15.7**	**17.6**	**19.4**	**29.6**	**44.6**	**29.2**
INCOME STATEMENT (IN MILLIONS):							
Total Revenues	36,903.0	33,702.0	30,951.0	27,757.0	25,371.0	23,516.0	21,311.0
Costs & Expenses	33,485.0	30,519.0	28,217.0	25,322.0	23,496.0	21,979.0	19,623.0
Depreciation & Amort.	940.0	854.0	780.0	693.0	650.0	594.0	548.0
Operating Income	2,478.0	2,329.0	1,954.0	1,742.0	1,225.0	943.0	1,140.0
Net Interest Inc./(Exp.)	d425.0	d393.0	d398.0	d416.0	d442.0	d442.0	d426.0
Income Before Income Taxes	2,053.0	1,936.0	1,556.0	1,326.0	783.0	501.0	714.0
Income Taxes	789.0	751.0	594.0	524.0	309.0	190.0	280.0
Net Income	1,264.0	1 1,185.0	1 962.0	1 802.0	1 474.0	311.0	434.0
Cash Flow	2,204.0	2,039.0	1,742.0	1,495.0	1,124.0	905.0	982.0
Average Shs. Outstg. (000)	913,000	931,400	934,600	927,400	874,800	867,200	864,000
BALANCE SHEET (IN MILLIONS):							
Cash & Cash Equivalents	356.0	220.0	255.0	211.0	201.0	175.0	147.0
Total Current Assets	7,304.0	6,483.0	6,005.0	5,561.0	5,440.0	4,955.0	4,959.0
Net Property	11,418.0	9,899.0	8,969.0	8,125.0	7,467.0	7,294.0	6,385.0
Total Assets	19,490.0	17,143.0	15,666.0	14,191.0	13,389.0	12,570.0	11,697.0
Total Current Liabilities	6,301.0	5,850.0	5,057.0	4,556.0	4,111.0	3,523.0	3,390.0
Long-Term Obligations	5,634.0	4,521.0	4,452.0	4,425.0	4,808.0	4,959.0	4,488.0
Net Stockholders' Equity	6,519.0	5,862.0	5,311.0	4,460.0	3,790.0	3,403.0	3,193.0
Net Working Capital	1,003.0	633.0	948.0	1,005.0	1,329.0	1,432.0	1,569.0
Year-end Shs. Outstg. (000)	911,683	911,682	823,618	875,600	868,000	864,000	864,000
STATISTICAL RECORD:							
Operating Profit Margin %	6.7	6.9	6.3	6.3	4.8	4.0	5.3
Net Profit Margin %	3.4	3.5	3.1	2.9	1.9	1.3	2.0
Return on Equity %	19.4	20.2	18.1	18.0	12.5	9.1	13.6
Return on Assets %	6.5	6.9	6.1	5.7	3.5	2.5	3.7
Debt/Total Assets %	28.9	26.4	28.4	31.2	35.9	39.5	38.4
Price Range	39.19-21.63	38.50-25.03	27.13-15.72	18.50-8.97	10.16-5.76	6.71-5.27	7.24-5.41
P/E Ratio	28.4-15.7	30.3-19.7	26.6-15.4	21.8-10.6	19.6-11.1	20.6-16.2	15.1-11.3
Average Yield %	0.7	0.6	0.8	1.2	1.9	2.4	2.2

Statistics are as originally reported. Adj. for 2-for-1 stk. split, 7/00 & 4/98; 3-for-1 stk. split, 7/96. 1 Bef. $41 mil ($0.05/sh) extraord. chg., 1/00; $27 mil ($0.03/sh) extraord chg., 1/99; $51 mil ($0.06/sh) extraord. chg. & incl. $45 mil pre-tax gain, 1/98; bef. $11 mil extraord. chg. & incl. $134 mil pre-tax chg., 1/97.

OFFICERS:
R. J. Ulrich, Chmn., C.E.O.
G. L. Storch, Vice-Chmn.
D. A. Scovanner, Exec. V.P., C.F.O.
J. T. Hale, Sr. V.P., Gen. Couns., Sec.

INVESTOR CONTACT: S.D. Kahn, V.P.-Invest. Rel., (612) 370-6736

PRINCIPAL OFFICE: 777 Nicollet Mall, Minneapolis, MN 55402-2055

TELEPHONE NUMBER: (612) 370-6948
FAX: (612) 370-5502
WEB: www.targetcorp.com

NO. OF EMPLOYEES: 252,000 (avg.)

SHAREHOLDERS: 14,660

ANNUAL MEETING: In May

INCORPORATED: MN, 1902

INSTITUTIONAL HOLDINGS:
No. of Institutions: 630
Shares Held: 740,807,319
% Held: 82.4

INDUSTRY: Variety stores (SIC: 5331)

TRANSFER AGENT(S): EquiServe, Jersey City, NJ

NYSE SYMBOL TCB
Rec. Pr. 38.03 (4/30/01)

TCF FINANCIAL CORPORATION

YIELD 2.6%
P/E RATIO 16.2

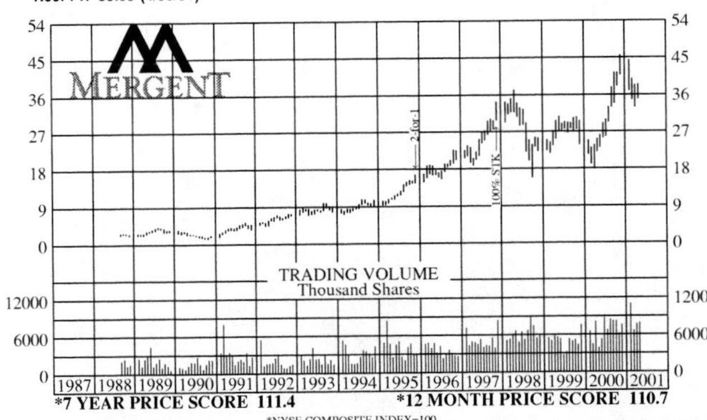

*7 YEAR PRICE SCORE 111.4 *12 MONTH PRICE SCORE 110.7

*NYSE COMPOSITE INDEX=100

INTERIM EARNINGS (Per Share):

Qtr.	Mar.	June	Sept.	Dec.
1997	0.40	0.42	0.43	0.43
1998	0.43	0.45	0.42	0.46
1999	0.44	0.49	0.52	0.55
2000	0.51	0.59	0.59	0.66

INTERIM DIVIDENDS (Per Share):

Amt.	Decl.	Ex.	Rec.	Pay.
0.212Q	4/26/00	5/05/00	5/09/00	5/31/00
0.212Q	7/17/00	8/02/00	8/04/00	8/31/00
0.212Q	10/23/00	11/01/00	11/03/00	11/30/00
0.25Q	1/17/01	1/31/01	2/02/01	2/28/01
0.25Q	4/30/01	5/09/01	5/11/01	5/31/01

Indicated div.: $1.00 (Div. Reinv. Plan)

CAPITALIZATION (12/31/00):

	($000)	(%)
Total Deposits	6,891,824	69.6
Long-Term Debt	2,098,925	21.2
Common & Surplus	910,220	9.2
Total	9,900,969	100.0

RECENT DEVELOPMENTS: For the year ended 12/31/00, net income jumped 12.2% to $186.2 million versus $166.0 million in the comparable period. Total interest income improved 9.9% to $826.7 million from $752.1 million in the preceding year. Net interest income increased 3.4% to $438.5 million compared with $424.2 million in the previous year. Total non-interest income grew 7.2% to $341.6 million versus $318.6 million in the comparable year.

PROSPECTS: Looking ahead, results should continue to benefit from new products introduced and an increase in supermarket banking. The Company plans to open 30 to 40 new supermarkets and traditional banking branches in 2001. In addition, the Company intends to enter into the discount brokerage business, which should promote cross selling and account growth opportunities while increasing fee income. The Company plans to launch this new business in the first half of 2001.

BUSINESS

TCF FINANCIAL CORPORATION, with $11.20 billion in assets as of 12/31/00, is the holding company of five federally chartered national banks and one bank holding company. TCB, through its affiliates, is engaged in community banking and lease financing activities and operates 352 banking offices, including 213 full-service supermarket branches, in Illinois, Indiana, Michigan, Minnesota, Wisconsin and Colorado. The Company's primary focus is lower- and middle-income customers and small- to medium-sized businesses in its markets. TCB emphasizes convenience in banking, open 12 hours a day, holidays and seven days a week. TCB's products include commercial, consumer and residential mortgage loan products, leasing, insurance and mutual funds, and some of its products, such as its commercial equipment and truck loans and leases, are offered in markets outside areas served by its bank subsidiaries.

ANNUAL FINANCIAL DATA

	12/31/00	12/31/99	12/31/98	12/31/97	12/31/96	12/31/95	12/31/94
Earnings Per Share	**2.35**	**2.00**	**1.76**	**1.69**	**4 1.21**	**1 2 3 0.86**	**1.16**
Tang. Book Val. Per Share	**9.29**	**7.78**	**7.74**	**7.94**	**7.36**	**6.84**	**6.20**
Dividends Per Share	**0.82**	**0.72**	**0.61**	**0.47**	**0.36**	**0.38**	**0.25**
Dividend Payout %	**35.1**	**36.2**	**34.8**	**27.7**	**29.7**	**43.9**	**21.6**
INCOME STATEMENT (IN MILLIONS):							
Total Interest Income	826.7	752.1	748.9	682.6	582.9	607.7	357.6
Total Interest Expense	388.1	327.9	323.2	289.0	242.7	288.5	152.5
Net Interest Income	438.5	424.2	425.7	393.6	340.1	319.2	205.1
Provision for Loan Losses	14.8	16.9	23.3	17.8	19.8	15.2	10.9
Non-Interest Income	325.2	306.6	280.3	215.0	147.8	126.5	112.3
Non-Interest Expense	462.5	452.8	428.7	361.6	341.1	317.3	213.9
Income Before Taxes	302.8	273.1	265.2	240.9	137.0	99.4	97.7
Net Income	186.2	166.0	156.2	145.1	4 85.7	1 2 3 61.7	57.4
Average Shs. Outstg. (000)	79,389	83,071	88,916	86,134	70,684	71,372	49,528
BALANCE SHEET (IN MILLIONS):							
Cash & Due from Banks	392.0	429.3	420.5	297.0	238.7	233.6	170.7
Securities Avail. for Sale	1,403.9	1,521.7	1,677.9	1,430.2	1,003.5	1,205.2	69.3
Total Loans & Leases	8,546.7	7,895.7	7,141.2	7,174.9	5,080.1	5,350.6	3,102.8
Allowance for Credit Losses	66.7	55.8	80.0	188.3	154.9	139.2	52.7
Net Loans & Leases	8,480.0	7,840.0	7,061.2	6,986.6	4,925.2	5,211.4	3,050.2
Total Assets	11,197.5	10,661.7	10,164.6	9,744.7	7,090.9	7,239.9	5,068.3
Total Deposits	6,891.8	6,584.8	6,715.1	6,907.3	4,977.6	5,191.6	3,819.6
Long-Term Obligations	2,098.9	2,073.9	2,093.8	1,614.7	1,200.1	1,003.0	698.1
Total Liabilities	10,287.2	9,852.7	9,319.1	8,791.0	6,541.4	6,712.2	4,741.1
Net Stockholders' Equity	910.2	809.0	845.5	953.7	549.6	527.9	327.6
Year-end Shs. Outstg. (000)	80,289	81,941	85,569	92,822	69,514	71,210	48,356
STATISTICAL RECORD:							
Return on Equity %	20.5	20.5	18.5	15.2	15.6	15.7	17.5
Return on Assets %	1.7	1.6	1.5	1.5	1.2	1.1	1.1
Equity/Assets %	8.1	7.6	8.3	9.8	7.8	7.3	6.5
Non-Int. Exp./Tot. Inc. %	61.6	63.5	62.9	60.8	70.3	71.4	67.4
Price Range	45.56-18.00	30.69-21.69	37.25-15.81	34.38-18.75	22.69-14.81	16.69-9.28	10.78-7.13
P/E Ratio	19.4-7.7	15.3-10.8	21.2-9.0	20.3-11.1	18.7-12.2	19.5-10.9	9.3-6.2
Average Yield %	2.6	2.8	2.3	1.8	1.9	2.9	2.8

Statistics are as originally reported. Adj. for stk. splits: 2-for-1, 12/97 & 12/95. 1 Bef. extraord. chrg., $963,000. 2 Incl. merger-related expenses, $21.7 mill. 3 Incl. cancel. costs early termination int.-rate exchg. chrg. $4.4 mill. 4 Incl. chrg. of $34.8 mill. for FDIC special assessment

OFFICERS:
W. A. Cooper, Chmn., C.E.O.
T. A. Cusick, Vice-Chmn., C.O.O.
L. A. Nagorske, Pres.
N. W. Brown, Exec. V.P., C.F.O., Treas.

INVESTOR CONTACT: Jason E. Korstange, Sr. V.P., Inv. Rel., (612) 745-2755

PRINCIPAL OFFICE: 801 Marquette Ave., Suite 302, Minneapolis, MN 55402

TELEPHONE NUMBER: (612) 661-6500
FAX: (612) 332-1753
WEB: www.tcfbank.com

NO. OF EMPLOYEES: 7,500 (approx.)

SHAREHOLDERS: 11,700 (approx.)

ANNUAL MEETING: In May

INCORPORATED: DE, Nov., 1987

INSTITUTIONAL HOLDINGS:
No. of Institutions: 208
Shares Held: 49,030,450
% Held: 62.3

INDUSTRY: Federal savings institutions (SIC: 6035)

TRANSFER AGENT(S): BankBoston, N.A., Boston, MA

NYSE SYMBOL TWE
Rec. Pr. 11.21 (4/30/01)

TD WATERHOUSE GROUP, INC.

YIELD ...
P/E RATIO 22.4

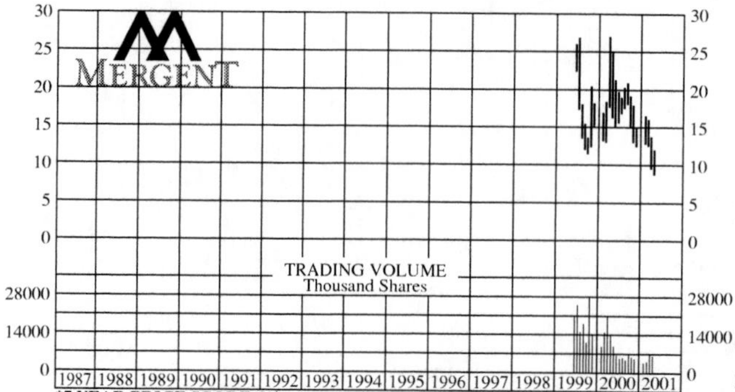

TRADING VOLUME
Thousand Shares

*7 YEAR PRICE SCORE N/A *12 MONTH PRICE SCORE 74.3
*NYSE COMPOSITE INDEX=100

INTERIM EARNINGS (Per Share):

Qtr.	Jan.	Apr.	July	Oct.
1998-99		0.28		
1999-00	0.15	0.20	0.09	0.11
2000-01	0.10	...	...	...

INTERIM DIVIDENDS (Per Share):

Amt.	Decl.	Ex.	Rec.	Pay.

No dividends paid.

CAPITALIZATION (10/31/00):

	($000)	(%)
Preferred Stock	11,948	0.5
Common & Surplus	2,211,975	99.5
Total	2,223,923	100.0

RECENT DEVELOPMENTS: For the quarter ended 1/31/01, net income declined 12.1% to $37.1 million from $42.2 million in the prior-year period. Total revenues fell 3.4% to $347.3 million. Commissions and fees revenues fell 4.7% to $196.3 million. Mutual fund and related revenue increased 3.2% to $41.6 million. Net interest revenue slipped 13.5% to $79.8 million. The number of on-line trades per day dropped 19.4% to 110,400. Total on-line accounts grew 67.5% to 2.4 million.

PROSPECTS: TWE announced expense and revenue initiatives to increase its pre-tax income by $200.0 million by fiscal 2001. TWE expects an annualized improvement of $175.0 million in pre-tax income by the end of the fourth quarter of fiscal 2001 through infrastructure expense reductions of $125.0 million and segmented pricing adjustments that will provide additional annual revenue of at least $50.0 million. TWE anticipates the remaining $25.0 million will be achieved during the first fiscal quarter of 2002.

BUSINESS

TD WATERHOUSE is a global on-line broker and a provider of on-line investing services and related financial products. TWE serves 4.6 million customer accounts in the U.S., Canada, the U.K., Australia, and Hong Kong. The firm also services customers in Japan, India and Luxembourg, through joint ventures in those countries. In addition to securities trading services, TWE also provides its customers with banking, mutual fund and other consumer financial products and services on an integrated basis, including investment news and clearing and execution services to correspondents and other broker-dealers. As of 11/5/00, TD Bank Financial Group held 88.6% of the outstanding share capital of TWE.

REVENUES

(10/31/2000)	($000)	(%)
Commissions & Fees	1,004,508	63.8
Mutual Fund & Related Rev	148,316	9.4
Net Interest Revenue	351,077	22.3
Other Revenues	71,514	4.5
Total	1,575,415	100.0

ANNUAL FINANCIAL DATA

	10/31/00	10/31/99	10/31/98	10/31/97	10/31/96
Earnings Per Share	**0.55**	**0.28**	**0.15**	...	...
Cash Flow Per Share	**0.77**	**0.43**	**0.27**	...	...
Tang. Book Val. Per Share	**3.71**	**3.45**	...	...	...
INCOME STATEMENT (IN MILLIONS):					
Total Revenues	1,575.4	960.1	614.5	446.6	167.4
Costs & Expenses	1,113.6	724.0	468.1	339.4	111.6
Depreciation & Amort.	80.3	53.6	42.9	28.6	1.6
Operating Income	381.6	182.5	103.5	78.6	54.2
Income Before Income Taxes	381.6	182.5	103.5	78.6	54.2
Income Taxes	171.3	85.2	54.8	42.4	24.6
Net Income	210.3	97.3	48.7	36.2	29.6
Cash Flow	290.6	151.0	91.6	64.9	31.3
Average Shs. Outstg. (000)	379,155	348,509	333,000	...	...
BALANCE SHEET (IN MILLIONS):					
Cash & Cash Equivalents	998.1	911.2	598.3	358.1	...
Total Current Assets	9,080.9	6,974.4	3,226.2	2,228.9	...
Net Property	140.6	73.5	27.6	19.8	...
Total Assets	10,989.3	8,591.8	4,298.7	2,946.6	...
Total Current Liabilities	8,395.0	6,424.6	3,206.6	2,232.9	...
Net Stockholders' Equity	2,223.9	1,952.1	995.1	619.5	...
Net Working Capital	685.9	549.8	19.6	d4.0	...
Year-end Shs. Outstg. (000)	379,789	376,419	...	...	...
STATISTICAL RECORD:					
Operating Profit Margin %	24.2	19.0	16.8	17.6	32.4
Net Profit Margin %	13.3	10.1	7.9	8.1	17.7
Return on Equity %	9.5	5.0	4.9	5.8	...
Return on Assets %	1.9	1.1	1.1	1.2	...
Price Range	27.00-12.44	26.88-11.44	...	...	...
P/E Ratio	49.1-22.6	95.9-40.8	...	...	...

Statistics are as originally reported. Total revenues include interest income, net of interest expense.

OFFICERS:
A. C. Baillie, Chmn.
J. G. See, Vice-Chmn.
S. D. McDonald, C.E.O.
F. J. Petrilli, Pres., C.O.O.

INVESTOR CONTACT: Kevin Sterns, Investor Relations, (212) 806-3500

PRINCIPAL OFFICE: 100 Wall Street, New York, NY 10005

TELEPHONE NUMBER: (212) 806-3500
WEB: www.tdwaterhouse.com

NO. OF EMPLOYEES: 8,298

SHAREHOLDERS: 233

ANNUAL MEETING: In Mar.

INCORPORATED: DE, 1999

INSTITUTIONAL HOLDINGS:
No. of Institutions: 63
Shares Held: 19,634,405
% Held: 5.2

INDUSTRY: Security brokers and dealers (SIC: 6211)

TRANSFER AGENT(S): Mellon Investor Services; CIBC Mellon Trust Company (Canada)

NYSE SYMBOL TE
Rec. Pr. 31.99 (4/30/01)

TECO ENERGY INC.

YIELD 4.3%
P/E RATIO 16.2

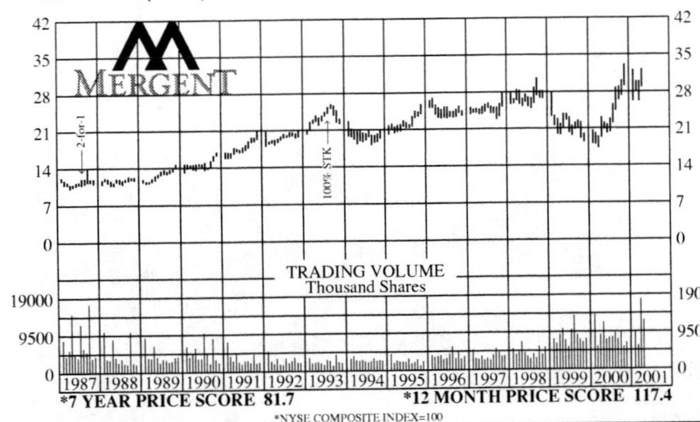

INTERIM EARNINGS (Per Share):

Qtr.	Mar.	June	Sept.	Dec.
1996	0.36	0.41	0.56	0.38
1997	0.37	0.39	0.51	0.31
1998	0.23	0.44	0.54	0.31
1999	0.37	0.39	0.42	0.32
2000	0.42	0.46	0.65	0.44

INTERIM DIVIDENDS (Per Share):

Amt.	Decl.	Ex.	Rec.	Pay.
0.335Q	4/19/00	4/27/00	5/01/00	5/15/00
0.335Q	7/19/00	7/28/00	8/01/00	8/15/00
0.335Q	10/18/00	10/30/00	11/01/00	11/15/00
0.335Q	1/18/01	1/30/01	2/01/01	2/15/01
0.345Q	4/18/01	4/27/01	5/01/01	5/15/01

Indicated div.: $1.38 (Div. Reinv. Plan)

CAPITALIZATION (12/31/00):

	($000)	(%)
Long-Term Debt	1,374,600	69.9
Deferred Income Tax	445,200	22.6
Redeemable Pfd. Stock	200,000	10.2
Common & Surplus	d52,600	-2.7
Total	1,967,200	100.0

RECENT DEVELOPMENTS: For the year ended 12/31/00, net income was $250.9 million versus income from continuing operations of $200.9 million in 1999. The 2000 results included an after-tax gain of $8.3 million associated with the formation of US Propane and after-tax nonrecurring charges totaling $9.0 million from adjusted values of leveraged leases and TECO Properties. Results for 1999 excluded a net loss of $14.8 million from discontinued operations. Revenues grew 15.7% to $2.30 billion.

PROSPECTS: On 3/20/01, TECO Power Services, a TE subsidiary, announced that it completed the acquisition of American Electric Power Company's Frontera Power Station, a 500-megawatt natural gas-fired combined-cycle plant located in the Rio Grande Valley in Texas, in a transaction valued at $265.0 million. The acquisition will expand TE's operating capacity in the southern U.S. with capabilities of selling power to the domestic and Mexican markets.

BUSINESS

TECO ENERGY, INC. is a diversified, energy-related holding company. Tampa Electric, which accounts for the majority of net income for TE, generates, purchases, transmits, distributes and sells electric energy to West Central Florida. The Peoples Gas System division purchases, distributes and markets natural gas for residential, commercial, industrial and electric power generation customers in Florida. TECO Transport Corp. transports, stores and transfers coal and other bulk dry commodities. TECO Coal Corp. owns mineral rights, owns or operates surface and underground mines, coal processing and loading facilities in Kentucky, Tennessee and Virginia. TECO Power Services Corp. is a wholesale power supplier that owns and operates independent power projects. TECO Coalbed Methane, Inc. produces natural gas from coalbeds. TECO Solutions offers various services through Bosek, Gibson and Associates, Inc. and BCH Mechanical, Inc. TECO Propane Ventures represents the Company's 38.0% interest in US Propane.

ANNUAL FINANCIAL DATA

	12/31/00	12/31/99	12/31/98	12/31/97	12/31/96	12/31/95	12/31/94
Earnings Per Share	[4] **1.97**	[2][3] **1.53**	[1][2] **1.52**	[2] **1.61**	**1.71**	**1.60**	[1] **1.32**
Cash Flow Per Share	**4.18**	**3.37**	**3.31**	**3.37**	**3.34**	**3.14**	**2.87**
Tang. Book Val. Per Share	...	...	...	...	**10.73**	**10.00**	**8.65**
Dividends Per Share	**1.33**	**1.28**	**1.23**	**1.17**	**1.10**	**1.05**	**1.00**
Dividend Payout %	**67.5**	**84.0**	**80.6**	**72.4**	**64.6**	**65.5**	**75.6**
INCOME STATEMENT (IN MILLIONS):							
Total Revenues	2,295.1	1,983.0	1,958.1	1,862.3	1,473.0	1,392.3	1,350.9
Costs & Expenses	1,464.1	1,192.8	1,197.6	1,104.2	847.3	793.7	800.3
Depreciation & Amort.	277.4	241.3	236.1	231.3	190.6	179.6	179.7
Maintenance Exp.	140.0	125.3	128.9	114.2	92.2	101.3	101.1
Operating Income	413.6	423.6	395.5	412.6	342.9	317.7	269.8
Net Interest Inc./(Exp.)	d166.9	d123.7	d104.3	d105.8	d86.9	d83.2	d77.1
Income Taxes	18.5	87.0	81.0	94.7	71.4	59.1	45.8
Net Income	[4] 250.9	[2][3] 200.9	[1][2] 200.4	[2] 211.4	200.7	186.1	[1] 153.2
Cash Flow	528.3	442.2	436.5	442.7	391.3	365.7	332.9
Average Shs. Outstg. (000)	126,300	131,200	131,700	131,200	117,200	116,500	115,923
BALANCE SHEET (IN MILLIONS):							
Gross Property	6,560.4	6,064.4	5,600.5	5,359.5	4,721.6	4,490.5	4,095.7
Accumulated Depreciation	2,590.3	2,436.6	2,292.9	2,123.0	1,765.0	1,616.2	1,475.5
Net Property	3,970.1	3,627.8	3,307.6	3,236.5	2,956.6	2,874.3	2,620.3
Total Assets	5,676.2	4,690.1	4,179.3	3,960.4	3,560.7	3,473.4	3,312.2
Long-Term Obligations	1,374.6	1,207.8	1,279.6	1,080.2	996.3	994.9	1,023.9
Net Stockholders' Equity	d52.6	d54.7	d61.4	d67.5	1,282.1	1,221.7	1,060.1
Year-end Shs. Outstg. (000)	119,300	126,700	132,000	130,900	117,600	116,700	116,199
STATISTICAL RECORD:							
Operating Profit Margin %	18.0	21.4	20.2	22.2	23.3	22.8	20.0
Net Profit Margin %	10.9	10.1	10.2	11.4	13.6	13.4	11.3
Net Inc./Net Property %	6.3	5.5	6.1	6.5	6.8	6.5	5.8
Net Inc./Tot. Capital %	12.8	12.1	11.7	14.2	7.4	7.1	6.2
Return on Equity %	...	...	...	...	15.7	15.2	14.4
Accum. Depr./Gross Prop. %	39.5	40.2	40.9	39.6	37.4	36.0	36.0
Price Range	33.19-17.25	28.00-18.38	30.63-24.75	28.00-22.75	27.00-23.00	25.75-20.00	22.63-18.13
P/E Ratio	16.8-8.8	18.3-12.0	20.1-16.3	17.4-14.1	15.8-13.4	16.1-12.5	17.1-13.7
Average Yield %	5.3	5.5	4.4	4.6	4.4	4.6	4.9

Statistics are as originally reported. [1] Incl. non-recurr. chrg. $16.1 mill., 1999; $25.9 mill., 1998; $25.0 mill. ($0.13/sh.), 1994 [2] Bef. disc. oper. loss $14.8 mill., 1999; gain $6.1 mill., 1998; loss $9.5 mill. ($0.07/sh.), 1997 [3] Incl. after-tax nonrecurr. chrgs. of $19.6 mill. ($0.15/sh.) [4] Incl. after-tax gain $8.3 mill. & nonrecurr. chrgs. $9.0 mill.

OFFICERS:
R. D. Fagan, Chmn., Pres., C.E.O.
G. L. Gillette, Sr. V.P., C.F.O.
S. M. McDevitt, V.P., General Counsel

INVESTOR CONTACT: Mark H. Tubb, Investor Relations, (800) 810-2032

PRINCIPAL OFFICE: Teco Plaza, 702 N. Franklin Street, Tampa, FL 33602

TELEPHONE NUMBER: (813) 228-4111
FAX: (813) 228-1670
WEB: www.tecoenergy.com

NO. OF EMPLOYEES: 5,872 (avg.)

SHAREHOLDERS: 23,933

ANNUAL MEETING: In Apr.

INCORPORATED: FL, Jan., 1981

INSTITUTIONAL HOLDINGS:
No. of Institutions: 324
Shares Held: 56,102,837
% Held: 41.3

INDUSTRY: Electric services (SIC: 4911)

TRANSFER AGENT(S): BankBoston, NA, Boston, MA.

NYSE SYMBOL TEK
Rec. Pr. 24.20 (4/30/01)

TEKTRONIX, INC.

YIELD ...
P/E RATIO 17.2

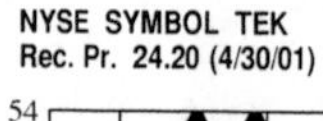

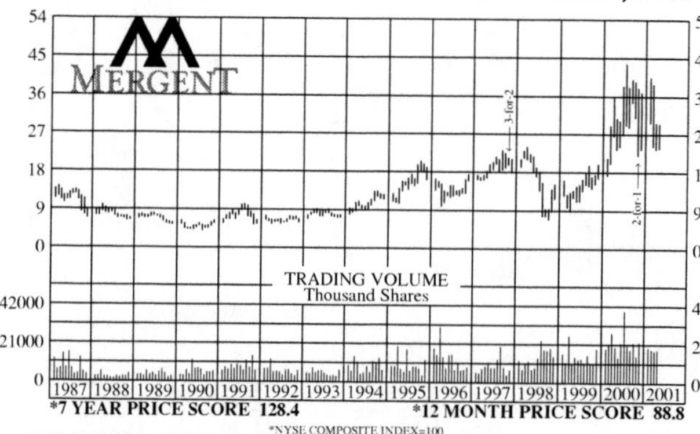

*7 YEAR PRICE SCORE 128.4 *12 MONTH PRICE SCORE 88.8

*NYSE COMPOSITE INDEX=100

INTERIM EARNINGS (Per Share):

Qtr.	Aug.	Nov.	Feb.	May
1996-97	0.23	0.27	0.29	0.04
1997-98	0.27	d0.21	0.34	0.42
1998-99	d0.05	d0.91	0.16	0.27
1999-00	d0.09	0.10	d0.18	0.32
2000-01	0.28	0.38	0.43	...

INTERIM DIVIDENDS (Per Share):

Amt.	Decl.	Ex.	Rec.	Pay.
0.12Q	6/24/99	7/07/99	7/09/99	7/26/99
0.12Q	9/23/99	10/06/99	10/08/99	10/25/99
0.12Q	12/17/99	1/12/00	1/14/00	1/31/00
2-for-1	9/21/00	11/01/00	10/10/00	10/31/00

Dividend suspended.

CAPITALIZATION (5/27/00):

	($000)	(%)
Long-Term Debt	150,369	13.3
Common & Surplus	977,594	86.7
Total	1,127,963	100.0

RECENT DEVELOPMENTS: For the quarter ended 2/24/01, net income rose to $41.0 million versus a loss from continuing operations of $16.8 million in 1999. Results for fiscal 2001 included non-recurring credits of $9.1 million. Results for fiscal 2000 included a gain of $5.5 million from the sale of a business and non-recurring charges of $36.6 million. Results for fiscal 2000 also excluded net income of $519.3 million from discontinued operations. Net sales rose 18.0% to $326.9 million.

PROSPECTS: TEK is beginning to experience a slowing order rate due to weakness in the market. Economic conditions have hampered many of the Company's core customers and TEK usually lags its customers in feeling the effects of a slowdown period. As a result, TEK expects orders to decrease by about 10.0% for the fourth quarter of fiscal 2001, while strong backlog should support revenue growth. Meanwhile, TEK has increased its investment in its India operations for future software development.

BUSINESS

TEKTRONIX, INC. is a test, measurement, and monitoring company providing measurement applications to the semiconductors, computers and telecommunications industries. TEK enables its customers to design, deploy, and manage next generation global communications networks and Internet technologies. Measurement business products include general purpose test instruments, RF and wireless instruments, telecommunications instruments, and television test instruments. The following is a sales breakdown for the year ended 5/27/00: measurement business, 96.5%; and video and networking, 3.5%. In January 2000, TEK sold its color printing business to Xerox Corporation.

ANNUAL FINANCIAL DATA

	5/27/00	5/29/99	5/31/98	5/31/97	5/25/96	5/27/95	5/28/94
Earnings Per Share	**[3] 0.13**	**[2] d0.53**	**0.80**	**[1] 1.16**	**1.00**	**0.88**	**0.67**
Cash Flow Per Share	**0.59**	**0.25**	**1.44**	**1.76**	**1.47**	**1.31**	**1.27**
Tang. Book Val. Per Share	**10.28**	**6.63**	**7.80**	**7.70**	**6.89**	**6.39**	**5.17**
Dividends Per Share	**0.24**	**0.24**	**0.21**	**0.20**	**0.20**	**0.20**	**0.20**
Dividend Payout %	**184.5**	**...**	**26.2**	**17.2**	**20.0**	**22.8**	**30.0**
INCOME STATEMENT (IN MILLIONS):							
Total Revenues	1,120.6	1,861.5	2,085.8	1,940.1	1,768.9	1,471.8	1,318.0
Costs & Expenses	1,074.9	1,846.6	1,907.1	1,717.0	1,583.4	1,320.2	1,174.8
Depreciation & Amort.	44.1	74.8	65.9	59.6	47.1	40.7	54.9
Operating Income	4.1	d69.1	115.3	165.0	143.4	115.2	86.7
Net Interest Inc./(Exp.)	7.2	d15.7	d10.1	d12.1	d14.0	d10.1	d10.0
Income Before Income Taxes	19.6	d75.2	122.8	168.8	142.3	109.9	85.9
Income Taxes	6.9	cr24.1	40.5	54.0	42.7	28.6	25.2
Equity Earnings/Minority Int.	2.5	d9.2	2.5	1.6	5.1	4.3	d1.6
Net Income	[3] 12.7	[2] d51.2	82.3	[1] 114.8	99.6	81.3	60.7
Cash Flow	56.9	23.6	148.2	174.4	146.7	122.0	115.6
Average Shs. Outstg. (000)	96,270	95,400	102,640	99,027	99,591	92,802	91,218
BALANCE SHEET (IN MILLIONS):							
Cash & Cash Equivalents	783.7	39.7	120.5	142.7	36.6	31.7	42.9
Total Current Assets	1,112.1	719.7	748.7	751.5	753.6	650.6	540.6
Net Property	188.5	442.3	425.2	343.1	307.6	251.9	223.3
Total Assets	1,534.6	1,359.4	1,376.8	1,316.7	1,328.5	1,209.7	991.1
Total Current Liabilities	330.2	497.0	349.8	304.1	365.3	380.7	275.8
Long-Term Obligations	150.4	150.7	150.7	151.6	403.9	210.0	104.1
Net Stockholders' Equity	977.6	621.6	784.9	771.3	675.3	602.7	469.5
Net Working Capital	781.8	222.6	398.9	447.4	388.2	269.9	264.8
Year-end Shs. Outstg. (000)	95,084	93,818	100,690	100,206	98,061	94,317	90,810
STATISTICAL RECORD:							
Operating Profit Margin %	0.4	...	5.5	8.5	8.1	7.8	6.6
Net Profit Margin %	1.1	...	3.9	5.9	5.6	5.5	4.6
Return on Equity %	1.3	...	10.5	14.9	14.7	13.5	12.9
Return on Assets %	0.8	...	6.0	8.7	7.5	6.7	6.1
Debt/Total Assets %	9.8	11.1	10.9	11.5	30.4	17.4	10.5
Price Range	20.00-8.78	24.09-6.84	23.21-16.08	17.42-9.92	20.63-10.46	13.50-7.88	9.29-6.71
P/E Ratio	153.7-67.5	...	29.0-20.1	15.0-8.5	20.6-10.5	15.4-9.0	13.9-10.1
Average Yield %	1.7	1.6	1.1	1.5	1.3	1.9	2.5

Statistics are as originally reported. Adj. for 3-for-2 split, 10/31/00 & 10/97. Fiscal year ends 5/31 of following year. [1] Incl. $40.5 mill. non-recur. restr. chg. for in-process R&D. [2] Incl. $84.4 mill. non-recur. chgs. [3] Incl. $31.6 mill. pre-tax chg. fr. sale of bus., $37.7 mill. non-recur. chg. & excl. $196.4 mill. fr. disc. ops.

OFFICERS:
J. J. Meyer, Chmn.
R. H. Wills, Pres., C.E.O.
C. L. Slade, V.P., C.F.O.

INVESTOR CONTACT: Colin Blade, (503) 627-7727

PRINCIPAL OFFICE: 14200 S.W. Karl Braun Drive, Beaverton, OR 97077

TELEPHONE NUMBER: (503) 627-7111
FAX: (503) 685-4104
WEB: www.tektronix.com

NO. OF EMPLOYEES: 4,276

SHAREHOLDERS: 3,249

ANNUAL MEETING: In Sept.

INCORPORATED: OR, Jan., 1946

INSTITUTIONAL HOLDINGS:
No. of Institutions: 262
Shares Held: 84,021,973
% Held: 89.6

INDUSTRY: Instruments to measure electricity (SIC: 3825)

TRANSFER AGENT(S): Mellon Investor Services, South Hackensack, NJ

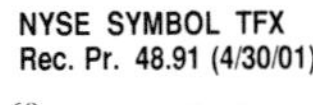

TELEFLEX INC.

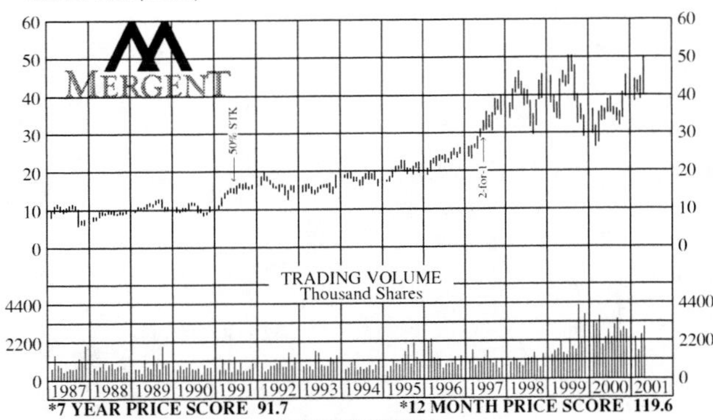

***7 YEAR PRICE SCORE 91.7** ***12 MONTH PRICE SCORE 119.6**

*NYSE COMPOSITE INDEX=100

INTERIM EARNINGS (Per Share):

Qtr.	Mar.	June	Sept.	Dec.
1997	0.45	0.49	0.36	0.56
1998	0.52	0.55	0.42	0.66
1999	0.60	0.67	0.49	0.71
2000	0.70	0.76	0.56	0.81

INTERIM DIVIDENDS (Per Share):

Amt.	Decl.	Ex.	Rec.	Pay.
0.15Q	8/07/00	8/23/00	8/25/00	9/15/00
0.15Q	10/30/00	11/21/00	11/24/00	12/15/00
0.15Q	1/29/01	2/22/01	2/26/01	3/15/01
0.17Q	4/27/01	5/23/01	5/25/01	6/15/01

Indicated div.: $0.68 (Div. Reinv. Plan)

CAPITALIZATION (12/31/00):

	($000)	(%)
Long-Term Debt	220,557	24.2
Common & Surplus	690,422	75.8
Total	910,979	100.0

RECENT DEVELOPMENTS: For the year ended 12/31/00, net income rose 14.7% to $109.2 million compared with $95.2 million in 1999. Revenues were $1.76 billion, up 10.2% from $1.60 billion in the prior year. Operating profit climbed 10.2% to $196.5 million compared with $178.3 million in the previous year. Sales in the commercial products segment rose 13.5% to $860.2 million, while sales in the medical products segment grew 10.6% to $411.8 million.

PROSPECTS: On 2/13/01, the Company completed the acquisition of Morse Controls, a global supplier of industrial and marine products, for $135.0 million in cash. The acquisition is strategically in line with the Company's plans to extend its industrial product lines through expanded global distribution and support. The transaction is expected to be accretive to full-year 2001 earnings. One way in which the Company plans to grow its businesses is through the introduction of new products into the marketplace.

BUSINESS

TELEFLEX INC. operates in three segments. Commercial Products (48.8% of 2000 sales and 44.3% of operating profit) designs and manufactures proprietary mechanical controls for the automotive market; mechanical, electrical and hydraulic controls, and electronics for the pleasure marine market; and proprietary products for fluid transfer and industrial applications. Medical Products (23.3%, 28.7%) manufactures and distributes a broad range of invasive disposable and reusable devices worldwide. Aerospace Products (27.9%, 27.0%) serves the aerospace and turbine engine markets. Its businesses design and manufacture precision controls and cargo systems for aviation; provide coating and repair services and manufactured components for users of both flight and land-based turbine engines.

ANNUAL FINANCIAL DATA

	12/31/00	12/26/99	12/27/98	12/28/97	12/29/96	12/31/95	12/25/94
Earnings Per Share	**2.83**	**2.47**	**2.15**	**1.86**	**1.58**	**1.38**	**1.18**
Cash Flow Per Share	**4.83**	**4.22**	**3.71**	**3.13**	**2.65**	**2.43**	**2.12**
Tang. Book Val. Per Share	**18.01**	**15.85**	**14.21**	**12.49**	**11.30**	**10.28**	**8.94**
Dividends Per Share	**0.58**	**0.51**	**0.45**	**0.39**	**0.34**	**0.30**	**0.26**
Dividend Payout %	**20.5**	**20.4**	**20.7**	**20.8**	**21.5**	**21.8**	**22.1**
INCOME STATEMENT (IN MILLIONS):							
Total Revenues	1,764.5	1,601.1	1,437.6	1,145.8	931.2	912.7	812.7
Costs & Expenses	1,508.1	1,373.2	1,235.7	977.0	791.8	782.7	698.3
Depreciation & Amort.	77.4	67.4	60.1	47.9	38.8	37.7	33.0
Operating Income	179.0	160.5	141.8	120.8	100.7	92.2	81.4
Net Interest Inc./(Exp.)	d20.8	d17.7	d17.1	d14.4	d13.9	d18.6	d18.4
Income Before Income Taxes	158.2	142.8	124.8	106.4	86.8	73.6	63.0
Income Taxes	49.0	47.5	42.2	36.3	29.6	24.7	21.8
Net Income	109.2	95.2	82.6	70.1	57.2	48.9	41.2
Cash Flow	186.6	162.6	142.7	118.0	95.9	86.6	74.2
Average Shs. Outstg. (000)	38,633	38,525	38,425	37,661	36,198	35,574	35,060
BALANCE SHEET (IN MILLIONS):							
Cash & Cash Equivalents	45.1	29.0	66.7	30.7	68.6	55.7	24.1
Total Current Assets	662.0	604.9	616.9	566.5	466.0	445.8	390.2
Net Property	489.5	465.9	431.8	364.0	291.8	271.8	264.3
Total Assets	1,401.3	1,263.4	1,215.9	1,079.2	857.9	785.2	710.8
Total Current Liabilities	383.9	329.4	311.5	294.9	196.7	193.2	169.7
Long-Term Obligations	220.6	246.2	275.6	237.6	195.9	196.8	190.5
Net Stockholders' Equity	690.4	602.6	534.5	463.8	409.2	355.4	309.0
Net Working Capital	278.2	275.5	305.5	271.6	269.4	252.7	220.5
Year-end Shs. Outstg. (000)	38,344	38,019	37,615	37,118	36,222	34,554	34,554
STATISTICAL RECORD:							
Operating Profit Margin %	10.1	10.0	9.9	10.5	10.8	10.1	10.0
Net Profit Margin %	6.2	5.9	5.7	6.1	6.1	5.4	5.1
Return on Equity %	15.8	15.8	15.4	15.1	14.0	13.8	13.3
Return on Assets %	7.8	7.5	6.8	6.5	6.7	6.2	5.8
Debt/Total Assets %	15.7	19.5	22.7	22.0	22.8	25.1	26.8
Price Range	45.38-26.13	50.44-28.88	46.38-29.50	39.75-23.19	26.13-18.94	22.88-17.19	20.13-15.88
P/E Ratio	16.0-9.2	20.4-11.7	21.6-13.7	21.4-12.5	16.5-12.0	16.6-12.5	17.1-13.5
Average Yield %	1.6	1.3	1.2	1.2	1.5	1.5	1.4

Statistics are as originally reported. Adj. for 2-for-1 split, 6/97.

OFFICERS:
L. K. Black, Chmn., C.E.O.
J. P. Black, Pres.

INVESTOR CONTACT: Janine Dusossoit, V.P., Investor Relations, (610) 834-6301

PRINCIPAL OFFICE: 630 West Germantown Pike, Suite 450, Plymouth Meeting, PA 19462

TELEPHONE NUMBER: (610) 834-6301
FAX: (610) 834-8228
WEB: www.teleflex.com

NO. OF EMPLOYEES: 16,600 (approx.)

SHAREHOLDERS: 1,300 (approx.)

ANNUAL MEETING: In Apr.

INCORPORATED: DE, June, 1943

INSTITUTIONAL HOLDINGS:
No. of Institutions: 213
Shares Held: 24,094,851
% Held: 62.7

INDUSTRY: Surgical and medical instruments (SIC: 3841)

TRANSFER AGENT(S): American Stock Transfer & Trust Company, New York, NY

NYSE SYMBOL TIN
Rec. Pr. 53.11 (5/31/01)

TEMPLE-INLAND INC.

YIELD 2.4%
P/E RATIO 13.9

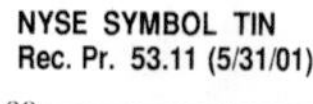

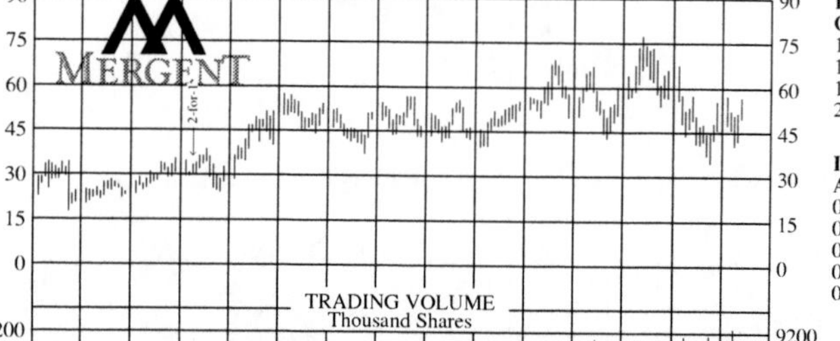

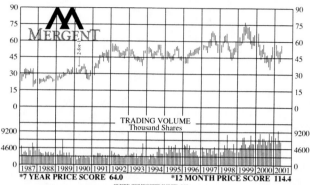

*7 YEAR PRICE SCORE 64.0 *12 MONTH PRICE SCORE 114.4

*NYSE COMPOSITE INDEX=100

INTERIM EARNINGS (Per Share):

Qtr.	Mar.	June	Sept.	Dec.
1997	0.24	0.28	0.22	0.17
1998	0.47	0.62	0.44	d0.32
1999	0.33	0.74	1.07	1.03
2000	1.04	1.20	0.87	0.72

INTERIM DIVIDENDS (Per Share):

Amt.	Decl.	Ex.	Rec.	Pay.
0.32Q	5/05/00	5/30/00	6/01/00	6/15/00
0.32Q	8/04/00	8/30/00	9/01/00	9/15/00
0.32Q	11/03/00	11/29/00	12/01/00	12/15/00
0.32Q	2/02/01	2/27/01	3/01/01	3/15/01
0.32Q	5/04/01	5/30/01	6/01/01	6/15/01

Indicated div.: $1.28 (Div. Reinv. Plan)

CAPITALIZATION (12/31/00):

	($000)	(%)
Long-Term Debt	5,055,000	70.6
Deferred Income Tax	272,000	3.8
Common & Surplus	1,833,000	25.6
Total	7,160,000	100.0

RECENT DEVELOPMENTS: For the year ended 12/30/00, net income advanced 2.1% to $195.0 million compared with income from continuing operations of $191.0 million in 1999. Results for 2000 included an after-tax special charge of $9.0 million. Total revenues were $4.29 billion, up 12.6% from $3.81 billion a year earlier. Operating income amounted to $462.0 million versus $45.0 milion a year earlier.

PROSPECTS: Going forward, TIN will focus on customers and improving operational efficiencies. Downtime is being taken in all product lines to balance inventories to customer orders. Meanwhile, domestic pricing for linerboard and boxes continues to be stable, although export markets for linerboard have declined. TIN's financial services operations continue to perform well reflecting growth in the bank's average loan portfolio.

BUSINESS

TEMPLE-INLAND INC. is a holding company. The Company is a major manufacturer of corrugated packaging and building products, with financial services operations in mortgage and consumer banking. The corrugated packaging operations consists of six linerboard mills, 41 corrugated packaging plants located throughout the U.S., Puerto Rico, Mexico and South America and eight specialty converting plants. TIN's Building Products Group manufactures a wide range of building products including lumber, plywood, particleboard, gypsum wallboard, and fiberboard. TIN's Financial Services Group consists of savings bank activities, mortgage banking, real estate development, and insurance brokerage. Forest resources include approximately 2.2 million acres of timberland in Texas, Louisiana, Georgia, and Alabama.

ANNUAL FINANCIAL DATA

	12/31/00	1/1/00	1/2/99	12/31/97	12/28/96	12/31/95	12/31/94
Earnings Per Share	**3 3.83**	**2 3.43**	**1 1.21**	**0.90**	**2.39**	**5.01**	**2.35**
Cash Flow Per Share	**8.80**	**7.01**	**7.85**	**6.19**	**7.39**	**9.20**	**6.27**
Tang. Book Val. Per Share	**37.28**	**35.55**	**35.94**	**36.32**	**36.37**	**35.27**	**31.84**
Dividends Per Share	**1.28**	**1.28**	**1.28**	**1.28**	**1.24**	**1.14**	**1.02**
Dividend Payout %	**33.4**	**37.3**	**105.8**	**142.2**	**51.9**	**22.8**	**43.4**
INCOME STATEMENT (IN MILLIONS):							
Total Revenues	4,286.0	3,682.0	3,740.0	3,625.0	3,460.0	3,460.0	2,938.0
Costs & Expenses	3,604.0	3,097.0	3,097.0	3,129.0	2,922.0	2,726.0	2,462.0
Depreciation & Amort.	253.0	200.0	372.0	297.0	277.0	234.0	220.0
Operating Income	414.0	385.0	224.0	199.0	261.0	500.0	256.0
Net Interest Inc./(Exp.)	d104.0	d95.0	d106.0	d110.0	d110.0	d73.0	d67.0
Income Before Income Taxes	320.0	306.0	124.0	95.0	156.0	431.0	193.0
Income Taxes	125.0	115.0	57.0	44.0	23.0	150.0	62.0
Net Income	3 195.0	2 191.0	1 67.0	51.0	133.0	281.0	131.0
Cash Flow	448.0	391.0	439.0	348.0	410.0	515.0	351.0
Average Shs. Outstg. (000)	50,900	55,800	55,900	56,200	55,500	56,000	56,000
BALANCE SHEET (IN MILLIONS):							
Cash & Cash Equivalents	322.0	51.0	244.0	188.0	228.0	358.0	315.0
Total Current Assets	884.0	682.0	869.0	804.0	847.0	979.0	1,245.0
Net Property	2,184.0	2,052.0	2,928.0	2,916.0	2,931.0	2,864.0	2,671.0
Total Assets	18,142.0	16,186.0	15,990.0	14,364.0	12,947.0	12,764.0	12,251.0
Total Current Liabilities	9,828.0	381.0	7,338.0	7,375.0	6,263.0	6,377.0	6,598.0
Long-Term Obligations	5,055.0	1,253.0	5,014.0	3,560.0	3,647.0	3,361.0	2,918.0
Net Stockholders' Equity	1,833.0	1,927.0	1,998.0	2,045.0	2,015.0	1,975.0	1,783.0
Net Working Capital	d8,944.0	301.0	d6,469.0	d6,571.0	d5,416.0	d5,398.0	d5,353.0
Year-end Shs. Outstg. (000)	49,174	54,200	55,600	56,300	55,400	56,000	56,000
STATISTICAL RECORD:							
Operating Profit Margin %	9.7	10.5	6.0	5.5	7.5	14.5	8.7
Net Profit Margin %	4.5	5.2	1.8	1.4	3.8	8.1	4.5
Return on Equity %	10.6	9.9	3.4	2.5	6.6	14.2	7.3
Return on Assets %	1.1	4.8	0.4	0.4	1.0	2.2	1.1
Debt/Total Assets %	27.9	31.8	31.4	24.8	28.2	26.3	23.8
Price Range	67.69-34.63	77.50-53.63	67.25-42.69	69.44-49.63	55.38-39.75	55.75-41.50	56.75-43.00
P/E Ratio	17.7-9.0	22.6-15.6	55.6-35.3	77.1-55.1	23.2-16.6	11.1-8.3	24.1-18.3
Average Yield %	2.5	2.0	2.3	2.2	2.6	2.3	2.0

Statistics are as originally reported. 1 Incl. nonrecur. charges of $32.1 mill. 2 Bef. discont. oper. of the bleached paperboard operation of $92.4 mill. 3 Incl. after-tax nonrecurr. chrg. of $9.0 mill.

OFFICERS:
K. M. Jastrow, II, Chmn., C.E.O.
R. D. Levy, C.F.O
D. W. Turpin, Treas.

INVESTOR CONTACT: C. Lynn Pavlic, Dir., Investor Relations, (512) 434-3737

PRINCIPAL OFFICE: 1300 Mopac Expressway South, Austin, TX 78746

TELEPHONE NUMBER: (512) 434-8000
FAX: (512) 434-8001
WEB: www.temple.com

NO. OF EMPLOYEES: 14,800 (approx.)

SHAREHOLDERS: 5,900 (approx.)

ANNUAL MEETING: In May

INCORPORATED: DE, 1983

INSTITUTIONAL HOLDINGS:
No. of Institutions: 239
Shares Held: 35,839,968
% Held: 72.8

INDUSTRY: Paperboard mills (SIC: 2631)

TRANSFER AGENT(S): First Chicago Trust Company of New York, Jersey City, NJ

NYSE SYMBOL THC
Rec. Pr. 44.64 (4/30/01)

TENET HEALTHCARE CORPORATION

YIELD . . .
P/E RATIO 27.1

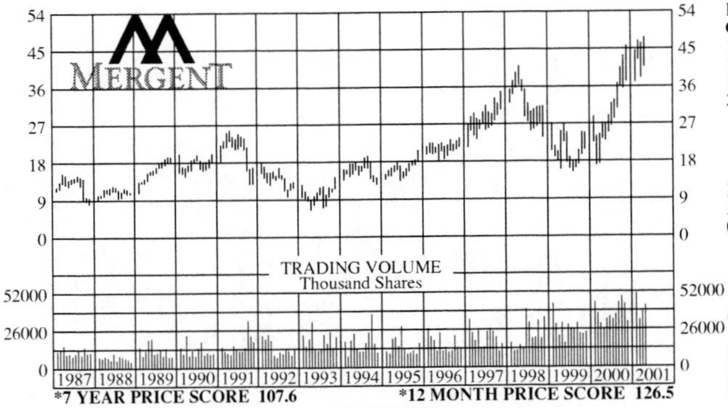

MERGENT

TRADING VOLUME
Thousand Shares

1987 1988 1989 1990 1991 1992 1993 1994 1995 1996 1997 1998 1999 2000 2001

*7 YEAR PRICE SCORE 107.6 *12 MONTH PRICE SCORE 126.5

*NYSE COMPOSITE INDEX=100

INTERIM EARNINGS (Per Share):

Qtr.	Aug.	Nov.	Feb.	May
1997-98	0.38	0.41	0.48	d0.08
1998-99	0.44	0.40	0.40	0.42
1999-00	0.41	0.43	0.12	0.51
2000-01	0.48	0.54	...	...

INTERIM DIVIDENDS (Per Share):

Amt.	Decl.	Ex.	Rec.	Pay.
0.01RR	3/06/00	3/13/00	3/15/00	3/24/00

CAPITALIZATION (5/31/00):

	($000)	(%)
Long-Term Debt	5,668,000	55.4
Deferred Income Tax	491,000	4.8
Common & Surplus	4,066,000	39.8
Total	10,225,000	100.0

RECENT DEVELOPMENTS: For the quarter ended 11/30/00, net income advanced 29.6% to $175.0 million versus $135.0 million in the comparable prior-year period. Earnings benefited from strong volumes, favorable pricing and cost controls. Net operating revenues rose 4.9% to $2.92 billion versus $2.78 billion in 1999. Same-facility admissions climbed 4.2% year over year, while same facility net patient revenue per admission grew 6.2%.

PROSPECTS: On 2/21/01, the Company made a minority equity investment in PatientKeeper, Inc. (formerly The Virtmed Corporation), a company that specializes in mobilizing medical information. PatientKeeper is creating an open architecture and universal platform for mobile healthcare computing, enabling any internal or third-party application to be available from one handheld device.

BUSINESS

TENET HEALTHCARE CORPORATION (formerly National Medical Enterprises, Inc.) is the nation's second largest for-profit operator of general hospitals. The Company's primary business is the operation of domestic and international general hospitals. The general hospitals offer acute-care services with fully-equipped operating and recovery rooms, radiology services, respiratory therapy services, pharmacies, clinical laboratories and most offer intensive care coronary care nursing units, physical therapy, orthopedic, oncology and outpatient services. As of 3/1/01, THC owned and operated 110 acute care hospitals with 26,914 licensed beds in 17 states. THC owns 21.0% of Broadlane, Inc., an on-line marketplace for high-volume hospital and medical supplies.

ANNUAL FINANCIAL DATA

	5/31/00	5/31/99	5/31/98	5/31/97	5/31/96	5/31/95	5/31/94
Earnings Per Share	[7] **1.08**	[1] **0.79**	[2] **1.22**	[3] **d0.24**	[4] **1.90**	[5] **1.10**	[6] **1.29**
Cash Flow Per Share	**2.77**	**2.57**	**2.69**	**1.22**	**3.44**	**2.20**	**2.48**
Tang. Book Val. Per Share	**2.35**	**1.51**	**0.47**	**0.26**	**0.07**	**...**	**7.31**
INCOME STATEMENT (IN MILLIONS):							
Total Revenues	11,414.0	10,880.0	9,895.0	8,691.0	5,559.0	3,318.0	2,967.0
Costs & Expenses	9,479.0	9,022.0	8,086.0	7,094.0	4,546.0	2,732.0	2,455.0
Depreciation & Amort.	533.0	556.0	460.0	443.0	321.0	195.0	198.0
Operating Income	1,047.0	939.0	1,128.0	414.0	692.0	391.0	314.0
Net Interest Inc./(Exp.)	d479.0	d485.0	d464.0	d417.0	d312.0	d138.0	d70.0
Income Before Income Taxes	618.0	474.0	647.0	d21.0	746.0	329.0	360.0
Income Taxes	278.0	225.0	269.0	52.0	348.0	135.0	144.0
Equity Earnings/Minority Int.	d21.0	d7.0	d22.0	d26.0	d2.0	19.0	...
Net Income	[7] 340.0	[1] 249.0	[2] 378.0	[3] d73.0	[4] 398.0	[5] 194.0	[6] 216.0
Cash Flow	873.0	805.0	838.0	370.0	719.0	389.0	414.0
Average Shs. Outstg. (000)	314,918	313,386	312,000	304,000	209,000	177,000	167,000
BALANCE SHEET (IN MILLIONS):							
Cash & Cash Equivalents	245.0	159.0	155.0	151.0	201.0	294.0	373.0
Total Current Assets	3,594.0	3,962.0	2,890.0	2,391.0	1,545.0	1,624.0	1,444.0
Net Property	5,894.0	5,839.0	6,014.0	5,490.0	3,648.0	3,319.0	1,764.0
Total Assets	13,161.0	13,771.0	12,833.0	11,705.0	8,332.0	7,918.0	3,697.0
Total Current Liabilities	1,912.0	2,022.0	1,767.0	1,869.0	1,134.0	1,356.0	1,640.0
Long-Term Obligations	5,668.0	6,391.0	5,829.0	5,022.0	3,191.0	3,273.0	223.0
Net Stockholders' Equity	4,066.0	3,870.0	3,558.0	3,224.0	2,636.0	1,986.0	1,320.0
Net Working Capital	1,682.0	1,940.0	1,123.0	522.0	411.0	268.0	d196.0
Year-end Shs. Outstg. (000)	313,460	311,024	309,000	303,000	219,000	200,000	166,000
STATISTICAL RECORD:							
Operating Profit Margin %	9.2	8.6	11.4	4.8	12.4	11.8	10.6
Net Profit Margin %	3.0	2.3	3.8	...	7.2	5.8	7.3
Return on Equity %	8.4	6.4	10.6	...	15.1	9.8	16.4
Return on Assets %	2.6	1.8	2.9	...	4.8	2.5	5.8
Debt/Total Assets %	43.1	46.4	45.4	42.9	38.3	41.3	6.0
Price Range	27.19-15.38	40.94-23.75	34.88-21.38	23.75-18.13	20.75-13.38	19.50-12.50	14.38-6.50
P/E Ratio	25.2-14.2	51.8-30.1	28.6-17.5	...	10.9-7.0	17.7-11.4	11.1-5.0

Statistics are as originally reported. [1] Incl. non-recurr. net chrg. $353.0 mill.; excl. an acctg. chrg. of $19.0 mill. [2] Incl. non-recurr. net chrg. $218.0 mill.; bef. extraord. chrg. $117.0 mill. [3] Incl. non-recurr. chrg. $758.0 mill.; bef. disc. loss $134.0 mill. & extraord. chrg. $47.0 mill. [4] Incl. gain on disp. $329.0 mill.; bef. disc. oper. loss $25.0 mill. & extraord. chrg. $23.0 mill. [5] Incl. non-recurr. chrg. $37.0 mill.; bef. disc. oper loss $9.0 mill. & extraord. chrg. $20.0 mill. [6] Bef. disc. oper. loss $701.0 mill. & acctg. chg. cr$60.0 mill. [7] Bef. acctg. chrg. of $19.0 mill. & disc. opers. loss of $19.0 mill.; Incl. non-recurr. net chrg. $344.0 mill.

OFFICERS:
J. C. Barbakow, Chmn., C.E.O.
D. L. Dennis, Pres., C.F.O., C.O.O.
S. D. Farber, V.P., Treas.

INVESTOR CONTACT: Paul J. Russell, V.P. Inv. Rel., (805) 563-7188

PRINCIPAL OFFICE: 3820 State Street, Santa Barbara, CA 93105

TELEPHONE NUMBER: (805) 563-6969
FAX: (888) 896-9016
WEB: www.tenethealth.com

NO. OF EMPLOYEES: 106,842 (approx.)

SHAREHOLDERS: 11,700 (approx.)

ANNUAL MEETING: In Oct.

INCORPORATED: CA, June, 1968; reincorp., NV, Dec., 1968

INSTITUTIONAL HOLDINGS:
No. of Institutions: 420
Shares Held: 284,686,500
% Held: 87.8

INDUSTRY: General medical & surgical hospitals (SIC: 8062)

TRANSFER AGENT(S): The Bank of New York, New York, NY

NYSE SYMBOL TNC
Rec. Pr. 43.08 (4/30/01)

TENNANT COMPANY

YIELD 1.9%
P/E RATIO 13.9

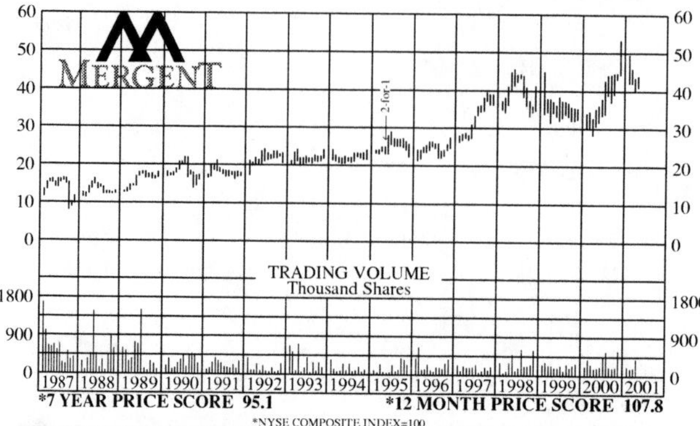

*7 YEAR PRICE SCORE 95.1 *12 MONTH PRICE SCORE 107.8

*NYSE COMPOSITE INDEX=100

INTERIM EARNINGS (Per Share):

Qtr.	Mar.	June	Sept.	Dec.
1995	0.39	0.53	0.47	0.59
1996	0.40	0.51	0.50	0.69
1997	0.44	0.64	0.60	0.75
1998	0.54	0.70	0.67	0.76
1999	0.53	0.66	0.35	0.61
2000	0.60	0.83	0.79	0.87

INTERIM DIVIDENDS (Per Share):

Amt.	Decl.	Ex.	Rec.	Pay.
0.19Q	5/04/00	5/30/00	6/01/00	6/15/00
0.20Q	8/10/00	8/30/00	9/01/00	9/15/00
0.20Q	11/16/00	12/13/00	12/15/00	12/29/00
0.20Q	2/23/01	3/01/01	3/05/01	3/15/01
0.20Q	5/03/01	5/30/01	6/01/01	6/15/01

Indicated div.: $0.80 (Div. Reinv. Plan)

CAPITALIZATION (12/31/00):

	($000)	(%)
Long-Term Debt	10,000	6.1
Common & Surplus	154,948	93.9
Total	164,948	100.0

RECENT DEVELOPMENTS: For the year ended 12/31/00, net earnings climbed 43.2% to $28.3 million from $19.7 million in 1999. Results for 1999 included restructuring charges of $6.7 million. Net sales increased 5.8% to $454.0 million from $429.4 million a year earlier, primarily due to market share gains and operating improvements, partially offset by unfavorable exchange rates mainly from the weak Euro. Operating margin grew to 9.6% from 7.3% the year before.

PROSPECTS: On 2/7/01, TNC announced that it plans to close a leased manufacturing facility in Waldhausen, Germany and transfer the related production to a contract manufacturer based in the Czech Republic. TNC expects to report about $3.8 million to $4.0 million in charges associated with this transfer. On 4/24/01, TNC and Johnson Wax Professional announced the formation of a joint venture company, NEXGEN FLOOR CARE SOLUTIONS™.

BUSINESS

TENNANT COMPANY specializes in the design, manufacture and sale of non-residential floor maintenance equipment and related products. The equipment manufactured consists mainly of motorized cleaning equipment and related products, including floor cleaning and preservation products, and is sold through a direct sales organization and independent distributors in more than 40 countries throughout the world. The Company has manufacturing operations in Holland, Michigan; Uden, The Netherlands; and Waldhausen, Germany. In January 1999, the Company acquired the business and assets of Paul Andra KG, a privately-owned manufacturer of commercial floor maintenance equipment in Germany.

QUARTERLY DATA

(12/31/2000)	REV ($000)	INC ($000)
First quarter	108,419	5,487
Second quarter	115,099	7,637
Third quarter	115,082	7,184
Fourth quarter	115,444	7,942

ANNUAL FINANCIAL DATA

	12/31/00	12/31/99	12/31/98	12/31/97	12/31/96	12/31/95	12/31/94
Earnings Per Share	**3.09**	**1 2.15**	**2.67**	**2.41**	**2.10**	**1.98**	**1.60**
Cash Flow Per Share	**5.11**	**4.20**	**4.51**	**4.15**	**3.73**	**3.40**	**2.94**
Tang. Book Val. Per Share	**15.16**	**13.06**	**12.68**	**12.12**	**10.57**	**8.86**	**10.10**
Dividends Per Share	**0.78**	**0.76**	**0.74**	**0.72**	**0.69**	**0.68**	**0.65**
Dividend Payout %	**25.2**	**35.3**	**27.7**	**29.9**	**32.9**	**34.3**	**40.6**
INCOME STATEMENT (IN THOUSANDS):							
Total Revenues	454,044	429,407	389,388	372,428	344,433	325,368	281,685
Costs & Expenses	392,129	379,478	334,489	318,872	296,415	281,096	244,440
Depreciation & Amort.	18,391	18,667	17,550	17,468	16,387	14,090	13,121
Operating Income	43,524	31,262	37,349	36,088	31,631	30,182	24,124
Net Interest Inc./(Exp.)	807	d1,097	1,479	2,678	1,768	1,492	2,130
Income Before Income Taxes	44,044	30,586	39,092	37,630	32,329	29,435	24,081
Income Taxes	15,794	10,893	13,767	13,425	11,302	9,773	8,346
Net Income	28,250	1 19,693	25,325	24,205	21,027	19,662	15,735
Cash Flow	46,641	38,360	42,875	41,673	37,414	33,752	28,856
Average Shs. Outstg.	9,135	9,140	9,500	10,032	10,021	9,916	9,826
BALANCE SHEET (IN THOUSANDS):							
Cash & Cash Equivalents	21,512	14,928	17,693	16,279	9,881	4,247	1,851
Total Current Assets	171,628	165,093	150,868	143,105	126,481	123,508	98,810
Net Property	66,713	66,306	66,640	65,111	65,384	63,724	56,552
Total Assets	263,285	257,533	239,098	233,870	219,180	215,750	182,834
Total Current Liabilities	67,255	74,999	60,809	56,115	7,898	17,969	66,065
Long-Term Obligations	10,000	16,003	23,038	20,678	21,824	23,149	6,300
Net Stockholders' Equity	154,948	135,915	131,267	134,086	123,106	107,067	118,687
Net Working Capital	104,373	90,094	90,059	86,990	118,583	105,539	32,745
Year-end Shs. Outstg.	9,053	8,989	9,123	9,699	9,965	9,952	9,839
STATISTICAL RECORD:							
Operating Profit Margin %	9.6	7.3	9.6	9.7	9.2	9.3	8.6
Net Profit Margin %	6.2	4.6	6.5	6.5	6.1	6.0	5.6
Return on Equity %	18.2	14.5	19.3	18.1	17.1	18.4	13.3
Return on Assets %	10.7	7.6	10.6	10.3	9.6	9.1	8.6
Debt/Total Assets %	3.8	6.2	9.6	8.8	10.0	10.7	3.4
Price Range	53.38-28.25	45.00-31.44	45.75-33.00	39.63-26.13	27.50-21.25	29.00-22.25	24.25-20.47
P/E Ratio	17.3-9.1	20.9-14.6	17.1-12.4	16.4-10.8	13.1-10.1	14.6-11.2	15.2-12.8
Average Yield %	1.9	2.0	1.9	2.2	2.8	2.7	2.9

Statistics are as originally reported. Adj. for stk. split: 2-for-1, 4/26/95 1 Incl. non-recurr. chrg. $6.7 mill.

OFFICERS:
J. M. Dolan, Pres., C.E.O.
A. T. Brausen, V.P., C.F.O., Treas.
P. J. O'Neill, Asst. Treas.
J. J. Seifert, V.P., Sec., Gen. Couns.

INVESTOR CONTACT: Anthony T. Brausen, V.P., C.F.O. & Treas., (763) 540-1553

PRINCIPAL OFFICE: 701 North Lilac Drive, P.O. Box 1452, Minneapolis, MN 55440

TELEPHONE NUMBER: (612) 540-1200
FAX: (612) 513-2142
WEB: www.tennantco.com

NO. OF EMPLOYEES: 2,391 (avg.)

SHAREHOLDERS: 3,500 (approx.)

ANNUAL MEETING: In May

INCORPORATED: MN, Jan., 1909

INSTITUTIONAL HOLDINGS:
No. of Institutions: 65
Shares Held: 5,345,168
% Held: 59.0

INDUSTRY: Service industry machinery, nec (SIC: 3589)

TRANSFER AGENT(S): Wells Fargo Bank Minnesota, N.A., St. Paul, Minnesota

NYSE SYMBOL TEN
Rec. Pr. 3.00 (4/30/01)

TENNECO AUTOMOTIVE, INC.

YIELD ...
P/E RATIO ...

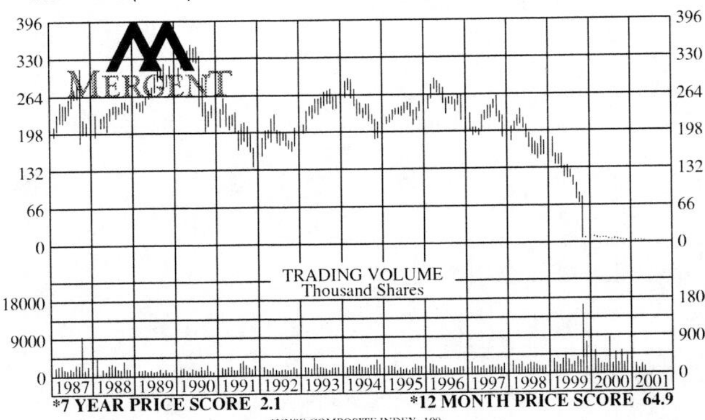

*7 YEAR PRICE SCORE 2.1 *12 MONTH PRICE SCORE 64.9

*NYSE COMPOSITE INDEX=100

INTERIM EARNINGS (Per Share):

Qtr.	Mar.	June	Sept.	Dec.
1997	2.20	3.05	3.10	2.20
1998	2.20	4.05	3.10	d1.80
1999	0.47	1.06	0.86	d4.25
2000	0.03	0.42	0.16	d1.74

INTERIM DIVIDENDS (Per Share):

Amt.	Decl.	Ex.	Rec.	Pay.
0.05Q	1/12/00	2/23/00	2/25/00	3/14/00
0.05Q	5/09/00	5/24/00	5/26/00	6/13/00
0.05Q	7/11/00	8/23/00	8/25/00	9/12/00
0.05Q	10/10/00	11/21/00	11/24/00	12/05/00

Div. payments suspended.

CAPITALIZATION (12/31/00):

	($000)	(%)
Long-Term Debt	1,435,000	74.6
Deferred Income Tax	144,000	7.5
Minority Interest	14,000	0.7
Common & Surplus	330,000	17.2
Total	1,923,000	100.0

RECENT DEVELOPMENTS: For the year ended 12/31/00, TEN incurred a loss of $41.0 million, before an extraordinary loss of $1.0 million, versus a loss of $63.0 million, before an accounting charge of $134.0 million, a loss from discontinued operations of $208.0 million, and an extraordinary loss of $18.0 million, in 1999. Earnings for 2000 included a one-time charge of $45.0 million. Net sales grew 8.2% to $3.55 billion.

PROSPECTS: As a result of increasingly difficult industry conditions, the Company intends to reduce its worldwide workforce by 1,105, or 22.0%, by the end of the first quarter of 2002. TEN expects this cost reduction plan to generate about $45.0 million in annual savings in 2001, and an additional $27.0 million by the end of the first quarter of 2002. TEN will also report cash charges related to the plan of up to $14.0 million in 2001.

BUSINESS

TENNECO AUTOMOTIVE, INC. (formerly Tenneco Inc.) is a worldwide producer and marketer of ride control and exhaust systems and products, which are sold under the Monroe® and Walker® global brand names. Among its products are Sensa-Trac® and Reflex™ shocks and struts, Rancho® shock absorbers, Walker® Quiet-Flow™ mufflers and DynoMax™ performance exhaust products, and Monroe® Clevite™ vibration control components. In addition, the Company serves OEMs on a global basis, including Ford, General Motors, Honda, Toyota, DaimlerChrysler, Volkswagen, BMW and Volvo. On 11/4/99, TEN completed the spin-off of Tenneco Packaging, now known as Pactiv Corporation.

GEOGRAPHIC DATA

(12/31/2000)	Rev(%)	Inc(%)
North America	55.4	62.8
Europe	35.1	28.8
Rest of World	9.5	10.2
Other	0.0	(1.8)
Total	100.0	100.0

ANNUAL FINANCIAL DATA

	12/31/00	12/31/99	12/31/98	12/31/97	12/31/96	12/31/95	12/31/94
Earnings Per Share	[6] **d1.18**	[5] **d1.87**	[4] **7.55**	[1] **10.55**	[2] [3] **6.40**	[3] **7.40**	[1] [2] [3] **6.60**
Cash Flow Per Share	3.14	2.38	20.80	21.23	15.06	12.70	10.22
Tang. Book Val. Per Share	...	...	25.75	27.97	37.94	60.69	...
Dividends Per Share	0.20	...	...	...	...	...	...
INCOME STATEMENT (IN MILLIONS):							
Total Revenues	3,549.0	3,292.0	7,605.0	7,318.0	6,648.0	5,260.0	4,164.0
Costs & Expenses	3,283.0	3,000.0	6,516.0	6,189.0	5,711.0	4,392.0	3,566.0
Depreciation & Amort.	151.0	144.0	448.0	365.0	309.0	196.0	142.0
Operating Income	120.0	148.0	641.0	764.0	628.0	672.0	456.0
Net Interest Inc./(Exp.)	d186.0	d106.0	d240.0	d216.0	d195.0	d160.0	d104.0
Income Before Income Taxes	d66.0	42.0	401.0	548.0	433.0	512.0	352.0
Income Taxes	cr27.0	82.0	116.0	163.0	194.0	231.0	114.0
Net Income	[6] d41.0	[5] d63.0	[4] 255.0	[1] 361.0	[2] [3] 218.0	[3] 258.0	[1] [2] [3] 238.0
Cash Flow	110.0	81.0	703.0	726.0	515.0	442.0	368.0
Average Shs. Outstg. (000)	35,000	34,000	33,800	34,200	34,200	34,800	36,000
BALANCE SHEET (IN MILLIONS):							
Cash & Cash Equivalents	35.0	84.0	36.0	41.0	62.0	354.0	...
Total Current Assets	1,109.0	1,201.0	2,157.0	2,115.0	1,923.0	1,946.0	...
Net Property	1,005.0	1,037.0	3,628.0	3,455.0	3,252.0	2,658.0	...
Total Assets	2,886.0	2,943.0	8,791.0	8,332.0	7,587.0	7,413.0	...
Total Current Liabilities	809.0	663.0	2,387.0	1,661.0	1,621.0	1,559.0	...
Long-Term Obligations	1,435.0	1,578.0	2,360.0	2,633.0	2,067.0	1,648.0	...
Net Stockholders' Equity	330.0	422.0	2,504.0	2,528.0	2,646.0	3,148.0	...
Net Working Capital	300.0	538.0	d230.0	454.0	302.0	387.0	...
Year-end Shs. Outstg. (000)	36,498	33,672	34,600	34,000	34,400	35,000	...
STATISTICAL RECORD:							
Operating Profit Margin %	3.4	4.5	8.4	10.4	9.4	12.8	11.0
Net Profit Margin %	...	...	3.4	4.9	3.3	4.9	5.7
Return on Equity %	...	...	10.2	14.3	8.2	8.2	...
Return on Assets %	...	...	2.9	4.3	2.9	3.5	...
Debt/Total Assets %	49.7	53.6	26.8	31.6	27.2	22.2	...
Price Range	11.50-2.50	186.25-7.00	237.50-147.50	260.63-186.57	292.50-216.88	251.88-209.38	293.75-185.00
P/E Ratio	...	...	31.5-19.5	24.7-17.7	45.7-33.9	34.0-28.3	44.5-28.0
Average Yield %	2.9	...	...	...	...	...	...

Statistics are as originally reported. Adj. for reverse 1-for-5 stk. split, 11/99. [1] Bef. acctg. chrg.: $46.0 mill., 1997; $39.0 mill., 1994. [2] Bef. extraord. chrg. $236.0 mill., 1996; $5.0 mill., 1994. [3] Bef. disc. oper. gain: $428.0 mill., 1996; $477.0 mill., 1995; $214.0 mill., 1994. [4] Incl. net pre-tax non-recurr. gains of $32.0 mill. [5] Bef. acctg. chrg. of $134.0 mill., extra. chrg. of $18.0 mill. & disc. oper. loss of $208.0 mill.; incl. after-tax restruct. exp. of $50.0 mill. & after-tax cost of $8.0 mill. to become a stand-alone public co. [6] Bef. extraord. chrg. of $1.0 mill.; incl. a one-time charge of $45.0 mill.

OFFICERS:
M. P. Frissora, Chmn., Pres., C.E.O.
M. A. McCollum, Sr. V.P., C.F.O.

INVESTOR CONTACT: Investor Relations, (847) 482-5042

PRINCIPAL OFFICE: 500 North Field Drive, Lake Forest, IL 60045

TELEPHONE NUMBER: (847) 482-5000
WEB: www.tenneco.com

NO. OF EMPLOYEES: 23,037 (approx.)

SHAREHOLDERS: 44,680 (approx., record)

ANNUAL MEETING: In May

INCORPORATED: DE, Aug., 1996

INSTITUTIONAL HOLDINGS:
No. of Institutions: 102
Shares Held: 18,119,374
% Held: 48.9

INDUSTRY: Motor vehicle parts and accessories (SIC: 3714)

TRANSFER AGENT(S): First Chicago Trust Company of New York, Jersey City, NJ

NYSE SYMBOL TER
Rec. Pr. 39.50 (4/30/01)

TERADYNE, INC.

YIELD ...
P/E RATIO 13.8

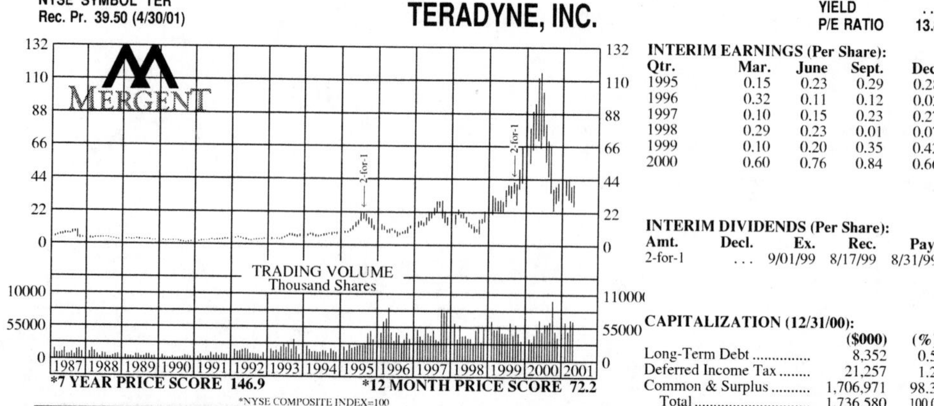

*7 YEAR PRICE SCORE 146.9 *12 MONTH PRICE SCORE 72.2

*NYSE COMPOSITE INDEX=100

INTERIM EARNINGS (Per Share):

Qtr.	Mar.	June	Sept.	Dec.
1995	0.15	0.23	0.29	0.28
1996	0.32	0.11	0.12	0.02
1997	0.10	0.15	0.23	0.27
1998	0.29	0.23	0.01	0.07
1999	0.10	0.20	0.35	0.42
2000	0.60	0.76	0.84	0.66

INTERIM DIVIDENDS (Per Share):

Amt.	Decl.	Ex.	Rec.	Pay.
2-for-1	...	9/01/99	8/17/99	8/31/99

CAPITALIZATION (12/31/00):

	($000)	(%)
Long-Term Debt	8,352	0.5
Deferred Income Tax	21,257	1.2
Common & Surplus	1,706,971	98.3
Total	1,736,580	100.0

RECENT DEVELOPMENTS: For the year ended 12/31/00, income was $517.8 million, before an accounting charge, versus net income of $191.7 million in 1999. Results for 2000 excluded the net cumulative effect of an accounting charge of $64.1 million. Net sales jumped 70.0% to $3.04 billion from $1.79 billion in the prior year. Sales were mainly driven by growth from TER's connections systems business and from the semiconductor test business, as well as improvements in TER's product positioning.

PROSPECTS: Market conditions in the semiconductor test industry are less favorable due to excess capacity, concerns about global economies and anticipated lower growth in many end markets. As a result, TER expects these conditions will affect its semiconductor test business in the foreseeable future. Meanwhile, conditions in the connections systems segment continue to be healthy. In regard, the Company will continue its aggressive growth plan as customers search for higher bandwidth applications.

BUSINESS

TERADYNE, INC. designs, manufactures, markets, and services electronic test systems and related software used by component manufacturers in the design and testing of their products and by electronic equipment manufacturers for the incoming inspection of components and for the design and testing of circuit boards and other assemblies. TER's electronic systems are also used by telephone operating companies for the testing and maintenance of their subscriber telephone lines and related equipment. TER also manufactures backplane connection systems, principally for the computer, telecommunications, and military/aerospace industries. RSW Software Inc., the Company's e-business division, offers Web-based testing applications through its e-TEST™ and EJB-test™ suite of products.

ANNUAL FINANCIAL DATA

	12/31/00	12/31/99	12/31/98	12/31/97	12/31/96	12/31/95	12/31/94
Earnings Per Share	**4 2.86**	**1.07**	**3 0.60**	**2 0.74**	**1 0.55**	**0.95**	**0.48**
Cash Flow Per Share	**3.42**	**1.56**	**1.04**	**1.08**	**0.85**	**1.20**	**0.72**
Tang. Book Val. Per Share	**9.89**	**6.77**	**6.13**	**5.62**	**5.10**	**4.60**	**3.39**
INCOME STATEMENT (IN MILLIONS):							
Total Revenues	3,043.9	1,790.9	1,489.2	1,266.3	1,171.6	1,191.0	677.4
Costs & Expenses	2,231.3	1,446.3	1,278.9	1,031.8	997.9	903.5	544.0
Depreciation & Amort.	101.9	86.4	76.3	59.2	50.9	43.1	35.3
Operating Income	710.8	258.2	133.9	175.3	122.8	244.4	98.1
Net Interest Inc./(Exp.)	28.9	15.7	11.9	18.0	16.9	11.2	4.7
Income Before Income Taxes	739.6	273.8	145.9	193.3	139.7	249.9	102.8
Income Taxes	221.9	82.2	43.8	65.7	46.1	90.6	31.9
Net Income	4 517.8	191.7	3 102.1	2 127.6	1 93.6	159.3	70.9
Cash Flow	619.6	278.1	178.4	186.8	144.5	202.4	106.2
Average Shs. Outstg. (000)	181,011	178,550	171,930	172,638	170,120	168,506	148,380
BALANCE SHEET (IN MILLIONS):							
Cash & Cash Equivalents	302.6	247.7	201.4	93.4	249.7	275.8	202.6
Total Current Assets	1,377.8	907.7	759.5	727.1	617.1	740.1	446.7
Net Property	733.8	497.7	435.0	343.1	273.5	257.0	183.6
Total Assets	2,355.9	1,568.2	1,312.8	1,251.7	1,096.8	1,023.8	655.9
Total Current Liabilities	619.3	392.3	255.7	278.0	225.3	229.6	139.2
Long-Term Obligations	8.4	8.9	13.2	13.1	15.7	18.7	8.8
Net Stockholders' Equity	1,707.0	1,153.0	1,026.4	937.1	842.0	759.9	493.3
Net Working Capital	758.5	515.4	503.9	449.1	391.9	510.6	307.5
Year-end Shs. Outstg. (000)	172,559	170,319	167,488	166,606	164,960	165,268	145,408
STATISTICAL RECORD:							
Operating Profit Margin %	23.4	14.4	9.0	13.8	10.5	20.5	14.5
Net Profit Margin %	17.0	10.7	6.9	10.1	8.0	13.4	10.5
Return on Equity %	30.3	16.6	9.9	13.6	11.1	21.0	14.4
Return on Assets %	22.0	12.2	7.8	10.2	8.5	15.6	10.8
Debt/Total Assets %	0.4	0.6	1.0	1.0	1.4	1.8	1.3
Price Range	115.44-23.00	66.00-20.63	24.22-7.50	29.59-11.81	13.88-5.56	21.44-8.03	8.56-5.09
P/E Ratio	40.4-8.0	61.7-19.3	40.7-12.6	40.0-16.0	25.2-10.1	22.7-8.5	17.9-10.7

Statistics are as originally reported. Adj. for 2-for-1 split, 8/99 & 8/95. 1 Incl. $10.8 mill. chg. rel. to workforce reduct. 2 Incl. $0.04/sh. non-recur. chg. 3 Incl. $23.0 mill. pre-tax chg. for excess raw material inventory. 4 Excl. $64.1 mill. net cumulative effect of acctg. chrg.

OFFICERS:
G. W. Chamillard, Chmn., Pres., C.E.O.
G. Beecher, V.P., C.F.O.
S. M. Osattin, V.P., Treas.

INVESTOR CONTACT: Tom Newman, V.P., Corp. Relations, (617) 422-2425

PRINCIPAL OFFICE: 321 Harrison Avenue, Boston, MA 02118

TELEPHONE NUMBER: (617) 482-2700
FAX: (617) 422-3915
WEB: www.teradyne.com

NO. OF EMPLOYEES: 10,200 (approx.)

SHAREHOLDERS: 2,406 (record)

ANNUAL MEETING: In May

INCORPORATED: MA, Sept., 1960

INSTITUTIONAL HOLDINGS:
No. of Institutions: 303
Shares Held: 141,446,824
% Held: 81.3

INDUSTRY: Instruments to measure electricity (SIC: 3825)

TRANSFER AGENT(S): BankBoston, N.A., c/o Boston EquiServe, Boston, MA

NYSE SYMBOL TSO
Rec. Pr. 14.90 (4/30/01)

TESORO PETROLEUM CORPORATION

YIELD	...
P/E RATIO	8.6

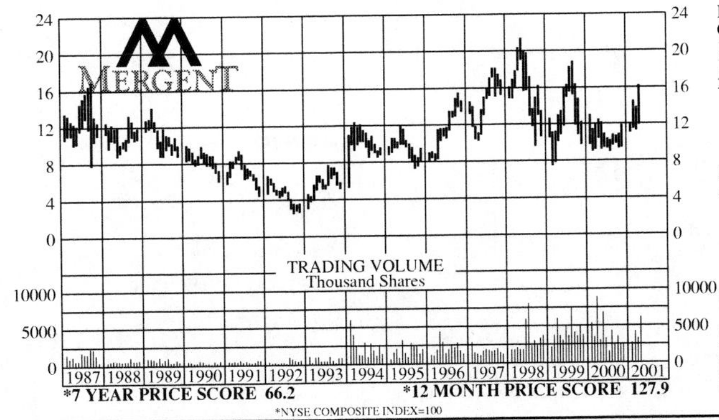

INTERIM EARNINGS (Per Share):

Qtr.	Mar.	June	Sept.	Dec.
1998		d0.86		
1999		1.92		
2000	0.20	0.35	0.60	0.59

INTERIM DIVIDENDS (Per Share):

Amt.	Decl.	Ex.	Rec.	Pay.
		No dividends paid.		

CAPITALIZATION (12/31/00):

	($000)	(%)
Long-Term Debt	306,800	28.3
Deferred Income Tax	107,200	9.9
Preferred Stock	165,000	15.2
Common & Surplus	504,900	46.6
Total	1,083,900	100.0

RECENT DEVELOPMENTS: For the year ended 12/31/00, net income amounted to $73.3 million versus income from continuing operations of $32.2 million in 1999. Revenues soared 70.1% to $5.10 billion compared with $3.00 billion the year before. Results for 1999 excluded an after-tax gain $42.8 million from discontinued operations. Results were driven by higher refined product margins and improved refinery throughput. Refining and Marketing operating income surged 51.2% to $189.1 million, while Marine Services operating income rose 76.3% to $10.4 million.

PROSPECTS: Near-term prospects are positive, reflecting refinery spreads that are benefiting from processing a greater percent of lower-cost, heavy crude oil and tight supply and demand conditions. As a result, TSO has deferred its planned turnaround of the Anacortes refinery until the first quarter of 2002 and now estimates that throughput for 2001 will average between 255,000 to 260,000 barrels per day. TSO noted that this will delay the start-up of the project to upgrade the fluid catalytic cracking unit until the first quarter of 2002.

BUSINESS

TESORO PETROLEUM CORPORATION is an independent refiner and marketer of petroleum products and provider of marine logistics services. The Company owns and operates three petroleum refineries with a combined capacity of 275,000 barrels per day and sells refined products to a wide variety of customers in the western U.S. and other countries on the Pacific Rim. As of 2/13/01, TSO's branded retail network was comprised of about 180 stations, of which approximately 90 were Company owned and operated. TSO also operates a network of terminals along the Texas and Louisiana Gulf Coast that provides fuel and logistical support services to the marine and offshore exploration and production industries. Refining and Marketing accounted for 96.3% of 2000 revenues; Marine Services, 3.7%.

ANNUAL FINANCIAL DATA

	12/31/00	12/31/99	12/31/98	12/31/97	12/31/96	12/31/95	12/31/94
Earnings Per Share	**1.75**	**[1] 1.92**	**[2][4] d0.86**	**[1] 1.14**	**[2][5] 2.90**	**[2][3] 2.29**	**[2][3] 0.77**
Cash Flow Per Share	**2.56**	**1.92**	**1.70**	**0.65**	**4.52**	**4.05**	**2.44**
Tang. Book Val. Per Share	**16.38**	**14.14**	**12.20**	**N.M.**	**11.51**	**8.74**	**6.59**
INCOME STATEMENT (IN MILLIONS):							
Total Revenues	5,104.4	3,000.3	1,490.3	853.1	1,039.8	1,002.9	877.2
Costs & Expenses	4,899.6	2,860.5	1,387.5	824.8	864.6	869.2	787.0
Depreciation & Amort.	45.5	42.9	71.1	15.1	43.1	44.2	38.8
Operating Income	199.5	131.0	59.3	26.8	144.8	105.9	51.3
Net Interest Inc./(Exp.)	d29.9	d36.4	d31.0	d6.5	d7.0	d19.1	d18.7
Income Before Income Taxes	123.5	51.2	d15.5	3.4	115.1	61.9	26.1
Income Taxes	50.2	19.0	cr0.5	1.0	38.3	4.4	5.6
Net Income	73.3	[1] 32.2	[2][4] d15.0	[1] 2.4	[2][5] 76.8	[2][3] 57.5	[2][3] 20.5
Cash Flow	106.9	63.1	50.1	17.5	119.9	101.7	56.6
Average Shs. Outstg. (000)	41,800	32,800	29,400	26,900	26,499	25,107	23,196
BALANCE SHEET (IN MILLIONS):							
Cash & Cash Equivalents	14.1	141.8	12.9	8,352.0	22.8	13.9	14.0
Total Current Assets	630.2	611.6	390.6	181,835.0	237.3	182.5	182.1
Net Property	781.4	731.6	894.6	413,823.0	316.5	261.7	273.3
Total Assets	1,543.6	1,486.5	1,428.4	627,808.0	582.6	519.2	484.4
Total Current Liabilities	382.4	321.6	208.2	107,495.0	137.9	104.9	96.2
Long-Term Obligations	306.8	390.2	531.4	115,314.0	79.3	155.0	192.2
Net Stockholders' Equity	669.9	623.1	559.2	332,964.0	304.1	216.5	160.7
Net Working Capital	247.8	290.0	182.4	74,340.0	99.5	77.5	85.9
Year-end Shs. Outstg. (000)	30,819	32,400	32,300	26,300	26,414	24,780	24,390
STATISTICAL RECORD:							
Operating Profit Margin %	3.9	4.4	4.0	3.1	13.9	10.6	5.9
Net Profit Margin %	1.4	1.1	...	0.3	7.4	5.7	2.3
Return on Equity %	10.9	5.2	...	...	25.3	26.6	12.7
Return on Assets %	4.7	2.2	...	...	13.2	11.1	4.2
Debt/Total Assets %	19.9	26.2	37.2	18.4	13.6	29.9	39.7
Price Range	13.00-8.94	18.81-7.44	21.38-9.56	18.19-10.25	15.50-8.00	12.00-7.25	12.38-5.25
P/E Ratio	7.4-5.1	9.8-3.9	...	16.0-9.0	5.3-2.8	5.2-3.2	16.1-6.8

Statistics are as originally reported. [1] Bef. inc. fr. disc. ops. of $42.8 mill., 1999; $28.3 mill., 1997 [2] Bef. extraord. loss $4.4 mill., 12/98; $2.3 mill., 12/96; $2.9 mill., 12/95; $4.8 mill., 12/94 [3] Incl. gain on sales of assets & oth. inc. of $32.7 mill., 1995; $2.4 mill., 1994 [4] Incl. write-downs of oil and gas properties of $68.3 mill. [5] Incl. inc. from settlement of natural gas contract of $60.0 mill. and gain on sales of assets & oth. inc. of $4.4 mill.

OFFICERS:
B. A. Smith, Chmn., Pres., C.E.O.
W. T. Van Kleef, Exec. V.P., C.O.O.
G. Wright, Sr. V.P., C.F.O.

INVESTOR CONTACT: Susan Pirotina, V.P., Communications, (210) 283-2631

PRINCIPAL OFFICE: 300 Concord Plaza Dr., San Antonio, TX 78216-6999

TELEPHONE NUMBER: (210) 828-8484
FAX: (210) 283-2003
WEB: www.tesoropetroleum.com
NO. OF EMPLOYEES: 2,100 (approx.)
SHAREHOLDERS: 2,800 (approx. record)
ANNUAL MEETING: In May
INCORPORATED: CA, Dec., 1939; reincorp., DE, Dec., 1968

INSTITUTIONAL HOLDINGS:
No. of Institutions: 103
Shares Held: 25,350,211
% Held: 82.0

INDUSTRY: Petroleum refining (SIC: 2911)

TRANSFER AGENT(S): Mellon Investor Services, Ridgefield Park, NJ

NYSE SYMBOL TX
Rec. Pr. 72.28 (4/30/01)

TEXACO INC.

YIELD 2.5%
P/E RATIO 15.5

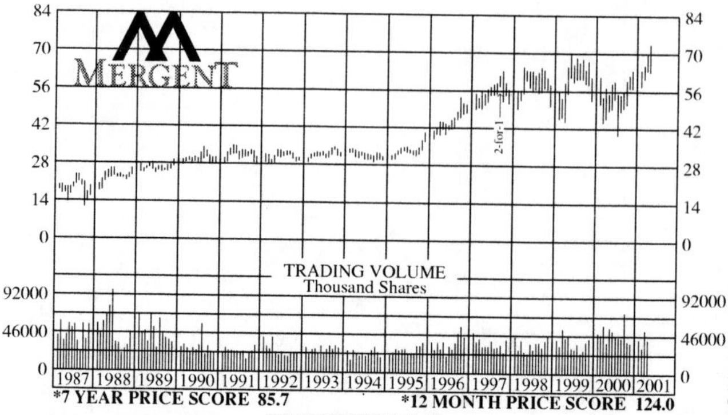

MERGENT

TRADING VOLUME
Thousand Shares

1987 1988 1989 1990 1991 1992 1993 1994 1995 1996 1997 1998 1999 2000 2001

*7 YEAR PRICE SCORE 85.7 *12 MONTH PRICE SCORE 124.0

*NYSE COMPOSITE INDEX=100

INTERIM EARNINGS (Per Share):

Qtr.	Mar.	June	Sept.	Dec.
1997	1.86	1.07	0.91	1.12
1998	0.46	0.61	0.38	d0.43
1999	0.35	0.50	0.71	0.58
2000	1.05	1.14	1.46	1.00

INTERIM DIVIDENDS (Per Share):

Amt.	Decl.	Ex.	Rec.	Pay.
0.45Q	7/21/00	8/04/00	8/08/00	9/08/00
0.45Q	10/27/00	11/06/00	11/08/00	12/08/00
0.45Q	1/19/01	2/06/01	2/08/01	3/09/01
0.45Q	4/24/01	5/04/01	5/08/01	6/08/01

Indicated div.: $1.80 (Div. Reinv. Plan)

CAPITALIZATION (12/31/00):

	($000)	(%)
Long-Term Debt	6,815,000	30.3
Deferred Income Tax	1,547,000	6.9
Minority Interest	713,000	3.2
Preferred Stock	300,000	1.3
Common & Surplus	13,144,000	58.4
Total	22,519,000	100.0

RECENT DEVELOPMENTS: For the year ended 12/31/00, net income surged to $2.54 billion versus $1.18 billion last year. Results for 2000 and 1999 included net non-recurring after-tax charges of $356.0 million and $37.0 million. Total revenues rose 43.2% to $50.10 billion. Exploration and production operating income soared to $2.60 billion from $1.01 billion in 1999, due to higher crude oil and natural gas prices; however, U.S. and international daily net production fell 10.2% and 7.3% to 574.0 and 537.0 thousand barrels of crude oil equivalent, respectively.

PROSPECTS: TX's near-term outlook is positive, reflecting healthy crude oil and natural gas prices. Production output should be enhanced by the second phase of the Captain field in the U.K. North Sea, which began production late in December 2000. Additionally, the Erskine field in the U.K. resumed production in December after being shut in for most of 2000 to replace a pipeline. Separately, TX's merger with Chevron Corporation continues to progress, with completion expected in mid 2001.

BUSINESS

TEXACO INC. and its subsidiaries are principally engaged in the worldwide exploration for and the production, transportation, refining and marketing of crude oil, natural gas liquids, natural gas and petroleum products, power generation, gasification and other energy technologies. TX's worldwide reserve base as of 12/31/00 included crude oil and natural gas liquids totaling 2.60 billion barrels, and natural gas totaling 8.14 trillion cubic feet.

ANNUAL FINANCIAL DATA

	12/31/00	12/31/99	12/31/98	12/31/97	12/31/96	12/31/95	12/31/94
Earnings Per Share	**6 4.65**	**5 2.14**	**1 1.04**	**2 4.87**	**3.76**	**3 1.29**	**4 1.72**
Cash Flow Per Share	**8.20**	**5.06**	**4.31**	**7.91**	**6.54**	**5.87**	**5.06**
Tang. Book Val. Per Share	**23.89**	**21.96**	**20.76**	**22.16**	**17.51**	**16.52**	**17.31**
Dividends Per Share	**1.80**	**1.80**	**1.80**	**1.75**	**1.65**	**1.60**	**1.60**
Dividend Payout %	**38.7**	**84.1**	**173.1**	**35.9**	**43.9**	**124.5**	**93.3**
INCOME STATEMENT (IN MILLIONS):							
Total Revenues	50,100.0	34,975.0	30,910.0	45,187.0	44,561.0	35,551.0	32,540.0
Costs & Expenses	44,412.0	31,782.0	28,795.0	41,227.0	40,556.0	32,879.0	29,872.0
Depreciation & Amort.	1,917.0	1,543.0	1,675.0	1,633.0	1,455.0	2,385.0	1,735.0
Operating Income	3,771.0	1,650.0	440.0	2,327.0	2,550.0	287.0	933.0
Net Interest Inc./(Exp.)	d458.0	d504.0	d480.0	d412.0	d434.0	d483.0	d498.0
Income Before Income Taxes	4,218.0	1,779.0	701.0	3,327.0	2,983.0	986.0	1,204.0
Income Taxes	1,676.0	602.0	98.0	663.0	965.0	258.0	225.0
Equity Earnings/Minority Int.	905.0	633.0	741.0	1,412.0	867.0	1,182.0	769.0
Net Income	6 2,542.0	5 1,177.0	1 603.0	2 2,664.0	2,018.0	3 728.0	4 979.0
Cash Flow	4,444.0	2,692.0	2,225.0	4,242.0	3,415.0	3,053.0	2,623.0
Average Shs. Outstg. (000)	543,952	537,860	529,000	543,000	522,000	520,000	518,000
BALANCE SHEET (IN MILLIONS):							
Cash & Cash Equivalents	253.0	448.0	271.0	395.0	552.0	536.0	464.0
Total Current Assets	7,053.0	5,963.0	5,636.0	6,432.0	7,665.0	6,458.0	6,019.0
Net Property	15,681.0	15,560.0	14,761.0	17,116.0	13,411.0	12,580.0	13,483.0
Total Assets	30,867.0	28,972.0	28,570.0	24,503.0	21,967.0	19,659.0	20,169.0
Total Current Liabilities	5,984.0	5,668.0	5,264.0	5,994.0	6,184.0	5,206.0	5,015.0
Long-Term Obligations	6,815.0	6,606.0	6,352.0	5,507.0	5,125.0	5,503.0	5,564.0
Net Stockholders' Equity	13,444.0	12,042.0	11,833.0	12,766.0	10,372.0	9,519.0	9,749.0
Net Working Capital	1,069.0	295.0	372.0	438.0	1,481.0	1,252.0	1,004.0
Year-end Shs. Outstg. (000)	550,163	534,601	535,000	542,000	548,000	528,000	516,000
STATISTICAL RECORD:							
Operating Profit Margin %	7.5	4.7	1.4	5.1	5.7	0.8	2.9
Net Profit Margin %	5.1	3.4	2.0	5.9	4.5	2.0	3.0
Return on Equity %	18.9	9.8	5.1	20.9	19.5	7.6	10.0
Return on Assets %	8.2	4.1	2.1	10.9	9.2	3.7	4.9
Debt/Total Assets %	22.1	22.8	22.2	22.5	23.3	28.0	27.6
Price Range	63.75-39.50	70.06-44.56	65.00-49.06	63.44-48.88	53.56-37.75	40.25-29.88	34.06-29.06
P/E Ratio	13.7-8.5	32.7-20.8	62.5-47.2	13.0-10.0	14.2-10.0	31.3-23.2	19.9-16.9
Average Yield %	3.5	3.1	3.2	3.1	3.6	4.6	5.1

Statistics are as originally reported. Adj. for 2-for-1 stk. split, 9/97 1 Bef. acctg. chrg. of $25.0 mill.; incls. non-recurr. chrgs. of $291.0 mill. 2 Incl. non-recurr. credit of $770.0 mill. 3 Bef. acctg. adj. chrg. of $121.0 mill. 4 Bef. disc. ops. income of $87.0 mill. 5 Incl. one-time chrgs. totaling $37.0 mill. 6 Incl. net special chrgs. of $356.0 mill.

OFFICERS:
G. F. Tilton, Chmn., C.E.O.
P. J. Lynch, Sr. V.P., C.F.O.

INVESTOR CONTACT: E. P. Smith, V.P., Inv. Rel. & Shrhld. Serv., (914) 253-4478

PRINCIPAL OFFICE: 2000 Westchester Ave., White Plains, NY 10650-0001

TELEPHONE NUMBER: (914) 253-4000
FAX: (914) 253-6286
WEB: www.texaco.com
NO. OF EMPLOYEES: 19,011
SHAREHOLDERS: 184,958
ANNUAL MEETING: In Apr.
INCORPORATED: DE, Aug., 1926

INSTITUTIONAL HOLDINGS:
No. of Institutions: 743
Shares Held: 362,884,398
% Held: 66.0

INDUSTRY: Petroleum refining (SIC: 2911)

TRANSFER AGENT(S): Mellon Investor Services, New York, NY

NYSE SYMBOL TXI
Rec. Pr. 32.75 (5/31/01)

TEXAS INDUSTRIES INC.

YIELD	0.9%
P/E RATIO	14.2

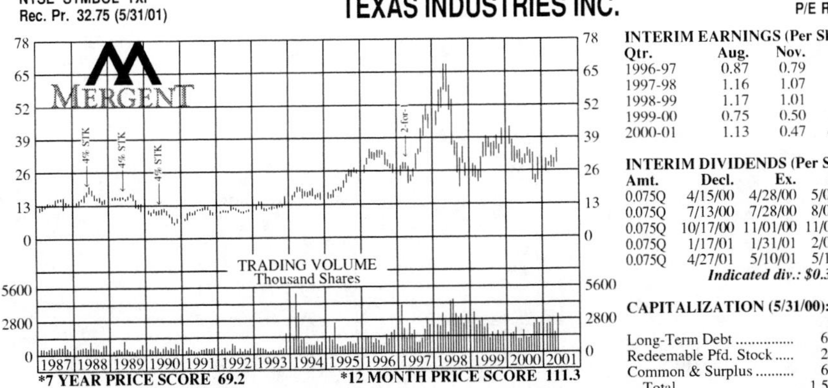

INTERIM EARNINGS (Per Share):

Qtr.	Aug.	Nov.	Feb.	May
1996-97	0.87	0.79	0.47	1.29
1997-98	1.16	1.07	0.85	1.60
1998-99	1.17	1.01	0.48	1.25
1999-00	0.75	0.50	0.64	1.26
2000-01	1.13	0.47	d0.55	...

INTERIM DIVIDENDS (Per Share):

Amt.	Decl.	Ex.	Rec.	Pay.
0.075Q	4/15/00	4/28/00	5/01/00	5/31/00
0.075Q	7/13/00	7/28/00	8/01/00	8/31/00
0.075Q	10/17/00	11/01/00	11/03/00	11/30/00
0.075Q	1/17/01	1/31/01	2/02/01	2/28/01
0.075Q	4/27/01	5/10/01	5/14/01	5/31/01

Indicated div.: $0.30

CAPITALIZATION (5/31/00):

	($000)	(%)
Long-Term Debt	623,284	41.0
Redeemable Pfd. Stock	200,000	13.1
Common & Surplus	698,026	45.9
Total	1,521,310	100.0

RECENT DEVELOPMENTS: For the quarter ended 2/27/01, the Company reported a net loss of $11.5 million compared with net income of $13.9 million in the equivalent 2000 quarter. Earnings for 2000 included an after-tax gain of $4.1 million from litigation recovery in steel operations. Results for 2001 and 2000 included after-tax dividends on preferred securities of $1.8 million in each year. Net sales declined 19.0% to $254.4 million compared with $314.3 million a year earlier.

PROSPECTS: Abnormal weather in TXI's markets severely limited shipments in the Company's cement, aggregate and concrete segment. In addition, lower realized product prices and increased costs, particularly in energy pressured marins. The steel segment faced competition from imports and high levels of customer inventories. Meanwhile, conditions are in place for domestic steel structural producers to begin regaining market share from imports.

BUSINESS

TEXAS INDUSTRIES INC., directly and through subsidiaries, is a producer of steel and cement/concrete products for the construction and manufacturing industries. The steel operation, conducted through TXI's Chaparral Steel Company located in Midlothian, Texas. Chaparral is an 84.5%-owned subsidiary as of 12/31/00. The division produces beams, rebar, channels, reinforcing bars, merchant quality rounds and special bar quality rounds. A major portion of TXI's shredded steel requirements is produced at its own steel mill. Products produced and supplied by the cement/concrete segment include cement, aggregates, ready-mix, block, brick and pipe. The cement/concrete facilities are concentrated in Texas and Louisiana.

ANNUAL FINANCIAL DATA

	5/31/00	5/31/99	5/31/98	5/31/97	5/31/96	5/31/95	5/31/94
Earnings Per Share	**3.15**	**3.92**	**4.69**	**3.40**	**3.52**	**1.94**	**1.15**
Cash Flow Per Share	**6.82**	**6.65**	**7.54**	**5.82**	**5.68**	**3.92**	**3.30**
Tang. Book Val. Per Share	**25.90**	**22.73**	**18.88**	**18.64**	**16.20**	**12.77**	**11.18**
Dividends Per Share	**0.30**	**0.30**	**0.30**	**0.20**	**0.20**	**0.10**	**0.10**
Dividend Payout %	**9.5**	**7.7**	**6.4**	**5.9**	**5.7**	**5.2**	**8.7**
INCOME STATEMENT (IN MILLIONS):							
Total Revenues	1,306.4	1,126.8	1,196.3	973.8	967.4	830.5	707.1
Costs & Expenses	1,080.9	920.1	971.2	789.7	776.3	690.8	597.0
Depreciation & Amort.	97.3	74.0	62.3	53.9	49.3	49.3	49.0
Operating Income	128.2	132.7	162.8	130.3	141.9	90.4	61.2
Net Interest Inc./(Exp.)	d32.7	d11.3	d20.5	d18.9	d20.0	d20.1	d26.2
Income Before Income Taxes	115.0	144.1	159.6	123.2	135.0	77.9	43.6
Income Taxes	38.0	48.3	53.1	41.2	47.3	25.7	15.6
Equity Earnings/Minority Int.	d7.1	d7.1	d4.4	d6.6	d7.8	d4.2	d2.3
Net Income	69.8	88.7	102.1	75.5	80.0	48.0	25.8
Cash Flow	167.1	162.8	164.4	129.4	129.2	97.3	74.7
Average Shs. Outstg. (000)	24,502	24,492	21,819	22,243	22,742	24,852	22,654
BALANCE SHEET (IN MILLIONS):							
Cash & Cash Equivalents	7.0	17.7	16.7	19.8	28.1	26.0	31.8
Total Current Assets	372.0	310.4	371.9	344.4	324.9	292.8	277.1
Net Property	1,229.1	1,006.2	616.5	398.8	375.3	347.1	344.9
Total Assets	1,815.7	1,531.1	1,185.8	847.9	801.1	753.1	749.1
Total Current Liabilities	168.3	148.0	144.9	101.4	105.6	105.2	115.7
Long-Term Obligations	623.3	456.4	405.7	176.1	160.2	185.3	171.3
Net Stockholders' Equity	698.0	632.6	553.3	452.8	420.0	343.1	352.7
Net Working Capital	203.7	162.4	227.0	243.0	219.3	187.6	161.4
Year-end Shs. Outstg. (000)	21,070	20,991	21,188	20,896	22,200	22,022	24,978
STATISTICAL RECORD:							
Operating Profit Margin %	9.8	11.8	13.6	13.4	14.7	10.9	8.7
Net Profit Margin %	5.3	7.9	8.5	7.8	8.3	5.8	3.6
Return on Equity %	10.0	14.0	18.5	16.7	19.0	14.0	7.3
Return on Assets %	3.8	5.8	8.6	8.9	10.0	6.4	3.4
Debt/Total Assets %	34.3	29.8	34.2	20.8	20.0	24.6	22.9
Price Range	42.56-21.63	68.25-19.56	52.00-20.88	34.63-25.06	27.31-15.06	19.88-14.75	16.25-10.56
P/E Ratio	13.5-6.9	17.4-5.0	11.1-4.5	10.2-7.4	7.8-4.3	10.2-7.6	14.2-9.2
Average Yield %	0.9	0.7	0.8	0.7	0.9	0.6	0.7

Statistics are as originally reported. Adj. for stk. splits and dividends: 2-for-1, 2/97. Incl. the results of Chaparral Steel on a consolidated basis.

OFFICERS:
G. R. Heffeman, Vice-Chmn.
R. D. Rogers, Pres., C.E.O.
R. M. Fowler, Exec. V.P., C.F.O.
K. R. Allen, V.P., Treas.

INVESTOR CONTACT: Ken Allen, Investor Relations, (972) 647-6730

PRINCIPAL OFFICE: 1341 West Mockingbird Lane, Suite 700W, Dallas, TX 75247-6913

TELEPHONE NUMBER: (972) 647-6700
FAX: (972) 647-3878
WEB: www.txi.com

NO. OF EMPLOYEES: 4,500 (avg.)

SHAREHOLDERS: 3,326 (approx.)

ANNUAL MEETING: In Oct.

INCORPORATED: DE, Apr., 1951

INSTITUTIONAL HOLDINGS:
No. of Institutions: 119
Shares Held: 17,304,598
% Held: 83.3

INDUSTRY: Blast furnaces and steel mills (SIC: 3312)

TRANSFER AGENT(S): Mellon Investor Services, New York, NY

NYSE SYMBOL TXN
Rec. Pr. 34.12 (5/31/01)

TEXAS INSTRUMENTS INC.

YIELD 0.2%
P/E RATIO 19.5

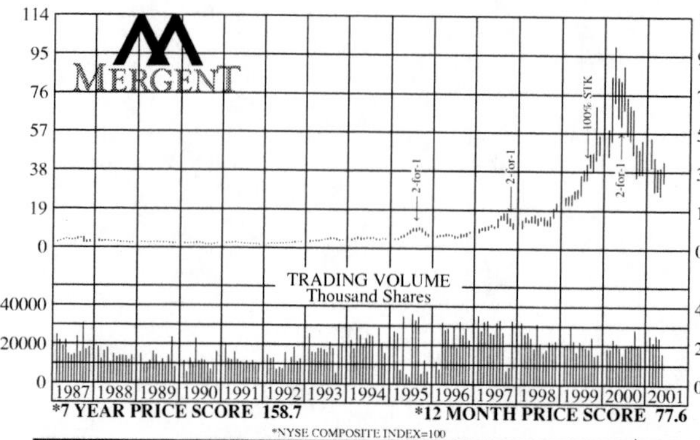

*7 YEAR PRICE SCORE 158.7 *12 MONTH PRICE SCORE 77.6

*NYSE COMPOSITE INDEX=100

INTERIM EARNINGS (Per Share):

Qtr.	Mar.	June	Sept.	Dec.
1996	0.11	0.05	d0.10	d0.03
1997	0.09	0.15	0.15	d0.17
1998	0.01	0.03	0.11	0.12
1999	0.15	0.20	0.24	0.26
2000	0.25	0.75	0.38	0.37

INTERIM DIVIDENDS (Per Share):

Amt.	Decl.	Ex.	Rec.	Pay.
2-for-1	4/20/00	5/23/00	5/01/00	5/22/00
0.021Q	7/20/00	7/27/00	7/31/00	8/21/00
0.021Q	10/19/00	10/27/00	10/31/00	11/20/00
0.021Q	1/18/01	1/29/01	1/31/01	2/12/01
0.021Q	4/18/01	4/26/01	4/30/01	5/21/01

Indicated div.: $0.09

CAPITALIZATION (12/31/00):

	($000)	(%)
Long-Term Debt	1,216,000	8.5
Deferred Income Tax	469,000	3.3
Common & Surplus	12,588,000	88.2
Total	14,273,000	100.0

RECENT DEVELOPMENTS: For the year ended 12/31/00, income from continuing operations amounted to $3.09 billion, before an accounting charge of $29.0 million, versus net income of $1.45 billion a year earlier. Earnings for 2000 and 1999 included non-recurring items that resulted in a net gain of $1.58 billion and a net charge of $217.0 million, respectively. Net revenues grew 21.7% to $11.88 billion from $9.76 billion the year before. Results for 1999 have been restated to reflect the acquisition of Burr Brown.

PROSPECTS: The Company initiated a cost reduction plan to limit the affect of reduced revenue on earnings. As part of its cost reduction plan, the Company is temporarily idling production at three manufacturing facilities, shortening workweeks at two other facilities and implementing cost controls for discretionary spending. Meanwhile, the Company lowered its capital spending plans for 2001 to $2.00 billion, a 30.0% reduction from last year's $2.80 billion.

BUSINESS

TEXAS INSTRUMENTS INC. is a global semiconductor company that designs and supplies digital signal processors and analog integrated circuits to the industrial, commercial and consumer markets. TXN also designs and manufactures other semiconductor products including standard logic devices, application-specific integrated circuits, reduced instruction-set computing microprocessors, microcontrollers and digital imaging devices. In addition to the semiconductor business, TXN operates two other segments, Sensors & Controls and Educational & Productivity Solutions (E&PS). Sensors & Controls sells electrical and electronic controls, sensors and radio-frequency identification systems to commercial and industrial markets. E&PS supplies educational and graphing calculators.

REVENUES

(12/31/00)	($000)	(%)
Semiconductor	10,284,000	86.6
Sensors & Controls	1,030,000	8.7
Educational & Productivity	446,000	3.8
Corporate Activities	3,000	0.0
Divested Activities	112,000	0.9
Total	11,875,000	100.0

ANNUAL FINANCIAL DATA

	12/31/00	12/31/99	12/31/98	12/31/97	12/31/96	12/31/95	12/31/94
Earnings Per Share	[5] **1.80**	[4] **0.84**	**0.26**	[3] **0.19**	[2] **d0.03**	[1] **0.70**	**0.45**
Cash Flow Per Share	**2.49**	**1.47**	**0.92**	**0.83**	**0.51**	**1.16**	**0.86**
Tang. Book Val. Per Share	**6.71**	**5.38**	**4.17**	**3.80**	**2.69**	**2.71**	**2.05**
Dividends Per Share	**0.09**	**0.09**	**0.09**	**0.09**	**0.09**	**0.07**	**0.05**
Dividend Payout %	**4.7**	**10.1**	**33.3**	**44.7**	**...**	**10.5**	**11.8**
INCOME STATEMENT (IN MILLIONS):							
Total Revenues	11,875.0	9,468.0	8,460.0	9,750.0	9,940.0	13,128.0	10,315.0
Costs & Expenses	8,160.0	6,717.0	6,917.0	8,026.0	9,062.0	10,778.0	8,567.0
Depreciation & Amort.	1,376.0	1,055.0	1,144.0	1,109.0	904.0	756.0	665.0
Operating Income	2,339.0	1,696.0	399.0	615.0	d26.0	1,594.0	1,083.0
Net Interest Inc./(Exp.)	d75.0	d75.0	16.0	d42.0	d84.0	d9.0	d39.0
Income Before Income Taxes	4,578.0	2,019.0	617.0	713.0	d23.0	1,619.0	1,042.0
Income Taxes	1,491.0	613.0	210.0	411.0	23.0	531.0	351.0
Net Income	[5] 3,087.0	[4] 1,406.0	332.0	[3] 208.0	[2] d119.0	[1] 1,040.0	646.0
Cash Flow	4,463.0	2,461.0	1,476.0	1,317.0	785.0	1,796.0	1,311.0
Average Shs. Outstg. (000)	1,791,630	1,673,520	1,604,000	1,590,908	1,536,936	1,549,048	1,526,840
BALANCE SHEET (IN MILLIONS):							
Cash & Cash Equivalents	4,003.0	2,662.0	2,249.0	3,020.0	978.0	1,553.0	1,290.0
Total Current Assets	8,115.0	6,055.0	4,846.0	6,103.0	4,454.0	5,518.0	4,017.0
Net Property	5,447.0	3,835.0	3,373.0	4,180.0	4,162.0	3,187.0	2,568.0
Total Assets	17,720.0	15,028.0	11,250.0	10,849.0	9,360.0	9,215.0	6,989.0
Total Current Liabilities	2,813.0	2,628.0	2,196.0	2,496.0	2,486.0	3,188.0	2,199.0
Long-Term Obligations	1,216.0	1,097.0	1,027.0	1,286.0	1,697.0	804.0	808.0
Net Stockholders' Equity	12,588.0	9,255.0	6,527.0	5,914.0	4,097.0	4,095.0	3,039.0
Net Working Capital	5,302.0	3,427.0	2,650.0	3,607.0	1,968.0	2,330.0	1,818.0
Year-end Shs. Outstg. (000)	1,732,052	1,625,783	1,564,000	1,557,996	1,522,024	1,512,000	1,482,928
STATISTICAL RECORD:							
Operating Profit Margin %	19.7	17.9	4.7	6.3	...	12.1	10.5
Net Profit Margin %	26.0	14.9	3.9	2.1	...	7.9	6.3
Return on Equity %	24.5	15.2	5.1	3.5	...	25.4	21.3
Return on Assets %	17.4	9.4	3.0	1.9	...	11.3	9.2
Debt/Total Assets %	6.9	7.3	9.1	11.9	18.1	8.7	11.6
Price Range	99.78-35.00	70.13-21.50	22.61-10.06	17.81-7.77	8.55-5.06	10.47-4.30	5.59-3.81
P/E Ratio	55.4-19.4	83.5-25.6	88.6-39.4	93.7-40.9	...	14.9-6.1	12.3-8.4
Average Yield %	0.1	0.2	0.5	0.7	1.2	1.0	1.1

Statistics are as originally reported. Adj. for stk. splits: 2-for-1, 5/00, 8/99, 11/97, 8/95. [1] Incl. restr. chgs. $132.0 mil. [2] Incl. $294.0 mil. chg. for acq. R&D, sev. costs & writdwns & bef. disc. ops. $109.0 mil. [3] Bef. disc. ops. gain $52.0 mil., gain $1.47 bil. fr. sale of ops. & $22.0 mil. chg. on exting. debt. [4] Incl. p-tax spec. chgs. $127.0 mil. & p-tax invest. gains $87.0 mil. [5] Bef. acctg. chg. of $29.0 mil.; incl. aft-tax non-recur. gain of $1.58 bil.

OFFICERS:
T. J. Engibous, Chmn., Pres., C.E.O.
W. A. Aylesworth, Sr. V.P., C.F.O., Treas.
J. F. Hubach, Sr. V.P., Gen. Couns.

INVESTOR CONTACT: Investor Relations, (972) 995-3773

PRINCIPAL OFFICE: 12500 TI Boulevard, P.O. Box 660199, Dallas, TX 75243-4136

TELEPHONE NUMBER: (972) 995-3773
FAX: (972) 995-4360
WEB: www.ti.com

NO. OF EMPLOYEES: 38,197

SHAREHOLDERS: 30,043

ANNUAL MEETING: In Apr.

INCORPORATED: DE, Dec., 1938

INSTITUTIONAL HOLDINGS:
No. of Institutions: 822
Shares Held: 1,070,806,453
% Held: 61.7

INDUSTRY: Semiconductors and related devices (SIC: 3674)

TRANSFER AGENT(S): Computershare Investor Services, LLC, Chicago, IL

NYSE SYMBOL TXT
Rec. Pr. 53.02 (4/30/01)

TEXTRON INC.

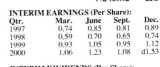

YIELD 2.5%
P/E RATIO 28.8

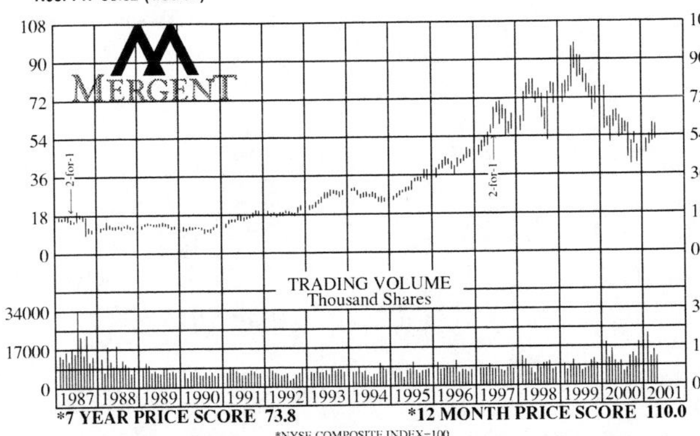

*7 YEAR PRICE SCORE 73.8 *12 MONTH PRICE SCORE 110.0

*NYSE COMPOSITE INDEX=100

INTERIM EARNINGS (Per Share):

Qtr.	Mar.	June	Sept.	Dec.
1997	0.74	0.85	0.81	0.89
1998	0.59	0.70	0.65	0.74
1999	0.93	1.05	0.95	1.12
2000	1.06	1.23	1.08	d1.53

INTERIM DIVIDENDS (Per Share):

Amt.	Decl.	Ex.	Rec.	Pay.
0.325Q	7/26/00	9/13/00	9/15/00	10/01/00
0.325Q	10/25/00	12/13/00	12/15/00	1/01/01
0.325Q	2/28/01	3/07/01	3/09/01	4/01/01
0.325Q	4/25/01	6/13/01	6/15/01	7/01/01

Indicated div.: $1.30 (Div. Reinv. Plan)

CAPITALIZATION (12/30/00):

	($000)	(%)
Long-Term Debt	6,136,000	56.0
Deferred Income Tax	315,000	2.9
Redeemable Pfd. Stock	512,000	4.7
Preferred Stock	12,000	0.1
Common & Surplus	3,982,000	36.3
Total	10,957,000	100.0

RECENT DEVELOPMENTS: For the year ended 12/30/00, TXT reported income of $277.0 million, before an accounting charge of $59.0 million, versus income of $623.0 million, before an extraordinary charge of $43.0 million, in 1999. Earnings for 2000 and 1999 included various pre-tax items that resulted in a charge of $483.0 million and a gain of $1.0 million, respectively. Results for 1999 excluded a gain of $1.65 billion from discontinued operations. Revenues grew 10.4% to $13.09 billion.

PROSPECTS: In 2001, TXT expects earnings to increase approximately 5.0%, excluding restructuring charges, compared with $4.65 per share reported in 2000. The after-tax cost of the restructuring plan is expected to be in the range of $85.0 million to $100.0 million. Annualized savings are expected to be between $100.0 million and $120.0 million, beginning in 2002, of which $50.0 million to $70.0 million should be realized in 2001.

BUSINESS

TEXTRON, INC. is a global, multi-industry company with manufacturing facilities in 30 countries. The Company operates in five industries: Aircraft, which includes commercial and military helicopters, tiltrotor aircraft, and business jets; Automotive, which includes interior and exterior trim, fuel systems and functional components; Industrial Products, which includes fluid and power systems, golf, turf-care and specialty products, light construction equipment, and electrical and video tools; Fastening Systems, which includes fasteners, fastening systems, engineered assemblies and installation tools; and Finance, which provides diversified commercial lending. Among the Company's products are Cessna Aircraft, Bell Helicopter, E-Z-GO golf cars, and Jacobsen and Ransomes turf-care equipment.

BUSINESS LINE ANALYSIS

(12/30/2000)	Rev (%)	Inc (%)
Aircraft	37.8	37.7
Automotive	20.3	14.6
Fastening Systems	14.7	10.0
Industrial Products	21.7	22.5
Finance	5.5	15.2
Total	100.0	100.0

ANNUAL FINANCIAL DATA

	12/30/00	1/1/00	1/2/99	⑤ 1/3/98	12/28/96	12/31/95	12/31/94
Earnings Per Share	**②⑦ 1.90**	**①③ 4.05**	**⑥ 2.68**	**3.29**	**③ 2.80**	**2.76**	**④ 2.40**
Cash Flow Per Share	**5.28**	**6.91**	**4.86**	**5.84**	**5.05**	**5.14**	**4.62**
Tang. Book Val. Per Share	**11.65**	**10.60**	**5.59**	**8.97**	**9.40**	**10.53**	**7.96**
Dividends Per Share	**1.30**	**1.26**	**1.10**	**0.97**	**0.85**	**0.76**	**0.68**
Dividend Payout %	**68.4**	**31.1**	**41.2**	**29.5**	**30.5**	**27.6**	**28.3**
INCOME STATEMENT (IN MILLIONS):							
Total Revenues	13,090.0	11,579.0	9,683.0	10,544.0	9,274.0	9,973.0	9,683.0
Costs & Expenses	11,016.0	9,877.0	8,268.0	8,435.0	7,329.0	7,932.0	7,866.0
Depreciation & Amort.	494.0	440.0	361.0	435.0	387.0	415.0	398.0
Operating Income	1,580.0	1,262.0	1,054.0	1,674.0	1,558.0	1,626.0	1,419.0
Net Interest Inc./(Exp.)	d486.0	d233.0	d301.0	d726.0	d731.0	d813.0	d665.0
Income Before Income Taxes	611.0	1,030.0	763.0	948.0	827.0	813.0	754.0
Income Taxes	308.0	381.0	294.0	364.0	322.0	321.0	308.0
Net Income	②⑦ 277.0	①③ 623.0	⑥ 443.0	558.0	③ 482.0	479.0	④ 433.0
Cash Flow	771.0	1,062.0	803.0	992.0	868.0	893.0	830.0
Average Shs. Outstg. (000)	146,150	153,754	165,374	170,000	172,000	174,000	180,000
BALANCE SHEET (IN MILLIONS):							
Cash & Cash Equivalents	289.0	209.0	53.0	931.0	867.0	6,025.0	5,343.0
Total Current Assets	3,921.0	3,752.0	4,377.0	13,426.0	13,567.0	17,448.0	15,839.0
Net Property	2,605.0	2,513.0	2,185.0	1,860.0	1,539.0	1,408.0	1,253.0
Total Assets	16,407.0	16,422.0	13,721.0	18,610.0	18,235.0	23,172.0	20,925.0
Total Current Liabilities	3,263.0	3,256.0	3,919.0	3,604.0	3,406.0	3,215.0	3,043.0
Long-Term Obligations	6,136.0	1,079.0	3,709.0	10,496.0	10,346.0	10,249.0	9,364.0
Net Stockholders' Equity	3,994.0	4,377.0	2,997.0	3,228.0	3,183.0	3,412.0	2,882.0
Net Working Capital	658.0	496.0	458.0	9,822.0	10,161.0	14,233.0	12,796.0
Year-end Shs. Outstg. (000)	140,933	147,002	154,742	163,000	166,000	170,000	170,000
STATISTICAL RECORD:							
Operating Profit Margin %	12.1	10.9	10.9	15.9	16.8	16.3	14.7
Net Profit Margin %	2.1	5.4	4.6	5.3	5.2	4.8	4.5
Return on Equity %	6.9	14.2	14.8	17.3	15.1	14.0	15.0
Return on Assets %	1.7	3.8	3.2	3.0	2.6	2.1	2.1
Debt/Total Assets %	37.4	6.6	27.0	56.4	56.7	44.2	44.8
Price Range	77.50-40.69	98.00-65.88	80.94-52.06	70.75-45.00	48.88-34.56	38.69-24.31	30.31-23.25
P/E Ratio	40.8-21.4	24.2-16.3	30.2-19.4	21.5-13.7	17.5-12.3	14.0-8.8	12.6-9.7
Average Yield %	2.2	1.5	1.7	1.7	2.0	2.4	2.5

Statistics are as originally reported. Adj. for 2-for-1 stk. split, 6/97. ① Bef. extraord. chrg. of $43.0 mill. ② Bef. acctg. chrg. of $59.0 mill., 12/00. ③ Bef. disc. opers. gain $1.65 bill., 4/99; loss $229.0 mill., 12/96. ④ Incl. a pre-tax net chrg. of $483.0 mill., 12/00; $9.0 mill.,12/94. ⑤ Incl. fin. & insur. subs. ⑥ Incl. special pre-tax charges of $87.0 mill. & a gain of $97.0 mill. fr. the sale of a div. ⑦ Incl. nonrecurr. chrg. of $483.0 mill.

OFFICERS:
L. B. Campbell, Chmn., C.E.O.
J. A. Janitz, Pres., C.O.O.

INVESTOR CONTACT: Doug Wilburne, Investor Relations, (401) 457-2353

PRINCIPAL OFFICE: 40 Westminster Street, Providence, RI 02903

TELEPHONE NUMBER: (401) 421-2800
FAX: (401) 421-2878
WEB: www.textron.com

NO. OF EMPLOYEES: 71,000 (approx.)

SHAREHOLDERS: 21,000 (approx.)

ANNUAL MEETING: In April

INCORPORATED: DE, July, 1967

INSTITUTIONAL HOLDINGS:
No. of Institutions: 337
Shares Held: 85,639,747
% Held: 60.7

INDUSTRY: Aircraft (SIC: 3721)

TRANSFER AGENT(S): First Chicago Trust Company of New York, Jersey City, NJ

ASE SYMBOL TMO
Rec. Pr. 26.36 (4/30/01)

THERMO ELECTRON CORPORATION

YIELD ...
P/E RATIO 73.2

TRADING VOLUME
Thousand Shares

*7 YEAR PRICE SCORE 67.0 *12 MONTH PRICE SCORE 102.4
*NYSE COMPOSITE INDEX=100

INTERIM EARNINGS (Per Share):

Qtr.	Mar.	June	Sept.	Dec.
1996	0.31	0.32	0.36	0.36
1997	0.35	0.37	0.41	0.40
1998	0.41	0.37	0.11	0.23
1999	0.17	d1.49	0.22	0.13
2000	0.09	0.13	0.04	0.10

INTERIM DIVIDENDS (Per Share):

Amt.	Decl.	Ex.	Rec.	Pay.

No dividends paid.

CAPITALIZATION (12/30/00):

	($000)	(%)
Long-Term Debt	1,528,483	37.3
Deferred Income Tax	10,691	0.3
Minority Interest	24,737	0.6
Common & Surplus	2,533,976	61.8
Total	4,097,887	100.0

RECENT DEVELOPMENTS: For the year ended 12/30/00, TMO posted income from continuing operations of $62.0 million versus $37.3 million a year earlier. Results for 2000 included restructuring and other unusual gains of $67.9 million, while results for 1999 included non-recurring charges of $37.3 million. Revenues fell to $2.28 billion from $2.29 billion in 1999. Separately, on 2/26/01, TMO announced it has acquired substantially all of the assets of Galactic Industries Corporation.

PROSPECTS: TMO's reorganization plan continues to move forward. In January 2001, TMO completed the sale of its Killam Group Inc. and Coleman Research businesses. On 2/13/01, TMO signed a definitive agreement to sell the assets of its wholly-owned Thermo Ecotek power-generation business to AES Corporation for about $195.0 million. Lastly, on 2/14/01, TMO announced that its Thermo Cardiosystems Inc. subsidiary completed its merger with Thoratec Corporation.

BUSINESS

THERMO ELECTRON CORPORATION provides technology-based instruments, components, and systems that offer solutions for markets ranging from life sciences to telecommunications to food, drug, and beverage production. The Company reports its business in three segments: Life Sciences develops products for the biotechnology and pharmaceutical markets, and clinical laboratory and healthcare industries. Optical Technologies Products are used in markets such as the scientific instrument, semiconductor, and telecommunications industries, to fabricate, analyze, and implement advanced materials. Measurement and Control provides a range of real-time, on-line sensors, monitors, and control systems for manufacturers.

REVENUES

(12/30/2000)	($000)	(%)
Life Sciences	780,020	33.9
Optical Technologies	480,014	20.9
Measurement & Control	1,037,331	45.2
Total	2,297,365	100.0

ANNUAL FINANCIAL DATA

	12/30/00	1/1/00	1/2/99	1/3/98	12/28/96	12/30/95	12/31/94
Earnings Per Share	**4 0.36**	**3 d0.11**	**1 1.07**	**2 1.41**	**2 1.35**	**1.10**	**0.93**
Cash Flow Per Share	**0.94**	**0.63**	**1.90**	**2.13**	**2.16**	**1.77**	**1.50**
Tang. Book Val. Per Share	**6.34**	**4.76**	**2.10**	**1.92**	**4.48**	**3.25**	**3.62**
Dividends Per Share	...	...	...	...	**0.01**	...	...
Dividend Payout %	...	...	...	...	**0.4**	...	...
INCOME STATEMENT (IN MILLIONS):							
Total Revenues	2,280.5	2,471.2	3,867.6	3,558.3	2,932.6	2,270.3	1,585.3
Costs & Expenses	1,917.0	2,258.5	3,374.0	3,016.8	2,570.9	1,960.1	1,343.9
Depreciation & Amort.	97.5	113.6	162.3	135.7	115.2	85.0	62.3
Operating Income	266.0	99.0	331.3	405.8	246.5	225.2	179.1
Net Interest Inc./(Exp.)	...	...	...	...	...	d15.7	d16.4
Income Before Income Taxes	184.8	37.5	391.5	488.5	374.6	298.8	203.6
Income Taxes	112.2	33.1	170.7	174.7	110.8	98.7	69.2
Equity Earnings/Minority Int.	d10.6	d19.0	d44.0	d74.4	d72.9	d60.7	d35.0
Net Income	4 62.0	3 d14.6	1 176.8	2 239.3	2 190.8	139.6	103.4
Cash Flow	159.5	99.1	339.1	375.1	306.0	224.6	165.7
Average Shs. Outstg. (000)	170,519	157,987	178,449	176,082	141,525	126,626	110,802
BALANCE SHEET (IN MILLIONS):							
Cash & Cash Equivalents	1,026.9	837.3	1,547.3	1,522.7	1,846.3	1,055.8	997.7
Total Current Assets	2,465.5	2,517.2	3,301.3	3,094.2	3,131.8	2,021.2	1,682.7
Net Property	285.9	510.6	833.0	789.0	704.4	712.8	614.0
Total Assets	4,863.0	5,181.8	6,331.6	5,795.9	5,141.2	3,744.9	3,019.9
Total Current Liabilities	728.6	1,066.3	1,138.3	1,092.2	913.2	714.8	536.5
Long-Term Obligations	1,528.5	1,566.0	2,025.5	1,742.9	1,550.3	1,116.0	1,049.8
Net Stockholders' Equity	2,534.0	2,014.5	2,248.1	1,997.9	1,754.4	1,299.8	990.3
Net Working Capital	1,737.0	1,450.9	2,163.0	2,002.0	2,218.6	1,306.4	1,146.2
Year-end Shs. Outstg. (000)	182,169	165,477	158,493	159,111	149,981	131,778	114,722
STATISTICAL RECORD:							
Operating Profit Margin %	11.7	4.0	8.6	11.4	8.4	9.9	11.3
Net Profit Margin %	2.7	...	4.6	6.7	6.5	6.1	6.5
Return on Equity %	2.4	...	7.9	12.0	10.9	10.7	10.4
Return on Assets %	1.3	...	2.8	4.1	3.7	3.7	3.4
Debt/Total Assets %	31.4	30.2	32.0	30.1	30.2	29.8	34.8
Price Range	31.24-14.00	20.25-12.50	44.25-13.56	44.00-28.38	44.38-29.75	34.67-15.94	21.28-16.00
P/E Ratio	86.8-38.9	...	41.4-12.7	31.2-20.1	32.9-22.0	31.5-14.5	22.8-17.1

Statistics are as originally reported. Adj. for all stk. splits thru 6/96 1 Incl. non-recurr. chrgs. of $23.6 mill.; bef. extraord. credit of $5.1 mill. 2 Incl. non-recurr. credit, 12/31/97, $78.8 mill.; credit 12/31/96, $2.8 mill. 3 Incl. restr. & non-recurr. chrgs. of $149.6 mill; bef. extraord. credit of $1.5 mill. & loss fr. discont. opers. of $161.5 mill. 4 Incl. restr. & oth. unusual gains of $67.9 mill.; bef. loss fr. disc. ops. of $85.8 mill. & extraord. gain of $532,000.

OFFICERS:
R. F. Syron, Chmn., C.E.O.
M. E. Dekkers, Pres., C.O.O.
T. Melas-Kyriazi, V.P., C.F.O.

INVESTOR CONTACT: T. Melas-Kyriazi, V.P., C.F.O., (781) 622-1111

PRINCIPAL OFFICE: 81 Wyman St., P.O. Box 9046, Waltham, MA 02454-9046

TELEPHONE NUMBER: (781) 622-1000
FAX: (781) 933-4476
WEB: www.thermo.com
NO. OF EMPLOYEES: 13,000 (approx.)
SHAREHOLDERS: 13,470 (record)
ANNUAL MEETING: In May
INCORPORATED: MA, 1956; reincorp., DE, Oct., 1960

INSTITUTIONAL HOLDINGS:
No. of Institutions: 298
Shares Held: 141,779,845
% Held: 77.6

INDUSTRY: Measuring & controlling devices, nec (SIC: 3829)

TRANSFER AGENT(S): BankBoston N.A., Boston, MA

NYSE SYMBOL TNB
Rec. Pr. 20.67 (4/30/01)

THOMAS & BETTS CORPORATION

YIELD 5.4%
P/E RATIO . . .

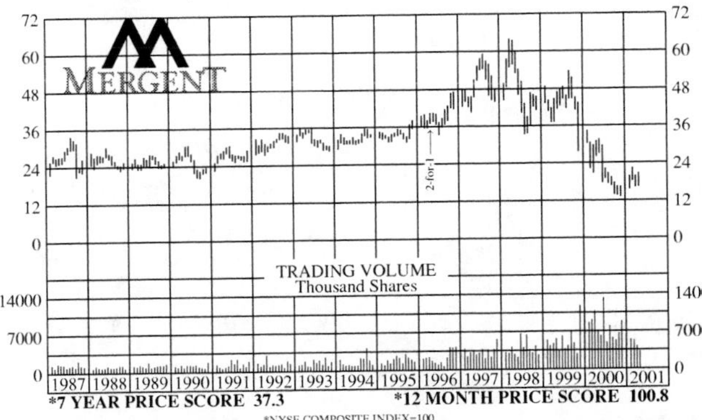

*7 YEAR PRICE SCORE 37.3 *12 MONTH PRICE SCORE 100.8

*NYSE COMPOSITE INDEX=100

INTERIM EARNINGS (Per Share):

Qtr.	Mar.	June	Sept.	Dec.
1997	0.55	0.70	0.73	0.83
1998	0.64	0.73	0.66	0.81
1999	0.67	0.76	0.82	0.40
2000	0.62	d2.87	d0.33	d1.20

INTERIM DIVIDENDS (Per Share):

Amt.	Decl.	Ex.	Rec.	Pay.
0.28Q	. . .	6/13/00	6/15/00	7/03/00
0.28Q	9/06/00	9/14/00	9/18/00	10/02/00
0.28Q	12/05/00	12/14/00	12/18/00	1/02/01
0.28Q	2/07/01	3/01/01	3/05/01	4/02/01
0.28Q	5/02/01	6/13/01	6/15/01	7/02/01

Indicated div.: $1.12 (Div. Reinv. Plan)

CAPITALIZATION (12/31/00):

	($000)	(%)
Long-Term Debt	669,983	42.2
Deferred Income Tax	12,520	0.8
Common & Surplus	905,910	57.0
Total	1,588,413	100.0

RECENT DEVELOPMENTS: For the year ended 12/31/00, TNB reported a net loss from continuing operations of $193.4 million versus income from continuing operations of $97.6 million in 1999. Results included pre-tax restructuring credits of $2.8 million and $1.5 million in 2000 and 1999, respectively. Results in 2000 also included a one-time pre-tax charge of $33.4 million from impairment of long-lived assets. Net sales fell 6.3% to $1.76 billion.

PROSPECTS: The Company is continuing to implement initiatives focused on lowering costs and improving efficiencies. New freight policies and procedures, expected to be in place by the second quarter of 2001, should begin to positively affect operating performance during the second half of 2001. The Company is consolidating shipments to customers in several key regional markets in an effort to reduce costs.

BUSINESS

THOMAS & BETTS CORPORATION is a global manufacturer of electrical and electronic connectors, components and systems. The electrical segment designs, manufactures and markets thousands of electrical connectors and components to the construction, maintenance and repair markets. The communications segment designs, manufactures and markets electromechanical components, subsystems and accessories used in the maintenance, construction and repair of cable television, telecommunication and data communications networks. Other products include heating products, steel poles and towers. On 7/2/00, the Company sold its electronic original equipment manufacturer business to Tyco International Ltd.

REVENUES

(12/31/2000)	($000)	(%)
Electrical	1,348,833	76.8
Communications	178,439	10.2
All Other	228,811	13.0
Total	1,756,083	100.0

ANNUAL FINANCIAL DATA

	12/31/00	1/2/00	1/3/99	12/28/97	12/29/96	12/31/95	1/1/95
Earnings Per Share	[4] d3.33	[3] 2.56	[3] 1.54	2.81	[2] 1.13	[1] 2.02	0.05
Cash Flow Per Share	d1.70	4.25	3.21	4.54	2.85	3.39	1.44
Tang. Book Val. Per Share	6.37	8.33	6.93	8.71	5.98	6.90	5.68
Dividends Per Share	1.12	1.12	1.12	1.12	1.12	1.12	1.12
Dividend Payout %	. . .	43.7	72.7	39.9	99.1	55.4	N.M.
INCOME STATEMENT (IN MILLIONS):							
Total Revenues	1,756.1	2,522.0	2,230.4	2,114.7	1,985.1	1,236.8	1,076.2
Costs & Expenses	1,909.8	2,232.4	1,980.5	1,760.3	1,702.1	1,044.7	998.1
Depreciation & Amort.	94.6	98.0	95.3	95.3	91.6	54.7	53.5
Operating Income	d248.4	191.6	154.5	259.1	130.4	137.5	24.6
Net Interest Inc./(Exp.)	d47.9	d61.0	d45.8	. . .	. . .	. . .	. . .
Income Before Income Taxes	d272.2	159.7	124.9	224.4	90.9	117.2	0.5
Income Taxes	cr78.8	11.4	37.4	69.6	31.0	36.3	cr1.4
Equity Earnings/Minority Int.	15.0	23.8	26.2	. . .	. . .	. . .	. . .
Net Income	[4] d193.4	[3] 148.3	[3] 87.5	154.9	[2] 59.9	[1] 80.9	1.9
Cash Flow	d98.8	246.4	182.8	250.2	151.4	135.6	55.4
Average Shs. Outstg. (000)	57,950	57,912	56,990	55,090	53,059	39,956	38,608
BALANCE SHEET (IN MILLIONS):							
Cash & Cash Equivalents	218.7	84.8	106.5	96.3	162.3	105.0	122.2
Total Current Assets	968.6	1,163.9	1,058.4	796.2	957.1	527.6	534.0
Net Property	425.5	666.5	631.0	569.8	539.9	338.2	275.5
Total Assets	2,087.8	2,652.7	2,499.6	2,038.7	2,131.2	1,259.4	1,208.2
Total Current Liabilities	419.3	513.4	587.5	439.8	491.9	282.9	280.3
Long-Term Obligations	670.0	935.7	791.0	502.8	645.1	327.8	319.5
Net Stockholders' Equity	905.9	1,094.1	1,015.1	977.4	868.4	600.6	553.0
Net Working Capital	549.3	650.5	470.9	356.3	465.2	244.7	253.6
Year-end Shs. Outstg. (000)	57,821	57,934	56,774	55,006	53,303	40,076	39,210
STATISTICAL RECORD:							
Operating Profit Margin %	. . .	7.6	6.9	12.3	6.6	11.1	2.3
Net Profit Margin %	. . .	5.9	3.9	7.3	3.0	6.5	0.2
Return on Equity %	. . .	13.6	8.6	15.8	6.9	13.5	0.3
Return on Assets %	. . .	5.6	3.5	7.6	2.8	6.4	0.2
Debt/Total Assets %	32.1	35.3	31.6	24.7	30.3	26.0	26.4
Price Range	34.38-13.06	53.69-27.56	64.00-33.31	59.25-40.38	47.25-33.25	38.13-31.00	35.63-29.06
P/E Ratio	. . .	21.0-10.8	41.6-21.6	21.1-14.4	41.8-29.4	18.9-15.3	711.1-580.1
Average Yield %	4.7	2.8	2.3	2.2	2.8	3.2	3.5

Statistics are as originally reported. Adj. for 2-for-1 stk. split, 4/96. [1] Bef. gain of $65.9 mill. fr. disc. opers.; Incl. restruct. chrg. $79.0 mill. [2] Incl. pre-tax chgs. totaling $97.1 mill. [3] Incl. pre-tax rec. for restruct. opers. of $11.6 mill., 1999; $62.1 mill, 1998. [4] Bef. net gain of $148.8 mill. ($2.56/sh) fr. disc. oper.; Incl. nonrecurr. chrgs. of $36.2 mill.

OFFICERS:
T. K. Dunnigan, Chmn., C.E.O.
J. P. Murphy, Sr. V.P., C.F.O.
J. Kronenberg, V.P., Gen. Couns., Sec.

INVESTOR CONTACT: Tricia Bergeren, Inv. Rel., (901) 252-8266

PRINCIPAL OFFICE: 8155 T & B Boulevard, Memphis, TN 38125

TELEPHONE NUMBER: (901) 252-8000
FAX: (901) 685-1988
WEB: www.tnb.com

NO. OF EMPLOYEES: 14,000 (approx.)

SHAREHOLDERS: 3,924

ANNUAL MEETING: In May

INCORPORATED: NJ, 1917; reincorp., TN, May, 1996

INSTITUTIONAL HOLDINGS:
No. of Institutions: 179
Shares Held: 46,533,829
% Held: 80.0

INDUSTRY: Current-carrying wiring devices (SIC: 3643)

TRANSFER AGENT(S): First Chicago Trust Company, Jersey City, NJ

NYSE SYMBOL TII
Rec. Pr. 27.25 (5/31/01)

THOMAS INDUSTRIES INC.

YIELD 1.2%
P/E RATIO 14.3

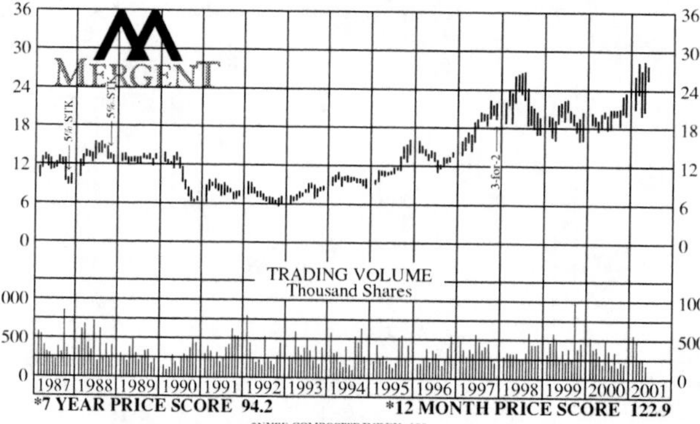

*7 YEAR PRICE SCORE 94.2 *12 MONTH PRICE SCORE 122.9

*NYSE COMPOSITE INDEX=100

INTERIM EARNINGS (Per Share):

Qtr.	March	June	Sept.	Dec.
1997	0.25	0.39	0.43	0.31
1998	0.32	0.42	0.43	0.33
1999	0.36	0.45	0.42	0.39
2000	0.45	0.53	0.48	0.45

INTERIM DIVIDENDS (Per Share):

Amt.	Decl.	Ex.	Rec.	Pay.
0.075Q	4/20/00	5/31/00	6/02/00	7/01/00
0.075Q	7/20/00	8/30/00	9/01/00	10/01/00
0.075Q	10/19/00	11/29/00	12/01/00	1/01/01
0.085Q	2/07/01	2/28/01	3/02/01	4/01/01
0.085Q	4/19/01	5/30/01	6/01/01	7/01/01

Indicated div.: $0.34 (Div. Reinv. Plan)

CAPITALIZATION (12/31/00):

	($000)	(%)
Long-Term Debt	40,727	15.2
Deferred Income Tax	9,415	3.5
Common & Surplus	217,357	81.3
Total	267,499	100.0

RECENT DEVELOPMENTS: For the year ended 12/31/00, net income advanced 15.0% to $30.1 million compared with $26.2 million in 1999. Results for 2000 included non-recurring, after-tax gains of $1.3 million. Net sales were $188.8 million, up 6.2% from $177.8 million a year earlier. Operating income for the pump and compressor segment increased 6.8% to $31.6 million, while operating income for the lighting segment rose 6.5% to $24.6 million.

PROSPECTS: TII's European Group plans to expand its product line to include miniature liquid pumps. GTG's sales should be bolstered in 2001 as GTG has become a supplier to Affiliated Distributors, the largest distributor marketing association of electrical equipment in North America. Separately, sales to customers for respiratory applications were flat in 2000. However, TII anticipates a resumption of growth in 2001.

BUSINESS

THOMAS INDUSTRIES INC. is involved in two businesses: compressors and vacuum pumps, and lighting. The Company designs, manufactures and sells compressors and vacuum pumps for use in global original equipment manufacturing applications as well as pneumatic construction equipment, leakage detection systems and laboratory equipment. Manufacturing facilities are located in North America and Europe, with additional sales and distribution operations located in Asia. The Company operates its lighting business through its 32.0% interest, as of 12/31/00, in the Genlyte Thomas Group LLC (GTG). GTG, which was formed in 1998, designs, manufactures, markets and sells lighting products principally in North America for consumer, commercial, industrial and outdoor applications.

ANNUAL FINANCIAL DATA

	12/31/00	12/31/99	12/31/98	12/31/97	12/31/96	12/31/95	12/31/94
Earnings Per Share	**[2] 1.91**	**1.62**	**1.50**	**1.38**	**1.09**	**0.83**	**[1] 0.70**
Cash Flow Per Share	**2.41**	**2.09**	**1.93**	**2.37**	**2.07**	**1.80**	**1.73**
Tang. Book Val. Per Share	**13.77**	**12.61**	**11.59**	**7.38**	**6.27**	**5.39**	**4.71**
Dividends Per Share	**0.30**	**0.30**	**0.30**	**0.27**	**0.27**	**0.27**	**0.27**
Dividend Payout %	**15.7**	**18.5**	**20.0**	**19.3**	**24.5**	**32.0**	**38.1**
INCOME STATEMENT (IN THOUSANDS):							
Total Revenues	188,824	176,382	177,220	547,702	510,111	490,573	456,565
Costs & Expenses	156,998	146,575	145,947	490,197	460,271	446,032	417,905
Depreciation & Amort.	7,907	7,671	7,176	16,049	15,682	14,803	15,524
Operating Income	48,494	45,283	44,420	41,456	34,158	29,738	23,136
Net Interest Inc./(Exp.)	d3,995	d4,601	d6,199	d6,480	d7,333	d8,242	d9,225
Income Before Income Taxes	48,298	42,209	39,406	35,644	27,688	21,053	18,198
Income Taxes	18,213	16,059	14,896	13,174	10,272	8,278	7,656
Equity Earnings/Minority Int.	24,575	23,147	20,323	...	...	...	...
Net Income	[2] 30,085	26,150	24,510	22,470	17,416	12,775	[1] 10,542
Cash Flow	37,992	33,821	31,686	38,519	33,098	27,578	26,066
Average Shs. Outstg.	15,777	16,182	16,383	16,272	16,022	15,350	15,090
BALANCE SHEET (IN THOUSANDS):							
Cash & Cash Equivalents	13,941	16,487	18,205	17,352	18,826	18,305	5,050
Total Current Assets	63,817	63,111	64,243	176,611	170,364	164,739	155,355
Net Property	39,521	36,152	34,001	80,197	77,795	75,710	75,962
Total Assets	308,120	293,976	282,359	327,639	319,650	313,533	305,071
Total Current Liabilities	33,185	33,373	34,403	84,353	84,526	83,902	77,797
Long-Term Obligations	40,727	40,513	48,298	55,006	62,632	70,791	79,693
Net Stockholders' Equity	217,357	209,482	190,687	173,405	157,702	143,177	133,766
Net Working Capital	30,632	29,738	29,840	92,258	85,838	80,837	77,558
Year-end Shs. Outstg.	15,051	15,759	15,742	15,859	15,789	15,179	15,122
STATISTICAL RECORD:							
Operating Profit Margin %	25.7	25.7	25.1	7.6	6.7	6.1	5.1
Net Profit Margin %	15.9	14.8	13.8	4.1	3.4	2.6	2.3
Return on Equity %	13.8	12.5	12.9	13.0	11.0	8.9	7.9
Return on Assets %	9.8	8.9	8.7	6.9	5.4	4.1	3.5
Debt/Total Assets %	13.2	13.8	17.1	16.8	19.6	22.6	26.1
Price Range	23.56-17.44	22.44-15.94	26.81-16.94	22.33-13.67	15.92-11.00	16.08-9.08	11.00-8.50
P/E Ratio	12.3-9.1	13.8-9.8	17.9-11.3	16.2-9.9	14.6-10.1	19.3-10.9	15.7-12.1
Average Yield %	1.5	1.6	1.4	1.5	2.0	2.1	2.7

Statistics are as originally reported. Adj. for stk. splits and div.: 3-for-2, 12/97. [1] Incl. a net gain of $3.0 mill. from the sale of divisions. [2] Incl. an after-tax nonrecurr. gain of $1.3 mill.

OFFICERS:
T. C. Brown, Chmn., Pres., C.E.O.
P. J. Stuecker, V.P., Fin., C.F.O., Sec.
R. D. Wiseman, Treas., Asst. Sec.

INVESTOR CONTACT: Phillip J. Stuecker, Corp. Sec., (502) 893-4600

PRINCIPAL OFFICE: 4360 Brownsboro Road, Louisville, KY 40207

TELEPHONE NUMBER: (502) 893-4600
FAX: (502) 895-6618
WEB: www.thomasind.com

NO. OF EMPLOYEES: 1,130 (approx.)

SHAREHOLDERS: 2,171

ANNUAL MEETING: In Apr.

INCORPORATED: DE, Aug., 1953

INSTITUTIONAL HOLDINGS:
No. of Institutions: 77
Shares Held: 10,099,715
% Held: 66.6

INDUSTRY: Lighting equipment, nec (SIC: 3648)

TRANSFER AGENT(S): National City Bank, Cleveland, OH

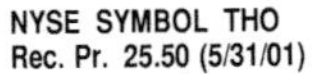

NYSE SYMBOL THO
Rec. Pr. 25.50 (5/31/01)

THOR INDUSTRIES, INC.

YIELD 0.3%
P/E RATIO 9.8

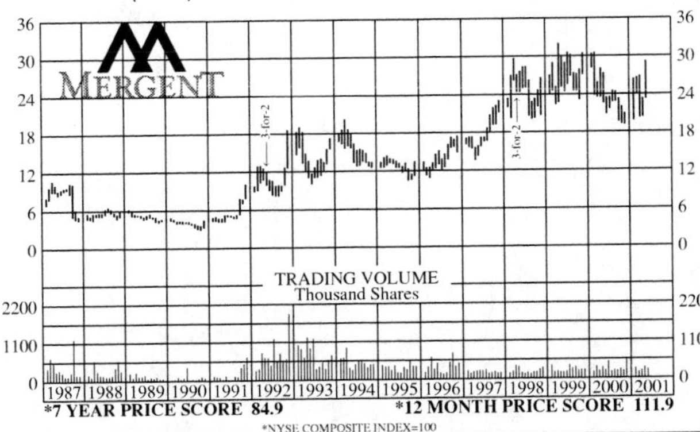

***7 YEAR PRICE SCORE 84.9** ***12 MONTH PRICE SCORE 111.9**

*NYSE COMPOSITE INDEX=100

INTERIM EARNINGS (Per Share):

Qtr.	Oct.	Jan.	April	July
1997	0.39	0.16	0.38	0.50
1998	0.45	0.28	0.50	0.35
1999	0.57	0.45	0.73	0.77
2000	0.80	0.55	0.83	0.80
2001	0.70	0.27	...	...

INTERIM DIVIDENDS (Per Share):

Amt.	Decl.	Ex.	Rec.	Pay.
0.02Q	5/22/00	6/14/00	6/16/00	7/05/00
0.02Q	9/26/01	9/27/00	9/29/00	10/10/00
0.02Q	11/16/01	12/20/00	12/22/00	1/03/01
0.02Q	2/26/01	3/14/01	3/16/01	4/02/01
0.02Q	5/29/01	6/13/01	6/15/01	7/05/01

Indicated div.: $0.08

CAPITALIZATION (7/31/00):

	($000)	(%)
Common & Surplus	195,204	100.0
Total	195,204	100.0

RECENT DEVELOPMENTS: For the quarter ended 1/31/01, net income fell 52.8% to $3.2 million compared with $6.7 million in the equivalent 2000 quarter. Results for 2000 included losses on divestment of subsidiary of $707.0 million. Net sales were $169.2 million, down 12.6% from $193.7 million a year earlier. Recreational vehicle backlog at 1/31/01 fell 41.0% to $69.8 million, while bus backlog at 1/31/01 jumped 61.0% to $205.1 million.

PROSPECTS: In March 2001, THO acquired certain assets of Ricon Corp.'s specialty vehicles division, which builds mini buses for the mobility-impaired. The transaction is expected to produce approximately $30.0 million in annual specialty vehicle sales, including chassis. In February 2001, THO announced that it has agreed to manufacture buses that integrate European styling and high performance components for ABC Bus Companies, Inc., a distributor of passenger coaches.

BUSINESS

THOR INDUSTRIES, INC. is the second-largest manufacturer of recreational vehicles (RVs) in North America and the largest builder of small and mid-size buses. The Company manufactures and sells a wide variety of RVs, as well as related parts and accessories, throughout the U.S. and Canada. Brand names include AIR STREAM, LAND YACHT, DUTCHMAN, SIGNATURE, FOUR WINDS, HURRICANE, FIFTH AVENUE, AEROLITE, CHATEAU, CITATION, CORSAIR, GENERAL COACH, KOMFORT, SKAMPER, WANDERER and TAHOE RVs, and ELDORADO NATIONAL and CHAMPIONS buses under model names such as AEROTECH, ESCORT, MST, TRANS MARK, E-Z RIDER, CHALLENGER, CONTENDER, and SOLO. Fiscal 2000 sales contributions were: RVs, 74.0%; bus products, 26.0%.

ANNUAL FINANCIAL DATA

	7/31/00	7/31/99	7/31/98	7/31/97	7/31/96	7/31/95	7/31/94
Earnings Per Share	**2.97**	**2.52**	**[2] 1.58**	**1.43**	**1.21**	**1.03**	**1.20**
Cash Flow Per Share	**3.36**	**2.82**	**1.94**	**1.79**	**1.60**	**1.39**	**1.54**
Tang. Book Val. Per Share	**15.14**	**12.34**	**9.89**	**8.30**	**7.38**	**6.21**	**5.32**
Dividends Per Share	**0.08**	**0.08**	**0.08**	**0.08**	**0.08**	**0.08**	**0.08**
Dividend Payout %	**2.7**	**3.2**	**5.1**	**5.6**	**6.6**	**7.7**	**6.7**
INCOME STATEMENT (IN THOUSANDS):							
Total Revenues	893,997	805,806	715,600	624,435	602,078	562,681	491,079
Costs & Expenses	829,868	750,508	676,135	590,299	570,225	535,857	459,598
Depreciation & Amort.	4,677	3,731	4,369	4,461	5,015	4,757	4,521
Operating Income	59,452	51,567	35,096	29,675	26,837	22,068	26,960
Net Interest Inc./(Exp.)	3,120	2,067	622	236	310	293	172
Income Before Income Taxes	60,873	52,436	33,051	30,010	27,243	22,551	26,796
Income Taxes	24,754	21,669	13,656	12,178	11,173	8,761	10,751
Net Income	36,119	30,766	[2] 19,395	17,832	16,070	13,790	16,045
Cash Flow	40,796	34,497	23,764	22,293	21,085	18,547	20,565
Average Shs. Outstg.	12,150	12,223	12,269	12,458	13,214	13,378	13,380
BALANCE SHEET (IN THOUSANDS):							
Cash & Cash Equivalents	77,963	68,866	43,532	13,380	13,062	6,821	13,564
Total Current Assets	225,287	202,124	173,705	132,900	130,036	104,515	102,049
Net Property	33,305	22,316	17,444	16,054	17,206	14,845	11,359
Total Assets	282,131	245,912	213,981	175,408	175,884	148,461	142,446
Total Current Liabilities	86,378	79,030	74,566	51,113	55,054	39,364	45,494
Net Stockholders' Equity	195,204	165,373	138,214	122,448	119,158	107,903	95,923
Net Working Capital	138,909	123,094	99,139	81,787	74,982	65,151	56,555
Year-end Shs. Outstg.	11,985	12,149	12,259	12,215	13,030	13,367	13,435
STATISTICAL RECORD:							
Operating Profit Margin %	6.7	6.4	4.9	4.8	4.5	3.9	5.5
Net Profit Margin %	4.0	3.8	2.7	2.9	2.7	2.5	3.3
Return on Equity %	18.5	18.6	14.0	14.6	13.5	12.8	16.7
Return on Assets %	12.8	12.5	9.1	10.2	9.1	9.3	11.3
Price Range	30.56-19.06	32.00-22.25	29.67-20.00	23.00-13.58	17.50-10.83	14.50-10.50	20.25-12.50
P/E Ratio	10.3-6.4	12.7-8.8	18.8-12.7	16.1-9.5	14.4-8.9	14.0-10.2	16.9-10.4
Average Yield %	0.3	0.3	0.3	0.4	0.6	0.6	0.5

Statistics are as originally reported. Adj. for stk. split: 50%, 5/92, 4/98. [1] Bef. an acctg. credit of $561,000. [2] Incl. loss of $2.7 mill. from divestment of Thor West and a gain of $1.3 million from sale of a subsidiary

OFFICERS:
W. F. Thompson, Chmn., Pres., C.E.O.
P. B. Orthwein, Vice-Chmn., Treas.
W. L. Bennett, Sr. V.P., C.F.O., Sec.

INVESTOR CONTACT: Investor Relations, (937) 596-6849

PRINCIPAL OFFICE: 419 West Pike Street, Jackson Center, OH 45334-0629

TELEPHONE NUMBER: (937) 596-6849
FAX: (937) 596-6539

NO. OF EMPLOYEES: 3,521 (approx.)

SHAREHOLDERS: 204

ANNUAL MEETING: In Dec.

INCORPORATED: NE, July, 1980; reincorp., DE, July, 1983

INSTITUTIONAL HOLDINGS:
No. of Institutions: 63
Shares Held: 5,041,920
% Held: 42.6

INDUSTRY: Motor homes (SIC: 3716)

TRANSFER AGENT(S): Computer Share Investor Services

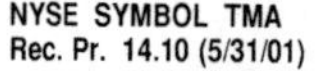

NYSE SYMBOL TMA
Rec. Pr. 14.10 (5/31/01)

THORNBURG MORTGAGE, INC.

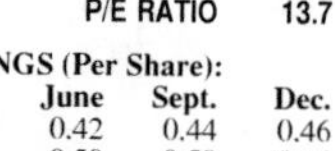

YIELD	8.5%
P/E RATIO	13.7

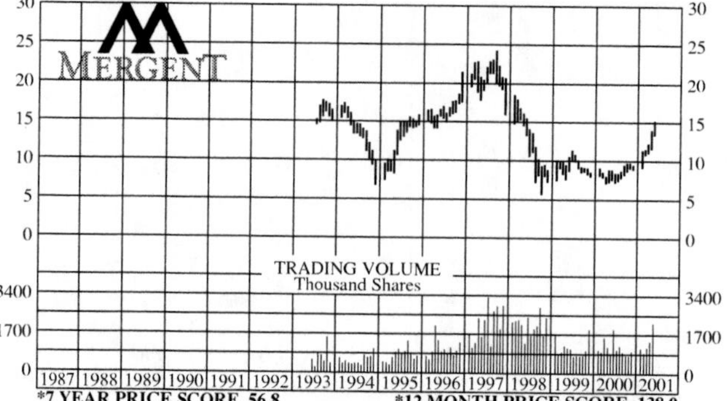

*7 YEAR PRICE SCORE 56.8 *12 MONTH PRICE SCORE 138.0

*NYSE COMPOSITE INDEX=100

INTERIM EARNINGS (Per Share):

Qtr.	Mar.	June	Sept.	Dec.
1996	0.42	0.42	0.44	0.46
1997	0.49	0.50	0.50	0.46
1998	0.42	0.27	0.14	d0.08
1999	0.14	0.25	0.26	0.24
2000	0.25	0.25	0.25	0.28

INTERIM DIVIDENDS (Per Share):

Amt.	Decl.	Ex.	Rec.	Pay.
0.23Q	4/17/00	5/02/00	5/04/00	5/17/00
0.23Q	7/18/00	8/02/00	8/04/00	8/17/00
0.25Q	10/17/00	11/02/00	11/06/00	11/17/00
0.25Q	1/25/01	2/06/01	2/08/01	2/20/01
0.30Q	4/18/01	5/02/01	5/04/01	5/21/01

Indicated div.: $1.20

CAPITALIZATION (12/31/00):

	($000)	(%)
Long-Term Debt	158,593	33.3
Preferred Stock	65,805	13.8
Common & Surplus	251,733	52.9
Total	476,131	100.0

RECENT DEVELOPMENTS: For the year ended 12/31/00, net income rose 14.0% to $29.2 million versus $25.6 million in 1999. Results for 2000 and 1999 included gains of $287,000 and $47,000, respectively, from the sale of adjustable rate mortgage securities. Results for 2000 and 1999 also included management fees of $4.2 million and $4.1 million, respectively, and a performance fee of $46,000 in 2000. Net interest income was $36.6 million, up 7.7% from $34.0 million the year before.

PROSPECTS: TMA plans to build its origination business in a cost effective way, including outsourcing its entire back-office operation to providers. These providers are paid on a loan-by-loan basis, which means they are paid only when the loan has been closed or serviced. This strategy is expected to be an efficient way to process loans and enhance TMA's portfolio and earnings. The expenses of this new business in 2001 should be modest due to TMA's outsourcing strategy and should be more than offset by expected overall earnings.

BUSINESS

THORNBURG MORTGAGE, INC. (formerly Thornburg Mortgage Asset Corp.) is a mortgage portfolio lending institution that invests in a portfolio of highly-rated adjustable-rate mortgage securities and high-quality adjustable-rate mortgage loans. The Company generates income both from its direct investment in these assets and the difference between the yield on its assets and the cost of its borrowings. As of 12/31/00, the Company held total assets of $4.19 billion, comprised mainly of adjustable-rate mortgage assets.

ANNUAL FINANCIAL DATA

	12/31/00	12/31/99	12/31/98	12/31/97	12/31/96	12/31/95	12/31/94
Earnings Per Share	**1.05**	**0.88**	**0.75**	**1.94**	**1.73**	**0.88**	**1.02**
Tang. Book Val. Per Share	**11.67**	**11.40**	**11.45**	**14.42**	**13.70**	**13.16**	**10.19**
Dividends Per Share	**0.94**	**0.92**	**1.41**	**1.92**	**1.58**	**0.70**	**0.99**
Dividend Payout %	**89.5**	**104.5**	**187.3**	**99.0**	**91.3**	**79.5**	**97.0**
INCOME STATEMENT (IN THOUSANDS):							
Interest Income	289,973	260,365	287,032	247,721	151,511	116,617	84,798
Total Income	290,260	260,412	286,754	248,910	151,883	116,049	85,661
Costs & Expenses	261,095	234,828	264,059	207,508	126,146	105,597	73,715
Net Income	29,165	25,584	22,695	41,402	25,737	10,452	11,946
Average Shs. Outstg.	21,506	21,490	21,488	18,158	14,874	11,927	11,758
BALANCE SHEET (IN THOUSANDS):							
Cash & Cash Equivalents	13,105	10,234	36,431	13,780	3,693	3,660	10,848
Total Assets	4,190,167	4,375,965	4,344,633	4,691,116	2,755,358	2,017,985	1,751,832
Long-Term Obligations	158,593	21,289	2,029	10,018	14,187	18,446	16,464
Total Liabilities	3,872,629	4,065,078	4,032,810	4,332,962	2,533,160	1,857,508	1,631,849
Net Stockholders' Equity	317,538	310,887	311,823	358,154	222,198	160,477	119,983
Year-end Shs. Outstg.	21,572	21,490	21,490	20,280	16,219	12,191	11,773
STATISTICAL RECORD:							
Net Inc.+Depr./Assets %	0.7	0.6	0.5	0.9	0.9	0.5	0.7
Return on Equity %	9.2	8.2	7.3	11.6	11.6	6.5	10.0
Return on Assets %	0.7	0.6	0.5	0.9	0.9	0.5	0.7
Price Range	9.81-7.06	11.38-7.44	18.50-5.63	24.25-15.88	21.50-14.13	15.88-7.38	17.38-6.75
P/E Ratio	9.3-6.7	12.9-8.5	24.7-7.5	12.5-8.2	12.4-8.2	18.0-8.4	17.0-6.6
Average Yield %	11.1	9.8	11.6	9.6	8.9	6.0	8.2

Statistics are as originally reported.

OFFICERS:
G. Thornburg, Chmn., C.E.O.
L. A. Goldstone, Pres., C.O.O.
R. P. Story, C.F.O., Treas.

INVESTOR CONTACT: Rick Story, Investor Relations, (505) 989-1900

PRINCIPAL OFFICE: 119 E. Marcy St., Suite 201, Santa Fe, NM 87501

TELEPHONE NUMBER: (505) 989-1900
FAX: (505) 989-8156
WEB: www.thornburgmortgage.com

NO. OF EMPLOYEES: N/A

SHAREHOLDERS: 1,792

ANNUAL MEETING: In April

INCORPORATED: MD, July, 1992

INSTITUTIONAL HOLDINGS:
No. of Institutions: 36
Shares Held: 1,767,560
% Held: 8.1

INDUSTRY: Real estate investment trusts (SIC: 6798)

TRANSFER AGENT(S): Continental Stock Transfer & Trust Company, New York, NY

NYSE SYMBOL TDW
Rec. Pr. 46.91 (5/31/01)

TIDEWATER INC.

YIELD 1.3%
P/E RATIO 34.5

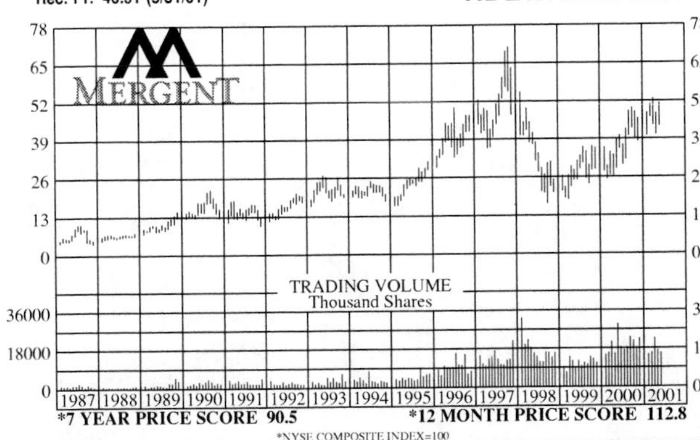

INTERIM EARNINGS (Per Share):

Qtr.	June	Sept.	Dec.	Mar.
1997-98	0.80	1.01	1.15	1.05
1998-99	1.05	0.98	0.71	0.93
1999-00	0.30	0.34	0.40	0.34
2000-01	0.15	0.47	0.40	...

INTERIM DIVIDENDS (Per Share):

Amt.	Decl.	Ex.	Rec.	Pay.
0.15Q	6/09/00	6/15/00	6/19/00	6/29/00
0.15Q	7/27/00	8/03/00	8/07/00	8/17/00
0.15Q	11/28/00	12/06/00	12/08/00	12/18/00
0.15Q	1/18/01	1/25/01	1/29/01	2/07/01
0.15Q	5/31/01	6/07/01	6/11/01	6/21/01

Indicated div.: $0.60

CAPITALIZATION (3/31/00):

	($000)	(%)
Deferred Income Tax	145,076	11.5
Common & Surplus	1,114,201	88.5
Total	1,259,277	100.0

RECENT DEVELOPMENTS: For the three months ended 12/31/00, net income rose slightly to $22.3 million compared with $22.2 million in the corresponding quarter a year earlier. Results included gains on sales of assets of $2.3 million and $2.1 million for 2000 and 1999, respectively. Results for 1999 also included a non-recurring credit of $5.0 million. Total revenues advanced 12.2% to $159.1 million from $141.8 million a year earlier.

PROSPECTS: On 1/10/01, TDW announced it has signed contracts for the construction of eight vessels as part of its new build program. TDW also announced that its subsidiary, Quality Shipyard L.L.C., will build a total of four vessels. Delivery of the new vessels will commence in December 2001 and will continue throughout 2002, with the final delivery expected in January 2003. These new vessels, coupled with expected solid demand going forward, reinforce TDW's positive future outlook.

BUSINESS

TIDEWATER INC. is a major provider of offshore supply vessels and marine support services serving the energy industry. The Company, through its fleet of over 570 vessels, serves most of the world's significant oil and gas exploration and production markets and provides services supporting all phases of offshore exploration, development and production. TDW's services include: the towing of and anchor-handling of mobile drilling rigs and equipment; transporting supplies and personnel necessary to sustain drilling, workover and production activities; and supporting pipelaying and other offshore construction activities. Principal markets served by TDW include the U.S. Gulf of Mexico, areas offshore Australia, Brazil, Egypt, India, Indonesian Malaysia, Mexico, Trinidad, Venezuela, West Africa, the North Sea and the Persian Gulf.

REVENUES

(03/31/00)	($000)	(%)
U.S. vessel	140,090	26.0
International vessel	398,427	74.0
Total	538,517	100.0

ANNUAL FINANCIAL DATA

	3/31/00	3/31/99	3/31/98	3/31/97	3/31/96	3/31/95	3/31/94
Earnings Per Share	**4 1.37**	**1 3.68**	**2 3.99**	**3 2.34**	**1.23**	**0.80**	**3 0.67**
Cash Flow Per Share	**2.85**	**5.33**	**5.49**	**3.67**	**2.55**	**2.42**	**2.25**
Tang. Book Val. Per Share	**12.82**	**11.90**	**10.80**	**12.40**	**11.57**	**10.43**	**10.49**
Dividends Per Share	**0.60**	**0.60**	**0.60**	**0.55**	**0.45**	**0.40**	**0.38**
Dividend Payout %	**43.8**	**16.3**	**15.0**	**23.5**	**36.6**	**50.0**	**56.0**
INCOME STATEMENT (IN MILLIONS):							
Total Revenues	574.8	969.0	1,060.2	803.0	643.4	538.8	522.1
Costs & Expenses	425.7	610.5	606.0	514.7	447.2	391.8	382.4
Depreciation & Amort.	82.5	94.8	91.4	82.3	82.4	86.6	83.7
Operating Income	66.6	263.7	362.7	206.1	113.8	60.4	56.1
Net Interest Inc./(Exp.)	d0.7	d2.4	d24.7	d1.0	d5.9	d4.7	d7.9
Income Before Income Taxes	105.3	276.7	356.5	216.5	110.9	67.4	57.7
Income Taxes	28.7	66.0	113.4	70.5	34.7	24.8	21.5
Equity Earnings/Minority Int.	8.5	5.9	5.1	3.6	4.5	1.7	0.7
Net Income	4 76.6	1 210.7	2 243.0	3 146.0	76.2	42.6	3 36.1
Cash Flow	159.1	305.5	334.4	228.3	158.6	129.2	119.8
Average Shs. Outstg. (000)	55,797	57,269	60,894	62,280	62,161	53,406	53,318
BALANCE SHEET (IN MILLIONS):							
Cash & Cash Equivalents	226.9	10.4	25.0	41.1	28.8	14.7	106.8
Total Current Assets	403.7	280.9	319.1	268.7	208.9	201.2	286.4
Net Property	556.0	638.2	705.6	681.1	659.8	605.9	448.2
Total Assets	1,432.3	1,394.5	1,492.8	1,039.0	978.2	902.2	809.9
Total Current Liabilities	74.8	82.3	204.2	94.7	85.7	101.5	130.3
Long-Term Obligations	...	...	25.0	...	...	100.0	...
Net Stockholders' Equity	1,114.2	1,067.7	998.8	769.7	738.8	580.2	557.0
Net Working Capital	328.9	198.5	114.9	174.0	123.3	99.7	156.1
Year-end Shs. Outstg. (000)	60,562	60,567	59,495	60,335	61,883	53,238	53,023
STATISTICAL RECORD:							
Operating Profit Margin %	11.6	27.2	34.2	25.7	17.7	11.2	10.7
Net Profit Margin %	13.3	21.7	22.9	18.2	11.8	7.9	6.9
Return on Equity %	6.9	19.7	24.3	19.0	10.3	7.3	6.5
Return on Assets %	5.3	15.1	16.3	14.1	7.8	4.7	4.5
Debt/Total Assets %	...	...	1.7	...	...	11.1	...
Price Range	36.50-18.31	55.19-17.06	70.50-35.88	50.00-29.38	31.63-16.50	25.00-18.00	27.00-16.38
P/E Ratio	26.6-13.4	15.0-4.6	17.7-9.0	21.4-12.6	25.7-13.4	31.2-22.5	40.3-24.4
Average Yield %	2.2	1.7	1.1	1.4	1.9	1.9	1.7

Statistics are as originally reported. 1 Incl. one-time gain of $5.1 mill. 2 Incl. one-time credit of $16.5 mill.; bef. gain of $61.7 mill. fr. disc. ops. 3 Incl. one-time credit 3/97, $6.4 mill.; credit 3/94, $4.6 mill. 4 Incl. gain on sale of assets of $19.4 mill.

OFFICERS:
W. C. O'Malley, Chmn., Pres., C.E.O.
J. K. Lousteau, C.F.O., Sr. V.P., Treas.
C. F. Laborde, Sr. V.P., Gen. Couns.

INVESTOR CONTACT: Keith Lousteau, Sr. V.P., C.F.O., (504) 568-1010

PRINCIPAL OFFICE: 601 Poydras St., Suite 1900, New Orleans, LA 70130

TELEPHONE NUMBER: (504) 568-1010
FAX: (504) 566-4582
WEB: www.tdw.com

NO. OF EMPLOYEES: 6,100 (approx.)

SHAREHOLDERS: 2,137 (approx.)

ANNUAL MEETING: In July

INCORPORATED: DE, Feb., 1956

INSTITUTIONAL HOLDINGS:
No. of Institutions: 249
Shares Held: 43,914,439
% Held: 78.6

INDUSTRY: Deep sea foreign trans. of freight (SIC: 4412)

TRANSFER AGENT(S): First National Bank of Boston, EquiServe, Boston, MA

NYSE SYMBOL TIF
Rec. Pr. 34.58 (5/31/01)

TIFFANY & CO.

YIELD 0.5%
P/E RATIO 27.4

*7 YEAR PRICE SCORE 160.6 *12 MONTH PRICE SCORE 97.4
*NYSE COMPOSITE INDEX=100

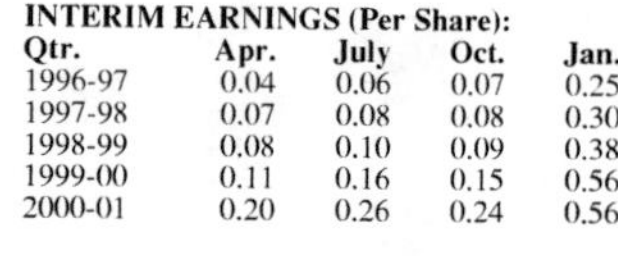

INTERIM EARNINGS (Per Share):

Qtr.	Apr.	July	Oct.	Jan.
1996-97	0.04	0.06	0.07	0.25
1997-98	0.07	0.08	0.08	0.30
1998-99	0.08	0.10	0.09	0.38
1999-00	0.11	0.16	0.15	0.56
2000-01	0.20	0.26	0.24	0.56

INTERIM DIVIDENDS (Per Share):

Amt.	Decl.	Ex.	Rec.	Pay.
100% STK	5/18/00	7/21/00	6/20/00	7/20/00
0.04Q	8/17/00	9/18/00	9/20/00	10/10/00
0.04Q	11/16/00	12/18/00	12/20/00	1/10/01
0.04Q	2/21/01	3/16/01	3/20/01	4/10/01
0.04Q	5/17/01	6/18/01	6/20/01	7/10/01

Indicated div.: $0.16

CAPITALIZATION (1/31/01):

	($000)	(%)
Long-Term Debt	242,157	20.7
Common & Surplus	925,483	79.3
Total	1,167,640	100.0

RECENT DEVELOPMENTS: For the year ended 1/31/01, net earnings jumped 30.8% to $190.6 million from $145.7 million a year earlier. Net sales increased 13.3% to $1.67 billion from $1.47 billion in the prior year. U.S. retail sales grew 12.0% to $833.2 million, international retail sales advanced 15.0% to $679.3 million, and direct marketing sales rose 13.0% to $155.6 million. Worldwide comparable-store sales were up 13.0% year-over-year. Gross profit was $948.4 million versus $821.7 million the year before.

PROSPECTS: Results in the second half of 2001 may benefit from improved consumer confidence sparked by lower interest rates. The Company is targeting long-term annual earnings growth of 15.0% to 20.0%, driven by 5.0% to 8.0% square footage growth and mid to high single-digit comparable-store sales. The Company is in the process of renovating its flagship store on Fifth Avenue in New York. The three-year project is expected to increase retail selling space at the store by 25.0%.

BUSINESS

TIFFANY & CO. is a designer, manufacturer, retailer and distributor offering an extensive array of fine jewelry, sterling silverware, china, crystal, timepieces, stationery, writing instruments, leather goods, scarves, and fragrances. The Company operates more than 100 retail stores and boutiques worldwide, including 41 stores in the U.S. Tiffany operates three channels of distribution: U.S. Retail includes retail sales in Company-operated stores in the U.S. and wholesale sales to independent retailers in North America; Direct Marketing includes corporate, catalog, and Internet sales; and International Retail includes retail sales through Company-operated stores and boutiques and corporate sales.

ANNUAL FINANCIAL DATA

	1/31/01	1/31/00	1/31/99	1/31/98	1/31/97	1/31/96	1/31/95
Earnings Per Share	**1.26**	**0.98**	**0.63**	**0.51**	**1 0.42**	**0.31**	**0.23**
Cash Flow Per Share	**1.56**	**1.25**	**0.83**	**0.66**	**0.57**	**0.45**	**0.36**
Tang. Book Val. Per Share	**6.34**	**5.22**	**3.72**	**3.18**	**2.70**	**2.02**	**1.71**
Dividends Per Share	**0.14**	**0.10**	**0.08**	**0.06**	**0.04**	**0.04**	**0.04**
Dividend Payout %	**11.1**	**10.8**	**12.8**	**11.9**	**10.2**	**11.5**	**15.1**
INCOME STATEMENT (IN MILLIONS):							
Total Revenues	1,668.1	1,461.9	1,169.2	1,017.6	922.1	803.3	682.8
Costs & Expenses	1,293.9	1,163.4	978.5	862.1	791.9	704.5	601.7
Depreciation & Amort.	46.7	41.5	29.7	22.1	20.8	18.8	16.5
Operating Income	327.4	256.9	161.1	133.4	109.4	80.0	64.7
Net Interest Inc./(Exp.)	d16.2	d15.0	d9.3	d8.0	d9.5	d12.3	d12.9
Income Before Income Taxes	317.6	248.1	155.6	127.8	102.9	69.0	51.6
Income Taxes	127.1	102.4	65.6	54.9	44.4	29.8	22.2
Net Income	190.6	145.7	90.1	72.8	1 58.4	39.2	29.3
Cash Flow	237.3	187.2	119.7	94.9	79.3	58.0	45.8
Average Shs. Outstg. (000)	151,816	149,666	143,936	144,416	139,812	128,936	127,184
BALANCE SHEET (IN MILLIONS):							
Cash & Cash Equivalents	195.6	216.9	188.6	107.3	117.2	82.0	44.3
Total Current Assets	1,004.8	891.7	815.6	631.1	569.0	501.4	401.8
Net Property	423.2	322.4	189.8	156.4	129.3	115.2	103.5
Total Assets	1,568.3	1,343.6	1,057.0	827.1	739.4	654.3	551.4
Total Current Liabilities	337.2	281.0	292.7	250.0	226.5	217.3	167.1
Long-Term Obligations	242.2	249.6	194.4	90.9	92.7	101.5	101.5
Net Stockholders' Equity	925.5	757.1	516.5	443.7	378.3	264.4	221.7
Net Working Capital	667.6	610.7	522.9	381.1	342.5	284.1	234.7
Year-end Shs. Outstg. (000)	145,897	144,952	138,932	139,720	138,116	127,904	125,624
STATISTICAL RECORD:							
Operating Profit Margin %	19.6	17.6	13.8	13.1	11.9	10.0	9.5
Net Profit Margin %	11.4	10.0	7.7	7.2	6.3	4.9	4.3
Return on Equity %	20.6	19.2	17.4	16.4	15.4	14.8	13.2
Return on Assets %	12.2	10.8	8.5	8.8	7.9	6.0	5.3
Debt/Total Assets %	15.4	18.6	18.4	11.0	12.5	15.5	18.4
Price Range	45.38-27.09	45.00-12.63	13.00-6.75	12.16-8.44	10.56-6.17	6.86-3.63	5.45-3.56
P/E Ratio	36.0-21.5	46.1-12.9	20.8-10.8	24.1-16.7	25.3-14.8	22.5-11.9	23.6-15.4
Average Yield %	0.4	0.4	0.8	0.6	0.5	0.7	0.8

Statistics are as originally reported. Adj. for 2-for-1 stk. splits, 7/00, 7/99 & 7/96. 1 Incl. $100,000 non-recur. net gain.

OFFICERS:
W. R. Chaney, Chmn.
J. E. Quinn, Vice-Chmn.
M. J. Kowalski, Pres., C.E.O.
J. N. Fernandez, Exec. V.P., C.F.O.

INVESTOR CONTACT: Mark L. Aaron, (212) 230-5301

PRINCIPAL OFFICE: 727 Fifth Ave., New York, NY 10022

TELEPHONE NUMBER: (212) 755-8000
FAX: (212) 605-4465
WEB: www.tiffany.com

NO. OF EMPLOYEES: 5,960 (avg.)

SHAREHOLDERS: 3,082

ANNUAL MEETING: In May

INCORPORATED: DE, Aug., 1984

INSTITUTIONAL HOLDINGS:
No. of Institutions: 321
Shares Held: 126,872,792
% Held: 87.0

INDUSTRY: Jewelry stores (SIC: 5944)

TRANSFER AGENT(S): Mellon Investor Services, Ridgefield Park, NJ

NYSE SYMBOL TKR
Rec. Pr. 17.70 (5/31/01)

TIMKEN COMPANY (THE)

YIELD 4.1%
P/E RATIO 23.3

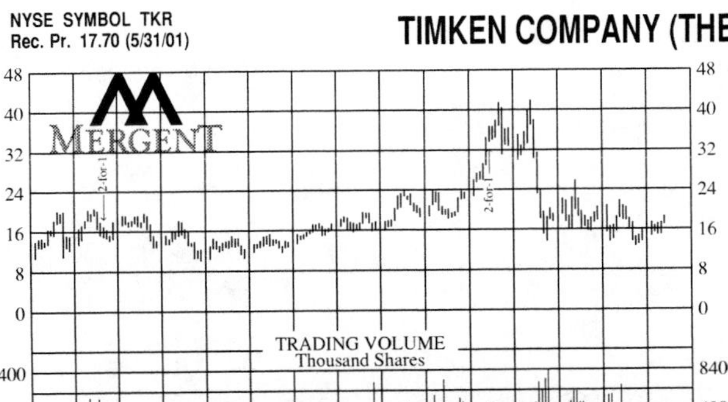

*7 YEAR PRICE SCORE 54.3 *12 MONTH PRICE SCORE 110.9

*NYSE COMPOSITE INDEX=100

INTERIM EARNINGS (Per Share):

Qtr.	Mar.	June	Sept.	Dec.
1996	0.54	0.55	0.51	0.63
1997	0.66	0.72	0.60	0.74
1998	0.78	0.61	0.22	0.21
1999	0.27	0.20	0.20	0.35
2000	0.26	0.35	0.13	0.02

INTERIM DIVIDENDS (Per Share):

Amt.	Decl.	Ex.	Rec.	Pay.
0.18Q	4/18/00	5/17/00	5/19/00	6/05/00
0.18Q	8/04/00	8/16/00	8/18/00	9/05/00
0.18Q	11/03/00	11/15/00	11/17/00	12/04/00
0.18Q	2/02/01	2/14/01	2/16/01	3/05/01
0.18Q	4/17/01	5/16/01	5/18/01	6/04/01

Indicated div.: $0.72 (Div. Reinv. Plan)

CAPITALIZATION (12/31/00):

	($000)	(%)
Long-Term Debt	305,181	23.1
Deferred Income Tax	11,742	0.9
Common & Surplus	1,004,682	76.0
Total	1,321,605	100.0

RECENT DEVELOPMENTS: For the year ended 12/31/00, net income fell 26.7% to $45.9 million from $62.6 million a year earlier. Results for 2000 included pre-tax nonrecurring charges totaling $27.8 million related to TKR's restructuring initiatives. Net sales were $2.64 billion, up 5.9% from $2.50 billion in 1999. Net sales to external customers for the bearings segment remained unchanged at $1.76 billion. Net sales for the steel segment advanced 19.7% to $879.7 million.

PROSPECTS: The Company has begun emphasizing a new manufacturing strategy that includes an aggressive reduction in its costs and asset base. Central to this initiative is achieving $100.0 million in annual cost savings and providing a stronger foundation for profitable growth. In an effort to achieve this goal, TKR intends to close bearing plants in Columbus, Ohio and Duston, England and to sell a tooling plant in Ashland, Ohio. The closures are expected to reduce positions by about 1,500 during the next two years.

BUSINESS

THE TIMKEN COMPANY is an international manufacturer of highly-engineered bearings and alloy steels. Products fall into two industry segments. The first includes tapered roller bearings used in a multitude of applications to reduce friction and conserve energy. The second classification is steel products of alloy, intermediate alloy, vacuum processed alloys, tool steel, carbon grades and custom-made steel products. Bearings are manufactured in the U.S., Brazil, Canada, France, South Africa, Australia and the U.K. Alloy mechanical tubing, alloy bars and high-alloy specialty steels are produced in the U.S. In 2000, 66.7% and 33.3% of net sales were derived from bearings and steel, respectively.

ANNUAL FINANCIAL DATA

	12/31/00	12/31/99	12/31/98	12/31/97	12/31/96	12/31/95	12/31/94
Earnings Per Share	**1 0.76**	**1.01**	**1.82**	**2.69**	**2.22**	**1.80**	**1.11**
Cash Flow Per Share	**3.24**	**3.43**	**4.05**	**4.79**	**4.23**	**3.78**	**3.03**
Tang. Book Val. Per Share	**12.75**	**14.58**	**14.65**	**14.20**	**12.73**	**11.46**	**10.33**
Dividends Per Share	**0.72**	**0.72**	**0.72**	**0.66**	**0.60**	**0.56**	**0.50**
Dividend Payout %	**94.7**	**71.3**	**39.6**	**24.5**	**27.1**	**30.8**	**45.2**
INCOME STATEMENT (IN MILLIONS):							
Total Revenues	2,643.0	2,495.0	2,679.8	2,617.6	2,394.8	2,230.5	1,930.4
Costs & Expenses	2,386.3	2,212.3	2,315.0	2,193.8	2,011.0	1,896.9	1,672.5
Depreciation & Amort.	151.0	149.9	139.8	134.4	126.5	123.4	119.3
Operating Income	105.6	132.8	225.0	289.3	257.3	210.2	138.6
Net Interest Inc./(Exp.)	d28.4	d24.1	d26.5	d21.4	d17.9	d19.8	d24.9
Income Before Income Taxes	70.6	99.0	185.4	266.6	225.3	180.2	111.3
Income Taxes	24.7	36.4	70.8	95.2	86.3	67.8	42.9
Net Income	1 45.9	62.6	114.5	171.4	138.9	112.4	68.5
Cash Flow	196.9	212.6	254.4	305.9	265.4	235.8	187.7
Average Shs. Outstg. (000)	60,723	62,026	62,810	63,804	62,776	62,388	61,900
BALANCE SHEET (IN MILLIONS):							
Cash & Cash Equivalents	10.9	7.9	0.3	9.8	5.3	7.3	12.1
Total Current Assets	898.5	833.5	850.3	855.2	793.6	710.3	657.2
Net Property	1,363.8	1,381.5	1,349.5	1,220.5	1,094.3	1,039.4	1,030.5
Total Assets	2,564.1	2,441.3	2,450.0	2,326.6	2,071.3	1,925.9	1,858.7
Total Current Liabilities	587.5	557.7	490.4	579.6	527.9	462.4	478.6
Long-Term Obligations	305.2	327.3	325.1	202.8	165.8	151.2	150.9
Net Stockholders' Equity	1,004.7	1,046.0	1,056.1	1,032.1	922.2	821.2	732.9
Net Working Capital	311.1	275.9	359.9	275.6	265.7	247.9	178.6
Year-end Shs. Outstg. (000)	59,965	61,196	61,848	62,880	62,646	62,700	62,122
STATISTICAL RECORD:							
Operating Profit Margin %	4.0	5.3	8.4	11.1	10.7	9.4	7.2
Net Profit Margin %	1.7	2.5	4.3	6.5	5.8	5.0	3.5
Return on Equity %	4.6	6.0	10.8	16.6	15.1	13.7	9.3
Return on Assets %	1.8	2.6	4.7	7.4	6.7	5.8	3.7
Debt/Total Assets %	11.9	13.4	13.3	8.7	8.0	7.8	8.1
Price Range	21.81-12.56	25.81-15.63	41.94-13.63	41.50-22.63	23.81-18.25	24.00-16.25	19.63-15.63
P/E Ratio	28.7-16.5	25.6-15.5	23.0-7.5	15.4-8.4	10.8-8.2	13.3-9.0	17.8-14.1
Average Yield %	4.2	3.5	2.6	2.1	2.9	2.8	2.8

Statistics are as originally reported. Adj. for stk. splits: 2-for-1, 5/97. 1 Incl. pre-tax restruct. and impair. chrgs. of $27.6 mill.

OFFICERS:
W. R. Timken Jr., Chmn., C.E.O.
J. W. Griffith, Pres., C.O.O.
S. B. Bailey, Treas.

INVESTOR CONTACT: Richard J. Mertes, Man., Invest. Rel., (330) 471-3378

PRINCIPAL OFFICE: 1835 Dueber Ave., S.W., Canton, OH 44706-2798

TELEPHONE NUMBER: (330) 438-3000
FAX: (330) 471-3452
WEB: www.timken.com

NO. OF EMPLOYEES: 20,474 (avg.)

SHAREHOLDERS: 42,661 (approx.); 8,366 (record)

ANNUAL MEETING: In Apr.

INCORPORATED: OH, 1904

INSTITUTIONAL HOLDINGS:
No. of Institutions: 174
Shares Held: 23,768,958
% Held: 39.6

INDUSTRY: Ball and roller bearings (SIC: 3562)

TRANSFER AGENT(S): First Chicago Trust Company of New York, Jersey City, NJ

NYSE SYMBOL TTN
Rec. Pr. 16.70 (4/30/01)

TITAN CORPORATION (THE)

YIELD ...
P/E RATIO ...

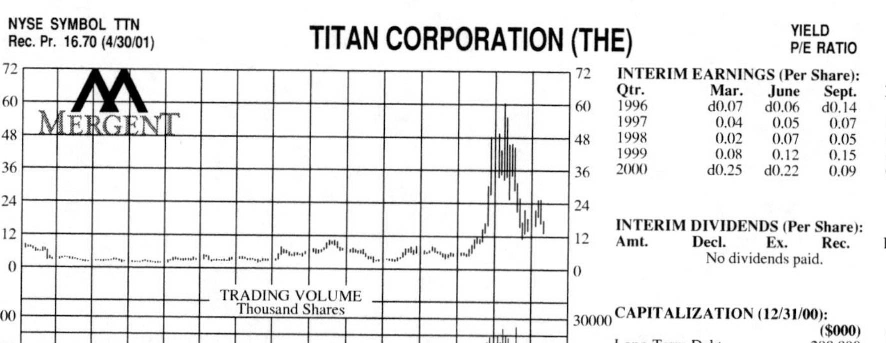

INTERIM EARNINGS (Per Share):

Qtr.	Mar.	June	Sept.	Dec.
1996	d0.07	d0.06	d0.14	Nil
1997	0.04	0.05	0.07	0.09
1998	0.02	0.07	0.05	0.03
1999	0.08	0.12	0.15	0.44
2000	d0.25	d0.22	0.09	0.05

INTERIM DIVIDENDS (Per Share):

Amt.	Decl.	Ex.	Rec.	Pay.

No dividends paid.

CAPITALIZATION (12/31/00):

	($000)	(%)
Long-Term Debt	298,890	41.1
Minority Interest	11,267	1.5
Redeemable Pfd. Stock	250,000	34.4
Preferred Stock	690	0.1
Common & Surplus	166,726	22.9
Total	727,573	100.0

RECENT DEVELOPMENTS: For the year ended 12/31/00, TTN reported a loss from continuing operations of $12.5 million versus income from continuing operations of $43.4 million in 1999. Results for 2000 included charges totaling $45.6 million and excluded losses totaling $6.3 million. Results for 1999 included a charge of $28.0 million and excluded a $5.6 million loss from discontinued operations. Revenues grew 27.7% to $1.03 billion from $809.1 million in 1999.

PROSPECTS: The Company announced plans to sell its commercial information assurance and network monitoring businesses. The sale is strategically in line with the Company's goal to focus on its core competencies. TTN expects to report a net gain from the disposition of these businesses. Meanwhile, in 2001, the Company plans to implement an initial public offering of one of its subsidiaries, sell its non-core assets, and focus on strengthening and growing its four core businesses.

BUSINESS

THE TITAN CORPORATION is a diversified technology company operating in five business segments. The Titan Systems segment provides information technology and communications services for defense, intelligence, and other U.S. and allied government agencies. The Cayenta segment provides comprehensive information technology services for its customers' business functions. The SureBeam segment manufactures food pasteurization systems using electronic radiation. The Titan Wireless segment designs, manufactures and installs satellite communication systems and provides services which support telephony and Internet access in developing countries. The Emerging Technologies and Businesses segment develops medical product sterilization systems and commercial applications for technologies created by the Company's other business segments.

ANNUAL FINANCIAL DATA

	12/31/00	12/31/99	12/31/98	12/31/97	12/31/96	12/31/95	12/31/94
Earnings Per Share	**1 d0.32**	**2 0.81**	**3 0.18**	**4 0.26**	**d0.27**	**5 d0.33**	**5 0.40**
Cash Flow Per Share	**0.58**	**1.01**	**0.37**	**0.48**	**0.11**	**d0.03**	**0.65**
Tang. Book Val. Per Share	...	...	**0.31**	**1.82**	**1.53**	**2.47**	**2.59**
INCOME STATEMENT (IN MILLIONS):							
Total Revenues	1,033.2	406.6	303.4	171.2	137.7	134.0	136.2
Costs & Expenses	974.1	329.0	277.9	151.8	134.1	133.8	123.1
Depreciation & Amort.	43.7	9.8	7.1	5.6	5.8	4.1	3.4
Operating Income	15.4	67.8	18.4	13.7	d2.2	d4.0	9.6
Net Interest Inc./(Exp.)	d36.0	d8.6	d7.0	d5.0	d3.0	d1.1	d0.6
Income Before Income Taxes	d20.6	59.2	11.4	8.7	d5.1	d5.0	9.0
Income Taxes	cr4.0	22.0	4.2	3.2	cr1.7	cr1.2	3.1
Equity Earnings/Minority Int.	4.1	...	...	...	...	...	...
Net Income	1 d12.5	2 37.2	3 7.2	4 5.5	d3.4	5 d3.8	5 6.0
Cash Flow	30.5	46.3	13.6	10.3	1.6	d0.4	8.7
Average Shs. Outstg. (000)	52,717	46,032	36,177	21,396	15,278	13,445	13,288
BALANCE SHEET (IN MILLIONS):							
Cash & Cash Equivalents	27.3	11.7	11.1	1.2	2.1	5.8	5.1
Total Current Assets	463.3	199.6	120.9	90.7	70.8	63.3	55.6
Net Property	88.1	35.4	25.7	19.2	21.0	18.3	12.9
Total Assets	959.4	406.2	192.6	138.1	127.8	95.2	81.9
Total Current Liabilities	195.5	122.2	56.5	36.8	29.7	43.4	34.2
Long-Term Obligations	298.9	137.7	70.3	37.3	40.1	4.3	0.8
Net Stockholders' Equity	167.4	110.7	50.7	53.4	46.6	38.6	38.8
Net Working Capital	267.8	77.5	64.5	53.9	41.1	19.9	21.4
Year-end Shs. Outstg. (000)	53,280	45,395	36,650	17,694	16,028	13,926	13,111
STATISTICAL RECORD:							
Operating Profit Margin %	1.5	16.7	6.0	8.0	...	...	7.1
Net Profit Margin %	...	9.2	2.4	3.2	...	...	4.4
Return on Equity %	...	33.6	14.2	10.3	...	...	15.4
Return on Assets %	...	9.2	3.7	4.0	...	...	7.3
Debt/Total Assets %	31.2	33.9	36.5	27.0	31.3	4.5	0.9
Price Range	60.50-11.13	48.38-4.75	8.25-3.81	8.38-2.75	7.75-2.38	10.38-5.38	8.00-2.88
P/E Ratio	...	59.7-5.9	45.8-21.2	32.2-10.6	...	...	20.0-7.2

Statistics are as originally reported. 1 Bef. $4.7 mill. extraord. chg., $55,000 foreign currency loss, & $1.5 mill. loss fr. disc. ops. and incl. $39.4 mill. acq.-rel. chg. & $6.2 mill. def. compensation chg. 2 Bef. $5.6 mil ($0.12/sh) loss fr disc opers & incl. $28.9 mil non-recur. gain. 3 Bef. $19.5 mil ($0.54/sh) acctg. chg., $7.4 mil ($0.21/sh) loss fr disc. opers. & incl. $9.9 mil pre-tax acquisition chg. 4 Bef. $343,000 ($0.01/sh) loss fr disc. opers. 5 Incl. $6.2 mil pre-tax restr. chg., 1995; $1.2 mil restr. credit, 1994.

OFFICERS:
G. W. Ray, Chmn., Pres., C.E.O.
M. W. Sopp, Sr. V.P., C.F.O.

INVESTOR CONTACT: Rochelle Bold, V.P., Investor Relations, (858) 552-9400

PRINCIPAL OFFICE: 3033 Science Park Rd., San Diego, CA 92121-1199

TELEPHONE NUMBER: (858) 552-9500
FAX: (858) 552-9645
WEB: www.titan.com

NO. OF EMPLOYEES: 7,670 (approx.)

SHAREHOLDERS: 3,540 (approx.)

ANNUAL MEETING: In May

INCORPORATED: IN, May, 1910; reincorp., DE, July, 1910

INSTITUTIONAL HOLDINGS:
No. of Institutions: 138
Shares Held: 30,614,265
% Held: 56.6

INDUSTRY: Computer integrated systems design (SIC: 7373)

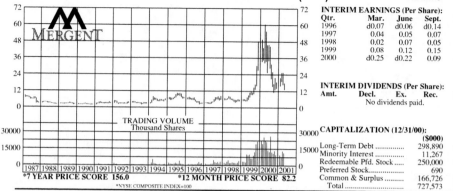

TRANSFER AGENT(S): Bank of America N.T. & S.A., Los Angeles, CA

NYSE SYMBOL TJX
Rec. Pr. 33.46 (5/31/01)

TJX COMPANIES, INC. (THE)

YIELD 0.5%
P/E RATIO 17.9

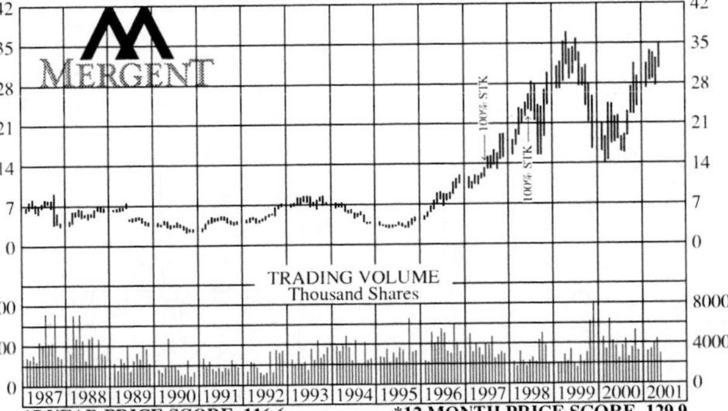

*7 YEAR PRICE SCORE 116.6 *12 MONTH PRICE SCORE 129.9

*NYSE COMPOSITE INDEX=100

INTERIM EARNINGS (Per Share):

Qtr.	Apr.	July	Oct.	Jan.
1997-98	0.14	0.15	0.31	0.29
1998-99	0.26	0.25	0.40	0.39
1999-00	0.39	0.36	0.50	0.44
2000-01	0.44	0.39	0.56	0.48

INTERIM DIVIDENDS (Per Share):

Amt.	Decl.	Ex.	Rec.	Pay.
0.04Q	6/06/00	8/08/00	8/10/00	8/31/00
0.04Q	9/06/00	11/07/00	11/09/00	11/30/00
0.04Q	12/06/00	2/06/01	2/08/01	3/01/01
0.045Q	4/12/01	5/08/01	5/10/01	5/31/01
0.045Q	6/05/01	8/07/01	8/09/01	8/30/01

Indicated div.: $0.18

CAPITALIZATION (1/27/01):

	($000)	(%)
Long-Term Debt	319,372	20.8
Common & Surplus	1,218,712	79.2
Total	1,538,084	100.0

RECENT DEVELOPMENTS: For the 52 weeks ended 1/27/01, net income totaled $538.1 million, up 2.1% compared with earnings of $526.8 million, before an accounting charge, the year before. Net sales climbed 8.9% to $9.58 billion from $8.80 billion a year earlier, driven primarily by the operation of 136 more stores than in fiscal 2000. Comparable-store sales increased 2.0% year-over-year. Operating income totaled $887.8 million, up 3.1% versus $861.3 million in the previous year.

PROSPECTS: TJX is accelerating its store expansion program to help fuel sales and earnings growth. During 2001, and over the next several years, TJX plans to grow its consolidated store base growth by 12.0%. Over the long term, the Company feels the U.S., Canadian and European markets will be able to support more than 4,000 stores of TJX's existing businesses. In an effort to support this increased store growth, TJX will increase its investment in its distribution center network.

BUSINESS

THE TJX COMPANIES, INC. (formerly Zayre Corp.) is the nation's largest off-price apparel retailer in terms of revenues. T.J. Maxx operates 662 stores, selling brand-name family apparel and accessories, women's shoes, domestic furnishings, jewelry and giftware. Marshalls is an off-price family apparel chain, operating 538 stores. Winners Apparel Ltd. is a Canadian off-price family apparel retailer, operating 117 stores. HomeGoods operates 85 off-price home fashion stores in a no-frills environment. T.K. Maxx is an off-price apparel concept operating 74 stores in the United Kingdom and Ireland. A.J. Wright operates 25 off-price family apparel stores. On 12/7/96, the Company sold its Chadwick's of Boston apparel mail-order catalog subsidiary to Brylane, L.P.

ANNUAL FINANCIAL DATA

	1/27/01	1/29/00	1/30/99	1/31/98	1/25/97	1/27/96	1/28/95
Earnings Per Share	**1.86**	**[1] 1.66**	**[5] 1.29**	**[4] 0.88**	**[3] 0.59**	**[2] 0.19**	**0.26**
Cash Flow Per Share	**2.47**	**2.16**	**1.69**	**1.20**	**0.90**	**0.48**	**0.52**
Tang. Book Val. Per Share	**2.72**	**3.09**	**3.17**	**2.77**	**2.39**	**0.85**	**1.41**
Dividends Per Share	**0.15**	**0.14**	**0.12**	**0.09**	**0.07**	**0.14**	**0.14**
Dividend Payout %	**8.3**	**8.1**	**8.9**	**10.5**	**11.9**	**75.6**	**53.8**
INCOME STATEMENT (IN MILLIONS):							
Total Revenues	9,579.0	8,795.3	7,949.1	7,389.1	6,689.4	4,447.5	3,842.8
Costs & Expenses	8,515.4	7,773.7	7,106.9	6,737.4	6,159.1	4,208.5	3,598.6
Depreciation & Amort.	175.8	160.4	136.5	124.9	126.8	85.9	76.5
Operating Income	887.8	861.3	705.7	526.8	403.5	153.1	167.7
Net Interest Inc./(Exp.)	d22.9	d7.3	d1.7	d4.5	d37.3	d44.2	d25.9
Income Before Income Taxes	864.9	853.9	704.0	522.3	366.1	108.9	141.8
Income Taxes	326.9	327.1	270.8	215.7	152.3	45.3	59.2
Net Income	538.1	[1] 526.8	[5] 433.2	[4] 306.6	[3] 213.8	[2] 63.6	82.6
Cash Flow	713.8	687.2	566.2	419.8	326.9	140.1	152.0
Average Shs. Outstg. (000)	289,196	317,791	334,648	349,612	362,500	292,532	293,868
BALANCE SHEET (IN MILLIONS):							
Cash & Cash Equivalents	132.5	371.8	461.2	404.4	474.7	209.2	41.6
Total Current Assets	1,721.9	1,700.6	1,743.1	1,682.6	1,662.3	1,686.7	1,046.2
Net Property	908.0	834.6	756.6	686.1	640.5	785.5	487.8
Total Assets	2,932.3	2,805.0	2,747.8	2,609.6	2,561.2	2,745.6	1,638.2
Total Current Liabilities	1,228.8	1,366.4	1,306.8	1,217.7	1,182.3	1,277.6	758.3
Long-Term Obligations	319.4	319.4	220.3	221.0	244.4	690.7	239.5
Net Stockholders' Equity	1,218.7	1,119.2	1,220.7	1,164.1	1,127.2	764.6	607.0
Net Working Capital	493.2	334.2	436.3	465.0	480.0	409.2	287.9
Year-end Shs. Outstg. (000)	380,379	299,979	322,141	319,802	318,304	289,944	289,604
STATISTICAL RECORD:							
Operating Profit Margin %	9.3	9.8	8.9	7.1	6.0	3.4	4.4
Net Profit Margin %	5.6	6.0	5.4	4.1	3.2	1.4	2.1
Return on Equity %	44.2	47.1	35.5	26.3	19.0	8.3	13.6
Return on Assets %	18.3	18.8	15.8	11.7	8.3	2.3	5.0
Debt/Total Assets %	10.9	11.4	8.0	8.5	9.5	25.2	14.6
Price Range	31.50-13.94	37.00-16.50	30.00-15.50	19.28-9.56	12.06-4.25	4.78-2.78	7.34-3.56
P/E Ratio	16.9-7.5	22.3-9.9	23.3-12.0	21.9-10.9	20.4-7.2	25.8-15.0	28.5-13.8
Average Yield %	0.7	0.5	0.5	0.6	0.9	3.7	2.5

Statistics are as originally reported. Adj. for 2-for-1 stk. split, 6/98 & 6/97. [2] Bef. $5.2 mil acctg. chg. [3] Bef. $3.3 mil extraord. chg. & $31.7 mil loss from disc. ops., & incl. $35 mil pre-tax chg. [4] Bef. $29.4 mil from disc. ops., $5.6 mil extraord. chg., & $125.6 mil gain from sale of opers. [5] Incl. $3.6 mil after-tax gain & bef. $1.8 mil extraord. chg. [6] Bef. $9.0 mil from disc. ops.

OFFICERS:
B. Cammarata, Chmn.
E. English, Pres., C.E.O.
D. G. Campbell, Exec. V.P., C.F.O.

INVESTOR CONTACT: Sherry Lang, V.P., Inv. & Pub. Rel., (508) 390-2323

PRINCIPAL OFFICE: 770 Cochituate Road, Framingham, MA 01701

TELEPHONE NUMBER: (508) 390-1000
FAX: (508) 390-2091
WEB: www.tjx.com

NO. OF EMPLOYEES: 77,000 (approx.)

SHAREHOLDERS: 40,300 (approx.)

ANNUAL MEETING: In June

INCORPORATED: DE, Apr., 1962

INSTITUTIONAL HOLDINGS:
No. of Institutions: 334
Shares Held: 246,945,743
% Held: 88.6

INDUSTRY: Family clothing stores (SIC: 5651)

TRANSFER AGENT(S): EquiServe Limited Partnership, Boston, MA

NYSE SYMBOL TOL
Rec. Pr. 32.65 (5/31/01)

TOLL BROTHERS, INC.

YIELD ...
P/E RATIO 7.6

MERGENT

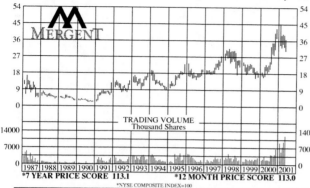

TRADING VOLUME
Thousand Shares

*7 YEAR PRICE SCORE 113.1 *12 MONTH PRICE SCORE 113.0

*NYSE COMPOSITE INDEX=100

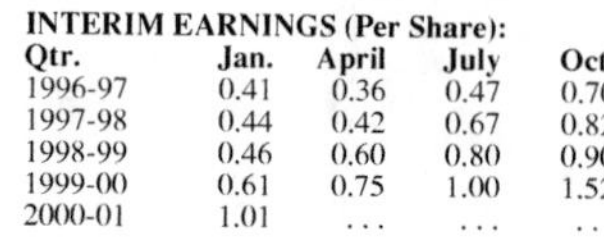

INTERIM EARNINGS (Per Share):

Qtr.	Jan.	April	July	Oct.
1996-97	0.41	0.36	0.47	0.70
1997-98	0.44	0.42	0.67	0.82
1998-99	0.46	0.60	0.80	0.90
1999-00	0.61	0.75	1.00	1.52
2000-01	1.01	...	...	...

INTERIM DIVIDENDS (Per Share):

Amt.	Decl.	Ex.	Rec.	Pay.
No dividends paid.				

CAPITALIZATION (10/31/00):

	($000)	(%)
Long-Term Debt	469,499	38.7
Common & Surplus	745,145	61.3
Total	1,214,644	100.0

RECENT DEVELOPMENTS: For the quarter ended 1/31/01, net income jumped 78.3% to $39.9 million compared with $22.4 million in the prior-year period. Revenues were $475.3 million, up 37.9% from $344.6 million a year earlier. Housing sales advanced 37.1% to $458.4 million, while land sales rose 20.9% to $10.9 million. The average price of homes delivered rose 12.9% to $472,000 from $418,000 in the prior-year period.

PROSPECTS: Results are being fueled by strong demographics supporting the luxury market. There are currently over 12.8 million affluent households to support the luxury market, and a large number of maturing baby boomers entering their move-up and empty-nester years. TOL currently has approximately 36,000 lots available at its disposal in growth-restricted affluent markets. TOL expects diluted earnings for fiscal 2001 to exceed $4.52 per share.

BUSINESS

TOLL BROTHERS, INC. builds customized single-family and attached homes, principally on land it develops and improves, for move-up and empty nester buyers in six regions of the country. TOL operates over 145 communities in 20 states as of 12/00. TOL offers various home designs with prices ranging from $132,000 to more than $832,000. TOL is developing country club, golf course communities in seven states and active-adult, age-qualified communities in Michigan, Connecticut, New Jersey and Virginia. TOL operates its own architectural, engineering, mortgage, title, land development and land sale, security, landscape, cable T.V. and broadband Internet delivery service, and house component assembly and manufacturing operations. TOL also operates its own lumber distribution. The Company acquires and develops commercial properties through its affiliate, Toll Brothers Realty Trust.

ANNUAL FINANCIAL DATA

	10/31/00	10/31/99	10/31/98	10/31/97	10/31/96	10/31/95	10/31/94
Earnings Per Share	**3.90**	**[1] 2.75**	**[1] 2.25**	**[1] 1.94**	**1.56**	**1.47**	**1.08**
Cash Flow Per Share	**4.13**	**2.93**	**2.38**	**2.06**	**1.65**	**1.56**	**1.16**
Tang. Book Val. Per Share	**20.12**	**16.64**	**14.23**	**11.24**	**9.28**	**7.63**	**6.11**
INCOME STATEMENT (IN MILLIONS):							
Total Revenues	1,814.4	1,464.1	1,210.8	971.7	760.7	646.3	504.1
Costs & Expenses	1,528.7	1,254.9	1,035.0	830.6	647.4	541.8	426.3
Depreciation & Amort.	8.5	6.6	5.6	4.1	3.3	2.9	2.7
Operating Income	277.1	202.7	170.2	137.0	110.0	101.6	75.0
Net Interest Inc./(Exp.)	d46.2	d39.9	d35.9	d29.4	d24.2	d22.2	d18.2
Income Before Income Taxes	231.0	162.8	134.3	107.6	85.8	79.4	56.8
Income Taxes	85.0	59.7	48.5	39.8	32.0	29.5	20.7
Net Income	145.9	[1] 103.0	[1] 85.8	[1] 67.8	53.7	49.9	36.2
Cash Flow	154.5	109.6	91.4	71.9	57.1	52.9	38.9
Average Shs. Outstg. (000)	37,413	37,436	38,360	34,918	34,492	33,909	33,626
BALANCE SHEET (IN MILLIONS):							
Cash & Cash Equivalents	161.9	96.5	80.1	147.6	22.9	27.8	41.7
Total Current Assets	1,987.3	1,627.2	1,238.7	1,101.0	822.1	676.6	570.7
Net Property	24.1	19.6	14.4	15.1	12.9	11.9	11.5
Total Assets	2,030.3	1,668.1	1,254.5	1,118.6	837.9	692.5	586.9
Total Current Liabilities	815.6	582.3	458.0	410.9	312.0	210.7	150.1
Long-Term Obligations	469.5	469.4	270.7	322.5	211.2	225.1	232.7
Net Stockholders' Equity	745.1	616.3	525.8	385.3	314.7	256.7	204.2
Net Working Capital	1,171.7	1,044.9	780.6	690.1	510.1	466.0	420.7
Year-end Shs. Outstg. (000)	37,028	37,035	36,935	34,275	33,919	33,638	33,423
STATISTICAL RECORD:							
Operating Profit Margin %	15.3	13.8	14.1	14.1	14.5	15.7	14.9
Net Profit Margin %	8.0	7.0	7.1	7.0	7.1	7.7	7.2
Return on Equity %	19.6	16.7	16.3	17.6	17.1	19.5	17.7
Return on Assets %	7.2	6.2	6.8	6.1	6.4	7.2	6.2
Debt/Total Assets %	23.1	28.1	21.6	28.8	25.2	32.5	39.6
Price Range	42.75-16.00	24.38-15.56	31.63-17.38	27.50-17.50	23.50-14.63	23.00-10.00	19.75-9.13
P/E Ratio	11.0-4.1	8.9-5.7	14.1-7.7	14.2-9.0	15.1-9.4	15.6-6.8	18.3-8.4

Statistics are as originally reported. [1] Bef. extraord. loss of $2.7 mill., 1997; $1.1 mill., 1998; and $1.5 mill., 1999.

OFFICERS:
R. I. Toll, Chmn., C.E.O.
B. E. Toll, Vice-Chmn.
Z. Barzilay, Pres., C.O.O.
J. H. Rassman, Sr. V.P., C.F.O., Treas.

INVESTOR CONTACT: Joseph R. Sicree, Dir., (215) 938-8000

PRINCIPAL OFFICE: 3103 Philmont Avenue, Huntingdon Valley, PA 19006-4298

TELEPHONE NUMBER: (215) 938-8000
FAX: (215) 938-8023
WEB: www.tollbrothers.com

NO. OF EMPLOYEES: 2,479

SHAREHOLDERS: 694 (approx.)

ANNUAL MEETING: In Mar.

INCORPORATED: DE, May, 1986

INSTITUTIONAL HOLDINGS:
No. of Institutions: 172
Shares Held: 21,642,586
% Held: 59.3

INDUSTRY: Operative builders (SIC: 1531)

TRANSFER AGENT(S): Mellon Investor Services, L.L.C, Ridgefield Park, NJ

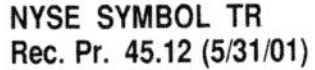

NYSE SYMBOL TR
Rec. Pr. 45.12 (5/31/01)

TOOTSIE ROLL INDUSTRIES, INC.

YIELD 0.6%
P/E RATIO 30.3

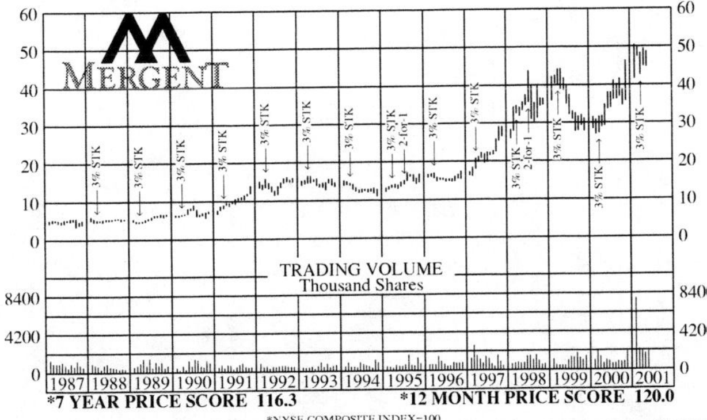

INTERIM EARNINGS (Per Share):

Qtr.	Mar.	June	Sept.	Dec.
1996	0.17	0.17	0.37	0.19
1997	0.17	0.23	0.48	0.26
1998	0.21	0.27	0.52	0.29
1999	0.23	0.28	0.56	0.29
2000	0.25	0.31	0.62	0.31

INTERIM DIVIDENDS (Per Share):

Amt.	Decl.	Ex.	Rec.	Pay.
0.07Q	9/11/00	9/27/00	9/29/00	10/10/00
0.07Q	12/04/00	12/14/00	12/18/00	1/05/01
0.07Q	2/21/01	3/02/01	3/06/01	4/05/01
3% STK	2/21/01	3/02/01	3/06/01	4/18/01
0.07Q	5/30/01	6/14/01	6/18/01	7/09/01

Indicated div.: $0.28

CAPITALIZATION (12/31/00):

	($000)	(%)
Long-Term Debt	7,500	1.6
Deferred Income Tax	12,422	2.6
Common & Surplus	458,696	95.8
Total	478,618	100.0

RECENT DEVELOPMENTS: For the twelve months ended 12/31/00, net earnings increased 6.2% to $75.7 million compared with $71.3 million a year earlier, primarily due to increased sales and ongoing cost control programs. Net sales advanced 7.6% to $427.1 million from $396.8 million in the previous year. The Company attributed the sales gain to additional sales from recently acquired brands and successful marketing and promotional programs, including pre-Halloween sales programs.

PROSPECTS: The Company's near-term prospects are positive, reflecting volume growth and product line extensions as well as new products. Recent product introductions include FRUIT SMOOTHIE POPS, a combination of fruit flavors and creamy yogurt flavors rolled together to taste like a fruit smoothie. Also, TR announced the introduction of HOT CHOCOLATE POPS for Fall 2001. Tootsie Hot Chocolate Pops are a chocolate flavored hard candy lollipop dipped in a marshmallow flavored caramel.

BUSINESS

TOOTSIE ROLL INDUSTRIES, INC. is engaged in the manufacture and sale of candy. Major products include: TOOTSIE ROLL, TOOTSIE ROLL POPS, CHILDS PLAY, CARAMEL APPLE POPS, CHARMS, BLOW-POPS and BLUE RAZZ. Other candy products include CELLAS CHERRIES, MASON DOTS, MASON CROWS, JUNIOR MINTS, CHARLESTON CHEW, SUGAR DADDY and SUGAR BABIES and FLUFFY STUFF COTTON CANDY. In September 1988, TR acquired Charms Co. for approximately $65.0 million. On 5/12/00, TR acquired the assets of Andes Candies Inc. The Company has manufacturing facilities in Chicago, New York, Tennessee, Massachusetts, Maryland, Canada and Mexico. TR celebrated its 100th anniversary in 1996.

GEOGRAPHIC DATA

(12/31/2000)	($000)	(%)
United States	394,545	92.4
Mexico & Canada	32,509	7.6
Total	427,054	100.0

ANNUAL FINANCIAL DATA

	12/31/00	12/31/99	12/31/98	12/31/97	12/31/96	12/31/95	12/31/94
Earnings Per Share	**1.49**	**1.38**	**1.29**	**1.15**	**0.89**	**0.76**	**0.71**
Cash Flow Per Share	**1.75**	**1.57**	**1.53**	**1.39**	**1.12**	**0.97**	**0.91**
Tang. Book Val. Per Share	**6.69**	**6.71**	**6.08**	**4.98**	**4.15**	**3.40**	**2.74**
Dividends Per Share	**0.25**	**0.21**	**0.17**	**0.14**	**0.11**	**0.10**	**0.08**
Dividend Payout %	**17.1**	**15.5**	**13.1**	**11.8**	**12.9**	**12.8**	**11.5**
INCOME STATEMENT (IN THOUSANDS):							
Total Revenues	427,054	396,750	388,659	375,594	340,909	312,660	296,932
Costs & Expenses	303,011	282,252	274,587	272,688	257,309	240,463	226,466
Depreciation & Amort.	13,314	9,979	12,807	12,819	12,068	10,794	10,478
Operating Income	110,729	104,519	101,265	90,087	71,532	61,403	59,988
Net Interest Inc./(Exp.)	...	...	...	...	2,389	1,646	d361
Income Before Income Taxes	117,808	111,447	106,063	95,361	75,098	64,038	61,167
Income Taxes	42,071	40,137	38,537	34,679	27,891	23,670	23,236
Net Income	75,737	71,310	67,526	60,682	47,207	40,368	37,931
Cash Flow	89,051	81,289	80,333	73,501	59,275	51,162	48,409
Average Shs. Outstg.	50,917	51,924	52,495	52,753	52,934	52,934	52,934
BALANCE SHEET (IN THOUSANDS):							
Cash & Cash Equivalents	132,487	159,506	163,920	142,280	144,157	103,450	62,370
Total Current Assets	203,211	224,532	228,539	206,961	201,513	164,949	118,887
Net Property	131,118	95,897	83,024	78,364	81,687	81,999	85,648
Total Assets	562,442	529,416	487,423	436,742	391,456	353,816	310,083
Total Current Liabilities	57,446	56,109	53,384	53,606	48,184	55,306	26,261
Long-Term Obligations	7,500	7,500	7,500	7,500	7,500	7,500	27,500
Net Stockholders' Equity	458,696	430,646	396,457	351,163	312,881	272,186	240,461
Net Working Capital	145,765	168,423	175,155	153,355	153,329	109,643	92,626
Year-end Shs. Outstg.	50,460	51,458	50,749	52,299	52,934	51,803	51,812
STATISTICAL RECORD:							
Operating Profit Margin %	25.9	26.3	26.1	24.0	21.0	19.6	20.2
Net Profit Margin %	17.7	18.0	17.4	16.2	13.8	12.9	12.8
Return on Equity %	16.5	16.6	17.0	17.3	15.1	14.8	15.8
Return on Assets %	13.5	13.5	13.9	13.9	12.1	11.4	12.2
Debt/Total Assets %	1.3	1.4	1.5	1.7	1.9	2.1	8.9
Price Range	46.42-26.98	44.25-27.69	43.82-25.85	29.05-16.07	17.42-14.61	17.17-12.10	15.25-10.98
P/E Ratio	31.2-18.2	32.2-20.1	34.0-20.0	25.2-13.9	19.6-16.5	22.6-15.9	21.4-15.4
Average Yield %	0.7	0.6	0.5	0.6	0.7	0.7	0.6

Statistics are as originally reported. Adj. for all stk. splits and divs. through 4/01.

OFFICERS:
M. J. Gordon, Chmn., C.E.O.
E. R. Gordon, Pres., C.O.O.
B. P. Bowen, Treas.

INVESTOR CONTACT: Investor Relations, (800) 851-9677

PRINCIPAL OFFICE: 7401 South Cicero Avenue, Chicago, IL 60629

TELEPHONE NUMBER: (773) 838-3400
WEB: www.tootsie.com

NO. OF EMPLOYEES: 1,950 (approx.)

SHAREHOLDERS: 9,500 (approx.)

ANNUAL MEETING: In May

INCORPORATED: VA, June, 1919

INSTITUTIONAL HOLDINGS:
No. of Institutions: 134
Shares Held: 11,179,577
% Held: 22.8

INDUSTRY: Candy & other confectionery products (SIC: 2064)

TRANSFER AGENT(S): Mellon Investor Services, LLC, Ridgefield Park, NJ

NYSE SYMBOL TMK
Rec. Pr. 37.89 (4/30/01)

TORCHMARK CORPORATION

YIELD 1.0%
P/E RATIO 13.4

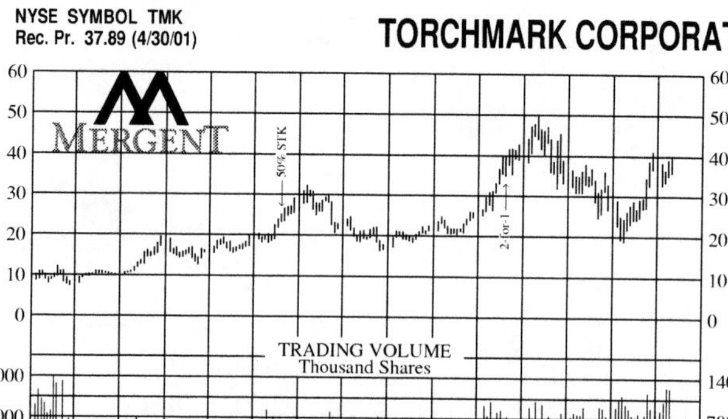

1987 1988 1989 1990 1991 1992 1993 1994 1995 1996 1997 1998 1999 2000 2001

***7 YEAR PRICE SCORE 79.9** ***12 MONTH PRICE SCORE 124.7**

*NYSE COMPOSITE INDEX=100

INTERIM EARNINGS (Per Share):

Qtr.	Mar.	June	Sept.	Dec.
1996	0.53	0.55	0.57	0.59
1997	0.56	0.54	0.67	0.67
1998	0.55	0.34	0.38	0.51
1999	0.59	0.27	0.55	0.52
2000	0.68	0.65	0.77	0.73

INTERIM DIVIDENDS (Per Share):

Amt.	Decl.	Ex.	Rec.	Pay.
0.09Q	5/04/00	7/05/00	7/07/00	8/01/00
0.09Q	7/20/00	10/06/00	10/11/00	11/01/00
0.09Q	10/24/00	1/05/01	1/09/01	2/01/01
0.09Q	3/08/01	4/04/01	4/06/01	5/01/01
0.09Q	4/27/01	7/03/01	7/06/01	8/01/01

Indicated div.: $0.36 (Div. Reinv. Plan)

CAPITALIZATION (12/31/00):

	($000)	(%)
Long-Term Debt	365,989	14.2
Common & Surplus	2,202,360	85.8
Total	2,568,349	100.0

RECENT DEVELOPMENTS: For the year ended 12/31/00, income was $361.8 million, before an extraordinary credit of $202,000, versus income of $258.9 million in the prior year. Results for 1999 excluded a loss on the disposal of discontinued operations of $1.1 million. Total revenues grew 13.0% to $2.52 billion from $2.23 billion the year before. Revenues for 2000 and 1999 included realized investment losses of $5.3 million and $111.0 million, respectively. Total premium revenue climbed 8.6% to $2.05 billion.

PROSPECTS: In 2001, the Company anticipates that all six of its distribution systems will experience continued growth in premium income. In addition, the Company expects administrative expenses to decrease as a percentage of premium income and estimates continued growth in its underwriting income. Furthermore, TMK will use the cash it generates within its operations to increase its invested assets, reduce its higher cost debt and repurchase shares of its common stock.

BUSINESS

TORCHMARK CORPORATION is a diversified insurance and financial services company. Through Liberty National Life Insurance Company, Globe Life & Accident Insurance Company, United American Insurance Company and United Investors Life Insurance Company. Torchmark's insurance subsidiaries write a variety of nonparticipating ordinary life insurance products. These include traditional and interest-sensitive whole-life insurance, term life insurance, and other life insurance. TMK also offers supplemental health insurance products classified as Medicare Supplement, cancer and other health policies. Annuity products include single-premium deferred annuities, flexible-premium deferred annuities, and variable annuities. For 2000, premiums revenue accounted for 81.3% of all revenues.

ANNUAL FINANCIAL DATA

	12/31/00	12/31/99	12/31/98	12/31/97	12/31/96	12/31/95	12/31/94
Earnings Per Share	**4 2.82**	**3 1.93**	**2 1.81**	**2.39**	**1 2.24**	**1 1.90**	**1.86**
Tang. Book Val. Per Share	**14.34**	**12.05**	**13.48**	**10.05**	**7.80**	**7.21**	**4.70**
Dividends Per Share	**0.36**	**0.36**	**0.58**	**0.58**	**0.58**	**0.56**	**0.56**
Dividend Payout %	**12.8**	**18.7**	**32.0**	**24.5**	**25.9**	**29.7**	**30.1**
INCOME STATEMENT (IN MILLIONS):							
Total Premium Income	2,046.2	1,884.1	1,753.6	1,678.0	1,609.9	1,546.3	1,388.9
Other Income	469.7	342.8	404.2	604.4	595.9	521.2	533.7
Total Revenues	2,515.9	2,226.9	2,157.9	2,282.5	2,205.8	2,067.5	1,922.6
Policyholder Benefits	1,339.5	1,236.5	1,150.3	1,108.9	1,058.1	1,009.3	921.3
Income Before Income Taxes	563.0	402.4	447.0	509.4	495.1	428.2	386.9
Income Taxes	190.8	134.3	154.3	178.5	180.6	157.5	124.3
Equity Earnings/Minority Int.	d10.3	d9.2	d36.9	6.8	4.0	1.3	10.6
Net Income	4 361.8	3 258.9	2 255.8	337.7	1 318.5	1 271.9	273.2
Average Shs. Outstg. (000)	128,353	141,431	141,352	141,431	142,460	143,188	144,192
BALANCE SHEET (IN MILLIONS):							
Cash & Cash Equivalents	135.6	114.6	80.8	148.7	103.4	86.0	115.5
Premiums Due	75.0	53.5	130.3	126.6	112.3	122.1	223.8
Invst. Assets: Fixed-term	5,949.5	5,679.8	5,768.4	5,859.7	5,328.3	5,210.2	4,392.3
Invst. Assets: Equities	0.5	29.2	9.8	12.4	8.9	10.6	31.5
Invst. Assets: Loans	374.0	339.2	357.8	300.7	271.3	246.2	200.0
Invst. Assets: Total	6,471.2	6,187.8	6,444.1	6,640.7	6,027.6	5,855.0	5,322.0
Total Assets	12,962.6	12,131.7	11,249.0	10,967.3	9,800.8	9,364.1	8,403.6
Long-Term Obligations	366.0	371.6	383.4	564.3	791.9	792.0	792.8
Net Stockholders' Equity	2,202.4	1,993.3	2,259.5	1,932.7	1,629.3	1,589.0	1,242.6
Year-end Shs. Outstg. (000)	126,389	131,996	136,849	140,040	139,666	143,334	143,068
STATISTICAL RECORD:							
Return on Revenues %	14.4	11.6	11.9	14.8	14.4	13.2	14.2
Return on Equity %	16.4	13.0	11.3	17.5	19.5	17.1	22.0
Return on Assets %	2.8	2.1	2.3	3.1	3.2	2.9	3.3
Price Range	41.19-18.75	38.00-24.56	49.81-31.81	42.81-25.00	26.06-20.13	22.63-17.13	24.75-16.19
P/E Ratio	14.6-6.6	19.7-12.7	27.5-17.6	17.9-10.5	11.7-9.0	11.9-9.0	13.3-8.7
Average Yield %	1.2	1.2	1.4	1.7	2.5	2.8	2.7

Statistics are as originally reported. Adj. for stk. split: 2-for-1, 8/97 1 Bef. disc. oper. loss 1996: $7.1 mill.; 1995: $128.7 mill. 2 Bef. disc. oper. loss $6.4 mill. and extraord. loss $5.0 mill. 3 Incl. non-recurr. chrg. $13.4 mill., net chrg. $72.1 mill. and gain $3.3 mill. on sale of assets. 4 Excl. extraord. gain of $202,000

OFFICERS:
C. B. Hudson, Chmn., Pres., C.E.O.
G. L. Coleman, Exec. V.P., C.F.O.

INVESTOR CONTACT: Joyce L. Lane, Inv. Rel., (972) 569-3627

PRINCIPAL OFFICE: 2001 Third Ave. South, Birmingham, AL 35233

TELEPHONE NUMBER: (205) 325-4200
FAX: (205) 325-4157
WEB: www.torchmarkcorp.com

NO. OF EMPLOYEES: 1,957 (avg.)

SHAREHOLDERS: 5,991

ANNUAL MEETING: In April

INCORPORATED: DE, Nov., 1979

INSTITUTIONAL HOLDINGS:
No. of Institutions: 283
Shares Held: 79,519,928
% Held: 63.1

INDUSTRY: Life insurance (SIC: 6311)

TRANSFER AGENT(S): First Chicago Trust Company of New York, Jersey City, NJ

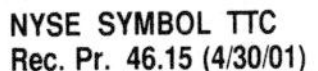

NYSE SYMBOL TTC
Rec. Pr. 46.15 (4/30/01)

TORO COMPANY (THE)

YIELD 1.0%
P/E RATIO 13.1

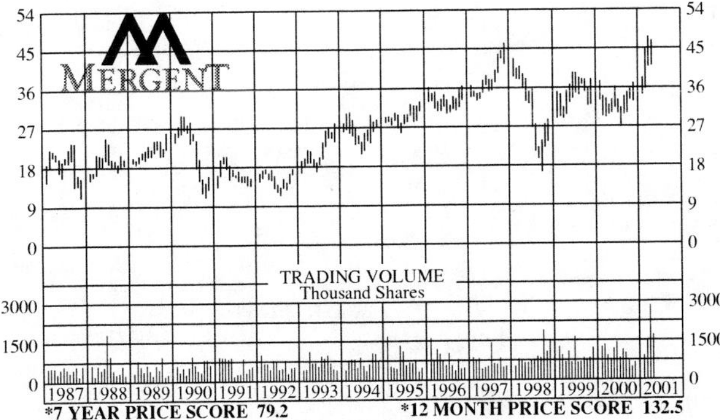

*7 YEAR PRICE SCORE 79.2 *12 MONTH PRICE SCORE 132.5

*NYSE COMPOSITE INDEX=100

INTERIM EARNINGS (Per Share):

Qtr.	1/31	4/30	7/31	10/31
1997	0.20	1.53	0.80	0.40
1998	d0.08	1.53	d0.20	d0.96
1999	0.06	1.83	0.78	d0.01
2000	0.07	2.08	1.26	0.08
2001	0.10	...	...	...

INTERIM DIVIDENDS (Per Share):

Amt.	Decl.	Ex.	Rec.	Pay.
0.12Q	5/18/00	6/20/00	6/22/00	7/12/00
0.12Q	9/15/00	9/22/00	9/26/00	10/12/00
0.12Q	12/07/01	12/14/00	12/18/00	1/12/01
0.12Q	3/14/01	3/22/01	3/26/01	4/12/01
0.12Q	5/24/01	6/20/01	6/22/01	7/12/01

Indicated div.: $0.48 (Div. Reinv. Plan)

CAPITALIZATION (10/31/00):

	($000)	(%)
Long-Term Debt	194,457	38.0
Common & Surplus	317,218	62.0
Total	511,675	100.0

RECENT DEVELOPMENTS: For the quarter ended 2/2/01, net earnings jumped 42.8% to $1.3 million versus $913,000 a year earlier. Results for 2000 included restructuring and other unusual income of $679,000. The Company attributed the earnings gains to foreign currency exchange issues, expense timing, and interest cost improvements. Net sales rose a modest 1.2% to $283.5 million from $280.2 million in the previous year.

PROSPECTS: Despite the uncertain economic climate, new product introductions from each of the Company's business units, coupled with cost and expense reductions and process improvements, should favorably affect TTC's near-term results. The new products include the Toro Flex 21® greensmower and three new consumer products, the Toro Timecutter® riding mower, the Toro Twister® utility vehicle, and the Lawn-boy® Easy Stride® lawn mover.

BUSINESS

THE TORO COMPANY designs, manufacturers and markets professional turf maintenance equipment, irrigation systems, landscaping equipment, and consumer products. Products include: gas-powered walk mowers, riding mowers, lawn and garden tractors, gas and electric snow throwers, trimmers, low-voltage lighting systems, irrigation products, and grooming and operating equipment for golf courses, parks, landscape contractors and schools. The Company currently distributes its products worldwide with sales and/or distribution offices in the U.S., Canada, Belguim, the U.K., Australia, Singapore, Japan and Italy.

REVENUES

(10/31/00)	($000)	(%)
Professional	868,486	65.0
Residential	429,491	32.1
Other	38,947	2.9
Total	1,336,924	100.0

ANNUAL FINANCIAL DATA

	10/31/00	10/31/99	10/31/98	10/31/97	10/31/96	[1] 10/31/95	7/31/95
Earnings Per Share	[5] 3.47	[4] 2.64	[3] 0.31	[2] 3.02	2.90	0.32	2.81
Cash Flow Per Share	6.39	5.59	3.21	5.57	4.35	0.60	4.14
Tang. Book Val. Per Share	25.24	22.25	20.63	19.78	17.75	15.69	15.40
Dividends Per Share	0.48	0.48	0.48	0.48	0.48	0.48	0.48
Dividend Payout %	13.8	18.2	154.8	15.9	16.6	150.0	17.1
INCOME STATEMENT (IN MILLIONS):							
Total Revenues	1,336.9	1,275.0	1,110.4	1,051.2	930.9	192.3	932.9
Costs & Expenses	1,201.6	1,161.0	1,048.5	948.0	849.3	182.0	850.8
Depreciation & Amort.	38.2	39.1	38.2	30.9	18.2	3.6	17.2
Operating Income	97.2	74.9	23.7	72.3	63.4	6.7	64.8
Net Interest Inc./(Exp.)	d26.4	d23.9	d25.4	d19.9	d13.6	d2.5	d11.9
Income Before Income Taxes	71.9	57.5	6.8	60.3	60.2	6.6	61.1
Income Taxes	26.6	22.4	2.7	23.8	23.8	2.6	24.4
Net Income	[5] 45.3	[4] 35.1	[3] 4.1	[2] 36.5	36.4	4.0	36.7
Cash Flow	83.4	74.2	42.3	67.4	54.6	7.6	53.9
Average Shs. Outstg. (000)	13,058	13,278	13,198	12,095	12,555	12,542	13,032
BALANCE SHEET (IN MILLIONS):							
Cash & Cash Equivalents	1.0	12.0	0.1	...	0.1	7.7	11.9
Total Current Assets	510.2	531.7	479.4	472.0	405.0	386.3	381.6
Net Property	132.9	124.2	127.1	116.9	73.8	70.0	70.1
Total Assets	779.4	787.2	724.0	661.6	496.9	472.7	468.3
Total Current Liabilities	260.9	305.8	258.2	237.8	207.9	221.2	212.7
Long-Term Obligations	194.5	195.6	196.8	177.7	53.0	53.4	64.9
Net Stockholders' Equity	317.2	279.7	263.4	241.2	213.6	190.9	185.5
Net Working Capital	249.3	225.9	221.2	234.2	197.1	165.1	169.0
Year-end Shs. Outstg. (000)	12,569	12,569	12,770	12,189	12,032	12,168	12,040
STATISTICAL RECORD:							
Operating Profit Margin %	7.3	5.9	2.1	6.9	6.8	3.5	6.9
Net Profit Margin %	3.4	2.7	0.4	3.5	3.9	2.1	3.9
Return on Equity %	14.3	12.5	1.6	15.1	17.0	2.1	19.8
Return on Assets %	5.8	4.5	0.6	5.5	7.3	0.8	7.8
Debt/Total Assets %	24.9	24.8	27.2	26.9	10.7	11.3	13.9
Price Range	37.50-27.25	39.50-28.75	42.75-16.50	46.31-33.00	36.50-30.00	32.88-25.63	32.88-25.63
P/E Ratio	10.8-7.9	15.0-10.9	137.9-53.2	15.3-10.9	12.6-10.3	102.7-80.1	11.7-9.1
Average Yield %	1.5	1.4	1.6	1.2	1.4	1.6	1.6

Statistics are as originally reported. [1] Results for 3 mos. only due to fiscal year-end change to 10/31 from 7/31. [2] Bef. extraord. chrg. of $1.7 mill. [3] Incls. non-recurr. pre-tax chrgs. of $15.0 mill. [4] Incls. one-time chrgs. of $1.7 mill. [5] Incls. one-time chrgs. of $2.0 mill.

OFFICERS:
K. B. Melrose, Chmn., C.E.O.
S. P. Wolfe, V.P., C.F.O., Treas.
J. L. McIntyre, V.P., Sec., Gen. Couns.

INVESTOR CONTACT: Investor Relations, (800) 468-9716

PRINCIPAL OFFICE: 8111 Lyndale Ave. South, Bloomington, MN 55420-1196

TELEPHONE NUMBER: (612) 888-8801
FAX: (612) 887-8258
WEB: www.toro.com

NO. OF EMPLOYEES: 4,976 (avg.)

SHAREHOLDERS: 5,850

ANNUAL MEETING: In Mar.

INCORPORATED: MN, Nov., 1935; reincorp., DE, Dec., 1983

INSTITUTIONAL HOLDINGS:
No. of Institutions: 117
Shares Held: 7,089,779
% Held: 55.8

INDUSTRY: Lawn and garden equipment (SIC: 3524)

TRANSFER AGENT(S): Wells Fargo Bank Minnesota, NA, St. Paul, MN

NYSE SYMBOL TOS
Rec. Pr. 46.05 (4/30/01)

TOSCO CORP.

YIELD	0.7%
P/E RATIO	13.3

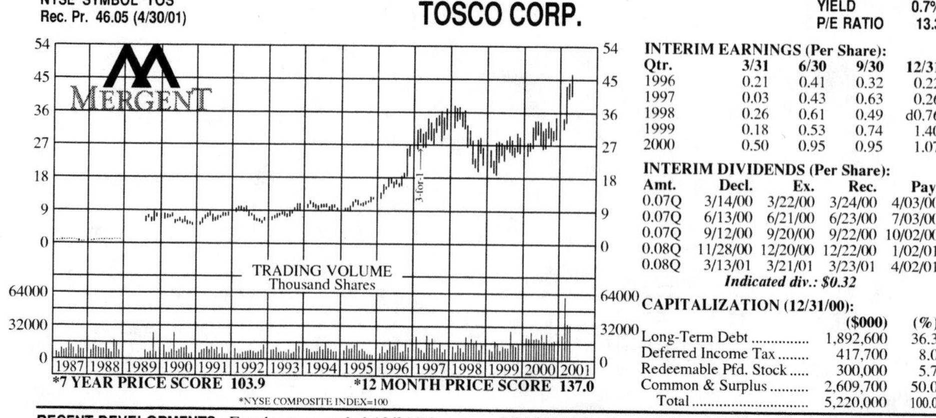

INTERIM EARNINGS (Per Share):

Qtr.	3/31	6/30	9/30	12/31
1996	0.21	0.41	0.32	0.22
1997	0.03	0.43	0.63	0.26
1998	0.26	0.61	0.49	d0.76
1999	0.18	0.53	0.74	1.40
2000	0.50	0.95	0.95	1.07

INTERIM DIVIDENDS (Per Share):

Amt.	Decl.	Ex.	Rec.	Pay.
0.07Q	3/14/00	3/22/00	3/24/00	4/03/00
0.07Q	6/13/00	6/21/00	6/23/00	7/03/00
0.07Q	9/12/00	9/20/00	9/22/00	10/02/00
0.08Q	11/28/00	12/20/00	12/22/00	1/02/01
0.08Q	3/13/01	3/21/01	3/23/01	4/02/01

Indicated div.: $0.32

CAPITALIZATION (12/31/00):

	($000)	(%)
Long-Term Debt	1,892,600	36.3
Deferred Income Tax	417,700	8.0
Redeemable Pfd. Stock	300,000	5.7
Common & Surplus	2,609,700	50.0
Total	5,220,000	100.0

RECENT DEVELOPMENTS: For the year ended 12/31/00, net income rose 19.9% to $529.4 million versus $441.7 million a year earlier. Results for 2000 included a pre-tax gain of $20.0 million on the sale of the Avon Refinery, while results for 1999 included net non-recurring pre-tax gains of $239.5 million. Sales surged 70.9% to $24.55 billion as refining sales jumped 79.0% to $15.30 billion and marketing sales advanced 59.0% to $9.24 billion.

PROSPECTS: On 2/4/01, Phillips Petroleum Company announced that it has agreed to purchase TOS in a $7.00 billion stock transaction. Under the terms of the agreement, Phillips will issue 0.8 Phillips shares for each TOS share and will also assume about $2.00 billion of TOS's debt. The transaction is expected to close by 9/30/01. Separately, on 1/10/01, 76 Lubricants Company, a division of TOS, announced that it has entered into an agreement to purchase Sunoco's Kendall motor oil brand.

BUSINESS

TOSCO CORP. is an independent refiner and marketer of petroleum products. TOS, through seven major facilities consisting of nine refineries, processed in 2000 approximately 1.1 million barrels per day of crude oil, feedstocks, and blendstocks into various petroleum products, chiefly light transportation fuels (gasoline, diesel, and jet fuel) and heating products. The Company's facilities are located on both the East and West Coasts and in the mid-Continent of the U.S. Through its retail distribution network, TOS sells about 6.70 billion gallons of fuel annually. As of 12/31/00, the Company's retail system included approximately 6,308 retail marketing locations operating under the BP, EXXONMOBIL, 76, and CIRCLE K tradenames. TOS acquired Circle K Corp. on 5/30/96. On 2/29/00, TOS acquired approximately 1,740 retail gasoline and convenience outlets from Exxon Corporation and Mobil Oil Corporation for $860.0 million plus inventories.

BUSINESS LINE ANALYSIS

(12/31/2000)	REV (%)	INC (%)
Refining	69.3	76.8
Marketing	30.7	23.2
Total	100.0	100.0

ANNUAL FINANCIAL DATA

	12/31/00	12/31/99	12/31/98	[1] 12/31/97	[3] 12/31/96	12/31/95	[4] 12/31/94
Earnings Per Share	[8] 3.47	[6][7] 2.83	[5] 0.67	[2] 1.37	[2] 1.16	[2] 0.69	0.76
Cash Flow Per Share	5.69	4.69	2.64	3.18	2.63	1.68	1.58
Tang. Book Val. Per Share	13.89	10.60	8.38	7.96	3.43	5.29	5.18
Dividends Per Share	0.28	0.26	0.24	0.24	0.21	0.16	0.21
Dividend Payout %	8.1	9.2	35.8	17.3	18.4	23.2	27.2
INCOME STATEMENT (IN MILLIONS):							
Total Revenues	24,545.2	14,362.1	12,021.5	13,281.6	9,922.6	7,284.1	6,365.8
Costs & Expenses	23,148.9	13,209.5	11,386.2	12,457.5	9,403.1	6,988.9	6,092.9
Depreciation & Amort.	354.2	308.4	313.9	303.5	184.5	111.4	84.9
Operating Income	1,042.1	844.2	321.5	520.5	335.0	183.7	188.0
Net Interest Inc./(Exp.)	d155.1	d118.8	d122.7	d139.7	d87.2	d56.3	d54.1
Income Before Income Taxes	896.7	755.7	188.7	370.7	247.4	127.4	133.8
Income Taxes	367.3	314.0	82.5	158.0	100.8	50.4	50.0
Net Income	[8] 529.4	[6][7] 441.7	[5] 106.2	[2] 212.7	[2] 146.6	[2] 77.1	83.8
Cash Flow	883.6	750.1	420.1	516.2	331.1	188.5	162.4
Average Shs. Outstg. (000)	155,400	159,900	159,122	162,474	125,842	112,442	102,643
BALANCE SHEET (IN MILLIONS):							
Cash & Cash Equivalents	97.8	82.1	80.9	78.2	129.7	48.3	54.6
Total Current Assets	3,086.5	1,644.5	1,519.0	1,812.3	1,042.5	881.4	859.4
Net Property	4,994.8	3,675.2	3,379.4	3,171.0	1,681.9	961.4	822.1
Total Assets	9,003.8	6,212.4	5,842.8	5,974.9	3,554.8	2,003.2	1,797.2
Total Current Liabilities	3,028.4	1,607.1	1,404.7	1,552.8	1,032.5	670.3	480.1
Long-Term Obligations	1,892.6	1,458.9	1,554.6	1,581.3	826.8	624.0	687.4
Net Stockholders' Equity	2,609.7	2,108.3	1,913.0	1,944.1	1,070.3	627.1	575.5
Net Working Capital	58.1	37.4	114.3	259.5	10.0	211.2	379.3
Year-end Shs. Outstg. (000)	144,900	143,900	152,142	156,266	131,015	111,195	111,150
STATISTICAL RECORD:							
Operating Profit Margin %	4.2	5.9	2.7	3.9	3.4	2.5	3.0
Net Profit Margin %	2.2	3.1	0.9	1.6	1.5	1.1	1.3
Return on Equity %	20.3	21.0	5.6	10.9	13.7	12.3	14.6
Return on Assets %	5.9	7.1	1.8	3.6	4.1	3.8	4.7
Debt/Total Assets %	21.0	23.5	26.6	26.5	23.3	31.2	38.2
Price Range	34.69-24.06	30.38-18.81	37.88-19.75	37.06-25.83	27.00-12.33	12.83-9.17	11.67-8.92
P/E Ratio	10.0-6.9	10.7-6.6	56.5-29.5	27.1-18.9	23.3-10.6	18.6-13.3	15.3-11.7
Average Yield %	1.0	1.1	0.8	0.8	1.1	1.5	2.0

Statistics are as originally reported. Adj. for 3-for-1 stk. split, 2/97 [1] Incl. ops. of 76 Products Co., acq. in 1997 [2] Incl. chrg. 12/31/97, $31.0 mil.; chrg. 12/31/96, $8.0 mil.; chrg. 12/31/95, $5.2 mil. [3] Incl. results of Circle K, acq. 5/96 [4] Refl. BP's acq. refining & retail ops. in Pacific Northwest [5] Incl. non-recurr. chrgs. of $280.0 mil. [6] Incl. chrgs. of $43.1 mil. [7] Incl. cr. of $282.6 mil. [8] Incl. aft.-tax gain of $11.9 mil. on sale of Avon Refinery

OFFICERS:
T. D. O'Malley, Chmn., C.E.O.
J. F. Allen, Pres., C.F.O.
W. McClave III, Exec. V.P., Gen. Couns.

INVESTOR CONTACT: Joseph D. Watson, Dir. of Investor Relations, (203) 977-1008

PRINCIPAL OFFICE: 1700 East Putnam Avenue, Old Greenwich, CT 06870

TELEPHONE NUMBER: (203) 698-7500
WEB: www.tosco.com

NO. OF EMPLOYEES: 21,300 full-time (approx.)

SHAREHOLDERS: 7,958

ANNUAL MEETING: In May

INCORPORATED: NV, Sept., 1955

INSTITUTIONAL HOLDINGS:
No. of Institutions: 281
Shares Held: 104,635,480
% Held: 67.9

INDUSTRY: Petroleum refining (SIC: 2911)

TRANSFER AGENT(S): BankBoston, N.A., Boston, MA

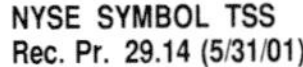

NYSE SYMBOL TSS
Rec. Pr. 29.14 (5/31/01)

TOTAL SYSTEM SERVICES, INC.

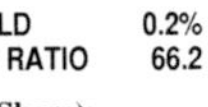

YIELD 0.2%
P/E RATIO 66.2

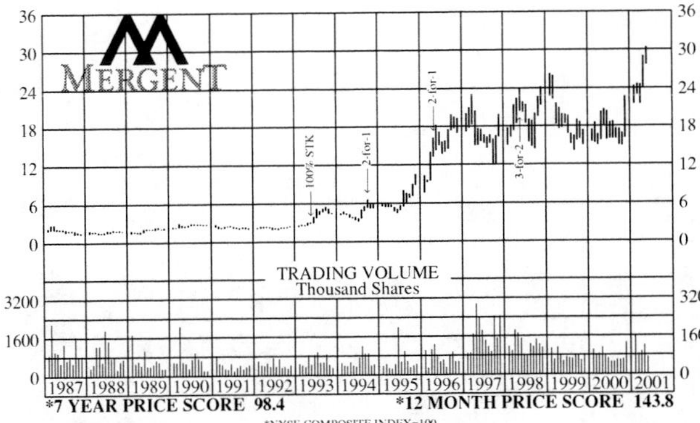

*7 YEAR PRICE SCORE 98.4 *12 MONTH PRICE SCORE 143.8

*NYSE COMPOSITE INDEX=100

INTERIM EARNINGS (Per Share):

Qtr.	Mar.	June	Sept.	Dec.
1996	0.03	0.04	0.06	0.07
1997	0.05	0.05	0.07	0.08
1998	0.05	0.06	0.08	0.09
1999	0.07	0.09	0.09	0.10
2000	0.11	0.12	0.10	0.11

INTERIM DIVIDENDS (Per Share):

Amt.	Decl.	Ex.	Rec.	Pay.
0.013Q	4/13/00	6/20/00	6/22/00	7/01/00
0.013Q	9/13/00	9/19/00	9/21/00	10/02/00
0.013Q	12/11/00	12/19/00	12/21/00	1/02/01
0.015Q	2/26/01	3/19/01	3/22/01	4/02/01
0.015Q	5/15/01	6/19/01	6/21/01	7/02/01

Indicated div.: $0.06

CAPITALIZATION (12/31/00):

	($000)	(%)
Deferred Income Tax	34,842	7.8
Minority Interest	2,584	0.6
Common & Surplus	409,014	91.6
Total	446,439	100.0

RECENT DEVELOPMENTS: For the year ended 12/31/00, net income improved 24.9% to $85.6 million compared with $68.6 million in the previous year. Total revenues jumped 12.6% to $601.3 million versus $533.9 million in the prior year. Revenue from value-added products and services rose 22.2% from the year before. Operating income rose 27.4% to $128.2 million from $100.6 million in 1999. The average number of cardholder accounts on file grew 7.9% to 194.6 million from 180.4 million the previous year.

PROSPECTS: Looking ahead, TSS expects internal growth of 10.0% to 12.0% for existing Visa and MasterCard consumer card clients and an approximate 50.0% increase in international revenues. Meanwhile, TSS will aggressively focus on expense control and productivity improvement, as well as expanding new product offerings and increasing the total cardholder base to approximately 220.0 million accounts. As a result, the Company expects an increase of approximately 20.0% in net income for 2001 over 2000.

BUSINESS

TOTAL SYSTEM SERVICES, INC. is an electronic payment processor of credit, debit, commercial stored value and retail cards. The Company provides the electronic link between buyers and sellers with a comprehensive on-line system of data processing services servicing issuing institutions throughout the United States, Canada, Honduras and the Caribbean, representing more than 195.0 million cardholder accounts on file as of December 31, 2000. TSS also offers value added products and services, such as credit evaluation, fraud control and marketing, to support its core processing services. As of 12/31/00, Synovus Financial Corp. owned 80.8% of TSS.

REVENUES

(12/31/2000)	($000)	(%)
Bankcard Data		
Processing.............	505,935	84.1
Other Services	95,358	15.9
Total	601,293	100.0

ANNUAL FINANCIAL DATA

	12/31/00	12/31/99	12/31/98	12/31/97	12/31/96	12/31/95	12/31/94
Earnings Per Share	**0.44**	**0.35**	**0.28**	**0.25**	**0.21**	**0.14**	**0.12**
Cash Flow Per Share	**0.70**	**0.61**	**0.47**	**0.39**	**0.32**	**0.25**	**0.20**
Tang. Book Val. Per Share	**1.35**	**1.21**	**1.05**	**0.93**	**0.73**	**0.55**	**0.43**
Dividends Per Share	**0.05**	**0.04**	**0.04**	**0.03**	**0.03**	**0.03**	**0.03**
Dividend Payout %	**10.2**	**11.4**	**12.5**	**12.1**	**14.5**	**21.0**	**21.3**
INCOME STATEMENT (IN MILLIONS):							
Total Revenues	601.3	533.9	396.2	361.5	311.6	249.7	187.6
Costs & Expenses	437.1	395.5	292.4	272.4	236.6	186.5	136.1
Depreciation & Amort.	51.6	50.2	37.5	29.1	23.1	20.3	16.4
Operating Income	128.2	100.6	79.3	69.3	59.0	42.9	35.1
Net Interest Inc./(Exp.)	5.0	2.2	2.5	2.3	1.4	0.8	0.3
Income Before Income Taxes	131.7	103.6	81.8	71.6	60.4	43.6	35.4
Income Taxes	46.1	35.0	27.0	24.1	21.0	16.0	12.9
Equity Earnings/Minority Int.	15.5	12.3	13.0	9.3	7.1	0.1	...
Net Income	85.6	68.6	54.8	47.5	39.4	27.7	22.5
Cash Flow	137.2	118.8	92.3	76.6	62.5	48.0	38.9
Average Shs. Outstg. (000)	195,265	195,479	194,669	194,239	193,931	193,895	193,889
BALANCE SHEET (IN MILLIONS):							
Cash & Cash Equivalents	80.1	54.9	9.6	44.3	32.5	18.8	14.7
Total Current Assets	211.0	179.7	119.7	132.4	98.3	77.8	58.6
Net Property	111.0	96.3	92.6	69.0	63.0	54.6	47.9
Total Assets	604.4	457.3	348.9	296.9	246.8	199.0	165.0
Total Current Liabilities	147.3	103.3	59.2	61.5	52.1	40.1	25.2
Long-Term Obligations	...	0.2	0.2	0.3	0.5	0.7	0.9
Net Stockholders' Equity	409.0	334.3	270.4	221.3	178.9	144.5	123.0
Net Working Capital	63.7	76.4	60.5	70.9	46.2	37.7	33.4
Year-end Shs. Outstg. (000)	194,739	194,862	194,045	193,995	193,935	194,192	193,894
STATISTICAL RECORD:							
Operating Profit Margin %	21.3	18.8	20.0	19.2	18.9	17.2	18.7
Net Profit Margin %	14.2	12.8	13.8	13.1	12.7	11.1	12.0
Return on Equity %	20.9	20.5	20.3	21.2	21.8	18.9	18.3
Return on Assets %	14.2	15.0	15.7	16.0	16.0	13.9	13.6
Debt/Total Assets %	...	...	0.1	0.1	0.2	0.3	0.5
Price Range	22.75-14.88	26.25-14.13	24.19-14.44	23.08-12.08	19.83-7.63	10.54-4.46	6.58-3.19
P/E Ratio	51.7-33.8	75.0-40.3	86.4-51.5	93.4-48.9	95.8-36.8	73.7-31.2	56.2-27.2
Average Yield %	0.3	0.2	0.2	0.2	0.2	0.4	0.5

Statistics are as originally reported. Adj. for 2-for-1 stk. spl., 4/96; 3-for-2 stk. spl., 5/98.

OFFICERS:
R. W. Ussery, Chmn., C.E.O.
P. W. Tomlinson, Pres.
J. B. Lipham, Exec. V.P., C.F.O.

INVESTOR CONTACT: Patrick A. Reynolds, Dir., Inv. Rel., (706) 649-5220

PRINCIPAL OFFICE: 1600 First Avenue, Columbus, GA 31901

TELEPHONE NUMBER: (706) 649-2204
FAX: (706) 649-2456
WEB: www.totalsystem.com

NO. OF EMPLOYEES: 4,542

SHAREHOLDERS: 11,313

ANNUAL MEETING: In Apr.

INCORPORATED: GA, Dec., 1982

INSTITUTIONAL HOLDINGS:
No. of Institutions: 60
Shares Held: 6,724,832
% Held: 3.5

INDUSTRY: Data processing and preparation (SIC: 7374)

TRANSFER AGENT(S): State Street Bank & Trust Co., Boston, MA

NYSE SYMBOL TWR
Rec. Pr. 10.60 (4/30/01)

TOWER AUTOMOTIVE, INC.

YIELD ...
P/E RATIO ...

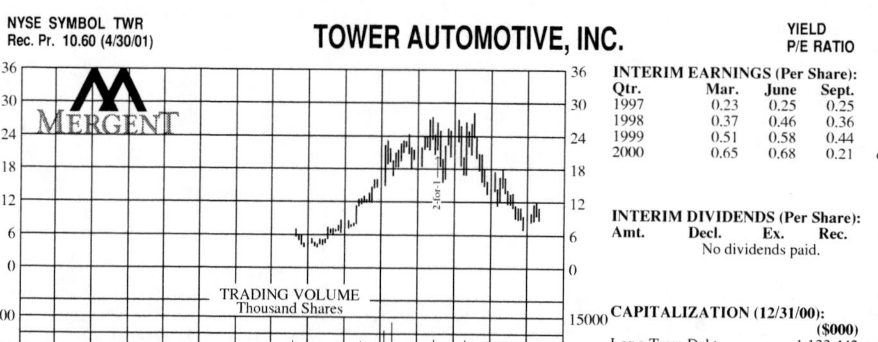

*7 YEAR PRICE SCORE N/A   *12 MONTH PRICE SCORE 100.3

*NYSE COMPOSITE INDEX=100

INTERIM EARNINGS (Per Share):

Qtr.	Mar.	June	Sept.	Dec.
1997	0.23	0.25	0.25	0.34
1998	0.37	0.46	0.36	0.50
1999	0.51	0.58	0.44	0.58
2000	0.65	0.68	0.21	d1.54

INTERIM DIVIDENDS (Per Share):

Amt.	Decl.	Ex.	Rec.	Pay.

No dividends paid.

CAPITALIZATION (12/31/00):

	($000)	(%)
Long-Term Debt	1,133,442	53.1
Capital Lease Obligations	8,458	0.4
Deferred Income Tax	33,884	1.6
Redeemable Pfd. Stock	258,750	12.1
Common & Surplus	700,095	32.8
Total	2,134,629	100.0

RECENT DEVELOPMENTS: For the twelve months ended 12/31/00, income was $16.4 million, before an extraordinary loss of $3.0 million, compared with net income of $117.1 million in the previous year. Results for 2000 included a pre-tax restructuring charge of $141.3 million. Revenues grew 16.7% to $2.53 billion from $2.17 billion the year before. Operating income fell 68.1% to $71.7 million from $225.1 million a year earlier. Gross profit rose 7.1% to $371.6 million from $346.9 million in 1999.

PROSPECTS: TWR's launch activity for the new Ford Explorer and the new Dodge Ram makes for a very challenging year. Add to this the public pressure for price reductions, along with the continued customer demand for capital investment by suppliers, and it becomes clear that TWR's business model must be changed. As a result, in 2001, TWR's focus will be to pay for required capital investments with operating cash flow, reduce debt and continue to be in compliance with debt obligations.

BUSINESS

TOWER AUTOMOTIVE, INC. is a designer and producer of structural components and assemblies used by automotive original equipment manufacturers, including Ford, Daimler-Chrysler, General Motors, Honda, Toyota, Nissan, Fiat, Kia, Hyundai, BMW and Volkswagen. The Company's current products include large structural stampings and assemblies, including exposed sheet metal components, lower vehicle structural stampings and assemblies, as well as suspension components and suspension modules.

REVENUES

(12/31/00)	($000)	(%)
Structural Components	1,769,778	69.9
Suspension Components	241,519	9.5
Modular Assemblies	276,206	10.9
Class A Surfaces	244,450	9.7
Total	2,531,953	100.0

ANNUAL FINANCIAL DATA

	12/31/00	12/31/99	12/31/98	12/31/97	12/31/96	12/31/95	12/31/94
Earnings Per Share	**[1] [2] 0.34**	**2.10**	**1.68**	**[1] 1.14**	**0.78**	**0.53**	**0.43**
Cash Flow Per Share	**3.39**	**3.57**	**2.94**	**2.14**	**1.24**	**0.80**	**0.66**
Tang. Book Val. Per Share	**...**	**3.03**	**4.00**	**2.33**	**3.24**	**2.10**	**1.58**
INCOME STATEMENT (IN MILLIONS):							
Total Revenues	2,532.0	2,170.0	1,836.5	1,235.8	399.9	222.8	165.5
Costs & Expenses	2,315.4	1,833.2	1,573.4	1,078.2	347.7	194.3	147.1
Depreciation & Amort.	144.8	111.6	87.4	48.0	12.8	6.5	4.1
Operating Income	71.7	225.1	175.7	109.7	39.4	21.9	14.3
Net Interest Inc./(Exp.)	d64.7	d38.0	d40.3	d29.0	d5.1	d1.8	d1.9
Income Before Income Taxes	7.0	187.2	135.4	80.7	34.3	20.1	12.4
Income Taxes	2.6	74.9	54.1	32.3	13.7	8.1	5.0
Equity Earnings/Minority Int.	12.0	4.8	6.8	0.2	...	...	...
Net Income	[1] [2] 16.4	117.1	88.0	[1] 48.7	20.6	12.1	7.4
Cash Flow	161.2	228.7	175.4	96.6	33.4	18.6	11.5
Average Shs. Outstg. (000)	47,560	63,974	59,711	45,202	26,846	23,394	17,440
BALANCE SHEET (IN MILLIONS):							
Cash & Cash Equivalents	3.4	3.6	3.4	...	39.6	1.0	0.1
Total Current Assets	548.5	558.1	436.1	371.3	137.0	61.8	59.8
Net Property	1,200.0	1,075.9	821.9	698.5	156.2	87.6	66.8
Total Assets	2,892.7	2,552.6	1,936.2	1,680.1	403.0	211.7	179.4
Total Current Liabilities	572.7	431.1	329.2	230.7	55.4	29.6	26.6
Long-Term Obligations	1,141.9	921.2	542.3	743.9	113.5	70.3	49.5
Net Stockholders' Equity	700.1	727.1	606.8	515.3	181.9	85.6	73.1
Net Working Capital	d24.2	126.9	106.9	140.6	81.5	32.2	33.1
Year-end Shs. Outstg. (000)	47,584	46,879	46,282	45,976	28,568	21,660	21,652
STATISTICAL RECORD:							
Operating Profit Margin %	2.8	10.4	9.6	8.9	9.9	9.8	8.6
Net Profit Margin %	0.6	5.4	4.8	3.9	5.2	5.4	4.4
Return on Equity %	2.3	16.1	14.5	9.4	11.3	14.1	10.1
Return on Assets %	0.6	4.6	4.5	2.9	5.1	5.7	4.1
Debt/Total Assets %	39.5	36.1	28.0	44.3	28.2	33.2	27.6
Price Range	17.88-6.94	28.25-13.38	27.50-15.50	24.34-14.88	16.13-7.19	8.75-3.69	7.06-3.69
P/E Ratio	52.6-20.4	13.5-6.4	16.4-9.2	21.4-13.0	20.8-9.3	16.7-7.0	16.4-8.6

Statistics are as originally reported. Adj. for 2-for-1 split, 6/98. [1] Bef. extraord loss of $3.0 mill., 2000; $2.4 mill., 1997; [2] Incl. pre-tax restruct. chrg. of $141.3 mill.

OFFICERS:
S. A. Johnson, Chmn.
D. K. Campbell, Pres., C.E.O.
A. A. Barone, V.P., C.F.O.

INVESTOR CONTACT: Judy Vijums, Inv. Rel., (612) 332-2335

PRINCIPAL OFFICE: 4508 IDS Center, Minneapolis, MN 55402

TELEPHONE NUMBER: (612) 342-2310
FAX: (612) 332-2012
WEB: www.towerautomotive.com

NO. OF EMPLOYEES: 16,000 (approx.)

SHAREHOLDERS: 2,951 (approx.)

ANNUAL MEETING: In May

INCORPORATED: DE, Mar., 1993

INSTITUTIONAL HOLDINGS:
No. of Institutions: 109
Shares Held: 37,306,642
% Held: 85.6

INDUSTRY: Metal stampings, nec (SIC: 3469)

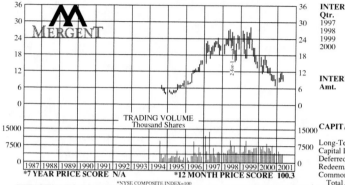

TRANSFER AGENT(S): First Chicago Trust Company, Jersey City, NJ

NYSE SYMBOL TOY
Rec. Pr. 27.70 (5/31/01)

TOYS "R" US, INC.

YIELD ...
P/E RATIO 15.0

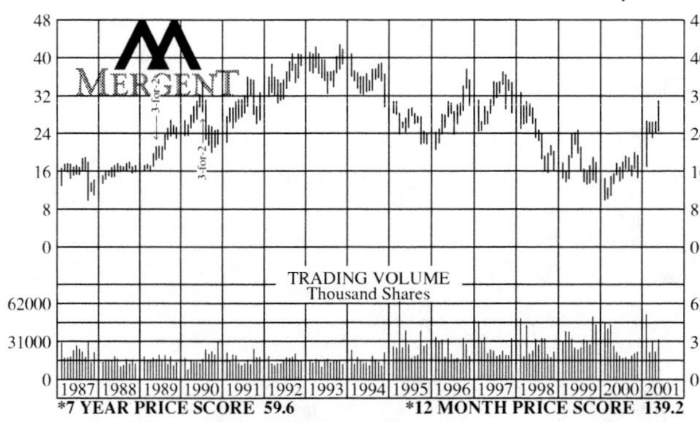

INTERIM EARNINGS (Per Share):

Qtr.	Apr.	July	Oct.	Jan.
1996-97	0.07	d0.03	0.12	1.37
1997-98	0.10	0.13	0.16	1.32
1998-99	0.07	0.06	d1.85	1.23
1999-00	0.07	0.05	0.06	0.98
2000-01	0.93	0.01	d0.32	1.23

INTERIM DIVIDENDS (Per Share):

Amt.	Decl.	Ex.	Rec.	Pay.

No dividends paid.

CAPITALIZATION (2/3/01):

	($000)	(%)
Long-Term Debt	1,567,000	28.7
Deferred Income Tax	402,000	7.4
Minority Interest	70,000	1.3
Common & Surplus	3,418,000	62.6
Total	5,457,000	100.0

RECENT DEVELOPMENTS: For the 53 weeks ended 2/3/01, net earnings totaled $404.0 million, up 44.8% versus $279.0 million in the corresponding 52-week period the year before. Results in the recent period included a one-time after-tax gain of $200.0 million from the April 2000 initial public offering of TOY's Japanese subsidiary. Net sales slid 4.5% to $11.33 billion. Sales in fiscal 2000 and fiscal 1999 included $277.0 million and $1.21 billion, respectively, in sales from Toys "R" Us - Japan, which was accounted for by the equity method since 4/24/00.

PROSPECTS: The Company is enjoying sharply higher sales of merchandise through its Toysrus.com Internet site, fueled by a strategic alliance with Amazon.com. Going forward, TOY plans to build on this sales momentum by adding further improvements to the site and converting its Babiesrus.com and Imaginarium.com sites to the Amazon platform. In 2001, the Company plans to convert approximately 250 existing U.S. toy stores to its C-3 format, which offers an easier-to-shop store layout with wider aisles and expanded merchandise selection.

BUSINESS

TOYS "R" US, INC., operates 710 toy stores in the U.S. and 492 international toy stores. These stores sell both children's and adult's toys, sporting goods, electronic and video games, books, infant and juvenile furniture, as well as educational and entertainment computer software for children. In addition, TOY operates 198 Kids "R" Us stores, which sell children's apparel. The Kids "R" Us stores, about 20,000 square feet in size, are divided into distinct areas for each age group. TOY also operates 148 Babies "R" Us stores, which offer everything for babies from diapers to baby furniture to clothing, and 38 Imaginarium stores that sell specialty toys. In addition, TOY sells merchandise through mail order catalogs and the Internet. On 2/3/97, TOY acquired Baby Superstore, Inc.

ANNUAL FINANCIAL DATA

	2/3/01	1/29/00	1/30/99	1/31/98	2/1/97	2/3/96	1/28/95
Earnings Per Share	**3 1.88**	**1.14**	**2 d0.50**	**1.70**	**2 1.54**	**1 0.53**	**1.85**
Cash Flow Per Share	**3.23**	**2.27**	**0.46**	**2.58**	**2.28**	**1.23**	**2.41**
Tang. Book Val. Per Share	**15.48**	**13.82**	**13.08**	**14.42**	**13.29**	**12.57**	**12.26**
INCOME STATEMENT (IN MILLIONS):							
Total Revenues	11,332.0	11,862.0	11,170.0	11,038.0	9,932.4	9,426.9	8,745.6
Costs & Expenses	10,647.0	11,064.0	10,928.0	9,941.0	8,971.7	8,883.7	7,672.2
Depreciation & Amort.	290.0	278.0	255.0	253.0	206.4	191.7	161.4
Operating Income	426.0	520.0	d13.0	844.0	754.3	351.5	912.0
Net Interest Inc./(Exp.)	d104.0	d80.0	d93.0	d72.0	d81.2	d85.9	d67.9
Income Before Income Taxes	637.0	440.0	d106.0	772.0	673.1	265.6	844.1
Income Taxes	233.0	161.0	26.0	282.0	245.7	117.5	312.3
Net Income	3 404.0	279.0	2 d132.0	490.0	2 427.4	1 148.1	531.8
Cash Flow	694.0	557.0	123.0	743.0	633.8	339.8	693.2
Average Shs. Outstg. (000)	215,000	245,400	265,400	288,400	277,500	276,900	287,415
BALANCE SHEET (IN MILLIONS):							
Cash & Cash Equivalents	275.0	584.0	410.0	214.0	760.9	202.7	369.8
Total Current Assets	2,907.0	2,873.0	2,597.0	2,904.0	3,159.6	2,418.9	2,530.7
Net Property	4,257.0	4,455.0	4,226.0	4,212.0	4,047.4	3,858.2	3,668.8
Total Assets	8,003.0	8,353.0	7,899.0	7,963.0	8,023.2	6,737.5	6,571.2
Total Current Liabilities	2,351.0	2,838.0	2,491.0	2,325.0	2,540.7	2,092.8	2,136.9
Long-Term Obligations	1,567.0	1,230.0	1,222.0	851.0	908.5	826.8	785.4
Net Stockholders' Equity	3,418.0	3,680.0	3,624.0	4,428.0	4,190.6	3,432.3	3,428.9
Net Working Capital	556.0	35.0	106.0	579.0	618.9	326.1	393.8
Year-end Shs. Outstg. (000)	197,500	239,300	250,600	282,400	287,800	273,100	279,790
STATISTICAL RECORD:							
Operating Profit Margin %	3.8	4.4	...	7.6	7.6	3.7	10.4
Net Profit Margin %	3.6	2.4	...	4.4	4.3	1.6	6.1
Return on Equity %	11.8	7.6	...	11.1	10.2	4.3	15.5
Return on Assets %	5.0	3.3	...	6.2	5.3	2.2	8.1
Debt/Total Assets %	19.6	14.7	15.5	10.7	11.3	12.3	12.0
Price Range	20.00-9.75	24.75-13.13	32.75-15.63	37.13-24.38	37.63-20.50	30.88-21.63	40.88-29.63
P/E Ratio	10.6-5.2	21.7-11.5	...	21.8-14.3	24.4-13.3	58.2-40.8	22.1-16.0

Statistics are as originally reported. 1 Incl. $270 mil restr. chg. 2 Incl. $508.0 mil after-tax restr. chg., 1999; $37.8 mil ($0.14/sh) after-tax chg. related to arbitration, 1997. 3 Incl. a one-time after-tax gain of $200.0 mil ($0.93/sh) from the 4/24/00 initial public offering of the Company's Japanese subsidiary.

OFFICERS:
M. Goldstein, Chmn.
J. H. Eyler, Jr., Pres., C.E.O.
L. Lipschitz, Exec. V.P., C.F.O.

INVESTOR CONTACT: Louis Lipschitz, Exec. V.P. & C.F.O., (201) 802-5548

PRINCIPAL OFFICE: 225 Summit Avenue, Montvale, NJ 07645

TELEPHONE NUMBER: (201) 802-5000
FAX: (201) 843-0973
WEB: www.toysrus.com

NO. OF EMPLOYEES: 69,000 (approx.)

SHAREHOLDERS: 30,207 (approx.)

ANNUAL MEETING: In June

INCORPORATED: DE, 1928

INSTITUTIONAL HOLDINGS:
No. of Institutions: 249
Shares Held: 192,672,587
% Held: 97.5

INDUSTRY: Hobby, toy, and game shops (SIC: 5945)

TRANSFER AGENT(S): American Stock Transfer & Trust Company, New York, NY

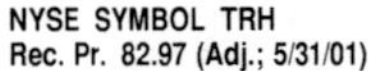
NYSE SYMBOL TRH
Rec. Pr. 82.97 (Adj.; 5/31/01)

TRANSATLANTIC HOLDINGS, INC.

YIELD 0.5%
P/E RATIO 20.6

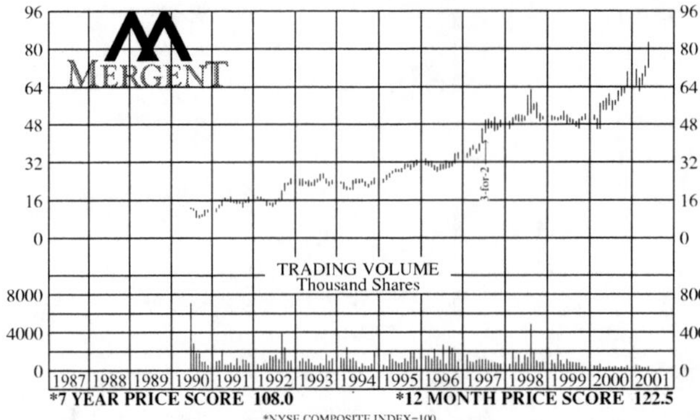

*7 YEAR PRICE SCORE 108.0 *12 MONTH PRICE SCORE 122.5

*NYSE COMPOSITE INDEX=100

INTERIM EARNINGS (Per Share):

Qtr.	Mar.	June	Sept.	Dec.
1997	0.80	0.83	0.92	1.01
1998	0.91	1.24	1.50	1.08
1999	1.42	1.13	0.69	0.34
2000	1.07	0.97	1.02	0.97

INTERIM DIVIDENDS (Per Share):

Amt.	Decl.	Ex.	Rec.	Pay.
0.135Q	9/21/00	11/28/00	11/30/00	12/14/00
0.135Q	11/30/00	2/27/01	3/01/01	3/15/01
0.135Q	3/22/01	5/30/01	6/01/01	6/15/01
50% STK	5/17/01	7/23/01	6/29/01	7/20/01
0.096Q	5/17/01	9/05/01	9/07/01	9/14/01

Indicated div.: $0.38

CAPITALIZATION (12/31/00):

	($000)	(%)
Common & Surplus	1,856,365	100.0
Total	1,856,365	100.0

RECENT DEVELOPMENTS: For the year ended 12/31/00, net income totaled $211.6 million, up 13.0% from $187.4 million in 1999. Total revenues climbed 8.8% to $1.87 billion versus $1.72 billion a year earlier. Net premiums written rose 10.7% to $1.66 billion from $1.50 billion in the prior year. Net premiums earned grew 9.9% to $1.63 billion, while net investment income rose 1.6% to $234.5 million. Results included realized capital gains of $33.1 million in 2000 and $82.8 million in 1999. The combined ratio for 2000 was 99.9 versus 105.2 for 1999.

PROSPECTS: On 1/8/01, Transatlantic Reinsurance Company (TRC) expanded its global presence by entering into a strategic partnership with Kuwait Reinsurance Company (KSC) located in Kuwait City, Kuwait. In connection with the partnership, TRC contributed $30.0 million to KSC in exchange for a 40.0% interest in the company. Established in 1972, KSC primarily provides property, casualty and life reinsurance products to clients in Middle Eastern and North African markets. This transaction should enable TRC to further develop business opportunities in the region.

BUSINESS

TRANSLANTIC HOLDINGS, INC., through its wholly-owned subsidiaries Transatlantic Reinsurance Company, Trans Re Zurich and Putnam Reinsurance Company, offers reinsurance capacity for a full range of property and casualty products on a treaty and facultative basis, directly and through brokers, to insurance and reinsurance companies, in both the domestic and international markets. The Company's principal lines of reinsurance include auto liability, other liability, accident and health, medical malpractice, marine and aviation, and surety and credit in the casualty lines, and fire and allied in the property lines. The Company has operations based in Chicago, Toronto, Miami (serving Latin America and the Caribbean), Buenos Aires, Rio de Janeiro, London, Paris, Zurich, Warsaw, Johannesburg, Sydney, Hong Kong, Shanghai and Tokyo.

ANNUAL FINANCIAL DATA

	12/31/00	12/31/99	12/31/98	12/31/97	12/31/96	12/31/95	12/31/94
Earnings Per Share	**4.03**	**3.58**	**4.73**	**3.56**	**4.49**	**3.83**	**2.96**
Tang. Book Val. Per Share	**35.59**	**31.53**	**30.96**	**26.17**	**32.95**	**28.71**	**22.20**
Dividends Per Share	**0.35**	**0.31**	**0.28**	**0.25**	**0.21**	**0.18**	**0.16**
Dividend Payout %	**8.6**	**8.8**	**5.9**	**7.1**	**4.7**	**4.6**	**5.4**
INCOME STATEMENT (IN MILLIONS):							
Net Premiums Earned	1,631.5	1,484.6	1,380.6	1,259.3	1,130.6	981.2	851.2
Net Investment Income	234.5	230.7	222.0	207.6	192.6	172.9	153.6
Total Revenues	1,866.0	1,715.4	1,602.6	1,466.9	1,323.3	1,154.1	1,004.8
Income Before Income Taxes	268.0	236.1	323.4	234.7	196.3	163.8	119.3
Income Taxes	56.3	48.7	75.8	49.2	41.5	31.9	17.6
Net Income	211.6	187.4	247.5	185.5	154.9	131.9	101.6
Average Shs. Outstg. (000)	52,476	52,323	52,298	52,127	34,475	34,409	34,353
BALANCE SHEET (IN MILLIONS):							
Cash & Cash Equivalents	157.3	110.0	95.6	87.5	136.7	60.7	76.3
Premiums Due	778.5	777.1	658.0	591.0	528.1	668.1	696.5
Invst. Assets: Fixed-term	3,427.8	3,462.1	3,533.5	3,440.9	3,060.8	2,666.1	2,259.9
Invst. Assets: Equities	545.7	537.1	511.4	458.2	386.7	255.1	155.3
Invst. Assets: Total	4,262.0	4,229.4	4,258.2	3,921.8	3,512.4	2,940.1	2,434.3
Total Assets	5,522.7	5,480.2	5,253.2	4,835.0	4,379.1	3,899.0	3,457.8
Net Stockholders' Equity	1,856.4	1,642.5	1,610.1	1,356.7	1,137.3	988.5	763.4
Year-end Shs. Outstg. (000)	52,160	52,092	52,000	51,845	34,520	34,425	34,389
STATISTICAL RECORD:							
Return on Revenues %	11.3	10.9	15.4	12.6	11.7	11.4	10.1
Return on Equity %	11.4	11.4	15.4	13.7	13.6	13.3	13.3
Return on Assets %	3.8	3.4	4.7	3.8	3.5	3.4	2.9
Price Range	70.58-45.83	53.67-46.04	63.00-45.83	51.04-33.89	36.11-27.72	32.83-23.22	25.50-20.17
P/E Ratio	17.5-11.4	15.0-12.9	13.3-9.7	14.3-9.5	8.0-6.2	8.6-6.1	8.6-6.8
Average Yield %	0.6	0.6	0.5	0.6	0.7	0.6	0.7

Statistics are as originally reported. Adj. for stk. splits: 50% div., 7/01; 3-for-2, 7/97

OFFICERS:
M. R. Greenberg, Chmn.
R. F. Orlich, Pres., C.E.O.
S. S. Skalicky, Exec. V.P., C.F.O.

INVESTOR CONTACT: Steven S. Skalicky, Exec. V.P., C.F.O., (212) 770-2040

PRINCIPAL OFFICE: 80 Pine Street, New York, NY 10005

TELEPHONE NUMBER: (212) 770-2000
FAX: (212) 785-7230
WEB: www.transre.com

NO. OF EMPLOYEES: 390 (approx.)

SHAREHOLDERS: 5,000 (approx.)

ANNUAL MEETING: In May

INCORPORATED: DE, 1986

INSTITUTIONAL HOLDINGS:
No. of Institutions: 95
Shares Held: 50,555,094 (Adj.)
% Held: 96.9

INDUSTRY: Fire, marine, and casualty insurance (SIC: 6331)

TRANSFER AGENT(S): American Stock Transfer & Trust Company, New York, NY

NYSE SYMBOL RIG
Rec. Pr. 53.45 (5/31/01)

TRANSOCEAN SEDCO FOREX INC.

YIELD 0.2
P/E RATIO 106.9

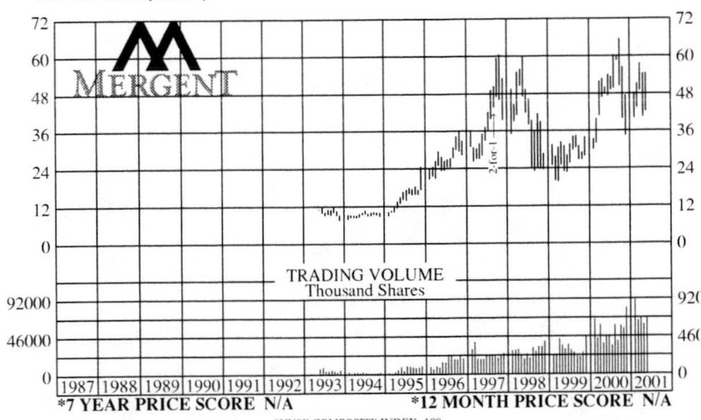

*7 YEAR PRICE SCORE N/A *12 MONTH PRICE SCORE N/A
*NYSE COMPOSITE INDEX=100

INTERIM EARNINGS (Per Share):

Qtr.	Mar.	June	Sept.	Dec.
1996	0.21	0.45	0.31	0.19
1997	0.27	0.28	0.39	0.46
1998	0.77	0.69	0.92	1.02
1999	0.85	0.56	0.46	d0.11
2000	0.15	0.17	0.22	d0.04

INTERIM DIVIDENDS (Per Share):

Amt.	Decl.	Ex.	Rec.	Pay.
0.03Q	8/09/00	8/30/00	9/01/00	9/15/00
0.03Q	11/09/00	11/29/00	12/01/00	12/15/00
0.03Q	2/08/01	2/28/01	3/02/01	3/16/01
0.03Q	5/10/01	5/30/01	6/01/01	6/15/01

Indicated div.: $0.12 (Div. Reinv. Plan)

CAPITALIZATION (12/31/00):

	($000)	(%)
Long-Term Debt	1,430,266	24.7
Deferred Income Tax	359,175	6.2
Common & Surplus	4,004,107	69.1
Total	5,793,548	100.0

RECENT DEVELOPMENTS: For the year ended 12/31/00, income was $107.1 million, before an after-tax extraordinary gain of $1.4 million, versus net income of $58.1 million in the prior-year period. Results for 2000 included after-tax charges of $42.2 million, partially offset by a gain of $17.8 million on the sale of assets. Results for 1999 included net charges totaling $42.0 million. Operating revenues totaled $1.23 billion versus $648.2 million in 1999. The 1999 results reflect only Sedco Forex.

PROSPECTS: On 1/31/01, RIG completed its acquisition of R&B Falcon Corporation in a transaction valued at $8.80 billion. The transaction created a company with a diverse rig fleet and broad geographic reach. Looking forward, RIG expects steady improvement throughout the drilling industry in 2001 as its customers increase exploration and production spending plans in response to the strong results generated by historically high crude oil and natural gas pricing.

BUSINESS

TRANSOCEAN SEDCO FOREX INC. (formerly Sedco Forex Holdings Ltd.) is an international provider of deepwater and harsh environment offshore contract drilling services for oil and gas exploration, development and production. RIG maintains 186 full or partially owned, chartered and managed mobile offshore drilling units, inland barges and other assets utilized in the support of offshore drilling activities worldwide. RIG's mobile offshore drilling fleet is comprised of 51 semisubmersible drilling rigs, including four newbuilds not yet active, 17 drillships and 59 jackup drilling rigs. On 12/31/99, Transocean Offshore Inc. completed its merger with Sedco Forex, which was spun off from Schlumberger Limited on 12/30/99. The Company completed its acquisition R&B Falcon Corporation on 1/31/01.

REVENUES

(12/31/2000)	($000)	(%)
United States	265,032	21.6
Norway & United Kingdom	407,365	33.1
Brazil	153,581	12.5
Nigeria	76,232	6.2
Indonesia	54,657	4.5
Angola & Austrilia	87,822	7.1
Rest of World	184,824	15.0
Total	1,229,513	100.0

ANNUAL FINANCIAL DATA

	12/31/00	12/31/99	12/31/98	12/31/97	[1] 12/31/96	12/31/95	12/31/94
Earnings Per Share	[4] 0.50	[3] 0.53	[2] 3.41	1.38	1.09	0.83	0.23
Cash Flow Per Share	1.78	1.49	4.56	2.38	1.73	1.30	0.66
Tang. Book Val. Per Share	14.08	13.53	12.96	9.29	8.39	6.40	5.66
Dividends Per Share	0.12	0.12	0.12	0.12	0.12	0.12	0.12
Dividend Payout %	24.0	22.6	3.5	8.7	11.1	14.5	53.3
INCOME STATEMENT (IN MILLIONS):							
Total Revenues	1,229.5	648.2	1,089.6	892.0	528.9	322.7	243.0
Costs & Expenses	827.5	493.6	512.5	571.5	374.7	243.6	197.6
Depreciation & Amort.	268.9	105.8	116.9	103.0	46.6	27.0	24.5
Operating Income	133.1	48.8	460.3	217.5	107.6	52.1	20.9
Net Interest Inc./(Exp.)	3.2	d4.8	d20.4	d21.0	d1.0	3.7	d0.4
Income Before Income Taxes	144.4	48.8	487.1	207.2	121.7	75.1	20.2
Income Taxes	36.7	cr9.3	143.7	65.3	43.6	28.2	7.5
Equity Earnings/Minority Int.	d0.6	...	...	...	...	...	...
Net Income	[4] 107.1	[3] 58.1	[2] 343.4	141.9	78.0	46.9	12.7
Cash Flow	376.0	163.9	460.3	245.0	124.6	73.9	37.2
Average Shs. Outstg. (000)	211,672	109,636	100,848	102,784	71,886	56,748	56,648
BALANCE SHEET (IN MILLIONS):							
Cash & Cash Equivalents	34.5	165.7	69.5	54.2	24.2	113.0	47.0
Total Current Assets	448.1	558.9	361.6	307.1	252.2	195.0	127.7
Net Property	4,695.0	4,344.5	2,128.1	1,668.0	1,370.3	303.5	326.1
Total Assets	6,358.8	6,140.2	3,250.9	2,755.1	2,443.2	542.3	493.5
Total Current Liabilities	495.2	528.5	192.4	185.2	231.5	62.1	48.5
Long-Term Obligations	1,430.3	1,187.6	814.0	728.3	392.3	30.0	30.0
Net Stockholders' Equity	4,004.1	3,910.1	1,978.6	1,621.2	1,627.7	363.6	321.1
Net Working Capital	d47.1	30.3	169.2	121.9	20.8	132.9	79.2
Year-end Shs. Outstg. (000)	210,710	210,120	100,551	99,917	103,046	56,830	56,722
STATISTICAL RECORD:							
Operating Profit Margin %	10.8	7.5	42.2	24.4	20.3	16.1	8.6
Net Profit Margin %	8.7	9.0	31.5	15.9	14.8	14.6	5.2
Return on Equity %	2.7	1.5	17.4	8.8	4.8	12.9	4.0
Return on Assets %	1.7	0.9	10.6	5.2	3.2	8.7	2.6
Debt/Total Assets %	22.5	19.3	25.0	26.4	16.1	5.5	6.1
Price Range	65.50-29.25	32.50-19.63	59.94-23.00	60.50-26.13	35.69-20.56	24.63-8.88	10.75-7.81
P/E Ratio	131.0-58.5	61.3-37.0	17.6-6.7	43.8-18.9	32.9-19.0	29.8-10.8	47.8-34.7
Average Yield %	0.3	0.5	0.3	0.3	0.4	0.7	1.3

Statistics are as originally reported. Adj. for 2-for-1 stk. split, 9/97. All figures for 1999 & earlier are for Transocean Offshore Inc. [1] Incl. ops. of Transocean ASA, acq. 9/96 [2] Incl. credits of $46.1 mil. [3] E.P.S. figures are pro-forma; incl. non-recur. chrgs. of $13.4 mil. [4] Incl. aft.-tax chrgs. of $42.2 mil. & asset sales gains of $17.8 mil.; bef. extraord. gain of $1.4 mil.

OFFICERS:
V. E. Grijalva, Chmn.
J. M. Talbert, Pres., C.E.O.
R. L. Long, Exec. V.P., C.F.O.

INVESTOR CONTACT: Jeffrey L. Chastain, (713) 232-7551

PRINCIPAL OFFICE: 4 Greenway Plaza, Houston, TX 77046

TELEPHONE NUMBER: (713) 232-7500
FAX: (713) 850-3834
WEB: www.deepwater.com

NO. OF EMPLOYEES: 7,300 (approx.)

SHAREHOLDERS: 15,600 (approx.)

ANNUAL MEETING: In May

INCORPORATED: DE, 1953

INSTITUTIONAL HOLDINGS:
No. of Institutions: 246
Shares Held: 63,348,979
% Held: 63.0

INDUSTRY: Drilling oil and gas wells (SIC: 1381)

TRANSFER AGENT(S): The Bank of New York, New York, NY

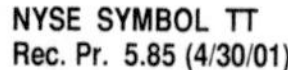

TRANSTECHNOLOGY CORPORATION

YIELD ...
P/E RATIO ...

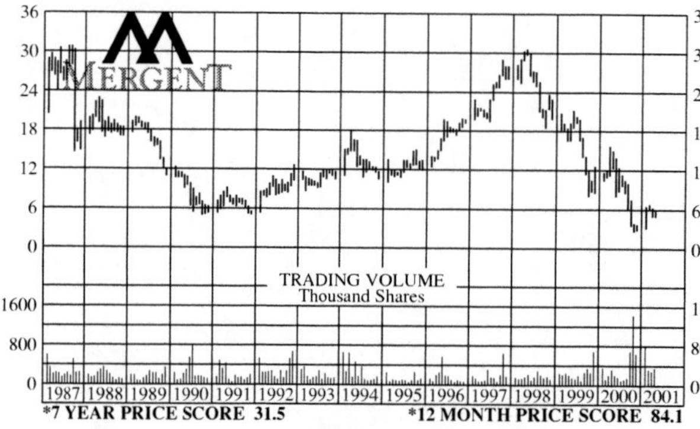

INTERIM EARNINGS (Per Share):

Qtr.	June	Sept.	Dec.	Mar.
1996-97	0.41	0.34	0.60	0.55
1997-98	0.46	0.45	0.57	0.63
1998-99	0.50	0.35	0.58	0.89
1999-00	0.35	d0.05	0.47	0.40
2000-01	d0.12	d0.28	d0.20	...

INTERIM DIVIDENDS (Per Share):

Amt.	Decl.	Ex.	Rec.	Pay.
0.065Q	10/12/99	11/10/99	11/15/99	12/01/99
0.065Q	1/13/00	2/10/00	2/14/00	3/01/00
0.065Q	4/12/00	5/11/00	5/15/00	6/01/00
0.065Q	7/13/00	8/11/00	8/15/00	9/01/00
0.065Q	10/12/00	11/13/00	11/15/00	12/01/00

Div. payments suspended.

CAPITALIZATION (3/31/00):

	($000)	(%)
Long-Term Debt	194,759	58.0
Deferred Income Tax	11,873	3.5
Common & Surplus	128,883	38.4
Total	335,515	100.0

RECENT DEVELOPMENTS: For the quarter ended 12/31/00, TT reported a net loss of $1.3 million versus net income of $2.9 million in the prior-year period. Net sales declined 8.8% to $78.3 million from $85.9 million in 1999. Sales from the Specialty Fasteners segment dropped 14.6% to $59.6 million due to lower foreign exchange rates and weaker product demand. Sales from the Aerospace segment increased 16.1% to $18.7 million.

PROSPECTS: The Company announced that it will become solely a manufacturer of niche aerospace products. TT will divest TransTechnology Engineered Components, a manufacturer of spring steel engineered fasteners and headlight adjusters. TT will also divest its cold-headed products, aerospace rivet, retaining ring, and hose clamp operations, with the proceeds going towards the retirement of $275.0 million of its debt.

BUSINESS

TRANSTECHNOLOGY CORPORATION is a multinational manufacturer of specialty fasteners and aerospace products with 14 manufacturing facilities in the U.S., Canada, England, Germany, and Brazil. The Company also maintains sales offices in Southfield, Michigan; Paris, France; and Barcelona, Spain. The Company's Engineered Components Group manufactures specialty fastener products, which include hose clamps, metal fasteners, and retaining rings. These products are manufactured by the following subsidiaries: Breeze Industrial Products, Palnut Company, and Industrial Retaining Ring. The Company's Aerospace Products Group manufactures rivets and externally threaded fasteners for the aerospace industry and specialty machined and cold-headed products.

ANNUAL FINANCIAL DATA

	3/31/00	3/31/99	3/31/98	3/31/97	3/31/96	3/31/95	3/31/94
Earnings Per Share	**[2][3] 1.16**	**[2] 2.30**	**[1] 2.11**	**[1] 1.92**	**[1] 1.67**	**[1] 1.45**	**[1] 1.34**
Cash Flow Per Share	**4.02**	**4.00**	**3.70**	**3.38**	**2.85**	**2.49**	**2.21**
Tang. Book Val. Per Share	**...**	**7.09**	**11.28**	**11.65**	**10.99**	**10.20**	**12.11**
Dividends Per Share	**0.26**	**0.26**	**0.26**	**0.26**	**0.26**	**0.25**	**0.24**
Dividend Payout %	**22.4**	**11.3**	**12.3**	**13.5**	**15.6**	**17.2**	**17.9**
INCOME STATEMENT (IN MILLIONS):							
Total Revenues	299.3	228.0	203.9	178.7	158.0	102.7	121.5
Costs & Expenses	246.8	191.8	169.0	150.4	133.2	83.7	104.3
Depreciation & Amort.	17.6	10.8	9.1	7.4	6.0	5.3	4.5
Operating Income	34.9	25.4	25.9	20.9	18.8	13.7	12.7
Net Interest Inc./(Exp.)	d19.4	d6.5	d6.2	d5.6	d5.3	d2.8	d1.6
Income Before Income Taxes	11.5	24.3	20.2	16.6	14.3	10.8	10.8
Income Taxes	4.4	9.7	8.2	6.9	5.8	3.5	3.9
Net Income	[2][3] 7.1	[2] 14.6	[1] 12.0	[1] 9.7	[1] 8.5	[1] 7.4	[1] 6.9
Cash Flow	24.8	25.4	21.0	17.1	14.5	12.7	11.4
Average Shs. Outstg. (000)	6,150	6,341	5,689	5,064	5,093	5,109	5,143
BALANCE SHEET (IN MILLIONS):							
Cash & Cash Equivalents	3.4	2.3	3.0	3.5	2.4	1.5	3.0
Total Current Assets	134.7	100.9	104.5	97.4	95.3	76.7	75.4
Net Property	106.0	76.4	63.7	58.6	60.6	29.5	36.0
Total Assets	482.8	279.7	236.1	199.1	199.4	129.4	125.9
Total Current Liabilities	133.0	29.8	48.1	38.3	37.9	23.6	21.6
Long-Term Obligations	194.8	102.5	51.4	67.5	72.6	37.0	33.2
Net Stockholders' Equity	128.9	123.7	115.8	77.4	72.5	64.5	66.0
Net Working Capital	1.8	71.1	56.4	59.1	57.3	53.1	53.8
Year-end Shs. Outstg. (000)	6,145	6,108	6,272	5,028	5,099	5,070	5,189
STATISTICAL RECORD:							
Operating Profit Margin %	11.7	11.1	12.7	11.7	11.9	13.3	10.4
Net Profit Margin %	2.4	6.4	5.9	5.4	5.4	7.2	5.7
Return on Equity %	5.5	11.8	10.4	12.6	11.7	11.4	10.4
Return on Assets %	1.5	5.2	5.1	4.9	4.3	5.7	5.5
Debt/Total Assets %	40.3	36.6	21.8	33.9	36.4	28.6	26.4
Price Range	21.25-8.00	30.63-18.44	29.00-19.38	19.88-12.38	15.13-10.00	17.88-10.50	12.00-8.63
P/E Ratio	18.3-6.9	13.3-8.0	13.7-9.2	10.4-6.4	9.1-6.0	12.3-7.2	9.0-6.4
Average Yield %	1.8	1.1	1.1	1.6	2.1	1.8	2.3

Statistics are as originally reported. [1] Bef. discont. oper.: d$924,000, 3/98; d$934,000, 3/97; d$1.1 mill., 3/96; d$4.9 mill., 3/95; cr$16,000, 3/94. [2] Bef. extraord. chrg. $541,000, 3/00; $781,000, 3/99. [3] Incl. a plant consolidation charge of $2.1 mill.

OFFICERS:
M. J. Berthelot, Chmn., Pres., C.E.O.
J. F. Spanier, V.P., C.F.O.
G. C. Harvey, V.P., Sec., Gen. Couns.
M. Aguirre, Asst. Sec.

INVESTOR CONTACT: Michael J. Berthelot, Chmn., Pres. & C.E.O., (908) 903-1600

PRINCIPAL OFFICE: 150 Allen Road, Liberty Corner, NJ 07938

TELEPHONE NUMBER: (908) 903-1600
FAX: (908) 903-1616
WEB: www.transtechnology.com

NO. OF EMPLOYEES: 2,581

SHAREHOLDERS: 1,824

ANNUAL MEETING: In July

INCORPORATED: CA, Jan., 1962; reincorp., DE, Jan., 1987

INSTITUTIONAL HOLDINGS:
No. of Institutions: 15
Shares Held: 1,902,595
% Held: 30.8

INDUSTRY: Hardware, nec (SIC: 3429)

TRANSFER AGENT(S): Boston EquiServe, L.P., Canton, MA

NYSE SYMBOL TRB
Rec. Pr. 42.14 (4/30/01)

TRIBUNE COMPANY

YIELD 1.0%
P/E RATIO 40.5

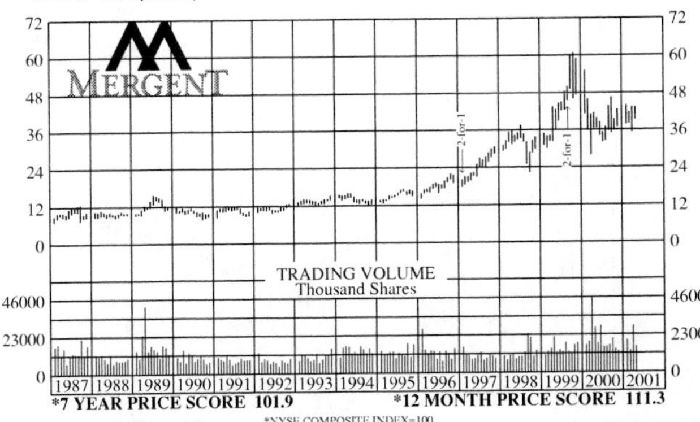

***7 YEAR PRICE SCORE 101.9** ***12 MONTH PRICE SCORE 111.3**

*NYSE COMPOSITE INDEX=100

INTERIM EARNINGS (Per Share):

Qtr.	Mar.	June	Sept.	Dec.
1997	0.25	0.43	0.41	0.41
1998	0.25	0.54	0.30	0.42
1999	1.31	3.39	0.45	0.48
2000	0.25	0.46	0.22	0.11

INTERIM DIVIDENDS (Per Share):

Amt.	Decl.	Ex.	Rec.	Pay.
0.10Q	7/18/00	8/29/00	8/31/00	9/14/00
0.10Q	10/24/00	11/28/00	11/30/00	12/14/00
0.11Q	2/13/01	2/21/01	2/23/01	3/08/01
0.11Q	5/08/01	5/29/01	5/31/01	6/14/01

Indicated div.: $0.44 (Div. Reinv. Plan)

CAPITALIZATION (12/31/00):

	($000)	(%)
Long-Term Debt	4,007,041	33.3
Deferred Income Tax	2,146,416	17.8
Preferred Stock	372,681	3.1
Common & Surplus	5,513,235	45.8
Total	12,039,373	100.0

RECENT DEVELOPMENTS: For the year ended 12/31/00, income from continuing operations fell 78.6% to $310.4 million compared with $1.45 billion in 1999. Results for 2000 included losses totaling $149.0 million and excluded a net loss of $86.0 million from discontinued operations. Results for 1999 included non-recurring gains totaling $1.76 billion and excluded gains totaling $18.7 million from discontinued operations. Total operating revenues rose 70.4% to $4.91 billion.

PROSPECTS: In the near-term, earnings may be affected by softer advertising spending. This trend will likely continue through mid 2001, with advertising revenue expected to improve during the second half of the year. For fiscal 2001, TRB expects consolidated revenues to grow 6.0% to 8.0% and operating cash flow to increase approximately 15.0% to $1.80 billion to $1.90 billion, on a pro forma basis. Moreover, earnings per share are expected to grow about 20.0% to $1.55.

BUSINESS

TRIBUNE COMPANY is a media company operating businesses in broadcasting, publishing and on the Internet. The Company owns and operates 22 major-market television stations and reaches nearly 80.0% of U.S. television households. Broadcasting properties also include four radio stations, Tribune Entertainment and the Chicago Cubs baseball team. In addition, TRB operates 11 daily newspapers, including THE BALTIMORE SUN, LOS ANGELES TIMES, THE HARTFORD COURANT, THE ADVOCATE, CHICAGO TRIBUNE, SUN SENTINEL, THE MORNING CALL, GREENWICH TIME, NEWSDAY, ORLANDO SENTINEL, and DAILY PRESS. The Company also distributes entertainment listings and syndicated content, and operates two 24-hour cable news channels. The Company's interactive segment operates news and information Web sites in 18 of the nation's top 30 markets. On 6/12/00, TRB completed the acquisition of Times Mirror for approximately $8.00 billion in cash and stock.

ANNUAL FINANCIAL DATA

	12/31/00	12/26/99	12/27/98	12/28/97	12/29/96	12/31/95	12/25/94
Earnings Per Share	**[5] 0.99**	**[4] 5.62**	**[3] 1.51**	**[3] 1.41**	**[1][2] 1.07**	**[1][2] 0.88**	**[1] 0.83**
Cash Flow Per Share	**2.20**	**6.44**	**2.21**	**2.23**	**1.66**	**1.34**	**1.26**
Tang. Book Val. Per Share	...	...	...	...	...	**0.27**	...
Dividends Per Share	**0.40**	**0.36**	**0.34**	**0.32**	**0.30**	**0.28**	**0.26**
Dividend Payout %	**40.4**	**3.1**	**10.9**	**10.9**	**27.9**	**32.0**	**31.3**
INCOME STATEMENT (IN MILLIONS):							
Total Revenues	4,910.4	3,221.9	2,980.9	2,719.8	2,405.7	2,244.7	2,154.9
Costs & Expenses	3,506.7	2,229.3	2,083.0	1,905.2	1,772.7	1,718.5	1,642.9
Depreciation & Amort.	370.6	222.2	195.6	172.5	142.9	121.0	115.4
Operating Income	1,033.0	770.4	702.3	642.0	490.1	405.2	396.6
Net Interest Inc./(Exp.)	d207.6	d65.6	d82.3	d60.2	d15.7	d7.3	d0.9
Income Before Income Taxes	597.1	2,440.1	705.1	659.0	474.4	412.5	428.7
Income Taxes	270.4	957.0	290.8	265.4	191.7	167.1	186.7
Equity Earnings/Minority Int.	d16.3	...	...	...	...	...	d6.4
Net Income	[5] 310.4	[4] 1,483.1	[3] 414.3	[3] 393.6	[1][2] 282.8	[1][2] 245.5	[1] 242.0
Cash Flow	658.0	1,686.6	591.1	547.3	406.9	347.6	338.8
Average Shs. Outstg. (000)	299,731	261,819	266,924	245,758	245,684	259,160	268,852
BALANCE SHEET (IN MILLIONS):							
Cash & Cash Equivalents	195.5	1,066.8	12.4	66.6	274.2	22.9	21.8
Total Current Assets	1,491.2	2,084.6	945.1	847.7	886.7	545.6	543.5
Net Property	1,743.8	712.5	676.7	650.4	642.7	640.7	641.0
Total Assets	14,676.2	8,797.7	5,935.6	4,777.6	3,700.9	3,288.3	2,785.8
Total Current Liabilities	1,449.2	860.6	828.1	706.2	673.1	557.2	529.7
Long-Term Obligations	4,007.0	2,694.2	1,616.3	1,521.5	979.8	757.4	411.2
Net Stockholders' Equity	5,885.9	3,469.9	2,356.6	1,826.0	1,539.5	1,379.9	1,333.0
Net Working Capital	41.9	1,224.0	117.0	141.5	213.6	d11.6	13.9
Year-end Shs. Outstg. (000)	299,518	237,791	238,004	163,734	245,890	250,208	266,804
STATISTICAL RECORD:							
Operating Profit Margin %	21.0	23.9	23.6	23.6	20.4	18.1	18.4
Net Profit Margin %	6.3	46.0	13.9	14.5	11.8	10.9	11.2
Return on Equity %	5.3	42.7	17.6	21.6	18.4	17.8	18.2
Return on Assets %	2.1	16.9	7.0	8.2	7.6	7.5	8.7
Price Range	55.19-27.88	60.88-30.16	37.53-22.38	30.75-17.75	22.06-14.16	17.22-12.69	16.13-12.22
P/E Ratio	55.7-28.2	10.8-5.4	24.9-14.8	21.8-12.6	20.5-13.2	19.7-14.5	19.4-14.7
Average Yield %	1.0	0.8	1.1	1.3	1.7	1.9	1.8

Statistics are as originally reported. Adj. for 2-for-1 split, 1/97 & 9/99. [1] Incl. $10.0 mill. after-tax non-recur. gains, 1996; $8.7 mill., 1995; $13.0 mill., 1994. [2] Bef. $89.3 mill. gain fr. disc. ops., 1996; $32.7 mill., 1995. [3] Incl. $119.1 mill. pre-tax non-recur. gains, 1998; $111.8 mill., 1997. [4] Incl. $1.76 bill. non-oper. gains & excl. d$3.1 mill. acct. chg. [5] Incl. a loss of $149.0 mill. from non-oper. items & excl. $86.0 mill. net loss fr. disc. ops.

OFFICERS:
J. W. Madigan, Chmn., Pres., C.E.O.
D. C. Grenesko, Sr. V.P., C.F.O.

INVESTOR CONTACT: Ruthelyn Musil, V.P., Corporate Relations, (312) 222-3787

PRINCIPAL OFFICE: 435 N. Michigan Ave., Chicago, IL 60611

TELEPHONE NUMBER: (312) 222-9100
FAX: (312) 222-4917
WEB: www.tribune.com
NO. OF EMPLOYEES: 22,700 (avg.)
SHAREHOLDERS: 7,301
ANNUAL MEETING: In May
INCORPORATED: IL, 1861; reincorp., DE, 1968

INSTITUTIONAL HOLDINGS:
No. of Institutions: 377
Shares Held: 167,693,261
% Held: 55.9

INDUSTRY: Newspapers (SIC: 2711)

TRANSFER AGENT(S): First Chicago Trust Company of New York, Jersey City, NJ

NYSE SYMBOL YUM
Rec. Pr. 44.82 (4/30/01)

TRICON GLOBAL RESTAURANTS, INC.

YIELD	...
P/E RATIO	16.2

MERGENT

TRADING VOLUME
Thousand Shares

1987 1988 1989 1990 1991 1992 1993 1994 1995 1996 1997 1998 1999 2000 2001

*7 YEAR PRICE SCORE N/A   *12 MONTH PRICE SCORE 127.6

*NYSE COMPOSITE INDEX=100

INTERIM EARNINGS (Per Share):

Qtr.	Mar.	June	Sept.	Dec.
1997		d0.73		
1998	0.35	0.78	0.82	0.95
1999	0.66	1.10	1.23	0.93
2000	0.80	0.71	0.40	0.86

INTERIM DIVIDENDS (Per Share):

Amt.	Decl.	Ex.	Rec.	Pay.

No dividends paid.

CAPITALIZATION (12/30/00):

	($000)	(%)
Long-Term Debt	2,397,000	115.0
Deferred Income Tax	10,000	0.5
Common & Surplus	d322,000	-15.4
Total	2,085,000	100.0

RECENT DEVELOPMENTS: For the year ended 12/30/00, net income fell 34.1% to $413.0 million compared with $627.0 million in the previous year. Results for 2000 included an after-tax gain on facility refranchising of $68.0 million and after-tax unusual charges totaling $106.0 million. Earnings for 1999 included nonrecurring items that resulted in a net gain of $197.0 million. Total revenues declined 9.3% to $7.09 billion versus $7.82 billion the year before. Operating profit fell 30.6% to $860.0 million.

PROSPECTS: During 2000, YUM opened 929 restaurants, including significant openings in China, Japan, Korea, Mexico, New Zealand, Thailand and the United Kingdom. For 2001, YUM expects similar levels of international restaurant openings. Meanwhile, YUM plans to rapidly expand its multibranding concept throughout the U.S. with the opening of 450 to 500 new multibranded locations. Going forward, YUM will focus on improving sales levels at its Taco Bell and KFC operations in the U.S.

BUSINESS

TRICON GLOBAL RESTAURANTS, INC. is comprised of four operating divisions organized around its three core concepts, KFC, Pizza Hut and Taco Bell. Each of the Company's four operating divisions is engaged in the operation, development, franchising and licensing of a system of both traditional and non-traditional quick-service-restaurant units. Non-traditional units include express units and kiosks, which have a more limited menu and operate in non-traditional locations like airports, gas and convenience stores, stadiums, amusement parks and colleges. The Company's domestic units by ownership as of 12/30/00 were: Pizza Hut, 1,801; KFC, 1,339 and Taco Bell, 1,162. In addition, there were nearly 1,200 units offering more than one concept. On 10/6/97, YUM was spun off from PepsiCo Inc.

REVENUES

(12/30/00)	($000)	(%)
Company Sales	6,305,000	88.9
Franchise & License Fees	788,000	11.1
Total	7,093,000	100.0

ANNUAL FINANCIAL DATA

	12/30/00	12/25/99	12/26/98	12/27/97	12/28/96	12/30/95	12/31/94
Earnings Per Share	[3] 2.77	[2] 3.92	2.84	[1] d0.73	...	...	...
Cash Flow Per Share	5.15	6.33	5.53	...	...	...	...
INCOME STATEMENT (IN MILLIONS):							
Total Revenues	7,093.0	7,822.0	8,468.0	9,681.0	10,232.0	10,250.0	9,565.0
Costs & Expenses	5,879.0	6,196.0	7,023.0	8,904.0	9,239.0	9,327.0	8,361.0
Depreciation & Amort.	354.0	386.0	417.0	536.0	621.0	671.0	622.0
Operating Income	860.0	1,240.0	1,028.0	241.0	372.0	252.0	582.0
Net Interest Inc./(Exp.)	d176.0	d202.0	d272.0	d276.0	d300.0	d355.0	d341.0
Income Before Income Taxes	684.0	1,038.0	756.0	d35.0	72.0	d103.0	241.0
Income Taxes	271.0	411.0	311.0	76.0	125.0	29.0	122.0
Net Income	[3] 413.0	[2] 627.0	445.0	[1] d111.0	[1] d53.0	d132.0	119.0
Cash Flow	767.0	1,013.0	862.0	425.0	568.0	539.0	741.0
Average Shs. Outstg. (000)	149,000	160,000	156,000	...	...	...	...
BALANCE SHEET (IN MILLIONS):							
Cash & Cash Equivalents	196.0	137.0	208.0	301.0	187.0	105.0	...
Total Current Assets	688.0	486.0	625.0	683.0	962.0	514.0	...
Net Property	2,540.0	2,531.0	2,896.0	3,261.0	4,050.0	4,448.0	...
Total Assets	4,149.0	3,961.0	4,531.0	5,098.0	6,520.0	6,908.0	...
Total Current Liabilities	1,216.0	1,298.0	1,473.0	1,579.0	1,416.0	1,478.0	...
Long-Term Obligations	2,397.0	2,391.0	3,436.0	4,551.0	231.0	260.0	...
Net Stockholders' Equity	d322.0	d560.0	d1,163.0	d1,620.0	4,239.0	4,575.0	...
Net Working Capital	d528.0	d812.0	d848.0	d896.0	d454.0	d964.0	...
Year-end Shs. Outstg. (000)	147,000	151,000	153,000	152,000	...	...	...
STATISTICAL RECORD:							
Operating Profit Margin %	12.1	15.9	12.1	2.5	3.6	2.5	6.1
Net Profit Margin %	5.8	8.0	5.3	...	...	...	1.2
Return on Assets %	10.0	15.8	9.8	...	...	...	...
Debt/Total Assets %	57.8	60.4	75.8	89.3	3.5	3.8	...
Price Range	38.56-23.56	73.88-35.00	50.88-25.06	40.00-27.88	...	...	...
P/E Ratio	13.9-8.5	18.8-8.9	17.9-8.8	...	...	...	...

Statistics are as originally reported. [1] Incl. non-recurr. chrg. 1997, $174.0 mill.; 1996, $246.0 mill. [2] Incl. after-tax net gain of $226.0 mill. ($1.41/sh.) & after-tax non-recurr. chrgs. totaling $29.0 mill. ($0.18/sh.) [3] Incl. after-tax net gain of $68.0 mill. & after-tax unusual chrgs. of $106.0 mill.

OFFICERS:
D. C. Novak, Chmn., Pres., C.E.O.
D. J. Deno, C.F.O.
C. L. Campbell, Sr. V.P., Gen. Couns., Sec.

INVESTOR CONTACT: Tim Jerzyk, V.P., Investor Relations, (502) 874-8617

PRINCIPAL OFFICE: 1441 Gardiner Lane, Louisville, KY 40213

TELEPHONE NUMBER: (502) 874-8300
FAX: (502) 454-2410
WEB: www.triconglobal.com

NO. OF EMPLOYEES: 57,000 full-time (approx.); 133,000 part-time (approx.)

SHAREHOLDERS: 144,000 (approx.)

ANNUAL MEETING: In May

INCORPORATED: NC, 1997

INSTITUTIONAL HOLDINGS:
No. of Institutions: 334
Shares Held: 107,914,539
% Held: 73.5

INDUSTRY: Eating places (SIC: 5812)

TRANSFER AGENT(S): Boston EquiServe, LP, Boston, MA

NYSE SYMBOL TGH
Rec. Pr. 56.99 (5/31/01)

TRIGON HEALTHCARE, INC.

YIELD	...
P/E RATIO	19.7

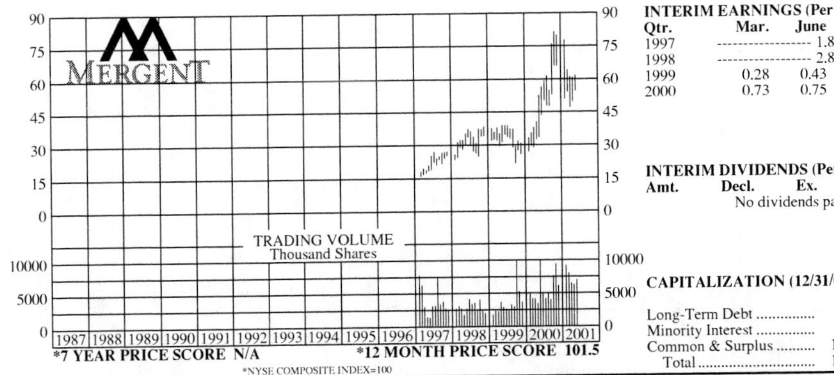

*7 YEAR PRICE SCORE N/A　　*12 MONTH PRICE SCORE 101.5

*NYSE COMPOSITE INDEX=100

INTERIM EARNINGS (Per Share):

Qtr.	Mar.	June	Sept.	Dec.
1997		1.86		
1998		2.88		
1999	0.28	0.43	d0.91	0.70
2000	0.73	0.75	0.88	0.54

INTERIM DIVIDENDS (Per Share):

Amt.	Decl.	Ex.	Rec.	Pay.

No dividends paid.

CAPITALIZATION (12/31/00):

	($000)	(%)
Long-Term Debt	275,448	21.1
Minority Interest	12,976	1.0
Common & Surplus	1,014,862	77.9
Total	1,303,286	100.0

RECENT DEVELOPMENTS: For the twelve months ended 12/31/00, net income skyrocketed to $112.0 million compared with $20.5 million in the comparable period of the previous year. Results for 2000 and 1999 included net realized losses on TGH's investment portfolio of $27.0 million and $22.0 million, respectively. Total revenues increased 11.3% to $2.61 billion from $2.35 billion a year earlier.

PROSPECTS: During the fourth quarter, the Company's subsidiary, Trigon Blue Cross Blue Shield reached agreements with Mid-Atlantic Health Alliance Inc. to provide increased access to physician services for Blue Cross and KeyCare members in the Fredricksburg, Virginia area. Looking ahead, the Company should continue to benefit from its PPO product, which increased membership by 29.0% year over year.

BUSINESS

TRIGON HEALTHCARE, INC. is a managed healthcare company in Virginia, serving nearly 2.0 million members primarily through statewide and regional provider networks. TGH divides its business into four segments: health insurance, government programs, investments and all other health-related business. TGH's health insurance segment provides a range of managed care products primarily through three network systems with a range of utilization and cost containment controls. The government programs segment includes the Federal Employee Program and claims processing for Medicare. All of the investment portfolios of the consolidated subsidiaries are managed and evaluated collectively within the investment segment. TGH's other health-related business includes disease management programs, third party administration for medical and workers compensation, health promotions and similar products.

REVENUES

(12/31/2000)	($000)	(%)
Health Insurance	2,036,225	80.7
Govt. Programs	464,303	18.4
All other services	21,339	0.9
Total	2,521,867	100.0

ANNUAL FINANCIAL DATA

	12/31/00	12/31/99	12/31/98	12/31/97	12/31/96	12/31/95	12/31/94
Earnings Per Share	**2.90**	**0.49**	**2.88**	**1.86**	**[1] [2] 0.94**	**[1] 0.83**	**[1] Nil**
Cash Flow Per Share	**2.95**	**0.65**	**2.90**	**2.44**	**5.05**	**1.48**	**...**
Tang. Book Val. Per Share	**26.63**	**24.15**	**23.84**	**21.05**	**15.69**	**16.96**	**...**
INCOME STATEMENT (IN MILLIONS):							
Total Revenues	2,611.6	2,346.4	2,236.4	2,063.6	1,922.5	1,724.9	1,563.7
Costs & Expenses	2,443.8	2,308.5	2,049.2	1,910.5	1,784.8	1,654.0	1,432.9
Depreciation & Amort.	2.0	6.4	0.4	8.4	17.1	11.0	12.2
Operating Income	165.8	31.5	186.8	144.7	120.6	60.0	118.5
Income Before Income Taxes	165.8	31.5	186.8	144.7	182.9	60.0	118.5
Income Taxes	50.1	8.3	63.2	49.6	cr13.6	8.3	24.6
Equity Earnings/Minority Int.	d3.7	d2.7	...	...	...	...	...
Net Income	112.0	20.5	123.6	95.1	[1] [2] 196.5	[2] 51.7	[1] 94.0
Cash Flow	114.0	26.9	123.9	103.5	213.7	62.7	106.2
Average Shs. Outstg. (000)	38,681	41,420	42,772	42,380	42,300	42,300	...
BALANCE SHEET (IN MILLIONS):							
Cash & Cash Equivalents	1,781.7	1,741.0	1,590.0	1,370.9	1,213.9	1,119.7	1,001.6
Total Current Assets	2,299.8	2,169.5	1,979.3	1,739.4	1,631.5	1,461.9	1,340.9
Net Property	69.8	51.2	47.9	43.9	49.5	44.8	43.9
Total Assets	2,448.5	2,314.1	2,174.2	1,928.8	1,833.1	1,565.3	1,403.1
Total Current Liabilities	1,026.0	1,003.5	875.1	747.8	890.8	738.1	669.9
Long-Term Obligations	275.4	248.0	89.3	90.1	87.5	...	...
Net Stockholders' Equity	1,014.9	937.0	1,071.2	958.7	739.8	740.1	655.9
Net Working Capital	1,273.8	1,166.0	1,104.3	991.6	740.7	723.8	671.0
Year-end Shs. Outstg. (000)	37,539	38,200	42,300	42,300	42,300	42,300	...
STATISTICAL RECORD:							
Operating Profit Margin %	6.3	1.3	8.4	7.0	6.3	3.5	7.6
Net Profit Margin %	4.3	0.9	5.5	4.6	10.2	3.0	6.0
Return on Equity %	11.0	2.2	11.5	9.9	26.6	7.0	14.3
Return on Assets %	4.6	0.9	5.7	4.9	10.7	3.3	6.7
Debt/Total Assets %	11.2	10.7	4.1	4.7	4.8	...	...
Price Range	81.50-26.88	39.00-21.50	38.38-23.50	27.25-15.88	...	...	...
P/E Ratio	28.1-9.3	79.6-43.9	13.3-8.2	14.6-8.5	...	...	...

Statistics are as originally reported. [1] Bef. extraord. chrg. of $644,000, 1994; $4.7 mill., 1995; $190.8 mill., 1996. [2] Incl. pre-tax gain of $62.3 mill. on sale of subsidiary.

OFFICERS:
T. G. Snead Jr., Chmn., C.E.O.
J. W. Coyle, Pres., C.O.O.
T. R. Byrd, Sr. V.P., C.F.O.
J. C. Wiltshire, Sr. V.P., Gen. Couns., Corp. Sec.

INVESTOR CONTACT: Chris Drake, Inv. Rel., (804) 354-3609

PRINCIPAL OFFICE: 2015 Staples Mill Road, Richmond, VA 23230

TELEPHONE NUMBER: (804) 354-7000
WEB: www.trigon.com

NO. OF EMPLOYEES: 3,917 full-time; 82 part-time

SHAREHOLDERS: 76,708

ANNUAL MEETING: In Apr.

INCORPORATED: VA, 1935

INSTITUTIONAL HOLDINGS:
No. of Institutions: 200
Shares Held: 24,563,792
% Held: 67.5

INDUSTRY: Hospital and medical service plans (SIC: 6324)

TRANSFER AGENT(S): The Bank of New York, New York, NY

NYSE SYMBOL TRN
Rec. Pr. 22.35 (5/31/01)

TRINITY INDUSTRIES, INC.

YIELD 3.2%
P/E RATIO . . .

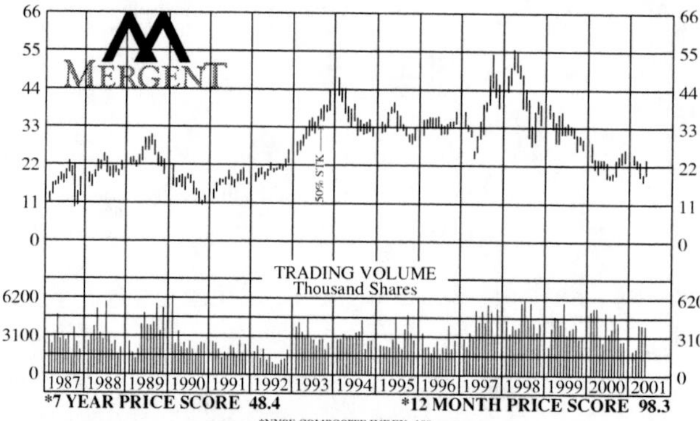

*7 YEAR PRICE SCORE 48.4 *12 MONTH PRICE SCORE 98.3

*NYSE COMPOSITE INDEX=100

INTERIM EARNINGS (Per Share):

Qtr.	June	Sept.	Dec.	Mar.
1996-97	0.80	0.81	0.80	0.80
1997-98	0.76	d0.17	0.88	0.89
1998-99	1.31	1.02	0.96	0.96
1999-00	1.10	1.16	1.02	0.87
2000-01	0.55	d0.35	d1.14	...

INTERIM DIVIDENDS (Per Share):

Amt.	Decl.	Ex.	Rec.	Pay.
0.18Q	3/10/00	4/12/00	4/14/00	4/28/00
0.18Q	6/08/00	7/12/00	7/14/00	7/31/00
0.18Q	9/14/00	10/11/00	10/13/00	10/31/00
0.18Q	12/14/00	1/10/01	1/15/01	1/31/01
0.18Q	3/08/01	4/10/01	4/13/01	4/30/01

Indicated div.: $0.72

CAPITALIZATION (3/31/00):

	($000)	(%)
Long-Term Debt [1]	95,400	8.2
Deferred Income Tax	58,500	5.0
Common & Surplus	1,015,100	86.8
Total	1,169,000	100.0

RECENT DEVELOPMENTS: For the quarter ended 12/31/00, TRN incurred a net loss of $42.4 million compared with net income of $40.3 million in 1999. Results for 2000 included after-tax charges of $42.0 million primarily related to write-downs of equity investments and wholly owned businesses, environmental liabilities and other charges. Revenues fell 42.8% to $401.2 million.

PROSPECTS: In March 2001, TRN announced its intention to discontinue and sell certain non-core assets. These assets include concrete mixers, concrete batch plants and component parts for the concrete related industries. Meanwhile, TRN expects earnings to be in the range of $1.20 to $1.50 per share in the next fiscal year.

BUSINESS

TRINITY INDUSTRIES, INC. is a diversified industrial growth company. Trinity principally operates in six business segments: the Railcar Group; Industrial Group; Highway Construction Products Group; Inland Barge Group; Parts & Service Group; and Concrete and Aggregate Group. TRN manufactures railroad freight cars, principally pressure and non-pressure tank cars, hopper cars, box cars, intermodal cars and gondola cars used for transporting a wide variety of liquids, gases and dry cargo. TRN is engaged in manufacturing metal containers for the storage and transportation of liquefied petroleum gas and anhydrous ammonia fertilizer. The highway construction products manufactured by TRN include highway guardrail and highway safety devices and related barrier products, and beams and girders. TRN produces river hopper barges, inland tank barges and fiberglass barge covers. TRN is engaged in the production and manufacturing of ready-mix concrete and aggregates primarily in Texas and Louisiana.

ANNUAL FINANCIAL DATA

	3/31/00	3/31/99	3/31/98	3/31/97	3/31/96	3/31/95	3/31/94
Earnings Per Share	**4.15**	**4.25**	**[4] 2.36**	**[3] 2.66**	**2.72**	**2.20**	**[2] 1.69**
Cash Flow Per Share	**6.16**	**5.90**	**4.03**	**4.71**	**4.53**	**3.65**	**3.10**
Tang. Book Val. Per Share	**26.37**	**23.22**	**20.40**	**18.83**	**17.93**	**15.95**	**14.37**
Dividends Per Share	**0.71**	**0.68**	**0.68**	**0.68**	**0.68**	**0.68**	**0.57**
Dividend Payout %	**17.1**	**16.0**	**28.8**	**25.6**	**25.0**	**30.9**	**33.7**
INCOME STATEMENT (IN MILLIONS):							
Total Revenues	2,740.6	2,926.9	2,473.0	2,234.3	2,496.0	2,314.9	1,784.9
Costs & Expenses	2,381.3	2,570.0	2,144.1	1,932.3	2,201.4	2,077.7	1,587.8
Depreciation & Amort.	80.3	72.0	73.0	87.8	75.9	58.6	56.8
Operating Income	279.0	284.9	255.9	214.2	201.2	157.5	116.6
Net Interest Inc./(Exp.)	d18.4	d15.9	d19.1	d20.9	d32.3	d32.5	d27.7
Income Before Income Taxes	262.9	296.4	165.9	181.3	186.3	147.5	114.2
Income Taxes	97.4	111.1	62.2	67.6	72.5	58.4	45.9
Net Income	165.5	185.3	[4] 103.7	[3] 113.7	113.8	89.1	[2] 68.3
Cash Flow	245.8	257.3	176.7	201.5	189.7	147.7	125.1
Average Shs. Outstg. (000)	39,900	43,600	43,900	42,800	41,900	40,500	40,300
BALANCE SHEET (IN MILLIONS):							
Cash & Cash Equivalents	16.9	13.5	3.1	12.2	15.4	15.3	8.7
Total Current Assets	727.3	768.0	736.2	563.6	712.6	680.6	602.4
Net Property	813.2	732.3	726.9	711.6	692.3	687.1	667.1
Total Assets	1,738.5	1,684.9	1,573.9	1,356.4	1,455.8	1,420.0	1,306.8
Total Current Liabilities	531.0	547.7	487.6	325.2	458.1	477.5	366.2
Long-Term Obligations	95.4	120.6	149.6	178.6	206.4	242.9	277.9
Net Stockholders' Equity	1,015.1	959.1	887.5	809.5	746.0	641.2	570.5
Net Working Capital	196.3	220.3	248.6	238.4	254.5	203.1	236.2
Year-end Shs. Outstg. (000)	38,500	41,300	43,500	43,000	41,600	40,200	39,700
STATISTICAL RECORD:							
Operating Profit Margin %	10.2	9.7	10.3	9.6	8.1	6.8	6.5
Net Profit Margin %	6.0	6.3	4.2	5.1	4.6	3.8	3.8
Return on Equity %	16.3	19.3	11.7	14.0	15.3	13.9	12.0
Return on Assets %	9.5	11.0	6.6	8.4	7.8	6.3	5.2
Debt/Total Assets %	5.5	7.2	9.5	13.2	14.2	17.1	21.3
Price Range	39.88-26.25	55.69-27.56	54.34-24.13	37.63-30.75	40.38-28.13	47.38-30.38	44.13-24.75
P/E Ratio	9.6-6.3	13.1-6.5	23.0-10.2	14.1-11.6	14.8-10.3	21.5-13.8	26.1-14.6
Average Yield %	2.1	1.6	1.7	2.0	2.0	1.7	1.7

Statistics are as originally reported. [1] Incl. leasing subsidiaries. [2] Bef. acctg. credit of $7.9 mill. ($0.20/sh.). [3] Bef. gain of $23.8 mill. in discont. opers. [4] Incl. $70.0 mill. pretax litigation settlement.

OFFICERS:
T. R. Wallace, Chmn., Pres., C.E.O.
J. L. Adams, Exec. V.P.
J. S. Ivy, V.P., C.F.O.
M. G. Fortado, V.P., Sec., Gen. Couns.

INVESTOR CONTACT: Michael E. Conley, Dir., Inv. Rel., (214) 589-8935

PRINCIPAL OFFICE: 2525 Stemmons Freeway, Dallas, TX 75207-2401

TELEPHONE NUMBER: (214) 631-4420
FAX: (214) 589-8501
WEB: www.trinityannual.net

NO. OF EMPLOYEES: 20,600 (approx.)

SHAREHOLDERS: 2,150 (approx.)

ANNUAL MEETING: In July

INCORPORATED: TX, 1933; reincorp., DE, Mar., 1987

INSTITUTIONAL HOLDINGS:
No. of Institutions: 143
Shares Held: 25,972,891
% Held: 70.5

INDUSTRY: Railroad equipment (SIC: 3743)

TRANSFER AGENT(S): The Bank of New York, New York, NY

NYSE SYMBOL TNO
Rec. Pr. 41.50 (5/31/01)

TRUE NORTH COMMUNICATIONS, INC.

YIELD 1.4%
P/E RATIO 29.6

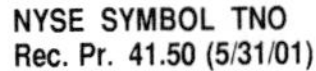

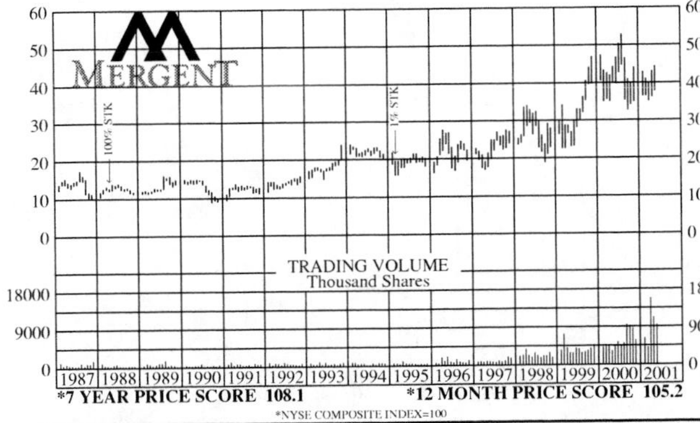

INTERIM EARNINGS (Per Share):

Qtr.	Mar.	June	Sept.	Dec.
1997	0.01	0.30	0.28	d1.73
1998	0.08	0.38	0.29	0.03
1999	0.15	0.43	d0.66	0.85
2000	0.20	0.54	0.47	0.19

INTERIM DIVIDENDS (Per Share):

Amt.	Decl.	Ex.	Rec.	Pay.
0.15Q	5/17/00	6/14/00	6/16/00	7/03/00
0.15Q	7/25/00	9/13/00	9/15/00	10/02/00
0.15Q	10/25/00	12/13/00	12/15/00	1/02/01
0.15Q	2/28/01	3/15/01	3/19/01	4/02/01
0.15Q	4/30/01	5/30/01	6/01/01	6/18/01

Indicated div.: $0.60 (Div. Reinv. Plan)

CAPITALIZATION (12/31/00):

	($000)	(%)
Long-Term Debt	26,730	6.2
Common & Surplus	404,983	93.8
Total	431,713	100.0

RECENT DEVELOPMENTS: For the year ended 12/31/00, net income soared to $61.6 million compared with $28.2 million in the previous year. Earnings for 2000 and 1999 included pre-tax restructuring and other charges of $16.9 million and $75.4 million, respectively, as well as a loss of $28.2 million and a gain of $2.4 million, respectively, from equity. Commissions and fees revenues increased 8.2% to $1.56 billion. Comparisons were made with restated prior-year figures.

PROSPECTS: On 3/19/01, the Company announced that it signed a definitive agreement to be acquired by The Interpublic Group of Companies, Inc. in a stock transaction valued at $2.10 billion. The combined company will have offices in more than 130 countries. Meanwhile, TNO continues to expand globally with the acquisition of Compagnia del Marketing Diretto, an Italian direct and digital marketing firm.

BUSINESS

TRUE NORTH COMMUNICATIONS INC. (formerly Foote, Cone & Belding Communications, Inc.), is a global advertising and communications holding company. It has three major global brands: FCB Worldwide, advertising; BSMG Worldwide, public relations; and Marketing Drive Worldwide, marketing services. TNO's U.S. brands include Bozell Group, New America Strategies Group, Temerlin McClain, Tierney Communications and TN Media. In the digital area, TNO's portfolio of brands includes R/GA Interactive, SixtyFootSpider and Stein Rogan + Partners. In addition, TNO has a stake in the German-based advertising agency, Springer & Jacoby. TNO also holds an approximately 44.0% interest in Modem Media Poppe Tyson, Inc., an internet marketing company.

QUARTERLY DATA

(12/31/2000)	REV	INC
1st Quarter	359,600	7,000
2nd Quarter	375,100	23,900
3rd Quarter	381,200	20,800
4th Quarter	441,000	9,900

ANNUAL FINANCIAL DATA

	12/31/00	12/31/99	12/31/98	[2] 12/31/97	12/31/96	12/31/95	12/31/94
Earnings Per Share	[5] 1.21	[5] 0.81	[4] 0.78	[3] d1.17	[1] 1.20	[1] 0.87	1.34
Cash Flow Per Share	2.66	1.98	1.75	d0.06	2.01	1.66	1.99
Tang. Book Val. Per Share	...	...	...	...	3.79	5.87	6.65
Dividends Per Share	0.60	0.60	0.60	0.45	0.75	0.60	0.60
Dividend Payout %	49.6	74.1	76.9	...	62.5	69.0	44.8
INCOME STATEMENT (IN MILLIONS):							
Total Revenues	1,556.8	1,439.4	1,242.3	1,204.9	493.1	439.1	403.7
Costs & Expenses	1,306.5	1,300.7	1,078.5	1,193.9	450.3	391.0	351.8
Depreciation & Amort.	74.0	56.3	45.1	47.5	19.0	17.8	14.9
Operating Income	176.4	82.3	118.7	d36.5	23.8	30.3	37.1
Net Interest Inc./(Exp.)	d17.2	d18.1	d22.0	d20.1	d8.6	d8.1	d7.0
Income Before Income Taxes	168.5	82.7	89.8	d46.1	19.2	14.8	36.0
Income Taxes	75.8	42.2	56.8	11.2	9.7	3.7	16.1
Net Income	[5] 61.6	[5] 38.8	[4] 36.1	[3] d50.0	[1] 27.8	[1] 19.7	30.3
Cash Flow	135.6	95.1	81.2	d2.5	46.8	37.4	45.2
Average Shs. Outstg. (000)	51,066	48,142	46,394	44,094	23,254	22,542	22,678
BALANCE SHEET (IN MILLIONS):							
Cash & Cash Equivalents	136.5	137.2	232.4	109.0	57.0	57.0	77.1
Total Current Assets	1,283.6	1,246.9	1,174.0	997.9	504.2	430.0	382.7
Net Property	166.1	156.8	128.3	124.3	61.4	54.6	45.7
Total Assets	2,063.3	2,005.3	1,779.0	1,674.4	932.7	766.1	673.7
Total Current Liabilities	1,486.5	1,394.8	1,334.8	1,232.3	553.2	476.5	399.5
Long-Term Obligations	26.7	36.6	15.3	35.9	31.5	5.4	5.5
Net Stockholders' Equity	405.0	366.4	307.4	267.8	241.3	222.1	207.8
Net Working Capital	d202.9	d147.8	d160.8	d234.4	d48.9	d46.5	d16.8
Year-end Shs. Outstg. (000)	50,119	48,857	45,021	43,952	23,668	23,368	22,842
STATISTICAL RECORD:							
Operating Profit Margin %	11.3	5.7	9.6	...	4.8	6.9	9.2
Net Profit Margin %	4.0	2.7	2.9	...	5.6	4.5	7.5
Return on Equity %	15.2	10.6	11.7	...	11.5	8.8	14.6
Return on Assets %	3.0	1.9	2.0	...	3.0	2.6	4.5
Debt/Total Assets %	1.3	1.8	0.9	2.1	3.4	0.7	0.8
Price Range	52.88-32.56	47.00-22.50	34.00-18.81	27.63-17.00	27.75-16.25	21.81-15.75	24.00-19.94
P/E Ratio	43.7-26.9	58.0-27.8	43.6-24.1	...	23.1-13.5	25.1-18.1	17.9-14.9
Average Yield %	1.4	1.7	2.3	2.0	3.4	3.2	2.7

Statistics are as originally reported. Adj. for a 2-for-1 stk splits, 2/95. [1] Incl. net pre-tax non-recurr. chrgs. of $1.4 mill., 1996; $10.2 mill., 1995. [2] Incl. operations of Bozell, Jacobs, Kenyon & Eckhardt, Inc. [3] Incl. pre-tax merger-rel. chrg. of $80.9 mill. [4] Incl. pre-tax restruct. & merger-rel. gain of $1.1 mill. & subsidiary restruct. chrg. of $4.3 mill. [5] Incl. pre-tax restruct. & other chrgs. of $16.9 mill., 2000; $76.4 mill., 1999.

OFFICERS:
D. A. Bell, Chmn., C.E.O.
K. J. Smith, Exec. V.P., C.F.O.
K. J. Ashley, V.P., Treas.

INVESTOR CONTACT: Susan Geanuleas, Vice-Pres., Corp. Commun., (312) 425-6570

PRINCIPAL OFFICE: 101 East Erie Street, Chicago, IL 60611-2897

TELEPHONE NUMBER: (312) 425-6500
FAX: (312) 425-6350
WEB: www.truenorth.com

NO. OF EMPLOYEES: 13,800 (approx.)

SHAREHOLDERS: 2,289 (record)

ANNUAL MEETING: In May

INCORPORATED: DE, Dec., 1942

INSTITUTIONAL HOLDINGS:
No. of Institutions: 159
Shares Held: 31,099,846
% Held: 61.2

INDUSTRY: Advertising agencies (SIC: 7311)

TRANSFER AGENT(S): First Chicago Trust Company, Jersey City, NJ

NYSE SYMBOL TRW
Rec. Pr. 38.46 (4/30/01)

TRW INC.

YIELD 3.6%
P/E RATIO 11.0

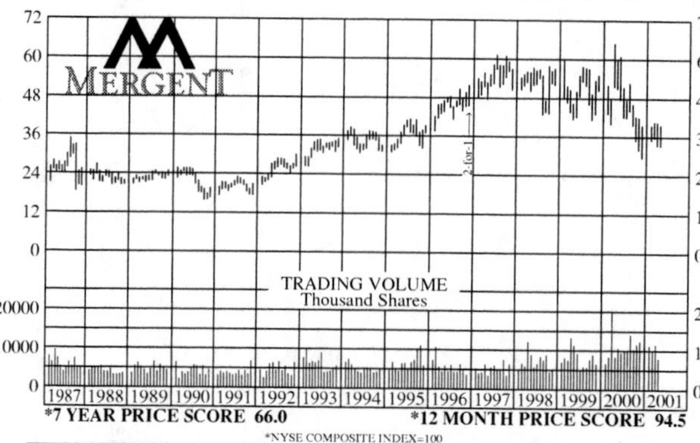

*7 YEAR PRICE SCORE 66.0 *12 MONTH PRICE SCORE 94.5

*NYSE COMPOSITE INDEX=100

INTERIM EARNINGS (Per Share):

Qtr.	Mar.	June	Sept.	Dec.
1997	0.93	1.05	0.86	d3.34
1998	1.03	1.00	0.85	0.96
1999	0.04	1.14	1.08	1.81
2000	1.68	1.59	0.26	d0.02

INTERIM DIVIDENDS (Per Share):

Amt.	Decl.	Ex.	Rec.	Pay.
0.33Q	4/26/00	5/10/00	5/12/00	6/15/00
0.33Q	7/26/00	8/09/00	8/11/00	9/15/00
0.35Q	10/25/00	11/08/00	11/10/00	12/15/00
0.35Q	12/13/00	2/07/01	2/09/01	3/15/01
0.35Q	4/25/01	5/09/01	5/11/01	6/15/01

Indicated div.: $1.40 (Div. Reinv. Plan)

CAPITALIZATION (12/31/00):

	($000)	(%)
Long-Term Debt	4,765,000	55.6
Deferred Income Tax	1,030,000	12.0
Minority Interest	123,000	1.4
Common & Surplus	2,651,000	30.9
Total	8,569,000	100.0

RECENT DEVELOPMENTS: For the year ended 12/31/00, net income declined 6.5% to $438.0 million compared with $468.8 million in the previous year. Earnings for 2000 and 1999 included unusual items resulting in net after-tax charges of $33.1 million and $99.6 million, respectively. Total sales grew 1.5% to $17.23 billion from $16.97 billion a year earlier. Sales for the Automotive segment fell 3.0% to $10.99 billion.

PROSPECTS: TRW will continue with efforts to reduce costs throughout 2001, and will attempt to sell non-core operations in its Automotive business. Separately, TRW was awarded a $78.7 million, five-year follow-on contract to provide technical support to the U.S. Air Force's Rocket Systems Launch Program. Meanwhile, TRW announced the creation of Picture PipeLine, LLC, a media management service company.

BUSINESS

TRW INC. provides high technology products and services for automotive, aerospace and information technology markets worldwide. Automotive products include steering, suspension, electronic and occupant restraint systems, engine valves and valve train parts, electro-mechanical assemblies, fasteners, and automotive electronic products. Aerospace and Information Technology designs and manufactures spacecraft and related equipment as well as software and systems engineering support services primarily for the U.S. Government. TRW has principal facilities in 25 countries. On 3/25/99, TRW acquired LucasVarity Plc.

REVENUES

(12/31/2000)	($000)	(%)
Occupant Safety	2,803,000	16.3
Chassis	5,681,000	33.0
Automotive Electronics	1,664,000	9.6
Other Automotive	846,000	4.9
Space & Electronics	1,880,000	10.9
Systems & Info. Technology	3,252,000	18.9
Aeronautical	1,105,000	6.4
Total	17,231,000	100.0

ANNUAL FINANCIAL DATA

	12/31/00	12/31/99	12/31/98	12/31/97	12/31/96	12/31/95	12/31/94
Earnings Per Share	**3 3.51**	**3 3.80**	**3.83**	**2 d0.40**	**1 1.37**	**3.35**	**2.53**
Cash Flow Per Share	**9.86**	**10.68**	**8.38**	**3.78**	**4.81**	**7.18**	**6.15**
Tang. Book Val. Per Share	...	...	**6.76**	**6.63**	**15.68**	**11.53**	**8.98**
Dividends Per Share	**1.34**	**1.32**	**1.26**	**1.24**	**1.14**	**1.02**	**0.97**
Dividend Payout %	**38.3**	**34.7**	**32.9**	...	**82.8**	**30.6**	**38.4**
INCOME STATEMENT (IN MILLIONS):							
Total Revenues	17,231.0	16,969.0	11,886.0	10,831.0	9,857.0	10,172.0	9,087.0
Costs & Expenses	15,438.0	15,068.0	10,497.0	10,016.0	8,949.0	8,849.0	7,962.0
Depreciation & Amort.	794.0	850.0	566.0	490.0	452.0	510.0	476.0
Operating Income	999.0	1,051.0	823.0	325.0	456.0	813.0	649.0
Net Interest Inc./(Exp.)	d524.0	d477.0	d114.0	d75.0	d84.0	d95.0	d105.0
Income Before Income Taxes	706.0	787.0	746.0	240.0	302.0	708.0	535.0
Income Taxes	268.0	318.0	269.0	289.0	120.0	262.0	202.0
Net Income	3 438.0	3 469.0	477.0	2 d23.0	1 182.0	446.0	333.0
Cash Flow	1,231.0	1,318.0	1,042.0	466.0	633.0	955.0	808.0
Average Shs. Outstg. (000)	124,900	123,500	124,400	123,700	131,700	133,200	131,600
BALANCE SHEET (IN MILLIONS):							
Cash & Cash Equivalents	267.0	228.0	83.0	70.0	386.0	59.0	109.0
Total Current Assets	3,967.0	5,199.0	2,703.0	2,435.0	2,781.0	2,336.0	2,215.0
Net Property	3,587.0	3,894.0	2,683.0	2,621.0	2,480.0	2,563.0	2,489.0
Total Assets	16,467.0	18,266.0	7,169.0	6,410.0	5,899.0	5,890.0	5,636.0
Total Current Liabilities	5,860.0	6,729.0	3,018.0	2,719.0	2,157.0	2,012.0	1,986.0
Long-Term Obligations	4,765.0	5,369.0	1,353.0	1,117.0	458.0	1,082.0	1,388.0
Net Stockholders' Equity	2,651.0	2,712.0	1,878.0	1,624.0	2,189.0	2,172.0	1,822.0
Net Working Capital	d1,893.0	d1,530.0	d315.0	d284.0	624.0	324.0	229.0
Year-end Shs. Outstg. (000)	124,200	110,400	119,900	122,500	126,100	131,200	129,800
STATISTICAL RECORD:							
Operating Profit Margin %	5.8	6.2	6.9	3.0	4.6	8.0	7.1
Net Profit Margin %	2.5	2.8	4.0	...	1.8	4.4	3.7
Return on Equity %	16.5	17.3	25.4	...	8.3	20.5	18.3
Return on Assets %	2.7	2.6	6.7	...	3.1	7.6	5.9
Debt/Total Assets %	28.9	29.4	18.9	17.4	7.8	18.4	24.6
Price Range	65.00-29.38	59.88-41.19	58.00-42.69	61.31-47.38	52.00-37.44	41.31-30.88	38.75-30.50
P/E Ratio	18.5-8.4	15.8-10.8	15.1-11.1	...	38.0-27.3	12.4-9.2	15.3-12.1
Average Yield %	2.9	2.6	2.5	2.3	2.5	2.8	2.8

Statistics are as originally reported. Adj. for 2-for-1 stk. split, 12/96. 1 Incl. $382.7 mill. in pre-tax restruct. chrgs. & excl. after-tax gain of $297.7 mill. from the sale of the Information Services unit. 2 Incl. $547.9 mill. in R&D chrgs. 3 Incl. net non-recurr. chrg. of $33.1mill., 2000; $99.6 mill., 1999.

OFFICERS:
J. T. Gorman, Chmn.
D. M. Cote, Pres., C.E.O

INVESTOR CONTACT: Joseph S. Cantle, Vice-Pres.-Inv. Rel., (216) 291-7506

PRINCIPAL OFFICE: 1900 Richmond Road, Cleveland, OH 44124

TELEPHONE NUMBER: (216) 291-7000
FAX: (216) 291-7321
WEB: www.trw.com

NO. OF EMPLOYEES: 103,000 (approx.)

SHAREHOLDERS: 22,325 (record)

ANNUAL MEETING: In April

INCORPORATED: OH, June, 1916

INSTITUTIONAL HOLDINGS:
No. of Institutions: 283
Shares Held: 70,191,151
% Held: 56.2

INDUSTRY: Motor vehicle parts and accessories (SIC: 3714)

TRANSFER AGENT(S): National City Bank, Cleveland, OH

NYSE SYMBOL TUP
Rec. Pr. 22.02 (4/30/01)

TUPPERWARE CORPORATION

YIELD 4.0%
P/E RATIO 17.1

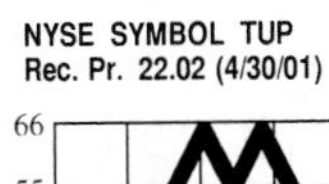

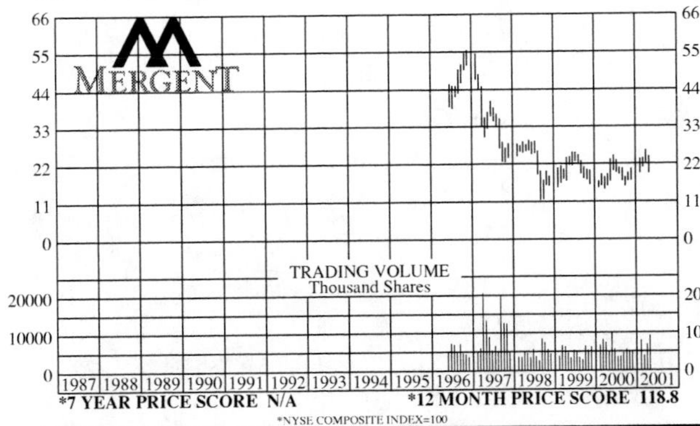

INTERIM EARNINGS (Per Share):

Qtr.	Mar.	June	Sept.	Dec.
1997	0.40	0.61	0.06	0.25
1998	0.26	0.39	d0.11	0.64
1999	0.31	0.25	0.06	0.75
2000	0.33	0.50	0.08	0.38

INTERIM DIVIDENDS (Per Share):

Amt.	Decl.	Ex.	Rec.	Pay.
0.22Q	5/11/00	6/14/00	6/16/00	6/30/00
0.22Q	8/10/00	9/13/00	9/15/00	10/02/00
0.22Q	11/14/00	12/14/00	12/18/00	1/05/01
0.22Q	3/13/01	3/21/01	3/23/01	4/06/01
0.22Q	5/17/01	6/14/01	6/18/01	7/02/01

Indicated div.: $0.88

CAPITALIZATION (12/30/00):

	($000)	(%)
Long-Term Debt	358,100	74.3
Common & Surplus	123,900	25.7
Total	482,000	100.0

RECENT DEVELOPMENTS: For the year ended 12/30/00, the Company reported net income of $74.9 million compared with income of $79.0 million in 1999. Results included re-engineering charges of $12.5 million in 2000 and $15.1 million in 1999. Sales were $1.07 billion, up slightly from $1.06 billion a year earlier. European sales fell 13.3% to $424.1 million. Asia Pacific's sales were flat at $242.0 million. Latin America's sales advanced 25.2% to $193.0 milllion.

PROSPECTS: Going forward, European sales may benefit from strenghening of the Euro. Asia Pacific's sales may continue to be negatively affected by softness in Japan and the Philippines. Latin America's sales should benefit from strong volume growth in Mexico and Brazil. For the full year, the target for sales is a low double-digit increase, and a high-teen increase in earnings, excluding foreign exchange and re-engineering costs.

BUSINESS

TUPPERWARE CORPORATION is a direct-selling multinational consumer products company engaged in the manufacture and sale of Tupperware products. The core of TUP's product line consists of a broad line of high-quality food storage containers that preserve freshness through the well-known Tupperware seals. The Company is a direct-seller of premium beauty and skin care products through its BeautiControl brand in North America. TUP also has an established line of food preparation and serving containers, kitchen gadgets, children's educational toys, microwave products and gifts. TUP's distribution system includes 1,846 distributors, 53,914 managers, and 1,036,651 dealers worldwide. The Company also sells its products via the Internet. Sales in 2000 were derived: European, 39%; Asia Pacific, 23%; Latin America, 18%; United States, 19%; and BeautiControl, 1%. The Company was spun off from Premark International, Inc. on 5/31/96.

ANNUAL FINANCIAL DATA

	12/30/00	12/25/99	12/26/98	12/27/97	12/28/96	12/30/95	12/31/94
Earnings Per Share	**2 1.29**	**2 1.37**	**1.18**	**1 1.32**	**2.70**	**2.55**	**Nil**
Cash Flow Per Share	**2.19**	**2.32**	**2.27**	**2.40**	**3.80**	**3.69**	...
Tang. Book Val. Per Share	**1.14**	**2.47**	**2.36**	**3.43**	**4.90**	...	...
Dividends Per Share	**0.88**	**0.88**	**0.88**	**0.88**	**0.22**	...	...
Dividend Payout %	**68.2**	**64.2**	**74.6**	**66.7**	**8.1**	...	...
INCOME STATEMENT (IN MILLIONS):							
Total Revenues	1,073.1	1,043.8	1,082.8	1,229.3	1,369.3	1,359.4	1,274.6
Costs & Expenses	884.7	866.3	904.6	1,028.5	1,049.2	1,073.7	1,027.9
Depreciation & Amort.	52.1	55.6	64.0	66.1	65.3	61.3	55.7
Operating Income	136.3	141.9	114.2	134.7	254.8	224.4	191.0
Net Interest Inc./(Exp.)	d21.0	d20.9	d22.7	d17.8	d8.0	1.9	0.2
Income Before Income Taxes	101.1	103.3	91.5	110.8	234.5	224.9	191.2
Income Taxes	26.2	24.3	22.4	28.8	59.8	53.5	42.0
Net Income	2 74.9	2 79.0	69.1	1 82.0	174.7	171.4	149.2
Cash Flow	127.0	134.6	133.1	148.1	240.0	232.7	204.9
Average Shs. Outstg. (000)	58,000	57,900	58,700	61,827	63,216	63,095	...
BALANCE SHEET (IN MILLIONS):							
Cash & Cash Equivalents	32.6	24.4	23.0	22.1	53.0	97.3	102.3
Total Current Assets	372.4	370.5	385.6	403.1	523.2	526.4	473.3
Net Property	233.1	242.9	271.0	293.0	331.0	317.7	310.2
Total Assets	849.4	796.1	823.4	847.2	978.5	944.0	882.6
Total Current Liabilities	275.8	309.2	290.1	299.8	379.8	438.3	400.4
Long-Term Obligations	358.1	248.5	300.1	236.7	215.3	0.4	0.5
Net Stockholders' Equity	123.9	145.3	135.8	214.2	305.5	415.6	395.1
Net Working Capital	96.6	61.3	95.5	103.3	143.4	88.1	72.9
Year-end Shs. Outstg. (000)	57,884	57,666	57,614	62,367	62,360	...	...
STATISTICAL RECORD:							
Operating Profit Margin %	12.7	13.6	10.5	11.0	18.6	16.5	15.0
Net Profit Margin %	7.0	7.6	6.4	6.7	12.8	12.6	11.7
Return on Equity %	60.5	54.4	50.9	38.3	57.2	41.2	37.8
Return on Assets %	8.8	9.9	8.4	9.7	17.9	18.2	16.9
Debt/Total Assets %	42.2	31.2	36.4	27.9	22.0	...	0.1
Price Range	24.50-14.56	25.50-15.06	29.00-11.44	54.50-22.50	55.50-38.25	...	...
P/E Ratio	19.0-11.3	18.6-11.0	24.6-9.7	41.3-17.0	20.6-14.2	...	...
Average Yield %	4.5	4.3	4.4	2.3	0.5	...	...

Statistics are as originally reported. 1 Incl. nonrecur. chrg. of $42.4 mill. 2 Incl. re-engineering chrg. of $15.1 mill., 1999; $12.5 mill., 2000.

OFFICERS:
E. V. Goings, Chmn., C.E.O.
A. D. Kennedy, Pres.
P. B. Van Sickle, Exec. V.P., C.F.O.

INVESTOR CONTACT: Michael Poteshman, (407) 826-4522

PRINCIPAL OFFICE: 14901 S. Orange Blossom Trail, Orlando, FL 32837

TELEPHONE NUMBER: (407) 826-5050
FAX: (407) 826-8849
WEB: www.tupperware.com

NO. OF EMPLOYEES: 7,000 (approx.)

SHAREHOLDERS: 11,532

ANNUAL MEETING: In May

INCORPORATED: DE, Feb., 1996

INSTITUTIONAL HOLDINGS:
No. of Institutions: 196
Shares Held: 40,606,185
% Held: 70.2

INDUSTRY: Toilet preparations (SIC: 2844)

TRANSFER AGENT(S): Wells Fargo Bank Minnesota, N.A., St Paul, MN

NYSE SYMBOL TW
Rec. Pr. 17.30 (4/30/01)

21ST CENTURY INSURANCE GROUP

YIELD 1.7%
P/E RATIO 115.3

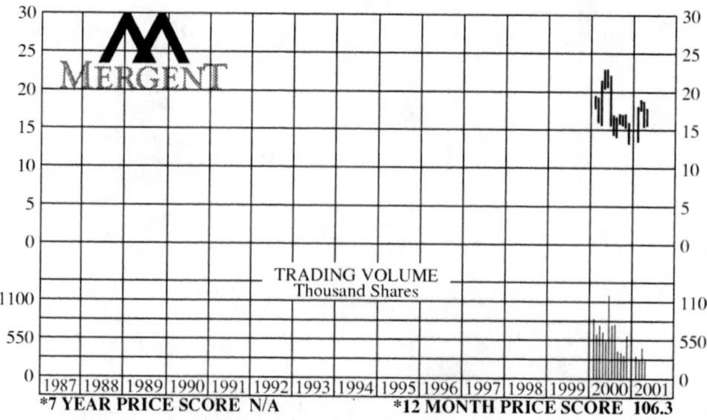

*7 YEAR PRICE SCORE N/A *12 MONTH PRICE SCORE 106.3

*NYSE COMPOSITE INDEX=100

INTERIM EARNINGS (Per Share):

Qtr.	Mar.	June	Sept.	Dec.
1998	0.34	0.49	0.44	d0.06
1999	0.33	0.38	0.21	0.08
2000	0.04	0.06	0.03	0.02

INTERIM DIVIDENDS (Per Share):

Amt.	Decl.	Ex.	Rec.	Pay.
0.16Q	5/30/00	6/13/00	6/15/00	6/28/00
0.08Q	9/14/00	9/21/00	9/25/00	10/05/00
0.08Q	11/14/00	11/27/00	11/29/00	12/14/00
0.08Q	2/28/01	3/13/01	3/15/01	3/30/01
0.08Q	6/06/01	6/14/01	6/18/01	6/29/01

Indicated div.: $0.32

CAPITALIZATION (12/31/00):

	($000)	(%)
Common & Surplus	720,561	100.0
Total	720,561	100.0

RECENT DEVELOPMENTS: For the year ended 12/31/00, net income declined to $12.9 million compared with $87.5 million in the previous year. Net premiums written jumped 8.2% to $832.1 million versus $768.8 million in the prior year. Underwriting loss totaled $42.5 million compared with income of $66.0 million in the previous year. Operating income declined to $7.4 million from $124.1 million in the preceding year.

PROSPECTS: Results for the year were dampened by lower underwriting results. Meanwhile, the Company will continue to focus on launching its marketing campaigns in selected markets following their initial introduction on December 26, 2000. These marketing campaigns highlight a variety of TW's low-cost products designed to have high-convenience services. Looking ahead, the Company expects steady improvement in underwriting results reflecting rate increases and product changes.

BUSINESS

21ST CENTURY INSURANCE GROUP is an insurance holding company. The Company, through its subsidiaries, 21st Century Insurance Company and 21st Century Casualty Company, directly markets and underwrites private passenger automobile, homeowners and personal umbrella insurance. The Company offers the following insurance coverages for private passenger automobiles: bodily injury liability, property damage, medical payments, uninsured and underinsured motorist, rental reimbursement, uninsured motorist property damage and collision deductible, towing, comprehensive, and collision.

REVENUES

(12/31/2000)	($000)	(%)
Premiums Earned	825,486	94.4
Investment Income	49,286	5.6
Total	874,772	0.0

ANNUAL FINANCIAL DATA

	12/31/00	12/31/99	12/31/98	12/31/97	12/31/96	12/31/95	12/31/94
Earnings Per Share	**0.15**	**1.00**	**1.19**	**1.37**	**0.92**	**0.88**	**d9.69**
Tang. Book Val. Per Share	**8.46**	**8.39**	**8.97**	**6.93**	**5.09**	**4.69**	**2.29**
Dividends Per Share	**0.48**	**0.64**	**0.58**	**0.25**	**0.05**	**...**	**0.32**
Dividend Payout %	**319.8**	**64.0**	**48.7**	**18.2**	**5.4**	**...**	**...**
INCOME STATEMENT (IN MILLIONS):							
Total Premium Income	825.5	770.4	772.9	786.0	856.6	963.8	1,034.0
Net Investment Income	49.3	62.7	75.1	73.5	73.2	81.7	84.8
Other Income	d5.0	d0.4	22.6	4.1	7.3	10.2	61.5
Total Revenues	869.8	832.7	870.7	863.5	937.1	1,055.7	1,180.3
Income Before Income Taxes	d1.1	121.2	155.4	168.1	108.4	101.2	d786.1
Income Taxes	cr14.0	33.7	54.3	57.2	34.4	31.6	cr288.1
Net Income	12.9	87.5	101.1	110.9	74.1	69.6	d498.0
Average Shs. Outstg. (000)	85,424	87,253	84,884	80,725	51,466	51,440	51,387
BALANCE SHEET (IN MILLIONS):							
Cash & Cash Equivalents	7.2	45.0	167.9	31.3	18.1	50.6	249.8
Premiums Due	129.1	127.4	137.7	141.5	150.5	139.1	164.3
Invst. Assets: Fixed-term	912.7	943.0	1,067.2	1,082.7	1,063.7	1,125.5	941.4
Invst. Assets: Equities	0.4	0.6	1.4	1.7	0.9	1.6	0.8
Invst. Assets: Total	913.1	943.5	1,068.6	1,084.5	1,064.6	1,127.1	942.2
Total Assets	1,338.1	1,379.3	1,593.2	1,482.5	1,513.8	1,608.9	1,702.8
Long-Term Obligations	...	67.5	112.5	157.5	175.0	175.0	160.0
Net Stockholders' Equity	720.6	720.8	785.6	583.0	487.7	466.6	317.9
Year-end Shs. Outstg. (000)	85,146	85,919	87,625	51,636	51,601	51,496	51,472
STATISTICAL RECORD:							
Return on Revenues %	1.5	10.5	11.6	12.8	7.9	6.6	...
Return on Equity %	1.8	12.1	12.9	19.0	15.2	14.9	...
Return on Assets %	1.0	6.3	6.3	7.5	4.9	4.3	...
Price Range	23.00-13.13	...	...	...	...	...	...
P/E Ratio	153.2-87.4	...	...	...	...	...	...
Average Yield %	2.7	...	...	...	...	...	...

Statistics are as originally reported.

OFFICERS:
R. M. Sandler, Chmn.
B. W. Marlow, Pres., C.E.O.
D. K. Howell, Sr. V.P., C.F.O.

INVESTOR CONTACT: Corporate Relations, (808) 704-3514

PRINCIPAL OFFICE: 6301 Owensmouth Ave., Suite 700, Woodland Hills, CA 91367

TELEPHONE NUMBER: (818) 704-3700
FAX: (818) 704-3485
WEB: my21st.com

NO. OF EMPLOYEES: 2,501 (avg.)

SHAREHOLDERS: 723 (approx.)

ANNUAL MEETING: In June

INCORPORATED: CA, May, 1969

INSTITUTIONAL HOLDINGS:
No. of Institutions: 52
Shares Held: 63,954,406
% Held: 75.1

INDUSTRY: Fire, marine, and casualty insurance (SIC: 6331)

TRANSFER AGENT(S): American Stock Transfer & Trust Company, New York, NY

NYSE SYMBOL TXU
Rec. Pr. 43.96 (4/30/01)

TXU CORPORATION

YIELD 5.5%
P/E RATIO 12.8

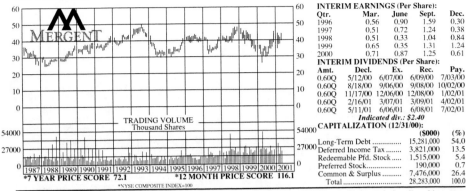

MERGENT

TRADING VOLUME
Thousand Shares

1987 1988 1989 1990 1991 1992 1993 1994 1995 1996 1997 1998 1999 2000 2001

*7 YEAR PRICE SCORE 72.1 *12 MONTH PRICE SCORE 116.1

*NYSE COMPOSITE INDEX=100

INTERIM EARNINGS (Per Share):

Qtr.	Mar.	June	Sept.	Dec.
1996	0.56	0.90	1.59	0.30
1997	0.51	0.72	1.24	0.38
1998	0.51	0.33	1.04	0.84
1999	0.65	0.35	1.31	1.24
2000	0.71	0.87	1.25	0.61

INTERIM DIVIDENDS (Per Share):

Amt.	Decl.	Ex.	Rec.	Pay.
0.60Q	5/12/00	6/07/00	6/09/00	7/03/00
0.60Q	8/18/00	9/06/00	9/08/00	10/02/00
0.60Q	11/17/00	12/06/00	12/08/00	1/02/01
0.60Q	2/16/01	3/07/01	3/09/01	4/02/01
0.60Q	5/11/01	6/06/01	6/08/01	7/02/01

Indicated div.: $2.40

CAPITALIZATION (12/31/00):

	($000)	(%)
Long-Term Debt	15,281,000	54.0
Deferred Income Tax	3,821,000	13.5
Redeemable Pfd. Stock	1,515,000	5.4
Preferred Stock	190,000	0.7
Common & Surplus	7,476,000	26.4
Total	28,283,000	100.0

RECENT DEVELOPMENTS: For the year ended 12/31/00, net income slipped 7.0% to $916.0 million versus $985.0 million in 1999. Results for 1999 included non-recurring net after-tax gains totaling $97.0 million. Operating revenues rose 28.6% to $22.01 billion versus $17.12 billion a year earlier. Results reflected strong revenue and customer growth, weather-driven energy sales, asset sales and significant mitigation of stranded costs. Net income from TXU's U.S. Gas segment tripled due to a revenue enhancement program and lower operating and maintenance expenses.

PROSPECTS: TXU Europe is currently in talks with a number of undisclosed parties to sell part of its 7,000 megawatts of U.K. generating capacity. TXU Europe aims to complete a deal by the end of the first half of 2001. Meanwhile, TXU Energy Services signed a ten-year multi-million dollar agreement with Aperian, Inc. to own, operate and maintain the mechanical and electrical energy equipment at Aperian's five data centers in the U.S. Going forward, the Company will continue to focus on building its portfolio of strategic assets and personnel.

BUSINESS

TXU CORPORATION (formerly Texas Utilities Company) is a holding company whose principal U.S. operations are conducted through TXU Electric Company, TXU Gas Company, and TXU Energy Industries Company. TXU's principal international operations are conducted through TXU International Holdings Limited, which owns TXU Europe Limited and TXU Australia Holdings L.P. TXU Australia Holdings' principal operating subsidiaries include Eastern Energy Limited, Kinetik Energy Pty. Ltd., and Westar Pty. Ltd. Through its subsidiaries, TXU is engaged in the generation, purchase, transmission, distribution and sale of electricity; the gathering, processing, transmission and distribution of natural gas; energy marketing; and telecommunications, retail energy services, international gas operations, power development and other businesses primarily in Texas, the U.K. and Australia. Financial results in 1998 were affected by the May 1998 acquisition of The Energy Group PLC.

ANNUAL FINANCIAL DATA

	12/31/00	12/31/99	12/31/98	12/31/97	12/31/96	12/31/95	12/31/94
Earnings Per Share	**3.43**	**[4] 3.53**	**[1][3] 2.79**	**[2] 2.85**	**3.35**	**[1] d0.61**	**2.40**
Cash Flow Per Share	**8.84**	**8.72**	**7.85**	**6.49**	**6.85**	**2.60**	**5.55**
Tang. Book Val. Per Share	**28.96**	**30.15**	**29.21**	**27.90**	**26.86**	**25.38**	**28.74**
Dividends Per Share	**2.40**	**2.30**	**2.20**	**2.10**	**2.00**	**3.08**	**3.08**
Dividend Payout %	**70.0**	**65.2**	**78.9**	**73.7**	**59.7**	**...**	**128.3**
INCOME STATEMENT (IN MILLIONS):							
Total Revenues	22,009.0	17,118.0	14,736.0	7,945.6	6,550.9	5,638.7	5,663.5
Costs & Expenses	18,113.0	13,076.0	10,933.0	5,200.3	3,759.6	3,125.4	3,304.8
Depreciation & Amort.	1,419.0	1,448.0	1,340.0	838.6	788.3	725.6	710.2
Operating Income	2,477.0	2,594.0	2,463.0	1,906.7	2,003.0	1,787.6	1,648.6
Net Interest Inc./(Exp.)	d1,327.0	d1,312.0	d1,152.0	d754.0	d786.6	d690.9	d715.6
Income Taxes	337.0	449.0	526.0	376.9	375.2	cr60.0	326.6
Net Income	916.0	[4] 985.0	[1][3] 740.0	[2] 660.5	753.6	[1] d138.6	542.8
Cash Flow	2,324.0	2,433.0	2,080.0	1,499.1	1,541.9	587.0	1,253.0
Average Shs. Outstg. (000)	264,000	279,000	265,000	230,958	225,160	225,841	225,834
BALANCE SHEET (IN MILLIONS):							
Gross Property	32,051.0	31,799.0	30,293.0	25,286.7	23,726.1	23,307.9	22,692.5
Accumulated Depreciation	8,750.0	8,159.0	7,426.0	6,715.7	6,127.6	5,562.2	5,023.0
Net Property	23,301.0	23,640.0	22,867.0	18,571.0	17,598.5	17,745.7	17,669.5
Total Assets	44,990.0	40,741.0	39,514.0	24,874.1	21,375.7	21,535.9	20,893.4
Long-Term Obligations	15,281.0	16,325.0	15,133.0	8,759.4	8,668.1	9,174.6	7,888.4
Net Stockholders' Equity	7,666.0	8,524.0	8,436.0	7,147.3	6,497.3	6,221.4	7,360.2
Year-end Shs. Outstg. (000)	258,109	276,407	282,333	245,238	224,603	225,841	225,841
STATISTICAL RECORD:							
Operating Profit Margin %	11.3	15.2	16.7	24.0	30.6	31.7	29.1
Net Profit Margin %	4.2	5.8	5.0	8.3	11.5	...	9.6
Net Inc./Net Property %	3.9	4.2	3.2	3.6	4.3	...	3.1
Net Inc./Tot. Capital %	3.2	3.3	2.6	3.3	4.1	...	2.9
Return on Equity %	11.9	11.6	8.8	9.2	11.6	...	7.4
Accum. Depr./Gross Prop. %	27.3	25.7	24.5	26.6	25.8	23.9	22.1
Price Range	45.25-25.94	47.19-32.75	48.06-38.38	42.00-31.50	43.75-38.50	41.25-30.13	43.13-29.63
P/E Ratio	13.2-7.6	13.4-9.3	17.2-13.8	14.7-11.1	13.1-11.5	...	18.0-12.3
Average Yield %	6.7	5.8	5.1	5.7	4.9	8.6	8.5

Statistics are as originally reported. [1] Incl. after-tax non-recurr. chrg. $31.0 mill., 1998; $802.0 mill., 1995 [2] Incl. $80.0 mill. rate settlement refund, $79.0 mill. fuel reconciliation disallowance and $12.0 mill. in interest related to fuel reconciliation and disallowance [3] Incl. non-recurr. after-tax restr. chg. & acq. costs $50.0 mill. [4] Incl. gain of $145.0 mill. from sale of PrimeCo & non-recurr. chrg. $48.0 mill.

OFFICERS:
E. Nye, Chmn., C.E.O.
H. J. Gibbs, Vice-Chmn.
D. W. Biegler, Pres.

INVESTOR CONTACT: David Anderson, Inv. Rel., (204) 812-4641

PRINCIPAL OFFICE: Energy Plaza, 1601 Bryan Street, Dallas, TX 75201-3411

TELEPHONE NUMBER: (214) 812-4600
FAX: (214) 812-4651
WEB: www.tu.com

NO. OF EMPLOYEES: 16,540

SHAREHOLDERS: 77,498

ANNUAL MEETING: In May

INCORPORATED: TX, Sept., 1945

INSTITUTIONAL HOLDINGS:
No. of Institutions: 401
Shares Held: 135,748,570
% Held: 52.6

INDUSTRY: Electric services (SIC: 4911)

TRANSFER AGENT(S): Texas Utilities Shareholder Services, Dallas, TX

NYSE SYMBOL TSN
Rec. Pr. 12.74 (5/31/01)

TYSON FOODS, INC.

YIELD 1.3%
P/E RATIO 23.6

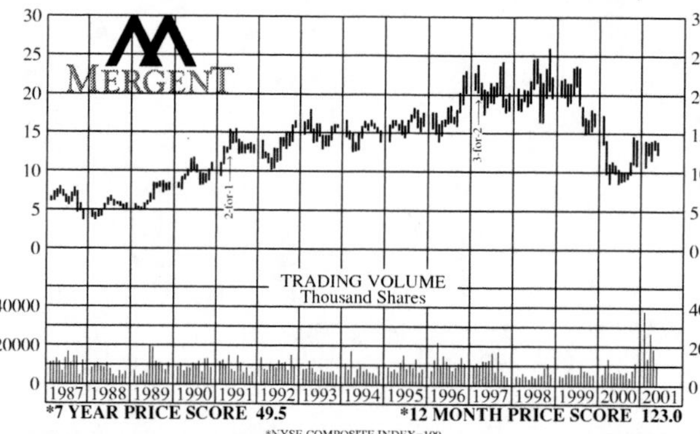

*7 YEAR PRICE SCORE 49.5 *12 MONTH PRICE SCORE 123.0

*NYSE COMPOSITE INDEX=100

INTERIM EARNINGS (Per Share):

Qtr.	Dec.	Mar.	June	Sept.
1996-97	0.20	0.22	0.21	0.22
1997-98	0.21	0.10	0.20	d0.39
1998-99	0.24	0.28	0.30	0.18
1999-00	0.25	0.16	0.18	0.08
2000-01	0.12	...	...	...

INTERIM DIVIDENDS (Per Share):

Amt.	Decl.	Ex.	Rec.	Pay.
0.04Q	5/08/00	8/30/00	9/01/00	9/15/00
0.04Q	8/11/00	11/29/00	12/01/00	12/15/00
0.04Q	11/20/00	2/27/01	3/01/01	3/15/01
0.04Q	1/12/01	5/30/01	6/01/01	6/15/01
0.04Q	5/04/01	8/29/01	9/01/01	9/15/01

Indicated div.: $0.16 (Div. Reinv. Plan)

CAPITALIZATION (9/30/00):

	($000)	(%)
Long-Term Debt	1,357,000	34.6
Deferred Income Tax	385,000	9.8
Common & Surplus	2,175,000	55.5
Total	3,917,000	100.0

RECENT DEVELOPMENTS: For the three months ended 12/30/00, net income totaled $27.0 million, down 52.6% compared with $57.0 million a year earlier. Sales slipped 2.0% to $1.74 billion from $1.78 billion the year before. Food Service segment sales slid 2.8% to $802.0 million, reflecting a 7.9% decrease in volume partially offset by a 5.6% increase in average sales prices. Consumer Products segment sales were down 1.7% to $529.0 million, due primarily to a 3.4% decline in average sales prices partially offset by a 1.8% increase in volume.

PROSPECTS: On 2/28/01, the Company announced it had decided to terminate its tender offer for 50.1% of IBP, Inc.'s common stock, reflecting a Securities and Exchange Commission investigation of accounting issues at IBP's DFG Foods subsidiary. The Company may consider pursuing a cash-election merger under which IBP shareholders will have the choice of either cash or TSN stock in exchange for their shares. Meanwhile, results are being hurt by higher grain prices, energy costs and weaker-than-expected pricing recovery.

BUSINESS

TYSON FOODS, INC. is a fully-integrated producer, processor and marketer of chicken and chicken-based food products, and other products such as flour and corn tortillas and chips under the MEXICAN ORIGINAL® brand. Additionally, TSN has animal feed and pet food ingredients operations that consist of breeding and rearing chickens, as well as processing and marketing of these food products. TSN's products are marketed and sold through retail grocery stores, warehouse stores, national and regional chain restaurants or their distributors, and food service operations such as plant and school cafeterias, convenience stores and hospitals. On 7/19/99, TSN sold its seafood division assets.

REVENUES

(9/30/2000)	($000)	(%)
Food Service	3,312,000	46.3
Consumer Products	2,250,000	31.4
International	657,000	9.2
Swine	157,000	2.2
Other	782,000	10.9
Total	7,158,000	100.0

ANNUAL FINANCIAL DATA

	9/30/00	10/2/99	10/3/98	9/27/97	9/28/96	9/30/95	10/1/94
Earnings Per Share	**2 0.67**	**2 1.00**	**1 0.11**	**0.86**	**0.40**	**1.01**	**d0.01**
Cash Flow Per Share	**1.97**	**2.26**	**1.32**	**1.92**	**1.50**	**1.95**	**0.84**
Tang. Book Val. Per Share	**5.50**	**5.10**	**4.05**	**4.17**	**3.72**	**3.04**	**2.51**
Dividends Per Share	**0.16**	**0.13**	**0.10**	**0.10**	**0.08**	**0.06**	**0.05**
Dividend Payout %	**23.9**	**13.0**	**90.8**	**11.6**	**20.0**	**6.0**	**...**
INCOME STATEMENT (IN MILLIONS):							
Total Revenues	7,158.0	7,362.9	7,414.1	6,355.7	6,453.8	5,511.2	5,110.3
Costs & Expenses	6,516.0	6,584.9	6,934.1	5,725.4	5,944.9	4,834.6	4,726.8
Depreciation & Amort.	294.0	291.1	276.4	230.4	239.3	204.9	188.3
Operating Income	348.0	486.9	203.6	399.9	269.6	471.7	195.2
Net Interest Inc./(Exp.)	d115.0	d124.0	d139.1	d110.4	d132.9	d114.9	d86.1
Income Before Income Taxes	234.0	371.0	71.0	329.7	132.6	343.6	118.6
Income Taxes	83.0	129.4	45.9	143.9	49.0	131.0	120.7
Equity Earnings/Minority Int.	...	d11.5	...	...	3.3	6.6	...
Net Income	2 151.0	2 230.1	1 25.1	185.8	86.9	219.2	d2.1
Cash Flow	445.0	521.2	301.5	416.2	326.2	424.1	186.2
Average Shs. Outstg. (000)	226,000	231,000	227,900	216,300	218,000	217,650	221,700
BALANCE SHEET (IN MILLIONS):							
Cash & Cash Equivalents	43.0	30.3	46.5	23.6	36.6	33.1	27.0
Total Current Assets	1,576.0	1,726.9	1,765.1	1,572.5	1,810.3	1,519.8	1,261.3
Net Property	2,141.0	2,184.5	2,256.5	1,924.8	1,869.2	2,013.5	1,610.0
Total Assets	4,854.0	5,082.7	5,242.5	4,411.0	4,544.1	4,444.3	3,668.0
Total Current Liabilities	886.0	987.0	831.0	721.0	685.8	865.8	539.8
Long-Term Obligations	1,357.0	1,515.2	1,966.6	1,558.2	1,806.4	1,620.5	1,381.5
Net Stockholders' Equity	2,175.0	2,128.0	1,970.4	1,621.5	1,541.7	1,467.7	1,289.4
Net Working Capital	690.0	739.9	934.1	851.5	1,124.5	654.0	721.5
Year-end Shs. Outstg. (000)	225,000	228,600	230,800	213,400	218,000	217,200	217,950
STATISTICAL RECORD:							
Operating Profit Margin %	4.9	6.6	2.7	6.3	4.2	8.6	3.8
Net Profit Margin %	2.1	3.1	0.3	2.9	1.3	4.0	...
Return on Equity %	6.9	10.8	1.3	11.5	5.6	14.9	...
Return on Assets %	3.1	4.5	0.5	4.2	1.9	4.9	...
Debt/Total Assets %	28.0	29.8	37.5	35.3	39.8	36.5	37.7
Price Range	17.38-8.50	23.75-14.88	26.00-16.31	24.25-17.38	23.08-13.83	18.33-13.83	16.67-12.50
P/E Ratio	25.9-12.7	23.7-14.9	236.1-148.2	28.2-20.2	57.7-34.6	18.2-13.7	...
Average Yield %	1.2	0.7	0.5	0.5	0.4	0.4	0.4

Statistics are as originally reported. Adj. for 3-for-2 stk. split, 2/97. 1 Incl. $142.2 mil asset impairment chg. 2 Incl. $24.2 mil chrg. from AmeriServe reorganization, 2000; $76.9 mil chrg. fr. sale of assets, 1999.

OFFICERS:
J. H. Tyson, Chmn., Pres., C.E.O.
S. Hankins, Exec. V.P., C.F.O.
G. Lee, V.P., C.O.O.

INVESTOR CONTACT: Louis C. Gottsponer, Jr., Dir., Investor Relations, (501) 290-4829

PRINCIPAL OFFICE: 2210 West Oaklawn Drive, Springdale, AR 72762-6999

TELEPHONE NUMBER: (501) 290-4000
FAX: (501) 290-4028
WEB: www.tyson.com
NO. OF EMPLOYEES: 75,400 (approx.)
SHAREHOLDERS: 36,079 (Cl. A); 17 (Cl. B)
ANNUAL MEETING: In Jan.
INCORPORATED: AR, Oct., 1947; reincorp., DE, Feb., 1986

INSTITUTIONAL HOLDINGS:
No. of Institutions: 135
Shares Held: 70,832,013
% Held: 31.9

INDUSTRY: Poultry slaughtering and processing (SIC: 2015)

TRANSFER AGENT(S): First Chicago Trust Company of New York, Jersey City, NJ

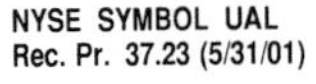

NYSE SYMBOL UAL
Rec. Pr. 37.23 (5/31/01)

UAL CORPORATION

YIELD 3.4%
P/E RATIO . . .

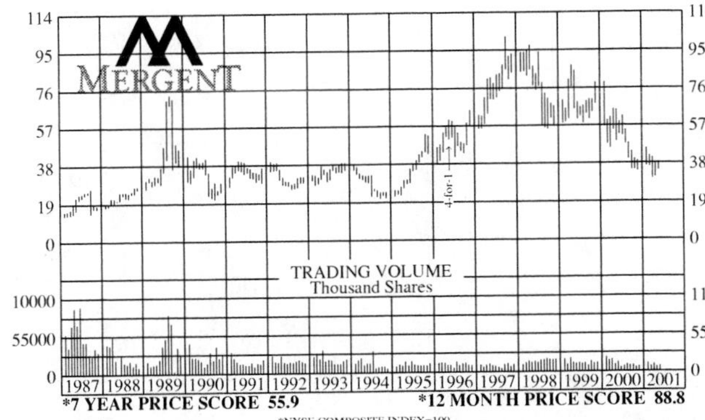

*7 YEAR PRICE SCORE 55.9 *12 MONTH PRICE SCORE 88.8
*NYSE COMPOSITE INDEX=100

INTERIM EARNINGS (Per Share):

Qtr.	Mar.	June	Sept.	Dec.
1997	0.92	2.31	5.61	0.12
1998	0.34	2.44	3.71	0.27
1999	0.44	5.80	2.89	0.84
2000	0.62	2.86	d2.17	d1.40

INTERIM DIVIDENDS (Per Share):

Amt.	Decl.	Ex.	Rec.	Pay.
0.313Q	6/28/00	7/12/00	7/14/00	8/01/00
0.313Q	9/28/00	10/12/00	10/16/00	11/01/00
0.313Q	12/14/00	1/11/01	1/16/01	2/01/01
0.313Q	3/22/01	4/11/01	4/16/01	5/01/01

Indicated div.: $1.25

CAPITALIZATION (12/31/00):

	($000)	(%)
Long-Term Debt	4,688,000	33.4
Capital Lease Obligations	2,261,000	16.1
Deferred Income Tax	1,241,000	8.8
Redeemable Pfd. Stock	670,000	4.8
Common & Surplus	5,190,000	36.9
Total	14,050,000	100.0

RECENT DEVELOPMENTS: For the year ended 12/31/00, earnings, before a $209.0 million accounting charge and a $6.0 million extraordinary charge, totaled $271.0 million versus earnings of $1.24 billion, before a $3.0 million extraordinary charge, the year before. Results included pre-tax non-recurring charges totaling $200.0 million and $17.0 million in 2000 and 1999, respectively. Earnings benefited from pre-tax gains of $109.0 million and $731.0 million in 2000 and 1999, respectively, from investment sales. Total operating revenues grew 7.4% to $19.35 billion.

PROSPECTS: UAL is continuing to work closely with the U.S. Department of Justice in an effort to complete its proposed $4.30 billion acquisition of US Airways Group, Inc. The transaction remains conditional pending regulatory clearance and other customary closing conditions. On 1/10/01, the Company and AMR Corp. entered into a $1.50 billion agreement, contingent on the consummation of the merger between United Airlines and US Airways, that enhances the competitive benefits of the acquisition and strategically addresses Department of Justice concerns.

BUSINESS

UAL CORPORATION is the parent company of United Airlines, Inc., which is the world's largest airline as measured by revenue passenger miles flown. During 2000, United carried, on average, more than 231,000 passengers per day and flew more than 126.93 billion revenue passenger miles. United has a global network of major connecting airports including Chicago, Denver, San Francisco, Los Angeles, Washington, D.C., Miami, Frankfurt, London, Tokyo, and Toronto. In October 1994, United began operating the United Shuttle® to compete with low-cost carriers on routes fewer than 750 miles. United Shuttle offers about 455 daily flights between 23 cities in the western U.S.

ANNUAL FINANCIAL DATA

	12/31/00	12/31/99	12/31/98	12/31/97	12/31/96	12/31/95	12/31/94
Earnings Per Share	[5] 1.89	[4] 9.97	6.83	[3] 9.04	[2] 5.96	[2] 5.47	[1] 0.19
Cash Flow Per Share	10.84	18.32	14.79	16.66	15.69	16.10	9.54
Tang. Book Val. Per Share	86.01	90.26	50.28	28.67	7.87	. . .	. . .
Dividends Per Share	0.94	. . .	. . .	. . .	. . .	. . .	. . .
Dividend Payout %	49.6	. . .	. . .	. . .	. . .	. . .	. . .
INCOME STATEMENT (IN MILLIONS):							
Total Revenues	19,352.0	18,027.0	17,561.0	17,378.0	16,362.0	14,943.0	13,950.0
Costs & Expenses	17,706.0	15,835.0	15,354.0	15,459.0	14,543.0	13,469.0	12,789.0
Depreciation & Amort.	992.0	801.0	729.0	660.0	696.0	645.0	640.0
Operating Income	654.0	1,391.0	1,478.0	1,259.0	1,123.0	829.0	521.0
Net Interest Inc./(Exp.)	d224.0	d219.0	d191.0	d130.0	d161.0	d259.0	d246.0
Income Before Income Taxes	431.0	1,942.0	1,256.0	1,524.0	970.0	621.0	171.0
Income Taxes	160.0	699.0	429.0	561.0	370.0	243.0	94.0
Net Income	[5] 271.0	[4] 1,243.0	827.0	[3] 963.0	[2] 600.0	[2] 378.0	[1] 77.0
Cash Flow	1,253.0	2,034.0	1,546.0	1,613.0	1,276.0	983.0	658.0
Average Shs. Outstg. (000)	116,500	111,600	105,200	97,400	82,600	63,548	75,168
BALANCE SHEET (IN MILLIONS):							
Cash & Cash Equivalents	2,344.0	689.0	815.0	845.0	697.0	1,143.0	1,532.0
Total Current Assets	4,779.0	2,935.0	2,908.0	2,948.0	2,682.0	3,043.0	3,192.0
Net Property	16,343.0	14,865.0	13,054.0	10,774.0	8,243.0	7,021.0	6,723.0
Total Assets	24,355.0	20,963.0	18,559.0	15,464.0	12,677.0	11,641.0	11,764.0
Total Current Liabilities	6,781.0	5,411.0	5,668.0	5,248.0	5,003.0	4,433.0	4,906.0
Long-Term Obligations	6,949.0	4,987.0	4,971.0	3,771.0	2,986.0	3,913.0	3,617.0
Net Stockholders' Equity	5,190.0	5,151.0	3,281.0	2,337.0	995.0	d239.0	d316.0
Net Working Capital	d2,002.0	d2,476.0	d2,760.0	d2,300.0	d2,321.0	d1,390.0	d1,714.0
Year-end Shs. Outstg. (000)	52,539	50,777	51,805	57,000	59,817	50,720	49,756
STATISTICAL RECORD:							
Operating Profit Margin %	3.4	7.7	8.4	7.2	6.9	5.5	3.7
Net Profit Margin %	1.4	6.9	4.7	5.5	3.7	2.5	0.6
Return on Equity %	5.2	24.1	25.2	41.2	60.3	. . .	. . .
Return on Assets %	1.1	5.9	4.5	6.2	4.7	3.2	0.7
Debt/Total Assets %	28.5	23.8	26.8	24.4	23.6	33.6	30.7
Price Range	79.00-34.06	87.38-58.13	97.50-55.25	101.75-55.38	64.75-38.56	52.97-21.91	37.50-20.78
P/E Ratio	41.8-18.0	8.8-5.8	14.3-8.1	11.3-6.1	10.9-6.5	9.7-4.0	197.3-109.3
Average Yield %	1.7	. . .	. . .	. . .	. . .	. . .	. . .

Statistics are as originally reported. [1] Bef. $26 mil acctg. chg., incl. $169 mil chg. [2] Bef. $67 mil loss, incl. $31 mil chg., 1996; $29 mil extraord. loss, incl. $13 mil chg., 1995. [3] Bef. $9 mil extraord. chg., incl. $235 mil gain. [4] Bef. $3 mil extraord. loss, incl. $468 mil gain. [5] Bef. $209 mil acctg. chg., $6 mil extraord. chg., incl. $200 mil chgs. & $109 mil gain.

OFFICERS:
J. E. Goodwin, Chmn., C.E.O.
A. P. Studdart, Exec. V.P., C.O.O.
D. A. Hacker, Exec. V.P., C.F.O.
INVESTOR CONTACT: Patricia Chaplinski, Investor Relations, (847) 700-7501
PRINCIPAL OFFICE: 1200 East Algonquin Road, Elk Grove Township, IL 60007

TELEPHONE NUMBER: (847) 700-4000
FAX: (847) 952-7325
WEB: www.ual.com
NO. OF EMPLOYEES: 102,000 (avg.)
SHAREHOLDERS: 23,542
ANNUAL MEETING: In May
INCORPORATED: DE, Dec., 1968

INSTITUTIONAL HOLDINGS:
No. of Institutions: 129
Shares Held: 34,049,818
% Held: 64.1
INDUSTRY: Air transportation, scheduled (SIC: 4512)
TRANSFER AGENT(S): Harris Trust and Savings Bank, Chicago, IL

NYSE SYMBOL UGI
Rec. Pr. 26.45 (4/30/01)

UGI CORPORATION

YIELD 6.0%
P/E RATIO 14.2

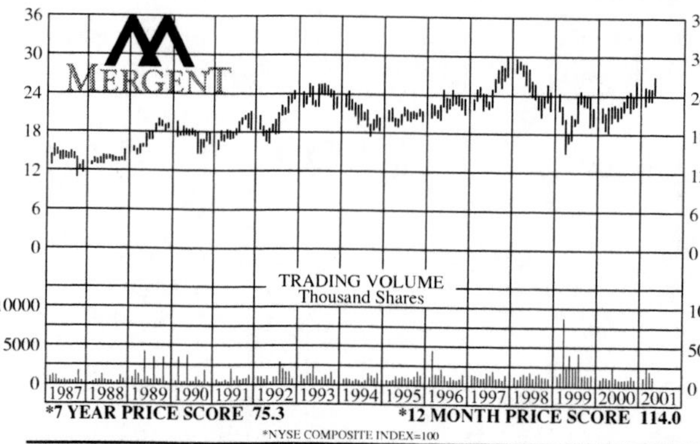

INTERIM EARNINGS (Per Share):

Qtr.	Dec.	Mar.	June	Sept.
1996-97	0.84	1.08	d0.04	d0.32
1997-98	0.75	0.94	d0.12	d0.36
1998-99	0.55	1.14	0.36	d0.31
1999-00	0.77	1.42	d0.17	d0.39
2000-01	1.00	...	...	...

INTERIM DIVIDENDS (Per Share):

Amt.	Decl.	Ex.	Rec.	Pay.
0.388Q	4/25/00	5/26/00	5/31/00	7/01/00
0.388Q	7/25/00	8/29/00	8/31/00	10/01/00
0.388Q	10/31/00	11/28/00	11/30/00	1/01/01
0.388Q	1/30/01	2/26/01	2/28/01	4/01/01
0.40Q	4/24/01	5/29/01	5/31/01	7/01/01

Indicated div.: $1.60 (Div. Reinv. Plan)

CAPITALIZATION (9/30/00):

	($000)	(%)
Long-Term Debt	1,029,700	53.3
Deferred Income Tax	172,900	9.0
Minority Interest	177,100	9.2
Redeemable Pfd. Stock	20,000	1.0
Common & Surplus	532,000	27.5
Total	1,931,700	100.0

RECENT DEVELOPMENTS: For the quarter ended 12/31/00, income rose 28.4% to $27.1 million, before an accounting change gain of $4.5 million, versus net income of $21.1 million a year earlier. Total revenues advanced 58.0% to $737.1 million. Operating income at UGI's AmeriGas Propane business increased 14.5% to $109.3 million, while gas utility operating income rose 19.9% to $89.0 million. Electric utility operating income fell 19.6% to $11.9 million.

PROSPECTS: On 3/27/01, UGI acquired an approximate 19.5% equity interest in Elf Antargaz, formerly the French propane distribution business of Total Fina Elf, SA. UGI joins a consortium consisting of Paribas Affaires Industrielles, which will own about 68.1% of Antargaz and Medit Mediterranea GPL, S.r.L., which will own an approximate 9.7% interest. In addition, certain members of management of Antargaz will own an approximate 2.7% interest.

BUSINESS

UGI CORPORATION is a holding company that operates propane distribution, gas and electric utility, energy marketing and related businesses through subsidiaries. The Company's majority-owned subsidiary, AmeriGas Partners, L.P., conducts a retail propane distribution business through its 98.99%-owned subsidiary, AmeriGas Propane, L.P. UGI Utilities, Inc., owns and operates a natural gas distribution utility and an electric distribution utility in eastern Pennsylvania. UGI Enterprises, Inc., conducts an energy marketing business. Through other subsidiaries, UGI owns and operates a propane distribution business in Austria, the Czech Republic, and Slovakia, owns and operates a heating, ventilation and air-conditioning service business and a retail hearth, spa and grill products business in the Mid Atlantic states, and participates in international propane joint-venture projects. Propane sales in 2000 were derived: 30% residential, 28% commercial-industrial, 11% motor fuel, 6% agricultural and 25% wholesale. Gas throughput was derived: 23% residential, 16% commercial/industrial, 60% transportation and 1% retail. Electric kilowatt-hour sales were residential 51%, commercial 35%, and industrial and other 14%. Revenues in 2000 were derived: 63.8% propane, 24.9% utilities, 8.4% energy services and 2.9% international propane.

ANNUAL FINANCIAL DATA

	9/30/00	9/30/99	9/30/98	9/30/97	9/30/96	9/30/95	9/30/94
Earnings Per Share	**1.64**	**[2] 1.74**	**1.22**	**1.57**	**1.19**	**[1] 0.24**	**1.17**
Cash Flow Per Share	**5.22**	**4.54**	**3.87**	**4.17**	**3.79**	**2.10**	**2.47**
Tang. Book Val. Per Share	...	...	...	...	...	...	**5.54**
Dividends Per Share	**1.52**	**1.47**	**1.45**	**1.43**	**1.41**	**1.39**	**1.36**
Dividend Payout %	**93.0**	**84.5**	**118.8**	**91.1**	**118.5**	**578.9**	**116.2**
INCOME STATEMENT (IN MILLIONS):							
Total Revenues	1,761.7	1,383.6	1,439.7	1,642.0	1,557.6	877.6	762.2
Costs & Expenses	1,473.0	1,118.0	1,181.7	1,356.0	1,311.9	738.4	603.5
Depreciation & Amort.	97.5	89.7	87.8	86.1	86.0	60.9	41.8
Operating Income	191.2	175.9	170.2	199.9	159.7	78.3	116.9
Net Interest Inc./(Exp.)	d98.5	d84.6	d84.4	d83.1	d79.5	d59.3	d43.3
Income Before Income Taxes	91.1	109.6	83.6	114.0	77.4	16.2	72.3
Income Taxes	40.1	43.2	34.4	43.6	33.6	22.7	33.6
Equity Earnings/Minority Int.	d6.3	d10.7	d8.9	d18.3	d4.3	14.4	d1.0
Net Income	44.7	[2] 55.7	40.3	52.1	39.5	[1] 7.9	37.7
Cash Flow	142.2	145.4	128.1	138.2	125.5	68.8	79.5
Average Shs. Outstg. (000)	27,255	32,016	33,123	33,132	33,142	32,710	32,200
BALANCE SHEET (IN MILLIONS):							
Cash & Cash Equivalents	101.7	55.6	148.4	129.4	97.1	132.7	77.4
Total Current Assets	426.1	290.9	350.6	403.9	381.6	367.3	179.0
Net Property	1,073.2	1,084.1	999.0	987.2	974.6	954.7	620.6
Total Assets	2,278.8	2,135.9	2,074.6	2,151.7	2,144.9	2,164.0	1,134.7
Total Current Liabilities	539.4	402.3	321.8	404.5	369.2	329.3	211.8
Long-Term Obligations	1,029.7	989.6	890.8	844.8	845.2	815.2	363.5
Net Stockholders' Equity	532.0	249.2	367.1	376.1	377.6	380.5	425.3
Net Working Capital	d113.3	d111.4	28.8	d0.6	12.4	38.0	d32.8
Year-end Shs. Outstg. (000)	26,994	27,270	32,823	33,199	33,136	32,917	32,393
STATISTICAL RECORD:							
Operating Profit Margin %	10.9	12.7	11.8	12.2	10.3	8.9	15.3
Net Profit Margin %	2.5	4.0	2.8	3.2	2.5	0.9	4.9
Return on Equity %	8.4	22.4	11.0	13.9	10.5	2.1	8.9
Return on Assets %	2.0	2.6	1.9	2.4	1.8	0.4	3.3
Debt/Total Assets %	45.2	46.3	42.9	39.3	39.4	37.7	32.0
Price Range	26.31-18.19	24.69-15.00	29.75-20.50	29.88-21.63	24.88-20.00	22.13-18.88	24.50-17.38
P/E Ratio	16.0-11.1	14.2-8.6	24.4-16.8	19.0-13.8	20.9-16.8	92.1-78.6	20.9-14.8
Average Yield %	6.9	7.4	5.8	5.6	6.3	6.8	6.5

Statistics are as originally reported. Incls. results of AP Propane on a consolidated basis. [1] Incl. non-recurr. chrgs. totaling $24.9 mill. [2] Incl. non-recurr. chrg. of $1.6 mill.

OFFICERS:
L. R. Greenberg, Chmn., Pres., C.E.O.
A. J. Mendicino, V.P., C.F.O.
B. P. Bovaird, V.P., Gen. Couns., Sec.

INVESTOR CONTACT: Robert W. Krick, Treas., (610) 337-1000

PRINCIPAL OFFICE: 460 North Gulph Road, King of Prussia, PA 19406

TELEPHONE NUMBER: (610) 337-1000
FAX: (610) 992-3254
WEB: www.ugicorp.com

NO. OF EMPLOYEES: 6,966

SHAREHOLDERS: 11,049

ANNUAL MEETING: In Feb.

INCORPORATED: PA, 1991

INSTITUTIONAL HOLDINGS:
No. of Institutions: 124
Shares Held: 14,745,892
% Held: 54.5

INDUSTRY: Gas and other services combined (SIC: 4932)

TRANSFER AGENT(S): Mellon Investor Services, Ridgefield Park, NJ

NYSE SYMBOL UDS
Rec. Pr. 45.11 (4/30/01)

ULTRAMAR DIAMOND SHAMROCK CORPORATION

YIELD	1.1%
P/E RATIO	8.8

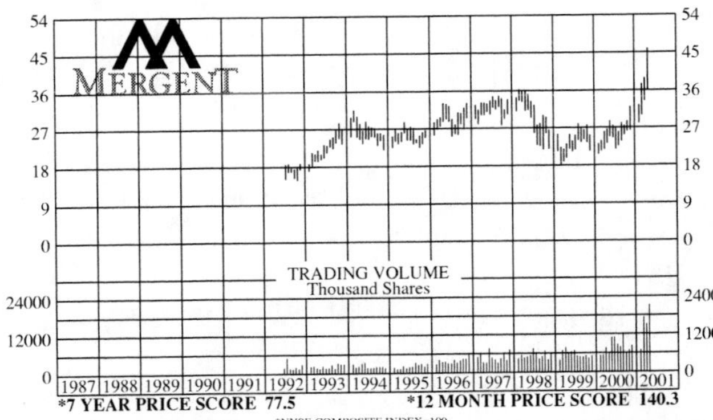

*7 YEAR PRICE SCORE 77.5   *12 MONTH PRICE SCORE 140.3

*NYSE COMPOSITE INDEX=100

INTERIM EARNINGS (Per Share):

Qtr.	Mar.	June	Sept.	Dec.
1996	0.28	0.61	0.17	d1.61
1997	0.35	0.60	0.72	0.32
1998	0.17	d0.36	0.29	d0.78
1999	0.18	0.56	0.97	0.29
2000	0.80	1.47	1.47	1.37

INTERIM DIVIDENDS (Per Share):

Amt.	Decl.	Ex.	Rec.	Pay.
0.275Q	5/02/00	5/16/00	5/18/00	6/01/00
0.275Q	8/01/00	8/15/00	8/17/00	8/31/00
0.275Q	10/04/00	11/17/00	11/21/00	12/05/00
0.275Q	2/08/01	2/14/01	2/19/01	3/05/01
0.125Q	4/30/01	5/16/01	5/18/01	6/06/01

Indicated div.: $0.50 (Div. Reinv. Plan)

CAPITALIZATION (12/31/00):

	($000)	(%)
Long-Term Debt	1,659,800	42.8
Deferred Income Tax	394,100	10.2
Common & Surplus	1,825,300	47.1
Total	3,879,200	100.0

RECENT DEVELOPMENTS: For the year ended 12/31/00, net income jumped to $444.3 million versus $173.2 million a year earlier. Results for 1999 included a non-recurring charge of $11.0 million. Revenues rose 22.4% to $17.06 billion. Refining segment operating income surged 96.5% to $881.7 million, reflecting improved refinery margins in the Northeast and the 8/31/00 acquisition of the Golden Eagle refinery. However, retail segment operating income fell 40.5% to $74.9 million due to lower fuel margins.

PROSPECTS: On 5/7/01, UDS and Valero Energy Corp. jointly announced an agreement for Valero to acquire UDS in a transaction valued at approximately $6.00 billion. The total consideration to be paid to UDS stockholders in the transaction includes a fixed exchange ratio of 1.228 shares of Valero common stock for about 50% of the outstanding shares of UDS common stock, and $55.00 in cash per share for the remaining shares. The acquisition is expected to close by the end of 2001.

BUSINESS

ULTRAMAR DIAMOND SHAMROCK CORPORATION, created through the merger of Diamond Shamrock Corporation and Ultramar Corporation on 12/3/96, is an independent refiner and retailer of refined products and convenience store merchandise. The Company's operations include seven refineries in the U.S. and Canada with a total throughput capacity of 850,000 barrels per day, convenience stores, pipelines and terminals, a home heating oil business, and petrochemical and natural gas liquids operations. UDS markets refined products and a range of convenience store merchandise in the U.S. and Northeast under the Diamond Shamrock®, Beacon®, Ultramar®, and Total® brand names through a network of about 4,600 convenience stores and 85 carlocks. UDS acquired the operations of Total Petroleum (North America) Ltd. in September 1997. On 8/31/00, UDS acquired the Golden Eagle Refinery for $807.7 million.

REVENUES

(12/31/2000)	($000)	(%)
Refining	10,273,300	60.2
Retail	6,625,100	38.8
Petrochemical/NGL	162,700	1.0
Total	17,061,100	100.0

ANNUAL FINANCIAL DATA

	12/31/00	12/31/99	12/31/98	[1] 12/31/97	[4] 12/31/96	12/31/95	12/31/94
Earnings Per Share	**5.11**	**[6] 2.00**	**[5] d0.89**	**[2][3] 1.94**	**[3] d0.54**	**1.18**	**1.56**
Cash Flow Per Share	**8.02**	**4.77**	**2.02**	**4.31**	**1.88**	**2.68**	**2.68**
Tang. Book Val. Per Share	**20.98**	**17.22**	**16.71**	**19.45**	**16.61**	**15.84**	**13.87**
Dividends Per Share	**1.10**	**1.10**	**1.10**	**1.10**	...	...	...
Dividend Payout %	**21.5**	**55.0**	...	**56.7**	...	...	...
INCOME STATEMENT (IN MILLIONS):							
Total Revenues	17,061.1	13,971.2	11,134.6	10,882.4	10,208.4	2,714.4	2,475.4
Costs & Expenses	15,995.9	13,301.3	10,834.4	10,297.9	9,958.6	2,540.1	2,296.4
Depreciation & Amort.	253.1	240.8	237.4	200.1	179.9	60.5	43.3
Operating Income	812.1	429.1	62.8	384.4	69.9	113.9	135.6
Net Interest Inc./(Exp.)	d113.1	d129.1	d133.8	d120.2	d110.1	d40.5	d40.8
Income Before Income Taxes	717.4	314.6	d64.0	275.2	d40.2	73.3	94.9
Income Taxes	262.8	131.1	3.8	110.2	cr4.3	25.7	33.9
Equity Earnings/Minority Int.	18.4	14.6	...	...	...	...	...
Net Income	444.3	[6] 173.2	[5] d78.1	[2][3] 159.6	[3] d35.9	47.6	61.0
Cash Flow	697.4	414.0	178.8	355.4	139.7	108.1	104.3
Average Shs. Outstg. (000)	87,002	86,742	88,555	82,424	74,400	40,340	38,972
BALANCE SHEET (IN MILLIONS):							
Cash & Cash Equivalents	197.1	92.8	176.1	92.0	197.9	126.9	55.1
Total Current Assets	1,853.3	1,396.8	1,505.8	1,610.8	1,399.3	642.7	607.9
Net Property	3,634.3	3,029.9	3,261.2	3,561.0	2,730.8	1,245.3	1,070.9
Total Assets	5,988.4	4,936.0	5,315.0	5,594.7	4,420.0	1,962.4	1,753.2
Total Current Liabilities	1,542.9	1,258.1	1,146.1	1,250.7	1,096.2	431.3	423.3
Long-Term Obligations	1,659.8	1,327.6	1,926.2	1,866.4	1,646.3	600.3	533.3
Net Stockholders' Equity	1,825.3	1,493.3	1,384.0	1,686.6	1,240.9	703.4	533.9
Net Working Capital	310.4	138.7	359.7	360.1	303.1	211.3	184.6
Year-end Shs. Outstg. (000)	86,987	86,700	82,800	86,700	74,700	44,414	38,506
STATISTICAL RECORD:							
Operating Profit Margin %	4.8	3.1	0.6	3.5	0.7	4.2	5.5
Net Profit Margin %	2.6	1.2	...	1.5	...	1.8	2.5
Return on Equity %	24.3	11.6	...	9.5	...	6.8	11.4
Return on Assets %	7.4	3.5	...	2.9	...	2.4	3.5
Debt/Total Assets %	27.7	26.9	36.2	33.4	37.2	30.6	30.4
Price Range	31.94-20.56	28.00-17.88	36.25-21.81	34.75-27.63	33.13-25.00	28.63-22.50	31.50-22.00
P/E Ratio	6.2-4.0	14.0-8.9	...	17.9-14.2	...	24.3-19.1	20.2-14.1
Average Yield %	4.2	4.8	3.8	3.5	...	...	...

Statistics are as originally reported. [1] Incl. ops. of Total Petroleum, acq. 9/97. [2] Bef. extraord. chrg. of $4.8 mill. [3] Incl. non-recurr. net pre-tax credit 12/31/97, $100,000; pre-tax chrg. 12/31/96, $77.4 mill. [4] Results & price chart prior to 1996 refl. opers. of Ultramar Corp. [5] Incl. non-recur. credits of $152.8 mill. [6] Incl. non-recur. exps. of $8.2 mill.

OFFICERS:
J. R. Gaulin, Chmn., Pres., C.E.O.
R. S. Shapard, Exec. V.P., C.F.O.

INVESTOR CONTACT: G. Spendlove, Dir., Investor Relations, (210) 592-4019

PRINCIPAL OFFICE: 6000 N. Loop 1604 West, San Antonio, TX 78249-1112

TELEPHONE NUMBER: (210) 592-2000
WEB: www.udscorp.com

NO. OF EMPLOYEES: 20,000 (approx.)

SHAREHOLDERS: 11,023

ANNUAL MEETING: In May

INCORPORATED: DE, Apr., 1992

INSTITUTIONAL HOLDINGS:
No. of Institutions: 230
Shares Held: 70,101,043
% Held: 98.6

INDUSTRY: Petroleum refining (SIC: 2911)

TRANSFER AGENT(S): Registrar and Transfer Company, Cranford, NJ

NYSE SYMBOL UFI
Rec. Pr. 5.98 (4/30/01)

UNIFI, INC.

YIELD ...
P/E RATIO 14.2

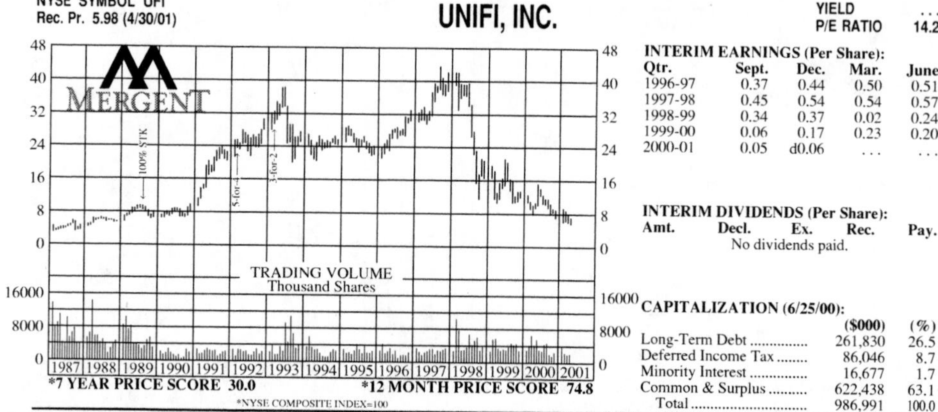

*7 YEAR PRICE SCORE 30.0 *12 MONTH PRICE SCORE 74.8

*NYSE COMPOSITE INDEX=100

INTERIM EARNINGS (Per Share):

Qtr.	Sept.	Dec.	Mar.	June
1996-97	0.37	0.44	0.50	0.51
1997-98	0.45	0.54	0.54	0.57
1998-99	0.34	0.37	0.02	0.24
1999-00	0.06	0.17	0.23	0.20
2000-01	0.05	d0.06	...	...

INTERIM DIVIDENDS (Per Share):

Amt.	Decl.	Ex.	Rec.	Pay.

No dividends paid.

CAPITALIZATION (6/25/00):

	($000)	(%)
Long-Term Debt	261,830	26.5
Deferred Income Tax	86,046	8.7
Minority Interest	16,677	1.7
Common & Surplus	622,438	63.1
Total	986,991	100.0

RECENT DEVELOPMENTS: For the quarter ended 12/24/00, the Company reported a net loss of $3.4 million compared with net income of $10.2 million in the equivalent prior-year quarter. Results for 2000 included a restructuring charge of $1.6 million. Net sales were $296.3 million, down 6.7% from $317.6 million in1999, reflecting weakness in retail sales of apparel during the holiday season, higher U.S. imports of fabric for home furnishings and the ongoing decrease in consumer demand for sheer hosiery and seamless apparel.

PROSPECTS: The Company expects near-term profitability to continue to suffer, based on current weak retail conditions, the lack of volume predictability, customer operating schedules and lower levels of consumer confidence. Meanwhile, the Company plans to eliminate 750 jobs worldwide, as well as take other restructuring measures such as manufacturing consolidation. These restructuring plans are expected to reduce costs by about $17.1 million in the U.S. and Europe.

BUSINESS

UNIFI, INC. is engaged in the business of processing yarns by the texturing of synthetic filament polyester and nylon fiber and the spinning of cotton and cotton blend fibers. UFI sells textured polyester yarns, nylon yarns, dyed yarns, covered yarns, spun yarns made of cotton, cotton and un-dyed synthetic blends, and cotton and pre-dyed polyester blends domestically and internationally to weavers and knitters who produce fabrics for the apparel, automotive upholstery, hosiery, home furnishings, industrial and other end-use markets. In August 1991, Macfield, Inc. merged with UFI.

ANNUAL FINANCIAL DATA

	6/25/00	6/27/99	6/28/98	6/29/97	6/30/96	6/25/95	6/26/94
Earnings Per Share	**0.65**	[3] **0.97**	[3] **2.08**	**1.81**	[1][2] **1.18**	**1.67**	[1] **1.08**
Cash Flow Per Share	**2.20**	**2.46**	**3.21**	**3.18**	**2.42**	**2.76**	**2.06**
Tang. Book Val. Per Share	**11.28**	**10.85**	**10.37**	**8.96**	**9.00**	**8.99**	**8.36**
Dividends Per Share	...	...	**0.28**	**0.50**	**0.48**	**0.46**	**0.48**
Dividend Payout %	...	...	**13.5**	**27.6**	**40.7**	**27.5**	**44.4**
INCOME STATEMENT (IN MILLIONS):							
Total Revenues	1,280.4	1,251.2	1,377.6	1,704.9	1,603.3	1,554.6	1,384.8
Costs & Expenses	1,093.1	1,042.1	1,123.4	1,432.0	1,370.8	1,297.7	1,155.7
Depreciation & Amort.	90.5	89.9	69.7	87.9	81.9	75.8	70.1
Operating Income	96.8	119.2	184.5	185.0	150.6	181.0	159.0
Net Interest Inc./(Exp.)	d27.5	d25.1	d14.7	d9.5	d7.8	d5.1	d10.0
Income Before Income Taxes	55.7	87.4	191.7	174.3	123.3	185.6	136.8
Income Taxes	17.7	28.4	62.8	58.6	44.9	69.4	60.3
Equity Earnings/Minority Int.	d12.5	d5.2	22.3	...	...	...	...
Net Income	38.0	[3] 59.0	[3] 128.9	115.7	[1][2] 78.4	116.2	[1] 76.5
Cash Flow	128.6	148.9	198.6	203.6	160.3	192.0	146.6
Average Shs. Outstg. (000)	58,511	60,570	61,856	63,935	66,211	69,542	71,020
BALANCE SHEET (IN MILLIONS):							
Cash & Cash Equivalents	18.8	44.4	8.4	9.5	24.5	146.2	152.1
Total Current Assets	383.4	362.1	369.2	379.7	361.9	503.0	456.6
Net Property	658.4	689.7	648.6	598.4	549.4	516.2	512.3
Total Assets	1,354.8	1,365.8	1,338.8	1,018.7	951.1	1,040.9	1,003.3
Total Current Liabilities	367.8	145.3	159.3	163.6	165.7	169.7	152.3
Long-Term Obligations	261.8	478.9	464.0	255.8	170.0	230.0	230.0
Net Stockholders' Equity	622.4	646.1	636.2	548.5	583.2	603.5	588.5
Net Working Capital	15.6	216.9	209.9	216.1	196.2	333.4	304.3
Year-end Shs. Outstg. (000)	55,163	59,548	61,355	61,210	64,831	67,140	70,433
STATISTICAL RECORD:							
Operating Profit Margin %	7.6	9.5	13.4	10.9	9.4	11.6	11.5
Net Profit Margin %	3.0	4.7	9.4	6.8	4.9	7.5	5.5
Return on Equity %	6.1	9.1	20.3	21.1	13.4	19.2	13.0
Return on Assets %	2.8	4.3	9.6	11.4	8.2	11.2	7.6
Debt/Total Assets %	19.3	35.1	34.7	25.1	17.9	22.1	22.9
Price Range	15.31-7.00	21.25-10.56	42.19-11.50	43.63-29.63	33.13-21.25	29.13-21.88	27.00-20.50
P/E Ratio	23.6-10.8	21.9-10.9	20.3-5.5	24.1-16.4	28.1-18.0	17.4-13.1	25.0-19.0
Average Yield %	...	...	1.0	1.4	1.8	1.8	2.0

Statistics are as originally reported. [1] Incl. non-recurr. chrg. $23.8 mill., 6/96; $13.4 mill., 6/94 [2] Bef. extraord. chrg. $5.9 mill. [3] Bef. acctg. change chrg. $2.8 mill., 6/99; $4.6 mill., 6/98

OFFICERS:
G. A. Mebane IV, Chmn.
B. R. Parke, Pres., C.E.O.
B. Moore, C.F.O., Exec. V.P.

INVESTOR CONTACT: Robert A. Ward, Exec. V.P., (910) 294-4410

PRINCIPAL OFFICE: 7201 West Friendly Avenue, Greensboro, NC 27410

TELEPHONE NUMBER: (336) 294-4410
FAX: (336) 316-5422
WEB: www.unifi-inc.com

NO. OF EMPLOYEES: 6,680 (approx.)

SHAREHOLDERS: 745 (approx.)

ANNUAL MEETING: In Oct.

INCORPORATED: NY, Jan., 1969

INSTITUTIONAL HOLDINGS:
No. of Institutions: 106
Shares Held: 35,782,086
% Held: 66.7

INDUSTRY: Throwing and winding mills (SIC: 2282)

TRANSFER AGENT(S): First Union National Bank, Charlotte, NC

NYSE SYMBOL UN
Rec. Pr. 55.59 (5/31/01)

UNILEVER, N.V.

YIELD ...
P/E RATIO 52.4

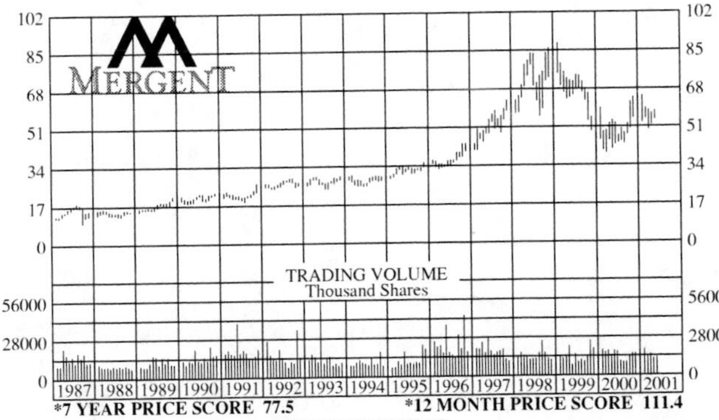

TRADING VOLUME
Thousand Shares

*7 YEAR PRICE SCORE 77.5 *12 MONTH PRICE SCORE 111.4
*NYSE COMPOSITE INDEX=100

INTERIM EARNINGS (Per Share):

Qtr.	Mar.	June	Sept.	Dec.
1998	0.62	0.65	0.99	0.63
1999	0.61	0.66	0.85	0.64
2000	0.63	0.54	0.83	d0.94

INTERIM DIVIDENDS (Per Share):

Amt.	Decl.	Ex.	Rec.	Pay.
0.416	...	11/10/99	11/15/99	12/17/99
0.772	...	5/08/00	5/10/00	5/30/00
0.415	...	11/08/00	11/10/00	12/18/00
0.839	...	5/14/01	5/16/01	5/29/01

CAPITALIZATION (12/31/00):

	($000)	(%)
Long-Term Debt	12,313,398	59.8
Minority Interest	582,403	2.8
Common & Surplus	7,698,466	37.4
Total	20,594,267	100.0

RECENT DEVELOPMENTS: For the year ended 12/31/00, net profit fell 62.7% to $1.04 billion compared with $2.79 billion in 1999. Results for 2000 and 1999 included exceptional losses of $1.83 billion and $287.0 million, respectively, and losses from amortization of goodwill and intangibles of $400.0 million and $24.0 million, respectively. Total revenues rose 9.8% to $45.30 billion from $41.26 billion in the previous year.

PROSPECTS: UN signed a definitive agreement to sell the Bestfoods Baking Company, a fresh baked goods company in the U.S., to George Weston Limited for $1.77 billion in cash. The transaction is expected to be completed in the second quarter of 2001. Meanwhile, UN sold several of its dry soup and sauces businesses in Europe to Campbell Soup Company for a debt free price of $1.00 billion euros.

BUSINESS

UNILEVER, N.V. is a worldwide producer of consumer products and foods. There are two parent companies: Unilever N.V. and Unilever PLC. These companies operate closely as a single entity. Products include consumer goods such as soaps and detergents, margarines, personal products and food and drinks. Other activities include specialty chemicals and agribusiness operations. In the U.S., Unilever N.V. is represented by Chesebrough-Pond's, Lever Brothers Co., Thomas J. Lipton, National Starch & Chemical, Ragu Foods and Elizabeth Arden. Revenues for 2000 were derived: Europe, 41.6%; North America, 24.4%; Africa and Middle East, 5.1%; Asia and Pacific, 16.9% and Latin America, 12.0%. On 5/12/00, UN acquired the Slim-Fast Food Companies for $2.30 billion.

ANNUAL FINANCIAL DATA

	12/31/00	12/31/99	12/31/98	12/31/97	12/31/96	12/31/95	12/31/94
Earnings Per Share	**2 0.99**	**2.65**	**3.05**	**1 4.73**	**2.15**	**8.25**	**8.94**
Tang. Book Val. Per Share	**...**	**12.21**	**8.59**	**19.14**	**13.51**	**...**	**...**
Dividends Per Share	**1.19**	**7.77**	**1.18**	**1.00**	**0.83**	**0.85**	**0.69**
Dividend Payout %	**120.2**	**293.3**	**38.7**	**21.1**	**38.4**	**10.3**	**7.7**
INCOME STATEMENT (IN MILLIONS):							
Total Revenues	45,297.4	41,255.6	46,826.0	47,355.3	50,315.3	49,567.3	47,580.1
Costs & Expenses	41,729.5	36,923.4	41,719.3	43,562.7	46,001.0	45,594.0	43,540.5
Operating Income	3,165.5	4,332.3	5,106.8	3,792.5	4,314.3	3,973.3	4,039.6
Net Interest Inc./(Exp.)	...	...	...	...	...	d380.6	d345.7
Income Before Income Taxes	2,566.2	4,370.5	5,330.3	7,723.8	3,988.8	3,646.8	3,821.8
Income Taxes	1,322.2	1,378.3	1,754.4	2,095.0	1,450.5	1,228.3	1,222.5
Equity Earnings/Minority Int.	d202.6	d202.4	d166.8	d154.2	d122.6	d102.0	d99.7
Net Income	2 1,041.4	2,789.8	3,409.2	1 5,474.6	2,415.6	2,316.6	2,499.7
Average Shs. Outstg. (000)	989,217	1,045,183	1,116,164	1,121,000	1,120,000	279,000	279,000
BALANCE SHEET (IN MILLIONS):							
Cash & Cash Equivalents	3,084.5	5,510.2	12,023.5	9,776.7	2,867.2	2,305.4	2,329.2
Total Current Assets	19,014.8	18,406.3	25,323.1	21,944.3	17,272.1	16,260.8	15,344.4
Net Property	9,272.3	...	...	10,035.5	13,473.0	13,484.0	12,764.1
Total Assets	54,319.9	28,077.6	35,305.1	32,144.0	30,970.3	29,968.7	28,406.9
Total Current Liabilities	26,730.2	...	8,415.2	9,282.1	9,985.7	9,794.3	9,356.4
Long-Term Obligations	12,313.4	2,956.0	2,692.4	1,571.4	2,093.0	1,834.6	1,676.5
Net Stockholders' Equity	7,698.5	7,813.8	5,498.2	12,381.8	8,797.1	8,699.8	8,346.0
Net Working Capital	d7,715.4	18,406.3	16,908.0	12,662.2	7,286.4	6,466.5	5,988.0
Year-end Shs. Outstg. (000)	571,576	640,000	640,000	640,000	640,000	...	...
STATISTICAL RECORD:							
Operating Profit Margin %	7.0	10.5	10.9	8.0	8.6	8.0	8.5
Net Profit Margin %	2.3	6.8	7.3	11.6	4.8	4.7	5.3
Return on Equity %	13.5	35.7	62.0	44.2	27.5	26.6	30.0
Return on Assets %	1.9	9.9	9.7	17.0	7.8	7.7	8.8
Debt/Total Assets %	22.7	10.5	7.6	4.9	6.8	6.1	5.9
Price Range	64.25-39.25	88.25-63.44	86.06-55.63	62.88-40.88	44.00-32.53	35.53-28.56	30.16-25.03
P/E Ratio	64.9-39.6	33.3-24.0	28.3-18.3	13.3-8.6	20.5-15.1	4.3-3.5	3.4-2.8
Average Yield %	2.3	10.2	1.7	1.9	2.2	2.6	2.5

Statistics are as originally reported. Adj. for stk. split: 4-for-1, 10/97. All figures are in U.S. dollars unless otherwise noted. Exchange rates: $1=ECU1.0611, 12/29/00; $1=ECU1.0068, 12/31/99; $1=ECU1.158, 12/31/98; $1=GLD1.9976, 12/31/97; GLD1.7449, 12/31/96; GLD1.6080, 12/31/95; GLD1.736, 12/31/94; GLD1.9409 1 Incl. net profit of $4.29 bill. on sale of chemicals businesses and $249.0 mill. loss on disposal of fixed assets. 2 Incl. $1.83 bill. exceptional item & $400.0 mill. amort. of goodwill & intangibles.

OFFICERS:
A. Burgmans, Chmn.
N. Fitzgerald, Vice-Chmn.

INVESTOR CONTACT: John T. Gald, Jr., Inv. Rel., (212) 906-4694

PRINCIPAL OFFICE: Weena 455, P.O. Box 760, Rotterdam, Netherlands

TELEPHONE NUMBER: (212) 906-4240
FAX: (212) 906-4666
WEB: www.unilever.com

NO. OF EMPLOYEES: 261,000 (avg.)

SHAREHOLDERS: N/A

ANNUAL MEETING: In May

INCORPORATED: NLD, Nov., 1927

INSTITUTIONAL HOLDINGS:
No. of Institutions: 384
Shares Held: 156,721,519
% Held: 24.5

INDUSTRY: Edible fats and oils, nec (SIC: 2079)

REGISTRAR(S): Morgan Guaranty Trust Company of New York, New York, NY

NYSE SYMBOL UNP
Rec. Pr. 56.89 (4/30/01)

UNION PACIFIC CORP.

YIELD 1.4%
P/E RATIO 17.1

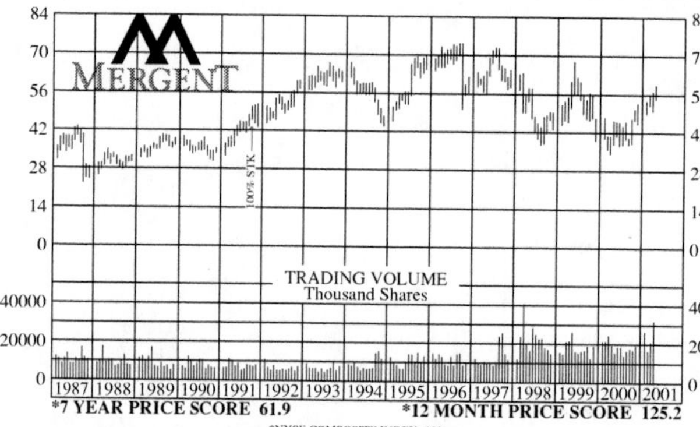

*7 YEAR PRICE SCORE 61.9 *12 MONTH PRICE SCORE 125.2

*NYSE COMPOSITE INDEX=100

INTERIM EARNINGS (Per Share):

Qtr.	Mar.	June	Sept.	Dec.
1997	0.52	0.87	0.96	d0.62
1998	d0.25	d0.91	0.13	d1.83
1999	0.52	0.77	0.86	0.95
2000	0.74	0.96	1.00	0.63

INTERIM DIVIDENDS (Per Share):

Amt.	Decl.	Ex.	Rec.	Pay.
0.20Q	2/24/00	3/13/00	3/15/00	4/03/00
0.20Q	5/25/00	6/12/00	6/14/00	7/03/00
0.20Q	8/03/00	9/11/00	9/13/00	10/02/00
0.20Q	11/16/00	12/11/00	12/13/00	1/02/01
0.20Q	2/22/01	3/12/01	3/14/01	4/02/01

Indicated div.: $0.80 (Div. Reinv. Plan)

CAPITALIZATION (12/31/00):

	($000)	(%)
Long-Term Debt	8,144,000	34.0
Deferred Income Tax	7,143,000	29.8
Common & Surplus	8,662,000	36.2
Total	23,949,000	100.0

RECENT DEVELOPMENTS: For the year ended 12/31/00, net income rose 7.5% to $842.0 million versus income from continuing operations of $783.0 million a year earlier. Results for 2000 included an after-tax charge of $72.0 million related to workforce reductions. Total operating revenues grew 5.7% to $11.88 billion. Commodity revenue gains were led by automotive, which rose 12.8% to $1.18 billion and intermodal, which advanced 10.7% to $1.91 billion.

PROSPECTS: UNP's near-term outlook is clouded by a combination of the slowing U.S. economy and the effect of higher fuel costs. Regarding the U.S. economy, slowdowns in key industries such as the automotive and chemicals industries could negatively affect the results of UNP's Union Pacific Railroad segment. On the positive side, the Company is benefiting from the introduction of new products and services, market expansion, and a profit turnaround in its Overnite Transportation unit.

BUSINESS

UNION PACIFIC CORPORATION is engaged primarily in rail transportation and trucking. Union Pacific Railroad is the largest railroad in North America, with over 33,000 route miles linking the Pacific Coast and Gulf Coast ports with the Midwest and eastern U.S. gateways. Major categories of freight are: agricultural products, automotive, chemicals, energy (primarily coal), industrial products and intermodal. Overnite Transportation Company is a major interstate trucking company serving all 50 states and portions of Canada and Mexico through 166 service centers located throughout the United States. Major categories of freight are: machinery, tobacco, textiles, plastics, electronics and paper products. On 9/11/96, UNP acquired Southern Pacific Rail Corporation.

QUARTERLY DATA

(12/31/00)($000)	REV	INC
1st Quarter	2,906,000	185
2nd Quarter	2,966,000	244
3rd Quarter	3,054,000	256
4th Quarter	2,952,000	157

ANNUAL FINANCIAL DATA

	12/31/00	12/31/99	12/31/98	12/31/97	[2] 12/31/96	12/31/95	12/31/94
Earnings Per Share	[6] 3.34	[5] 3.12	[4] d2.57	[1] 1.74	[1][3] 3.36	[3] 3.01	4.66
Cash Flow Per Share	7.36	6.92	1.78	5.95	6.86	6.12	9.53
Tang. Book Val. Per Share	35.09	32.29	29.93	30.79	42.76	27.35	20.45
Dividends Per Share	0.80	0.80	1.03	1.72	1.72	1.72	1.63
Dividend Payout %	24.0	25.6	...	98.8	51.2	57.1	35.0
INCOME STATEMENT (IN MILLIONS):							
Total Revenues	11,878.0	11,273.0	10,553.0	11,079.0	8,786.0	7,486.0	7,798.0
Costs & Expenses	8,835.0	8,386.0	9,654.0	8,783.0	6,491.0	5,503.0	5,198.0
Depreciation & Amort.	1,140.0	1,083.0	1,070.0	1,043.0	762.0	642.0	1,005.0
Operating Income	1,903.0	1,804.0	d171.0	1,253.0	1,533.0	1,341.0	1,595.0
Net Interest Inc./(Exp.)	d723.0	d733.0	d714.0	d605.0	d468.0	d407.0	d325.0
Income Before Income Taxes	1,310.0	1,202.0	d696.0	676.0	1,113.0	933.0	1,419.0
Income Taxes	468.0	419.0	cr63.0	244.0	380.0	314.0	461.0
Net Income	[6] 842.0	[5] 783.0	[4] d633.0	[1] 432.0	[1][3] 733.0	[3] 619.0	958.0
Cash Flow	1,982.0	1,866.0	437.0	1,475.0	1,495.0	1,261.0	1,963.0
Average Shs. Outstg. (000)	269,450	269,800	246,000	248,000	218,000	206,000	206,000
BALANCE SHEET (IN MILLIONS):							
Cash & Cash Equivalents	105.0	175.0	176.0	90.0	191.0	230.0	121.0
Total Current Assets	1,285.0	1,314.0	1,502.0	1,415.0	1,334.0	1,679.0	1,822.0
Net Property	28,196.0	27,519.0	26,939.0	25,977.0	25,044.0	14,105.0	12,271.0
Total Assets	30,499.0	29,888.0	29,374.0	28,764.0	27,914.0	19,446.0	15,942.0
Total Current Liabilities	2,962.0	2,885.0	2,932.0	3,247.0	3,056.0	1,899.0	2,505.0
Long-Term Obligations	8,144.0	8,426.0	8,511.0	8,285.0	7,900.0	6,232.0	4,090.0
Net Stockholders' Equity	8,662.0	8,001.0	7,393.0	8,225.0	8,225.0	6,364.0	5,131.0
Net Working Capital	d1,677.0	d1,571.0	d1,430.0	d1,832.0	d1,722.0	d220.0	d683.0
Year-end Shs. Outstg. (000)	246,820	247,783	247,000	247,000	176,000	206,000	205,000
STATISTICAL RECORD:							
Operating Profit Margin %	16.0	16.0	...	11.3	17.4	17.9	20.5
Net Profit Margin %	7.1	6.9	...	3.9	8.3	8.3	12.3
Return on Equity %	9.7	9.8	...	5.3	8.9	9.7	18.7
Return on Assets %	2.8	2.6	...	1.5	2.6	3.2	6.0
Debt/Total Assets %	26.7	28.2	29.0	28.8	28.3	32.0	25.7
Price Range	52.81-34.25	67.88-39.00	63.75-37.31	72.98-56.25	74.50-50.00	70.13-45.63	67.13-43.75
P/E Ratio	15.8-10.3	21.8-12.5	...	41.9-32.3	22.2-14.9	23.3-15.2	14.4-9.4
Average Yield %	1.8	1.5	2.0	2.7	2.8	3.0	2.9

Statistics are as originally reported. [1] Incl. non-recurr. chrg. 12/31/97, $555.0 mill.; chrg. 12/31/96, $2.0 mill. [2] Incl. ops. of Southern Pacific Rail Corp., acq. 9/96 [3] Bef. disc. ops. inc. 12/31/96, $171.0 mill.; inc. 12/31/95, $327.0 mill. [4] Incl. pre-tax merg.-rel. chrgs. of $69.0 mill. & goodwill impair. of $547.0 mill. [5] Bef. disc. oper. gain of $27.0 mill. [6] Incl. aft.-tax wrkfrc. reduct. chrg. of $72.0 mill. ($0.27/sh.)

OFFICERS:
R. K. Davidson, Chmn., Pres., C.E.O.
J. R. Young, Exec. V.P., C.F.O.
C. W. von Bernuth, Sr V.P., Couns., Sec.

INVESTOR CONTACT: M. Sanders Jones, V.P., Treas., (402) 271-6111

PRINCIPAL OFFICE: 1416 Dodge Street, Omaha, NE 68179

TELEPHONE NUMBER: (402) 271-5777
WEB: www.up.com

NO. OF EMPLOYEES: 63,000 (avg.)

SHAREHOLDERS: 39,150 (approx.)

ANNUAL MEETING: In Apr.

INCORPORATED: UT, Feb., 1969

INSTITUTIONAL HOLDINGS:
No. of Institutions: 461
Shares Held: 203,199,777
% Held: 82.1

INDUSTRY: Railroads, line-haul operating (SIC: 4011)

TRANSFER AGENT(S): Computershare Investor Services, Chicago, IL

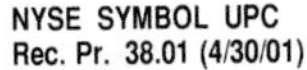

NYSE SYMBOL UPC
Rec. Pr. 38.01 (4/30/01)

UNION PLANTERS CORPORATION

YIELD 5.3%
P/E RATIO 12.7

TRADING VOLUME
Thousand Shares

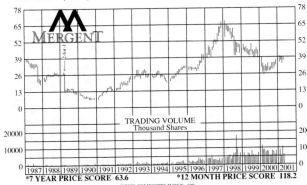

*7 YEAR PRICE SCORE 63.6 *12 MONTH PRICE SCORE 118.2
*NYSE COMPOSITE INDEX=100

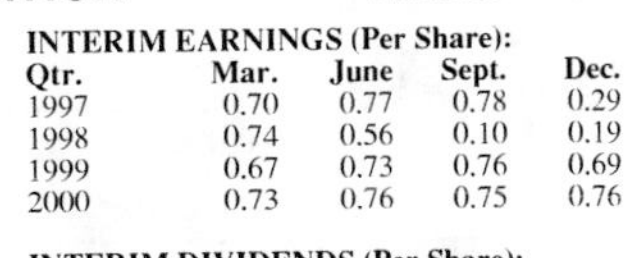

INTERIM EARNINGS (Per Share):

Qtr.	Mar.	June	Sept.	Dec.
1997	0.70	0.77	0.78	0.29
1998	0.74	0.56	0.10	0.19
1999	0.67	0.73	0.76	0.69
2000	0.73	0.76	0.75	0.76

INTERIM DIVIDENDS (Per Share):

Amt.	Decl.	Ex.	Rec.	Pay.
0.50Q	4/21/00	4/27/00	5/01/00	5/15/00
0.50Q	7/20/00	7/28/00	8/01/00	8/15/00
0.50Q	10/19/00	10/30/00	11/01/00	11/15/00
0.50Q	1/18/01	1/30/01	2/01/01	2/15/01
0.50Q	4/19/01	4/27/01	5/01/01	5/15/01

Indicated div.: $2.00 (Div. Reinv. Plan)

CAPITALIZATION (12/31/00):

	($000)	(%)
Total Deposits	23,113,383	82.8
Long-Term Debt	1,878,971	6.7
Preferred Stock	19,691	0.1
Common & Surplus	2,900,363	10.4
Total	27,912,408	100.0

RECENT DEVELOPMENTS: For the year ended 12/31/00, net earnings fell to $409.3 million from $410.0 million in 1999. Net interest income fell 2.0% to $1.23 billion. Provision for losses on loans rose 4.1% to $77.1 million. Total non-interest income, including investment securities gains of $381,000 in 2000 and $2.1 million in 1999, grew 9.1% to $559.4 million. Non-interest expense increased 2.5% to $1.10 billion.

PROSPECTS: On 2/12/01, the Company announced that it acquired Jefferson Savings Bancorp, Inc. of Ballwin, Missouri for approximately $140.0 million. The transaction allows the Company to strengthen its presence in the St. Louis market. The Company expects continued loan growth while maintaining credit quality in 2001, as the markets served by UPC generally have a good economic outlook.

BUSINESS

UNION PLANTERS CORPORATION is a $34.72 billion (12/31/00) multi-state bank holding company headquartered in Tennessee. The principal banking markets of the Company are Alabama, Arkansas, Florida, Kentucky, Illinois, Indiana, Iowa, Louisiana, Mississippi, Missouri, Tennessee, and Texas. The Company's existing market areas are served by its 847 banking offices and 1,065 ATMs. The mortgage operations of UPC's subsidiary, Union Planter Bank, N.A., operate through 25 mortgage production offices in Alabama, Arizona, California, Colorado, Florida, Georgia, Louisiana, Mississippi, Nevada, North Carolina, Ohio, Tennessee, Texas, and Washington, in addition to mortgage production offices located in its branch banking locations. On 7/1/98, the Company acquired People's First Corporation for $1.43 billion.

ANNUAL FINANCIAL DATA

	12/31/00	12/31/99	[1] 12/31/98	12/31/97	12/31/96	12/31/95	12/31/94
Earnings Per Share	**3.00**	**2.85**	**1.58**	**2.45**	**1.95**	**2.82**	**1.25**
Tang. Book Val. Per Share	**13.54**	**11.97**	**17.42**	**19.33**	**17.79**	**17.95**	**14.76**
Dividends Per Share	**2.00**	**2.00**	**2.00**	**1.50**	**1.08**	**0.98**	**0.88**
Dividend Payout %	**66.7**	**70.2**	**126.6**	**61.0**	**55.4**	**34.8**	**70.4**
INCOME STATEMENT (IN MILLIONS):							
Total Interest Income	2,527.7	2,297.9	2,314.4	1,416.7	1,180.6	836.7	664.1
Total Interest Expense	1,296.5	1,041.4	1,107.1	646.3	574.6	389.3	275.8
Net Interest Income	1,231.1	1,256.5	1,207.2	770.4	606.0	447.4	388.3
Provision for Loan Losses	77.1	74.0	204.1	113.6	57.4	22.2	3.6
Non-Interest Income	559.4	512.7	568.8	361.6	226.3	157.7	93.6
Non-Interest Expense	1,102.8	1,076.4	1,200.0	697.7	570.6	382.2	398.8
Income Before Taxes	610.6	618.8	371.9	320.7	204.3	200.7	79.4
Net Income	409.3	410.0	225.6	208.8	133.7	135.4	58.6
Average Shs. Outstg. (000)	136,656	143,983	142,693	85,195	64,987	45,008	40,055
BALANCE SHEET (IN MILLIONS):							
Cash & Due from Banks	1,018.3	1,127.9	1,271.6	816.5	594.5	432.9	488.7
Securities Avail. for Sale	7,077.5	7,788.2	8,577.7	3,435.1	3,181.6	2,896.8	156.0
Total Loans & Leases	23,982.2	21,474.5	19,611.2	12,687.1	10,464.2	7,100.1	5,980.6
Allowance for Credit Losses	360.2	370.4	355.8	253.9	197.0	163.7	153.5
Net Loans & Leases	23,622.0	21,104.1	19,255.4	12,433.2	10,267.2	6,936.4	5,827.0
Total Assets	34,720.7	33,280.4	31,692.0	18,105.1	15,222.6	11,277.1	10,015.1
Total Deposits	23,113.4	23,372.1	24,896.5	13,440.3	11,490.3	9,447.7	8,417.8
Long-Term Obligations	1,879.0	1,057.8	1,333.7	1,414.9	1,273.7	485.3	341.0
Total Liabilities	31,800.7	30,504.2	28,707.9	16,358.2	13,869.7	10,310.8	9,284.4
Net Stockholders' Equity	2,920.1	2,776.1	2,984.1	1,746.9	1,352.9	966.3	730.7
Year-end Shs. Outstg. (000)	134,735	138,487	141,925	81,651	64,927	45,447	40,179
STATISTICAL RECORD:							
Return on Equity %	14.0	14.8	7.6	12.0	9.9	14.0	8.0
Return on Assets %	1.2	1.2	0.7	1.2	0.9	1.2	0.6
Equity/Assets %	8.4	8.3	9.4	9.6	8.9	8.6	7.3
Non-Int. Exp./Tot. Inc. %	61.6	60.9	67.2	61.7	68.9	63.2	79.4
Price Range	39.69-25.25	49.63-38.25	67.94-40.13	67.13-38.25	41.50-28.13	32.50-20.50	28.88-19.50
P/E Ratio	13.1-8.4	17.4-13.4	43.0-25.4	27.4-15.6	21.3-14.4	11.5-7.3	23.1-15.6
Average Yield %	6.2	4.6	3.7	2.8	3.1	3.7	3.6

Statistics are as originally reported. [1] Reflects the acq. of People's First Corporation on 7/1/98.

OFFICERS:
J. W. Moore, Chmn., C.E.O.
B. L. Doxey, Sr. Exec. V.P., C.F.O.

INVESTOR CONTACT: Bobby L. Doxey, Exec. V.P. & C.F.O., (901) 580-6781

PRINCIPAL OFFICE: 7130 Goodlett Farms Pkwy, Memphis, TN 38018

TELEPHONE NUMBER: (901) 580 6000
FAX: (901) 383 2396
WEB: www.unionplanters.com

NO. OF EMPLOYEES: 11,632 full-time; 2,368 part-time

SHAREHOLDERS: 34,100 approx.

ANNUAL MEETING: In April

INCORPORATED: TN, Nov., 1971

INSTITUTIONAL HOLDINGS:
No. of Institutions: 239
Shares Held: 41,782,648
% Held: 30.5

INDUSTRY: National commercial banks (SIC: 6021)

TRANSFER AGENT(S): Union Planters Bank, N.A., Belleville, IL

NYSE SYMBOL UB
Rec. Pr. 30.54 (4/30/01)

UNIONBANCAL CORP.

YIELD 3.3%
P/E RATIO 11.3

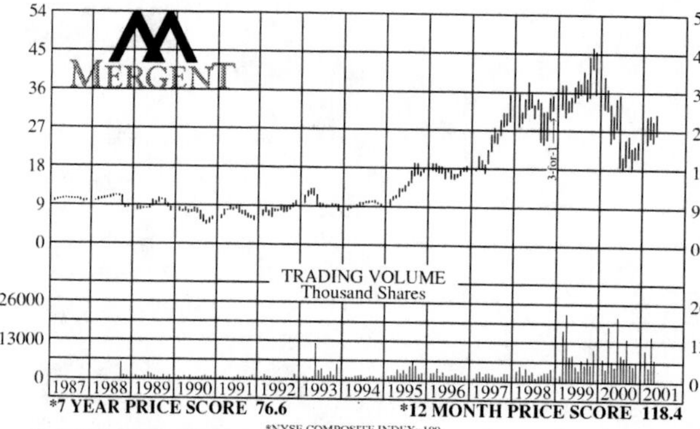

*7 YEAR PRICE SCORE 76.6 *12 MONTH PRICE SCORE 118.4

*NYSE COMPOSITE INDEX=100

INTERIM EARNINGS (Per Share):

Qtr.	Mar.	June	Sept.	Dec.
1998	0.54	0.62	0.84	0.65
1999	0.69	0.69	0.43	0.83
2000	0.96	0.87	0.82	0.05

INTERIM DIVIDENDS (Per Share):

Amt.	Decl.	Ex.	Rec.	Pay.
0.25Q	5/09/00	6/07/00	6/09/00	7/07/00
0.25Q	7/26/00	9/06/00	9/09/00	10/06/00
0.25Q	10/26/00	12/06/00	12/08/00	1/12/01
0.25Q	2/28/01	3/07/01	3/09/01	4/06/01
0.25Q	4/25/01	6/06/01	6/08/01	7/06/01

Indicated div.: $1.00 (Div. Reinv. Plan)

CAPITALIZATION (12/31/00):

	($000)	(%)
Total Deposits	27,283,183	88.9
Long-Term Debt	200,000	0.7
Common & Surplus	3,211,565	10.5
Total	30,694,748	100.0

RECENT DEVELOPMENTS: For the year ended 12/31/00, net income fell to $439.9 million from $441.7 million in 1999. Results included a restructuring credit of $19.0 million in 2000 versus a charge of $85.0 million in 1999. Net interest income improved 11.9% to $1.58 billion. Provision for credit losses increased sharply to $440.0 million versus $65.0 million in 1999. Noninterest rose 10.3% to $647.2 million.

PROSPECTS: In 2001, UB will continue to focus on growth in the consumer asset portfolio, expanding wealth management services, and extending the small business franchise. As a result, UB expects operating earnings to increase more than 25.0% from the $2.54 per diluted share in 2000. In addition, UB anticipates that the provision for credit losses will be in the range of $250.0 million to $300.0 million in 2001, down from $440.0 million in 2000.

BUSINESS

UNIONBANCAL CORPORATION is a commercial bank holding company based in San Francisco with consolidated assets of $35.20 billion as of 12/31/00. The Company's principal subsidiary, Union Bank of California, N.A., has 242 banking offices in California, 6 banking offices in Oregon and Washington, and 18 overseas facilities. The Company is 64.0%-owned by The Bank of Tokyo-Mitsubishi, Ltd. and was formed as a result of the combination of Union Bank with BanCal Tri-State Corporation on 4/1/96.

LOAN DISTRIBUTION

(12/31/00)	($000)	(%)
Commercial, Financial & Industrial	13,748,838	52.9
Construction	939,302	3.6
Mortgage	6,642,737	25.5
Consumer	2,410,729	9.3
Lease financing	1,134,440	4.4
Foreign Originated	1,134,352	4.4
Total	26,010,398	100.0

ANNUAL FINANCIAL DATA

	12/31/00	12/31/99	12/31/98	12/31/97	12/31/96	12/31/95	12/31/94
Earnings Per Share	**[2] 2.72**	**[2] 2.64**	**[1] 2.65**	**2.30**	**1.37**	**1.79**	**0.60**
Tang. Book Val. Per Share	**20.17**	**18.18**	**17.45**	**16.40**	**14.40**	**11.84**	**10.22**
Dividends Per Share	**1.00**	**0.76**	**0.56**	**0.49**	**0.23**	...	...
Dividend Payout %	**36.8**	**28.8**	**21.1**	**21.3**	**17.0**	...	...
INCOME STATEMENT (IN MILLIONS):							
Total Interest Income	2,501.1	2,161.9	2,085.2	2,033.5	1,927.3	1,302.3	1,021.3
Total Interest Expense	916.6	746.1	767.0	801.8	758.7	469.9	308.0
Net Interest Income	1,584.4	1,415.8	1,318.2	1,231.7	1,168.6	832.4	713.3
Provision for Loan Losses	440.0	65.0	45.0	...	40.0	57.0	80.0
Non-Interest Income	647.2	586.8	533.5	463.0	418.7	247.5	225.1
Non-Interest Expense	1,130.2	1,282.0	1,135.2	1,044.7	1,134.9	681.2	752.9
Income Before Taxes	661.4	655.6	671.5	650.0	412.4	341.7	120.6
Net Income	[2] 439.9	[2] 441.7	[1] 466.5	411.3	249.5	207.3	75.3
Average Shs. Outstg. (000)	161,989	167,149	175,737	165,018	164,220	109,236	106,518
BALANCE SHEET (IN MILLIONS):							
Cash & Due from Banks	2,957.1	2,142.0	2,135.4	2,541.7	2,268.8	1,749.7	1,014.4
Securities Avail. for Sale	4,467.4	3,390.0	3,906.3	3,092.8	2,781.7	1,461.3	717.8
Total Loans & Leases	26,010.4	25,913.0	24,296.1	22,581.3	20,898.1	14,392.4	12,360.9
Allowance for Credit Losses	613.9	470.4	459.3	451.7	523.9	332.4	316.8
Net Loans & Leases	25,396.5	25,442.6	23,836.8	22,129.6	20,374.2	14,060.0	12,044.1
Total Assets	35,162.5	33,684.8	32,276.3	30,585.3	29,234.1	19,518.1	16,761.1
Total Deposits	27,283.2	26,256.6	24,507.9	23,296.4	21,533.0	14,867.1	12,834.7
Long-Term Obligations	200.0	298.0	298.0	348.0	382.0	331.4	415.9
Total Liabilities	31,950.9	30,697.3	29,218.1	27,906.0	26,739.1	17,984.5	15,527.6
Net Stockholders' Equity	3,211.6	2,987.5	3,058.2	2,702.2	2,500.4	1,533.6	1,233.5
Year-end Shs. Outstg. (000)	159,234	164,283	175,260	164,748	164,289	109,608	107,472
STATISTICAL RECORD:							
Return on Equity %	13.7	14.8	15.3	15.2	10.0	13.5	6.1
Return on Assets %	1.3	1.3	1.4	1.3	0.9	1.1	0.4
Equity/Assets %	9.1	8.9	9.5	8.8	8.6	7.9	7.4
Non-Int. Exp./Tot. Inc. %	50.6	64.0	61.3	61.6	71.5	63.1	80.2
Price Range	39.69-17.94	46.44-30.13	38.31-23.63	35.50-16.94	19.19-15.44	19.25-8.94	10.50-8.06
P/E Ratio	14.6-6.6	17.6-11.4	14.5-8.9	15.4-7.4	14.0-11.3	10.7-5.0	17.5-13.5
Average Yield %	3.5	2.0	1.8	1.9	1.3	...	...

Statistics are as originally reported. Adj. for stk. split: 3-for-1, 12/21/98. [1] Incl. after-tax cr. $44.8 mill. fr. red. in CA tax liab. [2] Incl. restruct. credit, 2000, $19.0 mill.; chrg., 1999, $85.0 mill.

OFFICERS:
K. Hayama, Chmn.
T. Moriguchi, Pres., C.E.O.
D. Matson, Exec. V.P., C.F.O.

INVESTOR CONTACT: John A. Rice, Jr., V.P. & Mgr., Inv. Rel., (415) 765-2969

PRINCIPAL OFFICE: 400 California Street, San Francisco, CA 94104-1476

TELEPHONE NUMBER: (415) 765-2969
FAX: (415) 765-2950
WEB: www.unionbancal.com

NO. OF EMPLOYEES: 8,715

SHAREHOLDERS: 2,200 (approx.)

ANNUAL MEETING: In Apr.

INCORPORATED: CA, Feb., 1953

INSTITUTIONAL HOLDINGS:
No. of Institutions: 125
Shares Held: 143,363,391
% Held: 90.5

INDUSTRY: National commercial banks (SIC: 6021)

TRANSFER AGENT(S): Computershare Investor Services, Los Angeles, CA

NYSE SYMBOL UNS
Rec. Pr. 23.21 (4/30/01)

UNISOURCE ENERGY CORP.

YIELD 1.7%
P/E RATIO 18.3

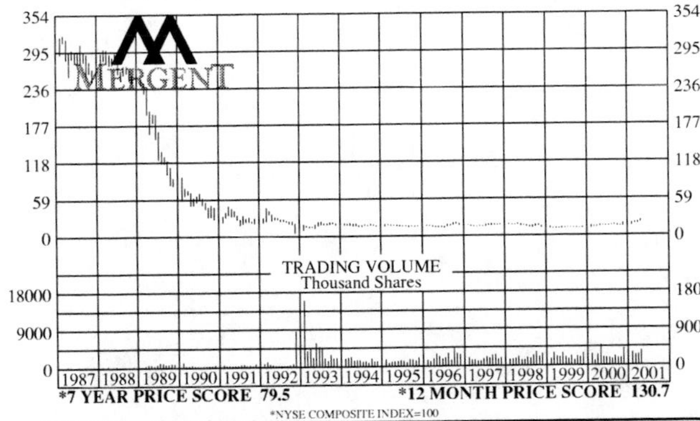

INTERIM EARNINGS (Per Share):

Qtr.	Mar.	June	Sept.	Dec.
1996	0.01	0.32	3.19	0.24
1997	0.36	0.93	1.35	d0.04
1998	d0.22	0.03	1.05	0.01
1999	d0.17	0.11	1.58	0.20
2000	0.01	0.32	0.52	0.42

INTERIM DIVIDENDS (Per Share):

Amt.	Decl.	Ex.	Rec.	Pay.
0.08Q	5/12/00	5/18/00	5/22/00	6/09/00
0.08Q	8/04/00	8/11/00	8/15/00	9/08/00
0.08Q	11/03/00	11/13/00	11/15/00	12/08/00
0.10Q	2/02/01	2/13/01	2/15/01	3/09/01
0.10Q	5/11/01	5/23/01	5/25/01	6/08/01

Indicated div.: $0.40

CAPITALIZATION (12/31/00):

	($000)	(%)
Long-Term Debt	1,132,395	53.2
Capital Lease Obligations	857,829	40.3
Deferred Income Tax	51,035	2.4
Common & Surplus	88,799	4.2
Total	2,130,058	100.0

RECENT DEVELOPMENTS: For the year ended 12/31/00, net income fell 25.9% to $41.9 million versus income of $56.5 million, before an extraordinary gain, in 1999. Earnings for 1999 included a non-recurring gain of $9.6 million from the sale of New Energy. Operating revenues improved 26.9% to $1.03 billion from $814.8 million the year before. Revenue from retail customers grew 5.5% to $664.6 million from $629.9 million in 1999. Sales for resale rocketed 110.0% to $359.8 million from $171.2 million a year earlier.

PROSPECTS: On 3/29/01, TEP signed a five-year wholesale contract to supply 60 megawatts of electricity to Phelps Dodge Energy Services. The contract calls for TEP, beginning in March of 2001, to supply the power at all times except during TEP's peak customer energy demand periods from July through September of each year. TEP expects the agreement to generate revenues of about $30.0 million annually. Going forward, earnings for the utility operations should continue to benefit from sales growth in the wholesale sector.

BUSINESS

UNISOURCE ENERGY CORPORATION is a holding company that conducts business through its wholly-owned subsidiaries Tucson Electric Power Company (TEP), a regulated utility, and Millennium Energy Holdings, Inc., consisting of unregulated energy businesses. TEP is an operating public utility that generates, purchases, transmits, distributes and sells electricity to over 338,700 retail customers as of 12/31/00 and to wholesale customers. TEP's retail service territory consists of a 1,155 square mile area of Southeastern Arizona. Millennium, an unregulated energy business, owns two-thirds of Advanced Energy Technologies, Inc., which owns Global Solar Energy, Inc., ION International, Inc., MEH Corporation, Nations Energy Corporation and Southwest Energy Solutions, Inc.

ANNUAL FINANCIAL DATA

	12/31/00	12/31/99	12/31/98	12/31/97	12/31/96	12/31/95	12/31/94
Earnings Per Share	**1.27**	[3] **1.74**	**0.87**	**2.59**	[2] **3.76**	[1] **1.71**	**0.65**
Cash Flow Per Share	**4.84**	**4.73**	**3.68**	**5.27**	**6.30**	**4.08**	**3.44**
Tang. Book Val. Per Share	**2.67**	**10.02**	**7.65**	**6.75**	**4.15**	**0.39**	...
Dividends Per Share	**0.32**	...	...	...	...	...	...
INCOME STATEMENT (IN MILLIONS):							
Total Revenues	1,033.7	803.8	768.7	729.9	715.9	670.6	691.5
Costs & Expenses	679.3	511.7	507.0	472.8	480.2	433.2	445.0
Depreciation & Amort.	117.2	97.7	90.4	86.4	81.7	76.3	89.9
Maintenance Exp.	39.7	36.9	36.1	36.7	36.4	38.9	42.1
Operating Income	197.4	157.4	135.2	134.0	117.6	122.1	114.4
Net Interest Inc./(Exp.)	d152.8	d114.4	d106.7	d95.6	d96.4	d100.5	d100.1
Income Taxes	...	...	...	cr41.4	cr91.9	cr29.4	cr4.8
Net Income	41.9	[3] 56.5	28.0	83.6	[2] 120.9	[1] 54.9	20.7
Cash Flow	159.1	154.2	118.4	170.0	202.6	131.2	110.6
Average Shs. Outstg. (000)	32,879	32,578	32,178	32,278	32,134	32,138	32,145
BALANCE SHEET (IN MILLIONS):							
Gross Property	3,225.8	3,139.7	3,224.8	3,159.6	3,096.5	3,039.6	2,987.1
Accumulated Depreciation	1,519.5	1,409.8	1,137.8	1,056.3	979.2	899.3	817.2
Net Property	1,706.3	1,729.9	1,915.6	1,935.5	1,953.9	1,978.1	2,007.4
Total Assets	2,671.4	2,656.3	2,634.2	2,634.4	2,568.5	2,530.9	2,701.9
Long-Term Obligations	1,990.2	2,016.2	2,074.0	2,105.4	2,118.9	2,105.4	2,304.7
Net Stockholders' Equity	88.8	324.2	246.6	216.9	133.3	12.5	d42.2
Year-end Shs. Outstg. (000)	33,219	32,349	32,258	32,139	32,135	32,134	32,145
STATISTICAL RECORD:							
Operating Profit Margin %	19.1	19.6	17.6	18.4	16.4	18.2	16.5
Net Profit Margin %	4.1	7.0	3.6	11.4	16.9	8.2	3.0
Net Inc./Net Property %	2.5	3.3	1.5	4.3	6.2	2.8	1.0
Net Inc./Tot. Capital %	2.0	2.4	1.2	3.5	5.1	2.4	0.9
Return on Equity %	47.2	17.4	11.4	38.5	90.7	439.7	...
Accum. Depr./Gross Prop. %	47.1	44.9	35.3	33.4	31.6	29.6	27.4
Price Range	19.31-10.81	13.94-10.38	18.94-12.25	18.25-13.88	20.75-12.25	18.75-13.13	20.63-14.38
P/E Ratio	...	...	21.8-14.1	7.0-5.4	5.5-3.3	11.0-7.7	31.7-22.1
Average Yield %	2.1	...	...	...	...	...	...

Statistics are as originally reported. [1] Incl. non-recurr. chrg. $12.2 mill. reduction in fuel exp. & $15.7 mill inc. tax benefit [2] Inc. one-time charge $13.6 mill. for workforce reduction [3] Bef. extraord. gain $22.6 mill.; but incl. pre-tax gain of $34.7 mill. on sale of NewEnergy.

OFFICERS:
J. S. Pignatelli, Chmn., Pres., C.E.O.
K. Larson, V.P., C.F.O.
D. R. Nelson, V.P., Gen. Couns., Sec.

INVESTOR CONTACT: Investor Relations, (520) 884-3968

PRINCIPAL OFFICE: 220 West Sixth Street, Tucson, AZ 85701

TELEPHONE NUMBER: (520) 571-4000
FAX: (520) 884-3934
WEB: www.unisourceenergy.com

NO. OF EMPLOYEES: 1,203 (avg.)

SHAREHOLDERS: 21,986

ANNUAL MEETING: In May

INCORPORATED: AZ, March, 1995

INSTITUTIONAL HOLDINGS:
No. of Institutions: 125
Shares Held: 21,634,601
% Held: 65.1

INDUSTRY: Electric services (SIC: 4911)

TRANSFER AGENT(S): The Bank of New York, New York, NY

NYSE SYMBOL UIS
Rec. Pr. 12.04 (4/30/01)

UNISYS CORP.

YIELD ...
P/E RATIO 15.4

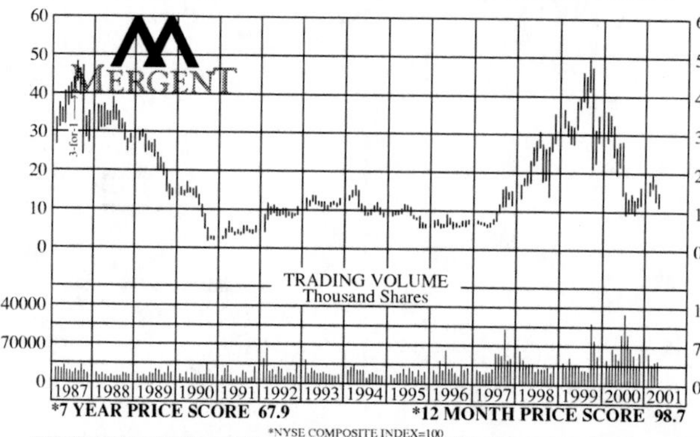

*7 YEAR PRICE SCORE 67.9 *12 MONTH PRICE SCORE 98.7

*NYSE COMPOSITE INDEX=100

INTERIM EARNINGS (Per Share):

Qtr.	Mar.	June	Sept.	Dec.
1995	0.02	0.06	d0.36	d4.06
1996	d0.25	d0.14	d0.09	0.15
1997	d0.06	0.08	0.14	d4.75
1998	0.14	0.24	0.26	0.42
1999	0.32	0.38	0.47	0.46
2000	0.34	0.18	0.14	0.12

INTERIM DIVIDENDS (Per Share):

Amt.	Decl.	Ex.	Rec.	Pay.
	No dividends paid.			

CAPITALIZATION (12/31/00):

	($000)	(%)
Long-Term Debt	536,300	19.7
Common & Surplus	2,186,100	80.3
Total	2,722,400	100.0

RECENT DEVELOPMENTS: For the year ended 12/31/00, income fell 53.2% to $244.8 million, before an extraordinary charge, versus $522.8 million in 1999. Results for 2000 and 1999 excluded extraordinary charges of $19.8 million and $12.1 million, respectively. Revenues were $6.89 billion, down 8.7% from $7.54 billion in the prior year. Operating income dropped 55.6% to $426.8 million versus $960.7 million the year before.

PROSPECTS: UIS expects future earnings to benefit from its strategic actions to concentrate on higher-growth, higher-margin business opportunities and de-emphasize commodity-based business. Meanwhile, UIS continues to make progress in realigning its cost base with a more focused business model. Recent personnel reductions should improve operating profit margins.

BUSINESS

UNISYS CORPORATION is an information management company that provides information services, technology, software and customer support on a worldwide basis. The Company operates in two business segments: Services and Technology. The Services segment consists of systems integration, including industry and custom applications, outsourcing, network services and multivendor maintenance. The Technology segment provides enterprise-class servers, specialized technologies and personal computers. Unisys services banks, airlines, newspapers, telecommunications, and government agencies. Revenues (and operating income percent) in 2000 were derived: Services, 68.9% (1.7%); and Technology, 31.1% (17.7%).

ANNUAL FINANCIAL DATA

	12/31/00	12/31/99	12/31/98	12/31/97	12/31/96	12/31/95	12/31/94
Earnings Per Share	[5] **0.77**	[5] **1.63**	**1.06**	[4] **d5.30**	[3] **d0.34**	[1][2] **d4.37**	[3] **d0.07**
Cash Flow Per Share	**1.65**	**2.62**	**2.05**	**1.39**	**1.57**	**d2.05**	**2.57**
Tang. Book Val. Per Share	**5.95**	**5.42**	...	...	...	...	...
INCOME STATEMENT (IN MILLIONS):							
Total Revenues	6,885.0	7,544.6	7,208.4	6,636.0	6,370.5	6,202.3	7,399.7
Costs & Expenses	6,187.2	6,318.7	6,131.8	5,798.6	5,713.4	6,504.8	6,643.5
Depreciation & Amort.	271.0	265.2	266.4	1,216.9	329.7	395.6	450.2
Operating Income	426.8	960.7	810.2	d379.5	327.4	d698.1	306.0
Net Interest Inc./(Exp.)	d79.8	d127.8	d171.7	d233.2	d249.7	d202.1	d203.7
Income Before Income Taxes	379.0	770.3	604.7	d758.8	93.7	d781.1	153.2
Income Taxes	134.2	247.5	217.7	94.8	31.9	cr153.8	45.0
Net Income	[5] 244.8	[5] 522.8	387.0	[4] d853.6	[3] 61.8	[1][2] d627.3	[3] 108.2
Cash Flow	515.8	751.3	546.9	252.2	270.7	d352.0	438.3
Average Shs. Outstg. (000)	313,115	287,290	266,944	182,016	172,601	171,958	170,752
BALANCE SHEET (IN MILLIONS):							
Cash & Cash Equivalents	378.0	464.0	604.3	803.0	1,029.2	1,119.7	884.6
Total Current Assets	2,587.0	2,845.7	2,816.7	2,886.5	3,133.1	3,218.6	3,141.5
Net Property	620.2	620.8	580.9	581.2	621.8	691.4	933.7
Total Assets	5,717.7	5,889.7	5,577.7	5,591.3	6,967.1	7,113.2	7,323.9
Total Current Liabilities	2,685.8	2,618.5	1,280.6	1,270.2	1,011.7	1,469.9	1,330.5
Long-Term Obligations	536.3	950.2	1,105.2	1,438.3	2,271.4	1,533.3	1,864.1
Net Stockholders' Equity	2,186.1	1,953.3	1,517.0	1,205.9	2,560.1	2,851.0	2,604.5
Net Working Capital	d98.8	227.2	1,536.1	1,616.3	2,121.4	1,748.7	1,811.0
Year-end Shs. Outstg. (000)	317,300	312,500	256,608	250,200	174,843	171,423	170,962
STATISTICAL RECORD:							
Operating Profit Margin %	6.2	12.7	11.2	...	5.1	...	4.1
Net Profit Margin %	3.6	6.9	5.4	...	1.0	...	1.5
Return on Equity %	11.2	26.8	25.5	...	3.8	...	4.2
Return on Assets %	4.3	8.9	6.9	...	0.9	...	1.5
Debt/Total Assets %	9.4	16.1	19.8	25.7	32.6	21.6	25.5
Price Range	36.06-9.13	49.69-20.94	35.38-13.31	16.50-5.75	9.13-5.38	11.75-5.50	16.50-8.25
P/E Ratio	46.8-11.8	30.5-12.8	33.4-12.6	...	...	...	...

Statistics are as originally reported. [1] Bef. $2.7 mill. ($0.02/sh.) inc. fr. disc. ops. [2] Incl. $581.9 mill. ($3.39/sh.) after-tax restr. chg. & $88.6 mill. ($0.51/sh.) after-tax chg. cov. loss prov. [3] Excl. $12.1 mill. ($0.07/sh.) extra. loss, 1996; $7.7 mill. ($0.04/sh.), 1994. [4] Bef. extra. loss of $19.8 mill. [5] Excl. $12.1 mill. extraord. chg., 1999; $19.8 mill., 2000.

OFFICERS:
L. A. Weinbach, Chmn., Pres., C.E.O.
H. S. Barron, Vice-Chmn.
J. B. Haugen, Sr. V.P., C.F.O.
S. A. Battersby, V.P., Treas.

INVESTOR CONTACT: Jack F. McHale, V.P. Investor Relations, (215) 986-6999

PRINCIPAL OFFICE: Unisys Way, Blue Bell, PA 19424

TELEPHONE NUMBER: (215) 986-4011
FAX: (215) 986-6850
WEB: www.unisys.com

NO. OF EMPLOYEES: 36,900 (approx.)

SHAREHOLDERS: 29,700

ANNUAL MEETING: In Apr.

INCORPORATED: MI, Jan., 1905; reincorp., DE, May, 1905

INSTITUTIONAL HOLDINGS:
No. of Institutions: 294
Shares Held: 187,910,836
% Held: 59.0

INDUSTRY: Electronic computers (SIC: 3571)

TRANSFER AGENT(S): Equiserve Trust Company, N.A., Jersey City, NJ

NYSE SYMBOL UAG
Rec. Pr. 14.01 (5/31/01)

UNITED AUTO GROUP, INC.

YIELD ...
P/E RATIO 11.9

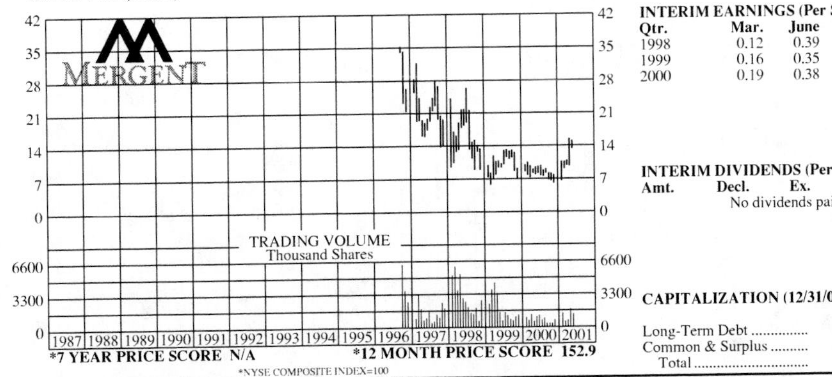

*7 YEAR PRICE SCORE N/A   *12 MONTH PRICE SCORE 152.9

*NYSE COMPOSITE INDEX=100

INTERIM EARNINGS (Per Share):

Qtr.	Mar.	June	Sept.	Dec.
1998	0.12	0.39	0.39	d0.22
1999	0.16	0.35	0.31	0.18
2000	0.19	0.38	0.40	0.21

INTERIM DIVIDENDS (Per Share):

Amt.	Decl.	Ex.	Rec.	Pay.

No dividends paid.

CAPITALIZATION (12/31/00):

	($000)	(%)
Long-Term Debt	442,463	48.9
Common & Surplus	461,670	51.1
Total	904,133	100.0

RECENT DEVELOPMENTS: For the year ended 12/31/00, earnings totaled $34.0 million, before a $4.0 million extraordinary charge, compared with earnings of $26.8 million, before an extraordinary credit of $732,000, the previous year. Total revenues climbed 21.4% to $4.88 billion from $4.02 billion a year earlier. Gross profit advanced 23.4% to $678.0 million, or 13.9% of total revenues, from $549.4 million, or 13.7% of total revenues, the year before.

PROSPECTS: On 5/30/01, the Company acquired two dealerships, Mercedes-Benz of Nanuet and KEA Honda, located in the New York metropolitan area. Revenues from these two dealerships is expected to be about $100.0 million annually, and will boost UAG's revenue in the New York market by approximately 12.0%. In March 2001, UAG acquired two dealerships in Virginia and Ohio, adding about $260.0 million in annual sales.

BUSINESS

UNITED AUTO GROUP, INC. operated, as of 5/30/01, 123 franchised automobile and light truck dealerships located in 18 states, Puerto Rico and Brazil. The Company's dealerships sell new and used vehicles, operate service and parts departments, as well as collision repair centers. In addition, UAG sells various aftermarket products, including finance, warranty, extended service and insurance contracts. As of 12/15/00, the Penske investment group, which includes Penske Corp., held approximately 55.0% of UAG's common stock.

REVENUES

(12/31/2000)	($000)	(%)
New Vehicles	2,971,468	60.8
Used Vehicles	1,227,597	25.1
Service & Parts	491,803	10.1
Finance & Insurance	193,121	4.0
Total	4,883,989	100.0

ANNUAL FINANCIAL DATA

	12/31/00	12/31/99	12/31/98	12/31/97	12/31/96	12/31/95	12/31/94
Earnings Per Share	[1] 1.16	[2] 1.01	[3] 0.64	d0.54	[1] 0.69	d0.63	d0.44
Cash Flow Per Share	1.98	1.73	1.43	d0.02	1.41	d0.12	0.14
Tang. Book Val. Per Share	...	...	...	...	...	0.18	3.77
INCOME STATEMENT (IN MILLIONS):							
Total Revenues	4,884.0	4,022.5	3,343.1	2,089.8	1,303.8	806.2	731.6
Costs & Expenses	4,721.6	3,899.1	3,274.8	2,075.5	1,273.8	808.1	725.8
Depreciation & Amort.	24.2	19.1	16.5	9.7	7.8	2.8	2.2
Operating Income	138.3	104.3	51.9	2.0	20.4	d5.3	3.6
Net Interest Inc./(Exp.)	d77.2	d58.0	d31.5	d15.1	d2.2	1.4	d0.9
Income Before Income Taxes	61.1	48.8	25.2	d15.5	17.1	d5.1	2.1
Income Taxes	26.6	21.4	11.6	cr5.5	6.3	cr2.1	...
Equity Earnings/Minority Int.	d0.5	d0.7	d0.3	d0.1	d3.4	d0.5	d3.8
Net Income	[1] 34.0	[2] 26.7	[3] 13.4	d10.1	[1] 7.5	d3.5	d1.7
Cash Flow	58.2	45.8	29.8	d0.5	15.3	d0.6	0.6
Average Shs. Outstg. (000)	29,415	26,526	20,932	18,607	10,851	5,482	3,873
BALANCE SHEET (IN MILLIONS):							
Cash & Cash Equivalents	7.4	19.8	38.5	99.5	69.6	5.2	0.8
Total Current Assets	1,903.2	1,358.7	1,181.4	1,068.7	601.8	283.8	237.1
Net Property	107.1	68.2	51.5	37.6	22.3	12.1	12.1
Total Assets	2,714.3	1,958.7	1,774.9	1,507.4	822.5	377.7	288.9
Total Current Liabilities	858.6	582.3	505.5	427.0	222.5	144.1	125.8
Long-Term Obligations	442.5	266.2	337.0	239.2	12.5	25.2	7.5
Net Stockholders' Equity	461.7	430.9	341.7	300.6	281.5	49.2	28.8
Net Working Capital	1,044.7	776.4	675.9	641.6	379.4	139.7	111.3
Year-end Shs. Outstg. (000)	18,556	21,321	19,690	18,293	16,690	2,583	1,529
STATISTICAL RECORD:							
Operating Profit Margin %	2.8	2.6	1.6	0.1	1.6	...	0.5
Net Profit Margin %	0.7	0.7	0.4	...	0.6	...	...
Return on Equity %	7.4	6.2	3.9	...	2.7	...	...
Return on Assets %	1.3	1.4	0.8	...	0.9	...	...
Debt/Total Assets %	16.3	13.6	19.0	15.9	1.5	6.7	2.6
Price Range	10.50-6.00	13.25-5.75	26.31-8.88	31.75-13.75	35.25-21.38	...	...
P/E Ratio	9.1-5.2	13.1-5.7	41.1-13.9	...	51.1-31.0	...	...

Statistics are as originally reported. [1] Bef. $4.0 mil ($0.14/sh) extraord. chg., 2000; $5.0 mil (0.46/sh), 1996. [2] Bef. $46,000 loss fr disc. ops & $732,000 extraord. gain [3] Bef. $12.9 mil loss fr disc. opers. & $1.2 mil extraord. chg.

OFFICERS:
R. S. Penske, Chmn., C.E.O.
S. X. DiFeo, Jr., Pres., C.O.O.
R. H. Kurnick, Jr., Exec. V.P., Gen. Couns., Sec.

INVESTOR CONTACT: Phil Hartz, Sr. V.P., Corp. Comm., (313) 592-5365

PRINCIPAL OFFICE: 13400 Outer Drive West, Detroit, MI 48239

TELEPHONE NUMBER: (313) 592-7311
FAX: (313) 592-7340
WEB: www.unitedauto.com

NO. OF EMPLOYEES: 7,500 (approx.)

SHAREHOLDERS: 106

ANNUAL MEETING: In May

INCORPORATED: DE, Dec., 1990

INSTITUTIONAL HOLDINGS:
No. of Institutions: 41
Shares Held: 8,689,202
% Held: 37.3

INDUSTRY: New and used car dealers (SIC: 5511)

TRANSFER AGENT(S): The Bank of Nova Scotia Trust Company of New York, New York, NY

NYSE SYMBOL UIC
Rec. Pr. 13.84 (4/30/01)

UNITED INDUSTRIAL CORPORATION

YIELD 2.9%
P/E RATIO 22.3

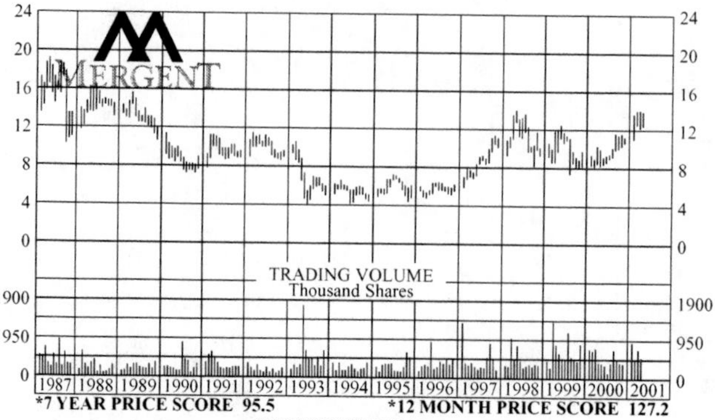

TRADING VOLUME
Thousand Shares

*7 YEAR PRICE SCORE 95.5 *12 MONTH PRICE SCORE 127.2

*NYSE COMPOSITE INDEX=100

INTERIM EARNINGS (Per Share):

Qtr.	Mar.	June	Sept.	Dec.
1997	0.14	0.14	0.54	0.37
1998	0.18	0.18	0.19	0.48
1999	0.19	0.11	0.17	0.03
2000	0.18	0.20	0.17	0.07

INTERIM DIVIDENDS (Per Share):

Amt.	Decl.	Ex.	Rec.	Pay.
0.10Q	4/26/00	5/09/00	5/11/00	5/31/00
0.10Q	7/24/00	8/08/00	8/10/00	8/31/00
0.10Q	10/19/00	11/01/00	11/03/00	11/28/00
0.10Q	2/12/01	2/21/01	2/23/01	3/01/01
0.10Q	4/26/01	5/14/01	5/16/01	5/31/01

Indicated div.: $0.40

CAPITALIZATION (12/31/00):

	($000)	(%)
Deferred Income Tax	9,182	7.4
Common & Surplus	114,893	92.6
Total	124,075	100.0

RECENT DEVELOPMENTS: For the year ended 12/31/00, net income increased 23.9% to $7.8 million compared with $6.3 million in the previous year. Earnings for 2000 included a gain of $3.9 million on the sale of the Company's subsidiary, Symtron Systems, Inc., and an insurance recovery of $2.3 million. Net sales advanced 18.1% to $256.4 million compared with $217.0 million in the previous year.

PROSPECTS: The Company expects to continue to grow significantly in its unmanned air vehicle business, as it continues to experience strong interest from potential overseas customers. In UIC's engineering and maintenance services business, the Company should continue to benefit from its contract with the U.S. Air Force. Moreover, the transportation business should benefit from restructured operations and new cost and oversight programs.

BUSINESS

UNITED INDUSTRIAL CORPORATION designs and produces defense, training, transportation, and energy systems. UIC's products include unmanned air vehicles, training and simulation systems, automated aircraft test and maintenance equipment, and ordnance systems. The Company also manufactures ground transportation components, as well as combustion equipment for biomass and refuse fuels. The Company's operations are conducted through two wholly-owned subsidiaries: AAI Corporation and Detroit Stoker Co. On 10/3/00, the Company sold Symtron Systems, Inc.

REVENUES

(12/31/2000)	($000)	(%)
Defense	200,743	78.3
Transportation	20,075	7.8
Energy	35,540	13.9
Total	256,358	100.0

ANNUAL FINANCIAL DATA

	12/31/00	12/31/99	12/31/98	12/31/97	12/31/96	12/31/95	12/31/94
Earnings Per Share	**[4] 0.62**	**0.50**	**[3] 1.03**	**[2] 1.19**	**[1] 0.52**	**[1] 0.07**	**0.43**
Cash Flow Per Share	**1.36**	**1.12**	**1.65**	**1.96**	**1.20**	**0.75**	**1.10**
Tang. Book Val. Per Share	**10.95**	**9.03**	**8.93**	**8.33**	**7.40**	**7.08**	**7.27**
Dividends Per Share	**0.40**	**0.40**	**0.40**	**0.29**	**0.20**	**0.26**	**0.28**
Dividend Payout %	**64.5**	**80.0**	**38.8**	**24.4**	**38.5**	**370.9**	**65.1**
INCOME STATEMENT (IN MILLIONS):							
Total Revenues	256.4	217.0	204.3	235.2	220.8	227.4	209.7
Costs & Expenses	248.5	199.7	186.2	210.0	200.9	215.1	193.5
Depreciation & Amort.	9.4	7.7	7.8	9.6	8.3	8.3	8.3
Operating Income	d2.1	9.6	10.2	15.6	11.7	4.0	7.9
Net Interest Inc./(Exp.)	8.8	1.7	3.5	0.5	d1.0	d1.2	d1.4
Income Before Income Taxes	11.5	9.1	15.9	30.6	10.6	2.6	8.4
Income Taxes	3.7	2.8	2.9	15.8	4.2	1.8	3.2
Net Income	[4] 7.8	6.3	[3] 13.0	[2] 14.8	[1] 6.4	[1] 0.9	5.2
Cash Flow	17.1	14.0	20.8	24.4	14.7	9.2	13.5
Average Shs. Outstg. (000)	12,609	12,509	12,609	12,420	12,211	12,193	12,242
BALANCE SHEET (IN MILLIONS):							
Cash & Cash Equivalents	11.4	13.1	25.8	29.2	13.4	11.9	6.1
Total Current Assets	164.6	110.0	97.5	117.6	100.4	101.0	109.9
Net Property	33.0	35.8	30.6	25.6	41.5	42.6	45.2
Total Assets	248.4	201.8	184.4	183.3	180.0	183.1	203.3
Total Current Liabilities	95.7	58.8	40.6	39.7	55.7	47.5	49.3
Long-Term Obligations	...	...	...	4.5	...	13.8	20.0
Net Stockholders' Equity	114.9	111.1	109.4	102.0	90.1	86.2	88.4
Net Working Capital	68.9	51.2	56.8	77.9	44.7	53.5	60.6
Year-end Shs. Outstg. (000)	10,496	12,294	12,250	12,249	12,174	12,171	12,167
STATISTICAL RECORD:							
Operating Profit Margin %	...	4.4	5.0	6.6	5.3	1.8	3.8
Net Profit Margin %	3.0	2.9	6.4	6.3	2.9	0.4	2.5
Return on Equity %	6.8	5.7	11.9	14.5	7.1	1.0	5.9
Return on Assets %	3.1	3.1	7.1	8.1	3.6	0.5	2.6
Debt/Total Assets %	...	...	...	2.4	...	7.5	9.8
Price Range	11.63-8.13	12.50-7.38	14.00-8.13	11.38-5.88	6.50-4.75	7.25-4.38	6.63-4.13
P/E Ratio	18.7-13.1	25.0-14.7	13.6-7.9	9.6-4.9	12.5-9.1	103.4-62.4	15.4-9.6
Average Yield %	4.1	4.0	3.6	3.4	3.6	4.5	5.2

Statistics are as originally reported. [1] Incl. after-tax write-off of certain inventories, recognition of reserves and chgs. rel. to resolvement of a dispute with the U.S. Navy: $5.1 mill., 1995; $2.6 mill., 1996. [2] Incl. after-tax gain of $8.5 mill. from the sale of bus. & $1.8 mill. fr. litig. settle. [3] Incl. pre-tax gain of $4.9 mill. fr. sale of assets. [4] Incl. a gain of $3.9 mill. fr. the sale of Symtron Systems, Inc. & an insurance recovery of $2.3 mill.

OFFICERS:
H. S. Gelb, Chmn.
R. R. Erkeneff, Pres., C.E.O.
J. H. Perry, V.P., C.F.O., Treas.

INVESTOR CONTACT: Investor Relations, (212) 752-8787

PRINCIPAL OFFICE: 570 Lexington Avenue, New York, NY 10022

TELEPHONE NUMBER: (212) 752-8787
FAX: (212) 838-4629
WEB: www.unitedindustrial.com

NO. OF EMPLOYEES: 1,700 (approx.)

SHAREHOLDERS: 2,200 (approx.)

ANNUAL MEETING: In May

INCORPORATED: DE, Sept., 1959

INSTITUTIONAL HOLDINGS:
No. of Institutions: 29
Shares Held: 4,016,074
% Held: 32.3

INDUSTRY: Special industry machinery, nec (SIC: 3559)

TRANSFER AGENT(S): American Stock Transfer and Trust Co., New York, NY

NYSE SYMBOL UPS
Rec. Pr. 57.45 (4/30/01)

UNITED PARCEL SERVICE, INC.

YIELD	1.3%
P/E RATIO	23.0

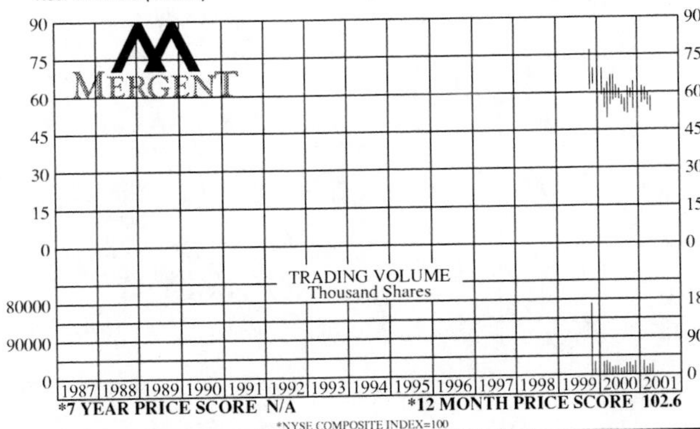

INTERIM EARNINGS (Per Share):

Qtrs.	Mar.	June	Sept.	Dec.
1997		0.81		
1998	0.32	0.42	0.40	0.43
1999	0.44	d0.77	0.52	0.56
2000	0.67	0.60	0.60	0.63

INTERIM DIVIDENDS (Per Share):

Amt.	Decl.	Ex.	Rec.	Pay.
0.17Q	5/18/00	5/25/00	5/30/00	6/09/00
0.17Q	...	8/24/00	8/28/00	9/08/00
0.17Q	11/16/00	11/22/00	11/27/00	1/05/01
0.19Q	2/20/01	2/22/01	2/26/01	3/09/01
0.19Q	5/16/01	5/25/01	5/30/01	6/08/01

Indicated div.: $0.76

CAPITALIZATION (12/31/00):

	($000)	(%)
Long-Term Debt	2,981,000	23.4
Common & Surplus	9,735,000	76.6
Total	12,716,000	100.0

RECENT DEVELOPMENTS: For the year ended 12/31/00, net income soared to $2.93 billion from $883.0 million in 1999. Earnings for 2000 included a nonrecurring net charge of $139.0 million. Earnings for 1999 included a net tax assessment gain of $1.44 billion. Total revenue increased 10.1% to $29.77 billion. U.S. domestic package revenue grew 7.6% to $24.00 billion, while international package revenue increased 11.7% to $4.17 billion. Operating profit improved 15.5% to $4.51 billion.

PROSPECTS: In January 2001, UPS agreed to acquire Fritz Companies, Inc., a provider of forwarding, customs brokerage and logistics services, for about $450.0 million. Separately, UPS entered into a definitive merger agreement under which UPS will acquire First International Bancorp, Inc. for about $78.0 million. First International primarily serves small and medium-sized businesses. Both acquisitions are expected to be non-dilutive to earnings per share in 2001 and modestly accretive in 2002.

BUSINESS

UNITED PARCEL SERVICE provides express delivery and logistics services, including comprehensive management of supply chains, for 1.8 million shipping customers per day throughout the United States and in over 200 other countries and territories. As of 12/31/00, the UPS airline is the 11th largest in the world, with 233 aircraft owned, 354 aircraft leased or chartered, 30 aircraft on order, and 91 aircraft under option. On 11/9/99, the Company brought to market an initial public offering of 109.4 million shares of Class B common stock at $50 per share.

GEOGRAPHIC DATA

(12/31/2000)	Rev (%)	Inc(%)
U.S. Domestic		
Package	80.6	87.1
International Package	14.0	6.1
Non-Package	5.4	6.8
Total	100.0	100.0

ANNUAL FINANCIAL DATA

	12/31/00	12/31/99	12/31/98	12/31/97
Earnings Per Share	**[2] 2.50**	**[1] 0.77**	**1.57**	**0.81**
Cash Flow Per Share	**3.50**	**1.77**	**2.57**	**1.77**
Tang. Book Val. Per Share	**8.58**	**10.50**	**6.42**	**5.42**
Dividends Per Share	**0.81**	...	...	...
Dividend Payout %	**32.4**	...	...	...
INCOME STATEMENT (IN MILLIONS):				
Total Revenues	29,771.0	27,052.0	24,788.0	22,458.0
Costs & Expenses	24,086.0	21,925.0	20,586.0	19,697.0
Depreciation & Amort.	1,173.0	1,139.0	1,112.0	1,063.0
Operating Income	4,512.0	3,988.0	3,090.0	1,698.0
Net Interest Inc./(Exp.)	d205.0	d228.0	d227.0	d187.0
Income Before Income Taxes	4,834.0	2,088.0	2,902.0	1,553.0
Income Taxes	1,900.0	1,205.0	1,161.0	644.0
Net Income	[2] 2,934.0	[1] 883.0	1,741.0	909.0
Cash Flow	4,107.0	2,022.0	2,853.0	1,972.0
Average Shs. Outstg. (000)	1,175,000	1,141,000	1,108,000	1,116,000
BALANCE SHEET (IN MILLIONS):				
Cash & Cash Equivalents	1,952.0	6,278.0	1,629.0	986.0
Total Current Assets	7,124.0	11,138.0	5,425.0	4,477.0
Net Property	12,329.0	11,579.0	11,384.0	11,007.0
Total Assets	21,662.0	23,043.0	17,067.0	15,912.0
Total Current Liabilities	4,501.0	4,198.0	3,717.0	3,398.0
Long-Term Obligations	2,981.0	1,912.0	2,191.0	2,583.0
Net Stockholders' Equity	9,735.0	12,474.0	7,173.0	6,087.0
Net Working Capital	2,623.0	6,940.0	1,708.0	1,079.0
Year-end Shs. Outstg. (000)	1,134,639	1,187,484	1,118,000	1,124,000
STATISTICAL RECORD:				
Operating Profit Margin %	15.2	14.7	12.5	7.6
Net Profit Margin %	9.9	3.3	7.0	4.0
Return on Equity %	30.1	7.1	24.3	14.9
Return on Assets %	13.5	3.8	10.2	5.7
Debt/Total Assets %	13.8	8.3	12.8	16.2
Price Range	69.75-49.50	76.94-61.00	...	...
P/E Ratio	27.9-19.8	99.9-79.2	...	...
Average Yield %	1.4	...	...	...

Statistics are as originally reported. Adj. for 2-for-1 merger exchange ratio as effected in connection with Co.'s initial public offering in 11/99. [1] Incl. tax assessment charge of $1.79 billion. [2] Incl. a net gain of $139.0 mill. from nonrecurr. items.

OFFICERS:
J. P. Kelly, Chmn., C.E.O.
M. L. Eskew, Vice-Chmn., Exec. V.P.
D. S. Davis, Sr. V.P., C.F.O., Treas.
T. Weidemeyer, Sr. V.P., C.O.O.

INVESTOR CONTACT: Kurt Kuehn, Investor Relations, (404) 828-6977

PRINCIPAL OFFICE: 55 Glenlake Parkway NE, Atlanta, GA 30328

TELEPHONE NUMBER: (404) 828-6000
FAX: (404) 828-6562
WEB: www.ups.com

NO. OF EMPLOYEES: 359,000 (avg.)

SHAREHOLDERS: 129,753 (class A); 10,280 (class B)

ANNUAL MEETING: In May

INCORPORATED: DE, July, 1999

INSTITUTIONAL HOLDINGS:
No. of Institutions: 370
Shares Held: 113,331,871
% Held: 10.1

INDUSTRY: Courier services, except by air (SIC: 4215)

TRANSFER AGENT(S): First Union National Bank, Charlotte, NC

NYSE SYMBOL UTX
Rec. Pr. 83.31 (5/31/01)

UNITED TECHNOLOGIES CORPORATION

YIELD 1.1%
P/E RATIO 23.4

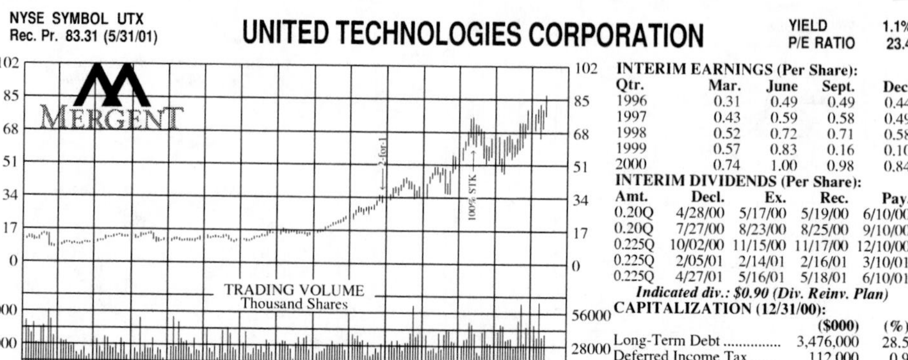

INTERIM EARNINGS (Per Share):

Qtr.	Mar.	June	Sept.	Dec.
1996	0.31	0.49	0.49	0.44
1997	0.43	0.59	0.58	0.49
1998	0.52	0.72	0.71	0.58
1999	0.57	0.83	0.16	0.10
2000	0.74	1.00	0.98	0.84

INTERIM DIVIDENDS (Per Share):

Amt.	Decl.	Ex.	Rec.	Pay.
0.20Q	4/28/00	5/17/00	5/19/00	6/10/00
0.20Q	7/27/00	8/23/00	8/25/00	9/10/00
0.225Q	10/02/00	11/15/00	11/17/00	12/10/00
0.225Q	2/05/01	2/14/01	2/16/01	3/10/01
0.225Q	4/27/01	5/16/01	5/18/01	6/10/01

Indicated div.: $0.90 (Div. Reinv. Plan)

CAPITALIZATION (12/31/00):

	($000)	(%)
Long-Term Debt	3,476,000	28.5
Deferred Income Tax	112,000	0.9
Minority Interest	497,000	4.1
Redeemable Pfd. Stock	432,000	3.5
Common & Surplus	7,662,000	62.9
Total	12,179,001	100.0

RECENT DEVELOPMENTS: For the year ended 12/31/00, net income totaled $1.81 billion compared with income from continuing operations of $841.0 million the year before. The 1999 results included pre-tax restructuring and other charges of $1.15 billion. Total revenues rose 10.2% to $26.58 billion from $24.13 billion a year earlier. Revenues at Carrier climbed 14.6% to $8.43 billion, while revenues at Pratt & Whitney slipped 4.0% to $7.37 billion. Revenues at Otis increased 8.8% to $6.15 billion, while revenues for the Flight Systems segment jumped 31.0% to $4.99 billion.

PROSPECTS: The Company is targeting revenue growth in the range of 7.0% and 10.0%, along with earnings per share growth of 15.0%, during 2001, driven by acquisitions and internal growth. UTX anticipates spending as much as $2.00 billion on acquisitions during 2001. In January, UTX acquired U.K.-based Claverham Group Ltd. The acquisition should help expand Hamilton Sundstrand's product offerings for European military aircraft. Also, the acquisition will enable UTX to expand into two new segments, missile flight control and railroad switching systems.

BUSINESS

UNITED TECHNOLOGIES CORP. provides high-technology products and support services to the aerospace, building and automotive industries. Carrier (31.3% of 2000 revenues) provides heating, ventilating and air conditioning equipment for commercial, industrial, and residential buildings. Pratt & Whitney (27.4%) consists of commercial and military aircraft engines, spare parts, and product support. Otis (22.8%) manufactures elevators, escalators, moving walks, and shuttle systems. Flight Systems (18.5%) includes Sikorsky military and commercial helicopters, and Hamilton Standard controls. The Company divested its Norden Systems subsidiary in 1994. On 5/4/99, UTX sold its automotive operations to Lear Corp. for $2.30 billion.

ANNUAL FINANCIAL DATA

	12/31/00	12/31/99	12/31/98	12/31/97	12/31/96	12/31/95	12/31/94
Earnings Per Share	**3.55**	**2 1.65**	**2.53**	**2.11**	**1.73**	**1.47**	**1 1.10**
Cash Flow Per Share	**5.19**	**3.33**	**4.27**	**3.72**	**3.31**	**3.24**	**2.66**
Tang. Book Val. Per Share	**1.52**	**3.11**	**7.23**	**7.84**	**7.61**	**7.68**	**6.44**
Dividends Per Share	**0.82**	**0.76**	**0.69**	**0.62**	**0.55**	**0.51**	**0.47**
Dividend Payout %	**23.2**	**46.1**	**27.5**	**29.5**	**31.9**	**34.9**	**43.2**
INCOME STATEMENT (IN MILLIONS):							
Total Revenues	26,583.0	24,127.0	25,715.0	24,713.0	23,512.0	22,802.0	21,197.0
Costs & Expenses	22,584.0	21,766.0	22,694.0	21,906.0	20,878.0	20,370.0	19,006.0
Depreciation & Amort.	859.0	844.0	854.0	848.0	853.0	844.0	840.0
Operating Income	3,140.0	1,517.0	2,167.0	1,959.0	1,781.0	1,588.0	1,351.0
Net Interest Inc./(Exp.)	d382.0	d260.0	d204.0	d195.0	d221.0	d244.0	d275.0
Income Before Income Taxes	2,758.0	1,257.0	1,963.0	1,764.0	1,560.0	1,344.0	1,076.0
Income Taxes	853.0	325.0	623.0	573.0	523.0	464.0	384.0
Equity Earnings/Minority Int.	d97.0	d91.0	d85.0	d119.0	d131.0	d130.0	d107.0
Net Income	1,808.0	2 841.0	1,255.0	1,072.0	906.0	750.0	1 585.0
Cash Flow	2,635.0	1,685.0	2,109.0	1,888.0	1,729.0	1,594.0	1,403.0
Average Shs. Outstg. (000)	508,010	506,700	494,000	508,000	522,000	492,000	528,000
BALANCE SHEET (IN MILLIONS):							
Cash & Cash Equivalents	748.0	957.0	550.0	755.0	1,127.0	900.0	386.0
Total Current Assets	10,662.0	10,627.0	9,355.0	9,248.0	9,611.0	8,952.0	8,228.0
Net Property	4,487.0	4,460.0	4,265.0	4,262.0	4,371.0	4,420.0	4,532.0
Total Assets	25,364.0	24,366.0	18,375.0	16,719.0	16,745.0	15,958.0	15,624.0
Total Current Liabilities	9,344.0	9,215.0	7,735.0	7,311.0	7,390.0	6,659.0	6,553.0
Long-Term Obligations	3,476.0	3,086.0	1,575.0	1,275.0	1,437.0	1,649.0	1,885.0
Net Stockholders' Equity	7,662.0	7,117.0	5,002.0	4,574.0	4,306.0	4,333.0	3,752.0
Net Working Capital	1,318.0	1,412.0	1,620.0	1,937.0	2,221.0	2,293.0	1,675.0
Year-end Shs. Outstg. (000)	584,306	474,546	450,000	458,000	476,000	488,000	492,000
STATISTICAL RECORD:							
Operating Profit Margin %	11.8	6.3	8.4	7.9	7.6	7.0	6.4
Net Profit Margin %	6.8	3.5	4.9	4.3	3.9	3.3	2.8
Return on Equity %	23.6	11.8	25.1	23.4	21.0	17.3	15.6
Return on Assets %	7.1	3.5	6.8	6.4	5.4	4.7	3.7
Debt/Total Assets %	13.7	12.7	8.6	7.6	8.6	10.3	12.1
Price Range	79.75-46.50	75.97-51.63	56.25-33.50	44.47-32.56	35.22-22.63	24.44-15.56	18.00-13.75
P/E Ratio	22.5-13.1	46.0-31.3	22.3-13.3	21.1-15.5	20.4-13.1	16.6-10.6	16.4-12.5
Average Yield %	1.3	1.2	1.5	1.6	1.9	2.6	3.0

Statistics are as originally reported. Adj. for 2-for-1 stk. split, 5/99 & 12/96. 1 Bef. $59 mil ($0.03/sh) chg. for acctg. adj. 2 Bef. $690 mil ($1.36/sh) after-tax gain from sale of UT Automotive & incl. $842 mil pre-tax restr. chg.

OFFICERS:
G. David, Chmn., C.E.O.
K. J. Krapek, Pres., C.O.O.
D. J. FitzPatrick, Sr. V.P., C.F.O., Treas.

INVESTOR CONTACT: Peter Murphy, (860) 728-7977

PRINCIPAL OFFICE: One Financial Plaza, Hartford, CT 06103

TELEPHONE NUMBER: (860) 728-7000
FAX: (860) 728-7028
WEB: www.utc.com

NO. OF EMPLOYEES: 153,800 (avg.)

SHAREHOLDERS: 24,000 (approx.)

ANNUAL MEETING: In Apr.

INCORPORATED: DE, July, 1934

INSTITUTIONAL HOLDINGS:
No. of Institutions: 680
Shares Held: 358,953,565
% Held: 76.3

INDUSTRY: Aircraft engines and engine parts (SIC: 3724)

TRANSFER AGENT(S): First Chicago Trust Company of New York, Jersey City, NJ

NYSE SYMBOL UNH
Rec. Pr. 65.48 (4/30/01)

UNITEDHEALTH GROUP INC.

YIELD ...
P/E RATIO 29.8

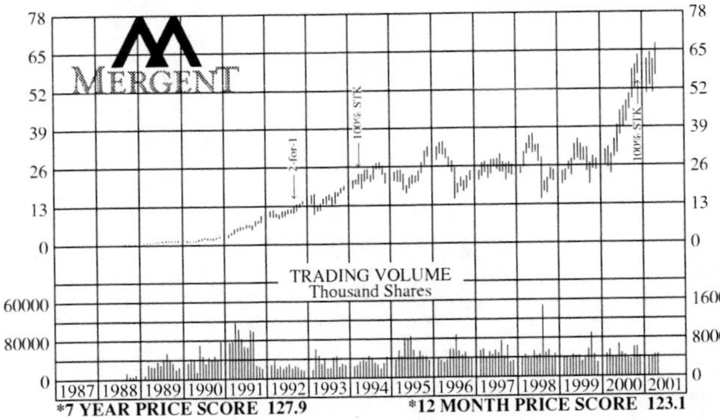

MERGENT

TRADING VOLUME
Thousand Shares

1987 1988 1989 1990 1991 1992 1993 1994 1995 1996 1997 1998 1999 2000 2001

*7 YEAR PRICE SCORE 127.9 *12 MONTH PRICE SCORE 123.1

*NYSE COMPOSITE INDEX=100

INTERIM EARNINGS (Per Share):

Qtr.	Mar.	June	Sept.	Dec.
1997	0.27	0.29	0.29	0.29
1998	0.32	d1.48	0.33	0.29
1999	0.36	0.38	0.41	0.46
2000	0.52	0.51	0.54	0.63

INTERIM DIVIDENDS (Per Share):

Amt.	Decl.	Ex.	Rec.	Pay.
0.03A	2/10/00	3/30/00	4/03/00	4/19/00
100% STK	10/25/00	12/26/00	12/01/00	12/22/00
0.03A	2/14/01	3/29/01	4/02/01	4/18/01

Indicated div.: $0.03 (Div. Reinv. Plan)

CAPITALIZATION (12/31/00):

	($000)	(%)
Long-Term Debt	650,000	15.0
Common & Surplus	3,688,000	85.0
Total	4,338,000	100.0

RECENT DEVELOPMENTS: For the year ended 12/31/00, net income advanced 29.6% to $736.0 million versus $568.0 million in the prior year. Results for 2000 included a net gain of $17.0 million from the disposition of UnitedHealth Capital investments. Total revenues were $21.12 billion, up 8.0% compared with $19.56 billion in 1999.

PROSPECTS: Revenues are being driven by strong demand for commercial health benefits, particularly in the UnitedHealthcare and Uniprise segments. During the twelve months ended 1/31/01, these segments combined increased the number of people served by a total of 2.1 million. For 2001, UNH anticipates earnings growth to be in the range of 18.0% to 20.0%.

BUSINESS

UNITEDHEALTH GROUP INC. offers health care coverage and related services through four lines of business. Health Care Services consists of the UnitedHealthcare and Ovations business units. UnitedHealthcare operates network-based health and well-being services including commercial, Medicare and Medicaid products for locally based employers and individuals in six broad regional markets. Ovations, which administers Medicare Supplement benefits on behalf of AARP, offers health and well-being services for Americans over 50. Uniprise provides network-based health and well-being services, business-to-business transactional infrastructure services, consumer connectivity and service, and technology support for large employers and health plans. Specialized Care Services is an expanding portfolio of health and well-being companies, each serving a specialized market need with a unique blend of benefits, provider networks, services and resources. Ingenix offers health care knowledge information of products and services.

ANNUAL FINANCIAL DATA

	12/31/00	12/31/99	12/31/98	12/31/97	12/31/96	12/31/95	12/31/94
Earnings Per Share	**5 2.19**	**1.60**	**4 d0.56**	**1.13**	**3 0.88**	**2 0.79**	**1 0.82**
Cash Flow Per Share	**2.92**	**2.26**	**d0.08**	**1.51**	**1.24**	**1.05**	**1.01**
Tang. Book Val. Per Share	**2.45**	**3.00**	**4.13**	**5.89**	**4.55**	**4.10**	**7.21**
Dividends Per Share	**0.02**	**0.02**	**0.02**	**0.02**	**0.02**	**0.02**	**0.02**
Dividend Payout %	**0.7**	**0.9**	**...**	**1.3**	**1.7**	**1.9**	**1.8**
INCOME STATEMENT (IN MILLIONS):							
Total Revenues	21,122.0	19,562.0	17,355.0	11,794.0	10,073.8	5,670.9	3,768.9
Costs & Expenses	19,675.0	18,386.0	17,212.0	10,906.0	9,344.2	5,115.6	3,198.8
Depreciation & Amort.	247.0	233.0	185.0	146.0	133.2	94.5	64.1
Operating Income	1,200.0	943.0	d42.0	742.0	596.4	460.8	506.0
Net Interest Inc./(Exp.)	d72.0	d49.0	d4.0	...	d0.6	d0.8	d2.2
Income Before Income Taxes	1,155.0	894.0	d46.0	742.0	580.9	460.0	467.9
Income Taxes	419.0	326.0	120.0	282.0	224.6	170.2	177.8
Equity Earnings/Minority Int.	...	...	...	...	d0.6	d3.8	d2.0
Net Income	5 736.0	568.0	4 d166.0	460.0	3 355.6	2 286.0	1 288.1
Cash Flow	983.0	801.0	d29.0	577.0	460.1	373.2	352.2
Average Shs. Outstg. (000)	336,500	355,000	382,000	382,000	371,690	354,886	350,418
BALANCE SHEET (IN MILLIONS):							
Cash & Cash Equivalents	1,619.0	2,151.0	1,814.0	1,256.0	1,647.3	1,803.9	1,654.3
Total Current Assets	4,405.0	4,568.0	4,280.0	2,193.0	2,739.7	2,867.1	1,908.2
Net Property	303.0	278.0	294.0	364.0	313.0	267.7	162.6
Total Assets	11,053.0	10,273.0	9,701.0	7,623.0	6,996.6	6,161.0	3,489.5
Total Current Liabilities	6,570.0	5,892.0	5,342.0	2,570.0	2,642.8	2,434.0	664.3
Long-Term Obligations	650.0	400.0	249.0	...	...	...	...
Net Stockholders' Equity	3,688.0	3,863.0	4,038.0	4,534.0	3,823.1	3,188.0	2,795.5
Net Working Capital	d2,165.0	d1,324.0	d1,062.0	d377.0	96.9	433.1	1,243.9
Year-end Shs. Outstg. (000)	317,235	334,940	367,860	382,222	369,730	350,430	345,662
STATISTICAL RECORD:							
Operating Profit Margin %	5.7	4.8	...	6.3	5.9	8.1	13.4
Net Profit Margin %	3.5	2.9	...	3.9	3.5	5.0	7.6
Return on Equity %	20.0	14.7	...	10.1	9.3	9.0	10.3
Return on Assets %	6.7	5.5	...	6.0	5.1	4.6	8.3
Debt/Total Assets %	5.9	3.9	2.6	...	...	...	...
Price Range	63.44-23.19	35.00-19.69	36.97-14.78	30.06-21.22	34.50-15.00	32.81-17.06	27.69-18.63
P/E Ratio	29.0-10.6	21.9-12.3	...	26.6-18.8	39.2-17.0	41.8-21.7	33.8-22.7
Average Yield %	...	0.1	0.1	0.1	0.1	0.1	0.1

Statistics are as originally reported. Adj. for 2-for-1 stock split, 12/00. 1 Incl. one-time chrg. of $35.9 mill. & bef. extraord. gain of $1.38 bill. 2 Incl. restruct. chrg. of $153.8 mill. 3 Excl. non-oper. costs of $14.9 mill. & prov. from losses of $45.0 mill. 4 Incl. pre-tax chrgs. of $900.0 mill. 5 Incl. net gain of $17.0 mill.

OFFICERS:
W. W. McGuire, Chmn., C.E.O.
S. J. Hemsley, Pres., C.O.O.
A. H. Kaplan, C.F.O.

INVESTOR CONTACT: John S. Penshorn, Investor Relations, (612) 936-1300

PRINCIPAL OFFICE: 9900 Bren Road East, Minnetonka, MN 55343

TELEPHONE NUMBER: (952) 936-1300
FAX: (952) 936-0044
WEB: www.unitedheathgroup.com

NO. OF EMPLOYEES: 30,000 (approx.)

SHAREHOLDERS: 13,279 (record)

ANNUAL MEETING: In May

INCORPORATED: MN, Jan., 1977

INSTITUTIONAL HOLDINGS:
No. of Institutions: 390
Shares Held: 271,297,705
% Held: 84.2

INDUSTRY: Hospital and medical service plans (SIC: 6324)

TRANSFER AGENT(S): Wells Fargo Shareowner Services, St. Paul, MN

NYSE SYMBOL UTR
Rec. Pr. 38.95 (5/31/01)

UNITRIN, INC.

YIELD	4.1%
P/E RATIO	29.7

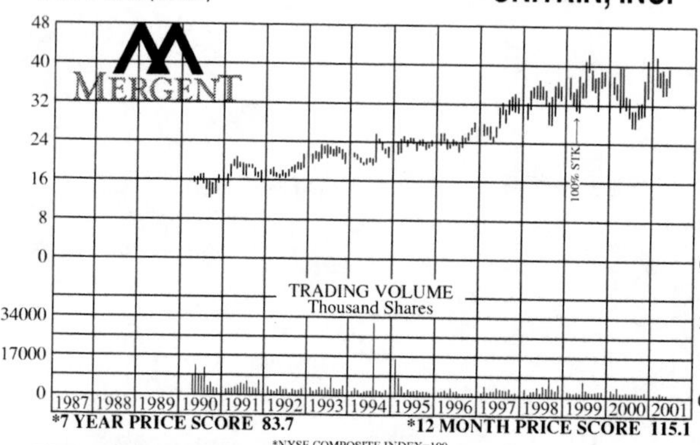

***7 YEAR PRICE SCORE 83.7** ***12 MONTH PRICE SCORE 115.1**

*NYSE COMPOSITE INDEX=100

INTERIM EARNINGS (Per Share):

Qtr.	Mar.	June	Sept.	Dec.
1996	0.33	0.39	0.51	0.53
1997	0.45	0.02	0.50	0.62
1998	1.00	0.46	4.35	0.60
1999	0.70	0.50	0.71	0.84
2000	0.60	0.37	d0.07	0.41

INTERIM DIVIDENDS (Per Share):

Amt.	Decl.	Ex.	Rec.	Pay.
0.375Q	5/03/00	5/12/00	5/16/00	5/30/00
0.375Q	8/09/00	8/18/00	8/22/00	9/05/00
0.375Q	11/01/00	11/10/00	11/14/00	11/30/00
0.40Q	2/07/01	2/14/01	2/19/01	3/02/01
0.40Q	5/02/01	5/10/01	5/14/01	5/25/01

Indicated div.: $1.60

CAPITALIZATION (12/31/00):

	($000)	(%)
Common & Surplus	1,701,200	100.0
Total	1,701,200	100.0

RECENT DEVELOPMENTS: For the year ended 12/31/00, net income declined 54.7% to $91.0 million from $201.0 million the previous year. Total revenues increased 7.7% to $1.95 billion from $1.81 billion a year earlier. Revenues from premiums grew 5.4% to $1.45 billion from $1.37 billion in 1999. Consumer Finance revenues jumped 14.6% to $141.7 million from $123.6 million in the previous year. Net investment income advanced 9.9% to $223.1 million. Net investment gains rose 23.6% to $140.5 million.

PROSPECTS: On 5/24/01, the Company announced that its common stock commenced trading on the New York Stock Exchange under the trading symbol: UTR. On 4/30/01, Unitrin Direct Auto Insurance, a subsidiary of UTR expanded its sales to the state of Florida. Separately, on 4/10/01 the Company announced that it has acquired certain securities of Northrop Grumman Corporation in exchange for all of UTR's holdings of Litton Industries, Inc. common stock pursuant to Northrop's acquisition of Litton.

BUSINESS

UNITRIN, INC. conducts its businesses through its subsidiaries, United Insurance Company of America, The Reliable Life Insurance Company, Trinity Universal Insurance Company, Fireside Securities Corporation and other indirect subsidiaries. The Company's subsidiaries are engaged in the property and casualty insurance, life and health insurance, direct market automobile insurance and consumer finance businesses. Insurance provided in the Property and Casualty Insurance segment consists of automobile, homeowner, commercial multi-peril, motorcycle, watercraft, fire, casualty, workers compensation and other related lines. The Life and Health Insurance segment includes both individual and group life, health and hospitalization insurance. In 2000, UNIT established the Direct Market Automobile Insurance segment to market and sell personal automobile insurance through direct mail, radio, television and the Internet. The Consumer Finance segment makes consumer loans primarily for the purchase of automobiles and offers savings accounts in the form of passbook accounts, investment certificates and money market accounts.

ANNUAL FINANCIAL DATA

	12/31/00	12/31/99	12/31/98	12/31/97	12/31/96	12/31/95	12/31/94
Earnings Per Share	**1.32**	**2.74**	**6.51**	**1.56**	**1.76**	**1.87**	**1.48**
Tang. Book Val. Per Share	**19.93**	**18.98**	**20.06**	**17.24**	**16.77**	**16.81**	**16.55**
Dividends Per Share	**1.50**	**1.40**	**1.30**	**1.20**	**1.10**	**1.00**	**0.75**
Dividend Payout %	**113.6**	**51.1**	**20.0**	**77.2**	**62.7**	**53.6**	**50.7**
INCOME STATEMENT (IN MILLIONS):							
Total Premium Income	1,447.9	1,373.3	1,228.3	1,222.0	1,220.3	1,099.1	1,048.8
Other Income	505.3	440.3	857.6	308.1	302.8	348.3	316.7
Total Revenues	1,953.2	1,813.6	2,085.9	1,530.1	1,523.1	1,447.4	1,365.5
Policyholder Benefits	1,039.6	889.1	781.8	780.1	799.7	717.5	654.4
Income Before Income Taxes	152.2	237.0	687.1	139.8	122.1	160.8	177.5
Income Taxes	54.4	77.9	238.6	47.1	40.2	55.3	62.9
Equity Earnings/Minority Int.	d6.8	41.9	62.3	25.2	50.6	45.1	33.8
Net Income	91.0	201.0	510.8	117.9	132.5	150.6	148.4
Average Shs. Outstg. (000)	68,800	73,100	78,200	75,200	75,442	80,800	100,226
BALANCE SHEET (IN MILLIONS):							
Cash & Cash Equivalents	23.3	24.1	8.6	14.5	17.0	9.1	23.3
Premiums Due	1,101.6	971.6	822.8	879.0	984.7	797.5	646.8
Invst. Assets: Fixed-term	2,733.2	2,651.8	2,557.3	2,315.4	2,207.4	2,457.1	2,442.9
Invst. Assets: Total	4,233.5	4,096.8	4,304.2	3,448.5	3,291.4	3,409.7	3,321.1
Total Assets	6,164.8	5,934.8	5,909.9	4,920.7	4,871.1	4,818.7	4,569.8
Net Stockholders' Equity	1,701.2	1,717.0	1,822.4	1,533.0	1,480.3	1,524.5	1,765.1
Year-end Shs. Outstg. (000)	67,648	70,993	76,000	75,170	74,682	76,980	94,106
STATISTICAL RECORD:							
Return on Revenues %	4.7	11.1	24.5	7.7	8.7	10.4	10.9
Return on Equity %	5.3	11.7	28.0	7.7	9.0	9.9	8.4
Return on Assets %	1.5	3.4	8.6	2.4	2.7	3.1	3.2
Price Range	41.13-27.19	42.38-30.50	37.06-27.78	34.25-24.25	28.19-22.13	25.25-21.50	25.75-19.25
P/E Ratio	31.2-20.6	15.5-11.1	5.7-4.3	22.0-15.6	16.1-12.6	13.5-11.5	17.4-13.0
Average Yield %	4.4	3.8	4.0	4.1	4.4	4.3	3.3

Statistics are as originally reported. Adj. for stk. splits: 2-for-1, 3/26/99

OFFICERS:
R. C. Vie, Chmn., Pres., C.E.O.
E. J. Draut, Sr. V.P., C.F.O., Treas.
S. Renwick, Sec., Gen. Couns.

INVESTOR CONTACT: Investor Relations, (312) 661-4930

PRINCIPAL OFFICE: One East Wacker Drive, Chicago, IL 60601

TELEPHONE NUMBER: (312) 661-4600
FAX: (312) 661-4690
WEB: www.unitrin.com

NO. OF EMPLOYEES: 7,500 (approx.)

SHAREHOLDERS: 8,000 (approx. record)

ANNUAL MEETING: In May

INCORPORATED: DE, Feb., 1990

INSTITUTIONAL HOLDINGS:
No. of Institutions: 149
Shares Held: 13,777,261
% Held: 20.4

INDUSTRY: Fire, marine, and casualty insurance (SIC: 6331)

TRANSFER AGENT(S): First Union National Bank, Charlotte, NC

NYSE SYMBOL UVV
Rec. Pr. 38.70 (4/30/01)

UNIVERSAL CORPORATION

YIELD 3.3%
P/E RATIO 10.0

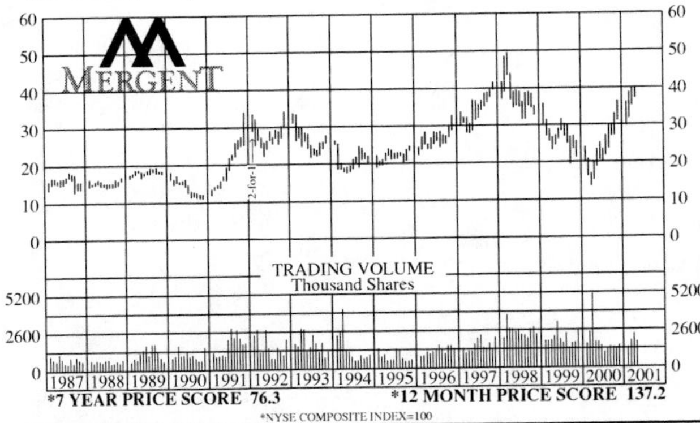

INTERIM EARNINGS (Per Share):

Qtr.	Sept.	Dec.	Mar.	June
1996-97	0.57	0.90	0.79	0.63
1997-98	0.63	1.08	1.18	1.10
1998-99	0.78	1.23	0.88	0.91
1999-00	0.93	0.85	1.29	0.69
2000-01	0.89	1.01	...	...

INTERIM DIVIDENDS (Per Share):

Amt.	Decl.	Ex.	Rec.	Pay.
0.31Q	5/03/00	7/06/00	7/10/00	8/14/00
0.31Q	8/10/00	10/04/00	10/09/00	11/13/00
0.32Q	12/08/00	1/04/01	1/08/01	2/12/01
0.32Q	2/01/01	4/05/01	4/09/01	5/14/01
0.32Q	5/03/01	7/05/01	7/09/01	8/13/01

Indicated div.: $1.28 (Div. Reinv. Plan)

CAPITALIZATION (6/30/00):

	($000)	(%)
Long-Term Debt	223,262	29.0
Deferred Income Tax	11,749	1.5
Minority Interest	36,837	4.8
Common & Surplus	497,779	64.7
Total	769,627	100.0

RECENT DEVELOPMENTS: For the quarter ended 12/31/00, net income increased 6.6% to $27.9 million versus $26.1 million a year earlier. Sales and other operating revenues declined 3.6% to $995.1 million from $1.03 billion in fiscal 1999. Tobacco revenues declined 1.3% to $758.1 million; however, operating income increased 10.3% to $58.4 million, primarily due to lower costs in the U.S. associated with operating fewer processing facilities.

PROSPECTS: UVV's near-term outlook is slowly improving. According to the Company, world market conditions are beginning to improve for tobacco as leaf demand appears to be strengthening and unsold leaf inventories are declining. Also, weakness in the U.S. dollar versus the euro should lead to more favorable earnings translations going forward at the Company's lumber and building products distribution business.

BUSINESS

UNIVERSAL CORPORATION is an independent leaf tobacco merchant with additional operations in agri-products and the distribution of lumber and building products. UVV's tobacco business involves selecting, buying, shipping, processing, packing, storing and financing leaf tobacco in the U.S. and other tobacco growing countries for the account of, or for resale to, manufacturers of tobacco products throughout the world. The agri-products operations involves the selecting, buying, shipping, processing, storing, financing, distribution, importing, and exporting of a number of products including tea, rubber, sunflower seeds, nuts, dried fruit, and canned and frozen foods. The lumber and building products operations involve distribution to the building and construction trade in the Netherlands and Belgium.

BUSINESS LINE ANALYSIS

(06/30/00)	Rev (%)	Inc (%)
Tobacco	69.7	84.7
Lumber & Building Product	16.0	9.9
Agri-products	14.3	5.5
Total	100.0	100.0

ANNUAL FINANCIAL DATA

	6/30/00	6/30/99	6/30/98	6/30/97	6/30/96	6/30/95	6/30/94
Earnings Per Share	**[5] 3.77**	**[4] 3.80**	**3.99**	**2.88**	**[3] 2.04**	**[2] 0.73**	**[1] 1.09**
Cash Flow Per Share	**5.49**	**5.38**	**5.43**	**4.35**	**3.54**	**2.12**	**2.35**
Tang. Book Val. Per Share	**13.04**	**12.47**	**11.71**	**9.37**	**7.64**	**6.87**	**6.46**
Dividends Per Share	**1.24**	**1.20**	**1.12**	**1.06**	**1.02**	**1.00**	**0.96**
Dividend Payout %	**32.9**	**31.6**	**28.1**	**36.8**	**50.0**	**137.0**	**88.1**
INCOME STATEMENT (IN MILLIONS):							
Total Revenues	3,402.0	4,004.9	4,287.2	4,112.7	3,570.2	3,280.9	2,975.1
Costs & Expenses	3,116.0	3,697.6	3,957.7	3,824.3	3,325.2	3,106.9	2,828.0
Depreciation & Amort.	52.0	52.8	51.1	51.6	52.5	48.6	44.9
Operating Income	233.9	254.6	278.4	236.8	192.5	125.4	102.2
Net Interest Inc./(Exp.)	d56.9	d56.8	d64.0	d64.9	d68.8	d69.6	d58.4
Income Before Income Taxes	189.6	211.8	248.0	171.9	123.7	55.8	43.8
Income Taxes	68.2	76.0	98.7	68.8	49.5	24.9	11.8
Equity Earnings/Minority Int.	5.0	5.5	8.8	d2.3	d2.9	d5.3	6.5
Net Income	[5] 113.8	[4] 127.3	141.3	100.9	[3] 71.4	[2] 25.6	[1] 38.6
Cash Flow	165.8	180.0	192.3	152.4	123.9	74.3	83.4
Average Shs. Outstg. (000)	30,205	33,477	35,388	35,076	35,038	35,014	35,502
BALANCE SHEET (IN MILLIONS):							
Cash & Cash Equivalents	61.4	92.8	79.8	109.1	214.8	158.1	164.5
Total Current Assets	1,088.2	1,170.3	1,430.3	1,431.2	1,329.0	1,262.4	1,186.0
Net Property	347.3	348.3	329.8	309.7	320.4	334.4	269.2
Total Assets	1,748.1	1,823.1	2,056.7	1,982.0	1,889.5	1,808.0	1,667.0
Total Current Liabilities	883.2	898.5	1,101.5	1,083.7	1,029.2	997.6	868.0
Long-Term Obligations	223.3	221.5	263.1	291.6	309.5	284.9	298.1
Net Stockholders' Equity	497.8	539.0	547.9	469.6	417.3	390.0	377.5
Net Working Capital	204.9	271.8	328.8	347.5	299.8	264.7	318.0
Year-end Shs. Outstg. (000)	28,147	32,091	34,866	35,139	35,056	35,030	35,001
STATISTICAL RECORD:							
Operating Profit Margin %	6.9	6.4	6.5	5.8	5.4	3.8	3.4
Net Profit Margin %	3.3	3.2	3.3	2.5	2.0	0.8	1.3
Return on Equity %	22.9	23.6	25.8	21.5	17.1	6.6	10.2
Return on Assets %	6.5	7.0	6.9	5.1	3.8	1.4	2.3
Debt/Total Assets %	12.8	12.2	12.8	14.7	16.4	15.8	17.9
Price Range	36.38-13.50	35.75-19.44	49.50-31.50	41.69-27.88	32.75-22.25	24.63-18.88	26.25-17.50
P/E Ratio	9.6-3.6	9.4-5.1	12.4-7.9	14.5-9.7	16.1-10.9	33.7-25.9	24.1-16.1
Average Yield %	5.0	4.3	2.8	3.0	3.7	4.6	4.4

Statistics are as originally reported. [1] Bef. acctg. change chrg. $29.4 mill. & incls. non-recurr. chrg. of $11.8 mill. [2] Incl. non-recurr. chrg. of $15.6 mill. [3] Bef. extraord. gain of $900,000. [4] Incl. gain of $16.7 mill. fr. sale of invest. [5] Incl. after-tax restruct. chrg. of $7.0 mill. ($0.23 per sh.)

OFFICERS:
H. H. Harrell, Chmn., C.E.O.
A. B. King, Pres., C.O.O.
H. H. Roper, V.P., C.F.O.

INVESTOR CONTACT: Karen M. L. Whelan, V.P., Treas., (804) 254-8689

PRINCIPAL OFFICE: 1501 North Hamilton Street, Richmond, VA 23260

TELEPHONE NUMBER: (804) 359-9311
FAX: (804) 254-3594
WEB: www.universalcorp.com

NO. OF EMPLOYEES: 32,000 (approx.)

SHAREHOLDERS: 2,882

ANNUAL MEETING: In Oct.

INCORPORATED: VA, Jan., 1918

INSTITUTIONAL HOLDINGS:
No. of Institutions: 135
Shares Held: 17,949,511
% Held: 66.1

INDUSTRY: Farm-product raw materials, nec (SIC: 5159)

TRANSFER AGENT(S): Wells Fargo Bank Minnesota, N.A. St. Paul, MN

NYSE SYMBOL UHS
Rec. Pr. 40.00 (Adj.; 5/31/01)

UNIVERSAL HEALTH SERVICES, INC.

YIELD	...
P/E RATIO	13.2

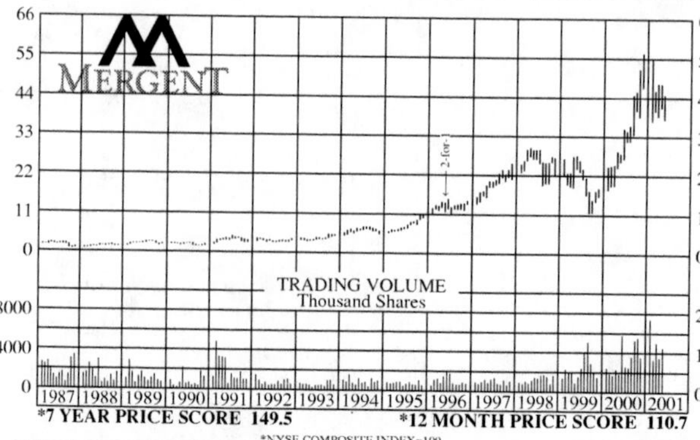

INTERIM EARNINGS (Per Share):

Qtr.	Mar.	June	Sept.	Dec.
1997	0.33	0.26	0.21	0.23
1998	0.39	0.31	0.20	0.31
1999	0.46	0.36	0.17	0.23
2000	0.46	0.38	0.36	0.31

INTERIM DIVIDENDS (Per Share):

Amt.	Decl.	Ex.	Rec.	Pay.
100% STK	4/17/01	6/04/01	5/16/01	6/01/01

CAPITALIZATION (12/31/00):

	($000)	(%)
Long-Term Debt	548,064	38.5
Deferred Income Tax	36,381	2.6
Minority Interest	120,788	8.5
Common & Surplus	716,574	50.4
Total	1,421,807	100.0

RECENT DEVELOPMENTS: For the year ended 12/31/00, net income increased 20.0% to $93.4 million versus $77.8 million in 1999. Results for 2000 and 1999 included pre-tax nonrecurring charges of $7.7 million and $5.3 million, respectively. Total revenues climbed 9.8% to $2.24 billion from $2.04 billion the year before. Revenue from acute care services rose 7.4% to $1.82 billion, while revenue from behavorial health services jumped 31.7% to $356.3 million.

PROSPECTS: UHS should continue to benefit from the completion of several acquistions. Moreover, UHS announced it has purchased an 80.0% interest in an operator of private hospitals in France for approximately $75.0 million. The new company formed by UHS to complete the transaction is named Medi-Partenaires. In 2001, UHS remains on track to achieve annual revenues of $2.60 billion and diluted earnings in the range of $3.65 to $3.80 per share.

BUSINESS

UNIVERSAL HEALTH SERVICES, INC. is principally engaged in the ownership and operation of acute care hospitals, behavioral health centers, ambulatory surgery centers, radiation oncology centers and women's centers. As of 12/31/00, UHS operated 59 hospitals, consisting of 23 acute care hospitals, 35 behavioral health centers, and a specialized women's health center in Arkansas, California, Delaware, the District of Columbia, Florida, Georgia, Illinois, Indiana, Kentucky, Louisiana, Massachusetts, Michigan, Mississippi, Missouri, Nevada, New Jersey, Oklahoma, Pennsylvania, Puerto Rico, South Carolina, Tennessee, Texas, Utah and Washington. UHS, through its Ambulatory Treatment Centers Division, owns outright, or in partnership with physicians, and operates or manages 25 surgery and radiation oncology centers located in 12 states and the District of Columbia.

REVENUES

(12/31/2000)	($000)	(%)
Acute Care Services	1,816,353	81.0
Behavioral Health Services	356,340	15.9
Other	69,751	3.1
Total	2,242,444	100.0

ANNUAL FINANCIAL DATA

	12/31/00	12/31/99	12/31/98	12/31/97	12/31/96	12/31/95	12/31/94
Earnings Per Share	[1] **1.51**	[1] **1.22**	**1.20**	**1.02**	[1] **0.82**	[1] **0.63**	[1] **0.51**
Cash Flow Per Share	**3.18**	**2.91**	**2.78**	**2.24**	**1.99**	**1.54**	**1.24**
Tang. Book Val. Per Share	**6.68**	**5.96**	**5.40**	**5.81**	**4.71**	**5.82**	**4.02**
INCOME STATEMENT (IN MILLIONS):							
Total Revenues	2,242.4	2,042.4	1,874.5	1,442.7	1,190.2	931.1	782.2
Costs & Expenses	1,932.2	1,772.8	1,609.8	1,236.7	1,012.9	804.0	676.8
Depreciation & Amort.	112.8	108.3	105.4	80.7	71.9	51.4	42.4
Operating Income	197.5	161.2	159.2	125.3	105.3	75.8	63.0
Net Interest Inc./(Exp.)	d29.9	d26.9	d27.1	d19.4	d21.3	d11.2	d6.3
Income Before Income Taxes	146.1	122.8	123.0	105.9	80.0	53.0	46.9
Income Taxes	52.7	45.0	43.5	38.6	29.3	17.5	18.2
Equity Earnings/Minority Int.	d13.7	d6.3	d9.1	...	...	...	...
Net Income	[1] 93.4	[1] 77.8	79.6	67.3	[1] 50.7	[1] 35.5	[1] 28.7
Cash Flow	206.2	186.1	185.0	148.0	122.6	86.9	71.1
Average Shs. Outstg. (000)	64,820	63,980	66,586	66,196	61,696	56,316	57,556
BALANCE SHEET (IN MILLIONS):							
Cash & Cash Equivalents	10.5	6.2	1.3	0.3	0.3	...	0.8
Total Current Assets	476.5	403.2	319.6	230.0	194.0	156.9	118.4
Net Property	875.6	777.1	808.8	663.1	567.6	393.0	331.6
Total Assets	1,742.4	1,498.0	1,448.1	1,085.3	965.8	748.1	521.5
Total Current Liabilities	248.8	217.2	170.1	160.5	140.1	135.0	103.8
Long-Term Obligations	548.1	419.2	418.2	272.5	275.6	237.1	85.1
Net Stockholders' Equity	716.6	641.6	627.0	526.6	453.0	297.7	260.6
Net Working Capital	227.6	186.0	149.6	69.6	53.9	21.9	14.6
Year-end Shs. Outstg. (000)	59,831	61,304	64,390	64,843	64,242	27,759	55,259
STATISTICAL RECORD:							
Operating Profit Margin %	8.8	7.9	8.5	8.7	8.8	8.1	8.0
Net Profit Margin %	4.2	3.8	4.2	4.7	4.3	3.8	3.7
Return on Equity %	13.0	12.1	12.7	12.8	11.2	11.9	11.0
Return on Assets %	5.4	5.2	5.5	6.2	5.2	4.7	5.5
Debt/Total Assets %	31.5	28.0	28.9	25.1	28.5	31.7	16.3
Price Range	56.47-18.06	27.56-11.56	29.88-19.22	25.41-13.88	15.38-10.81	11.13-5.63	7.41-4.78
P/E Ratio	37.5-12.0	22.7-9.5	25.0-16.1	25.0-13.7	18.7-13.2	17.7-8.9	14.7-9.5

Statistics are as originally reported. Adj. for 100% stk. div., 6/01. [1] Incl. pre-tax nonrecurr. chrgs. of $7.7 mill, 2000; $5.3 mill., 1999; $4.1 mill., 1996; $11.6 mill., 1995; $9.8 mill., 1994

OFFICERS:
A. B. Miller, Chmn., Pres., C.E.O.
K. E. Gorman, Sr. V.P., C.F.O.
S. G. Filton, V.P., Contr., Sec.

INVESTOR CONTACT: Kirk E. Gorman, Sr. Vice-Pres. & CFO, (610) 768-3300

PRINCIPAL OFFICE: Universal Corporate Center, 367 South Gulph Road, King Of Prussia, PA 19406-0958

TELEPHONE NUMBER: (610) 768-3300
FAX: (610) 768-3336
WEB: www.uhsinc.com

NO. OF EMPLOYEES: 17,920 full-time; 7,680 part-time

SHAREHOLDERS: 752

ANNUAL MEETING: In May

INCORPORATED: DE, Sep., 1978

INSTITUTIONAL HOLDINGS:
No. of Institutions: 227
Shares Held: 54,728,298 (Adj.)
% Held: 91.3

INDUSTRY: General medical & surgical hospitals (SIC: 8062)

TRANSFER AGENT(S): Mellon Investor Services, Ridgefield Park, NJ

NYSE SYMBOL UVN
Rec. Pr. 43.71 (4/30/01)

UNIVISION COMMUNICATIONS INC.

YIELD ...
P/E RATIO 87.4

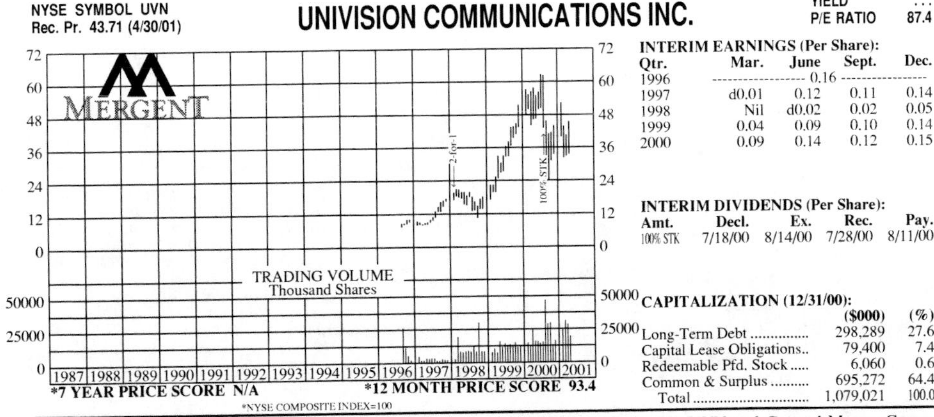

*7 YEAR PRICE SCORE N/A *12 MONTH PRICE SCORE 93.4
*NYSE COMPOSITE INDEX=100

INTERIM EARNINGS (Per Share):

Qtr.	Mar.	June	Sept.	Dec.
1996		0.16		
1997	d0.01	0.12	0.11	0.14
1998	Nil	d0.02	0.02	0.05
1999	0.04	0.09	0.10	0.14
2000	0.09	0.14	0.12	0.15

INTERIM DIVIDENDS (Per Share):

Amt.	Decl.	Ex.	Rec.	Pay.
100% STK	7/18/00	8/14/00	7/28/00	8/11/00

CAPITALIZATION (12/31/00):

	($000)	(%)
Long-Term Debt	298,289	27.6
Capital Lease Obligations	79,400	7.4
Redeemable Pfd. Stock	6,060	0.6
Common & Surplus	695,272	64.4
Total	1,079,021	100.0

RECENT DEVELOPMENTS: For the year ended 12/31/00, net income advanced 40.0% to $116.9 million compared with income of $83.5 million, before an extraordinary loss, in 1999. Results included a special charge of $2.0 million related to an executive's resignation. Net revenues were $863.5 million, up 24.6% from $693.1 million a year earlier. Net revenues for UVN's Internet business were $500,000 versus nil in 1999. Operating income amounted to $261.3 million, up 27.8% from $204.5 million the year before.

PROSPECTS: On 2/8/01, UVN and General Motors Corporation (GM) announced an on-line, one-year strategic marketing alliance. According to the agreement, GM will sponsor several content areas on Univision.com, including The Vida Channel (The Lifestyle Channel) and Aventuras Del Camino (Adventures On The Road), a new content area featuring automobile-related travel content and safety tips. On 4/18/01, UVN acquired a 50% interest in Mexico-based Disa Records, S.A. de C.V., the second largest independent Spanish-language record label in the world.

BUSINESS

UNIVISION COMMUNICATIONS INC. is a major Spanish-language television broadcaster in the United States, reaching more than 92% of all Hispanic households and having an 84% average share of the U.S. Spanish-language network television audience in 2000. Univision Television Group owns and operates 12 full-power and seven low-power television stations. UVN's Network, which is the most watched television network (English- or Spanish-language) among Hispanic households, provides the Company's broadcast and cable affiliates with 24 hours per day of Spanish-language programming with a prime-time schedule of substantially all first-run programming throughout the year. UVN also owns Galavision, a Spanish-language cable network that had approximately 3.6 million Hispanic subscribers as of 12/31/00, representing approximately 65% of all Hispanic households that subscribed to cable television in 2000.

ANNUAL FINANCIAL DATA

	12/31/00	12/31/99	12/31/98	12/31/97	12/31/96	12/31/95	12/31/94
Earnings Per Share	[5] **0.57**	[3] **0.36**	**0.05**	[4] **0.36**	[3] **0.16**	...	...
Cash Flow Per Share	**0.77**	**0.62**	**0.32**	**0.61**	**13.39**	...	...
Tang. Book Val. Per Share	**0.77**	...	...	...	...	...	...
INCOME STATEMENT (IN MILLIONS):							
Total Revenues	863.5	693.1	577.1	459.7	244.9	173.1	139.0
Costs & Expenses	534.0	424.6	379.8	295.1	135.3	91.8	68.0
Depreciation & Amort.	68.1	64.0	66.1	60.3	42.5	37.4	37.1
Operating Income	261.3	204.5	131.2	104.4	67.1	43.9	33.9
Net Interest Inc./(Exp.)	d31.5	d28.9	d37.5	d41.8	d44.6	d44.1	d42.7
Income Before Income Taxes	225.0	175.1	50.3	63.7	24.3	d9.4	d8.8
Income Taxes	108.1	91.5	40.3	cr19.5	5.7	...	0.1
Equity Earnings/Minority Int.	...	...	...	...	1.9	d7.3	1.2
Net Income	[5] 116.9	[3] 83.5	9.9	[4] 83.2	[3] 18.6	[2] d9.4	[1] d7.7
Cash Flow	184.5	147.0	75.4	142.9	58.2	28.0	29.4
Average Shs. Outstg. (000)	238,964	236,237	232,418	232,690	4,560	13,054	20
BALANCE SHEET (IN MILLIONS):							
Cash & Cash Equivalents	54.5	22.6	13.0	10.8	11.7	14.0	5.9
Total Current Assets	249.9	177.9	154.0	138.8	111.8	55.0	42.6
Net Property	247.2	205.2	144.5	123.9	103.4	25.6	21.3
Total Assets	1,448.3	974.5	938.3	967.8	884.4	545.9	565.9
Total Current Liabilities	363.0	141.9	152.9	144.0	120.4	131.3	127.6
Long-Term Obligations	377.7	303.1	377.4	460.8	498.5	471.3	454.0
Net Stockholders' Equity	695.3	513.8	394.6	346.2	262.2	d77.1	d29.2
Net Working Capital	d113.1	36.0	1.1	d5.3	d8.6	d76.2	d84.9
Year-end Shs. Outstg. (000)	206,065	203,355	180,904	170,598	170,448	20	20
STATISTICAL RECORD:							
Operating Profit Margin %	30.3	29.5	22.7	22.7	27.4	25.3	24.4
Net Profit Margin %	13.5	12.1	1.7	18.1	7.6	...	...
Return on Equity %	16.8	16.3	2.5	24.0	7.1	...	...
Return on Assets %	8.1	8.6	1.1	8.6	2.1	...	...
Debt/Total Assets %	26.1	31.1	40.2	47.6	56.4	86.3	80.2
Price Range	62.69-24.00	51.59-17.06	21.00-10.53	17.44-7.94	10.06-7.38	...	...
P/E Ratio	110.0-42.1	145.3-48.0	465.6-233.5	49.1-22.4	62.9-46.1	...	...

Statistics are as originally reported. Adj. for 100% stk. split, 8/00. [1] Excl. extraord. loss of $4.3 mill. [2] Incl. nonrecurr. exp. of $1.8 mill. [3] Excl. extraord. loss of $8.2 mill., 1996; $2.6 mill., 1999. [4] Incl. nonrecurr. reversal of $1.1 mill. [5] Incl. nonrecurr. chrg. of $2.0 mill.

OFFICERS:
A. J. Perenchio, Chmn., C.E.O.
H. Cisneros, Pres., C.O.O.
G. W. Blank, Exec. V.P., C.F.O.

INVESTOR CONTACT: Andrew Hobson, Investor Relations, (310) 556-7690

PRINCIPAL OFFICE: 1999 Avenue Of The Stars, Suite 3050, Los Angeles, CA 90067

TELEPHONE NUMBER: (310) 556-7676
FAX: (310) 556-3568
WEB: www.unvision.net

NO. OF EMPLOYEES: 2,260 (approx.)

SHAREHOLDERS: 178 (approx.)

ANNUAL MEETING: In May

INCORPORATED: DE, April, 1992

INSTITUTIONAL HOLDINGS:
No. of Institutions: 243
Shares Held: 134,018,678
% Held: 65.0

INDUSTRY: Television broadcasting stations (SIC: 4833)

TRANSFER AGENT(S): The Bank of New York, New York, NY

NYSE SYMBOL UCL
Rec. Pr. 38.65 (5/31/01)

UNOCAL CORP.

YIELD 2.1%
P/E RATIO 13.2

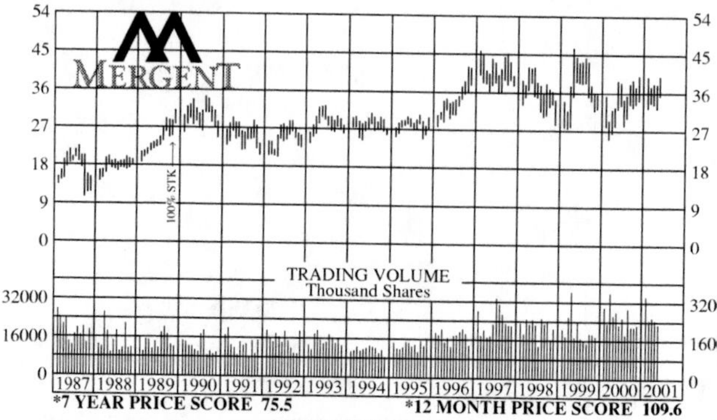

MERGENT

TRADING VOLUME
Thousand Shares

*7 YEAR PRICE SCORE 75.5 *12 MONTH PRICE SCORE 109.6

*NYSE COMPOSITE INDEX=100

INTERIM EARNINGS (Per Share):

Qtr.	Mar.	June	Sept.	Dec.
1996	0.47	0.92	0.69	0.01
1997	0.75	0.63	0.71	0.59
1998	0.08	0.43	0.15	d0.12
1999	0.03	0.04	0.10	0.40
2000	0.51	1.00	0.71	0.70

INTERIM DIVIDENDS (Per Share):

Amt.	Decl.	Ex.	Rec.	Pay.
0.20Q	5/22/00	7/06/00	7/10/00	8/10/00
0.20Q	9/25/00	10/05/00	10/10/00	11/10/00
0.20Q	12/05/00	1/08/01	1/10/01	2/09/01
0.20Q	3/27/01	4/06/01	4/10/01	5/10/01
0.20Q	5/21/01	7/06/01	7/10/01	8/10/01

Indicated div.: $0.80 (Div. Reinv. Plan)

CAPITALIZATION (12/31/00):

	($000)	(%)
Long-Term Debt	2,392,000	36.0
Deferred Income Tax	618,000	9.3
Minority Interest	392,000	5.9
Redeemable Pfd. Stock	522,000	7.9
Common & Surplus	2,719,000	40.9
Total	6,643,001	100.0

RECENT DEVELOPMENTS: For the year ended 12/31/00, earnings from continuing operations totaled $723.0 million compared with $113.0 million in the previous year. Results for 2000 and 1999 included non-recurring charges of $75.0 million and $36.0 million, respectively. Results excluded earnings from discontinued operations of $37.0 million and $24.0 million for 2000 and 1999, respectively. Total revenues increased 54.4% to $9.20 billion from $5.96 billion in 1999.

PROSPECTS: Prospects are positive, reflecting higher commodity prices and rising production. UCL's Lower 48 natural gas production should benefit from a full year of production from the new Muni field on the Ship Shoal 295 lease offshore Louisiana, which started up production early in the fourth quarter of 2000, as well as various recent acquisitions. Meanwhile, longer-term results could benefit substantially from UCL's exploration program, which includes its first deepwater wells offshore Brazil and Gabon.

BUSINESS

UNOCAL CORP. is an independent oil and gas exploration and production company, with major activities in North America, including the Gulf of Mexico region, Alaska and Canada, and in Asia, including Thailand, Indonesia, and Bangladesh. UCL is also pursuing exploration programs in West Africa and Brazil. In addition, the Company produces geothermal energy and manufactures and markets nitrogen-based fertilizers, petroleum coke, graphites and specialty minerals. In 2000, net proved reserves were: crude oil, 632 million barrels; and natural gas, 6,540 billion cubic feet. Sales and operating revenues were derived: Exploration and Production, 20.9%; Global Trade, 75.1%; Pipeline, 0.4%; Geothermal & Power, 1.7%; and Carbon & Mineral, 1.9%.

GEOGRAPHIC DATA

(12/31/2000)	($000)	(%)
United States	6,956,000	78.0
Canada	168,000	1.9
Thailand	735,000	8.2
Indonesia	689,000	7.7
Other Foreign	365,000	4.1
Corporate	1,000	0.1
Total	8,914,000	100.0

ANNUAL FINANCIAL DATA

	12/31/00	12/31/99	12/31/98	12/31/97	12/31/96	12/31/95	12/31/94
Earnings Per Share	**[5] 2.93**	**[4] 0.46**	**0.54**	**[1][2] 2.65**	**[1] 1.76**	**0.91**	**[3] 0.36**
Cash Flow Per Share	**6.62**	**3.71**	**4.12**	**6.23**	**6.01**	**5.04**	**4.26**
Tang. Book Val. Per Share	**11.70**	**9.42**	**9.14**	**9.67**	**9.28**	**9.97**	**9.65**
Dividends Per Share	**0.80**	**0.80**	**0.80**	**0.80**	**0.80**	**0.80**	**0.80**
Dividend Payout %	**27.3**	**173.9**	**148.1**	**30.2**	**45.5**	**87.9**	**222.2**
INCOME STATEMENT (IN MILLIONS):							
Total Revenues	9,202.0	6,057.0	5,479.0	6,064.0	5,328.0	8,425.0	7,965.0
Costs & Expenses	6,886.0	4,742.0	4,097.0	4,115.0	3,222.0	6,649.0	6,449.0
Depreciation & Amort.	971.0	833.0	867.0	962.0	1,059.0	1,022.0	947.0
Operating Income	1,345.0	482.0	515.0	987.0	1,047.0	754.0	569.0
Net Interest Inc./(Exp.)	d210.0	d199.0	d177.0	d183.0	d279.0	d291.0	d275.0
Income Before Income Taxes	1,236.0	250.0	305.0	771.0	758.0	463.0	294.0
Income Taxes	497.0	121.0	175.0	102.0	302.0	203.0	170.0
Equity Earnings/Minority Int.	d16.0	d16.0	...	...	...	...	...
Net Income	[5] 723.0	[4] 113.0	130.0	[1][2] 669.0	[1] 456.0	260.0	[3] 124.0
Cash Flow	1,694.0	946.0	997.0	1,631.0	1,497.0	1,246.0	1,035.0
Average Shs. Outstg. (000)	256,000	255,000	242,000	262,000	249,000	247,000	243,000
BALANCE SHEET (IN MILLIONS):							
Cash & Cash Equivalents	235.0	332.0	238.0	338.0	217.0	94.0	148.0
Total Current Assets	1,802.0	1,631.0	1,388.0	1,501.0	3,228.0	1,576.0	1,528.0
Net Property	6,433.0	5,980.0	5,276.0	4,816.0	4,590.0	7,109.0	6,823.0
Total Assets	10,010.0	8,967.0	7,952.0	7,530.0	9,123.0	9,891.0	9,337.0
Total Current Liabilities	1,845.0	1,559.0	1,376.0	1,160.0	1,622.0	1,316.0	1,257.0
Long-Term Obligations	2,392.0	2,853.0	2,558.0	2,169.0	2,940.0	3,698.0	3,461.0
Net Stockholders' Equity	2,719.0	2,184.0	2,202.0	2,350.0	2,329.0	2,976.0	2,867.0
Net Working Capital	d43.0	72.0	12.0	341.0	1,606.0	260.0	271.0
Year-end Shs. Outstg. (000)	232,422	231,818	241,000	243,000	251,000	247,000	244,000
STATISTICAL RECORD:							
Operating Profit Margin %	14.6	8.0	9.4	16.3	19.7	8.9	7.1
Net Profit Margin %	7.9	1.9	2.4	11.0	8.6	3.1	1.6
Return on Equity %	26.6	5.2	5.9	28.5	19.6	8.7	4.3
Return on Assets %	7.2	1.3	1.6	8.9	5.0	2.6	1.3
Debt/Total Assets %	23.9	31.8	32.2	28.8	32.2	37.4	37.1
Price Range	40.13-25.00	46.63-27.50	42.13-28.31	45.88-36.13	42.13-27.75	30.50-24.75	30.75-24.38
P/E Ratio	13.7-8.5	101.3-59.8	78.0-52.4	17.3-13.6	23.9-15.8	33.5-27.2	85.4-67.7
Average Yield %	2.5	2.2	2.3	2.0	2.3	2.9	2.9

Statistics are as originally reported. [1] Bef. disc. ops. loss $50.0 mil. 12/97; $420.0 mil., 12/96 [2] Bef. extraord. chrg. $38.0 mil. [3] Bef. acctg. adj. chrg. of $277.0 mil. [4] Bef. inc. fr. disc. opers. $24.0 mil. [5] Incl. non-recur. chrg. of $75.0 mil.; bef. inc. fr. disc. ops. of $37.0 mil.

OFFICERS:
J. W. Creighton Jr., Chmn.
C. R. Williamson, C.E.O.
T. H. Ling, Pres., C.O.O.

INVESTOR CONTACT: Robert E. Wright, V.P., Investor Relations, (310) 726-7665

PRINCIPAL OFFICE: 2141 Rosecrans Avenue, Suite 4000, El Segundo, CA 90245

TELEPHONE NUMBER: (310) 726-7600
WEB: www.unocal.com

NO. OF EMPLOYEES: 6,800 (avg.)

SHAREHOLDERS: 24,625 (approx.)

ANNUAL MEETING: In May

INCORPORATED: DE, Mar., 1983

INSTITUTIONAL HOLDINGS:
No. of Institutions: 377
Shares Held: 189,631,408
% Held: 78.0

INDUSTRY: Crude petroleum and natural gas (SIC: 1311)

TRANSFER AGENT(S): Mellon Investor Services, Ridgefield Park, NJ

NYSE SYMBOL UNA
Rec. Pr. 3.20 (4/30/01)

UNOVA, INC.

YIELD ...
P/E RATIO ...

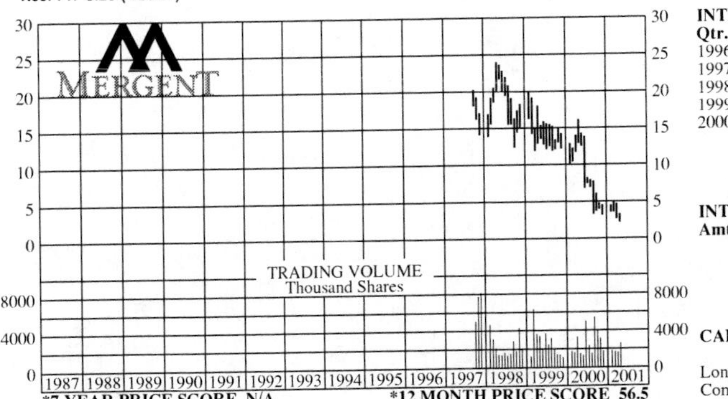

*7 YEAR PRICE SCORE N/A   *12 MONTH PRICE SCORE 56.5

*NYSE COMPOSITE INDEX=100

INTERIM EARNINGS (Per Share):

Qtr.	Mar.	June	Sept.	Dec.
1996		0.78		
1997	0.21	d3.51	0.22	d0.10
1998	0.14	0.17	0.24	0.72
1999	0.06	0.06	0.17	0.24
2000	d0.01	0.29	d0.13	d0.86

INTERIM DIVIDENDS (Per Share):

Amt.	Decl.	Ex.	Rec.	Pay.

No dividends paid.

CAPITALIZATION (12/31/00):

	($000)	(%)
Long-Term Debt	213,503	23.7
Common & Surplus	687,784	76.3
Total	901,287	100.0

RECENT DEVELOPMENTS: For the year ended 12/31/00, UNA posted a net loss of $39.8 million versus net earnings of $29.6 million a year earlier. Results for 2000 included pre-tax charges of $33.7 million and a non-recurring gain of $44.7 million. Sales and service revenues fell 12.8% to $1.84 billion. Separately, on 2/9/01, UNA announced that it has reached an agreement with its banks to amend its principal secured credit lines. The agreement, which expires on 11/8/01, allows UNA to draw up to $400.0 million based on its planned cash requirements.

PROSPECTS: The Company's near-term outlook is uncertain. On the plus side, Intermec, a unit of UNA's Automated Data Systems segment, is experiencing improvement in orders and activity from the "Direct-Store-Delivery" market and is expecting further industry progress throughout 2001. However, the Industrial Automation Systems segment is suffering from slower capital investments in new engine programs for the automotive industry. Also, the markets of the Advanced Manufacturing Equipment unit have not yet recovered from their slowdown.

BUSINESS

UNOVA, INC. is a global supplier of mobile computing and wireless network products of non-office applications and of manufacturing systems technologies primarily for automotive and aerospace industries. The Company operates in two primary businesses: The Automated Data Systems segment is comprised of mobile computing and wireless communication systems products and services, principally serving the industrial market. Customers are global distribution and transportation companies, food and beverage operations, manufacturing industries, health care providers and government agencies. The Industrial Automation Systems segment is comprised of an Integrated Production Systems division, including body welding and assembly systems, and precision grinding and abrasives operations, primarily serving the worldwide automotive, off-road vehicle, and diesel engine industries. The Advanced Manufacturing Equipment division is comprised machining systems and stand-alone machine tools primarily serving the aerospace and manufacturing industries. In June 1998, UNA acquired R&B Machine Tool. In October 1998, UNA acquired the machine tool business of Cincinnati Milacron, renamed Cincinnati Machine, for about $187.3 million.

ANNUAL FINANCIAL DATA

	12/31/00	12/31/99	12/31/98	[1] 12/31/97	12/31/96	12/31/95	12/31/94
Earnings Per Share	[2] d0.71	0.54	1.27	d3.17	0.78	...	...
Cash Flow Per Share	0.49	1.73	2.32	d2.42	1.28	...	...
Tang. Book Val. Per Share	5.60	5.98	5.48	4.10	...	...	...
INCOME STATEMENT (IN MILLIONS):							
Total Revenues	1,837.8	2,108.7	1,662.7	1,426.2	1,164.7	942.9	971.1
Costs & Expenses	1,856.8	1,955.4	1,494.5	1,517.3	1,060.5	863.3	889.8
Depreciation & Amort.	67.3	66.0	57.0	40.7	27.0	26.1	28.7
Operating Income	d86.3	87.3	111.2	d131.7	77.1	53.4	52.6
Net Interest Inc./(Exp.)	d30.6	d38.0	d25.7	d16.7	d7.1	d9.3	d15.7
Income Before Income Taxes	d72.1	49.3	117.0	d148.4	70.0	44.0	36.9
Income Taxes	cr32.3	19.7	47.3	23.0	28.0	17.8	15.4
Net Income	[2] d39.8	29.6	69.7	d171.4	42.0	26.2	21.6
Cash Flow	27.5	95.6	126.8	d130.7	69.1	52.3	50.3
Average Shs. Outstg. (000)	55,714	55,120	54,703	54,057	53,892	...	...
BALANCE SHEET (IN MILLIONS):							
Cash & Cash Equivalents	106.8	25.2	17.7	13.7	149.5	103.5	...
Total Current Assets	895.1	1,110.3	1,179.5	749.1	695.8	546.5	...
Net Property	228.2	270.9	286.2	157.7	132.5	137.3	...
Total Assets	1,720.7	1,903.5	1,979.2	1,356.4	1,073.8	919.0	...
Total Current Liabilities	717.2	662.5	787.3	471.3	429.8	351.8	...
Long-Term Obligations	213.5	365.4	366.5	216.9	14.5	14.1	...
Net Stockholders' Equity	687.8	731.3	701.4	589.5	574.5	502.7	...
Net Working Capital	177.9	447.8	392.2	277.8	266.0	194.7	...
Year-end Shs. Outstg. (000)	56,793	55,551	54,942	54,513	...	...	...
STATISTICAL RECORD:							
Operating Profit Margin %	...	4.1	6.7	...	6.6	5.7	5.4
Net Profit Margin %	...	1.4	4.2	...	3.6	2.8	2.2
Return on Equity %	...	4.0	9.9	...	7.3	5.2	...
Return on Assets %	...	1.6	3.5	...	3.9	2.9	...
Debt/Total Assets %	12.4	19.2	18.5	16.0	1.4	1.5	...
Price Range	16.13-3.13	20.00-11.88	24.00-12.38	20.31-14.13	...	...	...
P/E Ratio	...	37.0-22.0	18.9-9.7	...	...	...	...

Statistics are as originally reported. [1] Results reflect the combined opers. of the Company and Western Atlas Inc. prior to the spin-off of the Company on 10/31/97. [2] Incl. one-time gain of $44.7 mill. on sale of Amtech transportation opers. & pre-tax chrgs. of $33.7 mill.

OFFICERS:
A. J. Brann, Chmn.
L. D. Brady, Pres., C.E.O.
M. E. Keane, Sr. V.P., C.F.O.

INVESTOR CONTACT: Dink Koerber, Investor Relations, (818) 992-2870

PRINCIPAL OFFICE: 21900 Burbank Boulevard, Woodland Hills, CA 91367-7418

TELEPHONE NUMBER: (818) 992-3000
FAX: (818) 992-2848
WEB: www.unova.com

NO. OF EMPLOYEES: 8,461 (approx.)

SHAREHOLDERS: 14,813 (approx.)

ANNUAL MEETING: In May

INCORPORATED: DE, 1997

INSTITUTIONAL HOLDINGS:
No. of Institutions: 74
Shares Held: 48,185,791
% Held: 84.9

INDUSTRY: Service industry machinery, nec (SIC: 3589)

TRANSFER AGENT(S): Mellon Investor Services, South Hackensack, NJ

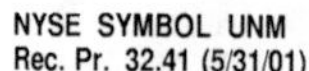

NYSE SYMBOL UNM
Rec. Pr. 32.41 (5/31/01)

UNUMPROVIDENT CORPORATION

YIELD 1.8%
P/E RATIO 13.9

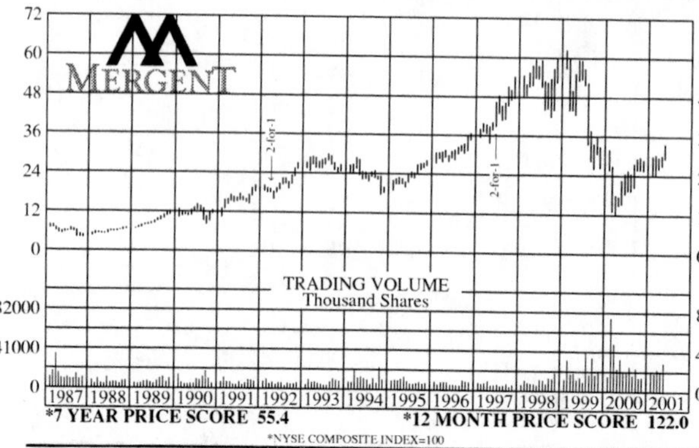

*7 YEAR PRICE SCORE 55.4 *12 MONTH PRICE SCORE 122.0

*NYSE COMPOSITE INDEX=100

INTERIM EARNINGS (Per Share):

Qtr.	Mar.	June	Sept.	Dec.
1996	0.50	0.51	0.30	0.33
1997	0.81	0.63	0.66	0.54
1998	0.66	0.70	0.74	0.47
1999	0.37	d0.80	d0.91	0.56
2000	0.56	0.59	0.57	0.62

INTERIM DIVIDENDS (Per Share):

Amt.	Decl.	Ex.	Rec.	Pay.
0.147Q	4/12/00	4/19/00	4/24/00	5/19/00
0.147Q	5/24/00	7/27/00	7/31/00	8/18/00
0.147Q	8/04/00	10/26/00	10/30/00	11/17/00
0.147Q	1/08/01	1/25/01	1/29/01	2/16/01
0.147Q	4/02/01	4/26/01	4/30/01	5/18/01

Indicated div.: $0.59 (Div. Reinv. Plan)

CAPITALIZATION (12/31/00):

	($000)	(%)
Long-Term Debt	1,615,500	20.4
Deferred Income Tax	430,800	5.4
Preferred Stock	300,000	3.8
Common & Surplus	5,575,500	70.4
Total	7,921,800	100.0

RECENT DEVELOPMENTS: For the year ended 12/31/00, net income was $564.2 million versus a net loss of $182.9 million in 1999. Total revenues were $9.43 billion, an increase of 1.1% versus $9.33 billion a year earlier. Revenues included net realized investment losses of $14.6 million in 2000 and net realized investment gains of $87.1 million in 1999. Premium income grew 3.1% to $7.06 billion from $6.84 billion in the prior year. Net investment income was flat at $2.06 billion versus the year before.

PROSPECTS: Operating results for the Employee Benefits segment and the Individual segment should continue to benefit from higher net investment income and a decline in total expenses. Moreover, operating improvements within the group life and group long-term care lines of business should help boost results. On 4/3/01, the Company acquired the assets of EmployeeLife.com, an Internet Capital Group partner company located in Mountain View, California.

BUSINESS

UNUMPROVIDENT CORPORATION (formerly UNUM Corporation), is a holding company for a group of insurance companies that collectively operate in all 50 states, the District of Columbia, Puerto Rico, and Canada. The Company was created from the merger between Unum Corporation and Provident Companies, Inc. as of 6/30/99. The Company's principal operating subsidiaries are Unum Life Insurance Company of America, Provident Life and Accident Insurance Company, The Paul Revere Life Insurance Company, and Colonial Life & Accident Insurance Company. The Company, through its subsidiaries, is the largest provider of group and individual disability insurance in North America, the United Kingdom, and Japan. UNM also provides a complementary portfolio of life insurance products, including long-term care insurance, life insurance, employer- and employee-paid group benefits, and related services.

REVENUES

(12/31/2000)	($000)	(%)
Premium Income	7,057,000	74.8
Net Investment Income	2,060,400	21.8
Net Realized Invest Gains	(14,600)	(0.1)
Other Income	329,500	3.5
Total	9,432,300	100.0

ANNUAL FINANCIAL DATA

	12/31/00	[2] 12/31/99	12/31/98	12/31/97	12/31/96	12/31/95	12/31/94
Earnings Per Share	**2.33**	**[3] d0.77**	**2.57**	**[1] 2.59**	**1.63**	**1.94**	**[1] 1.05**
Tang. Book Val. Per Share	**20.29**	**17.79**	**19.74**	**17.61**	**15.76**	**15.77**	**13.23**
Dividends Per Share	**0.59**	**0.59**	**0.58**	**0.56**	**0.55**	**0.52**	**0.46**
Dividend Payout %	**25.3**	**...**	**22.8**	**21.8**	**33.4**	**26.7**	**44.0**
INCOME STATEMENT (IN MILLIONS):							
Total Premium Income	7,057.0	6,843.2	3,841.7	3,188.7	3,120.4	3,018.2	2,732.4
Other Income	2,375.3	2,486.4	799.7	888.0	922.3	1,104.7	891.3
Total Revenues	9,432.3	9,329.6	4,641.4	4,076.7	4,042.7	4,122.9	3,623.7
Policyholder Benefits	6,407.5	6,787.6	2,886.2	2,395.3	2,324.7	2,493.0	2,248.1
Income Before Income Taxes	865.6	d165.5	517.4	536.4	341.6	381.9	198.6
Income Taxes	301.4	17.4	154.0	166.1	103.6	100.8	43.9
Net Income	564.2	[3] d182.9	363.4	[1] 370.3	238.0	281.1	[1] 154.7
Average Shs. Outstg. (000)	242,061	239,081	141,400	142,923	146,000	145,354	148,316
BALANCE SHEET (IN MILLIONS):							
Cash & Cash Equivalents	386.5	613.9	296.7	147.6	200.4	939.2	328.0
Premiums Due	7,897.8	5,505.9	2,288.1	1,664.8	1,366.2	645.2	189.7
Invst. Assets: Fixed-term	22,588.9	22,356.7	7,896.9	7,310.9	6,942.7	9,135.4	7,867.8
Invst. Assets: Equities	24.5	38.4	31.0	30.7	31.3	25.2	627.9
Invst. Assets: Loans	3,562.3	3,595.0	1,441.0	1,259.5	1,365.0	1,382.6	1,417.3
Invst. Assets: Total	26,604.1	26,549.3	9,837.7	8,934.1	8,724.7	11,692.5	10,433.8
Total Assets	40,363.9	38,447.5	15,182.9	13,200.3	15,467.5	14,787.8	13,127.2
Long-Term Obligations	1,615.5	1,166.5	881.8	635.8	526.9	583.8	428.7
Net Stockholders' Equity	5,875.5	5,282.2	2,737.7	2,434.8	2,263.1	2,302.9	1,915.4
Year-end Shs. Outstg. (000)	241,135	240,339	138,709	138,272	143,600	146,016	144,826
STATISTICAL RECORD:							
Return on Revenues %	6.0	...	7.8	9.1	5.9	6.8	4.3
Return on Equity %	9.6	...	13.3	15.2	10.5	12.2	8.1
Return on Assets %	1.4	...	2.4	2.8	1.5	1.9	1.2
Price Range	31.94-11.94	62.50-26.00	60.06-41.75	54.25-33.63	36.75-27.38	28.25-18.81	29.00-17.56
P/E Ratio	13.7-5.1	...	23.4-16.2	20.9-13.0	22.5-16.8	14.6-9.7	27.7-16.8
Average Yield %	2.7	1.3	1.1	1.3	1.7	2.2	2.0

Statistics are as originally reported. Adj. for stk. split: 2-for-1, 6/97 [1] Incl. non-recurr. chrg. 1997, $43.6 mill.; 1994, $134.5 mill. [2] Results through 1st quarter of 1999 are for UNUM Corp. only [3] Incl. pre-tax non-recurr. chrgs. $874.5 mill.

OFFICERS:
J. H. Chandler, Chmn., Pres., C.E.O.
F. D. Copeland, Exec. V.P., Gen. Couns.

INVESTOR CONTACT: Kent M. Mohnkern, V.P. Inv. Relations, (207) 770-4330

PRINCIPAL OFFICE: 2211 Congress Street, Portland, ME 04122

TELEPHONE NUMBER: (423) 755-1011
WEB: www.unum.com

NO. OF EMPLOYEES: 12,400 (approx.)

SHAREHOLDERS: 22,086

ANNUAL MEETING: In May

INCORPORATED: DE, Jan., 1985

INSTITUTIONAL HOLDINGS:
No. of Institutions: 319
Shares Held: 168,479,589
% Held: 69.8

INDUSTRY: Accident and health insurance (SIC: 6321)

TRANSFER AGENT(S): First Chicago Trust Company of New York, Jersey City, NJ

NYSE SYMBOL URS
Rec. Pr. 21.50 (4/30/01)

URS CORPORATION

YIELD	...
P/E RATIO	9.4

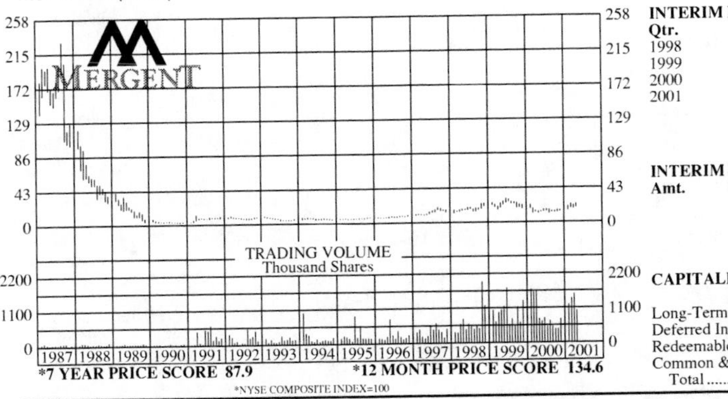

*7 YEAR PRICE SCORE 87.9 *12 MONTH PRICE SCORE 134.6
*NYSE COMPOSITE INDEX=100

INTERIM EARNINGS (Per Share):

Qtr.	Jan.	Apr.	July	Oct.
1998	0.27	0.31	0.40	0.45
1999	0.35	0.42	0.53	0.68
2000	0.40	0.51	0.64	0.72
2001	0.42	...	...	...

INTERIM DIVIDENDS (Per Share):

Amt.	Decl.	Ex.	Rec.	Pay.

No dividends paid.

CAPITALIZATION (10/31/00):

	($000)	(%)
Long-Term Debt	603,128	60.0
Deferred Income Tax	33,157	3.3
Redeemable Pfd. Stock	111,013	11.0
Common & Surplus	257,794	25.6
Total	1,005,092	100.0

RECENT DEVELOPMENTS: For the quarter ended 1/31/01, net income improved 9.5% to $9.4 million versus $8.6 million in the previous year quarter. Revenues increased slightly to $515.6 million compared with $512.9 million in the corresponding 2000 quarter. Results were dampened by the continuing tight labor market for professional engineers. Income before taxes increased 8.1% to $17.0 million versus $15.7 million in the prior-year quarter.

PROSPECTS: On 5/1/01, the Company announced that it has been awarded 15 new contracts that are expected to generate a total of approximately $225.0 million in additional revenues. The new contract includes large energy, air and surface transportation, water resources, facilities and environmental projects, and will contribute to the Company's revenues over the next several years.

BUSINESS

URS CORPORATION is an engineering services firm that provides a broad range of planning, design and program and construction management services. The Company provides these services in seven markets: surface transportation, air transportation, railroads/mass transit, industrial process/petrochemical, general building and facilities, water/wastewater and hazardous waste. The Company offers services to state, local and Federal government agencies, as well as to private clients in the chemical, pharmaceutical, manufacturing, forest products, energy, oil, gas, mining, healthcare, water supply, retail and commercial development, telecommunications and utilities industries. URS conduct business through approximately 319 principal offices located throughout the world, including the United States, Europe and the Asia/Pacific region.

ANNUAL FINANCIAL DATA

	10/31/00	10/31/99	10/31/98	10/31/97	10/31/96	10/31/95	10/31/94
Earnings Per Share	2.27	1.98	1.43	1.06	0.82	0.68	0.60
Cash Flow Per Share	3.94	3.63	2.35	1.79	1.33	0.95	0.82
Tang. Book Val. Per Share	...	...	2.41	3.23	1.90	4.42	4.16
INCOME STATEMENT (IN MILLIONS):							
Total Revenues	2,205.6	1,418.5	805.9	406.5	305.5	179.8	164.1
Costs & Expenses	1,996.8	1,283.9	741.1	374.5	284.2	168.9	155.4
Depreciation & Amort.	45.3	33.8	14.6	7.9	5.3	3.1	2.6
Operating Income	163.5	100.9	50.2	24.0	16.0	7.7	6.1
Net Interest Inc./(Exp.)	d71.9	d34.6	d8.8	d4.8	d3.9	d1.4	d1.2
Income Before Income Taxes	91.6	66.3	41.5	19.2	12.1	6.4	4.9
Income Taxes	41.7	29.7	18.8	7.7	4.7	1.3	0.5
Net Income	49.9	36.6	22.7	11.5	7.4	5.1	4.4
Cash Flow	86.9	67.0	37.2	19.4	12.7	8.2	7.0
Average Shs. Outstg. (000)	22,020	18,484	15,808	10,883	9,498	8,632	8,556
BALANCE SHEET (IN MILLIONS):							
Cash & Cash Equivalents	23.7	45.7	36.5	22.1	22.4	8.8	9.5
Total Current Assets	776.6	745.8	286.2	149.4	127.9	59.7	54.3
Net Property	88.7	93.2	29.5	17.8	15.8	5.8	5.5
Total Assets	1,427.1	1,437.5	451.7	212.7	185.6	74.1	65.2
Total Current Liabilities	382.0	386.7	155.2	86.2	70.3	23.4	20.6
Long-Term Obligations	603.1	649.0	95.0	41.4	55.4	10.0	9.3
Net Stockholders' Equity	257.8	207.2	166.4	77.2	56.7	39.5	34.0
Net Working Capital	394.6	147.1	53.1	25.5	34.0	23.1	19.9
Year-end Shs. Outstg. (000)	16,547	15,206	15,206	10,741	8,640	7,167	7,019
STATISTICAL RECORD:							
Operating Profit Margin %	7.4	7.1	6.2	5.9	5.2	4.3	3.7
Net Profit Margin %	2.3	2.6	2.8	2.8	2.4	2.8	2.7
Return on Equity %	19.4	11.8	13.6	14.9	13.0	12.8	13.1
Return on Assets %	3.5	2.5	5.0	5.4	4.0	6.8	6.8
Price Range	21.81-10.75	29.56-15.50	23.69-11.31	19.06-9.00	9.88-6.25	7.38-5.13	8.00-4.75
P/E Ratio	9.6-4.7	14.9-7.8	16.6-7.9	18.0-8.5	12.0-7.6	10.8-7.5	13.3-7.9

Statistics are as originally reported.

OFFICERS:
M. M. Koffel, Chmn., C.E.O.
K. P. Ainsworth, Exec. V.P., C.F.O., Sec.
D. C. Nelson, V.P., Treas.
J. Masters, V.P., Gen. Couns.

INVESTOR CONTACT: Investor Relations, (415) 774-2700

PRINCIPAL OFFICE: 100 California Street, Suite 500, San Francisco, CA 94111-4529

TELEPHONE NUMBER: (415) 774-2700
FAX: (415) 398-1905
WEB: www.urscorp.com

NO. OF EMPLOYEES: 15,900 (approx.)

SHAREHOLDERS: 4,591 (approx. record)

ANNUAL MEETING: In Mar.

INCORPORATED: CA, May, 1957; reincorp., DE, May, 1976

INSTITUTIONAL HOLDINGS:
No. of Institutions: 76
Shares Held: 11,946,731
% Held: 70.0

INDUSTRY: Engineering services (SIC: 8711)

TRANSFER AGENT(S): Mellon Investor Services LLC, San Francisco, CA

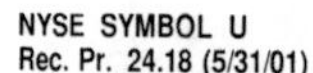

NYSE SYMBOL U
Rec. Pr. 24.18 (5/31/01)

US AIRWAYS GROUP, INC.

YIELD ...
P/E RATIO ...

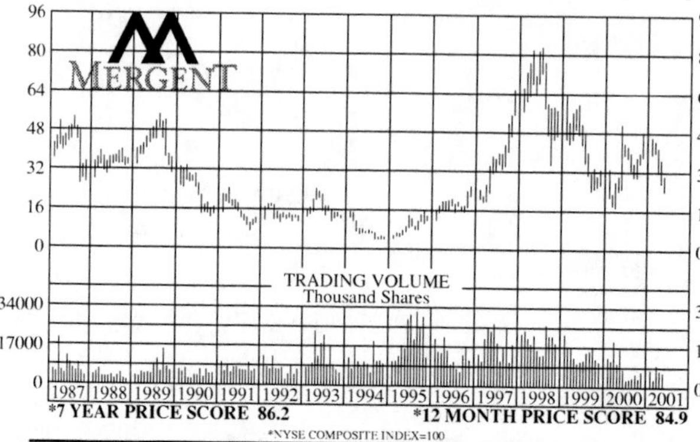

*7 YEAR PRICE SCORE 86.2 *12 MONTH PRICE SCORE 84.9

*NYSE COMPOSITE INDEX=100

INTERIM EARNINGS (Per Share):

Qtr.	Mar.	June	Sept.	Dec.
1996	d0.86	2.71	0.69	0.08
1997	2.00	2.46	2.04	4.66
1998	0.96	1.95	1.51	1.18
1999	0.56	4.26	d1.19	d1.16
2000	d1.72	1.17	d0.45	d1.50

INTERIM DIVIDENDS (Per Share):

Amt.	Decl.	Ex.	Rec.	Pay.

No dividends paid.

CAPITALIZATION (12/31/00):

	($000)	(%)
Long-Term Debt	2,688,000	115.4
Common & Surplus	d358,000	-15.4
Total	2,330,000	100.0

RECENT DEVELOPMENTS: For the year ended 12/31/00, the Company reported a loss of $166.0 million, before an accounting charge, versus net income of $197.0 million a year earlier. The 1999 results included a one-time pre-tax gain of $274.0 million from the sale of an investment. Total operating revenues were up 7.8% to $9.27 billion from $8.60 billion the prior year. Operating loss was $53.0 million versus operating income of $136.0 million the year before. US Airways' passenger load factor, or percentage of seats filled, improved to 70.3% versus 69.9% in 1999.

PROSPECTS: The Company is experiencing weakness in business travel bookings, reflecting slowing economic conditions in the U.S. and declining consumer confidence levels. In addition, increased competition from both lower cost and large network airlines in the eastern U.S. are negatively affecting US Airways' revenue growth. Meanwhile, U is continuing to work closely with the U.S. Department of Justice in an effort to complete its pending merger with UAL Corporation. On 1/12/01, the transaction was approved by the European Commission.

BUSINESS

US AIRWAYS GROUP, INC. (formerly USAir Group, Inc.) is the holding company for US Airways, which operates 417 aircraft that serve over 107 airports in the continental United States, Canada, Mexico, France, Germany, Italy, Spain, the United Kingdom and the Caribbean. Major hubs are located in Charlotte, Philadelphia and Pittsburgh. The Company also owns Allegheny Airlines, Piedmont Airlines, PSA Airlines, and other aviation subsidiaries. On 12/30/97, US Airways purchased Shuttle, Inc., which focuses on commuter travel, with many daily roundtrips from New York to Boston and Washington D.C. US Airways also launched a low-fare carrier, MetroJet, on 6/1/98.

ANNUAL FINANCIAL DATA

	12/31/00	12/31/99	12/31/98	12/31/97	12/31/96	12/31/95	12/31/94
Earnings Per Share	[3] **d2.47**	[1] **2.64**	**5.60**	[1] **9.87**	[2] **2.69**	[1] **0.55**	[1] **d12.73**
Cash Flow Per Share	**2.39**	**7.59**	**8.54**	**12.93**	**7.23**	**5.75**	**d6.37**
INCOME STATEMENT (IN MILLIONS):							
Total Revenues	9,269.0	8,595.0	8,688.0	8,513.8	8,142.0	7,474.3	6,997.2
Costs & Expenses	8,996.0	8,090.0	7,384.0	7,556.7	7,417.0	6,828.0	7,107.4
Depreciation & Amort.	326.0	369.0	290.0	372.8	288.0	324.6	381.2
Operating Income	d53.0	136.0	1,014.0	584.3	437.0	321.7	d491.4
Net Interest Inc./(Exp.)	d142.0	d89.0	d109.0	d135.3	d184.0	d242.2	d243.2
Income Before Income Taxes	d223.0	345.0	902.0	672.0	275.0	128.3	d684.9
Income Taxes	cr57.0	148.0	364.0	cr352.7	12.0	9.0	...
Equity Earnings/Minority Int.	...	...	1.0	30.6	37.0	34.5	26.5
Net Income	[3] d166.0	[1] 197.0	538.0	[1] 1,024.7	[2] 263.0	[1] 119.3	[1] d684.9
Cash Flow	160.0	566.0	822.0	1,334.3	463.0	359.0	d381.8
Average Shs. Outstg. (000)	66,855	74,603	96,211	103,180	64,021	62,430	59,915
BALANCE SHEET (IN MILLIONS):							
Cash & Cash Equivalents	1,316.0	870.0	1,210.0	1,964.3	1,586.8	901.7	451.7
Total Current Assets	2,592.0	2,096.0	2,364.0	2,777.4	2,310.2	1,583.1	1,116.5
Net Property	4,989.0	4,049.0	3,660.0	3,725.1	3,918.0	4,041.4	4,331.8
Total Assets	9,127.0	7,685.0	7,870.0	8,372.4	7,531.4	6,955.0	6,808.0
Total Current Liabilities	2,918.0	2,501.0	2,269.0	2,528.3	2,848.7	2,484.7	2,260.1
Long-Term Obligations	2,688.0	2,113.0	1,955.0	2,425.8	2,615.8	2,717.1	2,895.4
Net Stockholders' Equity	d358.0	d117.0	593.0	725.3	d584.4	d835.8	d896.9
Net Working Capital	d326.0	d405.0	95.0	249.1	d538.5	d901.6	d1,143.5
Year-end Shs. Outstg. (000)	67,006	81,819	83,755	91,442	64,306	63,449	61,088
STATISTICAL RECORD:							
Operating Profit Margin %	...	1.6	11.7	6.9	5.4	4.3	...
Net Profit Margin %	...	2.3	6.2	12.0	3.2	1.6	...
Return on Equity %	...	...	90.7	141.3	...	...	...
Return on Assets %	...	2.6	6.8	12.2	3.5	1.7	...
Debt/Total Assets %	29.5	27.5	24.8	29.0	34.7	39.1	42.5
Price Range	51.50-17.44	64.00-24.13	83.25-34.75	65.75-19.25	25.88-11.75	15.88-4.25	15.38-3.88
P/E Ratio	...	24.2-9.1	14.9-6.2	6.7-2.0	9.6-4.4	28.9-7.7	...

Statistics are as originally reported. [1] Incl. $181.0 mil non-recur. after-tax gain, 1999; $394.9 mil net gain, 1997; $4.1 mil non-recur. gain, 1995; & $226.1 mil chg., 1994. [2] Incl. approx. $163.1 mil in expenses & a $29.5 mil non-recur. gain. [3] Bef. $103.0 mil ($1.55/sh.) acctg. chg.

OFFICERS:
S. M. Wolf, Chmn.
R. Gangwal, Pres., C.E.O.
T. A. Mutryn, Sr. V.P., C.F.O.

INVESTOR CONTACT: Juliette C. Heintze, V.P., Investor Relations, (703) 872-5306

PRINCIPAL OFFICE: 2345 Crystal Dr., Arlington, VA 22227

TELEPHONE NUMBER: (703) 872-7000
FAX: (703) 418-7098
WEB: www.usairways.com

NO. OF EMPLOYEES: 48,100

SHAREHOLDERS: 23,000

ANNUAL MEETING: In May

INCORPORATED: DE, Feb., 1983

INSTITUTIONAL HOLDINGS:
No. of Institutions: 170
Shares Held: 38,193,428
% Held: 57.0

INDUSTRY: Air transportation, scheduled (SIC: 4512)

TRANSFER AGENT(S): The Bank of New York, New York, NY

NYSE SYMBOL USB
Rec. Pr. 22.30 (5/31/01)

U.S. BANCORP

YIELD	3.4%
P/E RATIO	10.5

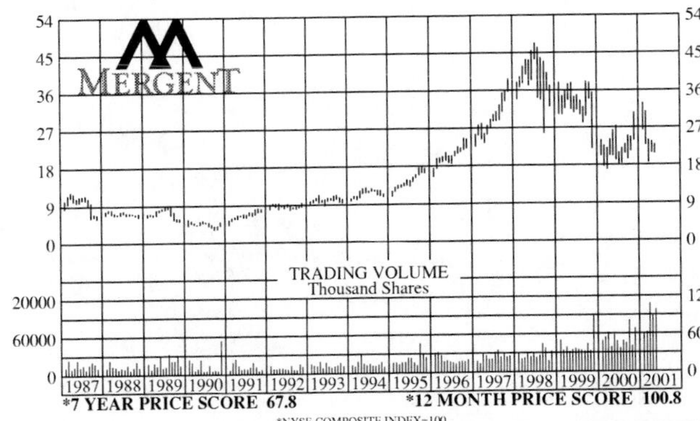

*7 YEAR PRICE SCORE 67.8 *12 MONTH PRICE SCORE 100.8

*NYSE COMPOSITE INDEX=100

INTERIM EARNINGS (Per Share):

Qtr.	Mar.	June	Sept.	Dec.
1997	0.39	0.41	d0.07	0.39
1998	0.44	0.43	0.44	0.48
1999	0.50	0.51	0.54	0.50
2000	0.51	0.52	0.54	0.56

INTERIM DIVIDENDS (Per Share):

Amt.	Decl.	Ex.	Rec.	Pay.
0.188Q	2/27/01	3/28/01	3/30/01	4/16/01

Indicated div.: $0.75 (Div. Reinv. Plan)

CAPITALIZATION (12/31/00):

	($000)	(%)
Total Deposits	53,257,000	66.2
Long-Term Debt	18,566,000	23.1
Common & Surplus	8,640,000	10.7
Total	80,463,000	100.0

RECENT DEVELOPMENTS: For the year ended 12/31/00, net income advanced 5.7% to $1.59 billion from $1.51 billion in 1999. Results for 2000 and 1999 included pre-tax merger-related charges of $61.3 million and $62.4 million, respectively. Net interest income increased 6.5% to $3.47 billion. Provision for credit losses grew 26.2% to $670.0 million. Total non-interest income improved 18.1% to $3.26 billion.

PROSPECTS: On 2/27/01, the Company acquired Firstar Corporation in a transaction valued at approximately $21.20 billion. As a result, USB is the eighth largest bank holding company in the U.S., with assets under management of $145.00 billion. On 5/7/01, USB signed a definitive agreement to acquire NOVA Corporation in a transaction valued at approximately $2.10 billion. NOVA specializes in the payment processing business.

BUSINESS

U.S. BANCORP, with over $160.00 billion in assets as of 2/27/01, is the eighth largest banking services holding company in the U.S. The Company operates 2,239 banking offices, approximately 5,200 branded ATMs, and provides a comprehensive line of banking, brokerage, insurance, investment, mortgage, trust and payments services and products to consumers, businesses and institutions throughout the Midwest and West. U.S. Bancorp is the parent company of Firstar Banks and U.S. Bank. On 9/20/99, USB completed the acquisition of Mercantile Bancorporation, Inc. On 2/27/01, USB completed the acquisition of Firstar Corporation.

LOAN DISTRIBUTION

(12/31/00)	($000)	(%)
Commercial	29,920,000	43.3
Real Est-Commercial Mtge	10,208,000	14.8
Real Estate-Construction	4,443,000	6.4
Lease Financing	4,096,000	5.9
Total Consumer	20,424,000	29.6
Total Loans	69,091,000	100.0

ANNUAL FINANCIAL DATA

	12/31/00	12/31/99	12/31/98	[1] 12/31/97	12/31/96	12/31/95	12/31/94
Earnings Per Share	[2] 2.13	[2] 2.06	[2] 1.78	[2][3] 1.11	[2][3] 1.78	[4] 1.40	[2][5] 0.74
Tang. Book Val. Per Share	7.11	6.07	5.50	5.96	7.55	6.86	6.21
INCOME STATEMENT (IN MILLIONS):							
Total Interest Income	6,707.1	5,676.7	5,407.4	5,293.6	2,653.9	2,545.2	2,288.1
Total Interest Expense	3,235.8	2,416.0	2,346.8	2,245.5	1,120.9	1,105.0	868.7
Net Interest Income	3,471.3	3,260.7	3,060.6	3,048.1	1,533.0	1,440.2	1,419.4
Provision for Loan Losses	670.0	531.0	379.0	460.3	136.0	115.0	123.6
Non-Interest Income	3,258.4	2,758.7	2,256.6	1,615.2	1,185.7	783.1	558.9
Non-Interest Expense	3,598.4	3,126.9	2,844.3	2,812.3	1,388.1	1,205.9	1,349.4
Income Before Taxes	2,461.3	2,361.5	2,093.9	1,390.7	1,194.6	902.4	505.3
Net Income	[2] 1,592.0	[2] 1,506.5	[2] 1,327.4	[2][3] 838.5	[2][3] 739.8	[4] 568.1	[2][5] 313.5
Average Shs. Outstg. (000)	747,900	732,990	744,178	742,914	412,248	401,808	408,825
BALANCE SHEET (IN MILLIONS):							
Cash & Due from Banks	4,142.0	4,036.0	4,772.0	4,739.0	2,413.0	1,837.0	1,707.0
Securities Avail. for Sale	5,035.0	5,488.0	6,114.0	7,080.0	3,701.0	3,342.0	5,262.0
Total Loans & Leases	69,091.0	62,885.0	59,122.0	54,708.0	27,128.0	26,400.0	24,550.0
Allowance for Credit Losses	1,067.0	995.0	1,001.0	1,009.0	517.0	474.0	475.0
Net Loans & Leases	68,024.0	61,890.0	58,121.0	53,699.0	26,611.0	25,926.0	24,075.0
Total Assets	87,336.0	81,530.0	76,438.0	71,295.0	36,489.0	33,874.0	34,128.0
Total Deposits	53,257.0	51,530.0	50,034.0	49,027.0	24,379.0	22,514.0	24,256.0
Long-Term Obligations	18,566.0	16,563.0	13,781.0	10,247.0	3,553.0	3,201.0	2,684.0
Total Liabilities	78,696.0	73,892.0	70,468.0	65,405.0	33,436.0	31,149.0	31,516.0
Net Stockholders' Equity	8,640.0	7,638.0	5,970.0	5,890.0	3,053.0	2,725.0	2,612.0
Year-end Shs. Outstg. (000)	752,060	753,330	725,762	739,932	404,610	382,005	401,496
STATISTICAL RECORD:							
Return on Equity %	18.4	19.7	22.2	14.2	24.2	20.8	12.0
Return on Assets %	1.8	1.8	1.7	1.2	2.0	1.7	0.9
Equity/Assets %	9.9	9.4	7.8	8.3	8.4	8.0	7.7
Non-Int. Exp./Tot. Inc. %	53.5	51.9	53.5	60.3	51.1	54.2	68.2
Price Range	30.50-16.88	38.06-21.88	47.31-25.63	38.88-22.50	24.67-15.33	17.92-10.88	13.00-9.79
P/E Ratio	14.3-7.9	18.5-10.6	26.6-14.4	35.0-20.3	13.9-8.6	12.8-7.8	17.6-13.3

Statistics are as originally reported. [1] Reflects the acq. of Business and Professional Bank of Sacramento, CA on 4/30/97. [2] Incl. pre-tax merger-rel. chrgs. of $61.3 mill., 2000; $62.4 mill., 1999; $216.5 mill., 1998; $511.6 mill., 1997; $69.9 mill., 1996; $31.0 mill., 1995; $122.7 mill., 1994. [3] Incl. a pre-tax gain fr. the sale of mtge. bank opers. of $9.4 mil., 1997; $45.8 mill., 1996. [4] Incl. a pre-tax gain fr. the sale of branches of $31.0 mill. [5] Bef. disc. opers. loss of $8.5 mill.

OFFICERS:
J. F. Grundhofer, Chmn., C.E.O.
D. M. Moffett, Vice-Chmn., C.F.O.
J. A. Grundhofer, Pres., C.E.O.

INVESTOR CONTACT: John R. Danielson, Senior Vice President of Investor & Corporate Relations, (612) 973-2261

PRINCIPAL OFFICE: First Bank Place, 601 Second Avenue South, Minneapolis, MN 55402-4302

TELEPHONE NUMBER: (612) 973-1111
FAX: (612) 370-4352
WEB: www.usbank.com

NO. OF EMPLOYEES: 28,949 (avg.)

SHAREHOLDERS: 47,094

ANNUAL MEETING: In Apr.

INCORPORATED: DE, Apr., 1929

INSTITUTIONAL HOLDINGS:
No. of Institutions: 617
Shares Held: 940,478,253
% Held: 0.0

INDUSTRY: National commercial banks (SIC: 6021)

TRANSFER AGENT(S): First Chicago Trust Company of New York, Jersey City, NJ

NYSE SYMBOL SLM
Rec. Pr. 71.10 (4/30/01)

USA EDUCATION, INC.

YIELD 1.0%
P/E RATIO 25.7

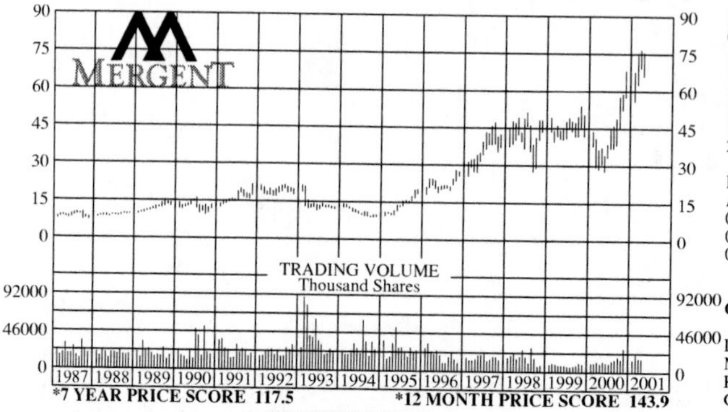

MERGENT

TRADING VOLUME
Thousand Shares

1987 1988 1989 1990 1991 1992 1993 1994 1995 1996 1997 1998 1999 2000 2001

***7 YEAR PRICE SCORE 117.5** ***12 MONTH PRICE SCORE 143.9**

*NYSE COMPOSITE INDEX=100

INTERIM EARNINGS (Per Share):

Qtr.	Mar.	June	Sept.	Dec.
1995	0.33	0.34	0.35	0.48
1996	0.50	0.51	0.51	0.57
1997	0.62	0.63	0.79	0.75
1998	0.80	0.84	0.64	0.66
1999	0.69	0.76	0.75	0.87
2000	0.93	0.73	0.55	0.56

INTERIM DIVIDENDS (Per Share):

Amt.	Decl.	Ex.	Rec.	Pay.
0.175Q	11/16/00	11/29/00	12/01/00	12/15/00
0.175Q	1/25/01	2/28/01	3/02/01	3/16/01
0.175Q	5/10/01	5/30/01	6/01/01	6/15/01

Indicated div.: $0.70

CAPITALIZATION (12/31/00):

	($000)	(%)
Long-Term Debt	14,910,939	90.1
Minority Interest	213,883	1.3
Preferred Stock	165,000	1.0
Common & Surplus	1,250,336	7.6
Total	16,540,158	100.0

RECENT DEVELOPMENTS: For the year ended 12/31/00, net income declined 7.2% to $465.0 million from $500.8 million in 1999. Results for 2000 included a one-time integration charge of $53.0 million. Results for 2000 and 1999 included gains on student loan securitizations of $91.8 million and $35.3 million, respectively, and gains on sales of securities of $18.6 million and $15.8 million, respectively. Total interest income rose 19.3% to $3.48 billion; however, net interest income fell 7.5% to $641.8 million.

PROSPECTS: Near-term prospects are favorable, reflecting the expected continued benefits of the Company's recent acquisitions of Student Loan Funding Resources, Inc. and USA Group, which were completed on 7/7/00 and 7/31/00, respectively. Going forward, these acquisitions should significantly increase the Company's managed portfolio, help to further diversify SLM's revenues sources and lead to increased market share.

BUSINESS

USA EDUCATION, INC. (formerly SLM Holding Corporation) is a state-chartered stockholder-owned corporation which was created to provide liquidity, primarily through instituting a secondary market and warehousing facilities for insured student loans made under state-sponsored student loan programs. These programs include the Guaranteed Student Loan Program, which encompasses Stafford loans, "PLUS" loans and Supplemental Loans for Students loans, as well as the Health Education Assistance Loan Program. SLM provides financial services to financial institutions, educational institutions, state agencies, and students. The services include loan purchases, funding and operational support. On 7/7/00, the Company acquired Student Loan Funding Resources, Inc. On 7/31/00, the Company completed the purchase of USA Group's guarantee servicing, student loan servicing and secondary market operations for $770.0 million in cash and stock.

ANNUAL FINANCIAL DATA

	12/31/00	12/31/99	12/31/98	12/31/97	12/31/96	12/31/95	12/31/94
Earnings Per Share	**[3] 2.76**	**3.06**	**2.95**	**[2] 2.80**	**[2] 2.13**	**[1][2] 2.14**	**[2] 2.01**
Tang. Book Val. Per Share	**7.62**	**4.29**	**3.98**	**3.67**	**3.63**	**6.01**	**4.06**
Dividends Per Share	**0.17**	...	...	...	...	...	...
Dividend Payout %	**6.3**	...	...	...	...	...	...
INCOME STATEMENT (IN MILLIONS):							
Total Interest Income	3,478.7	2,808.6	2,576.3	3,283.8	3,449.3	3,693.7	2,851.6
Total Interest Expense	2,836.9	2,114.8	1,925.0	2,526.2	2,582.9	3,020.6	2,142.5
Net Interest Income	641.8	693.8	651.3	757.7	866.4	673.0	709.1
Provision for Loan Losses	32.1	34.4	28.6	...	...	...	...
Non-Interest Income	687.6	450.8	477.0	500.9	146.9	...	...
Non-Interest Expense	585.7	358.6	360.9	493.8	405.7	160.6	130.4
Income Before Taxes	711.6	751.7	750.1	764.8	607.7	512.5	578.6
Equity Earnings/Minority Int.	d10.7	d10.7	d10.7	d10.7	d10.7	...	...
Net Income	[3] 465.0	500.8	490.1	[2] 511.2	[2] 413.5	[1][2] 371.2	[2] 412.1
Average Shs. Outstg. (000)	164,355	163,158	170,066	182,941	194,466	...	...
BALANCE SHEET (IN MILLIONS):							
Total Loans & Leases	39,485.8	35,879.3	31,005.6	32,764.3	38,016.3	39,513.5	39,351.2
Net Loans & Leases	39,485.8	35,879.3	31,005.6	32,764.3	38,016.3	39,513.5	39,351.2
Total Assets	48,791.8	44,024.8	37,210.0	39,908.8	47,629.9	50,001.7	53,361.3
Long-Term Obligations	14,910.9	4,496.3	8,810.6	14,541.3	22,606.2	30,082.6	34,319.4
Total Liabilities	47,376.5	43,183.9	36,556.4	39,234.2	46,795.9	48,920.5	51,489.6
Net Stockholders' Equity	1,415.3	840.9	653.6	674.6	833.9	1,081.2	1,471.2
Year-end Shs. Outstg. (000)	164,145	157,577	164,127	183,633	229,934	144,265	309,610
STATISTICAL RECORD:							
Return on Equity %	32.9	59.6	75.0	75.8	49.6	34.3	28.0
Return on Assets %	1.0	1.1	1.3	1.3	0.9	0.7	0.8
Equity/Assets %	2.9	1.9	1.8	1.7	1.8	2.2	2.8
Non-Int. Exp./Tot. Inc. %	44.1	31.3	32.0	39.2	40.0	23.9	18.4
Price Range	68.25-27.81	53.94-39.50	51.38-27.50	47.18-25.43	28.07-18.07	20.25-9.39	14.25-8.93
P/E Ratio	24.7-10.1	17.6-12.9	17.4-9.3	16.8-9.1	13.2-8.5	9.5-4.4	7.1-4.4
Average Yield %	0.4	...	...	...	...	...	...

Statistics are as originally reported. Adj. for stk split: 7-for-2, 1/98 [1] Bef. acctg. change chrg. of $130.1 mill. [2] Bef. chrgs. on debt extinguished, $3.3 mill., 1997; $4.8 mill., 1996; $4.9 mill., 1995;$9.3 mill., 1994; $137.4 mill., 1993; $93.1 mill., 1992 [3] Incl. one-time integration chrg. $53.0 mill

OFFICERS:
E. A. Fox, Chmn.
A. L. Lord, C.E.O.
J. F. Remondi, Exec. V.P., C.F.O.

INVESTOR CONTACT: Jefffrey R. Heinz, Asst. V.P., (703) 810-7743

PRINCIPAL OFFICE: 11600 Sallie Mae Drive, Reston, VA 20193

TELEPHONE NUMBER: (703) 810-3000
WEB: www.salliemae.com

NO. OF EMPLOYEES: 6,712 (avg.)

SHAREHOLDERS: 612 (approx.)

ANNUAL MEETING: In May

INCORPORATED: DE, Feb., 1997

INSTITUTIONAL HOLDINGS:
No. of Institutions: 325
Shares Held: 152,374,238
% Held: 93.5

INDUSTRY: Personal credit institutions (SIC: 6141)

TRANSFER AGENT(S): Mellon Investor Services, New York, NY

NYSE SYMBOL USG
Rec. Pr. 8.36 (5/31/01)

USG CORP.

YIELD 1.2%
P/E RATIO . . .

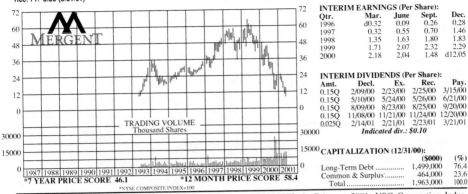

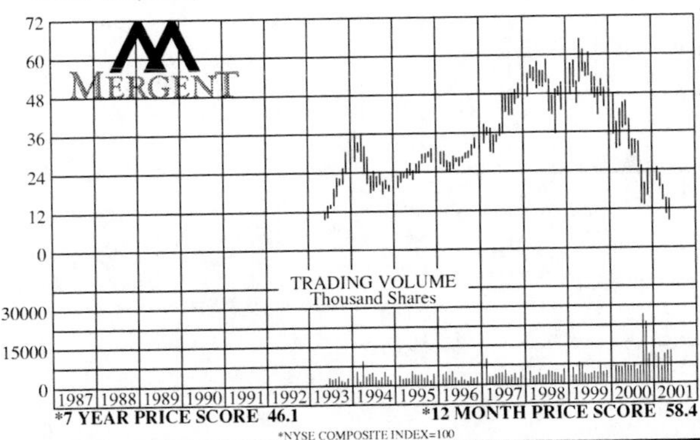

INTERIM EARNINGS (Per Share):

Qtr.	Mar.	June	Sept.	Dec.
1996	d0.32	0.09	0.26	0.28
1997	0.32	0.55	0.70	1.46
1998	1.35	1.63	1.80	1.83
1999	1.71	2.07	2.32	2.29
2000	2.18	2.04	1.48	d12.05

INTERIM DIVIDENDS (Per Share):

Amt.	Decl.	Ex.	Rec.	Pay.
0.15Q	2/09/00	2/23/00	2/25/00	3/15/00
0.15Q	5/10/00	5/24/00	5/26/00	6/21/00
0.15Q	8/09/00	8/23/00	8/25/00	9/20/00
0.15Q	11/08/00	11/21/00	11/24/00	12/20/00
0.025Q	2/14/01	2/21/01	2/23/01	3/21/01

Indicated div.: $0.10

CAPITALIZATION (12/31/00):

	($000)	(%)
Long-Term Debt	1,499,000	76.4
Common & Surplus	464,000	23.6
Total	1,963,000	100.0

RECENT DEVELOPMENTS: For the year ended 12/31/00, USG reported a net loss of $259.0 million from net income of $421.0 million in 1999. Results for 2000 included a nonrecurring charge of $900.0 million. The decline in earnings was also attributed to significantly lower market prices for gypsum wallboard and higher production costs associated with increased energy prices. Net sales were $3.78 billion, down slightly from $3.81 billion. Comparisons were made with restated 1999 results.

PROSPECTS: In February 2001, USG Corporation Industrial Products, a division of USG, formed a joint venture with Bindan Corporation to market and distribute a wide range of industrial products in architectural, road repair and statuary applications. On 1/11/01, USG announced a restructuring, which included a workforce reduction and the closing of additional high-cost wallboard capacity. Annual savings from restructuring initiatives are estimated at $40.0 million.

BUSINESS

USG CORPORATION is a manufacturer and distributor of building materials producing a wide range of products for use in new residential, new nonresidential and repair and remodel construction, as well as products used in certain industrial processes. USG's operations are organized into three operating segments: North American Gypsum, Worldwide Ceilings and Building Products Distribution. North American Gypsum, which manufactures and markets gypsum and related products in the United States, Canada and Mexico, includes U.S. Gypsum in the United States, the gypsum business of CGC, Inc. in Canada, and Yeso Panamericano S.A. de C.V. in Mexico. Worldwide Ceilings, which manufactures and markets interior systems products worldwide, includes USG Interiors, Inc., the international interior systems business managed as USG International, and the ceilings business of CGC. Building Products Distribution consists of L&W Supply.

REVENUES

(12/31/00)	($000)	(%)
North American Gypsum	2,298,000,000	52.5
Worldwide Ceilings	705,000,000	16.1
Building Products Distribution	1,373,000,000	31.4
Total	4,376,000,000	100

ANNUAL FINANCIAL DATA

	12/31/00	12/31/99	12/31/98	12/31/97	12/31/96	12/31/95	12/31/94
Earnings Per Share	**[1] d5.62**	**8.39**	**6.61**	**3.03**	**0.31**	**d0.71**	**d2.14**
Cash Flow Per Share	**d3.55**	**10.20**	**8.26**	**7.04**	**5.19**	. . .	. . .
Tang. Book Val. Per Share	**10.69**	**17.74**	**10.57**	**3.13**	. . .	. . .	. . .
Dividends Per Share	**0.60**	**0.45**	**0.11**	. . .	. . .	. . .	. . .
Dividend Payout %	. . .	**5.4**	**1.7**	. . .	. . .	. . .	. . .
INCOME STATEMENT (IN MILLIONS):							
Total Revenues	3,781.0	3,600.0	3,130.0	2,874.0	2,590.0	2,444.0	2,290.0
Costs & Expenses	4,054.0	2,779.0	2,464.0	2,298.0	2,148.0	2,018.0	1,933.0
Depreciation & Amort.	96.0	91.0	81.0	197.0	234.0	236.0	253.0
Operating Income	d369.0	730.0	585.0	379.0	208.0	190.0	104.0
Net Interest Inc./(Exp.)	d47.0	d43.0	d48.0	d57.0	d73.0	d93.0	d139.0
Income Before Income Taxes	d420.0	684.0	534.0	320.0	132.0	65.0	d38.0
Income Taxes	cr161.0	263.0	202.0	172.0	117.0	97.0	54.0
Net Income	[1] d259.0	421.0	332.0	148.0	15.0	d32.0	d92.0
Cash Flow	d163.0	512.0	413.0	345.0	249.0	204.0	161.0
Average Shs. Outstg. (000)	45,972	50,216	50,000	49,000	47,510	45,120	43,243
BALANCE SHEET (IN MILLIONS):							
Cash & Cash Equivalents	70.0	197.0	152.0	72.0	44.0	70.0	197.0
Total Current Assets	876.0	873.0	797.0	640.0	503.0	491.0	644.0
Net Property	1,830.0	1,568.0	1,214.0	982.0	887.0	842.0	755.0
Total Assets	3,214.0	2,773.0	2,357.0	1,926.0	1,818.0	1,890.0	2,124.0
Total Current Liabilities	896.0	491.0	429.0	376.0	395.0	383.0	455.0
Long-Term Obligations	1,499.0	577.0	561.0	610.0	706.0	865.0	1,077.0
Net Stockholders' Equity	464.0	867.0	518.0	147.0	d23.0	d37.0	d8.0
Net Working Capital	d20.0	382.0	368.0	264.0	108.0	108.0	189.0
Year-end Shs. Outstg. (000)	43,401	48,860	49,000	47,000	45,000	45,000	45,000
STATISTICAL RECORD:							
Operating Profit Margin %	. . .	20.3	18.7	13.2	8.0	7.8	4.5
Net Profit Margin %	. . .	11.7	10.6	5.1	0.6	. . .	. . .
Return on Equity %	. . .	48.6	64.1	100.7	. . .	. . .	. . .
Return on Assets %	. . .	15.2	14.1	7.7	0.8	. . .	. . .
Debt/Total Assets %	46.6	20.8	23.8	31.7	38.8	45.8	50.7
Price Range	48.00-13.13	65.00-41.13	58.75-35.50	51.50-29.63	34.50-24.00	31.38-19.25	36.00-17.25
P/E Ratio	. . .	7.7-4.9	8.9-5.4	17.0-9.8	111.3-77.4	. . .	. . .
Average Yield %	2.0	0.8	0.2	. . .	. . .	. . .	. . .

Statistics are as originally reported. [1] Incl. pre-tax prov. for asbestos claims chrg. of $850.0 mill. & prov. for restruct. exp. of $50.0 mill.

OFFICERS:
W. C. Foote, Chmn., Pres., C.E.O.
P. J. O'Bryan, Vice-Chmn.
R. H. Fleming, Exec. V.P., C.F.O.
D. R. Lowes, V.P., Treas.

INVESTOR CONTACT: Investor Relations, (312) 606-4125

PRINCIPAL OFFICE: 125 S. Franklin St., Chicago, IL 60606-4678

TELEPHONE NUMBER: (312) 606-4000
FAX: (312) 606-4093
WEB: www.usgcorp.com

NO. OF EMPLOYEES: 14,900 (avg.)

SHAREHOLDERS: 4,773

ANNUAL MEETING: In May

INCORPORATED: DE, Oct., 1984

INSTITUTIONAL HOLDINGS:
No. of Institutions: 145
Shares Held: 32,179,893
% Held: 74.1

INDUSTRY: Gypsum products (SIC: 3275)

TRANSFER AGENT(S): Computershare Investor Services, Chicago, IL

NYSE SYMBOL UST
Rec. Pr. 30.10 (4/30/01)

UST, INC.

YIELD 6.1%
P/E RATIO 11.1

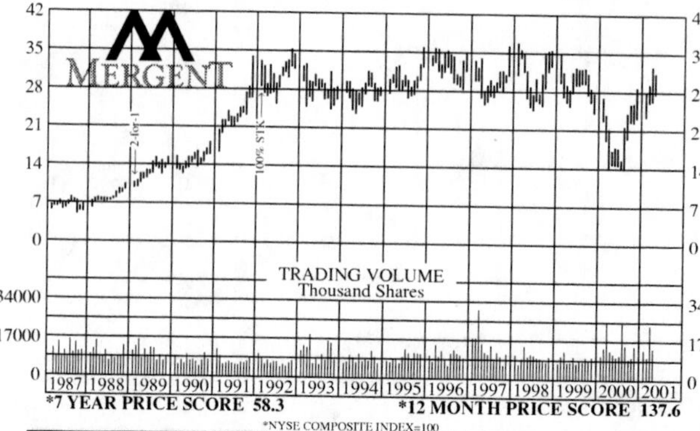

INTERIM EARNINGS (Per Share):

Qtr.	Mar.	June	Sept.	Dec.
1996	0.55	0.62	0.65	0.61
1997	0.55	0.64	0.62	0.57
1998	0.60	0.64	0.63	0.57
1999	0.60	0.70	0.69	0.70
2000	0.62	0.69	0.69	0.70

INTERIM DIVIDENDS (Per Share):

Amt.	Decl.	Ex.	Rec.	Pay.
0.44Q	5/01/00	5/31/00	6/02/00	6/15/00
0.44Q	7/28/00	8/30/00	9/01/00	9/15/00
0.44Q	10/26/00	11/29/00	12/01/00	12/15/00
0.46Q	2/15/01	3/13/01	3/15/01	3/30/01
0.46Q	5/01/01	6/13/01	6/15/01	6/29/01

Indicated div.: $1.84 (Div. Reinv. Plan)

CAPITALIZATION (12/31/00):

	($000)	(%)
Long-Term Debt	869,175	65.5
Deferred Income Tax	186,559	14.1
Common & Surplus	270,572	20.4
Total	1,326,306	100.0

RECENT DEVELOPMENTS: For the year ended 12/31/00, net earnings fell 5.8% to $441.9 million versus $469.3 million a year earlier. Net sales rose 2.3% to $1.55 billion. Tobacco segment sales gained 2.6% to $1.34 billion, while operating income fell 1.1% to $768.8 million. Moist smokeless tobacco net unit volume was unchanged at 633.0 million cans; however, premium can sales fell 3.2% reflecting the SKOAL LONG CUT value conversion from 1.0 oz. to 1.2 oz. of tobacco per can.

PROSPECTS: For 2001, UST continues to project an increase of 10.0% for net sales, net earnings and earnings per share. Contributing factors may include improved can sale comparisons of SKOAL LONG CUT after the first quarter, as the increased value conversion is lapped. In addition, COPENHAGEN BLACK, a bourbon-flavored product, will roll-out nationally and ROOSTER and RED SEAL line extensions will launch regionally. Fiscal 2001 also includes an extra shipping day that could amount to 10.0 million cans.

BUSINESS

UST INC. is a holding company, and through its subsidiaries is a manufacturer of smokeless tobacco products with COPENHAGEN, COPENHAGEN LONG CUT, SKOAL, SKOAL LONG CUT, SKOAL BANDITS, ROOSTER and RED SEAL as principal brands. Other consumer products made and marketed by UST subsidiaries include premium wines sold nationally under the CHATEAU STE. MICHELLE, COLUMBIA CREST and VILLA MT. EDEN labels, as well as sparkling wine produced under the DOMAINE STE. MICHELLE label and premium cigars including DON THOMAS, DON THOMAS SPECIAL EDITION, ASTRAL and HABANO PRIMERO. UST also produces and markets beers under the brand BERT GRANT'S ALE.

REVENUES

(12/31/2000)	($000)	(%)
Smokeles Tobacco	1,343,779	86.8
Wine	174,472	11.3
All Other	29,393	1.9
Total	1,547,644	100.0

ANNUAL FINANCIAL DATA

	12/31/00	12/31/99	12/31/98	12/31/97	12/31/96	12/31/95	12/31/94
Earnings Per Share	**2.70**	**[2] 2.68**	**[3] 2.44**	**[1] 2.37**	**2.48**	**2.16**	**1.87**
Cash Flow Per Share	**2.94**	**2.89**	**2.61**	**2.53**	**2.63**	**2.30**	**2.00**
Tang. Book Val. Per Share	**1.32**	**0.96**	**2.25**	**2.37**	**1.53**	**1.63**	**1.84**
Dividends Per Share	**1.76**	**1.68**	**1.62**	**1.62**	**1.48**	**1.30**	**1.12**
Dividend Payout %	**65.2**	**62.7**	**66.4**	**68.4**	**59.7**	**60.2**	**59.9**
INCOME STATEMENT (IN MILLIONS):							
Total Revenues	1,547.6	1,512.3	1,423.2	1,401.7	1,371.7	1,325.4	1,223.0
Costs & Expenses	755.3	698.8	659.2	659.9	592.5	588.5	554.1
Depreciation & Amort.	39.6	37.0	31.7	30.5	28.3	29.1	28.2
Operating Income	752.7	776.5	732.3	711.3	750.9	707.8	640.7
Net Interest Inc./(Exp.)	d34.3	d13.5	2.2	d7.5	d6.4	d3.2	d0.1
Income Before Income Taxes	718.4	762.9	734.5	703.9	744.5	704.6	640.6
Income Taxes	276.5	293.7	279.2	264.7	280.5	274.8	253.1
Net Income	441.9	[2] 469.3	[3] 455.3	[1] 439.1	464.0	429.8	387.5
Cash Flow	481.5	506.3	487.0	469.6	492.3	458.9	415.7
Average Shs. Outstg. (000)	163,506	175,114	186,880	185,602	187,386	199,246	207,504
BALANCE SHEET (IN MILLIONS):							
Cash & Cash Equivalents	96.0	75.0	33.2	6.9	54.5	69.4	50.7
Total Current Assets	691.4	580.0	507.2	441.8	450.6	425.6	381.9
Net Property	358.6	361.9	338.7	326.7	300.9	294.8	305.9
Total Assets	1,646.4	1,015.6	913.3	826.7	807.4	784.8	741.2
Total Current Liabilities	169.6	261.3	197.3	166.5	306.6	280.7	160.8
Long-Term Obligations	869.2	411.0	100.0	100.0	100.0	100.0	125.0
Net Stockholders' Equity	270.6	200.8	468.3	437.9	282.0	293.6	361.7
Net Working Capital	521.8	318.7	309.9	275.3	144.0	144.8	221.2
Year-end Shs. Outstg. (000)	204,743	208,937	208,096	184,789	183,856	180,526	196,110
STATISTICAL RECORD:							
Operating Profit Margin %	48.6	51.3	51.5	50.7	54.7	53.4	52.4
Net Profit Margin %	28.6	31.0	32.0	31.3	33.8	32.4	31.7
Return on Equity %	163.3	233.7	97.2	100.3	164.5	146.4	107.1
Return on Assets %	26.8	46.2	49.8	53.1	57.5	54.8	52.3
Debt/Total Assets %	52.8	40.5	10.9	12.1	12.4	12.7	16.9
Price Range	28.88-13.88	34.94-24.06	36.88-24.56	36.31-25.50	35.88-28.25	36.00-26.50	31.50-23.63
P/E Ratio	10.7-5.1	13.0-9.0	15.1-10.1	15.3-10.8	14.5-11.4	16.7-12.3	16.8-12.6
Average Yield %	8.2	5.7	5.3	5.2	4.6	4.2	4.1

Statistics are as originally reported. [1] Incl. non-recurr. chrg. of $5.0 mill. [2] Incl. net chrg. of $9.4 mill. [3] Incl. net chrg. of $31.7 mill.

OFFICERS:
V. A. Gierer Jr., Chmn., Pres., C.E.O.
R. T. D'Alessandro, Sr. V.P., C.F.O.
R. H. Verheij, Exec. V.P., Gen. Couns.

INVESTOR CONTACT: Investor Relations, (203) 661-1100

PRINCIPAL OFFICE: 100 West Putnam Ave., Greenwich, CT 06830

TELEPHONE NUMBER: (203) 661-1100
FAX: (203) 661-1129
WEB: www.ustshareholder.com

NO. OF EMPLOYEES: 4,855 (avg.)

SHAREHOLDERS: 8,000 (approx.)

ANNUAL MEETING: In Jan.

INCORPORATED: DE, Dec., 1986

INSTITUTIONAL HOLDINGS:
No. of Institutions: 261
Shares Held: 118,068,413
% Held: 72.5

INDUSTRY: Chewing and smoking tobacco (SIC: 2131)

TRANSFER AGENT(S): BankBoston N.A., Boston, MA

NYSE SYMBOL MRO
Rec. Pr. 32.35 (5/31/01)

USX-MARATHON GROUP

YIELD 2.8%
P/E RATIO 23.3

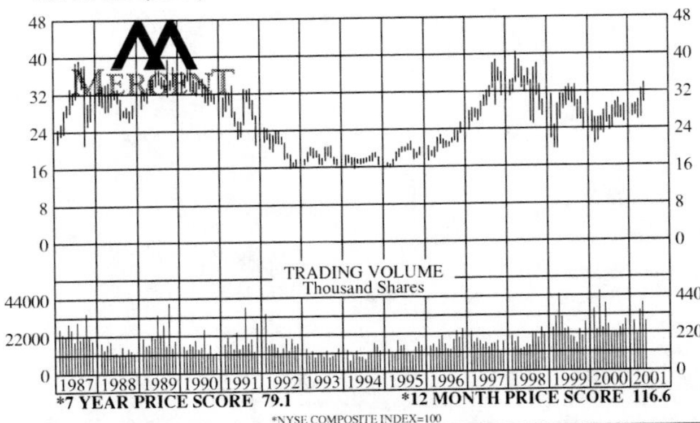

*7 YEAR PRICE SCORE 79.1 *12 MONTH PRICE SCORE 116.6
*NYSE COMPOSITE INDEX=100

INTERIM EARNINGS (Per Share):

Qtr.	Mar.	June	Sept.	Dec.
1996	0.75	0.43	0.57	0.58
1997	0.37	0.41	0.66	0.13
1998	0.63	0.56	0.17	d0.29
1999	0.38	0.43	0.74	0.55
2000	0.81	1.18	0.38	d1.00

INTERIM DIVIDENDS (Per Share):

Amt.	Decl.	Ex.	Rec.	Pay.
0.21Q	4/25/00	5/15/00	5/17/00	6/10/00
0.23Q	7/25/00	8/14/00	8/16/00	9/09/00
0.23Q	10/31/00	11/14/00	11/16/00	12/09/00
0.23Q	1/30/01	2/16/01	2/21/01	3/10/01
0.23Q	4/24/01	5/14/01	5/16/01	6/09/01

Indicated div.: $0.92 (Div. Reinv. Plan)

CAPITALIZATION (12/31/00):

	($000)	(%)
Long-Term Debt	1,937,000	19.1
Deferred Income Tax	1,354,000	13.3
Minority Interest	1,840,000	18.1
Redeemable Pfd. Stock	184,000	1.8
Common & Surplus	4,845,000	47.7
Total	10,160,001	100.0

RECENT DEVELOPMENTS: For the year ended 12/31/00, net income declined 33.9% to $432.0 million versus $654.0 million a year earlier. Results for 2000 and 1999 included after-tax net non-recurring charges of $876.0 million and $220.0 million, respectively. Total revenues rose 43.5% to $33.86 billion from $23.59 billion in 1999. The Company's operations benefited from consistently strong worldwide liquid hydrocarbon and natural gas prices combined with solid Midwest refined-product margins.

PROSPECTS: On 4/24/01, USX Corporation said that it would proceed with a reorganization plan, expected to be implemented by year end, that involves a tax-free spin-off of the steel and steel-related business of USX Corporation into a freestanding, publicly traded company to be known as United States Steel Corporation (USSC). Holders of current USX-U.S. Steel Group common stock would become holders of USSC common stock. Holders of current USX-Marathon Group common stock would become holders of Marathon Oil Company common stock.

BUSINESS

USX-MARATHON GROUP, a unit of USX Corporation, was formed as a result of USX Corp. splitting its stock into separate steel and energy securities. Shareholders received one fifth of a share of U.S. Steel and one share of Marathon Oil stock for each USX Corp. share held. Marathon's operations include worldwide exploration and production of crude oil and natural gas; domestic refining, marketing and transportation of petroleum products primarily through Marathon Ashland Petroleum LLC, owned 62% by Marathon; and other energy related businesses. In 2000, worldwide exploration and production operations contributed 13.3% of revenues; refining, marketing and transportation operations, 81.9%; and other energy related businesses, 4.8%. Net proved reserves in 2000 was: liquid hydrocarbons, 717.0 million barrels; natural gas, 3.09 trillion cubic feet. In February 2001, the Company acquired Pennaco Energy Inc. in a transaction valued at approximately $500.0 million.

BUSINESS LINE ANALYSIS

(12/31/2000)	Rev	Inc (%)
Exploration & Production	13.3	53.9
Refining, Marketing & Transporation	81.9	44.8
Other Energy Related	4.8	1.3
Total	100.0	100.0

ANNUAL FINANCIAL DATA

	12/31/00	12/31/99	12/31/98	12/31/97	12/31/96	12/31/95	12/31/94
Earnings Per Share	**[5] 1.39**	**[4] 2.11**	**[3] 1.05**	**[1] 1.58**	**[1] 2.33**	**[2] d0.31**	**1.10**
Cash Flow Per Share	**5.38**	**5.18**	**4.27**	**3.85**	**4.74**	**2.54**	**3.61**
Tang. Book Val. Per Share	**15.72**	**15.50**	**13.95**	**12.52**	**11.60**	**10.01**	**11.02**
Dividends Per Share	**0.88**	**0.84**	**0.84**	**0.76**	**0.70**	**0.68**	**0.68**
Dividend Payout %	**63.3**	**39.8**	**80.0**	**48.1**	**30.0**	**...**	**61.8**
INCOME STATEMENT (IN MILLIONS):							
Total Revenues	33,859.0	24,327.0	22,075.0	15,754.0	16,332.0	13,871.0	12,757.0
Costs & Expenses	30,966.0	21,664.0	20,196.0	14,158.0	14,405.0	12,949.0	11,452.0
Depreciation & Amort.	1,245.0	950.0	941.0	664.0	693.0	817.0	721.0
Operating Income	1,648.0	1,713.0	938.0	932.0	1,234.0	105.0	584.0
Net Interest Inc./(Exp.)	d236.0	d288.0	d237.0	d260.0	d284.0	d318.0	d285.0
Income Before Income Taxes	914.0	978.0	452.0	672.0	991.0	d190.0	476.0
Income Taxes	482.0	324.0	142.0	216.0	320.0	cr107.0	155.0
Equity Earnings/Minority Int.	d498.0	d447.0	d249.0	...	...	...	...
Net Income	[5] 432.0	[4] 654.0	[3] 310.0	[1] 456.0	[1] 671.0	[2] d83.0	321.0
Cash Flow	1,677.0	1,604.0	1,251.0	1,120.0	1,364.0	730.0	1,036.0
Average Shs. Outstg. (000)	311,761	309,696	293,000	291,000	288,000	287,000	287,000
BALANCE SHEET (IN MILLIONS):							
Cash & Cash Equivalents	340.0	111.0	137.0	36.0	32.0	77.0	28.0
Total Current Assets	4,985.0	4,102.0	2,976.0	2,018.0	2,046.0	1,888.0	1,737.0
Net Property	9,375.0	10,293.0	10,429.0	7,566.0	7,298.0	7,521.0	8,471.0
Total Assets	15,232.0	15,705.0	14,544.0	10,565.0	10,151.0	10,109.0	10,951.0
Total Current Liabilities	4,012.0	3,149.0	2,610.0	2,262.0	2,142.0	2,025.0	1,712.0
Long-Term Obligations	1,937.0	3,320.0	3,456.0	2,476.0	2,642.0	3,367.0	3,983.0
Net Stockholders' Equity	4,845.0	4,800.0	4,312.0	3,618.0	3,340.0	2,872.0	3,241.0
Net Working Capital	973.0	953.0	366.0	d244.0	d96.0	d137.0	25.0
Year-end Shs. Outstg. (000)	308,300	309,696	309,000	289,000	288,000	287,000	287,000
STATISTICAL RECORD:							
Operating Profit Margin %	4.9	7.0	4.2	5.9	7.6	0.8	4.6
Net Profit Margin %	1.3	2.7	1.4	2.9	4.1	...	2.5
Return on Equity %	8.9	13.6	7.2	12.6	20.1	...	9.9
Return on Assets %	2.8	4.2	2.1	4.3	6.6	...	2.9
Debt/Total Assets %	12.7	21.1	23.8	23.4	26.0	33.3	36.4
Price Range	30.38-20.69	33.44-19.63	40.50-25.00	38.88-23.75	25.50-17.25	21.50-15.75	19.13-15.63
P/E Ratio	21.9-14.9	15.8-9.3	38.6-23.8	24.6-15.0	10.9-7.4	...	17.4-14.2
Average Yield %	3.4	3.2	2.6	2.4	3.3	3.7	3.9

Statistics are as originally reported. Chart prices prior to May, 1991 are for USX Corp. [1] Incl. chrg. 12/31/97, $284.0 mil; cr. 12/31/96, $137.0 mil [2] Bef. acctg. adj. chrg. of $659.0 mil [3] Incl. $267.0 mil inv. mkt. val. cr. [4] Incl. gain of $220.0 mil [5] Incl. net chrgs. of $876.0 mil

OFFICERS:
C. P. Cazalot Jr., Pres.
J. L. Frank, Exec. V.P.
J. T. Mills, Sr. V.P.

INVESTOR CONTACT: Charles D. Williams, V.P., Inv. Rel., (212) 826-8413

PRINCIPAL OFFICE: 600 Grant Street, Pittsburgh, PA 15219-4776

TELEPHONE NUMBER: (412) 433-1121
FAX: (412) 433-4818
WEB: www.usx.com

NO. OF EMPLOYEES: 31,515 (avg.)

SHAREHOLDERS: 65,000

ANNUAL MEETING: In Apr.

INCORPORATED: DE, 1965

INSTITUTIONAL HOLDINGS:
No. of Institutions: 411
Shares Held: 232,082,791
% Held: 75.2

INDUSTRY: Oil and gas exploration services (SIC: 1382)

TRANSFER AGENT(S): USX Corporation, Shareholder Services, Pittsburgh, PA

NYSE SYMBOL X
Rec. Pr. 19.52 (5/31/01)

USX-U.S. STEEL GROUP

YIELD 2.0%
P/E RATIO 21.0

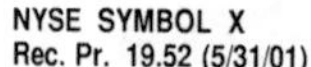

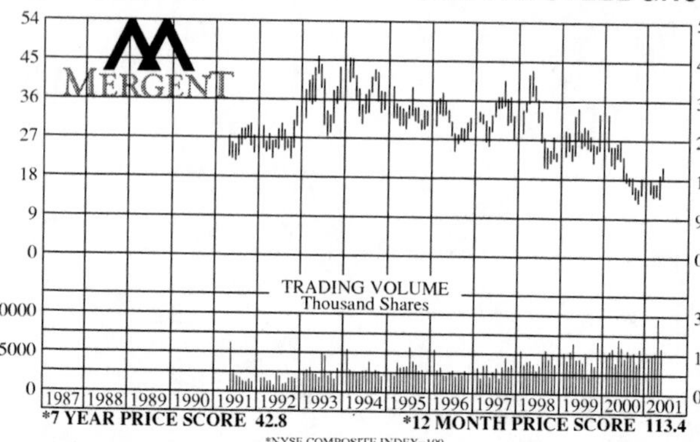

*7 YEAR PRICE SCORE 42.8 *12 MONTH PRICE SCORE 113.4

*NYSE COMPOSITE INDEX=100

INTERIM EARNINGS (Per Share):

Qtr.	Mar.	June	Sept.	Dec.
1997	0.96	1.23	1.32	1.64
1998	0.95	1.46	0.71	0.81
1999	d0.13	0.59	d0.32	0.35
2000	0.45	0.62	0.19	d0.33

INTERIM DIVIDENDS (Per Share):

Amt.	Decl.	Ex.	Rec.	Pay.
0.25Q	4/25/00	5/15/00	5/17/00	6/10/00
0.25Q	7/25/00	8/14/00	8/16/00	9/09/00
0.25Q	10/31/00	11/14/00	11/16/00	12/09/00
0.25Q	1/30/01	2/16/01	2/21/01	3/10/01
0.10Q	4/24/01	5/14/01	5/16/01	6/09/01

Indicated div.: $0.40 (Div. Reinv. Plan)

CAPITALIZATION (12/31/00):

	($000)	(%)
Long-Term Debt	2,236,000	44.1
Deferred Income Tax	666,000	13.1
Redeemable Pfd. Stock	249,000	4.9
Preferred Stock	2,000	0.0
Common & Surplus	1,917,000	37.8
Total	5,070,000	100.0

RECENT DEVELOPMENTS: For the year ended 12/31/00, X incurred a net loss of $21.0 million compared with income of $51.0 million, before an extraordinary loss, in 1999. Earnings included nonrecurring items that resulted in net after-tax charges of $98.0 million in 2000 and $39.0 million in 1999. Total revenues were $6.13 billion, up 12.1% from $5.47 billion a year earlier. Income from operations fell 30.7% to $104.0 million.

PROSPECTS: The Company expects sheet and plate pricing will continue to be depressed. Steel imports are continuing at high levels across all product lines. Domestically, X's order book continues to be weak, the economy continues to soften and natural gas prices remain extraordinarily high. For the full year 2001, domestic shipments are expected to be approximately 11.0 million net tons, excluding any shipments from the potential acquisition of LTV Tin.

BUSINESS

THE U.S. STEEL GROUP, a business unit of USX Corp., is the largest integrated steel producer in the United States. U.S. Steel is primarily engaged in the production and sale of steel mill products, coke and taconite pellets. The Company is also involved in the management of mineral resources, domestic coal mining, real estate development, engineering and consulting services. Certain business activities are conducted through joint ventures and partially-owned companies, such as USS-POSCO Industries, PRO-TEC Coating Company, Transtar, Inc., Clairton 1314B Partnership, and Republic International, LLC. The U.S. Steel Group contributed 15.0% to USX consolidated sales in 2000.

ANNUAL FINANCIAL DATA

	12/31/00	12/31/99	12/31/98	12/31/97	12/31/96	12/31/95	12/31/94
Earnings Per Share	**3 d0.33**	**2 0.48**	**3.92**	**4.88**	**1 3.00**	**1 3.53**	**2.35**
Cash Flow Per Share	**3.74**	**3.91**	**7.33**	**8.00**	**6.49**	**9.06**	**6.53**
Tang. Book Val. Per Share	**21.60**	**23.23**	**24.02**	**20.45**	**18.34**	**16.11**	**12.01**
Dividends Per Share	**1.00**	**1.00**	**1.00**	**1.00**	**1.00**	**1.00**	**1.00**
Dividend Payout %	**...**	**208.3**	**25.5**	**20.5**	**33.3**	**28.3**	**42.6**
INCOME STATEMENT (IN MILLIONS):							
Total Revenues	6,132.0	5,314.0	6,283.0	6,941.0	6,547.0	6,575.0	6,066.0
Costs & Expenses	5,668.0	4,860.0	5,421.0	5,865.0	5,895.0	5,657.0	5,439.0
Depreciation & Amort.	360.0	304.0	283.0	303.0	292.0	318.0	314.0
Operating Income	104.0	150.0	579.0	773.0	360.0	481.0	313.0
Net Interest Inc./(Exp.)	d105.0	d74.0	d42.0	d87.0	d116.0	d129.0	d140.0
Income Before Income Taxes	d1.0	76.0	537.0	686.0	367.0	453.0	248.0
Income Taxes	20.0	25.0	173.0	234.0	92.0	150.0	47.0
Net Income	3 d21.0	2 51.0	364.0	452.0	1 275.0	1 422.0	201.0
Cash Flow	331.0	346.0	638.0	752.0	545.0	716.0	490.0
Average Shs. Outstg. (000)	88,613	88,396	87,000	94,000	84,000	79,000	75,000
BALANCE SHEET (IN MILLIONS):							
Cash & Cash Equivalents	219.0	22.0	9.0	18.0	23.0	52.0	20.0
Total Current Assets	2,717.0	1,981.0	1,275.0	1,531.0	1,428.0	1,444.0	1,780.0
Net Property	2,739.0	2,516.0	2,500.0	2,496.0	2,551.0	2,512.0	2,536.0
Total Assets	8,711.0	7,525.0	6,693.0	6,694.0	6,580.0	6,521.0	6,480.0
Total Current Liabilities	1,391.0	1,266.0	1,016.0	1,334.0	1,299.0	1,519.0	1,267.0
Long-Term Obligations	2,236.0	902.0	464.0	456.0	1,014.0	923.0	1,432.0
Net Stockholders' Equity	1,919.0	2,056.0	2,093.0	1,782.0	1,566.0	1,344.0	945.0
Net Working Capital	1,326.0	715.0	259.0	197.0	129.0	d75.0	513.0
Year-end Shs. Outstg. (000)	88,767	88,392	87,000	87,000	85,000	83,000	76,000
STATISTICAL RECORD:							
Operating Profit Margin %	1.7	2.8	9.2	11.1	5.5	7.3	5.2
Net Profit Margin %	...	1.0	5.8	6.5	4.2	6.4	3.3
Return on Equity %	...	2.5	17.4	25.4	17.6	31.4	21.3
Return on Assets %	...	0.7	5.4	6.8	4.2	6.5	3.1
Debt/Total Assets %	25.7	12.0	6.9	6.8	15.4	14.2	22.1
Price Range	32.94-12.69	34.25-21.75	43.06-20.44	40.75-25.38	37.88-24.13	39.13-29.13	45.63-30.25
P/E Ratio	...	71.3-45.3	11.0-5.2	8.4-5.2	12.6-8.0	11.1-8.3	19.4-12.9
Average Yield %	4.4	3.6	3.1	3.0	3.2	2.9	2.6

Statistics are as originally reported. 1 Bef. an extraord. loss of $2.0 mill. from the exting. of debt. 2 Bef. $5.0 mill. extraord. loss on the extinguishment of debt. 3 Incl. nonrecur. after-tax chrgs. of $98.0 mill.

OFFICERS:
T. J. Usher, Chmn., C.E.O.
R. M. Hernandez, Vice-Chmn., C.F.O.
P. J. Wilhelm, Pres.
S. K. Todd, Gen. Couns.

INVESTOR CONTACT: Investor Relations, (212) 826-8413

PRINCIPAL OFFICE: 600 Grant Street, Pittsburgh, PA 15219-4776

TELEPHONE NUMBER: (412) 433-1121
FAX: (412) 433-4818
WEB: www.usx.com

NO. OF EMPLOYEES: 18,784

SHAREHOLDERS: 49,940 (approx.)

ANNUAL MEETING: In Apr.

INCORPORATED: DE, May, 1991

INSTITUTIONAL HOLDINGS:
No. of Institutions: 207
Shares Held: 49,645,411
% Held: 55.9

INDUSTRY: Petroleum refining (SIC: 2911)

TRANSFER AGENT(S): USX Corporation Shareholder Services, Pittsburgh, PA

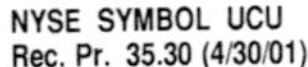

NYSE SYMBOL UCU
Rec. Pr. 35.30 (4/30/01)

UTILICORP UNITED INC.

YIELD	3.4%
P/E RATIO	16.0

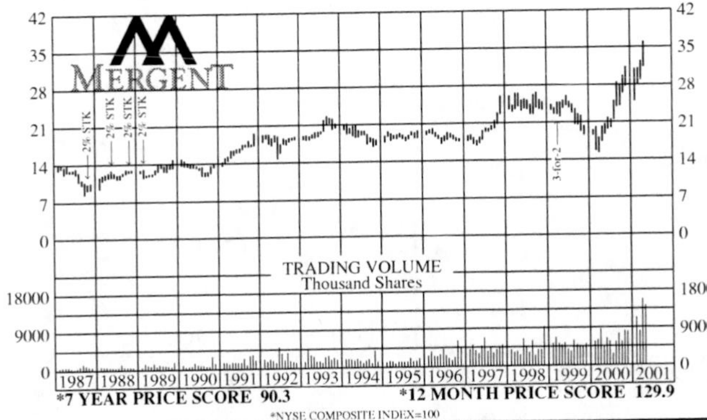

*7 YEAR PRICE SCORE 90.3 *12 MONTH PRICE SCORE 129.9

*NYSE COMPOSITE INDEX=100

INTERIM EARNINGS (Per Share):

Qtr.	Mar.	June	Sept.	Dec.
1997	0.71	0.25	0.31	0.23
1998	0.53	0.29	0.36	0.45
1999	0.57	0.27	0.46	0.45
2000	0.59	0.31	0.80	0.50

INTERIM DIVIDENDS (Per Share):

Amt.	Decl.	Ex.	Rec.	Pay.
0.30Q	8/02/00	8/18/00	8/22/00	9/12/00
0.30Q	11/08/00	11/20/00	11/22/00	12/12/00
0.30Q	2/07/01	2/20/01	2/22/01	3/12/01
0.30Q	5/02/01	5/18/01	5/22/01	6/12/01

Indicated div.: $1.20 (Div. Reinv. Plan)

CAPITALIZATION (12/31/00):

	($000)	(%)
Long-Term Debt	2,345,900	44.8
Deferred Income Tax	625,200	11.9
Minority Interest	18,100	0.3
Redeemable Pfd. Stock	350,000	6.7
Preferred Stock	100,000	1.9
Common & Surplus	1,799,600	34.4
Total	5,238,800	100.0

RECENT DEVELOPMENTS: For the year ended 12/31/00, net income grew 28.8% to $206.8 million from $160.5 million a year earlier. Results for 2000 included impairment-related charges of $27.2 million. Sales jumped 55.6% to $28.97 billion from $18.62 billion in 1999. Results reflected increased contributions from international businesses and substantial gains from UCU's Aquila segment, as earnings before interest and taxes from wholesale services soared to $144.2 million versus $27.5 million in the prior year.

PROSPECTS: Near-term prospects are positive, reflecting continued strength from the Company's Aquila segment, as energy marketing activities are benefiting from a stronger pricing environment and solid execution. Accordingly, the Company expects consolidated earnings per share for 2001 to experience 15.0% growth compared with $2.21 earnings in 2000. Meanwhile, the Company discontinued its efforts to sell its utility network construction and maintenance business and related assets.

BUSINESS

UTILICORP UNITED INC. is a multinational energy company serving approximately 4.0 million customers across the United States, Canada, the United Kingdom, New Zealand and Australia. Through its Aquila Energy subsidiary, UCU markets natural gas and electricity to industrial and wholesale customers in nearly all of the contiguous 48 states and much of Canada. Aquila also provides wholesale energy services in the U.K. and has a presence in Scandinavia, Germany and Spain. Through its Aquila Gas Pipeline Corporation subsidiary, Aquila also gathers, transports and processes natural gas and gas liquids in Texas and Oklahoma. The Company serves electric and gas utility customers in Missouri, Kansas, Nebraska, Colorado, Michigan and Minnesota. On 12/31/00, UCU completed the acquisition of St. Joseph Light & Power Company.

ANNUAL FINANCIAL DATA

	12/31/00	12/31/99	[4] 12/31/98	12/31/97	12/31/96	12/31/95	12/31/94
Earnings Per Share	[5] 2.21	1.75	1.63	[3] 1.51	[2] 1.47	[1] 1.15	1.39
Cash Flow Per Share	4.61	3.85	3.48	3.25	3.27	3.45	3.62
Tang. Book Val. Per Share	17.94	16.30	15.82	14.49	14.49	13.72	13.55
Dividends Per Share	1.20	1.20	1.20	1.17	1.17	1.15	1.13
Dividend Payout %	54.3	68.6	73.6	77.9	80.0	100.0	81.7
INCOME STATEMENT (IN MILLIONS):							
Total Revenues	28,974.9	18,621.5	12,563.4	8,926.3	4,332.3	2,798.5	1,514.6
Costs & Expenses	28,417.7	18,100.0	12,172.6	8,553.4	3,981.1	2,417.8	1,087.7
Depreciation & Amort.	225.0	193.7	150.0	129.6	127.8	155.6	147.1
Maintenance Exp.	...	...	...	...	...	...	49.3
Operating Income	332.2	327.8	240.8	243.3	223.4	225.1	230.5
Net Interest Inc./(Exp.)	d215.0	d185.3	d132.6	d135.3	d135.6	d120.7	d105.1
Income Taxes	118.2	68.2	86.6	89.7	80.7	52.0	49.3
Equity Earnings/Minority Int.	159.5	69.5	119.5	68.8	83.9	15.1	...
Net Income	[5] 206.8	160.5	132.2	[3] 134.1	[2] 105.8	[1] 79.8	94.4
Cash Flow	431.8	354.2	282.2	263.4	231.5	233.3	238.5
Average Shs. Outstg. (000)	93,750	92,110	81,180	81,000	70,815	67,620	65,955
BALANCE SHEET (IN MILLIONS):							
Gross Property	5,929.6	5,209.9	4,762.1	3,800.7	3,657.9	3,410.6	2,556.6
Accumulated Depreciation	2,274.7	1,544.8	1,448.2	1,320.4	1,251.2	1,131.0	923.0
Net Property	3,654.9	3,665.1	3,313.9	2,480.3	2,406.7	2,279.6	2,414.9
Total Assets	14,115.6	7,538.6	5,991.5	5,113.5	4,704.9	3,885.9	3,111.1
Long-Term Obligations	2,345.9	2,202.3	1,375.8	1,358.6	1,470.7	1,355.4	976.9
Net Stockholders' Equity	1,899.6	1,525.4	1,446.0	1,163.6	1,183.0	971.7	932.2
Year-end Shs. Outstg. (000)	100,311	93,606	91,416	80,279	79,941	68,949	66,900
STATISTICAL RECORD:							
Operating Profit Margin %	1.1	1.8	1.9	2.7	5.2	8.0	15.2
Net Profit Margin %	0.7	0.9	1.1	1.5	2.4	2.9	6.2
Net Inc./Net Property %	5.7	4.4	4.0	5.4	4.4	3.5	3.9
Net Inc./Tot. Capital %	3.9	3.5	3.8	4.4	3.4	2.9	4.3
Return on Equity %	10.9	10.5	9.1	11.5	8.9	8.2	10.1
Accum. Depr./Gross Prop. %	38.4	29.7	30.4	34.7	34.2	33.2	36.1
Price Range	31.31-15.19	26.00-18.56	26.63-22.50	26.04-16.75	20.17-17.17	19.75-17.58	21.25-16.75
P/E Ratio	14.2-6.9	14.9-10.6	16.3-13.8	17.3-11.1	13.7-11.7	17.2-15.3	15.3-12.1
Average Yield %	5.2	5.4	4.9	5.5	6.3	6.1	6.0

Statistics are as originally reported. Adj. for stk. split: 3-for-2, 3/99 [1] Incl. charge $19.6 mill [2] Inc. gain $11.8 mill. & net charge $6.8 mill. [3] Incl. gain $53.0 mill. for merger terminate. fee, a pre-tax chrg. $26.5 mill. for asset impairs., & a pre-tax chrg. $6.5 mill. for add. reserves; excl. a net extraord. chrg. $7.2 mill. & a net acctg. change chrg. of $4.8 mill. [4] Refl. increased interest in Power New Zealand to 78.6%. [5] Incls. impair. chrgs. of $27.2 mill.

OFFICERS:
R. C. Green Jr., Chmn., C.E.O.
R. K. Green, Pres., C.O.O.
P. Lowe, Sr. V.P., C.F.O.

INVESTOR CONTACT: Jerry Myers, Investor Relations, (816) 467-3552

PRINCIPAL OFFICE: 20 West Ninth Street, Kansas City, MO 64105

TELEPHONE NUMBER: (816) 421-6600
FAX: (816) 467-3435
WEB: www.utilicorp.com
NO. OF EMPLOYEES: 8,228 (avg.)
SHAREHOLDERS: 44,017
ANNUAL MEETING: In May
INCORPORATED: MO, April, 1950; reincorp., DE, April, 1987

INSTITUTIONAL HOLDINGS:
No. of Institutions: 239
Shares Held: 35,272,488
% Held: 31.3

INDUSTRY: Electric and other services combined (SIC: 4931)

TRANSFER AGENT(S): First Chicago Trust Company of New York, Jersey City, NJ

NYSE SYMBOL VCI
Rec. Pr. 35.35 (4/30/01)

VALASSIS

YIELD ...
P/E RATIO 15.6

MERGENT

TRADING VOLUME
Thousand Shares

*7 YEAR PRICE SCORE 105.3 *12 MONTH PRICE SCORE 106.6
*NYSE COMPOSITE INDEX=100

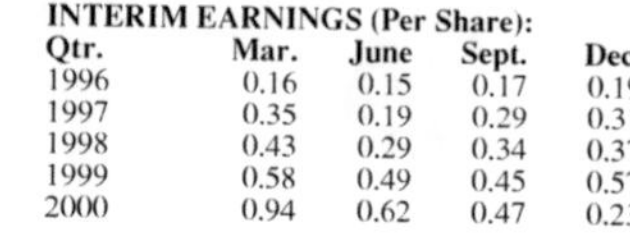

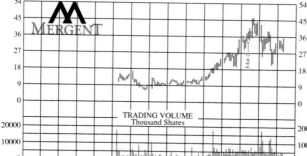

INTERIM EARNINGS (Per Share):

Qtr.	Mar.	June	Sept.	Dec.
1996	0.16	0.15	0.17	0.19
1997	0.35	0.19	0.29	0.31
1998	0.43	0.29	0.34	0.37
1999	0.58	0.49	0.45	0.57
2000	0.94	0.62	0.47	0.23

INTERIM DIVIDENDS (Per Share):

Amt.	Decl.	Ex.	Rec.	Pay.

No dividends paid.

CAPITALIZATION (12/31/00):

	($000)	(%)
Long-Term Debt	325,490	212.8
Common & Surplus	d172,504	-112.8
Total	152,986	100.0

RECENT DEVELOPMENTS: For the year ended 12/31/00, the Company reported net earnings of $125.7 million compared with earnings of $121.1 million, before an after-tax extraordinary loss of $6.9 million, in the previous year. Earnings for 2000 and 1999 included losses of $25.9 million and $1.4 million, respectively, on investments and reserves against impaired assets. Total revenue increased 8.6% to $863.1 million.

PROSPECTS: The Company expects earnings per share growth in 2001 to range from 10.0% to 15.0%, with approximately $9.0 million to $11.0 million in pre-tax losses from investments. Results should be enhanced by an increase in the Company's Free-Standing Inserts business due to the success of new contracts, an expected reduction in paper costs, and the conclusion of newspaper insertion rate negotiations.

BUSINESS

VALASSIS (formerly Valassis Communications, Inc.) provides a wide range of strategic marketing services for manufacturers and retailers. The Company generates most of its revenues by printing and publishing cents-off coupons and other consumer purchase incentives primarily for packaged goods manufacturers. The Company also prints and publishes refund offers, premiums, sweepstakes and contests distributed to households throughout the United States.

QUARTERLY DATA

(12/31/2000)($000)	REV	INC
1st Quarter	239,037	53,411
2nd Quarter	211,085	34,383
3rd Quarter	191,073	25,662
4th Quarter	221,926	12,243

ANNUAL FINANCIAL DATA

	12/31/00	12/31/99	12/31/98	12/31/97	12/31/96	12/31/95	12/31/94
Earnings Per Share	3 2.27	2 2.09	2 1.42	1.13	0.67	1 0.15	2 0.03
Cash Flow Per Share	...	2.31	1.69	1.38	...	0.44	0.18
INCOME STATEMENT (IN MILLIONS):							
Total Revenues	863.1	794.6	741.4	675.5	659.1	613.8	279.0
Costs & Expenses	626.8	567.0	554.6	506.6	533.2	531.7	245.6
Depreciation & Amort.	11.3	12.9	15.8	15.6	15.2	19.0	9.7
Operating Income	225.0	214.6	171.0	153.3	110.7	63.1	23.7
Net Interest Inc./(Exp.)	d22.9	d26.0	d34.4	d38.3	d39.6	d40.5	d19.6
Income Before Income Taxes	202.1	188.7	136.5	115.0	71.1	22.6	4.1
Income Taxes	76.4	67.5	52.2	45.1	28.2	13.0	2.1
Net Income	3 125.7	2 121.1	2 84.3	69.9	42.9	1 9.6	2 1.9
Cash Flow	137.0	134.0	100.1	85.5	58.1	28.6	11.6
Average Shs. Outstg. (000)	...	58,084	59,309	61,962	...	64,955	64,955
BALANCE SHEET (IN MILLIONS):							
Cash & Cash Equivalents	11.1	11.1	6.9	35.4	60.2	34.4	21.2
Total Current Assets	167.7	142.3	143.1	151.1	177.8	155.1	109.3
Net Property	60.0	52.8	46.4	40.2	34.8	34.9	41.3
Total Assets	325.7	247.2	232.0	240.9	273.7	258.9	234.3
Total Current Liabilities	171.1	169.6	158.6	148.5	161.4	148.8	130.7
Long-Term Obligations	325.5	291.4	340.5	367.1	395.9	416.0	417.9
Net Stockholders' Equity	d172.5	d215.6	d268.5	d277.0	d286.6	d309.3	d319.0
Net Working Capital	d3.4	d27.3	d15.5	2.6	16.4	6.3	d21.4
Year-end Shs. Outstg. (000)	53,563	56,128	57,589	59,274	63,116	64,955	64,955
STATISTICAL RECORD:							
Operating Profit Margin %	26.1	27.0	23.1	22.7	16.8	10.3	8.5
Net Profit Margin %	14.6	15.2	11.4	10.4	6.5	1.6	0.7
Return on Assets %	38.6	49.0	36.3	29.0	15.7	3.7	0.8
Debt/Total Assets %	99.9	117.9	146.7	152.4	144.6	160.7	178.3
Price Range	42.63-20.50	46.50-29.04	34.50-19.42	23.92-12.00	14.08-9.75	12.42-9.08	13.17-7.00
P/E Ratio	18.8-9.0	22.2-13.9	24.3-13.7	21.2-10.6	21.1-14.6	84.4-61.8	485.9-258.3

Statistics are as originally reported. Adj. for 3-for-2 stk. split, 5/99. 1 Incl. gain of $16.9 mill. from the sale of a business. 2 Bef. extraord. loss of $6.9 mill., 1999; $13.6 mill., 1998; $4.2 mill., 1994. 3 Incl. a loss of $25.9 mill. on investments and reserves against impaired assets.

OFFICERS:
A. F. Schultz, Chmn., Pres. & C.E.O.
B. P. Hoffman, Exec. V.P., Gen. Couns.
R. L. Recchia, Exec. V.P., C.F.O.

INVESTOR CONTACT: Lynn Liddle, V.P.-Inv. & Pub. Rel., (734) 591-7374

PRINCIPAL OFFICE: 19975 Victor Parkway, Livonia, MI 48152

TELEPHONE NUMBER: (734) 591-3000
FAX: (313) 591-4938
WEB: www.valassis.com

NO. OF EMPLOYEES: 1,400 (avg.)

SHAREHOLDERS: 251 (approx. record)

ANNUAL MEETING: In May

INCORPORATED: DE, Oct., 1986

INSTITUTIONAL HOLDINGS:
No. of Institutions: 181
Shares Held: 50,878,895
% Held: 95.3

INDUSTRY: Advertising, nec (SIC: 7319)

TRANSFER AGENT(S): American Stock Transfers & Trust Company, New York, NY

NYSE SYMBOL VLO
Rec. Pr. 44.09 (5/31/01)

VALERO ENERGY CORPORATION

YIELD 0.7%
P/E RATIO 7.9

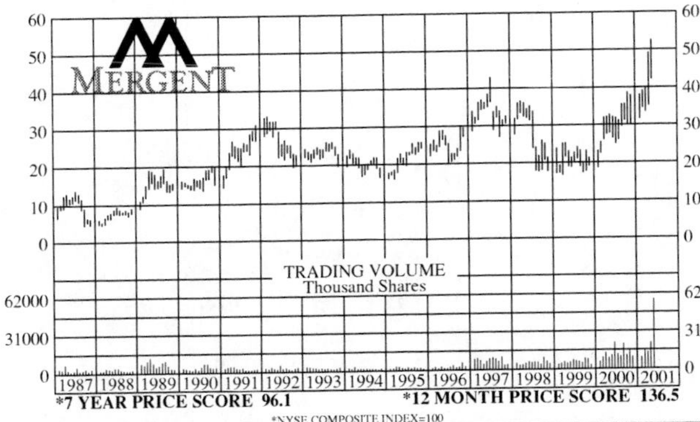

INTERIM EARNINGS (Per Share):

Qtr.	Mar.	June	Sept.	Dec.
1996	0.39	0.41	0.23	0.37
1997	0.29	0.55	0.93	0.22
1998	d0.11	0.70	0.08	d1.53
1999	d0.05	d0.39	0.40	0.29
2000	0.54	1.51	2.01	1.47

INTERIM DIVIDENDS (Per Share):

Amt.	Decl.	Ex.	Rec.	Pay.
0.08Q	5/04/00	5/25/00	5/30/00	6/14/00
0.08Q	7/20/00	8/14/00	8/16/00	9/13/00
0.08Q	10/19/00	11/13/00	11/15/00	12/13/00
0.08Q	1/18/01	2/12/01	2/14/01	3/14/01
0.08Q	5/10/01	5/24/01	5/29/01	6/13/01

Indicated div.: $0.32

CAPITALIZATION (12/31/00):

	($000)	(%)
Long-Term Debt	1,042,417	33.1
Deferred Income Tax	406,634	12.9
Redeemable Pfd. Stock	172,500	5.5
Common & Surplus	1,527,055	48.5
Total	3,148,606	100.0

RECENT DEVELOPMENTS: For the year ended 12/31/00, net income surged to $339.1 million versus $14.3 million a year earlier. Results benefited from the contribution of the Benicia refinery and retail assets, which were acquired from ExxonMobil on 5/15/00. Also, strong distillate margins, primarily resulting from low inventories and cold weather in November and December 2000, and substantial discounts on the Company's sour crude oil feedstocks had a favorable effect on earnings. Operating revenues rose 84.3% to $14.67 billion from $7.96 billion in 1999.

PROSPECTS: On 5/7/01, VLO and Ultramar Diamond Shamrock Corp. jointly announced an agreement for Valero Energy Corporation to acquire Ultramar Diamond Shamrock in a transaction valued approximately $6.00 billion. With this acquisition, the Company will have annual revenues of $32.00 billion and total assets of more than $10.00 billion. The acquisition, which is expected to close by the end of 2001, is expected to be highly accretive to earnings and cash flow.

BUSINESS

VALERO ENERGY CORPORATION is one of the largest independent petroleum refining and marketing companies in the United States. VLO currently owns and operates six refineries in California, Texas, Louisiana and New Jersey with a combined throughput capacity of approximately 1.0 million barrels per day. Operations are involved in the production of premium petroleum products such as reformulated gasoline, low-sulfur diesel and oxygenates, and gasoline meeting specifications of the California Air Resources Board, or CARB gasoline. VLO also produces middle distillates, jet fuel and petrochemicals. The Company markets its products in 34 states through an extensive wholesale bulk and rack marketing network, and in California through approximately 80 Company-owned retail and 270 retail distributor locations. On 7/31/97, VLO sold its natural gas related business to PG&E Corp. On 5/15/00, VLO acquired the Benicia Refinery and certain Exxon-branded supplier relationships for about $1.05 billion.

ANNUAL FINANCIAL DATA

	[3] 12/31/00	12/31/99	12/31/98	12/31/97	12/31/96	12/31/95	12/31/94
Earnings Per Share	**5.60**	**0.25**	**[2] d0.84**	**[1] 2.03**	**1.40**	**1.10**	**0.40**
Cash Flow Per Share	**8.46**	**2.70**	**1.41**	**3.62**	**4.55**	**4.20**	**2.82**
Tang. Book Val. Per Share	**25.10**	**19.35**	**19.40**	**20.64**	**24.49**	**23.56**	**23.85**
Dividends Per Share	**0.32**	**0.32**	**0.32**	**0.42**	**0.52**	**0.52**	**0.52**
Dividend Payout %	**5.7**	**127.9**	**...**	**20.7**	**37.1**	**47.3**	**130.0**
INCOME STATEMENT (IN MILLIONS):							
Total Revenues	14,671.1	7,961.2	5,539.3	5,756.2	4,990.7	3,019.8	1,837.4
Costs & Expenses	13,887.1	7,753.0	5,464.0	5,452.8	4,651.4	2,695.7	1,606.6
Depreciation & Amort.	173.1	139.0	126.5	92.4	138.4	135.3	104.9
Operating Income	611.0	69.1	d51.2	211.0	200.9	188.8	125.9
Net Interest Inc./(Exp.)	d76.2	d55.4	d32.5	d42.5	d95.2	d101.2	d76.9
Income Before Income Taxes	528.2	20.2	d83.1	175.6	113.7	95.1	42.8
Income Taxes	189.1	5.9	cr35.8	63.8	41.0	35.3	15.9
Equity Earnings/Minority Int.	...	...	...	...	...	...	d10.7
Net Income	339.1	14.3	[2] d47.3	[1] 111.8	72.7	59.8	26.9
Cash Flow	512.2	153.3	79.3	199.6	199.8	183.3	122.3
Average Shs. Outstg. (000)	60,525	56,758	56,078	55,129	43,926	43,651	43,370
BALANCE SHEET (IN MILLIONS):							
Cash & Cash Equivalents	14.6	60.1	11.2	9.9	57.6	64.7	61.7
Total Current Assets	1,285.1	828.9	639.7	789.0	888.2	621.5	532.9
Net Property	2,676.7	1,984.5	1,959.3	1,592.5	2,093.9	2,075.4	2,141.2
Total Assets	4,307.7	2,979.3	2,725.7	2,493.0	3,149.6	2,876.7	2,831.4
Total Current Liabilities	1,039.0	719.0	497.7	597.3	875.2	471.3	460.8
Long-Term Obligations	1,042.4	785.5	822.3	430.2	868.3	1,035.6	1,021.8
Net Stockholders' Equity	1,527.1	1,084.8	1,085.3	1,158.8	1,085.4	1,033.8	1,039.9
Net Working Capital	246.1	109.9	142.0	191.7	13.0	150.3	72.1
Year-end Shs. Outstg. (000)	60,838	56,067	55,937	56,136	44,186	43,732	43,465
STATISTICAL RECORD:							
Operating Profit Margin %	4.2	0.9	...	3.7	4.0	6.3	6.9
Net Profit Margin %	2.3	0.2	...	1.9	1.5	2.0	1.5
Return on Equity %	22.2	1.3	...	9.6	6.7	5.8	2.6
Return on Assets %	7.9	0.5	...	4.5	2.3	2.1	0.9
Debt/Total Assets %	24.2	26.4	30.2	17.3	27.6	36.0	36.1
Price Range	38.63-18.50	25.31-16.69	36.50-17.63	43.00-26.94	30.00-20.25	25.88-16.00	24.13-16.50
P/E Ratio	6.9-3.3	101.2-66.7	...	21.2-13.3	21.4-14.5	23.5-14.5	60.3-41.2
Average Yield %	1.1	1.5	1.2	1.2	2.1	2.5	2.6

Statistics are as originally reported. [1] Bef. disc. ops. loss of $15.7 mill. [2] Incl. a pre-tax chrg. of $170.9 mill. [3] Incl. results from the Benicia refinery & retail assets that were acq. from ExxonMobil on 5/15/00.

OFFICERS:
W. E. Greehey, Chmn., Pres., C.E.O.
J. D. Gibbons, Exec. V.P., C.F.O.
G. C. King, Exec. V.P., C.O.O.

INVESTOR CONTACT: Lee Bailey, Dir., Inv. Rel., (210) 370-2139

PRINCIPAL OFFICE: One Valero Place, San Antonio, TX 78212-0500

TELEPHONE NUMBER: (210) 370-2000
FAX: (210) 246-2646
WEB: www.valero.com

NO. OF EMPLOYEES: 3,180 (avg.)

SHAREHOLDERS: 3,101 (record)

ANNUAL MEETING: In May

INCORPORATED: DE, Nov., 1955

INSTITUTIONAL HOLDINGS:
No. of Institutions: 234
Shares Held: 53,756,814
% Held: 88.1

INDUSTRY: Petroleum refining (SIC: 2911)

TRANSFER AGENT(S): Computershare, Chicago, IL

NYSE SYMBOL VHI
Rec. Pr. 10.60 (4/30/01)

VALHI, INC.

YIELD 2.3%
P/E RATIO 16.1

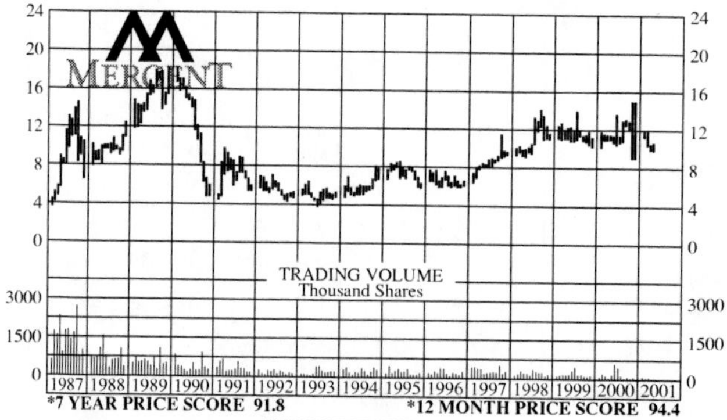

MERGENT

TRADING VOLUME
Thousand Shares

1987 1988 1989 1990 1991 1992 1993 1994 1995 1996 1997 1998 1999 2000 2001

*7 YEAR PRICE SCORE 91.8 *12 MONTH PRICE SCORE 94.4

*NYSE COMPOSITE INDEX=100

INTERIM EARNINGS (Per Share):

Qtr.	Mar.	June	Sept.	Dec.
1997	d0.20	0.02	0.02	0.34
1998	1.76	d0.02	0.11	0.09
1999	0.02	0.53	0.07	d0.22
2000	0.09	0.30	0.11	0.16

INTERIM DIVIDENDS (Per Share):

Amt.	Decl.	Ex.	Rec.	Pay.
0.05Q	5/11/00	6/13/00	6/15/00	6/30/00
0.05Q	8/25/00	9/15/00	9/19/00	9/29/00
0.06Q	10/26/00	12/12/00	12/14/00	12/29/00
0.06Q	2/14/01	3/21/01	3/23/01	3/30/01
0.06Q	5/10/01	6/13/01	6/15/01	6/29/01

Indicated div.: $0.24

CAPITALIZATION (12/31/00):

	($000)	(%)
Long-Term Debt	595,354	35.6
Deferred Income Tax	294,371	17.6
Minority Interest	156,278	9.3
Common & Surplus	628,235	37.5
Total	1,674,238	100.0

RECENT DEVELOPMENTS: For the year ended 12/31/00, VHI reported income of $77.1 million, before an extraordinary charge of $500,000, versus income of $47.4 million in 1999. Earnings for 2000 included a pre-tax net legal settlement gain of $69.5 million. Earnings for 1999 included a net pre-tax one-time gain of $40.0 million. Earnings for 1999 excluded a gain of $2.0 million from discontinued operations. Net sales rose 8.7% to $1.32 billion.

PROSPECTS: On 3/20/01, NL Industries, Inc. suffered a fire at its Leverkusen, Germany TiO2 facility. As a result, NL aniticipates its TiO2 sales and production volumes for 2001 will be lower compared with 2000. Moreover, NL expects its operating income, excluding fire-related insurance recoveries, will be lower than 2000 primarily due to lower sales and production volumes and higher operating costs, particularly for energy.

BUSINESS

VALHI, INC. is a holding company that operates through its subsidiaries and affiliates in the chemicals, component products, titanium metals and waste management industries. VHI's diverse product offerings include titanium dioxide pigments, components for office furniture and other products, and various titanium products. As of 12/31/00, VHI owns 60.0% of NL Industries Inc., a worldwide producer of titanium dioxide; 90.0% of Waste Control Specialists; 68.0% of CompX International Inc., a components products company; and 80.0% of Tremont Corporation, a holding company that owns 20% of NL Industries Inc. and 39% of Titanium Metals Corp. Contran Corp. owns approximately 93.0% of VHI.

BUSINESS LINE ANALYSIS

(12/31/2000)	REV(%)	INC(%)
Chemicals	85.6	82.9
Component Products	14.4	17.1
Total	100.0	100.0

ANNUAL FINANCIAL DATA

	12/31/00	12/31/99	12/31/98	12/31/97	12/31/96	[3] 12/31/95	12/31/94
Earnings Per Share	[6] 0.66	[1] 0.41	[5] 1.94	[4] 0.24	[2] 0.04	0.60	[2] 0.17
Cash Flow Per Share	1.27	0.96	2.45	0.77	0.65	1.42	0.43
Tang. Book Val. Per Share	2.33	2.02	2.78	1.11	0.40	0.19	...
Dividends Per Share	0.21	0.20	0.20	0.20	0.20	0.12	0.08
Dividend Payout %	31.8	48.8	10.3	83.3	498.8	20.0	47.0
INCOME STATEMENT (IN MILLIONS):							
Total Revenues	1,319.0	1,213.7	1,538.3	1,217.9	1,232.2	1,994.3	842.4
Costs & Expenses	955.0	964.7	889.8	969.3	1,051.1	1,663.4	723.3
Depreciation & Amort.	71.1	64.7	59.0	62.3	69.9	93.9	29.6
Operating Income	222.5	112.3	498.3	67.5	11.1	237.0	89.5
Net Interest Inc./(Exp.)	d70.4	d72.0	d91.2	d118.9	d100.2	d126.2	d35.3
Income Before Income Taxes	215.2	55.1	490.2	54.8	14.7	110.2	29.1
Income Taxes	94.4	cr71.3	192.2	27.6	3.5	41.1	9.5
Equity Earnings/Minority Int.	d51.0	d136.1	d80.3	d12.7	d3.3	d1.2	d25.1
Net Income	[6] 77.1	[1] 47.4	[5] 225.8	[4] 27.1	[2] 4.2	68.5	[2] 19.7
Cash Flow	148.2	112.1	284.8	89.4	74.1	162.5	49.3
Average Shs. Outstg. (000)	116,270	116,194	116,126	115,881	114,622	114,437	114,303
BALANCE SHEET (IN MILLIONS):							
Cash & Cash Equivalents	204.3	175.0	224.6	360.4	398.2	170.9	220.0
Total Current Assets	667.1	638.1	675.5	750.7	837.7	931.6	936.1
Net Property	537.5	565.4	527.3	541.7	690.2	874.7	807.7
Total Assets	2,256.8	2,235.2	2,242.2	2,178.1	2,145.0	2,572.2	2,480.7
Total Current Liabilities	398.0	352.2	352.6	324.1	563.7	662.3	656.2
Long-Term Obligations	595.4	609.3	630.6	1,008.1	844.5	1,084.3	1,086.7
Net Stockholders' Equity	628.2	589.4	578.5	384.9	303.9	274.3	198.4
Net Working Capital	269.1	285.9	322.9	426.6	274.0	269.2	279.9
Year-end Shs. Outstg. (000)	115,160	115,066	114,976	115,203	114,642	114,530	114,398
STATISTICAL RECORD:							
Operating Profit Margin %	16.9	9.3	32.4	5.5	0.9	11.9	10.6
Net Profit Margin %	5.8	3.9	14.7	2.2	0.3	3.4	2.3
Return on Equity %	12.3	8.0	39.0	7.0	1.4	25.0	9.9
Return on Assets %	3.4	2.1	10.1	1.2	0.2	2.7	0.8
Debt/Total Assets %	26.4	27.3	28.1	46.3	39.4	42.2	43.8
Price Range	15.00-9.00	14.00-10.19	14.13-9.06	11.50-6.38	7.75-5.88	8.63-5.75	8.13-4.75
P/E Ratio	22.7-13.6	34.1-24.8	7.3-4.7	47.9-26.6	193.3-146.5	14.4-9.6	47.8-27.9
Average Yield %	1.8	1.7	1.7	2.2	2.9	1.7	1.2

Statistics are as originally reported. [1] Bef. extraord. chrg. of $54,000 and disc. opers. gain of $2.0 mill., 1999. [2] Bef. disc. opers. gain of $37.8 mill., 1996; loss of $8.1 mill., 1994. [3] Incl. consol. results of NL Industries. [4] Bef. disc. opers. gain of $33.6 mill. & extraord. chrg. of $4.3 mill. [5] Bef. extraord. chrg. of $6.2 mill. & incl. net non-recurr. gains of $398.1 mill. [6] Incl. pre-tax legal settlement gain of $69.5 mill.

OFFICERS:
H. C. Simmons, Chmn., C.E.O.
G. R. Simmons, Vice-Chmn.
S. L. Watson, Pres.

INVESTOR CONTACT: Investor Relations, (972) 233-1700

PRINCIPAL OFFICE: 5430 LBJ Freeway, Suite 1700, Dallas, TX 75240-2697

TELEPHONE NUMBER: (972) 233-1700
FAX: (972) 448-1445

NO. OF EMPLOYEES: 7,110 (approx.)

SHAREHOLDERS: 2,500 (approx.)

ANNUAL MEETING: In May

INCORPORATED: DE, Mar., 1987

INSTITUTIONAL HOLDINGS:
No. of Institutions: 28
Shares Held: 2,436,033
% Held: 2.1

INDUSTRY: Chemicals & allied products, nec (SIC: 5169)

TRANSFER AGENT(S): Computershare Investor Services, Chicago, IL

NYSE SYMBOL VLY
Rec. Pr. 27.43 (4/30/01)

VALLEY NATIONAL BANCORP

YIELD	3.9%
P/E RATIO	15.7

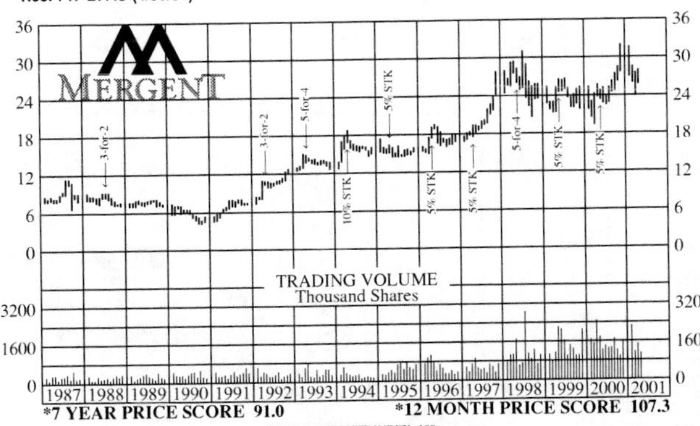

INTERIM EARNINGS (Per Share):

Qtr.	Mar.	June	Sept.	Dec.
1997	0.44	0.43	0.46	0.47
1998	0.39	0.41	0.41	0.39
1999	0.41	0.39	0.43	0.42
2000	0.43	0.44	0.44	0.44

INTERIM DIVIDENDS (Per Share):

Amt.	Decl.	Ex.	Rec.	Pay.
0.26Q	8/17/00	9/06/00	9/08/00	10/02/00
0.26Q	11/29/00	12/06/00	12/08/00	1/02/01
0.26Q	2/22/01	3/07/01	3/09/01	4/02/01
5% STK	4/04/01	5/02/01	5/04/01	5/18/01
0.265Q	5/30/01	6/04/01	6/06/01	7/02/01

Indicated div.: $1.06 (Div. Reinv. Plan)

CAPITALIZATION (12/31/00):

	($000)	(%)
Total Deposits	5,123,717	81.8
Long-Term Debt	591,808	9.5
Common & Surplus	545,074	8.7
Total	6,260,599	100.0

RECENT DEVELOPMENTS: For the year ended 12/31/00, net income increased slightly to $106.8 million from $106.3 million in 1999. Results included net gain on sale of loans of $2.2 million and $2.5 million in 2000 and 1999, respectively. Results for 1999 included merger-related charges of $3.0 million. Total interest income grew 7.8% to $460.9 million. Total non-interest income rose 7.7% to $50.9 million.

PROSPECTS: On 1/19/01, the Company completed the acquisition of Merchants New York Bancorp, Inc. for approximately $375.0 million. The Company will continue to operate the former Merchants branches in Manhattan as The Merchants Bank of New York, a division of VLY. The Company expects this acquisition to generate sufficient cost savings and to be accretive to earnings in 2001.

BUSINESS

VALLEY NATIONAL BANCORP, with over $6.20 billion in assets as of 12/31/00, is a bank holding company. The Company's principal subsidiary is Valley National Bank (VNB). VNB is a national banking association, which provides a full range of commercial and retail banking services through 118 branch offices located in 78 communities serving 10 counties throughout northern New Jersey. These services include the following: the acceptance of demand, savings and time deposits; extension of consumer, real estate, Small Business Administration and other commercial credits; title insurance; investment services; and full personal and corporate trust, as well as pension and fiduciary services. On 1/19/01, the Company acquired Merchants New York Bancorp, Inc. for $375.0 million.

LOAN DISTRIBUTION

(12/31/2000)	($000)	(%)
Commercial	530,351	11.4
Mortgage	2,692,042	57.8
Consumer	1,439,021	30.8
Total	4,661,414	100.0

ANNUAL FINANCIAL DATA

	12/31/00	12/31/99	12/31/98	12/31/97	12/31/96	12/31/95	12/31/94
Earnings Per Share	**3 1.67**	**2 1.65**	**2 1.59**	**1.81**	**1.59**	**1.45**	**1.62**
Tang. Book Val. Per Share	**8.65**	**8.83**	**9.12**	**10.18**	**9.04**	**8.91**	**8.16**
Dividends Per Share	**0.97**	**0.90**	**0.81**	**0.71**	**0.64**	**0.61**	**0.55**
Dividend Payout %	**54.8**	**51.2**	**39.1**	**40.4**	**42.3**	**34.3**	**28.3**
INCOME STATEMENT (IN MILLIONS):							
Total Interest Income	460.9	427.5	389.7	368.3	324.3	316.7	242.9
Total Interest Expense	202.8	169.2	160.1	156.0	145.5	143.3	93.8
Net Interest Income	258.1	258.4	229.6	212.3	178.8	173.4	149.1
Provision for Loan Losses	6.1	9.1	12.4	12.3	2.4	2.7	3.5
Non-Interest Income	50.9	47.3	43.1	42.3	26.3	21.0	22.5
Non-Interest Expense	141.0	137.9	134.8	123.2	101.2	90.2	79.0
Income Before Taxes	161.8	158.5	125.5	119.2	101.4	101.5	89.0
Net Income	3 106.8	2 106.3	2 97.3	85.0	67.5	62.6	59.0
Average Shs. Outstg. (000)	64,164	64,371	61,307	46,931	42,473	43,291	36,665
BALANCE SHEET (IN MILLIONS):							
Cash & Due from Banks	186.7	161.6	175.8	148.2	162.9	167.3	154.6
Securities Avail. for Sale	1,035.8	1,005.4	929.1	1,017.2	950.2	1,146.3	458.2
Total Loans & Leases	4,661.4	4,554.8	3,977.9	3,622.3	3,177.4	2,794.1	2,184.7
Allowance for Credit Losses	53.7	55.1	49.9	46.4	41.4	40.6	37.9
Net Loans & Leases	4,607.7	4,499.6	3,928.0	3,576.0	3,136.0	2,753.5	2,146.8
Total Assets	6,425.8	6,360.4	5,541.2	5,090.7	4,686.7	4,585.8	3,739.4
Total Deposits	5,123.7	5,051.3	4,674.7	4,403.0	4,176.2	4,083.9	3,334.0
Long-Term Obligations	591.8	564.9	...	...	...	...	...
Total Liabilities	5,880.8	5,806.9	4,985.4	4,615.3	4,290.1	4,185.6	3,443.8
Net Stockholders' Equity	545.1	553.5	555.8	475.4	396.5	400.2	300.2
Year-end Shs. Outstg. (000)	63,039	62,678	63,977	49,037	44,248	45,806	38,631
STATISTICAL RECORD:							
Return on Equity %	19.6	19.2	17.5	17.9	17.0	15.6	19.7
Return on Assets %	1.7	1.7	1.8	1.7	1.4	1.4	1.6
Equity/Assets %	8.5	8.7	10.0	9.3	8.5	8.7	8.0
Non-Int. Exp./Tot. Inc. %	45.6	45.1	49.4	48.4	49.3	46.4	46.1
Price Range	32.02-19.22	26.76-21.17	31.10-20.52	27.90-16.70	19.58-14.89	17.46-14.42	18.86-12.69
P/E Ratio	19.2-11.5	17.1-13.5	20.6-13.6	16.1-9.7	12.9-9.8	12.7-10.5	12.3-8.2
Average Yield %	3.8	3.8	3.1	3.2	3.7	3.8	3.5

Statistics are as originally reported. Adj. for 5% stk. spl., 5/00, 5/99, 5/97, 5/96, 5/95; 5-for-4 stk. spl., 5/98. 1 Excl. an acctg. change chrg. $402,000. 2 Incl. merger-related chrg., 1999, $3.0 mill.; 1998, $4.5 mill. 3 Incl. net gain on sale of loans of $2.0 mill.

OFFICERS:
G. H. Lipkin, Chmn., Pres., C.E.O.
P. Southway, Vice-Chmn.
A. D. Eskow, Exec. V.P., C.F.O.

INVESTOR CONTACT: Investor Relations, (800) 522-4100-3380

PRINCIPAL OFFICE: 1455 Valley Road, Wayne, NJ 07474-0558

TELEPHONE NUMBER: (973) 305-8800
WEB: www.valleynationalbank.com

NO. OF EMPLOYEES: 1,858

SHAREHOLDERS: 8,371 (record)

ANNUAL MEETING: In April

INCORPORATED: NJ, 1982

INSTITUTIONAL HOLDINGS:
No. of Institutions: 95
Shares Held: 11,134,424
% Held: 14.2

INDUSTRY: National commercial banks (SIC: 6021)

TRANSFER AGENT(S): American Stock Transfer & Trust Company, New York, NY

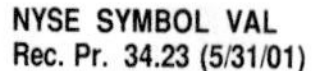

NYSE SYMBOL VAL
Rec. Pr. 34.23 (5/31/01)

VALSPAR CORP. (THE)

YIELD 1.6%
P/E RATIO 18.6

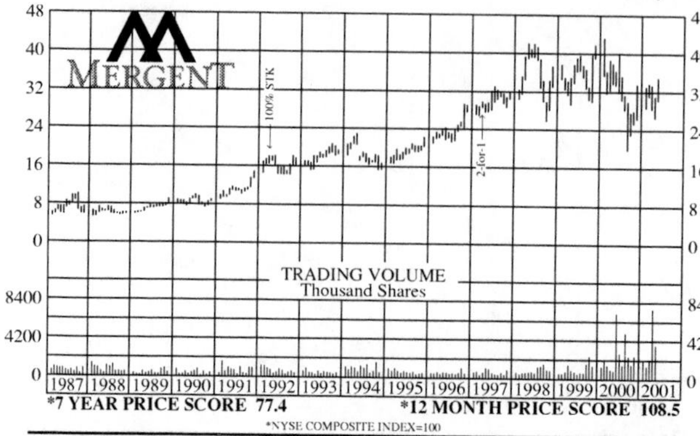

*7 YEAR PRICE SCORE 77.4 *12 MONTH PRICE SCORE 108.5
*NYSE COMPOSITE INDEX=100

INTERIM EARNINGS (Per Share):

Qtr.	Jan.	Apr.	July	Oct.
1996-97	0.18	0.39	0.47	0.46
1997-98	0.20	0.45	0.50	0.48
1998-99	0.22	0.51	0.59	0.55
1999-00	0.26	0.59	0.59	0.56
2000-01	0.10	...	...	...

INTERIM DIVIDENDS (Per Share):

Amt.	Decl.	Ex.	Rec.	Pay.
0.13Q	2/23/00	3/29/00	3/31/00	4/14/00
0.13Q	6/21/00	6/29/00	7/03/00	7/14/00
0.13Q	8/16/00	9/28/00	10/02/00	10/13/00
0.135Q	12/12/00	12/27/00	12/29/00	1/15/01
0.135Q	2/28/01	3/29/01	4/02/01	4/16/01

Indicated div.: $0.54 (Div. Reinv. Plan)

CAPITALIZATION (10/27/00):

	($000)	(%)
Long-Term Debt	300,300	39.5
Deferred Income Tax	22,366	2.9
Common & Surplus	437,571	57.6
Total	760,237	100.0

RECENT DEVELOPMENTS: For the quarter ended 1/26/01, net income dropped 61.1% to $4.5 million compared with $11.5 million in the equivalent 2000 quarter. Results reflected a slowdown in the economy, which pressured sales for architectural and industrial products. Net sales were $337.0 million, up 4.1% from $323.7 million a year earlier. Revenues for the current period included one month of domestic revenues from Lilly Industries.

PROSPECTS: Currently, VAL is experiencing some improvement in architectural coatings sales, and packaging coatings sales remain healthy. Meanwhile, VAL expects earnings dilution from the acquisition of Lilly Industries to moderate in response to aggressive operating and raw material cost-reductions. As a result, VAL is on track to achieve its cost-reduction goal of $70.0 million within the next two years.

BUSINESS

THE VALSPAR CORPORATION is a multinational paint and coatings manufacturer with operations in two segments: Coatings (90.0% of 2000 sales) and Coating Intermediates (10.0%). The Company manufactures and distributes a broad portfolio of coatings products. The Architectural, Automotive and Specialty product line includes interior and exterior decorative paints and aerosols, automotive and fleet refinish coatings and high performance floor coatings. The Packaging product line includes coatings and inks for rigid packaging containers. The Industrial product line includes decorative and protective coatings for metal, wood and plastic substrates. Coating Intermediates, primarily resins and colorants, are used by the Company and itself to other coatings manufacturers.

ANNUAL FINANCIAL DATA

	10/27/00	10/29/99	10/30/98	10/31/97	10/25/96	10/27/95	10/28/94
Earnings Per Share	**(4) 2.00**	**(3) 1.87**	**1.63**	**1.49**	**1.26**	**(2) 1.08**	**(1) 1.04**
Cash Flow Per Share	**3.05**	**2.78**	**2.32**	**2.07**	**1.76**	**1.54**	**1.48**
Tang. Book Val. Per Share	**5.39**	**4.07**	**5.70**	**5.68**	**5.79**	**4.82**	**4.03**
Dividends Per Share	**0.52**	**0.46**	**0.42**	**0.36**	**0.33**	**0.30**	**0.26**
Dividend Payout %	**26.0**	**24.6**	**25.8**	**24.2**	**26.2**	**27.9**	**25.0**
INCOME STATEMENT (IN MILLIONS):							
Total Revenues	1,483.3	1,387.7	1,155.1	1,017.3	859.8	790.2	786.8
Costs & Expenses	1,274.1	1,202.9	1,002.7	879.5	742.5	687.2	688.8
Depreciation & Amort.	45.2	39.8	30.7	25.8	22.3	20.3	19.1
Operating Income	163.9	145.0	121.7	112.0	95.0	82.7	78.9
Net Interest Inc./(Exp.)	d22.0	d19.1	d10.7	d5.3	d3.0	d4.2	d2.5
Income Before Income Taxes	141.7	135.1	118.8	109.2	93.0	79.2	75.8
Income Taxes	55.3	52.9	46.7	43.3	37.2	31.7	30.3
Net Income	(4) 86.5	(3) 82.1	72.1	65.9	55.9	(2) 47.5	(1) 45.5
Cash Flow	131.7	121.9	102.9	91.6	78.2	67.8	64.6
Average Shs. Outstg. (000)	43,196	43,836	44,320	44,233	44,402	44,182	43,646
BALANCE SHEET (IN MILLIONS):							
Cash & Cash Equivalents	20.9	33.2	15.0	11.1	7.1	4.9	2.4
Total Current Assets	533.9	514.9	426.1	356.8	275.2	236.9	220.9
Net Property	298.7	312.1	233.5	185.7	153.8	130.4	107.0
Total Assets	1,125.0	1,110.7	801.7	615.5	486.4	398.2	363.4
Total Current Liabilities	334.3	374.7	268.0	259.4	179.1	145.9	134.8
Long-Term Obligations	300.3	298.9	164.8	35.8	31.9	21.7	35.3
Net Stockholders' Equity	437.6	393.8	340.2	295.1	253.7	212.1	174.1
Net Working Capital	199.6	140.2	158.1	97.4	96.1	91.0	86.1
Year-end Shs. Outstg. (000)	42,481	42,983	43,418	43,678	43,854	43,978	43,164
STATISTICAL RECORD:							
Operating Profit Margin %	11.1	10.4	10.5	11.0	11.0	10.5	10.0
Net Profit Margin %	5.8	5.9	6.2	6.5	6.5	6.0	5.8
Return on Equity %	19.8	20.9	21.2	22.3	22.0	22.4	26.1
Return on Assets %	7.7	7.4	9.0	10.7	11.5	11.9	12.5
Debt/Total Assets %	26.7	26.9	20.6	5.8	6.6	5.4	9.7
Price Range	43.31-19.75	41.88-29.25	42.13-25.75	33.06-26.81	29.31-20.94	22.31-16.69	22.94-15.25
P/E Ratio	21.7-9.9	22.4-15.6	25.8-15.8	22.2-18.0	23.3-16.6	20.8-15.5	22.1-14.7
Average Yield %	1.6	1.3	1.2	1.2	1.3	1.5	1.4

Statistics are as originally reported. Adj. for stk. split: 2-for-1, 3/97. (1) Incl. pretax chrg. of $2.5 mill. from the writedown of a plant. (2) Reflects the acquisition of Sunbelt Coatings on a pooling of interests basis. (3) Incl. restruct. chrg. of $8.3 mill. (4) Incl. restr. credit of $1.2 mill.

OFFICERS:
R. M. Rompala, Chmn., Pres., C.E.O.
P. C. Reyelts, Sr. V.P., C.F.O.
R. Engh, Sr. V.P., Sec., Gen. Couns.

INVESTOR CONTACT: Rolf Engh, Sr. V.P., Sec., Gen. Couns., (612) 332-7371

PRINCIPAL OFFICE: 1101 Third Street South, Minneapolis, MN 55415

TELEPHONE NUMBER: (612) 332-7371
FAX: (612) 375-7723
WEB: www.valspar.com

NO. OF EMPLOYEES: 6,500 (avg.)

SHAREHOLDERS: 1,731 (record)

ANNUAL MEETING: In Feb.

INCORPORATED: DE, Dec., 1934

INSTITUTIONAL HOLDINGS:
No. of Institutions: 137
Shares Held: 18,020,822
% Held: 42.3

INDUSTRY: Paints and allied products (SIC: 2851)

TRANSFER AGENT(S): Mellon Investor Services, Ridgefield Park, NJ

NYSE SYMBOL VRC
Rec. Pr. 24.09 (5/31/01)

VARCO INTERNATIONAL INC.

YIELD	...
P/E RATIO	114.7

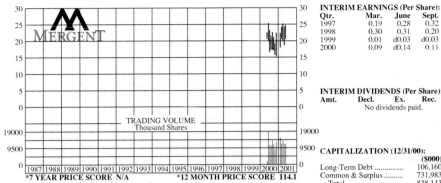

*7 YEAR PRICE SCORE N/A *12 MONTH PRICE SCORE 114.1

*NYSE COMPOSITE INDEX=100

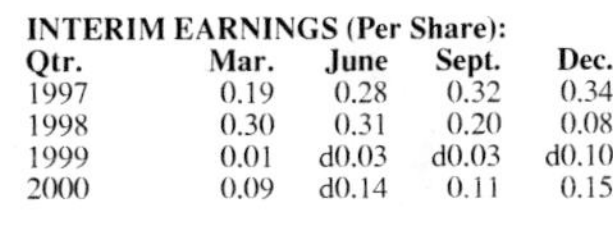

INTERIM EARNINGS (Per Share):

Qtr.	Mar.	June	Sept.	Dec.
1997	0.19	0.28	0.32	0.34
1998	0.30	0.31	0.20	0.08
1999	0.01	d0.03	d0.03	d0.10
2000	0.09	d0.14	0.11	0.15

INTERIM DIVIDENDS (Per Share):

Amt.	Decl.	Ex.	Rec.	Pay.

No dividends paid.

CAPITALIZATION (12/31/00):

	($000)	(%)
Long-Term Debt	106,160	12.7
Common & Surplus	731,983	87.3
Total	838,143	100.0

RECENT DEVELOPMENTS: For the year ended 12/31/00, net income totaled $21.1 million, a decrease of 29.4% from $29.8 million in the comparable period. Results included after-tax merger and transaction costs of $22.4 million and $5.1 million in 2000 and 1999, respectively. Total revenue declined 11.2% to $866.6 million versus $975.8 million in the previous year. Operating profit declined 9.6% to $60.9 million from $67.3 million the year before.

PROSPECTS: Going forward, VRC anticipates an increase in future orders for its equipment and services, as customers announce new builds or consider new builds or upgrades. Meanwhile, in March 2001, VRC announced the acquisitions of Chimo Equipment Ltd., a provider of drilling rig instrumentation equipment and services, and Bradon Industries, a manufacturer of coiled tubing units and provider of industrial plant services and construction.

BUSINESS

VARCO INTERNATIONAL, INC. is a manufacturer and supplier of drilling equipment and rig instrumentation, oilfield tubular inspections and internal coating techniques, solids control systems and services, and coiled tubing and pressure control equipment for both land and offshore drilling operations. The Company also provides in-service pipeline inspections, manufacturers high pressure fiberglass tubulars, sells and leases advanced in-line inspection equipment to makers of oil country tubular goods, and offers quality assurance and inspection services to a diverse range of industries. In May 2000, the Company merged with Tuboscope Inc.

REVENUES

(12/31/00)	($000)	(%)
Drilling Equipment Sales	283,360	32.7
Tubular Services	248,099	28.6
Drilling Services	250,229	28.9
Coiled Tubing & Wireless	84,927	9.8
Total	866,615	100.0

ANNUAL FINANCIAL DATA

	12/31/00	12/31/99	12/31/98	12/31/97	12/31/96	12/31/95	12/31/94
Earnings Per Share	**[5] 0.22**	**[4] d0.16**	**0.89**	**[3] 1.14**	**[1] d1.17**	**0.44**	**[1] 0.41**
Cash Flow Per Share	**0.81**	**0.60**	**1.54**	**1.68**	**d0.71**	**1.23**	**1.14**
Tang. Book Val. Per Share	**4.93**	**2.28**	**2.32**	**1.68**	**1.54**	**2.39**	**1.75**
INCOME STATEMENT (IN THOUSANDS):							
Total Revenues	866,615	385,474	567,701	525,231	341,431	190,015	192,175
Costs & Expenses	749,186	340,660	450,121	398,548	345,591	147,833	151,062
Depreciation & Amort.	56,518	33,779	30,499	25,758	17,121	14,722	14,065
Operating Income	60,911	11,035	87,081	100,925	d21,281	27,460	27,048
Net Interest Inc./(Exp.)	d11,908	d17,865	d17,521	d14,125	d12,944	d12,118	d12,533
Income Before Income Taxes	45,847	d7,884	67,111	84,949	d34,988	15,205	14,289
Income Taxes	24,792	cr728	25,166	31,845	8,238	6,386	6,001
Equity Earnings/Minority Int.	...	d293	d721	d629	d741	d652	d680
Net Income	[5] 21,055	[4] d7,156	41,945	[3] 53,104	[1] d43,226	8,819	[1] 8,288
Cash Flow	77,573	26,623	72,444	78,862	d26,280	22,841	20,967
Average Shs. Outstg.	95,356	44,314	46,913	46,946	36,809	18,530	18,447
BALANCE SHEET (IN THOUSANDS):							
Cash & Cash Equivalents	12,176	5,258	8,735	12,593	10,407	9,394	8,531
Total Current Assets	455,706	198,630	230,468	247,716	166,233	84,753	80,994
Net Property	343,673	242,825	241,826	210,561	181,380	140,038	149,895
Total Assets	1,076,982	676,039	712,172	686,167	505,165	306,679	317,027
Total Current Liabilities	192,328	111,808	116,369	166,422	91,840	40,130	45,068
Long-Term Obligations	106,160	199,449	219,438	187,803	168,229	107,055	123,851
Net Stockholders' Equity	731,983	333,497	339,074	300,033	218,902	121,441	113,424
Net Working Capital	263,378	86,822	114,099	81,294	74,393	44,623	35,926
Year-end Shs. Outstg.	94,821	44,628	44,091	44,236	41,612	18,546	18,467
STATISTICAL RECORD:							
Operating Profit Margin %	7.0	2.9	15.3	19.2	...	14.5	14.1
Net Profit Margin %	2.4	...	7.4	10.1	...	4.6	4.3
Return on Equity %	2.9	...	12.4	17.7	...	7.3	7.3
Return on Assets %	2.0	...	5.9	7.7	...	2.9	2.6
Debt/Total Assets %	9.9	29.5	30.8	27.4	33.3	34.9	39.1
Price Range	25.38-15.25	...	...	...	...	...	...
P/E Ratio	115.3-69.3	...	...	...	...	...	...

Statistics are as originally reported. [1] Excl. extraord. chrg., 1996, $6.4 mill.; 1994, $764,000. [2] Incl. restruct. chrg., $13.3 mill. [3] Incl. write-off of long lived assets of $63.1 mill., Drexel transaction costs of $11.3 mill., transaction costs & write-offs of $2.2 mill. [4] Incl. transaction write-off costs of $7.8 mill. [5] Incl. merger and transaction costs of $22.4 mill.

OFFICERS:
G. I. Boyadjieff, Chmn., C.E.O.
J. F. Lauletta, Pres., C.O.O.
J. C. Winkler, Exec. V.P., C.F.O., Treas.

INVESTOR CONTACT: Investor Relations, (713) 799-5100

PRINCIPAL OFFICE: 2835 Holmes Road, Houston, TX 77051

TELEPHONE NUMBER: (713) 799-5100
FAX: (713) 799-1460
WEB: www.tuboscope.com

NO. OF EMPLOYEES: 6,660 (avg.)

SHAREHOLDERS: 1,270 (approx.)

ANNUAL MEETING: In May

INCORPORATED: DE, March, 1988

INSTITUTIONAL HOLDINGS:
No. of Institutions: 157
Shares Held: 66,336,139
% Held: 69.3

INDUSTRY: Oil and gas field services, nec (SIC: 1389)

TRANSFER AGENT(S): Mellon Investor Services, Ridgefield Park, NJ

NYSE SYMBOL VAR
Rec. Pr. 68.90 (4/30/01)

VARIAN MEDICAL SYSTEMS, INC.

YIELD ...
P/E RATIO 39.6

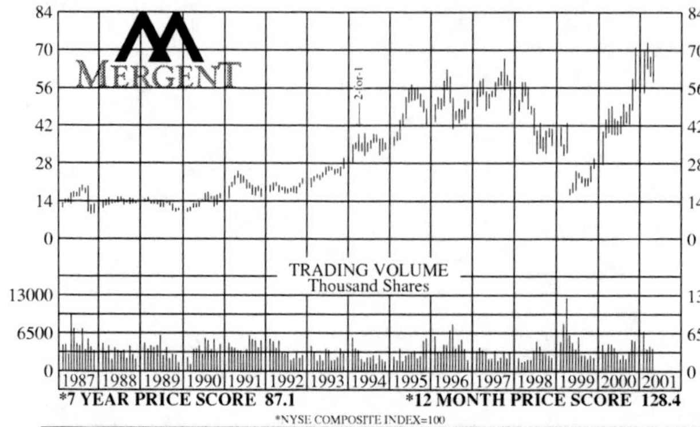

INTERIM EARNINGS (Per Share):

Qtr	Dec.	Mar.	June	Sept.
1997-98	0.64	0.75	0.61	0.42
1998-99	d0.08	d0.34	0.21	0.41
1999-00	0.17	0.32	0.43	0.71
2000-01	0.28	...	...	...

INTERIM DIVIDENDS (Per Share):

Amt.	Decl.	Ex.	Rec.	Pay.

No dividends paid.

CAPITALIZATION (9/29/00):

	($000)	(%)
Long-Term Debt	58,500	17.8
Common & Surplus	270,359	82.2
Total	328,859	100.0

RECENT DEVELOPMENTS: For the quarter ended 12/29/00, income was $9.3 million, before an acounting credit of $100,000, compared with net income $5.2 million in the previous year. Sales increased 14.2% to $161.4 million from $141.3 million in the year-earlier quarter. Operating earnings soared 48.5% to $14.7 million from $9.9 million in 1999. Net orders advanced 14.3% to $193.2 million, while order backlog improved 17.9% to $504.5 million.

PROSPECTS: On 1/19/01, VAR announced the launch of an on-line store for fast, easy, and convenient access to VAR's full line of medical X-ray tubes. Separately, VAR has renewed several multi-year agreements to supply customers with advanced radiotherapy systems for treating cancer. The contracts cover VAR's equipment and software for SmartBeam™ intensity modulated radiation therapy.

BUSINESS

VARIAN MEDICAL SYSTEMS, INC. (formerly Varian Associates, Inc.) is a manufacturer of integrated cancer therapy systems. More than 4,200 Varian CLINAC® medical linear accelerators and XIMATRON® simulators systems are in service around the world, treating an estimated 100,000 cancer patients per day. VAR is also a major supplier of x-ray tubes for diagnostic imaging applications. VAR is involved in several high-growth product development opportunities, including its advanced brachytherapy system for cancer treatment and the world's first real-time, digital X-ray fluoroscopic imager. In addition, VAR is pursuing technologies and products based on molecular medicine. VAR has manufacturing sites in North America and Europe and 40 sales and support offices around the world. In April 1999, VAR completed the spin-off of the instruments and semiconductor equipment businesses.

REVENUES

(09/29/2000)	$(000)	(%)
Oncology Systems	534,000	77.4
X-ray Products	136,000	19.7
Other	20,000	2.9
Total	690,000	100.0

ANNUAL FINANCIAL DATA

	9/29/00	[4] 10/1/99	10/2/98	9/26/97	9/27/96	9/29/95	9/30/94
Earnings Per Share	**[5] 1.64**	**[3] 0.27**	**2.43**	**[2] 3.66**	**3.81**	**[1] 3.01**	**2.22**
Cash Flow Per Share	**2.41**	**1.49**	**3.83**	**5.10**	**5.24**	**4.59**	**3.70**
Tang. Book Val. Per Share	**8.51**	**6.05**	**18.75**	**17.42**	**15.27**	**12.72**	**13.23**
Dividends Per Share	...	**0.10**	**0.39**	**0.35**	**0.31**	**0.27**	**0.23**
Dividend Payout %	...	**37.0**	**16.0**	**9.6**	**8.1**	**9.0**	**10.4**
INCOME STATEMENT (IN MILLIONS):							
Total Revenues	689.7	590.4	1,422.1	1,425.8	1,599.4	1,575.7	1,552.5
Costs & Expenses	580.0	528.7	1,264.3	1,250.3	1,363.2	1,353.2	1,370.0
Depreciation & Amort.	22.0	37.4	42.7	45.6	46.1	55.6	52.5
Operating Income	87.7	24.3	115.2	129.9	190.1	166.9	130.0
Net Interest Inc./(Exp.)	d2.8	d6.1	d2.4	d3.2	d0.8	d1.6	d2.0
Income Before Income Taxes	84.9	18.2	112.7	177.8	189.2	165.3	128.0
Income Taxes	31.8	10.0	38.9	62.2	67.2	59.5	48.6
Net Income	[5] 53.0	[3] 8.2	73.8	[2] 115.6	122.1	[1] 105.8	79.4
Cash Flow	75.0	45.6	116.5	161.2	168.1	161.4	131.9
Average Shs. Outstg. (000)	31,104	30,527	30,419	31,587	32,075	35,202	35,676
BALANCE SHEET (IN MILLIONS):							
Cash & Cash Equivalents	83.3	25.1	149.7	142.3	82.7	122.7	78.9
Total Current Assets	450.6	382.2	839.8	813.5	743.9	757.7	668.8
Net Property	80.1	80.3	214.2	195.6	212.1	191.9	235.3
Total Assets	602.6	539.2	1,218.3	1,104.3	1,019.0	1,003.8	962.4
Total Current Liabilities	249.9	269.8	504.9	464.3	450.0	500.7	431.8
Long-Term Obligations	58.5	58.5	111.1	73.2	60.3	60.3	60.4
Net Stockholders' Equity	270.4	185.0	557.5	524.6	467.9	394.9	449.5
Net Working Capital	200.7	112.4	334.9	349.2	293.9	257.0	236.9
Year-end Shs. Outstg. (000)	31,769	30,563	29,743	30,108	30,646	31,052	33,979
STATISTICAL RECORD:							
Operating Profit Margin %	12.7	4.1	8.1	9.1	11.9	10.6	8.4
Net Profit Margin %	7.7	1.4	5.2	8.1	7.6	6.7	5.1
Return on Equity %	19.6	4.4	13.2	22.0	26.1	26.8	17.7
Return on Assets %	8.8	1.5	6.1	10.5	12.0	10.5	8.2
Debt/Total Assets %	9.7	10.8	9.1	6.6	5.9	6.0	6.3
Price Range	71.00-27.50	43.00-16.25	58.38-31.56	67.00-45.88	62.88-40.50	57.38-34.50	39.25-28.25
P/E Ratio	43.3-16.8	159.2-60.2	24.0-13.0	18.3-12.5	16.5-10.6	19.1-11.5	17.7-12.7
Average Yield %	...	0.3	0.9	0.6	0.6	0.6	0.7

Statistics are as originally reported. Adj. for stk. split: 2-for-1, 3/94 [1] Bef. disc. opers. gain $33.5 mill. ($0.95/sh.) [2] Incl. net gain on sale of assets $29.2 mill. ($0.96/sh.) [3] Bef. disc. oper. loss of $30.8 mill., but incl. non-recurr. chrgs. $31.0 mill. [4] Reflects spin-off of instruments and semiconductor equipment businesses. [5] Incl. non-recurr. chrgs. $2.2 mill.

OFFICERS:
R. M. Levy, Pres., C.E.O.
E. W. Finney, V.P., C.F.O., Treas.
J. B. Phair, V.P., Gen. Couns., Sec.

INVESTOR CONTACT: Stockholder Relations, (650) 424-5855

PRINCIPAL OFFICE: 3100 Hansen Way, Palo Alto, CA 94304-1038

TELEPHONE NUMBER: (650) 493-4000
FAX: (650) 493-0307
WEB: www.varian.com

NO. OF EMPLOYEES: 2,374 (avg.)

SHAREHOLDERS: 4,474 (approx.)

ANNUAL MEETING: In Feb.

INCORPORATED: CA, Apr., 1948; reincorp., DE, Jan., 1976

INSTITUTIONAL HOLDINGS:
No. of Institutions: 199
Shares Held: 26,908,066
% Held: 82.1

INDUSTRY: Special industry machinery, nec (SIC: 3559)

TRANSFER AGENT(S): First Chicago Trust Company of New York, Jersey City, NJ

NYSE SYMBOL VRC
Rec. Pr. 24.09 (5/31/01)

VARCO INTERNATIONAL INC.

YIELD ...
P/E RATIO 114.7

TRADING VOLUME
Thousand Shares

*7 YEAR PRICE SCORE N/A *12 MONTH PRICE SCORE 114.1

*NYSE COMPOSITE INDEX=100

INTERIM EARNINGS (Per Share):

Qtr.	Mar.	June	Sept.	Dec.
1997	0.19	0.28	0.32	0.34
1998	0.30	0.31	0.20	0.08
1999	0.01	d0.03	d0.03	d0.10
2000	0.09	d0.14	0.11	0.15

INTERIM DIVIDENDS (Per Share):

Amt.	Decl.	Ex.	Rec.	Pay.

No dividends paid.

CAPITALIZATION (12/31/00):

	($000)	(%)
Long-Term Debt	106,160	12.7
Common & Surplus	731,983	87.3
Total	838,143	100.0

RECENT DEVELOPMENTS: For the year ended 12/31/00, net income totaled $21.1 million, a decrease of 29.4% from $29.8 million in the comparable period. Results included after-tax merger and transaction costs of $22.4 million and $5.1 million in 2000 and 1999, respectively. Total revenue declined 11.2% to $866.6 million versus $975.8 million in the previous year. Operating profit declined 9.6% to $60.9 million from $67.3 million the year before.

PROSPECTS: Going forward, VRC anticipates an increase in future orders for its equipment and services, as customers announce new builds or consider new builds or upgrades. Meanwhile, in March 2001, VRC announced the acquisitions of Chimo Equipment Ltd., a provider of drilling rig instrumentation equipment and services, and Bradon Industries, a manufacturer of coiled tubing units and provider of industrial plant services and construction.

BUSINESS

VARCO INTERNATIONAL, INC. is a manufacturer and supplier of drilling equipment and rig instrumentation, oilfield tubular inspections and internal coating techniques, solids control systems and services, and coiled tubing and pressure control equipment for both land and offshore drilling operations. The Company also provides in-service pipeline inspections, manufacturers high pressure fiberglass tubulars, sells and leases advanced in-line inspection equipment to makers of oil country tubular goods, and offers quality assurance and inspection services to a diverse range of industries. In May 2000, the Company merged with Tuboscope Inc.

REVENUES

(12/31/00)	($000)	(%)
Drilling Equipment		
Sales	283,360	32.7
Tubular Services........	248,099	28.6
Drilling Services........	250,229	28.9
Coiled Tubing &		
Wireless.................	84,927	9.8
Total	866,615	100.0

ANNUAL FINANCIAL DATA

	12/31/00	12/31/99	12/31/98	12/31/97	12/31/96	12/31/95	12/31/94
Earnings Per Share	**[5] 0.22**	**[4] d0.16**	**0.89**	**[3] 1.14**	**[1] d1.17**	**0.44**	**[1] 0.41**
Cash Flow Per Share	**0.81**	**0.60**	**1.54**	**1.68**	**d0.71**	**1.23**	**1.14**
Tang. Book Val. Per Share	**4.93**	**2.28**	**2.32**	**1.68**	**1.54**	**2.39**	**1.75**
INCOME STATEMENT (IN THOUSANDS):							
Total Revenues	866,615	385,474	567,701	525,231	341,431	190,015	192,175
Costs & Expenses	749,186	340,660	450,121	398,548	345,591	147,833	151,062
Depreciation & Amort.	56,518	33,779	30,499	25,758	17,121	14,722	14,065
Operating Income	60,911	11,035	87,081	100,925	d21,281	27,460	27,048
Net Interest Inc./(Exp.)	d11,908	d17,865	d17,521	d14,125	d12,944	d12,118	d12,533
Income Before Income Taxes	45,847	d7,884	67,111	84,949	d34,988	15,205	14,289
Income Taxes	24,792	cr728	25,166	31,845	8,238	6,386	6,001
Equity Earnings/Minority Int.	...	d293	d721	d629	d741	d652	d680
Net Income	[5] 21,055	[4] d7,156	41,945	[3] 53,104	[1] d43,226	8,819	[1] 8,288
Cash Flow	77,573	26,623	72,444	78,862	d26,280	22,841	20,967
Average Shs. Outstg.	95,356	44,314	46,913	46,946	36,809	18,530	18,447
BALANCE SHEET (IN THOUSANDS):							
Cash & Cash Equivalents	12,176	5,258	8,735	12,593	10,407	9,394	8,531
Total Current Assets	455,706	198,630	230,468	247,716	166,233	84,753	80,994
Net Property	343,673	242,825	241,826	210,561	181,380	140,038	149,895
Total Assets	1,076,982	676,039	712,172	686,167	505,165	306,679	317,027
Total Current Liabilities	192,328	111,808	116,369	166,422	91,840	40,130	45,068
Long-Term Obligations	106,160	199,449	219,438	187,803	168,229	107,055	123,851
Net Stockholders' Equity	731,983	333,497	339,074	300,033	218,902	121,441	113,424
Net Working Capital	263,378	86,822	114,099	81,294	74,393	44,623	35,926
Year-end Shs. Outstg.	94,821	44,628	44,091	44,236	41,612	18,546	18,467
STATISTICAL RECORD:							
Operating Profit Margin %	7.0	2.9	15.3	19.2	...	14.5	14.1
Net Profit Margin %	2.4	...	7.4	10.1	...	4.6	4.3
Return on Equity %	2.9	...	12.4	17.7	...	7.3	7.3
Return on Assets %	2.0	...	5.9	7.7	...	2.9	2.6
Debt/Total Assets %	9.9	29.5	30.8	27.4	33.3	34.9	39.1
Price Range	25.38-15.25	...	...	...	...	...	...
P/E Ratio	115.3-69.3	...	...	...	...	...	...

Statistics are as originally reported. [1] Excl. extraord. chrg., 1996, $6.4 mill.; 1994, $764,000. [2] Incl. restruct. chrg., $13.3 mill. [3] Incl. write-off of long lived assets of $63.1 mill., Drexel transaction costs of $11.3 mill., transaction costs & write-offs of $2.2 mill. [4] Incl. transaction write-off costs of $7.8 mill. [5] Incl. merger and transaction costs of $22.4 mill.

OFFICERS:
G. I. Boyadjieff, Chmn., C.E.O.
J. F. Lauletta, Pres., C.O.O.
J. C. Winkler, Exec. V.P., C.F.O., Treas.

INVESTOR CONTACT: Investor Relations, (713) 799-5100

PRINCIPAL OFFICE: 2835 Holmes Road, Houston, TX 77051

TELEPHONE NUMBER: (713) 799-5100
FAX: (713) 799-1460
WEB: www.tuboscope.com

NO. OF EMPLOYEES: 6,660 (avg.)

SHAREHOLDERS: 1,270 (approx.)

ANNUAL MEETING: In May

INCORPORATED: DE, March, 1988

INSTITUTIONAL HOLDINGS:
No. of Institutions: 157
Shares Held: 66,336,139
% Held: 69.3

INDUSTRY: Oil and gas field services, nec (SIC: 1389)

TRANSFER AGENT(S): Mellon Investor Services, Ridgefield Park, NJ

NYSE SYMBOL VAR
Rec. Pr. 68.90 (4/30/01)

VARIAN MEDICAL SYSTEMS, INC.

YIELD . . .
P/E RATIO 39.6

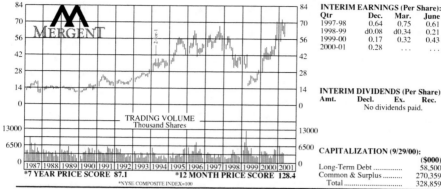

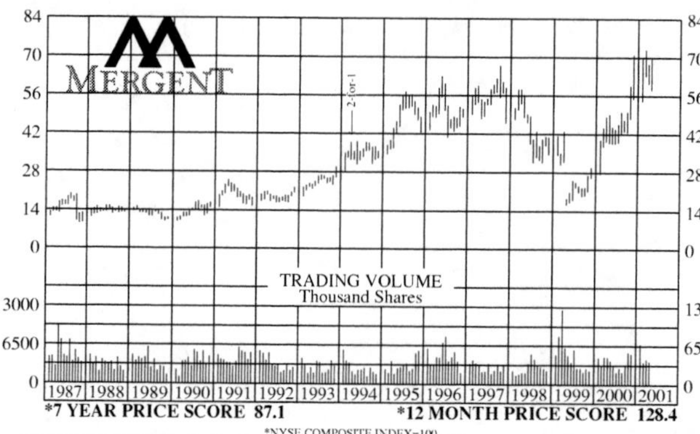

INTERIM EARNINGS (Per Share):

Qtr	Dec.	Mar.	June	Sept.
1997-98	0.64	0.75	0.61	0.42
1998-99	d0.08	d0.34	0.21	0.41
1999-00	0.17	0.32	0.43	0.71
2000-01	0.28	. . .	. . .	. . .

INTERIM DIVIDENDS (Per Share):

Amt.	Decl.	Ex.	Rec.	Pay.

No dividends paid.

CAPITALIZATION (9/29/00):

	($000)	(%)
Long-Term Debt	58,500	17.8
Common & Surplus	270,359	82.2
Total	328,859	100.0

RECENT DEVELOPMENTS: For the quarter ended 12/29/00, income was $9.3 million, before an acounting credit of $100,000, compared with net income $5.2 million in the previous year. Sales increased 14.2% to $161.4 million from $141.3 million in the year-earlier quarter. Operating earnings soared 48.5% to $14.7 million from $9.9 million in 1999. Net orders advanced 14.3% to $193.2 million, while order backlog improved 17.9% to $504.5 million.

PROSPECTS: On 1/19/01, VAR announced the launch of an on-line store for fast, easy, and convenient access to VAR's full line of medical X-ray tubes. Separately, VAR has renewed several multi-year agreements to supply customers with advanced radiotherapy systems for treating cancer. The contracts cover VAR's equipment and software for SmartBeam™ intensity modulated radiation therapy.

BUSINESS

VARIAN MEDICAL SYSTEMS, INC. (formerly Varian Associates, Inc.) is a manufacturer of integrated cancer therapy systems. More than 4,200 Varian CLINAC® medical linear accelerators and XIMATRON® simulators systems are in service around the world, treating an estimated 100,000 cancer patients per day. VAR is also a major supplier of x-ray tubes for diagnostic imaging applications. VAR is involved in several high-growth product development opportunities, including its advanced brachytherapy system for cancer treatment and the world's first real-time, digital X-ray fluoroscopic imager. In addition, VAR is pursuing technologies and products based on molecular medicine. VAR has manufacturing sites in North America and Europe and 40 sales and support offices around the world. In April 1999, VAR completed the spin-off of the instruments and semiconductor equipment businesses.

REVENUES

(09/29/2000)	$(000)	(%)
Oncology Systems	534,000	77.4
X-ray Products	136,000	19.7
Other	20,000	2.9
Total	690,000	100.0

ANNUAL FINANCIAL DATA

	9/29/00	[4] 10/1/99	10/2/98	9/26/97	9/27/96	9/29/95	9/30/94
Earnings Per Share	**[5] 1.64**	**[3] 0.27**	**2.43**	**[2] 3.66**	**3.81**	**[1] 3.01**	**2.22**
Cash Flow Per Share	**2.41**	**1.49**	**3.83**	**5.10**	**5.24**	**4.59**	**3.70**
Tang. Book Val. Per Share	**8.51**	**6.05**	**18.75**	**17.42**	**15.27**	**12.72**	**13.23**
Dividends Per Share	. . .	**0.10**	**0.39**	**0.35**	**0.31**	**0.27**	**0.23**
Dividend Payout %	. . .	**37.0**	**16.0**	**9.6**	**8.1**	**9.0**	**10.4**
INCOME STATEMENT (IN MILLIONS):							
Total Revenues	689.7	590.4	1,422.1	1,425.8	1,599.4	1,575.7	1,552.5
Costs & Expenses	580.0	528.7	1,264.3	1,250.3	1,363.2	1,353.2	1,370.0
Depreciation & Amort.	22.0	37.4	42.7	45.6	46.1	55.6	52.5
Operating Income	87.7	24.3	115.2	129.9	190.1	166.9	130.0
Net Interest Inc./(Exp.)	d2.8	d6.1	d2.4	d3.2	d0.8	d1.6	d2.0
Income Before Income Taxes	84.9	18.2	112.7	177.8	189.2	165.3	128.0
Income Taxes	31.8	10.0	38.9	62.2	67.2	59.5	48.6
Net Income	[5] 53.0	[3] 8.2	73.8	[2] 115.6	122.1	[1] 105.8	79.4
Cash Flow	75.0	45.6	116.5	161.2	168.1	161.4	131.9
Average Shs. Outstg. (000)	31,104	30,527	30,419	31,587	32,075	35,202	35,676
BALANCE SHEET (IN MILLIONS):							
Cash & Cash Equivalents	83.3	25.1	149.7	142.3	82.7	122.7	78.9
Total Current Assets	450.6	382.2	839.8	813.5	743.9	757.7	668.8
Net Property	80.1	80.3	214.2	195.6	212.1	191.9	235.3
Total Assets	602.6	539.2	1,218.3	1,104.3	1,019.0	1,003.8	962.4
Total Current Liabilities	249.9	269.8	504.9	464.3	450.0	500.7	431.8
Long-Term Obligations	58.5	58.5	111.1	73.2	60.3	60.3	60.4
Net Stockholders' Equity	270.4	185.0	557.5	524.6	467.9	394.9	449.5
Net Working Capital	200.7	112.4	334.9	349.2	293.9	257.0	236.9
Year-end Shs. Outstg. (000)	31,769	30,563	29,743	30,108	30,646	31,052	33,979
STATISTICAL RECORD:							
Operating Profit Margin %	12.7	4.1	8.1	9.1	11.9	10.6	8.4
Net Profit Margin %	7.7	1.4	5.2	8.1	7.6	6.7	5.1
Return on Equity %	19.6	4.4	13.2	22.0	26.1	26.8	17.7
Return on Assets %	8.8	1.5	6.1	10.5	12.0	10.5	8.2
Debt/Total Assets %	9.7	10.8	9.1	6.6	5.9	6.0	6.3
Price Range	71.00-27.50	43.00-16.25	58.38-31.56	67.00-45.88	62.88-40.50	57.38-34.50	39.25-28.25
P/E Ratio	43.3-16.8	159.2-60.2	24.0-13.0	18.3-12.5	16.5-10.6	19.1-11.5	17.7-12.7
Average Yield %	. . .	0.3	0.9	0.6	0.6	0.6	0.7

Statistics are as originally reported. Adj. for stk. split: 2-for-1, 3/94 [1] Bef. disc. opers. gain $33.5 mill. ($0.95/sh.) [2] Incl. net gain on sale of assets $29.2 mill. ($0.96/sh.) [3] Bef. disc. oper. loss of $30.8 mill., but incl. non-recurr. chrgs. $31.0 mill. [4] Reflects spin-off of instruments and semiconductor equipment businesses. [5] Incl. non-recurr. chrgs. $2.2 mill.

OFFICERS:
R. M. Levy, Pres., C.E.O.
E. W. Finney, V.P., C.F.O., Treas.
J. B. Phair, V.P., Gen. Couns., Sec.

INVESTOR CONTACT: Stockholder Relations, (650) 424-5855

PRINCIPAL OFFICE: 3100 Hansen Way, Palo Alto, CA 94304-1038

TELEPHONE NUMBER: (650) 493-4000
FAX: (650) 493-0307
WEB: www.varian.com

NO. OF EMPLOYEES: 2,374 (avg.)

SHAREHOLDERS: 4,474 (approx.)

ANNUAL MEETING: In Feb.

INCORPORATED: CA, Apr., 1948; reincorp., DE, Jan., 1976

INSTITUTIONAL HOLDINGS:
No. of Institutions: 199
Shares Held: 26,908,066
% Held: 82.1

INDUSTRY: Special industry machinery, nec (SIC: 3559)

TRANSFER AGENT(S): First Chicago Trust Company of New York, Jersey City, NJ

NYSE SYMBOL Z
Rec. Pr. 13.30 (5/31/01)

VENATOR GROUP, INC.

YIELD ...
P/E RATIO 19.9

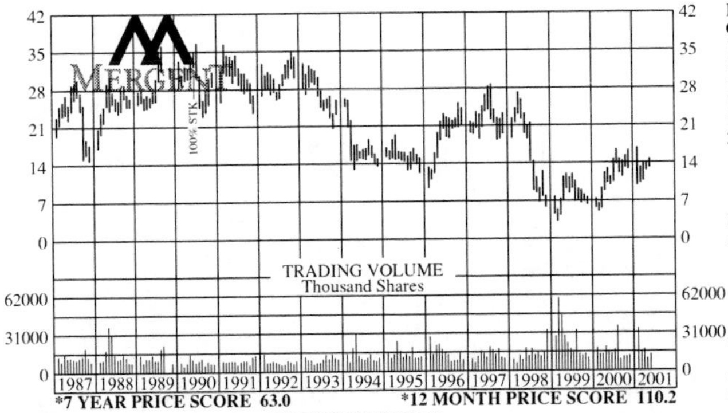

TRADING VOLUME
Thousand Shares

*7 YEAR PRICE SCORE 63.0 *12 MONTH PRICE SCORE 110.2

*NYSE COMPOSITE INDEX=100

INTERIM EARNINGS (Per Share):

Qtr.	Apr.	July	Oct.	Jan.
1995-96	d0.60	d0.09	0.26	d0.80
1996-97	d0.17	0.17	0.52	0.74
1997-98	0.01	0.19	0.41	0.85
1998-99	d0.04	d0.09	d0.29	0.21
1999-00	d0.08	d0.30	0.05	0.44
2000-01	0.11	0.07	0.18	0.31

INTERIM DIVIDENDS (Per Share):

Amt.	Decl.	Ex.	Rec.	Pay.

Last dist. $0.15Q, 3/1/95

CAPITALIZATION (2/3/01):

	($000)	(%)
Capital Lease Obligations..	259,000	20.4
Common & Surplus	1,013,000	79.6
Total	1,272,000	100.0

RECENT DEVELOPMENTS: For the 53 weeks ended 2/3/01, income from continuing operations was $107.0 million versus income from continuing operations of $59.0 million in the corresponding 52-week period a year earlier. Results included pre-tax restructuring charges of $1.0 million and $85.0 million in 2000 and 1999, respectively. Sales rose 2.2% to $4.36 billion. Comparable-store sales were up 11.5% year over year. Comparisons were made with restated prior-year figures.

PROSPECTS: On 3/29/01, Z announced plans to close its 323 Northern Reflections stores in the U.S. The divestiture of these operations, which is expected to be completed by the end of the second quarter in fiscal 2001, should help the Company focus on growing its athletic business going forward. Following the closing of its U.S. operations, Z's Northern Group will consist of 195 Northern Reflections and Northern Traditions stores, 112 Northern Getaway stores and 63 Northern Elements stores in Canada.

BUSINESS

VENATOR GROUP, INC. (formerly Woolworth Corporation) is primarily a mall-based retailer of athletic apparel and footwear. As of 2/3/01, Z operated 3,582 stores in 14 countries in North America, Europe and Australia, under the names Foot Locker, Lady Foot Locker, Kids Foot Locker and Champs Sports, as well as Footlocker.com/Eastbay, the Company's Internet and catalog operations. The Company is in the process of divesting its chain of apparel stores operating under the names Northern Reflections, Northern Traditions, Northern Getaway and Northern Elements. In 1998, the Company sold its 357-store German General Merchandise business, its six-store nursery chain, and divested its Specialty Footwear segment, comprised of 467 Kinney shoe stores and 103 Footquarters stores. In 1999, Z sold its 768-store Afterthoughts fashion accessory chain.

ANNUAL FINANCIAL DATA

	2/3/01	1/29/00	1/30/99	1/31/98	1/25/97	1/27/96	1/28/95
Earnings Per Share	**[7] 0.77**	**[6] 0.13**	**[5] 0.02**	**[4] 1.57**	**[3] 1.26**	**[2] d1.23**	**[1] 0.36**
Cash Flow Per Share	**1.85**	**1.43**	**1.14**	**2.81**	**2.66**	**0.56**	**2.12**
Tang. Book Val. Per Share	**6.27**	**7.18**	**6.39**	**9.41**	**9.96**	**9.24**	**10.29**
Dividends Per Share	...	...	...	...	...	**0.15**	**0.88**
Dividend Payout %	...	...	...	...	...	...	**244.4**
INCOME STATEMENT (IN MILLIONS):							
Total Revenues	4,356.0	4,647.0	4,555.0	6,624.0	8,092.0	8,224.0	8,238.0
Costs & Expenses	4,023.0	4,603.0	4,499.0	6,103.0	7,587.0	7,901.0	7,857.0
Depreciation & Amort.	151.0	182.0	152.0	168.0	187.0	239.0	233.0
Operating Income	182.0	d138.0	d96.0	353.0	318.0	84.0	148.0
Net Interest Inc./(Exp.)	d22.0	d57.0	d44.0	d44.0	d73.0	d119.0	d107.0
Income Before Income Taxes	176.0	28.0	d39.0	338.0	280.0	d233.0	96.0
Income Taxes	69.0	11.0	cr42.0	125.0	111.0	cr69.0	49.0
Net Income	[7] 107.0	[6] 17.0	[5] 3.0	[4] 213.0	[3] 169.0	[2] d164.0	[1] 47.0
Cash Flow	258.0	199.0	155.0	381.0	356.0	75.0	280.0
Average Shs. Outstg. (000)	139,100	138,800	135,900	135,800	134,000	133,000	132,000
BALANCE SHEET (IN MILLIONS):							
Cash & Cash Equivalents	109.0	162.0	193.0	116.0	321.0	13.0	72.0
Total Current Assets	1,000.0	1,089.0	1,275.0	1,459.0	1,823.0	1,618.0	2,069.0
Net Property	684.0	809.0	974.0	1,053.0	1,058.0	1,225.0	1,521.0
Total Assets	2,232.0	2,515.0	2,876.0	3,182.0	3,476.0	3,506.0	4,173.0
Total Current Liabilities	629.0	777.0	964.0	756.0	856.0	841.0	1,710.0
Long-Term Obligations	259.0	312.0	511.0	535.0	580.0	619.0	309.0
Net Stockholders' Equity	1,013.0	1,139.0	1,038.0	1,271.0	1,334.0	1,229.0	1,358.0
Net Working Capital	371.0	312.0	311.0	703.0	967.0	777.0	359.0
Year-end Shs. Outstg. (000)	138,691	137,665	135,700	135,000	134,000	133,000	132,000
STATISTICAL RECORD:							
Operating Profit Margin %	4.2	...	...	5.3	3.9	1.0	1.8
Net Profit Margin %	2.5	0.4	0.1	3.2	2.1	...	0.6
Return on Equity %	10.6	1.5	0.3	16.8	12.7	...	3.5
Return on Assets %	4.8	0.7	0.1	6.7	4.9	...	1.1
Debt/Total Assets %	11.6	12.4	17.8	16.8	16.7	17.7	7.4
Price Range	16.50-5.00	12.00-3.19	27.25-5.81	28.75-18.25	25.25-9.38	19.38-12.25	26.25-12.88
P/E Ratio	21.4-6.5	92.2-24.5	1,355.7-289.2	18.3-11.6	20.0-7.4	...	72.9-35.8
Average Yield %	...	...	...	...	...	0.9	4.5

Statistics are as originally reported. [1] Incl. $30 mil prov for disp. of ops. & incl. $41 mil gain. [2] Incl. $170 mil chg. for writedown of assets & sale of ops. [3] Incl. $10 mil net loss fr disp of ops. & sale of real est. [4] Incl. $9 mil net gain & bef. $223 mil net loss fr disc. ops. [5] Bef. $139.0 mil disc. ops. loss. [6] Incl. $144 mil restr. chg. & bef. $23 mil inc. fr. disc. ops. & $8 mil acctg. gain. [7] Bef. $346 mil loss fr. disc. ops., $1 mil acctg. chrg. & incl. $1 mil restr. chg.

OFFICERS:
J. C. Bacot, Chmn.
M. D. Serra, Pres., C.E.O.
B. L. Hartman, Sr. V.P., C.F.O.

INVESTOR CONTACT: Juris Pagrabs, Dir., Investor Relations, (212) 553-2600

PRINCIPAL OFFICE: 112 West 34th Street, New York, NY 10120

TELEPHONE NUMBER: (212) 720-3700
FAX: (212) 553-7026
WEB: www.venatorgroup.com
NO. OF EMPLOYEES: 48,815
SHAREHOLDERS: 32,398
ANNUAL MEETING: In June
INCORPORATED: NY, Dec., 1911; reincorp., NY, 1989

INSTITUTIONAL HOLDINGS:
No. of Institutions: 156
Shares Held: 112,980,068
% Held: 81.5

INDUSTRY: Men's footwear, except athletic (SIC: 3143)

TRANSFER AGENT(S): EquiServe, Jersey City, NJ

NYSE SYMBOL VZ
Rec. Pr. 55.07 (4/30/01)

VERIZON COMMUNICATIONS

YIELD 2.8%
P/E RATIO 14.0

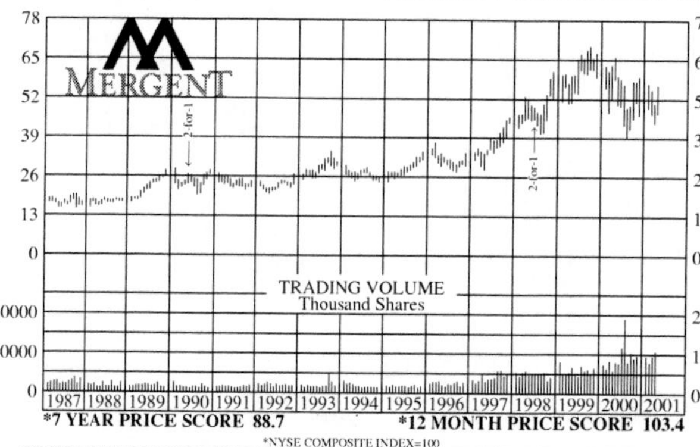

INTERIM EARNINGS (Per Share):

Qtr.	Mar.	June	Sept.	Dec.
1997	0.45	0.57	d0.05	0.60
1998	1.13	0.65	d0.01	0.65
1999	0.72	0.74	0.74	0.45
2000	0.46	1.79	0.97	0.70

INTERIM DIVIDENDS (Per Share):

Amt.	Decl.	Ex.	Rec.	Pay.
0.047Q	6/30/00	7/06/00	7/10/00	8/01/00
0.385Q	9/07/00	10/05/00	10/10/00	11/01/00
0.385Q	12/07/00	1/08/01	1/10/01	2/01/01
0.385Q	3/05/01	4/06/01	4/10/01	5/01/01
0.385Q	6/07/01	7/06/01	7/10/01	8/01/01

Indicated div.: $1.54

CAPITALIZATION (12/31/00):

	($000)	(%)
Long-Term Debt	42,491,000	37.2
Deferred Income Tax	15,260,000	13.4
Minority Interest	21,830,000	19.1
Common & Surplus	34,578,000	30.3
Total	114,159,000	100.0

RECENT DEVELOPMENTS: For the year ended 12/31/00, income from continuing operations was $10.81 billion versus $8.30 billion a year earlier. Results for 2000 and 1999 included net gains on the sale of assets of $3.79 billion and $1.38 billion, respectively. Results also included a $664.0 million credit and a $664.0 million charge in 2000 and 1999, respectively, on mark-to-market adjustments. Total revenues rose 11.2% to $64.71 billion.

PROSPECTS: Results are being fueled by continued strong demand for wireless and data services. Looking forward, VZ is aiming to serve between 1.2 million and 1.3 million digital subscriber line customers by 12/31/01, up from 540,000 a year earlier. Also, Verizon Wireless expects to deploy by year end the first phase of its third generation or 3G wireless technology, which is expected to allow substantially higher Internet access speeds.

BUSINESS

VERIZON COMMUNICATIONS (formerly Bell Atlantic Corp.), formed by the merger of Bell Atlantic Corporation and GTE Corp. on 6/30/00, is a provider of high-growth communications services. VZ is among the largest providers of wireline and wireless communications in the United States, with nearly 109.0 million access line equivalents and more than 27.5 million wireless customers and 4.9 million long-distance customers as of 2/1/01. VZ also provides print and online directory information. VZ's global presence extends to 40 countries in the Americas, Europe, Asia and the Pacific. As of 12/31/00, the Company owned 55.0% of Verizon Wireless, which was formed in April 2000 through the combination of Bell Atlantic's and Vodafone AirTouch's U.S. wireless assets.

BUSINESS LINE ANALYSIS

(12/31/2000)	REV (%)	INC (%)
Domestic Telecom	68.0	68.0
Domestic Wireless	22.4	5.9
International	3.1	9.7
Information Services	6.5	16.4
Total	100.0	100.0

ANNUAL FINANCIAL DATA

	12/31/00	12/31/99	12/31/98	12/31/97	12/31/96	12/31/95	12/31/94
Earnings Per Share	**[8] 3.95**	**[7] 2.66**	**[1] 1.87**	**1.57**	**[3] 1.98**	**[4][5] 2.13**	**[6] 1.61**
Cash Flow Per Share	**8.43**	**6.49**	**5.52**	**5.23**	**4.93**	**5.12**	**4.64**
Tang. Book Val. Per Share	**...**	**10.23**	**9.31**	**8.82**	**9.52**	**8.81**	**7.73**
Dividends Per Share	**1.54**	**1.54**	**1.54**	**1.49**	**1.43**	**1.40**	**1.37**
Dividend Payout %	**39.0**	**57.9**	**82.3**	**94.9**	**72.2**	**65.6**	**85.4**
INCOME STATEMENT (IN MILLIONS):							
Total Revenues	64,707.0	33,174.0	31,565.9	[2] 30,193.9	13,081.4	13,429.5	13,791.4
Costs & Expenses	35,688.0	18,609.0	19,188.7	19,098.3	7,550.2	7,716.2	8,334.7
Depreciation & Amort.	12,261.0	6,070.0	5,750.0	5,754.1	2,594.6	2,627.1	2,652.1
Operating Income	16,758.0	8,495.0	6,627.2	5,341.5	2,936.6	3,086.2	2,804.6
Net Interest Inc./(Exp.)	d3,490.0	d1,263.0	d1,335.4	d1,230.0	d477.9	d561.0	d582.1
Income Before Income Taxes	17,819.0	6,765.0	4,998.9	3,984.1	2,750.6	3,009.4	2,286.8
Income Taxes	7,009.0	2,557.0	2,008.1	1,529.2	1,011.2	1,147.6	884.9
Equity Earnings/Minority Int.	3,576.0	143.0	d414.6	d124.1	327.9	152.5	41.1
Net Income	[8] 10,810.0	[7] 4,208.0	[1] 2,990.8	2,454.9	[3] 1,739.4	[4][5] 1,861.8	[6] 1,401.9
Cash Flow	23,061.0	10,278.0	8,708.5	8,209.0	4,334.0	4,488.9	4,054.0
Average Shs. Outstg. (000)	2,737,000	1,583,000	1,578,300	1,571,000	879,200	876,600	874,400
BALANCE SHEET (IN MILLIONS):							
Cash & Cash Equivalents	2,370.0	1,936.0	1,022.9	1,043.4	424.2	356.8	142.9
Total Current Assets	22,121.0	10,596.0	9,082.3	9,000.8	3,948.0	3,872.7	3,783.3
Net Property	69,504.0	39,299.0	36,815.5	35,039.4	15,915.7	15,921.3	16,938.1
Total Assets	164,735.0	62,614.0	55,143.9	53,964.1	24,856.2	24,156.8	24,271.8
Total Current Liabilities	34,236.0	13,467.0	10,531.2	13,664.2	8,605.5	8,096.5	8,314.1
Long-Term Obligations	42,491.0	18,463.0	17,646.4	13,265.0	5,960.2	6,407.2	6,805.7
Net Stockholders' Equity	34,578.0	15,880.0	14,453.8	13,895.9	8,339.8	7,715.4	6,742.9
Net Working Capital	d12,115.0	d2,871.0	d1,448.9	d4,663.4	d4,657.5	d4,223.8	d4,530.8
Year-end Shs. Outstg. (000)	2,751,651	1,552,677	1,553,300	1,576,052	875,632	875,344	872,372
STATISTICAL RECORD:							
Operating Profit Margin %	25.9	25.6	21.0	17.7	22.4	23.0	20.3
Net Profit Margin %	16.7	12.7	9.5	8.1	13.3	13.9	10.2
Return on Equity %	31.3	26.5	20.7	17.7	20.9	24.1	20.8
Return on Assets %	6.6	6.7	5.4	4.5	7.0	7.7	5.8
Debt/Total Assets %	25.8	29.5	32.0	24.6	24.0	26.5	28.0
Price Range	66.00-39.06	69.50-50.63	61.19-40.44	45.88-28.38	37.44-27.56	34.44-24.19	29.81-24.19
P/E Ratio	16.7-9.9	26.1-19.0	32.7-21.6	29.3-18.1	18.9-13.9	16.2-11.4	18.6-15.1
Average Yield %	2.9	2.6	3.0	4.0	4.4	4.8	5.1

Statistics are as originally reported. Results for 12/31/99 & earlier are for Bell Atlantic Corp. Adj. for 2-for-1 stk. split, 5/98. [1] Bef. extraord. chrg. of $25.5 mil. [2] Refl. 8/97 acq. of NYNEX Corp. [3] Bef. actg. chrg. of $19.8 mil. [4] Bef. extraord. chrg. of $3.5 mil. [5] Incl. cr. of $160.0 mil. [6] Bef. extraord. gain & actg. chrgs. of $2.16 mil. [7] Bef. extraord. chrg. of $6.0 mil. [8] Incl. gains of $4.45 bil.; bef. extraord. gain of $1.03 bil. & acctg. chrg. of $40.0 mil.

OFFICERS:
C. R. Lee, Chmn., Co-C.E.O.
I. Seidenberg, Pres., Co-C.E.O.
F. V. Salerno, Vice Chmn., C.F.O.

INVESTOR CONTACT: Shareholder Relations, (212) 395-1525

PRINCIPAL OFFICE: 1095 Avenue of the Americas, New York, NY 10036

TELEPHONE NUMBER: (212) 395-2121
FAX: (212) 921-2917
WEB: www.verizon.com

NO. OF EMPLOYEES: 260,000 (approx.)

SHAREHOLDERS: 1,335,000 (record)

ANNUAL MEETING: In Apr.

INCORPORATED: DE, Oct., 1983

INSTITUTIONAL HOLDINGS:
No. of Institutions: 1,065
Shares Held: 1,182,288,062
% Held: 43.7

INDUSTRY: Telephone communications, exc. radio (SIC: 4813)

TRANSFER AGENT(S): EquiServe, Boston, MA

NYSE SYMBOL VFC
Rec. Pr. 41.36 (5/31/01)

VF CORPORATION

YIELD 2.2%
P/E RATIO 18.3

TRADING VOLUME
Thousand Shares

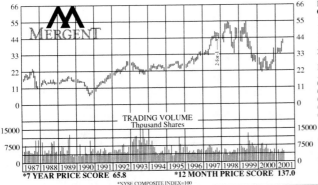

***7 YEAR PRICE SCORE 65.8** ***12 MONTH PRICE SCORE 137.0**

*NYSE COMPOSITE INDEX=100

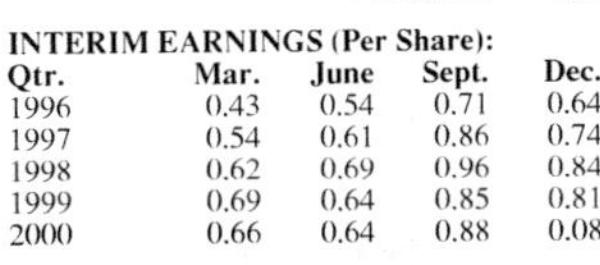

INTERIM EARNINGS (Per Share):

Qtr.	Mar.	June	Sept.	Dec.
1996	0.43	0.54	0.71	0.64
1997	0.54	0.61	0.86	0.74
1998	0.62	0.69	0.96	0.84
1999	0.69	0.64	0.85	0.81
2000	0.66	0.64	0.88	0.08

INTERIM DIVIDENDS (Per Share):

Amt.	Decl.	Ex.	Rec.	Pay.
0.22Q	4/25/00	6/07/00	6/09/00	6/19/00
0.22Q	7/18/00	9/06/00	9/10/00	9/20/00
0.23Q	10/18/00	12/06/00	12/08/00	12/18/00
0.23Q	2/06/01	3/07/01	3/09/01	3/19/01
0.23Q	4/24/01	6/06/01	6/08/01	6/18/01

Indicated div.: $0.92 (Div. Reinv. Plan)

CAPITALIZATION (12/30/00):

	($000)	(%)
Long-Term Debt	905,036	28.8
Redeemable Pfd. Stock	48,483	1.5
Common & Surplus	2,191,813	69.7
Total	3,145,332	100.0

RECENT DEVELOPMENTS: For the year ended 12/30/00, income declined 27.1% to $267.1 million, before an accounting charge of $6.8 million, compared with net income of $366.2 million a year earlier. Results for 2000 included restructuring costs of $119.9 million for actions that were implemented to improve future profitability. Net sales advanced 3.5% to $5.75 billion from $5.55 billion in the previous year.

PROSPECTS: VFC's near-term outlook is mixed. On the plus side, the Company's core jeanswear, playwear, daypack, knitwear and international businesses are performing well. In addition, new brands, new product introductions, and an improved cost structure should lead to sales gains and better profitability. VFC expects earnings per share to range from $3.21 to $3.28 and sales to rise slightly above 2000 levels.

BUSINESS

VF CORPORATION designs, manufactures and markets branded jeanswear, intimate apparel, children's playwear, occupational apparel, knitwear and other apparel. Apparel is manufactured and marketed under the following brands: LEE, WRANGLER, RUSTLER, RIDERS, and BRITTANIA jeanswear; LEE CASUAL, and TIMBER CREEK BY WRANGLER casual/sportswear; VANITY FAIR, VASSARETTE, LILY OF FRANCE, OSCAR DE LA RENTA, and NIKE intimate apparel; RED KAP and BULWARK occupational apparel; JANTZEN and NIKE swimwear; and HEALTHTEX, LEE, and NIKE children's apparel. Jeanswear is manufactured and marketed internationally under the LEE, WRANGLER, MAVERICK and OLD AXE brands, and intimate apparel is marketed under various labels. On 5/20/00, VFC acquired the Eastpak branded business and the CHIC jeans brand. On 8/16/00, VFC completed the acquisition of The North Face, Inc.

REVENUES

(12/30/2000)	($000)	(%)
Consumer Apparel	4,227,997	73.6
Occupational Apparel	661,635	11.5
All Other Revenue	858,247	14.9
Total	5,747,879	100.0

ANNUAL FINANCIAL DATA

	12/30/00	1/1/00	1/2/99	1/3/98	1/4/97	12/31/95	12/31/94
Earnings Per Share	**[1] 2.27**	**2.99**	**3.10**	**2.70**	**2.32**	**1.21**	**2.10**
Cash Flow Per Share	**3.76**	**4.37**	**4.40**	**3.91**	**3.61**	**2.55**	**3.35**
Tang. Book Val. Per Share	**12.56**	**10.08**	**9.33**	**8.68**	**8.68**	**6.97**	**6.41**
Dividends Per Share	**0.89**	**0.85**	**0.81**	**0.77**	**0.73**	**0.69**	**0.65**
Dividend Payout %	**39.2**	**28.4**	**26.1**	**28.5**	**31.5**	**57.3**	**31.0**
INCOME STATEMENT (IN MILLIONS):							
Total Revenues	5,747.9	5,551.6	5,478.8	5,222.2	5,137.2	5,062.3	4,971.7
Costs & Expenses	5,064.5	4,731.6	4,633.3	4,460.9	4,419.3	4,547.2	4,274.4
Depreciation & Amort.	173.4	167.4	161.4	156.3	160.6	167.7	158.5
Operating Income	510.0	652.6	684.2	605.1	557.3	347.4	538.8
Net Interest Inc./(Exp.)	d81.0	d62.5	d55.9	d25.9	d49.4	d66.2	d71.0
Income Before Income Taxes	431.5	595.6	631.6	585.9	508.4	284.1	455.7
Income Taxes	164.4	229.3	243.3	234.9	208.9	126.8	181.1
Net Income	[1] 267.1	366.2	388.3	350.9	299.5	157.3	274.5
Cash Flow	437.2	530.1	546.0	503.4	456.1	320.9	428.8
Average Shs. Outstg. (000)	117,218	122,258	124,995	129,720	127,292	127,486	129,240
BALANCE SHEET (IN MILLIONS):							
Cash & Cash Equivalents	118.9	79.9	63.2	124.1	270.6	84.1	59.7
Total Current Assets	2,110.1	1,877.4	1,848.2	1,601.5	1,706.3	1,667.6	1,551.2
Net Property	776.0	804.4	776.1	706.0	721.5	749.9	767.0
Total Assets	4,358.2	4,026.5	3,836.7	3,322.8	3,449.5	3,447.1	3,335.6
Total Current Liabilities	1,006.2	1,113.5	1,033.0	765.9	766.3	868.3	912.3
Long-Term Obligations	905.0	517.8	521.7	516.2	519.1	614.2	516.7
Net Stockholders' Equity	2,191.8	2,163.8	2,066.3	1,866.8	1,973.7	1,771.5	1,734.0
Net Working Capital	1,103.9	763.9	815.1	835.6	940.1	799.3	638.8
Year-end Shs. Outstg. (000)	86,807	116,205	119,466	121,225	127,816	126,878	128,330
STATISTICAL RECORD:							
Operating Profit Margin %	8.9	11.8	12.5	11.6	10.8	6.9	10.8
Net Profit Margin %	4.6	6.6	7.1	6.7	5.8	3.1	5.5
Return on Equity %	12.2	16.9	18.8	18.8	15.2	8.9	15.8
Return on Assets %	6.1	9.1	10.1	10.6	8.7	4.6	8.2
Debt/Total Assets %	20.8	12.9	13.6	15.5	15.0	17.8	15.5
Price Range	36.90-20.94	55.00-27.44	54.69-33.44	48.25-32.25	34.94-23.81	28.56-23.38	26.88-22.13
P/E Ratio	16.3-9.2	18.4-9.2	17.6-10.8	17.9-11.9	15.1-10.3	23.7-19.4	12.8-10.5
Average Yield %	3.1	2.1	1.8	1.9	2.5	2.7	2.7

Statistics are as originally reported. Adj. for stk. split: 2-for-1, 11/97 [1] Incls. restruct. costs of $119.9 mill.; bef. acctg. chge. chrg. of $6.8 mill.

OFFICERS:
M. J. McDonald, Chmn., Pres., C.E.O.
R. K. Shearer, V.P., C.F.O.
F. C. Pickard III, V.P., Treas.

INVESTOR CONTACT: Cindy Knoebel, CFA, Dir., Inv. & Corp. Comm., (336) 547-6192

PRINCIPAL OFFICE: 628 Green Valley Road, Suite 500, Greensboro, NC 27408

TELEPHONE NUMBER: (336) 547-6000
FAX: (336) 547-7630
WEB: www.threads.vfc.com

NO. OF EMPLOYEES: 75,000 (approx.)

SHAREHOLDERS: 6,667 (record)

ANNUAL MEETING: In April

INCORPORATED: PA, Dec., 1889

INSTITUTIONAL HOLDINGS:
No. of Institutions: 235
Shares Held: 98,601,531
% Held: 88.0

INDUSTRY: Men's and boys' clothing, nec (SIC: 2329)

TRANSFER AGENT(S): First Chicago Trust Company of New York, Jersey City, NJ

NYSE SYMBOL VIA
Rec. Pr. 57.85 (5/31/01)

VIACOM INC.

YIELD ...
P/E RATIO ...

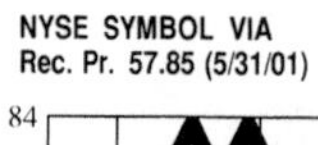

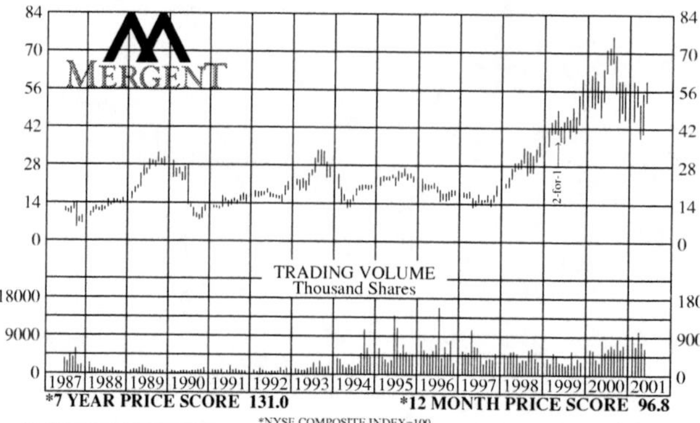

INTERIM EARNINGS (Per Share):

Qtr.	Mar.	June	Sept.	Dec.
1996	0.01	0.01	0.12	0.01
1997	d0.06	d0.33	0.01	0.80
1998	0.05	d0.40	0.10	0.15
1999	0.08	0.08	0.16	0.19
2000	0.11	d0.41	0.02	0.02

INTERIM DIVIDENDS (Per Share):

Amt.	Decl.	Ex.	Rec.	Pay.
2-for-1	2/26/99	4/15/99	3/01/99	3/31/99

CAPITALIZATION (12/31/00):

	($000)	(%)
Long-Term Debt	12,473,800	18.5
Minority Interest	7,040,200	10.4
Common & Surplus	47,966,900	71.1
Total	67,480,900	100.0

RECENT DEVELOPMENTS: For the year ended 12/31/00, VIA reported a loss of $363.8 million, before an accounting change charge, versus income of $371.7 million, before an extraordinary loss, in the prior year. Results for 2000 included after-tax merger-related charges totaling $505.0 million. Revenues were $20.04 billion, up 55.9% from $12.86 billion in 1999. Television revenues more than doubled to $5.38 billion. Video revenues rose 11.1% to $4.96 billion, while cable networks revenues climbed 27.9% to $3.90 billion.

PROSPECTS: On 1/23/01, the Company acquired BET Holdings II, Inc., which owns the Black Entertainment Television cable network, for $3.00 billion. On 2/21/01, VIA completed its purchase of the 37.0% of Infinity Broadcasting Corporation that it did not already own for about $12.00 billion. Going forward, VIA expects results will benefit from strong operating performance at its popular cable networks, along with the continued success of the CBS hit show "Survivor."

BUSINESS

VIACOM INC. is a diversified entertainment company. VIA's operations include Infinity Broadcasting, CBS, Nickelodeon, VH1, TNN, CMT, Blockbuster, MTV Networks, BET, Paramount Pictures, Showtime Networks, and Simon & Schuster. VIA also owns Spelling Entertainment Group and the UPN television network, as well as half-interests in Comedy Central, and UCI. National Amusements, Inc., a closely-held corporation which operates about 1,300 screens in the U.S., the U.K. and South America, is the parent company of Viacom. On 5/4/00, VIA acquired CBS Corp. The Company acquired BET Holdings II, Inc. on 1/23/01 and Infinity Broadcasting Corporation on 2/21/01.

ANNUAL FINANCIAL DATA

	12/31/00	12/31/99	12/31/98	12/31/97	12/31/96	12/31/95	12/31/94
Earnings Per Share	**[3][4] d0.30**	**[1] 0.51**	**[1][2] d0.10**	**[2][3] 0.45**	**[2][3] 0.15**	**[2] 0.21**	**[1][2] 0.13**
Cash Flow Per Share	**1.53**	**1.72**	**1.02**	**1.82**	**1.26**	**1.30**	**1.18**
INCOME STATEMENT (IN MILLIONS):							
Total Revenues	20,043.7	12,858.8	12,096.1	13,206.1	12,084.2	11,688.7	7,363.2
Costs & Expenses	16,481.4	10,751.4	10,551.1	11,476.4	9,992.3	9,375.0	6,289.2
Depreciation & Amort.	2,241.4	860.1	793.4	976.9	817.6	820.4	465.7
Operating Income	1,320.9	1,247.3	751.6	752.8	1,274.3	1,493.3	608.3
Net Interest Inc./(Exp.)	d769.1	d421.2	d599.0	d763.0	d798.0	d821.4	d494.1
Income Before Income Taxes	560.6	843.9	137.3	1,222.7	480.5	689.2	376.7
Income Taxes	729.8	411.4	138.7	689.6	295.5	417.0	279.7
Equity Earnings/Minority Int.	d194.6	d60.8	d42.1	d158.6	d14.3	d57.3	33.5
Net Income	[3][4] d363.8	[1] 371.7	[1][2] d43.5	[2][3] 374.5	[2][3] 170.7	[2] 214.9	[1][2] 130.5
Cash Flow	1,877.6	1,219.4	722.7	1,291.4	928.3	975.3	521.2
Average Shs. Outstg. (000)	1,225,300	709,500	708,700	708,600	734,800	750,200	440,000
BALANCE SHEET (IN MILLIONS):							
Cash & Cash Equivalents	934.5	680.8	767.3	292.3	209.0	464.1	597.7
Total Current Assets	7,832.4	5,198.4	4,595.8	4,778.7	4,794.4	4,295.9	4,424.3
Net Property	6,601.8	3,425.3	3,079.5	3,197.7	3,155.8	3,217.9	2,583.1
Total Assets	82,646.1	24,486.4	23,613.1	28,288.7	28,834.0	29,026.0	28,273.7
Total Current Liabilities	7,758.2	4,399.7	5,632.6	5,052.5	4,268.7	4,098.6	4,131.2
Long-Term Obligations	12,473.8	5,697.7	3,813.4	7,423.0	9,855.7	10,712.1	10,402.4
Net Stockholders' Equity	47,966.9	11,132.0	12,049.6	13,383.6	12,594.4	12,093.8	11,791.6
Net Working Capital	74.2	798.7	d1,036.8	d273.8	525.7	197.3	293.1
Year-end Shs. Outstg. (000)	1,495,900	697,800	695,000	695,800	704,000	739,400	717,400
STATISTICAL RECORD:							
Operating Profit Margin %	6.6	9.7	6.2	5.7	10.5	12.8	8.3
Net Profit Margin %	...	2.9	...	2.8	1.4	1.8	1.8
Return on Equity %	...	3.3	...	2.8	1.4	1.8	1.1
Return on Assets %	...	1.5	...	1.3	0.6	0.7	0.5
Debt/Total Assets %	15.1	23.3	16.5	27.1	35.3	38.1	37.9
Price Range	78.88-44.31	60.44-35.38	37.13-20.25	21.13-12.63	23.81-14.88	27.13-20.13	22.50-10.88
P/E Ratio	...	118.5-69.2	...	46.9-28.4	155.7-98.7	131.9-100.0	198.8-97.9

Statistics are as originally reported. Adj. for stk. 2-for-1 split, 3/99 [1] Bef. extraord. chrg. 1999, $37.7 mill.; 1998, $74.7 mill.; 1994, $20.4 mill. [2] Bef. disc. oper. loss 1998, $4.2 mill.; gain 1997, $419.1 mill.; 1996, $1.08 bill.; loss 1995, $7.6 mill.; 1994, $20.5 mill. [3] Incl. non-recurr. chrg. 2000, $505.0 mill.; 1997, $323.0 mill.; 1996, $88.9 mill. [4] Bef. acctg. change chrg. $452.3 mill.

OFFICERS:
S. M. Redstone, Chmn., C.E.O.
P. P. Dauman, Deputy Chmn., Exec. V.P.
T. E. Dooley, Deputy Chmn., Exec. V.P.
M. Karmazin, Pres., C.O.O.

PRINCIPAL OFFICE: 1515 Broadway, New York, NY 10036

TELEPHONE NUMBER: (212) 258-6000
FAX: (212) 258-6358
WEB: www.viacom.com
NO. OF EMPLOYEES: 133,830 (approx.)
SHAREHOLDERS: 7,721 (approx. class A com.); 82,067 (approx. class B com.)
ANNUAL MEETING: In May
INCORPORATED: DE, Nov., 1986

INSTITUTIONAL HOLDINGS:
No. of Institutions: 159
Shares Held: 34,290,534
% Held: 0.0

INDUSTRY: Motion picture & video production (SIC: 7812)

TRANSFER AGENT(S): First Chicago Trust Company of New York, New York, NY

NYSE SYMBOL VVI
Rec. Pr. 25.25 (5/31/01)

VIAD CORPORATION

YIELD 1.4%
P/E RATIO 16.0

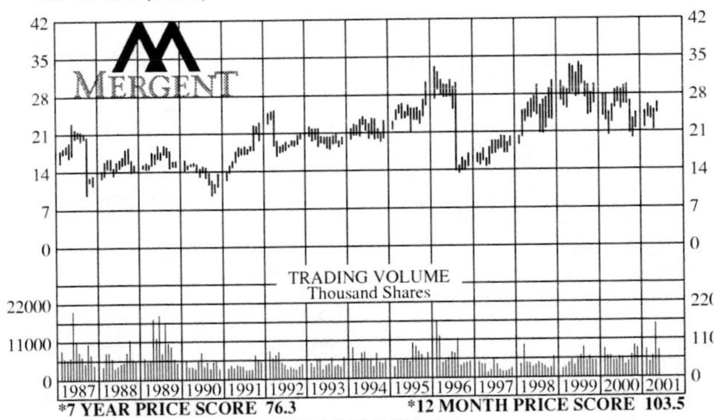

*7 YEAR PRICE SCORE 76.3 *12 MONTH PRICE SCORE 103.5
*NYSE COMPOSITE INDEX=100

INTERIM EARNINGS (Per Share):

Qtr.	Mar.	June	Sept.	Dec.
1997	0.11	0.28	0.36	0.28
1998	0.15	0.41	0.58	0.38
1999	0.20	0.33	0.42	0.49
2000	0.28	0.46	0.48	0.36

INTERIM DIVIDENDS (Per Share):

Amt.	Decl.	Ex.	Rec.	Pay.
0.09Q	5/09/00	5/31/00	6/02/00	7/03/00
0.09Q	8/16/00	8/31/00	9/05/00	10/02/00
0.09Q	11/16/00	12/06/00	12/08/00	1/02/01
0.09Q	2/15/01	3/07/01	3/09/01	4/02/01
0.09Q	5/08/01	5/30/01	6/01/01	7/02/01

Indicated div.: $0.36

CAPITALIZATION (12/31/00):

	($000)	(%)
Long-Term Debt	377,306	32.8
Minority Interest	4,263	0.4
Redeemable Pfd. Stock	6,658	0.6
Common & Surplus	763,156	66.3
Total	1,151,383	100.0

RECENT DEVELOPMENTS: For the year ended 12/31/00, net income advanced 12.4% to $144.5 million versus income from continuing operations of $128.6 million in 1999. Results included non-recurring income of $877,000 in 2000 and $6.1 million in 1999. Revenues were $1.73 billion, up 9.2% from $1.58 billion a year earlier. Operating income of Payment Services increased 24.6% to $160.1 million.

PROSPECTS: On 3/1/01, the Company's subsidiary, MoneyGram Payment Systems, Inc., was selected as the exclusive money transfer affiliate of Poste Italiane, the Italian Post Office. Poste Italiane will initially install the MoneyGram service in approximately 1,200 of its locations, with expansion expected into additional locations later in 2001.

BUSINESS

VIAD CORPORATION (formerly The Dial Corporation) was formed after the spin-off of Dial's consumer products group in August 1996. The Company is a diversified business that provides services to businesses for use by their customers. Accordingly, VVI markets its payments services through more than 100,000 retail and financial locations (payment services), to numerous tradeshow organizers and exibitors (convention and event services), and others. The Company's convention and event services are provided by VVI's GES Exposition Services and Exhibitgroup/ Giltspur companies. The Company's Payment Services business is conducted by the Travelers Express group of companies. VVI's Travel and Recreation Services are provided by the Brewster Transport and ProDine business units. Net sales (and operating income) for 2000 were derived from the following: Convention and Event Services, 58.1% (31.3%); Payment Services, 37.8% (61.4%); and Travel and Recreation Services, 4.1% (7.3%). On 7/1/99, VVI completed the sale of its airline catering business, conducted by Dobbs International Services, Inc.

ANNUAL FINANCIAL DATA

	12/31/00	12/31/99	12/31/98	12/31/97	12/31/96	12/31/95	12/31/94
Earnings Per Share	[6] **1.58**	[5] **1.32**	[4] **1.52**	[3] **1.03**	[2] **0.74**	[1] **d0.20**	**1.61**
Cash Flow Per Share	**2.34**	**1.99**	**2.40**	**1.88**	**1.57**	**1.31**	**2.89**
Tang. Book Val. Per Share	**1.25**	**0.84**	...	...	...	...	...
Dividends Per Share	**0.36**	**0.34**	**0.32**	**0.32**	**0.56**	...	...
Dividend Payout %	**22.8**	**25.8**	**21.1**	**31.1**	**75.7**	...	...
INCOME STATEMENT (IN MILLIONS):							
Total Revenues	1,726.8	1,581.2	2,542.1	2,417.5	2,263.2	3,575.1	3,546.8
Costs & Expenses	1,463.5	1,330.4	2,217.7	2,116.4	1,984.4	3,347.3	3,106.8
Depreciation & Amort.	68.6	63.0	85.9	78.5	74.4	114.9	109.9
Operating Income	194.8	187.8	238.6	222.6	204.4	112.8	330.2
Net Interest Inc./(Exp.)	d25.3	d26.9	d40.8	d48.7	d53.0	d76.0	d61.2
Income Before Income Taxes	173.2	163.6	217.7	138.9	111.0	d10.7	221.7
Income Taxes	28.7	35.0	67.0	41.2	41.9	cr11.9	81.4
Equity Earnings/Minority Int.	d1.7	d2.1	d2.2	d1.2	d1.8	d4.3	d3.4
Net Income	[6] 144.5	[5] 128.6	[4] 150.6	[3] 97.8	[2] 69.1	[1] 1.1	140.3
Cash Flow	213.1	191.5	236.5	176.3	143.5	116.1	250.2
Average Shs. Outstg. (000)	90,925	96,396	98,367	93,786	91,637	88,707	86,646
BALANCE SHEET (IN MILLIONS):							
Cash & Cash Equivalents	1,279.4	731.5	566.5	632.4	674.7	809.5	694.5
Total Current Assets	1,551.0	922.2	843.4	925.8	1,023.8	1,372.0	1,244.2
Net Property	290.0	313.6	467.6	470.1	473.0	857.9	813.4
Total Assets	6,300.2	5,210.9	4,802.8	3,730.3	3,453.3	4,225.2	3,780.9
Total Current Liabilities	4,939.0	3,921.2	3,396.4	2,636.0	2,352.8	2,449.3	2,056.8
Long-Term Obligations	377.3	342.6	531.3	377.8	518.8	814.3	721.7
Net Stockholders' Equity	763.2	708.6	645.9	529.2	432.2	548.2	555.1
Net Working Capital	d3,388.0	d2,999.0	d2,553.1	d1,710.2	d1,329.0	d1,077.3	d812.5
Year-end Shs. Outstg. (000)	99,740	94,243	99,395	99,223	95,946	94,231	92,789
STATISTICAL RECORD:							
Operating Profit Margin %	11.3	11.9	9.4	9.2	9.0	3.2	9.3
Net Profit Margin %	8.4	8.1	5.9	4.0	3.1	...	4.0
Return on Equity %	18.9	18.1	23.3	18.5	16.0	0.2	25.3
Return on Assets %	2.3	2.5	3.1	2.6	2.0	...	3.7
Debt/Total Assets %	6.0	6.6	11.1	10.1	15.0	19.3	19.1
Price Range	29.81-19.75	33.88-24.00	30.56-18.56	20.38-14.63	33.25-13.38	30.38-20.88	24.00-19.25
P/E Ratio	18.9-12.5	25.7-18.2	20.1-12.2	19.8-14.2	44.9-18.1	...	14.9-12.0
Average Yield %	1.5	1.2	1.3	1.8	2.4	...	...

Statistics are as originally reported. Adj. for stk. split: 2-for-1, 7/94. [1] Incl. nonrecur. chrg. of $130.0 mill. [2] Excl. inc. fr. discont. oper. of $40.7 mill. Incl. nonrecur. chrg. of $2.5 mill. [3] Excl. extraord. chrg. of $8.5 mill. [4] Incl. nonrecurr. after-tax gains of $32.9 mill. and a $6.9 mill. after-tax charge for a proposed litigation settlement. [5] Excl. inc. fr. discont. oper. of $219.0 mill., incl. non-recurr. gain of $6.1 mill. [6] Incl. non-recur. inc. of $877,000.

OFFICERS:
R. H. Bohannon, Chmn., Pres., C.E.O.
K. A. Fracalossi, C.F.O., Treas.
S. E. Sayre, V.P., Sec., Gen. Couns.

INVESTOR CONTACT: Kim Fracalossi, C.F.O., Treas., (602) 207-5988

PRINCIPAL OFFICE: 1850 N. Central Ave., Suite 0815, Phoenix, AZ 85077

TELEPHONE NUMBER: (602) 207-4000
FAX: (602) 207-5900
WEB: www.viad.com

NO. OF EMPLOYEES: 7,300 (approx.)

SHAREHOLDERS: 30,666 (of record)

ANNUAL MEETING: In May

INCORPORATED: DE, Dec., 1991

INSTITUTIONAL HOLDINGS:
No. of Institutions: 186
Shares Held: 62,024,808
% Held: 70.5

INDUSTRY: Functions related to deposit banking (SIC: 6099)

TRANSFER AGENT(S): Wells Fargo Shareholder Services, St. Paul, MN

NYSE SYMBOL VSH
Rec. Pr. 20.60 (5/31/01)

VISHAY INTERTECHNOLOGY, INC.

YIELD ...
P/E RATIO 5.5

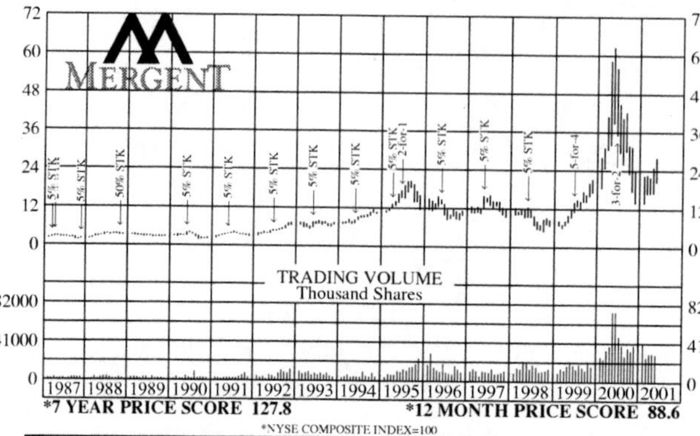

INTERIM EARNINGS (Per Share):

Qtr.	Mar.	June	Sept.	Dec.
1996	0.23	0.03	0.12	0.05
1997	0.16	0.17	0.17	0.06
1998	0.13	0.13	0.09	d0.29
1999	0.01	0.16	0.20	0.28
2000	0.56	0.96	1.22	1.01

INTERIM DIVIDENDS (Per Share):

Amt.	Decl.	Ex.	Rec.	Pay.
5-for-4	5/21/99	6/23/99	6/01/99	6/22/99
3-for-2	5/18/00	6/12/00	5/30/00	6/09/00

CAPITALIZATION (12/31/00):

	($000)	(%)
Long-Term Debt	140,467	6.6
Deferred Income Tax	79,109	3.7
Minority Interest	63,480	3.0
Common & Surplus	1,833,855	86.6
Total	2,116,911	100.0

RECENT DEVELOPMENTS: For the twelve months ended 12/31/00, net income skyrocketed to $517.9 million compared with $83.2 million in the previous year. The 2000 results included a pre-tax gain of $8.4 million on the sale of Lite-On Power Semiconductor Corporation and a pre-tax gain of $8.9 million on the termination of an interest rate swap. Net sales jumped 40.1% to $2.47 billion from $1.76 billion in the prior year. Gross profit more than doubled to $1.01 billion versus $460.4 million the year before.

PROSPECTS: On 5/25/01, VSH commenced an offer to exchange 1.5 shares of common stock for each share of common stock of Siliconix Incorporated not already owned by VSH. As of 5/25/01, VSH owned about 80.4% of the outstanding shares of Siliconix. Looking ahead, the Company appears to be prepared and poised for growth. Separately, VSH announced that as a result of overcapacity, VHS expects earnings per share for 2001 to be in the range of $2.50 to $2.75 per share.

BUSINESS

VISHAY INTERTECHNOLOGY, INC. is a manufacturer of passive and active electronic components, resistors, capacitors, inductors and a producer of discrete semiconductors, diodes, optoelectronics, transistors, infrared communication devices, and power and analog switching integrated circuits. The Company's components can be found in products manufactured in a broad range of industries worldwide. The Company operates in 64 plants in the U.S., Mexico, Germany, Austria, the U.K., France, Portugal, the Czech Republic, Hungary, Israel, Taiwan, China and the Philippines.

BUSINESS LINE ANALYSIS

(12/31/00)	REV	INC (%)
Passive	66.0	72.8
Active	34.0	27.2
Total	100.0	100.0

ANNUAL FINANCIAL DATA

	12/31/00	12/31/99	12/31/98	12/31/97	12/31/96	12/31/95	12/31/94
Earnings Per Share	[6] **3.77**	[5] **0.65**	[4] **0.06**	[3] **0.42**	[2] **0.42**	[1] **0.78**	**0.55**
Cash Flow Per Share	**4.79**	**1.74**	**1.07**	**1.07**	**1.02**	**1.38**	**1.09**
Tang. Book Val. Per Share	**11.15**	**4.83**	**4.49**	**5.31**	**6.70**	**6.52**	**3.46**
INCOME STATEMENT (IN MILLIONS):							
Total Revenues	2,465.1	1,760.1	1,572.7	1,125.2	1,098.0	1,224.4	987.8
Costs & Expenses	1,627.7	1,426.7	1,321.6	920.2	934.9	1,002.5	832.1
Depreciation & Amort.	140.8	139.7	127.9	81.9	77.2	69.5	57.7
Operating Income	696.5	193.7	93.9	108.6	85.8	152.4	98.0
Net Interest Inc./(Exp.)	d25.2	d53.3	d49.0	d18.8	d17.4	d29.4	d24.8
Income Before Income Taxes	690.2	134.7	38.8	87.5	70.4	123.0	74.1
Income Taxes	148.2	36.9	30.6	34.2	17.7	30.3	15.2
Equity Earnings/Minority Int.	d24.2	d14.5	...	...	...	...	...
Net Income	[6] 517.9	[5] 83.2	[4] 8.2	[3] 53.3	[2] 52.6	[1] 92.7	58.9
Cash Flow	658.7	222.9	136.2	135.2	129.9	162.2	116.7
Average Shs. Outstg. (000)	137,463	128,232	126,797	126,904	126,702	117,923	106,570
BALANCE SHEET (IN MILLIONS):							
Cash & Cash Equivalents	337.2	105.2	113.7	55.3	20.9	19.6	26.9
Total Current Assets	1,474.9	926.7	956.6	646.0	623.2	640.2	560.6
Net Property	973.6	930.5	997.1	709.1	710.7	669.2	532.3
Total Assets	2,783.7	2,323.8	2,462.7	1,719.6	1,556.0	1,543.3	1,334.0
Total Current Liabilities	417.7	345.2	316.8	190.8	189.0	228.9	232.2
Long-Term Obligations	140.5	656.9	814.8	347.5	229.9	228.6	402.3
Net Stockholders' Equity	1,833.9	1,013.6	1,002.5	959.6	945.2	907.9	565.1
Net Working Capital	1,057.2	581.5	639.8	455.1	434.2	411.3	328.3
Year-end Shs. Outstg. (000)	137,927	127,023	126,879	126,760	111,066	105,716	97,989
STATISTICAL RECORD:							
Operating Profit Margin %	28.3	11.0	6.0	9.7	7.8	12.4	9.9
Net Profit Margin %	21.0	4.7	0.5	4.7	4.8	7.6	6.0
Return on Equity %	28.2	8.2	0.8	5.6	5.6	10.2	10.4
Return on Assets %	18.6	3.6	0.3	3.1	3.4	6.0	4.4
Debt/Total Assets %	5.0	28.3	33.1	20.2	14.8	14.8	30.2
Price Range	62.67-13.88	21.33-5.93	12.51-4.90	16.19-9.37	15.78-8.41	20.45-10.59	11.49-6.87
P/E Ratio	16.6-3.7	33.0-9.2	195.1-76.5	38.4-22.2	37.9-20.2	26.1-13.5	20.8-12.4

Statistics are as originally reported. Adj. for all stk. dividends and splits through 6/00 [1] Incl. charge $4.2 mill. ($0.04/sh.) [2] Incl. charge $38.0 mill. for restruc. [3] Inc. pre-tax chrg. $12.6 mill. for restruc., a pre-tax charge $1.9 mill. for an unusual expense, and a pre-tax charge of $7.2 million for amort. of goodwill. [4] Incl. non-cash special charges of $55.3 million. [5] Incl. non-recurr. chrg. $14.6 mill. & loss on disp. of sub. $10.1 mill. [6] Incl. a pre-tax gain of $8.9 mill. on term. of int. swap. & incl. gain of $8.4 mill. on sale of Lite-On Power.

OFFICERS:
F. Zandman, Chmn., C.E.O.
A. D. Eden, Vice-Chmn., Exec. V.P.
G. Paul, Pres., C.O.O.
R. N. Grubb, Exec. V.P., C.F.O., Treas.

INVESTOR CONTACT: Robert A. Freece, Sr. V.P., (610) 644-1300

PRINCIPAL OFFICE: 63 Lincoln Highway, Malvern, PA 19355-2120

TELEPHONE NUMBER: (610) 644-1300
FAX: (610) 296-0657
WEB: www.vishay.com

NO. OF EMPLOYEES: 22,418 (approx.)

SHAREHOLDERS: 2,067 (approx.)

ANNUAL MEETING: In May

INCORPORATED: DE, July, 1962

INSTITUTIONAL HOLDINGS:
No. of Institutions: 248
Shares Held: 66,715,619
% Held: 48.4

INDUSTRY: Electronic resistors (SIC: 3676)

TRANSFER AGENT(S): American Stock Transfer & Trust, New York, NY

NYSE SYMBOL VVI
Rec. Pr. 25.25 (5/31/01)

VIAD CORPORATION

YIELD 1.4%
P/E RATIO 16.0

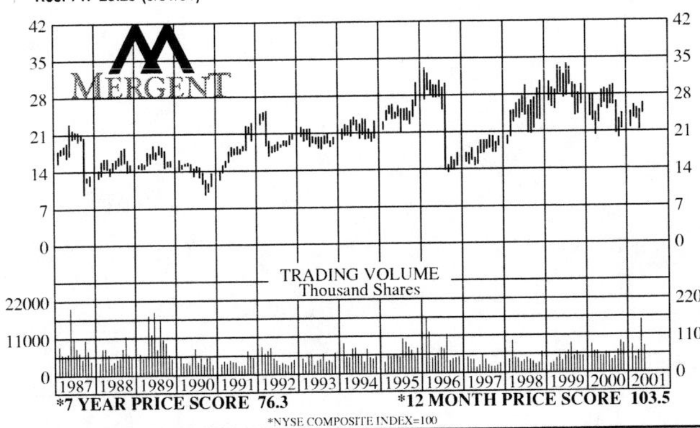

INTERIM EARNINGS (Per Share):

Qtr.	Mar.	June	Sept.	Dec.
1997	0.11	0.28	0.36	0.28
1998	0.15	0.41	0.58	0.38
1999	0.20	0.33	0.42	0.49
2000	0.28	0.46	0.48	0.36

INTERIM DIVIDENDS (Per Share):

Amt.	Decl.	Ex.	Rec.	Pay.
0.09Q	5/09/00	5/31/00	6/02/00	7/03/00
0.09Q	8/16/00	8/31/00	9/05/00	10/02/00
0.09Q	11/16/00	12/06/00	12/08/00	1/02/01
0.09Q	2/15/01	3/07/01	3/09/01	4/02/01
0.09Q	5/08/01	5/30/01	6/01/01	7/02/01

Indicated div.: $0.36

CAPITALIZATION (12/31/00):

	($000)	(%)
Long-Term Debt	377,306	32.8
Minority Interest	4,263	0.4
Redeemable Pfd. Stock	6,658	0.6
Common & Surplus	763,156	66.3
Total	1,151,383	100.0

RECENT DEVELOPMENTS: For the year ended 12/31/00, net income advanced 12.4% to $144.5 million versus income from continuing operations of $128.6 million in 1999. Results included non-recurring income of $877,000 in 2000 and $6.1 million in 1999. Revenues were $1.73 billion, up 9.2% from $1.58 billion a year earlier. Operating income of Payment Services increased 24.6% to $160.1 million.

PROSPECTS: On 3/1/01, the Company's subsidiary, MoneyGram Payment Systems, Inc., was selected as the exclusive money transfer affiliate of Poste Italiane, the Italian Post Office. Poste Italiane will initially install the MoneyGram service in approximately 1,200 of its locations, with expansion expected into additional locations later in 2001.

BUSINESS

VIAD CORPORATION (formerly The Dial Corporation) was formed after the spin-off of Dial's consumer products group in August 1996. The Company is a diversified business that provides services to businesses for use by their customers. Accordingly, VVI markets its payments services through more than 100,000 retail and financial locations (payment services), to numerous tradeshow organizers and exibitors (convention and event services), and others. The Company's convention and event services are provided by VVI's GES Exposition Services and Exhibitgroup/ Giltspur companies. The Company's Payment Services business is conducted by the Travelers Express group of companies. VVI's Travel and Recreation Services are provided by the Brewster Transport and ProDine business units. Net sales (and operating income) for 2000 were derived from the following: Convention and Event Services, 58.1% (31.3%); Payment Services, 37.8% (61.4%); and Travel and Recreation Services, 4.1% (7.3%). On 7/1/99, VVI completed the sale of its airline catering business, conducted by Dobbs International Services, Inc.

ANNUAL FINANCIAL DATA

	12/31/00	12/31/99	12/31/98	12/31/97	12/31/96	12/31/95	12/31/94
Earnings Per Share	**6 1.58**	**5 1.32**	**4 1.52**	**3 1.03**	**2 0.74**	**1 d0.20**	**1.61**
Cash Flow Per Share	**2.34**	**1.99**	**2.40**	**1.88**	**1.57**	**1.31**	**2.89**
Tang. Book Val. Per Share	**1.25**	**0.84**	...	...	...	...	...
Dividends Per Share	**0.36**	**0.34**	**0.32**	**0.32**	**0.56**	...	...
Dividend Payout %	**22.8**	**25.8**	**21.1**	**31.1**	**75.7**	...	...
INCOME STATEMENT (IN MILLIONS):							
Total Revenues	1,726.8	1,581.2	2,542.1	2,417.5	2,263.2	3,575.1	3,546.8
Costs & Expenses	1,463.5	1,330.4	2,217.7	2,116.4	1,984.4	3,347.3	3,106.8
Depreciation & Amort.	68.6	63.0	85.9	78.5	74.4	114.9	109.9
Operating Income	194.8	187.8	238.6	222.6	204.4	112.8	330.2
Net Interest Inc./(Exp.)	d25.3	d26.9	d40.8	d48.7	d53.0	d76.0	d61.2
Income Before Income Taxes	173.2	163.6	217.7	138.9	111.0	d10.7	221.7
Income Taxes	28.7	35.0	67.0	41.2	41.9	cr11.9	81.4
Equity Earnings/Minority Int.	d1.7	d2.1	d2.2	d1.2	d1.8	d4.3	d3.4
Net Income	6 144.5	5 128.6	4 150.6	3 97.8	2 69.1	1 1.1	140.3
Cash Flow	213.1	191.5	236.5	176.3	143.5	116.1	250.2
Average Shs. Outstg. (000)	90,925	96,396	98,367	93,786	91,637	88,707	86,646
BALANCE SHEET (IN MILLIONS):							
Cash & Cash Equivalents	1,279.4	731.5	566.5	632.4	674.7	809.5	694.5
Total Current Assets	1,551.0	922.2	843.4	925.8	1,023.8	1,372.0	1,244.2
Net Property	290.0	313.6	467.6	470.1	473.0	857.9	813.4
Total Assets	6,300.2	5,210.9	4,802.8	3,730.3	3,453.3	4,225.2	3,780.9
Total Current Liabilities	4,939.0	3,921.2	3,396.4	2,636.0	2,352.8	2,449.3	2,056.8
Long-Term Obligations	377.3	342.6	531.3	377.8	518.8	814.3	721.7
Net Stockholders' Equity	763.2	708.6	645.9	529.2	432.2	548.2	555.1
Net Working Capital	d3,388.0	d2,999.0	d2,553.1	d1,710.2	d1,329.0	d1,077.3	d812.5
Year-end Shs. Outstg. (000)	99,740	94,243	99,395	99,223	95,946	94,231	92,789
STATISTICAL RECORD:							
Operating Profit Margin %	11.3	11.9	9.4	9.2	9.0	3.2	9.3
Net Profit Margin %	8.4	8.1	5.9	4.0	3.1	...	4.0
Return on Equity %	18.9	18.1	23.3	18.5	16.0	0.2	25.3
Return on Assets %	2.3	2.5	3.1	2.6	2.0	...	3.7
Debt/Total Assets %	6.0	6.6	11.1	10.1	15.0	19.3	19.1
Price Range	29.81-19.75	33.88-24.00	30.56-18.56	20.38-14.63	33.25-13.38	30.38-20.88	24.00-19.25
P/E Ratio	18.9-12.5	25.7-18.2	20.1-12.2	19.8-14.2	44.9-18.1	...	14.9-12.0
Average Yield %	1.5	1.2	1.3	1.8	2.4	...	...

Statistics are as originally reported. Adj. for stk. split: 2-for-1, 7/94. 1 Incl. nonrecur. chrg. of $130.0 mill. 2 Excl. inc. fr. discont. oper. of $40.7 mill. Incl. nonrecur. chrg. of $2.5 mill. 3 Excl. extraord. chrg. of $8.5 mill. 4 Incl. nonrecurr. after-tax gains of $32.9 mill. and a $6.9 mill. after-tax charge for a proposed litigation settlement. 5 Excl. inc. fr. discont. oper. of $219.0 mill., incl. non-recurr. gain of $6.1 mill. 6 Incl. non-recur. inc. of $877,000.

OFFICERS:
R. H. Bohannon, Chmn., Pres., C.E.O.
K. A. Fracalossi, C.F.O., Treas.
S. E. Sayre, V.P., Sec., Gen. Couns.

INVESTOR CONTACT: Kim Fracalossi, C.F.O., Treas., (602) 207-5988

PRINCIPAL OFFICE: 1850 N. Central Ave., Suite 0815, Phoenix, AZ 85077

TELEPHONE NUMBER: (602) 207-4000
FAX: (602) 207-5900
WEB: www.viad.com

NO. OF EMPLOYEES: 7,300 (approx.)

SHAREHOLDERS: 30,666 (of record)

ANNUAL MEETING: In May

INCORPORATED: DE, Dec., 1991

INSTITUTIONAL HOLDINGS:
No. of Institutions: 186
Shares Held: 62,024,808
% Held: 70.5

INDUSTRY: Functions related to deposit banking (SIC: 6099)

TRANSFER AGENT(S): Wells Fargo Shareholder Services, St. Paul, MN

NYSE SYMBOL VSH
Rec. Pr. 20.60 (5/31/01)

VISHAY INTERTECHNOLOGY, INC.

YIELD ...
P/E RATIO 5.5

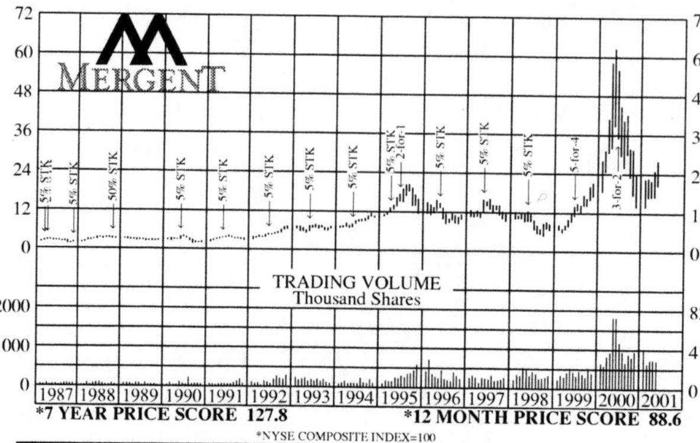

*7 YEAR PRICE SCORE 127.8 *12 MONTH PRICE SCORE 88.6
*NYSE COMPOSITE INDEX=100

INTERIM EARNINGS (Per Share):

Qtr.	Mar.	June	Sept.	Dec.
1996	0.23	0.03	0.12	0.05
1997	0.16	0.17	0.17	0.06
1998	0.13	0.13	0.09	d0.29
1999	0.01	0.16	0.20	0.28
2000	0.56	0.96	1.22	1.01

INTERIM DIVIDENDS (Per Share):

Amt.	Decl.	Ex.	Rec.	Pay.
5-for-4	5/21/99	6/23/99	6/01/99	6/22/99
3-for-2	5/18/00	6/12/00	5/30/00	6/09/00

CAPITALIZATION (12/31/00):

	($000)	(%)
Long-Term Debt	140,467	6.6
Deferred Income Tax	79,109	3.7
Minority Interest	63,480	3.0
Common & Surplus	1,833,855	86.6
Total	2,116,911	100.0

RECENT DEVELOPMENTS: For the twelve months ended 12/31/00, net income skyrocketed to $517.9 million compared with $83.2 million in the previous year. The 2000 results included a pre-tax gain of $8.4 million on the sale of Lite-On Power Semiconductor Corporation and a pre-tax gain of $8.9 million on the termination of an interest rate swap. Net sales jumped 40.1% to $2.47 billion from $1.76 billion in the prior year. Gross profit more than doubled to $1.01 billion versus $460.4 million the year before.

PROSPECTS: On 5/25/01, VSH commenced an offer to exchange 1.5 shares of common stock for each share of common stock of Siliconix Incorporated not already owned by VSH. As of 5/25/01, VSH owned about 80.4% of the outstanding shares of Siliconix. Looking ahead, the Company appears to be prepared and poised for growth. Separately, VSH announced that as a result of overcapacity, VHS expects earnings per share for 2001 to be in the range of $2.50 to $2.75 per share.

BUSINESS

VISHAY INTERTECHNOLOGY, INC. is a manufacturer of passive and active electronic components, resistors, capacitors, inductors and a producer of discrete semiconductors, diodes, optoelectronics, transistors, infrared communication devices, and power and analog switching integrated circuits. The Company's components can be found in products manufactured in a broad range of industries worldwide. The Company operates in 64 plants in the U.S., Mexico, Germany, Austria, the U.K., France, Portugal, the Czech Republic, Hungary, Israel, Taiwan, China and the Philippines.

BUSINESS LINE ANALYSIS

(12/31/00)	REV	INC (%)
Passive	66.0	72.8
Active	34.0	27.2
Total	100.0	100.0

ANNUAL FINANCIAL DATA

	12/31/00	12/31/99	12/31/98	12/31/97	12/31/96	12/31/95	12/31/94
Earnings Per Share	[6] **3.77**	[5] **0.65**	[4] **0.06**	[3] **0.42**	[2] **0.42**	[1] **0.78**	**0.55**
Cash Flow Per Share	**4.79**	**1.74**	**1.07**	**1.07**	**1.02**	**1.38**	**1.09**
Tang. Book Val. Per Share	**11.15**	**4.83**	**4.49**	**5.31**	**6.70**	**6.52**	**3.46**
INCOME STATEMENT (IN MILLIONS):							
Total Revenues	2,465.1	1,760.1	1,572.7	1,125.2	1,098.0	1,224.4	987.8
Costs & Expenses	1,627.7	1,426.7	1,321.6	920.2	934.9	1,002.5	832.1
Depreciation & Amort.	140.8	139.7	127.9	81.9	77.2	69.5	57.7
Operating Income	696.5	193.7	93.9	108.6	85.8	152.4	98.0
Net Interest Inc./(Exp.)	d25.2	d53.3	d49.0	d18.8	d17.4	d29.4	d24.8
Income Before Income Taxes	690.2	134.7	38.8	87.5	70.4	123.0	74.1
Income Taxes	148.2	36.9	30.6	34.2	17.7	30.3	15.2
Equity Earnings/Minority Int.	d24.2	d14.5	...	...	...	...	...
Net Income	[6] 517.9	[5] 83.2	[4] 8.2	[3] 53.3	[2] 52.6	[1] 92.7	58.9
Cash Flow	658.7	222.9	136.2	135.2	129.9	162.2	116.7
Average Shs. Outstg. (000)	137,463	128,232	126,797	126,904	126,702	117,923	106,570
BALANCE SHEET (IN MILLIONS):							
Cash & Cash Equivalents	337.2	105.2	113.7	55.3	20.9	19.6	26.9
Total Current Assets	1,474.9	926.7	956.6	646.0	623.2	640.2	560.6
Net Property	973.6	930.5	997.1	709.1	710.7	669.2	532.3
Total Assets	2,783.7	2,323.8	2,462.7	1,719.6	1,556.0	1,543.3	1,334.0
Total Current Liabilities	417.7	345.2	316.8	190.8	189.0	228.9	232.2
Long-Term Obligations	140.5	656.9	814.8	347.5	229.9	228.6	402.3
Net Stockholders' Equity	1,833.9	1,013.6	1,002.5	959.6	945.2	907.9	565.1
Net Working Capital	1,057.2	581.5	639.8	455.1	434.2	411.3	328.3
Year-end Shs. Outstg. (000)	137,927	127,023	126,879	126,760	111,066	105,716	97,989
STATISTICAL RECORD:							
Operating Profit Margin %	28.3	11.0	6.0	9.7	7.8	12.4	9.9
Net Profit Margin %	21.0	4.7	0.5	4.7	4.8	7.6	6.0
Return on Equity %	28.2	8.2	0.8	5.6	5.6	10.2	10.4
Return on Assets %	18.6	3.6	0.3	3.1	3.4	6.0	4.4
Debt/Total Assets %	5.0	28.3	33.1	20.2	14.8	14.8	30.2
Price Range	62.67-13.88	21.33-5.93	12.51-4.90	16.19-9.37	15.78-8.41	20.45-10.59	11.49-6.87
P/E Ratio	16.6-3.7	33.0-9.2	195.1-76.5	38.4-22.2	37.9-20.2	26.1-13.5	20.8-12.4

Statistics are as originally reported. Adj. for all stk. dividends and splits through 6/00 [1] Incl. charge $4.2 mill. ($0.04/sh.) [2] Incl. charge $38.0 mill. for restruc. [3] Inc. pre-tax chrg. $12.6 mill. for restruc., a pre-tax charge $1.9 mill. for an unusual expense, and a pre-tax charge of $7.2 million for amort. of goodwill. [4] Incl. non-cash special charges of $55.3 million. [5] Incl. non-recurr. chrg. $14.6 mill. & loss on disp. of sub. $10.1 mill. [6] Incl. a pre-tax gain of $8.9 mill. on term. of int. swap. & incl. gain of $8.4 mill. on sale of Lite-On Power.

OFFICERS:
F. Zandman, Chmn., C.E.O.
A. D. Eden, Vice-Chmn., Exec. V.P.
G. Paul, Pres., C.O.O.
R. N. Grubb, Exec. V.P., C.F.O., Treas.

INVESTOR CONTACT: Robert A. Freece, Sr. V.P., (610) 644-1300

PRINCIPAL OFFICE: 63 Lincoln Highway, Malvern, PA 19355-2120

TELEPHONE NUMBER: (610) 644-1300
FAX: (610) 296-0657
WEB: www.vishay.com

NO. OF EMPLOYEES: 22,418 (approx.)

SHAREHOLDERS: 2,067 (approx.)

ANNUAL MEETING: In May

INCORPORATED: DE, July, 1962

INSTITUTIONAL HOLDINGS:
No. of Institutions: 248
Shares Held: 66,715,619
% Held: 48.4

INDUSTRY: Electronic resistors (SIC: 3676)

TRANSFER AGENT(S): American Stock Transfer & Trust, New York, NY

NYSE SYMBOL VC
Rec. Pr. 16.53 (4/30/01)

VISTEON CORPORATION

YIELD 1.5%
P/E RATIO 7.9

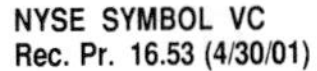

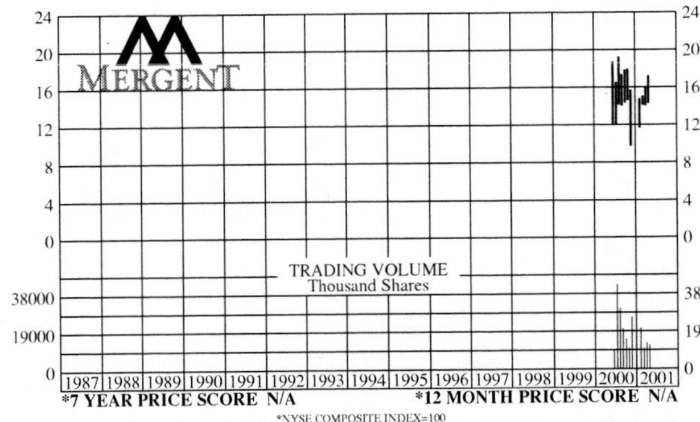

*7 YEAR PRICE SCORE N/A *12 MONTH PRICE SCORE N/A

*NYSE COMPOSITE INDEX=100

INTERIM EARNINGS (Per Share):

Qtr.	Mar.	June	Sept.	Dec.
1997		3.93		
1998		5.41		
1999		5.65		
2000	1.13	1.25	0.37	d0.67

INTERIM DIVIDENDS (Per Share):

Amt.	Decl.	Ex.	Rec.	Pay.
0.06Q	7/14/00	7/31/00	8/02/00	9/01/00
0.06Q	10/11/00	10/30/00	11/01/00	12/01/00
0.06Q	1/10/01	1/26/01	1/30/01	3/01/01
0.06Q	4/11/01	4/30/01	5/02/01	6/01/01

Indicated div.: $0.24 (Div. Reinv. Plan)

CAPITALIZATION (12/31/00):

	($000)	(%)
Long-Term Debt	1,397,000	28.4
Deferred Income Tax	18,000	0.4
Common & Surplus	3,505,000	71.2
Total	4,920,000	100.0

RECENT DEVELOPMENTS: For the year ended 12/31/00, net income fell 63.3% to $270.0 million from $735.0 million the year before. Results for 2000 included a pre-tax non-cash impairment charge of $220.0 million due to a reduction of the net book value of VC's glass segment. Earnings were also affected by a one-time 5.0% price realignment that resulted from VC's separation from Ford Motor Co. Total revenues rose slightly to $19.47 billion versus $19.37 billion in the previous year.

PROSPECTS: VC will focus on reducing costs through collaboration with its customers, suppliers, competitors and non-automotive partners. VC has developed over 24 partnerships with companies such as Microsoft, Agere, Raytheon and Kayaba. Meanwhile, revenues should benefit from secured contracts with Ford, VW Group, Hyundai, General Motors, DaimlerChrysler, PSA Peugeot Citron, Renault, Honda, Fiat and Kia. The combined contracts should add revenues of $2.60 billion in new business.

BUSINESS

VISTEON CORPORATION is a major supplier of automotive systems, modules and components to global vehicle manufacturers. The Company operates in three business segments. The Dynamics and Energy Conversion segment focuses on leveraging vehicle dynamics and includes the energy transformation and chassis product groups. The Comfort, Communication and Safety segment includes the climate control, interior/exterior systems, telematics and multimedia systems product groups. The Glass segment includes the vehicle glazing and commercial glass product groups. VC operates a delivery system of more than 130 technical, manufacturing, sales and service facilities located in 25 countries. On 6/12/00, VC was spun off from Ford Motor Company.

REVENUES

(12/31/00)	($000)	(%)
Dynamics & Energy Conversion	8,939,000	46.0
Comfort, Communication & Safety	9,782,000	50.2
Glass	746,000	3.8
Total	19,467,000	100.0

ANNUAL FINANCIAL DATA

	12/31/00	12/31/99	12/31/98	12/31/97
Earnings Per Share	**1 2.08**	**5.65**	**5.41**	**3.93**
Cash Flow Per Share	**7.28**	...	...	...
Tang. Book Val. Per Share	**26.76**	**108.62**	...	...
Dividends Per Share	**0.12**	...	...	...
Dividend Payout %	**5.8**	...	...	...
INCOME STATEMENT (IN MILLIONS):				
Total Revenues	19,467.0	19,366.0	17,762.0	17,220.0
Costs & Expenses	18,350.0	17,526.0	16,063.0	15,779.0
Depreciation & Amort.	676.0	651.0	565.0	590.0
Operating Income	441.0	1,189.0	1,134.0	851.0
Net Interest Inc./(Exp.)	d58.0	d64.0	d44.0	d65.0
Income Before Income Taxes	439.0	1,172.0	1,116.0	815.0
Income Taxes	143.0	422.0	416.0	305.0
Equity Earnings/Minority Int.	30.0	32.0	29.0	30.0
Net Income	1 270.0	735.0	703.0	511.0
Cash Flow	946.0	1,386.0	1,268.0	1,101.0
Average Shs. Outstg. (000)	130,000	...	...	...
BALANCE SHEET (IN MILLIONS):				
Cash & Cash Equivalents	1,477.0	1,849.0	542.0	...
Total Current Assets	5,005.0	5,196.0	3,191.0	...
Net Property	5,497.0	5,789.0	5,391.0	...
Total Assets	11,325.0	12,449.0	9,373.0	...
Total Current Liabilities	3,804.0	5,475.0	3,164.0	...
Long-Term Obligations	1,397.0	1,358.0	816.0	...
Net Stockholders' Equity	3,505.0	1,499.0	1,655.0	...
Net Working Capital	1,201.0	d279.0	27.0	...
Year-end Shs. Outstg. (000)	131,000	13,800	...	...
STATISTICAL RECORD:				
Operating Profit Margin %	2.3	6.1	6.4	4.9
Net Profit Margin %	1.4	3.8	4.0	3.0
Return on Equity %	7.7	49.0	42.5	...
Return on Assets %	2.4	5.9	7.5	...
Debt/Total Assets %	12.3	10.9	8.7	...
Price Range	19.25-9.75	...	...	...
P/E Ratio	9.3-4.7	...	...	...
Average Yield %	0.8	...	...	...

Statistics are as originally reported. 1 Incl. non-cash impairment chrg. of $220.0 mill.

OFFICERS:
P. J. Pestillo, Chmn., C.E.O.
M. F. Johnston, Pres., C.O.O.
D. R. Coulson, Exec. V.P., C.F.O.
S. L. Fox, Sr. V.P., Sec., Gen. Couns.

INVESTOR CONTACT: Derek Fiebig, Dir. Inv. Rel., (800) 847-8366

PRINCIPAL OFFICE: 5500 Auto Club Drive, Dearborn, MI 48126

TELEPHONE NUMBER: (800) 847-8366
WEB: www.visteon.com

NO. OF EMPLOYEES: 82,000 (approx.)

SHAREHOLDERS: 138,661

ANNUAL MEETING: In May

INCORPORATED: DE, Jan., 2000

INSTITUTIONAL HOLDINGS:
No. of Institutions: 311
Shares Held: 68,880,322
% Held: 52.6

INDUSTRY: Motor vehicle supplies and new parts (SIC: 5013)

TRANSFER AGENT(S): EquiServe Trust Company, N.A., Jersey City, NJ

NYSE SYMBOL EYE
Rec. Pr. 20.85 (5/31/01)

VISX, INC.

YIELD ...
P/E RATIO 37.9

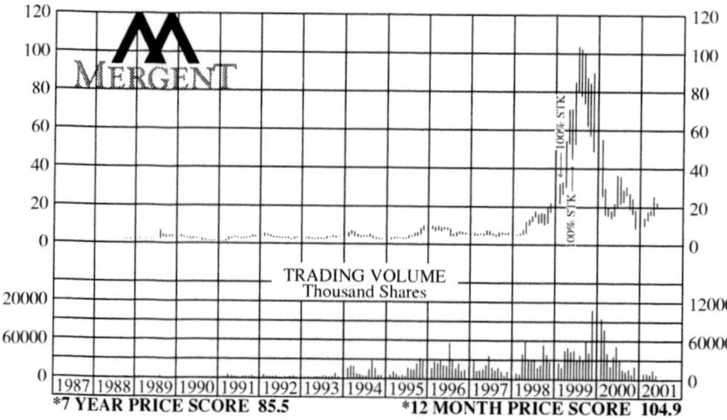

TRADING VOLUME
Thousand Shares

*7 YEAR PRICE SCORE 85.5 *12 MONTH PRICE SCORE 104.9

*NYSE COMPOSITE INDEX=100

INTERIM EARNINGS (Per Share):

Qtr.	Mar.	June	Sept.	Dec.
1997	0.05	d0.01	0.08	0.11
1998	0.15	d0.26	0.23	0.26
1999	0.15	0.32	0.36	0.38
2000	0.30	0.07	0.19	d0.01

INTERIM DIVIDENDS (Per Share):

Amt.	Decl.	Ex.	Rec.	Pay.

No dividends paid.

CAPITALIZATION (12/31/00):

	($000)	(%)
Common & Surplus	268,772	100.0
Total	268,772	100.0

RECENT DEVELOPMENTS: For the year ended 12/31/00, net income decreased 61.6% to $35.2 million from $91.7 million in the previous year. The 2000 results included a pre-tax litigation settlement expense of $11.8 million. Total revenues declined 26.2% to $200.2 million from $271.3 million a year earlier. Revenues from system sales fell 20.5% to $60.6 million, while license, service and other revenue dropped 29.1% to $139.5 million.

PROSPECTS: The Company's outlook is promising as the U.S. laser vision correction procedure market should experience continued strong growth over the next four years. In light of the weakness in the current economic environment, EYE projects about 20.0% growth in this market during 2001. However, the Company expects that this growth will accelerate in the future as the economy recovers.

BUSINESS

VISX, INCORPORATED is engaged in the design and development of proprietary technologies and systems for laser vision correction. The Company's principal product, the VISX STAR Laser System, utilizes an excimer laser to reshape the surface of the cornea to treat nearsightedness, astigmatism and farsightedness, and is intended to reduce or eliminate the patient's dependence on corrective lenses. The device is also intended to treat other eye disorders, such as opacities and superficial scars. Use of the VISX System is controlled by a proprietary optical memory card which is sold separately. The VisionKey® card is encoded with proprietary technology which is required to operate the VISX System. It also provides the user with access to software upgrades and can facilitate the collection of patient data. The WaveScan™ Wavefront System, which allows physicians to instantly measure refractive aberrations using highly advanced optics.

REVENUES

(12/31/2000)	($000)	(%)
System sales	60,678	30.3
License, service & other	139,570	69.7
Total	200,248	100.0

ANNUAL FINANCIAL DATA

	12/31/00	12/31/99	12/31/98	12/31/97	12/31/96	12/31/95	12/31/94
Earnings Per Share	**[2] 0.55**	**1.35**	**0.39**	**[1] 0.22**	**0.27**	**d0.30**	**d0.15**
Cash Flow Per Share	**0.61**	**1.39**	**0.42**	**0.25**	**0.29**	**d0.29**	**d0.14**
Tang. Book Val. Per Share	**4.42**	**4.88**	**2.26**	**1.79**	**1.61**	**1.32**	**0.33**
INCOME STATEMENT (IN THOUSANDS):							
Total Revenues	200,248	271,252	133,750	68,631	69,664	16,703	17,896
Costs & Expenses	140,741	126,022	72,447	51,257	54,123	26,798	24,621
Depreciation & Amort.	3,515	3,132	2,083	1,854	1,195	610	609
Operating Income	55,992	142,098	59,220	15,520	14,346	d10,705	d7,334
Net Interest Inc./(Exp.)	14,080	10,848	5,536	4,999	4,265	1,340	472
Income Before Income Taxes	58,216	152,946	29,756	16,019	18,611	...	d6,264
Income Taxes	22,995	61,178	4,166	1,922	1,303	...	...
Net Income	[2] 35,221	91,768	25,590	[1] 14,097	17,308	d14,765	d6,264
Cash Flow	38,736	94,900	27,673	15,951	18,503	d14,155	d5,655
Average Shs. Outstg.	63,778	68,119	65,398	63,272	63,896	49,244	41,488
BALANCE SHEET (IN THOUSANDS):							
Cash & Cash Equivalents	229,453	258,359	116,539	100,833	88,990	75,219	11,161
Total Current Assets	298,397	349,474	166,638	123,933	113,295	88,862	18,067
Net Property	4,996	5,681	4,318	4,032	3,621	1,565	1,450
Total Assets	321,507	362,721	176,619	130,352	119,689	91,078	20,627
Total Current Liabilities	52,735	45,928	37,630	20,053	20,417	11,197	6,225
Net Stockholders' Equity	268,772	316,793	138,989	110,299	99,272	79,881	13,993
Net Working Capital	245,662	303,546	129,008	103,880	92,878	77,665	11,842
Year-end Shs. Outstg.	60,756	64,888	61,598	61,448	61,620	60,696	42,100
STATISTICAL RECORD:							
Operating Profit Margin %	28.0	52.4	44.3	22.6	20.6	...	...
Net Profit Margin %	17.6	33.8	19.1	20.5	24.8	...	...
Return on Equity %	13.1	29.0	18.4	12.8	17.4	...	...
Return on Assets %	11.0	25.3	14.5	10.8	14.5	...	...
Price Range	55.25-8.75	103.88-21.50	22.00-4.88	7.63-4.47	9.88-4.44	10.03-2.50	7.19-2.50
P/E Ratio	100.4-15.9	76.9-15.9	56.4-12.5	34.2-20.0	36.6-16.4	...	...

Statistics are as originally reported. Adj. for stk. split: 2-for-1, 5/12/99; 2-for-1, 1/13/99 [1] Incl. non-recurr. chrg. $4.5 mill. [2] Incl. pre-tax chrg. of $11.8 mill. for litigation settle. exp.

OFFICERS:
M. B. Logan, Chmn.
E. H. Davila, Pres., C.E.O.
T. R. Maier, Exec. V.P., C.F.O., Treas.
J. F. Runkel Jr., V.P., Sec., General Couns.

INVESTOR CONTACT: Investor Relations, (408) 773-7022

PRINCIPAL OFFICE: 3400 Central Expressway, Santa Clara, CA 95051

TELEPHONE NUMBER: (408) 773-7022
FAX: (408) 773-7300
WEB: www.visx.com

NO. OF EMPLOYEES: 390

SHAREHOLDERS: 765 (record); (approx.)

ANNUAL MEETING: In May

INCORPORATED: DE, Jun., 1988

INSTITUTIONAL HOLDINGS:
No. of Institutions: 125
Shares Held: 30,972,661
% Held: 54.8

INDUSTRY: Electromedical equipment (SIC: 3845)

TRANSFER AGENT(S): EquiServe LP, Canton, MA

NYSE SYMBOL VNO
Rec. Pr. 36.72 (4/30/01)

VORNADO REALTY TRUST

YIELD 5.8%
P/E RATIO 16.8

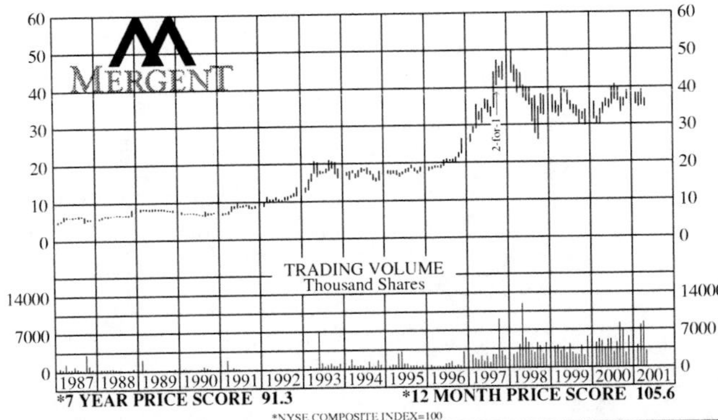

INTERIM EARNINGS (Per Share):

Qtr.	Mar.	June	Sept.	Dec.
1998	0.35	0.37	0.46	0.40
1999	0.49	0.49	0.51	0.45
2000	0.54	0.53	0.65	0.47

INTERIM DIVIDENDS (Per Share):

Amt.	Decl.	Ex.	Rec.	Pay.
0.48Q	4/28/00	5/04/00	5/08/00	5/16/00
0.48Q	7/28/00	8/03/00	8/07/00	8/15/00
0.53Q	10/27/00	11/02/00	11/06/00	11/14/00
0.53Q	1/26/01	2/01/01	2/05/01	2/13/01
0.53Q	4/27/01	5/03/01	5/07/01	5/15/01

Indicated div.: $2.12

CAPITALIZATION (12/31/00):

	($000)	(%)
Long-Term Debt	2,656,897	42.9
Minority Interest	1,456,159	23.5
Preferred Stock	481,460	7.8
Common & Surplus	1,597,260	25.8
Total	6,191,776	100.0

RECENT DEVELOPMENTS: For the year ended 12/31/00, income totaled $235.1 million, before an extraordinary charge of $1.1 million, versus net income of $202.5 million in the previous year. Total revenues improved 18.6% to $826.5 million compared with $697.0 million in the prior year. Operating income jumped 23.8% to $360.4 million from $291.1 million in 1999. VNO completed $404.1 million in real estate acquisitions and investments in 2000.

PROSPECTS: On 3/19/01, the Company announced that it has been unable to reach a final agreement with the Port Authority of New York and New Jersey to conclude a net lease of the World Trade Center Company. Separately on 5/17/01, the Company announced that it has completed the sale of its 50.0%-owned office building at 570 Lexington Avenue to Bernard H. Mendik for $60.0 million. The Company reported a gain on the sale of approximately $10.0 million.

BUSINESS

VORNADO REALTY TRUST is a fully integrated real estate investment trust. The Company operates in five business segments: Office, Retail, Merchandise Mart, Temperature Controlled Logistics and other investments. The office segment is comprised of all or portions of 22 office properties in the New York City totaling approximately 14.4 million sq. ft. Also, VNO owns a 34.0% limited partnership interest in Charles E. Smith Commercial Realty L.P. The retail properties segment consists of 55 shopping center totaling approximately 11.3 million sq. ft. in six states and Puerto Rico. The Merchandise Mart Properties contain approximately 8.1 million square feet, including the 3.4 million square foot Merchandise Mart in Chicago. The Temperature Controlled Logistics segment consists of a 60.0% interest in partnerships that own 88 warehouse facilities nationwide. Other real estate investments include a 33.1% of the common stock of Alexander's, Inc.; the Hotel Pennsylvania in New York City; eight dry warehouse/industrial properties in New Jersey and other real estate interests.

ANNUAL FINANCIAL DATA

	12/31/00	12/31/99	12/31/98	12/31/97	12/31/96	12/31/95	12/31/94
Earnings Per Share	**[3] 2.20**	**1.94**	**[1] 1.59**	**0.79**	**[2] 2.49**	**[2] 2.25**	**[2] 0.95**
Tang. Book Val. Per Share	**18.40**	**18.26**	**17.63**	**14.33**	**10.41**	**8.01**	**5.39**
Dividends Per Share	**1.97**	**1.81**	**1.64**	**1.36**	**1.22**	**1.12**	**1.00**
Dividend Payout %	**89.5**	**93.1**	**103.1**	**172.1**	**49.0**	**49.8**	**105.3**
INCOME STATEMENT (IN MILLIONS):							
Rental Income	695.1	590.8	425.5	168.3	87.4	80.4	70.8
Total Income	826.5	697.0	509.9	209.1	116.9	108.7	94.0
Costs & Expenses	366.3	322.3	235.8	88.3	41.6	39.0	36.7
Depreciation	99.8	83.6	59.2	45.9	13.7	10.8	10.0
Interest Expense	170.3	141.7	114.7	42.9	16.7	16.4	14.2
Income Before Income Taxes	324.4	195.1	149.7	53.2	59.7	55.0	41.2
Equity Earnings/Minority Int.	d89.3	7.4	3.1	7.9	1.7	d2.0	...
Net Income	[3] 235.1	202.5	[1] 152.9	61.0	[2] 61.4	[2] 53.0	[2] 41.2
Average Shs. Outstg. (000)	88,692	93,302	82,656	57,217	24,603	23,580	21,854
BALANCE SHEET (IN MILLIONS):							
Cash & Cash Equivalents	471.7	249.7	289.2	417.5	117.2	90.1	110.8
Total Assets	6,370.3	5,479.2	4,425.8	2,524.1	565.2	491.5	393.5
Long-Term Obligations	2,656.9	2,048.8	2,051.0	956.7	232.4	233.4	234.2
Total Liabilities	4,291.6	3,423.9	2,643.1	1,210.3	288.9	297.2	276.9
Net Stockholders' Equity	2,078.7	2,055.4	1,782.7	1,313.8	276.3	194.3	116.7
Year-end Shs. Outstg. (000)	86,804	86,336	85,077	72,165	26,548	24,247	21,654
STATISTICAL RECORD:							
Net Inc.+Depr./Assets %	5.3	5.2	4.8	4.2	13.3	13.0	13.0
Return on Equity %	11.3	9.9	8.6	4.6	22.2	27.3	35.3
Return on Assets %	3.7	3.7	3.5	2.4	10.9	10.8	10.5
Price Range	40.75-29.88	40.00-29.69	49.81-26.00	47.38-25.38	26.44-17.81	19.50-16.31	18.88-15.13
P/E Ratio	18.5-13.6	20.6-15.3	31.3-16.4	60.0-32.1	10.6-7.2	8.7-7.2	19.9-15.9
Average Yield %	5.6	5.2	4.3	3.7	5.5	6.3	5.9

Statistics are as originally reported. Adj. for 2-for-1 stk. spl., 10/97 [1] Incl. a net gain from insurance settlement & condemn. of $9.6 mill. [2] Incl. gain on marketable secs., 1996, $913,000; 1995, $294,000; 1994, $643,000. [3] Bef. extraord. chrg., $1.1 mill.

OFFICERS:
S. Roth, Chmn., C.E.O.
M. D. Fascitelli, Pres.

INVESTOR CONTACT: Investor Relations, (212) 894-7000

PRINCIPAL OFFICE: 888 Seventh Avenue, New York, NY 10019

TELEPHONE NUMBER: (212) 894-7000
FAX: (201) 587-0600
WEB: www.vno.com

NO. OF EMPLOYEES: 1,300 (approx.)

SHAREHOLDERS: 2,500 (approx.)

ANNUAL MEETING: In May

INCORPORATED: MD, May, 1993

INSTITUTIONAL HOLDINGS:
No. of Institutions: 163
Shares Held: 56,131,394
% Held: 64.7

INDUSTRY: Real estate investment trusts (SIC: 6798)

TRANSFER AGENT(S): First Union National Bank, Charlotte, NC

NYSE SYMBOL VMC
Rec. Pr. 46.23 (4/30/01)

VULCAN MATERIALS COMPANY

YIELD 1.9%
P/E RATIO 21.4

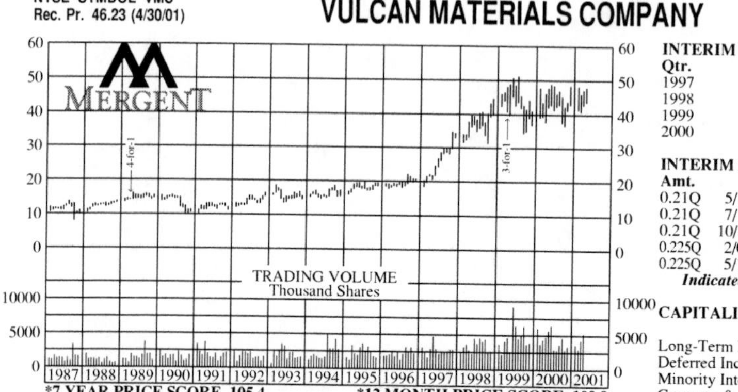

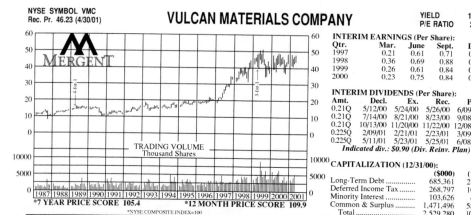

*7 YEAR PRICE SCORE 105.4 *12 MONTH PRICE SCORE 109.9
*NYSE COMPOSITE INDEX=100

INTERIM EARNINGS (Per Share):

Qtr.	Mar.	June	Sept.	Dec.
1997	0.21	0.61	0.71	0.50
1998	0.36	0.69	0.88	0.58
1999	0.26	0.61	0.84	0.64
2000	0.23	0.75	0.84	0.34

INTERIM DIVIDENDS (Per Share):

Amt.	Decl.	Ex.	Rec.	Pay.
0.21Q	5/12/00	5/24/00	5/26/00	6/09/00
0.21Q	7/14/00	8/21/00	8/23/00	9/08/00
0.21Q	10/13/00	11/20/00	11/22/00	12/08/00
0.225Q	2/09/01	2/21/01	2/23/01	3/09/01
0.225Q	5/11/01	5/23/01	5/25/01	6/08/01

Indicated div.: $0.90 (Div. Reinv. Plan)

CAPITALIZATION (12/31/00):

	($000)	(%)
Long-Term Debt	685,361	27.1
Deferred Income Tax	268,797	10.6
Minority Interest	103,626	4.1
Common & Surplus	1,471,496	58.2
Total	2,529,280	100.0

RECENT DEVELOPMENTS: For the year ended 12/31/00, net earnings decreased 8.3% to $219.9 million from $239.7 million in 1999. Earnings for 2000 included a charge of $23.0 million from an arbitration assessment. Net sales rose 5.8% to $2.49 billion. Construction material net sales grew 4.2% to $1.89 billion, despite severe winter weather in November and December of 2000. Chemical net sales increased 11.1% to $605.8 million.

PROSPECTS: In 2001, VMC expects earnings per share to range from $2.85 to $3.00. Barring an economic recession, earnings are expected to range from $425.0 million to $450.0 million in the construction materials business and $70.0 million to $80.0 million in the chemicals business. Separately, VMC signed a letter of intent to acquire from Empresas ICA Sociedad Controladora its 50.0% share of the Vulcan/ICA joint venture for $121.0 million.

BUSINESS

VULCAN MATERIALS COMPANY is engaged in the production, distribution and sale of construction materials and industrial and specialty chemicals. The Company is a producer of construction aggregates and other construction materials. The Company is also a chemicals manufacturer, supplying chloralkali and other industrial and specialty chemicals. Construction materials accounted for 75.7% of 2000 sales, while chemicals, such as chlorinated hydrocarbons, caustic soda and anhydrous ammonia, accounted for 24.3%.

REVENUES

(12/31/2000)	($000)	(%)
Construction materials	1,885,900	75.7
Chemicals	605,800	24.3
Total	2,491,700	100.0

ANNUAL FINANCIAL DATA

	12/31/00	12/31/99	12/31/98	12/31/97	12/31/96	12/31/95	12/31/94
Earnings Per Share	**[3] 2.16**	**2.35**	**2.50**	**2.03**	**[2] 1.79**	**[2] 1.54**	**[1] 0.89**
Cash Flow Per Share	**4.43**	**4.37**	**3.85**	**3.21**	**2.85**	**2.57**	**1.86**
Tang. Book Val. Per Share	**9.00**	**8.63**	**11.47**	**9.81**	**8.42**	**7.59**	**6.79**
Dividends Per Share	**0.84**	**0.78**	**0.69**	**0.63**	**0.56**	**0.49**	**0.44**
Dividend Payout %	**38.9**	**33.2**	**27.7**	**30.8**	**31.3**	**31.5**	**49.4**
INCOME STATEMENT (IN MILLIONS):							
Total Revenues	2,491.7	2,355.8	1,776.4	1,678.6	1,568.9	1,461.0	1,253.4
Costs & Expenses	1,918.9	1,790.6	1,295.8	1,274.4	1,181.9	1,100.2	1,009.
Depreciation & Amort.	232.4	207.1	137.8	120.6	112.6	110.7	106
Operating Income	340.5	358.1	342.9	283.6	274.5	250.1	137
Net Interest Inc./(Exp.)	d43.4	d44.2	d0.1	d3.7	d5.5	d10.0	d
Income Before Income Taxes	312.2	351.6	374.8	300.5	285.6	258.4	1
Income Taxes	92.3	111.9	118.9	91.4	97.0	92.2	
Net Income	[3] 219.9	239.7	255.9	209.1	[2] 188.6	[2] 166.2	[1]
Cash Flow	452.3	446.8	393.7	329.8	301.2	276.9	
Average Shs. Outstg. (000)	102,012	102,190	102,177	102,849	105,519	107,799	1
BALANCE SHEET (IN MILLIONS):							
Cash & Cash Equivalents	55.3	52.8	180.6	128.6	50.8	21.9	.7
Total Current Assets	694.5	624.7	576.4	487.1	394.0	362.1	6.8
Net Property	1,848.6	1,639.7	895.8	808.4	764.5	698.0	01.8
Total Assets	3,228.6	2,839.5	1,658.6	1,449.2	1,320.6	1,215.	81.1
Total Current Liabilities	572.2	386.6	211.5	207.7	194.7	177	211.3
Long-Term Obligations	685.4	698.9	76.5	81.9	85.5	9	97.4
Net Stockholders' Equity	1,471.5	1,323.7	1,153.7	991.5	883.7	79	731.6
Net Working Capital	122.3	238.1	364.9	279.4	199.4	1	125.5
Year-end Shs. Outstg. (000)	101,044	100,735	100,596	101,061	104,913	104	107,721
STATISTICAL RECORD:							
Operating Profit Margin %	13.7	15.2	19.3	16.9	17.5		11.0
Net Profit Margin %	8.8	10.2	14.4	12.5	12.0	4	7.8
Return on Equity %	14.9	18.1	22.2	21.1	21.3	.9	13.4
Return on Assets %	6.8	8.4	15.4	14.4	14.3	3.7	8.3
Debt/Total Assets %	21.2	24.6	4.6	5.7	6.5	7.4	8.2
Price Range	48.88-36.50	51.25-34.31	44.66-31.33	34.64-18.41	22.16-17.71	16.04	18.83-14.67
P/E Ratio	22.6-16.9	21.8-14.6	17.9-12.5	17.0-9.1	12.4-9.	-10.4	21.2-16.5
Average Yield %	2.0	1.8	1.8	2.4	2.	2.7	2.6

Statistics are as originally reported. Adj. for stk. splits: 3-for-1, 2 [1] Incl. a pre-tax gain of $4.2 mill. on the sale of Co.'s industrial sand oper. [2] Incl. gain fr es of assets: $5.2 mill., 1996; $16.5 mill., 1995. [3] Incl. a chrg. of $23.0 mill. from an arbitr settlement.

OFFICERS:
D. M. James, Chmn., C.E.O.
M. E. Tomkins, Sr. V.P., C.F.O.

INVESTOR CONTACT: Charles R. Brown, Investor Relations, (205) 298-3191

PRINCIPAL OFFICE: 1200 Urban Center Drive, Birmingham, AL 35242

TELEPHONE NUMBER: (205) 298-3000
FAX: (205) 298-2963
WEB: www.vulcanmaterials.com

NO. OF EMPLOYEES: 9,315 (approx.)

SHAREHOLDERS: 3,450 (approx.)

ANNUAL MEETING: In May

INCORPORATED: NJ, Sept., 1956

INSTITUTIONAL HOL S:
No. of Institutions:
Shares Held: 65,5 3
% Held: 64.9

INDUSTRY: Cru nd broken limestone (SIC: 1422)

TRANSFER A S): First Chicago Trust Company of York, Jersey City, NJ

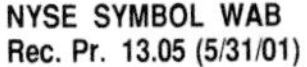

NYSE SYMBOL WAB
Rec. Pr. 13.05 (5/31/01)

WABTEC CORPORATION

YIELD 0.3%
P/E RATIO 22.5

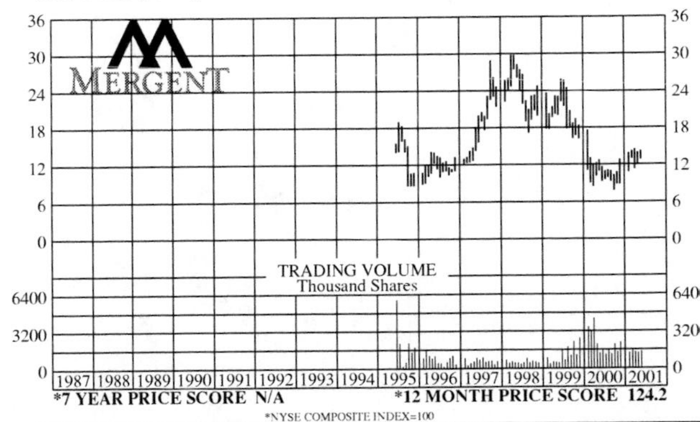

INTERIM EARNINGS (Per Share):

Qtr.	Mar.	June	Sept.	Dec.
1996	0.27	0.29	0.28	0.31
1997	0.34	0.37	0.35	0.37
1998	0.42	0.45	0.42	0.45
1999	0.48	0.51	0.48	0.39
2000	0.38	0.18	d0.08	0.10

INTERIM DIVIDENDS (Per Share):

Amt.	Decl.	Ex.	Rec.	Pay.
0.01Q	5/08/00	5/11/00	5/15/00	5/31/00
0.01Q	8/08/00	8/11/00	8/15/00	8/31/00
0.01Q	10/24/00	11/13/00	11/15/00	11/30/00
0.01Q	2/14/01	2/13/01	2/15/01	2/28/01
0.01Q	5/22/01	5/11/01	5/15/01	5/31/01

Indicated div.: $0.04

CAPITALIZATION (12/31/00):

	($000)	(%)
Long-Term Debt	539,446	71.6
Deferred Income Tax	17,110	2.3
Common & Surplus	196,371	26.1
Total	752,927	100.0

RECENT DEVELOPMENTS: For the twelve months ended 12/31/00, net income dropped 33.1% to $25.4 million versus income of $37.9 million, before an extraordinary charge of $1.3 million, in the previous year. Results for 2000 included a pre-tax restructuring charge of $27.1 million and a $5.1 million write-off of deferred tax assets. Net sales fell 8.3% to $1.03 billion from $1.12 billion in 1999. Freight Group segment sales fell 15.1% to $749.7 million while Transit Group segment sales rose 16.8% to $278.3 million.

PROSPECTS: The Company's subsidiary, Wabtec Rail Ltd., was awarded a $21.0 million contract to supply 190 specialty freight cars to Railtrack Plc., which owns and operates Britain's railway infrastructure. The cars will be delivered during 2001. Meanwhile, WAB expects earnings to show double-digit growth for the year, which implies full-year diluted earnings of about $1.25 per share, excluding a first-quarter merger restructuring charge of about $5.0 million.

BUSINESS

WABTEC CORPORATION (formerly Westinghouse Air Brake Company) is a manufacturer of equipment for locomotives, railway freight cars and passenger transit vehicles. WAB's products are sold to both original equipment manufacturers and the aftermarket. WAB also provides outsource services to the railroad and passenger transit aftermarkets. On 11/19/99, the Company acquired MotivePower Industries.

BUSINESS LINE ANALYSIS

(12/31/00)	Rev (%)	Inc (%)
Freight Group	73.2	79.8
Transit Group	26.8	20.2
Total	100.0	100.0

ANNUAL FINANCIAL DATA

	12/31/00	12/31/99	12/31/98	12/31/97	12/31/96	12/31/95	12/31/94
Earnings Per Share	**3 0.59**	**2 0.86**	**1.75**	**1.42**	**1.15**	**1 1.32**	**0.92**
Cash Flow Per Share	**1.55**	**1.82**	**2.73**	**2.36**	**1.93**	**2.02**	**1.32**
Tang. Book Val. Per Share	...	...	...	...	...	...	**0.56**
Dividends Per Share	**0.04**	**0.04**	**0.04**	**0.04**	**0.04**	**0.01**	...
Dividend Payout %	**6.8**	**4.7**	**2.3**	**2.8**	**3.5**	**0.8**	...
INCOME STATEMENT (IN MILLIONS):							
Total Revenues	1,028.0	1,121.1	670.9	564.4	453.5	425.0	347.5
Costs & Expenses	896.8	962.4	541.0	449.8	351.5	317.0	257.8
Depreciation & Amort.	41.7	42.6	25.2	24.6	22.2	18.6	16.1
Operating Income	89.5	116.0	104.7	90.0	79.7	89.3	73.6
Net Interest Inc./(Exp.)	d45.5	d44.4	d31.2	d29.7	d26.2	d31.0	d10.9
Income Before Income Taxes	47.6	71.5	72.5	60.6	53.6	58.5	62.5
Income Taxes	22.2	33.6	27.6	23.3	20.9	23.4	25.6
Net Income	3 25.4	2 37.9	45.0	37.3	32.7	1 35.1	36.8
Cash Flow	67.1	80.6	70.2	61.9	55.0	53.7	52.9
Average Shs. Outstg. (000)	43,382	44,234	25,708	26,173	28,473	26,639	40,000
BALANCE SHEET (IN MILLIONS):							
Cash & Cash Equivalents	6.1	7.1	3.3	0.8	0.6	0.2	1.0
Total Current Assets	447.6	437.2	263.0	180.5	150.2	106.7	90.7
Net Property	214.6	222.7	125.0	108.4	95.8	72.8	67.3
Total Assets	984.0	996.7	596.2	410.9	363.2	263.4	187.7
Total Current Liabilities	190.7	194.2	167.6	131.8	102.0	70.0	43.8
Long-Term Obligations	539.4	567.8	437.2	332.3	312.0	283.5	78.1
Net Stockholders' Equity	196.4	181.9	d33.9	d79.3	d76.2	d108.7	46.8
Net Working Capital	256.9	243.0	95.4	48.7	48.2	36.7	46.9
Year-end Shs. Outstg. (000)	42,842	51,529	33,895	33,683	37,489	37,643	40,000
STATISTICAL RECORD:							
Operating Profit Margin %	8.7	10.3	15.6	15.9	17.6	21.0	21.2
Net Profit Margin %	2.5	3.4	6.7	6.6	7.2	8.3	10.6
Return on Equity %	12.9	20.9	...	...	...	...	78.7
Return on Assets %	2.6	3.8	7.5	9.1	9.0	13.3	19.6
Debt/Total Assets %	54.8	57.0	73.3	80.9	85.9	107.6	41.6
Price Range	17.56-7.81	25.94-16.19	29.81-17.13	28.94-12.13	14.13-8.88	19.00-8.63	...
P/E Ratio	29.8-13.2	30.2-18.8	17.0-9.8	20.4-8.5	12.3-7.7	14.4-6.5	...
Average Yield %	0.3	0.2	0.2	0.2	0.3	0.1	...

Statistics are as originally reported. 1 Bef. extraord. chrg. ot $1.4 mill. ($0.50/sh) 2 Incl. merger and restructure chrg. $43.6 mill. & excl. net extraord. loss of $1.3 mill. 3 Incl. merger and restructure chrg. $27.1 mill.

OFFICERS:
W. E. Kassling, Chmn.
G. T. Davies, Pres., C.E.O.
R. J. Brooks, Exec. V.P., C.F.O.

INVESTOR CONTACT: T.R. Wesley, V.P., Inv. Rel. & Corp. Comm. (412) 825-1000

PRINCIPAL OFFICE: 1001 Air Brake Ave., Wilmerding, PA 15148

TELEPHONE NUMBER: (412) 825-1000
FAX: (412) 825-1019
WEB: www.wabtec.com

NO. OF EMPLOYEES: 6,244 (avg.)

SHAREHOLDERS: 1,104

ANNUAL MEETING: In May

INCORPORATED: DE, 1989

INSTITUTIONAL HOLDINGS:
No. of Institutions: 91
Shares Held: 36,587,330
% Held: 85.2

INDUSTRY: Railroad equipment (SIC: 3743)

TRANSFER AGENT(S): Mellon Investor Services, Pittsburgh, PA

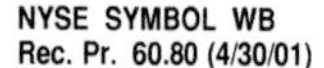
NYSE SYMBOL WB
Rec. Pr. 60.80 (4/30/01)

WACHOVIA CORPORATION

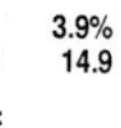
YIELD 3.9%
P/E RATIO 14.9

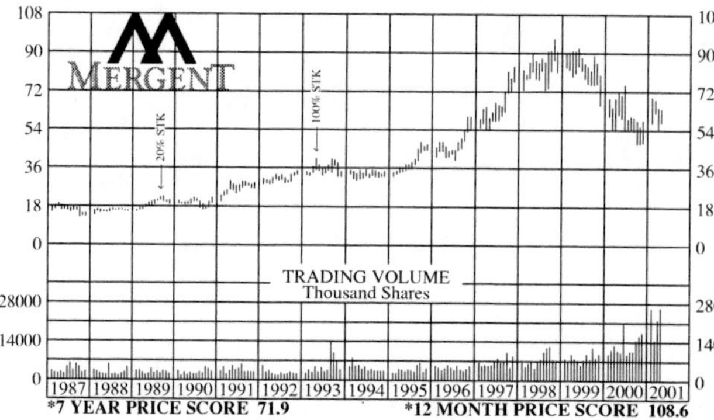

*7 YEAR PRICE SCORE 71.9 *12 MONTH PRICE SCORE 108.6

*NYSE COMPOSITE INDEX=100

INTERIM EARNINGS (Per Share):

Qtr.	Mar.	June	Sept.	Dec.
1997	0.99	1.01	1.04	0.02
1998	0.93	1.00	1.09	1.19
1999	1.18	1.19	1.25	1.28
2000	1.20	0.67	1.00	1.20

INTERIM DIVIDENDS (Per Share):

Amt.	Decl.	Ex.	Rec.	Pay.
0.54Q	4/28/00	5/09/00	5/11/00	6/01/00
0.60Q	7/28/00	8/08/00	8/10/00	9/01/00
0.60Q	10/27/00	11/07/00	11/09/00	12/01/00
0.60Q	1/26/01	2/06/01	2/08/01	3/01/01
0.60Q	4/27/01	5/08/01	5/10/01	6/01/01

Indicated div.: $2.40 (Div. Reinv. Plan)

CAPITALIZATION (12/31/00):

	($000)	(%)
Total Deposits	44,412,182	72.2
Long-Term Debt	10,808,218	17.6
Common & Surplus	6,284,539	10.2
Total	61,504,939	100.0

RECENT DEVELOPMENTS: For the year ended 12/31/00, net income declined 17.7% to $832.3 million from $1.01 billion in the prior year. Earnings for 2000 and 1999 included pre-tax merger-related charges of $29.0 million and $19.3 million, respectively. Results for 2000 also included various charges of $127.5 million. Net interest income increased 1.8% to $2.52 billion. Total non-interest income grew 19.1% to $1.93 billion, while total non-interest expenses rose 14.7% to $2.58 billion.

PROSPECTS: On 4/16/01, the Company and First Union Corporation (FTU) signed a definitive agreement under which FTU will acquire WB in a transaction valued at approximately $13.40 billion. The combined company, which will be known as Wachovia Corporation, will have total assets of $324.00 billion. On 5/14/01, the Company received an offer from SunTrust Banks, Inc. under which SunTrust would acquire WB for approximately $14.70 billion.

BUSINESS

WACHOVIA CORPORATION is one of the largest interstate bank holding companies in the Southeast, with $74.03 billion in assets as of 12/31/00. Wachovia operates more than 650 full-service offices and 1,350 Automatic Teller Machines (ATMs) throughout Florida, Georgia, North Carolina, South Carolina and Virginia. Wachovia offers full-service banking, investment banking, mortgage banking, trust, investment, insurance and several other services. At 12/31/00, the loan portfolio consisted of: commercial loans, 33.2%; retail, 19.8%; real estate, 39.3%; lease financing and foreign, 7.7%. On 4/1/99, WB completed its acquisition of Interstate/Johnson Lane, Inc.

ANNUAL FINANCIAL DATA

	12/31/00	12/31/99	12/31/98	12/31/97	12/31/96	12/31/95	12/31/94
Earnings Per Share	**[2][3] 4.07**	**[2] 4.90**	**[2] 4.18**	**[2] 2.94**	**3.81**	**[1] 3.50**	**3.13**
Tang. Book Val. Per Share	**24.72**	**28.04**	**26.30**	**25.13**	**22.96**	**22.15**	**19.23**
Dividends Per Share	**2.28**	**2.06**	**1.86**	**1.68**	**1.52**	**1.38**	**1.23**
Dividend Payout %	**56.0**	**42.0**	**44.5**	**57.1**	**39.9**	**39.4**	**39.3**
INCOME STATEMENT (IN MILLIONS):							
Total Interest Income	5,345.4	4,666.8	4,665.2	4,262.4	3,227.3	3,019.7	2,362.3
Total Interest Expense	2,829.6	2,196.7	2,314.2	2,168.8	1,672.6	1,579.1	1,038.4
Net Interest Income	2,515.7	2,470.1	2,351.0	2,093.6	1,554.7	1,440.6	1,323.9
Provision for Loan Losses	588.5	298.1	299.5	264.9	149.9	103.8	71.8
Non-Interest Income	1,931.3	1,621.0	1,248.6	1,007.2	787.7	735.6	607.8
Non-Interest Expense	2,583.0	2,250.6	1,996.3	1,966.7	1,257.5	1,203.6	1,098.4
Income Before Taxes	1,275.5	1,542.4	1,303.8	869.1	934.9	868.9	761.5
Net Income	[2][3] 832.3	[2] 1,011.2	[2] 874.2	[2] 592.8	644.6	[1] 602.5	539.1
Average Shs. Outstg. (000)	204,450	206,192	209,153	201,901	169,097	172,089	172,339
BALANCE SHEET (IN MILLIONS):							
Cash & Due from Banks	3,727.4	3,475.0	3,800.3	4,221.8	3,367.7	2,692.3	2,670.1
Securities Avail. for Sale	8,532.5	7,966.1	8,648.5	9,908.7	7,946.2	8,524.8	4,428.2
Total Loans & Leases	55,001.7	49,621.2	45,719.2	44,194.4	31,283.2	29,261.2	25,890.8
Allowance for Credit Losses	822.6	554.8	548.0	544.7	409.3	408.8	406.1
Net Loans & Leases	54,179.2	49,066.4	45,171.2	43,649.7	30,873.9	28,852.3	25,484.7
Total Assets	74,031.7	67,352.5	64,122.8	65,397.1	46,904.5	44,981.3	39,188.0
Total Deposits	44,412.2	41,786.4	40,994.7	42,653.8	27,250.1	26,368.8	23,069.3
Long-Term Obligations	10,808.2	7,814.3	7,596.7	5,934.1	6,466.9	5,423.0	4,790.5
Total Liabilities	67,747.1	61,694.1	58,784.6	60,222.8	43,142.7	41,207.6	35,901.5
Net Stockholders' Equity	6,284.5	5,658.5	5,338.2	5,174.3	3,761.8	3,773.8	3,286.5
Year-end Shs. Outstg. (000)	203,424	201,812	202,986	205,927	163,844	170,359	170,934
STATISTICAL RECORD:							
Return on Equity %	13.2	17.9	16.4	11.5	17.1	16.0	16.4
Return on Assets %	1.1	1.5	1.4	0.9	1.4	1.3	1.4
Equity/Assets %	8.5	8.4	8.3	7.9	8.0	8.4	8.4
Non-Int. Exp./Tot. Inc. %	58.1	55.2	55.8	63.5	53.8	56.8	57.0
Price Range	75.25-47.44	92.31-65.44	96.81-72.75	83.94-53.50	60.25-39.63	48.25-32.00	35.38-30.13
P/E Ratio	18.5-11.7	18.8-13.4	23.2-17.4	28.5-18.2	15.8-10.4	13.8-9.1	11.3-9.6
Average Yield %	3.7	2.6	2.2	2.4	3.0	3.4	3.8

Statistics are as originally reported. [1] Incl. after-tax gain of $30.7 mill. from non-recurr. items. [2] Incl. pre-tax merger-rel. chrgs.: $29.0 mill., 2000; $19.3 mill., 1999; $85.3 mill., 1998; $220.3 mill., 1997. [3] Incl. a pre-tax restruct. chrg. of $107.5 mill. & a pre-tax litig. chrg. of $20.0 mill.

OFFICERS:
L. M. Baker Jr., Chmn., C.E.O.
R. S. McCoy Jr., Vice-Chmn., C.F.O., Treas.
J. Prendergast, Pres., C.O.O.

INVESTOR CONTACT: H. Jo Barlow, Vice-President, (336) 732-5787

PRINCIPAL OFFICE: 100 North Main Street, Winston-Salem, NC 27101

TELEPHONE NUMBER: (336) 770-5000
FAX: (336) 732-2281
WEB: www.wachovia.com

NO. OF EMPLOYEES: 20,325

SHAREHOLDERS: 50,581

ANNUAL MEETING: In April

INCORPORATED: NC, July, 1985

INSTITUTIONAL HOLDINGS:
No. of Institutions: 417
Shares Held: 105,691,411
% Held: 51.8

INDUSTRY: National commercial banks (SIC: 6021)

TRANSFER AGENT(S): EquiServe, Boston, MA

NYSE SYMBOL WAK
Rec. Pr. 16.05 (5/31/01)

WACKENHUT CORPORATION (THE)

YIELD	...
P/E RATIO	12.8

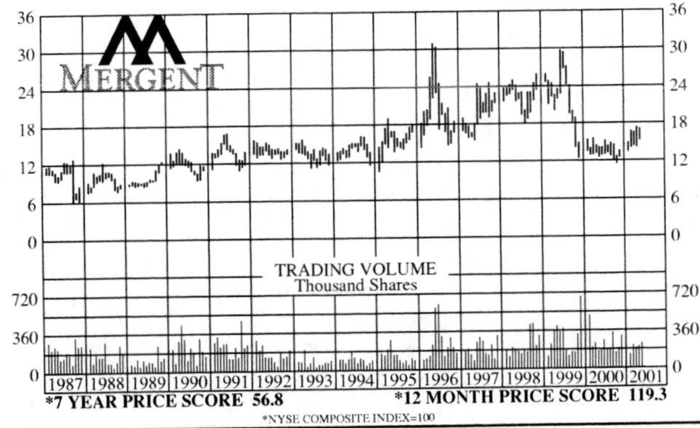

INTERIM EARNINGS (Per Share):

Qtr.	Mar.	June	Sept.	Dec.
1996	0.08	0.15	0.21	0.22
1997	0.13	0.17	0.23	d0.53
1998	0.17	0.23	0.29	0.33
1999	0.26	0.30	0.35	0.37
2000	0.28	0.33	0.27	0.37

INTERIM DIVIDENDS (Per Share):

Amt.	Decl.	Ex.	Rec.	Pay.

No dividends paid.

CAPITALIZATION (12/31/00):

	($000)	(%)
Long-Term Debt	11,400	4.6
Minority Interest	58,100	23.5
Common & Surplus	177,800	71.9
Total	247,300	100.0

RECENT DEVELOPMENTS: For the year ended 12/31/00, income declined 10.2% to $17.6 million, before the cumulative effect of an accounting charge, compared with net income of $19.6 million in 1999. Results for 2000 included a non-recurring pre-tax charge of $3.8 milion. Revenues were $2.51 billion, up 16.4% from $2.15 billion a year earlier. Global security services group revenues rose 12.2% to $1.17 billion.

PROSPECTS: On 2/1/01, WAK announced that it has been awarded a five-year contract by Exelon Corporation to provide security services at eleven nuclear power generating facilities in three states: Pennsylvania, Illinois, and New Jersey. WAK's Nuclear Services Division has been contracted for security services at the sites for varying periods of time. The value of the contract is approximately $195.0 million.

BUSINESS

THE WACKENHUT CORPORATION is a provider of services outsourced by business and government. The security-related support services include base operations, facility management, fire and emergency medical services and food service to private and publicly managed correctional facilities. Wackenhut International provides a variety of services internationally, which include electronic security systems, central station monitoring, cash-in-transit, satellite tracking of vehicles and cargo, building maintenance, secure storage of documents, postal services and distribution logistics. WAK, through its approximately 56.0%-owned public subsidiary, Wackenhut Corrections Corporation, designs, constructs, finances and manages correctional, detention and public sector mental health facilities and performs separate correctional-related services. Contributions to revenues in 2000 were: Global Security Services, 47.0%; Correctional Services, 21.0%; and Staffing Services, 32.0%.

ANNUAL FINANCIAL DATA

	12/31/00	1/2/00	1/3/99	12/28/97	12/29/96	12/31/95	1/1/95
Earnings Per Share	**[2][3] 1.15**	**1.28**	**[3] 1.03**	**[2] 0.01**	**[2] 0.66**	**0.60**	**[1] 0.19**
Cash Flow Per Share	**2.88**	**2.81**	**2.21**	**1.19**	**1.68**	**1.60**	**1.18**
Tang. Book Val. Per Share	**8.51**	**7.54**	**10.08**	**9.89**	**10.04**	**5.18**	**4.76**
Dividends Per Share	**...**	**0.15**	**0.29**	**0.26**	**0.27**	**0.32**	**0.36**
Dividend Payout %	**...**	**11.7**	**28.2**	**N.M.**	**40.9**	**52.5**	**187.4**
INCOME STATEMENT (IN MILLIONS):							
Total Revenues	2,505.1	2,152.3	1,755.1	1,126.8	906.1	796.7	747.7
Costs & Expenses	2,444.3	2,091.5	1,705.2	1,106.0	875.9	768.8	729.2
Depreciation & Amort.	25.9	22.9	17.5	17.5	13.8	12.2	11.9
Operating Income	34.9	37.9	32.4	3.3	16.3	15.8	15.3
Net Interest Inc./(Exp.)	d1.6	2.0	2.2	2.8	1.6	d2.0	d3.6
Income Before Income Taxes	33.3	39.9	34.6	6.0	17.9	13.7	3.0
Income Taxes	13.3	15.9	13.7	2.3	6.3	4.7	...
Equity Earnings/Minority Int.	d2.4	d4.4	d5.0	d3.7	d2.5	d1.7	d0.7
Net Income	[2][3] 17.6	19.6	[3] 15.9	[2] 0.1	[2] 9.1	7.3	[1] 2.3
Cash Flow	43.5	42.5	33.4	17.6	22.9	19.4	14.2
Average Shs. Outstg. (000)	15,100	15,100	15,100	14,746	13,636	12,132	12,066
BALANCE SHEET (IN MILLIONS):							
Cash & Cash Equivalents	60.8	67.0	43.5	45.2	52.8	20.2	13.8
Total Current Assets	328.5	299.1	255.7	251.9	220.6	122.2	137.6
Net Property	79.4	68.2	59.9	56.5	34.5	19.3	30.8
Total Assets	570.3	525.7	453.0	404.4	323.9	197.9	212.8
Total Current Liabilities	197.9	179.8	168.7	135.0	72.5	70.3	65.6
Long-Term Obligations	11.4	16.5	3.3	13.3	5.9	5.4	39.0
Net Stockholders' Equity	177.8	163.9	149.2	146.8	148.2	62.9	57.5
Net Working Capital	130.6	119.3	87.0	116.9	148.1	51.9	72.1
Year-end Shs. Outstg. (000)	15,000	14,800	14,800	14,854	14,761	12,132	12,066
STATISTICAL RECORD:							
Operating Profit Margin %	1.4	1.8	1.8	0.3	1.8	2.0	2.0
Net Profit Margin %	0.7	0.9	0.9	...	1.0	0.9	0.3
Return on Equity %	9.9	12.0	10.7	0.1	6.1	11.5	4.0
Return on Assets %	3.1	3.7	3.5	...	2.8	3.7	1.1
Debt/Total Assets %	2.0	3.1	0.7	3.3	1.8	2.7	18.3
Price Range	15.56-11.44	29.75-12.38	26.00-18.00	24.69-15.38	31.00-14.25	19.00-10.50	16.25-11.50
P/E Ratio	13.5-9.9	23.2-9.7	25.2-17.5	2,444.4-1,522.3	47.0-21.6	31.7-17.5	84.6-59.9
Average Yield %	...	0.7	1.3	1.3	1.2	2.1	2.6

Statistics are as originally reported. Adj. for stk. splits: 25%, 1/95 & 1/96. [1] Incl. a pretax chrg. of $8.7 mill. from the write-down of assets and bef. an extraord. chrg. of $887,000 from early exting. of debt. [2] Incl. nonrecur. chrg. of $750,000, 1996; $18.3 mill., 1997; $3.8 mill., 2000. [3] Bef. acctg. change chrg. of $6.6 mill., 1998; $800,000, 2000.

OFFICERS:
G. R. Wackenhut, Chmn.
R. R. Wackenhut, Vice-Chmn., Pres., C.E.O.
P. L. Maslowe, Exec. V.P., C.F.O.

INVESTOR CONTACT: Patrick F. Cannan, Dir. Corp. Comm., (561) 691-6643

PRINCIPAL OFFICE: 4200 Wackenhut Drive, #100, Palm Beach Gardens, FL 33410-4243

TELEPHONE NUMBER: (561) 622-5656
FAX: (561) 662-7406
WEB: www.wackenhut.com

NO. OF EMPLOYEES: 100,200 (approx.)

SHAREHOLDERS: 555 (approx. series A com.); 585 (approx. series B com.)

ANNUAL MEETING: In May

INCORPORATED: FL, Dec., 1958

INSTITUTIONAL HOLDINGS:
No. of Institutions: 32
Shares Held: 1,471,409
% Held: 14.6

INDUSTRY: Detective & armored car services (SIC: 7381)

TRANSFER AGENT(S): Mellon Investor Services, L.L.C., Ridgefield Park, NJ

NYSE SYMBOL WDR
Rec. Pr. 30.42 (4/30/01)

WADDELL & REED FINANCIAL, INC.

YIELD 1.2%
P/E RATIO 22.7

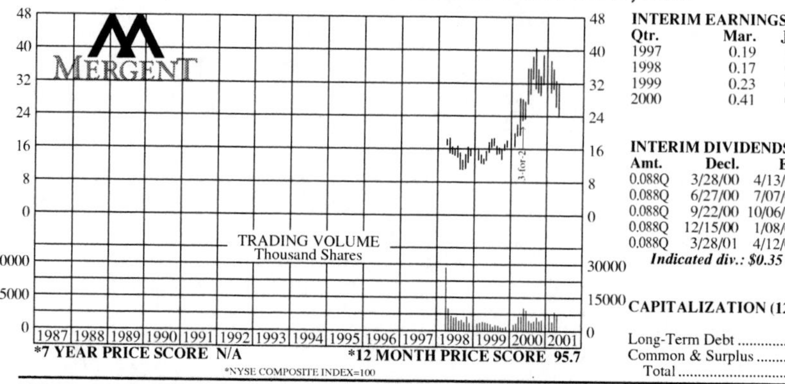

*7 YEAR PRICE SCORE N/A *12 MONTH PRICE SCORE 95.7
*NYSE COMPOSITE INDEX=100

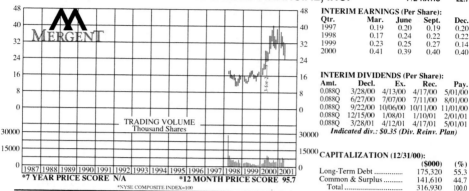

INTERIM EARNINGS (Per Share):

Qtr.	Mar.	June	Sept.	Dec.
1997	0.19	0.20	0.19	0.20
1998	0.17	0.24	0.22	0.22
1999	0.23	0.25	0.27	0.14
2000	0.41	0.39	0.40	0.40

INTERIM DIVIDENDS (Per Share):

Amt.	Decl.	Ex.	Rec.	Pay.
0.088Q	3/28/00	4/13/00	4/17/00	5/01/00
0.088Q	6/27/00	7/07/00	7/11/00	8/01/00
0.088Q	9/22/00	10/06/00	10/11/00	11/01/00
0.088Q	12/15/00	1/08/01	1/10/01	2/01/01
0.088Q	3/28/01	4/12/01	4/17/01	5/01/01

Indicated div.: $0.35 (Div. Reinv. Plan)

CAPITALIZATION (12/31/00):

	($000)	(%)
Long-Term Debt	175,320	55.3
Common & Surplus	141,610	44.7
Total	316,930	100.0

RECENT DEVELOPMENTS: For the year ended 12/31/00, net income advanced 44.2% to $139.0 million from $96.4 million in 1999. Earnings for 1999 excluded a pre-tax net nonrecurring charge of $23.6 million. Total operating revenues increased 46.0% to $520.7 million from $346.5 million the year before. Investment management fees grew 42.1% to $253.8 million. Underwriting and distribution fees rose 60.6% to $202.9 million.

PROSPECTS: On 4/30/01, the Company combined its two classes of common stock by converting its shares of Class B Common Stock into shares of Class A Common Stock on a one-for-one basis. Separately, WDR sold its two home office buildings to Mesirow Realty Sale-Leaseback. The sale resulted in a realized gain of approximately $1.8 million, which will be deferred and amortized over the term of the operating lease.

BUSINESS

WADDELL & REED FINANCIAL, INC., with assets under management of $36.70 billion as of 12/31/00, is the holding company of Waddell & Reed, Inc., Waddell & Reed Investment Management Company, and Waddell & Reed Services Company. Waddell & Reed, Inc. is a registered broker-dealer and registered investment advisor that acts as the nationwide distributor and underwriter for the shares of mutual funds and distributor of insurance products issued primarily by United Investors Life Insurance Company. Waddell & Reed Investment Management Company is a registered investment advisor that provides investment management and advisory services to WDR's mutual funds and to institutions and other private clients. Waddell & Reed Services Company provides transfer agency and accounting services to the funds and their shareholders. On 3/31/00, WDR acquired The Legend Group.

REVENUES

(12/31/2000)	($000)	%
Investment Management Fees..	253,774	48.7
Underwriting & Dist. Fees........................	202,879	39.0
Shareholder Service Fees........................	53,436	10.3
Investment & Other...	10,613	2.0
Total	520,702	100.0

ANNUAL FINANCIAL DATA

	12/31/00	12/31/99	12/31/98	12/31/97	12/31/96	12/31/95
Earnings Per Share	**1.60**	[1] **0.89**	**0.85**	**0.73**	...	...
Cash Flow Per Share	**1.71**	**0.95**	**0.89**	**0.78**	...	...
Tang. Book Val. Per Share	...	**0.15**	**1.18**	...	**2.06**	...
Dividends Per Share	**0.35**	**0.35**	**0.27**	...	...	...
Dividend Payout %	**22.1**	**39.6**	**31.3**	...	...	...
INCOME STATEMENT (IN MILLIONS):						
Total Revenues	520.7	356.7	287.3	241.8	221.0	183.5
Costs & Expenses	283.5	219.2	140.3	122.4	111.0	94.0
Depreciation & Amort.	9.3	5.4	4.8	4.2	4.7	4.8
Operating Income	227.9	132.0	142.2	115.1	105.3	84.7
Net Interest Inc./(Exp.)	...	...	d6.7	...	3.9	3.9
Income Before Income Taxes	227.9	132.0	135.5	115.1	109.2	88.6
Income Taxes	88.9	50.3	51.8	44.9	42.5	35.1
Net Income	139.0	[1] 81.8	83.7	70.3	66.7	53.5
Cash Flow	118.7	55.2	62.1	22.8	70.4	58.3
Average Shs. Outstg. (000)	86,895	91,548	99,269	96,000	...	...
BALANCE SHEET (IN MILLIONS):						
Cash & Cash Equivalents	125.7	151.2	133.3	92.8	79.0	...
Total Current Assets	166.1	185.5	172.5	130.1	110.1	...
Net Property	55.5	27.6	20.6	12.1	10.4	...
Total Assets	422.2	335.1	327.2	447.0	429.3	...
Total Current Liabilities	93.7	198.6	109.8	155.9	62.7	...
Long-Term Obligations	175.3	...	...	509.2	124.1	...
Net Stockholders' Equity	141.6	126.3	207.1	d229.9	232.6	...
Net Working Capital	72.3	d13.1	62.7	d25.8	47.5	...
Year-end Shs. Outstg. (000)	83,411	86,450	94,228	63,450	63,450	...
STATISTICAL RECORD:						
Operating Profit Margin %	43.8	37.0	49.5	47.6	47.7	46.2
Net Profit Margin %	26.7	22.9	29.1	29.1	30.2	29.2
Return on Equity %	98.2	64.7	40.4	...	28.7	...
Return on Assets %	32.9	24.4	25.6	15.7	15.5	...
Debt/Total Assets %	41.5	...	...	113.9	28.9	...
Price Range	40.50-16.54	18.67-12.38	18.67-10.96	...	...	...
P/E Ratio	25.3-10.3	20.9-13.9	22.0-12.9	...	...	...
Average Yield %	1.2	2.3	1.8	...	...	...

Statistics are as originally reported. Adj. for 3-for-2 stk. split, 4/00. [1] Incl. loss on sale of real estate of $4.6 mill. & write-off of deferred acq. costs of $19.0 mill.

OFFICERS:
K. A. Tucker, Chmn., C.E.O.
H. J. Herrmann, Pres.
J. E. Sundeen Jr., Sr. V.P., C.F.O., Treas.
D. C. Schulte, V.P., Sec., Gen. Couns.

INVESTOR CONTACT: D. Tyler Towery, (913) 236-1880

PRINCIPAL OFFICE: 6300 Lamar Avenue, Overland Park, KS 66202

TELEPHONE NUMBER: (913) 236-2000
FAX: (913) 236-2017
WEB: www.waddell.com

NO. OF EMPLOYEES: 1,341

SHAREHOLDERS: 3,908 (class A com.); 4,117 (class B com.)

ANNUAL MEETING: In April

INCORPORATED: DE, Dec., 1981

INSTITUTIONAL HOLDINGS:
No. of Institutions: 189
Shares Held: 39,337,845
% Held: 49.4

INDUSTRY: Security brokers and dealers (SIC: 6211)

TRANSFER AGENT(S): First Chicago, EquiServe Division, Jersey City, NJ

NYSE SYMBOL WMT
Rec. Pr. 51.75 (5/31/01)

WAL-MART STORES, INC.

YIELD 0.5%
P/E RATIO 36.4

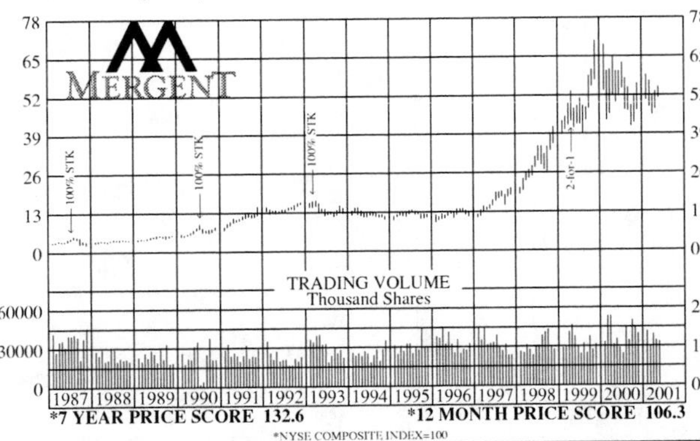

*7 YEAR PRICE SCORE 132.6 *12 MONTH PRICE SCORE 106.3

*NYSE COMPOSITE INDEX=100

INTERIM EARNINGS (Per Share):

Qtr.	Apr.	July	Oct.	Jan.
1997-98	0.15	0.18	0.18	0.29
1998-99	0.19	0.23	0.23	0.35
1999-00	0.25	0.28	0.29	0.43
2000-01	0.30	0.36	0.31	0.45

INTERIM DIVIDENDS (Per Share):

Amt.	Decl.	Ex.	Rec.	Pay.
0.06Q	8/10/00	9/13/00	9/15/00	10/10/00
0.06Q	11/16/00	12/20/00	12/22/00	1/08/01
0.07Q	3/09/01	3/21/01	3/23/01	4/09/01
0.07Q	5/31/01	6/20/01	6/22/01	7/09/01

Indicated div.: $0.28 (Div. Reinv. Plan)

CAPITALIZATION (1/31/01):

	($000)	(%)
Long-Term Debt	12,501,000	26.0
Capital Lease Obligations	3,154,000	6.6
Minority Interest	1,140,000	2.4
Common & Surplus	31,343,000	65.1
Total	48,138,000	100.0

RECENT DEVELOPMENTS: For the year ended 1/31/01, net income was $6.30 billion, up 12.9% versus earnings of $5.58 billion, before an accounting charge, the previous year. Net sales advanced 15.9% to $191.33 billion from $165.01 billion the year before. Net sales in the Wal-Mart Stores segment, including Supercenters, climbed 12.1% to $121.89 billion, while net sales in the Sam's Club segment grew 8.1% to $26.80 billion. International segment net sales jumped 41.2% to $32.10 billion, while McLane's net sales leapt 20.3% to $10.54 billion.

PROSPECTS: The Company anticipates earnings will grow by a single-digit percentage in the first half of 2001, increasing to a double-digit percentage during the second half of the year. In 2001, WMT's domestic store-expansion plans include the opening of about 40 new discount department stores, 170 to 180 new Supercenters, 40 to 50 Sam's Club locations, and 15 to 20 Neighborhood Markets. Also, WMT plans to open between 100 and 110 units in existing international markets in 2001, and may enter Japan as early as 2002.

BUSINESS

WAL-MART STORES, INC. operates 1,724 discount department stores, 910 Supercenters, 475 Sam's Clubs and 19 Neighborhood Markets in the United States. WMT also operates 501 Wal-Mart stores in Mexico, 241 in the United Kingdom, 174 in Canada, 95 in Germany, 20 in Brazil, 16 in Puerto Rico, 11 in Argentina, and six in Korea. WMT also operates eleven stores in China under joint venture agreements. WMT stores offer one-stop shopping by providing a wide assortment of merchandise to satisfy most of the clothing, home, recreational and convenience needs of the family. Supercenters combine food, general merchandise, and services including pharmacy, dry cleaning, portrait studios, photo finishing, hair salons, and optical shops. WMT also operates McLane and Western, a specialty distribution subsidiary, serving over 35,000 convenience stores, mass merchandisers and quick-service restaurants.

ANNUAL FINANCIAL DATA

	1/31/01	1/31/00	1/31/99	1/31/98	1/31/97	1/31/96	1/31/95
Earnings Per Share	**1.40**	**[1] 1.25**	**0.99**	**0.78**	**0.67**	**0.60**	**0.59**
Cash Flow Per Share	**2.04**	**1.78**	**1.41**	**1.14**	**0.99**	**0.88**	**0.82**
Tang. Book Val. Per Share	**4.99**	**3.69**	**4.18**	**4.13**	**3.75**	**3.22**	**2.77**
Dividends Per Share	**0.23**	**0.189**	**0.15**	**0.128**	**0.104**	**0.096**	**0.08**
Dividend Payout %	**16.4**	**15.1**	**15.2**	**16.4**	**15.5**	**16.0**	**13.6**
INCOME STATEMENT (IN MILLIONS):							
Total Revenues	193,295.0	166,809.0	139,208.0	119,299.0	106,146.0	94,749.0	83,412.0
Costs & Expenses	178,937.0	154,329.0	129,216.0	111,162.0	98,988.0	88,211.0	77,374.0
Depreciation & Amort.	2,868.0	2,375.0	1,872.0	1,634.0	1,463.0	1,304.0	1,070.0
Operating Income	11,490.0	10,105.0	8,120.0	6,503.0	5,695.0	5,234.0	4,968.0
Net Interest Inc./(Exp.)	d1,374.0	d1,022.0	d797.0	d784.0	d845.0	d888.0	d706.0
Income Before Income Taxes	10,116.0	9,083.0	7,323.0	5,719.0	4,850.0	4,346.0	4,262.0
Income Taxes	3,692.0	3,338.0	2,740.0	2,115.0	1,794.0	1,606.0	1,581.0
Equity Earnings/Minority Int.	d129.0	d170.0	d153.0	d78.0	...	...	...
Net Income	6,295.0	[1] 5,575.0	4,430.0	3,526.0	3,056.0	2,740.0	2,681.0
Cash Flow	9,163.0	7,950.0	6,302.0	5,160.0	4,519.0	4,044.0	3,751.0
Average Shs. Outstg. (000)	4,484,000	4,474,000	4,485,000	4,533,000	4,592,000	4,598,000	4,582,000
BALANCE SHEET (IN MILLIONS):							
Cash & Cash Equivalents	2,054.0	1,856.0	1,879.0	1,447.0	883.0	83.0	45.0
Total Current Assets	26,555.0	24,356.0	21,132.0	19,352.0	17,993.0	17,331.0	15,338.0
Net Property	40,934.0	35,969.0	25,973.0	23,606.0	20,324.0	18,894.0	15,874.0
Total Assets	78,130.0	70,349.0	49,996.0	45,384.0	39,604.0	37,541.0	32,819.0
Total Current Liabilities	28,949.0	25,803.0	16,762.0	14,460.0	10,957.0	11,454.0	9,973.0
Long-Term Obligations	15,655.0	16,674.0	9,607.0	9,674.0	10,016.0	10,600.0	9,709.0
Net Stockholders' Equity	31,343.0	25,834.0	21,112.0	18,503.0	17,143.0	14,756.0	12,726.0
Net Working Capital	d2,394.0	d1,447.0	4,370.0	4,892.0	7,036.0	5,877.0	5,365.0
Year-end Shs. Outstg. (000)	4,470,000	4,457,000	4,448,000	4,482,000	4,570,000	4,586,000	4,594,000
STATISTICAL RECORD:							
Operating Profit Margin %	5.9	6.1	5.8	5.5	5.4	5.5	6.0
Net Profit Margin %	3.3	3.3	3.2	3.0	2.9	2.9	3.2
Return on Equity %	20.1	21.6	21.0	19.1	17.8	18.6	21.1
Return on Assets %	8.1	7.9	8.9	7.8	7.7	7.3	8.2
Debt/Total Assets %	20.0	23.7	19.2	21.3	25.3	28.2	29.6
Price Range	69.00-41.44	70.25-38.69	41.38-18.78	20.97-11.00	14.13-9.55	13.81-10.25	14.63-10.50
P/E Ratio	49.3-29.6	56.2-30.9	41.8-19.0	26.9-14.1	21.2-14.4	23.2-17.2	25.0-17.9
Average Yield %	0.4	0.3	0.5	0.8	0.9	0.8	0.6

Statistics are as originally reported. Adj. for 100% stk. div., 4/99. [1] Bef. $198.0 mil ($0.04/sh) acctg. chg.

OFFICERS:
S. R. Walton, Chmn.
H. L. Scott, Jr., Pres., C.E.O.
T. M. Schoewe, Exec. V.P., C.F.O.

PRINCIPAL OFFICE: 702 Southwest 8th Street, Bentonville, AR 72716-8611

TELEPHONE NUMBER: (501) 273-4000
FAX: (501) 273-1986
WEB: www.wal-mart.com

NO. OF EMPLOYEES: 1,244,000 (avg.)

SHAREHOLDERS: 362,000

ANNUAL MEETING: In June

INCORPORATED: DE, Oct., 1969

INSTITUTIONAL HOLDINGS:
No. of Institutions: 997
Shares Held: 1,584,363,577
% Held: 35.4

INDUSTRY: Variety stores (SIC: 5331)

TRANSFER AGENT(S): EquiServe First Chicago Trust Co., Jersey City, NJ

NYSE SYMBOL WAG
Rec. Pr. 40.19 (5/31/01)

WALGREEN CO.

YIELD 0.3%
P/E RATIO 47.8

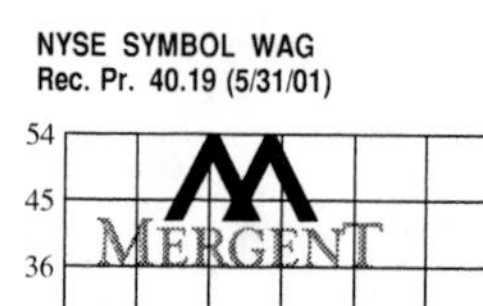

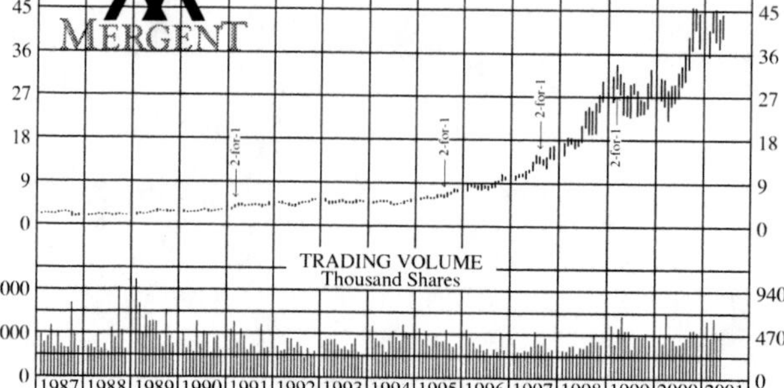

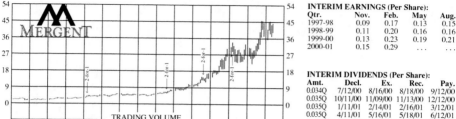

*7 YEAR PRICE SCORE 152.8 *12 MONTH PRICE SCORE 113.9

*NYSE COMPOSITE INDEX=100

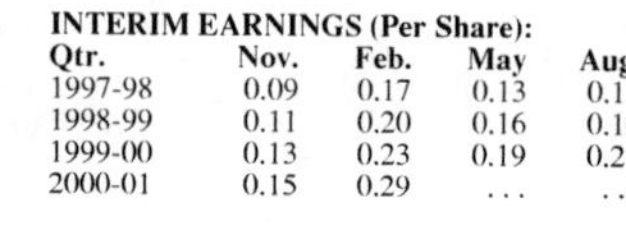

INTERIM EARNINGS (Per Share):

Qtr.	Nov.	Feb.	May	Aug.
1997-98	0.09	0.17	0.13	0.15
1998-99	0.11	0.20	0.16	0.16
1999-00	0.13	0.23	0.19	0.21
2000-01	0.15	0.29	...	...

INTERIM DIVIDENDS (Per Share):

Amt.	Decl.	Ex.	Rec.	Pay.
0.034Q	7/12/00	8/16/00	8/18/00	9/12/00
0.035Q	10/11/00	11/09/00	11/13/00	12/12/00
0.035Q	1/11/01	2/14/01	2/16/01	3/12/01
0.035Q	4/11/01	5/16/01	5/18/01	6/12/01

Indicated div.: $0.14 (Div. Reinv. Plan)

CAPITALIZATION (8/31/00):

	($000)	(%)
Deferred Income Tax	101,600	2.3
Common & Surplus	4,234,000	97.7
Total	4,335,600	100.0

RECENT DEVELOPMENTS: For the quarter ended 2/28/01, net earnings advanced 24.3% to $296.9 million from $238.9 million the previous year. Results in the recent period included a $22.1 million pre-tax gain from a partial payment of the Company's share of the brand name prescription drug antitrust litigation settlement. Net sales climbed 14.6% to $6.43 billion from $5.61 billion the year before. Comparable-store sales increased 8.7% year over year.

PROSPECTS: The Company anticipates spending $1.40 billion for capital expenditures during fiscal 2001, including the opening of 500 new stores and for technology improvements and distribution expansion. Two new distribution centers are currently under construction in West Palm Beach, Florida and in the Dallas, Texas metropolitan area. Another center is planned in northern Ohio and several existing centers are expected to be expanded.

BUSINESS

WALGREEN COMPANY operated 3,343 drugstores located in 43 states and Puerto Rico as of 2/28/01. The drugstores sell prescription and nonprescription drugs in addition to other products including general merchandise, cosmetics, toiletries, household items, food and beverages. Customer prescription purchases can be made at the drugstores as well as through the mail, telephone and the Internet. The Company's retail drugstore operations are supported by nine distribution centers and a mail service facility located in Beaverton, Oregon. Prescription drugs comprised 55% of fiscal 2000 total sales; general merchandise, 26%; nonprescription drugs, 11%; and cosmetics and toiletries, 8%.

ANNUAL FINANCIAL DATA

	8/31/00	8/31/99	8/31/98	8/31/97	8/31/96	8/31/95	8/31/94
Earnings Per Share	**2 0.76**	**0.62**	**1 0.54**	**0.44**	**0.38**	**0.33**	**0.29**
Cash Flow Per Share	**0.99**	**0.82**	**0.72**	**0.60**	**0.52**	**0.46**	**0.40**
Tang. Book Val. Per Share	**4.19**	**3.47**	**2.86**	**2.40**	**2.08**	**1.82**	**1.60**
Dividends Per Share	**0.14**	**0.131**	**0.126**	**0.12**	**0.11**	**0.10**	**0.09**
Dividend Payout %	**17.9**	**21.1**	**23.3**	**27.6**	**30.0**	**31.0**	**30.9**
INCOME STATEMENT (IN MILLIONS):							
Total Revenues	21,206.9	17,838.8	15,307.0	13,363.0	11,778.4	10,395.1	9,235.0
Costs & Expenses	19,752.7	16,613.3	14,283.0	12,491.0	11,027.0	9,743.5	8,661.2
Depreciation & Amort.	230.1	210.1	189.0	164.0	147.3	131.5	118.1
Operating Income	1,224.1	1,015.4	835.0	708.0	604.1	520.0	455.6
Net Interest Inc./(Exp.)	5.7	11.9	5.0	4.0	2.9	3.7	2.8
Income Before Income Taxes	1,263.3	1,027.3	877.0	712.0	606.9	523.7	458.4
Income Taxes	486.4	403.2	340.0	276.0	235.2	203.0	176.5
Net Income	2 776.9	624.1	1 537.0	436.0	371.7	320.8	281.9
Cash Flow	1,007.0	834.2	726.0	600.0	519.1	452.3	400.0
Average Shs. Outstg. (000)	1,019,889	1,014,282	1,005,692	996,670	993,744	990,108	989,168
BALANCE SHEET (IN MILLIONS):							
Cash & Cash Equivalents	12.8	141.8	144.0	73.0	8.8	22.2	108.4
Total Current Assets	3,550.1	3,221.7	2,623.0	2,326.0	2,019.0	1,812.9	1,672.8
Net Property	3,428.2	2,593.9	2,144.0	1,754.0	1,448.4	1,249.0	1,085.5
Total Assets	7,103.7	5,906.7	4,902.0	4,207.0	3,633.6	3,252.6	2,908.7
Total Current Liabilities	2,303.7	1,923.8	1,580.0	1,439.0	1,182.0	1,077.8	1,050.7
Long-Term Obligations	...	...	...	...	10.1	10.3	...
Net Stockholders' Equity	4,234.0	3,484.3	2,849.0	2,373.0	2,043.1	1,792.6	1,573.6
Net Working Capital	1,246.4	1,297.9	1,043.0	887.0	837.1	735.2	622.1
Year-end Shs. Outstg. (000)	1,010,819	1,004,022	996,488	987,580	984,564	984,564	984,568
STATISTICAL RECORD:							
Operating Profit Margin %	5.8	5.7	5.5	5.3	5.1	5.0	4.9
Net Profit Margin %	3.7	3.5	3.5	3.3	3.2	3.1	3.1
Return on Equity %	18.3	17.9	18.8	18.4	18.2	17.9	17.9
Return on Assets %	10.9	10.6	11.0	10.4	10.2	9.9	9.7
Debt/Total Assets %	...	...	...	...	0.3	0.3	...
Price Range	45.75-22.06	33.94-22.69	30.22-14.78	16.81-9.63	10.91-7.28	7.84-5.41	5.67-4.22
P/E Ratio	60.2-29.0	54.7-36.6	56.5-27.6	38.2-21.9	29.1-19.4	24.1-16.6	19.9-14.8
Average Yield %	0.4	0.5	0.6	0.9	1.2	1.5	1.8

Statistics are as originally reported. Adj. for 2-for-1 stk. split, 2/99, 8/97, & 7/95. 1 Bef. $26.4 mil ($0.03/sh) chg. for acctg. adj. & incl. $23.0 mil ($0.03/sh) after-tax gain. 2 Incl. $33.5 mil ($0.02/sh) pre-tax gain from partial payment of a prescription-drug antitrust settlement.

OFFICERS:
L. D. Jorndt, Chmn., C.E.O.
D. W. Bernauer, Pres., C.O.O.
R. L. Polark, Sr. V.P., C.F.O.
M. A. Wagner, Treas.

INVESTOR CONTACT: John M. Palizza, Asst. Treas., (847) 940-2935

PRINCIPAL OFFICE: 200 Wilmot Rd., Deerfield, IL 60015

TELEPHONE NUMBER: (847) 940-2500
FAX: (847) 914-2654
WEB: www.walgreens.com

NO. OF EMPLOYEES: 74,000 full-time (approx.); 42,000 part-time (approx.)

SHAREHOLDERS: 88,526

ANNUAL MEETING: In Jan.

INCORPORATED: IL, Feb., 1909

INSTITUTIONAL HOLDINGS:
No. of Institutions: 668
Shares Held: 585,457,726
% Held: 57.5

INDUSTRY: Drug stores and proprietary stores (SIC: 5912)

TRANSFER AGENT(S): Computershare Investor Services, Chicago, IL

NYSE SYMBOL WCS
Rec. Pr. 17.14 (5/31/01)

WALLACE COMPUTER SERVICES, INC.

YIELD 3.9%
P/E RATIO 25.6

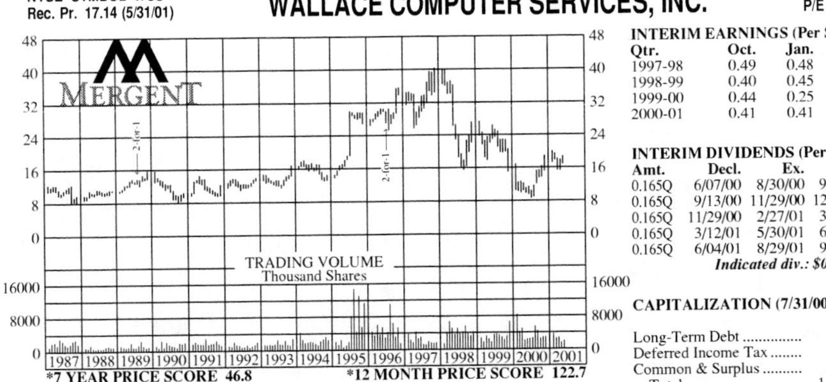

***7 YEAR PRICE SCORE 46.8** ***12 MONTH PRICE SCORE 122.7**

*NYSE COMPOSITE INDEX=100

INTERIM EARNINGS (Per Share):

Qtr.	Oct.	Jan.	Apr.	July
1997-98	0.49	0.48	0.41	0.33
1998-99	0.40	0.45	0.49	0.46
1999-00	0.44	0.25	d0.41	0.26
2000-01	0.41	0.41	...	...

INTERIM DIVIDENDS (Per Share):

Amt.	Decl.	Ex.	Rec.	Pay.
0.165Q	6/07/00	8/30/00	9/01/00	9/20/00
0.165Q	9/13/00	11/29/00	12/01/00	12/20/00
0.165Q	11/29/00	2/27/01	3/01/01	3/20/01
0.165Q	3/12/01	5/30/01	6/01/01	6/20/01
0.165Q	6/04/01	8/29/01	9/03/01	9/20/01

Indicated div.: $0.66

CAPITALIZATION (7/31/00):

	($000)	(%)
Long-Term Debt	389,413	38.6
Deferred Income Tax	69,912	6.9
Common & Surplus	549,537	54.5
Total	1,008,862	100.0

RECENT DEVELOPMENTS: For the quarter ended 1/31/01, net income advanced 64.8% to $16.9 million from $10.3 million a year earlier. Results in the recent period included a pre-tax restructuring charge of $302,000. Net sales grew 9.4% to $420.5 million from $384.2 million the year before. Integrated Graphics segment sales climbed 14.4% to $217.9 million, while sales for the Forms and Labels segment rose 4.6% to $202.6 million.

PROSPECTS: Increased pricing pressures are hurting profitability in the Company's Integrated Graphics segment. Going forward, WCS will focus on implementing initiatives to help boost operating profitability in this segment. Meanwhile, the Company's restructuring and cost-control initiatives are positively affecting operating results in the Forms & Labels segment despite slightly lower sales primarily related to increased competition.

BUSINESS

WALLACE COMPUTER SERVICES, INC. is engaged primarily in the computer services and supply industry. The Company operates in two business segments, Forms and Labels, and Integrated Graphics. The principal products and services supplied by the Forms and Labels segment include the design, manufacture and sales of both paper based and electronic business forms, the manufacture of both electronic data processing labels and prime labels, and the manufacture and distribution of a standard line of office products. The Integrated Graphics segment includes the design and manufacture of high-color, high quality marketing and promotional materials, and the manufacture of direct response printing materials.

ANNUAL FINANCIAL DATA

	7/31/00	7/31/99	7/31/98	7/31/97	7/31/96	7/31/95	7/31/94
Earnings Per Share	**3 0.55**	**2 1.80**	**1.71**	**1.88**	**2 1.60**	**1.23**	**1 1.07**
Cash Flow Per Share	**2.42**	**3.58**	**3.26**	**3.01**	**2.59**	**2.06**	**1.81**
Tang. Book Val. Per Share	**6.26**	**6.56**	**5.94**	**10.06**	**10.25**	**9.47**	**8.81**
Dividends Per Share	**0.66**	**0.65**	**0.63**	**0.57**	**0.46**	**0.39**	**0.33**
Dividend Payout %	**120.0**	**35.8**	**36.5**	**30.6**	**28.9**	**31.3**	**31.2**
INCOME STATEMENT (IN MILLIONS):							
Total Revenues	1,565.2	1,530.5	1,356.1	906.3	862.3	712.8	588.2
Costs & Expenses	1,410.0	1,299.1	1,143.8	722.0	700.3	590.5	483.5
Depreciation & Amort.	77.6	75.4	67.5	49.2	45.0	37.3	33.0
Operating Income	77.7	155.9	144.7	135.1	116.9	85.0	71.6
Net Interest Inc./(Exp.)	d31.2	d29.2	d21.4	d0.7	1.6	2.4	2.2
Income Before Income Taxes	49.7	126.8	123.4	134.4	118.5	87.5	73.9
Income Taxes	27.1	50.7	49.2	53.1	45.5	32.2	26.6
Net Income	3 22.6	2 76.1	74.2	81.3	2 73.0	55.3	1 47.3
Cash Flow	100.2	151.5	141.7	130.5	118.0	92.6	80.3
Average Shs. Outstg. (000)	41,338	42,375	43,397	43,322	45,582	44,980	44,386
BALANCE SHEET (IN MILLIONS):							
Cash & Cash Equivalents	4.5	8.0	3.5	15.9	62.6	41.1	77.0
Total Current Assets	442.8	448.4	426.8	290.5	304.1	258.9	248.2
Net Property	412.8	437.0	454.4	301.5	288.9	256.5	232.9
Total Assets	1,249.3	1,297.7	1,257.5	720.4	695.9	592.7	538.6
Total Current Liabilities	196.1	191.9	189.9	141.3	97.9	65.7	64.8
Long-Term Obligations	389.4	416.7	428.2	24.5	30.6	25.6	23.5
Net Stockholders' Equity	549.5	583.6	547.5	493.2	510.4	456.1	410.1
Net Working Capital	246.7	256.5	236.9	149.2	206.2	193.2	183.4
Year-end Shs. Outstg. (000)	40,404	42,307	43,268	43,070	45,587	45,378	44,786
STATISTICAL RECORD:							
Operating Profit Margin %	5.0	10.2	10.7	14.9	13.6	11.9	12.2
Net Profit Margin %	1.4	5.0	5.5	9.0	8.5	7.8	8.0
Return on Equity %	4.1	13.0	13.6	16.5	14.3	12.1	11.5
Return on Assets %	1.8	5.9	5.9	11.3	10.5	9.3	8.8
Debt/Total Assets %	31.2	32.1	34.1	3.4	4.4	4.3	4.4
Price Range	18.94-8.56	27.25-14.94	40.00-15.44	40.38-25.63	35.63-25.25	30.00-13.75	18.13-12.94
P/E Ratio	34.4-15.6	15.1-8.3	23.4-9.0	21.5-13.6	22.3-15.8	24.4-11.2	17.0-12.1
Average Yield %	4.8	3.1	2.3	1.7	1.5	1.8	2.1

Statistics are as originally reported. Adj. for 2-for-1 stk. split, 7/96. 1 Bef. $663,000 ($0.03/sh) gain from acctg. adj. 2 Incl. $1.6 mil ($0.02/sh) non-recur. chg. rel to inv. adj., 1999; & $6.2 mil ($0.14/sh) non-recur. chg. rel. to takeover exp., 1996. 3 Incl. $41.6 mil pre-tax restr. chg.

OFFICERS:
M. D. Jones, Chmn., C.E.O.
M. O. Duffield, Pres., C.O.O.
V. L. Avril, Sr. V.P., C.F.O.
R. J. Kelderhouse, V.P., Treas.

INVESTOR CONTACT: Tamaryn Wiggins, Dir., Investor Relations, (630) 588-5397

PRINCIPAL OFFICE: 2275 Cabot Drive, Lisle, IL 60532

TELEPHONE NUMBER: (630) 588-5000
FAX: (630) 449-1161
WEB: www.wallace.com

NO. OF EMPLOYEES: 8,167 (avg.)

SHAREHOLDERS: 2,892

ANNUAL MEETING: In Nov.

INCORPORATED: DE, June, 1963

INSTITUTIONAL HOLDINGS:
No. of Institutions: 150
Shares Held: 32,141,937
% Held: 78.5

INDUSTRY: Manifold business forms (SIC: 2761)

TRANSFER AGENT(S): Boston EquiServe, L.P., Boston, MA

NYSE SYMBOL WAC
Rec. Pr. 0.69 (4/30/01)

WARNACO GROUP, INC. (THE)

YIELD ...
P/E RATIO ...

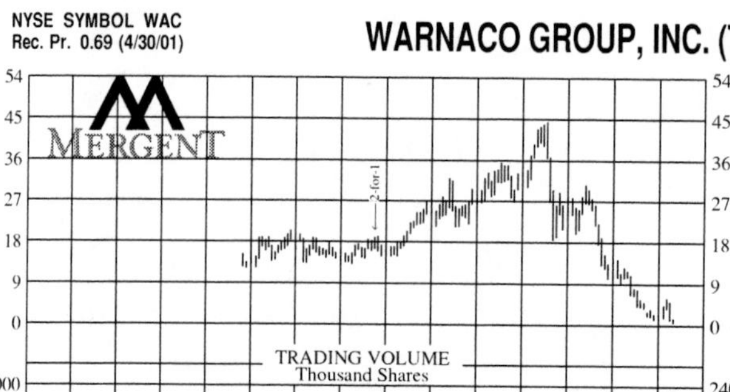

1987 1988 1989 1990 1991 1992 1993 1994 1995 1996 1997 1998 1999 2000 2001

*7 YEAR PRICE SCORE 14.1 *12 MONTH PRICE SCORE 53.0

*NYSE COMPOSITE INDEX=100

INTERIM EARNINGS (Per Share):

Qtr.	Mar.	June	Sept.	Dec.
1997-98	0.34	0.32	0.60	d0.77
1998-99	0.10	0.20	0.43	d0.54
1999-00	0.39	0.49	0.80	0.05
2000-01	0.51	d1.20	d1.77	d3.79

INTERIM DIVIDENDS (Per Share):

Amt.	Decl.	Ex.	Rec.	Pay.
0.09Q	8/19/99	8/31/99	9/02/99	10/07/99
0.09Q	11/23/99	12/03/99	12/07/99	1/06/00
0.09Q	2/20/00	3/07/00	3/09/00	4/04/00
0.09Q	5/11/00	6/13/00	6/15/00	7/06/00
0.09Q	8/20/00	9/01/00	9/06/00	10/05/00

Dividend suspended.

CAPITALIZATION (12/30/00):

	($000)	(%)
Redeemable Pfd. Stock	103,387	57.3
Common & Surplus	77,104	42.7
Total	180,491	100.0

RECENT DEVELOPMENTS: For the year ended 12/30/00, the Company reported loss of $331.1 million, before an accounting change charge of $13.1 million versus net income of $97.8 million in 1999. Net revenues improved 6.4% to $2.25 billion versus $2.11 billion in the prior year. Operating loss totaled $174.5 million versus operating income of $212.2 million in 1999. Results included the operations of Authentic Fitness and A.B.S., acquired in December 1999 and September 1999, respectively.

PROSPECTS: On 6/11/01, WAC filed for Chapter 11 bankruptcy protection primarily due to its high debt level and a softening retail environment. Under the protection of Chapter 11, the Company will seek to increase operating liquidity and continue the operational and financial restructuring it began in 2000. Going forward, the Company expects revenue growth to continue to be dampened by the retail slowdown and inventory reductions among the Company's largest customers.

BUSINESS

WARNACO GROUP, INC. (THE) and its subsidiaries design, manufacture and market a broad line of women's intimate apparel, such as bras, panties, sleepwear, shapewear and daywear; men's apparel, such as sportswear, jeanswear, khakis, underwear and accessories; women's and junior's apparel, such as sportswear and jeanswear; and active apparel, such as swimwear, swim accessories and fitness apparel, all of which are sold under a variety of internationally owned and licensed brand names. The Company operates in three business segments: Intimate Apparel, Sportswear and Accessories and Retail Stores.

BUSINESS LINE ANALYSIS

(12/30/2000)	REV (%)	INC (%)
Intimate Apparel	35.9	23.8
Sportsware & Accessories	54.5	77.7
Retail Stores	9.6	(1.5)
Total	100.0	100.0

ANNUAL FINANCIAL DATA

	12/30/00	1/1/00	1/2/99	1/3/98	1/4/97	1/6/96	1/7/95
Earnings Per Share	**[1] d6.27**	**1.72**	**[1] 0.22**	**0.42**	**d0.16**	**[2] 1.10**	**[3] 1.53**
Cash Flow Per Share	**d4.09**	**2.90**	**1.04**	**1.35**	**0.42**	**1.60**	**1.99**
Tang. Book Val. Per Share	...	...	...	**1.46**	**2.45**	**5.43**	...
Dividends Per Share	**0.36**	**0.36**	**0.36**	**0.31**	**0.28**	**0.14**	...
Dividend Payout %	...	**20.9**	**163.6**	**73.8**	...	**12.7**	...
INCOME STATEMENT (IN MILLIONS):							
Total Revenues	2,249.9	2,114.2	1,950.3	1,435.7	1,063.8	916.2	788.8
Costs & Expenses	2,309.5	1,817.1	1,813.2	1,302.2	1,007.8	779.7	670.8
Depreciation & Amort.	115.0	67.2	51.5	50.7	30.1	22.6	18.8
Operating Income	d174.5	229.9	85.6	82.8	26.0	113.9	99.2
Net Interest Inc./(Exp.)	d172.2	d81.0	d63.8	d45.9	d32.4	d33.9	d32.5
Income Before Income Taxes	d309.9	148.9	21.8	36.9	d6.5	80.0	63.7
Income Taxes	21.2	51.1	7.7	13.9	1.8	30.4	0.4
Net Income	[1] d331.1	97.8	[1] 14.1	23.0	d8.2	[2] 49.6	[3] 63.3
Cash Flow	d216.1	165.0	65.6	73.7	21.8	72.3	82.1
Average Shs. Outstg. (000)	52,783	56,796	63,005	54,821	51,707	45,278	41,285
BALANCE SHEET (IN MILLIONS):							
Cash & Cash Equivalents	11.3	82.2	9.5	12.0	11.8	6.2	3.8
Total Current Assets	662.9	1,197.7	707.5	879.8	650.5	542.4	420.5
Net Property	329.2	326.4	224.3	130.4	121.5	106.3	80.9
Total Assets	2,343.1	2,763.0	1,783.1	1,727.6	1,142.9	941.1	780.6
Total Current Liabilities	2,096.6	879.5	679.1	450.5	439.9	234.9	316.1
Long-Term Obligations	...	1,188.0	411.9	354.3	215.8	194.3	206.8
Net Stockholders' Equity	77.1	563.3	578.1	808.1	475.7	500.3	240.5
Net Working Capital	d1,433.7	318.1	28.4	429.3	210.6	307.5	104.5
Year-end Shs. Outstg. (000)	53,169	53,229	57,207	61,919	51,862	41,734	41,734
STATISTICAL RECORD:							
Operating Profit Margin %	...	10.9	4.4	5.8	2.4	12.4	12.6
Net Profit Margin %	...	4.6	0.7	1.6	...	5.4	8.0
Return on Equity %	...	17.4	2.4	2.9	...	9.9	26.3
Return on Assets %	...	3.5	0.8	1.3	...	5.3	8.1
Debt/Total Assets %	...	43.0	23.1	20.5	18.9	20.6	26.5
Price Range	14.44-1.25	30.63-10.13	44.44-18.50	35.56-26.63	32.00-21.25	26.88-14.88	19.25-13.13
P/E Ratio	...	17.8-5.9	201.9-84.1	84.7-63.4	...	24.4-13.5	12.6-8.6
Average Yield %	4.6	1.8	1.1	1.0	1.1	0.7	...

Statistics are as originally reported. [1] Bef. acctg. change charge, 2000, $13.1 mill.; 1999, $46.3 mill. [2] Bef. extraord. chrg., 1996, $3.1 mill. [3] Incl. non-recurr. exp., 1995, $3.0 mill.

OFFICERS:
L. J. Wachner, Chmn., Pres., C.E.O.
P. Terenzio, Sr. V.P., C.F.O.
C. J. Deddens, V.P., Treas.

PRINCIPAL OFFICE: 90 Park Avenue, New York, NY 10016

TELEPHONE NUMBER: (212) 661-1300
FAX: (212) 687-6771

NO. OF EMPLOYEES: 21,440 (avg.)

SHAREHOLDERS: 266

ANNUAL MEETING: In May

INCORPORATED: DE, Mar., 1986

INSTITUTIONAL HOLDINGS:
No. of Institutions: 57
Shares Held: 15,151,721
% Held: 28.7

INDUSTRY: Bras, girdles, and allied garments (SIC: 2342)

TRANSFER AGENT(S): The Bank of New York, New York, NY

NYSE SYMBOL WM
Rec. Pr. 35.62 (5/31/01)

WASHINGTON MUTUAL, INC.

YIELD	2.5%
P/E RATIO	15.0

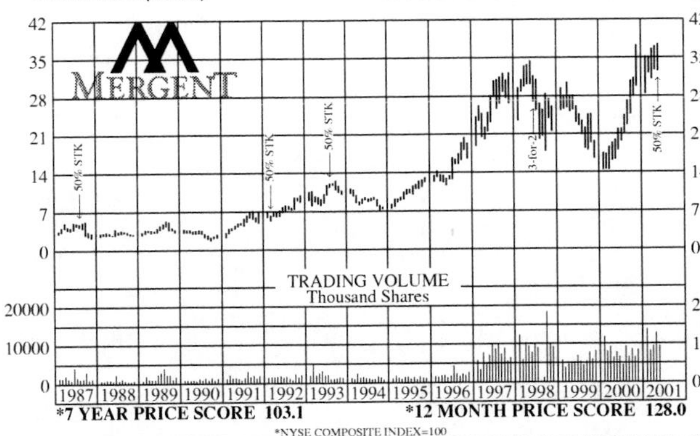

***7 YEAR PRICE SCORE 103.1** ***12 MONTH PRICE SCORE 128.0**

*NYSE COMPOSITE INDEX=100

INTERIM EARNINGS (Per Share):

Qtr.	Mar.	June	Sept.	Dec.
1997	0.41	0.43	d0.24	0.43
1998	0.45	0.47	0.49	0.19
1999	0.51	0.52	0.56	0.53
2000	0.56	0.61	0.57	0.63

INTERIM DIVIDENDS (Per Share):

Amt.	Decl.	Ex.	Rec.	Pay.
0.29Q	7/19/00	7/27/00	7/31/00	8/15/00
0.30Q	10/18/00	10/27/00	10/31/00	11/15/00
0.31Q	1/16/01	1/29/01	1/31/01	2/15/01
50% STK	4/17/01	5/16/01	4/30/01	5/15/01
0.22Q	4/17/01	4/26/01	4/30/01	5/15/01

Indicated div.: $0.88 (Div. Reinv. Plan)

CAPITALIZATION (12/31/00):

	($000)	(%)
Total Deposits	79,574,000	50.5
Long-Term Debt	67,785,000	43.0
Common & Surplus	10,166,000	6.5
Total	157,525,000	100.0

RECENT DEVELOPMENTS: For the year ended 12/31/00, net income increased 4.5% to $1.90 billion from $1.82 billion in the prior year. Earnings for 2000 and 1999 included a pre-tax gain of $261.6 million and $109.4 million, respectively, from the sale of loans. Results for 1999 also included a transaction-related expense of $95.7 million. Net interest income decreased 3.1% to $4.31 billion from $4.45 billion a year earlier.

PROSPECTS: On 4/2/01, WM announced an agreement to acquire Fleet Mortgage Corporation for about $660.0 million. This transaction, along with its acquisitions of Bank United Corporation and the mortgage operations of The PNC Financial Services Group, Inc. in February 2001, will increase WM's residential mortgage servicing portfolio to $451.50 billion. As a result, WM will be the nation's second largest mortgage servicing business.

BUSINESS

WASHINGTON MUTUAL, INC. is a holding company for both banking and nonbanking subsidiaries. WM's primary banking subsidiaries are Washington Mutual Bank, FA (formerly Washington Mutual Savings Bank), Washington Mutual Bank and Washington Mutual Bank fsb. These organizations provide consumer banking, full-service securities brokerage, mutual fund management, and travel and insurance underwriting services. As of 12/31/00, WM and its subsidiaries had assets of $194.72 billion and operated more than 2,000 offices nationwide. On 7/1/97, WM acquired Great Western Financial Corp. On 10/1/98, WM acquired H.F. Ahmanson & Co. In February 2001, WM acquired the residential mortgage banking business of PNC Financial Services Group and Bank United Corp.

LOAN DISTRIBUTION

(12/31/2000)	($000)	(%)
Single-Family		
Residential (SFR)	83,113,000	67.6
SFR Construction	1,431,000	1.2
Second Mtge	10,478,000	8.5
Special Mtge Fin	7,254,000	5.9
Commercial Business	2,274,000	1.8
Commercial Real		
Estate	18,480,000	15.0
Total	123,030,000	100.0

ANNUAL FINANCIAL DATA

	12/31/00	12/31/99	[7] 12/31/98	[6] 12/31/97	12/31/96	12/31/95	12/31/94
Earnings Per Share	[5] 2.36	[4] 2.11	[3] 1.71	[2] 0.83	[1] 0.38	1.10	1.13
Tang. Book Val. Per Share	9.96	8.41	8.85	7.97	7.98	8.84	7.99
Dividends Per Share	0.76	0.65	0.55	0.47	0.40	0.34	0.31
Dividend Payout %	32.2	31.0	32.0	57.0	105.8	31.2	27.6
INCOME STATEMENT (IN MILLIONS):							
Total Interest Income	13,783.0	12,062.2	11,221.5	6,811.0	3,149.2	2,916.1	1,207.8
Total Interest Expense	9,472.0	7,610.4	6,929.7	4,154.5	1,958.2	1,923.4	636.6
Net Interest Income	4,311.0	4,451.8	4,291.7	2,656.5	1,191.0	992.6	571.2
Provision for Loan Losses	185.0	167.1	162.0	207.1	201.5	75.0	20.0
Non-Interest Income	1,984.0	1,509.0	1,577.0	750.9	259.3	208.3	107.8
Non-Interest Expense	3,126.0	2,909.6	3,337.3	2,299.1	1,025.3	700.5	384.3
Income Before Taxes	2,984.0	2,884.2	2,369.5	901.1	223.5	425.5	274.8
Equity Earnings/Minority Int.	...	...	...	...	d13.6	d15.8	...
Net Income	[5] 1,899.0	[4] 1,817.1	[3] 1,486.9	[2] 481.8	[1] 114.3	289.9	172.3
Average Shs. Outstg. (000)	804,695	861,830	867,843	555,852	253,933	247,374	136,114
BALANCE SHEET (IN MILLIONS):							
Securities Avail. for Sale	...	34.7	39.1	23.4	1.6	0.2	0.6
Total Loans & Leases	119,626.0	113,745.7	107,612.2	67,810.7	30,694.2	24,428.1	12,534.6
Allowance for Credit Losses	1,014.0	1,041.9	1,067.8	670.5	590.8	319.0	128.0
Net Loans & Leases	118,612.0	112,703.7	106,544.4	67,140.2	30,103.4	24,109.1	12,406.6
Total Assets	194,716.0	186,513.6	165,493.3	96,981.1	44,551.9	41,471.4	18,457.7
Total Deposits	79,574.0	81,129.8	85,492.1	50,986.0	24,080.1	24,463.0	9,777.9
Long-Term Obligations	67,785.0	63,297.3	45,198.1	22,991.3	7,918.5	5,306.0	3,816.7
Total Liabilities	184,550.0	177,461.0	156,148.9	91,672.0	42,154.0	39,484.9	17,153.1
Net Stockholders' Equity	10,166.0	9,052.7	9,344.4	5,309.1	2,397.9	2,541.7	1,304.6
Year-end Shs. Outstg. (000)	809,784	857,384	890,112	579,510	283,820	269,298	139,435
STATISTICAL RECORD:							
Return on Equity %	18.7	20.1	15.9	16.6	4.8	11.4	13.2
Return on Assets %	1.0	1.0	0.9	0.5	0.3	0.7	0.9
Equity/Assets %	5.2	4.9	5.6	5.5	5.4	6.1	7.1
Non-Int. Exp./Tot. Inc. %	49.7	48.8	56.9	67.5	70.7	58.3	56.6
Price Range	37.29-14.42	30.50-16.46	34.45-17.83	32.28-18.78	20.39-11.61	13.11-7.39	11.11-7.00
P/E Ratio	15.8-6.1	14.5-7.8	20.2-10.4	39.0-22.7	53.9-30.7	11.9-6.7	9.8-6.2
Average Yield %	2.9	2.8	2.1	1.8	2.5	3.3	3.4

Statistics are as originally reported. Adj. for stk. 3-for-2 splits: 5/01, 6/98. [1] Incl. various pre-tax net exps. of $256.7 mill. [2] Incl. transact.-rel. exp. of $531.1 mill. [3] Incl. net pre-tax non-recurr. gains of $316.0 mill. & a write-down of $52.9 mill. [4] Incl. trans.-rel. exp. of $95.7 mill. [5] Incl. a pre-tax gain on the sale of loans of $261.6 mill. [6] Reflects the acq. of Great Western Financial Corp. on 7/1/97. [7] Reflects acq. of H. F. Ahmanson & Co. on 10/1/98.

OFFICERS:
K. K. Killinger, Chmn., Pres., C.E.O.
W. A. Longbrake, Vice-Chmn., C.F.O.
F. L. Chapman, Sr. Exec. V.P., Gen. Couns.

INVESTOR CONTACT: Ruthanne King, Inv. Rel., (206) 461-6421

PRINCIPAL OFFICE: 1201 Third Avenue, Suite 1500, Seattle, WA 98101

TELEPHONE NUMBER: (206) 461-2000
FAX: (206) 554-2778
WEB: www.wamu.com

NO. OF EMPLOYEES: 28,798

SHAREHOLDERS: 35,207

ANNUAL MEETING: In April

INCORPORATED: WA, Nov., 1994

INSTITUTIONAL HOLDINGS:
No. of Institutions: 602
Shares Held: 663,792,236 (Adj.)
% Held: 75.7

INDUSTRY: Savings institutions, except federal (SIC: 6036)

TRANSFER AGENT(S): Mellon Investor Services, Ridgefield Park, NJ

NYSE SYMBOL WPO
Rec. Pr. 581.00 (4/30/01)

WASHINGTON POST COMPANY (THE)

YIELD 1.0%
P/E RATIO 40.6

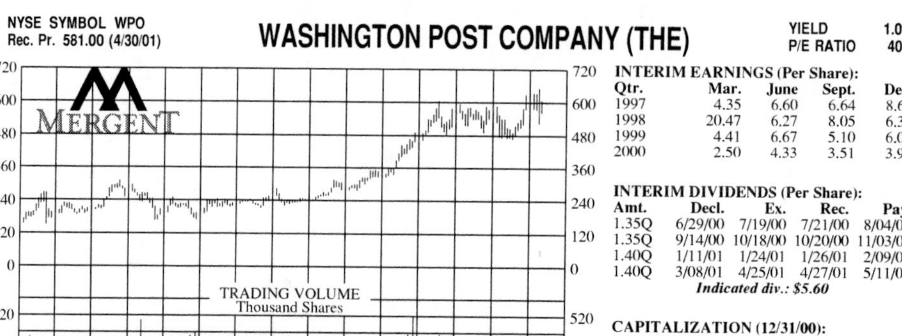

INTERIM EARNINGS (Per Share):

Qtr.	Mar.	June	Sept.	Dec.
1997	4.35	6.60	6.64	8.63
1998	20.47	6.27	8.05	6.30
1999	4.41	6.67	5.10	6.09
2000	2.50	4.33	3.51	3.98

INTERIM DIVIDENDS (Per Share):

Amt.	Decl.	Ex.	Rec.	Pay.
1.35Q	6/29/00	7/19/00	7/21/00	8/04/00
1.35Q	9/14/00	10/18/00	10/20/00	11/03/00
1.40Q	1/11/01	1/24/01	1/26/01	2/09/01
1.40Q	3/08/01	4/25/01	4/27/01	5/11/01

Indicated div.: $5.60

CAPITALIZATION (12/31/00):

	($000)	(%)
Long-Term Debt	873,267	35.1
Deferred Income Tax	117,731	4.7
Redeemable Pfd. Stock	13,148	0.5
Common & Surplus	1,481,007	59.6
Total	2,485,153	100.0

RECENT DEVELOPMENTS: For the year ended 12/31/00, net income fell 39.6% to $136.5 million versus $225.8 million in 1999. Results for 2000 included a one-time after-tax charge of $16.5 million from an early retirement program and a non-operating charge of $19.8 million from the write-downs of certain of WPO's e-commerce instruments. Results for 1999 included a non-operating gain of $21.4 million. Total operating revenues were $2.41 billion, up 8.9% from $2.22 billion in the previous year.

PROSPECTS: The Company's Kaplan, Inc. subsidiary plans to expand its services in Korea with J EduLine, the educational subsidiary of Joongang Ilbo, a Korean media corporation. EduLine introduced a new "Kaplan Center Korea" in Seoul in May 2001. Meanwhile, Kaplan Canada Ltd., a wholly-owned subsidiary of Kaplan, Inc., acquired The Study Seminar for Financial Analysts, a provider of preparatory seminars for the Chartered Financial Analyst examination.

BUSINESS

THE WASHINGTON POST COMPANY operates principally in the areas of newspaper publishing, television broadcasting, magazine publishing, cable television and education services. Newspaper operations include THE WASHINGTON POST, the HERALD, which is published in Everett, Washington, and Gazette Newspapers, Inc. Broadcast operations are conducted primarily through six VHF stations. Magazine operations consist of the publication of a weekly news magazine, NEWSWEEK, which has one domestic and three international editions. Cable television operations provides services to about 735,000 subscribers in 19 states. Education services includes Kaplan, Inc., which provides a wide range of educational services. WPO also has a 50% interest in the International Herald Tribune, S.A.S., a French company.

ANNUAL FINANCIAL DATA

	12/31/00	1/2/00	1/3/99	12/28/97	12/29/96	12/31/95	1/1/95
Earnings Per Share	**[4] 14.32**	**22.30**	**[3] 41.10**	**[2] 26.23**	**20.05**	**[1] 17.15**	**[1] 14.65**
Cash Flow Per Share	**33.41**	**38.45**	**54.84**	**33.00**	**28.70**	**25.92**	**24.08**
Tang. Book Val. Per Share	**50.03**	**51.03**	**69.84**	**42.64**	**85.25**	**62.96**	**54.16**
Dividends Per Share	**5.40**	**5.20**	**5.00**	**4.80**	**4.60**	**4.40**	**4.20**
Dividend Payout %	**37.7**	**23.3**	**12.2**	**18.3**	**22.9**	**25.7**	**28.7**
INCOME STATEMENT (IN MILLIONS):							
Total Revenues	2,412.2	2,215.6	2,110.4	1,956.3	1,853.4	1,719.4	1,614.0
Costs & Expenses	1,891.7	1,664.3	1,592.3	1,469.9	1,421.3	1,351.2	1,229.9
Depreciation & Amort.	180.6	162.8	139.1	105.0	94.9	97.3	109.2
Operating Income	339.9	388.5	378.9	381.4	337.2	271.0	274.9
Net Interest Inc./(Exp.)	d53.8	d25.7	d10.4	2.2	3.8	2.4	3.6
Income Before Income Taxes	229.9	375.4	668.1	463.1	360.2	311.4	286.9
Income Taxes	93.4	149.6	250.8	181.5	139.4	121.3	117.3
Equity Earnings/Minority Int.	d36.5	d8.8	d5.1	10.0	19.7	24.5	7.3
Net Income	[4] 136.5	225.8	[3] 417.3	[2] 281.6	220.8	[1] 190.1	[1] 169.7
Cash Flow	316.0	387.6	555.4	385.7	315.1	287.4	278.9
Average Shs. Outstg. (000)	9,460	10,082	10,129	10,733	10,980	11,086	11,582
BALANCE SHEET (IN MILLIONS):							
Cash & Cash Equivalents	31.3	112.7	86.9	21.1	102.3	159.7	141.8
Total Current Assets	405.1	476.2	404.9	308.5	382.6	406.6	375.9
Net Property	927.1	854.9	841.1	653.8	511.4	457.4	411.4
Total Assets	3,200.7	2,986.9	2,729.7	2,077.3	1,870.4	1,732.9	1,696.9
Total Current Liabilities	408.8	822.5	389.1	608.8	281.6	308.2	273.1
Long-Term Obligations	873.3	397.6	395.0	...	...	...	50.3
Net Stockholders' Equity	1,481.0	1,367.8	1,588.1	1,184.1	1,322.8	1,184.2	1,126.9
Net Working Capital	d3.7	d346.4	15.8	d300.3	101.0	98.4	102.8
Year-end Shs. Outstg. (000)	9,460	9,439	10,093	11,828	9,131	11,307	11,346
STATISTICAL RECORD:							
Operating Profit Margin %	14.1	17.5	18.0	19.5	18.2	15.8	17.0
Net Profit Margin %	5.7	10.2	19.8	14.4	11.9	11.1	10.5
Return on Equity %	9.2	16.5	26.3	23.8	16.7	16.1	15.1
Return on Assets %	4.3	7.6	15.3	13.6	11.8	11.0	10.0
Debt/Total Assets %	27.3	13.3	14.5	...	...	...	3.0
Price Range	628.75-467.25	594.50-490.13	605.50-462.00	491.06-325.13	351.75-276.75	315.00-237.50	284.00-221.75
P/E Ratio	43.9-32.6	26.7-22.0	14.7-11.2	18.7-12.4	17.5-13.8	18.4-13.8	19.4-15.1
Average Yield %	1.0	1.0	0.9	1.2	1.5	1.6	1.7

Statistics are as originally reported. [1] Incl. $2.8 mill. ($0.24/sh.) net after-tax gain, 12/31/95; $8.1 mill. ($0.70/sh.), 1/1/95. [2] Incl. $44.5 mill. non-recur. gain. [3] Incl. $194.4 mill. gain fr. disp. of int. in Cowles Media, sale of 14 cable systems & disp. of Junglee. [4] Incl. $16.5 mill. one-time after-taxchg. & $19.8 mill. non-oper. chg.

OFFICERS:
D. E. Graham, Chmn., C.E.O.
K. Graham, Chmn. of Exec. Comm.
D. M. Daniels, V.P., Gen. Couns.

INVESTOR CONTACT: Daniel Lynch, Treas., (202) 334-6000

PRINCIPAL OFFICE: 1150 15th Street N.W., Washington, DC 20071

TELEPHONE NUMBER: (202) 334-6000
FAX: (202) 334-1031
WEB: www.washpostco.com
NO. OF EMPLOYEES: 10,700 (approx.)
SHAREHOLDERS: 23 (Class A); 1,125 (Class B)
ANNUAL MEETING: In May
INCORPORATED: DE, 1947

INSTITUTIONAL HOLDINGS:
No. of Institutions: 185
Shares Held: 5,234,399
% Held: 55.3

INDUSTRY: Newspapers (SIC: 2711)

TRANSFER AGENT(S): EquiServe First Chicago Trust Division, Jersey City, NJ

NYSE SYMBOL WMI
Rec. Pr. 24.41 (4/30/01)

WASTE MANAGEMENT, INC.

YIELD ...
P/E RATIO ...

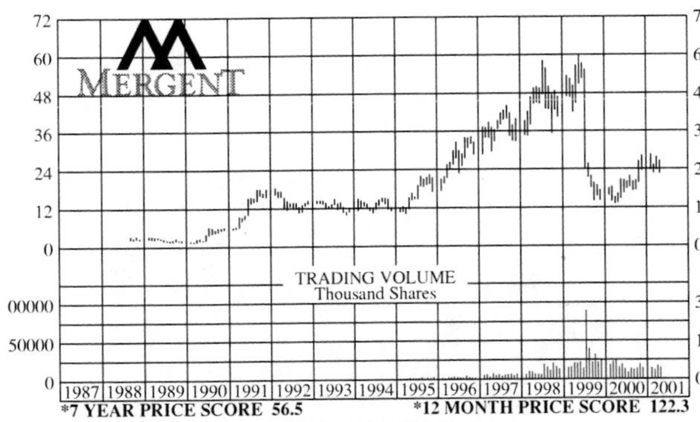

*7 YEAR PRICE SCORE 56.5 *12 MONTH PRICE SCORE 122.3
*NYSE COMPOSITE INDEX=100

INTERIM EARNINGS (Per Share):

Qtr.	Mar.	June	Sept.	Dec.
1997	0.32	0.43	0.12	0.39
1998	0.55	0.53	d2.21	0.10
1999	0.58	0.50	d1.53	d0.18
2000	0.09	Nil	d0.31	0.06

INTERIM DIVIDENDS (Per Share):

Amt.	Decl.	Ex.	Rec.	Pay.
0.01A	9/14/99	9/28/99	9/30/99	10/19/99
0.01A	8/15/00	9/27/00	9/30/00	10/16/00

Indicated div.: $0.01 (Div. Reinv. Plan)

CAPITALIZATION (12/31/00):

	($000)	(%)
Long-Term Debt	8,372,000	59.5
Deferred Income Tax	879,000	6.2
Minority Interest	15,000	0.1
Common & Surplus	4,801,000	34.1
Total	14,067,000	100.0

RECENT DEVELOPMENTS: For the year ended 12/31/00, WMI reported a net loss of $97.0 million compared with a loss of $395.0 million, before an extraordinary loss, in 1999. Results included asset impairments and unusual charges of $749.0 million in 2000 and $739.0 million in 1999. Results for 1999 also included charges of $45.0 million for merger and acquisition related costs. Operating revenues were $12.49 billion, down 4.8% from $13.13 billion a year earlier.

PROSPECTS: In 2001, WMI plans to execute four major initiatives. The initiatives include conversion from WMI's existing financial information systems to PeopleSoft systems; implemention of WMI's procurement strategy; roll-out of the Local Market Strategy initiative in 31 service areas where the Company operates; and roll-out WMI's Service Machine initiative to create value through an increased focus on customer service.

BUSINESS

WASTE MANAGEMENT, INC. (formerly USA Waste Services, Inc.) is a global company that provides integrated waste management services. In North America, WMI provides solid waste management services collection, transfer, recycling and resource recovery services, and disposal services, including the landfill disposal of hazardous wastes. In addition, WMI is a developer, operator and owner of waste-to-energy facilities in the U.S. WMI also engages in other hazardous waste management services throughout North America, as well as low-level and other radioactive waste services. Internationally, WMI operates throughout Europe, the Pacific Rim, South America and other select international markets. On 7/16/98, WMI completed the acquisition of Waste Management Holdings, Inc. (formerly Waste Management, Inc.).

REVENUES

(12/31/2000)	($000)	(%)
North America Solid Waste	11,218,000	89.8
WM International Waste	809,000	6.5
Non-solid Waste	465,000	3.7
Total	12,492,000	100.0

ANNUAL FINANCIAL DATA

	12/31/00	12/31/99	12/31/98	12/31/97	12/31/96	12/31/95	12/31/94
Earnings Per Share	[3] **d0.16**	[6] **d0.64**	[5] **d1.31**	[4] **1.26**	[3] **0.24**	[2] **0.55**	[1] **d1.55**
Cash Flow Per Share	**2.14**	**1.99**	**1.25**	**2.47**	**1.33**	**1.32**	**d0.41**
Tang. Book Val. Per Share	...	...	...	**4.51**	**4.57**	**5.14**	**1.43**
Dividends Per Share	**0.01**	**0.01**	**0.01**	...	...	...	...
INCOME STATEMENT (IN MILLIONS):							
Total Revenues	12,492.0	13,126.9	12,703.5	2,613.8	1,313.4	457.1	434.2
Costs & Expenses	10,025.0	10,972.8	11,365.1	1,764.8	1,049.9	345.9	341.5
Depreciation & Amort.	1,429.0	1,614.2	1,498.7	303.2	153.2	56.4	56.1
Operating Income	1,038.0	540.0	d160.4	545.7	110.3	54.9	36.6
Net Interest Inc./(Exp.)	d717.0	d731.2	d654.6	d96.6	d40.3	d38.7	d31.4
Income Before Income Taxes	321.0	d162.7	d699.9	463.3	78.1	18.9	d72.4
Income Taxes	418.0	232.3	66.9	189.9	45.1	cr11.4	3.9
Equity Earnings/Minority Int.	d23.0	d24.2	d24.3	...	...	...	...
Net Income	[3] d97.0	[6] d395.1	[5] d766.8	[4] 273.3	[3] 32.9	[2] 30.3	[1] d76.3
Cash Flow	1,332.0	1,219.1	731.9	576.6	186.1	86.6	d20.7
Average Shs. Outstg. (000)	621,257	612,932	584,301	233,371	139,740	65,836	50,408
BALANCE SHEET (IN MILLIONS):							
Cash & Cash Equivalents	94.0	181.4	88.7	51.2	23.5	13.2	30.2
Total Current Assets	2,457.0	6,220.5	3,881.4	655.4	340.0	120.1	119.1
Net Property	10,126.0	10,303.8	11,637.7	3,955.0	1,810.3	593.3	523.6
Total Assets	18,565.0	22,681.4	22,715.2	6,622.8	2,830.5	908.0	785.6
Total Current Liabilities	2,937.0	7,489.5	4,293.7	568.7	320.0	105.2	86.4
Long-Term Obligations	8,372.0	8,399.3	11,114.2	2,724.4	1,158.3	334.9	363.9
Net Stockholders' Equity	4,801.0	4,402.6	4,372.5	2,629.0	1,155.3	402.8	164.3
Net Working Capital	d480.0	d1,268.9	d412.3	86.7	20.0	14.9	32.7
Year-end Shs. Outstg. (000)	622,650	627,210	608,244	217,782	139,586	55,270	49,671
STATISTICAL RECORD:							
Operating Profit Margin %	8.3	4.1	...	20.9	8.4	12.0	8.4
Net Profit Margin %	...	...	...	10.5	2.5	6.6	...
Return on Equity %	...	...	...	10.4	2.9	7.5	...
Return on Assets %	...	...	...	4.1	1.2	3.3	...
Debt/Total Assets %	45.1	37.0	48.9	41.1	40.9	36.9	46.3
Price Range	28.31-13.00	60.00-14.00	58.19-34.44	44.13-28.63	34.25-17.25	22.50-10.00	15.13-10.38
P/E Ratio	...	...	...	35.0-22.7	142.6-71.8	40.9-18.2	...

Statistics are as originally reported. [1] Incl. non-recurr. chrg. $92.0 mill. [2] Incl. non-recurr. chrg. $29.8 mill. [3] Incl. non-recurr. chrg. $184.5 mill., 1996; $749.0 mill., 2000. [4] Bef. extraord. loss $6.3 mill., but incl. non-recurr. chrg. $134.1 mill. [5] Bef. extraord. loss $3.9 mill., but incl. non-recurr. chrg. $2.67 bill. [6] Bef. extraord. loss $2.5 mill., but incl. non-recurr. chrg. $783.5 mill.

OFFICERS:
A. M. Myers, Chmn., C.E.O., Pres.
L. O'Donnel, III, Sr. V.P., Couns., Sec.
W. L. Trubeck, Sr. V.P., C.F.O.

INVESTOR CONTACT: Cherle Rice, Investor Relations, (713) 512-6548

PRINCIPAL OFFICE: 1001 Fannin Street, Suite 4000, Houston, TX 77002

TELEPHONE NUMBER: (713) 512-6200
FAX: (713) 512-6299
WEB: www.wmx.com

NO. OF EMPLOYEES: 57,000 (approx.)

SHAREHOLDERS: 31,501 (record)

ANNUAL MEETING: In May

INCORPORATED: OK, Sept., 1987; reincorp., DE, June, 1995

INSTITUTIONAL HOLDINGS:
No. of Institutions: 389
Shares Held: 540,301,742
% Held: 86.4

INDUSTRY: Refuse systems (SIC: 4953)

TRANSFER AGENT(S): Computershare Investor Services, Chicago, IL

NYSE SYMBOL WAT
Rec. Pr. 52.20 (4/30/01)

WATERS CORPORATION

YIELD ...
P/E RATIO 45.0

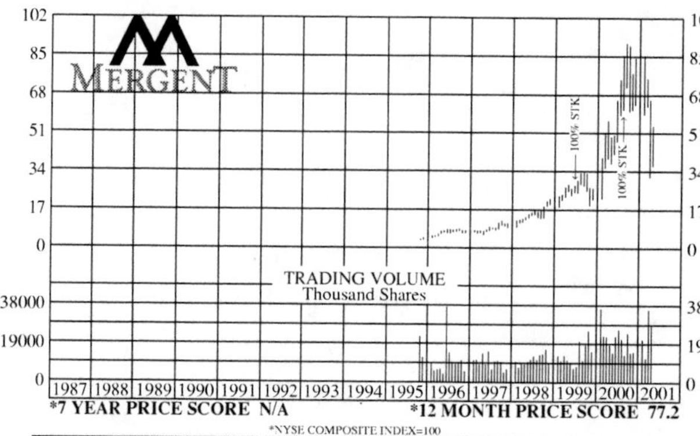

*7 YEAR PRICE SCORE N/A *12 MONTH PRICE SCORE 77.2

*NYSE COMPOSITE INDEX=100

INTERIM EARNINGS (Per Share):

Qtr.	Mar.	June	Sept.	Dec.
1995	d0.01	0.05	0.09	0.02
1996	0.07	d0.08	0.05	0.12
1997	0.10	0.12	d0.32	0.05
1998	Nil	0.15	0.17	0.25
1999	0.18	0.22	0.22	0.32
2000	0.23	0.28	0.28	0.37

INTERIM DIVIDENDS (Per Share):

Amt.	Decl.	Ex.	Rec.	Pay.
100% STK	2/26/99	6/11/99	5/27/99	6/10/99
100% STK	7/13/00	8/28/00	8/04/00	8/25/00

CAPITALIZATION (12/31/00):

	($000)	(%)
Common & Surplus	451,781	100.0
Total	451,781	100.0

RECENT DEVELOPMENTS: For the year ended 12/31/00, income, before the cumulative effect of an accounting charge of $10.8 million, rose 27.6% to $156.1 million compared with $122.3 million in 1999. Net sales were $795.1 million, up 12.9% from $704.4 million in the prior year. Sales benefited from strong demand from life science customers and sales of mass spectrometry products. Gross profit climbed 13.3% to $506.8 million from $447.3 million in the previous year.

PROSPECTS: Going forward, the Company plans to introduce a range of new products in its liquid chromatography, mass spectrometry and thermal analysis technology platforms. The introduction of these new products should have a positive effect on top-line growth. Separately, the Company signed a license and research agreement with Sandia National Laboratories. Under a multi-year cooperative research and development agreement, the companies will jointly develop further microfluidics technology.

BUSINESS

WATERS CORPORATION provides instruments in three complementary analytical technologies: high performance liquid chromatography (HPLC), thermal analysis and mass spectrometry. HPLC, the largest product segment in the Company, is utilized to detect, identify, monitor, and measure the chemical, physical, and biological composition of materials, and to purify a full range of compounds. Waters' products are primarily used by pharmaceutical, industrial, university research, and development of laboratories. WAT is also engaged in thermal analysis, a prevalent and complementary technique used in the analysis of polymers, through its wholly-owned subsidiary, TA Instruments, Inc. In 1997, WAT acquired Micromass Limited, a market leader in mass spectrometry, and YMC, Inc., a manufacturer and distributor of chromatography chemicals and supplies.

ANNUAL FINANCIAL DATA

	12/31/00	12/31/99	12/31/98	12/31/97	12/31/96	12/31/95	[1] 12/31/94
Earnings Per Share	[5] 1.14	0.92	[4] 0.57	[3] d0.08	[2] 0.15	[2] 0.14	...
Cash Flow Per Share	1.36	1.14	0.79	0.10	0.29	0.30	...
Tang. Book Val. Per Share	2.21	0.98	...	...	...	...	...
INCOME STATEMENT (IN MILLIONS):							
Total Revenues	795.1	704.4	618.8	465.5	391.1	333.0	131.1
Costs & Expenses	554.8	498.2	470.5	423.2	327.5	270.1	193.3
Depreciation & Amort.	29.4	29.7	28.5	21.1	17.8	16.5	5.4
Operating Income	210.8	176.5	119.8	21.2	45.8	46.4	d66.7
Net Interest Inc./(Exp.)	0.1	d8.9	d18.3	d13.7	d14.7	d30.3	d12.1
Income Before Income Taxes	211.0	167.6	101.5	7.5	31.1	17.2	d78.7
Income Taxes	54.8	45.2	27.1	15.8	11.2	3.1	1.5
Net Income	[5] 156.1	122.3	[4] 74.4	[3] d8.3	[2] 19.9	[2] 14.1	d80.2
Cash Flow	185.6	151.6	101.9	11.9	36.7	29.7	d74.8
Average Shs. Outstg. (000)	136,743	132,632	129,284	116,508	126,512	98,328	...
BALANCE SHEET (IN MILLIONS):							
Cash & Cash Equivalents	75.5	3.8	5.5	3.1	0.6	3.2	12.7
Total Current Assets	343.8	247.3	251.6	216.5	144.0	127.3	151.7
Net Property	102.6	91.8	89.0	88.7	74.8	70.3	71.1
Total Assets	692.3	584.4	577.7	552.1	365.5	299.8	327.6
Total Current Liabilities	220.5	197.8	185.6	170.7	82.8	70.9	68.4
Long-Term Obligations	...	81.1	218.3	305.3	210.5	158.5	270.0
Net Stockholders' Equity	451.8	292.2	150.1	62.3	57.8	58.1	d16.3
Net Working Capital	123.3	49.5	66.1	45.8	61.2	56.4	83.3
Year-end Shs. Outstg. (000)	129,811	124,518	121,188	118,332	115,692	115,184	...
STATISTICAL RECORD:							
Operating Profit Margin %	26.5	25.1	19.4	4.6	11.7	13.9	...
Net Profit Margin %	19.6	17.4	12.0	...	5.1	4.2	...
Return on Equity %	34.6	41.9	49.6	...	34.4	24.3	...
Return on Assets %	22.5	20.9	12.9	...	5.4	4.7	...
Debt/Total Assets %	...	13.9	37.8	55.3	57.6	52.9	82.4
Price Range	90.94-21.97	33.84-18.13	21.88-9.13	12.11-5.78	8.41-4.19	4.56-3.31	...
P/E Ratio	79.8-19.3	36.8-19.7	38.5-16.1	...	56.0-27.9	33.8-24.5	...

Statistics are as originally reported. Adj. for 2-for-1 split, 6/99 & 8/00. [1] Partial year, from 8/19/94 (date of inception). [2] Bef. $22.3 mill. ($0.71/sh.) extraord. loss, 1996; and $12.1 mill. ($0.49/sh.) extraord. loss, 1995. [3] Incl. $55.0 mill. non-recur. chg. fr. in-process R&D and $16.5 mill. non-recur. chg. fr. revaluation of Micromass inventory. [4] Incl. $16.5 mill. non-recur. chg. rel. to acq. of Micromass Limited. [5] Excl. $10.8 mill. cumulative effect of acctg. chg.

OFFICERS:
D. A. Berthiaume, Chmn., Pres., C.E.O.
J. Ornell, Sr. V.P., C.F.O.

INVESTOR CONTACT: Brian K. Mazar, V.P., Investor Relations, (508) 482-2193

PRINCIPAL OFFICE: 34 Maple Street, Milford, MA 01757

TELEPHONE NUMBER: (508) 478-2000
FAX: (508) 872-1990
WEB: www.waters.com

NO. OF EMPLOYEES: 3,200 (approx.)

SHAREHOLDERS: 259 (approx.)

ANNUAL MEETING: In May

INCORPORATED: DE, Aug., 1994

INSTITUTIONAL HOLDINGS:
No. of Institutions: 301
Shares Held: 119,638,975
% Held: 91.7

INDUSTRY: Analytical instruments (SIC: 3826)

TRANSFER AGENT(S): BankBoston, N.A., c/o Boston EquiServe, Boston, MA

NYSE SYMBOL WPI
Rec. Pr. 49.80 (4/30/01)

WATSON PHARMACEUTICALS, INC.

YIELD ...
P/E RATIO 26.8

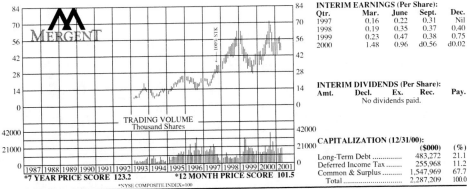

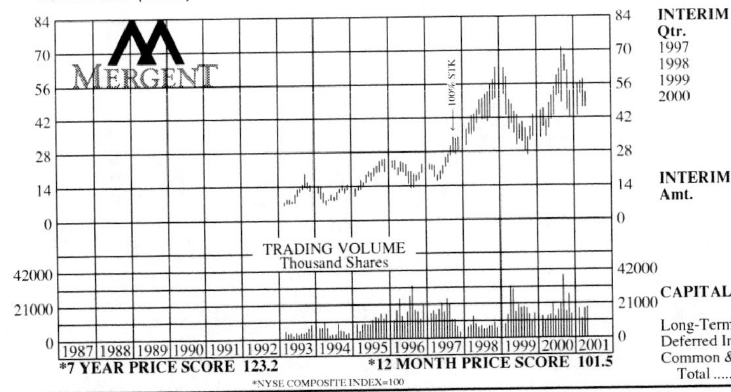

INTERIM EARNINGS (Per Share):

Qtr.	Mar.	June	Sept.	Dec.
1997	0.16	0.22	0.31	Nil
1998	0.19	0.35	0.37	0.40
1999	0.23	0.47	0.38	0.75
2000	1.48	0.96	d0.56	d0.02

INTERIM DIVIDENDS (Per Share):

Amt.	Decl.	Ex.	Rec.	Pay.

No dividends paid.

CAPITALIZATION (12/31/00):

	($000)	(%)
Long-Term Debt	483,272	21.1
Deferred Income Tax	255,968	11.2
Common & Surplus	1,547,969	67.7
Total	2,287,209	100.0

RECENT DEVELOPMENTS: For the year ended 12/31/00, income was $170.7 million, before an extraordinary charge of $1.2 million and accounting charge of $12.0 million, versus net income of $182.7 million in 1999. The 2000 results included pre-tax charges totaling $147.4 million and a pre-tax gain of $358.6 million for the sale of Andrx common stock. Net revenues increased 15.1% to $811.5 million.

PROSPECTS: The Company announced the launch of four new brand pharmaceutical products by its newly realigned and refocused branded sales forces. Three new pain management products are MAXIDONE™, NORCO™ 5.0 mg and NORCO™ 7.5 mg will represent an estimated $40.0 million in revenues for 2001. The fourth product, UNITHROID™, represents an estimated $15.0 million in revenues for 2001.

BUSINESS

WATSON PHARMACEUTICALS, INC. is engaged in the development, production, marketing and distribution of branded and off-patent pharmaceutical products. The Company's products include therapeutic and preventive agents generally sold by prescription or over-the-counter for the treatment of human diseases and disorders. The Company's branded pharmaceutical business operates primarily in three specialty areas: Dermatology, Women's Health and General Products. The Company is also engaged in the development, manufacture and sale of off-patent pharmaceutical products.

BUSINESS LINE ANALYSIS

(12/31/2000)	REV (%)	INC (%)
Branded Pharm. Products	52.1	76.9
Generic Pharm. Products	45.7	19.1
Other	2.2	4.0
Total	100.0	100.0

ANNUAL FINANCIAL DATA

	12/31/00	12/31/99	12/31/98	12/31/97	12/31/96	12/31/95	12/31/94
Earnings Per Share	**[2] 1.65**	**[1] 1.83**	**1.32**	**1.01**	**0.98**	**0.65**	**0.53**
Cash Flow Per Share	**2.34**	**2.28**	**1.66**	**1.17**	**1.07**	**0.73**	**0.63**
Tang. Book Val. Per Share	**0.98**	**5.00**	**3.08**	**3.14**	**5.20**	**3.97**	**3.25**
INCOME STATEMENT (IN MILLIONS):							
Total Revenues	811.5	689.2	556.1	338.3	194.1	152.9	87.1
Costs & Expenses	731.9	407.8	332.1	201.4	104.3	94.3	54.4
Depreciation & Amort.	71.4	44.0	31.3	14.6	7.1	6.3	3.8
Operating Income	8.2	237.4	192.8	122.3	82.7	52.3	28.9
Net Interest Inc./(Exp.)	d8.9	d6.6	d0.5	11.6	8.6	11.6	1.1
Income Before Income Taxes	357.9	275.1	192.3	133.9	91.3	50.0	30.0
Income Taxes	184.7	93.7	78.2	54.4	35.9	24.9	11.3
Equity Earnings/Minority Int.	d2.5	d2.6	6.8	10.7	17.9	22.8	...
Net Income	[2] 170.7	[1] 178.9	120.8	90.2	73.3	47.9	18.7
Cash Flow	242.1	222.9	152.1	104.8	80.4	54.2	22.5
Average Shs. Outstg. (000)	103,575	97,780	91,593	89,325	75,328	74,286	35,662
BALANCE SHEET (IN MILLIONS):							
Cash & Cash Equivalents	237.6	115.9	72.7	114.9	211.0	118.3	56.5
Total Current Assets	831.3	434.7	293.3	252.3	279.6	197.6	87.1
Net Property	194.5	138.8	109.1	88.0	73.6	70.0	41.6
Total Assets	2,579.9	1,438.8	1,070.0	760.5	419.6	322.1	130.3
Total Current Liabilities	280.4	129.2	94.8	99.8	21.4	28.8	12.0
Long-Term Obligations	483.3	149.5	149.9	2.4	2.9	3.6	5.1
Net Stockholders' Equity	1,548.0	1,054.6	750.5	565.0	382.7	289.0	111.0
Net Working Capital	550.9	305.5	198.5	152.5	258.2	168.8	75.0
Year-end Shs. Outstg. (000)	105,600	96,133	89,508	87,882	73,666	72,738	34,168
STATISTICAL RECORD:							
Operating Profit Margin %	1.0	34.4	34.7	36.2	42.6	34.2	33.2
Net Profit Margin %	21.0	26.0	21.7	26.7	37.8	31.3	21.5
Return on Equity %	11.0	17.0	16.1	16.0	19.2	16.6	16.8
Return on Assets %	6.6	12.4	11.3	11.9	17.5	14.9	14.3
Debt/Total Assets %	18.7	10.4	14.0	0.3	0.7	1.1	3.9
Price Range	71.50-33.69	62.94-26.50	63.00-30.50	34.13-16.00	24.75-13.00	25.25-10.00	14.75-6.38
P/E Ratio	43.3-20.4	34.4-14.5	47.7-23.1	33.8-15.8	25.4-13.3	39.1-15.5	28.1-12.1

Statistics are as originally reported. Adj. for 100% stk. split, 10/97 [1] Incl. a pre-tax merger-rel. chrg. of $20.5 mill. [2] Bef. extra. loss of $1.2 mill. & acctg. chrg. of $12.0 mill.; incl. a pre-tax non-recurr. gain of $358.6 mill. & one-time chrgs. of $147.4 mill.

OFFICERS:
A. Y. Chao Ph.D., Chmn., Pres., C.E.O.
M. E. Boxer, Sr. V.P., C.F.O.
R. C. Funsten, Sr. V.P., Sec., Gen. Couns.

INVESTOR CONTACT: Investor Relations, (909) 270-1400

PRINCIPAL OFFICE: 311 Bonnie Circle, Corona, CA 92880-2882

TELEPHONE NUMBER: (909) 270-1400
FAX: (909) 270-1096
WEB: www.watsonpharm.com

NO. OF EMPLOYEES: 3,000 (approx.)

SHAREHOLDERS: 80,000 (approx.)

ANNUAL MEETING: In May

INCORPORATED: CA, 1983; reincorp., NV, 1985

INSTITUTIONAL HOLDINGS:
No. of Institutions: 318
Shares Held: 67,641,983
% Held: 63.9

INDUSTRY: Pharmaceutical preparations (SIC: 2834)

TRANSFER AGENT(S): American Stock Transfer & Trust Company, New York, NY

NYSE SYMBOL WTS
Rec. Pr. 16.45 (4/30/01)

WATTS INDUSTRIES, INC.

YIELD 1.5%
P/E RATIO 14.1

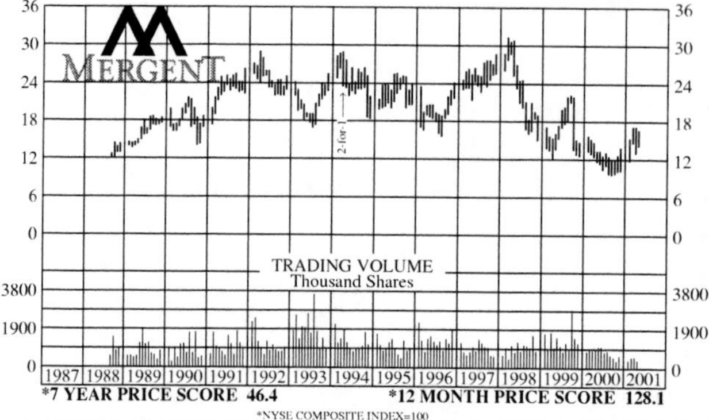

*7 YEAR PRICE SCORE 46.4 *12 MONTH PRICE SCORE 128.1

*NYSE COMPOSITE INDEX=100

INTERIM EARNINGS (Per Share):

Qtr.	Sept.	Dec.	Mar.	June
1997-98	0.50	0.50	0.51	0.44
1998-99	0.46	0.27	0.26	0.27
1999-00	0.34	...	...	...
Qtr.	**Mar.**	**June**	**Sept.**	**Dec.**
1999	...	...	...	0.61
2000	0.30	0.30	0.29	0.28

INTERIM DIVIDENDS (Per Share):

Amt.	Decl.	Ex.	Rec.	Pay.
0.06Q	7/25/00	8/31/00	9/05/00	9/18/00
0.06Q	10/23/00	11/30/00	12/04/00	12/15/00
0.06Q	2/06/01	3/01/01	3/05/01	3/16/01
0.06Q	4/25/01	5/31/01	6/04/01	6/15/01

Indicated div.: $0.24

CAPITALIZATION (12/31/00):

	($000)	(%)
Long-Term Debt	105,377	29.3
Deferred Income Tax	15,463	4.3
Minority Interest	6,775	1.9
Common & Surplus	232,542	64.6
Total	360,157	100.0

RECENT DEVELOPMENTS: For the year ended 12/31/00, income from continuing operations climbed 1.5% to $31.2 million versus $30.7 million in 1999. Results for 2000 and 1999 excluded after-tax losses of $7.2 million and $3.1 million, respectively, from discontinued operations. Results for 1999 included a restructuring charge of $1.5 million. Net sales were $516.1 million, up 1.3% from $509.7 million in 1999. Acquisitions and cost reduction efforts helped offset the negative effects of the soft housing market.

PROSPECTS: The Company acquired Dumser Metallbau GmbH & Co. KG of Landau, Germany. Dumser produces brass, steel, and stainless steel manifolds used as the prime distribution device in hydronic heating systems, and boiler sets, which is a wall-mounted cabinet installed in the vicinity of the boiler, containing the factory assembled set of the circulation pump, pressure, temperature, and flow controls. The acquisition strengthens WTS' position in the European hydronic heating industry.

BUSINESS

WATTS INDUSTRIES, INC. designs, manufactures and sells a line of valves for the plumbing and heating, water quality, industrial, and oil and gas industries. The Company's product lines include safety relief valves, regulators, thermostatic mixing valves, ball valves and flow control valves for water service primarily in residential and commercial environments, and metal and plastic water supply/drainage products for residential construction and home repair and remodeling. On 10/18/99, WTS completed the spin-off of its industrial, oil and gas subsidiary, CIRCOR International, Inc., to shareholders.

ANNUAL FINANCIAL DATA

	12/31/00	[2] 12/31/99	6/30/99	6/30/98	6/30/97	6/30/96	6/30/95
Earnings Per Share	**[4] 1.17**	**[3] 0.61**	**[1] 1.10**	**[1] 1.95**	**[1] 1.77**	**[1] d1.82**	**1.54**
Cash Flow Per Share	**1.93**	**0.95**	**1.75**	**2.79**	**2.53**	**d1.09**	**2.36**
Tang. Book Val. Per Share	**5.08**	**4.71**	**11.02**	**13.75**	**8.24**	**8.51**	**8.67**
Dividends Per Share	**0.27**	**0.35**	**0.35**	**0.35**	**0.31**	**0.28**	**0.25**
Dividend Payout %	**22.9**	**57.4**	**31.8**	**17.9**	**17.5**	...	**16.2**
INCOME STATEMENT (IN MILLIONS):							
Total Revenues	516.1	261.0	474.5	730.0	720.3	640.9	657.7
Costs & Expenses	436.0	222.2	405.2	616.2	613.1	658.5	549.1
Depreciation & Amort.	20.1	9.2	17.5	23.2	20.8	21.6	24.6
Operating Income	60.0	29.6	51.8	90.6	86.4	d39.2	84.0
Net Interest Inc./(Exp.)	d9.1	d4.1	d5.2	d8.8	d9.7	d9.3	d8.7
Income Before Income Taxes	49.2	25.4	44.9	81.1	75.6	d49.4	73.6
Income Taxes	18.0	8.9	15.5	27.7	27.1	4.4	27.9
Net Income	[4] 31.2	[3] 16.5	[1] 29.5	[1] 53.4	[1] 48.5	[1] d53.8	45.7
Cash Flow	51.2	25.7	46.9	76.6	69.3	d32.2	70.3
Average Shs. Outstg. (000)	26,551	27,081	26,799	27,423	27,433	29,527	29,755
BALANCE SHEET (IN MILLIONS):							
Cash & Cash Equivalents	15.2	13.0	12.8	10.7	14.4	...	8.7
Total Current Assets	249.2	252.8	367.1	371.7	345.6	416.2	355.1
Net Property	125.8	130.2	129.2	161.5	152.7	148.0	168.4
Total Assets	482.0	487.1	637.7	665.8	622.1	656.3	690.0
Total Current Liabilities	112.1	111.1	99.2	134.3	120.9	129.9	113.1
Long-Term Obligations	105.4	124.0	118.9	115.4	125.9	160.2	132.8
Net Stockholders' Equity	232.5	219.5	387.7	374.0	333.6	319.6	406.0
Net Working Capital	137.1	141.7	267.9	237.4	224.7	286.2	242.0
Year-end Shs. Outstg. (000)	26,461	26,374	26,444	27,156	27,013	28,222	29,623
STATISTICAL RECORD:							
Operating Profit Margin %	11.6	11.3	10.9	12.4	12.0	...	12.8
Net Profit Margin %	6.0	6.3	6.2	7.3	6.7	...	7.0
Return on Equity %	13.4	7.5	7.6	14.3	14.5	...	11.3
Return on Assets %	6.5	3.4	4.6	8.0	7.8	...	6.6
Debt/Total Assets %	21.9	25.5	18.6	17.3	20.2	24.4	19.3
Price Range	15.75-9.56	22.25-12.06	22.25-12.06	31.38-14.94	28.69-21.25	24.25-15.50	25.63-19.75
P/E Ratio	13.5-8.2	36.5-19.8	20.2-11.0	16.1-7.7	16.2-12.0	...	16.6-12.8
Average Yield %	2.1	2.8	2.0	1.5	1.2	1.4	1.1

Statistics are as originally reported. [1] Excl. net gain fr. disc. ops. of $3.5 mill., 1996; $79,000, 1997; $25.2 mill., 1998; $6.5 mill., 1999. [2] For the transition period from 6/30/99 to 12/31/99. [3] Excl. loss of $1.2 mill. fr. disc. ops. & incl. restr. chgs. of $1.5 mill. [4] Excl. $7.2 mill. income fr. disc. ops.

OFFICERS:
T. P. Horne, Chmn., Pres., C.E.O.
W. C. McCartney, C.F.O., Treas., Sec.
L. J. Taufen, Gen. Couns., Asst. Sec.

INVESTOR CONTACT: William C. McCartney, (978) 688-1811

PRINCIPAL OFFICE: 815 Chestnut Street, North Andover, MA 01845

TELEPHONE NUMBER: (978) 688-1811
FAX: (978) 688-5841
WEB: www.wattsind.com

NO. OF EMPLOYEES: 3,400 (approx.)

SHAREHOLDERS: 154 (cl. A com.); 3200 (approx. cl A beneficial); 9 (cl. B com.)

ANNUAL MEETING: In Oct.

INCORPORATED: DE, 1985

INSTITUTIONAL HOLDINGS:
No. of Institutions: 76
Shares Held: 13,915,003
% Held: 52.6

INDUSTRY: Industrial valves (SIC: 3491)

TRANSFER AGENT(S): The First National Bank of Boston, Boston, MA

NYSE SYMBOL WFT
Rec. Pr. 58.23 (4/30/01)

WEATHERFORD INTERNATIONAL, INC.

YIELD . . .
P/E RATIO . . .

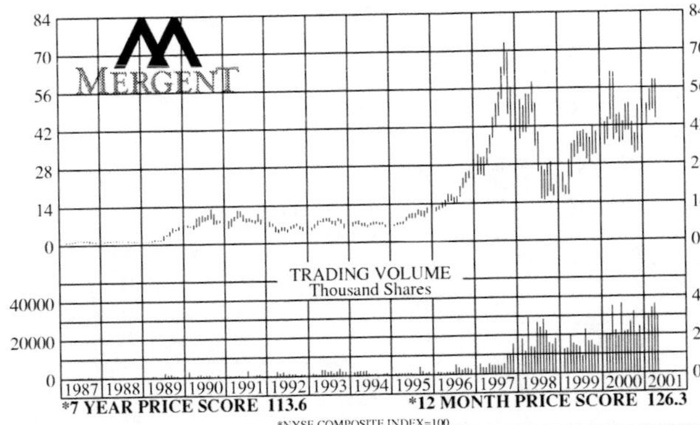

*7 YEAR PRICE SCORE 113.6 *12 MONTH PRICE SCORE 126.3

*NYSE COMPOSITE INDEX=100

INTERIM EARNINGS (Per Share):

Qtr.	Mar.	June	Sept.	Dec.
1996	0.07	0.11	0.16	0.23
1997	0.31	0.41	0.49	0.57
1998	0.63	d0.15	0.44	d0.25
1999	0.04	0.02	0.03	0.07
2000	0.09	0.12	0.19	d0.76

INTERIM DIVIDENDS (Per Share):

Amt.	Decl.	Ex.	Rec.	Pay.

No dividends paid.

CAPITALIZATION (12/31/00):

	($000)	(%)
Long-Term Debt	730,176	30.0
Deferred Income Tax	164,451	6.8
Minority Interest	198,523	8.2
Common & Surplus	1,338,458	55.0
Total	2,431,608	100.0

RECENT DEVELOPMENTS: For the year ended 12/31/00, WFT posted a loss from continuing operations of $38.9 million versus income of $16.2 million a year earlier. Results for 2000 included charges of $67.2 million related to the disposal of the Company's compression business and an accompanying $65.9 million income tax charge. Results for 2000 and 1999 excluded losses of $3.5 million and $37.1 million, respectively, from discontinued operations. Net revenues rose 46.3% to $1.81 billion.

PROSPECTS: Going forward, the Company should benefit from the introduction of new products and services as well as the addition of new capacity to meet rising demand. Separately, on 2/12/01, WFT completed the exchange of Weatherford Global Compression Services for a 48.0% interest in Universal Compression Holdings, Inc. On 3/12/01, the Company announced the purchase of Tesco Corporation's underbalanced drilling business for about $33.0 million.

BUSINESS

WEATHERFORD INTERNATIONAL, INC. (formerly EVI, Inc.) is a provider of equipment and services used for the drilling, completion and production of oil and natural gas wells. WFT's products and services are divided into four principal operating business divisions. Drilling and intervention services (48.6% of 2000 revenues) provides fishing and rental services, well installation services, cementing products and underbalanced drilling and specialty pipeline services. Completion systems (12.2%) provides a range of completion products and services. Artificial lift systems (24.2%) offers all forms of artificial lift used for the production of oil and gas. Compression services (15.0%) offers a complete range of products and services from complete field compression management to single sales and rentals of compressor units, compressor packaging and field maintenance and repair. On 5/27/98, the Company acquired Weatherford Enterra, Inc. On 4/14/00, WFT spun off its Grant Prideco drilling products business to shareholders.

REVENUES

(12/31/2000)	($000)	(%)
Products	797,146	43.9
Services & Rentals	1,017,115	56.1
Total	1,814,261	100.0

ANNUAL FINANCIAL DATA

	12/31/00	12/31/99	12/31/98	12/31/97	12/31/96	12/31/95	12/31/94
Earnings Per Share	[7] **d0.36**	[6] **0.16**	[5] **0.66**	[4] **1.77**	[3] **0.60**	[2] **0.09**	[1] **0.19**
Cash Flow Per Share	**1.53**	**1.78**	**2.41**	**2.48**	**1.01**	**0.51**	**0.75**
Tang. Book Val. Per Share	**2.61**	**7.78**	**7.01**	**2.63**	**7.66**	**5.19**	**3.76**
INCOME STATEMENT (IN MILLIONS):							
Total Revenues	1,814.3	1,240.2	2,010.7	892.3	478.0	271.7	248.5
Costs & Expenses	1,490.7	1,009.3	1,693.6	716.6	415.0	241.3	214.8
Depreciation & Amort.	206.6	166.7	170.7	33.7	16.8	12.4	14.3
Operating Income	120.3	66.8	149.0	142.0	46.3	18.0	19.5
Net Interest Inc./(Exp.)	d48.0	d41.7	d51.5	d17.4	d14.3	d16.3	d13.5
Income Before Income Taxes	71.3	28.4	99.4	128.7	31.5	2.4	6.4
Income Taxes	109.5	8.5	34.6	45.0	7.0	cr0.2	1.8
Equity Earnings/Minority Int.	2.7	d1.1	2.7	. . .	. . .	. . .	. . .
Net Income	[7] d38.9	[6] 16.2	[5] 64.8	[4] 83.7	[3] 24.5	[2] 2.6	[1] 4.6
Cash Flow	167.7	182.9	235.6	117.3	41.3	15.0	18.9
Average Shs. Outstg. (000)	109,457	102,889	97,757	47,367	40,706	29,448	25,258
BALANCE SHEET (IN MILLIONS):							
Cash & Cash Equivalents	153.8	44.4	40.2	31.9	247.8	2.9	3.1
Total Current Assets	1,241.6	869.1	1,082.4	631.0	558.7	309.2	164.8
Net Property	973.0	899.0	838.3	301.7	172.7	100.2	150.9
Total Assets	3,461.6	3,513.8	2,831.7	1,366.1	852.8	453.1	350.7
Total Current Liabilities	462.7	666.1	556.8	314.2	233.1	78.3	70.5
Long-Term Obligations	730.2	226.6	229.7	43.2	126.7	124.2	125.7
Net Stockholders' Equity	1,338.5	1,833.4	1,493.9	527.2	454.1	228.1	110.9
Net Working Capital	778.9	203.1	525.6	316.9	325.6	230.9	94.3
Year-end Shs. Outstg. (000)	109,960	108,242	97,404	47,190	45,930	37,044	25,320
STATISTICAL RECORD:							
Operating Profit Margin %	6.6	5.4	7.4	15.9	9.7	6.6	7.8
Net Profit Margin %	. . .	1.3	3.2	9.4	5.1	1.0	1.9
Return on Equity %	. . .	0.9	4.3	15.9	5.4	1.1	4.2
Return on Assets %	. . .	0.5	2.3	6.1	2.9	0.6	1.3
Debt/Total Assets %	21.1	6.4	8.1	3.2	14.9	27.4	35.8
Price Range	62.00-31.75	42.13-16.75	58.44-15.00	73.00-23.88	25.75-11.13	12.63-5.94	8.13-5.63
P/E Ratio	. . .	263.1-104.6	88.5-22.7	41.2-13.5	42.9-18.5	140.1-65.9	43.9-30.4

Statistics are as originally reported. [1] Bef. extraord. chrg. of $4.0 mil. ($0.15/sh.) [2] Bef. inc. of $8.8 mil. ($0.30/sh.) fr. disc. ops. [3] Bef. net gain of $74.4 mil. ($1.83/sh.) fr. disc. ops. & extraord. chrg. of $731,000 ($0.02/sh.) [4] Incl. gain of $3.4 mil. on sale of mkt. sec.; bef. extraord. chrg. of $9.0 mil. ($0.19/sh.) [5] Incl. merger & oth. chrgs. of $144.1 mil. [6] Bef. loss of $37.1 mil. ($0.36/sh.) fr. disc. ops. [7] Incl. $67.2 mil. chrg. rel. to disp. of bus. & inc. tax chrg. of $65.9 mil. rel. to disp. of bus.; bef. loss of $3.5 mill. ($0.03/sh.) fr. disc. ops.

OFFICERS:
B. J. Duroc-Danner, Chmn., Pres., C.E.O.
C. W. Huff, Exec. V.P., C.F.O.
B. F. Longaker, Jr., Exec. V.P.

INVESTOR CONTACT: Shareholder Relations, (713) 693-4000

PRINCIPAL OFFICE: 515 Post Oak Boulevard, Houston, TX 77027-3415

TELEPHONE NUMBER: (713) 693-4000
FAX: (713) 297-8488
WEB: www.weatherford.com

NO. OF EMPLOYEES: 11,900 (approx.)

SHAREHOLDERS: 3,056

ANNUAL MEETING: In June

INCORPORATED: MA, 1972; reincorp., DE, Sep., 1972

INSTITUTIONAL HOLDINGS:
No. of Institutions: 275
Shares Held: 100,448,965
% Held: 91.1

INDUSTRY: Oil and gas field machinery (SIC: 3533)

TRANSFER AGENT(S): American Stock Transfer & Trust Company, New York, NY

NYSE SYMBOL WBB
Rec. Pr. 37.65 (5/31/01)

WEBB (DEL) CORPORATION

YIELD ...
P/E RATIO 8.1

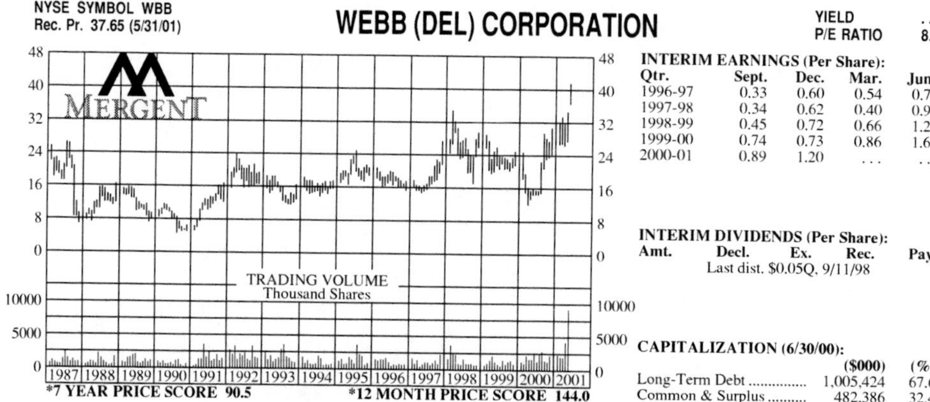

*7 YEAR PRICE SCORE 90.5 *12 MONTH PRICE SCORE 144.0

*NYSE COMPOSITE INDEX=100

INTERIM EARNINGS (Per Share):

Qtr.	Sept.	Dec.	Mar.	June
1996-97	0.33	0.60	0.54	0.75
1997-98	0.34	0.62	0.40	0.94
1998-99	0.45	0.72	0.66	1.27
1999-00	0.74	0.73	0.86	1.67
2000-01	0.89	1.20	...	...

INTERIM DIVIDENDS (Per Share):

Amt.	Decl.	Ex.	Rec.	Pay.

Last dist. $0.05Q, 9/11/98

CAPITALIZATION (6/30/00):

	($000)	(%)
Long-Term Debt	1,005,424	67.6
Common & Surplus	482,386	32.4
Total	1,487,810	100.0

RECENT DEVELOPMENTS: For the quarter ended 12/31/00, net earnings jumped 65.4% to $22.6 million from $13.7 million a year earlier. Revenues totaled $489.0 million, down 1.3% versus $495.6 million in 1999. Home closings fell 20.5% to 1,687 units from 2,122 units in the prior year, offset somewhat as average revenue per home closing grew 15.6% year-over-year. The backlog of homes under contract slid 4.7% to 3,503 units, representing an aggregate contract amount of $948.0 million. However, average contract sales amount per home rose 8.4% to $271,000.

PROSPECTS: On 5/1/01, the Company announced that it has entered into a definitive agreement to be acquired by Pulte Homes, a homebuilder with operations in 41 markets across the U.S., Argentina, Puerto Rico and Mexico, for about $1.80 billion, including the assumption of approximately $1.00 billion of WBB's debt. The combination is expected to generate annual cost savings of about $50.0 million. The transaction is anticipated to be completed by the end of July 2001, subject to shareholder and regulatory approvals.

BUSINESS

DEL WEBB CORPORATION designs, develops and markets large-scale, master-planned residential communities for active adults age 55 and over, controlling all phases of the master plan development process from land selection through the construction and sale of homes. The Company's geographic presence continues to expand with Sun Cities in Phoenix and Tucson, AZ, Las Vegas, NV, Palm Desert and Lincoln, CA, Hilton Head, SC, Georgetown, TX, Ocala, FL, and Chicago, IL. The Company also builds family and country club communities in Phoenix and Las Vegas. Coventry Homes, a conventional homebuilding operation, was purchased in 1991.

ANNUAL FINANCIAL DATA

	6/30/00	6/30/99	6/30/98	6/30/97	6/30/96	6/30/95	6/30/94
Earnings Per Share	**4.00**	**3.11**	**2.30**	**1 2.22**	**2 d0.44**	**1.87**	**1.13**
Cash Flow Per Share	**36.19**	**26.36**	**20.07**	**20.50**	**16.81**	**16.74**	**10.01**
Tang. Book Val. Per Share	**26.27**	**22.22**	**19.09**	**17.07**	**15.10**	**15.37**	**13.70**
Dividends Per Share	...	...	**0.15**	**0.20**	**0.20**	**0.20**	**0.20**
Dividend Payout %	...	...	**6.5**	**9.0**	...	**10.7**	**17.7**
INCOME STATEMENT (IN MILLIONS):							
Total Revenues	2,040.0	1,466.2	1,177.8	1,186.3	1,050.7	803.1	510.1
Costs & Expenses	1,247.7	881.2	737.1	748.4	654.7	502.0	332.4
Depreciation & Amort.	597.1	435.0	327.9	326.4	300.6	226.1	133.5
Operating Income	195.3	149.9	112.7	111.5	95.4	75.0	44.2
Net Interest Inc./(Exp.)	d85.6	d59.2	d46.2	d49.5	d42.4	d31.2	d18.0
Income Before Income Taxes	109.6	90.8	66.5	62.0	d11.9	43.8	26.2
Income Taxes	35.5	32.7	23.9	22.3	cr4.2	15.3	9.2
Net Income	74.2	58.1	42.5	1 39.7	2 d7.8	28.5	17.0
Cash Flow	671.3	493.1	370.5	366.1	292.9	254.6	150.5
Average Shs. Outstg. (000)	18,550	18,705	18,458	17,862	17,425	15,209	15,036
BALANCE SHEET (IN MILLIONS):							
Cash & Cash Equivalents	21.0	22.7	14.4	24.7	18.3	18.9	6.5
Total Current Assets	1,776.4	1,645.3	1,127.7	964.4	918.2	847.7	669.1
Net Property	96.6	72.4	33.3	20.9	27.6	29.3	36.8
Total Assets	1,980.8	1,866.8	1,310.5	1,086.7	1,024.8	925.1	758.4
Total Current Liabilities	492.9	421.4	260.8	223.8	245.3	204.5	161.4
Long-Term Obligations	1,005.4	1,040.6	703.9	563.1	514.7	491.3	395.7
Net Stockholders' Equity	482.4	404.8	345.8	299.8	264.8	229.3	201.3
Net Working Capital	1,283.5	1,223.9	866.9	740.6	672.8	643.2	507.7
Year-end Shs. Outstg. (000)	18,360	18,221	18,108	17,567	17,538	14,921	14,697
STATISTICAL RECORD:							
Operating Profit Margin %	9.6	10.2	9.6	9.4	9.1	9.3	8.7
Net Profit Margin %	3.6	4.0	3.6	3.3	...	3.5	3.3
Return on Equity %	15.4	14.4	12.3	13.2	...	12.4	8.5
Return on Assets %	3.7	3.1	3.2	3.7	...	3.1	2.2
Debt/Total Assets %	50.8	55.7	53.7	51.8	50.2	53.1	52.2
Price Range	30.69-12.00	29.00-19.56	34.88-17.06	27.38-14.75	20.75-15.25	25.00-16.63	18.38-13.63
P/E Ratio	7.7-3.0	9.3-6.3	15.2-7.4	12.3-6.6	...	13.4-8.9	16.3-12.1
Average Yield %	...	...	0.6	0.9	1.1	1.0	1.3

Statistics are as originally reported. 1 Bef. $1.3 mil ($0.07/sh) extraord. chg. 2 Incl. $42.3 mil ($2.35/sh) after-tax chg.

OFFICERS:
P. J. Dion, Chmn.
L. C. Hanneman, Jr., Pres., C.E.O.
J. A. Spencer, Exec. V.P., C.F.O.

INVESTOR CONTACT: Investor Relations Dept., (800) 545-9322

PRINCIPAL OFFICE: 6001 North 24th Street, Phoenix, AZ 85016

TELEPHONE NUMBER: (602) 808-8000
FAX: (602) 808-8097
WEB: www.delwebb.com
NO. OF EMPLOYEES: 4,700 (avg.)
SHAREHOLDERS: 2,595 (approx.)
ANNUAL MEETING: In Nov.
INCORPORATED: AR, Mar., 1946; reincorp., DE, 1994

INSTITUTIONAL HOLDINGS:
No. of Institutions: 101
Shares Held: 11,374,880
% Held: 61.1

INDUSTRY: Operative builders (SIC: 1531)

TRANSFER AGENT(S): Wells Fargo Bank Minnesota, N.A., South St. Paul, MN

NYSE SYMBOL WMK
Rec. Pr. 34.98 (5/31/01)

WEIS MARKETS, INC.

YIELD 3.1%
P/E RATIO 19.8

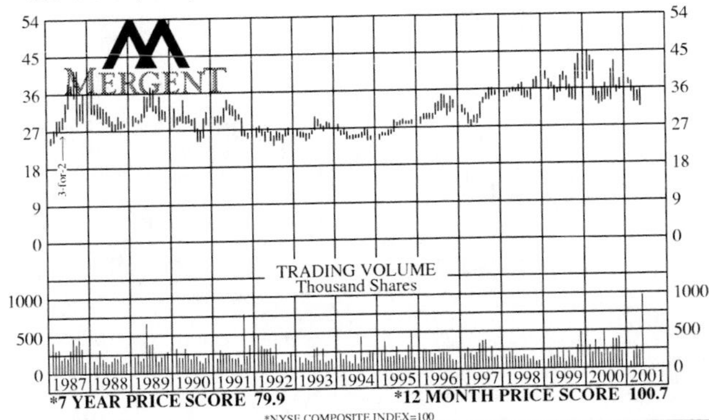

***7 YEAR PRICE SCORE 79.9** ***12 MONTH PRICE SCORE 100.7**

*NYSE COMPOSITE INDEX=100

INTERIM EARNINGS (Per Share):

Qtr.	Mar.	June	Sept.	Dec.
1996	0.46	0.46	0.47	0.48
1997	0.43	0.46	0.46	0.52
1998	0.64	0.40	0.44	0.52
1999	0.51	0.46	0.46	0.48
2000	0.43	0.52	0.46	0.36

INTERIM DIVIDENDS (Per Share):

Amt.	Decl.	Ex.	Rec.	Pay.
0.27Q	6/06/00	8/03/00	8/07/00	8/24/00
0.27Q	10/30/00	11/01/00	11/03/00	11/17/00
0.27Q	1/29/01	1/31/01	2/02/01	2/16/01
0.27Q	4/20/01	4/26/01	4/30/01	5/14/01

Indicated div.: $1.08 (Div. Reinv. Plan)

CAPITALIZATION (12/30/00):

	($000)	(%)
Deferred Income Tax	17,731	1.8
Common & Surplus	947,886	98.2
Total	965,617	100.0

RECENT DEVELOPMENTS: For the 53 weeks ended 12/30/00, net income totaled $73.8 million, down 7.4% compared with $79.7 million in the corresponding 52-week period the previous year. Results in 2000 were negatively affected by a fourth-quarter pre-tax charge of $4.9 million related to a litigation settlement. The 1999 earnings included a one-time pre-tax gain of $3.4 million from the sale of an investment. Net sales climbed 2.8% to $2.06 billion from $2.00 billion a year earlier.

PROSPECTS: Profits continue to be squeezed by increased costs for wages, benefits and fuel. Going forward, the Company will focus on opening new stores and remodeling or expanding existing locations in an effort to spur sales growth. In 2000, the Company opened nine superstores, including five new stores and four replacement units, remodeled or expanded six stores, and closed four smaller, under-performing locations.

BUSINESS

WEIS MARKETS, INC. operates 163 supermarkets in Pennsylvania, New Jersey, New York, Maryland, Virginia and West Virginia. The Company supplies its retail stores from distribution centers in Sunbury, Northumberland, and Milton, PA. Many of WMK's private label products are supplied by the Company's ice cream manufacturing plant, fresh meat processing plant, and milk processing plant. The Company also owns SuperPetz, an operator of 33 pet supply stores in 11 states. On 4/8/00, the Company completed the sale of Weis Food Service, its regional food service division.

QUARTERLY DATA

(12/30/2000)($000)	REV	INC
1st Quarter	519,750	17,878
2nd Quarter	508,957	21,658
3nd Quarter	485,875	19,103
4rd Quarter	546,394	15,184

ANNUAL FINANCIAL DATA

	12/30/00	12/25/99	12/26/98	12/27/97	12/28/96	12/30/95	12/31/94
Earnings Per Share	**1 1.77**	**1 1.91**	**1 2.00**	**1.87**	**1.87**	**1.84**	**1.75**
Cash Flow Per Share	**2.99**	**3.02**	**3.11**	**2.91**	**2.77**	**2.61**	**2.45**
Tang. Book Val. Per Share	**22.74**	**22.03**	**21.33**	**20.28**	**19.47**	**18.61**	**17.53**
Dividends Per Share	**1.06**	**1.02**	**0.98**	**0.94**	**0.88**	**0.80**	**0.74**
Dividend Payout %	**59.9**	**53.4**	**49.0**	**50.3**	**47.1**	**43.5**	**42.3**
INCOME STATEMENT (IN MILLIONS):							
Total Revenues	2,061.0	2,004.9	1,867.5	1,818.8	1,753.2	1,646.4	1,556.7
Costs & Expenses	1,930.0	1,865.6	1,744.8	1,690.2	1,624.5	1,527.1	1,446.1
Depreciation & Amort.	50.9	46.3	46.3	43.5	38.1	33.2	30.6
Operating Income	80.1	93.0	76.4	85.1	90.6	86.2	80.0
Income Before Income Taxes	116.8	124.0	134.5	118.6	120.7	121.7	117.2
Income Taxes	43.0	44.3	50.8	40.4	41.9	42.3	40.9
Equity Earnings/Minority Int.	...	...	...	...	...	0.2	...
Net Income	1 73.8	1 79.7	1 83.7	78.2	78.9	79.4	76.3
Cash Flow	124.7	126.0	130.0	121.7	117.0	112.6	106.9
Average Shs. Outstg. (000)	41,695	41,718	41,776	41,843	42,280	43,083	43,662
BALANCE SHEET (IN MILLIONS):							
Cash & Cash Equivalents	413.6	389.2	411.1	377.3	390.7	435.5	457.0
Total Current Assets	617.2	602.6	608.2	575.8	590.6	606.5	617.8
Net Property	441.8	439.4	398.4	365.2	343.9	286.0	245.3
Total Assets	1,085.9	1,058.2	1,029.2	971.8	966.3	923.2	892.1
Total Current Liabilities	120.3	120.8	118.7	104.3	127.4	115.3	112.3
Net Stockholders' Equity	947.9	918.5	890.6	847.3	818.5	791.6	762.4
Net Working Capital	496.9	481.7	489.5	471.6	463.3	491.1	505.4
Year-end Shs. Outstg. (000)	41,688	41,692	41,756	41,773	42,041	42,534	43,484
STATISTICAL RECORD:							
Operating Profit Margin %	3.9	4.6	4.1	4.7	5.2	5.2	5.1
Net Profit Margin %	3.6	4.0	4.5	4.3	4.5	4.8	4.9
Return on Equity %	7.8	8.7	9.4	9.2	9.6	10.0	10.0
Return on Assets %	6.8	7.5	8.1	8.0	8.2	8.6	8.5
Price Range	45.25-32.00	44.31-32.88	38.88-33.25	36.25-26.88	34.88-27.75	29.00-24.00	28.00-23.88
P/E Ratio	25.6-18.1	23.2-17.2	19.4-16.6	19.4-14.4	18.6-14.8	15.8-13.0	16.0-13.6
Average Yield %	2.7	2.6	2.7	3.0	2.8	3.0	2.9

Statistics are as originally reported. 1 Incl. $4.9 mil pre-tax litigation chg., 2000; $3.4 mil pre-tax gain fr. sale of asset, 1999; $8.3 mil ($0.20/sh) after-tax gain from sale of stk., 1998.

OFFICERS:
R. F. Weis, Chmn., Treas.
N. S. Rich, Pres.
R. P. Hermanns, V.P., C.O.O.
W. R. Mills, V.P.-Fin., Sec.

PRINCIPAL OFFICE: 1000 South Second Street, P.O. Box 471, Sunbury, PA 17801-0471

TELEPHONE NUMBER: (570) 286-4571
FAX: (570) 286-3286
WEB: www.weismarkets.com

NO. OF EMPLOYEES: 20,700 (approx.)

SHAREHOLDERS: 5,951 (approx.)

ANNUAL MEETING: In June

INCORPORATED: PA, Dec., 1924

INSTITUTIONAL HOLDINGS:
No. of Institutions: 72
Shares Held: 4,763,780
% Held: 11.4

INDUSTRY: Grocery stores (SIC: 5411)

TRANSFER AGENT(S): American Stock Transfer & Trust Company, New York, NY

NYSE SYMBOL WLM
Rec. Pr. 18.65 (4/30/01)

WELLMAN, INC.

YIELD 1.9%
P/E RATIO 21.2

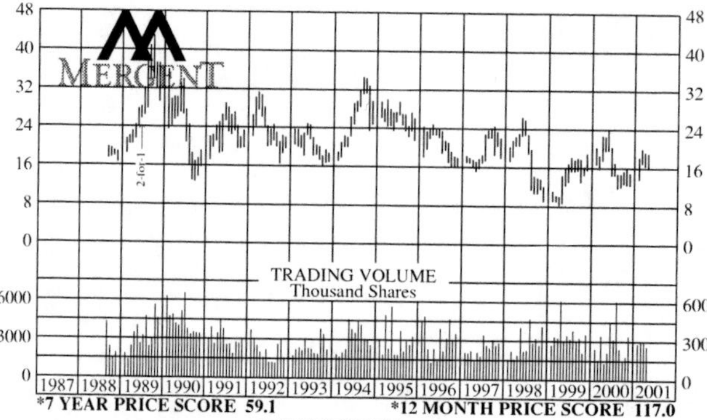

*7 YEAR PRICE SCORE 59.1 *12 MONTH PRICE SCORE 117.0

*NYSE COMPOSITE INDEX=100

INTERIM EARNINGS (Per Share):

Qtr.	Mar.	June	Sept.	Dec.
1996	0.35	0.35	d0.09	0.19
1997	0.28	0.17	0.31	0.21
1998	0.41	0.46	0.25	d0.74
1999	0.06	d0.34	d0.13	0.11
2000	0.13	0.22	0.26	0.27

INTERIM DIVIDENDS (Per Share):

Amt.	Decl.	Ex.	Rec.	Pay.
0.09Q	5/16/00	5/30/00	6/01/00	6/15/00
0.09Q	8/11/00	8/30/00	9/01/00	9/15/00
0.09Q	11/09/00	11/29/00	12/01/00	12/15/00
0.09Q	2/20/01	2/27/01	3/01/01	3/15/01
0.09Q	5/16/01	5/30/01	6/01/01	6/15/01

Indicated div.: $0.36

CAPITALIZATION (12/31/00):

	($000)	(%)
Long-Term Debt	371,672	37.1
Common & Surplus	629,609	62.9
Total	1,001,281	100.0

RECENT DEVELOPMENTS: For the year ended 12/31/00, net income was $27.8 million compared with a net loss of $9.3 million, before an accounting charge, in 1999. Results included restructuring income of $800,000 in 2000 and a restructuring charge of $17.4 million in 1999. Net sales were $1.12 billion, up 19.4% from $935.4 million a year earlier.

PROSPECTS: Looking ahead, WLM expects earnings for its PET resins businesses to improve in 2001; however, this may be mitigated by lower margins in the domestic fiber businesses. The domestic fibers business continues to be negatively affected by weak demand, primarily resulting from imports throughout the textile chain. However, the Company expects business conditions to improve as the year progresses.

BUSINESS

WELLMAN, INC. manufactures and markets polyester products, including Fortrel® brand polyester textile fibers, polyester fibers made from recycled raw materials and PermaClear® PET (polyethylene terephthalate) packaging resins and EcoClear® brand PET packaging made from 100% recycled postconsumer PET beverage containers. The Company currently has annual capacity to manufacture approximately 1.10 billion pounds of fiber and 1.10 billion pounds of resins worldwide at six major production facilities in the U.S. and Europe. The world's largest PET plastic recycler, Wellman utilizes a significant amount of recycled raw materials in its manufacturing operations. The Company operates through two segments: the Fibers and Recycled Products Group (FRPG) and the Packaging Products Group (PPG). In 2000, FRPG contributed 56.0% of sales; and PPG, 44.0%.

REVENUES

(12/31/2000)	($000)	(%)
Fibers & Recycled Product	620,062	55.5
Packaging Products ...	496,644	44.5
Total	1,116,706	100.0

ANNUAL FINANCIAL DATA

	12/31/00	12/31/99	12/31/98	12/31/97	12/31/96	12/31/95	12/31/94
Earnings Per Share	**[5] 0.87**	**[4] d0.29**	**[1] 0.37**	**[3] 0.97**	**0.81**	**[2] 2.20**	**1.94**
Cash Flow Per Share	**3.03**	**1.95**	**2.63**	**3.29**	**2.88**	**4.14**	**3.72**
Tang. Book Val. Per Share	**12.28**	**11.54**	**12.17**	**11.71**	**10.72**	**10.62**	**8.33**
Dividends Per Share	**0.36**	**0.36**	**0.36**	**0.35**	**0.31**	**0.27**	**0.23**
Dividend Payout %	**41.4**	**...**	**97.3**	**36.1**	**38.3**	**12.3**	**11.9**
INCOME STATEMENT (IN MILLIONS):							
Total Revenues	1,116.7	935.4	968.0	1,083.2	1,098.8	1,109.4	936.1
Costs & Expenses	993.1	865.1	847.2	941.5	962.7	911.1	754.9
Depreciation & Amort.	68.7	70.1	70.8	72.4	67.9	65.4	59.5
Operating Income	54.9	0.2	50.0	69.3	68.1	132.9	121.7
Net Interest Inc./(Exp.)	d18.0	d13.3	d8.3	d12.2	d14.0	d11.7	d13.7
Income Before Income Taxes	36.9	d13.1	18.4	51.2	54.1	115.7	108.0
Income Taxes	9.1	cr3.8	6.7	20.8	27.6	41.7	43.2
Net Income	[5] 27.8	[4] d9.3	[1] 11.7	[3] 30.4	26.5	[2] 74.1	64.8
Cash Flow	96.5	60.8	82.4	102.7	94.5	139.4	124.3
Average Shs. Outstg. (000)	31,884	31,203	31,391	31,269	32,774	33,699	33,417
BALANCE SHEET (IN MILLIONS):							
Cash & Cash Equivalents	...	...	...	...	2.1	3.9	21.6
Total Current Assets	276.8	264.5	304.3	283.6	297.0	364.3	272.2
Net Property	792.3	815.6	917.2	754.5	597.6	527.6	447.9
Total Assets	1,334.1	1,344.0	1,493.5	1,319.2	1,203.9	1,210.7	1,040.6
Total Current Liabilities	139.5	162.3	253.1	112.9	105.5	145.8	84.3
Long-Term Obligations	371.7	375.7	410.7	394.5	319.4	272.9	256.3
Net Stockholders' Equity	629.6	611.4	643.3	634.4	623.9	650.3	577.6
Net Working Capital	137.3	102.2	51.2	170.7	191.6	218.5	187.9
Year-end Shs. Outstg. (000)	31,757	31,439	31,316	31,138	31,112	33,441	33,192
STATISTICAL RECORD:							
Operating Profit Margin %	4.9	...	5.2	6.4	6.2	12.0	13.0
Net Profit Margin %	2.5	...	1.2	2.8	2.4	6.7	6.9
Return on Equity %	4.4	...	1.8	4.8	4.3	11.4	11.2
Return on Assets %	2.1	...	0.8	2.3	2.2	6.1	6.2
Debt/Total Assets %	27.9	28.0	27.5	29.9	26.5	22.5	24.6
Price Range	24.00-11.81	19.00-8.25	26.44-9.00	24.56-15.13	24.88-15.88	30.00-21.50	34.63-17.13
P/E Ratio	27.6-13.6	...	71.4-24.3	25.3-15.6	30.7-19.6	13.6-9.8	17.8-8.8
Average Yield %	2.0	2.6	2.0	1.8	1.5	1.0	0.9

Statistics are as originally reported. Adj. for stk. split: 2-for-1, 6/98. [1] Incl. restruct. chrg. of $6.9 mill. [2] Incl. $3.4 mill. net loss on divestitures. [3] Incl. chrg. of $8.1 mill. ($0.26/sh.) of unusual & nonrecur. items. [4] Incl. restr. chrg. of $17.4 mill.; bef. an acctg. change chrg. of $1.8 mill. [5] Incl. restruct. income of $800,000.

OFFICERS:
T. M. Duff, Chmn., C.E.O.
C. J. Christenson, Pres., C.O.O.
K. R. Phillips, V.P., C.F.O., Treas.
M. J. Rosenblum, V.P., C.A.O., Contr.

INVESTOR CONTACT: Dennis Sabourin, Inv. Rel. Mgr., (732) 935-7321

PRINCIPAL OFFICE: 595 Shrewsbury Avenue, Shrewsbury, NJ 07702

TELEPHONE NUMBER: (732) 212-3300
WEB: www.wellmaninc.com

NO. OF EMPLOYEES: 2,600 (approx.)

SHAREHOLDERS: 856 (approx.)

ANNUAL MEETING: In May

INCORPORATED: DE, July, 1985

INSTITUTIONAL HOLDINGS:
No. of Institutions: 106
Shares Held: 27,063,149
% Held: 85.2

INDUSTRY: Organic fibers, noncellulosic (SIC: 2824)

TRANSFER AGENT(S): Continental Stock Transfer and Trust Company, New York, NY

NYSE SYMBOL WLP
Rec. Pr. 98.25 (4/30/01)

WELLPOINT HEALTH NETWORKS, INC.

YIELD	...
P/E RATIO	18.6

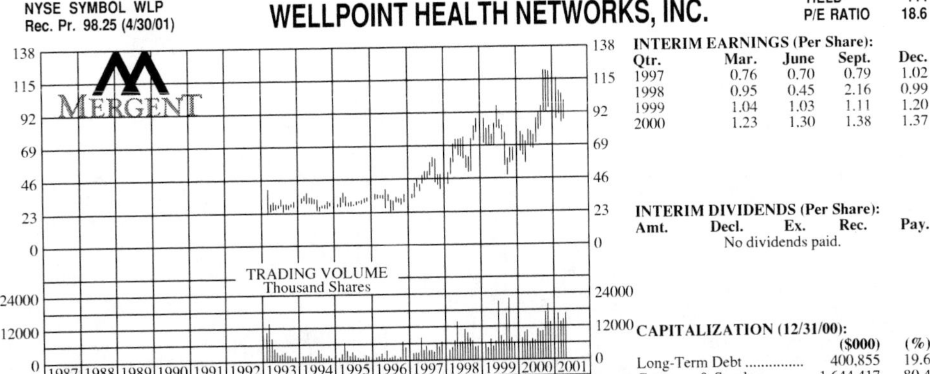

*7 YEAR PRICE SCORE 124.3 *12 MONTH PRICE SCORE 108.4

*NYSE COMPOSITE INDEX=100

INTERIM EARNINGS (Per Share):

Qtr.	Mar.	June	Sept.	Dec.
1997	0.76	0.70	0.79	1.02
1998	0.95	0.45	2.16	0.99
1999	1.04	1.03	1.11	1.20
2000	1.23	1.30	1.38	1.37

INTERIM DIVIDENDS (Per Share):

Amt.	Decl.	Ex.	Rec.	Pay.

No dividends paid.

CAPITALIZATION (12/31/00):

	($000)	(%)
Long-Term Debt	400,855	19.6
Common & Surplus	1,644,417	80.4
Total	2,045,272	100.0

RECENT DEVELOPMENTS: For the year ended 12/31/00, the Company reported net income of $342.3 million compared with income of $297.2 million, before an extraordinary gain of $1.9 million and an accounting charge of $20.6 million, in the previous year. Total revenues advanced 23.3% to $9.23 billion from $7.49 billion in the prior year. Operating income was $634.2 million, up 15.7% from $548.3 million the year before.

PROSPECTS: On 3/12/01, the Company announced that it acquired Cerulean Companies, Inc., the parent company of Blue Cross and Blue Shield of Georgia, in a $700.0 million all-cash transaction. The acquisition will allow WLP to offer innovative hybrid products that combine features of its open-access and managed care plans to an additional 1.88 billion members of Blue Cross and Blue Shield of Georgia.

BUSINESS

WELLPOINT HEALTH NETWORKS, INC. offers a broad range of network-based health products, including preferred provider organizations (PPOs), health maintenance organizations (HMOs) and point-of-service (POS) and other hybrid plans and indemnity plans to the large and small employer, individual, Medicaid and senior markets. WLP serves more than 7.9 million medical members and 40.0 million specialty members nationally through Blue Cross of California and UNICARE Life and Health Insurance Company throughout other parts of the country. In addition, WLP offers a variety of specialty and other products and services, including pharmacy, dental, vision, utilization management, long term care insurance, life insurance, preventive care, disability insurance, behavioral health, COBRA and flexible benefits account administration. The Company offers managed care services for self-funded employers, including underwriting, actuarial services, network access, medical cost management and claims processing.

ANNUAL FINANCIAL DATA

	12/31/00	12/31/99	12/31/98	12/31/97	12/31/96	12/31/95	12/31/94
Earnings Per Share	**5.29**	[1][2] **4.38**	[4] **4.55**	[3] **3.27**	**3.04**	[3] **1.81**	**2.14**
Cash Flow Per Share	**6.35**	**5.31**	**5.26**	**4.03**	**3.56**	**2.03**	**2.35**
Tang. Book Val. Per Share	**16.89**	**14.28**	**13.19**	**7.52**	**4.78**	**15.53**	**12.83**
INCOME STATEMENT (IN MILLIONS):							
Total Revenues	9,229.0	7,485.4	6,478.4	5,826.4	4,169.8	3,107.1	2,791.7
Costs & Expenses	8,523.8	6,872.8	5,981.4	5,320.8	3,738.4	2,769.6	2,411.4
Depreciation & Amort.	71.0	64.3	50.2	52.7	35.2	22.0	20.3
Operating Income	634.2	548.3	446.8	453.0	396.3	315.5	360.0
Net Interest Inc./(Exp.)	d24.0	d20.2	d26.9	d36.7	d36.6	...	...
Income Before Income Taxes	564.3	487.3	392.0	382.2	339.5	302.8	352.0
Income Taxes	222.0	190.1	72.4	154.8	137.5	122.8	138.9
Net Income	342.3	[1][2] 297.2	[4] 319.5	[3] 227.4	202.0	[3] 180.0	213.2
Cash Flow	413.3	361.6	369.7	280.1	237.2	202.0	233.5
Average Shs. Outstg. (000)	65,109	68,096	70,259	69,462	66,527	99,500	99,500
BALANCE SHEET (IN MILLIONS):							
Cash & Cash Equivalents	3,663.2	3,150.4	2,661.0	2,836.6	2,041.6	2,245.0	371.4
Total Current Assets	4,500.4	3,816.0	3,434.4	3,505.8	2,538.5	2,469.1	586.2
Net Property	151.0	125.9	131.5	115.2	82.7	43.0	33.9
Total Assets	5,504.7	4,593.2	4,225.8	4,533.4	3,405.5	2,685.6	2,385.6
Total Current Liabilities	3,072.9	2,527.3	2,182.9	2,344.3	1,545.5	840.3	874.8
Long-Term Obligations	400.9	347.9	300.0	388.0	625.0	...	...
Net Stockholders' Equity	1,644.4	1,312.7	1,315.2	1,223.2	870.5	1,670.2	1,418.9
Net Working Capital	1,427.5	1,288.7	1,251.6	1,161.5	993.0	1,628.7	d288.6
Year-end Shs. Outstg. (000)	62,825	63,626	67,119	69,774	66,527	99,500	99,500
STATISTICAL RECORD:							
Operating Profit Margin %	6.9	7.3	6.9	7.8	9.5	10.2	12.9
Net Profit Margin %	3.7	4.0	4.9	3.9	4.8	5.8	7.6
Return on Equity %	20.8	22.6	24.3	18.6	23.2	10.8	15.0
Return on Assets %	6.2	6.5	7.6	5.0	5.9	6.7	8.9
Debt/Total Assets %	7.3	7.6	7.1	8.6	18.4	...	...
Price Range	121.50-56.94	97.00-48.25	87.88-42.06	61.13-32.50	39.13-23.38	37.00-27.00	37.00-24.25
P/E Ratio	23.0-10.8	22.1-11.0	19.3-9.2	18.7-9.9	12.9-7.7	20.4-14.9	17.3-11.3

Statistics are as originally reported. [1] Bef. extraord. gain of $1.9 mill. [2] Bef. acctg. chrg. of $20.6 mill. [3] Incl. nonrecurr. chrg. of $14.5 mill., 1997; $57.1 mill., 1995. [4] Bef. a loss of $88.3 mill. fr. disposal of workers' compensation.

OFFICERS:
L. D. Schaeffer, Chmn., C.E.O.
D. C. Colby, Exec. V.P., C.F.O.
T. C. Geiser, Exec. V.P., Gen. Couns., Sec.

INVESTOR CONTACT: John Cygul, V.P., Inv. Rel., Corp. Comm., (805) 557-6786

PRINCIPAL OFFICE: 1 Wellpoint Way, Thousand Oaks, CA 91362

TELEPHONE NUMBER: (818) 234-4000
WEB: www.wellpoint.com

NO. OF EMPLOYEES: 10,900 (approx.)

SHAREHOLDERS: 660 (approx.)

ANNUAL MEETING: In May

INCORPORATED: DE, Aug., 1992

INSTITUTIONAL HOLDINGS:
No. of Institutions: 306
Shares Held: 58,854,061
% Held: 93.3

INDUSTRY: Health and allied services, nec (SIC: 8099)

TRANSFER AGENT(S): Mellon Investor Services, Ridgefield, NJ

NYSE SYMBOL WFC
Rec. Pr. 46.97 (4/30/01)

WELLS FARGO & COMPANY

YIELD 2.0%
P/E RATIO 18.6

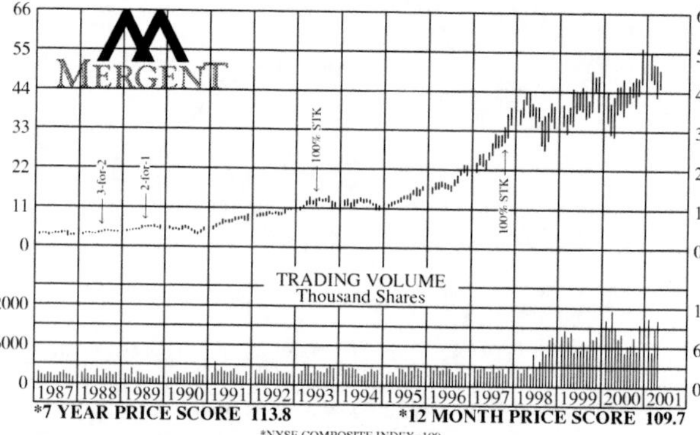

*7 YEAR PRICE SCORE 113.8 *12 MONTH PRICE SCORE 109.7

*NYSE COMPOSITE INDEX=100

INTERIM EARNINGS (Per Share):

Qtr.	Mar.	June	Sept.	Dec.
1997	0.42	0.43	0.45	0.46
1998	0.41	0.44	0.45	d0.12
1999	0.53	0.55	0.57	0.58
2000	0.61	0.63	0.64	0.65

INTERIM DIVIDENDS (Per Share):

Amt.	Decl.	Ex.	Rec.	Pay.
0.22Q	4/25/00	5/03/00	5/05/00	6/01/00
0.22Q	7/25/00	8/02/00	8/04/00	9/01/00
0.24Q	10/23/00	11/01/00	11/03/00	12/01/00
0.24Q	1/23/01	1/31/01	2/02/01	3/01/01
0.24Q	4/24/01	5/02/01	5/04/01	6/01/01

Indicated div.: $0.96 (Div. Reinv. Plan)

CAPITALIZATION (12/31/00):

	($000)	(%)
Total Deposits	169,559,000	74.3
Long-Term Debt	32,046,000	14.0
Preferred Stock	385,000	0.2
Common & Surplus	26,103,000	11.4
Total	228,093,000	100.0

RECENT DEVELOPMENTS: For the year ended 12/31/00, net income increased to $4.03 billion from $4.01 billion in 1999. Results for 2000 and 1999 included pre-tax net gains of $58.0 million and $16.0 million, respectively, on dispositions of premises and equipment. Net interest income rose 7.4% to $10.87 billion. Total non-interest income increased 10.9% to $8.84 billion. Total non-interest expense, including the above gains, grew 11.2% to $11.83 billion.

PROSPECTS: On 3/8/01, WFC announced that it has signed a definitive agreement to acquire ACO Brokerage Holdings Corporation, parent of Acordia, which ranks fifth largest among all U.S. insurance agencies. Acordia reported more than $400.0 million in annual revenue and operates 112 offices in 29 states. The transaction is expected to close in the second quarter of 2001. Separately, WFC acquired Conseco Finance Vendor Services, a leasing company.

BUSINESS

WELLS FARGO & COMPANY (formerly Norwest Corporation), with $272.43 billion in assets as of 12/31/00, is a diversified financial services company providing banking, insurance, investments, mortgage and consumer finance through more than 5,400 financial services stores and the Internet across North America and elsewhere internationally. In early November 1998, the former Wells Fargo & Company merged with WFC Holdings, a subsidiary of Norwest Corp., with WFC Holdings as the surviving corporation. In connection with the merger, Norwest changed its name to Wells Fargo & Company. On 10/25/00, WFC acquired First Security, creating the largest banking franchise in the western region of the U.S.

LOAN DISTRIBUTION

(12/31/00)	($000)	(%)
Commercial	50,518	26.9
Real Estate 1-4 Family	18,464	9.8
Other Real Estate	23,972	12.7
Real Estate Construction	7,715	4.0
Total Consumer	29,101	15.4
Foreign	48,808	25.9
Lease Financing	10,023	5.3
Total	188,601	100.0

ANNUAL FINANCIAL DATA

	12/31/00	12/31/99	② 12/31/98	12/31/97	12/31/96	12/31/95	12/31/94
Earnings Per Share	④ 2.33	④ 2.23	③ 1.17	1.75	① 1.54	1.38	1.23
Tang. Book Val. Per Share	9.11	7.87	6.71	8.90	7.88	7.05	5.34
Dividends Per Share	0.90	0.79	0.70	0.61	0.53	0.45	0.38
Dividend Payout %	38.6	35.2	59.8	35.1	34.2	32.6	31.2
INCOME STATEMENT (IN MILLIONS):							
Total Interest Income	18,725.0	14,375.0	14,055.0	6,697.4	6,318.3	5,717.3	4,393.7
Total Interest Expense	7,860.0	5,020.0	5,065.0	2,664.0	2,617.0	2,448.0	1,590.1
Net Interest Income	10,865.0	9,355.0	8,990.0	4,033.4	3,701.3	3,269.3	2,803.6
Provision for Loan Losses	1,329.0	1,045.0	1,545.0	524.7	394.7	312.4	164.9
Non-Interest Income	8,843.0	7,420.0	6,427.0	2,962.3	2,564.6	1,865.0	1,638.3
Non-Interest Expense	11,830.0	9,782.0	10,579.0	4,421.3	4,089.7	3,399.1	3,096.4
Income Before Taxes	6,549.0	5,948.0	3,293.0	2,049.7	1,781.5	1,422.8	1,180.6
Net Income	④ 4,026.0	④ 3,747.0	③ 1,950.0	1,351.0	① 1,153.9	956.0	800.4
Average Shs. Outstg. (000)	1,718,400	1,665,200	1,641,800	750,059	739,400	663,358	630,184
BALANCE SHEET (IN MILLIONS):							
Cash & Due from Banks	16,978.0	13,250.0	12,731.0	4,912.1	4,856.6	4,320.3	3,431.2
Securities Avail. for Sale	38,655.0	38,518.0	31,997.0	18,470.8	16,433.6	15,393.6	13,774.1
Total Loans & Leases	161,124.0	119,464.0	107,994.0	44,634.1	41,154.2	37,830.7	33,703.6
Allowance for Credit Losses	3,719.0	3,170.0	3,134.0	3,346.4	2,814.0	2,594.8	1,917.5
Net Loans & Leases	157,405.0	116,294.0	104,860.0	41,287.7	38,340.2	35,235.9	31,786.1
Total Assets	272,426.0	218,102.0	202,475.0	88,540.2	80,175.4	72,134.4	59,315.9
Total Deposits	169,559.0	132,708.0	136,788.0	55,457.1	50,130.2	42,028.8	36,424.0
Long-Term Obligations	32,046.0	23,375.0	19,709.0	12,766.7	13,082.2	13,676.8	9,186.3
Total Liabilities	245,938.0	195,971.0	181,716.0	81,518.0	74,111.2	66,822.3	55,469.5
Net Stockholders' Equity	26,488.0	22,131.0	20,759.0	7,022.2	6,064.2	5,312.1	3,846.4
Year-end Shs. Outstg. (000)	1,714,646	1,626,850	1,644,058	758,619	737,406	705,520	621,284
STATISTICAL RECORD:							
Return on Equity %	15.2	16.9	9.4	19.2	19.0	18.0	20.8
Return on Assets %	1.5	1.7	1.0	1.5	1.4	1.3	1.3
Equity/Assets %	9.7	10.1	10.3	7.9	7.6	7.4	6.5
Non-Int. Exp./Tot. Inc. %	60.0	58.3	68.6	63.2	65.3	66.2	69.7
Price Range	56.38-31.38	49.94-32.19	43.88-27.50	39.50-21.38	23.44-15.25	17.38-11.31	14.13-10.50
P/E Ratio	24.2-13.5	22.4-14.4	37.5-23.5	22.6-12.2	15.3-9.9	12.6-8.2	11.5-8.6
Average Yield %	2.1	1.9	2.0	2.0	2.7	3.1	3.1

Statistics are as originally reported. Adj. for 2-for-1 stock split, 10/97. ① Incl. one-time SAIF pre-tax chg. of $19.0 mill. ② Reflects 11/98 merger with Norwest Corp. & subsequent name change to Wells Fargo & Co. Years prior to 12/31/98 represent the results of Norwest Corp. only. ③ Incl. $1.20 bill. in merger-related & other chgs., a $320.0 mill. prov. for loan losses, & a pre-tax net loss of $325.0 mill. on the disposition of premises & equip. ④ Incl. pre-tax net gain on dispositions of premises & equipment of $58.0 mill., 2000; $16.0 mill., 1999.

OFFICERS:
R. M. Kovacevich, Chmn., Pres., C.E.O.
L. S. Biller, Vice-Chmn., C.O.O.
R. J. Kari, Exec. V.P., C.F.O.

INVESTOR CONTACT: Robert S. Strickland, Sr Vice President, (415) 396-0523

PRINCIPAL OFFICE: 420 Montgomery Street, San Francisco, CA 94163

TELEPHONE NUMBER: (800) 411-4932
WEB: www.wellsfargo.com

NO. OF EMPLOYEES: 92,178

SHAREHOLDERS: 90,277

ANNUAL MEETING: In April

INCORPORATED: DE, Jan., 1929

INSTITUTIONAL HOLDINGS:
No. of Institutions: 871
Shares Held: 1,078,800,400
% Held: 62.9

INDUSTRY: National commercial banks (SIC: 6021)

TRANSFER AGENT(S): Wells Fargo Shareowner Services, St. Paul, MN

NYSE SYMBOL WEN
Rec. Pr. 25.33 (4/30/01)

WENDY'S INTERNATIONAL, INC.

YIELD 0.9%
P/E RATIO 17.7

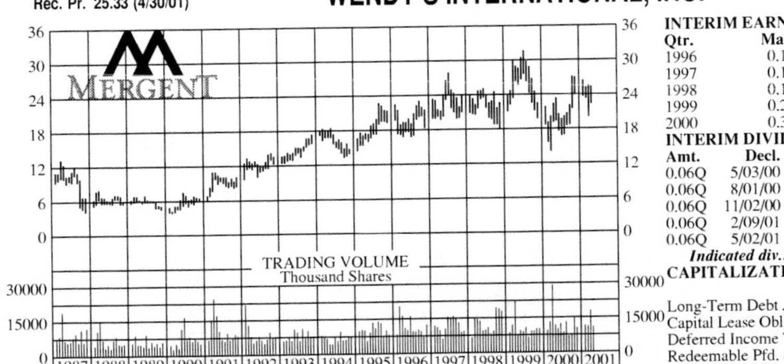

*7 YEAR PRICE SCORE 76.4 *12 MONTH PRICE SCORE 113.3
*NYSE COMPOSITE INDEX=100

INTERIM EARNINGS (Per Share):

Qtr.	Mar.	June	Sept.	Dec.
1996	0.16	0.38	0.36	0.30
1997	0.19	0.42	0.39	d0.03
1998	0.18	0.34	0.33	0.09
1999	0.25	0.39	0.35	0.33
2000	0.30	0.43	0.41	0.29

INTERIM DIVIDENDS (Per Share):

Amt.	Decl.	Ex.	Rec.	Pay.
0.06Q	5/03/00	5/11/00	5/15/00	5/26/00
0.06Q	8/01/00	8/09/00	8/11/00	8/25/00
0.06Q	11/02/00	11/09/00	11/13/00	11/28/00
0.06Q	2/09/01	2/15/01	2/20/01	3/06/01
0.06Q	5/02/01	5/10/01	5/14/01	5/25/01

Indicated div.: $0.24 (Div. Reinv. Plan)

CAPITALIZATION (12/31/00):

	($000)	(%)
Long-Term Debt	204,027	12.4
Capital Lease Obligations	44,357	2.7
Deferred Income Tax	72,750	4.4
Redeemable Pfd. Stock	200,000	12.1
Common & Surplus	1,126,143	68.4
Total	1,647,277	100.0

RECENT DEVELOPMENTS: For the twelve months ended 12/31/00, net income inched up 1.8% to $169.6 million compared with $166.6 million in the previous year. Total revenues climbed 8.2% to $2.24 billion from $2.07 billion in the prior year. Retail sales jumped 8.5% to $1.81 billion, while franchise revenues rose 7.1% to $429.1 million. WEN's domestic operating margin slipped 20 basis points to 16.5% from 1999, mainly due to higher average wages.

PROSPECTS: WEN expects same-store sales growth at Wendy's® U.S. company restaurants to range from 3.0% to 3.5% and same-store sales growth for Tim Horton® restaurants in Canada to range between 5.0% and 6.0%. Meanwhile, WEN will continue to focus on its proven Service Excellence® program, quality of products and balanced marketing initiatives. Unit development for 2001 is expected to be 515 to 555 restaurants systemwide.

BUSINESS

WENDY'S INTERNATIONAL, INC., is the third-largest quick service hamburger restaurant chain with $7.70 billion in systemwide sales during 2000. The Company owns 1,153 Wendy's restaurants and franchises an additional 4,639 units, as of 12/31/00. Wendy's menu includes hamburgers, chicken sandwiches, hot stuffed baked potatoes, pita sandwiches and desserts. The Super Value Menu offers several products each priced at $0.99. Breakfast products are offered at some units. Also, the Company and its franchises own and operate more than 2,000 Tim Hortons restaurants, which sell coffee and baked goods in Canada and the U.S.

REVENUES

(12/31/00)	($000)	(%)
Retail sales	1,807,841	80.8
Franchise revenues	429,105	19.2
Total revenues	2,236,946	100.0

ANNUAL FINANCIAL DATA

	12/31/00	1/2/00	1/3/99	12/28/97	12/29/96	12/31/95	1/1/95
Earnings Per Share	**1.44**	**1.32**	**0.95**	**0.97**	**1.20**	**[1] 0.90**	**0.93**
Cash Flow Per Share	**2.31**	**2.06**	**1.63**	**1.67**	**1.91**	**1.59**	**1.64**
Tang. Book Val. Per Share	**9.48**	**8.60**	**8.20**	**9.77**	**8.89**	**7.46**	**6.60**
Dividends Per Share	**0.24**	**0.24**	**0.24**	**0.24**	**0.24**	**0.24**	**0.24**
Dividend Payout %	**16.7**	**18.2**	**25.3**	**24.7**	**20.0**	**26.7**	**25.8**
INCOME STATEMENT (IN MILLIONS):							
Total Revenues	2,236.9	2,072.2	1,948.2	2,037.3	1,897.1	1,746.3	1,397.9
Costs & Expenses	1,813.1	1,683.2	1,601.8	1,702.8	1,541.2	1,434.2	1,164.8
Depreciation & Amort.	113.5	103.0	100.2	104.5	95.0	84.5	73.7
Operating Income	310.4	286.0	246.3	230.0	260.9	227.6	159.4
Net Interest Inc./(Exp.)	d15.1	d10.2	d2.0	d3.6	d6.8	d10.2	d9.9
Income Before Income Taxes	271.4	268.7	207.7	219.5	254.8	165.1	149.5
Income Taxes	101.8	102.1	84.3	89.0	98.9	55.1	52.3
Net Income	169.6	166.6	123.4	130.5	155.9	[1] 110.1	97.2
Cash Flow	283.1	269.6	223.6	235.0	250.9	194.5	170.9
Average Shs. Outstg. (000)	122,483	131,039	137,089	140,738	131,290	122,041	104,238
BALANCE SHEET (IN MILLIONS):							
Cash & Cash Equivalents	169.7	210.8	160.7	234.3	223.8	213.8	142.9
Total Current Assets	319.1	349.8	313.7	381.6	337.0	321.3	232.6
Net Property	1,497.1	1,389.2	1,280.8	1,265.5	1,207.9	1,006.7	865.2
Total Assets	1,957.7	1,883.6	1,837.9	1,941.7	1,781.4	1,509.2	1,214.8
Total Current Liabilities	296.4	284.2	249.4	212.6	207.8	295.9	286.1
Long-Term Obligations	248.4	249.0	246.0	249.8	241.8	337.2	173.1
Net Stockholders' Equity	1,126.1	1,065.4	1,068.1	1,184.2	1,056.8	818.8	701.9
Net Working Capital	22.7	65.6	64.3	168.9	129.2	25.4	d53.5
Year-end Shs. Outstg. (000)	114,210	118,230	124,005	115,946	113,019	103,993	101,758
STATISTICAL RECORD:							
Operating Profit Margin %	13.9	13.8	12.6	11.3	13.8	13.0	11.4
Net Profit Margin %	7.6	8.0	6.3	6.4	8.2	6.3	7.0
Return on Equity %	15.1	15.6	11.5	11.0	14.8	13.4	13.8
Return on Assets %	8.7	8.8	6.7	6.7	8.8	7.3	8.0
Debt/Total Assets %	12.7	13.2	13.4	12.9	13.6	22.3	14.3
Price Range	27.13-14.00	31.69-19.69	25.19-18.13	27.94-19.63	23.00-16.75	22.75-14.38	18.50-13.25
P/E Ratio	18.8-9.7	24.0-14.9	26.5-19.1	28.8-20.2	19.2-14.0	25.3-16.0	19.9-14.2
Average Yield %	1.2	0.9	1.1	1.0	1.2	1.3	1.5

Statistics are as originally reported. [1] Incl. non-recurr. chrg. $33.9 mill., 12/31/98; $49.7 mill., 12/31/95

OFFICERS:
R. D. Thomas, Senior Chmn., Founder
J. T. Schuessler, Chmn., Pres., C.E.O.
K. B. Anderson, Exec. V.P., C.F.O.
J. F. Brownley, Sr. V.P., Treas.

INVESTOR CONTACT: J. D. Barker, V.P. Inv. Rel., (614) 764-3044

PRINCIPAL OFFICE: P.O. Box 256, 4288 West Dublin-Granville Road, Dublin, OH 43017-0256

TELEPHONE NUMBER: (614) 764-3100
FAX: (614) 764-3330
WEB: www.wendys.com

NO. OF EMPLOYEES: 44,000 (avg.)

SHAREHOLDERS: 82,000 (approx.)

ANNUAL MEETING: In May

INCORPORATED: OH, Dec., 1969

INSTITUTIONAL HOLDINGS:
No. of Institutions: 256
Shares Held: 70,174,876
% Held: 61.7

INDUSTRY: Eating places (SIC: 5812)

TRANSFER AGENT(S): American Stock Transfer & Trust Company, New York, NY

NYSE SYMBOL WCC
Rec. Pr. 8.35 (5/31/01)

WESCO INTERNATIONAL, INC.

YIELD ...
P/E RATIO 11.9

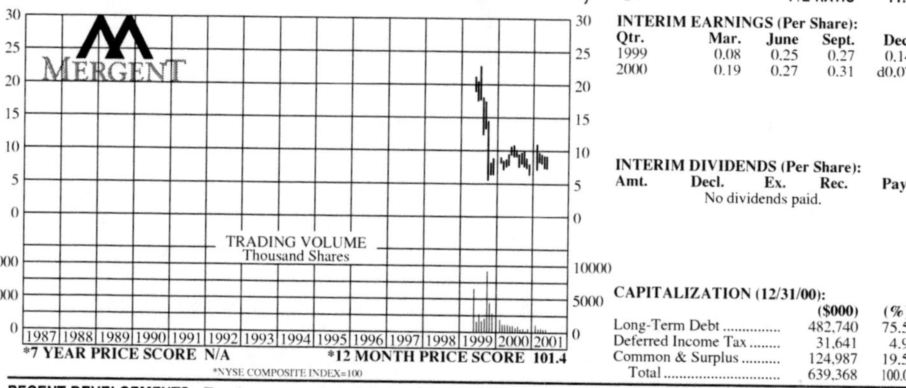

INTERIM EARNINGS (Per Share):

Qtr.	Mar.	June	Sept.	Dec.
1999	0.08	0.25	0.27	0.14
2000	0.19	0.27	0.31	d0.07

INTERIM DIVIDENDS (Per Share):

Amt. Decl. Ex. Rec. Pay.

No dividends paid.

CAPITALIZATION (12/31/00):

	($000)	(%)
Long-Term Debt	482,740	75.5
Deferred Income Tax	31,641	4.9
Common & Surplus	124,987	19.5
Total	639,368	100.0

RECENT DEVELOPMENTS: For the year ended 12/31/00, net income totaled $33.4 million, down 4.9% compared with income of $35.1 million, before an extraordinary charge of $10.5 million, a year earlier. Results for 2000 included a $9.4 million pre-tax restructuring charge. Net sales rose 13.4% to $3.88 billion from $3.42 billion in the previous year. Gross profit was $684.1 million, or 17.6% of net sales, versus $616.6 million, or 18.0% of net sales, the year before.

PROSPECTS: Sluggish sales growth is being partially offset by WCC's initiatives focused on controlling costs and improving gross margins. Going forward, sales growth should be fueled by a significant increase in new customer programs, as well as from expected improvement in the U.S. economy. In March 2001, WCC acquired Herning Underground Supply, Inc. and Alliance Utility Products, Inc., distributors of gas, lighting and communications utility products with net sales of about $112.0 million in 2000.

BUSINESS

WESCO INTERNATIONAL, INC. is a major provider of electrical products and other industrial maintenance, repair, and operating supplies and services in North America. WCC operates approximately 360 branches and five distribution centers located in 48 states, nine Canadian provinces, Puerto Rico, Mexico, Guam, the United Kingdom and Singapore. The Company offers more than one million products from over 23,000 suppliers to its customers, which include a wide variety of industrial companies; contractors for industrial, commercial and residential projects; utility companies; and commercial, institutional and governmental customers.

REVENUES

(12/31/2000)	($000)	(%)
United States	3,494,527	90.0
Canada	319,823	8.3
Other Foreign	66,746	1.7
Total	3,881,096	100.0

ANNUAL FINANCIAL DATA

	12/31/00	12/31/99	12/31/98	12/31/97
Earnings Per Share	1 0.70	2 0.75	1 d0.02	0.55
Cash Flow Per Share	1.26	1.29	0.33	0.79
Tang. Book Val. Per Share	...	...	...	2.14
INCOME STATEMENT (IN MILLIONS):				
Total Revenues	3,881.1	3,420.1	3,025.4	2,594.8
Costs & Expenses	3,728.9	3,269.2	2,947.0	2,498.2
Depreciation & Amort.	26.7	25.9	22.4	16.6
Operating Income	125.4	125.0	56.0	80.1
Net Interest Inc./(Exp.)	d43.8	d47.0	d45.1	d20.1
Income Before Income Taxes	56.7	58.5	0.8	59.9
Income Taxes	23.3	23.3	8.5	23.7
Net Income	1 33.4	2 35.1	1 d7.7	36.2
Cash Flow	60.2	61.1	14.6	52.8
Average Shs. Outstg. (000)	47,747	47,525	45,052	66,679
BALANCE SHEET (IN MILLIONS):				
Cash & Cash Equivalents	21.1	8.8	8.1	7.6
Total Current Assets	764.2	653.8	582.1	696.8
Net Property	123.5	116.6	107.6	95.1
Total Assets	1,170.0	1,028.8	950.5	870.9
Total Current Liabilities	523.8	454.8	466.5	360.5
Long-Term Obligations	482.7	422.5	579.2	294.3
Net Stockholders' Equity	125.0	117.3	d142.6	184.5
Net Working Capital	240.4	199.0	115.6	336.3
Year-end Shs. Outstg. (000)	44,770	47,944	25,210	53,944
STATISTICAL RECORD:				
Operating Profit Margin %	3.2	3.7	1.9	3.1
Net Profit Margin %	0.9	1.0	...	1.4
Return on Equity %	26.8	30.0	...	19.6
Return on Assets %	2.9	3.4	...	4.2
Debt/Total Assets %	41.3	41.1	60.9	33.8
Price Range	10.88-6.31	22.88-5.50	...	...
P/E Ratio	15.5-9.0	30.5-7.3	...	...

Statistics are as originally reported. 1 Incl. $9.4 mil. pre-tax restr. chg., 2000; $51.8 mil. pre-tax recapitalization chg., 1998. 2 Bef. $10.5 mil. ($0.22/sh) extraord. chg.

OFFICERS:
R. W. Haley, Chmn., C.E.O.
S. A. Van Oss, V.P., C.F.O.
D. A. Brailer, Sec., Treas.

PRINCIPAL OFFICE: Commerce Court, Four Station Square, Suite 700, Pittsburgh, PA 15219

TELEPHONE NUMBER: (412) 454-2200
FAX: (412) 454-2595
WEB: www.wescodirect.com

NO. OF EMPLOYEES: 6,000 (approx.)

SHAREHOLDERS: 123 (approx.)

ANNUAL MEETING: In May

INCORPORATED: DE, 1999

INSTITUTIONAL HOLDINGS:
No. of Institutions: 41
Shares Held: 10,702,517
% Held: 23.9

INDUSTRY: Electrical apparatus and equipment (SIC: 5063)

TRANSFER AGENT(S): Mellon Investor Services, Ridgefield Park, NJ

NYSE SYMBOL WST
Rec. Pr. 26.91 (5/31/01)

WEST PHARMACEUTICAL SERVICES, INC.

YIELD 2.7%
P/E RATIO 244.6

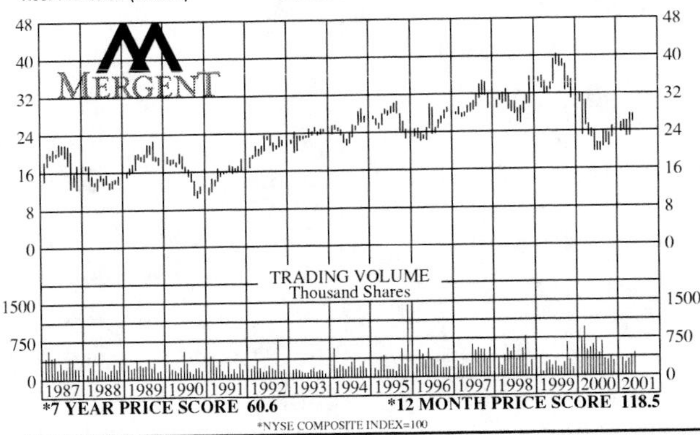

INTERIM EARNINGS (Per Share):

Qtr.	Mar.	June	Sept.	Dec.
1996	d0.49	0.50	0.40	0.60
1997	0.51	0.61	1.05	0.51
1998	d1.19	0.58	0.38	0.66
1999	0.63	0.69	0.57	0.68
2000	0.35	0.35	0.32	d0.91

INTERIM DIVIDENDS (Per Share):

Amt.	Decl.	Ex.	Rec.	Pay.
0.17Q	3/27/00	4/17/00	4/19/00	5/03/00
0.17Q	6/20/00	7/17/00	7/19/00	8/02/00
0.18Q	8/01/00	10/16/00	10/18/00	11/01/00
0.18Q	12/12/00	1/22/01	1/24/01	2/07/01
0.18Q	3/12/01	4/16/01	4/18/01	5/02/01

Indicated div.: $0.72

CAPITALIZATION (12/31/00):

	($000)	(%)
Long-Term Debt	195,800	43.3
Deferred Income Tax	51,000	11.3
Minority Interest	1,000	0.2
Common & Surplus	204,800	45.2
Total	452,600	100.0

RECENT DEVELOPMENTS: For the year ended 12/31/00, net income was $1.6 million compared with $38.7 million in 1999. The decline in earnings was primarily attributed to soft market conditions and project delays, as well as continued inventory reductions by select customers in the U.S. Results for 2000 and 1999 included restructuring charges of $20.8 million and $700,000, respectively. Net sales were $430.1 million, down 8.3% from $469.1 million a year earlier.

PROSPECTS: WST announced that it is closing its contract packaging facility and its plastic device manufacturing plant in Puerto Rico, as well as its Site Management Office in Cleveland, during the first half of 2001. In addition, WST will also dispose of the assets related to its sterile-fill operation in Lakewood, New Jersey. As a result of its cost containment initiatives, WST is optimistic that its earnings performance will improve in 2001 as industry conditions become more favorable.

BUSINESS

WEST PHARMACEUTICAL SERVICES, INC. (formerly The West Company, Inc.) is engaged in the design, development, manufacture and marketing of closures, stoppers, containers, medical device components and assemblies made from elastomers, metal, glass and plastic that meet the unique filling, sealing, dispensing and delivery needs of the pharmaceutical, health care and consumer products markets. The Company also manufactures related packaging machinery. WST's products include pharmaceutical packaging components (stoppers, seals, caps, containers and dropper bulbs), components for medical devices (parts for syringes and components for blood sampling and analysis devices and for intravenous administration sets) and packaging components for consumer products.

REVENUES

(12/31/2000)	($000)	(%)
Devices		
Development Prod.	361,900	84.1
Contract Services	66,700	15.5
Drug Delivery R&D	1,800	0.4
Total	430,400	100.0

ANNUAL FINANCIAL DATA

	12/31/00	12/31/99	12/31/98	12/31/97	12/31/96	12/31/95	12/31/94
Earnings Per Share	**[3] 0.11**	**[3] 2.57**	**[2] 0.40**	**2.68**	**[1] 1.00**	**1.73**	**1.70**
Cash Flow Per Share	**2.68**	**4.94**	**2.36**	**4.60**	**2.87**	**3.52**	**3.14**
Tang. Book Val. Per Share	**10.65**	**11.23**	**11.24**	**13.65**	**11.79**	**11.50**	**11.75**
Dividends Per Share	**0.69**	**0.65**	**0.61**	**0.57**	**0.53**	**0.49**	**0.45**
Dividend Payout %	**626.7**	**25.3**	**152.5**	**21.3**	**53.0**	**28.3**	**26.5**
INCOME STATEMENT (IN MILLIONS):							
Total Revenues	430.1	469.1	449.7	452.5	458.8	412.9	365.1
Costs & Expenses	377.9	366.5	382.4	357.6	395.4	333.5	296.6
Depreciation & Amort.	37.0	35.7	32.3	31.9	30.7	29.6	23.1
Operating Income	15.2	66.9	35.0	63.0	32.7	49.8	45.4
Net Interest Inc./(Exp.)	d13.1	d10.4	d7.2	d5.6	d6.9	d7.3	d3.3
Income Before Income Taxes	2.1	56.5	27.8	57.4	25.8	42.5	42.1
Income Taxes	1.5	18.4	21.2	13.3	10.8	13.9	13.4
Equity Earnings/Minority Int.	1.0	0.6	0.1	0.3	1.4	0.1	d1.4
Net Income	[3] 1.6	[3] 38.7	[2] 6.7	44.4	[1] 16.4	28.7	27.3
Cash Flow	38.6	74.4	39.0	76.3	47.1	58.3	50.4
Average Shs. Outstg. (000)	14,409	15,048	16,504	16,572	16,418	16,557	16,054
BALANCE SHEET (IN MILLIONS):							
Cash & Cash Equivalents	42.7	45.3	31.3	52.3	27.3	17.4	27.2
Total Current Assets	173.1	184.7	159.7	170.7	156.7	148.4	136.7
Net Property	235.8	227.6	220.3	202.2	210.3	229.3	192.2
Total Assets	557.4	551.8	505.6	477.9	477.4	480.1	397.4
Total Current Liabilities	79.3	104.0	104.2	58.0	65.6	61.8	86.3
Long-Term Obligations	195.8	141.5	105.0	87.4	95.5	104.5	35.9
Net Stockholders' Equity	204.8	231.2	230.1	277.7	252.0	254.1	227.3
Net Working Capital	93.8	80.7	55.5	112.7	91.1	86.6	50.4
Year-end Shs. Outstg. (000)	14,310	14,664	15,026	16,568	16,383	16,621	16,464
STATISTICAL RECORD:							
Operating Profit Margin %	3.5	14.3	7.8	13.9	7.1	12.1	12.4
Net Profit Margin %	0.4	8.2	1.5	9.8	3.6	7.0	7.5
Return on Equity %	0.8	16.7	2.9	16.0	6.5	11.3	12.0
Return on Assets %	0.3	7.0	1.3	9.3	3.4	6.0	6.9
Debt/Total Assets %	35.1	25.6	20.8	18.3	20.0	21.8	9.0
Price Range	31.88-19.63	40.44-30.88	35.69-25.75	35.06-27.00	30.00-22.13	30.63-22.63	29.13-21.25
P/E Ratio	289.5-178.2	15.7-12.0	89.2-64.4	13.1-10.1	30.0-22.1	17.7-13.1	17.1-12.5
Average Yield %	2.7	1.8	2.0	1.8	2.0	1.8	1.8

Statistics are as originally reported. [1] Incl. restruct. chrg. of $700,000 [2] Incl. nonrecurr. chrgs. of $32.2 mill. [3] Incl. one-time chrgs. of $700,000, 1999; $20.8 mill., 2000.

OFFICERS:
W. G. Little, Chmn., C.E.O.
S. A. Ellers, Exec. V.P., C.F.O.
J. R. Gailey, III, V.P., Gen. Couns., Sec.

INVESTOR CONTACT: Stephen M. Heumann, V.P., Treas., (610) 594-3346

PRINCIPAL OFFICE: 101 Gordon Drive, P.O. Box 645, Lionville, PA 19341-0645

TELEPHONE NUMBER: (610) 594-2900
FAX: (610) 594-3000
WEB: www.westpharma.com

NO. OF EMPLOYEES: 4,700

SHAREHOLDERS: 1,780; 2200 (nominee holders)

ANNUAL MEETING: In May

INCORPORATED: PA, 1923

INSTITUTIONAL HOLDINGS:
No. of Institutions: 64
Shares Held: 8,342,071
% Held: 58.2

INDUSTRY: Fabricated rubber products, nec (SIC: 3069)

TRANSFER AGENT(S): American Stock Transfer and Trust Company, New York, NY

NYSE SYMBOL WE
Rec. Pr. 22.92 (5/31/01)

WESTCOAST ENERGY INC.

YIELD ...
P/E RATIO ...

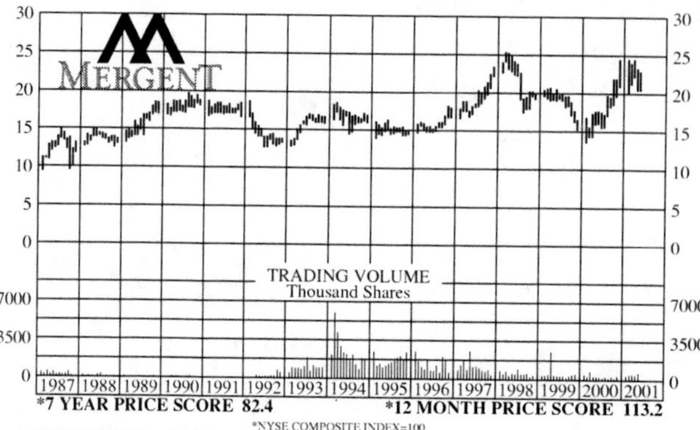

*7 YEAR PRICE SCORE 82.4 *12 MONTH PRICE SCORE 113.2
*NYSE COMPOSITE INDEX=100

INTERIM EARNINGS (Per Share②):

Qtr.	Mar.	June	Sept.	Dec.
1996	1.32	0.16	d0.06	0.54
1997	1.20	0.31	1.34	0.72
1998	0.99	0.01	d0.06	0.59
1999	1.08	0.05	0.44	0.38
2000	1.01	0.51	0.20	0.98

INTERIM DIVIDENDS (Per Share②):

Amt.	Decl.	Ex.	Rec.	Pay.
0.32Q	4/26/00	6/07/00	6/09/00	6/30/00
0.32Q	7/27/00	9/06/00	9/08/00	9/30/00
0.32Q	10/25/00	12/06/00	12/08/00	12/31/00
0.34Q	2/21/01	3/07/01	3/09/01	3/31/01
0.34Q	4/25/01	6/06/01	6/08/01	6/30/01

Indicated div.: $1.36 (Div. Reinv. Plan)

CAPITALIZATION (12/31/00):

	($000)	(%)
Long-Term Debt	3,983,851	56.1
Deferred Income Tax	587,136	8.3
Minority Interest	110,755	1.6
Preferred Stock	577,128	8.1
Common & Surplus	1,844,141	26.0
Total	7,103,011	100.0

RECENT DEVELOPMENTS: For the year ended 12/31/00, net income rose 45.3% to C$388.0 million ($258.9 million) versus C$267.0 million ($184.9 million) a year earlier. Results for 1999 included an after-tax gain on the sale of Centra Gas Manitoba of C$59.0 million ($39.0 million.) Operating revenues rose 41.0% to C$8.96 billion ($5.97 billion). Results for 2000 were driven by gains from the energy marketing division and energy services businesses, and increased contributions from new pipeline and international projects.

PROSPECTS: On 1/16/01, WE announced that it has exercised its option to sell its remaining 49.0% interest in NGX Canada to OM Gruppen, effective 1/1/01. Meanwhile, WE will continue to pursue a number of core investment opportunities including expansion at Maritimes & Northeast Pipeline, further development of independent power projects, increased storage and transmission capacity at the Company's natural gas utility business, and British Columbia facilities expansion.

BUSINESS

WESTCOAST ENERGY INC. is engaged in the exploration, transportation and distribution of natural gas for Canadian and U.S. markets. WE operates a natural gas transportation system which consists of 33,099 miles of pipe and gathering lines throughout British Columbia and the western U.S. The Company owns Westcoast Petroleum Ltd. and holds the majority interest in Canadian Roxy Petroleum Ltd., both of which explore for and produce oil and natural gas. Principal joint ventures are Foothills Pipe Lines Ltd. and Empire State Pipeline (50%-owned). WE also holds a controlling interest in Pacific Northern Gas Ltd. and Saratoga Processing Company. Transmission & field services accounted for 9.2% of 2000 revenues; gas distribution, 20.7%; power generation, 1.4%; international, 1.4%; and services, 67.2%.

ANNUAL FINANCIAL DATA

	12/31/00	12/31/99	12/31/98	12/31/97	12/31/96	12/31/95	12/31/94
Earnings Per Share	**1.80**	**1.23**	**1.01**	**1.43**	① **1.43**	**1.47**	**1.30**
Cash Flow Per Share	**3.68**	**2.98**	**3.30**	**3.68**	**3.63**	**3.80**	**3.13**
Tang. Book Val. Per Share	**15.19**	**14.44**	**13.89**	**13.87**	**13.68**	**12.84**	**12.00**
② **Dividends Per Share**	**1.28**	**1.28**	**1.26**	**1.20**	**1.05**	**0.93**	**0.89**
INCOME STATEMENT (IN MILLIONS):							
Total Revenues	5,974.8	4,337.9	4,874.8	5,092.8	3,564.1	3,052.5	2,646.3
Costs & Expenses	5,146.8	3,628.9	4,204.6	4,311.3	2,770.9	2,309.4	2,081.0
Depreciation & Amort.	284.2	277.7	240.6	229.1	217.9	201.5	156.8
Operating Income	543.8	431.4	429.6	552.3	575.4	541.6	408.5
Net Interest Inc./(Exp.)	d344.3	d345.5	d322.5	d316.2	d327.5	d328.3	d244.5
Income Before Income Taxes	304.2	223.6	166.5	256.3	245.6	238.9	207.5
Income Taxes	38.7	31.9	31.7	85.7	84.1	79.9	69.2
Equity Earnings/Minority Int.	22.7	d6.9	d4.0	d4.9	d6.6	d14.7	5.7
Net Income	258.9	184.9	130.9	165.8	① 155.0	144.4	123.3
Cash Flow	511.1	431.4	347.0	375.4	359.0	330.5	268.8
Average Shs. Outstg. (000)	139,000	145,000	105,000	102,000	99,000	87,000	86,000
BALANCE SHEET (IN MILLIONS):							
Cash & Cash Equivalents	122.8	69.9	70.7	41.8	21.2	...	...
Total Current Assets	2,365.9	1,161.2	1,054.8	1,096.3	970.9	709.4	725.7
Net Property	6,249.7	6,306.4	5,663.3	5,589.4	5,703.3	5,478.4	4,293.1
Total Assets	10,092.7	8,154.4	7,150.9	7,017.2	6,991.5	6,440.7	5,291.1
Total Current Liabilities	2,581.4	1,587.7	1,278.8	1,424.3	1,109.1	1,037.1	1,252.6
Long-Term Obligations	3,983.9	3,842.8	3,500.8	3,441.4	3,467.6	3,376.5	2,223.5
Net Stockholders' Equity	2,421.3	2,257.2	2,038.2	1,829.0	1,707.1	1,332.4	1,231.9
Net Working Capital	d215.5	d426.5	d224.0	d328.1	d138.2	d327.6	d526.8
Year-end Shs. Outstg. (000)	121,443	114,848	112,671	103,246	101,000	88,000	86,000
STATISTICAL RECORD:							
Operating Profit Margin %	9.1	9.9	8.8	10.8	16.1	17.7	15.4
Net Profit Margin %	4.3	4.3	2.7	3.3	4.3	4.7	4.7
Return on Equity %	10.7	8.2	6.4	9.1	9.1	10.8	10.0
Return on Assets %	2.6	2.3	1.8	2.4	2.2	2.2	2.3
Debt/Total Assets %	39.5	47.1	49.0	49.0	49.6	52.4	42.0
Price Range	24.50-13.50	20.81-15.19	25.44-17.38	23.50-16.50	18.25-14.63	16.38-13.88	18.63-14.38
P/E Ratio	13.6-7.5	16.9-12.3	25.2-17.2	16.4-11.5	12.7-10.2	11.1-9.4	14.3-11.0

Statistics are as originally reported. All figures are in U.S. dollars unless otherwise noted. Exchange rates are as follows: 0.6672, 12/31/00; 0.6924, 12/31/99; 0.6609, 12/31/98; 0.6965, 12/31/97; 0.7311, 12/31/96; 0.7329, 12/31/95; 0.7129, 12/31/94. ① Incl. one-time chrgs. of $15.0 mill. ② In Canadian dollars

OFFICERS:
M. E. Phelps, Chmn., C.E.O.
G. M. Wilson, Exec. V.P., C.F.O.

INVESTOR CONTACT: Thomas M. Merinsky, Mgr., Investor Relations, (604) 488-8021

PRINCIPAL OFFICE: 1333 West Georgia Street, Vancouver, British Columbia, Canada

TELEPHONE NUMBER: (604) 488-8000
FAX: (604) 488-8500
WEB: www.westcoastenergy.com
NO. OF EMPLOYEES: 5,455 (avg.)
SHAREHOLDERS: 8,047
ANNUAL MEETING: In Apr.
INCORPORATED: Canada, Apr., 1949

INSTITUTIONAL HOLDINGS:
No. of Institutions: 45
Shares Held: 17,106,840
% Held: 14.0

INDUSTRY: Crude petroleum and natural gas (SIC: 1311)

TRANSFER AGENT(S): Computershare Trust Company of Canada

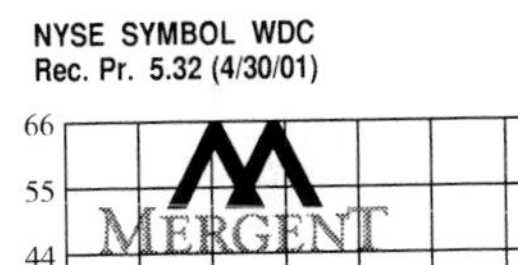

NYSE SYMBOL WDC
Rec. Pr. 5.32 (4/30/01)

WESTERN DIGITAL CORPORATION

YIELD ...
P/E RATIO ...

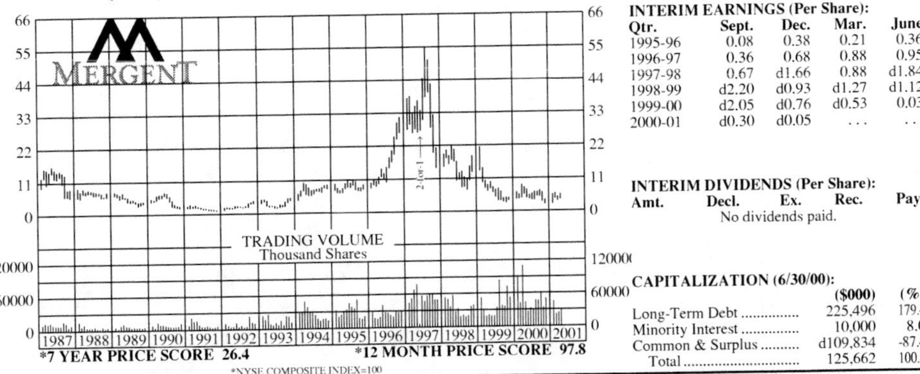

INTERIM EARNINGS (Per Share):

Qtr.	Sept.	Dec.	Mar.	June
1995-96	0.08	0.38	0.21	0.36
1996-97	0.36	0.68	0.88	0.95
1997-98	0.67	d1.66	0.88	d1.84
1998-99	d2.20	d0.93	d1.27	d1.12
1999-00	d2.05	d0.76	d0.53	0.03
2000-01	d0.30	d0.05	...	...

INTERIM DIVIDENDS (Per Share):

Amt.	Decl.	Ex.	Rec.	Pay.

No dividends paid.

CAPITALIZATION (6/30/00):

	($000)	(%)
Long-Term Debt	225,496	179.4
Minority Interest	10,000	8.0
Common & Surplus	d109,834	-87.4
Total	125,662	100.0

RECENT DEVELOPMENTS: For the quarter ended 12/29/00, the Company reported a loss of $8.8 million, before an extraordinary item, compared with a loss of $91.5 million in 1999. Results for 2000 and 1999 excluded extraordinary credits of $10.6 million and $76.3 million, respectively, from the redemption of debentures. Results for 1999 included restructuring charges totaling $25.5 million. Total revenues slipped 5.3% to $530.7 million from $560.2 million in the previous year.

PROSPECTS: On 3/12/01, WDC formed a new company, SANavigator Inc., from its Connex subsidiary to exclusively focus on the storage area network management software market. SANavigator Inc. will continue to develop its storage area network management software, pursue strategic acquisitions and market products through specific sales channels. Separately, WDC announced the availability of its highest capacity performance desktop hard drive, a 7,200 random processing memory, three-disk model.

BUSINESS

WESTERN DIGITAL CORPORATION designs, manufactures, and sells hard drives for the personal computer market. WDC is one of the three largest independent manufacturers of hard drives. WDC's principal drive products are 3.5-inch form factor hard drives for the desktop PC market with storage capacities from 7.5 gigabytes to 45.0 gigabytes (GB). The hard drives utilize the enhanced integrated drive electronics interface. With the introduction of product lines for the mobile and enterprise storage markets, WDC now designs, manufactures, and sells hard drives across the entire spectrum of the hard drive market. Geographic revenues for 2000 were derived: U.S., 45.2%; Europe, 11.3%; and Asia, 43.5%.

ANNUAL FINANCIAL DATA

	6/30/00	7/3/99	6/27/98	6/28/97	6/29/96	7/1/95	6/30/94
Earnings Per Share	**[4] d2.89**	**[3] d5.51**	**[2] d3.32**	**2.86**	**[1] 1.01**	**1.28**	**0.89**
Cash Flow Per Share	**d2.25**	**d4.04**	**d2.73**	**3.54**	**1.54**	**1.73**	**1.44**
Tang. Book Val. Per Share	...	...	**3.60**	**7.22**	**5.21**	**4.69**	**3.21**
INCOME STATEMENT (IN MILLIONS):							
Total Revenues	1,957.6	2,767.2	3,541.5	4,177.9	2,865.2	2,130.9	1,539.7
Costs & Expenses	2,258.4	3,112.9	3,785.7	3,812.8	2,736.1	1,954.2	1,401.6
Depreciation & Amort.	78.5	131.1	51.6	63.5	51.6	43.6	46.2
Operating Income	d379.3	d476.8	d295.8	301.6	77.5	133.0	91.9
Net Interest Inc./(Exp.)	4.9	d15.9	3.8	13.2	13.1	12.0	d5.8
Income Before Income Taxes	d374.4	d492.7	d292.0	314.8	107.9	145.0	86.0
Income Taxes	cr19.5	...	cr1.8	47.2	11.0	21.7	12.9
Net Income	[4] d354.9	[3] d492.7	[2] d290.2	267.6	[1] 96.9	123.3	73.1
Cash Flow	d276.5	d361.6	d238.6	331.1	148.5	166.9	119.3
Average Shs. Outstg. (000)	122,624	89,478	87,525	93,521	96,248	96,396	82,726
BALANCE SHEET (IN MILLIONS):							
Cash & Cash Equivalents	184.0	226.1	459.8	208.3	219.2	307.7	243.5
Total Current Assets	451.4	688.3	1,052.1	1,017.9	794.3	730.1	537.5
Net Property	99.0	237.9	347.0	247.9	148.3	88.6	73.4
Total Assets	615.6	1,022.4	1,442.7	1,307.1	984.1	858.8	640.5
Total Current Liabilities	445.1	626.6	588.6	653.7	514.0	369.6	275.7
Long-Term Obligations	225.5	534.1	519.2	...	...	...	58.6
Net Stockholders' Equity	d109.8	d153.8	317.8	620.0	453.9	473.4	288.2
Net Working Capital	6.3	61.7	463.5	364.2	280.2	360.5	261.7
Year-end Shs. Outstg. (000)	153,335	90,611	88,293	85,896	87,142	100,964	89,790
STATISTICAL RECORD:							
Operating Profit Margin %	...	...	...	7.2	2.7	6.2	6.0
Net Profit Margin %	...	...	...	6.4	3.4	5.8	4.8
Return on Equity %	...	...	...	43.2	21.3	26.0	25.4
Return on Assets %	...	...	...	20.5	9.8	14.4	11.4
Debt/Total Assets %	36.6	52.2	36.0	...	...	...	9.2
Price Range	8.81-2.19	21.44-2.75	22.06-7.13	54.75-14.50	31.69-8.06	11.06-6.56	10.19-4.31
P/E Ratio	...	...	...	19.1-5.1	31.4-8.0	8.6-5.1	11.5-4.9

Statistics are as originally reported. Adj. for 2-for-1 split, 6/97. [1] Incl. $17.3 mill. pre-tax gain fr. sale of bus. [2] Incl. $148.0 mill. spl. chgs. & about $22.0 mill. cost rel. to new tech. agreement with IBM. [3] Incl. $61.0 mill. restr. chgs. [4] Incl. $85.8 mill. restr. chgs. & excl. $166.9 mill. extraord. gain.

OFFICERS:
T. E. Pardun, Chmn.
M. H. Massengill, Pres., C.E.O.
T. A. Hopp, Sr. V.P., C.F.O.
S. M. Slavin, V.P., Taxes, Treas.

INVESTOR CONTACT: Robert L. Erickson, V.P., Law and Secretary

PRINCIPAL OFFICE: 8105 Irvine Center Drive, Irvine, CA 92618

TELEPHONE NUMBER: (949) 932-5000
FAX: (949) 932-5612
WEB: www.westerndigital.com

NO. OF EMPLOYEES: 7,321

SHAREHOLDERS: 3,902 (approx.)

ANNUAL MEETING: In Nov.

INCORPORATED: CA, Apr., 1970; reincorp., DE, Jan., 1987

INSTITUTIONAL HOLDINGS:
No. of Institutions: 90
Shares Held: 84,411,173
% Held: 48.4

INDUSTRY: Computer storage devices (SIC: 3572)

TRANSFER AGENT(S): American Stock Transfer & Trust Company, New York, NY

NYSE SYMBOL WGR
Rec. Pr. 38.10 (5/31/01)

WESTERN GAS RESOURCES, INC.

YIELD 0.5%
P/E RATIO 27.4

MERGENT

TRADING VOLUME
Thousand Shares

1987 1988 1989 1990 1991 1992 1993 1994 1995 1996 1997 1998 1999 2000 2001

*7 YEAR PRICE SCORE 110.4 *12 MONTH PRICE SCORE 148.2

*NYSE COMPOSITE INDEX=100

INTERIM EARNINGS (Per Share):

Qtr.	Mar.	June	Sept.	Dec.
1996	0.30	0.11	0.01	0.24
1997	0.25	d0.05	0.07	d0.55
1998	0.33	d0.16	d0.23	d2.35
1999	d0.15	d0.54	d0.05	d0.12
2000	0.32	0.24	0.36	0.47

INTERIM DIVIDENDS (Per Share):

Amt.	Decl.	Ex.	Rec.	Pay.
0.05Q	6/01/00	6/28/00	6/30/00	8/11/00
0.05Q	9/15/00	9/27/00	9/30/00	11/14/00
0.05Q	12/07/00	12/27/00	12/31/00	2/14/01
0.05Q	2/28/01	3/28/01	3/30/01	5/14/01
0.05Q	6/01/01	6/27/01	6/30/01	8/13/01

Indicated div.: $0.20

CAPITALIZATION (12/31/00):

	($000)	(%)
Long-Term Debt	358,700	43.9
Deferred Income Tax	67,680	8.3
Preferred Stock	416	0.1
Common & Surplus	391,118	47.8
Total	817,914	100.0

RECENT DEVELOPMENTS: For the year ended 12/31/00, income was $57.8 million, before an after-tax extraordinary loss of $1.7 million, compared with a loss of $16.0 million, before an after-tax extraordinary loss of $1.1 million, in the previous year. Results included an after-tax gain of $5.7 million in 2000 and an after-tax loss of $22.7 million in 1999, respectively, from the sale of assets. Total revenues jumped 71.8% to $3.28 billion versus $1.91 billion in the prior year.

PROSPECTS: On 1/4/00, WGR announced the sale of its subsidiary, Pinnacle Gas Treating, Inc. to Anadarko Petroleum Corporation for about $38.0 million. The sale completes the Company's plan to divest underperforming assets that began approximately two years ago. WGR plans to invest as much as $100.0 million in acquisitions and other growth projects to expand its gas gathering and production in the Rocky Mountain region and Canada, while maintaining a debt-to-capital level of 50.0% or less for 2001.

BUSINESS

WESTERN GAS RESOURCES, INC. is an independent gas gatherer and processor, producer, transporter and energy marketer. The Company designs, constructs, owns and operates 18 natural gas gathering and processing facilities in major gas-producing basins in the Rocky Mountain, Mid-Continent, Gulf Coast and Southwestern regions of the U.S. The Company markets natural gas and natural gas liquids nationwide and in Canada, providing risk management, transportation and other services to a variety of customers. The Company also owns certain producing properties, and explores and develops gas reserves, primarily in Wyoming, in support of its gathering and processing facilities.

REVENUES

(12/31/00)	($000)	(%)
Gas	2,624,409	80.0
Natural Gas Liquids	590,936	18.0
Processing, transporation	53,156	1.6
Other	13,487	0.4
Total	3,281,988	100.0

ANNUAL FINANCIAL DATA

	12/31/00	12/31/99	12/31/98	12/31/97	12/31/96	12/31/95	12/31/94
Earnings Per Share	[6] **1.39**	[5] **d0.86**	[4] **d2.42**	[3] **d0.28**	[2] **0.66**	[1] **d0.84**	**d0.19**
Cash Flow Per Share	**3.21**	**0.76**	**d0.57**	**1.57**	**3.04**	**1.70**	**2.76**
Tang. Book Val. Per Share	**12.10**	**10.86**	**11.97**	**14.55**	**14.95**	**14.42**	**16.97**
Dividends Per Share	**0.20**	**0.20**	**0.20**	**0.20**	**0.20**	**0.20**	**0.20**
Dividend Payout %	**14.4**	...	...	...	**30.3**	...	...
INCOME STATEMENT (IN MILLIONS):							
Total Revenues	3,282.0	1,910.7	2,133.6	2,385.3	2,091.0	1,257.0	1,063.5
Costs & Expenses	3,108.6	1,822.0	2,146.2	2,296.3	1,951.7	1,162.7	956.5
Depreciation & Amort.	57.9	51.0	59.3	59.2	63.2	65.4	63.6
Operating Income	115.4	37.8	d72.0	29.7	76.1	28.9	43.4
Net Interest Inc./(Exp.)	d33.5	d33.2	d33.6	d27.5	d34.4	d37.2	d31.9
Income Taxes	33.6	cr9.2	cr38.4	0.7	13.7	cr2.2	4.2
Net Income	[6] 57.8	[5] d16.0	[4] d67.2	[3] 1.5	[2] 27.9	[1] d6.1	7.4
Cash Flow	105.3	24.5	d18.3	50.3	80.7	43.8	59.6
Average Shs. Outstg. (000)	32,835	32,151	32,147	32,138	26,520	25,754	25,696
BALANCE SHEET (IN MILLIONS):							
Gross Property	1,054.4	952.4	1,152.1	1,251.1	1,118.9	1,049.8	1,062.2
Accumulated Depreciation	306.7	260.1	305.6	294.4	252.6	200.2	179.5
Net Property	747.7	692.3	846.5	956.7	866.3	849.6	882.7
Total Assets	1,431.4	1,049.5	1,219.4	1,348.3	1,361.6	1,194.0	1,167.4
Long-Term Obligations	358.7	378.3	504.9	441.4	379.5	454.5	418.0
Net Stockholders' Equity	391.5	349.7	385.2	468.1	480.5	371.9	436.7
Year-end Shs. Outstg. (000)	32,336	32,162	32,148	32,146	32,109	25,770	25,712
STATISTICAL RECORD:							
Operating Profit Margin %	3.5	2.0	...	1.2	3.6	2.3	4.1
Net Profit Margin %	1.8	...	...	0.1	1.3	...	0.7
Net Inc./Net Property %	7.7	...	...	0.2	3.2	...	0.8
Net Inc./Tot. Capital %	7.1	...	...	0.2	3.0	...	0.8
Return on Equity %	14.8	...	...	0.3	5.8	...	1.7
Accum. Depr./Gross Prop. %	29.1	27.3	26.5	23.5	22.6	19.1	16.9
Price Range	34.69-10.63	20.00-3.88	22.13-5.31	25.56-14.88	19.88-11.13	24.25-15.00	35.38-17.88
P/E Ratio	25.0-7.6	...	...	...	30.1-16.9	...	...
Average Yield %	0.9	1.7	1.5	1.0	1.3	1.0	0.8

Statistics are as originally reported. [1] Incl. a net restruct. chg. of $1.3 mill. and a net chg. of $12.4 mill. for impair. of assets. [2] Incl. a net gain of $1.2 mill. fr. sale of gas processing facility. [3] Incl. a net gain of about $1.2 mill. fr. sale of gas processing facility & incl. a net chg. of $22.0 mill. for the impair. of assets. [4] Incl. a net impair. chg. of $69.0 mill. & a net gain of $10.5 mill. fr. sale of assets. [5] Bef. extraord. loss of $1.1 mill.; Incl. loss fr. sale of assets of $29.8 mill. and impair. chrgs. of $1.2 mill. [6] Bef. extraord. loss of $1.7 mill. & incl. an after-tax gain of $5.7 mill. fr. asset sales

OFFICERS:
B. G. Wise, Chmn.
W. L. Stonehocker, Vice-Chmn.
L. F. Outlaw, Pres, C.E.O., C.O.O.

INVESTOR CONTACT: Ron Wirth, Director of Investor Relations, (800) 933-5603

PRINCIPAL OFFICE: 12200 N. Pecos St., Denver, CO 80234-3439

TELEPHONE NUMBER: (303) 452-5603
FAX: (303) 252-6150
WEB: www.westerngas.com

NO. OF EMPLOYEES: 616 (approx.)

SHAREHOLDERS: 235

ANNUAL MEETING: In May

INCORPORATED: DE, Oct., 1989

INSTITUTIONAL HOLDINGS:
No. of Institutions: 106
Shares Held: 17,199,203
% Held: 52.9

INDUSTRY: Natural gas transmission (SIC: 4922)

TRANSFER AGENT(S): Equiserve, L.P., Boston, MA

NYSE SYMBOL WR
Rec. Pr. 24.77 (4/30/01)

WESTERN RESOURCES, INC.

YIELD 4.8%
P/E RATIO 17.9

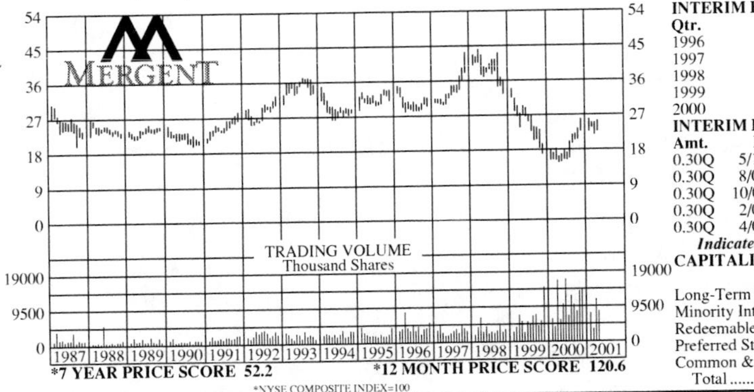

*7 YEAR PRICE SCORE 52.2 *12 MONTH PRICE SCORE 120.6

*NYSE COMPOSITE INDEX=100

INTERIM EARNINGS (Per Share):

Qtr.	Mar.	June	Sept.	Dec.
1996	0.66	0.40	0.87	0.48
1997	0.61	0.36	7.77	d1.23
1998	0.45	0.50	1.10	d1.21
1999	0.31	0.27	0.72	d1.31
2000	0.61	0.36	0.80	d0.39

INTERIM DIVIDENDS (Per Share):

Amt.	Decl.	Ex.	Rec.	Pay.
0.30Q	5/17/00	6/07/00	6/09/00	7/03/00
0.30Q	8/02/00	9/06/00	9/08/00	10/02/00
0.30Q	10/04/00	12/06/00	12/08/00	1/02/01
0.30Q	2/09/01	3/07/01	3/09/01	4/02/01
0.30Q	4/04/01	6/06/01	6/08/01	7/02/01

Indicated div.: $1.20 (Div. Reinv. Plan)

CAPITALIZATION (12/31/00):

	($000)	(%)
Long-Term Debt	3,237,849	58.1
Minority Interest	184,591	3.3
Redeemable Pfd. Stock	220,000	3.9
Preferred Stock	24,858	0.4
Common & Surplus	1,906,562	34.2
Total	5,573,860	100.0

RECENT DEVELOPMENTS: For the year ended 12/31/00, income totaled $91.1 million, before an extraordinary gain of $49.2 million and accounting change charge of $3.8 million. This compares with income of $2.6 million, before an extraordinary gain of $11.7 million, in the previous year. Results for 1999 included non-recurring charges of $88.1 million. Total sales climbed 16.7% to $2.37 billion from $2.03 billion the year before. Energy sales advanced 27.9% to $1.83 billion, while monitored services sales slid 10.2% to $537.9 million.

PROSPECTS: On 12/15/00, Wenstar Industries Inc., WR's unregulated subsidiary, sold its preferred interest in Paradigm Direct LLC, a direct marketing services company, for $51.0 million. On 11/9/00, WR announced that Public Service Company of New Mexico (PNM) will acquire the Company's electric utility operations for about $1.50 billion in stock. Under the terms of the agreement, PNM and WR will both become subsidiaries of a new holding company to be named at a future date. The companies expect the transaction to be completed in late 2001 or early 2002.

BUSINESS

WESTERN RESOURCES, INC. (formerly The Kansas Power and Light Company) is a publicly traded consumer services company. WR is engaged in the business of providing electric generation, transmission and distribution services to approximately 636,000 customers in Kansas and providing monitored services to approximately 1.4 million customers in North America, the United Kingdom and Europe. The Company owns a 45.0% interest in ONEOK, Inc., a natural gas transmission and distribution company with about 1.4 million customers in Oklahoma and Kansas. Regulated electric service is provided by KPL, a division of WR, and Kansas Gas and Electric Company, a wholly-owned subsidiary. In addition, WR owns an 85.0% interest in Protection One, Inc., a security alarm company.

ANNUAL FINANCIAL DATA

	12/31/00	12/31/99	12/31/98	12/31/97	12/31/96	12/31/95	12/31/94
Earnings Per Share	**3 1.30**	**1 2 d0.01**	**1 2 0.65**	**1 7.51**	**1 2.41**	**2.71**	**2.82**
Cash Flow Per Share	**7.32**	**5.88**	**4.92**	**11.45**	**5.77**	**5.65**	**5.59**
Tang. Book Val. Per Share	**13.28**	**11.47**	**11.38**	**17.73**	**25.14**	**24.71**	**23.93**
Dividends Per Share	**1.67**	**2.14**	**2.13**	**2.09**	**2.05**	**2.01**	**1.97**
Dividend Payout %	**128.5**	...	**327.6**	**27.8**	**85.1**	**74.2**	**69.9**
INCOME STATEMENT (IN MILLIONS):							
Total Revenues	2,368.5	2,036.2	2,034.1	2,151.8	2,046.8	1,572.1	1,617.9
Costs & Expenses	1,728.3	1,366.5	1,522.9	1,752.1	1,340.4	916.6	969.1
Depreciation & Amort.	414.5	395.2	280.7	256.7	214.2	182.9	170.4
Maintenance Exp.	...	...	...	...	99.1	108.6	113.2
Operating Income	225.6	274.5	230.5	142.9	304.0	275.4	269.5
Net Interest Inc./(Exp.)	d289.6	d370.3	d226.1	d193.2	d149.3	d119.6	d116.0
Income Taxes	46.1	cr33.4	14.6	378.6	89.1	88.5	95.6
Equity Earnings/Minority Int.	8.6	12.9	0.4	4.7	...	...	...
Net Income	3 91.1	1 2 0.7	1 2 46.2	1 494.1	1 169.0	181.7	187.4
Cash Flow	504.5	394.8	323.2	745.9	368.3	351.2	344.5
Average Shs. Outstg. (000)	68,962	67,080	65,634	65,128	63,834	62,157	61,618
BALANCE SHEET (IN MILLIONS):							
Gross Property	6,290.8	6,032.3	5,786.4	5,644.9	6,376.7	6,228.9	6,048.7
Accumulated Depreciation	2,328.2	2,170.9	2,030.8	1,899.1	2,058.6	1,926.5	1,790.3
Net Property	3,993.4	3,889.4	3,795.1	3,786.5	4,356.5	4,356.4	4,298.3
Total Assets	7,767.2	8,008.2	7,951.4	6,977.0	6,647.8	5,490.7	5,189.6
Long-Term Obligations	3,237.8	2,883.1	3,063.1	2,181.9	1,681.6	1,391.3	1,357.0
Net Stockholders' Equity	1,931.4	1,900.3	1,962.8	2,089.1	1,649.5	1,578.0	1,499.3
Year-end Shs. Outstg. (000)	70,082	67,402	65,909	65,410	64,625	62,856	61,618
STATISTICAL RECORD:							
Operating Profit Margin %	9.5	13.5	11.3	6.6	14.9	17.5	16.7
Net Profit Margin %	3.8	...	2.3	23.0	8.3	11.6	11.6
Net Inc./Net Property %	2.3	...	1.2	13.0	3.9	4.2	4.4
Net Inc./Tot. Capital %	1.6	...	0.8	10.6	3.6	4.1	4.7
Return on Equity %	4.7	...	2.4	23.7	10.2	11.5	12.5
Accum. Depr./Gross Prop. %	37.0	36.0	35.1	33.6	32.3	30.9	29.6
Price Range	25.88-14.69	33.88-16.81	44.19-32.56	43.44-29.75	34.88-28.00	34.00-28.63	34.88-26.13
P/E Ratio	19.9-11.3	...	68.0-50.1	5.8-4.0	14.5-11.6	12.5-10.6	12.4-9.3
Average Yield %	8.2	8.4	5.6	5.7	6.5	6.4	6.5

Statistics are as originally reported. 1 Incl. net non-recurr. chrgs. $88.1 mill., 12/99; $98.9 mill., 12/98; $776.1 mill., 12/97; $18.2 mill., 12/96. 2 Bef. extraord. gain $11.7 mill., 12/99; $1.6 mill., 12/98. 3 Bef. $49.2 mill. ($0.71/sh) extraord. gain & $3.8 mill. ($0.05/sh) acctg. chg.

OFFICERS:
D. C. Wittig, Chmn., Pres., C.E.O.
C. Koupal, Exec. V.P., C.A.O.
R. D. Terrill, Exec. V.P., Gen. Couns.

INVESTOR CONTACT: Carl A. Ricketts, V.P., Inv. Rel., (785) 575-8424

PRINCIPAL OFFICE: 818 S. Kansas Avenue, P.O. Box 889, Topeka, KS 66601-0889

TELEPHONE NUMBER: (785) 575-6300
FAX: (785) 575-8061
WEB: www.wr.com
NO. OF EMPLOYEES: 8,300 (approx.)
SHAREHOLDERS: 39,546
ANNUAL MEETING: In June
INCORPORATED: KS, March, 1924

INSTITUTIONAL HOLDINGS:
No. of Institutions: 175
Shares Held: 29,213,594
% Held: 34.6

INDUSTRY: Electric and other services combined (SIC: 4931)

TRANSFER AGENT(S): Western Resources, Inc., Topeka, KS

NYSE SYMBOL WXS
Rec. Pr. 6.47 (4/30/01)

WESTPOINT STEVENS INC.

YIELD 1.2%
P/E RATIO . . .

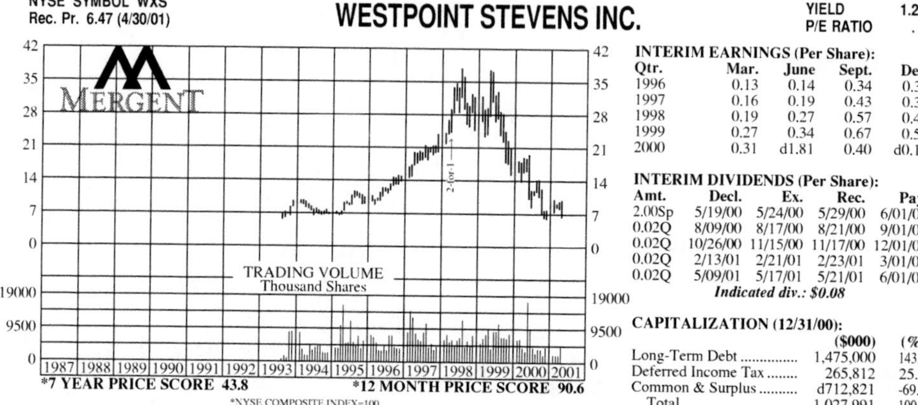

INTERIM EARNINGS (Per Share):

Qtr.	Mar.	June	Sept.	Dec.
1996	0.13	0.14	0.34	0.31
1997	0.16	0.19	0.43	0.38
1998	0.19	0.27	0.57	0.49
1999	0.27	0.34	0.67	0.56
2000	0.31	d1.81	0.40	d0.18

INTERIM DIVIDENDS (Per Share):

Amt.	Decl.	Ex.	Rec.	Pay.
2.00Sp	5/19/00	5/24/00	5/29/00	6/01/00
0.02Q	8/09/00	8/17/00	8/21/00	9/01/00
0.02Q	10/26/00	11/15/00	11/17/00	12/01/00
0.02Q	2/13/01	2/21/01	2/23/01	3/01/01
0.02Q	5/09/01	5/17/01	5/21/01	6/01/01

Indicated div.: $0.08

CAPITALIZATION (12/31/00):

	($000)	(%)
Long-Term Debt	1,475,000	143.5
Deferred Income Tax	265,812	25.9
Common & Surplus	d712,821	-69.3
Total	1,027,991	100.0

RECENT DEVELOPMENTS: For the year ended 12/31/00, net loss totaled $63.3 million compared with net income of $104.1 million in the prior year. Results for 2000 included after-tax restructuring and impairment charges of $130.1 million. Net sales slipped 3.6% to $1.82 billion from $1.88 billion the year before, reflecting continued weak demand for home fashion products and significant inventory reduction by certain major retailers. Operating earnings amounted to $34.9 million versus $268.1 million a year earlier.

PROSPECTS: On 1/5/01, the Company completed its acquisition of CMI Industries, Inc.'s Chatham Consumer Products division, which is a manufacturer and wholesaler of woven blankets with estimated annual sales of $35.0 million. Looking ahead, WXS is targeting sales growth of 10.0% or more in 2001. This sales growth is expected to be fueled by the Company's expanded Ralph Lauren business, new Walt Disney license shipments and additional sales from the Chatham acquisition.

BUSINESS

WESTPOINT STEVENS INC. manufactures and markets home fashions consumer products. The Company manufactures and markets a broad range of bed and bath products including: decorative sheets, accessories and towels; designer sheets, accessories and towels; sheets, accessories and towels for the hospitality industry; blankets; private label sheets, accessories and towels; bedskirts; bedspreads; comforters; duvet covers; drapes; valances; throw pillows; bed pillows; mattress pads; shower curtains and table covers. Home Fashions trademarks include GRAND PATRICIAN®, MARTEX®, PATRICIAN®, UTICA®, STEVENS®, LADY PEPPERELL® and VELLUX®. Also, certain products are manufactured and sold under licensing agreements that include, among others, RALPH LAUREN HOME, DISNEY HOME, SANDERSON, DESIGNERS GUILD, JOE BOXER, GLYNDA TURLEY and SERTA PERFECT SLEEPER.

ANNUAL FINANCIAL DATA

	12/31/00	12/31/99	12/31/98	12/31/97	12/31/96	12/31/95	12/31/94
Earnings Per Share	[2] **d1.28**	**1.84**	**1.51**	[1] **1.11**	**0.91**	**d1.98**	**d3.01**
Cash Flow Per Share	**0.35**	**3.33**	**2.85**	**2.34**	**2.12**	**1.96**	**1.77**
Dividends Per Share	**2.08**	**0.06**	. . .	. . .	. . .	. . .	. . .
Dividend Payout %	. . .	**3.3**	. . .	. . .	. . .	. . .	. . .
INCOME STATEMENT (IN MILLIONS):							
Total Revenues	1,815.9	1,883.3	1,779.0	1,657.5	1,723.8	1,649.9	1,596.8
Costs & Expenses	1,700.1	1,531.1	1,450.1	1,365.4	1,451.3	1,386.8	1,339.4
Depreciation & Amort.	80.8	84.1	80.6	77.2	77.0	258.1	323.1
Operating Income	34.9	268.1	248.3	214.9	195.6	5.0	d65.8
Net Interest Inc./(Exp.)	d122.3	d102.4	d105.7	d102.2	d102.4	d101.3	d102.1
Income Before Income Taxes	d98.8	162.9	141.7	110.2	90.4	d99.4	d180.8
Income Taxes	cr35.4	58.8	51.1	41.0	32.7	30.5	22.6
Net Income	[2] d63.3	104.1	90.6	[1] 69.3	57.7	d129.8	d203.4
Cash Flow	17.5	188.2	171.1	146.5	134.7	128.2	119.7
Average Shs. Outstg. (000)	49,635	56,598	59,949	62,654	63,566	65,398	67,550
BALANCE SHEET (IN MILLIONS):							
Cash & Cash Equivalents	0.2	0.2	0.5	17.4	14.0	8.0	2.0
Total Current Assets	548.9	548.3	469.7	473.5	395.6	430.9	393.2
Net Property	772.0	840.7	776.9	707.2	706.0	684.2	665.6
Total Assets	1,458.4	1,540.7	1,391.2	1,286.1	1,157.0	1,143.0	1,270.2
Total Current Liabilities	368.9	315.2	291.5	261.3	254.7	315.2	270.4
Long-Term Obligations	1,475.0	1,375.0	1,275.0	1,146.3	1,075.0	1,075.0	1,035.0
Net Stockholders' Equity	d712.8	d498.0	d487.5	d423.0	d450.4	d505.9	d337.2
Net Working Capital	180.1	233.1	178.2	212.2	140.9	115.7	122.7
Year-end Shs. Outstg. (000)	49,414	52,241	56,285	59,401	61,704	63,952	67,312
STATISTICAL RECORD:							
Operating Profit Margin %	1.9	14.2	14.0	13.0	11.3	0.3	. . .
Net Profit Margin %	. . .	5.5	5.1	4.2	3.3	. . .	. . .
Return on Assets %	. . .	6.8	6.5	5.4	5.0	. . .	. . .
Debt/Total Assets %	101.1	89.2	91.6	89.1	92.9	94.1	81.5
Price Range	19.63-5.94	37.56-15.19	37.88-21.75	23.88-14.50	15.13-8.75	11.75-6.56	9.75-6.38
P/E Ratio	. . .	20.4-8.3	25.1-14.4	21.5-13.1	16.7-9.7	. . .	. . .
Average Yield %	16.3	0.2	. . .	. . .	. . .	. . .	. . .

Statistics are as originally reported. Adj. for stk. split: 2-for-1, 3/2/98 [1] Bef. disc. oper. gain $8.8 mill. ($0.14/sh.) [2] Incl. $130.1 mill. ($2.62/sh) after-tax restr. chrg.

OFFICERS:
H. T. Green, Jr., Chmn., C.E.O.
M. L. Fontenot, Pres., C.O.O.
D. C. Meek, Exec. V.P., C.F.O.

INVESTOR CONTACT: Glenda Strong, Inv. Rel., (706) 645-4000

PRINCIPAL OFFICE: 507 West Tenth Street, West Point, GA 31833

TELEPHONE NUMBER: (706) 645-4000
FAX: (706) 645-4396
WEB: www.westpointstevens.com

NO. OF EMPLOYEES: 16,286 (approx.)

SHAREHOLDERS: 278 (record)

ANNUAL MEETING: In May

INCORPORATED: DE, 1987

INSTITUTIONAL HOLDINGS:
No. of Institutions: 84
Shares Held: 22,308,901
% Held: 45.1

INDUSTRY: Housefurnishings, nec (SIC: 2392)

TRANSFER AGENT(S): The Bank of New York, New York, NY

NYSE SYMBOL W
Rec. Pr. 26.38 (4/30/01)

WESTVACO CORPORATION

YIELD 3.3%
P/E RATIO 11.2

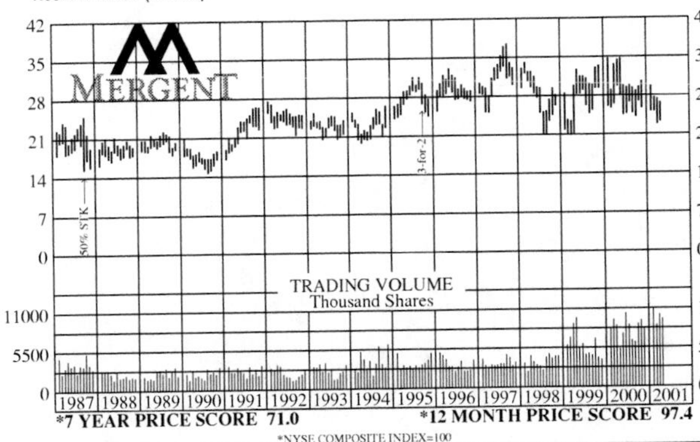

INTERIM EARNINGS (Per Share):

Qtr.	Jan.	April	July	Oct.
1996-97	0.35	0.37	0.37	0.51
1997-98	0.32	0.34	0.31	0.33
1998-99	0.25	0.27	0.35	0.24
1999-00	0.50	0.70	0.53	0.80
2000-01	0.33	...	...	...

INTERIM DIVIDENDS (Per Share):

Amt.	Decl.	Ex.	Rec.	Pay.
0.22Q	5/23/00	5/31/00	6/02/00	7/03/00
0.22Q	8/22/00	8/30/00	9/01/00	10/02/00
0.22Q	11/28/00	12/06/00	12/08/00	1/02/01
0.22Q	2/27/01	3/07/01	3/09/01	4/02/01
0.22Q	5/22/01	5/30/01	6/01/01	7/02/01

Indicated div.: $0.88 (Div. Reinv. Plan)

CAPITALIZATION (10/31/00):

	($000)	(%)
Long-Term Debt [1]	2,686,674	45.3
Deferred Income Tax	907,739	15.3
Common & Surplus	2,332,593	39.4
Total	5,927,006	100.0

RECENT DEVELOPMENTS: For the quarter ended 1/31/01, net income decreased 33.7% to $33.3 million compared with $50.2 million in the equivalent 2000 quarter. The decline in earnings was primarily attributed to the rapid deceleration in U.S. economic growth and related lower demand for coated papers and bleached paperboard. Total revenues were $937.7 million, up 15.5% from $812.0 million a year earlier.

PROSPECTS: Looking ahead, W plans to continue to focus on product innovation, new technologies, cost control, and strategic acquisitions in global markets. Paper segment revenues may continue to be negatively affected by lower sales of coated paper for commercial printing and label applications and competition from imported coated paper. However, the chemical segment may benefit from higher sales of activated carbon for automotive emission controls and resins used in printing inks and other products.

BUSINESS

WESTVACO CORPORATION is a producer of paper, packaging and specialty chemicals. International business accounts for about 25% of sales and involves customers in more than 70 nations. In addition to exporting a wide range of products from the United States, the Company further supports its global packaging business with wholly-owned manufacturing operations in Brazil and the Czech Republic. Westvaco owns 1.5 million acres of timberlands in the United States and Brazil. Dividends have been paid since 1895.

BUSINESS LINE ANALYSIS

(10/31/2000)	Rev (%)	Inc (%)
Packaging Products	59.4	63.1
Paper Products	31.8	25.3
Chemical Products	8.8	11.6
Total	100.0	100.0

ANNUAL FINANCIAL DATA

	10/31/00	10/31/99	10/31/98	10/31/97	10/31/96	10/31/95	10/31/94
Earnings Per Share	**[4][3] 2.53**	**[4] 1.11**	**1.30**	**1.60**	**2.09**	**[3] 2.80**	**[2] 1.03**
Cash Flow Per Share	**5.63**	**3.90**	**4.06**	**4.23**	**4.45**	**5.08**	**3.21**
Tang. Book Val. Per Share	**23.17**	**21.65**	**22.39**	**22.35**	**21.69**	**20.49**	**18.48**
Dividends Per Share	**0.88**	**0.88**	**0.88**	**0.88**	**0.88**	**0.77**	**0.73**
Dividend Payout %	**34.8**	**79.3**	**67.7**	**55.0**	**42.1**	**27.5**	**71.2**
INCOME STATEMENT (IN MILLIONS):							
Total Revenues	3,719.9	2,831.2	2,904.7	3,011.0	3,074.5	3,302.7	2,613.2
Costs & Expenses	2,794.2	2,200.5	2,309.1	2,402.0	2,408.1	2,501.9	2,122.9
Depreciation & Amort.	313.9	280.5	281.0	269.2	240.4	230.3	219.3
Operating Income	611.8	350.3	314.6	339.9	426.0	570.5	271.0
Net Interest Inc./(Exp.)	d192.1	d123.5	d110.2	d93.3	d90.1	d100.2	d109.1
Income Before Income Taxes	403.6	148.0	204.4	246.6	336.0	470.3	161.9
Income Taxes	148.9	36.8	72.4	83.9	123.8	186.9	58.3
Net Income	[4][3] 254.7	[4] 111.2	132.0	162.7	212.2	[3] 283.4	[2] 103.6
Cash Flow	568.6	391.6	413.0	431.9	452.6	513.7	322.9
Average Shs. Outstg. (000)	100,916	100,495	101,788	101,978	101,737	101,190	100,581
BALANCE SHEET (IN MILLIONS):							
Cash & Cash Equivalents	225.3	108.8	105.1	175.4	115.4	151.8	75.0
Total Current Assets	1,063.7	738.0	739.2	805.2	716.1	787.0	630.6
Net Property	4,196.6	3,581.4	3,802.4	3,684.4	3,353.7	3,140.1	3,063.4
Total Assets	6,569.9	4,896.7	5,008.7	4,898.8	4,437.5	4,252.7	3,983.0
Total Current Liabilities	566.9	425.1	467.1	405.6	418.9	428.7	361.6
Long-Term Obligations	2,686.7	...	...	...	...	...	...
Net Stockholders' Equity	2,332.6	2,171.3	2,246.4	2,278.6	2,209.7	2,080.6	1,862.0
Net Working Capital	496.8	312.9	272.1	399.6	297.2	358.3	269.0
Year-end Shs. Outstg. (000)	100,662	100,292	100,326	101,930	101,891	101,551	100,750
STATISTICAL RECORD:							
Operating Profit Margin %	16.4	12.4	10.8	11.3	13.9	17.3	10.4
Net Profit Margin %	6.8	3.9	4.5	5.4	6.9	8.6	4.0
Return on Equity %	10.9	5.1	5.9	7.1	9.6	13.6	5.6
Return on Assets %	3.9	2.3	2.6	3.3	4.8	6.7	2.6
Debt/Total Assets %	40.9	...	...	...	...	...	...
Price Range	34.75-24.06	33.50-20.81	34.13-21.00	37.50-25.00	33.13-25.38	31.67-24.08	26.50-19.75
P/E Ratio	13.7-9.5	30.2-18.7	26.2-16.2	23.4-15.6	15.8-12.1	11.3-8.6	25.7-19.2
Average Yield %	3.0	3.2	3.2	2.8	3.0	2.8	3.2

Statistics are as originally reported. [1] Incl. capital lease obligations. [2] Incl. net gains of $6.0 mill. from sale of assets. [3] Bef. extraord. chrg. $2.6 mill., 1995; $8.8 mill., 2000. [4] Incl. restruct. chrg. of $80.5 mill., 1999; $16.1 mill., 2000.

OFFICERS:
J. A. Luke, Jr., Chmn., Pres., C.E.O.
K. R. Osar, Sr. V.P., C.F.O
W. L. Wilkie, II, Sr. V.P., Gen. Couns.

INVESTOR CONTACT: Roger A. Holmes, (203) 461-7537

PRINCIPAL OFFICE: 299 Park Avenue, New York, NY 10171

TELEPHONE NUMBER: (212) 688-5000
FAX: (212) 318-5104
WEB: www.westvaco.com

NO. OF EMPLOYEES: 17,100 (approx.)

SHAREHOLDERS: 13,890 (approx.)

ANNUAL MEETING: In Feb.

INCORPORATED: DE, July, 1899

INSTITUTIONAL HOLDINGS:
No. of Institutions: 249
Shares Held: 77,742,107
% Held: 77.2

INDUSTRY: Paper mills (SIC: 2621)

TRANSFER AGENT(S): The Bank of New York, New York, NY

NYSE SYMBOL WON
Rec. Pr. 26.25 (4/30/01)

WESTWOOD ONE, INC.

YIELD ...
P/E RATIO 70.9

MERGENT

TRADING VOLUME
Thousand Shares

2-for-1

*7 YEAR PRICE SCORE 126.1 *12 MONTH PRICE SCORE 100.8
*NYSE COMPOSITE INDEX=100

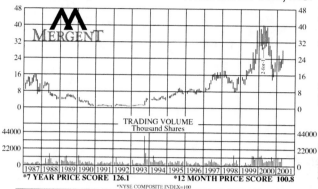

INTERIM EARNINGS (Per Share):

Qtr.	Mar.	June	Sept.	Dec.
1998	Nil	0.06	0.06	0.08
1999	d0.01	0.07	0.08	0.12
2000	0.03	0.09	0.09	0.16

INTERIM DIVIDENDS (Per Share):

Amt.	Decl.	Ex.	Rec.	Pay.
2-for-1	1/27/00	3/23/00	3/08/00	3/22/00

CAPITALIZATION (12/31/00):

	($000)	(%)
Long-Term Debt	168,000	14.8
Deferred Income Tax	15,568	1.4
Common & Surplus	949,892	83.8
Total	1,133,460	100.0

RECENT DEVELOPMENTS: For the year ended 12/31/00, net income jumped 77.0% to $42.3 million compared with $23.9 million in the previous year. Net revenues improved 54.5% to $553.7 million due primarily to higher net revenues at the Company's traffic operations and continued growth at the Company's core advertising business. Operating income improved 70.2% to $103.5 million versus $60.8 million the year before.

PROSPECTS: Going forward, WON should continue to post revenue growth in 2001. In addition, WON's core business continues to be strong excluding the Internet advertising segment. Meanwhile, WON will continue to focus on expanding its new business efforts in an attempt to replace the decline in revenue from the Internet advertisers segment. Separately, WON signed a three-year renewal agreement with the MTV Radio Network. Under the agreement, MTV will provide programming in the form of three daily news and prep services.

BUSINESS

WESTWOOD ONE, INC. offers over 150 news, sports, music, talk, entertainment programs, features, live events and 24 hour/seven days a week formats. Through its subsidiaries, Metro Networks/Shadow Broadcast Services, the Company provides local content to the radio and TV industries including news, sports, weather, traffic, video news services and other information. SmartRoute Systems manages update information centers for state and local departments of transportation, and markets traffic and travel content to wireless, Internet, in-vehicle navigation systems and voice portal customers. The Company serves more than 7,500 radio stations. The Company is managed by Infinity Broadcasting Corporation

QUARTERLY DATA

(12/31/2000)($000)	Rev	Inc
1st Quarter	122,102	3,956
2nd Quarter	136,501	10,644
3rd Quarter	139,014	9,870
4th Quarter	156,076	17,813

ANNUAL FINANCIAL DATA

	12/31/00	12/31/99	12/31/98	12/31/97	12/31/96	12/31/95	[3] 12/31/94
Earnings Per Share	**0.36**	**0.30**	**[4] 0.20**	**0.37**	**0.26**	**0.14**	**[1][2] d0.04**
Cash Flow Per Share	**0.90**	**0.69**	**0.47**	**0.56**	**0.44**	**0.34**	**0.26**
INCOME STATEMENT (IN MILLIONS):							
Total Revenues	553.7	358.3	259.3	240.8	171.8	145.7	136.3
Costs & Expenses	388.1	267.3	207.5	191.9	132.2	112.7	112.2
Depreciation & Amort.	62.1	30.2	18.4	13.0	12.3	13.8	18.2
Operating Income	103.5	60.8	33.4	35.9	27.3	19.3	6.0
Net Interest Inc./(Exp.)	d10.8	d12.1	d10.3	d8.5	d8.7	d9.5	d8.8
Income Before Income Taxes	93.4	49.3	23.4	27.7	18.8	10.2	d2.5
Income Taxes	51.1	25.4	10.4	2.2	1.3	0.5	0.2
Net Income	42.3	23.9	[4] 13.0	25.5	17.5	9.7	[1][2] d2.7
Cash Flow	104.4	54.1	31.5	38.5	29.8	23.4	15.4
Average Shs. Outstg. (000)	115,864	78,930	66,868	69,302	67,126	68,620	58,828
BALANCE SHEET (IN MILLIONS):							
Cash & Cash Equivalents	6.8	10.6	2.5	2.8	2.7	0.3	2.4
Total Current Assets	153.9	169.3	85.7	77.9	48.4	41.9	46.2
Net Property	58.1	56.0	24.4	15.5	16.1	15.6	16.7
Total Assets	1,285.6	1,334.9	345.3	335.9	273.0	245.6	260.1
Total Current Liabilities	138.2	128.0	78.6	65.8	52.0	35.3	38.5
Long-Term Obligations	168.0	158.0	170.0	115.0	130.4	107.9	115.4
Net Stockholders' Equity	949.9	1,019.8	77.2	124.7	86.8	94.1	95.5
Net Working Capital	15.7	41.3	7.1	12.2	d3.6	6.6	7.7
Year-end Shs. Outstg. (000)	129,300	127,898	57,334	63,438	59,844	62,502	62,010
STATISTICAL RECORD:							
Operating Profit Margin %	18.7	17.0	12.9	14.9	15.9	13.3	4.4
Net Profit Margin %	7.6	6.7	5.0	10.6	10.2	6.6	...
Return on Equity %	4.5	2.3	16.9	20.4	20.2	10.3	...
Return on Assets %	3.3	1.8	3.8	7.6	6.4	3.9	...
Debt/Total Assets %	13.1	11.8	49.2	34.2	47.8	44.0	44.4
Price Range	40.38-13.75	38.00-11.41	18.25-7.75	17.50-8.19	9.50-6.75	9.75-4.81	5.81-3.56
P/E Ratio	112.1-38.2	126.6-38.0	93.5-39.7	47.3-22.1	36.5-26.0	69.6-34.4	...

Statistics are as originally reported. Adj. for stk. split: 2-for-1, 3/00 [1] Incl. restruct. costs, $2.4 mill. [2] Bef. extraord. loss, $590,000 [3] Fiscal year-end changed from 11/30 to 12/31 [4] Incl. non-recurr. chrg., $551,000

OFFICERS:
N. J. Pattiz, Chmn.
J. Hollander, Pres., C.E.O.
F. Suleman, Exec. V.P., C.F.O., Sec.

INVESTOR CONTACT: Farid Suleman, Exec. V.P., C.F.O., Sec., (212) 641-2000

PRINCIPAL OFFICE: 40 West 57th Street, 5th Floor, New York, NY 10019

TELEPHONE NUMBER: (212) 641-2000
WEB: www.westwoodone.com

NO. OF EMPLOYEES: 2,900 (approx.)

SHAREHOLDERS: 340 (approximately)

ANNUAL MEETING: In May

INCORPORATED: CA, 1974; reincorp., DE, July, 1985

INSTITUTIONAL HOLDINGS:
No. of Institutions: 171
Shares Held: 70,580,138
% Held: 65.2

INDUSTRY: Communication services, nec (SIC: 4899)

TRANSFER AGENT(S): City National Bank, Beverly Hills, CA

NYSE SYMBOL WY
Rec. Pr. 57.21 (5/31/01)

WEYERHAEUSER COMPANY

YIELD 2.8%
P/E RATIO 15.4

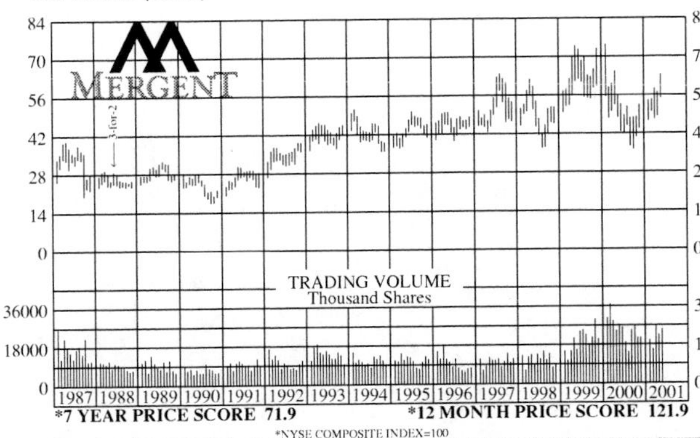

*7 YEAR PRICE SCORE 71.9 *12 MONTH PRICE SCORE 121.9

*NYSE COMPOSITE INDEX=100

INTERIM EARNINGS (Per Share):

Qtr.	March	June	Sept.	Dec.
1997	0.10	0.56	0.53	0.49
1998	0.43	0.34	0.56	0.15
1999	0.21	0.81	1.18	0.79
2000	1.04	0.89	0.90	0.89

INTERIM DIVIDENDS (Per Share):

Amt.	Decl.	Ex.	Rec.	Pay.
0.40Q	4/18/00	5/03/00	5/05/00	5/30/00
0.40Q	7/06/00	7/26/00	7/28/00	8/28/00
0.40Q	10/12/00	11/01/00	11/03/00	12/04/00
0.40Q	1/09/01	1/31/01	2/02/01	3/05/01
0.40Q	4/17/01	5/02/01	5/04/01	6/04/01

Indicated div.: $1.60 (Div. Reinv. Plan)

CAPITALIZATION (12/31/00):

	($000)	(%)
Long-Term Debt	4,336,000	32.0
Deferred Income Tax	2,377,000	17.5
Common & Surplus	6,832,000	50.4
Total	13,545,000	100.0

RECENT DEVELOPMENTS: For the year ended 12/31/00, net income advanced 36.4% to $840.0 million. Results included nonrecurring charges of $186.0 million in 2000 and $134.0 million in 1999 for the integration and closure of facilities. Total net sales and revenues were $15.98 billion, up 25.0% from $12.78 billion a year earlier. Operating income rose 30.9% to $1.49 billion from $1.14 billion the year before. Comparisons were made with restated prior-year figures.

PROSPECTS: In 2001, WY will continue to focus on improving operational efficiencies and streamlining the delivery of internal support services. Meanwhile, on 5/7/01, the Company announced that it increased the price of its tender offer for all outstanding shares of Willamette Industries, Inc. to $50.00 per share from $48.00 per share. Also, the date of the expiration of the tender offer was extended to await the results of the Willamette shareholder vote for its board of directors.

BUSINESS

WEYERHAEUSER COMPANY is a grower and harvester of timber and a manufacturer, distributor and seller of forest products, real estate development and construction, and other real estate related activities. WY has offices or operations in 17 countries. WY owns 5.9 million acres and leases 500,000 acres of commercial forest land in the U.S. and British Columbia, most of it highly productive and located well to serve both domestic and international markets. WY also has license arrangements in Canada covering about 31.6 million acres (of which 20.0 million acres are considered to be productive forestland). Sales breakdown in 2000 was: Timberlands, 7.0%; Wood Products, 43.0%; Pulp, Paper, and Packaging, 41.0%; and Real Estate and related assets, 9.0%. In 1997, the Company sold its mortgage banking business. Financial Services has been combined with Real Estate to form one segment.

ANNUAL FINANCIAL DATA

	12/31/00	12/26/99	12/27/98	12/28/97	12/31/96	12/31/95	12/25/94
Earnings Per Share	**[4] 3.72**	**[1][3] 2.98**	**[1] 1.47**	**[1] 1.71**	**2.34**	**[2] 3.93**	**2.86**
Cash Flow Per Share	**7.53**	**6.08**	**4.93**	**4.88**	**5.45**	**6.98**	**5.46**
Tang. Book Val. Per Share	**26.56**	**28.23**	**22.74**	**23.30**	**23.21**	**22.57**	**20.86**
Dividends Per Share	**1.60**	**1.60**	**1.60**	**1.60**	**1.60**	**1.50**	**1.20**
Dividend Payout %	**43.0**	**53.7**	**108.8**	**93.6**	**68.4**	**38.2**	**42.0**
INCOME STATEMENT (IN MILLIONS):							
Total Revenues	15,980.0	12,262.0	10,766.0	11,210.0	11,114.0	11,788.0	10,398.0
Costs & Expenses	13,630.0	10,494.0	9,423.0	9,813.0	9,427.0	9,564.0	8,644.0
Depreciation & Amort.	859.0	640.0	616.0	628.0	617.0	621.0	534.0
Operating Income	1,491.0	1,128.0	656.0	769.0	1,070.0	1,603.0	1,220.0
Net Interest Inc./(Exp.)	d351.0	d277.0	d273.0	d297.0	d319.0	d315.0	d277.0
Income Before Income Taxes	1,194.0	905.0	492.0	556.0	778.0	1,315.0	962.0
Income Taxes	483.0	354.0	169.0	197.0	257.0	445.0	331.0
Equity Earnings/Minority Int.	129.0	65.0	42.0	d17.0	d58.0	d71.0	d42.0
Net Income	[4] 840.0	[1][3] 616.0	[1] 365.0	[1] 342.0	463.0	[2] 799.0	589.0
Cash Flow	1,699.0	1,256.0	981.0	970.0	1,080.0	1,420.0	1,123.0
Average Shs. Outstg. (000)	225,608	206,626	198,914	198,967	198,318	203,525	205,543
BALANCE SHEET (IN MILLIONS):							
Cash & Cash Equivalents	115.0	1,640.0	28.0	100.0	33.0	34.0	67.0
Total Current Assets	3,288.0	4,543.0	2,170.0	2,294.0	2,324.0	2,327.0	2,006.0
Net Property	11,965.0	11,094.0	9,458.0	9,721.0	10,046.0	9,356.0	8,815.0
Total Assets	18,195.0	18,339.0	12,834.0	13,075.0	13,596.0	13,253.0	13,007.0
Total Current Liabilities	2,704.0	2,934.0	1,499.0	1,384.0	1,483.0	1,603.0	1,667.0
Long-Term Obligations	4,336.0	4,453.0	4,098.0	4,515.0	5,083.0	4,736.0	4,666.0
Net Stockholders' Equity	6,832.0	7,173.0	4,526.0	4,649.0	4,604.0	4,486.0	4,290.0
Net Working Capital	584.0	1,609.0	671.0	910.0	841.0	724.0	339.0
Year-end Shs. Outstg. (000)	213,898	226,039	199,009	199,486	198,336	198,770	205,618
STATISTICAL RECORD:							
Operating Profit Margin %	9.3	9.2	6.1	6.9	9.6	13.6	11.7
Net Profit Margin %	5.3	5.0	3.4	3.1	4.2	6.8	5.7
Return on Equity %	12.3	8.6	8.1	7.4	10.1	17.8	13.7
Return on Assets %	4.6	3.4	2.8	2.6	3.4	6.0	4.5
Debt/Total Assets %	23.8	24.3	31.9	34.5	37.4	35.7	35.9
Price Range	74.50-36.06	73.94-49.56	62.00-36.75	63.94-42.63	49.88-39.50	50.38-36.88	51.25-35.75
P/E Ratio	20.0-9.7	24.8-16.6	42.2-25.0	37.4-24.9	21.3-16.9	12.8-9.4	17.9-12.5
Average Yield %	2.9	2.6	3.2	3.0	3.6	3.4	2.8

Statistics are as originally reported. [1] Incl. a net nonrecurr. restruct. chrgs. $9.0 mill., 1997; & $45.0 mill., 1998; $65.0 mill., 1999. [2] Incl. spec. chrgs. of $184.0 mill. [3] Bef. acctg. adj. chrg. of $89.0 mill. [4] Incl. chrg. of $56.0 mill. for the closure of facilities & chrg. for settlement of hardboard siding claims of $130.0 mill.

OFFICERS:
S. R. Rogel, Chmn., Pres., C.E.O.
W. C. Stivers, Exec. V.P., C.F.O.

INVESTOR CONTACT: Richard J. Taggart, Inv. Rel., (253) 924-2058

PRINCIPAL OFFICE: 33663 Weyerhaeuser Way South, Federal Way, WA 98003

TELEPHONE NUMBER: (253) 924-2345
FAX: (253) 924-3332
WEB: www.weyerhaeuser.com

NO. OF EMPLOYEES: 47,200 (approx.)

SHAREHOLDERS: 17,437

ANNUAL MEETING: In Apr.

INCORPORATED: WA, Jan., 1900

INSTITUTIONAL HOLDINGS:
No. of Institutions: 388
Shares Held: 152,547,283
% Held: 71.1

INDUSTRY: Sawmills and planing mills, general (SIC: 2421)

TRANSFER AGENT(S): Mellon Investor Services, L.L.C. Ridgefield Park, NJ

NYSE SYMBOL WGL
Rec. Pr. 28.60 (4/30/01)

WGL HOLDINGS, INC.

YIELD 4.4%
P/E RATIO 14.2

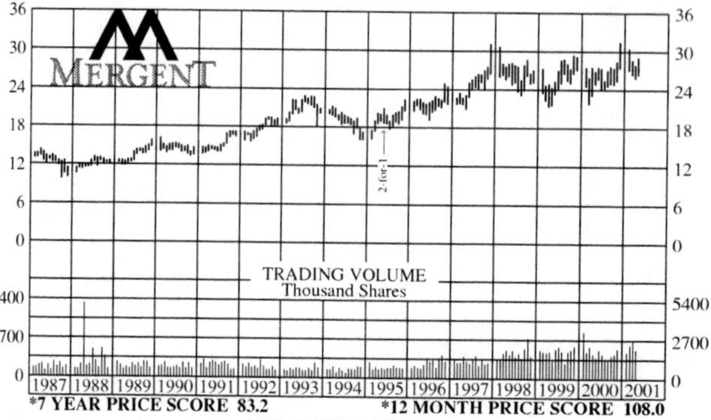

INTERIM EARNINGS (Per Share):

Qtr.	Dec.	Mar.	June	Sept.
1997-98	0.87	1.22	d0.17	d0.38
1998-99	0.55	1.39	d0.15	d0.31
1999-00	0.85	1.39	d0.12	d0.33
2000-01	1.08	...	...	...

INTERIM DIVIDENDS (Per Share):

Amt.	Decl.	Ex.	Rec.	Pay.
0.31Q	3/03/00	4/06/00	4/10/00	5/01/00
0.31Q	6/28/00	7/06/00	7/10/00	8/01/00
0.31Q	9/27/00	10/05/00	10/10/00	11/01/00
0.31Q	12/15/00	1/08/01	1/10/01	2/01/01
0.315Q	3/02/01	4/06/01	4/10/01	5/01/01

Indicated div.: $1.26 (Div. Reinv. Plan)

CAPITALIZATION (12/31/00):

	($000)	(%)
Long-Term Debt	559,576	38.1
Deferred Income Tax	169,442	11.5
Preferred Stock	28,173	1.9
Common & Surplus	711,496	48.4
Total	1,468,687	100.0

RECENT DEVELOPMENTS: For the quarter ended 12/31/00, net income advanced 27.8% to $50.4 million versus $39.4 million in 1999. Results for the 1999 period included a pre-tax nonrecurring gain of $365,000 from the sale of non-utility assets. Total revenues grew 77.0% to $647.0 million from $365.6 million the year before. Higher revenues resulted from a 34.2% increase in the number of degree days over the same quarter of 1999.

PROSPECTS: During the recent quarter, Washington Gas Energy Services, Inc., WGL's retail energy marketing subsidiary, began selling electricity for the first time to about 8,000 accounts in Maryland and Virginia. The electricity operations reported a net loss due to start-up costs associated with initial customer acquisitions and transmission arrangements. Earnings from WGL's operations are expected to improve during the remainder of 2001.

BUSINESS

WGL HOLDINGS, INC., a holding company, distributes natural gas to Washington D.C. and adjoining areas through three divisions: District of Columbia Natural Gas, Maryland Natural Gas and Northern Virginia Natural Gas. WGL also has four active subsidiaries: Shenandoah Gas, Frederick Gas and Hampshire Gas, which provide gas service to areas in Virginia; Crab Run Gas, which is involved in the exploration and development of natural gas prospects; and Washington Resources Group, which conducts WGL's non-gas investments including real estate, energy-related services and equity holdings in emerging growth companies. The 1,607 million therms delivered in 2000 were derived as follows: 69% firm customers, 31.0% interruptible customers.

REVENUES

(9/30/2000)	($000)	(%)
Utility Revenues	1,031,105	82.5
Retail Energy Marketing	166,705	13.4
Heating, Vent & Air Condi	47,473	3.8
Consumer Financing	2,962	0.2
Other Non-utlity	947	0.1
Total	1,249,192	100.0

ANNUAL FINANCIAL DATA

	12/31/00	9/30/99	9/30/98	9/30/97	9/30/96	9/30/95	9/30/94
Earnings Per Share	**4 1.79**	**3 1.47**	**2 1.54**	**1.85**	**1 1.85**	**1.45**	**1.42**
Cash Flow Per Share	**3.27**	**2.88**	**2.90**	**3.13**	**3.09**	**2.65**	**2.56**
Tang. Book Val. Per Share	**15.31**	**14.72**	**13.83**	**13.48**	**12.79**	**11.95**	**11.51**
Dividends Per Share	**1.24**	**1.22**	**1.20**	**1.18**	**1.14**	**1.12**	**1.10**
Dividend Payout %	**69.0**	**82.6**	**77.6**	**63.8**	**61.3**	**77.1**	**78.1**
INCOME STATEMENT (IN MILLIONS):							
Total Revenues	1,248.0	1,112.2	1,040.6	1,055.8	969.8	828.7	914.9
Costs & Expenses	969.6	861.1	802.8	799.8	720.7	616.4	701.5
Depreciation & Amort.	68.9	65.2	59.4	55.9	53.5	51.3	48.0
Maintenance Exp.	31.2	35.6	38.5	36.9	33.1	31.3	35.8
Operating Income	128.9	107.8	140.0	163.1	162.4	129.7	129.6
Net Interest Inc./(Exp.)	d43.7	d37.0	d37.7	d34.1	d30.6	d31.9	d32.1
Income Taxes	49.3	42.5	38.0	47.9	49.4	37.5	37.3
Net Income	4 84.6	3 68.8	2 68.6	82.0	1 81.6	62.9	60.5
Cash Flow	152.2	132.6	126.7	136.6	133.8	112.9	107.1
Average Shs. Outstg. (000)	46,473	45,984	43,691	43,706	43,360	42,575	41,836
BALANCE SHEET (IN MILLIONS):							
Gross Property	2,225.3	2,114.1	1,992.8	1,846.5	1,722.0	1,608.5	1,516.2
Accumulated Depreciation	765.0	711.3	673.3	629.3	591.4	552.5	521.2
Net Property	1,460.3	1,402.7	1,319.5	1,217.1	1,130.6	1,056.1	995.0
Total Assets	1,939.8	1,766.7	1,682.4	1,552.0	1,464.6	1,360.1	1,333.0
Long-Term Obligations	559.6	506.1	428.6	431.6	353.9	329.1	342.3
Net Stockholders' Equity	739.7	712.5	636.2	617.5	587.2	541.5	514.0
Year-end Shs. Outstg. (000)	46,470	46,473	43,955	43,700	43,704	42,932	42,186
STATISTICAL RECORD:							
Operating Profit Margin %	10.3	9.7	13.5	15.5	16.8	15.7	14.2
Net Profit Margin %	6.8	6.2	6.6	7.8	8.4	7.6	6.6
Net Inc./Net Property %	5.8	4.9	5.2	6.7	7.2	6.0	6.1
Net Inc./Tot. Capital %	5.8	5.0	5.7	6.9	7.6	6.3	6.2
Return on Equity %	11.4	9.7	10.8	13.3	13.9	11.6	11.8
Accum. Depr./Gross Prop. %	34.4	33.6	33.8	34.1	34.3	34.3	34.4
Price Range	31.50-21.75	29.44-21.31	30.75-23.06	31.13-20.88	25.00-19.13	22.38-16.13	21.25-16.00
P/E Ratio	17.6-12.2	20.0-14.5	20.0-15.0	16.8-11.3	13.5-10.3	15.4-11.1	15.0-11.3
Average Yield %	4.6	4.8	4.4	4.5	5.1	5.8	5.9

Statistics are as originally reported. Adjusted for 2-for-1 stock split 5/95. 1 Incl. a nonrecurr. after-tax chg. of $3.8 mill. assoc. with the Company's reorganization. 2 Incl. a net gain of $1.6 mill. from the sale of investments in venture capital funds. 3 Incl. a nonrecurr. gain of $100,000. 4 Incl. a nonrecurr. gain of $711,000 mill. fr. the sale of assets.

OFFICERS:
J. H. DeGraffenreidt Jr., Chmn., Pres., C.E.O.
F. M. Kline, V.P., C.F.O.
S. C. Jennings, Treas.

INVESTOR CONTACT: Craig Gilbert, Mgr. Inv. Rel., (202) 624-6410

PRINCIPAL OFFICE: 1100 H Street, N.W., Washington, DC 20080

TELEPHONE NUMBER: (703) 750-4440
FAX: (202) 624-6196
WEB: www.washgas.com

NO. OF EMPLOYEES: 2,048

SHAREHOLDERS: 20,029

ANNUAL MEETING: In Mar.

INCORPORATED: DC, Mar., 1957

INSTITUTIONAL HOLDINGS:
No. of Institutions: 158
Shares Held: 19,240,202
% Held: 41.4

INDUSTRY: Natural gas distribution (SIC: 4924)

TRANSFER AGENT(S): The Bank of New York, New York, NY

NYSE SYMBOL WHR
Rec. Pr. 62.89 (5/31/01)

WHIRLPOOL CORPORATION

YIELD 2.2%
P/E RATIO 12.2

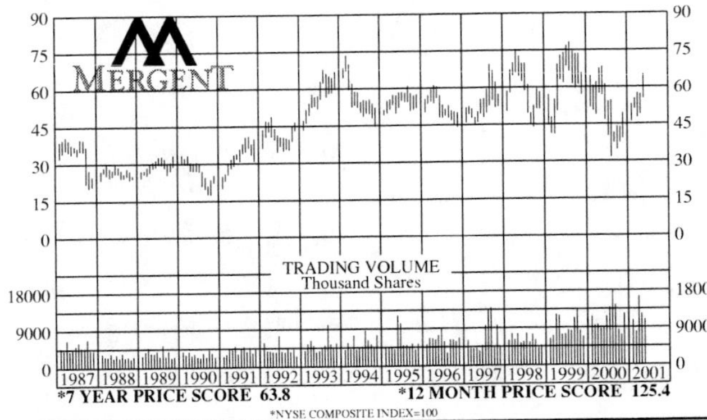

*7 YEAR PRICE SCORE 63.8 *12 MONTH PRICE SCORE 125.4
*NYSE COMPOSITE INDEX=100

INTERIM EARNINGS (Per Share):

Qtr.	Mar.	June	Sept.	Dec.
1996	0.50	0.70	0.28	0.60
1997	0.62	0.86	d2.69	0.66
1998	0.90	1.05	1.02	1.09
1999	0.36	1.30	1.40	1.51
2000	1.52	1.66	0.98	1.00

INTERIM DIVIDENDS (Per Share):

Amt.	Decl.	Ex.	Rec.	Pay.
0.34Q	4/18/00	5/16/00	5/18/00	6/15/00
0.34Q	8/15/00	8/28/00	8/30/00	9/15/00
0.34Q	10/17/00	11/29/00	12/01/00	12/31/00
0.34Q	2/20/01	2/28/01	3/02/01	3/15/01
0.34Q	4/17/01	5/15/01	5/17/01	6/15/01

Indicated div.: $1.36 (Div. Reinv. Plan)

CAPITALIZATION (12/31/00):

	($000)	(%)
Long-Term Debt	795,000	28.4
Deferred Income Tax	175,000	6.2
Minority Interest	147,000	5.2
Common & Surplus	1,684,000	60.1
Total	2,801,000	100.0

RECENT DEVELOPMENTS: For the year ended 12/31/00, net earnings totaled $367.0 million, up 5.8% compared with $347.0 million in the prior year. Net sales slipped 1.8% to $10.33 billion from $10.51 billion a year earlier, due primarily to unfavorable foreign currency exchange rates. Operating profit was down 7.8% to $807.0 million from $875.0 million the year before. For the quarter ended 12/31/00, net earnings slid 40.7% to $67.0 million from $113.0 million the previous year. Net sales declined 4.1% to $2.58 billion from $2.69 billion in 1999.

PROSPECTS: In January 2001, the Company implemented a new restructuring program focused on streamlining its worldwide operations, including the elimination of up to 6,000 positions. Initiatives under the program will be implemented in phases on a quarter-by-quarter basis and are expected to be completed within 12 to 18 months. Annual cost savings generated by the restructuring program are anticipated to be in the range of $225.0 million and $250.0 million, with pre-tax charges of between $300.0 million and $350.0 million when fully implemented.

BUSINESS

WHIRLPOOL CORPORATION and its consolidated subsidiaries manufacture and market a full line of major home appliances and other related products. The principal products include home laundry appliances, home refrigeration and room air conditioning equipment. The Company manufactures products in 13 countries and markets products in more than 170 countries. WHR markets its products under 11 brand names including WHIRLPOOL, KITCHENAID, ROPER, ESTATE, BAUKNECHT, IGNIS, LADEN and INGLIS. The Company is also the principal supplier to Sears, Roebuck and Co. of many products marketed under the KENMORE brand name.

REVENUES

(12/31/2000)	($000)	(%)
Home Refrigerators & Freezers	3,165,000	30.7
Home Laundry Appliances	3,094,000	29.9
Home Cooking Appliances	1,636,000	15.9
Other Revenues	2,430,000	23.5
Total	10,325,000	100.0

ANNUAL FINANCIAL DATA

	12/31/00	12/31/99	12/31/98	12/31/97	12/31/96	12/31/95	12/31/94
Earnings Per Share	**5.20**	**4.56**	**[1] 4.06**	**[3] d0.62**	**[2] 2.08**	**2.80**	**[2] 2.10**
Cash Flow Per Share	**10.86**	**10.16**	**9.87**	**4.15**	**6.79**	**6.95**	**5.92**
Tang. Book Val. Per Share	**13.91**	**16.00**	**13.92**	**11.25**	**14.08**	**12.61**	**13.42**
Dividends Per Share	**1.36**	**1.36**	**1.36**	**1.36**	**1.36**	**1.36**	**1.22**
Dividend Payout %	**26.2**	**29.8**	**33.5**	**...**	**65.4**	**48.6**	**58.1**
INCOME STATEMENT (IN MILLIONS):							
Total Revenues	10,325.0	10,511.0	10,323.0	8,617.0	8,696.0	8,347.0	8,104.0
Costs & Expenses	9,118.0	9,219.0	9,197.0	8,250.0	8,043.0	7,639.0	7,475.0
Depreciation & Amort.	400.0	417.0	438.0	356.0	353.0	312.0	292.0
Operating Income	807.0	875.0	688.0	11.0	300.0	396.0	397.0
Net Interest Inc./(Exp.)	d180.0	d166.0	d260.0	d168.0	d165.0	d141.0	d114.0
Income Before Income Taxes	577.0	514.0	564.0	d171.0	130.0	242.0	292.0
Income Taxes	200.0	197.0	209.0	cr9.0	81.0	100.0	176.0
Equity Earnings/Minority Int.	d10.0	30.0	d45.0	116.0	107.0	67.0	42.0
Net Income	367.0	347.0	[1] 310.0	[3] d46.0	[2] 156.0	209.0	[2] 158.0
Cash Flow	767.0	764.0	748.0	310.0	509.0	521.0	450.0
Average Shs. Outstg. (000)	70,600	75,200	75,800	74,700	75,000	75,000	76,000
BALANCE SHEET (IN MILLIONS):							
Cash & Cash Equivalents	114.0	261.0	636.0	578.0	129.0	149.0	72.0
Total Current Assets	3,237.0	3,177.0	3,882.0	4,281.0	3,812.0	3,541.0	3,078.0
Net Property	2,134.0	2,178.0	2,418.0	2,375.0	1,798.0	1,779.0	1,440.0
Total Assets	6,902.0	6,826.0	7,935.0	8,270.0	8,015.0	7,800.0	6,655.0
Total Current Liabilities	3,303.0	2,892.0	3,267.0	3,676.0	4,022.0	3,829.0	2,988.0
Long-Term Obligations	795.0	714.0	1,087.0	1,074.0	955.0	983.0	885.0
Net Stockholders' Equity	1,684.0	1,867.0	2,001.0	1,771.0	1,926.0	1,877.0	1,723.0
Net Working Capital	d66.0	285.0	615.0	605.0	d210.0	d288.0	90.0
Year-end Shs. Outstg. (000)	66,265	74,463	76,089	75,262	74,415	74,081	73,845
STATISTICAL RECORD:							
Operating Profit Margin %	7.8	8.3	6.7	0.1	3.4	4.7	4.9
Net Profit Margin %	3.6	3.3	3.0	...	1.8	2.5	1.9
Return on Equity %	21.8	18.6	15.5	...	8.1	11.1	9.2
Return on Assets %	5.3	5.1	3.9	...	1.9	2.7	2.4
Debt/Total Assets %	11.5	10.5	13.7	13.0	11.9	12.6	13.3
Price Range	68.31-31.50	78.25-40.94	75.25-43.69	69.50-45.25	61.00-44.25	60.88-49.25	73.50-44.63
P/E Ratio	13.1-6.1	17.2-9.0	18.5-10.8	...	29.3-21.3	21.7-17.6	35.0-21.2
Average Yield %	2.7	2.3	2.3	2.4	2.6	2.5	2.1

Statistics are as originally reported. [1] Bef. $15 mil ($0.19/sh) inc. fr. discont. opers. [2] Incl. $19 mil ($0.25/sh) after-tax chg., 1996; $190 mil pre-tax chg., 1994. [3] Bef. $11 mil ($0.16/sh) inc. fr. discont. opers. & incl. $252 mil ($3.35/sh) net chg.

OFFICERS:
D. R. Whitwam, Chmn., C.E.O.
J. M. Fettig, Pres., C.O.O.
M. E. Brown, Exec. V.P., C.F.O.

INVESTOR CONTACT: Thomas C. Filstrup, Dir., Investor Relations, (616) 923-3189

PRINCIPAL OFFICE: 2000 North M-63, Benton Harbor, MI 49022-2692

TELEPHONE NUMBER: (616) 923-5000
FAX: (616) 923-3978
WEB: www.whirlpoolcorp.com
NO. OF EMPLOYEES: 60,695 (avg.)
SHAREHOLDERS: 11,688 (approx.)
ANNUAL MEETING: In Apr.
INCORPORATED: DE, Aug., 1955

INSTITUTIONAL HOLDINGS:
No. of Institutions: 239
Shares Held: 59,487,684
% Held: 89.3

INDUSTRY: Household appliances, nec (SIC: 3639)

TRANSFER AGENT(S): First Chicago Trust Company of New York, Jersey City, NJ

NYSE SYMBOL JWA
Rec. Pr. 20.20 (5/31/01)

WILEY (JOHN) & SONS INC.

YIELD 0.8%
P/E RATIO 21.7

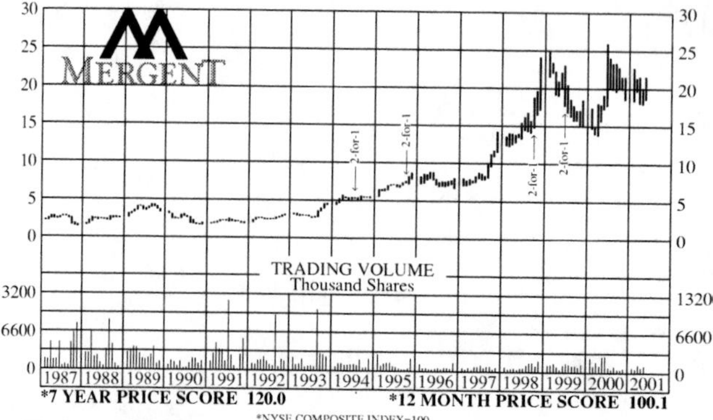

INTERIM EARNINGS (Per Share):

Qtr.	July	Oct.	Jan.	Apr.
1997-98	0.13	0.09	0.28	0.07
1998-99	0.16	0.15	0.20	0.10
1999-00	0.20	0.22	0.26	0.13
2000-01	0.26	0.27	0.27	...

INTERIM DIVIDENDS (Per Share):

Amt.	Decl.	Ex.	Rec.	Pay.
0.036Q	3/15/00	3/30/00	4/03/00	4/17/00
0.04Q	6/23/00	7/05/00	7/07/00	7/21/00
0.04Q	9/21/00	9/29/00	10/03/00	10/17/00
0.04Q	12/07/00	12/20/00	12/22/00	1/18/01
0.04Q	3/14/01	3/29/01	4/02/01	4/17/01

Indicated div.: $0.16

CAPITALIZATION (4/30/00):

	($000)	(%)
Long-Term Debt	95,000	33.5
Deferred Income Tax	15,440	5.5
Common & Surplus	172,738	61.0
Total	283,178	100.0

RECENT DEVELOPMENTS: For the quarter ended 1/31/01, net income increased 3.3% to $17.3 million from $16.7 million in the comparable 2000 quarter. Revenues grew 1.6% to $161.0 million from $158.4 million in the previous year. Revenues in the domestic professional/trade segment increased 3.6% to $43.1 million. Domestic scientific, technical, and medical segment revenues grew 4.7% to $36.2 million.

PROSPECTS: Going forward, the Company expects to achieve earnings per share growth ranging from 10.0% to 12.0% in fiscal year 2001. However, JWA experienced an unusally strong fourth quarter in 2000, which will make the year-to-year comparison difficult. Separately, JWA launched BoldIdeas, an on-line collection of forty of the Company's top business and environmental management publications.

BUSINESS

JOHN WILEY & SONS, INC. develops, publishes and markets textbooks, reference works, consumer books, periodicals, including journals and other subscription-based products and electronic media products, to colleges and universities, libraries, bookstores, professional groups, industrial organizations, government agencies and individuals in the United States and abroad. In addition, the Company imports, adapts, markets and distributes books from other publishers. The Company also develops and markets computer software and electronic databases for educational use and professional research and training.

REVENUES

(04/30/00)	REV	INC
Scientific, Tech., & Medical..................	241,618	40.6
Professional/Trade.....	198,544	33.4
Educational................	154,653	26.0
Total	594,815	100.0

ANNUAL FINANCIAL DATA

	4/30/00	4/30/99	4/30/98	4/30/97	4/30/96	4/30/95	4/30/94
Earnings Per Share	**0.81**	**0.60**	**3 0.56**	**0.31**	**2 0.37**	**1 0.28**	**0.19**
Cash Flow Per Share	**1.63**	**1.21**	**1.18**	**0.83**	**0.78**	**0.63**	**...**
Tang. Book Val. Per Share	**...**	**...**	**...**	**...**	**1.02**	**0.71**	**0.61**
Dividends Per Share	**0.14**	**0.12**	**0.11**	**0.09**	**0.08**	**0.07**	**0.07**
Dividend Payout %	**16.7**	**20.0**	**19.1**	**30.2**	**22.2**	**26.1**	**36.2**
INCOME STATEMENT (IN MILLIONS):							
Total Revenues	594.8	508.4	467.1	432.0	362.7	331.1	294.3
Costs & Expenses	452.6	404.2	363.5	362.9	302.7	281.3	251.6
Depreciation & Amort.	53.2	40.6	41.4	34.3	27.0	23.0	23.8
Operating Income	89.0	63.7	62.2	34.8	33.0	26.9	18.9
Net Interest Inc./(Exp.)	d8.4	d7.3	d7.9	d6.2	d0.4	d2.9	d3.6
Income Before Income Taxes	82.6	62.0	58.1	30.9	38.8	25.8	17.1
Income Taxes	30.2	22.3	21.5	10.5	14.1	7.5	4.9
Net Income	52.4	39.7	3 36.6	20.3	2 24.7	1 18.3	12.1
Cash Flow	105.6	80.3	78.0	54.6	51.7	41.3	35.9
Average Shs. Outstg. (000)	64,825	66,513	65,952	65,612	66,256	65,396	...
BALANCE SHEET (IN MILLIONS):							
Cash & Cash Equivalents	42.3	149.0	127.4	79.1	55.3	34.4	57.5
Total Current Assets	177.1	256.0	237.6	204.1	170.6	141.2	153.6
Net Property	38.2	34.7	34.3	32.7	23.0	21.2	19.6
Total Assets	569.3	528.6	506.9	457.9	284.5	247.5	243.9
Total Current Liabilities	254.1	195.1	178.4	164.4	139.1	130.0	118.6
Long-Term Obligations	95.0	125.0	125.0	125.0	...	...	26.0
Net Stockholders' Equity	172.7	162.2	160.8	129.0	118.0	98.8	82.3
Net Working Capital	d76.9	60.9	59.3	39.8	31.5	11.2	35.1
Year-end Shs. Outstg. (000)	60,712	62,382	63,992	63,640	64,500	63,676	63,000
STATISTICAL RECORD:							
Operating Profit Margin %	15.0	12.5	13.3	8.1	9.1	8.1	6.4
Net Profit Margin %	8.8	7.8	7.8	4.7	6.8	5.5	4.1
Return on Equity %	30.3	24.5	22.8	15.8	20.9	18.5	14.7
Return on Assets %	9.2	7.5	7.2	4.4	8.7	7.4	5.0
Debt/Total Assets %	16.7	23.6	24.7	27.3	...	...	10.7
Price Range	24.91-14.94	24.16-12.25	14.25-7.03	8.88-6.66	8.75-5.47	5.75-4.38	4.63-2.63
P/E Ratio	30.7-18.4	40.3-20.4	25.7-12.7	28.6-21.5	23.5-14.7	20.5-15.6	24.3-13.8
Average Yield %	0.7	0.7	1.0	1.2	1.2	1.4	1.9

Statistics are as originally reported. Adj. for 2-for-1 stk. split: 5/99, 10/98, 10/95 & 6/94. 1 Incl. a $2.6 mill. after-tax gain from a favorable resolution of amended tax return claims. 2 Incl. $4.4 mill. in amortization & financing exps. related to the acq. of VCH Publishing Group in June 1996. 3 Incl. $21.3 mill. gain on sale of publishing assets.

OFFICERS:
B. Wiley II, Chmn.
W. J. Pesce, Pres., C.E.O.
R. D. Wilder, Exec. V.P., C.F.O., C.O.O.

INVESTOR CONTACT: Susan Spilka, Investor Relations, (212) 850-6147

PRINCIPAL OFFICE: 605 Third Avenue, New York, NY 10158-0012

TELEPHONE NUMBER: (212) 850-6000
FAX: (212) 850-6088
WEB: www.wiley.com

NO. OF EMPLOYEES: 2,300

SHAREHOLDERS: 1,245 (Class A); 175(Class B).

ANNUAL MEETING: In Sept.

INCORPORATED: NY, Jan., 1904

INSTITUTIONAL HOLDINGS:
No. of Institutions: 96
Shares Held: 31,468,680
% Held: 51.6

INDUSTRY: Book publishing (SIC: 2731)

TRANSFER AGENT(S): Registrar and Transfer Company, Cranford, NJ

NYSE SYMBOL WLL
Rec. Pr. 50.23 (5/31/01)

WILLAMETTE INDUSTRIES, INC.

YIELD 1.8%
P/E RATIO 16.1

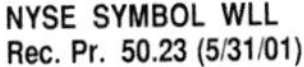
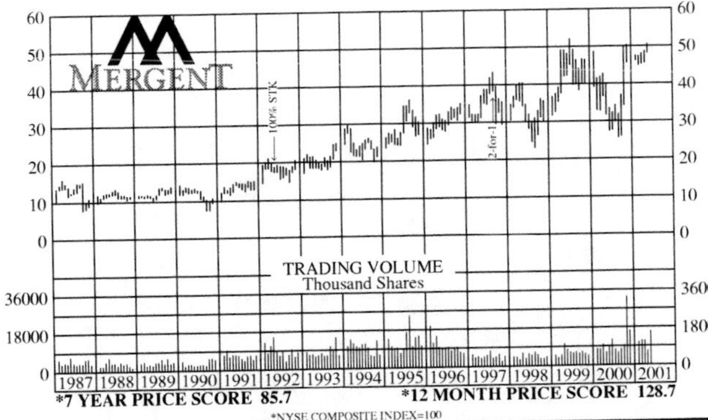

INTERIM EARNINGS (Per Share):

Qtr.	Mar.	June	Sept.	Dec.
1997	0.12	0.16	0.19	0.19
1998	0.20	0.21	0.32	0.07
1999	0.28	0.57	0.73	0.75
2000	0.76	0.82	0.76	0.78

INTERIM DIVIDENDS (Per Share):

Amt.	Decl.	Ex.	Rec.	Pay.
0.21Q	4/18/00	5/24/00	5/29/00	6/14/00
0.21Q	8/03/00	8/24/00	8/28/00	9/14/00
0.21Q	11/09/00	11/22/00	11/27/00	12/14/00
0.23Q	2/08/01	2/22/01	2/26/01	3/14/01
0.23Q	5/14/01	5/24/01	5/29/01	6/14/01

Indicated div.: $0.92 (Div. Reinv. Plan)

CAPITALIZATION (12/31/00):

	($000)	(%)
Long-Term Debt	1,542,926	34.3
Deferred Income Tax	568,273	12.7
Common & Surplus	2,381,043	53.0
Total	4,492,242	100.0

RECENT DEVELOPMENTS: For the year ended 12/31/00, net income increased 32.4% to $344.9 million from $260.5 million in 1999. The improvement in earnings was primarily attributed to improved pricing for white paper and lower raw material costs for WLL's brown paper operations. Results included non-recurring and other unusual expenses of $19.7 million in 2000 and $11.7 million in 1999. Net sales were $4.65 billion, up 8.9% from $4.27 billion. Comparisons were made with restated 1999 results.

PROSPECTS: The Company is continuing to resist the alleged hostile takeover bid by Weyerhaeuser Co., which recently revised its tender offer to purchase WLL for $50.00 per share in cash. Separately, WLL is facing economic and market pressures, as well as rising energy costs. However, management believes that it remains well-positioned in the forest products industry. This position is enhanced by the Company's recent capital projects.

BUSINESS

WILLAMETTE INDUSTRIES, INC. is an integrated, geographically diverse forest products company with 105 plants with manufacturing facilities in 24 states, France, Ireland and Mexico. The Company's paper group manufactures brown paper, corrugated containers and sheets, preprinted linerboard, kraft bags and sacks, inks and printing plates, communications papers, white paper and market pulp and cut sheets and other converting products. The Company's building materials group produces plywood and oriented strand board, lumber, particleboard, medium density fiberboard and engineered wood products. The Company owns 1.7 million acres of timberlands in the northwestern and southern United States.

ANNUAL FINANCIAL DATA

	12/31/00	12/31/99	12/31/98	12/31/97	12/31/96	12/31/95	12/31/94
Earnings Per Share	**1 3.12**	**1 2.33**	**1 0.80**	**0.65**	**1.74**	**4.67**	**1.62**
Cash Flow Per Share	**5.56**	**4.62**	**3.63**	**3.22**	**4.09**	**6.70**	**3.41**
Tang. Book Val. Per Share	**21.76**	**19.75**	**18.04**	**17.91**	**17.85**	**16.72**	**12.61**
Dividends Per Share	**0.84**	**0.70**	**0.64**	**0.64**	**0.62**	**0.57**	**0.48**
Dividend Payout %	**26.9**	**30.0**	**80.0**	**98.4**	**35.6**	**12.2**	**29.7**
INCOME STATEMENT (IN MILLIONS):							
Total Revenues	4,651.8	4,078.0	3,700.3	3,438.7	3,425.2	3,873.6	3,007.9
Costs & Expenses	3,728.3	3,270.2	3,300.7	2,926.2	2,770.6	2,755.4	2,443.7
Depreciation & Amort.	270.2	257.5	316.8	286.3	259.6	224.1	197.4
Operating Income	633.5	550.3	264.8	226.2	395.0	894.1	366.8
Net Interest Inc./(Exp.)	d119.1	d125.3	d132.0	d117.0	d92.8	d71.0	d71.5
Income Before Income Taxes	514.4	413.3	132.8	111.3	306.1	823.8	288.9
Income Taxes	169.5	152.8	43.8	38.3	114.0	309.0	111.3
Net Income	1 344.9	1 260.5	1 89.0	73.0	192.1	514.8	177.6
Cash Flow	615.1	518.0	405.7	359.3	451.6	738.9	375.1
Average Shs. Outstg. (000)	110,717	112,001	111,747	111,550	110,536	110,292	110,038
BALANCE SHEET (IN MILLIONS):							
Cash & Cash Equivalents	24.3	25.6	31.4	27.6	22.2	18.0	12.8
Total Current Assets	992.8	889.6	794.3	766.2	859.6	774.8	604.7
Net Property	3,017.6	2,751.2	2,707.1	2,566.3	2,330.5	2,054.9	1,863.5
Total Assets	5,117.7	4,797.9	4,697.7	4,811.1	4,720.7	3,413.6	3,033.4
Total Current Liabilities	596.7	432.1	427.5	458.1	570.4	415.6	466.1
Long-Term Obligations	1,542.9	1,628.8	1,821.1	1,916.0	1,766.9	790.2	915.8
Net Stockholders' Equity	2,381.0	2,203.7	2,002.4	1,994.5	1,976.3	1,846.9	1,387.9
Net Working Capital	396.1	457.5	366.8	308.1	289.1	359.3	138.5
Year-end Shs. Outstg. (000)	109,417	111,587	110,981	111,357	110,708	110,448	110,072
STATISTICAL RECORD:							
Operating Profit Margin %	13.6	13.5	6.8	6.6	11.5	23.1	12.2
Net Profit Margin %	7.4	6.4	2.3	2.1	5.6	13.3	5.9
Return on Equity %	14.5	11.8	4.4	3.7	9.7	27.9	12.8
Return on Assets %	6.7	5.4	1.9	1.5	4.1	15.1	5.9
Debt/Total Assets %	30.1	33.9	38.8	39.8	37.4	23.1	30.2
Price Range	50.50-25.50	52.13-31.50	40.50-23.00	43.50-29.25	35.13-24.38	36.38-23.38	29.75-19.78
P/E Ratio	16.2-8.2	22.4-13.5	50.6-28.7	66.9-45.0	20.2-14.0	7.8-5.0	18.4-12.2
Average Yield %	2.2	1.7	2.0	1.8	2.1	1.9	1.9

Statistics are as originally reported. 1 Incl. non-recurring chrg. of approximately $1.0 mill., 1998; $10.0 mill., 1999; $19.7 mill., 2000.

OFFICERS:
W. Swindells, Chmn.
D. C. McDougall, Pres., C.E.O.
G. W. Hawley, Exec. V.P., C.F.O., Treas., Sec.

INVESTOR CONTACT: E. Jane Sinnema, Dir., Inv. Rel., (503) 227-5581

PRINCIPAL OFFICE: 1300 S.W. Fifth Ave., Suite 3800, Portland, OR 97201

TELEPHONE NUMBER: (503) 227-5581
FAX: (503) 227-5604
WEB: www.wii.com

NO. OF EMPLOYEES: 14,975 (approx.)

SHAREHOLDERS: 34,700 (approx. beneficial)

ANNUAL MEETING: In June

INCORPORATED: OR, Mar., 1906

INSTITUTIONAL HOLDINGS:
No. of Institutions: 251
Shares Held: 64,432,987
% Held: 58.8

INDUSTRY: Paper mills (SIC: 2621)

TRANSFER AGENT(S): Mellon Investor Services, Ridgefield Park, NJ

NYSE SYMBOL WCG
Rec. Pr. 4.52 (4/30/01)

WILLIAMS COMMUNICATIONS GROUP, INC.

YIELD . . .
P/E RATIO . . .

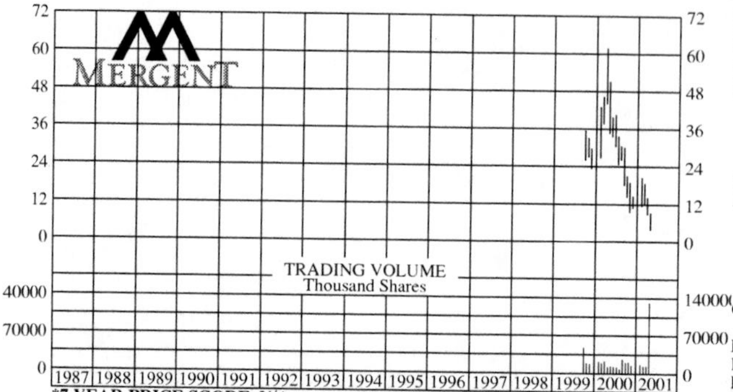

TRADING VOLUME
Thousand Shares

*7 YEAR PRICE SCORE N/A *12 MONTH PRICE SCORE 46.7

*NYSE COMPOSITE INDEX=100

INTERIM EARNINGS (Per Share):

Qtr.	Mar.	June	Sept.	Dec.
1998	d0.07	d0.04	d0.16	d0.20
1999	d0.19	d0.31	d0.22	d0.16
2000	d0.18	0.03	d0.32	d0.13

INTERIM DIVIDENDS (Per Share):

Amt.	Decl.	Ex.	Rec.	Pay.
		No dividends paid.		

CAPITALIZATION (12/31/00):

	($000)	(%)
Long-Term Debt	4,526,706	75.1
Minority Interest	45,028	0.7
Preferred Stock	240,722	4.0
Common & Surplus	1,213,272	20.1
Total	6,025,728	100.0

RECENT DEVELOPMENTS: For the year ended 12/31/00, WCG posted a loss from continuing operations of $277.7 million versus a loss of $328.3 million a year earlier. Total revenues rose 39.5% to $839.1 million. Results have been restated to report the Company's Williams Communications Solutions segment as discontinued operations. On 4/23/01, The Williams Companies, Inc. (WMB) completed its spinoff of WCG through a tax-free distribution of 398.5 million shares to WMB shareholders.

PROSPECTS: The Company should benefit from completion of its 33,000-mile next-generation network connecting 125 cities. Meanwhile, in March 2001, in a move to strengthen the Company's focus on the rapidly growing broadband market, WCG sold its Solutions division (U.S., Mexico and Canadian professional services operations) to Platinum Equity Holdings. WCG also signed a contract with TELUS to sell its Canadian enterprise services business unit, Williams Communications Canada. Financial terms of the transactions were not disclosed.

BUSINESS

WILLIAMS COMMUNICATIONS GROUP, INC. owns, operates and is extending a nationwide fiber-optic network focused on providing voice, data, Internet and video services to communications services providers. WCG also provides integrated fiber-optic, satellite and teleport video transmission services for the broadcast industry. The Company is organized into three operating segments: Network, which includes a publicly traded Australian telecommunications company and various other investments that drive bandwidth usage on the WCG network; Broadband Media; and Strategic Investments. As of 12/31/00, Strategic Investments' foreign investments were all located in South America. As of 4/24/01, The Williams Companies, Inc. held approximately 5.0% of the Company's stock.

REVENUES

(12/31/2000)	($000)	(%)
Network	705,020	84.1
Broadband Media	168,761	20.0
Eliminations	(34,704)	(4.1)
Total	839,077	100.0

ANNUAL FINANCIAL DATA

	12/31/00	12/31/99	12/31/98	12/31/97	12/31/96
Earnings Per Share	**3 d0.61**	**d0.87**	**d0.40**	**2 d0.08**	**1 d0.01**
Cash Flow Per Share	**d0.19**	**d0.55**	**d0.21**	**0.11**	**0.06**
Tang. Book Val. Per Share	**2.37**	**3.78**	**577.12**	. . .	. . .
INCOME STATEMENT (IN MILLIONS):					
Total Revenues	839.1	2,023.0	1,733.5	1,428.5	705.2
Costs & Expenses	1,102.7	2,194.9	1,839.6	1,413.6	672.9
Depreciation & Amort.	185.0	132.4	87.1	71.9	32.4
Operating Income	d448.7	d304.4	d193.2	d56.9	d0.1
Net Interest Inc./(Exp.)	d161.5	d97.6	d7.3	d0.4	d17.5
Income Before Income Taxes	d610.1	d401.9	d200.5	d12.8	d1.8
Income Taxes	cr34.1	cr7.8	cr5.1	2.0	0.4
Equity Earnings/Minority Int.	298.3	34.5	9.7	d15.2	d1.3
Net Income	3 d277.7	d359.7	d185.7	2 d30.0	1 d3.5
Cash Flow	d87.7	d227.3	d98.6	41.8	28.9
Average Shs. Outstg. (000)	464,145	412,620	460,000	395,435	460,000
BALANCE SHEET (IN MILLIONS):					
Cash & Cash Equivalents	213.9	494.3	42.0	11.3	. . .
Total Current Assets	1,206.4	2,830.6	841.4	560.2	. . .
Net Property	5,139.0	2,149.5	712.4	413.5	. . .
Total Assets	7,409.3	6,377.9	2,338.5	1,511.8	. . .
Total Current Liabilities	929.7	982.1	557.0	409.2	. . .
Long-Term Obligations	4,526.7	980.8	620.7	. . .	. . .
Net Stockholders' Equity	1,454.0	2,112.6	1,007.7	868.5	. . .
Net Working Capital	276.8	1,848.5	284.4	151.0	. . .
Year-end Shs. Outstg. (000)	468,600	463,600	1,000	. . .	1,000
STATISTICAL RECORD:					
Debt/Total Assets %	61.1	15.4	26.5	. . .	. . .
Price Range	61.81-9.50	35.44-23.25	. . .	. . .	. . .

Statistics are as originally reported. 1 Incls. gain on sale of assets of $15.7 mill. 2 Incls. gain on sale of interest in subsidiary of $44.5 mill. 3 Bef. loss fr. disc. ops. of $540.0 mill. ($1.16/sh.)

OFFICERS:
K. E. Bailey, Chmn.
H. E. Janzen, Pres., C.E.O.
S. E. Schubert, Sr. V.P., C.F.O.

INVESTOR CONTACT: Patricia Kraft, Investor Relations, (918) 573-3142

PRINCIPAL OFFICE: One Williams Center, Tulsa, OK 74172

TELEPHONE NUMBER: (918) 573-2000
FAX: (918) 573-1895
WEB: www.williams communications.com
NO. OF EMPLOYEES: 10,642 (approx.)
SHAREHOLDERS: 707 (approx. record)
ANNUAL MEETING: In May
INCORPORATED: DE, Dec., 1994

INSTITUTIONAL HOLDINGS:
No. of Institutions: 116
Shares Held: 24,850,286
% Held: 5.1

INDUSTRY: Telephone communications, exc. radio (SIC: 4813)

TRANSFER AGENT(S): The Bank of New York, New York, NY

NYSE SYMBOL WMB
Rec. Pr. 42.17 (4/30/01)

WILLIAMS COMPANIES, INC. (THE)

YIELD 1.4%
P/E RATIO 21.8

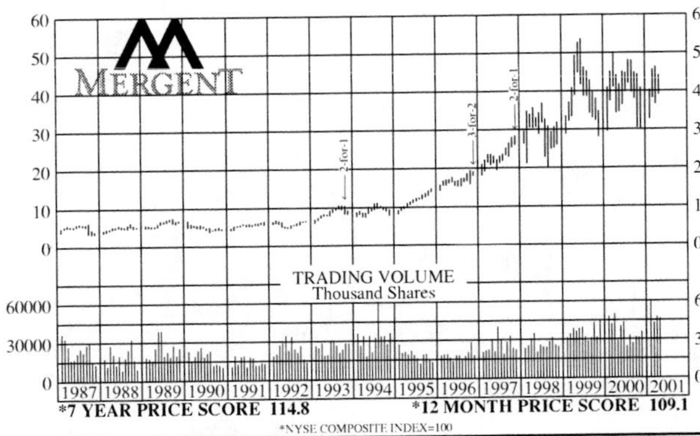

*7 YEAR PRICE SCORE 114.8 *12 MONTH PRICE SCORE 109.1

*NYSE COMPOSITE INDEX=100

INTERIM EARNINGS (Per Share):

Qtr.	Mar.	June	Sept.	Dec.
1997	0.32	0.32	0.19	0.21
1998	0.16	0.14	0.07	d0.02
1999	0.12	0.04	0.03	0.12
2000	0.28	0.79	0.29	0.57

INTERIM DIVIDENDS (Per Share):

Amt.	Decl.	Ex.	Rec.	Pay.
0.15Q	5/19/00	6/07/00	6/09/00	6/26/00
0.15Q	7/24/00	8/23/00	8/25/00	9/11/00
0.15Q	11/16/00	12/06/00	12/08/00	12/25/00
0.15Q	1/22/01	3/07/01	3/09/01	3/26/01
0.15Q	5/21/01	6/06/01	6/08/01	6/25/01

Indicated div.: $0.60

CAPITALIZATION (12/31/00):

	($000)	(%)
Long-Term Debt	10,342,400	50.0
Deferred Income Tax	2,828,100	13.7
Minority Interest	1,440,400	7.0
Redeemable Pfd. Stock	189,900	0.9
Common & Surplus	5,892,000	28.5
Total	20,692,800	100.0

RECENT DEVELOPMENTS: For the year ended 12/31/00, income from continuing operations soared to $873.2 million versus $172.4 million a year earlier. Revenues surged to $10.40 billion from $7.17 billion in 1999. Results were driven by WMB's Energy Services segment, increased natural gas liquids margins and volumes and higher natural gas production prices. On 4/23/01, WMB completed the spin-off of Williams Communications through a tax-free distribution of 398.5 million shares to WMB shareholders.

PROSPECTS: Prospects are positive, reflecting continue strength at the Company's Energy Services segment. Separately, on 2/22/01, WMB announced a 10-year, fixed-price power agreement with the California Department of Water Resources to provide up to 1,400 megawatts to California. On 2/20/01, WMB announced a 16-year agreement to supply fuel to and market 3,300 megawatts of capacity for six natural gas-fired generation facilities to be developed by Kinder Morgan Power Company over the next four years.

BUSINESS

THE WILLIAMS COMPANIES, INC. is engaged in natural gas transmission, energy services and telecommunications. The Gas Pipeline segment is comprised of five interstate natural gas pipelines, including Williams Gas Pipelines Central, Kern River Gas Transmission, Northwest Pipeline, Texas Gas Transmission, and Transcontinental Gas Pipe Line. The Energy Services segment includes the Energy Marketing & Trading, Exploration & Production, Midstream & Liquids and Petroleum Services businesses. The Communications segment consists of three operating units, including Network, Broadband Media and Strategic Investments.

BUSINESS LINE ANALYSIS

(12/31/2000)	REV (%)	INC (%)
Gas Pipelines	17.4	39.9
Energy Services	73.5	83.8
Communications	7.8	(24.7)
Other	1.3	1.0
Total	100.0	100.0

ANNUAL FINANCIAL DATA

	12/31/00	12/31/99	12/31/98	12/31/97	12/31/96	12/31/95	12/31/94
Earnings Per Share	**6 1.95**	**5 0.36**	**4 0.32**	**1 1.04**	**2 2.17**	**2 1.86**	**3 1.52**
Cash Flow Per Share	**3.79**	**2.04**	**1.82**	**2.49**	**4.71**	**4.27**	**2.99**
Tang. Book Val. Per Share	**13.26**	**11.59**	**8.34**	**9.50**	**20.70**	**29.04**	**14.85**
Dividends Per Share	**0.60**	**0.60**	**0.60**	**0.54**	**0.47**	**0.36**	**0.28**
Dividend Payout %	**30.8**	**166.6**	**187.4**	**51.9**	**21.7**	**19.4**	**18.4**
INCOME STATEMENT (IN MILLIONS):							
Total Revenues	10,398.0	8,593.1	7,658.3	4,409.6	3,531.2	2,855.7	1,751.1
Costs & Expenses	7,796.0	7,002.5	6,286.8	2,983.7	2,218.4	1,857.0	1,258.5
Depreciation & Amort.	831.9	742.0	646.3	499.5	411.4	369.4	150.3
Operating Income	1,770.1	848.6	725.2	926.4	901.4	670.7	342.3
Net Interest Inc./(Exp.)	d793.5	d598.2	d484.5	d388.6	d353.0	d263.4	d139.8
Income Taxes	554.0	161.2	110.4	178.0	183.1	102.0	81.7
Equity Earnings/Minority Int.	d12.0	7.2	9.6	d14.0	...	...	...
Net Income	6 873.2	5 161.8	4 146.6	1 350.5	2 362.3	2 299.4	3 164.9
Cash Flow	1,705.1	901.0	785.8	840.2	763.3	653.5	306.4
Average Shs. Outstg. (000)	449,320	441,512	431,816	337,539	162,118	153,069	102,470
BALANCE SHEET (IN MILLIONS):							
Gross Property	24,589.5	19,249.8	16,215.6	12,284.4	11,212.3	9,478.7	4,311.1
Accumulated Depreciation	4,921.7	4,094.3	3,621.0	2,228.8	1,826.0	1,464.0	1,187.1
Net Property	19,667.8	15,155.5	12,594.6	10,055.6	9,386.3	8,014.7	3,124.0
Total Assets	40,197.0	25,288.5	18,637.3	13,879.0	12,418.8	10,561.2	5,226.1
Long-Term Obligations	10,342.4	9,235.3	6,366.4	4,565.3	4,376.9	2,874.0	1,307.8
Net Stockholders' Equity	5,892.0	5,920.3	4,257.4	3,571.7	3,421.0	3,187.1	1,505.5
Year-end Shs. Outstg. (000)	444,300	444,500	428,300	315,307	157,477	103,765	94,626
STATISTICAL RECORD:							
Operating Profit Margin %	17.0	9.9	9.5	21.0	25.5	23.5	19.5
Net Profit Margin %	8.4	1.9	1.9	7.9	10.3	10.5	9.4
Net Inc./Net Property %	7 4.4	1.1	1.2	3.5	3.9	3.7	5.3
Net Inc./Tot. Capital %	4.2	0.9	1.1	3.5	3.8	3.9	4.7
Return on Equity %	14.8	2.7	3.4	9.8	10.6	9.4	11.0
Accum. Depr./Gross Prop. %	20.0	21.3	22.3	18.1	16.3	15.4	27.5
Price Range	49.75-29.50	53.75-28.00	36.94-20.00	28.38-18.06	19.50-14.17	14.83-8.17	11.13-7.38
P/E Ratio	25.5-15.1	149.3-77.8	115.4-62.5	27.3-17.4	9.0-6.5	8.0-4.4	7.3-4.9
Average Yield %	1.5	1.5	2.1	2.3	2.8	3.1	3.0

Statistics are as originally reported. Adj. for 2-for-1 stk. split, 12/97; 3-for-2, 12/96. 1 Incl. non-recur. cr. of $44.5 mil.; bef. extraord. chrg. of $79.1 mil. ($0.24/sh.) 2 Incl. non-recur. pre-tax cr. 12/31/96, $15.7 mil.; aft.-tax cr. 12/31/95, $14.0 mil. 3 Bef. gain of $94.0 mil. fr. disc. ops. & extraord. cr. of $12.2 mil. 4 Incl. one-time chrg. of $80.0 mil.; bef. disc. oper. loss of $14.3 mil.; bef. extraord. chrg. of $4.8 mil. 5 Bef. extraord. gain of $65.2 mil.; bef acctg. chrg. of $5.6 mil. 6 Bef. loss fr. disc. ops. of $348.9 mil. ($0.78/sh.)

OFFICERS:
K. E. Bailey, Chmn., Pres., C.E.O.
J. D. McCarthy, Sr. V.P., C.F.O.
W. G. von Glahn, Sr. V.P., Gen. Couns.

INVESTOR CONTACT: Rick Rodekohr or Richard George, (800) 600-3782

PRINCIPAL OFFICE: One Williams Center, Tulsa, OK 74172

TELEPHONE NUMBER: (918) 573-2000
FAX: (918) 588-2334
WEB: www.williams.com
NO. OF EMPLOYEES: 24,100 (approx.)
SHAREHOLDERS: 14,272 (approx. record)
ANNUAL MEETING: In May
INCORPORATED: NE, Feb., 1949; reincorp., DE, Feb., 1987

INSTITUTIONAL HOLDINGS:
No. of Institutions: 561
Shares Held: 281,571,706
% Held: 58.3

INDUSTRY: Natural gas transmission (SIC: 4922)

TRANSFER AGENT(S): First Chicago Trust Company of New York, Jersey City, NJ

NYSE SYMBOL WSM
Rec. Pr. 33.68 (5/31/01)

WILLIAMS-SONOMA, INC.

YIELD ...
P/E RATIO 33.7

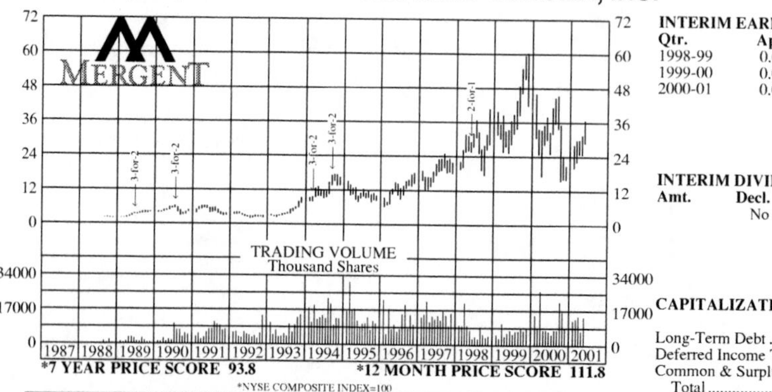

INTERIM EARNINGS (Per Share):

Qtr.	Apr.	July	Oct.	Jan.
1998-99	0.04	0.07	0.09	0.75
1999-00	0.06	0.12	0.16	0.82
2000-01	0.08	0.09	0.04	0.79

INTERIM DIVIDENDS (Per Share):

Amt.	Decl.	Ex.	Rec.	Pay.

No dividends paid.

CAPITALIZATION (1/28/01):

	($000)	(%)
Long-Term Debt	135,875	23.6
Deferred Income Tax	12,231	2.1
Common & Surplus	427,458	74.3
Total	575,564	100.0

RECENT DEVELOPMENTS: For the 52 weeks ended 1/28/01, net earnings slipped 16.6% to $56.8 million from $68.1 million a year earlier. Results in the prior-year period included a $4.0 million pre-tax gain from the sale of assets. Net revenue climbed 25.3% to $1.83 billion from $1.46 billion the previous year. Comparable-store sales rose 5.5% year over year. Retail sales increased 19.6% to $1.04 billion, while direct-to-customer sales jumped 33.1% to $685.2 million. As a percentage of net revenue, gross profit was 37.9% versus 38.8% the year before.

PROSPECTS: During 2001, WSM anticipates opening 57 new stores, including its first locations in Canada, while closing 24 stores. The Company's capital spending program is expected to range between $135.0 million and $150.0 million in fiscal 2001. Results in the second half of 2001 could benefit from new merchandise selections and improved economic conditions in the U.S. The Company is targeting sales growth between 15.0% and 18.0%, comparable-store sales growth of 2.0% to 3.0%, and earnings of between $1.17 and $1.23 per share in fiscal 2001.

BUSINESS

WILLIAMS-SONOMA, INC. is a specialty retailer of products for the home. As of 1/28/01, the Company operated 382 retail stores including 200 Williams-Sonoma, 136 Pottery Barn, 26 Hold Everything, 12 outlet stores, and eight Pottery Barn Kids. Williams-Sonoma stores offer a selection of culinary and serving equipment, including cookware, cookbooks, cutlery, informal dinnerware, glassware and table linen, along with a variety of foods including gourmet coffees and pasta sauces. Pottery Barn stores feature an assortment of items in casual home furnishings, flatware and table accessories from around the world, while Hold Everything stores provide products for household storage needs. The Company also sells merchandise through six mail-order catalogs and three e-commerce web sites.

ANNUAL FINANCIAL DATA

	1/28/01	1/30/00	1/31/99	2/1/98	2/2/97	1/28/96	1/29/95
Earnings Per Share	**0.99**	**[1] 1.16**	**0.96**	**0.75**	**0.44**	**0.05**	**0.38**
Cash Flow Per Share	**1.89**	**1.78**	**1.41**	**1.15**	**0.83**	**0.33**	**0.58**
Tang. Book Val. Per Share	**7.66**	**6.80**	**5.42**	**3.74**	**2.86**	**2.39**	**2.33**
INCOME STATEMENT (IN MILLIONS):							
Total Revenues	1,829.5	1,384.0	1,104.0	933.3	811.8	644.7	528.5
Costs & Expenses	1,678.4	1,238.3	985.4	835.4	746.7	621.2	483.3
Depreciation & Amort.	51.5	36.5	26.4	24.0	20.9	14.5	10.5
Operating Income	99.5	109.2	92.1	73.8	44.2	8.9	34.7
Net Interest Inc./(Exp.)	d7.2	d2.4	d1.4	d3.8	d5.0	d4.5	d1.3
Income Before Income Taxes	92.3	110.7	90.7	70.0	39.2	4.4	33.4
Income Taxes	35.5	42.6	35.8	28.7	16.5	1.8	13.9
Net Income	56.8	[1] 68.1	54.9	41.3	22.7	2.5	19.6
Cash Flow	108.3	104.6	81.3	65.4	43.6	17.1	30.1
Average Shs. Outstg. (000)	57,460	58,612	57,655	56,666	52,572	52,276	52,254
BALANCE SHEET (IN MILLIONS):							
Cash & Cash Equivalents	19.7	92.8	107.3	97.2	78.8	4.2	17.5
Total Current Assets	392.9	409.9	326.8	270.2	226.0	161.2	128.1
Net Property	490.5	313.2	243.1	201.0	172.1	147.3	79.4
Total Assets	891.9	738.9	576.2	477.2	404.4	319.1	217.9
Total Current Liabilities	311.3	215.8	153.9	135.6	129.5	122.1	78.6
Long-Term Obligations	135.9	131.3	117.0	145.9	128.9	75.3	21.0
Net Stockholders' Equity	427.5	383.3	302.0	193.2	146.0	121.7	118.2
Net Working Capital	81.6	194.1	172.9	134.5	96.6	39.1	49.5
Year-end Shs. Outstg. (000)	55,803	56,379	55,772	51,681	51,088	50,854	50,684
STATISTICAL RECORD:							
Operating Profit Margin %	5.4	7.9	8.3	7.9	5.4	1.4	6.6
Net Profit Margin %	3.1	4.9	5.0	4.4	2.8	0.4	3.7
Return on Equity %	13.3	17.8	18.2	21.4	15.6	2.1	16.6
Return on Assets %	6.4	9.2	9.5	8.7	5.6	0.8	9.0
Debt/Total Assets %	15.2	17.8	20.3	30.6	31.9	23.6	9.7
Price Range	46.00-15.50	60.31-25.25	40.75-17.44	25.00-12.25	18.19-6.25	15.19-7.81	17.63-7.89
P/E Ratio	46.5-15.7	52.0-21.8	42.4-18.2	33.3-16.3	41.8-14.4	303.2-155.9	47.0-21.0

Statistics are as originally reported. Adj. for stk. splits: 2-for-1, 5/98; 3-for-2, 9/94 & 2/94. [1] Incl. $4.0 mil pre-tax gain fr. sale of assets.

OFFICERS:
W. H. Lester, Chmn.
D. W. Hilpert, C.E.O.
S. L. McCollam, Sr. V.P., C.F.O.

INVESTOR CONTACT: Bryn Richardson, Dir., Inv. Rel., (415) 616-7856

PRINCIPAL OFFICE: 3250 Van Ness Avenue, San Francisco, CA 94109

TELEPHONE NUMBER: (415) 421-7900
FAX: (415) 434-0881
WEB: www.williams-sonoma.com
NO. OF EMPLOYEES: 5,600 full-time (approx.); 16,400 part-time (approx.)
SHAREHOLDERS: 565 (approx.)
ANNUAL MEETING: In May
INCORPORATED: CA, Apr., 1973

INSTITUTIONAL HOLDINGS:
No. of Institutions: 178
Shares Held: 38,091,837
% Held: 68.1

INDUSTRY: Misc. homefurnishings stores (SIC: 5719)

TRANSFER AGENT(S): Mellon Investor Services, San Francisco, CA

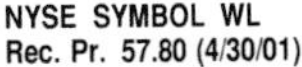

NYSE SYMBOL WL
Rec. Pr. 57.80 (4/30/01)

WILMINGTON TRUST CORPORATION

YIELD 3.3%
P/E RATIO 15.6

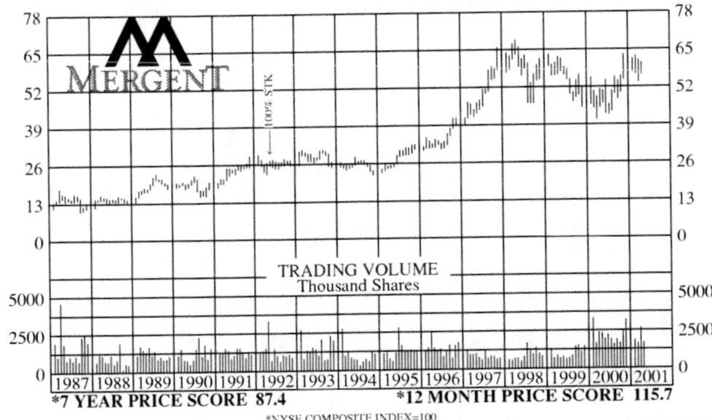

*7 YEAR PRICE SCORE 87.4 *12 MONTH PRICE SCORE 115.7

*NYSE COMPOSITE INDEX=100

INTERIM EARNINGS (Per Share):

Qtr.	Mar.	June	Sept.	Dec.
1997	0.72	0.77	0.79	0.80
1998	0.79	0.82	0.86	0.87
1999	0.87	0.89	0.92	0.53
2000	0.94	0.94	0.95	0.87

INTERIM DIVIDENDS (Per Share):

Amt.	Decl.	Ex.	Rec.	Pay.
0.45Q	4/20/00	4/27/00	5/01/00	5/15/00
0.45Q	7/20/00	7/28/00	8/01/00	8/15/00
0.45Q	10/19/00	10/30/00	11/01/00	11/15/00
0.45Q	1/18/01	1/30/01	2/01/01	2/15/01
0.48Q	4/19/01	4/27/01	5/01/01	5/15/01

Indicated div.: $1.92 (Div. Reinv. Plan)

CAPITALIZATION (12/31/00):

	($000)	(%)
Total Deposits	5,286,016	87.4
Long-Term Debt	168,000	2.8
Common & Surplus	591,900	9.8
Total	6,045,916	100.0

RECENT DEVELOPMENTS: For the year ended 12/31/00, net income rose 4.4% to $120.9 million versus $115.9 million a year earlier. Net interest income improved 3.8% to $255.1 million from $245.9 million in 1999. Provision for loan losses grew 25.1% to $21.9 million. Total loans were $5.19 billion, reflecting the strength of the diversified economy in the Delaware Valley and new business momentum in the Philadelphia region.

PROSPECTS: On 1/25/01, the Company announced the remodeling of its wealth management and financial services Web site, wilmingtontrust.com. The Web site offers visitors news and financial information, and a variety of planning and wealth management tools. Users can access their account and portfolio information, and communicate through an ongoing e-mail dialogue with WL's planning and investment experts.

BUSINESS

WILMINGTON TRUST CORPORATION, with assets of $7.32 billion as of 12/31/00, is a financial services company with offices in California, Delaware, Florida, Maryland, Nevada, New York, Pennsylvania, London, and the Cayman and Channel Islands. The Company provides wealth management, corporate trust, and commercial banking services to clients throughout the United States and in more than 50 other countries.

LOAN DISTRIBUTION

(12/31/2000)	($000)	(%)
Commercial, Financial & Agriculture	1,622,654	31.3
Real Estate-Construction	372,702	7.2
Mortgage-Commercial	990,433	19.0
Mortgage-Residential	925,938	17.9
Install To Individuals	1,277,291	24.6
Total	5,189,018	100.0

ANNUAL FINANCIAL DATA

	12/31/00	12/31/99	12/31/98	12/31/97	12/31/96	12/31/95	12/31/94
Earnings Per Share	**3.70**	**3.21**	**3.34**	**3.08**	**2.83**	**2.56**	**2.37**
Tang. Book Val. Per Share	**12.96**	**10.34**	**12.14**	**15.03**	**13.71**	**13.09**	**11.80**
Dividends Per Share	**1.77**	**1.65**	**1.53**	**1.41**	**1.29**	**1.17**	**1.06**
Dividend Payout %	**47.8**	**51.4**	**45.8**	**45.8**	**45.6**	**45.7**	**44.7**
INCOME STATEMENT (IN MILLIONS):							
Total Interest Income	530.5	462.2	456.9	430.6	402.9	377.3	307.9
Total Interest Expense	275.3	216.3	219.2	200.6	188.6	180.0	123.6
Net Interest Income	255.1	245.9	237.7	230.0	214.2	197.4	184.3
Provision for Loan Losses	21.9	17.5	20.0	21.5	16.0	12.3	4.6
Non-Interest Income	223.7	156.7	158.3	131.1	115.5	108.2	93.9
Non-Interest Expense	272.2	258.2	230.1	207.7	192.3	181.0	172.0
Income Before Taxes	184.8	161.7	171.5	158.4	144.1	131.7	120.8
Net Income	120.9	107.3	114.3	106.0	97.3	90.0	85.2
Average Shs. Outstg. (000)	32,680	33,383	34,275	34,466	34,399	35,213	35,990
BALANCE SHEET (IN MILLIONS):							
Cash & Due from Banks	223.8	225.1	204.6	239.4	231.2	252.8	203.5
Securities Avail. for Sale	1,440.1	1,686.3	1,298.7	1,316.4	798.5	910.2	253.2
Total Loans & Leases	5,189.0	4,821.6	4,324.4	4,004.8	3,783.9	3,527.6	3,283.0
Allowance for Credit Losses	77.3	78.4	76.7	74.6	66.8	55.6	51.6
Net Loans & Leases	5,111.7	4,743.2	4,247.7	3,930.1	3,717.1	3,472.0	3,231.4
Total Assets	7,321.6	7,201.9	6,300.6	6,122.4	5,564.4	5,372.2	4,742.4
Total Deposits	5,286.0	5,369.5	4,536.8	4,169.0	3,913.7	3,587.6	3,308.8
Long-Term Obligations	168.0	168.0	168.0	43.0	43.0	28.0	...
Total Liabilities	6,729.7	6,703.7	5,754.4	5,619.3	5,099.7	4,912.8	4,324.1
Net Stockholders' Equity	591.9	498.2	546.2	503.0	464.7	459.4	418.2
Year-end Shs. Outstg. (000)	32,393	32,353	33,329	33,478	33,893	35,090	35,449
STATISTICAL RECORD:							
Return on Equity %	20.4	21.5	20.9	21.1	20.9	19.6	20.4
Return on Assets %	1.7	1.5	1.8	1.7	1.7	1.7	1.8
Equity/Assets %	8.1	6.9	8.7	8.2	8.4	8.6	8.8
Non-Int. Exp./Tot. Inc. %	56.8	64.3	59.1	57.5	58.5	59.7	61.4
Price Range	63.38-40.56	63.50-44.75	68.50-46.38	66.00-39.25	41.75-30.25	32.50-22.75	28.50-22.00
P/E Ratio	17.1-11.0	19.8-13.9	20.5-13.9	21.4-12.7	14.8-10.7	12.7-8.9	12.0-9.3
Average Yield %	3.4	3.0	2.7	2.7	3.6	4.2	4.2

Statistics are as originally reported. Adj. for stk. split: 2-for-1, 5/18/92.

OFFICERS:
T. T. Cecala, Chmn., C.E.O.
R. V. Harra Jr., Pres., C.O.O., Treas.
D. R. Gibson, Sr. V.P., C.F.O.
M. A. Digregorio, V.P., Sec.

INVESTOR CONTACT: Ellen Roberts, Media & Investor Relations, (302) 651-8069

PRINCIPAL OFFICE: Rodney Square North, 1100 North Market St., Wilmington, DE 19890-0001

TELEPHONE NUMBER: (302) 651-1000
FAX: (302) 651-8010
WEB: www.wilmingtontrust.com

NO. OF EMPLOYEES: 2,299

SHAREHOLDERS: 9,189

ANNUAL MEETING: In May

INCORPORATED: DE, Mar., 1901

INSTITUTIONAL HOLDINGS:
No. of Institutions: 199
Shares Held: 14,023,786
% Held: 43.2

INDUSTRY: State commercial banks (SIC: 6022)

TRANSFER AGENT(S): Wells Fargo Shareowner Services, South St. Paul, MN

NYSE SYMBOL WIN
Rec. Pr. 26.61 (5/31/01)

WINN-DIXIE STORES, INC.

YIELD 3.8%
P/E RATIO . . .

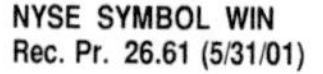

*7 YEAR PRICE SCORE 47.2 *12 MONTH PRICE SCORE 156.1
*NYSE COMPOSITE INDEX=100

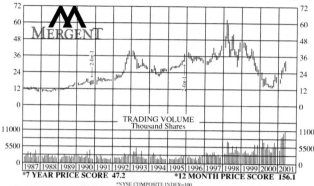

INTERIM EARNINGS (Per Share):

Qtr.	Sept.	Dec.	Mar.	June
1996-97	0.31	0.32	0.38	0.35
1997-98	0.32	0.38	0.41	0.22
1998-99	0.10	0.35	0.40	0.38
1999-00	0.15	d0.13	0.07	d1.70
2000-01	0.07	0.09	. . .	. . .

INTERIM DIVIDENDS (Per Share):

Amt.	Decl.	Ex.	Rec.	Pay.
0.085M	1/02/01	2/13/01	2/15/01	3/01/01
0.085M	1/02/01	3/13/01	3/15/01	4/02/01
0.085M	4/02/01	4/11/01	4/16/01	5/01/01
0.085M	4/02/01	5/11/01	5/15/01	6/01/01
0.085M	4/02/01	6/13/01	6/15/01	7/02/01

Indicated div.: $1.02 (Div. Reinv. Plan)

CAPITALIZATION (6/28/00):

	($000)	(%)
Capital Lease Obligations..	32,239	3.6
Common & Surplus	867,835	96.4
Total	900,074	100.0

RECENT DEVELOPMENTS: For the 16 weeks ended 1/10/01, net earnings totaled $12.2 million compared with a net loss of $18.8 million in the prior year. Results in the recent period included after-tax non-recurring charges totaling $24.0 million primarily related to restructuring. Net sales slipped 7.5% to $3.96 billion from $4.28 billion a year earlier. Comparable-store sales, which include replacement stores, were down 3.9% year-over-year. Gross profit declined 9.3% to $1.06 billion, or 26.8% of net sales, from $1.17 billion, or 27.4% of net sales, the year before.

PROSPECTS: Sales are being hampered by construction disruptions from 537 store retrofits, including the elimination of several unprofitable departments such as salad bars, melon bars and dry cleaners. However, operating profitability is beginning to benefit from cost savings generated by 217 store retrofits that have been completed. On 1/11/01, WIN completed the acquisition of 68 grocery stores and 32 gas stations, which generate about $625.0 million in annual sales, from Jitney-Jungle Stores of America, Inc. for approximately $80.2 million plus inventory.

BUSINESS

WINN-DIXIE STORES, INC. operates a chain of 1,089 retail self-service food stores in 14 states and the Bahamas that offer a broad line of groceries, meats, seafood, fresh produce, deli/bakery, pharmaceuticals and general merchandise items. Stores operate under the names WINN-DIXIE, WINN-DIXIE MARKETPLACE, THRIFTWAY, BUDDIES, and THE CITY MEAT MARKETS. The Company also operates support facilities, including 18 distribution centers and 20 manufacturing and processing plants. At 6/28/00, the Davis family owned approximately 41.8% of the Company's common stock.

ANNUAL FINANCIAL DATA

	6/28/00	6/30/99	6/24/98	6/25/97	6/26/96	6/28/95	6/29/94
Earnings Per Share	**1 d1.57**	**1.23**	**1 1.33**	**1.36**	**1.69**	**1.56**	**1.45**
Cash Flow Per Share	**0.19**	**3.19**	**3.55**	**3.30**	**3.32**	**2.90**	**2.50**
Tang. Book Val. Per Share	**6.03**	**9.50**	**9.22**	**8.98**	**8.85**	**8.21**	**7.13**
Dividends Per Share	**1.02**	**1.02**	**1.02**	**0.98**	**0.93**	**0.81**	**0.74**
Dividend Payout %	**. . .**	**82.9**	**76.7**	**72.4**	**54.7**	**52.2**	**51.4**
INCOME STATEMENT (IN MILLIONS):							
Total Revenues	13,697.5	14,136.5	13,617.5	13,218.7	12,955.5	11,787.8	11,082.2
Costs & Expenses	13,806.3	13,636.8	13,056.1	12,705.4	12,416.7	11,325.5	10,660.1
Depreciation & Amort.	256.7	292.4	330.4	291.2	248.3	200.9	157.4
Operating Income	d365.4	207.3	230.9	222.1	290.5	261.4	264.7
Net Interest Inc./(Exp.)	d47.1	d29.6	d28.5	d22.1	d21.2	d14.3	d14.3
Income Before Income Taxes	d302.4	296.5	317.8	319.4	387.3	354.0	348.5
Income Taxes	cr73.5	114.1	119.2	115.0	131.7	121.8	132.4
Net Income	1 d228.9	182.3	1 198.6	204.4	255.6	232.2	216.1
Cash Flow	27.8	474.7	529.0	495.7	503.9	433.1	373.5
Average Shs. Outstg. (000)	145,445	148,680	148,866	150,289	151,577	149,434	149,288
BALANCE SHEET (IN MILLIONS):							
Cash & Cash Equivalents	29.6	24.7	23.6	14.1	32.2	30.4	31.5
Total Current Assets	1,471.9	1,798.0	1,735.8	1,588.0	1,500.9	1,455.7	1,361.2
Net Property	1,034.5	1,222.6	1,169.8	1,128.7	998.8	897.8	706.8
Total Assets	2,747.1	3,149.1	3,068.7	2,921.4	2,648.6	2,482.8	2,146.6
Total Current Liabilities	1,421.6	1,547.3	1,507.2	1,392.6	1,112.2	1,030.1	873.2
Long-Term Obligations	32.2	38.5	48.6	54.0	60.9	77.7	85.4
Net Stockholders' Equity	867.8	1,411.1	1,368.9	1,337.5	1,342.3	1,241.2	1,057.5
Net Working Capital	50.4	250.7	228.6	195.4	388.7	425.5	488.0
Year-end Shs. Outstg. (000)	140,830	148,577	148,531	148,876	151,685	151,122	148,352
STATISTICAL RECORD:							
Operating Profit Margin %	. . .	1.5	1.7	1.7	2.2	2.2	2.4
Net Profit Margin %	. . .	1.3	1.5	1.5	2.0	2.0	2.0
Return on Equity %	. . .	12.9	14.5	15.3	19.0	18.7	20.4
Return on Assets %	. . .	5.8	6.5	7.0	9.7	9.4	10.1
Debt/Total Assets %	1.2	1.2	1.6	1.8	2.3	3.1	4.0
Price Range	24.75-13.44	46.63-22.31	62.81-28.63	44.00-29.88	39.00-31.00	37.63-25.56	29.19-21.31
P/E Ratio	. . .	37.9-18.1	47.2-21.5	32.4-22.0	23.1-18.3	24.1-16.4	20.1-14.7
Average Yield %	5.3	3.0	2.2	2.7	2.6	2.6	3.0

Statistics are as originally reported. Adj. for 2-for-1 stk. split, 11/95. 1 Incl. $304.1 mil ($2.09/sh) after-tax non-recur. chg., 2000; $11 mil ($0.07/sh), 1998.

OFFICERS:
A. D. Davis, Chmn., C.E.O.
A. R. Rowland, Pres., C.E.O.
R. P. McCook, Sr. V.P., C.F.O.
E. E. Zahra, Sr. V.P., Gen. Couns.

PRINCIPAL OFFICE: 5050 Edgewood Court, Jacksonville, FL 32254-3699

TELEPHONE NUMBER: (904) 783-5000
FAX: (904) 783-5548
WEB: www.winn-dixie.com
NO. OF EMPLOYEES: 53,000 full-time; 67,000 part-time
SHAREHOLDERS: 45,668
ANNUAL MEETING: In Oct.
INCORPORATED: FL, Dec., 1928

INSTITUTIONAL HOLDINGS:
No. of Institutions: 178
Shares Held: 29,995,939
% Held: 21.4

INDUSTRY: Grocery stores (SIC: 5411)

TRANSFER AGENT(S): First Chicago Trust Company of New York, Jersey City, NJ

NYSE SYMBOL WGO
Rec. Pr. 19.04 (5/31/01)

WINNEBAGO INDUSTRIES, INC.

YIELD	1.1%
P/E RATIO	10.2

*7 YEAR PRICE SCORE 91.7 *12 MONTH PRICE SCORE 128.0

*NYSE COMPOSITE INDEX=100

INTERIM EARNINGS (Per Share):

Qtr.	Nov.	Feb.	May	Aug.
1995-96	0.12	0.09	0.21	0.16
1996-97	0.11	d0.15	0.15	0.15
1997-98	0.21	0.18	0.31	0.32
1998-99	0.43	0.45	0.65	0.44
1999-00	0.55	0.54	0.74	0.37
2000-01	0.45	0.30	...	...

INTERIM DIVIDENDS (Per Share):

Amt.	Decl.	Ex.	Rec.	Pay.
0.10S	3/18/99	6/02/99	6/04/99	7/02/99
0.10S	10/08/99	12/08/99	12/10/99	1/10/00
0.10S	3/16/00	6/07/00	6/09/00	7/10/00
0.10S	10/12/00	12/06/00	12/08/00	1/08/01
0.10S	3/14/01	6/06/01	6/08/01	7/09/01

Indicated div.: $0.20

CAPITALIZATION (8/26/00):

	($000)	(%)
Common & Surplus	174,909	100.0
Total	174,909	100.0

RECENT DEVELOPMENTS: For the quarter ended 2/24/01, net income decreased 47.8% to $6.2 million compared with $11.9 million in the equivalent 2000 quarter. Net revenues were $142.5 million, down 24.8% from $189.6 million a year earlier. Operating income fell 49.7% to $8.6 million versus $17.0 million in 2000. Shipments of Class A motor homes slipped 33.7% to 1,127, while shipments of Class C motor homes decreased 24.2% to 677.

PROSPECTS: WGO expects results for the remainder of the fiscal year to be hampered by the slowdown in the economy, particularly from factors such as higher interest rates and decreased consumer confidence levels. However, WGO continues to gain market share and has no long-term debt. WGO's market share grew to 17.1% of the Class A and Class C motor home retail market for calendar 2000 from 15.8% for calendar 1997.

BUSINESS

WINNEBAGO INDUSTRIES, INC. is a major manufacturer of motor homes that are self-contained recreation vehicles used primarily in leisure travel and outdoor recreation activities. Motor home sales by the Company represented at least 87% of its revenues in each of the past five fiscal years. These vehicles are sold through dealer organizations primarily under the WINNEBAGO®, ITASCA®, RIALTA® and ULTIMATE® brand names. Other products manufactured by WGO consist principally of extruded aluminum, commercial vehicles, and a variety of component products for other manufacturers. Finance revenues consist of revenues from floor plan unit financing for a limited number of WGO's dealers.

QUARTERLY DATA

(08/26/2000)($000)	REV	INC
1st Quarter	182,551	12,381
2nd Quarter	187,144	11,851
3rd Quarter	211,137	16,257
4th Quarter	162,491	7,910

ANNUAL FINANCIAL DATA

	8/26/00	8/28/99	8/29/98	8/30/97	8/31/96	8/26/95	8/27/94
Earnings Per Share	**2.20**	**1.96**	**1.00**	**[3] 0.26**	**[2] 0.57**	**1.11**	**[1] 0.69**
Cash Flow Per Share	**2.50**	**2.22**	**1.23**	**0.51**	**0.95**	**1.45**	**1.00**
Tang. Book Val. Per Share	**8.22**	**6.70**	**5.11**	**4.79**	**4.15**	**3.96**	**3.16**
Dividends Per Share	**0.20**	**0.20**	**0.20**	**0.20**	**0.20**	**0.40**	**...**
Dividend Payout %	**9.1**	**10.2**	**20.0**	**76.9**	**35.1**	**36.0**	**...**
INCOME STATEMENT (IN THOUSANDS):							
Total Revenues	743,323	667,650	525,094	438,132	484,804	460,129	452,116
Costs & Expenses	666,047	597,920	486,535	426,516	454,395	433,374	427,088
Depreciation & Amort.	6,622	5,748	5,582	6,468	9,700	8,863	7,798
Operating Income	70,654	63,982	32,977	5,148	20,709	17,892	16,794
Net Interest Inc./(Exp.)	3,338	2,627	2,950	1,844	354	2,114	d661
Income Before Income Taxes	73,992	66,609	35,927	6,992	21,063	20,006	16,133
Income Taxes	25,593	22,349	11,543	416	6,639	cr7,912	cr1,312
Equity Earnings/Minority Int.	...	...	...	...	...	...	d174
Net Income	48,399	44,260	24,384	[3] 6,576	[2] 14,424	27,918	[1] 17,445
Cash Flow	55,021	50,008	29,966	13,044	24,124	36,781	25,243
Average Shs. Outstg.	22,011	22,537	24,314	25,435	25,349	25,286	25,187
BALANCE SHEET (IN THOUSANDS):							
Cash & Cash Equivalents	51,443	48,160	53,859	32,130	5,113	10,652	4,148
Total Current Assets	213,518	203,681	154,521	141,161	126,617	120,904	110,887
Net Property	45,455	38,371	32,912	33,593	39,929	39,257	41,598
Total Assets	308,686	285,889	230,612	213,475	220,596	211,630	183,959
Total Current Liabilities	71,835	79,961	62,602	41,226	64,462	51,210	52,364
Long-Term Obligations	...	...	...	...	1,692	3,810	4,140
Net Stockholders' Equity	174,909	149,384	116,523	123,882	105,311	100,448	79,710
Net Working Capital	141,683	123,720	91,919	99,935	62,155	69,694	58,523
Year-end Shs. Outstg.	21,274	22,299	22,813	25,854	25,349	25,341	25,239
STATISTICAL RECORD:							
Operating Profit Margin %	9.5	9.6	6.3	1.2	4.3	3.9	3.7
Net Profit Margin %	6.5	6.6	4.6	1.5	3.0	6.1	3.9
Return on Equity %	27.7	29.6	20.9	5.3	13.7	27.8	21.9
Return on Assets %	15.7	15.5	10.6	3.1	6.5	13.2	9.5
Debt/Total Assets %	...	...	...	...	0.8	1.8	2.3
Price Range	21.75-10.75	28.75-12.88	16.38-8.25	9.63-6.25	10.38-6.75	10.75-7.38	13.88-7.63
P/E Ratio	9.9-4.9	14.7-6.6	16.4-8.2	37.0-24.0	18.2-11.8	9.7-6.6	20.1-11.0
Average Yield %	1.2	1.0	1.6	2.5	2.3	4.4	...

Statistics are as originally reported. [1] Bef. a chrg. of $20.4 mill. for acctg. changes. [2] Bef. income from discont. oper. of $593,000 and loss on disposal of electronic component assembly segment of $2.6 mill. [3] Bef. gain from sale of discont. oper. of $16.5 mill. ($0.65/sh.).

OFFICERS:
B. D. Hertzke, Chmn., Pres., C.E.O.
E. F. Barker, V.P., C.F.O.
R. M. Beebe, V.P., Gen. Couns., Sec.

INVESTOR CONTACT: Edwin F. Barker, V.P., C.F.O., (641) 585-6141

PRINCIPAL OFFICE: 605 West Crystal Lake Road, P.O. Box 152, Forest City, IA 50436-0152

TELEPHONE NUMBER: (641) 585-3535
FAX: (641) 585-6966
WEB: www.winnebagoind.com

NO. OF EMPLOYEES: 3,300 (approx.)

SHAREHOLDERS: 5,932

ANNUAL MEETING: In Jan.

INCORPORATED: IA, Feb., 1958

INSTITUTIONAL HOLDINGS:
No. of Institutions: 74
Shares Held: 6,999,635
% Held: 34.1

INDUSTRY: Motor homes (SIC: 3716)

TRANSFER AGENT(S): Wells Fargo Bank Minnesota, N.A., St. Paul, MN

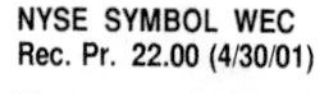

NYSE SYMBOL WEC
Rec. Pr. 22.00 (4/30/01)

WISCONSIN ENERGY CORPORATION

YIELD	3.6%
P/E RATIO	17.3

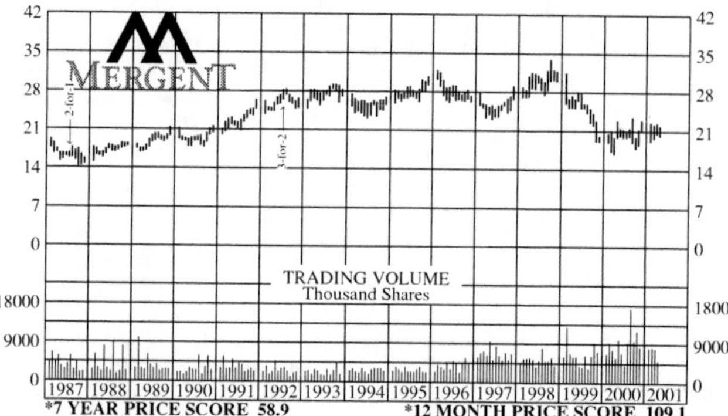

INTERIM EARNINGS (Per Share):

Qtr.	Mar.	June	Sept.	Dec.
1996	0.57	0.41	0.48	0.51
1997	0.40	d0.09	0.21	0.02
1998	0.43	0.25	0.50	0.45
1999	0.46	0.42	0.59	0.32
2000	0.42	0.25	0.36	0.24

INTERIM DIVIDENDS (Per Share):

Amt.	Decl.	Ex.	Rec.	Pay.
0.39Q	4/27/00	5/10/00	5/12/00	6/01/00
0.39Q	7/28/00	8/10/00	8/14/00	9/01/00
0.20Q	10/25/00	11/10/00	11/14/00	12/01/00
0.20Q	2/07/01	2/12/01	2/14/01	3/01/01
0.20Q	5/02/01	5/10/01	5/14/01	6/01/01

Indicated div.: $0.80 (Div. Reinv. Plan)

CAPITALIZATION (12/31/00):

	($000)	(%)
Long-Term Debt	2,732,700	49.1
Deferred Income Tax	587,100	10.5
Redeemable Pfd. Stock	200,000	3.6
Preferred Stock	30,400	0.5
Common & Surplus	2,016,800	36.2
Total	5,567,000	100.0

RECENT DEVELOPMENTS: For the twelve months ended 12/31/00, net income decreased 26.2% to $154.2 million compared with $209.0 million in the previous year. Total operating revenues soared 47.6% to $3.35 billion from $2.27 billion the year before. Utility energy revenues rose 24.7% to $2.56 billion. Non-utility energy revenues rocketed 93.0% to $372.8 million. Manufacturing revenues were $374.2 million, while other operating revenues surged 74.7% to $51.0 million from $29.2 million in 1999.

PROSPECTS: WEC signed a definitive agreement with NRG Energy, Inc. for the sale of two fossil-fueled power plants operated by Wisvest Connecticut, LLC, which have a combined generating capacity of more than 1,000 megawatts. WEC expects gross proceeds from the sale, which is expected to close by mid 2001, to be about $350.0 million. On 5/11/01, WEC sold FieldTech to Invensys Management Services for $18.0 million. Meanwhile, WEC expects 2001 earnings to be about $2.00 to $2.25 per share.

BUSINESS

WISCONSIN ENERGY CORPORATION is a Milwaukee-based holding company with subsidiaries in utility and non-utility businesses. The Company serves more than 1.0 million electric and 940,000 natural gas customers in Wisconsin and Michigan's Upper Peninsula through its subsidiaries, Wisconsin Electric, Wisconsin Gas and Edison Sault Electric. WEC's non-utility subsidiaries include energy services and development, pump manufacturing, waste-to-energy and real estate businesses. On 4/26/00, the Company acquired WICOR, a Milwaukee-based diversified holding company, for $1.20 billion in cash.

REVENUES

(12/31/00)	($000)	(%)
Utility	2,556,700	76.2
Non-Utility	372,800	11.1
Manfacturing	374,200	11.2
Other	51,000	1.5
Total	3,354,700	100.0

ANNUAL FINANCIAL DATA

	12/31/00	12/31/99	12/31/98	12/31/97	12/31/96	12/31/95	12/31/94
Earnings Per Share	**1.27**	[3] **1.79**	**1.65**	[2] **0.54**	**1.97**	**2.13**	[1] **1.67**
Cash Flow Per Share	**4.57**	**7.53**	**6.83**	**5.67**	**6.86**	**6.97**	**6.36**
Tang. Book Val. Per Share	**10.03**	**16.89**	**16.46**	**16.51**	**17.42**	**16.89**	**16.01**
Dividends Per Share	**1.37**	**1.56**	**1.55**	**1.53**	**1.51**	**1.46**	**1.40**
Dividend Payout %	**107.9**	**87.1**	**94.2**	**284.2**	**76.5**	**68.3**	**83.6**
INCOME STATEMENT (IN MILLIONS):							
Total Revenues	3,354.7	2,272.6	1,980.0	1,789.6	1,773.8	1,770.5	1,742.2
Costs & Expenses	2,509.6	1,144.5	940.9	877.5	822.1	797.4	848.5
Depreciation & Amort.	400.2	318.8	284.7	265.6	247.2	228.1	220.0
Maintenance Exp.	...	...	169.3	135.1	103.0	112.4	124.6
Operating Income	444.9	456.4	276.7	199.5	305.8	329.0	263.3
Net Interest Inc./(Exp.)	d223.3	d111.1	d92.1	d88.2	d88.4	d93.5	d90.5
Income Taxes	125.9	111.1	cr2.6	cr26.8	cr1.3	cr2.5	cr1.2
Net Income	154.2	[3] 562.0	496.5	[2] 372.7	513.8	537.6	[1] 466.7
Cash Flow	554.4	880.8	781.2	638.3	761.0	765.7	686.7
Average Shs. Outstg. (000)	121,200	117,019	114,315	112,570	110,983	109,850	108,025
BALANCE SHEET (IN MILLIONS):							
Gross Property	7,831.0	6,814.2	6,435.6	5,925.2	5,552.3	5,271.3	5,155.2
Accumulated Depreciation	3,912.9	3,250.0	3,007.7	2,700.8	2,442.0	2,288.1	2,134.5
Net Property	4,152.4	3,846.6	3,515.6	3,314.6	3,185.8	3,042.5	3,077.4
Total Assets	8,406.1	6,233.1	5,361.8	5,037.7	4,810.8	4,560.7	4,408.3
Long-Term Obligations	2,732.7	2,134.6	1,749.0	1,532.4	1,416.1	1,367.6	1,283.7
Net Stockholders' Equity	2,047.2	2,038.2	1,933.6	1,893.4	1,975.8	1,901.7	1,775.0
Year-end Shs. Outstg. (000)	118,645	118,904	115,607	112,866	111,679	110,819	108,940
STATISTICAL RECORD:							
Operating Profit Margin %	13.3	20.1	14.0	11.1	17.2	18.6	15.1
Net Profit Margin %	4.6	24.7	25.1	20.8	29.0	30.4	26.8
Net Inc./Net Property %	3.7	14.6	14.1	11.2	16.1	17.7	15.2
Net Inc./Tot. Capital %	2.8	11.2	11.7	9.4	13.2	14.3	13.2
Return on Equity %	7.5	27.6	25.7	19.7	26.0	28.3	26.3
Accum. Depr./Gross Prop. %	50.0	47.7	46.7	45.6	44.0	43.4	41.4
Price Range	23.56-16.81	31.56-19.06	34.00-27.00	29.06-23.00	32.00-26.00	30.88-25.75	27.50-23.13
P/E Ratio	18.6-13.2	17.6-10.6	20.6-16.4	53.8-42.6	16.2-13.2	14.5-12.1	16.5-13.8
Average Yield %	6.8	6.2	5.1	5.9	5.2	5.1	5.5

Statistics are as originally reported. [1] Incl. non-recurr chrg. $190.1 mill. related to restructuring. [2] Incl. non-recurr chrg. $36.9 mill. [3] Incl. non-recurr. after-tax chrg. $10.8 mill. related to the settlement of litigation.

OFFICERS:
R. A. Abdoo, Chmn., Pres., C.E.O.
G. E. Wardeberg, Vice-Chmn.
P. Donovan, Sr. V.P., C.F.O.

INVESTOR CONTACT: Colleen Henderson, Man. Inv. Rel., (414) 221-2592

PRINCIPAL OFFICE: 231 West Michigan Street, P.O. Box 2949, Milwaukee, WI 53201

TELEPHONE NUMBER: (414) 221-2345
FAX: (414) 221-2172
WEB: www.wisenergy.com

NO. OF EMPLOYEES: 10,191 full-time; 267 part-time

SHAREHOLDERS: 77,051

ANNUAL MEETING: In May

INCORPORATED: WI, June, 1981

INSTITUTIONAL HOLDINGS:
No. of Institutions: 235
Shares Held: 57,459,613
% Held: 48.8

INDUSTRY: Electric and other services combined (SIC: 4931)

TRANSFER AGENT(S): EquiServe, Canton, MA

NYSE SYMBOL WWW
Rec. Pr. 17.00 (5/31/01)

WOLVERINE WORLD WIDE, INC.

YIELD 0.9%
P/E RATIO 65.4

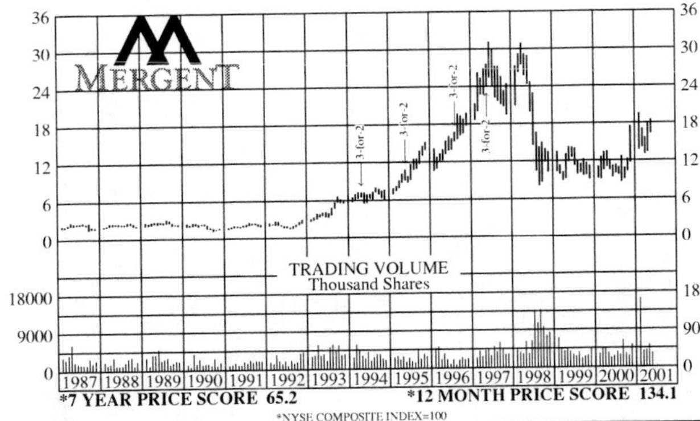

***7 YEAR PRICE SCORE 65.2** ***12 MONTH PRICE SCORE 134.1**

*NYSE COMPOSITE INDEX=100

INTERIM EARNINGS (Per Share):

Qtr.	Mar.	June	Sept.	Dec.
1996	0.08	0.13	0.17	0.39
1997	0.11	0.17	0.21	0.47
1998	0.15	0.21	0.25	0.36
1999	0.09	d0.07	0.28	0.48
2000	0.12	0.18	d0.37	0.33

INTERIM DIVIDENDS (Per Share):

Amt.	Decl.	Ex.	Rec.	Pay.
0.035Q	4/14/00	6/29/00	7/03/00	8/01/00
0.035Q	7/17/00	9/28/00	10/02/00	11/01/00
0.035Q	12/15/00	12/28/00	1/02/01	2/01/01
0.04Q	3/06/01	3/29/01	4/02/01	5/01/01
0.04Q	5/15/01	6/28/01	7/02/01	8/01/01

Indicated div.: $0.16

CAPITALIZATION (12/30/00):

	($000)	(%)
Long-Term Debt	87,878	20.2
Deferred Income Tax	9,431	2.2
Common & Surplus	337,238	77.6
Total	434,547	100.0

RECENT DEVELOPMENTS: For the twelve months ended 12/30/00, net income plummeted 67.0% to $10.7 million from $32.4 million in the previous year. Earnings were negatively affected by a lackluster holiday season and the effect of $45.1 million in nonrecurring charges. Net sales and other operating income rose 5.4% to $701.3 million from $665.6 million in the prior year. Gross profit inched up 1.6% to $224.0 million from $220.3 million a year earlier. Operating income decreased 58.7% to $25.0 million from $60.6 million the year before.

PROSPECTS: The Company recently launched a 24-hour customer service via a new business-to-business Web site. The site provides WWW's retail customers and sales representatives with the ability to check order status, track shipments, check stock availability, place orders and browse the product catalogs for all of WWW's nine consumer brands. Meanwhile, future revenues should benefit from higher incoming orders for WWW's Merrell and Harley-Davidson footwear brands and its U.S. Hush Puppies business.

BUSINESS

WOLVERINE WORLD WIDE, INC. manufactures and markets branded footwear and performance leather. WWW operates domestic retail shoe stores, selling both WWW's manufactured footwear and footwear made by unaffiliated companies. Major branded products include: BATES® UNIFORM FOOTWEAR; CATERPILLAR® FOOTWEAR; COLEMAN® FOOTGEAR; HARLEY-DAVIDSON® FOOTWEAR; HUSH PUPPIES® shoes, slippers, and accessories; HUSH PUPPIES® college clogs, JOE BOXER® slippers and TURTLE FUR® slippers; HY-TEST® safety footwear; MERRELL® performance outdoor footwear; WOLVERINE® work, sport and rugged outdoor footwear, apparel and accessories; STANLEY footwear and WOLVERINE® ALL SEASON WEATHER LEATHERS™. WWW's comfort technologies include: AIR PARADISE™BOUNCE®, COMFORT CURVE®, WOLVERINE DURASHOCKS® and DURASHOCKS MOTION CONTROL™, WOLVERINE FUSION™ and ZEROG™.

ANNUAL FINANCIAL DATA

	12/30/00	1/1/00	1/2/99	1/3/98	12/28/96	12/30/95	12/31/94
Earnings Per Share	**2 0.26**	**0.78**	**0.97**	**2 0.96**	**0.77**	**0.63**	**1 0.49**
Cash Flow Per Share	**0.68**	**1.14**	**1.27**	**1.17**	**0.93**	**0.77**	**0.64**
Tang. Book Val. Per Share	**7.77**	**7.65**	**6.88**	**6.20**	**5.46**	**4.98**	**3.64**
Dividends Per Share	**0.14**	**0.12**	**0.10**	**0.08**	**0.07**	**0.06**	**0.04**
Dividend Payout %	**51.9**	**15.1**	**10.7**	**8.6**	**9.0**	**9.2**	**8.9**
INCOME STATEMENT (IN THOUSANDS):							
Total Revenues	701,291	665,576	669,329	665,125	511,029	413,957	378,473
Costs & Expenses	658,576	590,100	587,093	592,455	455,569	370,697	343,451
Depreciation & Amort.	17,695	14,881	13,036	9,151	7,147	5,765	5,664
Operating Income	25,020	60,595	69,200	63,519	48,313	37,495	29,358
Net Interest Inc./(Exp.)	d9,909	d10,346	d7,279	d4,610	d1,595	d3,678	d3,337
Income Before Income Taxes	15,015	49,546	61,808	61,081	47,667	34,114	25,423
Income Taxes	4,325	17,166	20,157	19,542	14,811	10,047	7,373
Net Income	2 10,690	32,380	41,651	2 41,539	32,856	24,067	1 18,050
Cash Flow	28,385	47,261	54,687	50,690	40,003	29,832	23,714
Average Shs. Outstg.	41,795	41,486	42,952	43,464	42,789	38,507	36,806
BALANCE SHEET (IN THOUSANDS):							
Cash & Cash Equivalents	8,434	1,446	6,203	5,768	8,534	27,088	2,949
Total Current Assets	325,086	349,301	340,978	303,861	264,628	214,875	168,536
Net Property	102,665	116,283	111,135	90,331	63,003	46,885	35,348
Total Assets	494,568	534,395	521,478	449,663	361,598	283,554	230,151
Total Current Liabilities	54,004	48,539	51,268	64,895	69,810	37,647	43,020
Long-Term Obligations	87,878	134,831	157,089	89,847	41,233	30,594	43,482
Net Stockholders' Equity	337,238	332,105	300,320	282,430	239,292	204,214	132,524
Net Working Capital	271,082	300,762	289,710	238,966	194,818	177,228	125,516
Year-end Shs. Outstg.	41,553	41,300	40,765	42,553	41,699	41,029	36,385
STATISTICAL RECORD:							
Operating Profit Margin %	3.6	9.1	10.3	9.5	9.5	9.1	7.8
Net Profit Margin %	1.5	4.9	6.2	6.2	6.4	5.8	4.8
Return on Equity %	3.2	9.7	13.9	14.7	13.7	11.7	13.7
Return on Assets %	2.2	6.1	8.0	9.2	9.1	8.5	7.8
Debt/Total Assets %	17.8	25.2	30.1	20.0	11.4	10.8	18.9
Price Range	17.50-8.56	14.25-8.88	30.94-8.06	31.13-18.58	19.75-10.56	15.17-6.85	8.04-5.48
P/E Ratio	67.3-32.9	18.3-11.4	31.9-8.3	32.4-19.4	25.7-13.8	24.2-10.9	16.4-11.2
Average Yield %	1.0	1.0	0.5	0.3	0.5	0.5	0.6

Statistics are as originally reported. Adj. for stk. splits: 3-for-2, 8/97; 8/96; 5/95; 4/94 1 Bef. disc. oper. loss, $1.5 mill. 2 Incl. non-recurr. chrgs. 2000, $45.1 mill.; 1997, $3.5 mill.

OFFICERS:
G. B. Bloom, Chmn.
T. J. O'Donovan, Pres., C.E.O.
S. L. Gulis Jr., Exec. V.P., C.F.O., Treas.

INVESTOR CONTACT: Stephen L. Gulis, Jr., Exec. V.P., C.F.O., (616) 866-5570

PRINCIPAL OFFICE: 9341 Courtland Drive, Rockford, MI 49351

TELEPHONE NUMBER: (616) 866-5500
FAX: (616) 866-0257
WEB: www.wolverineworldwide.com

NO. OF EMPLOYEES: 4,903 (approx.)

SHAREHOLDERS: 1,975

ANNUAL MEETING: In April

INCORPORATED: DE, June, 1969

INSTITUTIONAL HOLDINGS:
No. of Institutions: 125
Shares Held: 33,053,120
% Held: 79.8

INDUSTRY: Footwear, except rubber, nec (SIC: 3149)

TRANSFER AGENT(S): Computershare Investor Services, Chicago IL

NYSE SYMBOL WOR
Rec. Pr. 11.50 (5/31/01)

WORTHINGTON INDUSTRIES, INC.

YIELD 5.6%
P/E RATIO 23.0

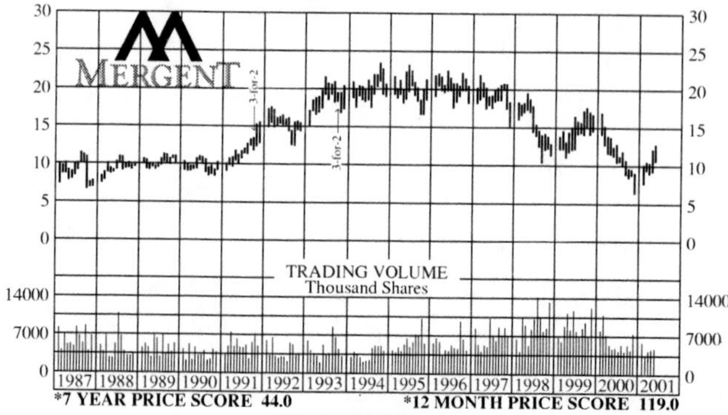

MERGENT

TRADING VOLUME
Thousand Shares

*7 YEAR PRICE SCORE 44.0 *12 MONTH PRICE SCORE 119.0

*NYSE COMPOSITE INDEX=100

INTERIM EARNINGS (Per Share):

Qtr.	Aug.	Nov.	Feb.	May
1996-97	0.22	0.23	0.23	0.28
1997-98	0.24	0.23	0.23	0.26
1998-99	0.18	0.20	0.21	0.31
1999-00	0.27	0.28	0.26	0.25
2000-01	0.15	0.08	0.02	...

INTERIM DIVIDENDS (Per Share):

Amt.	Decl.	Ex.	Rec.	Pay.
0.16Q	5/22/00	6/13/00	6/15/00	6/29/00
0.16Q	8/25/00	9/13/00	9/15/00	9/29/00
0.16Q	11/16/00	12/13/00	12/15/00	12/29/00
0.16Q	2/22/01	3/13/01	3/15/01	3/29/01
0.16Q	5/19/01	6/13/01	6/15/01	6/29/01

Indicated div.: $0.64 (Div. Reinv. Plan)

CAPITALIZATION (5/31/00):

	($000)	(%)
Long-Term Debt	362,190	29.8
Deferred Income Tax	125,942	10.4
Minority Interest	53,586	4.4
Common & Surplus	673,354	55.4
Total	1,215,072	100.0

RECENT DEVELOPMENTS: For the quarter ended 2/28/01, net income fell 92.3% to $1.8 million versus $23.2 million in 2000. Results for 2000 included a restructuring charge of $6.5 million. Total net sales were $418.7 million, up 13.9% from $486.5 million a year earlier. Processed steel products reported an operating loss of $239,000 versus operating income of $21.2 million, reflecting declining demand, particularly in the automotive sector, while metal framing segment operating earnings fell 65.6% to $3.7 million.

PROSPECTS: On 2/1/01, WOR announced the shutdown of a portion of its Malvern, PA Worthington Steel facility. This transaction is part of WOR's ongoing strategy to maximize the use of capacity and cut costs. Malvern will continue to operate its coating lines, which produce nickel, zinc and painted products. Separately, WOR's subsidiary Dietrich Metal Framing has expanded its operations to manufacture residential and commercial framing components in Kapolei, Hawaii and Renton, Washington.

BUSINESS

WORTHINGTON INDUSTRIES, INC. is a diversified steel processor that focuses on steel processing and metals-related businesses. WOR operates 57 facilities in 11 countries. The Company is involved in three business segments: Processed Steel Products, Metal Framing and Pressure Cylinders. The Processed Steel Products segment includes The Worthington Steel Company business unit and The Gerstenslager Company business unit. The Metal Framing segment is made up of Dietrich Industries, Inc. and the Pressure Cylinders segment consists of Worthington Cylinder Corporation. In addition, the Company holds an equity position in seven joint ventures.

ANNUAL FINANCIAL DATA

	5/31/00	5/31/99	5/31/98	5/31/97	5/31/96	5/31/95	5/31/94
Earnings Per Share	[4] **1.06**	[1][2] **0.90**	[1][3] **0.85**	**0.97**	**1.01**	**1.29**	**0.94**
Cash Flow Per Share	**1.86**	**1.74**	**1.48**	**1.50**	**1.44**	**1.66**	**1.30**
Tang. Book Val. Per Share	**6.92**	**6.74**	**7.08**	**6.38**	**6.32**	**6.50**	**5.56**
Dividends Per Share	**0.59**	**0.55**	**0.51**	**0.47**	**0.43**	**0.39**	**0.34**
Dividend Payout %	**55.7**	**61.1**	**60.0**	**48.4**	**42.6**	**30.2**	**36.5**
INCOME STATEMENT (IN MILLIONS):							
Total Revenues	1,962.6	1,763.1	1,624.4	1,911.7	1,477.8	1,483.6	1,285.1
Costs & Expenses	1,722.1	1,538.4	1,427.5	1,706.1	1,312.5	1,295.6	1,133.3
Depreciation & Amort.	71.0	78.5	61.5	51.4	39.2	34.1	32.4
Operating Income	169.5	146.2	135.5	154.2	126.1	153.8	119.4
Net Interest Inc./(Exp.)	d39.8	d43.1	d25.6	d18.4	d8.3	d6.0	d3.0
Income Before Income Taxes	123.8	108.3	111.3	136.8	118.7	148.4	116.8
Income Taxes	56.5	49.1	48.3	57.2	56.5	70.0	50.8
Equity Earnings/Minority Int.	26.8	24.5	19.3	13.8	29.1	38.3	18.9
Net Income	[4] 94.2	[1][2] 83.6	[1][3] 82.3	93.3	91.3	116.7	84.9
Cash Flow	165.1	162.1	143.8	144.7	130.6	150.8	117.2
Average Shs. Outstg. (000)	88,598	93,106	96,949	96,557	90,812	90,730	90,378
BALANCE SHEET (IN MILLIONS):							
Cash & Cash Equivalents	0.5	7.6	3.8	7.2	19.0	2.0	13.3
Total Current Assets	624.2	624.3	643.0	594.1	476.0	451.9	413.1
Net Property	862.5	871.3	933.2	691.0	512.3	334.9	307.6
Total Assets	1,673.9	1,687.0	1,842.3	1,561.2	1,220.1	917.0	798.6
Total Current Liabilities	433.3	427.7	410.0	246.8	151.3	179.2	180.5
Long-Term Obligations	362.2	365.8	439.6	450.4	298.7	53.5	54.1
Net Stockholders' Equity	673.4	689.6	780.3	715.5	639.5	590.3	503.9
Net Working Capital	191.0	196.5	233.0	347.3	324.8	272.7	232.6
Year-end Shs. Outstg. (000)	85,755	89,949	96,657	96,711	90,830	90,840	90,561
STATISTICAL RECORD:							
Operating Profit Margin %	8.6	8.3	8.3	8.1	8.5	10.4	9.3
Net Profit Margin %	4.8	4.7	5.1	4.9	6.2	7.9	6.6
Return on Equity %	14.0	12.1	10.5	13.0	14.3	19.8	16.8
Return on Assets %	5.6	5.0	4.5	6.0	7.5	12.7	10.6
Debt/Total Assets %	21.6	21.7	23.9	28.8	24.5	5.8	6.8
Price Range	17.69-11.06	19.56-10.38	22.00-15.13	22.50-17.50	23.25-16.63	23.50-17.50	21.67-15.00
P/E Ratio	16.7-10.4	21.7-11.5	25.9-17.8	23.2-18.0	23.0-16.5	18.2-13.6	23.0-16.0
Average Yield %	4.1	3.7	2.7	2.4	2.2	1.9	1.9

Statistics are as originally reported. [1] Bef. disc. oper. loss 5/31/99: $20.9 mill.; gain 5/31/98: $17.3 mill. [2] Bef. acctg. change chrg. $7.8 mill. [3] Bef. extraord. credit $18.8 mill. [4] Incl. restruct. chrg. of $6.5 mill.

OFFICERS:
J. P. McConnell, Chmn., C.E.O.
J. S. Christie, Pres., C.O.O.
J. T. Baldwin, V.P., C.F.O.

INVESTOR CONTACT: Allison McFerren Sanders, Dir., Inv. Rel., (614) 840-3133

PRINCIPAL OFFICE: 1205 Dearborn Drive, Columbus, OH 43085

TELEPHONE NUMBER: (614) 438-3210
FAX: (614) 438-3256
WEB: www.worthingtonindustries.com

NO. OF EMPLOYEES: 8,000 (approx.)

SHAREHOLDERS: 11,134 (approx. record)

ANNUAL MEETING: In Sept.

INCORPORATED: OH, June, 1955; reincorp., OH, Sept., 1998

INSTITUTIONAL HOLDINGS:
No. of Institutions: 180
Shares Held: 29,412,805
% Held: 34.5

INDUSTRY: Cold finishing of steel shapes (SIC: 3316)

TRANSFER AGENT(S): Fleet National Bank, Boston, MA

NYSE SYMBOL WPS
Rec. Pr. 33.01 (4/30/01)

WPS RESOURCES CORPORATION

YIELD 6.2%
P/E RATIO 13.0

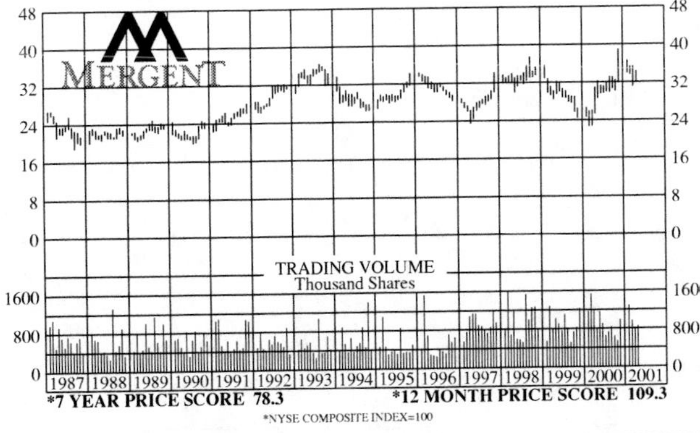

INTERIM EARNINGS (Per Share):

Qtr.	Mar.	June	Sept.	Dec.
1996	0.98	0.42	0.43	0.17
1997	0.76	0.40	0.54	0.55
1998	0.72	0.41	0.45	0.24
1999	0.86	0.38	0.52	0.48
2000	1.10	0.43	0.49	0.51

INTERIM DIVIDENDS (Per Share):

Amt.	Decl.	Ex.	Rec.	Pay.
0.505Q	4/13/00	5/26/00	5/31/00	6/20/00
0.515Q	7/13/00	8/29/00	8/31/00	9/20/00
0.515Q	10/12/00	11/28/00	11/30/00	12/20/00
0.515Q	2/08/01	2/26/01	2/28/01	3/20/01
0.515Q	4/12/01	5/29/01	5/31/01	6/20/01

Indicated div.: $2.06 (Div. Reinv. Plan)

CAPITALIZATION (12/31/00):

	($000)	(%)
Long-Term Debt	587,017	41.8
Capital Lease Obligations	72,955	5.2
Deferred Income Tax	100,463	7.2
Redeemable Pfd. Stock	50,000	3.6
Preferred Stock	51,168	3.6
Common & Surplus	542,777	38.6
Total	1,404,380	100.0

RECENT DEVELOPMENTS: For the year ended 12/31/00, net income climbed 12.5% to $67.0 million versus $59.6 million in the previous year. Earnings benefited from profitable operations at WPS Energy Services, Inc. and strong sales volumes at Wisconsin Public Service Corporation. Operating revenues soared 77.7% to $1.95 billion from $1.10 billion in the prior year. Electric utility operating revenue climbed 8.9% to $642.7 million.

PROSPECTS: WPS expects to see continued earnings growth from its non-regulated subsidiaries and strong performance from its utilities in 2001. WPS estimates earnings for the year to be in the range of $2.55 to $2.65 per share. Over the long-term, WPS should benefit from the acquisition of Wisconsin Fuel and Light Company, which was completed on 4/2/01.

BUSINESS

WPS RESOURCES CORPORATION (formerly Wisconsin Public Service Corp.) operates as a holding company with both regulated utility and non-regulated business units. The Company's principal wholly-owned subsidiaries are: Wisconsin Public Service Corporation (WPSC), a regulated electric and gas utility in Wisconsin and Michigan; Upper Peninsula Power Company, a regulated electric utility in Michigan; and WPS Energy Services, Inc. and WPS Power Development, Inc., both non-regulated subsidiaries. As of 12/31/00, WPSC served 395,063 electric retail and 235,470 gas retail customers.

ANNUAL FINANCIAL DATA

	12/31/00	12/31/99	12/31/98	12/31/97	12/31/96	12/31/95	12/31/94
Earnings Per Share	**2.53**	**2.24**	**1.76**	**2.25**	**2.00**	**2.32**	**2.21**
Cash Flow Per Share	**7.05**	**5.94**	**5.63**	**6.11**	**5.92**	**6.46**	**5.76**
Tang. Book Val. Per Share	**20.21**	**19.97**	**19.48**	**20.00**	**19.56**	**19.39**	**18.69**
Dividends Per Share	**2.04**	**2.00**	**1.96**	**1.92**	**1.88**	**1.84**	**0.46**
Dividend Payout %	**80.6**	**89.3**	**111.4**	**85.3**	**94.0**	**79.3**	**20.6**
INCOME STATEMENT (IN MILLIONS):							
Total Revenues	1,951.6	1,098.5	1,063.7	878.3	858.3	719.8	673.8
Costs & Expenses	1,646.1	819.5	808.3	644.4	617.2	461.6	432.8
Depreciation & Amort.	119.6	98.7	102.5	92.2	93.9	99.1	85.2
Maintenance Exp.	73.0	60.6	52.8	41.7	48.8	50.8	50.0
Operating Income	112.8	119.7	100.0	100.1	98.3	108.4	105.8
Net Interest Inc./(Exp.)	d50.8	d32.8	d28.6	d26.4	d25.3	d25.5	d25.3
Income Taxes	6.0	29.7	23.4	29.3	24.4	30.8	29.5
Equity Earnings/Minority Int.	...	...	0.6	0.8	0.3	...	...
Net Income	67.0	59.6	46.6	53.7	47.5	55.2	52.4
Cash Flow	186.6	158.3	149.2	145.9	141.4	154.3	137.6
Average Shs. Outstg. (000)	26,463	26,644	26,511	23,873	23,891	23,897	23,897
BALANCE SHEET (IN MILLIONS):							
Gross Property	2,547.7	2,429.2	2,197.6	1,899.4	1,825.8	1,760.0	1,690.8
Accumulated Depreciation	1,365.4	1,293.4	1,206.1	1,032.1	952.3	905.4	846.5
Net Property	1,198.3	1,150.9	1,010.2	886.4	892.9	868.9	863.8
Total Assets	2,816.1	1,816.5	1,510.4	1,299.6	1,330.7	1,266.7	1,217.3
Long-Term Obligations	660.0	584.5	343.0	304.0	611.6	613.2	619.9
Net Stockholders' Equity	593.9	587.5	568.4	529.0	518.7	514.6	497.7
Year-end Shs. Outstg. (000)	26,851	26,851	26,551	23,897	23,897	23,897	23,897
STATISTICAL RECORD:							
Operating Profit Margin %	5.8	10.9	9.4	11.4	11.5	15.1	15.7
Net Profit Margin %	3.4	5.4	4.4	6.1	5.5	7.7	7.8
Net Inc./Net Property %	5.6	5.2	4.6	6.1	5.3	6.4	6.1
Net Inc./Tot. Capital %	4.8	4.5	4.3	5.6	3.8	4.4	4.2
Return on Equity %	11.3	10.1	8.2	10.2	9.2	10.7	10.5
Accum. Depr./Gross Prop. %	53.6	53.2	54.9	54.3	52.2	51.4	50.1
Price Range	39.00-22.63	35.75-24.44	37.50-29.94	34.25-23.38	34.38-28.25	34.25-26.75	33.63-26.25
P/E Ratio	15.4-8.9	16.0-10.9	21.3-17.0	15.2-10.4	17.2-14.1	14.8-11.5	15.2-11.9
Average Yield %	6.6	6.6	5.8	6.7	6.0	6.0	1.5

Statistics are as originally reported.

OFFICERS:
L. L. Weyers, Chmn., Pres., C.E.O.
D. P. Bittner, Sr. V.P., C.F.O.
R. G. Baeten, V.P., Treas.

INVESTOR CONTACT: Ralph G. Baeten, Vice Pres-Treasurer, (920) 433-1449

PRINCIPAL OFFICE: 700 North Adams Street, P.O. Box 19001, Green Bay, WI 54307-9001

TELEPHONE NUMBER: (920) 433-4901
FAX: (920) 433-1526
WEB: www.wpsr.com

NO. OF EMPLOYEES: 3,030

SHAREHOLDERS: 24,029

ANNUAL MEETING: In May

INCORPORATED: WI, July, 1883

INSTITUTIONAL HOLDINGS:
No. of Institutions: 116
Shares Held: 8,323,709
% Held: 29.6

INDUSTRY: Electric and other services combined (SIC: 4931)

TRANSFER AGENT(S): Firstar Bank, N.A., Milwaukee, WI

NYSE SYMBOL WWY
Rec. Pr. 48.31 (4/30/01)

WRIGLEY (WILLIAM) JR. CO.

YIELD 1.6%
P/E RATIO 33.1

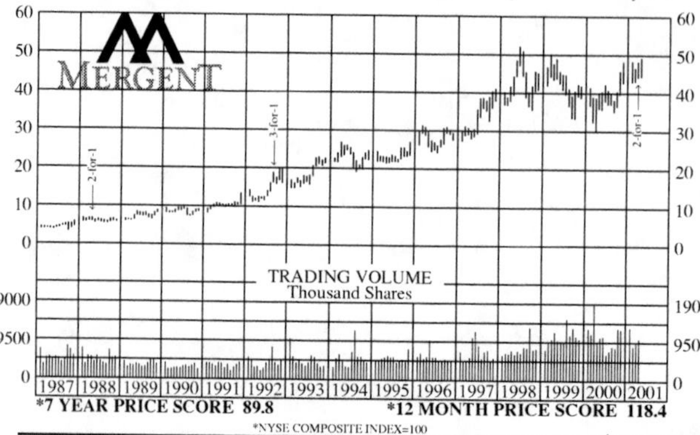

*7 YEAR PRICE SCORE 89.8 *12 MONTH PRICE SCORE 118.4

*NYSE COMPOSITE INDEX=100

INTERIM EARNINGS (Per Share):

Qtr.	Mar.	June	Sept.	Dec.
1996	0.25	0.25	0.27	0.24
1997	0.27	0.33	0.30	0.27
1998	0.33	0.37	0.32	0.31
1999	0.30	0.38	0.34	0.32
2000	0.33	0.41	0.37	0.35

INTERIM DIVIDENDS (Per Share):

Amt.	Decl.	Ex.	Rec.	Pay.
0.35Q	8/16/00	10/12/00	10/16/00	11/01/00
0.35Q	10/25/00	1/10/01	1/12/01	2/01/01
2-for-1	1/23/01	3/01/01	2/06/01	2/28/01
0.19Q	1/23/01	4/10/01	4/13/01	5/01/01
0.19Q	5/24/01	7/11/01	7/13/01	8/01/01

Indicated div.: $0.76 (Div. Reinv. Plan)

CAPITALIZATION (12/31/00):

	($000)	(%)
Deferred Income Tax	40,144	3.4
Common & Surplus	1,132,897	96.6
Total	1,173,041	100.0

RECENT DEVELOPMENTS: For the year ended 12/31/00, net earnings rose 6.7% to $328.9 million compared with $308.2 million a year earlier. Total revenues increased 4.1% to $2.15 billion from $2.06 billion in 1999. Americas sales, principally the U.S., advanced 6.0% to $906.0 million, while overseas sales gained 2.7% to $1.24 billion. WWY noted that the full-year overseas sales gain was reduced by more than 75.0% in consolidation due to the strength of the U.S. dollar.

PROSPECTS: On 3/15/01, WWY announced that it has signed a definitive agreement to acquire selected assets of Gum Tech International for $25.0 million cash and the purchase of 200,000 shares of Gum Tech's stock. The acquisition is expected to help strengthen WWY's Wrigley Healthcare division, which was formed in October 2000. Wrigley Healthcare recently introduced its first product, SURPASS® antacid chewing gum pellets.

BUSINESS

WM. WRIGLEY JR. CO. is the world's largest chewing gum producer. Main brands are WRIGLEYS SPEARMINT, DOUBLEMINT, JUICY FRUIT, WINTERFRESH, BIG RED, EXTRA, FREEDENT, ECLIPSE, and HUBBA BUBBA bubble gum. Additional brands manufactured and marketed internationally are ORBIT, AIR WAVES, ICEWHITE and EXCEL. Through its Amurol Confections Company subsidiary, WWY also manufactures and markets various non-gum items, such as a line of suckers, dextrose candy, liquid gel candy and hard roll candies. Wrigley brands are produced in 14 factories, including three plants in the U.S. plus 11 others outside the U.S. Sales for 2000 were derived from North America, 42.2%; Europe, 42.4%; Asia, 11.4%; Pacific, 3.3%; other, 0.7%. WWY's largest non-U.S. markets by shipments were Australia, Canada, China, France, Germany, Philippines, Poland, Russia, Taiwan and the United Kingdom. In October 2000, WWY formed the Wrigley Healthcare division.

QUARTERLY DATA

(12/31/2000)($000)	REV	INC
1st Quarter	503,291	74,605
2nd Quarter	570,224	92,103
3rd Quarter	533,294	83,842
4th Quarter	538,897	78,392

ANNUAL FINANCIAL DATA

	12/31/00	12/31/99	12/31/98	12/31/97	12/31/96	12/31/95	12/31/94
Earnings Per Share	**1.45**	**1.33**	**2 1.32**	**1 1.17**	**1 1.00**	**0.97**	**1 0.99**
Cash Flow Per Share	**1.70**	**1.59**	**1.55**	**1.39**	**1.20**	**1.15**	**1.17**
Tang. Book Val. Per Share	**5.02**	**4.97**	**4.98**	**4.25**	**3.87**	**3.43**	**2.96**
Dividends Per Share	**0.70**	**0.67**	**0.65**	**0.58**	**0.51**	**0.48**	**0.45**
Dividend Payout %	**48.3**	**50.0**	**49.4**	**50.0**	**51.3**	**49.7**	**45.4**
INCOME STATEMENT (IN MILLIONS):							
Total Revenues	2,145.7	2,079.2	2,023.4	1,954.2	1,850.6	1,769.7	1,661.3
Costs & Expenses	1,624.6	1,572.9	1,526.1	1,508.5	1,443.1	1,373.8	1,265.4
Depreciation & Amort.	57.9	61.2	55.8	50.4	47.3	43.8	41.1
Operating Income	463.2	445.1	441.5	395.2	360.2	352.2	354.8
Net Interest Inc./(Exp.)	...	d0.7	d0.6	d1.0	d1.1	d2.0	d1.5
Income Before Income Taxes	479.3	444.4	440.9	394.2	359.1	350.2	353.3
Income Taxes	150.4	136.2	136.4	122.6	128.8	126.5	122.7
Net Income	328.9	308.2	2 304.5	1 271.6	1 230.3	223.7	1 230.5
Cash Flow	386.8	369.4	360.3	322.1	277.6	267.5	271.6
Average Shs. Outstg. (000)	227,036	231,722	231,928	231,928	231,966	232,132	232,716
BALANCE SHEET (IN MILLIONS):							
Cash & Cash Equivalents	329.9	306.9	351.7	327.4	300.6	231.7	230.2
Total Current Assets	828.7	803.7	843.2	797.7	729.4	672.1	623.3
Net Property	607.0	559.1	520.1	430.5	388.1	347.5	289.4
Total Assets	1,574.7	1,547.7	1,520.9	1,343.1	1,233.5	1,099.2	978.8
Total Current Liabilities	288.2	251.8	218.6	225.8	218.2	213.4	209.9
Net Stockholders' Equity	1,132.9	1,138.8	1,157.0	985.4	897.4	796.9	688.5
Net Working Capital	540.5	551.9	624.5	571.9	511.3	458.7	413.4
Year-end Shs. Outstg. (000)	225,524	228,992	232,220	231,938	231,940	232,004	232,418
STATISTICAL RECORD:							
Operating Profit Margin %	21.6	21.4	21.8	20.2	19.5	19.9	21.4
Net Profit Margin %	15.3	14.8	15.0	13.9	12.4	12.6	13.9
Return on Equity %	29.0	27.1	26.3	27.6	25.7	28.1	33.5
Return on Assets %	20.9	19.9	20.0	20.2	18.7	20.4	23.6
Price Range	48.31-29.94	50.31-33.25	52.16-35.47	41.03-27.28	31.44-24.19	27.00-21.44	26.94-19.06
P/E Ratio	33.3-20.6	37.8-25.0	39.7-27.0	35.1-23.3	31.6-24.3	28.0-22.2	27.2-19.3
Average Yield %	1.8	1.6	1.5	1.7	1.8	2.0	2.0

Statistics are as originally reported. Adj. for 2-for-1 stk. split, 2/01 1 Incls. non-recurring net chrg. 12/31/97: $3.3 mill.; chrg. 12/31/96: $13.0 mill.; credit 12/31/94: $24.8 mill. 2 Incls. one-time gain of $10.4 mill.

OFFICERS:
W. Wrigley Jr., Pres., C.E.O.
R. V. Waters, Sr. V.P., C.F.O.
A. J. Schneider, Treas.

INVESTOR CONTACT: Christopher Perille, Dir., Corp. Comm., (312) 644-2121

PRINCIPAL OFFICE: 410 North Michigan Avenue, Chicago, IL 60611

TELEPHONE NUMBER: (312) 644-2121
FAX: (312) 645-4083
WEB: www.wrigley.com

NO. OF EMPLOYEES: 9,800 (approx.)

SHAREHOLDERS: 37,321 (common); 3,397 (class B common)

ANNUAL MEETING: In Mar.

INCORPORATED: DE, Oct., 1927

INSTITUTIONAL HOLDINGS:
No. of Institutions: 355
Shares Held: 79,175,235
% Held: 35.1

INDUSTRY: Chewing gum (SIC: 2067)

TRANSFER AGENT(S): EquiServe Trust Company, Jersey City, NJ

NYSE SYMBOL WYN
Rec. Pr. 1.96 (4/30/01)

WYNDHAM INTERNATIONAL, INC.

YIELD ...
P/E RATIO ...

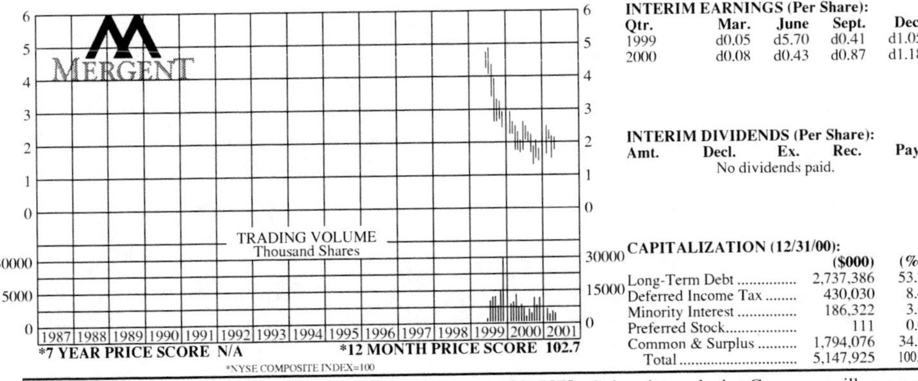

INTERIM EARNINGS (Per Share):

Qtr.	Mar.	June	Sept.	Dec.
1999	d0.05	d5.70	d0.41	d1.05
2000	d0.08	d0.43	d0.87	d1.18

INTERIM DIVIDENDS (Per Share):

Amt.	Decl.	Ex.	Rec.	Pay.

No dividends paid.

CAPITALIZATION (12/31/00):

	($000)	(%)
Long-Term Debt	2,737,386	53.2
Deferred Income Tax	430,030	8.4
Minority Interest	186,322	3.6
Preferred Stock	111	0.0
Common & Surplus	1,794,076	34.9
Total	5,147,925	100.0

RECENT DEVELOPMENTS: For the year ended 12/31/00, net loss was $324.7 million versus a loss of $1.06 billion, before an extraordinary charge, in 1999. Results included non-recurring charges of $526.6 million and $446.6 million in 2000 and 1999, respectively. Revenues remained flat at $2.50 billion. During the year, the Company disposed of $418.8 million in non-strategic assets, exceeding its 2000 plan to sell $300.0 million in assets.

PROSPECTS: Going forward, the Company will concentrate on the remaining two years of its program to sell off all non-core, non-strategic assets in an attempt to reduce leverage and focus more on the Wyndham brand. As a result, the Company plans to dispose of or swap approximately $500.0 million in non-core, non-strategic assets in 2001.

BUSINESS

WYNDHAM INTERNATIONAL INC. is a fully integrated and multi-branded hotel enterprise that operates primarily in the upscale and luxury segments in the United States, Canada, Mexico, the Caribbean and Europe. The Company classifies its business into proprietary owned brands and non-proprietary brand hotel divisions under which it manages the business. Among its proprietary branded hotels are Wyndham Hotels & Resorts, Wyndham Luxury Resorts, Wyndham Gardens, Summerfield Suites by Wyndham. Non-proprietary branded properties include all properties which are not Wyndham hotel properties, resort properties, all suite properties or other proprietary branded properties. The properties consist of Crowne Plaza, Embassy Suites, Marriott, Courtyard by Marriott, Sheraton and independents.

QUARTERLY DATA

(12/31/2000) ($000)	REV	INC
1st Quarter	653,626	11,597
2nd Quarter	662,995	(46,517)
3rd Quarter	574,466	(119,339)
4th Quarter	607,508	(170,412)

ANNUAL FINANCIAL DATA

	12/31/00	12/31/99	12/31/98	12/31/97	12/31/96	12/31/95	12/31/94
Earnings Per Share	[2] **d2.56**	[2][3] **d7.14**	[3] **d2.34**	[3] **0.01**	[1] **d0.07**	**0.38**	**0.38**
Cash Flow Per Share	**d0.57**	**d4.46**	**1.01**	**1.12**	**0.08**	**0.52**	**0.53**
Tang. Book Val. Per Share	**8.07**	**10.52**	**9.60**	**11.79**	**1.93**	**2.08**	**2.05**
INCOME STATEMENT (IN MILLIONS):							
Total Revenues	2,498.6	2,495.3	2,056.3	335.0	53.9	50.7	51.6
Costs & Expenses	2,319.6	2,282.0	1,652.5	226.3	52.7	44.4	45.1
Depreciation & Amort.	332.6	343.7	265.8	60.1	1.7	1.6	1.7
Operating Income	d153.6	d130.4	138.1	48.7	d0.5	4.7	4.8
Net Interest Inc./(Exp.)	d371.9	d353.2	d260.1	d50.5	...	...	...
Income Before Income Taxes	d525.5	d483.6	d122.0	d1.9	d0.5	4.7	4.8
Income Taxes	cr205.9	571.4	17.1	0.5	0.3	0.5	0.5
Equity Earnings/Minority Int.	d5.1	d7.1	12.7	2.7	...	...	...
Net Income	[2] d324.7	[2][3] d1,062.1	[3] d126.4	[3] 0.4	[1] d0.8	4.2	4.2
Cash Flow	d95.6	d788.1	110.3	60.5	0.9	5.8	5.9
Average Shs. Outstg. (000)	167,308	161,255	137,764	54,201	11,105	11,100	11,086
BALANCE SHEET (IN MILLIONS):							
Cash & Cash Equivalents	150.5	246.8	159.0	47.4	9.1	18.6	20.3
Total Current Assets	1,571.6	477.6	6,229.4	2,258.4	10.2	21.4	21.8
Net Property	...	...	...	...	17.2	16.2	14.5
Total Assets	6,066.9	7,003.5	7,415.7	2,507.9	27.7	37.9	36.8
Total Current Liabilities	911.1	491.8	4,205.7	1,238.5	6.2	7.6	5.8
Long-Term Obligations	2,737.4	3,513.4	...	...	...	...	...
Net Stockholders' Equity	1,794.2	2,137.7	2,603.0	989.9	21.5	23.1	22.7
Net Working Capital	660.5	d14.2	2,023.7	1,019.9	3.9	13.8	16.0
Year-end Shs. Outstg. (000)	167,416	167,194	213,522	73,277	11,105	11,105	11,086
STATISTICAL RECORD:							
Operating Profit Margin %	...	...	6.7	14.5	...	9.2	9.2
Net Profit Margin %	...	...	...	0.1	...	8.3	8.2
Return on Equity %	...	...	...	...	...	18.2	18.5
Return on Assets %	...	...	...	...	...	11.1	11.5
Debt/Total Assets %	45.1	50.2	...	...	...	...	...
Price Range	2.94-1.31	4.88-2.44	...	...	...	...	...

Statistics are as originally reported. [1] Incl. merger related costs, $4.0 mill. [2] Incl. non-recurr. chrg., 2000,$526.6 mill.; 1999, $446.6 mill. [3] Bef. extraord. loss, 1999, $9.8 mill.; 1998, $31.8 mill.; 1997, $2.5 mill.

OFFICERS:
F. J. Kleisner, Chmn., C.E.O.
T. Teng, Pres., C.O.O.
R. Smith, Exec. V.P., C.F.O.

INVESTOR CONTACT: Investor Relations, (212) 863-1265

PRINCIPAL OFFICE: 1950 Stemmons Freeway, Suite 6001, Dallas, TX 75207

TELEPHONE NUMBER: (214) 863-1000
FAX: (214) 863-1527
WEB: www.wyndhamintl.com

NO. OF EMPLOYEES: 28,000 (approx.)

SHAREHOLDERS: 20,500

ANNUAL MEETING: In May

INCORPORATED: DE, 1983

INSTITUTIONAL HOLDINGS:
No. of Institutions: 73
Shares Held: 56,312,524
% Held: 33.5

INDUSTRY: Hotels and motels (SIC: 7011)

TRANSFER AGENT(S): American Stock Transfer & Trust Company, New York, NY

NYSE SYMBOL XEL
Rec. Pr. 31.20 (4/30/01)

XCEL ENERGY, INC.

YIELD 4.8%
P/E RATIO 21.2

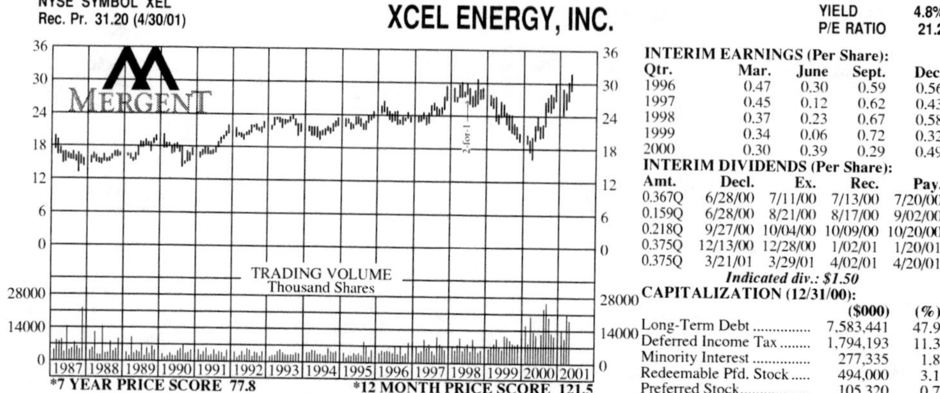

INTERIM EARNINGS (Per Share):

Qtr.	Mar.	June	Sept.	Dec.
1996	0.47	0.30	0.59	0.56
1997	0.45	0.12	0.62	0.43
1998	0.37	0.23	0.67	0.58
1999	0.34	0.06	0.72	0.32
2000	0.30	0.39	0.29	0.49

INTERIM DIVIDENDS (Per Share):

Amt.	Decl.	Ex.	Rec.	Pay.
0.367Q	6/28/00	7/11/00	7/13/00	7/20/00
0.159Q	6/28/00	8/21/00	8/17/00	9/02/00
0.218Q	9/27/00	10/04/00	10/09/00	10/20/00
0.375Q	12/13/00	12/28/00	1/02/01	1/20/01
0.375Q	3/21/01	3/29/01	4/02/01	4/20/01

Indicated div.: $1.50

CAPITALIZATION (12/31/00):

	($000)	(%)
Long-Term Debt	7,583,441	47.9
Deferred Income Tax	1,794,193	11.3
Minority Interest	277,335	1.8
Redeemable Pfd. Stock	494,000	3.1
Preferred Stock	105,320	0.7
Common & Surplus	5,562,124	35.2
Total	15,816,413	100.0

RECENT DEVELOPMENTS: For the year ended 12/31/00, income was $545.8 million, before an extraordinary charge of $19.0 million, compared with net income of $570.9 million in the previous year. Results for 2000 and 1999 included special charges of $241.0 million and $31.1 million, respectively. Total revenues jumped 48.3% to $11.59 billion from $7.82 billion the year before. Comparisons were made with restated 1999 figures.

PROSPECTS: The Company and Northern Alternative Energy, Inc. recently executed power purchase agreements that will result in the installation of 650 megawatts of wind and combustion turbine energy, to be developed at five sites in Minnesota, Iowa and Wisconsin. Looking ahead, the Company expects to invest significant amounts of capital in nonregulated projects and is involved in seven pending acquisitions slated for competitor in the first half of 2001 through NRG Energy.

BUSINESS

XCEL ENERGY, INC. (formerly Northern States Power Company), is a public utility holding company formed on 8/18/00 upon the merger of New Century Energies and Northern States Power Company. The Company provides a portfolio of energy-related products and services to 3.0 million electricity customers and 1.5 million natural gas customers. The Company, with operations in 12 Western and Midwestern states, has six public utility subsidiaries: Southwestern Public Service Company, Public Service Company of Colorado, Cheyenne Light, Fuel and Power Company, Northern States Power Company Minnesota, Northern States Power Company Wisconsin, and Black Mountain Gas Company. The Company operates numerous non-utility subsidiaries and owns 82.0% of NRG Energy, Inc., as of 1/31/01.

ANNUAL FINANCIAL DATA

	12/31/00	[2] 12/31/99	12/31/98	12/31/97	12/31/96	12/31/95	12/31/94
Earnings Per Share	[4] 1.54	[3] 1.43	1.84	[1] 1.61	1.91	1.96	1.73
Cash Flow Per Share	4.14	7.24	7.70	7.81	8.12	8.63	4.35
Tang. Book Val. Per Share	16.32	15.97	15.62	15.27	14.71	14.24	13.57
Dividends Per Share	1.47	1.44	1.42	1.40	1.36	1.33	1.30
Dividend Payout %	95.4	100.7	77.2	86.6	71.5	68.3	75.4
INCOME STATEMENT (IN MILLIONS):							
Total Revenues	11,591.8	3,188.2	3,130.5	3,043.7	2,955.4	2,894.2	2,486.5
Costs & Expenses	9,162.6	1,553.9	1,539.2	1,498.5	1,449.8	1,366.8	1,657.9
Depreciation & Amort.	858.1	473.9	423.2	398.9	381.4	372.1	350.1
Maintenance Exp.	...	178.6	181.1	164.5	155.8	158.2	170.1
Operating Income	1,571.1	343.5	364.3	361.8	366.0	345.9	308.3
Net Interest Inc./(Exp.)	d641.2	d440.9	d325.5	d289.5	d261.4	d245.8	d214.4
Income Taxes	304.9	cr61.0	cr40.6	cr48.1	cr14.6	5.1	...
Equity Earnings/Minority Int.	d40.5	...	...	...	31.0	29.2	35.9
Net Income	[4] 545.8	[3] 642.3	742.4	[1] 712.6	746.2	804.2	243.5
Cash Flow	1,399.6	1,110.8	1,160.0	1,100.5	1,115.4	1,163.8	581.2
Average Shs. Outstg. (000)	338,111	153,443	150,743	140,870	137,358	134,832	133,690
BALANCE SHEET (IN MILLIONS):							
Gross Property	24,032.2	9,783.9	9,424.2	9,062.3	8,741.3	8,406.9	8,109.2
Accumulated Depreciation	8,759.3	5,332.5	5,028.9	4,701.0	4,403.4	4,096.6	3,835.5
Net Property	15,272.9	4,451.5	4,395.2	4,361.3	4,337.9	4,310.3	4,273.7
Total Assets	21,768.8	9,767.7	7,396.3	7,144.1	6,636.9	6,228.6	5,953.6
Long-Term Obligations	7,583.4	3,453.4	1,851.1	1,878.9	1,592.6	1,542.3	1,463.4
Net Stockholders' Equity	5,667.4	2,662.9	2,586.6	2,572.1	2,376.3	2,267.9	2,137.4
Year-end Shs. Outstg. (000)	340,834	153,041	152,697	149,236	138,126	136,352	133,844
STATISTICAL RECORD:							
Operating Profit Margin %	13.6	10.8	11.6	11.9	12.4	12.0	12.4
Net Profit Margin %	4.7	20.1	23.7	23.4	25.3	27.8	9.8
Net Inc./Net Property %	3.6	14.4	16.9	16.3	17.2	18.7	5.7
Net Inc./Tot. Capital %	3.5	9.0	13.6	13.1	15.6	17.3	5.5
Return on Equity %	9.6	24.1	28.7	27.7	31.4	35.5	11.4
Accum. Depr./Gross Prop. %	36.4	54.5	53.4	51.9	50.4	48.7	47.3
Price Range	30.00-16.13	27.94-19.31	30.81-25.69	29.44-22.25	26.69-22.25	24.75-21.25	23.50-19.38
P/E Ratio	19.5-10.5	19.5-13.5	16.7-14.0	18.3-13.8	14.0-11.6	12.7-10.9	13.6-11.2
Average Yield %	6.4	6.1	5.0	5.4	5.6	5.8	6.1

Statistics are as originally reported. Adj. for stk. split: 2-for-1, 6/1/98 [1] Incl. non-recurr. chrg. $29.0 mill. fr. termination of merger. [2] Results for 12/31/99 and prior are for Northern States Power Company. [3] Incl. spec. chrgs. of $31.1 mill. [4] Incl. spec. chrgs. rel. to merger of $241.0 mill, excl. extraord. item of $19.0 mill.

OFFICERS:
J. J. Howard, Chmn.
W. H. Brunetti, Pres., C.E.O.
E. J. McIntyre, V.P., C.F.O.

INVESTOR CONTACT: Richard J. Kolkmann, Dir. Investor Relations, (612) 215-4559

PRINCIPAL OFFICE: 8000 Nicollet Mall, Minneapolis, MN 55402

TELEPHONE NUMBER: (612) 330-5500
FAX: (612) 330-5688
WEB: www.xcelenergy.com

NO. OF EMPLOYEES: 15,812 (avg.)

SHAREHOLDERS: 134,616

ANNUAL MEETING: In April

INCORPORATED: MN, June, 1909

INSTITUTIONAL HOLDINGS:
No. of Institutions: 354
Shares Held: 138,236,292
% Held: 40.4

INDUSTRY: Electric and other services combined (SIC: 4931)

TRANSFER AGENT(S): Wells Fargo Shareowner Services, South St. Paul, MN

NYSE SYMBOL XRX
Rec. Pr. 9.91 (5/31/01)

XEROX CORPORATION

YIELD 2.0%
P/E RATIO . . .

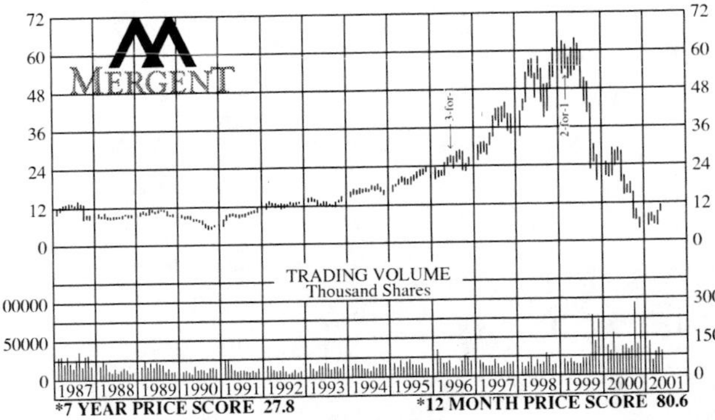

*7 YEAR PRICE SCORE 27.8 *12 MONTH PRICE SCORE 80.6
*NYSE COMPOSITE INDEX=100

INTERIM EARNINGS (Per Share):

Qtr.	Mar.	June	Sept.	Dec.
1996	0.34	0.43	0.36	0.63
1997	0.39	0.50	0.46	0.73
1998	0.42	d1.10	0.53	0.85
1999	0.48	0.62	0.47	0.41
2000	d0.38	0.19	d0.26	d0.19

INTERIM DIVIDENDS (Per Share):

Amt.	Decl.	Ex.	Rec.	Pay.
0.20Q	2/07/00	3/01/00	3/03/00	4/01/00
0.20Q	5/18/00	5/31/00	6/02/00	7/01/00
0.20Q	7/10/00	8/30/00	9/01/00	10/01/00
0.05Q	10/09/00	11/29/00	12/01/00	1/01/01
0.05Q	2/05/01	2/28/01	3/02/01	4/01/01

Indicated div.: $0.20 (Div. Reinv. Plan)

CAPITALIZATION (12/31/00):

	($000)	(%)
Long-Term Debt	15,404,000	75.8
Minority Interest	141,000	0.7
Redeemable Pfd. Stock	638,000	3.1
Preferred Stock	647,000	3.2
Common & Surplus	3,493,000	17.2
Total	20,323,000	100.0

RECENT DEVELOPMENTS: For the year ended 12/31/00, net loss totaled $257.0 million versus net income of $1.34 billion the year before. Results for 2000 included net pre-tax charges of $758.0 million and one-time pre-tax gains totaling $221.0 million, primarily from the sale of XRX's China operations. Total revenues slid 4.4% to $18.70 billion from $19.57 billion a year earlier. Comparisons were made with restated prior-year results reflecting certain accounting irregularities at XRX's Mexican operations.

PROSPECTS: The Company is implementing a strategic restructuring plan that should help boost cash flow, improve operating profitability and strengthen XRX's balance sheet. The plan includes a series of asset dispositions, valued between $2.00 billion and $4.00 billion, and cost-control initiatives, which are expected to reduce expenses by more than $1.00 billion in 2001. Going forward, XRX will focus on growing its core businesses, including document services, high-end printing and color products.

BUSINESS

XEROX CORPORATION is engaged in the developing, manufacturing, marketing and servicing of document processing products and systems. XRX distributes its products in the Western Hemisphere through divisions and wholly-owned subsidiaries, and in Europe, Africa, the Middle East and parts of Asia through Xerox Limited. In the Pacific Rim, Australia and New Zealand, Xerox products are distributed by Fuji Xerox Co. Ltd., an unconsolidated joint venture equally owned by Fuji Photo Film Co., Ltd. of Japan and Xerox Limited.

ANNUAL FINANCIAL DATA

	12/31/00	12/31/99	12/31/98	12/31/97	12/31/96	12/31/95	12/31/94
Earnings Per Share	[3] d0.44	1.96	[2] 0.80	2.02	1.75	[1] 1.70	1.12
Cash Flow Per Share	1.04	3.20	2.08	3.03	2.88	2.69	2.30
Tang. Book Val. Per Share	2.88	4.79	4.76	5.54	5.74	5.02	6.12
Dividends Per Share	0.80	0.78	0.70	0.63	0.56	0.50	0.50
Dividend Payout %	. . .	39.8	87.5	30.9	32.1	29.4	44.6
INCOME STATEMENT (IN MILLIONS):							
Total Revenues	18,701.0	19,228.0	19,449.0	18,166.0	17,378.0	16,611.0	17,837.0
Costs & Expenses	18,017.0	15,960.0	17,620.0	15,187.0	14,639.0	13,969.0	15,372.0
Depreciation & Amort.	948.0	935.0	821.0	739.0	715.0	660.0	681.0
Operating Income	d264.0	2,333.0	1,008.0	2,240.0	2,024.0	1,982.0	1,784.0
Income Before Income Taxes	d384.0	2,036.0	763.0	2,141.0	1,944.0	1,847.0	1,470.0
Income Taxes	cr109.0	631.0	207.0	728.0	700.0	615.0	551.0
Equity Earnings/Minority Int.	18.0	19.0	29.0	39.0	d38.0	d58.0	d125.0
Net Income	[3] d257.0	1,424.0	[2] 585.0	1,452.0	1,206.0	[1] 1,174.0	794.0
Cash Flow	638.0	2,305.0	1,350.0	2,134.0	1,862.0	1,789.0	1,402.0
Average Shs. Outstg. (000)	667,581	737,400	675,000	722,000	666,000	666,000	642,000
BALANCE SHEET (IN MILLIONS):							
Cash & Cash Equivalents	1,741.0	126.0	79.0	75.0	104.0	130.0	8,440.0
Total Current Assets	13,022.0	11,985.0	12,475.0	10,766.0	10,152.0	9,833.0	22,046.0
Net Property	2,495.0	2,456.0	2,366.0	2,377.0	2,256.0	2,092.0	2,108.0
Total Assets	29,475.0	28,814.0	30,024.0	27,732.0	26,818.0	25,969.0	38,585.0
Total Current Liabilities	6,268.0	7,950.0	8,507.0	7,692.0	7,204.0	6,999.0	6,838.0
Long-Term Obligations	15,404.0	10,994.0	10,867.0	8,779.0	8,697.0	8,148.0	8,021.0
Net Stockholders' Equity	4,140.0	5,580.0	5,544.0	5,690.0	5,088.0	4,641.0	5,009.0
Net Working Capital	6,754.0	4,035.0	3,968.0	3,074.0	2,948.0	2,834.0	15,208.0
Year-end Shs. Outstg. (000)	665,156	665,156	657,000	652,000	652,000	648,000	636,000
STATISTICAL RECORD:							
Operating Profit Margin %	. . .	12.1	5.2	12.3	11.6	11.9	10.0
Net Profit Margin %	. . .	7.4	3.0	8.0	6.9	7.1	4.5
Return on Equity %	. . .	25.5	10.6	25.5	23.7	25.3	15.9
Return on Assets %	. . .	4.9	1.9	5.2	4.5	4.5	2.1
Debt/Total Assets %	52.3	38.2	36.2	31.7	32.4	31.4	20.8
Price Range	29.31-3.75	63.94-19.00	60.81-33.09	44.00-25.75	29.13-19.90	24.10-16.08	18.79-14.63
P/E Ratio	. . .	32.6-9.7	76.0-41.4	21.8-12.7	16.7-11.4	14.2-9.5	16.7-13.0
Average Yield %	4.8	1.9	1.5	1.8	2.3	2.5	3.0

Statistics are as originally reported. Adj. for stk. splits: 2-for-1, 2/99; 3-for-1, 6/96. [1] Bef. $1.65 bil gain fr. disc. ops. & incl. $98 mil Brazilian tax benefit. [2] Bef. $190 mil after-tax chg. fr. disc. ops. & incl. $1.11 bil after-tax restr. chg. [3] Incl. $540 mil pre-tax restr. chg.; $101 mil pre-tax chg. rel. to XRX's Mexican ops.; $90 mil pre-tax inv. chgs.; $27 mil pre-tax chg. for in-process R&D; $200 mil pre-tax gain fr. sale of China ops.; & $21 mil gain fr. sale of stk.

OFFICERS:
P. A. Allaire, Chmn., C.E.O.
B. D. Romeril, Vice-Chmn., C.F.O.
A. M. Mulcahy, Pres., C.O.O.

INVESTOR CONTACT: Leslie F. Varon, Dir., Investor Relations, (203) 968-4406

PRINCIPAL OFFICE: 800 Long Ridge Road, Stamford, CT 06904-1600

TELEPHONE NUMBER: (203) 968-3000
FAX: (203) 968-4566
WEB: www.xerox.com

NO. OF EMPLOYEES: 94,600

SHAREHOLDERS: 55,297

ANNUAL MEETING: In May

INCORPORATED: NY, Apr., 1906

INSTITUTIONAL HOLDINGS:
No. of Institutions: 333
Shares Held: 354,056,804
% Held: 53.0

INDUSTRY: Photographic equipment and supplies (SIC: 3861)

TRANSFER AGENT(S): BankBoston, N.A., Boston, MA

NYSE SYMBOL XTR
Rec. Pr. 50.70 (4/30/01)

XTRA CORP.

YIELD	...
P/E RATIO	9.9

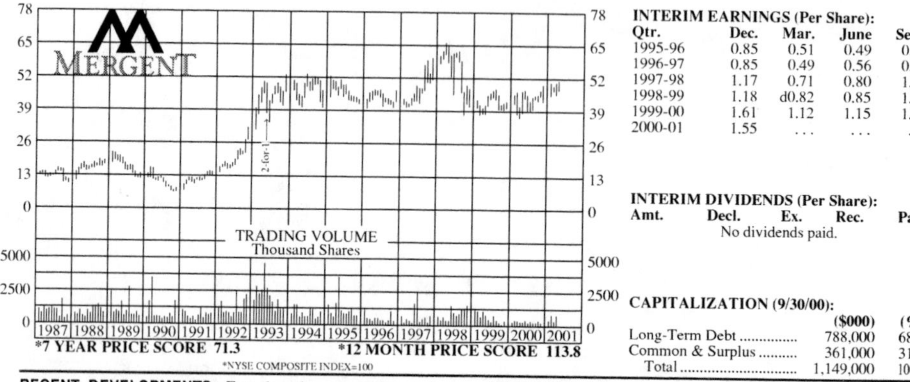

*7 YEAR PRICE SCORE 71.3 *12 MONTH PRICE SCORE 113.8
*NYSE COMPOSITE INDEX=100

INTERIM EARNINGS (Per Share):

Qtr.	Dec.	Mar.	June	Sept.
1995-96	0.85	0.51	0.49	0.71
1996-97	0.85	0.49	0.56	0.88
1997-98	1.17	0.71	0.80	1.20
1998-99	1.18	d0.82	0.85	1.28
1999-00	1.61	1.12	1.15	1.31
2000-01	1.55	...	...	...

INTERIM DIVIDENDS (Per Share):

Amt.	Decl.	Ex.	Rec.	Pay.
No dividends paid.				

CAPITALIZATION (9/30/00):

	($000)	(%)
Long-Term Debt	788,000	68.6
Common & Surplus	361,000	31.4
Total	1,149,000	100.0

RECENT DEVELOPMENTS: For the three months ended 12/31/00, net income slipped 10.0% to $18.0 million compared with $20.0 million in the corresponding quarter of 1999. Results for 2000 included pre-tax income of $2.0 million from an acquisition break-up fee received from a leasing acquisition target. Total revenues were $123.0 million, down 3.1% from $127.0 million in the prior-year period. Operating income decreased 12.5% to $42.0 million compared with $48.0 million the year before.

PROSPECTS: The Company is experiencing utilization decreases in all of its divisions that go beyond the normal seasonal softening. However, the Company has not seen any indication of an improvement in 2001, and attributes the reduction in freight demand being experienced by its customers to the slowing U.S. economy. As a result of the ongoing weak demand, XTR expects its operating performance for fiscal 2001 will lag its performance in 2000.

BUSINESS

XTRA CORPORATION leases, primarily on an operating basis, freight transportation equipment such as over-the-road trailers, marine containers, including intermodal trailers, chassis and domestic containers. XTR leases over-the-road and intermodal equipment throughout North America, predominately within the U.S., to private fleet owners, railroads, contract and common carriers, as well as marine containers that are leased worldwide to steamship lines. Customers lease equipment primarily to cover cyclical, seasonal and geographical shortages and as a substitute for purchasing. Revenues are primarily a function of lease rates and working units, which are dependent on fleet size and equipment utilization. At 9/30/00, XTR managed a diverse fleet of approximately 275,000 units.

ANNUAL FINANCIAL DATA

	9/30/00	9/30/99	9/30/98	9/30/97	9/30/96	9/30/95	9/30/94
Earnings Per Share	**5.20**	**1 2.49**	**3.88**	**2.77**	**2.56**	**3.39**	**3.38**
Cash Flow Per Share	**17.54**	**13.38**	**13.64**	**12.40**	**11.63**	**9.92**	**9.21**
Tang. Book Val. Per Share	**30.39**	**26.30**	**26.54**	**23.56**	**21.96**	**21.65**	**19.51**
Dividends Per Share	...	...	**0.44**	**0.80**	**0.72**	**0.64**	**0.56**
Dividend Payout %	...	...	**11.3**	**28.9**	**28.1**	**18.9**	**16.6**
INCOME STATEMENT (IN MILLIONS):							
Total Revenues	477.0	464.0	461.0	435.0	422.5	377.7	355.3
Costs & Expenses	162.0	197.0	151.0	153.0	140.8	127.7	123.8
Depreciation & Amort.	151.0	151.0	150.0	148.0	146.2	110.6	99.2
Operating Income	164.0	116.0	160.0	134.0	135.5	139.4	132.3
Net Interest Inc./(Exp.)	d58.0	d58.0	d58.0	d63.0	d66.0	d41.4	d33.9
Income Before Income Taxes	105.0	58.0	99.0	71.0	69.1	98.0	98.4
Income Taxes	42.0	23.0	39.0	28.0	28.0	40.7	40.8
Net Income	63.0	1 35.0	60.0	43.0	41.1	57.3	57.6
Cash Flow	214.0	186.0	210.0	191.0	187.3	167.9	156.8
Average Shs. Outstg. (000)	12,200	13,900	15,400	15,400	16,100	16,925	17,021
BALANCE SHEET (IN MILLIONS):							
Cash & Cash Equivalents	2.0	4.0	3.0	4.0	7.7	6.3	43.2
Total Current Assets	118.0	120.0	109.0	112.0	101.7	103.9	138.5
Net Property	1,432.0	1,439.0	1,452.0	1,454.0	1,407.0	1,398.3	845.7
Total Assets	1,566.0	1,573.0	1,575.0	1,585.0	1,536.8	1,523.0	1,004.9
Total Current Liabilities	67.0	75.0	78.0	81.0	76.4	129.4	74.2
Long-Term Obligations	788.0	852.0	802.0	892.0	892.0	841.1	434.6
Net Stockholders' Equity	361.0	337.0	408.0	360.0	341.5	358.8	330.5
Net Working Capital	51.0	45.0	31.0	31.0	25.3	d25.5	64.4
Year-end Shs. Outstg. (000)	11,880	12,812	15,373	15,277	15,550	16,569	16,940
STATISTICAL RECORD:							
Operating Profit Margin %	34.4	25.0	34.7	30.8	32.1	36.9	37.2
Net Profit Margin %	13.2	7.5	13.0	9.9	9.7	15.2	16.2
Return on Equity %	17.5	10.4	14.7	11.9	12.0	16.0	17.4
Return on Assets %	4.0	2.2	3.8	2.7	2.7	3.8	5.7
Debt/Total Assets %	50.3	54.2	50.9	56.3	58.0	55.2	43.2
Price Range	49.50-36.38	47.81-37.50	66.06-37.50	60.00-40.25	47.38-39.75	52.50-41.63	53.25-40.00
P/E Ratio	9.5-7.0	19.2-15.1	17.0-9.7	21.7-14.5	18.5-15.5	15.5-12.3	15.8-11.8
Average Yield %	...	...	0.8	1.6	1.7	1.4	1.2

Statistics are as originally reported. 1 Incl. $13.0 mill. restr. chgs., $1.0 mill. unusual chg. rel. to term. of merger, & $25.0 mill. revenue equip. write-down.

OFFICERS:
R. B. Goergen, Chmn.
L. Rubin, Pres., C.E.O.
S. L. Johnson, V.P., Treas.

INVESTOR CONTACT: Investor Relations, (203) 221-1005

PRINCIPAL OFFICE: 200 Nyala Farms Road, Westport, CT 06880

TELEPHONE NUMBER: (203) 221-1005
WEB: www.xtra.com

NO. OF EMPLOYEES: 722 (avg.)

SHAREHOLDERS: 605 (approx.)

ANNUAL MEETING: In Jan.

INCORPORATED: DE, Dec., 1976

INSTITUTIONAL HOLDINGS:
No. of Institutions: 78
Shares Held: 10,368,585
% Held: 88.9

INDUSTRY: Equipment rental & leasing, nec (SIC: 7359)

TRANSFER AGENT(S): BankBoston, N.A., c/o Boston EquiServe, Boston, MA

NYSE SYMBOL YRK
Rec. Pr. 35.25 (5/31/01)

YORK INTERNATIONAL CORPORATION

YIELD 1.7%
P/E RATIO 12.6

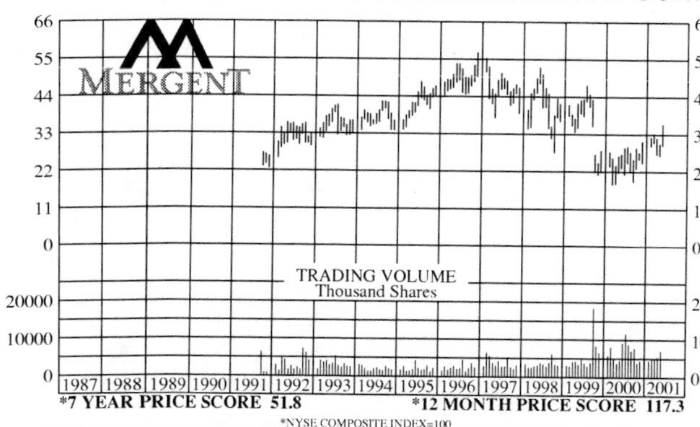

INTERIM EARNINGS (Per Share):

Qtr.	Mar.	June	Sept.	Dec.
1996	0.55	1.05	0.88	0.89
1997	0.34	0.97	0.55	d0.81
1998	0.36	1.03	1.16	0.81
1999	0.44	1.01	0.09	0.36
2000	0.60	1.20	0.40	0.59

INTERIM DIVIDENDS (Per Share):

Amt.	Decl.	Ex.	Rec.	Pay.
0.15Q	5/26/00	6/19/00	6/21/00	6/30/00
0.15Q	8/30/00	9/18/00	9/20/00	9/29/00
0.15Q	11/30/00	12/18/00	12/20/00	12/29/00
0.15Q	3/09/01	3/19/01	3/21/01	3/30/01
0.15Q	5/25/01	6/18/01	6/20/01	6/29/01

Indicated div.: $0.60 (Div. Reinv. Plan)

CAPITALIZATION (12/31/00):

	($000)	(%)
Long-Term Debt	831,354	52.6
Common & Surplus	748,976	47.4
Total	1,580,330	100.0

RECENT DEVELOPMENTS: For the year ended 12/31/00, net income was $106.6 million versus income of $76.8 million before an accounting change charge the previous year. Results included pre-tax acquisition, integration, restructuring and other charges totaling $49.7 million and $54.5 million in 2000 and 1999, respectively. Results also included pre-tax gains from divestitures of $26.9 million and $9.6 million in 2000 and 1999, respectively. Net sales rose to $3.90 billion from $3.87 billion the year before.

PROSPECTS: In 2001, the Company is targeting revenue growth of about 3.0% and earnings from operations in the range of $3.25 to $3.50 per share. Increased revenues from service business growth and new product introductions are expected to be partially offset by unfavorable foreign currency exchange rates and revenue declines related to plant and product line rationalizations. YRK's ongoing implementation of cost-control initiatives is expected to generate cost savings of $25.0 million to $30.0 million in 2001.

BUSINESS

YORK INTERNATIONAL CORPORATION is a full-line, global manufacturer of heating, ventilating, air conditioning and refrigeration (HVA&R) products. Products fall into four business categories. Engineered Systems products (38% of 2000 sales) consist of large institutional heating, air conditioning, process cooling, industrial and thermal storage equipment. Refrigeration products (25%) include refrigeration and gas-compression equipment serving the food, beverage, marine, chemical and petrochemical processing industries. Unitary products (24%) include central air conditioning systems, heat pumps, gas and oil furnaces, and indoor air quality accessories. Bristol compressors (13%) are used in air conditioning and heat pump systems. On 9/30/99, YRK sold its performance contracting business, Viron Corp.

QUARTERLY DATA

(12/31/00)($000)	REV	INC
1st Quarter	897,004	23,095
2nd Quarter	1,066,397	45,687
3rd Quarter	948,967	15,256
4th Quarter	985,035	22,569

ANNUAL FINANCIAL DATA

	12/31/00	12/31/99	12/31/98	12/31/97	12/31/96	12/31/95	12/31/94
Earnings Per Share	**[2] 2.78**	**[1] [2] 1.93**	**3.36**	**[3] 1.10**	**3.37**	**[2] d2.36**	**2.40**
Cash Flow Per Share	**5.18**	**4.14**	**5.20**	**2.70**	**4.89**	**d0.85**	**3.73**
Tang. Book Val. Per Share	**1.44**	**...**	**9.84**	**7.44**	**9.86**	**6.37**	**3.52**
Dividends Per Share	**0.60**	**0.60**	**0.48**	**0.48**	**0.36**	**0.24**	**0.16**
Dividend Payout %	**21.6**	**31.1**	**14.3**	**43.6**	**10.7**	**...**	**6.7**
INCOME STATEMENT (IN MILLIONS):							
Total Revenues	3,897.4	3,866.6	3,289.2	3,193.7	3,218.5	2,929.9	2,421.9
Costs & Expenses	3,636.6	3,614.4	2,985.7	3,010.9	2,913.2	2,890.1	2,200.2
Depreciation & Amort.	91.6	88.3	74.8	68.8	67.0	61.5	49.7
Operating Income	169.3	163.9	228.7	114.0	238.4	d21.7	172.0
Net Interest Inc./(Exp.)	d81.6	d61.1	d41.5	d40.9	d34.5	d41.4	d29.2
Income Before Income Taxes	121.0	118.1	187.3	78.5	204.5	d70.8	144.4
Income Taxes	14.4	41.3	50.8	31.1	56.6	25.3	54.7
Equity Earnings/Minority Int.	6.4	5.7	0.1	5.3	0.6	d7.7	1.7
Net Income	[2] 106.6	[1] [2] 76.8	136.5	[3] 47.4	147.9	[2] d96.1	89.8
Cash Flow	198.2	165.1	211.3	116.1	214.9	d34.6	139.4
Average Shs. Outstg. (000)	38,281	39,832	40,622	43,040	43,950	40,630	37,397
BALANCE SHEET (IN MILLIONS):							
Cash & Cash Equivalents	26.4	39.5	22.7	12.2	11.5	8.8	5.9
Total Current Assets	1,457.8	1,490.4	1,310.5	1,221.6	1,291.3	1,179.5	850.5
Net Property	484.3	499.7	374.7	368.6	360.4	332.1	274.4
Total Assets	2,774.2	2,874.5	2,106.5	1,996.3	2,074.8	1,927.0	1,588.0
Total Current Liabilities	918.0	1,005.1	789.5	686.5	767.1	786.4	614.1
Long-Term Obligations	831.4	854.5	362.7	452.3	313.6	314.2	280.6
Net Stockholders' Equity	749.0	731.9	730.8	646.3	780.4	624.8	526.9
Net Working Capital	539.8	485.2	521.1	535.1	524.1	393.1	236.4
Year-end Shs. Outstg. (000)	38,372	38,362	39,995	40,628	43,622	43,073	32,969
STATISTICAL RECORD:							
Operating Profit Margin %	4.3	4.2	7.0	3.6	7.4	...	7.1
Net Profit Margin %	2.7	2.0	4.1	1.5	4.6	...	3.7
Return on Equity %	14.2	10.5	18.7	7.3	19.0	...	17.0
Return on Assets %	3.8	2.7	6.5	2.4	7.1	...	5.7
Debt/Total Assets %	30.0	29.7	17.2	22.7	15.1	16.3	17.7
Price Range	30.88-18.13	47.50-21.00	52.75-27.50	55.38-37.63	57.00-43.88	48.50-34.13	42.50-33.88
P/E Ratio	11.1-6.5	24.6-10.9	15.7-8.2	50.3-34.2	16.9-13.0	...	17.7-14.1
Average Yield %	2.4	1.8	1.2	1.0	0.7	0.6	0.4

Statistics are as originally reported. [1] Bef. $442,000 acctg. chg. [2] Incl. $26.9 mil pre-tax gain fr sale of Northfield Freezing & other pre-tax chgs. of $49.7 mil, 2000; $54.5 mil pre-tax acq-rel. chg. & $9.6 mil pre-tax gain on sale of Viron Corp., 1999; & $244.5 mil chg. for impair. loss, 1995. [3] Incl. $75.1 mil chg. for facil. closings & downsizing of German opers.

OFFICERS:
G. C. McDonough, Chmn.
M. R. Young, Pres., C.E.O.
C. D. Myers, V.P., C.F.O.

INVESTOR CONTACT: David Myers, (717) 771-6183

PRINCIPAL OFFICE: 631 South Richland Ave., York, PA 17403

TELEPHONE NUMBER: (717) 771-7890
FAX: (717) 771-7381
WEB: www.york.com

NO. OF EMPLOYEES: 24,600 (approx.)

SHAREHOLDERS: 5,326

ANNUAL MEETING: In May

INCORPORATED: DE, 1874

INSTITUTIONAL HOLDINGS:
No. of Institutions: 148
Shares Held: 32,707,714
% Held: 85.2

INDUSTRY: Refrigeration and heating equipment (SIC: 3585)

TRANSFER AGENT(S): Mellon Investors Services, Ridgefield Park, NJ

NYSE SYMBOL ZNT
Rec. Pr. 27.05 (5/31/01)

ZENITH NATIONAL INSURANCE CORP.

YIELD 3.7%
P/E RATIO . . .

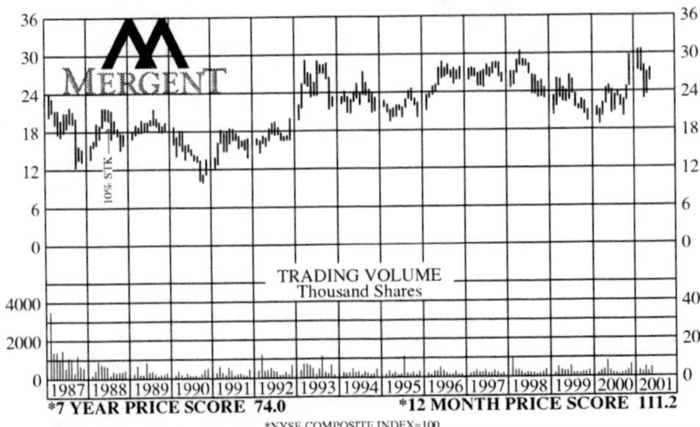

INTERIM EARNINGS (Per Share):

d0.61	Mar.	June	Sept.	Dec.
1996	0.70	0.60	0.51	0.30
1997	0.40	0.44	0.44	0.28
1998	0.42	0.44	0.20	0.20
1999	6.09	d0.20	d2.17	d0.56
2000	d0.31	d1.14	d0.71	d0.61

INTERIM DIVIDENDS (Per Share):

Amt.	Decl.	Ex.	Rec.	Pay.
0.25Q	5/18/00	7/27/00	7/31/00	8/14/00
0.25Q	9/07/00	10/27/00	10/31/00	11/14/00
0.25Q	12/11/00	1/29/01	1/31/01	2/14/01
0.25Q	2/13/01	4/26/01	4/30/01	5/15/01
0.25Q	5/24/01	7/27/01	7/31/01	8/14/01

Indicated div.: $1.00

CAPITALIZATION (12/31/00):

	($000)	(%)
Long-Term Debt	58,374	13.5
Redeemable Pfd. Stock	65,618	15.1
Common & Surplus	309,776	71.4
Total	433,768	100.0

RECENT DEVELOPMENTS: For the year ended 12/31/00, the Company reported a loss of $47.8 million, before an extraordinary gain of $993,000, compared with net income of $54.1 million in the previous year. Results for 2000 included a realized loss on investments of $15.5 million, while results for 1999 included a realized gain on investments of $7.7 million and a gain of $160.3 million from the sale of CalFarm Insurance Company. Total revenues fell 6.6% to $459.6 million from $492.1 million the year before.

PROSPECTS: Operating results for 2000 were affected by continuing underwriting losses in the workers' compensation operations, and the adverse reserve development of 1999 reinsurance losses. However, the Company believes that it has weathered the worst of the recent turmoil of competitive markets and has the financial strength to take advantage of more positive pricing. Looking ahead, ZEN remains positive that its workers' compensation results will improve with increases in both volume and prices.

BUSINESS

ZENITH NATIONAL INSURANCE CORP. is a holding company engaged through its wholly-owned insurance subsidiaries Zenith Insurance Company, ZNAT Insurance Company and Zenith Star Insurance Company, in the property-casualty insurance business. Zenith also conducts real estate operations through a wholly-owned subsidiary which develops land and constructs private residences for sale in Las Vegas, Nevada. On 12/31/96, Zenith Insurance acquired Associated General Commerce Self-Insurers' Trust Fund, a Florida workers' compensation self-insurers' fund. On 4/1/98, Zenith Insurance acquired RISCORP, Inc. On 3/31/99, ZNT sold CalFarm Insurance Co. Reliance Insurance Co. owns about 38% of ZNT's stock. Contributions to property/casualty premiums earned in 2000 were as follows: workers' compensation, 88.8% and reinsurance, 11.2%.

REVENUES

(12/31/00)	($000)	(%)
Premium Earned	338,752	73.6
Net Investment Income	51,766	11.2
Realized Loss on Invests.	(15,467)	(3.4)
Real Estate Sales	84,518	18.6
Total	459,569	100.0

ANNUAL FINANCIAL DATA

	12/31/00	12/31/99	12/31/98	12/31/97	12/31/96	12/31/95	12/31/94
Earnings Per Share	**3 d2.78**	**2 3.15**	**1.11**	**1.57**	**2.11**	**1 1.08**	**1.99**
Tang. Book Val. Per Share	**16.47**	**19.32**	**18.73**	**19.66**	**19.17**	**18.58**	**16.25**
Dividends Per Share	**1.00**	**1.00**	**1.00**	**1.00**	**1.00**	**1.00**	**1.00**
Dividend Payout %	. . .	**31.7**	**90.1**	**63.7**	**47.4**	**92.6**	**50.2**
INCOME STATEMENT (IN MILLIONS):							
Total Premium Income	338.8	369.4	529.9	488.7	452.9	437.5	463.2
Other Income	120.8	122.7	106.9	111.8	103.5	81.5	131.9
Total Revenues	459.6	492.1	636.8	600.5	556.4	519.0	595.1
Policyholder Benefits	1.5	0.6	0.5	0.4	2.5	5.7	98.9
Income Before Income Taxes	d72.3	83.1	28.8	43.5	57.1	29.4	57.6
Income Taxes	cr24.5	29.0	9.7	15.4	19.5	9.7	19.7
Net Income	3 d47.8	2 54.1	19.1	28.1	37.6	1 19.7	37.9
Average Shs. Outstg. (000)	17,269	17,172	17,158	17,886	17,834	18,364	19,090
BALANCE SHEET (IN MILLIONS):							
Cash & Cash Equivalents	174.5	195.5	189.1	222.3	118.8	144.0	134.7
Premiums Due	434.6	452.9	532.0	198.8	230.0	149.5	133.4
Invst. Assets: Fixed-term	595.0	654.9	770.4	589.4	659.0	623.5	1,224.6
Invst. Assets: Equities	27.3	25.6	26.9	23.4	22.8	22.7	19.4
Invst. Assets: Loans	. . .	. . .	. . .	. . .	. . .	. . .	45.3
Invst. Assets: Total	852.7	901.7	1,048.7	880.0	852.8	835.2	1,463.0
Total Assets	1,472.2	1,573.8	1,818.7	1,252.2	1,242.7	1,115.4	1,840.8
Long-Term Obligations	58.4	74.7	74.6	74.5	74.4	74.2	74.1
Net Stockholders' Equity	309.8	354.6	347.0	361.9	337.5	330.4	309.9
Year-end Shs. Outstg. (000)	17,443	17,150	17,148	17,819	17,604	17,784	18,950
STATISTICAL RECORD:							
Return on Revenues %	. . .	11.0	3.0	4.7	6.8	3.8	6.4
Return on Equity %	. . .	15.3	5.5	7.8	11.1	6.0	12.2
Return on Assets %	. . .	3.4	1.1	2.2	3.0	1.8	2.1
Price Range	29.75-18.75	26.69-19.25	30.50-22.88	28.75-24.63	28.88-21.13	24.63-19.38	27.38-20.63
P/E Ratio	. . .	8.5-6.1	27.5-20.6	18.3-15.7	13.7-10.0	22.8-17.9	13.8-10.4
Average Yield %	4.1	4.4	3.7	3.7	4.0	4.5	4.2

Statistics are as originally reported. 1 Bef. disc. oper. loss $13.1 mill. 2 Incl. $160.3 million gain from sale of CalFarm Insurance Co., chrg. $34.8 mill. associated with RISCORP-related adj. & chrg. $2.3 mill. for catastrophe losses. 3 Excl. extraord. gain $993,000

OFFICERS:
S. R. Zax, Chmn., Pres.
W. J. Owen, Sr. V.P., C.F.O.
J. J. Tickner, Sr. V.P., Sec.

INVESTOR CONTACT: William J. Owen, Sr. V.P., C.F.O., (818) 713-1000

PRINCIPAL OFFICE: 21255 Califa Street, Woodland Hills, CA 91367-5021

TELEPHONE NUMBER: (818) 713-1000
FAX: (818) 713-0177
WEB: www.zenithnational.com

NO. OF EMPLOYEES: 1,100 (approx.)

SHAREHOLDERS: 268

ANNUAL MEETING: In May

INCORPORATED: DE, June, 1971

INSTITUTIONAL HOLDINGS:
No. of Institutions: 69
Shares Held: 7,781,601
% Held: 44.5

INDUSTRY: Fire, marine, and casualty insurance (SIC: 6331)

TRANSFER AGENT(S): Mellon Investor Services, Los Angeles, CA